P9-DGU-941

The Norton Anthology of Theory and Criticism

THIRD EDITION

William E. Cain
MARY JEWETT GAISER PROFESSOR OF ENGLISH AND AMERICAN STUDIES
WELLESLEY COLLEGE

Laurie A. Finke
PROFESSOR OF WOMEN'S AND GENDER STUDIES
KENYON COLLEGE

John McGowan
JOHN W. AND ANNA HANES DISTINGUISHED PROFESSOR
OF ENGLISH AND COMPARATIVE LITERATURE
UNIVERSITY OF NORTH CAROLINA, CHAPEL HILL

T. Denean Sharpley-Whiting
GERTRUDE CONAWAY VANDERBILT DISTINGUISHED PROFESSOR
OF AFRICAN AMERICAN AND DIASPORA STUDIES AND FRENCH
VANDERBILT UNIVERSITY

Jeffrey J. Williams
PROFESSOR OF LITERARY AND CULTURAL STUDIES
CARNEGIE MELLON UNIVERSITY

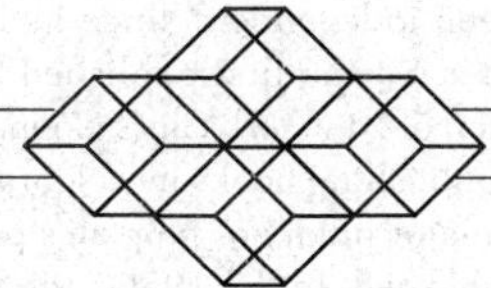

The Norton Anthology of Theory and Criticism

THIRD EDITION

Vincent B. Leitch, *General Editor*
GEORGE LYNN CROSS RESEARCH PROFESSOR EMERITUS
PAUL AND CAROL DAUBE SUTTON CHAIR EMERITUS IN ENGLISH
UNIVERSITY OF OKLAHOMA

W • W • NORTON & COMPANY • New York • London

W. W. Norton & Company has been independent since its founding in 1923, when William Warder Norton and Mary D. Herter Norton first published lectures delivered at the People's Institute, the adult education division of New York City's Cooper Union. The firm soon expanded its program beyond the Institute, publishing books by celebrated academics from America and abroad. By mid-century, the two major pillars of Norton's publishing program—trade books and college texts—were firmly established. In the 1950s, the Norton family transferred control of the company to its employees, and today—with a staff of four hundred and a comparable number of trade, college, and professional titles published each year—W. W. Norton & Company stands as the largest and oldest publishing house owned wholly by its employees.

Printed in the United States of America.

The text of this book is composed in Fairfield Medium
with the display set in Bernhard Modern
Composition by Westchester Book Group
Manufacturing by LSC Crawfordsville

Editor: Peter Simon
Associate Editor: Gerra Goff
Editorial Assistant: Katie Pak
Managing Editor, College: Marian Johnson
Manuscript Editor: Alice Falk
Project Editor: Sujin Hong
Production Manager: Sean Mintus
Text Design: Antonina Krass
Permissions Manager: Megan Schindel
Permissions Clearing: Margaret Gorenstein

Library of Congress Cataloging-in-Publication Data

Names: Leitch, Vincent B., date- author, editor. | Cain, William E., author. | Finke, Laurie A., author. | McGowan, John. | Sharpley-Whiting, T. Denean. | Williams, Jeffrey J.
Title: The Norton anthology of theory and criticism/Vincent B. Leitch, General Editor, George Lynn Cross Research Professor, Paul and Carol Daube Sutton, Chair in English, University of Oklahoma; William E. Cain, Mary Jewett Gaiser Professor of English and American Studies, Wellesley College; Laurie A. Finke, Professor of Women's and Gender Studies, Kenyon College; John McGowan, John W. and Anna Hanes, Distinguished Professor of English and Comparative Literature, University of North Carolina, Chapel Hill; T. Denean Sharpley-Whiting, Distinguished Professor of African American and Diaspora Studies and French, Vanderbilt University; Jeffrey J. Williams, Professor of Literary and Cultural Studies, Carnegie Mellon University.
Description: Third edition. | New York; London: W. W. Norton & Company, [2018]
Identifiers: LCCN 2018006310 | ISBN 9780393602951 (hardcover)
Subjects: LCSH: Criticism. | Literature—History and criticism—Theory, etc.
Classification: LCC PN86 .N67 2018 | DDC 801/.95—dc23 LC record available at https://lccn.loc.gov/2018006310

W. W. Norton & Company, Inc., 500 Fifth Avenue, New York, NY 10110
wwnorton.com

W. W. Norton & Company Ltd., 15 Carlisle Street, London W1D 3BS

1 2 3 4 5 6 7 8 9 0

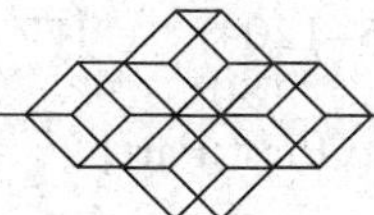

Contents

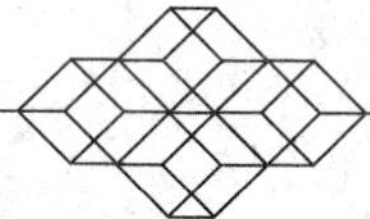

Alternative Table of Contents

Part I: Modern and Contemporary Schools and Movements

Part II: Genres

Part III: Historical Periods

Part IV: Issues and Topics

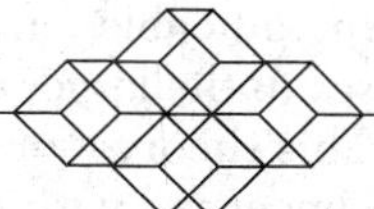

Preface

A wide-ranging and comprehensive collection, *The Norton Anthology of Theory and Criticism* offers one or more selections from 159 figures, representing major developments from ancient to recent times, from Gorgias and Plato to Judith Butler, Franco Moretti, and Sianne Ngai. It provides selections from previously underrepresented fields, such as rhetoric, new historicisms, media studies, and affect theory, along with a full complement of works from canonical figures such as Aristotle, Immanuel Kant, Karl Marx, Cleanth Brooks, Michel Foucault, and Edward W. Said. From canonical authors, it includes classic texts as well as selections newly revalued. The standard works of Western theory and criticism from the ancient Greeks to the present are represented, as are texts from "forgotten" figures such as Moses Maimonides, Baruch Spinoza, and Friedrich Schleiermacher. The anthology is particularly rich in modern and contemporary theory, providing materials from more than a hundred writers and covering all the main schools and movements, ranging from Marxism, psychoanalysis, and formalism to poststructuralism, cultural studies, race and ethnicity studies, queer theory, and many more. We have also drawn from today's most vital currents, including body studies, narrative theory, postcolonial studies, and ecocriticism, plus popular culture studies. This anthology consolidates the many gains won through the expansion of theory in recent decades.

In the third edition, contemporary selections from Adūnīs (Arabic), Hamid Dabashi (Persian), Karatani Kōjin (Japanese), Li Zehou (Chinese), and C. D. Narasimhaiah (Indian) represent illuminating intersections of non-European and Western theoretical and literary traditions. These pieces join non-European materials included in the earlier editions from Chinua Achebe, Frantz Fanon, and Ngugi wă Thiong'o.

In view of current changes, it is worth pausing to consider the configuration and meaning of "theory." Today the term encompasses significant works not only of poetics, theory of criticism, and aesthetics as of old, but also of rhetoric, media studies, race and ethnicity theory, gender theory, and theories of popular culture as well as globalization and modernity. But theory in its newer sense means still more than this broadly expanded body of topics and texts. It entails a mode of questioning and analysis that moves beyond earlier formalist research into the "literariness" of literature without giving up formalist techniques of close reading. Because of the effects of poststructuralism, cultural studies, and the social movements that emerged in the 1960s and have developed in profound ways since then, especially ongoing women's and civil rights movements, contemporary theory entails skepticism toward systems, institutions, and norms; a readiness to take critical stands and to engage in resistance; an interest in blind spots, contradictions, and distortions (often discovered to be ineradicable); and a habit of linking local and personal practices and responses to the larger economic, political, historical, and ethical forces of culture. This theory—or cultural critique, as it is more descriptively termed—is less concerned with elaborating conditions of possibility, as is Kantian critique, than with investigating and criticizing values, practices, representations, and affects embedded in cultural texts and surrounding institutions. To its critics such theory looks like advocacy rather than impartial objective inquiry into poetics and the history of literature. This difference between so-called surface and symptomatic reading highlights one among other long-standing fault lines in the field of criticism and theory discussed in the Introduction.

The Table of Contents lists figures and texts in chronological order. An Alternative Table of Contents recasts the chronological order, providing lists of figures in four categories commonly used in studying theory: schools and movements; major genres; historical periods; and key issues and topics. Additional ways of organizing the history and subject matter of theory and criticism are possible, to be sure. Other figures in the anthology could be included in the existing categories. We decided against combining proponents and opponents in the popular schools and movements categories, as is sometimes done. Thus, for example, Mikhail Bakhtin does not appear under "Formalism" as one of its most celebrated critics. To list together antagonists and advocates would have created confusion and unduly multiplied the number of figures in our categories. Within each school and movement, of course, readers will encounter differences and disputes. One of the risks of the categories we employ in the Alternative Table of Contents is that their groupings of figures and topics from different periods and moments unavoidably deemphasize historical conflicts, evolution, and differences. That noted, the editors believe our readers will find the Alternative Table of Contents suggestive and useful.

The Introduction to Theory and Criticism that follows the two Tables of Contents consists of eighteen brief, semiautonomous sections that introduce students to the field of theory through its main historical periods, its major modern and contemporary schools and movements, its perennial issues and problems, and its key terms. Here we provide a quick and wide-ranging overview of the history and nature of the field. Sections have been subtitled for easy reference in making assignments and in following the trajectory of the discussion.

Each selection in the anthology is annotated so that students may focus on the texts and not have to consult reference sources for basic information. Headnotes to each figure cover a range of topics. To begin with, they provide biographical information and historical background. They discuss sources and critical reception as well as the relevance of the selections for theoretical questions. They highlight each selection's main arguments, where necessary defining key terms and concepts and pointing out related perennial problems in the field. They refer to other works by the authors and note problems identified by later critics. They position the authors in relation to other figures in the anthology, picturing the history of theory not as a string of isolated pearls but as a mosaic in which each work fits into larger frames of ongoing discussions and arguments. Finally, an annotated bibliography, located at the back of the book, is given for each figure, covering main texts and editions, biographical sources (when available), useful secondary sources and criticism, and bibliographies related to the author's works (when available).

In choosing the selections the editors have been guided by a range of criteria. We have looked for readable and teachable texts that reflect the scope of the history of theory. This does not mean, however, that challenging and difficult texts are missing. We have favored complete works and self-contained excerpts; snippets are the exception. Yet in a number of cases we have edited texts to focus on topics germane to the field and to save space for other selections. We have sought out reliable editions and translations. From the outset we have followed the practice that no figure or selection could make it into the anthology without the agreement of at least half the editors. We consulted with colleagues, including a hundred past users who completed a survey. We have made quite a few selections with an eye to pairing or triangulating—for example, we chose the famous closing section on writing from Plato's *Phaedrus*, having in mind Derrida's landmark critique of that text in his *Dissemination*. When they occur, such fruitful counterpoints are indicated in the headnotes and in the Alternative Table of Contents. Of course, innumerable combinations and permutations are possible, and our accounts cannot be exhaustive. But we have noted typographically all cross-references in the headnotes and footnotes by putting in small capitals the names of theorists and critics appearing in the anthology. While we have privileged standard works and contemporary classics of theory, we have also sought to present overlooked as well as forgotten texts.

In past editions we included a general bibliography of criticism and theory as a supplement, but given the vast profusion of sources and online bibliographical tools, we have decided to forgo it. However, we continue to offer discursive bibliographies of each author, which we now publish together in the final section of the anthology. For convenience in this edition, we have added to all 200 selections Keywords derived from our Alternative Table of Contents. This change of format takes the place of a Subject Index, affording coherence, focus, and economy.

In putting this anthology together, we have faced a number of challenges. One difficulty was coping with the impossibility of including every significant theorist. Our original lists of several hundred figures had to be shortened to 159: even a long book such as this one imposes limits. Some of the lengthiest selections—by Longinus, Sir Philip Sidney, Percy Bysshe Shelley, Adrienne Rich, and Jacques Derrida, for instance—had to be trimmed, and each editor had favorite figures omitted. The enclosure of post–World War II theory in the university and its increased professionalization have meant that contemporary nonacademic critics, literary journalists, and writers have been largely excluded from the theory canon. While theory remains Eurocentric, our selections from Africa, Asia, and the Middle East begin the opening to wider horizons.

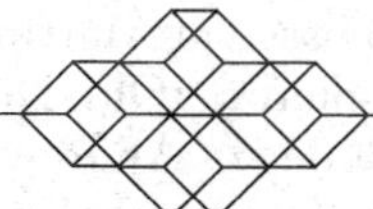

Acknowledgments to the Third Edition

We appreciate assistance from the following people: Eve Tavor Bannet (University of Oklahoma), Megan Becker-Leckrone (University of Nevada, Las Vegas), Michael Bérubé (Pennsylvania State University), Paul Bowman (Cardiff University), William Christopher Brown (University of Minnesota Crookston), Danny C. Campbell (Chowan College), Rey Chow (Duke University), Tim Conley (Brock University), William Covey (Slippery Rock University), Jonathan Culler (Cornell University), Daniel Darvay (Colorado State University–Pueblo), Richard Dienst (Rutgers University), Jeffrey R. Di Leo (University of Houston–Victoria), Nancy El Gendy (University of Nevada, Reno), Bruce Gardiner (University of Sydney), William Germano (Cooper Union), Peter Gilgen (Cornell University), Larry Grossberg (University of North Carolina at Chapel Hill), Carolin Hahnemann (Kenyon College), Ann C. Hall (Ohio Dominican University), Brian K. Hudson (Central New Mexico Community College), Walter Kalaidjian (Emory University), John Kirby (Miami University), Reinhold Kramer (Brandon University), Mitchell Lewis (Elmira College), James Liner (University of Washington Tacoma), John Lisovsk, Jennifer Lombard, Hans Lottenbach (Kenyon College), Derek Lowe (University of Southern Alabama), Steven Mailloux (Loyola Marymount University), Regina Martin (Denison University), Luiz Fernando Martins (Brazil), Günter Meckenstock (University of Kiel), Susan Hollis Merritt, Arash Moradi (Shahid Beheshi University), Christian Moraru (University of North Carolina at Greensboro), Timothy Murphy (Oklahoma State University), Pashmina Murthy (Kenyon College), Patrick O'Donnell (Michigan State University), Bruce Robbins (Columbia University), Barry Sarchett (Colorado College), Ronald Schleifer (University of Oklahoma), Anne H. Stevens (University of Nevada, Las Vegas), Tauan Fernandes Tinti (University of Campinas), György Túry (Budapest Metropolitan University), Gregory Ulmer (University of Florida), H. Aram Veeser (City University of New York), Ariana Vigil (University of North Carolina at Chapel Hill), Shunzhu Wang (Rider University), James P. Warren (Washington and Lee University), Charles Whitney (University of Nevada, Las Vegas), and Gang Zhu (Nanjing University).

For special help we thank both William Covey and John Kirby.

Gratitude goes to our consultants on non-Western theory and criticism: Terri DeYoung (University of Washington), Ming Dong Gu (University of Texas at Dallas), Feroza Jussawalla (University of New Mexico), Indra Levy (Stanford University), and Kamran Talattof (University of Arizona).

We express our appreciation to reviewers and commentators on the second edition, including Stacy Alaimo (University of Texas, Arlington), Lynn

Alexander (University of Tennessee at Martin), Brigitte Anderson (University of Pikeville), Sarah Appleton (Old Dominion University), Robert Archambeau (Lake Forest College), Andrew Armond (Oklahoma Baptist University), Gretchen Bartels (California Baptist University), Wesley Beal (Lyon College), Rebecca Belcher-Rankin (Olivet Nazarene University), Florence Boos (University of Iowa), Christopher K. Brooks (Wichita State University), David Buehrer (Valdosta State University), Amee Carmines (Hampton University), Laura Carroll (Abilene Christian University), Ranita Chatterjee (California State University, Northridge), Chih-Ping Chen (Alma College), Francis X. Connor (Wichita State University), Sarah Davis (Hunter College), Anthony Dawahare (California State University, Northridge), Robin DeRosa (Plymouth State Universtiy), Molly Desjardins (University of Northern Colorado), Eric d'Evegnee (Brigham Young University, Idaho), George Drake (Central Washington University), Julie Dugger (Western Washington University), Elizabeth Duquette (Gettysburg College), Gary Eddy (Winona State University), Marian Eide (Texas A&M University), Gregory Eiselein (Kansas State University), Nikolai Endres (Western Kentucky University), Aden Evens (Fairhaven College of Interdisciplinary Studies), Cassandra Falke (Norges Arktiske Universitet), Lianna Farber (University of Minnesota), Michael Faris (Texas Tech University), Thomas Festa (SUNY New Paltz), Ellen Friedman (The College of New Jersey), Michael Lee Gardin (University of Texas at San Antonio), Laura George (Eastern Michigan University), Joshua Gooch (D'Youville College), Robert Gorsch (Saint Mary's College of California), Evan Gottlieb (Oregon State University), Eric Gray (St. Gregory's University), Willard P. Greenwood II (Hiram College), Heather Hathaway (Marquette University), Chene Heady (Longwood University), Burgsbee Lee Hobbs (Saint Leo University), Jane Hoogestraat (Missouri State University), Matt Hooley (Texas Tech University), Heidi Hosey (Mercyhurst University), Kelly Hurley (University of Colorado, Boulder), Amy Jamgochian (University of California, Berkeley), David Kaloustian (Bowie State University), Gerard Killeen (Marylhurst University), Mary Klages (University of Colorado, Boulder), James Knapp (Loyola University of Chicago), Lesley Kordecki (DePaul University), Joseph Kronick (Louisiana State University), Tonya Krouse (Northern Kentucky University), Barry Laga (Colorado Mesa University), Stephen Lehigh (California State University, San Bernardino), Richard Mace (Pace University), Gregory Maertz (St. John's University), Susan Jaret McKinstry (Carleton College), Richard Menke (University of Georgia), Gretchen Michlitsch (Winona State University), Debra Monroe (Texas State University), Mary Mullen (Villanova University), Joanne Myers (Gettysburg College), Ode Ogede (North Carolina Central University), Matthew Potolsky (University of Utah), Timothy Richardson (University of Texas, Arlington), Benjamin Robertson (University of Colorado, Boulder), Valerie Rohy (University of Vermont), Arnold Sanders (Goucher College), Stephen Schillinger (Oberlin College & Conservatory), Scott Shershow (University of California, Davis), Anne Stevens (University of Nevada, Las Vegas), Meghan Sweeney (University of North Carolina at Wilmington), Sharon Talley (Texas A&M University, Corpus Christi), Slater Juan Thompson (University of Wisconsin, Eau Claire), Alan Vardy (Hunter College), Robyn Warhol (Ohio State University), James P. Warren (Washington and Lee University), Jolanta Wawrzycka (Radford University), John Wells

(Virginia Commonwealth University), Toby Widdicombe (University of Alaska Anchorage), Tyrone Williams (Xavier University), Sarah Winter (University of Connecticut), Sean Witters (University of Vermont), Jessica Wohlschlaeger (Missouri Baptist University), and Nancy Workman (Lewis University).

Thanks are due to the following research assistants: Adam Ahlgrim, Terrance Dean, Andrea Lechleitner, and Souri Sompanith. Special thanks go to John-Mark Hart, who spent several years on this project.

The editors wish to thank W. W. Norton Associate Editor Gerra Goff, who guided this edition through production, and especially Editor Peter Simon, who has shepherded this book through three editions.

The Norton Anthology of Theory and Criticism

THIRD EDITION

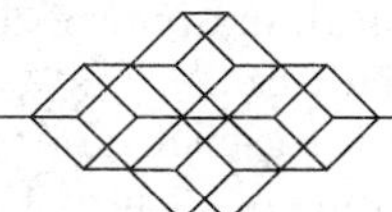

Introduction to Theory and Criticism

In recent times, theory and criticism have become central to literary and cultural studies, treated less as aids to the study of literature and culture than as ends in themselves. As Jonathan Culler noted in *Framing the Sign: Criticism and Its Institutions* (1988), "Formerly the history of criticism was part of the history of literature (the story of changing conceptions of literature advanced by great writers), but . . . now the history of literature is part of the history of criticism." This dramatic reversal, which occurred gradually over the course of the twentieth century, means that the history of criticism and theory increasingly provides the general framework for studying literature and culture in colleges and universities. Some literary scholars and writers deplore the shift toward "theory," regarding it as a turn away from literature and its central concerns. These "antitheorists," as they are called, advocate a return to studying literature for itself—yet however sensible this position may at first appear, it has problems: it itself presupposes a definition of literature, and it promotes a certain way of scrutinizing literature ("for itself"). In other words, the antitheory position turns out to rely on unexamined—and debatable—theories of literature and criticism. What theory demonstrates, in this case and in others, is that there is no position free of theory, not even the one called "common sense."

The history of theory and criticism from ancient times to the present is one of contending ideas and opinions about such apparently self-evident topics as "literature" and "interpretation." Historically, interpretation has been conceptualized in a number of different ways: as, for example, objective textual analysis or moral assessment or emotional response or literary evaluation or cultural critique. The same is also true of literature, which has been defined in terms of its ability to represent reality, or to express its author's inner being, or to teach morality, or to cleanse our emotions, to name only a few common but conflicting formulations. The history of criticism and theory contains many such arguments. Taken together, the antitheorists themselves adhere to very different, often contradictory understandings of literature and interpretation. Such conflict points to the vitality, the excitement, and the complexity of the field of theory and criticism, whose expansive universe of issues and problems engages ideas not only about literature, language, interpretation, genre, style, meaning, and tradition but also about subjectivity, ethnicity, race, gender, sexuality, class, culture, nationality, ideology, institutions, and historical periods. In this anthology, students new to literary and cultural studies will discover a wide-ranging interdisciplinary and comparative field whose practitioners examine, formulate, and assess all manner of theories and problems related to the study of literature and culture.

In addition, students new to criticism and theory will encounter a rich array of technical terms and concepts, critical approaches and schools, and literary and cultural theories and theorists. From *signifier* to *deconstruction* to *cultural studies*, from Aristotle to Foucault, the field of theory and criticism is marked by a multitude of signposts sometimes unfamiliar to even the most widely read students. In this introduction as well as in the headnotes to each author, we help students make sense of this complex but rewarding area. We begin by surveying an array of notable answers to two central questions—what is interpretation? and what is literature?—in order to establish our bearings. Shifting direction, we then survey the historical development of theory and criticism, from the classical to the Romantic periods, after which we provide brief overviews of major schools and movements of the last century, plus finally the disaggregation of the field in the twenty-first century. Along the way, we discuss many of the theorists in this anthology, explain perennial problems and issues, define key concepts and terms, and illuminate the underlying structure of the field of theory and criticism, including its most significant conflicts.

WHAT IS INTERPRETATION?

Within the field of theory and criticism, various terms and concepts are applied to the encounter between the reader and the text. This transaction, which we will provisionally call "reading" or "interpretation," typically involves such activities as personal response, appreciation, evaluation, historical reception, explication, exegesis, and critique. Not surprisingly, the master words *interpretation* and *reading* are themselves debatable. In fact, in choosing a term or terms to characterize the encounter between text and reader, one takes a specific theoretical position regarding the exact nature of reading and interpretation.

Consider a few such key terms. Whereas *explication* and *exegesis* stress the objective labor of deciphering a text in a methodical way (line by line, in the case of a short poem), *personal response* and *appreciation* emphasize the intimate, casual, and subjective aspects of reading. *Critique* and *historical reception*, in turn, accentuate the distances in values and time between the interpreter and the work. An exegesis of a text is not the same as an appreciation or a critique. Exegesis presumes a dense and enigmatic text in need of elaborate explanation; appreciation implies a reader-friendly work just waiting to be enjoyed here and now; and critique presupposes a hidden set of questionable or dangerous premises and values undergirding a complex document. In the case of exegesis an interpreter needs to be a knowledgeable puzzle solver; appreciation positions the reader as an eager and sympathetic hedonist; and critique calls for a critic at once suspicious and ethical, committed to a set of values different from, or directly opposed to, those expressed in the text. In depicting the critical encounter, theories of reading and interpretation invariably assign characteristics to texts and allocate particular roles and tasks to readers.

Many of the selections in this anthology differ markedly in how they characterize interpretation and reading. For instance, Friedrich Schleiermacher draws a detailed account of interpretation both as historically informed grammatical explication and as psychological identification with the author. His view contrasts with the perspective of Fredric Jameson, who advocates an elaborate three-phase process of interpretation focused specifically on ideology critique of social contradictions, class antagonisms, and historical stages of social development manifested in texts. And Paul de Man instead pictures reading as a mode of exegesis wherein the reader's rewriting or restaging of the text replaces the original with an interpretive allegory: reading for him unavoidably becomes "misreading." That highly competent theorists can propose completely different models of reading fuels continued theoretical debate about interpretation.

One of the most famous ways of reading is the mode of textual analysis developed by the New Critics, particularly Cleanth Brooks. During the mid-twentieth century, the New Criticism became the dominant critical practice in many North American and British universities, and it remains influential today, especially in the introductory literature classroom. To interpret as a New Critic is to demonstrate through multiple (re)readings of poetic texts the intricacy of artistic forms. "Meaning" is found neither in a simple paraphrase of the text, nor in propositions extracted from it, but in carefully orchestrated and unified textual elements (for example, images, tropes, tones, and symbols). The literary work is (pre)conceived as an autonomous, highly coherent, dramatic artifact (a "well-wrought urn") separate from and above the life of the author and reader as well as separate from its social context and from everyday language. Textual inconsistencies are harmonized by being valorized as artful literary ambiguities, paradoxes, or ironies.

Yet there are problems with this seemingly sensible "formalist" method. Some theorists have complained that it posits an overly aestheticized, narrow theory of meaning. The "close reading" or "practical criticism" advocated rules out a great deal, including personal response, authorial intention, propositional meaning, social and historical context, and ideology. It values retrospective analysis rather than the risky ongoing experience or actual process of trying to make sense of a work. It privileges both freestanding spatial form over temporal flow and critical distance over the reader's personal participation. It makes textual unity mandatory, finessing gaps and loose ends. It favors well-made and compact rather than sprawling works and genres. The reading practice of New Criticism is an explicit emptying out of literary interpretation in order to highlight intrinsic artistic craft and form while ruling out such extrinsic matters as morality, psychology, and politics.

Even without sampling further the many theories of reading and interpretation presented in this anthology, we can see that there are no easy answers to the question "what is interpretation?" New Criticism has been singled out to demonstrate how a practice of reading might be questioned, but many of the other theories in this anthology could have served equally well. The relationship between interpretation and reading continues to be a major preoccupation in the field of criticism and theory. All who think critically have an opportunity to engage various theories of reading and to define their own views.

WHAT IS LITERATURE?

Another major question—"what is literature?"—can be, and regularly is, answered by associating literature with such keywords as representation, expression, knowledge, poetic or rhetorical language, genre, text, or discourse.

In our ordinary understanding, literature represents life; it holds up, as it were, a mirror to nature and is thus "mimetic." The expressive theory of literature, which regards literature as stemming from the author's inner being, similarly depends on a notion of mirroring, though here literature reflects the inner soul rather than the external world of the writer. The didactic theory, which sees literature as a source of knowledge, insight, wisdom, purgation, and perhaps prophecy, is compatible with both the mimetic and the expressive theory: literature can depict external and internal realities while at the same time disseminating valuable knowledge and clarifying emotions. The dominant view of literature as both mimetic and didactic, still alive today, arose with the ancient Greeks and was challenged by the Romantics and then the moderns. Though the theory of literature—or "poetics," as it is sometimes called—has been a contested topic throughout history, the debate has been especially fierce from the late nineteenth century to the present.

Modern theorists often insist that the language of literature, unlike that of newspapers and science, foregrounds poetic effects (particularly tropes and figures) that range from alliteration, assonance, metaphor, and paradox to rhythm and rhyme. In this formalist theory of literature or poetics, neither depiction of external or internal reality nor knowledge about existence or refined emotion distinguishes literature from ordinary and scientific discourse: instead, "literariness" (or "poeticity") renders literature distinctive and special.

This theory first emerged during the nineteenth century when poets such as Edgar Allan Poe and Gerard Manley Hopkins started exploring, sometimes extravagantly, the constituent materials of literature (especially sound effects), turning away from the notion of literature as simply a reliable recorder of nature or source of morality. A similar transformation followed in the visual arts; the postimpressionist painters focused on paint textures, brush strokes, and color intensities rather than seeking photographic realities. Writers and theorists at the time often felt that to justify literature by pointing to its accuracy and realism was to put it in competition with the sciences, social sciences, journalism, and photography—a competition they believed it could not win. Conversely, by emphasizing the literariness of literature, they would accord it a distinctive and elevated aesthetic status over competing domains and fields, ensuring its survival and dignity in challenging times. Such a formalist theory of literature prevailed in the early and mid-twentieth century among Anglo-American New Critics and Slavic formalists, some of whom are represented in this anthology.

A well-known heuristic device conveniently summarizes all the accounts of literature discussed up to this point. Developed by M. H. Abrams in *The Mirror and the Lamp: Romantic Theory and the Critical Tradition* (1953), this study aid pictures the literary "work" at the center of a triangular structure; the outer three points are occupied by the "universe," the "artist," and the "audience." Mimetic theory emphasizes the relations between the work

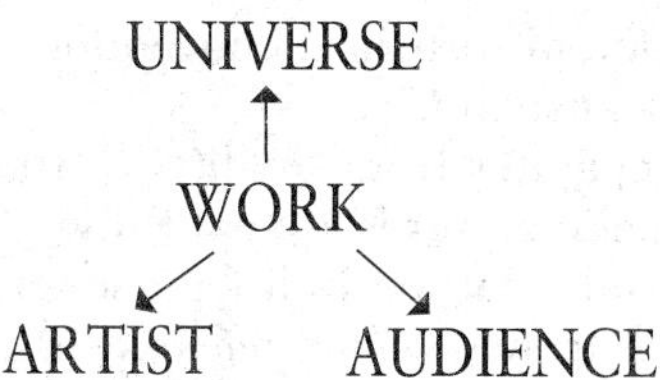

and the universe; expressive theory foregrounds the link between work and artist; didactic theory highlights the tie between work and audience. Formalist theory focuses on the work itself; as we have just seen, it deemphasizes connections between the text and the universe, artist, or audience. Until the early Romantic era, literary theory dealt with the poem's relationship to the universe and the audience; in the nineteenth century it focused on the artist; and in the twentieth century it turned to the work itself. Most theories of criticism and literature, argues Abrams, juggle these four major elements and orientations, tending to privilege one.

This classification scheme and its lessons have proven useful, especially in illustrating basic theoretical orientations and in delineating broad historical trends. But the famous diagram has limitations, as any theorist will tell you. Perhaps the most serious is that it stops with modernism: it predates the appearance of such influential postmodern theoretical movements as structuralism, poststructuralism, feminism, queer theory, postcolonial theory, and cultural studies. Abrams maps a progression from mimesis and didacticism to expressionism to formalism, but recent theory and criticism of literature have moved on to cultural critique. In the process, theorists have focused in turn on the imitation of reality and its lessons, on inner truths and visions, on poetic techniques and their orchestrations, and on sociohistorical and political representations and their values. In this historical development the "old" problems recede from view but never disappear; instead, they undergo reconfiguration and occupy new conceptual relations.

Consider, for instance, the structuralist or semiotic theory of literature that fits all literary texts into genre classifications. According to this perspective, a genre is defined by arbitrary sets of conventions, such as those governing the haiku—a poem of seventeen syllables in three lines of five, seven, and five syllables, respectively. These conventions distance literary writing from ordinary reality, even when the conventions are calculated to give the appearance of direct reportage. In seeing literature as genre consisting of complex sets of codes, the structuralist retains the formalist view of literature as a separate mode of discourse that follows its own artistic rules but adds the sociological concept of *convention*. Because conventions are not only literary but also linguistic and cultural, literature and society are reconnected through discourse.

Poststructuralist and deconstructive accounts of literature go one step further by problematizing the notion of mirroring, which, as we have seen, undergirds expressive, didactic, and mimetic theories of literature. They do so through a close and technically complex examination of the workings of language—seen as distant and different from reality, for it necessarily contains distorting rhetorical and genre devices. Language is not a simple transparent medium. Any use of language, no matter how typical or everyday, employs *some* combination of historical conventions and figurative devices, which compromises its transparency.

Moreover, language separates from "reality" at the very basic level of the sign because, strictly speaking, words are not things. The four letters *b, i, r, d* are not an actual feathered creature. In linguistic terminology, neither *signifiers* (words) nor *signifieds* (concepts) are *referents* (things). Because language consists of "floating signifiers" that are detached from reality, it simulates or summons things. Language deals in effects rather than things. The gaps between signifiers, signifieds, and referents render the truthfulness and reliability of language *undecidable* (a technical term from mathematics borrowed by poststructuralism).

Language is thus, to employ technical deconstructive terms, *text* or *textuality*, meaning a complex interweaving of self-referential, undecidable relationships. In extreme forms, this challenging postmodern theory of literature as textuality views language as thoroughly divorced from reality; in more moderate forms, language maintains a relation to reality, albeit a more or less uncertain one. At stake is literature's ability to reflect reality or impart reliable knowledge—and the uncertainty raises doubts about its truth claims and about earlier theories of literature. This area of inquiry is commonly labeled the "crisis of reference" (or "referentiality").

The dizzying deconstructive view of literature as textuality has been opposed by the widespread poststructuralist theory of literature as *discourse*, a term associated with the influential work of Michel Foucault. Discourse theorists trace the language of literature to its source in the spoken language of everyday social life. Conceived by its many advocates as anti-elitist, this materialist theory of discourse—whether it stems from Foucault, Mikhail M. Bakhtin, black aestheticians, New Historicists, cultural materialists, queer theorists, psychoanalytic critics, or cultural studies scholars (all allotted space in this anthology and discussed later in the introduction)—insists that language is uttered by embodied subjects who are situated historically in contentious social spheres that are regulated by powerful institutions. Significantly, this theory of the *social text*—of language use as dialogical—gives new life to earlier views of literature as mimetic, expressive, and didactic.

Literature, according to these recent discourse theories of the social text, re-presents and refracts reality. Indeed, language itself constitutes reality; it also produces distortions. This is mimesis with a difference: literature represents reality; but reality is grounded in convention, not nature, and it is subject to illusion. Similarly, discourse theorists affirm that literature expresses the inner life of authors, but life is understood to be a regulated *social* phenomenon that differs with the time, location, and group of the author. In place of the solitary poet giving unique expression to truths universal to all humankind, we find in recent discourse theories an embattled "scriptor" creatively mixing and matching cultural codes derived from her or his situation, community, and tradition.

In this account literature retains didactic as well as mimetic and expressive powers. In addition, the knowledge it conveys is of the "cultural unconscious"—that is, of the archive of historical words, symbols, codes, instincts, wishes, and conflicts characteristic of a people and its era. To treat discourse as social text pluralizes the theory of literature, making a single universal or totalizing humanist theory of literature, good for all times and places, appear reductive. In posthumanist thinking, literatures replace literature.

Theories of literature and theories of reading have affinities with one another. Here are four instances. First, the formalist idea of literature as a well-made artistic object corresponds to the notion of reading as careful explication and evaluation of dense poetic style. Second, when viewed as the spiritual expression of a gifted seer, poetry elicits a biographical approach to criticism focused on the poet's inner development. Third, dense historical symbolic works presuppose a theory of reading as exegesis or decipherment. Fourth, literature conceived as social text or dialogical discourse calls for cultural critique. While we can separate theories of literature from theories of interpretation, they often work hand in hand.

CLASSICAL THEORY AND CRITICISM

Anthologies covering the history of theory and criticism usually begin with the classical theorists, and rightly so, because their influence on its development has continued up to the present. The most influential classical theorists in Western culture are Plato and Aristotle, followed distantly by Horace. Recently, a renewed interest in rhetoric has brought Gorgias, Quintilian, and others into the picture—a change that illustrates the mutability of the canon of theory. Taken together, the classical theorists represent a wide range of opinions about literature and its significance developed over a millennium (from the fifth century B.C.E. to the fifth century C.E.). To sample their groundbreaking work, we will consider here some of their opinions on two leading, often interrelated issues of their time: literary mimesis and didacticism.

On these two issues, Plato and his student Aristotle present the best-known views. Both agree that *mimēsis* (imitation or representation) is a key feature of poetry, but they conceive of and evaluate it differently. Plato has his spokesperson Socrates disapprove of poetry's imitation of reality on the grounds that poetry cannot depict truth and teach morality and that it is irrational—based on inspiration, not knowledge. As an idealist philosopher, he locates reality in a transcendent world of eternal Forms or Ideas that only reason can properly apprehend; this world is distinct from the illusory phenomenal world of our senses, which poetry represents. For Plato, the material world is at best an imperfect copy of the original transcendent world of Ideas, and poetry is but a degraded copy of a copy. He concludes that poetic representation threatens social stability by offering false images and unsuitable role models. In *Republic*, therefore, he has Socrates recommend that it be banished from the ideal society, except perhaps for poetry that praises the gods and avoids representing them in an unseemly fashion.

Plato takes this severe position in part because he is reacting against the views of earlier sophists such as Gorgias and Thrasymachus, whom he represents as concerned less with truth than with persuasion. They saw language as not simply representing reality but in effect producing reality by shaping the beliefs of an audience. As a result, in oratory as well as in poetry, what matters most is bringing a particular audience to hold a specific point of view, not imitating an absolute truth. Some sophists even boasted that in a debate they could argue any side of an issue and win. Later rhetoricians such as Quintilian emphasized that the good orator was also a morally good person, but truth and honesty apparently mattered little to fifth-century Greek sophists, who significantly influenced the formation of Plato's ethical position.

Less transcendental than Plato and Socrates, and more concerned with truth than the sophists, Aristotle asserts that poetic imitation can reveal truth precisely because it does not passively copy appearances: it is a more creative act. Poetry in this view is an organized whole, whose parts are organically related and subordinated to a single objective. Because he focuses on tragic drama, Aristotle takes plot as the major example of the organization of poetry. For him, plot is not a random sequence of incidents but a unified whole with a beginning, middle, and end structured by logical necessity. Unlike history, which is built on accidental details, poetry rises above the description of particulars to represent universal truths about nature. This new view of imitation springs from Aristotle's belief that human beings have a natural instinct for imitation, which is generally pleasurable and connected with learning.

Later developments in classical theory and criticism build on the groundbreaking work of the Greek rhetoricians, Plato, and Aristotle. Horace, a Roman poet, follows Aristotle in asserting that poets can and must imitate nature, adding that it is also important for young poets to imitate great writers. As he approves of poetic imitation, Horace stresses morality and decorum. For him, the pleasures of imitation are best yoked with moral teaching: he declares that the primary function of poetry is to combine "pleasure with usefulness." This famous Horatian maxim has exerted considerable influence on all subsequent theorizing.

MEDIEVAL THEORY AND CRITICISM

Spanning the course of a millennium (from the fifth through the fifteenth century), medieval theory and criticism contain numerous documents related to the practices of reading and interpretation, to the theory of language, and to the nature and use of literature.

Much medieval literary theory evolved out of the interpretation of sacred Scriptures. Drawing on the Neoplatonism of Plotinus and his disciple Proclus, medieval writers explored how to read the Book of God's Word (the Bible) as a divinely authorized representation of the Book of God's Works (nature). Hugh of St. Victor, for instance, describes interpretation as the reflection, or imitation, of God's works in his words. For Hugh, the whole visible world is a book written by the finger of God. Thus, in reading one discovers not a pale imitation of nature, as Plato believed, but the ways in which reading a text and reading the world are parallel activities.

This medieval theory of hermeneutics (the art and science of interpretation) is grounded in Augustine's notion that human language is a divinely ordained reflection of the Logos (the Word of God), which is said to guarantee the unity of meaning in the Bible and the book of nature, even when that meaning is not readily discernible. Language truthfully portrays the world as it is, in spite of the confusion caused by the multiplication of tongues at

Babel. According to Augustine, language exists only to convey a meaning that preexists it; it cannot be reflexive or playful (as it may be in poetry); and it must efface itself in pointing to the preexistent truth it represents. Language is "transparent."

Most medieval writers accepted the Augustinian theory of language, and they also shared Augustine's deep distrust of poetic fables and figurative language. But they faced serious theoretical contradictions. Try as they might to assert the "truth" of language and the uselessness of poetic fictions, medieval writers could not overlook the presence of both poetry and fables in the master text of Christianity, the Bible. The most common if still not entirely satisfactory response was to argue that the transcendental majesty of God could be represented only indirectly, through poetic or figurative language. In this view, the heroic songs and psalms of the Old Testament, as well as Christ's parables in the New Testament, function as metaphoric mediations, creating similitudes between this world and the next. Such similitudes are necessary, Augustine argues, so that "by means of corporeal and temporal things we may comprehend the eternal and spiritual." Ultimately, the medieval defense of poetry was based on Macrobius's distinction between fables that "merely gratify the ear" and those that "encourage the reader to good works."

In exploring such issues, medieval writers relied primarily on the textual techniques of exegesis. Particularly important were the exegetical genres of the gloss and the commentary, derived from the works of ancient grammarians and expanded for explication of the Bible. Glosses are elucidations of individual words or phrases, written in the margins or between the lines of a text; commentaries are much more extensive textual expositions, appearing at first as local and marginal remarks (like footnotes) but later produced as freestanding continuous texts (for example, Bernardus Sylvestris's twelfth-century *Commentary on the First Six Books of Virgil's "Aeneid"*). Known as the *enarratio poetarum* (exposition of the poets), these interpretive genres shaped the basic approach to all authoritative texts, which were transmitted in manuscripts filled with glosses and commentary that retained space for future textual exegesis.

The dominant technique of medieval gloss and commentary is allegory, a method of reading texts for their underlying esoteric meanings. Quintilian's definition of allegory as meaning "one thing in the words, another in the senses" was the basis of medieval definitions of allegory; but what was for him a figure of speech became, when combined with the Augustinian belief that poetry is a revelation of an otherwise inaccessible transcendent world, a critical tool to explain and control the dissemination of meanings in sacred Scriptures. Only later would it become a literary genre. Following Quintilian, medieval writers eventually elaborated four levels of allegorical interpretation to be used in the study of the Bible: the *literal*, or historical; the *allegorical*, or spiritual; the *tropological*, or moral; and the *anagogical*, or mystical. In the New Testament story of Christ's raising of Lazarus from the dead, for example, the medieval exegete would recognize first that, on the literal level, the story is a record of an event that actually took place. On the allegorical level, the story prefigures Christ's death, descent into hell, and resurrection. On the tropological level, it represents the sacrament of Penance, whereby the individual soul is raised from the death of sin. And on the anagogical level, it portrays the resurrection of the body after the Last Judgment.

By the twelfth century, medieval writers had extended allegorical biblical interpretation to the study of pagan mythologies and great classical works of art, such as Virgil's epic poem, the *Aeneid*. Medieval Christians could not literally accept pagan gods, nor could they simply read the stories as "fables," but they could see them as expressions of philosophical ideas. Eventually, allegorical interpretation was applied to contemporary writing, as in Dante's reading of his *Divine Comedy* in "Letter to Can Grande." Although it slowly passed out of favor after the Middle Ages, allegorical interpretation reemerged as a significant influence in the late twentieth century—for example, in the work of Northrop Frye and Fredric Jameson, both of whom developed schemes for interpreting texts based on multiple levels of interpretation.

Medieval theory and criticism, significantly, are also concerned with prescriptive poetics: that is, with how to write poetry. Inspired by Horace's *Ars Poetica*, this pragmatic criticism synthesizes classical views on rhetoric, grammar, and style, often taking the form of guides to composition. For instance, the medieval Horatian poet-critic Geoffrey of Vinsauf adopts and revises Horace's fundamental principle of decorum for a medieval audience. For Geoffrey, the poet's objective is not to invent new subject matter but to develop new ways of treating traditional themes. In this regard, the poet is like the medieval exegete, who preserves the past and develops intricate ways of extending it. The poet has definite roles to play in the pursuit of innovation as well as traditional craft.

RENAISSANCE AND NEOCLASSICAL THEORY AND CRITICISM

While Renaissance and neoclassical literary theory and criticism display a renewed interest in Greek and Latin classics, they also manifest a new concern with vernacular languages and national literatures. Spanning the sixteenth, seventeenth, and eighteenth centuries, the debates between the ancients and the moderns began in Italy and extended throughout western Europe, setting the framework for much of the theory and criticism of the time—and addressing problems that are still with us today.

The defenders of the ancients directed attention to classical genres such as tragic drama and epic, holding them up as models for composition. At first, the ideal was not just to imitate the genres of antiquity but to use their languages, especially Latin. The argument for strictly adhering to classical forms grew out of a unique synthesis of Aristotle's *Poetics* and Horace's *Ars Poetica*. From the *Poetics*, Renaissance critics developed an appreciation for isolating and distinguishing genres, which they tended to treat prescriptively rather than descriptively. The most famous instance is the doctrine of the "three unities" (action, place, and time), which extrapolates from Aristotle's notion of the unity of action to demand that dramas have not only one action but also one setting and a brief span of fictional time (not exceeding one day). Here Aristotle's original description of a body of preexisting Greek tragedies is turned into a set of rules for the writing of plays. This position, which first emerged in the commentaries on Aristotle by the Italian Renaissance critic Ludovico Castelvetro, found its most influential expression a century later in the critical writings of the neoclassical French dramatist Pierre Corneille and the English poet John Dryden—both of whom in their creative works were dedicated to their native languages and literatures and thus combined modern and ancient perspectives.

Joined to the doctrine of the three unities was a special Horatian concern with "verisimilitude." In practice, this meant depicting historical realities and facts and excluding fantastic beings and events, except those that could be explained by Christian beliefs, such as the actions of God and demons. Critics often pointed to significant passages in Horace that stressed the importance of decorum and of copying the techniques and strategies of one's accomplished literary predecessors. The general sense was that by imitating classics, modern Renaissance and neoclassical writers were also imitating nature. This position was strongly advocated by the Italian critic Julius Caesar Scaliger and was later summed up memorably in one of the many witty neoclassical couplets of Alexander Pope's *An Essay on Criticism*. Pope notes that the youthful poet Virgil scorned to represent anything except nature when he set out to write the *Aeneid*: "But when t'examine ev'ry Part he came, / *Nature* and *Homer* were, he found, the *same*." Pope concludes from Virgil's example, "Learn hence for Ancient *Rules* a just Esteem; / To copy *Nature* is to copy *Them*."

In contrast to the ancients, the moderns in the debates not only appreciated but championed new literary forms that departed from the various classical genres. One among many examples is Giambattista Giraldi's defense of the new Renaissance romantic epic, epitomized by Ludovico Ariosto's *Orlando Furioso* and later by Edmund Spenser's *Faerie Queene*. Critics of these long poems pointed out that they lacked unity and verisimilitude and that they deviated markedly from the classical epic, but Giraldi praised the variety of Ariosto's poem as well as its "marvelous" incidents, claiming that it constituted a new genre not subject to classical rules. In a parallel move, Giacopo Mazzoni supported Dante's dream allegory in the *Divine Comedy*, stressing the importance of purely imaginary imitation. Informing both Mazzoni's and Giraldi's arguments is a view of the poet's creative powers as unbounded. Sir Philip Sidney captured the essence of this position, which set the stage for Shakespeare, when he stated, "Nature never set forth the earth in so rich tapestry as divers poets have done, neither with so pleasant rivers, fruitful trees, sweet-smelling flowers, nor whatsoever else may make the too-much-loved earth more lovely: her world is brazen, the poets only deliver a golden."

With this defense by the moderns of the unfettered powers of the poet also came a defense of the use of vernacular languages in place of Latin. Critics and poets began to believe that they could rival the great literary achievements of Greece and Rome with their respective native languages. This trend began as early as Dante, whose *Divine Comedy* was composed in Italian, but in the Renaissance it spread across western Europe. The Italian language was defended by Giraldi and Mazzoni, the French language by Joachim du Bellay and Pierre de Ronsard, and the English language by Sidney and George Puttenham. The turn to the vernacular reflected the growing national consciousness of the time and an increasing preoccupation with distinct national literary traditions.

ROMANTIC THEORY AND CRITICISM

The Romantic movement in the arts developed in the latter half of the eighteenth century, inspired in part by the American and French Revolutions, and it flourished in the early nineteenth century, spreading throughout Europe and the New World. Although it manifests a variety of forms in specific social and historical contexts, the major characteristic of Romanticism is arguably its focus on the individual. Romantic theory was influenced by the philosopher Immanuel Kant's attention to the ways in which subjectivity determines our apprehension of the world. It was also influenced by the developing regard for individual sensibility and originality, a concern first manifested during the mid-eighteenth century.

In Romantic theory and criticism, emphasis on the individual led to an unprecedented focus on poetry as the personal expression of the poet—a development that aimed to counter the decorum, traditionalism, and preoccupation with genre that was characteristic of neoclassicism. Romantic poets such as Johann Wolfgang von Goethe, William Wordsworth, and Percy Bysshe Shelley all saw their art as intimately bound up with their personal impressions, moods, feelings, and sentiments, while Romantic critics such as Schleiermacher called for readers' sympathetic identification with the author.

In discussions of poetry, Romantics drew attention to how the imagination transforms and synthesizes discrete sense perceptions, creating unique organic poems. Perhaps the most celebrated instance of this focus appears in *Biographia Literaria*, where Samuel Taylor Coleridge claims that the poet "diffuses a tone and spirit of unity, that blends, and (as it were) *fuses*, each into each, by that synthetic and magical power, to which we have exclusively appropriated the name of imagination." This Romantic view of the poem as an organic form developed by the individual imagination was contrary to the neoclassical dictate that artists must imitate previous works of art and follow the rules of their genre. As exemplified by Coleridge, Elizabeth Robinson Montagu, and others, it led to a renewed appreciation of the unique creative genius of Shakespeare, whose unusual and irregular plays were often criticized by neoclassical theorists for ignoring the unities of action, time, and place. Later, the Romantic concept of organic form, shorn of theorizing about the author, would inspire early twentieth-century formalist theories of intricate poetic structure and coherence.

The Romantic fascination with the synthesizing power of the imagination paralleled an abiding concern with the symbol, displayed most famously in the writings of Coleridge and Ralph Waldo Emerson. For the Romantics, the poetic symbol expressed universal ideas through particular concrete details, images, and metaphors. Unlike allegory, which they condemned as a mechanical imposition of meaning and morality onto poetry, the poetic symbol manifested its meaning organically, providing aesthetic pleasure and beauty as well as moral truth. According to Friedrich von Schiller, the process of reading a poem was an experience of "play"—a serious play that reconciled the particular and the general and brought an uplifting sense of freedom to the reader and the poet, saving them from the alienation and despair of the modern world. For the Romantics, poetry—through the symbol—humanized an increasingly dehumanized world.

The genre of choice during the Romantic era in England was the lyric poem, which displaced the epic poem favored by neoclassical writers. Long Romantic poems tended to be arrangements of lyric pieces, as in Wordsworth's *Prelude*. Of all the available genres, the lyric poem was best suited for the expression of individual emotion. Not uncommonly, the lyric appeared as a "fragment," a technique that further stressed the break with neoclassicism, which valued unity, wholeness, and rational design. Some lyrics aimed to attain the sublime, associated with robust imaginative grandeur, infinity, irrationality, plus fear and terror, which was achieved less through sophisticated style and rhetoric (as in the classical writer Longinus, the earliest theorist of the sublime) than by the force of individual genius.

The long struggle of the novel to be regarded as a serious literary form as yet had little effect on theory and criticism, though this genre (especially the Gothic novel) thrived during the Romantic period. The classical hierarchy of literary genres—epic followed by tragic drama and then by lyric poetry—left little room for the novel until Victorian times. Even today the novel often cedes pride of place in literary history to epic poetry and tragic drama, though perhaps no longer to lyric poetry.

A final significant trait of Romantic theory was an emphasis on historical stages of development. The changing social, political, and economic conditions around them prompted many thinkers to ponder literary and cultural history. In theory and criticism, such attention led to repeated attempts—by Jean-Jacques Rousseau, G. W. F. Hegel, Germaine de Staël, and others—to correlate specific forms of literature and the arts to specific historical periods. Often, poetry was identified—as it had earlier been by Giambattista Vico—with "primitive" forms of society, in which people were purportedly less rational and more intuitive. This concern with the dynamics of history was to have a significant impact on the influential work of Karl Marx.

MARXISM

From ancient times, literature and the arts have portrayed, and criticism and theory have discussed, differences in people's social class and history. But with the spread and maturation of capitalism through its various stages, economic and other disparities have more visibly polarized wealthy and poor classes, city residents and ghetto dwellers, inhabitants of the first and third worlds, whites and people of color, men and women. Class formations, class consciousness, and class tensions form part of the historical experience of modernization, and theory and criticism have been grappling with these and related issues for several centuries now.

Many of the current concepts, terms, and issues related to social class derive from Marxist criticism, a diverse and influential source for literary and cultural theory that stems from the work of the nineteenth-century German philosopher and economist Karl Marx. One of its grounding concepts is Marx's theory of "modes of production." According to Marxism, human history is divided into seven successive historical modes of production—tribal hordes, Neolithic kinship societies, oriental despotism, ancient slaveholding societies, feudalism, capitalism, and communism. Class conflict within a specific mode of production follows a basic overall pattern. The capitalist or bourgeois mode of modern times has been characterized mainly by the conflict between the industrial working class (the *proletariat*, or labor) and the owners and manipulators of the means of production (the *bourgeoisie*). Other classes, including the unemployed and criminals (the *lumpenproletariat*) as well as the dwindling aristocracy, watch this conflict from the historical sidelines. Sooner or later, Marx predicted, international labor will win and the communist mode of production will emerge triumphant, leading to a society free from rampant inequality, exploitation, and class struggle.

According to Marxist theory, the socioeconomic elements of society constitute its base (or foundation), while its cultural spheres—specifically its politics, law, religion, philosophy, and arts—compose its superstructure. *Ideology* consists of the ideas, beliefs, forms, and values of the ruling class that circulate through all the cultural spheres. Members of the working class who subscribe to bourgeois ideas and values exhibit "false consciousness," since such values ignore the socioeconomic realities of their own working-class lives. *Hegemony* designates the continuous ideological domination of all classes by the ruling bloc through such nonviolent stabilizing and consensus-building institutions as church, school, family, the media, the mainstream arts, trade unions, business interests, and technoscientific establishments. These institutions are what Louis Althusser, a leading Marxist theorist, calls "Ideological State Apparatuses" (ISAs): they manage instability and conflict to impose and maintain social order, working for the most part outside of official state power.

Culture and the arts in the Marxist view are neither innocent entertainment nor independent of social forces; they play a significant role in transmitting ideology and shoring up the hegemonic order. This is not to say that artists and intellectuals are merely mouthpieces of the dominant social class or bloc, because many explicitly protest the ruling systems and implicitly address their contradictions and shortcomings. The ideological orientations of a literary work can be complicated: a text often contains mixed and contradictory messages that reflect its broad social milieu rather than simply its author's personal philosophy. From a Marxist perspective, artistic works frequently present fugitive, alternative, and counterhegemonic images sometimes suggesting liberatory possibilities and lending them a socially critical undertone.

Viewed from the vantage point of stylistics (the branch of linguistics that analyzes literary style), the conflicts of classes and groups in society produce what Bakhtin famously called "heteroglossia"—that is, the complex stratification of a language like English into different dialects, generational slangs, professional argots, speech genres, group codes, literary genres, and class mannerisms. Many novels (for example, James Joyce's *Ulysses*) incorporate such social conflicts in the form of heteroglot discourse, a carnivalization of different "languages" that revolt against official style.

With the rise of consumer and multinational capitalism, many have found Karl Marx's concepts of the *commodity, commodity fetishism,* and *commodification* increasingly useful for understanding culture and society, and thus the terms often appear in the writings of contemporary critics and theorists. Commodities are goods or services produced primarily for monetary exchange and profit—a carpenter may, for example, build a table to sell, not to use. For him or her, this commodity has exchange value, not use value. Labor itself has come to be bought and sold in a money economy; rather than being applied by isolated workers during the production of goods for personal use, it is more typically used in the service of another to earn and then exchange money for items necessary for subsistence.

The fetishism of the commodity describes both our fascination as we stand before a glittering array of products in a store and our forgetting the paid labor of workers that went into the products. This displacement of use value from the commodity—its transformation into cash exchange—results in the alienation of workers from their own labor: carpenters in the factory care little about the tables they assemble. Moreover, the extraction of high rates of profit by owners from their workers' labor results in exploitation, which is a key element of commodity exchange. The term *commodification* names this whole accelerating phenomenon of producing goods and services not for their use value but their exchange value, a phenomenon that threatens to overtake every sphere of life in our time. From pollution credits to underground fashion and music to sexual mates, everything and anything can be purchased as a commodity.

Marxist critics complain that commodification promotes reification, the tendency to view people and human relations as things or objects with price tags. In the arts, for instance, commodification leads artists to hawk their works anxiously to gain profits in an impersonal, competitive market, and it has positioned critics as the hired advisers to moneyed collectors. Observing this process, theorists wonder if criticism and the arts can any longer possess a socially critical dimension.

Contemporary Marxist critics and cultural studies scholars (who are indebted to Marxism) increasingly worry about the co-optation by the market (and the media) of every form of resistance, ranging across the arts and popular culture. If outrageous radical vanguard movements such as surrealism, punk, and gangsta rap can become profitable commodities, is opposition to hegemony possible? The agencies of commodification and hegemonic incorporation threaten to defuse the radical force of all subversive artistic practices, transforming them into hot news stories and merchandise destined for the market economy. Marxist criticism and cultural studies aim their critical inquiries at this system and its dynamics.

PSYCHOANALYSIS

It is often said that Sigmund Freud discovered the unconscious, but it is more accurate to say that he and other psychoanalysts mapped its spaces and mechanisms. The findings of psychoanalysis have filtered into literary and cultural criticism and theory, providing a battery of terms, concepts, and problems that reach beyond those critics who describe themselves as psychoanalytic.

According to psychoanalysis, the human psyche consists of unconscious and conscious spheres, with most of its contents lodged out of sight in the unconscious and covered over by a relatively smaller and less dense consciousness. The keys to the dark and inaccessible unconscious lie, psychoanalysts say, in free association, fantasies, slips of the tongue (so-called Freudian slips), and especially dreams, all of which reveal deeply buried, repressed, and self-censored wishes. The techniques used to interpret such unconscious materials, particularly dreams, have been useful to literary and cultural critics as well as psychoanalysts, since they are all in the business of deciphering cryptic symbolic texts.

The nightly formation of dreams, or the *dream-work* in Freudian terminology, involves the censorship of unconscious wishes (frequently sexual) that undergo four kinds of deliberate, positive distortion on their way to consciousness: condensation, displacement, symbolization, and secondary revision or elaboration. These unconscious processes explain why dreams usually emerge as garbled "nonsense." The task of the psychoanalyst is, with the help of the patient, to make sense of dream texts. Here, psychoanalysis asserts that nonsense is meaningful and that distortion is inescapable and creative. Both assertions are taken seriously by many critics and theorists as they work to understand texts, especially since literary discourses are sometimes as seemingly nonsensical and distorted as dreams. Psychoanalytic decoding of symbols has proved particularly illuminating to critics, including those followers of Carl Jung who have made inventories of archetypes—universal symbols such as the garden and the desert, water and fire, the hero and the monster, the river journey and the ordeal, birth and death—that they believe are stored in humanity's collective unconscious.

Many highly influential modern and postmodern theories of literature are indebted to psychoanalysis and its foundational concept of the unconscious. Two examples of such psychopoetics—Harold Bloom's "anxiety of influence" and French feminism's *écriture féminine*—illustrate the richness and complexity of psychoanalytic theories. According to Bloom, each major poet in the Anglo-American tradition from the early Romantics to the late modernists has suffered a devastating yet productive anxiety of influence, as the newcomer poet selects a role model both to imitate and to compete against, wishing ultimately to emerge as a major poet who triumphs over (but triumphs because of) the poetic precursor. Prior to the neoclassical and Romantic periods, literary influence was almost entirely beneficial (as in the case, say, of Spenser's influence on Milton). With the rise of the subjective lyric poem as a major genre, influence became baleful, involving the aspiring poet's primal repression of the precursor plus a series of later psychological defenses against this parent figure, including masochistic reversals, sublimations, introjections, regressions, and projections. These entail what Bloom calls "misprision" (mistaking, misreading, misinterpreting), the inescapable and necessary creative distortion enacted unconsciously in the newcomer's poems in imitation of, and competition with, the loved but hated precursor. Bloom has been criticized for focusing on competition instead of collaboration, for favoring canonical poets over less well known poets, and for omitting nearly all writing by women, but Bloom's critics have rarely questioned the usefulness of his theoretical understanding of distortion or of unconscious repression, two psychoanalytical concepts widely used in the field of theory and criticism.

The literary theory of *écriture féminine* (feminine/female writing) derives from the work of the celebrated psychoanalyst Jacques Lacan, as creatively revised by the French feminist Hélène Cixous. According to Lacan's challenging theory, an infant moves during its earliest psychosocial development from an "Imaginary order"—a mother-centered, nonsubjugated, presymbolic, pre-oedipal space of bodily drives and rhythms (linked with the unconscious)—to a "Symbolic order" of separation between self and (m)other, of law and patriarchal social codes, and of loss and associated desire (linked with consciousness). *Écriture féminine* is a radical, disruptive mode of "feminine" writing that is opposed to patriarchal discourse with its rigid grammar, boundaries, and categories; tapping into the Imaginary, it gives voice to the unconscious, the body, the nonsubjective, and polymorphous drives. Even though such feminine writing can be produced by male as well as female writers (for example, by Jean Genet and James Joyce), it is a psychopoetics positioned by Cixous explicitly against patriarchal values and practices.

In both the anxiety of influence and *écriture féminine*, as in psychoanalysis generally, Freud's theory of the "Oedipus complex" plays a central role. According to this theory, an infant must successfully complete various stages of development (oral, anal, oedipal) to ensure later psychological well-being. In the oedipal stage, the (male) child must separate from the mother and identify with the father on his way to entering the Symbolic order. The Oedipus complex is displayed by those males whose failure to negotiate the oedipal stage of development leaves them deeply attached to their mothers and often feeling rivalry with their fathers. Bloom's theory of the anxiety of influence presents a parallel rivalry with the father. And *écriture féminine* is a feminist effort to reconceive the pre-oedipal sphere as a highly positive source of creativity and liberation, rather than simply an infantile domain of irrational instincts that we must abandon.

Perhaps the most famous contemporary revision of Freudian oedipal theory appears in Gilles Deleuze and Félix Guattari's Marxist and psychoanalytical *Anti-Oedipus*, a book that criticizes many aspects of Freud's work—notably, the bourgeois presupposition that the nuclear family is the universal framework for all normal human development. According to Deleuze and Guattari, Freudian theory subjugates the disruptive unconscious—with its often antisocial desires and flows—to the hegemonic order of the patriarchal family, the rule of law, and the capitalist economy. Freud's psychoanalysis, focused as it is on the oedipal triangle, is unable to acknowledge the truly complex nature of subjectivity, seen by Deleuze and Guattari as an open-ended process of becoming in which multiple contradictory positions and roles coexist and clash.

FORMALISM

Formalist criticism rose to prominence in the early twentieth century, usually defining itself as objective in opposition to subjectivist theories of literature such as critical impressionism, which was perceived to be both solipsistic and relativistic. Formalist criticism is not interested in the feelings of poets, the individual responses of readers, or representations of "reality"; instead, it attends to artistic structure and form. It privileges the work over against the artist, audience, and universe. The two best-known schools of formalist criticism are Anglo-American New Criticism and Russian formalism.

As discussed above, New Critics approach literature—particularly poetry—as an autonomous entity. They focus on the form of the literary object, self-consciously separating literary criticism from the study of sources, biography, reception, social and historical contexts, politics, and other "extrinsic" matters. They depersonalize poetry and attribute its speaking not to the poet but to the so-called *persona* (an abstract dramatic character internal to the work). They advocate "intrinsic" analysis or "close reading" (explication) that avoids paraphrase and thematic statements, examining instead the complex stylistic orchestrations that compose poetry. What New Critics seek in their studies of poetic form is a set of "organic" relationships of literary elements (images, symbols, tropes, features of genre and style, settings, and tones), whose overall unity often depends on artful ambiguity, paradox, or irony. This special state of aesthetic suspension that underwrites the all-important unity—reminiscent of Kant's earlier "purposiveness without purpose" and Coleridge's "balance or reconciliation of opposite or discordant qualities"—is for them a defining feature of poetry. It distinguishes the literary from the more ordinary uses of language found in journalism, everyday speech, scientific writing, and so on, where direct communication, not highly wrought aesthetic form, is most important.

Similarly, Russian formalist critics such as Roman Jakobson and Boris Eichenbaum distinguish between the literary and the nonliterary. They view literature primarily as a verbal art, rather than as a reflection of reality or an expression of emotions. Separating literary criticism from such fields as psychology, sociology, and intellectual history, they focus on the distinguishing features of literature, its "literariness." What most separates literature from other modes of discourse is that it draws attention to its own medium, that is, to a complex texture of formal devices and strategies that include versification, style, and narrative structure. Whereas New Critics study the artful convergence of elements in a literary structure (aesthetic unity), Russian formalists examine the creative deviation of elements from the historical background of literary norms and conventions.

The importance of formalism, especially the Anglo-American variety, cannot be underestimated in Anglophone spheres. Because it is a dominant mode of modern criticism against which much later postmodern theory typically defines itself in whole or in part, we refer to it later in this introduction to develop a fuller account.

RECEPTION THEORY AND HERMENEUTICS

Contemporary critical theory offers a rich panoply of types of readers—ideal readers, superreaders, implied readers, virtual readers, real readers, historical readers, resisting readers, critical readers, and more. Such terms are usually found in reader-response theory and reception aesthetics, realms that focus on theories of readers and meaning.

In reading a novel, we can sometimes extrapolate from it an implied reader, a figure whom the text seems to be addressing and who occasionally functions as a character in the work (for example, the characters to whom Marlow tells his story in Joseph Conrad's *Heart of Darkness*). An implied reader differs both from a virtual reader, to whom the text is vaguely addressed by the author, and from a historical reader, who actually reads the text at the time of its publication. The hypothetical perfect decoder of the work, who knows everything necessary to make sense of it, is the ideal reader; but the most original and innovative texts require a superreader, a special ideal reader endowed not only with extensive linguistic and literary knowledge but also with superior aesthetic sensibility. Both the critical and the resisting reader, situated in definite historical moments and possessing strong values and interests, find themselves opposing and interrogating texts (imagine an average American or Briton today reading Hitler's *Mein Kampf*). Real readers are people whose actual responses to novels, plays, poems, and other texts have been recorded by theorists and, in some cases, analyzed for their individual styles and for the personal psychological quirks that they reveal.

Theories of meaning accompany these accounts of various readers. Some reader-response theories construe meaning as an entity located in the text or in a paraphrase of the text and thus view readers as discovering objective textual meanings. But other reader-response theories argue that insofar as reading occurs through time and involves the continuous adjustment of perceptions, ideas, feelings, and evaluations, the meaning of a work is the moment-by-moment experience of it, not something separate or left over. Meaning is therefore a process, not a product; it is an event, not a retrospective reconstruction or intellectual reformulation. This subjectivist theory of meaning has limitations, however: it endorses the idea of reading as private consumption, and it construes *experience* as a straightforward, unconditioned, conscious, and knowable process.

Some reception theorists see meaning as a production dependent on preexisting social codes and protocols of interpretation. In this view, every interpretive community—for example, psychoanalytical critics—employs a particular set of interpretive strategies for (re)writing (that is, producing) texts and for constituting their properties, intentions, and meanings. Such preestablished strategies determine the shape of meaning, which is neither prior to nor independent of the act of interpretation.

The New Critics approach meaning differently. They famously warn against the "heresy of paraphrase," emphasizing that it is a mistake for a reader to paraphrase a work's content in order to distill its propositional meaning. Textual paraphrases usually end up being moral or utilitarian statements, putting literature on a level and in competition with other disciplines such as philosophy, religion, or politics. By invoking the "affective fallacy" and "intentional fallacy," two related and equally famous New Critical concepts, they forbid us to locate meaning in the emotional responses of the reader or in the intentions of the author, respectively. According to the New Critics, the literary artifact does not need the support of such external agents if it is well made. The sense of *meaning* becomes complex and abstract for these formalists. On the one hand, it is a secondary, relatively unimportant feature of literary structure; on the other, it is an aesthetic concept of organic unity that reconciles textual incongruities with the aid of irony, paradox, and ambiguity. New Criticism is celebrated for telling us what meaning is not: it is not propositional truth, nor the author's intention, nor a reader's response.

To clarify the concept, some theorists, such as the hermeneuticist E. D. Hirsch Jr., have added the notion of significance. While significance changes, meaning does not. Here meaning is construed as a fixed, self-identical, reproducible object derived from the author's intention. Significance, which builds on meaning, adds the reader's personal associations, interests, values, and contexts. Over time a text may come to have a different significance but not a different meaning. The reader therefore operates on two levels, one subjective and one objective, with the latter seen as higher according to Hirsch.

Meaning is often understood as having multiple levels, with the reader playing different roles as part of one complicated task. Consider approaches as different as the medieval hermeneutical division of textual meaning into four levels (literal, allegorical, moral, mystical), which emphasizes the spiritual realm, and Fredric Jameson's Marxist attention to three horizons of meaning (social stratification, class struggle, mode of production), which aims to discover the critical utopian elements of cultural texts. Such levels or horizons inevitably are set in hierarchies, a process that leads to disagreements among theorists as they argue over which should take priority.

Hermeneutics is a discipline that studies understanding and textual interpretation, including scriptural, literary, and legal discourses. Though it spans classical to contemporary times, the dominant tradition stems from modern German philosophy, notably the works of Schleiermacher, Dilthey, Heidegger, and Gadamer. The conservative philological tradition of Schleiermacher and Hirsch regards meaning as both stable and changeable, the result of objective and personal interpretations, textual reconstruction, and psychological identifications. But priority is placed firmly on objective historical reconstruction and fixed meaning, not on secondary private associations. The liberal phenomenological tradition, on the other hand, considers meaning an intimate encounter, an open-ended performance, an interested and careful interaction rooted in life experience and expectations. It has interest neither in impersonal, objective textual reconstruction nor in the quest for valid methods to ensure the one correct interpretation.

A very influential contribution of hermeneutics to contemporary theory of interpretation is Paul Ricoeur's distinction between negative suspicious and positive restorative interpretation. Associated with Marxism, psychoanalysis, and poststructuralism, the "hermeneutics of suspicion" aims to demystify illusions—for example, to uncover unconscious motivations, to reveal ideology, to deconstruct traditional binary concepts. Conversely, positive hermeneutics seeks to provide access to essential sources of life, such as utopian impulses, possibilities of happiness, communal dialogue. Near the end of *The Political Unconscious*, Jameson extends Ricoeur and declares that "a Marxist negative hermeneutic, a Marxist practice of ideological analysis proper, must in the practical work of reading and interpretation be exercised *simultaneously* with a Marxist positive hermeneutic, or a decipherment of the Utopian impulses of these same still ideological cultural texts." To the scrupulous, attentive, historically positioned general reader of hermeneutics, philological and phenomenological, Jameson adds the future-oriented political reader.

With the turn of literary studies to cultural studies in recent decades, reader-response criticism and theory morphed into broader reception and audience studies. Here the focus is on nonacademic, nonelite vernacular interpretive communities and the reading strategies they deploy. Typical groups investigated include women's reading clubs dedicated to popular literature (e.g., romance novels), fan subcultures devoted to specific television series or movies such as *Star Trek*, and 'zine communities built up around particular music bands. In this work, cultural studies researchers use ethnographic and participant-observer methods borrowed from sociology, privileging sympathetic insider's views of underground, alternative, and deviant reading communities. In studying a reading club of forty-two lower-middle-class heterosexual women from the Midwest in *Reading the Romance*, Janice Radway documented a wide range of nonacademic reading practices. Consumers of romance novels, it turns out, read rapidly, often skip to the end, pay no attention to literary style, ignore critical distance and objectivity, identify strongly with characters (especially heroines), and care most about story and plot line. They share strong dislikes, which is to say they have prescriptive criteria: no violent heroes, weak heroines, pornography, unhappy or ambiguous endings. Such vernacular readers possess standards that enable them to distinguish good from bad romance. For the members of this group, meaning fuses public and private feelings connected to the compensatory utopian dimensions of romance fiction. This genre of literature is set against a world of often nonexpressive, ungentle husbands preoccupied with work and sports. Here meaning is tied up not only with fantasy, pleasure, escape, and therapy but also with relaxation, restoration, and leisure in the context of being on call 24/7. Speaking hermeneutically, meaning and significance become inseparable in this setting.

At the start of the twenty-first century a number of literary theorists launched complaints about the dominance of suspicious negative hermeneutics and symptomatic reading associated with Marxism, feminism, psychoanalysis, and cultural studies. Especially prominent were various new formalist advocates of "surface reading," who construe cultural critique as paranoid and call for reparative and positive, descriptive and appreciative "looking at" rather than "looking through" literature.

STRUCTURALISM AND SEMIOTICS

Pioneering concepts and methods of structural linguistics and anthropology strongly influenced how modern theory and criticism understand cultural phenomena. From structuralist methodology has come the discipline of semiotics or semiology, a field that studies sign systems, codes, and conventions of all kinds, ranging from human to animal languages, the language of fashion to the lexicon of food, the codes of diagnostic medicine to those of written literature. By extension, literary semiotics construes its primary object of analysis to be literature as a system, while social (or cultural) semiotics explores culture as a set of interlocking systems and subsystems.

The model for structuralist thinking is Ferdinand de Saussure's linguistics, which centers not on individual utterances but on the underlying rules and conventions that enable language to operate. Saussurean structuralism analyzes the social or collective dimensions of language, focusing on grammar rather than usage, rules rather than actual expressions, and *langue* (the system of language) rather than *parole* (actual speech). This linguistics is concerned with the infrastructure of language common to all speakers at a given time (which operates on an unconscious level), and not with surface phenomena or historical change. Thus it attends to the synchronic (that which exists now), not the diachronic (that which exists and changes over time).

In valuing deep structure over surface phenomena, structuralism resembles Marxism and psychoanalysis, both of which examine underlying causes and transpersonal forces of complex systems, shifting attention away from individual human consciousness and choice. Structuralism thereby shares in the widespread and ongoing modern antihumanism and posthumanism that decenter the individual, portraying the self as a construct and a consequence of impersonal systems. Individuals neither originate nor control the conventions of their social existence, mental life, or mother tongue. Rather, they are created by social and cultural systems, within which they are subjects. For this reason, many contemporary theorists, especially structuralist, Marxist, and psychoanalytical critics, prefer the terms *subject* and *subjectivity* to *person* or *individual*.

To get a sense of the kinds of projects that structuralism and semiotics might undertake, consider the fashion system. As members of a society, people know which items of clothing, textures, colors, and styles go with which. In most Western societies today, sneakers don't properly fit with a tuxedo, a top hat doesn't work with jeans and a T-shirt, and a pair of red shoes, an orange skirt, and a purple blouse simply don't go together. Few people would be able to supply a complete written description of all the unconscious but well-known rules of dress, but such a list could be created—by structuralists and semioticians.

Similarly, sophisticated literary readers as well as authors possess a considerable amount of knowledge in the form of not-quite-explicit conventions and rules of reading, which structuralist poetics aims to chart. Most stories can be reduced to one of a few underlying basic plots, and most characters are variations on a few types, which structuralist narratology aims to inventory. Like language, literature is a system of conventions most noticeable in the rules of genres.

POSTSTRUCTURALISM AND DECONSTRUCTION

In the late twentieth century, poststructuralism set the terms and the agenda for many of the major developments and debates in the field of theory and criticism. It played, and continues to play, a significant role in shaping the direction of other schools and movements, particularly feminist criticism, postcolonial theory, cultural studies, film studies, and queer theory. Originally a vanguard movement of French literary intellectuals and philosophers who came into prominence during the 1960s and 1970s and who were critical of yet indebted to structuralism, it quickly spread to intellectuals around the globe. By the close of the twentieth century, poststructuralism had become the leading edge of postmodernism and was often labeled "postmodern theory."

We have already touched on many of the main features of poststructuralism. They include the problematizing of linguistic referentiality, an emphasis on heteroglossia, the decentering of the subject, the rejection of "reason" as universal or foundational, the criticism of humanism, a stress on difference over sameness, and the theory of the social text.

Some poststructuralist accounts of literature derive from deconstructive theory, especially its three interconnected concepts of textuality (or floating signifiers), rhetoricity, and intertextuality. Because the signifier (word) is disconnected from the signified (concept) and the referent (thing), language floats or slides in relation to reality, a condition made more severe with the additional sliding introduced by figurative language, such as metaphors and metonymies. Such rhetoricity adds layers of substitutions and supplements (more differences) to floating signifiers. Textuality and rhetoricity are conditioned by a third sliding or differential element, intertextuality—a text's dependence on prior words, concepts, connotations, codes, conventions, unconscious practices, and texts. Every text is an intertext that borrows, knowingly or not, from the immense archive of previous culture. The term *(inter)textuality*, with the parentheses, captures the sense of textuality as being conditioned by this inescapable historical intertext.

The technical term *dissemination* is commonly employed to name the deconstructive concept of textual meaning; rather than being simply ambiguous or paradoxical, as in earlier New Criticism, meaning here is sliding, abyssal, undecidable. The linguistic, rhetorical, and intertextual properties of language undermine or deconstruct stable meaning. Poststructuralist theories of language, whether they focus on floating signifiers, rhetoricity, intertextuality, dissemination, *écriture féminine*, or elsewhere, bring traditional mimetic, expressive, didactic, and formalist theories into crisis but do not invalidate their claims. This "undecidability," a hallmark of Jacques Derrida's and Paul de Man's deconstruction, galvanizes opponents—particularly when joined to the related poststructuralist claim of the "death of the author," which disconnects the text from any sure grounding in authorial intention or psychology.

Deconstructive conceptions of reading as both misreading and misprision, discussed earlier, do not signal an end to textual interpretation but change its grounds. The redoubled reading typical of much deconstruction often rests on claims of interest and insight, not of validity or truth. A reading or interpretation of a text does not prove but persuades: it is more or less compelling, productive, original, or useful.

Deconstruction originated in the name of a special difference (or *différance*), stemming from both structural linguistics and phenomenological philosophy. It denotes the structure of differences that defines both the sliding (differential) operation of the signifier-signified complex and, more abstractly, the existence of entities that are already differentiated and divided because they necessarily exist in space and in time. Each bluebird is singular. Leftist-oriented poststructuralism extends these concepts of ontological difference and differential meaning, adding sociopolitical differences in class, gender, sexuality, race, ethnicity, and nationality. There is no more multifaceted term in contemporary poststructuralist theory than *difference*.

Deconstruction is not just a school and branch of poststructuralism but also an analytic procedure developed by Derrida, a historian of philosophy, that quickly became a methodological instrument widely used by literary and cultural theorists and critics. "A deconstruction" involves *inversion* and *reinscription* of a traditional philosophical opposition. First, one locates in a chosen text a significant conceptual opposition (for example, nature/culture, purity/contamination, animality/humanity, or male/female) at a moment of maximum instability. To invert the binary pair, one shows how the belated second term is actually indispensable and constitutively prior to the primary term. For instance, it is from the vantage point of culture that nature is named and defined; similarly, the idea of purity depends on the prior possibility of contamination. Second, to reinscribe the terms of the opposition, one must destabilize and transform—deconstruct—the usual understanding of the concepts, especially their temporal and hierarchical relations. Thus Derrida famously deconstructed the speech/writing opposition by showing how writing precedes speech; characteristically, he reinscribes the concept of writing (*écriture* in French) to mean any and all forms of inscription in any medium. In doing so, he undercuts the privileging of speech as face-to-face spontaneous utterance.

Certain branches and strands of poststructuralism focus on desire, the body, and subjectivity rather than on textuality, rhetoricity, and deconstruction. Two cases mentioned earlier (in the discussion of psychoanalytic criticism) are the theories of *écriture féminine* and anti-Oedipus. In this domain—where psychoanalysis, gender studies, cultural studies, and poststructuralism intersect—the problems of subject formation, gender identity, and political resistance link poststructuralism not only with cultural studies and feminist theory but also with postcolonial criticism, queer theory, and related movements and schools. To its opponents, the deconstructive strands of poststructuralism concerned with the rhetoricity and undecidability of literary texts seem narrowly focused, conservative, formalistic, and apolitical. Poststructuralism in its political form is also interested in popular culture, minority literatures, radical politics, "deviant" subjectivities, and the dynamics of hegemonic institutions. A great deal of common ground, therefore, is shared by political poststructuralism, Marxism, and postmodern social activism such as the feminist, lesbian, gay, and ethnic rights movements. The fusion of approaches, disciplines, and movements can be confusing, but it has produced some interesting and original criticism and theory, and is arguably a leading trait of postmodern culture.

FEMINISM

Feminist criticism is part of the broader feminist political movement that seeks to rectify sexist discrimination and inequalities. Its broad goals include exposing masculinist stereotypes, distortions, and omissions in male-dominated literature; studying female creativity, genres, styles, themes, careers, and literary traditions; discovering and evaluating lost and neglected literary works by women; developing feminist theoretical concepts and methods; examining the forces that shape women's lives, literature, and criticism, ranging across psychology and politics, biology and cultural history; and creating new ideas of and roles for women, including new institutional arrangements. Feminist theory and criticism have brought revolutionary change to literary and cultural studies by expanding the canon, by critiquing sexist representations and values, by stressing the importance of gender and sexuality, and by advocating institutional and social reforms.

Theorists of a "feminist aesthetic" argue that women have a literature of their own, possessing its own images, themes, characters, forms, styles, and canons. In Elaine Showalter's pioneering account of British novelists from the early nineteenth century to the 1970s, for example, women writers form a subculture sharing distinctive economic, political, and professional realities, all of which determine specific problems and artistic preoccupations that mark women's literature. Sandra M. Gilbert and Susan Gubar propose that nineteenth-century women writers had to negotiate alienation and psychological disease in order to attain literary authority, which they achieved by reclaiming the heritage of female creativity, remembering their lost foremothers, and refusing the debilitating cultural roles of *angel* and *monster* assigned to them by patriarchal society. Countering Harold Bloom's masculinist "anxiety of influence," Gilbert and Gubar's "anxiety of authorship" depicts the precursor poet as a sister or mother whose example enables the creativity of the latecomer writer to develop collaboratively against the confining and sickening backdrop of forbidding male literary authority. Diseases common among women in male-dominated, misogynistic societies include agoraphobia, anorexia, bulimia, claustrophobia, hysteria, and madness in general, and they recur in the images, themes, and characters of women's literature.

Judith Fetterley states in *The Resisting Reader: A Feminist Approach to American Fiction* that women read differently than men. She examines classic American fiction from Irving and Hawthorne to Hemingway and Mailer and points out that this is not "universal" but masculine literature, which forces women readers to identify against themselves. Such literature neither expresses nor legitimates women's experiences, and in reading it women have to think as men, identify with male viewpoints, accept male values and interests, and tolerate sexist hostility and oppression. Under such conditions, women must become "resisting readers" rather than assenting ones, using feminist criticism and critique as a way both to challenge male domination of the institutions of literature and to change society.

As concepts such as the anxiety of authorship, *écriture féminine*, and the matriarchal potential of the Imaginary order suggest, psychoanalysis is fundamental to much feminist theory and criticism. However, feminist psychoanalysis is typically revisionist: it has had to work through and criticize the "phallocentric" presuppositions and prejudices of Sigmund Freud, Jacques Lacan, and other pioneering psychoanalysts. The feminine anxiety of authorship—in its opposition to the masculine anxiety of influence—reconfigures the "oedipal" relationship between writers as cooperative and nurturing rather than competitive and rivalrous. Similarly, *écriture féminine* transforms Lacan's idea of the Imaginary, casting it not simply as an infantile sphere of primary drives superseded on the way to the patriarchal Symbolic order but as a liberating domain of bodily rhythms and pulsations associated with the mother that permeates literature—for example, modern experimental poetry. Moreover, the pre-Symbolic Imaginary order, a realm of bisexual/androgynous/polymorphous sexuality, opens the possibility of sexual liberation from the suffocating confines of the "compulsory heterosexuality" that dominates patriarchal culture.

Within feminist circles, there are political differences and conflicts of interest among women of color and white women, women from different classes, women of different sexualities, women belonging to different nations and regions, and women who are liberals, conservatives, radicals, and revolutionaries. Black women have asserted that white middle-class women, in academia as well as in the mass media, often end up speaking for feminism or for all women, even though they tend to represent only their own interests.

Third world women, abroad and at home (Latinas, Aboriginals, Asian women), feel silenced and unrepresented in mainstream social agendas, which rarely consider their needs or issues. Lesbian women have likewise organized themselves to ensure that their voices are heard. The "politics of difference" opens into a world of differences and multiple identities among and within women themselves.

A key flash point among feminist critics has been identity politics, by which is meant a politics of difference based on some fixed or definable feature(s) of identity (as in a middle-class white woman, a working-class black woman, a third world brown woman, and so on). Critics of such identity politics have several major points of contention. To begin with, defining feminist identity by giving priority to race or class or geography tends to essentialize these features, reducing people to social indicators whose "real essence" is determined by race or class or country of origin. Moreover, an emphasis on the multiplicity of female identities undermines the solidarity and united front of feminists. Advocates of the politics of difference respond, in turn, that the act of herding all women into one homogeneous category (Woman) is a reductive totalization and very unlikely to disturb the dominant order. They argue that alliances and coalitions, in strategic cooperation with other new social movements, will best and most democratically address issues of equality and recognition. In the spheres of theory and criticism, the micropolitics of difference challenges universal notions of traditional humanism and promotes two key ideas: there are many women's literatures across the globe, and there are many modes of resistance and of resisting reading.

QUEER THEORY

An influential field that has built on ideas from feminism, gender studies, women's studies, and lesbian and gay studies is queer theory. While it is sometimes defined broadly to include all non-straight sexualities, a more focused view exists. It begins by criticizing the dominant heterosexual binary, masculine/feminine, which enthrones "the" two sexes and which casts other sexualities as abnormal, illicit, or criminal. It attacks the homophobic and patriarchal bases of heterosexuality. But it aims beyond lesbian and gay rights philosophies to study other so-called perverse, deviant, and alternative sexualities. For example, queer theorists investigate the historical developments of such categories as *sodomite, hermaphrodite*, and *homosexual*, as well as *woman* and *man*, stressing the socially constructed character and hierarchy of sexualities. Of particular interest are transgressive phenomena such as drag, camp, cross-dressing, and transsexuality, all of which highlight the nonbiological, performative aspects of gender construction. To be "masculine" or "feminine" requires practicing an array of rituals, which cross-dressers faithfully mimic and parody in the production of gender identity.

Queer theorists point out that heteronormativity is an ideology embedded in social institutions ranging from the family, church, and school to the law, media, and politics. Its functioning relies on the firmness and continuous policing of the binary opposition normal/abnormal, which enables sexual minorities to be stigmatized and criminalized as well as pathologized. Foucault's work, especially *The History of Sexuality*, highlights the instability and arbitrariness of this crucial binary. In addition, French feminists deconstruct it in their explorations of the pre-oedipal sphere of the Imaginary order, a primordial realm of polysexuality. Like all identity, sexual identity is a social construct subject to regulations and norms set against instabilities and fluidities. It is, moreover, enmeshed with other social differences, including race and ethnicity, social class, and nationality.

Queer theory grapples with internal disputes over politics and activism. Such disputes take various forms—for example, street protest versus ivory tower theory, queer separatism versus assimilation (evident in debates over the "join them" strategy of gay marriage), queers of color versus white queers. At the same time, the ongoing worldwide criminalization of queer sexualities, plus the HIV/AIDS crisis during an era of resurgent religious fundamentalisms, has presented to queer people a threatening and punitive social order, subject to moral panics and waves of intolerance. Not surprisingly, much queer activism and politics rests less on fixed identities than on affinities.

Throughout the history of literature, there have been many queer writers, literary characters, and themes. One of the aims of queer theory and criticism is to recover this literature as well as to criticize omissions, distortions, and stereotypes present in mainstream criticism and literature. Another key aim is the broad critique of heteronormative ideology and culture.

POSTCOLONIAL STUDIES AND RACE AND ETHNICITY STUDIES

Postcolonial studies, an interdisciplinary field, examines the global impact of mainly European colonialism, from its beginnings in the fifteenth century to the present. Broadly speaking, it aims to describe the mechanisms of colonial power, to recover excluded or marginalized "subaltern" voices, and to theorize the complexities of colonial, neocolonial, and postcolonial identity, national belonging, and globalization. In our new century, it has branched out to investigate the long histories of other imperial empires across the globe.

One major issue concerns the nature of representation. Following the groundbreaking example of Edward Said's *Orientalism*, postcolonial critics have investigated the ways in which Western representations of third world countries serve the political interests of their makers. Postcolonial critics problematize "objective" perception, pointing out the unbalanced power relations that typically shape the production of knowledge. They have argued that the West has constructed the third world as an "Other." Such ideological projections become the negative terms of binary oppositions in which the positive terms are normative representations of the West. Further, these damaging stereotypes continue to circulate through anthropological, historical, and literary texts, as well as mass media such as newspapers, television, and the Internet.

A related line of inquiry in postcolonial theory studies how institutions of education function in the spread of imperialism. Historical documents such as Thomas Babington Macaulay's notorious "Minute on Indian Education"

(1835) show that education—including here the study of English literature and the English language—plays a strategic part in ruling over colonized peoples. As it inculcates Western Eurocentric values, literary education supports a kind of cultural colonization, creating a class of colonial subjects often burdened by a double consciousness and by divided loyalties. It helps Western colonizers rule by consent rather than by violence. The nature of this enterprise has led some—for example, Ngugi wă Thiong'o, Henry Owuor Anyumba, and Taban lo Liyong in "On the Abolition of the English Department"—to call for the dismantling of institutions of Western education in the third world.

The realization of the extent to which the cultures of colonizers and colonized interact has prompted reflections on the hybrid nature of identity and culture. No culture, one argument goes, is ever pure. This insight is everywhere evident in our own era of globalized postindustrial or neoliberal capitalism: the nationalism that undergirds notions of pure culture is daily called into question by the international flows of commodities, money, information, technology, and people. These dynamics of globalization, hybridization, and nationalism preoccupy scholars of postcolonial studies.

Postcolonial literary criticism focuses on literatures produced by subjects in the context of colonial domination: for instance, in Africa, Asia, and the Caribbean. Built on knowledge of the institutions of colonial education and the hybrid nature of culture, the analysis of postcolonial literature explores the complex interactions and antagonisms between native, indigenous, "precolonial" cultures and the imperial cultures imposed on them.

The concerns of postcolonial literary studies overlap with those of race and ethnicity studies, a broad field that examines a wide array of topics (including literature) related to minority ethnic groups; in North America, for example, these would include African, Asian, Hispanic, and Native peoples, among others. Consider the case of the 43 million African Americans today, whose history has included deportation, slavery, oppression, and struggle. Some scholars argue that the black community in the United States has evolved a distinctive and separate way of life, neither Anglo-Saxon nor African. The character of African American arts is communal rather than individualistic, the psychology is repudiative rather than accommodative of racism, and the tradition is oral-musical rather than textual. African Americans, the argument goes, possess their own values, styles, customs, themes, techniques, and genres. In the past, mainstream white critics have found the black arts to be grotesque, humorous, entertaining, inferior. African American artists have responded variously—sometimes adopting white values and forms, or rejecting them outright, or blending them into a hybrid. Literary critics engaged in race and ethnicity studies analyze the nature and dynamics of minority literatures, usually focusing on one group's literature but often in the context of dominant cultures (thereby overlapping with postcolonial studies).

Among the issues of long-standing concern among ethnic and race critics are racial purity (essence) and mixed blood; the status of racial experience and memory; internal differences of class, gender, and sexual orientation; national versus transnational identities and loyalties; the aesthetic as opposed to the sociological value of literature and the arts; and the place of theory. To what extent do differences of class, gender, sexuality, and skin color (or blood quantum), as well as ties to home, internally divide ethnic and racial communities? What roles do political separatism, integrationism, and transnational solidarity play? Is racial experience a personal social construction, an inherited and shared legacy, a paranoid projection? Is it reliable as a basis for solidarity and unity? What is the epistemological status of testimony, autobiography, and biography? A great deal of personal criticism has been written by ethnic intellectuals. Why? Is theory sometimes a tool of white Europeans employed to distract ethnic intellectuals? Do academic ethnic intellectuals have a special obligation to go public and address society rather than remaining in their labs and libraries engaged in professional discourse and advancement? Or must they work on both fronts?

What is perhaps most worth remarking in this context is the pioneering methodological richness of race and ethnicity studies: it draws from historicism, Marxism, psychoanalysis, formalism, structuralism and poststructuralism, feminism, queer theory, postcolonial criticism, and cultural studies. As in so much other contemporary criticism and theory, we encounter in race and ethnic studies innumerable crossovers, the mixing and matching of different strands and traditions of theory.

NEW HISTORICISMS

Those who write contemporary criticism and theory often turn toward history. Among the schools and movements that regularly historicize their topics of inquiry are Marxism, feminism, postcolonial criticism, ethnic and race studies, and queer theory. Reception aesthetics and hermeneutics also construe their objects of study historically. With the contemporary addition to the canon of long-lost literary works by women, people of color, and queers, archival research continues to play a productive role in criticism and theory. A great deal of the social history of minorities is nowadays written from the margins: it is usefully labeled "history from below." Not surprisingly, minorities feel compelled to (re)discover and (re-)create usable pasts. Such work often produces counterhistories set against weighty mainstream traditions and accounts. This is history with a critical edge. Capitalism has a history, dating back to the early Renaissance. So too do colonialisms. New chapters in these histories come forth regularly from contemporary critics and theorists. Jameson's influential story about postmodern third-stage late capitalism and Said's narrative of modern Western Orientalism are two prominent examples of contemporary historicism.

Some contemporary historical critics and theorists exhibit admiration for philology, the study of culture through linguistic analysis. Developed by Vico, Schleiermacher, and others during the Enlightenment, it has been extended in more recent times by Erich Auerbach and Hans Robert Jauss as well as Said and Jameson. Unlike history from below, philologically oriented history aspires to objectivity and uses the broadest possible canvas. Its scope is global rather than regional, and it stands in contrast to more narrowly gauged institutional history, such as we find in Richard Ohmann's account of the postwar New York publishing business and in Terry Eagleton's investigation of the late nineteenth-century British discipline of English studies. On a different note, psychohistory typically creates a sequence of case studies (psychological profiles) strung together to illustrate a historical thesis. Consider, for instance, the psychohistories of nineteenth- and twentieth-century Anglo-American male poets and women writers produced, respectively, by Bloom and by Gilbert and Gubar. One argues for an epochal anxiety of influence and the other for a countervailing anxiety of authorship. Both are broad historical claims.

Many contemporary literary scholars have fused the concerns of history from below, of Marxist history, of institutional history, and of psychohistory, examining the evolution of racial and gender codes, class conflict, and hegemonic institutions. They turn to such texts as Shakespeare's plays, Dickens's novels, and Whitman's poetry. Noteworthy in this regard is the American critical movement known as New Historicism, a term coined in the 1980s by Stephen Greenblatt.

New Historicists study literary texts not as autonomous objects but as material artifacts made in interaction with specific social, cultural, and political forces. This view of literature breaks down the traditional distinction between literary and nonliterary texts and forms. Inspired by Michel Foucault, New Historicists, who are specialists in traditional literary periods, provide thick descriptions of contending social forces not only surrounding but circulating through cultural discourses, notably literary works. They use literary texts as lenses to focus on social questions of authority, agency, and institutional power. Their major preoccupation is the dynamics of social containment and subversion. A favorite formula is "author and theme"—for instance, Shakespeare and exorcism—as they self-consciously use surprise and provocation in establishing new points of view and in designing innovative critical projects.

CULTURAL STUDIES

Theories concerned with literature and its interpretation inevitably touch on ideas about culture. If we define *culture* as the aggregate of language, knowledge, belief, morality, law, custom, and art collectively acquired by human beings, then it is easy to see how the contents and forms of culture supply the materials and procedures of literature and criticism. As a way of life and sphere of struggle, culture encompasses elements not only of elite but also of popular and mass arts and practices. Yet the contemporary recognition of "low-" and "middle-brow" culture is something new in the long history of Western modern cultural criticism, which for several centuries has focused mainly on exceptional and elite forms. Beginning in the 1960s, cultural critics started to pay serious attention to mass, popular, and everyday materials, usually in the context of their ideologies (dominant ideas and values). Those in the discipline called cultural studies, in particular, study such discourses as television, cinema, advertising, rap music, magazines, minority literatures, and popular literature (thrillers, science fiction, romances, westerns, Gothic fiction), focusing on how such materials are produced, distributed, and consumed.

While researchers in cultural studies employ various methods, including surveys, field-based studies, textual interpretations, historical background studies, and participant observations, institutional analysis and ideology critique have been especially important. Critics interested in present-day popular romances, for instance, have examined the practices of institutions such as publishing companies in shaping and maintaining the rules of the romance genre as well as in packaging and promoting successful reproductions of the form. Since institutions overlap and connect with satellite institutions, an investigation into one often leads to another. In the case of romance, a critic who began by scrutinizing the genre's presence in television soap operas and women's magazines would soon find links to publishers, literary agents, booksellers, television programmers, magazine editors, and authors. Because circuits of institutions perform such important roles in creating, conditioning, and commodifying cultural discourses, their analysis is central to the enterprise of cultural studies.

Ideology critique critically examines the ideas, feelings, beliefs, values, and representations embedded in, and promoted by, the artifacts and practices of a culture or a group. It overlaps with institutional analysis. In *English in America*, Richard Ohmann describes how the institution of English studies itself disseminates not only the practical skills of analysis, organization, and literacy but also the values of detachment, caution, and cooperation, all of which aid the smooth operation of contemporary capitalist societies. Associated with the professional managerial classes, such attitudes and manners (ideology) are invisible yet ever present in English classrooms, as well as in places of employment.

Some conservative literary critics have opposed cultural studies, criticizing the twin displacements of the canon (the body of works traditionally accepted as "great") by popular culture and of formalist poetic explication by sociological analyses, especially ideology critique. Because cultural studies deals with issues of conflict, domination, class struggle, minorities, state power, and ideology, they fault it for politicizing the field. Often this debate, part of contemporary culture wars, sets multiculturalism and analysis attentive to race, class, and gender against literary appreciation and close reading. Some accuse cultural studies of displaying "political correctness" rather than critical independence.

Cultural studies advocates argue that what counts as literature changes from one time, place, and group to another. Before the eighteenth century in western Europe, the word *literature* designated all books and writing. Only during the late Enlightenment and Romantic eras did literature come to be more narrowly defined as belles lettres. Perhaps postmodern debates over the concept of literature may be seen as staging a return to the older definition; in any case, they explicitly contest the aestheticizing or refining of literature typical of the modern age.

Cultural studies offers distinctive answers to the two key questions with which we began—what is interpretation? what is literature? First, literature consists of popular, mass, and minority genres as well as elite canonical works. It includes a wide array of discourses, from writings in standard literary genres to rap lyrics, blues poems, oral legends, diaries, magazines, movies, posters, romances, soap operas, video games (narratives), and so on. With a different population or in another time or place, literary discourse would be differently defined. There is one constant in this culturally relative definition: literature is symptomatic of the state of its society. Second, interpretation employs institutional analysis, ideology critique, and field-based research, as well as textual explication, exegesis, aesthetic appreciation, and personal response.

For cultural studies, personhood (or subjectivity) involves three things: the operations of our unconscious, the effects of surrounding sociohistorical forces, and the multiple subject positions that each individual occupies. This complex view of subjectivity applies to the author, not just the critic: authored texts by definition contain unconscious and socially symptomatic materials unique to specific times, places, and persons. It is thus no surprise that cultural studies and formalist literary criticisms are sometimes seen as diametrically opposed, antagonistic critical projects—one expansive and wide-ranging, the other contracted and tightly focused; one engaged with psychology, sociology, and politics, the other wedded to aesthetics and poetics and viewing extrinsic concerns as misplaced.

THEORY FRACTALIZED

In the early twenty-first century, theory has increasingly fractalized into niches and now comprises many separate subfields (see Theory Map on pages 34–35). Arguably, among the most noteworthy subfields are body studies, disability studies, ecocritical studies, globalization studies, indigenous studies, media studies, narrative studies, popular culture studies, science and technology studies, transatlantic and transpacific studies, trauma studies, and whiteness studies. Most of these areas are semiautonomous, having their own recognized leading figures, histories and major texts, publication outlets, and repertoires of issues and concepts. Significantly, the studies model is replacing the long-standing schools and movements model in accounts of the structure and history of the domain of contemporary criticism and theory. However, contemporary schools and movements remain important today as sources and resources for practical criticism and for learning theory.

When cultural studies started in the 1990s to replace poststructuralism and deconstruction as the newest thing in Anglophone spheres, some critics began to talk excitedly of a new posttheory moment. The term *posttheory* refers to two concurrent phenomena: the receding of poststructuralism into the background, along with the rise and dissemination of a multifaceted cultural studies across all fields and periods of literary theory and criticism. While posttheory designates a time "after theory," where *theory* is synonymous with poststructuralism, it does not mean the death of theory or a movement beyond theory if the word retains its usual meanings: presuppositions and principles; modern and contemporary schools, movements, and subfields; critical practices and methods (professional know-how). Theory in these ordinary senses lives on, and it has come to designate via shorthand the field of criticism and theory. In *After Theory*, Terry Eagleton resolutely declares on the opening page: "Those to whom the title of this book suggests that 'theory' is now over, and that we can all relievedly return to an age of pre-theoretical innocence, are in for a disappointment. There can be no going back. . . ." Jonathan Culler puts it more tersely near the close of *The Literary in Theory*: "We are inexorably in theory, whether we champion or deplore it."

There are very good reasons that contemporary theory continues to frame the study of literature and culture in academic institutions. Theory raises and answers questions about a broad array of fundamental issues, some old and some new, pertaining to reading and interpretive strategies, literature and culture, tradition and nationalism, genre and gender, meaning and paraphrase, originality and intertextuality, authorial intention and the unconscious, literary education and social hegemony, standard language and heteroglossia, poetics and rhetoric, representation and truth, and so on. In addition, theory opens literary and cultural studies to neighboring disciplines and numerous national traditions. It reinvigorates the field not only by reexamining the canonical list of great works and the tool kit of basic concepts and methods but also by recasting the received interpretations of old texts and frameworks and by revealing interesting new zones of meaning and possibilities for future critical inquiry.

Theorists are fond of pointing out that everyone theorizes, about the world as well as about literature and interpretation, and that theories must be examined, debated, and tested. Plato suggested long ago that the unexamined life is not worth living, providing a worthy maxim for philosophers—and for students of theory and criticism.

Twenty-First-Century

Empire
Postcolonial Studies
Border Studies

GLOBALIZATION

Diaspora Studies
Multiculturalism
New American Studies

Neoliberalism
Late Capitalism
The New Economic Criticism
Patronage Studies

POLITICAL ECONOMY

Subaltern Studies
Working-Class Studies
The Multitude
Debt Studies

Resistance Studies
Surveillance and Security Studies
Body Studies
Cyborg Studies

BIOPOLITICS

Gender Studies
Disability Studies
Age Studies
Leisure Studies

Cognitive Theory
Object Studies
Technoscience Studies

ECOCRITICISM

Animal Studies
Food Studies
Geocriticism

New Southern U.S. Studies
Whiteness Studies
Indigenous Studies
Ethnic Studies

IDENTITY

Women's Studies
Queer Studies
Masculinity Studies
Sexuality Studies

Sinaphone
Lusophone
Hispanophone
Francophone
Anglophone

LITERARY COMPARATIVISMS

Black Atlantic
Transatlantic
Transpacific
Multilingual
Translation Studies

THEORY MAP

Archive Studies
Professionalization Studies
Publishing Histories
Canonization Studies

INSTITUTIONAL STUDIES

Critical Pedagogy
Academic Labor Studies
Corporate University
Digital Humanities

Celebrity Studies
Public Intellectuals
Public Sphere
Subcultures

POPULAR CULTURE

Popular Music
Fashion Studies
Sport Studies
Gaming Studies

Electronic Literature
Religion and Literature
Popular Poetries
Pulp Fiction
Performance Studies

GENRE

Narrative Studies
New History of Novel
Life Writing
Oratures
Outsider Arts

Sound Studies
Visual Culture Studies
TV Studies
Film Studies

MEDIA STUDIES

Book History
Periodical Studies
New Media
Social Media

Affect Theory
Testimony
Sentimentality

AFFECT STUDIES

Trauma Studies
Memory Studies
Holocaust Studies

Literacy Studies
Discourse Analysis
Composition Studies
History of Rhetoric

RHETORIC

Tropology
Orality
Cognitive Poetics
Reception Studies

Theory and Criticism

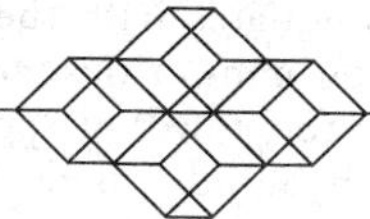

GORGIAS OF LEONTINI
ca. 483–376 B.C.E.

With its observations on the power of speech (*logos*), Gorgias's "Encomium of Helen" develops a classical rhetoric antithetical to Platonic poetics, one that anticipates JACQUES DERRIDA's twentieth-century critique of PLATO. Where Plato commends moral content, Gorgias praises elegant form; where Plato is didactic, Gorgias aims to persuade through performance; where Plato—and those who followed him, like AUGUSTINE—condemns rhetoric as dangerously false, Gorgias embraces it. Speech, Gorgias wrote in another fragment, "summons whoever wishes [to compete], but crowns the one who is able." The highly wrought style for which he is justly famous, with its frequent use of paradox, antithesis, balancing clauses, and rhyme, has its closest modern parallel in OSCAR WILDE's celebrated epigrammatic style. Like Wilde, Gorgias raises significant issues about the radical contingency of all truth claims, issues that have been central to contemporary theoretical debates.

Gorgias came from a Greek colony in Sicily and, by all accounts, lived to be more than one hundred years old. Nothing is known of his life until he came to Athens in 427 B.C.E. as part of an embassy from his native Leontini. There his dazzling oratorical style, whose force is difficult to capture in translation, made him something of a sensation; he quickly became one of the most influential of the sophists, a group of itinerant teachers who went from city to city earning their living by instructing others in subtle argumentation. Although later writers would credit them with philosophical doctrines, in particular a skepticism about the claims of reason to arrive at truth, the sophists were members of a profession and not a school of thought. That we today use the term *sophistry* to refer to plausible but fallacious arguments reflects the influence of the sophists' critics, most notably Plato.

Gorgias confined himself almost exclusively to the teaching of oratory—rhetoric—which was the main road to success in Greek city-states. In the *Meno*, Plato writes that he admired Gorgias because he did not claim to be a teacher of *aretē*, or virtue; "in fact, he laughs at others he hears making such promises. He thinks one should make men skillful at speaking." Only fragments of Gorgias's rhetorical works survive, primarily in the form of commonplaces, or rhetorical exercises that were used to instruct others. The "Encomium of Helen" is an example of this genre, as is the longer fragment in defense of Palamides, a minor Greek hero at Troy. Gorgias concludes his defense of Helen, "I wished to write this speech for Helen's encomium and my amusement," suggesting that like the other fragments of his speeches that survive, it was an epideictic composition—a display piece intended to demonstrate the principles of rhetoric to his pupils, presumably accompanied by a verbal commentary that has not survived.

The extant "Encomium of Helen" illustrates Gorgias's flamboyant style, which Plato later parodied in Agathon's speech in the *Symposium*. The defense of Helen of

Troy, a character long vilified by poets, proves a fitting challenge for even the most accomplished rhetorician. But it also serves as a pretext for a discussion of the power of speech, which Gorgias equates with the force of compulsion—an argument developed in modern times by many critics, most notably FRIEDRICH NIETZSCHE and PAUL DE MAN. Gorgias likens the power of speech to persuade to the power of magical charms or drugs to alter the mind or body. He has none of Plato's firm belief that right reasoning will ultimately lead to truth. Speech is as likely to lead to "evil persuasion" as to correct action. The elaborate antitheses and paradoxes of Gorgias's style may express the belief that since truth exists but is contingent, a clear expression of contrasts and alternatives is needed if one is to sift through the competing claims of persuasive speech. In the history of theory and criticism, rhetoric continually raises such problems as the truth status of language, the power and pleasure of persuasive discourse, and the reliability of figures and tropes.

"Encomium of Helen" Keywords: Classical Theory, Language, Rhetoric

From Encomium of Helen[1]

[1] For a city the finest adornment (*kosmos*) is a good citizenry, for a body beauty, for a soul wisdom, for an action *aretē*,[2] and for a speech truth; and the opposites of these are indecorous. A man, woman, speech, deed, city or action that is worthy of praise should be honored with acclaim, but the unworthy should be branded with blame. For it is equally error and ignorance to blame the praiseworthy and praise the blameworthy. [2] The man who speaks correctly what ought to be said has a duty to refute those who find fault with Helen. Among those who listen to the poets a single-voiced, single-minded conviction has arisen about this woman, the notoriety of whose name is now a reminder of disasters. My only wish is to bring reason to the debate, eliminate the cause of her bad reputation, demonstrate that her detractors are lying, reveal the truth, and put an end to ignorance.

[3] That the woman I speak of is by nature and birth the foremost of the foremost, men or women, is well known by all.[3] Clearly her mother was Leda and her father in fact a god, but in story a mortal: Zeus and Tyndareus. One was thought to be her father because he was, the other was reported to be because he said he was; one was mightiest of men, the other tyrant of all. [4] Born from such as these, she equaled the gods in beauty, not concealed but revealed. Many were the erotic passions she aroused in many men, and her one body brought many bodies full of great ambition for great deeds; some had abundant wealth, some the glory of an old noble lineage, some the vigor of personal valor, and some the power of acquired wisdom. All came for love that desires to conquer and from unconquerable

1. Translated by Michael Gagarin and Paul Woodruff, who occasionally include the Greek in parentheses.
2. Excellence or virtue (Greek).
3. According to the Greek myth, Helen was the daughter of Zeus, who took the form of a swan before raping her mother, Leda. Before he would give her in marriage, Helen's human father, Tyndareus, made all the Greek princes swear an oath that if any wrong were done to her husband they would come to his aid. Thus the Trojan prince Paris's abduction of Helen from her husband, Menelaus, precipitated the Trojan War. Paris had been asked to judge the beauty of three goddesses; he declared the fairest to be Aphrodite, goddess of love, who had promised him the love of the world's most beautiful woman (i.e., Helen) if he chose her.

desire for honor. [5] Who it was or why or how he took Helen and fulfilled his love, I shall not say. For to tell those who know something they know carries conviction, but does not bring pleasure. Now that my speech has passed over the past, it is to the beginning of my future speech that I proceed and propose the likely reasons for Helen's journey to Troy.

[6] Either she did what she did because of the will of fortune and the plan of the gods and the decree of necessity, or she was seized by force, or persuaded by words, <or captured by love>. If she left for the first reason, then any who blame her deserve blame themselves, for a human's anticipation cannot restrain a god's inclination. For by nature the stronger is not restrained by the weaker but the weaker is ruled and led by the stronger: the stronger leads, the weaker follows. Now, a god is stronger than a human in strength, in wisdom, and in other respects; and so if blame must be attached to fortune and god, then Helen must be detached from her ill repute.

[7] If she was forcibly abducted and unlawfully violated and unjustly assaulted, it is clear that her abductor, her assaulter, engaged in crime; but she who was abducted and assaulted encountered misfortune. Thus, the undertaking undertaken by the barbarian was barbarous in word and law and deed and deserves blame in word, loss of rights in law, and punishment in deed. But she who was violated, from her country separated, from her friends isolated, surely (*eikotōs*) deserves compassion rather than slander. For he did and she suffered terrible things. It is right to pity her but hate him.

[8] If speech (*logos*) persuaded and deluded her mind, even against this it is not hard to defend her or free her from blame, as follows: speech is a powerful master and achieves the most divine feats with the smallest and least evident body.[4] It can stop fear, relieve pain, create joy, and increase pity. How this is so, I shall show; [9] and I must demonstrate this to my audience to change their opinion.

Poetry (*poiēsis*) as a whole I deem and name "speech (*logos*) with meter." To its listeners poetry brings a fearful shuddering, a tearful pity, and a grieving desire, while through its words the soul feels its own feelings for good and bad fortune in the affairs and lives of others. Now, let me move from one argument to another. [10] Sacred incantations with words inject pleasure and reject pain, for in associating with the opinion of the mind, the power of an incantation enchants, persuades, and alters it through bewitchment. The twin arts of witchcraft and magic have been discovered, and these are illusions of mind and delusions of judgment. [11] How many men on how many subjects have persuaded and do persuade how many others by shaping a false speech! For if all men on all subjects had memory of the past, <understanding> of the present, and foresight into the future, speech would not be the same in the same way;[5] but as it is, to remember the past, to examine the present, or to prophesy the future is not easy; and so most men on most subjects make opinion an adviser to their minds. But opinion is perilous and uncertain, and brings those who use it to perilous and uncertain good fortune. [12] What reason is there, then, why Helen did not

4. Gorgias seems to be describing speech as if it were a physical body, so small it cannot be seen, moving from person to person.

5. Text uncertain, but the sense clearly is "the same as it is now" [translators' note].

go just as unwillingly under the influence of speech as if she were seized by the violence of violators? For persuasion expelled her thought—persuasion, which has the same power, but not the same form as compulsion (*anankē*). A speech persuaded a soul that was persuaded, and forced it to be persuaded by what was said and to consent to what was done. The persuader, then, is the wrongdoer, because he compelled her, while she who was persuaded is wrongly blamed, because she was compelled by the speech. [13] To see that persuasion, when added to speech, indeed molds the mind as it wishes, one must first study the arguments of astronomers, who replace opinion with opinion: displacing one but implanting another, they make incredible, invisible matters apparent to the eyes of opinion. Second, compulsory debates with words,[6] where a single speech to a large crowd pleases and persuades because written with skill (*technē*), not spoken with truth. Third, contests of philosophical arguments, where it is shown that speed of thought also makes it easy to change a conviction based on opinion. [14] The power of speech has the same effect on the disposition of the soul as the disposition of drugs on the nature of bodies. Just as different drugs draw forth different humors from the body—some putting a stop to disease, others to life—so too with words: some cause pain, others joy, some strike fear, some stir the audience to boldness, some benumb and bewitch the soul with evil persuasion.

[15] The case has been made: if she was persuaded by speech, her fortune was evil, not her action. The fourth reason, I discuss in my fourth argument. If it was love that did all these things, she will easily escape blame for the error that is said to have occurred.

* * *

[19] So if Helen's eye, pleased by Alexander's[7] body, transmitted to her soul an eagerness and striving for love, why is that surprising? If love is a god, with the divine power of gods, how could a weaker person refuse and reject him? But if love is a human sickness and a mental weakness, it must not be blamed as mistake, but claimed as misfortune. For it came, as it came, snared by the mind, not prepared by thought, under the compulsion of love, not the provision of art (*technē*).

[20] How then can the blame of Helen be considered just? Whether she did what she did, invaded by love, persuaded by speech, impelled by force or compelled by divine necessity, she escapes all blame entirely.

[21] With my speech I have removed this woman's ill repute; I have abided by the rule laid down at the beginning of my speech; I have tried to dispel the injustice of blame and the ignorance of opinion; I wished to write this speech for Helen's encomium and my amusement.

ca. 400 B.C.E.

6. This expression probably designates speeches in law courts [translators' note].

7. Paris's.

PLATO
ca. 427–ca. 347 B.C.E.

A monumental figure in the history of Western philosophy, Plato looms nearly as large in the history of European literary theory. Indeed, for many literary scholars he marks the beginning of the tradition of literary theory, although his choice of the dialogue format, in which historical personages convey particular arguments, suggests that the issues he raises had already been debated before he took them up—as do the extant fragments of the writings of the pre-Socratic philosophers. The several dozen dialogues attributed to Plato engage almost every issue that interests philosophers: the nature of being; the question of how we come to know things; the proper ordering of human society; and the nature of justice, truth, the good, love, and beauty. Although Plato did not set out to write systematic literary theory—unlike his student ARISTOTLE, who produced a treatise on poetics—his consideration of philosophical issues in several of the dialogues leads him to reflect on poetry, and those reflections have often set the terms of literary debate in the West.

What binds together Plato's various discussions of poetry is a distrust of *mimēsis* (representation or imitation). According to Plato, all art—including poetry—is a mimesis of nature, a copy of objects in the physical world. But those objects in the material world, according to the idealist philosophy that Plato propounds, are themselves only mutable copies of timeless universals, called Forms or Ideas. Poetry is merely a copy of a copy, leading away from the truth rather than toward it. Philosophers and literary critics ever since, from Plotinus in the third century C.E. to JACQUES DERRIDA in the late twentieth century, have wrestled with the terms of Plato's critique of poetry, revising it or attempting to point out inconsistencies in his argument.

Plato was born about four years after the beginning of the twenty-five-year-long Peloponnesian War between Athens and Sparta and just after the death of the great Athenian statesman Pericles, who had overseen the city's artistic golden age. His parents both came from distinguished Athenian families, and his stepfather, an associate of Pericles, was an active participant in the political and cultural life of fifth-century Athens. Plato had two older brothers, Glaucon and Adeimantus, who appear as characters in his longest dialogue, *Republic* (ca. 375 B.C.E.). As a young man, growing up in a city at war and in constant political turmoil, he seems to have been destined for a political career. But after the Peloponnesian War ended in 405 with the defeat and humiliation of Athens, the excesses of Athenian political life under the oligarchical rule (404–403) of the so-called Thirty Tyrants and under the restored democracy left Plato disillusioned with political life. The execution in 399 of Socrates, on charges of impiety and corrupting the young, was a turning point in his life. The older philosopher was a close friend of Plato's family, and Plato's writings attest to Socrates' great influence on him. Indeed, the position of Socrates in European philosophy is unique. Though he apparently never wrote a word, his influence on subsequent thought through his followers, Plato in particular, is incalculable.

After Socrates' death Plato retired from Athenian political life and traveled for a number of years. In 388 he journeyed to Italy and Sicily, where he became the friend of Dionysius I, the ruler of Syracuse, and his brother-in-law Dion. The following year Plato returned to Athens, where he founded the Academy, an institution devoted to research and instruction in philosophy and the sciences; he taught there for the rest of his life. Plato envisioned the Academy as a school for statesmen where he could train a new kind of philosopher-ruler (or "guardian") according to the principles set forth in his *Republic*. Unlike the older sophist GORGIAS or Plato's contemporary rival Isocrates, who both taught the arts of rhetoric and persuasion, Plato focused primarily in the Academy on mathematics, logic, and philosophy. However, when Dionysius died in 367, Dion invited Plato to return to Syracuse to undertake the philosophical education of the new ruler, Dionysius II. Plato went, perhaps with the hope of putting the theory of *Republic* into practice; but philosophy proved no match for local politics and Dionysius's suspicions. Indeed, a return visit resulted in Plato's brief imprisonment; by 360 he was back at the Academy for good.

Plato is recognized as a master of the dialogue form and as one of the great prose stylists of the Greek language. His published writings, apparently all of which are preserved, consist of some twenty-six dramatic dialogues on philosophical and related themes. The central problematic posed by this form is that it becomes virtually impossible to attribute any statement directly to Plato: he never speaks in his own person. The only exceptions are a series of thirteen letters (whose authenticity is still a matter of scholarly debate) written in the last decades of Plato's life, most addressing the political situation in Syracuse. Only the seventh—and longest—letter takes up philosophical issues. For the most part, Plato places his arguments in the mouths of characters who may or may not be based on historical persons. The speakers can never be assumed to be voicing Plato's own views or the views of those whose names they bear. In almost all the dialogues, Socrates is the focal character and Plato's mouthpiece, but Plato's Socrates is not the historical Socrates. These complications, which thwart efforts to fix Plato's thought within a series of propositional statements, have attracted much attention, especially from contemporary Continental philosophers like Derrida.

The chronology of Plato's dialogues is highly controversial, but most scholars divide the works roughly into three periods. The earliest works, begun after 399, include the *Apology of Socrates* and *Crito*, in which Plato defends Socrates against the charges that led to his death; *Gorgias*, in which Socrates' opponent is the sophist Gorgias; and *Ion*, which examines poetry as a kind of divine madness. Characteristic of these early Platonic dialogues is Socrates' disarming claim of ignorance and a formal technique of cross-examination called *elenchus*, a method of questioning designed to lead a learner through stages of reasoning and to expose the contradictions in an opponent's original statement. The middle period, from 380 to 367, includes the *Symposium*, *Cratylus*, and *Republic*, all begun after the founding of the Academy; they develop the theory of Forms or Ideas anticipated in the early dialogues. The Forms constitute a realm of unchanging being to which the world of individual mutable objects is subordinate. Because the Forms are immutable, they are more real—and more true—than the changeable material world. The Form of the Good enjoys a unique status, for it is responsible for the being and intelligibility of the world as a whole. Plato's famous "Allegory of the Cave" in book 7 of *Republic* (one of our selections) provides a memorable introduction to the Platonic theory of Forms, which is reiterated in book 10's equally well known critique of artistic imitation. *Cratylus* is of interest to theorists of language because the dispute in this dialogue concerns the "correctness" of names: do they point unproblematically to the "nature of things"—that is, to the Forms—as Hermogenes contends, or are they merely a matter of convention, as Cratylus argues? Socrates concludes that the matter is unresolvable, but that "no one with any understanding will commit himself or the education of his soul to names, or trust them or their givers to the point of firmly stating that he knows something." To the late period (366–360) belong *Timaeus*, which throughout the Middle Ages was Plato's most widely known work; *Critias;* and *Sophist*. *Phaedrus*, our final selection, with its notorious attack on writing, is usually classified as transitional, falling between the middle and late periods, with themes characteristic of both.

In *Ion*, our opening selection, Plato's Socrates engages Ion in a debate about the nature of the rhapsode's knowledge of poetry, about the nature of poetry, and about the status of knowledge itself. Poetry, Socrates maintains, is not an art but instead a form of divine madness: "the poet is an airy thing, winged and holy, and he is not able to make poetry until he becomes inspired and goes out of his mind." This debate between the claims of inspiration and those of art would subsequently have a long history in European literary criticism. Is poetry primarily a craft with a set of rules that can be taught and learned, as HORACE, the medieval rhetorician Geoffrey of Vinsauf (ca. 1200), and ALEXANDER POPE argue, or is it primarily the result of inspiration or genius, as LONGINUS, the Neoplatonist Plotinus (205–270), FRIEDRICH VON SCHILLER, WILLIAM WORDSWORTH, RALPH WALDO EMERSON, and others, following Plato, have maintained?

Plato's Socrates goes a step further. Not only is poetry a form of divinely inspired madness, but so is criticism. "You are powerless to speak about Homer," he tells Ion, "on the basis of knowledge or mastery." Socrates uses the image of a magnet as a metaphor for divine inspiration: as a magnet attracts iron and passes that attraction along, so the gods inspire the artist, who inspires the interpreter, who, in tum, inspires the audience. For Plato's Socrates, the work of poet and critic is not divided between inspiration and rational analysis, as it is for most modem critics (see, for instance, MATTHEW ARNOLD and the New Critic CLEANTH BROOKS); rather, it lies on a continuum. The work of the critic is no more rational than that of the poet, the critic's knowledge no more truthful.

However, it is helpful when reading Plato to remember that his dialogues do not always present a straightforward argument or arrive at a single unambiguous conclusion. The process of elenchus and Socrates' persistent irony often make it difficult to pin him down to any one position. In *Ion*, is Socrates making fun of the pomposity of the rhapsode, or does he seriously believe that whatever truth emerges from poetry and the interpretation of poetry results only from divine madness? This method of "emptying out" the question by Socrates to reveal his opponents' ignorance is evident in our second selection, which brings together those places in *Republic* in which Plato discusses the "ancient quarrel between philosophy and poetry" (books 2, 3, and 10).

As Socrates and his interlocutors, Adeimantus in book 2 and Glaucon in books 3 and 10, consider the role that literature or "stories" should play in the education of the future rulers or "guardians" of his ideal republic, Plato's Socrates argues that because poets lie they ought to be banished from the republic—or, at the very least, heavily censored. Plato's polemic against literature hinges on the nature of its mimesis or imitation of the world. At the simplest level of imitation, Plato raises questions about literature's content. If it is to be part of the education of young malleable minds, literature must encourage only virtue. It must represent a world in which virtue is rewarded and even the punishment of evil serves virtuous ends. Not surprisingly, whether epic, lyric, or tragedy, the literature Socrates cites falls short of this standard. Literature, however, fails at the level not only of content but also of form. Because its stories are fictional, made up, literature is dangerous; it produces only lies. Furthermore, because mimesis presents us with an inferior copy of a copy, poetry—performed rather than read in Plato's time—takes its listeners away from rather than toward the ideal Forms.

Both the Allegory of the Cave (book 7) and *Republic* 10's infamous critique of mimesis explore the nature of knowledge and its proper objects, the Forms. The world we perceive through the senses, the world that poetry imitates, Socrates argues, is illusory and deceptive. It depends on a prior realm of separately existing Forms, organized beneath the Form of Good. The realm of Forms is accessible not through the senses, as is the world of appearances, but only through rigorous philosophic discussion and thought, based on mathematical reasoning. For Plato's Socrates, measuring, counting, and weighing all bring us closer to the realm of Forms than do poetry's pale representations of nature. All art and poetry, because they represent what is already an inferior representation of the true original (the Forms), can only lead further away from the truth, and further into a world of illusion and deception. Virtually every subsequent defense of poetry (memorable examples include those by Aristotle, SIR PHILIP SIDNEY, APHRA BEHN, and PERCY BYSSHE SHELLEY) has had to come to terms with Plato's devastating attack on poetry as inferior and deceptive mimesis.

Plato's *Phaedrus* (from which our final selection is taken) has been of interest to contemporary literary theory for its discussion of the evils of writing. There Plato has Socrates relate the story of the invention of writing by the Egyptian god Theuth (Thoth), who offers it to King Thamus. Thamus declines the offer, deciding that humans are better off without writing because it substitutes an alien inscription—lifeless signs—for the authentic living presence of spoken language. Far from aiding memory, writing will cause it to atrophy. For Plato, the only good memory is *anamnēsis*, the recollection of spiritual truths through genuine, living wisdom: that is, through philosophy. Plato reiterates this point in his Seventh Letter, where he says: "anyone who is seriously studying high matters will be the last to write about them and thus expose his thought to the envy and criticism of men . . . [W]henever we see a book, whether the laws of a legislator or a composition on any other subject, we can be sure that if the author is really serious, the book does not contain his best thoughts; they are stored away with the fairest of his possessions. And if he has committed these serious thoughts to writing, it is because men, not the gods, 'have taken his wits away.'" Yet Plato's use of a myth in *Phaedrus* to frame his philosophical objections to writing raises questions of its own, since presumably myths suffer from the same defects as the texts of the sophists, rhetoricians, poets, and other purveyors of false wisdom whom Plato criticizes elsewhere. Derrida offers a celebrated unraveling of the logic of Plato's argument against writing in his *Dissemination* (see below), which may be the most significant encounter between a twentieth-century philosopher and Plato.

Plato is the progenitor of Western didactic criticism and theory: the idea that literature should serve moral and social functions. *Republic*, where he describes an ideal well-regulated community in which the educational curriculum promotes respect for law, reason, authority, self-discipline, and piety, has been especially influential. Although Plato's Socrates loves and regularly cites Homer's *Iliad* and *Odyssey*, he calls for the censorship of many passages in these works that represent sacrilegious, sentimental, unlawful, and irrational behavior. Above all else, he requires that literature teach goodness and grace. Plato's relentless application of this standard to all literature marks one of the most noteworthy beginnings of the ancient quarrel between philosophy and poetry.

***Ion* Keywords:** Affect, Classical Theory, Epic, Ethics, Poetry, Representation, Rhetoric
***The Republic* Keywords:** Aesthetics, Affect, Classical Theory, Drama, Epic, Ethics, Poetry, Religion, Representation
***Phaedrus* Keywords:** Classical Theory, Language, Rhetoric

Ion[1]

[530] SOCRATES:[2] Ion! Hello. Where have you come from to visit us this time? From your home in Ephesus?

ION: No, no, Socrates. From Epidaurus, from the festival of Asclepius.[3]

1. Translated by Paul Woodruff, who sometimes adds clarifying words or phrases in square brackets. Also in square brackets in the text are the Stephanus numbers used almost universally in citing Plato's works: they refer to the pages of a 1578 edition published by Henri Estienne.

2. Greek philosopher (469–399 B.C.E.) and Plato's spokesperson.

3. Greco-Roman hero and god of healing; he had a famous 4th-century B.C.E. temple in Epidaurus, a small Greek state on a peninsula of the Saronic Gulf.

SOCRATES: Don't tell me the Epidaurians hold a contest for *rhapsodes*[4] in honor of the god?

ION: They certainly do! They do it for every sort of poetry and music.

SOCRATES: Really! Did you enter the contest? And how did it go for you?

ION: First prize, Socrates! We carried it off.

SOCRATES: That's good to hear. Well, let's see that we win the big games at Athens, next.

ION: We'll do it, Socrates, god willing.

SOCRATES: You know, Ion, many times I've envied you rhapsodes your profession. Physically, it is always fitting for you in your profession to be dressed up to look as beautiful as you can; and at the same time it is necessary for you to be at work with poets—many fine ones, and with Homer[5] above all, who's the best poet and the most divine—and you have to learn his thought, not just his verses! Now that is something to envy! I mean, no one would ever get to be a good rhapsode if he didn't understand what is meant by the poet. A rhapsode must come to present the poet's thought to his audience; and he can't do that beautifully unless he knows what the poet means. So this all deserves to be envied.

ION: That's true, Socrates. And that's the part of my profession that took the most work. I think I speak more beautifully than anyone else about Homer; neither Metrodorus of Lampsacus nor Stesimbrotus of Thasos nor Glaucon[6] nor anyone else past or present could offer as many beautiful thoughts about Homer as I can.

SOCRATES: That's good to hear, Ion. Surely you won't begrudge me a demonstration?

ION: Really, Socrates, it's worth hearing how well I've got Homer dressed up. I think I'm worthy to be crowned by the Sons of Homer[7] with a golden crown.

SOCRATES: Really, I shall make time to hear that later. Now I'd just like an answer to this: [531] Are you so wonderfully clever about Homer alone—or also about Hesiod and Archilochus?[8]

ION: No, no. Only about Homer. That's good enough; I think.

SOCRATES: Is there any subject on which Homer and Hesiod both say the same things?

ION: Yes, I think so. A good many.

SOCRATES: Then, on those subjects, would you explain Homer's verse better and more beautifully than Hesiod's?

ION: Just the same Socrates, on those subjects, anyway, where they say the same things.

SOCRATES: And how about the subjects on which they do not say the same things? Divination, for example. Homer says something about it and so does Hesiod.

ION: Certainly.

4. Professional orators who recited poetry, especially that of Homer and the other epic poets.

5. Greek epic poet (ca. 8th c. B.C.E.), to whom the *Iliad* and the *Odyssey* are attributed.

6. Plato had an elder brother with this name. Metrodorus (ca. 330–ca. 277 B.C.E.), a follower and friend of the Athenian philosopher Epicurus and one of the most important teachers of Epicureanism. Stesimbrotus (active late 5th c. B.C.E.), a biographer of Homer.

7. The sons of Homer were a guild of rhapsodes who originally claimed to be descendants of Homer [translator's note].

8. Earliest Greek lyric poet (active ca. 650 B.C.E.). Hesiod (active ca. 700 B.C.E.), Greek epic didactic poet.

Socrates: Well. Take all the places where those two poets speak of divination, both where they agree and where they don't: who would explain those better and more beautifully, you, or one of the diviners if he's good?

Ion: One of the diviners.

Socrates: Suppose *you* were a diviner: if you were really able to explain the places where the two poets agree, wouldn't you also know how to explain the places where they disagree?

Ion: That's clear.

Socrates: Then what in the world is it that you're clever about in Homer but not in Hesiod and the other poets? Does Homer speak of any subjects that differ from those of *all* the other poets? Doesn't he mainly go through tales of war, and of how people deal with each other in society—good people and bad, ordinary folks and craftsmen? And of the gods, how *they* deal with each other and with men? And doesn't he recount what happens in heaven and in hell, and tell of the births of gods and heroes? Those are the subjects of Homer's poetry-making, aren't they?

Ion: That's true, Socrates.

Socrates: And how about the other poets? Did they write on the same subjects?

Ion: Yes, but Socrates, they didn't do it the way Homer did.

Socrates: How, then? Worse?

Ion: Much worse.

Socrates: And Homer does it better?

Ion: *Really* better.

Socrates: Well now, Ion, dear heart, when a number of people are discussing arithmetic, and one of them speaks best, I suppose *someone* will know how to pick out the good speaker.

Ion: Yes.

Socrates: Will it be the same person who can pick out the bad speakers, or someone else?

Ion: The same, of course.

Socrates: And that will be someone who has mastered arithmetic, right?

Ion: Yes.

Socrates: Well. Suppose a number of people are discussing healthy nutrition, and one of them speaks best. Will one person know that the best speaker speaks best, and another that an inferior speaker speaks worse? Or will the same man know both?

Ion: Obviously, the same man.

Socrates: Who is he? What do we call him?

Ion: A doctor.

Socrates: So, to sum it up, this is what we're saying: when a number of people speak on the same subject, it's always the same person who will know how to pick out good speakers and bad speakers. [532] If he doesn't know how to pick out a bad speaker, he certainly won't know a good speaker—on the same subject, anyway.

Ion: That's so.

Socrates: Then it turns out that the same person is "wonderfully clever" about both speakers.

Ion: Yes.

SOCRATES: Now *you* claim that Homer and the other poets (including Hesiod and Archilochus) speak on the same subjects, but not equally well. *He's* good, and they're inferior.

ION: Yes, and it's true.

SOCRATES: Now if you really do know who's speaking well, you'll know that the inferior speakers are speaking worse.

ION: Apparently so.

SOCRATES: You're superb! So if we say that Ion is equally clever about Homer and the other poets, we'll make no mistake. Because you agree yourself that the same person will be an adequate judge of all who speak on the same subjects, and that almost all the poets *do* treat the same subjects.

ION: Then how in the world do you explain what *I* do, Socrates? When someone discusses another poet I pay no attention, and I have no power to contribute anything worthwhile: I simply doze off. But let someone mention Homer and right away I'm wide awake and I'm paying attention and I have plenty to say.

SOCRATES: *That's* not hard to figure out, my friend. Anyone can tell that you are powerless to speak about Homer on the basis of knowledge or mastery. Because if your ability came by mastery, you would be able to speak about all the other poets as well. Look, there is an art of poetry as a whole, isn't there?

ION: Yes.

SOCRATES: And now take the whole of *any* other subject: won't it have the same discipline throughout? And this goes for every subject that can be mastered. Do you need me to tell you what I mean by this, Ion?

ION: Lord, yes, I do, Socrates. I love to hear you wise men talk.

SOCRATES: I wish that were true, Ion. But wise? Surely you are the wise men, you rhapsodes and actors, you and the poets whose work you sing. As for me, I say nothing but the truth, as you'd expect from an ordinary man. I mean, even this question I asked you—look how commonplace and ordinary a matter it is. Anybody could understand what I meant: don't you use the same discipline throughout whenever you master the whole of a subject? Take this for discussion—painting is a subject to be mastered as a whole, isn't it?

ION: Yes.

SOCRATES: And there are many painters, good and bad, and there have been many in the past.

ION: Certainly.

SOCRATES: Have you ever known anyone who is clever at showing what's well painted and what's not in the work of Polygnotus[9] but who's powerless to do that for other painters? [533] Someone who dozes off when the work of other painters is displayed, and is lost, and has nothing to contribute—but when he has to give judgment on Polygnotus or any other painter (so long as it's just *one*), he's wide awake and he's paying attention and he has plenty to say—have you ever known anyone like that?

ION: Good lord no, of course not!

9. Greek painter from Thasos (ca. 500–ca. 440 B.C.E.), later an Athenian citizen.

Socrates: Well. Take sculpture. Have you ever known anyone who is clever at explaining which statues are well made in the case of Daedalus, son of Metion, or Epeius, son of Panopeus, or Theodorus of Samos,[1] or any other *single* sculptor, but who's lost when he's among the products of other sculptors, and he dozes off and has nothing to say?

Ion: Good lord no. I haven't.

Socrates: And further, it is my opinion, you've never known anyone ever—not in flute-playing, not in cithara-playing, not in singing to the cithara, and not in rhapsodizing—you've never known a man who is clever at explaining Olympus or Thamyrus or Orpheus or Phemius,[2] the rhapsode from Ithaca, but who has nothing to contribute about Ion, the rhapsode from Ephesus, and cannot tell when he does his work well and when he doesn't—you've never known a man like that.

Ion: I have nothing to say against you on that point, Socrates. But *this* I know about myself: I speak about Homer more beautifully than anybody else and I have lots to say; and everybody says I do it well. But about the other poets I do not. Now see what that means.

Socrates: I do see, Ion, and I'm going to announce to you what I think that is. As I said earlier, that's not a subject you've mastered—speaking well about Homer; it's a divine power that moves you, as a "Magnetic" stone moves iron rings. (That's what Euripides called it; most people call it "Heraclean."[3]) This stone not only pulls those rings, if they're iron, it also puts power *in* the rings, so that they in turn can do just what the stone does—pull other rings—so that there's sometimes a very long chain of iron pieces and rings hanging from one another. And the power in all of them depends on this stone. In the same way, the Muse[4] makes some people inspired herself, and then through those who are inspired a chain of other enthusiasts is suspended. You know, none of the epic poets, if they're good, are masters of their subject; they are inspired, possessed, and that is how they utter all those beautiful poems. The same goes for lyric poets if they're good: just as the Corybantes[5] are not in their right minds when they dance, [534] lyric poets, too, are not in their right minds when they make those beautiful lyrics, but as soon as they sail into harmony and rhythm they are possessed by Bacchic frenzy. Just as Bacchus worshippers when they are possessed draw honey and milk from rivers,[6] but not when they are in their right minds—the soul of a lyric poet does this too, as they say themselves. For of course poets tell us that they gather songs at honey-flowing springs, from glades and gardens of the Muses, and that they bear songs to us as bees carry honey, flying like bees. And what

1. Greek architect and sculptor (active ca. 550 B.C.E.). Daedalus: in Greek mythology, a consummately skilled Athenian artisan and artist. Epeius: mythological builder of the Trojan horse.
2. Court singer in the palace of Odysseus, king of Ithaca, in Homer's *Odyssey*. Olympus: Greek mountain, famed as the home of the gods. Thamyras: mythological Thracian bard who challenged the Muses. Orpheus: Greek musician unrivaled among mortals.
3. Natural magnets apparently came from Magnesia and Heraclia in Caria in Asia Minor, and were called after those places [translator's note]. Euripides (ca. 485–ca. 406 B.C.E.), Athenian tragedian; the phrase appears in a fragment of a lost play.
4. One of the 9 daughters of Memory who preside over the arts and all intellectual pursuits.
5. Priests of the goddess Cybele, the Great Mother of the gods (whose worship spread west from Asia Minor); her followers engaged in wild and sometimes bloody dances.
6. Bacchus worshippers apparently danced themselves into a frenzy in which they found streams flowing with honey and milk (Euripides, *Bacchae* 708–11) [translator's note]. Bacchus: another name for Dionysus, god of wine and of fertility.

they say is true. For a poet is an airy thing, winged and holy, and he is not able to make poetry until he becomes inspired and goes out of his mind and his intellect is no longer in him. As long as a human being has his intellect in his possession he will always lack the power to make poetry or sing prophecy. Therefore because it's not by mastery that they make poems or say many lovely things about their subjects (as you do about Homer)—but because it's by a divine gift—each poet is able to compose beautifully only that for which the Muse has aroused him: one can do dithyrambs, another encomia, one can do dance songs, another, epics, and yet another, iambics;[7] and each of them is worthless for the other types of poetry. You see, it's not mastery that enables them to speak those verses, but a divine power, since if they knew how to speak beautifully on one type of poetry by mastering the subject, they could do so for all the others also. That's why the god takes their intellect away from them when he uses them as his servants, as he does prophets and godly diviners, so that we who hear should know that *they* are not the ones who speak those verses that are of such high value, for their intellect is not in them: the god himself is the one who speaks, and he gives voice through them to us. The best evidence for this account is Tynnichus from Chalcis,[8] who never made a poem anyone would think worth mentioning, *except* for the praise-song everyone sings, almost the most beautiful lyric-poem there is, and simply, as he says himself, "an invention of the Muses." In this more than anything, then, I think, the god is showing us, so that we should be in no doubt about it, that these beautiful poems are not human, not even *from* human beings, but are divine and from gods; that poets are nothing but representatives of the gods, possessed by whoever possesses them. To show *that*, the god deliberately sang the most beautiful lyric poem through the most worthless poet. [535] Don't you think I'm right, Ion?

Ion: Lord yes, *I* certainly do. Somehow you touch my soul with your words, Socrates, and I do think it's by a divine gift that good poets are able to present these poems to us from the gods.

Socrates: And you rhapsodes in turn present what the poets say.

Ion: That's true too.

Socrates: So you turn out to be representatives of representatives.

Ion: Quite right.

Socrates: Hold on, Ion; tell me this. Don't keep any secrets from *me*. When you recite epic poetry well and you have the most stunning effect on your spectators, either when you sing of Odysseus[9]—how he leapt into the doorway, his identity now obvious to the suitors, and he poured out arrows at his feet—or when you sing of Achilles charging at Hector, or when you sing a pitiful episode about Andromache or Hecuba or Priam,[1] are you at that time in your right mind, or do you get beside yourself? And doesn't your soul, in its enthusiasm, believe that it is present at the

7. A meter based on the syllabic pattern short-long; iambic trimeter was regularly used in the dialogue and set speeches of tragedy. "Dithyrambs": choral poems originally sung in honor of Dionysus, later associated with highly excited music and impassioned language. "Encomia": hymns of praise.

8. Greek poet known solely for his paean to Apollo, which does not survive.

9. The hero of Homer's *Odyssey*; he pours out arrows in *Odyssey* 22, attacking the men who had been pursuing his wife during his long absence.

1. King of Troy; he appears in Homer's *Iliad*. Achilles: greatest Greek warrior of the Trojan War and central character of the *Iliad*. Hector: oldest son of Priam and Hecuba and the greatest of the Trojan warriors, slain by Achilles (see *Iliad* 22); his wife was Andromache.

actions you describe, whether they're in Ithaca or in Troy or wherever the epic actually takes place?

Ion: What a vivid example you've given me, Socrates! I won't keep secrets from *you*. Listen, when *I* tell a sad story, my eyes are full of tears; and when I tell a story that's frightening or awful, my hair stands on end with fear and my heart jumps.

Socrates: Well, Ion, should we say this man is in his right mind at times like these: when he's at festivals or celebrations, all dressed up in fancy clothes, with golden crowns, and he weeps, though he's lost none of his finery—or when he's standing among millions of friendly people and he's frightened, though no one is undressing him or doing him any harm? Is he in his right mind then?

Ion: Lord no, Socrates. Not at all, to tell the truth.

Socrates: And you know that you have the same effects on most of your spectators too, don't you?

Ion: I know very well that we do. I look down at them every time from up on the rostrum, and they're crying and looking terrified, and as the stories are told they are filled with amazement. You see I must keep my wits and pay close attention to them: if I start them crying, *I* will laugh as I take their money, but if *they* laugh, I shall cry at having lost money.

Socrates: And you know that this spectator is the last of the rings, don't you—the ones that I said take their power from each other by virtue of the Heraclean stone [the magnet]? The middle ring is you, [536] the rhapsode or actor, and the first one is the poet himself. The god pulls people's souls through all these wherever he wants, looping the power down from one to another. And just as if it hung from that stone, there's an enormous chain of choral dancers and dance teachers and assistant teachers hanging off to the sides of the rings that are suspended from the Muse. One poet is attached to one Muse, another to another (we say he is "possessed," and that's near enough, for he is *held*). From these first rings, from the poets, *they* are attached in their turn and inspired, some from one poet, some from another: some from Orpheus, some from Musaeus,[2] and many are possessed and held from Homer. You are one of *them*, Ion, and you are possessed from Homer. And when anyone sings the work of another poet, you're asleep and you're lost about what to say; but when any song of that poet is sounded, you are immediately awake, your soul is dancing, and you have plenty to say. You see it's not because you're a master of knowledge about Homer that you can say what you say, but because of a divine gift, because you are possessed. That's how it is with the Corybantes, who have sharp ears only for the specific song that belongs to whatever god possesses them; they have plenty of words and movements to go with *that* song; but they are quite lost if the music is different. That's how it is with you, Ion: when anyone mentions Homer, you have plenty to say, but if he mentions the others you are lost; and the explanation of this, for which you ask me—why it is that you have plenty to say about Homer but not about the others—is that it's not mastering the subject, but a divine gift, that makes you a wonderful singer of Homer's praises.

2. Mythical singer, closely connected with Orpheus.

ION: You're a good speaker, Socrates. Still, I would be amazed if you could speak well enough to convince me that I am possessed or crazed when I praise Homer. I don't believe you'd think so if you heard me speaking on Homer.

SOCRATES: And I really do want to hear you, but not before you answer me this: on which of Homer's subjects do you speak well? I don't suppose you speak well on *all* of them.

ION: I do, Socrates, believe me, on every single one!

SOCRATES: Surely not on those subjects you happen to know nothing about, even if Homer does speak of them.

ION: And these subjects Homer speaks of, but I don't know about—what are they?

[537] SOCRATES: But doesn't Homer speak about professional subjects in many places, and say a great deal? Chariot driving, for example, I'll show you, if I can remember the lines.

ION: No, I'll recite them. I *do* remember.

SOCRATES: Then tell me what Nestor says to his son Antilochus, when he advises him to take care at the turning post in the horse race they held for Patroclus'[3] funeral.

ION: "Lean," he says,

> Lean yourself over on the smooth-planed chariot
> Just to the left of the pair. Then the horse on the right—
> Goad him, shout him on, easing the reins with your hands.
> At the post let your horse on the left stick tight to the turn
> So you seem to come right to the edge, with the hub
> Of your welded wheel. But escape cropping the stone . . . [4]

SOCRATES: That's enough. Who would know better, Ion, whether Homer speaks correctly or not in these particular verses—a doctor or a charioteer?

ION: A charioteer, of course.

SOCRATES: Is that because he is a master of that profession, or for some other reason?

ION: No. It's because he's a master of it.

SOCRATES: Then to each profession a god has granted the ability to know a certain function. I mean, the things navigation teaches us—we won't learn them from medicine as well, will we?

ION: Of course not.

SOCRATES: And the things medicine teaches us we won't learn from architecture.

ION: Of course not.

SOCRATES: And so it is for every other profession: what we learn by mastering one profession we won't learn by mastering another, right? But first, answer me this. Do you agree that there are different professions—that one is different from another?

ION: Yes.

3. Achilles' dearest friend, slain by Hector. Nestor: the oldest of the Greek generals at Troy; in the *Iliad*, he often gives advice.

4. *Iliad* 23.335–40 [translator's note].

SOCRATES: And is this how you determine which ones are different? When *I* find that the knowledge [involved in one case] deals with different subjects from the knowledge [in another case], then I claim that one is a different profession from the other. Is that what you do?

ION: Yes.

SOCRATES: I mean if there is some knowledge of the same subjects, then why should we say there are two different professions?—Especially when each of them would allow us to know the same subjects! Take these fingers: I know there are five of them, and you know the same thing about them than I do. Now suppose I asked you whether it's the same profession—arithmetic—that teaches you and me the same things, or whether it's two different ones. Of course you'd say it's the same one.

ION: Yes.

[538] SOCRATES: Then tell me now what I was going to ask you earlier. Do you think it's the same way for every profession—the same profession must teach the same subjects, and a different profession, if it *is* different, must teach not the same subjects, but different ones?

ION: That's how I think it is, Socrates.

SOCRATES: Then a person who has not mastered a given profession will not be able to be a good judge of the things which belong to that profession, whether they are things said or things done.

ION: That's true.

SOCRATES: Then who will know better whether or not Homer speaks beautifully and well in the lines you quoted? You, or a charioteer?

ION: A charioteer.

SOCRATES: That's because you're a rhapsode, of course, and not a charioteer.

ION: Yes.

SOCRATES: And the rhapsode's profession is different from the charioteer's.

ION: Yes.

SOCRATES: If it's different, then its knowledge is of different subjects also.

ION: Yes.

SOCRATES: Then what about the time Homer tells how Hecamede, Nestor's woman, gave barley-medicine to Machaon[5] to drink? He says something like this—

> Over wine of Pramnos she grated goat's milk cheese
> With a brazen grater. . . . And onion relish for the drink . . .[6]

Is Homer right or not: would a fine diagnosis here come from a doctor's profession or a rhapsode's?

ION: A doctor's.

SOCRATES: And what about the time Homer says:

> Leaden she plunged to the floor of the sea like a weight
> That is fixed to a field cow's horn. Given to the hunt
> It goes among ravenous fish, carrying death.[7]

5. A fighter and healer in the *Iliad*.
6. *Iliad* 11.639–40 with 630 [translator's note].
7. *Iliad* 24.80–82 [translator's note].

Should we say it's for a fisherman's profession or a rhapsode's to tell whether or not he describes this beautifully and well?

ION: That's obvious, Socrates. It's for a fisherman's.

SOCRATES: All right, look. Suppose you were the one asking questions, and you asked me, "Socrates, since you're finding out which passages belong to each of the professions Homer treats—which are the passages that each profession should judge—come tell me this: which are the passages that belong to a diviner and to divination, passages he should be able to judge as to whether they're well or badly composed?" Look how easily I can give you a true answer. Often, in the *Odyssey*, he says things like what Theoclymenus says—the prophet of the sons of Melampus:[8]

[539] Are you mad? What evil is this that's upon you? Night
Has enshrouded your hands, your faces, and down to your knees.
Wailing spreads like fire, tears wash your cheeks.
Ghosts fill the dooryard, ghosts fill the hall, they rush
To the black gate of hell, they drop below darkness. Sunlight
Has died from a sky run over with evil mist.[9]

And often in the *Iliad*, as in the battle at the wall.[1] There he says:

There came to them a bird as they hungered to cross over.
An eagle, a high-flier, circled the army's left
With a blood-red serpent carried in its talons, a monster,
Alive, still breathing, it has not yet forgotten its warlust,
For it struck its captor on the breast, by the neck;
It was writhing back, but the eagle shot it groundwards
In agony of pain, and dropped it in the midst of the throng,
Then itself, with a scream, soared on a breath of the wind.[2]

I shall say that these passages and those like them belong to a diviner. They are for him to examine and judge.

ION: That's a true answer, Socrates.

SOCRATES: Well, *your* answers are true, too, Ion. Now *you* tell me—just as I picked out for you, from the *Odyssey* and the *Iliad*, passages that belong to a diviner and ones that belong to a doctor and ones that belong to a fisherman—in the same way, Ion, since you have more experience with Homer's work than I do, you pick out for me the passages that belong to the rhapsode and to his profession, the passages a rhapsode should be able to examine and to judge better than anyone else.

ION: My answer, Socrates, is "all of them."

SOCRATES: That's not *your* answer, Ion. Not "all of them." Or are you really so forgetful? But no, it would not befit a *rhapsode* to be forgetful.

[540] ION: What do you think I'm forgetting?

SOCRATES: Don't you remember you said that a rhapsode's profession is different from a charioteer's?

ION: I remember.

8. Legendary seer who ruled in Argos and progenitor of the so-called Sons of Melampus, one of the four clans of seers in ancient Greece. They included Theoclymenus, seer of Argos; he appears in the *Odyssey*, prophesying for Telemachus, Odysseus's son.

9. *Odyssey* 20.351–57; line 354 is omitted by Plato [translator's note].

1. The city wall of Troy.

2. *Iliad* 12.200–207 [translator's note].

SOCRATES: And didn't you agree that because they are different they will know different subjects?

ION: Yes.

SOCRATES: So a rhapsode's profession, on *your* view, will not know everything, and neither will a rhapsode.

ION: But things like that are exceptions, Socrates.

SOCRATES: By "things like that" you mean that almost all the subjects of the other professions are exceptions, don't you? But then what sort of thing *will* a rhapsode know, if not everything?

ION: My opinion, anyhow, is that he'll know what it's fitting for a man or a woman to say—or for a slave or a freeman, or for a follower or a leader.

SOCRATES: So—what should a leader say when he's at sea and his ship is hit by a storm—do you mean a rhapsode will know better than a navigator?

ION: No, no. A navigator will know *that*.

SOCRATES: And when he is in charge of a sick man, what should a leader say—will a rhapsode know better than a doctor?

ION: Not that, either.

SOCRATES: But he *will* know what a slave should say. Is that what you mean?

ION: Yes.

SOCRATES: For example, what should a slave who's a cowherd say to calm down his cattle when they're going wild—will a rhapsode know what a cowherd does not?

ION: Certainly not.

SOCRATES: And what a woman who spins yarn should say about working with wool?

ION: No.

SOCRATES: And what a man should say, if he's a general, to encourage his troops?

ION: Yes! That's the sort of thing a rhapsode will know.

SOCRATES: What? Is a rhapsode's profession the same as a general's?

ION: Well, *I* certainly would know what a general should say.

SOCRATES: Perhaps that's because you're also a general by profession, Ion. I mean, if you were somehow both a horseman and a cithara-player at the same time, you would know good riders from bad. But suppose I asked you: "Which profession teaches you good horsemanship—the one that makes you a horseman, or the one that makes you a cithara-player?"

ION: The horseman, I'd say.

SOCRATES: Then if you also knew good cithara-players from bad, the profession that taught you *that* would be the one which made you a cithara-player, not the one that made you a horseman. Wouldn't you agree?

ION: Yes.

SOCRATES: Now, since you know the business of a general, do you know this by being a general or by being a good rhapsode?

ION: I don't think there's any difference.

[541] SOCRATES: What? Are you saying there's no difference? On your view is there one profession for rhapsodes and generals, or two?

ION: One, I think.

SOCRATES: So anyone who is a good rhapsode turns out to be a good general too.

ION: Certainly, Socrates.

SOCRATES: It also follows that anyone who turns out to be a good general is a good rhapsode too.

ION: No. This time I don't agree.

SOCRATES: But you do agree to this: anyone who is a good rhapsode is a good general too.

ION: I quite agree.

SOCRATES: And aren't you the best rhapsode in Greece?

ION: By far, Socrates.

SOCRATES: Are you also a general, Ion? Are you the best in Greece?

ION: Certainly, Socrates. That, too, I learned from Homer's poetry.

SOCRATES: Then why in heaven's name, Ion, when you're both the best general *and* the best rhapsode in Greece, do you go around the country giving rhapsodies but not commanding troops? Do you think Greece really needs a rhapsode who is crowned with a golden crown? And does not need a general?[3]

ION: Socrates, *my* city is governed and commanded by you [by Athens]; we don't need a general. Besides, neither your city nor Sparta would choose me for a general. You think you're good enough for that yourselves.

SOCRATES: Ion, you're superb. Don't you know Apollodorus of Cyzicus?

ION: What does *he* do?

SOCRATES: He's a foreigner who has often been chosen by Athens to be their general. And Phanosthenes of Andros and Heraclides of Clazomenae—they're also foreigners; they've demonstrated that they are worth noticing, and Athens appoints them to be generals or other sorts of officials. And do you think that *this* city, that makes such appointments, would not select Ion of Ephesus and honor him, if they thought he was worth noticing? Why? Aren't you people from Ephesus Athenians of long standing?[4] And isn't Ephesus a city that is second to none?

But *you*, Ion, you're doing me wrong, if what you say is true that what enables you to praise Homer is knowledge or mastery of a profession. You assured me that you knew many lovely things about Homer, you promised to give a demonstration; but you're cheating me, you're a long way from giving a demonstration. You aren't even willing to tell me what it is that you're so wonderfully clever *about*, though I've been begging you for ages. Really, you're just like Proteus,[5] you twist up and down and take many different shapes, till finally you've escaped me altogether by turning yourself into a general, [542] so as to avoid proving how wonderfully wise you are about Homer.

If you're really a master of your subject, and if, as I said earlier, you're cheating me of the demonstration you promised about Homer, then you're doing me wrong. But if you're not a master of your subject, if you're possessed by a divine gift from Homer, so that you make many lovely speeches about the poet without knowing anything—as *I* said about you—then

3. The memory of Athens' defeat in the Peloponnesian War (which ended in 404 B.C.E.) was perhaps still fresh in Plato's mind when he wrote this dialogue.

4. For most of the 5th century, Ephesus, an important center of trade founded by Ionian colonists on the west coast of Asia Minor, belonged to an alliance led by Athens against the Persians.

5. Proteus was a servant of Poseidon [god of the sea]. He had the power to take whatever shape he wanted in order to avoid answering questions (*Odyssey* 4.385ff.) [translator's note].

you're not doing me wrong. So choose, how do you want us to think of you—as a *man* who does wrong, or as someone *divine*?

ION: There's a great difference, Socrates. It's much lovelier to be thought divine.

SOCRATES: Then *that* is how we think of you, Ion, the lovelier way: it's as someone divine, and not as master of a profession, that you are a singer of Homer's praises.

ca. 390 B.C.E.

From The Republic[1]

From *Book II*

* * *

The question of education is clearly relevant to our inquiry.

In that case, my dear Adeimantus,[2] we must not give up on it even though it should detain us for some time.

Let us face the question.

I suggest we proceed with our guardians' education in a spirit of leisure. We shall tell tales and recount fables that will serve to educate them.

Good.

And what better education than that which has been for so long part of our own heritage? That would mean, I suppose, gymnastic for the body and music for the soul.[3]

Yes.

And education in music should begin earlier than gymnastic?

It should.

And we understand music to include poetry and stories, do we not?

Of course.

And these, in turn, are of two kinds. They are either true or false.[4]

Yes.

[377] And our students will have to be educated to understand both, beginning with the false?

I don't understand.

But surely you realize that we always begin by telling children fables. Of course, the fables contain some elements of truth, but by and large they are false. And so the child is exposed to fable before he is old enough to learn gymnastic. That is what I meant by saying that we must start with music before taking up gymnastic.

1. Translated by Richard W. Sterling and William C. Scott. The numbers in square brackets are the Stephanus numbers used almost universally in citing Plato's works; they refer to the pages of a 1578 edition published by Henri Estienne.

2. At this point in *Republic*, the philosopher Socrates (469–399 B.C.E., Plato's spokesperson) and Adeimantus are discussing what education the future rulers (or "guardians") of the perfect state should have. Socrates (speaking here) leads the discussion and Adeimantus follows (Socrates' other interlocutor in our selections from *Republic* books 3 and 7 is Adeimantus's brother Glaucon).

3. The education Plato describes here is consonant with the kind of education available in 5th-century Athens, which would include physical education for the body (gymnastic), education for character though reading, writing, and arithmetic (*grammata*), and music. Poetry would be taught as part of the music curriculum.

4. Either fiction or nonfiction.

I understand now.

Then you will also understand that the most important part of any work is its beginning. This is especially true for the education of young children. At this tender age they are the most impressionable and therefore most likely to adopt any and all models set before them.

True.

Then we can hardly afford to let the children listen to just any tales or fables recounted by just any teachers who happen along. We surely don't want the children to adopt opinions and beliefs that might be largely contrary to the kinds of values we deem desirable for them to have when they become adults.

Certainly not.

Then our program of education must begin with censorship. The censors will approve the fables and stories they deem good and ban those they consider to be harmful. We shall persuade mothers and nurses to tell the children stories from the approved list, assuring them that the training of the soul is far more important than the training of the body. If we apply this criterion, most of the stories they tell now will have to be discarded.

Which stories?

Let us consider the greatest stories; that will help us to understand the less renowned stories as well. The spirit and pattern will be the same in both. Don't you think so?

It is likely. But I have yet to understand what you mean by the greatest stories.

Those that have come down to us from Hesiod and Homer[5] and the other poets. Men have heard these stories again and again. We still hear them, and I believe that they are false.

Which stories do you mean? What fault do you find in them?

The most serious fault of all. They tell lies. Still worse, the lies they tell are malevolent.

How can we tell when they are lying?

Whenever they tell a tale that plays false with the true nature of gods[6] and heroes. Then they are like painters whose portraits bear no resemblance to their models.

Such things are surely blameworthy. But be specific. What do you mean in particular?

First of all, I mean the greatest and most malevolent lies about matters of the greatest concern: what Hesiod said Uranus did to his son Cronos and how Cronos revenged himself on his father. [378] Then there is the tale of Cronos's further doings and how he suffered in his turn at the hands of his own son, Zeus.[7] Even were these stories true, they ought not to be told indis-

5. Greek epic poet (ca. 8th c. B.C.E.), to whom the *Iliad* and the *Odyssey* are attributed. Hesiod (active ca. 700 B.C.E.), Greek epic didactic poet.

6. Because of the basic polytheism of Greek religion, the word for god occurs commonly in both singular and plural. We have consistently spelled the word without capitalization. A reader should be aware that differing conceptions of divinity underlie the ensuing discussion [translators' note].

7. Hesiod tells the story of the cosmic battle among members of three successive generations of gods in which the sons overthrew their fathers. First, Cronos castrated his father Uranus. Cronos then swallowed each of his children as Rhea gave birth to them. But Zeus she bore secretly and gave him to others to raise. To Cronos she gave a stone wrapped in swaddling clothes to swallow in place of the baby. When fully grown, Zeus forced Cronos to vomit up the stone and his other offspring, who joined with their liberator Zeus to form the final generation of ruling gods (Hesiod, *Theogony* 154–210 and 453–506) [translators' note].

criminately to young and thoughtless persons. It would be best if they could be buried in silence. If they absolutely must be retold, it should be only to a chosen few under conditions of total secrecy. And this only after performing a sacrifice not of an ordinary pig[8] but of some huge and usually unprocurable victim. That should help cut down the number of listeners.

I must admit that the stories you cite are extremely objectionable.

Yes, they are, Adeimantus, and they are not to be told in our city. No young man should be given to understand that even in the most outrageous crimes there is nothing outrageous. Nor should the child be taught to believe that in abandoning all restraint in order to punish the misdeeds of his father he will only be following the example of the first and greatest gods.

By Zeus, I agree. These stories are not fit to be told.

Nor can we permit it to be said that gods plot against gods and make war upon each other—which is in any case false—if we want our future guardians to abhor even the thought of quarreling among themselves. Still less shall we make up stories of battles among gods or giants; nor shall we permit the various episodes of their wars to be embroidered on our garments.[9] We shall follow the same policy concerning all the other endless quarrels of gods and heroes with their friends and relatives. If we could get them to believe us, we would tell our future guardians that quarreling is a blasphemy, and we would say that to this day there has never been a quarrel among citizens.

Now this is the sort of thing that the old men and the old women ought to be telling the children right from the start. As the children grow older, the poets must be compelled to write for them in a similar vein. But the story of Hera put in chains by her own son Hephaestus is inadmissible.[1] So is the story of these two on another occasion when Zeus hurled Hephaestus down from heaven for taking his mother's part when she was being beaten.[2] Once again, the battles of the gods in Homer's verse have no place in our city, whether they purport to be allegories or not. Young minds are not able to discriminate between what is allegorical and what is literal. At that age, whatever their minds absorb is likely to become fixed and unalterable. This may be the most important reason why tales for the very young should epitomize the fairest thoughts of virtue.

I agree with you there. But were someone to ask where we should find these desirable kinds of stories or themes, how should we reply?

Adeimantus, at this particular moment we are not poets but founders of a state. [379] Now it is proper that founders of states should be cognizant of the norms governing the general content of poetic compositions and the limits beyond which the poets must not go. But it is not the business of founders to compose the fables themselves.

Yes, but that's the whole point. What are the norms that should govern the telling of tales about the gods?

8. A sacrifice usual before initiation into the Eleusinian mysteries, secret cults at Eleusis in honor of Demeter, goddess of grain, and her daughter Persephone.

9. The battle of the giants against the gods—the Gigantomachia—was depicted on the robe woven for the statue of Athena at the Parthenon.

1. Hera was bound to a throne containing concealed chains given to her by her son Hephaestus [translators' note], the Greek god of fire and metalworking.

2. According to one legend, Hephaestus was lamed when Zeus cast him out of heaven for defending Hera, queen of the gods (see *Iliad* 1.591–97). Hera was Zeus's wife and sister.

Well, they should be something like this. Whether portrayed in epic, lyric, or tragic form, deity should always be depicted as it truly is.

Agreed.

And is god not always good? Should he not always be represented as such?

Yes.

Further, no good thing is harmful?

No.

And what is not harmful cannot harm?

Of course not.

And that which does no harm also does no evil?

It does no evil.

Can that which does no evil itself cause evil?

Impossible.

Then good produces good and is the source of happiness.

Yes.

It follows that the good is not the cause of all things but only of good things. It cannot be blamed for those things which are evil.

Quite right.

If god is good, then, he cannot be the source of all things, as the multitude is prone to say. In the affairs of men god acts as cause but rarely; of most things he is not the cause. This must be true because in human life good things are few and evils are many. The good we receive we must attribute to god alone; for the causes of evil we must look elsewhere.

I think what you say is true.

Then we cannot countenance the follies and errors in the poets' descriptions of the gods. Homer, for instance, says:

> Two urns stand on the palace floor of Zeus
> filled with destinies he allots,
> one containing good things and the other evil.

He who receives from Zeus both kinds

> chances upon evil one day and good the next.

But when Zeus does not blend the lots and instead gives a man unmixed evil,

> Hunger drives him, a wanderer everywhere on earth.

So we must not have it said that

> good and evil are alike bestowed by Zeus.[3]

Nor shall we approve if anyone tries to saddle Zeus or Athena with blame for the broken oaths and treaties that were really Pandarus's own doing.[4] Further, it is inadmissible to assert that Zeus and Themis[5] fomented discord

3. *Iliad* 24.527–32.
4. During a truce in the Trojan War, Athena, disguised as Laodocus [a Trojan warrior], appeared to Pandarus, another Trojan warrior, and persuaded him to shoot an arrow at Menelaus—an action that broke the truce and re-ignited the war (*Iliad* 4.86–103) [translators' note]. Athena: Greek goddess of wisdom and war, and the patron god of Athens. Menelaus: king of Sparta, and a central figure in the Trojan War as Helen of Troy's husband.
5. Greek goddess of justice, wisdom, and good counsel.

and strife among the gods. [380] And our young people must not be permitted to hear these words of Aeschylus:

> When a god would utterly destroy a house
> he implants in men the guilty cause.

Such verse the poet uses in writing of the sorrows of Niobe.[6] But if he or any poet must concern himself with these and similar themes when recalling the house of Pelops[7] or the Trojan War, we must make him conform to one of two requirements. Either he agrees not to ascribe the woes of men to the acts of gods, or he must provide some such explanation as we now are looking for ourselves. That is, what the gods did was just and righteous punishment, and those mortals upon whom it was inflicted benefited from it. But if instead they are portrayed as having been made miserable by the penalty and the gods declared to be the authors of their misery, this is something no poet will be allowed to say. On the other hand, if a poet should say that the wicked are miserable because they need to be punished and that the gods benefit them by providing the penalty, that we shall allow.

The proposition that a god, who is good, should cause evil to anyone is something we must strenuously deny. In a well-governed city it is something neither young nor old will assert or listen to. It must not be said or sung in verse or prose. It is a contradictory, profitless, and impious fiction.

I agree. I would vote to make your words law.

Then let this be one of the laws and principles in our city concerning the gods to which our speakers and poets must conform: a god is not the author of all things but only of good things.

Good.

We must consider a further proposition. Do you think that god is a wizard? Do you think he would play insidious games with us, assuming one shape at one time and another at another? Would he actually change himself and pass from his own form into many forms? Or would he deceive us by sometimes only feigning such transformations? Or is god simple? In that case, he would be less likely than any other being to depart from his own true form.

I shall need to think about that.

But what do you say to this? If something changes its form, it must either have changed itself or else there must have been some external cause.

Necessarily.

And is it not also true that things in their best condition are least likely to be affected or changed by external causes? The healthy human body, for example, is least likely to suffer adverse effects from food or drink or exer-

6. Niobe had boasted that she, with her twelve children, was the equal of Leto, who had only two divine children, Apollo and Artemis. The two gods killed all twelve of Niobe's children and left her sorrowing for her lost family [translators' note]. Aeschylus (525–456 B.C.E.), Greek tragedian; the quotation is from his *Niobe* (a lost play).

7. The curse on the house of Pelops was applied to successive generations. Myrtilus, Hermes' son, cursed Pelops as he threw him into the sea, and this curse was carried out first upon Pelops's sons, Atreus and Thyestes. Thyestes seduced Atreus's wife, but Atreus chopped up several of Thyestes' children and served them to their father in a stew. Atreus's children are Menelaus, whose wife Helen is given to Paris by Aphrodite, the extramarital gift that provoked the Trojan War; and Agamemnon, who is slain by his wife Clytemnestra and her lover Aegisthus (a surviving son of Thyestes). The children of Agamemnon and Clytemnestra are Orestes and Electra, who must arrange the murder of their mother at the command of Apollo [translators' note]. When writing plays, many Greek tragedians drew on this complex of myths.

tion. With plants it is the same. Those in full vigor will be the last to be damaged by high winds or the heat of the sun [381] or any other cause.

I agree.

Then we can adduce that the soul that is bravest and wisest will be least vulnerable to confusion or disorders originating from external sources?

Yes.

By analogy, I suppose, the same principle applies to men's artifacts—furniture, clothing, and houses. Those that are well made are least liable to be changed by time and other influences.

True.

Then we ought to be able to assert a universal truth: everything that is well made in nature or in art is best able to withstand change from without.

Apparently.

Now, could we agree that god, and everything that belongs to him, is in every way perfect?

Of course.

It follows that it would be the least of all possibilities that god should be compelled by external pressures to take on many forms.

Least indeed.

Still, he could will to change and transform himself?

Of course.

Will he change himself into something better and more beautiful or will the change be in the direction of the bad and the ugly?

If god changes, it must necessarily be for the worse, for we cannot suppose him to be initially deficient in any way in either goodness or beauty.

Well said, Adeimantus. Now another question: would anyone, whether god or man, willingly make himself worse?

Impossible.

Then it is impossible for a god even to wish to change himself. Intrinsically good and beautiful, a god abides simply and forever in his own form.

I think that is an unavoidable conclusion.

Then, my good friend, we must not suffer any poet to tell us that

> The gods appear as strangers from far lands
> and roam men's cities in many guises.[8]

Let no one fabricate falsehoods about Proteus and Thetis.[9] Neither let anyone in tragic or other kind of verse introduce Hera disguised as a priestess appealing for alms for the life-giving sons of Inachos,[1] the river of Argos. Many other such lies must also be suppressed. Further, we must not permit mothers under the influence of poets to frighten their children with wrong versions of myths that say certain gods masquerade as strangers from strange lands and haunt the night. Instead, we will make them take heed lest they speak evil of the gods and make cowards of their children.

8. *Odyssey* 17.485–86.

9. Proteus, the old man of the sea, is able to change into a variety of shapes. In the *Odyssey* (4.455–59) he turns into a lion, a snake, a leopard, a boar, flowing water, a tree, and finally back into a man. Thetis [mother of the hero Achilles] turned into a fire, a lion, and several more elusive forms in order to escape the embrace of Peleus [Achilles' father] (Pindar, *Nemean Ode* 4.62ff., and Ovid, *Metamorphoses* 9.238–46) [translators' note].

1. Both a river in Argos, a city-state on the Peloponnese, and a river god. The "sons" are presumably the river's tributaries with their "life-giving" water.

There can be no sanction for any such behavior.

Well, then, another question. If we are agreed that the gods are unchanging and do not will to change, could it nonetheless be true that by witchcraft and sorcery they could make us believe the illusion that they do indeed appear in many forms?

Perhaps.

[382] But do you really believe that a god would lie in word or deed or would seek to victimize us with illusions?

I don't know.

Don't you know that the true lie, if one can use such an expression, is hated by men and gods alike?

What do you mean?

I mean the lie that finds lodging in the inmost part of men's souls and remains there to deceive them about all the things most important to their lives. This is the lie that has no friends. Men hate and fear it above all others.

I still don't understand.

That is because you think I am trying to say something profound. All I mean is that every man loathes the thought that he might be taken captive by a lie which would prevent him from distinguishing between reality and unreality. That his soul should be possessed by a lie whereby he is continually deceived and irrevocably ignorant is something no man wants to accept.

Now I understand, and I agree.

Then it must be correct to say that what I have called the true lie is ignorance in the soul of the man deceived. The lie in words, on the other hand, does no more than imitate what the true lie does to the soul. It bears only a somewhat shadowy resemblance to the true lie and is not altogether false. Is that not right?

Quite right.

We have said, then, that the true lie is hated by both gods and men.

I agree.

Now what about the lie in words? Could it sometimes be useful to some people and therefore not be considered hateful? Would it be advantageous in dealing with enemies? And how about those we call friends? Should any of these be bent on doing wrong by some act of folly or madness, might not the lie in words be helpful as a sort of medicine, as a means by which we try to divert them and prevent the deed from being done? Consider also the fables and stories from the past that we have just been discussing. Because of our ignorance of the truth about the ancient times, our only recourse is to tell fables, patterning the false on the true as best we can so that our stories may have some use.

Yes, we men do all these things.

But would god find these kinds of lies useful? Would he lie about the past, for example, because he does not know the truth about it?

Such a notion would be absurd.

Then in god there is no lying poet.

No.

Well, then, would he lie because he fears his enemies?

Inconceivable.

But he may have friends who are mad or given over to folly?

Fools and madmen are not friends of god.

Then god has no motive for lying?

None.

May we conclude that in all things deity and the divine are entirely free from falsehood?

Yes.

Then god is simple and true in deed and word. He is unchanging and unchangeable. He doesn't lie. Whether men wake or whether men dream, god never deceives them with visions or with words or by signs.

[383] This is also what I think, when I hear you say it.

You would also concur, I assume, in a second law or principle to govern representations of the gods in poetry and prose. That is, the gods are neither wizards who confound us by transformations, nor do they deceive us by word or deed.

I concur.

Despite our esteem for Homer, then, we cannot admire the dream of lies that Zeus imparts to the sleeping Agamemnon.[2] Nor can we commend the verse of Aeschylus wherein Thetis alleged that Apollo sang at her wedding,

> Foretelling the fair fortunes of her progeny:
> Long would be their days and free from pain and ills.
> He made complete the tale of heaven's blessings,
> singing a joyous hymn and gladdening my heart.
> I believed that Phoebus would not lie,
> that a prophet would utter only truth.
> But he himself who sang that wedding night,
> he himself who feasted with us,
> he himself who promised these fair things,
> himself is now the slayer of my son.[3]

We shall be angry with a poet who writes such lines about the gods and shall forbid their presentation in public. Nor can we permit teachers to make use of such poets in instructing the young if our guardians are to become god-fearing men, and indeed godlike, insofar as that is possible for men.

I agree. I accept these laws and principles.

* * *

From *Book III*

[386] From childhood onward, then, these are the kinds of things we shall permit or forbid our guardians to hear about the gods, so that they will honor the gods and their mothers and fathers, and be true friends to each other.

I think these are good principles.

What next? If they are to be courageous they must learn still other lessons. They must learn not to fear death—or do you think anyone could be brave who is afraid of death?

No, I don't.

2. The dream deceiving Agamemnon tells him to muster the Greeks for battle because the gods have not agreed that Troy can be taken (*Iliad* 2.1–15) [translators' note]. Agamemnon: king of Mycenae and commander of the Greek expedition against Troy.

3. From a lost play. Phoebus: Apollo, god of prophecy as well as healing and music.

What about any man who believes the underworld is real and terrible? Will he be likely to be fearless? In battle, will he prefer death to defeat and slavery?

He will not.

Then we must expand our supervision to those who write and tell stories about these matters, too. We must ask them to speak better of Hades[4] rather than worse, for what they tell us now is not true, nor is it edifying for those who are going to be warriors.

You are right.

Let us begin, then, by expunging the verse that follows and all other writings and sayings of the same ilk:

> I would rather be a poor serf
> on the land of one himself penurious,
> than be monarch of all who ever died.

and this:

> Lest to mortals and immortals
> the houses of the dead be conjured up,
> dark, hideous, dank,
> and abhorrent to the gods themselves.

and this:

> Ah, woe! So it is true:
> in Hades' house are souls and apparitions,
> but all intelligence is gone.

and:

> He was alone with his wisdom and wit.
> All the others were shadows and wraiths.

and:

> Unwillingly his soul went forth from his body
> to bewail its doom in Hades
> and lament lost manliness and youth.

[387] and:

> Shrilling and gibbering,
> the soul slipped down like a vapor
> and vanished underneath the earth.

and:

> Like bats hanging in a darkened cave
> will cling to a rock together and shriek
> for the one that falls from the cluster,
> so their souls will screech and falter.[5]

4. The Greek underworld.
5. From *Odyssey* 11.489–91; *Iliad* 20.64–66, 23.103–4; *Odyssey* 10.495; *Iliad* 16.856–57, 23.100–101; and *Odyssey* 24.6–9.

We shall beg Homer and the other poets not to be angry if we ban these and all similar passages. Our objection is not that they are not poetic; nor is it that they do not please most hearers. Rather it is because the more poetic they are, the less they are suited to the ears of boys and men being schooled to be free and so to fear slavery more than death.

Further, we must suppress the entire vocabulary of terror and fear customarily used to describe the world below. Styx, the tide of hate, Cocytus, the river of lamentation,[6] charnel house, withered shades—all such terms that make men tremble will have to go. Horror stories may be all right for other purposes, but our purpose is to prevent our guardians becoming hotheaded from such stories or else degenerate in nerves and heart.

Your concern is well taken.

Then let us do away with them.

Agreed.

And we must require the contrary sentiments in poetry and prose?

Clearly.

Surely we should expunge the wailing and laments of famous men?

They must go with the rest.

Consider, however, whether we shall indeed do right in getting rid of them. Our purpose is to affirm that a good man will not think death a terrible thing even should it befall another good man and comrade.

That is our purpose.

Then he would not lament his friend as if something terrible had happened to him.

No.

Further, we would say of him that of all men he is most sufficient to himself in leading the good life. He has least need of anybody else.

True.

So he finds it less terrible than others to endure the loss of a son, a brother, a fortune, or anything else?

That follows.

And when misfortune overtakes him, he will lament but little and bear his sorrow in moderation?

Yes.

Then we shall do well to delete the lamentations of famous men. We can attribute them to women—and not to the better sort of women either—and to men of lesser account. [388] We do this so that those we educate to be guardians of the city will disdain such behavior.

We shall be right in doing so.

Then we must turn once again to Homer and the other poets and ask them not to portray Achilles, himself the son of a goddess,

> lying on his side, then on his back,
> and again face down,
> then rising up distraught and quivering
> on a beach of the waste and barren sea,

6. Two of the four rivers of Hades.

nor scooping up ashes with both hands and pouring them on his head,[7] nor giving way to grief and tears in Homer's various descriptions. Neither should Priam, close kin to the gods, be described in supplication,

> calling aloud and rolling in the dung,
> entreating each man by name.[8]

Most particularly shall we entreat Homer and the others at least to spare us from those descriptions that have the gods themselves given over to lamentation and wailing:

> Alas! Ah, woe is me, unhappy mother,
> who gave birth to the bravest, and now to my sorrow.[9]

If they insist on characterizing the gods in this way, they should at least not dare to misrepresent Zeus, greatest of the gods, by putting such words as these into his mouth:

> Oh, woe! My heart is afflicted
> that I should behold a man most dear to me
> being chased around the city of Troy.

or these:

> Oh, Sarpedon, dearest of men to me.
> Oh, sorrow, he is fated to be slain
> by Patroclus, Menoetius's son.[1]

Now, my dear Adeimantus, supposing our youth should take seriously such nonsense about the gods instead of laughing at it? Would any of them in that case be likely to think such conduct unworthy of themselves? Would they not reflect that they are only men and therefore have no cause to rebuke themselves for behaving in the way the gods themselves behave? Would they not be likely to abandon shame and self-control, starting to wail and chant dirges at the slightest provocation?

Without doubt.

But our previous reasoning has shown that this is the sort of thing we ought not to permit. And I think we better stick to this position until somebody shows us a better one.

I agree.

Nor must our young men be too fond of laughter. Anyone who gives way to excessive laughter almost always provokes a violent reaction.

So it seems.

It follows that persons of importance ought not to be described as overcome by laughter. [389] Still less should we sanction similar representations of the gods.

7. *Iliad* 24.10–13 and 18.23–24. Achilles: the greatest of the Greek warriors at Troy and the central figure of the *Iliad*.

8. *Iliad* 22.414–15. Priam: the last king of Troy, descended from Zeus.

9. *Iliad* 18.54. The speaker is Thetis.

1. *Iliad* 22.168–69 (Hector is being chased by Achilles), 16.433–34. Sarpedon: a son of Zeus who fought with the Trojans. Patroclus: the dearest friend of Achilles.

Just as you say: such representations of the gods are still less acceptable.

Then these sayings of Homer about the gods are also unacceptable:

> Irrepressible laughter spread among the blessed gods
> as they saw their Hephaestus bustling about the palace.[2]

No, we cannot accept them, according to your view.

If you choose to call it my view. At any rate, we must repudiate them.

Further: we must prize truth. We said before that gods have no use for lies. If that is right, and if it is also right that lies are useful to men only as a kind of medicine or remedy, then only doctors should be permitted to use them. Lay persons have no business lying.

Obviously.

Only the rulers of the city—and no others—may tell lies. And their lies, whether directed to enemies or citizens, will be legitimate only if their purpose is to serve the public interest. But no private person may tell lies to rulers. To do so would be a great transgression—greater even than if a patient were to deceive his doctor about the true condition of his body, or if an athlete were to practice a like deception with his trainer. Or, to draw a further analogy, we may liken it to a case where a man conceals from the captain the true conditions prevailing aboard the ship and lies about how he and his fellow sailors fare.

I agree.

Now if the ruler of a city catches anybody lying—besides himself—any of the craftsmen,

> whether priest, carpenter, or doctor of medicine,[3]

he will punish them for subversive practice, as damaging to a city as to a ship.

He will, if words are as good as deeds.

Next, our young people must learn moderation.

Certainly.

And would you agree that the main issues for the multitude concerning moderation are obedience to the rulers and self-rule in regard to the bodily appetites?

I think so.

Then we shall commend what Homer has Diomedes say:

> Friend, be quiet and obey my word,[4]

and also what follows:

> The Greeks marched forward with valor,
> silent, in fear of their captains,[5]

and all similar passages.

2. *Iliad* 1.599–600.
3. *Odyssey* 17.383–84.
4. *Iliad* 4.412. Diomedes: a lord of Argos who was one of the best Greek fighters at Troy.
5. This couplet combines *Iliad* 3.8 and 4.431.

Yes, these are well said.

But what of these lines and those following them?

> Oh, you, heavy with wine, timorous as a deer,
> cringing like a dog—[6]

[390] Are these and similar impertinences addressed to rulers by private citizens well said or ill?

They are ill said.

Certainly they are ill suited to prepare the young for the practice of moderation and self-control. But, on the other hand, if listening to such things provides some pleasure, we ought not to be surprised. Or what is your opinion?

The same as yours.

And here we have the wisest of men saying what he thinks the fairest thing in all the world:

> Tables laden with bread and meat,
> the cup bearer drawing wine from the bowl
> and filling our goblets.[7]

Will these words be conducive to temperance in a young man? Or these?

> Hunger is the worst of destinies and deaths.[8]

The same question applies to the tale of Zeus, alone and awake, devising plans while men and the other gods slept, only to forget them in a moment when roused by his lust for Hera. So overcome was he by the sight of her that he did not even want to go to the house, and they made love right there upon the ground. Zeus said to Hera he had not felt so fierce a passion even during their courting days when "deceiving their dear parents."[9]

Nor will self-control among our youth be strengthened if they hear the same theme recounted in the story of Hephaestus fastening together the bodies of Ares and Aphrodite.[1]

By Zeus, I think you are right.

But, ah, the words and deeds of famous men enduring against great odds—these are the kinds of things suitable for our young people to see and hear. Consider this example:

> He smote his breast and admonished thus his heart:
> Endure, my heart; far worse hast thou endured.[2]

Excellent.

Next, our men ought not to covet gifts or money.

Certainly not.

Then they must not hear it sung that

6. These words of insult are spoken by Achilles to Agamemnon, the leader of the Greeks at Troy (*Iliad* 1.225) [translators' note].
7. *Odyssey* 9.8–10. The lines are spoken by Odysseus, who is often described as clever or scheming.
8. *Odyssey* 12.342.
9. See *Iliad* 14.294–351 (quotation, 296).
1. The story of Hephaestus's magical bed which entrapped Ares [god of war] and Aphrodite in the act of adultery is told in Book 8 of Homer's *Odyssey* [translators' note]. Aphrodite, the goddess of love and beauty, was Hephaestus's wife.
2. *Odyssey* 20.17–18.

Gifts persuade the gods, gifts persuade dread kings.[3]

Neither can we endorse the counsel Phoenix urged upon his pupil Achilles: that he should accept gifts from the Greeks and help them, but if they offered no gifts, he should continue to show them his anger. Neither shall we say or believe of Achilles himself that he was so greedy as to accept gifts from Agamemnon or that he demanded payment to yield up a corpse [391] and would otherwise refuse to do so.[4]

Such conduct must not be condoned.

My regard for Homer makes me hesitate to charge him with outright impiety when he imputes such deeds and sentiments to Achilles. But he does not persuade me. Nor do others who say the same things. I cannot believe, for example, that Achilles would say to Apollo:

> You have impeded me, O most malignant of the gods.
> King of the bowmen, I would take revenge upon you,
> had I the power.[5]

Neither do I trust those stories of his disobedience to the river god and his readiness to fight with him.[6] Nor will I credit the allegation that he promised and consecrated the locks of his hair to the other river god, Spercheus, and then offered them up instead to the dead Patroclus.[7]

That Achilles actually did all these things is something we must not believe. We shall reject the charges that he dragged Hector's body around the tomb of Patroclus and slew living victims on the funeral pyre.[8] We must not suffer our youth to suppose that Achilles, pupil of the most wise Chiron[9]—Achilles, son of a goddess and of Peleus, the most chaste of men and grandson of Zeus—could be so at odds with himself as to suffer from two contradictory maladies: greed such as becomes no free man and a brazen arrogance toward both gods and men.

No. These sorts of things we shall neither sanction nor believe.

Let us also adopt the same posture concerning those dreadful stories of rape that are told about Theseus, son of Poseidon, and Pirithous, the son of Zeus himself.[1] Let us refuse to believe that any other child of a god—or any hero—would dare to do such wicked deeds as people tell us nowadays. What we must do is either to require our poets to deny that such deeds were ever done or else to deny that children of the gods did them. They may speak of the deeds or of the doers, but must not join one to the other. We will not have poets attempting to persuade our youth that the gods beget evil and that heroes are no better than men. As we said earlier, such views are both sacrilegious and false. Or am I not right in saying we have already proved that gods cannot possibly cause evil?

3. A proverb.
4. The incident alluded to is Achilles' agreement to release the body of Hector to his father Priam, a story told in Book 24 of the *Iliad*. It should be noted, however, that Achilles does not demand gifts; he is prepared to return the body in response to the command of the gods [translators' note].
5. *Iliad* 22.15, 20.
6. Homer relates that Achilles ignored the urging of the Scamander River to stop bloodying its waters by the slaughter of so many Trojans (*Iliad* 21.214ff.) [translators' note].
7. Achilles' father Peleus had vowed to offer locks of hair from his son's head when Achilles returned from Troy safely. Instead Achilles placed them on the pyre of his fallen friend Patroclus because he knew that he would never return home (*Iliad* 23.138–51) [translators' note].
8. *Iliad* 24.14–18, 23.175–77.
9. A wise centaur, whose pupils included many great heroes of Greek mythology.
1. Theseus and Pirithous joined to carry off Helen, Menelaus's wife, and Persephone, the queen of the underworld [translators' note].

You are right.

Furthermore, these views are harmful to those who hear them. A person will not fail to be lenient with himself and his own trespasses if he believes that the kinds of shameful deeds we have just been discussing are acts of

> the gods' own kin, the relatives of Zeus,
> of those whose ancestral altar
> flames high atop Mount Ida
> and in whose blood line courses still
> the flame of immortality.[2]

So let us put an end to all these stories lest our youth [392] sink into moral turpitude.

Yes, let us do so.

Well, then, what is there still to talk about in the matter of censorship and storytelling? Have we omitted anything? We have already considered gods, daemons, heroes, and the netherworld.

We have.

Then what we have still to discuss are the stories about men.

Right.

But, my friend, this is something we cannot possibly do at this point.

Why not?

Because I suppose we shall again be saying that writers of both poetry and prose speak falsely of men, and in matters of the greatest moment. They will offer numerous examples of unjust men who are happy and just men who are wretched. They will assert that there is profit in injustice if it can be concealed, while justice is invariably your loss and another man's gain. I presume that we shall forbid them to say these things and then compel them to say and sing to the contrary. Do you concur?

I am sure of it.

* * *

Then we can say that good words, good harmony, good grace, and good rhythm follow from the good order and disposition of the soul. By "good disposition" we don't mean "good-natured," a term so often used as indulgent description of someone who is simple-minded. We mean to describe instead a soul in which reason has been educated to govern in goodness and truth.

I agree.[3]

Are these not the things our youth must strive for if they are to fulfill their own true purposes?

This is what they must do.

[401] And are not many of these things to be found in painting and in all similar arts—weaving, embroidery, furniture making, and architecture? So too in the natural world of animals and plants. In all of these we can find grace and gracelessness. Gracelessness, disharmony, and discord are closely linked to evil words and an evil temper. The opposite qualities are bound together in the same way.

You are right.

2. From the *Niobe* of Aeschylus.

3. Glaucon is speaking here.

Should we conclude, then, that our supervision should be confined only to poets, compelling them to summon up the image of goodness in their poems or else to forgo writing poetry among us? Or should we extend our guidance to those in the other arts and forbid representations of any kind of evil disposition—of what is licentious, illiberal, and graceless—whether in living creatures, in buildings, or in any other product of the arts of man? Here, too, we would penalize disobedience by excluding them from the practice of their art in our city. In this way we could protect our guardians from growing up in the presence of evil, in a veritable pasture of poisonous herbs where by grazing at will, little by little and day by day, they should unwittingly accumulate a huge mass of corruption in their souls.

By the same token, we should seek out artists and craftsmen whose natural gifts enable them to discern true beauty and grace. Then we shall have a salubrious climate in which our young may dwell and benefit from all their surroundings, where works of beauty are conveyed to eye and ear like breezes bringing health from wholesome places. In this way, from early childhood on, they would easily live in harmony and friendship with beauty and reason, coming finally to resemble them.

A truly noble concept of education.

That is why education in poetry and music is first in importance, Glaucon. Rhythm and harmonies have the greatest influence on the soul; they penetrate into its inmost regions and there hold fast. If the soul is rightly trained, they bring grace. If not, they bring the contrary. One who is properly educated in these matters would most quickly perceive and deplore the absence or perversion of beauty in art or nature. With true good taste he would instead delight in beautiful things, praising them and welcoming them into his soul. He would nourish them and would himself come to be beautiful and good. [402] While still young and still unable to understand why, he will reject and hate what is ugly. Then, later, when reason comes to one so educated, his affinity for what is good and beautiful will lead him to recognize and welcome her.

You have given the best possible reasons for studying poetry and music.

Do you also see that this way of studying them resembles the way we learned to read? We could not become proficient in reading until we knew the individual letters of the alphabet and recognized each of them in all the various word combinations in which they appear. So we learned that it was necessary to pay attention to everything—great or small—and disregard nothing in our texts if we were ever to become letter-perfect and so fully literate.

True.

Supposing we had seen some letters reflected in a mirror or in water? We should never have known what they were unless we had previously come to know them in their original forms. But is it not also true that knowledge of both original and likeness is attained through one and the same kind of study and discipline?

Yes.

By the gods, then, I am right. We can have no truly educated men—no true musicians whether we speak of ourselves or of those we want to train to be guardians—unless we can understand the nature of such things as courage, temperance, generosity, or nobility, both in their original essential forms and in the resemblances of the forms. We must understand their opposites as well, also in form and image. We must understand them in all the combinations in which they appear—great or small—paying attention to everything and disregarding nothing. And once again we must recognize that we attain this kind of understanding through one and the same kind of study and discipline.

You make a compelling case.

Then wherever there is a correspondence between beauty in the soul and in the body, both reflecting beauty in its original form, will that not be the fairest sight of all for those who can see?

Surely the fairest.

And the fairest is the most beloved?

Of course.

Then the well-educated man, the true musician, would love this kind of person. But where there is disharmony, there he would not love.

He would not love if the defect were in the soul. But if it were a defect of the body, he would not turn away; he would love nonetheless.

I understand. You know whereof you speak, and I agree. But let me put another question: can there be any connection between temperance and the extremes of pleasure?

How could there be? After all, we know that extreme pleasure drives a man out of his mind no less than extreme pain.

And his bonds with virtue are severed?

[403] Yes.

But there are links between pleasure, insolence, and license?

Yes.

Do you know of any pleasure more exciting and sensuous than sex?

No. Nor any more likely to drive a man mad.

But is not true love temperate and harmonious, a love of beauty and order?

Indeed.

So nothing of madness or license must be allowed to intrude upon true love?

No.

Then mad or intemperate pleasure cannot be sanctioned. Lover and beloved who love rightly must not have anything to do with it.

No, Socrates, they must not.

I assume, then, that in the city we are founding you would propose a law whereby a lover is permitted to kiss and touch his beloved with honorable purpose like a father would his son, if the beloved consents thereto. But he would be allowed to go no further; otherwise, by manifesting a want of taste and culture, he would court disgrace.

Quite right.

Would you also agree that our discussion of music is now finished? What could be more fitting than to complete our analysis by showing that the purpose of poetry and music is to cultivate the love of beauty?

It is a fitting conclusion.

* * *

From *Book VII*

[514] Here allegory may show us best how education—or the lack of it—affects our nature. Imagine men living in a cave with a long passageway stretching between them and the cave's mouth, where it opens wide to the light. Imagine further that since childhood the cave dwellers have had their legs and necks shackled so as to be confined to the same spot. They are further constrained by blinders that prevent them from turning their heads; they can see only directly in front of them. Next, imagine a light from a fire some distance behind them and burning at a higher elevation. Between the prisoners and the fire is a raised path along whose edge there is a low wall like the partition at the front of a puppet stage. The wall conceals the puppeteers while they manipulate their puppets above it.

So far I can visualize it.[4]

Imagine, further, men behind the wall carrying all sorts of objects along its length and holding them above it. The objects include human and animal images made of stone and wood [515] and all other material. Presumably, those who carry them sometimes speak and are sometimes silent.

You describe a strange prison and strange prisoners.

Like ourselves. Tell me, do you not think those men would see only the shadows cast by the fire on the wall of the cave? Would they have seen anything of themselves or of one another?

How could they if they couldn't move their heads their whole life long?

Could they see the objects held above the wall behind them or only the shadows cast in front?

Only the shadows.

If, then, they could talk with one another, don't you think they would impute reality to the passing shadows?

Necessarily.

Imagine an echo in their prison, bouncing off the wall toward which the prisoners were turned. Should one of those behind the wall speak, would the prisoners not think that the sound came from the shadows in front of them?

No doubt of it.

By every measure, then, reality for the prisoners would be nothing but shadows cast by artifacts.

It could be nothing else.

Imagine now how their liberation from bondage and error would come about if something like the following happened. One prisoner is freed from his shackles. He is suddenly compelled to stand up, turn around, walk, and look toward the light. He suffers pain and distress from the glare of the light. So dazzled is he that he cannot even discern the very objects whose shadows he used to be able to see. Now what do you suppose he would answer if he were told that all he had seen before was illusion but that now he was nearer reality, observing real things and therefore seeing more truly? What if someone pointed to the objects being carried above the wall, questioning him as to what each one is? Would he not be at a loss? Would he not

4. Glaucon is Socrates' interlocutor here.

regard those things he saw formerly as more real than the things now being shown him?

He would.

Again, let him be compelled to look directly at the light. Would his eyes not feel pain? Would he not flee, turning back to those things he was able to discern before, convinced that they are in every truth clearer and more exact than anything he has seen since?

He would.

Then let him be dragged away by force up the rough and steep incline of the cave's passageway, held fast until he is hauled out into the light of the sun. Would not such a rough passage be painful? Would he not resent the experience? [516] And when he came out into the sunlight, would he not be dazzled once again and unable to see what he calls realities?

He could not see even one of them, at least not immediately.

Habituation, then, is evidently required in order to see things higher up. In the beginning he would most easily see shadows; next, reflections in the water of men and other objects. Then he would see the objects themselves. From there he would go on to behold the heavens and the heavenly phenomena—more easily the moon and stars by night than the sun by day.

Yes.

Finally, I suppose, he would be able to look on the sun itself, not in reflections in the water or in fleeting images in some alien setting. He would look at the sun as it is, in its own domain, and so be able to see what it is really like.

Yes.

It is at this stage that he would be able to conclude that the sun is the cause of the seasons and of the year's turning, that it governs all the visible world and is in some sense also the cause of all visible things.

This is surely the next step he would take.

Now, supposing he recalled where he came from. Supposing he thought of his fellow prisoners and of what passed for wisdom in the place they were inhabiting. Don't you think he would feel pity for all that and rejoice in his own change of circumstance?

He surely would.

Suppose there had been honors and citations those below bestowed upon one another. Suppose prizes were offered for the one quickest to identify the shadows as they go by and best able to remember the sequence and configurations in which they appear. All these skills, in turn, would enhance the ability to guess what would come next. Do you think he would covet such rewards? More, would he envy and want to emulate those who hold power over the prisoners and are in turn reverenced by them? Or would he not rather hold fast to Homer's words that it is "better to be the poor servant of a poor master,"[5] better to endure anything, than to believe those things and live that way?

I think he would prefer anything to such a life.

Consider, further, if he should go back down again into the cave and return to the place he was before, would not his eyes now go dark after so abruptly leaving the sunlight behind?

They would.

5. *Odyssey* 11.489.

Suppose he should then have to compete once more in shadow watching with those who never left the cave. And this before his eyes had become accustomed to the dark [517] and his dimmed vision still required a long period of habituation. Would he not be laughed at? Would it not be said that he had made the journey above only to come back with his eyes ruined and that it is futile even to attempt the ascent? Further, if anyone tried to release the prisoners and lead them up and they could get their hands on him and kill him, would they not kill him?

Of course.

Now, my dear Glaucon, we must apply the allegory as a whole to all that has been said so far. The prisoners' cave is the counterpart of our own visible order, and the light of the fire betokens the power of the sun. If you liken the ascent and exploration of things above to the soul's journey through the intelligible order, you will have understood my thinking, since that is what you wanted to hear. God only knows whether it is true. But, in any case, this is the way things appear to me: in the intelligible world the last thing to be seen—and then only dimly—is the idea of the good. Once seen, however, the conclusion becomes irresistible that it is the cause of all things right and good, that in the visible world it gives birth to light and its sovereign source, that in the intelligible world it is itself sovereign and the author of truth and reason, and that the man who will act wisely in private and public life must have seen it.

I agree, insofar as I can follow your thinking.

Come join me, then, in this further thought. Don't be surprised if those who have attained this high vision are unwilling to be involved in the affairs of men. Their souls will ever feel the pull from above and yearn to sojourn there. Such a preference is likely enough if the assumptions of our allegory continue to be valid.

Yes, it is likely.

By the same token, would you think it strange if someone returning from divine contemplation to the miseries of men should appear ridiculous? What if he were still blinking his eyes and not yet readjusted to the surrounding darkness before being compelled to testify in court about the shadows of justice or about the images casting the shadows? What if he had to enter into debate about the notions of such matters held fast by people who had never seen justice itself?

It would not be strange.

[518] Nonetheless, a man with common sense would know that eyesight can be impaired in two different ways by dint of two different causes, namely, transitions from light into darkness and from darkness into light. Believing that the soul also meets with the same experience, he would not thoughtlessly laugh when he saw a soul perturbed and having difficulty in comprehending something. Instead he would try to ascertain whether the cause of its faded vision was the passage from a brighter life to unaccustomed darkness or from the deeper darkness of ignorance toward the world of light, whose brightness then dazzled the soul's eye. He will count the first happy, and the second he will pity. Should he be minded to laugh, he who comes from below will merit it more than the one who descends from the light above.

A fair statement.

* * *

From *Book X*

[595] Indeed. And many other things about our city convince me that we have built it truly. When I say this, I think particularly of the role we assigned to poetry.

What do you mean?[6]

We barred any kind of poetry that is imitative;[7] under no circumstances can it be admitted to the city. The reason for excluding it should be still more evident than before now that we have examined the soul's several parts.

What do you mean?

Well, don't go tattling to the tragic poets and all the other mimics. But, between ourselves, it appears to me that their art corrupts the minds of all who hearken to them, save only those whose knowledge of reality provides an antidote.

What do you have in mind when you say that?

My love and reverence for Homer since I was a boy makes me hesitate. Yet I must speak out: he seems to have been the first teacher and originator of all these beautiful tragedies. Honoring truth must take precedence over honoring the man. Hence my conviction that one must speak his mind.

That much is certain.

Then listen. Or, rather, answer.

Then ask.

Could you tell me in general what imitation is? I myself am hardly able to understand its nature and purpose.

Then how should I be able to understand it?

Nothing to wonder at. You know that men with duller vision [596] often see things before those with keener sight.

True. But in your presence I find myself unwilling to say just anything that occurs to me. So speak up yourself.

Very well. Shall we begin the inquiry by following our customary procedure? I think we have generally followed the practice of subsuming multiplicities under a single form or idea and then calling them collectively by a single name.[8] Do you understand?

I understand.

Then consider some multiplicity of your choice. For example, there are many beds and tables.

Of course.

But among these furnishings, I suppose, there are only two forms: one of a bed and one of a table.

Agreed.

Is it not also our custom to say that the carpenter who makes a bed or table or some other piece of useful furniture looks to the form of each? Presumably no craftsman produces the form itself. How could he?

He could not.

Now, what would you call this next kind of craftsman?

What kind?

6. Glaucon is Socrates' interlocutor here.
7. Tragedy and epic; insofar as they are imitative, they are by definition removed from reality. The total ban here seems to contradict *Republic* 2 and 3, where Socrates encourages literary representation of behavior that is appropriate and good.
8. That is, the Idea or Form.

The one who can make all the things that each class of artisan considers its own specialty.

I would call him a clever and wonderful man.

Wait. Soon you will say even more. Not only is this craftsman able to construct all practical contrivances. He also breeds all plants and animals, including himself. Still more, he creates the earth and sky, the gods and all things in heaven and in Hades under the earth.

Now I would call him a wonderful sophist.[9]

Are you skeptical? Tell me, do you think no such craftsman could exist? Or do you think it possible that in some sense there could be one who makes all these objects but in another sense not? Or don't you realize that in a certain way you yourself could be the maker of all things?

And what way is that?

The way is not difficult. It can be quickly managed anywhere on earth—most quickly if you are prepared to carry a mirror with you wherever you go. Quickly you will produce the sun and the things of heaven; quickly the earth; quickly yourself; quickly all the animals, plants, contrivances, and every other object we just mentioned.

But only in appearance; not in reality.

Excellent. You advance the argument at just the right moment. Now, the painter is one kind of craftsman, is he not?

Of course.

I suppose you will say that what he creates is unreal. Still, in a certain way, he does make a bed, doesn't he?

Yes. He makes something resembling a bed.

[597] Once again, how about the carpenter? Weren't you just saying that he also does not make a real bed? He simply makes a particular bed and not what we call the real bed, the form of a bed.

Yes. I said that.

Then he is not making something real but only a facsimile. That is not reality. So if someone should say that the carpenter's work (or that of other artisans) is the same as reality, he could hardly be called truthful.

At least, that would be the view of people who devote their time to these kinds of arguments.

No wonder, then, that the one who makes beds also offers only a dim reflection of the truth.

No wonder.

Shall we now apply these examples to aid us in finding out what an imitator really is?

If you wish.

Well, then, it turns out there are three kinds of beds. One exists in nature. I suppose we would say god created it. Who else could?

No one else, I should think.

And then the bed the carpenter made.

Yes.

And the one made by the painter. Right?

All right.

9. An itinerant teacher of the 5th century B.C.E.; sophists were Greece's first professional teachers (see GORGIAS).

So we have the painter, the carpenter, and god. These three produce three kinds of beds.

Three. Right.

God, then, whether he willed it or because he felt some constraint not to make more than one bed, did in fact make only one bed, the real bed. Never were two or more beds made by god, nor would they ever be.

Why not?

I shall explain. Even if he had made only two beds, a third would unavoidably appear. That would be the real bed, of which the other two would only be copies.

Right.

God, I suppose, knowing this and wishing to be the real creator of the real bed and not some particular craftsman making some particular bed, wrought in nature only one bed.

Apparently.

Shall we call him something like its true and natural creator?

That would be fitting since he has created this and everything else in nature.

What about the carpenter? Does he not make a bed?

Yes.

And the painter? Does he not also create a bed?

Certainly not.

Then what relationship does he have with the bed?

I think it would be most fair to call him an imitator of things that others create.

So one who makes something at third remove from nature you call an imitator?

Indeed I do.

And the maker of tragedies is also thrice removed, as it were, from the king and the truth. He is therefore an imitator like all other imitators?

It seems so.

Then we agree about the imitator. Now let us return to the painter. [598] Is it his habit to imitate the original in nature or the craftsmen's products?

What the craftsmen make.

As they are or as they appear to be? This is a distinction still to be made.

What do you mean?

This. If you look at a bed from the side or the front or from any other angle, is it any different? Or does it remain the same in fact but different in appearance—and does this not hold for everything else?

The latter is true. It looks different, but it's not different.

This, then, is the point we want to consider. Does painting imitate reality or appearance? Does it imitate illusion or truth?

Illusion.

Then imitation is surely far from truth. This probably explains why the imitator will put his hand to anything; he grasps only a small fragment of whatever it is he works with, and even that is unreal. The painter, for example, will portray a shoemaker, a carpenter, or other craftsmen without any understanding of the arts they use. Nonetheless, if he is a good artist and displays his portrait of the carpenter from a distance, he would deceive children and unreasoning men into believing that they were seeing a real carpenter.

Why not?

At any rate, my friend, I think this is what we should keep in mind in all such matters. When anyone tells us that he has met some person who knows all the arts and everything else known to man—that there is nothing he does not know better than everybody else—we must tell him that he is gullible and must have met a magician and been deceived. He was duped into thinking such a person omniscient because of his own inability to test and verify the difference between knowledge, ignorance, and imitation.

That is certain.

Now let us consider tragedy and Homer as its master. Some say the tragic poets know all the arts, all things human, all things pertaining to virtue and vice, all things divine. They claim that the good poet writing good poetry must know what he is writing about; otherwise he would not be able to be a poet. Therefore we must ask whether those who talk this way may have been keeping company with imitators who deceived them; whether, in consequence, they looked at the works of poets [599] but did not understand that they were thrice removed from reality and could easily be produced without any knowledge of truth. For poets contrive appearances and not reality. Or is there something in what they say? Do good poets really know what many think they say so well?

The question certainly requires examination.

Then if a man were able to produce both realities and illusions, do you think he would choose to work with illusions and devote himself to them as the best that life could offer?

No.

I would suppose, if he actually knew the things he imitates, he would do those things and leave off imitating. Would he not try to leave as his memorial a tangible record of many splendid deeds? Would he not rather be the one who is praised than the one who praises?

I should think he would. In deeds there is far greater honor and profit.

Well, let us not demand an accounting from Homer or any of the other poets whether any of them were really doctors or whether they merely copied off medical language. Nor will we ask whether any poet, past or present, has ever healed men as Asclepius[1] healed them; nor whether he has left behind heirs to his medical knowledge the way Asclepius did. And we shall forgo questions about any of the other arts. But surely it is fair to inquire of Homer concerning the greatest and most estimable things he undertook to speak of: wars, military skills, the governing of cities, and the education of men.

"Beloved Homer," we could say, "if your words about virtue are not at third remove from the truth, if you don't fit our definition of the imitator as an inventor of dreams—if you are instead next neighbor to truth and can identify the kinds of behavior that make men better or worse in both private and public life—then tell us what city has ever been better governed thanks to you. Sparta owes thanks to Lycurgus. Many other cities, small and great, owe a similar debt of thanks.[2] What city gives you credit for having been a

1. Hero and god of healing (in the *Iliad*, a mortal).
2. The next several lines contain the names of a series of lawgivers who gained fame for their success in designing successful constitutions [translators' note]. Lycurgus: traditional founder of the Spartan political, social, and legal systems.

good lawgiver or benefactor? In Italy and Sicily, Charondas is so credited; among us it is Solon.[3] Who credits you?" Will there be any he can name?

I don't suppose so. Even Homer's followers have never mentioned any.

[600] Can we recall any war in Homer's time won under his command or as a result of his advice?

None.

What about the inventions and practical devices that we expect from men skilled in crafts? Thales the Milesian and Anacharsis from Scythia are credited with many.[4] How about Homer?

None.

Well, if Homer has no record of public service, what report do we have of him as a private educator around whom men gathered because they cherished his teachings? Did he and they pass on to posterity a kind of Homeric way of life after the manner of Pythagoras?[5] Such a legacy is counted among Pythagoras's greatest achievements. Even now his successors use the term *Pythagorean* to denote a certain way of life that many of our contemporaries look upon with respect.

Once again, Socrates, there is no report. To look on his companion Creophylus as representative of Homeric culture might turn out to be a more promising subject for ridicule than the name Creophylus itself.[6] For if the things said about Homer are true, he was neglected by that child of the flesh during most of his lifetime.

So tradition tells us. Don't you suppose then, Glaucon, that if Homer had really been able to educate men and make them better because he was a man of real knowledge and not an imitator, he would have had many companions and been loved and honored by them? After all, Protagoras of Abdera and Prodicus of Ceos[7] and others are able to attract many of their contemporaries to their private lessons, where they impress upon their listeners that without instruction from them they will be able to govern neither their cities nor their own homes. This is the wisdom that makes them so beloved that their students all but carry them about on their shoulders. If Homer had helped men to achieve excellence, surely his contemporaries would not have let him and Hesiod live as itinerant reciters of poetry. Would they not sooner have parted with gold than with their poets? Would they not have insisted that they stay with them and dwell in their homes? Failing that, would they not have followed and attended them until they were able to receive from them an adequate education?

I think your questions are to the point, Socrates.

Then we should be prepared to declare that the entire tribe of poets—beginning with Homer—are mere imitators of illusions of virtue and imita-

3. Athenian statesman and poet (ca. 638–559 B.C.E.), who reformed the city's constitution. Charondas (6th c. B.C.E.), lawgiver of Catana and other colonies of Chalcis in Sicily.

4. Thales and Anacharsis are both counted among the seven sages of antiquity. Thales was a philosopher, statesman, and mathematician; his most famous exploit was his calculation of an eclipse that occurred on May 28, 585 B.C.E. Anacharsis is reported to have invented the anchor and the potter's wheel [translators' note].

5. Pythagoras [6th c. B.C.E.] based his philosophical and religious beliefs on mathematical formulations. He provided an education for his followers based on his "way of life." In southern Italy he founded a religious brotherhood in the city of Croton [translators' note].

6. Creophylus literally means "of the beef tribe"; he is supposed to have been a friend of Homer and an epic poet [translators' note].

7. Greek sophist, a contemporary of Socrates. Protagoras (5th c. B.C.E.), Greek philosopher, one of the most successful of the sophists.

tors as well of the other things they write about. They don't lay a hand on truth. Instead, as we said a moment ago, they are like the painter who knows nothing about cobbling [601] but who creates what seems to be a shoemaker in the eyes of those who also know nothing of the subject and who judge simply in terms of shape and color.

You are right.

I suppose we may say the same of the poet himself. He only knows how to imitate, daubing the several arts with words and phrases but understanding nothing. His imitations speak to those who are equally ignorant and who see things only through words. The poet will use meter, rhythm, and harmony; and no matter whether his subject matter concerns generals or shoemakers, his hearers will call everything praiseworthy. It is true that these embellishments have great charm. But once the poet's words are said alone, without the accompanying music and color, I think you know what kind of showing they make. Surely you have observed for yourself.

I have.

Are his words not like faces that once were young but never beautiful and from which youth is now departed?

Exactly.

Now consider still another proposition: The imitator, the one who creates illusions, does not understand reality but only what reality appears to be. Would you agree to that?

Yes.

All right. But we mustn't leave the matter at midpoint. It ought to be discussed fully.

Go ahead.

Well, we might say that the painter paints reins and a bit.

Yes?

But they are manufactured by a cobbler and a smith?

Of course.

Does the painter know the true characteristics of reins and bit? Or is it not true that even the artisans, the cobbler and the smith, fail to understand their nature? Is it not true that only the horseman understands how to use them?

That is true.

Then we can say that the same holds true for everything.

What?

Everything finds expression in three arts: the art that uses, the art that creates, and the art that imitates.

Yes?

But judgments about what is true, beautiful, or good in any living thing, any human action, or any human art ought to be made only in terms of the use that nature or the artisan intended them for.

True.

Then the conclusion must necessarily follow that he who uses anything is the one who knows most about it. He draws on his experience in reporting its merits and defects to the maker. For example, a flutist will tell the flute maker which of his flutes performs best in concert; he will order accordingly, and the flute maker will do his bidding.

You are right.

He who possesses knowledge, then, will make judgments concerning the degree of excellence of the flutes; the other will heed him and make the flutes accordingly.

Yes.

So the user will have true knowledge. But the maker will also trust his own judgment concerning the merits and defects of the instrument because he associates with, [602] and hence is compelled to listen to, the man who knows.

True.

But what about the imitator? Will experience or application teach the painter what is beautiful and real? Were he compelled to keep company with the man who knows and who tells him what to paint, would he be persuaded?

No.

Then neither knowledge nor opinion can help the imitator to arrive at valid judgments about his own imitations.

It seems not.

So far as understanding his own work, then, the situation of poet and imitator must be truly delightful.

Not at all. Quite the reverse.

Nonetheless, he will keep on imitating, and never will he understand why something is bad or good. And what he will imitate is all too evident: whatever pleases the ignorant masses.

Of course.

So it seems that we are all but agreed on these matters: the imitator knows hardly anything about the things he imitates; imitation is a kind of game and not to be taken seriously; and those who write tragedies, either in iambic or heroic verse,[8] are the most extravagant of all the imitators.

Agreed.

By heaven, then, it follows that imitation must be concerned with things at the third remove from truth.

Agreed.

And which part of man responds to imitation's power?

What do you mean?

Let me illustrate. I assume you would agree that the mass of any magnitude looks different when viewed from near and then from far?

I agree.

And that straight things appear bent when seen underwater? And that color can distort our vision so that concave becomes convex? The source of all these illusions is plainly to be found in some part of our souls. There is where we shall find the flaw in our nature that the imitators exploit, where they manipulate light and dark so that their conjuror's tricks and marionette shows appear to be nothing short of magic.

True.

Now the full beauty of man's capacity to weigh, to measure, and to number comes to light. All are antidotes to error. They liberate our souls from illusory perceptions of what is greater or less or more or heavier, so that we may be governed by those things that we can weigh, measure, and reckon.

That is unquestionably true.

8. The meter of epics (heroic verse) is dactylic hexameter (a 6-foot line based on the syllabic patterns long-short-short); iambic trimeter (a 3-foot line based on the syllabic pattern short-long) was the most common meter of dialogue and set speeches in tragedies.

And these would obviously be functions of that part of the soul that reasons and calculates.

Clearly.

But when the reasoning part measures and demonstrates that some things are equal, some are larger, and some smaller, won't it often be contradicted by appearance, by the way these same things seem to be?

Yes.

And didn't we judge it impossible that one could simultaneously hold contradictory opinions about the same thing?

We did, and rightly so.

[603] Then that part of the soul that rejects the evidence of measurement and the part that affirms it cannot be the same.

True.

Further: the best part of the soul is that which relies on calculation and measurement?

Clearly.

And the contrary part is to be found among the lesser elements of the soul?

Necessarily.

This is the point I was getting at when I said that the works produced by painting and imitation are generally far from truth. Such arts appeal to that part in us which is far removed from intelligence. They cannot be our companions or friends for any good or healthy purpose.

Very true.

Hence imitation is a defective art. It mates with what is also defective, and so it produces defective offspring as well.

Apparently.

Does all this apply only to vision? Or does it also apply to hearing and hence to poetry?

It probably applies to both.

But we ought not to rely only on the plausibility of the analogy we drew from painting. Let us instead consider directly that part of the mind to which imitative poetry makes its specific appeal. We must discover whether this part of the mind is superior or inferior.

We have an obligation to try.

Put it this way. Let us say that imitation simulates the actions of human beings, whether the acts be freely willed or performed under compulsion. It also reports the actors' judgments whether the results were good or ill, and whether they felt joy or sorrow. Is there anything else to say?

Nothing.

In all of this, then, is any man of one mind? Or are confusion and contradiction evident here just as they were when we were discussing the phenomenon of vision? Is a man ever of two minds about the same thing? When it comes to action, is he divided against himself? Does he experience internal strife? But I realize that there is now no need for us to come to an agreement about these matters. We found sufficient agreement in previous discussions[9] that our souls are always teeming with ten thousand such contradictions.

We were right in making the agreement.

9. In *Republic* 4.439b–444a, where Socrates argues that each mind or soul is divided into three distinct and sometimes warring parts (the rational, the spirited, and the desiring).

Yes. But I think we omitted something then that must be considered now.

What is it?

We surely said it before this: a good man who has the misfortune to lose a son or suffer some other kind of loss of something most dear to him will bear what he has to bear with greater composure than others.

Of course.

Now consider this. Will he feel no pain? Or, since that could not be, will he be temperate in giving vent to his grief?

The latter is closer to truth.

[604] Now tell me this. When will he make the greater effort to fight back and endure the pain? When he is among others or when he is by himself?

His struggle will be greater when he is seen by others.

But when he is alone, I should think he would dare to utter many things he would be ashamed of were others to hear them? He would do many things that he would rather not have others see him do?

True enough.

Do not law and reason sustain the will to endure? Is it not the suffering itself that goads a man to give way to his grief?

Yes.

So when we observe two contradictory impulses simultaneously at work within a man, must we not infer the presence of two distinct motives?

Clearly.

One of which is ready to follow the precepts of the law?

What do you mean?

The law, I should imagine, admonishes us to maintain our equanimity in adversity, insofar as that is possible. It bids us shun discontent because we cannot know what is truly good or evil in such situations. No one benefits from despondency, and nothing in mortal life deserves that much concern. Finally, grief prevents us from attaining the thing we need the most and as quickly as possible.

What is that?

Thought. We need to think about what has happened to us. One must accept the way the dice fall and then order one's life according to the dictates of reason. One ought not to behave like children who have stumbled, wasting time wailing and pressing one's hands to the injured part. Instead, the soul should learn to remedy the hurt forthwith, to restore what has fallen, and to remedy the complaint with the appropriate medicine.

Surely that is the best way to deal with whatever chance may bring.

The best part of us, we have said, is willing to follow these rules of reason?

Clearly.

Then must we not also say that the part of us which leads us to dwell on past sufferings and positively revels in lamentation is our idle and irrational side and the very author of cowardice?

We will say that.

Then that part of our personality given to despondency presents many and diverse occasions for imitation. Much different is our disposition to be reasonable and intelligent. It remains relatively constant and is not easy to imitate. Nor would the imitation be easy to understand (especially by some disorderly mob in a theater) because it would be reflecting a disposition alien to the crowd.

[605] Very true.

It should be evident that the imitative poet is far removed from the better disposition of our souls. Since he covets applause from the multitude, his pursuit of wisdom leads in a different direction. He devotes himself to unstable or choleric characters because they are easier to imitate.

That is also true.

Hence we would be justified in laying hold of the poet and setting him down as the counterpart of the painter. Like the painter, his works are distant from reality. Poet and painter also resemble one another in their appeal to the inferior part of the soul and their neglect of the best part. At last, then, we have arrived at a justification for not admitting the poet to a well-ordered state. Because he calls forth the worst elements in the soul and then nourishes them and makes them strong, he destroys the soul's reasoning part. All this finds a parallel in any city where someone makes the wicked mighty, appoints them the city's governors, and corrupts the city's best elements. The imitative poet has exactly the same impact on the private individual. He corrupts the individual's character with fabrications far removed from reality and panders to the soul's fool that cannot even distinguish big from little.

Well said.

But the gravest indictment remains to be discussed. The poet's power to corrupt even the best men—with rare exceptions—is surely the most serious cause for alarm.

If the effect is what you say, it surely is.

Listen and consider this. When Homer or one of the other tragic poets imitates a grieving hero and causes him to utter extended lamentations or has him chant and beat his breast, you know that even the best of us enjoy it. We are held captive by the imitation; we suffer with the hero, and whoever can most powerfully evoke this mood in us we call the best poet.

Of course. I know that.

When we experience personal sorrow ourselves, however, quite the contrary occurs. We pride ourselves if we are able to maintain our equanimity and bear the burden. We reckon this to be a man's behavior. But what we found favor with just now in the poem we generally consider to be the behavior of women.

I recognize that.

Is it right that we should respond in this manner? We see a man impersonate the kind of character that we would despise and reject in ourselves. Yet we do not disapprove; instead, we enjoy ourselves and praise the performance.

By Zeus! That certainly doesn't seem reasonable.

[606] It will seem reasonable enough if we consider what follows.

What?

Consider how in our own misfortunes we forcibly constrain that part of our soul that hungers for tears and the satisfaction of a cry. This is the part whose nature it is to desire these things; this is the part that finds satisfaction and enjoyment in the poets. And the best part of us, when it observes the suffering of others and has not been sufficiently educated by either reason or habit, will relax its control over the sentiments. After all, there is no disgrace in comforting and pitying what is evidently a good man when he gives way to an excess of grief. Instead, to do so would be counted as a vicarious pleasure and pure gain, something one would not willingly forgo by disdaining to hear the whole poem. That happens, I suppose, because only a few men will reflect that the vicarious enjoyment of other people's sufferings has an effect upon one's own. Lavishing pity on others makes it hard to contain pity when it comes to our own sufferings.

That is true.

Must we not apply the same principle to the things that make us laugh? Are there not jokes you would be ashamed to repeat but which provide you with much amusement when you hear them privately or at a comedy? In these circumstances you see no disgrace in laughing at them just as in the other example there seemed no cause for disgrace in giving vent to pity. Here, too, your reason is at work admonishing the comic in you so that you will not gain the reputation of a buffoon. But when others joke, you let your comic sense run loose. Indulging it, you return to your own affairs and discover that you have unwittingly become a comic poet.

Right again.

Sex, anger, and all the desires, as well as all the pleasures and pains that make their presence felt in whatever we do—on all these poetry has the same effect. It makes them grow great instead of drying them up. It establishes them as our governors when instead they should be the ones governed if we are to become men who are better and happier instead of worse and more miserable.

I can't dispute you.

So then, Glaucon, when you encounter admirers of Homer who say that this poet is the tutor of Greece, that to study him is to refine human conduct and culture, and that we should order our entire lives in accordance with his precepts, [607] you must welcome them and love them as people who are doing the best they can. You can certainly agree that Homer is the greatest of poets and first among tragedians. But you must hold firm to the position that our city will admit no poetry except hymns to the gods and fair words about good men. Once entry is permitted to the honey-tongued Muse, whether in lyric or epic form, pleasure and pain will become kings of the city, law will be displaced, and so will that governing reason which time and opinion have approved.

I concur.

Having returned to the subject of poetry, let us make her an apology: we acted properly when we exiled her from the city earlier on. Reason constrained us to do so. And lest we be convicted of a certain harshness and parochialism, let us remind her that there is an old quarrel between philosophy and poetry. "The bitch that yelps and bays at her master," "great in the conversation of simpletons," "a company of overwise fools," and "refined thinkers who are really beggars"—these and many other reproaches mark the ancient antagonism.[1] Even so, we shall declare that if poetry that is imitative and aims to provide pleasure can show cause why it should find a place in a well-governed city, we should be glad to welcome its return from exile. We, too, are very aware of its charms. Of course, we must not be guilty of impiety by betraying what we think is true. But don't you yourself feel the magic of poetry, especially when Homer is the poet?

1. The identity of these poets who attacked philosophy is unknown [translators' note].

It affects me deeply.

Then if poetry, in turn, would make her defense in lyric or some other meter, would it not be just if she should return to us from exile?

It certainly would be.

And we would certainly offer her partisans—not poets themselves but those who love poetry—an opportunity to plead her case in prose without meter and to argue that poetry is not only delightful but also a blessing to the life of men and well-governed cities. And we shall hear them kindly, for we shall surely be the gainers if the case can be made that poetry is a source of goodness as well as pleasure.

It would be a very great gain.

But, my friend, if the verdict goes the other way, we must be like men who once loved but now know that their love has played them false. Hard though it is, they will hold themselves aloof. So we, loving this kind of poetry bred into us by the education we have received from our noble cities, [608] will rejoice if poetry appears at its best and truest. But so long as she is unable to offer a tenable defense, we shall chant to ourselves the arguments we have already considered. They will serve as a talisman to protect us from being seduced once again by the rude passions of the masses. In any case, we have learned that this kind of poetry does not deserve to be taken seriously in any meaningful effort to seek truth. On the contrary, one who listens to it must fear for the governance of his soul and must hold to all we have said about poetry.

You are right. I agree.

My dear Glaucon, we are engaged in a great struggle, a struggle greater than it seems. The issue is whether we shall become good or bad. And neither money, office, honor, nor poetry itself must be allowed to persuade us to neglect justice or any other virtue.

After all that we have discussed I am ready to join you in saying that. I should think anyone else would do the same.

* * *

ca. 375 B.C.E.

From Phaedrus[1]

* * *

SOCRATES: Is this enough on the subject of rhetorical expertise and its lack?

PHAEDRUS: Of course.

SOCRATES: But don't we still have to discuss whether or not writing is desirable—what makes it acceptable and what makes it undesirable?

1. Translated by Robin Waterfield. The participants in the dialogue are the philosopher Socrates (469–399 B.C.E., Plato's spokesperson) and Phaedrus (ca. 450–400 B.C.E.), a Socratic philosopher. The numbers in square brackets are the Stephanus numbers used almost universally in citing Plato's works; they refer to the pages of a 1578 edition published by Henri Estienne. Except as indicated, all subsequent notes are Waterfield's, abridged.

PHAEDRUS: Yes.

SOCRATES: So do you know the best way for either a theoretical or a practical approach to speech to please god?

PHAEDRUS: No, I don't. Do you?

SOCRATES: Well, I can pass on something I've heard from our predecessors. Only they know the truth of the matter, but if we had made this discovery by ourselves, would we any longer have the slightest interest in mere human conjectures?

PHAEDRUS: What an absurd question! Please tell me what you say you've heard.

SOCRATES: All right. The story I heard is set in Naucratis in Egypt,[2] where there was one of the ancient gods of Egypt—the one to whom the bird they call the 'ibis' is sacred, whose name is Theuth.[3] This deity was the inventor of number, arithmetic, geometry, and astronomy, of games involving draughts and dice—and especially of writing. At the time, the king of the whole of Egypt around the capital city of the inland region (the city the Greeks call 'Egyptian Thebes'[4]), was Thamous, or Amon, as the Greeks call him.[5] Theuth came to Thamous and showed him the branches of expertise he had invented, and suggested that they should be spread throughout Egypt. Thamous asked him what good each one would do, and subjected Theuth's explanations to criticism if he thought he was going wrong and praise if thought he was right. The story goes that Thamous expressed himself at length to Theuth about each of the branches of expertise, both for and against them. It would take a long time to go through all Thamous' views, but when it was the turn of writing, Theuth said, 'Your highness, this science will increase the intelligence of the people of Egypt and improve their memories. For this invention is a potion for memory and intelligence.' But Thamous replied, 'You are most ingenious, Theuth. But one person has the ability to bring branches of expertise into existence, another to assess the extent to which they will harm or benefit those who use them. The loyalty you feel to writing, as its originator, [275] has just led you to tell me the opposite of its true effect. It will atrophy people's memories. Trust in writing will make them remember things by relying on marks made by others, from outside themselves, not on their own inner resources, and so writing will make the things they have learnt disappear from their minds. Your invention is a potion for jogging the memory, not for remembering. You provide your students with the appearance of intelligence, not real intelligence. Because your students will be widely read, though without any contact with a teacher, they will seem to be men of

2. The story is another Platonic invention. He sets it in Egypt because the Egyptians were famous for their records of the ancient past. Naucratis was a Greek trading station in Egypt, established in the sixth century according to Herodotus [Greek historian (ca. 484–ca. 425 B.C.E.), chiefly of the Persian Wars; sometimes called "the father of history"—editor's note].

3. Better known as Thoth (or Tahuti), the ibis-headed Egyptian equivalent to the god Hermes, in his capacity as god of scribes and communication. Plato perhaps uses the name "Theuth" to remind his readers of the end of the Greek name "Prometheus," because Prometheus was the inventor of writing in Greek myth.

4. To distinguish it from the main city of Boeotia on the Greek mainland, which had (and still has) the same name.

5. Not the name of any known Egyptian king, and perhaps a corruption of "Amous" or Amon (Amun), the god who became identified with Ra, the Sun-god, and became the chief deity of Egypt.

wide knowledge, when they will usually be ignorant. And this spurious appearance of intelligence will make them difficult company.'

PHAEDRUS: Socrates, it doesn't take much for you to make up stories from Egypt and anywhere else in the world you feel like.

SOCRATES: Well, my friend, the people at the sanctuary of Zeus at Dodona say that the original prophecies there were spoken by an oak.[6] In those days people weren't as clever as you young ones nowadays, and they were so foolish that they happily listened to oak and rock, as long as they told the truth. But perhaps it matters to you who the speaker is, or what country he's from, because you are not concerned only with whether or not he is right.

PHAEDRUS: You're right to have told me off—and, yes, I think the Theban king was correct about writing.

SOCRATES: So anyone who thinks he can get a branch of expertise to survive by committing it to writing—and also anyone who inherits the work with the assumption that writing will give him something clear and reliable—would be behaving in a thoroughly foolish manner and really would be ignorant of Amon's prediction, if he supposed that written words could do more than jog the memory of someone who already knows the topic that has been written about.

PHAEDRUS: Quite so.

SOCRATES: Yes, because there's something odd about writing, Phaedrus, which makes it exactly like painting. The offspring of painting stand there as if alive, but if you ask them a question they maintain an aloof silence.[7] It's the same with written words: you might think they were speaking as if they had some intelligence, but if you want an explanation of any of the things they're saying and you ask them about it, they just go on and on for ever giving the same single piece of information. Once any account has been written down, you find it all over the place, hobnobbing with completely inappropriate people no less than with those who understand it, and completely failing to know who it should and shouldn't talk to. And faced with rudeness and unfair abuse it always needs its father to come to its assistance, since it is incapable of defending or helping itself.

PHAEDRUS: Again, you're quite right.

[276] SOCRATES: Well, is there any other way of using words? Does the written word have a legitimate brother? Can we see how it is born, and how much better and stronger it grows than its brother?

PHAEDRUS: What is this way of using words? How is it born, do you think?

SOCRATES: It is the kind that is written along with knowledge in the soul of a student. It is capable of defending itself, and it knows how to speak to those it should and keep silent in the company of those to whom it shouldn't speak.

PHAEDRUS: You're talking about the living, ensouled speech of a man of knowledge. We'd be right to describe the written word as a mere image of this.

SOCRATES: Absolutely. So here's another question for you. Consider a sensible farmer who cares for his seeds and wants to see them come to

6. In a trance, the priestesses would interpret the rustling of the leaves of an oak tree. [Dodona: town in Epirus, in northwest Greece—editor's note.]

7. One might also add that the written word ignores all the unspoken aspects such as body language, tone of voice, and so on, which constitute a major proportion of communication.

fruition. Do you think he'd happily spend time and effort planting them in the summer in gardens of Adonis,[8] and watch them grow up in eight days, or would he do this, if at all, as a diversion and for the sake of a festival? Don't you think that for seeds he was serious about he'd draw on his skill as a farmer, sow them in the appropriate soil, and be content if what he sowed reached maturity in the eighth month?

PHAEDRUS: Yes, that's what he'd do, Socrates. He'd take care of the one lot of seeds and treat the others differently, just as you said.

SOCRATES: So are we to say that someone who knows about right and fine and good activities is less sensible than our farmer where his own seeds are concerned?

PHAEDRUS: Of course not.

SOCRATES: Then he won't spend time and effort writing what he knows in water—in black water[9]—and sowing them with his pen by means of words which can neither speak in their own defence nor come up with a satisfactory explanation of the truth.

PHAEDRUS: No, it's hardly likely that he will.

SOCRATES: No. He'll probably sow and write his gardens of letters for amusement, if at all, as a way of storing up things to jog his own memory when 'he reaches the age of forgetfulness', and also the memory of anyone else who is pursuing the same course as him. He'll happily watch these delicate gardens growing, and he'll presumably spend his time diverting himself with them rather than the symposia[1] and so on with which other people amuse themselves.

PHAEDRUS: What a wonderful kind of diversion you're describing, Socrates—that of a person who can amuse himself with words, as he tells stories about justice and the other things you mentioned—compared with the trivial pastimes of others!

SOCRATES: Yes, that's right, my dear Phaedrus. But it's far better, in my opinion, to treat justice and so on seriously, which is what happens when an expert dialectician takes hold of a suitable soul and uses his knowledge to plant and sow the kinds of words which are capable of defending both themselves and the one who planted them. So far from being barren, [277] these words bear a seed from which other words grow in other environments. This makes them capable of giving everlasting life to the original seed, and of making the man who has them as happy as it is possible for a mortal man to be.

PHAEDRUS: Yes, this is certainly far better.

SOCRATES: With this conclusion in place, Phaedrus, we are at last in a position to reach a verdict about the other issue.

PHAEDRUS: What other issue?

SOCRATES: The one that brought us here. We wanted to investigate why Lysias[2] was abused for writing speeches, and the expert or inexpert

8. "Gardens of Adonis" were pots in which plants were forced to mature in time for his festival, when they would wither and die in the midsummer sun to represent the death of Adonis, or the passing of youth. [Adonis: a Greek mythological figure whose cult was associated with vegetation and fertility—editor's note.]

9. To write in or on water was proverbially futile. "Black water" is of course ink.

1. Drinking parties [editor's note].

2. Athenian orator (ca. 456–ca. 380 B.C.E.), whose oration on love provides the occasion for the discussion in *Phaedrus* [editor's note].

composition of the actual speeches. Well, I think we've made it fairly clear what makes for expertise and its lack.

PHAEDRUS: I thought so, but could you remind me again?

SOCRATES: First, someone has to know the truth of every matter he's speaking or writing about, which is to say that he has to be capable of defining a whole as it is in itself and then know how to divide it up class by class until he reaches something indivisible. He also has to be able to distinguish souls in the same sort of way, discover the kind of speech which naturally fits each kind of soul, and organize and arrange his speeches accordingly—offering a complex soul a complex speech which covers the whole range of modes, and a simple soul a simple speech. Until he can do all this he will be incapable of tackling speeches in as much of a professional manner as their nature allows, either for teaching or for persuasion. This is what the whole of our earlier discussion has shown us.

PHAEDRUS: Yes, absolutely. That's pretty much what we found.

SOCRATES: So what about the question whether or not it is acceptable to deliver or write speeches, and under what circumstances it would or would not be fair to describe it as a shameful activity? Haven't our recent conclusions shown . . .

PHAEDRUS: What conclusions?

SOCRATES: . . . that if Lysias or anyone else who has in the past written a speech, or will write one in the future, for private or public consumption—that is, in the latter case, when proposing legislation and so composing a political speech—thinks there is any great degree of reliability and clarity in it, this is a source of shame for the author, whether or not anyone has ever said as much to him. For, awake or asleep, ignorance about what activities are right and wrong and good and bad cannot, when seen aright, fail to be a matter for reproach, even if the general mass of people approve of it.

PHAEDRUS: I quite agree.

SOCRATES: But consider someone who thinks that, whatever the subject, a written speech is bound to be largely a source of amusement, and that no speech which has ever been written in verse or in prose deserves to be taken seriously; that the same goes for the declamations of rhapsodes,[3] which are designed to produce conviction, but allow no cross-examination and contain no element of teaching; that in actual fact [278] the best speeches do no more than jog the memories of men of knowledge; that clarity and perfection and something worth taking seriously are to be found only in words which are used for explanation and teaching, and are truly written in the soul, on the subject of right and fine and good activities; that, while he ignores all the rest, words of this kind should be attributed to him as his legitimate sons—above all the words within himself, if he has found them and they are there, but secondly the words that are at once the offspring and the brothers of these internal ones of his, and have duly grown in others' souls. It looks, Phaedrus, as though anyone with these views has attained the condition you and I can only pray for.

PHAEDRUS: I have no hesitation at all in wishing and praying for what you've said.

3. Professional reciters of poetry, especially the Homeric epics, and lecturers on the topic.

SOCRATES: So now we've diverted ourselves for long enough on the subject of speeches. It's up to you to go and tell Lysias of our excursion to the Nymphs' spring and the Muses'[4] shrine. Explain to him how we listened to speeches which commanded us to tell Lysias (and any other composer of speeches), Homer (and any other author of poetry, whether accompanied or unaccompanied by music), and thirdly Solon[5] (and anyone else who writes legislation, as he calls it—which is to say, written compositions in the form of political speeches) that if he has written from a position of knowledge of how things truly are, if he can mount a defence when challenged on the content of his work, and if he can produce arguments of his own to prove the unimportance of what he has written, then he does not deserve a title derived from these pursuits,[6] but a description based on the things he takes seriously.

PHAEDRUS: What names are you thinking of giving him?

SOCRATES: I think it's too much to call him 'wise', Phaedrus: only the gods deserve that label. But it would suit him better and be more appropriate to call him a lover of wisdom,[7] or something like that.

PHAEDRUS: Yes, that would fit the bill.

SOCRATES: On the other hand, wouldn't you be right to use the titles 'poet' or 'speech-writer' or 'law-writer' for someone who has nothing more valuable than the composition or piece of writing he has arrived at by a lengthy process of turning upside down, and by cutting and pasting the various parts into different relations with one another?

PHAEDRUS: Of course.

SOCRATES: Then this is what you should tell your friend.

PHAEDRUS: And what about you? What are you going to do? After all, we surely shouldn't ignore your friend as well.

SOCRATES: Who's that?

PHAEDRUS: The beautiful Isocrates.[8] What are you going to tell him, Socrates? What shall we call him?

SOCRATES: Isocrates is still young, Phaedrus, but I'd like to tell you what I guess [279] the future holds for him.

PHAEDRUS: What?

SOCRATES: He strikes me as being naturally more talented than Lysias and his crowd, and also to have a nobler temperament. So it wouldn't surprise me at all if, as he matured, he came to stand out among everyone else who has ever undertaken speech-writing, as an adult among children and more so—and that's considering the kinds of speeches he is currently engaged on. I think he'd stand out even more if he wasn't content with his present work, and some more divine impulse were to guide him towards greater things. For he does innately have a certain philosophical cast to his mind, my friend. So that's the message I shall

4. In Greek mythology, 9 daughters of Memory who preside over the arts and all intellectual pursuits. Nymphs: goddesses of lower rank, often associated with aspects of nature (the ocean, trees, etc.) [editor's note].

5. Athenian statesman and poet (ca. 638–559 B.C.E.), who reformed the city's constitution. Homer (ca. 8th c. B.C.E.), Greek epic poet to whom the *Iliad* and *Odyssey* are attributed [editor's note].

6. That is, he should not be called a "speech-writer," for instance, which Phaedrus said earlier was used as a term of abuse.

7. In Greek, *philosophos*—a philosopher.

8. Athenian orator, rhetorician, and teacher (436–338 B.C.E.), whose school attracted pupils from all over Greece and greatly influenced later methods of education [editor's note].

bring Isocrates, as my beloved, from the gods of this place, and you already know what to tell your beloved Lysias.

PHAEDRUS: All right. But let's go, now that the weather has cooled down.

SOCRATES: Shouldn't one first pray to the gods here before setting off?

PHAEDRUS: Of course.

SOCRATES: Dear Pan[9] and all gods here, grant that I may become beautiful within and that my external possessions may be congruent with my inner state. May I take wisdom for wealth, and may I have just as much gold as a moderate person, and no one else, could bear and carry by himself. Have I missed anything out, Phaedrus? This prayer will do for me.

PHAEDRUS: Say the prayer for me too. For friends share everything.[1]

SOCRATES: Let's go.

370 B.C.E.

9. God of shepherds and small-game hunting, a pastoral deity, and therefore named earlier as one of the deities who might have inspired Socrates in these rural surroundings.

1. A proverb quite often quoted by Plato.

ARISTOTLE
384–322 B.C.E.

Alongside his teacher PLATO, Aristotle is the great founding figure of Western philosophy and literary theory. Aristotle invented the scientific method of analysis and, in a wide-ranging series of treatises, codified the divisions of knowledge into disciplines and subdisciplines that carry on to the present day, such as physics, chemistry, zoology, biology, botany, psychology, politics, logic, and epistemology. Unlike Plato, who uses the dialogue to dramatize paths of thinking in a conversational literary form, Aristotle relies in his extant works on categorization and logical differentiation in a straightforward propositional manner. He focuses on the distinctive qualities of any given object of study, whether of plants or of plays, systematically describing their specific features and construction.

Plato and other ancient writers often commented on literary works, but Aristotle inaugurated the systematic discipline of literary criticism and theory with the *Poetics*. It is perhaps the most influential work in the history of criticism and theory, shaping future considerations of genre, prosody, style, structure, and form. Its modern impact began in the Renaissance, when it was rediscovered from fragmentary manuscript sources and taken as a rule book for literary composition. Its descriptions of formal unity influenced seventeenth-century European writers, such as the French dramatist PIERRE CORNEILLE, and eighteenth-century writers reviving its precepts as "neoclassicism." In twentieth-century literary theory the *Poetics* was foundational for formalist methods, which apply objective modes of analysis to linguistic artifacts and discern the structural attributes of literary works; it influenced a wide array of critics, such as the American New Critics (like WILLIAM K. WIMSATT JR. and MONROE C. BEARDSLEY), the archetypal critics (notably NORTHROP FRYE), and the French structuralists (like TZVETAN TODOROV).

Aristotle's *On Rhetoric* suggests a different avenue for the study of literature. Rather than seeing literary works in terms of their distinctive features and internal construction, it opens for consideration their affective and political dimensions as forms of public speech. Because of its focus on types of public speaking, *Rhetoric*'s influence on literary study has been less direct than that of the *Poetics*, but its emphasis on audience response undergirds subsequent theoretical approaches concerned with the reader, interpretation, and the political effects of literature. Although Aristotle himself does not favor one avenue of investigation over another, his distinction between poetics and rhetoric reflects a perennial division in literary theory: the split between theories concerned with the internal properties of literature and those concerned with literature's external effects, especially on readers and society.

Aristotle was born in Stagira in northern Greece, which was under the rule of Macedonia. His father, Nicomachus, was the personal physician to and a friend of Amyntus II, the king of Macedonia. Scholars speculate that his father's practice as a physician inculcated in Aristotle a pragmatic interest in biology and the natural world, and Aristotle's ties to the Macedonian court affected his subsequent career. In 367 B.C.E. Aristotle went to study at Plato's Academy in Athens, where he distinguished himself as one of Plato's best students and eventually became a teacher himself. In 347, around the time of Plato's death, Aristotle left Athens; he traveled first to Assos in Asia Minor, where he taught in a colony of Platonists for three years, and then to the island of Lesbos, where he did the biological research that grounded his later scientific treatises. In 344 or 343, Amyntas's son, King Philip, invited Aristotle to tutor his heir, Alexander (later known as Alexander the Great), who was then about thirteen years old. While he had contact with and received the patronage of Alexander until his death, Aristotle concluded his tutoring in 340, after which he probably lived in Macedonia or Stagira, perhaps then completing *On Rhetoric*. In 335, when Alexander acceded to the throne and departed for his campaigns in Asia, Aristotle returned to Athens and began his own school at the Lyceum. He taught poetics, rhetoric, politics, ethics, and metaphysics, and probably at this time worked on his famous treatises, including the *Politics*, the *Nicomachean Ethics*, and the *Poetics*. After the death of Alexander in 323, when public sentiment against Macedonia was rising, Aristotle left Athens to live in Chalcis on the island of Euboea, where he died in 322. For Aristotle the life of the philosopher was not reclusive but unfolded in the midst of public affairs.

Only about a fifth of Aristotle's 150 reported works survive—transmitted, usually imperfectly, through manuscript copies in the Middle Ages. His treatises are known as "esoteric" works, because they were not copied by scribes to be distributed but were available only in libraries for study by others; some seem to be lecture notes or study guides rather than polished works. This accounts for their compressed style and sometimes abrupt transitions, frequent repetitions, and shorthand references to other works or writers. It also makes the works particularly difficult to date, since they were probably composed and revised over a period of time. The *Poetics*, very likely gathered from a set of incomplete notes, survived only in a few faulty copies. Scholars speculate that we have just half the original text and that the missing second half dealt with comedy.

Aristotle's early writings, now known only by the reports of ancient writers, were written in the form of dialogues, obviously showing the influence of Plato. His more mature works, however, depart from his teacher's model in a number of significant ways. Stylistically, he replaces the literary approach with systematic expositions of particular subjects, more in the form of technical manuals than dramatic accounts. Methodologically, Aristotle operates through analysis, which in its root sense entails examining objects by studying their component parts, and through differentiation and classification. For instance, in biology Aristotle starts with the most general category—living organisms; he then examines them according to what differentiates them—as plants, animals, and so on; further classifies them into particular species; and catalogues their distinctive traits. Philosophically, Aristotle grounds his research on a more empirical basis than Plato, looking at nature and the objects of the real world. In so doing, he tacitly rejects Plato's fundamental concept of transcendent Ideas or Forms that govern and generate reality. In his own terms, Aristotle often works from induction, drawing his general conclusions from the particular objects he observes, whereas Plato usually works from deduction, drawing particular conclusions from his general metaphysical concept of being.

The *Poetics*, our first selection, demonstrates Aristotle's analytical method, which parallels that of his examinations of biology or zoology. Aristotle turns to the various categories of human artifacts, differentiating those made in language and eventually focusing on poetry and especially on the species-specific traits of epic and tragedy. He assumes a distinction between the wide class of objects that are humanly made and those that are naturally produced—between, say, a chair and a tree. (The Greek word for "poetry," *poiēsis*, is itself based on the verb "to make.") In treating poetry as a craft, Aristotle differs from Plato, who discusses poetry in terms of inspiration and the emotive transport of the poet—a strain that continues in nineteenth-century Romanticism, exemplified by WILLIAM WORDSWORTH's definition of poetry as "the spontaneous overflow of emotion." Aristotle limits his study of poetry to its observable kinds and its formal construction, more or less ignoring questions about its affective origins, which he regards as falling under the auspices of other pursuits, such as psychology or rhetoric.

Drawing on a wide range of literary examples, especially Sophocles' celebrated tragedy *Oedipus Rex*, Aristotle adduces six salient parts of tragedy, in order of their importance—plot, character, thought, diction, music, and spectacle. He spends the most time on the first, specifying the key features of good plots. Central to Aristotle is imitation (*mimēsis*), and he judges the best plots to have verisimilitude: they must be plausible (even if impossible). He also stresses a logically connected order (an appropriate starting point, elaboration, and a dramatic end or resolution), centered on one unified action rather than depicting multiple, divergent, or unnecessary actions. The best kind of resolution is one that shows a reversal (*peripeteia*) of position for the main character, as well as the character's recognition (*anagnōrisis*) of his or her fate. Aristotle reasons that the characters in tragedy should come from high positions, otherwise their tragic circumstances would not be remarkable; he also prescribes that their fates be linked to their own error (*hamartia*, literally "missing the mark," though frequently translated as "flaw"), rather than from some accident or wickedness. Aristotle concludes somewhat technically by classifying parts of speech (in his discussion of diction), sketching solutions to problems of interpretation, and comparing the genres of tragedy and epic.

Though rooted in the literature of its time (and focusing especially on a form of drama quite different from ours), the extant *Poetics* has continued to influence criticism. Aristotle's systematic categorization of genus and species and his comparison of tragedy and epic underlie all genre theory. Notably, they undergird modern considerations of the historical movement from epic to the novel, such as those of GYÖRGY LUKÁCS and MIKHAIL M. BAKHTIN. Perhaps most decisively, Aristotle's systematic description of plot and its component parts ground contemporary narrative theory, in particular the technical field of narratology.

His scientific examination of poetry has been championed by the New Critics Wimsatt and CLEANTH BROOKS as "Aristotle's answer" to Plato, responding both to Plato's view of poetry as a degraded imitation twice removed from the reality of eternal Ideas or Forms and to his suspicion of poetry as stirring emotions in a way that is dangerous for society. Instead of directly disagreeing with Plato, Aristotle implicitly validates poetry by examining it as a legitimate branch of study. Countering Plato's notion of poetry as degraded imitation, Aristotle sees poetry as a source of universal knowledge of human behavior: unlike history, which produces knowledge only of specific situations, poetry describes the actions of characters who might be any humans. Moreover, he claims that good poetry has a positive emotional effect on its audience, which he calls *katharsis*—perhaps the most important and variously interpreted word in the *Poetics*. Some commentators have interpreted the term in a medical sense, as a purgative that flushes out the audience's unwieldy emotion; others see it in terms of moral purification. More recently, critics have equated catharsis with ethical and intellectual clarification.

In other treatises, Aristotle analyzes natural objects in terms of four component "causes," schematized as material, formal, efficient, and final. If we apply this rubric to poetry, the material cause of a poem would be its raw material—language; the formal cause, the shape of the resulting object—the poem; its efficient cause, what makes it—the poet; and the final cause, the end use—its effects on an audience, emotionally as well as educationally and politically. Although Aristotle alludes to audience response in his discussion of catharsis, in the *Poetics* he is most concerned with the material and formal causes of poetry. This concentrated focus has strongly marked modern literary criticism—notably that of the New Critics, who explicitly disallow considerations of the audience as "the affective fallacy," in the phrase of Wimsatt and Beardsley. However, Aristotle is by no means so dismissive. Instead, he treats considerations of the audience—the final cause—as a different line of research, taken up in his *On Rhetoric*.

We have come to understand rhetoric as the study of figures of speech, following the medieval and Renaissance traditions (and the modern practice of writers like PAUL DE MAN), but Aristotle defines it more broadly as the ability to see the available means of persuasion. In typical Aristotelian fashion, *On Rhetoric* begins in book 1 by differentiating three elements of persuasion in public speech: the arguments a speaker uses, the *ēthos* or character of the speaker, and the disposition of the audience. Additionally, it differentiates three species of public speeches: deliberative, which deal with future events, as in politics; judicial, which concern past events, as in law courts; and epideictic, which are concerned with the present as they praise or blame a person, as in a eulogy or declamatory attack. Aristotle stresses the importance of argument in part to challenge the then prevalent teachings of the sophists, such as GORGIAS in an earlier generation, who he believed used rhetoric irresponsibly, lacking concern for valid reasoning.

However, Aristotle also acknowledges the elements of persuasion outside the realm of reasoning, paying particular attention to the emotions that speeches induce in their audiences. In book 2, he adduces the first systematic study of affect, differentiating emotions such as anger, calmness, fear, confidence, shame, pity, indignation, envy, and emulation. In book 3, paralleling his examination of diction in the *Poetics*, Aristotle concludes with a discussion of *lexis* (variously translated as "style," "word choice," or "form of expression"). Perhaps the most important term in *On Rhetoric* is *telos*—the final cause, end, objective, or goal of persuasion—effected through emotion and style as well as argument. *On Rhetoric* highlights the public ends of language rather than its formal properties.

Although its influence has not been as sustained or decisive as that of the *Poetics*, *On Rhetoric* considers how response is a factor in interpretation. In its delineations of emotions, it presages the aesthetic tradition, whose concern is the affective dimensions of literary works, and it provides a grounding for reader-response theory, which centers on subjective audience interaction rather than the objective features of the work itself. Perhaps most significantly, it suggests the historical and political significance of literature in its role as public discourse.

Whether acknowledged or not, Aristotle's seminal distinction between poetics and rhetoric has been crucial in contemporary debates over the proper object of literary criticism. Against the tendency fostered by the New Critics and later by certain deconstructive critics who advocated a narrow linguistic study of literature, recent decades have witnessed a "rhetorical turn" toward methods favoring attention to the personal, historical, and social effects of literary texts. Some object that such approaches address topics outside the purview of literary study. That is, they urge a strict poetic view, arguing that literary criticism should focus on the distinctive attributes of literary works. But when we take account of *On Rhetoric* alongside the *Poetics*, we see that Aristotle does not disallow these other topics; he opens literary study to a consideration of its pedagogical and social ends as well as its distinctive formal properties.

***Poetics* Keywords:** Classical Theory, Drama, Epic, Formalism, Language, Narrative Theory, Poetry, Representation
***On Rhetoric* Keywords:** Affect, Classical Theory, Language, Reception Theory, Rhetoric

Poetics[1]

[1, 1447a] The art of poetry, both in its general nature and in its various specific forms, is the subject here proposed for discussion. And with regard to each of the poetic forms, I wish to consider what characteristic effect it has, how its plots should be constructed if the poet's work is to be good, and also the number and nature of the parts of which the form consists. Such other matters as may be relevant to this field of study will likewise be included. Let us, then, follow the order of nature, and begin by taking up that which is by nature first.

Epic poetry and Tragedy, also Comedy, the Dithyramb,[2] and most of the music performed on the flute and the lyre are all, in a collective sense, Imitations.[3] However, they differ from one another in three ways—either (1) by using different means [or media] of imitation; or (2) by imitating different objects; or (3) by imitating in a different manner and not in the same mode of presentation.

Just as certain persons, by rule of art or mere practice, make likenesses of various objects by imitating them in colors and forms, and others again imitate by means of the voice, so, taken as a whole, the arts I have mentioned have as their means of imitation rhythm, language, and melody. These, however, they employ either separately or in combination. For example, the arts of the flutist and citharist employ only rhythm and melody, as do other arts of similar effect such as that of the panpipes; and rhythm alone without melody is the medium of the dance—dancers simply by means of a rhythmical pattern of movement succeed in imitating men's characters, emotions, and actions.

The art that imitates in language alone, in prose or in [nonlyrical] verse [1447b] (whether combining different meters or using only one of them), remains to this day without a name. For there is no common name under which we can bring the prose mimes of Sophron and Xenarchus and the Socratic dialogues,[4] nor would there be even if the imitation they embody

1. Translated by James Hutton, who adds clarifying words or phrases in square brackets and includes Greek terms in parentheses. Also in square brackets in the text are both the traditional chapter divisions inserted by Renaissance editors and the Bekker numbers, used almost universally in citing Aristotle's works; they refer to the page numbers and columns of an 1831 edition by Immanuel Bekker.
2. Greek choral poetry originally sung in honor of Dionysus, the god of wine and fertility worshipped in an ecstatic cult.
3. From the Greek *mimēsis*, translated as "imitation" or "representation."
4. The philosophical works of PLATO (ca. 427–ca. 347 B.C.E.), which are written as dialogues usually featuring his teacher, Socrates (469–399 B.C.E.), and one or more interlocutors. "Mimes": imitative performances usually featuring short scenes from daily life. Sophron of Syracuse (5th c. B.C.E.) wrote mimes in rhythmic prose; his son Xenarchus also wrote mimes.

were made in iambic trimeters, elegiac couplets,[5] or any other such verse—except, indeed, that people in general attach the word "poet" to the name of a particular meter and speak, for example, of elegiac poets and epic poets, calling them poets, not on the basis of imitation, but indiscriminately according to the meter they use. This is customary even when what is produced is a versified treatise on medicine or natural science. But Homer and Empedocles[6] have nothing in common except just their meter, and it is right, therefore, to call the one a poet and the other a physical philosopher rather than a poet. Similarly, anyone who produces an imitation, even if it is in a mixture of all the verse forms, as in the case of Chaeremon's[7] *Centaur*, which is a mixed rhapsody in all the meters, must in virtue of his imitation be called a poet. In these matters, then, the distinctions thus made may suffice.

There are, however, certain arts that make use of all the stated media, viz., rhythm, song, and metrical language, and among these are dithyrambic poetry, nomic poetry,[8] tragedy, and comedy. Here the distinction is that dithyramb and nome employ all three media continuously throughout, while tragedy and comedy employ first one means and then the other.

This completes what I have to say about the differences among the arts in respect to the means they employ in effecting the imitation.

[2, 1448a] Since the objects that the imitators represent are persons engaged in action, and since these persons will necessarily be persons of either a higher or a lower moral type (for this is the one division that characters submit to almost without exception, goodness and badness being universal criteria of character), they represent them accordingly as either better than we are or worse or about the same. For example, among painters, Polygnotus portrayed men better than we are, Pauson men inferior to the norm, and Dionysius[9] men like ourselves. And clearly, each of the aforementioned kinds of imitation will have these variations, and will be different by virtue of imitating objects that differ in this way. Thus it is possible for these differences to arise in dancing and in flute and lyre playing, and also in the art that employs prose and unsung verse. Homer, for example, represents men better than we are, Cleophon men like ourselves, and Hegemon of Thasos, the inventor of parodies, and Nicochares,[1] author of the *Deiliad*, men worse than the norm. Similarly, one could represent different types in dithyrambs and nomes, as . . . Timotheus and Philoxenus do in their treatment of the Cyclops.[2] And it is upon the same point of difference also that tragedy parts company with comedy, since comedy prefers to imitate persons who are worse, tragedy persons who are better, than the present generation.

5. A verse form consisting of couplets whose first line is in dactylic hexameter (i.e., a 6-foot line based on the syllabic pattern long-short-short), the meter of epic, and whose second line replaces the 3rd and 6th foot with one long syllable. "Iambic trimeters": the verse form of most dialogue and set speeches in tragedies (a 3-foot line based on the syllabic pattern short-long).
6. Pre-Socratic Greek natural philosopher (ca. 493–433 B.C.E.), who wrote in epic meter (dactylic hexameter). Homer (ca. 8th c. B.C.E.), Greek epic poet to whom is attributed the *Iliad* and the *Odyssey*; the ancient Greeks also credited him with a number of lost shorter epics, including the comic *Margites*.
7. Greek tragedian (mid-4th c. B.C.E.).
8. Originally, melodies (for lyre or flute) created to accompany epic texts; later, choral compositions.
9. Painter from Colophon. Polygnotus (ca. 500–ca. 440 B.C.E.), one of the first great Greek painters. Pauson (late 5th c. B.C.E.), Athenian caricaturist.
1. Athenian comic poet (active ca. 390 B.C.E.), whose *Deiliad* (*deilos* means "cowardly") parodied heroic epic. Cleophon (4th c. B.C.E.), Athenian tragic poet. Hegemon (5th c. B.C.E.), poet whose parodies won competitions in Athens.
2. Mythical one-eyed giants. Timotheus of Miletus (ca. 450–ca. 360 B.C.E.) and Philoxenus of Cythera (ca. 435–ca. 380 B.C.E.) were both Greek dithyrambic poets.

[3] The third difference in these arts has to do with the manner in which any one of these objects may be imitated; for it is possible to represent the same objects in the same medium but in different modes. Thus they may be imitated either in narration (whether the narrator speaks at times in an assumed role, which is Homer's way, or always in his own person without change) or in a mode in which all the characters are presented as functioning and in action.

It is in these three ways, then, as we said at the beginning, that imitation is differentiated—by the means, by the objects, and by the manner of presentation. So in one way Sophocles would be the same kind of imitator as Homer, in that both represent noble characters, and in another way the same as Aristophanes,[3] since both present their characters as acting and doing.

Indeed, some say that dramas are so called, because their authors represent the characters as "doing" them (*drôntes*). And it is on this basis that the Dorians[4] lay claim to the invention of both tragedy and comedy. For comedy is claimed by the Megarians[5] here in Greece, who say it began among them at the time when they became a democracy, and by the Megarians of Sicily on the grounds that the poet Epicharmus came from there and was much earlier than Chionides and Magnes;[6] while tragedy is claimed by certain Dorians of the Peloponnese. They offer the words as evidence, noting that outlying villages, called *dêmoi* by the Athenians, are called *kômai* by them, and alleging that *kômôdoi* [comedians] acquired their name, not from *kômazein* [to revel], but from the fact that, being expelled in disgrace from the city, they wandered from village to village. [1448b] The Dorians further point out that their word for "to do" is *drân*, whereas the Athenians use *prattein*.

Let this be our account, then, of the number and nature of the differences imitation admits of.

[4] For the beginnings of poetry in general, there appear to have been two causes, both rooted in human nature. Thus from childhood it is instinctive in human beings to imitate, and man differs from the other animals as the most imitative of all and getting his first lessons by imitation, and by instinct also all human beings take pleasure in imitations. We have evidence of this in actual experience, for the forms of those things that are distressful to see in reality—for example, the basest animals and corpses—we contemplate with pleasure when we find them represented with perfect realism in images. For this again the reason is that the experience of learning things is highly enjoyable, not only for philosophers but for other people as well, only their share in it is limited; when they enjoy seeing images, therefore, it is because as they look at them they have the experience of learning and reasoning out what each thing represents, concluding, for example, that "this figure is so and so"; for if the image depicts something one has not seen before, the pleasure it gives will not be that of an imitation but will come from its workmanship or coloring or some other such source. Imitation, then, being something that we have by nature, and the

3. Greatest poet of Greek Old Comedy (450–385 B.C.E.). Sophocles (ca. 496–406 B.C.E.), great Greek tragedian.
4. A people (probably originally from southwest Macedonia) that invaded Greece ca. 1100–1000 B.C.E., reaching south into the Peloponnese.
5. Residents of a Dorian city on the Isthmus of Corinth (west of Athens); it was a democracy in the 6th century B.C.E.
6. Aristotle names three early comic poets: Epicharmus was Sicilian (active early 5th ca. B.C.E.) and wrote in Doric Greek, while Chionides (active ca. 485 B.C.E.) and Magnes (active ca. 470 B.C.E.) were Athenian.

same being true of melody and rhythm (verses clearly are segments of the various rhythms), at the outset, persons who had a special aptitude for these things, making improvements bit by bit, produced out of their improvisations the beginnings of poetry.

And in accordance with their individual types of character, poetry split into two kinds; for the graver spirits tended to imitate noble actions and noble persons performing them, and the more frivolous poets the doings of baser persons, and as the more serious poets began by composing hymns and encomia, so these began with lampoons. To be sure, we cannot mention any poem of this type by a pre-Homeric poet, though doubtless many composed them, but beginning with Homer we can—his own *Margites*, for example, among other similar works. In these invectives the iambic meter came into use as something suited to their character—in fact, we now call this particular meter iambic because it was the meter in which men lampooned (iambized) one another.

Thus among the early poets, some became poets of heroic verse and others again of iambic verse. Homer was not only the master poet of the serious vein, unique in the general excellence of his imitations and especially in the dramatic quality he imparts to them, but was also the first to give a glimpse of the idea of comedy by avoiding personal abuse and giving dramatic treatment to the ridiculous; for his *Margites* is analogous to the comedies just as the *Iliad* and the *Odyssey* are to the tragedies. [1449a] And once tragedy and comedy had made their appearance, those who were drawn to one or the other of the branches of poetry, true to their natural bias, became either comic poets instead of iambic poets or tragic poets instead of epic poets because the new types were more important—i.e., got more favorable attention, than the earlier ones.

Whether tragedy has, then, fully realized its possible forms or has not yet done so is a question the answer to which both in the abstract and in relation to the audience [or the theater] may be left for another discussion. Its beginnings, certainly, were in improvisation, as were also those for comedy, tragedy originating in impromptus by the leaders of the dithyrambic chorus, and comedy in those of the leaders of the phallic performances which still remain customary in many cities. Little by little tragedy grew greater as the poets developed whatever they perceived of its emergent form, and after passing through many changes, it came to a stop, being now in possession of its specific nature.

It was Aeschylus[7] who first increased the number of the actors from one to two and reduced the role of the chorus, giving first place to the dialogue. Sophocles [added] the third actor and [introduced] painted scenery. Again, [there was a change] in magnitude; from little plots and ludicrous language (since the change was from the satyr play[8]), tragedy came only late in its development to assume an air of dignity, and its meter changes from the trochaic tetrameter[9] to the iambic trimeter. Indeed, the reason why they

7. The earliest of the 3 great Greek tragedians (525–456 B.C.E.).

8. A type of play that formed part of the spring festival of Dionysus in early 5th-century B.C.E. Athens. Each of the poets competing wrote three tragedies and one satyr play; the latter presented grotesque versions of ancient legends, with the chorus dressed as satyrs (half-man, half-goat, and wearing a phallus).

9. A 4-foot line based on the syllabic pattern long-short; though occasionally used for dialogue in tragedies, this fast-moving line was thought less stately than iambic meter. The choruses in tragedies used other meters.

used the tetrameter at first was that their form of poetry was satiric [i.e., for "satyrs"] and hence more oriented toward dancing; but as the spoken parts developed, natural instinct discovered the appropriate meter, since of all the metrical forms the iambic trimeter is best adapted for speaking. (This is evident, since in talking with one another we very often utter iambic trimeters, but seldom dactylic hexameters, or if we do we depart from the tonality of normal speech. Again, [there was a change] in the number of episodes[1]—but as for this and the way in which reportedly each of the other improvements came about, let us take it all as said, since to go through the several details would no doubt be a considerable task.

[5] Comedy, as we have said, is an imitation of persons worse than the average. Their badness, however, does not extend to the point of utter depravity; rather, ridiculousness is a particular form of the shameful and may be described as the kind of error and unseemliness that is not painful or destructive. Thus, to take a ready example, the comic mask is unseemly and distorted but expresses no pain.

(While the changes marking the development of tragedy, and the persons responsible for them, did not pass unnoticed, no attention was paid to comedy in its early stages because comedy was not regarded as important; [1449b] only rather late in its history did the archon[2] begin granting a chorus of comedians, the performers having previously been volunteers. Thus when there begins to be any record of comic poets, so designated, comedy already possessed its general outlines, and we do not know who introduced masks or prologues or the accepted number of actors or anything of that sort. However, the practice of composing comic plots originally came from Sicily, and in Athens Crates[3] was the first to discard the abusive mode and construct a universalized type of plot or fable.)

Epic poetry followed tragedy to the extent of being an imitation of good men in the medium of metrical language; where they differ is in the narrative manner of epic and its use of a single meter. There is also a difference in length: tragedy endeavors as far as possible to keep within one revolution of the sun, or to exceed this limit but little, whereas the epic is without restriction as to time and herein differs from tragedy, although at first the treatment of time in tragedies was just the same as in epic poems. Their constituent parts are the same, except that there are two [Music and Spectacle] which are peculiar to tragedy; and consequently anyone who knows how to distinguish good tragedy from bad can do the same with epic, since tragedy has all the parts that epic has, but epic not all those that make up tragedy.

[6] The mimetic art in hexameters [epic poetry] and comedy will be discussed later on; but at this point I wish to speak about tragedy and to begin by gathering up from what I have already said the definition of its nature that emerges from that. Thus, Tragedy is an imitation of an action that is serious, complete, and possessing magnitude; in embellished language, each kind of which is used separately in the different parts, in the mode of action and not narrated; and effecting through pity and fear [what we call] the *catharsis*[4] of

1. The sections of a tragedy that are positioned between two choruses.
2. The chief magistrate in ancient Greek city-states.
3. Athenian comic poet (active ca. 450–ca. 430 B.C.E.).
4. A much-debated Greek term, related to a verb meaning "to cleanse" or "purify"; usually left untranslated and understood as "purgation," it can also mean "clarification."

such emotions. By "embellished language" I mean language having rhythm and melody, and by "separately in different parts" I mean that some parts of a play are carried on solely in metrical speech while others again are sung.

Since the imitation is carried out in the dramatic mode by the personages themselves, it necessarily follows, first, that the arrangement of Spectacle will be a part of tragedy, and next, that Melody and Language will be parts, since these are the media in which they effect the imitation. By "language" I mean precisely the composition of the verses, by "melody" only that which is perfectly obvious. And since tragedy is the imitation of an action and is enacted by men in action, these persons must necessarily possess certain qualities of Character and Thought, since these are the basis for our ascribing qualities to the actions themselves [1450a]—character and thought are natural causes of actions—and it is in their actions that men universally meet with success or failure. The imitation of the action is the Plot. By plot I here mean the combination of the events; Character is that in virtue of which we say that the personages are of such and such a quality; and Thought is present in everything in their utterances that aims to prove a point or that expresses an opinion. Necessarily, therefore, there are in tragedy as a whole, considered as a special form, six constituent elements, viz. Plot, Character, Language, Thought, Spectacle, and Melody. Of these elements, two [Language and Melody] are the *media* in which they effect the imitation, one [Spectacle] is the *manner*, and three [Plot, Character, Thought] are the *objects* they imitate; and besides these there are no other parts. So then they employ these six forms, not just some of them so to speak; for every drama has spectacle, character, plot, language, melody, and thought in the same sense, but the most important of them is the organization of the events [the plot].

For tragedy is not an imitation of men but of actions and of life. It is in action that happiness and unhappiness are found, and the end we aim at is a kind of activity, not a quality, in accordance with their characters men are of such and such a quality, in accordance with their actions they are fortunate or the reverse. Consequently, it is not for the purpose of presenting their characters that the agents engage in action, but rather it is for the sake of their actions that they take on the characters they have. Thus, what happens—that is, the plot—is the end for which a tragedy exists, and the end or purpose is the most important thing of all. What is more, without action there could not be a tragedy, but there could be without characterization. In fact, the tragedies of most of our recent playwrights are lacking in the ethical element, and generally speaking many poets [of all kinds] show a similar tendency. So too among painters, Zeuxis[5] stands in contrast with Polygnotus, the latter being an excellent portrayer of character, whereas there is no delineation of character at all in the painting of Zeuxis. And again, merely by stringing together a succession of speeches full of character and well composed in point of language and thought, one will never create the effect we said was proper to tragedy, but this effect is much more apt to be achieved with a tragedy possessing a plot and coordinated events, even though it may be relatively deficient in its treatment of these other elements.

A further point: the principal means by which tragedy exerts its fascination are parts of the plot, that is to say reversals and recognitions. Finally, it

5. Greek painter from Heraclea in southern Italy; he was in Athens ca. 400 B.C.E.

is significant that beginning authors are able to attain proficiency in language and character portrayal sooner than in plot construction—a point that may also be illustrated from nearly all the early dramatists. Clearly, then, the first principle and, as it were, the soul of tragedy is the plot, and second in importance is character. In painting, too, it is much the same [1450b]—a painter who smeared on the most beautiful colors at random would give less pleasure than he would by making a likeness of something in black and white. Tragedy is an imitation of an action, and it is an imitation of the agents chiefly owing to the action.

Third in order of importance comes the element of Thought. This is the ability to say what it is possible and appropriate to say [on any subject], which in oratory is the function of the arts of statesmanship and rhetoric. [I name both], since the early poets made their personages speak in the manner of statesmen, whereas those of our time make theirs speak rhetorically. [Thought must be distinguished from Character.] "Character" is whatever reveals a person's habit of moral choice—whatever he tends to choose or reject when the choice is not obvious—and this element is, therefore, absent from speeches in which there is absolutely no choosing or rejecting of anything by the speaker. "Thought," on the other hand, is present whenever speakers are engaged in proving that something is so or not so, or when they are making some general pronouncement.

The fourth element is Language. I define Language, as I said earlier, to be the expression of meaning by the use of words, and the definition is as valid for verse as for prose. Of the remaining elements, Melody is the most important of the pleasurable accessories, while Spectacle, though fascinating in itself, is of all the parts the least technical in the sense of being least germane to the art of poetry. For tragedy fulfills its function even without a public performance and actors, and, besides, in the realization of the spectacular effects the art of the property man counts for more than the art of the poets.

[7] Now that the parts are established, let us next discuss what qualities the plot should have, since plot is the primary and most important part of tragedy. I have posited that tragedy is an imitation of an action that is a whole and complete in itself and of a certain magnitude—for a thing may be a whole, and yet have no magnitude to speak of. Now a thing is a whole if it has a beginning, a middle, and an end. A beginning is that which does not come necessarily after something else, but after which it is natural for another thing to exist or come to be. An end, on the contrary, is that which naturally comes after something else, either as its necessary sequel or as its usual [and hence probable] sequel, but itself has nothing after it. A middle is that which both comes after something else and has another thing following it. A well-constructed plot, therefore, will neither begin at some chance point nor end at some chance point, but will observe the principles here stated.

Now as for magnitude: In order to be beautiful, a living creature or anything else made up of parts not only must have its parts organized but must also have just the size that properly belongs to it. Beauty depends on size and order; hence an extremely minute creature could not be beautiful, for our vision becomes blurred as it approaches the point of imperceptibility, nor could an utterly huge creature be beautiful, for, [1451a] unable to take it in all at once, the viewer finds that its unity and wholeness have escaped his field of vision—if, for example, it were an animal a thousand miles long. Therefore, just as organized bodies and animals, if they are to be beautiful, must have size and such size as to be easily taken in by the eye, so plot, for the same reason, must have length and such length as to be easily held in the memory. The limit of length considered in relation to the public contests and production in sensible form has nothing to do with the art of poetry—if a hundred tragedies had to be presented in the contest, the performance would be timed by water clocks, as was actually done at one time, they say. But considered in relation to the very nature of the thing itself, the limit is this: Invariably, the larger the plot is, while still remaining perspicuous, the more beautiful it is in virtue of its magnitude. Or, to express it in a simple formulation: If the length is sufficient to permit a change from bad fortune to good or from good fortune to bad to come about in an inevitable or probable sequence of events, this is a satisfactory limit of magnitude.

[8] Contrary to what some people think, a plot is not ipso facto a unity if it revolves about one man. Many things, indeed an endless number of things, happen to any one man some of which do not go together to form a unity, and similarly among the actions one man performs there are many that do not go together to produce a single unified action. Those poets seem all to have erred, therefore, who have composed a *Heracleid*, a *Theseid*,[6] and other such poems, it being their idea evidently that since Heracles was one man, their plot was bound to be unified. But Homer, just as he excels in every other respect, seems in this matter also, either by art or natural instinct, to have taken the right view. In composing his *Odyssey*, he did not put into it every event that had befallen Odysseus[7]—his being wounded on Mount Parnassus, for example, and his feigning madness when the host was assembling, neither of which events was at all a necessary or probable consequence of the other—but instead he constructed the *Odyssey* around a single action such as I am describing, and he did the same with the *Iliad*. Consequently, just as in the other mimetic arts an imitation is unified when it is the imitation of a unified object, so in poetry the plot, since it is the imitation of an action, must be the imitation of a unified action comprising a whole; and the events which are the parts of the plot must be so organized that if any one of them is displaced or taken away, the whole will be shaken and put out of joint; for if the presence or absence of a thing makes no discernible difference, that thing is not part of the whole.

[9] From what has already been said, it will be evident that the poet's function is not to report things that have happened, but rather to tell of such things as might happen, things that are possibilities by virtue of being in themselves inevitable or probable. Thus the difference between [1451b] the historian and the poet is not that the historian employs prose and the poet verse—the work of Herodotus[8] could be put into verse, and it would be no less a history with verses than without them; rather the difference is that the one tells of things that have been and the other of such things as might be. Poetry, therefore, is a more philosophical and a higher thing than

6. In ancient Greece, there were several epic *Heracleids* and *Theseids*—poems depicting, respectively, the heroes Heracles and Theseus.

7. The wily king of Ithaca whose efforts to return home to Greece after the Trojan War are chronicled in the *Odyssey*.

8. Greek historian (ca. 484–ca. 425 B.C.E.), chiefly of the Persian Wars; sometimes called "the father of history."

history, in that poetry tends rather to express the universal, history rather the particular fact. A universal is: The sort of thing that (in the circumstances) a certain kind of person will say or do either probably or necessarily, which in fact is the universal that poetry aims for (with the addition of names for the persons); a particular, on the other hand is: What Alcibiades[9] did or had done to him. This [generalizing tendency] has now come out clearly in the case of comedy, where the poets, having constructed their plots out of probable incidents, then supply any names that may occur to them, and do not, like the iambic poets, take a particular individual as their subject. In tragedy, however, the historical names are retained. Basically this is because possibility means credibility; until something happens we remain uncertain of its possibility, but what has happened obviously is possible, since if impossible, it would not have happened. Yet as a matter of fact there are some tragedies in which only one or two of the well-known names occur, the rest being invented, and other tragedies again in which there are no famous names at all. An example is Agathon's[1] *Antheus*. In this play, plot and names alike are invented, and yet it gives no less pleasure on that account. So there certainly is no need to make a point of adhering to the traditional stories on which tragedies are based. Indeed, it would be absurd to do so, since the well-known tales are well known only to a few, and nevertheless they give pleasure to all.

It is clear, then, from the foregoing remarks that the poet should be a maker of plots more than a maker of verses, in that he is a poet by virtue of his imitation and he imitates actions. So even if on occasion he takes real events as the subject of a poem, he is none the less a poet, since nothing prevents some of the things that have actually happened from being of the sort that might probably or possibly happen, and it is in accordance with this that he is their poet.

Among plots and actions of the simple type, the episodic form is the worst. I call episodic a plot in which the episodes follow one another in no probable or inevitable sequence. Plots of this kind are constructed by bad poets on their own account, and by good poets on account of the actors; since they are composing entries for a competitive exhibition, they stretch the plot beyond what it can bear and [1452a] are often compelled, therefore, to dislocate the natural order. And it is not only an action complete in itself that tragedy represents; it also represents incidents involving pity and fear, and such incidents are most effective when they come unexpectedly and yet occur in a causal sequence in which one thing leads to another. For occurring in this way, they will have more of the marvelous about them than if they came to pass of themselves and by accident. (Indeed, things that actually do happen by accident seem most marvelous when they appear to be intentional, as when at Argos the statue of Mitys[2] killed the man who had caused Mitys' death by falling down on him as he stood looking at it. It is hard to believe that such things happen without design.) Plots of this kind, therefore, are necessarily better than others.

[10] Some plots are simple, others complex; indeed the actions of which the plots are imitations are at once so differentiated to begin with. Assuming the action to be continuous and unified, as already defined, I call that action

9. Athenian politician and general (ca. 450–404 B.C.E.).

1. Innovative Athenian tragedian (d. ca. 401 B.C.E.); fewer than 40 lines of his works remain.

2. Mitys's murderer was killed in this fashion ca. 374 B.C.E.

simple in which the change of fortune takes place without a reversal or recognition, and that action complex in which the change of fortune involves a recognition or a reversal or both. These events [recognitions and reversals] ought to be so rooted in the very structure of the plot that they follow from the preceding events as their inevitable or probable outcome; for there is a vast difference between following from and merely following after.

[11] Reversal (Peripety) is, as aforesaid, a change from one state of affairs to its exact opposite, and this, too, as I say, should be in conformance with probability or necessity. For example, in *Oedipus*,[3] the messenger comes to cheer Oedipus by relieving him of fear with regard to his mother, but by revealing his true identity, does just the opposite of this. In *Lynceus*[4] again, Lynceus is brought on expecting to die and Danaüs follows intending to put him to death, but as a result of what has gone before, it turns out that Danaüs is put to death and Lynceus is saved.

Recognition, as the word itself indicates, is a change from ignorance to knowledge, leading either to friendship or to hostility on the part of those persons who are marked for good fortune or bad. The best form of recognition is that which is accompanied by a reversal, as in the example from *Oedipus*. There are, to be sure, other forms of recognition—and, indeed, what I have just said may occur in reference to inanimate objects or anything whatever, and it is possible to discover that someone has or has not done something—but the form that has most to do with the plot, and most to do with the action, is the one I have mentioned; for a recognition joined thus with a reversal [1452b] will be fraught with pity or with fear (the type of action tragedy is presumed to imitate) because misery and happiness alike will come to be realized in recognitions of this kind. Now since recognition involves more than one person, there are cases in which one of two persons already knows the other and the recognition is on one side only, and other cases in which recognition has to take place on both sides. Iphigeneia, for example, was recognized by Orestes[5] from the sending of her letter, but a second recognition was required to reveal his identity to her.

Two elements of the tragic plot, then, are Reversal and Recognition. A third element is Suffering (*pathos*). We have said what reversal and recognition are; Suffering is an action of a destructive or painful description, such as the deaths that take place in the open [and not behind the scenes], agonies of pain, wounds, and so on.

[12] Earlier I spoke of the parts of tragedy that are to be employed as formative elements. The following are the parts or separate sections into which it is divided quantitatively: Prologue, Episode, Exode, and Choral part, this last again being divided into Parodos and Stasimon, which are found in all tragedies, and songs from the stage[6] and Kommoi, found only in some. The

3. *Oedipus Rex* (ca. 430 B.C.E.), by Sophocles—a play to which Aristotle frequently refers as a model for his definition of tragedy. Unknowingly, Oedipus kills his father, Laius; takes his father's place as king of Thebes; and marries his mother, Jocasta. When he learns that he has not escaped the fate foretold, he gouges out his eyes and banishes himself, hence undergoing a reversal from king to outcast.

4. Lost tragedy by the orator and tragic poet Theodectes (ca. 375–334 B.C.E.), about the daughters of King Danaus of Argos, who ordered them to kill their husbands (all obeyed except Hypermnestra, whose husband was Lynceus).

5. In *Iphigenia in Tauris* (ca. 413 B.C.E.), by Euripides (ca. 485–ca. 406 B.C.E.), the youngest of the three great Greek tragedians; the two are siblings.

6. That is, songs sung by the actors (not the chorus).

Prologue is the whole section preceding the entrance song (Parodos) of the chorus; an Episode a whole section between two complete choral odes; and the Exode the whole section after which there is no choral ode. In the choral part, the Parodos is the first continuous utterance of the chorus; a Stasimon is a choral ode without anapaestic and trochaic lines;[7] a Kommos is a lament in which chorus and actors both take part. Earlier I spoke of the parts of tragedy that are to be employed as formative elements; these are the parts or separate sections into which it is divided quantitatively.

[13] Next in order after the points I have just dealt with, it would seem necessary to specify what one should aim at and what avoid in the construction of plots, and what it is that will produce the effect proper to tragedy.

Now since in the finest kind of tragedy the structure should be complex and not simple, and since it should also be a representation of terrible and piteous events (that being the special mark of this type of imitation), in the first place, it is evident that good men ought not to be shown passing from prosperity to misfortune, for this does not inspire either pity or fear, but only revulsion; nor evil men rising from ill fortune to prosperity, for this is the most untragic plot of all—it lacks every requirement, in that it neither elicits human sympathy nor stirs pity or fear. [1453a] And again, neither should an extremely wicked man be seen falling from prosperity into misfortune, for a plot so constructed might indeed call forth human sympathy, but would not excite pity or fear, since the first is felt for a person whose misfortune is undeserved and the second for someone like ourselves—pity for the man suffering undeservedly, fear for the man like ourselves—and hence neither pity nor fear would be aroused in this case. We are left with the man whose place is between these extremes. Such is the man who on the one hand is not preeminent in virtue and justice, and yet on the other hand does not fall into misfortune through vice or depravity, but falls because of some mistake, one among the number of the highly renowned and prosperous, such as Oedipus and Thyestes[8] and other famous men from families like theirs.

It follows that the plot which achieves excellence will necessarily be single in outcome and not, as some contend, double, and will consist in a change of fortune, not from misfortune to prosperity, but the opposite, from prosperity to misfortune, occasioned not by depravity, but by some great mistake on the part of one who is either such as I have described or better than this rather than worse. (What actually has taken place confirms this; for though at first the poets accepted whatever myths came to hand, today the finest tragedies are founded upon the stories of only a few houses, being concerned, for example, with Alcmeon, Oedipus, Orestes, Meleager, Thyestes, Telephus,[9] and such others as have chanced to suffer terrible things or to do them.) So, then, tragedy having this construction is the finest kind of tragedy from an

7. Lines based on the syllabic pattern short-short-long (often used in the parados) or long-short.

8. Like Oedipus, a popular subject for Greek tragedy, though none survives; his story has numerous variants. He unknowingly ate the flesh of his own sons, served by his brother Atreus; and following the advice of an oracle, he committed incest with his daughter to beget the son who would avenge him.

9. Few of the tragedies involving these characters survive. Telephus, fated to kill his great-uncles, is exposed by his grandfather (a tragedy by Euripides told of Telephus's wound, received from Achilles as the Greeks were preparing to sail for Troy, that would not heal); Alcmeon and Orestes kill their mothers, Eriphyle and Clytemnestra, to avenge their fathers' deaths and are driven mad by the Furies (female demons who punish kin-murderers); and Meleager kills his uncles, and as a result his mother kills him.

artistic point of view. And consequently, those persons fall into the same error who bring it as a charge against Euripides that this is what he does in his tragedies and that most of his plays have unhappy endings. For this is in fact the right procedure, as I have said; and the best proof is that on the stage and in the dramatic contests, plays of this kind seem the most tragic, provided they are successfully worked out, and Euripides, even if in everything else his management is faulty, seems at any rate the most tragic of the poets.

Second to this is the kind of plot that some persons place first, that which like the *Odyssey* has a double structure and ends in opposite ways for the better characters and the worse. If it seems to be first, that is attributable to the weakness of the audience, since the poets only follow their lead and compose the kind of plays the spectators want. The pleasure it gives, however, is not that which comes from tragedy, but is rather the pleasure proper to comedy; for in comedy those who in the legend are the worst of enemies—Orestes and Aegisthus,[1] for example—end by leaving the scene as friends, and nobody is killed by anybody.

[14, 1453b] The effect of fear and pity may be created by spectacle; but it may also be created by the very structure of the events, and this method has priority and is the way of a better poet. For the plot should be so constructed that even without seeing the play, anyone who merely hears the events unfold will shudder and feel pity as a result of what is happening—which is precisely what one would experience in listening to the plot of *Oedipus*. To procure this effect by means of spectacle is less artistic in that it calls for external apparatus, while those who produce through spectacle something that is not terrifying but only portentous in effect have no part in tragedy at all, for not every sort of pleasure is to be sought from tragedy, but only that which properly belongs to it. And since the pleasure the poet is to provide is that which comes from pity and fear through an imitation, clearly this effect must be embodied in the events of the plot.

Let us consider, therefore, the kinds of occurrences that seem terrible or pitiful. Actions of this sort must, of course, happen between persons who are either friends to one another or enemies or neither. Now if enemy harms enemy, there is nothing to excite pity either in his doing the deed or in his being on the point of doing it—nothing, that is, but the actual suffering; and the same is true if the parties are neither friends nor enemies. When, however, the tragic event occurs within the sphere of the natural affections—when, for instance, a brother kills or is on the point of killing his brother, or a son his father, or a mother her son, or a son his mother, or something equally drastic is done—that is the kind of event a poet must try for. There is, of course, no possibility of altering the traditional stories—I mean Clytemnestra being murdered by Orestes and Eriphyle by Alcmeon—but it is the poet's duty to find a way of using even these traditional subjects well.

Let me say more clearly what I mean by using them well. It is possible to have the action occur with full knowledge and awareness on the part of those involved, as the early poets used to do and as Euripides does when he has Medea[2] kill her children. It is possible also to do the awful thing, but to

1. Clytemnestra's lover (and Agamemnon's cousin), whom (in the version told in Aeschylus's *Agamemnon*) Orestes also kills.

2. A sorceress from Colchis. In *Medea* (431 B.C.E.), to avenge herself on Jason, who has deserted her for the daughter of a king, she kills his—and her—children.

do it in ignorance and then discover the relationship of the victim later, as Sophocles' Oedipus does. In this case, to be sure, the deed is done outside the play, but it is done in the tragedy itself, for example, by the Alcmeon of Astydamas and by Telegonus in *Odysseus Wounded*.[3] A third possibility is for one who is about to do one of these atrocious deeds in ignorance to discover the relationship before he does it. There are no other possibilities, for the deed has either to be done or not done and with knowledge or without knowledge. Of these situations, the worst is for someone to be on the point of doing the deed with knowledge, and then not do it. This is revolting in itself, and is not tragic, since no suffering is involved. It is not employed, therefore, by the poets [1454a] except occasionally, as when Haemon in *Antigone*[4] fails to kill Creon. The doing of the deed comes next in order. The better way is for it to be done in ignorance, with the recognition following afterward; there is then nothing revolting in the act, and the recognition astounds us. The best situation, however, is the last mentioned. It is exemplified in *Chresphontes*, where Merope is on the point of murdering her son, when she recognizes him and desists, and in *Iphigeneia*, where the sister is about to slay her brother; and in *Helle*,[5] where the son is about to give his mother up to the enemy when he learns who she is.

These considerations account for the fact mentioned earlier, that not many families provide subjects for tragedies. The poets, that is, in seeking out tragic situations, discovered more by luck than lore how to contrive in their plots the kind of situation we have described. And this obliges them to keep returning for subjects to those few houses that have had such dire events befall them.

Enough, then, has now been said about the construction of the events and what the plots should be like in tragedy; [and hence we turn next to Character].

[15] With regard to the Characters there are four things to aim at. First and foremost is that the characters be good. The personages will have character if, as aforesaid, they reveal in speech or in action what their moral choices are, and a good character will be one whose choices are good. It is possible to portray goodness in every class of persons; a woman may be good and a slave may be good, though perhaps as a class women are inferior and slaves utterly base. The second requisite is to make the character appropriate. Thus it is possible to portray any character as manly, but inappropriate for a female character to be manly or formidable in the way I mean. Third is to make the characters lifelike, which is something different from making them good and appropriate, as described above. Fourth is to make them consistent. Even if the person being imitated is inconsistent and this is what the character is supposed to be, he should nevertheless be portrayed as consistently inconsistent.

There is an example of unnecessary baseness in the character of Menelaus in *Orestes*,[6] of the unsuitable and inappropriate in the lamentation of Odysseus

3. A lost play by Sophocles in which Telegonus, the son of Odysseus and Circe, fatally wounds his father without knowing his victim's identity. Astydamas (active ca. 390 B.C.E.), a prolific Athenian tragedian; *Alcmeon* (and all but a few lines of his works) is lost.

4. By Sophocles (ca. 441 B.C.E.). Haemon, who loves Antigone, tries to kill his father (Creon, king of Thebes), who is responsible for her suicide.

5. Nothing more is known of this play. The *Chresphontes* (now lost) and *Iphigenia in Tauris* are both by Euripides.

6. In Euripides' play *Orestes* (408 B.C.E.), Menelaus basely refuses to help his nephew.

in *Scylla* and in the declamation of Melanippe;[7] and of inconsistency in *Iphigeneia in Aulis*,[8] where the Iphigeneia who begs to be spared bears no resemblance to the Iphigeneia who appears thereafter.

In the characters and the plot construction alike, one must strive for that which is either necessary or probable, so that whatever a character of any kind says or does may be the sort of thing such a character will inevitably or probably say or do and the events of the plot may follow one after another either inevitably or with probability. (Obviously, then, the denouement of the plot should arise from the plot itself and not be brought about "from the machine," [1454b] as it is in *Medea* and in the embarkation scene in the *Iliad*.[9] The machine is to be used for matters lying outside the drama, either antecedents of the action which a human being cannot know, or things subsequent to the action that have to be prophesied and announced; for we accept it that the gods see everything. Within the events of the plot itself, however, there should be nothing unreasonable, or if there is, it should be kept outside the play proper, as is done in the *Oedipus* of Sophocles.)

Inasmuch as tragedy is an imitation of persons who are better than the average, the example of good portrait painters should be followed. These, while reproducing the distinctive appearance of their subjects in a recognizable likeness, make them handsomer in the picture than they are in reality. Similarly, the poet when he comes to imitate men who are irascible or easygoing or have other defects of character should depict them as such and yet as good men at the same time. An example involving harshness is the way Agathon and Homer portray Achilles.[1]

These, then, are matters to be carefully observed, as also are matters appertaining to the sense perceptions that the poet's art necessarily entails, for in respect to these, too, it is often possible to miss the mark. A sufficient account of them has been given in my published discourse.[2]

[16] What Recognition is in general has already been explained. To turn now to its several species, first (1) there is the form that is least artistic and, from poverty of invention, the one they use most—that is, recognition by marks or tokens. Such marks are sometimes congenital, as "the lance the earth-born bear," or the "stars" in Carcinus'[3] *Thyestes*, and sometimes acquired, either something on the person, like a scar, or external tokens such as necklaces or the boat in *Tyro*.[4] Even these, however, can be used in better or worse ways. Thus Odysseus is recognized by means of his scar in one way by the nurse and in another way by the swineherds.[5] The recognitions by the herdsmen, and

7. In *Melanippe the Wise*, a lost play by Euripides, the heroine apparently argues with a philosophical sophistication inappropriate for a woman. *Scylla*: a lost dithyramb by Timotheus, in which Odysseus weeps in an unmanly way for his crew members killed by the monster Scylla.

8. A play by Euripides set at Aulis (ca. 405 B.C.E.), depicting Iphigenia about to be sacrificed by her father, Agamemnon, so that the Greeks may have fair winds as they sail to Troy; according to one version of the myth, she was saved by Artemis and transported far away to Tauris, where she becomes high priestess (and where Orestes later arrives).

9. In *Iliad* 8.155–81, only the arbitrary intervention of the goddess Athena prevents the Greeks from giving up the fight at Troy and going home. In *Medea*, after killing her children Medea flies off in the chariot of the sun god Helios, her grandfather; this is the "god from the (theatrical) machine" (in Latin, the *deus ex machina*), an unexpected event that resolves the plot.

1. The greatest warrior among the Greeks and the central character of the *Iliad*.

2. Presumably referring to the dialogue *On Poets*, esp. fragments 4–7.

3. Prolific Greek tragic poet (early 4th c. B.C.E.). The preceding quotation may be from Euripides' lost *Antigone*.

4. A lost play by Sophocles; Tyro's sons are abandoned in a small boat that leads to their later recognition.

5. Odysseus is recognized artfully (because inevitably) by his nurse when she notices his scar in the "bath scene" (*Odyssey* 19.386–475); but his declaration of his identity to the swineherds, when he shows them the scar as proof (21.205–25), is manufactured by the poet.

all such recognitions as use tokens as proofs of identity, are artistically worse, while those that occur spontaneously like the one in the Bath Scene are better. Second (2) are recognitions obviously managed by the poet and inartistic for that reason. An instance is the way Orestes in *Iphigeneia* gets himself recognized as Orestes: Iphigeneia is spontaneously recognized through the letter, but Orestes speaks for himself in terms imposed by the poet and not by the plot. The fault here is close to the one just mentioned, since he might just as well have had a few marks or tokens on him. Another example is the "voice of the shuttle" in Sophocles' *Tereus*.[6] A third type of recognition (3) is that which comes about through memory—i.e., a person's reaction upon seeing something. [1455a] Thus in Dicaeogenes' *Cyprians*, the hero bursts into tears upon seeing the picture, and in the Alcinous[7] episode Odysseus, when he hears the minstrel, is reminded of the past and weeps, therewith in both cases they are recognized. Fourth (4) is recognition through reasoning. This is exemplified in the *Choephori*:[8] "Someone resembling me has come; no one but Orestes resembles me; therefore Orestes has come." Another example is the recognition suggested for *Iphigeneia* by Polyidus the Sophist.[9] It would be natural, he said, for Orestes to reflect that his sister had been sacrificed and here he was himself about to be sacrificed in turn. Again, in the *Tydeus* of Theodectes, the father says that he had come in search of his son only to meet with death himself. In the *Phinidae*,[1] the women upon seeing the place drew this conclusion about their fate: that here they were doomed to die, since this was the place where they had been exposed in infancy. There is also (5) a composite kind of recognition resulting from faulty inference by one party or the other. For instance, in *Odysseus the False Messenger*,[2] the point that Odysseus and no one else can string the bow[3] is something set up by the poet and is the basic premise, [and it remains so] even if the messenger did say that he would know the bow which he had not seen; but having him gain recognition by this second means [i.e., by identifying the bow] on the assumption that he was going to be recognized by the first means [stringing the bow] is a fallacy.

Of all the forms of recognition, however, the best is that which springs from the events themselves, the shock of surprise having thus a probable basis. Such are the recognitions in the *Oedipus* of Sophocles and in *Iphigeneia*: it is probable that Iphigeneia should wish to send a letter. Only recognitions of this kind escape the artificiality of tokens and necklaces. Next best are recognitions that result from reasoning.

[17] The poet, as he constructs his plots and is working them out complete with language, should as far as possible place the action before his eyes; for in this way, seeing the events with the utmost vividness, as if they were taking place in his very presence, he will discern what is appropriate and will be least likely to overlook discrepancies. Witness to this point is the mistake that brought censure upon Carcinus. Amphiaraus came back

6. A lost play. Philomela tells her sister the story of her rape by Tereus—her brother-in-law, who has torn out her tongue to silence her—by weaving a picture of it.
7. King of the Phaeacians and Odysseus's host in *Iliad* 7–12 (for the telltale weeping, see 8.521–34). Dicaeogenes (late 5th c. B.C.E.), a minor Greek tragedian.
8. Aeschylus's *Choephori*, or *Libation Bearers* (458 B.C.E.), lines 168–234.
9. Polyidus (early 4th c. B.C.E.), perhaps the poet and critic Polyidus of Selymbria.
1. Lost, as is *Tydeus*.
2. A lost play by an unknown author.
3. For Odysseus's bow, see *Odyssey* 21.

from the sanctuary.[4] This was not noticed if one did not visualize the action, but on the stage the play collapsed when the audience would not tolerate the oversight. Also the poet should as far as possible work out the play with the appropriate dramatic gestures, for among poets of equal ability, those who themselves are in the emotional states they depict are the most convincing; that is, one who is in the throes of distress conveys distress and one who is in a rage conveys anger most truthfully and accurately. For this reason, poetry is the art of a man of genius or of one having a touch of madness—the first sort are versatile, the second excitable.

Whether one is using a traditional story or an invented story and composing it oneself, [1455b] one should first set it down in a general outline, and only then proceed to expand it by fashioning the episodes. What I mean by taking this general view of the whole may be illustrated from *Iphigeneia*, thus:

> A certain young girl who had been offered in sacrifice vanished mysteriously from the sight of the sacrificers, and having been set down in another country where it was the custom to sacrifice foreigners to the goddess, became the priestess of this rite. Some time later it happened that the priestess's brother arrived. (The fact that he went there because the oracle for a certain reason commanded it, and what he went for, are matters external to the plot.) Upon his arrival, he was seized and was on the point of being sacrificed when he revealed who he was (either in Euripides' way of managing it, or in that of Polyidus with the quite natural remark that evidently not only his sister but he also had to be sacrificed); and thereby his life was saved.

This done, it is now time to put in the characters' names and to fashion the episodes, taking care to see that the episodes are appropriate, as are, for example, in *Orestes* the fit of madness that leads to Orestes' capture and the ritual cleansing that leads to the escape. Note that in drama the episodes are short, whereas in epic poetry episodes are used to give the poem length. Thus the argument of the Odyssey is not long:

> A certain man has been absent from home for many years; he is kept under hostile surveillance by Poseidon;[5] and he is alone. Besides, the situation at home is that suitors are dissipating his property and plotting against his son. But after suffering from storms at sea, the man returns, reveals himself to certain persons, and attacking his enemies comes off safe himself and destroys them.

This is the essential story; and all the rest consists of episodes.

[18] In every tragedy there is first the Complication and then the Denouement. The complication comprises the events outside the play itself and often also some of the events within the play, and the remainder is the denouement. I mean that the complication extends from the beginning up to the last moment before the change to good or bad fortune occurs, and that the denouement begins with that change and extends to the end of the

4. In a lost play; Amphiaraus, a ruler in Argos, was a seer and was one of the Seven against Thebes, who unsuccessfully sought to help one of Oedipus's sons take the rule of Thebes from the other.

5. Greek god of the sea and the father of the Cyclops, whom Odysseus blinded and mocked.

play. For example, in the *Lynceus* of Theodectes, the complication includes the antecedent events and, within the play, the seizure of the child and that in turn of [the parents]; the denouement extends from the indictment for murder to the end.

There are four types of tragedy, corresponding in number to the "parts" already mentioned. There is complex tragedy, the whole of which consists of reversal and recognition; tragedy of passion—for example, the various plays entitled *Ajax* or [1456a] *Ixion*;[6] tragedy of character, such as the *Women of Phthia* and *Peleus*;[7] and fourth ***, such as the *Daughters of Phorcys* and *Prometheus*[8] and all plays the scene of which is in Hades. One should by all means endeavor to have all these types at his command, or at least most of them and the most important—especially in view of the way they harass the poets nowadays; good poets having existed in each case in the past, they now expect the single poet to surpass each one of these in his point of excellence.

The right way to compare tragedy with tragedy is to consider no feature so much as the plot—that is, in plays having the same complication and denouement. Many poets do well with the complication, only to fail with the denouement, but the one capacity should be brought into line with the other.

One must bear in mind also what has been said repeatedly, and not construct a tragedy on the plan of an epic poem (by epic I mean, having a multiplicity of stories)—as if, for example, someone were to dramatize the story of the *Iliad* in its entirety. In the epic, thanks to the length of the poem, the parts all assume their due proportions, but in plays the result of such a multiplicity is far from what was expected. One has only to note that those who have dramatized the *Sack of Troy* entire, instead of taking one part at a time as Euripides did, or the whole Niobe story[9] instead of doing as Aeschylus did, invariably either have their plays hissed off or make but a poor showing in the competition. In fact, the one occasion when even Agathon was driven from the stage was when he did this.

It is remarkable how both in peripeties [i.e., complex plots] and in simple plots the poets keep their aim fixed on the effects they wish to produce—the tragic effect, that is, and the effect of human sympathy. The latter is our feeling when a clever but villainous man is outwitted, Sisyphus[1] for example, or when a brave but unjust man is defeated. This even has a kind

6. No play of this name survives. In Greek mythology, Ixion was the first to murder kin and attempted to rape Hera, queen of the gods; as punishment for the second crime, he is chained forever to a wheel in Hades, the underworld. *Ajax*: Sophocles' play (ca. 445 B.C.E.) tells the story of the Greek warrior who, after being driven mad by Athena, commits suicide out of shame.

7. Both lost works revolve around the family of Achilles, who was the son of Peleus and came from Phthia. *Women of Phthia* is by Sophocles; both Sophocles and Euripides wrote plays titled *Peleus*.

8. Perhaps Aeschylus's *Prometheus Bound*, whose hero speaks while bound to the rocks in the Caucasus. *Daughters of Phorcys*: perhaps by Aeschylus. Phorcys was a sea god, and his daughters were monsters: the 3 Graeae, old women who shared one tooth and one eye, and the 3 serpent-haired Gorgons, the sight of whom turned humans to stone.

9. There are no known epics concerning Niobe; Aeschylus's *Niobe* is lost. *Sack of Troy*: a poem in the epic cycle, by Lesches of Mytiline (ca. 7th c. B.C.E.) or Arctinus of Miletus (ca. 8th c. B.C.E.). Euripides treated some of the same events in his *Trojan Women* and *Hecuba*.

1. A sly trickster who murdered travelers and once even chained the god of death, he is punished eternally for betraying Zeus's secrets; he tries to roll a stone over the top of a steep hill, but always fails and must try again from the bottom. Aeschylus, Sophocles, and Euripides all wrote plays on Sisyphus.

of probability, if only in the sense of Agathon's comment,[2] for it is probable that many improbable things will happen.

The chorus ought to be regarded as one of the actors, and as being part of the whole and integrated into performance, not in Euripides' way but in that of Sophocles. In the other poets, the choral songs have no more relevance to the plot than if they belonged to some other play. And so nowadays, following the practice introduced by Agathon, the chorus merely sings interludes. But what difference is there between the singing of interludes and taking a speech or even an entire episode from one play and inserting it into another?

[19] Now that the other elements have been discussed, it remains to speak of Language and Thought. As for Thought, this subject may best find its place in my discussion of rhetoric,[3] since it belongs more properly to that field of study. Under Thought come all the effects that are to be obtained through speech, and these fall under the heads of proving and refuting, stirring up emotions [1456b] (pity, fear, anger, and the rest), and enlarging or belittling the importance of things. Obviously, in their actions as well as in their utterances, the personages will employ Thought in these same categories whenever they have to inspire pity or terror or convey a sense of importance or plausibility simply by what they do; the only difference being that the acts must make their impression immediately without verbal explanation, while the effects of the speech must be procured by the speaker and be the result of what he says, for if the intended impression were to be made independently of the speech and not by means of it, what need would there be for the speaker?

To come to Language, one technical study relating to it concerns the Forms of Expression, knowledge of which properly belongs to the art of Elocution and to the specialist in that sort of thing—what is a command, what is a prayer, a statement, a question, an answer, and the like. A poet's knowledge or ignorance of these matters is not a point on which criticism of any consequence is directed against his art. For what error would anyone suppose there to be in the words "Sing, goddess, the wrath," which Protagoras,[4] however, criticizes on the grounds that Homer thinks he is uttering a prayer when he is really giving an order. According to Protagoras, to bid someone do or not do something is a command. Let us, therefore, leave this technicality aside as belonging to some other art and not to the art of poetry.

[20] Language, taken as a whole, is divisible into the following parts: the single letter, the syllable, the connective particle, the article[?], the noun, the verb, the inflection, the unified uterance.

A letter is an indivisible sound—not every such sound, however, but one capable of uniting with others in a complex sound; the lower animals utter indivisible sounds, but not what I call a letter. These primary sounds are divided into vowels, semivowels, and mutes. A vowel is a letter having audible sound without the application [of the tongue or lips]; a semivowel is one having audible sound with such application—e.g., S and R; a mute—e.g., G and D—is one which, though made by application [of these organs], has no

2. Agathon's comment occurred in a play, and is quoted in its original form in Aristotle's *On Rhetoric* 1402a: "Perhaps someone may say that this is probable, that many things may befall mortals that are not probable" [translator's note].
3. For Aristotle's discussion of types of argument, see *On Rhetoric* 1356a–1358a (see below).
4. Pre-Socratic philosopher (5th c. B.C.E.), who was one of the most successful of the sophists, or itinerant teachers. "Sing . . .": the first words of the *Iliad*.

sound by itself but becomes audible when combined with letters having a sound. The letters owe their variety to their being produced by different conformations of the mouth or the different parts of it, to their being aspirated or not aspirated, to their being long or short, and, finally, to their being uttered with acute, grave, or intermediate tones. Detailed study of these matters belongs to the subject of metrics.

A syllable is a nonsignificant sound composed of a mute and a letter having sound [vowel or semivowel]; for GR without A is a syllable as well as GRA. But differences of syllables is also a subject for metrics.

The Connective Particle is (a) a nonsignificant sound—e.g. *men, êtoi, de*—which neither prevents [1457a] nor causes formation of one significant sound [expression] out of two or more others, and which cannot correctly stand by itself at the beginning of a phrase; or (b) it is a nonsignificant sound, such as *amphi, peri,*[5] etc., which functions to make one significant sound [expression] out of two or more significant sounds.

An Article[?] is a nonsignificant sound which marks the beginning or end or a division [of an expression].

A Noun is a composite significant sound, not indicating time, no part of the composite being by itself significant; for even when a noun is composed of two others we do not treat these as separately significant; e.g., in the name Theodore *-dore* ["gift"] is not significant.

A Verb is a composite significant sound, indicating time, no part of the composite being by itself significant, just as in nouns. Thus "men" or "white" gives no indication of "when," but "walks" and "has walked" add to their meaning the indication respectively of present and past time.

Inflection applies to nouns or verbs, as when the meaning is "of" or "to" something, and so forth; or when the reference is to one or more than one, as "man" and "men"; or again it may be a mode of utterance, for example, a question or a command: "walked?" and "Walk!" being inflections of the verb in these two forms of utterance.

A unified utterance is a composite significant sound, some parts of which have independent meaning. Not every such utterance is a combination of nouns and verbs; it can exist without verbs, as, for example, the definition of man. However, it will always include a member having independent meaning, as "Cleon" in "Cleon walks." The unified utterance is a unit in either of two ways, either because what it signifies is itself a unit or because it is a combination of several parts. Thus the *Iliad* is unified by combination, the definition of man by signifying one thing.

[21] Words are of two kinds, simple words—those like *gê* (earth) that are not compounds of significant parts—and double words. The latter are compounds consisting either of a significant and a nonsignificant part (though in the compound these are not recognized as significant or nonsignificant), or of two parts both of which have meaning. There may also be triple and quadruple words and indeed multiple words, as, for example, most of the names of the people of Marseilles [? in a mock heroic poem]—Hermocaicoxanthus.[6] [1457b]

5. Around, about; in Greek, these are both prepositions and prefixes.
6. A comical name compounded from the names of three rivers (Hermus, Caïcus, and Xanthus) in western Asia Minor, where the founders of Marseilles (then called Massalia) originated.

Every word is either (1) the ordinary current word, or (2) a foreign word, or (3) a metaphor, or (4) an ornamental word, or (5) a coined word, or a word (6) lengthened or (7) curtailed or (8) otherwise altered in form.

By "current word" I mean a word used by everyone [in any particular region], and by "foreign word" a word used by others elsewhere. Obviously, the same word may be both current and foreign, but not for the same people; *sigynon* (lance) is a current word in Cyprus but a foreign word for us.[7]

Metaphor is the application to one thing of the name belonging to another. We may apply (a) the name of a genus to one of its species, or (b) the name of a species to its genus, or (c) the name of one species to another of the same genus, or (d) the transfer may be based on a proportion. Examples:

(a) From genus to species: "Here stands my ship," since *to be at anchor* is a special form of *standing still*.

(b) From species to genus: "Truly *ten thousand* noble deeds hath Odysseus done," for *ten thousand* is a large number and is here used in place of the generic *many*.

(c) From species to species: "*drawing* off the life with bronze" and "*cutting* off [streams of water?] with unwearied bronze [vessels?]," where "drawing off" is put for "cutting off" and "cutting off" for "drawing off," both expressions being species of the genus "take away."

(d) The meaning of metaphor by analogy [or proportional metaphor] is that when among four things the second is related to the first as the fourth is related to the third, one may substitute the fourth for the second or the second for the fourth. And sometimes the term related to the proper term in the analogy is added to the metaphor, thus: The wine cup is to Dionysus as the shield is to Ares,[8] and therefore one may call a wine cup "the shield of Dionysus" and the shield "the wine cup of Ares." Again, old age is to life what evening is to day; and one may speak of evening as "the old age of the day" (either thus or as Empedocles puts it) and of old age as "the evening of life" or "the sunset of life." In some cases there are terms of the proportion for which actually we have no word but which nevertheless will find expression in metaphor. Thus to cast seed is to sow, but there is no special word for the casting of its rays by the sun; this, however, is to sunlight what sowing is to seed, and hence the expression: "sowing a god-created flame." There is still another way in which this type of metaphor may be used. Having called one thing by the name of another, we can deny it some special attribute of this thing—as one might call a shield not the wine cup "of Ares," but the "wineless" wine cup.

A coined word is a word not used at all by any group of speakers but simply invented by the poet; for apparently there are some words of this kind, as *ernygas* ("sprouters"?) for *kerata* ("horns") and *arêtêr* ("supplicator") for *hiereus* ("priest").

An Expanded [1458a] Word is one in which a vowel that is usually short is treated as long, or one in which an extra syllable has been inserted. A Curtailed Word is one from which some part has been taken away. Examples of expanded words: *polêos* for *poleôs, Pêlêïadeô* for *Pêleidou*; of curtailed words: *krî* (for *krithe*), *dô* (for *dôma*), and *ops* (for *opsis*) in *mia ginetai amphoterôn*

7. That is, though speaking Greek, those on the island of Cyprus speak a different dialect.

8. Greek god of war.

ops.[9] A word is Altered when part of the usual form is kept and part is refashioned. Example, *dexiteron kata mazon* for *dexion*.[1]

Nouns themselves are masculine or feminine, or else intermediate between these.[2] Masculine [and not feminine] are all that end in nu, rho, or sigma or compounds of sigma (i.e., psi and ksi); feminine are those ending in vowels that are always long (i.e., eta and omega) or in alpha among vowels that may be long or short. Thus the masculine and feminine terminations are equal in number, the compounds psi and ksi counting as sigma. No noun ends in a mute or in an invariably short vowel [epsilon or omicron]; only three end in iota, namely *meli* (honey), *kommi* (gum), and *peperi* (pepper); and five end in upsilon: <*pôu* (flock), *nâpu* (mustard), *gonu* (knee), *doru* (spear), *astu* (town)>. The intermediates end in these vowels and in nu and sigma.

[22] Of Diction the prime virtue is to be clear without being commonplace. Diction is at its clearest when composed of words in everyday use, but then it is commonplace, as is exemplified by the poetry of Cleophon and Sthenelus.[3] On the other hand, an impressive diction, one that escapes the ordinary, results from the use of strange words, by which I mean foreign words, metaphors, expanded words, and whatever departs from normal usage. However, anything composed entirely in such language will either be a riddle or a barbarism—a riddle if composed in metaphors, a barbarism if in foreign words alone. In fact, the very idea of a riddle is to describe a given object by means of a string of absurdities, a thing that cannot of course be done by any combination of the proper terms, but can be done if you combine the corresponding metaphors, as in "I saw a man welding bronze on another man with fire,"[4] and similar riddles. In like manner, a combination of foreign words produces a barbarism.

What is needed, therefore, is a blend, so to speak, of these ingredients, since the unfamiliar element (the foreign word, the metaphor, the ornamental word, and the other types mentioned) will save the diction from being commonplace and drab, while the colloquial element will ensure its clarity. [1458b] By no means least important in what they contribute at once to clarity and to unfamiliarity are the expanded, curtailed, and altered forms of words. These will provide the element of unfamiliarity insofar as deviation from the normal forms makes them unusual, while the fact that they are in part ordinary words will ensure clarity. Unwarranted, therefore, are the objections of those who censure this kind of expression and hold the poet up to ridicule for using it, as for instance the elder Eucleides[5] does. Making poetry is easy, he says, if they let you stretch out the words as much as you please, and therewith he produces some burlesque lines in the style in question.

Epicharên eidon Marathônade badizonta,

and

9. One vision (*ops*, "face," "eye") comes into being from two [eyes] (quoted from a fragment of Empedocles). The expanded words mean "of the city," "son of Peleus"; the curtailed words mean "barley," "mansion," and "seeing."

1. The Greek literally means "in the righter [instead of 'right'] breast" (*Iliad* 5.393).

2. Some editors condemn this paragraph (which contains much that is inaccurate) as spurious.

3. Probably a tragic poet whose poor style is ridiculed by Aristophanes.

4. In *On Rhetoric* 1405b, Aristotle uses the same example and explains that it refers to the process of cupping.

5. Identity unknown, although both an Athenian magistrate and a Megaran philosopher of that name were active ca. 400 B.C.E.

Ouk an g'eramenos [?] ton ekeinou elleboron.[6]

Agreed that too obvious a use of lengthened words becomes ridiculous, but moderation has its place in all the stylistic devices, and Eucleides might have achieved the same effect with metaphors, foreign words, and the rest, if he had treated them abusively with the express purpose of raising a laugh. Try substituting the normal words in a verse of epic poetry, and you will realize what a difference the lengthened forms make when handled properly. The same with foreign words, metaphors, and the other forms, anyone who replaced them with the regular words would see that what I say is right.

To illustrate: The same iambic line is found both in Aeschylus and in Euripides, but Euripides has altered just one word, putting a strange word in place of a common everyday one, and as a result his line seems fine and the other poor in comparison. Aeschylus in his *Philoctetes* has it thus:

phagedaina hê mou sarkas esthiei podos[7]

and what Euripides did was to change *ἐσθίει* ("eats") to *θοινᾶται* ("feasts on"). Again, in the line,

nun de m'eôn oligos te kai outidanos kai aeikês[8]

suppose one were to substitute the ordinary words and say:

nun de m'eôn mikros te kai asthenikos kai aeikês[9]

and similarly in

diphron aeikelion katatheis oligên te trapezan

Say:

diphron mochthêrou katatheis mikran te trapezan.[1]

And suppose *êiones boôsin* ("the sea beaches bellow") to be replaced by *êiones krazousin* ("the sea beaches cry out"). Also, Ariphrades[2] made fun of the tragic poets for using locutions that no one would employ in ordinary speech, such as *dômatôn apo* ("from the houses away") instead of *apo dômatôn* ("away from the houses") and *sethen* ("of thine") and *ego de nin* [where *nin* is an archaic third-person pronoun] [1459a] and *Achilleôs peri* ("Achilles about") for *peri Achilleôs* ("about Achilles"), and so on. But all such expressions, just because they are not in the current vocabulary, give distinction to the poet's language; and that is what Ariphrades failed to understand.

To give appropriate treatment to the kinds of words here discussed, including compounds and foreign words, is in every case important, but

6. The first line translates as "I saw Epichares walking to Marathon" and the second, only fragmentary, "would not, in love(?) . . . that man's hellebore." The two phrases are unrelated; both contain words with arbitrarily lengthened syllables. Epichares: a common name in Athens. Marathon: a large Attic city on the northeast coast. "Hellebore": an herb thought to be a cure for madness.

7. "The gnawing ulcer that eats the flesh of my foot," from a lost play by Euripides. The *Philoctetes* of Sophocles but not Euripides survives, in which Philoctetes, an outstanding archer who used the bow and arrows of Heracles, sailed with Greeks for Troy but was left behind on an island because a wound on his foot, caused by snakebite, produced a horrible smell.

8. "But now a paltry man, a weakling, in aspect ill-favored (has blinded me)" (*Odyssey* 9.515).

9. "But now a little man, a man who is weak and unpleasing."

1. "A wretched stool and a little table"; the first line, "Having placed (for him) an unseemly stool and a paltry table," is from *Odyssey* 20.259.

2. An unknown comic poet.

most important by far is to have an aptitude for metaphor. This alone cannot be had from another but is a sign of natural endowment; since being good at making metaphors is equivalent to being perceptive of resemblances. And among these verbal forms, compounds are best fitted for dithyrambs, foreign words for heroic verse,[3] and metaphors for iambic verse. In heroic verse all the forms may be used; but in iambic verse, where the aim is to imitate the spoken language as closely as possible, only those forms are appropriate which would also be used in prose—that is, the current word, the metaphor, and the ornamental word.

Let us regard the foregoing as a sufficient account of tragedy and of imitation in the mode of direct action.

[23] But as for the imitative art that is narrative [in manner] and employs metrical language [as its medium],[4] it is evident that, just as in tragedies, its plots should be dramatic in structure—that is, should involve a single action, whole and complete in itself, having a beginning, a middle, and an end, so that like one whole living creature it may produce its appropriate pleasure—and that its structure should not resemble histories, which necessarily present not a single action but a single period of time with all that happened therein to one or more persons, no matter how little relation one event may have had with another. (Thus though occurring at the same time, the naval battle at Salamis and the battle with the Carthaginians in Sicily did not converge to a common end,[5] and similarly in a time sequence there are cases in which one event follows another without uniting in a single issue.) Yet perhaps the majority of the poets do precisely that. Hence on this point also, Homer, as we have said of him before, might seem divine compared with the others, in that, though the war had indeed a beginning and an end, even so he did not attempt to make the whole of it the subject of his poem, since he realized that if he did so, the narrative was going to be too vast to be easily embraced in one view, or if he limited its extent, the variety of incidents would make it too complicated. As it is, he has selected one part of the war as his theme and used many of the other parts as episodes, the Catalogue of Ships,[6] for example, and the other episodes with which he spaces out his poem. The others make their poems about one man, or about one period of time, or else about one action that has many parts, as is done by the authors of the [1459b] *Cypria* and the *Little Iliad*.[7] And so, while the *Iliad* and the *Odyssey* each furnish the subject for but a single tragedy, or at most for two, the *Cypria* has furnished themes for many tragedies and the *Little Iliad* themes for more than eight—an *Award of the Arms*, a *Philoctetes*, a *Neoptolemus*, a *Eurypylus*, a *Beggary*, a *Laconian Women*, a *Sack of Troy*, a *Sailing of the Fleet*, a *Sinon*, and a *Trojan Women*.[8]

[24] Likewise, epic poetry should include the same types as tragedy—the simple, the complex, the poem of character, and the poem of passion; and should have the same essential elements, except music and spectacle, since an epic poem needs reversals and recognitions and sufferings, and ought

3. That is, verses in the meter of epic (dactylic hexameter).
4. Aristotle turns here from drama to epic.
5. According to Herodotus (7.166.1), the victory of the Greek fleet over the Persians at Salamis and the victory of the Sicilian Greeks led by Gelon over the Carthaginians occurred on the same day in 480 B.C.E.
6. *Iliad* 2.484–759.
7. Poems in the epic cycle, of unknown authorship: the *Cypria* related the origins of the Trojan War; the *Little Iliad*, events after the end of the *Iliad*.
8. Only Sophocles' *Philoctetes* and Euripides' *Trojan Women* are extant; some editors doubt that Aristotle is responsible for all the titles in this list.

also to have a good quality of thought and language. All these things Homer was the first to use, and he used them fully; for his two poems are complementary in structure, the *Iliad* being simple in plot and a poem of passion, and the *Odyssey* complex (it has recognitions throughout) and a poem of character; moreover they surpass all other poems in excellence of language and thought.

However, epic poetry differs from tragedy in the length of the composition and in meter. As to length, the formulation we have already made is valid—that it should be possible to embrace the beginning and the end in one view. Such would be the case if the poems were shorter than the old epic poems and approached the length of the group of tragedies presented at a single hearing. Yet relative to its extension in magnitude, epic poetry has a very distinct advantage in that in tragedy it is not possible to represent various parts [of the story] as being enacted simultaneously, but only the one that the players have in hand on the stage, whereas in epic the narrative form makes it possible to describe many parts as completed within the same time, and through these, if they are appropriate, the bulk of the poem is enlarged. This, accordingly, is an advantage that epic poetry has, making for grandeur and the diversion of the hearer through the introduction of episodes of dissimilar character; for uniformity soon palls and is a reason for failure in the case of tragedies.

As for the meter, the heroic [hexameter] proved, as the result of trial, to be the fitting one. Indeed, it would seem out of keeping if anyone were to compose a narrative imitation in some other meter or in a combination of meters, since in comparison with the other verse forms the heroic [hexameter] is the most deliberate and weighty. (These qualities make it especially receptive of foreign words and metaphors—for in this respect narrative imitation goes beyond the other kinds.) The iambic trimeter and the trochaic tetrameter, [1460a] on the other hand, are verses of movement, the latter being proper to the dance and the former to [dramatic] action. To combine these meters, as Chaeremon does, would be still more out of place in epic. No one, therefore, has ever composed a long poem in any other meter than the heroic; but nature herself, as we have said, teaches us to choose the meter appropriate to it.

In addition to the many other reasons why Homer deserves admiration, there is this in particular, that he alone among the epic poets has not failed to understand the part the poet himself should take in his poem. The poet should, in fact, speak as little as possible in his own person, since in what he himself says he is not an imitator. Now the other poets are themselves on the scene throughout their poems, and their moments of imitation are few and far between, but Homer, after a few introductory words, at once brings on a man or a woman or some other personage, and not one of them characterless but each with a character of his own.

The marvelous is an element that should of course be embodied in tragedies, but that which is a prime source of the marvelous—namely, the irrational—can be more freely introduced in epic poetry where we do not have the performer of the act directly before our eyes; for the Pursuit of Hector[9] would seem ridiculous if it took place on the stage—the army just standing by and taking no part in the chase and Achilles shaking his head

9. *Iliad* 22.131–207; Hector, eldest son of the king of Troy and the greatest Trojan warrior, initially flees Achilles.

at them—but in the poem the absurdity goes unnoticed. And the marvelous is enjoyable; note how everyone in reporting a piece of news adds his own embellishments with the idea of pleasing the listener.

It is Homer especially who has taught the other poets how to tell lies as they should be told. This is done by the use of paralogism. That is, when the existence of one thing entails the existence of a second thing, or one occurrence entails a second occurrence, people assume that if this second thing exists, the antecedent also exists or occurs; but this is not so. If, then, the antecedent is a lie, but there is something else that would necessarily exist or happen if it were the truth, one should add this thing to the lie, for knowing this second thing to be true, our mind wrongly infers that the antecedent is true also. The Bath Scene provides an example.[1]

What is impossible yet probable should be preferred to that which is possible but incredible; plots should never be constructed out of irrational parts. Best that there should not be anything irrational in them at all, but if there is, let it be outside the story told, as, in *Oedipus Tyrannus*, Oedipus's not knowing how Laius died, and not something in the play, as their reporting of the Pythian Games in *Electra* or in the *Mysians*[2] the man's having come all the way from Tegea to Mysia without uttering a word. To argue that without the part in question the plot would be ruined is ridiculous; no such plots should be constructed in the first place. If, however, such a part has been included, and is made to appear relatively plausible, it may be accepted in spite of its absurdity; since, even in the *Odyssey*, the irrational features of the Landing Scene[3] would in themselves not have been tolerable, [1460b] as would be apparent if a bad poet were to handle them, but as it is, with the aid of the other good features, the poet obliterates these and mitigates the absurdity.

The place for elaborate diction is in the less vital passages—that is, passages not intended to reveal either character or thought; for, the other way round, where character and thought are to be revealed, too brilliant a diction will obscure them.

[25] Critical problems and their solutions fall into different classes, the number and nature of which will be made clear by the considerations that follow.

Since the poet is an imitator, exactly like a painter or any other maker of images, he must necessarily in every case be imitating one of three objects: things as they once were or now are; or things as people say or suppose they were or are; or things as they ought to be. The language in which these things are narrated will include foreign words and metaphors and various abnormalities of diction, for this is a license we grant to the poets. And further, correctness in politics is not the same thing as correctness in poetry, nor is correctness in any other art the same as in poetry, but in poetry itself error is of two kinds, that which involves the art itself and that which is incidental. Thus the art itself is involved if one has decided to imitate [a certain object

1. That is, Penelope's false inference, from the disguised Odysseus's accurate description of some clothing, that his tale of being a Cretan who met her husband Odysseus is true (*Odyssey* 19.165–250).

2. A play of Aeschylus or Sophocles; Tegea in the Peloponnese is distant from Mysia in northwest Asia Minor. *Electra*: Sophocles' tragedy (ca. 414 B.C.E.) contains a false account (lines 680–763) of Orestes' death in a chariot crash in the Pythian Games, which were founded centuries after the events of the play.

3. *Odyssey* 13.116–25. After the Phaeacians rowed the sleeping Odysseus home to Ithaca with magical speed, he remained asleep as they lifted him out of the ship when it landed.

and fails to represent it correctly through] incompetence; but it is a nonessential error if one decides by mistake to represent a horse with both right legs thrown forward, or if the fault involves a particular art, medicine, for example, or any other art whatsoever. So then, it is in the light of the foregoing postulates that one should examine the criticisms that fall within the general problems, and find the answers to them.

First, criticisms relating to the art itself:

1. "The thing represented is impossible." That is indeed a fault, but it is justified if doing so achieves the artistic purpose—this has already been stated: if doing so makes this or some other part of the poem more exciting. An example is the Pursuit of Hector. It is not justified, however, if the end could have been achieved equally well or better in strict conformity with the special art there relevant; for, if possible, no mistakes should be made at all.

2. Also we should inquire whether the mistake involves the art itself or is incidental. Thus, the error is less if the artist did not know that female deer have no horns than if he failed to draw a recognizable picture.

3. Again, if something is criticized as not being true to fact, the answer may be: Yes, but that is how it ought to be—just as Sophocles, too, said that he portrayed men as they ought to be, while Euripides portrayed them as they are.

4. But if the representation is neither true to fact nor an idealization, the solution may be that it accords with what men say. So with what [the poets] tell about the gods; this is perhaps neither the better way of speaking about them, nor the truth; it may be [as reprehensible; 1461a] as Xenophanes[4] thought it was—still, it is what men say.

5. In other cases, perhaps not "better than mere fact" but "thus it once was" is the answer. So in the problem about the arms—"Their spears stood pointed upward, butts in the ground"[5] that was the custom in those days—and still is the custom in Illyria.

6. In dealing with the question whether that which has been said or done by someone is right or wrong, we must not only have regard to the moral quality, good or bad, of the act or utterance in and for itself, but must consider who says or does it, to whom it is said or done, on what occasion, how, and from what motive—whether, for example, the purpose is to bring about a greater good or to avert a greater evil.

In meeting other criticisms, one should pay attention to the use of language.

7. The criticism may be met by applying the category "foreign word." Thus in *οὐρῆας μὲν πρῶτον* [the mules first of all], perhaps by *οὐρῆας* Homer does not mean "mules" but "sentinels."[6] And his description of Dolon,[7] ὅς ῥ' *ἦ τοι εἶδος μὲν ἔην κακός* [who indeed was ill favored in form], may mean, not misshapen in body, but having an ugly face, since in Crete "well formed" (*εὐειδής*) is the regular word for "fair-faced" (*εὐπρόσωπος*). And "mix the drink" (*ζωρότερον*) may not mean to mix it "stronger," as for heavy drinkers, but "faster."

4. Pre-Socratic philosopher and poet (ca. 570–ca. 480 B.C.E.) who denounced immoral tales of Greek gods.

5. *Iliad* 10.152–53.

6. *Iliad* 1.50, where the Greek word *ourēas* may derive either from *oreus* (mule) or from *ouros* (sentinel). All the following examples in this passage come from the *Iliad*, sometimes abbreviating the original.

7. A Trojan scout killed by the Greeks (*Iliad* 10.314–457).

8. Again, the expression may be explained as metaphorical. So in "Now all the gods and men slept throughout the night" followed presently by "whenever he [Agamemnon] looked toward the Trojan plain, [he was amazed at] the din of flutes and pipes," the word "all" is used metaphorically for "many," since "all" is a species of the genus "many." And "alone without a share" is metaphorical, since the best-known instance is taken for the only one.

9. The solution may lie in a change of accent. In this way, Hippias of Thasos solved the difficulty in *δίδομεν δέ οἱ εὐχος ἀρέσθαι* and again in *τὸ μὲν οὐ καταπύθεται ὄμβρῳ*.[8]

10. In other cases, punctuation may provide the answer, as in Empedocles' sentence: "Suddenly things became mortal that before had learnt to be immortal and things unmixed before mixed."

11. In others, we must take account of an ambiguity, as in "night is more than two thirds gone and a third remains," where "more than" is ambiguous, [since the word *πλέω* may also mean "fully"].

12. In others again, we may appeal to a habitual mode of speech. As a mixture of wine and water is called simply "wine," so, analogously, the poet speaks of "a greave of newly wrought tin." And on the same principle by which iron workers are always called "braziers," Ganymede[9] is said to be "the wine pourer of Zeus," though gods do not drink wine. But this might also be explained as metaphorical.

Whenever a particular word involves an apparent contradiction, the thing to do is to consider all the possible meanings it may have in the passage in question. For example, in "there the brazen spear was stopped" we should consider all the possible meanings "to be checked there" admits of, trying it in this sense and that sense, for the best understanding of it. This method of procedure is just the opposite of that which [1461b] Glaucon[1] describes. Certain critics, he says, begin with an unlikely assumption about some point, then condemn the meaning they have themselves assumed and give reasons against it, and they censure the poet for having said what they imagine he has said, if this is in contradiction to what they and only they have thought. The question of Icarius has been treated in this way. They assume that Icarius was a Laconian; therefore it is an absurdity that Telemachus,[2] on his visit to Lacedaemon, does not meet him there. But perhaps it is rather as the Cephalonians say, for by their account it was in their country that Odysseus married and the name is not Icarius but Icadius; and hence very likely the problem arises from a [textual] error.

In general, we should justify the Impossible by referring it to poetic effect, or to the principle of enhancement, or to received opinion. Thus in reference to poetic effect, a convincing impossibility is preferable to that which, though possible, is unconvincing. And [in reference to enhancement, if it is impossible] that there should be men such as, for example, Zeuxis portrayed, then it may be a case of betterment—the ideal should surpass the reality. The Improbable [or Irrational] should be justified by "what men say," and also by the fact that sometimes the thing in question is not improbable—"it is probable that

8. The phrases translate as "but grant that he gain his prayer" and "part rotted by rain." Hippias of Thasos: an unknown figure (possibly an individual who died in Athens in 404 B.C.E.).
9. A beautiful young Trojan prince seized and carried to Olympus by Zeus's eagle; he became a minor Greek god.
1. Perhaps the interpreter of Homer named by Plato in *Ion* 530d; see above.
2. Odysseus's son (for this visit, see *Odyssey* 4). Icarius: Penelope's father, from Sparta (Lacedaemonia).

something improbable will happen." In examining Contradictions we should proceed as one does when testing [possible fallacious] refutations in a debate—i.e., "whether the same thing and in relation to the same thing and in the same sense"—applying these tests to the poet also [as well as to the debater] either in reference to the things he actually says or to what a reasonable person would suppose him to mean. But censure on the grounds of Improbability or of Depravity is justified if the poet brings them in when there is no need for them at all, as Euripides' Aegeus[3] is needlessly improbable and his Menelaus in the *Orestes* needlessly base.

Thus there are just five classes of problems from which critics draw their strictures, since whenever they object to something it is always because they find it either (1) Impossible, or (2) Improbable, or (3) Immoral, or (4) Contradictory, or (5) Incorrect as regards a special art. And we in turn must proceed from the same five classes of objections when we look for solutions. The solutions themselves are twelve in number.

[26] Someone might raise the question whether the epic or the tragic form of imitation is better. Thus:—if the less vulgar form is the better and that form which is addressed to the better audience is always the less vulgar, clearly the form that relies entirely on imitation is too vulgar by far; for convinced that the spectators never comprehend what is meant unless the actor adds something on his own, the players keep up a vast stir of activity and common flutists, for example, will go reeling about if they have to represent the throwing of a discus, or will clutch at the chorus leader if their music depicts Scylla. Tragedy, then, is of such a character; it is like what the older generation of actors thought about those who came after them—Mynniscus used to call Callipides an ape for what he regarded as his extravagant style of acting, while much the same was said of Pindarus,[4] [1462a] and as these later actors stand in relation to the earlier ones, so the tragic art as a whole stands in relation to epic. In short, epic poetry, they tell us, is addressed to a superior audience who have no need of gestures and postures, tragedy to the common crowd. Therefore, if tragedy is vulgar, obviously it will be inferior.

Now in the first place, the complaint does not bear on the art of poetry, it bears on the art of acting, since it is also possible for a rhapsode to overdo the gesticulation when reciting epic poetry, as Sosistratus did, and for the singer in a singing contest to do so, as did Mnasitheus of Opus.[5] Then, too, not every form of bodily movement is to be condemned, unless we are to condemn the dance itself, but only the attitudes and gestures of ignoble persons—which is just the objection formerly made to Callipides and repeated nowadays about other actors, that their women are anything but ladies. And again, tragedy succeeds in producing its proper effect even without any movement at all, just as epic poetry does, since when it is merely read the tragic force is clearly manifested. So then, if it is superior in all other respects, this at least is no necessary part of it.

In the next place, [tragedy is in fact the better form] because (1) it has everything that epic poetry has (for it can even employ the epic meter), and

3. In *Medea* (lines 663–758). Aegeus, king of Athens, happens to pass through Corinth and see Medea; he promises her future asylum.

4. Presumably an actor. Mynniscus of Chalcis (active ca. 460–420 B.C.E.), an actor known for roles in Aeschylus's plays. Callipides (active ca. 427–400 B.C.E.), a Greek actor.

5. Both unknown.

has in addition an element of no small importance in its music, which intensifies our pleasure in the highest degree, then also (2) it has the advantage of vividness both when read and when acted; again (3) it excels because in tragedy the imitation fulfils its purpose [1462b] in shorter compass—that which is more concentrated gives greater pleasure than that which is dispersed over a great length of time: I mean, for example, if someone were to lay out the *Oedipus* of Sophocles in the same number of lines as the *Iliad*; and again (4) the epic poets have a less unified type of imitation (witness the fact that any such poem supplies subjects for several tragedies), and consequently if ever they do make a poem of unified plot, either the tale will be concisely told and create a sense of abruptness, or it will conform to the normal epic length and seem watery; and I mean that the latter will be the case if the poem is put together out of a plurality of actions, as, for example, the *Iliad* has many such parts, and the *Odyssey* also, each part having a magnitude of its own; and yet these particular poems are as well constructed as an epic poem can be, and come as near as possible to being imitations of a single action. So, then, if tragedy is superior to epic poetry in all these respects, and excels it besides in [performing] the function for which the art exists (for these imitations should give us not just any pleasure but precisely the pleasure we have indicated), it is clear that tragedy is the better form of the two inasmuch as it succeeds better than the epic in achieving the end in view.

Let this then be our account of Tragedy and Epic Poetry—their general nature; the number and variety of their species and constituent parts; the causes of success or failure; and critical problems with their solutions . . .

ca. 330 B.C.E.

From On Rhetoric[1]

From *Book I*

FROM CHAPTER 2

Let rhetoric be [defined as] an ability, in each [particular] case, to see the available means of persuasion. This is the function of no other art;[2] for each of the others is instructive and persuasive about its own subject: for example, medicine about health and disease and geometry about the properties of magnitudes and arithmetic about numbers and similarly in the case of the other arts and sciences. But rhetoric seems to be able to observe the persuasive about "the given," so to speak. That, too, is why we say it does not include technical knowledge of any particular, defined genus [of subjects].

Of the *pisteis*,[3] some are atechnic ("non-artistic"), some entechnic ("embodied in art, artistic"). I call *atechnic* those that are not provided by "us" [i.e.,

1. Translated by George A. Kennedy, who sometimes adds clarifying words or phrases in square brackets. Also in square brackets in the text are the Bekker numbers used almost universally in citing Aristotle's works; they refer to the page numbers and columns of an 1831 edition by Immanuel Bekker.

2. In Greek, *technē*. Aristotle distinguishes between human arts, such as rhetoric or poetics, and sciences, such as physics or logic, which adduce verifiable results.

3. Proofs or means of persuasion (Greek).

the potential speaker] but are preexisting: for example, witnesses, testimony from torture, contracts, and such like; and *entechnic*[4] whatever can be prepared by method and by "us"; thus, one must use the former and invent the latter. [1356a] Of the *pisteis* provided through speech there are three species; for some are in the character [*ēthos*] of the speaker, and some in disposing the listener in some way, and some in the speech [*logos*] itself, by showing or seeming to show something.

[There is persuasion] through character whenever the speech is spoken in such a way as to make the speaker worthy of credence; for we believe fair-minded people to a greater extent and more quickly [than we do others], on all subjects in general and completely so in cases where there is not exact knowledge but room for doubt. And this should result from the speech, not from a previous opinion that the speaker is a certain kind of person; for it is not the case, as some of the handbook writers propose in their treatment of the art, that fair-mindedness on the part of the speaker makes no contribution to persuasiveness; rather, character is almost, so to speak, the most authoritative form of persuasion.

[There is persuasion] through the hearers when they are led to feel emotion [*pathos*] by the speech; for we do not give the same judgment when grieved and rejoicing or when being friendly and hostile. To this and only this we said contemporary technical writers try to give their attention. The details on this subject will be made clear when we speak about the emotions.

Persuasion occurs through the arguments when we show the truth or the apparent truth from whatever is persuasive in each case.

* * *

FROM CHAPTER 3

The species of rhetoric are three in number; for such is the number [of classes] to which the hearers of speeches belong. A speech consists of three things: a speaker and a subject on which he speaks and someone addressed, [1358b] and the objective[5] of the *speech* relates to the last (I mean the hearer). Now it is necessary for the hearer to be either an observer or a judge, and [in the latter case] a judge of either past or future happenings. A member of a democratic assembly is an example of one judging about future happenings, a juror an example of one judging the past. An observer is concerned with the ability [of the speaker]. Thus, there would necessarily be three genera of rhetorics: deliberative, judicial, demonstrative.[6] Deliberative advice is either protreptic ["exhortation"] or apotreptic ["dissuasion"]; for both those advising in private and those speaking in public always do one or the other of these. In the law courts there is either accusation or defense; for it is necessary for the disputants to offer one or the other of these. In epideictic, there is either praise or blame. Each of these [species] has its own "time"; for the deliberative speaker, the future (for whether exhorting or dissuading he advises about future events); for the speaker in court, the past (for he always prosecutes or defends concerning what has been done); in epideictic the present is the most important; for all

4. Also translated as "artistic," made by men.
5. In Greek, *telos*, also translated as "end" or "goal."
6. In Greek, *epideiktikon*, also translated as "epideictic."

speakers praise or blame in regard to existing qualities, but they often also make use of other things, both reminding [the audience] of the past and projecting the course of the future. The "end" of each of these is different, and there are three ends for three [species]: for the deliberative speaker [the end] is the advantageous and the harmful (for someone urging something advises it as the better course and one dissuading dissuades on the ground that it is worse), and he includes other factors as incidental: whether it is just or unjust, or honorable or disgraceful; for those speaking in the law courts [the end] is the just and the unjust, and they make other considerations incidental to these; for those praising and blaming [the end] is the honorable and the shameful, and these speakers bring up other considerations in reference to these qualities. Here is a sign that the end of each [species of rhetoric] is what has been said: sometimes one would not dispute other factors; for example, a judicial speaker [might not deny] that he has done something or done harm, but he would never agree that he has [intentionally] done wrong; for [if he admitted that,] there would be no need of a trial. Similarly, deliberative speakers often advance other facts, but they would never admit that they are advising things that are not advantageous [to the audience] or that they are dissuading [the audience] from what is beneficial; and often they do not insist that it is not unjust to enslave neighbors or those who have done no wrong. And similarly, those who praise or blame do not consider whether someone has done actions that are advantageous or harmful [to himself] [1359a] but often they include it even as a source of praise that he did what was honorable without regard to the cost to himself; for example, they praise Achilles because he went to the aid of his companion Patroclus[7] knowing that he himself must die, though he could have lived. To him, such a death was more honorable; but life was advantageous.

* * *

From *Book II*

FROM CHAPTER 1

These [topics, set forth in book 1] are the proper sources of exhortation and dissuasion, praise and blame, and prosecution and defense, and the kinds of opinions and propositions useful for their persuasive expression; for enthymemes[8] are concerned with these matters and drawn from these sources, so the result is speaking in a specific way in each genus of speeches. But since rhetoric is concerned with making a judgment (people judge what is said in deliberation, and judicial proceedings are also a judgment), it is necessary not only to look to the argument, that it may be demonstrative and persuasive but also [for the speaker] to construct a view of himself as a certain kind of person and to prepare the judge; for it makes much difference in regard to persuasion (especially in deliberations but also in trials) that the speaker seem to be a certain kind of person and that his hearers suppose him to be disposed toward them in a certain way and in addition if

7. In stories of the Trojan War, Achilles' closest friend; Achilles rejoined the battle to avenge his death at the hands of the Trojan hero Hector.

8. Rhetorical arguments by deduction, applying general principles to specific cases, that leave one of their premises unstated. Enthymemes use a looser form of reasoning than syllogisms, which are technical logical arguments that follow a rigid 3-part procedure.

they, too, happen to be disposed in a certain way [favorably or unfavorably to him]. For the speaker to seem to have certain qualities is more useful in deliberation; for the audience to be disposed in a certain way [is more useful] in lawsuits, for things do not seem the same to those who are friendly and those who are hostile, nor [the same] to the angry and the calm but either altogether different or different in importance: [1378a] to one who is friendly, the person about whom he passes judgment seems not to do wrong or only in a small way; to one who is hostile, the opposite; and to a person feeling strong desire and being hopeful, if something in the future is a source of pleasure, it appears that it will come to pass and will be good, but to an unemotional person and one in a disagreeable state of mind, the opposite.

There are three reasons why speakers themselves are persuasive; for there are three things we trust other than logical demonstration. These are practical wisdom [*phronēsis*] and virtue and good will, for speakers make mistakes in what they say through [failure to exhibit] either all or one of these; for either through lack of practical sense they do not form opinions rightly; or though forming opinions rightly they do not say what they think because of a bad character; or they are prudent and fair-minded but lack good will, so that it is possible for people not to give the best advice although they know [what] it [is]. These are the only possibilities. Therefore, a person seeming to have all these qualities is necessarily persuasive to the hearers. The means by which one might appear prudent and good are to be grasped from analysis of the virtues; for a person would present himself as being of a certain sort from the same sources that he would use to present another person; and good will and friendliness need to be described in a discussion of the emotions.

The emotions are those things through which, by undergoing change, people come to differ in their judgments and which are accompanied by pain and pleasure, for example, anger, pity, fear, and other such things and their opposites. There is need to divide the discussion of each into three headings. I mean, for example, in speaking of anger, what is their *state of mind* when people are angry and against *whom* are they usually angry and for what sort of *reasons*; for if we understood one or two of these but not all, it would be impossible to create anger [in someone]. And similarly, in speaking of the other emotions.

* * *

From *Book III*

FROM CHAPTER 2

[1404b] Let the matters just discussed be regarded as understood, and let the virtue of style[9] be defined as "to be clear" (speech is a kind of sign, so if it does not make clear it will not perform its function)—and neither flat nor above the dignity of the subject, but appropriate. The poetic style is hardly flat, but it is not appropriate for speech.

The use of nouns and verbs in their prevailing meaning makes for clarity; other kinds of words, as discussed in the *Poetics*,[1] make the style ornamented rather than flat. To deviate [from prevailing usage] makes language seem more elevated; for people feel the same in regard to word usage as they do in

9. In Greek, *lexis*, literally "speech"; the word is variously translated "language," "word choice," and "expression," as well as "style."

1. See *Poetics* 21–22, 1457a–1459a (above).

regard to strangers compared with citizens. As a result, one should make the language unfamiliar, for people are admirers of what is far off, and what is marvelous is sweet. Many [kinds of words] accomplish this in verse and are appropriate there; for what is said [in poetry] about subjects and characters is more out of the ordinary, but in prose much less so; for the subject matter is less remarkable, since even in poetry it would be rather inappropriate if a slave used fine language or if a man were too young for his words, or if the subject were too trivial, but in these cases, too, propriety is a matter of contraction or expansion [of what is being said]. As a result, authors should compose without being noticed and should seem to speak not artificially but naturally. (The latter is persuasive, the former the opposite; for people become resentful, as at someone plotting against them, just as they are at those adulterating wines.) An example is the success of Theodorus'[2] voice when contrasted with that of other actors; for his seems the voice of the actual character, but the others' those of somebody else. The "theft" is well done if one composes by choosing words from ordinary language. Euripides[3] does this and first showed the way.

* * *

ca. 340 B.C.E.

2. Renowned Athenian tragic actor (active ca. 370 B.C.E.).

3. Greek tragedian (ca. 485–ca. 406 B.C.E.).

HORACE
65–8 B.C.E.

It would be impossible to overestimate the importance of Horace's *Ars Poetica* (*Art of Poetry*) for the subsequent history of literary criticism. Since its composition in the first century B.C.E., this epigrammatic and sometimes enigmatic critical poem has exerted an almost continual influence over poets and literary critics alike—perhaps because its dicta, phrased in verse form, are so eminently quotable. Horace's injunction that poetry should both "instruct and delight" has been repeated so often that it has come be to known as the Horatian platitude. His practical approach to poetry as a craft, or *ars*, contrasts markedly with the more theoretical bent of his predecessors, especially ARISTOTLE and PLATO. In fact, unlike Plato, Horace holds the poet in very high regard, as his "Epistle to Augustus" suggests: "The poet forms the young child's stammering mouth, and turns his ear at a timely hour from obscene discourse; next he also shapes his heart with friendly precepts, castigating harshness, resentment, and wrath. He tells of deeds honorably done, instructs rising generations by the examples of famous men, and consoles the sick and helpless."

Horace describes himself in his youth as the impoverished son of a freed slave, yet he rose to great prominence in Rome, becoming both a leading member of the illustrious circle of poets patronized by the emperor Augustus (63 B.C.E.–14 C.E.) and one of Rome's greatest poets and satirists. Quintus Horatius Flaccus was born in Venusia, a Roman military colony in southeastern Italy on the border between Apulia and

Lucania. His father worked as an auctioneer and had a small landholding. It is possible that in his poetry (our main source for his biography) Horace somewhat exaggerates his family's poverty. His father was apparently wealthy enough to send his son to Rome for his schooling. At the age of nineteen Horace went to Athens to the university. There Marcus Brutus convinced him to join in his futile attempt to reestablish the Republic. He accompanied Brutus to Asia Minor and was appointed to the high post of military tribune. After the defeat of Brutus and Cassius at Philippi in 42 B.C.E. at the hands of Octavian—the future Augustus who would one day be the poet's patron—Horace returned to Rome, to find that his father's home and land had been confiscated. Despite this setback, he was able to obtain a pardon for his part in the rebellion and to purchase a position as *scriba quaestorius*, a keeper of records in the treasury. At this time, he also began his career as a poet. His abilities were recognized by Gaius Maecenas, a wealthy aristocrat and the most prominent literary patron in Rome, to whom he was introduced by the poet Virgil. He maintained a close friendship with Maecenas until the latter's death. Around 38 B.C.E., through Maecenas, Horace became a member of the small circle of writers who enjoyed the patronage of Octavian, whose power was growing; he would take full control (and the title "Augustus") in 27 B.C.E. Though he declined an offer to become the emperor's secretary, the emperor's support enabled Horace to do nothing but write poetry for the rest of his life. He died of a sudden illness on November 27, 8 B.C.E., only two months after the death of his patron and friend Maecenas, next to whose tomb he was buried.

Horace is celebrated for his poetry; between 39 and 10 B.C.E., he produced numerous epodes (lyric poems), odes, satires, and verse epistles (letters). Many of the epistles deal with the subject of poetry: the best-known are the "Epistle to Florus"; the "Epistle to Augustus," which examines the role of poetry in the state and asserts the merits of contemporary (that is, Augustan) poetry; and the famous "Epistle to the Pisones."

The Roman rhetorician Quintilian (ca. 30/35–ca. 100 C.E.) was the first to give the title *ars poetica* (art of poetry) or *liber de arte poetica* (book of the poetic art) to Horace's letter to the Pisones, a prominent Roman family with interests in poetry and literary criticism. The *Ars Poetica* was written perhaps as late as 10 B.C.E., although the date remains controversial, as do the identities of the members of the Piso family—father and sons—whom the poem addresses. Most likely the senior Piso is Lucius Calpurnius Piso (48 B.C.E.–32 C.E.); the sons have not been identified. The *Ars Poetica* is less a formal verse epistle, however—the trappings of the letter form are superficial at best—than a long conversational poem about poetry, written by an experienced and famous poet of the day. This form was widely imitated by later poets—most notably by Geoffrey of Vinsauf in the twelfth century, Pierre de Ronsard in the sixteenth, Nicolas Boileau in the seventeenth, ALEXANDER POPE in the eighteenth, Lord Byron in the nineteenth, and Wallace Stevens in the twentieth. The genre of literary theory in verse form presents many challenges. Because of the requirements of versification, the structure of Horace's text—its organization and transitions—is often dictated less by logical argumentation than by verbal association and rhetorical tone. Translation of the *Ars Poetica* (476 lines long) is notoriously difficult. Many English translations imitate Horace's hexameter lines by using rhymed couplets, which tend to reduce Horace's urbane wit at best to a string of epigrammatic statements held together by the meter, at worst to doggerel. For this reason, we have chosen a prose translation here.

While heavily indebted to Greek literature, and in particular to Aristotle (especially the *Poetics* and *On Rhetoric*), the *Ars Poetica* is neither a systematic exposition of a coherent theory of poetic composition nor a comprehensive textbook for aspiring writers. Instead, it is an argument for poetry as a craft. Poetry is not merely inspired madness (as in Plato) or genius; it is an art and, as such, has rules and conventions that require both instruction and practice. Horace understands the concept of *ars* in three ways: as a practiced mastery of a craft, as a systematic knowledge of theory and technique, and as a capacity for objective self-criticism. His urbane text counsels the aspiring young poet, in this case probably the elder Piso son, that the craft of poetry will require painstaking work and self-sacrifice to acquire.

Another key principle that dominates the whole of the *Ars Poetica* is decorum. Briefly defined, decorum is the discernment and use of appropriateness, propriety, proportion, and unity in the arts, whether in painting, sculpture, or poetry. This is the Horatian principle that most appealed to later French and English neoclassical critics (see, for example, Pope, below), who often applied standards of decorum more rigidly than Horace himself would have. For Horace, decorum required that the poet fit the part to the whole, the subject to the appropriate genre, and meter and language to both character and circumstance. A skillful poet, knowledgeable in the craft of poetry and observant of the principles of decorum, would produce the kind of poetry able to "delight and instruct" its audiences.

Among the many dicta for which Horace's text is most famous are the warning against the "purple patch" (*purpureus pannus*) and the declarations that "poetry resembles painting" (*ut pictura poesis*), "even Homer sometimes sleeps" (*idem dormitat Homerus*), and poetry should be "pleasing" and "useful" (*dulce et utile*). Purple patches are inappropriately placed ornate passages that violate the principle of decorum and thus should be avoided by writers. Later critics have built on Horace's likening of poetry to painting to explore the spatial as well as the temporal dimensions of literature (see below, for example, SIR PHILIP SIDNEY, G. E. LESSING, and ERICH AUERBACH). Because sometimes even a poet as great as Homer errs, Horace counsels tolerance of occasional small faults. The pleasures of poetry for readers and theater audiences should be joined to practical and moral instruction embodied in the work, though Horace seems more preoccupied with delight and careful craft than with moral uplift. It is to these and other pithy and suggestive observations that modern critics often turn when considering Horace.

Horace's critics have complained that the long epistle is disorganized, that it sometimes sacrifices sense for the sake of wit, and that it lacks grandeur, being preoccupied with audience response. Since its appearance, however, the *Ars Poetica* has appealed to those literary critics interested in codifying the principles of poetic composition, in arguing the relative merits of craft and genius in poetry, and in debating whether the primary goal of literature is pleasure or instruction.

***Ars Poetica* Keywords:** Aesthetics, Authorship, The Canon/Tradition, Classical Theory, Drama, Literary History, Poetry

Ars Poetica[1]

Imagine a painter wanting to attach a horse's neck to a human head, assemble limbs from everywhere, and add feathers of various colours, so that a woman beautiful above the waist tailed into a revolting black fish! Could you hold back your laughter, my friends, if admitted to view it? Believe me, Pisos, a book could be very like such a canvas, its images just empty inventions like a sick man's dreams: neither foot nor head would be rendered in a single form.—"Painters and poets alike have always had an equal prerogative to venture anything," you say?—We know. This is a concession we both ask for,

1. Translated by Ross S. Kilpatrick. Numbers in square brackets refer to line numbers in Horace's Latin poem. Horace addresses this epistle to the Piso family, father and sons; scholars largely agree on the identification of the elder Piso as Lucius Calpurnius Piso (48 B.C.E.–32 C.E.), though none of the sons has been positively identified.

and make in return. But not to the point where savage beasts mate with the meek, where serpents twin with birds and lambs with tigers! When weighty works professing greatness are under way, one or two purple patches are stitched in to give them far-seen brilliance, as when the grove and altar of Diana[2] are described, and the windings of water rushing through pleasant fields, or the River Rhine, or a rainbow. (But this is not the place for such considerations). Perhaps you do know how to draw a cypress tree. What is the good of that, if what's wanted is a man (painted *ex voto*[3] for a fee) swimming hopelessly away from his shattered ships? An amphora[4] began to take shape. So why does a jug emerge as the wheel races on? The point is, whatever you're making, it should be unified and coherent.

[21] The majority of us bards, Father (and you, young men, so worthy of your father), are taken in by what appear to be correct principles. I strive for brevity only to become obscure; I pursue smoothness but nerve and spirit fail me. Aiming at grandeur, you become turgid; over-cautious and fearful of the storm, you creep along the ground. One who lavishes variety on a single subject paints a dolphin in the woods or a boar in the waves. In avoiding blame you produce a flaw, if *ars*[5] is lacking. Down near the school of Aemilius,[6] one workman will mould fingernails and represent the softest hair, both in bronze. But the sum total is unhappy, since he won't ever know how to lay out his entire work. As for me, if I wanted to compose something I would no more desire to be that man than go through life with a crooked nose—though I might attract glances with my black eyes and hair!

[38] When you write, choose material to match your strengths, and long consider what your shoulders refuse to bear and what they will. The writer who selects according to his abilities will lack neither style nor a clear arrangement. The virtue and charm of arrangement will be found, if I'm not mistaken, here: in saying right now what ought to be said right now, and deferring the rest for later. In weaving words together be sparing and careful. Let the author of a promised poem favour one approach, and scorn another. You will have spoken in an uncommon way if a clever collocation renders a familiar word new. Should it be necessary to explain obscure matters in fresh terms (and give shape to matters unheard of by the loinclad Cethegi![7]), such licence is available, and will be given if exercised with restraint. New and recently fashioned words will gain acceptance if they tumble from the well-spring of Greek by judicious diversion. But why will a Roman grant Caecilius and Plautus what he denies to Vergil and Varius?[8] Why is it I am begrudged the few words I can garner, when the tongue of Cato, and of Ennius,[9] has enriched our native speech and endowed it with

2. Roman goddess of the hunt, the moon, and childbirth.
3. Literally "from the vow" (Latin), an offering to a divinity to fulfill a vow.
4. A type of container, usually for wine, often with a pointed base to allow upright storage.
5. Art (Latin).
6. A school for gladiators, near the shops of bronze workers.
7. An old patrician family that persisted in wearing old-fashioned garb.
8. Roman poet (ca. 74–14 B.C.E.), friend of Virgil and Horace; his works included the tragedy *Thyestes*. Caecilius Statius (d. ca. 168 B.C.E.), former slave from Gaul who wrote Latin comedies. Plautus (d. ca. 184 B.C.E.), Roman comic dramatist whose plays were modeled on Greek New Comedy originals (the social satires of ca. 320–mid-3d c. B.C.E.). Vergil or Virgil (70–19 B.C.E.), Roman poet, author of the *Aeneid* and friend of Horace.
9. Roman tragic and epic poet (ca. 239–169 B.C.E.) who tried to refine the Latin language according to Greek example. Cato (234–149 B.C.E.), Roman statesman, moralist, and prolific writer of treatises and history.

new names for things? It has always been permissible and always will be, to produce a word stamped with today's date.

[60] Just as woods change their leaves in the fullness[1] of the years, falling one by one . . . so perish words with age, after flourishing and thriving when newly born, like youths. We ourselves, and our works, are debts owed to death. Whether Neptune[2] protects the fleets in the land's embrace from the North Winds, a kingly task, or the marsh, long-unproductive and suitable for oars, sustains cities nearby and feels the weight of a plough, or the stream (now taught a better course) has changed a course threatening crops, such things made by mortal men shall perish. Much less likely is it that the esteem and favour granted to modes of speech could live and endure [69]. Many terms shall grow back which now have fallen away, and those now held in esteem shall fall, if our poetic practice so approves. Such is the criterion by which the judgement, rules, and standards for speech expression are to be discovered.

[73] The metre for handling the exploits of captains and kings and grim wars has been shown by Homer.[3] Lamentation was the first to be couched in verses unequally linked, then afterward the expression of prayer as well.[4] But as for who originated the slender elegy, well, the critics are debating this and the case is awaiting their judgement. Rage armed Archilochus with his characteristic iambus,[5] the foot which comic socks and grand tragic buskins[6] seized upon as suited to argument and the suppression of popular clamour. It was born to represent action. The Muse assigned the gods and sons of gods to the lyre, along with the victorious boxer, winning race-horse, youthful longings and wine's liberating power. If in producing my works I cannot observe (and don't know) the required genres and styles, why am I hailed as "Poet"? Why prefer wanton ignorance to learning?

[87] Comic material resists presentation in tragic verse. Likewise the "Feast of Thyestes"[7] resents poetry that is conversational and worthy almost of the comic sock. Let each discrete detail keep the place allotted. From time to time, though, comedy does raise its voice too, as Chremes[8] delivers accusations with his swollen mouth. A tragic actor frequently grieves in plain discourse; Telephus and Peleus,[9] both poor and exiled, cast aside bombast and foot-and-a-half words if concerned to touch the heart of the spectator effectively with their lamentation.

1. Several markings denoting editorial emendations of the Latin text have been deleted.
2. Roman god of the sea.
3. Greek epic poet (ca. 8th c. B.C.E.) to whom the *Iliad* and *Odyssey* are traditionally attributed. The meter of epic is dactylic hexameter (a 6-foot line based on the syllabic pattern long-short-short).
4. Inscriptions accompanying dedications or prayers to gods, which, like lamentation, are written in elegiac couplets: a line of dactylic hexameter followed by a line replacing the 3d and 6th foot with one long syllable. The shorter second line gives the couplet a sense of falling off, thought to impart melancholy.
5. Metrical foot made of one short and one long syllable; iambic trimeter was the measure used in dialogue in both Greek comedies and Greek tragedies. Archilochus (ca. 7th c. B.C.E.), Ionian lyric poet thought to be the earliest writer of iambic verse.
6. Symbols of comedy and tragedy. In Greek theater, tragic actors wore a boot that elevated them, while comic actors wore a thin shoe called a sock.
7. In Greek mythology, Atreus murdered the sons of his brother Thyestes and served them to Thyestes, who had seduced Atreus's wife.
8. Miserly character in the comedies of Terence (Roman dramatist, ca. 190–ca. 159 B.C.E.).
9. Father of the Greek hero Achilles, the central character in the *Iliad*; as a young man, Peleus was banished from his homeland. Telephus: son of Heracles and Auge, wounded by Achilles' spear and cured by its rust. Both are characters in plays by the Greek tragedian Euripides (ca. 485–ca. 406 B.C.E.).

[99] It is not enough that poetry be noble: it should impart delight, and transport the listener as it likes. As people's faces respond with laughter to those who laugh, so do they cry in response to those who cry. If you want me to cry, you must first cry yourself. Then, Telephus (or you, Peleus), will your misfortunes make me suffer. If you speak your assigned parts badly I shall either nod or laugh. Grim words are appropriate to a gloomy countenance; words full of threat, to the angry; wanton, to the playful; serious in delivery, to the severe. First, you see, Nature shapes us within for every aspect of life's fortunes. She gives us pleasure, or drives us to wrath, or brings us to earth with the profound anguish of grief. Afterwards she brings out the heart's emotions with the tongue as their interpreter. If a speaker's words are not consonant with his fortunes, the people (both horse and foot)[1] will burst out laughing!

[114] It will make a lot of difference whether a god is speaking or a hero; a mature old man or one still in flower of youth; a strong-minded dame or a busy nurse, a far-travelled merchant or a cultivator of a green farm, a Colchian or Assyrian, or someone reared at Thebes or Argos.[2]

[119] Either follow a legend when writing, or make up details consistent with themselves. If, say, you are putting the illustrious Achilles back on stage, let him be unyielding, wrathful, inexorable, savage; have him say that by nature laws are not for him, never failing to appeal to a judgement of arms. Medea should be fierce and invincible, Ino tearful, Ixion faithless, Io wandery, Orestes grim.[3] If you are putting something untried on stage, and trying to shape a new character, let him be the same from the beginning to the last detail, just as he was when he entered, and remain true to himself. [127] It is hard to make unique poetry out of the commonplace; you do better if you spin out a canto of the *Iliad* into episodes than be the first to present something unfamiliar and unworked.

[131] Public domain will become private right if you don't dally on the trivial and broad track, faithfully rendering word for word like a translator, leaping in your imitation into some narrow hole from which propriety or the law of the genre forbids you even to budge. You don't begin this way (as a cyclic writer[4] once did): "Priam's fortune shall I sing, and a war far-famed." What will he produce by promising something worthy of so great an utterance? The mountains shall labour—a ridiculous mouse come forth! How much better did he begin who constructed nothing ineptly: "Tell me, O Muse, of the man who after the time of Troy's capture saw the manners of many men as well as their cities."[5] His plan is not to give out smoke from the flash but light from the smoke, to produce striking tales of wonder from it:

1. The Latin here, *equites peditesque*, refers to soldiers, mounted and on foot, and by extension to people high- and lowborn.
2. The Argive Agamemnon shows reserve and dignity, while the Theban Creon is a headstrong tyrant. The Assyrian would be effeminate, as compared with the Colchian, but both would be barbarians (Assyria was an ancient empire of west Asia; Colchis bordered the Black Sea).
3. Son of Agamemnon and Clytemnestra who avenges his father's murder by killing his mother and her lover; he is gloomy because the Furies hound him for the crime of matricide. Medea: enchantress of Greek myth who helps Jason gain the Golden Fleece and, after he abandons her, murders their children in revenge. Ino: daughter of Cadmus, wife of Athamas; pursued by her enraged husband after plotting against her stepchildren, she leaped into the sea with her son. Ixion: king who slew his father-in-law and is bound to a perpetually revolving wheel in the underworld as punishment for his attempted seduction of Hera, Zeus's wife. Io: daughter of Inachus who was loved by Zeus and subsequently transformed into a cow, goaded by gadflies sent by the angry Hera.
4. That is, one of the writers of the epic cycle, writing works that complete the story told by Homer.
5. The opening lines of the *Odyssey*.

Antiphates, and Scylla and Charbydis along with the Cyclops![6] He doesn't begin "The Return of Diomede" with the death of Meleager, or "The Trojan War" with the twin egg![7] He is ever rushing towards the issue, carrying the listener into the midst of events as if they were known to him. He leaves out what he despairs of handling with brilliance, telling his lies and mixing the true with the false in such a way that the middle harmonizes with the beginning, and the end with the middle.

[153] Listen to what I long for (and the public along with me), if you wish someone to stay in the hall to applaud, sitting till that moment when the piper says: "Applause, please!"[8] You have to observe the characteristics of each age, and attribute proper behaviour to impulsive natures and years. The boy who now knows how to respond in words and press the earth with steady foot loves to play with his mates; he gathers his rage only to lay it aside again, and changes by the hour. The beardless youth, free from watchful eye at last, rejoices in horses and hounds and the sunny campus turf. He can be shaped to vice like wax; caustic with those who give him advice, slow to look ahead to future advantage, wasteful of money, high-spirited, passionate in his desires, and quick to abandon his fancies. When his pursuits change, the age and spirit of manhood seeks out wealth and friendships, pays service to honour, and is wary of doing what he may soon strive to change. Many handicaps swarm around an old man, whether he is seeking gain (but wretched even when he finds what he wants, for he shuns it and is afraid to enjoy it) or managing all his affairs with numbing fear—a putter-off of hope, tedious, helpless, fearful of the future, difficult, complaining, praising the good old days when he was a lad, correcting and censuring the young. The years bring many blessings with them as they come, and bear many away as they go. So don't let the part of an old man be assigned to a youth, and that of a man to a boy. A character will always dwell upon what is inseparable from, and suited to, his age.

[179] Action either takes place on stage or is narrated afterward.[9] Those actions that reach us via the ear strike the mind less forcefully than what comes before our trusty eyes and what the spectator conveys to himself. But actions which ought to be performed off stage you must not bring on stage, and many you'll remove from view so that the full force of eloquence may relate them. Medea is not to slay her boys in public, nor the wicked Atreus cook human entrails in full view, nor Procne turn into a bird or Cadmus[1] into a snake! Whatever you show me thus I view with disbelief and revulsion.

6. Characters from Homer's *Odyssey*: Antiphates, king of the Laestrygones; Cyclops, Greek mythological giant with one eye; Scylla, half-human sea monster that takes men from passing ships; Charybdis, a dangerous whirlpool in the waters between Sicily and Italy, personified as a female monster.

7. The offspring of Leda and Zeus were twins, Clytemnestra and Helen (born from an "egg" because Zeus came to Leda in the form of a swan); the seizure of Helen, taken from her husband by the Trojan prince Paris, is usually considered by poets to be the immediate cause of the Trojan War. Meleager: uncle of Diomedes, a Greek hero in the *Iliad*; his death years before had no bearing on the Diomedes' difficulties in returning home from Troy.

8. The comedies of the Roman playwrights Plautus and Terence close with *plaudite* (applaud!) or an equivalent request.

9. Most of the precepts enumerated in this section may be found in ARISTOTLE's *Poetics* (see above).

1. In Greek mythology, the founder of Thebes; both Cadmus and his wife were changed into serpents at the end of their lives. Atreus: father of Agamemnon and Menelaus; he arranged the feast of Thyestes. Procne: wife of Tereus, who punished him for raping her sister by killing her own child and serving him to her husband; as he pursued the sisters, all three were turned into birds.

[189] A play that really seeks to be in demand and then, once seen, revived, is not to be shorter or more extended than five acts.[2] And a god is not to intervene unless a knot be encountered worthy of such a deliverer.[3] A fourth actor is not to attempt to speak.

[193] Let the chorus preserve its role and forceful function as an actor, and not break in between acts with a song contributing nothing to the plot, nor fitting properly. Let it favour the good, and give friendly advice; control the angry and support those afraid to hope. Let it praise the modest table, the benefits of justice and laws, and Peace with her opened gates; let it conceal acts done, and pray to the gods that Fortune may return to the wretched and depart from the proud. A simple, slender pipe[4] with only a few holes used to support choruses effectively, accompanying them with its breath and filling the seats (not as yet too crowded) with its blast. (It was not, as now, bound with orichalc,[5] rivaling trumpets.) It was for that kind of performance, of course, that the people would gather in manageable numbers (only a few, one might guess), honest, righteous, and modest. After they began to extend their domains victoriously, with a wider wall on the way to embracing the city and their Genius[6] lawfully placated with wine each day in daytime festivals, a greater licence was added to rhythms and modes. For what discernment would they, untaught, have had in their leisure, as rustic mingled with urban, base with honourable? So the piper added movement (and decadence) to an ancient art, and he wandered over the stage with his robe trailing behind. So also did notes increase on the austere lyres, and forceful eloquence bring an unwonted style of delivery. And keen on the scent of useful information, and prophetically inspired, choral utterance rivaled that of Delphic oracles.[7]

[220] Next, someone competing in tragic song for a paltry goat[8] stripped down his rustic satyrs,[9] and in rough manner (but with some dignity intact) tried some jokes. The reason was that the listener had to be caught by enticements and novel delights when the rituals were over and he was tipsy and free of the law's restraint. But it will be appropriate to present your mocking chattering satyrs agreeably, and relieve the serious with the playful. Let no god or hero, once introduced in royal gold and purple, move into shady taverns with vulgar speech. Nor is he to grasp at clouds and nonsense in contempt for the earth. Tragedy despises all chatter in light verses, and will be too ashamed (like a matron bidden to dance on holidays) to mix with wanton satyrs! If I compose "Satyrs" I won't be one to favour only unadorned and prevailing words and expressions, Pisos. Nor will I so strive to avoid a

2. This 5-act structure is not Aristotelian but may have developed from Greek New Comedy, especially from the comedies of Menander (ca. 342–ca. 292 B.C.E.).
3. The *deus ex machina* (literally, "god from the machine"; Latin) was a divine character lowered from above the stage to resolve the action at the end of a play.
4. That is, a flute.
5. Yellow copper ore (a precious and highly prized metal), and the brass made from it. Horace describes here more than one pipe bound together with metal, creating a sound to rival trumpets.
6. The guardian deity of a place.
7. Pronouncements of the oracle of Apollo at Delphi, the most important oracle in ancient Greece.
8. Horace believes that the Greek term *tragoidia*—literally, "goat song"—took its name from the prize of a goat.
9. Woodland spirits, usually part human, part goat. Horace is describing satyr plays, a type of Greek drama that featured choruses of satyrs and made fun of episodes from myths. Although their style and meter were those of tragedy rather than comedy, the plays included drunkenness, phallic sexuality, pranks, and jokes. At Greek festivals a satyr play was commonly performed after three tragedies.

tragic tone that it makes no difference whether Davus is speaking or bold Pythias (having bilked a talent out of the sharp-scented Simo)[1] or Silenus,[2] the guardian and personal servant of his divine charge. My object will be poetry so fashioned from the familiar that anyone may hope to achieve the same for himself—and in vain attempt waste much sweat and labour! This shows how important are poetic texture and combination, and how much honour accrues to material drawn from the common store. When Fauns[3] are brought out from the woods they should, in my view, avoid acting as if born at some crossroads, regular denizens of the forum, or forever playing some adolescent part with vapid verses, or babbling in filthy and ignominious speech. For some people take offence at it (those with steed,[4] ancestry and property). If some individual buying shelled peas and nuts expresses approval of a work, they don't just suffer it gladly and give it the crown!

[251] A long syllable following closely upon a short is called an iambus, a rapid foot; hence its name was also extended to iambic trimeters, though for not that long a time. It had been producing six pulses, each first to last like itself. To bring itself a little more slowly and sedately to the ear it admitted a steadying spondee[5] with obliging tolerance to its adoptive rights, but not to the point of yielding the second and fourth place in the partnership. This foot rarely appears even in Accius' noble trimeters; and the verses of Ennius,[6] when put ponderously upon the stage, are condemned on the serious charge of either too much hasty and careless work, or an ignorance of craft.

[263] Not every critic sees faulty rhythm in poetry, and favour has been given undeservedly to poets who are Roman. Am I therefore to hive off and write as I please? Or suppose that everyone will see my mistakes, but still be less watchful and cautious because they will (I hope) make allowances? In short, while avoiding censure, I earn no praise. You must unroll Greek originals in your hand night and day. (You say your forebears praised Plautine[7] metres and wit? They admired both with an excess of tolerance, not to say foolishness, if you and I know how to separate coarseness from refinement in speech, and our fingers and ears are trained in the laws of sound!)

[275] They say the unknown genre of the tragic Muse was discovered by Thespis,[8] who wheeled his poems about on wagons for men to sing and act, their faces well stained with lees.[9] After him, as inventor of the mask and the noble robe, Aeschylus[1] laid out a stage with modest-sized beams, producing plays which resounded grandly and strode on the buskin.[2] Old Comedy[3] succeeded that, meeting with much approval. But excessive freedom led to abuse

1. Three common names of type characters in New Comedy, representing respectively the slave, maid or prostitute, and old man. "Talent": an ancient denomination of money (of varying but high value).
2. A satyr, later represented as a cheerful old drunk, who was the adviser and instructor of Dionysus, god of wine (his "divine charge").
3. That is, satyrs.
4. The *equites* (horsemen or "knights"), who in the Roman Republic formed a wealthy class almost equal to senators in social standing.
5. A metrical foot formed by two long syllables.
6. Quintus Ennius (ca. 239–ca. 169 B.C.E.), early Roman poet and dramatist. Lucius Accius (170–90 B.C.E.), Roman playwright and literary critic.
7. Characteristic of the Roman comic playwright Plautus.
8. Pioneer of Greek tragedy (6th c. B.C.E.), credited with introducing the actor's reply to the chorus.
9. Sediment remaining after the fermentation of wine.
1. Greek dramatist (525–456 B.C.E.) who introduced the third actor to the Greek stage.
2. Knee- or calf-length boot worn by actors in tragedies.
3. The first phase of ancient Greek comedy (ca. 5th c. B.C.E.); its greatest writer was Aristophanes (ca. 450–ca. 385 B.C.E.).

and a degree of violence that deserved to be curbed by law. The law was enforced, and the chorus fell basely silent, its right to injure removed.

[285] Our poets have left nothing untried, and not the least glory is due to those with the courage to abandon the Greeks' footsteps and celebrate things done at home, or produce either *praetextae* or *togatae*.[4] Nor would Latium[5] have greater might in virtue's field or arms' renown than with its tongue, if all our poets were not repelled by labour and patience with the file. As for you, O offspring of Pompilian[6] blood, rebuke the poem not disciplined through many a day and many an erasure, and not trimmed off and ten times smoothed to the nail!

[295] Democritus[7] believed that talent is a more fortunate thing than base craftsmanship, and because he excluded the "sane" from Helicon,[8] a good part of our poets ignore fingernails and beard, heading for secret haunts and avoiding the baths. It seems that the prize and the name of "poet" will be gained by the one who does not entrust his head (three Anticyras full of hellebore[9] could not cure it!) to Licinus the barber. (Oh how gauche am I then, purging *my* bile just before the spring season! No one else could have made better poetry—but it's not worth all that!) My function shall be that of a whetstone, therefore, able to render iron sharp, while not endowed itself for cutting. Though not engaged in writing myself, I shall teach its function and obligations; where its stores are secured, what fosters and shapes the poet; what is appropriate for him, what is not; where excellence takes him, where error.

[309] Correct writing finds its beginning and source in discernment. Socratic scrolls[1] can show you your subject matter, and when that has been planned ahead, the words will follow without reluctance. The person who has learned what he owes to country and friends—what regard he should have for parent, brother, and guest, what a senator's duty is and a judge's, the role of a general sent into battle—certainly knows how to assign the appropriate qualities to each character. When he's trained in imitation I'll advise him to examine a pattern of life and mores, and draw living voices from this. From time to time a piece which has splendid maxims and a fine moral tone, even though lacking charm and without weight and craftsmanship, will give more pleasure and interest to people than verses devoid of substance, and musical trifles. To the Greeks the Muse gave talent and a full-throated utterance. (The Greeks are a people greedy for nothing if not praise.) *Roman* children learn to divide a copper into a hundred parts with lengthy calculations: "Albinus[2] Minor! Take one-twelfth from five-twelfths! What's the difference?—"One third."—"Très bien![3] You'll know how to preserve your capital. Now add one-twelfth. What's the answer?"—"One half!"

4. Plays on themes drawn from common life; the term refers to the toga worn by ordinary people. *Praetextae*: a Roman dramatic genre that dealt with Roman historical figures rather than Greek myth; the term refers to the type of toga worn by Roman magistrates.
5. Area of central Italy that included Rome.
6. Descendants of Numa Pompilius, half-legendary second king of Rome (traditional dates, 715–673 B.C.E.).
7. Greek philosopher (460–370 B.C.E.).
8. Mountain sacred to the Muses (in Greek mythology, 9 daughters of Memory who preside over the arts and all intellectual pursuits) in Boeotia, northwest of the Gulf of Corinth.
9. Proverbially a cure for madness; a major source of hellebore in antiquity was the Greek port city of Anticyra, on the north coast of the Gulf of Corinth.
1. The Greek philosopher Socrates (469–399 B.C.E.) left no writings, but he was the most important speaker in the dialogues of his greatest pupil, PLATO (ca. 427–ca. 347 B.C.E.).
2. Roman family name; the translator adds "minor" to stress the boy's youth.
3. Excellent (French; in Horace, this interjection is in Greek).

When such corroding concern for private hoard has stained their hearts, can there be any hope of our fashioning poems worth dressing with cedar oil and storing in smooth cypress?

[333] Poets wish either to benefit or delight, or else say things at once pleasant and suited to life. Whatever your precepts, be brief, so that people's minds may grasp what you say quickly and easily and retain it faithfully. All excess overflows from a mind that's full. Things fashioned to give pleasure should be very close to reality. A story should not demand belief in absolutely anything, or draw a live boy out of a Lamia's[4] belly after lunch! Our divisions of elder citizens condemn anything devoid of "profit"; the disdainful Ramnes[5] pass rough poetry by. Mingling the "useful" with the "sweet" wins every point, by alike delighting and advising the reader. That is a book worth its price at the shop of the Sosii;[6] there is the one to cross the sea too, and greatly prolong the life of its author's fame.

[347] Some offences, though, we are willing to forgive. For instance, a string does not render the sound wanted by hand and brain [and when you demand a flat it quite frequently gives a sharp];[7] nor will the bow always strike the target it points at. But when the bright places in a poem are more numerous I am not one to be offended by a few blemishes that carelessness has let in or human nature failed to avoid. What am I getting at? Just as a copyist is not to be excused if he persistently makes the same mistake in spite of being warned, and a lyrist is laughed to scorn if he makes a series of blunders on the same string, so, in my view, one who fails badly becomes a "Choerilus."[8] I greet his one or two nice touches with laughter and astonishment! Yet I am the very one to resent it whenever good Homer nods. The fact remains, sleep is ordained to steal over a long work.

[361] A poem is like a picture. One will captivate you if you stand closer, one if you stand further away. This one favours shadow; that one will want to be seen in daylight if it is not to dread the edge of a critic's tongue. This one pleased just once, this one will after ten visits.

[365b] O elder youth,[9] though bred to the true by your father's words and possessing a natural sense of discernment, take hold of what I say to you here and remember it. An average and an adequate quality is rightly allowed in certain things. The average barrister and attorney is far removed from the force of Messalla's eloquence and lacks the knowledge of Cascellius Aulus[1]—but he does have his value, nonetheless. That poets should ever be "average" is not a concession allowed by man, gods, or the stalls. As an out-of-tune orchestra, and gooey unguent, and poppy seed with Sardinian honey[2] spoil the pleasure of banquet tables (the dinner could have gone on without them), so a poem, created and revealed to give our hearts delight, approaches the worst if it falls short of the best.

4. A mythical female monster of Libya who ate children; ancient Greek parents invoked her name to scare their children into good behavior.
5. Young nobles.
6. Brothers who were well-known booksellers and Horace's publishers.
7. The square brackets here indicate a corrupted manuscript line.
8. Minor epic poet of the 4th c. B.C.E. who accompanied Alexander the Great on his campaigns and was paid to celebrate him.
9. Another reference to the Pisos, to whom the poem was addressed.
1. Famous lawyer of Horace's time. Messalla Corvinus (64 B.C.E.–8 C.E.), Roman political leader, orator, author, soldier, and a patron of the arts.
2. Poppy seeds, when roasted and served with honey, were considered a delicacy; but they were spoiled if the honey had a bitter flavor.

[379] A man who does not know how to compete stays clear of athletic gear, and if he has no training in ball, discus and hoop, stays on the sidelines, so the encircling crowd won't be entitled to break out laughing. Yet one who doesn't have the knowledge still has the audacity to fashion verses! (So what? you say? He is free—and free-born—and most of all, given equestrian rank by his cash. And he's far removed from every vice!)

[385] Don't utter or fashion anything over Minerva's[3] objections. There's a criterion. There's an attitude of mind. But if you do write something, let it find the ears of Maecius[4] to be judged, and your father's, and mine. And keep it shut up for nine years right inside its parchment wrapper. What you haven't published may be destroyed: the uttered word is beyond recall!

[391] Woodland folk were frightened away from their slaughtered fare by Orpheus,[5] a holy man and a prophet of the gods. Hence his reputation for taming tigers and furious lions. So too was Amphion, founder of the city of Thebes, described as moving rocks by the sound of his tortoise[6] and the charm of his entreaty, leading them wherever he wished. Once upon a time such things as these were counted for discernment: distinguishing public from private, sacred from profane; restraining promiscuity, giving rules for marriage, building towns, carving laws on wood. Honour and renown came thus to inspired bards and their songs. After them came renowned Homer and Tyrtaeus,[7] whetting manly hearts for martial wars with their verses. Oracles were told through poems; a way of life was shown, and the favour of kings sought through Pierian[8] measures. And play was discovered, and an end to lengthy labours. So don't be ashamed of the lyre-skilled Muse and Apollo[9] the singer!

[408] The question was raised whether a praiseworthy poem comes about by nature or by craft. For my part I don't see what dedication can achieve without a rich vein of talent—or, for that matter, untrained inspiration. The one calls for the resources of the other and makes a friendly collaboration with it. A youthful runner dedicated to touching the longed-for goal has endured and achieved much: sweating and shivering, abstaining from women and wine. Any piper who plays at the Pythian games[1] first learned how, trembling in fear of his master. These days, it seems, one may just say, "I compose marvellous poetry. Let the devil take the hindmost! I would be ashamed to be left behind, and forced to admit complete ignorance of what I have not learned!"

[419] Like a hawker collecting a crowd to buy his wares, the poet for his own profit—though wealthy in property and capital put out at interest—orders his claques[2] to show up. Even if he is one who can afford a rich spread (and do it right) and put up a bond for some poor nobody and rescue

3. Roman goddess of handicrafts and war, whose attributes became conflated with those of the Greek goddess Athena.
4. Roman author of 12 epigrams of whom nothing else is known except his name. The sense here is that Maecius is a judicious critic, worthy of imitation.
5. A holy man because he was credited with founding a Greek mystery religion, Orphism. His extraordinary musical powers—said to be able to charm not only wild beasts but also rocks and trees—made Orpheus a model of the poet.
6. That is, his lyre, which was fashioned from tortoise shell. Amphion: son of Zeus and Antiope, responsible in part for the miraculous construction of the walls of Thebes.
7. Poet of the 7th c. B.C.E.—according to tradition, a lame Attic schoolmaster—who composed war songs and martial elegies for the Spartans, who sang them while marching.
8. Belonging to a spring sacred to the Muses, so a source of knowledge. See, for instance, ALEXANDER POPE in "An Essay on Criticism" (below): "A *little Learning* is a dang'rous Thing; / Drink deep, or taste not the *Pierian* Spring."
9. Son of Zeus and Leto, god of music and poetry.
1. Quadrennial competitions held at Delphi in honor of Apollo; they included musical as well as athletic contests.
2. Groups hired to applaud at a performance.

one entangled in an awkward court case, I'll be surprised if (for all his blessings) he knows how to distinguish a false friend from a true. So whether you've presented a gift to someone or will intend to give one, don't introduce him to your verses when he's sated with happiness. "Beautiful! Fine! Excellent!" he'll shout. He'll grow pale over them, and trickle dew from his dear eyes, leap up, thump the earth with his foot! Just as hired mourners at a funeral say and do more than those who are grieving from the heart, in the same way a mocker makes more of a show than the man whose praise is sincere. Kings are said to ply with many a goblet someone whose worthiness of their friendship they are striving to assess, and rack him with strong wine. If you compose poems, the sentiments that lurk beneath the skin should never deceive you.

[438] Whenever you recited something to Quintilius,[3] he would say: "Correct this, please, and that." If, after two or three vain attempts you continued to insist that you could do no better, he would just tell you to delete it and put your ill-turned verses back on the anvil. If you preferred to defend a mistake, rather than change it, he would not burden himself with any further word or useless effort to stop you being sole unchallenged lover of yourself and your work! The good and wise man will rebuke verses lacking craftsmanship, fault harsh ones, put a black oblique stroke of the pen next to your sloppy ones, cut back ambitious adornment, force you to illuminate what is unclear, reproach you for an ambiguous statement, censure what should be altered. He will become an "Aristarchus,"[4] and will not say, "Why offend a friend in trifles?" Such "trifles" will get that friend into serious trouble once he has been laughed at and unfavourably received!

[453] Like one attacked by a bad case of scabies, or the royal disease, or aberrant frenzy and a wrathful Diana,[5] men of discernment are afraid to touch a "mad" poet and they avoid him. The young and impetuous flush him out and chase after him. If thus belching and raving sublime verses he falls down a well or pit like a fowler intent on blackbirds, let him long shout, "Help, Citizens! Save me!" But no one will be bothered to lift him out. If someone should be concerned enough to bring help and let down a rope, I would suggest that he just may have thrown himself down there on purpose, and not want to be saved!—and recount the demise of the poet of Sicily.

[464b] In the throes of passion for immortality, Empedocles leapt in cold blood into Aetna's[6] flames. Poets should have that right—*let* them perish! To save someone against his will is like murder. Not just once has he done this, nor will he behave normally if he is restrained and lays aside his passion for a glorious death. Nor is it quite clear why he goes on scribbling verses. He may have pissed on his father's ashes or disturbed some grim enclosure in an unholy way! He is unquestionably mad, and like a bear whose might has smashed the confining bars of his cage he routs the unlearned and learned alike with fierce recitation! Anyone he seizes he

3. Quintilius Varus (d. 24 B.C.E.), native of Cremona and an eminent critic, was a friend of both Horace and Virgil; the name is used here to denote someone with taste.

4. Aristarchus of Samothrace (ca. 220–145 B.C.E.), distinguished Alexandrian scholar, particularly known for his scrupulous work marking spurious or doubtful lines in Homer.

5. Lunacy (as the word's derivation from *luna* suggests) was supposed to be caused by the moon goddess, Diana. "Royal disease": jaundice.

6. Mount Etna in Sicily, Europe's highest active volcano. Empedocles (ca. 493–ca. 433 B.C.E.), Greek philosopher, poet, and statesman born in Sicily; the actual place and manner of his death is disputed.

grips and murders with his reading—a leech with no intention of letting go his skin, until he's full of gore!

ca. 10 B.C.E.

LONGINUS
first century C.E.

Since the eighteenth century, the ancient Greek text *On Sublimity* has maintained a reputation as one of the most influential classical works in the tradition of European criticism, despite the uncertainty that surrounds its authorship and date of composition. A distinctive feature of this famous treatise is its favorable commentary on the role of emotion (*pathos*) in the practices of writing, oratory, and reading. According to the author of *On Sublimity* (*Peri Hupsous* in Greek), whom critics refer to as "Longinus," the presence of noble passion is essential for achieving sublimity (*hupsos*), by which he means an elevated and lofty style of writing that rises above the ordinary. From Longinus's author-centered perspective, writers and orators achieve greatness not just by rhetorical techniques but also by deep feelings, profound thoughts, and natural genius: "Sublimity is the echo of a noble mind." Often the experience of reading a great author or listening to a great speech leads us to a feeling of ecstasy or transport (*ekstasis*), which is distinct from the more rational effects of persuasion, the goal of rhetoric. For Longinus, sublimity uplifts the spirit of the reader, filling him or her with unexpected astonishment and pride, arousing noble thoughts, and suggesting more than words can convey.

The extant text of *On Sublimity* derives from a tenth-century medieval manuscript that offers conflicting statements as to the identity of the treatise's creator. For unknown reasons, the table of contents attributes the text to either "Dionysius or Longinus," while the title of the manuscript itself simply indicates that a certain "Dionysius Longinus" is the author. The first attribution suggests that the author is either the Augustan Age Dionysius of Halicarnassus or Cassius Longinus, the third-century pupil of Plotinus. For various detailed reasons, neither of these alternatives has convinced scholars. The principal argument against Dionysius is that *On Sublimity* does not comport with the style and general approach of his other works, whose authorship is not in question. The main point of contention against Longinus, who in the eighteenth century was universally held to be the author, is that textual evidence taken from the concluding chapter on the decline of literature suggests a date of composition no later than 100 C.E., thus ruling out a third-century author. The title of the manuscript offers no solution either, for nothing is known of a Dionysius Longinus. One of the few things that can be determined with some certainty is that the author must have been a Hellenized Jew or at least in contact with Jewish culture, since the opening of Genesis is cited as a worthy example of sublimity. Such a reference is quite distinctive: no other known pagan writer employs the Bible in this manner. While scholars continue to attribute *On Sublimity* to Cassius Longinus, they do so as a matter of convenience.

Despite seven lengthy gaps that make up approximately one-third of the original text, the intended organization of *On Sublimity* is reasonably certain. After the formal preface addressed to Postumius Terentianus (about whom we know nothing) and the enumeration of common faults that arise when authors attempt to achieve sublimity, Longinus provides some general marks of true sublimity. Then, in the eighth chapter, he proceeds to enumerate the five sources of sublimity: great thoughts, strong emotion, certain figures of thought and speech, noble diction, and dignified word arrangement. The remainder of the treatise, except for the anomalous short final chapter on the decline of literature (not included in our selection), concerns itself with detailed analytical discussion of each source in the order in which they are first listed, with illustrative digressions on Homer (8th c. B.C.E.), Demosthenes (384–322 B.C.E.), and PLATO (ca. 427–ca. 347 B.C.E.), among others. While the text on the second source, strong emotion, is no longer extant, the author's understanding of it is clear from many comments scattered throughout the treatise.

Often cited as a peak moment in *On Sublimity* is the digression on Plato and the orator Lysias (ca. 459–ca. 380 B.C.E.) near the end of the treatise, following the discussion of metaphors. The digression on genius, as it is known, is important because it provides a detailed and eloquent account of sublimity through a series of concise comparisons in which Homer, Plato, and Demosthenes figure as exemplary geniuses. (Many other classical writers are mentioned in the text.) Longinus is prompted by the preference of Caecilius, a rival theorist of the sublime (1st c. C.E.), for Lysias over Plato. Lysias, Caecilius claims, is a more faultless, pure, and correct writer than Plato, who often gets carried away with his metaphors. Longinus responds by saying that flawless or impeccable mediocrity, which never reaches the heights of sublimity, is not to be preferred over erratic genius. The former, which concerns itself with exactitude, minutia, and correctness, remains within the domain of the familiar, the humble, the charming, and the customary; the latter ranges freely over the grandeur, the loftiness, and the vastness of nature, admiring such awe-inspiring phenomena as the Nile, the Danube, the Rhine, or indeed the ocean, rather than the lesser streams. For Longinus, the faults that geniuses sometimes manifest are excusable because they are inevitable in the pursuit of sublimity, which expresses the boundless thought of human beings and raises them to the "spiritual greatness of god." Freedom from error, per se, Longinus concludes, does not achieve the emotional intensity of sublimity, which strikes suddenly like the brilliance of lightning. Because of the grand manner in which Longinus makes his case here and throughout the treatise, ALEXANDER POPE would later say that Longinus "*Is himself* that great Sublime he draws."

On Sublimity differs fundamentally from Platonic doctrine, which distrusted the frenzied and irrational flights of poetic inspiration and banned poetry from the ideal republic. Cleverly, Longinus points out that Plato does not practice what he preaches. In citing Plato as an example of a sublime writer, Longinus reinterprets the philosopher, highlighting the unconscious ways in which he too is "carried away by a sort of literary madness." *On Sublimity* also differs from HORACE, who in the *Ars Poetica* coolly stresses rhetorical strategies rather than the erratic genius of authors; Horace would have felt comfortable with the last three sources of the sublime, centered as they are on rhetoric, but probably not with the first two, which depend on the mind and heart of the author. In some respects, Longinus's treatise is more like ARISTOTLE's *Poetics*, for they both take note of the formal techniques and psychological effects of literature, Aristotle famously focusing on the emotional "catharsis" that an audience experiences during the performance of a tragedy. An important distinction between the two is that Longinus considers the emotional psychology of the author as well as that of the audience.

Longinus's text appears not to have been read during ancient or medieval times, perhaps because it was lost. It reemerged as an important text first in the Renaissance, with the Italian translation of Niccolò da Falgano in 1560, but especially with Nicolas Boileau's 1674 French rendering. The latter made *On Sublimity* a central text in European criticism throughout the eighteenth century and set the stage for many discussions of the sublime, including those by JOSEPH ADDISON, EDMUND BURKE, and, most notably, IMMANUEL KANT. With Kant's *Critique of Judgment* (1790), the theory of the sublime reached a level of analytical rigor considerably beyond that of Longinus, who, by comparison, is content merely to enact the sublime and work intuitively. Still, Longinus manages to anticipate many of Kant's major themes, especially his fascination with the uplifting sense of the "supersensible" (the transcendent). He also anticipates Romantic theories of literature, which focus on the creative genius of the author.

From a contemporary perspective, Longinus's view of the sublime has limitations. It focuses mainly on the profound feelings and thoughts of geniuses and audiences, without attending to the ways in which they are structured or determined by language. Longinus does discuss figurative language, rhetoric, and composition, but the ideas and emotions of the genius precede such linguistic "ornamentation." The audience's experience, moreover, is said to transcend words. Such a view contrasts with the influential rhetorical reading of the sublime by the deconstructive theorist PAUL DE MAN, who—especially in his "Phenomenality and Materiality in Kant" (1984)—underscores the figurative or tropological determination of consciousness. For some schools of contemporary theory, Longinus's emphasis on spiritual transcendence would also be considered a limitation. For example, late twentieth-century theorists of postmodern culture, including FREDRIC JAMESON and JEAN-FRANÇOIS LYOTARD, conceive the sublime in materialist cultural terms—as disorienting experiences of unrepresentable new global systems and networks and as inconceivable cataclysmic modern historical events (such as the Holocaust). Such theorizing, however, could not have taken place without Longinus's groundbreaking analysis in *On Sublimity*, which thus will continue to be a key text for understanding the sublime.

***On Sublimity* Keywords:** Aesthetics, Affect, Authorship, Classical Theory, Language, Rhetoric, Tradition

From On Sublimity[1]

Preface

My dear Postumius Terentianus,[2]

[1.1] You will recall that when we were reading together Caecilius'[3] monograph *On Sublimity*, we felt that it was inadequate to its high subject, and failed to touch the essential points. Nor indeed did it appear to offer the reader much practical help, though this ought to be a writer's principal object. Two things are required of any textbook: first, that it should explain what its subject is; second, and more important, that it should explain how and by what methods we can achieve it. Caecilius tries at immense length to explain to us what sort of thing 'the sublime' is, as though we did not know; but he has somehow passed over as unnecessary the question how we can develop our nature to some degree of greatness. [1.2] However, we ought perhaps not so much to blame our author for what he has left out as to commend him for his originality and enthusiasm.

1. Translated by D. A. Russell, who has also supplied the headings in the text. The chapter and section numbers, included in square brackets, date to the 16th century.
2. Nothing is known of Postumius Terentianus.
3. Caecilius of Calacte in Sicily (1st c. C.E.), Greek rhetorician. His monograph on sublimity is lost, but later references in Longinus's text suggest that the author neglected the role of strong noble emotion and generous use of metaphor, valuing the even tone of impeccably correct and faultless writers over the ecstasy, wonder, and astonishment of erratic geniuses.

You have urged me to set down a few notes on sublimity for your own use. Let us then consider whether there is anything in my observations which may be thought useful to public men. You must help me, my friend, by giving your honest opinion in detail, as both your natural candour and your friendship with me require. It was well said that what man has in common with the gods is 'doing good and telling the truth'.

[1.3] Your education dispenses me from any long preliminary definition. Sublimity is a kind of eminence or excellence of discourse. It is the source of the distinction of the very greatest poets and prose writers and the means by which they have given eternal life to their own fame. [1.4] For grandeur produces ecstasy rather than persuasion in the hearer; and the combination of wonder and astonishment always proves superior to the merely persuasive and pleasant. This is because persuasion is on the whole something we can control, whereas amazement and wonder exert invincible power and force and get the better of every hearer. Experience in invention and ability to order and arrange material cannot be detected in single passages; we begin to appreciate them only when we see the whole context. Sublimity, on the other hand, produced at the right moment, tears everything up like a whirlwind, and exhibits the orator's whole power at a single blow.

[2.1] Your own experience will lead you to these and similar considerations. The question from which I must begin is whether there is in fact an art of sublimity or profundity. Some people think it is a complete mistake to reduce things like this to technical rules. Greatness, the argument runs, is a natural product, and does not come by teaching. The only art is to be born like that. They believe moreover that natural products are very much weakened by being reduced to the bare bones of a textbook.

[2.2] In my view, these arguments can be refuted by considering three points:

(i) Though nature is on the whole a law unto herself in matters of emotion and elevation, she is not a random force and does not work altogether without method.

(ii) She is herself in every instance a first and primary element of creation, but it is method that is competent to provide and contribute quantities and appropriate occasions for everything, as well as perfect correctness in training and application.

(iii) Grandeur is particularly dangerous when left on its own, unaccompanied by knowledge, unsteadied, unballasted, abandoned to mere impulse and ignorant temerity. It often needs the curb as well as the spur.

[2.3] What Demosthenes[4] said of life in general is true also of literature: good fortune is the greatest of blessings, but good counsel comes next, and the lack of it destroys the other also. In literature, nature occupies the place of good fortune, and art that of good counsel. Most important of all, the very fact that some things in literature depend on nature alone can itself be learned only from art.

If the critic of students of this subject will bear these points in mind, he will, I believe, come to realize that the examination of the question before us is by no means useless or superfluous.

* * *

4. *Orations* 23.113 [translator's note]. Demosthenes (384–322 B.C.E.), the greatest Athenian orator.

Some Marks of True Sublimity

At this stage, the question we must put to ourselves for discussion is how to avoid the faults which are so much tied up with sublimity. [6.1] The answer, my friend, is: by first of all achieving a genuine understanding and appreciation of true sublimity. This is difficult; literary judgement comes only as the final product of long experience. However, for the purposes of instruction, I think we can say that an understanding of all this can be acquired. I approach the problem in this way:

[7.1] In ordinary life, nothing is truly great which it is great to despise; wealth, honour, reputation, absolute power—anything in short which has a lot of external trappings—can never seem supremely good to the wise man because it is no small good to despise them. People who could have these advantages if they chose but disdain them out of magnanimity are admired much more than those who actually possess them. It is much the same with elevation in poetry and literature generally. We have to ask ourselves whether any particular example does not give a show of grandeur which, for all its accidental trappings, will, when dissected, prove vain and hollow, the kind of thing which it does a man more honour to despise than to admire. [7.2] It is our nature to be elevated and exalted by true sublimity. Filled with joy and pride, we come to believe we have created what we have only heard. [7.3] When a man of sense and literary experience hears something many times over, and it fails to dispose his mind to greatness or to leave him with more to reflect upon than was contained in the mere words, but comes instead to seem valueless on repeated inspection, this is not true sublimity; it endures only for the moment of hearing. Real sublimity contains much food for reflection, is difficult or rather impossible to resist, and makes a strong and ineffaceable impression on the memory. [7.4] In a word, reckon those things which please everybody all the time as genuinely and finely sublime. When people of different trainings, ways of life, tastes, ages, and manners all agree about something, the judgement and assent of so many distinct voices lends strength and irrefutability to the conviction that their admiration is rightly directed.

The Five Sources of Sublimity; The Plan of the Book

[8.1] There are, one may say, five most productive sources of sublimity. (Competence in speaking is assumed as a common foundation for all five; nothing is possible without it.)

(i) The first and most important is the power to conceive great thoughts; I defined this in my work on Xenophon.[5]

(ii) The second is strong and inspired emotion. (These two sources are for the most part natural; the remaining three involve art.)

(iii) Certain kinds of figures. (These may be divided into figures of thought and figures of speech.)

(iv) Noble diction. This has as subdivisions choice of words and the use of metaphorical and artificial language.[6]

5. Athenian historian and essayist (ca. 428–ca. 354 B.C.E.).

6. Or "and coined words" [translator's note].

(v) Finally, to round off the whole list, dignified and elevated word-arrangement.

Let us now examine the points which come under each of these heads. I must first observe, however, that Caecilius has omitted some of the five—emotion, for example. [8.2] Now if he thought that sublimity and emotion were one and the same thing and always existed and developed together, he was wrong. Some emotions, such as pity, grief, and fear, are found divorced from sublimity and with a low effect. Conversely, sublimity often occurs apart from emotion. Of the innumerable examples of this I select Homer's bold account of the Aloadae:[7]

> Ossa upon Olympus they sought to heap; and on Ossa
> Pelion with its shaking forest, to make a path to heaven—

and the even more impressive sequel—

> and they would have finished their work . . .[8]

[8.3] In orators, encomia[9] and ceremonial or exhibition pieces always involve grandeur and sublimity, though they are generally devoid of emotion. Hence those orators who are best at conveying emotion are least good at encomia, and conversely the experts at encomia are not conveyers of emotion. [8.4] On the other hand, if Caecilius thought that emotion had no contribution to make to sublimity and therefore thought it not worth mentioning, he was again completely wrong. I should myself have no hesitation in saying that there is nothing so productive of grandeur as noble emotion in the right place. It inspires and possesses our words with a kind of madness and divine spirit.

(i) Greatness of Thought

[9.1] The first source, natural greatness, is the most important. Even if it is a matter of endowment rather than acquisition, we must, so far as is possible, develop our minds in the direction of greatness and make them always pregnant with noble thoughts. You ask how this can be done. [9.2] I wrote elsewhere something like this: 'Sublimity is the echo of a noble mind.' This is why a mere idea, without verbal expression, is sometimes admired for its nobility—just as Ajax's silence in the Vision of the Dead is grand and indeed more sublime than any words could have been.[1] [9.3] First then we must state where sublimity comes from: the orator must not have low or ignoble thoughts. Those whose thoughts and habits are trivial and servile all their lives cannot possibly produce anything admirable or worthy of eternity. Words will be great if thoughts are weighty.

* * *

7. In Greek mythology, two giants: the sons of Poseidon (god of the sea) and Iphimedeia, wife of Aloeus.
8. *Odyssey* 11.315–17 [translator's note]. Ossa, Olympus, and Pelion are all mountains in northeastern Greece. The *Odyssey* and *Iliad* (ca. 8th c. B.C.E.) are epic poems attributed to Homer.
9. Formal poems (odes) or speeches in praise of a living person, object, or event, but not a god, delivered before a special audience. See, for example, GORGIAS's *Encomium of Helen* (above).
1. *Odyssey* 11.563. Note that this is not an example, but a simile illustrating the point that ideas in themselves can be grand [translator's note].

Selection and Organization of Material

[10.1] Now have we any other means of making our writing sublime? Every topic naturally includes certain elements which are inherent in its raw material. It follows that sublimity will be achieved if we consistently select the most important of these inherent features and learn to organize them as a unity by combining one with another. The first of these procedures attracts the reader by the selection of details, the second by the density of those selected.

Consider Sappho's[2] treatment of the feelings involved in the madness of being in love. She uses the attendant circumstances and draws on real life at every point. And in what does she show her quality? In her skill in selecting the outstanding details and making a unity of them:

> [10.2] To me he seems a peer of the gods, the man who sits facing you and hears your sweet voice
> and lovely laughter; it flutters my heart in my breast. When I see you only for a moment, I cannot speak;
> my tongue is broken, a subtle fire runs under my skin; my eyes cannot see, my ears hum;
> cold sweat pours off me; shivering grips me all over; I am paler than grass; I seem near to dying;
> but all must be endured . . .[3]

[10.3] Do you not admire the way in which she brings everything together—mind and body, hearing and tongue, eyes and skin? She seems to have lost them all, and to be looking for them as though they were external to her. She is cold and hot, mad and sane, frightened and near death, all by turns. The result is that we see in her not a single emotion, but a complex of emotions. Lovers experience all this; Sappho's excellence, as I have said, lies in her adoption and combination of the most striking details.

A similar point can be made about the descriptions of storms in Homer, who always picks out the most terrifying aspects. [10.4] The author of the *Arimaspea* on the other hand expects these lines to excite terror:

> This too is a great wonder to us in our hearts:
> there are men living on water, far from land, on the deep sea:
> miserable they are, for hard is their lot;
> they give their eyes to the stars, their lives to the sea;
> often they raise their hands in prayer to the gods,
> as their bowels heave in pain.[4]

Anyone can see that this is more polished than awe-inspiring. Now compare it with Homer [10.5] (I select one example out of many):

> He fell upon them as upon a swift ship falls a wave,
> huge, wind-reared by the clouds. The ship
> is curtained in foam, a hideous blast of wind

2. Greek lyric poet (b. ca. 612 B.C.E.).
3. Sappho, frag. 31 Lobel-Page.
4. From a lost poem attributed to Aristeas of Proconnesus, a prophet of Apollo said to have traveled in Siberia in the 7th c. B.C.E. The lines perhaps express the surprised comment of innocent continentals, deep in Asia, on the tales they have heard about ships and seagoing [translator's note].

roars in the sail. The sailors shudder in terror:
they are carried away from under death, but only just.[5]

[10.6] Aratus[6] tried to transfer the same thought:

A little plank wards off Hades.

But this is smooth and unimpressive, not frightening. Moreover, by saying 'a plank wards off Hades', he has got rid of the danger. The plank *does* keep death away. Homer, on the other hand, does not banish the cause of fear at a stroke; he gives a vivid picture of men, one might almost say, facing death many times with every wave that comes. Notice also the forced combination of naturally uncompoundable prepositions: *hupek*, 'from under'. Homer has tortured the words to correspond with the emotion of the moment, and expressed the emotion magnificently by thus crushing words together. He has in effect stamped the special character of the danger on the diction: 'they are carried away from under death'.

[10.7] Compare Archilochus on the shipwreck, and Demosthenes on the arrival of the news ('It was evening . . .').[7]

In short, one might say that these writers have taken only the very best pieces, polished them up and fitted them together. They have inserted nothing inflated, undignified, or pedantic. Such things ruin the whole effect, because they produce, as it were, gaps or crevices, and so spoil the impressive thoughts which have been built into a structure whose cohesion depends upon their mutual relations.

Amplification

[11.1] The quality called 'amplification' is connected with those we have been considering. It is found when the facts or the issues at stake allow many starts and pauses in each section. You wheel up one impressive unit after another to give a series of increasing importance. There are innumerable varieties of amplification: [11.2] it may be produced by commonplaces, by exaggeration or intensification of facts or arguments, or by a build-up of action or emotion. The orator should realize, however, that none of these will have its full effect without sublimity. Passages expressing pity or disparagement are no doubt an exception; but in any other instance of amplification, if you take away the sublime element, you take the soul away from the body. Without the strengthening influence of the sublimity, the effective element in the whole loses all its vigour and solidity.

[11.3] What is the difference between this precept and the point made above about the inclusion of vital details and their combination in a unity?

5. *Odyssey* 15.624–28 [translator's note].
6. *Phaenomena* 299 [translator's note]. Aratus (ca. 315–ca. 240 B.C.E.), Greek poet who often wrote on philosophy and natural science.
7. The example from Archilochus cannot be certainly identified. That from Demosthenes (*On the Crown* 169) describes the alarm at Athens when news arrived of Philip's occupation of Elatea (339 B.C.E.): "It was evening when somebody brought the *prutaneis* [city magistrates] the news that Elatea was captured. Some of them got up in the middle of dinner and began to drive the traders from the stalls in the *agora* [marketplace] and burn the wicker hurdles. Others sent for the generals and gave instructions to the trumpeter. The town was full of uproar" [translator's note]. Archilochus (7th c. B.C.E.), earliest Greek lyric poet whose work survives. Philip II (reigned 359–336 B.C.E.), king of Macedon. Elatea: strategically located town, three days' march from Athens.

What in general is the difference between amplification and sublimity? I must define my position briefly on these points, in order to make myself clear.

[12.1] I do not feel satisfied with the definition given by the rhetoricians: 'amplification is expression which adds grandeur to its subject'. This might just as well be a definition of sublimity or emotion or tropes. All these add grandeur of some kind. The difference lies, in my opinion, in the fact that sublimity depends on elevation, whereas amplification involves extension; sublimity exists often in a single thought, amplification cannot exist without a certain quantity and superfluity. [12.2] To give a general definition, amplification is an aggregation of all the details and topics which constitute a situation, strengthening the argument by dwelling on it; it differs from proof in that the latter demonstrates the point made . . .

* * *

Imitation of Earlier Writers as a Means to Sublimity

[13.2] Plato,[8] if we will read him with attention, illustrates yet another road to sublimity, besides those we have discussed. This is the way of imitation and emulation of great writers of the past. Here too, my friend, is an aim to which we must hold fast. Many are possessed by a spirit not their own. It is like what we are told of the Pythia[9] at Delphi: she is in contact with the tripod near the cleft in the ground which (so they say) exhales a divine vapour, and she is thereupon made pregnant by the supernatural power and forthwith prophesies as one inspired. Similarly, the genius of the ancients acts as a kind of oracular cavern, and effluences flow from it into the minds of their imitators. Even those previously not much inclined to prophesy become inspired and share the enthusiasm which comes from the greatness of others. [13.3] Was Herodotus the only 'most Homeric' writer? Surely Stesichorus[1] and Archilochus earned the name before him. So, more than any, did Plato, who diverted to himself countless rills from the Homeric spring. (If Ammonius[2] had not selected and written up detailed examples of this, I might have had to prove the point myself.) [13.4] In all this process there is no plagiarism. It resembles rather the reproduction of good character in statues and works of art.[3] Plato could not have put such a brilliant finish on his philosophical doctrines or so often risen to poetical subjects and poetical language, if he had not tried, and tried wholeheartedly, to compete for the prize against Homer, like a young aspirant challenging an admired master. To break a lance in this way may well have been a brash and contentious thing to do, but the competition proved anything but valueless. As Hesiod says, 'this strife is good for men.'[4] Truly it is a noble contest and prize of honour, and one well worth winning, in which to be defeated by one's elders is itself no disgrace.

8. Greek philosopher (ca. 427–ca. 347 B.C.E.). For PLATO's comments on poetry, see above.
9. A priestess of Apollo and the most famous of his oracles (located on the slopes of Mt. Parnassus near the Greek city Delphi).
1. Greek choral poet (ca. 630–555 B.C.E.) who wrote narratives on epic themes. Herodotus (ca. 484–ca. 425 B.C.E.), Greek historian.
2. Head of the Alexandrian library (2d c. B.C.E.) and author of commentaries on Homer and other Greek authors.
3. Text uncertain: perhaps "the reproduction of beauty of form . . ." [translator's note].
4. *Works and Days* 24: healthy rivalry contrasted with the strife that produces war [translator's note]. Hesiod (active ca. 700 B.C.E.), Greek didactic poet.

[14.1] We can apply this to ourselves. When we are working on something which needs loftiness of expression and greatness of thought, it is good to imagine how Homer would have said the same thing, or how Plato or Demosthenes or (in history) Thucydides[5] would have invested it with sublimity. These great figures, presented to us as objects of emulation and, as it were, shining before our gaze, will somehow elevate our minds to the greatness of which we form a mental image. [14.2] They will be even more effective if we ask ourselves 'How would Homer or Demosthenes have reacted to what I am saying, if he had been here? What would his feelings have been?' It makes it a great occasion if you imagine such a jury or audience for your own speech, and pretend that you are answering for what you write before judges and witnesses of such heroic stature. [14.3] Even more stimulating is the further thought: 'How will posterity take what I am writing?' If a man is afraid of saying anything which will outlast his own life and age, the conceptions of his mind are bound to be incomplete and abortive; they will miscarry and never be brought to birth whole and perfect for the day of posthumous fame.

Visualization (Phantasia)

[15.1] Another thing which is extremely productive of grandeur, magnificence and urgency, my young friend, is visualization (*phantasia*). I use this word for what some people call image-production. The term *phantasia* is used generally for anything which in any way suggests a thought productive of speech;[6] but the word has also come into fashion for the situation in which enthusiasm and emotion make the speaker *see* what he is saying and bring it *visually* before his audience. [15.2] It will not escape you that rhetorical visualization has a different intention from that of the poets: in poetry the aim is astonishment, in oratory it is clarity. Both, however, seek emotion and excitement.

> Mother, I beg you, do not drive them at me,
> the women with the blood in their eyes and the snakes—
> they are here, they are here, jumping right up to me.[7]

Or again:

> O! O! She'll kill me. Where shall I escape?[8]

The poet himself saw the Erinyes,[9] and has as good as made his audience see what he imagined.

* * *

[15.8] The poetical examples, as I said, have a quality of exaggeration which belongs to fable and goes far beyond credibility. In an orator's visualizations, on the other hand, it is the element of fact and truth which makes for success; when the content of the passage is poetical and fabulous and does

5. Greek historian (ca. 455–ca. 400 B.C.E.).
6. A Stoic definition [translator's note]. The philosophical school of Stoicism, founded in Athens by Zeno of Citium (335–263 B.C.E.), had widespread influence in Greece and Rome.
7. Euripides, *Orestes* 255–57. Orestes sees the Furies [translator's note]. The Furies: hideous spirits who avenge wrongs done to kindred, especially murder; Orestes has killed his mother, Clytemnestra. Euripides (ca. 485–ca. 406 B.C.E.), Greek tragedian.
8. Euripides, *Iphigenia in Tauris* 291. Again Orestes and the Furies [translator's note].
9. That is, the Furies.

not shrink from any impossibility, the result is a shocking and outrageous abnormality. This is what happens with the shock orators of our own day; like tragic actors, these fine fellows *see* the Erinyes, and are incapable of understanding that when Orestes says

> Let me go; you are one of my Erinyes,
> you are hugging me tight, to throw me into Hell,[1]

he visualizes all this *because he is mad.*

[15.9] What then is the effect of rhetorical visualization? There is much it can do to bring urgency and passion into our words; but it is when it is closely involved with factual arguments that it enslaves the hearer as well as persuading him. 'Suppose you heard a shout this very moment outside the court, and someone said that the prison had been broken open and the prisoners had escaped—no one, young or old, would be so casual as not to give what help he could. And if someone then came forward and said "This is the man who let them out", our friend would never get a hearing; it would be the end of him.'[2] [15.10] There is a similar instance in Hyperides' defence of himself when he was on trial for the proposal to liberate the slaves which he put forward after the defeat.[3] 'It was not the proposer', he said, 'who drew up this decree: it was the battle of Chaeronea.' Here the orator uses a visualization actually in the moment of making his factual argument, with the result that his thought has taken him beyond the limits of mere persuasiveness. [15.11] Now our natural instinct is, in all such cases, to attend to the stronger influence, so that we are diverted from the demonstration to the astonishment caused by the visualization, which by its very brilliance conceals the factual aspect. This is a natural reaction: when two things are joined together, the stronger attracts to itself the force of the weaker.

[15.12] This will suffice for an account of sublimity of thought produced by greatness of mind, imitation, or visualization.[4]

(iii) Figures: An Example to Illustrate the Right Use of Figures[5]

[16.1] The next topic is that of figures. Properly handled, figures constitute, as I said, no small part of sublimity. It would be a vast, or rather infinite, labour to enumerate them all; what I shall do is to expound a few of those which generate sublimity, simply in order to confirm my point.

[16.2] Here is Demosthenes putting forward a demonstrative argument on behalf of his policy.[6] What would have been the natural way to put it? 'You have not done wrong, you who fought for the liberty of Greece; you have examples to prove this close at home: the men of Marathon, of Salamis, of Plataea did not do wrong.' But instead of this he was suddenly inspired to give voice to the oath by the heroes of Greece: 'By those who risked their lives at Marathon, you have not done wrong!' Observe what he effects by this single

1. Euripides, *Orestes* 264–65 [translator's note].
2. Demosthenes, *Orations* 24.208 [translator's note].
3. I.e., after Philip's victory at Chaeronea (338 B.C.E.). The speech is not extant [translator's note]. Hyperides (389–322 B.C.E.), Greek orator, professional speech writer, and prosecutor. Chaeronea: northernmost town of Boeotia, where Philip defeated the Athenians and the Thebans.
4. Note that this is not a complete summary of chaps. 9–15 [translator's note].
5. The section on the second source of the sublime, strong emotion, is missing from the extant Greek manuscript.
6. The passage discussed is in *Orations* 18.208 [translator's note].

figure of conjuration, or 'apostrophe' as I call it here. He deifies his audience's ancestors, suggesting that it is right to take an oath by men who fell so bravely, as though they were gods. He inspires the judges with the temper of those who risked their lives. He transforms his demonstrations into an extraordinary piece of sublimity and passion, and into the convincingness of this unusual and amazing oath. At the same time he injects into his hearers' minds a healing specific, so as to lighten their hearts by these paeans of praise and make them as proud of the battle with Philip as of the triumphs[7] of Marathon and Salamis. In short, the figure enables him to run away with his audience.

* * *

The Relation between Figures and Sublimity

[17.1] At this point, my friend, I feel I ought not to pass over an observation of my own. It shall be very brief: figures are natural allies of sublimity and themselves profit wonderfully from the alliance. I will explain how this happens.

Playing tricks by means of figures is a peculiarly suspect procedure. It raises the suspicion of a trap, a deep design, a fallacy. It is to be avoided in addressing a judge who has power to decide, and especially in addressing tyrants, kings, governors, or anybody in a high place. Such a person immediately becomes angry if he is led astray like a foolish child by some skilful orator's figures. He takes the fallacy as indicating contempt for himself. He becomes like a wild animal. Even if he controls his temper, he is now completely conditioned against being convinced by what is said. A figure is therefore generally thought to be best when the fact that it is a figure is concealed.

[17.2] Thus sublimity and emotion are a defence and a marvellous aid against the suspicion which the use of figures engenders. The artifice of the trick is lost to sight in the surrounding brilliance of beauty and grandeur, and it escapes all suspicion. 'By the men of Marathon . . .' is proof enough. For how did Demosthenes conceal the figure in that passage? By sheer brilliance, of course. As fainter lights disappear when the sunshine surrounds them, so the sophisms of rhetoric are dimmed when they are enveloped in encircling grandeur. [17.3] Something like this happens in painting: when light and shadow are juxtaposed in colours on the same plane, the light seems more prominent to the eye, and both stands out and actually appears much nearer. Similarly, in literature, emotional and sublime features seem closer to the mind's eye, both because of a certain natural kinship and because of their brilliance. Consequently, they always show up above the figures, and overshadow and eclipse their artifice.

* * *

7. At Marathon, the Athenians aided by the Plataeans became the first Greeks to defeat the Persians (490 B.C.E.); near the island of Salamis, the Persian fleet was routed by combined Greek forces (480 B.C.E.).

Hyperbaton

* * *

[22.1] Hyperbaton is an arrangement of words or thoughts which differs from the normal sequence . . .[8] It is a very real mark of urgent emotion. People who in real life feel anger, fear, or indignation, or are distracted by jealousy or some other emotion (it is impossible to say how many emotions there are; they are without number), often put one thing forward and then rush off to another, irrationally inserting some remark, and then hark back again to their first point. They seem to be blown this way and that by their excitement, as if by a veering wind. They inflict innumerable variations on the expression, the thought, and the natural sequence. Thus hyperbaton is a means by which, in the best authors, imitation approaches the effect of nature. Art is perfect when it looks like nature, nature is felicitous when it embraces concealed art. Consider the words of Dionysius of Phocaea in Herodotus:[9] 'Now, for our affairs are on the razor's edge, men of Ionia, whether we are to be free or slaves—and worse than slaves, runaways—so if you will bear hardships now, you will suffer temporarily but be able to overcome your enemies.' [22.2] The natural order of thought would have been: 'Men of Ionia, now is the time for you to bear hardships, for our affairs are on the razor's edge.' The speaker has displaced 'men of Ionia'; he begins with the cause of fear, as though the alarm was so pressing that he did not even have time to address the audience by name. He has also diverted the order of thought. Before saying that they must suffer hardship themselves (that is the gist of his exhortation), he first gives the reason why it is necessary, by saying 'our affairs are on the razor's edge'. The result is that he seems to be giving not a premeditated speech but one forced on him by the circumstances.

[22.3] It is even more characteristic of Thucydides to show ingenuity in separating by transpositions even things which are by nature completely unified and indivisible.

Demosthenes is less wilful in this than Thucydides, but no one uses this kind of effect more lavishly. His transpositions produce not only a great sense of urgency but the appearance of extemporization, as he drags his hearers with him into the hazards of his long hyperbata. [22.4] He often holds in suspense the meaning which he set out to convey and, introducing one extraneous item after another in an alien and unusual place before getting to the main point, throws the hearer into a panic lest the sentence collapse altogether, and forces him in his excitement to share the speaker's peril, before, at long last and beyond all expectation, appositely paying off at the end the long due conclusion; the very audacity and hazardousness of the hyperbata add to the astounding effect. There are so many examples that I forbear to give any.

* * *

8. Probably a few words are missing here [translator's note].

9. *Histories* 6.11 [translator's note]. Dionysius of Phocaea: commander of the Greek fleet in the battle of Lade (494 B.C.E.), which the Persians won. In the ancient world, defeated peoples were often enslaved.

Conclusion of the Section on Figures

[29.2] So much, my dear Terentianus, by way of digression on the theory of the use of those figures which conduce to sublimity. They all make style more emotional and excited, and emotion is as essential a part of sublimity as characterization is of charm.

(iv) Diction: General Remarks

[30.1] Thought and expression are of course very much involved with each other. We have therefore next to consider whether any topics still remain in the field of diction. The choice of correct and magnificent words is a source of immense power to entice and charm the hearer. This is something which all orators and other writers cultivate intensely. It makes grandeur, beauty, old-world charm, weight, force, strength, and a kind of lustre bloom upon our words as upon beautiful statues; it gives things life and makes them speak. But I suspect there is no need for me to make this point; you know it well. It is indeed true that beautiful words are the light that illuminates thought.

[30.2] Magniloquence, however, is not always serviceable: to dress up trivial material in grand and solemn language is like putting a huge tragic mask on a little child. In poetry and history, however . . . [1]

Use of Everyday Words

* * *

[31.1] Theopompus'[2] much-admired phrase seems to me to be particularly expressive because of the aptness of the analogy, though Caecilius manages to find fault with it: 'Philip was excellent at stomaching facts.' An idiomatic phrase is sometimes much more vivid than an ornament of speech, for it is immediately recognized from everyday experience, and the familiar is inevitably easier to credit. 'To stomach facts' is thus used vividly of a man who endures unpleasantness and squalor patiently, and indeed with pleasure, for the sake of gain. [31.2] There are similar things in Herodotus: 'Cleomenes in his madness cut his own flesh into little pieces with a knife till he had sliced himself to death', 'Pythes continued fighting on the ship until he was cut into joints.'[3] These phrases come within an inch of being vulgar, but they are so expressive that they avoid vulgarity.

Metaphors

[32.1] As regards number of metaphors, Caecilius seems to agree with the propounders of the rule that not more than two or at most three may be used of the same subject. Here too Demosthenes is our canon. The right occasions are when emotions come flooding in and bring the multiplication of

1. Lacuna equivalent to about four pages [translator's note].
2. Greek historian (b. ca. 378 B.C.E.).
3. *Histories* 6.75, 7.181 [translator's note]. Cleomenes: king of Sparta (reigned ca. 519–480 B.C.E.). Pythes: soldier who fought against the Persians ca. 480 B.C.E.

metaphors with them as a necessary accompaniment. [32.2] 'Vile flatterers, mutilators of their countries, who have given away liberty as a drinking present, first to Philip and now to Alexander, measuring happiness by the belly and the basest impulses, overthrowing liberty and freedom from despotism, which Greeks of old regarded as the canons and standards of the good.'[4] In this passage the orator's anger against traitors obscures the multiplicity of his metaphors.

[32.3] This is why Aristotle and Theophrastus[5] say that there are ways of softening bold metaphors—namely by saying 'as if', 'as it were', 'if I may put it so', or 'if we may venture on a bold expression'. Apology, they say, is a remedy for audacity. [32.4] I accept this doctrine, but I would add—and I said the same about figures—that strong and appropriate emotions and genuine sublimity are a specific palliative for multiplied or daring metaphors, because their nature is to sweep and drive all these other things along with the surging tide of their movement. Indeed it might be truer to say that they *demand* the hazardous. They never allow the hearer leisure to count the metaphors, because he too shares the speaker's enthusiasm.

[32.5] At the same time, nothing gives distinction to commonplaces and descriptions so well as a continuous series of tropes.[6] This is the medium in which the description of man's bodily tabernacle is worked out so elaborately in Xenophon and yet more superlatively by Plato.[7] Thus Plato calls the head the 'citadel' of the body; the neck is an 'isthmus' constructed between the head and the chest; the vertebrae, he says, are fixed underneath 'like pivots'. Pleasure is a 'lure of evil' for mankind; the tongue is a 'taste-meter'. The heart is a 'knot of veins' and 'fountain of the blood that moves impetuously round', allocated to the 'guard-room'. The word he uses for the various passages of the canals is 'alleys'. 'Against the throbbing of the heart,' he continues, 'in the expectation of danger and in the excitation of anger, when it gets hot, they contrived a means of succour, implanting in us the lungs, soft, bloodless, and with cavities, a sort of cushion, so that when anger boils up in the heart, the latter's throbbing is against a yielding obstacle, so that it comes to no harm.' Again: he calls the seat of the desires 'the women's quarters', and the seat of anger 'the men's quarters'. The spleen is for him 'a napkin for the inner parts, which therefore grows big and festering through being filled with secretions'. 'And thereafter', he says again, 'they buried the whole under a canopy of flesh', putting the flesh on 'as a protection against dangers from without, like felting.' Blood he called 'fodder of the flesh'. For the purpose of nutrition, he says also, 'they irrigated the body, cutting channels as in gardens, so that the streams of the veins might flow as it were from an incoming stream, making the body an aqueduct'. Finally: when the end is at hand, the soul's 'ship's cables' are 'loosed', and she herself 'set free'.

[32.6] The passage contains countless similar examples; but these are enough to make my point, namely that tropes are naturally grand, that metaphors conduce to sublimity, and that passages involving emotion and description are the most suitable field for them. [32.7] At the same time, it is plain without my saying it that the use of tropes, like all other good things in lit-

4. Demosthenes 18.296 [translator's note].
5. Greek philosopher and naturalist (ca. 370–ca. 285 B.C.E.), pupil and successor of ARISTOTLE.
6. Figures of speech.
7. Xenophon, *Memorabilia* 1.4.5ff.; Plato, *Timaeus* 65c–85e ("Longinus" picks various details out of this long passage, and runs them together) [translator's note].

erature, always tempts one to go too far. This is what people ridicule most in Plato, who is often carried away by a sort of literary madness into crude, harsh metaphors or allegorical fustian. 'It is not easy to understand that a city ought to be mixed like a bowl of wine, wherein the wine seethes with madness, but when chastened by another, sober god, and achieving a proper communion with him, produces a good and moderate drink.'[8] To call water 'a sober god', says the critic, and mixture 'chastening', is the language of a poet who is far from sober himself.

Digression: Genius versus Mediocrity

[32.8] Faults of this kind formed the subject of Caecilius' attack in his book on Lysias,[9] in which he had the audacity to declare Lysias in all respects superior to Plato. He has in fact given way without discrimination to two emotions: loving Lysias more deeply than he loves himself, he yet hates Plato with an even greater intensity. His motive, however, is desire to score a point, and his assumptions are not, as he believed, generally accepted. In preferring Lysias to Plato he thinks he is preferring a faultless and pure writer to one who makes many mistakes. But the facts are far from supporting his view.

[33.1] Let us consider a really pure and correct writer. We have then to ask ourselves in general terms whether grandeur attended by some faults of execution is to be preferred, in prose or poetry, to a modest success of impeccable soundness. We must also ask whether the greater *number* of good qualities or the greater good qualities ought properly to win the literary prizes. These questions are relevant to a discussion of sublimity, and urgently require an answer.

[33.2] I am certain in the first place that great geniuses are least 'pure'. Exactness in every detail involves a risk of meanness; with grandeur, as with great wealth, there ought to be something overlooked. It may also be inevitable that low or mediocre abilities should maintain themselves generally at a correct and safe level, simply because they take no risks and do not aim at the heights, whereas greatness, just because it is greatness, incurs danger.

[33.3] I am aware also of a second point. All human affairs are, in the nature of things, better known on their worse side; the memory of mistakes is ineffaceable, that of goodness is soon gone. [33.4] I have myself cited not a few mistakes in Homer and other great writers, not because I take pleasure in their slips, but because I consider them not so much voluntary mistakes as oversights let fall at random through inattention and with the negligence of genius. I do, however, think that the greater good qualities, even if not consistently maintained, are always more likely to win the prize—if for no other reason, because of the greatness of spirit they reveal. Apollonius makes no mistakes in the *Argonautica*; Theocritus[1] is very felicitous in the *Pastorals*, apart from a few passages not connected with the theme; but would you rather be Homer or Apollonius? [33.5] Is the Eratosthenes[2] of that

8. *Laws* 773c–d [translator's note].
9. Greek orator (ca. 459–ca. 380 B.C.E.) who reacted against the grandiose manner of Gorgias, striving for common language, pure diction, and lucidity rather than powerful emotional appeals.
1. Greek poet (ca. 300–ca. 260 B.C.E.) whose works are the earliest example of pastoral poetry. Apollonius of Rhodes (b. ca. 295 B.C.E.), head of the Alexandrian library and poet; his *Argonautica* is the great epic of the Alexandrian period.
2. Eratosthenes of Cyrene (ca. 275–194 B.C.E.), Greek poet, critic, geographer, and astronomer.

flawless little poem *Erigone* a greater poet than Archilochus, with his abundant, uncontrolled flood, that bursting forth of the divine spirit which is so hard to bring under the rule of law? Take lyric poetry: would you rather be Bacchylides or Pindar?[3] Take tragedy: would you rather be Ion of Chios or Sophocles?[4] Ion and Bacchylides are impeccable, uniformly beautiful writers in the polished manner; but it is Pindar and Sophocles who sometimes set the world on fire with their vehemence, for all that their flame often goes out without reason and they collapse dismally. Indeed, no one in his senses would reckon all Ion's works put together as the equivalent of the one play *Oedipus*.

[34.1] If good points were totted up, not judged by their real value, Hyperides would in every way surpass Demosthenes. He is more versatile, and has more good qualities. He is second-best at everything, like a pentathlon competitor; always beaten by the others for first place, he remains the best of the non-specialists. [34.2] In fact, he reproduces all the good features of Demosthenes, except his word-arrangement, and also has for good measure the excellences and graces of Lysias. He knows how to talk simply where appropriate; he does not deliver himself of everything in the same tone, like Demosthenes. His expression of character has sweetness and delicacy. Urbanity, sophisticated sarcasm, good breeding, skill in handling irony, humour neither rude nor tasteless but flavoured with true Attic salt,[5] an ingenuity in attack with a strong comic element and a sharp sting to its apt fun—all this produces inimitable charm. He has moreover great talents for exciting pity, and a remarkable facility for narrating myths with copiousness and developing general topics with fluency. For example, while his account of Leto is in his more poetic manner, his Funeral Speech is an unrivalled example of the epideictic style.[6] [34.3] Demosthenes, by contrast, has no sense of character. He lacks fluency, smoothness, and capacity for the epideictic manner; in fact he is practically without all the qualities I have been describing. When he forces himself to be funny or witty, he makes people laugh at him rather than with him. When he wants to come near to being charming, he is furthest removed from it. If he had tried to write the little speech on Phryne or that on Athenogenes,[7] he would have been an even better advertisement for Hyperides. [34.4] Yet Hyperides' beauties, though numerous, are without grandeur: 'inert in the heart of a sober man', they leave the hearer at peace. Nobody feels frightened reading Hyperides.

But when Demosthenes begins to speak, he concentrates in himself excellences finished to the highest perfection of his sublime genius—the intensity of lofty speech, living emotions, abundance, acuteness, speed where

3. Major Greek lyric poet (518–438 B.C.E.), known for his elaborate odes (encomia) celebrating victories in athletic and music contests. Bacchylides (ca. 524–ca. 452 B.C.E.), Greek lyric poet also known for his odes.
4. One of the great Greek tragedians (ca. 496–406 B.C.E.), best known for his Oedipus trilogy. Ion of Chios (ca. 490–ca. 421 B.C.E.), Greek poet famed chiefly for his tragedies, none of which has survived.
5. Elegant wit.
6. The speech (*Deliacus*) in which the myth of Leto was told is lost; the Funeral Speech is extant (*Oration* 2) [translator's note]. "The epideictic style": speech designed for delivery at festivals and funeral orations; it is distinguished from forensic oratory (for law courts) and deliberative (political) oratory. Leto: the mother of the Greek deities Apollo and Artemis.
7. The first is lost; the second is *Oration* 3 (5) [translator's note]. Phryne (4th c. B.C.E.), celebrated Greek courtesan. Athenogenes: Athenian businessman who was the subject of Hyperides' "Against Athenogenes."

speed is vital, all his unapproachable vehemence and power. He concentrates it all in himself—they are divine gifts, it is almost blasphemous to call them human—and so outpoints all his rivals, compensating with the beauties he has even for those which he lacks. The crash of his thunder, the brilliance of his lightning make all other orators, of all ages, insignificant. It would be easier to open your eyes to an approaching thunderbolt than to face up to his unremitting emotional blows.

[35.1] To return to Plato and Lysias, there is, as I said, a further difference between them. Lysias is much inferior not only in the importance of the good qualities concerned but in their number; and at the same time he exceeds Plato in the number of his failings even more than he falls short in his good qualities.

[35.2] What then was the vision which inspired those divine writers who disdained exactness of detail and aimed at the greatest prizes in literature? Above all else, it was the understanding that nature made man to be no humble or lowly creature, but brought him into life and into the universe as into a great festival, to be both a spectator and an enthusiastic contestant in its competitions. She implanted in our minds from the start an irresistible desire for anything which is great and, in relation to ourselves, supernatural.

[35.3] The universe therefore is not wide enough for the range of human speculation and intellect. Our thoughts often travel beyond the boundaries of our surroundings. If anyone wants to know what we were born for, let him look round at life and contemplate the splendour, grandeur, and beauty in which it everywhere abounds. [35.4] It is a natural inclination that leads us to admire not the little streams, however pellucid and however useful, but the Nile, the Danube, the Rhine, and above all the Ocean. Nor do we feel so much awe before the little flame we kindle, because it keeps its light clear and pure, as before the fires of heaven, though they are often obscured. We do not think our flame more worthy of admiration than the craters of Etna,[8] whose eruptions bring up rocks and whole hills out of the depths, and sometimes pour forth rivers of the earth-born, spontaneous fire. [35.5] A single comment fits all these examples: the useful and necessary are readily available to man, it is the unusual that always excites our wonder.

[36.1] So when we come to great geniuses in literature—where, by contrast, grandeur is not divorced from service and utility—we have to conclude that such men, for all their faults, tower far above mortal stature. Other literary qualities prove their users to be human; sublimity raises us towards the spiritual greatness of god. Freedom from error does indeed save us from blame, but it is only greatness that wins admiration. [36.2] Need I add that every one of those great men redeems all his mistakes many times over by a single sublime stroke? Finally, if you picked out and put together all the mistakes in Homer, Demosthenes, Plato, and all the other really great men, the total would be found to be a minute fraction of the successes which those heroic figures have to their credit. Posterity and human experience—judges whose sanity envy cannot question—place the

8. An active volcano in Sicily.

crown of victory on their heads. They keep their prize irrevocably, and will do so

so long as waters flow and tall trees flourish.[9]

[36.3] It has been remarked that 'the failed Colossus is no better than the Doryphorus of Polyclitus'.[1] There are many ways of answering this. We may say that accuracy is admired in art and grandeur in nature, and it is *by nature* that man is endowed with the power of speech; or again that statues are expected to represent the human form, whereas, as I said, something higher than human is sought in literature.

[36.4] At this point I have a suggestion to make which takes us back to the beginning of the book. Impeccability is generally a product of art; erratic excellence comes from natural greatness; therefore, art must always come to the aid of nature, and the combination of the two may well be perfection.

It seemed necessary to settle this point for the sake of our inquiry; but everyone is at liberty to enjoy what he takes pleasure in.

* * *

(v) Word-Arrangement or Composition

[39.1] There remains the fifth of the factors contributing to sublimity which we originally enumerated. This was a certain kind of composition or word-arrangement. Having set out my conclusions on this subject fully in two books, I shall here add only so much as is essential for our present subject.

Effect of Rhythm

Harmony is a natural instrument not only of conviction and pleasure but also to a remarkable degree of grandeur and emotion. [39.2] The *aulos*[2] fills the audience with certain emotions and makes them somehow beside themselves and possessed. It sets a rhythm, it makes the hearer move to the rhythm and assimilate himself to the tune, 'untouched by the Muses though he be'.[3] The notes of the lyre, though they have no meaning, also, as you know, often cast a wonderful spell of harmony with their varied sounds and blended and mingled notes. [39.3] Yet all these are but spurious images and imitations of persuasion, not the genuine activities proper to human nature of which I spoke.[4] Composition, on the other hand, is a harmony of words, man's natural instrument, penetrating not only the ears but the very soul. It arouses all kinds of conceptions of words and thoughts and objects, beauty and melody—all things native and natural to mankind. The combination and variety of its sounds convey the speaker's emotions to the minds of those around him and make the hearers share them.

9. "Epigram on the tomb of Midas," ascribed to Homer: see Plato, *Phaedrus* 264d [translator's note].

1. It is not certain whether "Longinus" means the Colossus of Rhodes or some other large statue. For the Doryphorus, famous for its proportions, see, e.g., G. M. A. Richter, *Handbook of Greek Art* (Phaidon, 1959), 110 [translator's note]. Polyclitus: a leading Greek sculptor of the second half of the 5th c. B.C.E. (a number of copies of his Doryphoros exist).

2. A reed instrument (often translated "pipe" or "flute").

3. Euripides, frag. 663 Nauck [translator's note].

4. Presumably in the work referred to in 39.1 [translator's note].

It fits his great thoughts into a coherent structure by the way in which it builds up patterns of words. Shall we not then believe that by all these methods it bewitches us and elevates to grandeur, dignity, and sublimity both every thought which comes within its compass and ourselves as well, holding as it does complete domination over our minds? It is absurd to question facts so generally agreed. Experience is proof enough.

* * *

Effect of Period Structure

[40.1] I come now to a principle of particular importance for lending grandeur to our words. The beauty of the body depends on the way in which the limbs are joined together, each one when severed from the others having nothing remarkable about it, but the whole together forming a perfect unity. Similarly great thoughts which lack connection are themselves wasted and waste the total sublime effect, whereas if they co-operate to form a unity and are linked by the bonds of harmony, they come to life and speak just by virtue of the periodic structure.[5] It is indeed generally true that, in periods, grandeur results from the total contribution of many elements.

[40.2] I have shown elsewhere that many poets and other writers who are not naturally sublime, and may indeed be quite unqualified for grandeur, and who use in general common and everyday words which carry with them no special effect, nevertheless acquire magnificence and splendour, and avoid being thought low or mean, solely by the way in which they arrange and fit together their words. Philistus, Aristophanes[6] sometimes, Euripides generally, are among the many examples. [40.3] Thus Heracles says after the killing of the children:

> I'm full of troubles, there's no room for more.[7]

This is a very ordinary remark, but it has become sublime, as the situation demands. If you re-arrange it, it will become apparent that it is in the composition, not in the sense, that Euripides' greatness appears.

[40.4] Dirce is being pulled about by the bull:

> And where it could, it writhed and twisted round,
> dragging at everything, rock, woman, oak,
> juggling with them all.[8]

The conception is fine in itself, but it has been improved by the fact that the word-harmony is not hurried and does not run smoothly; the words are propped up by one another and rest on the intervals between them; set wide apart like that, they give the impression of solid strength.

* * *

5. A sentence (i.e., a "period") composed of intricately balanced main and dependent clauses, often artfully arranged to create a sense of anticipation.
6. Major Greek comic dramatist (ca. 450–ca. 385 B.C.E.). Philistus (ca. 430–356 B.C.E.), Greek historian of Sicily.
7. Euripides, *Hercules Furens* 1245 [translator's note].
8. From Euripides' lost *Antiope* (frag. 221 Nauck) [translator's note]. The quote describes how the mythical Dirce died. She was tied to the tail of a bull by Antiope's sons, who were attempting to avenge the mistreatment Dirce had inflicted on their mother.

Conclusion

[43.6] There is no urgent need to enumerate in detail features which produce a low effect. We have explained what makes style noble and sublime; the opposite qualities will obviously make it low and undignified.

* * *

1st century C.E.

AUGUSTINE OF HIPPO
354–430

"Scripture enjoins nothing but love, and censures nothing but lust." Although this critical touchstone, articulated by St. Augustine in *On Christian Teaching*, may strike modern readers as more theological than literary, it involved Augustine in some remarkably modern literary issues: for example, how signs function, how readers make meaning of texts, and how interpretations are validated. He offers a generally Christian response to the problem of intentionality when he says of love in the Scriptures, "Anyone who derives from them an idea which is useful for supporting this love but fails to say what the writer demonstrably meant in the passage has not made a fatal error, and is certainly not a liar."

Augustine was born in a North African Roman province in present-day Algeria—a backwater of the Roman Empire. Although his mother, Monica, was a devout Christian, his father was a pagan and thus their son was not baptized. He studied in the rhetoric schools of Carthage, where he was attracted to Manichaeism, an early Christian philosophy noted for its extreme metaphysical and moral dualism and its belief that evil is as powerful as good. The other great influence on his intellectual development was Greek philosophy, most notably the works of such Neoplatonists as Plotinus. Augustine taught in Carthage for seven years, from 376 to 383. He then went to Rome, where he set up as a teacher of rhetoric. By 384, at the age of thirty, he was a prominent enough scholar to be appointed municipal professor of rhetoric by the city of Milan. There, profoundly moved by the preaching of Ambrose, the bishop of Milan, he was baptized in 387. He resigned his position and returned to North Africa, where, in 391, he became a priest. In 395 he was appointed bishop of Hippo, a position he held until his death.

Augustine was an extremely prolific writer (his bibliography numbers over one thousand works). Besides his celebrated *Confessions*, written around 400, and his magisterial philosophy of history, *City of God* (413–26), undertaken in the wake of the sack of Rome, he wrote many commentaries on the Bible and polemics against prominent heresies of the time, including Manichaeism. One treatise that deals with the theory of criticism and biblical interpretation—*On Christian Teaching* (*De doctrina christiana* in Latin)—was written after his appointment as bishop of Hippo. *On Christian Teaching*, whose first three books were written around 395 (book 4 was added in 427), is a central text of medieval philosophy and aesthetics.

Augustine wrote at a time when Christianity was just beginning to establish itself, a time when there was no agreement on a fixed text for its Scriptures. The

Bible consisted of scattered manuscript fragments (complete Bibles were rare), written variously in Hebrew, Greek, and Latin. Because of his early experiences with Manichaeism, Augustine recognized the need for some way to authorize the interpretation of Scriptures to prevent Christianity from fragmenting into sects. The existing hodgepodge of unconnected and sometimes contradictory narratives (and translations) could not simply be taken as a group of literal documents. Only a method of interpreting figurative language could unravel the many difficult and obscure passages contained in various Scriptures, but to argue for a figurative reading of the sacred texts of Christianity required mechanisms to limit meaning to authorized interpretations. Drawing from many sources, including classical Platonic thinking about language (see PLATO), the rhetorical tradition in which he was trained, the epistles of St. Paul, and the early traditions of biblical criticism pioneered by Origen (180–254) in Greek and Sts. Jerome (ca. 347–420) and Ambrose (ca. 340–397) in Latin, Augustine fashioned a theory of signification that would dominate Western hermeneutics for ten centuries after his death. In the later Middle Ages, Augustinian sign theory would be further developed into a system of exegesis (a method for interpreting texts allegorically) by writers such as Hugh of St. Victor (1097–1141) and THOMAS AQUINAS, as well as by vernacular poets such as DANTE.

Augustine's originality lay in linking the theory of signs to a theory of language, which to this point had been considered separately, and in bringing both theories to bear on the practice of interpreting Scriptures. His first principles, the basic elements of signification, were transmitted almost unchanged to the modern linguist FERDINAND DE SAUSSURE. In books 1 and 2 of *On Christian Teaching*, Augustine distinguishes between signs and things: "For a sign is a thing which of itself makes some other thing come to mind, besides the impression that it presents to the senses." He further differentiates between natural and conventional (or "given") signs: natural signs, such as smoke or the tracks of an animal, signify without intending to; conventional signs, such as words, are used by living beings to convey things they have sensed or understood. Conventional signs may be further distinguished as literal and figurative; for instance, "ox" may conventionally refer to a four-legged draft animal, but in the New Testament it also figuratively symbolizes one of the four evangelists. This careful survey of assumptions might seem, at first glance, somewhat obvious and simple, but it is necessary so that Augustine can posit a stable one-to-one correspondence between signs and the things they signify. Augustine's concern is to create a method and rules by which readers can correctly interpret difficult passages of Scriptures whose meaning might be obscure. Difficulties are created because signs (primarily words) are either unknown or ambiguous. Book 2 details the learning necessary to understand unknown or unfamiliar signs encountered in reading Scriptures. This learning includes a knowledge not only of languages and translation but more generally of history, philosophy, logic, mathematics, music, the sciences, and rhetoric (which he takes up in more detail in book 4). In book 3 he turns to ambiguous signs, which present a different set of interpretive challenges. Here Augustine develops a method for close reading that stresses the importance of attending to punctuation, to grammar and syntax, and to metaphor for correct interpretations of biblical texts.

The development of an adequate theory of conventional signs, especially of tropes, is one of the goals of Augustinian hermeneutics—as it is for much subsequent theory of interpretation, including modern semiotics. It is, however, a project undermined by signs' ability to carry multiple meanings (to function in richly figurative ways), a problem Augustine addressed but never adequately resolved.

***On Christian Teaching* Keywords:** The Canon/Tradition, Hermeneutics, Interpretation Theory, Language, Medieval Theory, Religion, Rhetoric, Semiotics

From On Christian Teaching[1]

From *Book Two*

When I was writing about things I began with the warning that attention should be paid solely to the fact that they existed, and not to anything besides themselves that they might signify. Now that I am discussing signs, I must say, conversely, that attention should not be paid to the fact that they exist, but rather to the fact that they are signs, or, in other words, that they signify.[2] For a sign is a thing which of itself makes some other thing come to mind, besides the impression that it presents to the senses. So when we see a footprint we think that the animal whose footprint it is has passed by; when we see smoke we realize that there is fire beneath it; when we hear the voice of an animate being we observe its feeling; and when the trumpet sounds soldiers know they must advance or retreat or do whatever else the state of the battle demands.

Some signs are natural, others given.[3] Natural signs are those which without a wish or any urge to signify cause something else besides themselves to be known from them, like smoke, which signifies fire. It does not signify fire because it wishes to do so; but because of our observation and consideration of things previously experienced it is realized that there is fire beneath it, even if nothing but smoke appears. The footprint of a passing animal also belongs to this category. The expression of an angry or depressed person signifies an emotional state even if there is no such wish on the part of the person who is angry or depressed, and likewise any other emotion is revealed by the evidence of the face even if we are not seeking to reveal it. It is not my intention to discuss this whole category now, but since it comes into my classification it could not be omitted altogether. So let the above remarks suffice.

Given signs are those which living things give to each other, in order to show, to the best of their ability, the emotions of their minds, or anything that they have felt or learnt. There is no reason for us to signify something (that is, to give a sign) except to express and transmit to another's mind what is in the mind of the person who gives the sign. It is this category of signs—to the extent that it applies to humans—that I have decided to examine and discuss, because even the divinely given signs contained in the holy scriptures have been communicated to us by the human beings who wrote them. Some animals, too, have signs among themselves by which they show the desires of their minds: a cockerel[4] on finding food gives a vocal sign to its hen to come quickly, and a dove calls to, or is called by, its mate by cooing. Many other such signs are observed regularly. Whether (as with a facial expression or a shout of pain) they accompany emotion without any desire to signify, or whether they are really given in order to signify something, is another question, and irrelevant to the matter in hand. I am excluding it from this work as not essential.

1. Translated by R. P. H. Green. Some of the translator's notes have been edited and some omitted.
2. In book 1, Augustine discusses "things," which, in and of themselves, do not signify anything. Here he turns his attention to the ways in which things can and do signify.
3. The Latin phrase Augustine uses here, *signa data*, is sometimes translated "conventional signs."
4. Rooster.

Some of the signs by which people communicate their feelings to one another concern the eyes; most of them concern the ears, and a very small number concern the other senses. When we nod, we give a sign just to the eyes of the person whom we want, by means of that sign, to make aware of our wishes. Particular movements of the hands signify a great deal. By the movement of all their limbs, actors give certain signs to the cognoscenti and converse with the spectators' eyes, as it were; and it is through the eyes that flags and standards convey the wishes of military commanders. All these things are, to coin a phrase, visible words. But most signs, as I said, and especially verbal ones, concern the ears. A trumpet, a flute, and a lyre generally produce not just a pleasant sound but one that is also significant. But these signs are very few compared with words. Words have gained an altogether dominant role among humans in signifying the ideas conceived by the mind that a person wants to reveal. It is true that our Lord gave a sign through the smell of the ointment by which his feet were anointed,[5] and that in the sacrament of his body and blood he signified his wishes through the sense of taste,[6] and that the healing of the woman who touched the border of his garment has its significance.[7] But an incalculable number of the signs by which people disclose their thoughts consist in words. I have been able to express in words all the various kinds of sign that I have briefly mentioned, but in no way could I have expressed all my words in terms of signs.

But spoken words cease to exist as soon as they come into contact with the air, and their existence is no more lasting than that of their sound; hence the invention, in the form of letters, of signs of words. In this way words are presented to the eyes, not in themselves, but by certain signs peculiar to them. These signs could not be shared by all nations, because of the sin of human disunity by which each one sought hegemony for itself. This pride is signified by the famous tower[8] raised towards heaven at the time when wicked men justly received incompatible languages to match their incompatible minds. Consequently even divine scripture, by which assistance is provided for the many serious disorders of the human will, after starting off in a single language,[9] in which it could have been conveniently spread throughout the world, was circulated far and wide in the various languages of translators and became known in this way to the Gentiles for their salvation. The aim of its readers is simply to find out the thoughts and wishes of those by whom it was written down and, through them, the will of God, which we believe these men followed as they spoke.

But casual readers are misled by problems and ambiguities of many kinds, mistaking one thing for another. In some passages they find no meaning at all that they can grasp at, even falsely, so thick is the fog created by some obscure phrases. I have no doubt that this is all divinely predetermined, so that pride may be subdued by hard work and intellects which tend to despise things that are easily discovered may be rescued from boredom and reinvigorated. Suppose someone were to make the following statements: that there exist holy and perfect men by whose lives and conduct the church of Christ tears away

5. In John 12.3–7, Mary Magdalene anoints Christ's feet with precious ointment. In book 3 of *On Christian Teaching*, Augustine interprets the "good odor" of the ointment as a sign of "good fame."

6. Matthew 26.26–28; Mark 14.22–24; Luke 22.15–20.

7. Matthew 9.20–22; Mark 5.25–29; Luke 8.43–44.

8. The Tower of Babel; see Genesis 11.1–9.

9. Hebrew for the Old Testament, Greek for the New [translator's note].

those who come to it from their various superstitions, and somehow, by inspiring them to imitate their goodness, incorporates them into itself; and that there exist servants of the true God, good and faithful men who, putting aside the burdens of this life, have come to the holy font of baptism, arise from it born again with the Holy Spirit, and then produce the fruit of a double love, that is love of God and love of their neighbour. Why is it, I wonder, that putting it like this gives less pleasure to an audience than by expounding in the same terms this passage from the Song of Songs, where the church is addressed and praised like a beautiful woman: 'Your teeth are like a flock of shorn ewes ascending from the pool, all of which give birth to twins, and there is not a sterile animal among them'?[1] Surely one learns the same lesson as when one hears it in plain words without the support of the imagery? And yet somehow it gives me more pleasure to contemplate holy men when I see them as the teeth of the church tearing men away from their errors and transferring them into its body, breaking down their rawness by biting and chewing. And it is with the greatest of pleasure that I visualize the shorn ewes, their worldly burdens set aside like fleeces, ascending from the pool (baptism) and all giving birth to twins (the two commandments of love), with none of them failing to produce this holy fruit. Exactly why this picture gives me greater pleasure than if no such imagery were presented by the divine books, since the topic is the same, and the lesson the same, it is difficult to say; this, however, is another question entirely. But no one disputes that it is much more pleasant to learn lessons presented through imagery, and much more rewarding to discover meanings that are won only with difficulty. Those who fail to discover what they are looking for suffer from hunger, whereas those who do not look, because they have it in front of them, often die of boredom. In both situations the danger is lethargy. It is a wonderful and beneficial thing that the Holy Spirit organized the holy scripture so as to satisfy hunger by means of its plainer passages and remove boredom by means of its obscurer ones. Virtually nothing is unearthed from these obscurities which cannot be found quite plainly expressed somewhere else.

* * *

There are two reasons why written texts fail to be understood: their meaning may be veiled either by unknown signs or by ambiguous signs. Signs are either literal or metaphorical. They are called literal when used to signify the things for which they were invented: as, for example, when we say *bovem* [ox], meaning the animal which we and all speakers of Latin call by that name. They are metaphorical when the actual things which we signify by the particular words are used to signify something else: when, for example, we say *bovem* and not only interpret these two syllables to mean the animal normally referred to by that name but also understand, by that animal, 'worker in the gospel', which is what scripture, as interpreted by the apostle Paul, means when it says, 'You shall not muzzle the ox that treads out the grain'.[2]

An important antidote to the ignorance of literal signs is the knowledge of languages. Users of the Latin language—and it is these that I have now undertaken to instruct—need two others, Hebrew and

1. Song of Solomon 4.2.
2. Deuteronomy 25.4. St. Paul interprets oxen as apostles, those "who labor in the word and doctrine," in 1 Corinthians 9.9 and 1 Timothy 5.18.

Greek,[3] for an understanding of the divine scriptures, so that recourse may be had to the original versions if any uncertainty arises from the infinite variety of Latin translators. Though we often find Hebrew words untranslated in the texts, like *amen, alleluia, raca, hosanna.*[4] In some cases, although they could be translated, the original form is preserved for the sake of its solemn authority (so *amen, alleluia*); in others, like the other two that I mentioned, they are said to be incapable of being translated into another language. There are certain words in particular languages which just cannot be translated into the idioms of another language. This is especially true of interjections, which signify emotion rather than an element of clearly conceived meaning: two such words, it is said, are *raca*, a word expressing anger, and *hosanna*, a word expressing joy. But it is not because of these few words, which it is easy enough to note down and ask other people about, but because of the aforementioned diversity of translators that a knowledge of languages is necessary. Translators of scripture from Hebrew into Greek can be easily counted, but not so translators into Latin, for in the early days of the faith any person who got hold of a Greek manuscript and fancied that he had some ability in the two languages went ahead and translated it.

This fact actually proves more of a help to interpretation than a hindrance, provided that readers are not too casual. Obscure passages are often clarified by the inspection of several manuscripts, like the passage in Isaiah[5] rendered by one translator as 'and do not despise the household of your own seed', but by another as 'and do not despise your own flesh'. Each one confirms the other. One is explained by the other, because 'flesh' can be taken literally—so that one may consider this a warning not to despise one's own body—and 'household of your seed' can be metaphorically understood as 'Christians', those spiritually born with us from the same seed of the word. But when the ideas of the translators are compared a more plausible idea suggests itself: that the command is literally about not despising your kinsfolk, since when you relate 'the household of your own seed' to the flesh your kinsfolk are what particularly comes to mind. This, I think, is the explanation of Paul's statement, 'If in any way I can arouse my flesh to jealousy, so that I may save some of them'[6] (in other words, so that they too may believe by jealously emulating those who believed earlier). By his flesh he meant the Jews, by virtue of his kinship with them. Another example, again from Isaiah:[7] one version has 'if you do not believe, you will not understand', another has 'if you do not believe, you will not stand fast'. It is not clear which of these represents the truth unless the versions in the original language are consulted. Yet both convey something important to those who read intelligently. It is difficult to find translators who diverge so much that they do not touch at some point. So because understanding concerns the vision of eternal things, whereas faith nourishes us with milk, so to speak, while we are babies in the cradle of this temporal life, and

3. Augustine himself admits to having little Greek and no Hebrew.
4. See, for example, Deuteronomy 27.15; Revelation 19.1; Matthew 5.22; John 12.13.
5. Isaiah 58.7. The first reading given is that of the Septuagint; the second a more literal translation used in the Vulgate [translator's note]. Septuagint: a translation of the Hebrew Bible into Greek, so called from the legend that it was done by 70 (*septuaginta*, Latin) superb Jewish scholars; references to it are abbreviated LXX. Vulgate: 4th-century Latin translation of the Bible that eventually became the official Latin version.
6. Romans 11.14.
7. Isaiah 7.9. The readings quoted are those of the Septuagint and of Symmachus respectively [translator's note]. Symmachus (ca. late 2d C.E.), an otherwise unknown scholar who translated the Old Testament into Greek.

because here and now 'we walk by faith, not sight',[8] and because if we do not walk by faith we cannot reach that vision which is not transient but eternal, and because we hold fast to the truth through a purified understanding—that is why one version says 'if you do not believe you will not stand fast' and the other 'if you do not believe you will not understand'.

Ambiguity in the original language often misleads a translator unfamiliar with the general sense of a passage, who may import a meaning which is quite unrelated to the writer's meaning. For example, some manuscripts have: 'their feet are sharp to shed blood' (the Greek adjective means both 'sharp' and 'quick').[9] The translator who wrote 'their feet are quick to shed blood' saw the meaning; but another was misled by the ambiguous sign and went astray. Any other translations of this are not obscure, but plain wrong. They differ from the above-mentioned examples, and our advice must be not to seek an interpretation of such texts, but an emendation. Another example: because *moschus* is 'calf' in Greek some translators did not interpret the word *moscheumata* as 'plants' but translated it as 'calves'.[1] This mistake has taken over so many manuscripts that an alternative reading is hard to find; and yet the meaning is quite obvious, because all is revealed in the words that follow. 'False plants do not put out deep roots' gives a better meaning here than 'calves', which are not rooted to the earth, but walk over it with their feet! This particular translation is guaranteed by the surrounding context.

Because the exact meaning which the various translators are trying to express, each according to his own ability and judgement, is not clear without an examination of the language being translated, and because a translator, unless very expert, often strays away from the author's meaning, we should aim either to acquire a knowledge of the languages from which the Latin scripture derives or to use the versions of those who keep excessively close to the literal meaning. Not that such translations are adequate, but they may be used to control the freedom or error of others who in their translations have chosen to follow the ideas rather than the words. Translators often meet not only individual words, but also whole phrases, which simply cannot be expressed in the idioms of the Latin language, at least not if one wants to maintain the usage of ancient speakers of Latin. Sometimes these translations lose nothing in intelligibility but trouble those people who take more delight in things when correct usage is observed in expressing the corresponding signs. What is called a solecism[2] is simply what results when words are not combined according to the rules by which our predecessors, who spoke with some authority, combined them. Whether you say *inter homines* or *inter hominibus*[3] does not matter to a student intent upon things. And again, what is a barbarism but a word articulated with letters or sounds that are not the same as those with which it was normally articulated by those who spoke Latin before us? Whether one says *ignoscere*[4] with a long or short third syllable is of little concern to someone who beseeches God to forgive his sins no matter how he may have managed to articulate the word.

* * *

8. 2 Corinthians 5.7.
9. Psalm 13.3 (LXX); cf. Romans 3.15 and Isaiah 59.7 (the latter does not use the ambiguous Greek adjective, *oxus*).
1. Wisdom 4.3.
2. An ungrammatical phrase.
3. The meaning is the same ("among men"), but only the first is good Latin [translator's note].
4. "To forgive." In what follows Augustine means "vowel," not "syllable" [translator's note].

As for metaphorical signs, any unfamiliar ones which puzzle the reader must be investigated partly through a knowledge of languages, and partly through a knowledge of things. There is a figurative significance and certainly some hidden meaning conveyed by the episode of the pool of Siloam,[5] where the man who had his eyes anointed by the Lord with mud made from spittle was ordered to wash his face. If the evangelist had not explained this name from an unfamiliar language, this important meaning would have remained hidden. So too, many of the Hebrew names not explained by the authors of these books undoubtedly have considerable significance and much help to give in solving the mysteries of the scriptures, if they can be explained at all. Various experts in the language have rendered no small service to posterity by explaining all these individual words from the scriptures and giving the meaning of the names Adam, Eve, Abraham, and Moses, and of place names such as Jerusalem, Zion, Jericho, Sinai, Lebanon, Jordan, and any other names in that language that are unfamiliar to us. Once these are clarified and explained many figurative expressions in scripture become quite clear.

Ignorance of things makes figurative expressions unclear when we are ignorant of the qualities of animals or stones or plants or other things mentioned in scripture for the sake of some analogy. The well-known fact about the snake, that it offers its whole body to assailants in place of its head, marvellously illustrates the meaning of the Lord's injunction to be as wise as serpents,[6] which means that in place of our head, which is Christ,[7] we should offer our body to persecutors, so that the Christian faith is not as it were killed within us when we spare our body and deny God. And the fact that a snake confined in its narrow lair puts off its old garment and is said to take on new strength chimes in excellently with the idea of imitating the serpent's astuteness and putting off the old man (to use the words of the apostle)[8] in order to put on the new, and also with that of doing so in a confined place, for the Lord said 'enter by the narrow gate'.[9] Just as a knowledge of the habits of the snake clarifies the many analogies involving this animal regularly given in scripture, so too an ignorance of the numerous animals mentioned no less frequently in analogies is a great hindrance to understanding. The same is true of stones, herbs, and anything that has roots. Even a knowledge of the carbuncle, a stone which shines in the dark, explains many obscure passages in scripture where it is used in an analogy; and ignorance of the beryl and adamant[1] often closes the door to understanding. It is easy to understand that unbroken peace is signified by the olive branch brought by the dove when it returned to the ark,[2] simply because we know that the smooth surface of oil is not easily broken by another liquid

5. John 9.7. The pool of Siloam is a rock-cut pool located just outside the walls of the Old City of Jerusalem; its name, according to John, means "sent." In "Lectures or Tractates on the Gospel According to St. John," Augustine explains: "Had He [Christ] not been sent, none of us would have been set free from iniquity. Accordingly he [the blind man] washed his eyes in that pool which is interpreted, Sent—he was baptized in Christ."
6. Matthew 10.16.
7. Ephesians 4.15.
8. Ephesians 4.22–24. The apostle is Paul.
9. Matthew 7.13.
1. A fabulous stone with the properties of diamonds and magnets; like the precious stones carbuncle and beryl, it was thought in the Middle Ages to have hidden, magical, or healing properties to which Christian writers added allegorical meanings. Beginning in the classical period, knowledge about rocks and stones and their meanings was systematically collected in books called *lapidaries*.
2. Genesis 8.11.

and also that the tree itself is in leaf all year round. And because of their ignorance about hyssop[3] many people, unaware of its power to cleanse the lungs or even (so it is said) to split rocks with its roots, in spite of its low and humble habit, are quite unable to discover why it is said, 'You will purge me with hyssop, and I shall be clean'.[4]

An unfamiliarity with numbers makes unintelligible many things that are said figuratively and mystically in scripture. An intelligent intellect (if I may put it thus) cannot fail to be intrigued by the meaning of the fact that Moses and Elijah and the Lord himself fasted for forty days.[5] The knotty problem of the figurative significance of this event cannot be solved except by understanding and considering the number, which is four times ten, and signifies the knowledge of all things woven into the temporal order. The courses of the day and the year are based on the number four: the day is divided into the hours of morning, afternoon, evening, and night, the year into the months of the spring, summer, autumn, and winter. While we live in the temporal order, we must fast and abstain from the enjoyment of what is temporal, for the sake of the eternity in which we desire to live, but it is actually the passage of time by which the lesson of despising the temporal and seeking the eternal is brought home to us. Then the number ten signifies the knowledge of the creator and creation: the Trinity[6] is the number of the creator, while the number seven symbolizes the creation because it represents life and the body. The former has three elements (hence the precept that God must be loved with the whole heart, the whole soul, and the whole mind),[7] and as for the body, the four elements of which it consists are perfectly obvious.[8] To live soberly according to this significance of the number ten—conveyed to us temporally (hence the multiplication by four)—and abstain from the pleasures of this world: this is the significance of the forty-day fast. This is enjoined by the law, as represented by Moses; by prophecy, as represented by Elijah; and by the Lord himself, who, to symbolize that he enjoyed the testimony of the law and the prophets, shone out in the midst of them on the mountain as the three amazed disciples looked on.[9] In the same way a solution may be found to explain how the number fifty, which enjoys particular authority in our religion because of Pentecost,[1] comes from the number forty; and how, when it is multiplied by three—either because of the three eras (before the law, under the law, under grace) or because of the name of the Father, the Son, and the Holy Spirit—and with the conspicuous addition of the Trinity, refers to the mystery of the fully purified church, matching the 153 fishes that were caught in the nets cast on the right-hand side of the boat after the Lord's resurrection.[2] In this way, expressed in a variety of numbers,

3. A medicinal plant native to southern Europe and the Middle East, commonly used as an antiseptic, cough reliever, and expectorant.
4. Psalm 50.7 LXX (51.7).
5. Exodus 24.18; 3 Kings LXX (1 Kings) 19.8; Matthew 4.2. Elijah: prophet of the Old Testament during the reign of Ahab, according to 1 and 2 Kings. In 1 Kings 19, Elijah travels 40 days and 40 nights to Mount Horeb, where Moses had received the Ten Commandments.
6. In Christian doctrine, the unity of the Father, the Son, and the Holy Spirit as three persons in one Godhead.
7. Matthew 22.37.
8. According to Greek philosophers from Empedocles (ca. 493–ca. 433 B.C.E.) on, all matter is composed of only four elements: earth, air, fire, and water.
9. Matthew 17.1–8; Mark 9.2–6.
1. The Christian holiday celebrating the descent of the Holy Spirit upon the apostles and followers of Christ. It occurs 50 days (in Greek, *pentēcostē* means "fiftieth") after Easter, falling on the 10th day after Ascension Thursday, which is itself 40 days after Easter.
2. John 21.6–11.

there are in the sacred books certain abstruse analogies which are inaccessible to readers without a knowledge of number.

Many passages are also made inaccessible and opaque by an ignorance of music. It has been elegantly demonstrated that there are some figurative meanings of things based on the difference between the psaltery and the lyre.[3] It is a matter of dispute among experts, not unreasonably, whether the psaltery of ten strings embodies some musical principle which obliges it to have this number of strings, or whether, if this is not so, the number should for that reason be understood rather in a special religious sense, either in terms of the Decalogue[4] (and if that number is investigated, it can only be related to the creator and the creation), or in terms of the number ten itself as expounded above. The number of years given in the gospel for the building of the Temple, forty-six,[5] has some musical overtones, and when related to the constitution of the Lord's body—which is why the Temple was mentioned—compels numerous heretics to admit that the Son of God took on a real human body, not an insubstantial one. Indeed we find both number and music mentioned with respect in several places in the holy scriptures.

* * *

From *Book Three*

The student who fears God earnestly seeks his will in the holy scriptures. Holiness makes him gentle, so that he does not revel in controversy; a knowledge of languages protects him from uncertainty over unfamiliar words or phrases, and a knowledge of certain essential things protects him from ignorance of the significance and detail of what is used by way of imagery. Thus equipped, and with the assistance of reliable texts derived from the manuscripts with careful attention to the need for emendation, he should now approach the task of analysing and resolving the ambiguities of the scriptures. To prevent himself from being misled by ambiguous signs, in so far as I can instruct him (it may indeed be the case that either because of great intellectual gifts or a clarity of mind that is the result of greater illumination than I have he scorns as elementary the methods which I wish to demonstrate)—but, as I began to say, in so far as I can instruct him, the student who is in the proper state of mind to accept my instruction should know that ambiguity in scripture resides either in literal or in metaphorical usages (as the terms were described in Book 2).

When it is literal usages that make scripture ambiguous, we must first of all make sure that we have not punctuated or articulated the passage incorrectly.[6] Once close consideration has revealed that it is uncertain how a passage should be punctuated and articulated, we must consult the rule of faith,[7] as it is perceived through the plainer passages of the scriptures and the authority of the church. (I dealt adequately with this matter when speaking of things in Book 1.) But if both interpretations, or indeed all of

3. Both are stringed instruments, similar to small harps, but with slightly different shapes and so different sounds.
4. The Ten Commandments (Exodus 20.2–17; Deuteronomy 5.6–21).
5. John 2.20. There John refers to the Second Temple, built ca. 350 B.C.E., after the Jews returned from Babylon. The Temple symbolically figures Christ's human body.
6. Ancient texts often lacked punctuation, accent marks, and sometimes even spaces.
7. By this Augustine (and AQUINAS after him) means the fundamentals of Christian doctrine [translator's note].

them, if there are several sides to the ambiguity, sound compatible with the faith, then it remains to consult the context—the preceding and following passages, which surround the ambiguity—in order to determine which of the several meanings that suggest themselves is supported by it, and which one lends itself to acceptable combinations with it.

Consider now the following examples. The well-known heretical punctuation[8] 'In the beginning was the Word, and the Word was with God, and there was God', giving a different sense in what follows ('This Word was in the beginning with God') refuses to acknowledge that the Word was God. This is to be refuted by the rule of faith, which lays down for us the equality of the members of the Trinity, and so we should say 'and the Word was God', and then go on, 'This was in the beginning with God.' The following ambiguous passage is not, on either interpretation, at odds with the faith, and therefore has to be resolved by its actual context. The apostle says, 'And I know not which to choose; I am torn in two directions having a desire to be dissolved and be with Christ, for that is much the best; to remain in the flesh is necessary on your account'.[9] It is not in fact clear whether we should read 'having a desire in two directions' or 'I am torn in two directions', followed by 'having a desire to be dissolved and be with Christ'. But since the phrase 'for that is much the best' follows, it is clear that he says he has a desire for that which is best, so that although torn in two directions he feels a desire to do the one but an obligation to do the other (that is, a desire to be with Christ, but an obligation to remain in the flesh). The ambiguity is resolved by the presence of the single word 'for'. Critics who remove this word have been led to the conclusion that he was apparently not only torn in two directions but also had a desire for two things.[1] So the punctuation must be: 'and I know not which to choose; I am torn in two directions' (pause) 'having a desire to be dissolved and be with Christ'. And then, as if he were being asked why he has a desire for this, he says, 'for it is much the best'. Why, then, is he torn in two directions? Because there is an obligation to remain, which he expresses thus: 'to remain in the flesh is necessary on your account'. Where an ambiguity can be resolved neither by an article of faith nor by the actual context there is no objection to any punctuation which follows one of the meanings that suggest themselves. Such is the passage in Corinthians: 'so having these promises, my dearest brethren, let us purify ourselves from all pollution of the flesh and the spirit, perfecting holiness in the fear of God. Welcome me; I have wronged no one'.[2] It is uncertain whether we should read 'let us purify ourselves from all pollution of the flesh and the spirit', on the analogy of the phrase 'so that she may be holy in body and spirit',[3] or 'let

8. The Arians are meant. As Augustine explains, their revised punctuation radically changed the theological significance of the passage [John 1.1–2; translator's note]. Arians: followers of a 3d-century heresy that rejected the doctrine of the Trinity, holding that Christ (the Son) is not equal to the Father.

9. Philippians 1.22–24; an English translation of these words cannot illustrate the ambiguity, because its word-order, unlike the Latin word-order, determines the meaning. The point here was important in debates with the Manichees, who saw in it evidence for the existence of two conflicting natures in the human soul [translator's note]. Manichaeism was a 3d-century heresy, to which Augustine subscribed early in his career: it espouses a dualism that divides the world between two equally powerful forces of good and evil.

1. The conclusion is not inescapable; the omission of *enim* ["for"; Latin] in the Vulgate did not close the question. In fact Augustine's first argument is the stronger one [translator's note].

2. 2 Corinthians 7.1–2; again an English translation inevitably removes the ambiguity under discussion [translator's note].

3. 1 Corinthians 7.34.

us purify ourselves from all pollution of the flesh', with a different sense emerging in what follows: 'and perfecting holiness of the spirit in the fear of God. Welcome me . . .' Such problems of punctuation are for the reader to resolve.

* * *

As well as these ambiguities we must consider in a similar way those which do not concern punctuation or reading aloud, like the one in Thessalonians' *Propterea consolati sumus fratres in vobis.*[4] It is not clear whether *fratres* is in the vocative case or the accusative;[5] neither reading would be contrary to the faith. But in Greek the corresponding case-forms are not identical, and so after inspecting the Greek we declare in favour of the vocative (equivalent to *o fratres*). If a translator had chosen to say *Propterea consolationem habuimus, fratres, in vobis*, he would have been less faithful to the wording, but there would be no doubt of his meaning. Or indeed *nostri*[6] might be added, for hardly anyone would doubt that the vocative was being used in the phrase *Propterea consolati sumus fratres nostri in vobis.* But it is rather dangerous to allow such changes. This has been done in Corinthians, where the apostle says *cotidie morior, per vestram gloriam, fratres, quam habeo in Christo Iesu:*[7] one translator actually wrote *cotidie morior, per vestram iuro gloriam*, because in Greek there is a clear and unambiguous word signifying an oath. In the field of literal expressions, then, as far as the books of holy scripture are concerned, it is very unusual, and very difficult, to find cases of ambiguity which cannot be resolved either by the particular details of the context—which are a pointer to the writer's intention—or by a comparison of Latin translations or an inspection of the original language.

But the ambiguities of metaphorical words, about which I must now speak, require no ordinary care and attention. To begin with, one must take care not to interpret a figurative expression literally. What the apostle says is relevant here: 'the letter kills but the spirit gives life'.[8] For when something meant figuratively is interpreted as if it were meant literally, it is understood in a carnal way. No 'death of the soul' is more aptly given that name than the situation in which the intelligence, which is what raises the soul above the level of animals, is subjected to the flesh by following the letter. A person who follows the letter understands metaphorical words as literal, and does not relate what the literal word signifies to any other meaning. On hearing the word 'sabbath', for example, he interprets it simply as one of the seven days which repeat themselves in a continuous cycle; and on hearing the word 'sacrifice' his thoughts do not pass beyond the rituals performed with sacrificial beasts or fruits of the earth. It is, then, a miserable kind of spiritual slavery to interpret signs as things, and to be incapable of raising the mind's eye above the physical creation so as to absorb the eternal light.

* * *

4. Therefore, brethren, we were comforted over you in all our affliction and distress by your faith (1 Thessalonians 3.7, King James Version [KJV]).
5. The case ending of a noun indicating its use in direct address ("Oh brethren") or as a direct object (the accusative). For *fratres*, they are identical.
6. Our (with *fratres*, this form could be vocative but not accusative).
7. I protest by your rejoicing which I have in Christ Jesus our Lord, I die daily (1 Corinthians 15.31, KJV). The second version might be translated "I swear by your rejoicing, I die daily." The apostle is Paul.
8. 2 Corinthians 3.6.

As well as this rule, which warns us not to pursue a figurative (that is, metaphorical) expression as if it were literal, we must add a further one: not to accept a literal one as if it were figurative. We must first explain the way to discover whether an expression is literal or figurative. Generally speaking, it is this: anything in the divine discourse that cannot be related either to good morals or to the true faith should be taken as figurative. Good morals have to do with our love of God and our neighbour, the true faith with our understanding of God and our neighbour. The hope that each person has within his own conscience is directly related to the progress that he feels himself to be making towards the love and understanding of God and s neighbour.

* * *

The literary-minded should be aware that our Christian authors used all the figures of speech which teachers of grammar call by their Greek name of tropes,[9] and that they did so more diversely and profusely than can be judged or imagined by those who are unfamiliar with scripture or who gained their knowledge of figures from other literature. Those who know about these tropes recognize them in sacred literature, and this knowledge to some extent helps them in understanding it. This would not be the proper place to present them to people not familiar with them; I do not wish to look as if I am giving a course on grammar. I recommend that they be learnt independently; as indeed I have recommended already, in Book 2, when discussing the importance of learning languages. (Letters, from which grammar actually takes its name—the Greek word for them is *grammata*—are of course the signs of the sounds involved in the articulation of the words which we use when speaking.) In the divine books we find not only examples of these tropes, as of everything else, but also the names of some of them, like 'allegory', 'enigma', and 'parable'.[1] Almost all these tropes, which are said to be acquired through one of the 'liberal' arts,[2] are also found in the utterances of those who have had no formal teaching in grammar and are content with the style of ordinary people. Don't we all say 'so may you flourish'? This is a metaphor. Don't we all refer to a swimming pool by the word *piscina*,[3] which takes its name from fish even though it does not contain fish and was not made for fish? This trope is called catachresis.[4]

It would take a long time to work through the others in the same way. Popular speech has even come to use some which are remarkable because what they mean is the opposite of what is said, like the figures of irony and antiphrasis.[5] In irony we indicate what is meant by means of our intonation, as when we say to a man who is doing something badly, 'you're doing a good job there'. In antiphrasis, on the other hand, we signify the opposite meaning, not by our intonation, but either by the use of particular words whose origin

9. Figures of speech (literally, "turns").
1. Teaching moral lessons by means of extended metaphors. "Allegory": a narrative relating one thing to mean another. "Enigma": allusive or obscure speech.
2. The arts or disciplines which it was considered worthwhile for a free man—or rather a man (sometimes woman) of some wealth and status—to learn [translator's note]. *Liber* means "free" in Latin.
3. Basin, pool, pond, tank, or other large container for water. A stock example among ancient grammarians [translator's note]. *Piscis* means "fish" in Latin.
4. This term denotes the use of a word in a context where strictly speaking it does not apply (e.g., "substantial" for "big," or "menu" and "mouse" in computer language) [translator's note].
5. From *anti* (reverse) and *phrasis* (diction): saying one thing and meaning the contrary.

derives from a contrary—for example, *lucus* [grove], which is so called because it has little light,[6] or by using certain customary expressions (though these can also be used without a contrary meaning). For example, when looking for something that is not available in a particular place, we may be told 'there's plenty';[7] or we may by adding words give what we say a contrary interpretation, as in 'beware of him, he's a good man'.[8] Are things of this kind not said by all the uneducated[9] and by people who are totally ignorant of the tropes and all their names? A knowledge of them is necessary for the resolution of ambiguities in scripture because when a meaning based on the literal interpretation of the words is absurd we must investigate whether the passage that we cannot understand is perhaps being expressed by means of one or other of the tropes. This is how most hidden meanings have been discovered.

ca. 395

6. Another old chestnut [translator's note].
7. Compare perhaps the modern "no problem" or (in some contexts) "I'm delighted" [translator's note].
8. It is not clear whether Augustine means that the meaning of "beware" is coloured by "good," and so means "look out for," or the reverse (so that "good" means "bad"), which would be more truly a contrary interpretation [translator's note].
9. The Roman rhetorician Quintilian (ca. 30/35–ca. 100 C.E.) points out (*Institutio Oratoria* 8.6.4) that metaphor was so natural a turn of speech that it was often employed by uneducated persons [translator's note]

MOSES MAIMONIDES (RABBI MOSES BEN MAIMON) 1135–1204

Moses Maimonides' *Guide of the Perplexed* brings into view what MATTHEW ARNOLD might call Hebraic ways of thinking about textual interpretation that continue to be relevant to literary theory today. As JACQUES DERRIDA declares in *Writing and Difference* (1967): "We live in the difference between the Jew and the Greek, which is perhaps the unity of what is called history." While Greek philosophy values the universal, the general, and the univocal, Jewish thought is more open to ambiguity, contradiction, and plurality of meaning. Where Greek thought separates interpretation from text, Jewish hermeneutics tends to see text and its interpretation as part of one process. Conflicts over these values have been central to contemporary debates, especially those on poststructuralism, even as the original theological issues that created them have become increasingly unfamiliar. Maimonides' importance for the Latin Middle Ages is twofold: he is among the handful of Jewish and Islamic scholars who reintroduced the works of ARISTOTLE, including Aristotelian literary criticism, to Europe; and he influenced Scholastic philosophers like THOMAS AQUINAS. But the significance of Jewish hermeneutics (the theory and practice of interpretation) for contemporary literary theory has not been as well understood as that of Christian hermeneutics, even though it is clear that Maimonides' methods of exegesis have strongly affected Jewish theorists who have shaped recent theoretical debates, such as SIGMUND FREUD, ERICH AUERBACH, LEO STRAUSS, HAROLD BLOOM, and Derrida.

Maimonides resembles AUGUSTINE when he insists on the need for an allegorical interpretation of the Torah (the Jewish Scriptures). Like other Western theorists of interpretation, Maimonides worries about three principal problems: discovering the author's original intention, warding off ingenious overinterpretation, and finding deep as opposed to superficial meaning. And he too argues that esoteric meanings exist, though they can often only be glimpsed before fading back into obscurity—which, he believes, is as it should be. The meaning of sacred texts is not always accessible to the vulgar but can be understood only by the perfect (virtuous) person, one who is prone to being perplexed. This is the reader that Maimonides addresses.

Maimonides' approach will seem somewhat alien to students of a Western literary criticism based on Greek methods of interpretation—and their Christian derivatives—which separate the literary text from its commentary and which strive for a univocal, single, "correct" interpretation. Jewish hermeneutics, as exemplified by Maimonides' *Guide of the Perplexed*, treats text and interpretation as dual aspects of the same revelation that remains open to multiple textual meanings.

Maimonides (also known by the acronym for his name, Rambam) was born into an influential Jewish family in Cordova, in Muslim Spain, near the end of the *convivi-encia*, the period from the eighth to the twelfth centuries when the three great religious cultures of the Middle Ages—Christian, Jewish, and Islamic—coexisted on the Iberian Peninsula. His father, from whom he received his rabbinic instruction, was a noted Talmudist (a scholar of the collection of ancient Jewish law) as well as a mathematician and astronomer. In addition, Maimonides received a secular education from the most distinguished Arabic scholars of his day. He was thirteen years old when Cordova was captured by the Almohads, members of a fundamentalist Islamic sect, and his family was compelled to choose between Islam and exile. They chose the latter; after wandering around Spain for ten years, they took up residence in Fez in Morocco, where Maimonides devoted himself to studies in theology and medicine. Fez was also under the rule of the Almohads, and for a while the family tried to pass as Muslims. But Maimonides' growing reputation as a scholar (by sixteen he had already published a treatise on logical terminology) brought him under the scrutiny of the authorities. He was even tried for having lapsed from Islam, a capital crime; he escaped death only because an Arab friend interceded. In 1165 the family set sail for the Holy Land, then held by Christians. They finally settled in Egypt, where Maimonides lived for the rest of his life. In Cairo he went into business in precious stones; but when his brother, his business partner, was lost at sea with the family fortune, Maimonides turned to medicine to support himself, becoming physician to the court of the grand vizier. He describes his work there as grueling, yet in his spare time he became the unofficial leader of the Jewish community of Cairo, studied the Torah, and worked on his comprehensive code of Jewish law. His widespread reputation for learning made him one of the most celebrated Jews of the Middle Ages; England's King Richard invited Maimonides to become his royal physician. Maimonides' death was publicly mourned throughout the Jewish world, and his body was moved to the Holy Land, where his grave has been a pilgrimage site ever since.

Maimonides' writings are extensive and eclectic; they include lengthy and ambitious works in medicine, theology, and philosophy. He wrote several commentaries on traditional Jewish law. He began his *Commentary on the Mishnah* (1168)—the great legal code composed during the period between 10 and 220 C.E. that was designed to organize and regulate Jewish oral law—when he was just twenty-three, completing it ten years later. A second collection, the massive *Mishneh Torah* (1178), was meant to provide a complete classification of rabbinic law. This alone would have been an unprecedented undertaking; but the *Mishneh Torah* is more than simply a law code. In it Maimonides also included many interpretations, passages of exegesis, historical surveys, and explanations of difficult phrases and concepts. *The Guide of the Perplexed* (1190) turns from the codification of religious law to "the science of the law in its true sense." In this wide-ranging and occasionally baffling treatise, Maimonides attempts to reconcile faith with philosophical reason, Judaism with a newly recovered Aristotelianism. More specifically, he wants to demonstrate that Judaism is not irreconcilable with the understanding of physics and metaphysics articulated by the twelfth-century Aristotelians. In the course of his introduction, he argues that when their "internal" sense is properly understood, the *Account of the Beginning* (the Genesis story) refers to "natural science" (physics) and *The Account of the Chariot* (Ezekiel 1 and 10) to "divine science" (metaphysics).

Ostensibly written for his disciple Joseph ben Judah, *The Guide* elucidates obscure parables and terms found in "the books of the prophets." Maimonides, whose interpretive skills were honed by his extensive investigations of the Mishnah, argues that to penetrate the meaning of Scriptures and the Talmud (the great collections of oral law compiled between the second and fifth centuries C.E.) requires a fully elaborated method of interpretation (a hermeneutic). In his introduction, he explains that the failures to understand (1) the polysemy (many meanings) of biblical language and (2) the biblical use of obscure parables (which maintain the secrets of divine knowledge) give rise to "perplexity" even in the learned. Significantly, biblical texts are full of terms that are difficult to understand because they are "equivocal"—they have more than one meaning; or "derivative"—they contain supplemental meanings derived from other terms; or "amphibolous"—they are understood as having sometimes one and sometimes many meanings. Maimonides illustrates his discussions with frequent quotations from the Bible.

A purely linguistic comprehension of the richness of biblical language, according to Maimonides, is insufficient for understanding the Torah and Talmud, for these texts are also full of parables designed to obscure the "secrets of the prophetic books." Such an understanding requires a more fully elaborated theory of narrative, which Maimonides sketches in his introduction, including a key distinction between those parables that must be interpreted word by word and those that must be interpreted holistically.

For Maimonides, contradictions, far from being philosophical flaws, are to be embraced and studied according to principles he sets forth at the end of the introduction, where he identifies seven types. Perhaps the most interesting of the contradictions in Maimonides' own hermeneutic is the essential tension in his introduction between the injunction to secrecy—his understanding that the secrets of that divine science "ought not to be taught even to one man, except if he be wise and able to understand by himself, in which case only the chapter headings may be transmitted to him"—and the need to pass those secrets from generation to generation by teaching them to others. In the context of a close-knit and homogeneous community, it might be possible to preserve secret knowledge by passing it on orally from teacher to student, master to disciple. But in the context of the Jewish Diaspora, which could separate teacher from pupil—as happened to Maimonides and his disciple Joseph—written texts become necessary for organizing and preserving such knowledge, even while running the risk that the teacher "in effect would be teaching them to thousands of men." To preserve from the ignorant and the vulgar "those truths especially requisite for [the pupil's] apprehension," Maimonides must adopt the very techniques of the texts he seeks to explain: he must conceal them by scattering them throughout the treatise and entangling them with contradictions so that the truths are "glimpsed and then again . . . concealed."

Insofar as Maimonides' interpretive method strikes the modern student of literary criticism as perhaps too esoteric to illuminate literary issues, that response may suggest the extent to which Greek modes of thinking have determined Western literary criticism. Yet Jewish hermeneutics has continued to exert at least a covert influence on the development of the dominant tradition. Although it was translated from its original Arabic into Hebrew and Latin during the Middle Ages, *The Guide of the Perplexed* was, ironically, not eagerly accepted within the Jewish community, because it advocated the study of philosophy alongside the more important study of the Torah.

But in the century following his death, Maimonides' influence spread widely among Jews and Christians alike. Maimonides and his famous predecessor Rashi (Rabbi Solomon ben Isaac, 1040–1105, a talmudic scholar from Troyes) were both important precursors of the Scholasticism of the High Middle Ages, affecting Christian exegetes such as Hugh of St. Victor and Thomas Aquinas. There are also elements in later Freudian analysis that elaborate and extend the rabbinic hermeneutics articulated by Maimonides. Finally, many of the issues that interest contemporary literary theorists such as Derrida and his Yale School disciples, most notably Harold Bloom—for example, the indeterminacy of interpretation or the continuity between literary text and interpretation—show the influence of Jewish approaches to interpretation.

***The Guide of the Perplexed* Keywords:** Hermeneutics, Interpretation Theory, Language, Medieval Theory, Philology, Religion

From The Guide of the Perplexed[1]

From [*Introduction to the First Part*]

Cause me to know the way wherein I should walk,
For unto Thee have I lifted my soul.[2]

Unto you, O men, I call,
And my voice is to the sons of men.[3]

Incline thine ear, and hear the words of the wise,
And apply thy heart unto my knowledge.[4]

The first purpose of this Treatise is to explain the meanings of certain terms occurring in books of prophecy. Some of these terms are equivocal; hence the ignorant attribute to them only one or some of the meanings in which the term in question is used. Others are derivative terms; hence they attribute to them only the original meaning from which the other meaning is derived. Others are amphibolous terms,[5] so that at times they are believed to be univocal and at other times equivocal. It is not the purpose of this Treatise to make its totality understandable to the vulgar or to beginners in speculation, nor to teach those who have not engaged in any study other than the science of the Law—I mean the legalistic study of the Law. For the purpose of this Treatise and of all those like it is the science of Law in its true sense.[6] Or rather its purpose is to give indications to a religious man for whom the validity of our Law has become established in his soul and has become actual in his belief—such a man being perfect in his religion and character, and having studied the sciences of the philosophers and come to know what they signify. The human intellect having drawn him on

1. Translated by Shlomo Pines, who occasionally supplies explanatory text in brackets.
2. Psalms 143.8.
3. Proverbs 8.4.
4. Proverbs 22.17.
5. Words understood as having sometimes one meaning and sometimes many meanings. "Equivocal": words with more than one meaning. "Derivative": words containing supplemental meanings derived from other words; words used figuratively.
6. In an earlier work, the *Mishneh Torah* (literally, "repetition of the Torah"), Maimonides collected, organized, and commented on the oral rabbinic law—called the Mishnah—that had evolved in the first centuries of the common era. In *The Guide of the Perplexed*, he turns his attention to the relationship between Jewish law and philosophy as well as to interpretive theory.

and led him to dwell within its province, he must have felt distressed by the externals of the Law and by the meanings of the above-mentioned equivocal, derivative, or amphibolous terms, as he continued to understand them by himself or was made to understand them by others. Hence he would remain in a state of perplexity and confusion as to whether he should follow his intellect, renounce what he knew concerning the terms in question, and consequently consider that he has renounced the foundations of the Law. Or he should hold fast to his understanding of these terms and not let himself be drawn on together with his intellect, rather turning his back on it and moving away from it, while at the same time perceiving that he had brought loss to himself and harm to his religion. He would be left with those imaginary beliefs to which he owes his fear and difficulty and would not cease to suffer from heartache and great perplexity.

This Treatise also has a second purpose: namely, the explanation of very obscure parables occurring in the books of the prophets, but not explicitly identified there as such. Hence an ignorant or heedless individual might think that they possess only an external sense, but no internal one. However, even when one who truly possesses knowledge considers these parables and interprets them according to their external meaning, he too is overtaken by great perplexity. But if we explain these parables to him or if we draw his attention to their being parables, he will take the right road and be delivered from this perplexity. That is why I have called this Treatise "The Guide of the Perplexed."

I do not say that this Treatise will remove all difficulties for those who understand it. I do, however, say that it will remove most of the difficulties, and those of the greatest moment. A sensible man thus should not demand of me or hope that when we mention a subject, we shall make a complete exposition of it, or that when we engage in the explanation of the meaning of one of the parables, we shall set forth exhaustively all that is expressed in that parable. An intelligent man would be unable to do so even by speaking directly to an interlocutor. How then could he put it down in writing without becoming a butt for every ignoramus who, thinking that he has the necessary knowledge, would let fly at him the shafts of his ignorance? We have already explained in our legal compilations some general propositions concerning this subject and have drawn attention to many themes. Thus we have mentioned there that the *Account of the Beginning*[7] is identical with natural science, and the *Account of the Chariot*[8] with divine science; and have explained the rabbinic saying: *The Account of the Chariot ought not to be taught even to one man, except if he be wise and able to understand by himself, in which case only the chapter headings may be transmitted to him.*[9] Hence you should not ask of me here anything beyond *the chapter headings*. And even those are not set down in order or arranged in coherent fashion in this Treatise, but rather are scattered and entangled with other subjects that are to be clarified. For my purpose is that the truths be glimpsed and then again be concealed, so as not to oppose that

7. Literally, the *Work of the Beginning* [translator's note]. That is, the Genesis story.
8. Literally, the *Work of the Chariot* [translator's note]. That is, Ezekiel 1 and 10.
9. From the Babylonian Talmud, Hagigah, 11b, 13a [translator's note]. The Babylonian Talmud is one of the two great Talmuds, or collections of oral law; it was compiled between the 2d and 5th centuries C.E. (the Jerusalem Talmud was compiled between 220 C.E. and the end of the 4th c.). It is divided into six Orders; each Order has a number of tractates. Hagigah is one of the tractates, which are further divided into chapters and then paragraphs.

divine purpose which one cannot possibly oppose and which has concealed from the vulgar among the people those truths especially requisite for His apprehension. As He has said: *The secret of the Lord is with them that fear Him.*[1] Know that with regard to natural matters as well, it is impossible to give a clear exposition when teaching some of their principles as they are. For you know the saying of [the Sages], *may their memory be blessed: The Account of the Beginning ought not to be taught in the presence of two men.*[2] Now if someone explained all those matters in a book, he in effect would be *teaching* them to thousands of men. Hence these matters too occur in parables in the books of prophecy. The *Sages, may their memory be blessed,* following the trail of these books, likewise have spoken of them in riddles and parables, for there is a close connection between these matters and the divine science, and they too are secrets of that divine science.

You should not think that these great *secrets* are fully and completely known to anyone among us. They are not. But sometimes truth flashes out to us so that we think that it is day, and then matter and habit in their various forms conceal it so that we find ourselves again in an obscure night, almost as we were at first. We are like someone in a very dark night over whom lightning flashes time and time again. Among us there is one[3] for whom the lightning flashes time and time again, so that he is always, as it were, in unceasing light. Thus night appears to him as day. That is the degree of the great one among the prophets, to whom it was said: *But as for thee, stand thou here by Me,*[4] and of whom it was said: *that the skin of his face sent forth beams, and so on.*[5] Among them there is one to whom the lightning flashes only once in the whole of his night; that is the rank of those of whom it is said: *they prophesied, but they did so no more.*[6] There are others between whose lightning flashes there are greater or shorter intervals. Thereafter comes he who does not attain a degree in which his darkness is illumined by any lightning flash. It is illumined, however, by a polished body or something of that kind, stones or something else that give light in the darkness of the night. And even this small light that shines over us is not always there, but flashes and is hidden again, as if it were the *flaming sword which turned every way.*[7] It is in accord with these states that the degrees of the perfect vary. As for those who never even once see a light, but grope about in their night, of them it is said: *They know not, neither do they understand; They go about in darkness.*[8] The truth, in spite of the strength of its manifestation, is entirely hidden from them, as is said of them: *And now men see not the light which is bright in the skies.*[9] They are the vulgar among the people. There is then no occasion to mention them here in this Treatise.

Know that whenever one of the perfect wishes to mention, either orally or in writing, something that he understands of these *secrets*, according to the degree of his perfection, he is unable to explain with complete clarity and coherence even the portion that he has apprehended, as he could do with the other sciences whose teaching is generally recognized. Rather there will befall him when teaching another that which he had undergone when learning

1. Psalm 25.14.
2. Babylonian Talmud, Hagigah, 11b.
3. Or: there are those [translator's note].
4. Deuteronomy 5.31.
5. Exodus 34.29.
6. Numbers 11.25.
7. Genesis 3.24.
8. Psalm 82.5.
9. Job 37.21.

himself. I mean to say that the subject matter will appear, flash, and then be hidden again, as though this were the nature of this subject matter, be there much or little of it. For this reason, all the Sages possessing knowledge of God the Lord, knowers of the truth, when they aimed at teaching something of this subject matter, spoke of it only in parables and riddles. They even multiplied the parables and made them different in species and even in genus. In most cases the subject to be explained was placed in the beginning or in the middle or at the end of the parable; this happened where a parable appropriate for the intended subject from start to finish could not be found. Sometimes the subject intended to be taught to him who was to be instructed was divided—although it was one and the same subject—among many parables remote from one another. Even more obscure is the case of one and the same parable corresponding to several subjects, its beginning fitting one subject and its ending another. Sometimes the whole is a parable referring to two cognate subjects within the particular species of science in question. The situation is such that the exposition of one who wishes to teach without recourse to parables and riddles is so obscure and brief as to make obscurity and brevity serve in place of parables and riddles. The men of knowledge and the sages[1] are drawn, as it were, toward this purpose by the divine will just as they are drawn by their natural circumstances. Do you not see the following fact? God, may His mention be exalted, wished us to be perfected and the state of our societies to be improved by His laws regarding actions. Now this can come about only after the adoption of intellectual beliefs, the first of which being His apprehension, may He be exalted, according to our capacity. This, in its turn, cannot come about except through divine science, and this divine science cannot become actual except after a study of natural science. This is so since natural science borders on divine science, and its study precedes that of divine science in time as has been made clear to whoever has engaged in speculation on these matters. Hence God, may He be exalted, caused His book to open with the *Account of the Beginning*, which, as we have made clear, is natural science. And because of the greatness and importance of the subject and because our capacity falls short of apprehending the greatest of subjects as it really is, we are told about those profound matters—which divine wisdom has deemed necessary to convey to us—in parables and riddles and in very obscure words. As [the Sages], *may their memory be blessed*, have said: *It is impossible to tell mortals*[2] *of the power of the Account of the Beginning. For this reason Scripture tells you obscurely: In the beginning God created, and so on.*[3] They thus have drawn your attention to the fact that the above-mentioned subjects are *obscure*. You likewise know *Solomon's* saying: *That which was is far off, and exceeding deep; who can find it out?*[4] That which is said about all this is in equivocal terms so that the multitude might comprehend them in accord with the capacity of their understanding and the weakness of their representation,

1. The Arabic term *al-ḥukamā*ʾ often designates the philosophers [translator's note].
2. Literally, flesh and blood [translator's note].
3. Cf. Midrash Shnei Ketubim, Batei Midrashoth, IV [translator's note]. Midrash: literally, "to seek out the meaning" (Hebrew); an explanation of a text from the Torah (the 5 books of Moses; known to Christians as the first 5 books of the Old Testament). The term may refer to a collection of such explanations or to a hermeneutic technique by which such explanations are produced. A midrash might explain a single word or a gap in the text. There are midrashim for every book of the Torah, and Maimonides here refers to a midrash on Genesis.
4. Ecclesiastes 7.24.

whereas the perfect man, who is already informed, will comprehend them otherwise.

We had promised in the Commentary on the *Mishnah* that we would explain strange subjects in the "Book of Prophecy" and in the "Book of Correspondence"—the latter being a book in which we promised to explain all the difficult passages in the *Midrashim*[5] where the external sense manifestly contradicts the truth and departs from the intelligible. They are all parables. However, when, many years ago, we began these books and composed a part of them, our beginning to explain matters in this way did not commend itself to us. For we saw that if we should adhere to parables and to concealment of what ought to be concealed, we would not be deviating from the primary purpose. We would, as it were, have replaced one individual by another of the same species. If, on the other hand, we explained what ought to be explained, it would be unsuitable for the vulgar among the people. Now it was to the vulgar that we wanted to explain the import of the *Midrashim* and the external meanings of prophecy. We also saw that if an ignoramus among the multitude of Rabbanites[6] should engage in speculation on these *Midrashim*, he would find nothing difficult in them, inasmuch as a rash fool, devoid of any knowledge of the nature of being, does not find impossibilities hard to accept. If, however, a perfect man of virtue should engage in speculation on them, he cannot escape one of two courses: either he can take the speeches in question in their external sense and, in so doing, think ill of their author and regard him as an ignoramus—in this there is nothing that would upset the foundations of belief; or he can attribute to them an inner meaning, thereby extricating himself from his predicament and being able to think well of the author whether or not the inner meaning of the saying is clear to him. With regard to the meaning of prophecy, the exposition of its various degrees, and the elucidation of the parables occurring in the prophetic books, another manner of explanation is used in this Treatise. In view of these considerations, we have given up composing these two books in the way in which they were begun. We have confined ourselves to mentioning briefly the foundations of belief and general truths, while dropping hints that approach a clear exposition, just as we have set them forth in the great legal compilation, *Mishneh Torah*.[7]

My speech in the present Treatise is directed, as I have mentioned, to one who has philosophized and has knowledge of the true sciences, but believes at the same time in the matters pertaining to the Law and is perplexed as to their meaning because of the uncertain terms and the parables. We shall include in this Treatise some chapters in which there will be no mention of an equivocal term. Such a chapter will be preparatory for another, or it will hint at one of the meanings of an equivocal term that I might not wish to mention explicitly in that place, or it will explain one of the parables or hint at the fact that a certain story is a parable. Such a chapter may contain

5. Maimonides uses here and subsequently the term *drashoth* [translator's note]. The Hebrew term (singular *derash* or *derasha*) refers to the meanings derived from the original text by means of a variety of rabbinic techniques.
6. Tenth-century teachers who began to use philosophy to supplement the written Torah and the oral Torah (Talmud) as a defense against rationalism. Though their philosophical thinking was not as sophisticated as Maimonides' use of Aristotle, they paved the way for him and other Jewish philosophers.
7. Maimonides' massive compilation of Jewish rabbinic law, written a decade before *The Guide of the Perplexed*.

strange matters regarding which the contrary of the truth sometimes is believed, either because of the equivocality of the terms or because a parable is taken for the thing being represented or vice versa.

As I have mentioned parables, we shall make the following introductory remarks: Know that the key to the understanding of all that the prophets, peace be on them, have said, and to the knowledge of its truth, is an understanding of the parables, of their import, and of the meaning of the words occurring in them. You know what God, may He be exalted, has said: *And by the ministry of the prophets have I used similitudes.*[8] And you know that He has said: *Put forth a riddle and speak a parable.*[9] You know too that because of the frequent use prophets make of parables, the prophet has said: *They say of me: Is he not a maker of parables?*[1] You know how *Solomon* began his book: *To understand a proverb, and a figure; The words of the wise, and their dark sayings.*[2] And it said in the *Midrash: To what were the words of the Torah to be compared before the advent of Solomon? To a well the waters of which are at a great depth and cool, yet no man could drink of them. Now what did one clever man do? He joined cord with cord and rope with rope and drew them up and drank. Thus did Solomon say one parable after another and speak one word after another until he understood the meaning of the words of the Torah.*[3] That is literally what they say. I do not think that anyone possessing an unimpaired capacity imagines that the *words of the Torah* referred to here that one contrives to understand through understanding the meaning of parables are ordinances concerning the building of *tabernacles*, the *lulab*, and the *law of four trustees.*[4] Rather what this text has in view here is, without any doubt, the understanding of obscure matters. About this it has been said: *Our Rabbis say: a man who loses a sela or a pearl in his house can find the pearl by lighting a taper worth an issar.*[5] *In the same way this parable in itself is worth nothing, but by means of it you can understand the words of the Torah.*[6] This too is literally what they say. Now consider the explicit affirmation of [the Sages], *may their memory be blessed*, that the internal meaning of the *words of the Torah* is a *pearl* whereas the external meaning of all parables *is* worth *nothing*, and their comparison of the concealment of a subject by its parable's external meaning to a man who let drop a pearl in his house, which was dark and full of furniture. Now this pearl is there, but he does not see it and does not know where it is. It is as though it were no longer in his possession, as it is impossible for him to derive any benefit from it until, as has been mentioned, he lights a lamp—an act to which an understanding of the meaning of the parable corresponds. The Sage has said: *A word fitly spoken is like apples of gold in settings [maskiyyoth] of silver.*[7] Hear now an elucidation

8. Hosea 12.10.
9. Ezekiel 17.2.
1. Ezekiel 20.49.
2. Proverbs 1.6. Proverbs is one of the books of the Bible traditionally ascribed to Solomon.
3. Cf. Midrash on the Song of Songs, 1.1 [translator's note].
4. Maimonides, contrasting those parts of the Torah that can be taken as parables with those that are completely straightforward (not in need of special interpretation), gives three examples of straightforward ordinances. "Tabernacle": a sukkah or building constructed during the holiday of Sukkoth, which occurs after the High Holy Days and commemorates the Jews' wandering in the desert. "Lulab": a wand of sorts, fashioned of palm leaves, willow, and myrtle and waved in four directions during the holiday of Sukkoth. "The law of the four trustees": the four categories of legal guardian over someone else's property, which are the unpaid guardian, the borrower, the paid guardian, and the hirer.
5. A coin; ninety-six *issar* were worth a *sela* [translator's note]. "A *sela*": a silver coin.
6. Cf. Midrash on the Song of Songs, 1.1 [translator's note].
7. Proverbs 25.11.

of the thought that he has set forth. The term *maskiyyoth* denotes filigree traceries; I mean to say traceries in which there are apertures with very small eyelets, like the handiwork of silversmiths. They are so called because a glance penetrates through them; for in the [Aramaic] *translation* of the Bible the Hebrew term *va-yashqeph*—meaning, he glanced—is translated *va-istekhe*.[8] The Sage accordingly said that a saying uttered with a view to two meanings is like an apple of gold overlaid with silver filigree-work having very small holes. Now see how marvellously this dictum describes a well-constructed parable. For he says that in a saying that has two meanings—he means an external and an internal one—the external meaning ought to be as beautiful as silver, while its internal meaning ought to be more beautiful than the external one, the former being in comparison to the latter as gold is to silver. Its external meaning also ought to contain in it something that indicates to someone considering it what is to be found in its internal meaning, as happens in the case of an apple of gold overlaid with silver filigree-work having very small holes. When looked at from a distance or with imperfect attention, it is deemed to be an apple of silver; but when a keen-sighted observer looks at it with full attention, its interior becomes clear to him and he knows that it is of gold. The parables of the prophets, peace be on them, are similar. Their external meaning contains wisdom that is useful in many respects, among which is the welfare of human societies, as is shown by the external meaning of *Proverbs* and of similar sayings. Their internal meaning, on the other hand, contains wisdom that is useful for beliefs concerned with the truth as it is.

Know that the prophetic parables are of two kinds. In some of these parables each word has a meaning, while in others the parable as a whole indicates the whole of the intended meaning. In such a parable very many words are to be found, not every one of which adds something to the intended meaning. They serve rather to embellish the parable and to render it more coherent or to conceal further the intended meaning; hence the speech proceeds in such a way as to accord with everything required by the parable's external meaning. Understand this well.

An example of the first kind of prophetic parable is the following text: *And behold a ladder set up on the earth, and so on*.[9] In this text, the word *ladder* indicates one subject; the words *set up on the earth* indicate a second subject; the words *and the top of it reached to heaven* indicate a third subject; the words *and behold the angels of God* indicate a fourth subject; the word *ascending* indicates a fifth subject; the words *and descending* indicate a sixth subject; and the words *And behold the Lord stood above it* indicate a seventh subject. Thus every word occurring in this parable refers to an additional subject in the complex of subjects represented by the parable as a whole.

An example of the second kind of prophetic parable is the following text: *For at the window of my house I looked forth through my lattice; And I beheld among the thoughtless ones, I discerned among the youths, A young man void of understanding, Passing through the street near her corner, And he went the way to her house; In the twilight, in the evening of the day, In the blackness of night and the darkness. And, behold, there met him a woman With the attire*

8. A verbal form deriving from the same root as the word *maskiyyoth*. Genesis 26.8 [translator's note].

9. Genesis 28.12–13. After the word *earth*, the verses read: *and the top of it reached to heaven; and behold the angels of God ascending and descending on it. And behold the Lord stood above it* [translator's note].

of a harlot, and wily of heart. She is riotous and rebellious, and so on.[1] *Now she is in the streets, now in the broad places, and so on.*[2] *So she caught him, and so on.*[3] *Sacrifices of peace-offerings were due from me, and so on.*[4] *Therefore came I forth to meet thee, and so on.*[5] *I have decked with the coverlets, and so on.*[6] *I have perfumed my bed, and so on.*[7] *Come, let us take our fill of love, and so on.*[8] *For my husband is not at home, and so on.*[9] *The bag of money, and so on.*[1] *With her much fair speech she causeth him to yield. With the blandishment of her lips she enticeth him away.*[2] The outcome of all this is a warning against the pursuit of bodily pleasures and desires. Accordingly he [Solomon] likens matter, which is the cause of all these bodily pleasures, *to a harlot* who is also a *married woman*. In fact his entire book is based on this allegory. And we shall explain in various chapters of this Treatise his wisdom in likening matter to a *married harlot*, and we shall explain how he concluded this book of his with a eulogy of the *woman* who is not a *harlot* but confines herself to attending to the welfare of her household and husband. For all the hindrances keeping man from his ultimate perfection, every deficiency affecting him and every disobedience, come to him from his matter alone, as we shall explain in this Treatise. This is the proposition that can be understood from this parable as a whole. I mean that man should not follow his bestial nature; I mean his matter, for the proximate matter of man is identical with the proximate matter of the other living beings. And as I have explained this to you and disclosed the secret of this parable, you should not hope [to find some signification corresponding to every subject occurring in the parable][3] so that you could say: what can be submitted for the words, *Sacrifices of peace-offerings were due from me; this day have I paid my vows?* What subject is indicated by the words, *I have decked my couch with coverlets?* And what subject is added to this general proposition by the words, *For my husband is not at home?* The same holds good for the other details in this *chapter*. For all of them only figure in the consistent development of the parable's external meaning, the circumstances described in it being of a kind typical for adulterers. Also the spoken words and other such details are of a kind typical of words spoken among adulterers. Understand this well from what I have said for it is a great and important principle with regard to matters that I wish to explain.

When, therefore, you find that in some chapter of this Treatise I have explained the meaning of a parable and have drawn your attention to the general proposition signified by it, you should not inquire into all the details occurring in the parable, nor should you wish to find significations corresponding to them. For doing so would lead you into one of two ways: either into turning aside from the parable's intended subject, or into assuming an

1. The omitted words are: *her feet abide not in her house* [translator's note].
2. The omitted words are: *and lieth in wait at every corner* [translator's note].
3. The omitted words are: *and kissed him, and with impudent face she said unto him* [translator's note].
4. The omitted words are: *this day have I paid my vows* [translator's note].
5. The omitted words are: *diligently to seek thy face, and I have found thee* [translator's note].
6. The omitted words are: *my bed, with striped cloths of the yarn of Egypt* [translator's note].
7. The omitted words are: *with myrrh, aloes and cinnamon* [translator's note].
8. The omitted words are: *until the morning; let us solace ourselves with loves* [translator's note].
9. The omitted words are: *he is gone a long journey* [translator's note].
1. The omitted words are: *he has taken with him, and will come home at the full moon* [translator's note].
2. Proverbs 7.6–21.
3. The words enclosed in brackets appear in Ibn Tibbon's Hebrew translation, but not in the printed Arabic text. There is little doubt that in this case Ibn Tibbon's text is more correct [translator's note].

obligation to interpret things not susceptible of interpretation and that have not been inserted with a view to interpretation. The assumption of such an obligation would result in extravagant fantasies such as are entertained and written about in our time by most of the sects of the world, since each of these sects desires to find certain significations for words whose author in no wise had in mind the significations wished by them. Your purpose, rather, should always be to know, regarding most parables, the whole that was intended to be known. In some matters it will suffice you to gather from my remarks that a given story is a parable, even if we explain nothing more; for once you know it is a parable, it will immediately become clear to you what it is a parable of. My remarking that it is a parable will be like someone's removing a screen from between the eye and a visible thing.

* * *

1190

THOMAS AQUINAS
1225–1274

Thomas Aquinas's *Summa Theologica*, also known as *Summa Theologiae*, with its compelling synthesis of faith and reason, of Platonism and Aristotelianism, of Hellenistic and Christian thought, marks the high point of the Scholastic philosophy and theology of the European Middle Ages. But it may be difficult to imagine that Aquinas, the medieval philosopher most widely read today, could have much to say about poetics, which he relegates in the *Summa* to "the least of all the sciences." Yet when read against the backdrop of the so-called commentary tradition, the tradition of allegorical interpretation of biblical and secular texts, Aquinas's writings on biblical exegesis force a reevaluation of our portrait of the saint as a prosaic logician. Early in the *Summa*, Aquinas wrestles with a problem that has continued to perplex both literary critics and philosophers of language: how to reconcile the indeterminacy of figurative language (such as poetic metaphor) with a belief in the ability of language to guarantee stable reference and access to truth and reality. If language cannot guarantee that the intentions of its author—whether divine or human—can be known, then how can it function as a vehicle of knowledge? The centrality of this question to contemporary debates over the nature of language and signification makes Aquinas's uneasy resolution of it—his insistence on both the multiplicity of meaning and the stability of reference in the biblical text—all the more interesting.

Thomas Aquinas (Tommaso d'Aquino) was born in his father's castle in Roccasecca in central Italy, the youngest son of a noble family. At the age of five he was sent to the Benedictine monastery of Monte Cassino to begin his education, and in 1236 he entered the University of Naples. Some time between 1240 and 1243, against his parents' wishes, he decided to join the Dominican friars, an order founded in 1205 and dedicated to learning and preaching. On the way to Rome he was abducted by his brothers and imprisoned for two years at the castle of San Giovanni, where his family tried everything—including hiring a prostitute to seduce him—to break his will. When his family finally relented, Thomas took his vows; he was sent to Cologne, Germany, in 1244 where he continued his education under the direction of Albertus Magnus, the most famous scholar of the order. Thomas's taciturnity as a student earned him a reputation for dullness, though Albertus, on hearing him defend a difficult thesis, is reported to have said, "We call this young man a dumb ox, but his bellowing in doctrine will one day resound throughout the world."

In 1245 Thomas accompanied Albertus to Paris as a student. In 1248, when a new *studium generale* (a school founded by the Dominicans for the teaching of theology) was opened in Cologne, Albertus returned as its master. Thomas went with him to serve as a bachelor, or subregent, under him. While in Cologne, in 1250, he was ordained a priest by the city's archbishop. In 1252 Thomas was sent to Paris to fill the position of bachelor at the *studium generale* in that city. His primary duty was teaching the *Sentences* of Peter Lombard (ca. 1100–1160), the basic textbook for all theology courses in the Middle Ages, and his commentaries on that book would later furnish the materials and plan for his chief work, the *Summa Theologica*. In 1257 Thomas took the degree of doctor in theology from the University of Paris and was subsequently appointed regent (or master) in theology, a position he held until 1259. The years between 1259 and 1265 are not well documented; most likely he spent them teaching, preaching, writing, and traveling throughout Europe. In 1265 he went to Rome to serve as regent of the *studium generale* founded there, and in 1268 the order sent him back to the University of Paris. In 1274, while traveling to the Council of Lyons, he fell ill. He was taken to the monastery of Fossanova, where he died on March 7. He was canonized a saint on July 18, 1323.

Aquinas composed more than sixty books on philosophy, theology, ethics, and exegesis. His exegetical works include commentaries on various books of the Bible, including Job, the Psalms, Isaiah, Jeremiah, the Epistles of St. Paul, and his *Catena Aurea* (a commentary on all four Gospels). His philosophical works include thirteen commentaries on ARISTOTLE, which were instrumental in the efforts of Christian scholarship to assimilate the Greek philosopher's newly discovered works. His *Summa contra Gentiles* (1261–64) was a defense of the Christian faith against the Jews and Muslims of Spain, whose scholarship was central to the recovery of Aristotle's writing in thirteenth-century Europe. This work reveals the breadth and depth of his understanding of the Jewish and Islamic philosophy of the period, especially that of MAIMONIDES (1135–1204) and the great Islamic philosopher Avicenna (980–1037). Far and away his greatest work, however, is the twenty-two-volume *Summa Theologica* (1265–73), an encyclopedic compendium, left unfinished at his death, designed to organize systematically and to explicate all of Christian theology and philosophy.

In his prologue to the *Summa*, Aquinas explains, "we shall endeavor, confiding in the Divine assistance, to treat of these things that pertain to sacred doctrine with brevity and clearness, in so far as the subject to be treated will permit." The fourfold method Aquinas follows, a method identified with Scholasticism, is first to pose a yes-or-no question, next to offer all of the arguments for the no position, then to present the contrary argument, and finally to supply a complete defense of his own position by replying to the objections outlined at the beginning. This form is illustrated in the selection below.

Very early in the *Summa*, in articles 9 and 10 of question 1, "On Sacred Doctrine: What Kind It Is and What It Covers," Aquinas deals with problems of interpretation that have occupied literary critics from ancient and medieval Christian and Jewish exegetes down to poststructuralist theorists like JACQUES DERRIDA. He wishes not only to explain the obscurities and ambiguities of biblical texts but also to understand the theoretical consequences of figurative language in a text that claims privileged authorship. Aquinas, like other medieval religious writers, has inherited the Platonic distrust of poetry—which is, in part, a distrust of the multiplicity of meaning and the instability of linguistic reference. The divine text, he argues, must "make truth clear," while figurative language obscures truth. Yet Scriptures use figurative language frequently; thus Aquinas must struggle to reconcile this kind of unstable language with the authority and infallibility of the sacred biblical word.

While poetry uses metaphors "for the sake of lively description," Aquinas argues, Scriptures use them of necessity. While poetry promotes deception, Scriptures reveal spiritual truths through corporeal metaphors. He offers three defenses of Scriptures' use of figurative language, which will find their way into the Italian poet-critic BOCCACCIO's defense of poetry in the fourteenth century. For Aquinas, the figurative language of Scriptures exercises the thoughtful mind, serves as a defense against the "ridicule of the impious," and preserves readers from error because it appeals to the senses to guide them to the intelligible. Like AUGUSTINE, Aquinas endorses the possibility that the Bible contains multiple meanings, while maintaining that such multiplicity does not lead to indeterminacy.

For Aquinas, as for such twelfth-century predecessors as Hugh of St. Victor (1097–1141) and Bernardus Silvestris (d. ca. 1160), biblical meanings are organized systematically and hierarchically on four levels that Aquinas enumerates in article 10: (1) the historical or literal; (2) the allegorical, which refers to the spiritual meaning in which the Old Law (Old Testament) prefigures the New (New Testament); (3) the tropological, which provides an edifying moral message; and (4) the anagogical, which refers to eschatology, or the end of time. While this system of biblical interpretation was first articulated by John Cassian in the fourth century and was introduced in the Latin West by Augustine in *On the Usefulness of Belief*, it reached the height of its popularity in the twelfth century in treatises like Hugh's *Didascalicon*. What sets Aquinas apart from his predecessors is his decidedly non-Platonic insistence that all interpretation of biblical texts must proceed from the literal sense alone. In fact, drawing on Augustine's *Usefulness of Belief*, Aquinas goes on to distinguish four different types of the literal sense of the Bible—history, etiology (the origin or cause of a statement), analogy (showing the agreement of the Old and New Testament), and parable. Aquinas's claim that nothing necessary to faith is conveyed through the allegorical senses of the Bible that is not conveyed clearly and openly through the literal sense would seem at odds with his endorsement of multiple meanings, since the obvious consequence of literal reading would be to render the techniques of *allēgorēsis* redundant. Indeed, there are some scholars who have argued that Aquinas's literal reading of Scriptures led to the rejection of allegorical readings of the Bible during the Reformation. Yet in their effort to come to terms with the difficulties of biblical language, Aquinas and other medieval exegetes developed conventions of interpretation that would influence all subsequent literary criticism long after the fourfold scheme of allegory was forgotten. Among these conventions is the practice of searching for "hidden" meanings in the text and the tendency to value literary texts for their multiplicity and complexity of meaning.

Aquinas occupies a pivotal position between the Neoplatonic exegetes of the twelfth century, philosopher-theologians such as Hugh of St. Victor and Bernardus Silvestris who wrote in Latin for a primarily clerical audience, and Italian poet-critics such as DANTE and Boccaccio, who, writing in Italian, would literally invent vernacular literary criticism in the fourteenth. Twelfth-century exegetes (Hugh may be the exception here) believed, with Augustine, that meaning had been hidden in the biblical text by God, so they subordinated the literal sense of the text to its allegorical senses in much the same way that Neoplatonists subordinated the material world to the transcendental world of forms (see PLATO). The revival of interest in Aristotle in the thirteenth century had profound consequences for the study of signification in both biblical and secular texts. Aquinas's more Aristotelian analyses of Scriptures privilege the literal over allegorical sense; and because the literal sense was identified with the expression of the author's intention, his remarks on biblical commentary set the stage for the appreciation of the individual poet's style apparent in the landmark fourteenth-century Italian criticism of Dante and Boccaccio.

Summa Theologica **Keywords:** Hermeneutics, Interpretation Theory, Language, Medieval Theory, Religion

From Summa Theologica[1]

From *Question I*

NINTH ARTICLE
WHETHER HOLY SCRIPTURE SHOULD USE METAPHORS?

We proceed thus to the Ninth Article:—

Objection 1. It seems that the Holy Scripture should not use metaphors. For that which is proper to the lowest science seems not to befit this science, which holds the highest place of all. But to proceed by the aid of various similitudes and figures is proper to poetry, the least of all the sciences. Therefore it is not fitting that this science should make use of such similitudes.

Obj. 2. Further, this doctrine seems to be intended to make truth clear. Hence a reward is held out to those who manifest it: *They that explain me shall have life everlasting.*[2] But by such similitudes truth is obscured. Therefore to put forward divine truths by likening them to corporeal things does not befit this science.

Obj. 3. Further, the higher creatures are, the nearer they approach to the divine likeness. If therefore any creature be taken to represent God, this representation ought chiefly to be taken from the higher creatures, and not from the lower; yet this is often found in the Scriptures.

On the contrary, It is written: *I have multiplied visions, and I have used similitudes by the ministry of the prophets.*[3] But to put forward anything by means of similitudes is to use metaphors. Therefore this sacred science may use metaphors.

I answer that, It is befitting Holy Writ to put forward divine and spiritual truths by means of comparisons with material things. For God provides for everything according to the capacity of its nature. Now it is natural to man to attain to intellectual truths through sensible objects, because all our knowledge originates from sense. Hence in Holy Writ spiritual truths are fittingly taught under the likeness of material things. This is what Dionysius says: *We cannot be enlightened by the divine rays except they be hidden within the covering of many sacred veils.*[4] It is also befitting Holy Writ, which is proposed to all without distinction of persons—*To the wise and to the unwise I am a debtor*[5]—that spiritual truths be expounded by means of figures taken from corporeal things, in order that thereby even the simple who are unable by themselves to grasp intellectual things may be able to understand it.

Reply Obj. 1. Poetry makes use of metaphors to produce a representation, for it is natural to man to be pleased with representations. But sacred doctrine makes use of metaphors as both necessary and useful.

Reply Obj. 2. The ray of divine revelation is not extinguished by the sensible imagery wherewith it is veiled, as Dionysius says;[6] and its truth so far

1. Translated by Fathers of the English Dominican Province.
2. Ecclesiasticus 24.31.
3. Hosea 12.10.
4. From *The Celestial Hierarchy* 1 [translator's note]. Its author, Pseudo-Dionysius, was a Neoplatonic writer of late 5th-century Syria who successfully passed himself off as Dionysius the Areopagite, whose conversion by St. Paul is recorded in Acts 17.34. His writing was influenced by Plotinus (ca. 204/5–270 C.E.), who is regarded as the founder of Neoplatonism.
5. Romans 1.14.
6. *Celestial Hierarchy* 1 [translator's note].

remains that it does not allow the minds of those to whom the revelation has been made, to rest in the metaphors, but raises them to the knowledge of truths; and through those to whom the revelation has been made others also may receive instruction in these matters. Hence those things that are taught metaphorically in one part of Scripture, in other parts are taught more openly. The very hiding of truth in figures is useful for the exercise of thoughtful minds, and as a defence against the ridicule of the impious, according to the words *Give not that which is holy to dogs*.[7]

Reply Obj. 3. As Dionysius says,[8] it is more fitting that divine truths should be expounded under the figure of less noble than of nobler bodies, and this for three reasons. Firstly, because thereby men's minds are the better preserved from error. For then it is clear that these things are not literal descriptions of divine truths, which might have been open to doubt had they been expressed under the figure of nobler bodies, especially for those who could think of nothing nobler than bodies. Secondly, because this is more befitting the knowledge of God that we have in this life. For what He is not is clearer to us than what He is. Therefore similitudes drawn from things farthest away from God form within us a truer estimate that God is above whatsoever we may say or think of Him. Thirdly, because thereby divine truths are the better hidden from the unworthy.[9]

TENTH ARTICLE
WHETHER IN HOLY SCRIPTURE A WORD MAY HAVE SEVERAL SENSES?

We proceed thus to the Tenth Article:—

Objection 1. It seems that in Holy Writ a word cannot have several senses, historical or literal, allegorical, tropological or moral, and anagogical. For many different senses in one text produce confusion and deception and destroy all force of argument. Hence no argument, but only fallacies, can be deduced from a multiplicity of propositions. But Holy Writ ought to be able to state the truth without any fallacy. Therefore in it there cannot be several senses to a word.

Obj. 2. Further, Augustine says that *the Old Testament has a fourfold division as to history, etiology, analogy, and allegory*.[1] Now these four seem altogether different from the four divisions mentioned in the first objection. Therefore it does not seem fitting to explain the same word of Holy Writ according to the four different senses mentioned above.

Obj. 3. Further, besides these senses, there is the parabolical,[2] which is not one of these four.

On the contrary, Gregory says: *Holy Writ by the manner of its speech transcends every science, because in one and the same sentence, while it describes a fact, it reveals a mystery*.[3]

7. Matthew 7.6.
8. *Celestial Hierarchy* 1 [translator's note].
9. In his reply to objection 3, Aquinas expresses some traditional justifications for using figurative language when speaking of God. Some, including the argument that such language obscures divine truths from the unworthy, are repeated in BOCCACCIO's defense of poetry in *Genealogy of the Gentile Gods* (1350–62; see below). There is a paradox involved in Aquinas's explanation that we know God better negatively through what he is *not* than through what he *is*, which we can never comprehend.
1. *On the Usefulness of Belief* 3 [translator's note]. AUGUSTINE (354–430), early Christian philosopher and theologian.
2. Expressed in a parable.
3. From *Moralia in Job* 20.1 [translator's note], by Pope Gregory I (540–604).

I answer that, The author of Holy Writ is God, in whose power it is to signify His meaning, not by words only (as man also can do), but also by things themselves. So, whereas in every other science things are signified by words, this science has the property that the things signified by the words have themselves also a signification. Therefore that first signification whereby words signify things belongs to the first sense, the historical or literal. That signification whereby things signified by words have themselves also a signification is called the spiritual sense, which is based on the literal, and presupposes it. Now this spiritual sense has a threefold division. For as the Apostle says the Old Law is a figure of the New Law,[4] and Dionysius says *the New Law itself is a figure of future glory.*[5] Again, in the New Law, whatever our Head has done is a type of what we ought to do. Therefore, so far as the things of the Old Law signify the things of the New Law, there is the allegorical sense; so far as the things done in Christ, or so far as the things which signify Christ, are types of what we ought to do, there is the moral sense. But so far as they signify what relates to eternal glory, there is the anagogical sense. Since the literal sense is that which the author intends, and since the author of Holy Writ is God, Who by one act comprehends all things by His intellect, it is not unfitting, as Augustine says, if, even according to the literal sense, one word in Holy Writ should have several senses.[6]

Reply Obj. 1. The multiplicity of these senses does not produce equivocation or any other kind of multiplicity, seeing that these senses are not multiplied because one word signifies several things; but because the things signified by the words can be themselves types of other things. Thus in Holy Writ no confusion results, for all the senses are founded on one—the literal—from which alone can any argument be drawn, and not from those intended in allegory, as Augustine says.[7] Nevertheless, nothing of Holy Scripture perishes on account of this, since nothing necessary to faith is contained under the spiritual sense which is not elsewhere put forward by the Scripture in its literal sense.

Reply Obj. 2. These three—history, etiology, analogy—are grouped under the literal sense. For it is called history, as Augustine expounds,[8] whenever anything is simply related; it is called etiology when its cause is assigned, as when Our Lord gave the reason why Moses allowed the putting away of wives—namely, on account of the hardness of men's hearts; it is called analogy whenever the truth of one text of Scripture is shown not to contradict the truth of another. Of these four, allegory alone stands for the three spiritual senses. Thus Hugh of St. Victor[9] includes the anagogical under the allegorical sense, laying down three senses only—the historical, the allegorical, and the tropological.

Reply Obj. 3. The parabolical sense is contained in the literal, for by words things are signified properly and figuratively. Nor is the figure itself, but that which is figured, the literal sense. When Scripture speaks of God's arm, the literal sense is not that God has such a member, but only what is signified by

4. A rough paraphrase of Hebrews 10.1.
5. *Celestial Hierarchy* 1 [translator's note].
6. *Confessions* 12.31.42 [translator's note].
7. *Epistles* 93.8.42 (Augustine's letter against the Donatists, a heretical Christian sect of the 4th and 5th centuries).
8. *Epistles* 93.8.24.
9. *De Sacramentis*, 4.4, prologue [translator's note]. Hugh of St. Victor (ca. 1097–1141), educator and biblical commentator.

this member, namely, operative power. Hence it is plain that nothing false can ever underlie the literal sense of Holy Writ.

1265–73

DANTE ALIGHIERI
1265–1321

The Divine Comedy (1307–21) secured Dante's reputation as the greatest poet of the Middle Ages; his literary criticism marks him as the first major theorist of European vernacular literature. Yet the relationship between Dante's masterpiece and his comments on poetics has vexed scholars throughout the modern period. How could a work as monumental and groundbreaking as *The Divine Comedy* be the product of as derivative and seemingly reductive a poetics as that described in his famous letter to Can Grande della Scala (1319)? Many have denied the authenticity of this letter, believing that the theologically driven allegory depicted there could not have been the basis for so great a poem. Such a position, however, neglects the subtleties of Dante's adaptation of the techniques of biblical exegesis to poetry. At the heart of these debates are questions about the nature and status of allegorical representation that have perennially engaged critics, including contemporary figures such as ERICH AUERBACH and PAUL DE MAN.

Much of Dante's literary criticism is derivative of the great twelfth- and thirteenth-century biblical scholars who preceded him—especially THOMAS AQUINAS, to whom he is most immediately indebted. But he is the first to make the intellectual achievements of medieval Latin culture accessible to those who did not know Latin and, just as significantly, to apply them to secular texts that could circulate among a growing audience of vernacular readers. In his *Eloquence in the Vernacular Tongue* (ca. 1304–08), Dante writes, "I see that such eloquence is unquestionably needed by almost everyone, for not only men, but even women and children (to the extent their nature allows) strive for it." His goal as a critic was to "enlighten the discernment of those who, like the blind, roam the streets thinking for the most part that what is really behind is in front." In fourteenth-century Europe, Dante's defense of Italian, his own vernacular, as an appropriate vehicle for poetry was innovative; indeed, the debate continued to rage long after—taken up, for example, by JOACHIM DU BELLAY in sixteenth-century France, JOHN DRYDEN in seventeenth-century England, and NGUGI WĂ THIONG'O in twentieth-century Kenya. In addition, Dante's remarks on the polysemous nature of poetic language continue to resound within present-day debates about allegory.

Dante Alighieri was born in Florence to a family that was neither wealthy nor especially prominent. His father, Alighiero di Bellincione d'Alighiero, was a member of the lesser nobility. Little is known about Dante's early education, though he probably received elementary instruction in grammar, language, and philosophy. Later he was a pupil of the Florentine encyclopedist, statesman, and poet Brunetto Latini, who, in the *The Divine Comedy*, is confined to the seventh circle of Hell for his sins against nature (sodomy). Under Latini's direction, Dante studied literature and rhetoric and associated himself with several respected Florentine poets, including Guido Cavalcanti. In 1283 he inherited a modest amount of money from his parents, and two years later he married Gemma Donati, who bore him four children. The death in 1290 of his childhood friend Beatrice Portinari proved to be a turning point in Dante's life, propelling him to begin an intense study of the philosophical works of Boethius (480–524 c.e.), Cicero (106–43 b.c.e.), and aristotle (384–322 b.c.e.). It also resulted in the appearance of his only work to be written in Florence. Dante's commemoration of Beatrice's death, *La Vita Nuova* (ca. 1295, *The New Life*), was a new, innovative approach to love poetry that equated love with mystical and spiritual revelation. His memorialization of Beatrice would continue in *The Divine Comedy*, where she serves as his guide to redemption in the concluding third volume, *Paradiso*.

In the last decade of the thirteenth century, Dante became involved in Florence's increasingly violent politics. For much of the late thirteenth century Italy was engulfed in a civil war between the Ghibellines (a party favoring imperial rule for Italy) and the Guelphs (a party advocating control by the papacy). By the time of Dante's birth, Florence had become a Guelph stronghold; but the Guelph party itself had split into two factions, the White and the Black, divided more by competing family loyalties than by opposing political philosophies. In 1295 Dante, a supporter of the White Guelphs, got entangled in the city's politics by enrolling in the Guild of Doctors and Pharmacists. A year later he participated in a citizen's government known as the Council of the Hundred. He was elected for a term as one of the six priors, or magistrates, of Florence in 1300. By 1302, however, the Black Guelphs had begun to displace the Whites in Florentine politics, and Dante was exiled on pain of death if he returned to Florence. He spent the next few years wandering around Italy, during which time he produced both *De Vulgari Eloquentia* (*Eloquence in the Vernacular Tongue*), a theoretical and practical defense of the literary uses of the vernacular (written, ironically, in Latin), and *Il Convivio* (1306–09, *The Banquet*), an encyclopedic collection of *canzoni* (or short poems) followed by related prose commentaries on philosophy. Both projects were abandoned before they were completed, probably because as early as 1306 Dante became caught up in the plan of *The Divine Comedy*.

By 1312 Dante took up residence in Verona, where he sought the patronage of that city's imperial vicar, Can Grande della Scala, a member of the powerful Scaliger family. There he wrote most of his greatest work, *The Divine Comedy*, dedicating its final volume, the *Paradiso*, to his patron. *De Monarchia*, a political treatise, was most likely written around 1317. Dante spent the last three years of his life in Ravenna; he died without having ever returned to his native Florence.

In our selections, Dante confronts the problem of how to understand and construe textual meaning. Both his encyclopedic treatise *Il Convivio* and his famous letter dedicating the *Paradiso* to his patron, Can Grande della Scala, examine the relationship between general critical principles and the detailed interpretation of specific parts of a text. Dante is remarkably consistent in his descriptions of how poetry is to be read and interpreted. He extends to vernacular poetry the four senses of allegorical interpretation—the literal, the allegorical, the moral, and the anagogical—articulated in earlier medieval commentaries on biblical texts. In doing so, he effects a synthesis between the "allegory of the poets," or the allegories that Christian writers such as Bernardus Silvestris (d. ca. 1160) attributed to pagan poets such as Virgil, and the "allegory of the theologians," or the interpretations of Scriptures developed by exegetes such as Hugh of St. Victor (ca. 1097–1141) and Aquinas. Although in classical rhetoric *allegory* involves saying one thing while meaning another, Dante insists that his allegories are not simple substitution codes (this is how Bernardus earlier understands Virgil's *Aeneid*). Instead, each of the four "senses" of the text inheres in and evokes the other three simultaneously. The text is polysemous: that is, it has many meanings—including the literal—that occur in a single imaginative act. Dante's commentaries demonstrate that textual exegesis (explication) was not expected to follow the theory of allegorical "senses" in any dogmatic or wooden way. That a poem could be interpreted literally and in three figurative senses (allegorical, moral, and anagogical) does not imply that every episode or every symbol must contain all four meanings. Dante offers a more subtle approach. Much of the richness of *The Divine Comedy*, for example, derives from the gap allegory opens up between the sign and what it might signify. The promise of stable signification seemingly held out by the allegorical method is offset by his claim that the text is polysemous, open to many meanings. This recurring paradox has also fascinated present-day critics of allegory, who are generally more interested than was Dante in the destabilization of meaning that accompanies the possibility of multiple meanings.

***Il Convivio* Keywords:** Hermeneutics, Interpretation Theory, Medieval Theory, Poetry, Religion
"The Letter to Can Grande" Keywords: Hermeneutics, Interpretation Theory, Medieval Theory, Poetry, Vernacular Language

From Il Convivio[1]

From *Book Two*

CHAPTER 1

Now that by way of a preface my bread has been sufficiently prepared in the preceding book through my own assistance, time calls and requires my ship to leave port; thus, having set the sail of my reason to the breeze of my desire, I enter upon the open sea with the hope of a smooth voyage and a safe and praiseworthy port at the end of my feast. But so that this food of mine may be more profitable, I wish to show, before it appears, how the first course must be eaten.[2]

As I stated in the first chapter, this exposition must be both literal and allegorical. To convey what this means, it is necessary to know that writings can be understood and ought to be expounded principally in four senses. The first is called the literal, and this is the sense that does not go beyond the surface of the letter, as in the fables of the poets. The next is called the allegorical, and this is the one that is hidden beneath the cloak of these fables, and is a truth hidden beneath a beautiful fiction. Thus Ovid says that with his lyre Orpheus tamed wild beasts and made trees and rocks move toward him,[3] which is to say that the wise man with the instrument of his voice makes cruel hearts grow tender and humble and moves to his will those who do not devote their lives to knowledge and art; and those who have no rational life whatsoever are almost like stones. Why this kind of concealment was devised by the wise will be shown in the penultimate book. Indeed the theologians take this sense otherwise than do the poets; but since it is my intention here to follow the method of the poets, I shall take the allegorical sense according to the usage of the poets.[4]

1. Translated by Richard H. Lansing.
2. In the allegorical framework of *Il Convivio*, Dante uses the conceit of a banquet to represent human knowledge. Like Boethius's *Consolation of Philosophy* (ca. 524 C.E.), *Il Convivio* employs a combination of verse and prose commentary called *prosimetrum*. In Dante's allegorical banquet, the "meat" is the *canzoni*, or verses, and the "bread" the commentaries on those verses.
3. Ovid (43 B.C.E.–17 C.E.), *Metamorphoses* 11.1–2. In Greek mythology, Orpheus was the greatest of all mortal musicians.
4. What Dante means by distinguishing between the allegory of the poets and the allegory of the theologians is not entirely clear and has given rise to endless speculation. The theologians insist on the veracity of all four levels of meaning, and conceived of the allegorical levels (the typological, tropological, and anagogical) to depend on a literal level which was historically true. In the allegory of the poets, as exemplified by the allusion to the myth of Orpheus, the literal level is a "bella menzongna," a beautiful fiction having no basis in historical reality. In the allegory of the theologians, moreover, the second level always refers to some aspect of Christ's historical being, of which he is the ideal type, which is not the case with the poets. The third and fourth levels are shared in common by both modes of allegory [translator's note].

The third sense is called moral, and this is the sense that teachers should intently seek to discover throughout the scriptures, for their own profit and that of their pupils; as, for example, in the Gospel we may discover that when Christ ascended the mountain to be transfigured, of the twelve Apostles he took with him but three, the moral meaning of which is that in matters of great secrecy we should have few companions.[5]

The fourth sense is called anagogical, that is to say, beyond the senses; and this occurs when a scripture is expounded in a spiritual sense which, although it is true also in the literal sense, signifies by means of the things signified a part of the supernal things of eternal glory, as may be seen in the song of the Prophet which says that when the people of Israel went out of Egypt, Judea was made whole and free.[6] For although it is manifestly true according to the letter, that which is spiritually intended is no less true, namely, that when the soul departs from sin it is made whole and free in its power. In this kind of explication, the literal should always come first, as being the sense in whose meaning the others are enclosed, and without which it would be impossible and illogical to attend to the other senses, and especially the allegorical. It would be impossible because in everything that has an inside and an outside it is impossible to arrive at the inside without first arriving at the outside; consequently, since in what is written down the literal meaning is always the outside, it is impossible to arrive at the other senses, especially the allegorical, without first arriving at the literal.

Moreover, it would be impossible because in every natural or artificial thing it is impossible to proceed to the form unless the subject on which the form must be imposed is prepared first—just as it is impossible for a piece of jewelry to acquire its form if the material (that is, its subject) is not first arranged and prepared, or a chest to acquire its form if the material (that is, the wood) is not first arranged and prepared. Consequently, since the literal meaning is always the subject and material of the other senses, especially of the allegorical, it is impossible to come to an understanding of them before coming to an understanding of it. Moreover, it would be impossible because in every natural or artificial thing it is impossible to proceed unless the foundation is laid first, as in a house or in studying; consequently, since explication is the building up of knowledge, and the explication of the literal sense is the foundation of the others, especially of the allegorical, it is impossible to arrive at the other senses without first arriving at it.

Moreover, even supposing it were possible, it would be illogical, that is to say out of order, and would therefore be carried out with great labor and much confusion. Consequently as the Philosopher says in the first book of the *Physics*,[7] nature wills that we proceed in due order in our learning, that is, by proceeding from that which we know better to that which we know not so well; I say that nature wills it since this way of learning is by nature innate in us. Therefore if the senses other than the literal are less understood (which they are, as is quite apparent), it would be illogical to proceed to explain them if the literal had not been explicated first. For these reasons, therefore, I shall on each occasion discuss first the literal meaning

5. The apostles Peter, James, and John; see Matthew 17.1–8, Mark 9.1–7, Luke 9.28–36 [translator's note].

6. Psalm 114; Dante refers to this same psalm in his "Letter to Can Grande" (below).

7. Aristotle, *Physics* 1.1, 184a17–21.

concerning each canzone, and afterwards I shall discuss its allegory (that is, the hidden truth), at times touching on the other senses, when opportune, as time and place deem proper.

1306–09

From The Letter to Can Grande[1]

* * *

[6] Therefore, if one should wish to present an introduction to a part of a work, it is necessary to present some conception of the whole work of which it is a part. For this reason I, who wish to present something in the form of an introduction to the above-mentioned part of the whole *Comedy*, have decided to preface it with some discussion of the whole work, in order to make the approach to the part easier and more complete.[2] There are six questions, then, which should be asked at the beginning about any doctrinal work: what is its subject, its form, its agent, its end, the title of the book, and its branch of philosophy. In three cases the answers to these questions will be different for the part of the work I propose to give you than for the whole, that is, in the cases of its subject, form, and title, while in the other three, as will be clear upon inspection, they will be the same. Thus these first three should be specifically asked in a discussion of the whole work, after which the way will be clear for an introduction to the part. Let us, then, ask the last three questions not only about the whole but also about the offered part itself.

[7] For the clarification of what I am going to say, then, it should be understood that there is not just a single sense in this work:[3] it might rather be called *polysemous*, that is, having several senses. For the first sense is that which is contained in the letter, while there is another which is contained in what is signified by the letter. The first is called literal, while the second is called allegorical, or moral or anagogical. And in order to make this manner of treatment clear, it can be applied to the following verses: "When Israel went out of Egypt, the house of Jacob from a barbarous people, Judea was made his sanctuary, Israel his dominion."[4] Now if we look at the letter alone, what is signified to us is the departure of the sons of Israel from Egypt during the time of Moses; if at the allegory, what is signified to us is our redemption through Christ; if at the moral sense, what is signified to us is the conversion of the soul from the sorrow and misery of sin to the state of grace; if at the anagogical, what is signified to us is the departure of the sanctified soul from bondage to the corruption of this world into the freedom of eternal glory. And although these mystical senses are called by various names, they may all be called allegorical, since they are all different from the literal or historical. For allegory is derived from the Greek *alleon*, which means in Latin *alienus* ("belonging to another") or *diversus* ("different").

1. Translated by Robert Haller. Can Grande della Scala (1287–1329), the imperial vicar of Verona, was Dante's patron; his name means "Big Dog."
2. Dante dedicated the third volume of *The Divine Comedy*, the *Paradiso*, to Can Grande; the letter serves as an introduction to that part of the poem.
3. *The Divine Comedy*.
4. Psalm 114.1–2; Dante uses the same psalm to illustrate the anagogical level of meaning in *Il Convivio* (see above).

[8] This being established, it is clear that the subject about which these two senses play must also be twofold. And thus it should first be noted what the subject of the work is when taken according to the letter, and then what its subject is when understood allegorically. The subject of the whole work, then, taken literally, is the state of souls after death, understood in a simple sense; for the movement of the whole work turns upon this and about this. If on the other hand the work is taken allegorically, the subject is man, in the exercise of his free will, earning or becoming liable to the rewards or punishments of justice.

* * *

[10] The title of the work is, "Here begins the Comedy of Dante Alighieri, a Florentine by birth but not in character." To understand the title, it must be known that comedy is derived from *comos*, "a village," and from *oda*, "a song," so that a comedy is, so to speak, "a rustic song."[5] Comedy, then, is a certain genre of poetic narrative differing from all others. For it differs from tragedy in its matter, in that tragedy is tranquil and conducive to wonder at the beginning, but foul and conducive to horror at the end, or catastrophe, for which reason it is derived from *tragos*, meaning "goat," and *oda*, making it, as it were, a "goat song," that is, foul as a goat is foul. This is evident in Seneca's[6] tragedies. Comedy, on the other hand, introduces a situation of adversity, but ends its matter in prosperity, as is evident in Terence's[7] comedies. And for this reason some writers have the custom of saying in their salutations, by way of greeting, "a tragic beginning and a comic ending to you." And, as well, they differ in their manner of speaking. Tragedy uses an elevated and sublime style, while comedy uses an unstudied and low style, which is what Horace implies in the *Art of Poetry* where he allows comic writers occasionally to speak like the tragic, and also the reverse of this:

> Yet sometimes even comedy elevates its voice,
> and angry Chremes rages in swelling tones;
> and in tragedy Telephus and Peleus often lament
> in prosaic speeches. . . .[8]

So from this it should be clear why the present work is called the *Comedy*. For, if we consider the matter, it is, at the beginning, that is, in Hell, foul and conducive to horror, but at the end, in Paradise, prosperous, conducive to pleasure, and welcome. And if we consider the manner of speaking, it is unstudied and low, since its speech is the vernacular, in which even women communicate. There are, besides these, other genres of poetic narrative, such as pastoral verse, elegy, satire, and the hymn of thanksgiving, as could also be gathered from Horace in his *Art of Poetry*. But there is no purpose to discussing these at this time.

* * *

1321

5. For a similar derivation of "comedy" (usually linked to the Greek *kōmos*, "revel," not *kōmē*, "village"), see ARISTOTLE, *Poetics* 3, 1448a (above).
6. Roman philosopher and author of several tragedies (ca. 4 B.C.E.–65 C.E.).
7. Roman comic dramatist (ca. 190–159 B.C.E.).
8. HORACE [65–8 B.C.E.], *Art of Poetry* 93–96 [translator's note]; reprinted above. Chremes: a character in Aristophanes' comedy *Ecclesiazusae* (ca. 392 B.C.E.). Telephus: in Greek mythology, a son of Heracles. Peleus: the father of the Greek hero Achilles.

GIOVANNI BOCCACCIO
1313–1375

Giovanni Boccaccio, author of the famous *Decameron* (1348–53), was, with DANTE and Petrarch, a pioneer of Italian vernacular literature and of the humanism that would become the philosophical basis of the Renaissance. Although Boccaccio's present-day reputation is based primarily on the bawdy tales of the *Decameron*, his romances and scholarly works were indispensible sources for poets throughout the Renaissance. His *Genealogia Deorum Gentilium* (1350–62, *Genealogy of the Gentile Gods*), an encyclopedic compendium in Latin of pagan mythology designed as a guide to the ancient poets, culminates in books 14 and 15 with a defense of poetry against the criticisms of it that reach back to PLATO's *Republic*. Like John of Salisbury in the twelfth century, Boccaccio defends poetry in terms that are unmistakably medieval. But he also stands in a long line of practicing poets who have written in defense of their art, ranging from HORACE (65–8 B.C.E.), JOACHIM DU BELLAY (ca. 1522–1560), and SIR PHILIP SIDNEY (1554–1586) to JOHN DRYDEN (1631–1700), ALEXANDER POPE (1688–1744), WILLIAM WORDSWORTH (1770–1850), and PERCY BYSSHE SHELLEY (1792–1822).

Boccaccio was born in Tuscany, the illegitimate son of a merchant, Boccaccino di Chelino, and raised in Florence. Having provided him with a grammatical and literary education, as well as practical business training, his father sent him in 1327 to serve an apprenticeship in Naples. Boccaccio, however, preferred the aristocratic intellectual circles of the court of Robert of Anjou to a life in commerce. He began to mingle in courtly society and to write stories in verse and prose. He fell in love with—and wrote about—an unattainable aristocratic woman he called Fiammetta, who has been identified as Maria d'Aquino, an illegitimate daughter of King Robert. His first literary works appeared during this period, including the allegorical poem *La caccia di Diana* (ca. 1334, *Diana's Hunt*) and two romances: *Filostrato* (ca. 1335)—a version of the story of Troilus and Criseida, later adapted by both Chaucer and Shakespeare—and *Teseida* (ca. 1339), a source of Chaucer's *Knight's Tale*. In 1341 Boccaccio returned to Florence, where he discovered a different kind of intellectual and artistic community, one that followed in the style of the recently deceased Dante. Under the influence of this literary tradition of allegorical didacticism that stressed the moral and symbolic dimensions of literature, he wrote the allegorical works *Comedy of the Florentine Nymphs* (1341–42) and *Fiammetta* (1343). By 1348, when the bubonic plague had reached Italy, Boccaccio began his greatest work, the hundred prose tales of the *Decameron*. The plague provides their framework—ten young people retreat to the country to escape the disease and tell ten stories each as a means of entertaining themselves during their confinement.

About 1350, around the same time that he began the *Genealogy of the Gentile Gods*, Boccaccio became involved in Florentine politics, serving on various ambassadorial missions. He also met Petrarch, beginning a friendship that would last until Petrarch's death in 1374. He turned from literature to scholarship, especially to the study of classical history, literature, and mythology, translating the Roman historian Livy, searching for ancient manuscripts, learning Greek, and attempting to establish an academic chair in Greek in Florence. Between 1350 and 1362 he wrote in Latin most of the *Genealogy*, as well as such scholarly collections as his *Fates of Illustrious Men* (1356, *De Casibus Virorum Illustrium*) and *Concerning Famous Women* (1361, *De Mulieribus Claris*), which was an important source for CHRISTINE DE PIZAN's famous *City of Ladies* (1405). In 1362 Boccaccio underwent a spiritual crisis during which he considered burning his secular writing and taking holy orders; he was dissuaded from both by Petrarch. A year later he retired to his native town, Certaldo, where he remained active in Florentine politics. By 1373 he had completed a biography, *Life of Dante*. In the same year, he is said to have met the English poet Chaucer in Florence. He died at Certaldo two years later.

Boccaccio intended *Genealogy of the Gentile Gods* as a monumental work of scholarship, a mythological sourcebook that would introduce readers to the study of the ancient poets. His decision to write in Latin rather than Italian is a measure of its seriousness as a scholarly project. Books 1–13, mostly completed by 1360, contain Boccaccio's allegorical interpretations of Greek mythology. By the 1360s, however, he seemed to feel that some kind of defense of the ancient poets was necessary as well, to show that they were, as he writes in the first chapter of book 15, "really men of wisdom, . . . their compositions full of profit and pleasure to the reader." Boccaccio's defense of poetry in books 14 and 15 compiles and arranges in a single document a series of arguments both for and against poetry that had been in circulation for more than a thousand years. Together with Plato's writing on poetry and ARISTOTLE's *Poetics* (which was not recovered in Europe until the fifteenth century), it provides the substance of Renaissance literary theory. The influence of the *Genealogy*'s defense of poetry during the Renaissance is easily discernible, for instance, in Sir Philip Sidney's *Defence of Poesy* (see below), published in England over two centuries later.

In chapter 5 of book 14 Boccaccio neutralizes the arguments of poetry's detractors, especially the philosophers who, since Plato, had been chief among those denouncing poetry as a distraction from the pursuit of truth. In the Middle Ages, the theologians had inherited the philosopher's mantle. Both philosophy and theology enjoyed enormous prestige in this period, beside which all other forms of knowledge, including poetry, were dismissed as trivial—especially in Italy, where the study of theology was more isolated from the other liberal arts than in the rest of Europe. Boccaccio borrows a scene from Dante's *Il Convivio* (see above), ultimately derived from Boethius's *Consolation of Philosophy* (ca. 524), opening chapter 5 with a vision of Lady Philosophy. Unlike either Dante or Boethius, however, Boccaccio puts poets in "high places," as Lady Philosophy's counselors, and relegates philosophers and other critics of poetry to the "noisy crowd" surrounding her. In a neat reversal, the text's allegory makes the poets the true followers of philosophy, while poetry's detractors are exposed as impostors. Placing the criticisms of poetry into the mouths of this crowd of pretenders robs them of their force; at the same time, poetry is redefined as proceeding, like philosophy, from "the bosom of God." Later in the text, Boccaccio concedes that philosophy does arrive at truth, but only by slow reason; poets do so by leaps of imagination.

Chapter 7 contains Boccaccio's most important ideas about poetry, ideas that draw both on his own experience as a poet and on critics who preceded him, including Horace, AUGUSTINE (354–430 C.E.), Macrobius (b. ca. 360 C.E.), Dante, and his friend Petrarch. He defines poetry as "fervid and exquisite invention" combined with "fervid expression, in speech or writing," insisting that inspiration, education in the liberal arts, and craft are equally important in its creation. Following Aristotle and the Roman orator Cicero (106–43 B.C.E.), Boccaccio carefully distinguishes poetry from rhetoric, countering a medieval tendency to subordinate poetry to both rhetoric and grammar. While the poet needs to master the rules and methods of rhetoric, poetry transcends it both in its "invention" and its "expression." Whereas rhetoricians are required to be "simple and clear," poets have license to invent wonders and to make language seem strange.

In chapter 12, Boccaccio takes on the charge that poets are often obscure, engaging in an argument that sounds remarkably similar to contemporary debates about theoretical jargon. If poets are obscure, so too, he argues, are philosophers such as Plato and Aristotle, who "abound in difficulties so tangled and involved that . . . they have yielded no clear nor consistent meaning." Holy Scriptures, he points out, are full of ambiguous and difficult passages, yet no critic would dare, for fear of blasphemy, accuse their author of deliberate obscurity for the sake of appearing clever. Obscurity, for Boccaccio, is both engaging and fruitful, as it is for MAIMONIDES (1135–1204). It protects poetry from vulgar people, while usefully prompting multiple interpretations from the learned.

True to his roots in medieval linguistics, which insists on a fundamental distinction between words used "properly" and those used "figuratively," Boccaccio never allows himself to question openly the notion of language as a transparent medium referring to an independent reality. For him, poetry is always subordinate to some higher reality—philosophy, theology, the divine. However, by insisting that poetry's "veil of fiction" "clothes" the naked truth, Boccaccio unwittingly challenges traditional assumptions about the referential nature of language and poetry, pointing toward the fundamentally figurative basis of all language.

***Genealogy of the Gentile Gods* Keywords:** The Canon/Tradition, Language, Medieval Theory, Poetry, Religion, Rhetoric

From Genealogy of the Gentile Gods[1]

From *Book 14*

V. OTHER CAVILLERS AT THE POETS AND THEIR IMPUTATIONS

There is also, O most serene of rulers,[2] as you know far better than I, a kind of house established in this world by God's gift, in the image of a celestial council, and devoted only to sacred studies. Within, on a lofty throne, sits Philosophy,[3] messenger from the very bosom of God, mistress of all knowledge. Noble is her mien and radiant with godlike splendor. There she sits arrayed in royal robes and adorned with a golden crown, like the Empress of all the World. In her left hand she holds several books, with her right hand she wields a royal sceptre, and in clear and fluent discourse she shows forth to such as will listen the truly praiseworthy ideals of human character, the forces of our Mother Nature, the true good, and the secrets of heaven. If you enter you do not doubt that it is a sanctuary full worthy of all reverence; and if you look about, you will clearly see there every opportunity for the higher pursuits of the human mind, both speculation and knowledge, and will gaze with wonder till you regard it not merely as one all-inclusive household, but almost the very image of the divine mind. Among other objects of great veneration there, behind the mistress of the household, are certain men seated in high places, few in number, of gentle aspect and utterance, who are so distinguished by their seriousness, honesty, and true humility, that you take them for gods not mortals. These men abound in the faith and doctrine of their mistress, and give freely to others of the fullness of their knowledge.

But there is also another group—a noisy crowd—of all sorts and conditions. Some of these have resigned all pride, and live in watchful obedience

1. Translated by Charles G. Osgood.
2. Boccaccio claims that his treatise was commissioned by Hugh IV of Cyprus, king of Cyprus and Jerusalem from 1324 to 1358. Hugh was dead by 1359; it is not clear why Boccaccio continues to address him.
3. The ultimate source for this image of Lady Philosophy is Boethius's *Consolation of Philosophy* (ca. 524 C.E.), Prose 1.3.

to the injunctions of their superiors, in hopes that their obsequious zeal may gain them promotion. But others there are who grow so elated with what is virtually elementary knowledge, that they fall upon their great mistress' robes as it were with their talons, and in violent haste tear away a few shreds as samples; then don various titles which they often pick up for a price; and, as puffed up as if they knew the whole subject of divinity, they rush forth from the sacred house, setting such mischief afoot among ignorant people as only the wise can calculate. Yet these rascals are sworn conspirators against all high arts. First they try to counterfeit a good man; they exchange their natural expression for an anxious, careful one. They go about with downcast eye to appear inseparable from their thoughts. Their pace is slow to make the uneducated think that they stagger under an excessive weight of high speculation. They dress unpretentiously, not because they are really modest, but only to mask themselves with sanctity. Their talk is little and serious. If you ask them a question they heave a sigh, pause a moment, raise their eyes to heaven, and at length deign to answer. They hope the bystanders will infer from this that their words rise slowly to their lips, not from any lack of eloquence, but because they are fetched from the remote sanctuary of heavenly secrets. They profess piety, sanctity, and justice, and often, forsooth, utter the words of the prophet,[4] "The zeal of God's house hath eaten me up."

Then they proceed to display their wonderful knowledge, and whatever they don't know they damn—to good effect too. This they do to avoid inquiry about subjects of which they are ignorant, or else to affect scorn and indifference in such matters as cheap, trivial, and obvious, while they have devoted themselves to things of greater importance. When they have caught inexperienced minds in traps of this sort, they proceed boldly to range about town, dabble in business, give advice, arrange marriages, appear at big dinners, dictate wills, act as executors of estates, and otherwise display arrogance unbecoming to a philosopher. Thus they blow up a huge cloud of popular reputation, and thereby so strut with vanity that, when they walk abroad, they want to have everybody's finger pointing them out, to overhear people saying that they are great masters of their subjects, and see how the grand folk rise to meet them in the squares of the city and call them "Rabbi,"[5] speak to them, invite them, give place and defer to them. Straightway they throw off all restraint and become bold enough for anything; they are not afraid to lay their own sickles to the harvest of another; and haply, while they are basely defiling other people's business, the talk may fall upon poetry and poets. At the sound of the word they blaze up in such a sudden fury that you would say their eyes were afire. They cannot stop; they go raging on by the very momentum of their wrath. Finally, like conspirators against a deadly enemy, in the schools, in public squares, in pulpits, with a lazy crowd, as a rule, for an audience, they break out into such mad denunciation of poets that the bystanders are afraid of the speakers themselves, let alone the harmless objects of attack.

They say poetry is absolutely of no account, and the making of poetry a useless and absurd craft; that poets are tale-mongers, or, in lower terms,

4. David, Psalms 69.9; John 2.17 [translator's note].

5. Literally, "my master," "my teacher" (Hebrew).

liars; that they live in the country among the woods and mountains because they lack manners and polish. They say, besides, that their poems are false, obscure, lewd, and replete with absurd and silly tales of pagan gods, and that they make Jove,[6] who was, in point of fact, an obscene and adulterous man, now the father of gods, now king of heaven, now fire, or air, or man, or bull, or eagle, or similar irrelevant things; in like manner poets exalt to fame Juno[7] and infinite others under various names. Again and again they cry out that poets are seducers of the mind, prompters of crime, and, to make their foul charge, fouler, if possible, they say they are philosophers' apes, that it is a heinous crime to read or possess the books of poets; and then, without making any distinction, they prop themselves up, as they say, with Plato's authority[8] to the effect that poets ought to be turned out-of-doors—nay, out of town, and that the Muses,[9] their mumming mistresses, as Boethius[1] says, being sweet with deadly sweetness, are detestable, and should be driven out with them and utterly rejected. But it would take too long to cite everything that their irritable spite and deadly hatred prompt these madmen to say. It is also before judges like these—so eminent, forsooth, so fair, so merciful, so well-inclined—that my work will appear, O glorious Prince; and I know full well they will gather about it like famished lions,[2] to seek what they may devour. Since my book has entirely to do with poetic material, I cannot look for a milder sentence from them than in their rage they thunder down upon poets. I am well aware that I offer my breast to the same missiles that their hatred has already employed; but I shall endeavor to ward them off.

O merciful God, meet now this foolish and ill-considered clamor of mad men, and oppose their rage. And thou, O best of kings, as I advance upon their line, support me with the strength of thy noble soul, and help me in my fight for thee; for courage and a stout heart must now be mine. Sharp and poisonous are their weapons, but weak withal. Foolish judges though they be, they are strong in other ways, and I tremble with fear before them, unless God, who deserteth not them that trust in Him, and thou, also, favor me. Slender is my strength and my mind weak, but great is my expectation of help; borne up by such hope, I shall rush upon them with justice at my right hand.

VII. THE DEFINITION OF POETRY, ITS ORIGIN, AND FUNCTION

This poetry, which ignorant triflers cast aside, is a sort of fervid and exquisite invention, with fervid expression, in speech or writing, of that which the mind has invented. It proceeds from the bosom of God, and few, I find, are the souls in whom this gift is born; indeed so wonderful a gift it is that true poets have always been the rarest of men. This fervor of poesy is sublime in its effects: it impels the soul to a longing for utterance; it brings forth strange and unheard-of creations of the mind; it arranges these meditations in a fixed order, adorns the whole composition with unusual interweaving of

6. Jupiter, the chief Roman god (identified with the Greek god Zeus).
7. Jupiter's wife and sister, the chief Roman goddess (identified with the Greek goddess Hera).
8. See PLATO, *Republic* 3.398a–b.
9. In Greek mythology, 9 daughters of Memory who preside over the arts and all intellectual pursuits.
1. Roman Christian philosopher (470–524). In *The Consolation of Philosophy*, Prose 1.1, Philosophy calls the Muses "play-acting prostitutes."
2. Like the Devil: 1 Peter 5.8 [translator's note].

words and thoughts; and thus it veils truth in a fair and fitting garment of fiction. Further, if in any case the invention so requires, it can arm kings, marshal them for war, launch whole fleets from their docks, nay, counterfeit sky, land, sea, adorn young maidens with flowery garlands, portray human character in its various phases, awake the idle, stimulate the dull, restrain the rash, subdue the criminal, and distinguish excellent men with their proper meed of praise: these, and many other such, are the effects of poetry. Yet if any man who has received the gift of poetic fervor shall imperfectly fulfil its function here described, he is not, in my opinion, a laudable poet. For, however deeply the poetic impulse stirs the mind to which it is granted, it very rarely accomplishes anything commendable if the instruments by which its concepts are to be wrought out are wanting—I mean, for example, the precepts of grammar and rhetoric, an abundant knowledge of which is opportune. I grant that many a man already writes his mother tongue admirably, and indeed has performed each of the various duties of poetry as such; yet over and above this, it is necessary to know at least the principles of the other Liberal Arts,[3] both moral and natural, to possess a strong and abundant vocabulary, to behold the monuments and relics of the Ancients, to have in one's memory the histories of the nations, and to be familiar with the geography of various lands, of seas, rivers and mountains.

Furthermore, places of retirement, the lovely handiwork of Nature herself, are favorable to poetry, as well as peace of mind and desire for worldly glory; the ardent period of life also has very often been of great advantage. If these conditions fail, the power of creative genius frequently grows dull and sluggish.

Now since nothing proceeds from this poetic fervor, which sharpens and illumines the powers of the mind, except what is wrought out by art,[4] poetry is generally called an art. Indeed the word poetry has not the origin that many carelessly suppose, namely *poio, pois*, which is but Latin *fingo, fingis*; rather it is derived from a very ancient Greek word *poetes*,[5] which means in Latin exquisite discourse (*exquisita locutio*). For the first men who, thus inspired, began to employ an exquisite style of speech, such, for example, as song in an age hitherto unpolished, to render this unheard-of discourse sonorous to their hearers, let it fall in measured periods; and lest by its brevity it fail to please, or, on the other hand, become prolix and tedious, they applied to it the standard of fixed rules, and restrained it within a definite number of feet and syllables. Now the product of this studied method of speech they no longer called by the more general term poesy, but poem. Thus as I said above, the name of the art, as well as its artificial product, is derived from its effect.

Now though I allege that this science of poetry has ever streamed forth from the bosom of God upon souls while even yet in their tenderest years,

3. The liberal arts in the Middle Ages included the trivium (grammar, rhetoric, and logic) and the quadrivium (arithmetic, geometry, music, and astronomy).

4. Conscious skill, technique, indispensable to poetic creation [translator's note].

5. Boccaccio's limitations in Greek have allowed him to follow Isidore of Seville—bad etymology and all—in this whole passage, as did writers before him who knew no Greek [translator's note]. Isidore of Seville (ca. 560–636), Spanish bishop and encyclopedist; see his *Etymologiarum* 8.7.2, "De poeta." The Greek *poieō* (which is, in fact, related to "poet") means "make, create"; the Latin *fingo* means "form, invent."

these enlightened cavillers will perhaps say that they cannot trust my words. To any fair-minded man the fact is valid enough from its constant recurrence. But for these dullards I must cite witnesses to it. If, then, they will read what Cicero,[6] a philosopher rather than a poet, says in his oration delivered before the senate in behalf of Aulus Licinius Archias,[7] perhaps they will come more easily to believe me. He says: "And yet we have it on the highest and most learned authority, that while other arts are matters of science and formula and technique, poetry depends solely upon an inborn faculty, is evoked by a purely mental activity, and is infused with a strange supernal inspiration."

But not to protract this argument, it is now sufficiently clear to reverent men, that poetry is a practical art,[8] springing from God's bosom and deriving its name from its effect, and that it has to do with many high and noble matters that constantly occupy even those who deny its existence. If my opponents ask when and in what circumstances, the answer is plain: the poets would declare with their own lips under whose help and guidance they compose their inventions when, for example, they raise flights[9] of symbolic steps to heaven, or make thick-branching trees[1] spring aloft to the very stars, or go winding about mountains to their summits. Haply, to disparage this art of poetry now unrecognized by them, these men will say that it is rhetoric which the poets employ. Indeed, I will not deny it in part, for rhetoric has also its own inventions. Yet, in truth, among the disguises of fiction rhetoric has no part, for whatever is composed as under a veil, and thus exquisitely wrought, is poetry and poetry alone.[2]

XII. THE OBSCURITY OF POETRY IS NOT JUST CAUSE FOR CONDEMNING IT

These cavillers further object that poetry is often obscure, and that poets are to blame for it, since their end is to make an incomprehensible statement appear to be wrought with exquisite artistry; regardless of the old rule of the orators, that a speech must be simple and clear. Perverse notion! Who but a deceiver himself would have sunk low enough not merely to hate what he could not understand, but incriminate it, if he could? I admit that poets are at times obscure. At the same time will these accusers please answer me? Take those philosophers among whom they shamelessly intrude; do they

6. Roman statesman, orator, and author (106–43 B.C.E.).
7. A Greek poet of Antioch, whose claim of Roman citizenship was successfully defended by Cicero; the greater part of his oration is devoted to glorifying literature (the quotation is from *Pro Archia* 8.18).
8. *Facultas* (ability, power, capacity, skill [Latin]) [translator's note].
9. Dante's mountain of Purgatory, and perhaps the steps from circle to circle (*Purgatorio* 11.40; 13.1; 17.65, 77; 25.8; etc.); or the three steps in *Purgatorio* 9.76ff.; or the mystic stairway of the Seventh Heaven (*Paradiso* 21.8; 22.68) [translator's note]. For DANTE ALIGHIERI (1265–1321), see above.
1. Like Pandarus and Bitias in Virgil's *Aeneid* [19 B.C.E.], 9.677–82: "While they within stand at the right and left / Before the turrets, armed, their lofty heads / Flashing with plumes. So by some river's bank, / Whether the Po or pleasant Athesis, / Two breezy oaks lift up their unshorn heads, / And nod their lofty tops" [translator's note].
2. According to Aristotle (*Rhetoric* 3.2) poetry can create wonder by strange matter and expression, as rhetoric should not. Cicero (*De Oratore* 1.16) says that the poet is more restricted than the orator by "numbers" but less in choice of words. Augustine (*De Ordine* 2.14.40) finds the grammarians rather than the rhetoricians are poetry's proper judges. In the Middle Ages the academic conception of poetry became debased and subordinated to rhetoric and grammar. Boccaccio obviously is protesting against the medieval opinion partly by appealing to the Ancients, but chiefly by consulting the fact of a poet's experience [translator's note]. For ARISTOTLE (384–322 B.C.E.) and the theologian AUGUSTINE (354–430 C.E.), see above.

always find their close reasoning as simple and clear as they say an oration should be? If they say yes, they lie; for the works of Plato and Aristotle, to go no further, abound in difficulties so tangled and involved that from their day to the present, though searched and pondered by many a man of keen insight, they have yielded no clear nor consistent meaning. But why do I talk of philosophers? There is the utterance of Holy Writ, of which they especially like to be thought expounders; though proceeding from the Holy Ghost, is it not full to overflowing with obscurities and ambiguities? It is indeed, and for all their denial, the truth will openly assert itself. Many are the witnesses, of whom let them be pleased to consult Augustine,[3] a man of great sanctity and learning, and of such intellectual power that, without a teacher, as he says himself, he learned many arts, besides all that the philosophers teach of the ten categories. Yet he did not blush to admit that he could not understand the beginning of Isaiah. It seems that obscurities are not confined to poetry. Why then do they not criticise philosophers as well as poets? Why do they not say that the Holy Spirit wove obscure sayings into his works, just to give them an appearance of clever artistry? As if He were not the sublime Artificer of the Universe![4] I have no doubt they are bold enough to say such things, if they were not aware that philosophers already had their defenders, and did not remember the punishment[5] prepared for them that blaspheme against the Holy Ghost. So they pounce upon the poets because they seem defenseless, with the added reason that, where no punishment is imminent, no guilt is involved. They should have realized that when things perfectly clear seem obscure, it is the beholder's fault. To a half-blind man, even when the sun is shining its brightest, the sky looks cloudy. Some things are naturally so profound that not without difficulty can the most exceptional keenness in intellect sound their depths; like the sun's globe, by which, before they can clearly discern it, strong eyes are sometimes repelled.[6] On the other hand, some things, though naturally clear perhaps, are so veiled by the artist's skill that scarcely anyone could by mental effort derive sense from them; as the immense body of the sun when hidden in clouds cannot be exactly located by the eye of the most learned astronomer. That some of the prophetic poems are in this class, I do not deny.

Yet not by this token is it fair to condemn them; for surely it is not one of the poet's various functions to rip up and lay bare the meaning which lies hidden in his inventions. Rather where matters truly solemn and memorable are too much exposed, it is his office by every effort to protect as well as he can and remove them from the gaze of the irreverent, that they cheapen not by too common familiarity. So when he discharges this duty and does it ingeniously, the poet earns commendation, not anathema.

Wherefore I again grant that poets are at times obscure, but invariably explicable if approached by a sane mind; for these cavillers view them with

3. Augustine, *Confessions* 4.16: "And what did it profit me that, when scarcely twenty years old, a book of Aristotle's entitled The Ten Predicaments [*Categories*] fell into my hands? . . . I read it alone and understood it . . . And what did it profit me that I . . . read unaided, and understood, all the books that I could get of the so-called liberal arts? . . . Whatever was written either on rhetoric or logic, geometry, music, or arithmetic, did I, without any great difficulty, and without the teaching of any man, understand." Cited by Petrarch, *Invectivae contra Medicum* [1355], 3, p. 1105 [translator's note].

4. Wisdom 7.21, 22 [translator's note].

5. Mark 3.29 [translator's note].

6. Perhaps a reminiscence of Dante, *Paradiso* 1.54ff. A favorite figure with Dante: cf. *Purgatorio* 32.11; *Paradiso* 25.118; etc. [translator's note].

owl eyes, not human. Surely no one can believe that poets invidiously veil the truth with fiction, either to deprive the reader of the hidden sense, or to appear the more clever; but rather to make truths which would otherwise cheapen by exposure the object of strong intellectual effort and various interpretation, that in ultimate discovery they shall be more precious. In a far higher degree is this the method of the Holy Spirit; nay, every right-minded man should be assured of it beyond any doubt. Besides it is established by Augustine in the *City of God*, Book Eleven, when he says:

"The obscurity of the divine word has certainly this advantage, that it causes many opinions about the truth to be started and discussed, each reader seeing some fresh meaning in it."

Elsewhere he says of Psalm 126:[7]

"For perhaps the words are rather obscurely expressed for this reason, that they may call forth many understandings, and that men may go away the richer, because they have found that closed which might be opened in many ways, than if they could open and discover it by one interpretation."

To make further use of Augustine's testimony (which so far is adverse to these recalcitrants), to show them how I apply to the obscurities of poetry his advice on the right attitude toward the obscurities of Holy Writ, I will quote his comment on Psalm 146:[8]

"There is nothing in it contradictory: somewhat there is which is obscure, not in order that it may be denied thee, but that it may exercise him that shall afterward receive it," etc.

But enough of the testimony of holy men on this point, I will not bore my opponents by again urging them to regard the obscurities of poetry as Augustine regards the obscurities of Holy Writ. Rather I wish that they would wrinkle their brows a bit, and consider fairly and squarely, how, if this is true of sacred literature addressed to all nations, in far greater measure is it true of poetry, which is addressed to the few.

If by chance in condemning the difficulty of the text, they really mean its figures of diction and oratorical colors and the beauty which they fail to recognize in alien words, if on this account they pronounce poetry obscure—my only advice is for them to go back to the grammar schools,[9] bow to the ferule, study, and learn what license ancient authority granted the poets in such matters, and give particular attention to such alien terms as are permissible beyond common and homely use. But why dwell so long upon the subject? I could have urged them in a sentence to put off the old mind,[1] and put on the new and noble; then will that which now seems to them obscure look familiar and open. Let them not trust to concealing their gross confusion of mind in the precepts of the old orators; for I am sure the poets were ever mindful of such. But let them observe that oratory is quite different, in

7. Augustine, *Enarratio: Patrilogia. Latina* 37.1675. Boccaccio's quotation immediately precedes the passage on the obscurity of Isaiah cited above [translator's note].
8. *Enarratio: Patrilogia. Latina* 37.1907. The preceding words are "Honor God's Scripture, honor God's Word, though it be not plain; in reverence wait for understanding. Be not wanton to accuse either the obscurity or seeming contradiction of Scripture" (trans. Coke) [translator's note].
9. The study of poetry was subject either to grammar or to rhetoric in the medieval scheme. See book 14, chapter 7. Though Boccaccio does not mention rhetoric in this passage, it is, like 14.7, a stroke on behalf of the liberation of poetry from technical bondage [translator's note].
1. Ephesians 4.22; Colossians 3.9 [translator's note].

arrangement of words, from fiction, and that fiction has been consigned to the discretion of the inventor as being the legitimate work of another art than oratory. "In poetic narrative above all, the poets maintain majesty of style and corresponding dignity." As saith Francis Petrarch[2] in the Third Book of his *Invectives*, contrary to my opponents' supposition, "Such majesty and dignity are not intended to hinder those who wish to understand, but rather propose a delightful task, and are designed to enhance the reader's pleasure and support his memory. What we acquire with difficulty and keep with care is always the dearer to us;" so continues Petrarch.[3] In fine, if their minds are dull, let them not blame the poets but their own sloth. Let them not keep up a silly howl against those whose lives and actions contrast most favorably with their own. Nay, at the very outset they have taken fright at mere appearances, and bid fair to spend themselves for nothing. Then let them retire in good time, sooner than exhaust their torpid minds with the onset and suffer a violent repulse.

But I repeat my advice to those who would appreciate poetry, and unwind its difficult involutions. You must read, you must persevere, you must sit up nights, you must inquire, and exert the utmost power of your mind. If one way does not lead to the desired meaning, take another; if obstacles arise, then still another; until, if your strength holds out, you will find that clear which at first looked dark. For we are forbidden by divine command[4] to give that which is holy to dogs, or to cast pearls before swine.

1350–62

2. Italian poet and humanist (1304–1374).
3. *Invectivae contra Medicum*, p. 1105. Petrarch has just been comparing the obscurity of poets with that of Holy Writ, not citing the difference between oratory and poetry. Boccaccio's quotation, either through his carelessness or corruption of his text, differs slightly from Petrarch [translator's note].
4. Matthew 7.6 [translator's note].

CHRISTINE DE PIZAN
ca. 1365–ca. 1429

The most prolific woman writer of the Middle Ages, Christine de Pizan was the first European woman to earn a living as a writer and, as such, she was acutely aware of the difficulty of reconciling the demands of writing with the occupations of women. In *Christine's Vision* (1405), a lengthy complaint against Fortune in the tradition of Boethius's *Consolation of Philosophy* (ca. 524), she laments that "although I was naturally inclined to scholarship from my birth, my occupation with the tasks common to married women and the burden of frequent childbearing had deprived me of it." The sheer volume of her literary output is all the more remarkable for a woman who was married and bearing children at the age of fifteen.

Christine was born in Venice around 1365. Shortly after, her father, Tommasso di Benvenuto da Pizzano, an astrologer-physician, received an offer of employment from Charles V of France—the age's greatest patron—and in 1368 he brought his family to Paris. Around 1380, at "the age when young girls are customarily assigned husbands" (according to *Christine's Vision*), Christine was married to Etienne de Castel. In the same year, the death of Charles V meant the loss of the royal patronage Tommasso had enjoyed; the family fortunes soon began to wane. In 1389 both Tommasso and Castel died, leaving Christine a twenty-five-year-old widow with three small children and a large household. Though her father and husband left her a small inheritance, they also left her with debts, which required many years of expensive litigation to settle. Fortunately, Christine's father had given her some education, so Christine turned to writing to support her family.

From 1399 until her death in 1429, Christine wrote more than twenty volumes in prose and verse, culminating in 1405 with *The Book of the City of Ladies*, the work for which she is best known. But Christine did not limit herself only to the defense of women, to the so-called *querelle des femmes* for which we remember her today. In 1404 she received her first large commission from Philip the Bold of Burgundy to write a biography of his father, Charles V. During her career, she wrote on subjects as diverse as good government (something sorely lacking in early fifteenth-century France), military strategy, religion, morality, and ethics. She died shortly after completing the *Ditié de Jehanne d'Arc* (1429, *Poem of Joan of Arc*).

In her earliest composition, *Epistle of the God of Love* (1399), Christine deplored the popularity of the *Roman de la Rose* (*Romance of the Rose*), one of the central works of medieval French literature, for its misogynistic representations of women. In 1402 she collected and published a series of letters by various hands that make up France's first literary debate—the so-called Quarrel of the *Rose*—over the merits of Jean de Meun's continuation of the poem begun by Guillaume de Lorris. In the course of this debate, Christine engaged with some of the most prominent fifteenth-century French intellectuals, including Jean Gerson, the chancellor of the University of Paris, who sided with Christine in condemning the poem, and Jean de Montreuil, the provost of Lille and a royal secretary, whose treatise in praise of the *Roman de la Rose* sparked the uproar. Our first selection, Christine's response to Montreuil's treatise, encapsulates the central issues of the debate. Christine objected to the obscene language used by some of the allegorical figures, most notably Reason's naming of the "secret parts" of the body and Genius's exhortation to procreate, and to the defamation of women in the speeches of the Duenna, the Jealous Husband, and Genius. One of the royal secretaries participating in the debate, Gontier Col, was so incensed by the criticism that he sharply attacked Christine for her presumption in contradicting Montreuil and called on her to retract her statements, a request she steadfastly refused. In Christine's mind, the two offenses—obscenity and misogyny—are linked. Some readers might see Christine's denunciation of the poem's obscenity as simply priggish; others might read it as a precursor to contemporary feminist arguments about pornography. However, she was engaging with members of the royal court in serious, age-old debates over the morality of literature and the duplicity of language.

In our second excerpt, from *The Book of the City of Ladies*, Christine continues the critique of misogyny begun in the Quarrel of the *Rose*. Her criticisms in both texts reveal a typically medieval distrust of the excesses of poetic language cut loose from proper signification. Misogynist writing is untrue because its authors have not understood the proper use of language. Christine's distrust of false representation reveals her indebtedness to theories of language pioneered by ST. AUGUSTINE, while her interest in allegory links her with writers such as Quintilian, Hugh of St. Victor, and DANTE, all of whom developed medieval notions of exegesis. Her attempt to counter the misogynist representations of the "philosophers and poets" with true representations of "good women" owes its largest debt to BOCCACCIO's *Concerning Famous Women* (1361), though she is far from being an uncritical reader of that text. While nearly three-quarters of the tales in the *City of Ladies* are found in Boccaccio's work, Christine's adaptations show her to be a resisting reader, her text a refutation of Boccaccio's often backhanded praise of women.

The opening of the *City of Ladies* illustrates some ways in which women read and write under the conditions of patriarchy. The predominance of "wicked insults" about women and their behavior in the books she reads prompts Christine to disregard everything she knows about women and to ask God why, if women were so evil, she could not have been born as a man. The process of building a "city of ladies" entails reeducating herself to read as a woman and to discern true from false representations of women. Christine's collection of stories about illustrious women might be read as an early attempt to counter what SANDRA M. GILBERT and SUSAN GUBAR in the twentieth century call the "anxiety of authorship" suffered by the woman writer, the fear that "because she can never become a precursor, the act of creation will isolate and destroy her." To clear the ground for a "city of ladies," Reason, her guide, must unpack the logical errors in misogynist discourse, articulating the reasons that so many learned men would slander women. But that is only a first step. The woman writer overcomes her anxiety of authorship only by actively seeking female precursors, the task that Christine sets herself in the *City of Ladies*. Like so many female critics who would follow her—for example, MARY WOLLSTONECRAFT and VIRGINIA WOOLF—Christine recognizes that because women have been denied education and thus kept ignorant, they have been unable to counter male images of female wickedness. Despite this spirited defense of women and her importance as a feminist precursor, we would be premature to call her a feminist writer. Her social vision of women's proper sphere is ultimately quite conservative, even for its time. Nevertheless, the *City of Ladies* remains an important document, an early voice of female resistance to the tradition of male misogyny.

"Christine's Reaction to Jean de Montreuil's Treatise on the *Roman de la Rose*" Keywords: The Canon/Tradition, Ethics, Feminist Criticism, Gender, Medieval Theory, Religion, Romance, Women's Literature
***The Book of the City of Ladies* Keywords:** The Canon/Tradition, Ethics, Feminist Criticism, Gender, Literary History, Medieval Theory, Women's Literature

Christine's Reaction to Jean de Montreuil's Treatise on the *Roman de la Rose*[1]

Christine
To a most skillful and learned person, Master Jean Johannes, Secretary to Our Lord the King and provost of Lille.[2]

To my lord the provost of Lille, with reverence, honor, and esteem. Dear lord and master who is wise in morals, steeped in learning, a trained clergyman, and an expert in rhetoric: I, Christine de Pizan, an ignorant woman of inadequate opinion—for this your wisdom may well hold the insignificance of my arguments in disdain—beg you to take into consideration my female weakness. Since you had the kindness, for which I thank you, to send me a small treatise[3] adorned with beautiful rhetoric and convincing arguments (where you say, it seems to me, that you can find no fault with any aspect of

1. Translated by Christine McWebb, whose notes have sometimes been abridged.
2. Christine's letter, written in June/July 1401, is a response to a treatise sent to her by Jean de Montreuil, whom she addresses as "secretary to our lord the king." Montreuil was a scholar of the late 14th to early 15th century and provost of Lille.
3. The small treatise refers to the *opusculum gallicum*, the treatise written by Jean de Montreuil about the *Roman* in May or June 1401, which is unfortunately lost to us today. Thanks to Christine's meticulous reply to this treatise, we have been provided, albeit implicitly, with a summary of its content [translator's note].

the compilation of the *Roman de la rose*,[4] which you support and approve as you do its authors, in particular de Meun), I, having read and reflected upon it and having understood it within the limits of my small intelligence, will reply because of my disagreement with you, although this treatise was not addressed to me, nor do you require my response. Rather, I agree with the skilled cleric to whom your text is addressed,[5] and wish to divulge and maintain openly that, with all due respect, you are mistaken in according unlimited praise to this work, which, I think, instead of being labeled useful should be called a work of idleness. As much as you reprimand your opponents and say that "it is important to understand that which is shown by another text if it is better written, longer, and well founded," etc., I shall not be accused of presumption for daring to repudiate and criticize this famous and very skilled author. However, take heed of my firm disagreement with certain elements which you express in your treatise. In truth, a mere assertion not rightfully justified can be contradicted without bias. Although I am neither learned nor eloquent in style (beautiful phrases and polite, elegant words would certainly make my arguments shine), I will nevertheless express my opinion plainly and in simple French, even if I cannot express it properly in adorned speech.[6]

Yet why did I say earlier that this book "ought rather be called a work of idleness . . ."? Without a doubt, it seems to me that a thing without use for anyone, regardless of how painstakingly it was done, may be called idle or worse than idle, even more so if it turns out to be harmful. When, some time ago and after I had acquired sufficient knowledge to understand such things, I wished to read this romance because of its great reputation, I read and thought about it at great length and tried to the best of my ability to understand it. It is true that I skipped the passages which were not to my liking, just as a rooster skips over hot embers: therefore, I did not read it in its entirety.[7] Nevertheless, I remember some things in it which I condemn very much. Moreover, I cannot approve of the praise coming from others for this work. It is also true that my limited understanding finds great beauty in many parts of the work, where he solemnly expresses what he wishes to say in very beautiful phrases and graceful leonine rhymes.[8] What he wished to say, he could not have said more skillfully, nor in a better rhyme. But in agreeing with the opinion which you contradict, there is no doubt in my mind that he sometimes speaks dishonorably, as when he speaks about the character whom he calls Reason, who calls the secret parts plainly by their

4. An allegorical poem in the form of a dream vision. The first 4,058 lines were written around 1230 by Guillaume de Lorris, a poet about whom little else is known. Around 1275, the poet and philosopher Jean de Meun (ca. 1250–ca. 1305) composed an additional 17,724 lines, his only extant work. The debate revolves primarily around certain notorious passages in de Meun's continuation.

5. This "especial clerc soubtil" has been identified as Nicolas de Clamanges [translator's note] (1360–1437), a member of the circle of Parisian theologians who participated in the debate over the *Roman de la Rose*.

6. Letter writers in the Middle Ages often included a formulaic expression of humility; while it is not to be taken too seriously, Christine frequently deploys it ironically against her interlocutors.

7. The fact that Christine admits she did not read the *Roman* in its entirety will later on become a significant point of contention in Pierre Col's reply to both Christine and Jean de Gerson [translator's note]. Gerson (1363–1429), a prominent theologian and chancellor of the University of Paris, was a participant in the debate over the *Roman de la Rose* who also condemned the poem. Col (ca. 1352–1416), another of Christine's opponents, was a royal secretary and canon of Paris and Tournai.

8. Traditionally defined as internal rhymes: that is, words that rhyme in the middle and end of a line. In *L'Art de dictier* (1392, *The Art of Writing Poetry*)—the first French treatise on versification—the poet Eustache Deschamps applied the term to a rhyme scheme that involves all a word's syllables (thus *timing/rhyming* is a leonine rhyme by his definition, while *singing/running* is not).

names.[9] You openly proclaim his view as logical and invoke—rightfully, I admit—that there is no ugliness in all things which God created, and consequently their names need not be hidden, because all things coming from Him are pure and clean, since in the state of innocence there was no ugliness in naming them. Yet through the corruption of sin mankind was ruined, and original sin has remained (as is shown in Holy Scripture). If I may argue by analogy: God made Lucifer the most beautiful among the angels and gave him a solemn and beautiful name,[1] which was later reduced to terrible ugliness through his sin. As a result, the name, beautiful as it may be in itself, terrifies those who hear it because of its association with the person.

You also quote Jesus Christ who, "when He spoke of the female sinners, called them *meretrix*," etc.[2] That He called them thus can be explained: It is not shameful to say the word *meretrix*, because it refers to an abject thing; words more abject than this could be used, even in Latin. What is shameful, however, is to speak in public of things of which Nature herself would be ashamed. With all due respect for the author and for you, I must say that you sin greatly against the noble virtue of shame, which by definition restrains obscenities and disgrace in word and deed. That this is a great vice and against honorable government and good custom is written in many places in Holy Scripture. And the word "which was merely called relics"[3] must be repudiated. I grant you, it is not the word which causes the disgrace of the thing, but the thing which renders the word disgraceful. It is for this reason, in my feeble opinion, that one must speak of these things only when absolutely necessary, such as in the case of an illness or for some other legitimate reason. Just as our first parents hid these parts naturally, so must we, in deed and in speech.

I cannot yet be silent about that which dissatisfies me immensely: He makes it Reason's task, whom he himself calls daughter of God, to propound such speech, and in the form of a dictum, as I note in the passage where she says to the Lover that "in the war of love . . . it is better to deceive than to be deceived."[4] In fact, I dare say that with this statement Master Jean de Meun's Reason has denounced her Father because He Himself taught her a very different lesson. And it cannot be that both statements are valid; this would mean that both are good. I think the opposite is true: Clearly, to be deceived is not as bad as to deceive, for the vice of pure perfidy is much worse than that of simple ignorance.

Now let us consider further the subject matter or manner of speech to which many would reasonably object. Good God! What disgust! What disgrace! And the exhortations which he teaches in the passage of the Duenna![5] By God! Who could possibly find anything but specious advice in them, full of insults and baseness? Hey, those of you who have beautiful daughters and

9. A central issue in the debate over the *Roman* is Lady Reason's defense of her practice of naming the testicles (7078–86), which Christine and Gerson both found "shameful."
1. Literally, "bringer of light"; in Christian theology, the name given to Satan before his fall from heaven.
2. That is, prostitute; see Matthew 21.31 and Luke 15.30 [translator's note].
3. In her discussion on words and their meaning, Lady Reason stresses the arbitrariness of the sign and the absence of relation between word and thing as she admits that "coilles" [testicles] could be called "reliques" [relics] or vice versa. Let us not forget that *reliques* is the term used later on in the narrative to describe the sacred, untouched vagina of the young virgin [translator's note].
4. *Roman de la Rose* 4261–62.
5. A chaperone or nurse. In the *Roman*, the Duenna acts as a go-between for the Lover; her account of her life (12710–4516) is filled with conventional misogynist themes.

wish to introduce them to an honorable life, give them—yes, ask for and give them—the *Roman de la rose* in order that they may learn how to distinguish good from bad. What am I saying? I mean bad from good! And to what end should anyone listen to such insults? Then, in the passage of the Jealous Husband,[6] my God, what could possibly be the benefit of such shameful and insulting speech, frequently uttered by those poor souls afflicted by this illness? What good example can this possibly set? And the insults of women—which can be found in that passage and which many dismiss by pointing out that it is the Jealous Husband speaking and that, indeed, this can be compared to God speaking through the mouth of Jeremiah![7] Yet surely, then, the other lies he added can in no way, God be thanked, lessen or worsen the situation for women. For when I remember the deceits, hypocrisies, and lies that occur in marriage or any other state which can be learned from this treatise, I certainly think that by comparison these are beautiful and good to hear!

And the character whom he calls the priest Genius[8] truly speaks wondrously: no doubt, Nature's works would have vanished entirely long ago, had he not so highly recommended them! By God, I would like to find someone who can explain to me the advantage of the long speech full of venom that he calls a "sermon," as if to deride holy preaching—delivered, he says, by this so-called Genius. In it such disgrace and specious words are used, fanning the flames of Nature's secrets, which ought to remain tacit and not be named, because it is impossible to see a work come to an end which logically cannot end: if the opposite were true, it would be advantageous for the continuation of humankind to find and utter fiery words and terms to encourage mankind to continue this work.

The author goes even further, if I remember correctly, though I cannot for the life of me understand to what purpose. In this sermon he uses metaphor to associate paradise and the joys that can be found there. He rightfully says that the virtuous will go there, and then announces that all men and women, without exception, should perform and carry out Nature's works[9]—no exception made, as if he wished to say (and, in fact, does say plainly)—that it is precisely these people who will be saved. It seems that he wishes to maintain that lechery is not a sin but, on the contrary, a virtue, which is wrong and against the law of God. Ha! What a notion, and what a doctrine! No good can possibly come of it! I think that many left the worldly life and have chosen to enter the monastic one, becoming hermits for the Holy Scripture, or have chosen to turn their backs on a sinful life, saving themselves from this kind of exhortation which, I dare tell those who will not like to hear it, will lead inevitably to immorality, decay, and vice, possibly causing great misfortune and sin.

And there is more, my God! Let us look a little further! How can his excessive, impetuous, and false accusations, insults, and defamation of women—whom he accuses of several great vices and perverse habits—possibly be valid

6. *Roman* 8437–9330.
7. According to the book of Jeremiah of the Old Testament, the prophet began his career in 627/26 [B.C.E.], the thirteenth year of King Josiah's reign. It is told there that he responded to Yahweh's call to prophesy by protesting, "I do not know how to speak, for I am only a youth" [translator's note].
8. An allegorical figure whose argument for the fecundity of nature (19475–20637) seems to Christine to advocate sexual license.
9. That is, engage in sexual intercourse. Genius wants to excommunicate and condemn "all those disloyal apostates, of high rank or low, who hold in despite the acts by which Nature is supported" (*Roman* 19500–502).

and purposeful? His appetite for such statements and examples seems insatiable. And if you wish to tell me that the Jealous Husband says these things out of anger, I do not understand why it is Genius's task to vehemently recommend and exhort that one share a bed with them [women] without refraining from the work he so praises. At the same time, however, he rants and raves about them, saying in fact, "Flee! Flee! Flee from the venomous serpent!"[1] Yet he goes on to say that one should not cease to follow them. This is a flagrant contradiction, to command one to flee from that which one is supposed to follow and follow that from which he wishes one to flee. Since women are so perverse, he should command men not to approach them at all, because one should always avoid the risk of encountering misfortune.

And since he so strongly forbids men to confide in women, who, he claims, are so eager to know their secrets[2]—though I do not know where the devil he found such rubbish and tainted speech, which he arranges in a long passage—I ask all those who believe that this is true to tell me when they have seen a man accused or killed, hanged, or reprimanded in the streets due to the indiscretion of his wife. I think they will be hard to find. That being said, it is always wise and noble to keep one's secrets hidden, because there is perfidy everywhere. As I heard tell not long ago, for example, there was someone who was accused and then hanged after being denounced by a friend in whom he had confided. Yet I think that neither the complaints nor the rumors of such terrible sins, disloyalties, and evil acts, which women purportedly commit in a mean spirit of complicity, will go very far in the court of law. In the end, a true secret is that which belongs to no one! I have already spoken about this in one of my poems, *L'Epistre au Dieu d'Amour.*[3] Where are the countries and kingdoms which have been exiled due to the great injustices caused by women? Let us not speak arbitrarily: Of which terrible crimes can even the worst and the most deceptive be accused? Truly, what can they do to betray you? If they ask for money from your purse, they will not simply steal it from you. So do not give it to them if you do not wish to! And if you say that they have made a fool of you, do not let them! Will they seek you out in your place of lodging, pleading with you or taking you by force? It would be nice to know how it is that they deceive you.

Moreover, he speaks unnecessarily and defamingly of married women who terribly betray their husbands, though he cannot know about the married state from experience,[4] and thus can only speak about it in general terms. What good does this do, and what can come of this? It can serve only to impede happiness and peace in marriage and to render husbands suspicious, who hear so much babbling and exaggeration and believe it, and it causes them to have little love for their wives. My God, what a biased exhortation! And, indeed, since he insults all women, I am forced to believe that he did not know nor was he acquainted with any honorable and virtuous woman, but, having known only fallen ones who led sinful lives, as the lecherous tend to do, he thought he knew—or claimed to know—that they must all be like this. And if he had only insulted the dishonorable ones and counseled men to flee them, he would have given a good lesson. But no, he accuses them all, without exception. Since he thinks they are deprived of reason and accuses them

1. A paraphrase of *Roman* 16548–86.
2. See *Roman* 16347–706.
3. *Epistle of the God of Love* (1399).
4. As a priest, he is celibate.

wrongfully, he himself should be blamed instead because he is so far from the truth; and his lie is not credible, since the contrary is so obviously true. For if he and all his partisans in this case had sworn that there were, are, and will be many worthy, honorable, educated, and even knowledgeable women who bring more good to the world than he ever did, even in worldly politics and in wise virtue, no harm will be done to anyone. Similarly, there were many who brought about reconciliation with their husbands and quietly kept the secret of their dealings and confidences and suffering even if their husbands were violent and bad lovers. Enough proof can be found of this in the Bible and in other ancient stories, such as in the lives of Sarah, Rebecca, Esther, Judith,[5] and many others. And even nowadays, there are many courageous and noble ladies of France, such as the holy and pious Queen Jeanne, Queen Blanche, the Duchess of Orléans (daughter of the King of France), and the Duchess of Anjou, now Queen of Sicily.[6] They are beautiful, chaste, honorable, and knowledgeable, as are many others. Further, there are many courageous bourgeois ladies such as my Lady of Ferté,[7] wife of Seigneur Pierre de Craon—she is to be praised—and others too numerous to mention here.

And you must believe me, dear sir, that I do not sustain these opinions in favor of women simply because I am myself a woman. For, to be sure, my purpose is simply to uphold the absolute truth because I know from experience that the truth is contrary to those things which I am denying. And as much as I am a woman, I am much better able to speak of these things than one who has no experience in this matter, and who thus can go only by mere assumption and guessing.

And then after all this, by God, let us consider the end of this treatise![8] As a certain proverb says, "Things finish in the end." Pay heed to the purpose of this very awful and shameful conclusion; what am I saying? Shameful? It is so shameful that I dare say that no one who loves virtue and honor will hear this shameful ruse without being ashamed and outraged, when Shame and Reason would not even allow decent people to think these disgraces, let alone listen to them. What is worse, I dare say that no one who loves virtue and honor will hear this shameful ruse without feeling ashamed and outraged, when Shame and Reason. . . . So why praise a text which no one will dare read nor tell in a proper setting—at the table of queens, princesses, or bourgeois ladies, for whom it would be appropriate to cover their faces, to blush with shame? And if you wish to excuse him claiming that it pleased him to use such images for the end of his love tale for the sake of embellishing it, I respond that he does not tell or teach us anything extraordinary whatsoever! Is it not known how men and women customarily copulate? If

5. This list of female biblical exempla will appear again in some of Christine's subsequent works, most notably in the *Livre de la cité des dames* [*Book of the City of Ladies*] (book 2, chapters 31, 32, 38, 39) [translator's note]. Judith: a Jewish widow who delivered the Jews from the Assyrians by beheading their commander, Holofernes (see Judith, an early book not included in the canonical Hebrew Bible). Sarah: wife of Abraham and mother of Isaac (Genesis 12–23). Rebecca: wife of Isaac and mother of Jacob and Esau (Genesis 24–27). Esther: queen of the Persian king Ahasuerus (Xerxes), who saved her fellow Jews from massacre (see Esther).

6. Marie de Châtillon (ca. 1343–1404), daughter of Charles de Blois, duke of Brittainy, who married Louis I of Anjou, younger brother of Charles V. Queen Jeanne (1310–1371), Jeanne d'Evreux, third wife of the French king Charles IV. Queen Blanche (1331–1398), Blanche of Navarre, the second wife of the French king Philip VI. Duchess of Orléans (1328–1392), Blanche of France, daughter of Charles IV and Jeanne d'Evreux, wife of Philip of Orleans (son of Philip VI).

7. Jeanne de Châtillon (ca. 1390–1426/27); her husband was lord of Sablé and La Ferté-Bernard in Brittany.

8. The poem ends with the male Lover's successful attack on the tower and his deflowering of the rose.

he had told us how bears, lions, or birds or other things behaved, and how they were created, it would have been funny because of the mockery, but he tells us nothing new. Surely, he could have used more pleasant and more courtly expressions, which would have pleased beautiful and honorable lovers better, as it would any other virtuous person.

Therefore, according to my limited intelligence and weak judgment and my lack of prolix language, though much more could be said and could be better expressed, I do not find this treatise useful in any way. Instead, it seems to me that great effort was undertaken for little gain. Despite my judgment, I admit that Master Jean de Meun was a very skilled and eloquent cleric who could have created a much more useful doctrine had he applied himself to it—which is a shame, but I suppose that instead of by usefulness, he was guided by his great love for carnality, which consumed him. After all, it is known that our actions reveal our inclinations. This said, I do not rebuke the *Roman de la rose* in its entirety, since without a doubt, it contains good and well-said things. In fact, the danger is all the greater because more credibility is given to the bad even if the good holds more authority and truth. Through this many errors have been planted, cleverly mixed in with truth and virtue. As his priest Genius says, "Flee, flee from women, the evil serpents hidden under the grass!" And he goes on: "Flee, flee the evil hidden beneath the shadow of good and virtue!"

So in conclusion, I say to you, dear sir, and to all your allies and partisans, who praise his work so highly that you are prepared to dare elevate it above all others, with all due respect, it is not worthy of such praise. You do not do other more worthy works justice, because a work without usefulness, which is harmful for the common good even if it is delightful and was painstakingly written, cannot be praised. Let us consider the example of the victorious Romans who, in former times, attributed no praise or honor to something which did not serve a public purpose. Then let us decide whether we are able to crown this romance with laurels.[9] After having considered these things and numerous others, I think it deserves to be buried in flames rather than crowned with laurels, although you claim it to be a "mirror for good living, a model for all estates to lead a life of wise social and moral conduct."[1] With all due respect: On the contrary, I call it an exhortation to vice, encouraging immoral life, a doctrine full of deceit; the path to damnation; a public defamer. It gives rise to suspicion and idolatry, to shame for many people, and possibly to heresy.[2]

I am convinced, however, since you protect him, that you will reply that the good is there to exhort others to practice it, and the bad is there to be avoided. If only I could persuade you that human nature, which is in itself inclined to sinfulness, does not need to be reminded of its limp in order to walk straight. And speaking of all the good which can be noted in this work, certainly more virtuous things, even things relating to social and moral conduct,

9. In the ancient world, laurel wreaths were given to the victors in Greek athletic games and in Roman battles; they were also associated with the triumphs of poets.

1. Jean de Meun proposes the term *Mirror for Lovers* as an alternative title for his continuation of the *Roman*. The term *mirror* inserts the *Roman* in the framework of this didactic genre alongside the numerous contemporary mirrors for princes and princesses. The reference here is to Jean de Montreuil's lost treatise; however, it does come up again in one of his Latin epistles [translator's note].

2. This is the first mention of a possible accusation of heresy by Christine, which will become a recurrent threat uttered by her and Jean Gerson [translator's note].

can be found in many other works by renowned philosophers such as Aristotle, Seneca, Saint Paul, Saint Augustine,[3] and so forth, who as you know attest to and teach the virtues and to flee vices much more effectively, eloquently, and profitably than ever was Jean de Meun able to do. But what will be remembered above all are the carnal pleasures, in the same way the invalid abuses his doctor's permission to drink, and out of gluttony believes that drinking will do him no harm. I am certain that you—to whom God allows it—and all the others onto whom God has bestowed clarity and a good conscience, untarnished by sin or its intention, will do penitence (the purpose of which is to bare the secrets of our conscience and to condemn our own will as judge of truth) and will judge the *Roman de la rose* properly and wish perhaps that you had never seen it. This will suffice.

I should not be accused of madness, arrogance, or pretentiousness in that I, a woman, dared to criticize such a skilled author and to diminish the praise of his work, when he alone dared to defame and to insult, without exception,[4] an entire sex.

1402

From The Book of the City of Ladies[1]

From *Part One*

1. HERE BEGINS THE BOOK OF THE CITY OF LADIES, WHOSE FIRST CHAPTER TELLS WHY AND FOR WHAT PURPOSE THIS BOOK WAS WRITTEN.

Following the practice that has become the habit of my life, namely the devoted study of literature, one day as I was sitting in my study, surrounded by books on many different subjects, my mind grew weary from dwelling at length on the weighty opinions of authors whom I had studied for so long. I looked up from my book, deciding then to leave subtle questions in peace and to read some lyric poetry for pleasure. With this intention, I searched for some small book, and by chance a strange volume came into my hands, not one of my own but one which had been given to me for safekeeping along with some others. When I held it open and saw from its title page that it was by Mathéolus,[2] I smiled, for though I had never seen it before, I had often heard that like other books it discussed respect for women. I thought I would browse through it to amuse myself. I had not been reading for very long when my good mother called me to refresh myself with some supper, for it was evening. Intending to look at it the next day, I put it down. The next morning, again seated in my study as was my habit, I remembered wanting to

3. For ARISTOTLE (384–322 B.C.E.) and AUGUSTINE (354–430 C.E.), see above. Seneca (ca. 4 B.C.E.–65 C.E.), Roman Stoic philosopher, statesman, and dramatist. Saint Paul (d. ca. 67 C.E.), Roman Jew whose conversion to Christianity is recorded in Acts of the New Testament, to whom all New Testament Epistles were attributed.

4. In this debate, Gontier Col, brother of Pierre, did in fact reprimand Christine for her "error and manifest foolishness which was caused by your pretentiousness, as a woman passionate about this matter."

1. Translated by Earl Jeffrey Richards.

2. The *Liber Lamentationum Matheoluli* (*The Book of the Lamentations of Mathéolus*), composed around 1300, translated from Latin into French in the last decades of the 14th century.

examine this book by Mathéolus. I started to read it and went on for a little while. Because the subject seemed to me not very pleasant for people who do not enjoy lies, and of no use in developing virtue or manners, given its lack of integrity in diction and theme, and after browsing here and there and reading the end, I put it down in order to turn my attention to more elevated and useful study. But just the sight of this book, even though it was of no authority, made me wonder how it happened that so many different men—and learned men among them—have been and are so inclined to express both in speaking and in their treatises and writings so many devilish and wicked thoughts about women and their behavior. Not only one or two and not even just this Mathéolus (for this book had a bad name anyway and was intended as a satire) but, more generally, judging from the treatises of all philosophers and poets and from all the orators—it would take too long to mention their names—it seems that they all speak from one and the same mouth. They all concur in one conclusion: that the behavior of women is inclined to and full of every vice. Thinking deeply about these matters, I began to examine my character and my conduct as a natural woman, and, similarly, I discussed this with other women whose company I frequently kept, princesses, great ladies, women of the middle and lower classes in great numbers, who graciously told me of their private experiences and intimate thoughts, in order to know in fact—judging in good conscience and without favor—whether the testimony of so many famous men could be true. To the best of my knowledge, no matter how long I confronted or dissected the problem, I could not see or realize how their claims could be true when compared to the natural behavior and character of women. Yet I still argued vehemently against women, saying that it would be impossible that so many famous men—such solemn scholars, possessed of such deep and great understanding, so clear-sighted in all things, as it seemed—could have spoken falsely on so many occasions that I could hardly find a book on morals where, even before I had read it in its entirety, I did not find several chapters or certain sections attacking women, no matter who the author was. This reason alone, in short, made me conclude that, although my intellect did not perceive my own great faults and, likewise, those of other women because of its simpleness and ignorance, it was however truly fitting that such was the case. And so I relied more on the judgment of others than on what I myself felt and knew. I was so transfixed in this line of thinking for such a long time that it seemed as if I were in a stupor. Like a gushing fountain, a series of authorities, whom I recalled one after another, came to mind, along with their opinions on this topic. And I finally decided that God formed a vile creature when He made woman, and I wondered how such a worthy artisan could have deigned to make such an abominable work which, from what they say, is the vessel as well as the refuge and abode of every evil and vice. As I was thinking this, a great unhappiness and sadness welled up in my heart, for I detested myself and the entire feminine sex, as though we were monstrosities in nature. And in my lament I spoke these words:

"Oh, God, how can this be? For unless I stray from my faith, I must never doubt that Your infinite wisdom and most perfect goodness ever created anything which was not good. Did You yourself not create woman in a very special way and since that time did You not give her all those inclinations which it pleased You for her to have? And how could it be that You could go wrong in anything? Yet look at all these accusations which have been judged, decided, and concluded against women. I do not know how to understand this repugnance. If it is so, fair Lord God, that in fact so many abominations abound in the female sex, for You Yourself say that the testimony of two or three witnesses lends credence,[3] why shall I not doubt that this is true? Alas, God, why did You not let me be born in the world as a male, so that all my inclinations would be to serve You better, and so that I would not stray in anything and would be as perfect as a male is said to be? But since Your kindness has not been extended to me, then forgive my negligence in Your service, most fair Lord God, and may it not displease You, for the servant who receives fewer gifts from his lord is less obliged in his service." I spoke these words to God in my lament and a great deal more for a very long time in sad reflection, and in my folly I considered myself most unfortunate because God had made me inhabit a female body in this world.[4]

* * *

4. HERE THE LADY EXPLAINS TO CHRISTINE THE CITY WHICH SHE HAS BEEN COMMISSIONED TO BUILD AND HOW SHE WAS CHARGED TO HELP CHRISTINE BUILD THE WALL AND ENCLOSURE, AND THEN GIVES HER NAME.

"Thus, fair daughter, the prerogative among women has been bestowed on you to establish and build the City of Ladies. For the foundation and completion of this City you will draw fresh waters from us as from clear fountains, and we will bring you sufficient building stone, stronger and more durable than any marble with cement could be. Thus your City will be extremely beautiful, without equal, and of perpetual duration in the world.

"Have you not read that King Tros founded the great city of Troy with the aid of Apollo, Minerva, and Neptune,[5] whom the people of that time considered gods, and also how Cadmus founded the city of Thebes with the admonition of the gods? And yet over time these cities fell and have fallen into ruin. But I prophesy to you, as a true sybil,[6] that this City, which you will found with our help, will never be destroyed, nor will it ever fall, but will remain prosperous forever, regardless of all its jealous enemies. Although it will be stormed by numerous assaults, it will never be taken or conquered.

"Long ago the Amazon kingdom[7] was begun through the arrangement and enterprise of several ladies of great courage who despised servitude, just as history books have testified. For a long time afterward they maintained it under the rule of several queens, very noble ladies whom they elected themselves, who governed them well and maintained their dominion with great strength. Yet, although they were strong and powerful and had conquered a large part of the entire Orient in the course of their rule and terrified all the neighboring lands (even the Greeks, who were then the flower of all countries in the world, feared them), nevertheless, after a time,

3. See Deuteronomy 17.6.
4. While she is engaged in this lamentation, three ladies appear to Christine, comforting her. The first speaks to her, telling her that with their help she will build a city of ladies, which would house "ladies who are of good reputation and worthy of praise."
5. Christine uses the Roman names of the Greek gods: Apollo, god of music and philosophy; Minerva (Athena), goddess of war and wisdom; and Neptune (Poseidon), god of the sea.
6. In ancient Greece, a female oracle.
7. In Greek mythology, a kingdom of female warriors.

the power of this kingdom declined, so that as with all earthly kingdoms, nothing but its name has survived to the present. But the edifice erected by you in this City which you must construct will be far stronger, and for its founding I was commissioned, in the course of our common deliberation, to supply you with durable and pure mortar to lay the sturdy foundations and to raise the large walls, all around, high, wide, and with mighty, entrenched towers, blockhouses, moats, and palisades,[8] just as is fitting for a city with a strong and lasting defense. Following our plan, you will set the foundations deep to last all the longer, and then you will raise the walls so high that they will not fear anyone. Daughter, now that I have told you the reason for our coming and so that you will more certainly believe my words, I want you to learn my name, by whose sound alone you will be able to learn and know that, if you wish to follow my commands, you have in me an administrator so that you may do your work flawlessly. I am called Lady Reason; you see that you are in good hands. For the time being then, I will say no more."[9]

* * *

8. HERE CHRISTINE TELLS HOW, UNDER REASON'S COMMAND AND ASSISTANCE, SHE BEGAN TO EXCAVATE THE EARTH AND LAY THE FOUNDATION.

Then Lady Reason responded and said, "Get up, daughter! Without waiting any longer, let us go to the Field of Letters. There the City of Ladies will be founded on a flat and fertile plain, where all fruits and freshwater rivers are found and where the earth abounds in all good things. Take the pick of your understanding and dig and clear out a great ditch wherever you see the marks of my ruler, and I will help you carry away the earth on my own shoulders."

I immediately stood up to obey her commands and, thanks to these three ladies, I felt stronger and lighter than before. She went ahead, and I followed behind, and after we had arrived at this field I began to excavate and dig, following her marks with the pick of cross-examination. And this was my first work:

"Lady, I remember well what you told me before, dealing with the subject of how so many men have attacked and continue to attack the behavior of women, that gold becomes more refined the longer it stays in the furnace, which means the more women have been wrongfully attacked, the greater waxes the merit of their glory. But please tell me why and for what reason different authors have spoken against women in their books, since I already know from you that this is wrong; tell me if Nature makes man so inclined or whether they do it out of hatred and where does this behavior come from?"

Then she replied, "Daughter, to give you a way of entering into the question more deeply, I will carry away this first basketful of dirt. This behavior most certainly does not come from Nature, but rather is contrary to Nature, for no connection in the world is as great or as strong as the great love

8. Defensive features of a medieval town. "Palisades": defensive walls enclosing a structure. "Blockhouses": small defensive forts, usually single buildings covering access to some strategic point.

9. The second and third ladies introduce themselves as Rectitude and Justice. Christine thanks the ladies for their comfort and promises to obey them in all things.

which, through the will of God, Nature places between a man and a woman. The causes which have moved and which still move men to attack women, even those authors in those books, are diverse and varied, just as you have discovered. For some have attacked women with good intentions, that is, in order to draw men who have gone astray away from the company of vicious and dissolute women, with whom they might be infatuated, or in order to keep these men from going mad on account of such women, and also so that every man might avoid an obscene and lustful life. They have attacked all women in general because they believe that women are made up of every abomination."

"My lady," I said then, "excuse me for interrupting you here, but have such authors acted well, since they were prompted by a laudable intention? For intention, the saying goes, judges the man."

"That is a misleading position, my good daughter," she said, "for such sweeping ignorance never provides an excuse. If someone killed you with good intention but out of foolishness, would this then be justified? Rather, those who did this, whoever they might be, would have invoked the wrong law; causing any damage or harm to one party in order to help another party is not justice, and likewise attacking all feminine conduct is contrary to the truth, just as I will show you with a hypothetical case. Let us suppose they did this intending to draw fools away from foolishness. It would be as if I attacked fire—a very good and necessary element nevertheless—because some people burnt themselves, or water because someone drowned. The same can be said of all good things which can be used well or used badly. But one must not attack them if fools abuse them, and you have yourself touched on this point quite well elsewhere in your writings.[1] But those who have spoken like this so abundantly—whatever their intentions might be—have formulated their arguments rather loosely only to make their point. Just like someone who has a long and wide robe cut from a very large piece of cloth when the material costs him nothing and when no one opposes him, they exploit the rights of others. But just as you have said elsewhere, if these writers had only looked for the ways in which men can be led away from foolishness and could have been kept from tiring themselves in attacking the life and behavior of immoral and dissolute women—for to tell the straight truth, there is nothing which should be avoided more than an evil, dissolute, and perverted woman, who is like a monster in nature, a counterfeit estranged from her natural condition, which must be simple, tranquil, and upright—then I would grant you that they would have built a supremely excellent work. But I can assure you that these attacks on all women—when in fact there are so many excellent women—have never originated with me, Reason, and that all who subscribe to them have failed totally and will continue to fail. So now throw aside these black, dirty, and uneven stones from your work, for they will never be fitted into the fair edifice of your City.

"Other men have attacked women for other reasons: such reproach has occurred to some men because of their own vices and others have been moved by the defects of their own bodies, others through pure jealousy, still others by the pleasure they derive in their own personalities from slander.

1. Reason may be referring to Christine's letters in the debate over *The Romance of the Rose* (see above).

Others, in order to show they have read many authors, base their own writings on what they have found in books and repeat what other writers have said and cite different authors.

* * *

From *Part Two*

36. AGAINST THOSE MEN WHO CLAIM IT IS NOT GOOD FOR WOMEN TO BE EDUCATED.

Following these remarks,[2] I, Christine, spoke, "My lady, I realize that women have accomplished many good things and that even if evil women have done evil, it seems to me, nevertheless, that the benefits accrued and still accruing because of good women—particularly the wise and literary ones and those educated in the natural sciences whom I mentioned above—outweigh the evil. Therefore, I am amazed by the opinion of some men who claim that they do not want their daughters, wives, or kinswomen to be educated because their mores[3] would be ruined as a result."

She responded, "Here you can clearly see that not all opinions of men are based on reason and that these men are wrong. For it must not be presumed that mores necessarily grow worse from knowing the moral sciences, which teach the virtues, indeed, there is not the slightest doubt that moral education amends and ennobles them. How could anyone think or believe that whoever follows good teaching or doctrine is the worse for it? Such an opinion cannot be expressed or maintained. I do not mean that it would be good for a man or a woman to study the art of divination[4] or those fields of learning which are forbidden—for the holy Church did not remove them from common use without good reason—but it should not be believed that women are the worse for knowing what is good.

"Quintus Hortensius, a great rhetorician and consumately skilled orator in Rome, did not share this opinion. He had a daughter, named Hortensia,[5] whom he greatly loved for the subtlety of her wit. He had her learn letters and study the science of rhetoric, which she mastered so thoroughly that she resembled her father Hortensius not only in wit and lively memory but also in her excellent delivery and order of speech—in fact, he surpassed her in nothing. As for the subject discussed above, concerning the good which comes about through women, the benefits realized by this woman and her learning were, among others, exceptionally remarkable. That is, during the time when Rome was governed by three men,[6] this Hortensia began to support the cause of women and to undertake what no man dared to undertake. There was a question whether certain taxes should be levied on women and on their jewelry during a needy period in Rome. This woman's eloquence was so compelling that she was listened to, no less readily than her father would have been, and she won her case.

2. Spoken by Christine's second guide, Rectitude.
3. Moral attitudes.
4. Occult practices.
5. Hortensia appears in BOCCACCIO's *Concerning Famous Women* (1361), chap. 82. Quintus Hortensius: dictator (in the Roman Republic, a temporary position of great power) appointed in 287 B.C.E.
6. Rome was usually governed by two men (consuls elected for 1-year terms); the third here is the dictator.

"Similarly, to speak of more recent times, without searching for examples in ancient history, Giovanni Andrea,[7] a solemn law professor in Bologna not quite sixty years ago, was not of the opinion that it was bad for women to be educated. He had a fair and good daughter, named Novella, who was educated in the law to such an advanced degree that when he was occupied by some task and not at leisure to present his lectures to his students, he would send Novella, his daughter, in his place to lecture to the students from his chair. And to prevent her beauty from distracting the concentration of her audience, she had a little curtain drawn in front of her. In this manner she could on occasion supplement and lighten her father's occupation. He loved her so much that, to commemorate her name, he wrote a book of remarkable lectures on the law which he entitled *Novella super Decretalium*,[8] after his daughter's name.

"Thus, not all men (and especially the wisest) share the opinion that it is bad for women to be educated. But it is very true that many foolish men have claimed this because it displeased them that women knew more than they did. Your father, who was a great scientist and philosopher, did not believe that women were worth less by knowing science; rather, as you know, he took great pleasure from seeing your inclination to learning. The feminine opinion of your mother, however, who wished to keep you busy with spinning and silly girlishness, following the common custom of women, was the major obstacle to your being more involved in the sciences. But just as the proverb already mentioned above says, 'No one can take away what Nature has given,' your mother could not hinder in you the feeling for the sciences which you, through natural inclination, had nevertheless gathered together in little droplets. I am sure that, on account of these things, you do not think you are worth less but rather that you consider it a great treasure for yourself; and you doubtless have reason to."

And I, Christine, replied to all of this, "Indeed, my lady, what you say is as true as the Lord's Prayer."

* * *

1405

7. Andrea (1275–1347) must have been known to Christine's father.

8. Literally, "new things about the decrees" (Latin).

JOACHIM DU BELLAY
ca. 1522–1560

Joachim du Bellay is known for having written one of the first theoretical defenses of a vernacular language against an imperial language. Contemporary postcolonial writers often attack the prestige of European languages, but those same European languages were once considered by Renaissance authors to be inferior to Latin and Greek. In *The Defense and Enrichment of the French Language* (1549), Joachim du Bellay argued that with careful cultivation, French was capable of equaling Greek and Latin as a literary language. But du Bellay's defense of the vernacular was paradoxically also an attack on the vernacular: French poetry, in his view, had to abandon its own popular forms in order to acquire the dignity of the classics.

Born in Anjou (France), a younger son in a minor branch of an ancient and noble French family, Joachim du Bellay possessed, from the beginning, both nobility and resentment. Impoverished, in poor health, and abandoned, du Bellay was to dream of a future as noble as the past—a nobility obtained through the pen rather than the sword. He was a frail child, and one of his long illnesses later left him nearly deaf. Both his parents had died by the time he was ten, leaving him in the care of an older brother. In one of the few references to his early years, Joachim berates his brother for indifference and for neglecting his education. Still, he did learn Latin and ultimately left home to study law at Poitiers, where he appears to have concentrated more on studying rhetoric and entering poetry competitions. His time at Poitiers is described by scholars as setting the scene for his entrance into the world of scholarship, poetry, and the life of the mind, the world that would become his legacy.

By all accounts, the turning point of du Bellay's life was the day he met Pierre de Ronsard, a distant cousin encountered by chance, apparently at a country inn. They were about the same age, with a common passion for learning and a shared love of poetry. Ronsard was a student in Paris at the Collège de Coqueret, a small, rundown boardinghouse that was one of many colleges that then formed the University of Paris. Du Bellay moved to Paris and enrolled at Coqueret in 1547.

Jean Dorat, the master at Coqueret, was a young, enthusiastic scholar of Greek philology, the historical and comparative study of the language, literature, and culture of ancient Greece. As master, he transformed the college into a center of humanism and rigorous scholarship. The handful of young noblemen who lived there studied literally around the clock, sometimes working in shifts to make the most efficient use of candles. They learned Greek, Latin, and Italian poetry and argued about translations, rhetoric, and the use of language. They soon began to see themselves as a unified group destined to bring about revolutionary changes in poetry. The group first called itself the Brigade but later chose a more peaceful, and more grandiose, name: the *Pléiade*, or constellation of seven poets (Pierre de Ronsard, Joachim du Bellay, Jean-Antoine de Baïf, Etienne Jodelle, Pontus de Tyard, Rémy Belleau, and Jean Dorat himself). Believing in the divine inspiration of poetry, they looked to the future, intent on creating a rich language that would benefit French poets to come.

Two years after his arrival in Paris, du Bellay wrote and published *The Defense and Enrichment of the French Language*. That same year he published a collection of love sonnets in French, *L'Olive* (the sonnet was one of the few vernacular forms approved by the Pléiade). In 1553 he accompanied Cardinal Jean du Bellay, his cousin, to Rome, where he served, grumblingly, as the cardinal's secretary. Two of his major works came out of his four-year stay in Italy: the sonnets in *Les Antiquitez de Rome* (1558) praise the glories of ancient Rome, while the poems in *Les Regrets* (1558) tell of the disillusionment he felt in the Rome of the present day. His failed love affair with a married Italian woman seems to have hastened his return to his newly appreciated homeland. Two years later, miserable, he died at the age of thirty-seven.

To understand du Bellay's argument in the *Defense*, we must recall the status of the French language during the sixteenth century. While Latin was the language of scholarship, legal documents, and poetry, the French vernacular suffered from an intellectual inferiority complex as the language of the masses, more frequently spoken than written. This two-language social order led to continual discord over the comparative value of languages, particularly French and Latin. During the 1530s and 1540s, scholars enthusiastically translated the texts of ancient Greece and Rome into the vernacular. However, because Latin was considered a richer, more poetic language, these same men composed their own poetry in Latin. The weighty presence of Latin in the church, in the academy, and in the poetry of French authors signified to some a linguistic enslavement. The question naturally arose as to what equips a language for eloquence. Was it the very nature of Greek and Latin that allowed a flourishing of scholarship? Or, rather, were all languages potentially equal?

The Defense and Enrichment of the French Language was written with a specific goal: to justify the French vernacular by establishing a new poetics to elevate the status of French and, in turn, France itself. A 1548 pamphlet had set the popular forms of French poetry on a par with Greek and Latin works, but the students at the Collège de Coqueret saw this declaration of victory in the battle for French as premature. French poetry required the enrichment provided by a study of classical authors. The Pléiade needed to respond with a manifesto, and du Bellay was the man for the job. As the pamphlet that provoked his treatise indicates, vernacular forms were already enjoying a lively reception through the efforts of poets of lowly birth such as Clément Marot, a rival of du Bellay's. Du Bellay was thus engaging in a class struggle with other French poets while defending French against Latin.

The *Defense* begins with a distinction between the natural and the cultural. Claiming that all languages are potentially equal in value, du Bellay points out the fundamental difference between plants and languages. While languages may appear to be of the same order as plants, they are, in fact, cultural constructs and thus not subject to the same *natural* variations of strength and weakness. The relative weakness of the French language is only temporary. Du Bellay supports this claim by discussing the rise of Latin: the Romans borrowed extensively from Greek authors but wrote in Latin; through imitation, they transformed Latin from a rather rough and brutish tongue to a language of literature and philosophy. Even the Greeks, he will later claim, drew from the wisdom of Egypt and India.

Although du Bellay begins his treatise by distinguishing between languages and plants, he goes on to employ a wide array of agricultural metaphors to describe the kinds of cultivation needed to transform a feeble language into a fruitful one. The metaphor of grafting seems ideal, conveying a process neither natural nor artificial: the grafting of one language onto another makes possible the development of robust new forms.

To enrich the vernacular, du Bellay recommends translation as a way of incorporating the knowledge of the ancients; but for highly rhetorical writings, especially poetry, translation cannot capture stylistic invention, which is specific to each language. Therefore, for poetry, imitation rather than translation is needed. The word du Bellay uses for a properly cultivated language is *copious*, which can be read as both "abundant" and "copied." But imitation should not be slavish: imitation can improve a natural genius but not create one. Without imitation, genius remains "wild"; without genius, imitation remains "apelike." What is to be imitated is the *spirit* of the original, not its external form.

Nevertheless, classical forms are inherently richer than popular forms, and French poets should adopt them, swallowing their classical predecessors whole and cannibalistically incorporating their genius. French poetry should abandon the ballades, rondelets, and virelays of the medieval popular tradition in favor of more learned forms: the ode (soon to be cultivated by Ronsard), the elegy, the eclogue, the sonnet. Du Bellay thus exhorts French poets to imitate and reincarnate the poets of Greece and Rome in order to demonstrate that French poetry can be as noble as the classics.

By trying to become something it was not, French poetry began to become what it is. The struggle between classical and popular forms gave rise to a kind of poetry that could not have been derived from either alone. Du Bellay's defense of French, ambivalent though it was about the popular roots of the vernacular, launched a poetic movement destined to stand as one of the golden moments of French poetry.

***The Defense and Enrichment of the French Language* Keywords:** Language, Literary History, Philology, Poetry, Rhetoric, Tradition, Vernacular Language

From The Defense and Enrichment of the French Language[1]

From *First Book*

CHAPTER 1
THE ORIGIN OF LANGUAGES

If Nature (of whom a person of great renown has, not without reason, wondered whether we should call her mother or stepmother[2]) had given all men the same desire and inclination, besides the innumerable benefits that would have resulted, human inconstancy would not have had to forge for itself so many ways of speaking. This diversity and confusion can rightly be called the Tower of Babel.[3] For languages are not born of themselves like herbs, roots, and trees, some of them sickly and weak in their kind, others healthy and robust and more capable of bearing the weight of human conceptions, but all their strength is born of the desire and will of mortals. That, it seems to me, is a great reason why we should not praise one language and blame another, since they all come from a single source and origin—that is, from the imagination of men—and have been shaped by the same judgment and for a single end—that is, to express among us the conceptions and apprehensions of the mind. It is true that with the passage of time some, from having been more carefully ordered, have become richer than others. But that should not be attributed to the natural superiority of those languages, but only to the artifice and industry of men. And therefore all things Nature has created, all the arts and learned disciplines in the four quarters of the world, are in themselves the same, but since men differ in their desires, they speak and write differently. Accordingly, I can not sufficiently blame the foolish arrogance and temerity of some of our fellow countrymen who, taking themselves for nothing less than Greeks or Romans, despise and reject with a more than Stoic haughtiness everything written in French. And I cannot sufficiently wonder at the strange opinion of some learned men, who think that our vulgar tongue is incapable of all good letters and erudition, as if an idea should be judged good or bad for its language alone. I do not aim to satisfy the first sort. I do wish (if I can do it) to change the opinion of the second with some arguments I hope briefly to develop, not that I feel myself more clear-sighted in this or in other things than they are, but because the affection they bear toward foreign languages does not allow them to reach a sound and impartial judgment concerning their vulgar tongue.

CHAPTER 2
THAT THE FRENCH LANGUAGE SHOULD NOT BE CALLED BARBAROUS

To begin, then, to broach the subject, as to the meaning of this word *barbarous*: in antiquity they were called barbarous who spoke Greek badly. For as

1. Translated by Richard Helgerson, whose notes have sometimes been slightly edited.
2. That is, kind or merciless; see *Natural History* 7.1, by the Roman writer Pliny the Elder (23–79 C.E.).
3. See Genesis 11, which describes how God responded to men's attempt to build this tower to heaven by confusing their language, thereby creating many different languages where there had been one for all people.

foreigners coming to Athens attempted to speak Greek, they often fell into this absurd sound *Barbaras*. Afterwards the Greeks transferred this term to brutal and cruel customs, calling all nations but Greece barbarous. This should in no way lessen the excellence of our language, seeing that this Greek arrogance, admiring only its own inventions, had neither the right nor the privilege thus to legitimate its nation and bastardize others. As Anacharsis said, the Scythians[4] were barbarians among the Athenians, but so were the Athenians among the Scythians. And even if the barbarity of the manners of our ancestors did rightly move them to call us barbarians, I do not see why we should be thought so now, since in civility of manners, equity of laws, greatness of courage, in short, in all forms and ways of living that are no less praiseworthy than beneficial, we are in nothing inferior to them, but rather superior, seeing that they are now such that we can justly call them by the name they gave others. That the Romans called us barbarians is of still less concern, given their ambition and insatiable hunger for glory, which strove not only to subjugate but to render all other nations vile and abject in comparison with them, especially the Gauls[5] from whom they suffered more shame and injury than from the others.

On this subject, often wondering how it happens that the deeds of the Roman people are so celebrated by everyone, indeed for so long preferred over those of all other nations together, I find no greater reason than this: it is because the Romans had such a great multitude of writers that most of their deeds (to say no worse) through the space of so many years—their eagerness in battle, their devastation of Italy, their foreign invasions—have been conserved intact to our times. The deeds of other nations, particularly of the Gauls before they fell to the power of the French,[6] and the deeds of the French themselves from the time they gave their name to the Gauls, have, on the contrary, been so poorly preserved, that we have nearly lost not only the glory of them but their very memory. This loss has been aggravated by the envy of the Romans, who, as if joined together to conspire against us, have diminished in every way they could our warlike praises, whose brilliance they could not endure. And not only have they wronged us in that, but to render us still more odious and contemptible, they have called us brutal, cruel, and barbarous. Someone will say, "Why did they spare the Greeks this name?" Because they would have done themselves still greater injury than to the Greeks, from whom they had borrowed everything good they had, at least with regard to the learned disciplines and the enrichment of their language. These reasons seem to me sufficient to make any equitable judge of things understand that our language (though we have been called barbarous either by our enemies or by those who had no right to give us this name) should not be scorned, especially by those to whom it belongs and is natural and who are in nothing inferior to the Greeks and Romans.

4. The Greek name for the nomadic peoples north of the Black Sea, in what is today Moldova, Ukraine, and western Russia. Anacharsis (6th c. B.C.E.), Scythian prince who traveled widely in Greece and was later credited with many pithy sayings.

5. Ancient Celtic peoples occupying the area that became modern France.

6. That is, the Franks, German tribes that entered the Roman provinces in the 3d century C.E. and overthrew the last Roman governor in Gaul in 486.

CHAPTER 3

WHY THE FRENCH LANGUAGE IS NOT AS RICH AS GREEK AND LATIN

And if our language is not as copious and rich as Greek or Latin, that should not be imputed to any defect in it, as though of itself it could never be other than poor and sterile, but should rather be attributed to the ignorance of our ancestors, who, holding (as someone[7] said, speaking of the ancient Romans) well-doing in higher esteem than fair speaking and preferring to leave to their posterity examples of virtue rather than precepts, denied themselves the glory of their high deeds and us the benefit of imitating them, and by the same means left us our language so poor and naked that it needs the ornaments and (so to speak) the feathers of others. But who would dare say that Greek and Latin were always at the level of excellence they attained at the time of Homer and of Demosthenes, of Virgil and of Cicero?[8] And had those authors judged that, whatever diligence and cultivation were applied to those languages, they would never be able to produce greater fruit, would they have made such great efforts to bring them to the height at which we now see them?

I can say as much of our language, which is just beginning to flower without bearing fruit, or rather, like a seedling and fresh shoot, has not yet flowered, much less yielded all the fruit it is capable of producing. That comes certainly not from any defect in its nature, as apt to engender as others, but through the fault of those who have had it in their care and have not sufficiently tended it; but like a wild plant in that same uncultivated place where it was born, they have let it grow old and nearly die, without ever watering it, pruning it, or protecting it from the bramble and thorns that shaded it. Had the ancient Romans been as negligent in the cultivation of their language when it first began to sprout, it would certainly not have become so great in such a brief time. But they, like good farmers, first transplanted it from a wild to a cultivated site. Then, so that it might yield fruit better and more quickly, pruning away the useless branches, they replaced them with fine and cultivated branches, taken in masterly fashion from the Greek language, which were rapidly so well grafted to their trunk and made to resemble it that from that time on they have no longer appeared adopted but natural. From this were born in the Latin language those flowers and those fruits colored with great eloquence, along with meter and the skillful blending of sound with sense, all of which every language produces not by its own nature but by art. Thus if the Greeks and Romans, more diligent in the cultivation of their languages than we are in that of ours, could not find in theirs, save as the result of great labor and industry, either grace or meter or indeed any eloquence, should we be surprised if our vulgar tongue is not as rich as it might be and take that as a reason to despise it as vile and worthless?

The time will perhaps come—and with the help of the good fortune of France, I have high hopes for it—when this noble and powerful kingdom will

7. The Roman historian Sallust (86–34 B.C.E.) in *Bellum Catalinae* 8.

8. Du Bellay chooses conventional representatives of excellence in Greek and Latin: in epic poetry, Homer (ca. 8th c. B.C.E.) and Virgil (70–19 B.C.E.); and in oratory, the Athenian Demosthenes (384–322 B.C.E.) and Cicero (106–43 B.C.E.).

in its turn seize the reins of universal dominion and when our language (if with Francis[9] the French language has not been wholly buried), which is just beginning to put down roots, will spring from the ground and grow to such height and girth that it will equal the Greeks and Romans themselves, producing, like them, Homers, Demosthenes, Virgils, and Ciceros, just as France has sometimes produced Pericles, Nicias, Alcibiades, Themistocles, Caesars, and Scipios.[1]

CHAPTER 4
THAT THE FRENCH LANGUAGE IS NOT AS POOR AS MANY JUDGE IT

I do not, however, consider our vulgar tongue, as it is now, to be as vile and abject as do those ambitious admirers of the Greek and Latin languages, who would not think, were they Pitho[2] herself, goddess of persuasion, that they could say anything of worth except in a foreign language not understood by the common people. And whoever wishes to look closely into the matter will find that our French language is not so poor that it cannot render faithfully what it borrows from others or so barren that it cannot produce on its own some fruit of good invention by means of the industry and diligence of its cultivators, if any are found who are such friends to their country and to themselves that they would apply themselves to it. But to whom, after God, shall we give thanks for such a benefit if not to our late good king and father Francis, the first of that name and first in all virtues? I say "first" inasmuch as he first in his noble kingdom restored all the good arts and learned disciplines to their former dignity and thus made our language, which was previously rude and unpolished, elegant and, if not as copious as it might be, at least a faithful interpreter of all others. And because of this, philosophers, historians, physicians, poets, Greek and Latin orators have learned to speak French. As, I might add, have the Hebrews: the Holy Scriptures[3] bear ample witness to what I say.

I will here leave aside the superstitious arguments of those who maintain that the mysteries of theology must not be laid bare and, as it were, profaned in a vulgar tongue,[4] as well as what they allege who hold the contrary opinion. For that controversy does not belong to what I have undertaken, which is only to show that our language did not at its birth have the gods and the stars so set against it that it could not one day achieve a level of excellence and perfection as well as any other, since all branches of learning can be faithfully and copiously treated in it, as may be seen from such a great number of Greek and Latin books, as well as Italian, Spanish, and others, translated into French by many excellent pens of our times.

9. Francis I (1494–1547), king of France (1515–47) and patron of the arts.
1. Du Bellay names famous statesmen and generals. The Greeks, all Athenians, were active during the 5th century B.C.E.—Pericles (ca. 495–429), Nicias (ca. 470–413), Alcibiades (ca. 450–404), and Themistocles (ca. 528–462). Julius Caesar (100–44 B.C.E.) and Scipio Africanus (ca. 236–184/3 B.C.E.) were statesmen as well as the most brilliant generals of Roman antiquity.
2. That is, Peitho (literally, "persuasion": Greek), in Greek mythology the personification of persuasion and seduction.
3. As allusion to biblical translations by, among others, Jacques Lefèvre d'Étaples in 1530 and Pierre-Robert Olivetan in 1535, to which objections of the sort du Bellay mentions in the following sentence were raised, especially by the theology faculty of the Sorbonne [translator's note].
4. Many within the Catholic Church resisted the publication of the Bible in French.

CHAPTER 5
THAT TRANSLATIONS ARE NOT SUFFICIENT TO GIVE PERFECTION TO THE FRENCH LANGUAGE

Nevertheless this very praiseworthy labor of translation does not seem to me the only or sufficient means to raise our vulgar tongue to be the equal—and the rival—of other more famous languages. I intend to prove this so clearly that no one (I believe) will wish to say the opposite, unless he is a manifest slanderer of truth. And first it is an accepted fact among all the best authors on rhetoric that there are five parts of speaking well: invention, elocution, disposition, memory, and pronunciation.[5] Now inasmuch as these last two are not so much learned by the benefit of languages as they are given to each person according to his innate talent, augmented and maintained by studious exercise and continual diligence, and inasmuch as disposition resides more in the discrimination and good judgment of the orator than in particular rules and precepts—since events of time, circumstances of place, conditions of persons, and diversity of occasions are innumerable—I will content myself with speaking of the first two: namely, invention and elocution.

The duty of the orator is then to speak elegantly and copiously on whatever topic is proposed.[6] Now, the ability to speak in this way of all things can only be acquired by a perfect knowledge of all branches of learning, which were first treated by the Greeks and then by their imitators, the Romans. It is thus necessary that those two languages be understood by anyone who wishes to attain that copiousness and richness of invention, which is the first and principal piece in the orator's armor. And with regard to this point, faithful translators can greatly aid and support those who have not the unique opportunity to devote themselves to foreign languages. But as for elocution, certainly the most difficult part of rhetoric and that without which all others remain useless, like a sword still enclosed in its sheath: elocution (I say), by which an orator is principally judged more excellent and one way of speaking thought better than another, being that from which eloquence is itself named, and whose virtue resides in appropriate words, familiar and not estranged from their common use, in metaphors, allegories, comparisons, similes, vivid descriptions,[7] and so many other figures and ornaments without which any writing in prose or verse is bare, maimed, and weak; I will never believe that one can learn all that from translators, for it is impossible to render a work with the same grace the author put into it, inasmuch as each language has an indescribable something that belongs to it alone, so that if you strive to express its inborn quality in another language, abiding by the law of translation, which is never to stray beyond the bounds of the author, your diction will be constrained, cold, and graceless. And as proof, just read a Latin Demosthenes and Homer, a French Cicero and Virgil, to see if they will beget such emotions in you—will, indeed, transform you like a Proteus[8] into differing kinds—as you feel reading those authors in their own languages. Going from the original to the translation, you will seem to pass from the burning

5. These divisions are standard in Greek and Latin handbooks of rhetoric.
6. See Cicero, *De Oratore* 1.6.20 [translator's note].
7. In French, *energies*, from the Greek *enargeia* or *energeia*, rhetorical terms for vivid description or description of things in motion [translator's note].
8. In Greek mythology a seer, son of Poseidon (god of the sea), who is able to assume different shapes at will.

mountain of Etna to the cold summit of the Caucasus.[9] And what I say of the Latin and Greek languages can be equally said of all the vulgar tongues, of which I will cite only Petrarch,[1] of whom I dare say that if a reborn Homer and Virgil undertook to translate him, they could not render him with the same grace and freshness that he has in his native Tuscan. Yet some in our time have tried to make him speak French.[2]

These, in brief, are the reasons that have made me think that the diligent service of translators, otherwise very useful in instructing those ignorant of foreign languages in the knowledge of things, is not sufficient to give our language that perfection and, as painters do with their paintings, that final touch we desire. And if the reasons I have provided do not appear strong enough, I will produce as my guarantors and defenders the ancient Roman authors, principally poets and orators, who (although Cicero translated several books of Xenophon and Aratus[3] and Horace offers precepts on good translating[4]) devoted themselves to this activity more for their study and individual benefit than to publish it for the amplification of their language, for their own glory, and for the use of others. If any have seen works of that time under the title of translations—I mean works of Cicero, of Virgil, and of the happy age of Augustus[5]—they can contradict what I say.

CHAPTER 6
OF BAD TRANSLATORS AND OF NOT TRANSLATING POETS

But what shall I say of some who truly deserve rather to be called traitors than translators?[6] For they betray those they undertake to reveal, denying them their glory and by the same means seduce ignorant readers, showing them white for black. To gain the name of learned men, they translate on credit languages, like Hebrew and Greek, of which they have never understood the first elements and to raise their standing still further, take on poets, a race of authors that, if I could or would translate, I would address as little as possible because of that divinity of invention they have more than others, that greatness of style, magnificence of words, gravity of thoughts, boldness and variety of figures, and a thousand other adornments of poetry; in short, that energy and indefinable spirit in their writings which the Latins would call *genius*.[7] All these things can be no more rendered in translation than a painter can represent the soul along with the body of the person he undertakes to portray from life.

What I say is not directed at those who by the order of princes and great lords translate the most famous Greek and Latin poets, for the obedience one

9. Mountain range between the Black and Caspian Seas. Etna: a volcano on the eastern coast of Sicily.
1. Italian poet and scholar (1304–1374).
2. Beginning early in the 16th century, several French translations of Petrarch appeared, most notably by the French poet Clément Marot (ca. 1496–1544), du Bellay's rival.
3. Greek poet (ca. 315–ca. 240 B.C.E.); his best-known work, a poem on astronomy titled *Phaenomena*, was translated by Cicero. Xenophon (ca. 428/27–ca. 354 B.C.E.), Athenian historian and general, author of the *Anabasis*, which significantly influenced Latin literature.
4. Du Bellay may have in mind the advice of the Roman poet HORACE (65–8 B.C.E.) in *Ars Poetica*, line 268, to "unroll Greek originals in your hand night and day."
5. The first emperor of Rome (63 B.C.E.–14 C.E.; proclaimed emperor, 27). He was a great patron of letters, and, after decades of civil war, his rule was a time of peace and prosperity.
6. The Italian proverb *traduttori, traditori*, (translators, traitors) is echoed in du Bellay's *traditeurs . . . traducteurs*.
7. The guardian spirit of a person or place.

owes such figures admits no excuse in this regard, but I mean rather to speak to those who from gaiety of heart (as they say) lightly undertake such things and accomplish them in the same way. O Apollo! O Muses![8] Thus to profane the sacred remains of antiquity! But I will say no more. Let him then who wishes to produce a work worthy to be valued in his own vulgar tongue leave the work of translating, especially of poets, to those who from a laborious task of little profit—one, I dare say again, useless and even harmful to the growth of their language—rightly earn more vexation than glory.

CHAPTER 7
HOW THE ROMANS ENRICHED THEIR LANGUAGE

If the Romans (someone will say) did not devote themselves to this labor of translation, then by what means were they able so to enrich their language, indeed to make it almost the equal of Greek? By imitating the best Greek authors, transforming themselves into them, devouring them, and, after having thoroughly digested them, converting them into blood and nourishment, selecting, each according to his own nature and the topic he wished to choose, the best author, all of whose rarest and most exquisite strengths they diligently observed and, like shoots, grafted them, as I said earlier, and adapted them to their own language. In doing this (I say) the Romans constructed all those fine writings we so ardently praise and admire, judging some to be the equal of the Greeks, preferring some as superior to them.

And of what I say Cicero and Virgil, whom willingly and with honor I always cite from the Latin language, provide good proof. The one gave himself entirely to the imitation of the Greeks, counterfeited and so vividly expressed the copiousness of Plato, the vehemence of Demosthenes, and the joyful sweetness of Isocrates that Molo of Rhodes,[9] once hearing him declaim, cried that he was bringing Greek eloquence to Rome. The other so well imitated Homer, Hesiod, and Theocritus[1] that since then it has been said of him that of those three he surpassed one, equaled one, and came so close to the other that, if the felicity of the subjects they treated had been the same, the prize would have been in doubt. Thus I ask you, you who undertake only translations, if these famous authors had diverted themselves in translating, would they have raised their language to the excellence and height where we now see it? Then do not think, whatever diligence and industry you may expend in that pursuit, that you can do enough for our language, which still crawls on all fours, for it to lift its head and get on its feet.

8. In Greek mythology, 9 daughters of Memory who preside over the arts and all intellectual pursuits. Apollo: the Greek and Roman god of music and prophecy.

9. Apollonius Molon (1st c. B.C.E.), rhetorician who lectured at Rhodes and visited Rome; he taught Cicero and other Romans. PLATO (ca. 427–ca. 347 B.C.E.), Greek philosopher; like him, Cicero wrote philosophical dialogues, including *De Republica*. Isocrates (436–338 B.C.E), Athenian orator, rhetorician, and teacher.

1. Greek poet (ca. 300–260 B.C.E.), whose pastoral poetry Virgil imitated in his *Eclogues*. Hesiod (active ca. 700 B.C.E.), Greek didactic poet whom Virgil imitated in his *Georgics*.

From *Second Book*

CHAPTER 3

THAT NATURAL TALENT IS NOT ENOUGH FOR HIM WHO IN POETRY WOULD PRODUCE A WORK WORTHY OF IMMORTALITY

But since there are good and bad models in all languages, I do not, Reader, want you to attach yourself without choice and judgment to the first comer. It would be far better to write without imitation than to resemble a bad author, seeing that even the most learned[2] agree that natural talent without the rules of art does more than rules without talent. Nevertheless, inasmuch as the amplification of our language (which is the subject I am addressing) cannot be accomplished without rules and erudition, I do want to warn those who aspire to that glory to imitate good Greek and Roman authors—indeed, even Italians, Spaniards, and others—or not to write at all, unless for yourself (as we say) and your Muses. Let no one answer me here by citing some of our writers who without any rules of art, or at most with no more than mediocre ones, have acquired great renown in our vulgar tongue.[3] Those who willingly admire petty things and disdain whatever exceeds their capacity will make as much of them as they want. But I know that the learned will put them in no other rank than that of those who speak French well and who have (as Cicero said of the earliest Roman authors) good wits but very little art. Nor let anyone claim that poets are born, for that can be assumed from the ardor and alacrity of mind which naturally motivates poets and without which all the rules of art would be lost on them and useless. Certainly it would be all too easy, and for that very reason contemptible, to win everlasting fame, if the felicity of nature that is granted even to the most ignorant were enough to do something worthy of immortality. He who wishes to fly through the hands and lips of men[4] must long dwell in his study. And he who desires to live in the memory of posterity must, as though dead unto himself, often sweat and tremble and, just as our courtier poets drink, eat, and sleep at their ease, endure hunger, thirst, and long vigils. These are the wings by which the writings of men soar to heaven.

But to return to the beginning of this topic, let our imitator first consider those he would imitate and what in them can and should be imitated, so as not to do as those who, wanting to resemble some great lord, will imitate rather a petty gesture of his or a vicious mode of behavior than his virtues and good graces. Above all, our imitator must have the judgment to know his own strength and to weigh how much his shoulders can bear. Let him diligently sound his own nature and adapt himself to the imitation of him to whom he feels closest. Otherwise his imitation will resemble that of an ape.

2. See Cicero, *Pro Archia* 7.15 and *De Oratore* 1.25.113; Quintilian, *Institutio Oratoria* (ca. 96 C.E.) 2.19.2 [translator's note].

3. The allusion is again to Clément Marot, who was a popular poet at the court of Francis I.

4. Here begins a passage lifted verbatim from one of du Bellay's Italian predecessors, Sperone Speroni (*Dialogo delle lingue*, 1542).

CHAPTER 4
WHAT KINDS OF POEMS THE FRENCH POET SHOULD CHOOSE

First then, O future Poet, read and reread. With nightly and daily hand, turn over the pages of Greek and Roman models. Then do me the favor of leaving to the Floral Games of Toulouse and the Confraternity of Rouen[5] all those old French poetic forms, such as rondels, ballads, virelays, royal airs, songs, and other such spices,[6] which corrupt the taste of our language and serve only as evidence of our ignorance. Give yourself over to those amusing epigrams, not as a host of new tale-tellers do today, who in a poem of ten lines are happy to have said nothing of worth in the first nine lines so long as there is a little joke in the tenth. But if lasciviousness does not please you, in imitation of a Martial[7] or some other of good reputation mix profit with pleasure.[8] Distill in a flowing and not harsh style those touching elegies, modeled after an Ovid, a Tibullus, and a Propertius,[9] weaving in from time to time some of those ancient myths, no small adornment of poetry. Sing me those odes,[1] still unknown to the French Muse, on a lute well tuned to the sound of the Greek and Roman lyre, and let there be no line in which some vestige of rare and ancient learning fails to appear. And for this, the praises of the gods and of virtuous men, the destined course of worldly things, the preoccupations of young men, such as love, free-flowing wine, and all good living, will supply you with matter. Above all, take care that this kind of poem be removed from the commonplace, enriched and illuminated with fit words and lively epithets, adorned with grave reflections, and varied with all sorts of poetic colors and ornaments, not like a "Laissez la verte couleur," "Amour avec Psyches," "O combien est heureuse,"[2] and other such works, worthier to be called vulgar songs than odes or lyric poems. As for epistles, this is not a kind of poem that can greatly enrich our vulgar tongue, since they are normally about familiar and domestic matters, unless you wanted to write them in imitation of elegies, like Ovid, or make them sententious and grave, like Horace.[3] I say much the same of satires, which the French, for I know not what reason, have called *coqs-à-l'âne*,[4] and which I advise you to practice just as infrequently, since I want you to avoid slander, unless, after the example of the ancients,

5. The oldest of several bourgeois fraternal societies established beginning in the 12th century to cultivate music and poetry. The Floral Games of Toulouse: an institution founded in 1323 by seven minstrel poets; during the 16th century, at the height of its glory, it was renamed the College of the Art and Science of Rhetoric.

6. Vernacular French medieval poetic genres.

7. Roman poet (ca. 40–ca. 104 C.E.), best known for his witty epigrams that depicted Roman society, high and low (sometimes in very coarse language).

8. Compare Horace, *Ars Poetica*, lines 342–43: "Mingling the 'useful' with the 'sweet' wins every point."

9. Roman poet (ca. 50–ca. 15 B.C.E.), one of the great masters of Latin love elegy (that is, a poem in elegiac couplets, a specific metrical form). Ovid (43 B.C.E.–17 C.E.) and Tibullus (ca. 50–19 B.C.E.) also wrote highly polished elegies.

1. The ode was the form in which du Bellay's friend Pierre Ronsard first distinguished himself with the publication in 1550, a little less than a year after the *Defense*, of his *First Four Books of Odes* [translator's note].

2. Three 16th-century French *chansons* (songs): "Leave the Green Color," "Love [or Cupid] with Psyche," and "Oh How Happy."

3. Horace's epistles are conversational, not grave; but the long poems of *Epistles* 2 concern literature. Ovid's elegiac epistles are his *Heroides* (letters from legendary women to their absent lovers or husbands) and his *Tristia* and *Letters from Pontus* (describing the hardships of the poet's exile and pleading for leniency).

4. From the expression *sauter du coq à l'âne* (to jump from the cock to the donkey); stories characterized by absurd associations.

you would spare the names of vicious persons and reprehend with moderation the vices of your time in heroic lines (that is, lines of ten or eleven syllables and not of eight or nine) under the name of *satire* and not that inept title of *coq-à-l'âne*. For this, you have the example of Horace, who, according to Quintilian,[5] holds first place among the satirists. Ring out for me those beautiful sonnets, a no less learned than pleasant Italian invention which agrees in name with the ode and differs from it only in that the sonnet has a certain number of lines of a fixed length, while the ode can run through all sorts of lines freely—can, indeed, invent them at will, after the example of Horace, who sang odes in nineteen kinds of lines, as the grammarians say. For the sonnet then, you have Petrarch and several modern Italians. With a resounding pipe and a well-joined flute, sing me those pleasant rustic eclogues[6] after the example of Theocritus and Virgil or seafaring ones after the example of Sannazaro,[7] a Neapolitan gentleman.

May it please the Muses that in all the kinds of poetry I have named we have many imitations like that eclogue on the birth of the son of Monseigneur the Dauphin, in my opinion one of the best little works that Marot[8] ever wrote. Adopt, too, into the French family those flowing and dainty hendecasyllabics, after the example of a Catullus, a Pontanus, and a Secundus,[9] which you could do, though not in quantitative meter, at least with regard to the number of syllables. As for comedies and tragedies, if kings and commonwealths would restore them to their ancient dignity, which farces and morality plays have usurped, I would surely think you should set yourself to them, and if you wished to do so for the adornment of your language, you know where you must find the models for them.

1549

5. Roman rhetorician and teacher of oratory (ca. 30/35–ca. 100 C.E.); he calls Horace the best satirist in *Institutio Oratoria* 10.1.94.
6. Short poems—often pastoral—in the form of a dialogue or soliloquy, particularly popular during the 15th and 16th centuries.
7. Jacopo Sannazaro (1458–1530), a poet born in Naples who was greatly admired by the poets of the Pléiade.
8. Clément Marot, official court poet. The Dauphin: Francis of Valois, the future King Francis II, born January 19, 1544.
9. Joannes Secundus (1511–1536), Latin name of the neo-Latin poet Jean Everaerts. Catullus (ca. 84–ca. 54 B.C.E.), Roman lyric poet who was the first to adopt Greek hendecasyllabics—11-syllable lines in a set pattern of "quantity" (i.e., syllable length)—to represent everyday Latin speech. Giovanni Pontano (1426–1503), neo-Latin prose writer and poet of the Italian Renaissance.

GIACOPO MAZZONI
1548–1598

In his *On the Defense of the "Comedy" of Dante* (1587, *Della difesa della "Comedia" di Dante*), the Italian Renaissance philosopher and scholar Giacopo Mazzoni set out to defend DANTE ALIGHIERI's great medieval poem from a growing number of detractors. As was also the case with the new Renaissance romantic epic, a genre defended by Mazzoni's elder contemporary Giambattista Giraldi, Dante's extended dream allegory was widely criticized as unrealistic. Instead of subscribing to the general preference for what Plato had called realistic ("icastic") imitation, Mazzoni chose to defend "phantastic" or purely imaginary imitation, claiming it to be the basis of Dante's *Divine Comedy.* In the process, Mazzoni developed an elaborate theory of the poetic "idol" (image or simulacrum), going well beyond the defense of a particular poem to formulate what many scholars believe to be the most fully developed system of literary aesthetics of the Renaissance.

Born in Cesena, Italy, Mazzoni as a young man was educated in Bologna, where he learned Hebrew, Greek, Latin, rhetoric, and poetics. In 1563 he entered the University of Padua to study philosophy and jurisprudence. Thereafter, he taught for brief periods at the universities in Rome, Pisa, and his native Cesena. He spent much of his time managing his family estates, but he often entered into public debates with many prominent public figures and made the acquaintance of such famous Italian writers as Sperone Speroni, Ludovico Castelvetro, and Torquato Tasso, among others. He was reputed to have an astoundingly good memory, able to recall at will any part of the works of Lucretius (ca. 94–55 B.C.E.), Virgil (70–19 B.C.E.), Dante, and Ludovico Ariosto (1474–1533), and he routinely defeated all opponents at public memory contests. He considered himself primarily a philosopher, an identification clearly reflected not only in the sophisticated argumentative structure of the *Defense* but also in his major work, *De Triplici Hominum Vita, Activa Nempe, Contemplativa, et Religiosa Methodi Tres* (1576, *On the Three Ways of Man's Life: The Active, the Contemplative, and the Religious*), a philosophical attempt in Latin to reconcile the views of Plato and Aristotle. In this work, as in the *Defense*, Mazzoni demonstrates a remarkable command of the history of philosophy, citing an impressive number of authorities and sources. His abiding concern with Dante scholarship is demonstrated by his having published before his *Defense* the polemical *Discorso in difesa della Commedia della divino poeta Dante* (1572, *The Discourse in Defense of the "Comedy" of the Divine Poet Dante*). Critics generally agree, however, that the earlier work is much less successful.

Taken from Mazzoni's book-length "Introduction and Summary" to his *Defense*, our selection has very few references to Dante, offering instead a straightforward presentation of Mazzoni's theory of poetry. Reflecting his celebrated memory, this text shows extensive reliance on a wide range of classical philosophers and rhetoricians, including Plato and Aristotle, as well as various Greek sophists and Neoplatonists, particularly Philostratus (active 3d c. C.E.) and Proclus (412–485 C.E.). Considered structurally, the "Introduction and Summary" presents three definitions of poetry one right after the other. Each definition views poetry from a different perspective, considering the poem as an artistic imitation, a game, and a game shaped by moral philosophy in order to promote social order.

Mazzoni indicates, to begin with, that poetry is an imitative art that has as its object the idol (simulacrum or image), not classical literary models, as other Renaissance theorists, such as Pierre de Ronsard, argued. The proper subject matter for poetic imitation, however, is *marvelous* scenes and events, whether these are strict imitations of reality or purely imaginative. As a result, poetry is a species of sophistic rhetoric in that it deals with what is credible and persuasive, not with what is necessarily true. Seen from the perspective of the audience, the goal of poetry is to move the reader to pleasure and delight in the perception of believable images (idols). Mazzoni argues, in addition, that the distinct pleasure of poetry should ultimately lead to its social utility or moral purpose. As an entertaining recreational game, poetry is a means of pleasantly interrupting the serious business of the world so that business may be later resumed with freshness and vigor. It does instruct, but in a concealed way; consequently it may be regarded at its best as regulated by the civil faculty (moral philosophy). Mazzoni's view here is summed up cryptically in his belief that Aristotle's "*Poetics* is the ninth book of [his] *Politics*."

A distinctive feature of Mazzoni's work is that it proceeds by continuous logical differentiation. Defining poetry for him requires making precise distinctions between similar but different phenomena. Perhaps the key distinction is the earliest, involving three types of objects: the idea, the work, and the idol, which conform to the observable, the fabricable, and the imitable. Here Mazzoni isolates the distinct traits of poetry by differentiating it from epistemology (the observable) and the practical arts (the fabricable). After subdividing the imitable into the phantastic and icastic, he goes on to assess these two forms of imitation in relation to ancient and "second" sophistic rhetoric. Since ancient sophistic used made-up names and second sophistic named real individuals, Mazzoni classifies the phantastic under the former and the icastic under the latter. In this differentiation he further emphasizes the autonomy and the imaginative or phantastic force of the image. Such complex sets of distinctions form the basis of Mazzoni's "Introduction and Summary," which tries to develop a complete and perfect definition of poetry.

Along the way Mazzoni distinguishes "poetics" from poetry, and he also develops a sociological theory of genre. Poetics examines a poem in relationship to the civil faculty, noting prescribed standards, rules, and laws, while poetry looks at a poem from the perspective of its making, attending to its form. As for genre, Mazzoni notes that there are three kinds of poetry: the comic, the heroic, and the tragic. Each of these is addressed to one of the three sorts of people whom Plato thought necessary for civil society: artisans, soldiers, and magistrates, respectively. (Artisans include lower- and middle-class citizens.) Mazzoni's point is that each genre regulates a particular social class, instilling civil obedience. The humor of comic poetry consoles artisans, resigning them to their low or modest estate, while the glorious battles of heroic poetry inspire soldiers to freely defend their country. Tragic poetry depicts the downfall of noble persons and, in so doing, encourages magistrates to take their duties seriously.

Some critics of Mazzoni have perceived contradictions in his definitions of poetry, particularly in his attempt to reconcile the pleasures of imitation with the lessons of the civil faculty. Moreover, some twentieth-century theory implicitly questioned his distinction between icastic and phantastic imitation, pointing out the artifice involved in even "realistic" modes of imitation. In spite of these criticisms, Mazzoni raises to a rigorous level of analysis the discussion of literary mimesis (imitation and representation) initiated by Plato and Aristotle. In emphasizing poetry's relationship to images and games, he also foreshadows later Romantic interest in theories of imagination and aesthetic play, as exemplified most influentially in the works, respectively, of SAMUEL TAYLOR COLERIDGE and FRIEDRICH VON SCHILLER.

On the Defense of the "Comedy" of Dante **Keywords:** Ethics, Poetry, Religion, Renaissance Theory, Representation, Rhetoric

From On the Defense of the "Comedy" of Dante

From *Introduction and Summary*[1]

It seems to me that before we proceed to discuss matters belonging to this defense, it would be well to offer first in briefer form what may be termed a summary notion of the art of poetry and of the defense of Dante,[2] bringing together some considerations scattered through the present volume and adding some others, the whole of which will serve not only as an opportune introduction to what I am going to say, but also as a brief compendium of what has been said.

1. Translated by Robert L. Montgomery, who occasionally adds clarifying words in brackets. The bracketed section numbers correspond to those of the 1587 first edition, which is not paginated.
2. The Italian poet DANTE ALIGHIERI (1265–1321).

It is the common opinion of all schools of philosophy that the arts and sciences are distinguished and separated from one another by means of a proper and particular object or subject. (I do not at this point differentiate between these two names around which each school constructs its discourse.) But no matter how this subject is handled, there is no agreement at all in opinion within the same school. For some (and the Bishop of Caserta[3] in his *Monomachia* followed this opinion) prefer to think that the objects of the arts and sciences are distinct according to a distinction between things insofar as they are things. And on the basis of this condition they are forced to admit two quite extraordinary conclusions. The first is that metaphysics is a comprehensive science, that which concerns itself (so to speak) with universal being, and that the other arts and sciences are a part of it, considering each of these some part of universal being. The second conclusion (if the first is correct) is that each particular art and science has for its subject some thing that could not then be the subject of any other art or science. And since both of these conclusions are quite false, as is shown elsewhere (we will discuss it briefly later), it must therefore be judged that the above opinion is not in any way conformable to the truth. [7] Passing on then to a better and truer opinion and following the Peripatetics,[4] I say, as they believe, that the arts and sciences derive their true and real distinctions from objects, not insofar as they are things, but insofar as they are (forgive me, all you strictly Tuscan writers, the necessity of this word) knowable[5] and, if one can speak so, artificiable.

* * *

[8] Since on this topic I find no doctrine more copious or sound than that of Plato[6] in the tenth book of the *Republic*, so, following in his footsteps, I say that there are three types of objects and that they have three ways in which they can be devised; as a consequence these constitute three species of arts in the first category. The objects are idea, work, and idol. The idea is the object of the ruling, or we might say, the governing arts. The work is the object of the fabricating arts, and the idol is the object of the imitating arts. Therefore the modes of the objects of the arts, insofar as they are capable of being differently treated by artifice will be three; that is, the observable, the fabricable, the imitable. The arts that only contemplate a thing pertinent to some object are the ruling arts, and they are founded in the idea. Such is the art of horsemanship when it deals with the bridle. For the art of horsemanship does not consist in making the bridle but is concerned only with the idea of how it has to work and prescribes to the bridle maker what he must hold to, to make it work. [9] The arts that make the bridle (which was first conceived by the ruling art) are those that have as object what is called the work. The arts that make what was first conceived by the ruling arts are the fabricating arts and have as object what is called the work, and such is bridlemaking, which makes the work of the bridle and nothing else. The imitating arts have been so named because they deal with the object only insofar as it is imitable; hence Plato said that it has an idol as object, which means the simulacrum or image of some other things.

3. Antonio Bernardi (1503–1565), bishop of Caserta from 1552 to 1554.

4. Followers of the Greek philosopher ARISTOTLE (384–322 B.C.E.).

5. Mazzoni uses the word *scibili*, a borrowing from Latin.

6. Greek philosopher (ca. 427–ca. 347 B.C.E.). For book 10 of *Republic*, see above.

Since, therefore, the same thing may be treated in different sciences under different modes of the knowable, so also the same thing can be submitted to different arts by different modes of artifice. And we have a clear example in the bridle: it belongs to the art of horsemanship when considered in its idea, to the art of bridlemaking when made as a work, and to painting when imitated as an idol.

But there may arise a doubt of some importance in thus distinguishing the imitative arts from other arts, for it would seem that the fabricating arts also deserve the name of imitation, since each one of these imitates in its work the model of the idea conceived by the ruling art. Thus, for example, the art of bridlemaking forms a bridle exactly in conformity to the idea conceived by horsemanship. Therefore it would seem that the fabricating arts are not very well distinguished from the imitating arts. I respond that (as has already been said) the distinction between arts derives from their objects insofar as they are capable of being devised variously and distinctly. [10] Now the artifice of the work is not only to represent the idea of the ruling art; it also has to serve other ends. And in this way we can say that bridlemaking forms the bridle in accordance with the idea conceived by horsemanship; still, this bridle is not made in order to represent the similitude of the idea, but rather so that it can be used in various ways in managing horses. Hence we see that the artifice of the fabricating arts aims at something other than just representing or resembling; therefore I say that the fabricating arts cannot be called imitative. But those arts that have the idol as object have an object that has no other end in its artifice but to represent and resemble; hence they are called imitative. And just as philosophers have come to call the logical faculty rational, not because it uses reason—for in this sense all the arts and all the faculties are rational—but because it has an object that takes all its being from reason and in reason; so we say that the imitative arts are so named, not because they use imitation—for in this sense all the arts involve more or less some kind of imitation—but because they have objects that have no other being or use except by reason of imitation or in imitation.

* * *

It can therefore be concluded that the imitative arts have been so named because they have as objects those things which are good for no other end or no other use than to represent or to resemble; and they are distinguished from the other arts that are not called imitative because their objects are good for other uses or other ends than representation or resemblance alone. In this way, then, the idol is the object of the imitative arts. [11] But in order to understand clearly what this idol, which is the true and sufficient object of the imitative arts, is, and in order to unravel all the complications that are wont to become involved in this subject, so that we may anticipate a perfect and settled account of it, it is necessary to begin at some distance.

* * *

[15] Coming now to our topic, I say that when we previously concluded that the idol is the object of the imitative arts, we did not mean that sort of idol that originates without human artifice, * * * but instead that which does have its origins in our artifice, arising only from our phantasy or our intellect by means of our choice and will, like the idols in painting, sculpture, and so

on. I conclude therefore that this species of idol is that which is a suitable object of human imitation and that when Aristotle said at the beginning of the *Poetics* that all the kinds of poetry are imitation,[7] he meant that sort of imitation which has as its object the idol that arises from human artifice in the way we have stated. Rather I will say further that all imitations that arise from human artifice insofar as they are imitations have the idol as object in this manner.

But it would seem that the words of Suidas[8] are contrary to this determination, for he shows himself believing that the idol that derives from human artifice is not an adequate object of the imitative arts, unless the idol is joined to some other different thing that he calls a similitude. Here are his words: "Idols are effigies of things that do not subsist, like tritons, sphinxes, or centaurs. But similitudes are the images of subsistent things, like beasts or men." [16] According to this statement of Suidas we see that there are two imitations. One of them represents the true, as a painter does when he represents with colors the effigy of a known man; and the other represents the caprice of the person who is doing the imitating, just as the painter does when he depicts according to the caprice of his phantasy. We see at the same time that the idol is the object of this second sort of imitation and at the same time that the similitude is the object of the first. Therefore, it is not true that the idol that is born of human artifice is an adequate object of every imitation.

We may respond that this statement of Suidas concerning the idol is too narrow and also in opposition to what other writers have said. Hesychius,[9] uttering other sentiments about the term "idol," speaks as follows: "The idol is similitude, image, and sign." He shows clearly then with these words that the idol is also taken as a similitude and as an image of something discovered. Ammonius in the *Etymology* and Favorinus[1] in the *Vocabulary* explaining the etymology of the idol have said that it derives "from the verb εἴδω, which means match or resemble," almost as if it meant that the idol is of things that are apparent but not found and of things that are found, of which it represents the likeness. Let us add to it what Plato left us in writing in the *Sophist* that imitation is of two species, one of which he names the icastic, and it is that which represents things that are really found or at least have been, and the other he called phantastic, of which we have examples in paintings made according to the caprice of the artist. And even he himself says the same thing in the tenth book of the *Republic*, namely that the idol is the object of every imitation. Therefore the idol must also be common to phantastic imitation.

* * *

I believe, then, that everyone is able to understand up to this point what imitative art is and how it is distinguished from other arts that are not imitative, and what the idol is, which is the object of imitation. Now I add that poetry ought to be placed under this imitative art or imitation, as a species

7. "Epic poetry and tragedy, comedy also and dithyrambic poetry, and the music of the flute and the lyre in most of their forms, are all in their general conception modes of imitation," *Poetics* 1 (trans. S. H. Butcher). In emphasizing imitation as the production of man-made images, Mazzoni seems to make a silent comment on Plato's theory of daemonic inspiration in *Ion* [translator's note]. For *Ion*, see above.

8. Greek lexicographer (late 10th c. C.E.).

9. Alexandrian grammarian (active 4th c. C.E.).

1. Rhetorician of Rome (ca. 80–ca. 150 C.E.). Ammonius (active 5th c. C.E.), Alexandrian philosopher, disciple of Proclus.

under its genus. Therefore, in beginning to define poetry one can say that it is imitation.

* * *

[29] Now let us sum up the discussion to this point concerning the nature of the imitative arts, their distinctiveness from the nonimitative arts, and the fact that poetry which is icastic or phantastic, dramatic or narrative, always has imitation for its genus, since it always forms idols and images in the ways mentioned.

The genus of poetry having been established, it remains for us to investigate the differences according to which it has come to be distinguished and separated from all the other imitative arts. And first of all it would seem that reason requires that we find the instrument proper to poetic imitation, and then its subject matter, and next its efficient cause, and then its final cause. In this fashion we will have established its definition completely and perfectly.

Now if we can find a genus that includes only three species, that is, harmony, number, and meter, we will by combining them with imitation have arrived at a proper instrument. But since such a genus is not to be found, we will compensate with rules taught by Aristotle at the beginning of the *Posterior Analytics*,[2] and instead of the general term we will take the names of all three species and say that poetry is an imitation made with harmony, with number, and with meter, singly or together.

* * *

[44] Now that we have found the genus, and the individuality of poetry—that is, its instrument[3]—we can be said to have discovered its entire form. Next it would appear that orderliness requires that we turn to inquire into its proper subject and material. In the opinion of many these are falsehood and lying, even though the verisimilar is a fitting subject of poetry. And they have let themselves be induced to believe this because they think that the true poet is one who by himself fabricates the invention of his poem, adding that he who takes it from a place other than his own invention does not deserve the name of a true poet. They suppose also that this is the opinion of Aristotle, who called Empedocles[4] more often a natural philosopher than a poet, because not his own invention but the truth of natural things was thought to exhibit itself in his verses.[5] And in another place he says that Herodotus's[6] history reduced to verse would still be history. And in this context I wish to mention that Euphronius in one of his comedies compared the poet to a cook in the following two lines cited by Athenaeus[7] in his *Banquet of the Wise Men*:

2. *Posterior Analytics* 1.2, 71b–72b. Aristotle here argues the case for syllogistically arriving at a general conclusion on the basis of premises that are certain and require no prior demonstration to establish their certainty. Moreover, the premises must be better known than the conclusion. Mazzoni will try to arrive at the distinctive generic description of poetry by using those attributes necessary to it, namely harmony, number, and meter. In other words, he will argue that poetry is a name given to a kind of imitation using these instruments, but as a genus its character is assumed rather than a previously given certainty [translator's note].

3. Mazzoni has just argued that the instruments of poetry are taken from music because they produce delight and because they reduce to order the immoderate pleasures that poetic imitation can instill.

4. Greek philosopher, poet, orator, physician, scientist, and statesman (ca. 493–ca. 433 B.C.E.).

5. *Poetics* 1, 1447b.

6. Greek historian (ca. 484–ca. 425 B.C.E.). See Aristotle, *Poetics* 9, 1451b.

7. Greek scholar (active ca. 200 C.E.). Euphronius (active mid–3d c. B.C.E.), an obscure Greek comic poet.

"The cook is no different from the poet, since both use wit to make art." * * * On account of all these authorities and others besides, it would be very easy to fall into the view of those who maintain that poetry has no subject other than the fabulous and false, but is yet linked to the verisimilar, since verisimilitude, according to the rule of Aristotle, is to be sought in the poets' fables.

[45] On the contrary, I maintain that this opinion does not conform to the truth for many reasons. Among these I am going to choose those which I think are most to the point. Therefore I will note first that the verisimilar false comes into some other arts that are different from that of the poets, such as rhetoric, which Aristides in the oration against the *Gorgias* of Plato and Philostratus[8] in the Proem to the *Lives of the Sophists* calls "praise" [*adulante*], that which always and everywhere impresses the verisimilar false on the minds of judges to turn them from the straight way of justice. And on this topic I recall having read a most splendid dialogue by Signor Camillo Paleotti, a most erudite gentleman and also the most illustrious Maecenas[9] of letters in this century, in which with very effective arguments and lively reasons he shows that the verisimilar false is, though greatly abused by the corrupt world, virtually the universal subject of the arts, the sciences, and education. Therefore it cannot be concluded that it is the proper and sufficient subject of the poets' art. Moreover, if it were to be the true subject of poetry, then poetry could not in any way be capable of truth; yet Plato wrote, Aristotle agreed, and reason persuades us that just the contrary is the case. Therefore Plato in the *Republic* and in the *Laws* having approved that kind of poetry which treats the Gods in conformity to the truth, has demonstrated that he believes that truth is not repugnant to poetry.[1] [46] Likewise Aristotle has confirmed this judgment in three places in the *Poetics*. The first is in these words: "And if it happens that anyone treats poetically of things that have actually happened, he would nevertheless be a poet. For nothing prevents anything that has actually happened from being such that it might happen and could happen in a verisimilar way, so that he who treats them is a poet." The second place is at the beginning of the defense of poets: "For either he represents things that have happened or are said to have happened or appear to have happened or ought to have happened." The third is a little after this where he writes: "And beyond this it will be objected that the things he has said are not true. But they are what ought to be true."[2] In all three places, and especially in the last two, we see manifestly that Aristotle has sometimes conceded that the poet may use the true as a subject and that from everything said before, the idol in icastic imitation is, in Aristotle's opinion, a poetic idol.

But in addition to the authority of Plato and Aristotle, there is also reason to prove that the poet sometimes utters what is true. For when he is recounting the wanderings of some hero, he can do no less many times than describe places in the countryside. In these he follows the facts of geography, so either it must be said that he occasionally loses his title of poet, which would be quite ridiculous, or we must confess that the true may sometimes be a

8. Greek sophist (b. ca. 170 C.E.). Aristides (2d c. C.E.), celebrated Greek sophist.
9. That is, patron; the Roman statesman Maecenas (d. 8 B.C.E.) was a great patron of letters. Paleotti (1552–1597), Catholic cardinal who wrote on law, religious subjects, and morality.
1. Cf. *Republic* 2.377–79 [see above] and *Laws* 7.801 [translator's note].
2. *Poetics* 9, 1451b; 25, 1460b; and 25, 1460b.

poetic subject. And we have already shown that idols and images can also be made from the true, both in narrative and in representation [i.e., drama].

From all these considerations it seems to me that we ought to affirm two conclusions as correct. The first of them is that the false is not always necessarily the subject of poetry. The second is that since the subject of poetry is sometimes true and sometimes false, there is consequently a need to constitute a poetic subject that by itself can be sometimes true and sometimes false. * * *

[47] Now if we remove the false and in its place put the true, we do not therefore destroy poetry, since we have already said that it can stand together with the true. The same can be said of the possible, for if the impossible is substituted in poetry, it will not therefore come to be corrupted or spoiled, if the impossible is credible. But if we take away the credible and in its place put the incredible, the nature of poetry is totally destroyed. And on the other hand taking the credible and at the same time removing the possible, we still have the poetic subject, as Aristotle has clearly testified in the following words: "As to what belongs to poetry, the credible impossible is more often to be preferred to the incredible and possible."[3] Therefore it ought to be said that among all these there is no more appropriate subject of poetry than the credible. And even more to the point, how much the credible by its very nature includes both the true and the false, for often not only the true but also the false is credible.

* * *

[51] Therefore, the credible is the object of that persuasion whose end is that which has now been demonstrated. And because it has already been decided on the authority of Aristotle that the credible is the subject of the art of the poets, it seems to me that we can draw three conclusions from what has been said. The first of them is that the poet being always concerned with the credible, he must as a necessary consequence treat everything in a fashion suitable to the credible, that is, always making use of singular and sensible means to represent the things he writes about whatever they may be. [52] And even if he treats things pertinent to contemplative doctrine, he must make every effort to represent them by idols and sensible simulacra, which Empedocles did not do. Hence, he was more often termed a physicist than a poet. In this matter Dante is really marvelous, as we will demonstrate more fully in the fifth book. For the present we must be content with this single example in which he speaks of the most holy and ineffable Trinity, writing:

Within the profound and clear substance
    Of the exalted light three circles appeared to me,
    Of three colors and one magnitude.
And one in the other, like a rainbow in a rainbow
    Seemed reflected, and the third seemed like
    Fire breathed forth equally from the one and the other.[4]

And for this reason it also happens that the poet uses such frequent comparisons and lengthy and specific parables. And whoever looks for the rea-

3. *Poetics* 24, 1460a.

4. *Paradiso* 33.115–20 [translator's note]. Dante's image uses "sensible means" to present the "contemplative doctrine" of the Son's eternal generation from the Father and the Spirit's eternal procession from the Father and the Son.

sons why the poet is obligated at the very least in his storytelling to use this mode of the credible may rest content with the following reason: because the poet must speak to the people, among whom are many rude and uneducated men, and if he were to discuss knowable things in a mode appropriate to the sciences, they would not understand. And so he treats his subject in a credible mode, that is, instructing by means of comparisons and similitudes taken from sensible things, and the people, who understand that in sensible things truth resides in a way that is revealed by the poet, easily believe for this reason that the same is true of intelligible things.

From this we are able to conclude that it is not denied to the poet to treat things pertinent to the sciences and the speculative intellect, but he treats them in a credible manner, making idols and poetic images, as Dante, with most marvelous and noble artifice, has certainly done in representing all intellectual nature and the intelligible world itself with idols and images most beautifully to all eyes.

I recall that Plato in the *Phaedrus*, exalting his own invention, wrote just to this point: "But of that place that is beyond the heavens, I do not know that any of the poets has ever treated or is likely to treat it in a manner worthy of the way it is."[5] And so on. But if he had seen Dante's third canticle, he would without any doubt have recognized his own invention as inferior and given the palm to Dante, and consequently to poets for knowing how to make idols and images appropriate to giving to the popular understanding the quality of the supercelestial world. Concerning this I have written at length in the fifth book where I also show with what tact Dante has at times introduced either a philosopher or a theologian to discuss matters pertinent to the contemplative sciences in an understandable fashion, never deviating from the credible. [53] The second conclusion is that, since the poet has the credible as his subject, he ought therefore to oppose credible things to the true and the false, the possible and the impossible, by which I mean that he ought to give more importance to the credible than to any of the others I have enumerated.

Therefore, if it should happen that two things should appear before the poet, one of them false but credible and the other true but incredible or at least not very credible, then the poet must leave the true and follow the credible. And if anyone wants an example, let him read what I have written in the seventy-third chapter of the third book, where it is shown that Ariosto[6] has described the mouths of the Ganges River according to credibility, departing totally from the truth. And if the Ganges were such that its mouths faced the south, as Ariosto has said, then it would also be necessary to say that Taprobana is New Zealand and not Sumatra.[7] And yet Ariosto, following the credible and leaving the true, has said that Sumatra is Taprobana. This is discussed in the thirtieth chapter of the third book.

The third and last conclusion, which is almost a corollary of the previous two, is that poetry, in order to give more importance to the credible than to the true, must be strictly categorized under the rational faculty named by the ancients "sophistic." [54] And for a complete understanding of this truth, which (unless I am mistaken) has until now remained mysterious, it must be understood that the poetic art may be taken in two modes, that is,

5. *Phaedrus* 247c.
6. Ludovico Ariosto (1474–1533), Italian poet.
7. A glance at the atlas will confirm Ariosto's superior knowledge of geography and the points of the compass [translator's note].

either according as it is concerned with the laws of the poetic idol, or according as it is concerned with fashioning or forming the poetic idol.

The first mode ought to be called "poetics" and the second "poetry." In the first mode is the ruling art, which uses the idol and is part of the civil faculty, as we will show a little further on. In the second mode is the art that forms and fabricates the idol and is a species of the rational faculty. As I have said, it ought to be included under sophistic, since it does not care about the true. I am aware that I may have offended the sensibilities of poets by fastening upon an art considered until now virtually divine and the title of sophistic, which has come to be thought repellent and scandalous. Yet to console them a bit I wish to dwell a bit upon the art of the sophists to show where it has or does not have positive or negative meanings. And for an easier understanding of what we have to say, I will set down here the words of Philostratus at the beginning of his *Lives of the Sophists*, which will be seen to contain a summary knowledge of the sophistic art very different from that commonly understood. Here then are the words of Philostratus:

> Ancient sophistic must be called philosophical rhetoric, since it argues the same things treated by philosophers. Those who bring forward questions and doubts about each little item, have neglected to understand the ancient sophists about whom they speak with such assurance. Even so, their introductions say, "I understand this," "I know this," "It is just a portion that I have considered." Or, "Nothing is permanent for men." Either this mode of beginning adds luster to an oration or it makes plainer what is going to be treated. It was part of human prophecy, which the Egyptians and the Chaldeans studied, and before them the Indians prophesied by means of the stars. It belonged to the oracles, as the Pythian oracle[8] said,
>
> "I know the number of grains of sand and how great the seas are."
>
> And this:
>
> "Of wood were the walls which Jove gave to Tritonia [Athena]." Also, both Orestes and Alcmeon[9] killing their mothers and many other things similarly fashioned were the subjects that the ancient sophists practised, and, drawing them out at length, they ornamented them everywhere with conceits, referring to the gods, heroes, justice, strength, and sometimes going even higher, they treated the creation of the world itself.

[55] In these words of Philostratus we have the proposition that sophistic is what treats everything rhetorically—that is, credibly—and reasons confidently with a certain vaunting of its propositions and takes feigned subjects like Orestes and Alcmeon, imitating the one or the other and representing them by idols. Now, that such representation by idols and images is proper to the sophistic art Plato has clearly shown in the *Sophist* where he names it Εἰδωλοποιητίκην, that is, "The making of idols,"[1] that which represents apparent reality. This was also confirmed by Alexander Aphrodisias[2] in his *Commentary on the Elenches of Aristotle*. Philostratus in the place cited above, seeking to prove that Prodicus Chio[3] was also a sophist, shows that

8. The most famous of Apollo's oracles, at Delphi; its priestess was the Pythia.
9. In Greek mythology, each avenged his father's death by killing his mother.
1. Plato's word is *eidōlopoiikē*; see especially *Sophist* 235b–236c, 268d.
2. Aristotelian commentator known as Exegetes (active 200 C.E.).
3. Prodicus of Chios (active 5th c. B.C.E.), a sophist concerned with precise diction and a friend of Socrates.

he wrote a book in which he dealt with a matter pertinent to moral philosophy, namely, the appetites for virtue and vice which are at war within young men, and made idols and images for them. [56] He then says, "And for this purpose Prodicus Chio wrote a pleasant speech in which virtue and vice in feminine guise stood around Hercules.[4] But he adorned and altered both of them as he saw fit and presented them to the young Hercules, here ease and softness and there discomfort and toil."

It seems to me therefore that one can reasonably say that poetry deserves to be placed under this ancient sophistic, since it also treats things credibly and speaks with such boldness as to profess to know all things by means of the Muses and Apollo.[5] Certainly Hesiod,[6] as a poet, became arrogant enough to pretend to know all things past, present, and future at once, and on this point I was pleased to see the opinion of a well-read commentator[7] on the *Poetics* who feels that it is not suitable to the poet in any way to use words or modes of speech which place in doubt the things he discusses, for, professing the credible more than others, he ought to utter things with great assurance and boldness. Thus on this condition also the poet deserves the name of sophist, and even more he deserves it as the maker of idols and as representing everything with images, as has been shown at sufficient length in the preceding discourse.

Philostratus also says that the ancient sophists willingly talked of gods and heroes, which material is held to be appropriate to poets. And therefore in this respect also it can be concluded that poetry is a species of ancient sophistic. But in order to understand perfectly everything pertinent to this discourse, it will be well to disclose all the other species of sophistic and then to see which are convenient to poetry, and which are not. Therefore, having discussed ancient sophistic in the words quoted above, Philostratus then shows that there is another species that he calls second sophistic, about which he writes in the following way: "Following this was one which does not suit the term new, for it also was ancient. But more often than not it favors and takes as its subjects the poor, the rich, gentlemen, or tyrants, giving them names, as in history. The old sophistic of Gorgias Leontinus originated in Thessaly, and the second sophistic of Aeschines,[8] son of Astrometus, was already in decline in the Athenian republic."

[57] We know by these words of Philostratus that the old sophistic was not different from the second in any other way, except that the old used made-up names and the second used real names. Whence it can be said that icastic poetry is a species of the second sophistic and phantastic poetry is a species of the ancient sophistic. Now I think that everyone should know that Philostratus believed the sophistic art to be that which set the true aside to behold the credible, and that he considered it worthy and noble, not low and scandalous, as Boethius[9] preferred to depict it, and perhaps also Aristotle and Plato. But to reconcile those authors who have condemned sophistic with those who have praised it, we have to understand that sophistic was considered in some way to partake of the rectitude of true philosophy.

4. The Roman name for Heracles, the greatest hero of classical mythology.
5. The ancient Greeks considered the Muses and Apollo to be the sources of inspiration for the arts and sciences.
6. Greek didactic poet (active ca. 700 B.C.E.).
7. Ludovico Castelvetro (ca. 1505–1571), Italian critic and philologist.
8. Famous Athenian orator (ca. 397–ca. 322 B.C.E.). GORGIAS (ca. 483–376 B.C.E), famous rhetor and sophist known for eloquence and skepticism.
9. Roman philosopher (ca. 480–524 C.E.).

Now only true philosophy directs the intellect by means of the true and the will by means of the good. Therefore only the sophistic totally contrary to true philosophy misdirects the intellect by means of the false and the will by means of evil. It was this sort of sophistic which was condemned by Plato and Aristotle and all their followers, and apparently Plato wanted to gather under this species of sophistic the poetry of Homer[1] as that which misdirected the intellect by representing false things about the gods and heroes and that which misdirected the will with that variety of imitation and immoderate augmenting of our feelings which were discussed just previously.[2] [58] And therefore one could say that any other poetry like that of Homer would have to be placed under the sophistic condemned by that philosopher, and not only was it banished from Plato's *Republic* but also from that of the Athenians, as Philostratus has written in the following words: "The Athenians, perceiving the eloquence of the sophists, chased them from the courts, on the grounds that they dominated the courts with unjust utterance and had too great a power over the law." Therefore the species of sophistic condemned by the philosopher is that which misdirects the intellect with falsehood and the will with injustice. Under which he also places that sort of poetry which produces the same disorders and which does not really deserve the name of poetry, since it does not form its idols according to the laws of poetic practice or theory, as was plainly discussed a little before.

The second species of sophistic is that which Philostratus called the old sophistic, which indeed sets feigned things before the intellect, yet does not mislead the will, so that it claims in every way to make it conformable to what is just. And that kind of sophistic was never condemned by the ancients. And if, even so, it should appear to someone that it deserves condemnation for misleading the intellect by some falsehood, I say that he should know that the ancient pagan philosophers (being at variance in this matter with the truth of sacred theology) have praised this misleading of the intellect in certain things, when it is directed to a legitimate end. And in this respect Plato preferred that the magistrate should be able to tell lies to his citizens for the sake of some public good.[3] I pass over the fact that this species of sophistic almost always contains some truth under the skin of a first appearance.

Now I maintain that phantastic poetry regulated by the proper laws belongs to that ancient sophistic, since it also offers feigned things to our intellects in order to regulate the appetite. And often it contains under the outer covering of fiction the truth of many noble concepts.

The third species of sophistic is that which Philostratus called the second sophistic, which does not employ feigned names and events, but rather true names and real actions on which are based discussions appropriate to the rules of justice. [59] And this was also much praised by the ancients: thus Demosthenes[4] and Aeschines professed to be most worthy and excellent in this kind, as Philostratus makes evident in the following words: "In this way Aeschines and Demosthenes publicly traded insults, when they were trying a case before the courts." And this was also called a species of sophistic, because even though it made use of true things in the cause of justice, yet

1. Greek epic poet (ca. 8th c. B.C.E.) to whom were attributed the *Iliad* and *Odyssey*, which were in effect the national poems of ancient Greece.
2. *Republic* 2.377–78 and *Protagoras* 316 [translator's note].
3. *Republic* 3.389b (see above).
4. Athenian orator and statesman (384–322 B.C.E.); his great rival was Aeschines.

it did so in a credible manner. For which reason the sophists sometimes departed from the truth if the false were a more credible or effective instrument in persuading those of what they wished. There is no better example than the following warning by Valerius Harpocration[5] about an oration of Demosthenes: "Demosthenes affirmed in his oration on the fleet that the revenue of the Athenian republic was six thousand talents[6] (a sum of three million six hundred thousand escudos), writing thus: 'He will hear that our fields yield us a revenue of six million talents.' This was either an error on the part of the scribe, or the orator spoke cleverly to make it appear that the republic had a greater ability to make war than the king of Persia."

Under the third species of sophistic we ought in my judgment to place icastic poetry, which represents true actions and persons but always in a credible way. [60] Therefore, on the basis of this entire discussion of sophistic with the fundamentals we have provided, everyone can understand that poetry is a rational faculty and that, among other rational faculties, it ought not to be placed with those that teach the truth, avoiding all other matters, but with those that employ all their power to examine the apparent credible, avoiding the true, and that this was the reason the ancients called it sophistic. To all these reasons may be added the authority of two most excellent writers. The first is Plato, who, as we have said, called the sophist a maker of idols, that is, a sophistic imitator. In the tenth book of the *Republic* where he discusses the imitator he calls him the "marvelous sophist," adding that he never represents the true, but always the apparent. "The painter," he says, "does not paint the real bed, only its appearance." And just after this he says clearly that an imitation is three stages removed from the truth, the first stage being the art of using, the second the art of making, and the third that of imitating. And then he concludes: "Therefore the imitator imitates at a distance from the truth, and, as we have seen, he is able to do all things because he touches only a small part of them, and that part is an image."[7] The second authority is Plutarch, who in the essay where he deals with how a young man ought to listen to poems, writes as follows: "But he who does not forget, but always keeps in mind the tricks of poetry in telling lies, will say to it at every turn, 'O clever device, whose hide is more varied than the lynx's, why when joking do you deceive with a serious brow, pretending to tell the truth?'"[8] And he has previously shown that poetry willingly accepts the lie in order better to please.

Therefore, I firmly conclude that poetry is a sophistic art and that through imitation, which is its proper genus, and the credible, which is its subject, and through delight, which is its end, when it is under that genus, and has that subject, and gains that end, it is many times forced to find room for the false. And although I have only cited Philostratus, Plato, and Plutarch on this point, a thousand others could be found whom I have left in the wings so as not to be too long.

And so the credible is the subject of poetry. But because it is also the subject of rhetoric we must necessarily see in what way it can be made to

5. Alexandrian lexicographer and scholar of oratory (active 2d c. c.e.).
6. About 340,000 lbs. (an Athenian talent was ca. 57 lbs.) of silver.
7. *Republic* 10.596d, 597e; 601d, 602c; 603a.
8. Plutarch, "How a Young Man Should Study Poetry," *Moralia*, Loeb ed., vol. 1, pp. 83–84 [translator's note]. Plutarch (ca. 50–ca. 120 c.e.), Greek biographer and moralist.

become proper to both poetry and rhetoric, since we will not fall into the error of those who accept the verisimilar false.

[61] I say therefore that the credible insofar as it is credible is the subject of rhetoric and the credible insofar as it is marvelous is the subject of poetry, for poetry must not only utter credible things but also marvelous things. And for this reason when it can do so credibly, it falsifies human and natural history and passes beyond them to impossible things, as I prove in the sixth chapter of the third book and in the others following, in which a full digression treats this material. So that, if two things equally credible were offered to the poet, one of them more marvelous than the other, though false, not just impossible, the poet ought to take it and refuse the other. And if anyone wants examples, let him read the abovementioned digression, in which, I am convinced, he will find many to the point in each of Aristotle's ten predicaments.[9]

But perhaps there is someone who might wonder why the credible marvelous is not found in company with the true. And he might also suppose that what was said before—that poetry sometimes admits the true—is wrong. I respond that sometimes true things are found in poetry which are often more marvelous than the false, not only in natural things, as Pliny the Younger[1] has shown in the eighth book of his *Letters* when he writes to Caninius Rufus, but also in human history, as that same Pliny has shown in the ninth book, writing to the same Caninius. [62] In the latter he explains that the war made on Dacia by the Emperor Trajan,[2] although true, was nevertheless a worthy subject for a poem because it was marvelous. Here are his words: "I greatly approve your plan of writing a poem on the Dacian war, for where could you have found a subject so fresh, so eventful, so broad, and, in short, so poetical; a subject which, although most true, is also marvelous. You will write of rivers turned into new channels, of bridges thrust across rivers for the first time, of camps pitched on precipitous mountains."[3] See how well Pliny demonstrates that the true can sometimes reach the marvelous. Concerning this topic there only remains to discuss that authority by which it seems to be proven that the false, insofar as it is verisimilar, is a poetic subject. I mention first of all that it is the case that Aristotle calls Empedocles more a physicist than a poet, and this is confirmed by Plutarch in the essay on understanding poems cited above: "I do not know of poetry without fable or fiction. For the verses of Empedocles and of Parmenides, the *Theriaca* of Nicander, and the sayings of Theognis[4] are more often than not sermons, so that as a vehicle to cast off the baseness of prose, I prefer the grandeur and measure of poetry."[5] Now as for the authority of Aristotle, we can respond to it in two ways, the first of which is that he has said that Empedocles is more often a physicist than a poet, but he has not by that statement said absolutely

9. The "predicaments" or predicables make up Aristotle's *Categories*. They are substance, quantity, quality, relation, place, time, position, state, action, and affection [translator's note].
1. Roman rhetorician (ca. 61–ca. 112 C.E.), nephew of the natural historian Pliny the Elder. Among his correspondents on literary subjects was Caninius Rufus, of whom little else is known.
2. Roman emperor, 98–117 C.E. (b. 53); he successfully conquered Dacia (roughly equivalent to modern Romania) in 105.
3. Pliny the Younger, *Letters*, book 8, letter 4. The reference to a natural marvel is in book 9, letter 33 [translator's note].
4. A Greek elegiac poet of Megara (active ca. 540 B.C.E.), known for his large fragmentary collection of gnomic verses. Parmenides (b. ca. 515 B.C.E.), Greek didactic poet and philosopher known for his *On Nature*, which contains the earliest Greek discussion of philosophical method. Nicander (2d c. B.C.E.), Greek poet and grammarian.
5. Plutarch, "How a Young Man Should Study Poetry," *Moralia*, Loeb ed., vol. 1, pp. 83–85 [translator's note].

that he is not a poet, so that affirming that he is more of a physicist than a poet, he has in some way said that he is a poet, since the grammarians tell us that the comparative assumes the positive.

The second way of answering Aristotle is that it could be said (as it was said above) that Empedocles did not merit the name of poet, not because he dealt with true things, for it has already been shown that poetry is able sometimes to treat the true; but because he dealt with things belonging to the sciences scientifically, when he was obligated as a poet to treat them credibly, that is, forming idols and images, matching his mode of instruction more often to the sensitive than to the intellectual powers. As for Plutarch, I say that either he is really speaking of the true and perfect poet, who (as it is said) ought more often to be placed under phantastic imitation, rather than icastic imitation, or his opinion is in opposition to that of Aristotle and Plato, that is, that poetry cannot in any fashion be made from the true. And this answer ought to suffice for the authority of Plutarch, which has been cited to the contrary. [63] To Aristotle's text where he writes that the history of Herodotus laid out in verse would still be history, and so not worthy of the name of poetry, I respond that it is true, but that it does not follow from this that one cannot in some way make a poem out of history, when it is represented as the credible marvelous in idols and particularized images. But if it were narrated in the mode appropriate to history, without making idols and images, even if it were laid out in verse, it would always remain history. And this was what Aristotle meant at that place [in the *Poetics*]. To the authority of Euphron,[6] I respond that the true can also be sweetened by narrating it in conformity with the credible, using idols and images.

For this reason I believe that icastic poetry, which takes a true subject from history, may nevertheless combine some things of its own in order to render that history more particularized. This is no doubt even more clearly evident in the dramatic-icastic than in the narrative-icastic.

As for the authority of Plato in the *Phaedo*, I say that he discussed phantastic poetry which always takes a fabulous subject, either forming one totally feigned or falsifying a true story. And for this reason he says in that place [the *Phaedo*] that the poet deserves his name more often for his inventing of fables than for his inventing of verses.[7] Or one might say that he takes the fable in the sense of every invention that can be suitable to the poem and names it fable, because for him such subjects are false and fabulous. [64] But it should not for this reason be said that he did not believe that the true could be a poetic subject, since in an infinite number of other places he says just the contrary, as has already been shown.

Therefore let us summarize what has been said on the poetic subject, that it ought to be credible and at the same time marvelous, and then joining this subject to the form already disclosed above, we can now say that *poetry is an imitation made with harmony, rhythm, and verses, singly or together, of things credible and marvelous*.

There remains for the completion of this definition that we find the efficient and final causes of poetry. Now as for the efficient cause, we might

6. Poet of Greek New Comedy (active 270 B.C.E.).
7. Apparently a somewhat inaccurate reference to *Phaedo* 61b.

dispatch it by saying that it is the human intellect. But this is a cause common to all the other arts, and we only wish to find one that is more appropriate to poetry and that, joined to its end, will reveal the proper origin and legitimate use of poetry.

Therefore in order to lay the foundation for this, I believe there is no surer way than to consider what that art is that discovers the use of poetry, because that, unless I deceive myself, will reveal the origin and the end of poetry. I think, then, that the civil faculty[8] is that which discovers not only the use of poetry but also explains the norm and the rules for the poetic idol. The following consideration presses me toward this belief, namely, that all the natural powers and the arts that are born of human reason are usually directed to contrary objects, as for example medicine, which not only deals with health and healthful potions but also with sickness and poisons. We can say also that the legal profession likewise not only professes to deal with justice but with injustice as well.

Now keeping this in mind, I say that the civil faculty not only professes to understand the justness of human actions but also the justness of the cessation of human actions, a justness that is opposed to the first justness as deprivation is opposed to habit. * * * [65] But the cessation of a process, as will be explained a little further on, must dispose and prepare men so that they are more apt and eager for the process. Therefore the same faculty will provide the rule for the activity and its cessation. [66] And note that I do not take cessation to be total privation or extinction or activity, but only cessation of serious and difficult activities, and so in the word *cessation* we include the activities of play and amusement which we do for recreation and entertainment. So it can be said that the contrariety of function and cessation is not only privation but (as was said above) also positive. It is privation insofar as the cessation indicates the absence of serious work. It is positive insofar as the cessation of serious work might contain some pleasant activity apt to restore the spirits fatigued by the more important function. This is clearly enough indicated by Aristotle in the tenth book of the *Ethics* and the eighth of the *Politics*, where discussing cessation (which he treats at length in the fifth chapter of the second book), the name is always ἀνάπαυσις and not σχολή[9] to make it clear that he does not take the otium that is the father of all vices as entertainment or the cessation of serious things, but rather some peaceful and gentle activity.[1]

So it appears to me that one can firmly say that in order for cessation to be the opposite of the privative and positive activity, it must necessarily be the concern of one art and a single faculty. But the civil faculty is that which considers the rightness of an activity, so it should also consider the rightness of its cessation. Within it, as I have said, are contained all the activities of amusement, that is, those performed in games. Therefore the consideration of the rightness of pleasure will without any doubt be pertinent in some way to the civil faculty and to moral philosophy. But among all games none is

8. By the civil faculty Mazzoni means, roughly speaking, ethics, or the mode of discourse that decides the social relevance of something [translator's note].

9. Both Greek terms can denote rest and repose, but the first (*anapausis*) suggests leisure and relaxation while the second (*scholē*) implies idleness.

1. *Nicomachean Ethics* 10.3; *Politics* 8 generally concerns education and leisure. The sixth chapter of the second book would seem more to Mazzoni's point than the fifth, which deals with a number of topics ranging from the justice system to political innovation [translator's note].

found more worthy, more noble, and more central than what the poets' work has made. Therefore the civil faculty takes care to consider principally among the other pleasures the standard and rightness of poetry.

Now, that the ancients believed that poetry was a game is shown in the abovementioned chapter of the second book on the authority of Virgil, Horace, Timocles[2] the comic poet, Plato in the tenth book of the *Republic*, and in the fifth of the *Laws*, and Eusebius of Caesarea[3] in the twelfth book of the *Evangelical Preparations*. To these can be added the authority of Aristotle, who in the seventh book of the *Politics* calls games "the imitations of those things you do seriously." And there is the authority of Plato who in the second book of the *Laws* says of poetic imitation: "Again I call it amusement and play."[4] From all these considerations it seems to me that it can be reasonably said that the civil faculty ought to be divided into two principal parts, one of which is concerned with the laws of activities and is given the general name of politics, that is the civil law. [67] The other is concerned with the laws of cessation or the laws of recreational activities, and is called poetics. And on this basis I believe that the *Poetics* is the ninth book of the *Politics*, and my view seems to me all the more correct in that I find in the eighth book of the *Politics* and at the beginning of the first chapter of the *Poetics* he commences to deal with music, in order to proceed step by step to discuss the recreation of the civil faculty. And so I say that the first seven books of the *Politics* speak of the civil faculty at work and the last two speak of the civil faculty (so to speak) at rest, a state we have just previously called poetics.[5]

Therefore poetics is part of the civil faculty and is what prescribes the standards, the rules, and the laws of the idol in poetry. So in a way it can be said that poetics deals with the idea of the idol and poetry with the making of it. Thus poetics will be in its genus the ruling art, using the idol made by poets to that end we have just previously mentioned. And in its genus poetry will be the fabricating art, the maker of the idol, which is then to be used by poetics and by the civil faculty.

[68] We can therefore add to the previous words concerning the definition of poetry its efficient cause and say: *Poetry is an imitation made with harmony, number, and verses, singly or together, of credible and marvelous things discovered by the civil faculty.*

Up to this point we have disclosed the form, the subject matter, and the making of poetry, so that it remains only to turn our hand to the discussion of its final cause. Ancient and modern writers have raised a great fuss about this, not knowing very well whether they should take usefulness or delight or both, or neither the one nor the other, as the end of poetry.

* * *

2. Greek poet of Middle Comedy (active ca. 330 B.C.E.). Virgil (70–19 B.C.E.), Roman poet. HORACE (65–8 B.C.E.), Roman lyric poet and satirist.
3. Bishop of Caesarea and historian of the early Christian church (ca. 260–340 C.E.).
4. Aristotle, *Politics* 7.1334a; Plato, *Laws* 2.667e [translator's note].
5. The latter part of book 7 and all of book 8 discuss liberal education, that is, the education appropriate to a free man. For Aristotle this means not just someone not a slave, but a citizen relieved from the compulsion to labor or earn a living by commerce. The civil faculty at rest or leisure thus concerns itself with contemplation and with the study and appreciation of certain kinds of elevated enjoyment such as music and poetry [translator's note].

[70] Now for a complete solution to the present questions, it is necessary to understand that it is not inappropriate for the same thing when considered in diverse ways to have diverse and different ends. And because in this matter I desire to be understood by everyone, it will not perhaps weigh against me to discuss the abovementioned proposition by means of some examples taken from natural things. Therefore I maintain that nature (as is demonstrated at length in the fifty-fifth chapter of the third book) forms the tongues of animals for one principal end, that is for taste, in order that by means of the delight taken in the tasting of food animals will be almost violently impelled to keep themselves alive. And therefore it can be said definitely that nature has formed the tongue in order to serve as an instrument of the vital powers and the concupiscible appetite. However (as Aristotle has declared in many places cited in the abovementioned chapter), nature has sometimes directed that same tongue to an end other than taste, since in men it has made it also an instrument of speech, and consequently as such it is not just an instrument of the vital power or the concupiscible appetite, but, rather, of the rational power and appetite. And at other times it has also been formed as an instrument of the irascible power, having been placed among their weapons of defense, as is seen in bees and in certain other insects.

Thus it can be said that the adequate and principal end that nature proposes in the fashioning of the tongue is taste, since the tongue is not found fashioned by nature unless it is directed to this end. [71] But for all this it can also be added that sometimes nature forms that same tongue to serve another end and consequently it is an instrument of other powers than the concupiscible or vital, and this is clearly seen in the tongues of bees and men. The first of these is an instrument not only of the concupiscible appetite but also of the irascible, and in this second mode it is not made for taste but for defense. The second is an instrument of the vital power and of the rational, and in the latter mode its end is human speech. Therefore, the tongue can be considered in three different manners, that is, as an instrument of the concupiscible, of the irascible, or of the rational appetites, and in each one of these modes it always has a different end—when used by the concupiscible power, it has taste as its end; when used by the irascible, offense; when used by the rational, speech—yet in such a way that taste seems always to be the more suitable and essential end among all the others.

In like fashion I say that poetry can be considered in three different modes, that is, as an imitative art, either as enjoyment or amusement simply, or as enjoyment or amusement directed, ruled, and defined by the civil faculty. If it is considered as an imitative art, I say that it has no other end than to represent or resemble correctly. And this is what Plato, Proclus, and Maximus of Tyre[6] meant in the passages cited above. [72] Now it should be understood that (as Aristotle has written in the tenth book of the *Ethics*) delight is an accident proper to some functions, and among them is without doubt most proper to imitation, since it seems in a way joined to it so that

6. Sophist (ca. 125–185 C.E.). Proclus (412–485 C.E.), Neoplatonic philosopher and systematizer known for his commentaries on Plato's works.

no mode of imitation can be found that does not at the same time bring both delight and pleasure. * * *

Since, therefore, imitation is always linked to delight, so it happens that all those who have attempted to produce games and enjoyment have produced them with some kind of imitation, as I have shown in discussing the ancient game of chess in the sixth chapter of the second book, and I may add here (to provide an example different from those two) the game of primero,[7] in which is represented the image of ochlocracy, that is, that republic in which the common people have the most power. For since in this kind of republic the aristocrats are weak and the common people strong, so in the game the cards commonly given the noblest names are of lesser value than the other cards that have the vulgar name of waste paper because of their baseness. Now since imitation itself can be considered as part of the above-mentioned game, in this mode it has no other end than to represent the image of ochlocracy and can be deemed a game and amusement, and in such a mode we recognize no other end than delight and pleasure. So I say that poetry can in the same way be thought of as an imitative art and as a game and amusement.

In the first mode it has as its end the correctness of the idol, that is, whether the thing has been imitated in an appropriate way. But in the second mode it contemplates delight and pleasure as its end, and these are joined to a good and perfect imitation. [73] Therefore, I conclude that poetry as an imitative art has the correctness of the idol as its end, but as a thing that should be used for play and amusement and to interrupt some more serious and rigorous business, it here proposes as its end delight born of appropriate imitation. Now this delight that poetry brings us can be looked at in two ways: that is, either as free and independent of any law, or as subject to and regulated by the civil faculty. In the first mode it is the end of that poetry which was classified under the kind of sophistic worthy of blame, because it disordered the appetite with immoderate delight, producing complete rebellion against reason and bringing on damage and loss to a virtuous life.

That was the sort of poetry banished from his republic by Plato, concerning the reason for which Maximus of Tyre has written in his eighth sermon that just as Mithecus, the most excellent cook, was banished by the Spartans, despite the fact that he was greatly esteemed among the other peoples of Greece, only because his art had no other end than to please the taste, which was totally repugnant to the sobriety of the Lacedaemonians;[8] so also did Plato banish poets from his republic as having regard for nothing other than delighting too freely. [74] And Proclus in the *Poetic Questions*, having admitted that this sort of poetry is truly enjoyable, supplies the reasons why it is damaging and harmful to civil life: "I will therefore suggest two reasons why Plato did not accept tragedy and comedy in a proper republic as worthy of the education of the young. One was the variety (as it is called) of the imitations; the other was the unlimited moving of the passions, which he wished to moderate however he could. To this can be added as a third the case of saying any sort of wickedness in those same genres about gods and heroes." And so on.

7. A card game, often called "prime" in Renaissance England [translator's note].

8. Citizens of Sparta (also called "Lacedaemon").

If, therefore, one has to reason about the end of this poetry, it can be definitely said that as an imitative art its end is the correctness of the idol, but that as recreation its only end is pleasure.

But if delight is considered insofar as it is regulated and defined by the civil faculty, we will necessarily have to say that it is directed toward the useful and consequently is that species of poetry which was placed under praiseworthy sophistic, that is, under that which orders the appetite and submits it to the reason, and, considered as game, defined by the civil faculty to have usefulness as its end. It is nevertheless true that I do not ascertain that this species of poetry is as rough and austere as Proclus claims in the first poetic questions, where he distinguishes two species of poetry, the good and the evil, in the following words: "But it is especially the job of the laws concerning the instruction of youth to keep an eye on such poetry as that which is genuinely enjoyable, pleasing, but not useful for teaching virtue, and which the more it is enjoyable, so the more it is harmful. And to the same laws belongs the choice of an austere muse that guides us to virtue by the right way. For we do not find the wonder of medicine in what is pleasant but in that which heals." In these words of Proclus we see that he believes poetry has to be more a medicine than an enjoyment and that consequently by giving it the useful as its end he does not mind if he separates it from any sort of delight. [75] But it is beyond doubt that in this he disagrees with Plato, who has clearly admitted in many places that poetry is the bringer of the useful to our minds by means of the delight it offers us under the species of enjoyment and recreation.

And to understand fully this favorable opinion of Plato's one has to know that there are three sorts of men to whom he apparently believed the civil faculty—by which we mean moral philosophy—could bring some betterment. These three sorts are: those disposed and habituated to the good, those who are wicked and habituated to evil, and those who are not disposed or in any way habituated either to good or evil. Among the first sort are the men who have learned to curb the disorderly movements of the appetites, and I think that these are the ones who practise moral philosophy well (as Plato himself writes in the *Protagoras* and the *Gorgias*) insofar as it is lawful, that is, insofar as it gives laws and precepts for living well and happily and free of passion. Of the second sort are impious men used to despising the decrees of the law, and for these he shows at length in the *Gorgias* that moral philosophy is useful, insofar as it is judicial, that is, insofar as evildoers are punished by penalties established in trials.[9] [76] Of the third sort are young girls and boys and all those who feel the tumult of passions, who, in addition, are not used to either good or evil, but who still can be taught the way of virtue and as well be instructed in the way of vice. And because these—as Aristotle has written at the beginning of the *Ethics*—are greatly agitated by their turbulent passions and violent affections, therefore, he believes, they are not apt listeners to the teaching of moral philosophy.[1] But Plato thinks that even these may be offered moral teachings seasoned with poetic sweetness. So it appears that Plato believes (according to what he writes in the second, third, and tenth

9. Cf. *Protagoras* 342–43 and *Gorgias* 476–77 [translator's note].

1. Aristotle, *Nicomachean Ethics* 1.4, 1095a [translator's note].

books of the *Republic*, but even more plainly in the second book of the *Laws*) that the poetic faculty is the civil faculty, or moral philosophy, and it gives instruction to those who are unfit for naked instruction, either because of their age or the strength of their passions. And so I conclude with Proclus that Plato sometimes calls poetry a medicine, like that which aims to make souls healthy, and thus has usefulness as its end.

But I disagree with Proclus because he does not recognize any sort of delight in poetry. Even Plato allows that it introduces the useful by means of delight, for thus he praises it and calls it play and wants to be so understood: "Because the more tender minds do not accept serious studies, their studies are called games and songs and are performed as play; so when men are physically ill, those who care for them spread their nourishment with sweet condiments, but they make unhealthful food unpleasant, so that they learn to accept the one and reject the other."[2]

* * *

[78] Now without any doubt I think that as regards the end of poetry this is a correct opinion, that is, that perfect poetry regards delight as the cause of the useful. And as proof of my opinion, I am going to make the following discussion a little different from that of Plato.

Therefore I say that perfect poetry is game and is modified by the civil faculty; insofar as it is recreation it has delight as its end, but insofar as it is modified or, so to speak, characterized by moral philosophy, it puts delight first in order to provide a later benefit. And from this it seems to me that the civil faculty has decided that everyone may enjoy the delight that comes from poetry. And it has been so established by Plato in his *Laws* and by other legislators. I say further that the Athenian Republic so valued the delight brought to the people by poets that they were not ashamed to give each year many hundreds of coins to its citizens to buy themselves seats in the theatre where they could more easily hear the comedies and tragedies acted. * * * [79] And if it should seem to anyone that it is necessary to set forth more in detail the mode and type of this benefit, I am pressed, in order to satisfy this desire, to say something briefly.

[80] Plato wanted his republic to be composed of three sorts of persons: artisans, soldiers, and magistrates. Proclus added that under the category of artisans Plato included all the lower- and middle-class citizens, and that under the category of magistrates he included all those more powerful people who had the government of the republic in their hands. Now based upon this supposition I say that there are, deriving from the providence of the civil faculty in the city, three principal kinds of poetry—the heroic, the tragic, and the comic, each one of which makes use of delight to benefit all the people; each principally aimed at the benefit of one of those three parts that are, according to Plato, necessary to civil community. And so we say that the heroic poem was principally directed at soldiers, since by means of the virtuous actions of the heroes represented in such poems, they would be as if spurred on by glory driven to imitate it. Tragedy principally looks to the utility and benefit of princes, magistrates, and the powerful and, so as to keep

2. *Laws* 2.659e–660a.

them always under the justice of the laws, represents freely the dreadful and terrible downfall of great persons, which comes almost to be a bridle to restrain and moderate the size of their fortune. Comedy has as its principal intention the benefit of persons of low or moderate estate, and to console them for their modest fortune it usually presents actions that always end happily. And in this way, I think, the civil faculty inclines to the understanding that the humble and popular life is so much more enjoyable and filled with greater contentment than the grand or regal life. * * *

[82] Since the civil faculty seeks to implant in the minds of humble citizens obedience to their superiors, so that out of desire for novelties they should not be moved to disobedience or rebellion, and so that they should always remain content with their condition, it gave birth to comedy, in which the humble life is shown to be happy, fortunate, and capable of infinite solace. On the other hand, since the more powerful and all those raised to the mastery of others have not had to pay too much attention to their fortune, and consequently have become insupportable and insolent in their rule, the civil faculty wished to create tragedy, which would function as an adequate counterweight to the insolence of prosperous fortune. Hence all those who find themselves in such a condition will be able to extract useful instruction in moderating the pride characteristic of their state. [83] This usefulness of tragedy, I believe, is clearly enough indicated by Dio Chrysostum[3] in these words: "Nor is it anyone poor that the tragic situation deals with. On the contrary, all tragedies concern the Atreides, the Agamemnons, and the Oedipuses,[4] who possess a great abundance of gold, silver, fields, and cattle. So they say that the golden fleece was the greatest of all misfortunes." And so on.

Now it seems to me that from what has been said before concerning the utility to be derived from comedy and tragedy, we can conclude that those two kinds of poems are directed by the civil faculty to the extinguishing of sedition and the preservation of peace. And because the civil faculty also has to keep military education in mind, in order that in times of war the republic may be capable of defending itself, it seems to me that it can probably be supposed that for this end the civil faculty created the heroic poem, in which is celebrated the highest strength of the heroes, and especially of those who generously disdain death for the sake of the country, to the end of reminding our soldiers of like examples so that they will consequently be more prone to despise the perils of death for the safety and increase of the public good. And in this way we see that these three species of poetry ruled by the civil faculty, in addition to delight, bring utility and benefit to the republic, instructing in an almost concealed way the three kinds of men, from which (according to Plato) the ideal order of citizens is made up. * * *

[84] Now to come to the end of this definition, I think it would be well to recapitulate in a brief epilogue what has been said before about the final cause of poetry. I say therefore that since language is always the instrument of the concupiscible power and has enjoyment as its end, but that, nevertheless considered as an instrument of the irascible power, it has as its end the defense of the sensitive soul; and if considered as an instrument of the

3. Rhetorician (ca. 40–ca. 120 c.e.), an adherent of Cynic-Stoic philosophy.

4. The sons of Atreus (i.e., the Atreides), Menelaus and Agamemnon, like Oedipus, were kings of Greek city-states.

rational power, its end is language. In the same way poetry is always an imitative art, and insofar as it is such, its end is always to represent the images of things correctly. Nevertheless, considered as a game, its end is delight; and considered as a game modified by the civil faculty, its immediate end is delight, but directed to profit.

On this premise, it seems to me that it can be concluded that poetry is capable of three definitions according as it is looked at in three different ways, that is, either as imitation, or purely as a game, or as a game modified by the civil faculty. In the first mode it can, perhaps, be defined this way: *Poetry is an art made with verse, number, and harmony, singly or together, imitative of the credible marvelous, and invented by the human intellect to represent the images of things suitably.* In the second mode this other definition would perhaps be appropriate: *Poetry is a game made with verse, number, and harmony, singly or together, imitating the credible marvelous, and invented by the human intellect in order to delight.* Now, since of poetry considered in the first mode we have come to understand all the authority that acknowledges correct imitation as the poetic end, so of poetry considered in the second mode we have expounded all the other authority that accepts only delight as poetic end[.] * * *

[85] In the third mode perhaps there is room for this last definition: *Poetry is a game made with verses, number, and harmony, singly or together, imitating the credible marvelous and invented by the civil faculty to delight the people in a useful way.* Of poetry considered in this mode, we have to understand fully all the authorities that attribute to it the end of usefulness by means of delight. [86] In this regard we should attend to the following words of Proclus, in which he talks of poetry more as a kind of learning than as imitation: "Now if it must be an imitation, as we have said, it also has to concern itself with worthy goodness. For I say that all its virtuous deeds, whether or not they are fashioned by imitation, have no more important end than the good."

From these three definitions there necessarily follow four corollaries. The first of these is that poetry taken in the first two modes is neither ruled nor governed by the civil faculty. The second is that only poetry in the third mode is that which is ruled and governed by moral philosophy or the civil faculty. The third is that the poetic that considers the idol in the first mode and that which likewise considers the idol in the second mode of poetry should not in any way be called a part of moral philosophy. The fourth and last corollary is that only the poetic that considers the idol in the third mode of poetry is that which really deserves to be called part of the civil faculty. And each good poet should put together his poems according to the rules of this mode of poetry, as Dante has done better than all the others.

* * *

1587

SIR PHILIP SIDNEY
1554–1586

Sir Philip Sidney embodied the aristocratic ideals of the Renaissance man: he was a courtier, soldier, statesman, amateur scholar, and poet—a legendary figure in his own lifetime. Author of the first English sonnet sequence, Sidney also wrote the first landmark of literary criticism in English. In 1579, a Puritan minister named Stephen Gosson published an attack on the theaters titled *The School of Abuse*, dedicating it, without permission, "to the right noble Gentleman, Master Philip Sidney, Esquire"; Sidney countered the following year with his work *The Defence of Poesy*, sometimes called *An Apology for Poetry* (1580–81). Though it responds to specific attacks, the *Defence* enjoys significance far beyond its occasion for its synthesis of the Renaissance understanding of classical literary theory, which set the terms of literary debate in England for the next two centuries, and for its formidable handling of its genre—the defense of poetry—which Sidney adapted from classical and medieval models.

Because Gosson's attack draws so heavily on PLATO's objections to poetry, Sidney's *Defence* reads like a reply to the *Republic*. Though his classicism is filtered through the Italian humanists of the fourteenth and fifteenth century (it echoes BOCCACCIO's defense of poetry in *Genealogy of the Gentile Gods*), Sidney relies particularly on ARISTOTLE's *Poetics* and HORACE's *Ars Poetica*. His remarks on the state of the English language and its poetry would define the significant literary issues for later English critics—including JOHN DRYDEN and APHRA BEHN in the seventeenth century and SAMUEL JOHNSON in the eighteenth—shaping the direction taken by post-Renaissance neoclassicism.

Sidney was born at Penshurst, the eldest son of Sir Henry Sidney and Mary Dudley, daughter of the duke of Northampton. His godfather, after whom he was named, was Philip II of Spain, husband of Queen Mary I. In 1564 he entered Shrewsbury school in Shropshire. By 1568 he was a student in Christ Church at Oxford University, though he left in 1571 without taking a degree, perhaps because of an outbreak of the plague. He departed England for the traditional "Grand Tour" of the Continent, arriving in Paris in 1572, in time to witness the infamous St. Bartholomew's Day Massacre of the Protestants.

In March 1575 Sidney returned to London, succeeding his father as Queen Elizabeth's cupbearer (a purely ceremonial position). The next year he traveled to Ireland with his father, the lord deputy, and the earl of Essex (Walter Devereux). Negotiations began for a marriage between Sidney, then twenty-three, and Essex's fourteen-year-old daughter Penelope. Sidney began writing sonnets addressed to her, calling her Stella and himself Astrophil, a literary exercise inspired by the sonnets of the Italian poet Petrarch (1304–1374) to Laura. Though in 1581 Penelope married another, the sonnets continued for many years, even after Sidney's own marriage.

Sidney, who was greatly admired both in England and on the Continent for his sophistication and learning, was for several years unable to find employment at court; he belonged to the faction led by his uncle Robert Dudley, the earl of Leicester, one of Queen Elizabeth's favorites. He divided his time between visits with his illustrious friends, among them the poet Edmund Spenser, and his own writing. When he fell out of favor with the queen, he retreated to his sister's estate and began work on the *Old Arcadia*, also known as *The Countess of Pembroke's Arcadia* (after his sister), a pastoral romance alternating prose and poetry that was completed about 1581. Two sonnet sequences followed, *Certain Sonnets* (1581) and *Astrophil and Stella* (1581–82). He also began, but did not complete, a revision of the *Arcadia*. In keeping with his sense of the decorum required of a courtier, none of Sidney's works, including the *Defence*, was published during his lifetime; instead, they circulated privately among his friends in manuscript.

By 1583 Sidney's fortunes seemed to be changing. He was knighted and finally given a government appointment. In the fall he married Frances Walsingham, daughter of Queen Elizabeth's secretary of state, and his father-in-law paid off his considerable debts. In 1585 the queen appointed him governor of Flushing in the Netherlands, where she had sent troops to fight against Spain in support of the Protestant cause. There, in September 1586, in a raid on a Spanish convoy at Zutphen, Sidney was wounded by a bullet in the left thigh. The wound became infected, and he died at Arnhem on October 17 at the age of thirty-two. All Europe mourned his loss, and after a lavish state funeral he was buried in St. Paul's Cathedral in London.

The Defence of Poesy is a classic statement of Renaissance literary theory primarily because of its scope, its typicality, and its wit. Unlike his English contemporary George Puttenham, Sidney displays little interest in formulating the technical rules of poetry or rhetoric; he treats the subject of poetry much more broadly. At the same time, Sidney's debts are clear; he is a synthesizer, not a trailblazer. *The Defence* is a veritable encyclopedia of Renaissance humanism. Though structured as a classical oration with the standard seven parts (exordium, proposition, division, examination, refutation, digression, peroration), Sidney's text is more usefully understood as treating three major topics. The first part defends the dignity of poetry, demonstrating its superiority to philosophy and history because it combines the moral precepts of the one with the entertaining examples of the other, all the while cloaking its lessons with the pleasurable devices of art. Along the way, Sidney discusses the ethics of genres, ranging from pastoral, elegy, and satire to comedy, tragedy, and epic. The second part deals with the specific objections raised against poetry, in particular the charge that the poet is a liar. Sidney follows Boccaccio on this point, famously declaring: "Now, for the poet, he nothing affirms, and therefore never lieth." Poets' imitations are not lies, as Plato charged, because poets make no truth claims. The third part of the essay examines the current state of English literature. Here Sidney, the practicing poet, offers some critical comments on genre, diction, poetic figures, meter, rhyme, rhythm, and the English vernacular compared to other languages. Of particular interest is Sidney's pointed criticism of the English drama for failing to adhere to the unities of time and place sketched in Aristotle's *Poetics*. This issue would occupy neoclassical critics of the drama from PIERRE CORNEILLE through Samuel Johnson.

A fundamental aesthetic problem of the late sixteenth century concerns the object and purpose of poetry's representation. Sidney's definition of poetry sets an agenda for the discussion of poetry that brings together many of the learned commonplaces of Renaissance criticism: "an art of imitation, . . . that is to say, a representing, counterfeiting or figuring forth—to speak metaphorically, a speaking picture—with this end: to teach and delight." This definition is less notable for its originality (it is drawn almost word for word from the Italian-born humanist Julius Caesar Scaliger's *Poetics* of 1561, which, in turn, was indebted to Aristotle's *Poetics* and Horace's *Ars Poetica*) than for the insights it gives into the critical controversies of the period. The definition, and Sidney's subsequent discussion of it, raises three issues—all derived from Plato's discussion of poetry in the *Republic*—that dominate literary criticism until the end of the eighteenth century: the nature of imitation, the problem of defining nature, and the injunction that poetry serve moral ends.

Although the principle of imitation reigned unchallenged in literary theory from the Renaissance to the end of the eighteenth century, not all critics meant the same thing by *imitation*, nor did they necessarily agree on what is imitated (compare GIACOPO MAZZONI's extremely elaborate contemporaneous views on the subject with Sidney's). At the center of the controversy over imitation was a debate about nature itself: what constituted nature and what was the status of representations of "reality"? Like the third-century C.E. philosopher Plotinus, Sidney uses the Platonic theory of

Forms to refute Plato's criticism of poetry. The Neoplatonic mimesis espoused by Sidney held that the nature the poet imitated was the ideal, not the material, world. In the Renaissance, the ideal of nature was God's cosmological plan. Sidney perhaps best represents this Christian viewpoint when he argues that "right poets" "imitate to teach and delight, and to imitate borrow nothing of what is, hath been or shall be, but range, only reined with learned discretion, into the divine consideration of what may be and should be." This view of mimesis is based on a religious belief in providential design; because the universe is the product of divine wisdom, the purpose of the poet is ultimately to affirm the rule of justice and order. The ideal that Sidney invokes—what may be or should be—is more "real" than what is. In the next century this view of nature runs head on into the scientific revolution, and the debate is recast in Dryden's *Essay of Dramatic Poesy* (see below) and elsewhere.

Critics of the *Defence*, especially modern ones, have argued that it is derivative, that Sidney is simply not an original theorist, and that the rhetorical play and intertextual abundance of his Renaissance prose is tiring. Yet so long as contemporary literary theorists continue to debate the status of nature and the ideological stakes involved in representation, Sidney's essay, with its elegant variation on Platonic mimesis, will repay close scrutiny.

***The Defence of Poesy* Keywords:** Affect, The Canon/Tradition, Drama, Ethics, Literary History, Poetry, Realism, Religion, Representation

From The Defence of Poesy

When the right virtuous Edward Wotton and I were at the Emperor's court together, we gave ourselves to learn horsemanship of John Pietro Pugliano, one that with great commendation had the place of an esquire in his stable.[1] And he, according to the fertileness of the Italian wit, did not only afford us the demonstration of his practice, but sought to enrich our minds with the contemplations therein, which he thought most precious. But with none I remember mine ears were at any time more loaden, than when (either angered with slow payment or moved with our learner-like admiration) he exercised his speech in the praise of his faculty.[2] He said soldiers were the noblest estate of mankind, and horsemen the noblest of soldiers. He said they were the masters of war and ornaments of peace, speedy goers and strong abiders,[3] triumphers both in camps and courts. Nay, to so unbelieved[4] a point he proceeded, as that no earthly thing bred such wonder to a prince as to be a good horseman—skill of government was but a *pedanteria*[5] in comparison. Then would he add certain praises by telling what a peerless beast the horse was, the only serviceable courtier without flattery, the beast

1. Sidney undertook a European tour between 1571 and 1575. Between autumn 1574 and spring 1575, at the court of the Holy Roman Emperor Maximilian II, he befriended Edward Wotton (1548–1626), secretary to the English embassy there. Sidney would already have been an accomplished horseman, but Vienna was a centre of more advanced equestrianism than was yet common in England: the celebrated Riding School, initially an adjunct of the imperial court and the probable scene of Sidney's encounter with Pugliano, was founded in 1572, and Pugliano, as Sidney indicates, would have been held in high esteem there (his office was one of considerable status) [except as indicated, all notes are Gavin Alexander's, sometimes abridged or otherwise edited]. [Esquire: officer in charge of a noble's horses and stables—editor's note.]
2. Profession, branch of knowledge.
3. Strong in sustaining an attack or standing their ground.
4. Unbelievable [editor's note].
5. Pedantry [Italian].

of most beauty, faithfulness, courage, and such more, that if I had not been a piece of a logician before I came to him, I think he would have persuaded me to have wished myself a horse.[6] But thus much at least with his no few words he drave into me, that self-love is better than any gilding to make that seem gorgeous wherein ourselves be parties. Wherein, if Pugliano's strong affection[7] and weak arguments will not satisfy you, I will give you a nearer example of myself, who (I know not by what mischance) in these my not old years and idlest times having slipped into the title of a poet am provoked to say something unto you in the defence of that my unelected vocation, which if I handle with more good will than good reasons, bear with me, since the scholar is to be pardoned that followeth the steps of his master. And yet I must say that, as I have more just cause to make a pitiful defence of poor poetry, which from almost the highest estimation of learning is fallen to be the laughing stock of children, so have I need to bring some more available proofs, since the former is by no man barred of his deserved credit, the silly latter[8] hath had even the names of philosophers used to the defacing of it, with great danger of civil war among the Muses.

* * *

But since the authors of most of our sciences were the Romans, and before them the Greeks, let us a little stand upon their authorities, but even so far as to see what names they have given unto this now scorned skill.

Among the Romans a poet was called *vates*, which is as much as a diviner, foreseer or prophet, as by his conjoined words *vaticinium* and *vaticinari* is manifest[9]—so heavenly a title did that excellent people bestow upon this heart-ravishing knowledge. And so far were they carried into the admiration thereof, that they thought in the chanceable hitting upon any such verses great foretokens of their following fortunes were placed. Whereupon grew the word of *Sortes Virgilianae*,[1] when by sudden opening Virgil's book they lighted upon any verse of his making, whereof the histories of the emperors' lives are full, as of Albinus the governor of our island, who in his childhood met with this verse, *arma amens capio; nec sat rationis in armis*, and in his age performed it.[2] Which, although it were a very vain and godless superstition (as also it was to think spirits were commanded by such verses, whereupon this word 'charms', derived of *carmina*,[3] cometh), so yet serveth it to show the great reverence those wits were held in, and altogether not without ground, since both the oracles of Delphos and Sibylla's prophecies were wholly delivered in verses;[4] for

6. Sidney was interested in contemporary developments in the theory of logic and had a reputation as a skilled disputant. The irony of this passage is enhanced by a habitual, though here submerged, play on words: Philip (phil-hippos) means "horse-lover."
7. Prejudice.
8. That is, poetry (characterized as deserving of compassion, "silly"); the "former" is horsemanship. To make sense of the syntax here the reader must imagine "*but* the latter" [editor's note].
9. *Vates* was the oldest Latin name for a poet but fell into disuse (*poeta*, derived from the Greek: *poiētēs* being preferred) until revived by Virgil (*Eclogues*, 7.27; 9.34) and HORACE (*Odes*, e.g. 1.1.35; 2.20.3). *Vaticinium* means "a prophesy," *vaticinari* "to foretell" or "to sing."

1. Virgilian lots (Latin), the practice of divining one's fortune by randomly selecting a line or passage from the Roman poet Virgil (70–19 B.C.E.) [editor's note].
2. "Frantic I seize arms; yet little purpose is there in arms." As a child Clodius [Albinus] was obsessed with the line from Virgil, *Aeneid* 2.314. Clodius [150–197 C.E.] was made governor of Britain, and was proclaimed emperor by his troops in 193 C.E.; he committed suicide after defeat by his rival Severus in 197.
3. Songs, incantations.
4. The oracles of the Pythian priestesses at Delphos, sacred to Apollo, were set down in hexameters. Oracles of the sibyl (or sibyls) were given in verse form.

that same exquisite observing of number and measure in the words, and that high-flying liberty of conceit[5] proper to the poet, did seem to have some divine force in it.

And may not I presume a little farther, to show the reasonableness of this word *vates*, and say that the holy David's Psalms are a divine poem?[6] If I do, I shall not do it without the testimony of great learned men both ancient and modern. But even the name of 'Psalms' will speak for me, which, being interpreted, is nothing but 'songs'; then, that it is fully written in metre, as all learned Hebricians agree, although the rules be not yet fully found;[7] lastly and principally, his handling his prophecy, which is merely[8] poetical. For what else is the awaking his musical instruments, the often and free changing of persons, his notable *prosopopoeias*[9] when he maketh you, as it were, see God coming in His majesty, his telling of the beasts' joyfulness and hills' leaping, but a heavenly poesy, wherein almost he showeth himself a passionate lover of that unspeakable and everlasting beauty, to be seen by the eyes of the mind, only cleared by faith? But, truly, now having named him, I fear me I seem to profane that holy name, applying it to poetry, which is among us thrown down to so ridiculous an estimation. But they that with quiet judgements will look a little deeper into it shall find the end and working of it such as, being rightly applied, deserveth not to be scourged out of the Church of God.

But now let us see how the Greeks named it, and how they deemed of it. The Greeks called him a 'poet', which name hath, as the most excellent, gone through other languages. It cometh of this word, *poiein*, which is 'to make', wherein, I know not whether by luck or wisdom, we Englishmen have met with the Greeks in calling him a 'maker', which name, how high and incomparable a title it is, I had rather were known by marking the scope of other sciences than by any partial allegation.[1]

There is no art delivered to mankind that hath not the works of nature for his[2] principal object, without which they could not consist,[3] and on which they so depend as they become actors and players, as it were, of what nature will have set forth. So doth the astronomer look upon the stars, and, by that he seeth, set down what order nature hath taken therein. So doth the geometrician and arithmetician in their divers sorts of quantities. So doth the musician in times[4] tell you which by nature agree, which not. The natural philosopher thereon hath his name, and the moral philosopher standeth upon the natural virtues, vices or passions of man: 'and follow nature,' saith he, 'therein, and thou shalt not err.' The lawyer saith what men have determined, the historian, what men have done. The grammarian speaketh only of the rules of speech, and the rhetorician and logician, considering what in nature will soonest prove and persuade, thereon give artificial rules,[5] which

5. Imagination.
6. The biblical King David is traditionally credited with writing the book of Psalms, thought to be divinely inspired [editor's note].
7. "Psalm" comes from the Greek *psalmos*, "song accompanied on the harp." St. Jerome [ca. 347–420 C.E.] and the 1st-century C.E. Jewish historian Josephus both claimed to find classical metrics and verse forms in the Psalms, and similar claims were made until the 20th century. The consensus now is that there is a system of patterning by clause length and word stress, but "the rules be not yet fully found."
8. Entirely.
9. The rhetorical figure *prosopopoeia* involves the personification of inanimate things and the giving of a voice to the absent or dead.
1. Biased assertion.
2. Its [editor's note].
3. Exist.
4. Units of metrical measurement. Renaissance music still lacked regular bar lines and time signatures.
5. That is, rules fashioned by skill [editor's note].

still are compassed within the circle of a question, according to the proposed matter. The physician weigheth the nature of man's body, and the nature of things helpful or hurtful unto it. And the metaphysic, though it be in the second and abstract notions, and therefore be counted supernatural,[6] yet doth he indeed build upon the depth of nature. Only the poet, disdaining to be tied to any such subjection, lifted up with the vigour of his own invention, doth grow in effect into another nature, in making things either better than nature bringeth forth or, quite anew, forms such as never were in nature, as the heroes, demigods, cyclopes, chimeras, furies[7] and such like. So as he goeth hand in hand with nature, not enclosed within the narrow warrant[8] of her gifts but freely ranging only within the zodiac of his own wit. Nature never set forth the earth in so rich tapestry as divers poets have done, neither with so pleasant rivers, fruitful trees, sweet-smelling flowers, nor whatsoever else may make the too-much-loved earth more lovely: her world is brazen, the poets only deliver a golden.[9]

But let those things alone and go to man, for whom as the other things are, so it seemeth in him her uttermost cunning is employed, and know whether she have brought forth so true a lover as Theagenes, so constant a friend as Pylades, so valiant a man as Orlando, so right a prince as Xenophon's Cyrus, so excellent a man every way as Virgil's Aeneas.[1] Neither let this be jestingly conceived, because the works of the one be essential, the other in imitation or fiction, for any understanding knoweth the skill of each artificer standeth in that *idea* or fore-conceit of the work, and not in the work itself.[2] And that the poet hath that *idea* is manifest by delivering them forth in such excellency as he had imagined them; which delivering forth also is not wholly imaginative, as we are wont to say by them that build castles in the air, but so far substantially it worketh, not only to make a Cyrus, which had been but a particular excellency as nature might have done, but to bestow a Cyrus upon the world to make many Cyruses, if they will learn aright why and how that maker made him.

Neither let it be deemed too saucy a comparison to balance the highest point of man's wit with the efficacy of nature, but rather give right honour to the heavenly Maker of that maker, who, having made man to His own likeness, set him beyond and over all the works of that second nature;[3] which in nothing he showeth so much as in poetry, when, with the force of a divine

6. Outside the physical world.
7. In Greek mythology, avenging deities who punish crimes both in this world and after death. "Heroes": in the Greek sense, individuals who are part human, part divine. "Demigods": offspring of a god and a mortal. "Cyclopes": one-eyed giants. "Chimeras": fire-breathing female monsters with a lion's head, goat's body, and serpent's tail [editor's note].
8. License, permission.
9. The myth of four (or five) ages goes back to the Greek poet Hesiod (active ca. 700 B.C.E.), *Works and Days*, lines 109–201; see also *Metamorphoses* 1.89–150 (ca. 10 C.E.), by the Roman poet Ovid. Traditionally, the first (and best) age is the golden age, followed by silver, brass or brazen (the generation of humans), and iron [editor's note].
1. Theagenes, the lover of Charikleia, is the hero of the 4th-century Greek prose romance, Heliodorus' *Aethiopica*. Pylades was the faithful friend of Orestes in Greek myth: see, e.g., Aeschylus' *Oresteia*; Orlando was Roland in the medieval chivalric romances and became Orlando in a series of 15th- and 16th-century Italian verse romances, culminating in Ariosto's *Orlando furioso* (1532). Xenophon wrote a fictional account of the education of the 6th-century B.C.E. Persian king Cyrus, admired founder of the Persian Empire, in the *Cyropaedia*. Aeneas is the hero of Virgil's epic the *Aeneid*.
2. Nature ("the one") and the poet ("the other") are aligned, both skilful artificers able to generate *ideas*, even though nature's ideas actually come into existence ("essential") whereas the poet's can only be represented on the page ("in imitation or fiction").
3. Man is made in God's image; as God presides over nature, man presides over an image of nature, the second nature which he has power to shape at will.

breath, he bringeth things forth surpassing her[4] doings—with no small arguments to the incredulous of that first accursed fall of Adam, since our erected wit maketh us know what perfection is, and yet our infected will keepeth us from reaching unto it. But these arguments will by few be understood, and by fewer granted. Thus much I hope will be given me, that the Greeks with some probability of reason gave him the name above all names of learning.

Now let us go to a more ordinary opening[5] of him, that the truth may be the more palpable; and so I hope, though we get not so unmatched a praise as the etymology of his names will grant, yet his very description, which no man will deny, shall not justly be barred from a principal commendation. Poesy, therefore, is an art of imitation, for so Aristotle termeth it in the word *mimēsis*, that is to say, a representing, counterfeiting or figuring forth—to speak metaphorically, a speaking picture—with this end: to teach and delight.[6] Of this have been three general kinds. The chief, both in antiquity and excellency, were they that did imitate the unconceivable excellencies of God. Such were David in his Psalms, Solomon in his Song of Songs, in his Ecclesiastes and Proverbs, Moses and Deborah in their Hymns, and the writer of Job, which, beside other, the learned Emanuel Tremellius and Franciscus Junius do entitle the poetical part of the Scripture.[7] Against these none will speak that hath the Holy Ghost in due holy reverence. In this kind, though in a full wrong divinity, were Orpheus, Amphion, Homer in his Hymns,[8] and many other both Greeks and Romans. And this poesy must be used by whosoever will follow St James' counsel[9] in singing psalms when they are merry, and I know is used with the fruit of comfort by some, when in sorrowful pangs of their death-bringing sins they find the consolation of the never-leaving goodness.

The second kind is of them that deal with matters philosophical, either moral, as Tyrtaeus, Phocylides, Cato;[1] or natural, as Lucretius and Virgil's *Georgics*;[2] or astronomical, as Manilius and Pontanus; or historical, as Lucan;[3] which who mislike, the fault is in their judgement quite out of taste, and not in the sweet food of sweetly uttered knowledge.

4. That is, nature. "He": i.e., the poet.
5. Exposition, definition.
6. See Horace, *Ars Poetica*, line 333: "Poets aim either to do good or to give pleasure" (see above). ARISTOTLE (384–322 B.C.E.) begins the *Poetics* by discussing the nature of poetic *mimēsis*, representation and imitation (see above) [editor's note].
7. Tremellius (1510–1580) and Junius (1545–1602) in their new Latin translation of the Bible from the Hebrew and Greek, *Biblia sacra* (1575), 2:4. [Solomon: the biblical king of Israel was traditionally viewed as the author of the books named. Moses: after the Egyptians pursuing the Israelites perished in the Red Sea, Moses sang a triumphal song of praise to God (Exodus 1.1–15). Deborah: a biblical prophet and judge of Israel who sang a famous song of triumph when the king of Canaan was defeated (Judges 5)—editor's note.]
8. The mythic poems known as the Homeric hymns were ascribed to Homer but were actually composed by various poets from the late 8th century B.C.E. onwards. [Homer (ca. 8th c. B.C.E.), Greek epic poet to whom the *Iliad* and the *Odyssey* are attributed. Orpheus: greatest poet and musician of Greek myth, whose songs could move trees and stones and enchant wild beasts. Amphion: son of Zeus and Antiope, who by singing and playing his lyre moved the stones to build the walls of Thebes—editor's note.]
9. James 5.13. Psalm singing was something of a Protestant craze in the 16th century.
1. Dionysus Cato, the reputed author of the Latin *Disticha de Moribus* (3d c. C.E., *Distichs on Morals*), a popular elementary textbook on morality in medieval and Elizabethan schools. Tyrtaeus (7th c. B.C.E.), Spartan general and poet whose writings include war songs and exhortations in elegiac verse. Phocylides (active 540s B.C.E.), an Ionian poet known for his aphoristic verse [editor's note].
2. A didactic poem that describes and celebrates agriculture (ca. 30 B.C.E.). Lucretius (ca. 94–55 B.C.E.), Roman poet who wrote an epic on Epicurean philosophy, *De rerum natura* (*On the Nature of Things*) [editor's note].
3. Roman statesman and poet (39–64 C.E.), author of a historical epic, *The Civil War*. Manilius (active ca. 20–30 C.E.), author of the *Astronomica*, a didactic poem on astronomy. Jovianus Pontanus (1426–1503), Latin name of the Italian poet, historian, and statesman Giovanni Pontano, author of a neo-Latin poem on the stars, *Urania* [editor's note].

But because this second sort is wrapped within the fold of the proposed subject, and takes not the course of his own invention, whether they properly be poets or no let grammarians dispute, and go to the third, indeed right poets, of whom chiefly this question ariseth, betwixt whom and these second is such a kind of difference as betwixt the meaner sort of painters, who counterfeit only such faces as are set before them, and the more excellent, who having no law but wit bestow that in colours upon you which is fittest for the eye to see—as the constant though lamenting look of Lucretia, when she punished in herself another's fault, wherein he painteth not Lucretia, whom he never saw, but painteth the outward beauty of such a virtue.[4] For these third be they which most properly do imitate to teach and delight, and to imitate borrow nothing of what is, hath been or shall be, but range, only reined with learned discretion, into the divine consideration of what may be and should be. These be they that, as the first and most noble sort may justly be termed *vates*, so these are waited on[5] in the excellentest languages and best understandings with the fore-described name of poets. For these indeed do merely make to imitate, and imitate both to delight and teach, and delight to move men to take that goodness in hand, which without delight they would fly as from a stranger, and teach to make them know that goodness whereunto they are moved—which being the noblest scope[6] to which ever any learning was directed, yet want there not idle tongues to bark at them.

These be subdivided into sundry more special denominations. The most notable be the heroic, lyric, tragic, comic, satiric, iambic, elegiac, pastoral and certain others, some of these being termed according to the matter they deal with, some by the sorts of verses they liked best to write in. For indeed the greatest part of poets have apparelled their poetical inventions in that numbrous[7] kind of writing which is called verse—indeed but apparelled, verse being but an ornament and no cause to poetry, since there have been many most excellent poets that never versified, and now swarm many versifiers that need never answer to the name of poets. For Xenophon, who did imitate so excellently as to give us *effigiem iusti imperii*—the portraiture of a just empire—under the name of Cyrus, as Cicero saith of him, made therein an absolute heroical poem.[8] So did Heliodorus in his sugared invention of that picture of love in Theagenes and Charikleia. And yet both these wrote in prose, which I speak to show that it is not rhyming and versing that maketh a poet (no more than a long gown maketh an advocate, who though he pleaded in armour should be an advocate and no soldier), but it is that feigning[9] notable images of virtues, vices or what else, with that delightful teaching, which must be the right describing note[1] to know a poet by; although indeed the senate of poets hath chosen verse as their fittest raiment, meaning, as in matter they passed all in all, so in manner to go beyond them, not speaking, table talk fashion, or like men in a dream, words as they chanceably fall from

4. In Roman legend, Lucretia was raped by Tarquin, the son of the last king of Rome; after telling her husband, she committed suicide (her story was often treated by Renaissance authors and artists) [editor's note].
5. Accompanied.
6. Object, purpose.
7. Metrical.
8. Sidney refers to Cicero's *Epistola ad Quintum* (*Letter to Quintus*), 1.1.8. [Cicero (106–43 B.C.E.), Roman statesman and orator; Quintus was his brother—editor's note.]
9. Sidney uses "feigning" and its cognates in a precise sense related to its etymology, from the Latin *fingere*, "to shape, form, make."
1. Name, distinguishing mark.

the mouth, but peising[2] each syllable of each word by just proportion, according to the dignity of the subject.

Now, therefore, it shall not be amiss first to weigh this latter sort of poetry by his works, and then by his parts, and if in neither of these anatomies he be condemnable, I hope we shall obtain a more favourable sentence. This purifying of wit, this enriching of memory, enabling of judgement, and enlarging of conceit,[3] which commonly we call learning, under what name soever it come forth, or to what immediate end soever it be directed, the final end is to lead and draw us to as high a perfection as our degenerate souls, made worse by their clayey lodgings, can be capable of. This, according to the inclination of the man, bred many-formed impressions. For some, that thought this felicity principally to be gotten by knowledge, and no knowledge to be so high or heavenly as acquaintance with the stars, gave themselves to astronomy; others, persuading themselves to be demigods if they knew the causes of things, became natural and supernatural philosophers. Some an admirable delight drew to music; and some the certainty of demonstration to the mathematics. But all, one and other, having this scope: to know, and by knowledge to lift up the mind from the dungeon of the body to the enjoying his own divine essence. But when by the balance of experience it was found that the astronomer, looking to the stars, might fall in a ditch,[4] that the inquiring philosopher might be blind in himself, and the mathematician might draw forth a straight line with a crooked heart, then, lo, did proof, the overruler of opinions, make manifest that all these are but serving sciences, which, as they have each a private end in themselves, so yet are they all directed to the highest end of the mistress-knowledge, by the Greeks called *architektonikē*, which stands as I think in the knowledge of a man's self, in the ethic and politic consideration, with the end of well-doing and not of well-knowing only[5]—even as the saddler's next[6] end is to make a good saddle, but his further end to serve a nobler faculty, which is horsemanship, so the horseman's to soldiery, and the soldier not only to have the skill but to perform the practice of a soldier. So that the ending end of all earthly learning being virtuous action, those skills that most serve to bring forth that have a most just title to be princes over all the rest.

Wherein, if we can, show we the poet's nobleness, by setting him before his other competitors. Among whom as principal challengers step forth the moral philosophers, whom me thinketh I see coming towards me with a sullen gravity, as though they could not abide vice by daylight, rudely clothed, for to witness outwardly their contempt of outward things, with books in their hands against glory, whereto they set their names, sophistically speaking against subtlety,[7] and angry with any man in whom they see the foul fault of anger. These men, casting largess as they go of definitions, divisions and distinctions,[8] with a scornful interrogative do soberly ask whether it be possible to find any path so ready to lead a man to virtue as that which

2. Weighing.
3. Understanding, power of thought.
4. A familiar anecdote from antiquity; see PLATO, *Theaetetus* 174a (where the philosopher is identified as Thales); Cicero, *On the Republic* 1.30 [editor's note].
5. Sidney follows Aristotle, *Nicomachean Ethics* 1.1–2, closely here. *Architektonikē* is the master-art or science, equated by Aristotle with the political science, that is, the art of living in society.
6. Nearest.
7. Sophistry.
8. Terms inherited from medieval scholasticism describing the stages of rhetorical and logical argument.

teacheth what virtue is, and teacheth it not only by delivering forth his very being, his causes and effects, but also by making known his enemy vice, which must be destroyed, and his cumbersome servant passion, which must be mastered, by showing the generalities that containeth it and the specialities that are derived from it;[9] lastly, by plain setting down how it extendeth itself out of the limits of a man's own little world to the government of families and maintaining of public societies.

The historian scarcely giveth leisure to the moralist to say so much, but that he—loaden with old mouse-eaten records, authorizing himself for the most part upon other histories whose greatest authorities are built upon the notable foundation of hearsay, having much ado to accord differing writers and to pick truth out of partiality, better acquainted with a thousand years ago than with the present age, and yet better knowing how this world goeth than how his own wit runneth, curious for antiquities and inquisitive of novelties, a wonder to young folks and a tyrant in table talk—denieth in a great chafe[1] that any man for teaching of virtue and virtuous actions is comparable to him. 'I am *testis temporum, lux veritatis, vita memoriae, magistra vitae, nuntia vetustatis.*[2] The philosopher,' saith he, 'teacheth a disputative[3] virtue, but I do an active. His virtue is excellent in the dangerless Academy[4] of Plato, but mine showeth forth her honourable face in the battles of Marathon, Pharsalia, Poitiers and Agincourt.[5] He teacheth virtue by certain abstract considerations, but I only bid you follow the footing of them that have gone before you. Old-aged experience goeth beyond the fine-witted philosopher, but I give the experience of many ages. Lastly, if he make the songbook, I put the learner's hand to the lute, and if he be the guide, I am the light.' Then would he allege[6] you innumerable examples, confirming story by stories, how much the wisest senators and princes have been directed by the credit of history, as Brutus, Alphonsus of Aragon,[7] and who not, if need be? At length, the long line of their disputation maketh a point[8] in this, that the one giveth the precept, and the other the example.

Now whom shall we find, since the question standeth for the highest form in the school of learning, to be moderator?[9] Truly, as me seemeth, the poet; and if not a moderator, even the man that ought to carry the title from them both, and much more from all other serving sciences. Therefore compare we the poet with the historian and with the moral philosopher, and if he go beyond them both, no other human skill can match him. For as for the divine, with all reverence it is ever to be excepted, not only for having his scope as far beyond any of these as eternity exceedeth a moment, but even

9. That is, an examination of genus and species.
1. Heart, rage.
2. Cicero, *De Oratore* 2.9.36 (Latin): "the witness of passing ages, the light of truth, the life of memory, the mistress of life, she who brings tidings of antiquity."
3. Theoretical.
4. Plato's school on the outskirts of Athens, founded ca. 385 B.C.E. [editor's note].
5. All sites of great victories: at Marathon, the Greeks defeated the Persians (490 B.C.E.); at Pharsalia, Julius Caesar defeated Pompey (48 B.C.E.); at Poitiers, the English led by Edward the Black Prince defeated the French (1356); and at Agincourt, the English led by Henry V again defeated the French (1415) [editor's note].
6. Cite.
7. Alphonso V of Aragon (1396–1458, also known as Alfonso I of Naples and Sicily) carried the Roman histories written by Livy and Caesar into battle with him. Marcus Brutus (85–42 B.C.E.), one of the conspirators against Caesar, was inspired by the thought of his ancestor Junius Brutus, who expelled the Tarquin kings [editor's note].
8. (Punning on) full stop, period.
9. Judge, chair. In logic and rhetoric the *quaestio* is the subject of debate, the central issue in an academic disputation. ["Form": grade level—editor's note.]

for passing each of these in themselves. And for the lawyer, though *ius*[1] be the daughter of justice, and justice the chief of virtues, yet because he seeketh to make men good rather *formidine poenae* than *virtutis amore*,[2] or, to say righter, doth not endeavour to make men good, but that their evil hurt not others, having no care, so he be a good citizen, how bad a man he be, therefore as our wickedness maketh him necessary, and necessity maketh him honourable, so is he not, in the deepest truth, to stand in rank with these who all endeavour to take naughtiness away and plant goodness even in the secretest cabinet of our souls. And these four are all that any way deal in the consideration of men's manners,[3] which being the supreme knowledge, they that best breed it deserve the best commendation.

The philosopher, therefore, and the historian are they which would win the goal, the one by precept, the other by example; but both, not having both, do both halt.[4] For the philosopher, setting down with thorny arguments the bare rule, is so hard of utterance, and so misty to be conceived, that one that hath no other guide but him shall wade in him till he be old before he shall find sufficient cause to be honest. For his knowledge standeth so upon the abstract and general, that happy is that man who may understand him, and more happy that can apply what he doth understand. On the other side, the historian, wanting[5] the precept, is so tied not to what should be but to what is, to the particular truth of things and not to the general reason of things, that his example draweth no necessary consequence, and therefore a less fruitful doctrine.

Now doth the peerless poet perform both, for whatsoever the philosopher saith should be done, he giveth a perfect picture of it in someone by whom he presupposeth it was done, so as he coupleth the general notion with the particular example. A perfect picture I say, for he yieldeth to the powers of the mind an image of that whereof the philosopher bestoweth but a wordish description, which doth neither strike, pierce nor possess the sight of the soul so much as that other doth. For as in outward things, to a man that had never seen an elephant or a rhinoceros, who should tell him most exquisitely all their shapes, colour, bigness and particular marks, or of a gorgeous palace an architector, with declaring the full beauties, might well make the hearer able to repeat, as it were by rote, all he had heard, yet should never satisfy his inward conceit with being witness to itself of a true lively[6] knowledge; but the same man, as soon as he might see those beasts well painted, or the house well in model, should straightways grow, without need of any description, to a judicial[7] comprehending of them: so no doubt the philosopher, with his learned definitions, be it of virtues or vices, matters of public policy or private government, replenisheth the memory with many infallible grounds of wisdom, which notwithstanding lie dark before the imaginative and judging power,[8] if they be not illuminated or figured forth by the speaking picture of poesy.

* * *

1. Right, law (Latin).
2. From fear of punishment . . . by the love of virtue (Latin); Horace, *Epistles* 1.16.52–53 [editor's note].
3. Morals.
4. Walk with a limp.
5. Lacking [editor's note].
6. Living, lifelike.
7. Judicious, just.
8. Here and elsewhere Sidney adopts the standard Renaissance tripartite division of mind (or "wit") into imagination (or "conceit"), judgment, and memory.

For the question is, whether the feigned image of poetry or the regular instruction of philosophy hath the more force in teaching. Wherein if the philosophers have more rightly showed themselves philosophers than the poets have attained to the high top of their profession (as in truth *mediocribus esse poetis / non di, non homines, non concessere columnae*)[9] it is, I say again, not the fault of the art, but that by few men that art can be accomplished.

* * *

For conclusion, I say the philosopher teacheth, but he teacheth obscurely, so as the learned only can understand him: that is to say, he teacheth them that are already taught. But the poet is the food for the tenderest stomachs; the poet is indeed the right popular philosopher. Whereof Aesop's tales give good proof, whose pretty allegories, stealing under the formal tales[1] of beasts, make many, more beastly than beasts, begin to hear the sound of virtue from these dumb speakers.

But now may it be alleged, that if this imagining of matters be so fit for the imagination, then must the historian needs surpass, who bringeth you images of true matters, such as indeed were done, and not such as fantastically or falsely may be suggested to have been done. Truly, Aristotle himself, in his discourse of poesy, plainly determineth this question, saying that poetry is *philosophōteron* and *spoudaioteron*—that is to say, it is more philosophical and more studiously serious than history.[2] His reason is, because poesy dealeth with *katholou*, that is to say with the universal consideration, and the history with *kath' hekaston*, the particular. Now, saith he, the universal weighs what is fit to be said or done, either in likelihood or necessity, which the poesy considereth in his imposed names; and the particular only marketh whether Alcibiades[3] did or suffered this or that. Thus far Aristotle: which reason of his, as all his, is most full of reason.

* * *

Now, to that which commonly is attributed to the praise of history, in respect of the notable learning is got by marking the success,[4] as though therein a man should see virtue exalted and vice punished, truly that commendation is peculiar to poetry, and far off from history; for indeed poetry ever sets virtue so out in her best colours, making fortune her well-waiting handmaid, that one must needs be enamoured of her. Well may you see Ulysses in a storm and in other hard plights,[5] but they are but exercises of patience and magnanimity,[6] to make them shine the more in the near-following prosperity. And of the contrary part, if evil men come to the stage, they ever go out (as the tragedy writer answered to one that misliked the show of such persons) so manacled as they little animate folks to follow them. But the history, being captived to the truth of a foolish world, is many times a terror from well-doing, and an encouragement to unbridled wickedness. For see we not valiant Miltiades rot in his fetters; the just Phocion and the accomplished

9. That poets should ever be "average" is not a concession allowed by man, gods, or the stalls (Latin); Horace, *Ars Poetica*, lines 372–73 [editor's note].
1. That is, the outward form of tales. The earliest surviving collection of fables ascribed to the 6th-century B.C.E. Aesop is a metrical version by Babrius, ca. 100 C.E.
2. See *Poetics* 9, 1451a36–1451b11 [editor's note].
3. Athenian general and politician (ca. 450–404 B.C.E.) [editor's note].
4. Outcome, upshot.
5. *Odyssey*, book 5. [Ulysses is the Latin name for Homer's Greek hero, Odysseus—editor's note.]
6. Fortitude, greatness of spirit.

Socrates put to death like traitors; the cruel Severus live prosperously; the excellent Severus miserably murdered; Sulla and Marius dying in their beds; Pompey and Cicero[7] slain then when they would have thought exile a happiness? See we not virtuous Cato driven to kill himself, and rebel Caesar so advanced that his name yet after sixteen hundred years lasteth in the highest honour?[8] And mark but even Caesar's own words of the forenamed Sulla (who in that only did honestly, to put down his dishonest tyranny), *literas nescivit,*[9] as if want of learning caused him to do well. He meant it not by poetry, which, not content with earthly plagues, deviseth new punishments in hell for tyrants, nor yet by philosophy, which teacheth *occidendos esse,*[1] but no doubt by skill in history, for that indeed can afford you Cypselus, Periander, Phalaris, Dionysius,[2] and I know not how many more of the same kennel, that speed[3] well enough in their abominable injustice of usurpation.

I conclude therefore that he excelleth history, not only in furnishing the mind with knowledge, but in setting it forward to that which deserveth to be called and accounted good, which setting forward and moving to well-doing indeed setteth the laurel crown upon the poets as victorious, not only of the historian, but over the philosopher, howsoever in teaching it may be questionable.[4] For suppose it be granted, that which I suppose with great reason may be denied, that the philosopher, in respect of his methodical proceeding, doth teach more perfectly than the poet; yet do I think that no man is so much *philophilosophos*[5] as to compare the philosopher in moving with the poet. And, that moving is of a higher degree than teaching, it may by this appear, that it is well nigh both the cause and effect of teaching. For who will be taught, if he be not moved with desire to be taught? And what so much good doth that teaching bring forth (I speak still of moral doctrine) as that it moveth one to do that which it doth teach? For, as Aristotle saith, it is not *gnōsis* but *praxis* must be the fruit;[6] and how *praxis* can be, without being moved to practise, it is no hard matter to consider.

7. Killed at the command of Antony (whom his orations defending the Republic had attacked) as he was trying to escape from Rome. Miltiades (ca. 550–489 B.C.E.), Athenian general and victor at Marathon later imprisoned by the Athenians. Phocian (4th c. B.C.E.)., Athenian general and statesman unjustly executed for treason because he had opposed the will of the people. Socrates (469–399 B.C.E.), Athenian philosopher immortalized in the writings of his pupil Plato and condemned to death on charges of impiety and corrupting youth. "Cruel Severus": Lucius Septimius Severus (145/6–221 C.E.), a strong emperor of Rome (193–211) who was ruthless in pursuit of his goals. "Excellent Severus": Alexander Severus (208/9–235 C.E.), a peaceful and religious emperor of Rome (225–235), slain by his troops. Sulla and Marius: Lucius Cornelius Sulla (ca. 138–78 B.C.E.) and Gaius Marius (157–86 B.C.E.), Roman generals whose struggle for military and political supremacy led to civil war (88–82 B.C.E.). Pompey: Pompey the Great (106–48 B.C.E.), Roman soldier and statesman defeated at Pharsalia by his former ally, Caesar, and murdered in Egypt [editor's note].

8. The rebellion of Julius Caesar (100–44 B.C.E.) against the Senate in 49 led to civil war and the end of the Roman Republic. Cato: Cato the Younger (95–46 B.C.E.), a defender of the Republic who committed suicide after it was clear that Caesar had won the day [editor's note].

9. He was ignorant of letters (Latin). ["Caesar's words" are recounted in Suetonius (b. ca. 69 C.E.), *Life of Julius Caesar* 77—editor's note.]

1. That they must fall (Latin).

2. All Greek "tyrants" (that is, rulers): Cypselus, in Corinth, ca. 657–625 B.C.E.; Periander, his son, in Corinth, 625–585 B.C.E.; Phalaris, whose rule in Acragas (Sicily), ca. 570–ca. 544 B.C.E., was notoriously cruel; and Dionysius I, in Syracuse, 405–367 B.C.E. [editor's note].

3. Prosper.

4. That is, who gets the crown for teaching alone may be debatable. [The crown is like those awarded to victors in the Greek athletic contests; laurel, because of the tree's association with Apollo, is linked to poetry—editor's note.]

5. A philosopher-lover (Greek).

6. See Aristotle, *Nicomachean Ethics* 1.3, 1095a: "The end is not knowledge (*gnōsis*) but action (*praxis*)" [editor's note].

The philosopher showeth you the way, he informeth you of the particularities, as well of the tediousness of the way, as of the pleasant lodging you shall have when your journey is ended, as of the many by-turnings that may divert you from your way. But this is to no man but to him that will read him, and read him with attentive, studious painfulness; which constant desire whosoever hath in him hath already passed half the hardness of the way, and therefore is beholding to the philosopher but for the other half. Nay truly, learned men have learnedly thought that where once reason hath so much overmastered passion as that the mind hath a free desire to do well, the inward light each mind hath in itself is as good as a philosopher's book, since in nature we know it is well to do well, and what is well and what is evil, although not in the words of art which philosophers bestow upon us; for out of natural conceit the philosophers drew it.[7] But to be moved to do that which we know, or to be moved with desire to know—*hoc opus, hic labor est*.[8]

Now therein of all sciences (I speak still of human, and according to the human conceit) is our poet the monarch. For he doth not only show the way, but giveth so sweet a prospect into the way as will entice any man to enter into it; nay, he doth as if your journey should lie through a fair vineyard—at the very first give you a cluster of grapes that, full of that taste, you may long to pass further. He beginneth not with obscure definitions, which must blur the margent[9] with interpretations and load the memory with doubtfulness,[1] but he cometh to you with words set in delightful proportion, either accompanied with or prepared for the well-enchanting skill of music, and with a tale, forsooth, he cometh unto you, with a tale which holdeth children from play and old men from the chimney corner; and pretending[2] no more, doth intend the winning of the mind from wickedness to virtue. Even as the child is often brought to take most wholesome things by hiding them in such other as have a pleasant taste, which if one should begin to tell them the nature of the aloes or rhabarbarum[3] they should receive, would sooner take their physic at their ears than at their mouth, so is it in men (most of which are childish in the best things till they be cradled in their graves): glad they will be to hear the tales of Hercules,[4] Achilles, Cyrus, Aeneas, and hearing them must needs hear the right description of wisdom, valour and justice, which if they had been barely (that is to say, philosophically) set out, they would swear they be brought to school again.

* * *

By these, therefore, examples and reasons I think it may be manifest that the poet with that same hand of delight doth draw the mind more effectually than any other art doth, and so a conclusion not unfitly ensue: that as virtue is the most excellent resting place for all worldly learning to make his end of, so poetry, being the most familiar[5] to teach it, and most princely to

7. The philosophers deduced moral laws, so why can't we?
8. "This is the labour, this is the toil." Virgil, *Aeneid* 6.129, on Aeneas' path back up from the underworld.
9. Margin of a book.
1. Ambiguity.
2. Claiming.
3. Aloes is a bitter purgative made from the leaves of several species of aloe; rhabarbarum is rhubarb or rhubarb-root, also used as a purgative.
4. Roman spelling of Heracles, greatest of the legendary Greek heroes [editor's note].
5. Courteous, friendly.

move towards it, in the most excellent work is the most excellent workman. But I am content not only to decipher him by his works (although works in commendation or dispraise must ever hold a high authority), but more narrowly will examine his parts, so that (as in a man), though all together may carry a presence full of majesty and beauty, perchance in some one defectuous[6] piece we may find blemish.

Now in his parts, kinds or species,[7] as you list to term them, it is to be noted that some poesies have coupled together two or three kinds: as the tragical and comical, whereupon is risen the tragi-comical. Some, in the manner, have mingled prose and verse, as Sannazaro and Boethius.[8] Some have mingled matters heroical and pastoral. But that cometh all to one in this question, for if severed they be good, the conjunction cannot be hurtful. Therefore, perchance forgetting some, and leaving some as needless to be remembered, it shall not be amiss in a word to cite the special kinds, to see what faults may be found in the right use of them.

Is it then the pastoral poem which is misliked?[9] (For perchance where the hedge is lowest they will soonest leap over.) Is the poor pipe disdained, which sometimes, out of Meliboeus' mouth, can show the misery of people under hard lords or ravening soldiers, and again, by Tityrus, what blessedness is derived to them that lie lowest from the goodness of them that sit highest;[1] sometimes, under the pretty tales of wolves and sheep, can include the whole considerations of wrongdoing and patience; sometimes show that contentions for trifles can get but a trifling victory, where perchance a man may see that even Alexander and Darius,[2] when they strave who should be cock of this world's dunghill, the benefit they got was that the after-livers may say:

> Haec memini, et victum frustra contendere Thyrsim.
> ex illo Corydon, Corydon est tempore nobis?[3]

Or is it the lamenting elegiac, which in a kind heart would move rather pity than blame; who bewails with the great philosopher Heraclitus[4] the weakness of mankind and the wretchedness of the world; who surely is to be praised, either for compassionate accompanying just causes of lamentations, or for rightly painting out how weak be the passions of woefulness? Is it the bitter but wholesome iambic,[5] who rubs the galled mind in making shame

6. Defective.
7. What we would now call "genres."
8. Influential examples of the *prosimetrum*, a work alternating verse and prose, include Boethius' [ca. 480–524] *Consolation of Philosophy* and DANTE's *La Vita Nuova* (*The New Life*). The *Arcadia* (1504) of Jacopo Sannazaro (1458–1530) is a rather limited pastoral narrative, its twelve prose sections alternating with twelve verse sections, but the work gave Sidney the title for his *Arcadia*.
9. Pastoral, the lowest ranking of the genres in the traditional lists, had the status of both the first type of poetry for a writer to publish and the first for a schoolboy to read.
1. Virgil, *Eclogues* 1, a dialogue between the dispossessed Meliboeus and the fortunate Tityrus.
2. The invading Alexander the Great (356–323 B.C.E.) twice defeated Darius III (ca. 380–330 B.C.E.), king of Persia, before Darius was deposed and finally murdered by his own soldiers [editor's note].
3. "This I remember, and how Thyrsis, vanquished, strove in vain. From that day it is Corydon, Corydon with us." The closing lines of Virgil, *Eclogues* 7.69–70, in which Meliboeus has narrated a contest between Corydon and Thyrsis.
4. The Greek philosopher of the 6th century, whose doctrine that everything is in a state of constant flux Sidney glances at here. [Heraclitus was known as "the weeping philosopher" because of his gloomy views—editor's note.]
5. Another genre named for a verse form. Sidney follows the Italian scholar and poet Julius Caesar Scaliger (1484–1558) in calling the direct and excoriating Juvenalian form of satire "iambic" and reserving the term "satiric" for the gentler, comic approach of Horace. ["The Juvenalian form": i.e., characteristic of the Roman satiric poet Juvenal (ca. 55–ca. 130 C.E.)—editor's note.]

the trumpet of villainy, with bold and open crying out against naughtiness? Or the satiric, who *omne vafer vitium ridenti tangit amico*;[6] who sportingly never leaveth till he make a man laugh at folly, and, at length ashamed, to laugh at himself, which he cannot avoid without avoiding the folly; who, while *circum praecordia ludit*,[7] giveth us to feel how many headaches a passionate life bringeth us to, how, when all is done, *est Ulubris, animus si nos non deficit aequus*?[8]

No? Perchance it is the comic, whom naughty play-makers and stage-keepers have justly made odious. To the arguments of abuse I will answer after; only thus much now is to be said—that the comedy is an imitation of the common errors of our life, which he representeth in the most ridiculous and scornful sort that may be, so as it is impossible that any beholder can be content to be such a one. Now, as in geometry the oblique must be known as well as the right,[9] and in arithmetic the odd as well as the even, so in the actions of our life who seeth not the filthiness of evil wanteth a great foil to perceive the beauty of virtue. This doth the comedy handle so in our private and domestical matters as, with hearing it, we get, as it were, an experience what is to be looked for of a niggardly Demea, of a crafty Davus, of a flattering Gnatho, of a vainglorious Thraso;[1] and not only to know what effects are to be expected, but to know who be such, by the signifying badge given them by the comedian.[2] And little reason hath any man to say that men learn the evil by seeing it so set out, since, as I said before, there is no man living, but, by the force truth hath in nature, no sooner seeth these men play their parts but wisheth them *in pistrinum*, although perchance the sack of his own faults lie so behind his back[3] that he seeth not himself dance the same measure;[4] whereto yet nothing can more open his eyes than to find his own actions contemptibly set forth.

So that the right use of comedy will, I think, by nobody be blamed. And much less of the high and excellent tragedy, that openeth the greatest wounds, and showeth forth the ulcers that are covered with tissue; that maketh kings fear to be tyrants, and tyrants manifest their tyrannical humours; that with stirring the affects of admiration[5] and commiseration teacheth the uncertainty of this world, and upon how weak foundations gilden roofs are builded; that maketh us know:

> qui sceptra saevus duro imperio regit
> timet timentes; metus in auctorem redit.[6]

6. The rascal probes his friend's every fault while making him laugh (Latin); slightly misquoted from Persius (34–62 C.E.), *Satires* 1.116–17 (a description of Horace) [editor's note].
7. He plays with his [friend's] heart (Latin); Persius 1.117 [editor's note].
8. [What we seek (i.e., to live well)] is in Ulubrae, if our equanimity doesn't fail us (Latin); slightly adapted from Horace, *Epistles* 1.1.30. Ulubrae was an uninspiring town surrounded by marshes [editor's note].
9. "Oblique" means "crooked," and "right" can mean "straight"; at the same time they are used in the technical sense of oblique and right angles.
1. Stock characters in the comedies of the Roman playwright Terence (ca. 190–159 B.C.E.).
2. The requirement of *decorum*, that characters be self-consistent and appropriate; cf. [Aristotle,] *Poetics* 1454a and Horace, *Ars Poetica*, lines 119–27.
3. In the Aesopic fable, man has two sacks, one filled with other men's faults, carried in front, one with his own, carried on his back where he cannot see it. *In pistrinum*: "in the mill," i.e., sentenced to hard labor.
4. Type of dance: i.e., "dance to the same tune."
5. Surprise, wonderment. "Affects": emotions.
6. "The tyrant who rules harshly fears those who fear him; terror rebounds on its agent." A popular tag [slightly misquoted] from Seneca, *Oedipus*, 705–6. [Seneca the Younger (ca. 4 B.C.E.–65 C.E.), Roman philosopher and playwright—editor's note.]

But how much it can move, Plutarch yieldeth a notable testimony of the abominable tyrant Alexander Pheraeus,[7] from whose eyes a tragedy well made and represented drew abundance of tears, who without all pity had murdered infinite numbers, and some of his own blood; so as he that was not ashamed to make matters for tragedies yet could not resist the sweet violence of a tragedy. And if it wrought no further good in him, it was that he, in despite of himself, withdrew himself from hearkening to that which might mollify[8] his hardened heart. But it is not the tragedy they do mislike, for it were too absurd to cast out so excellent a representation of whatsoever is most worthy to be learned.

Is it the lyric that most displeaseth, who with his tuned lyre and well-accorded voice giveth praise, the reward of virtue, to virtuous acts; who gives moral precepts and natural problems;[9] who sometime raiseth up his voice to the height of the heavens in singing the lauds of the immortal God? Certainly I must confess my own barbarousness: I never heard the old song of Percy and Douglas that I found not my heart moved more than with a trumpet, and yet is it sung but by some blind crowder,[1] with no rougher voice than rude style—which being so evil apparelled in the dust and cobwebs of that uncivil age, what would it work trimmed in the gorgeous eloquence of Pindar?[2] In Hungary I have seen it the manner at all feasts and other such meetings to have songs of their ancestors' valour, which that right soldierlike nation think one of the chiefest kindlers of brave courage.[3] The incomparable Lacedemonians[4] did not only carry that kind of music ever with them to the field, but even at home, as such songs were made, so were they all content to be singers of them, when the lusty men were to tell what they did, the old men what they had done, and the young what they would do. And where a man may say that Pindar many times praiseth highly victories of small moment, matters rather of sport than virtue, as it may be answered, it was the fault of the poet and not of the poetry, so indeed the chief fault was in the time and custom of the Greeks, who set those toys at so high a price that Philip of Macedon reckoned a horserace won at Olympus among his three fearful felicities.[5] But as the unimitable Pindar often did, so is that kind most capable and most fit to awake the thoughts from the sleep of idleness to embrace honourable enterprises.

There rests the heroical,[6] whose very name I think should daunt all backbiters. For by what conceit can a tongue be directed to speak evil of that which draweth with him no less champions than Achilles, Cyrus, Aeneas, Turnus,

7. Ruler of Pherae in Thessaly, 369–358 B.C.E.; in his *Life of Pelopidas*, Plutarch (ca. 50–120 C.E.) records that Alexander, whose savagery he details, wept at the sufferings of Hecuba and Andromache in the Greek playwright Euripides' *Troades* (415 B.C.E.) [editor's note].
8. Soften.
9. Questions posed for academic discussion [editor's note].
1. Fiddler, minstrel. Some form of the ballad of Chevy Chase, dating from the 15th century, which tells of the enmity between Percy (of Northumberland) and the Scottish Douglas; both die in battle.
2. Greek lyric poet (ca. 518–438 B.C.E.), known for his elaborate odes honoring victors in athletic contests. "Uncivil age": the Middle Ages [editor's note].
3. Sidney spent several weeks in Hungary in 1573.
4. Spartans.
5. Mistaking, as was common, Mount Olympus for Olympia, site of the Games. The three "felicities" were reported to Philip on the same day; the other two were a victory against the Illyrians and the birth of his son Alexander, later the Great (Plutarch's *Life of Alexander* 3). "Toys": trifles. "Fearful": inspiring awe, reverence; ominous.
6. The heroical, or epic, was acknowledged to be the foremost literary kind by almost all authorities, only comparable to tragedy for the dignity of its subject matter, and preferable for its greater scope.

Tydeus and Rinaldo;[7] who doth not only teach and move to a truth, but teacheth and moveth to the most high and excellent truth; who maketh magnanimity and justice shine through all misty fearfulness and foggy desires; who, if the saying of Plato and Tully be true, that who could see virtue would be wonderfully ravished with the love of her beauty[8]—this man sets her out to make her more lovely in her holiday apparel[9] to the eye of any that will deign not to disdain until they understand? But if anything be already said in the defence of sweet poetry, all concurreth to the maintaining the heroical, which is not only a kind, but the best and most accomplished kind of poetry. For as the image of each action stirreth and instructeth the mind, so the lofty image of such worthies most inflameth the mind with desire to be worthy, and informs with counsel how to be worthy. Only let Aeneas be worn in the tablet of your memory[1]—how he governeth himself in the ruin of his country, in the preserving his old father, and carrying away his religious ceremonies;[2] in obeying God's commandment to leave Dido,[3] though not only all passionate kindness but even the human consideration of virtuous gratefulness would have craved other of him; how in storms, how in sports, how in war, how in peace, how a fugitive, how victorious, how besieged, how besieging, how to strangers, how to allies, how to enemies, how to his own; lastly, how in his inward self, and how in his outward government—and I think in a mind not prejudiced with a prejudicating humour he will be found in excellency fruitful, yea even as Horace saith, *melius Chrysippo et Crantore*.[4]

But truly I imagine it falleth out with these poet-whippers as with some good women, who often are sick but in faith they cannot tell where—so the name of poetry is odious to them, but neither his cause nor effects, neither the sum that contains him nor the particularities descending from him, give any fast handle to their carping dispraise.

Since then poetry is of all human learnings the most ancient, and of most fatherly antiquity, as from whence other learnings have taken their beginnings; since it is so universal that no learned nation doth despise it, nor barbarous nation is without it; since both Roman and Greek gave such divine names unto it, the one of prophesying, the other of making, and that indeed that name of making is fit for him, considering that where all other arts retain themselves within their subject, and receive, as it were, their being from it, the poet, only, only bringeth his own stuff, and doth not learn a conceit out of a

7. Achilles is the hero of Homer's *Iliad* and the *Achilleis* of Statius (ca. 45–96 C.E.); Tydeus is mentioned in Homer and is one of the seven against Thebes in Statius, *Thebais*; Rinaldo figures in Ariosto's *Orlando furioso*, and in Torquato Tasso's *Rinaldo* (1562) and *Gerusalemme liberata* (1580–81, *Jerusalem Delivered*). [Turnus: legendary king of Italy, defeated by Aeneas in single combat in Virgil's *Aeneid*—editor's note.]

8. Plato, *Phaedrus* 250d, followed in Cicero, *De finibus* (*On Ends*) 2.16.52 and *De officiis* (*On Duties*) 1.5.14. [Tully: another name for Cicero, whose full name is Marcus Tullius Cicero—editor's note.]

9. As opposed to the work clothes in which she is dressed by philosophers.

1. The image of the mind as a wax tablet (e.g., *tabula rasa* in Latin, a blank tablet) was common in Sidney's day. "Tables" or "tablets" were also boards on which portraits were painted; the image is thus closely related to the thread of visual metaphors centred on the "speaking picture." Sidney's list alludes to all the central matter of the *Aeneid*.

2. Virgil, *Aeneid* 2.705–20. "Ceremonies": religious objects (here, the household gods) [editor's note].

3. The queen of Carthage, whom Jupiter orders Aeneas to leave so that he may fulfill his destiny in Italy. As he departs, she commits suicide; see *Aeneid* 4 [editor's note].

4. Better than Chrysippus and Crantor (Latin); Horace, *Epistles* 1.2.4, referring to the poet Homer, who conveys what is beautiful, shameful, useful, and not useful better than do two philosophers, the Stoic Chrysippus (ca. 280–207 B.C.E.) and the commentator on Plato Crantor (ca. 335– ca. 275 B.C.E.) [editor's note].

matter but maketh matter for a conceit;[5] since, neither his description nor end containing any evil, the thing described cannot be evil; since his effects be so good as to teach goodness and to delight the learners; since therein (namely in moral doctrine, the chief of all knowledges) he doth not only far pass the historian, but for instructing is well nigh comparable to the philosopher, for moving leaves him behind him; since the Holy Scripture (wherein there is no uncleanness) hath whole parts in it poetical, and that even our Saviour Christ vouchsafed to use the flowers of it; since all his kinds are not only in their united forms but in their severed dissections fully commendable—I think (and think I think rightly) the laurel crown appointed for triumphant captains doth worthily of all other learnings honour the poet's triumph.[6]

* * *

Now then go we to the most important imputations laid to the poor poets. For ought I can yet learn, they are these. First, that there being many other more fruitful knowledges, a man might better spend his time in them than in this. Secondly, that it is the mother of lies. Thirdly, that it is the nurse of abuse, infecting us with many pestilent desires, with a siren's sweetness drawing the mind to the serpent's tail of sinful fancies[7] (and herein especially comedies give the largest field to ear,[8] as Chaucer saith); how both in other nations and in ours, before poets did soften us, we were full of courage, given to martial exercises, the pillars of manlike liberty, and not lulled asleep in shady idleness with poets' pastimes. And lastly and chiefly, they cry out with open mouth as if they had overshot Robin Hood, that Plato banished them out of his commonwealth.[9] Truly this is much, if there be much truth in it.

First, to the first. That a man might better spend his time is a reason indeed, but it doth, as they say, but *petere principium*.[1] For if it be, as I affirm, that no learning is so good as that which teacheth and moveth to virtue, and that none can both teach and move thereto so much as poetry, then is the conclusion manifest, that ink and paper cannot be to a more profitable purpose employed. And certainly, though a man should grant their first assumption, it should follow (methinks) very unwillingly that good is not good because better is better. But I still and utterly deny that there is sprung out of earth a more fruitful knowledge.

To the second, therefore, that they should be the principal liars, I answer paradoxically but truly, I think truly, that of all writers under the sun the poet is the least liar—and though[2] he would, as a poet can scarcely be a liar. The

5. Does not take his fore-conceit [preconception] from events but creates events which will form a satisfying fore-conceit.
6. A triumph was "the entrance of a victorious commander with his army and spoils in solemn procession into Rome, permission for which was granted by the senate in honour of an important achievement in war" (*Oxford English Dictionary*). The victorious commander would then be crowned with laurel. In 1341, the poet Petrarch was given a triumph and crowned with laurel; thereafter dignified poets were crowned literally or figuratively with laurel (hence "poet laureate").
7. Fantasies. The sirens lured passing sailors to their deaths with their music; they were half woman, half bird, though Sidney has preferred the later tradition of depicting them as mermaids, perhaps because of the lure of the tale/tail pun.
8. To plow; the English poet Chaucer (ca. 1343–1400) uses the phrase "a large feeld to ere" in the *Knight's Tale, Canterbury Tales* 1.886 [editor's note].
9. Cf. the proverb: "Many speak of Robin Hood that never shot with his bow," i.e., people repeat Plato's argument who know nothing of his philosophy. [For Plato's expulsion of the poets, see *Republic* 3.398a–b, 10.595a–608b—editor's note.]
1. Beg the question (Latin).
2. Even if.

astronomer with his cousin the geometrician can hardly escape when they take upon them to measure the height of the stars. How often, think you, do the physicians lie, when they aver things good for sicknesses which afterwards send Charon a great number of souls drowned in a potion before they come to his ferry?[3] And no less of the rest which take upon them to affirm. Now, for the poet, he nothing affirms, and therefore never lieth, for, as I take it, to lie is to affirm that to be true which is false. So as the other artists, and especially the historian, affirming many things, can in the cloudy knowledge of mankind hardly escape from many lies. But the poet, as I said before, never affirmeth; the poet never maketh any circles about your imagination,[4] to conjure you to believe for true what he writes; he citeth not authorities of other histories, but even for his entry calleth the sweet Muses to inspire into him a good invention[5]—in troth, not labouring to tell you what is or is not, but what should or should not be. And therefore, though he recount things not true, yet because he telleth them not for true, he lieth not, without we will say that Nathan lied in his speech before-alleged to David,[6] which as a wicked man durst scarce say, so think I none so simple would say that Aesop lied in the tales of his beasts—for who thinks that Aesop wrote it for actually true were well worthy to have his name chronicled among the beasts he writeth of. What child is there, that coming to a play and seeing 'Thebes' written in great letters upon an old door doth believe that it is Thebes? If then a man can arrive to that child's age to know that the poet's persons and doings are but pictures what should be and not stories what have been, they will never give the lie[7] to things not affirmatively but allegorically and figuratively written; and therefore, as in history, looking for truth, they may go away full fraught with falsehood, so in poesy, looking but for fiction, they shall use the narration but as an imaginative ground-plot of a profitable invention.[8]

* * *

Their third is, how much it abuseth men's wit, training it to wanton sinfulness and lustful love: for indeed that is the principal, if not only, abuse I can hear alleged. They say the comedies rather teach than reprehend amorous conceits.[9] They say the lyric is larded with passionate sonnets, the elegiac weeps the want of his mistress, and that even to the heroical Cupid[1] hath ambitiously climbed. Alas, Love, I would thou couldst as well defend thyself as thou canst offend others; I would those on whom thou dost attend could either put thee away or yield good reason why they keep thee. But grant love of beauty to be a beastly fault (although it be very hard, since only man and no beast hath that gift to discern beauty); grant that lovely name of love to deserve all hateful reproaches (although even some of my masters the

3. In the Greek underworld, Charon was the ferryman who transported the souls of the dead across the river Styx.
4. The magic circles drawn on the ground by necromancers defined the area within which the magic worked.
5. The traditional epic invocation, as in Homer ("Sing, Muse, of the wrath of Achilles," *Iliad*, 1.1); "invention" is the matter of the narrative or oration. "Entry": opening words.
6. King of Israel (d. ca. 970 B.C.E.); according to the Bible, God sent the prophet Nathan to reprimand him for committing adultery with Bathsheba (2 Samuel 12) [editor's note].
7. Make an accusation of lying.
8. "Narration" meant "story" and, in rhetoric, "statement of facts of the case"; "ground-plot" meant either "foundation" or "ground-plan"; "invention," another rhetorical term, is the finding of the matter for the poem or oration.
9. Minds, ideas.
1. Roman god of love (the equivalent of the Greek Eros, whose name means "Love") [editor's note].

philosophers spent a good deal of their lamp oil in setting forth the excellency of it);[2] grant, I say, whatsoever they will have granted, that not only love but lust, but vanity, but—if they list—scurrility possesseth many leaves of the poets' books: yet think I, when this is granted, they will find their sentence may with good manners put the last words foremost, and not say that poetry abuseth man's wit, but that man's wit abuseth poetry.

For I will not deny but that man's wit may make poesy, which should be *eikastikē*, which some learned have defined figuring forth good things, to be *phantastikē*, which doth contrariwise infect the fancy with unworthy objects,[3] as the painter that should give to the eye either some excellent perspective, or some fine picture, fit for building or fortification,[4] or containing in it some notable example, as Abraham sacrificing his son Isaac, Judith killing Holofernes, David fighting with Goliath,[5] may leave those and please an ill-pleased[6] eye with wanton shows of better-hidden matters. But what, shall the abuse of a thing make the right use odious? Nay, truly, though I yield that poesy may not only be abused, but that being abused, by the reason of his sweet charming force, it can do more hurt than any other army of words, yet shall it be so far from concluding that the abuse should give reproach to the abused, that contrariwise it is a good reason, that whatsoever, being abused, doth most harm, being rightly used (and upon the right use each thing conceiveth his title[7]) doth most good. Do we not see skill of physic, the best rampire[8] to our often assaulted bodies, being abused, teach poison, the most violent destroyer? Doth not knowledge of law, whose end is to even and right all things, being abused, grow the crooked fosterer of horrible injuries? Doth not (to go to the highest) God's word abused breed heresy, and His name abused become blasphemy? Truly, a needle cannot do much hurt, and as truly (with leave of ladies be it spoken) it cannot do much good. With a sword thou mayst kill thy father, and with a sword thou mayst defend thy prince and country. So that, as in their calling poets fathers of lies they said nothing, so in this their argument of abuse they prove the commendation.

They allege herewith, that before poets began to be in price,[9] our nation had set their heart's delight upon action and not imagination, rather doing things worthy to be written than writing things fit to be done. What that before-time was, I think scarcely Sphinx[1] can tell, since no memory is so ancient that hath the precedence of poetry. And certain it is, that in our plainest homeliness yet never was the Albion[2] nation without poetry. Marry, this argument, though it be levelled against poetry, yet is it indeed a chain

2. Sidney is principally aiming at Plato's *Symposium* and *Phaedrus*.
3. Plato makes this distinction in *Sophist*. Icastic or "likeness-making" art occurs "whenever someone produces an imitation by keeping to the proportions of length, breadth and depth of his model, and also by keeping to the appropriate colours of his parts" (235d–e). Fantastic art produces "appearances that aren't likenesses" (236c), either by representing things which do not exist or by inaccurately representing those which do.
4. The early Renaissance painters were almost invariably skilled mathematicians and architects.
5. All biblical references: Abraham prepares to sacrifice Isaac in Genesis 22; Judith kills Holofernes, a general of Nebuchadnezzer who is besieging her city, after tricking him into a drunken stupor, in Judith 12 (a book of the Apocrypha); David fights and slays the Philistine giant Goliath in 1 Samuel 17 [editor's note].
6. Pleased by ill things.
7. Right, entitlement.
8. Rampart, defensive mound of earth. ["Physic": medicine—editor's note.]
9. Esteem.
1. In Greek mythology, the riddling monster bested by Oedipus [editor's note].
2. Britain. Albion was an ancient name, supposedly predating "Britain."

shot[3] against all learning, or bookishness as they commonly term it. Of such mind were certain Goths,[4] of whom it is written, that having in the spoil of a famous city taken a fair library, one hangman, belike fit to execute the fruits of their wits, who had murdered a great number of bodies, would have set fire in it. 'No,' said another, very gravely, 'take heed what you do, for while they are busy about these toys, we shall with more leisure conquer their countries.'[5] This indeed is the ordinary doctrine of ignorance, and many words sometimes I have heard spent in it. But because this reason is generally against all learning as well as poetry, or rather all learning but poetry; because it were too large a digression to handle it, or at least too superfluous, since it is manifest that all government of action is to be gotten by knowledge, and knowledge best by gathering many knowledges, which is reading—I only with Horace, to him that is of that opinion, *iubeo stultum esse libenter.*[6]

* * *

But now indeed my burden is great, now Plato's name is laid upon me, whom, I must confess, of all philosophers I have ever esteemed most worthy of reverence; and with good reason, since of all philosophers he is the most poetical. Yet if he will defile the fountain out of which his flowing streams have proceeded, let us boldly examine with what reasons he did it. First, truly, a man might maliciously object that Plato, being a philosopher, was a natural enemy of poets. For indeed, after the philosophers had picked out of the sweet mysteries of poetry the right discerning true points of knowledge, they forthwith putting it in method, and making a school art of that which the poets did only teach by a divine delightfulness, beginning to spurn at their guides, like ungrateful prentices were not content to set up shops for themselves, but sought by all means to discredit their masters; which, by the force of delight, being barred them, the less they could overthrow them, the more they hated them. For indeed, they found for Homer seven cities strave who should have him for their citizen, where many cities banished philosophers as not fit members to live among them.[7] For only repeating certain of Euripides' verses many Athenians had their lives saved of the Syracusans, where the Athenians themselves thought many philosophers unworthy to live.[8] Certain poets, as Simonides and Pindarus, had so prevailed with Hiero the First,[9] that of a tyrant they made him a just king; where Plato could do so little with Dionysius,[1] that he himself of a philosopher was made

3. Cannon shot of two balls joined by a chain.
4. East Germanic tribes; some, in the 5th century C.E., occupied Italy and beseiged and sacked Rome; others sacked and burned Athens in the 3d century and again at the end of the 4th century [editor's note].
5. This story of the sack of Athens in 267 C.E. is told by Petrus Patricius in his continuation of Dio Cassius, *Roman Histories* 54, 17. [Patricius (6th c. C.E.), Byzantine historian. Dio (ca. 155–ca. 235 C.E.), Roman administrator and historian who wrote in Greek—editor's note.]
6. "Cheerfully bid him be a fool." Adapted from Horace, *Satires* 1.1.63: "Bid him be miserable."
7. The Homeric anecdote is repeated by Cicero, *Pro Archia poeta* [the oration *On Behalf of the Poet Archias*] 8.19, and became very popular. Among banished philosophers were Empedocles [ca. 493–ca. 433 B.C.E.] from his native town Acragas, and Anaxagoras [ca. 500–428 B.C.E.] and Protagoras [5th c. B.C.E.] the Sophist from Athens.
8. For "Euripides' verses" see Plutarch, *Life of Nicias*. Socrates was the most celebrated philosopher condemned to death by Athenians.
9. Tyrant (ruler) of Syracuse (478–467/66 B.C.E.), whose court was visited by Pindar in 476. Simonides (ca. 556–468 B.C.E.), Greek lyric and elegiac poet who also visited the court of Hieron about 476 [editor's note].
1. Dionysius II (b. ca. 397 B.C.E.), who became tyrant of Syracuse in 367. Invited to Sicily by an influential Syracusan, Plato tried with little success to mold Dionysius into a philosopher-king. After Dionysius tricked Plato into returning in 361, he temporarily imprisoned the philosopher [editor's note].

a slave.[2] But who should do thus, I confess, should requite the objections made against poets with like cavillations[3] against philosophers, as likewise one should do that should bid one read *Phaedrus* or *Symposium* in Plato,[4] or the discourse of love in Plutarch,[5] and see whether any poet do authorize abominable filthiness as they do. Again, a man might ask out of what commonwealth Plato did banish them: in sooth, thence where he himself alloweth community of women.[6] So as belike this banishment grew not for effeminate wantonness, since little should poetical sonnets be hurtful when a man might have what woman he listed. But I honour philosophical instructions, and bless the wits which bred them, so as they be not abused, which is likewise stretched to poetry.

St Paul himself (who yet, for the credit of poets, allegeth twice two poets, and one of them by the name of a prophet) setteth a watchword upon philosophy—indeed upon the abuse.[7] So doth Plato upon the abuse, not upon poetry. Plato found fault that the poets of his time filled the world with wrong opinions of the gods, making light tales of that unspotted essence, and therefore would not have the youth depraved with such opinions.[8] Herein may much be said; let this suffice. The poets did not induce such opinions, but did imitate those opinions already induced. For all the Greek stories can well testify that the very religion of that time stood upon many, and many-fashioned,[9] gods, not taught so by the poets, but followed according to their nature of imitation. Who list may read in Plutarch the discourses of Isis and Osiris, of the cause why oracles ceased, of the divine providence,[1] and see whether the theology of that nation stood not upon such dreams, which the poets indeed superstitiously observed; and truly, since they had not the light of Christ, did much better in it than the philosophers who, shaking off superstition, brought in atheism. Plato therefore, whose authority I had much rather justly construe than unjustly resist, meant not in general of poets, in those words of which Julius Scaliger saith *qua authoritate barbari quidam atque hispidi abuti velint ad poetas e republica exigendos*,[2] but only meant to drive out those wrong opinions of the Deity (whereof now, without further law,[3] Christianity hath taken away all the hurtful belief), perchance, as he thought, nourished by the then esteemed poets. And a man need go no further than to Plato himself to know his meaning, who in his dialogue called *Ion*[4] giveth high and rightly divine commendation unto poetry. So as Plato, banishing the abuse, not the thing—not banishing it, but giving due honour unto it—shall be our patron and not our adversary. For indeed I had much

2. The story that Plato was sold into slavery by the Spartan ambassador to whom Dionysius I (ca. 430–367 B.C.E.) had given him is told by Cicero [in *Pro Rabiro Postumo* 9.23]; the Spartans were famous scorners of philosophy.
3. Cavils, petty objections.
4. The sections on love in both *Phaedrus* and *Symposium* concern the love of older for younger men, a key part of educated Greek culture.
5. Plutarch's *Amatorius*, a dialogue that relies heavily on Plato's [editor's note].
6. *Republic* 5 [457c–461e], arguing that women and children should not be considered the property of individual men.
7. St. Paul [early Christian apostle, d. ca. 67 C.E.] twice cites poets, quotes them three times, and demonstrates knowledge of four.
8. *Republic* 2.377–3.392. "Light": wanton, lascivious.
9. In many forms; able to change their shapes.
1. Essays in Plutarch's *Moralia*: "On Isis and Osiris," "On the Failure of Oracles," "On Divine Vengeance." ["List": wishes—editor's note.]
2. Whose authority certain barbarous and uncouth men seek to use in order to expel poets from the republic (Latin); *Poetices* 1.2.
3. Ado, or philosophical legislation (pun).
4. *Ion* [see above] is a short and beguilingly ironic dialogue between Socrates and the rhapsode (performer of poetry) Ion, in which Socrates develops a theory of poetic inspiration, but only in order to show that the poet and rhapsode know nothing about anything.

rather, since truly I may do it, show their mistaking of Plato, under whose lion's skin they would make an ass-like braying against poesy,[5] than go about[6] to overthrow his authority, whom the wiser a man is, the more just cause he shall find to have in admiration, especially since he attributeth unto poesy more than myself do, namely to be a very inspiring of a divine force far above man's wit, as in the forenamed dialogue is apparent.

Of the other side, who would show the honours have been by the best sort of judgements granted them, a whole sea of examples would present themselves: Alexanders, Caesars, Scipios,[7] all favourers of poets; Laelius, called the Roman Socrates, himself a poet, so as part of *Heautontimoroumenos* in Terence was supposed to be made by him;[8] and even the Greek Socrates, whom Apollo confirmed to be the only wise man, is said to have spent part of his old time in putting Aesop's fables into verses.[9] And, therefore, full evil should it become his scholar Plato to put such words in his master's mouth against poets. But what need more? Aristotle writes the Art of Poesy—and why, if it should not be written? Plutarch teacheth the use to be gathered of them—and how, if they should not be read? And who reads Plutarch's either history or philosophy shall find he trimmeth both their garments with guards[1] of poesy. But I list not to defend poesy with the help of his underling historiography. Let it suffice to have showed it is a fit soil for praise to dwell upon, and what dispraise may set upon it is either easily overcome, or transformed into just commendation.

So that since the excellencies of it may be so easily and so justly confirmed, and the low creeping objections so soon trodden down—it not being an art of lies, but of true doctrine; not of effeminateness, but of notable stirring of courage; not of abusing man's wit, but of strengthening man's wit; not banished, but honoured by Plato—let us rather plant more laurels for to engarland the poets' heads (which honour of being laureate, as besides them only triumphant captains were, is a sufficient authority to show the price they ought to be held in) than suffer the ill-savoured breath of such wrong-speakers once to blow upon the clear springs of poesy.

But since I have run so long a career[2] in this matter, methinks, before I give my pen a full stop, it shall be but a little more lost time to inquire why England, the mother of excellent minds, should be grown so hard a step-mother to poets, who certainly in wit ought to pass all other, since all only proceedeth from their wit, being indeed makers of themselves, not takers of others.

* * *

5. In the Aesopian fable the ass puts on a lion's skin and passes for a fearsome lion until the wind blows it off, or in another version, until a fox who had earlier heard him braying calls his bluff.
6. Aim, endeavour.
7. Scipio Africanus (ca. 236–184/83 B.C.E.), great Roman general who defeated Hannibal and the Carthaginians [editor's note].
8. Gaius Laelius (born ca. 190 B.C.E.), nicknamed Sapiens ("wise"), appears as a speaker in several of Cicero's dialogues [in *De officiis* 1.90, he is compared to Socrates]. Cicero also records that Terence's plays were ascribed to him by many; Terence alludes to a debt in the prologues to *Heautontimorumenos* (*The Self-Tormentor*).
9. Socrates was confirmed to be the wisest man by the Delphic oracle [of Apollo], according to Plato (*Apology* 21a). In Plato's *Phaedro* (60d–61b) he is represented as versifying Aesop in prison.
1. Ornamental trimmings.
2. Most of the early meanings of "career" concern horses—a gallop at full stretch, a racehorse, the jousting area of a tiltyard; Sidney is horse or rider in this image.

Marry, they that delight in poesy itself should seek to know what they do and how they do, and especially look themselves in an unflattering glass of reason, if they be inclinable unto it. For poesy must not be drawn by the ears: it must be gently led, or rather it must lead, which was partly the cause that made the ancient learned affirm it was a divine gift and no human skill, since all other knowledges lie ready for any that hath strength of wit. A poet no industry can make, if his own genius be not carried into it, and therefore is it an old proverb—*orator fit, poeta nascitur.*[3] Yet confess I always, that as the fertilest ground must be manured, so must the highest-flying wit have a Daedalus[4] to guide him. That Daedalus, they say, both in this and in other, hath three wings to bear itself up into the air of due commendation: that is, art, imitation and exercise. But these, neither artificial rules nor imitative patterns, we much cumber ourselves withal. Exercise indeed we do, but that very fore-backwardly, for where we should exercise to know, we exercise as having known, and so is our brain delivered of much matter which never was begotten by knowledge. For, there being two principal parts, matter to be expressed by words and words to express the matter, in neither we use art or imitation rightly. Our matter is *quodlibet*:[5] indeed, though wrongly, performing Ovid's verse, *quicquid conabor dicere, versus erit*;[6] never marshalling it into any assured rank,[7] that almost the readers cannot tell where to find themselves.

Chaucer, undoubtedly, did excellently in his *Troilus and Criseyde*,[8] of whom truly I know not whether to marvel more, either that he in that misty time could see so clearly, or that we in this clear age go so stumblingly after him. Yet had he great wants, fit to be forgiven in so reverent an antiquity. I account the *Mirror of Magistrates* meetly furnished of beautiful parts; and in the Earl of Surrey's[9] lyrics many things tasting of a noble birth, and worthy of a noble mind. The *Shepheardes Calender* hath much poetry in his eclogues, indeed worthy the reading, if I be not deceived. That same framing of his style to an old rustic language I dare not allow, since neither Theocritus in Greek, Virgil in Latin, nor Sannazaro in Italian did affect it.[1] Besides these, I do not remember to have seen but few (to speak boldly) printed that have poetical sinews in them. For proof whereof, let but most of the verses be put in prose, and then ask the meaning; and it will be found that one verse did but beget another, without ordering at the first what should be at the last, which becomes a confused mass of words, with a tingling sound of rhyme, barely accompanied with reason.

3. The orator is made, the poet is born (Latin) [editor's note].
4. In Greek mythology, a consummately skilled Athenian artisan; he fashioned wings of feather and wax so that he and his son, Icarus, could escape King Minos of Crete, but Icarus ignored his warnings, flew too close to the sun, and perished [editor's note].
5. Whatever we want (Latin).
6. Anything I try to say will come out as poetry (Latin); adapting Ovid, *Tristia* (*Sad Things*) 4.10.26 (from past to future tense).
7. Order.
8. The most popular of the poems of Geoffrey Chaucer with the Elizabethans.
9. Henry Howard, earl of Surrey (1517–1547), English poet. *A Mirror for Magistrates* (1559), a collection of Elizabethan poems on the fall of great men in English history (each told in the first person) [editor's note].
1. [Edmund] Spenser's *The Shepheardes Calender* was published anonymously in 1579 and dedicated to Sidney. The language is both archaic and rustic; it was in fact thought that both the Greek poet Theocritus (ca. 300–ca. 250 B.C.E.) in his *Idylls* and Virgil in the *Eclogues* were aiming at a similar effect. Sannazaro, the author of *Arcadia*, was also admired for his *Piscatory Eclogues* (1526).

Our tragedies and comedies not without cause cried out against, observing rules neither of honest civility nor skilful poetry—excepting *Gorboduc* (again, I say, of those that I have seen) which, notwithstanding as it is full of stately speeches and well-sounding phrases, climbing to the height of Seneca's style, and as full of notable morality, which it doth most delightfully teach, and so obtain the very end of poesy, yet in truth it is very defectuous in the circumstances, which grieveth me, because it might not remain as an exact model of all tragedies.[2] For it is faulty both in place and time, the two necessary companions of all corporal actions. For where the stage should always represent but one place, and the uttermost time presupposed in it should be, both by Aristotle's precept and common reason, but one day, there is both many days and many places inartificially[3] imagined. But if it be so in *Gorboduc*, how much more in all the rest, where you shall have Asia of the one side and Afric of the other, and so many other under-kingdoms, that the player, when he cometh in, must ever begin with telling where he is, or else the tale will not be conceived? Now you shall have three ladies walk to gather flowers, and then we must believe the stage to be a garden. By and by we hear news of shipwreck in the same place, and then we are to blame if we accept it not for a rock. Upon the back of that comes out a hideous monster with fire and smoke, and then the miserable beholders are bound to take it for a cave. While in the meantime two armies fly in, represented with four swords and bucklers,[4] and then what hard heart will not receive it for a pitched field?

Now, of time they are much more liberal. For ordinary it is that two young princes fall in love, after many traverses[5] she is got with child, delivered of a fair boy, he is lost, groweth a man, falls in love, and is ready to get another child—and all this in two hours' space, which how absurd it is in sense, even sense may imagine, and art hath taught, and all ancient examples justified, and at this day the ordinary players in Italy will not err in.[6] Yet will some bring in an example of *Eunuchus* in Terence, that containeth matter of two days,[7] yet far short of twenty years. True it is, and so was it to be played in two days, and so fitted to the time it set forth. And though Plautus have in one place done amiss, let us hit with him, and not miss with him.[8]

But they will say, 'How then shall we set forth a story which containeth both many places and many times?' And do they not know that a tragedy is tied to the laws of poesy and not of history, not bound to follow the story, but having liberty either to feign a quite new matter or to frame the history to the most tragical conveniency?[9] Again, many things may be told which cannot be showed, if they know the difference betwixt reporting and representing: as,

2. *Gorboduc* was a tragedy in blank verse by Thomas Sackville (1536–1608), who also contributed to *A Mirror for Magistrates*, and Thomas Norton (1532–1584); first presented in 1561, it was printed in 1565. The tragedies of Lucius Annaeus Seneca were used in schools, and their lofty and moralizing language was taken up by earlier Elizabethan dramatists.

3. Inartistically.

4. Shields.

5. Misfortunes. ["Princes": sovereigns of either sex—editor's note.]

6. Sidney may have witnessed the performance of popular comedies when he was in Padua and Venice in 1574.

7. Sidney confuses *Eunuchus* with another play, probably *Heautontimorumenos*.

8. Scaliger criticizes Plautus' *Captives* for spanning too much time (6.3). [Plautus (d. ca. 184 B.C.E.), Roman comic playwright—editor's note.]

9. Propriety, decorum.

for example, I may speak, though I am here, of Peru, and in speech digress from that to the description of Calicut;[1] but in action I cannot represent it without Pacolet's horse.[2] And so was the manner the ancients took, by some *nuntius*[3] to recount things done in former time or other place. Lastly, if they will represent an history, they must not (as Horace saith) begin *ab ovo*,[4] but they must come to the principal point of that one action which they will represent.

By example this will be best expressed. I have a story of young Polydorus,[5] delivered for safety's sake, with great riches, by his father Priamus to Polymnestor, King of Thrace, in the Trojan war time; he, after some years, hearing the overthrow of Priamus, for to make the treasure his own, murdereth the child; the body of the child is taken up by Hecuba; she, the same day, findeth a sleight[6] to be revenged most cruelly of the tyrant. Where now would one of our tragedy writers begin, but with the delivery of the child? Then should he sail over into Thrace, and so spend I know not how many years, and travel numbers of places. But where doth Euripides? Even with the finding of the body, the rest leaving to be told by the spirit of Polydorus. This need no further to be enlarged; the dullest wit may conceive it.

But besides these gross absurdities, how all their plays be neither right tragedies nor right comedies, mingling kings and clowns, not because the matter so carrieth it, but thrust in the clown by head and shoulders to play a part in majestical matters, with neither decency nor discretion, so as neither the admiration and commiseration nor the right sportfulness is by their mongrel tragicomedy obtained. I know Apuleius did somewhat so, but that is a thing recounted with space of time, not represented in one moment.[7] And I know the ancients have one or two examples of tragicomedies, as Plautus hath *Amphitryo*;[8] but if we mark them well, we shall find that they never, or very daintily,[9] match hornpipes and funerals. So falleth it out that, having indeed no right comedy in that comical part of our tragedy, we have nothing but scurrility unworthy of any chaste ears, or some extreme show of doltishness, indeed fit to lift up a loud laughter, and nothing else, where the whole tract[1] of a comedy should be full of delight, as the tragedy should be still maintained in a well-raised admiration.

But our comedians think there is no delight without laughter, which is very wrong, for though laughter may come with delight, yet cometh it not of delight, as though delight should be the cause of laughter; but well may one thing breed both together. Nay, rather in themselves they have, as it were, a kind of contrariety. For delight we scarcely do, but in things that have a conveniency[2] to ourselves or to the general nature; laughter almost ever cometh of things most disproportioned to ourselves and nature. Delight hath a joy in it, either permanent or present; laughter hath only a scornful tickling. For

1. Calicut (modern Kozhikode), on the west coast of India, was a major trading port.
2. The flying horse of the enchanter Pacolet in the popular late-medieval romance *Valentine and Orson*.
3. Messenger (Latin).
4. From the egg (Latin). See Horace's *Ars Poetica*, line 147 [editor's note].
5. The story and characters appear in Euripides, *Hecuba* (ca. 424 B.C.E.); Hecuba, Priam's wife, was enslaved after the fall of Troy [editor's note].
6. Trick, stratagem.
7. Apuleius was the 2d-century C.E. author of the *Metamorphosis* (known as *The Golden Ass*), a fantastical story with many inset narratives which influenced Sidney's *Arcadia*.
8. In the prologue to *Amphitryo*, Plautus explicitly describes his play as a tragicomedy.
9. Sparingly, deftly.
1. Course, duration.
2. Suitability, congruity.

example, we are ravished with delight to see a fair woman, and yet are far from being moved to laughter. We laugh at deformed creatures, wherein certainly we cannot delight. We delight in good chances; we laugh at mischances. We delight to hear the happiness of our friends or country, at which he were worthy to be laughed at that would laugh. We shall, contrarily, laugh sometimes to find a matter quite mistaken and go down the hill against the bias in the mouth of some such men as, for the respect of them, one shall be heartily sorry he cannot choose but laugh, and so is rather pained than delighted with laughter.[3] Yet deny I not, but that they may go well together. For as in Alexander's picture well set out we delight without laughter, and in twenty mad antics[4] we laugh without delight, so in Hercules painted with his great beard and furious countenance in a woman's attire, spinning at Omphale's commandment,[5] it breedeth both delight and laughter: for the representing of so strange a power in love procureth delight, and the scornfulness of the action stirreth laughter. But I speak to this purpose, that all the end of the comical part be not upon such scornful matters as stir laughter only, but, mixed with it, that delightful teaching which is the end of poesy. And the great fault even in that point of laughter, and forbidden plainly by Aristotle,[6] is that they stir laughter in sinful things, which are rather execrable than ridiculous; or in miserable, which are rather to be pitied than scorned. For what is it to make folks gape at a wretched beggar, and a beggarly clown;[7] or, against law of hospitality, to jest at strangers, because they speak not English so well as we do? What do we learn, since it is certain *nil habet infelix paupertas durius in se, / quam quod ridiculus homines facit?*[8] But rather a busy loving courtier, and a heartless threatening Thraso, a self-wise-seeming schoolmaster, a wry-transformed traveller:[9] these if we saw walk in stage names, which we play naturally—therein were delightful laughter and teaching delightfulness, as, in the other, the tragedies of Buchanan[1] do justly bring forth a divine admiration. But I have lavished out too many words of this play matter. I do it because, as they are excelling parts of poesy, so is there none so much used in England, and none can be more pitifully abused; which, like an unmannerly daughter showing a bad education, causeth her mother Poesy's honesty[2] to be called in question.

Other sort of poetry almost have we none, but that lyrical kind of songs and sonnets, which, Lord, if He gave us so good minds, how well it might be employed, and with how heavenly fruits, both private and public, in singing the praises of the immortal beauty, the immortal goodness of that God who

3. The gist of this rather perplexing sentence is that sometimes one will laugh rather painfully when people one respects drop clangers or speak with unintended irony. "Against the bias": metaphor from bowls, the slope of the ground counteracting the swerve of the ball.
4. Grotesque plays or characters.
5. Following a prophecy, Hercules had to sell himself into slavery to cure his madness. He was bought by Omphale, queen of Lydia, and a love affair developed; while Omphale wore Hercules' lionskin, Hercules wore dresses and wove or span at her feet. "Furious": mad.
6. See Aristotle, *Nicomachean Ethics* 4.8, 1128a [editor's note].
7. Peasant.
8. Of all the woes of luckless poverty none is harder to endure than this, that it exposes men to ridicule (Latin); Juvenal, *Satires* 3.152–53.
9. Thraso is a braggart in Terence. Sidney created a "self-wise-seeming schoolmaster" in Rombus, in his brief entertainment the *Lady of May* (1578 or 1579). The other character types came to be familiar in the plays of Shakespeare and his contemporaries. "Wry-transformed": diverted, twisted from a natural course.
1. George Buchanan (1506–1582), Scottish humorist and author, tutor to Mary, Queen of Scots, and James VI of Scotland [editor's note].
2. Honour, chastity.

giveth us hands to write and wits to conceive; of which we might well want words, but never matter, of which we could turn our eyes to nothing, but we should ever have new-budding occasions. But truly, many of such writings as come under the banner of unresistible love, if I were a mistress, would never persuade me they were in love, so coldly they apply fiery speeches, as men that had rather read lovers' writings, and so caught up certain swelling phrases (which hang together like a man that once told my father that the wind was at northwest and by south, because he would be sure to name winds enough), than that in truth they feel those passions; which easily, as I think, may be bewrayed by that same forcibleness or *energeia*[3] (as the Greeks call it) of the writer. But let this be a sufficient, though short, note that we miss the right use of the material point of poesy.

Now, for the outside of it, which is words or (as I may term it) diction, it is even well worse, so is that honey-flowing matron Eloquence apparelled, or rather disguised, in a courtesan-like painted affectation: one time with so far-fet words that may seem monsters but must seem strangers to any poor Englishman; another time with coursing of a letter, as if they were bound to follow the method of a dictionary;[4] another time with figures and flowers extremely winter-starved. But I would this fault were only peculiar to versifiers, and had not as large possession among prose-printers, and, which is to be marvelled, among many scholars, and, which is to be pitied, among some preachers. Truly, I could wish, if at least I might be so bold to wish in a thing beyond the reach of my capacity, the diligent imitators of Tully and Demosthenes,[5] most worthy to be imitated, did not so much keep Nizolian paper-books of their figures and phrases as, by attentive translation,[6] as it were, devour them whole, and make them wholly theirs. For now they cast sugar and spice upon every dish that is served to the table, like those Indians, not content to wear earrings at the fit and natural place of the ears, but they will thrust jewels through their nose and lips, because they will be sure to be fine.[7]

* * *

But what? Methinks I deserve to be pounded[8] for straying from poetry to oratory. But both have such an affinity in the wordish consideration, that I think this digression will make my meaning receive the fuller understanding, which is not to take upon me to teach poets how they should do, but only, finding myself sick among the rest, to show some one or two spots of the common infection grown among the most part of writers, that acknowledging ourselves somewhat awry, we may bend to the right use both of matter and manner; whereto our language giveth us great occasion, being indeed capable of any excellent exercising of it. I know some will say it is a mingled language.[9] And why not so much the better, taking the best of both

3. A vigour of style "inwardly working to stir to the mind." "Bewrayed": betrayed.
4. Sidney describes the passion for alliteration prevalent in early Elizabethan poetry. "Coursing": hunting.
5. Athenian statesman (384–322 B.C.E.) considered the greatest Greek orator, as Cicero (Tully) was considered the greatest Roman orator [editor's note].
6. Transformation, adaptation. ["Nizolian paper-books": commonplace books like those of the Italian lexicographer Marius Nizolius (16th c.)—editor's note.]
7. This picture is based on early reports from travellers to South America.
8. Impounded, shut up in a pound like a stray animal.
9. That is, mixed of Anglo-Saxon and Norman French, as well as absorbing many Latin loan words.

the other?[1] Another will say it wanteth grammar. Nay, truly, it hath that praise that it wants not grammar: for grammar it might have, but it needs it not, being so easy in itself, and so void of those cumbersome differences of cases, genders, moods, and tenses, which I think was a piece of the Tower of Babylon's curse,[2] that a man should be put to school to learn his mother tongue. But for the uttering sweetly and properly the conceits of the mind, which is the end of speech, that hath it equally with any other tongue in the world, and is particularly happy in compositions of two or three words together, near the Greek, far beyond the Latin, which is one of the greatest beauties can be in a language.

Now, of versifying there are two sorts, the one ancient, the other modern. The ancient marked the quantity of each syllable, and according to that framed his verse. The modern observing only number,[3] with some regard of the accent, the chief life of it standeth in that like sounding of the words which we call rhyme. Whether of these be the more excellent would bear many speeches: the ancient no doubt more fit for music, both words and time[4] observing quantity, and more fit lively to express divers passions by the low or lofty sound of the well-weighed syllable; the latter likewise with his rhyme striketh a certain music to the ear, and in fine, since it doth delight, though by another way, it obtains the same purpose, there being in either sweetness and wanting in neither majesty. Truly, the English, before any vulgar[5] language I know, is fit for both sorts. For, for the ancient, the Italian is so full of vowels that it must ever be cumbered with elisions; the Dutch[6] so, of the other side, with consonants that they cannot yield the sweet sliding fit for a verse; the French in his whole language hath not one word that hath his accent in the last syllable saving two, called *antepenultima*; and little more hath the Spanish, and therefore very gracelessly may they use dactyls.[7] The English is subject to none of these defects. Now, for the rhyme,[8] though we do not observe quantity, yet we observe the accent very precisely, which other languages either cannot do, or will not do so absolutely. That *caesura*, or breathing place, in the midst of the verse neither Italian nor Spanish have; the French and we never almost fail of. Lastly, even the very rhyme itself, the Italian cannot put it in the last syllable, by the French named the masculine rhyme, but still[9] in the next to the last, which the French call the female, or the next before that, which the Italian term *sdrucciola*:[1] the example of the former is 'buono' / 'suono', of the *sdrucciola* is 'femina' / 'semina'. The French, of the other side, hath both the male, as 'bon' / 'son', and the female, as 'plaise' / 'taise', but the *sdrucciola* he hath not; where the English hath all three, as 'due' / 'true', 'father' / 'rather', 'motion' / 'potion'. With much more which might be said, but that already I find the triflingness of this discourse is much too much enlarged.

1. That is, Anglo-Saxon and French.
2. The curse was that the one language of the people be confounded, so "that they may not understand one another's speech"; the story of the Tower of Babel (the Hebrew name for Babylon) is told in Genesis 11 [editor's note].
3. Syllable count as opposed to syllable length (or quantity) [editor's note].
4. That is, musical measure.
5. Vernacular.
6. German (Deutsch).
7. The dactyl is a foot consisting of three syllables, the first long or stressed, the following two short or unstressed; it is the constituent unit of dactylic hexameter, the vehicle of epic verse [in Greek and Latin].
8. That is, the modern (accentual-)syllabic system.
9. Always.
1. Literally, "slippery": that is, the easy sliding together of rhymes of three or more syllables [editor's note].

So that since the ever-praiseworthy poesy is full of virtue-breeding delightfulness, and void of no gift that ought to be in the noble name of learning; since the blames laid against it are either false or feeble; since the cause why it is not esteemed in England is the fault of poet-apes,[2] not poets; since, lastly, our tongue is most fit to honor poesy, and to be honoured by poesy, I conjure you all that have had the evil luck to read this ink-wasting toy of mine, even in the name of the nine Muses, no more to scorn the sacred mysteries of poesy, no more to laugh at the name of poets, as though they were next inheritors to fools, no more to jest at the reverent title of a rhymer, but to believe with Aristotle that they were the ancient treasures of the Grecians' divinity; to believe with Bembus[3] that they were first bringers-in of all civility; to believe with Scaliger that no philosopher's precepts can sooner make you an honest man than the reading of Virgil; to believe with Clauserus, the translator of Cornutus, that it pleased the heavenly Deity, by Hesiod[4] and Homer, under the veil of fables to give us all knowledge, logic, rhetoric, philosophy natural and moral and *quid non?*;[5] to believe with me that there are many mysteries contained in poetry which of purpose were written darkly,[6] lest by profane wits it should be abused; to believe with Landin[7] that they are so beloved of the gods, that whatsoever they write proceeds of a divine fury; lastly, to believe themselves when they tell you they will make you immortal by their verses. Thus doing, your name shall flourish in the printers' shops; thus doing, you shall be of kin to many a poetical preface; thus doing, you shall be most fair, most rich, most wise, most all—you shall dwell upon superlatives; thus doing, though you be *libertino patre natus*, you shall suddenly grow *Herculea proles—si quid mea carmina possunt*;[8] thus doing, your soul shall be placed with Dante's Beatrix or Virgil's Anchises.[9] But if (fie of such a but) you be born so near the dull-making cataract of Nilus that you cannot hear the planet-like music of poetry;[1] if you have so earth-creeping a mind that it cannot lift itself up to look to the sky of poetry, or rather by a certain rustical disdain will become such a mome as to be a Momus of poetry;[2] then, though I will not wish unto you the ass's ears of Midas,[3] nor to be driven by a poet's verses, as Bubonax[4] was, to hang himself, nor to be rhymed to death, as is said to be done in Ireland;[5] yet thus much

2. Poetasters, rhymesters.
3. Pietro Bembo (1470–1560), Italian Renaissance grammarian and an editor and author of poetry [editor's note].
4. Greek didactic epic poet (active ca. 700 B.C.E.). Clauserus: Conrad Clauser (16th c.), German humanist. Lucius Annaeus Cornutus (b. ca. 20 C.E.), teacher of rhetoric and Stoic philosophy at Rome [editor's note].
5. What not? (Latin).
6. Obscurely, allegorically.
7. Christoforo Landino (1424–1504), influential Florentine humanist, editor of Dante's *Divina commedia*.
8. A descendant of Hercules—if my songs can achieve anything (Latin); Virgil, *Aeneid* 9.446. *Libertino patre natus*: son of a freedman (Latin); Horace, *Satires* 1.6.6.
9. That is, with the blessed dead; Dante meets Beatrice in heaven in the *Divine Comedy*, and Aeneas finds his father, Anchises, in the Elysian Fields during his journey to the underworld (*Aeneid* 6) [editor's note].
1. Cicero, *Somnium Scipionis* (*Dream of Scipio*) 5.13, likens the inability to hear the music of the spheres (the machinery of cosmic harmony echoed in the hearts of ordered men and the forms of ordered poetry), even though it fills everyone's ears, to the deafness of those who live near the waterfalls [cataract] of the Nile.
2. From the Greek *mōmos*, ridicule, a personification of ridicule, sarcasm and carping criticism, the son or daughter of Night, and a popular character in poetical prefaces. "Mome": blockhead, fool.
3. Legendary king of Phrygia; when Midas judged Pan the winner of a musical contest with Apollo, Apollo gave him ass's ears (according to the version told in Ovid, *Metamorphoses* 11.146–93) [editor's note].
4. Sidney fuses the names of two 6th-century B.C.E. Greek figures in a well-known story: Bupalus created a statue caricaturing the poet Hipponax, whose bitter satire in response led the sculptor to hang himself [editor's note].
5. The use of verse charms to kill vermin and people was widely attested in Elizabethan accounts of Ireland.

curse I must send you in the behalf of all poets; that while you live, you live in love, and never get favour for lacking skill of a sonnet, and when you die, your memory die from the earth for want of an epitaph.

1580–81 1595

PIERRE CORNEILLE
1606–1684

Pierre Corneille provoked literary quarrels, infuriated critics, and delighted audiences for the better part of the seventeenth century. Decidedly not a courtly *dramatist*, Corneille was a *playwright*. A member of the emerging bourgeoisie, he wrote plays for money and to please audiences, not to curry favor with the royal or the literary establishment. It is therefore ironic that he is often seen today as the spokesman and exemplar of French classical theater. His promotion of classical "rules" is in part a plea for the value of not taking them too literally.

Corneille was born in the Normandy town of Rouen, France, where his father was a minor administrative official. After undergoing a rigorous and regulated Jesuit education, in which he excelled in Latin, he began legal studies in 1622; two years later he enrolled at the bar of Rouen. He argued only one case, with disastrous results: he stumbled over his words and stuttered, and at the age of nineteen he abandoned a legal career that had just begun. His father then bought him two modest magisterial posts in Rouen, in the department of rivers and forests. In 1629 a troupe of actors passed through Rouen, and Corneille showed them the script for a five-act comedy, *Mélite*. No one quite knows when he composed the play, or what may have inspired him to launch himself suddenly into the world of theater. The troupe took the play to Paris, where it was performed that winter and was the hit of the 1629–30 season. For the next several years, he wrote a new play each season—mostly comedies, but also tragicomedies and tragedies.

In 1637 Corneille's most famous play, *Le Cid* (based on a Spanish original; its title derived from the Arab word for "lord"), appeared and incited a flurry of critical attention that became known as the "Quarrel of *The Cid*." The Quarrel originated in the tension between Corneille's two audiences: the public and the critics. The public loved *Le Cid*, whose success was demonstrated even at the level of language: a new expression, "beau comme *Le Cid*" (as fine as *Le Cid*), entered the Parisian vernacular. The critics, on the other hand, sought to demonstrate the moral threat posed by the play, and in a series of pamphlets they attacked it and its author. In *Le Cid* a young woman, torn between love and duty, seems about to marry the man who has just killed her father. Such behavior, the critics argued, offends both reason and moral values. Drawing on the classical authority of both ARISTOTLE and HORACE, they insisted on the didactic function of the theater. A play's moral instruction, they claimed, was achieved by strict adherence to the rules of classical theater; these included the unities of time, place, and action and—more important—the need for both verisimilitude (*vraisemblance*) and decorum (*bienséance*). The critics held that a play should not only please, but please according to the rules. Louis XIII's chief minister, Cardinal de Richelieu, considered the stage the site for enacting a universal public virtue. He had founded the Académie Française (the French Academy) just two years before the staging of *Le Cid*, and the Quarrel offered him the public forum to assert his public moral authority. After a year of literary skirmishes—pamphlets and protests on the subversive nature of art and the need for public virtue—Richelieu, who had once included Corneille among his privileged "Five Authors," stepped in: with the authority of absolutism and the Académie, he proclaimed *Le Cid* contrary to the rules of *vraisemblance*. Corneille retreated to Rouen and indirectly answered the attacks by composing two tragedies on Roman themes, *Horace* (1639) and *Cinna* (1642). Both works adhere to the classical rules of composition.

In his conformity to the very rules that had been invoked against him, Corneille was implicitly siding with his critics and using the controversy to rethink his own baroqueness. The term *baroque*, derived from the artistic extravagance originally associated with the architecture of Catholic Spain and Italy, refers to a recurrent stylistic tendency rather than simply to a period, art form, or culture. In France the baroque is seen as extending the exuberance of the Renaissance, while classicism is seen as taming it. The baroque is based on energy, antithesis, exaggeration, and the stretching and transgressing of boundaries; the classical is based on balance and on the intensity of restraint. To the French, paradoxically, Shakespeare is too "baroque"—mixed, impure, multileveled, imperfect. In French classical theater, the forces of the baroque are internalized and held in precarious equilibrium within the self. Corneille succeeded in finding within classical rules a framework more suitable for his dramas of subjective conflict than that offered by the more diffuse and extravagant spectacles of the baroque theater that had inspired his earlier works. In 1642 he also wrote *Polyeucte martyr*, treating a Christian subject in the style of a classical work. The four plays of this period (*Le Cid*, *Horace*, *Cinna*, and *Polyeucte*) constitute what was later termed Corneille's tetralogy.

The luxuriant growth of the French language called for a century earlier by the poets JOACHIM DU BELLAY and Pierre de Ronsard had undergone a severe pruning in the early seventeenth century by a strict legislator of classical verse forms, François de Malherbe, and the golden age of French classical theater (called "neoclassical" in England) had begun. Malherbe prescribed the decorum of verse, which was followed quite faithfully for the next two centuries, both in theater and in lyric poetry: the twelve-syllable line, called an "alexandrine," was expected to break in the middle and not run on to the next line without a grammatical justification; in addition, rhyme should alternate between "masculine" and "feminine" endings. Corneille continued to be an anomalous champion of this theatrical and poetic regulation.

By the mid-1640s, Corneille was clearly the master of the French stage; he continued to live in Rouen, while traveling frequently to Paris. Married in 1641, he led the life of a provincial Catholic bourgeois with his wife and, eventually, seven children. In 1644 his first collection of plays was published. Now under the new political regime, the regency of Anne of Austria and her prime minister, Cardinal Mazarin (both Richelieu and Louis XIII had died), Corneille continued in his fame. In 1647, when he was considered for the third time, Corneille was elected to the French Academy.

During the revolt (known as "La Fronde") of a group of powerful nobles against the monarchy, Corneille's plays waned somewhat in popularity, though he wrote several "machine plays" that delighted crowds with their spectacular special effects and settings. Whenever a play of his was not well received, Corneille tended to retreat from public life. During one of his retreats he translated and published Thomas à Kempis's fifteenth-century Latin treatise *The Imitation of Jesus Christ* (1656); while it was obviously a radical shift from theatrical comedies, the translation was a great popular success.

His plays of the 1660s—mostly tragedies—were less popular than his earlier works. Times had changed: Corneille was still respected, but two younger playwrights—Racine and Molière—were beginning to steal the hearts of audiences and the favor of the court of the "Sun King," Louis XIV. Racine began his career by attacking Corneille, and the rivalry reached a head when, in 1670, Corneille and Racine were each urged to write a tragedy on the same topic (the doomed love between a Roman emperor and the queen of Palestine), unaware of the other's intention. Racine's *Bérénice* was deemed superior to Corneille's *Tite et Bérénice*, and Racine subsequently went on to write his greatest plays. Corneille continued to write, too, but with diminishing success; his last play, *Suréna, général des Parthes*, was produced in 1675. He died in 1684; in the following year his younger brother, Thomas Corneille, also a playwright, was given his seat in the French Academy, with the blessing of the belatedly gracious Racine.

More than twenty years after the Quarrel of *Le Cid*, Corneille wrote and published a defense of his dramatic style. The defense took the form of *Trois Discours sur le poème dramatique* (1660, *Three Discourses on Dramatic Poetry*), which was published in the seventh edition of his theatrical works. His discourses had a double aim: on the one hand, he needed to uphold the authority of Aristotle and the "ancients" against the frenzy and formlessness of the baroque; on the other, he needed to defend his theatrical practices against the rigid interpretation of that same Aristotle, whose authority had underpinned the Academy's criticism of *Le Cid*. Although he is often seen as a rigid apologist for classical form, Corneille actually argues for flexibility, for a practical adaptation of the sometimes unclear statements made in the *Poetics*, suiting the spirit but not always the letter of Aristotle's description of a well-made tragedy.

Corneille's *Trois Discours* directly responded to the publication in 1657 of the Abbé d'Aubignac's *Pratique du théâtre (The Practice of Theater)*, but the essays were obviously part of a much larger critical dialogue that had been going on throughout Corneille's career—a dialogue that had in many ways begun the year *Le Cid* opened in Paris. In *An Essay of Dramatic Poesy* (1668; see below), the English dramatist JOHN DRYDEN took up the issues with equal intensity. In the *Discourses*, written to introduce the three volumes of Corneille's own plays (the play printed under the author's supervision being a relatively recent departure from ancient practice), Corneille cites only himself among living dramatists, referring often to the ancients. The three essays each endorse Aristotelian ideas but argue that the strict rules of French classical theater are based on an overly literal interpretation of the *Poetics*. Again and again, Corneille claims that everyone agrees with Aristotle—they just don't agree on what he means.

Corneille opens the first discourse by quoting Aristotle's declaration that the sole purpose of drama is to please the spectator, and he repeatedly demonstrates that this desire to please the spectator will serve as his first axiom, to which the other rules of classical theater will often, but not always, be subordinate. The moralists of the seventeenth century, citing Aristotle, argued that the classical conventions necessarily led to didactic theater. But Corneille makes the didactic function secondary to entertainment. Though citing the same sources—Aristotle and Horace—he interprets them to challenge received ideas and to serve his own aesthetic ends. For example, in the first *Discours*, on the matter of *bienséance*, he views Aristotle's statement that a character's morals must be "good" not as a call for "naive depiction of vices and virtues," but rather as an insistence on character development: each character must be true to his or her history. To support his claim, he lists many examples from classical Greek theater of heroes who are adulterers or killers; here, says Corneille, classical theater transcends the simplistic idea that audiences need moral heroes to be "good" and adulterers and killers to be "bad" and therefore punished. It is more important to portray human behavior as it is, in keeping with a character's birth, family, and social status, than to offer flawless paragons of moral behavior.

In the second *Discours*, Corneille discusses the Aristotelian ideas on the nature of tragedy, especially the ways in which the tragic hero elicits pity and fear from the audience, which in turn leads to a purging, or catharsis, of those passions. He argues that human emotions are complicated and that the oppositions inherent in human nature, such as the contradictory forces of love and duty, will evoke pity and empathy from the audience. While classical theory prescribes that all actions should be both probable and necessary, some of the most intense tragic effects are created by predicaments that are not, at least according to *bienséance*, probable. Yet these unlikely events can nevertheless reveal something fundamental about human nature.

"Of the Three Unities of Action, Time, and Place," our selection, continues in the tone of the first two discourses. Using many examples from his own plays and quoting liberally from Aristotle's *Poetics*, Corneille in this third *Discours* both justifies his own dramatic works and explains the theories behind them. Above all, he is a pragmatist—a successful playwright and seasoned craftsman who has refused to submit to the prescriptive dicta of theatrical critics of his time. He knows that a play must please, even dazzle the audience.

Here he shows how the three unities can, at times, assist in the overall aim of theater. He begins by discussing the unity of action, which, for Corneille, does not require only one action on stage. "One complete action" may contain several other less-developed actions, which may or may not take place on the stage. He allows for some action to take place offstage between acts, and he also allows for particular actions that do not necessarily bring about the principal action. He does advise the writer to avoid actions that have happened before the time of the play, since such narrations of prior events will burden the spectator's memory, and he criticizes the multiple subplots that characterize Shakespearean drama.

The unity of time is founded on Aristotle's statement that the action of a play should be contained "within a single circuit of the sun." Corneille dismisses the argument as to whether Aristotle's maxim referred to a twelve-hour day or a twenty-four-hour day, offering instead the principle of proportion. A portrait will "gain in excellence" as it closely resembles reality. Since a play lasts about two hours, the action represented should come as close to two hours as possible. Yet precision in this unity may make the spectator aware of an unnatural need to compress the action; therefore, as with most theatrical strictures, Corneille wishes to allow latitude, and above all to "leave the matter of duration to the imagination of the spectators."

Corneille similarily calls for a judicious approach to the unity of place. Baroque plays, which sometimes spanned continents, were clearly in violation of *vraisemblance*. But a confined space like that of the theater itself—royal apartments, for example—might turn out to be overly restrictive (Shakespeare could be said to have gotten around this by staging his plays in a theater called the Globe). The concentration provided by a spatial confinement approaching that of the theater itself should always make sense. One should seek unity as much as possible, but at the same time recognize that not every subject can be adapted to its demands.

Within the strictures derived from Aristotle, then, Corneille is arguing for a loosening, not a tightening, of classical rules. His discussion of the unities, often taken to be prescriptive, is really a defense of flexibility. True, he brandishes Aristotle's authority against the exuberance of baroque forms. But his Aristotle can be adapted to fit a wide range of theatrical practices. The point, he concludes, is "to make the ancient rules agree with modern pleasures." Corneille would have been surprised to find that for later playwrights, especially in Germany during the early eighteenth century, he had become the epitome of the cold nobility and rigid formalism of the same classical theater into which he had constantly attempted to breathe life.

"Of the Three Unities of Action, Time, and Place" Keywords: Drama, Formalism, Language, Tradition

Of the Three Unities of Action, Time, and Place[1]

The two preceding discourses and the critical examination of the plays which my first two volumes contain have furnished me so many opportunities to explain my thoughts on these matters[2] that there would be little left for me to say if I absolutely forbade myself to repeat.

I hold then, as I have already said, that in comedy, unity of action consists in the unity of plot or the obstacle to the plans of the principal actors, and in tragedy in the unity of peril, whether the hero falls victim to it or escapes. It is not that I claim that several perils cannot be allowed in the latter or several plots or obstacles in the former, provided that one passes necessarily from one to the other; for then escape from the first peril does not make the action complete since the escape leads to another danger; and the resolution of one plot does not put the actors at rest since they are confounded afresh in another. My memory does not furnish me any ancient examples of this multiplicity of perils linked each to each without the destruction of the unity of action; but I have noted independent double action as a defect in *Horace* and in *Théodore*,[3] for it is not necessary that the first kill his sister upon gaining his victory nor that the other give herself up to martyrdom after having escaped prostitution; and if the death of Polyxène and that of Astyanax in Seneca's[4] *Trojan Women* do not produce the same irregularity I am very much mistaken.

In the second place, the term unity of action does not mean that tragedy should show only one action on the stage. The one which the poet chooses for his subject must have a beginning, a middle, and an end;[5] and not only are these three parts separate actions which find their conclusion in the principal one, but, moreover, each of them may contain several others with the same subordination. There must be only one complete action, which leaves the mind of the spectator serene; but that action can become complete only through several others which are less perfect and which, by serving as preparation, keep the spectator in a pleasant suspense. This is what must be contrived at the end of each act in order to give continuity to the action. It is not necessary that we know exactly what the actors are doing in the intervals which separate the acts, nor even that they contribute to the action when they do not appear on the stage; but it is necessary that each act leave us in the expectation of something which is to take place in the following one.

If you asked me what Cléopâtre is doing in *Rodogune*[6] between the time when she leaves her two sons in the second act until she rejoins Antiochus in the fourth, I should be unable to tell you, and I do not feel obliged to

1. Translated by Donald Schier.
2. The principles Corneille had derived from ARISTOTLE's *Poetics* (see above). The first two discourses were "On the Uses and Elements of Dramatic Poetry" and "Discourse on Tragedy and of the Methods of Treating It, according to Probability and Necessity." Each play also had an *examen* (critical examination) appended by Corneille.
3. Two tragedies by Corneille, written respectively in 1640 and 1645.
4. Seneca the Younger (ca. 4 B.C.E.–65 C.E.), Roman philosopher, statesman, and tragedian.
5. See Aristotle, *Poetics* 7, 1450b.
6. *Rodogune, Princesse des Parthes* (1644), a tragedy by Corneille in which Cleopatra, queen of Syria, promises the throne to the one of her two sons, Antiochus and Seleucus, who will bring to her the head of Rodogune, with whom both are in love. When Seleucus is killed, Cleopatra prepares to poison Antiochus and Rodogune, but ends up drinking the poison herself.

account for her; but the end of this second act prepares us to see an amicable effort by the two brothers to rule and to hide Rodogune from the venomous hatred of their mother. The effect of this is seen in the third act, whose ending prepares us again to see another effort by Antiochus to win back these two enemies one after the other and for what Séleucus does in the fourth, which compels that unnatural mother [Cléopâtre] to resolve upon what she tries to accomplish in the fifth, whose outcome we await with suspense.

In *Le Menteur*[7] the actors presumably make use of the whole interval between the third and fourth acts to sleep; their rest, however, does not impede the continuity of the action between those two acts because the third does not contain a complete event. Dorante ends it with his plan to seek ways to win back the trust of Lucrèce, and at the very beginning of the next he appears so as to be able to talk to one of her servants and to her, should she show herself.

When I say that it is not necessary to account for what the actors do when they are not on stage, I do not mean that it is not sometimes very useful to give such an accounting, but only that one is not forced to do it, and that one ought to take the trouble to do so only when what happens behind the scenes is necessary for the understanding of what is to take place before the spectators. Thus I say nothing of what Cléopâtre did between the second and the fourth acts, because during all that time she can have done nothing important as regards the principal action which I am preparing for; but I point out in the very first lines of the fifth act that she has used the interval between these latter two for the killing of Séleucus, because that death is part of the action. This is what leads me to state that the poet is not required to show all the particular actions which bring about the principal one; he must choose to show those which are the most advantageous, whether by the beauty of the spectacle or by the brilliance or violence of the passions they produce, or by some other attraction which is connected with them, and to hide the others behind the scenes while informing the spectator of them by a narration or by some other artistic device; above all, he must remember that they must all be so closely connected that the last are produced by the preceding and that all have their source in the protasis[8] which ought to conclude the first act. This rule, which I have established in my first *Discourse*, although it is new and contrary to the usage of the ancients, is founded on two passages of Aristotle. Here is the first of them: "There is a great difference," he says, "between events which succeed each other and those which occur because of others."[9] The Moors come into the *Cid*[1] after the death of the Count and not because of the death of the Count; and the fisherman comes into *Don Sanche*[2] after Charles is suspected of being the Prince of Aragon and not because he is suspected of it; thus both are to be criticized. The second passage is even more specific and says precisely "that everything that happens in tragedy must arise necessarily or probably from what has gone before."[3]

7. *The Liar* (1643), a comedy by Corneille in which a provincial fabulator, Dorante, seeks to impress two Parisian women, Lucrèce and Clarice.

8. The introductory act or exposition of classical Greek drama (literally, "that which is put forward"; Greek), a term of late antiquity.

9. Aristotle, *Poetics* 10, 1452a.

1. *Le Cid* (1637), a tragedy by Corneille.

2. *Don Sanche d'Aragon* (1649), a heroic comedy by Corneille.

3. Aristotle, *Poetics* 10, 1452a.

The linking of the scenes which unites all the individual actions of each act and of which I have spoken in criticizing *La Suivante*[4] is a great beauty in a poem and one which serves to shape continuity of action through continuity of presentation; but, in the end, it is only a beauty and not a rule. The ancients did not always abide by it although most of their acts have but two or three scenes. This made things much simpler for them than for us, who often put as many as nine or ten scenes into each act. I shall cite only two examples of the scorn with which they treated this principle: one is from Sophocles,[5] in *Ajax*, whose monologue before he kills himself has no connection with the preceding scene; the other is from the third act of Terence's[6] *The Eunuch*, where Antipho's soliloquy has no connection with Chremes and Pythias who leave the stage when he enters. The scholars of our century, who have taken the ancients for models in the tragedies they have left us, have even more neglected that linking than did the ancients, and one need only glance at the plays of Buchanan, Grotius, and Heinsius,[7] of which I spoke in the discussion of *Polyeucte*,[8] to agree on that point. We have so far accustomed our audiences to this careful linking of scenes that they cannot now witness a detached scene without considering it a defect; the eye and even the ear are outraged by it even before the mind has been able to reflect upon it. The fourth act of *Cinna*[9] falls below the others through this flaw; and what formerly was not a rule has become one now through the assiduousness of our practice.

I have spoken of three sorts of linkings in the discussion of *La Suivante*: I have shown myself averse to those of sound, indulgent to those of sight, favorable to those of presence and speech; but in these latter I have confused two things which ought to be separated. Links of presence and speech both have, no doubt, all the excellence imaginable; but there are links of speech without presence and of presence without speech which do not reach the same level of excellence. An actor who speaks to another from a hiding-place without showing himself forms a link of speech without presence which is always effective; but that rarely happens. A man who remains on stage merely to hear what will be said by those whom he sees making their entrance forms a link of presence without speech; this is often clumsy and falls into mere pretense, being contrived more to accede to this new convention which is becoming a precept than for any need dictated by the plot of the play. Thus, in the third act of *Pompée*,[1] Achorée, after having informed Charmion of the reception Caesar gave to the king when he presented to him the head of that hero, remains on the stage where he sees the two of them come together

4. *The Lady's Maid* (1633), a comedy by Corneille; his earlier criticism was in the *examen* to the play.
5. Greek tragic dramatist (ca. 496–406 B.C.E.). *Ajax* (ca. 441) is generally regarded as the earliest of his extant plays.
6. Roman comic dramatist (ca. 190–ca. 159 B.C.E.); *Eunuchus* was produced in 161.
7. Daniël Heinsius (1580–1655), Dutch poet and classical scholar; he published an edition of Aristotle's *Poetics* (1611), and his *De Tragoediae Constitutione* (1611) decisively influenced French classical theater. George Buchanan (1506–1582), Scottish humanist, educator, and man of letters who taught Latin in Paris and was known throughout Europe as a scholar and a Latin poet. Hugo Grotius (1583–1645), Dutch jurist whose writings also included a number of tragedies.
8. *Polyeucte martyr* (1640), a Christian tragedy by Corneille; this earlier discussion was in the *examen* to the play.
9. *Cinna, ou la clémence d'Auguste* (1641, *Cinna, or the Clemency of Augustus*), a tragedy by Corneille. In an effort to avenge her father, Emilie incites her beloved Cinna to overthrow the emperor, Augustus. He is betrayed by a fellow conspirator, Maxime, also in love with Emilie; the conspirators are, in the end, all pardoned by a merciful Augustus.
1. *La mort de Pompée* (1642, *The Death of Pompey*), a tragedy by Corneille.

merely to hear what they will say and report it to Cléopâtre. Ammon does the same thing in the fourth act of *Andromède*[2] for the benefit of Phinée, who retires when he sees the king and all his court arriving. Characters who become mute connect rather badly scenes in which they play little part and in which they count for nothing. It is another matter when they hide in order to find out some important secret from those who are speaking and who think they are not overheard, for then the interest which they have in what is being said, added to a reasonable curiosity to find out what they cannot learn in any other way, gives them an important part in the action despite their silence; but in these two examples Ammon and Achorée lend so cold a presence to the scenes they overhear that, to be perfectly frank, whatever feigned reason I give them to serve as pretext for their action, they remain there only to connect the scenes with those that precede, so easily can both plays dispense with what they do.

Although the action of the dramatic poem must have its unity, one must consider both its parts: the complication and the resolution. "The complication is composed," according to Aristotle, "in part of what has happened off stage before the beginning of the action which is there described, and in part from what happens on stage; the rest belongs to the resolution. The change of fortune forms the separation of these two parts. Everything which precedes it is in the first part, and this change, with what follows it, concerns the other."[3] The complication depends entirely upon the choice and industrious imagination of the poet and no rule can be given for it, except that in it he ought to order all things according to probability or necessity, a point which I have discussed in the second *Discourse*; to this I add one piece of advice, which is that he involve himself as little as possible with things which have happened before the action he is presenting. Such narrations are annoying, usually because they are not expected, and they disturb the mind of the spectator, who is obliged to burden his memory with what has happened ten or twelve years before in order to understand what he is about to see; but narrations which describe things which happen and take place behind the scenes once the action has started always produce a better effect because they are awaited with some curiosity and are a part of the action which is being shown. One of the reasons why so many illustrious critics favor *Cinna* above anything else I have done is that it contains no narration of the past, the one Cinna makes in describing his plot to Emilie being rather an ornament which tickles the mind of the spectators than a necessary marshaling of the details they must know and impress upon their memories for the understanding of what is to come. Emilie informs them adequately in the first two scenes that he is conspiring against Augustus in her favor, and if Cinna merely told her that the plotters are ready for the following day he would advance the action just as much as by the hundred lines he uses to tell both what he said to them and the way in which they received his words. There are plots which begin at the very birth of the hero like that of *Héraclius*,[4] but these great efforts of the imagination demand an

2. A successful "machine play" (extravagant spectacle) (1650) by Corneille.

3. Aristotle, *Poetics* 18, 1455b.

4. *Héraclius, empereur d'Orient* (1647), a tragedy by Corneille. In this complicated drama of near-incest and mistaken identity, the main characters are Héraclius, the legitimate prince; Phocas, the usurping ruler; Martian, son (unbeknownst to him) of Phocas; and Pulchérie, sister of Héraclius.

extraordinary attention of the spectator and often keep him from taking a real pleasure in the first performances, so much do they weary him.

In the resolution I find two things to avoid: the mere change of intention and the machine.[5] Not much skill is required to finish a poem when he who has served as the obstacle to the plans of the principal actors for four acts desists in the fifth without being constrained to do so by any remarkable event; I have spoken of this in the first *Discourse* and I shall add nothing to that here. The machine requires no more skill when it is used only to bring down a god who straightens everything out when the actors are unable to do so. It is thus that Apollo functions in the *Orestes*:[6] this prince and his friend Pylades, accused by Tyndarus and Menelaus of the death of Clytemnestra and condemned after prosecution by them, seize Helen and Hermione; they kill, or think they kill the first, and threaten to do the same with the other if the sentence pronounced against them is not revoked. To smooth out these difficulties Euripides seeks nothing subtler than to bring Apollo down from heaven, and he, by absolute authority, orders that Orestes marry Hermione and Pylades Electra; and lest the death of Helen prove an obstacle to this, it being improbable that Hermione would marry Orestes since he had just killed her mother, Apollo informs them that she is not dead, that he has protected her from their blows and carried her off to heaven at the moment when they thought they were killing her. This use of the machine is entirely irrelevant, being founded in no way on the rest of the play, and makes a faulty resolution. But I find a little too harsh the opinion of Aristotle, who puts on the same level the chariot Medea uses to flee from Corinth after the vengeance she has taken on Creon.[7] It seems to me there is a sufficient basis for this in the fact that she has been made a magician and that actions of hers as far surpassing natural forces as that one have been mentioned in the play. After what she did for Jason at Colchis and after she had made his father Aeson young again following his return, and after she had attached invisible fire to the gift she gave to Creusa, the flying chariot is not improbable and the poem has no need of other preparation for that extraordinary effect. Seneca gives it preparation by this line which Medea speaks to her nurse:

> Tuum quoque ipsa corpus hinc mecum aveham;[8]

and I by this one which she speaks to Aegeus

> I shall follow you tomorrow by a new road.[9]

5. That is, the *deus ex machina* (god from a machine; Latin); in some Greek tragedies, a sort of crane lowered a god from the sky to provide a quick resolution to an entangled plot.
6. A drama (408 b.c.e.) by Euripides (ca. 485–ca. 406 b.c.e.), the Greek playwright who used the *deus ex machina* most frequently. In the Greek myth, Orestes kills his mother, Clytemnestra, to avenge her murder of his father, Agamemnon. Tyndareus is the father of Clytemnestra and of Helen (of Troy), whose husband is Menelaus; Hermione is Helen's daughter, and Electra is Orestes' sister. Apollo is the Greek god of music and prophecy.
7. At the end of Euripides' *Medea* (431 b.c.e.); see *Poetics* 15, 1454b. At Colchis, Medea, a sorceress, helps Jason steal the Golden Fleece, and later marries him; when he chooses to marry the daughter of Creon, king of Corinth (unnamed in Euripides' play, named Creusa in Seneca's), she sends Jason's new wife a robe covered in a deadly ointment and kills Jason's and her two children, escaping in the dragon-drawn chariot of Helios (the sun), her grandfather.
8. Seneca, *Medea*, line 975: "I'll also carry away your corpse from here with me" (Medea is addressing her dead child).
9. Corneille, *Médée* (1635); Aegeus is a legendary king of Athens, whom Medea marries after fleeing Corinth.

Thus the condemnation of Euripides, who took no precautions, may be just and yet not fall on Seneca or on me: and I have no need to contradict Aristotle in order to justify myself on this point.

From the action I turn to the acts, each of which ought to contain a portion of it, but not so equal a portion that more is not reserved for the last than for the others and less given to the first than to the others. Indeed, in the first act one may do no more than depict the moral nature of the characters and mark off how far they have got in the story which is to be presented. Aristotle does not prescribe the number of the acts; Horace limits it to five;[1] and although he prohibits having fewer, the Spaniards are obstinate enough to stop at three and the Italians often do the same thing. The Greeks used to separate the acts by the chanting of the chorus, and since I think it reasonable to believe that in some of their poems they made it chant more than four times, I should not want to say they never exceeded five. This way of distinguishing the acts was less handy than ours, for either they paid attention to what the chorus was chanting or they did not; if they did, the mind of the spectators was too tense and had no time in which to rest; if they did not, attention was too much dissipated by the length of the chant, and when a new act began, an effort of memory was needed to recall to the imagination what had been witnessed and at what point the action had been interrupted. Our orchestra presents neither of these two inconveniences; the mind of the spectator relaxes while the music is playing and even reflects on what he has seen, to praise it or to find fault with it depending on whether he has been pleased or displeased; and the short time the orchestra is allowed to play leaves his impressions so fresh that when the actors return he does not need to make an effort to recall and resume his attention.

The number of scenes in each act has never been prescribed by rule, but since the whole act must have a certain number of lines which make its length proportionate to that of the others, one may include in it more or fewer scenes depending on whether they are long or short to fill up the time which the whole act is to consume. One ought, if possible, to account for the entrance and exit of each actor; I consider this rule indispensable, especially for the exit, and think there is nothing so clumsy as an actor who leaves the stage merely because he has no more lines to speak.

I should not be so rigorous for the entrances. The audience expects the actor, and although the setting represents the room or the study of whoever is speaking, yet he cannot make his appearance there unless he comes out from behind the tapestry, and it is not always easy to give a reason for what he has just done in town before returning home, since sometimes it is even probable that he has not gone out at all. I have never seen anybody take offense at seeing Emilie begin *Cinna* without saying why she has come to her room; she is presumed to be there before the play begins, and it is only stage necessity which makes her appear from behind the scenes to come there. Thus I should willingly dispense from the rigors of the rule the first scene of each act but not the others, because once an actor is on the stage anyone who enters must have a reason to speak to him or, at least, must profit from the opportunity to do so when it offers. Above all, when an actor enters twice in one act, in comedy or in tragedy, he must either lead one to

1. The Roman poet HORACE (65–8 B.C.E.), *Ars Poetica*, lines 189–90 (see above).

expect that he will soon return when he leaves the first time, like Horace in the second act and Julie in the third act of *Horace*, or explain on returning why he has come back so soon.

Aristotle wishes the well-made tragedy to be beautiful and capable of pleasing without the aid of actors and quite aside from performance.[2] So that the reader may more easily experience that pleasure, his mind, like that of the spectator, must not be hindered, because the effort he is obliged to make to conceive and to imagine the play for himself lessens the satisfaction which he will get from it. Therefore, I should be of the opinion that the poet ought to take great care to indicate in the margin the less important actions which do not merit being included in the lines, and which might even mar the dignity of the verse if the author lowered himself to express them. The actor easily fills this need on the stage, but in a book one would often be reduced to guessing and sometimes one might even guess wrong, unless one were informed in this way of these little things. I admit that this is not the practice of the ancients; but you must also allow me that because they did not do it they have left us many obscurities in their poems which only masters of dramatic art can explain; even so, I am not sure they succeed as often as they think they do. If we forced ourselves to follow the method of the ancients completely, we should make no distinction between acts and scenes because the Greeks did not. This failure on their part is often the reason that I do not know how many acts there are in their plays, nor whether at the end of an act the player withdraws so as to allow the chorus to chant, or whether he remains on stage without any action while the chorus is chanting, because neither they nor their interpreters have deigned to give us a word of indication in the margin.

We have another special reason for not neglecting that helpful little device as they did: this is that printing puts our plays in the hands of actors who tour the provinces and whom we can thus inform of what they ought to do, for they would do some very odd things if we did not help them by these notes. They would find themselves in great difficulty at the fifth act of plays that end happily, where we bring together all the actors on the stage (a thing which the ancients did not do); they would often say to one what is meant for another, especially when the same actor must speak to three or four people one after the other. When there is a whispered command to make, like Cléopâtre's to Laonice which sends her to seek poison,[3] an aside would be necessary to express this in verse if we were to do without the marginal indications, and that seems to me much more intolerable than the notes, which give us the real and only way, following the opinion of Aristotle, of making the tragedy as beautiful in the reading as in performance, by making it easy for the reader to imagine what the stage presents to the view of the spectators.

The rule of the unity of time is founded on this statement of Aristotle "that the tragedy ought to enclose the duration of its action in one journey of the sun or try not to go much beyond it."[4] These words gave rise to a famous dispute as to whether they ought to be understood as meaning a natural day of twenty-four hours or an artificial day of twelve; each of the two opinions has important partisans, and, for myself, I find that there are subjects so difficult

2. Aristotle, *Poetics* 6, 1450b.
3. In *Rodogune*.
4. Aristotle, *Poetics* 5, 1449b.

to limit to such a short time that not only should I grant the twenty-four full hours but I should make use of the license which the philosopher gives to exceed them a little and should push the total without scruple as far as thirty. There is a legal maxim which says that we should broaden the mercies and narrow the rigors of the law, *odia restringenda, favores ampliandi*; and I find that an author is hampered enough by this constraint which forced some of the ancients to the very edge of the impossible. Euripides in *The Suppliants*[5] makes Theseus leave Athens with an army, fight a battle beneath the walls of Thebes, which was ten or twelve leagues away, and return victorious in the following act; and between his departure and the arrival of the messenger who comes to tell the story of his victory, the chorus has only thirty-six lines to speak. That makes good use of such a short time. Aeschylus[6] makes Agamemnon come back from Troy with even greater speed. He had agreed with Clytemnestra, his wife, that as soon as the city was taken he would inform her by signal fires built on the intervening mountains, of which the second would be lighted as soon as the first was seen, the third at the sight of the second, and so on; by this means she was to learn the great news the same night. However, scarcely had she learned it from the signal fires when Agamemnon arrives, whose ship, although battered by a storm, if memory serves, must have traveled as fast as the eye could see the lights. *The Cid* and *Pompée*, where the action is a little precipitate, are far from taking so much license; and if they force ordinary probability in some way, at least they do not go as far as such impossibilities.

Many argue against this rule, which they call tyrannical, and they would be right if it were founded only on the authority of Aristotle; but what should make it acceptable is the fact that common sense supports it. The dramatic poem is an imitation, or rather a portrait of human actions, and it is beyond doubt that portraits gain in excellence in proportion as they resemble the original more closely. A performance lasts two hours and would resemble reality perfectly if the action it presented required no more for its actual occurrence. Let us then not settle on twelve or twenty-four hours, but let us compress the action of the poem into the shortest possible period, so that the performance may more closely resemble reality and thus be more nearly perfect. Let us give, if that is possible, to the one no more than the two hours which the other fills. I do not think that *Rodogune* requires much more, and perhaps two hours would be enough for *Cinna*. It we cannot confine the action within the two hours, let us take four, six, or ten, but let us not go much beyond twenty-four for fear of falling into lawlessness and of so far reducing the scale of the portrait that it no longer has its proportionate dimensions and is nothing but imperfection.

Most of all, I should like to leave the matter of duration to the imagination of the spectators and never make definite the time the action requires unless the subject needs this precision, but especially not when probability is a little forced, as in the *Cid*, because precision serves only to make the crowded action obvious to the spectator. Even when no violence is done to a poem by the necessity of obeying this rule, why must one state at the beginning that the sun is rising, that it is noon at the third act, and that the

5. A tragedy first performed ca. 422 B.C.E.

6. Greek tragic dramatist (525–456 B.C.E.); Corneille describes the beginning of his *Agamemnon* (458).

sun is setting at the end of the last act? This is only an obtrusive affectation; it is enough to establish the possibility of the thing in the time one gives to it and that one be able to determine the time easily if one wishes to pay attention to it, but without being compelled to concern oneself with the matter. Even in those actions which take no longer than the performance it would be clumsy to point out that a half hour has elapsed between the beginning of one act and the beginning of the next.

I repeat what I have said elsewhere,[7] that when we take a longer time, as, for instance, ten hours, I should prefer that the eight extra be used up in the time between the acts and that each act should have as its share only as much time as performance requires especially when all scenes are closely linked together. I think, however, that the fifth act, by special privilege, has the right to accelerate time so that the part of the action which it presents may use up more time than is necessary for performance. The reason for this is that the spectator is by then impatient to see the end, and when the outcome depends on actors who are off stage, all the dialogue given to those who are on stage awaiting news of the others drags and action seems to halt. There is no doubt that from the point where Phocas exits in the fifth act of *Héraclius* until Amyntas enters to relate the manner of his death, more time is needed for what happens off stage than for the speaking of the lines in which Héraclius, Martian, and Pulchérie complain of their misfortune. Prusias and Flaminius, in the fifth act of *Nicomède*,[8] do not have the time they would need to meet at sea, take counsel with each other, and return to the defense of the queen; and the Cid has not enough time to fight a duel with Don Sanche during the conversations of the Infanta with Léonor and of Chimène with Elvire. I was aware of this and yet have had no scruples about this acceleration of which, perhaps, one might find several examples among the ancients, but the laziness of which I have spoken will force me to rest content with this one, which is from the *Andria*[9] of Terence. Simo slips his son Pamphilus into the house of Glycerium in order to get the old man, Crito, to come out and to clear up with him the question of the birth of his mistress, who happens to be the daughter of Chremes. Pamphilus enters the house, speaks to Crito, asks him for the favor and returns with him; and during this exit, this request, and this re-entry, Simo and Chremes, who remain on stage, speak only one line each, which could not possibly give Pamphilus more than time enough to ask where Crito is, certainly not enough to talk with him and to explain to him the reasons for which he should reveal what he knows about the birth of the unknown girl.

When the conclusion of the action depends on actors who have not left the stage and about whom no one is awaiting news, as in *Cinna* and *Rodogune*, the fifth act has no need of this privilege because then all the action takes place in plain sight, as does not happen when part of it occurs off stage after the beginning of the act. The other acts do not merit the same freedom. If there is not time enough to bring back an actor who has made his exit, or to indicate what he has done since that exit, the accounting can be postponed to the following act; and the music, which separates the two acts, may use up as much time as is necessary; but in the fifth act no postponement is possible: attention is exhausted and the end must come quickly.

7. In the *Examen de Mélite*, which precedes the present Discourse in the edition published by Corneille [translator's note].

8. A tragedy (1651) by Corneille.

9. *The Maid of Andros* (166 B.C.E.), Terence's first play.

I cannot forget that although we must reduce the whole tragic action to one day, we can nevertheless make known by a narration or in some other more artful way what the hero of the tragedy has been doing for several years, because there are plays in which the crux of the plot lies in an obscurity of birth which must be brought to light, as in *Oedipus*.[1] I shall not say again that the less one burdens oneself with past actions, the more favorable the spectator will be, because of the lesser degree of trouble he is given when everything takes place in the present and no demands are made on his memory except for what he has seen; but I cannot forget that the choice of a day both illustrious and long-awaited is a great ornament to a poem. The opportunity for this does not always present itself, and in all that I have written until now you will find only four of that kind: the day in *Horace* when two nations are to decide the question of supremacy of empire by a battle; and the ones in *Rodogune, Andromède*, and *Don Sanche*. In *Rodogune* it is a day chosen by two sovereigns for the signature of a treaty of peace between the hostile crowns, for a complete reconciliation of the two rival governments through a marriage, and for the elucidation of a more than twenty-year-old secret concerning the right of succession of one of the twin princes on which the fate of the kingdom depends, as does the outcome of both their loves. The days in *Andromède* and *Don Sanche* are not of lesser importance, but, as I have just said, such opportunities do not often present themselves, and in the rest of my works I have been able to choose days remarkable only for what chance makes happen on them and not by the use to which public arrangements destined them long ago.

As for the unity of place, I find no rule concerning it in either Aristotle or Horace. This is what leads many people to believe that this rule was established only as a consequence of the unity of one day, and leads them to imagine that one can stretch the unity of place to cover the points to which a man may go and return in twenty-four hours. This opinion is a little too free, and if one made an actor travel post-haste, the two sides of the theater might represent Paris and Rouen. I could wish, so that the spectator is not at all disturbed, that what is performed before him in two hours might actually be able to take place in two hours, and that what he is shown in a stage setting which does not change might be limited to a room or a hall depending on a choice made beforehand; but often that is so awkward, if not impossible, that one must necessarily find some way to enlarge the place as also the time of the action. I have shown exact unity of place in *Horace, Polyeucte*, and *Pompée*, but for that it was necessary to present either only one woman, as in *Polyeucte*; or to arrange that the two who are presented are such close friends and have such closely related interests that they can be always together, as in *Horace*; or that they may react as in *Pompée* where the stress of natural curiosity drives Cléopâtre from her apartments in the second act and Cornélie in the fifth; and both enter the great hall of the king's palace in anticipation of the news they are expecting. The same thing is not true of *Rodogune*: Cléopâtre and she have interests which are too divergent to permit them to express their most secret thoughts in the same place. I might say of that play what I have said of

1. The *Oedipus Rex* (ca. 430 B.C.E.) of Sophocles is the best-known treatment of the story (an *Oedipus* of Seneca is also extant); at the climax of the play Oedipus learns that he has unknowingly killed his father and married his mother. Corneille wrote his *Oedipe* in 1659.

Cinna, where, in general, everything happens in Rome and, in particular, half of the action takes place in the quarters of Auguste and half of it in Emilie's apartments. Following that arrangement, the first act of this tragedy would be laid in Rodogune's antechamber, the second, in Cléopâtre's apartments, the third, in Rodogune's; but if the fourth act can begin in Rodogune's apartments it cannot finish there, and what Cléopâtre says to her two sons one after the other would be badly out of place there. The fifth act needs a throne room where a great crowd can be gathered. The same problem is found in *Héraclius*. The first act could very well take place in Phocas's quarters, the second, in Léontine's apartments; but if the third begins in Pulchérie's rooms, it cannot end there, and it is outside the bounds of probability that Phocas should discuss the death of her brother in Pulchérie's apartments.

The ancients, who made their kings speak in a public square, easily kept a rigorous unity of place in their tragedies. Sophocles, however, did not observe it in his *Ajax*, when the hero leaves the stage to find a lonely place in which to kill himself and does so in full view of the people; this easily leads to the conclusion that the place where he kills himself is not the one he has been seen to leave, since he left it only to choose another.

We do not take the same liberty of drawing kings and princesses from their apartments, and since often the difference and the opposition on the part of those who are lodged in the same palace do not allow them to take others into their confidence or to disclose their secrets in the same room, we must seek some other compromise about unity of place if we want to keep it intact in our poems; otherwise we should have to decide against many plays which we see succeeding brilliantly.

I hold, then, that we ought to seek exact unity as much as possible, but as this unity does not suit every kind of subject, I should be very willing to concede that a whole city has unity of place. Not that I should want the stage to represent the whole city, that would be somewhat too large, but only two or three particular places enclosed within its walls. Thus the scene of *Cinna* does not leave Rome, passing from the apartments of Auguste to the house of Emilie. *Le Menteur* takes place in the Tuileries and in the Place Royale at Paris, and *La Suite*[2] shows us the prison and Mélisse's house at Lyons. *The Cid* increases even more the number of particular places without leaving Seville; and since the close linking of scenes is not observed in that play, the stage in the first act is supposed to represent Chimène's house, the Infante's apartments in the king's palace, and the public square; the second adds to these the king's chamber. No doubt there is some excess in this freedom. In order to rectify in some way this multiplication of places when it is inevitable, I should wish two things done: first, that the scene should never change in a given act but only between the acts, as is done in the first three acts of *Cinna*; the other, that these two places should not need different stage settings and that neither of the two should ever be named, but only the general place which includes them both, as Paris, Rome, Lyons, Constantinople, and so forth. This would help to deceive the spectator, who, seeing nothing that would indicate the difference in the places, would not notice the change, unless it was maliciously and critically pointed out, a thing which few are capable of doing, most spectators being warmly intent upon

2. *La Suite du Menteur* (1643, *Sequel to the Liar*), a comedy by Corneille.

the action which they see on the stage. The pleasure they take in it is the reason why they do not seek out its imperfections lest they lose their taste for it; and they admit such an imperfection only when forced, when it is too obvious, as in *Le Menteur* and *La Suite*, where the different settings force them to recognize the multiplicity of places in spite of themselves.

But since people of opposing interests cannot with verisimilitude unfold their secrets in the same place, and since they are sometimes introduced into the same act through the linking of scenes which the unity of place necessarily produces, one must find some means to make it compatible with the contradiction which rigorous probability finds in it, and consider how to preserve the fourth act of *Rodogune* and the third of *Héraclius*, in both of which I have already pointed out the contradiction which lies in having enemies speak in the same place. Jurists allow legal fictions, and I should like, following their example, to introduce theatrical fictions by which one could establish a theatrical place which would not be Cléopâtre's chamber nor Rodogune's, in the play of that name, nor that of Phocas, of Léontine or of Pulchérie in *Héraclius*, but a room contiguous to all these other apartments, to which I should attribute these two privileges: first, that each of those who speaks in it is presumed to enjoy the same secrecy there as if he were in his own room; and second, that whereas in the usual arrangement it is sometimes proper for those who are on stage to go off, in order to speak privately with others in their rooms, these latter might meet the former on stage without shocking convention, so as to preserve both the unity of place and the linking of scenes. Thus Rodogune, in the first act, encounters Laonice, whom she must send for so as to speak with her; and, in the fourth act, Cléopâtre encounters Antiochus on the very spot where he has just moved Rodogune to pity, even though in utter verisimilitude the prince ought to seek out his mother in her own room since she hates the princess too much to come to speak to him in Rodogune's, which, following the first scene, would be the locus of the whole act, if one did not introduce that compromise which I have mentioned into the rigorous unity of place.

Many of my plays will be at fault in the unity of place if this compromise is not accepted, for I shall abide by it always in the future when I am not able to satisfy the ultimate rigor of the rule. I have been able to reduce only three plays, *Horace, Polyeucte,* and *Pompée*, to the requirements of the rule. If I am too indulgent with myself as far as the others are concerned, I shall be even more so for those which may succeed on the stage through some appearance of regularity. It is easy for critics to be severe; but if they were to give ten or a dozen plays to the public, they might perhaps slacken the rules more than I do, as soon as they have recognized through experience what constraint their precision brings about and how many beautiful things it banishes from our stage. However that may be, these are my opinions, or if you prefer, my heresies concerning the principal points of the dramatic art, and I do not know how better to make the ancient rules agree with modern pleasures. I do not doubt that one might easily find better ways of doing that, and I shall be ready to accept them when they have been put into practice as successfully as, by common consent, mine have been.

1660

JOHN DRYDEN
1631–1700

John Dryden worked expertly in poetry, drama, criticism, and translation. He was a true literary professional, an eminent (if controversial) public writer who took pride in his craft and prepared the way for later writers who built upon what he had done—ALEXANDER POPE and SAMUEL JOHNSON in particular. He occupies a central place in the history of English criticism.

Biographical evidence suggests that Dryden's middle-class parents supported the Puritan cause and Parliament. Dryden was educated at Westminster School and at Trinity College, Cambridge, receiving his degree in 1654.

His first important poem, *Heroic Stanzas* (1658, published 1659), eulogized Oliver Cromwell, the Puritan religious, military, and political leader and the lord protector of England (1653–58). Dryden was present at Cromwell's funeral, as were the Puritan poets John Milton and Andrew Marvell. In 1660, when Charles II assumed the throne eleven years after the execution of his father, Charles I, Dryden celebrated the event in his poem *Astraea Redux* ("justice restored"). This and later shifts in his political and religious positions led many critics to charge that he was an opportunist; but as Johnson noted in his *Life of Dryden*, "if he changed, he changed with the nation."

Annus Mirabilis ("year of wonders," 1667), a historical poem that describes two events of 1666, the English defeat of the Dutch naval fleet and the Great Fire in London that destroyed two-thirds of the city, helped win Dryden the poet laureateship in 1668. Other celebrated poems include the mock-heroic "Mac Flecknoe" (1682), a model for Pope's *Dunciad*; the political satires *Absalom and Achitophel* (1681) and *The Medal* (1682); and two religious poems, "Religio Laici" ("a layman's religion," 1682), which is a defense of Anglicanism, and *The Hind and the Panther* (1687), which criticizes the Anglican Church and reflects Dryden's conversion to Catholicism.

Dryden also was the major dramatist of his day. His best comedy is *Marriage à la Mode* (1671), and his most noteworthy tragedies are *Aureng-Zebe* (in rhymed couplets, 1675) and *All for Love, or The World Well Lost* (in blank verse, 1677). The last of these, influenced by French neoclassical theory, adapts Shakespeare's *Antony and Cleopatra* to the three unities of action, place, and time (see PIERRE CORNEILLE). In addition to plays and dramatic criticism, Dryden produced skillful translations of such classical authors as Persius, Juvenal, Plutarch, and Virgil; some scholars have judged his *Fables, Ancient and Modern* (1700), consisting of translations and paraphrases of Ovid, BOCCACCIO, and Chaucer, to be his finest achievement. Dryden's critical writings also form a significant and serious body of work. From his defenses, prefaces, dedications, prologues, and epilogues—and his poems on or to other writers and artists—we can piece together his literary and critical views.

Dryden occupies a key place in the history of English prose and criticism. His relaxed, conversational style, MATTHEW ARNOLD stated in the nineteenth century, is "such as we would all gladly use if we only knew how." Dryden examined the nature of comedy and tragedy, satire, poetry, and translation. He knew well, and was influenced by, Greek, Roman, and neoclassical French texts and theories; at the same time, he valued English writers from Chaucer to Ben Jonson and Shakespeare and sought to mediate among classical, modern, and national literary traditions.

Dryden's judgments are solid and sensible. "A man should have a reasonable, philosophical, and in some measure mathematical head to be a complete and excellent poet," he once observed, "and besides this should have experience in all sorts of humors and manners of men; should be thoroughly skilled in conversation and should have a great knowledge of mankind in general." His formulations are frequently witty and his advice cogent, as in his preface to the *Fables*: "An Author is not to write all he can, but only all he ought." Dryden respects authority and precedent without being weighed down by them: "If the plays of the Ancients are more correctly plotted, ours are more beautifully written. . . . 'Tis not enough that Aristotle has said so, for Aristotle drew his models of tragedy from Sophocles and Euripides; and if he had seen ours, might have changed his mind." His tone is urbane, cultured, and civilized; and like that of Arnold and T. S. ELIOT, his criticism benefits from his own wide range of experience in creative writing.

Dryden's strengths and limits as a critic are displayed in his best-known critical work, the lengthy conversation *An Essay of Dramatic Poesy* (1668; rev. 1684), from which we take our selection. His stated purpose is "to vindicate the honor of our English writers from the censure of those who unjustly prefer the French before them." Through his four speakers, he treats the relationship between the ancients and the moderns, French dramatic theory and English practice, and the use of rhyme in drama, commenting along the way, as in our excerpt, on Shakespeare, Jonson, and other authors. Samuel Johnson maintained of the *Essay* that "modern English prose begins here"; he identifies Dryden as "the father of English criticism." But while the *Essay* is confident, leisurely, graceful, exploratory, and spirited, it is nonetheless a little slow and sometimes pedantic. Dryden favors balance, counterpoint, argument; he uses the "essay" form to undertake a tentative inquiry. He seeks to break down and complicate distinctions, opening up such apparently fixed terms as *propriety* and *decorum.* But the *Essay* overall lacks the energy, boldness, and edge of Dryden's best satiric poems.

Dryden is an informed, judicious critic who made important contributions to the understanding and study of literary tradition, genre, and translation. Perhaps he could even be identified as the first modern critic, in his effort to make literary criticism and dramatic theory more analytical, comparative, speculative, and scientific. Dryden's work as a playwright sharpened his sense of literature as an institution always undergoing development and change—he was keenly aware of the diverse, evolving interests of the audiences and readers whom he sought to delight and teach. For all his knowledge of Greek and Roman texts and respect for cultural and literary authority, Dryden was not bound to the past. His criticism was connected to his creative work—he sought to explain and defend it, including the new principles that it exemplified. Dryden is a leader in the distinguished line of England's poet-critics that begins with SIR PHILIP SIDNEY and includes Johnson, SAMUEL TAYLOR COLERIDGE, Arnold, and Eliot.

***An Essay of Dramatic Poesy* Keywords:** Drama, The Canon/Tradition, Enlightenment Theory, Language, Poetry, Vernacular Language

From An Essay of Dramatic Poesy

* * *

"To begin, then, with Shakspeare.[1] He was the man who of all modern, and perhaps ancient poets, had the largest and most comprehensive soul. All the images of nature were still present to him, and he drew them, not laboriously, but luckily; when he describes anything, you more than see it, you feel it too. Those who accuse him to have wanted learning, give him the greater commendation: he was naturally learned; he needed not the spectacles of

1. In this excerpt, Neander (the Dryden character) is speaking and weighing the merits of Shakespeare.

books to read nature; he looked inwards, and found her there. I cannot say he is everywhere alike; were he so, I should do him injury to compare him with the greatest of mankind. He is many times flat, insipid; his comic wit degenerating into clenches,[2] his serious swelling into bombast. But he is always great, when some great occasion is presented to him; no man can say he ever had a fit subject for his wit, and did not then raise himself as high as above the rest of poets,

Quantum lenta solent inter viburna cupressi.[3]

The consideration of this made Mr. Hales of Eaton[4] say, that there was no subject of which any poet ever writ, but he would produce it much better done in Shakspeare; and however others are now generally preferred before him, yet the age wherein he lived, which had contemporaries with him Fletcher and Jonson,[5] never equalled them to him in their esteem: and in the last king's court,[6] when Ben's reputation was at highest, Sir John Suckling,[7] and with him the greater part of the courtiers, set our Shakspeare far above him.

"Beaumont and Fletcher, of whom I am next to speak, had, with the advantage of Shakspeare's wit, which was their precedent, great natural gifts, improved by study: Beaumont especially being so accurate a judge of plays, that Ben Jonson, while he lived, submitted all his writings to his censure, and, 'tis thought, used his judgment in correcting, if not contriving, all his plots. What value he had for him, appears by the verses he writ to him;[8] and therefore I need speak no farther of it. The first play that brought Fletcher and him in esteem was their *Philaster*:[9] for before that, they had written two or three very unsuccessfully, as the like is reported of Ben Jonson, before he writ *Every Man in his Humour*.[1] Their plots were generally more regular than Shakspeare's, especially those which were made before Beaumont's death; and they understood and imitated the conversation of gentlemen much better; whose wild debaucheries, and quickness of wit in repartees, no poet before them could paint as they have done. Humour,[2] which Ben Jonson derived from particular persons, they made it not their business to describe: they represented all the passions very lively, but above all, love. I am apt to believe the English language in them arrived to its highest perfection: what words have since been taken in, are rather superfluous than ornamental. Their plays are now the most pleasant and frequent entertainments of the stage; two of theirs being acted through the year for one of Shakspeare's or Jonson's: the reason is, because there is a certain gaiety in their comedies, and pathos in their more serious plays, which suit generally with all men's humours. Shakspeare's language is likewise a little obsolete, and Ben Jonson's wit comes short of theirs.

2. Puns, quibbles.
3. As do cypresses among the bending shrubs (Latin). From Virgil, *Eclogues* 1.125 (37 B.C.E.).
4. John Hales (1584–1656), a fellow of Eton, one of England's most famous endowed boarding schools (founded in 1440).
5. Ben Jonson (1572–1637), English dramatist and poet. John Fletcher (1579–1625), English dramatist who collaborated with Francis Beaumont (1584–1616) on a number of plays from 1606 to 1613 (each also wrote plays on his own).
6. Charles I (1600–1649, reigned 1625–49).
7. English poet and courtier (1609–1642).
8. The epigram "To Francis Beaumont" (1616).
9. Produced in 1608 or 1609.
1. Produced in 1598.
2. That is, a dominating passion or propensity; the phrase "comedy of humours" was applied to Jonson's comic dramas and characters.

"As for Jonson, to whose character I am now arrived, if we look upon him while he was himself (for his last plays were but his dotages),[3] I think him the most learned and judicious writer which any theatre ever had. He was a most severe judge of himself, as well as others. One cannot say he wanted wit, but rather that he was frugal of it. In his works you find little to retrench or alter. Wit, and language, and humour also in some measure, we had before him; but something of art was wanting to the drama till he came. He managed his strength to more advantage than any who preceded him. You seldom find him making love in any of his scenes, or endeavouring to move the passions; his genius was too sullen and saturnine[4] to do it gracefully, especially when he knew he came after those who had performed both to such an height. Humour was his proper sphere; and in that he delighted most to represent mechanic people.[5] He was deeply conversant in the ancients, both Greek and Latin, and he borrowed boldly from them: there is scarce a poet or historian among the Roman authors of those times whom he has not translated in *Sejanus* and *Catiline*.[6] But he has done his robberies so openly, that one may see he fears not to be taxed by any law. He invades authors like a monarch; and what would be theft in other poets is only victory in him. With the spoils of these writers he so represents old Rome to us, in its rites, ceremonies, and customs, that if one of their poets had written either of his tragedies, we had seen less of it than in him. If there was any fault in his language, 'twas that he weaved it too closely and laboriously, in his comedies[7] especially: perhaps, too, he did a little too much Romanise our tongue, leaving the words which he translated almost as much Latin as he found them: wherein, though he learnedly followed their language, he did not enough comply with the idiom of ours. If I would compare him with Shakspeare, I must acknowledge him the more correct poet, but Shakspeare the greater wit. Shakspeare was the Homer, or father of our dramatic poets; Jonson was the Virgil, the pattern of elaborate writing;[8] I admire him, but I love Shakspeare. To conclude of him; as he has given us the most correct plays, so in the precepts which he has laid down in his *Discoveries*,[9] we have as many and profitable rules for perfecting the stage, as any wherewith the French can furnish us."[1]

* * *

1668, 1684

3. Dryden is referring here to such late and mediocre plays as *The New Inn* (1629) and *A Tale of a Tub* (1633).
4. Heavy, melancholy, sullen.
5. Manual workers, artisans.
6. Jonson's two Roman plays, 1603 and 1611.
7. In the first edition of the *Essay*, Dryden wrote "in his serious plays."
8. The *Iliad* and the *Odyssey*, attributed to the Greek poet Homer (ca. 8th c. B.C.E.), provided the model for later epic poetry, and Virgil (70–19 B.C.E.) was highly self-conscious about his relation to his predecessor when he wrote the *Aeneid*, the Roman national epic.
9. Jonson's *Timber, or Discoveries Made upon Men and Matter* (1640) is a series of notes and extracts on writing and other subjects.
1. Most notably in PIERRE CORNEILLE's "Of the Three Unities" (1660; see above).

BARUCH SPINOZA
1632–1677

Modern secularism and postmodern philosophies of immanence are both indebted to the seventeenth-century philosopher Baruch Spinoza. Usually classified (along with his near contemporaries René Descartes and Gottfried Leibniz) as one of the "rationalist" philosophers, Spinoza's stringent monism contests the Cartesian dualisms of body and spirit, subject and object. For Spinoza, God is identified with nature. Rather than existing in some transcendental, heavenly sphere, he dwells within creation—a creation that is rational through and through, and thus comprehensible to humans if their reason is properly exercised. No revelation through sacred scripture is required to apprehend the divine (or the nature of the universe), since reason is adequate to that task. It follows that Spinoza approaches the Bible as one would any other book produced by humans, and that approach has had profound consequences for subsequent theories of interpretation.

Born in Amsterdam, Spinoza was a member of the Marrano community of Jews who had fled the persecutions inflicted on them in Portugal in the early 1600s. (The term *marrano* is derived from an Arabic word meaning "forbidden," or "anathematized.") The Marranos had come to Portugal from Spain after that country expelled its entire Jewish population in 1492. To live in Portugal, these exiles had to convert to Christianity—and Spinoza's parents had been arrested and charged with secretly carrying on Jewish practices. They left Portugal in 1615, eventually making their way to Amsterdam; there, in 1627, they joined a growing Marrano community that was trying to reestablish its traditional religion after a century of disuse. Spinoza spoke Portuguese at home, used Spanish as his primary reading language, studied Hebrew in the religious schools he attended, and spoke Dutch in his encounters with his non-Jewish compatriots. His family was reasonably prosperous, and he received a strict religious education within the tight-knit Marrano community, which was tolerated by but not assimilated into Dutch society. His mother, stepmother, and father had all died by the time Spinoza was twenty-one, and he went into the family's import business with his elder brother.

His business affairs and his intellectual interests had already brought Spinoza into contact with Amsterdam's non-Jewish citizens, especially various radical Protestant sectarians, prior to his (in)famous excommunication from the Jewish community when he was twenty-three. Speculation about the reasons for his banishment has been endless, but there are no extant documents detailing its cause. The text of the 1656 excommunication itself is often quoted: "By decree of the angels and by command of the holy men, we excommunicate, expel, curse and damn Baruch de Espinoza, with the consent of God. . . . We warn that none may contact him orally or in writing, nor do him any favor, nor stay under the same roof with him, nor read any paper he made or wrote." Though the language sounds remarkably harsh, it was in fact standard for such writs and not crafted specifically against Spinoza. More important, such excommunications—which were fairly common (more than one hundred were issued in the seventy years from 1630 to 1700)—were usually temporary, and reprobates could reconcile with the community in various ways. What makes Spinoza's case distinctive is that he left the community, lived the rest of his life among non-Jews, and did not (as far as we know) make any effort at reconciliation.

After his expulsion, Spinoza lived with the radical thinker and bookseller Franciscus van den Enden, from whom he learned Latin, the language he used in all his philosophical writings. By 1658, Spinoza had begun putting down his philosophical thoughts in several pieces that he never finished; these have survived and now form part of his complete works. He had also moved out of Amsterdam to the village of Rijnsburg, after having been attacked on the streets of Amsterdam. There he took up the craft of grinding lenses, which would provide his livelihood for the rest of his life. His first published work, *Principles of Cartesian Philosophy* (1663), already shows him struggling against Cartesian dualism. In this same period, he began work on *Ethics*, the major statement of his full philosophical system. He interrupted work on *Ethics* to write the *Theological-Political Treatise*, a book he apparently thought would persuade (even placate) those who thought him a dangerous radical. He did take the precaution of publishing the book anonymously (in 1670)—and with a false title page in order to protect the printer from prosecution. Spinoza's faith in rational argument was not borne out by the reception to his book: it was roundly condemned even as the secret of its authorship was soon uncovered. But Spinoza was not arrested, and the book itself was not banned until shortly after his death. However, the furor it caused led Spinoza to circulate the finished *Ethics* only among a very limited circle, while providing instructions for its publication after his death.

Even though Spinoza was condemned as a dangerous freethinker and published hardly anything during his lifetime, he was fairly well-known in contemporary philosophical circles in England, France, and Germany, as well as in Holland. Leibniz knew of his work and even made a pilgrimage to visit him; in 1673 the University of Heidelberg offered him a chair in philosophy, which he declined. Spinoza moved to The Hague in 1671, and he died of tuberculosis six years later at the age of forty-four.

As Jonathan Israel among contemporary Spinozists has conclusively shown, in his time Spinoza's monistic identification of God with nature was deemed heretically atheist, pantheist, or both. It stood at the center of the "radical Enlightenment" that developed a thoroughgoing revision of the received Judeo-Christian tradition (especially in its Aristotelian form as developed most fully by THOMAS AQUINAS). Israel's work, along with the debates around the meaning of "secularism" sparked by Charles Taylor's *A Secular Age* (2007), is partially responsible for the heightened interest in Spinoza in our own time. For writers such as GILLES DELEUZE and ANTONIO NEGRI, Spinoza's denial of a transcendent divine—or of any extraterrestrial force or power—has provided an opening toward an alternative metaphysics. Furthermore, Spinoza's denial of mind-body dualism has inspired contemporary neuroscientists, even as his long discussion of the emotions in *Ethics* has been revisited by contemporary theorists interested in affect and the emotions.

Our selection, from the *Theological-Political Treatise*, highlights a different aspect of Spinoza's legacy: his contribution to the theory of interpretation. Broadly speaking, literary criticism as a practice and an academic discipline in the West draws on two sources: the Greco-Roman tradition encapsulated in works by ARISTOTLE, LONGINUS, and HORACE (among others); and the Judeo-Christian tradition articulated by writers such as AUGUSTINE OF HIPPO, MOSES MAIMONIDES, and DANTE ALIGHIERI. Where the classical writers mostly emphasize matters of form, genre, and rhetorical effect, the Judeo-Christian writers are focused on meaning. Their work is concerned with interpretation of the Bible, a sacred text whose import is not immediately manifest. A method of interpretation, a hermeneutics, is required to discern the meaning of biblical passages, which are often understood to be allegorical or symbolic. They claim that the text does not speak straightforwardly, and will yield its meaning only to a skilled (and learned) interpreter, often a scholar or a priest.

Spinoza is clearly in this Judeo-Christian tradition, not only because his primary text to interpret is the Bible but also because he assumes that interpretation is a complex affair. However, the method of interpretation he demonstrates in reading the Bible challenges received orthodox doctrines about the Bible's provenance and meaning. Most provocatively, he denies the long-established claim that Moses is the author of the Pentateuch (the first five books of the Bible). Indeed, he insists that the Bible is the work of human authors, written by them over a period of years. More generally, Spinoza begins what comes to be known as the "historical" interpretation of the Bible, a practice that rests on the insistence that knowing the text's origins, its historical context, and the ways its words were understood in the writer's time are crucial elements for an accurate understanding of its meaning. His approach takes interpretation of the Bible out of the control of religious authorities and hands it over to skilled philologists—scholar-linguists steeped in the history of cultures. Spinoza treats this sacred text as he would any humanly produced work. Hence Spinoza's work is connected to the secularization often deemed characteristic of the move from the Middle Ages into modernity.

Irrespective of the religious controversies in which Spinoza was embedded, his description of how to go about interpreting a text still resonates with the practice of critics concerned that interpretation be accurate. Spinoza emphasizes that readers must not let their preconceived notions influence what they understand the text to be saying. To correctly read a text requires an act of historical imagination, wedded to a scholarly knowledge of historical facts. No special revelation is necessary: our own native abilities as reasoners, as readers, provide us with everything we need to interpret accurately. But Spinoza does not mean (and here he is arguing against the views of Maimonides) that we should assume the text in front of us to be reasonable. We should not impose on the text our view of what makes rational sense: we are trying to discover what its author thought or meant, not what we think. We are not going to be aided by divine revelation, but we need to be using our native reason in a way that curbs its desire to make things plausible or logical according to our present sense of rightness. Instead, we have to learn everything we can about the author, about the context in which he or she was writing, about the status of the language used at the time of writing, and about the prevailing beliefs and accepted knowledge of that time. All of this depends on learning the exact provenance of the text in question. Who wrote it and when? Has it been transmitted to us in its original form—or has it been changed in the process of transmission or through translation? Has its institutional status—as canonical (authorized) or apocryphal (unauthorized)—altered its presentation or its reception? And do we have the philological skills to understand the words deployed, since a language changes over time? The Hebrew that hardly existed as a spoken tongue in seventeenth-century Amsterdam is not the same language that the authors of the Hebrew Bible used.

Spinoza keeps telling us that we can successfully interpret texts, despite the manifold difficulties he identifies. His confidence is rooted in the successes of the science of his time. Just as science uncovers the mysteries of Nature, he tells us, a reason-driven method of interpretation can uncover many mysteries of the Bible. He meant this assurance to be comforting, wildly underestimating the hostility to the idea that a sacred text like the Bible should be treated scientifically, that it should be examined just as we might a body in the anatomy theater. At the same time, he also hedges his historical approach, claiming that the Bible's pronouncements on "moral conduct," presumably because they are held to be universally true for all time, do not pose the same kinds of obstacles to interpretation that the rest of the text does. It does not require scrupulous and scholarly hermeneutics to understand the Bible's moral messages. He sees fairly clearly, in other words, that his historical method implies (at the very least) a kind of relativism against which he needs to guard. Later writers concerned with hermeneutics, such as FRIEDRICH SCHLEIERMACHER and Hans-Georg Gadamer, would struggle with this issue of the extent to which our ability to understand writers from radically different times and cultures is limited by the prejudices that inform our thinking in the present.

Spinoza's compelling description of what is required to engage and understand a text from another era sets the terms of a challenge that literary criticism continually has to face.

Theological-Political Treatise **Keywords**: Authorship, The Canon/Tradition, Enlightenment Theory, Hermeneutics, Interpretation Theory, Language, Modernity, Philology, Religion

From Theological-Political Treatise[1]

Chapter 7. Of the Interpretation of Scripture

On every side we hear men saying that the Bible is the Word of God, teaching mankind true blessedness, or the path to salvation. But the facts are quite at variance with their words, for people in general seem to make no attempt whatsoever to live according to the Bible's teachings. We see that nearly all men parade their own ideas as God's Word, their chief aim being to compel others to think as they do, while using religion as a pretext. We see, I say, that the chief concern of theologians on the whole has been to extort from Holy Scripture their own arbitrarily invented ideas, for which they claim divine authority. In no other field do they display less scruple and greater temerity than in the interpretation of Scripture, the mind of the Holy Spirit, and if while so doing they feel any misgivings, their fear is not that they may be mistaken in their understanding of the Holy Spirit and may stray from the path to salvation, but that others may convict them of error, thus annihilating their personal prestige and bringing them into contempt.

Now if men were really sincere in what they profess with regard to Holy Scripture, they would conduct themselves quite differently; they would not be racked by so much quarrelling and such bitter feuding, and they would not be gripped by this blind and passionate desire to interpret Scripture and to introduce innovations in religion. On the contrary, they would never venture to accept as Scriptural doctrine what was not most clearly taught by Scripture itself. And finally, those sacrilegious persons who have had the hardihood to alter Scripture in several places would have been horrified at the enormity of the crime and would have stayed their impious hands. But ambition and iniquity have reached such a pitch that religion takes the form not so much of obedience to the teachings of the Holy Spirit as of defending what men have invented. Indeed, religion is manifested not in charity but in spreading contention among men and in fostering the bitterest hatred, under the false guise of zeal in God's cause and a burning enthusiasm. To these evils is added superstition, which teaches men to despise reason and Nature, and to admire and venerate only that which is opposed to both. It is therefore not surprising that, to make Scripture appear more wonderful and awe-inspiring, they endeavour to explicate it in such a way that is seems diametrically opposed both to reason and to Nature. So they imagine

1. Translated by Samuel Shirley.

that the most profound mysteries lie hidden in the Bible, and they exhaust themselves in unraveling these absurdities while ignoring other things of value. They ascribe to the Holy Spirit whatever their wild fancies have invented, and devote their utmost strength and enthusiasm to defending it. For human nature is so constituted that what men conceive by pure intellect, they defend only by intellect and reason, whereas the beliefs that spring from the emotions are emotionally defended.

In order to escape from this scene of confusion, to free our minds from the prejudices of theologians and to avoid the hasty acceptance of human fabrications as divine teachings, we must discuss the true method of Scriptural interpretation and examine it in depth; for unless we understand this we cannot know with any certainty what the Bible or the Holy Spirit intends to teach. Now to put it briefly, I hold that the method of interpreting Scripture is no different from the method of interpreting Nature, and is in fact in complete accord with it. For the method of interpreting Nature consists essentially in composing a detailed study of Nature from which, as being the source of our assured data, we can deduce the definitions of the things of Nature. Now in exactly the same way the task of Scriptural interpretation requires us to make a straightforward study of Scripture, and from this, as the source of our fixed data and principles, to deduce by logical inference the meaning of the authors of Scripture. In this way—that is, by allowing no other principles or data for the interpretation of Scripture and study of its contents except those that can be gathered only from Scripture itself and from a historical study of Scripture—steady progress can be made without any danger of error, and one can deal with matters that surpass our understanding with no less confidence than those matters which are known to us by the natural light of reason.

But to establish clearly that this is not merely a sure way, but the only way open to us, and that it accords with the method of interpreting Nature, it should be observed that Scripture frequently treats of matters that cannot be deduced from principles known by the natural light; for it is chiefly made up of historical narratives and revelation. Now an important feature of the historical narratives is the appearance of miracles; that is, as we showed in the previous chapter,[2] stories of unusual occurrences in Nature, adapted to the beliefs and judgment of the historians who recorded them. The revelations, too, were adapted to the beliefs of the prophets, as we showed in chapter 2;[3] and these do, indeed, surpass human understanding. Therefore knowledge of all these things—that is, of almost all the contents of Scripture—must be sought from Scripture alone, just as knowledge of Nature must be sought from Nature itself.

As for the moral doctrines that are also contained in the Bible, although these themselves can be demonstrated from accepted axioms, it cannot be

2. Chapter 6, where Spinoza claims that because God does not contravene natural laws, a miracle must be understood "simply [as] an event whose natural cause we . . . cannot explain by comparison with any other normal event."

3. Spinoza argues that the authors of the various biblical books held the accepted scientific views of their times, though such views would be understood as mistaken by later readers. The Hebrew prophets, who lived from ca. 1000 B.C.E. to ca. 450 B.C.E., were religious leaders of the Jewish people (*prophētēs* in Greek means "advocate") and authors of the "prophetic books" (the books in the Hebrew Bible that bear their names). Among the prominent prophets are Isaiah, Ezekiel, Samuel, and Jeremiah.

proved from such axioms that Scripture teaches these doctrines: this can be established only from Scripture itself. Indeed, if we want to testify, without any prejudgment, to the divinity of Scripture, it must be made evident to us from Scripture alone that it teaches true moral doctrine; for it is on this basis alone that its divinity can be proved. We have shown that the chief characteristic which established the certainty of the prophets was that their minds were directed to what was right and good; hence this must be made evident to us, too, before we can have faith in them. We have already shown that miracles can never give proof of God's divinity, apart from the fact that they could be wrought even by a false prophet. Therefore the divinity of Scripture must be established solely from the fact that it teaches true virtue. Now this can be established only from Scripture. If this could not be done, our acceptance of Scripture and our witness to its divinity would argue great prejudice on our part. Therefore all knowledge of Scripture must be sought from Scripture alone.

Finally, Scripture does not provide us with definitions of the things of which it speaks, any more than Nature does. Therefore, just as definitions of the things of Nature must be inferred from the various operations of Nature, in the same way definitions must be elicited from the various Biblical narratives as they touch on a particular subject. This, then, is the universal rule for the interpretation of Scripture, to ascribe no teaching to Scripture that is not clearly established from studying it closely. What kind of study this should be, and what are the chief topics it should include, must now be explained.

1. It should inform us of the nature and properties of the language in which the Bible was written and which its authors were accustomed to speak. Thus we should be able to investigate, from established linguistic usage, all the possible meanings of any passage. And since all the writers of both the Old and the New Testaments were Hebrews, a study of the Hebrew language must undoubtedly be a prime requisite not only for an understanding of the books of the Old Testament, which were written in that language, but also for the New Testament. For although the latter books were published in other languages,[4] their idiom is Hebraic.

2. The pronouncements made in each book should be assembled and listed under headings, so that we can thus have to hand all the texts that treat of the same subject. Next, we should note all those that are ambiguous or obscure, or that appear to contradict one another. Now here I term a pronouncement obscure or clear according to the degree of difficulty with which the meaning can be elicited from the context, and not according to the degree of difficulty with which its truth can be perceived by reason. For the point at issue is merely the meaning of the texts, not their truth. I would go further: in seeking the meaning of Scripture we should take every precaution against the undue influence, not only of our own prejudices, but of our faculty of reason insofar as that is based on the principles of natural cognition. In order to avoid confusion between true meaning and truth of fact, the former must be sought simply from linguistic usage, or from a process of reasoning that looks to no other basis than Scripture.

4. The 27 books of the New Testament are written in Hellenistic Greek (Koine). Jesus and the apostles are believed to have spoken Aramaic, a Semitic language related to Hebrew.

For further clarification, I shall give an example to illustrate all that I have here said. The sayings of Moses,[5] "God is fire," and "God is jealous," are perfectly clear as long as we attend only to the meanings of the words; and so, in spite of their obscurity from the perspective of truth and reason, I classify these sayings as clear. Indeed, even though their literal meaning is opposed to the natural light of reason, this literal meaning must nevertheless be retained unless it is in clear opposition to the basic principles derived from the study of Scripture. On the other hand, if these statements in their literal interpretation were found to be in contradiction with the basic principles derived from Scripture, they would have to be interpreted differently (that is, metaphorically) even though they were in complete agreement with reason. Therefore the question as to whether Moses did or did not believe that God is fire must in no wise be decided by the rationality or irrationality of the belief, but solely from other pronouncements of Moses. In this particular case, since there are several other instances where Moses clearly tells us that God has no resemblance to visible things in heaven or on the earth or in the water, we must hence conclude that either this statement or all those others must be explained metaphorically. Now since one should depart as little as possible from the literal meaning, we should first enquire whether this single pronouncement, 'God is fire,' admits of any other than a literal meaning; that is, whether the word 'fire' can mean anything other than ordinary natural fire. If the word 'fire' is not found from linguistic usage to have any other meaning, then neither should this statement be interpreted in any other way, however much it is opposed to reason, and all other passages should be made to conform with it, however much they accord with reason. If this, too, should prove impossible on the basis of linguistic usage, then these pronouncements would have to be regarded as irreconcilable, and we should therefore suspend judgment regarding them. However, since the word 'fire' is also used in the sense of anger or jealousy (Job ch. 31 v. 12), Moses' pronouncements are easily reconciled, and we can properly conclude that these two statements, 'God is fire' and 'God is jealous' are one and the same statement.

Again, as Moses clearly teaches that God is jealous and nowhere tells us that God is without passions or emotions, we must evidently conclude that Moses believed this, or at least that he intended to teach this, however strongly we may be convinced that this opinion is contrary to reason. For, as we have shown, it is not permissible for us to manipulate Scripture's meaning to accord with our reason's dictates and our preconceived opinions; all knowledge of the Bible is to be sought from the Bible alone.

3. Finally, our historical study should set forth the circumstances relevant to all the extant books of the prophets, giving the life, character and pursuits of the author of every book, detailing who he was, on what occasion and at what time and for whom and in what language he wrote. Again, it should relate what happened to each book, how it was first received, into whose hands it fell, how many variant versions there were, by whose decision

5. Jewish leader, to whom the first five books of the Hebrew Bible (the Pentateuch) are traditionally attributed; for the sayings, see Deuteronomy 4.24. Theologians still dispute whether Moses is a mythical figure or actually existed (with dates for his life ranging from 1500 B.C.E. to 1300 B.C.E.). Spinoza's denial that Moses is the author of the Pentateuch, a denial based on internal evidence from those five books, is highly unorthodox.

it was received into the canon, and, finally, how all the books, now universally regarded as sacred, were united into a single whole. All these details, I repeat, should be available from a historical study of Scripture; for in order to know which pronouncements were set forth as laws and which as moral teaching, it is important to be acquainted with the life, character and interests of the author. Furthermore, as we have a better understanding of a person's character and temperament, so we can more easily explain his words. Again, to avoid confusing teachings of eternal significance with those which are of only temporary significance or directed only to the benefit of a few, it is also important to know on what occasion, at what period, and for what nation or age all these teachings were written down. Finally, it is important to know the other details we have listed so that, in addition to the authenticity of each book, we may also discover whether or not it may have been contaminated by spurious insertions, whether errors have crept in, and whether these have been corrected by experienced and trustworthy scholars. All this information is needed by us so that we may accept only what is certain and incontrovertible, and not be led by blind impetuosity to take for granted whatever is set before us.

Now when we possess this historical account of Scripture and are firmly resolved not to assert as the indubitable doctrine of the prophets anything that does not follow from this study or cannot be most clearly inferred from it, it will then be time to embark on the task of investigating the meaning of the prophets and the Holy Spirit. But for this task, too, we need a method and order similar to that which we employ in interpreting Nature from the facts presented before us. Now in examining natural phenomena we first of all try to discover those features that are most universal and common to the whole of Nature, to wit, motion-and-rest and the rules and laws governing them which Nature always observes and through which she constantly acts; and then we advance gradually from these to other less universal features. In just the same way we must first seek from our study of Scripture that which is most universal and forms the basis and foundation of all Scripture; in short, that which is commended in Scripture by all the prophets, as doctrine eternal and most profitable for all mankind. For example, that God exists, one alone and omnipotent, who alone should be worshipped, who cares for all, who loves above all others those who worship him and love their neighbours as themselves. These and similar doctrines, I repeat, are taught everywhere in Scripture so clearly and explicitly that no one has ever been in any doubt as to its meaning on these points. But what God is, in what way he sees and provides for all things and similar matters, Scripture does not teach formally, and as eternal doctrine. On the contrary, we have clearly shown that the prophets themselves were not in agreement on these matters, and therefore on topics of this kind we should make no assertion that claims to be the doctrine of the Holy Spirit, even though the natural light of reason may be quite decisive on that point.

Having acquired a proper understanding of this universal doctrine of Scripture, we must then proceed to other matters which are of less universal import but affect our ordinary daily life, and which flow from the universal doctrine like rivulets from their source. Such are all the specific external actions of true virtue which need a particular occasion for their exercise. If there be found in Scripture anything ambiguous or obscure regarding such matters, it must be explained and decided on the basis of the universal doctrine of Scripture. If any passages are found to be in contradiction with one another, we should consider on what occasion, at what time, and for whom they were written. For example, when Christ says, "Blessed are they that mourn, for they shall be comforted,"[6] we do not know from this text what kind of mourners are meant. But as Christ thereafter teaches that we should take thought for nothing save only the kingdom of God and His righteousness, which he commends as the highest good (Matth. ch. 6 v. 33), it follows that by mourners he means only those who mourn for man's disregard of the kingdom of God and His righteousness; for only this can be the cause of mourning for those who love nothing but the kingdom of God, or justice, and utterly despise whatever else fortune has to offer.

So, too, when Christ says, "But if a man strike you on the right cheek, turn to him the left also"[7] and the words that follow, if he were laying this command on judges in the role of lawgiver, this precept would have violated the law of Moses. But he expressly warns against this (Matth. ch. 5 v. 17). Therefore we should consider who said this, to whom, and at what time. This was said by Christ, who was not ordaining laws as a lawgiver, but was expounding his teachings as a teacher, because (as we have already shown) he was intent on improving men's minds rather than their external actions. Further, he spoke these words to men suffering under oppression, living in a corrupt commonwealth where justice was utterly disregarded, a commonwealth whose ruin he saw to be imminent. Now we see that this very same teaching, which Christ here expounds when the ruin of the city was imminent, was also given by Jeremiah[8] in similar circumstances at the first destruction of the city (Lamentations ch. 3 v. 30). Thus it was only at the time of oppression that the prophets taught this doctrine which was nowhere set forth as law; whereas Moses (who did not write at a time of oppression, but—please note—was concerned to found a good commonwealth), although he likewise condemned revenge and hatred against one's neighbour, yet demanded an eye for an eye. Therefore it clearly follows simply on Scriptural grounds that this teaching of Christ and Jeremiah concerning the toleration of injury and total submission to the wicked applies only in situation where justice is disregarded and at times of oppression, but not in a good commonwealth. Indeed, in a good commonwealth where justice is upheld, everyone who wants to be accounted as just has the duty to go before a judge and demand justice for wrongdoing (Lev. ch. 5 v. 1), not out of revenge (Lev. ch. 19 v. 17, 18), but with the purpose of upholding justice and the laws of his country, and to prevent the wicked from rejoicing in their wickedness. All this plainly in accord with the natural reason. I could produce many more similar examples, but I think this is sufficient to explain my meaning and the usefulness of this method, which is my only object at present.

Now up to this point we have confined our investigation to those Scriptural pronouncements which are concerned with moral conduct, and which

6. Matthew 5.6.
7. Matthew 5.39.
8. Jewish prophet (active 626/27–ca. 580 B.C.E.). "The city" is Jerusalem, destroyed by the Babylonians in 586 B.C.E.

can be the more easily elucidated because on such subjects there has never been any real difference of opinion among the writers of the Bible. But other biblical passages which belong only to the field of philosophical speculation do not yield so easily to investigation. The approach is more difficult, for the prophets differed among themselves in matters of philosophical speculation (as we have already shown) and their narratives conform especially to the prejudices of their particular age. So we are debarred from deducing and explaining the meaning of one prophet from some clearer passages in another, unless it is most plainly established that they were of one and the same mind. I shall therefore briefly explain how in such cases we should elicit the meaning of the prophets from the study of Scripture. Here, again, we must begin from considerations of a most general kind, first of all seeking to establish from the clearest Scriptural pronouncements what is prophecy or revelation and what is its essential nature; then what is a miracle, and so on with other subjects of a most general nature. Thereafter we must move on to the beliefs of individual prophets, and from there finally to the meaning of each particular revelation or prophecy, narrative and miracle. We have already pointed out with many apposite examples what great caution we should exercise in these matters to avoid confusing the minds of the prophets and historians with the mind of the Holy Spirit and with factual truth, and so I do not think it necessary to say any more on this subject. But with regard to the meaning of revelation, it should be observed that this method only teaches us how to discover what the prophets really saw or heard, and not what they intended to signify or represent by the symbols in question. The latter we can only guess at, not infer with certainty from the basis of Scripture.

We have thus set out our plan for interpreting Scripture, at the same time demonstrating that this is the only sure road to the discovery of its true meaning. I do indeed admit that those are better informed (if there are any) who are in possession of a sure tradition or true explanation transmitted from the prophets themselves, as the Pharisees[9] claim, or those who have a pontiff whose interpretation of Scripture is infallible, as the Roman Catholics boast. However, as we cannot be sure either of the tradition in question or of the authority of the pontiff, we cannot base any certain conclusion on them. The latter is denied by the earliest Christians, the former by the most ancient sects of the Jews; and if, furthermore, we examine the succession of years (to mention nothing else) through which this tradition is traced right back to Moses, which the Pharisees have accepted from their Rabbis, we shall find that it is incorrect, as I prove elsewhere. Therefore such a tradition should be regarded with the utmost suspicion; and although our method requires us to accept as uncorrupted a certain tradition of the Jews—namely, the meaning of the words of the Hebrew language, which we have accepted from them—we can be quite sure of the one while doubting the other. For while it may occasionally have been in someone's interest to alter the meaning of some passage, it could never

9. Members of a Jewish religious party (ca. 160 B.C.E.–ca. 70 C.E.) who relied on an oral tradition of scriptural interpretation for their understanding of the Bible; their rivals the Sadducees, in contrast, refused to go beyond the written Torah. By comparing the Pharisees to the Roman Catholics and their infallible pope, Spinoza makes clear his distaste for their position.

have been to anyone's interest to change the meaning of a word. Indeed, this is very difficult to accomplish, for whoever would try to change the meaning of a word would also have to explain all the writers who wrote in that language and used that word in its accepted meaning, in each case taking account of the character or intention of the writer; or else he would have to falsify the text, a task requiring much circumspection. Then again, a language is preserved by the learned and unlearned alike, whereas books and the meaning of their contents are preserved only by the learned. Therefore we can readily conceive that the learned may have altered or corrupted the meaning of some passage in a rare book which they had in their possession, but not the meaning of words. Besides which, if anyone should wish to change the customary meaning of a word, he would find it difficult to maintain consistency thereafter both in his writing and in his speaking.

For these and other reasons we may readily assume that it could never have entered anyone's mind to corrupt a language, whereas there may frequently have been an intention to corrupt the meaning of a writer by altering what he wrote or by giving it a wrong interpretation. Therefore, since our method (based on the principle that knowledge of Scripture must be sought only from Scripture) is the only true method, if there is anything that it cannot achieve for us in our pursuit of a complete understanding of Scripture, we must regard this as quite unattainable.

At this point I have to discuss any difficulties and shortcomings in our method which may stand in the way of our acquiring a complete and assured knowledge of the Holy Bible. The first important difficulty in our method is this, that it demands a thorough knowledge of the Hebrew language. Where is this now to be obtained? The men of old who used the Hebrew language have left to posterity no information concerning the basic principles and study of this language. At any rate, we possess nothing at all from them, neither dictionary nor grammar nor textbook on rhetoric. The Hebrew nation has lost all its arts and embellishments (little wonder, in view of the disasters and persecutions it has suffered) and has retained only a few remnants of its language and of its books, few in number. Nearly all the words for fruits, birds, fishes have perished with the passage of time, together with numerous other words. Then again, the meanings of many nouns and verbs occurring in the Bible are either completely unknown or subject to dispute. We are deprived not only of these, but more especially of the knowledge of Hebrew phraseology. The idiom and modes of speech peculiar to the Hebrew nation have almost all been consigned to oblivion by the ravages of time. So we cannot always discover to our satisfaction all the possible meanings which a particular passage can yield from linguistic usage; and there are many passages where the sense is very obscure and quite incomprehensible although the component words have a clearly established meaning.

Besides our inability to present a complete account of the Hebrew language, there is the further problem presented by the composition and nature of that language. This gives rise to so many ambiguities as to render it impossible to devise a method[1] that can teach us with certainty how to

1. That is, impossible for us who are not used to this language and lack a systematic account of its phraseology [Spinoza's note].

discover the true meaning of all Scriptural passages; for apart from the sources of ambiguity that are common to all languages, there are others peculiar to Hebrew which give rise to many ambiguities. These I think it worth listing here.

First, ambiguity and obscurity in the Bible are often caused by the fact that letters involving the same organ of speech are substituted one for another. The Hebrews divide all letters of the alphabet into five classes in accordance with the five oral instruments employed in their pronunciation, namely, the lips, the tongue, the teeth, the palate and the throat. For example, ה, ע, ח, א[2] *alef, ḥet, 'ayin, hē* are called gutturals, and are used one in place of another without any distinction apparent to us. For instance, אל *el*, which means 'to', is often used for על *'al*, which means 'above', and vice-versa. As a result, any parts of a text may often be rendered ambiguous or appear to be meaningless utterances.

A second ambiguity arises from the multiple meanings of conjunctions and adverbs. For example, ו *vav* serves indiscriminately to join and to separate, and can mean 'and', 'but', 'because', 'however' and 'then'. כ *ki* has seven or eight meanings: 'because', 'although', 'if', 'when', 'just as', 'that', 'a burning' and so on. This is the case with almost all particles.

Thirdly—and the source of many ambiguities—verbs in the Indicative mood lack the Present, the Past Imperfect, the Pluperfect and the Future Perfect, and other tenses in common use in other languages. In the Imperative and Infinitive Moods verbs lack all the tenses except the Present, and in the Subjunctive there are no tenses at all. And although all the tenses and moods thus lacking could have been supplied, with ease and even with great elegance, by definite rules deduced from the fundamental principles of language, the writers of old showed complete disregard for such rules, and indiscriminately used Future for Present and Past, and contrariwise Past for Future, and furthermore used Indicative for Imperative and Subjunctive, to the great detriment of clarity.

Besides these three sources of ambiguity in Hebrew there remain two more to be noted, both of which are of far greater importance. First, the Hebrews do not have letters for vowels. Secondly, it was not their custom to punctuate their texts, nor to give them force or emphasis; and although vowels and punctuation thus lacking are usually supplied by points and accents, these cannot satisfy us, having been devised and instituted by men of a later age whose authority should carry no weight with us. The ancient writers did not employ points (that is, vowels and accents), as is abundantly testified; men of later ages added both of these in accordance with their own interpretation of the Bible. Therefore the accents and points that we now have are merely contemporary interpretations, and deserve no more credibility and authority than other commentaries. Those who fail to realise this do not understand the justification of the author of the Epistle to the Hebrews (ch. 11 v. 21) in giving an interpretation of the text of Genesis ch. 47 v. 31 very different from that of the pointed Hebrew text—as if the Apostle ought to have been taught the meaning of Scripture by those who inserted points! In my opinion it is the latter who should be regarded as at

2. Spinoza names these letters from right to left (the normal reading order in Hebrew).

fault. To make this clear to all, and to show how different interpretations arise simply from the absence of vowels, I shall here set down both interpretations.

Those who inserted the points interpreted the passage as follows: 'and to Israel bent over (or, changing ע *'ayin* into א *alef*, a letter of the same organ, towards) the head of the bed.' The author of the Epistle reads 'and Israel bent over the head of his staff,' reading 'mate' for '*mita*', the only difference being in the vowels. Now since in this part of the story there is only a question of Jacob's age, and not of his illness which is mentioned in the next chapter, it seems more probable that the historian intended to say that Jacob bent over the head of his staff (which men of advanced age employ to support themselves), not of the bed; and this is especially so because this interpretation does not require the substitution of one letter for another. Now my purpose in giving this example is not only to harmonise the passage in the Epistle to the Hebrews with the text of Genesis, but also to show how little confidence is to be placed in modern points and accents. Thus he who would interpret Scripture without any prejudice is in duty bound to hold these in doubt and to examine them afresh.

To return to our theme, such being the structure and nature of the Hebrew language, it is quite understandable that such a number of ambiguities must arise that no method can be devised for deciding them all. For we have no grounds for expecting that this can be completely achieved from a comparison of different passages, which we have shown to be the only way to elicit the true meaning from the many senses which a particular passage can yield with linguistic justification. It is only by chance that a comparison of passages can throw light on any particular passage, since no prophets wrote with the deliberate purpose of explaining another's words, or his own. And furthermore, we can draw no conclusion as to the meaning of one prophet or apostle from the meaning of another except in matters of moral conduct, as we have already convincingly demonstrated; no such conclusions can be drawn when they are dealing with philosophical questions, or are narrating miracles or history. I could bring further examples to prove this point, that there are many inexplicable passages in Scripture; but I prefer to leave this subject for the present, and I shall proceed to a consideration of the points that still remain: the further difficulties we encounter in this true method of Scriptural interpretation, or in what way it falls short.

One further difficulty consequent upon this method is this, that it requires an account of the history of all the biblical books, and this for the most part we cannot provide. As I shall make clear at some length at a later stage, we either have no knowledge at all or but doubtful knowledge of the authors—or if you prefer the expression, the writers—of many of the books. Again, we do not even know on what occasion or at what time these books of unknown authorship were written. Furthermore, we do not know into whose hands all these books fell, or in whose copies so many different readings were found, nor yet again whether there were not many other versions in other hands. When I touched on this topic I did make a brief reference to the importance of knowing all these details, but there I deliberately passed over certain considerations which must now be taken up.

If we read a book relating events which are incredible or incomprehensible, or which is written in a very obscure style, and if we do not know the author or the time or the occasion of its composition, it will be vain for us to try to achieve a greater understanding of its true meaning. Deprived of all these facts we cannot possibly know what was, or could have been, the author's intention. But if we are fully informed of these facts, we are in a position to form an opinion free from all danger of mistaken assumptions; that is to say, we ascribe to the author, or to him for whom he wrote, no more and no less than his just meaning, concentrating our attention on what the author could have had in mind, or what the time and the occasion demanded. I imagine that everyone is agreed on this; for it often happens that we read in different books stories that are much alike, and form very different judgments of them according to our opinions of the writers. I remember once having read a book about a man named Orlando Furioso[3] who used to ride a winged monster in the sky, fly over any regions he chose and singlehanded slay huge numbers of men and giants, together with other similar fantastic happenings which are quite incomprehensible in respect to our intellect. Now I had read a similar story in Ovid about Perseus, and another story in the books of Judges and Kings about Samson, who singlehanded and unarmed slew thousands of men, and of Elijah,[4] who flew through the air and finally went to heaven in a chariot and horses of fire. These stories, I repeat, are obviously similar, yet we form a very different judgment of each. The first writer was concerned only to amuse, the second had a political motive, the third a religious motive, and it is nothing else but our opinion of the writers that brings us to make these judgments. It is therefore evident that in the case of obscure or incomprehensible writings, it is essential for us to have some knowledge of the authors if we seek to interpret their writings. And for the same reasons, to choose the correct reading out of the various readings of unclear narratives, we have to know in whose manuscript these different readings are found, and whether there were ever some other versions supported by men of greater authority.

In the case of certain books of the Bible, our method of interpretation involves the further difficulty that we do not possess them in the language in which they were first written. The Gospel according to Matthew and undoubtedly the Epistle to the Hebrews were written in Hebrew, it is commonly held, but are not extant in that form. There is some doubt as to the language in which the Book of Job was written. Ibn Ezra,[5] in his commentaries, asserts that it was translated into Hebrew from another language, and that this is the reason for its obscurity. I say nothing of the apocryphal books,[6] since their authority is of a very different kind.

Such then, is a full account of the difficulties involved in this method of interpreting Scripture from its own history, such as we possess. These difficulties, which I undertook to recount, I consider so grave that I have no hesitation in affirming that in many instances we either do not know the

3. Hero of the epic poem *Orlando Furioso* (published 1532) by Italian poet Ludovico Ariosto.

4. Hebrew prophet (9th c. B.C.E.) whose story is told in 1 Kings 17–19 and 2 Kings 1–2. Ovid (43 B.C.E.–17 C.E.), Roman poet who told the story of the legendary Greek hero Perseus in *Metamorphoses* 4.603–5.249. Samson: legendary Jewish warrior and judge (see Judges 13–16).

5. Abraham ben Meir ibn Ezra (ca. 1090–1167), Spanish poet, scholar, and biblical exegete.

6. Writings not included in authorized or canonical editions of the Bible (e.g., Judith, the Wisdom of Solomon).

true meaning of Scripture or we can do no more than make conjecture. But on the other hand I must again emphasise, with regard to all these difficulties, that they can prevent us from grasping the meaning of the prophets only in matters beyond normal comprehension, which can merely be imagined; it is not true of matters open to intellectual perception, whereof we can readily form a clear conception.[7] For things which of their own nature are readily apprehended can never be so obscurely worded that they are not easily understood; as the proverb says, 'a word to the wise is enough.' Euclid, whose writings are concerned only with things exceedingly simple and perfectly intelligible, is easily made clear by anyone in any language; for in order to grasp his thought and to be assured of his true meaning there is no need to have a thorough knowledge of the language in which he wrote. A superficial and rudimentary knowledge is enough. Nor need we enquire into the author's life, pursuits and character, the language in which he wrote, and for whom and when, nor what happened to his book, nor its different readings, nor how it came to be accepted and by what council. And what we here say of Euclid can be said of all who have written on matters which of their very nature are capable of intellectual apprehension.

Thus we can conclude that, with the help of such a historical study of Scripture as is available to us, we can readily grasp the meanings of its moral doctrines and be certain of their true sense. For the teachings of true piety are expressed in quite ordinary language, and being directed to the generality of people they are therefore straightforward and easy to understand. And since true salvation and blessedness consist in true contentment of mind and we find our true peace only in what we clearly understand, it most evidently follows that we can understand the meaning of Scripture with confidence in matters relating to salvation and necessary to blessedness. Therefore we have no reason to be unduly anxious concerning the other contents of Scripture; for since for the most part they are beyond the grasp of reason and intellect, they belong to the sphere of the curious rather than the profitable.

I consider that I have now displayed the true method of Scriptural interpretation and have sufficiently set forth my opinion on this matter. Furthermore, I have no doubt that it is now obvious to all that this method demands no other light than the natural light of reason. For the nature and virtue of that light consists essentially in this, that by a process of logical deduction that which is hidden is inferred and concluded from what is known, or given as known. This is exactly what our method requires. And although we grant that our method does not suffice to explain with certainty everything that is found in the Bible, this is the consequence not

7. By things comprehensible I mean not only those which can be logically proved but also those which we are wont to accept with moral certainty and to hear without surprise, although they can by no means be proved. Anyone can comprehend Euclid's propositions before they are proved. Similarly, I call comprehensible those narratives, whether of future or past events, that do not exceed human belief, and likewise laws, institutions and customs, although they cannot be proved with mathematical certainty. But mysterious symbols, and narratives that exceed all human belief, I call incomprehensible. Yet even among these there are many that yield to examination by our method, so that we can perceive the author's meaning [Spinoza's note]. Euclid (active ca. 300 B.C.E.), Greek mathematician whose treatise on geometry, the *Elements*, was used as a textbook into the 19th century.

of the defectiveness of the method but of the fact that the path which it tells us is the true and correct one has never been pursued nor trodden by men, and so with the passage of time has become exceedingly difficult and almost impassable. This I imagine is quite clear from the very difficulties I have recounted.

It now remains for me to examine the views of those who disagree with me. The first to be considered is held by those who maintain that the natural light of reason does not have the power to interpret Scripture, and that a supernatural light is absolutely essential for this task. What they mean by this light that is beyond the natural light I leave them to explain. For my own part, I can only surmise that they wish to admit, using rather obscure terminology, that they too are for the most part in doubt as to the true meaning of Scripture; for if we consider their explanations, we find that they contain nothing of the supernatural—indeed, nothing but the merest conjectures. Let them be compared if you please, with the explanations of those who frankly admit that they possess no other light but the natural light. They will be found to be remarkably similar; that is to say, their explanations are human, the fruit of long thought, and elaborately devised. As to their assertions that the natural light is insufficient for this task, that is plainly false, for two reasons. In the first place, we have already proved that the difficulty of interpreting Scripture arises not from the lack of power of the natural light, but from the negligence (not to say malice) of those who failed to compile a historical study of Scripture while that was still possible. Secondly, everyone will admit, I imagine, that this supernatural light is a divine gift granted only to the faithful. Now the prophets and the apostles preached not only to the faithful, but especially to unbelievers and the impious. So their audiences must have been capable of understanding the meaning of the prophets and the apostles; otherwise these latter would have appeared to be preaching to children and babies, not to men endowed with reason. Moses, too, would have ordained his laws in vain if they could have been understood only by the faithful, who stand in no need of law. Therefore those who look to a supernatural light to understand the meaning of the prophets and the apostles are sadly in need of the natural light; and so I can hardly think that such men possess a divine supernatural gift.

1670

APHRA BEHN
1640–1689

In *A Room of One's Own* (1929), VIRGINIA WOOLF writes that "All women together ought to let flowers fall upon the tomb of Aphra Behn, . . . for it was she who earned them the right to speak their minds." Behn was the first Englishwoman to earn a living as a writer. As such, she became the model for the commercial woman writer operating outside the narrow circle of mainstream propriety while trying to gain a place within it. In her critical writing, she reveals the obstacles faced by a woman striving to earn a living in a profession dominated by men. She describes her exclusion from the polite society that would underwrite and support her plays, as well as the different standards applied to her as a woman. Perhaps because of her sex, her literary criticism tells us more about the everyday difficulties faced by practicing dramatists than do the writings of any literary critic of the time. The prefaces to her plays are peopled by theater managers and licensors who threaten to suppress her plays, critics who find them obscene, and audiences who shout them down; there are directors who rewrite her lines and actors who mangle them. Her critical writing, unburdened by the classical university education that was denied to her, undermines the commonplaces of seventeenth-century criticism by setting her practical experience as a playwright against the "rules" of neoclassical orthodoxy articulated by earlier critics such as SIR PHILIP SIDNEY, PIERRE CORNEILLE, and JOHN DRYDEN.

Although the circumstances of Behn's birth remain mired in controversy, she was most probably born Aphra Johnson, and may have been the daughter of Bartholomew Johnson and Elizabeth Denham, baptized in Harbledown outside of Canterbury, England, on December 14, 1640. In her early twenties, Behn went with her family to Suriname (Dutch Guiana), then an English possession, where her father or a relative of her father was nominated to the post of lieutenant-governor. He died en route, but the family settled in Suriname anyway; they remained there until 1664, when England resigned the colony to the Dutch. She describes her life in Suriname in her famous novel *Oroonoko* (1688). On her return to England, she married a city merchant named Behn, a gentleman of Dutch extraction about whom little is known. Her married life was brief: by 1666 her husband was dead, perhaps one of the victims of the plague that swept London in 1665–66, and she was forced to earn a living on her own. In 1666 she was persuaded by Thomas Killegrew, then licensee of the King's Theater, to act as a spy in the second Anglo-Dutch War. But the English government failed to pay even Behn's living expenses while she was in Holland, and she had to borrow money to survive. When she returned to London in 1667, she was imprisoned for failure to pay her debts. Somehow she regained her freedom, and by 1670 she had begun her career as a dramatist with the successful production of *The Forced Marriage* at Lincoln's Inn Fields. She went on to become one of the most prolific writers of the late seventeenth century, surpassed in output only by John Dryden, England's poet laureate.

Behn wrote during the Restoration, which began in 1660 when Charles II returned from exile in France to take the throne after a twenty-year interregnum. The Puritans had closed the theaters at the beginning of the English Civil War, in the early 1640s; the two that now reopened were very different from those of Shakespeare's day, a generation earlier. The most revolutionary change was that women, not boys, played women's roles. The presence of actresses in the Restoration theater undoubtedly enabled Behn to make a successful living writing plays, though women playwrights, like actresses, were never considered quite respectable.

During her career Behn wrote at least eighteen plays, as well as many poems and prose works. In addition she is considered one of the "mothers" of the English novel. Her best and most successful plays were *The Rover* (1677) and *The Lucky Chance* (1687). Though her sex alone was enough to make her a controversial writer, she did not shy away from the political controversies of her day, remaining all her life a staunch royalist. In 1682 she was briefly arrested and charged with "abusive reflections upon persons of quality" for an epilogue she had written chastising the duke of Monmouth, the illegitimate son of Charles II, for his rebellion against his father. She also wrote the first antislavery novel, *Oroonoko,* which was later made into a play by Thomas Southern. On April 16, 1689, Aphra Behn died and was buried in Westminster Abbey—not among the poets in Poets' Corner, but in the cloister. Her epitaph is attributed to her former lover John Hoyle: "Here lies proof that wit can never be / Defence enough against mortality."

Behn's work as a literary critic—which is limited primarily to the prefaces and dedicatory letters she wrote for her plays—falls into two periods, each marked by a sustained piece of critical writing: the "Epistle to the Reader" prefacing her third play, *The Dutch Lover* (1673), and the preface to *The Lucky Chance*, written toward the end of her career. In these two selections we can see the development of Behn's critical attitudes toward the fashionable literary debates of her day, especially those about propriety and decorum in the drama.

The "Epistle to the Reader" was written when Behn was trying to establish a name for herself in the extremely competitive world of the theater. With characteristic acerbic wit, her "Epistle" exposes the elitist underpinnings of late seventeenth-century literary theory. She is the first English critic to reject outright HORACE's platitude that literature must instruct and delight. Most English writers responded to earlier Puritan attacks on the theater by arguing that plays were a means of inculcating morality, but Behn rejects this approach. She argues that poetry—and drama in particular—rarely if ever improves anyone's morality, nor indeed are plays written with such an end in mind. Their purpose is to entertain, and that is the sole measure of their success. Behn's "apology" for her art does not draw on the authority of the classical tradition embodied by venerable critics such as ARISTOTLE and Horace. Unlike Dryden, who in *An Essay of Dramatic Poesy* (1668) charts the evolution of the modern stage from classical antiquity, sprinkling his argument liberally with Latin and Greek quotations, Behn has everything to gain from separating her profession—playwriting—from literary activities that required a university education and knowledge of languages to which she was denied access because of her sex. Stripping away the "Academick frippery" that surrounded the debate over the "musty rules of Unity," she suggests that more important than the structural unity of a play's action, time, and plot is the competence of the actors who perform it. Not preoccupied by the classical defense of poetry, she is able to discuss with scathing honesty the realities of competing in the theatrical world of the late seventeenth century.

Behn's prose style is more difficult than is usual even for a seventeenth-century text. In "Epistle to the Reader," she mimics the philosophically dense and incomprehensible language of fashionable intellectual debate as well as the modish slang of the day. Unable to call on the shared intellectual tradition that shaped the literary criticism of contemporaries like Dryden, Behn's criticism is immersed in the day-to-day culture of the fashionable society she hoped would support her efforts as a writer, and these references sometimes seem obscure to all but historians of the period.

Moving from the bantering wit and dense style of the "Epistle" to the later preface to *The Lucky Chance*, a more orthodox statement about literature and a defense against charges of impropriety, one is struck by the difference in tone and content. Perhaps chastened by her imprisonment, or simply reflecting her position in 1687 as a more successful, less marginalized, dramatist, Behn expresses her desire to "tread in those successful Paths my Predecessors have so long thriv'd in, to take those Measures that both the Ancient and Modern Writers have set me," thus linking herself with the tradition she had rejected in her earlier essay. Nevertheless, Behn still eloquently and forthrightly defends her right to compete as a writer on equal terms with men. She attacks the overt sexual biases and double standards of the criticism of her day that condemned a play simply because of the sex of its author, exposing what the late twentieth-century feminist Mary Ellmann, in *Thinking about Women* (1968), called criticism by sexual analogy. Such criticism treats books by women as if they *were* women, indulging in an "intellectual measuring of busts and hips." In pleading for "my Masculine Part the Poet in me," Behn anticipates the feminist analyses of critics such as SANDRA M. GILBERT and SUSAN GUBAR, who argue that the Western tradition of literature has gendered authorship as a masculine activity, thereby creating, in women, an "anxiety of authorship."

It would be a mistake, however, to make too great a claim for Behn's feminism. Her libertine pose masked a conservative royalist politics and a desire for access to the elite society that excluded her. She saw herself as an exception to the rule of women's exclusion from the profession of writing rather than as a pathbreaker demonstrating the error of that rule. Her outspokenness and her refusal to conform politely to the dictates of modesty and propriety led later generations of critics, like Dr. John Doran, writing in his *Annals of the English Stage* (1864), to dismiss her as "a mere harlot who danced through uncleanness and dared them to follow," but these same qualities have made her a figure of great interest to feminist critics.

***The Dutch Lover* Keywords:** Drama, Enlightenment Theory, Feminist Criticism, Gender, Women's Literature
"Preface to *The Lucky Chance*" Keywords: Drama, Enlightenment Theory, Feminist Criticism, Gender, Women's Literature

From The Dutch Lover

Epistle to the Reader

Good, Sweet, Honey, Sugar-candied
READER[1]

(Which I think is more than any one has call'd you yet.) I must have a word or two with you before you do advance into the Treatise; but 'tis not to beg your pardon for diverting you from your affairs, by such an idle Pamphlet as this is, for I presume you have not much to do, and therefore are to be obliged to me for keeping you from worse imployment, and if you have a better, you may get you gone about your business: but if you will mispend your time, pray lay the fault upon your self; for I have dealt pretty fairly in the matter, and told you in the Title Page what you are to expect within. Indeed, had I hung out a sign of the Immortality of the Soul, of the Mystery of Godliness, or of Ecclesiastical Policie, and then had treated you with Indiscerpibility, and Essential Spissitude (words,[2] which though I am no competent Judge of, for want of Languages, yet I fancy strongly ought to mean just nothing) with a company of Apocryphal midnight tales cull'd out of the choicest insignificant Authors; If I had only prov'd in Folio that *Apollonius*[3] was a naughty Knave, or had presented you with two or three of the worst principles transcrib'd out of the peremptory and ill natur'd, (though prettily ingenious) Doctor of *Malmsbury*[4] undigested, and ill manag'd by

1. In the prefaces to the printed texts of plays, the habit of mocking readers often complemented the mockery of audiences in prologues [except as indicated, all notes are Janet M. Todd's].
2. The habit of confounding the public with difficult words was much mocked.
3. Apollonius is probably Apollonius of Tyana, a Greek philosopher following Pythagoras (6th c. B.C.E.). He was born at the beginning of the Christian era, and to some skeptics such as Charles Blount (and later Voltaire [1694–1778]) he represented a coherent and admirable moral alternative to Christ and his teaching. "In Folio" indicated a full sized sheet of paper or parchment folded only once, therefore a volume of the largest size.
4. Thomas Hobbes (1588–1679), born in Wiltshire, was an influential materialist whose avoidance of Christian concepts provoked much abuse and argument. [Malmsbury: Malmesbury, a town in Wiltshire—editor's note.]

a silly, fancy, ignorant, impertinent,[5] ill educated Chaplain, I were then indeed sufficiently in fault; but having inscrib'd Comedy on the beginning of my Book, you may guess pretty near what peny-worths you are like to have, and ware[6] your money and your time accordingly.

I would not yet be understood to lessen the dignity of Playes, for surely they deserve a place among the middle, if not the better sort of Books, for I have heard that most of that which bears the name of Learning, and which has abused such quantities of Ink and Paper, and continually imploys so many ignorant, unhappy souls for ten, twelve, twenty years in the University[7] (who yet poor wretches think they are doing something all the while) as Logick, &c. and several other things (that shall be nameless, lest I should mispel them) are much more absolutely nothing than the errantest Play that e're was writ. Take notice, Reader, I do not assert this purely upon my own knowledge, but I think I have known it very fully prov'd, both sides being fairly heard, and seen some ingenious opposers of it most abominably baffled in the Argument: Some of which I have got so perfectly by rote, that if this were a proper place for it, I am apt to think myself could almost make it clear; and as I would not undervalue Poetry, so neither am I altogether of their judgement, who believe no wisdom in the world beyond it. I have often heard indeed (and read) how much the World was anciently oblig'd to it for most of that which they call'd Science, which my want of letters makes me less assur'd of than others happily may be: but I have heard some wise men say, that no considerable part of the useful knowledge was this way communicated, and on the other way, that it hath serv'd to propagate so many idle superstitions, as all the benefits it hath or can be guilty of, can never make sufficient amends for, which unaided by the unluckey charms of Poetry, could never have possest a thinking Creature such as man. However true this is, I am my self well able to affirm that none of all our English Poets, and least the Dramatique (so I think you call them) can be justly charg'd with too great reformation of mens minds or manners, and for that I may appeal to general experiment, if those who are the most assiduous Disciples of the Stage, do not make the fondest[8] and the lewdest crew about this Town; for if you should unhappily converse [with] them through the year, you will not find one dram of sence amongst a Club of them, unless you will allow for such a little Link-Boys[9] Ribaldry, thick larded with unseasonable oaths, & impudent defiance of God, and all things serious, and that at such a senceless damn'd unthinking rate, as, if 'twere well distributed, would spoil near half the Apothecaries trade, and save the sober people of the Town the charge of Vomits;[1] And it was smartly said, (how prudently I cannot tell) by a late learned Doctor, who, though himself no great asserter of a Deity, (as you'l believe by that which follows) yet was observed to be continually perswading of this sort of men (if I for once may call them so) of the necessity and truth of our Religion; and being ask'd how he came to bestir himself so much this way, made answer, that it was because their ignorance and indiscreet debauch made them a scandal to the profession of

5. Rude [editor's note].
6. Spend [editor's note].
7. The colleges at Oxford and Cambridge University followed a very traditional curriculum, which Behn more than once criticized [editor's note].
8. Most foolish, most idiotic [editor's note].
9. Boys employed to carry torches to light people through the streets.
1. Purges [editor's note].

Atheism. And for their wisdom and design, I never knew it reach beyond the invention of some notable expedient, for the speedier ridding them of their estate, (a devilish clog to Wit and Parts) than other grouling[2] Mortals know, or battering half a dozen fair new Windows in a Morning after their debauch, whilst the dull unjantee[3] Rascal they belong to is fast asleep. But I'l proceed no farther in their character, because that miracle of Wit (in spight of Academick frippery) the mighty *Echard*[4] hath already done it to my satisfaction; and whoever undertakes a Suppliment to any thing he hath discourst, had better for their reputation be doing nothing.

Besides, this Theam is worn too thread-bare by the whiffling[5] would-be Wits of the Town, and of both the stone-blind-eyes of the Kingdom. And therefore to return to that which I before was speaking of, I will have leave to say that in my judgement the increasing number of our latter Plays have not done much more towards the amending of mens Morals, or their Wit, than hath the frequent Preaching, which this last age hath been pester'd with, (indeed without all Controversie they have done less harm) nor can I once imagine what temptation any one can have to expect it from them: for, sure I am, no Play was ever writ with that design.[6] If you consider Tragedy, you'l find their best of characters unlikely patterns for a wise man to pursue: For he that is the Knight of the Play, no sublunary feats must serve his Dulcinea;[7] for if he can't bestrid the Moon, he'l ne'er make good his business to the end, and if he chance to be offended, he must without considering right or wrong confound all things he meets, and put you half a score likely tall fellows into each pocket; and truly if he come not something near this pitch, I think the Tragedies not worth a farthing; for Playes were certainly intended for the exercising of mens passions, not their understandings, and he is infinitely far from wise, that will bestow one moments private meditation on such things: And as for Comedie, the finest folks you meet with there, are still unfitter for your imitation, for though within a leaf or two of the Prologue, you are told that they are people of Wit, good Humour, good Manners, and all that: yet if the Authors did not kindly add their proper names, you'd never know them by their characters; for whatsoe'er's the matter, it hath happen'd so spightfully in several Playes, which have been prettie well receiv'd of late, that even those persons that were meant to be the ingenious Censors of the Play, have either prov'd the most debauch'd, or most unwittie people in the Companie: nor is this error very lamentable, since as I take it Comedie was never meant, either for a converting or confirming Ordinance:[8] In short, I think a Play the best divertisement[9] that wise men have; but I do also think them nothing so, who do discourse as formallie about the rules of it, as if 'twere the grand affair of

2. Growling [editor's note].
3. Dull, not showy [editor's note].
4. John Eachard mocked the university education of the clergy. [Eachard (1637–1697), college head and satirist—editor's note.]
5. Moving inconstantly, "as if driven by a puff of wind," *Johnson's Dictionary* [published in 1755 by SAMUEL JOHNSON].
6. Throughout the century the stage had been attacked by Puritans as a pernicious influence on the morals of the spectators. Many playwrights including Dryden sought to counter this by urging the ethical and moral base of their work. [JOHN DRYDEN (1631–1700), English playwright, poet, and critic—editor's note.]
7. A reference to Cervantes' *Don Quixote* [1605, 1616], where the hero's beloved is called Dulcinea. Don Quixote was famous for his lofty but unrealisable ideals. ["Sublunary": terrestrial, of this world—editor's note.]
8. Authoritative direction.
9. Entertainment [editor's note].

humane life. This being my opinion of Plays, I studied only to make this as entertaining as I could, which whether I have been successful in, my gentle Reader, you may for your shilling judge.[1] To tell you my thoughts of it, were to little purpose, for were they very ill, you may be sure I would not have expos'd it; nor did I so till I had first consulted most of those who have a reputation for judgement of this kind; who were at least so civil (if not kind) to it as did incourage me to venture it upon the Stage, and in the Press: Nor did I take their single word for it, but us'd their reasons as a confirmation of my own.

Indeed that day 'twas Acted first, there comes me into the Pit, a long, lither, phlegmatick, white, ill-favour'd, wretched Fop,[2] an officer in Masquerade newly transported with a Scarfe & Feather[3] out of *France*, a sorry Animal that has nought else to shield it from the uttermost contempt of all mankind, but that respect which we afford to Rats and Toads, which though we do not well allow to live, yet when considered as a part of God's Creation, we make honourable mention of them. A thing, Reader——but no more of such a Smelt:[4] This thing, I tell ye, opening that which serves it for a mouth, out issued such a noise as this to those that sate about it, that they were to expect a woful Play, God damn him, for it was a womans. Now how this came about I am not sure, but I suppose he brought it piping hot from some, who had with him the reputation of a villanous Wit: for Creatures of his size of sence talk without all imagination, such scraps as they pick up from other folks. I would not for a world be taken arguing with such a propertie as this; but if I thought there were a man of any tolerable parts, who could upon mature deliberation distinguish well his right-hand from his left, and justly state the difference between the number of sixteen and two, yet had this prejudice upon him; I would take a little pains to make him know how much he errs. For waving the examination,[5] why women having equal education with men, were not as capable of knowledge, of whatever sort as well as they: I'l only say as I have touch'd before, that Plays have no great room for that which is mens great advantage over women, that is Learning: We all well know that the immortal *Shakespears* Playes (who was not guilty of much more of this than often falls to womens share)[6] have better pleas'd the World than *Johnsons* works, though by the way 'tis said that *Benjamin* was no such Rabbi neither, for I am inform'd his Learning was but Grammer high;[7] (sufficient indeed to rob poor *Salust*[8] of his

1. Costs of seats in the theatre varied but on the whole the cheapest seats in the gallery went for a shilling. In the pit a seat was about half a crown [i.e., 2½ shillings] and in the boxes four shillings.
2. Lither means lazy or sluggish according to Elisha Coles' *An English Dictionary* (1676); phlegmatic means "full of Phlegme, the cold and moist humour of the body"; a fop is a foolish dandy. [Coles (1640–1680), a schoolmaster who was among the earliest English lexicographers—editor's note.]
3. Military dandyism.
4. A simpleton [editor's note].
5. Refraining from an investigation into [editor's note].
6. Much was made of Shakespeare's lack of university education which allowed him to be a useful predecessor for a female playwright. See Dryden's *An Essay of Dramatic Poesy* (1668): "He was naturally learn'd; he needed not the spectacles of books to read Nature. . . ."
7. In the Restoration Ben Jonson [1572–1637] was the most esteemed of the dramatists writing before the Interregnum. "Grammer high" indicated the level achieved at a grammar school, where learned languages were grammatically taught. ["The Interregnum": 1649–60, the period between Charles I's execution and the Restoration of the monarchy and the accession of Charles II—editor's note.]
8. Sallust (86–34 B.C.E.) was a Roman historian whose works on the Catiline conspiracy [in 63 B.C.E.] provided many plots for English playwrights. Jonson's *Catiline* was performed in 1611.

best Orations) and it hath been observ'd, that they are apt to admire him most confoundedly, who have just such a scantling of it as he had; and I have seen a man the most severe of *Johnsons* Sect,[9] sit with his Hat remov'd less than a hairs breadth from one sullen posture for almost three hours at the Alchymist; who at that excellent Play of *Harry* the Fourth[1] (which yet I hope is far enough from Farce) hath very hardly kept his Doublet whole; but affectation hath always had a greater share both in the actions and discourse of men than truth and judgement have: and for our Modern ones, except our most unimitable Laureat,[2] I dare to say I know of none that write at such a formidable rate, but that a woman may well hope to reach their greatest hights. Then for their musty rules of Unity,[3] and God knows what besides, if they meant any thing, they are enough intelligible, and as practible by a woman; but really methinks they that disturb their heads with any other rules of Playes besides the making them pleasant, and avoiding of scurrility, might much better be imploy'd in studying how to improve mens too too imperfect knowledge of that ancient English Game, which hight long Laurence:[4] And if Comedy should be the Picture of ridiculous mankind, I wonder any one should think it such a sturdy task, whilst we are furnish'd with such precious Originals as him, I lately told you of; if at least that Character do not dwindle into Farce, and so become too mean an entertainment for those persons who are us'd to think. Reader, I have a complaint or two to make to you, and I have done; Know then this Play was hugely injur'd in the Acting, for 'twas done so imperfectly as never any was before, which did more harm to this than it could have done to any of another sort; the Plot being busie (though I think not intricate) and so requiring a continual attention, which being interrupted by the intolerable negligence of some that acted in it, must needs much spoil the beauty on't. My Dutch Lover[5] spoke but little of what I intended for him, but supply'd it with a deal of idle stuff, which I was wholly unacquainted with, till I had heard it first from him; so that Jack-pudding[6] ever us'd to do: which though I knew before, I gave him yet the part, because I knew him so acceptable to most o'th' lighter Periwigs about the Town, and he indeed did vex me so, I could almost be angry: Yet, but Reader, you remember, I suppose, a fusty

9. A reference to those believing in the rules of drama such as Thomas Shadwell [1643–1692], who had had success with *The Sullen Lovers* (1688) and *The Humourists* (1671). In his preface to the printed text of the former he praised the three unities and declared that all playwrights should imitate Jonson in the creation of humour characters, "though none are like to come near; he being the onely person that appears to me to have made perfect Representations of Humane Life."

1. *The Alchemist* by Jonson and *Henry IV* by Shakespeare. The line between proper comedy and farce was frequently drawn. For example in his preface to *An Evening's Love* (1671) Dryden wrote, "Comedy consists . . . of natural actions and characters; . . . Farce . . . of forced humours, and unnatural events."

2. John Dryden became poet laureate in 1668 [editor's note].

3. The three unities of time, place, and action; see above SIR PHILIP SIDNEY, PIERRE CORNEILLE, and Dryden [editor's note].

4. A Long Lawrence was an instrument marked with signs about three inches long like a short ruler or totem with eight sides. Each side had a different set of markings of strokes, zigzags and crosses. A game of chance was played especially at Christmas, each player rolling the Long Lawrence and losing or winning pins or tokens according to which side came up. The term "Lawrence" may have come from the marks, seeming like the bars of a gridiron on which St. Lawrence was martyred. See Alice Bertha Gomme, *The Traditional Games of England, Scotland, and Ireland* (London, 1894).

5. Behn may be referring to the famous comic actor Edward Angel when she blamed the actor playing Haunce [the Dutch Lover] for ad-libbing instead of following her lines.

6. Low-class buffoon [editor's note].

piece of Latine that has past from hand to hand this thousand years they say (and how much longer I can't tell) in favour of the dead.[7] I intended him a habit much more notably ridiculous, which if it can ever be important was so here, for many of the Scenes in the three last Acts depended upon the mistakes of the Colonel for *Haunce*, which the ill-favour'd likeness of their Habits is suppos'd to cause. Lastly, my Epilogue was promis'd me by a Person[8] who had surely made it good, if any, but he failing of his word, deputed one, who has made it as you see, and to make out your penyworth you have it here. The Prologue is by misfortune lost. Now, Reader, I have eas'd my mind of all I had to say, and so sans farther complyment, Adieu.

1673

Preface to *The Lucky Chance*

The little Obligation I have to some of the witty Sparks[1] and Poets of the Town, has put me on a Vindication of this Comedy from those Censures that Malice, and ill Nature have thrown upon it, tho in vain: The Poets I heartily excuse, since there is a sort of Self-Interest in their Malice, which I shou'd rather call a witty Way they have in this Age, of Railing at every thing they find with pain successful, and never to shew good Nature and speak well of any thing; but when they are sure 'tis damn'd, then they afford it that worse Scandal, their Pity. And nothing makes them so throughstitcht an Enemy as a full Third Day,[2] that's Crime enough to load it with all manner of Infamy; and when they can no other way prevail with the Town, they charge it with the old never failing Scandal——That's 'tis not fit for the Ladys: As if (if it were as they falsly give it out) the Ladys were oblig'd to hear Indecencys only from their Pens and Plays; and some of them have ventur'd to treat 'em as Coursely as 'twas possible, without the least Reproach from them; and in some of their most Celebrated Plays have entertained 'em with things, that if I should here strip from their Wit and Occasion that conducts 'em in and makes them proper, their fair Cheeks would perhaps wear a natural Colour[3] at the reading them: yet are never taken Notice of, because a Man writ them, and they may hear that from them they blush at from a Woman——But I make a Challenge to any Person of common Sense and Reason——that is not wilfully bent on ill Nature, and will in spight of Sense wrest a double *Entendre* from every thing, lying upon the Catch for a Jest or a Quibble, like a Rook for a Cully;[4] but any unprejudic'd Person that knows not the Author, to read any of my Comedys

7. The proverb is *De mortuis nil nisi bonum*, Speak well of the dead.
8. Possibly a reference to Edward Ravenscroft with whom Behn was friendly at the time. His failure might have been due to a bout of venereal disease. Ravenscroft wrote the epilogue for Behn's *The Town-Fopp* (1676). [Ravenscroft (ca. 1654–1707), British playwright—editor's note.]
1. Fops, dandies [except as indicated, all subsequent notes are Janet M. Todd's].
2. Good payment from the third night's profits, the traditional recompense for the playwright; through-stitcht: complete, from a stitch that went right through the cloth.
3. A blush rather than cosmetic paint.
4. A card-sharper or a cheat for a victim. ["Quibble": a pun—editor's note.]

and compare 'em with others of this Age, and if they find one Word that can offend the chastest Ear, I will submit to all their peevish Cavills; but Right or Wrong they must be Criminal because a Woman's; condemning them without having the Christian Charity, to examine whether it be guilty or not, with reading, comparing, or thinking; the Ladies taking up any Scandal on Trust from some conceited Sparks, who will in spight of Nature be Wits and *Beaus*; then scatter it for Authentick all over the Town and Court, poysoning of others Judgment with their false Notions, condemning it to worse than Death, Loss of Fame. And to fortifie their Detraction, charge me with all the Plays that have ever been offensive; though I wish with all their Faults I had been the Author of some of those they have honour'd me with.

For the farther Justification of this Play; it being a Comedy of Intrigue, Dr. *Davenant*[5] out of Respect to the Commands he had from Court, to take great Care that no Indecency should be in Plays, sent for it and nicely look't it over, putting out any thing he but imagin'd the Criticks would play with. After that, Sir *Roger L'Estrange*[6] read it and licens'd it, and found no such Faults as 'tis charg'd with: Then Mr. *Killigrew*,[7] who more severe than any, from the strict Order he had, perus'd it with great Circumspection; and lastly the Master Players, who you will I hope in some Measure esteem Judges of Decency and their own Interest, having been so many Years Prentice to the Trade of Judging.

I say, after all these Supervisors the Ladys may be convinc'd, they left nothing that cou'd offend, and the Men of their unjust Reflections on so many Judges of Wit and Decencys. When it happens that I challenge any one, to point me out the least Expression of what some have made their Discourse, they cry, *That Mr.* Leigh[8] *opens his Night Gown, when he comes into the Bride-chamber*; if he do, which is a Jest of his own making, and which I never saw, I hope he has his Cloaths on underneath? And if so, where is the Indecency? I have seen in that admirable Play of *Oedipus*,[9] the Gown open'd wide, and the Man shown in his Drawers and Wastecoat, and never thought it an Offence before. Another crys, *Why we know not what they mean, when the Man takes a Woman off the Stage, and another is thereby cuckolded*; is that any more than you see in the most Celebrated of your Plays? as the *City Politicks*, the *Lady Mayoress*, and the *Old Lawyers Wife*,[1] who goes with a Man she never saw before, and comes out again the joyfull'st Woman alive, for having made her Husband a Cuckold with such Dexterity, and yet I see nothing unnatural nor obscene: 'tis proper for the Characters. So in that lucky Play of the *London Cuckolds*,[2] not to recite Particulars. And in that good Comedy of

5. Charles Davenant (1656–1714), eldest son of Sir William Davenant, who received the patent for the Duke's Company after the Restoration. Charles was co-owner of the United Company, which put on *The Lucky Chance*; he was also an M.P. and helped in the licensing of plays. ["M.P.": member of Parliament—editor's note.]

6. Licenser of published works throughout most of the Restoration and a man much admired by Behn for his propagandist efforts for the royal government [1616–1704].

7. Charles Killigrew (1655–1725), co-owner of the United Company and Master of the Revels. He was responsible for the content of performed plays.

8. Anthony Leigh [d. 1692], the famous comic actor. The offending action is specified in the stage directions.

9. A play of 1678 by Nathaniel Lee and Dryden; in act 2, scene I, Oedipus enters sleepwalking in his shirt. [JOHN DRYDEN (1631–1700), English playwright, poet, and critic—editor's note.]

1. *City Politicks*: John Crowne's Tory play performed in the season of 1682–83. The Lady Mayoress and the Old Lawyers Wife are two characters who make their husbands cuckolds.

2. A popular play of Behn's friend, Edward Ravenscroft, performed in 1681. It has three cuckolds in it.

Sir Courtly Nice,[3] the *Taylor to the young Lady*——in the fam'd Sir *Fopling*, *Dorimont* and *Bellinda*,[4] see the very Words——In *Valentinian*,[5] see the Scene between the *Court Bawds*. And *Valentinian* all loose and rufl'd a Moment after the Rape, and all this you see without scandal, and a thousand others. The *Moor* of *Venice* in many places. The *Maids Tragedy*——see the Scene of undressing the Bride, and between the *King* and *Amintor*, and after between the *King* and *Evadne*[6]——All these I Name as some of the best Plays I know; If I should repeat the Words exprest in these Scenes I mention, I might justly be charg'd with coarse ill Manners, and very little Modesty, and yet they so naturally fall into the places they are design'd for, and so are proper for the Business, that there is not the least Fault to be found with them; though I say those things in any of mine wou'd damn the whole Peice, and alarm the Town. Had I a Day or two's time, as I have scarce so many Hours to write this in (the Play, being all printed off and the Press waiting,) I would sum up all your Beloved Plays, and all the things in them that are past with such Silence by; because written by Men: such Masculine Strokes in me, must not be allow'd. I must conclude those Women (if there be any such) greater Criticks in that sort of Conversation than my self, who find any of that sort of mine, or any thing that can justly be reproach't. But 'tis in vain by dint of Reason or Comparison to convince the obstinate Criticks, whose Business is to find Fault, if not by a loose and gross Imagination to create them, for they must either find the Jest, or make it; and those of this sort fall to my share, they find Faults of another kind for the Men Writers. And this one thing I will venture to say, though against my Nature, because it has a Vanity in it: That had the Plays I have writ come forth under any Mans Name, and never known to have been mine; I appeal to all unbyast Judges of Sense, if they had not said that Person had made as many good Comedies, as any one Man that has writ in our Age; but a Devil on't the Woman damns the Poet.

Ladies, for its further Justification to you, be pleas'd to know, that the first Copy of this Play was read by several Ladys of very great Quality, and unquestioned Fame, and received their most favourable Opinion, not one charging it with the Crime, that some have been pleas'd to find in the Acting. Other Ladys who saw it more than once, whose Quality and Vertue can sufficiently justifie any thing they design to favour, were pleas'd to say, they found an Entertainment in it very far from scandalous; and for the Generality of the Town, I found by my Receipts it was not thought so Criminal. However, that shall not be an Incouragement to me to trouble the Criticks with new Occasion of affronting me, for endeavouring at least to divert;

3. John Crowne's comedy from 1685, *The Taylor to the Young Lady,* uses double entendres in his talk with the young woman and her aunt in act 2, scene 2.

4. Etherege's *Man of Mode; or, Sir Fopling Flutter* (1676). The hero, Dorimant, sleeps with Belinda and then describes the pleasure. [George Etherege (1635–1692), English comic playwright—editor's note.]

5. Edward Hyde, Lord Rochester's 1684 revision of Francis Beaumont (ca. 1584–1616) and John Fletcher's (1579–1625) earliest play, which concerns the rape of Lucina by the emperor Valentinian. Beaumont and Fletcher were younger contemporaries of Shakespeare, known for their popular collaborations [editor's note].

6. *The Maid's Tragedy* was a popular play by Beaumont and Fletcher, revived in the Restoration; in it the King forces a marriage between Amintor and Evadne his mistress and indulges in bawdy remarks about the wedding night and the failure of consummation. The *Moor of Venice*: Shakespeare's *Othello* [1603–04], one of the first plays to be performed on the Restoration stage.

and at this rate, both the few Poets that are left, and the Players who toil in vain, will be weary of their Trade.

I cannot omit to tell you, that a Wit of the Town, a Friend of mine at *Wills* Coffee House,[7] the first Night of the Play, cry'd it down as much as in him lay, who before had read it and assured me he never saw a prettier Comedy. So complaisant one pestilent Wit will be to another, and in the full Cry make his Noise too; but since 'tis to the witty Few I speak, I hope the better Judges will take no Offence, to whom I am oblig'd for better Judgments; and those I hope will be so kind to me, knowing my Conversation not at all addicted to the Indecencys alledged, that I would much less practice it in a Play, that must stand the Test of the censuring World. And I must want common Sense, and all the Degrees of good Manners, renouncing my Fame, all Modesty and Interest for a silly Sawcy fruitless Jest, to make Fools laugh, and Women blush, and wise Men asham'd; My self all the while, if I had been guilty of this Crime charg'd to me, remaining the only stupid, insensible. Is this likely, is this reasonable to be believ'd by any body, but the wilfully blind? All I ask, is the Priviledge for my Masculine Part the Poet in me, (if any such you will allow me) to tread in those successful Paths my Predecessors have so long thriv'd in, to take those Measures that both the Ancient and Modern Writers have set me, and by which they have pleas'd the World so well. If I must not, because of my Sex, have this Freedom, but that you will usurp all to your selves; I lay down my Quill, and you shall hear no more of me, no not so much as to make Comparisons, because I will be kinder to my Brothers of the Pen, than they have been to a defenceless Woman; for I am not content to write for a Third day only. I value Fame as much as if I had been born a *Hero*; and if you rob me of that, I can retire from the ungrateful World, and scorn its fickle Favours.

1687

7. A famous London coffeehouse in Covent Garden kept by Will Unwin.

GIAMBATTISTA VICO
1668–1744

The Italian philosopher Giambattista Vico is noted for his original insights into the origins and development of language and culture. An advocate of a holistic philological approach to the study of society, centered on language, he produced wide-ranging analyses that addressed issues not only in history and sociology but also in jurisprudence, philosophy, theology, politics, rhetoric, and poetics. His most celebrated accomplishment, from the perspective of the twenty-first century, is his monumental *Scienza nuova* (*New Science*), which he issued in three editions (1725, 1730, 1744). Anticipating the developmental theories of G. W. F. HEGEL and KARL MARX, this work presents the now-famous theory of the three periods of social development, which he terms the ages of the gods, heroes, and men. Among the distinctive features of each period are differences in language and literature as well as in government and law.

Vico's Theory of Ideal Eternal History

Three Ages	Three Types of Government	Three Types of Language	Three Types of Jurisprudence
Age of gods	Divine government exercised through auspices and oracle	Wordless (hieroglyphic) language using gestures and physical objects	Mystic theology
Age of heroes	Heroes' government based on presumed natural superiority	Heroic emblems (symbolic language) using similes, metaphors, images, and descriptions of nature	Civil equity
Age of men	Human government through democracies and monarchies	Civilized (epistolary, vernacular) language established by popular convention over which the people are absolute lords	Natural equity

The general sense, as in Hegel and Marx, is that human nature is not absolute but historical, a product of changing social institutions and material configurations. For literary theory, the most important claims of Vico's *New Science* are its arguments for the origin of human society in the prerational poetic nature of human beings and for the primordial status of four "master tropes" of rhetoric: metaphor, synecdoche, metonymy, and irony.

Born in Naples, Vico was the son of a bookseller. He received an education in Scholastic philosophy and in rhetoric from a series of Neapolitan clergymen, becoming proficient in Latin literature. By the age of seventeen, Vico was applying himself to the study of civil and canon (church) law while writing poetry on the side as a pleasant diversion. He became accomplished enough as a poet that for much of his life he was often called on by the aristocracy to write occasional verse for important public events, such as weddings or funerals. He briefly studied law at the University of Naples, but he relied mostly on local tutors and self-education. As a young man, he befriended a group of "modern" intellectuals, known as the Investigators, who critiqued or rejected the authority of the "ancients." Central to this controversial group was the new philosophy of Galileo Galilei (1564–1642), Francis Bacon (1561–1626), and René Descartes (1596–1650), as well as the "alternative" classical views of the Greek philosopher Epicurus (341–270 B.C.E.) and the Roman poet Lucretius (ca. 94–55 B.C.E.). Reflecting the widespread intellectual changes in Europe that have come to be known as the Enlightenment, the group was largely concerned with putting science and philosophy on a rational and empirical foundation.

In 1699 Vico became professor of rhetoric at the University of Naples, a position he held for more than forty years. His early annual orations, now available in *On Humanistic Education* (1993), address the proper methods and functions of education. During this time he joined the Palatine Academy, an eclectic group of modern intellectuals committed to the emerging values of the Enlightenment. As befitted his education and intellectual associations, Vico was interested in a wide variety of subjects, including the physical sciences and mathematics. In 1710 he published his first major work, *De antiquissima Italorum sapientia* (*On the Most Ancient Wisdom of the Italians*), which attempts to reconstruct the nonrationalistic philosophy of a pre-Roman civilization via the etymological study of Latin words. Here and in his other works, Vico strove to be a persuasive philologist, as he studied cultures and their histories through languages, especially etymologies. His philological work was not valued in his own time, but it was later admired by such leading twentieth-century critics as ERICH AUERBACH and EDWARD W. SAID. Vico's next important publication, *Il diritto universale* (1720–22, *Universal Right*), focused on the historical origin and development of jurisprudence. In chronological order, it traced the emergence of different types of society, identifying a particular form of law with each while also making important links to various linguistic, literary, and religious forms. Later, at the invitation of a nobleman, Vico also published his autobiography (1725–28), the first modern example of its kind.

In 1725 Vico published the first edition of his *New Science*. As a study of the nonrationalistic origins and historical development of "pagan" (pre-Christian, non-Jewish) societies, it strongly resembles the two major works that preceded it. He considered the *New Science* his most important work, which would reveal the underlying order in the diversity of the pagan nations just as Isaac Newton's *Principia Mathematica* (1687) had unveiled the eternal laws of nature. Vico was deeply disappointed by the book's reception, however, which tended to be unfavorable when not indifferent. Feeling misunderstood and unacknowledged, he described himself as "a foreigner in his own country." In 1735 he was appointed the official historian to Charles Bourbon, then king of Naples and Sicily, but he remained primarily concerned with revising his *New Science*. He published a second edition in 1730 and prepared a third, which appeared shortly after his death in 1744.

Our selections, taken from the third edition, begin with Vico's discussion of the historical stages that pagan nations have traversed. Comparing the various ancient histories of the Egyptians, Chaldeans, Scythians, Phoenicians, Greeks, and Romans, he reveals an underlying universal pattern—the expression of a divine providence working in the world, reducing multiplicity to order. The necessary course (*corso*) that the nations must run passes through the ages of the gods, heroes, and men. Each age is characterized by a particular kind of nature, custom, jurisprudence, government, and language. A distinctive feature of Vico's sequence of ages—unlike the classical movement from golden to iron age—is its susceptibility to what he calls a "recourse" (*ricorso*) or recurrence, which suggests that a nation may retraverse a previous stage or all three.

One of Vico's main concerns is the poetic nature of the first human beings in the age of the gods, the "master key" of his science. As he explains it, the first human beings apprehended the world in a "poetic" manner. With vigorous imaginations and robust senses, but feeble powers of reasoning, they responded to their unknown world with passionate fear and wonder, creating sublime images of nature. In this regard, Vico's portrait of the early poets is different from LONGINUS's classical theory of sublimity, locating the sources of great writing in the lack of rationality rather than in individual genius. A bit later, Jean-Jacques Rousseau (1712–1778) would make a similar argument about the origin of languages. The point, for Vico, is that the poetic nature of the first human beings inaugurated their world. In support of this view, he notes that the first poets anthropomorphized nature and accounted for the unknown in human and metaphorical terms. Vico's famous examples include the "primitive" human response to the terror of lighting and thunder, as well as the mythical belief in the ancient existence of giants. While the former led to the imaginative creation of an angry sky god, Jupiter, the latter illustrates the etymological origin of Roman nobles, derived from the Greek and Latin words for indigenous people (*autochthones* and *indigenae*).

Vico suggests that the religions—as well as the logic, morals, economics, politics, physics, cosmography, astronomy, geography, and history—of the pagan nations are rooted in poetic and rhetorical responses to nature. In some sense the foundations of civil society can be said to reside in the modifications of the minds and institutions of human beings. But such modifications are not so much analytical or rational as they are poetic or, more precisely, rhetorical. Metaphor, synecdoche, metonymy, and irony, Vico's four master figures, shape human beings' apprehension of the world.

Vico's thought exerted significant influence on nineteenth- and twentieth-century cultural theorists. Karl Marx refers approvingly to Vico's fundamentally historical understanding of human nature in a famous footnote to *Capital* (1867), and the critique of dominant Enlightenment forms of rationalism built into Vico's poetic and rhetorical theory of culture has inspired critics of modernity such as Isaiah Berlin. (In this latter regard, Vico's work bears comparison with MARTIN HEIDEGGER's later theories of poetry: both thinkers assign poetry a fundamental role in world building.) Many contemporary theorists would reject Vico's totalizing idea of "ideal eternal history" as well as the privileged position of Christianity in his providentialist historiography. However, Edward W. Said credits Vico as a major influence who offers a corrective of Western tendencies to devalue the Orient. According to Said, Vico stresses the organic interconnectedness of all cultures (Eastern and Western) and makes the important point that humans create their own knowledge and history. Finally, Vico pioneers the concern with rhetorical tropes as foundational to human life developed by such twentieth-century thinkers as ROMAN JAKOBSON, HAYDEN WHITE, PAUL DE MAN, and HAROLD BLOOM, a great admirer of Vichian poetics.

***New Science* Keywords:** Enlightenment Theory, Language, Literary History, Philology, Poetry, Religion, Rhetoric, Vernacular Language

From New Science[1]

* * *

[31] Thus, by studying the common nature of nations in the light of divine providence, my *New Science*, or new metaphysics, discovers the origins of divine and human institutions in the pagan nations.[2] And on the basis of these origins, my Science establishes a system of the natural law of the nations, which progresses with great regularity and consistency in all three ages through which the Egyptians said they had passed in the entire course of world history. These three ages are the following:

(1) The age of the gods, when the pagan peoples believed that they were living under divine government, and that all their actions were commanded by auspices[3] and oracles, which are the most ancient institutions in secular history.

(2) The age of the heroes, when heroes ruled everywhere in aristocratic states by virtue of their presumed natural superiority to the plebeians.

(3) And finally, the age of men, when all recognized their equality in human nature, so that they first established democracies and later monarchies, which are the two forms of human government.

1. Translated by David Marsh.
2. Heathen peoples; pre-Christian non-Hebrew gentile societies.
3. Those who prophesy from the flight of birds.

[32] Corresponding to these three types of nature and government, three kinds of language were spoken, which constitute the lexicon of my New Science:

(1) The first dates from the age of families when pagan peoples had just embraced civilization. We find that it was a mute or wordless language which used gestures or physical objects bearing a natural relationship to the ideas they wanted to signify.

(2) The second language used heroic emblems—such as similes, comparisons, images, metaphors, and descriptions of nature—as the principal lexicon of its heroic language, which was spoken in the age when heroes ruled.

(3) The third language was the human or civilized language which used vocabulary agreed on by popular convention, and of which the people are the absolute lords. This language is proper to democracies and monarchies, for in those states it is the people who determine the meaning of the laws, which are binding for nobles and plebeians alike. Hence, once the laws of any nation are written in the common speech, knowledge of them is no longer in the hands of the nobility. Previously, the nobles of every nation, who were also priests, kept their laws in a secret language like a sacred object. This is the natural reason for the secrecy in which the Roman patricians kept their laws before popular liberty was established.

These are precisely the three languages which the Egyptians said had been spoken earlier in their world, corresponding exactly in both number and order to the three ages through which their world had passed:

(1) The first was the *hieroglyphic* language, a sacred and secret language using mute gestures, as befits religions, in which observance is more important than speech.

(2) The second was the *symbolic* language using resemblances, like the heroic language I have just described.

(3) Finally, the third was the *epistolary* or vernacular language, which was used for the common business of everyday life. These three kinds of language were found among the Chaldaeans, Scythians, Egyptians, Germanic peoples, and all the other nations of pagan antiquity. (Hieroglyphic writing persisted later among the Egyptians simply because they were closed to foreign nations longer, which also explains why the Chinese still use ideograms. But the use of hieroglyphics by other nations proves that the Egyptians' presumption of their own remote antiquity is groundless.)

[33] My Science sheds light on the origins of both languages and letters, which were previously the despair of historians and philologists,[4] whose bizarre and grotesque opinions I shall review. The unfortunate reason for their error is obvious: they simply assumed that nations developed languages first, and then letters. Yet languages and letters were born as twins and developed at the same pace through all three kinds. We find precise evidence for such origins in the stages of the Latin language which I discovered in the first edition of my *New Science*. (Earlier, I remarked that this work contains three sections which I do not regret writing; this is the second of them.) This evidence has offered me many discoveries about the history, government, and law of the ancient Romans, as the reader will find in countless passages of

4. Those who study culture and its history through languages, especially through historical and comparative linguistics.

the present work. Following my example, scholars of Oriental languages, of Greek, and especially of German among the modern languages, which is a mother tongue, will be able to make discoveries about antiquities that surpass their expectations and mine.

[34] In seeking the basic principle of the common origins of languages and letters, we find that the first peoples of pagan antiquity were, by a demonstrable necessity of their nature, *poets* who spoke by means of *poetic symbols*. This discovery provides the master key of my New Science, but making it has cost me nearly an entire scholarly career spent in tireless researches. For to our more civilized natures, the poetic nature of the first people is utterly impossible to imagine, and can be understood only with the greatest effort. Their symbols were certain *imaginative general categories*, or archetypes. These were largely images of animate beings, such as gods and heroes, which they formed in their imagination, and to which they assigned all the specifics and particulars comprised by each generic category. (In precisely this way, the myths of civilized ages, such as the plots of the New Comedy,[5] are rational archetypes derived from moral philosophy; and from these myths, our comic poets create in their characters these imaginative archetypes, which are simply the most complete ideas of human types in each genre.) We find, then, that the divine and heroic symbols were true myths, or true mythical speech. And we discover that, in describing the early age of the Greek peoples, the meaning of their allegories is based on identity rather than analogy, and is thus historical rather than philosophical.

These archetypes—which is what myths are in essence—were created by people endowed with vigorous imaginations but feeble powers of reasoning. So they prove to be true poetic statements, which are feelings clothed in powerful passions, and thus filled with sublimity and arousing wonder. We further find that poetic expression springs from two sources: the poverty of language, and the need to explain and be understood. This engendered the vividness of heroic speech, which was the direct successor of the mute language of the divine age, which had conveyed ideas through gestures and objects naturally related to them. Eventually, following the inevitable natural course of human institutions, the Assyrians, Syrians, Phoenicians, Egyptians, Greeks, and Romans developed languages, which began with heroic verse, then passed to iambics,[6] and finally ended in prose. This progression is confirmed by the history of ancient poetry. And it explains why we find so many natural versifiers are born in German-speaking lands, particularly in the peasant region of Silesia; and why the first authors in Spanish, French, and Italian wrote in verse.

[35] From these three languages, we may derive a conceptual dictionary, which properly defines words in all the different articulate languages. In this work, I shall refer, when necessary, to this dictionary, of which the reader will find a detailed sample in the first edition of my Science. In that passage, I studied the timeless attributes of the fathers who lived in the age when lan-

5. A genre of Greek drama from about 320 B.C.E. to the mid-3d century B.C.E. that offers a mildly satiric view of contemporary Athenian society, focusing especially on family life.

6. Poetic metrical feet (each composed of a short and a long syllable) that approximate the rhythm of conversation. "Heroic verse": the formal dactylic hexameter (a 6-foot line, based on the syllable pattern long-short-short) of Greek and Latin epic.

guages were formed, both in the state of families and in the first heroic cities. Then, in fifteen different languages, both living and dead, I derived proper definitions of the words for father, which varied according to their different attributes. (Of the three sections in that edition which satisfy me, this is the third.) This lexicon proves necessary if we are to learn the language of the ideal eternal history through which the histories of all nations in time pass. And it is necessary if we are to be scientific in citing authorities that confirm our observations about the natural law of nations, and about particular kinds of jurisprudence.

[36] There were, then, *three* languages, proper to *three* ages in which *three* kinds of government ruled, conforming to *three* kinds of civil natures, which change as nations follow their course. And we find that these languages were accompanied by an appropriate kind of jurisprudence, which in each age followed the same order.[7]

* * *

[51] We have reviewed the vain opinions held by the pagan nations, and especially the Egyptians, concerning their own antiquity as a necessary preamble to all our knowledge of the pagan world. We proceed in two ways: (1) by seeking to determine methodically this important starting-point, the precise time and place in which pagan civilization began in the world; and (2) by seeking to offer human reasons to support our Christian faith. (This faith begins from the truth that the first people in the world were the Jews, descended from Adam, who was created by the true God at the world's creation.) Accordingly, the first science we must study is mythology, meaning the interpretation of myths: for all pagan histories have mythical origins, and the myths of the pagan nations were their first histories. By applying this method, we shall discover the beginnings of the sciences as well as of the nations: for the sciences could only arise within nations that were already formed. Throughout my New Science, I show that the sciences sprang from institutions necessary or useful to humankind, which were later perfected as ingenious individuals refined them. This must be the starting-point of universal history, whose origins and principles were previously lacking, as all scholars agree.

* * *

[331] Still, in the dense and dark night which envelops remotest antiquity, there shines an eternal and inextinguishable light. It is a truth which cannot be doubted: *The civil world*[8] *is certainly the creation of humankind.* And consequently, the principles of the civil world can and must be discovered *within the modifications of the human mind.* If we reflect on this, we can only wonder why all the philosophers have so earnestly pursued a knowledge of the world of nature, which only God can know as its creator, while they neglected to study the world of nations, or civil world, which people can in fact know because they created it. The cause of this paradox

7. The three types of jurisprudence are mystic theology, civil equity (reason of state), and natural equity.

8. The totality of institutions constituting pagan human societies governed by law.

is that infirmity of the human mind noted in Axiom 63.[9] Because it is buried deep within the body, the human mind naturally tends to notice what is corporeal, and must make a great and laborious effort to understand itself, just as the eye sees all external objects, but needs a mirror to see itself.

* * *

[342] In its first principal aspect, then, my New Science must be a *rational civil theology of divine providence*, which was previously lacking in philosophy. For some philosophers were completely unaware of the existence of providence. The Epicureans[1] said that human affairs are set in motion by the blind collision of atoms; and the Stoics[2] said they are drawn along by an inexorable chain of causes and effects. And other philosophers merely considered providence within the order of natural things, calling their metaphysics a 'natural theology'. While contemplating the providential aspect of God, they confirmed its existence through the physical order of nature, which they observed in the motions of physical bodies like the spheres and the elements, as well as in the final cause revealed in lesser natural phenomena.

By contrast, the philosophers should have discussed providence as revealed in the economy of civil institutions. This is clear from the proper meaning of the word 'divinity', which was applied to providence. This noun derives from the Latin verb *divinari*, to divine: in other words, to understand either what is hidden from men, meaning the future, or what is hidden within them, meaning their conscience. Properly speaking, then, divinatory providence is the first and principal part of the subject of jurisprudence, or divine institutions; while the second and complementary part of jurisprudence, or human institutions, must derive from divinatory institutions. My New Science is therefore a demonstration, as it were, of *providence as historical fact*. That is, it must provide a history of the orders and institutions which providence bestowed on the great polity of humankind without the knowledge or advice of humankind, and often contrary to human planning. For although by its creation our world is temporal and particular, the orders which providence establishes in it are universal and eternal.

* * *

[349] Thus, my New Science also traces the *ideal eternal history* through which the history of every nation passes in time; and it follows each nation in its birth, growth, maturity, decline, and fall. Now, according to the first irrefutable principle stated above, the world of nations is clearly a human creation, and its nature reflected in the human mind. Hence, I would venture to say that anyone who studies my Science will retrace this ideal eternal history for himself, recreating it by the criterion that it *had to, has to, and will have to* be so. For there can be no more certain history than that which is recounted

9. Vico's notion of axioms, which form the base of his philosophical system developed across *New Science*, is not derived wholly through pure reasoning; it is rooted in probability and circumstance. Axiom 63 states, "Because of the senses, the human mind naturally tends to view itself externally in the body, and it is only with great difficulty that it can understand itself by means of reflection. This axiom offers us this universal principle of etymology in all languages: words are transferred from physical objects and their properties to signify what is conceptual and spiritual." In subsequent references to his axioms, Vico contextualizes and defines their meaning.

1. Followers of the Greek philosopher Epicurus (341–270 B.C.E.).

2. Followers of the Greek philosopher Zeno (335–263 B.C.E.).

by its creator. In this way, my Science proceeds like geometry which, by constructing and contemplating its basic elements, creates its own world of measurable quantities. So does my Science, but with greater reality, just as the orders of human affairs are more real than points, lines, surfaces, and figures. This is an indication that my proofs are divine and should afford my reader something like divine pleasure. For in God knowledge and creation are the same thing.

* * *

[361] In the axioms, we established that all the histories of the pagan nations had mythical origins; that among the Greeks, who are the source of all our knowledge of pagan antiquity, the first wise men were theological poets; and that all temporal institutions by nature have crude origins. When we turn to poetic wisdom, we must regard its origins in the same light. Poetic wisdom has come down to us exalted by a supreme and sovereign esteem which springs both from the conceit of the nations and, to a greater extent, from the conceit of scholars.[3] For it was the conceit of scholars that led the Egyptian high priest Manetho[4] to convert all of Egypt's mythical history into a sublime natural theology, as Axiom 55 states, just as it led the Greeks to convert their myths into philosophy. These two peoples did this not only because they had both inherited extremely filthy stories, as Axiom 54 states, but also for the five following reasons.

[362] The first reason was their reverence for religion, for it was by their myths that the pagan nations were everywhere founded on the basis of religion. The second was the great effect of their religion, namely the civil world, which is so wisely ordered that it can only be the result of superhuman wisdom. The third reason was the opportunity which their myths, bolstered by a religious veneration and believed to contain great wisdom, offered the philosophers for investigating and pondering lofty philosophical topics, as we shall see later. The fourth reason was the facility with which philosophers could express their sublime philosophical meditations in language they happily inherited from the poets. The fifth and final reason, which stands for all the others, was that the philosophers could confirm their theories by appealing to the authority of religion and the wisdom of the poets. Of these five reasons, the first two inspired the praise which the philosophers, even in their error, bestowed on divine providence for ordering the world of nations; while by the fifth they bore witness to this same providence. The third and fourth reasons are illusions which divine providence tolerated so that philosophers could understand and recognize providence for what it truly is, an attribute of the true God.

[363] Throughout this work, I shall show that everything that the poets sensed in their popular wisdom was later understood by the philosophers in their esoteric wisdom. We may say, then, that the poets were the *sense* of

3. Conceits are forms of excessively high regard for one's own worth or virtue. Among nations conceit is demonstrated by the claim of nearly every pagan nation to have been the origin of civilization; among scholars it is manifested in the attribution of one's own knowledge and wisdom to various kinds of ancient writings.

4. Egyptian priest and historian (active ca. 280 B.C.E.); his *History of Egypt*, which covered rulers from mythical times to 323, became the basis of our conventional numbering of dynasties.

mankind, and the philosophers its *intellect*. Thus, what Aristotle[5] said in particular about the individual is also true in general about humankind: 'Nothing is found in the intellect which was not found first in the senses', *Nihil est in intellectu quin prius fuerit in sensu*. This means that the human mind can only understand a thing after the senses have furnished an impression of it, which is what today's metaphysicians call an occasion. For the mind uses the intellect whenever it 'gathers' something insensible from a sense impression, and this act of gathering is the proper meaning of the Latin verb *intelligere*, to understand.

[364] Before discussing poetic wisdom, we must consider what wisdom is in general. Wisdom is the faculty governing all the disciplines that teach the arts and sciences which perfect our humanity. Plato[6] defines wisdom as the perfecter of humankind. People essentially consist of mind and spirit, or (we may say) of intellect and will. Wisdom must perfect both these parts, beginning with the intellect. For once the mind is illuminated by a knowledge of what is highest, it will lead the spirit to choose what is best. The highest institutions in the universe are those we call divine, because they turn our reason and understanding towards God. The best institutions are those we call human, because they serve the well-being of the entire human race. Hence, true wisdom must teach us the knowledge of divine institutions in order to direct human institutions towards the highest good. Indeed, I believe that Marcus Terentius Varro,[7] who deserved to be called 'the most learned of the Romans', followed this two-part plan in constructing his *Divine and Human Institutions*, a great work which we have regrettably lost through the injustice of time. In my Science, I shall discuss these same topics as best I can, given the imperfections of my learning and the poverty of my erudition.

[365] Among the pagans, wisdom began with the Muse, whom Homer,[8] in a golden passage of the *Odyssey*, defines as the knowledge of good and evil, or what was later called divination. (By contrast, God founded the true religion of the Jews—from which Christianity arose—on the natural prohibition of divination, which is naturally denied to people, as Axiom 24 states.) At first, the Muse must properly have been the science of divining by the auspices, which was the popular wisdom of all nations. This popular wisdom contemplated God in the attribute of His providence, so that from *divinari*, to divine, His essence was called divinity. And we shall soon see that the theological poets, who clearly founded the civilization of Greece, were experts in this wisdom, which is why the Romans called judicial astrologers 'professors of wisdom'. Next, wisdom was ascribed to people who were famous for the useful counsels they gave to humankind: hence the so-called Seven Sages, or Wise Men, of Greece.[9] Later, wisdom was broadened to include people who wisely ordered and governed commonwealths for the good of their peoples and nations. Still later, the term was extended to the knowledge

5. Greek philosopher (384–322 B.C.E.; see above); the reference is to *On the Soul* 3.8, 432a.
6. Greek philosopher (ca. 427–ca. 347 B.C.E.; see above).
7. Roman scholar (116–27 B.C.E.).
8. Greek epic poet (ca. 8th c. B.C.E.). Homer's *Iliad* begins "Sing, Muse, . . ."
9. Seven statesmen and thinkers of the early 5th century B.C.E., credited with formulating pithy aphorisms (e.g., "Know thyself"; "Avoid extremes"). Plato (*Protagoras* 343a) names them as Solon of Athens, Chilon of Sparta, Thales of Miletus, Bias of Priene, Cleobulus of Lindus, Pittacus of Mitylene, and Myson of Chen.

of divine things in nature, or metaphysics, which is accordingly called a divine science. (In seeking to know man's mind in God, metaphysics recognizes God as the source of all truth, and hence as the regulator of all good. Thus, metaphysics essentially serves the good of the human race, whose survival depends on its universal belief in the *provident* nature of divinity. Plato perhaps deserved to be called divine because he demonstrated this providence. By contrast, any doctrine which denies the providential aspect of God should be called folly rather than wisdom.) Finally, among the Jews and then among us Christians, the knowledge of the eternal things revealed by God was called wisdom. Perhaps because they regarded such wisdom as the knowledge of true good and true evil, the early Tuscans called it 'science in divinity'.

[366] We must, then, distinguish three kinds of theology: (1) poetic theology, which was proper to the theological poets, and was the civil theology of all the pagan nations; (2) natural theology, which is proper to the metaphysicians; and (3) our Christian theology, which combines civil and natural theology with the highest revealed theology. (This division is truer than the one proposed by Varro, who regarded poetic theology as the third kind. In fact, the poetic theology of the pagans was the same as their civil theology. But since Varro was misled by the common error that the myths contained profound mysteries of sublime philosophy, he thought that poetic theology combined both the civil and natural kinds.) All three kinds of theology are connected by their contemplation of divine providence, and in fact divine providence directed human institutions so that poetic and natural theology prepared the nations for revealed theology. For poetic theology governed them through certain sensible signs, which they believed to be divine counsels sent by the gods to humankind; while natural theology demonstrates providence by eternal and insensible arguments. Hence, these two disposed the nations to accept revealed theology by virtue of a supernatural faith, which is superior not only to our senses but to human reason itself.

[367] Our discussion of poetic wisdom starts from the following three propositions. (1) Metaphysics is the sublime science which assigns specific subjects to the sciences we call subordinate. (2) The wisdom of the ancients was that of the theological poets, who were undoubtedly the first wise men of the pagan world, as Axiom 44 states. (3) And by nature all things must have crude origins. These three propositions lead us to trace the beginnings of poetic wisdom to a crude metaphysics, from which various sciences branch out as if from a tree trunk. On one side, we find the branches of logic, ethics, economics, and politics, which are all poetic sciences. On the other, we find further poetic sciences: physics, with her daughters cosmography and astronomy; and astronomy's two daughters, chronology and geography, whom she endows with certainty.

With these sciences in mind, I shall trace clearly and distinctly how the founders of pagan civilization used their poetic wisdom. We shall see how they used their natural theology or metaphysics to imagine the gods; their logic to invent languages; their ethics to create heroes; their household economy to found families; and their politics to found cities. We shall see how they used their physics to establish the divine principles of all things; their human physiology to create themselves, in a certain sense;

their cosmography to envision a universe of gods; and their astronomy to transfer planets and constellations from the earth to the heavens. And we shall see how they used their chronology to establish the starting-point of time reckoning; and how the Greeks, to cite one example, used their geography to describe the entire world within their own homeland.

[368] In this way, my New Science simultaneously offers a *history of the ideas, customs, and deeds of humankind*. From these three topics, we shall derive the principles of the history of human nature, which are the principles of universal history that we previously seemed to lack.

[369] The founders of pagan antiquity must have descended from the races of Ham, Japheth, and Shem, who one by one gradually renounced the true religion of their common father Noah.[1] This religion was the only bond which kept them within human society, both in the union of marriage and hence in their family groups. When they renounced it and began to couple promiscuously, they dissolved their marriages and dispersed their families. In this way, they began to wander like brutes through the earth's great forest. (The race of Ham wandered through southern Asia into Egypt and the rest of Africa; that of Japheth through northern Asia, or Scythia, into Europe; and that of Shem through central Asia to the Near East.) They were scattered widely as they fled from the wild beasts which abounded in the great forest, and as they pursued women who in that state were wild, timid, and intractable. And they were further separated as they sought pasture and water.

Since mothers abandoned their children, they grew up without hearing any human speech, or learning any human behaviour, and sank to an utterly bestial and brutish state. In this state, mothers merely nursed their infants and let them wallow naked in their own faeces, abandoning them for ever once they were weaned. Wallowing in their faeces (whose nitrous salts wondrously enriched the soil), these children struggled to make their way through the great forest, now grown dense after the recent flood. And as their muscles expanded and contracted in this struggle, the children absorbed more and more nitrous salts. At the same time, these children lacked that fear of gods, fathers, and teachers which tempers the most exuberant phase of childhood. As a result, their flesh and bones must have grown inordinately large, and they became so vigorous and robust that they turned out to be giants.

(This upbringing was even more brutish than that to which Caesar and Tacitus[2] attribute the gigantic stature of the Germans, as Axiom 26 states. This upbringing also explains the gigantic stature of the Goths reported by Procopius,[3] and that of the Patagonians,[4] who are said to live near the Strait of Magellan. On this subject, natural scientists have written numerous absurdities, which have been assembled by Jean Chassagnon[5] in his

1. The builder of the biblical ark; all humans born after the Flood were descended from his sons (Genesis 6–9).
2. Roman historian (ca. 55–ca. 120 C.E.), author of *Germania*. Julius Caesar (100–44 B.C.E.), Roman military and political leader who wrote about the Germans in his *Commentaries on the Gallic War*.
3. Byzantine historian (ca. 500–ca. 565), who observed and wrote about Justinian's war against the Goths—East Germanic tribes who had occupied Italy in the 3d and 4th centuries—in his *History of the Wars*.
4. Native tribes of Patagonia, the southernmost region of South America.
5. Jean Chassanion (1531–1598), French author of *De gigantibus* (1580).

treatise *On Giants*. Great skulls and bones of an enormous size have been found and are still being found today, for the most part in the mountains—which is an important fact to which I shall return. The size of these remains is further exaggerated by popular traditions, for reasons I shall discuss in their place.)

[370] After the flood, these giants were scattered throughout the earth. We have seen that such giants are found in Greek mythology; and Latin historians unwittingly confirm their existence in ancient Italy. For they write that the most ancient peoples of Italy, known as the Aborigines, called themselves 'autochthonous', which is synonymous with 'sons of Earth', which to the Greeks and Romans meant nobles. Appropriately, the Greeks called the sons of Earth 'giants', just as their myths called the Earth the mother of giants. Hence, we should translate the Greek *autochthones* in Latin as *indigenae*, indigenous people, which properly means the native sons of a land. For in Latin the native gods of a people or nation were called *dii indigetes*, as if to say *inde geniti*, born there, or as we now say more succinctly ingeniti, inborn. (The syllable *de* is one of the redundancies of the early languages which I shall discuss later. Thus, the early Latins said *induperator* for *imperator*, commander; and the Law of the Twelve Tables[6] reads *endoiacito* for *iniicito*, to lay hands on. This may be why armistices came to be called *induciae*, truces, as if from *iniiciae*: for to make a peace treaty was *icere foedus*, to strike an agreement.) To return to my point, from *indigena* the Romans derived *ingenuus*, whose first and proper meaning was noble—as in the *artes ingenuae*, noble arts. Eventually, the adjective came to mean free. (Still, the phrase *artes liberales*, liberal arts, retained the sense of noble arts.) For the nobles alone made up the free populations of the first cities; whereas the plebeians in them were slaves or the precursors of slaves.

* * *

[374] In reasoning about the wisdom of the ancient pagans, all the philosophers and philologists should have begun with these first men, who were stupid, insensate, and horrid beasts, that is, giants in the proper sense I have just described. (In *The Church Before the Law*, Father Jacques Boulduc[7] says that the biblical term giants means 'pious, venerable, and illustrious men'. But this can be true only of the noble giants who established pagan religions by divination and gave their name to the age of giants.) And these scholars should have begun with metaphysics, since it finds its proofs not in the external world, but within the modifications of the reflective mind. The world of nations was clearly a human creation, and hence its principles should have been sought within the human mind. And to the extent that human nature coincides with that of animals, it must rely on the senses as the sole means of knowing things.

[375] As the first wisdom of the pagan world, poetic wisdom must have begun with a metaphysics which, unlike the rational and abstract metaphysics of today's scholars, sprang from the senses and imagination of the first people. For they lacked the power of reason, and were entirely guided

6. The earliest Roman law codes, drawn up in 450–451 B.C.E.

7. French priest and author (ca. 1575–1646).

by their vigorous sensations and vivid imaginations, as Axiom 36 states. This metaphysics was their own poetry, which sprang from an innate poetic faculty: for they were naturally endowed with sense and imagination. Their poetry also sprang naturally from their ignorance of causes. For, as Axiom 35 states, ignorance is the mother of wonder; and being ignorant of all things, the first people were amazed by everything. In them, poetry began as literally *divine*. For whenever something aroused their feelings of wonder, they imagined its cause as a god. And at the same time, whatever aroused their wonder they endowed with a substantial being based on their own ideas. This is the nature of children, whom we see picking up inanimate objects in play and talking with them as if they were living persons, as Axiom 37 states.

Lactantius[8] observed how early people saw gods in the objects of their wonder, as Axiom 38 states. This is now confirmed by the behaviour of the American Indians, who call gods all the things that exceed their limited understanding. To them, we may add the ancient Germans who lived near the Arctic Ocean. According to Tacitus, they said they could *hear* the sun at night as it passed by sea from west to east, and they claimed to *see* the gods.[9] Such crude and simple nations give us a clearer understanding of the founders of the pagan world who are discussed here.

[376] In this manner, the earliest people of the pagan nations created things according to their own ideas: for they were the children of the nascent human race, as Axiom 37 states. Yet their act of creation was infinitely removed from the creation of God, who by his perfect understanding knows things and creates them in this knowledge. In their robust ignorance, the earliest people could create only by using their imagination, which was grossly physical. Yet this very physicality made their creation wonderfully sublime, and this sublimity was so great and powerful that it excited their imaginations to ecstasy. By virtue of this imaginative creation, they were called poets, which in Greek means creators. Great poetry has three tasks: (1) *to invent sublime myths* which are suited to the popular understanding; (2) *to excite to ecstasy*[1] so that poetry attains its purpose; and this purpose is (3) *to teach the masses to act virtuously*, just as the poets have taught themselves. The natural origin of this human institution gave rise to that invariable property, nobly expressed by Tacitus, that frightened people vainly 'imagine a thing and at once believe it', *fingunt simul creduntque*.[2]

[377] Now, this was clearly the nature of the first founders of pagan civilization when the heavens thundered for the first time since the flood. This happened in Mesopotamia a century after the flood,[3] and in the rest of the world two centuries after it. For that much time was necessary for the moisture of the universal flood to dry out, so that the earth could send into the air any dry exhalations or flammable matter that might have generated lightning. As was inevitable when such a violent phenomenon filled the sky for the first time, the heavens now produced the most frightening thunderclaps and light-

8. Firmianus Lactantius (ca. 240–ca. 320 C.E.), Roman Christian writer and rhetorician. Vico refers to *Divine Institutions* 1.15.

9. A reference to Tacitus, *Germania* 45.

1. Vico uses *eccesso* in the Latin sense of *excessus mentis*, "ecstasy" [translator's note].

2. Tacitus, *Annales* 5.10.

3. That is, Noah's Flood (Genesis 7).

ning bolts. At this time, a few giants, who must have been the most robust, were living scattered through the forests of the mountain heights, which is where the most robust animals have their lairs. Suddenly frightened and thunderstruck by this inexplicably great phenomenon, they raised their eyes and observed the heavens. In this state, such people by nature possessed only robust physical strength and expressed their violent passions by shouting and grunting. So they imagined the heavens as a great living body, and in this manifestation, they called the sky Jupiter. (The nature of the human mind in such cases leads it to attribute its own nature to an external phenomenon, as Axiom 32 states.) And they thought that Jupiter, the first god of the so-called greater clans, was trying to speak to them through the whistling of his bolts and the crashing of his thunder.

The giants now began to exercise that natural curiosity which is the daughter of ignorance and the mother of knowledge, and which is born when wonder arouses the human mind, as Axiom 39 states. This natural trait still persists tenaciously among the common people. When they see a comet, parhelion,[4] or any unusual natural phenomenon, especially in the heavens, they grow curious and then quite anxious to learn its significance, as Axiom 39 states. And when they wonder at the marvellous effect of a magnet on iron, they arrive at the conclusion that the magnet has a secret sympathy for iron—and this in the present age, when our minds are keener and even enlightened by philosophy. Indeed, they view all of nature as a vast living body that feels passions and emotions, as Axiom 32 states.

[378] The countless abstract expressions which permeate our languages today have divorced our civilized thought from the senses, even among the common people. The art of writing has greatly refined the nature of our thought; and the use of numbers has intellectualized it, so to speak, even among the masses, who know how to count and reckon. As a result, we are by nature incapable of forming the vast image of that mistress which some call 'Sympathetic Nature'. (In fact, people who mouth this expression have literally nothing in mind; for a mental falsehood is nothing, and the imagination is powerless to form vast images of falsity.) We are likewise incapable of entering into the vast imaginative powers of the earliest people. Their minds were in no way abstract, refined, or intellectualized; rather, they were completely sunk in their senses, numbed by their passions, and buried in their bodies. This is why I said earlier that we can barely understand, and by no means imagine, the thinking of the early people who founded pagan antiquity.

[379] In this manner, the first theological poets invented the first divine myth, which was the greatest myth ever invented: Jupiter, the king and father of gods and men, in the act of hurling a thunderbolt. The figure of Jupiter was so poetic—that is, popular, exciting, and instructive—that its inventors at once believed it, and they feared, revered, and worshipped Jupiter in frightful religions, which I shall discuss later. These people now believed that everything they saw, imagined, or even did themselves was Jupiter—which illustrates the trait of the human mind noted by Tacitus in

4. A bright spot tinged with color that can appear on a parhelic circle (a luminous halo parallel to the horizon at the altitude of the sun).

Axiom 34. And they endowed all the universe and its parts with the being of an animate substance. This is the civil and historical meaning of the poetic tag 'all things are full of Jupiter', *Iovis omnia plena*.[5] Later, Plato interpreted this to mean the ether that permeates and fills everything in the universe.[6] But in fact, the theological poets thought that Jupiter was no higher than the mountain tops. And since these early people communicated by signs, they naturally believed that lightning bolts and thunderclaps were signs made to them by Jupiter. (Later, from Latin *nuo*, to make a sign by nodding, they derived *numen*, divine will, by an idea which is utterly sublime and worthy to express divine majesty.) They believed that Jupiter commanded by signs, that these signs were physical words, and that nature was Jupiter's language.

The science of this language the pagans universally believed to be divination, which the Greeks called theology, meaning the science of the gods' speech. This is how Jupiter was assigned to the fearful kingdom of lightning, which made him the king of gods and men. He acquired two titles: *optimus*, best, meaning *fortissimus*, strongest (in early Latin *fortis* meant the same as classical *bonus*, good); and *maximus*, greatest, alluding to his body, which was as vast as the heavens. Because he did not destroy the human race with his bolts, he acquired the title Soter or Saviour. (This first beneficent act gave rise to religion, which is the first of the three basic principles of my New Science.) And because he stayed the giants from their brutish wandering, so that they became the rulers of the nations, he acquired the title Stator, or Stayer. (Latin historians give too restricted a meaning to this title when they cite a single historical event, and observe that, during a battle with the Sabines, Jupiter was invoked by Romulus and 'stayed' the Romans from flight.)[7]

[380] This is the origin of those many Jupiters, whose existence amazes the philologists. Each pagan nation had its own Jupiter, and the Egyptians in their conceit said that their Jupiter Ammon was the oldest of all, as Axiom 3 states. In fact, all these Jupiters are mythical references to natural history, which show that the flood was universal, as Axiom 42 states.

[381] Thus, if we bear in mind the principles of poetic archetypes formulated in Axioms 47–49, we see that Jupiter was born naturally in poetry as a *divine archetype* or *imaginative universal*, to whom the ancient pagans with their poetic nature referred every aspect of divination. In this way, their poetic wisdom began with the poetic metaphysics of contemplating God in his attribute of providence. And they called themselves theological poets, meaning wise men or sages who understood the speech of the gods expressed in Jupiter's auspices. They were also properly called divines in the sense of diviners, from the Latin verb *divinari*, which properly means to divine or predict. Their science was called the Muse, which Homer defines as the knowledge of good and evil. (This meant divination, which God prohibited to Adam when he established the true religion, as Axiom 24 states.) And for their mystical theology, the poets were in Greek called *mystae*, initi-

5. Virgil, *Eclogues* 3.60 (ca. 37 B.C.E.).
6. Plato, *Cratylus* 412d.
7. Romulus, mythical founder of Rome, procured wives for his citizens by inviting the Sabines, a group of neighboring tribes, to a festival and seizing the women; this led to a series of wars (which ended with Romulus as king). For Jupiter Stator, see, e.g., Livy 1.12.6.

ates, a term which Horace[8] learnedly translates as 'interpreters of the gods', for they explained the divine mysteries of the auspices and oracles. In this science, every pagan nation had its own sibyl, and we find mention of twelve of them. Sibyls[9] and oracles are the most ancient institutions of the pagan world.

[382] All these remarks tally with the passage from Lactantius,[1] cited in Axiom 38, who describes the origins of idolatry by saying that the earliest people, being simple and uncouth, invented gods 'in terror of their manifest power'. Thus, it was fear that invented gods in the world; and not fear inspired by other people, but fear born within their own minds, as Axiom 40 states. This origin of idolatry also reveals the origin of divination, since they were born as twins. In turn, these institutions were followed by sacrifices, which were offered to 'procure' the auspices, that is, to interpret them correctly.

[383] We find confirmation of this origin of poetry in this invariable property: the proper subject of poetry is a believable impossibility. Thus, while it is impossible that physical objects have intelligence, people believed that the thundering heavens were Jupiter. This is why poets are so fond of singing the wonders created by the spells of sorceresses. To explain this, we must posit a hidden sense that nations have of God's omnipotence. This sense in turn engenders another by which all peoples are naturally led to offer infinite honours to divinity. This was the manner in which the poets founded religions among the pagans.

[384] These remarks overturn all the previous theories about the origins of poetry, from Plato and Aristotle in antiquity to our own Francesco Patrizi, Julius Caesar Scaliger, and Ludovico Castelvetro.[2] Unlike them, we have discovered that poetry was born sublime precisely because it lacked rationality. This is why no later discipline—philosophy, poetics, or criticism—ever equalled or surpassed the sublimity of poetry. Hence, it is Homer's privilege to be the foremost of all the sublime or heroic poets, in terms of both merit and age. My discovery of the true origins of poetry dispels the common belief in the *incomparable wisdom* of the ancients, which scholars have eagerly sought to discover, from Plato to Bacon in his *Wisdom of the Ancients*.[3] For this wisdom was in fact the *popular wisdom* of the lawgivers who founded mankind, rather than the *esoteric wisdom* of a few lofty philosophers. Hence, as in the case of Jupiter, we shall judge absurd all the *mystical senses* of profound philosophy which scholars have given to Greek myths and Egyptian hieroglyphics. By contrast, we shall judge natural the *historical sense* which they naturally preserved.

* * *

[400] Metaphysics contemplates things in all the categories of their being, but it becomes logic when it considers them in the categories by

8. Roman poet and satirist (65–8 B.C.E.). Vico refers to *Ars Poetica*, line 391 (see above).
9. That is, female prophets (the most famous in Italy was at Cumae, west of modern Naples).
1. Lactantius, *Divine Institutions* 1.15.
2. Vico names three Italian Renaissance philosophers noted for their critical engagement with classical literary theory, particularly Aristotle's *Poetics*: Francesco Patrizzi (1529–1597), Julius Caesar Scaliger (1484–1558), and Lodovico Castelvetro (1505–1571).
3. *On the Wisdom of the Ancients* (1609), by the English philosopher Francis Bacon (1561–1626).

which they are signified. Hence, now that we have considered poetry as a poetic metaphysics, by which the theological poets imagined most physical objects to be divine substances, we may consider it as a *poetic logic*, by which it signifies those substances.

[401] The word logic comes from Greek *logos*, which at first properly meant fable, or *fabula* in Latin, which later changed into Italian *favella*, speech. In Greek, a fable was also called *mythos*, myth, from which is derived Latin *mutus*, mute. For speech was born in the mute age as a mental language, which Strabo[4] in a golden passage says existed before any spoken or articulated language: this is why in Greek *logos* means both word and idea. Appropriately, divine providence ordained that this language arose in a religious age, for it is the invariable property of religion that meditation is more important than speech. As Axiom 57 states, the first language employed by the nations in their mute age must have originated with signs, gestures, or physical objects which had a natural relation to the ideas expressed. Hence, Greek *logos* also meant thing, and the Hebrew word for word (translated by Greek *logos* and Latin *verbum*) also meant deed, as Thomas Gataker[5] observes in *The Style of the New Testament*. We find that *mythos* was also defined as *vera narratio*, or true narration. According to Plato and later Iamblichus,[6] this is the natural speech which was once spoken in the world; but as Axiom 57 notes, this was mere conjecture on their part. Hence, Plato's effort to discover this speech in his dialogue *Cratylus* proved vain, and he was criticized for it by Aristotle and Galen.[7] In fact, the earliest speech, that of the theological poets, did not use words which suited the nature of the things they expressed. (This was the sacred language invented by Adam, on whom God bestowed divine *onomatothesia*, nomenclature, which is the art of assigning names to things according to their nature.)[8] Rather, their first speech was a *fantastic speech based on animate substances*, most of which they imagined to be divine.

[402] For example, the theological poets understood Jupiter, Cybele or Berecynthia, and Neptune[9] in this way. At first, pointing mutely, they interpreted them as the substances of the sky, earth, and sea, which they imagined to be animate deities; and, trusting the truth of their senses, they believed they were gods. In this way, they used these three deities to explain everything related to the sky, earth, and sea, which is the function of poetic archetypes explained in Axioms 47–9. And they used other deities to signify various subspecies of each major god: for example, Flora for flowers and Pomona for fruits. Today we reverse this mental process when we deal with intellectual notions, such as the faculties of the human mind, the emotions, virtues, vices, sciences, and arts. For we generally imagine them as feminine personifications, to which we refer their various properties, causes, and effects. And when we wish to express our understanding of intellectual notions, our imagination must assist us in explaining them and in giving them human form, as

4. Greek geographer (ca. 64 B.C.E.–ca. 23 C.E.).
5. English Puritan churchman (1574–1654); he published *De Novi Instrumenti Stylo, Dissertatio* in 1648.
6. Greek Neoplatonic philosopher (ca. 250–ca. 325 C.E.).
7. Greek physician and philosopher (129–ca. 199 C.E.).
8. See Genesis 2.19–20.
9. Roman god of the sea. Cybele and Berecynthia: two names for the same goddess, the Greco-Roman "Great Mother" worshipped in cult.

painters of allegories do. By contrast, the theological poets could not use their understanding, and so performed the contrary operation, which is far more sublime. They attributed senses and emotions to physical bodies, even bodies as vast as the sky, earth, and sea, as we have just seen. Later, as their vast imaginations diminished and their powers of abstraction increased, these deities shrank to diminutive symbols of themselves. Since the origins of these human institutions were buried in obscurity, metonymy[1] dressed these symbols in the learned guise of allegory. Jupiter grew so small and light that an eagle now carries him in its flight. Neptune rides the sea in a dainty coach. And Cybele is seated on a lion.

* * *

[404] All the primary figures of speech are corollaries of poetic logic. The most luminous figure, and hence the most basic and common, is metaphor. Metaphor is especially prized when, by the metaphysics just described, it confers sense and emotion on insensate objects. The first poets attributed to physical bodies the being of animate substances, endowed with limited powers of sense and emotion like their own. In this way, they created myths about them; and every such metaphor is a miniature myth. This gives us a criterion for dating the origin of metaphors in various languages. For example, all metaphors based on analogies between physical objects and the products of abstract thought must date from an age in which philosophies were just beginning to take shape. We find proof of this in the fact that in every language the terms used in the fine arts and advanced sciences are of rustic origin.

[405] Noteworthy too is the fact that in all languages most expressions for inanimate objects employ metaphors derived from the human body and its parts, or from human senses and emotions. Thus, we say *head* for top or beginning; *front* or *brow*, and *shoulders* or *back*, for before and behind; *eyes* of vines [Latin *oculi*, buds]; *lights* [Italian *lumi*] for entrances to a house; *mouth* for any opening; *lip* for the rim of a pitcher or other container. We speak of the *tooth* of a plough, rake, saw, or comb; the *beards* of plants and their roots; a *tongue* of the sea; the *throat* of rivers and mountains [French *gorge*]; a *neck* of land; and the *arm* of a river. We say *hand* for a small number; *lap* of the sea for a gulf [Latin *sinus*, bay]; and *flanks* and *sides* for lateral portions. We speak of the *coast* [Italian *costiera*, rib] of the sea, and the *leg* or *foot* of countries. We say *heart* for the centre (as the Romans said *umbilicus*, navel); *foot* for end, and *plan* [Latin *planta*, footprint] for base or foundation. We speak of the *flesh* and the *bones* [English *stones*] of fruit; a *vein* of water, rock, or ore; the *blood* of the vine, meaning wine; and the *bowels* of the earth. Similarly, the sky or sea *smiles* on us; the wind *whistles*; the waves *murmur*, and a body *groans* under a great weight. In antiquity, the farmers in Latium used to say that the fields were *thirsty*, the crops were *distressed*, and grains *ran riot*. Even today farmers say that plants *fall in love*, vines *go mad*, and fir-trees *weep* with sap. And countless other examples can be cited in any language.

1. A rhetorical trope or figure of speech in which one word is substituted for another to which it is related in some way other than resemblance (e.g., by contiguity, as in "crown" used for "king").

All this follows from Axiom 1: 'In his ignorance, man makes himself the measure of the universe.' And in the examples cited, man has reduced the entire world to his own body. Now, rational metaphysics teaches us that man becomes all things through understanding, *homo intelligendo fit omnia*. But with perhaps greater truth, this imaginative metaphysics shows that man becomes all things by not understanding, *homo non intelligendo fit omnia*. For when man understands, he extends his mind to comprehend things; but when he does not understand, he makes them out of himself and, by transforming himself, becomes them.

[406] Using their poetic logic, which was a product of poetic metaphysics, the early poetic peoples named things in two ways: (1) by using sensible ideas, which are the source of metonymy; and (2) by using particular ideas, which are the source of synecdoche.[2]

(1) Metonymy which substitutes the author for the work originated because authors were more often named than their works. Metonymy which substitutes the object for its form and accidents originated because they could not abstract forms and qualities, as Axiom 49 states. And metonymy of cause for effect created miniature myths, in which causes were imagined as feminine personifications clothed in their effects, such as ugly Poverty, sad Old Age, and pale Death.

[407] (2) Synecdoche became metaphor when people raised particulars to universals or united parts to form wholes. At first, only human beings were properly called mortals, since they were the only ones who sensed their mortality. The use of 'head' for man or person, so common in vernacular Latin, reflects the age when people lived in woodlands and only a man's head could be seen at a distance. (By contrast, the word 'man' is an abstraction, a sort of philosophical category comprising the body and its parts, the mind and its faculties, and the heart and its feelings.) Similarly, Latin *tignum*, beam, and *culmen*, stalk of straw, must have properly meant rafter and straw when houses were thatched. Later, as cities became more ornate, *tignum* came to mean all construction materials, and *culmen* the completion of a building. Thus, *tectum*, roof, came to mean the entire house, because in the earliest times a covering overhead was all that was needed to make a house. And *puppis*, poop, came to mean a ship, because its height made it the first part visible to people ashore; just as people said 'sail' for ship during the medieval return of barbarism. Thus, *mucro*, point, came to mean a sword, since it was the point which early people felt and which aroused their fright. (By contrast, the word 'sword' is an abstraction, a general category comprising pommel, hilt, edge, and point.) Similarly, the material meant the whole thing formed from it—witness 'iron' for sword—because they could not abstract the form from its material.

In Ovid,[3] we find the poetic phrase, 'It was the third harvest', *Tertia messis erat*, which combines synecdoche and metonymy. This combination was doubtless born of natural necessity, since it must have taken more than a thousand years for this astronomical idea to arise among the nations. Even today, farmers outside Florence say 'We have reaped so many times' to indi-

2. A rhetorical trope or figure of speech in which a part is substituted for a whole or vice versa, as in "all hands on deck."

3. Roman poet (43 B.C.E.–17 C.E.). Vico quotes *Heroides* 6.59.

cate a number of years. Likewise, Virgil joins two synecdoches and a metonymy in his verse, 'After several ears of grain I shall marvel seeing my kingdoms', *Post aliquot, mea regna videns, mirabor aristas.*[4] This phrase exposes the awkward way in which people of the early rustic age expressed themselves. They signified years by saying 'ears of grain', *aristas*, which is more particular than 'harvest'. But because the phrase is so awkward, textbooks have judged it a rhetorical extravagance.

[408] Irony could clearly arise only in an age capable of reflection, because it consists of a falsehood which reflection disguises in a mask of truth. From this emerges an important principle of human institutions, which confirms the origin of poetry discovered in my Science. Since the pagan world's earliest people were as simple as children, who are by nature truthful, they could invent nothing false in their early myths. These myths must therefore have been *true narratives*, as we have defined them.

[409] All figures of speech may be reduced to these four types—metaphor, metonymy, synecdoche, and irony—which were previously thought to be the ingenious inventions of writers. But my discussion of them proves that they were in fact necessary modes of expression in all the early poetic nations, and originally had natural and proper meanings. These expressions became figurative only later, as the human mind developed and invented words which signified abstract forms, that is, generic categories comprising various species, or relating parts to a whole. Knowing this, we may begin to demolish two common errors of the grammarians: that prose is the proper form of speech, and poetic speech improper; and that men spoke first in prose and later in verse.

* * *

[779] We have seen that poetic wisdom justly deserves supreme and sovereign praise on two counts. (1) As is clearly and consistently recognized, poetic wisdom founded pagan civilization. Even while striving to affirm this, the conceits of nations and scholars have in fact denied it. For the nations have imagined poetic wisdom as a vain magnificence, while scholars have distorted it with incongruous philosophical wisdom. (2) As popular tradition relates, poetic wisdom created sages who were equally great as philosophers, lawmakers, generals, historians, orators, and poets. But in creating them, this wisdom formed them only roughly: this is how we see them in their myths, in which we perceive the embryonic outlines, as it were, of all esoteric wisdom. We may conclude that in their myths the nations used crude and physical language to describe the principles of the world of sciences. Later, this was elucidated by the specialized researches of scholars who used rational argument and general rules. All this confirms the thesis of [this book], that the theological poets were the sense of human wisdom, as the philosophers were its intellect.

1725, 1744

4. *Eclogues* 1.69, by the Roman poet Virgil (70–19 B.C.E.).

JOSEPH ADDISON
1672–1719

The English poet, dramatist, and essayist Joseph Addison is best known as the coauthor with Richard Steele of an influential series of periodical essays, published in *The Tatler* (April 12, 1709–January 2, 1711) and *The Spectator* (first series, March 1, 1711–December 6, 1712; second series, 1714). He is distinguished for his clear, orderly prose style, which did much to elevate the status of the essay as a literary form, and for his skillful descriptions of character, which helped prepare the way for later eighteenth-century pioneers in a new English genre, the novel. Addison was an important cultural and literary figure, particularly for middle-class readers. As he explained in *Spectator* No. 10: "It was said of Socrates that he brought philosophy down from heaven to inhabit among men; and I shall be ambitious to have it said of me that I have brought philosophy out of closets and libraries, schools and colleges, to dwell in clubs and assemblies, at tea-tables and in coffeehouses." Addison achieved this goal and became a model for generations of critics and essayists.

Addison was educated at Oxford, where he excelled in classical studies and composed Latin verse that JOHN DRYDEN admired. By his early twenties, Addison had already published poetry, but he was as intent on political advancement as on literary success. He used his literary talents to praise leading statesmen of the Whig political party, which sought to limit royal power. His career reached its height in 1713, when his neoclassical tragedy *Cato* was produced in London; it focuses on the Roman republican Cato (95–46 B.C.E.), who chose suicide rather than submit to the dictator Julius Caesar. SAMUEL JOHNSON judged *Cato* "rather a poem in dialogue than a drama," and modern scholars have found it tedious; but it was a popular success and was frequently performed, in part because many interpreted it as a commentary on the English political scene.

Successful in both literature and politics, Addison was appointed undersecretary of state (1706); secretary to Lord Wharton, the lord lieutenant in Ireland (1709); and chief secretary for Ireland (1715). He served as lord commissioner for trade (1716), and on retirement he was rewarded with a generous pension. He had entered Parliament as a Whig in 1708 and held his seat until his death in 1719.

Addison's partnership with the Irish writer and Whig supporter Steele—whom he had known since their school days together—began in 1709. He contributed 42 essays to Steele's *Tatler*, and collaborated with Steele on 36 others; he wrote even more—274 essays of a total of 555—for their joint venture *The Spectator. The Tatler* appeared three times a week, *The Spectator* every day except Sunday (both were later published in book form). These periodicals gave Addison a means to fulfill his cultural mission. He concurred with the ideal that Steele defined for *The Tatler*, which was "to enliven Morality with Wit, and to temper Wit with Morality," thereby offering men and women a guide to virtue. But together with urbane, witty sketches of fictional characters (notably the eccentric, kindly country gentleman Sir Roger de Coverley) and advice on conduct were essays devoted to the writings of John Locke, John Milton, and others. Addison claimed that each copy that was purchased was in turn passed on to twenty people or more, and he hoped that his lucid treatment of important topics in literature and philosophy would significantly influence the public's critical judgment and taste.

In our first selection, *Spectator* No. 62, Addison examines the nature of wit, one of the most complex, shifting terms in poetics. In a broad sense, it means the natural ability to perceive and understand, keen intelligence, quick and subtle perception; but it refers more specifically to the capacity of writers to perceive and express relationships between seemingly disparate or incongruous things in striking, paradoxical, surprising figures of speech. From the seventeenth through the eighteenth centuries, wit was a central topic in literary theory and criticism. ALEXANDER POPE defined it most memorably—"*True Wit* is *Nature* to Advantage drest, / What oft was *Thought*, but ne'er so well *Exprest*" (*An Essay on Criticism*, 1711; see below)—but Dryden and Johnson also discuss it in detail.

For the Romantics and Victorians, wit mattered less than imagination. Sometimes too, in this period and even earlier, wit was simultaneously praised and devalued, taken as a sign of quickness in repartee but not necessarily of serious or profound reflection. As Voltaire remarked in his *Philosophical Dictionary* (1764), "he who cannot shine by thought, seeks to bring himself into notice by a witticism." In this sense, it was frequently associated with satire, comedy, and humor. But in the modern period, T. S. ELIOT, F. R. LEAVIS, and CLEANTH BROOKS reinvigorated the serious meanings of wit and enriched critical understanding of the play of irony and paradox, linking it to the best in the English poetical tradition.

Addison begins by quoting John Locke's distinction between *wit*, which emphasizes congruity and resemblance, and *judgment*, which stresses distinction and difference. But he adds that true wit requires a verbal effect that delights and surprises the reader. The resemblance must not be unduly common or familiar, nor wholly verbal—ideas as well as words are involved. Most of Addison's discussion treats such "mixed wit," but he ends by moving outward from the writer's use of language to the responses of readers, anticipating the intricate issues of aesthetics probed later in the century by DAVID HUME, IMMANUEL KANT, and other philosophers and theorists. Like Dryden and the French critic Jean Regnauld de Segrais (1624–1701), Addison aims to teach readers to value wit in its best forms and not to rest content with simpler uses, however appealing at first these might be; indeed, he connects wit with the quality of humanity.

In our second selection, from *Spectator* No. 412, Addison examines the imagination. He reiterates his point about the uncommon and the new, describing the pleasure that we receive when our sight is refreshed by a surprising and gratifying view of an object or scene that gives us a new idea of something that we thought we already understood. Addison's discussion of "greatness" reflects the interest in the sublime sparked by the French critic Nicolas Boileau's 1674 translation of *On Sublimity*, a Greek text attributed to LONGINUS (first century C.E.; see above). Like wit, *the sublime* is a complex term and literary category. It connotes majesty, awe, nobility, and spiritual, moral, and intellectual excellence. In some discussions, it chiefly refers to something *in* natural scenes and landscapes. At the same time, the term often evokes the response of viewers—their sensations and feelings that Nature creates, their pleasurable anxiety and incomprehension—a topic that Kant later explored in his *Critique of Judgment* (1790; see below).

For his part, Addison appears especially interested in the viewer, audience, reader—in what one might call the psychology of the sublime. In other papers (e.g., *Spectator* No. 416), he extends his inquiry into the sublime and the beautiful by distinguishing between the primary and secondary pleasures of the imagination; in the first, the viewer responds directly to an object, whereas in the second, he or she is returned to that object through a work of literature or art. Addison suggests that the writer or artist can thus kindle pleasures that rival or exceed those that Nature itself provides.

Addison's brief critical and theoretical papers, while lucid, are rarely profound or deep. Dryden is the more pioneering critic and theorist, and Pope the more brilliantly adroit: Addison does not operate at their level. Nor does he show the sophistication and depth that later critics (including EDMUND BURKE, Johnson, and SAMUEL TAYLOR COLERIDGE) display in treating the same topics. But Addison remains significant for the influential cultural work—the work of the public intellectual—that he undertook. He read widely in literature and philosophy (both English and French), summarized well what he had discovered, and successfully brought it into the public sphere. In defining terms and making distinctions, Addison gave his readers the critical vocabulary that they needed to sort and categorize the relationship between words and ideas, between the world they inhabited and the literature they consumed. Though he is not as central to the tradition of theory and criticism as are Johnson and Coleridge, Addison is a key influence on both of them.

The Spectator, No. 62 [True and False Wit] **Keywords:** Aesthetics, Enlightenment Theory, Language, Literary History, Poetry
The Spectator, No. 412 [On the Sublime] **Keywords:** Aesthetics, Enlightenment Theory, Language, Poetry

The Spectator, No. 62 [True and False Wit]

Scribendi recte sapere est et principium et fons.[1]
—Horace, *Ars Poetica*, 310

Mr. Locke[2] has an admirable reflection upon the difference of wit and judgment, whereby he endeavours to show the reason why they are not always the talents of the same person. His words are as follow: 'And hence, perhaps, may be given some reason of that common observation, that men who have a great deal of wit and prompt memories, have not always the clearest judgment, or deepest reason. For wit lying most in the assemblage of ideas, and putting those together with quickness and variety, wherein can be found any resemblance or congruity, thereby to make up pleasant pictures and agreeable visions in the fancy; judgment, on the contrary, lies quite on the other side, in separating carefully one from another, ideas wherein can be found the least difference, thereby to avoid being misled by similitude, and by affinity to take one thing for another. This is a way of proceeding quite contrary to metaphor and allusion; wherein, for the most part, lies that entertainment and pleasantry of wit which strikes so lively on the fancy, and is therefore so acceptable to all people.'

This is, I think, the best and most philosophical account that I have ever met with of wit, which generally, though not always, consists in such a resemblance and congruity of ideas as this author mentions. I shall only add to it, by way of explanation, that every resemblance of ideas is not that which we call wit, unless it be such an one that gives delight and surprise to the reader. These two properties seem essential to wit, more particularly the last of them. In order therefore that the resemblance in the ideas be wit, it is necessary that the ideas should not lie too near one another in the nature of things; for where the likeness is obvious, it gives no surprise. To compare one man's singing to that of another, or to represent the whiteness of any object by that of milk and snow, or the variety of its colours by

1. Wisdom is the starting point and source of correct writing (Latin). From *Ars Poetica* (see above) by the Roman lyric poet HORACE (65–8 B.C.E.).

2. John Locke (1632–1704), English philosopher. The "reflection" is in his *Essay Concerning Human Understanding* (1690), 2.11.2.

those of the rainbow, cannot be called wit, unless, besides this obvious resemblance, there be some further congruity discovered in the two ideas that is capable of giving the reader some surprise. Thus when a poet tells us, the bosom of his mistress is as white as snow, there is not wit in the comparison; but when he adds, with a sigh, that it is as cold too, it then grows into wit. Every reader's memory may supply him with innumerable instances of the same nature. For this reason, the similitudes in heroic poets, who endeavour rather to fill the mind with great conceptions, than to divert it with such as are new and surprising, have seldom anything in them that can be called wit. Mr. Locke's account of wit, with this short explanation, comprehends most of the species of wit, as metaphors, similitudes, allegories, enigmas, mottoes, parables, fables, dreams, visions, dramatic writings, burlesque, and all the methods of allusion: as there are many other pieces of wit (how remote soever they may appear at first sight from the foregoing description) which upon examination will be found to agree with it.

As true wit generally consists in this resemblance and congruity of ideas, false wit chiefly consists in the resemblance and congruity sometimes of single letters, as in anagrams, chronograms, lipograms,[3] and acrostics; sometimes of syllables, as in echoes and doggerel rhymes; sometimes of words, as in puns and quibbles; and sometimes of whole sentences or poems, cast into the figures of eggs, axes, or altars:[4] nay, some carry the notion of wit so far, as to ascribe it even to external mimicry; and to look upon a man as an ingenious person, that can resemble the tone, posture, or face of another.

As true wit consists in the resemblance of ideas, and false wit in the resemblance of words, according to the foregoing instances; there is another kind of wit which consists partly in the resemblance of ideas, and partly in the resemblance of words; which for distinction's sake I shall call mixed wit. This kind of wit is that which abounds in Cowley, more than in any author that ever wrote. Mr. Waller[5] has likewise a great deal of it. Mr. Dryden is very sparing in it. Milton had a genius much above it. Spenser[6] is in the same class with Milton. The Italians, even in their epic poetry, are full of it. Monsieur Boileau,[7] who formed himself upon the ancient poets, has everywhere rejected it with scorn. If we look after mixed wit among the Greek writers, we shall find it nowhere but in the epigrammatists. There are indeed some strokes of it in the little poem ascribed to Musæus,[8] which by that, as well as many other marks, betrays itself to be a modern composition. If we look into the Latin writers, we find none of this mixed wit in Virgil, Lucretius,

3. Compositions in which all words containing a certain letter or letters are omitted. "Chronograms": phrases in which certain letters express a date (e.g., capitalized letters that stand for Roman numerals).

4. Famous examples of such pattern or shaped poems include "The Altar" and "Easter Wings" by George Herbert (1593–1633).

5. Edmund Waller (1606–1687), English poet admired for his development of the heroic couplet. Abraham Cowley (1618–1667), English metaphysical poet. Unusual metaphor is characteristic of metaphysical poetry.

6. Edmund Spenser (ca. 1552–1599), English poet whose works include the unfinished epic *The Faerie Queene*. John Dryden (1631–1700), English poet, dramatist, and critic. John Milton (1608–1674), English poet and prose writer; his masterpiece is the epic *Paradise Lost*.

7. Nicolas Boileau (1636–1711), French poet, dramatist, and critic; author of *The Art of Poetry*, a treatise in verse (1674).

8. Greek poet (probably late 5th c. C.E.). "The little poem": *Hero and Leander*, translated in 1635.

or Catullus;[9] very little in Horace, but a great deal of it in Ovid, and scarce anything else in Martial.[1]

Out of the innumerable branches of mixed wit, I shall choose one instance which may be met with in all the writers of this class. The passion of love in its nature has been thought to resemble fire; for which reason the words fire and flame are made use of to signify love. The witty poets therefore have taken an advantage from the doubtful meaning of the word fire, to make an infinite number of witticisms. Cowley observing the cold regard of his mistress's eyes,[2] and at the same time their power of producing love in him, considers them as burning-glasses made of ice; and finding himself able to live in the greatest extremities of love, concludes the torrid zone to be habitable. When his mistress has read his letter written in juice of lemon by holding it to the fire, he desires her to read it over a second time by love's flames. When she weeps, he wishes it were inward heat that distilled those drops from the limbec.[3] When she is absent he is beyond eighty, that is, thirty degrees nearer the pole[4] than when she is with him. His ambitious love is a fire that naturally mounts upwards; his happy love is the beams of heaven, and his unhappy love flames of hell. When it does not let him sleep, it is a flame that sends up no smoke; when it is opposed by counsel and advice, it is a fire that rages the more by the wind's blowing upon it. Upon the dying of a tree in which he had cut his loves, he observes that his written flames had burned up and withered the tree. When he resolves to give over his passion, he tells us that one burnt like him for ever dreads the fire. His heart is an Ætna, that instead of Vulcan's shop encloses Cupid's forge in it.[5] His endeavouring to drown his love in wine, is throwing oil upon the fire. He would insinuate to his mistress, that the fire of love, like that of the sun (which produces so many living creatures) should not only warm but beget. Love in another place cooks pleasure at his fire. Sometimes the poet's heart is frozen in every breast, and sometimes scorched in every eye. Sometimes he is drowned in tears, and burnt in love, like a ship set on fire in the middle of the sea.

The reader may observe in every one of these instances, that the poet mixes the qualities of fire with those of love; and in the same sentence speaking of it both as a passion, and as real fire, surprises the reader with those seeming resemblances or contradictions that make up all the wit in this kind of writing. Mixed wit therefore is a composition of pun and true wit, and is more or less perfect as the resemblance lies in the ideas or in the words: its foundations are laid partly in falsehood and partly in truth: reason puts in her claim for one half of it, and extravagance for the other. The only province therefore for this kind of wit, is epigram, or those little occasional poems that in their own nature are nothing else but a tissue of epi-

9. All poets of the Latin "Golden Age," writing in varied genres on a range of subjects: eclogues, georgics, and epic (Virgil, 70–19 B.C.E.); philosophy (Lucretius, ca. 94–55 B.C.E.); and love lyrics and elegy (Catullus, ca. 84–ca. 54 B.C.E.).

1. Roman poet (ca. 40–ca. 104 C.E.), known for his epigrams. Ovid (43 B.C.E.–17 C.E.), Roman poet of outstanding verbal brilliance, author of love poetry and a highly mannered epic, the *Metamorphoses*.

2. In "The Mistress, or Several Copies of Love-Verses" (1647).

3. Alembic: that is, an apparatus used in distillation.

4. That is, 30 degrees nearer than in England, which is roughly 50 degrees north of the equator.

5. Mt. Etna, a volcano in Sicily, was supposed to be the workshop of Vulcan, the Roman god of fire, who had a forge; Cupid, son of Vulcan and Venus, was the Roman boy-god of love.

grams. I cannot conclude this head of mixed wit, without owning that the admirable poet out of whom I have taken the examples of it, had as much true wit as any author that ever writ; and indeed all other talents of an extraordinary genius.

It may be expected, since I am upon this subject, that I should take notice of Mr. Dryden's definition of wit; which, with all the deference that is due to the judgment of so great a man, is not so properly a definition of wit, as of good writing in general. Wit, as he defines it, is 'a propriety of words and thoughts adapted to the subject.'[6] If this be a true definition of wit, I am apt to think that Euclid[7] was the greatest wit that ever set pen to paper: it is certain there never was a greater propriety of words and thoughts adapted to the subject, than what that author has made use of in his elements. I shall only appeal to my reader, if this definition agrees with any notion he has of wit: if it be a true one, I am sure Mr. Dryden was not only a better poet, but a greater wit than Mr. Cowley; and Virgil a much more facetious man than either Ovid or Martial.

Bouhours,[8] whom I look upon to be the most penetrating of all the French critics, has taken pains to show that it is impossible for any thought to be beautiful which is not just, and has not its foundation in the nature of things; that the basis of all wit is truth; and that no thought can be valuable, of which good sense is not the ground-work. Boileau has endeavoured to inculcate the same notion in several parts of his writings, both in prose and verse. This is that natural way of writing, that beautiful simplicity, which we so much admire in the compositions of the ancients; and which nobody deviates from, but those who want strength of genius to make a thought shine in its own natural beauties. Poets who want this strength of genius to give that majestic simplicity to nature, which we so much admire in the works of the ancients, are forced to hunt after foreign ornaments, and not to let any piece of wit of what kind soever escape them. I look upon these writers as Goths[9] in poetry, who, like those in architecture, not being able to come up to the beautiful simplicity of the old Greeks and Romans, have endeavoured to supply its place with all the extravagances of an irregular fancy. Mr. Dryden makes a very handsome observation on Ovid's writing a letter from Dido to Æneas,[1] in the following words: 'Ovid (says he, speaking of Virgil's fiction of Dido and Æneas) takes it up after him, even in the same age, and makes an ancient heroine of Virgil's new-created Dido; dictates a letter for her just before her death to the ungrateful fugitive; and, very unluckily for himself, is for measuring a sword with a man so much superior in force to him, on the same subject. I think I may be judge of this, because I have translated both.

6. Dryden, preface to *The State of Innocence* (1674, 1677): "The definition of wit . . . is only this: that it is a propriety of thoughts and words; or, in other terms, thoughts and words elegantly adapted to the subject."

7. Greek mathematician (active ca. 300 B.C.E.), author of a 13-volume treatise on mathematics, the *Elements*.

8. Dominique Bouhours (1628–1702), Jesuit teacher and grammarian; one of his works was translated into English in 1705 as *The Art of Criticism*.

9. Germanic peoples who invaded the Roman Empire in the early centuries of the Christian era. "Gothic" at this time has several meanings: Germanic; medieval, not classical; barbarous, crude. It also refers to a medieval architectural style not derived from Greek or Roman models.

1. In one of Ovid's *Heroides* (ca. 16 B.C.E.), which were verse letters between mythological lovers. Dryden's observation is from the dedication to his translation of Virgil's *Aeneid* (1697), Ovid's source for the story of Dido, the legendary founder and queen of Carthage, who killed herself when Aeneas, the legendary founder of Rome, deserted her.

The famous author of the art of love[2] has nothing of his own; he borrows all from a greater master in his own profession, and, which is worse, improves nothing which he finds: nature fails him, and being forced to his old shift, he has recourse to witticism. This passes indeed with his soft admirers, and gives him the preference to Virgil in their esteem.'

Were not I supported by so great an authority as that of Mr. Dryden, I should not venture to observe, that the taste of most of our English poets, as well as readers, is extremely Gothic. He quotes Monsieur Segrais[3] for a threefold distinction of the readers of poetry: in the first of which he comprehends the rabble of readers, whom he does not treat as such with regard to their quality, but to their numbers and the coarseness of their taste. His words are as follow: 'Segrais has distinguished the readers of poetry, according to their capacity of judging, into three classes. (He might have said the same of writers too, if he had pleased.) In the lowest form he places those whom he calls *les petits esprits*,[4] such things as are our upper-gallery audience in a play-house; who like nothing but the husk and rind of wit, prefer a quibble, a conceit, an epigram, before solid sense and elegant expression: these are mob-readers. If Virgil and Martial stood for parliament-men, we know already who would carry it.[5] But though they make the greatest appearance in the field, and cry the loudest, the best on't is they are but a sort of French Huguenots, or Dutch boors,[6] brought over in herds, but not naturalised; who have not lands of two pounds per annum in Parnassus,[7] and therefore are not privileged to poll.[8] Their authors are of the same level, fit to represent them on a mountebank's stage, or to be masters of the ceremonies in a bear-garden:[9] yet these are they who have the most admirers. But it often happens, to their mortification, that as their readers improve their stock of sense (as they may by reading better books, and by conversation with men of judgment) they soon forsake them.'

I must not dismiss this subject without observing, that as Mr. Locke in the passage above mentioned has discovered the most fruitful source of wit, so there is another of a quite contrary nature to it, which does likewise branch itself out into several kinds. For not only the resemblance but the opposition of ideas does very often produce wit; as I could show in several little points, turns, and antitheses, that I may possibly enlarge upon in some future speculation.

1711

2. *The Art of Love* is a didactic poem by Ovid.
3. Jean Regnauld de Segrais (1624–1701), French poet who translated Virgil's *Aeneid* and *Georgics*; Dryden quotes from an essay prefixed to that translation.
4. The small-minded (French).
5. That is, the witty Martial would defeat the solemn Virgil in an election.
6. Peasants. Addison here names the largest groups of immigrants in England.
7. Greek mountain sacred to Apollo and the Muses, and thus associated with poetry.
8. Vote. Only those who met certain property requirements could vote.
9. The site of bearbaiting (setting dogs on a chained bear for entertainment).

From The Spectator, No. 412 [On the Sublime]

—Divisum sic breve fiet opus.[1]

—Martial, *Epigrams*, 4.83

I shall first consider those pleasures of the imagination which arise from the actual view and survey of outward objects. And these, I think, all proceed from the sight of what is great, uncommon, or beautiful. There may, indeed, be something so terrible or offensive, that the horror or loathsomeness of an object may overbear the pleasure which results from its greatness, novelty, or beauty; but still there will be such a mixture of delight in the very disgust it gives us, as any of these three qualifications are most conspicuous and prevailing.

By greatness, I do not only mean the bulk of any single object, but the largeness of a whole view, considered as one entire piece. Such are the prospects of an open champian[2] country, a vast uncultivated desert, of huge heaps of mountains, high rocks and precipices, or a wide expanse of waters, where we are not struck with the novelty or beauty of the sight, but with that rude kind of magnificence which appears in many of these stupendous works of Nature. Our imagination loves to be filled with an object, or to grasp at anything that is too big for its capacity. We are flung into a pleasing astonishment at such unbounded views, and feel a delightful stillness and amazement in the soul at the apprehension of them. The mind of man naturally hates everything that looks like a restraint upon it, and is apt to fancy itself under a sort of confinement, when the sight is pent up in a narrow compass, and shortened on every side by the neighbourhood of walls or mountains. On the contrary, a spacious horizon is an image of liberty, where the eye has room to range abroad, to expatiate[3] at large on the immensity of its views, and to lose itself amidst the variety of objects that offer themselves to its observation. Such wide and undetermined[4] prospects are as pleasing to the fancy, as the speculations of eternity or infinitude are to the understanding. But if there be a beauty or uncommonness joined with this grandeur, as in a troubled ocean, a heaven adorned with stars and meteors, or a spacious landscape cut out into rivers, woods, rocks, and meadows, the pleasure still grows upon us, as it arises from more than a single principle.

Everything that is new or uncommon raises a pleasure in the imagination, because it fills the soul with an agreeable surprise, gratifies its curiosity, and gives it an idea of which it was not before possessed. We are, indeed, so often conversant with one set of objects, and tired out with so many repeated shows of the same things, that whatever is new or uncommon contributes a little to vary human life, and to divert our minds, for a while, with the strangeness of its appearance: it serves us for a kind of refreshment, and takes off from that satiety we are apt to complain of in our usual and ordinary entertainments. It is this that bestows charms on a

1. Divided thus, the work will be made brief (Latin). From the Roman poet Martial (ca. 40–ca. 104 C.E.), *Epigrams*.

2. Unbroken level plain.

3. Range freely.

4. Open.

monster, and makes even the imperfections of nature please us. It is this that recommends variety, where the mind is every instant called off to something new, and the attention not suffered to dwell too long, and waste itself on any particular object. It is this, likewise, that improves what is great or beautiful, and makes it afford the mind a double entertainment. Groves, fields, and meadows are at any season of the year pleasant to look upon, but never so much as in the opening of the spring, when they are all new and fresh with their first gloss upon them, and not yet too much accustomed and familiar to the eye. For this reason there is nothing that more enlivens a prospect than rivers, jetteaus,[5] or falls of water, where the scene is perpetually shifting, and entertaining the sight every moment with something that is new. We are quickly tired with looking upon hills and valleys, where everything continues fixed and settled in the same place and posture, but find our thoughts a little agitated and relieved at the sight of such objects as are ever in motion, and sliding away from beneath the eye of the beholder.

But there is nothing that makes its way more directly to the soul than beauty, which immediately diffuses a secret satisfaction and complacency through the imagination, and gives a finishing to anything that is great or uncommon. The very first discovery of it strikes the mind with an inward joy, and spreads a cheerfulness and delight through all its faculties. There is not, perhaps, any real beauty or deformity more in one piece of matter than another, because we might have been so made that whatsoever now appears loathsome to us might have shown itself agreeable; but we find by experience that there are several modifications of matter which the mind, without any previous consideration, pronounces at first sight beautiful or deformed. Thus we see that every different species of sensible[6] creatures has its different notions of beauty, and that each of them is most affected with the beauties of its own kind. This is nowhere more remarkable than in birds of the same shape and proportion, where we often see the male determined in his courtship by the single grain[7] or tincture of a feather, and never discovering any charms but in the colour of its species.[8]

* * *

There is a second kind of beauty that we find in the several products of art and nature which does not work in the imagination with that warmth and violence as the beauty that appears in our proper species, but is apt, however, to raise in us a secret delight, and a kind of fondness for the places or objects in which we discover it. This consists either in the gaiety or variety of colours, in the symmetry and proportion of parts, in the arrangement and disposition of bodies, or in a just mixture and concurrence of all together. Among these several kinds of beauty the eye takes most delight in colours. We nowhere meet with a more glorious or pleasing show in nature than what appears in the heavens at the rising and setting of the sun, which is wholly made up of those different stains of light that show themselves in clouds of a different situation. For this reason we find the poets, who are always addressing themselves to the imagination, borrowing more of their epithets from colours than from any other topic.

5. Fountains or jets of water.
6. Endowed with sensation.
7. Hue.
8. We have omitted here 19 lines of Latin verse, probably by Addison himself, describing the courtship of birds.

As the fancy delights in everything that is great, strange, or beautiful, and is still more pleased the more it finds of these perfections in the same object, so it is capable of receiving a new satisfaction by the assistance of another sense. Thus any continued sound, as the music of birds, or a fall of water, awakens every moment the mind of the beholder, and makes him more attentive to the several beauties of the place that lie before him. Thus if there arises a fragrancy of smells or perfumes, they heighten the pleasures of the imagination, and make even the colours and verdure of the landscape appear more agreeable; for the ideas of both senses recommend each other, and are pleasanter together than when they enter the mind separately, as the different colours of a picture, when they are well disposed, set off one another, and receive an additional beauty from the advantage of their situation.

1712

ALEXANDER POPE
1688–1744

Scholars have noted dozens of sources—the Roman writers HORACE and Quintilian (ca. 30/35–100 C.E.), the French poet-critic Nicolas Boileau (1636–1711), his English contemporary JOHN DRYDEN, and many more—for Alexander Pope's versified "art of poetry," *An Essay on Criticism* (1711); but their labors, though valuable, miss the central point. Pope advanced no claims for the originality of the views he presented, and in the final analysis his poem is memorable less for its doctrine than for the brilliance of its style, which revitalizes familiar teachings and makes them sparkle. It delightfully illustrates Pope's own view of literary "borrowing": that "poets, like merchants, should repay with something of their own what they take from others, not, like pirates, make prize of all they meet." The *Essay* is a sophisticated, witty poem, a compendium of critical principles, with much reading and reflection behind it—from an author who was astonishingly young when it was written.

Pope was born in London in 1688, the year of the Glorious Revolution, when the Catholic King James II was deposed in favor of Protestant William III and Mary II. He was the son of a linen merchant who was Roman Catholic, and thus suffered from the controls of England's anti-Catholic laws. While not always strictly enforced, these laws were onerous. Catholics were prevented from practicing their religion freely; they could not legally reside within ten miles of London; they were not allowed to attend the universities, vote, or hold public offices or seats in Parliament. In 1711 Pope's family moved to Binfield in Windsor Forest, thirty miles outside London, a place that Pope described evocatively in one of his best early poems, "Windsor-Forest" (1713).

A local priest taught Greek and Latin to Pope, and he picked up French and Italian during a short term of study in London. Pope's father encouraged him to write verse, insisting that his son's rhymes be perfect, and Pope early on crafted "imitations" of Chaucer (ca. 1343–1400), Edmund Spenser (1552–1599), Edmund Waller (1606–1687), and Abraham Cowley (1618–1667). Limitations not simply legal but also physical encouraged him to focus on his literary efforts. Tuberculosis of the bones in childhood had curved Pope's spine and stunted his growth—he was only four and a half feet tall—and throughout his life he suffered from frequent and severe headaches.

In addition to *An Essay on Criticism* and "Windsor-Forest," Pope's major poems include "The Rape of the Lock" (1712; enlarged ed., 1714); *The Dunciad*, targeting Pope's literary enemies (first published anonymously in 1728; enlarged eds. 1742, 1743); *Moral Essays* (1731–35); *Imitations of Horace* (1733–38) and their prologue, "An Epistle to Dr. Arbuthnot" (1735); and *An Essay on Man* (1733–34), a philosophical poem designed to "vindicate the ways of God to Man" (1.16). Pope also produced a magnificent translation of the *Iliad* (1715–20), co-translated the *Odyssey* (1725–26), and edited the works of Shakespeare (1725). He had concerns outside literature; his keen interests in painting, sculpture, architecture, and horticulture were expressed in the garden and grotto that he built at Twickenham, a five-acre villa he rented on the Thames, where he moved with his mother after his father's death in 1718.

An Essay on Criticism was published anonymously on May 15, 1711, a week before the poet's twenty-third birthday. The manuscript we have is dated in Pope's hand, "Written in the year 1709," but elsewhere he put the date of composition as early as 1706. And though he claimed to have written the *Essay* quickly, the manuscript shows that he revised his poem carefully. For later editions, Pope provided a table of contents and divided the 750-line poem into three parts—the second starting at line 201 and the third at line 560.

Pope means his lively heroic couplets to remind readers of principles they already should know. Like many writers in the seventeenth and eighteenth centuries, he judges literature to be plagued by ill-informed, careless, proud, and pompous critics, whose mistaken evaluations of texts mislead authors as well as readers. John Dryden, in "The Author's Apology for Heroic Poetry" (1677), similarly laments that he and his fellow authors have "fallen into an age of illiterate, censorious, and detracting people, who, thus qualified, set up for critics." In the *Essay* Pope writes that the dismaying state of criticism reflects a broad historical decline from the Greek and Roman past—the golden age of art, when critics generously sought to advise authors and to instruct readers on how to appreciate them.

The best works of art, Pope maintains, derive from a deeply felt, well-reasoned study of Nature; and studying the great works of the past leads one to see their reliance on the stable principles of harmony and order that Nature itself teaches. This is Pope's and his age's neoclassicism—to imitate the ancient authors and adopt the critical precepts that these authors and their texts embody. Like Jonathan Swift, JOSEPH ADDISON, and other significant writers of the early to mid–eighteenth century, Pope particularly admired the authors, notably Virgil, Ovid, and Horace, who had flourished during the reign of the Roman emperor Augustus (27 B.C.E.–14 C.E.), and he sought through his writing to make his own era similarly "Augustan" in its literary production. Reading Homer and Virgil, Pope believed, sharpens taste and judgment and enables us to perceive the intimate relationship between art and Nature. The classic texts are, like Nature, a standard and a guide. Their balance, harmony, and good proportion are evident in their parts as well as demonstrated in the whole. In the prosody of a poem, for example, the sound and meter in a well-proportioned and well-regulated work enact the actions and the sense conveyed (see lines 364–73).

At moments, as when Pope rebukes pride and envy (e.g., lines 201–18), the *Essay* might strike some readers today as less about literature and criticism than about morality. But as Pope sees it, good authors or critics must truly know themselves and possess a finely developed moral sense and purpose. Such people know and abide by the limits of human aspiration, seek models for right aesthetic and moral conduct, and guard against the self-delusion and self-destructiveness of overweening pride.

Some critics contend that Pope uses his chief terms, such as *Nature, wit,* and *judgment*, too loosely, and they have claimed that the *Essay* lacks a coherent structure. It is, like Horace's *Ars Poetica*, more associative than logical. It offers encouragement and advice in a sequence of briskly paced observations on the nature of art, the value of the ancients, the importance of the rules, the need to observe decorum in word selection, the connection between artistic creation and criticism, and other topics. The key words are invoked in different passages to enliven the specific point at hand. Rather than using them loosely, Pope deliberately draws on all of their senses.

For example, *wit* (from the Old English *witan*, "to know") is a complex, multivalent word, difficult to pin down, and Pope capitalizes on its range of meanings and implications. It means, first, the mind or the understanding, the faculty of reasoning and thinking. In his *Dictionary* (1755), SAMUEL JOHNSON gives as its "original signification" "the powers of the mind; the mental faculties; the intellects." But wit can also refer, he notes, to a poetic conceit, figure of speech, felicitous phrasing, common sense, inventiveness, astuteness of perception, the capacity to see resemblance in apparently unlike things, cleverness, fancy, genius; it can mean the imaginative power that judgment must temper and control (see, e.g., lines 82–83), even as it also implies judgment itself—wit curbing excessive wit. Pope offers his own definition in perhaps the best-known couplets of the *Essay*:

> *True Wit* is *Nature* to Advantage drest,
> What oft was *Thought*, but ne'er so well *Exprest*,
> *Something*, whose Truth convinc'd at Sight we find,
> That gives us back the Image of our Mind. (lines 297–300)

Wit *is* Nature; it instances something that we have all thought, but whose sheer truth the poet now makes compelling through his or her language. True wit is subtle, sharp, and, above all, surprising—a striking image, a vivid metaphor, a paradoxical figure of speech. Addison and Johnson also delve into the nature of wit, but it is Pope who exemplifies the meanings of this complex word and idea more inventively than any other writer in the canon of eighteenth-century English literature and criticism.

The most memorable assessment of the *Essay* remains Samuel Johnson's: "[The *Essay*] exhibits every mode of excellence that can embellish or dignify didactick composition, selection of matter, novelty of arrangement, justness of precept, splendour of illustration, and propriety of digression." It is a hopeful work, all the more affecting in light of the political quarrels and ferocious literary feuds in which Pope engaged later in his career. These climaxed in his gigantic satire of literary idiocy, *The Dunciad, in Four Books*, published in its final form in October 1743. In this great last text of his poetic career, Pope describes the sublime awfulness of hordes of pedants, false poets, and dunces. His dazzling punitive wit here takes on the grotesque grandeur of mock-epic, on a scale eclipsing that displayed in the elegant, highly cultivated early work. *The Dunciad* shows Pope's angry realization of the difficulty in winning wide acceptance for the neoclassical views that he had advocated and had described with both power and grace in *An Essay on Criticism*.

***An Essay on Criticism* Keywords:** Aesthetics, Authorship, The Canon/Tradition, Defense of Criticism, Enlightenment Theory, Poetry

From An Essay on Criticism

———Si quid novisti rectius istis,
Candidus imperti; si non, his utere mecum.
—Horat[1]

'Tis hard to say, if greater Want of Skill
Appear in *Writing* or in *Judging* ill;
But, of the two, less dang'rous is th' Offence,
To tire our *Patience*, than mis-lead our *Sense*:
Some few in *that*, but Numbers err in *this*,
Ten Censure[2] wrong for one who Writes amiss;
A *Fool* might once *himself* alone expose,
Now *One* in *Verse* makes many more in *Prose*.
'Tis with our *Judgments* as our *Watches*, none
Go just *alike*, yet each believes his own.
In *Poets* as true *Genius* is but rare,
True *Taste* as seldom is the *Critick's* Share;
Both must alike from Heav'n derive their Light,
These *born* to Judge, as well as those to Write.
Let such teach others who themselves excell,
And *censure freely* who have *written well*.
Authors are partial to their *Wit*, 'tis true,
But are not *Criticks* to their *Judgment* too?
Yet if we look more closely, we shall find
Most have the *Seeds* of Judgment in their Mind;
Nature affords at least a *glimm'ring Light*;
The *Lines*, tho' touch'd but faintly, are drawn right.
But as the slightest Sketch, if justly trac'd,
Is by ill *Colouring* but the more disgrac'd,
So by *false Learning* is *good Sense* defac'd;
Some are bewilder'd in the Maze of Schools,
And some made *Coxcombs*[3] Nature meant but *Fools*.
In search of *Wit* these lose their *common Sense*,
And then turn Criticks in their own Defence.
Each burns alike, who can, or cannot write,
Or with a *Rival*'s, or an *Eunuch*'s spite.
All *Fools* have still an Itching to deride,
And fain *wou'd* be upon the *Laughing Side*:
If *Mævius* Scribble in *Apollo*'s[4] spight,
There are, who *judge* still *worse* than he can *write*.
Some have at first for *Wits*, then *Poets* past,
Turn'd *Criticks* next, and prov'd plain *Fools* at last;
Some neither can for *Wits* nor *Criticks* pass,

1. HORACE (65–8 B.C.E.), *Epistles* 1.6.67–68: "If you know any maxims better than these, be so good as to let me know them; if not, use these as I do."
2. Judge.
3. Pretenders to learning, conceited asses.
4. Greek and Roman god of poetry. Maevius (1st c. B.C.E.), a bad poet to whom both Virgil (*Eclogue* 3) and Horace (*Epode* 10) allude.

As heavy Mules are neither *Horse* nor *Ass*.
Those half-learn'd Witlings, num'rous in our Isle,
As half-form'd Insects on the Banks of *Nile*;[5]
Unfinish'd Things, one knows not what to call,
Their Generation's so *equivocal*:
To tell[6] 'em, wou'd a *hundred Tongues* require,
Or *one vain Wit's*, that might a hundred tire.
  But *you* who seek to *give* and *merit* Fame,
And justly bear a Critick's noble Name,
Be sure *your self* and your own *Reach* to know,
How far your *Genius, Taste*, and *Learning* go;
Launch not beyond your Depth, but be discreet,
And mark *that Point* where Sense and Dulness *meet*.
  Nature to all things fix'd the Limits fit,
And wisely curb'd proud Man's pretending Wit:
As on the *Land* while *here* the *Ocean* gains,
In *other Parts* it leaves wide sandy Plains;
Thus in the *Soul* while *Memory* prevails,
The solid Pow'r of *Understanding* fails;
Where Beams of warm *Imagination* play,
The *Memory*'s soft Figures melt away.
One *Science*[7] only will one *Genius* fit;
So *vast* is Art,[8] so *narrow* Human Wit:
Not only bounded to *peculiar Arts*,
But oft in *those*, confin'd to *single Parts*.
Like Kings we lose the Conquests gain'd before,
By vain Ambition still to make them more:
Each might his *sev'ral Province* well command,
Wou'd all but *stoop* to what they *understand*.
  First follow NATURE,[9] and your Judgment frame
By her just Standard, which is still the same:[1]
Unerring Nature, still divinely bright,
One *clear, unchang'd*, and *Universal* Light,
Life, Force, and Beauty, must to all impart,
At once the *Source*, and *End*, and *Test* of *Art*.
Art from that Fund each *just Supply* provides,
Works *without Show*,[2] and *without Pomp* presides:
In some fair Body thus th' informing Soul
With Spirits feeds, with Vigour fills the whole,
Each Motion guides, and ev'ry Nerve sustains;
It self unseen, but in th' *Effects*, remains.

5. The ancients believed that forms of animal and insect life were spontaneously generated on the banks of the Nile River.
6. Count.
7. Branch of learning.
8. Pope alludes to a maxim attributed to Hippocrates (ca. 460–ca. 377 B.C.E.), celebrated Greek physician: "Life is short, but art [sometimes translated 'science'] is long, opportunity fleeting, experiment dangerous, judgment difficult."
9. The term encompasses the physical world, the sum of human experiences, and the principle of order and coherence in the universe.
1. Compare JOHN DRYDEN's claim in *Parallel betwixt Poetry and Painting* (1695): "For Nature is still the same in all ages, and can never be contrary to herself."
2. Pope here recalls the familiar Latin maxim *ars est celare artem* (the art is to conceal the art).

Some, to whom Heav'n in Wit has been profuse,
Want as much more, to turn it to its use;
For *Wit*[3] and *Judgment* often are at strife,
Tho' meant each other's Aid, like *Man* and *Wife*.
'Tis more to *guide* than *spur* the Muse's Steed;[4]
Restrain his Fury, than provoke his Speed;
The winged Courser, like a gen'rous[5] Horse,
Shows most true Mettle when you *check* his Course.

* * *

Of all the Causes which conspire to blind
Man's erring Judgment, and misguide the Mind,
What the weak Head with strongest Byass[6] rules,
Is *Pride*, the *never-failing Vice of Fools*.
Whatever Nature has in *Worth* deny'd,
She gives in large Recruits[7] of *needful Pride*;
For as in *Bodies*, thus in *Souls*, we find
What wants in *Blood* and *Spirits*, swell'd with *Wind*;
Pride, where Wit fails, steps in to our Defence,
And fills up all the *mighty* Void of Sense!
If once right Reason drives *that Cloud* away,
Truth breaks upon us with *resistless Day*;
Trust not your self; but your Defects to know,
Make use of ev'ry *Friend*—and ev'ry *Foe*.
A *little Learning* is a dang'rous Thing;
Drink deep, or taste not the *Pierian*[8] Spring:
There *shallow Draughts* intoxicate the Brain,
And drinking *largely* sobers us again.
Fir'd at first Sight with what the *Muse* imparts,
In *fearless Youth* we tempt[9] the Heights of Arts,
While from the bounded *Level* of our Mind,
Short Views we take, nor see the *Lengths behind*,
But *more advanc'd*, behold with strange Surprize
New, distant Scenes of *endless* Science rise!
So pleas'd at first, the towring *Alps* we try,
Mount o'er the Vales, and seem to tread the Sky;
Th' Eternal Snows appear already past,
And the first *Clouds* and *Mountains* seem the last:
But *those attain'd*, we tremble to survey
The growing Labours of the lengthen'd Way,
Th' *increasing* Prospect *tires* our wandring Eyes,

3. *Wit* has a range of meanings, including reasoning power, intelligence, mental soundness, sanity, astuteness of perception or judgment, and the ability to see relationships between seemingly disparate things. It also can refer to a person of sound judgment and perception.
4. Pegasus, the winged horse of classical mythology, identified with inspiration. Muse: one of the 9 daughters of Memory who preside over the arts and all intellectual pursuits.
5. High spirited, noble.
6. Bias, a term from lawn bowling: the irregularity in the shape of the ball that causes it to swerve.
7. Supplies, troops, reinforcements.
8. Belonging to the Pierides, another name for the Muses (the spring is Hippocrene—located on Mt. Helicon, in central Greece—which was sacred to the Muses).
9. Attempt, dare.

Hills peep o'er Hills, and *Alps* on *Alps* arise!
A perfect Judge will *read* each Work of Wit
With the same Spirit that its Author *writ*,
Survey the Whole, nor seek slight Faults to find,
Where *Nature moves*, and *Rapture warms* the Mind;
Nor lose, for that malignant dull Delight,
The *gen'rous Pleasure* to be charm'd with Wit.
But in such Lays[1] as neither *ebb*, nor *flow*,
Correctly cold, and *regularly low*,
That shunning Faults, one quiet *Tenour* keep;
We cannot *blame* indeed—but we may *sleep*.
In Wit, as Nature, what affects our Hearts
Is not th' Exactness of peculiar Parts;
'Tis not a Lip, or *Eye*, we Beauty call,
But the joint Force and full *Result* of *all*.
Thus when we view some well-proportion'd Dome,[2]
(The *World's* just Wonder, and ev'n *thine* O *Rome*!)
No single Parts unequally surprize;
All comes *united* to th' admiring Eyes;
No monstrous Height, or Breadth, or Length appear;
The *Whole* at once is *Bold*, and *Regular*.
Whoever thinks a faultless Piece to see,
Thinks what ne'er was, nor is, nor e'er shall be.
In ev'ry Work regard the *Writer's End*,
Since none can compass more than they *Intend*;
And if the *Means* be just, the *Conduct* true,
Applause, in spite of trivial Faults, is due.[3]
As Men of Breeding, sometimes Men of Wit,
T' avoid *great Errors*, must the *less* commit,
Neglect the Rules each *Verbal Critick* lays,
For *not* to know some Trifles, is a Praise.
Most Criticks, fond of some subservient Art,
Still make the *Whole* depend upon a *Part*,
They talk of *Principles*, but Notions prize,
And All to one lov'd Folly Sacrifice.
Once on a time, *La Mancha*'s Knight,[4] they say,
A certain *Bard* encountring on the Way,
Discours'd in Terms as just, with Looks as Sage,
As e'er cou'd *Dennis*,[5] of the *Grecian* Stage;
Concluding all were desp'rate Sots and Fools,
Who durst depart from *Aristotle*'s Rules.[6]

1. Songs; narrative poems or ballads.
2. Specifically, the dome of St. Peter's Basilica in Rome (16th c.).
3. Compare John Dryden, "The Author's Apology for Heroic Poetry" (1677): "'Tis malicious and unmannerly to snarl at the little lapses of a pen, from which Virgil [Roman poet (70–19 B.C.E.), author of the greatest Latin epic, the *Aeneid*] himself stands not exempted."
4. Don Quixote, title character of the work by Miguel de Cervantes (1605, 1615); but Pope's story is taken from a spurious sequel to *Don Quixote* written by Don Alonzo Fernandez de Avellaneda (trans. 1705).
5. John Dennis (1657–1734), English critic and playwright.
6. That is, the "rules" for tragedy and epic derived from his *Poetics* (see above); because ARISTOTLE (384–322 B.C.E.) was born in Stagira (in Macedonia), he was sometimes called "the Stagyrite."

Our Author, happy in a Judge so nice,[7]
Produc'd his Play, and beg'd the Knight's Advice,
Made him observe the *Subject* and the *Plot*,
The *Manners, Passions, Unities*,[8] what not?
All which, exact to *Rule* were brought about,
Were but a *Combate in the Lists*[9] left out.
What! Leave the Combate out? Exclaims the Knight;
Yes, or we must renounce the *Stagyrite*.
Not so by Heav'n (he answers in a Rage)
Knights, Squires, and Steeds, must enter on the Stage.
So vast a Throng the Stage can ne'er contain.
Then build a New, or act it in a Plain.
   Thus Criticks, of less Judgment than *Caprice*,
Curious,[1] not *Knowing*, not *exact*, but *nice*,
Form *short Ideas*; and offend in *Arts*
(As most in *Manners*) by a *Love to Parts*.
   Some to *Conceit*[2] alone their Taste confine,
And glitt'ring Thoughts struck out[3] at ev'ry Line;
Pleas'd with a Work where nothing's just or fit;
One *glaring Chaos* and *wild Heap* of *Wit*:
Poets like Painters, thus, unskill'd to trace
The *naked Nature* and the *living Grace*,
With *Gold* and *Jewels* cover ev'ry Part,
And hide with *Ornaments* their *Want of Art*.
True Wit is *Nature* to Advantage drest,
What oft was *Thought*, but ne'er so well *Exprest*,
Something, whose Truth convinc'd at Sight we find,
That gives us back the Image of our Mind:
As Shades more sweetly recommend the Light,
So modest Plainness sets off sprightly Wit:
For *Works* may have more *Wit* than does 'em good,
As *Bodies* perish through Excess of *Blood*.[4]
   Others for *Language* all their Care express,
And value *Books*, as Women *Men*, for *Dress*:
Their Praise is still—*The Stile is excellent*:
The *Sense*, they humbly take upon Content.[5]
Words are like *Leaves*; and where they most abound,
Much *Fruit of Sense* beneath is rarely found.
False Eloquence, like the *Prismatic Glass*,
Its gawdy Colours spreads on *ev'ry place*;[6]
The Face of Nature we no more Survey,
All glares *alike*, without *Distinction* gay:
But true *Expression*, like th' unchanging *Sun*,

7. Precise, overrefined.
8. The neoclassical unities (of action, time, and place) thought to govern drama; see PIERRE CORNEILLE, "Of the Three Unities" (1660; above).
9. Field for jousting.
1. Particular, difficult to satisfy.
2. The extravagant use of similes and metaphors.
3. Produced by a stroke of invention.
4. Standard medical practice of Pope's time included bleeding patients to reduce their "excess of blood."
5. Accept on authority.
6. An allusion to Isaac Newton's *Optics* (1703), which discusses the prism and spectrum.

Clears, and *improves* whate'er it shines upon,
It *gilds* all Objects, but it *alters* none.
Expression is the *Dress* of *Thought*, and still
Appears more *decent* as more *suitable*;
A vile Conceit in pompous Words exprest,
Is like a Clown in regal Purple drest;
For diff'rent *Styles* with diff'rent *Subjects* sort,
As several Garbs with Country, Town, and Court.
Some by *Old Words* to Fame have made Pretence;
Ancients in *Phrase*, meer Moderns in their *Sense*!
Such *labour'd Nothings*, in so *strange* a Style,
Amaze th'unlearn'd, and make the Learned *Smile*.
Unlucky, as *Fungoso*[7] in the Play,
These Sparks with aukward Vanity display
What the Fine Gentleman wore *Yesterday*!
And but so mimick ancient Wits at best,
As Apes our Grandsires in their *Doublets drest*.
In *Words*, as *Fashions*, the same Rule will hold;
Alike Fantastick, if *too New*, or *Old*;
Be not the *first* by whom the *New* are try'd,
Nor yet the *last* to lay the *Old* aside.
    But most by *Numbers*[8] judge a Poet's Song,
And *smooth* or *rough*, with them, is *right* or *wrong*;
In the bright *Muse* tho' thousand *Charms* conspire,
Her Voice is all these tuneful Fools admire,
Who haunt *Parnassus* but to please their Ear,
Not mend their Minds; as some to *Church* repair,
Not for the *Doctrine*, but the *Musick* there.
These *Equal Syllables* alone require,
Tho' oft the Ear the open *Vowels* tire,[9]
While *Expletives*[1] their feeble Aid *do* join,
And ten low Words oft creep in one dull Line,
While they ring round the same *unvary'd Chimes*,
With sure *Returns* of still *expected Rhymes*.
Where-e'er you find the cooling *Western Breeze*,
In the next Line, it *whispers thro' the Trees*;
If *Chrystal Streams with pleasing Murmurs creep*,
The Reader's threaten'd (not in vain) with *Sleep*.
Then, at the *last*, and *only* Couplet fraught
With some *unmeaning* Thing they call a *Thought*,
A *needless Alexandrine*[2] ends the Song,
That like a wounded Snake, drags its slow length along.
Leave such to tune their own dull Rhimes, and know

7. A poor student in Ben Jonson's play *Every Man out of His Humour* (1599), who tries without success to keep up with the fashions.
8. Meters.
9. That is, when a word ending in a vowel is followed by a word beginning with one (e.g., "the open"). Throughout this passage, Pope exemplifies in his verse the fault or virtue discussed.
1. Words used to complete the number of feet needed in a line of verse without adding to the sense.
2. A line of 12 syllables (rather than the usual 10), like line 357.

What's *roundly smooth*, or *languishingly slow*;
And praise the *Easie Vigor* of a Line,
Where *Denham*'s Strength, and *Waller*'s Sweetness join.[3]
True Ease in Writing comes from Art, not Chance,
As those move easiest who have learn'd to dance.
'Tis not enough no Harshness gives Offence,
The *Sound* must seem an *Eccho* to the *Sense*.
Soft is the Strain when *Zephyr*[4] gently blows,
And the *smooth Stream* in *smoother Numbers* flows;
But when loud Surges lash the sounding Shore,
The *hoarse, rough Verse* shou'd like the *Torrent* roar.
When *Ajax*[5] strives, some Rock's vast Weight to throw,
The Line too *labours*, and the Words move *slow*;
Not so, when swift *Camilla*[6] scours the Plain,
Flies o'er th'unbending Corn, and skims along the Main.
Hear how *Timotheus'*[7] vary'd Lays surprize,
And bid Alternate Passions fall and rise!
While, at each Change, the Son of *Lybian Jove*[8]
Now *burns* with Glory, and then *melts* with Love;
Now his *fierce Eyes* with *sparkling Fury* glow;
Now *Sighs* steal out, and *Tears begin to flow*:
Persians and *Greeks* like *Turns of Nature*[9] found,
And the *World's Victor* stood subdu'd by *Sound*!
The Pow'r of Musick all our Hearts allow;
And what *Timotheus* was, is *Dryden* now.
   Avoid *Extreams*; and shun the Fault of such,
Who still are pleas'd *too little*, or *too much*.
At ev'ry Trifle scorn to take Offence,
That always shows *Great Pride*, or *Little Sense*;
Those *Heads* as *Stomachs* are not sure the best
Which nauseate all, and nothing can digest.
Yet let not each gay *Turn* thy Rapture move,
For Fools *Admire*, but Men of Sense *Approve;*[1]
As things seem *large* which we thro' *Mists* descry,
Dulness is ever apt to *Magnify*.
   Some *foreign* Writers, some our *own* despise;
The *Ancients* only, or the *Moderns* prize:
(Thus *Wit*, like *Faith*, by each Man is apply'd
To *one small Sect*, and All are *damn'd beside*.)

3. Pope, like Dryden before him, admired the English poets John Denham (1615–1669) and, especially, Edmund Waller (1606–1687) for having improved English versification (in particular, the heroic couplet, the form used in this poem).
4. The west wind; a gentle breeze.
5. A Greek hero in the *Iliad*, known for his great strength.
6. A woman warrior who fought against the Trojans in Italy. In *Aeneid* 7.808–11, Virgil describes her ability to skim over ears of wheat (i.e., "corn") and over the sea.
7. Alexander the Great's musician; presented in Dryden's ode "Alexander's Feast" (1697) as modulating Alexander's moods through the shifts in his music.
8. Alexander the Great (356–323 B.C.E.), who liked to claim that Zeus (identified with the Roman Jupiter) was his father. Priests of the celebrated oracle of Zeus Ammon in Siwa, north of the Libyan desert, greeted Alexander as the son of Zeus.
9. Alternations of feelings.
1. Judge with discrimination (vs. wonder at without comprehension).

Meanly they seek the Blessing to confine,
And force *that Sun* but on a *Part* to Shine;
Which not alone the Southern Wit sublimes,[2]
But ripens Spirits in cold *Northern Climes*;
Which from the first has shone on *Ages past*,
Enlights the *present*, and shall warm the *last*:
(Tho' *each* may feel *Increases* and *Decays*,
And see now *clearer* and now *darker Days*)
Regard not then if Wit be *Old* or *New*,
But blame the *False*, and value still the *True*.
   Some ne'er advance a Judgment of their own,
But *catch* the *spreading Notion* of the Town;
They reason and conclude by *Precedent*,
And own *stale Nonsense* which they ne'er invent.
Some judge of Authors' *Names*, not *Works*, and then
Nor praise nor blame the *Writings*, but the *Men*.
Of all this *Servile Herd* the worst is He
That in *proud Dulness* joins with *Quality*,[3]
A constant Critick at the Great-man's Board,
To *fetch and carry* Nonsense for my Lord.
What *woful stuff* this Madrigal wou'd be,
In some starv'd Hackny Sonneteer,[4] or me?
But let a *Lord* once own the *happy Lines*,
How the *Wit brightens*! How the *Style refines*!
Before *his* sacred Name flies ev'ry Fault,
And each *exalted* Stanza *teems* with *Thought*!
   The *Vulgar* thus through *Imitation* err;
As oft the *Learn'd* by being *Singular*;
So much they scorn the Crowd, that if the Throng
By *Chance* go right, they *purposely* go wrong;
So Schismatics[5] the *plain Believers* quit,
And are but damn'd for having *too much Wit*.
   Some praise at Morning what they blame at Night;
But always think the *last* Opinion *right*.
A Muse by these is like a Mistress us'd,
This hour she's *idoliz'd*, the next *abus'd*,
While their weak Heads, like Towns unfortify'd,
'Twixt Sense and Nonsense daily change their Side.
Ask them the Cause; *They're wiser still*, they say;
And still to Morrow's wiser than to Day.
We think our *Fathers* Fools, so *wise* we grow;
Our *wiser Sons*, no doubt, will think *us* so.
Once *School-Divines*[6] this zealous Isle o'erspread;
Who knew most *Sentences*[7] was *deepest read*;

2. Raises up.
3. People of high rank.
4. Hireling poet.
5. Sectarians in religion.
6. Medieval theologians.
7. A reference to Peter Lombard's *Four Books of Sentences* (ca. 1145–51), which in a long series of questions presents the views of the fathers and doctors of the church on complex doctrinal matters; it became the standard theological text of the Middle Ages.

Faith, Gospel, All, seem'd made to be *disputed*,
And none had *Sense enough to be Confuted*.
Scotists and *Thomists*,[8] now, in Peace remain,
Amidst their *kindred Cobwebs* in *Duck-Lane*.[9]
If *Faith* it self has *diff'rent Dresses* worn,
What wonder *Modes* in *Wit* shou'd take their Turn?
Oft, leaving what is Natural and fit,
The *current Folly* proves the *ready Wit*,[1]
And Authors think their Reputation safe,
Which lives as long as *Fools* are pleas'd to *Laugh*.
Some valuing those of their own *Side*, or *Mind*,
Still make themselves the measure of Mankind;
Fondly[2] we think we honour Merit then,
When we but praise *Our selves* in *Other Men*.
Parties in *Wit* attend on those of *State*,
And publick Faction doubles private Hate.
Pride, Malice, Folly, against *Dryden* rose,
In various Shapes of *Parsons, Criticks, Beaus*;[3]
But Sense surviv'd, when *merry Jests* were past;
For rising Merit will *buoy up* at last.
Might he return, and bless once more our Eyes,
New *Blackmores* and new *Milbourns*[4] must arise;
Nay shou'd great *Homer* lift his awful[5] Head,
Zoilus[6] again would start up from the Dead.
Envy will *Merit* as its *Shade* pursue,
But like a Shadow, proves the *Substance* true;
For envy'd Wit, like *Sol*[7] Eclips'd, makes known
Th' *opposing Body's* Grossness, not its *own*.
When first that Sun too powerful Beams displays,
It draws up Vapours which obscure its Rays;
But ev'n those Clouds at last adorn its Way,
Reflect new Glories, and augment the Day.

* * *

LEARN then what MORALS Criticks ought to show,
For 'tis but *half a Judge's Task*, to *Know*.
'Tis not enough, Taste, Judgment, Learning, join;
In all you speak, let Truth and Candor[8] shine:

8. The two main schools of medieval philosophy were the followers of Duns Scotus (ca. 1270–1308) and of THOMAS AQUINAS (1225–1274).
9. A London street where old books were sold.
1. Facile, clever expression.
2. Foolishly.
3. That is, beaux: fops, dandies, men overly concerned about their dress and appearance. Pope has in mind John Wilmot (1647–1680), second earl of Rochester, and George Villiers (1627–1687), second duke of Buckingham. "Parsons": these included Jeremy Collier (1650–1726), whose *Short View of the Immorality and Profaneness of the English Stage* (1698) targeted Dryden. "Criticks": these included Thomas Shadwell (ca. 1642–1692), an English dramatist and poet who savagely attacked Dryden in the 1680s.
4. Luke Milbourne (1649–1720), a clergyman whose *Notes on Dryden's Virgil* (1698) criticized the translation. Sir Richard Blackmore (1654–1729), physician and poet who criticized Dryden in *Satire against Wit* (1700).
5. Awe-inspiring. Homer (ca. 8th c. B.C.E.), Greek poet to whom the *Iliad* and *Odyssey* are ascribed.
6. A 4th-century B.C.E. philosopher and grammarian notorious for his bitter attacks on the *Iliad* and the *Odyssey*.
7. The sun.
8. Impartiality.

That not alone what to your *Sense* is due,
All may allow; but seek your *Friendship* too.
Be *silent* always when you *doubt* your Sense;
And *speak*, tho' *sure*, with *seeming Diffidence*:
Some positive persisting Fops we know,
Who, if *once wrong*, will needs be *always so*;
But you, with Pleasure own your Errors past,
And make each Day a *Critick* on[9] the last.
'Tis not enough your Counsel still be *true*,
Blunt Truths more Mischief than *nice Falshoods* do;
Men must be *taught* as if you taught them *not*;
And Things *unknown* propos'd as Things *forgot*:
Without *Good Breeding, Truth* is disapprov'd;
That only makes *Superior* Sense *belov'd*.
Be Niggards of Advice on no Pretence;
For the *worst Avarice* is that of *Sense*:
With mean Complacence[1] ne'er betray your Trust,
Nor be so *Civil* as to prove *Unjust*;
Fear not the Anger of the Wise to raise;
Those best can *bear Reproof*, who *merit Praise*.
'Twere well, might Criticks still this Freedom take;
But *Appius*[2] reddens at each Word you speak,
And *stares, Tremendous*! with a *threatning Eye*,
Like some *fierce Tyrant* in *Old Tapestry*!
Fear most to tax an *Honourable* Fool,
Whose Right it is, *uncensur'd* to be dull;
Such without *Wit* are Poets when they please,
As without *Learning* they can take *Degrees*.[3]
Leave dang'rous *Truths* to unsuccessful *Satyrs*,[4]
And *Flattery* to fulsome *Dedicators*,
Whom, when they *Praise*, the World believes no more,
Than when they promise to give *Scribling* o'er.
'Tis best sometimes your Censure to restrain,
And *charitably* let the Dull be *vain*:
Your Silence there is better than your *Spite*,
For who can *rail* so long as they can *write*?
Still humming on, their drowzy Course they keep,
And *lash'd* so long, like *Tops*, are lash'd *asleep*.[5]
False Steps but help them to renew the Race,
As after *Stumbling*, Jades[6] will *mend* their Pace.
What Crouds of these, impenitently bold,
In *Sounds* and jingling *Syllables* grown old,
Still *run on* Poets in a raging Vein,

9. Critique of, commentary on.
1. Desire to please.
2. John Dennis; Appius, in his tragedy *Appius and Virginia* (1709), was highly sensitive to criticism. Dennis frequently used the word "tremendous."
3. Those in certain positions (e.g., privy councillors) could receive university degrees without fulfilling any requirements.
4. Satires.
5. When tops spin rapidly they "sleep," seeming not to move.
6. Worn-out horses.

Ev'n to the Dregs and *Squeezings* of the *Brain*;
Strain out the last, dull droppings of their Sense,
And Rhyme with all the *Rage* of *Impotence*!
  Such shameless *Bards* we have; and yet 'tis true,
There are as mad, abandon'd *Criticks* too.
The Bookful Blockhead, ignorantly read,
With *Loads* of *Learned Lumber* in his Head,
With his own Tongue still edifies his Ears,
And always *List'ning to Himself* appears.
All Books he reads, and all he reads assails,
From *Dryden's Fables* down to *Durfey's Tales*.[7]
With *him*, most Authors steal their Works, or buy;
Garth[8] did not write his own *Dispensary*.
Name a new *Play*, and *he's* the Poet's *Friend*,
Nay show'd his Faults—but when wou'd Poets mend?
No Place so Sacred from such Fops is barr'd,
Nor is *Paul's Church* more safe than *Paul's Church-yard*:[9]
Nay, fly to *Altars*; *there* they'll talk you dead;
For Fools rush in where *Angels* fear to tread.
Distrustful *Sense* with modest Caution speaks;
It still *looks home*, and *short Excursions* makes;
But *ratling Nonsense* in full *Vollies* breaks;
And never shock'd, and never turn'd aside,
Bursts out, resistless, with a thundring Tyde!
  But where's the Man, who Counsel *can* bestow,
Still *pleas'd* to *teach*, and yet not *proud* to *know*?
Unbiass'd, or[1] by *Favour* or by *Spite*;
Not *dully prepossest*, nor *blindly right*;
Tho' Learn'd, well-bred; and tho' well-bred, sincere;
Modestly bold, and Humanly severe?
Who to a *Friend* his Faults can freely show,
And gladly praise the Merit of a *Foe*?
Blest with a *Taste* exact, yet unconfin'd;
A *Knowledge* both of *Books* and *Humankind*;
Gen'rous Converse;[2] a *Soul* exempt from *Pride*;
And *Love to Praise*, with *Reason* on his Side?
  Such once were *Criticks*, such the Happy *Few*,
Athens and *Rome* in better Ages knew.
The mighty *Stagyrite* first left the Shore,
Spread all his Sails, and durst the Deeps explore;
He steer'd securely, and discover'd far,
Led by the Light of the *Mæonian*[3] *Star*.
Poets, a *Race* long unconfin'd and free,

7. *Tales Tragical and Comical* (1704), by Thomas D'Urfey (1653–1723). Dryden's *Fables Ancient and Modern* (1700), a set of verse translations.
8. Sir Samuel Garth (1661–1719), later a friend of Pope's, was (wrongly) accused of falsely claiming authorship of the mock-heroic *The Dispensary* (1699).
9. Where booksellers had stalls.
1. Either.
2. Well-bred conversation.
3. Of Maeonia (region of Asia Minor), where Homer was said to have been born.

Still fond and proud of *Savage Liberty*,
Receiv'd his Laws,[4] and stood convinc'd 'twas fit
Who conquer'd *Nature*, shou'd preside o'er *Wit*.
Horace still charms with graceful Negligence,
And without Method *talks* us into Sense,
Will like a *Friend* familiarly convey
The *truest Notions* in the *easiest way*.[5]
He, who Supream in Judgment, as in Wit,
Might boldly censure, as he boldly writ,
Yet *judg'd* with *Coolness* tho' he sung with *Fire*;
His *Precepts* teach but what his *Works* inspire.
Our Criticks take a contrary Extream,
They *judge* with *Fury*, but they *write* with *Fle'me*:[6]
Nor suffers *Horace* more in wrong *Translations*
By *Wits*, than *Criticks* in as wrong *Quotations*.
See *Dionysius*[7] *Homer's* Thoughts refine,
And call new Beauties forth from ev'ry Line!
Fancy and Art in gay *Petronius*[8] please,
The *Scholar's Learning*, with the *Courtier's Ease*.
In grave *Quintilian's*[9] copious Work we find
The justest *Rules*, and clearest *Method* join'd;
Thus *useful Arms* in Magazines[1] we place,
All rang'd in *Order*, and dispos'd with *Grace*,
But less to please the Eye, than arm the Hand,
Still fit for Use, and ready at Command.
Thee, bold *Longinus*![2] all the Nine[3] inspire,
And bless *their Critick* with a *Poet's Fire*.
An ardent *Judge*, who Zealous in his Trust,
With *Warmth* gives Sentence, yet is always *Just*;
Whose *own Example* strengthens all his Laws,
And *Is himself* that great Sublime he draws.
Thus long succeeding Criticks justly reign'd,
License repress'd, and *useful Laws* ordain'd;
Learning and *Rome* alike in Empire grew
And *Arts* still *follow'd* where her *Eagles*[4] *flew*;
From the same Foes, at last, both felt their Doom,
And the same Age saw *Learning* fall, and *Rome*.
With *Tyranny*, then *Superstition* join'd,
As that the *Body*, this enslav'd the *Mind*;
Much was *Believ'd*, but little *understood*,

4. Rules for literary composition.
5. Least formal, highly accessible.
6. Phlegm, thought to cause sluggishness and indifference; it was one of the four humors in early physiology.
7. Dionysius of Halicarnassus, Greek rhetor and historian active in Rome ca. 30–7 B.C.E.
8. Petronius Arbiter, the author of the *Satyricon* (1st c. C.E.); he may have been the courtier Petronius who was the judge on questions of taste at the court of Nero (emperor 54–68).
9. Roman rhetorician (ca. 30/35–100 C.E.); his "copious work" is the 12-volume *Institutio Oratoria*.
1. Storehouses.
2. Greek rhetorican (1st c. C.E.), to whom the treatise *On Sublimity* is attributed (see above).
3. The 9 Muses.
4. Emblems on the Roman army's banners.

And to be *dull* was constru'd to be *good*;
A *second* Deluge Learning thus o'er-run,
And the *Monks* finish'd what the *Goths* begun.[5]
At length, *Erasmus*,[6] that *great, injur'd* Name,
(The *Glory* of the Priesthood, and the *Shame*!)
Stemm'd the *wild Torrent* of a *barb'rous Age*,
And drove those *Holy Vandals* off the Stage.
But see! each *Muse*, in *Leo's*[7] Golden Days,
Starts from her Trance, and trims her wither'd Bays!
Rome's ancient *Genius*,[8] o'er its *Ruins* spread,
Shakes off the *Dust*, and rears his rev'rend Head!
Then *Sculpture* and her *Sister-Arts* revive;
Stones leap'd to *Form*, and *Rocks* began to *live*;
With *sweeter Notes* each *rising Temple* rung;
A *Raphael* painted, and a *Vida*[9] sung!
Immortal *Vida*! on whose honour'd Brow
The Poet's *Bays* and Critick's *Ivy*[1] grow:
Cremona[2] now shall ever boast thy Name,
As next in Place to *Mantua*, next in Fame.
But soon by Impious Arms from *Latium*[3] chas'd,
Their *ancient Bounds* the banish'd Muses past;
Thence Arts o'er all the *Northern World* advance;
But *Critic Learning* flourish'd most in *France*.
The *Rules*, a Nation born to serve, obeys,
And *Boileau*[4] still in Right of *Horace* sways.
But *we*, brave *Britons*, *Foreign Laws* despis'd,
And kept *unconquer'd*, and *unciviliz'd*,
Fierce for the *Liberties of Wit*, and bold,
We still defy'd the *Romans*, as *of old*.
Yet *some* there were, among the *sounder Few*
Of those who *less presum'd*, and *better knew*,
Who durst assert the *juster Ancient Cause*,
And here *restor'd* Wit's *Fundamental Laws*.
Such was the Muse, whose Rules and Practice tell,
Nature's chief Master-piece is writing well.[5]
Such was *Roscomon*[6]—not more *learn'd* than *good*,
With Manners gen'rous as his Noble Blood;

5. That is, the medieval theologians put the finishing touches on the damage done to learning by the Goths and Vandals, the Germanic peoples who had earlier sacked Rome.
6. Dutch scholar and philosopher (1466–1536), author of *The Praise of Folly*, a humanist satire on the abuses of learning. He was "the glory of the priesthood" because of his erudition and goodness, and its "shame" in that he was persecuted.
7. Pope Leo X (1475–1521), a patron of learning and the arts during the Italian Renaissance.
8. Guardian or protective spirit of a place.
9. Marco Girolamo Vida (ca. 1480–1566), Italian poet who wrote in Latin. Raphael: Raffaello Sanzio (1483–1520), Italian painter.
1. Symbol of poetry and learning. Bays, or laurel, are strongly associated with Apollo.
2. City in northern Italy. (Vida's birth place, as Mantua was Virgil's).
3. Italy. Rome was sacked by Hapsburg mercenaries in 1527; Pope suggests that learning then fled to other parts of Europe, especially France.
4. Nicolas Boileau (1636–1711), French critic and poet; his works include the poem *L'Art poétique* (1674).
5. Quoted from the *Essay on Poetry* (1682), by Pope's friend and supporter John Sheffield (1647–1721).
6. Wentworth Dillon (ca. 1633–1685), fourth earl of Roscommon, poet and critic; author of the *Essay on Translated Verse* (1684).

To him the Wit of *Greece* and *Rome* was known,
And ev'ry Author's *Merit*, but his own.
Such late was *Walsh*,[7]—the Muse's Judge and Friend,
Who justly knew to blame or to commend;
To Failings *mild*, but *zealous* for Desert;[8]
The *clearest Head*, and the *sincerest Heart*.
This humble Praise, lamented *Shade!* receive,
This Praise at least a grateful Muse may give!
The Muse, whose early Voice you taught to Sing,
Prescrib'd her Heights, and prun'd her tender Wing,
(Her Guide now lost) no more attempts to *rise*,
But in low Numbers short Excursions tries:
Content, if hence th' Unlearn'd their Wants may view,
The Learn'd reflect on what before they knew:
Careless of *Censure*, nor too fond of *Fame*,
Still pleas'd to *praise*, yet not afraid to *blame*,
Averse alike to *Flatter*, or *Offend*,
Not *free* from Faults, nor yet too vain to *mend*.

1711

7. William Walsh (1663–1708), whom Dryden praised as "the best critic of our nation"; he was Pope's friend and mentor.

8. Degree of merit or demerit, excellence, reward.

SAMUEL JOHNSON
1709–1784

As countless anecdotes attest, Samuel Johnson was cantankerous and dogmatic. He inveighed against the philosopher George Berkeley's (1685–1753) apparent denial of the reality of the external world by kicking a stone and declaring, "I refute him *thus*." And he coined many mordant aphorisms, such as "The road to hell is paved with good intentions" and "Patriotism is the last refuge of a scoundrel." Theatrical, deliberately provocative, and beloved by many friends and admired by fellow writers, Johnson is one of the most influential critics in English literary history. "The best part of every author," Johnson affirmed, "is in general to be found in his book," and this is true in his own case. Though he often chastised himself for indolence, fearful that salvation would be denied to him because he was not fully using his great gifts, he was in fact astonishingly productive, and in many genres. His literary labors include a monumental *Dictionary of the English Language*, a comprehensive edition of Shakespeare, and the *Lives of the English Poets*, a set of insightful, vividly written biographical and literary portraits of seventeenth- and eighteenth-century authors.

Johnson was born in Lichfield, Staffordshire, a town about 100 miles northwest of London. His father was a bookseller, and his education consisted largely of the volumes in his father's bookshop and the lessons "whipped" into him by the master of the grammar school in Lichfield. He attended Pembroke College at Oxford for only a year, leaving in December 1729 because he lacked the funds to continue. At Oxford, he later recounted, "I was miserably poor, and I thought to fight my way by my literature and my wit"; the fight, continuing in later years, would leave him in poverty for most of his life.

Johnson was an intense, discerning reader; as the economist Adam Smith recalled, "Johnson knew more books than any man alive." While at Oxford, he pored over the popular devotional tract *A Serious Call to a Devout and Holy Life* (1729), by the schoolmaster and minister William Law. He termed Law's book "the finest piece of hortatory theology in any language," and it is the foundation for the prayers and meditations that he composed later in his life.

In July 1735 Johnson married Elizabeth Jervis Porter, a forty-six-year-old widow and mother of three children. With money from her, Johnson opened a school in Edial, near Lichfield, in 1736. One of his students was David Garrick, who became a poet, essayist, and acclaimed actor. While there, Johnson worked on a historical tragedy, *Irene*, which recounts the story of the love of Sultan Mahomet for the lovely Irene, a Christian slave captured in Constantinople—this play was not performed until 1749, in a production that Garrick organized. The school soon proved a failure, however, in part because Johnson lacked the credential of a university degree.

In 1737 Johnson and Garrick traveled to London; with a population between 650,000 and 700,000, it had become the largest city in Europe. Johnson found it captivating and later famously professed: "Why, Sir, you find no man, at all intellectual, who is willing to leave London. No, Sir, when a man is tired of London, he is tired of life; for there is in London all that life can afford." Once settled there, he began his association with the *Gentleman's Magazine*, contributing to it not only prose and poetry but also, from 1741 to 1744, a series of speeches purporting to represent debates in the House of Commons: he re-created them, relying solely on notes and reports.

Johnson was working on and planning larger projects as well. In 1745 he wrote "Miscellaneous Observations on the Tragedy of Macbeth," along with a proposal for an edition of Shakespeare; in the following year, he outlined his "Plan of a Dictionary of the English Language." His major prose publication of this period was *An Account of the Life of Mr. Richard Savage* (1744), a book that details the trials of a failed poet whom Johnson knew and the tribulations of Grub Street, the address of many literary hacks and desperate writers. In verse his central achievement was "The Vanity of Human Wishes," published in 1749. This solemn, disquieting rumination on the futility of worldly hopes and endeavors was the first composition that Johnson issued under his own name.

In the 1750s Johnson wrote many periodical essays. The best of this work appeared in *The Rambler*, which was published twice weekly from March 1750 to March 1752. The twentieth-century critic Walter Jackson Bate has described these pieces as "saturated with thought to an extent unexceeded by any other writer of English prose since Francis Bacon." Johnson's wife Elizabeth told him at the time: "I thought very well of you before this; but I did not imagine you could have written any thing equal to this." She died on March 17, 1752, three days after the publication of its last number. Johnson also contributed essays to his friend John Hawkesworth's periodical *The Adventurer*; and from 1758 to 1760, he wrote yet another series of essays, titled *The Idler*, which were published in a weekly newspaper, *The Universal Chronicle*. But Johnson's greatest accomplishment of the decade was *A Dictionary of the English Language*, published in two large folio volumes in April 1755. Nine years in the making, and compiled by Johnson and six assistants, it consists of 40,000 defined words and 114,000 quotations that illustrate the meanings.

In one week's time in January 1759, Johnson wrote his only long fictional work, *Rasselas*, so that he could pay for his mother's funeral and settle her debts. Three years later he received from King George III an annual pension of 300 pounds, winning at last a measure of economic security. Soon after, he met the Scotsman James Boswell, a twenty-two-year-old lawyer less interested in law than in literature and politics. Boswell cultivated Johnson's friendship; watched him in action at literary clubs with Adam Smith, the painter Joshua Reynolds, EDMUND BURKE, and other luminaries; sparred with him in conversation; and gathered facts and anecdotes about him. Boswell made Johnson the subject of what is often called the greatest biography in English, *The Life of Samuel Johnson, LL.D.* (1791).

Johnson's eight-volume edition of Shakespeare was published in October 1765. The much-delayed work was flawed: Johnson neither performed the complete collation of texts he had promised nor examined carefully the sources that Shakespeare had drawn on. He ignored the sonnets and poems, and (like the Romantic critics) treats the plays not as works for the stage but as texts to be read. Nonetheless, the preface—one of our selections—and the many interpretive notes amount to a compelling assessment. Johnson celebrates Shakespeare's gifts in portraying character and revealing truths about human nature and, more important, defends the playwright against charges of violating the dramatic unities of time and place and improperly mixing the genres of tragedy and comedy. Johnson was not the first to propose that authors be granted freedom to depart from classical rules and prescriptions for literary composition, but his authority and formidable style gave this position its irresistible legitimacy. SAMUEL TAYLOR COLERIDGE, William Hazlitt, and other critics in the early 1800s balked at (even as they oversimplified) Johnson's neoclassical principles and disputed his evaluations of authors, yet his support for rule-breaking innovation, in the preface to *Shakespeare* and elsewhere, helped to prepare the literary and cultural ground for the Romantic revolution.

In 1777 Johnson, then sixty-seven, was approached by London booksellers to contribute brief prefaces to a multivolume edition of English poets. Though the original plan was scaled back (instead of including all reputable poets from Chaucer on, the survey began in the seventeenth century with Cowley), Johnson did much more than required, producing in all about 400,000 words of biographical and interpretive text on the fifty-two poets (all male). Each preface follows a three-part plan, as Johnson recounts the author's biography, summarizes the main features of his character, and critically examines the writings; the essays on Cowley, Milton, DRYDEN, POPE, and ADDISON expanded into panoramic studies of the writer's life and works.

The *Lives of the English Poets* (1783) is not a grand act of personal canon making. While Johnson proposed several additions, the choices generally were not his own. He believed in an English literary canon—one that surpassed the literatures of other nations—but this canon could not be determined by any single critic. Unlike such modern critics as T. S. ELIOT, F. R. LEAVIS, and HAROLD BLOOM, who seek through robust arguments to reorder literary rankings that they view as dated and objectionable, Johnson found the test of time decisive. As he explained in the preface to *Shakespeare*, "What has been longest known has been most considered, and what is most considered is best understood."

For Johnson, the best contemporary literature resembles the great literature of the past in its fidelity to the facts of unchanging human nature and in its concern for moral instruction—for guidance in how best to live (that is, how best to bear life's pain). "Nothing can please many," he wrote, "and please long, but just representations of general nature." Thus in our selection from *Rasselas* Johnson emphasizes that "the business of the poet . . . is to examine, not the individual, but the species; to remark general properties and large appearances." "Great thoughts," he observes in the *Life of Cowley* (our final selection), "are always general." Such an appeal to shared values does not entirely preclude literary originality. As "On Fiction," our selection from *The Rambler*, indicates, Johnson could accept the emerging genre of the novel as long as its practitioners stayed alert to their moral duty to readers. Frequently in his criticism he commends poets for their capacity to delight or surprise us, for their powers of verbal invention. But by originality,

Johnson meant what was new and unexpected *and* deeply recognizable—the refreshed, reawakened expression of truths with which readers would already be familiar.

Johnson proposed writing a "History of Criticism as it relates to judging of authours, from Aristotle to the present age," but he never undertook this daunting project; his general attitude toward critics and criticism must be pieced together from essays, letters, and parts of the preface to *Shakespeare* and the *Lives of the English Poets*. In *Rambler* 92, Johnson comes as close as he does anywhere to defining the work of the critic, stressing "principles," "rational deduction," and "science" and concluding: "Criticism reduces those regions of literature under the dominion of science, which have hitherto known only the anarchy of ignorance, the caprices of fancy, and the tyranny of prescription." Yet on this topic, as often in his writing, Johnson calls attention to facets of literary experience that undercut the positions he elsewhere advocates: he is his own sharpest, most cogent critic. In the preface to *Shakespeare*, he acknowledges the limitations of "the rules of criticism": "there is always an appeal open from criticism to nature." Generic categories and literary conventions matter; critics must consider how well or badly an author abides by them. But historical context, Johnson realizes, must be considered as well; as he explains in his *Life of Dryden*, "That which is easy at one time was difficult at another." Thus even such a highly principled critic could contend, in his *Life of Pope*, that we err when we "judge by principles rather than perception."

Johnson possessed a strong sense of the power and responsibility of writers; as he emphasizes in *Rambler* 4, novelists must use their talents to correct error and teach good conduct: they should not describe persons and situations—however true-to-life these might be—that could corrupt the minds of readers, particularly the young and inexperienced. The poet has an equal burden. Offended by the mixture of sacred and profane elements in Milton's pastoral elegy "Lycidas," Johnson calls the poem vulgar and disgusting, indecent and impious. This assault on "Lycidas" is notorious, yet it is significant less for the stridency of Johnson's judgment than for the strength of his response, the intensity of his experience as a reader.

The motions of Johnson's mind are more supple, balanced (if precariously at times), and even contradictory than might be predicted of a voice that is so confident and proud. We should heed his performance as a writer—the behavior of his language, the turns and tones of his subtle and complex sentences and paragraphs—in order to appreciate him fully. The final two paragraphs of the *Life of Cowley*, in which Johnson sums up the achievements of the metaphysical poets after having criticized them, illustrate his flexibility of mind. For modern readers, Johnson's style and point of view may require some getting accustomed to. But as MATTHEW ARNOLD concluded ("Johnson's *Lives*," 1878) in a formulation still pertinent today: "The more we study Johnson, the higher will be our esteem for the power of his mind, the width of his interests, the largeness of his knowledge, the freshness, fearlessness, and strength of his judgments."

The Rambler, No. 4 [On Fiction] **Keywords:** Enlightenment Theory, Narrative Theory, The Novel, Realism
The History of Rasselas, Prince of Abyssinia **Keywords:** Aesthetics, Authorship, Enlightenment Theory, Poetry
"Preface to *Shakespeare*" Keywords: Authorship, The Canon/Tradition, Drama, Enlightenment Theory, Literary History, Realism
Lives of the English Poets **Keywords:** Enlightenment Theory, Language, Literary History, Poetry

The Rambler, No. 4 [On Fiction]

Simul et jucunda et idonea dicere vitae.[1]
—Horace, *Ars Poetica*, l. 334

And join both profit and delight in one.
—Creech[2]

The works of fiction, with which the present generation seems more particularly delighted,[3] are such as exhibit life in its true state, diversified only by accidents that daily happen in the world, and influenced by passions and qualities which are really to be found in conversing with mankind.

This kind of writing may be termed not improperly the comedy of romance,[4] and is to be conducted nearly by the rules of comic poetry. Its province is to bring about natural events by easy means, and to keep up curiosity without the help of wonder: it is therefore precluded from the machines and expedients of the heroic romance, and can neither employ giants to snatch away a lady from the nuptial rites, nor knights to bring her back from captivity; it can neither bewilder its personages in desarts,[5] nor lodge them in imaginary castles.

I remember a remark made by Scaliger upon Pontanus,[6] that all his writings are filled with the same images; and that if you take from him his lillies and his roses, his satyrs and his dryads,[7] he will have nothing left that can be called poetry. In like manner, almost all the fictions of the last age will vanish, if you deprive them of a hermit and a wood, a battle and a shipwreck.

Why this wild strain of imagination found reception so long, in polite and learned ages, it is not easy to conceive; but we cannot wonder that, while readers could be procured, the authors were willing to continue it: for when a man had by practice gained some fluency of language, he had no further care than to retire to his closet, let loose his invention, and heat his mind with incredibilities;[8] a book was thus produced without fear of criticism, without the toil of study, without knowledge of nature, or acquaintance with life.

The task of our present writers is very different; it requires, together with that learning which is to be gained from books, that experience which can never be attained by solitary diligence, but must arise from general converse, and accurate observation of the living world. Their performances have, as Horace expresses it, *plus oneris quantum veniae minus*,[9] little indulgence, and

1. Poets wish either to benefit or delight, or else say things at once pleasant and suited to life (Latin). HORACE (65–8 B.C.E.), Roman poet; for the *Ars Poetica*, see above.
2. Thomas Creech (1659–1700), English classical scholar. Here he translates the epigraph above.
3. Possibly Tobias Smollett's *Roderick Random* (1748) and Henry Fielding's *Tom Jones* (1749).
4. An entertaining story of love and adventure, which includes elements of fantasy and myth.
5. Deserts.
6. Jovanius Pontanus (1426–1503), Italian poet. The remark was by Julius Caesar Scaliger, an Italian-born French scholar (1484–1558), in his *Poetics* 5.4.
7. In classical mythology, wood nymphs. "Satyrs": goatlike sylvan deities.
8. Things that cannot be believed. "Closet": "a small room of privacy and retirement" (Johnson's *Dictionary*).
9. Slightly misquoted from Horace, *Epistles* 2.1.170 (translated by Johnson).

therefore more difficulty. They are engaged in portraits of which every one knows the original, and can detect any deviation from exactness of resemblance. Other writings are safe, except from the malice of learning, but these are in danger from every common reader; as the slipper ill executed was censured by a shoemaker who happened to stop in his way at the Venus of Apelles.[1]

But the fear of not being approved as just copyers of human manners, is not the most important concern that an author of this sort ought to have before him. These books are written chiefly to the young, the ignorant, and the idle, to whom they serve as lectures of conduct, and introductions into life. They are the entertainment of minds unfurnished with ideas, and therefore easily susceptible of impressions; not fixed by principles, and therefore easily following the current of fancy; not informed by experience, and consequently open to every false suggestion and partial account.

That the highest degree of reverence should be paid to youth, and that nothing indecent should be suffered to approach their eyes or ears; are precepts extorted by sense and virtue from an ancient writer,[2] by no means eminent for chastity of thought. The same kind, tho' not the same degree of caution, is required in every thing which is laid before them, to secure them from unjust prejudices, perverse opinions, and incongruous combinations of images.

In the romances formerly written, every transaction and sentiment was so remote from all that passes among men, that the reader was in very little danger of making any applications to himself; the virtues and crimes were equally beyond his sphere of activity; and he amused himself with heroes and with traitors, deliverers and persecutors, as with beings of another species, whose actions were regulated upon motives of their own, and who had neither faults nor excellencies in common with himself.

But when an adventurer is levelled with the rest of the world, and acts in such scenes of the universal drama, as may be the lot of any other man; young spectators fix their eyes upon him with closer attention, and hope by observing his behavior and success to regulate their own practices, when they shall be engaged in the like part.

For this reason these familiar histories may perhaps be made of greater use than the solemnities of professed morality, and convey the knowledge of vice and virtue with more efficacy than axioms and definitions. But if the power of example is so great, as to take possession of the memory by a kind of violence, and produce effects almost without the intervention of the will, care ought to be taken that, when the choice is unrestrained, the best examples only should be exhibited; and that which is likely to operate so strongly, should not be mischievous or uncertain in its effects.

The chief advantage which these fictions have over real life is, that their authors are at liberty, tho' not to invent, yet to select objects, and to cull from the mass of mankind, those individuals upon which the attention ought most to be employ'd; as a diamond, though it cannot be made, may be polished by

1. Greek painter (4th c. B.C.E.). The story of the shoemaker correcting the artist's representation comes from the Roman writer Pliny the Elder (23/4–79 C.E.), *Natural History* 35.84.

2. Juvenal (ca. 55–ca. 140 C.E.), Roman poet; see *Satire* 14.

art, and placed in such a situation, as to display that lustre which before was buried among common stones.

It is justly considered as the greatest excellency of art, to imitate nature; but it is necessary to distinguish those parts of nature, which are most proper for imitation: greater care is still required in representing life, which is so often discoloured by passion, or deformed by wickedness. If the world be promiscuously[3] described, I cannot see of what use it can be to read the account; or why it may not be as safe to turn the eye immediately upon mankind, as upon a mirror which shows all that presents itself without discrimination.

It is therefore not a sufficient vindication of a character, that it is drawn as it appears, for many characters ought never to be drawn; nor of a narrative, that the train of events is agreeable to observation and experience, for that observation which is called knowledge of the world, will be found much more frequently to make men cunning than good. The purpose of these writings is surely not only to show mankind, but to provide that they may be seen hereafter with less hazard; to teach the means of avoiding the snares which are laid by Treachery for Innocence, without infusing any wish for that superiority with which the betrayer flatters his vanity; to give the power of counteracting fraud, without the temptation to practise it; to initiate youth by mock encounters in the art of necessary defence, and to increase prudence without impairing virtue.

Many writers, for the sake of following nature, so mingle good and bad qualities in their principal personages, that they are both equally conspicuous; and as we accompany them through their adventures with delight, and are led by degrees to interest ourselves in their favour, we lose the abhorrence of their faults, because they do not hinder our pleasure, or, perhaps, regard them with some kindness for being united with so much merit.

There have been men indeed splendidly wicked, whose endowments threw a brightness on their crimes, and whom scarce any villainy made perfectly detestable, because they never could be wholly divested of their excellencies; but such have been in all ages the great corrupters of the world, and their resemblance ought no more to be preserved, than the art of murdering without pain.

Some have advanced, without due attention to the consequences of this notion, that certain virtues have their correspondent faults, and therefore that to exhibit either apart is to deviate from probability. Thus men are observed by Swift to be "grateful in the same degree as they are resentful."[4] This principle, with others of the same kind, supposes man to act from a brute impulse, and persue a certain degree of inclination, without any choice of the object; for, otherwise, though it should be allowed that gratitude and resentment arise from the same constitution of the passions, it follows not that they will be equally indulged when reason is consulted; yet unless that consequence be admitted, this sagacious maxim becomes an empty sound, without any relation to practice or to life.

3. In a mixed, disorderly fashion.

4. These are the words of the English poet and critic ALEXANDER POPE (1688–1744), not the Anglo-Irish satirist and poet Jonathan Swift (1667–1745). The contemporary source is the Swift-Pope *Miscellanies* 2 (1727): 354. "Grateful": pleasing, agreeable.

Nor is it evident, that even the first motions to these effects are always in the same proportion. For pride, which produces quickness of resentment, will obstruct gratitude, by unwillingness to admit that inferiority which obligation implies; and it is very unlikely, that he who cannot think he receives a favour will acknowledge or repay it.

It is of the utmost importance to mankind, that positions of this tendency should be laid open and confuted; for while men consider good and evil as springing from the same root, they will spare the one for the sake of the other, and in judging, if not of others at least of themselves, will be apt to estimate their virtues by their vices. To this fatal error all those will contribute, who confound the colours of right and wrong, and instead of helping to settle their boundaries, mix them with so much art, that no common mind is able to disunite them.

In narratives, where historical veracity has no place, I cannot discover why there should not be exhibited the most perfect idea of virtue; of virtue not angelical, nor above probability, for what we cannot credit we shall never imitate, but the highest and purest that humanity can reach, which, exercised in such trials as the various revolutions of things shall bring upon it, may, by conquering some calamities, and enduring others, teach us what we may hope, and what we can perform. Vice, for vice is necessary to be shewn, should always disgust; nor should the graces of gaiety, or the dignity of courage, be so united with it, as to reconcile it to the mind. Wherever it appears, it should raise hatred by the malignity of its practices, and contempt by the meanness of its stratagems; for while it is supported by either parts or spirit, it will be seldom heartily abhorred. The Roman tyrant[5] was content to be hated, if he was but feared; and there are thousands of the readers of romances willing to be thought wicked, if they may be allowed to be wits. It is therefore to be steadily inculcated, that virtue is the highest proof of understanding, and the only solid basis of greatness; and that vice is the natural consequence of narrow thoughts, that it begins in mistake, and ends in ignominy.

1750

From The History of Rasselas, Prince of Abyssinia

Chapter X.

Imlac's History Continued. A Dissertation upon Poetry

"Wherever I[1] went, I found that Poetry was considered as the highest learning, and regarded with a veneration somewhat approaching to that which man would pay to the Angelick Nature. And it yet fills me with wonder, that, in almost all countries, the most ancient poets are considered as the best: whether it be that every other kind of knowledge is an acquisition gradually attained, and poetry is a gift conferred at once; or that the first

5. The emperor Gaius Julius Caesar Germanicus (12–41 C.E.), known as "Caligula." See Suetonius (ca. 69–after 122 C.E.), *Life of Caligula* 30.1.

1. Johnson's spokesman is the philosopher and poet Imlac, who is addressing Prince Rasselas, son of the emperor of Abyssinia.

poetry of every nation surprised them as a novelty, and retained the credit by consent which it received by accident at first: or whether, as the province of poetry is to describe Nature and Passion, which are always the same, the first writers took possession of the most striking objects for description, and the most probable occurrences for fiction, and left nothing to those that followed them, but transcription of the same events, and new combinations of the same images. Whatever be the reason, it is commonly observed that the early writers are in possession of nature, and their followers of art: that the first excel in strength and invention, and the latter in elegance and refinement.[2]

"I was desirous to add my name to this illustrious fraternity. I read all the poets of Persia and Arabia, and was able to repeat by memory the volumes,[3] that are suspended in the mosque of Mecca. But I soon found that no man was ever great by imitation. My desire of excellence impelled me to transfer my attention to nature and to life. Nature was to be my subject, and men to be my auditors: I could never describe what I had not seen: I could not hope to move those with delight or terrour, whose interests and opinions I did not understand.

"Being now resolved to be a poet, I saw every thing with a new purpose; my sphere of attention was suddenly magnified: no kind of knowledge was to be overlooked. I ranged mountains and deserts for images and resemblances, and pictured upon my mind every tree of the forest and flower of the valley. I observed with equal care the crag of the rock and the pinnacles of the palace. Sometimes I wandered along the mazes of the rivulet, and sometimes watched the changes of the summer clouds. To a poet nothing can be useless. Whatever is beautiful, and whatever is dreadful, must be familiar to his imagination: he must be conversant with all that is awfully vast or elegantly little.[4] The plants of the garden, the animals of the wood, the minerals of the earth, and meteors of the sky, must all concur to store his mind with inexhaustible variety: for every idea is useful for the inforcement or decoration of moral or religious truth;[5] and he, who knows most, will have most power of diversifying his scenes, and of gratifying his reader with remote allusions and unexpected instruction.

"All the appearances of nature I was therefore careful to study, and every country which I have surveyed has contributed something to my poetical powers."

"In so wide a survey, said the prince, you must surely have left much unobserved. I have lived, till now, within the circuit of those mountains, and yet cannot walk abroad without the sight of something which I had never beheld before, or never heeded."

"The business of a poet, said Imlac, is to examine, not the individual, but the species: to remark general properties and large appearances: he does not number the streaks of the tulip, or describe the different shades in the

2. Johnson's observations here are connected to debates in the period about what constituted poetic originality and whether modern authors could achieve it.
3. Illuminated manuscripts of sacred texts, "suspended" or hung in mosques.
4. Johnson is drawing on EDMUND BURKE's account of the sublime in *A Philosophical Enquiry into the Origin of Our Ideas of the Sublime and Beautiful* (1757; see below).
5. In "A Defence of 'An Essay of Dramatic Poesy'" (1668), JOHN DRYDEN states: "moral truth is the mistress of the poet as much as of the philosopher; poesy must resemble natural truth, but it must *be* ethical."

verdure of the forest. He is to exhibit in his portraits of nature such prominent and striking features, as recall the original to every mind; and must neglect the minuter discriminations, which one may have remarked, and another have neglected, for those characteristicks which are alike obvious to vigilance and carelessness.

"But the knowledge of nature is only half the task of a poet; he must be acquainted likewise with all the modes of life. His character requires that he estimate the happiness and misery of every condition; observe the power of all the passions in all their combinations, and trace the changes of the human mind as they are modified by various institutions and accidental influences of climate or custom, from the spriteliness of infancy to the despondence of decrepitude. He must divest himself of the prejudices of his age or country; he must consider right and wrong in their abstracted and invariable state; he must disregard present laws and opinions, and rise to general and transcendental[6] truths, which will always be the same: he must therefore content himself with the slow progress of his name; contemn the applause of his own time, and commit his claims to the justice of posterity. He must write as the interpreter of nature, and the legislator of mankind, and consider himself as presiding over the thoughts and manners of future generations; as a being superiour to time and place.

"His labour is not yet at an end: he must know many languages and many sciences; and, that his stile may be worthy of his thoughts, must, by incessant practice, familiarize to himself every delicacy of speech and grace of harmony."

1759

From Preface to *Shakespeare*

That praises are without reason lavished on the dead, and that the honours due only to excellence are paid to antiquity, is a complaint likely to be always continued by those, who, being able to add nothing to truth, hope for eminence from the heresies of paradox; or those, who, being forced by disappointment upon consolatory expedients, are willing to hope from posterity what the present age refuses, and flatter themselves that the regard which is yet denied by envy, will be at last bestowed by time.

Antiquity, like every other quality that attracts the notice of mankind, has undoubtedly votaries that reverence it, not from reason, but from prejudice. Some seem to admire indiscriminately whatever has been long preserved, without considering that time has sometimes co-operated with chance; all perhaps are more willing to honour past than present excellence; and the mind contemplates genius through the shades of age, as the eye surveys the sun through artificial opacity. The great contention of criticism is to find the faults of the moderns, and the beauties of the ancients. While an authour is yet living we estimate his powers by his worst performance, and when he is dead, we rate them by his best.

6. "General; pervading many particulars" (Johnson's *Dictionary*).

To works, however, of which the excellence is not absolute and definite, but, gradual and comparative; to works not raised upon principles demonstrative and scientifick, but appealing wholly to observation and experience, no other test can be applied than length of duration and continuance of esteem. What mankind have long possessed they have often examined and compared; and if they persist to value the possession, it is because frequent comparisons have confirmed opinion in its favour. As among the works of nature no man can properly call a river deep, or a mountain high, without the knowledge of many mountains, and many rivers; so in the productions of genius, nothing can be stiled excellent till it has been compared with other works of the same kind. Demonstration[1] immediately displays its power, and has nothing to hope or fear from the flux of years; but works tentative and experimental must be estimated by their proportion to the general and collective ability of man, as it is discovered in a long succession of endeavours. Of the first building that was raised, it might be with certainty determined that it was round or square; but whether it was spacious or lofty must have been referred to time. The Pythagorean scale of numbers[2] was at once discovered to be perfect; but the poems of *Homer*[3] we yet know not to transcend the common limits of human intelligence, but by remarking, that nation after nation, and century after century, has been able to do little more than transpose his incidents, new-name his characters, and paraphrase his sentiments.

The reverence due to writings that have long subsisted arises therefore not from any credulous confidence in the superior wisdom of past ages, or gloomy persuasion of the degeneracy of mankind, but is the consequence of acknowledged and indubitable positions, that what has been longest known has been most considered, and what is most considered is best understood.

The Poet, of whose works I have undertaken the revision,[4] may now begin to assume the dignity of an ancient, and claim the privilege of established fame and prescriptive veneration. He has long outlived his century, the term commonly fixed as the test of literary merit.[5] Whatever advantages he might once derive from personal allusions, local customs, or temporary opinions, have for many years been lost; and every topick of merriment, or motive of sorrow, which the modes of artificial life afforded him, now only obscure the scenes which they once illuminated. The effects of favour and competition are at an end; the tradition of his friendships and his enmities has perished; his works support no opinion with arguments, nor supply any faction with invectives; they can neither indulge vanity nor gratify malignity; but are read without any other reason than the desire of pleasure, and are therefore praised only as pleasure is obtained; yet, thus unassisted by interest or passion, they have past through variations of taste and changes of manners, and, as they devolved from one generation to another, have received new honours at every transmission.

But because human judgment, though it be gradually gaining upon certainty, never becomes infallible; and approbation, though long continued, may yet be only the approbation of prejudice or fashion; it is proper to inquire,

1. "The highest degree of deducible or argumental evidence" (Johnson's *Dictionary*).
2. The Greek philosopher and mathematician Pythagoras (6th c. B.C.E.) is thought to have discovered the musical ratios of the octave (2:1), the fifth (3:2), and the fourth (4:3).
3. That is, the *Iliad* and the *Odyssey*, attributed to the Greek poet Homer (ca. 8th c. B.C.E.).
4. That is, the process of editing.
5. See HORACE (65–8 B.C.E.), *Epistles* 2.1.39.

by what peculiarities of excellence *Shakespeare* has gained and kept the favour of his countrymen.

Nothing can please many, and please long, but just representations of general nature. Particular manners can be known to few, and therefore few only can judge how nearly they are copied. The irregular combinations of fanciful invention may delight a-while, by that novelty of which the common satiety of life sends us all in quest; but the pleasures of sudden wonder are soon exhausted, and the mind can only repose on the stability of truth.

Shakespeare is above all writers, at least above all modern writers, the poet of nature; the poet that holds up to his readers a faithful mirrour of manners and of life.[6] His characters are not modified by the customs of particular places, unpractised by the rest of the world; by the peculiarities of studies or professions, which can operate but upon small numbers; or by the accidents of transient fashions or temporary opinions: they are the genuine progeny of common humanity, such as the world will always supply, and observation will always find. His persons act and speak by the influence of those general passions and principles by which all minds are agitated, and the whole system of life is continued in motion. In the writings of other poets a character is too often an individual; in those of *Shakespeare* it is commonly a species.

It is from this wide extension of design that so much instruction is derived. It is this which fills the plays of *Shakespeare* with practical axioms and domestick wisdom. It was said of *Euripides*,[7] that every verse was a precept; and it may be said of *Shakespeare*, that from his works may be collected a system of civil and oeconomical[8] prudence. Yet his real power is not shewn in the splendour of particular passages, but by the progress of his fable,[9] and the tenour of his dialogue; and he that tries to recommend him by select quotations, will succeed like the pedant in *Hierocles*,[1] who, when he offered his house to sale, carried a brick in his pocket as a specimen.

It will not easily be imagined how much *Shakespeare* excells in accommodating his sentiments to real life, but by comparing him with other authours. It was observed of the ancient schools of declamation, that the more diligently they were frequented, the more was the student disqualified for the world, because he found nothing there which he should ever meet in any other place. The same remark may be applied to every stage but that of *Shakespeare*. The theatre, when it is under any other direction, is peopled by such characters as were never seen, conversing in a language which was never heard, upon topicks which will never arise in the commerce of mankind. But the dialogue of this authour is often so evidently determined by the incident which produces it, and is pursued with so much ease and simplicity, that it seems scarcely to claim the merit of fiction, but to have been gleaned by diligent selection out of common conversation, and common occurrences.

Upon every other stage the universal agent is love, by whose power all good and evil is distributed, and every action quickened or retarded. To bring a

6. Hamlet counsels the players to remember that the purpose of acting "is to hold as 'twere the mirror up to nature"; *Hamlet* (ca. 1600), 3.2.20.
7. Greek tragedian (ca. 485–ca. 406 B.C.E.).
8. That is, pertaining to political economy.
9. "The series or contexture of events which constitute a poem epic or dramatic" (Johnson's *Dictionary*).
1. Hierocles of Alexander (5th c. C.E.), Greek Neoplatonic philosopher and author of a book of humorous anecdotes that Johnson translated in 1741.

lover, a lady and a rival into the fable; to entangle them in contradictory obligations, perplex them with oppositions of interest, and harrass them with violence of desires inconsistent with each other; to make them meet in rapture and part in agony; to fill their mouths with hyperbolical joy and outrageous sorrow; to distress them as nothing human ever was distressed; to deliver them as nothing human ever was delivered; is the business of a modern dramatist. For this probability is violated, life is misrepresented, and language is depraved. But love is only one of many passions; and as it has no great influence upon the sum of life, it has little operation in the dramas of a poet, who caught his ideas from the living world, and exhibited only what he saw before him. He knew, that any other passion, as it was regular or exorbitant, was a cause of happiness or calamity.

Characters thus ample and general were not easily discriminated and preserved, yet perhaps no poet ever kept his personages more distinct from each other. I will not say with *Pope*,[2] that every speech may be assigned to the proper speaker, because many speeches there are which have nothing characteristical; but perhaps, though some may be equally adapted to every person, it will be difficult to find, any that can be properly transferred from the present possessor to another claimant. The choice is right, when there is reason for choice.

Other dramatists can only gain attention by hyperbolical or aggravated characters, by fabulous and unexampled excellence or depravity, as the writers of barbarous romances invigorated the reader by a giant and a dwarf; and he that should form his expectations of human affairs from the play, or from the tale, would be equally deceived. *Shakespeare* has no heroes; his scenes are occupied only by men, who act and speak as the reader thinks that he should himself have spoken or acted on the same occasion: Even where the agency is supernatural the dialogue is level with life. Other writers disguise the most natural passions and most frequent incidents; so that he who contemplates them in the book will not know them in the world: *Shakespeare* approximates the remote, and familiarizes the wonderful; the event which he represents will not happen, but if it were possible, its effects would probably be such as he has assigned; and it may be said, that he has not only shewn human nature as it acts in real exigencies, but as it would be found in trials, to which it cannot be exposed.

This therefore is the praise of *Shakespeare*, that his drama is the mirrour of life; that he who has mazed[3] his imagination, in following the phantoms which other writers raise up before him, may here be cured of his delirious extasies, by reading human sentiments in human language, by scenes from which a hermit may estimate the transactions of the world, and a confessor predict the progress of the passions.

His adherence to general nature has exposed him to the censure of criticks, who form their judgments upon narrower principles. *Dennis* and *Rhymer* think his *Romans* not sufficiently *Roman*; and *Voltaire*[4] censures his kings as

2. In preface to *Shakespeare* (1725), edited by ALEXANDER POPE (1688–1744).

3. That is, followed the complex and winding paths.

4. The pen name of François Marie Arouet (1694–1778), French Enlightenment writer and critic, who assailed Shakespeare for breaking the classical rules of drama. John Dennis (1657–1734), English playwright and critic. Thomas Rymer (ca. 1642–1713), English critic and historian.

not completely royal. *Dennis* is offended, that *Menenius*,[5] a senator of *Rome*, should play the buffoon; and *Voltaire* perhaps thinks decency violated when the *Danish* Usurper[6] is represented as a drunkard. But *Shakespeare* always makes nature predominate over accident; and if he preserves the essential character, is not very careful of distinctions superinduced and adventitious. His story requires Romans or kings, but he thinks only on men. He knew that *Rome*, like every other city, had men of all dispositions; and wanting a buffoon, he went into the senate-house for that which the senate-house would certainly have afforded him. He was inclined to shew an usurper and a murderer not only odious but despicable, he therefore added drunkenness to his other qualities, knowing that kings love wine like other men, and that wine exerts its natural power upon kings. These are the petty cavils of petty minds; a poet overlooks the casual distinction of country and condition, as a painter, satisfied with the figure, neglects the drapery.

The censure which he has incurred[7] by mixing comick and tragick scenes, as it extends to all his works, deserves more consideration. Let the fact be first stated, and then examined.

Shakespeare's plays are not in the rigorous and critical sense either tragedies or comedies, but compositions of a distinct kind; exhibiting the real state of sublunary[8] nature, which partakes of good and evil, joy and sorrow, mingled with endless variety of proportion and innumerable modes of combination; and expressing the course of the world, in which the loss of one is the gain of another; in which, at the same time, the reveller is hasting to his wine, and the mourner burying his friend; in which the malignity of one is sometimes defeated by the frolick of another; and many mischiefs and many benefits are done and hindered without design.

Out of this chaos of mingled purposes and casualties the ancient poets, according to the laws which custom had prescribed, selected some the crimes of men, and some their absurdities; some the momentous vicissitudes of life, and some the lighter occurrences; some the terrours of distress, and some the gayeties of prosperity. Thus rose the two modes of imitation, known by the names of *tragedy* and *comedy*, compositions intended to promote different ends by contrary means, and considered as so little allied, that I do not recollect among the *Greeks* or *Romans* a single writer who attempted both.

Shakespeare has united the powers of exciting laughter and sorrow not only in one mind, but in one composition. Almost all his plays are divided between serious and ludicrous characters, and, in the successive evolutions of the design, sometimes produce seriousness and sorrow, and sometimes levity and laughter.

That this is a practice contrary to the rules of criticism will be readily allowed; but there is always an appeal open from criticism to nature. The end of writing is to instruct; the end of the poetry is to instruct by pleasing.[9] That the mingled drama may convey all the instruction of tragedy or comedy cannot be denied, because it includes both in its alternations of exhibition and approaches nearer than either to the appearance of life, by shewing how great machinations and slender designs may promote or obviate one another,

5. A character in Shakespeare's *Coriolanus* (1608).
6. Claudius, the murderer of Hamlet's father, the king.
7. From Voltaire.
8. Beneath the moon; of this world, earthly.
9. See Horace, *Ars Poetica*, lines 343–44 (above).

and the high and the low co-operate in the general system by unavoidable concatenation.

It is objected, that by this change of scenes the passions are interrupted in their progression, and that the principal event, being not advanced by a due gradation of preparatory incidents, wants at last the power to move, which constitutes the perfection of dramatick poetry. This reasoning is so specious, that it is received as true even by those who in daily experience feel it to be false. The interchanges of mingled scenes seldom fail to produce the intended vicissitudes of passion. Fiction cannot move so much, but that the attention may be easily transferred; and though it must be allowed that pleasing melancholy be sometimes interrupted by unwelcome levity, yet let it be considered likewise, that melancholy is often not pleasing, and that the disturbance of one man may be the relief of another; that different auditors have different habitudes; and that, upon the whole, all pleasure consists in variety.

The players,[1] who in their edition divided our authour's works into comedies, histories, and tragedies, seem not to have distinguished the three kinds by any very exact or definite ideas.

An action which ended happily to the principal persons, however serious or distressful through its intermediate incidents, in their opinion, constituted a comedy. This idea of a comedy continued long amongst us; and plays were written, which, by changing the catastrophe,[2] were tragedies to-day, and comedies to-morrow.

Tragedy was not in those times a poem of more general dignity or elevation than comedy; it required only a calamitous conclusion, with which the common criticism of that age was satisfied, whatever lighter pleasure it afforded in its progress.

History was a series of actions, with no other than chronological succession, independent on each other, and without any tendency to introduce or regulate the conclusion. It is not always very nicely distinguished from tragedy. There is not much nearer approach to unity of action in the tragedy of *Antony and Cleopatra*, than in the history of *Richard the Second*. But a history might be continued through many plays; as it had no plan, it had no limits.

Through all these denominations of the drama, *Shakespeare*'s mode of composition is the same; an interchange of seriousness and merriment, by which the mind is softened at one time, and exhilarated at another. But whatever be his purpose, whether to gladden or depress, or to conduct the story, without vehemence or emotion, through tracts of easy and familiar dialogue, he never fails to attain his purpose; as he commands us, we laugh or mourn, or sit silent with quiet expectation, in tranquillity without indifference.

When *Shakespeare*'s plan is understood, most of the criticisms of *Rhymer* and *Voltaire* vanish away. The play of *Hamlet* is opened, without impropriety, by two sentinels; *Iago*[3] bellows at *Brabantio*'s window, without injury to the scheme of the play, though in terms which a modern audience would not easily endure; the character of *Polonius*[4] is seasonable and useful; and the Grave-diggers themselves may be heard with applause.

1. John Heminges (d. 1630) and Henry Condell (d. 1627), members of Shakespeare's acting company, produced the Shakespeare First Folio, published in 1623.
2. The climax of a dramatic action.
3. In *Othello* (1603–04).
4. A meddling figure of comedy in *Hamlet*; the gravediggers appear to comic effect later in the play.

Shakespeare engaged in dramatick poetry with the world open before him; the rules of the ancients were yet known to few; the publick judgment was unformed; he had no example of such fame as might force him upon imitation, nor criticks of such authority as might restrain his extravagance: He therefore indulged his natural disposition, and his disposition, as *Rhymer* has remarked, led him to comedy. In tragedy he often writes, with great appearance of toil and study, what is written at last with little felicity; but in his comick scenes, he seems to produce without labour, what no labour can improve. In tragedy he is always struggling after some occasion to be comick; but in comedy he seems to repose, or to luxuriate, as in a mode of thinking congenial to his nature. In his tragick scenes there is always something wanting, but his comedy often surpasses expectation or desire. His comedy pleases by the thoughts and the language, and his tragedy for the greater part by incident and action. His tragedy seems to be skill, his comedy to be instinct.

The force of his comick scenes has suffered little diminution from the changes made by a century and a half, in manners or in words. As his personages act upon principles arising from genuine passion, very little modified by particular forms, their pleasures and vexations are communicable to all times and to all places; they are natural, and therefore durable; the adventitious peculiarities of personal habits, are only superficial dies, bright and pleasing for a little while, yet soon fading to a dim tinct, without any remains of former lustre; but the discriminations of true passion are the colours of nature; they pervade the whole mass, and can only perish with the body that exhibits them. The accidental compositions of heterogeneous modes are dissolved by the chance which combined them; but the uniform simplicity of primitive qualities neither admits increase, nor suffers decay. The sand heaped by one flood is scattered by another, but the rock always continues in its place. The stream of time, which is continually washing the dissoluble fabricks of other poets, passes without injury by the adamant[5] of *Shakespeare*.

If there be, what I believe there is, in every nation, a style which never becomes obsolete, a certain mode of phraseology so consonant and congenial to the analogy and principles of its respective language as to remain settled and unaltered; this style is probably to be sought in the common intercourse of life, among those who speak only to be understood, without ambition of elegance. The polite are always catching modish innovations, and the learned depart from established forms of speech, in hope of finding or making better; those who wish for distinction forsake the vulgar, when the vulgar is right; but there is a conversation above grossness and below refinement, where propriety resides, and where this poet seems to have gathered his comick dialogue. He is therefore more agreeable to the ears of the present age than any other authour equally remote, and among his other excellencies deserves to be studied as one of the original masters of our language.

These observations are to be considered not as unexceptionably constant, but as containing general and predominant truth. *Shakespeare*'s familiar dialogue is affirmed to be smooth and clear, yet not wholly without rugged-

5. An impregnable and surpassingly hard substance.

ness or difficulty; as a country may be eminently fruitful, though it has spots unfit for cultivation: His characters are praised as natural, though their sentiments are sometimes forced, and their actions improbable; as the earth upon the whole is spherical, though its surface is varied with protuberances and cavities.

Shakespeare with his excellencies has likewise faults, and faults sufficient to obscure and overwhelm any other merit. I shall shew them in the proportion in which they appear to me, without envious malignity or superstitious veneration. No question can be more innocently discussed than a dead poet's pretensions to renown; and little regard is due to that bigotry which sets candour higher than truth.

His first defect is that to which may be imputed most of the evil in books or in men. He sacrifices virtue to convenience, and is so much more careful to please than to instruct, that he seems to write without any moral purpose. From his writings indeed a system of social duty may be selected, for he that thinks reasonably must think morally; but his precepts and axioms drop casually from him; he makes no just distribution of good or evil, nor is always careful to shew in the virtuous a disapprobation of the wicked; he carries his persons indifferently through right and wrong, and at the close dismisses them without further care, and leaves their examples to operate by chance. This fault the barbarity of his age cannot extenuate; for it is always a writer's duty to make the world better, and justice is a virtue independant on[6] time or place.

The plots are often so loosely formed, that a very slight consideration may improve them, and so carelessly pursued, that he seems not always fully to comprehend his own design. He omits opportunities of instructing or delighting which the train of his story seems to force upon him, and apparently rejects those exhibitions which would be more affecting, for the sake of those which are more easy.

It may be observed, that in many of his plays the latter part is evidently neglected. When he found himself near the end of his work, and, in view of his reward, he shortened the labour to snatch the profit. He therefore remits his efforts where he should most vigorously exert them, and his catastrophe is improbably produced or imperfectly represented.

He had no regard to distinction of time or place, but gives to one age or nation, without scruple, the customs, institutions, and opinions of another, at the expence not only of likelihood, but of possibility. These faults *Pope* has endeavoured, with more zeal than judgment, to transfer to his imagined interpolators.[7] We need not wonder to find *Hector* quoting *Aristotle*, when we see the loves of *Theseus* and *Hippolyta*[8] combined with the *Gothick* mythology of fairies. *Shakespeare*, indeed, was not the only violator of chronology, for in the same age *Sidney*, who wanted not the advantages of learning, has, in his *Arcadia*,[9] confounded the pastoral with the feudal

6. Independent of.
7. In his *Preface to Shakespeare*, Pope maintained that "the many blunders and illiteracies of the first publishers of [Shakespeare's] works" explain why the texts are marred by errors and anachronisms.
8. Figures from Greek mythology who are characters in *A Midsummer Night's Dream* (ca. 1595). Hector: a character in *Troilus and Cressida* (1601–02; see 2.2.165–66); the Greek philosopher ARISTOTLE (384–322 B.C.E.) lived centuries after the events in that play are presumed to have occurred.
9. A prose romance (1590) by SIR PHILIP SIDNEY (1554–1586).

times, the days of innocence, quiet and security, with those of turbulence, violence, and adventure.

In his comick scenes he is seldom very successful, when he engages his characters in reciprocations of smartness and contests of sarcasm; their jests are commonly gross, and their pleasantry licentious; neither his gentlemen nor his ladies have much delicacy, nor are sufficiently distinguished from his clowns by any appearance of refined manners. Whether he represented the real conversation of his time is not easy to determine; the reign of *Elizabeth*[1] is commonly supposed to have been a time of stateliness, formality and reserve; yet perhaps the relaxations of that severity were not very elegant. There must, however, have been always some modes of gayety preferable to others, and a writer ought to chuse the best.

In tragedy his performance seems constantly to be worse, as his labour is more. The effusions of passion which exigence forces out are for the most part striking and energetick; but whenever he solicits his invention, or strains his faculties, the offspring of his throes is tumour,[2] meanness, tediousness, and obscurity.

In narration he affects a disproportionate pomp of diction, and a wearisome train of circumlocution, and tells the incident imperfectly in many words, which might have been more plainly delivered in few. Narration in dramatick poetry is naturally tedious, as it is unanimated and inactive, and obstructs the progress of the action; it should therefore always be rapid, and enlivened by frequent interruption. *Shakespeare* found it an encumbrance, and instead of lightening it by brevity, endeavoured to recommend it by dignity and splendour.

His declamations or set speeches are commonly cold and weak, for his power was the power of nature; when he endeavoured, like other tragick writers, to catch opportunities of amplification, and instead of inquiring what the occasion demanded, to show how much his stores of knowledge could supply, he seldom escapes without the pity or resentment of his reader.

It is incident[3] to him to be now and then entangled with an unwieldy sentiment, which he cannot well express, and will not reject; he struggles with it a while, and if it continues stubborn, comprises it in words such as occur, and leaves it to be disentangled and evolved[4] by those who have more leisure to bestow upon it.

Not that always where the language is intricate the thought is subtle, or the image always great where the line is bulky; the equality of words to things is very often neglected, and trivial sentiments and vulgar ideas disappoint the attention, to which they are recommended by sonorous epithets and swelling figures.[5]

But the admirers of this great poet have never less reason to indulge their hopes of supreme excellence, than when he seems fully resolved to sink them in dejection, and mollify them with tender emotions by the fall of greatness, the danger of innocence, or the crosses of love. He is not long soft and pathetick without some idle conceit, or contemptible equivocation. He no sooner begins to move, than he counteracts himself; and terrour and

1. Elizabeth I (1533–1603; reigned 1558–1603).
2. "Affected pomp; false magnificence; puffy grandeur" (Johnson's *Dictionary*).
3. Likely to happen.
4. Deduced, worked out. "Comprises": sums up.
5. Figures of speech.

pity, as they are rising in the mind, are checked and blasted by sudden frigidity.

A quibble[6] is to *Shakespeare*, what luminous vapours are to the traveller; he follows it at all adventures; it is sure to lead him out of his way, and sure to engulf him in the mire. It has some malignant power over his mind, and its fascinations are irresistible. Whatever be the dignity or profundity of his disquisition, whether he be enlarging knowledge or exalting affection, whether he be amusing attention with incidents, or enchaining it in suspense, let but a quibble spring up before him, and he leaves his work unfinished. A quibble is the golden apple for which he will always turn aside from his career,[7] or stoop from his elevation. A quibble, poor and barren as it is, gave him such delight, that he was content to purchase it, by the sacrifice of reason, propriety and truth. A quibble was to him the fatal *Cleopatra* for which he lost the world, and was content to lose it.[8]

It will be thought strange, that, in enumerating the defects of this writer, I have not yet mentioned his neglect of the unities;[9] his violation of those laws which have been instituted and established by the joint authority of poets and of criticks.

For his other deviations from the art of writing I resign him to critical justice, without making any other demand in his favour, than that which must be indulged to all human excellence: that his virtues be rated with his failings: But, from the censure which this irregularity may bring upon him, I shall, with due reverence to that learning which I must oppose, adventure to try how I can defend him.

His histories, being neither tragedies nor comedies are not subject to any of their laws; nothing more is necessary to all the praise which they expect, than that the changes of action be so prepared as to be understood, that the incidents be various and affecting, and the characters consistent, natural, and distinct. No other unity is intended, and therefore none is to be sought.

In his other works he has well enough preserved the unity of action. He has not, indeed, an intrigue regularly perplexed and regularly unravelled: he does not endeavour to hide his design only to discover it, for this is seldom the order of real events, and *Shakespeare* is the poet of nature: But his plan has commonly what *Aristotle* requires, a beginning, a middle, and an end;[1] one event is concatenated with another, and the conclusion follows by easy consequence. There are perhaps some incidents that might be spared, as in other poets there is much talk that only fills up time upon the stage; but the general system makes gradual advances, and the end of the play is the end of expectation.

To the unities of time and place he has shewn no regard; and perhaps a nearer view of the principles on which they stand will diminish their value, and withdraw from them the veneration which, from the time of

6. "A low conceit depending on the sound of words; a pun" (Johnson's *Dictionary*).
7. Course. In Greek mythology, Atalanta lost a footrace to Hippomenes (who thereby won her in marriage) because she paused to pick up three golden apples that he dropped in her path.
8. In Shakespeare's tragedy *Antony and Cleopatra* (1606–07), the renowned soldier Mark Antony is willing to trade his eminent position for the love of the Egyptian queen Cleopatra, the last ruler in the Ptolemaic dynasty.
9. That is, the neoclassical unities of time, place, and action.
1. Aristotle, *Poetics* 7 (see above).

Corneille,[2] they have very generally received, by discovering that they have given more trouble to the poet, than pleasure to the auditor.

The necessity of observing the unities of time and place arises from the supposed necessity of making the drama credible. The criticks hold it impossible, that an action of months or years can be possibly believed to pass in three hours; or that the spectator can suppose himself to sit in the theatre, while ambassadors go and return between distant kings, while armies are levied and towns besieged, while an exile wanders and returns, or till he whom they saw courting his mistress, shall lament the untimely fall of his son. The mind revolts from evident falsehood, and fiction loses its force when it departs from the resemblance of reality.

From the narrow limitation of time necessarily arises the contraction of place. The spectator, who knows that he saw the first act at *Alexandria*, cannot suppose that he sees the next at *Rome*, at a distance to which not the dragons of *Medea*[3] could, in so short a time, have transported him; he knows with certainty that he has not changed his place, and he knows that place cannot change itself; that what was a house cannot become a plain; that what was *Thebes* can never be *Persepolis*.

Such is the triumphant language with which a critick exults over the misery of an irregular poet, and exults commonly without resistance or reply. It is time therefore to tell him by the authority of *Shakespeare*, that he assumes, as an unquestionable principle, a position, which, while his breath is forming it into words, his understanding pronounces to be false. It is false, that any representation is mistaken for reality; that any dramatick fable in its materiality was ever credible, or, for a single moment, was ever credited.

The objection arising from the impossibility of passing the first hour at *Alexandria*, and the next at *Rome*, supposes, that when the play opens, the spectator really imagines himself at *Alexandria*, and believes that his walk to the theatre has been a voyage to *Egypt*, and that he lives in the days of *Antony* and *Cleopatra*. Surely he that imagines this may imagine more. He that can take the stage at one time for the palace of the *Ptolemies*, may take it in half an hour for the promontory of *Actium*.[4] Delusion, if delusion be admitted, has no certain limitation; if the spectator can be once persuaded, that his old acquaintance are *Alexander* and *Caesar*, that a room illuminated with candles is the plain of *Pharsalia*, or the bank of *Granicus*,[5] he is in a state of elevation above the reach of reason, or of truth, and from the heights of empyrean poetry, may despise the circumscriptions of terrestrial nature. There is no reason why a mind thus wandering in extasy should count the clock, or why an hour should not be a century in that calenture[6] of the brains that can make the stage a field.

2. PIERRE CORNEILLE (1606–1684), French tragic dramatist whose very popular play *Le Cid* was criticized for violating the three unities. See his "Of the Three Unities of Action, Time, and Place" (1660; above).

3. According to Greek mythology, after avenging herself on her unfaithful husband, Jason, by murdering their children, Medea departed in a chariot drawn by dragons.

4. On the western coast of Greece, where a naval battle in 31 B.C.E. ended with Antony's final defeat.

5. A river in Asia Minor (near the site of Troy) that gave its name to a famous battle at which Alexander the Great (356–323 B.C.E.) routed the Persians (334 B.C.E.). Pharsalia: at Pharsalus, in 48 B.C.E., Julius Caesar (100–44 B.C.E.) defeated his Roman rival Pompey (106–48 B.C.E.).

6. A delirium (specifically, a delusion suffered by sailors who imagine that the sea is a green field).

The truth is, that the spectators are always in their senses, and know, from the first act to the last, that the stage is only a stage, and that the players are only players. They came to hear a certain number of lines recited with just gesture and elegant modulation. The lines relate to some action, and an action must be in some place; but the different actions that compleat a story may be in places very remote from each other; and where is the absurdity of allowing that space to represent first *Athens*, and then *Sicily*, which was always known to be neither *Sicily* nor *Athens*, but a modern theatre?

By supposition, as place is introduced, time may be extended; the time required by the fable elapses for the most part between the acts; for, of so much of the action as is represented, the real and poetical duration is the same. If, in the first act, preparations for war against *Mithridates*[7] are represented to be made in *Rome*, the event of the war may, without absurdity, be represented, in the catastrophe, as happening in *Pontus*; we know that there is neither war, nor preparation for war; we know that we are neither in *Rome* nor *Pontus*; that neither *Mithridates* nor *Lucullus* are before us. The drama exhibits successive imitations of successive actions; and why may not the second imitation represent an action that happened years after the first, if it be so connected with it, that nothing but time can be supposed to intervene? Time is, of all modes of existence, most obsequious to the imagination; a lapse of years is as easily conceived as a passage of hours. In contemplation we easily contract the time of real actions, and therefore willingly permit it to be contracted when we only see their imitation.

It will be asked, how the drama moves, if it is not credited. It is credited with all the credit due to a drama. It is credited, whenever it moves, as a just picture of a real original; as representing to the auditor what he would himself feel, if he were to do or suffer what is there feigned to be suffered or to be done. The reflection that strikes the heart is not, that the evils before us are real evils, but that they are evils to which we ourselves may be exposed. If there be any fallacy, it is not that we fancy the players, but that we fancy ourselves unhappy for a moment; but we rather lament the possibility than suppose the presence of misery, as a mother weeps over her babe, when she remembers that death may take it from her. The delight of tragedy proceeds from our consciousness of fiction; if we thought murders and treasons real, they would please no more.

Imitations produce pain or pleasure, not because they are mistaken for realities, but because they bring realities to mind. When the imagination is recreated by a painted landscape, the trees are not supposed capable to give us shade, or the fountains coolness; but we consider, how we should be pleased with such fountains playing beside us, and such woods waving over us. We are agitated in reading the history of *Henry* the Fifth, yet no man takes his book for the field of *Agencourt*.[8] A dramatick exhibition is a book recited with concomitants that encrease or diminish its effect. Familiar

7. King of Pontus (reigned 120–63 B.C.E.), in what is now Turkey, who engaged in 3 wars with Rome; the Roman general Lucullus (ca. 117–57/56 B.C.E.) drove him out of Pontus in 72.

8. Agincourt, a village in France near which an English army under Henry V defeated a much larger French force in 1415.

comedy is often more powerful on the theatre, than in the page; imperial tragedy is always less. The humour of *Petruchio* may be heightened by grimace; but what voice or what gesture can hope to add dignity or force to the soliloquy of *Cato*?[9]

A play read, affects the mind like a play acted. It is therefore evident, that the action is not supposed to be real; and it follows, that between the acts a longer or shorter time may be allowed to pass, and that no more account of space or duration is to be taken by the auditor of a drama, than by the reader of a narrative, before whom may pass in an hour the life of a hero, or the revolutions of an empire.

Whether *Shakespeare* knew the unities, and rejected them by design, or deviated from them by happy ignorance, it is, I think, impossible to decide, and useless to enquire. We may reasonably suppose, that, when he rose to notice, he did not want[1] the counsels and admonitions of scholars and criticks, and that he at last deliberately persisted in a practice, which he might have begun by chance. As nothing is essential to the fable, but unity of action, and as the unities of time and place arise evidently from false assumptions, and, by circumscribing the extent of the drama, lessen its variety, I cannot think it much to be lamented, that they were not known by him, or not observed: Nor, if such another poet could arise, should I very vehemently reproach him, that his first act passed at *Venice*, and his next in *Cyprus*.[2] Such violations of rules merely positive,[3] become the comprehensive genius of *Shakespeare*, and such censures are suitable to the minute and slender criticism of *Voltaire:*

Non usque adeo permiscuit imis
Longus summa dies, ut non, si voce Metelli
Serventur leges, malint a Caesare tolli.[4]

Yet when I speak thus slightly of dramatick rules, I cannot but recollect how much wit and learning may be produced against me; before such authorities I am afraid to stand, not that I think the present question one of those that are to be decided by mere authority, but because it is to be suspected, that these precepts have not been so easily received but for better reasons than I have yet been able to find. The result of my enquiries, in which it would be ludicrous to boast of impartiality, is, that the unities of time and place are not essential to a just drama, that though they may sometimes conduce to pleasure, they are always to be sacrificed to the nobler beauties of variety and instruction; and that a play, written with nice[5] observation of critical rules, is to be contemplated as an elaborate curiosity, as the product of superfluous and ostentatious art, by which is shewn, rather what is possible, than what is necessary.

9. The title character of a tragedy by JOSEPH ADDISON (1713); his soliloquy on immortality (5.1.1–40), delivered just before he kills himself, was admired in the 18th century as an expression of noble sentiment. Petruchio: the hero in Shakespeare's comedy *The Taming of the Shrew* (ca. 1592).
1. Lack.
2. Places that figure in Shakespeare's tragedy *Othello*.
3. Arbitrary; not natural.
4. The course of time has not wrought such confusion that the laws would not rather be trampled on by Caesar than saved by Metellus (Latin; trans. J. D. Duff). From Lucan, *Civil War* (ca. 63 C.E.), 3.138–40. Metellus (d. 46 B.C.E.), a Roman politician who committed suicide after his defeat by Julius Caesar, a far superior general.
5. Precise.

He that, without diminution of any other excellence, shall preserve all the unities unbroken, deserves the like applause with the architect, who shall display all the orders of architecture[6] in a citadel, without any deduction from its strength; but the principal beauty of a citadel is to exclude the enemy; and the greatest graces of a play, are to copy nature and instruct life.

Perhaps, what I have here not dogmatically but deliberately written, may recal the principles of the drama to a new examination. I am almost frighted at my own temerity; and when I estimate the fame and the strength of those that maintain the contrary opinion, am ready to sink down in reverential silence; as *Æneas* withdrew from the defence of *Troy*, when he saw *Neptune* shaking the wall, and *Juno* heading the besiegers.[7]

Those whom my arguments cannot persuade to give their approbation to the judgment of *Shakespeare*, will easily, if they consider the condition of his life, make some allowance for his ignorance.

Every man's performances, to be rightly estimated, must be compared with the state of the age in which he lived, and with his own particular opportunities; and though to the reader a book be not worse or better for the circumstances of the authour, yet as there is always a silent reference of human works to human abilities, and as the enquiry, how far man may extend his designs, or how high he may rate his native force, is of far greater dignity than in what rank we shall place any particular performance, curiosity is always busy to discover the instruments, as well as to survey the workmanship, to know how much is to be ascribed to original powers, and how much to casual and adventitious help. The palaces of *Peru* or *Mexico* were certainly mean and incommodious habitations, if compared to the houses of *European* monarchs; yet who could forbear to view them with astonishment, who remembered that they were built without the use of iron?

* * *

1765

From Lives of the English Poets

From *Cowley*[1]

* * *

[ON METAPHYSICAL WIT]

Cowley, like other poets who have written with narrow views and, instead of tracing intellectual pleasure to its natural sources in the mind of man, paid their court to temporary prejudices, has been at one time too much praised and too much neglected at another.

6. Building styles, characterized by the type of classical column used.

7. See Virgil, *Aeneid* (19 B.C.E.) 2.610–14. Aeneas is a heroic warrior, but Neptune and Juno are gods.

1. The English poet and essayist Abraham Cowley (1618–1667).

Wit, like all other things subject by their nature to the choice of man, has its changes and fashions, and at different times takes different forms. About the beginning of the seventeenth century appeared a race of writers that may be termed the metaphysical poets,[2] of whom in a criticism on the works of Cowley it is not improper to give some account.

The metaphysical poets were men of learning, and to shew their learning was their whole endeavour; but, unluckily resolving to shew it in rhyme, instead of writing poetry they only wrote verses, and very often such verses as stood the trial of the finger better than of the ear; for the modulation was so imperfect that they were only found to be verses by counting the syllables.

If the father of criticism[3] has rightly denominated poetry τέχνη μιμητική, *an imitative art*, these writers will without great wrong lose their right to the name of poets, for they cannot be said to have imitated any thing: they neither copied nature nor life; neither painted the forms of matter nor represented the operations of intellect.

Those however who deny them to be poets allow them to be wits. Dryden confesses of himself and his contemporaries that they fall below Donne in wit, but maintains that they surpass him in poetry.

If Wit be well described by Pope as being 'that which has been often thought, but was never before so well expressed,'[4] they certainly never attained nor ever sought it, for they endeavoured to be singular in their thoughts, and were careless of their diction. But Pope's account of wit is undoubtedly erroneous; he depresses it below its natural dignity, and reduces it from strength of thought to happiness of language.

If by a more noble and more adequate conception that be considered as Wit which is at once natural and new, that which though not obvious is, upon its first production, acknowledged to be just; if it be that, which he that never found it, wonders how he missed; to wit of this kind the metaphysical poets have seldom risen. Their thoughts are often new, but seldom natural; they are not obvious, but neither are they just; and the reader, far from wondering that he missed them, wonders more frequently by what perverseness of industry they were ever found.

But Wit, abstracted from its effects upon the hearer, may be more rigorously and philosophically considered as a kind of *discordia concors*;[5] a combination of dissimilar images, or discovery of occult resemblances in things apparently unlike. Of wit, thus defined, they have more than enough. The most heterogeneous ideas are yoked by violence together; nature and art are ransacked for illustrations, comparisons, and allusions; their learning instructs, and their subtilty surprises; but the reader commonly thinks his improvement dearly bought, and, though he sometimes admires, is seldom pleased.

2. A term probably taken from JOHN DRYDEN's complaint about the poetry of John Donne (1572–1631) in *A Discourse Concerning the Original and Progress of Satire* (1693): "He affects the metaphysics . . . and perplexes the minds of the fair sex with nice speculations of philosophy, when he should engage their hearts, and entertain them with the softness of love." See also T. S. ELIOT, "The Metaphysical Poets" (1921; below).

3. The Greek philosopher ARISTOTLE (384–322 B.C.E.).

4. Slightly misquoted from *An Essay on Criticism* (1711), line 298, by ALEXANDER POPE (1688–1744; see above).

5. Harmonious disharmony (Latin).

From this account of their compositions it will be readily inferred that they were not successful in representing or moving the affections. As they were wholly employed on something unexpected and surprising they had no regard to that uniformity of sentiment, which enables us to conceive and to excite the pains and the pleasure of other minds: they never enquired what on any occasion they should have said or done, but wrote rather as beholders than partakers of human nature; as beings looking upon good and evil, impassive and at leisure; as Epicurean[6] deities making remarks on the actions of men and the vicissitudes of life, without interest and without emotion. Their courtship was void of fondness and their lamentation of sorrow. Their wish was only to say what they hoped had been never said before.

Nor was the sublime[7] more within their reach than the pathetick; for they never attempted that comprehension and expanse of thought which at once fills the whole mind, and of which the first effect is sudden astonishment, and the second rational admiration. Sublimity is produced by aggregation, and littleness by dispersion. Great thoughts are always general, and consist in positions not limited by exceptions, and in descriptions not descending to minuteness. It is with great propriety that subtlety, which in its original import means exility[8] of particles, is taken in its metaphorical meaning for nicety of distinction. Those writers who lay on the watch for novelty could have little hope of greatness; for great things cannot have escaped former observation. Their attempts were always analytick: they broke every image into fragments, and could no more represent by their slender conceits and laboured particularities the prospects of nature or the scenes of life, than he who dissects a sun-beam with a prism can exhibit the wide effulgence of a summer noon.

What they wanted[9] however of the sublime they endeavoured to supply by hyperbole; their amplification had no limits: they left not only reason but fancy behind them, and produced combinations of confused magnificence that not only could not be credited, but could not be imagined.

Yet great labour directed by great abilities is never wholly lost: if they frequently threw away their wit upon false conceits, they likewise sometimes struck out unexpected truth: if their conceits were far-fetched, they were often worth the carriage.[1] To write on their plan it was at least necessary to read and think. No man could be born a metaphysical poet, nor assume the dignity of a writer by descriptions copied from descriptions, by imitations borrowed from imitations, by traditional imagery and hereditary similes, by readiness of rhyme and volubility of syllables.

In perusing the works of this race of authors the mind is exercised either by recollection or inquiry; either something already learned is to be retrieved, or something new is to be examined. If their greatness seldom elevates, their acuteness often surprises; if the imagination is not always gratified, at least the powers of reflection and comparison are employed; and in the mass of materials, which ingenious absurdity has thrown together, genuine wit

6. That is, free from disturbance. The Greek philosopher Epicurus (341–270 B.C.E.) taught that personal happiness is the highest good, best attained through austere living and the study of philosophy.

7. On the sublime, see the writings of JOSEPH ADDISON (1672–1719; above) and EDMUND BURKE (1729–1797; below).

8. Smallness in number or size.

9. Lacked.

1. That is, worth the trouble of carrying them so far.

and useful knowledge may be sometimes found, buried perhaps in grossness of expression, but useful to those who know their value, and such as, when they are expanded to perspicuity and polished to elegance, may give lustre to works which have more propriety though less copiousness of sentiment.

* * *

1783

DAVID HUME
1711–1776

The Scottish philosopher and historian David Hume responded to and developed the empiricist work of his predecessors John Locke (1632–1704) and George Berkeley (1685–1753). He, too, opposed the rationalist belief in innate ideas and held that knowledge derives from experience. But he moved beyond them toward a position of radical skepticism, denying the possibility of certain knowledge and maintaining that the mind itself is a bundle of sensations. Hume reached the conclusion that we cannot derive and prove a theory of reality at all; we can know only experience and must base our beliefs upon it. The selection below, "Of the Standard of Taste," develops this view in a provocative way, tracing uncertain linkages between human capacities, personal experiences, and standards.

Hume is one of the major figures of the Enlightenment. Many criticized his skeptical views as extremist and alarming, especially because they challenged religious orthodoxy; yet many others acclaimed him as one of Scotland's and Europe's foremost thinkers. In the words of the modern scholar Walter Jackson Bate, "in Hume's writings, human reason was dissected with such devastating effect that philosophy has never since quite recovered the traditional classical confidence in reason." This achievement is all the more fascinating from a man described by one friend, the Scottish economist Adam Smith, "as approaching as nearly to the idea of a perfectly wise and virtuous man, as perhaps the nature of human frailty will admit."

Hume's major philosophical and moral writings include *A Treatise of Human Nature* (1739–40), usually regarded as his masterpiece and an extraordinary achievement for an author in his mid-twenties; *Essays, On Moral and Political Subjects* (1741); *An Enquiry Concerning Human Understanding*—a simplified version of the *Treatise* (1748); and *An Enquiry Concerning the Principles of Morals* (1751, "of all my writings incomparably the best"). He also wrote *Political Discourses* (1752), *The Natural History of Religion* (1755), and the *History of England* (6 vols., 1754–62), which for decades was the standard work in the field. The extent of Hume's skepticism is reflected in his late writings on religion, where he disputes all claims for any rational or natural theology; knowing that these ideas would be controversial, he withheld the text of *The Dialogues Concerning Natural Religion* (1779) until after his death.

Born in Edinburgh, David Hume attended the university there. In 1734 he journeyed to Anjou, in northwest France, where he studied and wrote. In 1739 he returned to England to help prepare his *Treatise* for publication. Later in life, Hume professed that this book was ill-argued and philosophically immature, yet it remains perhaps his most widely read work (particularly the first section, on morals). The poor response to the *Treatise* deeply disappointed him—he remarked that it "fell dead-born from the press"—but the greater success of the later *Essays* led him to hope that he might be selected for the chair of moral philosophy at the University of Edinburgh in 1744. His critics, however, protested that his views were heretical and even atheistic. For example, Hume argued that "the idea of God, as meaning an infinitely intelligent, wise, and good Being, arises from reflecting on the operations of our own mind, and augmenting, without limit, those qualities of goodness and wisdom." Men and women, so it seems, make their Maker; and Hume's own calm in the face of such observations disturbed his detractors all the more.

Having failed to receive the academic position he sought, Hume then took leave of Edinburgh for a long period, traveling and serving in a number of educational, military, and diplomatic posts in Scotland, England, and Europe. In 1748 he published his *Enquiry Concerning Human Understanding*, which revised and popularized book 1 of his *Treatise*. Two new sections, "Of Miracles" and "Of a Particular Providence and of a Future State," show Hume's dissent from religious belief and doctrine, as does, less directly, the slightly later *Enquiry Concerning the Principles of Morals*. For Hume, sentiments and not the decrees of God are the basis for morality.

From the early 1750s to the mid-1760s, Hume spent most of his time in Edinburgh. In 1752 he was made keeper of the Advocates Library, a post that enabled him to concentrate on the historical research and writing that led to his *History*. In 1763 he took a diplomatic position in Paris, where—admired for his intellectual gifts and personality—he became friends with aristocrats and literary men. Hume spent his final years mostly in Edinburgh, revising and correcting his works. His friends Adam Smith, the writer and playwright S. J. Pratt, and Samuel Johnson's biographer James Boswell all described how Hume, without a belief in an afterlife, prepared for death—thereby sparking yet more charges of apostasy. The publication in 1779 of Hume's *Dialogues* and, in 1782, of two essays on suicide and immortality renewed these accusations and criticisms.

Hume is skeptical, but he is also intellectually curious, lucid in his prose, and cogent and complicated in his thought; he is sometimes perplexing and contradictory, but never obscure, in argument. We can gain some sense of the nature of his skepticism by pondering the connection, as he sees it, between one event and another. The *cause* of their connection, Hume argues, is something for which we have no impression and thus no idea; as a result, we ourselves infer this causal link. But while we cannot see or prove the connection, we can say we know that it exists, because of the cause-and-effect relationship that we draw from our experience, which leads us to expect that it will recur.

Our selection, "Of the Standard of Taste," is a celebrated literary performance, and it bears suggestively on modern and contemporary debates about standards in criticism, reader-response theory, interpretive communities, and canon formation. The essay itself has an unusual origin. In 1756 Hume had prepared a new book for publication, to be titled *Five Dissertations*; its five essays were "The Natural History of Religion," "Of the Passions," "Of Tragedy," "Of Suicide," and "Of the Immortality of the Soul." The antireligious thrust of the final two essays, however, made Hume's publisher fearful, and he was in fact threatened with prosecution should they appear in print. Hume replaced the two troublesome essays with "Of the Standard of Taste," and the book—retitled *Four Dissertations*—was published early in 1757.

Hume begins with the fact of critical disagreement, the wide variations in "taste" that testify both to the different observations that persons make and to the different terms—or differing meanings attached to the same terms—that they use to describe what they have experienced. In light of all this, he asks, can we ever hope to identify a "standard of taste"? The first answer seems to be that we cannot. As we ponder the idea of a standard, we find ourselves inclined to say that merit or value is always in the eye of the beholder—thus one person praises an object as beautiful that another, or most others, would say is ugly. How can this atypical view be disputed or, in Hume's word, "regulated"? We are left with differences in taste, and no standard for discriminating among them in any final sense.

Hume then queries the position that he has just seemed to endorse. Does not common sense tell us all that in poetry John Milton is superior to John Ogilby, and in prose Joseph Addison is superior to John Bunyan? The epic poems of Homer, which gave pleasure to auditors in preclassical times, continue to do the same for readers in England and France in the eighteenth century. His poetry has endured when that by many others (whose compositions once enjoyed a high reputation) has not. Hume therefore proposes that each person has the capacity for recognizing true beauty, which offers after all the prospect of a "true standard of taste and sentiment." Of course, not all capacities are realized; as Hume puts it, some people lack "*delicacy* of imagination" and are therefore unable to feel the "proper sentiment of beauty."

More experience: this is Hume's main remedy for the shortcomings in aesthetic response that afflict some persons. He recommends that they practice an art and reexamine its works, making their taste finer, more subtle and discriminating. Hume stresses the need for comparisons among a range of works only to insist, a moment later, that we examine the object at hand free from "prejudice." Here, as elsewhere, Hume may appear to be contradicting himself on a point that he seemed to judge crucial. Such shifts are part of the open, flexible, and exploratory nature of his approach.

The slighting reference to the Qur'an in Hume's essay is unacceptable, and he takes for granted judgments (e.g., Addison's superiority to Bunyan) that many today would quarrel with—a point that exposes his reliance on the "common sense" of his time. Moreover, his argument has a circularity that is hard to overlook. Some persons, he says, have a finer taste than others. How do we know this? Because it is universally acknowledged to be so.

Though Hume's style marks him as a writer of the eighteenth century, in some respects his views anticipate certain disquieting ironies of poststructuralist theory. The scholar James Engell has described Hume's position in this essay in terms that evoke JACQUES DERRIDA: "The standard of taste becomes a presence that is, in a sense, an absence. . . . Hume is saying that in matters of taste, although there is very definitely at any given time in history a center or a standard, we cannot define or find that center—at least we cannot precisely agree what it is. It is always, for us, decentered." As a philosopher Hume is close to us; we read him often with a shock of recognition.

"Of the Standard of Taste" Keywords: Aesthetics, The Canon/Tradition, Defense of Criticism, Enlightenment Theory, Interpretation Theory, Literary History

Of the Standard of Taste

The great variety of Taste, as well as of opinion, which prevails in the world, is too obvious not to have fallen under every one's observation. Men of the most confined knowledge are able to remark[1] a difference of taste in the nar-

1. Observe, notice.

row circle of their acquaintance, even where the persons have been educated under the same government, and have early imbibed the same prejudices. But those, who can enlarge their view to contemplate distant nations and remote ages, are still more surprized at the great inconsistence and contrariety. We are apt to call *barbarous* whatever departs widely from our own taste and apprehension: But soon find the epithet of reproach retorted on us. And the highest arrogance and self-conceit is at last startled, on observing an equal assurance on all sides, and scruples, amidst such a contest of sentiment, to pronounce positively in its own favour.

As this variety of taste is obvious to the most careless enquirer; so will it be found, on examination, to be still greater in reality than in appearance. The sentiments of men often differ with regard to beauty and deformity of all kinds, even while their general discourse is the same. There are certain terms in every language, which import blame, and others praise; and all men, who use the same tongue, must agree in their application of them. Every voice is united in applauding elegance, propriety, simplicity, spirit in writing; and in blaming fustian, affectation, coldness, and a false brilliancy: But when critics come to particulars, this seeming unanimity vanishes; and it is found, that they had affixed a very different meaning to their expressions. In all matters of opinion and science, the case is opposite: The difference among men is there oftener found to lie in generals than in particulars; and to be less in reality than in appearance. An explanation of the terms commonly ends the controversy; and the disputants are surprized to find, that they had been quarrelling, while at bottom they agreed in their judgment.

Those who found morality on sentiment, more than on reason, are inclined to comprehend ethics under the former observation, and to maintain, that, in all questions, which regard conduct and manners, the difference among men is really greater than at first sight it appears. It is indeed obvious, that writers of all nations and all ages concur in applauding justice, humanity, magnanimity, prudence, veracity; and in blaming the opposite qualities. Even poets and other authors, whose compositions are chiefly calculated to please the imagination, are yet found from HOMER down to FENELON,[2] to inculcate the same moral precepts, and to bestow their applause and blame on the same virtues and vices. This great unanimity is usually ascribed to the influence of plain reason; which, in all these cases, maintains similar sentiments in all men, and prevents those controversies, to which the abstract sciences are so much exposed. So far as the unanimity is real, this account may be admitted as satisfactory: But we must also allow that some part of the seeming harmony in morals may be accounted for from the very nature of language. The word *virtue*, with its equivalent in every tongue, implies praise; as that of *vice* does blame: And no one, without the most obvious and grossest impropriety, could affix reproach to a term, which in general acceptation is understood in a good sense; or bestow applause, where the idiom requires disapprobation. HOMER's general precepts, where he delivers any such, will never be contro-

2. François Fénelon (1651–1715), French churchman and writer, author of a didactic romance of Homeric characters, *The Adventures of Telemachus* (1699). Telemachus is the son of Odysseus and Penelope. Homer: the epics the *Iliad* (whose central figure is Achilles) and the *Odyssey* (centered on Odysseus, or Ulysses) were often taken as the starting point of Western literature (ca. 8th c. B.C.E.).

verted; but it is obvious, that, when he draws particular pictures of manners, and represents heroism in ACHILLES and prudence in ULYSSES, he intermixes a much greater degree of ferocity in the former, and of cunning and fraud in the latter, than FENELON would admit of. The sage ULYSSES in the GREEK poet seems to delight in lies and fictions, and often employs them without any necessity or even advantage: But his more scrupulous son, in the FRENCH epic writer, exposes himself to the most imminent perils, rather than depart from the most exact line of truth and veracity.

The admirers and followers of the ALCORAN[3] insist on the excellent moral precepts interspersed throughout that wild and absurd performance. But it is to be supposed, that the ARABIC words, which correspond to the ENGLISH, equity, justice, temperance, meekness, charity, were such as, from the constant use of that tongue, must always be taken in a good sense; and it would have argued the greatest ignorance, not of morals, but of language, to have mentioned them with any epithets, besides those of applause and approbation. But would we know, whether the pretended prophet had really attained a just sentiment of morals? Let us attend to his narration; and we shall soon find, that he bestows praise on such instances of treachery, inhumanity, cruelty, revenge, bigotry, as are utterly incompatible with civilized society. No steady rule of right seems there to be attended to; and every action is blamed or praised, so far only as it is beneficial or hurtful to the true believers.

The merit of delivering true general precepts in ethics is indeed very small. Whoever recommends any moral virtues, really does no more than is implied in the terms themselves. That people, who invented the word *charity*, and used it in a good sense, inculcated more clearly and much more efficaciously, the precept, *be charitable*, than any pretended legislator or prophet, who should insert such a *maxim* in his writings. Of all expressions, those, which, together with their other meaning, imply a degree either of blame or approbation, are the least liable to be perverted or mistaken.

It is natural for us to seek a *Standard of Taste*; a rule, by which the various sentiments of men may be reconciled; at least, a decision, afforded, confirming one sentiment, and condemning another.

There is a species of philosophy, which cuts off all hopes of success in such an attempt, and represents the impossibility of ever attaining any standard of taste. The difference, it is said, is very wide between judgment and sentiment. All sentiment is right; because sentiment has a reference to nothing beyond itself, and is always real, wherever a man is conscious of it. But all determinations of the understanding are not right; because they have a reference to something beyond themselves, to wit, real matter of fact; and are not always conformable to that standard. Among a thousand different opinions which different men may entertain of the same subject, there is one, and but one, that is just and true; and the only difficulty is to fix and ascertain it. On the contrary, a thousand different sentiments, excited by the same object, are all right: Because no sentiment represents what is really in the object. It only marks a certain conformity or relation between the object and the organs or faculties of the mind; and if that con-

3. The Qur'an, which collects and records the revelations of the Prophet Muhammad (570–632).

formity did not really exist, the sentiment could never possibly have being. Beauty is no quality in things themselves: It exists merely in the mind which contemplates them; and each mind perceives a different beauty. One person may even perceive deformity, where another is sensible of beauty; and every individual ought to acquiesce in his own sentiment, without pretending to regulate those of others. To seek the real beauty, or real deformity, is as fruitless an enquiry, as to pretend to ascertain the real sweet or real bitter. According to the disposition of the organs, the same object may be both sweet and bitter; and the proverb has justly determined it to be fruitless to dispute concerning tastes. It is very natural, and even quite necessary, to extend this axiom to mental, as well as bodily taste; and thus common sense, which is so often at variance with philosophy, especially with the sceptical kind, is found, in one instance at least, to agree in pronouncing the same decision.

But though this axiom, by passing into a proverb, seems to have attained the sanction of common sense; there is certainly a species of common sense which opposes it, at least serves to modify and restrain it. Whoever would assert an equality of genius and elegance between OGILBY and MILTON, or BUNYAN and ADDISON,[4] would be thought to defend no less an extravagance, than if he had maintained a mole-hill to be as high as TENERIFFE,[5] or a pond as extensive as the ocean. Though there may be found persons, who give the preference to the former authors; no one pays attention to such a taste; and we pronounce without scruple the sentiment of these pretended critics to be absurd and ridiculous. The principle of the natural equality of tastes is then totally forgot, and while we admit it on some occasions, where the objects seem near an equality, it appears an extravagant paradox, or rather a palpable absurdity, where objects so disproportioned are compared together.

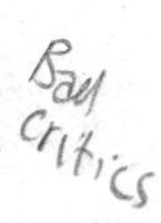

It is evident that none of the rules of composition are fixed by reasonings *a priori*, or can be esteemed abstract conclusions of the understanding, from comparing those habitudes[6] and relations of ideas, which are eternal and immutable. Their foundation is the same with that of all the practical sciences, experience; nor are they any thing but general observations, concerning what has been universally found to please in all countries and in all ages. Many of the beauties of poetry and even of eloquence are founded on falsehood and fiction, on hyperboles, metaphors, and an abuse or perversion of terms from their natural meaning. To check the sallies of the imagination, and to reduce every expression to geometrical truth and exactness, would be the most contrary to the laws of criticism; because it would produce a work, which, by universal experience, has been found the most insipid and disagreeable. But though poetry can never submit to exact truth, it must be confined by rules of art, discovered to the author either by genius or observation. If some negligent or irregular writers have pleased, they have not pleased by their transgressions of rule or order, but in spite of these transgressions: They have possessed other beauties, which were conformable to

4. Hume pairs two poets, John Ogilby (1600–1676) and John Milton (1608–1674), and two prose writers, John Bunyan (1628–1688) and JOSEPH ADDISON (1672–1719).

5. Largest of the Canary Islands and site of a volcanic peak.

6. Habits.

just criticism; and the force of these beauties has been able to overpower censure, and give the mind a satisfaction superior to the disgust arising from the blemishes. ARIOSTO[7] pleases; but not by his monstrous and improbable fictions, by his bizarre mixture of the serious and comic styles, by the want of coherence in his stories, or by the continual interruptions of his narration. He charms by the force and clearness of his expression, by the readiness and variety of his inventions, and by his natural pictures of the passions, especially those of the gay and amorous kind: And however his faults may diminish our satisfaction, they are not able entirely to destroy it. Did our pleasure really arise from those parts of his poem, which we denominate faults, this would be no objection to criticism in general: It would only be an objection to those particular rules of criticism, which would establish such circumstances to be faults, and would represent them as universally blameable. If they are found to please, they cannot be faults; let the pleasure, which they produce, be ever so unexpected and unaccountable.

But though all the general rules of art are founded only on experience and on the observation of the common sentiments of human nature, we must not imagine, that, on every occasion, the feelings of men will be conformable to these rules. Those finer emotions of the mind are of a very tender and delicate nature, and require the concurrence of many favourable circumstances to make them play with facility and exactness, according to their general and established principles. The least exterior hindrance to such small springs, or the least internal disorder, disturbs their motion, and confounds the operation of the whole machine. When we would make an experiment of this nature, and would try the force of any beauty or deformity, we must choose with care a proper time and place, and bring the fancy to a suitable situation and disposition. A perfect serenity of mind, a recollection of thought, a due attention to the object; if any of these circumstances be wanting, our experiment will be fallacious, and we shall be unable to judge of the catholic and universal beauty. The relation, which nature has placed between the form and the sentiment, will at least be more obscure; and it will require greater accuracy to trace and discern it. We shall be able to ascertain its influence not so much from the operation of each particular beauty, as from the durable admiration, which attends those works, that have survived all the caprices of mode and fashion, all the mistakes of ignorance and envy.

The same HOMER, who pleased at ATHENS and ROME two thousand years ago, is still admired at PARIS and at LONDON. All the changes of climate, government, religion, and language, have not been able to obscure his glory. Authority or prejudice may give a temporary vogue to a bad poet or orator; but his reputation will never be durable or general. When his compositions are examined by posterity or by foreigners, the enchantment is dissipated, and his faults appear in their true colours. On the contrary, a real genius, the longer his works endure, and the more wide they are spread, the more sincere is the admiration which he meets with. Envy and jealousy have too much place in a narrow circle; and even familiar acquaintance with his person may diminish the applause due to his performances: But

7. Lodovico Ariosto (1474–1533), Italian poet; his masterpiece is the romantic epic *Orlando Furioso* (1516).

when these obstructions are removed, the beauties, which are naturally fitted to excite agreeable sentiments, immediately display their energy; and while the world endures, they maintain their authority over the minds of men.

It appears then, that, amidst all the variety and caprice of taste, there are certain general principles of approbation or blame, whose influence a careful eye may trace in all operations of the mind. Some particular forms or qualities, from the original structure of the internal fabric, are calculated to please, and others to displease; and if they fail of their effect in any particular instance, it is from some apparent defect or imperfection in the organ. A man in a fever would not insist on his palate as able to decide concerning flavours; nor would one, affected with the jaundice, pretend to give a verdict with regard to colours.[8] In each creature, there is a sound and a defective state; and the former alone can be supposed to afford us a true standard of taste and sentiment. If, in the sound state of the organ, there be an entire or a considerable uniformity of sentiment among men, we may thence derive an idea of the perfect beauty; in like manner as the appearance of objects in day-light, to the eye of a man in health, is denominated their true and real colour, even while colour is allowed to be merely a phantasm of the senses.

Many and frequent are the defects in the internal organs, which prevent or weaken the influence of those general principles, on which depends our sentiment of beauty or deformity. Though some objects, by the structure of the mind, be naturally calculated to give pleasure, it is not to be expected, that in every individual the pleasure will be equally felt. Particular incidents and situations occur, which either throw a false light on the objects, or hinder the true from conveying to the imagination the proper sentiment and perception.

One obvious cause, why many feel not the proper sentiment of beauty, is the want of that *delicacy* of imagination, which is requisite to convey a sensibility of those finer emotions. This delicacy every one pretends to: Every one talks of it; and would reduce every kind of taste or sentiment to its standard. But as our intention in this essay is to mingle some light of the understanding with the feelings of sentiment, it will be proper to give a more accurate definition of delicacy, than has hitherto been attempted. And not to draw our philosophy from too profound a source, we shall have recourse to a noted story in DON QUIXOTE.[9]

It is with good reason, says SANCHO to the squire with the great nose, that I pretend to have a judgment in wine: This is a quality hereditary in our family. Two of my kinsmen were once called to give their opinion of a hogshead, which was supposed to be excellent, being old and of a good vintage. One of them tastes it; considers it; and after mature reflection pronounces the wine to be good, were it not for a small taste of leather, which he perceived in it. The other, after using the same precautions, gives also his verdict in favour of the wine; but with the reserve of a taste of iron, which he could easily distinguish. You cannot imagine how much they were

8. It was thought that to a person whose eye was discolored by jaundice, everything would look yellow.

9. The novel *Don Quixote* (1605, 1615), by Miguel de Cervantes; this story comes from part 2, chapter 13.

both ridiculed for their judgment. But who laughed in the end? On emptying the hogshead, there was found at the bottom, an old key with a leathern thong tied to it.

The great resemblance between mental and bodily taste will easily teach us to apply this story. Though it be certain, that beauty and deformity, more than sweet and bitter, are not qualities in objects, but belong entirely to the sentiment, internal or external; it must be allowed, that there are certain qualities in objects, which are fitted by nature to produce those particular feelings. Now as these qualities may be found in a small degree, or may be mixed and confounded with each other, it often happens, that the taste is not affected with such minute qualities, or is not able to distinguish all the particular flavours, amidst the disorder, in which they are presented. Where the organs are so fine, as to allow nothing to escape them; and at the same time so exact as to perceive every ingredient in the composition: This we call delicacy of taste, whether we employ these terms in the literal or metaphorical sense. Here then the general rules of beauty are of use; being drawn from established models, and from the observation of what pleases or displeases, when presented singly and in a high degree: And if the same qualities, in a continued composition and in a smaller degree, affect not the organs with a sensible delight or uneasiness, we exclude the person from all pretensions to this delicacy. To produce these general rules or avowed patterns of composition is like finding the key with the leathern thong; which justified the verdict of SANCHO's kinsmen, and confounded those pretended judges who had condemned them. Though the hogshead had never been emptied, the taste of the one was still equally delicate, and that of the other equally dull and languid: But it would have been more difficult to have proved the superiority of the former, to the conviction of every by-stander. In like manner, though the beauties of writing had never been methodized, or reduced to general principles; though no excellent models had ever been acknowledged; the different degrees of taste would still have subsisted, and the judgment of one man been preferable to that of another; but it would not have been so easy to silence the bad critic, who might always insist upon his particular sentiment, and refuse to submit to his antagonist. But when we show him an avowed principle of art; when we illustrate this principle by examples, whose operation, from his own particular taste, he acknowledges to be conformable to the principle; when we prove, that the same principle may be applied to the present case, where he did not perceive or feel its influence: He must conclude, upon the whole, that the fault lies in himself, and that he wants the delicacy, which is requisite to make him sensible of every beauty and every blemish, in any composition or discourse.

It is acknowledged to be the perfection of every sense or faculty, to perceive with exactness its most minute objects, and allow nothing to escape its notice and observation. The smaller the objects are, which become sensible to the eye, the finer is that organ, and the more elaborate its make and composition. A good palate is not tried by strong flavours; but by a mixture of small ingredients, where we are still sensible of each part, notwithstanding its minuteness and its confusion with the rest. In like manner, a quick and acute perception of beauty and deformity must be the perfection of our mental taste; nor can a man be satisfied with himself while he suspects, that any excellence or blemish in a discourse has passed him unobserved. In this case, the perfection of the man, and the perfection of the sense or feeling, are found to be united. A very delicate palate, on many occasions, may be a great inconvenience both to a man himself and to his friends: But a delicate taste of wit or beauty must always be a desirable quality; because it is the source of all the finest and most innocent enjoyments, of which human nature is susceptible. In this decision the sentiments of all mankind are agreed. Wherever you can ascertain a delicacy of taste, it is sure to meet with approbation; and the best way of ascertaining it is to appeal to those models and principles, which have been established by the uniform consent and experience of nations and ages.

But though there be naturally a wide difference in point of delicacy between one person and another, nothing tends further to encrease and improve this talent, than *practice* in a particular art, and the frequent survey or contemplation of a particular species of beauty. When objects of any kind are first presented to the eye or imagination, the sentiment, which attends them, is obscure and confused; and the mind is, in a great measure, incapable of pronouncing concerning their merits or defects. The taste cannot perceive the several excellencies of the performance; much less distinguish the particular character of each excellency, and ascertain its quality and degree. If it pronounce the whole in general to be beautiful or deformed, it is the utmost that can be expected; and even this judgment, a person, so unpractised, will be apt to deliver with great hesitation and reserve. But allow him to acquire experience in those objects, his feeling becomes more exact and nice:[1] He not only perceives the beauties and defects of each part, but marks the distinguishing species of each quality, and assigns it suitable praise or blame. A clear and distinct sentiment attends him through the whole survey of the objects; and he discerns that very degree and kind of approbation or displeasure, which each part is naturally fitted to produce. The mist dissipates, which seemed formerly to hang over the object: The organ acquires greater perfection in its operations; and can pronounce, without danger of mistake, concerning the merits of every performance. In a word, the same address and dexterity, which practice gives to the execution of any work, is also acquired by the same means, in the judging of it.

So advantageous is practice to the discernment of beauty, that, before we can give judgment on any work of importance, it will even be requisite, that that very individual performance be more than once perused by us, and be surveyed in different lights with attention and deliberation. There is a flutter or hurry of thought which attends the first perusal of any piece, and which confounds the genuine sentiment of beauty. The relation of the parts is not discerned: The true characters of style are little distinguished: The several perfections and defects seem wrapped up in a species of confusion, and present themselves indistinctly to the imagination. Not to mention, that there is a species of beauty, which, as it is florid and superficial, pleases at first; but being found incompatible with a just expression either of reason

1. Refined.

or passion, soon palls upon the taste, and is then rejected with disdain, at least rated at a much lower value.

It is impossible to continue in the practice of contemplating any order of beauty, without being frequently obliged to form *comparisons* between the several species and degrees of excellence, and estimating their proportion to each other. A man, who has had no opportunity of comparing the different kinds of beauty, is indeed totally unqualified to pronounce an opinion with regard to any object presented to him. By comparison alone we fix the epithets of praise or blame, and learn how to assign the due degree of each. The coarsest daubing contains a certain lustre of colours and exactness of imitation, which are so far beauties, and would affect the mind of a peasant or Indian with the highest admiration. The most vulgar ballads are not entirely destitute of harmony or nature; and none but a person, familiarized to superior beauties, would pronounce their numbers[2] harsh, or narration uninteresting. A great inferiority of beauty gives pain to a person conversant in the highest excellence of the kind, and is for that reason pronounced a deformity: As the most finished object, with which we are acquainted, is naturally supposed to have reached the pinnacle of perfection, and to be entitled to the highest applause. One accustomed to see, and examine, and weigh the several performances, admired in different ages and nations, can alone rate the merits of a work exhibited to his view, and assign its proper rank among the productions of genius.

But to enable a critic the more fully to execute this undertaking, he must preserve his mind free from all *prejudice*,[3] and allow nothing to enter into his consideration, but the very object which is submitted to his examination. We may observe, that every work of art, in order to produce its due effect on the mind, must be surveyed in a certain point of view, and cannot be fully relished by persons, whose situation, real or imaginary, is not conformable to that which is required by the performance. An orator addresses himself to a particular audience, and must have a regard to their particular genius,[4] interests, opinions, passions, and prejudices; otherwise he hopes in vain to govern their resolutions, and inflame their affections. Should they even have entertained some prepossessions against him, however unreasonable, he must not overlook this disadvantage; but, before he enters upon the subject, must endeavour to conciliate their affection, and acquire their good graces. A critic of a different age or nation, who should peruse this discourse, must have all these circumstances in his eye, and must place himself in the same situation as the audience, in order to form a true judgment of the oration. In like manner, when any work is addressed to the public, though I should have a friendship or enmity with the author, I must depart from this situation; and considering myself as a man in general, forget, if possible, my individual being and my peculiar circumstances. A person influenced by prejudice, complies not with this condition; but obstinately maintains his natural position, without placing himself in that point of

2. Metrical structure.

3. Unreasonable preconceived judgment or conviction; an opinion without just grounds or sufficient knowledge.

4. Disposition.

view, which the performance supposes. If the work be addressed to persons of a different age or nation, he makes no allowance for their peculiar views and prejudices; but, full of the manners of his own age and country, rashly condemns what seemed admirable in the eyes of those for whom alone the discourse was calculated. If the work be executed for the public, he never sufficiently enlarges his comprehension, or forgets his interest as a friend or enemy, as a rival or commentator. By this means, his sentiments are perverted; nor have the same beauties and blemishes the same influence upon him, as if he had imposed a proper violence on his imagination, and had forgotten himself for a moment. So far his taste evidently departs from the true standard; and of consequence loses all credit and authority.

It is well known, that in all questions, submitted to the understanding, prejudice is destructive of sound judgment, and perverts all operations of the intellectual faculties: It is no less contrary to good taste; nor has it less influence to corrupt our sentiment of beauty. It belongs to *good sense* to check its influence in both cases; and in this respect, as well as in many others, reason, if not an essential part of taste, is at least requisite to the operations of this latter faculty. In all the nobler productions of genius, there is a mutual relation and correspondence of parts; nor can either the beauties or blemishes be perceived by him, whose thought is not capacious enough to comprehend all those parts, and compare them with each other, in order to perceive the consistence and uniformity of the whole. Every work of art has also a certain end or purpose, for which it is calculated; and is to be deemed more or less perfect, as it is more or less fitted to attain this end. The object of eloquence is to persuade, of history to instruct, of poetry to please by means of the passions and the imagination. These ends we must carry constantly in our view, when we peruse any performance; and we must be able to judge how far the means employed are adapted to their respective purposes. Besides, every kind of composition, even the most poetical, is nothing but a chain of propositions and reasonings; not always, indeed, the justest and most exact, but still plausible and specious, however disguised by the colouring of the imagination. The persons introduced in tragedy and epic poetry, must be represented as reasoning, and thinking, and concluding, and acting, suitably to their character and circumstances; and without judgment, as well as taste and invention, a poet can never hope to succeed in so delicate an undertaking. Not to mention, that the same excellence of faculties which contributes to the improvement of reason, the same clearness of conception, the same exactness of distinction, the same vivacity of apprehension, are essential to the operations of true taste, and are its infallible concomitants. It seldom, or never happens, that a man of sense, who has experience in any art, cannot judge of its beauty; and it is no less rare to meet with a man who has a just taste without a sound understanding.

Thus, though the principles of taste be universal, and nearly, if not entirely the same in all men; yet few are qualified to give judgment on any work of art, or establish their own sentiment as the standard of beauty. The organs of internal sensation are seldom so perfect as to allow the general principles their full play, and produce a feeling correspondent to those principles. They either labour under some defect, or are vitiated by some disorder; and by that means, excite a sentiment, which may be pronounced erroneous. When the critic has no delicacy, he judges without any distinction, and is only affected by the grosser and more palpable qualities of the object: The finer touches pass unnoticed and disregarded. Where he is not aided by practice, his verdict is attended with confusion and hesitation. Where no comparison has been employed, the most frivolous beauties, such as rather merit the name of defects, are the object of his admiration. Where he lies under the influence of prejudice, all his natural sentiments are perverted. Where good sense is wanting, he is not qualified to discern the beauties of design and reasoning, which are the highest and most excellent. Under some or other of these imperfections, the generality of men labour; and hence a true judge in the finer arts is observed, even during the most polished ages, to be so rare a character: Strong sense, united to delicate sentiment, improved by practice, perfected by comparison, and cleared of all prejudice, can alone entitle critics to this valuable character; and the joint verdict of such, wherever they are to be found, is the true standard of taste and beauty.

But where are such critics to be found? By what marks are they to be known? How distinguish them from pretenders? These questions are embarrassing; and seem to throw us back into the same uncertainty, from which, during the course of this essay, we have endeavoured to extricate ourselves.

But if we consider the matter aright, these are questions of fact, not of sentiment. Whether any particular person be endowed with good sense and a delicate imagination, free from prejudice, may often be the subject of dispute, and be liable to great discussion and enquiry: But that such a character is valuable and estimable will be agreed in by all mankind. Where these doubts occur, men can do no more than in other disputable questions, which are submitted to the understanding: They must produce the best arguments, that their invention suggests to them; they must acknowledge a true and decisive standard to exist somewhere, to wit, real existence and matter of fact; and they must have indulgence to such as differ from them in their appeals to this standard. It is sufficient for our present purpose, if we have proved, that the taste of all individuals is not upon an equal footing, and that some men in general, however difficult to be particularly pitched upon, will be acknowledged by universal sentiment to have a preference above others.

But in reality the difficulty of finding, even in particulars, the standard of taste, is not so great as it is represented. Though in speculation, we may readily avow a certain criterion in science and deny it in sentiment, the matter is found in practice to be much more hard to ascertain in the former case than in the latter. Theories of abstract philosophy, systems of profound theology, have prevailed during one age: In a successive period, these have been universally exploded: Their absurdity has been detected: Other theories and systems have supplied their place, which again gave place to their successors: And nothing has been experienced more liable to the revolutions of chance and fashion than these pretended decisions of science. The case is not the same with the beauties of eloquence and poetry. Just expressions of passion and nature are sure, after a little time, to gain public applause, which they maintain for ever. ARISTOTLE, and PLATO, and EPICURUS, and DESCARTES,[5] may successively yield to each other: But TERENCE and VIRGIL[6] maintain an universal, undisputed empire over the minds of men. The abstract philosophy of CICERO[7] has lost its credit: The vehemence of his oratory is still the object of our admiration.

Though men of delicate taste be rare, they are easily to be distinguished in society, by the soundness of their understanding and the superiority of their faculties above the rest of mankind. The ascendant, which they acquire, gives a prevalence to that lively approbation, with which they receive any productions of genius, and renders it generally predominant. Many men, when left to themselves, have but a faint and dubious perception of beauty, who yet are capable of relishing any fine stroke, which is pointed out to them. Every convert to the admiration of the real poet or orator is the cause of some new conversion. And though prejudices may prevail for a time, they never unite in celebrating any rival to the true genius, but yield at last to the force of nature and just sentiment. Thus, though a civilized nation may easily be mistaken in the choice of their admired philosopher, they never have been found long to err, in their affection for a favourite epic or tragic author.

But notwithstanding all our endeavours to fix a standard of taste, and reconcile the discordant apprehensions of men, there still remain two sources of variation, which are not sufficient indeed to confound all the boundaries of beauty and deformity, but will often serve to produce a difference in the degrees of our approbation or blame. The one is the different humours of particular men; the other, the particular manners and opinions of our age and country. The general principles of taste are uniform in human nature: Where men vary in their judgments, some defect or perversion in the faculties may commonly be remarked; proceeding either from prejudice, from want of practice, or want of delicacy; and there is just reason for approving one taste, and condemning another. But where there is such a diversity in the internal frame or external situation as is entirely blameless on both sides, and leaves no room to give one the preference above the other; in that case a certain degree of diversity in judgment is unavoidable, and we seek in vain for a standard, by which we can reconcile the contrary sentiments.

A young man, whose passions are warm, will be more sensibly touched with amorous and tender images, than a man more advanced in years, who takes pleasure in wise, philosophical reflections concerning the conduct of life and moderation of the passions. At twenty, OVID may be the favourite author; HORACE at forty; and perhaps TACITUS[8] at fifty. Vainly would we, in such cases, endeavour to enter into the sentiments of others, and divest ourselves of those propensities, which are natural to us. We choose our favourite author as we do our friend, from a conformity of humour and disposition. Mirth or passion, sentiment or reflection; whichever of these most

5. Hume names four philosophers: the Greeks ARISTOTLE (384–322 B.C.E.), PLATO (ca. 427–ca. 347 B.C.E.), and Epicurus (341–270 B.C.E.), and the French René Descartes (1596–1650).

6. Roman poet (70–19 B.C.E.). Terence (ca. 190–159 B.C.E.), Roman comic playwright.

7. Roman statesman and orator (106–43 B.C.E.).

8. Roman public official and historian (ca. 55–ca. 120 C.E.). Ovid (43 B.C.E.–17 C.E.), Roman poet best known for his love poetry. HORACE (65–8 B.C.E.), Roman lyric poet and satirist whose works often reflected his own life.

predominates in our temper, it gives us a peculiar sympathy with the writer who resembles us.

One person is more pleased with the sublime; another with the tender; a third with raillery. One has a strong sensibility to blemishes, and is extremely studious of correctness: Another has a more lively feeling of beauties, and pardons twenty absurdities and defects for one elevated or pathetic[9] stroke. The ear of this man is entirely turned towards conciseness and energy; that man is delighted with a copious, rich, and harmonious expression. Simplicity is affected by one; ornament by another. Comedy, tragedy, satire, odes, have each its partizans, who prefer that particular species of writing to all others. It is plainly an error in a critic, to confine his approbation to one species or style of writing, and condemn all the rest. But it is almost impossible not to feel a predilection for that which suits our particular turn and disposition. Such preferences are innocent and unavoidable, and can never reasonably be the object of dispute, because there is no standard, by which they can be decided.

For a like reason, we are more pleased, in the course of our reading, with pictures and characters, that resemble objects which are found in our own age or country, than with those which describe a different set of customs. It is not without some effort, that we reconcile ourselves to the simplicity of ancient manners, and behold princesses carrying water from the spring, and kings and heroes dressing their own victuals. We may allow in general, that the representation of such manners is no fault in the author, nor deformity in the piece; but we are not so sensibly touched with them. For this reason, comedy is not easily transferred from one age or nation to another. A FRENCHMAN or ENGLISHMAN is not pleased with the ANDRIA of TERENCE, or CLITIA of MACHIAVEL;[1] where the fine lady, upon whom all the play turns, never once appears to the spectators, but is always kept behind the scenes, suitably to the reserved humour of the ancient GREEKS and modern ITALIANS. A man of learning and reflection can make allowance for these peculiarities of manners; but a common audience can never divest themselves so far of their usual ideas and sentiments, as to relish pictures which no wise resemble them.

But here there occurs a reflection, which may, perhaps, be useful in examining the celebrated controversy concerning ancient and modern learning; where we often find the one side excusing any seeming absurdity in the ancients from the manners of the age, and the other refusing to admit this excuse, or at least, admitting it only as an apology for the author, not for the performance. In my opinion, the proper boundaries in this subject have seldom been fixed between the contending parties. Where any innocent peculiarities of manners are represented, such as those above mentioned, they ought certainly to be admitted; and a man, who is shocked with them, gives an evident proof of false delicacy and refinement. The poet's *monument more durable than brass*,[2] must fall to the ground like common brick

9. That is, full of pathos or feeling.
1. Niccolò Machiavelli (1469–1527), Italian political theorist; he wrote the play *Clizia* in 1525. In *Andria* (166 B.C.E.), the young woman at the center of the action never speaks a word.
2. Horace, *Odes* 3.30.1.

or clay, were men to make no allowance for the continual revolutions of manners and customs, and would admit of nothing but what was suitable to the prevailing fashion. Must we throw aside the pictures of our ancestors, because of their ruffs and fardingales?[3] But where the ideas of morality and decency alter from one age to another, and where vicious manners are described, without being marked with the proper characters of blame and disapprobation; this must be allowed to disfigure the poem, and to be a real deformity. I cannot, nor is it proper I should, enter into such sentiments; and however I may excuse the poet, on account of the manners of his age, I never can relish the composition. The want of humanity and of decency, so conspicuous in the characters drawn by several of the ancient poets, even sometimes by HOMER and the GREEK tragedians, diminishes considerably the merit of their noble performances, and gives modern authors an advantage over them. We are not interested in the fortunes and sentiments of such rough heroes: We are displeased to find the limits of vice and virtue so much confounded: And whatever indulgence we may give to the writer on account of his prejudices, we cannot prevail on ourselves to enter into his sentiments, or bear an affection to characters, which we plainly discover to be blameable.

The case is not the same with moral principles, as with speculative opinions of any kind. These are in continual flux and revolution. The son embraces a different system from the father. Nay, there scarcely is any man, who can boast of great constancy and uniformity in this particular. Whatever speculative errors may be found in the polite writings of any age or country, they detract but little from the value of those compositions. There needs but a certain turn of thought or imagination to make us enter into all the opinions, which then prevailed, and relish the sentiments or conclusions derived from them. But a very violent effort is requisite to change our judgment of manners, and excite sentiments of approbation or blame, love or hatred, different from those to which the mind from long custom has been familiarized. And where a man is confident of the rectitude of that moral standard, by which he judges, he is justly jealous of it, and will not pervert the sentiments of his heart for a moment, in complaisance to any writer whatsoever.

Of all speculative errors, those, which regard religion, are the most excusable in compositions of genius; nor is it ever permitted to judge of the civility or wisdom of any people, or even of single persons, by the grossness or refinement of their theological principles. The same good sense, that directs men in the ordinary occurrences of life, is not hearkened to in religious matters, which are supposed to be placed altogether above the cognizance of human reason. On this account, all the absurdities of the pagan system of theology must be overlooked by every critic, who would pretend to form a just notion of ancient poetry; and our posterity, in their turn, must have the same indulgence to their forefathers. No religious principles can ever be imputed as a fault to any poet, while they remain merely principles, and

3. Farthingales: supports (such as hoops) that expanded skirts to extend them at the hip line. "Ruffs": stiff collars.

take not such strong possession of his heart, as to lay him under the imputation of *bigotry* or *superstition*. Where that happens, they confound the sentiments of morality, and alter the natural boundaries of vice and virtue. They are therefore eternal blemishes, according to the principle abovementioned: nor are the prejudices and false opinions of the age sufficient to justify them.

It is essential to the ROMAN catholic religion to inspire a violent hatred of every other worship, and to represent all pagans, mahometans,[4] and heretics as the objects of divine wrath and vengeance. Such sentiments, though they are in reality very blameable, are considered as virtues by the zealots of that communion, and are represented in their tragedies and epic poems as a kind of divine heroism. This bigotry has disfigured two very fine tragedies of the FRENCH theatre, POLIEUCTE and ATHALIA;[5] where an intemperate zeal for particular modes of worship is set off with all the pomp imaginable, and forms the predominant character of the heroes. "What is this," says the sublime JOAD to JOSABET, finding her in discourse with MATHAN, the priest of BAAL, "Does the daughter of DAVID speak to this traitor? Are you not afraid, lest the earth should open and pour forth flames to devour you both? Or lest these holy walls should fall and crush you together? What is his purpose? Why comes that enemy of God hither to poison the air, which we breathe, with his horrid presence?" Such sentiments are received with great applause on the theatre of PARIS; but at LONDON the spectators would be full as much pleased to hear ACHILLES tell AGAMEMNON, that he was a dog in his forehead, and a deer in his heart, or JUPITER threaten JUNO with a sound drubbing, if she will not be quiet.[6]

RELIGIOUS principles are also a blemish in any polite composition, when they rise up to superstition, and intrude themselves into every sentiment, however remote from any connection with religion. It is no excuse for the poet, that the customs of his country had burthened[7] life with so many religious ceremonies and observances, that no part of it was exempt from that yoke. It must for ever be ridiculous in PETRARCH[8] to compare his mistress, LAURA, to JESUS CHRIST. Nor is it less ridiculous in that agreeable libertine, BOCCACE,[9] very seriously to give thanks to GOD ALMIGHTY and the ladies, for their assistance in defending him against his enemies.

1757

4. Muslims.
5. *Athalie* (1691), by Jean Racine; Hume quotes from 3.5. *Polyeucte* (1641–42), play by PIERRE CORNEILLE.
6. See Homer, *Iliad* 1.225, 565–67. Hume's point is that English audiences are unmoved by the tragedies' Catholic sentiments.
7. Burdened.
8. Francesco Petrarca (1304–1374), Italian poet, scholar, and humanist; Laura is the subject of a series of love lyrics titled *Canzoniere* or *Rima* (see, e.g., no. 3 for the comparison to Jesus).
9. GIOVANNI BOCCACCIO (1313–1375), Italian poet and writer. His most famous work, the *Decameron* (1351–53), is a collection of 100 tales supposedly told over 10 days; Hume refers here to the introduction to "The Fourth Day."

IMMANUEL KANT
1724–1804

Immanuel Kant's massive contributions to modern metaphysics, epistemology, and ethics aside, his *Critique of Judgment* (1790) ranks with ARISTOTLE's *Poetics* among our most influential philosophical treatises on art. Kant's book is a compendium of the beliefs about and ideals for art that have come to be called *aestheticism* (the separation of artistic concerns and values into their own sphere, which is seen as superior to all others). The branch of philosophy dealing with the nature of beauty, art, and taste first arose in the mid-eighteenth century in the work of Edmund Alexander Baumgarten, DAVID HUME, and EDMUND BURKE. Kant's *Critique of Judgment* responds to and augments their earlier work while giving art an exalted place within human existence, a place that justifies the new philosophical interest in art as a distinct sphere of human activity. The specifics of Kant's characterization of art resonate throughout the Romantic and modernist periods and have become a frequent target of contemporary theorists and philosophers.

Kant was born in Königsberg, East Prussia, where he attended the university, became a professor at that same university, and died shortly after his retirement. He never married and he never traveled outside of East Prussia. His regular, uneventful life is summed up in the legend that Königsberg residents set their clocks by his appearance for his afternoon walk at precisely the same time each day. His early work was mostly in the natural sciences, with one excursion into aesthetics: *Observations on the Feeling of the Beautiful and Sublime* (1764). In this work, he argues that such feelings are purely subjective, precisely the position he sets himself against when later revisiting the same terrain in his *Critique of Judgment*.

Kant's major work begins with the *Critique of Pure Reason* (1781), in which he develops his "critical philosophy" to overcome David Hume's subjectivist skepticism. This "first critique" was followed by two others: the *Critique of Practical Reason* (1788) and the *Critique of Judgment*. The three books cover the true, the good, and the beautiful, respectively. By *critique* Kant meant a delineation of the fundamental or "transcendental" conditions necessary to any particular mental process. Thus the *Critique of Pure Reason* presents the mental forms (or categories) that must be in place within the perceiving subject for any successful apprehension of the external world. He insists that these universals (for example, cause and effect, or unity) are implanted within every human being and underwrite the very possibility of "understanding" (that is, the ability to process, organize, and comprehend the data given to our senses by the outside world). We can never directly know what he calls "things-in-themselves," because we process sensory data through preexisting mental categories.

The *Critique of Practical Reason* attempts to provide a universal foundation for morals, which concern nonphysical ideas, not material realities. Kant's basic claim is that practical reason in each individual dictates the same fundamental moral dictum, which he called the categorical (i.e., unconditional) imperative: never do anything that you could not willingly endorse being done by everyone else in the world.

The first two critiques create a gap between the physical (sensible) and nonphysical (supersensible) worlds. Understanding deals with the physical world of cause and effect, where each occurrence has been determined by prior events. Reason emanates from a supersensible realm of freedom. Pure reason names the "forms" or "categories" through which understanding grasps sensible things. Practical reason provides the maxims, notably the famous categorical imperative, through which the self legislates to itself the laws of proper conduct. The ability to reason makes humans free, but they are also physical creatures subject to physical causality. *The Critique of*

Judgment exists to bridge this gap between what Kant sees as two aspects of human nature. The very word *aesthetic*, whose Greek root means "of the senses," aids Kant's effort to connect the sensory to the supersensible. Beauty is experienced through the senses, but points us beyond mere sensation. Aesthetic ideas, Kant tells us in §49, combine the images we gather from the sensible world with "much that is ineffable, but the feeling of which quickens our cognitive powers and connects language, which otherwise would be mere letters, with spirit." Thus Kant describes "the use of imagination for cognition" in the standard eighteenth-century way: cognitive imagination produces mental images of absent realities. But he also introduces an "aesthetic" imagination, one that creates sensible forms through which to communicate to others content that is spiritual, emotional, and otherwise well-nigh unnameable. And this imagination, like beauty itself, is represented as free "from any instruction by rules, but still as purposive." By bodying forth ideas, the aesthetic joins the physical and nonphysical worlds.

That Kant fixes on the aesthetic experience of beauty to solve a pressing problem in his own large-scale system has been irrelevant to many of the artists and writers who subsequently adopted or adapted his characterization of art. The literature on the *Critique of Judgment* divides into two traditions, one focusing on Kant's overall philosophical project and the other focusing on the theory of art that can be derived from Kant's work; our selection is slanted toward the latter, but to understand Kant's way of approaching the whole topic of art we must also take into account his broader philosophical goal and system.

Kant's primary aim is to establish the "subjective universality" of the judgment that something is beautiful or sublime. Judgment in general is the determination of whether a particular instance qualifies as one thing or another. For example, given the number "10," I judge it to be an even number because I recognize that it is divisible by 2. Or when I judge the object in front of me to be a table, I am (Kant says) simply "subsuming" a particular thing under the general concept of table, a concept I already possess. Such judgments are "determinative" and "objective." Since the concepts *even number* and *table* already exist and unambiguously provide the rule my judgment follows, there is little room for error or disagreement.

The statements "it's beautiful" and "it's a table" are identical in form, yet we are much more likely to disagree over the former. Why? Kant's answer has two parts. On the one hand, by saying "it's beautiful" rather than "I think it's beautiful," I am making a claim to validity beyond my individual, subjective preferences. On the other hand, *beautiful* is not a determinative concept like *table* or *even number*: judgments about beauty are instead "reflective," occurring in the absence of a firm rule or standard, and hence are more likely to generate disagreement. The beautiful is often original, surprising, and a departure from the norm (conversely, the norm can seem too regular, boring, and academic). The ability to judge well amid such uncertainties is called *taste*—and some people have better taste than others (though Kant would insist that everyone has the potential to achieve the highest possible taste).

In considering the notion of taste, Kant is (once again) engaging with David Hume. While accepting Hume's contention that taste is something learned, Kant believes that he failed in "Of the Standard of Taste" (1757; see above) to defend against the possible conclusion that it is culturally relative. Kant's solution is to distinguish between what is "agreeable," what is "good," and what is "beautiful." (As a rule of thumb, reading Kant becomes much easier when one pays attention to what distinctions he draws and why.) The good is a matter of reason—and of what we *should* desire. The agreeable is a matter of the senses—and of what we physically desire. The beautiful mixes the sensible with the nonsensible—and involves no desire whatsoever: thus Kant calls judgments of beauty "disinterested." Perhaps nothing Kant advanced has been as influential as this severance of the beautiful from interest. His basic notion is that a sensory experience of pleasure can move from the subjective ("that is pleasing to me") to the objective ("that should please everyone") only if purged of its individual, interested elements.

Kant uses the example of the difference between taste in food and taste in flowers. My daughter and I can agree that cotton candy is sweet, but she likes and desires it while I dislike and do not desire it. There is no disputing taste in such matters precisely because it is tied to idiosyncratic, physiological appetites. But Kant believes that things change when we perceive a field of flowers—or a painting of flowers. The flowers have no purpose in relation to my life or my physical needs. I can contemplate them disinterestedly, and thus my judgment about their beauty is not connected to their gratifying my personal sensibility. My statement "they are beautiful" solicits, Kant says, the agreement of everyone else in a way that my statement "I like green beans" does not.

The understanding of art that follows from this analysis was widely adopted. MATTHEW ARNOLD's "Function of Criticism at the Present Time" (1864; see below) is an important attempt to extend the ideal of disinterestedness to criticism; more recent critics have attempted to refute the notion (see our selections by PIERRE BOURDIEU and TERRY EAGLETON). Crucially, Kant's argument leads him to elevate artistic form over matter. Because he is trying to demote the physical appeal of the aesthetic, he claims that the formal properties of the observed object, not its physical and material properties, most influence judgments of beauty. Sensual responses are subjective (later writers also consider them vulgar), failing to rise above the level of the agreeable. This distinction is still used today by some to distinguish pornography from art with sexual content. In addition, the valorization of form over matter resurfaces in the various modernist versions of "abstract" and "nonrepresentational" art that emerge between 1850 (Flaubert's desire to write a novel about nothing) and 1950 (abstract expressionism).

Disinterestedness as an aesthetic ideal also entails distinguishing between the useful and the nonutilitarian work of art. At its most extreme, it generates the credo of aestheticism: "art for art's sake" (for example, see our selections from WALTER PATER and OSCAR WILDE). The beautiful object should not be tainted with any mundane purpose. The troubled relationship between art and commerce stems in part from this dream of an art that can transcend all petty worldly concerns. Kant expresses this aim in a famous formula: the beautiful object reveals "purposiveness without purpose." That is, the object is comprehensible only if we assume it was made by a purposive agent (an a priori condition of aesthetic judgment that Kant's "critique" reveals), even though it has no particular, determinative purpose. The formal coherence of flowers is incomprehensible apart from a general assumption of their "purposiveness," although we can ascribe no particular purpose to them. Art objects aspire to general purposiveness in the absence of any concrete purpose.

As we apprehend such objects, we respond with "free play" of the mind (a notion further developed by FRIEDRICH VON SCHILLER, among many others). The aesthetic therefore provides an experience of freedom within the physical world of causal determination. Aesthetic experience is crucial to Kant because it makes possible a "harmony" between our human freedom and our physical immersion in the world—the feeling that is the true foundation of our experiences of beauty. And because such harmony is available to all humans, I can solicit their agreement with my particular judgments of beauty. But in any particular case, I may not succeed in gaining others' agreement. Kant is careful to say that beauty is only an "ideal," not a "concept." The example is singular, but it carries a general significance. Each artwork, like every judgment about beauty, solicits its audience's approval both as a particular and as an example of a kind, a genre, or an act of criticism. For that reason, there is no rule of beauty: its validity for everyone will always be "exemplary."

For Kant, beauty intimates the harmony within our dual human nature as free and physical beings. Beauty ultimately refers to the subjective experience of this harmony rather than to any property in the object that promotes that experience. Hence aesthetic experience is "subjective"; but because all humans are susceptible to the experience of harmony, this response possesses a "universality" usually absent in subjective judgments. Kant goes even further when he calls beauty "the symbol of morality" (§59) and comes close to providing beauty a purpose and an interest. His own interests in writing the third critique certainly come to light in this statement: he wants the experience of the beautiful to signify that humans live in an "intelligible" universe, that the ideas and precepts generated by human reason are in tune with the nature of the universe itself. The experience of beauty tells us that mind and world fit.

The sublime, in contrast, shows us a misfit between mind and world. When we experience a hurricane or an earthquake, nature appears to dwarf human concerns and capabilities. Kant distinguishes between two types of sublimity. The mathematical sublime is anything so large that the imagination cannot encompass it; we thus cannot form an adequate image of this "absolutely great" thing. The dynamical sublime reveals a power beyond human scope; it dwarfs our capacities and inspires fear or, even better, respect. The sublime, according to Kant, allows us to glimpse things beyond comprehension and to experience the limits of the sensible, physical world, generating feelings of awe and terror. This experience of the limits of the sensible, of its inability to encompass aspects of our mental world, reminds us of "the superiority of the rational vocation of our cognitive powers over the greatest power of sensibility" (§27). But even while performing this important function of pointing us away from the sensible toward the mysterious supersensible, the sublime remains disquieting because in doing so it indicates a split between the two. It is just this experience of disjunction that Kant needs to subsume within the grander overarching experience of harmony that comes with the beautiful. Thus he writes "that the concept of the sublime in nature is not nearly as important and rich in implications as that of the beautiful in nature" (§23).

Kant inherits the notion of the sublime as a central feature of the aesthetic from LONGINUS and Burke, but he addresses it mostly to contain it. Thus, his sensibility is noticeably at odds with the Romantic and postmodernist writers for whom the sublime registers the gulf between human aspirations and what the world renders possible, or the recurrent artistic experience of struggling to express the ineffable with the limited material resources (sound, paint, words, stone) afforded to the arts. Such writers as JEAN-FRANÇOIS LYOTARD and PAUL DE MAN have found Kant's reflections on the sublime suggestive even while criticizing his attempts to retain beauty's elevation over the sublime.

In fact, attitudes toward Kant are something of a litmus test among contemporary theorists. Section 40 encapsulates what we might call Kant's liberal optimism—his belief that disinterested judgments can enable "unprejudiced," "broadened" thinking and pave the way toward "enlightenment" and agreement. The *sensus communis*, an understanding shared by all humans, serves as both the guarantor (since everyone potentially possesses it) and the end result of the discussions surrounding differing judgments. Anti-Kantians (often proponents of the sublime) deny the possibility of such common ground for discussion and eventual agreement, arguing that the translation of different viewpoints into a common language always already erases or represses the very differences that constitute the disagreement.

It might seem surprising that the *Critique of Judgment* has been an extraordinarily influential text on art. After all, in some ways, the book is hardly about art at all. Most of Kant's examples come from nature, and *aesthetic* in his usage refers more to what is experienced through the senses than to something specifically artistic. Like Aristotle, he focuses on the spectator's response rather than on artistic production, but without Aristotle's interest in the elements or properties of the art object. Kant apparently believes that it makes no difference whether the object is natural or human-made. Even when he does distinguish art from nature in §43, Kant is more concerned with preserving art's freedom—aligning it with beauty against the determined world of science and the utilitarian concerns of craft—than with examining the consequences of art's being (by definition) artificial. He never considers why the beauties offered by nature do not suffice, or what art can do that nature cannot.

Not surprisingly, Kant's influential description of the genius (the creative artist) highlights freedom above all else. The genius has a natural gift, a talent, which enables the production of exemplary and original beautiful works in the absence of any preexisting formula or rule for that production. Art is valued, in part, because the genius expresses "what is ineffable" in such a way as to make it "universally communicable." The creative imagination, in other words, produces artistic images that body forth mental states (judgments and feelings) that resist determinate expression. Because communicability is so central for Kant, genius must be tempered, even disciplined, by taste, which brings genius's originality back into contact with common sense (*sensus communis*).

Although there were always dissenters, Kant's general account of the aesthetic as formal, free, nonutilitarian, disinterested, and nonsensory was the prevailing orthodoxy for almost two centuries. That so many contemporary theorists have written against the *Critique of Judgment* testifies to the continuing importance of the understanding of art that it enshrines and that they have attempted to revise.

Critique of Judgment **Keywords:** Aesthetics, Enlightenment Theory, Formalism, Representation

From Critique of Judgment[1]

From *Introduction*

Judgment in general is the ability to think the particular as contained under the universal. If the universal (the rule, principle, law) is given, then judgment, which subsumes the particular under it, is *determinative* (even though [in its role] as transcendental judgment it states a priori the conditions that must be met for subsumption under that universal to be possible). But if only the particular is given and judgment has to find the universal for it, then this power is merely *reflective*.

* * *

ON THE AESTHETIC PRESENTATION OF THE PURPOSIVENESS[2] OF NATURE

What is merely subjective in the presentation of an object, i.e., what constitutes its reference to the subject and not to the object, is its aesthetic character; but whatever in it serves, or can be used, to determine the object

1. Translated by Werner S. Pluhar, who occasionally retains the original German words or adds information in brackets in the text. Unless otherwise specified, parenthetical terms are in Latin and are translated in the text.

2. The general sense that a thing was formed by a purposive hand, although without a specific function or purpose (a key term in Kant's aesthetic theory). "Aesthetic": pertaining to an individual's sensory experiences.

(for cognition)[3] is its logical validity. In the cognition of an object of sense these two references [to the subject and to the object] occur together.

* * *

[T]hat subjective [feature] of a presentation *which cannot at all become an element of cognition* is the *pleasure* or *displeasure* connected with that presentation. For through this pleasure or displeasure I do not cognize anything in the object of the presentation, though it may certainly be the effect of some cognition. Now a thing's purposiveness, insofar as it is presented in the perception of the thing, is also not a characteristic of the object itself (for no such characteristic can be perceived), even though it can be inferred from a cognition of things. Therefore, the subjective [feature] of the presentation which cannot at all become an element of cognition is the purposiveness that precedes the cognition of an object and that we connect directly with this presentation even if we are not seeking to use the presentation of the object for cognition. Therefore, in this case we call the object purposive only because its presentation is directly connected with the feeling of pleasure, and this presentation itself is an aesthetic presentation of purposiveness. The only question is whether there is such a presentation of purposiveness at all.

When pleasure is connected with mere apprehension (*apprehensio*) of the form of an object of intuition, and we do not refer the apprehension to a concept so as to give rise to determinate cognition, then we refer the presentation not to the object but solely to the subject; and the pleasure cannot express anything other than the object's being commensurate with the cognitive powers that are, and insofar as they are, brought into play when we judge reflectively, and hence [expresses] merely a subjective formal purposiveness of the object. For this apprehension of forms by the imagination could never occur if reflective judgment did not compare them, even if unintentionally, at least with its ability [in general] to refer intuitions to concepts. Now if in this comparison a given presentation unintentionally brings the imagination (the power of a priori intuitions) into harmony with the understanding (the power of concepts), and this harmony arouses a feeling of pleasure, then the object must thereupon be regarded as purposive for the reflective power of judgment. A judgment of this sort is an aesthetic judgment about the object's purposiveness; it is not based on any concept we have of the object, nor does it provide such a concept. When the form of an object (rather than what is material in its presentation, viz., in sensation) is judged in mere reflection on it (without regard to a concept that is to be acquired from it) to be the basis of a pleasure in such an object's presentation, then the presentation of this object is also judged to be connected necessarily with this pleasure, and hence connected with it not merely for the subject apprehending this form but in general for everyone who judges [it]. The object is then called beautiful, and our ability to judge by such a pleasure (and hence also with universal validity) is called taste.

* * *

3. The process in which sense data plus the categories of understanding ("pure reason") combine in our ability to apprehend and name objects in the external world.

From *Book I. Analytic of the Beautiful*

§1. A JUDGMENT OF TASTE IS AESTHETIC

If we wish to decide whether something is beautiful or not, we do not use understanding to refer the presentation to the object so as to give rise to cognition; rather, we use imagination[4] (perhaps in connection with understanding) to refer the presentation to the subject and his feeling of pleasure or displeasure. Hence a judgment of taste is not a cognitive judgment and so is not a logical judgment but an aesthetic one, by which we mean a judgment whose determining basis *cannot be other* than *subjective*. But any reference of presentations, even of sensations, can be objective (in which case it signifies what is real [rather than formal] in an empirical presentation); excepted is a reference to the feeling of pleasure and displeasure—this reference designates nothing whatsoever in the object, but here the subject feels himself, [namely] how he is affected by the presentation.

To apprehend a regular, purposive building with one's cognitive power (whether the presentation is distinct or confused) is very different from being conscious of this presentation with a sensation of liking. Here the presentation is referred only to the subject, namely, to his feeling of life, under the name feeling of pleasure or displeasure, and this forms the basis of a very special power of discriminating and judging. This power does not contribute anything to cognition, but merely compares the given presentation in the subject with the entire presentational power, of which the mind becomes conscious when it feels its own state. The presentations given in a judgment may be empirical (and hence aesthetic), but if we refer them to the object, the judgment we make by means of them is logical. On the other hand, even if the given presentations were rational, they would still be aesthetic if, and to the extent that, the subject referred them, in his judgment, solely to himself (to his feeling).

§2. THE LIKING THAT DETERMINES A JUDGMENT OF TASTE IS DEVOID OF ALL INTEREST

Interest is what we call the liking we connect with the presentation of an object's existence. Hence such a liking always refers at once to our power of desire, either as the basis that determines it, or at any rate as necessarily connected with that determining basis. But if the question is whether something is beautiful, what we want to know is not whether we or anyone cares, or so much as might care, in any way, about the thing's existence, but rather how we judge it in our mere contemplation of it (intuition or reflection). Suppose someone asks me whether I consider the palace I see before me beautiful. I might reply that I am not fond of things of that sort, made merely to be gaped at. Or I might reply like that Iroquois *sachem* who said that he liked nothing better in Paris than the eating-houses.[5] I might even

4. The ability to represent in thought the features experienced in the sense perception of the external world.

go on, as *Rousseau*[6] would, to rebuke the vanity of the great who spend the people's sweat on such superfluous things. I might, finally, quite easily convince myself that, if I were on some uninhabited island with no hope of ever again coming among people, and could conjure up such a splendid edifice by a mere wish, I would not even take that much trouble for it if I already had a sufficiently comfortable hut. The questioner may grant all this and approve of it; but it is not to the point. All he wants to know is whether my mere presentation of the object is accompanied by a liking, no matter how indifferent I may be about the existence of the object of this presentation. We can easily see that, in order for me to say that an object is *beautiful*, and to prove that I have taste, what matters is what I do with this presentation within myself, and not the [respect] in which I depend on the object's existence. Everyone has to admit that if a judgment about beauty is mingled with the least interest then it is very partial and not a pure judgment of taste. In order to play the judge in matters of taste, we must not be in the least biased in favor of the thing's existence but must be wholly indifferent about it.

There is no better way to elucidate this proposition, which is of prime importance, than by contrasting the pure disinterested liking that occurs in a judgment of taste with a liking connected with interest, especially if we can also be certain that the kinds of interest I am about to mention are the only ones there are.

§3. A LIKING *FOR THE AGREEABLE* IS CONNECTED WITH INTEREST

Agreeable *is what the senses like in sensation.*

* * *

Now, that a judgment by which I declare an object to be agreeable expresses an interest in that object is already obvious from the fact that, by means of sensation, the judgment arouses a desire for objects of that kind, so that the liking presupposes something other than my mere judgment about the object: it presupposes that I have referred the existence of the object to my state insofar as that state is affected by such an object. This is why we say of the agreeable not merely that we *like* it but that it *gratifies* us. When I speak of the agreeable, I am not granting mere approval: the agreeable produces an inclination. Indeed, what is agreeable in the liveliest way requires no judgment at all about the character of the object, as we can see in people who aim at nothing but enjoyment (this is the word we use to mark the intensity of the gratification): they like to dispense with all judging.

5. Kant's reference has been traced to Pierre François Xavier de Charlevoix, *History and General Description of New France* (Paris, 1744) [translator's note]. Charlevoix (1682–1761), French Jesuit explorer.

6. Jean-Jacques Rousseau (1712–1778), Swiss-born French political philosopher and novelist.

§4. A LIKING *FOR THE GOOD* IS CONNECTED WITH INTEREST

Good is what, by means of reason, we like through its mere concept. We call something (viz., if it is something useful) *good for* [this or that] if we like it only as a means. But we call something *intrinsically good* if we like it for its own sake. In both senses of the term, the good always contains the concept of a purpose, consequently a relation of reason to a volition (that is at least possible), and hence a liking for the existence of an object or action. In other words, it contains some interest or other.

In order to consider something good, I must always know what sort of thing the object is [meant] to be, i.e., I must have a [determinate] concept of it. But I do not need this in order to find beauty in something. Flowers, free designs, lines aimlessly intertwined and called foliage: these have no significance, depend on no determinate concept, and yet we like [*gefallen*] them. A liking [*Wohlgefallen*] for the beautiful must depend on the reflection, regarding an object, that leads to some concept or other (but it is indeterminate which concept this is). This dependence on reflection also distinguishes the liking for the beautiful from [that for] the agreeable, which rests entirely on sensation.[7]

It is true that in many cases it seems as if the agreeable and the good are one and the same. Thus people commonly say that all gratification (especially if it lasts) is intrinsically good, which means roughly the same as to be (lastingly) agreeable and to be good are one and the same. Yet it is easy to see that in talking this way they are merely substituting one word for another by mistake, since the concepts that belong to these terms are in no way interchangeable. Insofar as we present an object as agreeable, we present it solely in relation to sense; but if we are to call the object good [as well], and hence an object of the will, we must first bring it under principles of reason, using the concept of a purpose. [So] if something that gratifies us is also called *good*, it has a very different relation to our liking. This is [also] evident from the fact that in the case of the good there is always the question whether it is good merely indirectly or good directly (i.e., useful, or intrinsically good), whereas in the case of the agreeable this question cannot even arise, since this word always signifies something that we like directly. (What we call beautiful is also liked directly.)

* * *

But despite all this difference between the agreeable and the good, they do agree in this: they are always connected with an interest in their object. This holds not only for the agreeable—see §3—and for what is good indirectly (useful), which we like as the means to something or other that is agreeable, but also for what is good absolutely and in every respect, i.e., the moral good, which carries with it the highest interest. For the good is the object of the will (a power of desire that is determined by reason). But to will something and to have a liking for its existence, i.e., to take an interest in it, are identical.

7. That is, the pleasure derived from beauty is related to the indeterminate concept of purposiveness; thus judgments of beauty stand between the pure sensuousness of the agreeable and the pure rationality of the good.

§5. COMPARISON OF THE THREE SORTS OF LIKING, WHICH DIFFER IN KIND

Both the agreeable and the good refer to our power of desire and hence carry a liking with them, the agreeable a liking that is conditioned pathologically by stimuli (*stimuli*), the good a pure practical liking that is determined not just by the presentation of the object but also by the presentation of the subject's connection with the existence of the object; i.e., what we like is not just the object but its existence as well. A judgment of taste, on the other hand, is merely *contemplative*, i.e., it is a judgment that is indifferent to the existence of the object: it [considers] the character of the object only by holding it up to our feeling of pleasure and displeasure. Nor is this contemplation, as such, directed to concepts, for a judgment of taste is not a cognitive judgment (whether theoretical or practical) and hence is neither *based* on concepts, nor directed to them as *purposes*.

Hence the agreeable, the beautiful, and the good designate three different relations that presentations have to the feeling of pleasure and displeasure, the feeling by reference to which we distinguish between objects or between ways of presenting them. The terms of approbation which are appropriate to each of these three are also different. We call *agreeable* what GRATIFIES us, *beautiful* what we just LIKE, good what we ESTEEM, or *endorse* [*billigen*], i.e., that to which we attribute [*setzen*] an objective value. Agreeableness holds for nonrational animals too; beauty only for human beings, i.e., beings who are animal and yet rational, though it is not enough that they be rational (e.g., spirits) but they must be animal as well; the good, however, holds for every rational being as such, though I cannot fully justify and explain this proposition until later. We may say that, of all these three kinds of liking, only the liking involved in taste for the beautiful is disinterested and *free*, since we are not compelled to give our approval by any interest, whether of sense or of reason. So we might say that [the term] liking, in the three cases mentioned, refers to *inclination*, or to *favor*, or to *respect*. For FAVOR is the only free liking. Neither an object of inclination, nor one that a law of reason enjoins on us as an object of desire, leaves us the freedom to make an object of pleasure for ourselves out of something or other. All interest either presupposes a need or gives rise to one; and, because interest is the basis that determines approval, it makes the judgment about the object unfree.

Consider, first, the interest of inclination, [which occurs] with the agreeable. Here everyone says: Hunger is the best sauce; and to people with a healthy appetite anything is tasty provided it is edible. Hence if people have a liking of this sort, that does not prove that they are selecting [*Wahl*] by taste. Only when their need has been satisfied can we tell who in a multitude of people has taste and who does not.

EXPLICATION OF THE BEAUTIFUL INFERRED FROM THE FIRST MOMENT[8]

Taste is the ability to judge an object, or a way of presenting it, by means of a liking or disliking *devoid of all interest*. The object of such a liking is called *beautiful*.

8. The "analytic of the beautiful" of book 1 is divided into four "moments," which treat beauty in terms of quality, quantity, purposes, and liking for the object, respectively.

§6. THE BEAUTIFUL IS WHAT IS PRESENTED WITHOUT CONCEPTS AS THE OBJECT OF A *UNIVERSAL* LIKING

This explication of the beautiful can be inferred from the preceding explication of it as object of a liking devoid of all interest. For if someone likes something and is conscious that he himself does so without any interest, then he cannot help judging that it must contain a basis for being liked [that holds] for everyone. He must believe that he is justified in requiring a similar liking from everyone because he cannot discover, underlying this liking, any private conditions, on which only he might be dependent, so that he must regard it as based on what he can presuppose in everyone else as well. He cannot discover such private conditions because his liking is not based on any inclination he has (nor on any other considered interest whatever): rather, the judging person feels completely *free* as regards the liking he accords the object. Hence he will talk about the beautiful as if beauty were a characteristic of the object and the judgment were logical (namely, a cognition of the object through concepts of it), even though in fact the judgment is only aesthetic and refers the object's presentation merely to the subject. He will talk in this way because the judgment does resemble a logical judgment inasmuch as we may presuppose it to be valid for everyone. On the other hand, this universality cannot arise from concepts. For from concepts there is no transition to the feeling of pleasure or displeasure (except in pure practical laws; but these carry an interest with them, while none is connected with pure judgments of taste). It follows that, since a judgment of taste involves the consciousness that all interest is kept out of it, it must also involve a claim to being valid for everyone, but without having a universality based on concepts. In other words, a judgment of taste must involve a claim to subjective universality.

§7. COMPARISON OF THE BEAUTIFUL WITH THE AGREEABLE AND THE GOOD IN TERMS OF THE ABOVE CHARACTERISTIC

As regards the *agreeable* everyone acknowledges that his judgment, which he bases on a private feeling and by which he says that he likes some object, is by the same token confined to his own person. Hence, if he says that canary wine is agreeable he is quite content if someone else corrects his terms and reminds him to say instead: It is agreeable to *me*. This holds moreover not only for the taste of the tongue, palate, and throat, but also for what may be agreeable to any one's eyes and ears. To one person the color violet is gentle and lovely, to another lifeless and faded. One person loves the sound of wind instruments, another that of string instruments. It would be foolish if we disputed about such differences with the intention of censuring another's judgment as incorrect if it differs from ours, as if the two were opposed logically. Hence about the agreeable the following principle holds: *Everyone has his own taste* (of sense).

It is quite different (exactly the other way round) with the beautiful. It would be ridiculous if someone who prided himself on his taste tried to justify [it] by saying: This object (the building we are looking at, the garment that man is wearing, the concert we are listening to, the poem put up to be judged) is beautiful *for me*. For he must not call it *beautiful* if [he means] only [that] *he* likes it. Many things may be charming and agreeable to him; no one cares about that. But if he proclaims something to be beautiful, then he requires the same liking from others; he then judges not just for himself but for everyone, and speaks of beauty as if it were a property of things. That is why he says: The *thing* is beautiful, and does not count on other people to agree with his judgment of liking on the ground that he has repeatedly found them agreeing with him; rather, he *demands* that they agree. He reproaches them if they judge differently, and denies that they have taste, which he nevertheless demands of them, as something they ought to have. In view of this [*sofern*], we cannot say that everyone has his own particular taste. That would amount to saying that there is no such thing as taste at all, no aesthetic judgment that could rightfully lay claim to everyone's assent.

* * *

§8. IN A JUDGMENT OF TASTE THE UNIVERSALITY OF THE LIKING IS PRESENTED ONLY AS SUBJECTIVE

* * *

We must begin by fully convincing ourselves that in making a judgment of taste (about the beautiful) we require [*ansinnen*] *everyone* to like the object, yet without this liking's being based on a concept (since then it would be the good), and that this claim to universal validity belongs so essentially to a judgment by which we declare something to be *beautiful* that it would not occur to anyone to use this term without thinking of universal validity; instead, everything we like without a concept would then be included with the agreeable. For as to the agreeable we allow everyone to be of a mind of his own, no one requiring [*zumuten*] others to agree with his judgment of taste. But in a judgment of taste about beauty we always require others to agree. Insofar as judgments about the agreeable are merely private, whereas judgments about the beautiful are put forward as having general validity (as being public), taste regarding the agreeable can be called taste of sense, and taste regarding the beautiful can be called taste of reflection, though the judgments of both are aesthetic (rather than practical) judgments about an object, [i.e.,] judgments merely about the relation that the presentation of the object has to the feeling of pleasure and displeasure. But surely there is something strange here. In the case of the taste of sense, not only does experience show that its judgment (of a pleasure or displeasure we take in something or other) does not hold universally, but people, of their own accord, are modest enough not even to require others to agree (even though there actually is, at times, very widespread agreement in these judgments too). Now, experience teaches us that the taste of reflection, with its claim that its judgment (about the beautiful) is universally valid for everyone, is also rejected often enough: What is strange is that the taste of reflection should nonetheless find itself able (as it actually does) to conceive of judgments that can demand such agreement, and that it does in fact require this agreement from everyone for each of its judgments. What the people who make these judgments dispute about is not whether such a claim is possible; they are merely unable to agree, in particular cases, on the correct way to apply this ability.

* * *

If we judge objects merely in terms of concepts, then we lose all presentation of beauty. This is why there can be no rule by which someone could be compelled to acknowledge that something is beautiful. No one can use reasons or principles to talk us into a judgment on whether some garment, house, or flower is beautiful. We want to submit the object to our own eyes, just as if our liking of it depended on that sensation. And yet, if we then call the object beautiful, we believe we have a universal voice, and lay claim to the agreement of everyone, whereas any private sensation would decide solely for the observer himself and his liking.

We can see, at this point, that nothing is postulated in a judgment of taste except such a *universal voice* about a liking unmediated by concepts. Hence all that is postulated is the *possibility* of a judgment that is aesthetic and yet can be considered valid for everyone. The judgment of taste itself does not *postulate* everyone's agreement (since only a logically universal judgment can do that, because it can adduce reasons); it merely *requires* this agreement from everyone, as an instance of the rule, an instance regarding which it expects confirmation not from concepts but from the agreement of others. Hence the universal voice is only an idea. (At this point we are not yet inquiring on what this idea rests.) Whether someone who believes he is making a judgment of taste is in fact judging in conformity with that idea may be uncertain; but by using the term beauty he indicates that he is at least referring his judging to that idea, and hence that he intends it to be a judgment of taste. For himself, however, he can attain certainty on this point, by merely being conscious that he is separating whatever belongs to the agreeable and the good from the liking that remains to him after that. It is only for this that he counts on everyone's assent, and he would under these conditions [always] be justified in this claim, if only he did not on occasion fail to observe these conditions and so make an erroneous judgment of taste.

§9. Investigation of the Question Whether in a Judgment of Taste the Feeling of Pleasure Precedes the Judging of the Object or the Judging Precedes the Pleasure

The solution of this problem is the key to the critique of taste and hence deserves full attention.

If the pleasure in the given object came first, and our judgment of taste were to attribute only the pleasure's universal communicability to the presentation of the object, then this procedure would be self-contradictory. For that kind of pleasure would be none other than mere agreeableness in the sensation, so that by its very nature it could have only private validity, because it would depend directly on the presentation by which the object *is given*.

Hence it must be the universal communicability of the mental state, in the given presentation, which underlies the judgment of taste as its subjective condition, and the pleasure in the object must be its consequence. Nothing, however, can be communicated universally except cognition, as well as presentation insofar as it pertains to cognition; for presentation is objective only insofar as it pertains to cognition, and only through this does it have a universal reference point with which everyone's presentational power is compelled to harmonize. If, then, we are to think that the judgment about this universal communicability of the presentation has a merely subjective determining basis, i.e., one that does not involve a concept of the object, then this basis can be nothing other than the mental state that we find in the relation between the presentational powers [imagination and understanding] insofar as they refer a given presentation to *cognition in general*.

When this happens, the cognitive powers brought into play by this presentation are in free play, because no determinate concept restricts them to a particular rule of cognition. Hence the mental state in this presentation must be a feeling, accompanying the given presentation, of a free play of the presentational powers directed to cognition in general. Now if a presentation by which an object is given is, in general, to become cognition, we need *imagination* to combine the manifold of intuition, and *understanding*[9] to provide the unity of the concept uniting the [component] presentations. This state of *free play* of the cognitive powers, accompanying a presentation by which an object is given, must be universally communicable; for cognition, the determination of the object with which given presentations are to harmonize (in any subject whatever) is the only way of presenting that holds for everyone.

But the way of presenting [which occurs] in a judgment of taste is to have subjective universal communicability without presupposing a determinate concept; hence this subjective universal communicability can be nothing but [that of] the mental state in which we are when imagination and understanding are in free play (insofar as they harmonize with each other as required for *cognition in general*). For we are conscious that this subjective relation suitable for cognition in general must hold just as much for everyone, and hence be just as universally communicable, as any determinate cognition, since cognition always rests on that relation as its subjective condition.

Now this merely subjective (aesthetic) judging of the object, or of the presentation by which it is given, precedes the pleasure in the object and is the basis of this pleasure, [a pleasure] in the harmony of the cognitive powers. But the universal subjective validity of this liking, the liking we connect with the presentation of the object we call beautiful, is based solely on the mentioned universality of the subjective conditions for judging objects.

* * *

Explication of the Beautiful Inferred from the Second Moment

Beautiful is what, without a concept, is liked universally.

* * *

9. The a priori mental categories. "The manifold of intuition": the sense data that we receive from the outside world.

§11. A JUDGMENT OF TASTE IS BASED ON NOTHING BUT THE *FORM OF PURPOSIVENESS* OF AN OBJECT (OR OF THE WAY OF PRESENTING IT)

Whenever a purpose is regarded as the basis of a liking, it always carries with it an interest, as the basis that determines the judgment about the object of the pleasure. Hence a judgment of taste cannot be based on a subjective purpose. But a judgment of taste also cannot be determined by a presentation of an objective purpose, i.e., a presentation of the object itself as possible according to principles of connection in terms of purposes, and hence it cannot be determined by a concept of the good. For it is an aesthetic and not a cognitive judgment, and hence does not involve a *concept* of the character and internal or external possibility of the object through this or that cause; rather, it involves merely the relation of the presentational powers to each other, insofar as they are determined by a presentation.

Now this relation, [present] when [judgment] determines an object as beautiful, is connected with the feeling of a pleasure, a pleasure that the judgment of taste at the same time declares to be valid for everyone. Hence neither an agreeableness accompanying the presentation, nor a presentation of the object's perfection and the concept of the good, can contain the basis that determines [such a judgment]. Therefore the liking that, without a concept, we judge to be universally communicable and hence to be the basis that determines a judgment of taste, can be nothing but the subjective purposiveness in the presentation of an object, without any purpose (whether objective or subjective), and hence the mere form of purposiveness, insofar as we are conscious of it, in the presentation by which an object is *given* us.

* * *

§13. A PURE JUDGMENT OF TASTE IS INDEPENDENT OF CHARM AND EMOTION

All interest ruins a judgment of taste and deprives it of its impartiality, especially if, instead of making the purposiveness precede the feeling of pleasure as the interest of reason does, that interest bases the purposiveness on the feeling of pleasure; but this is what always happens in an aesthetic judgment that we make about something insofar as it gratifies or pains us. Hence judgments affected in this way can make either no claim at all to a universally valid liking, or a claim that is diminished to the extent that sensations of that kind are included among the bases determining the taste. Any taste remains barbaric if its liking requires that *charms* and *emotions* be mingled in, let alone if it makes these the standard of its approval.

And yet, (though beauty should actually concern only form), charms are frequently not only included with beauty, as a contribution toward a universal aesthetic liking, but are even themselves passed off as beauties, so that the matter of the liking is passed off as the form.[1] This is a misunderstand-

1. That is, material embellishments are mistakenly thought to be the source of beauty.

ing that, like many others having yet some basis in truth, can be eliminated by carefully defining these concepts.

A *pure judgment of taste* is one that is not influenced by charm or emotion (though these may be connected with a liking for the beautiful), and whose determining basis is therefore merely the purposiveness of the form.

§14. Elucidation by Examples

Aesthetic judgments, just like theoretical (i.e., logical) ones, can be divided into empirical and pure. Aesthetic judgments are empirical if they assert that an object or a way of presenting it is agreeable or disagreeable; they are pure if they assert that it is beautiful. Empirical aesthetic judgments are judgments of sense (material aesthetic judgments); only pure aesthetic judgments (since they are formal) are properly judgments of taste.

Hence a judgment of taste is pure only insofar as no merely empirical liking is mingled in with the basis that determines it. But this is just what happens whenever charm or emotion have a share in a judgment by which something is to be declared beautiful.

Here again some will raise objections, trying to make out, not merely that charm is a necessary ingredient in beauty, but indeed that it is sufficient all by itself to [deserve] being called beautiful.

* * *

But the view that the beauty we attribute to an object on account of its form is actually capable of being heightened by charm is a vulgar error that is very prejudicial to genuine, uncorrupted, solid [*gründlich*] taste. It is true that charms may be added to beauty as a supplement: they may offer the mind more than that dry liking, by also making the presentation of the object interesting to it, and hence they may commend to us taste and its cultivation, above all if our taste is still crude and unpracticed. But charms do actually impair the judgment of taste if they draw attention to themselves as [if they were] bases for judging beauty. For the view that they contribute to beauty is so far off the mark that it is in fact only as aliens that they must, indulgently, be granted admittance when taste is still weak and unpracticed, and only insofar as they do not interfere with the beautiful form.

In painting, in sculpture, indeed in all the visual arts, including architecture and horticulture insofar as they are fine arts, *design* is what is essential; in design the basis for any involvement of taste is not what gratifies us in sensation, but merely what we like because of its form. The colors that illuminate the outline belong to charm. Though they can indeed make the object itself vivid to sense, they cannot make it beautiful and worthy of being beheld. Rather, usually the requirement of beautiful form severely restricts [what] colors [may be used], and even where the charm [of colors] is admitted it is still only the form that refines the colors.

All form of objects of the senses (the outer senses or, indirectly, the inner sense as well) is either *shape* or *play*; if the latter, it is either play of shapes (in space, namely, mimetic art and dance), or mere play of sensations (in time). The *charm* of colors or of the agreeable tone of an instrument may be added, but it is the *design* in the first case and the *composition* in the second that constitute the proper object of a pure judgment of taste; that the purity of the colors and of the tones, or for that matter their variety and contrast, seem to contribute to the beauty, does not mean that, because they themselves are agreeable, they furnish us, as it were, with a supplement to, and one of the same kind as, our liking for the form. For all they do is to make the form intuitable more precisely, determinately, and completely, while they also enliven the presentation by means of their charm, by arousing and sustaining the attention we direct toward the object itself.

Even what we call *ornaments* (*parerga*[2]), i.e., what does not belong to the whole presentation of the object as an intrinsic constituent, but [is] only an extrinsic addition, does indeed increase our taste's liking, and yet it too does so only by its form, as in the case of picture frames, or drapery on statues, or colonnades around magnificent buildings. On the other hand, if the ornament itself does not consist in beautiful form but is merely attached, as a gold frame is to a painting so that its charm may commend the painting for our approval, then it impairs genuine beauty and is called *finery*.

Emotion, a sensation where agreeableness is brought about only by means of a momentary inhibition of the vital force followed by a stronger outpouring of it, does not belong to beauty at all. But sublimity (with which the feeling of emotion is connected) requires a different standard of judging from the one that taste uses as a basis. Hence a pure judgment of taste has as its determining basis neither charm nor emotion, in other words, no sensation, which is [merely] the matter of an aesthetic judgment.

* * *

§16. A JUDGMENT OF TASTE BY WHICH WE DECLARE AN OBJECT BEAUTIFUL UNDER THE CONDITION OF A DETERMINATE CONCEPT IS NOT PURE

There are two kinds of beauty, free beauty (*pulchritudo vaga*) and merely accessory beauty (*pulchritudo adhaerens*). Free beauty does not presuppose a concept of what the object is [meant] to be. Accessory beauty does presuppose such a concept, as well as the object's perfection in terms of that concept. The free kinds of beauty are called (self-subsistent) beauties of this or that thing. The other kind of beauty is accessory to a concept (i.e., it is conditioned beauty) and as such is attributed to objects that fall under the concept of a particular purpose.

Flowers are free natural beauties. Hardly anyone apart from the botanist knows what sort of thing a flower is [meant] to be; and even he, while recognizing it as the reproductive organ of a plant, pays no attention to this natural purpose when he judges the flower by taste. Hence the judgment is based on no perfection of any kind, no intrinsic purposiveness to which the combination of the manifold might refer. Many birds (the parrot, the humming-bird, the bird of paradise) and a lot of crustaceans in the sea are [free] beauties themselves [and] belong to no object determined by concepts as to its purpose, but we like them freely and on their own account. Thus design *à la grecque*,[3] the foliage on borders or on wallpaper, etc., mean

2. Byworks, subordinate things (Greek).
3. The phrase *à la grecque* [in the style of the Greeks; French] was apparently used in the eighteenth century—and is still used by some present-day French art historians—to characterize the classicism in what is now called the Louis XVI style [translator's note].

nothing on their own: they represent [*vorstellen*] nothing, no object under a determinate concept, and are free beauties. What we call fantasias in music (namely, music without a topic [*Thema*]), indeed all music not set to words, may also be included in the same class.

When we judge free beauty (according to mere form) then our judgment of taste is pure. Here we presuppose no concept of any purpose for which the manifold is to serve the given object, and hence no concept [as to] what the object is [meant] to represent; our imagination is playing, as it were, while it contemplates the shape, and such a concept would only restrict its freedom.

* * *

§17. ON THE IDEAL OF BEAUTY

There can be no objective rule of taste, no rule of taste that determines by concepts what is beautiful. For any judgment from this source [i.e., taste] is aesthetic, i.e., the basis determining it is the subject's feeling and not the concept of an object. If we search for a principle of taste that states the universal criterion of the beautiful by means of determinate concepts, then we engage in a fruitless endeavor, because we search for something that is impossible and intrinsically contradictory. The universal communicability of the sensation (of liking or disliking)—a universal communicability that is indeed not based on a concept—[I say that] the broadest possible agreement among all ages and peoples regarding this feeling that accompanies the presentation of certain objects is the empirical criterion [for what is beautiful]. This criterion, although weak and barely sufficient for a conjecture, [does suggest] that a taste so much confirmed by examples stems from [a] deeply hidden basis, common to all human beings, underlying their agreement in judging the forms under which objects are given them.

That is why we regard some products of taste as *exemplary*. This does not mean that taste can be acquired by imitating someone else's. For taste must be an ability one has oneself; and although someone who imitates a model may manifest skill insofar as he succeeds in this, he manifests taste only insofar as he can judge that model himself. From this, however, it follows that the highest model, the archetype of taste, is a mere idea, an idea which everyone must generate within himself and by which he must judge any object of taste, any example of someone's judging by taste, and even the taste of everyone [else].

Idea properly means a rational concept, and *ideal* the presentation of an individual being as adequate to an idea. Hence that archetype of taste, which does indeed rest on reason's indeterminate idea of a maximum, but which still can be presented not through concepts but only in an individual exhibition, may more appropriately be called the ideal of the beautiful. Though we do not have such an ideal in our possession, we do strive to produce it within us. But it will be merely an ideal of the imagination, precisely because it does not rest on concepts but rests on an exhibition, and the power of exhibition is the imagination.

* * *

Explication of the Beautiful Inferred from the Third Moment

Beauty is an object's form of *purposiveness* insofar as it is perceived in the object *without the presentation of a purpose*.[4]

§18. What the Modality of a Judgment of Taste Is

About any presentation I can say at least that there is a *possibility* for it (as a cognition) to be connected with a pleasure. About that which I call *agreeable* I say that it *actually* gives rise to pleasure in me. But we think of the *beautiful* as having a *necessary* reference to liking. This necessity is of a special kind. It is not a theoretical objective necessity, allowing us to cognize a priori that everyone *will feel* this liking for the object I call beautiful. Nor is it a practical objective necessity, where, through concepts of a pure rational will that serves freely acting beings as a rule, this liking is the necessary consequence of an objective law and means nothing other than that one absolutely (without any further aim) ought to act in a certain way. Rather, as a necessity that is thought in an aesthetic judgment, it can only be called *exemplary*, i.e., a necessity of the assent of *everyone* to a judgment that is regarded as an example of a universal rule that we are unable to state. Since an aesthetic judgment is not an objective and cognitive one, this necessity cannot be derived from determinate concepts and hence is not apodeictic.[5] Still less can it be inferred from the universality of experience (from a thorough agreement among judgments about the beauty of a certain object). For not only would experience hardly furnish a sufficient amount of evidence for this, but a concept of the necessity of these judgments cannot be based on empirical judgments.

§19. The Subjective Necessity That We Attribute to a Judgment of Taste Is Conditioned

A judgment of taste requires everyone to assent; and whoever declares something to be beautiful holds that everyone *ought* to give his approval to the object at hand and that he too should declare it beautiful. Hence the *ought* in an aesthetic judgment, even once we have [*nach*] all the data needed for judging, is still uttered only conditionally. We solicit everyone else's assent because we have a basis for it that is common to all. Indeed, we could count on that assent, if only we could always be sure that the instance had been subsumed correctly under that basis, which is the rule for the approval.

* * *

4. It might be adduced as a counterinstance to this explication that there are things in which we see a purposive form without recognizing a purpose in them [but which we nevertheless do not consider beautiful]. Examples are the stone utensils sometimes excavated from ancient burial mounds, which are provided with a hole as if for a handle. Although these clearly betray in their shape a purposiveness whose purpose is unknown, we do not declare them beautiful on that account. And yet, the very fact that we regard them as work[s] of art already forces us to admit that we are referring their shape to some intention or other and to some determinate purpose. That is also why we have no direct liking whatever for their intuition. A flower, on the other hand, e.g., a tulip, is considered beautiful, because in our perception of it we encounter a certain purposiveness that, given how we are judging the flower, we do not refer to any purpose whatever [Kant's note].

5. Absolutely certain.

§22. The Necessity of the Universal Assent That We Think in a Judgment of Taste Is a Subjective Necessity That We Present as Objective by Presupposing a Common Sense

Whenever we make a judgment declaring something to be beautiful, we permit no one to hold a different opinion, even though we base our judgment only on our feeling rather than on concepts; hence we regard this underlying feeling as a common rather than as a private feeling. But if we are to use this common sense in such a way, we cannot base it on experience; for it seeks to justify us in making judgments that contain an ought: it does not say that everyone *will* agree with my judgment, but that he *ought* to. Hence the common sense, of whose judgment I am at that point offering my judgment of taste as an example, attributing to it *exemplary* validity on that account, is a mere ideal standard. With this standard presupposed, we could rightly turn a judgment that agreed with it, as well as the liking that is expressed in it for some object, into a rule for everyone. For although the principle is only subjective, it would still be assumed as subjectively universal (an idea necessary for everyone); and so it could, like an objective principle, demand universal assent insofar as agreement among different judging persons is concerned, provided only we were certain that we had subsumed under it correctly.

That we do actually presuppose this indeterminate standard of a common sense is proved by the fact that we presume to make judgments of taste. But is there in fact such a common sense, as a constitutive principle of the possibility of experience, or is there a still higher principle of reason that makes it only a regulative principle for us, [in order] to bring forth in us, for higher purposes, a common sense in the first place? In other words, is taste an original and natural ability, or is taste only the idea of an ability yet to be acquired and [therefore] artificial, so that a judgment of taste with its requirement for universal assent is in fact only a demand of reason to produce such agreement in the way we sense? In the latter case the *ought*, i.e., the objective necessity that everyone's feeling flow along with the particular feeling of each person, would signify only that there is a possibility of reaching such agreement; and the judgment of taste would only offer an example of the application of this principle. These questions we neither wish to nor can investigate at this point. For the present our task is only to analyze the power of taste into its elements, and to unite these ultimately in the idea of a common sense.

Explication of the Beautiful Inferred from the Fourth Moment

Beautiful is what without a concept is cognized as the object of a *necessary* liking.

General Comment on the First Division[6] of the Analytic

If we take stock of the above analyses, we find that everything comes down to the concept of taste, namely, that taste is an ability to judge an object in reference to the *free lawfulness* of the imagination. Therefore, in a judgment of taste the imagination must be considered in its freedom. This

6. That is, the first book—the analytic of the beautiful.

implies, first of all, that this power is here not taken as reproductive, where it is subject to the laws of association, but as productive and spontaneous (as the originator of chosen forms of possible intuitions). Moreover, [second,] although in apprehending a given object of sense the imagination is tied to a determinate form of this object and to that extent does not have free play (as it does [e.g.] in poetry), it is still conceivable that the object may offer it just the sort of form in the combination of its manifold as the imagination, if it were left to itself [and] free, would design in harmony with the *understanding's lawfulness* in general. And yet, to say that the *imagination* is *free* and yet *lawful of itself*, i.e., that it carries autonomy with it, is a contradiction. The understanding alone gives the law. But when the imagination is compelled to proceed according to a determinate law, then its product is determined by concepts (as far as its form is concerned); but in that case the liking, as was shown above, is a liking not for the beautiful but for the good (of perfection, at any rate, formal perfection), and the judgment is not a judgment made by taste. It seems, therefore, that only a lawfulness without a law, and a subjective harmony of the imagination with the understanding without an objective harmony—where the presentation is referred to a determinate concept of an object—is compatible with the free lawfulness of the understanding (which has also been called purposiveness without a purpose) and with the peculiarity of a judgment of taste.

From *Book II. Analytic of the Sublime*

§23. Transition from the Power of Judging the Beautiful to that of Judging the Sublime

The beautiful and the sublime are similar in some respects. We like both for their own sake, and both presuppose that we make a judgment of reflection rather than either a judgment of sense or a logically determinative one. Hence in neither of them does our liking depend on a sensation, such as that of the agreeable, nor on a determinate concept, as does our liking for the good; yet we do refer the liking to concepts, though it is indeterminate which concepts these are. Hence the liking is connected with the mere exhibition or power of exhibition, i.e., the imagination, with the result that we regard this power, when an intuition is given us, as harmonizing with the *power of concepts*, i.e., the understanding or reason, this harmony furthering [the aims of] these. That is also why both kinds of judgment are *singular* ones that nonetheless proclaim themselves universally valid for all subjects, though what they lay claim to is merely the feeling of pleasure, and not any cognition of the object.

But some significant differences between the beautiful and the sublime are also readily apparent. The beautiful in nature concerns the form of the object, which consists in [the object's] being bounded. But the sublime can also be found in a formless object, insofar as we present *unboundedness*, either [as] in the object or because the object prompts us to present it, while yet we add to this unboundedness the thought of its totality. So it seems that we regard the beautiful as the exhibition of an indeterminate concept of the understanding, and the sublime as the exhibition of an indeterminate concept of reason.[7] Hence in the case of the beautiful our liking is connected with the presentation of *quality*, but in the case of the sublime with the presentation of *quantity*. The two likings are also very different in kind. For the one liking ([that for] the beautiful) carries with it directly a feeling of life's being furthered, and hence is compatible with charms and with an imagination at play. But the other liking (the feeling of the sublime) is a pleasure that arises only indirectly: it is produced by the feeling of a momentary inhibition of the vital forces followed immediately by an outpouring of them that is all the stronger. Hence it is an emotion, and so it seems to be seriousness, rather than play, in the imagination's activity. Hence, too, this liking is incompatible with charms, and, since the mind is not just attracted by the object but is alternately always repelled as well, the liking for the sublime contains not so much a positive pleasure as rather admiration and respect, and so should be called a negative pleasure.

But the intrinsic and most important distinction between the sublime and the beautiful is presumably the following. If, as is permissible, we start here by considering only the sublime in natural objects (since the sublime in art is always confined to the conditions that [art] must meet to be in harmony with nature), then the distinction in question comes to this: (Independent) natural beauty carries with it a purposiveness in its form, by which the object seems as it were predetermined for our power of judgment, so that this beauty constitutes in itself an object of our liking. On the other hand, if something arouses in us, merely in apprehension and without any reasoning on our part, a feeling of the sublime, then it may indeed appear, in its form, contrapurposive for our power of judgment, incommensurate with our power of exhibition, and as it were violent to our imagination, and yet we judge it all the more sublime for that.

We see from this at once that we express ourselves entirely incorrectly when we call this or that *object of nature* sublime, even though we may quite correctly call a great many natural objects beautiful; for how can we call something by a term of approval if we apprehend it as in itself contrapurposive? Instead, all we are entitled to say is that the object is suitable for exhibiting a sublimity that can be found in the mind. For what is sublime, in the proper meaning of the term, cannot be contained in any sensible form but concerns only ideas of reason, which, though they cannot be exhibited adequately, are aroused and called to mind by this very inadequacy, which can be exhibited in sensibility. Thus the vast ocean heaved up by storms cannot be called sublime. The sight of it is horrible; and one must already have filled one's mind with all sorts of ideas if such an intuition is to attune it to a feeling that is itself sublime, inasmuch as the mind is induced to abandon sensibility and occupy itself with ideas containing a higher purposiveness.

Independent natural beauty reveals to us a technic of nature that allows us to present nature as a system in terms of laws whose principle we do not find anywhere in our understanding: the principle of a purposiveness directed to our use of judgment as regards appearances. Under this principle,

7. *Reason* refers to our mental work with nonphysical ideas; *understanding* refers to apprehension and cognition of the physical world.

appearances must be judged as belonging not merely to nature as governed by its purposeless mechanism, but also to [nature considered by] analogy with art. Hence even though this beauty does not actually expand our cognition of natural objects, it does expand our concept of nature, namely, from nature as mere mechanism to the concept of that same nature as art, and that invites us to profound investigations about [how] such a form is possible. However, in what we usually call sublime in nature there is such an utter lack of anything leading to particular objective principles and to forms of nature conforming to them, that it is rather in its chaos that nature most arouses our ideas of the sublime, or in its wildest and most ruleless disarray and devastation, provided it displays magnitude and might. This shows that the concept of the sublime in nature is not nearly as important and rich in implications as that of the beautiful in nature, and that this concept indicates nothing purposive whatever in nature itself but only in what *use* we can make of our intuitions of nature so that we can feel a purposiveness within ourselves entirely independent of nature. For the beautiful in nature we must seek a basis outside ourselves, but for the sublime a basis merely within ourselves and in the way of thinking that introduces sublimity into our presentation of nature. This is a crucial preliminary remark, which separates our ideas of the sublime completely from the idea of a purposiveness of *nature*, and turns the theory of the sublime into a mere appendix to our aesthetic judging of the purposiveness of nature. For through these ideas we do not present a particular form in nature, but only develop [the] purposive use that the imagination makes of the presentation of nature.

* * *

§25. EXPLICATION OF THE TERM SUBLIME

We call *sublime* what is *absolutely [schlechthin] large*. To be large [*groß*] and to be a magnitude [*Größe*] are quite different concepts (*magnitudo* and *quantitas*). Also, *saying simply [schlechtweg]* (*simpliciter*) that something is large is quite different from saying that it is *absolutely large* (*absolute, non comparative magnum*[8]). The latter is *what is large beyond all comparison*.

* * *

The above explication can also be put as follows: *That is sublime in comparison with which everything else is small*. We can easily see here that nothing in nature can be given, however large we may judge it, that could not, when considered in a different relation, be degraded all the way to the infinitely small, nor conversely anything so small that it could not, when compared with still smaller standards, be expanded for our imagination all the way to the magnitude of a world; telescopes have provided us with a wealth of material in support of the first point, microscopes in support of the second. Hence, considered on this basis, nothing that can be an object of the senses is to be called sublime. [What happens is that] our imagination strives to progress toward infinity, while our reason demands absolute totality as a real idea, and so [the imagination,] our power of estimating the

8. Absolutely, not comparatively, large (Latin).

magnitude of things in the world of sense, is inadequate to that idea. Yet this inadequacy itself is the arousal in us of the feeling that we have within us a supersensible power; and what is absolutely large is not an object of sense, but is the use that judgment makes naturally of certain objects so as to [arouse] this (feeling), and in contrast with that use any other use is small. Hence what is to be called sublime is not the object, but the attunement[9] that the intellect [gets] through a certain presentation that occupies reflective judgment.

Hence we may supplement the formulas already given to explicate the sublime by another one: *Sublime is what even to be able to think proves that the mind has a power surpassing any standard of sense.*

§26. On Estimating the Magnitude of Natural Things, as We Must for the Idea of the Sublime

* * *

In order for the imagination to take in a quantum intuitively, so that we can then use it as a measure or unity in estimating magnitude by numbers, the imagination must perform two acts: *apprehension (apprehensio)*, and *comprehension (comprehensio aesthetica)*. Apprehension involves no problem, for it may progress to infinity. But comprehension becomes more and more difficult the farther apprehension progresses, and it soon reaches its maximum, namely, the aesthetically largest basic measure for an estimation of magnitude. For when apprehension has reached the point where the partial presentations of sensible intuition that were first apprehended are already beginning to be extinguished in the imagination, as it proceeds to apprehend further ones, the imagination then loses as much on the one side as it gains on the other; and so there is a maximum in comprehension that it cannot exceed.

This serves to explain a comment made by *Savary* in his report on Egypt:[1] that in order to get the full emotional effect from the magnitude of the pyramids one must neither get too close to them nor stay too far away. For if one stays too far away, then the apprehended parts (the stones on top of one another) are presented only obscurely, and hence their presentation has no effect on the subject's aesthetic judgment; and if one gets too close, then the eye needs some time to complete the apprehension from the base to the peak, but during that time some of the earlier parts are invariably extinguished in the imagination before it has apprehended the later ones, and hence the comprehension is never complete. Perhaps the same observation can explain the bewilderment or kind of perplexity that is said to seize the spectator who for the first time enters St. Peter's Basilica in Rome. For he has the feeling that his imagination is inadequate for exhibiting the idea of a whole, [a feeling] in which imagination reaches its maximum, and as it strives to expand that maximum, it sinks back into itself, but consequently comes to feel a liking [that amounts to an] emotion [*rührendes Wohlgefallen*].

I shall say nothing for now regarding the basis of this liking, a liking connected with a presentation from which one would least expect it, namely, a presentation that makes us aware of its own inadequacy and hence also of its

9. That is, the mental sensation that attends perceiving an object that exceeds the capacity of our senses.

1. *Lettres sur l'Égypte* (1785–86, *Letters on Egypt*), by Claude-Étienne Savary (1750–1788), French traveler and Orientalist.

subjective unpurposiveness for the power of judgment in its estimation of magnitude. Here I shall only point out that if the aesthetic judgment in question is to be *pure* (*unmixed with any teleological* and hence rational judgment), and if we are to give an example of it that is fully appropriate for the critique of *aesthetic* judgment, then we must point to the sublime not in products of art (e.g., buildings, columns, etc.), where both the form and the magnitude are determined by a human purpose, nor in natural things *whose very concept carries with it a determinate purpose* (e.g., animals with a known determination in nature), but rather in crude nature (and even in it only insofar as it carries with it no charm, nor any emotion aroused by actual danger), that is, merely insofar as crude nature contains magnitude. For in such a presentation nature contains nothing monstrous (nor anything magnificent or horrid); it does not matter how far the apprehended magnitude has increased, just as long as our imagination can comprehend it within one whole. An object is *monstrous* if by its magnitude it nullifies the purpose that constitutes its concept. And *colossal* is what we call the mere exhibition of a concept if that concept is almost too large for any exhibition (i.e., if it borders on the relatively monstrous); for the purpose of exhibiting a concept is hampered if the intuition of the object is almost too large for our power of apprehension. A pure judgment about the sublime, on the other hand, must have no purpose whatsoever of the object as the basis determining it, if it is to be aesthetic and not mingled with some judgment of understanding or of reason.

* * *

Since the presentation of anything that our merely reflective power of judgment is to like without an interest must carry with it a purposiveness that is subjective and yet universally valid, but since in the sublime (unlike the beautiful) our judging is not based on a purposiveness of the *form* of the object, the following questions arise: What is this subjective purposiveness, and how does it come to be prescribed as a standard, thereby providing a basis for a universally valid liking accompanying the mere estimation of magnitude—an estimation that has been pushed to the point where the ability of our imagination is inadequate to exhibit the concept of magnitude?

When the imagination performs the combination [*Zusammensetzung*] that is required to present a magnitude, it encounters no obstacles and on its own progresses to infinity, while the understanding guides it by means of numerical concepts, for which the imagination must provide the schema; and in this procedure, which is involved in the logical estimation of magnitude, there is indeed something objectively purposive under the concept of a purpose (since any measuring is a purpose).

* * *

The infinite, however, is absolutely large (not merely large by comparison). Compared with it everything else (of the same kind of magnitudes) is small. But—and this is most important—to be able even to think the infinite as *a whole* indicates a mental power that surpasses any standard of sense. For [thinking the infinite as a whole while using a standard of sense] would require a comprehension yielding as a unity a standard that would have a determinate relation to the infinite, one that could be stated in numbers; and this is impossible. If the human mind is nonetheless to *be able even to think* the given infinite without contradiction, it must have within itself a power that is supersensible, whose idea of a noumenon[2] cannot be intuited but can yet be regarded as the substrate underlying what is mere appearance, namely, our intuition of the world. For only by means of this power and its idea do we, in a pure intellectual estimation of magnitude, comprehend the infinite in the world of sense *entirely under* a concept, even though in a mathematical estimation of magnitude by *means of numerical concepts* we can never think it in its entirety. Even a power that enables us to think the infinite of supersensible intuition as given (in our intelligible substrate) surpasses any standard of sensibility. It is large beyond any comparison even with the power of mathematical estimation—not, it is true, for [the pursuit of] a theoretical aim on behalf of our cognitive power, but still as an expansion of the mind that feels able to cross the barriers of sensibility with a different (a practical) aim.

Hence nature is sublime in those of its appearances whose intuition carries with it the idea of their infinity. But the only way for this to occur is through the inadequacy of even the greatest effort of our imagination to estimate an object's magnitude. In the mathematical estimation of magnitude, however, the imagination is equal to the task of providing, for any object, a measure that will suffice for this estimation, because the understanding's numerical concepts can be used in a progression and so can make any measure adequate to any given magnitude. Hence it must be the *aesthetic* estimation of magnitude where we feel that effort, our imagination's effort to perform a comprehension that surpasses its ability to encompass [*begreifen*] the progressive apprehension in a whole of intuition, and where at the same time we perceive the inadequacy of the imagination—unbounded though it is as far as progressing is concerned—for taking in and using, for the estimation of magnitude, a basic measure that is suitable for this with minimal expenditure on the part of the understanding. Now the proper unchangeable basic measure of nature is the absolute whole of nature, which, in the case of nature as appearance, is infinity comprehended. This basic measure, however, is a self-contradictory concept (because an absolute totality of an endless progression is impossible). Hence that magnitude of a natural object to which the imagination fruitlessly applies its entire ability to comprehend must lead the concept of nature to a supersensible substrate (which underlies both nature and our ability to think), a substrate that is large beyond any standard of sense and hence makes us judge as *sublime* not so much the object as the mental attunement in which we find ourselves when we estimate the object.

Therefore, just as the aesthetic power of judgment in judging the beautiful refers the imagination in its free play to the *understanding* so that it will harmonize with the understanding's *concepts* in general (which concepts they are is left indeterminate), so in judging a thing sublime it refers the imagination to *reason* so that it will harmonize subjectively with reason's *ideas* (which ideas they are is indeterminate), i.e., so that it will produce a mental attunement that conforms to and is compatible with the one that an influence by determinate (practical) ideas would produce on feeling.

2. Something as it is in itself (which Kant sets against *phenomenon*, a "mere appearance" grasped through the senses).

This also shows that true sublimity must be sought only in the mind of the judging person, not in the natural object the judging of which prompts this mental attunement. Indeed, who would want to call sublime such things as shapeless mountain masses piled on one another in wild disarray, with their pyramids of ice, or the gloomy raging sea? But the mind feels elevated in its own judgment of itself when it contemplates these without concern for their form and abandons itself to the imagination and to a reason that has come to be connected with it—though quite without a determinate purpose, and merely expanding it—and finds all the might of the imagination still inadequate to reason's ideas.

* * *

§27. On the Quality of Liking in Our Judging of the Sublime

The feeling that it is beyond our ability to attain to an idea *that is a law for us* is RESPECT. Now the idea of comprehending every appearance that may be given us in the intuition of a whole is an idea enjoined on us by a law of reason, which knows no other determinate measure that is valid for everyone and unchanging than the absolute whole. But our imagination, even in its greatest effort to do what is demanded of it and comprehend a given object in a whole of intuition (and hence to exhibit the idea of reason), proves its own limits and inadequacy, and yet at the same time proves its vocation to [obey] a law, namely, to make itself adequate to that idea. Hence the feeling of the sublime in nature is respect for our own vocation. But by a certain subreption[3] (in which respect for the object is substituted for respect for the idea of humanity within our[selves, as] subject[s]) this respect is accorded an object of nature that, as it were, makes intuitable for us the superiority of the rational vocation of our cognitive powers over the greatest power of sensibility.

Hence the feeling of the sublime is a feeling of displeasure that arises from the imagination's inadequacy, in an aesthetic estimation of magnitude, for an estimation by reason, but is at the same time also a pleasure, aroused by the fact that this very judgment, namely, that even the greatest power of sensibility is inadequate, is [itself] in harmony with rational ideas, insofar as striving toward them is still a law for us. For it is a law (of reason) for us, and part of our vocation, to estimate any sense object in nature that is large for us as being small when compared with ideas of reason; and whatever arouses in us the feeling of this supersensible vocation is in harmony with that law. Now the greatest effort of the imagination in exhibiting the unity [it needs] to estimate magnitude is [itself] a reference to something *large absolutely*, and hence also a reference to reason's law to adopt only this something as the supreme measure of magnitude. Hence our inner perception that every standard of sensibility is inadequate for an estimation of magnitude by reason is [itself] a harmony with laws of reason, as well as a displeasure that arouses in us the feeling of our supersensible vocation, according to which finding that every standard of sensibility is inadequate to the ideas of reason is purposive and hence pleasurable.

3. A misrepresentation; a misunderstanding derived from such a misrepresentation.

In presenting the sublime in nature the mind feels *agitated*, while in an aesthetic judgment about the beautiful in nature it is in *restful* contemplation. This agitation (above all at its inception) can be compared with a vibration, i.e., with a rapid alternation of repulsion from, and attraction to, one and the same object. If a [thing] is excessive for the imagination (and the imagination is driven to [such excess] as it apprehends [the thing] in intuition), then [the thing] is, as it were, an abyss in which the imagination is afraid to lose itself. Yet, at the same time, for reason's idea of the supersensible [this same thing] is not excessive but conforms to reason's law to give rise to such striving by the imagination. Hence [the thing] is now attractive to the same degree to which [formerly] it was repulsive to mere sensibility. The judgment itself, however, always remains only aesthetic here. For it is not based on a determinate concept of the object, and presents merely the subjective play of the mental powers themselves (imagination and reason) as harmonious by virtue of their contrast. For just as, when we judge the beautiful, imagination and *understanding* give rise to a subjective purposiveness of the mental powers by their *accordance*, so do imagination and *reason* here give rise to such a purposiveness by their *conflict*, namely, to a feeling that we have a pure and independent reason, or a power for estimating magnitude, whose superiority cannot be made intuitable by anything other than the inadequacy of that power which in exhibiting magnitudes (of sensible objects) is itself unbounded.

* * *

§28. ON NATURE AS A MIGHT

Might is an ability that is superior to great obstacles. It is called *dominance* [*Gewalt*] if it is superior even to the resistance of something that itself possesses might. When in an aesthetic judgment we consider nature as a might that has no dominance over us, then it is *dynamically sublime*.

If we are to judge nature as sublime dynamically, we must present it as arousing fear. (But the reverse does not hold: not every object that arouses fear is found sublime when we judge it aesthetically.) For when we judge [something] aesthetically (without a concept), the only way we can judge a superiority over obstacles is by the magnitude of the resistance. But whatever we strive to resist is an evil, and it is an object of fear if we find that our ability [to resist it] is no match for it. Hence nature can count as a might, and so as dynamically sublime, for aesthetic judgment only insofar as we consider it as an object of fear.

We can, however, consider an object *fearful* without being afraid *of* it, namely, if we judge it in such a way that we merely *think* of the case where we might possibly want to put up resistance against it, and that any resistance would in that case be utterly futile. Thus a virtuous person fears God without being afraid of him. For he does not think of wanting to resist God and his commandments as a possibility that should worry *him*. But for every such case, which he thinks of as not impossible intrinsically, he recognizes God as fearful.

Just as we cannot pass judgment on the beautiful if we are seized by inclination and appetite, so we cannot pass judgment at all on the sublime in nature if we are afraid. For we flee from the sight of an object that scares us, and it is impossible to like terror that we take seriously. That is why the agreeableness that arises from the cessation of a hardship is *gladness*. But since this gladness involves our liberation from a danger, it is accompanied by our resolve never to expose ourselves to that danger again. Indeed, we do not even like to think back on that sensation, let alone actively seek out an opportunity for it.

On the other hand, consider bold, overhanging and, as it were, threatening rocks, thunderclouds piling up in the sky and moving about accompanied by lightning and thunderclaps, volcanoes with all their destructive power, hurricanes with all the devastation they leave behind, the boundless ocean heaved up, the high waterfall of a mighty river, and so on. Compared to the might of any of these, our ability to resist becomes an insignificant trifle. Yet the sight of them becomes all the more attractive the more fearful it is, provided we are in a safe place. And we like to call these objects sublime because they raise the soul's fortitude above its usual middle range and allow us to discover in ourselves an ability to resist which is of a quite different kind, and which gives us the courage [to believe] that we could be a match for nature's seeming omnipotence.

For although we found our own limitation when we considered the immensity of nature and the inadequacy of our ability to adopt a standard proportionate to estimating aesthetically the magnitude of nature's *domain*, yet we also found, in our power of reason, a different and nonsensible standard that has this infinity itself under it as a unit; and since in contrast to this standard everything in nature is small, we found in our mind a superiority over nature itself in its immensity. In the same way, though the irresistibility of nature's might makes us, considered as natural beings, recognize our physical impotence, it reveals in us at the same time an ability to judge ourselves independent of nature, and reveals in us a superiority over nature that is the basis of a self-preservation quite different in kind from the one that can be assailed and endangered by nature outside us. This keeps the humanity in our person from being degraded, even though a human being would have to succumb to that dominance [of nature]. Hence if in judging nature aesthetically we call it sublime, we do so not because nature arouses fear, but because it calls forth our strength (which does not belong to nature [within us]), to regard as small the [objects] of our [natural] concerns: property, health, and life, and because of this we regard nature's might (to which we are indeed subjected in these [natural] concerns) as yet not having such dominance over us, as persons, that we should have to bow to it if our highest principles were at stake and we had to choose between upholding or abandoning them. Hence nature is here called sublime [*erhaben*] merely because it elevates [*erhebt*] our imagination, [making] it exhibit those cases where the mind can come to feel its own sublimity, which lies in its vocation and elevates it even above nature.

This self-estimation loses nothing from the fact that we must find ourselves safe in order to feel this exciting liking, so that (as it might seem), since the danger is not genuine, the sublimity of our intellectual ability might also not be genuine. For here the liking concerns only our ability's *vocation*, revealed in such cases, insofar as the predisposition to this ability is part of our nature, whereas it remains up to us, as our obligation, to develop and exercise this ability. And there is truth in this, no matter how conscious of his actual present impotence man may be when he extends his reflection thus far.

I admit that this principle seems farfetched and the result of some subtle reasoning, and hence high-flown [*überschwenglich*] for an aesthetic judgment. And yet our observation of man proves the opposite, and proves that even the commonest judging can be based on this principle, even though we are not always conscious of it. For what is it that is an object of the highest admiration even to the savage? It is a person who is not terrified, not afraid, and hence does not yield to danger but promptly sets to work with vigor and full deliberation. Even in a fully civilized society there remains this superior esteem for the warrior, except that we demand more of him: that he also demonstrate all the virtues of peace—gentleness, sympathy, and even appropriate care for his own person—precisely because they reveal to us that his mind cannot be subdued by danger. Hence, no matter how much people may dispute, when they compare the statesman with the general, as to which one deserves the superior respect, an aesthetic judgment decides in favor of the general. Even war has something sublime about it if it is carried on in an orderly way and with respect for the sanctity of the citizens' rights. At the same time it makes the way of thinking of a people that carries it on in this way all the more sublime in proportion to the number of dangers in the face of which it courageously stood its ground. A prolonged peace, on the other hand, tends to make prevalent a mere[ly] commercial spirit, and along with it base selfishness, cowardice, and softness, and to debase the way of thinking of that people.

* * *

§29. ON THE MODALITY OF A JUDGMENT ABOUT THE SUBLIME IN NATURE

Beautiful nature contains innumerable things about which we do not hesitate to require everyone's judgment to agree with our own, and can in fact expect such agreement without being wrong very often. But we cannot with the same readiness count on others to accept our judgment about the sublime in nature. For it seems that, if we are to pass judgment on that superiority of [such] natural objects, not only must our aesthetic power of judgment be far more cultivated, but also so must the cognitive powers on which it is based.

In order for the mind to be attuned to the feeling of the sublime, it must be receptive to ideas. For it is precisely nature's inadequacy to the ideas—and this presupposes both that the mind is receptive to ideas and that the imagination strains to treat nature as a schema for them—that constitutes what both repels our sensibility and yet attracts us at the same time, because it is a dominance [*Gewalt*] that reason exerts over sensibility only for the sake of expanding it commensurately with reason's own domain (the practical one) and letting it look outward toward the infinite, which for sensibility is an abyss. It is a fact that what is called sublime by us, having been prepared through culture, comes across as merely repellent to a person who is uncultured and lacking in the development of moral ideas. In all the evidence of nature's destructive force [*Gewalt*], and in the large scale of its might, in contrast to which his own is nonexistent, he will see only the hardship, danger, and misery that would confront anyone forced to live in such a place. Thus (as Mr. de Saussure[4] relates) the good and otherwise sensible Savoyard peasant did not hesitate to call anyone a fool who fancies glaciered mountains. He might even have had a point, if Saussure had acted merely from fancy, as most travelers tend to, in exposing himself to the dangers involved in his observations, or in order that he might some day be able to describe them with pathos. In fact, however, his intention was to instruct mankind, and that excellent man got, in addition, the soul-stirring sensation and gave it into the bargain to the readers of his travels.

But the fact that a judgment about the sublime in nature requires culture (more so than a judgment about the beautiful) still in no way implies that it was initially produced by culture and then introduced to society by way of (say) mere convention. Rather, it has its foundation in human nature: in something that, along with common sense, we may require and demand of everyone, namely, the predisposition to the feeling for (practical) ideas, i.e., to moral feeling.

This is what underlies the necessity—which we include in our judgment about the sublime—of the assent of other people's judgment to our own. For just as we charge someone with a lack of *taste* if he is indifferent when he judges an object of nature that we find beautiful, so we say that someone has no *feeling* if he remains unmoved in the presence of something we judge sublime. But we demand both taste and feeling of every person, and, if he has any culture at all, we presuppose that he has them. But we do so with this difference: taste we demand unhesitatingly from everyone, because here judgment refers the imagination merely to the understanding, our power of concepts; in the case of feeling, on the other hand, judgment refers the imagination to reason, our power of ideas, and so we demand feeling only under a subjective presupposition (though we believe we are justified and permitted to require [fulfillment of] this presupposition in everyone): we presuppose moral feeling in man. And so we attribute necessity to this [kind of] aesthetic judgment as well.

* * *

§40. On Taste as a Kind of *Sensus Communis*

We often call the power of judgment a sense, when what we notice is not so much its reflection as merely its result. We then speak of a sense of truth, a sense of decency, of justice, etc. We do this even though we know, or at least properly ought to know, that a sense cannot contain these concepts, let alone have the slightest capacity to pronounce universal rules, but that a conception of truth, propriety, beauty, or justice could never enter our thoughts if we were not able to rise above the senses to higher cognitive powers. [This] *common human understanding*, which is merely man's sound ([but] not yet cultivated) understanding, is regarded as the very least

4. Horace Bénédict de Saussure (1740–1799), Swiss geologist and botanist [translator's note].

that we are entitled to expect from anyone who lays claim to the name of human being; and this is also why it enjoys the unfortunate honor of being called common sense (*sensus communis*), and this, indeed, in such a way that the word common (not merely in our language, where it is actually ambiguous, but in various others as well) means the same as *vulgar*—i.e., something found everywhere, the possession of which involves no merit or superiority whatever.

Instead, we must [here] take *sensus communis* to mean the idea of a sense *shared* [by all of us], i.e., a power to judge that in reflecting takes account (a priori), in our thought, of everyone else's way of presenting [something], in order *as it were* to compare our own judgment with human reason in general and thus escape the illusion that arises from the ease of mistaking subjective and private conditions for objective ones, an illusion that would have a prejudicial influence on the judgment. Now we do this as follows: we compare our judgment not so much with the actual as rather with the merely possible judgments of others, and [thus] put ourselves in the position of everyone else, merely by abstracting from the limitations that [may] happen to attach to our own judging; and this in turn we accomplish by leaving out as much as possible whatever is matter, i.e., sensation, in the presentational state, and by paying attention solely to the formal features of our presentation or of our presentational state. Now perhaps this operation of reflection will seem rather too artful to be attributed to the ability we call *common* sense. But in fact it only looks this way when expressed in abstract formulas. Intrinsically nothing is more natural than abstracting from charm and emotion when we seek a judgment that is to serve as a universal rule.

[Let us compare with this *sensus communis*] the common human understanding, even though the latter is not being included here as a part of the critique of taste. The following maxims may serve to elucidate its principles: (1) to think for oneself; (2) to think from the standpoint of everyone else; and (3) to think always consistently. The first is the maxim of an *unprejudiced*, the second of a *broadened*, the third of a *consistent* way of thinking. The first is the maxim of a reason that is never *passive*. A propensity to a passive reason, and hence to a heteronomy of reason, is called *prejudice*; and the greatest prejudice of all is *superstition*, which consists in thinking of nature as not subject to rules which the understanding through its own essential law lays down as the basis of nature. Liberation from superstition is called *enlightenment*; for although liberation from prejudices generally may also be called enlightenment, still superstition deserves to be called a prejudice preeminently (*in sensu eminenti*[5]), since the blindness that superstition creates in a person, which indeed it even seems to demand as an obligation, reveals especially well the person's need to be guided by others, and hence his state of a passive reason. As for the second maxim concerning [a person's] way of thinking, it seems that we usually [use a negative term and] call someone limited (of a *narrow* mind as opposed to a *broad* mind) if his talents are insufficient for a use of any magnitude (above all for intensive use). But we are talking here not about the power of cognition, but about the *way of thinking* [that involves] putting this power

5. In the prominent sense [of the term] (Latin).

to a purposive use; and this, no matter how slight may be the range and the degree of a person's natural endowments, still indicates a man with a *broadened way of thinking* if he overrides the private subjective conditions of his judgment, into which so many others are locked, as it were, and reflects on his own judgment from a *universal standpoint* (which he can determine only by transferring himself to the standpoint of others). The third maxim, the one concerning a *consistent* way of thinking, is hardest to attain and can in fact be attained only after repeated compliance with a combination of the first two has become a skill. We may say that the first of these maxims is the maxim of the understanding, the second that of judgment, the third that of reason.

Resuming now the thread from which I just digressed, I maintain that taste can be called a *sensus communis* more legitimately than can sound understanding, and that the aesthetic power of judgment deserves to be called a shared sense more than does the intellectual one, if indeed we wish to use the word *sense* to stand for an effect that mere reflection has on the mind, even though we then mean by sense the feeling of pleasure. We could even define taste as the ability to judge something that makes our feeling in a given presentation *universally communicable* without mediation by a concept.

The aptitude that human beings have for communicating their thoughts to one another also requires that imagination and understanding be related in such a way that concepts can be provided with accompanying intuitions, and intuitions in turn with accompanying concepts, these intuitions and concepts joining to [form] cognition. But here the harmony of the two mental powers is *law-governed*, under the constraint of determinate concepts. Only where the imagination is free when it arouses the understanding, and the understanding, without using concepts, puts the imagination into a play that is regular [i.e., manifests regularity], does the presentation communicate itself not as a thought but as the inner feeling of a purposive state of mind.

Hence taste is our ability to judge a priori the communicability of the feelings that (without mediation by a concept) are connected with a given presentation.

* * *

§43. ON ART IN GENERAL

(1) *Art* is distinguished from *nature* as doing (*facere*) is from acting or operating in general (*agere*); and the product or result of art is distinguished from that of nature, the first being a work (*opus*), the second an effect (*effectus*).

By right we should not call anything art except a production through freedom, i.e., through a power of choice that bases its acts on reason. For though we like to call the product that bees make (the regularly constructed honeycombs) a work of art, we do so only by virtue of an analogy with art; for as soon as we recall that their labor is not based on any rational deliberation on their part, we say at once that the product is a product of their nature (namely, of instinct), and it is only to their creator that we ascribe it as art.

[It is true that] if, as sometimes happens when we search through a bog, we come across a piece of hewn wood, we say that it is a product of art, rather than of nature, i.e., that the cause which produced it was thinking of a purpose to which this object owes its form. Elsewhere too, I suppose, we see art in everything that is of such a character that before it became actual its cause must have had a presentation of it (as even in the case of bees), yet precisely without the cause's having [in fact] *thought* of that effect. But if we simply call something a work of art in order to distinguish it from a natural effect, then we always mean by that a work of man.

(2) *Art*, as human skill, is also distinguished from *science* ([i.e., we distinguish] *can* from *know*), as practical from theoretical ability, as technic from theory (e.g., the art of surveying from geometry). That is exactly why we refrain from calling anything art that we *can* do the moment we *know* what is to be done, i.e., the moment we are sufficiently acquainted with what the desired effect is. Only if something [is such that] even the most thorough acquaintance with it does not immediately provide us with the skill to make it, then to that extent it belongs to art. *Camper*[6] describes with great precision what the best shoe would have to be like, yet he was certainly unable to make one.

(3) *Art* is likewise distinguished from *craft*. The first is also called *free art*, the second could also be called *mercenary art*. We regard free art [as an art] that could only turn out purposive (i.e., succeed) if it is play, in other words, an occupation that is agreeable on its own account; mercenary art we regard as labor, i.e., as an occupation that on its own account is disagreeable (burdensome) and that attracts us only through its effect (e.g., pay), so that people can be coerced into it. To judge whether, in a ranking of the guilds, watchmakers should be counted as artists but smiths as craftsmen, we would have to take a viewpoint different from the one adopted here: we would have to compare [*Proportion*] the talents that each of these occupations presupposes. Whether even among the so-called seven free arts[7] a few may not have been included that should be numbered with the sciences, as well as some that are comparable to crafts, I do not here wish to discuss. It is advisable, however, to remind ourselves that in all the free arts there is yet a need for something in the order of a constraint, or, as it is called, a *mechanism*. (In poetry, for example, it is correctness and richness of language, as well as prosody and meter.) Without this the *spirit*, which in art must be *free* and which alone animates the work, would have no body at all and would evaporate completely. This reminder is needed because some of the more recent educators believe that they promote a free art best if they remove all constraint from it and convert it from labor into mere play.

* * *

§46. FINE ART IS THE ART OF GENIUS

Genius is the talent (natural endowment) that gives the rule of art. Since talent is an innate productive ability of the artist and as such belongs itself to nature, we could also put it this way: *Genius* is the innate mental predisposition (*ingenium*) *through which* nature gives the rule to art.

6. Peter Camper (1722–1789), Dutch anatomist and naturalist [translator's note].
7. That is, the liberal arts of medieval education, made up of the trivium (grammar, logic, and rhetoric) and the more advanced quadrivium (music, arithmetic, geometry, and astronomy). *Liber* means "free" in Latin.

Whatever the status of this definition may be, and whether or not it is merely arbitrary, or rather adequate to the concept that we usually connect with the word *genius* (these questions will be discussed in the following section), still we can prove even now that, in terms of the meaning of the word genius adopted here, fine arts must necessarily be considered arts of *genius*.

For every art presupposes rules, which serve as the foundation on which a product, if it is to be called artistic, is thought of as possible in the first place. On the other hand, the concept of fine art does not permit a judgment about the beauty of its product to be derived from any rule whatsoever that has a *concept* as its determining basis, i.e., the judgment must not be based on a concept of the way in which the product is possible. Hence fine art cannot itself devise the rule by which it is to bring about its product. Since, however, a product can never be called art unless it is preceded by a rule, it must be nature in the subject (and through the attunement of his powers) that gives the rule to art; in other words, fine art is possible only as the product of genius.

What this shows is the following: (1) Genius is a *talent* for producing something for which no determinate rule can be given, not a predisposition consisting of a skill for something that can be learned by following some rule or other; hence the foremost property of genius must be *originality*. (2) Since nonsense too can be original, the products of genius must also be models, i.e., they must be *exemplary*; hence, though they do not themselves arise through imitation, still they must serve others for this, i.e., as a standard or rule by which to judge. (3) Genius itself cannot describe or indicate scientifically how it brings about its products, and it is rather as *nature* that it gives the rule. That is why, if an author owes a product to his genius, he himself does not know how he came by the ideas for it; nor is it in his power [*Gewalt*] to devise such products at his pleasure, or by following a plan, and to communicate [his procedure] to others in precepts that would enable them to bring about like products. (Indeed, that is presumably why the word genius is derived from [Latin] *genius*, [which means] the guardian and guiding spirit that each person is given as his own at birth, and to whose inspiration [*Eingebung*] those original ideas are due.) (4) Nature, through genius, prescribes the rule not to science but to art, and this also only insofar as the art is to be fine art.

* * *

§48. ON THE RELATION OF GENIUS TO TASTE

Judging beautiful objects to be such requires *taste*; but fine art itself, i.e., *production* of such objects, requires *genius*.

If we consider genius as the talent for fine art (and the proper meaning of the word implies this) and from this point of view wish to analyze it into the powers that must be combined in order to constitute such a talent, then we must begin by determining precisely how natural beauty, the judging of which requires only taste, differs from artistic beauty, whose possibility (which we must also bear in mind when we judge an object of this sort) requires genius.

A natural beauty is a *beautiful thing*; artistic beauty is a *beautiful presentation* of a thing.

* * *

§49. ON THE POWERS OF THE MIND WHICH CONSTITUTE GENIUS

Of certain products that are expected to reveal themselves at least in part to be fine art, we say that they have no *spirit*, even though we find nothing to censure in them as far as taste is concerned. A poem may be quite nice and elegant and yet have no spirit. A story may be precise and orderly and yet have no spirit. An oration may be both thorough and graceful and yet have no spirit. Many conversations are entertaining, but they have no spirit. Even about some woman we will say that she is pretty, communicative, and polite, but that she has no spirit. Well, what do we mean here by spirit?

Spirit [*Geist*] in an aesthetic sense is the animating principle in the mind. But what this principle uses to animate [or quicken] the soul, the material it employs for this, is what imparts to the mental powers a purposive momentum, i.e., imparts to them a play which is such that it sustains itself on its own and even strengthens the powers for such play.

Now I maintain that this principle is nothing but the ability to exhibit *aesthetic ideas*; and by an aesthetic idea I mean a presentation of the imagination which prompts much thought, but to which no determinate thought whatsoever, i.e., no [determinate] *concept*, can be adequate, so that no language can express it completely and allow us to grasp it. It is easy to see that an aesthetic idea is the counterpart (pendant) of a *rational idea*, which is, conversely, a concept to which no *intuition* (presentation of the imagination) can be adequate.

For the imagination ([in its role] as a productive cognitive power) is very mighty when it creates, as it were, another nature out of the material that actual nature gives it. We use it to entertain ourselves when experience strikes us as overly routine. We may even restructure experience; and though in doing so we continue to follow analogical laws, yet we also follow principles which reside higher up, namely, in reason (and which are just as natural to us as those which the understanding follows in apprehending empirical nature). In this process we feel our freedom from the law of association (which attaches to the empirical use of the imagination); for although it is under that law that nature lends us material, yet we can process that material into something quite different, namely, into something that surpasses nature.

Such presentations of the imagination we may call *ideas*. One reason for this is that they do at least strive toward something that lies beyond the bounds of experience, and hence try to approach an exhibition of rational concepts (intellectual ideas), and thus [these concepts] are given a semblance of objective reality. Another reason, indeed the main reason, for calling those presentations ideas is that they are inner intuitions to which no concept can be completely adequate. A poet ventures to give sensible expression to rational ideas of invisible beings, the realm of the blessed, the realm of hell, eternity, creation, and so on. Or, again, he takes [things] that are indeed exemplified in experience, such as death, envy, and all the other vices, as well as love, fame, and so on; but then, by means of an imagination that emulates the example of reason in reaching [for] a maximum, he ventures to give these sensible expression in a way that goes beyond the limits of experience, namely, with a completeness for which no example can be found in nature. And it is actually in the art of poetry that the power [i.e., faculty] of aesthetic ideas can manifest itself to full extent. Considered by itself, however, this power is actually only a talent (of the imagination).

Now if a concept is provided with [*unterlegen*] a presentation of the imagination such that, even though this presentation belongs to the exhibition of the concept, yet it prompts, even by itself, so much thought as can never be comprehended within a determinate concept and thereby the presentation aesthetically expands the concept itself in an unlimited way, then the imagination is creative in [all of] this and sets the power of intellectual ideas (i.e., reason) in motion: it makes reason think more, when prompted by a [certain] presentation, than what can be apprehended and made distinct in the presentation (though the thought does pertain to the concept of the object [presented]).

* * *

In a word, an aesthetic idea is a presentation of the imagination which is conjoined with a given concept and is connected, when we use imagination in its freedom, with such a multiplicity of partial presentations that no expression that stands for a determinate concept can be found for it. Hence it is a presentation that makes us add to a concept the thoughts of much that is ineffable, but the feeling of which quickens our cognitive powers and connects language, which otherwise would be mere letters, with spirit.

So the mental powers whose combination (in a certain relation) constitutes *genius* are imagination and understanding. One qualification is needed, however. When the imagination is used for cognition, then it is under the constraint of the understanding and is subject to the restriction of adequacy to the understanding's concept. But when the aim is aesthetic, then the imagination is free, so that, over and above that harmony with the concept, it may supply, in an unstudied way, a wealth of undeveloped material for the understanding which the latter disregarded in its concept. But the understanding employs this material not so much objectively, for cognition, as subjectively, namely, to quicken the cognitive powers, though indirectly this does serve cognition too. Hence genius actually consists in the happy relation—one that no science can teach and that cannot be learned by any diligence—allowing us, first, to discover ideas for a given concept, and, second, to hit upon a way of *expressing* these ideas that enables us to communicate to others, as accompanying a concept, the mental attunement that those ideas produce. The second talent is properly the one we call spirit. For in order to express what is ineffable in the mental state accompanying a certain presentation and to make it universally communicable—whether the expression consists in language or painting or plastic art—we need an ability [viz., spirit] to apprehend the imagination's rapidly passing play and to unite it in a concept that can be communicated without the constraint of rules (a concept that on that very account is original, while at the same time it reveals a new rule that could not have been inferred from any earlier principles or examples).

If, after this analysis, we look back to the above explication of what we call *genius*, we find: *First*, genius is a talent for art, not for science, where we must start from distinctly known rules that determine the procedure we must use in it. *Second*, since it is an artistic talent, it presupposes a determinate concept of the product, namely, its purpose; hence genius presupposes understanding, but also a presentation (though an indeterminate one) of the material, i.e., of the intuition, needed to exhibit this concept, and hence presupposes a relation of imagination to understanding. *Third*, it manifests itself not so much in the fact that the proposed purpose is achieved in exhibiting a determinate concept, as, rather, in the way *aesthetic ideas*, which contain a wealth of material [suitable] for that intention, are offered or expressed; and hence it presents the imagination in its freedom from any instruction by rules, but still as purposive for exhibiting the given concept. Finally, *fourth*, the unstudied, unintentional subjective purposiveness in the imagination's free harmony with the understanding's lawfulness presupposes such a proportion and attunement of these powers as cannot be brought about by any compliance with rules, whether of science or of mechanical imitation, but can be brought about only by the subject's nature.

These presuppositions being given, genius is the exemplary originality of a subject's natural endowment in the *free* use of his cognitive powers. Accordingly, the product of a genius (as regards what is attributable to genius in it rather than to possible learning or academic instruction) is an example that is meant not to be imitated, but to be followed by another genius. (For in mere imitation the element of genius in the work—what constitutes its spirit—would be lost.) The other genius, who follows the example, is aroused by it to a feeling of his own originality, which allows him to exercise in art his freedom from the constraint of rules, and to do so in such a way that art itself acquires a new rule by this, thus showing that the talent is exemplary. But since a genius is nature's favorite and so must be regarded as a rare phenomenon, his example gives rise to a school for other good minds, i.e., a methodical instruction by means of whatever rules could be extracted from those products of spirit and their peculiarity; and for these [followers] fine art is to that extent imitation, for which nature, through a genius, gave the rule.

But this imitation becomes *aping* if the pupil *copies* everything, including even the deformities that the genius had to permit only because it would have been difficult to eliminate them without diminishing the force of the idea. This courage [to retain deformities] has merit only in a genius. A certain *boldness* of expression, and in general some deviation from the common rule, is entirely fitting for a genius; it is however not at all worthy of imitation, but in itself always remains a defect that [any]one must try to eliminate, though the genius has, as it were, a privilege to allow the defect to remain [anyway], because the inimitable [element] in the momentum of his spirit would be impaired by timorous caution.

* * *

§59. ON BEAUTY AS THE SYMBOL OF MORALITY

* * *

Now I maintain that the beautiful is the symbol of the morally good; and only because we refer [*Rücksicht*] the beautiful to the morally good (we all do so [*Beziehung*] naturally and require all others also to do so, as a duty) does our liking for it include a claim to everyone else's assent, while the mind is also conscious of being ennobled, by this [reference], above a mere receptivity for pleasure derived from sense impressions, and it assesses the value of other people too on the basis of [their having] a similar maxim in their power of judgment. The morally good is the intelligible that taste has in view, as I indicated in the preceding section;[8] for it is with this intelligible that even our higher cognitive powers harmonize, and without this intelligible contradictions would continually arise from the contrast between the nature of these powers and the claims that taste makes. In this ability [taste], judgment does not find itself subjected to a heteronomy from empirical laws, as it does elsewhere in empirical judging—concerning objects of such a pure liking it legislates to itself, just as reason does regarding the power of desire. And because the subject has this possibility within him, while outside [him] there is also the possibility that nature will harmonize with it, judgment finds itself referred to something that is both in the subject himself and outside him, something that is neither nature nor freedom and yet is linked with the basis of freedom, the supersensible, in which the theoretical and the practical power are in an unknown manner combined and joined into a unity. I shall now bring up a few points of this analogy [between the beautiful and the morally good], noting at the same time what difference there is between them.

(1) The beautiful we like *directly* (but only in intuition reflect[ed upon], not in its concept, as we do morality). (2) We like it *without any interest*. (Our liking for the morally good is connected necessarily with an interest, but with an interest that does not precede our judgment about the liking but is produced by this judgment in the first place.) (3) In judging the beautiful, we present the *freedom* of the imagination (and hence [of] our power [of] sensibility) as harmonizing with the lawfulness of the understanding. (In a moral judgment we think the freedom of the will as the will's harmony with itself according to universal laws of reason.) (4) We present the subjective principle for judging the beautiful as *universal*, i.e., as valid for everyone, but as unknowable through any universal concept. (The objective principle of morality we also declare to be universal[ly valid], i.e., [valid] for all subjects, as well as for all acts of the same subject, but also declare to be knowable through a universal concept.) Hence not only is a moral judgment capable of [having] determinate constitutive principles, but its possibility *depends* on our basing the[se] maxims on those principles and their universality.

The common understanding also habitually bears this analogy in mind, and beautiful objects of nature or of art are often called by names that seem to presuppose that we are judging [these objects] morally. We call buildings or trees majestic and magnificent, or landscapes cheerful and gay; even colors are called innocent, humble, or tender, because they arouse sensations in us that are somehow analogous to the consciousness we have in a mental state produced by moral judgments. Taste enables us, as it were, to make the transition from sensible charm to a habitual moral interest without making too violent a leap; for taste presents the imagination as admitting, even in its freedom, of determination that is purposive for the understanding, and it teaches us to like even objects of sense freely, even apart from sensible charm.

1790

8. Section 58, omitted from our selection.

EDMUND BURKE
1729–1797

The sublime, which Edmund Burke examines in his major work *A Philosophical Enquiry into the Origins of Our Ideas of the Sublime and Beautiful* (1757), is one of the most intriguing terms in the history of literary criticism and theory. When invoked to name the defining quality of a great literary or artistic work, it usually suggests grandeur, vastness, awe, immense power. But the concept has a complex history, and critics and theorists have for centuries explored its meanings. It was first described in the treatise *On Sublimity,* written in the first century C.E. by a Greek rhetorician known (because of an early misattribution) as LONGINUS; in this text, the sublime is defined as "excellence in language" and as the "expression of a great spirit." It is associated as well with frightening, huge phenomena in nature—volcanoes, storms, the surging seas. Here already are signs of the tensions and ambiguities that Burke, and others in the eighteenth and nineteenth centuries, inquired into. Is the sublime a fact about nature or art, or both? Is the sublime a property of the work of literature itself? Or is it, instead, less in the work than in the soul, mind, or character of the genius who produces the work? Or—yet another variation—is it an extraordinary experience brought about by the power of the perceiver, and thus testimony not to the work or to the author but to something in the reader, something special in the intensity of the reader's response?

Burke's contribution to aesthetics is significant, although he is best known as a political theorist and statesman. He was born in Dublin, Ireland; his father, a lawyer, was a Protestant, and his mother was a Roman Catholic. He attended Trinity College in Dublin from 1743 to 1748 and then in 1750 began the study of law at the Middle Temple in London. His first publication, a satiric work titled *A Vindication of Natural Society,* was published anonymously in 1756. It was followed the next year by the *Enquiry,* also published anonymously, and this book won praise from scholars and critics in England and abroad. Burke soon became friends with a number of accomplished writers and artists, including Oliver Goldsmith, SAMUEL JOHNSON, and Joshua Reynolds; Johnson called Burke's work on the sublime "an example of true criticism." Beginning in 1758, Burke was also the editor (anonymously) of *The Annual Register,* a survey of world affairs; he held the position for three decades.

In 1765 Burke was appointed secretary to the marquess of Rockingham, a notable Whig political leader, and he became a member of Parliament. He took an active role in debates over the relationship between Parliament and the king, as George III attempted to increase the power of the monarchy; the Whigs sought to limit royal authority. In his pamphlet *Thoughts on the Cause of the Present Discontents* (1770), Burke criticized George's choice of ministers and presented a new conception of political "party." Traditionally, political parties had been seen as inherently subversive and unpatriotic, as well as sources of factionalism; but Burke viewed parties as collectives brought together on the basis of shared public principles. Rightly conceived, "party" was a "constitutional link between king and parliament, providing consistency and strength in administration, or principled criticism in opposition."

In addition to his efforts to limit the power of the king, Burke was involved in the 1760s and 1770s in the disputes about how best to govern the American colonies, a question considered in *Thoughts.* He delivered a number of speeches on this issue, faulting the policies of the British government for being rigid, contradictory, and unworkable. He called for "conciliation"—not an end to imperial authority but a more pragmatic exercise of it that would take into serious account the reasons for the colonists' complaints about taxation and lack of representation.

Burke was also an angry, incisive critic of the French Revolution, which broke out in 1789 and which many British writers, including WILLIAM WORDSWORTH and SAMUEL TAYLOR COLERIDGE, initially welcomed and supported. In his classic text *Reflections on the Revolution in France* (1790), Burke inveighed against unfettered democracy and dangerous appeals to the universal "rights of man" as he defended tradition, monarchy, and hereditary aristocracy. He resisted abstract speculation and (as he defined them) systems and schemes for social and political change that ignored the long history and organic interrelatedness of sociopolitical life, culture, and institutions. Society, for Burke, means a "partnership" between "those who are living, those who are dead, and those who are yet to be born." It is dangerously wrong to interfere with this partnership, however alluring the ideals brought forward as justification.

In our selection, we see Burke writing as a literary theorist, taking up a subject that previous critics had discussed and that resonated in the verse of contemporary poets. He is indebted, for example, to JOSEPH ADDISON's essays on taste, the imagination, and the sublime (see above) and to DAVID HUME's "Of the Standard of Taste" (1757; see above). Like these writers, he operates within the empirical tradition that John Locke had established in *An Essay Concerning Human Understanding* (1690)—that knowledge derives from sense experience and that simple ideas are combined into more complex ones. Burke has also absorbed the melancholy, reflective, sometimes ominous and disquieting poetry of Edward Young ("Night Thoughts," 1742), Thomas Gray ("Elegy Written in a Country Churchyard," 1751), and others. He is interested in the psychological and physical nature of our emotional responses to the exalted and the fearful, the terrible and terrifying, both in art and in nature.

In the excerpt below, Burke begins with a cogent account of the limitations of curiosity and novelty. These at first might strike us as positive terms—and to an extent they are, as Burke describes them. But, he explains, the problem with curiosity is that it is fickle, taking us all too quickly from one object of attention to another as it offers us the promise of some novelty, of something new and unusual that momentarily rouses us from the sense of familiarity with which we experience life as a whole. Yet to keep us from restlessness, anxiety, and weariness—Burke's words—our minds require the stimulation of other types of powers and passions, an observation that leads Burke to an inquiry into the more profound sensations of pain and pleasure.

Before Burke can depict the complex emotion surrounding the special experience of the sublime, he must briefly rehearse a psychology of relevant emotions. He maps them into two main groups. The social affects of pleasure and joy, linked with life and health, contrast sharply with the private sensations of pain and danger, which are tied to illness, death, and self-preservation. The former, observes Burke, have a weak impact on our emotions in comparison with the latter, more powerful passions. In his account, the king of personal terrors is death. Burke associates the aesthetic experience of the sublime with the most powerful private emotions, provided they are faced at a safe "aesthetic distance."

These early sections might prompt us to compare Burke with other philosophers and writers of the eighteenth century interested in similar ideas, such as Samuel Johnson and David Hume; with the poets and critics of the Romantic era who took issue with them; and with the theorists who spoke either for or against affective response and reader response in the twentieth century. But these sections are a preparation for section VII, where Burke introduces his understanding of "the sublime," which is, he maintains, "the strongest emotion which the mind is capable of feeling." The meaning of the sublime and the difference between the sublime and the beautiful, which Burke highlights here and develops in detail in later chapters, are the most significant features of his book.

Used as an adjective, "sublime" (from the Latin *sublimis*, "on high, uplifted, raised up") in the sixteenth and seventeenth centuries meant grand, elevated, lofty. By the middle of the eighteenth century, it also suggested the highest moral, intellectual, or emotional level, as well as great nobility of character. Late in the century, it was used as both an adjective and a noun to refer, as it does today, to a sensation—overwhelming awe, astonishment, fear, terror—produced by great scenes in nature and powerful works of literature and art.

Though Burke read Longinus's text when he was a student at Trinity, he seems already to have been fascinated by the idea and experience of the sublime. For example, while in his teens he commented in a letter on a flood he saw from a distance: "It gives me pleasure to see nature in these great though terrible scenes. It fills the mind with grand ideas, and turns the soul in upon itself." In his *Essay on Criticism* (1711; see above), ALEXANDER POPE had highlighted the order, harmony, and proportion that characterized Nature—and that writers should seek to embody in their work. But in this letter and in his book on the sublime, Burke is getting at an irrational element in both nature and art, something not captured by terms such as *reason, order, proportion*, and *balance*. The experience of the sublime, in all of its intensity, does partake of the irrational. But if we experienced it only as the irrational, we would feel only terror, not delight. Our perspective should exist at a distance, sufficiently detached from the experience that we are able to enjoy, contemplate, and reflect upon it. As we engage with sublime literary works, by maintaining an aesthetic distance we can perceive their status as representations of reality, not as reality itself.

Burke thus delves into the response of the reader or viewer to the sublime, and in his attention to the psychological nature of response he looks forward to the philosopher IMMANUEL KANT in his *Critique of Judgment* (1790), the German dramatist and critic G. E. LESSING, Coleridge, and RALPH WALDO EMERSON. Coleridge and Emerson, and, later, Walt Whitman, discover the sublime in the commonplace and everyday through the power of the perceiving mind—the capacity to recognize and voice, as Whitman does, the awe-inspiring infinite meaningfulness of a leaf of grass. Burke's influence on the understanding of the "terror" associated with the sublime is also apparent in the theory and practice of the Gothic novel; in *The Mysteries of Udolpho* (1794), Ann Radcliffe describes the impact of terror on the mind in Burkean terms: "A terror of this nature, as it occupies and expands the mind, and elevates it to a high expectation, is purely sublime, and leads us, by a kind of fascination, to seek even the object from which we appear to shrink."

Unlike some theorists of the era, though like Kant later in the century, Burke makes a distinction between the sublime and the beautiful. The sublime he connects to terror, obscurity, vastness, infinity; the beautiful he associates with smallness, brightness of color, the finite. His book stands roughly midway between the elegant neoclassicism of JOHN DRYDEN and Pope and the transcendence-seeking Romantic poetry and criticism of Wordsworth and Coleridge. Burke was one of the central figures in the challenge to the tradition that Dryden and Pope represented, and he prepared the way for the literary revolution of the 1790s—which coincided with the French Revolution that he despised. In yet another irony, for the deconstructionists PAUL DE MAN, JACQUES DERRIDA, and their followers, the sublime came to signify the plurality in language that keeps meaning from ever achieving a fixed form: dizzying, disorienting, and disorder-generating, it is dramatically at odds with the values that Burke in his political writing so eloquently defended.

A Philosophical Enquiry into the Origin of Our Ideas of the Sublime and Beautiful **Keywords:** Aesthetics, Affect, The Body, Enlightenment Theory, Interpretation Theory, Language

From A Philosophical Enquiry into the Origin of Our Ideas of the Sublime and Beautiful

From *Part I*

SECTION I. NOVELTY

The first and the simplest emotion which we discover in the human mind, is Curiosity. By curiosity, I mean whatever desire we have for, or whatever pleasure we take in novelty. We see children perpetually running from place to place to hunt out something new; they catch with great eagerness, and with very little choice, at whatever comes before them; their attention is engaged by every thing, because every thing has, in that stage of life, the charm of novelty to recommend it. But as those things which engage us merely by their novelty, cannot attach us for any length of time, curiosity is the most superficial of all the affections; it changes its object perpetually; it has an appetite which is very sharp, but very easily satisfied; and it has always an appearance of giddiness, restlessness and anxiety. Curiosity from its nature is a very active principle; it quickly runs over the greatest part of its objects, and soon exhausts the variety which is commonly to be met with in nature; the same things make frequent returns, and they return with less and less of any agreeable effect. In short, the occurrences of life, by the time we come to know it a little, would be incapable of affecting the mind with any other sensations than those of loathing and weariness, if many things were not adapted to affect the mind by means of other powers besides novelty in them, and of other passions besides curiosity in ourselves. These powers and passions shall be considered in their place. But whatever these powers are, or upon what principle soever they affect the mind, it is absolutely necessary that they should not be exerted in those things which a daily and vulgar use have brought into a stale unaffecting familiarity. Some degree of novelty must be one of the materials in every instrument which works upon the mind; and curiosity blends itself more or less with all our passions.

SECTION II. PAIN AND PLEASURE

It seems then necessary towards moving the passions of people advanced in life to any considerable degree, that the objects designed for that purpose, besides their being in some measure new, should be capable of exciting pain or pleasure from other causes. Pain and pleasure are simple ideas, incapable of definition. People are not liable to be mistaken in their feelings, but they are very frequently wrong in the names they give them, and in their reasonings about them. Many are of the opinion, that pain arises necessarily from the removal of some pleasure; as they think pleasure does from the ceasing or diminution of some pain. For my part I am rather inclined to imagine, that pain and pleasure in their most simple and natural manner of affecting, are each of a positive nature, and by no means necessarily dependent on each other for their existence. The human mind is often, and I think it is for the most part, in a state neither of pain nor pleasure, which I call a state of indifference. When I am carried from this state into a state of actual pleasure, it does not appear necessary that I should pass through the medium of any sort of pain. If in such a state of indifference, or ease, or tranquillity, or call it what you please, you were to be suddenly entertained with a concert of music; or suppose some object of a fine shape, and bright lively colours to be presented before you; or imagine your smell is gratified with the fragrance of a rose; or if without any previous thirst you were to drink of some pleasant kind of wine; or to taste of some sweetmeat without being hungry; in all the several senses, of hearing, smelling, and tasting, you undoubtedly find a pleasure; yet if I enquire into the state of your mind previous to these gratifications, you will hardly tell me that they found you in any kind of pain; or having satisfied these gratifications, you will hardly tell me that they found you in any kind of pain; or having satisfied these several senses with their several pleasures, will you say that any pain has succeeded, though the pleasure is absolutely over? Suppose on the other hand, a man in the same state of indifference, to receive a violent blow, or to drink of some bitter potion, or to have his ears wounded with some harsh and grating sound; here is no removal of pleasure; and yet here is felt, in every sense which is affected, a pain very distinguishable. It may be said perhaps, that the pain in these cases had its rise from the removal of the pleasure which the man enjoyed before, though that pleasure was of so low a degree as to be perceived only by the removal. But this seems to me a subtilty, that is not discoverable in nature. For if, previous to the pain, I do not feel any actual pleasure, I have no reason to judge that any such thing exists; since pleasure is only pleasure as it is felt. The same may be said of pain, and with equal reason. I can never persuade myself that pleasure and pain are mere relations, which can only exist as they are contrasted: but I think I can discern clearly that there are positive pains and pleasures, which do not at all depend upon each other. Nothing is more certain to my own feelings than this. There is nothing which I can distinguish in my mind with more clearness than the three states, of indifference, of pleasure, and of pain. Every one of these I can perceive without any sort of idea of its relation to any thing else. Caius is afflicted with a fit of the cholic;[1] this man is actually in pain; stretch Caius upon the rack, he will feel a much greater pain; but does this pain of the rack arise from the removal of any pleasure? or is the fit of the cholic a pleasure or a pain just as we are pleased to consider it?

SECTION III. THE DIFFERENCE BETWEEN THE REMOVAL OF PAIN AND POSITIVE PLEASURE

We shall carry this proposition yet a step further. We shall venture to propose, that pain and pleasure are not only, not necessarily dependent for their existence on their mutual diminution or removal, but that, in reality, the diminution or ceasing of pleasure does not operate like positive pain; and that the removal or diminution of pain, in its effect has very little resemblance to positive pleasure.[2] The former of these propositions will, I believe, be much more readily allowed than the latter; because it is very evident that pleasure, when it has run its career, sets us down very nearly where it found us. Pleasure of every kind quickly satisfies; and when it is over, we relapse into indif-

1. That is, colic: severe abdominal pain.
2. Mr. Locke thinks that the removal or lessening of a pain is considered and operates as a pleasure, and the loss or diminishing of pleasure as a pain. It is this opinion which we consider here [Burke's note]. Burke quotes "this opinion" directly from *An Essay Concerning Human Understanding* (1690), 2.20.16, by the English philosopher John Locke (1632–1704).

ference, or rather we fall into a soft tranquillity, which is tinged with the agreeable colour of the former sensation. I own, it is not at first view so apparent, that the removal of a great pain does not resemble positive pleasure: but let us recollect in what state we have found our minds upon escaping some imminent danger, or on being released from the severity of some cruel pain. We have on such occasions found, if I am not much mistaken, the temper of our minds in a tenor very remote from that which attends the presence of positive pleasure; we have found them in a state of much sobriety, impressed with a sense of awe, in a sort of tranquillity shadowed with horror. The fashion of the countenance and the gesture of the body on such occasions is so correspondent to this state of mind, that any person, a stranger to the cause of the appearance, would rather judge us under some consternation, than in the enjoyment of any thing like positive pleasure.

ὡς δ' ὅτ' ἂν ἄνδρ' ἄτη πυκινὴ λάβῃ, ὅς τ' ἐνὶ πάτρῃ
φῶτα κατακτείνας ἄλλων ἐξίκετο δῆμον,
ἀνδρὸς ἐς ἀφνειοῦ, θάμβος δ' ἔχει εἰσορόωντας,[3]

As when a wretch, who conscious of his crime,
Pursued for murder from his native clime,
Just gains some frontier, breathless, pale, amaz'd;
All gaze, all wonder!

Iliad, 24

This striking appearance of the man whom Homer supposes to have just escaped an imminent danger, the sort of mixt passion of terror and surprize, with which he affects the spectators, paints very strongly the manner in which we find ourselves affected upon occasions any way similar. For when we have suffered from any violent emotion, the mind naturally continues in something like the same condition, after the cause which first produced it has ceased to operate. The tossing of the sea remains after the storm; and when this remain of horror has entirely subsided, all the passion, which the accident raised, subsides along with it; and the mind returns to its usual state of indifference. In short, pleasure (I mean any thing either in the inward sensation, or in the outward appearance like pleasure from a positive cause) has never, I imagine, its origin from the removal of pain or danger.

SECTION IV. OF DELIGHT AND PLEASURE, AS OPPOSED TO EACH OTHER

But shall we therefore say, that the removal of pain or its diminution is always simply painful? or affirm that the cessation or the lessening of pleasure is always attended itself with a pleasure? by no means. What I advance is no more than this; first, that there are pleasures and pains of a positive and independent nature; and secondly, that the feeling which results from the ceasing or diminution of pain does not bear a sufficient resemblance to positive pleasure to have it considered as of the same nature, or to entitle it to be known by the same name; and thirdly, that upon the same principle the removal or qualification of pleasure has no resemblance to positive pain. It is

3. Homer (ca. 8th c. B.C.E.), *Iliad* 24.480–82. The English version, slightly misquoted, is from ALEXANDER POPE's translation (1715–20).

certain that the former feeling (the removal or moderation of pain) has something in it far from distressing, or disagreeable in its nature. This feeling, in many cases so agreeable, but in all so different from positive pleasure, has no name which I know; but that hinders not its being a very real one, and very different from all others. It is most certain, that every species of satisfaction or pleasure, how different soever in its manner of affecting, is of a positive nature in the mind of him who feels it. The affection is undoubtedly positive; but the cause may be, as in this case it certainly is, a sort of *Privation*. And it is very reasonable that we should distinguish by some term two things so distinct in nature, as a pleasure that is such simply, and without any relation, from that pleasure, which cannot exist without a relation, and that too a relation to pain. Very extraordinary it would be, if these affections, so distinguishable in their causes, so different in their effects, should be confounded with each other, because vulgar use has ranged them under the same general title. Whenever I have occasion to speak of this species of relative pleasure, I call it *Delight;* and I shall take the best care I can, to use that word in no other sense. I am satisfied the word is not commonly used in this appropriated signification; but I thought it better to take up a word already known, and to limit its signification, than to introduce a new one which would not perhaps incorporate so well with the language. I should never have presumed the least alteration in our words, if the nature of the language, framed for the purposes of business rather than those of philosophy, and the nature of my subject that leads me but of the common track of discourse, did not in a manner necessitate me to it. I shall make use of this liberty with all possible caution. As I make use of the word *Delight* to express the sensation which accompanies the removal of pain or danger; so when I speak of positive pleasure, I shall for the most part call it simply *Pleasure*.

SECTION V. JOY AND GRIEF

It must be observed, that the cessation of pleasure affects the mind three ways. If it simply ceases, after having continued a proper time, the effect is *indifference*; if it be abruptly broken off, there ensues an uneasy sense called *disappointment*; if the object be so totally lost that there is no chance of enjoying it again, a passion arises in the mind, which is called *grief*. Now there is none of these, not even grief, which is the most violent, that I think has any resemblance to positive pain. The person who grieves, suffers his passion to grow upon him; he indulges it, he loves it: but this never happens in the case of actual pain, which no man ever willingly endured for any considerable time. That grief should be willingly endured, though far from a simply pleasing sensation, is not so difficult to be understood. It is the nature of grief to keep its object perpetually in its eye, to present it in its most pleasurable views, to repeat all the circumstances that attend it, even to the last minuteness; to go back to every particular enjoyment, to dwell upon each, and to find a thousand new perfections in all, that were not sufficiently understood before; in grief, the *pleasure* is still uppermost; and the affliction we suffer has no resemblance to absolute pain, which is always odious, and which we endeavour to shake off as soon as possible. The *Odyssey* of Homer, which abounds with so many natural and affecting images, has none more striking than those which Menelaus[4] raises of the calamitous fate of his friends, and his own manner of feeling it. He owns indeed, that he often gives himself some intermission from such melancholy reflections, but he observes too, that melancholy as they are, they give him pleasure.

> ἀλλ' ἔμπης πάντας μὲν ὀδυρόμενος καὶ ἀχεύων
> πολλάκις ἐν μεγάροισι καθήμενος ἡμετέροισιν
> ἄλλοτε μέν τε γόῳ φρένα τέρπομαι, ἄλλοτε δ' αὖτε
> παύομαι· αἰψηρὸς δὲ κόρος κρυεροῖο γόοιο.[5]

> *Still in short intervals of* pleasing woe,
> *Regardful of the friendly dues I owe,*
> *I to the glorious dead, for ever dear,*
> Indulge *the tribute of a* grateful *tear.*
>
> *Odyssey*, 4

On the other hand, when we recover our health, when we escape an imminent danger, is it with joy that we are affected? The sense on these occasions is far from that smooth and voluptuous satisfaction which the assured prospect of pleasure bestows. The delight which arises from the modifications of pain, confesses the stock from whence it sprung, in its solid, strong, and severe nature.

SECTION VI. OF THE PASSIONS WHICH BELONG TO SELF-PRESERVATION

Most of the ideas which are capable of making a powerful impression on the mind, whether simply of Pain or Pleasure, or of the modifications of those, may be reduced very nearly to these two heads, *self-preservation* and *society*; to the ends of one or the other of which all our passions are calculated to answer. The passions which concern self-preservation, turn mostly on *pain* or *danger.* The ideas of *pain, sickness,* and *death,* fill the mind with strong emotions of horror; but *life* and *health,* though they put us in a capacity of being affected with pleasure, they make no such impression by the simple enjoyment. The passions therefore which are conversant about the preservation of the individual, turn chiefly on *pain* and *danger,* and they are the most powerful of all the passions.

SECTION VII. OF THE SUBLIME

Whatever is fitted in any sort to excite the ideas of pain, and danger, that is to say, whatever is in any sort terrible, or is conversant about terrible objects, or operates in a manner analogous to terror, is a source of the *sublime*; that is, it is productive of the strongest emotion which the mind is capable of feeling. I say the strongest emotion, because I am satisfied the ideas of pain are much more powerful than those which enter on the part of pleasure. Without all doubt, the torments which we may be made to suffer, are much greater in their effect on the body and mind, than any pleasures which the most learned voluptuary could suggest, or than the liveliest imagination, and the most

4. King of Sparta; though he returned safely from Troy after the object of the Trojan War was achieved (the retrieval of his wife, Helen), many Greeks died in battle or on their way home.

5. Homer, *Odyssey* 4.100–103. The English version is from Pope's translation (1715–20).

sound and exquisitely sensible body could enjoy. Nay I am in great doubt, whether any man could be found who would earn a life of the most perfect satisfaction, at the price of ending it in the torments, which justice inflicted in a few hours on the late unfortunate regicide in France.[6] But as pain is stronger in its operation than pleasure, so death is in general a much more affecting idea than pain; because there are very few pains, however exquisite, which are not preferred to death; nay, what generally makes pain itself, if I may say so, more painful, is, that it is considered as an emissary of this king of terrors. When danger or pain press too nearly, they are incapable of giving any delight, and are simply terrible; but at certain distances, and with certain modifications, they may be, and they are delightful, as we every day experience.[7] The cause of this I shall endeavour to investigate hereafter.

SECTION VIII. OF THE PASSIONS WHICH BELONG TO SOCIETY

The other head under which I class our passions, is that of *society*, which may be divided into two sorts. I. The society of the *sexes*, which answers the purposes of propagation; and next, that more *general society*, which we have with men and with other animals, and which we may in some sort be said to have even with the inanimate world. The passions belonging to the preservation of the individual, turn wholly on pain and danger; those which belong to *generation*, have their origin in gratifications and *pleasures*; the pleasure most directly belonging to this purpose is of a lively character, rapturous and violent, and confessedly the highest pleasure of sense; yet the absence of this so great an enjoyment, scarce amounts to an uneasiness; and except at particular times, I do not think it affects at all. When men describe in what manner they are affected by pain and danger; they do not dwell on the pleasure of health and the comfort of security, and then lament the *loss* of these satisfactions: the whole turns upon the actual pains and horrors which they endure. But if you listen to the complaints of a forsaken lover, you observe, that he insists largely on the pleasures which he enjoyed, or hoped to enjoy, and on the perfection of the object of his desires; it is the *loss* which is always uppermost in his mind. The violent effects produced by love, which has sometimes been even wrought up to madness, is no objection to the rule which we seek to establish. When men have suffered their imaginations to be long affected with any idea, it so wholly engrosses them as to shut out by degrees almost every other, and to break down every partition of the mind which would confine it. Any idea is sufficient for the purpose, as is evident from the infinite variety of causes which give rise to madness: but this at most can only prove, that the passion of love is capable of producing very extraordinary effects, not that its extraordinary emotions have any connection with positive pain.

From *Part III*

SECTION XXVII. THE SUBLIME AND BEAUTIFUL COMPARED

On closing this general view of beauty, it naturally occurs, that we should compare it with the sublime; and in this comparison there appears a remark-

6. Robert-François Damiens (1715–1757), who attempted to kill Louis XV on January 5, 1757, was tortured to death on March 26.

7. Here Burke touches on the key notion of aesthetic distance.

able contrast. For sublime objects are vast in their dimensions, beautiful ones comparatively small; beauty should be smooth, and polished; the great, rugged and negligent; beauty should shun the right line, yet deviate from it insensibly; the great in many cases loves the right line, and when it deviates, it often makes a strong deviation; beauty should not be obscure; the great ought to be dark and gloomy; beauty should be light and delicate; the great ought to be solid, and even massive. They are indeed ideas of a very different nature, one being founded on pain, the other on pleasure; and however they may vary afterwards from the direct nature of their causes, yet these causes keep up an eternal distinction between them, a distinction never to be forgotten by any whose business it is to affect the passions. In the infinite variety of natural combinations we must expect to find the qualities of things the most remote imaginable from each other united in the same object. We must expect also to find combinations of the same kind in the works of art. But when we consider the power of an object upon our passions, we must know that when any thing is intended to affect the mind by the force of some predominant property, the affection produced is like to be the more uniform and perfect, if all the other properties or qualities of the object be of the same nature, and tending to the same design as the principal;

If black and white blend, soften, and unite
A thousand ways, are there no black and white?[8]

If the qualities of the sublime and beautiful are sometimes found united, does this prove that they are the same, does it prove that they are any way allied, does it prove even that they are not opposite and contradictory? Black and white may soften, may blend, but they are not therefore the same. Nor when they are so softened and blended with each other, or with different colours, is the power of black as black, or of white as white, so strong as when each stands uniform and distinguished.

1757, 1759

8. Slightly misquoted from Pope, *An Essay on Man* (1733–34), 2.213–14.

GOTTHOLD EPHRAIM LESSING
1729–1781

Gotthold Ephraim Lessing is known for having questioned one of the most famous statements never meant. In HORACE's *Ars Poetica*, the Latin phrase *ut pictura poesis* (as painting, so poetry) was taken by many generations of critics to be prescriptive ("poetry *should* be like painting") rather than analogical ("poetry, like painting, does the following . . ."). Regardless of Horace's intent, the prescription has been immensely productive for poetry; but in *Laocoön* (1766) Lessing attacks this presumption of equivalence between poetry and painting, spelling out the differences between the visual and the verbal arts.

Born in Kamenz, Saxony, to a country pastor, Lessing was the first of twelve children (five died in childhood). After acquiring a solid education in languages and sciences, he enrolled at the University of Leipzig and soon fell under the spell of a more worldly and freethinking friend. His parents, alarmed by this influence and by Lessing's familiarity with the theater, called him home. When he explained to them that the hostility between church and theater could be overcome by improving the theater, he was allowed to return to Leipzig, where he became actively involved with a theatrical company, writing and producing plays. Unfortunately, the company failed, leaving Lessing to cover the debts; he fled, first to Wittenberg, then to Berlin.

Once in Berlin, he declared financial independence; working as a translator, reviewer, and playwright, he became the first German author to live by his pen. He found intellectual companionship with several close friends, especially the philosopher Moses Mendelssohn, who was introduced to Lessing as a chess partner and who influenced many of Lessing's aesthetic ideas.

In Berlin Lessing developed his gifts for both drama and debate. To him, the recommendation that German theater imitate seventeenth-century French classical drama (an idea promoted by Johann Christoph Gottsched) seemed a terrible mistake. The French had literalized ARISTOTLE and tied the theater to an overly formal set of rules. In his play *Miss Sara Sampson* (1755), Lessing attempted something quite different from PIERRE CORNEILLE, the epitome of classicism. He wrote the first German bourgeois tragedy—that is, a tragedy involving not the court but a middle-class family. He also entered the first of several intense polemical exchanges on unlikely topics by writing *Vademecum* (1754), a critique of a translation of Horace written by a pastor who was, unfortunately for Lessing, a protégé of Frederick II of Prussia. Frederick later repaid him by not appointing him to the post of royal librarian in Berlin.

Though he was barely supporting himself, the next few years were very productive: he wrote fables and a treatise on fables, plays, and a life of Sophocles, and he collaborated on the *Letters Concerning the Most Recent Literature* (1759–81) with his friends Mendelssohn and Gotthold Samuel Nicolai. In these letters, Lessing continued his campaign to free drama from French classicism, arguing that it should take its inspiration from Shakespeare. He also became close friends with a poet and military man who later served as the model for the hero of his comedy of honor, *Minna von Barnhelm* (1767). In 1760 Lessing took up a post as secretary to a general in Breslau. His excellent salary enabled him to send money to his family and to buy books. It was during this period that he wrote *Laokoon, oder Über die Grenzen der Malerei und Poesie* (*Laocoön, or On the Limits of Painting and Poetry*), from which our selection is taken.

Thwarted in his hopes to become the royal librarian in Berlin, he became dramatist and consultant to a repertory theater in Hamburg. There he began publishing the periodical the *Hamburg Dramaturgy* (which contained views far more radical than any he could practice), invested in a publishing house, and engaged again in a polemic—this time with the antiquarian Christian Adolphe Klotz, who had attacked his *Laocoön*. In response, he wrote *Letters of Antiquarian Content* (1768–69) and *How the Ancients Portrayed Death* (1769). Finally, unable to extricate himself from the dispute, frustrated with the constraints of the theater, and unsuccessful in business, he took refuge in the post of librarian at the Ducal Library in Wolfenbüttel.

Lessing was well suited for the job, though the library was dilapidated and isolated. As he put it in order, he corresponded with scholars and, in 1773, began publishing some of the library's holdings. He also began a correspondence with the recently widowed Eva König (whose family he had known in Hamburg), whom he married in 1776; a year later Eva gave birth to a child, and both died within days.

Lessing continued his work in drama, completing *Emilia Galotti*, a political tragedy, in 1772. *Nathan the Wise*, a dramatic poem about religious tolerance, was performed at Easter 1778; it stirred controversy by putting its message of universal brotherhood in the mouth of a noble Jew. Lessing went on publishing his library discoveries as well, and the fragments from Heinrich Samuel Reimarus's thesis on natural religion embroiled him in his final, and most intense, polemical exchange. His main attacker was Johann Melchior Goeze, and Lessing's angry *Anti-Goeze* pamphlets of 1778 and other writings on religion led to his being censored: he had to submit his later writings to the duke for approval. His provocative argument was that the truth of religion could never be captured in any fixed form; even the Bible was full of errors and contradictions. It was the *search* for truth and not any one Truth that proved the value of humanity. Little wonder that Lessing fell so readily into polemic: for him, such exchanges did not lead to truth but enacted it. In his last work, *The Education of the Human Race* (1780), Lessing continued to analyze the relation between reason and faith, education and revelation. Furious with all existing religions, Lessing was equally furious with smug atheism or complacent freethinking. His health declined after 1778, and he died at Wolfenbüttel at the age of fifty-two.

In spite of the variety of his interests and writings, Lessing's importance for literary criticism in English rests almost exclusively on the impact of his 1766 *Laocoön*. He begins it by discussing the role of the critic, whose duty with respect to the work of art is to make distinctions and discern causes rather than simply to register effects. While endorsing the well-known saying of the early fifth-century B.C.E. poet Simonides that painting is mute poetry and poetry a speaking picture, he argues that although the two arts are similar in *aim* (imitation) and in *effect* (pleasure), they differ greatly in *means* (visual versus verbal). Lessing goes on to analyze their differences.

In the course of his essay, Lessing takes on a veritable bookshelf of other writings, most notably Count Caylus's *Tableaux tirés de l'Iliade, de l'Odyssée d'Homère et de l'Enéide de Virgile, avec des observations générales sur le costume* (1757, *Scenes from Homer's Iliad and Odyssey and Virgil's Aeneid, with General Comments about Costume*); Joseph Spence's 1747 dialogues on visual and verbal art called *Polymetis;* and, most important, Johann Joachim Winckelmann's 1754 *Gedanken über die Nachahmung der greichischen Werke* (*Thoughts on the Imitation of Greek Works*). It is Winckelmann's concept of classical Greek "noble simplicity and quiet grandeur" that Lessing wishes to combat, not in the visual arts (where, he argues, it belonged) but in the verbal arts: epic and (implicitly) tragedy. The cold formalism of classical French drama was too much like sculpture; Lessing wants to make sure that the art of imitation in drama draws on Aristotle (plot is the "imitation of an *action*") rather than PLATO (mimesis is the imitation of a *form*). Winckelmann's idealization of Greek beauty had a powerful appeal; indeed, it was still being attacked a century later by FRIEDRICH NIETZSCHE in *The Birth of Tragedy* (1872; see below).

Laocoön stands as the first modern contribution to what we might call "media studies," in the sense that Lessing attempts to describe the limits and possibilities of the visual and verbal *media*. Our selection highlights the lines of the analysis and minimizes the polemical digressions and extended classical allusions, emphasizing the argument—which runs as follows. Painting is more similar to its subject than poetry is: in painting, both the medium and the thing imitated are visual, whereas poetry can use only words, arbitrary designations, to convey things that do not resemble words at all. In addition, visual art is static while verbal art unfolds through succession. Visual art is an art of *space;* verbal art is an art of *time*. Verbal art cannot equal the instant vividness of sculpture or painting, but it can depict things that visual art cannot capture: invisibility, negation, rhetoric. Visual art, in order to achieve maximum dynamism, has to choose the "pregnant moment," the moment most suggestive of the entire situation.

The word "pregnant" has come to have a life of its own in Lessing criticism in English; it was used by many translators (though not ours) to render the German *fruchtbar* ("fruitful"—here translated "effective") and *prägnant* (from the verb *prägen*, "to stamp, emboss, impress"; the adjective does mean "pregnant," but only figuratively, as "pregnant with meaning"—here translated "suggestive"). Behind the German word lies a Latin one (*praegnans*, "pregnant"). This phantom pregnancy is a good symbol of what Lessing is describing: the moment most likely to contain forces that can be continued in the imagination of the spectator. In visual art, therefore, a covert narrative force is always present. The same force exists in verbal descriptions of purely visual phenomena; even when poetry depicts an object rather than an action, it moves along the object in time as if from the standpoint of the object's maker rather than of its passive viewer.

Lessing's distinction between the arts has often been contested. In his 1957 essay on Lessing, the art historian E. H. Gombrich points out that visual art itself is conventional, not natural. In 1945 the literary critic Joseph Frank protested that a literary work of art exists not just in time but also in space. And many art historians have objected that a painting cannot be viewed all at once; it must be experienced through time. Taking an opposite tack, some theorists of ecphrasis (the depiction of a work of visual art in a poem) have felt that Lessing opens up possibilities he doesn't pursue. Far from being impossible in poetry, ecphrasis constitutes an interesting poetic challenge.

Because of his persistent fascination with what could *not* be visualized, Lessing is a particularly useful theorist of verbal art. In his discussion of fables, he points out that the test of a good fable is the impossibility of illustrating it. In his last writings about religion, he argues that even writing has too positive an existence to convey what escapes representation altogether. Perhaps this dissatisfaction with *every* medium is what makes his writings so suggestive for literary and aesthetic theory.

***Laocoön* Keywords:** Aesthetics, Language, Media, Poetry

From Laocoön[1]

From *Preface*

The first person to compare painting with poetry was a man of fine feeling who observed that both arts produced a similar effect upon him. Both, he felt, represent absent things as being present and appearance as reality. Both create an illusion, and in both cases the illusion is pleasing.

A second observer, in attempting to get at the nature of this pleasure, discovered that both proceed from the same source. Beauty, a concept which we first derive from physical objects, has general rules applicable to a number of things: to actions and thoughts as well as to forms.

A third, who examined the value and distribution of these general rules, observed that some of them are more predominant in painting, others in poetry. Thus, in the one case poetry can help to explain and illustrate painting, and in the other painting can do the same for poetry.

The first was the amateur, the second the philosopher, and the third the critic.

The first two could not easily misuse their feelings or their conclusions. With the critic, however, the case was different. The principal value of his observations depends on their correct application to the individual case. And since for every one really discerning critic there have always been fifty clever ones, it would have been a miracle if this application had always been made with the caution necessary to maintain a proper balance between the two arts.

* * *

1. Translated by Edward Allen McCormick (who sometimes adds clarifying words or phrases in square brackets); the full title is *Laocoön, or On the Limits of Painting and Poetry*.

From *Chapter One*

The general and distinguishing characteristics of the Greek masterpieces of painting and sculpture are, according to Herr Winckelmann,[2] noble simplicity and quiet grandeur, both in posture and in expression. "As the depths of the sea always remain calm," he says "however much the surface may be agitated, so does the expression in the figures of the Greeks reveal a great and composed soul in the midst of passions."

> Such a soul is depicted in Laocoön's[3] face—and not only in his face—under the most violent suffering. The pain is revealed in every muscle and sinew of his body, and one can almost feel it oneself in the painful contraction of the abdomen without looking at the face or other parts of the body at all. However, this pain expresses itself without any sign of rage either in his face or in his posture. He does not raise his voice in a terrible scream, which Virgil describes his Laocoön as doing;[4] the way in which his mouth is open does not permit it. Rather he emits the anxious and subdued sigh described by Sadolet.[5] The pain of body and the nobility of soul are distributed and weighed out, as it were, over the entire figure with equal intensity. Laocoön suffers, but he suffers like the Philoctetes of Sophocles[6]; his anguish pierces our very soul, but at the same time we wish that we were able to endure our suffering as well as this great man does.
>
> Expressing so noble a soul goes far beyond the formation of a beautiful body. This artist must have felt within himself that strength of spirit which he imparted to his marble. In Greece artists and philosophers were united in one person, and there was more than one Metrodorus.[7] Philosophy extended its hand to art and breathed into its figures more than common souls. . . .[8]

The remark on which the foregoing comments are based, namely that the pain in Laocoön's face is not expressed with the same intensity that its violence would lead us to expect, is perfectly correct. It is also indisputable that this very point shows truly the wisdom of the artist. Only the ill-informed observer would judge that the artist had fallen short of nature and had not attained the true pathos of suffering.

2. Johann Joachim Winckelmann (1717–1768), German classical scholar whose *Thoughts on the Imitation of Greek Works in Painting and Sculpture* (1754) prompted Lessing's response.
3. A Trojan priest. The best-known version of his story is found in the *Aeneid*, by the Roman poet Virgil (70–19 B.C.E.), who describes how when Laocoön unsuccessfully tries to warn his countrymen against the Greek "gift" of the Trojan horse, the goddess Athena sends two huge serpents to strangle him and his two sons (2.40–56, 199–227). The famous sculpture described by Winckelmann represents the three dying figures in the grip of the snakes; discovered in 1506, it is thought to be a collaborative work of the 2d century B.C.E. Laocoön is thus depicted in both sculpture and poetry, giving Lessing the pivot on which he will differentiate between the arts.
4. *Aeneid* 2.222.
5. Jacopo Sadoleto (1477–1547), Italian prelate and poet, who wrote a poem about the Laocoön group when it was discovered.
6. Greek tragedian (ca. 496–406 B.C.E.); *Philoctetes* was performed in 409. The Greek hero Philoctetes used the bow and arrows of Heracles; he sailed for Troy but was left behind on an island because a wound on his foot, caused by snakebite, produced a horrible smell. He remained alone for 10 years, until on the advice of an oracle he and his bow were brought to Troy.
7. An Athenian (2d c. B.C.E.) who, according to Pliny the Elder (23/24–79 C.E.; see *Natural History* 35.135), was both a painter and a philosopher.
8. Winckelmann, *Thoughts on the Imitation of Greek Works*, pp. 21, 22 [Lessing's note]. Some of the author's notes have been edited, and some omitted.

But as to the reasons on which Herr Winckelmann bases this wisdom, and the universality of the rule which he derives from it, I venture to be of a different opinion.

* * *

[I]f, according to the ancient Greeks, crying aloud when in physical pain is compatible with nobility of soul, then the desire to express such nobility could not have prevented the artist from representing the scream in his marble. There must be another reason why he differs on this point from his rival the poet,[9] who expresses this scream with deliberate intention.

From *Chapter Two*

Whether it be fact or fiction that Love inspired the first artistic effort in the fine arts,[1] this much is certain: she never tired of guiding the hands of the old masters. Painting, as practiced today, comprises all representations of three-dimensional bodies on a plane. The wise Greek, however, confined it to far narrower limits by restricting it to the imitation of beautiful bodies only. The Greek artist represented only the beautiful, and ordinary beauty, the beauty of a lower order, was only his accidental subject, his exercise, his relaxation. The perfection of the object itself in his work had to give delight, and he was too great to demand of his audience that they be satisfied with the barren pleasure that comes from looking at a perfect resemblance, or from consideration of his skill as a craftsman. Nothing in his art was dearer to him or seemed nobler than its ultimate purpose.

"Who would want to paint you when no one even wants to look at you?" an old epigrammatist[2] asks of an exceedingly deformed man. Many an artist of our time would say, "Be as ugly as possible, I will paint you nevertheless. Even though no one likes to look at you, they will still be glad to look at my picture, not because it portrays you but because it is a proof of my art, which knows how to present such a monster so faithfully."

* * *

The law of the Olympic judges sprang from the same idea of the beautiful. Every victor in the Olympic games received a statue, but only the three-time winner had a portrait-statue erected in his honor. This was to prevent the increase of mediocre portraits among works of art, for a portrait, although admitting idealization, is dominated by likeness. It is the ideal of one particular man and not of man in general.

We laugh when we hear that among the ancients even the arts were subject to the civil code. But we are not always right when we do so. Unquestionably, laws must not exercise any constraint on the sciences, for the ultimate goal of knowledge is truth. Truth is a necessity to the soul, and it is tyranny to impose the slightest constraint on the satisfaction of this essential need. But the ultimate goal of the arts is pleasure, and this pleasure is not indispens-

9. That is, Virgil.
1. Lessing alludes to the story of a Corinthian maid who, saddened by her lover's impending departure, drew his outline on a wall while he slept (see Pliny the Elder, *Natural History* 35.151); her father, a potter, filled in the outline with clay and thus invented bas-relief.
2. Antiochus of Syracuse (5th c. B.C.E.).

able. Hence it may be for the lawmaker to determine what kind of pleasure and how much of each kind he will permit.

The plastic arts in particular—aside from the inevitable influence they exert on the character of a nation—have an effect that demands close supervision by the law. If beautiful men created beautiful statues, these statues in turn affected the men, and thus the state owed thanks also to beautiful statues for beautiful men. (With us the highly susceptible imagination of mothers seems to express itself only in producing monsters.)

From this point of view I believe I can find some truth in some of the ancient tales which are generally rejected as outright lies. The mothers of Aristomenes, Aristodamas, Alexander the Great, Scipio, Augustus, and Galerius[3] all dreamed during pregnancy that they had relations with a serpent. The serpent was a symbol of divinity, and the beautiful statues and paintings depicting Bacchus, Apollo, Mercury, or Hercules[4] were seldom without one. Those honest mothers had feasted their eyes on the god during the day, and their confused dreams recalled the image of the reptile. Thus I save the dream and abandon the interpretation born of the pride of their sons and the impudence of the flatterer. For there must be some reason why the adulterous fantasy was always a serpent.

But I am digressing. I wanted simply to establish that among the ancients beauty was the supreme law of the visual arts. Once this has been established, it necessarily follows that whatever else these arts may include must give way completely if not compatible with beauty, and, if compatible, must at least be subordinate to it.

Let us consider expression. There are passions and degrees of passion which are expressed by the most hideous contortions of the face and which throw the whole body into such unnatural positions as to lose all the beautiful contours of its natural state. The ancient artists either refrained from depicting such emotions or reduced them to a degree where it is possible to show them with a certain measure of beauty.

* * *

If we apply this now to the Laocoön, the principle which I am seeking becomes apparent. The master strove to attain the highest beauty possible under the given condition of physical pain. The demands of beauty could not be reconciled with the pain in all its disfiguring violence, so it had to be reduced. The scream had to be softened to a sigh, not because screaming betrays an ignoble soul, but because it distorts the features in a disgusting manner. Simply imagine Laocöon's mouth forced wide open, and then judge! Imagine him screaming, and then look! From a form which inspired pity because it possessed beauty and pain at the same time, it has now become an ugly, repulsive figure from which we gladly turn away. For the sight of pain provokes distress; however, the distress should be transformed, through beauty, into the tender feeling of pity.

3. This list mixes the legendary (the first 2 are Greek heroes) and the historical—the great general Alexander of Macedonia (356–323 B.C.E.), the Roman general Scipio Africanus (236–184/83 B.C.E.), and the Roman emperors Augustus (63 B.C.E.–14 C.E.) and Galerius (ca. 250–ca. 311 C.E.).

4. The Roman name for Heracles, the greatest of the Greek heroes. Bacchus: Greek and Roman god of wine and a name of Dionysus, whose cult was orgiastic. Apollo: Greek and Roman god of music, healing, and prophecy. Mercury: Roman messenger of the gods.

The wide-open mouth, aside from the fact that the rest of the face is thereby twisted and distorted in an unnatural and loathsome manner, becomes in painting a mere spot and in sculpture a cavity, with most repulsive effect.

* * *

From *Chapter Three*

As I have already said, art has been given a far wider scope in modern times. It is claimed that representation in the arts covers all of visible nature, of which the beautiful is but a small part. Truth and expression are art's first law, and as nature herself is ever ready to sacrifice beauty for the sake of higher aims, so must the artist subordinate it to his general purpose and pursue it no farther than truth and expression permit. It is enough that truth and expression transform the ugliest aspects of nature into artistic beauty.

But even if we were willing to leave these ideas for the moment unchallenged as to their value, we would still have to consider, quite independently of these ideas, why the artist must nevertheless set certain restraints upon expression and never present an action at its climax.

The single moment of time to which art must confine itself by virtue of its material limitations will lead us, I believe, to such considerations.

If the artist can never make use of more than a single moment in ever-changing nature, and if the painter in particular can use this moment only with reference to a single vantage point, while the works of both painter and sculptor are created not merely to be given a glance but to be contemplated—contemplated repeatedly and at length—then it is evident that this single moment and the point from which it is viewed cannot be chosen with too great a regard for its effect. But only that which gives free rein to the imagination is effective.[5] The more we see, the more we must be able to imagine. And the more we add in our imaginations, the more we must think we see. In the full course of an emotion, no point is less suitable for this than its climax. There is nothing beyond this, and to present the utmost to the eye is to bind the wings of fancy and compel it, since it cannot soar above the impression made on the senses, to concern itself with weaker images, shunning the visible fullness already represented as a limit beyond which it cannot go. Thus, if Laocoön sighs, the imagination can hear him cry out; but if he cries out, it can neither go one step higher nor one step lower than this representation without seeing him in a more tolerable and hence less interesting condition. One either hears him merely moaning or else sees him dead.

Furthermore, this single moment, if it is to receive immutable permanence from art, must express nothing transitory. According to our notions, there are phenomena, which we conceive as being essentially sudden in their beginning and end and which can be what they are only for a brief moment. However, the prolongation of such phenomena in art, whether agreeable or otherwise, gives them such an unnatural appearance that they make a weaker impression the more often we look at them, until they finally

5. In German, *fruchtbar*: "fruitful."

fill us with disgust or horror. La Mettrie,[6] who had himself portrayed in painting and engraving as a second Democritus, seems to be laughing only the first few times we look at him. Look at him more often and the philosopher turns into a fop. His laugh becomes a grin. The same holds true for screaming. The violent pain which extorts the scream either soon subsides or else destroys the sufferer. When a man of firmness and endurance cries out he does not do so unceasingly, and it is only the seeming perpetuity of such cries when represented in art that turns them into effeminate helplessness or childish petulance. This, at least, the artist of the Laocoön had to avoid, even if screaming had not been detrimental to beauty, and if his art had been allowed to express suffering without beauty.

Among the ancient painters Timomachus[7] seems to have been the one most fond of subjects that display extreme passion. His raving Ajax and his infanticide Medea[8] were famous paintings, but from the descriptions we have of them it is clear that he thoroughly understood and was able to combine two things: that point or moment which the beholder not so much sees as adds in his imagination, and that appearance which does not seem so transitory as to become displeasing through its perpetuation in art. Timomachus did not represent Medea at the moment when she was actually murdering her children, but a few moments before, when a mother's love was still struggling with her vengefulness. We can foresee the outcome of this struggle; we tremble in anticipation of seeing Medea as simply cruel, and our imagination takes us far beyond what the painter could have shown us in this terrible moment. But for this very reason we are not offended at Medea's perpetual indecision, as it is represented in art, but wish it could have remained that way in reality. We wish that the duel of passions had never been decided, or at least had continued long enough for time and reflection to overcome rage and secure the victory for maternal feelings. This wisdom on the part of Timomachus has earned him lavish and frequent praise and raised him far above another, unknown painter who was foolish enough to depict Medea at the height of her rage, thus endowing her brief instant of madness with a permanence that is an affront to all nature.

* * *

From *Chapter Nine*

If we wish to compare the painter and the poet in particular instances, we must first know whether they both enjoyed complete freedom; whether, that is to say, they could work toward producing the greatest possible effect in their respective arts without any external constraint.

6. Julien Offroy de La Mettrie (1709–1751), French physician and philosopher, whose *L'Homme machine* (1747) made him the most notorious materialist of his day. The Greek Democritus (ca. 460–ca. 370 B.C.E.) was also a materialist (he argued that everything, including the soul, is composed of atoms); he was known as the "laughing philosopher," perhaps because he believed that individuals were responsible for their own well-being.

7. Painter of Byzantium (1st c. B.C.E.) mentioned by Pliny the Elder (35.11).

8. A sorceress from Colchis who took revenge on her husband Jason (for deserting her to marry a king's daughter) by killing his (and her) two children. Ajax: one of the greatest Greek warriors at Troy; driven mad by Athena, he killed animals believing that he was attacking the Greek leaders who had refused to give him the armor of the dead Achilles (when he regained his senses, he killed himself). Both figures were often treated in art and tragedies.

Religion often represented just such an external constraint on the classical artist. His work, destined for worship and devotion, could not always be as perfect as it would have been if he had had as his sole aim the pleasure of his spectators. But superstition overloaded the gods with symbols, and the most beautiful gods were not always honored as such.

In the temple at Lemnos, from which the pious Hypsipyle[9] rescued her father in the disguise of the god, Bacchus was represented with horns. No doubt he appeared this way in all his temples since the horns were symbolic and one of his necessary attributes. Only the free artist, who did not have to create his Bacchus for some temple, omitted this symbol; and if we find none with horns among the extant statues of him, we may perhaps take this as proof that none of them belongs among the consecrated ones under which he was actually worshiped. Besides this, it is highly probable that the wrath of pious iconoclasts during the first centuries of Christianity fell in great part on these latter. Only seldom did they spare a work of art, because it had not been desecrated by adoration.

However, since pieces of both kinds are to be found among the excavated objects of antiquity, I should prefer that only those be called works of art in which the artist had occasion to show himself as such and in which beauty was his first and ultimate aim. None of the others, which betray too obvious traces of religious conventions, deserves this name because in their case the artist did not create for art's sake,[1] but his art was merely a handmaid of religion, which stressed meaning more than beauty in the material subjects it allotted to art for execution. By this I do not mean to say that religion has not also frequently sacrificed meaning for beauty, or, out of consideration for art and the more refined taste of the period, has ceased to emphasize it to such a degree that beauty alone would seem to be the sole object.

* * *

From *Chapter Ten*

I comment on an expression of astonishment in Spence[2] which clearly shows how little thought he must have given to the limits of poetry and painting. "As to the muses in general," he says, "it is strange that the poets are so brief in describing them, far briefer in fact than might be expected for goddesses to whom they are so greatly indebted."[3]

What can this mean but that he is amazed that when poets speak of the muses they do not use the mute language of painters? To the poets Urania is the muse of astronomy; we recognize her office from her name and her functions. The artist, in order to make her recognizable, must show her pointing with a wand to a celestial globe. The wand, the globe, and the pointing position are his letters, from which he lets us spell out the name Urania. But when the poet wishes to say that Urania had foreseen his death long ago in the stars,

9. Daughter of King Thoas, the son of Dionysus; the women of the island of Lemnos killed all the other men, who had left their wives for Thracian women.

1. Possibly the first use of the expression "art for art's sake."

2. Joseph Spence (1699–1768), an Oxford professor whose *Polymetis* (1747), written in dialogues, is one of the targets of Lessing's criticism.

3. *Polymetis,* Dialogue VIII, p. 91 [Lessing's note]. "Muses": in Greek mythology, the 9 daughters of memory who preside over the arts and all intellectual pursuits.

Ipsa diu positis lethum praedixerat astris Uranie . . .[4]

why should he, out of respect for the painter, add: "Urania, her wand in hand, the celestial globe before her"? It is as though a man who can and may speak were at the same time using those signs which the mutes in the Turkish seraglio[5] invented among themselves for lack of a voice.

Spence again expresses the same astonishment when speaking of the moral beings, those divinities whom the ancients made preside over the virtues and the conduct of human life. "It should be remarked," he says, "that the Roman poets have far less to say about the best of these moral beings than one would expect. On this point the artists are much more complete, and whoever wants to know what appearance each of them made need only look at the coins of the Roman emperors. The poets, to be sure, often speak of these beings as persons, but of their attributes, their clothing and their appearance in general they have little to say."[6]

When the poet personifies abstractions, he characterizes them sufficiently by their names and the actions he has them perform.

The artist lacks these means and must therefore add to his personified abstractions symbols by which they may be recognized. But because these symbols are something different and mean something different, they make the figures allegorical.

The female figure with a bridle in her hand; another leaning against a pillar—these are, in art, allegorical figures. For the poet, however, Moderation and Constancy are not allegorical beings but simply personified abstractions.

Necessity invented these symbols for the artist, for only through them can he make it understood what this or that figure is supposed to represent. But why should the poet have forced upon him what the artist had to accept of necessity; a necessity which he himself has no part of?

The very thing which so surprised Spence should be prescribed to poets as a general law. They must not convert the necessities of painting into a part of their own wealth. Nor must they regard the means that art has invented in order to keep up with poetry as perfections which should give them reason for envy. When the artist adorns a figure with symbols, he raises what was a mere figure to a higher being; but if the poet employs these artistic trimmings, he turns that higher being into a puppet.

* * *

Chapter Twelve

Homer[7] treats of two kinds of beings and actions, visible and invisible. This distinction cannot be made in painting, where everything is visible and visible in but one way. Hence, when Count Caylus[8] makes the pictures of invisible actions follow the visible ones in an unbroken sequence, and when in his paintings showing mixed actions, i.e., those in which both visible and invis-

4. Statius, *Thebaid* 8.551 [Lessing's note]; the preceding clause translates the Latin. Statius (ca. 46–96 C.E.), Roman poet.

5. The harem, women's quarters overseen at courts by eunuchs and, in Lessing's account, mutes.

6. *Polymetis*, Dialogue X, pp. 137, 139 [Lessing's note].

7. Greek epic poet (ca. 8th c. B.C.E.) to whom the *Iliad* and the *Odyssey* are attributed.

8. Philippe de Tubières (1692–1765), French art critic; his book of criticism *Scenes from Homer's Iliad and Odyssey and Virgil's Aeneid* (1757) is the third of Lessing's targets.

ible beings take part, he does not and perhaps cannot specify how the latter (which only we who look at the picture are supposed to discover in it) are to be introduced so that the figures in the painting do not see them (or at least appear not to see them)—when Count Caylus does this, I say, the series as a whole as well as a number of single pictures necessarily become extremely confused, incomprehensible, and self-contradictory.

Still, with the book before us it would be possible to remedy this fault. The worst of it is that when painting erases the distinction between visible and invisible beings it simultaneously destroys all those characteristic features by which this latter, higher order is raised above the lower one.

For example, when the gods, who are divided as to the fate of the Trojans, finally come to blows, the entire battle is represented in the poem as being invisible.[9] This invisibility gives the imagination free rein to enlarge the scene and envisage the persons and actions of the gods on a grander scale than the measure of ordinary man. But painting must adopt a visible scene, whose various indispensable parts become the scale for the figures participating in it—a scale which the eye has ready at hand and whose lack of proportion to the higher beings makes them appear monstrous on the artist's canvas.

Minerva, whom Mars[1] ventures to attack first in this battle, steps back and with her mighty hand seizes a large, black, rough stone which the united strength of men had rolled there for a landmark in times past:

> ἣ δ' ἀναχασσαμένη λίθον εἵλετο χειρὶ παχείῃ
> κείμενον ἐν πεδίῳ, μέλανα, τρηχύν τε μέγαν τε,
> τόν ῥ' ἄνδρες πρότεροι θέσαν ἔμμεναι οὖρον αρούρης·[2]

In order to form a proper estimate of the size of this stone we should remember that Homer makes his heroes twice as strong as the strongest men of his own time but tells us that these again were surpassed in strength by the men whom Nestor[3] knew in his youth. Now I ask, if Minerva hurls a stone which no one man, not even one from Nestor's youth, could set up as a landmark—if Minerva hurls such a stone at Mars, of what stature is the goddess supposed to be? If her stature is in proportion to the size of the stone, then the element of the marvelous disappears. A man three times my size naturally ought to be able to hurl a stone three times as large as I can. But if the stature of the goddess is not in proportion to the size of the stone, an improbability for the eye arises in the painting whose offensiveness is not removed by the cold calculation that a goddess must possess superhuman strength. Wherever I see a greater effect, I also expect to see a greater cause.

And Mars, thrown to the ground by this mighty stone,

> ἑπτὰ δ' ἐπέσχε πέλεθρα πεσὼν,[4]

covered seven acres of land. It is impossible for the painter to give the god this extraordinary size, and yet if he does not do so, it is no longer Mars—or at least not the Homeric Mars—who is lying on the ground, but a common warrior.

9. *Iliad* 21.385 [Lessing's note].
1. Ares, Greek god of war. Minerva: Athena, Greek goddess of war and wisdom.
2. But Athene giving back caught up in her heavy hand a stone / that lay in the plain, black and rugged and huge, one which men / of a former time had set there as boundary mark of the cornfield; *Iliad* 21.403–5 (trans. Richmond Lattimore) [translator's note]. "Corn" here refers to grain.
3. The oldest of the Greek generals who fought at Troy.
4. Falling, he covered seven *plethra*; *Iliad* 21.407. One *plethron* was 10,000 square feet.

Longinus[5] says that it seemed to him now and then as though Homer raised his men to gods and reduced his gods to men. Painting carries out this reduction. In it everything which in the poem raises the gods above godlike human creatures vanishes altogether. Size, strength, and swiftness—qualities which Homer always has in store for his gods in a higher and more extraordinary degree than that bestowed on his finest heroes—must in the painting sink to the common level of humanity. Jupiter and Agamemnon, Apollo and Achilles, Ajax and Mars[6] all become exactly the same kind of beings, recognizable by nothing more than their outward conventional symbols.

The means which painting uses to convey to us that this or that object must be thought of as invisible is a thin cloud veiling the side of the object that is turned toward the other persons in the pictures. It appears that this cloud was borrowed from Homer, for when in the tumult of battle one of the more important heroes runs into great danger, from which only a divine power can save him, the poet has the protecting divinity envelop him in a thick cloud, or in darkness, and so carry him away, as Paris is carried off by Venus, or Idaeus by Neptune, or Hector by Apollo.[7] And Caylus never fails to recommend heartily this mist or cloud to the artist when he outlines for him a painting of such occurrences. And yet who can fail to see that concealment by cloud or night is, for the poet, nothing more than a poetic expression for rendering a thing invisible? For that reason it has always been a source of surprise to me to see this poetic expression actually used and a real cloud introduced in the painting, behind which the hero stands hidden from his enemy as behind a screen. That was not what the poet intended. It exceeds the limits of painting, for in this case the cloud is a true hieroglyphic, a mere symbol, which does not render the rescued hero invisible, but says to the spectators: you must imagine to yourselves that he is invisible. It is no better than the scrolls that issue from the mouths of figures in old Gothic paintings.

It is true that when Apollo rescues Hector from Achilles, Homer has the latter make three further thrusts with his spear into the thick mist (τρὶς δ' ἠέρα τύψε βαθεῖαν).[8] But in the language of poetry this means only that Achilles was so enraged that he made the three additional thrusts before realizing that his enemy was no longer before him. Achilles did not see an actual mist, and the power of the gods to render invisible did not lie in any mist, but in their ability to bear the object away swiftly. It was only to show that this abduction took place too quickly for the human eye to follow the disappearing body that the poet first conceals it in a mist or cloud. And it was not because a cloud appeared in place of the abducted body, but because we think of that which is wrapped in mist as being invisible. Accordingly, Homer sometimes inverts the case, and instead of rendering the object invisible, causes the subject to be struck blind. For example, Neptune blinds Achilles when he rescues Aeneas from his murderous hands by suddenly

5. The name given the 1st century C.E. author of *On Sublimity* (see above); the reference is to section 7.

6. Lessing pairs each god with an appropriate man. Jupiter: Zeus, king of the Gods. Agamemnon: king of Mycenae and leader of the Greeks at Troy. Achilles: the greatest Greek warrior at Troy and the focus of the *Iliad*.

7. All episodes from the *Iliad* (3.380–82, 5.23, 20.443–44). Paris: prince of Troy who was awarded the most beautiful woman in the world by Aphrodite (Venus), goddess of love, for naming her the most beautiful of 3 goddess. Idaeus: son of a Trojan priest of Hephaestus who is in fact saved by Hephaestus, the god of the forge, and not Poseidon (Neptune), the god of the sea. Hector: oldest prince of Troy and the greatest of the Trojan warriors (Apollo favored the Trojans).

8. *Iliad* 20.446 [Lessing's note].

snatching him out of the thick of the fight and placing him in the rear.[9] Actually, however, Achilles' eyes are no more blinded than, in the former example, the abducted heroes are wrapped in a cloud. The poet merely makes this or that addition in order to make more palpable to our senses that extreme rapidity of abduction which we call disappearance.

However, painters have appropriated the Homeric mist not only in those cases where Homer himself used it, or would have used it (namely, in rendering persons invisible or causing them to disappear), but in every instance where the spectator is supposed to see something in the painting which the characters themselves, or some of them, cannot see. Minerva became visible to Achilles alone when she prevented him from assaulting Agamemnon.[1] I know of no other way to express this, says Caylus, than by concealing her from the rest of the council by a cloud. But this is in complete violation of the spirit of the poet! Invisibility is the natural condition of his gods; no blindfolding, no interruption of the rays of light is needed to prevent them from being seen; but an enlightenment, an increased power of mortal vision is required, if they are intended to be seen. Thus it is not only that in painting the cloud is an arbitrary and not a natural sign; but this arbitrary sign does not even possess the definite distinctness which it could have as such, for it is used both to render the visible invisible and the invisible visible.

Chapter Fifteen

As experience shows, the poet can raise to this degree of illusion the representation of objects other than those that are visible. Consequently, whole categories of pictures which the poet claims as his own must necessarily be beyond the reach of the artist. Dryden's *Song for St. Cecelia's Day*[2] is full of musical pictures which leave the painter's brush idle. But I do not want to stray too far from my subject with such examples, from which in the final analysis we learn little more than that colors are not sounds and ears not eyes.[3]

I will confine myself rather to the consideration of pictures of visible objects only, which are common to both poet and painter. Why is it that a number of poetic pictures of this kind are of no use to the painter and, conversely, many real pictures lose most of their effect when treated by the poet? Example may guide me here. I repeat: the picture of Pandarus[4] in the fourth book of the *Iliad* is one of the most elaborate and graphic in all of Homer. From the seizing of the bow to the flight of the arrow every moment is painted, and all these moments follow in such close succession and yet are so distinct, one from the other, that if we did not know how a bow should be handled, we would be able to learn it from this description alone. Pandarus takes out his bow, strings it, opens the quiver, chooses an unused, well-feathered arrow, adjusts the arrow's notch to the string and draws

9. *Iliad*, 20.321–29 [Lessing's note]. Aeneas: Trojan ally, a son of Aphrodite and later the founder of the colony that became Rome.
1. *Iliad* 1.194–98.
2. Also called *Alexander's Feast*, this ode was written in 1687 and set to music by Handel in 1739 [translator's note]. JOHN DRYDEN (1631–1700), English poet, dramatist, and critic.
3. An allusion to a quotation in Caylus from Jean de la Fontaine (1621–1695), French author of fables.
4. An ally of the Trojans who broke the truce between the Greeks and Trojans in the passage described (*Iliad* 4.105–26).

both back; the string is brought close to the breast, the metal point of the arrow comes close to the bow, the great round bow springs open again with a clang, the string vibrates, and the arrow has sped away, flying eagerly toward its mark.

Caylus cannot have overlooked this splendid picture. What, then, did he find there to make him consider it unable to afford material to his artists? And why was it that the council of deliberating and drinking gods seemed to him better suited for his purpose? The subjects are visible in both cases, and what more than visible subjects does the painter need to fill his canvas?

The difficulty must be this: although both subjects, being visible, are equally suitable for actual painting, there is still this essential difference between them: in the one case the action is visible and progressive, its different parts occurring one after the other in a sequence of time, and in the other the action is visible and stationary, its different parts developing in co-existence in space. But if painting, by virtue of its symbols or means of imitation, which it can combine in space only, must renounce the element of time entirely, progressive actions, by the very fact that they are progressive, cannot be considered to belong among its subjects. Painting must be content with coexistent actions or with mere bodies which, by their position, permit us to conjecture an action. Poetry, on the other hand. . . .

From *Chapter Sixteen*

But I shall attempt now to derive the matter from its first principles.

I reason thus: if it is true that in its imitations painting uses completely different means or signs than does poetry, namely figures and colors in space rather than articulated sounds in time, and if these signs must indisputably bear a suitable relation to the thing signified, then signs existing in space can express only objects whose wholes or parts coexist, while signs that follow one another can express only objects whose wholes or parts are consecutive.

Objects or parts of objects which exist in space are called bodies. Accordingly, bodies with their visible properties are the true subjects of painting.

Objects or parts of objects which follow one another are called actions. Accordingly, actions are the true subjects of poetry.

However, bodies do not exist in space only, but also in time. They persist in time, and in each moment of their duration they may assume a different appearance or stand in a different combination. Each of these momentary appearances and combinations is the result of a preceding one and can be the cause of a subsequent one, which means that it can be, as it were, the center of an action. Consequently, painting too can imitate actions, but only by suggestion through bodies.

On the other hand, actions cannot exist independently, but must be joined to certain beings or things. Insofar as these beings or things are bodies, or are treated as such, poetry also depicts bodies, but only by suggestion through actions.

Painting can use only a single moment of an action in its coexisting compositions and must therefore choose the one which is most suggestive[5] and

5. In German, *den prägnantesten wählen*: "choose the most pregnant (with meaning)."

from which the preceding and succeeding actions are most easily comprehensible.

Similarly, poetry in its progressive imitations can use only one single property of a body. It must therefore choose that one which awakens the most vivid image of the body, looked at from the point of view under which poetry can best use it. From this comes the rule concerning the harmony of descriptive adjectives and economy in description of physical objects.

I should put little faith in this dry chain of reasoning did I not find it completely confirmed by the procedure of Homer, or rather if it had not been just this procedure that led me to my conclusions. Only on these principles can the grand style of the Greek be defined and explained, and only thus can the proper position be assigned to the opposite style of so many modern poets, who attempt to rival the painter at a point where they must necessarily be surpassed by him.

I find that Homer represents nothing but progressive actions. He depicts bodies and single objects only when they contribute toward these actions, and then only by a single trait. No wonder, then, that where Homer paints, the artist finds little or nothing to do himself; and no wonder that his harvest can be found only where the story assembles a number of beautiful bodies in beautiful positions and in a setting favorable to art, however sparingly the poet himself may paint these bodies, these positions, and this setting. If we go through the whole series of paintings as Caylus proposes them, one by one, we find that each is a proof of this remark.

* * *

From *Chapter Seventeen*

But the objection will be raised that the symbols of poetry are not only successive but are also arbitrary; and, as arbitrary symbols, they are of course able to represent bodies as they exist in space. Examples of this might be taken from Homer himself. We need only to recall his shield of Achilles[6] to have the most decisive instance of how discursively and yet at the same time poetically a single object may be described by presenting its coexistent parts.

I shall reply to this twofold objection. I call it twofold because a correct deduction must hold good even without examples; and, conversely, an example from Homer is of importance to me even when I am unable to justify it by means of deduction.

It is true that since the symbols of speech are arbitrary, the parts of a body may, through speech, be made to follow one another just as readily as they exist side by side in nature. But this is a peculiarity of speech and its signs in general and not as they serve the aims of poetry. The poet does not want merely to be intelligible, nor is he content—as is the prose writer—with simply presenting his image clearly and concisely. He wants rather to make the ideas he awakens in us so vivid that at that moment we believe that we feel the real impressions which the objects of these ideas would produce on us. In this moment of illusion we should cease to be conscious of the means which the poet uses for this purpose, that is, his words. This

6. Forged by the god Hephaestus to replace the armor borrowed by his friend Patroclus, whom Hector killed; its intricate work is described at length (*Iliad* 18.478–608).

was the substance of the definition of a poetical painting given above. But the poet is always supposed to paint, and we shall now see how far bodies with their coexistent parts adapt themselves to this painting.

* * *

From *Chapter Eighteen*

And yet should Homer himself have lapsed into this lifeless description of material objects? I do hope that there are but few passages which one can find to support this; and I feel certain that these few passages are of such a nature as to confirm the rule to which they seem to be the exception.

It remains true that succession of time is the province of the poet just as space is that of the painter.

It is an intrusion of the painter into the domain of the poet, which good taste can never sanction, when the painter combines in one and the same picture two points necessarily separate in time, as does Fra Mazzuoli[7] when he introduces the rape of the Sabine women[8] and the reconciliation effected by them between their husbands and relations, or as Titian[9] does when he presents the entire history of the prodigal son, his dissolute life, his misery, and his repentance.

It is an intrusion of the poet into the domain of the painter and a squandering of much imagination to no purpose when, in order to give the reader an idea of the whole, the poet enumerates one by one several parts or things which I must necessarily survey at one glance in nature if they are to give the effect of a whole.

But as two equitable and friendly neighbors do not permit the one to take unbecoming liberties in the heart of the other's domain, yet on their extreme frontiers practice a mutual forbearance by which both sides make peaceful compensation for those slight aggressions which, in haste and from force of circumstance, the one finds himself compelled to make on the other's privilege: so also with painting and poetry.

To support this I will not cite the fact that in great historical paintings the single moment is always somewhat extended, and that perhaps there is not a single work comprising a wealth of figures in which each one of them is in exactly that motion and position it should be in at the moment of the main action; some are represented in the attitude of a somewhat earlier, others in that of a somewhat later moment. This is a liberty which the master must justify by certain refinements in the arrangement—in the way he uses his figures and places them closer to or more distant from the main action—which permits them to take a more or less momentary part in what is going on. I shall merely make use of a remark made by Mengs concerning Raphael's[1] drapery. "In his paintings," he says, "there is a reason for every fold,

7. Francesco Mazzuoli (1503–1540), Italian painter.

8. A famous legend of early Rome. Romulus, its mythical founder, gained wives for the men he had gathered to his new city by inviting neighboring peoples to a festival and seizing the women. The war that followed between Romans and Sabines ended when the Sabine women thrust themselves onto the battlefield between their fathers and their new husbands, leading to peace and the union of the foes under a single government.

9. Tiziano Vecelli (1488/90–1576), Italian painter. For the story of the prodigal son, see Luke 15.11–32.

1. Raffaello Santi (1483–1520), Italian painter. Anton Raphael Mengs (1728–1779), German painter and art critic; a close friend of Winckelmann.

whether it be because of its own weight or because of the movement of the limbs. Sometimes we can tell from them how they were before, and Raphael even tried to attach significance to this. We can see from the folds whether an arm or a leg was in a backward or forward position prior to its movement; whether the limb had moved or is moving from contraction to extension, or whether it had been extended and is now contracted."[2] It is indisputable that in this case the artist is combining two different moments into one. For since that part of the drapery which lies on the foot immediately follows it in its forward motion—unless the drapery be of very stiff material and hence entirely unsuitable for painting—there is no moment in which the garment can form any other fold whatsoever except that which the actual position of the limb requires. However, if it is permitted to form a different fold, then the drapery is represented at the moment preceding and the limb at the following. Nevertheless, who would be so particular with the artist who finds it advantageous to show us these two moments at the same time? Who would not praise him rather for having had the understanding and the courage to commit such a minor error for the sake of obtaining greater perfection of expression?

The poet deserves the same forbearance. His progressive imitation actually allows him to allude to only one side, only one characteristic of his material objects at one time. But when the happy structure of his language permits him to do this in a single word, why should he not be allowed to add a second word now and then? And why not even a third, if it is worth the trouble? Or even a fourth? I have already said that for Homer a ship is only a black ship, or a hollow ship, or a swift ship, or at the most a well-manned black ship. This is to be understood of his style in general. Here and there we find a passage in which he adds a third descriptive epithet. Καμπύλα κύκλα, χάλκεα, ὀκτάκνημα[3] round, bronze, eight-spoked wheels. And also a fourth: ἀσπίδα πάντοσ' ἐΐσην, καλὴν, χαλκείην, ἐξήλατον,[4] a uniformly smooth, beautiful, embossed bronze shield. Who would censure him for this? Who would not rather thank him for this little extravagance when he feels what a good effect it can have in some few suitable passages?

But I shall not allow the particular justification of either poet or painter to be based on the above-mentioned analogy of the two friendly neighbors. A mere analogy neither proves nor justifies anything. The following consideration must be their real justification: just as in the painter's art two different moments border so closely on one another that we can, without hesitation, accept them as one, so in the poet's work do the several features representing the various parts and properties in space follow one another in such rapid succession that we believe we hear them all at once.

It is in this, I say, that the excellence of Homer's language aids him unusually well. It not only allows him the greatest possible freedom in the accumulation and combination of epithets, but it finds such a happy arrangement for these accumulated adjectives that the awkward suspension of their noun disappears. Modern languages are lacking entirely in one or more of these advantages. For example, the French must paraphrase the καμπύλα κύκλα, χάλκεα, ὀκτάκνημα with "the round wheels, which were of bronze and had

2. *Thoughts about Beauty and Taste in Painting* [1771], p. 69 [Lessing's note].

3. *Iliad* 5.722–23.

4. *Iliad* 12.294–95.

eight spokes." They give the meaning but destroy the picture. Yet the picture is everything here and the meaning nothing; and without the former the latter turns the liveliest of poets into a tiresome bore, a fate which has often befallen our good Homer under the pen of the conscientious Madame Dacier.[5] The German language, on the other hand, can usually translate Homer's epithets with equally short equivalent adjectives, although it is unable to imitate the advantageous arrangement of Greek. We can say, to be sure, *die runden, ehernen, achtspeichigten* . . . [the round, brazen, eight-spoked], but *Räder* [wheels] drags behind. Who does not feel that three different predicates, before we learn the subject, can produce only an indistinct and confused picture? The Greek combines the subject and the first predicate, and leaves the others to follow. He says, "round wheels, brazen, eight-spoked." And so we know immediately what he is speaking of. In conformity with the natural order of thought, we first become acquainted with the thing itself and then with its accidents. Our [German] language does not enjoy this advantage. Or should I say, it does enjoy it but can seldom make use of it without ambiguity? Both amount to the same thing. For if we place the adjectives after the subject, they must stand *in statu absoluto*, i.e., in uninflected form. Hence, we must say *runde Räder, ehern und achtspeichigt* (round wheels, brazen and eight-spoked). However, in this *statu* the German adjectives are identical with the German adverbs, and if we take them as such with the next verb that is predicated of the subject, they not infrequently produce a completely false, and in any case a very uncertain meaning.

But I am lingering over trifles and it may appear as if I were going to forget the shield, the shield of Achilles, that is—the famous picture which more than anything else caused Homer to be considered by the ancients a master of painting.[6] A shield, it will be said, is a single material object which the poet cannot present by describing its coexistent parts. And yet Homer, in more than a hundred splendid verses, has described this shield, its material, its form, all the figures which filled its enormous surface, so exactly and in such detail that it was not difficult for modern artists to produce a drawing of it exact in every part.

My answer to this particular objection is that I have already answered it. Homer does not paint the shield as finished and complete, but as a shield that is being made. Thus, here too he has made use of that admirable artistic device: transforming what is coexistent in his subject into what is consecutive, and thereby making the living picture of an action out of the tedious painting of an object. We do not see the shield, but the divine master as he is making it. He steps up to the anvil with hammer and tongs, and after he has forged the plates out of the rough, the pictures which he destines for the shield's ornamentation rise before our eyes out of the bronze, one after the other, beneath the finer blows of his hammer. We do not lose sight of him until all is finished. Now the shield is complete, and we marvel at the work. But it is the believing wonder of the eyewitness who has seen it forged.

* * *

5. Anne Lefèvre Dacier (ca. 1650–1720), well-known French translator of Greek and Latin works, including both the *Iliad* (1699) and the *Odyssey* (1708).

6. Dionysius Halicarnassus, *Vita Homeri*, in Thomas Gale, *Opuscula mythologica* [1671], p. 401 [Lessing's note].

From *Chapter Twenty-One*

We might ask whether poetry does not lose too much when we take from her all depictions of physical beauty? But who would do this? If we dissuade her from taking one particular way to attain such pictures, and from following confusedly the footsteps of a sister art without ever reaching the same goal, do we thereby exclude her from every other path where art in turn must see poetry take the lead?

The same Homer, who so assiduously refrains from detailed descriptions of physical beauties, and from whom we scarcely learn in passing that Helen had white arms and beautiful hair,[7] nevertheless knows how to convey to us an idea of her beauty which far surpasses anything art is able to accomplish toward that end. Let us recall the passage where Helen steps before an assembly of Trojan elders. The venerable old men see her, and one says to the other:

οὐ νέμεσις Τρῶας καὶ ἐϋκνήμιδας Ἀχαιοὺς
τοιῇδ' ἀμφὶ γυναικὶ πολὺν χρόνον ἄλγεα πάσχειν·
αἰνῶς ἀθανάτῃσι θεῇς εἰς ὦπα ἔοικεν·[8]

What can convey a more vivid idea of beauty than to let cold old age acknowledge that she is indeed worth the war which had cost so much blood and so many tears?

What Homer could not describe in all its various parts he makes us recognize by its effect. Paint for us, you poets, the pleasure, the affection, the love and delight which beauty brings, and you have painted beauty itself.

* * *

1766

7. *Iliad* 3.329; "white arms" 121 [Lessing's note]. Helen: in Greek mythology, daughter of Zeus and Leda and wife of Menelaus; her abduction by Paris led to the Trojan War.
8. *Iliad* 3.156–58 [Lessing's note]. "Surely there is no blame on Trojans and strong-greaved Achaians / if for long time they suffer hardship for a woman like this one. / Terrible is the likeness of her face to immortal goddesses" (trans. Lattimore).

FRIEDRICH VON SCHILLER
1759–1805

Friedrich von Schiller was one of the foremost German writers of the late eighteenth and early nineteenth centuries. Perhaps best known for his dramas, he was also an editor, a journalist, a writer of vivid letters (especially to Goethe and to the German philologist and diplomat Wilhelm von Humboldt), a historian, a translator of Euripides, Shakespeare, and Racine, a poet, and a literary theorist.

Born in Marbach, Germany, Schiller became an army medical officer in Stuttgart in 1780. But soon he began seriously working on poetry and drama, choosing a literary career. He published *Die Räuber* (1781, *The Robbers*) at his own expense, and its performance in 1782 was a landmark in German theatrical history. Romantic writers in England, especially SAMUEL TAYLOR COLERIDGE and the critic William

Hazlitt, admired *The Robbers* for its presentation of the themes of liberty, abuse of power, and authoritarianism.

On the recommendation of Goethe, Schiller was named professor of history at the University of Jena in 1789, and in 1797–98 they worked together on a collection of ballads, a collaboration contemporaneous with that of WILLIAM WORDSWORTH and Coleridge in England.

Many readers admire Schiller's lyrics and ballads, though his long didactic poems (e.g., *The Artists,* 1789, on the power of art to civilize and bring compassion to mankind) are more famous; best known to English-speaking audiences is his "Ode to Joy," which Beethoven set to music in his monumental Ninth Symphony.

In several influential texts on literary and dramatic theory, aesthetics, and the sublime, Schiller explored the relations between art, politics, and history. He looked primarily to IMMANUEL KANT's *Critique of Judgment* (1790; see above), and his development of and response to Kant's ideas later influenced the literary theory of the German Romantic writers and of Coleridge.

In *On the Aesthetic Education of Man* (1795), Schiller was writing in the immediate aftermath of the French regicide and Reign of Terror, during which thousands were executed. The sufferings and shocks of the French Revolution inform his inquiry into the role of art: how can humankind achieve freedom when the failure of political solutions is so graphically displayed? In this text, which grew from a series of actual letters to a benefactor (our selection contains three letters), Schiller explains that freedom can occur only through education, and the key to education is the experience of beauty—the elevation of mind and soul through art. Beauty allows persons to ennoble their nature; each of us can become a "beautiful soul" (*schöne Seele*) harmonizing duty and inclination through art, which Schiller associates with the "play impulse" or "play drive" that makes reconciliation and transcendence possible.

Schiller's *On Naive and Reflective Poetry* (1795–96), a companion piece, contrasts the ancients and the moderns, their different attitudes toward nature, and their performances in poetry. (Often the title's second adjective is given as "sentimental," but this term does not adequately translate *sentimentalisch.*) Modern poets, Schiller states, will never regain the naive—that is, the immediate and unconscious—relationship to nature that the ancients enjoyed. He focuses not on rules to be obeyed or ignored but rather on different types of consciousness. As in *On the Aesthetic Education of Man,* his primary concern is the author's conception of self and of the ideals and purposes of art—the motivating power that informs and imparts life to the text.

Schiller's broad sense of a break between a harmonious past and the divided or disrupted present in which artists perceive the difficulty, if not the impossibility, of embodying their hopes and desires in their actual work, is echoed in the poetry and criticism of MATTHEW ARNOLD, T. S. ELIOT, and many other nineteenth- and twentieth-century writers. They may disagree on the timing, but all emphasize that this shift in consciousness—a dissociation of sensibility—manifests itself in the operations of individual thought and feeling and in the style and structure of poetry.

In the selection below from *On the Aesthetic Education of Man,* Schiller touches on the sense of acute modern cultural crisis that impels his arguments about the priority of the aesthetic. He summons up an optimistic vision of the artist preparing "the shape of things to come," even as he testifies to the ordeal of being an artist in a hostile environment. Defy the world's opinion: this is Schiller's advice to those wondering whether they can endure in the midst of an unsympathetic and corrupt age. The artist should be true to the heart's "noble impulses": "Impart to the world you would influence a *Direction* towards the good, and the quiet rhythm of time will bring it to fulfilment." Through our inner potential, we revitalize ourselves and reinvigorate (and sometimes disturb and unsettle) others.

The weakness of this position is that Schiller separates "the rhythm of time" (which he trusts) from the very different rhythm of the world of Utility that, he concedes, now rules but that he believes can be transcended. Others grappled more directly with the comprehensive changes driven by the accelerating power of capitalism, described by the Scottish-born historian (and biographer of Schiller) Thomas Carlyle in "Signs of the Times" (1829): "Not the external and the physical alone is now managed by machinery, but the internal and spiritual also. . . . Men are grown mechanical in head and in heart, as well as in hand." Not just KARL MARX and FRIEDRICH ENGELS but the Victorian critics and social reformers John Ruskin and William Morris responded to this alienation in ways that Schiller—whose aesthetic works are grounded less in historical reference and analysis than in idealization of the harmonious wholeness of the ancient Greeks—could not.

Yet Schiller, a prophet of the alienation that would pain many later authors, believed that this alienation could be overcome through the civilizing power of literature, enabling a higher Ideal to triumph over the degraded principles and practices to which persons were currently (and mistakenly) loyal. A passionate advocate for individual and political freedom, Schiller gave everything to his art; "the Muses drained me dry," he wrote to Goethe (1795), and, after a long period of poor health, he died in his mid-forties.

***On the Aesthetic Education of Man* Keywords:** Aesthetics, Defense of Criticism, Modernity, Poetry, Romantic Theory

From On the Aesthetic Education of Man[1]

Second Letter

1. But should it not be possible to make better use of the freedom you accord me than by keeping your attention fixed upon the domain of the fine arts? Is it not, to say the least, untimely to be casting around for a code of laws for the aesthetic world at a moment when the affairs of the moral offer interest of so much more urgent concern, and when the spirit of philosophical inquiry is being expressly challenged by present circumstances to concern itself with that most perfect of all the works to be achieved by the art of man: the construction of true political freedom?

2. I would not wish to live in a century other than my own, or to have worked for any other. We are citizens of our own Age no less than of our own State. And if it is deemed unseemly, or even inadmissible, to exempt ourselves from the morals and customs of the circle in which we live, why should it be less of a duty to allow the needs and taste of our own epoch some voice in our choice of activity?

3. But the verdict of this epoch does not, by any means, seem to be going in favour of art, not at least of the kind of art to which alone my inquiry will be directed. The course of events has given the spirit of the age a direction which threatens to remove it ever further from the art of the Ideal. This kind of art must abandon actuality, and soar with becoming boldness above our wants and needs; for Art is a daughter of Freedom, and takes her orders

1. Translated by E. M. Wilkinson and L. A. Willoughby. These letters were originally addressed to Schiller's benefactor Friedrich Christian (1745–1814), duke of Augustenburg.

from the necessity inherent in minds, not from the exigencies of matter. But at the present time material needs reign supreme and bend a degraded humanity beneath their tyrannical yoke. *Utility* is the great idol of our age, to which all powers are in thrall and to which all talent must pay homage. Weighed in this crude balance, the insubstantial merits of Art scarce tip the scale, and, bereft of all encouragement, she shuns the noisy market-place of our century. The spirit of philosophical inquiry[2] itself is wresting from the imagination one province after another, and the frontiers of art contract the more the boundaries of science expand.

4. Expectantly the gaze of philosopher and man of the world alike is fixed on the political scene, where now, so it is believed, the very fate of mankind is being debated. Does it not betray a culpable indifference to the common weal not to take part in this general debate? If this great action is, by reason of its cause and its consequences, of urgent concern to every one who calls himself man, it must, by virtue of its method of procedure, be of quite special interest to every one who has learnt to think for himself. For a question which has hitherto always been decided by the blind right of might, is now, so it seems, being brought before the tribunal of Pure Reason[3] itself, and anyone who is at all capable of putting himself at the centre of things, and of raising himself from an individual into a representative of the species, may consider himself at once a member of this tribunal, and at the same time, in his capacity of human being and citizen of the world, an interested party who finds himself more or less closely involved in the outcome of the case. It is, therefore, not merely his own cause which is being decided in this great action; judgement is to be passed according to laws which he, as a reasonable being, is himself competent and entitled to dictate.

5. How tempting it would be for me to investigate such a subject in company with one who is as acute a thinker as he is a liberal citizen of the world! And to leave the decision to a heart which has dedicated itself with such noble enthusiasm to the weal of humanity. What an agreeable surprise if, despite all difference in station, and the vast distance which the circumstances of the actual world make inevitable, I were, in the realm of ideas, to find my conclusions identical with those of a mind as unprejudiced as your own! That I resist this seductive temptation, and put Beauty before Freedom, can, I believe, not only be excused on the score of personal inclination, but also justified on principle. I hope to convince you that the theme I have chosen is far less alien to the needs of our age than to its taste. More than this: if man is ever to solve that problem of politics in practice he will have to approach it through the problem of the aesthetic, because it is only through Beauty that man makes his way to Freedom. But this cannot be demonstrated without my first reminding you of the principles by which Reason is in any case guided in matters of political legislation.

2. Pertaining not only to the study of fundamental principles but also to the empirical investigation into practical things.

3. See IMMANUEL KANT, *The Critique of Pure Reason* (1781). In the preface, Kant states that his goal is to "assure to reason its lawful claims, and dismiss all groundless pretensions, not by despotic decrees, but in accordance with its own eternal and unalterable laws."

Sixth Letter

1. Have I not perhaps been too hard on our age in the picture I have just drawn? That is scarcely the reproach I anticipate. Rather a different one: that I have tried to make it prove too much. Such a portrait, you will tell me, does indeed resemble mankind as it is today; but does it not also resemble any people caught up in the process of civilization, since all of them, without exception, must fall away from Nature by the abuse of Reason before they can return to her by the use of Reason?

2. Closer attention to the character of our age will, however, reveal an astonishing contrast between contemporary forms of humanity and earlier ones, especially the Greek. The reputation for culture and refinement, on which we otherwise rightly pride ourselves *vis-à-vis* humanity in its *merely* natural state, can avail us nothing against the natural humanity of the Greeks. For they were wedded to all the delights of art and all the dignity of wisdom, without however, like us, falling a prey to their seduction. The Greeks put us to shame not only by a simplicity to which our age is a stranger; they are at the same time our rivals, indeed often our models, in those very excellences with which we are wont to console ourselves for the unnaturalness of our manners. In fullness of form no less than of content, at once philosophic and creative, sensitive and energetic, the Greeks combined the first youth of imagination with the manhood of reason in a glorious manifestation of humanity.

3. At that first fair awakening of the powers of the mind, sense and intellect did not as yet rule over strictly separate domains; for no dissension had as yet provoked them into hostile partition and mutual demarcation of their frontiers. Poetry had not as yet coquetted with wit, nor speculation prostituted itself to sophistry. Both of them could, when need arose, exchange functions, since each in its own fashion paid honour to truth. However high the mind might soar, it always drew matter lovingly along with it; and however fine and sharp the distinctions it might make, it never proceeded to mutilate. It did indeed divide human nature into its several aspects, and project these in magnified form into the divinities of its glorious pantheon; but not by tearing it to pieces; rather by combining its aspects in different proportions, for in no single one of their deities was humanity in its entirety ever lacking. How different with us Moderns! With us too the image of the human species is projected in magnified form into separate individuals—but as fragments, not in different combinations, with the result that one has to go the rounds from one individual to another in order to be able to piece together a complete image of the species. With us, one might almost be tempted to assert, the various faculties appear as separate in practice as they are distinguished by the psychologist in theory, and we see not merely individuals, but whole classes of men, developing but one part of their potentialities, while of the rest, as in stunted growths, only vestigial traces remain.

4. I do not underrate the advantages which the human race today, considered as a whole and weighed in the balance of intellect, can boast in the

face of what is best in the ancient world. But it has to take up the challenge in serried ranks, and let whole measure itself against whole. What individual Modern could sally forth and engage, man against man, with an individual Athenian for the prize of humanity?

5. Whence this disadvantage among individuals when the species as a whole is at such an advantage? Why was the individual Greek qualified to be the representative of his age, and why can no single Modern venture as much? Because it was from all-unifying Nature that the former, and from the all-dividing Intellect that the latter, received their respective forms.

6. It was civilization itself which inflicted this wound upon modern man. Once the increase of empirical knowledge, and more exact modes of thought, made sharper divisions between the sciences inevitable, and once the increasingly complex machinery of State necessitated a more rigorous separation of ranks and occupations, then the inner unity of human nature was severed too, and a disastrous conflict set its harmonious powers at variance. The intuitive and the speculative understanding now withdrew in hostility to take up positions in their respective fields, whose frontiers they now began to guard with jealous mistrust; and with this confining of our activity to a particular sphere we have given ourselves a master within, who not infrequently ends by suppressing the rest of our potentialities. While in the one a riotous imagination ravages the hard-won fruits of the intellect, in another the spirit of abstraction stifles the fire at which the heart should have warmed itself and the imagination been kindled.

7. This disorganization, which was first started within man by civilization and learning, was made complete and universal by the new spirit of government. It was scarcely to be expected that the simple organization of the early republics should have survived the simplicity of early manners and conditions; but instead of rising to a higher form of organic existence it degenerated into a crude and clumsy mechanism. That polypoid[4] character of the Greek States, in which every individual enjoyed an independent existence but could, when need arose, grow into the whole organism, now made way for an ingenious clock-work, in which, out of the piecing together of innumerable but lifeless parts, a mechanical kind of collective life ensued. State and Church, laws and customs, were now torn asunder; enjoyment was divorced from labour, the means from the end, the effort from the reward. Everlastingly chained to a single little fragment of the Whole, man himself develops into nothing but a fragment; everlastingly in his ear the monotonous sound of the wheel that he turns, he never develops the harmony of his being, and instead of putting the stamp of humanity upon his own nature, he becomes nothing more than the imprint of his occupation or of his specialized knowledge. But even that meagre, fragmentary participation, by which individual members of the State are still linked to the Whole, does not depend upon forms which they spontaneously prescribe for themselves (for how could one entrust to their freedom

4. That is, like a polyp: a small, simple water animal that is attached to a surface (such as coral), or a small mass of cells that grows in the body.

of action a mechanism so intricate and so fearful of light and enlightenment?); it is dictated to them with meticulous exactitude by means of a formulary which inhibits all freedom of thought. The dead letter takes the place of living understanding, and a good memory is a safer guide than imagination and feeling.

8. When the community makes his office the measure of the man; when in one of its citizens it prizes nothing but memory, in another a mere tabularizing[5] intelligence, in a third only mechanical skill; when, in the one case, indifferent to character, it insists exclusively on knowledge, yet is, in another, ready to condone any amount of obscurantist[6] thinking as long as it is accompanied by a spirit of order and law-abiding behaviour; when, moreover, it insists on special skills being developed with a degree of intensity which is only commensurate with its readiness to absolve the individual citizen from developing himself in extensity—can we wonder that the remaining aptitudes of the psyche are neglected in order to give undivided attention to the one which will bring honour and profit? True, we know that the outstanding individual will never let the limits of his occupation dictate the limits of his activity. But a mediocre talent will consume in the office assigned him the whole meagre sum of his powers, and a man has to have a mind above the ordinary if, without detriment to his calling, he is still to have time for the chosen pursuits of his leisure. Moreover, it is rarely a recommendation in the eyes of the State if a man's powers exceed the tasks he is set, or if the higher needs of the man of parts constitute a rival to the duties of his office. So jealously does the State insist on being the sole proprietor of its servants that it will more easily bring itself (and who can blame it?) to share its man with the Cytherean, than with the Uranian, Venus.[7]

9. Thus little by little the concrete life of the Individual is destroyed in order that the abstract idea of the Whole may drag out its sorry existence, and the State remains for ever a stranger to its citizens since at no point does it ever make contact with their feeling. Forced to resort to classification in order to cope with the variety of its citizens, and never to get an impression of humanity except through representation at second hand, the governing section ends up by losing sight of them altogether, confusing their concrete reality with a mere construct of the intellect; while the governed cannot but receive with indifference laws which are scarcely, if at all, directed to them as persons. Weary at last of sustaining bonds which the State does so little to facilitate, positive society begins (this has long been the fate of most European States) to disintegrate into a state of primitive morality, in which public authority has become but one party *more*, to be hated and circumvented by those who make authority necessary, and only obeyed by such as are capable of doing without it.

10. With this twofold pressure upon it, from within and from without, could humanity well have taken any other course than the one it actually

5. Making lists or tables.

6. Opposed to enlightenment or the spread of knowledge; deliberately making something obscure or withholding knowledge from the general public.

7. Uranian Venus presides over sacred love; Cytherean Venus presides over profane love.

took? In its striving after inalienable possessions in the realm of ideas, the spirit of speculation could do no other than become a stranger to the world of sense, and lose sight of matter for the sake of form. The practical spirit, by contrast, enclosed within a monotonous sphere of material objects, and within this uniformity still further confined by formulas, was bound to find the idea of an unconditioned Whole receding from sight, and to become just as impoverished as its own poor sphere of activity. If the former was tempted to model the actual world on a world conceivable by the mind, and to exalt the subjective conditions of its own perceptual and conceptual faculty into laws constitutive of the existence of things, the latter plunged into the opposite extreme of judging all experience whatsoever by one particular fragment of experience, and of wanting to make the rules of its *own* occupation apply indiscriminately to all others. The one was bound to become the victim of empty subtilities, the other of narrow pedantry; for the former stood too high to discern the particular, the latter too low to survey the Whole. But the damaging effects of the turn which mind thus took were not confined to knowledge and production; it affected feeling and action no less. We know that the sensibility of the psyche depends for its intensity upon the liveliness, for its scope upon the richness, of the imagination. The preponderance of the analytical faculty must, however, of necessity, deprive the imagination of its energy and warmth, while a more restricted sphere of objects must reduce its wealth. Hence the abstract thinker very often has a *cold* heart, since he dissects his impressions, and impressions can move the soul only as long as they remain whole; while the man of practical affairs often has a *narrow* heart, since his imagination, imprisoned within the unvarying confines of his own calling, is incapable of extending itself to appreciate other ways of seeing and knowing.

11. It was part of my procedure to uncover the disadvantageous trends in the character of our age and the reasons for them, not to point out the advantages which Nature offers by way of compensation. I readily concede that, little as individuals might benefit from this fragmentation of their being, there was no other way in which the species as a whole could have progressed. With the Greeks, humanity undoubtedly reached a maximum of excellence, which could neither be maintained at that level nor rise any higher. Not maintained, because the intellect was unavoidably compelled by the store of knowledge it already possessed to dissociate itself from feeling and intuition in an attempt to arrive at exact discursive understanding; not rise any higher, because only a specific degree of clarity is compatible with a specific fullness and warmth. This degree the Greeks had attained; and had they wished to proceed to a higher stage of development, they would, like us, have had to surrender their wholeness of being and pursue truth along separate paths.

12. If the manifold potentialities in man were ever to be developed, there was no other way but to pit them one against the other. This antagonism of faculties and functions is the great instrument of civilization—but it is only the instrument; for as long as it persists, we are only on the way to becoming civilized. Only through individual powers in man becoming isolated, and arrogating to themselves exclusive authority, do they come into conflict with

the truth of things, and force the Common Sense, which is otherwise content to linger with indolent complacency on outward appearance, to penetrate phenomena in depth. By pure thought usurping authority in the world of sense, while empirical thought is concerned to subject the usurper to the conditions of experience, both these powers develop to their fullest potential, and exhaust the whole range of their proper sphere. And by the very boldness with which, in the one case, imagination allows her caprice to dissolve the existing world-order, she does, in the other, compel Reason to rise to the ultimate sources of knowing, and invoke the law of Necessity against her.

13. One-sidedness in the exercise of his powers must, it is true, inevitably lead the individual into error; but the species as a whole to truth. Only by concentrating the whole energy of our mind into a *single* focal point, contracting our whole being into a single power, do we, as it were, lend wings to this individual power and lead it, by artificial means, far beyond the limits which Nature seems to have assigned to it. Even as it is certain that all individuals taken together would never, with the powers of vision granted them by Nature alone, have managed to detect a satellite of Jupiter which the telescope reveals to the astronomer, so it is beyond question that human powers of reflection would never have produced an analysis of the Infinite or a Critique of Pure Reason,[8] unless, in the individuals called to perform such feats, Reason had separated itself off, disentangled itself, as it were, from all matter, and by the most intense effort of abstraction armed their eyes with a glass for peering into the Absolute. But will such a mind, dissolved as it were into pure intellect and pure contemplation, ever be capable of exchanging the rigorous bonds of logic for the free movement of the poetic faculty, or of grasping the concrete individuality of things with a sense innocent of preconceptions and faithful to the object? At this point Nature sets limits even to the most universal genius, limits which he cannot transcend; and as long as philosophy has to make its prime business the provision of safeguards against error, truth will be bound to have its martyrs.

14. Thus, however much the world as a whole may benefit through this fragmentary specialization of human powers, it cannot be denied that the individuals affected by it suffer under the curse of this cosmic purpose. Athletic bodies can, it is true, be developed by gymnastic exercises; beauty only through the free and harmonious play of the limbs. In the same way the keying up of individual functions of the mind can indeed produce extraordinary human beings; but only the equal tempering of them all, happy and complete human beings. And in what kind of relation would we stand to either past or future ages, if the development of human nature were to make such sacrifice necessary? We would have been the serfs of mankind; for several millennia we would have done slaves' work for them, and our mutilated nature would bear impressed upon it the shameful marks of this servitude. And all this in order that a future generation might in blissful indolence attend to the care of its moral health, and foster the free growth of its humanity!

8. That is, Kant's *Critique of Pure Reason*.

15. But can Man really be destined to miss himself for the sake of any purpose whatsoever? Should Nature, for the sake of her own purposes, be able to rob us of a completeness which Reason, for the sake of hers, enjoins upon us? It must, therefore, be wrong if the cultivation of individual powers involves the sacrifice of wholeness. Or rather, however much the law of Nature tends in that direction, it must be open to us to restore by means of a higher Art the totality of our nature which the arts themselves have destroyed.

Ninth Letter

1. But is this not, perhaps, to argue in a circle? Intellectual education is to bring about moral education, and yet moral education is to be the condition of intellectual education? All improvement in the political sphere is to proceed from the ennobling of character—but how under the influence of a barbarous constitution is character ever to become ennobled? To this end we should, presumably, have to seek out some instrument not provided by the State, and to open up living springs which, whatever the political corruption, would remain clear and pure.

2. I have now reached the point to which all my preceding reflections have been tending. This instrument is Fine Art; such living springs are opened up in its immortal exemplars.

3. Art, like Science, is absolved from all positive constraint and from all conventions introduced by man; both rejoice in absolute *immunity* from human arbitrariness. The political legislator may put their territory out of bounds; he cannot rule within it. He can proscribe the lover of truth; Truth itself will prevail. He can humiliate the artist; but Art he cannot falsify. True, nothing is more common than for both, science as well as art, to pay homage to the spirit of the age, or for creative minds to accept the critical standards of prevailing taste. In epochs where character becomes rigid and obdurate, we find science keeping a strict watch over its frontiers, and art moving in the heavy shackles of rules; in those where it becomes enervated and flabby, science will strive to please, and art to gratify. For whole centuries thinkers and artists will do their best to submerge truth and beauty in the depths of a degraded humanity; it is they themselves who are drowned there, while truth and beauty, with their own indestructible vitality, struggle triumphantly to the surface.

4. The artist is indeed the child of his age; but woe to him if he is at the same time its ward or, worse still, its minion! Let some beneficent deity snatch the suckling betimes from his mother's breast, nourish him with the milk of a better age, and suffer him to come to maturity under a distant Grecian sky. Then, when he has become a man, let him return, a stranger, to his own century; not, however, to gladden it by his appearance, but rather, terrible like Agamemnon's son,[9] to cleanse and to purify it. His theme he

9. Orestes, who "cleansed" his home on his return by killing his mother Clytemnestra and her lover Aegisthus, who had murdered Agamemnon (a myth often treated in Greek tragedy, most notably in Aeschylus's *Oresteia* trilogy, 458 B.C.E.).

will, indeed, take from the present; but his form he will borrow from a nobler time, nay, from beyond time altogether, from the absolute, unchanging, unity of his being. Here, from the pure aether[1] of his genius, the living source of beauty flows down, untainted by the corruption of the generations and ages wallowing in the dark eddies below. The theme of his work may be degraded by vagaries of the public mood, even as this has been known to ennoble it; but its form, inviolate, will remain immune from such vicissitudes. The Roman of the first century had long been bowing the knee before his emperors when statues still portrayed him erect; temples continued to be sacred to the eye long after the gods had become objects of derision; and the infamous crimes of a *Nero* or a *Commodus*[2] were put to shame by the noble style of the building whose frame lent them cover. Humanity has lost its dignity; but Art has rescued it and preserved it in significant stone. Truth lives on in the illusion of Art, and it is from this copy, or after-image, that the original image will once again be restored. Just as the nobility of Art *survived* the nobility of Nature, so now Art goes before her, a voice rousing from slumber and preparing the shape of things to come. Even before Truth's triumphant light can penetrate the recesses of the human heart, the poet's imagination will intercept its rays, and the peaks of humanity will be radiant while the dews of night still linger in the valley.

5. But how is the artist to protect himself against the corruption of the age which besets him on all sides? By disdaining its opinion. Let him direct his gaze upwards, to the dignity of his calling and the universal Law, not downwards towards Fortune and the needs of daily life. Free alike from the futile busyness which would fain set its mark upon the fleeting moment, and from the impatient spirit of enthusiasm which applies the measure of the Absolute to the sorry products of Time, let him leave the sphere of the actual to the intellect, which is at home there, whilst he strives to produce the Ideal out of the union of what is possible with what is necessary. Let him express this ideal both in semblance and in truth, set the stamp of it upon the play of his imagination as upon the seriousness of his conduct, let him express it in all sensuous and spiritual forms, and silently project it into the infinity of time.

6. But not everyone whose soul glows with this ideal was granted either the creative tranquillity or the spirit of long patience required to imprint it upon the silent stone, or pour it into the sober mould of words, and so entrust it to the executory hands of time. Far too impetuous to proceed by such unobtrusive means, the divine impulse to form often hurls itself directly upon present-day reality and upon the life of action, and undertakes to fashion anew the formless material presented by the moral world. The misfortunes of the human race speak urgently to the man of feeling; its degradation more urgently still; enthusiasm is kindled, and in vigorous souls ardent longing drives impatiently on towards action. But did he ever ask himself whether those disorders in the moral world offend his reason, or whether they do not rather wound his self-love? If he does not yet know the answer, he will detect

1. For the Greeks, the clear air beyond the clouds; the element breathed by the gods.

2. Both were notoriously cruel emperors of Rome: Nero (37–68 C.E.), emperor 54–68; Commodus (161–192), emperor 180–92. Under the Republic, which ended in the 1st century B.C.E., Romans did not "bow the knee."

it by the zeal with which he insists upon specific and prompt results. The pure moral impulse is directed towards the Absolute. For such an impulse time does not exist, and the future turns into the present from the moment that it is seen to develop with inevitable Necessity out of the present. In the eyes of a Reason which knows no limits, the Direction is at once the Destination, and the Way[3] is completed from the moment it is trodden.

7. To the young friend of truth and beauty who would inquire of me how, despite all the opposition of his century, he is to satisfy the noble impulses of his heart, I would make answer: Impart to the world you would influence a *Direction* towards the good, and the quiet rhythm of time will bring it to fulfilment. You will have given it this direction if, by your teaching, you have elevated its thoughts to the Necessary and the Eternal, if, by your actions and your creations, you have transformed the Necessary and the Eternal into an object of the heart's desire. The edifice of error and caprice will fall—it must fall, indeed it has already fallen—from the moment you are certain that it is on the point of giving way. But it is in man's inner being that it must give way, not just in the externals he presents to the world. It is in the modest sanctuary of your heart that you must rear victorious truth, and project it out of yourself in the form of beauty, so that not only thought can pay it homage, but sense, too, lay loving hold on its appearance. And lest you should find yourself receiving from the world as it is the model you yourself should be providing, do not venture into its equivocal company without first being sure that you bear within your own heart an escort from the world of the ideal. Live with your century; but do not be its creature. Work for your contemporaries; but create what they need, not what they praise. Without sharing their guilt, yet share with noble resignation in their punishment, and bow your head freely beneath the yoke which they find as difficult to dispense with as to bear. By the steadfast courage with which you disdain their good fortune, you will show them that it is not through cowardice that you consent to share their sufferings. Think of them as they ought to be, when called upon to influence them; think of them as they are, when tempted to act on their behalf. In seeking their approval appeal to what is best in them, but in devising their happiness recall them as they are at their worst; then your own nobility will awaken theirs, and their unworthiness not defeat your purpose. The seriousness of your principles will frighten them away, but in the play of your semblance they will be prepared to tolerate them; for their taste is purer than their heart, and it is here that you must lay hold of the timorous fugitive. In vain will you assail their precepts, in vain condemn their practice; but on their leisure hours you can try your shaping hand. Banish from their pleasures caprice, frivolity, and coarseness, and imperceptibly you will banish these from their actions and, eventually, from their inclinations too. Surround them, wherever you meet them, with the great and noble forms of genius, and encompass them about with the symbols of perfection, until Semblance conquer Reality, and Art triumph over Nature.

1795

3. See John 14.6 (KJV): "Jesus saith unto him, I am the way, the truth, and the life: no man cometh unto the Father, but by me."

MARY WOLLSTONECRAFT
1759–1797

Mary Wollstonecraft wrote one of the first treatises of modern feminism. *A Vindication of the Rights of Woman* (1792) inserts an analysis of the relations between the sexes into a wholesale revolutionary attack on hereditary privilege of all sorts—birth, wealth, rank, *and* gender. Of course, not every revolutionary theorist in the 1790s would include male privilege on such a list: the French National Assembly's Declaration of the Rights of Man in 1789 said nothing about the rights of women. Yet Wollstonecraft's argument for rational education for both sexes was based on the promise of freedom enthusiastically greeted by many English writers in the early days of the French Revolution.

Wollstonecraft had previously written *A Vindication of the Rights of Men* (1790), one of the first polemical responses to EDMUND BURKE's conservative *Reflections on the Revolution in France* (1790). Months before Thomas Paine's perhaps better-known *Rights of Man* (1791–92), Wollstonecraft composed the first *Vindication* at white heat; it was printed anonymously. For Wollstonecraft, Burke's defense of the charms of existing arrangements was of a piece with the implicit gendering of his earlier aesthetic distinction between the beautiful and the sublime in his *Philosophical Enquiry into the Origin of Our Ideas of the Sublime and Beautiful* (1757; see above). Beauty was a property of weaker entities than man; sublimity, of stronger. Women's beauty was thus synonymous with women's inferiority. In both her *Vindications*, Wollstonecraft skillfully demystifies all arguments designed to justify inequality on the basis of existing arrangements, customs, or feelings alone.

As the second-born and first daughter of six children, she experienced firsthand the preference accorded men in both property and dignity. Her older brother was the only grandchild to inherit part of his grandfather's fortune (made in the silk industry), much of which was consumed by Mary's father as he attempted to lead the life of a gentleman farmer. As his finances worsened, he appropriated money that had been set aside for the other children and seems to have become increasingly brutal. At age nineteen Mary decided to strike out on her own.

In addition to trying her hand at several of the positions open to middle-class women without resources (lady's companion, governess, seamstress), Wollstonecraft opened a school at Newington Green with her two younger sisters and a dear friend, Fanny Blood. Although Mary's formal education had ended when she was fifteen, she was an avid reader and later taught herself French, German, Dutch, and Italian. The school failed, but the experience gave rise to Wollstonecraft's first publication, *Thoughts on the Education of Daughters* (1786), and to an acquaintance with antiestablishment thinkers, especially the dissenter Dr. Richard Price (whose sermon on the anniversary of England's Glorious Revolution of 1688 was soon to provoke Burke's *Reflections*).

While working as a governess for the Kingsborough family in Ireland, Wollstonecraft wrote her first novel—*Mary, A Fiction* (1788); when dismissed by the Kingsboroughs (for reasons that are unclear), she returned to London, where her sympathetic publisher, Joseph Johnson, put her to work doing translations and reviews for his new *Analytical Review*. Around his table gathered some of the most interesting intellectuals of the day, including the radical thinker Thomas Paine, the painter Henry Fuseli, the political philosopher and novelist William Godwin, and the poet William Blake.

When the Bastille prison was stormed by a Paris mob in 1789, inaugurating the French Revolution, English radicals looked to France with great enthusiasm. As

WILLIAM WORDSWORTH would later put it in his poem "French Revolution" (1809), "Bliss was it in that dawn to be alive[.] . . . What temper at the prospect did not wake / To happiness unthought of?" (also included in *The Prelude* [1805] 10.692–707). It was in this climate that Mary Wollstonecraft composed her *Vindications*. To the promise of liberty and equality for all men, Wollstonecraft added the simple but radical idea that women, too, had a right to develop their faculties freely, that the laws subjecting them to fathers or husbands could be changed, and that their existing defects (and indeed their charms) were largely a result of social conditioning, and could be modified. By comparing women to military men—both are fond of dress, trained in obedience, and not expected to think for themselves—she implies that education and socialization account for more differences than does gender alone.

At the time of writing *A Vindication of the Rights of Woman*, Wollstonecraft was just beginning to experience the additional complications that a life of passion could create for an independent woman attempting to live by her reason. She fell in love with Henry Fuseli and horrified his wife by suggesting that the three of them might live together. Soon thereafter, she went to Paris alone.

Once in France, she wrote about the French Revolution (her *Historical and Moral View of the Origin and Progress of the French Revolution, and the Effect It Has Produced in Europe* was published in 1794), observed the Reign of Terror with increasing recoil, and fell in love with a dashing American, Gilbert Imlay, who, when British citizens were being rounded up, registered her as his wife for her protection. She conceived a child with him, whom she named Fanny, after Fanny Blood. Though the birth was without complications, Wollstonecraft's life was not. Imlay was often absent on "business," and on two occasions when Wollstonecraft was to join him in London, she discovered evidence of his infidelities. She twice attempted suicide; between attempts, she offered to journey to Scandinavia to investigate some business dealings for Imlay, and, traveling with a toddler and an attendant, wrote letters detailing her travels (later published as *Letters Written during a Short Residence in Norway, Denmark, and Sweden*, 1796). But the relationship with Imlay was over. As VIRGINIA WOOLF memorably surmised in her 1929 short essay on Wollstonecraft (reprinted in *The Second Common Reader*): "Tickling minnows he had hooked a dolphin, and the creature rushed him through the waters till he was dizzy and only wanted to escape."

Wollstonecraft reentered the circle of intellectuals around Joseph Johnson, and this time she found a great deal to discuss with the forty-year-old William Godwin, who was now at the peak of his career (having published *Political Justice* in 1793 and the novel *Caleb Williams* in 1794). Soon "it was friendship melting into love," as Godwin later described it. Both of them were opposed to marriage on principle—he felt that all formal commitments violate the feelings that inspire them, and she felt that marriage laws disadvantage women. Nevertheless, when Mary found herself pregnant again, they married at the beginning of 1797 so that the child would be legitimate. Ironically, many "respectable" acquaintances who had wanted to believe that Mary was married to Imlay broke off relations when this gesture of propriety revealed the earlier illegitimacy.

The author of *A Vindication of the Rights of Woman* was happily working on a novel titled *Maria, or The Wrongs of Woman* (the play—and lack of symmetry—between universal "rights" and gender-specific "wrongs" sums up the differences between Wollstonecraft's treatises and her novels) while she awaited the birth of "William." But she and Godwin had little chance to test their marital experiment. On September 10, 1797, she died of an infection contracted during unsuccessful attempts to remove her broken and unexpelled placenta, eleven days after giving birth to a daughter—the future Mary Shelley, author of a Gothic novel of education (*Frankenstein*) and wife of a passionate disciple of both Godwin and Wollstonecraft, PERCY BYSSHE SHELLEY.

Unlike other middle-class women, whose husbands, fathers, wealth, or connections veiled their legal powerlessness, Mary Wollstonecraft clearly saw the damage caused by sexual inequality. She was socialized for but she never experienced a life of respectable dependency. The first readers of *A Vindication of the Rights of Woman* applauded her apparent commitment to bourgeois respectability, but when Godwin published in his *Memoirs of Mary Wollstonecraft* (1798) a frank account of her subsequent sexual life, the increasingly conservative public reacted to her lack of deference (for which modern feminists applaud her) with horror. Her freedom and independence were seen as proof of licentiousness and immorality.

Mary Wollstonecraft was a cultural and not a literary critic, but as an acute reader of the contradictions inherent in the literary tradition she is a forerunner of "ideological" reading. Literature was central to her work in several fundamental ways. In her novels, she plumbs the conflicts between reason and emotion ("sensibility"), or within reason itself, neither of which are dealt with in her treatises. In her reply to Burke, she does not separate his aesthetic from his political theory. And she finds at the heart of the literary canon the same sexual inequality and incoherence she is arguing against in society at large.

In the extract printed below, for example, Wollstonecraft begins by pointing out two incompatible moments in Milton's *Paradise Lost*: Adam's plea to God for an equal and Eve's birth as an unequal. How are these to be reconciled? If God exists, she argues, and if humans are all characterized by their capacity for immortality, then one God fits all, and virtue must be the same in kind, if not in degree, for both sexes. The obedience and secondariness expected of women ("He for God only, she for God in him," as Milton put it) make a mockery of true companionship, giving women access only to a reflection of the light of reason that they should seek for themselves. In good Enlightenment fashion, Wollstonecraft comes close to taking the Serpent's role, arguing Eve out of blind obedience and into independent thinking.

Wollstonecraft is particularly concerned with the education of women, entering a larger discussion concerning education in general during the period. Jean-Jacques Rousseau's *Emile* (1762) had argued that men should have *less* rather than *more* education. Society needed to return to, preserve, and nurture man's natural goodness. Wollstonecraft agreed with much that Rousseau wrote about fresh air, exercise, and natural reason, but she vigorously criticized his differentiation between the educations of Emile and of Sophie. While Emile was expected to develop all his faculties, Sophie was expected to develop only in such a way as to remain "pleasing" to men. Wollstonecraft was not alone in calling for change—she had reviewed with approval Catharine Macauley Graham's *Letters on Education* (1790), and her treatise was dedicated to Charles-Maurice de Talleyrand-Périgord, who had promoted women's education in a 1791 report to the French National Assembly—but her logic was particularly incisive.

Today Wollstonecraft is celebrated for her early advocacy of women's equality and rationality and for arguing against the degradation and subjugation of women justified by "the arbitrary power of beauty." Her unblinking accounts of existing female defects in mind, body, and character—which sometimes sound misogynist themselves—were in the service of the new forms of freedom and education sought by proponents of Enlightenment reason and revolutionary change.

A Vindication of the Rights of Woman **Keywords:** Enlightenment Theory, Feminist Criticism, Gender, Women's Literature

From A Vindication of the Rights of Woman

From *Chapter II.* *The Prevailing Opinion of a Sexual Character Discussed*

To account for, and excuse the tyranny of man, many ingenious arguments have been brought forward to prove, that the two sexes, in the acquirement of virtue, ought to aim at attaining a very different character: or, to speak explicitly, women are not allowed to have sufficient strength of mind to acquire what really deserves the name of virtue. Yet it should seem, allowing them to have souls, that there is but one way appointed by Providence to lead *mankind* to either virtue or happiness.

If then women are not a swarm of ephemeron[1] triflers, why should they be kept in ignorance under the specious name of innocence? Men complain, and with reason, of the follies and caprices of our sex, when they do not keenly satirize our headstrong passions and groveling vices.—Behold, I should answer, the natural effect of ignorance! The mind will ever be unstable that has only prejudices to rest on, and the current will run with destructive fury when there are no barriers to break its force. Women are told from their infancy, and taught by the example of their mothers, that a little knowledge of human weakness, justly termed cunning, softness of temper, *outward* obedience, and a scrupulous attention to a puerile kind of propriety, will obtain for them the protection of man; and should they be beautiful, every thing else is needless, for, at least, twenty years of their lives.

Thus Milton[2] describes our first frail mother; though when he tells us that women are formed for softness and sweet attractive grace, I cannot comprehend his meaning, unless, in the true Mahometan[3] strain, he meant to deprive us of souls, and insinuate that we were beings only designed by sweet attractive grace, and docile blind obedience, to gratify the senses of man when he can no longer soar on the wing of contemplation.

How grossly do they insult us who thus advise us only to render ourselves gentle, domestic brutes! For instance, the winning softness so warmly, and frequently, recommended, that governs by obeying. What childish expressions, and how insignificant is the being—can it be an immortal one? who will condescend to govern by such sinister methods! "Certainly," says Lord Bacon, "man is of kin to the beasts by his body; and if he be not of kin to God by his spirit, he is a base and ignoble creature!"[4] Men, indeed, appear to me to act in a very unphilosophical manner when they try to secure the good conduct of women by attempting to keep them always in a state of childhood. Rousseau[5] was more consistent when he wished to stop the progress of reason in both sexes, for if men eat of the tree of knowledge, women will come in for a taste;[6] but, from the imperfect cultivation which their understandings now receive, they only attain a knowledge of evil.

1. Short-lived (literally, living only one day).
2. John Milton (1608–1674), English poet whose epic poem, *Paradise Lost* (1667), tells the biblical story of the fall of humankind; Wollstonecraft refers to 4.298.
3. Muslim. Islam was thought to deny that women have souls.
4. Francis Bacon (1561–1626), *Essays or Counsels Civil and Moral* (1625), Essay 16, "Of Atheism" [D. L. Macdonald and Kathleen Scherf's note].
5. Jean-Jacques Rousseau (1712–1778), Swiss-born French political philosopher; author of *Emile, or, On Education* (1762). All references to Rousseau in this selection are to book 5 of *Emile*, unless otherwise specified.
6. See Genesis 2–3. The story of "man's first disobedience" (1.1) in eating this fruit forms the center of Milton's *Paradise Lost*.

Children, I grant, should be innocent; but when the epithet is applied to men, or women, it is but a civil term for weakness. For if it be allowed that women were destined by Providence to acquire human virtues, and by the exercise of their understandings, that stability of character which is the firmest ground to rest our future hopes upon, they must be permitted to turn to the fountain of light, and not forced to shape their course by the twinkling of a mere satellite.[7] Milton, I grant, was of a very different opinion; for he only bends to the indefeasible right of beauty, though it would be difficult to render two passages which I now mean to contrast, consistent. But into similar inconsistencies are great men often led by their senses.

> "To whom thus Eve with *perfect beauty* adorn'd.
> My Author and Disposer, what thou bidst
> *Unargued* I obey; so God ordains;
> God is *thy law, thou mine*: to know no more
> Is Woman's *happiest* knowledge and her *praise*."[8]

These are exactly the arguments that I have used to children; but I have added, your reason is now gaining strength, and, till it arrives at some degree of maturity, you must look up to me for advice—then you ought to *think*, and only rely on God.

Yet in the following lines Milton seems to coincide with me; when he makes Adam thus expostulate with his Maker.

> "Hast thou not made me here thy substitute,
> And these inferior far beneath me set?
> Among *unequals* what society
> Can sort, what harmony or true delight?
> Which must be mutual, in proportion due
> Giv'n and receiv'd; but in *disparity*
> The one intense, the other still remiss
> Cannot well suit with either, but soon prove
> Tedious alike: of *fellowship* I speak
> Such as I seek, fit to participate
> All rational delight—"[9]

In treating, therefore, of the manners of women, let us, disregarding sensual arguments, trace what we should endeavour to make them in order to co-operate, if the expression be not too bold, with the supreme Being.

By individual education, I mean, for the sense of the word is not precisely defined, such an attention to a child as will slowly sharpen the senses, form the temper, regulate the passions as they begin to ferment, and set the understanding to work before the body arrives at maturity; so that the man may only have to proceed, not to begin, the important task of learning to think and reason.

To prevent any misconstruction, I must add, that I do not believe that a private education can work the wonders which some sanguine writers have attributed to it. Men and women must be educated, in a great degree, by the opinions and manners of the society they live in. In every age there has been

7. That is, women should turn to the sun, not the moon.
8. Milton, *Paradise Lost* 4.634–38 (Wollstonecraft's italics).
9. *Paradise Lost* 8.381–91 (Wollstonecraft's italics). "Participate": partake of.

a stream of popular opinion that has carried all before it, and given a family character, as it were, to the century. It may then fairly be inferred, that, till society be differently constituted, much cannot be expected from education. It is, however, sufficient for my present purpose to assert, that, whatever effect circumstances have on the abilities, every being may become virtuous by the exercise of its own reason; for if but one being was created with vicious inclinations, that is positively bad, what can save us from atheism? or if we worship a God, is not that God a devil?

Consequently, the most perfect education, in my opinion, is such an exercise of the understanding as is best calculated to strengthen the body and form the heart. Or, in other words, to enable the individual to attain such habits of virtue as will render it independent. In fact, it is a farce to call any being virtuous whose virtues do not result from the exercise of its own reason. This was Rousseau's opinion respecting men:[1] I extend it to women, and confidently assert that they have been drawn out of their sphere by false refinement, and not by an endeavour to acquire masculine qualities. Still the regal homage which they receive is so intoxicating, that till the manners of the times are changed, and formed on more reasonable principles, it may be impossible to convince them that the illegitimate power, which they obtain, by degrading themselves, is a curse, and that they must return to nature and equality, if they wish to secure the placid satisfaction that unsophisticated affections impart. But for this epoch we must wait—wait, perhaps, till kings and nobles, enlightened by reason, and, preferring the real dignity of man to childish state, throw off their gaudy hereditary trappings: and if then women do not resign the arbitrary power of beauty—they will prove that they have *less* mind than man.

I may be accused of arrogance; still I must declare what I firmly believe, that all the writers who have written on the subject of female education and manners from Rousseau to Dr. Gregory,[2] have contributed to render women more artificial, weak characters, than they would otherwise have been; and, consequently, more useless members of society. I might have expressed this conviction in a lower key; but I am afraid it would have been the whine of affection, and not the faithful expression of my feelings, of the clear result, which experience and reflection have led me to draw. When I come to that division of the subject, I shall advert to the passages that I more particularly disapprove of, in the works of the authors I have just alluded to; but it is first necessary to observe, that my objection extends to the whole purport of those books, which tend, in my opinion, to degrade one half of the human species, and render women pleasing at the expence of every solid virtue.

Though, to reason on Rousseau's ground, if man did attain a degree of perfection of mind when his body arrived at maturity, it might be proper, in order to make a man and his wife *one*, that she should rely entirely on his understanding; and the graceful ivy, clasping the oak that supported it, would form a whole in which strength and beauty would be equally conspicuous. But, alas! husbands, as well as their helpmates, are often only overgrown children; nay, thanks to early debauchery, scarcely men in their outward

1. Expressed early in *Emile*.
2. John Gregory (1724–1773), *A Father's Legacy to His Daughters* (1774). Wollstonecraft included substantial excerpts from Gregory in *The Female Reader* ([compiled in] 1789) [Macdonald and Scherf's note].

form—and if the blind lead the blind, one need not come from heaven[3] to tell us the consequence.

Many are the causes that, in the present corrupt state of society, contribute to enslave women by cramping their understandings and sharpening their senses. One, perhaps, that silently does more mischief than all the rest, is their disregard of order.

To do every thing in an orderly manner, is a most important precept, which women, who, generally speaking, receive only a disorderly kind of education, seldom attend to with that degree of exactness that men, who from their infancy are broken into method, observe. This negligent kind of guess-work, for what other epithet can be used to point out the random exertions of a sort of instinctive common sense, never brought to the test of reason? prevents their generalizing matters of fact—so they do to-day, what they did yesterday, merely because they did it yesterday.

This contempt of the understanding in early life has more baneful consequences than is commonly supposed; for the little knowledge which women of strong minds attain, is, from various circumstances, of a more desultory kind than the knowledge of men, and it is acquired more by sheer observations on real life, than from comparing what has been individually observed with the results of experience generalized by speculation. Led by their dependent situation and domestic employments more into society, what they learn is rather by snatches; and as learning is with them, in general, only a secondary thing, they do not pursue any one branch with that persevering ardour necessary to give vigour to the faculties, and clearness to the judgment. In the present state of society, a little learning is required to support the character of a gentleman; and boys are obliged to submit to a few years of discipline. But in the education of women, the cultivation of the understanding is always subordinate to the acquirement of some corporeal accomplishment; even while enervated by confinement and false notions of modesty, the body is prevented from attaining that grace and beauty which relaxed half-formed limbs never exhibit. Besides, in youth their faculties are not brought forward by emulation; and having no serious scientific study, if they have natural sagacity it is turned too soon on life and manners. They dwell on effects, and modifications, without tracing them back to causes; and complicated rules to adjust behaviour are a weak substitute for simple principles.

As a proof that education gives this appearance of weakness to females, we may instance the example of military men, who are, like them, sent into the world before their minds have been stored with knowledge or fortified by principles. The consequences are similar; soldiers acquire a little superficial knowledge, snatched from the muddy current of conversation, and, from continually mixing with society, they gain, what is termed a knowledge of the world; and this acquaintance with manners and customs has frequently been confounded with a knowledge of the human heart. But can the crude fruit of casual observation, never brought to the test of judgment, formed by comparing speculation and experience, deserve such a distinction? Soldiers, as well as women, practise the minor virtues with punctilious politeness. Where is then the sexual difference, when the education has

3. That is, be Jesus; in Matthew 15.14 he declares that "if the blind lead the blind, both shall fall into the ditch."

been the same? All the difference that I can discern, arises from the superior advantage of liberty, which enables the former to see more of life.

It is wandering from my present subject, perhaps, to make a political remark; but, as it was produced naturally by the train of my reflections, I shall not pass it silently over.

Standing armies can never consist of resolute, robust men; they may be well disciplined machines, but they will seldom contain men under the influence of strong passions, or with very vigorous faculties. And as for any depth of understanding, I will venture to affirm, that it is as rarely to be found in the army as amongst women; and the cause, I maintain, is the same. It may be further observed, that officers are also particularly attentive to their persons, fond of dancing, crowded rooms, adventures, and ridicule.[4] Like the *fair* sex, the business of their lives is gallantry.—They were taught to please, and they only live to please. Yet they do not lose their rank in the distinction of sexes, for they are still reckoned superior to women, though in what their superiority consists, beyond what I have just mentioned, it is difficult to discover.

The great misfortune is this, that they both acquire manners before morals, and a knowledge of life before they have, from reflection, any acquaintance with the grand ideal outline of human nature. The consequence is natural; satisfied with common nature, they become a prey to prejudices, and taking all their opinions on credit, they blindly submit to authority. So that, if they have any sense, it is a kind of instinctive glance, that catches proportions, and decides with respect to manners; but fails when arguments are to be pursued below the surface, or opinions analyzed.

May not the same remark be applied to women? Nay, the argument may be carried still further, for they are both thrown out of a useful station by the unnatural distinctions established in civilized life. Riches and hereditary honours have made cyphers of women to give consequence to the numerical figure;[5] and idleness has produced a mixture of gallantry and despotism into society, which leads the very men who are the slaves of their mistresses to tyrannize over their sisters, wives, and daughters. This is only keeping them in rank and file, it is true. Strengthen the female mind by enlarging it, and there will be an end to blind obedience; but, as blind obedience is ever sought for by power, tyrants and sensualists are in the right when they endeavour to keep women in the dark, because the former only want slaves, and the latter a play-thing. The sensualist, indeed, has been the most dangerous of tyrants, and women have been duped by their lovers, as princes by their ministers, whilst dreaming that they reigned over them.

I now principally allude to Rousseau, for his character of Sophia is, undoubtedly, a captivating one, though it appears to me grossly unnatural; however it is not the superstructure, but the foundation of her character, the principles on which her education was built, that I mean to attack; nay, warmly as I admire the genius of that able writer, whose opinions I shall

4. Why should women be censured with petulant acrimony, because they seem to have a passion for a scarlet coat? Has not education placed them more on a level with soldiers than any other class of men? [Wollestonecraft's note]. "Ridicule": that which is ridiculous.

5. That is, women are merely zeroes ("ciphers") to add to the family name, inflating its value but being nothing in themselves.

often have occasion to cite, indignation always takes place of admiration, and the rigid frown of insulted virtue effaces the smile of complacency, which his eloquent periods[6] are wont to raise, when I read his voluptuous reveries. Is this the man, who, in his ardour for virtue, would banish all the soft arts of peace, and almost carry us back to Spartan discipline? Is this the man who delights to paint the useful struggles of passion, the triumphs of good dispositions, and the heroic flights which carry the glowing soul out of itself?—How are these mighty sentiments lowered when he describes the pretty foot and enticing airs of his little favourite! But, for the present, I wave[7] the subject, and, instead of severely reprehending the transient effusions of overweening sensibility, I shall only observe, that whoever has cast a benevolent eye on society, must often have been gratified by the sight of humble mutual love, not dignified by sentiment, or strengthened by a union in intellectual pursuits. The domestic trifles of the day have afforded matters for cheerful converse, and innocent caresses have softened toils which did not require great exercise of mind or stretch of thought: yet, had not the sight of this moderate felicity excited more tenderness than respect? An emotion similar to what we feel when children are playing, or animals sporting,[8] whilst the contemplation of the noble struggles of suffering merit has raised admiration, and carried our thoughts to that world where sensation will give place to reason.

Women are, therefore, to be considered either as moral beings, or so weak that they must be entirely subjected to the superior faculties of men.

Let us examine this question. Rousseau declares that a woman should never, for a moment, feel herself independent, that she should be governed by fear to exercise her *natural* cunning, and made a coquetish slave in order to render her a more alluring object of desire, a *sweeter* companion to man, whenever he chooses to relax himself. He carries the arguments, which he pretends to draw from the indications of nature, still further, and insinuates that truth and fortitude, the corner stones of all human virtue, should be cultivated with certain restrictions, because, with respect to the female character, obedience is the grand lesson which ought to be impressed with unrelenting rigour.

What nonsense! when will a great man arise with sufficient strength of mind to puff away the fumes which pride and sensuality have thus spread over the subject! If women are by nature inferior to men, their virtues must be the same in quality, if not in degree, or virtue is a relative idea; consequently, their conduct should be founded on the same principles, and have the same aim.[9]

Connected with man as daughters, wives, and mothers, their moral character may be estimated by their manner of fulfilling those simple

6. Sentences.
7. Waive.
8. Similar feelings has Milton's pleasing picture of paradisiacal happiness ever raised in my mind; yet, instead of envying the lovely pair, I have, with conscious dignity, or Satanic pride, turned to hell for sublimer objects. In the same style, when viewing some noble monument of human art, I have traced the emanation of the Deity in the order I admired, till, descending from that giddy height, I have caught myself contemplating the grandest of all human sights;—for fancy quickly placed, in some solitary recess, an outcast of fortune, rising superior to passion and discontent [Wollestonecraft's note].
9. Rousseau argues that men's and women's virtues are essentially different [Macdonald and Scherf's note].

duties; but the end, the grand end of their exertions should be to unfold their own faculties and acquire the dignity of conscious virtue. They may try to render their road pleasant; but ought never to forget, in common with man, that life yields not the felicity which can satisfy an immortal soul. I do not mean to insinuate, that either sex should be so lost in abstract reflections or distant views, as to forget the affections and duties that lie before them, and are, in truth, the means appointed to produce the fruit of life; on the contrary, I would warmly recommend them, even while I assert, that they afford most satisfaction when they are considered in their true, sober light.

Probably the prevailing opinion, that woman was created for man, may have taken its rise from Moses's poetical story;[1] yet, as very few, it is presumed, who have bestowed any serious thought on the subject, ever supposed that Eve was, literally speaking, one of Adam's ribs, the deduction must be allowed to fall to the ground; or, only be so far admitted as it proves that man, from the remotest antiquity, found it convenient to exert his strength to subjugate his companion, and his invention to shew that she ought to have her neck bent under the yoke, because the whole creation was only created for his convenience or pleasure.

Let it not be concluded that I wish to invert the order of things; I have already granted, that, from the constitution of their bodies, men seem to be designed by Providence to attain a greater degree of virtue. I speak collectively of the whole sex; but I see not the shadow of a reason to conclude that their virtues should differ in respect to their nature. In fact, how can they, if virtue has only one eternal standard? I must therefore, if I reason consequentially, as strenuously maintain that they have the same simple direction, as that there is a God.

It follows then that cunning should not be opposed to wisdom, little cares to great exertions, or insipid softness, varnished over with the name of gentleness, to that fortitude which grand views alone can inspire.

I shall be told that woman would then lose many of her peculiar graces, and the opinion of a well known poet might be quoted to refute my unqualified assertion. For Pope has said, in the name of the whole male sex,

> "Yet ne'er so sure our passion to create,
> As when she touch'd the brink of all we hate."[2]

In what light this sally places men and women, I shall leave to the judicious to determine; meanwhile I shall content myself with observing, that I cannot discover why, unless they are mortal,[3] females should always be degraded by being made subservient to love or lust.

To speak disrespectfully of love is, I know, high treason against sentiment and fine feelings; but I wish to speak the simple language of truth, and rather to address the head than the heart. To endeavour to reason love out of the world, would be to out Quixote[4] Cervantes, and equally offend against

1. Moses was traditionally credited with writing the first 5 books of the Bible; see Genesis 2.18–25.
2. ALEXANDER POPE (1688–1744), *Epistle II, To a Lady: Of the Characters of Women* (1735), 51–52.
3. That is, unless they are not as capable as men of immortal life.
4. That is, to be more foolishly impractical than Don Quixote, the overly idealistic title character of the novel (1605, 1615) by Miguel de Cervantes (1547–1616).

common sense; but an endeavour to restrain this tumultuous passion, and to prove that it should not be allowed to dethrone superior powers, or to usurp the sceptre which the understanding should ever coolly wield, appears less wild.

Youth is the season for love in both sexes; but in those days of thoughtless enjoyment provision should be made for the more important years of life, when reflection takes place of sensation. But Rousseau, and most of the male writers who have followed his steps, have warmly inculcated that the whole tendency of female education ought to be directed to one point:—to render them pleasing.

Let me reason with the supporters of this opinion who have any knowledge of human nature, do they imagine that marriage can eradicate the habitude of life? The woman who has only been taught to please will soon find that her charms are oblique sunbeams, and that they cannot have much effect on her husband's heart when they are seen every day, when the summer is passed and gone. Will she then have sufficient native energy to look into herself for comfort, and cultivate her dormant faculties? or, is it not more rational to expect that she will try to please other men; and, in the emotions raised by the expectation of new conquests, endeavour to forget the mortification her love or pride has received? When the husband ceases to be a lover—and the time will inevitably come, her desire of pleasing will then grow languid, or become a spring of bitterness; and love, perhaps, the most evanescent of all passions, gives place to jealousy or vanity.

I now speak of women who are restrained by principle or prejudice; such women, though they would shrink from an intrigue with real abhorrence, yet, nevertheless, wish to be convinced by the homage of gallantry that they are cruelly neglected by their husbands; or, days and weeks are spent in dreaming of the happiness enjoyed by congenial souls till their health is undermined and their spirits broken by discontent. How then can the great art of pleasing be such a necessary study? it is only useful to a mistress; the chaste wife, and serious mother, should only consider her power to please as the polish of her virtues, and the affection of her husband as one of the comforts that render her task less difficult and her life happier.—But, whether she be loved or neglected, her first wish should be to make herself respectable, and not to rely for all her happiness on a being subject to like infirmities with herself.

* * *

1792

GERMAINE NECKER DE STAËL
1766–1817

Mme de Staël is one of the few women writers without whom the history of French literature cannot be told. Bridging the gap between the old regime and the Revolution, between national and comparative literatures, and between classical aesthetics and *littérature engagée*, her writings were an advance justification of both Romanticism and realism in France. Celebrated for her conversation, condemned for her sexuality, and alternately lauded and vilified for her politics, she embodied the kind of freedom that revolutionary theorists seldom imagined for women. She was a child of the Enlightenment and never abandoned the principles of self-realization it entailed. "The only reason to fear women's wit," she wrote in 1800, "would be some sort of scrupulous anxiety about their happiness. And indeed, by developing their rational minds one might well be enlightening them as to the misfortunes often connected with their fate; but the same reasoning would apply to the effect of the enlightenment on the happiness of the human race in general, a question which seems to me to have been decided once and for all."

Germaine de Staël was born in Paris to Swiss Protestant parents. Her father, Jacques Necker, had amassed a fortune in banking, thanks to French laws that prevented most Catholics from lending money at high interest. Her mother, Suzanne (née Curchod), maintained a celebrated salon. Germaine seems not to have inherited her mother's great beauty, but her childhood was spent in the company of famous Enlightenment figures such as Edward Gibbon, chronicler of the fall of the Roman Empire and former suitor of Suzanne Curchod; Denis Diderot and Jean d'Alembert, authors of the *Encyclopédie*; and many others. Her father, appointed to act as Louis XVI's finance minister in 1777, was lionized by both the king, whose treasury he restored, and the people, whom he fed. Indeed, it was his dismissal by the king in 1789 that led to the storming of the Bastille.

At age nineteen, Germaine Necker was one of the wealthiest heiresses in Europe. Her parents, seeking a son-in-law who was not Catholic, briefly considered William Pitt the Younger, but she was unwilling to move to England. In 1786 she settled on a young Swedish suitor very much in favor with the French and the Swedish courts. Erik Magnus de Staël-Holstein, a penniless nobleman, had had his eye on Germaine's fortune since she was twelve. King Gustavus III made him Swedish ambassador to France for life (in a complicated bargain in which France gave Sweden the Caribbean Island of St. Barthélémy), and Germaine was assured she would never have to live in Sweden.

Germaine de Staël supplemented this marriage of convenience through passionate involvements with some of the most interesting men of the century. Her lovers were numerous; among the best known were Charles-Maurice de Talleyrand, then bishop of Autun; Count Louis de Narbonne, whose ambivalence during the early revolutionary period led him to support both Lafayette and the royal family; Benjamin Constant, whose brilliant conversation matched her own and who fictionalized their affair in his novel *Adolphe* (1816); and Adolphe Ribbing, who masterminded the assassination of the same Swedish king who had brought about her marriage. August Wilhelm von Schlegel was central to her intellectual life and preceptor to her children (she gave birth to five, and only the first—who died in infancy—was conceived within marriage). Her last love was a younger man and a commoner, John Rocca, with whom at forty-five she bore a mentally disabled son and whom she secretly married before she died (Erik having died in 1802). On reading Mme de Staël's first novel, *Delphine* (1802), and recognizing the autobiographical elements in it, Talleyrand quipped: "Mme de Staël has disguised both herself and me as women in her novel." De Staël's mother, influenced by Jean-Jacques Rousseau's theories of education in his *Emile* (1762) but switching the gender roles presented in that work, had brought her daughter up with the independence of an Emile, not the compliance of a Sophie.

Although she wanted nothing more than to live in Paris, Mme de Staël spent most of her adult life elsewhere—not just in France but also in England, Germany, Italy, Sweden, Russia, Austria, and, most important, Switzerland, where her parents, in and out of favor in France, had bought the château of Coppet in 1784. Her exile by Napoleon in 1803 to "forty leagues from Paris" was only the most official of her banishments by political forces on the left and on the right. Her defense of a constitutional monarchy was too royalist for the revolutionary Jacobins, and her defense of a republic was too revolutionary for the aristocratic *émigrés*. A moderate in favor of both liberty and property, she offended everyone. The authors of the French constitution frequented her Paris salon, but she wrote in defense of Queen Marie Antoinette. Napoleon, neither constitutional nor republican, was a worthy opponent for fourteen years. He not only exiled her from Paris but also planted spies in her entourage, had her correspondence read, took offense at all her writings, and stopped publication of her *On Germany* in 1810. Yet her opposition to Napoleon did not prevent a certain identification: in his final days, she informed him of a plot on his life. In 1815, when Napoleon was at last defeated, she hoped for a constitutional monarchy but rallied to the support of the restoration of Louis XVIII; she was reimbursed, in the process, for the two million francs her father had lent the royal treasury.

Wherever she lived, Mme de Staël configured a brilliant salon around her. Her passion for intellectual conversation both seduced and exhausted her guests, whom she received, in the manner of the old regime, from the moment she awoke to the moment she retired (a day whose length grew as her insomnia worsened). Conversations within the "Groupe de Coppet" (Coppet Group) revolved around liberal opposition to Napoleon and around Romantic ideals of literature and human progress. Leading figures such as Johann Wolfgang von Goethe, Wilhelm von Humboldt, Lord Byron, Simonde de Sismondi, and Juliette Récamier fueled Mme de Staël's changing sense of the possibilities. Her château at Coppet has remained a gathering place for scholars and writers; colloquia on her work regularly take place there, where she was laid to rest next to her parents.

De Staël's early "Essay on Fictions," published in 1795 (our first selection), makes the case, in her characteristic epigrammatic style, for what was eventually to become the nineteenth-century realist novel. Novels, she claims, should broaden their range to include every human predicament, not simply romantic love. Novels can give the creative intellect the space to explore every intractable problem facing postrevolutionary man and woman. Fictions in which "nothing is true and everything is likely" will challenge novel writers to represent what they take to be the real. Unlike philosophical allegories, which subordinate fiction to ideas, and historical fictions, which subordinate fiction to facts, the novel can re-create the world as it is and, in the process, change it. Useless if merely accurate or merely imaginary, literature has the power to move, to awaken, to inform, to distract, and to console. Far from being outside of history, the novel can come to grips with everything that *makes* history.

On Literature Considered in Its Relationship to Social Institutions (1800), from which our second selection is taken, is a fitting monument to the turn from the eighteenth to the nineteenth century. Deeply connected to the fate of the French Revolution, which had just passed through the Reign of Terror (during which Mme de Staël lost many friends and was almost executed herself), *On Literature* describes history as an ongoing process that, whatever its setbacks, ultimately heads toward human progress and perfectibility. As a domain in which the mind can stretch itself to the utmost, literature is an intimate part of that process. When, in later conversation, Mme de Staël was introduced to Goethe's views on art for art's sake, she found this Weimar aesthetic contrary to all she hoped for from literature, but so dialectical was her mind that she loved to find an idea she could resist. As Goethe later reported, "My obstinate contrariness often drove her to despair, but it was then that she was at her most amiable and that she displayed her mental and verbal agility most brilliantly."

Romanticism in France is rooted in the writings of Rousseau, another Swiss, but by all accounts the decisive turn was taken when Mme de Staël introduced German Romanticism to the French. In her book *On Germany* (1810), she offered Europe and particularly France an alternative to the empire of Napoleon with his taste for classicism and absolutism. Her division between northern literature (melancholy, medieval, Christian, emotional, misty—Romantic) and southern literature (sunny, rational, sensual, pagan—classical) was both cosmopolitan and nationalist in an age when modern nationalism was just taking shape. All of the categories were problematic, but despite the rhetorical force of Mme de Staël's oppositions, their thrust was less essential ("the German soul," "the French mind") than dialectical. Within the French tradition, the seeds of Romanticism already existed: all that was needed was to make them grow. And German thinkers would provide the nutrients.

In addition to her theoretical and political writings, de Staël is famous for two novels—*Delphine* (1802) and *Corinne, or Italy* (1807). The latter paints a portrait of a celebrated, independent woman artist; her art is deepened by her love for an Englishman who, initially attracted by her talent, eventually abandons her for a less complex partner. Corinne, who is half English and half Italian, combines the genius of the Mediterranean with the sensitivity of the North in her poetry, but she suffers, in the end, from culture's inability to incorporate superior and complex women. Mme de Staël had much to say about the plight of the woman intellectual, whether living in a monarchy or in a republic, a plight that is nowhere more cogently analyzed than in our selection from *On Literature*. The category of "exceptional woman," a term invented by French culture both to counteract and to appropriate women like Mme de Staël, continued to function well into the twentieth century, as SIMONE DE BEAUVOIR was to find out. By separating the exception from the condition of women in general, society recognizes and benefits from female talent without having to change its view—often shared by the exceptional woman herself—of women as such.

"Essay on Fictions" Keywords: Literary History, The Novel, Realism
***On Literature Considered in Its Relationship to Social Institutions* Keywords:** Gender, Institutional Studies, Literary History, Women's Literature

From Essay on Fictions[1]

Introduction

Man's most valuable faculty is his imagination. Human life seems so little designed for happiness that we need the help of a few creations, a few images, a lucky choice of memories to muster some sparse pleasure on this earth and struggle against the pain of all our destinies—not by philosophical force, but by the more efficient force of distraction. The dangers of imagination have been discussed a good deal, but there is no point in looking up what impotent mediocrity and strict reason have said on this topic over and

1. Translated by Vivian Folkenflik.

over again. The human race is not about to give up being stimulated, and anyone who has the gift of appealing to people's emotions is even less likely to give up the success promised by such talent. The number of necessary and evident truths is limited; it will never be enough for the human mind or heart. The highest honor may well go to those who discover such truths, but the authors of books producing sweet emotions or illusions have also done useful work for humanity. Metaphysical precision cannot be applied to man's affections and remain compatible with his nature. Beginnings are all we have on this earth—there is no limit. Virtue is actual and real, but happiness floats in space; anyone who tries to examine happiness inappropriately will destroy it, as we dissolve the brilliant images of the mist if we walk straight through them. And yet the advantage of fictions is not the pleasure they bring. If fictions please nothing but the eye, they do nothing but amuse; but if they touch our hearts, they can have a great influence on all our moral ideas. This talent may be the most powerful way there is of controlling behavior and enlightening the mind. Man has only two distinct faculties: reason and imagination. All the others, even feeling, are simply results or combinations of these two. The realm of fiction, like that of imagination, is therefore vast. Fictions do not find obstacles in passions: they make use of them. Philosophy may be the invisible power in control of fictions, but if she is the first to show herself, she will destroy all their magic.

When I talk about fictions, I will therefore be considering them from two perspectives of content and charm: this kind of writing may contain pleasure without useful purpose, but never vice versa. Fictions are meant to attract us; the more moral or philosophical the result one is trying to achieve, the more they have to be decked out with things to move us, leading us to the goal without advance warning. In mythological fictions I will consider only the poet's talent; these fictions could well be examined in the light of their religious influence, but such a point of view is absolutely foreign to my subject. I will be discussing the writings of the ancients according to the impression they create in our times, so my concern must be with their literary talent rather than their religious beliefs.

Fictions can be divided into three groups: (1) marvelous and allegorical fictions, (2) historical fictions, (3) fictions in which everything is both invented and imitated, where nothing is true and everything is likely.[2]

This topic should really be discussed in an extensive treatise including most existing literary works and involving thoughts on almost every topic, since the complete exposition of any one idea is connected to the whole chain of ideas. But I am only trying to prove that the most useful kind of fiction will be novels taking life as it is, with delicacy, eloquence, depth, and morality, and I have excluded everything irrelevant to that goal from this essay.

III

The third and last part of this essay must deal with the usefulness of natural fictions, as I call them, where everything is both invented and imitated, so that nothing is true but everything looks true to life. Tragedies with completely imaginary subjects will not be included here; they portray a more

2. That is, realist novels, discussed under heading III.

lofty nature, an extraordinary situation at an extraordinary level. The verisimilitude of such plays depends on events that are extremely rare, and morally applicable to very few people. Comedies and other dramas are in the theater what novels are to other fiction: their plots are taken from private life and natural circumstances. However, the conventions of the theater deprive us of the commentary which gives examples of reflections their individuality. Dramas are allowed to choose their characters among people other than kings and heroes, but they can show only broadly defined situations, because there is no time for nuance. And life is not concentrated like that—does not happen in contrasts—is not really theatrical in the way plays have to be written. Dramatic art has different effects, advantages, and means which might well be discussed separately, but I think only the modern novel is capable of achieving the constant, accurate usefulness we can get from the picture of our ordinary, habitual feelings. People usually make a separate case of what they call philosophical novels; all novels should be philosophical, as they should all have a moral goal. Perhaps, however, we are not guided so inevitably toward this moral goal when all the episodes narrated are focused on one principal idea, exempting the author from all probability in the way one situation follows another. Each chapter then becomes a kind of allegory—its events are only there to illustrate the maxim at the end. The novels *Candide, Zadig,* and *Memnon,*[3] while delightful in other respects, would be much more useful if they were not marvelous, if they offered an example instead of an emblem and if, as I say, the whole story did not have to relate to the same goal. Such novels are at the same disadvantage as teachers: children never believe them, because they make everything that happens relate to the lesson at hand. Children unconsciously know already that there is less regularity than that in real life. Events are also invented in novels like Richardson's and Fielding's,[4] where the author is trying to keep close to life by following with great accuracy the stages, developments, and inconsistencies of human history, and the way the results of experience always come down to the morality of actions and the advantages of virtue, nonetheless. In these novels, however, the feelings are so natural that the reader often believes he is being spoken to directly, with no artifice but the tactfulness of changing the names.

The art of novel-writing does not have the reputation it deserves because of a throng of bad writers overwhelming us with their colorless productions; in this genre, perfection may require the greatest genius, but mediocrity is well within everyone's grasp. This infinite number of colorless novels has almost used up the passion portrayed in them; one is terrified of finding the slightest resemblance in one's own life to the situations they describe. It has taken the very greatest masters to bring this genre back again, despite the writers who have degraded it. And others have dragged it even lower by including disgusting scenes of vice. Despite the fact that fiction's main advantage is to gather around man everything in nature that might be useful to him as a lesson or model, some writers supposed we might have some kind of use for these detestable paintings of evil habits. As if such fictions

3. Tales by Voltaire: *Zadig* was published in 1747; *Memnon* in 1749, *Candide* in 1759 [translator's note].

4. Samuel Richardson (1689–1761) and Henry Fielding (1707–1754), English novelists.

could ever leave a heart that rejected them in the same state of purity as a heart that had never known them! The novel as we conceive of it, however—as we have a few examples of it—is one of the most beautiful creations of the human mind, and one of the most influential on individual morality, which is what ultimately determines the morality of the public.

There is a very good reason why public opinion does not have enough respect for the writing of good novels, however. This is because novels are considered to be exclusively devoted to the portrayal of love—the most violent, universal, and true passion of them all, but also the passion which inspires no interest at any other time of life than youth, since youth is all it influences. We may well believe that all deep and tender feelings belong to the nature of love, and that hearts which have neither known nor pardoned love cannot feel enthusiasm in friendship, devotion in misery, worship of one's parents, passion for one's children. One can feel respect for one's duties, but no delight or self-surrender in their accomplishment, if one has not loved with all the strength of one's soul, ceasing to be one's self to live entirely in another. The destiny of women and the happiness of men who are not called upon to govern empires often depend for the rest of their lives on the role they gave to the influence of love in their youth. Nevertheless, when people reach a certain age, they completely forget the impression love made on them. Their character changes; they devote themselves to other goals, other passions; and these new interests are what we should extend the subjects of novels to include. A new career would then be open to authors who have the talent to paint all the emotions of the human heart, and are able to use their intimate knowledge of it to involve us. Ambition, pride, greed, vanity could be the primary topic of novels which would have situations as varied as those arising from love, and fresher plots. Will people object that such a tableau of men's passions exists in history, and that we should look for it there? History does not reach the lives of private men, feelings and characters that do not result in public events. History does not act on you with sustained moral interest. Reality often fails to make an effect; and the commentary needed to make a lasting impression would stop the essential quick narrative pace, and give dramatic form to a work that should have a very different sort of merit. And the moral of history can never be completely clear. This may be because one cannot always show with any degree of certainty the inner feelings that punish the wicked in their prosperity and reward the virtuous in their misery, or perhaps because man's destiny is not completed in this life. Practical morality is founded on the advantages of virtue, but the reading of history does not always put it in the limelight.

Great historians (especially Tacitus)[5] do try to attach some moral to every event they relate, making us envy the dying Germanicus, and hate Tiberius at the pinnacle of his grandeur. But they can still portray only those feelings certified by facts. What stays with us from a reading of history is more likely to be the influence of talent, the brilliance of glory, the advantages of power, than the quiet, subtle, gentle morality which is the basis of individual happi-

5. Roman historian (ca. 55–ca. 120 C.E.). In *Annales* 2, Tacitus recounts the strains between Tiberius (42 B.C.E.–37 C.E.; emperor, 14 C.E.–37 C.E.) and his nephew Germanicus (15 B.C.E.–19 C.E.), whom he adopted but whose popularity he perceived as a threat; given command of the eastern provinces, Germanicus died (probably poisoned) in Syria.

ness and the relationship between individuals. Everyone would think me ridiculous if I said I set no value on history, and that I preferred fictions—as if fictions did not arise from experience, and as if the delicate nuances shown in novels did not come from the philosophical results and mother-ideas presented by the great panorama of public events! However, the morality of history only exists in bulk. History gives constant results by means of the recurrence of a certain number of chances: its lessons apply to nations, not individuals. Its examples always fit nations, because if one considers them in a general way they are invariable; but it never explains the exceptions. These exceptions can seduce each man as an individual; the exceptional circumstances consecrated by history leave vast empty spaces into which the miseries and wrongs that make up most private destinies could easily fall. On the other hand, novels can paint characters and feeling with such force and detail that they make more of an impression of hatred for vice and love for virtue than any other kind of reading. The morality of novels belongs more to the development of the internal emotions of the soul than to the events they relate. We do not draw a useful lesson from whatever arbitrary circumstance the author invents as punishment for the crime; what leaves its indelible mark on us comes from the truthful rendition of the scenes, the gradual process or sequence of wrongdoing, the enthusiasm for sacrifices, the sympathy for misfortune. Everything is so true to life in such novels that we have no trouble persuading ourselves that everything could happen just this way—not past history, but often, it seems, the history of the future.

Novels give a false idea of mankind, it has been said. This is true of bad novels, as it is true of paintings which imitate nature badly. When novels are good, however, nothing gives such an intimate knowledge of the human heart as these portrayals of the various circumstances of private life and the impressions they inspire. Nothing gives so much play to reflection, which finds much more to discover in details than in generalities. Memoirs would be able to do this if their only subjects were not, as in history, famous men and public events. If most men had the wit and good faith to give a truthful, clear account of what they had experienced in the course of their lives, novels would be useless—but even these sincere narratives would not have all the advantages of novels. We would still have to add a kind of dramatic effect to the truth; not deforming it, but condensing it to set it off. This is the art of the painter: far from distorting objects, it represents them in a way that makes them more immediately apprehended. Nature sometimes shows us things all on the same level, eliminating any contrasts; if we copy her too slavishly we become incapable of portraying her. The most truthful account is always an imitative truth: as a tableau, it demands a harmony of its own. However remarkable a true story may be for its nuances, feelings, and characters, it cannot interest us without the talent necessary for the composition of fiction. But despite our admiration for the genius that lets us penetrate the recesses of the human heart, it is impossible to bear all those minute details with which even the most famous novels are burdened. The author thinks they add to the picture's verisimilitude, blind to the fact that anything that slows down the interest destroys the only truth fiction has: the impression it produces. To put everything that happens in a room onstage is to destroy theatrical illusion completely. Novels have dramatic conventions also: the only thing necessary in an invention is what adds to the effect one is creating. If a glance, a movement, or an unnoticed circumstance helps paint a character or develop our understanding of a feeling, the simpler the means, the greater the merit in catching it—but a scrupulously detailed account of an ordinary event diminishes verisimilitude instead of increasing it. Thrown back on a positive notion of what is true by the kind of details that belong only to truth, you soon break out of the illusion, weary of being unable to find either the instruction of history or the interest of a novel.

The greatest power of fiction is its talent to touch us; almost all moral truths can be made tangible if they are shown in action. Virtue has so much influence on human happiness or misery that one can make most of life's situations depend on it. Some severe philosophers condemn all emotions, wanting moral authority to rule by a simple statement of moral duty. Nothing is less suited to human nature. Virtue must be brought to life if she is to fight the passions with any chance of winning; a sort of exaltation must be aroused for us to find any charm in sacrifice; misfortune must be embellished for us to prefer it to the great charm of guilty enticement; and the touching fictions which incite the soul to generous feelings make it unconsciously engage itself in a promise that it would be ashamed to retract in similar circumstances. But the more real power there is in fiction's talent for touching us, the more important it becomes to widen its influence to the passions of all ages, and the duties of all situations. The primary subject of novels is love, and characters who have nothing to do with it are present only as accessories. It would be possible to find a host of new subjects if one followed a different plan. *Tom Jones*[6] has the most general moral of any novel: love appears in it as only one of many means of showing the philosophical result. The real aim of *Tom Jones* is to show the uncertainty of judgments founded on appearances, proving the superiority of natural and what we may call involuntary virtues over reputations based on mere respect for external etiquette. And this is one of the most useful, most deservedly famous of all novels. *Caleb Williams*, by Mr. Godwin,[7] is a recent novel which, despite some tedious passages and oversights, seems to give a good idea of this inexhaustible genre. Love plays no part in this fiction; the only motives for the action are the hero's unbridled passion for the world's respect and Caleb's overpowering curiosity, leading him to discover whether or not Falkland deserves the esteem he enjoys. We read this story with all the absorption inspired by romantic interest and the reflection commanded by the most philosophical tableau.

Some successful fictions do give pictures of life unrelated to love: several *Moral Tales* of Marmontel, a few chapters of *Sentimental Journey*, various anecdotes from the *Spectator*[8] and other books on morality, some pieces taken from German literature, whose superiority is growing every day. There is still, however, no new Richardson devoting himself to paint men's other passions in a novel completely exploring the progress and consequences of these passions. The success of such a work would come from the truth of its

6. *The History of Tom Jones, a Foundling* (1749), a novel by Fielding.
7. William Godwin (1756–1836), English novelist and political theorist, married to MARY WOLLSTONECRAFT; *Caleb Williams* was published in 1794.
8. A periodical (1711–12) written by JOSEPH ADDISON and Richard Steele. Jean-François Marmontel (1723–1799), French author whose *Moral Tales* (1761–86) appeared first in a journal. *Sentimental Journey through England and France*: a 1768 narrative by Laurence Sterne.

characters, the force of its contrasts and the energy of its situations, rather than from that feeling which is so easy to paint, so quick to arouse interest, pleasing women by what it makes them remember even if it cannot attract them by the greatness or novelty of the scenes it presents. What beautiful things we would find in the Lovelace[9] of ambition! What philosophical developments, if we were eager to explain and analyze all the passions, as novels have already done for love! Let no one object that books on morality are enough to teach us a knowledge of our duties; such books cannot possibly go into all the nuances of delicacy, or detail the myriad resources of the passions. We can glean a morality purer and higher from novels than from any didactic work on virtue; didactic works are so dry that they have to be too indulgent. Maxims have to be generally applicable, so they never achieve that heroic delicacy we may offer as a model but cannot reasonably impose as a duty. Where is the moralist who could say: "If your whole family wants you to marry a detestable man, and you are prompted by their persecution to give a few signs of the most innocent interest to the man you find attractive, you are going to bring death and dishonor upon yourself"? This, however, is the plot of *Clarissa*; this is what we read with admiration, without a word of protest to the author who touches us and holds us captive. What moralist would claim that it is better to abandon oneself to deep despair, the sort of despair that threatens life and disturbs the mind, rather than marry the most virtuous man in the world if his religion is different from your own? Well, we need not approve of the superstitious opinions of *Clementina*,[1] but love struggling against a scruple of conscience and duty winning out over passion are a sight that moves and touches even loose-principled people who would have rejected such a conclusion disdainfully if it had been a maxim preceding the tableau instead of an effect that followed it. In novels of a less sublime genre, there are so many subtle rules for women's conduct! We could support this opinion by quoting from masterpieces like *The Princess of Clèves, The Count of Comminge, Paul and Virginia, Cecilia*, most of the writings of Madame Riccoboni, *Caroline*, whose charm is felt by everyone, the touching episode of Caliste, the letters of Camilla,[2] in which the mistakes of a woman and their miserable consequences give a more moral and severe picture than the spectacle of virtue itself, and many other French, English, and German works. Novels have the right to offer the severest morality without revolting our hearts; they have captured feeling, the only thing that can successfully plead for indulgence. Pity for misfortune or interest in passion often win the struggle against books of morality, but good novels have the art of putting this emotion itself on their side and using it for their own ends.

There is still one serious objection to love stories: that they paint love in such a way as to arouse it, and that there are moments in life when this dan-

9. The villain-hero who seduces the title character in Richardson's *Clarissa, or The History of a Young Lady* (1747–48).

1. The Italian woman who renounces the eponymous hero of Richardson's *History of Sir Charles Grandison* (1753–54) [shortened translator's note].

2. All these works are novels. *The Princess of Clèves* is by Mme de La Fayette (1678); *The Count of Comminge* (1735) is by Mme de Tencin; *Paul and Virginia* (1787) is by Jacques-Henri Bernadin de Saint-Pierre; *Cecilia* (1782) and *Camilla* (1796) are by Fanny Burney; Marie-Jeanne Riccoboni (1713–1792) wrote a number of novels in the mid-18th century. *Caroline* is probably *Caroline de Litchfield* (1785), by Isabelle de Montolieu. Isabelle de Charrière, later [Benjamin] Constant's intimate friend, wrote *Caliste* (1787) [translator's note].

ger wins out over every kind of advantage. This drawback could not exist in novels about any other human passion, however. By recognizing the most fleeting symptoms of a dangerous inclination from the very beginning, one could turn oneself as well as others away from it. Ambition, pride, and avarice often exist without the least consciousness on the part of those they rule. Love feeds on the portrait of its own feelings, but the best way to fight the other passions is to make them be recognized. If the features, tricks, means, and results of these passions were as fully shown and popularized by novels as the history of love, society would have more trustworthy rules and more scrupulous principles about all the transactions of life. Even if purely philosophical writings could predict and detail all the nuances of actions, as do novels, dramatic morality would still have the great advantage of arousing indignant impulses, and exaltation of soul, a sweet melancholy—the various effects of fictional situations, and a sort of supplement to existence. This impression resembles the one we have of real facts we might have witnessed, but it is less distracting for the mind than the incoherent panorama of events around us, because it is always directed toward a single goal. Finally, there are men over whom duty has no influence, and who could still be preserved from crime by developing within them the ability to be moved. Characters capable of adopting humanity only with the help of such a faculty of emotion, the physical pleasure of the soul, would naturally not deserve much respect; nevertheless, if the effect of these touching fictions became widespread enough among the people, it might give us some assurance that we would no longer have in our country those beings whose character poses the most incomprehensible moral problem that has ever existed. The gradual steps from the known to the unknown stop well before we reach any understanding of the emotions which rules the executioners of France. Neither events nor books can have developed in them the least trace of humanity, the memory of a single sensation of pity, any mobility within the mind itself for them to remain capable of that constant cruelty, so foreign to all the impulses of nature—a cruelty which has given mankind its first limitless concept, the complete idea of crime.

There are writings whose principal merit is the eloquence of passion, such as the "Epistle of Abelard" by Pope, *Werther*, the *Portuguese Letters*, and especially *The New Héloïse*.[3] The aim of such works is often moral, but what remains with us more than anything else is the absolute power of the heart. We cannot classify such novels. Every century has one soul and one genius capable of achieving this—it cannot be a genre, it cannot be a goal. Who would want to proscribe these miracles of the word, these deep impressions which satisfy all the emotions of the passionate? Readers enthusiastic about such talent are very few in number; these works always do their admirers good. Let ardent, sensitive souls admire them; they cannot make their language understood by anyone else. The feelings that disturb such beings are rarely understood; constantly condemned, they would believe themselves

3. *Julie, or The New Heloise* (1761), an epistolary novel by Jean-Jacques Rousseau. "Epistle of Abelard": *Eloisa to Abelard* (1717), by ALEXANDER POPE (1688–1744); Héloïse fell in love with and secretly married her tutor, the 11th-century theologian Pierre Abélard (on discovery, she was sent to a convent and he became a monk). *Werther*: *The Sorrows of Young Werther* (1774), by Johann Wolfgang von Goethe. *The Portuguese Letters*: letters (published 1699) said to have been written by a Portuguese nun to her lover, a French officer, but probably written by their French "translator," Gabriel Joseph de Lavergne, vicomte de Guilleragues.

alone in the world, they would soon hate their own nature for isolating them, if a few passionate, melancholy works did not make them hear a voice in the desert of life, letting them find in solitude a few rays of the happiness that escapes them in the middle of society. The pleasure of retreat is refreshing after the vain attempts of disappointed hope; far from this unfortunate creature, the entire universe may be in motion, but such eloquent, tender writing stays near him as his most faithful friend, the one who understands him best. Yes, a book must be right if it offers even one day's distraction from pain; it helps the best of men. Of course there are also sorrows that come from one's own character flaws, but so many of them come from superiority of mind or sensitivity of heart! and there are so many that would be easier to bear if one had fewer good qualities! I respect the suffering heart, even when it is unknown to me; I take pleasure in fictions whose only effect might be to comfort this heart by capturing its interest. In this life, which we pass through rather than feel, the distributor of the only real happiness of which human nature is capable would be someone who distracts man from himself and others, suspending the action of the passions by substituting independent pleasures for them—if the influence of his talent could only last.

1795

From On Literature Considered in Its Relationship to Social Institutions[1]

On Women Writers (2.4)

> Unhappiness is like the black mountain of Bember, at the edge of the blazing kingdom of Lahor. As long as you are climbing it, you see nothing ahead of you but sterile rocks; but once you are at the peak, heaven is at your head, and at your feet the kingdom of Cashmere.
>
> —*The Indian Hut*, by Bernadin de Saint-Pierre[2]

The existence of women in society is still uncertain in many ways. A desire to please excites their minds; reason recommends obscurity; and their triumphs and failures are equally and completely arbitrary.

I believe a day will come when philosophical legislators will give serious attention to the education of women, to the laws protecting them, to the duties which should be imposed on them, to the happiness which can be guaranteed them. At present, however, most women belong neither to the natural nor to the social order. What succeeds for some women is the ruin of others; their good points may do them harm, their faults may prove useful. One minute they are everything, the next nothing. Their destiny resembles that of freedmen under the emperors: if they try to gain any influence, this unofficial power is called criminal, while if they remain slaves their destiny is crushed.

1. Translated by Vivian Folkenflik.
2. French naturalist and author (1737–1814), heavily influenced by the writings of Jean-Jacques Rousseau (1712–1788); his novel *The Indian Hut* was published in 1791. "Lahor" and "Cashmere," now better known as Lahore and Kashmir, are regions of northern India (in 1947 Lahore was divided between India and Pakistan).

It would no doubt be generally preferable for women to devote themselves entirely to the domestic virtues, but the peculiar thing about men's judgments of women is that they are much likelier to forgive women for neglecting these duties than for attracting attention by unusual talent. Men are quite willing to tolerate women's degradation of the heart, so long as it is accompanied by mediocrity of mind. The best behavior in the world can scarcely obtain forgiveness for real superiority.

I am now going to discuss the various causes of this peculiar phenomenon, beginning with the condition of women writers in monarchies, then in republics. I am interested in the differences these political situations make in the destinies of women who set their minds upon literary celebrity; I will then consider more generally the sort of happiness fame can promise these women.

In monarchies, women have ridicule to fear; in republics, hatred.

In a monarchy, the sense of the right and proper is so acute that any unusual act or impulse to change one's situation looks ridiculous right away. Anything your rank or position forces you to do finds a thousand admirers; everything you invent spontaneously, with no obligation, is judged severely and in advance. The jealousy natural to all men calms down only if you can apologize for success under cover of some obligation. Unless you cover fame itself with the excuse of your situation and practical interests, if people think your only motive is a need to distinguish yourself, you will annoy those whom ambition is leading in the same direction as yourself.

Men can always hide their vanity or their craving for applause under the appearance or reality of stronger, nobler passions; but women who write are generally assumed to be primarily inspired by a wish to show off their wit. As a result, the public is very reluctant to grant its approval, and the public's sense that women cannot do without this approval is precisely what tempts it to deny it. In every walk of life, as soon as a man sees your obvious need of him, his feelings for you almost always cool down. A woman publishing a book makes herself so dependent on public opinion that those who mete it out make her harshly aware of their power.

These general causes, acting more or less uniformly in all countries, are reinforced by various circumstances peculiar to the French monarchy. The spirit of chivalry, still lingering on in France, was opposed in some respects to the overeager cultivation of letters even by men; it must have aroused all the more dislike for women concentrating on literary studies and turning their thoughts away from their primary concern, the sentiments of the heart. The niceties of the code of honor might well make men averse from submitting themselves to the motley criticism attracted by publicity. How much more must they have disliked seeing the creatures entrusted to their protection—their wives, sisters, daughters—running the gauntlet of public criticism, or even giving the public the right to make a habit of talking about them!

Great talent could triumph over all these considerations, but it was still hard for women to bear reputations as authors nobly, simultaneously combining them with the independence of high rank and keeping up the dignity, grace, ease, and unself-consciousness that were supposed to distinguish their habitual style and manners.

Women were certainly allowed to sacrifice household occupations to a love of society and its pleasures; serious study, however, was condemned as pedantic. If from the very first moment one did not rise above the teasing which went on from all sides, this teasing would end by discouraging talent and poisoning the well of confidence and exaltation.

Some of these disadvantages are not found in republics, especially if one of the goals of the republic is the encouragement of enlightenment. It might perhaps be natural for literature to become women's portion in such a state, and for men to devote themselves entirely to higher philosophy.

The education of women has always followed the spirit of the constitutions established in free countries. In Sparta, women were accustomed to the exercises of war; in Rome, they were expected to have austere and patriotic virtues. If we want the moving principle of the French Republic to be the emulation of enlightenment and philosophy, it is only reasonable to encourage women to cultivate their minds, so that men can talk with them about ideas that would hold their interest.

Nevertheless, ever since the Revolution men have deemed it politically and morally useful to reduce women to a state of the most absurd mediocrity. They have addressed women only in a wretched language with no more delicacy than wit. Women have no longer any motive to develop their minds. This has been no improvement in manners or morality. By limiting the scope of ideas we have not succeeded in bringing back the simplicity of primitive life: the only result of less wit has been less delicacy, less respect for public opinion, fewer ways to endure solitude. And this applies to everything else in the current intellectual climate too: people invariably think that enlightenment is the cause of whatever is going wrong, and they want to make up for it by making reason go backward. Either morality is a false concept, or the more enlightened we are the more attached to morality we become.

If Frenchmen could give their wives all the virtues of Englishwomen, including retiring habits and a taste for solitude, they would do very well to prefer such virtues to the gifts of brilliant wit. All the French will manage to do this way, however, is to make their women read nothing, know nothing, and become incapable of carrying on a conversation with an interesting idea, or an apt expression, or eloquent language. Far from being kept at home by this happy ignorance, Frenchwomen unable to direct their children's education would become less fond of them. Society would become more necessary to these women—and also more dangerous, because no one could talk to them of anything but love, and this love would not even have the delicacy that can stand in for morality.

If such an attempt to make women completely insipid and frivolous ever succeeded, there would be several important losses to national morality and happiness. Women would have fewer ways to calm men's furious passions. They would no longer have any useful influence over opinion—and women are the ones at the heart of everything relating to humanity, generosity, delicacy. Women are the only human beings outside the realm of political interest and the career of ambition, able to pour scorn on base actions, point out ingratitude, and honor even disgrace if that disgrace is caused by noble sentiments. The opinion of society would no longer have any power over men's actions at all if there were no women left in France enlightened enough to make their judgments count, and imposing enough to inspire genuine respect.

I firmly believe that under the ancien régime, when opinion exerted such wholesome authority, this authority was the work of women distinguished by character and wit. Their eloquence was often quoted when they were inspired by some generous scheme or defending the unfortunate; if the expression of some sentiment demanded courage because it would offend those in power.

These are the same women who gave the strongest possible proofs of devotion and energy during the course of the Revolution.

Men in France will never be republican enough to manage without the independence and pride that comes naturally to women. Women may indeed have had too much influence on public affairs under the ancien régime; but they are no less dangerous when bereft of enlightenment, and therefore of reason. Their influence then turns to an inordinate craving for luxury, undiscerning choices, indelicate recommendations. Such women debase the men they love, instead of exalting them. And is the state the better off for it? Should the very limited risk of meeting a woman whose superiority is out of line with the destiny of her sex deprive the republic of France's reputation for the art of pleasing and living in society? Without any women, society can be neither agreeable nor amusing; with women bereft of wit, or the kind of conversational grace which requires the best education, society is spoiled rather than embellished. Such women introduce a kind of idiotic chatter and cliquish gossip into the conversation, alienating all the superior men and reducing brilliant Parisian gatherings to young men with nothing to do and young women with nothing to say.

We can find disadvantages to everything in life. There are probably disadvantages to women's superiority—and to men's; to the vanity of clever people; to the ambition of heroes; to the imprudence of kind hearts, the irritability of independent minds, the recklessness of courage, and so forth. But does that mean we should use all our energy to fight natural gifts, and direct our social institutions toward humbling our abilities? It is hardly as if there were some guarantee that such degradation would promote familial or governmental authority. Women without the wit for conversation or writing are usually just that much more skillful at escaping their duties. Unenlightened countries may not understand how to be free, but they are able to change their masters with some frequency.

Enlightening, teaching, and perfecting women together with men on the national and individual level: this must be the secret for the achievement of every reasonable goal, as well as the establishment of any permanent social or political relationships.

The only reason to fear women's wit would be some sort of scrupulous anxiety about their happiness. And indeed, by developing their rational minds one might well be enlightening them as to the misfortunes often connected with their fate; but that same reasoning would apply to the effect of enlightenment on the happiness of the human race in general, a question which seems to me to have been decided once and for all.

If the situation of women in civil society is so imperfect, what we must work toward is the improvement of their lot, not the degradation of their minds. For women to pay attention to the development of mind and reason would promote both enlightenment and the happiness of society in general. The cultivated education they deserve could have only one really unfortunate result: if some few of them were to acquire abilities distinguished enough to make them hungry for glory. Even this risk, however, would do society no harm, and would only be unfortunate for the very limited number of women whom nature might dedicate to the torture of useless superiority.

And if there were to be some woman seduced by intellectual celebrity and insistent on achieving it! How easy it would be to divert her, if she were caught in time! She could be shown the dreadful destiny to which she was on the verge of committing herself. Examine the social order, she would be told; you will soon see it up in arms against any woman trying to raise herself to the height of masculine reputation.

As soon as any woman is pointed out as a person of distinction, the general public is prejudiced against her. The common people judge according to a few common rules which can be followed without taking any risks. Whatever goes beyond the habitual immediately offends people who consider daily routine the safeguard of mediocrity. A superior man is enough to startle them; a superior woman, straying even farther from the beaten track, must surprise and annoy them even more. A distinguished man almost always has some important career as his field of action, so his talents may turn out to be useful to the interests of even those who least value the delights of the mind. The man of genius may become a man of power, so envious and silly people humor him. But a clever woman is only called upon to offer them new ideas and lofty sentiments, about which they could not care less; her celebrity seems to them much ado about nothing.

Even glory can be a source of reproach to a woman, because it contrasts with her natural destiny. Strict virtue condemns the celebrity even of something which is good in itself, because it damages the perfection of modesty. Men of wit are so astounded by the existence of women rivals that they cannot judge them with either an adversary's generosity or a protector's indulgence. This is a new kind of combat, in which men follow the laws of neither kindness nor honor.

Suppose, as a crowning misfortune, a woman were to acquire celebrity in a time of political dissension. People would think her influence unbounded, even if she had no influence at all; accuse her of all her friends' actions; and hate her for everything she loved. It is far preferable to attack a defenseless target than a dangerous one.

Nothing lends itself more quickly to vague assumptions than the dubious life of a woman with a famous name and an obscure career. An empty-witted man may inspire ridicule, a man of bad character may drop under the weight of contempt, a mediocre man may be cast aside—but everyone would much rather attack the unknown power they call a woman. When the plans of the ancients did not work out, they used to convince themselves that fate had thwarted them. Our modern vanity also prefers to attribute its failures to secret causes instead of to itself; in time of need, what stands in for fatality is the supposed power of famous women.

Women have no way to show the truth, no way to throw light on their lives. The public hears the lie; only their intimate friends can judge the truth. What real way is there for a woman to disprove slanderous accusations? A man who had been slandered lets his actions answer the universe, saying, "My life is a witness: it too must be heard."[3] But where can a woman find any such witness? A few private virtues, hidden favors, feelings locked into the narrow circle of her situation, writings which may make her known in places where she does not live, in times when she will no longer exist.

A man can refute calumny in his work itself, but self-defense is an additional handicap for women. For a woman to justify herself is a new topic for gossip. Women feel there is something pure and delicate in their nature, quickly withered by the very gaze of the public. Wit, talent, passion in the soul may make them emerge from this mist which should always be surrounding them, but they will always yearn for it as their true refuge.

However distinguished women may be, the sight of ill will makes them tremble. Courageous in misfortune, they are cowards against dislike; thought uplifts them, but their character is still weak and sensitive. Most women whose superior abilities make them want renown are like Erminia dressed in armor.[4] Warriors see the helmet, the lance, the bright plume of feathers, and think they are up against strength, so they attack with violence; with the very first blows, they have struck at the heart.

Such injustices can not only spoil a woman's happiness and peace of mind, but also alienate even the most important objects of her affection. Who can be sure that a libelous portrayal will not strike at the truth of memory? Who knows whether or not slanderers, having wreaked havoc with life, will rob death itself of the tender, regretful feelings that should be associated with the memory of a beloved woman?

So far I have portrayed only the unfairness of men: but what about the threat of injustice from other women? Do not women secretly arouse the malevolence of men? Do women ever form an alliance with a famous woman, sustaining her, defending her, supporting her faltering steps?

And that is still not all. Public opinion seems to release men from every duty toward a recognizably superior woman. Men can be ungrateful to her, unfaithful, even wicked, without making public opinion responsible for avenging her. "Is she not an extraordinary woman?" That says it all; she is abandoned to her own strength, and left to struggle with misery. She lacks both the sympathy inspired by a woman and the power protecting a man. Like the pariahs of India,[5] such a woman parades her peculiar existence among classes she cannot belong to, which consider her as destined to exist on her own, the object of curiosity and perhaps a little envy: what she deserves, in fact, is pity.

1800

3. No source has been identified; but the quoted sentence is written in the French classical alexandrine (12-syllable) meter.

4. In Tasso's *Jerusalem Delivered* (1581), the princess Erminia wears borrowed armor to seek her love Tancred in the Christian camp [translator's note].

5. Those who are at the bottom or outside of the traditional caste system of India (the words in the epigraph from *The Indian Hut* are spoken by a pariah).

FRIEDRICH SCHLEIERMACHER
1768–1834

German philosopher, classical philologist, and leading liberal Protestant theologian, Friedrich Schleiermacher is best known as a founder of modern general hermeneutics: that is, the art of understanding and interpreting discourse through systematic procedures. His most important contribution to the history of theory and criticism is arguably his "Outline of the 1819 Lectures," a fragmentary document produced in midcareer and published from handwritten notes after his death in *Hermeneutics* (1959; 2d ed., 1974). In this pioneering depiction of the processes of textual understanding, Schleiermacher argued that to understand a text fully one must understand simultaneously the entire thought of a writer as well as the whole language he or she employs, keeping in mind that the language and the author's thought reciprocally modify each other. The two major tasks of textual interpretation, according to Schleiermacher, are to comprehend the language and historical culture of a text (grammatical interpretation) and to reconstruct an author's purpose (psychological or "technical" interpretation). With these insights Schleiermacher laid the foundation of modern hermeneutics, preparing the way for such important yet widely divergent twentieth-century theorists of interpretation as MARTIN HEIDEGGER and Hans-Georg Gadamer (1900–2002).

Schleiermacher was born in Breslau, Prussia, and studied at two Moravian Brethren schools and at the University of Halle. During the late 1790s he began his celebrated translation into German of almost all of Plato's works (still in print); he was active in the Berlin circle of Romanticists, being a close associate and briefly roommate of Friedrich Schlegel, to whose vanguard journal, *Athenaeum,* he was an early contributor. He served as chaplain and professor of theology and philosophy at Halle between 1804 and 1806, later taking a position at the University of Berlin (1810–34), which he co-founded. Schleiermacher regularly preached at Trinity Church in Berlin, advocating the right of union for Reformed and Lutheran groups in Prussia, freedom of the church from the state, shorter working hours, social insurance, and women's rights.

Schleiermacher's theology reflects the influence of Romanticism and Moravian pietism, especially in his two most famous works, *On Religion: Speeches to Its Cultured Despisers* (1799) and *The Christian Faith* (1821–22), which argue that religion is an intuitive feeling for and dependence on the infinite realm, not a set of moral or metaphysical principles; religion needed no external justification. It was to convince his fellow German Romantics that they were not as far from religion as they believed that he undertook the first book, a confession of faith that gained him a national reputation overnight. Today he is often regarded as one of the most significant Protestant theologians since Luther. In his time his influence was wide, reaching such figures as RALPH WALDO EMERSON, who also devalued doctrine in favor of intuitive dependence on the infinite.

His interest in understanding the Bible led to Schleiermacher's concern with hermeneutics. In his "Outline of the 1819 Lectures," our selection, he expands on his basic distinction between grammatical and psychological interpretation, noting that the latter involves two distinct methods. Using the first, divinatory interpretation, one seeks to identify intuitively with the author; Schleiermacher sees this as representing a feminine dimension of our knowledge of human nature. (This mode of interpretation echoes his notions about religion as an intuitive feeling.) Using the second method, comparative interpretation, one works to understand a text as a type or historical genre; it is purportedly a masculine force.

Both psychological and grammatical interpretation primarily seek to isolate the text's central idea, procedure, or motivating principle in light of which all textual details can be gauged. Artful interpretation requires such centering and also multiple rigorous readings. But problems do arise, some of which are avoidable and some not. Interpretation necessarily gets caught up in various circularities. Readers early in the process intuit the meaning of a text, which then predetermines the directions of meaning. This is one version of the celebrated "hermeneutic circle" of interpretation, identified by Schleiermacher and later explored by leading hermeneuticists, especially Heidegger and Gadamer. To understand the whole text, Schleiermacher points out, one must understand each part; but to understand each part, one must understand the whole. He expands this circle by requiring that to understand an individual text, an interpreter must understand the complete historical context and vocabulary of a language—foreknowledge derived paradoxically from individual texts.

Schleiermacher catalogues several types of avoidable misunderstanding, which result from bias, mistaking a text's meaning, or misjudging the value of a segment of text. (Under the influence of FRIEDRICH NIETZSCHE and SIGMUND FREUD, contemporary critics such as HAROLD BLOOM and PAUL DE MAN, unlike Schleiermacher, have come to conceive "misunderstanding" as an ineradicable, productive element of all understanding.) Moreover, for Schleiermacher allegorical interpretation—that is, reading symbolically—risks erroneously discovering everything in everything, unless the text itself legitimates the approach with an allusion appropriate to both the contextual and the central textual ideas. Finally, historical interpretation can run into trouble by construing an ancient text in terms of modern conditions instead of uncovering its writer's relationship to his or her milieu and language.

Schleiermacher posits two broad categories of texts. "Objective texts" such as histories and epics require a minimum of psychological interpretation and a maximum of grammatical interpretation, whereas "subjective texts" such as personal letters and lyrics call for more psychological than grammatical interpretation. The goal of hermeneutics in either case is—as he famously declared—"to understand the discourse just as well and even better than its creator." We have no way of knowing the creator's purpose other than through reconstruction, but "No individual inspection of a work ever exhausts its meaning."

Helpfully, Schleiermacher outlines four types of positive hermeneutical reconstruction. There are two types of grammatical or objective reconstruction—historical and divinatory—and two types of psychological or subjective reconstruction—historical and divinatory. In brief, objective historical reconstruction examines how language shapes the text, objective divinatory reconstruction analyzes how the text itself developed that language, subjective historical reconstruction explores the text as the product of the author's soul, and subjective divinatory reconstruction attempts to determine how the process of writing affects the writer's inner thoughts. Interpretation for Schleiermacher is at once psychological and grammatical, intuitive and comparative. It is an art of understanding, not just explaining, the act of a living, intuiting person gifted with foreknowledge and experience of life as well as linguistic and cultural competence—an art that always requires a leap into the midst of textual complexities and circularities.

Earlier German hermeneutics, as practiced in the contexts of theology, law, and literature, focused narrowly on philology, particularly its penchant for interpretive procedures and rules of validation. Schleiermacher here broadens its scope toward a phenomenological philosophy attentive to the roles of intuition, understanding, and foreknowledge in the lived world of human beings. This shift was variously amplified by his greatest successors, Wilhelm Dilthey (1833–1911), Heidegger, and Gadamer. Schleiermacher is generally credited with grounding hermeneutics in human understanding, with according language a foundational role in interpretation, and with highlighting the interdependence of mind and medium, subject and object, divination and comparison.

However much successors and followers admire and build on Schleiermacher's work, they find problems with his hermeneutic theory. In the various editions of his *Truth and Method—Outline for a Philosophical Hermeneutics* (1960), Gadamer characterizes the principle of divination as hopelessly Romantic. He faults Schleiermacher for not taking into account the historical context and prejudices of the interpreter, which, he shrewdly argues, are essential constituents of understanding. Intuition assumes uniform human experience; prejudices arise in a world of antagonistic standpoints. And the leading modern French hermeneuticist, Paul Ricoeur (1913–2005), contends that Schleiermacher does not sufficiently distinguish between the author and the ideas governing the work; Ricoeur sees the latter as the true object of interpretation. Schleiermacher vacillates, too, on what constitutes the "text" (or object of inquiry)—it is sometimes the author's oeuvre (complete works), sometimes a particular work, and sometimes a genre or cultural archive.

Various critics, moreover, have noted Schleiermacher's tendency, especially in his late works, to "psychologize": that is, to pass through language to the supposed prelinguistic mental processes and intentions of the author, forgetting that grammar and psychology are interdependent. When this happens, Schleiermacher's hermeneutics turns into psychological reconstruction, which is the direction taken by Dilthey. A similar path is staked out by E. D. Hirsch Jr. (b. 1928), who, however, turns to interpretive reconstruction as a way to rectify the rampant critical subjectivism and relativism that he believes plague contemporary literary criticism, including much hermeneutics.

In spite of criticisms, Schleiermacher's contributions to hermeneutics should not be underestimated. His psychological notion of divination enabled him to explicitly correct and complement earlier Enlightenment concepts of rationality. He usefully jettisoned the old rigid separations of hermeneutics into specialized biblical, legal, and literary kinds, developing a self-conscious project for a general hermeneutics. Like his important contemporaries FRIEDRICH SCHILLER and SAMUEL TAYLOR COLERIDGE, he attempted to reconcile well-entrenched inherited philosophical oppositions, especially subject/object, finite/infinite, individual/social, and psychology/grammar. He construed understanding as an act of dialogue, not verification. Lastly, he pictured the act of interpretation as antiauthoritarian and nonhierarchical, in keeping with the radical social forces of his time (committed to toppling monarchical regimes and feudal class arrangements, manifested especially in the French Revolution) and with the dynamics of early democracy and capitalism. All these elements, which marked Schleiermacher historically as a Romantic, significantly influenced the work of later philosophical hermeneutics.

***Hermeneutics* Keywords:** Hermeneutics, Interpretation, Phenomenology, Philology, Religion, Romantic Theory

From Hermeneutics

From *Outline of the 1819 Lectures*[1]

INTRODUCTION[2]

1. Hermeneutics as the art of understanding does not yet exist in general; rather, only various specialized hermeneutics exist.

1. Edited and translated by Jan Wojcik and Roland Haas, who occasionally insert the original German or explanatory words or phrases in brackets.

2. The Outline consists of an "Introduction," "First Part: The Grammatical Exposition," and "Second Part: The Technical (or Psychological) Interpretation." The headings are somewhat misleading. The "Introduction" gives a systematic exposition of principles for analyzing the language and psychological manifestations of a literary text. The "First Part" elaborates the principles for the analysis of language; the "Second Part" extends the "Introduction" in describing how the two parts of interpretation work together in the "divination" of a text. We limit our translation to the "Introduction" and the "Second Part" which comprise the heart of Schleiermacher's hermeneutical principles. We have referred to the marginal notes Schleiermacher added to the manuscript in 1828 only when they clarified ambiguities in the text [translators' note].

1. [We speak of] only the art of understanding, not the exposition of the understanding. The latter would only be a specialized part of the art of speaking and writing that could only be dependent on the general principles of hermeneutics.

2. This refers as well to difficult points in foreign-language texts. In reading them, one more often presumes familiarity with the subject matter and the language. When one is familiar with both, the distinction between them becomes difficult to make because one has perhaps not understood properly the more apparent. Only an artistic understanding consistently grasps the discourse [*Reden*] of a text [*Schrift*].[3]

3. Usually one supposes that one could rely on a healthy knowledge of human nature for formulating the general principles of interpretation. But then there is the danger that one would also tend to rely on a healthy feeling about the exceptional qualities of a text in determining what they meant.

2. It is very difficult to determine the exact nature of a general hermeneutics.

1. For a long time it was handled as a supplement to logic, but as one had to give up all logical tenets in its practice, this had to cease. The philosopher has no inclination to establish a theory about hermeneutics because he believes that it is more important to be understood than to understand.

2. Philology[4] has made positive contributions throughout history. But its method of hermeneutics is simply to aggregate observations.

3. [Hermeneutics is] the art of relating discourse [*Reden*] and understanding [*Verstehen*] to each other; discourse, however, being on the outer sphere of thought, requires that one must think of hermeneutics as an art, and thus as philosophical.

1. Thus the art of exposition depends on their composition. They are mutually dependent to the point that where discourse is without art, so is the understanding of it.

4. Discourse is the mediation of shareable thought. As a result both rhetoric and hermeneutics share a common relationship to the dialectic.[5]

1. Discourse is of course also a mediation of thought among individuals. Thought becomes complete only through interior discourse, and in this respect discourse could be considered manifested thought. But where the thinker thinks original thoughts, he himself requires the art of discourse to transform them into expressions that afterwards require exposition [*Auslegung*].

2. The unity of hermeneutics and rhetoric results from the fact that every act of understanding is the obverse of an act of discourse, in that one must come to grasp the thought which was at the base of the discourse.

3. The dependence of both on the dialectic results from the fact that all development of knowledge is dependent on both discourse and understanding.

3. Discourse (*Reden*) is Schleiermacher's term for the discursive sense of a text, shaped by the particular language the author uses to express his inner thoughts (see 4–6). Here he makes a distinction between the literal meaning of a text (*Schrift*) and the discursive meaning (*Reden*) that is most obvious when one reads a somewhat unfamiliar foreign language (see 14.2) [translators' note].

4. The scholarly discipline dedicated to the historical understanding of foreign cultures through linguistic and comparative analysis of texts.

5. That part of logic concerned with thinking, notably thinking embodied in discourse.

5. As every discourse has a two-part reference, to the whole language and to the entire thought of its creator, so all understanding of speech consists of two elements [*Momenten*]—understanding the speech as it derives from the language and as it derives from the mind of the thinker.

1. Every speech derives from a given language. One can also turn this around and say that originally and continuously language only comes into being through discourse; at any rate, communication presupposes the accessibility of the language; that is, a shared knowledge of the same. When something comes between unmediated discourse and communication, the art of discourse begins, for one must take into consideration the possibility that the listener might find something strange in someone else's use of language.

2. Every discourse depends on earlier thought. One can also turn this around, of course, but in relation to communication it remains true, since the art of understanding only has to do with progressive thinking.

3. It follows that every person is on one hand a locus in which a given language is formed after an individual fashion and, on the other, a speaker who is only able to be understood within the totality of the language. In the same way, he is also a constantly developing spirit, while his discourse remains an object within the context of other intellection.

6. Understanding is only an interaction of these two elements.

1. Discourse can only be understood as a fact of the spirit if it is understood as a characteristic of the language, because the innateness of the language modifies the spirit.

2. It can also only be understood as a modification of the language if it is understood as a fact of the spirit, because all influences of individuals on the language are manifested through discourse.

7. Both stand completely equal, and one could only with injustice claim that the grammatical interpretation is the inferior and the psychological the superior.

1. The psychological is the superior only if one views language as the means by which the individual communicates his thoughts; the grammatical is then merely a cleaning away of temporary difficulties.

2. The grammatical is the superior if one views language as stipulating the thinking of all individuals and the individual's discourse only as a locus at which the language manifests itself.

3. Only by means of such a reciprocity could one find both to be completely similar.

8. The essential hermeneutical task is to handle every part in such a way that the handling of the other parts will produce no change in the results, or, in other words, every part must be handled as a discrete unit with equal respect paid to all other parts.

1. This reciprocity is important even if one part predominates over the other according to what was said in paragraph six.

2. But each is only complete if it makes the other redundant and contributes to construing the other, because indeed language [*Sprache*] can only be learned inasmuch as its discourse [*Rede*] can be understood; and in the same way, the inner cohesion of humanity can only be understood as it manifests itself externally through its discourse.

9. Exposition [*Auslegung*] is an art.

1. Every part stands by itself. Every composition is a finite certainty out of the infinite uncertainty. Language is an infinite because every element can be determined in a specific manner only through the other elements. And this is also true for the psychological part because every perspective of an individual is infinite; and the outside influences on people extend into the disappearing horizon. A composition composed of such elements cannot be defined by rules, which carry with them the security of their application.

2. Should the grammatical part be considered by itself, one would need in some cases a complete knowledge of the language, or, in others, a complete knowledge of the person. As neither can ever be complete, one must go from one to the other, and it is not possible to give any rules as to how this should be done.

10. The successful performance of the art depends on a linguistic talent and a talent for assessing individual human nature.

1. By the first point we do not mean the facility for learning foreign languages—the difference between the mother tongue and a foreign language does not come into consideration here for the time being; rather, a sense for the contemporaneity of a language, for analogy, difference, etc. One could mean by this that rhetoric and hermeneutics must always be together. Just as hermeneutics requires other talents, so also does rhetoric, if not always the same ones. The linguistic talent, at any rate, is shared, even if the hermeneutical method develops it differently than the rhetorical method does.

2. The knowledge of human nature is here the superior of those subjective elements in the development of discourse. No less importantly, hermeneutics and artistic human presentation are always together. But a great number of hermeneutical mistakes are based on the deficiency of linguistic talent, or in its faulty application.

3. Inasmuch as these talents are generally given by nature, so hermeneutics is a commonsense endeavor. Inasmuch as a person is missing one talent, he is crippled, and the other talents can only serve to help him adjudicate about that which all together would have permitted him to know directly.

11. Not all discourse is on an equal footing for exposition. Certain discourses have no value for it, others an absolute value; the majority lie between these two points.

1. Something of no value might excite no interest as an entity, but would still be important in the language as a reiteration which language requires for the preservation of its continuity. But that which repeats only already available things is worth nothing in itself. Like talking about the weather. Alone, this is not an absolute nothing, only minimal. For it developed itself in the same way as significant things.

2. When the grammatical aspect predominates in a work, even the most imaginative, we call it classical. When the psychological aspect predominates, we call it original. And, of course, one part could absolutely dominate the other only if the author was an absolute genius.

3. To be classical, a work must be more than transitory; it must determine subsequent production. No less so the original. And even the best work cannot be free from influence.

12. When both aspects of interpretation—the analysis of the grammatical and the psychological part of a text—are used equally throughout, they are nevertheless always used in different proportions.

1. This follows from the fact that something of grammatical insignificance does not necessarily have to be of psychological insignificance, and vice versa; and insignificancy in one does not imply insignificancy in the other.

2. A minimum of psychological interpretation is needed with a predominately objective subject. [To this belongs] pure history, especially of specific individuals, as comprehensive studies tend more to draw on subjective conclusions; also epics, commercial discussions which want to become history, and strictly didactic writings of every kind. The interpreter's subjectivity should not enter the exposition; rather, it should be affected by the exposition. A minimum of grammatical interpretation accompanies a maximum of psychological in the exposition of personal letters, especially when they transmit didactic advice or historical information. (Lyrics or polemics too?)

13. There is no other diversity in the methods of exposition aside from those cited above.

1. As an example, we can take the wonderful perspective which comes from the argument over the historical exposition of the New Testament, based on the question whether there are special modes of interpretation reserved for it alone. In this debate the assertion of the historical school is the only correct one, that the New Testament authors are products of their age. The only danger in their reasoning is their tendency to overlook the power of Christianity to create new concepts and forms of expression; they tend to explain everything in light of available concepts and forms. To correct the historical style of interpretation one has to resist this one-sidedness. Correct interpretation requires a relationship of the grammatical and psychological interpretation, since new concepts can arise out of new emotional experiences.

2. One would also err if one thought of a historical interpretation as simply a retrospective view of the textual events. One must keep in mind that what was written was often written in a different day and age from the one in which the interpreter lives; it is the primary task of interpretation not to understand an ancient text in view of modern thinking, but to rediscover the original relationship between the writer and his audience.

3. The Allegorical Interpretation. First of all, it is not an interpretation of an allegory, where the only purpose is to understand the figurative meaning without reference to whether there is truth at the base of it or not. Examples of allegories would be the parable of the sower, or the story of the rich man.[6] Rather, allegorical interpretation begins with a presupposition that the meaning is lacking in the immediate context, and so one needs to supply a figurative one. With this supposition one is unsatisfied with the general principle that every speech can have only one grammatical meaning. The dissatisfaction arises, perhaps, from the correct assessment that an allusion in a text does point to a second meaning; one who does not comprehend it could completely follow the whole context, but would still be missing one meaning situated within the discourse. The danger is that one could find an

6. Both in the New Testament: for the sower, see Matthew 13.1–9, 18–23; for the rich man, see Luke 16.19–31.

allusion which is not situated within the discourse. Then one would dissect the discourse improperly. The test for a proper allusion is this: to see whether it seems entwined as one of the contextual ideas within the main line of thought, to assess whether the explicit thoughts inspire the implicit. But the contextual ideas are not therewith to be considered merely individual and insignificant. Rather, just as the whole world is made up of many men, each idea contributes to its whole sense, even if it appears only as its dark shadow.

There is, after all, a parallelism in many various lines of thought, so that something could inspire something else; for example, there is parallelism between the physical and ethical, and between the musical and the visual arts. One should be careful, however, to detect whether there are any indications for the figurative expressions one seems to detect. The allegorical interpretations which have been made without such indication, especially in traditional interpretations of Homer and the Bible, all depend on a special assumption. This is that the books of Homer[7] and the Old Testament are special compendiums, the Old Testament above all, which contains all wisdom in some form or another. Along with this, both of them have appeared to have a mystical content compounded of sententious philosophy on the one hand and history on the other.

With myths, however, no technical interpretation is possible, since one cannot focus on an individual text[8] and alternatively compare the literal and the figurative meaning. There is certainly a different situation regarding the New Testament which leads to two kinds of blunders. First, its association with the Old Testament encourages the use of the same methods often associated with the Old Testament interpretation. Second, the New Testament interpreters tend more than their Old Testament counterparts to view the Holy Spirit as the book's author. But the Holy Spirit cannot be thought of as a temporally contingent and characteristic consciousness. From this false view springs the inclination to find everything foreshadowed everywhere. Common sense, or precise instructions on how texts should be read, can protect texts from this inclination, but isolated passages which seem to be unmeaningful in themselves seem to encourage it.

4. Here the question occasionally intrudes upon us, whether the holy books of the Holy Spirit must be handled differently than others. We must not be concerned with dogmatic decisions about inspiration, since they themselves derive from interpretation. We must not distinguish between the preaching and the writing of the apostles, since their future church had to be built on the preaching. And it follows from this that we must not believe that the whole of Christianity directly developed from the writings, since they are all aimed at specific communities and could also not have been understood by subsequent readers if they had not been understood by the original audience. Each community simply sought out the specific characteristics of the Jesus story according to its own given particular focus on the many details. Therefore, we must expose it to the same method and consider that even if the authors were no more than dead tools, still the Holy Spirit could only have spoken through them as they themselves would have spoken.

5. The most dangerous deviation from this principle is encouraged by the cabalistic[9] style of exposition which directs its endeavors to find

7. The *Iliad* and the *Odyssey* (ca. 8th c. B.C.E.), each divided into 24 books.

8. Myths have no single author and no single established text; therefore technical (psychological) interpretation is impossible.

9. Esoteric, mystical.

everything in everything. Only their interpretive endeavors which respect the diversity which results from the various relationships of both constructed parts can rightfully be called exposition.

14. The difference between artful and crude exposition has nothing to do with whether the work is familiar or strange, or with the discourse or the text, but solely with whether one wants to understand certain things exactly or not.

1. If it were only foreign and old texts that needed the art, the original readers would not have needed it, and the art would then depend on the differences between them and us. This difference must first be resolved, of course, through a knowledge of language and history; the exposition begins only after a successful identification of the text's original meaning. The difference between interpreting an old foreign text and a local contemporary one is only that with the old text the process of discovering its relevance to its milieu cannot completely precede the identification of its meaning; rather, both must be integrated from the beginning.

2. The text [*Schrift*] is not always the focus of attention either. Otherwise the art would only become necessary through the difference between text and discourse; that is to say, by the absence of the living voice and by the inaccessibility of other personal influences. These things, however, require exposition themselves, while they always remain somewhat nebulous. A living voice can certainly facilitate understanding a great deal, but even the writer must take into consideration that writing is not the same as speaking. If it were, then the art of exposition would be superfluous, which is, of course, not the case. Consequently, the need for exposition depends on the difference between written and spoken discourse, when the latter does not accompany the former.

3. Thus, when discourse and text behave so that no other difference remains between them save the one indicated, it follows that the artfully correct exposition has no other goal than that which we have in hearing every common spoken discourse.

15. The careless practice of the art results from the fact that understanding is pursued in the light of a negative goal: that misunderstanding should be avoided.

1. Careless interpretation tends to limit its understanding to obtaining certain easy-to-attain goals.

2. But even it must avail itself of the art in difficult cases; and thus hermeneutics can even arise from the artless practice. But since it only sees difficulties as isolated problems, it becomes an aggregate of observations. And for the same reason tends to consider itself a specialized hermeneutics because it brings special methods to the solving of difficult problems. This is how the theological, the juristic, and the philological methods originated, and what they consider to be their special purposes.

3. The basis for their view is the peculiarity of their special languages and the peculiar manner in which their speakers communicate to their hearers.

16. Strict interpretation begins with misunderstanding and searches out a precise understanding.

1. This results from its beginning with an assumption about what the meaning is that properly should only be discovered in the way the language and intention present it.

2. Careless interpretation distinguishes only the [predetermined] sense from the manner of expression, which in fact depend on each other for their mutual identity, the determination of which is the minimum requirement for avoiding artless practice.[1]

17. Two things should be avoided: qualitatively misunderstanding the content, and quantitatively misunderstanding nuance.

1. Examined objectively, qualitative misunderstanding is mistaking the place of a part of a discourse in the language with that of another one, as, for example, the confusion of the meaning of a word with that of another. The qualitative misunderstanding is subjective, the mistaking of the meaning of an expression, so that one gives the same thing a different meaning than the speaker gave to it in his sphere.

2. Quantitative misunderstanding arises from a subjective response to the value of the elaboration a speaker gives to a part of the text, or by analogy from an objective response to a part taken out of context.

3. The quantitative, which is normally taken little into account, always leads to the qualitative.

4. These negative expressions cover all interpretive operations. But one could not develop the rules from their negativity alone; rather, one must develop them positively, with a constant eye on the negative.

5. One must also distinguish the difference between passive and active misunderstanding. The latter is timidity which, however it might be the consequence of a bias that nothing can appear certain unless it is very obvious, can still entertain very false assumptions.

18. The art can only develop its rules from a positive formula, and this is the historical and the divinatory [prophetic], objective and subjective reconstruction [*Nachkonstruieren*] of the given discourse.

1. Objective historical reconstruction considers how the discourse behaves in the totality of the language, and considers a text's self-contained knowledge as a product of the language. Objective divinatory reconstruction assesses how the discourse itself developed the language. Without both of these, one cannot avoid qualitative and quantitative misunderstanding.

2. Subjective historical reconstruction considers a discourse as a product of the soul; subjective divinatory assesses how the process of writing affects the writer's inner thoughts. Without both, just as was the case above, misunderstanding is once again unavoidable.

3. The task is this, to understand the discourse just as well and even better than its creator. Since we have no unmediated knowledge of that which is within him, we must first seek to become conscious of much which he could have remained unconscious of, unless he had become self-reflectingly his own reader. For objective reconstruction he has no more data than we do.

4. Posed in this manner, the task is an infinite one, because there is an infinity of the past and the future that we wish to see in the moment of

1. Paraphrase: artful interpretation begins with a hunch about a text's meaning which it continuously corrects and refines; careless interpretation begins with a prejudice about a text's meaning which it forces the text to support [translators' note].

discourse. Hence, this art is just as capable of inspiration as any other. In fact, a text has no meaning unless it can give rise to this inspiration. However, the decision on how far one wishes to pursue an approach must be, in any case, determined practically, and actually is a question for a specialized hermeneutics and not for a general one.

19. One must first equate oneself with the author by objective and subjective reconstruction before applying the art.

1. With objective reconstruction one proceeds through a knowledge of the language as the author used it. It must be more exact than even the original readers possessed, who themselves had to put themselves in the place of the author. With subjective reconstruction one proceeds through the knowledge of the author's inner and outer life.

2. But both can only be completely secured through a similarly complete exposition. For only from a reading of all of an author's works can one become familiar with his vocabulary, his character, and his circumstances.

20. The vocabulary and the history of the period in which an author works constitute the whole within which his texts must be understood with all their peculiarities.

1. This complete knowledge is contained within an apparent circle,[2] so that every extraordinary thing can only be understood in the context of the general of which it is a part, and vice versa. And all knowledge can only be scientific to the extent that it is complete.

2. This circle makes possible an identification with the author, and thus it follows that, first, the more complete knowledge we possess, the better bolstered we are for exposition, and, second, no material for exposition can be understood in isolation; rather, every reading makes us better suited for understanding by enriching our previous knowledge. We can only be satisfied with immediate understanding when dealing with the meaningless.

21. If the knowledge of the particular vocabulary can only be amassed during the exposition through lexical help and through individual observation, there can exist no self-sufficient exposition.

1. Only an independent knowledge of the actual life of a language gives one a source independent of the exposition for the knowledge of the vocabulary. For this reason we have only an incomplete understanding of what Greek and Latin words mean. Hence, the first lexical task in such cases is to consider the whole literature as a context for understanding the individual linguistic item. These complementary tasks balance each other through the exposition itself, contributing to an artful exposition.

2. Under the term *vocabulary* I subsume the dialect, period, and the mode—prose or poetry.

3. Even first impressions should be based on lexical meaning, for spontaneous interpretation can only rest on prior knowledge [*Vorkenntnisse*], but even all decisions about the language in dictionaries and in explanatory notes proceed from special and other perhaps unreliable expositions.

2. The troubling yet unavoidable "hermeneutic circle" of interpretation.

4. In the area of the New Testament, one can say with certainty that the unreliability and arbitrariness of the exposition rests largely on this fault. This is because contrasting analogies always develop from individual observations. For example, the development of New Testament vocabulary is rooted in classical antiquity and developed through Macedonian Greek through its use by the profane Jewish writers and by Josephus and Philo, by the deuterocanonical writers, and by the writers of the Septuagint,[3] who flavored their Greek with Hebrewisms.

22. Even if the necessary knowledge of history comes only from prolegomena, there can still exist no self-sufficient exposition.

1. Such prolegomena are the sort of critical helps it is the duty of a publisher who desires to be a mediator to use. But they must depend on a knowledge of the whole literary circle a work belongs to, and the whole development of an author himself. Thus they are themselves dependent on exposition, and so are all reckonings whose beginnings are not determined by a specific goal. The exact expositor must, however, gradually glean everything from the sources themselves, and it is because of this that his task can only progress from easy to more difficult. But the dependency becomes most injurious if one brings in such notes in the prolegomena that actually could only be derived from the interpreted work itself.

2. The New Testament has given birth to a special discipline: the writing of the introduction. This is not an actual organic component of the theological discipline; but it is a practical expedient, partly for the beginner, partly for the master, since it is easier to bring together all of the relevant examinations in one place. But the expositor should always contribute to it so as to augment and relate the great mass of evidence.

23. An individual element can only be understood in light of its place in the whole text; and therefore, a cursory reading for an overview of the whole must precede the exact exposition.

1. Understanding appears to go in endless circles, for a preliminary understanding of even the individuals themselves comes from a general knowledge of the language.

2. Synopses that the author gives himself are too dry to engage even the technical aspect of interpretation, and with summaries like those publishers authorize for prefaces one comes under the influence of their interpretations.

3. The aim is to find the main idea in light of which the others must be measured, and this goes as well for the technical aspect—to find the main procedure from which the others can more easily be found. It is similarly indispensable for grammatical interpretation, which is obvious from the various forms of misunderstanding it often raises.

4. One can omit it easier when dealing with the unmeaningful, and although with difficult works it appears to be less helpful, it is actually all the more indispensable. A general summary is characteristically the least help in understanding difficult writers.

Should the exposition be done partially, one would eventually have to connect both aspects in the execution of the interpretation, but in theory

3. A Greek translation of the Hebrew Scriptures by Jewish scholars (ca. 3d c. B.C.E.). Flavius Josephus (b. 37/8 C.E.) and Philo Judaeus (ca. 20 B.C.E.–ca. 50 C.E.): secular Jewish writers of history and philosophy, respectively. "Deuterocanonical writers": authors of books of the Scriptures contained in the Septuagint but not in the Hebrew canon.

one must divide and handle each specially, even if afterwards one must endeavor to develop each so completely that the other becomes indispensable, or, what is more important, so that its result coincides with the first. The grammatical interpretation leads the way.

PART TWO
THE TECHNICAL INTERPRETATION

1. The common beginning for both the technical and the grammatical interpretation is the general overview which grasps the unity of the work and the main features of the composition. The unity of the work, the theme, will be viewed here as the writer's motivating principle, and the foundation of the composition as his peculiar nature as it is manifested in each motif.

The unity of the work derives from the manner in which the grammatical constructions available in the language are composed or connected. The author sets a verbal object in motion as communication. The difference between popular and scientific works is that the author of the former arranges the subject according to his peculiar style, which mirrors itself in his ordering. Because each author has minor conceptions each of which is determined by his peculiarities, one can recognize them from among analogous omissions and anomalous inclusions.

I perceive the author as he functions in the language: partly bringing forth new things by his use of language, partly retaining qualities of language which he repeats and transmits. In the same way, from a knowledge of an area of speech, I can perceive the author's language as its product and see how he operates under its aegis. Both methods are the same process begun from different starting points.

2. The ultimate goal of the psychological [technical] exposition is nothing other than to perceive the consequences of the beginning; that is to say, to consider the work as it is formed by its parts, and to perceive every part in light of the work's overall subject as its motivation; this is also to say that the form is seen to be shaped by the subject matter.

When I have looked at everything individually, there is nothing left over to understand. It is also obvious in itself that the apparent contrast between understanding the individual parts and understanding the whole disappears when every part receives the same treatment as the whole. But the goal [of good interpretation] is only achieved in the continuity of both perspectives. Even when much is only to be understood grammatically, it is not understood fully unless one can make an intrinsic analysis which never loses sight of the genesis of the work.

3. The goal of good interpretation is to understand the style completely.

We are accustomed to understanding style as the handling of language. We presume that thought and language intertwine throughout, and the specific manner with which one understands the subject requires an understanding of the arrangement of words: i.e., the handling of language.

The peculiarity of an individual conception results from what is missing or added to a conventional conception. Whatever peculiarity results from imitation or habit results in a bad style.

4. Good interpretation can only be approximated.

We are, considering all advances in hermeneutical theory, still far from making it a perfect art, as the perennial fights over the writings of Homer and over the comparative merits of the three tragic writers[4] show.

No individual inspection of a work ever exhausts its meaning; interpretation can always be rectified. Even the best is only an approximation of the meaning. Because interpretation so seldom succeeds, and because even the superior critic is open to criticism, we can see that we are still far from the goal of making hermeneutics a perfect art.

5. Before beginning the technical exposition, we must know the manner in which the subject occurred to the originator, and how he acquired his language, and anything else one can learn about his mannerisms.

First, one must consider the prior development of the genre of the work at the time when it was written; second, one must consider the use made of the genre typically in the place where the writer worked and in adjacent areas; finally, no exact understanding of the development and usage is possible without a knowledge of the related contemporary literature and especially the works the author might have used as a model. Such a cohesive study is indispensable.

The third goal raises very troublesome problems. We could say that the interpretive process as a whole is only as easy as this step is to take. But because even this step requires a judgment which can also be anticipated in the previous steps, it is possible that one might be able to omit it. Biographies of the author were originally annexed to their works for this purpose; nowadays this connection is overlooked. The best sort of prolegomena attends to the first two points.

With these contextualizations [*Vorkenntnissen*] in hand one can gain an excellent perception of the essential characteristic of a work upon a first reading.

6. The whole task requires the use of two methods, the divinatory and the comparative, which, however, as they constantly refer back to each other, must not be separated.

Using the divinatory, one seeks to understand the writer intimately [*unmittelbar*] to the point that one transforms oneself into the other. Using the comparative, one seeks to understand a work as a characteristic type, viewing the work, in other words, in light of others like it. The one is the feminine force in the knowledge of human nature; the other is the masculine.

Both refer back to each other. The first depends on the fact that every person has a susceptibility to intuiting others, in addition to his sharing many human characteristics. This itself appears to depend on the fact that everyone shares certain universal traits; divination consequently is inspired as the reader compares himself with the author.

But how does the comparative come to subsume the subject under a general type? Obviously, either by comparing, which could go on infinitely, or by divination.

4. That is, the Greek tragedians Aeschylus, Sophocles, and Euripides (all active 5th c. B.C.E.). "Perennial fights": over whether the *Iliad* and *Odyssey* were by a single poet or were collections of short works put together from various sources.

Neither may be separated from the other, because divination receives its security first from an affirmative comparison, without which it might become outlandish. But the comparative of itself cannot yield a unity. The general and specific must permeate each other, and this can only happen by means of divination.

7. The idea of the work, by which the author's fundamental purpose [*Wille*] reveals itself, can only be understood in terms of the convergence of the basic material and its peculiarity of his developments.

The basic material by itself stipulates no set manner of execution. As a rule it is easy enough to determine, even if it is not exactly specified; but for all that, one can be mistaken. One finds the purpose of the work most precisely in its peculiar or characteristic development of its material. Often the characteristic motif has only a limited influence on certain sections of a work, but nonetheless shapes the character of the work by its influence on others. The interpretive knack is to somehow intuit the meaning while being cautiously aware of how the intuition in some ways predetermines the process of validating it.

1819, 1828 1959, 1974

GEORG WILHELM FRIEDRICH HEGEL
1770–1831

IMMANUEL KANT (1724–1804) and G. W. F. Hegel are the ARISTOTLE and PLATO of modern Continental philosophy, the two dominant figures from whom everything else flows. Hegel is a great synthesizer, a system builder who bequeaths to modern thought the conviction that an individual entity's meaning rests not in itself but in the relationship of that thing to other things within an all-encompassing, ever-changing whole. Where the part is *situated* is crucial. All modern criticism that stresses the historical and social context of utterances or artworks is Hegelian to some degree.

Hegel was the son of a minor court official in the duchy of Württemburg, in what is now Germany. He studied theology at the University of Tübingen, where he became friends with the poet Friedrich Hölderlin and the philosopher Friedrich von Schelling. After graduating in 1793, Hegel worked as a private tutor until he began teaching at the University of Jena in 1801, the year he published his first book. In 1807 he published *Phenomenology of Spirit*, the first version of his grand philosophical vision and one of the great philosophical masterpieces of all time. A sexual scandal (he had a child with his landlord's wife) forced Hegel to leave Jena in 1807, and he would not teach in a university again until 1816. He reached the height of his fame and influence with his lectures at the University of Berlin, which he delivered regularly from 1818 until his death. Many of these series were published either by Hegel himself or from the notes taken by his students, as was *Lectures on Fine Art* (1835–38).

Hegel is usually associated with the *dialectic*, which entails the confrontation of any thesis with its opposite (antithesis), and the resultant synthesis of the two through a process of "overcoming" (*aufgehoben* in German). We might call the dialectic the motor of the Hegelian system, stressing movement and change over stasis. This system, which places individual elements in relation to one another, is in constant motion. Meaning and truth are never fixed, because they are always in process. The world possesses not determinate being but only momentary resting places on the stages of becoming. Hegel does believe that there will be stasis and perfection at the end of history, and at times he appears to believe that his philosophy is that end, the moment when consciousness fully understands its own nature—its essential unity with all that exists. Spirit (*Geist*) is the name Hegel most often uses to designate this fundamental unity, and the goal of philosophy is to gain the "absolute knowledge" that would consist of Spirit recognizing the world as its own emanation. The changes of history, its dialectical path, would then come to an end. The dream of such completion has proven extraordinarily alluring yet often dangerous. Shorn of that dream, Hegel's philosophy gives us a dynamic world of interrelationships in which the various elements contend with one another through dialectical struggle. Hegel's most famous disciple, KARL MARX, adopts both the vision of struggle and the dream of an end to strife. But Hegelian themes also echo, in a different key, throughout the work of poststructuralists such as MICHEL FOUCAULT and JULIA KRISTEVA.

Our first selection presents the most famous instance of dialectical confrontation in Hegel, the so-called Master-Slave ("lord" and "bondsman" in our translation) dialectic. Although dense and abstract, this section of *Phenomenology of Spirit* has been very influential, especially in France, where, by way of Alexandre Kojève's celebrated *Introduction to the Reading of Hegel* (1947), it shaped the thought of Jean-Paul Sartre, SIMONE DE BEAUVOIR, JACQUES LACAN, and JACQUES DERRIDA, among others. The question Hegel asks is this: how does a human being come to consciousness of itself as a self (a consciousness that animals lack)? Hegel assumes that humans are not born with the sense "I am John Smith, and this is what I believe and am like." How then do we acquire self-consciousness? Only in meeting with something that is not the self, according to Hegel. Confrontation with my limits, with the not-self, enables me to identify what is self, what belongs to me. The reality of this discovered self depends on two things: I must have the consciousness that I am a self (which Hegel calls "being-for-self"), and my existence must be acknowledged or recognized by other human beings ("being-for-others"). In Hegel's words, "Self-consciousness exists in and for itself when, and by the fact that, it so exists for another; that is, it exists only in being acknowledged."

Most interpreters have seen Hegel as demonstrating that selfhood is a social fact. The child develops a sense of self largely because others treat it as a self—and the self will be socially constructed in different ways, depending on how it is treated. Selves are not born but made, in a dialectical social process of interrelationships among selves. This ongoing process proceeds through "moments" that Hegel then identifies as stages on the way toward full self-consciousness. Just as the self develops consciousness over time, so the human species as a whole passes through moments in history on the path to absolute knowledge. *Phenomenology of Spirit* traces this movement of humans through time to the culminating moment of the full self-consciousness of Spirit.

In the Master-Slave dialectic, the counterposed selves who are coming to consciousness have so much at stake that their relationships are a constant source of strife, "such that they prove themselves and each other through a life-and-death struggle." Selves do not take their fundamental dependence on others kindly. Here power enters the discussion, as Hegel imagines that each individual would prefer to guarantee continued recognition from the other, while not extending that recognition in turn. Such imbalance, taken to its extreme, is figured by Hegel as the relationship between a master and a slave, which is established in a battle that ends when the Slave grants recognition and service to the Master in return for continued life. (Both the Master and Slave stake their life in the battle, but the loser becomes a slave by choosing a life of servitude over death at the hand of the victor.)

The Master, however, finds victory hollow. Recognition, like love, has value only when it is freely given, when it comes from someone who is like me in status. If the other acknowledges my existence only because forced to do so, how can that calm my lurking doubt about who I am? (Hegel not only anticipates the processes of self-formation described by SIGMUND FREUD but also describes the existential anxiety that haunts any attachment to "identity.") The Master's access to his own selfhood is mediated through his relationship to the Slave; and since that Slave is "not an independent consciousness, but a dependent one," the Master "is, therefore, not certain of *being-for-self* as the truth of himself." By obliterating the Slave's independence, the Master has removed the very "other" that must be encountered to achieve selfhood.

Meanwhile, the Slave moves from the "dread . . . it has experienced" in the face of "death, the absolute Lord [or Master]" to a fairly satisfactory self-consciousness achieved through work. (The Hegelian description of labor as redemptive greatly influenced Marx.) The Slave gains a sense of self because his labor has an effect on a material world of resistant objects. The Master has lost contact with the non-self (except with the Slave) because he has left all physical interaction with the world to the Slave. This ironic reversal of the Master-Slave relationship points toward the reciprocity of dependence that Hegel sees as characterizing human relationships: "They *recognize* themselves as *mutually recognizing* one another." Only if I am willing to acknowledge that the other is also a self, who has a need and a right to be a being-for-self, can I satisfactorily establish my own selfhood.

This account provides a memorable and persuasive model for understanding the complex dynamics of intersubjective relationships. Selfhood is a social product that individuals crave; identity has to be constructed through contentious interaction with and relation to others; this process makes us dependent on others, and thus inclined to resent and fear them; and such dependence involves forms of psychological and social power that are distinct from physical force or the power afforded by superior wealth. Whenever modern literary theorists and critics have been interested in questions of identity and of the self's confrontation with the other (however understood), Hegel's famous account of the Master-Slave dialectic has hovered in the background.

Our second selection consists of excerpts from the introduction to *Lectures on Fine Art*—Hegel's contribution to philosophical aesthetics, the field that seeks to define the aims of the arts, the features of art objects, the activity of artists, and the effects of the arts on audiences. Aesthetics dates from the 1750s, but Hegel clearly echoes Plato on the arts. For Hegel, the fundamental goal of humanity is to come to full consciousness of the Idea (or Spirit), and philosophy is the golden road to that goal. Yet, unlike Plato, he wants to praise art, not condemn it. Because Hegel accepts the superiority of spirit over matter, truth over appearance, universal over particular, intellectual over sensual, and logic over feeling, he must argue that art, understood correctly, is not merely a sensuous, material, singular thing; instead, it contributes to human understanding of the Idea.

Hegel takes the line of argument suggested by his model of thinking. Just as the self in the Master-Slave dialectic can come to self-consciousness only through encountering an other, so thinking needs to encounter an object. The Spirit or Idea dwells within humans, but as "a *thinking* consciousness" a person "draws out of himself and puts *before himself* what . . . is." After art has given Spirit a concrete form, it can be apprehended. This account makes art part of the philosophical project of coming to full consciousness—and provides Hegel with firm answers to a number of problems that bedevil aesthetics.

In the first part of our selection, Hegel reviews previous notions of the arts, steering a middle path between accounts that emphasize rules and those that rely on pure inspiration. More important, Hegel asserts the superiority of human-made artistic objects to God-made natural ones by appealing to their spiritual purpose. Spirit dwells in nature as well as in humans, but only humans are conscious of reaching an awareness of spirit. A man needs art "to lift the inner and outer world into his spiritual consciousness as an object in which he recognizes again his own self." In Hegel's quasi-religious philosophy, human life reaches its highest form when we recognize that the spirit of the creator permeates all of the created world, including ourselves. To discover this true self, to align ourselves with spirit, is to attain "free rationality."

True to his historicist convictions, in the second part of our selection Hegel presents the movement to full self-consciousness as occurring in stages. Symbolic, classical, and romantic art form a dialectical triad. Symbolic art, tied to "perceived natural objects," attempts but fails to attach a spiritual significance to those objects. This failure has its uses, since at least "the foreignness of the Idea to natural phenomena" is made manifest. The gap here between the natural and the spiritual is, Hegel tells us, "sublime," a striking revision of a category invoked in antiquity by LONGINUS and in the eighteenth century by JOSEPH ADDISON, EDMUND BURKE, and Kant.

The failure of primitive symbolic art, associated with the ancient Near East, generates its antithesis, classical art; and what Hegel sees as the higher, Western tradition begins. By focusing on "the human form," the Greeks gave the Idea an adequate material embodiment. Since humans are a potent example of the union of spirit and body, Hegel finds ingenious the classical solution to the problem of "bring[ing] the spiritual before our eyes in a sensuous manner." But it too has a defect—the opposite of that of symbolic art, which could not give the Idea a local habitation and name. Classical art fails because it "determine[s]" spirit "as particular and human," thus obscuring its "absolute and eternal" essence.

This "defect . . . demands a transition to a higher form," the Romantic. The threat of classical art lies in its sensuousness. Romantic art, even as it utilizes sensuous forms, must move both artist and audience (by irony and sublimity) toward "the *inwardness of self-consciousness*," toward the indwelling spirit. As a synthesis and overcoming of symbolic and classical art, Romantic art dissociates the idea from the sensuous form (as does symbolic art) even as it presents the sensuous form (as does classical art). Romantic art stages the "inadequacy" of the material embodiment so that "the Idea . . . appear[s] *perfected* in itself as spirit and heart."

Thus Hegel is a champion of Romantic art. In the move from sensuous form to inwardness, he places the expression of "subjective inner depth" and "reflective emotion" at the center of the artistic enterprise. This notion of art as expression is the cornerstone of Romantic aesthetics—WILLIAM WORDSWORTH, PERCY BYSSHE SHELLEY, and RALPH WALDO EMERSON are among the nineteenth-century writers who espouse some version of an expressivist aesthetic—and it continues to dominate popular understandings of art, especially poetry. But Hegel's historicism also suggests a broader expressivist understanding of art, in which the artwork is viewed as an expression of an era, zeitgeist, culture, or nation rather than of the artist's self. In both cases, artistic representation is tied not to some visible thing imitated by the artist but to some invisible ideas, emotions, attitudes, values, or spirit.

While much contemporary critical practice, knowingly or not, is Hegelian, postmodern theory has self-consciously struggled (sometimes desperately) to slough off Hegelian habits. The great problem is Hegel's will to totality, the movement of his philosophy, through dialectical overcoming and synthesis, to include everything. Postmodern theorists resist this philosophical imperialism, this "totalizing impulse," insisting that inclusion through the dialectic always comes at the price of overcoming what is most singular and different in the incorporated other. The problem with subsuming everything into a totalizing system is the erasure of difference. Hence, in our selection Hegel makes art safe for philosophy by downplaying or explaining away everything that makes art different from and even antithetical to thinking.

By highlighting the different and the singular, postmodernists question Hegel's placing of everything into a relational, systematic whole. But since postmodern theory does accept that meaning is the product of systematic, though differential, relations, Hegel has been hard to negate. Because he can be neither banished nor embraced, Hegel remains a figure to whom much contemporary theory obsessively returns.

***Phenomenology of Spirit* Keywords:** Identity, Marxism, Phenomenology, Poststructuralism, Subjectivity

***Lectures on Fine Art* Keywords:** Aesthetics, Ethics, Phenomenology, Religion, Romantic Theory

From Phenomenology of Spirit[1]

[*The Master-Slave Dialectic*]

178. Self-consciousness exists in and for itself when, and by the fact that, it so exists for another; that is, it exists only in being acknowledged [*als ein Anerkanntes*]. The Notion of this its unity in its duplication embraces many and varied meanings. Its moments, then, must on the one hand be held strictly apart, and on the other hand must in this differentiation at the same time also be taken and known as not distinct, or in their opposite significance. The twofold significance of the distinct moments has in the nature of self-consciousness to be infinite, or directly the opposite of the determinateness in which it is posited. The detailed exposition of the Notion of this spiritual unity in its duplication will present us with the process of Recognition [*Anerkennen*].

179. Self-consciousness is faced by another self-consciousness; it has come *out of itself*. This has a twofold significance: first, it has lost itself, for it finds itself as an *other* being; secondly, in doing so it has superseded the other, for it does not see the other as an essential being, but in the other sees its own self.

180. It must supersede this otherness of itself. This is the supersession of the first ambiguity, and is therefore itself a second ambiguity. First, it must proceed to supersede the *other* independent being in order thereby to become certain of *itself* as the essential being; secondly, in so doing it proceeds to supersede its *own* self, for this other is itself.

181. This ambiguous supersession of its ambiguous otherness is equally an ambiguous return *into itself*. For first, through the supersession, it receives back its own self, because, by superseding *its* otherness, it again becomes equal to itself; but secondly, it equally gives the other self-consciousness back again to itself, for it saw itself in the other, but supersedes this being of itself in the other and thus lets the other again go free.

182. Now, this movement of self-consciousness in relation to another self-consciousness has in this way been represented as the action of *one* self-consciousness, but this action of the one has itself the double significance of being both its own action and the action of the other as well. For the other is equally independent and self-contained, and there is nothing in it of which it is not itself the origin. The first does not have the object before it merely as it exists primarily for desire, but as something that has an independent existence of its own, which, therefore, it cannot utilize for its own purposes, if that object does not of its own accord do what the first does to it. Thus the movement is simply the double movement of the two self-consciousnesses. Each sees the *other* do the same as it does; each does itself what it demands of the other, and therefore also does what it does only in so far as the other does the same. Action by one side only would be useless because what is to happen can only be brought about by both.

1. Translated by A. V. Miller, who sometimes retains the original German or adds clarifying words or phrases in brackets and has added the paragraph numbers.

183. Thus the action has a double significance not only because it is directed against itself as well as against the other, but also because it is indivisibly the action of one as well as of the other.

184. In this movement we see repeated the process which presented itself as the play of Forces, but repeated now in consciousness. What in that process was *for us*, is true here of the extremes themselves. The middle term is self-consciousness which splits into the extremes; and each extreme is this exchanging of its own determinateness and an absolute transition into the opposite. Although, as consciousness, it does indeed come *out of itself*, yet, though out of itself, it is at the same time kept back within itself, is *for itself*, and the self outside it, is for *it*. It is aware that it at once is, and is not, another consciousness, and equally that this other is *for itself* only when it supersedes itself as being for itself, and is for itself only in the being-for-self of the other. Each is for the other the middle term, through which each mediates itself with itself and unites with itself; and each is for itself, and for the other, an immediate being to its own account, which at the same time is such only through this mediation.[2] They *recognize* themselves as *mutually recognizing* one another.

185. We have now to see how the process of this pure Notion of recognition, of the duplicating of self-consciousness in its oneness, appears to self-consciousness. At first, it will exhibit the side of the inequality of the two, or the splitting-up of the middle term into the extremes which, as extremes, are opposed to one another, one being only *recognized*, the other only *recognizing*.

186. Self-consciousness is, to begin with, simple being-for-self, self-equal through the exclusion from itself of everything else. For it, its essence and absolute object is 'I'; and in this immediacy, or in this [mere] being, of its being-for-self, it is an *individual*. What is 'other' for it is an unessential, negatively characterized object. But the 'other' is also a self-consciousness; one individual is confronted by another individual. Appearing thus immediately on the scene, they are for one another like ordinary objects, *independent* shapes, individuals submerged in the being [or immediacy] of *Life*—for the object in its immediacy is here determined as Life. They are, *for each other*, shapes of consciousness which have not yet accomplished the movement of absolute abstraction, of rooting-out all immediate being, and of being merely the purely negative being of self-identical consciousness; in other words, they have not as yet exposed themselves to each other in the form of pure being-for-self, or as self-consciousness. Each is indeed certain of its own self, but not of the other, and therefore its own self-certainty still has no truth. For it would have truth only if its own being-for-self had confronted it as an independent object, or, what is the same thing, if the object had presented itself as this pure self-certainty. But according to the Notion of recognition this is possible only when each is for the other what the other is for it, only when each in its own self through its own action, and again through the action of the other, achieves this pure abstraction of being-for-self.

187. The presentation of itself, however, as the pure abstraction of self-consciousness consists in showing itself as the pure negation of its objective

2. That is, the encounter with the other is necessary for self-consciousness.

mode, or in showing that it is not attached to any specific *existence*, not to the individuality common to existence as such, that it is not attached to life. This presentation is a twofold action: action on the part of the other, and action on its own part. In so far as it is the action of the *other*, each seeks the death of the other. But in doing so, the second kind of action, action on its own part, is also involved; for the former involves the staking of its own life. Thus the relation of the two self-conscious individuals is such that they prove themselves and each other through a life-and-death struggle. They must engage in this struggle, for they must raise their certainty of being *for themselves* to truth, both in the case of the other and in their own case. And it is only through staking one's life that freedom is won; only thus is it proved that for self-consciousness, its essential being is not [just] being, not the *immediate* form in which it appears, not its submergence in the expanse of life, but rather that there is nothing present in it which could not be regarded as a vanishing moment, that it is only pure *being-for-self*. The individual who has not risked his life may well be recognized as a *person*, but he has not attained to the truth of this recognition as an independent self-consciousness. Similarly, just as each stakes his own life, so each must seek the other's death, for it values the other no more than itself; its essential being is present to it in the form of an 'other', it is outside of itself and must rid itself of its self-externality. The other is an *immediate* consciousness entangled in a variety of relationships, and it must regard its otherness as a pure being-for-self or as an absolute negation.

188. This trial by death, however, does away with the truth which was supposed to issue from it, and so, too, with the certainty of self generally. For just as life is the *natural* setting of consciousness, independence without absolute negativity, so death is the *natural* negation of consciousness, negation without independence, which thus remains without the required significance of recognition. Death certainly shows that each staked his life and held it of no account, both in himself and in the other; but that is not for those who survived this struggle. They put an end to their consciousness in its alien setting of natural existence, that is to say, they put an end to themselves, and are done away with as *extremes* wanting to be *for themselves*, or to have an existence of their own. But with this there vanishes from their interplay the essential moment of splitting into extremes with opposite characteristics; and the middle term collapses into a lifeless unity which is split into lifeless, merely immediate, unopposed extremes; and the two do not reciprocally give and receive one another back from each other consciously, but leave each other free only indifferently, like things. Their act is an abstract negation, not the negation coming from consciousness, which supersedes in such a way as to preserve and maintain what is superseded, and consequently survives its own supersession.[3]

189. In this experience, self-consciousness learns that life is as essential to it as pure self-consciousness. In immediate self-consciousness the simple 'I' is the absolute object which, however, for us or in itself is absolute mediation, and has as its essential moment lasting independence. The dissolution of that simple unity is the result of the first experience; through this there is posited a pure self-consciousness, and a consciousness which is not purely for itself

3. This description of "the negation coming from consciousness" encapsulates the dialectic.

but for another, i.e. is a merely *immediate* consciousness, or consciousness in the form of *thinghood*. Both moments are essential. Since to begin with they are unequal and opposed, and their reflection into a unity has not yet been achieved, they exist as two opposed shapes of consciousness; one is the independent consciousness whose essential nature is to be for itself, the other is the dependent consciousness whose essential nature is simply to live or to be for another. The former is lord [*Herr*], the other is bondsman [*Knecht*].[4]

190. The lord is the consciousness that exists *for itself*, but no longer merely the Notion of such a consciousness. Rather, it is a consciousness existing *for itself* which is mediated with itself through another consciousness, i.e. through a consciousness whose nature it is to be bound up with an existence that is independent, or thinghood in general. The lord puts himself into relation with both of these moments, to a *thing* as such, the object of desire, and to the consciousness for which thinghood is the essential characteristic. And since he is (a) *qua* the Notion of self-consciousness an immediate relation of *being-for-self*, but (b) is now at the same time mediation, or a being-for-self which is for itself only through another, he is related (a) immediately to both, and (b) mediately to each through the other. The lord relates himself mediately to the bondsman through a being [a thing] that is independent, for it is just this which holds the bondsman in bondage; it is his chain from which he could not break free in the struggle, thus proving himself to be dependent, to possess his independence in thinghood. But the lord is the power over this thing, for he proved in the struggle that it is something merely negative; since he is the power over this thing and this again is the power over the other [the bondsman], it follows that he holds the other in subjection. Equally, the lord relates himself mediately to the thing through the bondsman; the bondsman, *qua* self-consciousness in general, also relates himself negatively to the thing, and takes away its independence; but at the same time the thing is independent *vis-à-vis* the bondsman, whose negating of it, therefore, cannot go to the length of being altogether done with it to the point of annihilation; in other words, he only *works* on it. For the lord, on the other hand, the *immediate* relation becomes through this mediation the sheer negation of the thing, or the enjoyment of it. What desire failed to achieve, he succeeds in doing, viz. to have done with the thing altogether, and to achieve satisfaction in the enjoyment of it. Desire failed to do this because of the thing's independence; but the lord, who has interposed the bondsman between it and himself, takes to himself only the dependent aspect of the thing and has the pure enjoyment of it. The aspect of its independence he leaves to the bondsman, who works on it.

191. In both of these moments the lord achieves his recognition through another consciousness; for in them, that other consciousness is expressly something unessential, both by its working on the thing, and by its dependence on a specific existence. In neither case can it be lord over the being of the thing and achieve absolute negation of it. Here, therefore, is present this moment of recognition, viz. that the other consciousness sets aside its own being-for-self, and in so doing itself does what the first does to it. Similarly, the other moment too is present, that this action of the second is the first's own action; for what the bondsman does is really the action of the

4. *Herr* and *Knecht* have often been translated "Master" and "Slave."

lord. The latter's essential nature is to exist only for himself; he is the sheer negative power for whom the thing is nothing. Thus he is the pure, essential action in this relationship, while the action of the bondsman is impure and unessential. But for recognition proper the moment is lacking, that what the lord does to the other he also does to himself, and what the bondsman does to himself he should also do to the other. The outcome is a recognition that is one-sided and unequal.

192. In this recognition the unessential consciousness is for the lord the object, which constitutes the *truth* of his certainty of himself. But it is clear that this object does not correspond to its Notion, but rather that the object in which the lord has achieved his lordship has in reality turned out to be something quite different from an independent consciousness. What now really confronts him is not an independent consciousness, but a dependent one. He is, therefore, not certain of *being-for-self* as the truth of himself. On the contrary, his truth is in reality the unessential consciousness and its unessential action.

193. The *truth* of the independent consciousness is accordingly the servile consciousness of the bondsman. This, it is true, appears at first *outside* of itself and not as the truth of self-consciousness. But just as lordship showed that its essential nature is the reverse of what it wants to be, so too servitude in its consummation will really turn into the opposite of what it immediately is; as a consciousness forced back into itself, it will withdraw into itself and be transformed into a truly independent consciousness.

194. We have seen what servitude is only in relation to lordship. But it is a self-consciousness, and we have now to consider what as such it is in and for itself. To begin with, servitude has the lord for its essential reality; hence the *truth* for it is the independent consciousness that it is *for itself*. However, servitude is not yet aware that this truth is implicit in it. But it does in fact contain within itself this truth of pure negativity and being-for-self, for it has experienced this its own essential nature. For this consciousness has been fearful, not of this or that particular thing or just at odd moments, but its whole being has been seized with dread; for it has experienced the fear of death, the absolute Lord. In that experience it has been quite unmanned, has trembled in every fibre of its being, and everything solid and stable has been shaken to its foundations. But this pure universal movement, the absolute melting-away of everything stable, is the simple, essential nature of self-consciousness, absolute negativity, *pure being-for-self*, which consequently is *implicit* in this consciousness. This moment of pure being-for-self is also *explicit* for the bondsman, for in the lord it exists for him as his *object*. Furthermore, his consciousness is not this dissolution of everything stable merely in principle; in his service he *actually* brings this about. Through his service he rids himself of his attachment to natural existence in every single detail; and gets rid of it by working on it.

195. However, the feeling of absolute power both in general, and in the particular form of service, is only implicitly this dissolution, and although the fear of the lord is indeed the beginning of wisdom, consciousness is not therein aware that it is a being-for-self. Through work, however, the bondsman becomes conscious of what he truly is. In the moment which corresponds to desire in the lord's consciousness, it did seem that the aspect of unessential relation to the thing fell to the lot of the bondsman, since in that

relation the thing retained its independence. Desire has reserved to itself the pure negating of the object and thereby its unalloyed feeling of self. But that is the reason why this satisfaction is itself only a fleeting one, for it lacks the side of objectivity and permanence. Work, on the other hand, is desire held in check, fleetingness staved off; in other words, work forms and shapes the thing. The negative relation to the object becomes its *form* and something *permanent*, because it is precisely for the worker that the object has independence. This *negative* middle term or the formative *activity* is at the same time the individuality or pure being-for-self of consciousness which now, in the work outside of it, acquires an element of permanence.[5] It is in this way, therefore, that consciousness, *qua* worker, comes to see in the independent being [of the object] its *own* independence.

196. But the formative activity has not only this positive significance that in it the pure being-for-self of the servile consciousness acquires an existence; it also has negative significance with respect to its first moment, *fear*. For, in fashioning the thing, the bondsman's own negativity, his being-for-self, becomes an object for him only through his setting at nought the existing *shape* confronting him. But this objective *negative* moment is none other than the alien being before which it has trembled. Now, however, he destroys this alien negative moment, posits *himself* as a negative in the permanent order of things, and thereby becomes *for himself*, someone existing on his own account. In the lord, the being-for-self is an 'other' for the bondsman, or is only *for* him [i.e. is not his own]; in fear, the being-for-self is present in the bondsman himself; in fashioning the thing, he becomes aware that being-for-self belongs to *him*, that he himself exists essentially and actually in his own right. The shape does not become something other than himself through being made external to him; for it is precisely this shape that is his pure being-for-self, which in this externality is seen by him to be the truth. Through this rediscovery of himself by himself, the bondsman realizes that it is precisely in his work wherein he seemed to have only an alienated existence that he acquires a mind of his own. For this reflection, the two moments of fear and service as such, as also that of formative activity, are necessary, both being at the same time in a universal mode. Without the discipline of service and obedience, fear remains at the formal stage, and does not extend to the known real world of existence. Without the formative activity, fear remains inward and mute, and consciousness does not become explicitly *for itself*. If consciousness fashions the thing without that initial absolute fear, it is only an empty self-centered attitude; for its form or negativity is not negativity *per se*, and therefore its formative activity cannot give it a consciousness of itself as essential being. If it has not experienced absolute fear but only some lesser dread, the negative being has remained for it something external, its substance has not been infected by it through and through. Since the entire contents of its natural consciousness have not been jeopardized, determinate being still *in principle* attaches to it; having a 'mind of one's own' is self-will, a freedom which is still enmeshed in servitude. Just as little as the pure form can become essential being for it, just as little is that form, regarded as extended to the

5. Work as "formative activity," according to Hegel, creates a stable object that comes to signify a similar stability for the consciousness that shapes that object.

particular, a universal formative activity, an absolute Notion; rather it is a skill which is master over some things, but not over the universal power and the whole of objective being.

1807

From Lectures on Fine Art[1]

From *Introduction*

* * *

THE WORK OF ART AS A PRODUCT OF HUMAN ACTIVITY

(*a*) As for the first point, that a work of art is a product of human activity, this view has given rise to the thought that this activity, being the *conscious* production of an external object, can also be *known* and expounded, and learnt and pursued by others. For what one man makes, another, it may seem, could make or imitate too, if only he were first acquainted with the manner of proceeding; so that, granted universal acquaintance with the rules of artistic production, it would only be a matter of everyone's pleasure to carry out the procedure in the same manner and produce works of art. It is in this way that the rule-providing theories, mentioned above, with their prescriptions calculated for practical application, have arisen. But what can be carried out on such directions can only be something formally regular and mechanical. For the mechanical alone is of so external a kind that only a purely empty exercise of will and dexterity is required for receiving it into our ideas and activating it; this exercise does not require to be supplemented by anything concrete, or by anything not prescribed in universal rules. This comes out most vividly when such prescriptions do not limit themselves to the purely external and mechanical, but extend to the significant and spiritual activity of the artist. In this sphere the rules contain only vague generalities, for example that 'the theme should be interesting, every character should speak according to his standing, age, sex, and situation'. But if rules are to satisfy here, then their prescriptions should have been drawn up at the same time with such precision that they could be observed just as they are expressed, without any further spiritual activity of the artist's. Being abstract in content, however, such rules reveal themselves, in their pretence of adequacy to fill the consciousness of the artist, as wholly inadequate, since artistic production is not a formal activity in accordance with given specifications. On the contrary, as spiritual activity it is bound to work from its own resources and bring before the mind's eye a quite other and richer content and more comprehensive individual creations [than formulae can provide]. Therefore, in so far as such rules do actually contain something specific and therefore of practical utility, they may apply in case of need, but still can afford no more than specifications for purely external circumstances.

(*b*) Thus, as it turns out, the tendency just indicated has been altogether abandoned, and instead of it the opposite one has been adopted to the same

1. Translated by T. M. Knox, who sometimes adds explanatory words or phrases in brackets.

extent. For the work of art was no longer regarded as a product of *general* human activity, but as a work of an entirely *specially gifted* spirit which now, however, is supposed to give free play simply and *only* to its own particular gift, as if to a specific natural force; it is to cut itself altogether loose from attention to universally valid laws and from a conscious reflection interfering with its own instinctive-like productive activity. Indeed it is supposed to be protected from such reflection, since its productions could only be contaminated and spoiled by such awareness. From this point of view the work of art has been claimed as a product of *talent* and *genius*, and the natural element in talent and genius has been especially emphasized. In a way, rightly, since talent is specific and genius universal capability, which man has not the power to give to himself purely and simply through his own self-conscious activity. On this topic we shall speak at greater length later.

Here we have only to mention the false aspect of this view, namely that in artistic production all consciousness of the artist's own activity is regarded as not merely superfluous but even deleterious. In that case production by talent and genius appears as only a *state* and, in particular, a state of *inspiration*. To such a state, it is said, genius is excited in part by an object, and in part can transpose itself into it by its own caprice, a process in which, after all, the good services of the champagne bottle are not forgotten. In Germany this notion became prominent at the time of the so-called *Period of Genius* which was introduced by Goethe's first poetical productions and then sustained by Schiller's.[2] In their earliest works these poets began afresh, setting aside all the rules then fabricated; they worked deliberately against these rules and thereby surpassed all other writers. However, I will not go further into the confusions which have been prevalent about the concept of inspiration and genius, and which prevail even today about the omnicompetence of inspiration as such. All that is essential is to state the view that, even if the talent and genius of the artist has in it a natural element, yet this element essentially requires development by thought, reflection on the mode of its productivity, and practice and skill in producing. For, apart from anything else, a main feature of artistic production is external workmanship, since the work of art has a purely technical side which extends into handicraft, especially in architecture and sculpture, less so in painting and music, least of all in poetry. Skill in technique is not helped by any inspiration, but only by reflection, industry, and practice. But such skill the artist is compelled to have in order to master his external material and not be thwarted by its intractability.

Now further, the higher the standing of the artist, the more profoundly should he display the depths of the heart and the spirit; these are not known directly but are to be fathomed only by the direction of the artist's own spirit on the inner and outer world. So, once again, it is study whereby the artist brings this content into his consciousness and wins the stuff and content of his conceptions.

* * *

2. Johann Wolfgang von Goethe (1749–1832) and FRIEDRICH VON SCHILLER (1759–1805) were the two most important poets of the Romantic period in Germany.

(*c*) A third view concerning the idea of the work of art as a product of human activity refers to the placing of the work of art in relation to the external phenomena of nature. Here the ordinary way of looking at things took easily to the notion that the human art-product ranked below the product of nature; for the work of art has no feeling in itself and is not through and through enlivened, but, regarded as an external object, is dead; but we are accustomed to value the living higher than the dead. That the work of art has no life and movement in itself is readily granted. What is alive in nature is, within and without, an organism purposefully elaborated into all its tiniest parts, while the work of art attains the appearance of life only on its surface; inside it is ordinary stone, or wood and canvas, or, as in poetry, an idea expressed in speech and letters. But this aspect—external existence—is not what makes a work into a product of fine art; a work of art is such only because, originating from the spirit, it now belongs to the territory of the spirit; it has received the baptism of the spiritual and sets forth only what has been formed in harmony with the spirit. Human interest, the spiritual value possessed by an event, an individual character, an action in its complexity and outcome, is grasped in the work of art and blazoned more purely and more transparently than is possible on the ground of other non-artistic things. Therefore the work of art stands higher than any natural product which has not made this journey through the spirit. For example, owing to the feeling and insight whereby a landscape has been represented in a painting, this work of the spirit acquires a higher rank than the mere natural landscape. For everything spiritual is better than any product of nature. Besides, no natural being is able, as art is, to present the divine Ideal.

Now on what the spirit draws from its own inner resources in works of art it confers permanence in their external existence too; on the other hand, the individual living thing in nature is transient, vanishing, changeable in outward appearance, while the work of art persists, even if it is not mere permanence which constitutes its genuine pre-eminence over natural reality, but its having made spiritual inspiration conspicuous.

But nevertheless this higher standing of the work of art is questioned by another idea commonly entertained. For nature and its products, it is said, are a work of God, created by his goodness and wisdom, whereas the art-product is a purely human work, made by human hands according to human insight. In this contrast between natural production as a divine creation and human activity as something merely finite there lies directly the misunderstanding that God does not work in and through men at all, but restricts the sphere of his activity to nature alone. This false opinion must be completely rejected if we are to penetrate to the true nature of art. Indeed, over against this view we must cling to the opposite one, namely that God is more honoured by what the spirit makes than by the productions and formations of nature. For not only is there something divine in man, but it is active in him in a form appropriate to the being of God in a totally different and higher manner than it is in nature. God is spirit, and in man alone does the medium, through which the Divine passes, have the form of conscious and actively self-productive spirit; but in nature this medium is the unconscious, the sensuous, and the external, which stands far below consciousness in worth. Now in art-production God is just as operative as he is in the phenomena of nature; but the Divine, as it discloses itself in the work of art, has been generated out of the spirit, and thus has won a suitable thoroughfare for its existence, whereas just being *there* in the unconscious sensuousness of nature is not a mode of appearance appropriate to the Divine.

(*d*) Now granted that the work of art is made by man as the creation of his spirit, a final question arises, in order to derive a deeper result from the foregoing [discussion], namely, what is man's *need* to produce works of art? On the one hand, this production may be regarded as a mere play of chance and fancies which might just as well be left alone as pursued; for it might be held that there are other and even better means of achieving what art aims at and that man has still higher and more important interests than art has the ability to satisfy. On the other hand, however, art seems to proceed from a higher impulse and to satisfy higher needs,—at times the highest and absolute needs since it is bound up with the most universal views of life and the religious interests of whole epochs and peoples.—This question about the non-contingent but absolute need for art, we cannot yet answer completely, because it is more concrete than an answer could turn out to be at this stage. Therefore we must content ourselves in the meantime with making only the following points.

The universal and absolute need from which art (on its formal side) springs has its origin in the fact that man is a *thinking* consciousness, i.e. that man draws out of himself and puts *before himself* what he is and whatever else is. Things in nature are only *immediate* and *single*, while man as spirit *duplicates* himself, in that (i) he *is* as things in nature are, but (ii) he is just as much *for* himself; he sees himself, represents himself to himself, thinks, and only on the strength of this active placing himself before himself is he spirit. This consciousness of himself man acquires in a two-fold way: *first, theoretically*, in so far as inwardly he must bring himself into his own consciousness, along with whatever moves, stirs, and presses in the human breast; and in general he must see himself, represent himself to himself, fix before himself what thinking finds as his essence, and recognize himself alone alike in what is summoned out of himself and in what is accepted from without. *Secondly*, man brings himself before himself by *practical* activity, since he has the impulse, in whatever is directly given to him, in what is present to him externally, to produce himself and therein equally to recognize himself. This aim he achieves by altering external things whereon he impresses the seal of his inner being and in which he now finds again his own characteristics. Man does this in order, as a free subject, to strip the external world of its inflexible foreignness and to enjoy in the shape of things only an external realization of himself. Even a child's first impulse involves this practical alteration of external things; a boy throws stones into the river and now marvels at the circles drawn in the water as an effect in which he gains an intuition of something that is his own doing. This need runs through the most diversiform phenomena up to that mode of self-production in external things which is present in the work of art. And it is not only with external things that man proceeds in this way, but no less with himself, with his own natural figure which he does not leave as he finds it but deliberately alters. This is the cause of all dressing up and adornment, even if it be barbaric, tasteless, completely disfiguring, or even pernicious like crushing the feet of Chinese ladies,[3] or slitting the ears and lips. For it is only among civilized people that alteration of figure, behaviour, and every sort and mode of external expression proceeds from spiritual development.

The universal need for art, that is to say, is man's rational need to lift the inner and outer world into his spiritual consciousness as an object in which he recognizes again his own self. The need for this spiritual freedom he satisfies, on the one hand, by making what is within him explicit to himself, but correspondingly by giving outward reality to this his explicit self, and thus in this duplication of himself by bringing what is in him into sight and knowledge for himself and others. This is the free rationality of man in which all acting and knowing, as well as art too, have their basis and necessary origin.

* * *

DEVELOPMENT OF THE IDEAL INTO THE PARTICULAR FORMS OF THE BEAUTY OF ART

But because the Idea is in this way a concrete unity, this unity can enter the art-consciousness only through the unfolding and then the reconciliation of the particularizations of the Idea,[4] and, through this development, artistic beauty acquires a *totality of particular stages and forms*. Therefore, after studying artistic beauty in itself and on its own account, we must see how beauty as a whole decomposes into its particular determinations. This gives, as the *second* part of our study, the doctrine of the *forms of art*. These forms find their origin in the different ways of grasping the Idea as content, whereby a difference in the configuration in which the Idea appears is conditioned. Thus the forms of art are nothing but the different relations of meaning and shape, relations which proceed from the Idea itself and therefore provide the true basis for the division of this sphere. For division must always be implicit in the concept, the particularization and division of which is in question.

We have here to consider *three* relations of the Idea to its configuration.

(*a*) *First*, art begins when the Idea, still in its indeterminacy and obscurity, or in bad and untrue determinacy, is made the content of artistic shapes. Being indeterminate, it does not yet possess in itself that individuality which the Ideal demands; its abstraction and one-sidedness leave its shape externally defective and arbitrary. The first form of art is therefore rather a *mere search* for portrayal than a capacity for true presentation; the Idea has not found the form even in itself and therefore remains struggling and striving after it. We may call this form, in general terms, the *symbolic* form of art. In it the abstract Idea has its shape outside itself in the natural sensuous material from which the process of shaping starts[5] and with which, in its appearance, this process is linked. Perceived natural objects are, on the one hand, primarily left as they are, yet at the same time the substantial Idea is imposed on them as their meaning so that they now acquire a vocation to express it and so are to be interpreted as if the Idea itself were present in them. A corollary of this is the fact that natural objects have in them an

3. That is, footbinding, a practice common among Chinese women from the 10th into the 20th century.
4. That is, the different historical forms of art.
5. An unknown block of stone may symbolize the Divine, but it does not represent it. Its natural shape has no connection with the Divine and is therefore external to it and not an embodiment of it. When shaping begins, the shapes produced are symbols, perhaps, but in themselves are fantastic and monstrous [Hegel's note].

aspect according to which they are capable of representing a universal meaning. But since a complete correspondence is not yet possible, this relation can concern only an *abstract* characteristic, as when, for example, in a lion strength is meant.

On the other hand, the abstractness of this relation brings home to consciousness even so the foreignness of the Idea to natural phenomena, and the Idea, which has no other reality to express it, launches out in all these shapes, seeks itself in them in their unrest and extravagance, but yet does not find them adequate to itself. So now the Idea exaggerates natural shapes and the phenomena of reality itself into indefiniteness and extravagance; it staggers round in them, it bubbles and ferments in them, does violence to them, distorts and stretches them unnaturally, and tries to elevate their phenomenal appearance to the Idea by the diffuseness, immensity, and splendour of the formations employed. For the Idea is here still more or less indeterminate and unshapable, while the natural objects are thoroughly determinate in their shape.

In the incompatibility of the two sides to one another, the relation of the Idea to the objective world therefore becomes a *negative* one, since the Idea, as something inward, is itself unsatisfied by such externality, and, as the inner universal substance thereof, it persists *sublime* above all this multiplicity of shapes which do not correspond with it. In the light of this sublimity, the natural phenomena and human forms and events are accepted, it is true, and left as they are, but yet they are recognized at the same time as incompatible with their meaning which is raised far above all mundane content.

These aspects constitute in general the character of the early artistic pantheism of the East, which on the one hand ascribes absolute meaning to even the most worthless objects, and, on the other, violently coerces the phenomena to express its view of the world whereby it becomes bizarre, grotesque, and tasteless, or turns the infinite but abstract freedom of the substance [i.e. the one Lord] disdainfully against all phenomena as being null and evanescent. By this means the meaning cannot be completely pictured in the expression and, despite all striving and endeavour, the incompatibility of Idea and shape still remains unconquered.—This may be taken to be the first form of art, the symbolic form with its quest, its fermentation, its mysteriousness, and its sublimity.

(*b*) In the *second* form of art which we will call the *classical*, the double defect of the symbolic form is extinguished. The symbolic shape is imperfect because, (i) in it the Idea is presented to consciousness only as indeterminate or determined *abstractly*, and, (ii) for this reason the correspondence of meaning and shape is always defective and must itself remain purely abstract. The classical art-form clears up this double defect; it is the free and adequate embodiment of the Idea in the shape peculiarly appropriate to the Idea itself in its essential nature. With this shape, therefore, the Idea is able to come into free and complete harmony. Thus the classical art-form is the first to afford the production and vision of the completed Ideal and to present it as actualized in fact.

Nevertheless, the conformity of concept and reality in classical art must not be taken in the purely *formal* sense of a correspondence between a content and its external configuration, any more than this could be the case with the Idea itself. Otherwise every portrayal of nature, every cast of features, every neighbourhood, flower, scene, etc., which constitutes the end and content of the representation, would at once be classical on the strength of such congruity between content and form. On the contrary, in classical art the peculiarity of the content consists in its being itself the concrete Idea, and as such the concretely spiritual, for it is the spiritual alone which is the truly inner [self]. Consequently, to suit such a content we must try to find out what in nature belongs to the spiritual in and for itself. The *original* Concept itself it must be which *invented* the shape for concrete spirit, so that now the *subjective* Concept—here the spirit of art—has merely *found* this shape and made it, as a natural shaped existent, appropriate to free individual spirituality. This shape, which the Idea as spiritual—indeed as individually determinate spirituality—assumes when it is to proceed out into a temporal manifestation, is the human form. Of course personification and anthropomorphism have often been maligned as a degradation of the spiritual, but in so far as art's task is to bring the spiritual before our eyes in a sensuous manner, it must get involved in this anthropomorphism, since spirit appears sensuously in a satisfying way only in its body. The transmigration of souls[6] is in this respect an abstract idea, and physiology should have made it one of its chief propositions that life in its development had necessarily to proceed to the human form as the one and only sensuous appearance appropriate to spirit.

But the human body in its forms counts in classical art no longer as a merely sensuous existent, but only as the existence and natural shape of the spirit, and it must therefore be exempt from all the deficiency of the purely sensuous and from the contingent finitude of the phenomenal world. While in this way the shape is purified in order to express in itself a content adequate to itself, on the other hand, if the correspondence of meaning and shape is to be perfect, the spirituality, which is the content, must be of such a kind that it can express itself completely in the natural human form, without towering beyond and above this expression in sensuous and bodily terms. Therefore here the spirit is at once determined as particular and human, not as purely absolute and eternal, since in this latter sense it can proclaim and express itself only as spirituality.

This last point in its turn is the defect which brings about the dissolution of the classical art-form and demands a transition to a higher form, the *third*, namely the *romantic*.

(c) The romantic form of art cancels again the completed unification of the Idea and its reality, and reverts, even if in a higher way, to that difference and opposition of the two sides which in symbolic art remained unconquered. The classical form of art has attained the pinnacle of what illustration by art could achieve, and if there is something defective in it, the defect is just art itself and the restrictedness of the sphere of art. This restrictedness lies in the fact that art in general takes as its subject-matter the spirit (i.e. the *universal*, infinite and concrete in its nature) in a *sensuously* concrete form, and classical art presents the complete unification of spiritual and sensuous existence as the *correspondence* of the two. But in this blending of the two, spirit is not in fact represented in its *true nature*. For spirit is the infinite subjectivity of the Idea, which as absolute inward-

6. Reincarnation, belief in which was widespread in Greek antiquity; it began with Greek Orphic cults and followers of the pre-Socratic philosopher Pythagoras (6th c. B.C.E.).

ness cannot freely and truly shape itself outwardly on condition of remaining moulded into a bodily existence as the one appropriate to it.[7]

Abandoning this [classical] principle, the romantic form of art cancels the undivided unity of classical art because it has won a content which goes beyond and above the classical form of art and its mode of expression. This content—to recall familiar ideas—coincides with what Christianity asserts of God as a spirit, in distinction from the Greek religion which is the essential and most appropriate content for classical art. In classical art the concrete content is *implicitly* the unity of the divine nature with the human, a unity which, just because it is only immediate and implicit, is adequately manifested also in an immediate and sensuous way. The Greek god is the object of naïve intuition and sensuous imagination, and therefore his shape is the bodily shape of man. The range of his power and his being is individual and particular. Contrasted with the individual he is a substance and power with which the individual's inner being is only implicitly at one but without itself possessing this oneness as inward subjective knowledge. Now the higher state is the *knowledge* of that *implicit* unity which is the content of the classical art-form and is capable of perfect presentation in bodily shape. But this elevation of the implicit into self-conscious knowledge introduces a tremendous difference. It is the infinite difference which, for example, separates man from animals. Man is an animal, but even in his animal functions, he is not confined to the implicit, as the animal is; he becomes conscious of them, recognizes them, and lifts them, as, for instance, the process of digestion, into self-conscious science. In this way man breaks the barrier of his implicit and immediate character, so that precisely because he *knows* that he is an animal, he ceases to be an animal and attains knowledge of himself as spirit.

Now if in this way what was implicit at the previous stage, the unity of divine and human nature, is raised from an *immediate* to a *known* unity, the *true* element for the realization of this content is no longer the sensuous immediate existence of the spiritual in the bodily form of man, but instead the *inwardness of self-consciousness*. Now Christianity brings God before our imagination as spirit, not as an individual, particular spirit, but as absolute in spirit and in truth. For this reason it retreats from the sensuousness of imagination into spiritual inwardness and makes this, and not the body, the medium and the existence of truth's content. Thus the unity of divine and human nature is a known unity, one to be realized only by *spiritual* knowing and *in spirit*. The new content, thus won, is on this account not tied to sensuous presentation, as if that corresponded to it, but is freed from this immediate existence which must be set down as negative, overcome, and reflected into the spiritual unity. In this way romantic art is the self-transcendence of art but within its own sphere and in the form of art itself.

We may, therefore, in short, adhere to the view that at this third stage the subject-matter of art is *free concrete spirituality*, which is to be manifested as *spirituality* to the spirituality inward. In conformity with this subject-matter, art cannot work for sensuous intuition. Instead it must, on the one hand, work for the inwardness which coalesces with its object simply as if with

7. In other words, thought is "inwardness" in the sense that thoughts are not outside one another in the way that parts of a body are. That is why the spirit cannot find an adequate embodiment in things but only in thoughts, or at least only in the inner life [Hegel's note].

itself, for subjective inner depth, for reflective emotion, for feeling which, as spiritual, strives for freedom in itself and seeks and finds its reconciliation only in the inner spirit. This *inner* world constitutes the content of the romantic sphere and must therefore be represented as this inwardness and in the pure appearance of this depth of feeling. Inwardness celebrates its triumph over the external and manifests its victory in and on the external itself, whereby what is apparent to the senses alone sinks into worthlessness.

On the other hand, however, this romantic form too, like all art, needs an external medium for its expression. Now since spirituality has withdrawn into itself out of the external world and immediate unity therewith, the sensuous externality of shape is for this reason accepted and represented, as in symbolic art, as something inessential and transient; and the same is true of the subjective finite spirit and will, right down to the particularity and caprice of individuality, character, action, etc., of incident, plot, etc. The aspect of external existence is consigned to contingency and abandoned to the adventures devised by an imagination whose caprice can mirror what is present to it, *exactly as it is*, just as readily as it can jumble the shapes of the external world and distort them grotesquely. For this external medium has its essence and meaning no longer, as in classical art, in itself and its own sphere, but in the heart which finds its manifestation in itself instead of in the external world and *its* form of reality, and this reconciliation with itself it can preserve or regain in every chance, in every accident that takes independent shape, in all misfortune and grief, and indeed even in crime.

Thereby the separation of Idea and shape, their indifference and inadequacy to each other, come to the fore again, as in symbolic art, but with this essential difference, that, in romantic art, the Idea, the deficiency of which in the symbol brought with it deficiency of shape, now has to appear *perfected* in itself as spirit and heart. Because of this higher perfection, it is not susceptible of an adequate union with the external, since its true reality and manifestation it can seek and achieve only within itself.

This we take to be the general character of the symbolic, classical, and romantic forms of art, as the three relations of the Idea to its shape in the sphere of art. They consist in the striving for, the attainment, and the transcendence of the Ideal as the true Idea of beauty.

1835–38

WILLIAM WORDSWORTH
1770–1850

"I am not a critic," William Wordsworth stated in 1830, "and set little value upon the art. The preface which I wrote long ago to my own Poems I was put upon to write by the urgent entreaties of a friend, and heartily regret I ever had anything to do with it; though I do not reckon the principles then advanced erroneous." Wordsworth defined himself as a poet above all, and he is less prolific and gifted as a literary theorist and critic than his friend SAMUEL TAYLOR COLERIDGE. Nevertheless, the preface that he wrote for the second edition of their book *Lyrical Ballads* (1800) is one of the most important documents in English criticism.

Wordsworth was born in Cockermouth, Cumberland, in the English Lake District. His mother died when he was eight; his father, an attorney, died less than six years later. Wordsworth was educated first at Hawkshead Grammar School, Westmorland, a boarding school noted for its training in mathematics and classics, and then at Cambridge University (1787–91), spending July–October 1790 on a walking tour of Europe. In France he was caught up in the excitement that followed the fall of the Bastille on July 14, 1789, and he became a fervent republican sympathizer.

Wordsworth's guardians wanted him to become an Anglican minister, but he persuaded them to support another twelve months of residence in France. When he was forced to return home in December 1792 by the threat of war between France and England, Wordsworth left behind the pregnant Annette Vallon; he supported her and their daughter in later years.

In 1793 Wordsworth's first works of poetry were published, *Descriptive Sketches* and *An Evening Walk*. In 1795 a legacy of £900 from a friend gave him the freedom to pursue a career as a poet. At this time he was living with his sister Dorothy; in 1797 they moved to Alfoxden in Somerset, with Coleridge (whom the poet had met in September 1795) a short distance away. There Wordsworth began to write the lyric and dramatic poems that many readers judge to be the central achievement of his career. The twentieth-century critic NORTHROP FRYE connects the poet's innovative descriptions to social and political critique: "In Wordsworth the existing social and educational structure is artificial, full of inert custom and hypocrisy. Nature is a better teacher than books, and one finds one's lost identity with nature in moments of feeling in which one is penetrated by the sense of nature's 'huge and mighty forms'" (quoting Wordsworth's *Prelude,* 1.398).

Wordsworth's early compositions, and his creative partnership with Coleridge, resulted in September 1798 in the anonymous publication of *Lyrical Ballads*. The volume opened with Coleridge's "Ancient Mariner" and closed with Wordsworth's "Tintern Abbey"; all but three of the intervening poems were Wordsworth's. A new edition of *Lyrical Ballads*, incorporating Wordsworth's Preface and many new poems, was issued in 1800; this edition gave Wordsworth's name on the title page but not Coleridge's (whose "Ancient Mariner" was moved back to become the penultimate poem in the collection). In the Preface, Wordsworth declared that the book's object was "to choose incidents and situations from common life and to relate or describe them . . . in a selection of language really used by men, . . . tracing in them . . . the primary laws of our nature." Still another edition was published in 1802, and it was reprinted in 1805.

In later decades, Wordsworth not only wrote new poems but also revised (not always for the better) his earlier work. A collected edition, which includes many of his best poems and two critical essays, was published in 1815. His collections culminated in the six-volume edition of 1849–50. In these years the poet enjoyed both personal happiness—marrying Mary Hutchinson in 1802 and winning recognition as a national figure (he was named poet laureate in 1843)—and painful losses, including the death at sea of his favorite brother in 1805, a long and never wholly ended estrangement from Coleridge, the deaths of two of his children in 1812, and the physical and mental decline of his sister Dorothy that began in the 1830s. An even earlier loss was of his liberal ideals, much to the dismay of such younger poets as Byron, Keats, and SHELLEY. Wordsworth was horrified by the bloody aftermath of the French Revolution and alarmed by the rise of the French military leader and emperor Napoleon; he became increasingly orthodox in his political, social, and religious beliefs.

The critic HAROLD BLOOM has said that in dramatizing the movements of the individual consciousness, Wordsworth made "the poet's own subjectivity" the "prevalent subject" of poetry. Wordsworth spurred writers to break free from the authority of neoclassical rules and conventions and to find inspiration instead in the emotions, experiences, and speech of ordinary persons. In valuing naturalness and spontaneity, Wordsworth was proposing not that poets abandon literary craft but that poetry should begin with acts of self-expression and self-exploration. There is much truth in the familiar generalization that Romantic poets are visionary, evocative describers of nature—its scenes, settings, landscapes. But the movement outward into the natural world is one dimension of an interior journey or quest into what Wordsworth called "the hiding-places of man's power." M. H. Abrams concisely explains this fundamental change, in his classic study *The Mirror and the Lamp: Romantic Theory and the Critical Tradition* (1953):

> The paramount cause of poetry is not, as in Aristotle, a formal cause, determined primarily by the human actions and qualities imitated; nor, as in neoclassic criticism, a final cause, the effect intended upon the audience; but instead an efficient cause—the impulse within the poet of feelings and desires seeking expression, or the compulsion of the "creative" imagination which, like God the creator, has its internal source of motion.

A number of the formulations in the preface have become widely known and are permanently linked to Wordsworth's name—for example, that the modern poems included in *Lyrical Ballads* fit to "metrical arrangement a selection of the real language of men in a state of vivid sensation," and that "good poetry is the spontaneous overflow of powerful feelings," "tak[ing] its origin from emotion recollected in tranquillity." Yet, as W. J. B. Owen and other scholars have noted, Wordsworth is less original than his bold tone and manner suggest; much of what he says about figurative language, poetic diction, and the relationship between poetry and prose draws on an array of eighteenth-century English writings on emotion, knowledge, and aesthetic theory. That we remember Wordsworth's words, not those of his sources, testifies both to the eloquence of his prose and to its association with a magnificent series of poems.

In his criticism, and in the Preface especially, Wordsworth seeks to explain and defend his own literary practice; in this respect, he is akin to fellow poets JOHN DRYDEN and T. S. ELIOT and the novelist HENRY JAMES, whose criticism fabricates frameworks through which their creative endeavors should be understood and appreciated. Like them, Wordsworth possesses a sharp sense of literary history and tradition; where he differs is in his refusal or failure to make the interpretation and evaluation of writers and texts an integral part of his literary project and identity. Overall his criticism—found in prefaces for his books of poems, a few essays, sentences and paragraphs in letters, and tossed-off opinions and asides in conversations with friends and acquaintances—is not impressive, nor are his judgments compelling. He misunderstood and devalued ALEXANDER POPE, SAMUEL JOHNSON, Goethe, and Byron and failed to perceive the genius of Thomas Carlyle and RALPH WALDO EMERSON. As he admitted himself, he was not much interested in the writing of his contemporaries; he cared little for novels, despite living in a period when the novel as a genre was coming to a new prominence. Instead, Wordsworth's mission is to return to basic, timeless truths—and thus he raises and confronts such questions as "What is a Poet?" and "To whom does he address himself?"

Like many important theoretical works by creative writers, Wordsworth's Preface is not always in accord with his actual practice. In the *Biographia Literaria* (1817), Coleridge makes exactly this point and states further that Wordsworth asserts without proof that the language of rural folk has a richer reality than that of city dwellers. There are other overemphases, ambiguities, and contradictions in Wordsworth's arguments as well. He stresses that poetry heals and restores the feelings of persons; but when one reviews his poetry and prose as a whole, particularly that of his later career, his point becomes hard to grasp: does Wordsworth mean that poetry will lead to a regenerated society, or that it will accommodate readers to their society as it is? Despite Wordsworth's insistence that the poet engage and employ the language "really used by men," and that such language is best located among those living a "low and rustic life," two of his own greatest literary heroes, as the scholar René Wellek has pointed out, were Spenser and Milton—"the most learned, even bookish poets of the English tradition."

The Preface is to some extent a political text as well as a literary position paper. Wordsworth's desire to select "incidents and situations from common life" blends into poetry the democratic sentiments that the French Revolution had inspired in him in the early 1790s. By advocating "the real language of men," Wordsworth cuts against the neoclassical view that the language of poetry must be more elevated than everyday speech. The rebelliousness in this stance helps us understand why the Romantic critic and essayist William Hazlitt connected Wordsworth's verse with "the revolutionary movement of our age": "His Muse," Hazlitt said, "is a levelling one." By directing attention to ballads, folklore, and other materials usually deemed nonliterary or unpoetical, Wordsworth expands the range of subjects for poetry. He honors children and common men and women, and even criminals and idiots: his poetry does not bestow dignity on them but expresses the dignity they already possess.

Wordsworth was actively concerned about the pressures that impinge on the lives of those living in newly industrialized cities, the pressures that threaten to reduce the mind "to a state of almost savage torpor" and that lead individuals to immerse themselves in reports and stories of sensational incidents. Here he looks forward to the opposition between high and mass or popular cultures that modern critics such as RAYMOND WILLIAMS later explored. Insofar as the Preface establishes the writer as an adversary to popular culture and the always-accelerating trends in social and cultural life, Wordsworth anticipates themes articulated by writers ranging from Shelley to D. H. Lawrence. The poet, he maintains in an important appendix added in 1802, "is the rock of defense of human nature; an upholder and preserver, carrying everywhere with him relationship and love." Moreover, as he discusses in some detail, poets in the future will be obliged to defend the worth of their activity against that of the scientists. This is a struggle to which MATTHEW ARNOLD, later in the nineteenth century, and I. A. Richards and the New Critics, in the twentieth century, return with even greater urgency.

"Preface to *Lyrical Ballads, with Pastoral and Other Poems*" Keywords: Aesthetics, Language, Literary History, Poetry, Romantic Theory, Vernacular Language

Preface to *Lyrical Ballads, with Pastoral and Other Poems* (1802)[1]

The first Volume of these Poems has already been submitted to general perusal. It was published, as an experiment, which, I hoped, might be of some use to ascertain, how far, by fitting to metrical arrangement a selection of the real language of men in a state of vivid sensation, that sort of pleasure and that quantity of pleasure may be imparted, which a Poet may rationally endeavour to impart.

I had formed no very inaccurate estimate of the probable effect of those Poems: I flattered myself that they who should be pleased with them would

1. This preface first appeared in the second edition of *Lyrical Ballads*, expanded to two volumes and dated 1800. For an edition published in 1802, Wordsworth revised the preface (he made more revisions for subsequent editions) and added an appendix; the important additions to the 1800 text are here given in brackets.

read them with more than common pleasure: and, on the other hand, I was well aware, that by those who should dislike them they would be read with more than common dislike. The result has differed from my expectation in this only, that I have pleased a greater number, than I ventured to hope I should please.

For the sake of variety, and from a consciousness of my own weakness, I was induced to request the assistance of a Friend,[2] who furnished me with the Poems of the ANCIENT MARINER, the FOSTER-MOTHER'S TALE, the NIGHTINGALE, and the Poem entitled LOVE. I should not, however, have requested this assistance, had I not believed that the Poems of my Friend would in a great measure have the same tendency as my own, and that, though there would be found a difference, there would be found no discordance in the colours of our style; as our opinions on the subject of poetry do almost entirely coincide.

Several of my Friends are anxious for the success of these Poems from a belief, that, if the views with which they were composed were indeed realized, a class of Poetry would be produced, well adapted to interest mankind permanently, and not unimportant in the multiplicity, and in the quality of its moral relations: and on this account they have advised me to prefix a systematic defence of the theory, upon which the poems were written. But I was unwilling to undertake the task, because I knew that on this occasion the Reader would look coldly upon my arguments, since I might be suspected of having been principally influenced by the selfish and foolish hope of *reasoning* him into an approbation of these particular Poems: and I was still more unwilling to undertake the task, because, adequately to display my opinions, and fully to enforce my arguments, would require a space wholly disproportionate to the nature of a preface. For to treat the subject with the clearness and coherence, of which I believe it susceptible, it would be necessary to give a full account of the present state of the public taste in this country, and to determine how far this taste is healthy or depraved; which, again, would not be determined, without pointing out, in what manner language and the human mind act and re-act on each other, and without retracing the revolutions, not of literature alone, but likewise of society itself. I have therefore altogether declined to enter regularly upon this defence; yet I am sensible, that there would be some impropriety in abruptly obtruding upon the Public, without a few words of introduction, Poems so materially different from those, upon which general approbation is at present bestowed.

It is supposed, that by the act of writing in verse an Author makes a formal engagement that he will gratify certain known habits of association; that he not only thus apprizes the Reader that certain classes of ideas and expressions will be found in his book, but that others will be carefully excluded. This exponent or symbol held forth by metrical language must in different areas of literature have excited very different expectations: for example, in the age of Catullus, Terence and Lucretius, and that of Statius or Claudian;[3] and in our own country, in the age of Shakespeare and

2. SAMUEL TAYLOR COLERIDGE (1772–1834), English poet and critic.

3. Wordsworth names Roman poets in different genres, before and after the common era (and thus writing in "Golden" vs. "Silver" Latin): Catullus (84–54 B.C.E.), lyric poet; Terence (ca. 190–159 B.C.E.), comic dramatist; Lucretius (ca. 94–55 B.C.E.), didactic poet; Statius (45–96 C.E.), epic poet; and Claudian (d. ca. 404 C.E.), an Alexandrian whose Latin poetry represents the end of the classical tradition.

Beaumont and Fletcher, and that of Donne and Cowley, or Dryden, or Pope.[4] I will not take upon me to determine the exact import of the promise which by the act of writing in verse an Author, in the present day, makes to his Reader; but I am certain, it will appear to many persons that I have not fulfilled the terms of an engagement thus voluntarily contracted. [They who have been accustomed to the gaudiness and inane phraseology of many modern writers, if they persist in reading this book to its conclusion, will, no doubt, frequently have to struggle with feelings of strangeness and aukwardness: they will look round for poetry, and will be induced to inquire by what species of courtesy these attempts can be permitted to assume that title.] I hope therefore the Reader will not censure me, if I attempt to state what I have proposed to myself to perform; and also, (as far as the limits of a preface will permit) to explain some of the chief reasons which have determined me in the choice of my purpose: that at least he may be spared any unpleasant feeling of disappointment, and that I myself may be protected from the most dishonourable accusation which can be brought against an Author, namely, that of an indolence which prevents him from endeavouring to ascertain what is his duty, or, when his duty is ascertained, prevents him from performing it.

The principal object, then, which I proposed to myself in these Poems was to [chuse incidents and situations from common life, and to relate or describe them, throughout, as far as was possible, in a selection of language really used by men; and, at the same time, to throw over them a certain colouring of imagination, whereby ordinary things should be presented to the mind in an unusual way; and, further, and above all, to make these incidents and situations interesting] by tracing in them, truly though not ostentatiously, the primary laws of our nature: chiefly, as far as regards the manner in which we associate ideas in a state of excitement. Low and rustic life was generally chosen, because in that condition, the essential passions of the heart find a better soil in which they can attain their maturity, are less under restraint, and speak a plainer and more emphatic language; because in that condition of life our elementary feelings co-exist in a state of greater simplicity, and, consequently, may be more accurately contemplated, and more forcibly communicated; because the manners of rural life germinate from those elementary feelings; and, from the necessary character of rural occupations, are more easily comprehended; and are more durable; and lastly, because in that condition the passions of men are incorporated with the beautiful and permanent forms of nature. The language, too, of these men is adopted (purified indeed from what appear to be its real defects, from all lasting and rational causes of dislike or disgust) because such men hourly communicate with the best objects from which the best part of language is originally derived; and because, from their rank in society and the sameness and narrow circle of their intercourse, being less under the influence of social vanity they convey their feelings and notions in simple and unelaborated expressions. Accordingly, such a language, arising out of repeated experience and regular feelings, is a more permanent, and a far

4. Wordsworth names three English dramatists—Shakespeare (1564–1616), Francis Beaumont (ca. 1584–1616), and John Fletcher (1579–1625); and four poets—John Donne (1572–1631), Abraham Cowley (1618–1667), JOHN DRYDEN (1631–1700), and ALEXANDER POPE (1688–1744). As their dates suggest, he focuses here less on chronology than on style.

more philosophical language, than that which is frequently substituted for it by Poets, who think that they are conferring honour upon themselves and their art, in proportion as they separate themselves from the sympathies of men, and indulge in arbitrary and capricious habits of expression, in order to furnish food for fickle tastes, and fickle appetites, of their own creation.[5]

I cannot, however, be insensible of the present outcry against the triviality and meanness both of thought and language, which some of my contemporaries have occasionally introduced into their metrical compositions; and I acknowledge that this defect, where it exists, is more dishonourable to the Writer's own character than false refinement or arbitrary innovation, though I should contend at the same time that it is far less pernicious in the sum of its consequences. From such verses the Poems in these volumes will be found distinguished at least by one mark of difference, that each of them has a worthy *purpose*. Not that I mean to say, that I always began to write with a distinct purpose formally conceived; but I believe that my habits of meditation have so formed my feelings, as that my descriptions of such objects as strongly excite those feelings, will be found to carry along with them a *purpose*. If in this opinion I am mistaken, I can have little right to the name of a Poet. For all good poetry is the spontaneous overflow of powerful feelings: but though this be true, Poems to which any value can be attached, were never produced on any variety of subjects but by a man, who being possessed of more than usual organic sensibility, had also thought long and deeply. For our continued influxes of feeling are modified and directed by our thoughts, which are indeed the representatives of all our past feelings; and, as by contemplating the relation of these general representatives to each other we discover what is really important to men, so, by the repetition and continuance of this act, our feelings will be connected with important subjects, till at length, if we be originally possessed of much sensibility, such habits of mind will be produced, that, by obeying blindly and mechanically the impulses of those habits, we shall describe objects, and utter sentiments, of such a nature and in such connection with each other, that the understanding of the being to whom we address ourselves, if he be in a healthful state of association, must necessarily be in some degree enlightened, and his affections ameliorated.

I have said that each of these poems has a purpose. I have also informed my Reader what this purpose will be found principally to be: namely, to illustrate the manner in which our feelings and ideas are associated in a state of excitement. But, speaking in language somewhat more appropriate, it is to follow the fluxes and refluxes of the mind when agitated by the great and simple affections of our nature. This object I have endeavoured in these short essays to attain by various means; by tracing the maternal passion through many of its more subtle windings, as in the poems of the IDIOT BOY and the MAD MOTHER; by accompanying the last struggles of a human being, at the approach of death, cleaving in solitude to life and society, as in the Poem of the FORSAKEN INDIAN; by showing, as in the Stanzas entitled WE ARE SEVEN, the perplexity and obscurity which in childhood attend our

5. It is worth while here to observe that the affecting parts of Chaucer [ca. 1343–1400] are almost always expressed in language pure and universally intelligible even to this day [Wordsworth's note].

notion of death, or rather our utter inability to admit that notion; or by displaying the strength of fraternal, or to speak more philosophically, of moral attachment when early associated with the great and beautiful objects of nature, as in THE BROTHERS; or, as in the Incident of SIMON LEE, by placing my Reader in the way of receiving from ordinary moral sensations another and more salutary impression than we are accustomed to receive from them. It has also been part of my general purpose to attempt to sketch characters under the influence of less impassioned feelings, as in the TWO APRIL MORNINGS, THE FOUNTAIN, THE OLD MAN TRAVELLING, THE TWO THIEVES, &c. characters of which the elements are simple, belonging rather to nature than to manners, such as exist now, and will probably always exist, and which from their constitution may be distinctly and profitably contemplated. I will not abuse the indulgence of my Reader by dwelling longer upon this subject; but it is proper that I should mention one other circumstance which distinguishes these Poems from the popular Poetry of the day; it is this, that the feeling therein developed gives importance to the action and situation, and not the action and situation to the feeling. My meaning will be rendered perfectly intelligible by referring my Reader to the Poems entitled POOR SUSAN and the CHILDLESS FATHER, particularly to the last Stanza of the latter Poem.

I will not suffer a sense of false modesty to prevent me from asserting, that I point my Reader's attention to this mark of distinction, far less for the sake of these particular Poems than from the general importance of the subject. The subject is indeed important! For the human mind is capable of being excited without the application of gross and violent stimulants; and he must have a very faint perception of its beauty and dignity who does not know this, and who does not further know, that one being is elevated above another, in proportion as he possesses this capability. It has therefore appeared to me, that to endeavour to produce or enlarge this capability is one of the best services in which, at any period, a Writer can be engaged; but this service, excellent at all times, is especially so at the present day. For a multitude of causes, unknown to former times, are now acting with a combined force to blunt the discriminating powers of the mind, and unfitting it for all voluntary exertion to reduce it to a state of almost savage torpor. The most effective of these causes are the great national events which are daily taking place,[6] and the encreasing accumulation of men in cities, where the uniformity of their occupations produces a craving for extraordinary incident, which the rapid communication of intelligence[7] hourly gratifies. To this tendency of life and manners the literature and theatrical exhibitions of the country have conformed themselves. The invaluable works of our elder writers, I had almost said the works of Shakespeare and Milton, are driven into neglect by frantic novels, sickly and stupid German Tragedies,[8] and deluges of idle and extravagant stories in verse.—When I

6. The French Revolution and the Napoleonic Wars, primarily between France and Great Britain (1799–1815), that grew out of it and out of the rise to power of the French general Napoléon Bonaparte (1769–1821), later emperor (1804–15).

7. Information, news (daily newspapers were spreading rapidly in England).

8. German melodramas by authors such as August von Kotzebue (1761–1819); in Jane Austen's novel *Mansfield Park* (1814), the Bertram family performs Elizabeth Inchbald's *Lovers' Vows*, which is based on von Kotzebue's *Das kind der Lieber*. "Frantic novels": Gothic novels, such as *The Mysteries of Udolpho* (1794) by Ann Radcliffe and *The Monk* (1796) by M. G. Lewis.

think upon this degrading thirst after outrageous stimulation, I am almost ashamed to have spoken of the feeble effort with which I have endeavoured to counteract it; and, reflecting upon the magnitude of the general evil, I should be oppressed with no dishonorable melancholy, had I not a deep impression of certain inherent and indestructible qualities of the human mind, and likewise of certain powers in the great and permanent objects that act upon it, which are equally inherent and indestructible; and did I not further add to this impression a belief, that the time is approaching when the evil will be systematically opposed, by men of greater powers, and with far more distinguished success.

Having dwelt thus long on the subjects and aim of these Poems, I shall request the Reader's permission to apprize him of a few circumstances relating to their *style*, in order, among other reasons, that I may not be censured for not having performed what I never attempted. [The Reader will find that personifications of abstract ideas rarely occur in these volumes; and, I hope, are utterly rejected as an ordinary device to elevate the style, and raise it above prose. I have proposed to myself to imitate, and, as far as is possible, to adopt the very language of men; and assuredly such personifications do not make any natural or regular part of that language. They are, indeed, a figure of speech occasionally prompted by passion, and I have made use of them as such; but I have endeavoured utterly to reject them as a mechanical device of style, or as a family language which Writers in metre seem to lay claim to by prescription.] I have wished to keep my Reader in the company of flesh and blood, persuaded that by so doing I shall interest him. I am, however, well aware that others who pursue a different track may interest him likewise; I do not interfere with their claim, I only wish to prefer a different claim of my own. There will also be found in these volumes little of what is usually called poetic diction; I have taken as much pains to avoid it as others ordinarily take to produce it; this I have done for the reason already alleged, to bring my language near to the language of men, and further, because the pleasure which I have proposed to myself to impart is of a kind very different from that which is supposed by many persons to be the proper object of poetry. I do not know how, without being culpably particular, I can give my Reader a more exact notion of the style in which I wished these poems to be written than by informing him that I have at all times endeavoured to look steadily at my subject, consequently, I hope that there is in these Poems little falsehood of description, and that my ideas are expressed in language fitted to their respective importance. Something I must have gained by this practice, as it is friendly to one property of all good poetry, namely good sense; but it has necessarily cut me off from a large portion of phrases and figures of speech which from father to son have long been regarded as the common inheritance of Poets. I have also thought it expedient to restrict myself still further, having abstained from the use of many expressions, in themselves proper and beautiful, but which have been foolishly repeated by bad Poets, till such feelings of disgust are connected with them as it is scarcely possible by any art of association to overpower.

If in a Poem there should be found a series of lines, or even a single line, in which the language, though naturally arranged, and according to the strict laws of metre, does not differ from that of prose, there is a numerous class of critics, who, when they stumble upon these prosaisms, as they call them, imagine that they have made a notable discovery, and exult over the Poet as over a man ignorant of his own profession. Now these men would establish a canon of criticism which the Reader will conclude he must utterly reject, if he wishes to be pleased with these volumes. And it would be a most easy task to prove to him, that not only the language of a large portion of every good poem, even of the most elevated character, must necessarily, except with reference to the metre, in no respect differ from that of good prose, but likewise that some of the most interesting parts of the best poems will be found to be strictly the language of prose, when prose is well written. The truth of this assertion might be demonstrated by innumerable passages from almost all the poetical writings, even of Milton himself. I have not space for much quotation; but, to illustrate the subject in a general manner, I will here adduce a short composition of Gray,[9] who was at the head of those who, by their reasonings, have attempted to widen the space of separation betwixt Prose and Metrical composition, and was more than any other man curiously elaborate in the structure of his own poetic diction.

> In vain to me the smiling mornings shine,
> And reddening Phoebus[1] lifts his golden fire:
> The birds in vain their amorous descant join,
> Or chearful fields resume their green attire.
> These ears, alas! for other notes repine;
> *A different object do these eyes require;*
> *My lonely anguish melts no heart but mine;*
> *And in my breast the imperfect joys expire*;
> Yet morning smiles the busy race to cheer,
> And new-born pleasure brings to happier men;
> The fields to all their wonted tribute bear;
> To warm their little loves the birds complain.
> *I fruitless mourn to him that cannot hear,*
> *And weep the more because I weep in vain.*

It will easily be perceived that the only part of this Sonnet which is of any value is the lines printed in Italics: it is equally obvious, that, except in the rhyme, and in the use of the single word 'fruitless' for fruitlessly, which is so far a defect, the language of these lines does in no respect differ from that of prose.

[By the foregoing quotation I have shewn that the language of Prose may yet be well adapted to Poetry; and I have previously asserted that a large portion of the language of every good poem can in no respect differ from that of good Prose. I will go further. I do not doubt that it may be safely affirmed, that there neither is, nor can be, any essential difference between the language of prose and metrical composition.] We are fond of tracing the resemblance between Poetry and Painting,[2] and, accordingly, we call them Sisters: but where shall we find bonds of connection sufficiently strict to

9. Thomas Gray (1716–1771); the poem quoted is "Sonnet on the Death of Richard West" (1775; West was a friend of Gray's at Eton). Gray, in a letter to West, had maintained that "the language of the age is never the language of poetry."

1. Apollo, Roman and Greek god of the sun, here identified with the sun.

2. A topic examined, for example, by the poets and critics HORACE, *Ars Poetica* (ca. 10 B.C.E.); Dryden, *A Parallel of Poetry and Painting* (1695); SIR PHILIP SIDNEY, *The Defence of Poesy* (1595); Pope, *An Essay on Criticism* (1711); GOTTHOLD EPHRAIM LESSING, *Laocöon* (1766); and SAMUEL JOHNSON, *Idler*, no. 34 (1758).

typify the affinity betwixt metrical and prose composition? They both speak by and to the same organs; the bodies in which both of them are clothed may be said to be of the same substance, their affections are kindred, and almost identical, not necessarily differing even in degree; Poetry[3] sheds no tears 'such as Angels weep,'[4] but natural and human tears; she can boast of no celestial Ichor[5] that distinguishes her vital juices from those of prose; the same human blood circulates through the veins of them both.

If it be affirmed that rhyme and metrical arrangement of themselves constitute a distinction which overturns what I have been saying on the strict affinity of metrical language with that of prose, and paves the way for other artificial distinctions which the mind voluntarily admits,[6] [I answer that the language of such Poetry as I am recommending is, as far as is possible, a selection of the language really spoken by men; that this selection, wherever it is made with true taste and feeling, will of itself form a distinction far greater than would at first be imagined, and will entirely separate the composition from the vulgarity and meanness of ordinary life; and, if metre be superadded thereto, I believe that a dissimilitude will be produced altogether sufficient for the gratification of a rational mind. What other distinction would we have? Whence is it to come? And where is it to exist? Not, surely, where the Poet speaks through the mouths of his characters: it cannot be necessary here, either for elevation of style, or any of its supposed ornaments; for, if the Poet's subject be judiciously chosen, it will naturally, and upon fit occasion, lead him to passions the language of which, if selected truly and judiciously, must necessarily be dignified and variegated, and alive with metaphors and figures. I forbear to speak of an incongruity which would shock the intelligent Reader, should the Poet interweave any foreign splendour of his own with that which the passion naturally suggests: it is sufficient to say that such addition is unnecessary. And, surely, it is more probable that those passages, which with propriety abound with metaphors and figures, will have their due effect, if, upon other occasions where the passions are of a milder character, the style also be subdued and temperate.

But, as the pleasure which I hope to give by the Poems I now present to the Reader must depend entirely on just notions upon this subject, and, as it is in itself of the highest importance to our taste and moral feelings, I cannot content myself with these detached remarks. And if, in what I am about to say, it shall appear to some that my labour is unnecessary, and that I am like a man fighting a battle without enemies, I would remind such persons that, whatever may be the language outwardly holden[7] by men, a practical faith in the opinions which I am wishing to establish is almost unknown. If my conclusions are admitted, and carried as far as they must be carried if admitted at all, our judgments concerning the works of the greatest Poets both ancient and modern will be far different from what they

3. I here use the word "Poetry" (though against my own judgment) as opposed to the word Prose, and synonymous with metrical composition. But much confusion has been introduced into criticism by this contradistinction of Poetry and Prose, instead of the more philosophical one of Poetry and Matter of Fact, or Science. The only strict antithesis to Prose is Metre; nor is this, in truth, a *strict* antithesis; because lines and passages of metre so naturally occur in writing prose, that it would be scarcely possible to avoid them, even if it were desirable [Wordsworth's note].
4. From John Milton, *Paradise Lost* (1667), 1.620.
5. In Greek mythology, the fluid that flows in the veins of the gods.
6. Here begins the longest and most important addition made in 1802; it contains 9 paragraphs.
7. Held.

are at present, both when we praise, and when we censure: and our moral feelings influencing, and influenced by these judgments will, I believe, be corrected and purified.

Taking up the subject, then, upon general grounds, I ask what is meant by the word Poet? What is a Poet? To whom does he address himself? And what language is to be expected from him? He is a man speaking to men: a man, it is true, endued with more lively sensibility, more enthusiasm and tenderness, who has a greater knowledge of human nature, and a more comprehensive soul, than are supposed to be common among mankind; a man pleased with his own passions and volitions, and who rejoices more than other men in the spirit of life that is in him; delighting to contemplate similar volitions and passions as manifested in the goings-on of the Universe, and habitually impelled to create them where he does not find them. To these qualities he has added a disposition to be affected more than other men by absent things as if they were present; an ability of conjuring up in himself passions, which are indeed far from being the same as those produced by real events, yet (especially in those parts of the general sympathy which are pleasing and delightful) do more nearly resemble the passions produced by real events, than any thing which, from the motions of their own minds merely, other men are accustomed to feel in themselves; whence, and from practice, he has acquired a greater readiness and power in expressing what he thinks and feels, and especially those thoughts and feelings which, by his own choice, or from the structure of his own mind, arise in him without immediate external excitement.

But, whatever portion of this faculty we may suppose even the greatest Poet to possess, there cannot be a doubt but that the language which it will suggest to him, must, in liveliness and truth, fall far short of that which is uttered by men in real life, under the actual pressure of those passions, certain shadows of which the Poet thus produces, or feels to be produced, in himself. However exalted a notion we would wish to cherish of the character of a Poet, it is obvious, that, while he describes and imitates passions, his situation is altogether slavish and mechanical, compared with the freedom and power of real and substantial action and suffering. So that it will be the wish of the Poet to bring his feelings near to those of the persons whose feelings he describes, nay, for short spaces of time perhaps, to let himself slip into an entire delusion, and even confound and identify his own feelings with theirs; modifying only the language which is thus suggested to him, by a consideration that he describes for a particular purpose, that of giving pleasure. Here, then, he will apply the principle on which I have so much insisted, namely, that of selection; on this he will depend for removing what would otherwise be painful or disgusting in the passion; he will feel that there is no necessity to trick out or elevate nature: and, the more industriously he applies this principle, the deeper will be his faith that no words, which his fancy or imagination can suggest, will be to be compared with those which are in the emanations of reality and truth.

But it may be said by those who do not object to the general spirit of these remarks, that, as it is impossible for the Poet to produce upon all occasions language as exquisitely fitted for the passion as that which the real passion itself suggests, it is proper that he should consider himself as in the situation of a translator, who deems himself justified when he substitutes excellences of another kind for those which are unattainable by him; and endeavours occasionally to surpass his original, in order to make some amends for the general inferiority to which he feels that he must submit. But this would be to encourage idleness and unmanly despair. Further, it is the language of men who speak of what they do not understand; who talk of Poetry as of a matter of amusement and idle pleasure; who will converse with us as gravely about a *taste* for Poetry, as they express it, as if it were a thing as indifferent as a taste for Rope-dancing, or Frontiniac[8] or Sherry. Aristotle, I have been told, hath said, that Poetry is the most philosophic of all writing:[9] it is so: its object is truth, not individual and local, but general, and operative; not standing upon external testimony, but carried alive into the heart by passion; truth which is its own testimony, which gives strength and divinity to the tribunal to which it appeals, and receives them from the same tribunal. Poetry is the image of man and nature. The obstacles which stand in the way of the fidelity of the Biographer and Historian, and of their consequent utility, are incalculably greater than those which are to be encountered by the Poet who has an adequate notion of the dignity of his art. The Poet writes under one restriction only, namely, that of the necessity of giving immediate pleasure to a human Being possessed of that information which may be expected from him, not as a lawyer, a physician, a mariner, an astronomer or a natural philosopher, but as a Man. Except this one restriction, there is no object standing between the Poet and the image of things; between this, and the Biographer and Historian there are a thousand.

Nor let this necessity of producing immediate pleasure be considered as a degradation of the Poet's art. It is far otherwise. It is an acknowledgment of the beauty of the universe, an acknowledgment the more sincere, because it is not formal, but indirect; it is a task light and easy to him who looks at the world in the spirit of love: further, it is a homage paid to the native and naked dignity of man, to the grand elementary principle of pleasure, by which he knows, and feels, and lives, and moves.[1] We have no sympathy but what is propagated by pleasure: I would not be misunderstood; but wherever we sympathize with pain it will be found that the sympathy is produced and carried on by subtle combinations with pleasure. We have no knowledge, that is, no general principles drawn from the contemplation of particular facts, but what has been built up by pleasure, and exists in us by pleasure alone. The Man of Science,[2] the Chemist and Mathematician, whatever difficulties and disgusts they may have had to struggle with, know and feel this. However painful may be the objects with which the Anatomist's knowledge is connected, he feels that his knowledge is pleasure; and where he has no pleasure he has no knowledge. What then does the Poet? He considers man and the objects that surround him as acting and re-acting upon each other, so as to produce an infinite complexity of pain and pleasure; he considers man in his own nature and in his ordinary life as contemplating this with a certain quantity of immediate knowledge, with certain convictions, intuitions, and deductions which by habit become of the nature of intuitions; he

8. A sweet wine.
9. See ARISTOTLE, *Poetics* 9, 1451b: "Poetry, therefore is a more philosophical and a higher thing than history, in that poetry tends rather to express the universal, history rather the particular fact."
1. Compare St. Paul's declaration that in God "we live, and move, and have our being" (Acts 17.28).
2. Wordsworth may have had in mind in particular the English chemist Humphrey Davy (1778–1829), who had lectured at the Royal Institution in London on January 21, 1802.

considers him as looking upon this complex scene of ideas and sensations, and finding every where objects that immediately excite in him sympathies which, from the necessities of his nature, are accompanied by an overbalance of enjoyment.

To this knowledge which all men carry about with them, and to these sympathies in which without any other discipline than that of our daily life we are fitted to take delight, the Poet principally directs his attention. He considers man and nature as essentially adapted to each other, and the mind of man as naturally the mirror of the fairest and most interesting qualities of nature. And thus the Poet, prompted by this feeling of pleasure which accompanies him through the whole course of his studies, converses with general nature with affections akin to those, which, through labour and length of time, the Man of Science has raised up in himself, by conversing with those particular parts of nature which are the objects of his studies. The knowledge both of the Poet and the Man of Science is pleasure; but the knowledge of the one cleaves to us as a necessary part of our existence, our natural and unalienable inheritance; the other is a personal and individual acquisition, slow to come to us, and by no habitual and direct sympathy connecting us with our fellow-beings. The Man of Science seeks truth as a remote and unknown benefactor; he cherishes and loves it in his solitude: the Poet, singing a song in which all human beings join with him, rejoices in the presence of truth as our visible friend and hourly companion. Poetry is the breath and finer spirit of all knowledge; it is the impassioned expression which is in the countenance of all Science. Emphatically may it be said of the Poet, as Shakespeare hath said of man, 'that he looks before and after.'[3] He is the rock of defence of human nature; an upholder and preserver, carrying every where with him relationship and love. In spite of difference of soil and climate, of language and manners, of laws and customs, in spite of things silently gone out of mind and things violently destroyed, the Poet binds together by passion and knowledge the vast empire of human society, as it is spread over the whole earth, and over all time. The objects of the Poet's thoughts are every where; though the eyes and senses of man are, it is true, his favorite guides, yet he will follow wheresoever he can find an atmosphere of sensation in which to move his wings. Poetry is the first and last of all knowledge—it is as immortal as the heart of man. If the labours of Men of Science should ever create any material revolution, direct or indirect, in our condition, and in the impressions which we habitually receive, the Poet will sleep then no more than at present, but he will be ready to follow the steps of the Man of Science, not only in those general indirect effects, but he will be at his side, carrying sensation into the midst of the objects of the Science itself. The remotest discoveries of the Chemist, the Botanist, or Mineralogist, will be as proper objects of the Poet's art as any upon which it can be employed, if the time should ever come when these things shall be familiar to us, and the relations under which they are contemplated by the followers of these respective Sciences shall be manifestly and palpably material to us as enjoying and suffering beings. If the time should ever come when what is now called Science, thus familiarized to men, shall be ready to put on, as it were, a form of flesh and blood, the Poet will lend his divine

3. *Hamlet* (ca. 1600), 4.4.36 ("Looking before and after").

spirit to aid the transfiguration, and will welcome the Being thus produced, as a dear and genuine inmate of the household of man.—It is not, then, to be supposed that any one, who holds that sublime notion of Poetry which I have attempted to convey, will break in upon the sanctity and truth of his pictures by transitory and accidental ornaments, and endeavour to excite admiration of himself by arts, the necessity of which must manifestly depend upon the assumed meanness of his subject.

What I have thus far said applies to Poetry in general; but especially to those parts of composition where the Poet speaks through the mouths of his characters; and upon this point it appears to have such weight that I will conclude, there are few persons of good sense, who would not allow that the dramatic parts of composition are defective, in proportion as they deviate from the real language of nature, and are coloured by a diction of the Poet's own, either peculiar to him as an individual Poet, or belonging simply to Poets in general, to a body of men who, from the circumstance of their compositions being in metre, it is expected will employ a particular language.

It is not, then, in the dramatic parts of composition that we look for this distinction of language; but still it may be proper and necessary where the Poet speaks to us in his own person and character. To this I answer by referring my Reader to the description which I have before given of a Poet. Among the qualities which I have enumerated as principally conducing to form a Poet, is implied nothing differing in kind from other men, but only in degree. The sum of what I have there said is, that the Poet is chiefly distinguished from other men by a greater promptness to think and feel without immediate external excitement, and a greater power in expressing such thoughts and feelings as are produced in him in that manner. But these passions and thoughts and feelings are the general passions and thoughts and feelings of men. And with what are they connected? Undoubtedly with our moral sentiments and animal sensations, and with the causes which excite these; with the operations of the elements and the appearances of the visible universe; with storm and sun-shine, with the revolutions of the seasons, with cold and heat, with loss of friends and kindred, with injuries and resentments, gratitude and hope, with fear and sorrow. These, and the like, are the sensations and objects which the Poet describes, as they are the sensations of other men, and the objects which interest them. The Poet thinks and feels in the spirit of the passions of men. How, then, can his language differ in any material degree from that of all other men who feel vividly and see clearly? It might be *proved* that it is impossible. But supposing that this were not the case, the Poet might then be allowed to use a peculiar language when expressing his feelings for his own gratification, or that of men like himself. But Poets do not write for Poets alone, but for men. Unless therefore we are advocates for that admiration which depends upon ignorance, and that pleasure which arises from hearing what we do not understand, the Poet must descend from this supposed height, and, in order to excite rational sympathy, he must express himself as other men express themselves. To this it may be added, that while he is only selecting from the real language of men, or, which amounts to the same thing, composing accurately in the spirit of such selection, he is treading upon safe ground, and we know what we are to expect from him. Our feelings are the same with respect to metre; for, as it may be proper to remind the Reader,] the distinction of metre is regular and uniform, and not like that which is produced by what is usually called poetic diction, arbitrary, and subject to infinite caprices upon which no calculation whatever can be made. In the one case, the Reader is utterly at the mercy of the Poet respecting what imagery or diction he may choose to connect with the passion, whereas, in the other, the metre obeys certain laws, to which the Poet and Reader both willingly submit because they are certain, and because no interference is made by them with the passion but such as the concurring testimony of ages has shown to heighten and improve the pleasure which co-exists with it.

It will now be proper to answer an obvious question, namely, Why, professing these opinions, have I written in verse? To this, in addition to such answer as is included in what I have already said, I reply in the first place, because, however I may have restricted myself, there is still left open to me what confessedly constitutes the most valuable object of all writing, whether in prose or verse, the great and universal passions of men, the most general and interesting of their occupations, and the entire world of nature, from which I am at liberty to supply myself with endless combinations of forms and imagery. Now, supposing for a moment that whatever is interesting in these objects may be as vividly described in prose, why am I to be condemned, if to such description I have endeavoured to superadd the charm which, by the consent of all nations, is acknowledged to exist in metrical language? To this, by such as are unconvinced by what I have already said, it may be answered, that a very small part of the pleasure given by Poetry depends upon the metre, and that it is injudicious to write in metre, unless it be accompanied with the other artificial distinctions of style with which metre is usually accompanied, and that by such deviation more will be lost from the shock which will be thereby given to the Reader's associations, than will be counterbalanced by any pleasure which he can derive from the general power of numbers.[4] In answer to those who still contend for the necessity of accompanying metre with certain appropriate colours of style in order to the accomplishment of its appropriate end, and who also, in my opinion, greatly under-rate the power of metre in itself, it might perhaps, as far as relates to these Poems, have been almost sufficient to observe, that poems are extant, written upon more humble subjects, and in a more naked and simple style than I have aimed at, which poems have continued to give pleasure from generation to generation. Now, if nakedness and simplicity be a defect, the fact here mentioned affords a strong presumption that poems somewhat less naked and simple are capable of affording pleasure at the present day; and, what I wished *chiefly* to attempt, at present, was to justify myself for having written under the impression of this belief.

But I might point out various causes why, when the style is manly, and the subject of some importance, words metrically arranged will long continue to impart such a pleasure to mankind as he who is sensible of the extent of that pleasure will be desirous to impart. The end of Poetry is to produce excitement in co-existence with an over-balance of pleasure. Now, by the supposition, excitement is an unusual and irregular state of the mind; ideas and feelings do not in that state succeed each other in accustomed order. But, if the words by which this excitement is produced are in themselves

4. Metrical language.

powerful, or the images and feelings have an undue proportion of pain connected with them, there is some danger that the excitement may be carried beyond its proper bounds. Now the co-presence of something regular, something to which the mind has been accustomed in various moods and in a less excited state, cannot but have great efficacy in tempering and restraining the passion by an intertexture of ordinary feeling, [and of feeling not strictly and necessarily connected with the passion. This is unquestionably true, and hence, though the opinion will at first appear paradoxical, from the tendency of metre to divest language in a certain degree of its reality, and thus to throw a sort of half consciousness of unsubstantial existence over the whole composition, there can be little doubt but that more pathetic situations and sentiments, that is, those which have a greater proportion of pain connected with them, may be endured in metrical composition, especially in rhyme, than in prose. The metre of the old Ballads is very artless; yet they contain many passages which would illustrate this opinion, and, I hope, if the following Poems be attentively perused, similar instances will be found in them.] This opinion may be further illustrated by appealing to the Reader's own experience of the reluctance with which he comes to the re-perusal of the distressful parts of Clarissa Harlowe, or the Gamester.[5] While Shakespeare's writings, in the most pathetic scenes, never act upon us as pathetic beyond the bounds of pleasure—an effect which, in a much greater degree than might at first be imagined, is to be ascribed to small, but continual and regular impulses of pleasurable surprise from the metrical arrangement.—On the other hand (what it must be allowed will much more frequently happen) if the Poet's words should be incommensurate with the passion, and inadequate to raise the Reader to a height of desirable excitement, then, (unless the Poet's choice of his metre has been grossly injudicious) in the feelings of pleasure which the Reader has been accustomed to connect with metre in general, and in the feeling, whether chearful or melancholy, which he has been accustomed to connect with that particular movement of metre, there will be found something which will greatly contribute to impart passion to the words, and to effect the complex end which the Poet proposes to himself.

If I had undertaken a systematic defence of the theory upon which these poems are written, it would have been my duty to develope the various causes upon which the pleasure received from metrical language depends. Among the chief of these causes is to be reckoned a principle which must be well known to those who have made any of the Arts the object of accurate reflection; I mean the pleasure which the mind derives from the perception of similitude in dissimilitude. This principle is the great spring of the activity of our minds, and their chief feeder. From this principle the direction of the sexual appetite, and all the passions connected with it, take their origin: it is the life of our ordinary conversation; and upon the accuracy with which similitude in dissimilitude, and dissimilitude in similitude are perceived, depend our taste and our moral feelings. It would not have been a useless employment to have applied this principle to the consideration of metre, and to have shown that metre is hence enabled to afford much pleasure, and

5. *The Gamester* (1753), a tragedy by Edward Moore (1712–1757) about gambling. *Clarissa Harlowe*: an epistolary novel (1747–48) by Samuel Richardson (1689–1761); the title character is abducted and raped, and she dies of grief.

to have pointed out in what manner that pleasure is produced. But my limits will not permit me to enter upon this subject, and I must content myself with a general summary.

I have said that Poetry is the spontaneous overflow of powerful feelings: it takes its origin from emotion recollected in tranquillity: the emotion is contemplated till by a species of reaction the tranquillity disappears, and an emotion, kindred to that which was before the subject of contemplation, is gradually produced, and does itself actually exist in the mind. In this mood successful composition generally begins, and in a mood similar to this it is carried on; but the emotion, of whatever kind and in whatever degree, from various causes is qualified by various pleasures, so that in describing any passions whatsoever, which are voluntarily described, the mind will upon the whole be in a state of enjoyment. Now, if Nature be thus cautious in preserving in a state of enjoyment a being thus employed, the Poet ought to profit by the lesson thus held forth to him, and ought especially to take care, that whatever passions he communicates to his Reader, those passions, if his Reader's mind be sound and vigorous, should always be accompanied with an overbalance of pleasure. Now the music of harmonious metrical language, the sense of difficulty overcome, and the blind association of pleasure which has been previously received from works of rhyme or metre of the same or similar construction, an indistinct perception perpetually renewed of language closely resembling that of real life, and yet, in the circumstance of metre, differing from it so widely, all these imperceptibly make up a complex feeling of delight, which is of the most important use in tempering the painful feeling which will always be found intermingled with powerful descriptions of the deeper passions. This effect is always produced in pathetic and impassioned poetry; while, in lighter compositions, the ease and gracefulness with which the Poet manages his numbers are themselves confessedly a principal source of the gratification of the Reader. I might perhaps include all which it is *necessary* to say upon this subject by affirming, what few persons will deny, that, of two descriptions, either of passions, manners, or characters, each of them equally well executed, the one in prose and the other in verse, the verse will be read a hundred times where the prose is read once. We see that Pope, by the power of verse alone, has contrived to render the plainest common sense interesting, and even frequently to invest it with the appearance of passion. In consequence of these convictions I related in metre the Tale of GOODY BLAKE AND HARRY GILL, which is one of the rudest of this collection. I wished to draw attention to the truth, that the power of the human imagination is sufficient to produce such changes even in our physical nature as might almost appear miraculous. The truth is an important one; the fact (for it is a *fact*) is a valuable illustration of it. And I have the satisfaction of knowing that it has been communicated to many hundreds of people who would never have heard of it, had it not been narrated as a Ballad, and in a more impressive metre than is usual in Ballads.

Having thus explained a few of the reasons why I have written in verse, and why I have chosen subjects from common life, and endeavoured to bring my language near to the real language of men, if I have been too minute in pleading my own cause, I have at the same time been treating a subject of general interest; and it is for this reason that I request the Reader's permission to add a few words with reference solely to these particular poems, and to some defects which will probably be found in them. I am sensible that my associations must have sometimes been particular instead of general, and that, consequently, giving to things a false importance, sometimes from diseased impulses I may have written upon unworthy subjects; but I am less apprehensive on this account, than that my language may frequently have suffered from those arbitrary connections of feelings and ideas with particular words and phrases, from which no man can altogether protect himself. Hence I have no doubt, that, in some instances, feelings even of the ludicrous may be given to my Readers by expressions which appeared to me tender and pathetic. Such faulty expressions, were I convinced they were faulty at present, and that they must necessarily continue to be so, I would willingly take all reasonable pains to correct. But it is dangerous to make these alterations on the simple authority of a few individuals, or even of certain classes of men; for where the understanding of an Author is not convinced, or his feelings altered, this cannot be done without great injury to himself: for his own feelings are his stay and support, and, if he sets them aside in one instance, he may be induced to repeat this act till his mind loses all confidence in itself, and becomes utterly debilitated. To this it may be added, that the Reader ought never to forget that he is himself exposed to the same errors as the Poet, and perhaps in a much greater degree: for there can be no presumption in saying, that it is not probable he will be so well acquainted with the various stages of meaning through which words have passed, or with the fickleness or stability of the relations of particular ideas to each other; and above all, since he is so much less interested in the subject, he may decide lightly and carelessly.

Long as I have detained my Reader, I hope he will permit me to caution him against a mode of false criticism which has been applied to Poetry in which the language closely resembles that of life and nature. Such verses have been triumphed over in parodies of which Dr. Johnson's stanza is a fair specimen.

'I put my hat upon my head,
And walk'd into the Strand,
And there I met another man
Whose hat was in his hand.'[6]

Immediately under these lines I will place one of the most justly admired stanzas of the '*Babes* in the Wood.'[7]

'These pretty Babes with hand in hand
Went wandering up and down;
But never more they saw the Man
Approaching from the Town.'

In both these stanzas the words, and the order of the words, in no respect differ from the most unimpassioned conversation. There are words in both,

6. Printed in the *London Magazine*, April 1785, parodying the ballad *The Hermit of Warkworth* (1771), by Thomas Percy. The Strand: a business street in central London.

7. A popular name for the old ballad "The Children in the Wood," which tells of two children cruelly treated by a wicked uncle. It is included in Thomas Percy's collection *Reliques of Ancient English Poetry* (3 vols., 1765), which Wordsworth valued highly.

for example, 'the Strand,' and 'the Town,' connected with none but the most familiar ideas; yet the one stanza we admit as admirable, and the other as a fair example of the superlatively contemptible. Whence arises this difference? Not from the metre, not from the language, not from the order of the words; but the *matter* expressed in Dr. Johnson's stanza is contemptible. The proper method of treating trivial and simple verses, to which Dr. Johnson's stanza would be a fair parallelism, is not to say, This is a bad kind of poetry, or This is not poetry; but This wants sense; it is neither interesting in itself, nor can *lead* to any thing interesting; the images neither originate in that sane state of feeling which arises out of thought, nor can excite thought or feeling in the Reader. This is the only sensible manner of dealing with such verses. Why trouble yourself about the species till you have previously decided upon the genus? Why take pains to prove that an ape is not a Newton,[8] when it is self-evident that he is not a man?

I have one request to make of my Reader, which is, that in judging these Poems he would decide by his own feelings genuinely, and not by reflection upon what will probably be the judgment of others. How common is it to hear a person say, 'I myself do not object to this style of composition, or this or that expression, but to such and such classes of people it will appear mean or ludicrous.' This mode of criticism, so destructive of all sound unadulterated judgment, is almost universal: I have therefore to request, that the Reader would abide independently by his own feelings, and that if he finds himself affected he would not suffer such conjectures to interfere with his pleasure.

If an Author by any single composition has impressed us with respect for his talents, it is useful to consider this as affording a presumption, that, on other occasions where we have been displeased, he nevertheless may not have written ill or absurdly; and, further, to give him so much credit for this one composition as may induce us to review what has displeased us with more care than we should otherwise have bestowed upon it. This is not only an act of justice, but, in our decisions upon poetry especially, may conduce in a high degree to the improvement of our own taste: for an *accurate* taste in poetry, and in all the other arts, as Sir Joshua Reynolds[9] has observed, is an *acquired* talent, which can only be produced by thought, and a long continued intercourse with the best models of composition. This is mentioned, not with so ridiculous a purpose as to prevent the most inexperienced Reader from judging for himself, (I have already said that I wish him to judge for himself;) but merely to temper the rashness of decision, and to suggest, that, if Poetry be a subject on which much time has not been bestowed, the judgment may be erroneous; and that in many cases it necessarily will be so.

I know that nothing would have so effectually contributed to further the end which I have in view, as to have shewn of what kind the pleasure is, and how that pleasure is produced, which is confessedly produced by metrical composition essentially different from that which I have here endeavoured to recommend: for the Reader will say that he has been pleased by such composition; and what can I do more for him? The power of any art is lim-

8. Sir Isaac Newton (1642–1727), English scientist and mathematician.

9. Portrait painter, essayist, and lecturer (1723–1792), author of annual *Discourses* (1769–90) on the arts delivered to students at the Royal Academy in London. See *Discourse* XII: "The habit of contemplating and brooding over the ideas of great geniuses, till you find yourself warmed by the contact, is the true method of forming an artist-like mind."

ited; and he will suspect, that, if I propose to furnish him with new friends, it is only upon condition of his abandoning his old friends. Besides, as I have said, the Reader is himself conscious of the pleasure which he has received from such composition, composition to which he has peculiarly attached the endearing name of Poetry; and all men feel an habitual gratitude, and something of an honorable bigotry for the objects which have long continued to please them; we not only wish to be pleased, but to be pleased in that particular way in which we have been accustomed to be pleased. There is a host of arguments in these feelings; and I should be the less able to combat them successfully, as I am willing to allow, that, in order entirely to enjoy the Poetry which I am recommending, it would be necessary to give up much of what is ordinarily enjoyed. But, would my limits have permitted me to point out how this pleasure is produced, I might have removed many obstacles, and assisted my Reader in perceiving that the powers of language are not so limited as he may suppose; and that it is possible that poetry may give other enjoyments, of a purer, more lasting, and more exquisite nature. This part of my subject I have not altogether neglected; but it has been less my present aim to prove, that the interest excited by some other kinds of poetry is less vivid, and less worthy of the nobler powers of the mind, than to offer reasons for presuming, that, if the object which I have proposed to myself were adequately attained, a species of poetry would be produced, which is genuine poetry; in its nature well adapted to interest mankind permanently, and likewise important in the multiplicity and quality of its moral relations.

From what has been said, and from a perusal of the Poems, the Reader will be able clearly to perceive the object which I have proposed to myself: he will determine how far I have attained this object; and, what is a much more important question, whether it be worth attaining: and upon the decision of these two questions will rest my claim to the approbation of the public.

Appendix to the Preface (1802)

As perhaps I have no right to expect from a Reader of an Introduction to a volume of Poems that attentive perusal without which it is impossible, imperfectly as I have been compelled to express my meaning, that what I have said in the Preface should throughout be fully understood, I am the more anxious to give an exact notion of the sense in which I use the phrase *poetic diction*; and for this purpose I will here add a few words concerning the origin of the phraseology which I have condemned under that name.—The earliest Poets of all nations generally wrote from passion excited by real events; they wrote naturally, and as men: feeling powerfully as they did, their language was daring, and figurative. In succeeding times, Poets, and men ambitious of the fame of Poets, perceiving the influence of such language, and desirous of producing the same effect, without having the same animating passion, set themselves to a mechanical adoption of those figures of speech, and made use of them, sometimes with propriety, but much more frequently applied them to feelings and ideas with which they had no natural connection whatsoever. A language was thus insensibly produced, differing materially from the real language of men in *any situation*. The Reader or Hearer of this distorted language found himself in a perturbed and unusual state of mind: when affected by the genuine language of passion he had been in a perturbed and unusual state of mind also: in both cases he was willing that his common judgment and understanding should be laid asleep, and he had no instinctive and infallible perception of the true to make him reject the false; the one served as a passport for the other. The agitation and confusion of mind were in both cases delightful, and no wonder if he confounded the one with the other, and believed them both to be produced by the same, or similar causes. Besides, the Poet spake to him in the character of a man to be looked up to, a man of genius and authority. Thus, and from a variety of other causes, this distorted language was received with admiration; and Poets, it is probable, who had before contented themselves for the most part with misapplying only expressions which at first had been dictated by real passion, carried the abuse still further, and introduced phrases composed apparently in the spirit of the original figurative language of passion, yet altogether of their own invention, and distinguished by various degrees of wanton deviation from good sense and nature.

It is indeed true that the language of the earliest Poets was felt to differ materially from ordinary language, because it was the language of extraordinary occasions; but it was really spoken by men, language which the Poet himself had uttered when he had been affected by the events which he described, or which he had heard uttered by those around him. To this language it is probable that metre of some sort or other was early superadded. This separated the genuine language of Poetry still further from common life, so that whoever read or heard the poems of these earliest Poets felt himself moved in a way in which he had not been accustomed to be moved in real life, and by causes manifestly different from those which acted upon him in real life. This was the great temptation to all the corruptions which have followed: under the protection of this feeling succeeding Poets constructed a phraseology which had one thing, it is true, in common with the genuine language of poetry, namely, that it was not heard in ordinary conversation; that it was unusual. But the first Poets, as I have said, spake a language which, though unusual, was still the language of men. This circumstance, however, was disregarded by their successors; they found that they could please by easier means: they became proud of a language which they themselves had invented, and which was uttered only by themselves; and, with the spirit of a fraternity, they arrogated it to themselves as their own. In process of time metre became a symbol or promise of this unusual language, and whoever took upon him to write in metre, according as he possessed more or less of true poetic genius, introduced less or more of this adulterated phraseology into his compositions, and the true and the false became so inseparably interwoven that the taste of men was gradually perverted; and this language was received as a natural language; and at length, by the influence of books upon men, did to a certain degree really become so. Abuses of this kind were imported from one nation to another, and with the progress of refinement this diction became daily more and more corrupt, thrusting out of sight the plain humanities of nature by a motley masquerade of tricks, quaintnesses, hieroglyphics, and enigmas.

It would be highly interesting to point out the causes of the pleasure given by this extravagant and absurd language: but this is not the place; it depends upon a great variety of causes, but upon none perhaps more than its influence in impressing a notion of the peculiarity and exaltation of the Poet's character, and in flattering the Reader's self-love by bringing him nearer to a sympathy with that character; an effect which is accomplished by unsettling ordinary habits of thinking, and thus assisting the Reader to approach to that perturbed and dizzy state of mind in which if he does not find himself, he imagines that he is *balked* of a peculiar enjoyment which poetry can, and ought to bestow.

The sonnet which I have quoted from Gray, in the Preface, except the lines printed in Italics, consists of little else but this diction, though not of the worst kind; and indeed, if I may be permitted to say so, it is far too common in the best writers, both antient and modern. Perhaps I can in no way, by positive example, more easily give my Reader a notion of what I mean by the phrase *poetic diction* than by referring him to a comparison between the metrical paraphrases which we have of passages in the old and new Testament, and those passages as they exist in our common Translation. See Pope's 'Messiah' throughout, Prior's 'Did sweeter sounds adorn my flowing tongue,'[1] &c. &c. 'Though I speak with the tongues of men and of angels,' &c. &c. See 1st Corinthians, chapter 13th. By way of immediate example, take the following of Dr. Johnson:[2]

'Turn on the prudent Ant thy heedless eyes,
Observe her labours, Sluggard, and be wise;
No stern command, no monitory voice,
Prescribes her duties, or directs her choice;
Yet, timely provident, she hastes away
To snatch the blessings of a plenteous day;
When fruitful Summer loads the teeming plain,
She crops the harvest and she stores the grain.
How long shall sloth usurp thy useless hours,
Unnerve thy vigour, and enchain thy powers?
While artful shades thy downy couch enclose,
And soft solicitation courts repose,
Amidst the drowsy charms of dull delight,
Year chases year with unremitted flight,
Till want now following, fraudulent and slow,
Shall spring to seize thee, like an ambushed foe.'

From this hubbub of words pass to the original. 'Go to the Ant, thou Sluggard, consider her ways, and be wise: which having no guide, overseer, or ruler, provideth her meat in the summer, and gathereth her food in the harvest. How long wilt thou sleep, O Sluggard? when wilt thou arise out of thy sleep? Yet a little sleep, a little slumber, a little folding of the hands to sleep. So shall thy poverty come as one that travaileth, and thy want as an armed man.' Proverbs, chap. 6th.

One more quotation and I have done. It is from Cowper's verses[3] supposed to be written by Alexander Selkirk:

1. "Charity. A Paraphrase on the Thirteenth Chapter of the First Epistle to the Corinthians" (1703), by Matthew Prior (1664–1721). "Messiah": a "sacred eclogue" (1712), imitating Virgil's Latin *Eclogue* 4 (ca. 37 B.C.E.).
2. "The Ant" (1766).
3. "Verses Supposed to be Written by Alexander Selkirk" (1782), stanzas 4–5, by William Cowper (1731–1800). Selkirk (1676–1721), a Scottish sailor who lived from 1704 to 1709 on an uninhabited island off the coast of Chile.

'Religion! what treasure untold
Resides in that heavenly word!
More precious than silver and gold,
Or all that this earth can afford.
But the sound of the church-going bell
These valleys and rocks never heard,
Ne'er sighed at the sound of a knell,
Or smiled when a sabbath appear'd.

Ye winds, that have made me your sport,
Convey to this desolate shore
Some cordial endearing report
Of a land I must visit no more.
My Friends, do they now and then send
A wish or a thought after me?
O tell me I yet have a friend,
Though a friend I am never to see.'

I have quoted this passage as an instance of three different styles of composition. The first four lines are poorly expressed; some Critics would call the language prosaic; the fact is, it would be bad prose, so bad, that it is scarcely worse in metre. The epithet 'church-going' applied to a bell, and that by so chaste[4] a writer as Cowper, is an instance of the strange abuses which Poets have introduced into their language till they and their Readers take them as matters of course, if they do not single them out expressly as objects of admiration. The two lines 'Ne'er sighed at the sound,' &c. are, in my opinion, an instance of the language of passion wrested from its proper use, and, from the mere circumstance of the composition being in metre, applied upon an occasion that does not justify such violent expressions; and I should condemn the passage, though perhaps few Readers will agree with me, as vicious poetic diction. The last stanza is throughout admirably expressed: it would be equally good whether in prose or verse, except that the Reader has an exquisite pleasure in seeing such natural language so naturally connected with metre. The beauty of this stanza tempts me here to add a sentiment which ought to be the pervading spirit of a system, detached parts of which have been imperfectly explained in the Preface,— namely, that in proportion as ideas and feelings are valuable, whether the composition be in prose or in verse, they require and exact one and the same language.

1800, 1802

4. Austere, ornament-free.

SAMUEL TAYLOR COLERIDGE
1772–1834

Samuel Taylor Coleridge has been praised as the premier English literary intellectual of his era and as the first modern critic, a writer who sought to integrate literary analysis with the insights of other disciplines and who labored (with less than complete success) to give literary criticism a philosophical foundation. But he has also been dismissed and derided in hostile tones rarely found in academic commentary. Was Coleridge a great original thinker? He drew on many eighteenth-century and contemporary authors, particularly German idealist and Romantic philosophers and critics, including IMMANUEL KANT, FRIEDRICH VON SCHILLER, Friedrich and A. W. Schlegel, and Friedrich von Schelling—and some scholars have commended him for introducing the best of German thought to an English readership. Less charitably, though with some reason, others have termed these literary debts, references, and borrowings to be nothing more than plagiarisms.

Coleridge has also been rebuked and mocked for the ambitious projects he proposed, launched, but left undone: an eight- to ten-volume history of literature, an epic poem on the origin of evil, and so on. He had extraordinary literary gifts, but was an undisciplined author who failed to make full use of his exceptional talents—as he himself knew well. Coleridge wrote in his copy of his book *The Statesman's Manual* (1816) that while he had produced a number of significant works, he stood in the world's eyes as "the wild eccentric Genius that has published nothing but fragments & splendid Tirades." With the possible exception of the *Biographia Literaria* (1817) and a handful of poems, none of his works holds together as an effective whole. Yet as a writer, and as a speaker (we have ample records of his conversations and lectures), he was, and still is, brilliantly impressive and stimulating.

Coleridge was born the son of the vicar of Ottery St. Mary, a small town in southwest England; but at age nine, following the death of his father, he was sent to school in London, attending Christ's Hospital as a charity student. In 1791 he enrolled in Jesus College, Cambridge University; two years later, plagued by debts, he enlisted in the Fifteenth Light Dragoons under the alias Silas Tomkyn Comberbache (S.T.C.). He was soon rescued from this mistake by his family and returned to the university, but he left in December 1794 without completing his degree.

In June 1794, while on a walking tour, Coleridge met the poet Robert Southey at Oxford, and the two concocted a plan for a "pantisocracy" (a society ruled by equals). They decided on a location (in Pennsylvania) and on the twelve men who, with their wives, would create this agricultural commune; but the only action taken was Coleridge's engagement (made necessary by the scheme) to Sara Fricker, the sister of Southey's fiancée. Though the plan collapsed, he married her in 1795.

In late 1794 Coleridge's first published poetry appeared—sonnets addressed to contemporary political radicals such as William Godwin and Joseph Priestley. In 1795 he worked as a journalist and lectured in Bristol on politics, religion, and history. Most scholars believe that he there first met WILLIAM WORDSWORTH, beginning an intense friendship that soon led to the most significant collaboration in English literary history. By May 1796 Coleridge was calling Wordsworth "a very dear friend of mine, who is in my opinion the best poet of the age," and his own first collection of poetry, *Poems on Various Subjects*, had just been published. In December, Coleridge and his wife Sara settled in Nether Stowey, and soon thereafter Wordsworth and his sister Dorothy moved nearby, to Alfoxden. Beginning in mid-1797 Coleridge and Wordsworth worked together on *Lyrical Ballads*, which they published anonymously in September 1798. Among the works of this period, Coleridge's high point as a poet, are "This Lime-Tree Bower My Prison," "The Rime of the Ancient Mariner," "Frost at Midnight," "Fears in Solitude," "The Nightingale," part I of "Christabel," and probably the fragment "Kubla Khan" as well.

Leaving his wife and two children behind, Coleridge accompanied the Wordsworths to Germany in September 1798, where he read and absorbed the philosophical and literary speculations of Kant, Schelling, the Schlegels, and Schiller (whose work he later translated).

On his return to England in mid-1799, Coleridge wrote political articles and made plans (unrealized) for a biography of the German critic and dramatist GOTTHOLD EPHRAIM LESSING and for a major book on Romantic metaphysics. The Coleridges followed the Wordsworths to the Lake District in 1800; and although the second edition of *Lyrical Ballads* (1800) appeared with only Wordsworth's name on the title page and with a long preface by Wordsworth that ignored Coleridge's poems, the men remained close. But Coleridge's personal life was in disarray. Already indifferent to his wife, he had fallen in love with Sara Hutchinson, whose sister, Mary, Wordsworth would marry in 1802; even worse, he had become dependent on laudanum (opium dissolved in alcohol, widely used to treat a number of disorders). Leaving his family behind, Coleridge spent two years traveling the Mediterranean and working in Malta; but he returned to England in 1806 still an addict. He lived for some months with the Wordsworths, and the relationship grew strained; the men finally broke on bitter terms in 1810.

Under the circumstances, Coleridge was surprisingly productive. In 1809 and 1810, he wrote and published *The Friend*, a periodical that ran for twenty-eight issues; and between 1808 and 1819, he lectured frequently on politics, religion, education, philosophy, and literature, offering especially incisive commentaries on Shakespeare and Milton. During the period from June to September 1815, he focused on the *Biographia Literaria*, which he dictated rather than wrote. From spring 1816 until his death in 1834, Coleridge lived in Highgate, a northern suburb of London, with and under the care of Dr. James Gillman, who helped control his drug addiction.

By this time known as the "Sage of Highgate," Coleridge published *Christabel and Other Poems* (1816); the first volume of his collected poems, *Sibylline Leaves* (1817; expanded 1828, 1834); and his *Poetical Works* (3 vols., 1828; 2d ed., 1829; 3d ed., 1834). His major prose works are *Lay Sermons* (1816, 1817), essays on national education and the structure of an organic society; *Biographia Literaria* (1817); "Treatise on Method" (included in the three-volume edition of *The Friend*, 1818); *Aids to Reflection* (1825; 2d ed., 1831); and *On the Constitution of the Church and State* (1829; 2d ed., 1830), in which he proposed the establishment of teachers, scholars, and priests as an independent estate of the realm, "the clerisy." In addition, *Table Talk* (edited by his nephew Henry Coleridge, 1836), which displays his skills in conversation; *Literary Remains* (1836), which contains an account of his 1818–19 lectures on "the history of philosophy" and the "general course of literature"; and *Anima Poetae* (1895), selections from his notebooks, all appeared after his death.

Coleridge frequently professed a commitment to system, logic, and method, but his own practice resists global theories and highly elaborated schemes and structures. It is the penetrating phrase or sentence, the powerful paragraph of speculation, and the shrewd, suggestive judgment that reveal Coleridge at his best. Still, for English and American critics in the early twentieth century, especially I. A. Richards, CLEANTH BROOKS, and other New Critics, the central Coleridge text is *Biographia Literaria*, where they found and built on Coleridge's theory of the imagination, his exposition of organic unity, and his treatment of poetry as the reconciliation of opposites.

Biographia Literaria, a hastily assembled work, mixes modes and genres. It includes autobiography, philosophy, literary theory, and analytical literary criticism, as well as a memoir of Wordsworth, a study of his poems, and a critique of his theory of poetic diction. At the center of Coleridge's project is his inquiry into and defense of the imagination. Coleridge's account, distinguishing between "fancy" and "imagination," lacks the splendor and breadth of PERCY BYSSHE SHELLEY's tribute to the imagination in *A Defence of Poetry* (written 1821; see below) as "the great instrument of moral good," but it has exercised a greater influence on later literary theory and criticism. Coleridge speaks first of the "primary" imagination: the "living power" of God, in the eternal act of creation, it is also the power of creation in each person. The "secondary" imagination echoes the primary; in conjunction with the will and understanding, it dissolves in order to re-create, making whole and harmonizing as a "synthetic and magical power." Fancy, in contrast, merely associates "fixities and definites."

This is an intriguing, if elusive, theory, over which commentators have puzzled. But the real importance of Coleridge's words is their departure from eighteenth-century neoclassical theory. SAMUEL JOHNSON, in his *Dictionary* (1765), offers "fancy" as one of the definitions of "imagination"; that Coleridge makes a distinction between the two has important implications for his conception of the poet and the poem. Neoclassical critics such as ALEXANDER POPE and Johnson could exempt only a great genius like Shakespeare from external rules of literary decorum, insisting that others rely on deliberate craft; but for Coleridge the creative work of every poet springs from an imaginative power at once available for analysis yet mysterious in its sources. He sees a poem as *organic*, true to itself, acquiring its shape like a plant from a seed and thereby growing according to its own internal law of development.

Coleridge's theory of the primary and secondary imagination honors the creative capacity of persons while remaining steadfast to the primacy of God; even more, Coleridge implies that each re-creative act that a poet performs is an act of worship. As modern scholars have pointed out, Coleridge was the most devout of all the major Romantic writers; his Christian faith is central to all his work. He sees "a similar union of the universal and the individual" in religion and in the fine arts. Yet implicit in Coleridge's theory of the imagination are both difficulty and failure, which take on added bleakness in this context. When he sets the imagination in contrast to a world of "essentially fixed and dead objects," does he mean that God has made a world that is dead—at least until awakened or renewed by a creative act?

Coleridge makes a similar distinction in his commentaries on allegory and symbol in *The Statesman's Manual*. Allegory, he indicates, is mechanical and formulaic, part of the larger problem of our degenerate age of triumphant "mechanic" philosophy; but symbol is organically unified, fusing the particular and the general, the temporal and the eternal. This distinction is crucial for Coleridge, yet, as PAUL DE MAN argues in "The Rhetoric of Temporality" (1969), his arguments do not sustain it: the more that Coleridge explores the distinction, the more he complicates and blurs its terms. Some of his best-known poetry ("The Rime of the Ancient Mariner," "Kubla Khan," "Christabel") has invited allegorical interpretation.

Coleridge's emphasis on the power of the imagination is at odds with much contemporary theory and historical and cultural criticism, which is suspicious of claims that appear to give certain individuals the power to create new worlds out of nothing but their imagination. The New Historicist STEPHEN GREENBLATT speaks, for example, not of the imaginative power and prowess of the author but of "social energy"; and it is true that Coleridge pays little attention to the social networks of signification in which an author's work takes shape. But recent theorists, reacting perhaps too sweepingly against the idea of the author as a Romantic genius, have tended to undervalue the creative power of the individual author, the agent of the imagination who, as Coleridge says of Shakespeare, demonstrates his authority and skill "not only in the general construction, but in all the detail."

***Biographia Literaria* Keywords:** Aesthetics, Authorship, Literary History, Poetry, Romantic Theory

From Biographia Literaria[1]

From *Volume 1*

FROM CHAPTER 1

* * *

As the result of all my reading and meditation, I abstracted two critical aphorisms, deeming them to comprize the conditions and criteria of poetic style; first, that not the poem which we have *read*, but that to which we *return*, with the greatest pleasure, possesses the genuine power, and claims the name of *essential poetry*. Second, that whatever lines can be translated into other words of the same language, without diminution of their significance, either in sense, or association, or in any worthy feeling, are so far vicious[2] in their diction. Be it however observed, that I excluded from the list of worthy feelings, the pleasure derived from mere novelty, in the reader, and the desire of exciting wonderment at his powers in the author. Oftentimes since then, in perusing French tragedies, I have fancied two marks of admiration at the end of each line, as hieroglyphics of the author's own admiration at his own cleverness. Our genuine admiration of a great poet is a continuous *under-current* of feeling; it is every where present, but seldom any where as a separate excitement. I was wont boldly to affirm, that it would be scarcely more difficult to push a stone out from the pyramids with the bare hand, than to alter a word, or the position of a word, in Milton or Shakespeare, (in their most important works at least) without making the author say something else, or something worse, than he does say. One great distinction, I appeared to myself to see plainly, between, even the characteristic faults of our elder poets, and the false beauty of the moderns. In the former, from DONNE to COWLEY,[3] we find the most fantastic out-of-the-way thoughts, but in the most pure and genuine mother English; in the latter, the most obvious thoughts, in language the most fantastic and arbitrary. Our faulty elder poets sacrificed the passion, and passionate flow of poetry, to the subtleties of intellect, and to the starts of wit; the moderns to the glare and glitter of a perpetual, yet broken and heterogeneous imagery, or rather to an amphibious something, made up, half of image, and half of abstract meaning. The one sacrificed the heart to the head; the other both heart and head to point and drapery.

* * *

1. The full title is *Biographia Literaria; Or, Biographical Sketches of My Literary Life and Opinions.* Footnotes by Coleridge have been omitted from this selection.
2. Defective.
3. Abraham Cowley (1618–1667), English satirist, poet, and essayist. John Donne (1572–1631), English poet. Both wrote so-called metaphysical poetry, reliant on complex metaphors and images.

FROM CHAPTER 4

* * *

This excellence,[4] which in all Mr. Wordsworth's writings is more or less predominant, and which constitutes the character of his mind, I no sooner felt, than I sought to understand. Repeated meditations led me first to suspect, (and a more intimate analysis of the human faculties, their appropriate marks, functions, and effects matured my conjecture into full conviction) that fancy and imagination were two distinct and widely different faculties, instead of being, according to the general belief, either two names with one meaning, or at furthest, the lower and higher degree of one and the same power. It is not, I own, easy to conceive a more opposite translation of the Greek *Phantasia*, than the Latin Imaginatio; but it is equally true that in all societies there exists an instinct of growth, a certain collective, unconscious good sense working progressively to desynonymize[5] those words originally of the same meaning, which the conflux of dialects had supplied to the more homogeneous languages, as the Greek and German: and which the same cause, joined with accidents of translation from original works of different countries, occasion in mixt languages like our own. The first and most important point to be proved is, that two conceptions perfectly distinct are confused under one and the same word, and (this done) to appropriate that word exclusively to one meaning, and the synonyme (should there be one) to the other. But if (as will be often the case in the arts and sciences) no synonyme exists, we must either invent or borrow a word. In the present instance the appropriation had already begun, and been legitimated in the derivative adjective: Milton had a highly *imaginative*, Cowley a very *fanciful* mind.[6] If therefore I should succeed in establishing the actual existences of two faculties generally different, the nomenclature would be at once determined. To the faculty by which I had characterized Milton, we should confine the term *imagination*; while the other would be contra-distinguished as *fancy*. Now were it once fully ascertained, that this division is no less grounded in nature, than that of delirium from mania, or Otway's

> Lutes, lobsters, seas of milk, and ships of amber,[7]

from Shakespeare's

> What! have his daughters brought him to this pass?[8]

or from the preceding apostrophe to the elements;[9] the theory of the fine arts, and of poetry in particular, could not, I thought, but derive some additional and important light. It would in its immediate effects furnish a torch

4. Coleridge has just claimed that it is the mark of genius "to represent familiar objects so as to awaken in the minds of others a kindred feeling concerning them." A considerable portion of the *Biographia Literaria* is devoted to a critical analysis of the English poet WILLIAM WORDSWORTH (1770–1850), Coleridge's friend and collaborator.

5. To differentiate in meaning words previously synonymous (so defined by the *Oxford English Dictionary*, which gives this as the first use of the word).

6. John Milton (1608–1674) was a contemporary of but far greater poet than Cowley.

7. *Venice Preserved* (1682), 5.2.151, by Thomas Otway (1652–1685). Coleridge uses the word "lobsters" where Otway had written "laurels."

8. *King Lear* (ca. 1604–05), 3.4.61 (Shakespeare begins the line "What, has").

9. That is, Lear's address to the storm, 3.2.1–9, 13–23.

of guidance to the philosophical critic; and ultimately to the poet himself. In energetic minds, truth soon changes by domestication into power; and from directing in the discrimination and appraisal of the product, becomes influence in the production. To admire on principle, is the only way to imitate without loss of originality.

* * *

FROM CHAPTER 13

* * *

The IMAGINATION then I consider either as primary, or secondary. The primary IMAGINATION I hold to be the living Power and prime Agent of all human Perception, and as a repetition in the finite mind of the eternal act of creation in the infinite I AM.[1] The secondary I consider as an echo of the former, co-existing with the conscious will, yet still as identical with the primary in the *kind* of its agency, and differing only in *degree*, and in the *mode* of its operation. It dissolves, diffuses, dissipates, in order to re-create; or where this process is rendered impossible, yet still at all events it struggles to idealize and to unify. It is essentially *vital*, even as all objects (*as* objects) are essentially fixed and dead.

FANCY, on the contrary, has no other counters to play with, but fixities and definites. The Fancy is indeed no other than a mode of Memory emancipated from the order of time and space; and blended with, and modified by that empirical phenomenon of the will, which we express by the word CHOICE. But equally with the ordinary memory it must receive all its materials ready made from the law of association.

* * *

From *Volume* 2

CHAPTER 14

During the first year that Mr. Wordsworth and I were neighbours,[2] our conversations turned frequently on the two cardinal points of poetry, the power of exciting the sympathy of the reader by a faithful adherence to the truth of nature, and the power of giving the interest of novelty by the modifying colours of imagination. The sudden charm, which accidents of light and shade, which moon-light or sun-set diffused over a known and familiar landscape, appeared to represent the practicability of combining both. These are the poetry of nature. The thought suggested itself (to which of us I do not recollect) that a series of poems might be composed of two sorts. In the one, the incidents and agents were to be, in part at least, supernatural; and the excellence aimed at was to consist in the interesting of the affections by the dramatic truth of such emotions, as would naturally accom-

1. See Exodus 3.14: "And God said unto Moses, I Am That I Am."
2. In 1797–98 Coleridge was living at Nether Stowey, and Wordsworth was nearby at Alfoxden, in southwest England.

pany such situations, supposing them real. And real in *this* sense they have been to every human being who, from whatever source of delusion, has at any time believed himself under supernatural agency. For the second class, subjects were to be chosen from ordinary life; the characters and incidents were to be such, as will be found in every village and its vicinity, where there is a meditative and feeling mind to seek after them, or to notice them, when they present themselves.

In this idea originated the plan of the "Lyrical Ballads;" in which it was agreed, that my endeavours should be directed to persons and characters supernatural, or at least romantic: yet so as to transfer from our inward nature a human interest and a semblance of truth sufficient to procure for these shadows of imagination that willing suspension of disbelief for the moment, which constitutes poetic faith. Mr. Wordsworth, on the other hand, was to propose to himself as his object, to give the charm of novelty to things of every day, and to excite a feeling analogous to the supernatural, by awakening the mind's attention from the lethargy of custom, and directing it to the loveliness and the wonders of the world before us; an inexhaustible treasure, but for which in consequence of the film of familiarity and selfish solicitude we have eyes, yet see not, ears that hear not, and hearts that neither feel nor understand.[3]

With this view I wrote the "Ancient Mariner," and was preparing among other poems, the "Dark Ladie," and the "Christabel," in which I should have more nearly realized my ideal, than I had done in my first attempt. But Mr. Wordsworth's industry had proved so much more successful[4] and the number of his poems so much greater, that my compositions, instead of forming a balance, appeared rather an interpolation of heterogeneous matter. Mr. Wordsworth added two or three poems written in his own character, in the impassioned, lofty, and sustained diction, which is characteristic of his genius. In this form the "Lyrical Ballads" were published; and were presented by him, as an *experiment*,[5] whether subjects, which from their nature rejected the usual ornaments and extra-colloquial style of poems in general, might not be so managed in the language of ordinary life as to produce the pleasureable interest, which it is the peculiar business of poetry to impart. To the second edition he added a preface of considerable length; in which notwithstanding some passages of apparently a contrary import, he was understood to contend for the extension of this style to poetry of all kinds, and to reject as vicious and indefensible all phrases and forms of style that were not included in what he (unfortunately, I think, adopting an equivocal expression) called the language of *real* life. From this preface, prefixed to poems in which it was impossible to deny the presence of original genius, however mistaken its direction might be deemed, arose the whole long continued controversy.[6] For from the conjunction of perceived

3. See Isaiah 6.9–10.
4. Wordsworth wrote 19 of the 23 poems in the first edition of *Lyrical Ballads* (1798).
5. See the brief advertisement to the first edition of *Lyrical Ballads*: "The majority of the following poems are to be considered as experiments. They were written chiefly with a view to ascertain how far the language of conversation in the middle and lower classes of society is adapted to the purposes of poetic pleasure."
6. That is, the controversy that arose over Wordsworth's theory and practice of poetry, especially in hostile essays by the critic Francis Jeffrey (1773–1850) in the *Edinburgh Review*. For Wordsworth's Preface to *Lyrical Ballads* (1800, 1802), see above.

power with supposed heresy I explain the inveteracy and in some instances, I grieve to say, the acrimonious passions, with which the controversy has been conducted by the assailants.

Had Mr. Wordsworth's poems been the silly, the childish things, which they were for a long time described as being; had they been really distinguished from the compositions of other poets merely by meanness of language and inanity of thought; had they indeed contained nothing more than what is found in the parodies and pretended imitations of them; they must have sunk at once, a dead weight, into the slough[7] of oblivion, and have dragged the preface along with them. But year after year increased the number of Mr. Wordsworth's admirers. They were found too not in the lower classes of the reading public, but chiefly among young men of strong sensibility and meditative minds; and their admiration (inflamed perhaps in some degree by opposition) was distinguished by its intensity, I might almost say, by its *religious* fervour. These facts, and the intellectual energy of the author, which was more or less consciously felt, where it was outwardly and even boisterously denied, meeting with sentiments of aversion to his opinions, and of alarm at their consequences, produced an eddy of criticism, which would of itself have borne up the poems by the violence, with which it whirled them round and round. With many parts of this preface in the sense attributed to them and which the words undoubtedly seem to authorize, I never concurred; but on the contrary objected to them as erroneous in principle, and as contradictory (in appearance at least) both to other parts of the same preface, and to the author's own practice in the greater number of the poems themselves. Mr. Wordsworth in his recent collection has, I find, degraded this prefatory disquisition to the end of his second volume, to be read or not at the reader's choice.[8] But he has not, as far as I can discover, announced any change in his poetic creed. At all events, considering it as the source of a controversy, in which I have been honored more, than I deserve, by the frequent conjunction of my name with his, I think it expedient to declare once for all, in what points I coincide with his opinions, and in what points I altogether differ. But in order to render myself intelligible I must previously, in as few words as possible, explain my ideas, first, of a POEM; and secondly, of POETRY itself, in *kind*, and in *essence*.

The office of philosophical *disquisition* consists in just *distinction*; while it is the priviledge of the philosopher to preserve himself constantly aware, that distinction is not division. In order to obtain adequate notions of any truth, we must intellectually separate its distinguishable parts; and this is the technical *process* of philosophy. But having so done, we must then restore them in our conceptions to the unity, in which they actually co-exist; and this is the *result* of philosophy. A poem contains the same elements as a prose composition; the difference therefore must consist in a different combination of them, in consequence of a different object proposed. According to the difference of the object will be the difference of the combination. It is possible, that the object may be merely to facilitate the recollection of any given facts or observations by artificial arrangement: and the composition will be a poem, merely because it is distinguished from prose by metre,

7. Soft, muddy ground.
8. For *Poems* (2 vols., 1815), Wordsworth moved the preface for *Lyrical Ballads* to an appendix and wrote a new preface and "supplementary" essay.

or by rhyme, or by both conjointly. In this, the lowest sense, a man might attribute the name of a poem to the well known enumeration of the days in the several months;

> Thirty days hath September,
> April, June, and November, &c.

and others of the same class and purpose. And as a particular pleasure is found in anticipating the recurrence of sounds and quantities, all compositions that have this charm superadded, whatever be their contents, *may* be entitled poems.

So much for the superficial *form*. A difference of object and contents supplies an additional ground of distinction. The immediate purpose may be the communication of truths; either of truth absolute and demonstrable, as in works of science; or of facts experienced and recorded, as in history. Pleasure, and that of the highest and most permanent kind, may *result* from the *attainment* of the end; but it is not itself the immediate end. In other works the communication of pleasure may be the immediate purpose; and though truth, either moral or intellectual, ought to be the *ultimate* end, yet this will distinguish the character of the author, not the class to which the work belongs. Blest indeed is that state of society, in which the immediate purpose would be baffled by the perversion of the proper ultimate end; in which no charm of diction or imagery could exempt the Bathyllus even of an Anacreon, or the Alexis of Virgil[9] from disgust and aversion.

But the communication of pleasure may be the immediate object of a work not metrically composed; and that object may have been in a high degree attained, as in novels and romances. Would then the mere superaddition of metre, with or without rhyme, entitle *these* to the name of poems? The answer is, that nothing can permanently please, which does not contain in itself the reason why it is so, and not otherwise.[1] If metre be superadded, all other parts must be made consonant with it. They must be such, as to justify the perpetual and distinct attention to each part, which an exact correspondent recurrence of accent and sound are calculated to excite. The final definition then, so deduced, may be thus worded. A poem is that species of composition, which is opposed to works of science, by proposing for its *immediate* object pleasure, not truth; and from all other species (having *this* object in common with it) it is discriminated by proposing to itself such delight from the *whole*, as is compatible with a distinct gratification from each component *part*.

Controversy is not seldom excited in consequence of the disputants attaching each a different meaning to the same word; and in few instances has this been more striking, than in disputes concerning the present subject. If a man chooses to call every composition a poem, which is rhyme, or measure, or both, I must leave his opinion uncontroverted. The distinction

9. The Roman poet (70–19 B.C.E.) whose *Eclogue* 2 (ca. 37 B.C.E.) is the shepherd Corydon's lovesick address to the male slave Alexis. Bathyllus: a beautiful boy of Samos to whom several odes of the Greek lyric poet Anacreon (b. ca. 570 B.C.E.) are addressed.

1. Coleridge's editors cite SAMUEL JOHNSON, *Rambler*, no. 154 (1751): "That which hopes to resist the blast of malignity, and stand firm against the attacks of time, must contain in itself some original principle of growth."

is at least competent to characterize the writer's intention. If it were subjoined, that the whole is likewise entertaining or affecting, as a tale, or as a series of interesting reflections, I of course admit this as another fit ingredient of a poem, and an additional merit. But if the definition sought for be that of a *legitimate* poem, I answer, it must be one, the parts of which mutually support and explain each other; all in their proportion harmonizing with, and supporting the purpose and known influences of metrical arrangement. The philosophic critics of all ages coincide with the ultimate judgement of all countries, in equally denying the praises of a just poem, on the one hand, to a series of striking lines or distichs,[2] each of which absorbing the whole attention of the reader to itself disjoins it from its context, and makes it a separate whole, instead of an harmonizing part; and on the other hand, to an unsustained composition, from which the reader collects rapidly the general result unattracted by the component parts. The reader should be carried forward, not merely or chiefly by the mechanical impulse of curiosity, or by a restless desire to arrive at the final solution; but by the pleasureable activity of mind excited by the attractions of the journey itself. Like the motion of a serpent, which the Egyptians made the emblem of intellectual power; or like the path of sound through the air; at every step he pauses and half recedes, and from the retrogressive movement collects the force which again carries him onward. Precipitandus est *liber* spiritus,[3] says Petronius Arbiter most happily. The epithet, *liber*, here balances the preceding verb; and it is not easy to conceive more meaning condensed in fewer words.

But if this should be admitted as a satisfactory character of a poem, we have still to seek for a definition of poetry. The writings of PLATO, and BISHOP TAYLOR, and the Theoria Sacra of BURNET,[4] furnish undeniable proofs that poetry of the highest kind may exist without metre, and even without the contradistinguishing objects of a poem. The first chapter of Isaiah (indeed a very large proportion of the whole book) is poetry in the most emphatic sense; yet it would be not less irrational than strange to assert, that pleasure, and not truth, was the immediate object of the prophet. In short, whatever *specific* import we attach to the word, poetry, there will be found involved in it, as a necessary consequence, that a poem of any length neither can be, or ought to be, all poetry. Yet if an harmonious whole is to be produced, the remaining parts must be preserved *in keeping* with the poetry; and this can be no otherwise effected than by such a studied selection and artificial arrangement, as will partake of *one*, though not a *peculiar*, property of poetry. And this again can be no other than the property of exciting a more continuous and equal attention, than the language of prose aims at, whether colloquial or written.

My own conclusions on the nature of poetry, in the strictest use of the word, have been in part anticipated in the preceding disquisition on the fancy and imagination.[5] What is poetry? is so nearly the same question with, what

2. Paired lines (in Greek and Latin verse, such couplets do not rhyme).
3. The free spirit must be hurried onward (Latin); from *Satyricon*, section 118, a novel by the Roman writer Petronius Arbiter (1st c. C.E.). *Liber* means "free," and the form of the preceding Latin verb shows necessity or obligation.
4. Thomas Burnet (1635–1735), an English clergyman who wrote *Telluris Theoria Sacra* (1681, *The Sacred Theory of the Earth*). Jeremy Taylor (1613–1667), Anglican religious writer whose sermons Coleridge esteemed. On the Greek philosopher PLATO (ca. 427–ca. 347 B.C.E.), see above.
5. In chapter 4.

is a poet? that the answer to the one is involved in the solution of the other. For it is a distinction resulting from the poetic genius itself, which sustains and modifies the images, thoughts, and emotions of the poet's own mind. The poet, described in *ideal* perfection, brings the whole soul of man into activity, with the subordination of its faculties to each other, according to their relative worth and dignity. He diffuses a tone, and spirit of unity, that blends, and (as it were) *fuses*, each into each, by that synthetic and magical power, to which we have exclusively appropriated the name of imagination. This power, first put in action by the will and understanding, and retained under their irremissive,[6] though gentle and unnoticed, control (*laxis effertur habenis*)[7] reveals itself in the balance or reconciliation of opposite or discordant qualities: of sameness, with difference; of the general, with the concrete; the idea, with the image; the individual, with the representative; the sense of novelty and freshness, with old and familiar objects; a more than usual state of emotion, with more than usual order; judgement ever awake and steady self-possession, with enthusiasm and feeling profound or vehement; and while it blends and harmonizes the natural and the artificial, still subordinates art to nature; the manner to the matter; and our admiration of the poet to our sympathy with the poetry. "Doubtless," as Sir John Davies[8] observes of the soul (and his words may with slight alteration be applied, and even more appropriately to the poetic IMAGINATION).

> Doubtless this could not be, but that she turns
> Bodies to spirit by sublimation strange,
> As fire converts to fire the things it burns,
> As we our food into our nature change.
>
> From their gross matter she abstracts their forms,
> And draws a kind of quintessence from things;
> Which to her proper nature she transforms
> To bear them light, on her celestial wings.
>
> Thus does she, when from individual states
> She doth abstract the universal kinds;
> Which then re-clothed in divers names and fates
> Steal access through our senses to our minds.

Finally, GOOD SENSE is the BODY of poetic genius, FANCY its DRAPERY, MOTION its LIFE, and IMAGINATION the SOUL that is every where, and in each; and forms all into one graceful and intelligent whole.

1817

6. Unremitting.
7. It is carried with loosened reins (Latin).
8. English poet (1569–1626). Coleridge slightly misquotes his poem *Nosce Teipsum* (1599; the title means "know thyself"), which explores the theme of immortality and the nature of the soul.

PERCY BYSSHE SHELLEY
1792–1822

Like the American poet Walt Whitman, Percy Bysshe Shelley has been revered by many readers for his haunting lyrics and, even more, for the radical views he expresses in both his poetry and prose. But more than any other nineteenth-century poet, he came in for relentless and mean-spirited abuse at the hands of major modernist poets and critics, including T. S. ELIOT, F. R. LEAVIS, JOHN CROWE RANSOM, and Allen Tate. For them, Shelley represented everything that modern poetry was seeking to move beyond, and they pummeled him for (as they saw it) the intersecting weaknesses of his poetry and his character: dreaminess, arrogance, self-absorption, irresponsibility. They judged his personal conduct offensive and his verse marred by muddled imagery and confused symbolism. Writing in 1950, the critic Leslie Fiedler reflected: "The only way to find out if a poet is immortal is to kill him; Milton and Wordsworth slain have risen; Cowley and Shelley are rotting in their tombs." Shelley seemed no more likely to recover his prestige than did the third-tier metaphysical poet with whom he was paired.

This downgrading of Shelley was already under way in the nineteenth century. In *Essays in Criticism* (1865, 1888), MATTHEW ARNOLD first declared that "the right sphere for Shelley's genius was the sphere of music, not of poetry," and later called him a "beautiful and ineffectual angel, beating in the void his luminous wings in vain." In *Literary Studies* (1884), the editor and essayist Walter Bagehot concluded: "He floats away into an imaginary Elysium or an expected Utopia; beautiful and excellent, of course, but having nothing in common with the absolute laws of the present world." This tone seemed to be justified by Shelley himself, who, for example, observed to his friend Edward Trelawny: "When my brain gets heated with thought it soon boils and throws off images and words faster than I can skim them off."

But Shelley's words to Trelawny bear witness to his creative energy and exhilaration, to his yearning to break free from constraint. Shelley's commitment to personal and social freedom perhaps provides the best context for understanding and valuing his writing. His poetry and prose attacked social and political tyranny, assailing the ways in which law and religion functioned to support an oppressive state. In phrasing that anticipated RALPH WALDO EMERSON's in *Nature* (1836), "The American Scholar" (1837), and other seminal American Transcendentalist texts, Shelley declared: "Let us believe in a kind of optimism in which we are our own gods" (letter, 1819). As he once said, he sought to call attention to the "else unfelt oppressions of this earth" ("Julian and Maddalo," line 450), that is, to make readers feel the nature and depth of human oppression and lift them to a higher conception of possibility. In doing this, he was performing the special office of the poet.

Shelley was born the son of a wealthy squire (and member of Parliament) near Horsham in Sussex, England. He was educated first at Syon House Academy, in Brentford, a western suburb of London, and then at Eton, the largest and most famous of England's public (i.e., endowed boarding) schools, where he was dubbed "mad Shelley" for his antics and "Eton atheist" for his skeptical views on religion. Imaginative and rebellious, he was already writing prose and poems while in his teens. He entered University College, Oxford University, in 1810; there he read such radical authors as William Godwin, author of the *Enquiry concerning Political Justice* (1793), and Thomas Paine, author of *The Rights of Man* (1791–92) and *The Age of Reason* (1793).

In March 1811, because Shelley had coauthored an empiricist pamphlet, *The Necessity of Atheism*, which he then mailed to the bishops and heads of the colleges at

Oxford, he was expelled from the university. His life became even more scandalous when he eloped to Edinburgh, Scotland, with sixteen-year-old Harriet Westbrook. This action, together with his refusal to renounce the pamphlet, caused a breach with his family that cost Shelley his inheritance.

After their marriage in August 1811, the young couple spent the next three years in England and Ireland, moving often. Shelley corresponded with Godwin, wrote addresses and proposals on such topics as Catholic emancipation, and was kept under watch by the civil authorities. His first important poem, *Queen Mab*, which exhibits his radical views on both religion and conventional morality, was privately printed in 1813. He wrote and lectured on a host of other subjects as well, from freedom of the press to vegetarianism. During this time, Harriet bore two children, but she and Shelley grew estranged.

When Shelley fell in love with Mary Godwin, the sixteen-year-old daughter of William Godwin and the English writer and reformer MARY WOLLSTONECRAFT, he acted according to his views on the primacy of love. Leaving his family behind, in 1814 he traveled to France with Mary (and her fifteen-year-old half-sister, Jane "Claire" Clairmont). After travels in France, Switzerland, and Germany, they returned to London; in spring 1815 Mary gave birth to a daughter who died prematurely, and in 1816 she bore a son, William. In Switzerland, with the Romantic poet Lord Byron as their companion during the summer of 1816, Mary began her famous novel *Frankenstein* while Percy worked on such major philosophical poems as "Hymn to Intellectual Beauty" and "Mont Blanc." They married, despite their objections to the institution of marriage, after Harriet drowned herself in 1816. Harriet's parents quickly secured a decree declaring Shelley unfit to have custody of his and Harriet's children, who were placed in foster care at his expense. In spring 1818 he left England for Italy, where he spent the rest of his life with Mary, their three children (two of whom died, within a nine-month period in 1818–19), Claire Clairmont, and her daughter (whose father was Byron).

While in Pisa, Shelley lived amid a circle of writers and adventurers, including Byron and Edward Trelawny. In April 1822 he moved to the village of Lerici on the Gulf of Spezia, and there he wrote a number of his best lyrics and vivid letters. Caught in a sudden storm while in a boat with his friend Edward Williams, he drowned in July 1822. Shelley left unfinished a political drama and "The Triumph of Life," a dream allegory that has figured significantly in contemporary criticism and theory (e.g., see the essays by HAROLD BLOOM, PAUL DE MAN, JACQUES DERRIDA, and others in *Deconstruction and Criticism*, 1997).

Shelley matters in literary history above all for his poetry, but his prose works are often powerful and remain undervalued. The best (and best-known) of them is *A Defence of Poetry*, which he wrote in response to his friend Thomas Love Peacock's "Four Ages of Poetry" (1820). Peacock presents a satiric, witty survey of the historical rise and decline of poetry that draws a parallel between the classical and modern periods. He traces English poetry's movement from the iron age of song, to the golden age of Shakespeare, then to the silver age of ALEXANDER POPE, and, finally, to the brass age of his Romantic contemporaries, whose work consists, he says, of "rant," "whining," and "cant." In reply, Shelley honors the activity of the poet and emphasizes that poetry has increased, rather than diminished, in importance in the modern era. Many of the ideas he presents are familiar, deriving from PLATO and, especially, from SIR PHILIP SIDNEY's *Defence of Poesy* (1595), which Shelley read as he prepared and planned his own work. Shelley gives them a fervent Romantic cast, particularly in the glowing images and passionate rhythms of his *Defence*'s final passages.

Peacock and Shelley had met in 1812, and they visited and corresponded with one another often. After Peacock's "Four Ages" appeared, Shelley wrote in a letter, January 1821, that he planned "an answer" to it: "It is very clever but, I think, very false." On March 21, he sent Peacock the first part of an essay meant to be its "antidote." In the original plan for the *Defence*, Shelley included a number of references to Peacock, but most of these were omitted when the text was prepared for publication after his death. Originally, too, the *Defence* was to have three parts: a general defense of poetry and its role in society, a survey of the development of English poetry, and a discussion of the literature of the day. Only the first part was completed.

Despite being an incomplete piece that draws on and adapts his own earlier writings—the prefaces to *The Revolt of Islam* and *Prometheus Unbound*, "Discourse on the Manners of the Ancient Greeks" (which prefaced his translation of Plato's *Symposium*), "Essay on Christianity," the first two chapters of *A Philosophical View of Reform*, and "Essay on the Devil"—the *Defence* is held together by the force of Shelley's personality and his literary and political convictions. Poetry, says Shelley, combines wisdom with delight; it is a source of pleasure; and it inculcates virtue, as readers seek to imitate the noble traits of character that Homer portrays in his heroes. Poetry kindles the sympathetic imagination, enabling us to locate ourselves "in the place of another"; it thereby unites individuals by breaking down the differences among them. It is so closely linked to the society from which it rises that its health serves as a barometer of society's health. It counterbalances the ascendant sciences of calculation and accumulation, which exacerbate inequality and selfishness. It is a universal spiritual force of evanescent inspiration, superseding logic and will and possessing prophetic power. At a memorable moment Shelley even envisions literature as one great poem that all poets have built up since time began.

There are tensions, even contradictions, in Shelley's text that his powerful prose cannot reconcile or explain. Thus, on the one hand, he presents much historical commentary on ancient Greek and Roman literary genres and on the literature of later periods. But, on the other hand, his highest flights of rhetoric pay tribute to the power of poetry to transcend history. There is a gap between the kind of historical particularity that Shelley provides in his literary and cultural comments and the general function that he assigns to poetry as "something divine" that "enlarges the circumference of the imagination."

In addition, Shelley's claims for the special qualities of the poet are problematic in his own terms. In exalting poets as the "best and happiest minds," the "unacknowledged legislators of the World," he paradoxically reinvokes the social distinctions, the ranking of persons, the law-giving from on high, that his works challenge. There may be a darker dimension to the vital, vigorous rhetoric that Shelley mobilizes in defense of literature. As RAYMOND WILLIAMS remarks in *Culture and Society* (1958), Shelley means the word *unacknowledged* to imply poets' importance—their great (albeit almost invisible) sociopolitical work. But the term also carries "the felt helplessness of a generation" as "a culture now dominated by science and industry [fails] to bestow upon poets the 'acknowledgment' that they merit." Williams also points out the mixed implications of Shelley's language about poets: their special high status both distinguishes and marginalizes them, separating them from the community to which Shelley insists they contribute so much.

The poet, Shelley maintains, is a power working for social and moral transformation—the chief influence in civilizing the community. Yet the poet, he also says, is "a nightingale, who sits in darkness and sings to cheer its own solitude with sweet sounds." Shelley's forthright testimonies on behalf of poetry and the tensions and contradictions that his rhetoric attempts to surmount continue to fascinate the *Defence*'s readers.

A *Defence of Poetry* Keywords: The Canon/Tradition, Epic, Ethics, Language, Literary History, Poetry, Religion, Romantic Theory

From A Defence of Poetry, or Remarks Suggested by an Essay Entitled "The Four Ages of Poetry"[1]

* * *

Poetry is ever accompanied with pleasure: all spirits on which it falls, open themselves to receive the wisdom which is mingled with its delight. In the infancy of the world, neither poets themselves nor their auditors are fully aware of the excellence of poetry: for it acts in a divine and unapprehended manner, beyond and above consciousness; and it is reserved for future generations to contemplate and measure the mighty cause and effect in all the strength and splendour of their union.[2] Even in modern times, no living poet ever arrived at the fulness of his fame; the jury which sits in judgement upon a poet, belonging as he does to all time, must be composed of his peers: it must be impanelled by Time from the selectest of the wise of many generations. A Poet is a nightingale, who sits in darkness and sings to cheer its own solitude with sweet sounds; his auditors are as men entranced by the melody of an unseen musician, who feel that they are moved and softened, yet know not whence or why. The poems of Homer and his contemporaries were the delight of infant Greece; they were the elements of that social system which is the column upon which all succeeding civilization has reposed. Homer embodied the ideal perfection of his age in human character; nor can we doubt that those who read his verses were awakened to an ambition of becoming like to Achilles, Hector and Ulysses:[3] the truth and beauty of friendship, patriotism and persevering devotion to an object, were unveiled to the depths in these immortal creations: the sentiments of the auditors must have been refined and enlarged by a sympathy with such great and lovely impersonations, until from admiring they imitated, and from imitation they identified themselves with the objects of their admiration. Nor let it be objected, that these characters are remote from moral perfection, and that they can by no means be considered as edifying patterns for general imitation. Every epoch under names more or less specious has deified its peculiar errors; Revenge is the naked Idol of the worship of a semi-barbarous age; and Self-deceit is the veiled Image of unknown evil before which luxury and satiety lie prostrate. But a poet considers the vices of his contemporaries as the temporary dress in which his creations must be arrayed, and which cover without concealing the eternal proportions of their beauty. An epic or dramatic personage is understood to wear them around his soul, as he may the antient armour or the modern uniform around his body; whilst it is easy to conceive a dress more graceful than either. The beauty of the internal nature cannot be so far concealed by its accidental vesture, but that the spirit of its form shall communicate itself to the very disguise, and indicate the shape it hides from the manner in which

1. "The Four Ages of Poetry" (1820), by Thomas Love Peacock (1785–1866), English writer and satirist.

2. This emphasis on the pleasure given by poetry echoes SIR PHILIP SIDNEY'S *Defence of Poesy* (1595). See also WILLIAM WORDSWORTH'S Preface to *Lyrical Ballads* (1800): "Nor let this necessity of producing immediate pleasure be considered as a degradation of the Poet's art. It is far otherwise."

3. Odysseus, the hero of the *Odyssey*. Achilles and Hector are the greatest warriors (Greek and Trojan, respectively) of the *Iliad*. These poems are the earliest Greek epics (ca. 8th c. B.C.E.).

it is worn. A majestic form and graceful motions will express themselves through the most barbarous and tasteless costume. Few poets of the highest class have chosen to exhibit the beauty of their conceptions in its naked truth and splendour; and it is doubtful whether the alloy of costume, habit, etc., be not necessary to temper this planetary music[4] for mortal ears.

The whole objection however of the immorality of poetry rests upon a misconception of the manner in which poetry acts to produce the moral improvement of man. Ethical science arranges the elements which poetry has created, and propounds schemes and proposes examples of civil and domestic life: nor is it for want of admirable doctrines that men hate, and despise, and censure, and deceive, and subjugate one another. But Poetry acts in another and diviner manner. It awakens and enlarges the mind itself by rendering it the receptable of a thousand unapprehended combinations of thought. Poetry lifts the veil from the hidden beauty of the world, and makes familiar objects be as if they were not familiar: it reproduces all that it represents, and the impersonations clothed in its Elysian[5] light stand thenceforward in the minds of those who have once contemplated them, as memorials of that gentle and exalted content which extends itself over all thoughts and actions with which it coexists. The great secret of morals is Love: or a going out of our own nature, and an identification of ourselves with the beautiful which exists in thought, action, or person, not our own.[6] A man, to be greatly good, must imagine intensely and comprehensively; he must put himself in the place of another and of many others; the pains and pleasures of his species must become his own. The great instrument of moral good is the imagination; and poetry administers to the effect by acting upon the cause. Poetry enlarges the circumference of the imagination by replenishing it with thoughts of ever new delight, which have the power of attracting and assimilating to their own nature all other thoughts, and which form new intervals and interstices whose void for ever craves fresh food. Poetry strengthens that faculty which is the organ of the moral nature of man, in the same manner as exercise strengthens a limb. A Poet therefore would do ill to embody his own conceptions of right and wrong, which are usually those of his place and time, in his poetical creations, which participate in neither. By this assumption of the inferior office of interpreting the effect, in which perhaps after all he might acquit himself but imperfectly, he would resign the glory in a participation in the cause. There was little danger that Homer, or any of the eternal poets, should have so far misunderstood themselves as to have abdicated this throne of their widest dominion. Those in whom the poetical faculty, though great, is less intense, as Euripides, Lucan, Tasso, Spenser,[7] have frequently affected a moral aim, and the effect of their poetry is diminished in exact proportion to the degree in which they compel us to advert to this purpose.

4. The music of the spheres: the beautiful sound said to be made by the movements of the planets.
5. Paradisiacal. According to classical mythology, after death the blessed dwell in the Elysian Fields.
6. Editors have noted the influence here of PLATO's *Symposium* (ca. 384 B.C.E.), which Shelley himself translated. He rendered one of its key sentences "Love, therefore, and every thing else that desires anything, desires that which is absent and beyond his reach, that which it has not, that which is not itself, that which it wants."
7. Edmund Spenser (1552–1599), English poet. Euripides (ca. 485–ca. 406 B.C.E.), Greek tragedian. Lucan (39–65 C.E.), Roman poet. Torquato Tasso (1544–1595), Italian poet.

Homer and the cyclic poets[8] were followed at a certain interval by the dramatic and lyrical Poets of Athens, who flourished contemporaneously with all that is most perfect in the kindred expressions of the poetical faculty; architecture, painting, music, the dance, sculpture, philosophy, and we may add the forms of civil life. For although the scheme of Athenian society was deformed by many imperfections[9] which the poetry existing in Chivalry and Christianity have erased from the habits and institutions of modern Europe; yet never at any other period has so much energy, beauty, and virtue, been developed: never was blind strength and stubborn form so disciplined and rendered subject to the will of man, or that will less repugnant to the dictates of the beautiful and the true, as during the century which preceded the death of Socrates.[1] Of no other epoch in the history of our species have we records and fragments stamped so visibly with the image of the divinity in man. But it is Poetry alone, in form, in action, or in language, which has rendered this epoch memorable above all others, and the storehouse of examples to everlasting time. For written poetry existed at the epoch simultaneously with the other arts, and it is an idle enquiry to demand which gave and which received the light, which all as from a common focus have scattered over the darkest periods of succeeding time. We know no more of cause and effect than a constant conjunction of events: Poetry is ever found to coexist with whatever other arts contribute to the happiness and perfection of man. I appeal to what has already been established to distinguish between the cause and the effect.

It was at the period here adverted to, that the Drama had its birth; and however a succeeding writer may have equalled or surpassed those few great specimens of the Athenian drama which have been preserved to us, it is indisputable that the art itself never was understood or practised according to the true philosophy of it, as at Athens. For the Athenians employed language, action, music, painting, the dance, and religious institutions, to produce a common effect in the representation of the highest idealisms of passion and of power; each division in the art was made perfect in its kind by artists of the most consummate skill, and was disciplined into a beautiful proportion and unity one towards another. On the modern stage a few only of the elements capable of expressing the image of the poet's conception are employed at once. We have tragedy without music and dancing; and music and dancing without the highest impersonations of which they are the fit accompaniment, and both without religion and solemnity. Religious institution has indeed been usually banished from the stage. Our system of divesting the actor's face of a mask, on which the many expressions appropriated to his dramatic character might be moulded into one permanent and unchanging expression, is favourable only to a partial and inharmonious effect; it is fit for nothing but a monologue, where all the attention may be directed to some great master of ideal mimicry. The modern practice of blending comedy with tragedy, though liable to great abuse in point of practice, is undoubtedly an extension of the dramatic circle; but the comedy

8. Poets after Homer who filled out the story of the Trojan War.

9. That is, slavery and the second-class status of women (Shelley explicitly names these "imperfections" below).

1. That is, the 5th century B.C.E., the golden age of Athenian politics and art (the philosopher Socrates was put to death in 399 B.C.E.).

should be as in King Lear, universal, ideal, and sublime. It is perhaps the intervention of this principle which determines the balance in favour of King Lear against the Œdipus Tyrannus or the Agamemnon, or, if you will, the trilogies with which they are connected;[2] unless the intense power of the choral poetry, especially that of the latter, should be considered as restoring the equilibrium. King Lear, if it can sustain this comparison, may be judged to be the most perfect specimen of the dramatic art existing in the world; in spite of the narrow conditions to which the poet was subjected by the ignorance of the philosophy of the Drama which has prevailed in modern Europe. Calderon[3] in his religious Autos has attempted to fulfill some of the high conditions of dramatic representation neglected by Shakespeare; such as the establishing a relation between the drama and religion, and the accommodating them to music and dancing; but he omits the observation of conditions still more important, and more is lost than gained by a substitution of the rigidly-defined and ever-repeated idealisms of a distorted superstition for the living impersonations of the truth of human passion.

But we digress.—The Author of the Four Ages of Poetry has prudently omitted to dispute on the effect of the Drama upon life and manners. For, if I know the knight by the device of his shield, I have only to inscribe Philoctetes[4] or Agamemnon or Othello upon mine to put to flight the giant sophisms which have enchanted him, as the mirror of intolerable light, though on the arm of one of the weakest of the Paladins,[5] could blind and scatter whole armies of necromancers and pagans. The connexion of scenic exhibitions with the improvement or corruption of the manners of men, has been universally recognized: in other words, the presence or absence of poetry in its most perfect and universal form has been found to be connected with good and evil in conduct and habit. The corruption which has been imputed to the drama as an effect, begins, when the poetry employed in its constitution, ends: I appeal to the history of manners whether the periods of the growth of the one and the decline of the other have not corresponded with an exactness equal to any other example of moral cause and effect.

The drama at Athens, or wheresoever else it may have approached to its perfection, coexisted with the moral and intellectual greatness of the age. The tragedies of the Athenian poets are as mirrors in which the spectator beholds himself, under a thin disguise of circumstance, stript of all but that ideal perfection and energy which every one feels to be the internal type of all that he loves, admires, and would become. The imagination is enlarged by a sympathy with pains and passions so mighty, that they distend in their conception the capacity of that by which they are conceived; the good affections are strengthened by pity, indignation, terror and sorrow;[6] and an exalted calm is prolonged from the satiety of this high exercise of them into

2. Sophocles' "trilogy" (the plays were not performed together) is *Oedipus Rex* (ca. 430 B.C.E.), *Oedipus Coloneus* (ca. 401), and *Antigone* (ca. 441); Aeschylus's Oresteian trilogy (458) comprises *Agamemnon, The Libation Bearers*, and *The Eumenides*. *King Lear* was first performed ca. 1605.

3. Pedro Calderón de la Barca (1600–1681), Spanish dramatist and poet; after he became a priest in 1651, he wrote only *autos sacramentales*, one-act religious dramas (usually allegorical).

4. Greek hero in the Trojan War and the subject of many tragedies; that by Sophocles (ca. 409 B.C.E.) survives.

5. The twelve peers of the court of Charlemagne (742–814), king of the Franks and founder of the first western European empire after the fall of Rome.

6. One interpretation of ARISTOTLE's idea of "catharsis" in tragedy, expressed in *Poetics* 6, 1449b (see above).

the tumult of familiar life; even crime is disarmed of half its horror and all its contagion by being represented as the fatal consequence of the unfathomable agencies of nature; error is thus divested of its wilfulness; men can no longer cherish it as the creation of their choice. In a drama of the highest order there is little food for censure or hatred; it teaches rather self-knowledge and self-respect. Neither the eye nor the mind can see itself, unless reflected upon that which it resembles. The drama, so long as it continues to express poetry, is as a prismatic and many-sided mirror, which collects the brightest rays of human nature and divides and reproduces them from the simplicity of these elementary forms, and touches them with majesty and beauty, and multiplies all that it reflects, and endows it with the power of propagating its like wherever it may fall.

But in periods of the decay of social life, the drama sympathizes with that decay. Tragedy becomes a cold imitation of the form of the great masterpieces of antiquity, divested of all harmonious accompaniment of the kindred arts; and often the very form misunderstood: or a weak attempt to teach certain doctrines, which the writer considers as moral truths; and which are usually no more than specious flatteries of some gross vice or weakness with which the author in common with his auditors are infected. Hence what has been called the classical and domestic drama. Addison's "Cato"[7] is a specimen of the one; and would it were not superfluous to cite examples of the other! To such purposes Poetry cannot be made subservient. Poetry is a sword of lightning, ever unsheathed, which consumes the scabbard that would contain it. And thus we observe that all dramatic writings of this nature are unimaginative in a singular degree; they affect sentiment and passion: which, divested of imagination, are other names for caprice and appetite. The period in our own history of the grossest degradation of the drama is the reign of Charles II[8] when all forms in which poetry had been accustomed to be expressed became hymns to the triumph of kingly power over liberty and virtue. Milton[9] stood alone illuminating an age unworthy of him. At such periods the calculating principle pervades all the forms of dramatic exhibition, and poetry ceases to be expressed upon them. Comedy loses its ideal universality: wit succeeds to humour; we laugh from self-complacency and triumph instead of pleasure; malignity, sarcasm and contempt, succeed to sympathetic merriment; we hardly laugh, but we smile. Obscenity, which is ever blasphemy against the divine beauty in life, becomes, from the very veil which it assumes, more active if less disgusting: it is a monster for which the corruption of society for ever brings forth new food, which it devours in secret.

The drama being that form under which a greater number of modes of expression of poetry are susceptible of being combined than any other, the connexion of poetry and social good is more observable in the drama than in whatever other form: and it is indisputable that the highest perfection of human society has ever corresponded with the highest dramatic excellence; and that the corruption or the extinction of the drama in a nation where it

7. The popular neoclassical tragedy (1713) about the Roman statesman Cato by the English poet and essayist JOSEPH ADDISON (1672–1719).

8. King of England (1630–1685; reigned 1660–85) during the Restoration, a period with a reputation for dissoluteness and frivolity.

9. The poet John Milton (1608–1674) was a supporter of the Puritan Revolution and a defender of the execution of Charles I (king of England from 1625 to 1649).

has once flourished, is a mark of a corruption of manners, and an extinction of the energies which sustain the soul of social life. But, as Machiavelli[1] says of political institutions, that life may be preserved and renewed, if men should arise capable of bringing back the drama to its principles. And this is true with respect to poetry in its most extended sense: all language, institution and form, require not only to be produced but to be sustained: the office and character of a poet participates in the divine nature as regards providence, no less than as regards creation.

Civil war, the spoils of Asia, and the fatal predominance first of the Macedonian,[2] and then of the Roman arms were so many symbols of the extinction or suspension of the creative faculty in Greece. The bucolic writers,[3] who found patronage under the lettered tyrants of Sicily and Egypt, were the latest representatives of its most glorious reign. Their poetry is intensely melodious: like the odour of the tuberose,[4] it overcomes and sickens the spirit with excess of sweetness; whilst the poetry of the preceding age was as a meadow-gale of June which mingles the fragrance of all the flowers of the field, and adds a quickening and harmonizing spirit of its own which endows the sense with a power of sustaining its extreme delight. The bucolic and erotic delicacy in written poetry is correlative with that softness in statuary, music, and the kindred arts, and even in manners and institutions which distinguished the epoch to which we now refer. Nor is it the poetical faculty itself, or any misapplication of it, to which this want of harmony is to be imputed. An equal sensibility to the influence of the senses and the affections is to be found in the writings of Homer and Sophocles: the former especially has clothed sensual and pathetic images with irresistible attractions. Their superiority over these succeeding writers consists in the presence of those thoughts which belong to the inner faculties of our nature, not in the absence of those which are connected with the external; their incomparable perfection consists in an harmony of the union of all. It is not what the erotic writers have, but what they have not, in which their imperfection consists. It is not inasmuch as they were Poets, but inasmuch as they were not Poets, that they can be considered with any plausibility as connected with the corruption of their age. Had that corruption availed so as to extinguish in them the sensibility to pleasure, passion and natural scenery, which is imputed to them as an imperfection, the last triumph of evil would have been achieved. For the end of social corruption is to destroy all sensibility to pleasure; and therefore it is corruption. It begins at the imagination and the intellect as at the core, and distributes itself thence as a paralyzing venom, through the affections into the very appetites, until all become a torpid mass in which sense hardly survives. At the approach of such a period, Poetry ever addresses itself to those faculties which are the last to be destroyed, and its voice is heard, like the footsteps of Astræa,[5] departing from the world. Poetry ever

1. Niccolò Machiavelli (1469–1527), Italian political philosopher; he discusses political institutions in *The Prince* (written 1513; published 1532), and *The Discourses* (ca. 1518).

2. Alexander the Great (356–323 B.C.E.), king of Macedonia, whose conquests extended to Egypt and India.

3. Greek pastoral poets, who wrote of shepherds and country folk; the first was Theocritus (ca. 300–ca. 260 B.C.E.), followed by Moschus (active ca. 150 B.C.E.) and Bion (active ca. 100 B.C.E.).

4. A plant with grasslike leaves; it is cultivated for its highly fragrant white flowers, which yield an oil formerly used in perfume.

5. The goddess of justice. She dwelled on earth during the Golden Age but was driven into heaven during the Iron Age by humanity's evil ways. See Ovid, *Metamorphoses* (ca. 10 C.E.), 1.149–50; Juvenal, *Satire* 6.19–20 (ca. 116 C.E.).

communicates all the pleasure which men are capable of receiving: it is ever still the light of life; the source of whatever of beautiful, or generous, or true can have place in an evil time. It will readily be confessed that those among the luxurious citizens of Syracuse and Alexandria who were delighted with the poems of Theocritus, were less cold, cruel and sensual than the remnant of their tribe. But corruption must have utterly destroyed the fabric of human society before Poetry can ever cease. The sacred links of that chain have never been entirely disjoined, which descending through the minds of many men is attached to those great minds, whence as from a magnet the invisible effluence is sent forth, which at once connects, animates and sustains the life of all. It is the faculty which contains within itself the seeds at once of its own and of social renovation. And let us not circumscribe the effects of the bucolic and erotic poetry within the limits of the sensibility of those to whom it was addressed. They may have perceived the beauty of those immortal compositions, simply as fragments and isolated portions: those who are more finely organized, or born in a happier age, may recognize them as episodes to that great poem, which all poets, like the co-operating thoughts of one great mind, have built up since the beginning of the world.

The same revolutions within a narrower sphere had place in antient Rome; but the actions and forms of its social life never seem to have been perfectly saturated with the poetical element. The Romans appear to have considered the Greeks as the selectest treasuries of the selectest forms of manners and of nature, and to have abstained from creating in measured language, sculpture, music or architecture, anything which might bear a particular relation to their own condition, whilst it should bear a general one to the universal constitution of the world. But we judge from partial evidence; and we judge perhaps partially. Ennius, Varro, Pacuvius, and Accius,[6] all great poets, have been lost. Lucretius is in the highest, and Virgil[7] in a very high sense, a creator. The chosen delicacy of the expressions of the latter is as a mist of light which conceals from us the intense and exceeding truth of his conceptions of nature. Livy[8] is instinct with poetry. Yet Horace, Catullus, Ovid,[9] and generally the other great writers of the Virgilian age, saw man and nature in the mirror of Greece. The institutions also and the religion of Rome were less poetical than those of Greece, as the shadow is less vivid than the substance. Hence poetry in Rome, seemed to follow rather than accompany the perfection of political and domestic society. The true Poetry of Rome lived in its institutions; for whatever of beautiful, true and majestic they contained could have sprung only from the faculty which creates the order in which they consist. The life of Camillus, the death of Regulus;[1] the expecta-

6. All pre-Augustan writers, whose work survives only in fragments: Ennius (239–169 B.C.E.), author of tragedies, comedies, prose, and an epic on Roman history, *Annales*; Varro (116–27 B.C.E.), the greatest scholar among the Romans, who wrote or edited hundreds of books (one on the Latin language survives in part, together with a volume of a work on farm management); Pacuvius (220–ca. 130 B.C.E.), author of tragedies and satires; and Accius (170–ca. 90 B.C.E.), author of tragedies and a 9-book poem on the history of literature, *Didascalica*.

7. Author (70–19 B.C.E.) of the *Aeneid*, generally considered the greatest Latin epic. Lucretius (ca. 94–55 B.C.E.), philosopher and author of a didactic Epicurean poem, *On the Nature of Things*.

8. Roman historian (59 B.C.E.–17 C.E.).

9. Author (43 B.C.E.–17 C.E.) of love poetry, fictional love letters, and the mock-heroic *Metamorphoses*. HORACE (65–8 B.C.E.), author of odes, satires, epistles, and the *Ars Poetica* (see above). Catullus (ca. 84–ca. 54 B.C.E.), author of lyric love poetry and elegy.

1. Marcus Atilius Regulus (d. ca. 249 B.C.E.), Roman general who, though himself held by the Carthaginians, persuaded the Roman Senate not to ransom him and the other soldiers; he

tion of the Senators, in their godlike state, of the victorious Gauls; the refusal of the Republic to make peace with Hannibal after the battle of Cannae,[2] were not the consequences of a refined calculation of the probable personal advantage to result from such a rhythm and order in the shews of life, to those who were at once the poets and the actors of the immortal dramas. The imagination beholding the beauty of this order, created it out of itself according to its own idea: the consequence was empire, and the reward ever-living fame. These things are not the less poetry, *quia carent vate sacro.*[3] They are the episodes of the cyclic poem written by Time upon the memories of men. The Past, like an inspired rhapsodist, fills the theatre of everlasting generations with their harmony.

At length the antient system of religion and manners had fulfilled the circle of its revolution. And the world would have fallen into utter anarchy and darkness, but that there were found poets among the authors of the Christian and Chivalric systems of manners and religion, who created forms of opinion and action never before conceived; which, copied into the imaginations of men, became as generals to the bewildered armies of their thoughts. It is foreign to the present purpose to touch upon the evil produced by these systems: except that we protest, on the ground of the principles already established, that no portion of it can be imputed to the poetry they contain.

It is probable that the astonishing poetry of Moses, Job, David, Solomon and Isaiah[4] had produced a great effect upon the mind of Jesus and his disciples. The scattered fragments preserved to us by the biographers of this extraordinary person, are all instinct with the most vivid poetry. But his doctrines seem to have been quickly distorted. At a certain period after the prevalence of a system of opinions founded upon those promulgated by him, the three forms into which Plato had distributed the faculties of mind[5] underwent a sort of apotheosis, and became the object of the worship of the civilized world. Here it is to be confessed that "Light seems to thicken," and

> The crow makes wing to the rooky wood,
> Good things of day begin to droop and drowze,
> And night's black agents to their preys do rouze.[6]

But mark how beautiful an order has sprung from the dust and blood of this fierce chaos! how the World, as from a resurrection, balancing itself on the golden wings of knowledge and of hope, has reassumed its yet unwearied flight into the Heaven of time. Listen to the music, unheard by outward ears, which is as a ceaseless and invisible wind, nourishing its everlasting course with strength and swiftness.

---

returned to Carthage and died in captivity (perhaps tortured to death; see Horace, *Odes* 3.5). Marcus Furius Camillus (d. ca. 365 B.C.E.), the second founder of Rome, who managed the city's military and political recovery after the Gallic invasion of 387/86 B.C.E.

2. Village in Apulia where in 216 B.C.E. the Romans suffered a major defeat by Hannibal, the great Carthaginian general (247–183/82 B.C.E.); the Romans ultimately won the war, however.

3. Because they lack a sacred poet (Latin); from Horace, *Odes* 4.9.28.

4. Job and Isaiah were once regarded as the authors of the books of the Bible given their names; Moses is traditionally credited with writing the entire Torah (the first five books of the Bible); David was thought to have composed most of the Psalms; Ecclesiastes, Proverbs, and the Song of Solomon were ascribed to Solomon.

5. Plato divided the human soul into three parts: the desiring, the rational, and the spirited (see *Republic* 4.439d–444a).

6. *Macbeth* (ca. 1606), 3.2.51–54, slightly misquoted.

The poetry in the doctrines of Jesus Christ, and the mythology and institutions of the Celtic conquerors of the Roman empire,[7] outlived the darkness and the convulsions connected with their growth and victory, and blended themselves into a new fabric of manners and opinion. It is an error to impute the ignorance of the dark ages to the Christian doctrines or the predominance of the Celtic nations. Whatever of evil their agencies may have contained sprung from the extinction of the poetical principle, connected with the progress of despotism and superstition. Men, from causes too intricate to be here discussed, had become insensible and selfish: their own will had become feeble, and yet they were its slaves, and thence the slaves of the will of others: lust, fear, avarice, cruelty and fraud, characterised a race amongst whom no one was to be found capable of *creating* in form, language, or institution. The moral anomalies of such a state of society are not justly to be charged upon any class of events immediately connected with them, and those events are most entitled to our approbation which could dissolve it most expeditiously. It is unfortunate for those who cannot distinguish words from thoughts, that many of these anomalies have been incorporated into our popular religion.

It was not until the eleventh century that the effects of the poetry of the Christian and Chivalric systems began to manifest themselves. The principle of equality had been discovered and applied by Plato in his Republic, as the theoretical rule of the mode in which the materials of pleasure and of power produced by the common skill and labour of human beings ought to be distributed among them. The limitations of this rule were asserted by him to be determined only by the sensibility of each, or the utility to result to all. Plato, following the doctrines of Timæus and Pythagoras,[8] taught also a moral and intellectual system of doctrine comprehending at once the past, the present, and the future condition of man. Jesus Christ divulged the sacred and eternal truths contained in these views to mankind, and Christianity, in its abstract purity, became the exoteric expression of the esoteric doctrines of the poetry and wisdom of antiquity. The incorporation of the Celtic nations with the exhausted population of the South, impressed upon it the figure of the poetry existing in their mythology and institutions. The result was a sum of the action and reaction of all the causes included in it; for it may be assumed as a maxim that no nation or religion can supersede any other without incorporating into itself a portion of that which it supersedes. The abolition of personal and domestic slavery, and the emancipation of women from a great part of the degrading restraints of antiquity were among the consequences of these events.

The abolition of personal slavery is the basis of the highest political hope that it can enter into the mind of man to conceive. The freedom of women produced the poetry of sexual love. Love became a religion, the idols of whose worship were ever present. It was as if the statues of Apollo and the Muses[9] had been endowed with life and motion and had walked forth among their worshippers; so that earth became peopled by the inhabitants

7. The Germanic tribes of northern Europe.
8. Greek philosopher and mathematician (ca. 6th c. B.C.E.). Timaeus: a Pythagorean, perhaps a fictional character, who is the key speaker in Plato's *Timaeus*.
9. In Greek mythology, 9 daughters of Memory who preside over the arts and all intellectual pursuits. Apollo: Greek and Roman god of poetry.

of a diviner world. The familiar appearance and proceedings of life became wonderful and heavenly; and a paradise was created as out of the wrecks of Eden. And as this creation itself is poetry, so its creators were poets; and language were the instrument of their art: "Galeotto fù il libro, e chi lo scrisse."[1] The Provençal Trouveurs, or inventors, preceded Petrarch,[2] whose verses are as spells, which unseal the inmost enchanted fountains of the delight which is in the grief of Love. It is impossible to feel them without becoming a portion of that beauty which we contemplate: it were superfluous to explain how the gentleness and the elevation of mind connected with these sacred emotions can render men more amiable, more generous, and wise, and lift them out of the dull vapours of the little world of self. Dante understood the secret things of love even more than Petrarch. His *Vita Nuova*[3] is an inexhaustible fountain of purity of sentiment and language: it is the idealized history of that period, and those intervals of his life which were dedicated to love. His apotheosis of Beatrice in Paradise and the gradations of his own love and her loveliness, by which as by steps he feigns himself to have ascended to the throne of the Supreme Cause, is the most glorious imagination of modern poetry. The acutest critics have justly reversed the judgement of the vulgar, and the order of the great acts of the "Divine Drama," in the measure of the admiration which they accord to the Hell, Purgatory and Paradise.[4] The latter is a perpetual hymn of everlasting love. Love, which found a worthy poet in Plato alone of all the antients, has been celebrated by a chorus of the greatest writers of the renovated world; and the music has penetrated the caverns of society, and its echoes still drown the dissonance of arms and superstition. At successive intervals, Ariosto, Tasso, Shakespeare, Spenser, Calderon, Rousseau,[5] and the great writers of our own age, have celebrated the dominion of love, planting as it were trophies in the human mind of that sublimest victory over sensuality and force. The true relation borne to each other by the sexes into which human kind is distributed has become less misunderstood; and if the error which confounded diversity with inequality of the powers of the two sexes has become partially recognized in the opinions and institutions of modern Europe, we owe this great benefit to the worship of which Chivalry was the law, and poets the prophets.

The poetry of Dante may be considered as the bridge thrown over the stream of time, which unites the modern and antient world. The distorted notions of invisible things which Dante and his rival Milton have idealized, are merely the mask and the mantle in which these great poets walk through eternity enveloped and disguised. It is a difficult question to determine how far they were conscious of the distinction which must have subsisted in their minds between their own creeds and that of the people. Dante at least appears to wish to mark the full extent of it by placing Riphæus, whom Virgil calls *justissimus unus*, in Paradise,[6] and observing a most heretical caprice

1. Gallehaut was the book and he who wrote it (Italian). From DANTE ALIGHIERI, *Inferno* (1321), 5.137.
2. Francesco Petrarca (1304–1374), Italian poet and scholar. "Provençal": the language of southern France. The troubadours of the south, 12th- and 13th-century poets, were the first to celebrate chivalric and courtly love.
3. *New Life* (ca. 1293), poetry and prose that tell of Dante's love for Beatrice.
4. The 3 books of Dante's *Divine Comedy*.
5. Jean-Jacques Rousseau (1712–1778), Swiss-born French philosopher and political theorist. Ludovico Ariosto (1474–1533), Italian epic poet.
6. Dante makes the Trojan warrior Riphaeus the only pagan in Paradise (see *Paradiso*, canto 20). *Justissimus unus*: the one most just [who was among the Trojans]; Virgil, *Aeneid* 2.426–27.

in his distribution of rewards and punishments. And Milton's poem contains within itself a philosophical refutation of that system of which, by a strange and natural antithesis, it has been a chief popular support. Nothing can exceed the energy and magnificence of the character of Satan as expressed in Paradise Lost.[7] It is a mistake to suppose that he could ever have been intended for the popular personification of evil. Implacable hate, patient cunning, and a sleepless refinement of device to inflict the extremest anguish on an enemy, these things are evil; and although venial in a slave are not to be forgiven in a tyrant; although redeemed by much that ennobles his defeat in one subdued, are marked by all that dishonours his conquest in the victor. Milton's Devil as a moral being is as far superior to his God as one who perseveres in some purpose which he has conceived to be excellent in spite of adversity and torture, is to one who in the cold security of undoubted triumph inflicts the most horrible revenge upon his enemy, not from any mistaken notion of inducing him to repent of a perseverance in enmity, but with the alleged design of exasperating him to deserve new torments. Milton has so far violated the popular creed (if this shall be judged to be a violation) as to have alleged no superiority of moral virtue to his God over his Devil. And this bold neglect of a direct moral purpose is the most decisive proof of the supremacy of Milton's genius. He mingled as it were the elements of human nature, as colours upon a single pallet, and arranged them into the composition of his great picture according to the laws of epic truth; that is, according to the laws of that principle by which a series of actions of the external universe and of intelligent and ethical beings is calculated to excite the sympathy of succeeding generations of mankind. The Divina Commedia and Paradise Lost have conferred upon modern mythology a systematic form; and when change and time shall have added one more superstition to the mass of those which have arisen and decayed upon the earth, commentators will be learnedly employed in elucidating the religion of ancestral Europe, only not utterly forgotten because it will have been stamped with the eternity of genius.

Homer was the first, and Dante the second epic poet: that is, the second poet the series of whose creations bore a defined and intelligible relation to the knowledge, and sentiment, and religion, and political conditions of the age in which he lived, and of the ages which followed it, developing itself in correspondence with their development. For Lucretius had limed the wings of his swift spirit in the dregs of the sensible world; and Virgil, with a modesty which ill became his genius, had affected the fame of an imitator even whilst he created anew all that he copied; and none among the flock of mock-birds, though their notes were sweet, Apollonius Rhodius, Quintus Calaber Smyrnæus, Nonnus, Lucan, Statius, or Claudian,[8] have sought

7. Shelley echoes the Romantic poet William Blake: "The reason Milton wrote in fetters when he wrote of Angels & God, and at liberty when of Devils & Hell, is because he was a true Poet and of the Devils party without knowing it," and "Energy is Eternal Delight" (*The Marriage of Heaven and Hell*, 1790). *Paradise Lost* was published in 1667.

8. Classical epic poets of varying quality, the first three writing in Greek and the others in Latin: Apollonius (3d c. B.C.E.), author of the *Argonautica*; Quintus Smyrnaeus (4th c. C.E.), author of a sequel to Homer's *Iliad*; Nonnus (5th c. C.E.), author of the 48-book *Dionysiaca*; Lucan, author of the *Civil War*; Statius (ca. 45–96 C.E.), author of the epic *Thebais*; and Claudian (d. 404 C.E.), a Greek-speaking Alexandrian whose poetry, including an unfinished epic, *The Rape of Proserpina*, marked the end of the classical tradition in Latin poetry.

even to fulfil a single condition of epic truth. Milton was the third Epic Poet. For if the title of epic in its highest sense be refused to the Æneid, still less can it be conceded to the Orlando Furioso, the Gerusalemme Liberata, the Lusiad, or the Fairy Queen.[9]

Dante and Milton were both deeply penetrated with the antient religion of the civilized world; and its spirit exists in their poetry probably in the same proportion as its forms survived in the unreformed worship of modern Europe. The one preceded and the other followed the Reformation at almost equal intervals. Dante was the first religious reformer, and Luther[1] surpassed him rather in the rudeness and acrimony, than in the boldness of his censures of papal usurpation. Dante was the first awakener of entranced Europe: he created a language in itself music and persuasion out of a chaos of inharmonious barbarisms. He was the congregator of those great spirits who presided over the resurrection of learning; the Lucifer[2] of that starry flock which in the thirteenth century shone forth from republican Italy, as from a heaven, into the darkness of the benighted world. His very words are instinct with spirit; each is as a spark, a burning atom of inextinguishable thought; and many yet lie covered in the ashes of their birth, and pregnant with a lightning which has yet found no conductor. All high poetry is infinite; it is as the first acorn, which contained all oaks potentially. Veil after veil may be undrawn, and the inmost naked beauty of the meaning never exposed. A great Poem is a fountain for ever overflowing with the waters of wisdom and delight; and after one person and one age has exhausted all its divine effluence which their peculiar relations enable them to share, another and yet another succeeds, and new relations are ever developed, the source of an unforeseen and an unconceived delight.

The age immediately succeeding to that of Dante, Petrarch, and Boccaccio,[3] was characterized by a revival of painting, sculpture, music, and architecture. Chaucer[4] caught the sacred inspiration, and the superstructure of English literature is based upon the materials of Italian invention.

But let us not be betrayed from a defence into a critical history of Poetry and its influence on Society. Be it enough to have pointed out the effects of poets, in the large and true sense of the word, upon their own and all succeeding times and to revert to the partial instances cited as illustrations of an opinion the reverse of that attempted to be established in the Four Ages of Poetry.

But poets have been challenged to resign the civic crown to reasoners and mechanists on another plea. It is admitted that the exercise of the imagination is most delightful, but it is alleged that that of reason is more useful. Let us examine as the grounds of this distinction, what is here meant by Utility.[5] Pleasure or good in a general sense, is that which the consciousness

9. Shelley names epics by, respectively, Ariosto (1516, 1532), Tasso (1581), the Portuguese Luis Vaz de Camões (1572), and Spenser (1590, 1596).

1. Martin Luther (1483–1546), German theologian and reformer, founder of the Reformation.

2. Literally, "light bearer" (Latin), the morning star. In Milton's *Paradise Lost*, Lucifer is the leader of the revolt of the angels against God, and is called Satan after his fall.

3. GIOVANNI BOCCACCIO (1313–1375), Italian writer and poet.

4. Geoffrey Chaucer (ca. 1343–1400), whose poetry drew strongly on the works of the three Italians named (especially Boccaccio).

5. Shelley replies here to the followers of Jeremy Bentham (1748–1832), English social reformer and philosopher, the founder of utilitarianism; he claimed that all conduct and legislation should aim at "the greatest happiness of the greatest number," and formulated a calculus of pleasure. Peacock argues in "The Four Ages of Poetry": "[Poetry] can never make a philosopher nor a statesman nor in any class of life a useful or rational man. It cannot claim the slightest share in any one of the comforts or utilities of life."

of a sensitive and intelligent being seeks, and in which when found it acquiesces. There are two kinds of pleasure, one durable, universal, and permanent; the other transitory and particular. Utility may either express the means of producing the former or the latter. In the former sense, whatever strengthens and purifies the affections, enlarges the imagination, and adds spirit to sense, is useful. But the meaning in which the Author of the Four Ages of Poetry seems to have employed the word utility is the narrower one of banishing the importunity of the wants of our animal nature, the surrounding men with security of life, the dispersing the grosser delusions of superstition, and the conciliating such a degree of mutual forbearance among men as may consist with the motives of personal advantage.

Undoubtedly the promoters of utility in this limited sense, have their appointed office in society. They follow the footsteps of poets, and copy the sketches of their creations into the book of common life. They make space, and give time. Their exertions are of the highest value so long as they confine their administration of the concerns of the inferior powers of our nature within the limits due to the superior ones. But whilst the sceptic destroys gross superstitions, let him spare to deface, as some of the French writers have defaced, the eternal truths charactered upon the imaginations of men. Whilst the mechanist abridges, and the political œconomist combines, labour, let them beware that their speculations, for want of correspondence with those first principles which belong to the imagination, do not tend, as they have in modern England, to exasperate at once the extremes of luxury and want. They have exemplified the saying, "To him that hath, more shall be given; and from him that hath not, the little that he hath shall be taken away."[6] The rich have become richer, and the poor have become poorer; and the vessel of the state is driven between the Scylla and Charybdis[7] of anarchy and despotism. Such are the effects which must ever flow from an unmitigated exercise of the calculating faculty.

It is difficult to define pleasure in its highest sense; the definition involving a number of apparent paradoxes. For, from an inexplicable defect of harmony in the constitution of human nature, the pain of the inferior is frequently connected with the pleasures of the superior portions of our being. Sorrow, terror, anguish, despair itself are often the chosen expressions of an approximation to the highest good. Our sympathy in tragic fiction depends on this principle; tragedy delights by affording a shadow of the pleasure which exists in pain. This is the source also of the melancholy which is inseparable from the sweetest melody. The pleasure that is in sorrow is sweeter than the pleasure of pleasure itself. And hence the saying, "It is better to go to the house of mourning, than to the house of mirth."[8] Not that this highest species of pleasure is necessarily linked with pain. The delight of love and friendship, the ecstasy of the admiration of nature, the joy of the perception and still more of the creation of poetry is often wholly unalloyed.

The production and assurance of pleasure in this highest sense is true utility. Those who produce and preserve this pleasure are Poets or poetical philosophers.

6. Mark 4.25.
7. That is, two equal dangers. In Greek mythology, Scylla and Charybdis are two monsters (who become a rock and whirlpool, respectively) that endanger sailors between Sicily and Italy.
8. Ecclesiastes 7.2.

The exertions of Locke, Hume, Gibbon, Voltaire, Rousseau,[9] and their disciples, in favour of oppressed and deluded humanity, are entitled to the gratitude of mankind. Yet it is easy to calculate the degree of moral and intellectual improvement which the world would have exhibited, had they never lived. A little more nonsense would have been talked for a century or two; and perhaps a few more men, women, and children, burnt as heretics. We might not at this moment have been congratulating each other on the abolition of the Inquisition in Spain.[1] But it exceeds all imagination to conceive what would have been the moral condition of the world if neither Dante, Petrarch, Boccaccio, Chaucer, Shakespeare, Calderon, Lord Bacon, nor Milton, had ever existed; if Raphael and Michael Angelo[2] had never been born; if the Hebrew poetry had never been translated; if a revival of the study of Greek literature had never taken place; if no monuments of antient sculpture had been handed down to us; and if the poetry of the religion of the antient world had been extinguished together with its belief. The human mind could never, except by the intervention of these excitements, have been awakened to the invention of the grosser sciences, and that application of analytical reasoning to the aberrations of society, which it is now attempted to exalt over the direct expression of the inventive and creative faculty itself.

We have more moral, political and historical wisdom, than we know how to reduce into practise; we have more scientific and œconomical knowledge than can be accommodated to the just distribution of the produce which it multiplies. The poetry in these systems of thought, is concealed by the accumulation of facts and calculating processes. There is no want of knowledge respecting what is wisest and best in morals, government, and political œconomy, or at least, what is wiser and better than what men now practise and endure. But we let "*I dare not* wait upon *I would*, like the poor cat i' the adage."[3] We want[4] the creative faculty to imagine that which we know; we want the generous impulse to act that which we imagine; we want the poetry of life: our calculations have outrun conception; we have eaten more than we can digest. The cultivation of those sciences which have enlarged the limits of the empire of man over the external world, has, for want of the poetical faculty, proportionally circumscribed those of the internal world; and man, having enslaved the elements, remains himself a slave. To what but a cultivation of the mechanical arts in a degree disproportioned to the presence of the creative faculty, which is the basis of all knowledge, is to be attributed the abuse of all invention for abridging and combining labour, to the exasperation of the inequality of mankind? From

9. I follow the classification adopted by the author of the Four Ages of Poetry. But Rousseau was essentially a poet. The others, even Voltaire, were mere reasoners [Shelley's note]. John Locke (1632–1704), English philosopher. DAVID HUME (1711–1776), Scottish empiricist philosopher, historian, and economist. Edward Gibbon (1737–1794), English historian best known as the author of *The History of the Decline and Fall of the Roman Empire* (6 vols., 1776–88). Voltaire: pen name of François-Marie Arouet (1694–1778), French writer and philosopher. These figures are apparently linked by their opposition, in different degrees, to Christianity.

1. The Spanish Inquisition, the harsh Roman Catholic tribunal for suppressing heresy, was established in 1478; it was not definitively abolished until the 1820 revolution led by reformist army officers.

2. Michelangelo [Buonarroti] (1475–1564), Italian Renaissance sculptor, painter, and architect. Francis Bacon (1561–1626), English philosopher and essayist. Raphael: Raffaello Sanzio (1483–1520), master painter of the Italian Renaissance.

3. *Macbeth*, 1.7.44–45.

4. Lack.

what other cause has it arisen that the discoveries which should have lightened, have added a weight to the curse imposed on Adam?[5] Poetry, and the principle of Self, of which money is the visible incarnation, are the God and the Mammon[6] of the world.

The functions of the poetical faculty are two-fold; by one it creates new materials of knowledge, and power and pleasure; by the other it engenders in the mind a desire to reproduce and arrange them according to a certain rhythm and order which may be called the beautiful and the good. The cultivation of poetry is never more to be desired than at periods when, from an excess of the selfish and calculating principle, the accumulation of the materials of external life exceed the quantity of the power of assimilating them to the internal laws of human nature. The body has then become too unwieldy for that which animates it.

Poetry is indeed something divine.[7] It is at once the centre and circumference of knowledge; it is that which comprehends all science, and that to which all science must be referred. It is at the same time the root and blossom of all other systems of thought; it is that from which all spring, and that which adorns all; and that which, if blighted, denies the fruit and the seed, and withholds from the barren world the nourishment and the succession of the scions[8] of the tree of life. It is the perfect and consummate surface and bloom of things; it is as the odour and the colour of the rose to the texture of the elements which compose it, as the form and the splendour of unfaded beauty to the secrets of anatomy and corruption. What were Virtue, Love, Patriotism, Friendship &c.—what were the scenery of this beautiful Universe which we inhabit—what were our consolations on this side of the grave—and what were our aspirations beyond it—if Poetry did not ascend to bring light and fire from those eternal regions where the owl-winged faculty of calculation dare not ever soar? Poetry is not like reasoning, a power to be exerted according to the determination of the will. A man cannot say, "I will compose poetry." The greatest poet even cannot say it: for the mind in creation is as a fading coal which some invisible influence, like an inconstant wind, awakens to transitory brightness: this power arises from within, like the colour of a flower which fades and changes as it is developed, and the conscious portions of our natures are unprophetic either of its approach or its departure. Could this influence be durable in its original purity and force, it is impossible to predict the greatness of the results; but when composition begins, inspiration is already on the decline, and the most glorious poetry that has ever been communicated to the world is probably a feeble shadow of the original conception of the poet. I appeal to the greatest Poets of the present day, whether it be not an error to assert that the finest passages of poetry are produced by labour and study. The toil and the delay recommended by critics can be justly interpreted to mean no more than a careful observation of the inspired moments, and an artificial connexion of the

5. That is, the need to labor for a living; imposed on Adam because he and Eve ate the forbidden fruit of the tree of knowledge: "In the sweat of thy face shalt thou eat bread, till thou return unto the ground" (Genesis 3.19).

6. The personification of avarice and lust for worldly gain; according to Matthew 6.24 and Luke 16.13, it is impossible to serve both God and Mammon.

7. Compare Sidney's reference, in *The Defence of Poesy*, to poetry as "a divine gift."

8. Young shoots or twigs of a plant, especially those cut for grafting or rooting.

spaces between their suggestions by the intertexture of conventional expressions; a necessity only imposed by a limitedness of the poetical faculty itself. For Milton conceived the Paradise Lost as a whole before he executed it in portions. We have his own authority also for the Muse having "dictated" to him the "unpremeditated song,"[9] and let this be an answer to those who would allege the fifty-six various readings of the first line of the Orlando Furioso. Compositions so produced are to poetry what mosaic is to painting. This instinct and intuition of the poetical faculty is still more observable in the plastic and pictorial arts: a great statue or picture grows under the power of the artist as a child in the mother's womb, and the very mind which directs the hands in formation is incapable of accounting to itself for the origin, the gradations, or the media of the process.

Poetry is the record of the best and happiest moments of the happiest and best minds. We are aware of evanescent visitations of thought and feeling sometimes associated with place or person, sometimes regarding our own mind alone, and always arising unforeseen and departing unbidden, but elevating and delightful beyond all expression; so that even in the desire and the regret they leave, there cannot but be pleasure, participating as it does in the nature of its object. It is as it were the interpenetration of a diviner nature through our own; but its footsteps are like those of a wind over a sea, which the coming calm erases, and whose traces remain only as on the wrinkled sand which paves it. These and corresponding conditions of being are experienced principally by those of the most delicate sensibility and the most enlarged imagination; and the state of mind produced by them is at war with every base desire. The enthusiasm of virtue, love, patriotism, and friendship is essentially linked with these emotions; and whilst they last, self appears as what it is, an atom to a Universe. Poets are not only subject to these experiences as spirits of the most refined organization, but they can colour all that they combine with the evanescent hues of this ethereal world; a word, a trait in the representation of a scene or a passion, will touch the enchanted chord, and reanimate, in those who have ever experienced these emotions, the sleeping, the cold, the buried image of the past. Poetry thus makes immortal all that is best and most beautiful in the world; it arrests the vanishing apparitions which haunt the interlunations[1] of life, and veiling them or in language or in form sends them forth among mankind, bearing sweet news of kindred joy to those with whom their sisters abide—abide, because there is no portal of expression from the caverns of the spirit which they inhabit into the universe of things. Poetry redeems from decay the visitations of the divinity in man.

Poetry turns all things to loveliness; it exalts the beauty of that which is most beautiful, and it adds beauty to that which is most deformed: it marries exultation and horror, grief and pleasure, eternity and change; it subdues to union under its light yoke all irreconcilable things. It transmutes all that it touches, and every form moving within the radiance of its presence is changed by wondrous sympathy to an incarnation of the spirit which it breathes; its secret alchemy turns to potable gold the poisonous waters which flow from death through life; it strips the veil of familiarity from the world, and lays bare the naked and sleeping beauty which is the spirit of its forms.

9. *Paradise Lost* 9.20–24.

1. Dark intervals.

All things exist as they are perceived: at least in relation to the percipient. "The mind is its own place, and of itself can make a heaven of hell, a hell of heaven."[2] But poetry defeats the curse which binds us to be subjected to the accident of surrounding impressions. And whether it spreads its own figured curtain or withdraws life's dark veil from before the scene of things, it equally creates for us a being within our being. It makes us the inhabitants of a world to which the familiar world is a chaos. It reproduces the common universe of which we are portions and percipients, and it purges from our inward sight the film of familiarity which obscures from us the wonder of our being.[3] It compels us to feel that which we perceive, and to imagine that which we know. It creates anew the universe after it has been annihilated in our minds by the recurrence of impressions blunted by reiteration. It justifies that bold and true word of Tasso—*Non merita nome di creatore, se non Iddio ed il Poeta.*[4]

A Poet, as he is the author to others of the highest wisdom, pleasure, virtue and glory, so he ought personally to be the happiest, the best, the wisest, and the most illustrious of men. As to his glory, let Time be challenged to declare whether the fame of any other institutor of human life be comparable to that of a poet. That he is the wisest, the happiest, and the best, inasmuch as he is a poet, is equally incontrovertible: the greatest poets have been men of the most spotless virtue, of the most consummate prudence, and, if we could look into the interior of their lives, the most fortunate of men: and the exceptions, as they regard those who possessed the poetic faculty in a high yet inferior degree, will be found on consideration to confirm rather than destroy the rule. Let us for a moment stoop to the arbitration of popular breath, and usurping and uniting in our own persons the incompatible characters of accuser, witness, judge and executioner, let us decide without trial, testimony, or form, that certain motives of those who are "there sitting where we dare not soar"[5] are reprehensible. Let us assume that Homer was a drunkard, that Virgil was a flatterer, that Horace was a coward, that Tasso was a madman, that Lord Bacon was a peculator,[6] that Raphael was a libertine, that Spenser was a poet laureate. It is inconsistent with this division of our subject to cite living poets, but Posterity has done ample justice to the great names now referred to. Their errors have been weighed and found to have been dust in the balance; if their sins "were as scarlet, they are now white as snow"; they have been washed in the blood of the mediator and the redeemer Time. Observe in what a ludicrous chaos the imputations of real or fictitious crime have been confused in the contemporary calumnies against poetry and poets; consider how little is, as it appears—or appears, as it is: look to your own motives, and judge not, lest ye be judged.[7]

2. Satan's defiant assertion in *Paradise Lost* 1.254–55, slightly misquoted.

3. Shelley echoes SAMUEL TAYLOR COLERIDGE in *Biographia Literaria* (1817), chap. 14, which describes Wordsworth's method as "awakening the mind's attention from the lethargy of custom, and directing it to the loveliness and the wonders of the world before us; an inexhaustible treasure, but for which in consequence of the film of familiarity and selfish solicitude we have eyes, yet see not, ears that hear not, and hearts that neither feel nor understand."

4. No one deserves the name of creator except God and the Poet (Italian). From Pierantonio Serassi's *Life of Torquato Tasso* (1785).

5. *Paradise Lost* 4.829, slightly misquoted.

6. Embezzler.

7. Shelley repeatedly echoes the Bible in this passage. Their errors have been weighed in the balance: Daniel 5.27; dust of the balance: Isaiah 40.15; were as scarlet: Isaiah 1.18; washed in the blood: Revelation 7.14; the mediator: Hebrews 9.15, 12.24; judge not: Matthew 7.1.

Poetry, as has been said, in this respect differs from logic, that it is not subject to the controul of the active powers of the mind, and that its birth and recurrence has no necessary connexion with consciousness or will. It is presumptuous to determine that these are the necessary conditions of all mental causation, when mental effects are experienced insusceptible of being referred to them. The frequent recurrence of the poetical power, it is obvious to suppose, may produce in the mind an habit of order and harmony correlative with its own nature and with its effects upon other minds. But in the intervals of inspiration, and they may be frequent without being durable, a poet becomes a man, and is abandoned to the sudden reflux of the influences under which others habitually live. But as he is more delicately organized than other men, and sensible to pain and pleasure, both his own and that of others, in a degree unknown to them, he will avoid the one and pursue the other with an ardour proportioned to this difference. And he renders himself obnoxious to calumny, when he neglects to observe the circumstances under which these objects of universal pursuit and flight have disguised themselves in one another's garments.

But there is nothing necessarily evil in this error, and thus cruelty, envy, revenge, avarice, and the passions purely evil, have never formed any portion of the popular imputations on the lives of poets.

I have thought it most favourable to the cause of truth to set down these remarks according to the order in which they were suggested to my mind by a consideration of the subject itself, instead of following that of the treatise that excited me to make them public. Thus although devoid of the formality of a polemical reply; if the view they contain be just, they will be found to involve a refutation of the Four Ages of Poetry, so far at least as regards the first division of the subject. I can readily conjecture what should have moved the gall of the learned and intelligent author of that paper; I confess myself like him unwilling to be stunned by the Theseids of the hoarse Codri[8] of the day. Bavius and Mævius[9] undoubtedly are, as they ever were, insufferable persons. But it belongs to a philosophical critic to distinguish rather than confound.

The first part of these remarks has related to Poetry in its elements and principles; and it has been shewn, as well as the narrow limits assigned them would permit, that what is called poetry, in a restricted sense, has a common source with all other forms of order and of beauty according to which the materials of human life are susceptible of being arranged, and which is poetry in an universal sense.

The second part will have for its object an application of these principles to the present state of the cultivation of Poetry, and a defence of the attempt to idealize the modern forms of manners and opinion, and compel them into a subordination to the imaginative and creative faculty. For the literature of England, an energetic development of which has ever preceded or accompanied a great and free development of the national will, has arisen as it were from a new birth. In spite of the low-thoughted envy which would under-

8. Juvenal begins *Satire* 1 by complaining about the *Theseid* (i.e., an epic poem on Theseus, the chief hero of Attica in ancient Greek legend) of "hoarse Codrus." Roman poets applied the name Codrus to bad writers fond of reading their work aloud.

9. Mediocre Latin poets (1st c. B.C.E.) satirized by Virgil (*Eclogue* 3); Horace's *Epode* 10 is an attack on Maevius.

value contemporary merit, our own will be a memorable age in intellectual achievements, and we live among such philosophers and poets as surpass beyond comparison any who have appeared since the last national struggle for civil and religious liberty.[1] The most unfailing herald, companion, and follower of the awakening of a great people to work a beneficial change in opinion or institution, is Poetry. At such periods there is an accumulation of the power of communicating and receiving intense and impassioned conceptions respecting man and nature. The persons in whom this power resides, may often, as far as regards many portions of their nature, have little apparent correspondence with that spirit of good of which they are the ministers. But even whilst they deny and abjure, they are yet compelled to serve, the Power which is seated upon the throne of their own soul. It is impossible to read the compositions of the most celebrated writers of the present day without being startled with the electric life which burns within their words. They measure the circumference and sound the depths of human nature with a comprehensive and all-penetrating spirit, and they are themselves perhaps the most sincerely astonished at its manifestations, for it is less their spirit than the spirit of the age. Poets are the hierophants[2] of an unapprehended inspiration, the mirrors of the gigantic shadows which futurity casts upon the present, the words which express what they understand not; the trumpets which sing to battle, and feel not what they inspire: the influence which is moved not, but moves. Poets are the unacknowledged legislators of the World.

1821 — 1840

1. That is, the English Civil War (1642–46, 1648–49).

2. Interpreters of sacred mysteries.

RALPH WALDO EMERSON
1803–1882

"Emerson is God," declared the literary theorist HAROLD BLOOM in an interview in 1993, in perhaps the most extravagant testimony yet to Emerson's impact on American literature and culture. Lecturer, poet, and essayist, and the leading exponent of New England Transcendentalism, Emerson's advocacy of self-reliance and nonconformity inspired American writers of his own time—notably, Henry David Thoreau, Margaret Fuller, Emily Dickinson, and Walt Whitman—and later. Emerson was significant as well for English and European intellectuals and philosophers, including George Eliot (1819–1880) and FRIEDRICH NIETZSCHE (1844–1900), and for the American philosophers William James (1842–1910) and John Dewey (1859–1952). A radical thinker and a shaper of striking sentences and aphorisms, Emerson made claims for himself (and, by extension, for readers) as daring as Bloom makes for Emerson. "The simplest person who in his integrity worships God," Emerson affirms in his essay "The Over-Soul" (1841), "becomes God."

In *Nature* (1836), the lecture "The American Scholar" (1837), the address before the Harvard Divinity School (1838), and two volumes of *Essays* (1841, 1844), Emerson announced and articulated nearly all of the central themes of Transcendentalism and, at the same time, subjected them to critique. He encouraged readers and audiences to feel the exaltation of their highest potential, to trust instinct and intuition (the signs of God's presence in persons), and to perceive Nature as a rich realm of truths more profound than any that human social orders made available. He expressed these themes in provocative, allusive prose, which proceeds with a rich if frequently discontinuous rhythm. At the same time, with regular self-questioning he maintained that there was no Transcendentalist party and no "pure" Transcendentalism at all.

Emerson attended the Boston Latin School and Harvard College (1817–21). While at Harvard, he began keeping a journal, and its stock of allusions, commentaries on his reading, and reflections on persons and events became the "Savings Bank"—annotated, cross-referenced, indexed—for his lectures, essays, and books. After graduation, Emerson taught school and then entered the Harvard Divinity School to prepare for the ministry, taking up a position at Boston's Second Unitarian Church in 1829. In September 1829 Emerson married the seventeen-year-old Ellen Louisa Tucker, but her health was poor, and she died from tuberculosis in February 1831.

Biographers have suggested that Emerson's grief led him to question his Unitarian faith, but his doubts about conventional Christian beliefs and his "antiquated" profession had been present in his journals and sermons for years. Later, he remarked that if his teachers at the Harvard Divinity School had been aware of his true thoughts and feelings, they would not have allowed him to graduate. In October 1832, saying he could no longer administer the sacrament of the Lord's Supper, Emerson resigned as minister of his Boston church. He explained, "It is my desire to do nothing which I cannot do with my whole heart."

In December 1832, Emerson traveled to Europe, and during his nine months abroad he met WILLIAM WORDSWORTH, SAMUEL TAYLOR COLERIDGE, and the Scottish-born essayist and historian Thomas Carlyle, with whom he corresponded for half a century. After returning to the United States, he lectured on natural history, biography, and history; settled in Concord, Massachusetts; remarried (Lydia Jackson in 1835); and worked on his first book, *Nature*, published anonymously (and at his own expense) in September 1836. Other important texts of this decade include "The American Scholar" and the Divinity School address, in which Emerson attacked religious tradition, doctrine, and the ministry for denying men and women the possibility for authentic self-discovery and religious fulfillment. "I think no man can go with his thoughts about him into one of our churches," he contended in the address, "without feeling that what hold the public worship had on men is gone, or going."

In the 1830s Emerson said, "I am a poet. . . . That is my nature & vocation," and he produced a number of difficult, gnomic poems that were collected in *Poems* (1847). But his real distinction lay in essays, journals, and books of cultural criticism and philosophy. Most scholars now agree that Emerson's best work is in the *Essays*, pointing especially to "History," "Self-Reliance," "The Over-Soul," "Circles," "The Poet," and "Experience." He followed the lectures and essays of the 1830s and 1840s with a series of books: *Representative Men* (1850), which contains studies of PLATO, Goethe, and others; *English Traits* (1856), a shrewd work of social criticism in which Emerson examines English life, tradition, and culture; and *The Conduct of Life* (1860), based on lectures he had presented in 1851 and including three major philosophical pieces—"Fate," "Power," and "Illusions."

Emerson played an active role in the meetings of the Transcendental Club, which the Unitarian clergyman F. H. Hedge organized in 1836 for the "exchange of thought among those interested in the new views in philosophy, theology, and literature." Like the other Transcendentalists, Emerson believed that all of creation is one, that men and women are inherently good, that intuition is the source of truth, and that individual perception illuminates and structures the world. "Nothing is at last sacred but the integrity of your own mind," Emerson professed, and this view led him to criticize the traditions, beliefs, and practices of the past that restricted the intellectual and moral development of persons in the present. God dwells within, according to Emerson, and thus each person should, he said early and late, establish an "original relation to the universe."

In his *Essay Concerning Human Understanding* (1690), John Locke had argued that the senses produce a register of impressions of the physical world on the blank tablet (the *tabula rasa*) of the mind; the understanding transforms them into abstractions and complex ideas. Emerson disagreed. Drawing on the writings of IMMANUEL KANT and, even more, Coleridge (the *Biographia Literaria*, 1817, and the religious and philosophical treatise *Aids to Reflection*, 1825), Emerson made "understanding"—the process by which the mind gathers the evidence of the senses and converts it into knowledge of the external world—subordinate to "reason," which he defined as the intuitive perception of truth. In *Nature*, Emerson affirmed, "I become a transparent eyeball; I am nothing; the currents of the Universal Being circulate through me; I am part or particle of God."

Emerson's reference to "Universal Being" points to the American version of Neoplatonism that he espoused. Each person must seek to regain communion with "Universal Being" or (Emerson's terms vary) Nature or Spirit. When it is lost, human beings view themselves as (and behave as if they were) isolated, powerless, alienated, corrupt. When it is restored, they sense their wholeness and enjoy a thrilling power and independence. This ecstatic feeling, Emerson suggests, is precious and precarious, astonishing and invigorating yet difficult for human beings to sustain. His philosophy is one of constant striving, of working to perfect and empower the self. Those (including HENRY JAMES) who take it for easy optimism are mistaken. In "Fate," Emerson emphasizes that "Nature is no sentimentalist,—does not cosset or pamper us. We must see that the world is rough and surly, and will not mind drowning a man or a woman, but swallows your ship like a grain of dust." In "The Poet," he pictures the imaginative seer as liberating us from ordinary life, which is characterized as miserable and prisonlike.

Our selections demonstrate Emerson's centrality for literary theory, philosophy (especially American pragmatism), and cultural criticism. The first, an excerpt from "The American Scholar," presents Emerson's mobile, and somewhat unnerving, account of the reading process. Truth, he suggests, does not lie in great books waiting for readers to extract it. "Creative reading," the right kind of reading, is instead the result of the truth that readers bring with them—a claim that would reemerge in the reader-response criticism of the 1970s and 1980s (without crediting Emerson). Reading should inspire us, Emerson states; but the genuine scholar, he implies, is occupied with reading only when there is nothing better to do. He is more concerned with writing, arguing that "each age must write its own books. . . . The books of an older period will not fit this." Emerson calls for truth-seekers—persons who look within themselves rather than in books for truth and who bear witness to their spiritual discoveries in books of their own.

As Emerson makes clear in "The Poet" (1844), our second selection, the writer reports passionately on personal experiences that will stimulate readers embarked on their own spiritual and intellectual journeys. All experience is meaningful; no "sensual fact" (that is, nothing that is perceived by the senses) lacks spiritual significance. The special office of the "poet" (i.e., the imaginative writer) is to be alert to the meanings that saturate all of existence; all persons have the potential to be poets (which is one way in which the poet is "representative"), but those who actually become poet-geniuses are "sovereign": they are potentates, emperors, liberating gods. Though Emerson found PERCY BYSSHE SHELLEY "wholly unaffecting," his grand vision of the poet's powers is akin to Shelley's in *A Defence of Poetry* (written

1821; see above). In Emerson's view, the more faithful the poet is to Nature, to Nature's harmonies, the better will be his or her art. Overall, he pays little attention to craft, style, technique. For Emerson, a poem is defined by a thought that is "passionately alive," not by its pattern of rhyme or meter or structure; he explicitly puts content before form.

Through most of the essay, Emerson speaks in universal terms; but toward its end, his commitment to literary and cultural nationalism becomes clear. He beckons for American poets who will take as a basis for their verse the facts, the experiences, and the sweep of the land itself. Though he honors the great writers of the past and of other lands, he emphasizes that present-day citizens of the new nation cannot find inspiration in them. He admits, however, "I look in vain for the poet whom I describe."

Emerson appeals for a literature that is American and modern, and at moments he anticipates major twentieth-century theorists and practitioners of literary modernism. T. S. ELIOT and Ezra Pound, for example, would seem to share Emerson's belief that the poet makes things new: "The poet, by an ulterior intellectual perception, gives them a power which makes their old use forgotten, and puts eyes and a tongue into every dumb and inanimate object." But the Romantic cast of Emerson's arguments ultimately made him more a foe than a friend for the modernists, with important exceptions (such as Gertrude Stein and Robert Frost). Eliot, in particularly strong terms, rejected the concept of the poet as inspired sage or spiritual seer and reaffirmed the sobering significance of tradition (see "Tradition and the Individual Talent," 1919; below). The immersion in the literature of the past that Eliot believed necessary for poets in order for them to find the stimulus for literary work of their own would have struck Emerson as a postponement of the individual's direct endeavor to hearken to the voice within, to the inner light (a phrase that Eliot despised).

For Emerson, what counts is who the poet is, which suggests why as a reader he preferred biography and history to poetry and fiction. He valued books that recounted a gifted individual's quest for freedom, power, and great achievement. Writing in his journal on January 10, 1832, he noted: "The difficulty is that we do not make a world of our own but fall into institutions already made & have to accommodate ourselves to them to be useful at all." Harold Bloom exaggerated when he called Emerson "God," but some critics have proposed, without exaggeration, that there was no truly American writing before Emerson, and that his presence has influenced everything written since.

"The American Scholar" Keywords: Interpretation Theory, Nationhood, Print Culture, Romantic Theory, Subjectivity
"The Poet" Keywords: Aesthetics, Nationhood, Poetry, Religion, Romantic Theory, Subjectivity, Vernacular Language

From The American Scholar[1]

* * *

The next great influence into the spirit of the scholar is the mind of the Past,—in whatever form, whether of literature, of art, of institutions, that mind is inscribed. Books are the best type of the influence of the past, and

1. First published as a pamphlet, with the title *An Oration, Delivered before the Phi Beta Society, at Cambridge, August 31, 1837.* Emerson chose the title "The American Scholar" when it was republished in *Nature, Addresses, and Lectures* (1849).

perhaps we shall get at the truth,—learn the amount of this influence more conveniently,—by considering their value alone.

The theory of books is noble. The scholar of the first age received into him the world around; brooded thereon; gave it the new arrangement of his own mind, and uttered it again. It came into him life; it went out from him truth. It came to him short-lived actions; it went out from him immortal thoughts. It came to him business; it went from him poetry. It was dead fact; now, it is quick thought. It can stand, and it can go. It now endures, it now flies, it now inspires. Precisely in proportion to the depth of mind from which it issued, so high does it soar, so long does it sing.

Or, I might say, it depends on how far the process had gone, of transmuting life into truth. In proportion to the completeness of the distillation, so will the purity and imperishableness of the product be. But none is quite perfect. As no air-pump can by any means make a perfect vacuum, so neither can any artist entirely exclude the conventional, the local, the perishable from his book, or write a book of pure thought, that shall be as efficient, in all respects, to a remote posterity, as to contemporaries, or rather to the second age. Each age, it is found, must write its own books; or rather, each generation for the next succeeding. The books of an older period will not fit this.

Yet hence arises a grave mischief. The sacredness which attaches to the act of creation, the act of thought, is transferred to the record. The poet chanting was felt to be a divine man: henceforth the chant is divine also. The writer was a just and wise spirit: henceforward it is settled the book is perfect; as love of the hero corrupts into worship of his statue. Instantly the book becomes noxious: the guide is a tyrant. The sluggish and perverted mind of the multitude, slow to open to the incursions of Reason, having once so opened, having once received this book, stands upon it, and makes an outcry if it is disparaged. Colleges are built on it. Books are written on it by thinkers, not by Man Thinking; by men of talent, that is, who start wrong, who set out from accepted dogmas, not from their own sight of principles. Meek young men grow up in libraries, believing it their duty to accept the views which Cicero, which Locke, which Bacon,[2] have given; forgetful that Cicero, Locke, and Bacon were only young men in libraries when they wrote these books.

Hence, instead of Man Thinking, we have the bookworm. Hence the book-learned class, who value books, as such; not as related to nature and the human constitution, but as making a sort of Third Estate[3] with the world and the soul. Hence the restorers of readings, the emendators,[4] the bibliomaniacs of all degrees.

Books are the best of things, well used; abused, among the worst. What is the right use? What is the one end which all means go to effect? They are for nothing but to inspire. I had better never see a book than to be warped by its attraction clean out of my own orbit, and made a satellite instead of a system. The one thing in the world, of value, is the active soul. This every man is entitled to; this every man contains within him, although in almost all men

2. Sir Francis Bacon (1561–1626), English statesman and writer, whose works include *The Advancement of Learning* (1605). Cicero (106–43 B.C.E.), Roman orator and statesman. John Locke (1632–1704), English philosopher, author of *An Essay Concerning Human Understanding* (1690).

3. In prerevolutionary France, the common people (the first estate or political order was the clergy, the second the nobility).

4. Editors of texts.

obstructed and as yet unborn. The soul active sees absolute truth and utters truth, or creates. In this action it is genius; not the privilege of here and there a favorite, but the sound estate of every man. In its essence it is progressive. The book, the college, the school of art, the institution of any kind, stop with some past utterance of genius. This is good, say they,—let us hold by this. They pin me down. They look backward and not forward. But genius looks forward: the eyes of man are set in his forehead, not in his hindhead: man hopes: genius creates. Whatever talents may be, if the man create not, the pure efflux of the Deity is not his;—cinders and smoke there may be, but not yet flame. There are creative manners, there are creative actions, and creative words; manners, actions, words, that is, indicative of no custom or authority, but springing spontaneous from the mind's own sense of good and fair.

On the other part, instead of being its own seer, let it receive from another mind its truth, though it were in torrents of light, without periods of solitude, inquest, and self-recovery, and a fatal disservice is done. Genius is always sufficiently the enemy of genius by over-influence. The literature of every nation bears me witness. The English dramatic poets have Shakspearized now for two hundred years.

Undoubtedly there is a right way of reading, so it be sternly subordinated. Man Thinking must not be subdued by his instruments. Books are for the scholar's idle times. When he can read God directly, the hour is too precious to be wasted in other men's transcripts of their readings. But when the intervals of darkness come, as come they must,—when the sun is hid and the stars withdraw their shining,—we repair to the lamps which were kindled by their ray, to guide our steps to the East again, where the dawn is. We hear, that we may speak. The Arabian proverb says, "A fig tree, looking on a fig tree, becometh fruitful."

It is remarkable, the character of the pleasure we derive from the best books. They impress us with the conviction that one nature wrote and the same reads. We read the verses of one of the great English poets, of Chaucer, of Marvell, of Dryden,[5] with the most modern joy,—with a pleasure, I mean, which is in great part caused by the abstraction of all *time* from their verses. There is some awe mixed with the joy of our surprise, when this poet, who lived in some past world, two or three hundred years ago, says that which lies close to my own soul, that which I also had well-nigh thought and said. But for the evidence thence afforded to the philosophical doctrine of the identity of all minds, we should suppose some preëstablished harmony, some foresight of souls that were to be, and some preparation of stores for their future wants, like the fact observed in insects, who lay up food before death for the young grub they shall never see.

I would not be hurried by any love of system, by any exaggeration of instincts, to underrate the Book. We all know, that as the human body can be nourished on any food, though it were boiled grass and the broth of shoes, so the human mind can be fed by any knowledge. And great and heroic men have existed who had almost no other information than by the printed page. I only would say that it needs a strong head to bear that diet. One must be an inventor to read well. As the proverb says, "He that would bring home the

5. John Dryden (1631–1700), poet, dramatist, and critic. Geoffrey Chaucer (ca. 1343–1400), author of *The Canterbury Tales*. Andrew Marvell (1621–1678), poet and satirist.

wealth of the Indies, must carry out the wealth of the Indies."[6] There is then creative reading as well as creative writing. When the mind is braced by labor and invention, the page of whatever book we read becomes luminous with manifold allusion. Every sentence is doubly significant, and the sense of our author is as broad as the world. We then see, what is always true, that as the seer's hour of vision is short and rare among heavy days and months, so is its record, perchance, the least part of his volume. The discerning will read, in his Plato[7] or Shakspeare, only that least part,—only the authentic utterances of the oracle;—all the rest he rejects, were it never so many times Plato's and Shakspeare's.

Of course there is a portion of reading quite indispensable to a wise man. History and exact science he must learn by laborious reading. Colleges, in like manner, have their indispensable office,—to teach elements. But they can only highly serve us when they aim not to drill, but to create; when they gather from far every ray of various genius to their hospitable halls, and by the concentrated fires, set the hearts of their youth on flame. Thought and knowledge are natures in which apparatus and pretension avail nothing. Gowns and pecuniary foundations, though of towns of gold, can never countervail the least sentence or syllable of wit. Forget this, and our American colleges will recede in their public importance, whilst they grow richer every year.

* * *

1837, 1849

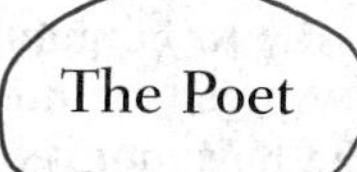

The Poet

Those who are esteemed umpires of taste are often persons who have acquired some knowledge of admired pictures or sculptures, and have an inclination for whatever is elegant; but if you inquire whether they are beautiful souls, and whether their own acts are like fair pictures, you learn that they are selfish and sensual. Their cultivation is local, as if you should rub a log of dry wood in one spot to produce fire, all the rest remaining cold. Their knowledge of the fine arts is some study of rules and particulars, or some limited judgment of color or form, which is exercised for amusement or for show. It is a proof of the shallowness of the doctrine of beauty as it lies in the minds of our amateurs, that men seem to have lost the perception of the instant dependence of form upon soul. There is no doctrine of forms in our philosophy. We were put into our bodies, as fire is put into a pan to be carried about; but there is no accurate adjustment between the spirit and the organ, much less is the latter the germination of the former. So in regard to other forms, the intellectual men do not believe in any essential dependence of the material world on thought and volition. Theologians think it a pretty air-castle to talk of the spiritual meaning of a ship or a cloud, of a city or a contract, but they prefer to come again to the solid ground of

6. Emerson likely found this proverb in James Boswell's *Life of Samuel Johnson, LL.D.* (1791), in the conversation for April 17, 1778.

7. On the Greek philosopher PLATO (ca. 427–ca. 347 B.C.E.), see above.

historical evidence; and even the poets are contented with a civil and conformed manner of living, and to write poems from the fancy, at a safe distance from their own experience. But the highest minds of the world have never ceased to explore the double meaning, or shall I say the quadruple or the centuple or much more manifold meaning, of every sensuous fact; Orpheus, Empedocles, Heraclitus, Plato, Plutarch, Dante, Swedenborg,[1] and the masters of sculpture, picture and poetry. For we are not pans and barrows,[2] nor even porters of the fire and torch-bearers, but children of the fire,[3] made of it, and only the same divinity transmuted and at two or three removes, when we know least about it. And this hidden truth, that the fountains whence all this river of Time and its creatures floweth are intrinsically ideal and beautiful, draws us to the consideration of the nature and functions of the Poet, or the man of Beauty; to the means and materials he uses, and to the general aspect of the art in the present time.

The breadth of the problem is great, for the poet is representative. He stands among partial men for the complete man, and apprises us not of his wealth, but of the common wealth. The young man reveres men of genius, because, to speak truly, they are more himself than he is. They receive of the soul as he also receives, but they more. Nature enhances her beauty, to the eye of loving men, from their belief that the poet is beholding her shows at the same time. He is isolated among his contemporaries by truth and by his art, but with this consolation in his pursuits, that they will draw all men sooner or later. For all men live by truth and stand in need of expression. In love, in art, in avarice, in politics, in labor, in games, we study to utter our painful secret. The man is only half himself, the other half is his expression.

Notwithstanding this necessity to be published, adequate expression is rare. I know not how it is that we need an interpreter, but the great majority of men seem to be minors, who have not yet come into possession of their own, or mutes, who cannot report the conversation they have had with nature. There is no man who does not anticipate a supersensual utility in the sun and stars, earth and water. These stand and wait[4] to render him a peculiar service. But there is some obstruction or some excess of phlegm[5] in our constitution, which does not suffer them to yield the due effect. Too feeble fall the impressions of nature on us to make us artists. Every touch should thrill. Every man should be so much an artist that he could report in conversation what had befallen him. Yet, in our experience, the rays or appulses[6] have sufficient force to arrive at the senses, but not enough to reach the quick and compel the reproduction of themselves in speech. The poet is the person in whom these powers are in balance, the man without impediment, who sees and handles that which others dream of, traverses the whole scale of experience, and is representative of man, in virtue of being the largest power to receive and to impart.

1. Emanuel Swedenborg (1688–1772), Swedish mystic and scientist. Orpheus: legendary Greek poet to whom hymns and fragments were attributed. Empedocles (ca. 493–ca. 433 B.C.E.), Heraclitus (active ca. 500 B.C.E.), and PLATO (ca. 427–ca. 347 B.C.E.): Greek philosophers. Plutarch (ca. 50–ca. 120 C.E.), Greek biographer and historian. DANTE ALIGHIERI (1265–1321), Italian poet, author of *The Divine Comedy*.
2. Carts for carrying a load. "Pans": containers, receptacles (e.g., for cooking).
3. A phrase derived from Heraclitus, who used fire to symbolize the process of change.
4. See John Milton, "When I Consider How My Light Is Spent" (written ca. 1652; published 1673): "They also serve who only stand and wait" (line 14).
5. One of the four "humors" of early physiology; said to cause sluggishness and lethargy.
6. Energetic motions toward something.

For the Universe has three children, born at one time, which reappear under different names in every system of thought, whether they be called cause, operation and effect; or, more poetically, Jove, Pluto, Neptune;[7] or, theologically, the Father, the Spirit and the Son; but which we will call here the Knower, the Doer and the Sayer. These stand respectively for the love of truth, for the love of good, and for the love of beauty. These three are equal. Each is that which he is, essentially, so that he cannot be surmounted or analyzed, and each of these three has the power of the others latent in him and his own, patent.

The poet is the sayer, the namer, and represents beauty. He is a sovereign, and stands on the centre. For the world is not painted or adorned, but is from the beginning beautiful; and God has not made some beautiful things, but Beauty is the creator of the universe. Therefore the poet is not any permissive potentate, but is emperor in his own right. Criticism is infested with a cant of materialism, which assumes that manual skill and activity is the first merit of all men, and disparages such as say and do not, overlooking the fact that some men, namely poets, are natural sayers, sent into the world to the end of expression, and confounds them with those whose province is action but who quit it to imitate the sayers. But Homer's words are as costly and admirable to Homer as Agamemnon's victories are to Agamemnon.[8] The poet does not wait for the hero or the sage, but, as they act and think primarily, so he writes primarily what will and must be spoken, reckoning the others, though primaries also, yet, in respect to him, secondaries and servants; as sitters or models in the studio of a painter, or as assistants who bring building-materials to an architect.

For poetry was all written before time was, and whenever we are so finely organized that we can penetrate into that region where the air is music, we hear those primal warblings and attempt to write them down, but we lose ever and anon a word or a verse and substitute something of our own, and thus miswrite the poem. The men of more delicate ear write down these cadences more faithfully, and these transcripts, though imperfect, become the songs of the nations. For nature is as truly beautiful as it is good, or as it is reasonable, and must as much appear as it must be done, or be known. Words and deeds are quite indifferent modes of the divine energy. Words are also actions, and actions are a kind of words.

The sign and credentials of the poet are that he announces that which no man foretold. He is the true and only doctor;[9] he knows and tells; he is the only teller of news, for he was present and privy to the appearance which he describes. He is a beholder of ideas and an utterer of the necessary and causal. For we do not speak now of men of poetical talents, or of industry and skill in metre, but of the true poet. I took part in a conversation the other day concerning a recent writer of lyrics,[1] a man of subtle mind, whose head appeared to be a music-box of delicate tunes and rhythms, and whose skill and command of language we could not sufficiently praise. But when the question arose whether he was not only a lyrist but a poet, we were obliged to confess that he is plainly a contemporary, not an eternal man. He

7. Three Roman gods: king of the gods (Jove), god of the dead and ruler of the underworld (Pluto), and god of the sea (Neptune).
8. Commander of the Greek army in Homer's epic poem the *Iliad* (ca. 8th c. B.C.E.).
9. Teacher.
1. Perhaps the English poet Alfred, Lord Tennyson (1809–1892).

does not stand out of our low limitations, like a Chimborazo under the line,[2] running up from a torrid base through all the climates of the globe, with belts of the herbage of every latitude on its high and mottled sides; but this genius is the landscape-garden of a modern house, adorned with fountains and statues, with well-bred men and women standing and sitting in the walks and terraces. We hear, through all the varied music, the ground-tone of conventional life. Our poets are men of talents who sing, and not the children of music. The argument is secondary, the finish of the verses is primary.

For it is not metres, but a metre-making argument that makes a poem,—a thought so passionate and alive that like the spirit of a plant or an animal it has an architecture of its own, and adorns nature with a new thing. The thought and the form are equal in the order of time, but in the order of genesis the thought is prior to the form. The poet has a new thought; he has a whole new experience to unfold; he will tell us how it was with him, and all men will be the richer in his fortune. For the experience of each new age requires a new confession, and the world seems always waiting for its poet. I remember when I was young how much I was moved one morning by tidings that genius had appeared in a youth who sat near me at table. He had left his work and gone rambling none knew whither, and had written hundreds of lines, but could not tell whether that which was in him was therein told; he could tell nothing but that all was changed,—man, beast, heaven, earth and sea. How gladly we listened! how credulous! Society seemed to be compromised. We sat in the aurora of a sunrise which was to put out all the stars. Boston seemed to be at twice the distance it had the night before, or was much farther than that. Rome,—what was Rome? Plutarch and Shakspeare were in the yellow leaf,[3] and Homer no more should be heard of. It is much to know that poetry has been written this very day, under this very roof, by your side. What! that wonderful spirit has not expired! These stony moments are still sparkling and animated! I had fancied that the oracles were all silent,[4] and nature had spent her fires; and behold! all night, from every pore, these fine auroras have been streaming. Every one has some interest in the advent of the poet, and no one knows how much it may concern him. We know that the secret of the world is profound, but who or what shall be our interpreter, we know not. A mountain ramble, a new style of face, a new person, may put the key into our hands. Of course the value of genius to us is in the veracity of its report. Talent may frolic and juggle; genius realizes and adds. Mankind in good earnest have availed so far in understanding themselves and their work, that the foremost watchman on the peak announces his news. It is the truest word ever spoken, and the phrase will be the fittest, most musical, and the unerring voice of the world for that time.

All that we call sacred history attests that the birth of a poet is the principal event in chronology. Man, never so often deceived, still watches for the arrival of a brother who can hold him steady to a truth until he has made it his own. With what joy I begin to read a poem which I confide in as an inspiration! And now my chains are to be broken; I shall mount above these

2. The equator. Chimborazo: a mountain in Ecuador, in the Andes range.

3. See the words of Macbeth, in *Macbeth* (ca. 1606), 5.3.23–24; "My way of life / Is fall'n into the sere, the yellow leaf." See also George Gordon, Lord Byron, "On This Day I Complete My Thirty-sixth Year" (1824): "My days are in the yellow leaf" (line 5).

4. See John Milton, "On the Morning of Christ's Nativity" (1645): "The oracles are dumb" (line 173).

clouds and opaque airs in which I live,—opaque, though they seem transparent,—and from the heaven of truth I shall see and comprehend my relations. That will reconcile me to life and renovate nature, to see trifles animated by a tendency, and to know what I am doing. Life will no more be a noise; now I shall see men and women, and know the signs by which they may be discerned from fools and satans. This day shall be better than my birthday: then I became an animal; now I am invited into the science of the real. Such is the hope, but the fruition is postponed. Oftener it falls that this winged man, who will carry me into the heaven, whirls me into mists, then leaps and frisks about with me as it were from cloud to cloud, still affirming that he is bound heavenward; and I, being myself a novice, am slow in perceiving that he does not know the way into the heavens, and is merely bent that I should admire his skill to rise like a fowl or a flying fish, a little way from the ground or the water; but the all-piercing, all-feeding and ocular air of heaven that man shall never inhabit. I tumble down again soon into my old nooks, and lead the life of exaggerations as before, and have lost my faith in the possibility of any guide who can lead me thither where I would be.

But, leaving these victims of vanity, let us, with new hope, observe how nature, by worthier impulses, has insured the poet's fidelity to his office of announcement and affirming, namely by the beauty of things, which becomes a new and higher beauty when expressed. Nature offers all her creatures to him as a picture-language. Being used as a type, a second wonderful value appears in the object, far better than its old value; as the carpenter's stretched cord, if you hold your ear close enough, is musical in the breeze. "Things more excellent than every image," says Jamblichus,[5] "are expressed through images." Things admit of being used as symbols because nature is a symbol, in the whole, and in every part. Every line we can draw in the sand has expression; and there is no body without its spirit or genius. All form is an effect of character; all condition, of the quality of the life; all harmony, of health; and for this reason a perception of beauty should be sympathetic, or proper only to the good. The beautiful rests on the foundations of the necessary.

The soul makes the body, as the wise Spenser teaches:—

"So every spirit, as it is more pure,
And hath in it the more of heavenly light,
So it the fairer body doth procure
To habit in, and it more fairly dight,
With cheerful grace and amiable sight.
For, of the soul, the body form doth take,
For soul is form, and doth the body make."[6]

Here we find ourselves suddenly not in a critical speculation but in a holy place, and should go very warily and reverently. We stand before the secret of the world, there where Being passes into Appearance and Unity into Variety.

The Universe is the externization of the soul. Wherever the life is, that bursts into appearance around it. Our science is sensual, and therefore superficial. The earth and the heavenly bodies, physics and chemistry, we

5. Iamblichus (ca. 250–ca. 325 C.E.), Neoplatonic philosopher of Syria; Emerson read his *Life of Pythagoras*.

6. "An Hymne in Honour of Beautie" (1596), lines 127–33, by the English poet Edmund Spenser (1552–1599). "Dight": clothed.

sensually treat, as if they were self-existent; but these are the retinue of that Being we have. "The mighty heaven," said Proclus,[7] "exhibits, in its transfigurations, clear images of the splendor of intellectual perceptions; being moved in conjunction with the unapparent periods of intellectual natures." Therefore science always goes abreast with the just elevation of the man, keeping step with religion and metaphysics; or the state of science is an index of our self-knowledge. Since every thing in nature answers to a moral power, if any phenomenon remains brute and dark it is because the corresponding faculty in the observer is not yet active.

No wonder then, if these waters be so deep, that we hover over them with a religious regard. The beauty of the fable proves the importance of the sense; to the poet, and to all others; or, if you please, every man is so far a poet as to be susceptible of these enchantments of nature; for all men have the thoughts whereof the universe is the celebration. I find that the fascination resides in the symbol. Who loves nature? Who does not? Is it only poets, and men of leisure and cultivation, who live with her? No; but also hunters, farmers, grooms and butchers, though they express their affection in their choice of life and not in their choice of words. The writer wonders what the coachman or the hunter values in riding, in horses and dogs. It is not superficial qualities. When you talk with him he holds these at as slight a rate as you. His worship is sympathetic; he has no definitions, but he is commanded in nature by the living power which he feels to be there present. No imitation or playing of these things would content him; he loves the earnest of the north wind, of rain, of stone and wood and iron. A beauty not explicable is dearer than a beauty which we can see to the end of. It is nature the symbol, nature certifying the supernatural, body overflowed by life which he worships with coarse but sincere rites.

The inwardness and mystery of this attachment drive men of every class to the use of emblems. The schools of poets and philosophers are not more intoxicated with their symbols than the populace with theirs. In our political parties, compute the power of badges and emblems. See the great ball which they roll from Baltimore to Bunker Hill![8] In the political processions, Lowell goes in a loom, and Lynn in a shoe, and Salem in a ship. Witness the cider-barrel, the log-cabin, the hickory-stick, the palmetto,[9] and all the cognizances of party. See the power of national emblems. Some stars, lilies, leopards, a crescent, a lion, an eagle, or other figure which came into credit God knows how, on an old rag of bunting, blowing in the wind on a fort at the ends of the earth, shall make the blood tingle under the rudest or the most conventional exterior. The people fancy they hate poetry, and they are all poets and mystics!

Beyond this universality of the symbolic language, we are apprised of the divineness of this superior use of things, whereby the world is a temple whose walls are covered with emblems, pictures and commandments of the

7. Greek Neoplatonic philosopher (412–485 C.E.).

8. In the Charlestown section of Boston. This stunt was undertaken by the Whig Party for their candidate William Henry Harrison during the presidential campaign in 1840 to illustrate that year's slogan, "Keep the ball a-rolling." Emerson then associates each Massachusetts town with its major product.

9. Emerson names symbols closely associated with politicians of the 1830s: the cider barrel and log cabin, with William Henry Harrison; the hickory stick, with "Old Hickory," Andrew Jackson (Democratic president, 1829–37); and the palmetto, with John C. Calhoun (Jackson's vice president), who was from South Carolina (the "palmetto state").

Deity,—in this, that there is no fact in nature which does not carry the whole sense of nature; and the distinctions which we make in events and in affairs, of low and high, honest and base, disappear when nature is used as a symbol. Thought makes everything fit for use. The vocabulary of an omniscient man would embrace words and images excluded from polite conversation. What would be base, or even obscene, to the obscene, becomes illustrious, spoken in a new connection of thought. The piety of the Hebrew prophets purges their grossness.[1] The circumcision is an example of the power of poetry to raise the low and offensive. Small and mean things serve as well as great symbols. The meaner the type by which a law is expressed, the more pungent it is, and the more lasting in the memories of men; just as we choose the smallest box or case in which any needful utensil can be carried. Bare lists of words are found suggestive to an imaginative and excited mind as it is related of Lord Chatham that he was accustomed to read in Bailey's[2] Dictionary when he was preparing to speak in Parliament. The poorest experience is rich enough for all the purposes of expressing thought. Why covet a knowledge of new facts? Day and night, house and garden, a few books, a few actions, serve us as well as would all trades and all spectacles. We are far from having exhausted the significance of the few symbols we use. We can come to use them yet with a terrible simplicity. It does not need that a poem should be long. Every word was once a poem. Every new relation is a new word. Also we use defects and deformities to a sacred purpose, so expressing our sense that the evils of the world are such only to the evil eye. In the old mythology, mythologists observe, defects are ascribed to divine natures, as lameness to Vulcan, blindness to Cupid,[3] and the like,—to signify exuberances.

For as it is dislocation and detachment from the life of God that makes things ugly, the poet, who re-attaches things to nature and the Whole,—re-attaching even artificial things and violation of nature, to nature, by a deeper insight,—disposes very easily of the most disagreeable facts. Readers of poetry see the factory-village and the railway, and fancy that the poetry of the landscape is broken up by these; for these works of art are not yet consecrated in their reading; but the poet sees them fall within the great Order not less than the beehive or the spider's geometrical web. Nature adopts them very fast into her vital circles, and the gliding train of cars she loves like her own. Besides, in a centred mind, it signifies nothing how many mechanical inventions you exhibit. Though you add millions, and never so surprising, the fact of mechanics has not gained a grain's weight. The spiritual fact remains unalterable, by many or by few particulars; as no mountain is of any appreciable height to break the curve of the sphere. A shrewd country-boy goes to the city for the first time, and the complacent citizen is not satisfied with his little wonder. It is not that he does not see all the fine houses and know that he never saw such before, but he disposes of them as easily as the poet finds place for the railway. The chief value of the new fact is to enhance the great and constant fact of Life,

1. Emerson may have in mind such passages as Ezekiel's comparison of Jerusalem to a harlot (15) and his description of the city's sins (22).
2. Nathan (or Nathaniel) Bailey (d. 1742), lexicographer and philologist, author of *An Universal Etymological English Dictionary* (1721). Lord Chatham, William Pitt (1708–1778), English statesman and orator.
3. The Roman god of love, son of Venus. Vulcan: the Roman god of fire and metalworking.

which can dwarf any and every circumstance, and to which the belt of wampum and the commerce of America are alike.

The world being thus put under the mind for verb and noun, the poet is he who can articulate it. For though life is great, and fascinates and absorbs; and though all men are intelligent of[4] the symbols through which it is named; yet they cannot originally use them. We are symbols and inhabit symbols; workmen, work, and tools, words and things, birth and death, all are emblems; but we sympathize with the symbols, and being infatuated with the economical uses of things, we do not know that they are thoughts. The poet, by an ulterior intellectual perception, gives them a power which makes their old use forgotten, and puts eyes and a tongue into every dumb and inanimate object. He perceives the independence of the thought on the symbol, the stability of the thought, the accidency and fugacity[5] of the symbol. As the eyes of Lyncæus[6] were said to see through the earth, so the poet turns the world to glass, and shows us all things in their right series and procession. For through that better perception he stands one step nearer to things, and sees the flowing or metamorphosis; perceives that thought is multiform; that within the form of every creature is a force impelling it to ascend into a higher form; and following with his eyes the life, uses the forms which express that life, and so his speech flows with the flowing of nature. All the facts of the animal economy, sex, nutriment, gestation, birth, growth, are symbols of the passage of the world into the soul of man, to suffer there a change and reappear a new and higher fact. He uses forms according to the life, and not according to the form. This is true science. The poet alone knows astronomy, chemistry, vegetation and animation, for he does not stop at these facts, but employs them as signs. He knows why the plain or meadow of space was strown with these flowers we call suns and moons and stars; why the great deep is adorned with animals, with men, and gods; for in every word he speaks he rides on them as the horses of thought.

By virtue of this science the poet is the Namer or Language-maker, naming things sometimes after their appearance, sometimes after their essence, and giving to every one its own name and not another's, thereby rejoicing the intellect, which delights in detachment or boundary. The poets made all the words, and therefore language is the archives of history, and, if we must say it, a sort of tomb of the muses. For though the origin of most of our words is forgotten, each word was at first a stroke of genius, and obtained currency because for the moment it symbolized the world to the first speaker and to the hearer. The etymologist finds the deadest word to have been once a brilliant picture. Language is fossil poetry. As the limestone of the continent consists of infinite masses of the shells of animalcules, so language is made up of images or tropes, which now, in their secondary use, have long ceased to remind us of their poetic origin. But the poet names the thing because he sees it, or comes one step nearer to it than any other. This expression or naming is not art, but a second nature, grown out of the first, as a leaf out of a tree. What we call nature is a certain self-regulated motion or change; and nature does all things by her own hands,

4. Acquainted with, versed in.
5. Transience, lack of enduring qualities. "Accidency": accidental or chance character.
6. In Greek mythology, the seaman with the keenest eyesight among those who sailed with Jason in quest of the Golden Fleece. See Apollonius of Rhodes (3d c. B.C.E.), *Argonautica* 1.155.

and does not leave another to baptize her but baptizes herself; and this through the metamorphosis again. I remember that a certain poet[7] described it to me thus:—

Genius is the activity which repairs the decays of things, whether wholly or partly of a material and finite kind. Nature, through all her kingdoms, insures herself. Nobody cares for planting the poor fungus; so she shakes down from the gills of one agaric countless spores, any one of which, being preserved, transmits new billions of spores to-morrow or next day. The new agaric of this hour has a chance which the old one had not. This atom of seed is thrown into a new place, not subject to the accidents which destroyed its parent two rods off. She makes a man; and having brought him to ripe age, she will no longer run the risk of losing this wonder at a blow, but she detaches from him a new self, that the kind may be safe from accidents to which the individual is exposed. So when the soul of the poet has come to ripeness of thought, she detaches and sends away from it its poems or songs,—a fearless, sleepless, deathless progeny, which is not exposed to the accidents of the weary kingdom of time; a fearless, vivacious offspring, clad with wings (such was the virtue of the soul out of which they came) which carry them fast and far, and infix them irrecoverably into the hearts of men. These wings are the beauty of the poet's soul. The songs, thus flying immortal from their mortal parent, are pursued by clamorous flights of censures, which swarm in far greater numbers and threaten to devour them; but these last are not winged. At the end of a very short leap they fall plump down and rot, having received from the souls out of which they came no beautiful wings. But the melodies of the poet ascend and leap and pierce into the deeps of infinite time.

So far the bard taught me, using his freer speech. But nature has a higher end, in the production of new individuals, than security, namely *ascension*, or the passage of the soul into higher forms. I knew in my younger days the sculptor who made the statue of the youth which stands in the public garden. He was, as I remember, unable to tell directly what made him happy or unhappy, but by wonderful indirections he could tell. He rose one day, according to his habit, before the dawn, and saw the morning break, grand as the eternity out of which it came, and for many days after, he strove to express this tranquillity, and lo! his chisel had fashioned out of marble the form of a beautiful youth, Phosphorus,[8] whose aspect is such that it is said all persons who look on it become silent. The poet also resigns himself to his mood, and that thought which agitated him is expressed, but *alter idem*,[9] in a manner totally new. The expression is organic, or the new type which things themselves take when liberated. As, in the sun, objects paint their images on the retina of the eye, so they, sharing the aspiration of the whole universe, tend to paint a far more delicate copy of their essence in his mind. Like the metamorphosis of things into higher organic forms is their change into melodies. Over everything stands its dæmon or soul, and, as the form of

7. Emerson himself, in his journal, paraphrasing Plato.
8. The Greek personification of the morning star (literally, "light-bearer"), sometimes represented as a youth bearing a torch.
9. A second self (Latin).

the thing is reflected by the eye, so the soul of the thing is reflected by a melody. The sea, the mountain-ridge, Niagara, and every flower-bed, pre-exist, or super-exist, in pre-cantations,[1] which sail like odors in the air, and when any man goes by with an ear sufficiently fine, he overhears them and endeavors to write down the notes without diluting or depraving them. And herein is the legitimation of criticism, in the mind's faith that the poems are a corrupt version of some text in nature with which they ought to be made to tally. A rhyme in one of our sonnets should not be less pleasing than the iterated nodes of a seashell, or the resembling difference of a group of flowers. The pairing of the birds is an idyl, not tedious as our idyls are; a tempest is a rough ode, without falsehood or rant; a summer, with its harvest sown, reaped and stored, is an epic song, subordinating how many admirably executed parts. Why should not the symmetry and truth that modulate these, glide into our spirits, and we participate the invention of nature?

This insight, which expresses itself by what is called Imagination, is a very high sort of seeing, which does not come by study, but by the intellect being where and what it sees; by sharing the path or circuit of things through forms, and so making them translucid to others. The path of things is silent. Will they suffer a speaker to go with them? A spy they will not suffer; a lover, a poet, is the transcendency of their own nature,—him they will suffer. The condition of true naming, on the poet's part, is his resigning himself to the divine *aura*[2] which breathes through forms, and accompanying that.

It is a secret which every intellectual man quickly learns, that beyond the energy of his possessed and conscious intellect he is capable of a new energy (as of an intellect doubled on itself), by abandonment to the nature of things; that beside his privacy of power as an individual man, there is a great public power on which he can draw, by unlocking, at all risks, his human doors, and suffering the ethereal tides to roll and circulate through him; then he is caught up into the life of the Universe, his speech is thunder, his thought is law, and his words are universally intelligible as the plants and animals. The poet knows that he speaks adequately then only when he speaks somewhat wildly, or "with the flower of the mind;"[3] not with the intellect used as an organ, but with the intellect released from all service and suffered to take its direction from its celestial life; or as the ancients[4] were wont to express themselves, not with intellect alone but with the intellect inebriated by nectar. As the traveller who has lost his way throws his reins on his horse's neck and trusts to the instinct of the animal to find his road, so must we do with the divine animal who carries us through this world. For if in any manner we can stimulate this instinct, new passages are opened for us into nature; the mind flows into and through things hardest and highest, and the metamorphosis is possible.

This is the reason why bards love wine, mead, narcotics, coffee, tea, opium, the fumes of sandalwood and tobacco, or whatever other procurers of animal exhilaration. All men avail themselves of such means as they

1. Enchantments, foretellings. Niagara: spectacular North American waterfalls.
2. Gentle breeze; intangible quality, atmosphere.
3. A translation of a Greek phrase from the "Chaldean Oracles" (2d c. C.E., though attributed to the Persian religious leader and prophet Zoroaster, ca. 7th c. B.C.E.), selections from which appeared in the Transcendentalist journal, *The Dial*, in 1844. Others have noted as a source *The True Intellectual System of the Universe* (1678), by the English Neoplatonist Ralph Cudworth (1617–1688).
4. The Neoplatonists Plotinus (ca. 204/5–270 C.E.) and Proclus (412–485 C.E.).

can, to add this extraordinary power to their normal powers; and to this end they prize conversation, music, pictures, sculpture, dancing, theatres, travelling, war, mobs, fires, gaming, politics, or love, or science, or animal intoxication,—which are several coarser or finer *quasi*-mechanical substitutes for the true nectar, which is the ravishment of the intellect by coming nearer to the fact. These are auxiliaries to the centrifugal tendency of a man, to his passage out into free space, and they help him to escape the custody of that body in which he is pent up, and of that jail-yard of individual relations in which he is enclosed. Hence a great number of such as were professionally expressers of Beauty, as painters, poets, musicians and actors, have been more than others wont to lead a life of pleasure and indulgence; all but the few who received the true nectar; and, as it was a spurious mode of attaining freedom, as it was an emancipation not into the heavens but into the freedom of baser places, they were punished for that advantage they won, by a dissipation and deterioration. But never can any advantage be taken of nature by a trick. The spirit of the world, the great calm presence of the Creator, comes not forth to the sorceries of opium or of wine. The sublime vision comes to the pure and simple soul in a clean and chaste body. That is not an inspiration, which we owe to narcotics, but some counterfeit excitement and fury. Milton says[5] that the lyric poet may drink wine and live generously, but the epic poet, he who shall sing of the gods and their descent unto men, must drink water out of a wooden bowl. For poetry is not 'Devil's wine,' but God's wine. It is with this as it is with toys. We fill the hands and nurseries of our children with all manner of dolls, drums and horses; withdrawing their eyes from the plain face and sufficing objects of nature, the sun and moon, the animals, the water and stones, which should be their toys. So the poet's habit of living should be set on a key so low that the common influences should delight him. His cheerfulness should be the gift of the sunlight; the air should suffice for his inspiration, and he should be tipsy with water. That spirit which suffices quiet hearts, which seems to come forth to such from every dry knoll of sere grass, from every pine stump and half-imbedded stone on which the dull March sun shines, comes forth to the poor and hungry, and such as are of simple taste. If thou fill thy brain with Boston and New York, with fashion and covetousness, and wilt stimulate thy jaded senses with wine and French coffee, thou shalt find no radiance of wisdom in the lonely waste of the pine woods.

If the imagination intoxicates the poet, it is not inactive in other men. The metamorphosis excites in the beholder an emotion of joy. The use of symbols has a certain power of emancipation and exhilaration for all men. We seem to be touched by a wand which makes us dance and run about happily, like children. We are like persons who come out of a cave or cellar into the open air. This is the effect on us of tropes,[6] fables, oracles and all poetic forms. Poets are thus liberating gods. Men have really got a new sense, and found within their world another world, or nest of worlds; for, the metamorphosis once seen, we divine that it does not stop. I will not now consider how much this makes the charm of algebra and the mathematics, which also have their tropes, but it is felt in every definition; as when Aristotle defines *space* to be an immovable vessel in which things are

5. In *Elegy VI* (1629), lines 55–78.

6. Figures of speech.

contained;[7]—or when Plato defines a *line* to be a flowing point; or *figure* to be a bound of solid;[8] and many the like. What a joyful sense of freedom we have when Vitruvius[9] announces the old opinion of artists that no architect can build any house well who does not know something of anatomy. When Socrates, in Charmides, tells us that the soul is cured of its maladies by certain incantations, and that these incantations are beautiful reasons, from which temperance is generated in souls; when Plato calls the world an animal, and Timæus affirms that the plants also are animals; or affirms a man to be a heavenly tree, growing with his root, which is his head, upward; and, as George Chapman, following him, writes,

> "So in our tree of man, whose nervie root
> Springs in his top;"—

when Orpheus speaks of hoariness as "that white flower which marks extreme old age;" when Proclus calls the universe the statue of the intellect; when Chaucer, in his praise of 'Gentilesse,' compares good blood in mean condition to fire, which, though carried to the darkest house betwixt this and the mount of Caucasus, will yet hold its natural office and burn as bright as if twenty thousand men did it behold; when John saw, in the Apocalypse, the ruin of the world through evil, and the stars fall from heaven as the fig tree casteth her untimely fruit; when Æsop reports the whole catalogue of common daily relations through the masquerade of birds and beasts;[1]—we take the cheerful hint of the immortality of our essence and its versatile habit and escapes, as when the gypsies say of themselves "it is in vain to hang them, they cannot die."[2]

The poets are thus liberating gods. The ancient British bards had for the title of their order, "Those who are free throughout the world." They are free, and they make free. An imaginative book renders us much more service at first, by stimulating us through its tropes, than afterward when we arrive at the precise sense of the author. I think nothing is of any value in books excepting the transcendental and extraordinary. If a man is inflamed and carried away by his thought, to that degree that he forgets the authors and the public and heeds only this one dream which holds him like an insanity, let me read his paper, and you may have all the arguments and histories and criticism. All the value which attaches to Pythagoras, Paracelsus, Cornelius Agrippa, Cardan, Kepler, Swedenborg, Schelling, Oken,[3] or any other who introduces questionable facts into his cosmogony, as angels, devils, magic, astrology, palmistry, mesmerism, and so on, is the certificate

7. Aristotle (384–322 B.C.E.), *Physics* 4.4, 212a.
8. Plato, *Meno* 76.
9. Roman engineer and architect (1st c. B.C.E.), best known for his work *On Architecture*.
1. In the allusion-filled preceding lines, Emerson's references to calling the world "an animal" and to "plants also are animals" are taken from Plato's dialogues *Charmides* (157) and *Timaeus* (30, 77); George Chapman (1559–1634), an English poet and translator of Homer, wrote the lines quoted in the dedication to Prince Henry at the beginning of his translation; Chaucer's praise of "gentilesse" is in "The Wife of Bath's Tale" (ca. 1400), lines 1139–45; for John's vision, see Revelation 6.13; Aesop wrote his beast fables in the 6th century B.C.E.
2. George Borrow, *The Zincali; or, An Account of the Gypsies of Spain* (1841).
3. Lorenz Oken (1779–1851), German naturalist and mystic philosopher. Pythagoras (6th c. B.C.E.), Greek philosopher and mathematician. Paracelsus (1493–1541), German alchemist and writer on occult subjects. Henricus Cornelius Agrippa van Nettesheim (1486–1535), German physician and magician. Girolamo Cardano (1501–1576), Italian physician, astrologer, and mathematician. Johann Kepler (1571–1630), German astronomer. Friedrich Wilhelm Joseph von Schelling (1775–1854), German philosopher.

we have of departure from routine, and that here is a new witness. That also is the best success in conversation, the magic of liberty, which puts the world like a ball in our hands. How cheap even the liberty then seems; how mean to study, when an emotion communicates to the intellect the power to sap and upheave nature; how great the perspective! nations, times, systems, enter and disappear like threads in tapestry of large figure and many colors; dream delivers us to dream, and while the drunkenness lasts we will sell our bed, our philosophy, our religion, in our opulence.

There is good reason why we should prize this liberation. The fate of the poor shepherd, who, blinded and lost in the snow-storm, perishes in a drift within a few feet of his cottage door, is an emblem of the state of man. On the brink of the waters of life and truth, we are miserably dying. The inaccessibleness of every thought but that we are in, is wonderful. What if you come near to it; you are as remote when you are nearest as when you are farthest. Every thought is also a prison; every heaven is also a prison. Therefore we love the poet, the inventor, who in any form, whether in an ode or in an action or in looks and behavior, has yielded us a new thought. He unlocks our chains and admits us to a new scene.

This emancipation is dear to all men, and the power to impart it, as it must come from greater depth and scope of thought, is a measure of intellect. Therefore all books of the imagination endure, all which ascend to that truth that the writer sees nature beneath him, and uses it as his exponent.[4] Every verse or sentence possessing this virtue will take care of its own immortality. The religions of the world are the ejaculations of a few imaginative men.

But the quality of the imagination is to flow, and not to freeze. The poet did not stop at the color or the form, but read their meaning; neither may he rest in this meaning, but he makes the same objects exponents of his new thought. Here is the difference betwixt the poet and the mystic, that the last nails a symbol to one sense, which was a true sense for a moment, but soon becomes old and false. For all symbols are fluxional; all language is vehicular and transitive, and is good, as ferries and horses are, for conveyance, not as farms and houses are, for homestead. Mysticism consists in the mistake of an accidental and individual symbol for an universal one. The morning-redness happens to be the favorite meteor to the eyes of Jacob Behmen,[5] and comes to stand to him for truth and faith; and, he believes, should stand for the same realities to every reader. But the first reader prefers as naturally the symbol of a mother and child, or a gardener and his bulb, or a jeweller polishing a gem. Either of these, or of a myriad more, are equally good to the person to whom they are significant. Only they must be held lightly, and be very willingly translated into the equivalent terms which others use. And the mystic must be steadily told,—All that you say is just as true without the tedious use of that symbol as with it. Let us have a little algebra, instead of this trite rhetoric,—universal signs, instead of these village symbols,—and we shall both be gainers. The history of hierarchies seems to show that all religious error consisted in making the symbol too stark and solid, and was at last nothing but an excess of the organ of language.

4. The means through which his beliefs are expounded.

5. Jakob Böhme (1575–1624), German theosophist and mystic, author of *Aurora: The Day-Spring, or, Dawning of the Day in the East: or, Morning-Redness in the Rising of the Sun* (1612).

Swedenborg, of all men in the recent ages, stands eminently for the translator of nature into thought. I do not know the man in history to whom things stood so uniformly for words. Before him the metamorphosis continually plays. Everything on which his eye rests, obeys the impulses of moral nature. The figs become grapes whilst he eats them. When some of his angels affirmed a truth, the laurel twig which they held blossomed in their hands. The noise which at a distance appeared like gnashing and thumping, on coming nearer was found to be the voice of disputants. The men in one of his visions, seen in heavenly light, appeared like dragons, and seemed in darkness; but to each other they appeared as men, and when the light from heaven shone into their cabin, they complained of the darkness, and were compelled to shut the window that they might see.

There was this perception in him which makes the poet or seer an object of awe and terror, namely that the same man or society of men may wear one aspect to themselves and their companions, and a different aspect to higher intelligences. Certain priests, whom he describes as conversing very learnedly together, appeared to the children who were at some distance, like dead horses; and many the like misappearances.[6] And instantly the mind inquires whether these fishes under the bridge, yonder oxen in the pasture, those dogs in the yard, are immutably fishes, oxen and dogs, or only so appear to me, and perchance to themselves appear upright men; and whether I appear as a man to all eyes. The Brahmins[7] and Pythagoras propounded the same question, and if any poet has witnessed the transformation he doubtless found it in harmony with various experiences. We have all seen changes as considerable in wheat and caterpillars. He is the poet and shall draw us with love and terror, who sees through the flowing vest the firm nature, and can declare it.

I look in vain for the poet whom I describe. We do not with sufficient plainness or sufficient profoundness address ourselves to life, nor dare we chaunt our own times and social circumstance. If we filled the day with bravery, we should not shrink from celebrating it. Time and nature yield us many gifts, but not yet the timely man, the new religion, the reconciler, whom all things await. Dante's praise is that he dared to write his autobiography in colossal cipher, or into universality.[8] We have yet had no genius in America, with tyrannous eye, which knew the value of our incomparable materials, and saw, in the barbarism and materialism of the times, another carnival of the same gods whose picture he so much admires in Homer; then in the Middle Age; then in Calvinism. Banks and tariffs, the newspaper and caucus, Methodism and Unitarianism, are flat and dull to dull people, but rest on the same foundations of wonder as the town of Troy and the temple of Delphi,[9] and are as swiftly passing away. Our log-rolling, our stumps and their politics, our fisheries, our Negroes and Indians, our boats and our repudiations,[1] the wrath of rogues and the pusillanimity of honest men, the northern trade, the southern planting, the western clearing, Oregon and Texas, are yet unsung. Yet America is a poem in our eyes; its ample geography dazzles

6. Each chapter of Swedenborg's *Apocalypse Revealed* (1766) concludes with "Memorable Revelations."
7. Members of the highest Hindu caste, from which priests and religious teachers are drawn.
8. In Dante's epic *Divine Comedy*, the poet himself plays a first-person role.
9. The site in Greece of the most important oracle of Apollo.
1. Refusals to pay debts. "Log-rolling": the exchange of political favors. "Stumps": speech platforms. "Boats": some editors print "boasts."

the imagination, and it will not wait long for metres. If I have not found that excellent combination of gifts in my countrymen which I seek, neither could I aid myself to fix the idea of the poet by reading now and then in Chalmers's collection of five centuries of English poets.[2] These are wits more than poets, though there have been poets among them. But when we adhere to the ideal of the poet, we have our difficulties even with Milton and Homer. Milton is too literary, and Homer too literal and historical.

But I am not wise enough for a national criticism, and must use the old largeness a little longer, to discharge my errand from the muse to the poet concerning his art.

Art is the path of the creator to his work. The paths or methods are ideal and eternal, though few men ever see them; not the artist himself for years, or for a lifetime, unless he come into the conditions. The painter, the sculptor, the composer, the epic rhapsodist, the orator, all partake one desire, namely to express themselves symmetrically and abundantly, not dwarfishly and fragmentarily. They found or put themselves in certain conditions, as, the painter and sculptor before some impressive human figures; the orator into the assembly of the people; and the others in such scenes as each has found exciting to his intellect; and each presently feels the new desire. He hears a voice, he sees a beckoning. Then he is apprised, with wonder, what herds of dæmons hem him in. He can no more rest; he says, with the old painter, "By God it is in me and must go forth of me." He pursues a beauty, half seen, which flies before him. The poet pours out verses in every solitude. Most of the things he says are conventional, no doubt; but by and by he says something which is original and beautiful. That charms him. He would say nothing else but such things. In our way of talking we say 'That is yours, this is mine;' but the poet knows well that it is not his; that it is as strange and beautiful to him as to you; he would fain hear the like eloquence at length. Once having tasted this immortal ichor,[3] he cannot have enough of it, and as an admirable creative power exists in these intellections, it is of the last importance that these things get spoken. What a little of all we know is said! What drops of all the sea of our science are baled[4] up! and by what accident it is that these are exposed, when so many secrets sleep in nature! Hence the necessity of speech and song; hence these throbs and heart-beatings in the orator, at the door of the assembly, to the end namely that thought may be ejaculated as Logos,[5] or Word.

Doubt not, O poet, but persist. Say 'It is in me, and shall out.' Stand there, balked and dumb, stuttering and stammering, hissed and hooted, stand and strive, until at last rage draw out of thee that *dream*-power which every night shows thee is thine own; a power transcending all limit and privacy, and by virtue of which a man is the conductor of the whole river of electricity. Nothing walks, or creeps, or grows, or exists, which must not in turn arise and walk before him as exponent of his meaning. Comes he to that power, his genius is no longer exhaustible. All the creatures by pairs and by tribes pour into his mind as into a Noah's ark, to come forth again to people a new

2. Alexander Chalmers (1759–1834), Scottish biographer and journalist, compiled *The Works of the English Poets, from Chaucer to Cowper* (21 vols., 1810).
3. In Greek myth, the blood of the gods. Emerson may mean nectar, the drink of the gods.
4. Bailed.
5. Word (Greek), the term used in John 1.1: "In the beginning was the word."

world. This is like the stock of air for our respiration or for the combustion of our fireplace; not a measure of gallons, but the entire atmosphere if wanted. And therefore the rich poets, as Homer, Chaucer, Shakspeare, and Raphael,[6] have obviously no limits to their works except the limits of their lifetime, and resemble a mirror carried through the street, ready to render an image of every created thing.

O poet! a new nobility is conferred in groves and pastures, and not in castles or by the sword-blade any longer. The conditions are hard, but equal. Thou shalt leave the world, and know the muse only. Thou shalt not know any longer the times, customs, graces, politics, or opinions of men, but shalt take all from the muse. For the time of towns is tolled from the world by funereal chimes, but in nature the universal hours are counted by succeeding tribes of animals and plants, and by growth of joy on joy. God wills also that thou abdicate a manifold and duplex life, and that thou be content that others speak for thee. Others shall be thy gentlemen and shall represent all courtesy and worldly life for thee; others shall do the great and resounding actions also. Thou shalt lie close hid with nature, and canst not be afforded to the Capitol or the Exchange.[7] The world is full of renunciations and apprenticeships, and this is thine; thou must pass for a fool and a churl for a long season. This is the screen and sheath in which Pan[8] has protected his well-beloved flower, and thou shalt be known only to thine own, and they shall console thee with tenderest love. And thou shalt not be able to rehearse the names of thy friends in thy verse, for an old shame before the holy ideal. And this is the reward; that the ideal shall be real to thee, and the impressions of the actual world shall fall like summer rain, copious, but not troublesome to thy invulnerable essence. Thou shalt have the whole land for thy park and manor, the sea for thy bath and navigation, without tax and without envy; the woods and the rivers thou shalt own, and thou shalt possess that wherein others are only tenants and boarders. Thou true land-lord! sea-lord! air-lord! Wherever snow falls or water flows or birds fly, wherever day and night meet in twilight, wherever the blue heaven is hung by clouds or sown with stars, wherever are forms with transparent boundaries, wherever are outlets into celestial space, wherever is danger, and awe, and love,—there is Beauty, plenteous as rain, shed for thee, and though thou shouldst walk the world over, thou shalt not be able to find a condition inopportune or ignoble.

1844

6. Raffaello Sanzio (1483–1520), Italian painter.
7. The stock exchange.
8. Greek god of the woods and fields.

EDGAR ALLAN POE
1809–1849

Edgar Allan Poe is a writer most American critics love to hate—or hate to love. In France, on the other hand, Poe has been considered a writer of genius by admirers from Charles Baudelaire to JACQUES LACAN. Is this discrepancy a sign that the French lack the finesse in English that the Americans possess? Or does it say something about two very different concepts of poetic language?

The American poet James Russell Lowell wrote in his *Fable for Critics* (1848):

> There comes Poe, with his Raven, like Barnaby Rudge,
> Three fifths of him genius and two fifths sheer fudge,
> Who talks like a book of iambs and pentameters,
> In a way to make people of common sense damn meters,
> Who has written some things quite the best of their kind,
> But the heart somehow seems all squeezed out by the mind.

For American readers, this view of Poe as excessively calculating exists side by side with a view of Poe as completely lacking control: he is seen as either sick (alcoholic, melancholic, necrophilic, impotent) or dissolute (alcoholic, immoral, untrustworthy, untruthful). Was it precisely this combination of craft and transgression that appealed to a poet like Baudelaire? Lowell was certainly right about one thing: genius or madman, visionary or drunk, seer or trickster, excessively in control or excessively out of control, Edgar Allan Poe was not made to please "people of common sense."

Born in Boston to the traveling actors David and Elizabeth Arnold Poe, Edgar lost both his father (who disappeared) and his mother (who died) by his third birthday. Edgar Poe was renamed "Edgar Allan" when he entered the home of the childless Frances and John Allan, although they never legally adopted him. As a self-made prosperous merchant in Richmond, Virginia, John Allan had little in common with his brilliant foster child, and the financial support he gave was always fraught and conditional. Edgar entered the University of Virginia in 1826 (a year after classes began at the college founded by Thomas Jefferson); but in an attempt to supplement his insufficient allowance, he gambled, lost money, and, when John Allan refused to make good the debt, left the university. Enlisting in the army in Boston under the name "Edgar A. Perry," he managed to pursue a double career: as a poet (his first book, *Tamerlane and Other Poems*, was signed "by a Bostonian") and as a military man. He asked for John Allan's financial help in attending the West Point military academy (grudgingly given) and in publishing his second book (denied); Edgar no sooner enrolled than deliberately got himself expelled in 1831 for disobeying orders.

Breaking with John Allan, Poe took up residence in Baltimore with the remnants of the Poe family: his father's mother, his older brother, his paternal aunt Maria Clemm, and her eight-year-old daughter, Virginia (whom he married in 1836, when she was not quite fourteen). He began submitting tales to writing contests and rose through the ranks of the *Southern Literary Messenger*, penning biting book reviews that increased the journal's circulation. His fierce originality and his desire for an American literary tradition not based on the "puffery" by which reviewers were expected to promote all American authors attracted both notice and misgivings: within two years he became the editor of the journal and then, in 1837, was fired. His would-be Southernness and his resentment of the Northern literary coteries through which writer's reputations were usually made gave him little tolerance for Northern ideals. He recoiled against literary didacticism in part out of irritation with the self-satisfactions of Northern abolitionist literature.

In 1838, still shy of his thirtieth birthday, Poe wrote and published a novel, *The Narrative of Arthur Gordon Pym*, and collected his *Tales of the Grotesque and Arabesque* a year later. Moving to Philadelphia and then to New York, he was a prolific reviewer for *Graham's Magazine*, the *Broadway Review*, and other journals. He became a popular success for two of his most unlikely feats of writing: his hoax about a balloon journey across the Atlantic and his poem "The Raven." "The Raven" is based on a combination of absurdity and inevitability: a bereaved lover admits a black bird into his chamber on a stormy night and, receiving from the bird an unexpected answer to a question, asks it whether he will ever see his beloved again: the bird can only repeat the same word, "nevermore." The poem was written in 1842; Poe's wife Virginia had just burst a blood vessel while singing and was to die of tuberculosis in 1847. Critics have thus noted the biographical sources of the poem in Poe's anticipated mourning, but Poe tells a very different story about the poem's origins in our selection, "The Philosophy of Composition" (1846).

In demand as a writer and lecturer, Poe attempted to raise money to start a new journal called *The Stylus*, which had been a dream of his since 1843. But he often alienated even those close to him with his intermittent drinking, his nervous depression, his delusions of persecution, and his campaigns against plagiarism (his accusations against Henry Wadsworth Longfellow in particular lost him the friendship of Lowell, for whom Poe's "sheer fudge" probably included false accusations). He died of "congestion of the brain" at age forty.

Fated even beyond the grave to depend on the resources of those who lacked benevolence toward him, Poe owed his negative posthumous reputation to the editorial skills and moral perspectives of his literary executor, Rufus Griswold. Griswold told Poe's story as a cautionary tale fit for a temperance tract: it was a life full of promise, ruined by drink and the lack of a moral compass. With the pathological base of Poe's genius established, the diagnostic strain of American criticism later moved to psychoanalysis: now Poe was not morally bankrupt but mad, a patient etherized upon the table of necrophilia, repetition, and impotence. In 1926 Joseph Wood Krutch published *Edgar Allan Poe: A Study in Genius*, a psychoanalytical study typical of this early phase of Freudian criticism.

But in mid-nineteenth-century France, it was the poets who noticed him. Charles Baudelaire was immediately smitten by the image of a poet rejected and misunderstood in his own country. He translated many of Poe's tales and introduced Poe to a privileged audience quite inclined to find value in whatever the small-minded, puritanical, and mediocre Americans could not understand.

Baudelaire's young admirer the French poet Stéphane Mallarmé, who claimed to have learned English only to read Poe, went on to translate the poems, which Baudelaire had largely left untranslated. Baudelaire and Mallarmé found in Poe a theory of poetry that privileged the aesthetic over the moral, the beautiful over the true, and artistic effect over authorial intention. "The Philosophy of Composition," published shortly after the success of "The Raven," is Poe's account of how he composed the poem "backwards" through sheer calculation. Often considered a mystification when read as a *record* of how Poe actually wrote "The Raven," the essay became for Baudelaire and Mallarmé (and later, for ROMAN JAKOBSON, who inherited Poe through the French symbolists) a superb *analysis* of its poetic language. In Poe's explanations, words and even letters—the signifier, not the signified—take the lead in creating the poetic effect. Like the intentionless repetition of a word by a bird made oracular only by the obsessed listener, the network of relations created by words alone is filled with meaning only by the reader. None of the essay's causal explanations can be taken at face value, but what Poe calls the "air of consequence" created by treating effects as causes situates the author's intention in the poem's design rather than in his own experience or sentiment. Which does not, of course, prevent readers from attributing a morbid state of mourning to the author, whose calculations are seen—perhaps rightly—as covering over raw feeling.

In the Freudian Marie Bonaparte's *Life and Works of Edgar Allan Poe* (1933; trans. 1949), the French poetic tradition met the psychoanalytic interpretation, and the status of Poe's poetry was lifted from symptom to dream. Later, in Jacques Lacan's celebrated "Seminar on 'The Purloined Letter'" (1966), Poe the patient was fully promoted to the position of analyst, ingeniously demonstrating, both in that story and in the mechanical repetitions depicted in "The Raven," an understanding of what FREUD would call the "repetition compulsion."

In a way, the two sides of Poe cannot be dissociated. Exploring the vast gap and tension between the unconscious and the intellect, Poe would never have gone so far if he had not known both madness and fabrication. What is seen as Poe's individual pathology, indeed, is often the revelation of aesthetic drives that are usually explained in another way. When Poe proclaims, in "The Philosophy of Composition," that "the death . . . of a beautiful woman is, unquestionably, the most poetical topic in the world," the generalization sounds pathological—until one remembers the many dead women in poetry whose authors cover up their attraction to the image by seeming only to lament it. In his stress on beauty, originality, and intense emotion, Poe is very much part of Romanticism; but in his emphasis on literary technique and construction; on details of meter, rhyme, and sound effects; and on fine calibration of scene, tone, and suspense, he is very much a forerunner of the modernism and its related formalism to come.

"The Philosophy of Composition" Keywords: Aesthetics, Affect, Authorship, Formalism, Language, Poetry

The Philosophy of Composition

Charles Dickens, in a note now lying before me, alluding to an examination I once made of the mechanism of "Barnaby Rudge,"[1] says—"By the way, are you aware that Godwin wrote his 'Caleb Williams'[2] backwards? He first involved his hero in a web of difficulties, forming the second volume, and then, for the first, cast about him for some mode of accounting for what had been done."

I cannot think this the *precise* mode of procedure on the part of Godwin—and indeed what he himself acknowledges,[3] is not altogether in accordance with Mr. Dickens' idea—but the author of "Caleb Williams" was too good an artist not to perceive the advantage derivable from at least a somewhat similar process. Nothing is more clear than that every plot, worth the name, must be elaborated to its *dénouement* before any thing be attempted with the pen. It is only with the *dénouement* constantly in view that we can give a plot its indispensable air of consequence, or causation, by making the incidents, and especially the tone at all points, tend to the development of the intention.

There is a radical error, I think, in the usual mode of constructing a story. Either history affords a thesis—or one is suggested by an incident of the day—or, at best, the author sets himself to work in the combination of striking events to form merely the basis of his narrative—designing, generally, to

1. An 1841 novel by Dickens (1812–1870), the most popular English novelist of the 19th century. Published serially, it presents a murder mystery whose solution Poe tried to guess from the early installments.
2. A 1794 novel by the English political theorist William Godwin (1756–1836).
3. In his preface to the 1832 edition.

fill in with description, dialogue, or autorial comment, whatever crevices of fact, or action, may, from page to page, render themselves apparent.

I prefer commencing with the consideration of an *effect*. Keeping originality *always* in view—for he is false to himself who ventures to dispense with so obvious and so easily attainable a source of interest—I say to myself, in the first place, "Of the innumerable effects, or impressions, of which the heart, the intellect, or (more generally) the soul is susceptible, what one shall I, on the present occasion, select?" Having chosen a novel, first, and secondly a vivid effect, I consider whether it can best be wrought by incident or tone—whether by ordinary incidents and peculiar tone, or the converse, or by peculiarity both of incident and tone—afterward looking about me (or rather within) for such combinations of event, or tone, as shall best aid me in the construction of the effect.

I have often thought how interesting a magazine paper might be written by any author who would—that is to say, who could—detail, step by step, the processes by which any one of his compositions attained its ultimate point of completion. Why such a paper has never been given to the world, I am much at a loss to say—but, perhaps, the autorial vanity has had more to do with the omission than any one other cause. Most writers—poets in especial—prefer having it understood that they compose by a species of fine frenzy—an ecstatic intuition[4]—and would positively shudder at letting the public take a peep behind the scenes, at the elaborate and vacillating crudities of thought—at the true purposes seized only at the last moment—at the innumerable glimpses of idea that arrived not at the maturity of full view—at the fully matured fancies discarded in despair as unmanageable—at the cautious selections and rejections—at the painful erasures and interpolations—in a word, at the wheels and pinions—the tackle for scene-shifting—the step-ladders and demon-traps—the cock's feathers, the red paint and the black patches, which, in ninety-nine cases out of the hundred, constitute the properties of the literary *histrio*.[5]

I am aware, on the other hand, that the case is by no means common, in which an author is at all in condition to retrace the steps by which his conclusions have been attained. In general, suggestions, having arisen pell-mell, are pursued and forgotten in a similar manner.

For my own part, I have neither sympathy with the repugnance alluded to, nor, at any time, the least difficulty in recalling to mind the progressive steps of any of my compositions; and, since the interest of an analysis, or reconstruction, such as I have considered a *desideratum*, is quite independent of any real or fancied interest in the thing analyzed, it will not be regarded as a breach of decorum on my part to show the *modus operandi* by which some one of my own works was put together. I select "The Raven,"[6] as the most generally known. It is my design to render it manifest that no one point in its composition is referrible either to accident or intuition—that the work proceeded, step by step, to its completion with the precision and rigid consequence of a mathematical problem.

Let us dismiss, as irrelevant to the poem *per se*, the circumstance—or say the necessity—which, in the first place, gave rise to the intention of composing a poem that should suit at once the popular and the critical taste.

4. A critical allusion to RALPH WALDO EMERSON'S essay "The Poet" (1844; see above).

5. Actor (Latin).

6. Still Poe's best-known poem (1845).

We commence, then, with this intention.

The initial consideration was that of extent. If any literary work is too long to be read at one sitting, we must be content to dispense with the immensely important effect derivable from unity of impression—for, if two sittings be required, the affairs of the world interfere, and every thing like totality is at once destroyed. But since, *ceteris paribus*, no poet can afford to dispense with *any thing* that may advance his design, it but remains to be seen whether there is, in extent, any advantage to counterbalance the loss of unity which attends it. Here I say no, at once. What we term a long poem is, in fact, merely a succession of brief ones[7]—that is to say, of brief poetical effects. It is needless to demonstrate that a poem is such, only inasmuch as it intensely excites, by elevating, the soul; and all intense excitements are, through a psychal necessity, brief. For this reason, at least one half of the "Paradise Lost"[8] is essentially prose—a succession of poetical excitements interspersed, *inevitably*, with corresponding depressions—the whole being deprived, through the extremeness of its length, of the vastly important artistic element, totality, or unity, of effect.

It appears evident, then, that there is a distinct limit, as regards length, to all works of literary art—the limit of a single sitting—and that, although in certain classes of prose composition, such as "Robinson Crusoe,"[9] (demanding no unity,) this limit may be advantageously overpassed, it can never properly be overpassed in a poem. Within this limit, the extent of a poem may be made to bear mathematical relation to its merit—in other words, to the excitement or elevation—again in other words, to the degree of the true poetical effect which it is capable of inducing; for it is clear that the brevity must be in direct ratio of the intensity of the intended effect:—this, with one proviso—that a certain degree of duration is absolutely requisite for the production of any effect at all.

Holding in view these considerations, as well as that degree of excitement which I deemed not above the popular, while not below the critical, taste, I reached at once what I conceived the proper *length* for my intended poem—a length of about one hundred lines. It is, in fact, a hundred and eight.

My next thought concerned the choice of an impression, or effect, to be conveyed: and here I may as well observe that, throughout the construction, I kept steadily in view the design of rendering the work *universally* appreciable. I should be carried too far out of my immediate topic were I to demonstrate a point upon which I have repeatedly insisted, and which, with the poetical, stands not in the slightest need of demonstration—the point, I mean, that Beauty is the sole legitimate province of the poem.[1] A few words, however, in elucidation of my real meaning, which some of my friends have evinced a disposition to misrepresent. That pleasure which is at once the most intense, the most elevating, and the most pure, is, I believe, found in the contemplation of the beautiful. When, indeed, men speak of Beauty, they mean, precisely, not a quality, as is supposed, but an effect—they refer,

7. Poe apparently has in mind the long, didactic poems of Henry Wadsworth Longfellow (1807–1882), an immensely popular American poet.

8. Long Christian epic (1667) by the English poet John Milton.

9. A 1719 novel by the English writer Daniel Defoe; because it is episodic, recounting the "life and adventures" of the title character, it need not be unified.

1. Poe's view of Beauty as universally pleasing was loosely derived from the German philosopher IMMANUEL KANT (1724–1804), probably via the English poet and critic SAMUEL TAYLOR COLERIDGE (1772–1834).

in short, just to that intense and pure elevation of *soul*—*not* of intellect, or of heart—upon which I have commented, and which is experienced in consequence of contemplating "the beautiful." Now I designate Beauty as the province of the poem, merely because it is an obvious rule of Art that effects should be made to spring from direct causes—that objects should be attained through means best adapted for their attainment—no one as yet having been weak enough to deny that the peculiar elevation alluded to, is *most readily* attained in the poem. Now the object, Truth, or the satisfaction of the intellect, and the object, Passion, or the excitement of the heart, are, although attainable, to a certain extent, in poetry, far more readily attainable in prose. Truth, in fact, demands a precision, and Passion, a *homeliness* (the truly passionate will comprehend me) which are absolutely antagonistic to that Beauty which, I maintain, is the excitement, or pleasurable elevation, of the soul. It by no means follows from any thing here said, that passion, or even truth, may not be introduced, and even profitably introduced, into a poem—for they may serve in elucidation, or aid the general effect, as do discords in music, by contrast—but the true artist will always contrive, first, to tone them into proper subservience to the predominant aim, and, secondly, to enveil them, as far as possible, in that Beauty which is the atmosphere and the essence of the poem.

Regarding, then, Beauty as my province, my next question referred to the *tone* of its highest manifestation—and all experience has shown that this tone is one of *sadness*. Beauty of whatever kind, in its supreme development, invariably excites the sensitive soul to tears. Melancholy is thus the most legitimate of all the poetical tones.

The length, the province, and the tone, being thus determined, I betook myself to ordinary induction, with the view of obtaining some artistic piquancy which might serve me as a key-note in the construction of the poem—some pivot upon which the whole structure might turn. In carefully thinking over all the usual artistic effects—or more properly *points*, in the theatrical sense—I did not fail to perceive immediately that no one had been so universally employed as that of the *refrain*. The universality of its employment sufficed to assure me of its intrinsic value, and spared me the necessity of submitting it to analysis. I considered it, however, with regard to its susceptibility of improvement, and soon saw it to be in a primitive condition. As commonly used, the *refrain*, or burden, not only is limited to lyric verse, but depends for its impression upon the force of monotone—both in sound and thought. The pleasure is deduced solely from the sense of identity—of repetition. I resolved to diversify, and so vastly heighten, the effect, by adhering, in general, to the monotone of sound, while I continually varied that of thought: that is to say, I determined to produce continuously novel effects, by the variation *of the application* of the *refrain*—the *refrain* itself remaining, for the most part, unvaried.

These points being settled, I next bethought me of the *nature* of my *refrain*. Since its application was to be repeatedly varied, it was clear that the *refrain* itself must be brief, for there would have been an insurmountable difficulty in frequent variations of application in any sentence of length. In proportion to the brevity of the sentence, would, of course, be the facility of the variation. This led me at once to a single word as the best *refrain*.

The question now arose as to the *character* of the word. Having made up my mind to a *refrain*, the division of the poem into stanzas was, of course, a corollary: the *refrain* forming the close to each stanza. That such a close, to have force, must be sonorous and susceptible of protracted emphasis, admitted no doubt: and these considerations inevitably led me to the long *o* as the most sonorous vowel, in connection with *r* as the most producible consonant.

The sound of the *refrain* being thus determined, it became necessary to select a word embodying this sound, and at the same time in the fullest possible keeping with that melancholy which I had predetermined as the tone of the poem. In such a search it would have been absolutely impossible to overlook the word "Nevermore." In fact, it was the very first which presented itself.

The next *desideratum* was a pretext for the continuous use of the one word "nevermore." In observing the difficulty which I at once found in inventing a sufficiently plausible reason for its continuous repetition, I did not fail to perceive that this difficulty arose solely from the pre-assumption that the word was to be so continuously or monotonously spoken by *a human* being—I did not fail to perceive, in short, that the difficulty lay in the reconciliation of this monotony with the exercise of reason on the part of the creature repeating the word. Here, then, immediately arose the idea of a *non*-reasoning creature capable of speech; and, very naturally, a parrot, in the first instance, suggested itself, but was superseded forthwith by a Raven, as equally capable of speech, and infinitely more in keeping with the intended *tone*.

I had now gone so far as the conception of a Raven—the bird of ill omen—monotonously repeating the one word, "Nevermore," at the conclusion of each stanza, in a poem of melancholy tone, and in length about one hundred lines. Now, never losing sight of the object *supremeness*, or perfection, at all points, I asked myself—"Of all melancholy topics, what, according to the *universal* understanding of mankind, is the *most* melancholy?" Death—was the obvious reply. "And when," I said, "is this most melancholy of topics most poetical?" From what I have already explained at some length, the answer, here also, is obvious—"When it most closely allies itself to *Beauty*: the death, then, of a beautiful woman is, unquestionably, the most poetical topic in the world—and equally is it beyond doubt that the lips best suited for such topic are those of a bereaved lover."

I had now to combine the two ideas; of a lover lamenting his deceased mistress and a Raven continuously repeating the word "Nevermore"—I had to combine these, bearing in mind my design of varying, at every turn, the *application* of the word repeated; but the only intelligible mode of such combination is that of imagining the Raven employing the word in answer to the queries of the lover. And here it was that I saw at once the opportunity afforded for the effect on which I had been depending—that is to say, the effect of the *variation of application*. I saw that I could make the first query propounded by the lover—the first query to which the Raven should reply "Nevermore"—that I could make this first query a commonplace one—the second less so—the third still less, and so on—until at length the lover, startled from his original *nonchalance* by the melancholy character of the word itself—by its frequent repetition—and by a consideration of the ominous reputation of the fowl that uttered it—is at length excited to superstition, and wildly propounds queries of a far different character—queries whose solution he has passionately at heart—propounds them half in superstition and half in that species of despair which delights in self-torture—propounds them not altogether because he believes in the prophetic or demoniac character of the bird (which, reason assures him, is merely repeating a lesson learned by rote) but because he experiences a phrenzied pleasure in so modeling his questions as to receive from the *expected* "Nevermore" the most delicious because the most intolerable of sorrow. Perceiving the opportunity thus afforded me—or, more strictly, thus forced upon me in the progress of the construction—I first established in mind the climax, or concluding query—that to which "Nevermore" should be in the last place an answer—that in reply to which this word "Nevermore" should involve the utmost conceivable amount of sorrow and despair.

Here then the poem may be said to have its beginning—at the end, where all works of art should begin—for it was here, at this point of my preconsiderations, that I first put pen to paper in the composition of the stanza:

"Prophet," said I, "thing of evil! prophet still if bird or devil!
By that heaven that bends above us—by that God we both adore,
Tell this soul with sorrow laden, if within the distant Aidenn.[2]
It shall clasp a sainted maiden whom the angels name Lenore—
Clasp a rare and radiant maiden whom the angels name Lenore."
Quoth the raven "Nevermore."

I composed this stanza, at this point, first that, by establishing the climax, I might the better vary and graduate, as regards seriousness and importance, the preceding queries of the lover—and, secondly, that I might definitely settle the rhythm, the metre, and the length and general arrangement of the stanza—as well as graduate the stanzas which were to precede, so that none of them might surpass this in rhythmical effect. Had I been able, in the subsequent composition, to construct more vigorous stanzas, I should, without scruple, have purposely enfeebled them, so as not to interfere with the climacteric effect.

And here I may as well say a few words of the versification. My first object (as usual) was originality. The extent to which this has been neglected, in versification, is one of the most unaccountable things in the world. Admitting that there is little possibility of variety in mere *rhythm*, it is still clear that the possible varieties of metre and stanza are absolutely infinite—and yet, *for centuries, no man, in verse, has ever done, or ever seemed to think of doing, an original thing*. The fact is, originality (unless in minds of very unusual force) is by no means a matter, as some suppose, of impulse or intuition. In general, to be found, it must be elaborately sought, and although a positive merit of the highest class, demands in its attainment less of invention than negation.

Of course, I pretend to no originality in either the rhythm or metre of the "Raven." The former is trochaic—the latter is octameter acatalectic, alternating with heptameter catalectic[3] repeated in the *refrain* of the fifth verse, and terminating with tetrameter catalectic. Less pedantically—the feet

2. Arabic term for paradise, *Adn* (Eden).
3. Lacking a syllable in the last foot (thus a line of 7½ feet, as Poe explains). "Trochaic": based on a metrical foot of the pattern long-short, or stressed-unstressed. "Acatalectic": complete in its syllables (literally, "not catalectic").

employed throughout (trochees) consist of a long syllable followed by a short: the first line of the stanza consists of eight of these feet—the second of seven and a half (in effect two-thirds)—the third of eight—the fourth of seven and a half—the fifth the same—the sixth three and a half. Now, each of these lines, taken individually, had been employed before, and what originality the "Raven" has, is in their *combination into stanza*; nothing even remotely approaching this combination has ever been attempted. The effect of this originality of combination is aided by other unusual, and some altogether novel effects, arising from an extension of the application of the principles of rhyme and alliteration.

The next point to be considered was the mode of bringing together the lover and the Raven—and the first branch of this consideration was the *locale*. For this the most natural suggestion might seem to be a forest, or the fields—but it has always appeared to me that a close *circumscription of space* is absolutely necessary to the effect of insulated incident:—it has the force of a frame to a picture. It has an indisputable moral power in keeping concentrated the attention, and, of course, must not be confounded with mere unity of place.

I determined, then, to place the lover in his chamber—in a chamber rendered sacred to him by memories of her who had frequented it. The room is represented as richly furnished—this in mere pursuance of the ideas I have already explained on the subject of Beauty, as the sole true poetical thesis.

The *locale* being thus determined, I had now to introduce the bird—and the thought of introducing him through the window, was inevitable. The idea of making the lover suppose, in the first instance, that the flapping of the wings of the bird against the shutter, is a "tapping" at the door, originated in a wish to increase, by prolonging, the reader's curiosity, and in a desire to admit the incidental effect arising from the lover's throwing open the door, finding all dark, and thence adopting the half-fancy that it was the spirit of his mistress that knocked.

I made the night tempestuous, first, to account for the Raven's seeking admission, and secondly, for the effect of contrast with the (physical) serenity within the chamber.

I made the bird alight on the bust of Pallas,[4] also for the effect of contrast between the marble and the plumage—it being understood that the bust was absolutely *suggested* by the bird—the bust of *Pallas* being chosen, first, as most in keeping with the scholarship of the lover, and, secondly, for the sonorousness of the word, Pallas, itself.

About the middle of the poem, also, I have availed myself of the force of contrast, with a view of deepening the ultimate impression. For example, an air of the fantastic—approaching as nearly to the ludicrous as was admissible—is given to the Raven's entrance. He comes in "with many a flirt and flutter."

Not the *least obeisance made he*—not a moment stopped or stayed he,
But with mien of lord or lady, perched above my chamber door.

In the two stanzas which follow, the design is more obviously carried out:—

4. A title of Athena, the Greek goddess of wisdom, the arts, and war.

Then this ebony bird beguiling my sad fancy into smiling
By the *grave and stern decorum of the countenance it wore,*
"Though thy *crest be shorn and shaven* thou," I said, "art sure no craven,
Ghastly grim and ancient Raven wandering from the nightly shore—
Tell me what thy lordly name is on the Night's Plutonian[5] shore!"
Quoth the Raven "Nevermore."

Much I marvelled *this ungainly fowl* to hear discourse so plainly,
Though its answer little meaning—little relevancy bore;
For we cannot help agreeing that no living human being
Ever yet was blessed with seeing bird above his chamber door—
Bird or beast upon the sculptured bust above his chamber door,
With such name as "Nevermore."

The effect of the *dénouement* being thus provided for, I immediately drop the fantastic for a tone of the most profound seriousness:—this tone commencing in the stanza directly following the one last quoted with the line,

But the Raven, sitting lonely on that placid bust, spoke only, etc.

From this epoch the lover no longer jests—no longer sees any thing even of the fantastic in the Raven's demeanor. He speaks of him as a "grim, ungainly, ghastly, gaunt, and ominous bird of yore," and feels the "fiery eyes" burning into his "bosom's core." This revolution of thought, or fancy, on the lover's part, is intended to induce a similar one on the part of the reader—to bring the mind into a proper frame for the *dénouement*—which is now brought about as rapidly and as *directly* as possible.

With the *dénouement* proper—with the Raven's reply, "Nevermore," to the lover's final demand if he shall meet his mistress in another world—the poem, in its obvious phase, that of a simple narrative, may be said to have its completion. So far, every thing is within the limits of the accountable—of the real. A raven, having learned by rote the single word "Nevermore," and having escaped from the custody of its owner, is driven, at midnight, through the violence of a storm, to seek admission at a window from which a light still gleams—the chamber-window of a student, occupied half in poring over a volume, half in dreaming of a beloved mistress deceased. The casement being thrown open at the fluttering of the bird's wings, the bird itself perches on the most convenient seat out of the immediate reach of the student, who, amused by the incident and the oddity of the visiter's demeanor, demands of it, in jest and without looking for a reply, its name. The raven addressed, answers with its customary word, "Nevermore"—a word which finds immediate echo in the melancholy heart of the student, who, giving utterance aloud to certain thoughts suggested by the occasion, is again startled by the fowl's repetition of "Nevermore." The student now guesses the state of the case, but is impelled, as I have before explained, by the human thirst for self-torture, and in part by superstition, to propound such queries to the bird as will bring him, the lover, the most of the luxury of sorrow, through the anticipated answer "Nevermore." With the indulgence, to the utmost extreme, of

5. Of or pertaining to Pluto, Roman god of the underworld.

this self-torture, the narration, in what I have termed its first or obvious phase, has a natural termination, and so far there has been no overstepping of the limits of the real.

But in subjects so handled, however skilfully, or with however vivid an array of incident, there is always a certain hardness or nakedness, which repels the artistical eye. Two things are invariably required—first, some amount of complexity, or more properly, adaptation; and, secondly, some amount of suggestiveness—some under current, however indefinite of meaning. It is this latter, in especial, which imparts to a work of art so much of that *richness* (to borrow from colloquy a forcible term) which we are too fond of confounding with *the ideal*. It is the *excess* of the suggested meaning—it is the rendering this the upper instead of the under current of the theme—which turns into prose (and that of the very flattest kind) the so called poetry of the so called transcendentalists.[6]

Holding these opinions, I added the two concluding stanzas of the poem—their suggestiveness being thus made to pervade all the narrative which has preceded them. The under current of meaning is rendered first apparent in the lines—

"Take thy beak from out *my heart*, and take thy form from off my door!"
Quoth the Raven "Nevermore!"

It will be observed that the words, "from out my heart," involve the first metaphorical expression in the poem. They, with the answer, "Nevermore," dispose the mind to seek a moral in all that has been previously narrated. The reader begins now to regard the Raven as emblematical—but it is not until the very last line of the very last stanza, that the intention of making him emblematical of *Mournful and Never-ending Remembrance* is permitted distinctly to be seen:

And the Raven, never flitting, still is sitting, still is sitting,
On the pallid bust of Pallas just above my chamber door;
And his eyes have all the seeming of a demon's that is dreaming,
And the lamplight o'er him streaming throws his shadow on the floor;
And my soul *from out that shadow* that lies floating on the floor
Shall be lifted—nevermore.

1846

6. A group of 19th-century writers and philosophers in New England; they viewed the individual soul as corresponding directly with the universe (thus eliminating language) and they located the truest source of knowledge in intuition, not experience. Emerson was one of the foremost Transcendentalists.

KARL MARX 1818–1883 / FRIEDRICH ENGELS 1820–1895

Karl Marx and Friedrich Engels are central figures in the history of literary criticism and theory and in the development of cultural studies, though neither produced a body of literary-critical work. The young Marx wrote lyrics, attempted drama and fiction, and read deeply in eighteenth- and nineteenth-century German philosophy and aesthetics, and the writings of Marx and Engels often refer to and quote literature from classical Greek drama to the novels of Charles Dickens. But as economic historians, social theorists, and revolutionaries seeking to change the world, their main work lay elsewhere, and their direct contributions to literary criticism are scattered and uneven. Yet perhaps this incompleteness makes their comments and observations about literature and criticism all the more suggestive, giving a long line of twentieth-century writers—including GYÖRGY LUKÁCS, Bertolt Brecht, WALTER BENJAMIN, GAYATRI CHAKRAVORTY SPIVAK, and FREDRIC JAMESON—much speculative and interpretive leeway in developing their own Marxist theories of literature.

To many it may seem perverse to study Marxist theory today, given the collapse between 1989 and 1991 of Communist governments in the Soviet Union and in the nations of Eastern Europe. But we must clearly distinguish between Marx and Engels as social theorists, philosophers, historians, and cultural critics and as revolutionaries—or, more accurately, as revolutionaries under whose name Communist leaders and parties seized power. The fall of particular regimes, "Marxist" more in name than in ideas, does little to lessen the impact of Marx's relentless, fascinated, shocked (and shocking) examination of capitalism and its costs to the men and women caught in its grasp. In brilliant passages such as our selection from *Capital* (1867) on the working day, his skillfully modulated prose can be powerfully moving.

For literary and cultural criticism, the seminal passage by Marx appears in his preface to *A Contribution to the Critique of Political Economy* (1858–59, excerpted below). Here, Marx emphasizes that he is concerned primarily with the "material conditions of life," the "economic structure of society." On this "foundation . . . rises a legal and political superstructure"; moreover, "The mode of production of material life conditions the social, political and intellectual life process in general. It is not the consciousness of men that determines their being, but, on the contrary, their social being that determines their consciousness." This formulation raises a number of questions: To what *degree* is consciousness socially and economically "determined"? What is the role of human agency? How closely connected are the base and the superstructure, and can the latter—which includes intellectual work and cultural institutions—affect the former? In the twentieth century, both LOUIS ALTHUSSER and RAYMOND WILLIAMS were later to wrestle directly with these questions.

The answers of Marx and Engels waver. As a famous passage (excerpted below) from the *Grundrisse* (1857–58, *Foundations* or *Outlines*) suggests, Marx found it difficult to explain the relationship between Greek art and the society within which it arose. Engels, too, recognized the limitations of the base / superstructure model. In a letter to Joseph Bloch (our final selection), Engels maintains that "According to the materialist conception of history, the *ultimately* determining element in history is the production and reproduction of real life," insisting that economics is not the only determinant and leaving room for the influence of "human minds."

Marx was born in Trier, Prussia (a region now part of Germany), the son of a Jewish lawyer who had converted to Protestantism to protect his job. Marx studied at the universities of Bonn, Berlin, and Jena, receiving his doctorate in April 1841 for a thesis on the Greek philosophers Democritus and Epicurus. In 1842 he edited a radical newspaper in Cologne, but the German authorities, angered by his criticisms, forced him to resign in 1843. He then traveled to Paris, where he and Engels, whom he had met in Cologne, began their collaboration. Engels, born in Barmen, in western Germany, was the son of a wealthy textile manufacturer; in the 1840s, he managed a factory in England that his father owned, and his horror at the harsh economic and social conditions in Manchester led him to write *The Condition of the Working Class in England in 1844* (1845). Engels later said that as he and Marx worked together in Paris, their "agreement in all theoretical fields became obvious."

Marx and Engels's joint work in the 1840s includes *The Holy Family* (1845) and *The German Ideology* (not published until 1932). In these texts, and in Marx's polemical pamphlet *The Poverty of Philosophy* (1847), they sought to prove that economic and social forces shape human consciousness. This materialism was meant to displace the idealist view that human consciousness shapes economic and social forces and forms. They based their interpretation of reality on *dialectical* materialism, believing that all change results from the constant conflict arising from the oppositions inherent in all ideas, movements, and events. They further argued that the internal tensions and contradictions in capitalism would lead inevitably to its demise.

Also important are Marx's writings collected in *Economic and Philosophic Manuscripts of 1844* (1932; trans. 1959), which contain much of his most passionate, incisive thinking about industrial conditions and the nature of consciousness under capitalism and present an excellent entry point into Marxist cultural analysis. Building on the work of the German philosopher Ludwig Feuerbach, author of *The Essence of Christianity* (1841), Marx is especially concerned here with the origin and impact of alienation. The industrial capitalist economy, says Marx, "alienates" individuals from the work that they do; unable to control their own labor, which they must "give" (sell) to another, they lack control and knowledge of themselves and never achieve their full human potential. However much they resent their situation, they believe—that is, they are conditioned to believe—that it cannot be changed, and that ultimately they have only themselves to blame for their discontent and failures.

Marx and Engels's most significant publication of the decade appeared in London in 1848: *Manifesto of the Communist Party* (soon known by and reprinted with the shorter title *The Communist Manifesto*). In this intense pamphlet Marx (who did the bulk of the writing) describes the triumphs of capitalism; the creation of a world market, world literature, and cosmopolitanism; the misery that capitalism imposes on the masses; the class struggle between the exploiters (owners) and the exploited (workers); the connection of people primarily via cash; the inevitability of revolution; and the dawn of a new, class-free society. Though specifically commissioned to state the principles and objectives of the Communist League (a secret organization composed primarily of German emigrés), it quickly became the position paper of militant working-class movements everywhere.

Because of his political writing and activity, Marx was expelled from both France and Germany in the late 1840s; in May 1849 he settled with his family in London. There, supported by Engels but nonetheless often in poverty, he resided for the remainder of his life. His major works during these decades are the *Grundrisse*, a manuscript of some 800 printed pages (1857–58, published 1939–41); the three book volume *Theories of Surplus Value* (1860s, published 1905–10); and above all *Das Kapital*, volume 1 of which appeared in 1867 (trans. 1886), with volumes 2 and 3, edited by Engels, published posthumously in 1885 and 1894 (trans. 1907, 1909). Volume 4 of *Das Kapital* is the aforementioned *Theories of Surplus Value*, edited and published by Karl Kautsky. Marx also wrote many articles for newspapers in the United States and Europe. Engels's writings include *Herr Eugen Dühring's Revolution in Science* (1878, usually referred to as *Anti-Dühring*), parts of which later appeared as a summary of the basics of socialism titled *Socialism: Utopian and Scientific* (1892); *The Origin of the Family, Private Property, and the State* (1884); and *Dialectics of Nature* (1925).

A literary theorist and critic reading Marx and Engels may raise questions that the texts do not answer. What roles do writers, critics, and intellectuals play? Do they illuminate for workers the nature of capitalist exploitation, or do they act at the service of those who already and best understand their true circumstances? Should writers be free to state the social and political facts as they see them, or must the goal of working-class revolution always shape their work—and if so, who sets the limits?

Marx has a simple but powerful reply: the answers will come only when the contradictions within capitalism produce them. Capitalism has no remedy for the worst social and economic problems that it creates and that will eventually rend it asunder. Marx is certain that capitalism will end, and why: but no one can know exactly what the roles of intellectuals and critics will be, and what the new society will look like, until the force of historical necessity brings them into being.

Meanwhile, Marxist critics have work to perform, practicing a discipline linked to the goal of radical social change. Thus they must approach literature, literary education, criticism, and theory as integral parts of economic and social life. In *The German Ideology*, as our selection indicates, Marx and Engels emphasize that we must study *real* men and women and *real* processes, not what has typically been said or thought by and about them.

Marx promotes "ideology critique," that is, the demystifying exposure of how class interests operate through cultural forms, whether political or legal, religious or philosophical, educational or literary. It is the nature of ideology to conceal the reality of class struggle from our perception and consciousness; and insofar as working-class people unconsciously absorb bourgeois values, they are unwitting carriers of "false consciousness."

The term *ideology* rarely appears in Marx's *Grundrisse* and *Capital*, but it is implicit in many of Marx's formulations of the difference between the surface and reality of capitalist society. Marxist critics are expected to investigate the systemic masking of the real methods and consequences of existing socioeconomic arrangements. Sometimes, however, Marx uses the term differently, as when he declares in *A Contribution to the Critique of Political Economy* that we grow aware of and fight the conflict between classes in "ideological forms."

Later Marxists have developed both the positive and negative senses of ideology. One dominant line of inquiry follows from the writings of ANTONIO GRAMSCI, who in his *Prison Notebooks* (published 1945–75) describes ideology as "the terrain on which men move, acquire consciousness of their position, struggle, etc."; he explores how a privileged social class can achieve cultural "hegemony," the manufactured assent to its beliefs and practices won peacefully through ideology. This concept of hegemony, developed by the British Marxist Raymond Williams (especially in *Marxism and Literature*, 1977) and by those he has influenced (notably STUART HALL and DICK HEBDIGE), has become fundamental to cultural studies. Critics use it in studying classic texts, the relationships and differences between canonical and noncanonical literature, popular culture, the media, education, and publishing—all outlets for ideology.

The power of ideology to mask and obscure is also at work in what Marx calls "the fetishism of commodities," which he discusses in our first selection from *Capital*. Under capitalism, human relations are increasingly characterized by more or less thoroughgoing alienation, monetization, and commodification. Relationships between workers and owners, buyers and sellers, are mediated through the things produced. These commodities become objects of fetishism—seeming to have an objective existence of their own that obscures the individual labor involved in their production. By being exchanged, they acquire a seemingly inherent value distinct from their use value or physical properties.

As a social and cultural theory, Marxism demands of its followers ongoing critical scrutiny and self-questioning of its own basic texts, which are suggestive but sometimes flawed and often incomplete. Marx and Engels underestimated, for example, the extraordinary power of capitalism to turn back and absorb opposition, and apparently they overlooked the damaging overstatements and reductiveness that mar their arguments. Moreover, though Marx was acutely responsive to the economic and political situation of workers, he appears incapable of actually seeing and making imaginative contact with them and their families, of conveying how they live, think, and feel. Even in his most illuminating work, Marx often mirrors the dehumanizing tendencies that his radical critiques of capitalism condemn. Individuals matter most to him as embodiments of ideas, as components of systems—a form of thinking that the best novelists of his time, such as Dickens and Balzac, brilliantly exposed and corrected.

On the "material conditions of life" and the "economic structure of society," Marx and Engels are sharp and compelling; on the subject of the creative and critical consciousness of persons and cultures, they falter. For foundational Marxist interpretations of cultural life, one must look instead to the work of such later theorists and critics as W. E. B. DU BOIS, Edmund Wilson (in his writings of the 1930s), THEODOR ADORNO, C. L. R. James, and Raymond Williams. They built upon but went beyond the insights that Marx and Engels provide, and their critical projects drew from the literary texts and cultural traditions that Marx and Engels admired but never fully engaged.

Economic and Philosophic Manuscripts of 1844 **Keywords:** Hegemony, Marxism, Religion, Subjectivity
The German Ideology **Keywords:** Ethics, Hegemony, Ideology, Marxism, Representation
The Communist Manifesto **Keywords:** Globalization, Hegemony, Ideology, Institutional Studies, Marxism, Modernity, Nationhood
Grundrisse **Keywords:** Aesthetics, Epic, Marxism
"Preface to *A Contribution to the Critique of Political Economy*" Keywords: Hegemony, Ideology, Marxism, Modernity
***Capital, Volume 1*, Keywords:** The Body, Hegemony, Marxism, Nationhood, Representation
"Letter from Friedrich Engels to Joseph Bloch" Keywords: Institutional Studies, Marxism, Nationhood, Religion

From Economic and Philosophic Manuscripts of 1844[1]

* * *

We have proceeded from the premises of political economy.[2] We have accepted its language and its laws. We presupposed private property, the separation of labour, capital and land, and of wages, profit of capital and rent of land—likewise division of labour, competition, the concept of

1. Translated by Martin Milligan.
2. The 19th-century social science concerned with the relations between political and economic processes (now often separated into political science and economics).

exchange-value, etc. On the basis of political economy itself, in its own words, we have shown that the worker sinks to the level of a commodity and becomes indeed the most wretched of commodities;[3] that the wretchedness of the worker is in inverse proportion to the power and magnitude of his production; that the necessary result of competition is the accumulation of capital in a few hands, and thus the restoration of monopoly in a more terrible form; that finally the distinction between capitalist and land-rentier,[4] like that between the tiller of the soil and the factory-worker, disappears and that the whole of society must fall apart into the two classes—the property-*owners* and the propertyless *workers*.

Political economy proceeds from the fact of private property, but it does not explain it to us. It expresses in general, abstract formulae the *material* process through which private property actually passes, and these formulae it then takes for *laws*. It does not *comprehend* these laws—i.e., it does not demonstrate how they arise from the very nature of private property. Political economy does not disclose the source of the division between labour and capital, and between capital and land. When, for example, it defines the relationship of wages to profit, it takes the interest of the capitalists to be the ultimate cause; i.e., it takes for granted what it is supposed to evolve. Similarly, competition comes in everywhere. It is explained from external circumstances. As to how far these external and apparently fortuitous circumstances are but the expression of a necessary course of development, political economy teaches us nothing. We have seen how, to it, exchange itself appears to be a fortuitous fact. The only wheels which political economy sets in motion are *avarice* and the *war amongst the avaricious—competition*.

Precisely because political economy does not grasp the connections within the movement, it was possible to counterpose, for instance, the doctrine of competition to the doctrine of monopoly, the doctrine of craft-liberty to the doctrine of the corporation, the doctrine of the division of landed property to the doctrine of the big estate—for competition, craft-liberty and the division of landed property were explained and comprehended only as fortuitous, premeditated and violent consequences of monopoly, the corporation, and feudal property, not as their necessary, inevitable and natural consequences.

Now, therefore, we have to grasp the essential connection between private property, avarice, and the separation of labour, capital and landed property; between exchange and competition, value and the devaluation of men, monopoly and competition, etc.; the connection between this whole estrangement and the *money*-system.

Do not let us go back to a fictitious primordial condition as the political economist does, when he tries to explain. Such a primordial condition explains nothing. He merely pushes the question away into a grey nebulous distance. He assumes in the form of fact, of an event, what he is supposed to deduce—namely, the necessary relationship between two things—between, for example, division of labour and exchange. Theology in the same way explains the origin of evil by the fall of man: that is, it assumes as a fact, in historical form, what has to be explained.

3. Because labor itself is sold to others, and at a very low price.

4. One who lives on income from land, stocks, or bonds.

We proceed from an *actual* economic fact.

The worker becomes all the poorer the more wealth he produces, the more his production increases in power and range. The worker becomes an ever cheaper commodity the more commodities he creates. With the *increasing value* of the world of things proceeds in direct proportion the *devaluation* of the world of men. Labour produces not only commodities; it produces itself and the worker as a *commodity*—and does so in the proportion in which it produces commodities generally.

This fact expresses merely that the object which labour produces—labour's product—confronts it as *something alien*, as a *power independent* of the producer. The product of labour is labour which has been congealed in an object, which has become material: it is the *objectification* of labour. Labour's realization is its objectification. In the conditions dealt with by political economy this realization of labour appears as *loss of reality* for the workers; objectification as *loss of the object* and *object-bondage*; appropriation as *estrangement*, as *alienation*.

So much does labour's realization appear as loss of reality that the worker loses reality to the point of starving to death. So much does objectification appear as loss of the object that the worker is robbed of the objects most necessary not only for his life but for his work. Indeed, labour itself becomes an object which he can get hold of only with the greatest effort and with the most irregular interruptions. So much does the appropriation of the object appear as estrangement that the more objects the worker produces the fewer can he possess and the more he falls under the dominion of his product, capital.

All these consequences are contained in the definition that the worker is related to the *product of his labour* as to an *alien* object. For on this premise it is clear that the more the worker spends himself, the more powerful the alien objective world becomes which he creates over-against himself, the poorer he himself—his inner world—becomes, the less belongs to him as his own. It is the same in religion. The more man puts into God, the less he retains in himself. The worker puts his life into the object; but now his life no longer belongs to him but to the object. Hence, the greater this activity, the greater is the worker's lack of objects. Whatever the product of his labour is, he is not. Therefore the greater this product, the less is he himself. The *alienation* of the worker in his product means not only that his labour becomes an object, an *external* existence, but that it exists *outside him*, independently, as something alien to him, and that it becomes a power of its own confronting him; it means that the life which he has conferred on the object confronts him as something hostile and alien.

Let us now look more closely at the *objectification*, at the production of the worker; and therein at the *estrangement*, the *loss* of the object, his product.

The worker can create nothing without *nature*, without the *sensuous external world*. It is the material on which his labor is manifested, in which it is active, from which and by means of which it produces.

But just as nature provides labor with the *means of life* in the sense that labour cannot *live* without objects on which to operate, on the other hand, it also provides the *means of life* in the more restricted sense—i.e., the means for the physical subsistence of the *worker* himself.

Thus the more the worker by his labour *appropriates* the external world, sensuous nature, the more he deprives himself of *means of life* in the double respect: first, that the sensuous external world more and more ceases to be an object belonging to his labour—to be his labour's *means of life*; and secondly, that it more and more ceases to be *means of life* in the immediate sense, means for the physical subsistence of the worker.

Thus in this double respect the worker becomes a slave of his object, first, in that he receives an *object of labour*, i.e., in that he receives *work*; and secondly, in that he receives *means of subsistence*. Therefore, it enables him to exist, first, as a *worker*; and, second, as a *physical subject*. The extremity of this bondage is that it is only as a *worker* that he continues to maintain himself as a *physical subject*, and that it is only as a *physical subject* that he is a *worker*.

(The laws of political economy express the estrangement of the worker in his object thus: the more the worker produces, the less he has to consume; the more values he creates, the more valueless, the more unworthy he becomes; the better formed his product, the more deformed becomes the worker; the more civilized his object, the more barbarous becomes the worker; the mightier labour becomes, the more powerless becomes the worker; the more ingenious labour becomes, the duller becomes the worker and the more he becomes nature's bondsman.)

Political economy conceals the estrangement inherent in the nature of labour by not considering the direct relationship between the worker (labour) *and production*. It is true that labour produces for the rich wonderful things—but for the worker it produces privation. It produces palaces—but for the worker, hovels. It produces beauty—but for the worker, deformity. It replaces labour by machines—but some of the workers it throws back to a barbarous type of labour, and the other workers it turns into machines. It produces intelligence—but for the worker idiocy, cretinism.[5]

The direct relationship of labour to its produce is the relationship of the worker to the objects of his production. The relationship of the man of means to the objects of production and to production itself is only a *consequence* of this first relationship—and confirms it. We shall consider this other aspect later.

When we ask, then, what is the essential relationship of labour we are asking about the relationship of the *worker* to production.

Till now we have been considering the estrangement, the alienation of the worker only in one of its aspects, i.e., the worker's *relationship to the products of his labour*. But the estrangement is manifested not only in the result but in the *act of production*—within the *producing activity* itself. How would the worker come to face the product of his activity as a stranger, were it not that in the very act of production he was estranging himself from himself? The product is after all but the summary of the activity of production. If then the product of labour is alienation, production itself must be active alienation, the alienation of activity, the activity of alienation. In the estrangement of the object of labour is merely summarized the estrangement, the alienation, in the activity of labour itself.

What, then, constitutes the alienation of labour?

5. That is, stunted physical and mental development.

First, the fact that labour is *external* to the worker, i.e., it does not belong to his essential being; that in his work, therefore, he does not affirm himself but denies himself, does not feel content but unhappy, does not develop freely his physical and mental energy but mortifies his body and ruins his mind. The worker therefore only feels himself outside his work, and in his work feels outside himself. He is at home when he is not working, and when he is working he is not at home. His labour is therefore not voluntary, but coerced; it is *forced labour.* It is therefore not the satisfaction of a need; it is merely a *means* to satisfy needs external to it. Its alien character emerges clearly in the fact that as soon as no physical or other compulsion exists, labour is shunned like the plague. External labour, labour in which man alienates himself, is a labour of self-sacrifice, of mortification. Lastly, the external character of labour for the worker appears in the fact that it is not his own, but someone else's, that it does not belong to him, that in it he belongs, not to himself, but to another. Just as in religion the spontaneous activity of the human imagination, of the human brain and the human heart, operates independently of the individual—that is, operates on him as an alien, divine or diabolical activity—in the same way the worker's activity is not his spontaneous activity. It belongs to another; it is the loss of his self.

As a result, therefore, man (the worker) no longer feels himself to be freely active in any but his animal functions—eating, drinking, procreating, or at most in his dwelling and in dressing-up, etc.; and in his human functions he no longer feels himself to be anything but an animal. What is animal becomes human and what is human becomes animal.

* * *

1844 1932

From The German Ideology[1]

* * *

The fact is, therefore, that definite individuals who are productively active in a definite way enter into these definite social and political relations. Empirical observation must in each separate instance bring out empirically, and without any mystification and speculation, the connection of the social and political structure with production. The social structure and the State are continually evolving out of the life process of definite individuals, but of individuals, not as they may appear in their own or other people's imagination, but as they *really* are; i.e., as they operate, produce materially, and hence as they work under definite material limits, presuppositions and conditions independent of their will.

The production of ideas, of conceptions, of consciousness, is at first directly interwoven with the material activity and the material intercourse of men, the language of real life. Conceiving, thinking, the mental intercourse of men, appear at this stage as the direct efflux of their material behaviour.[2]

1. Translated by S. Ryazanskaya, based on an earlier translation by W. Lough.

2. That is, the actions that human beings take in their relationship to the productive forces of their society.

The same applies to mental production as expressed in the language of politics, laws, morality, religion, metaphysics, etc., of a people. Men are the producers of their conceptions, ideas, etc.—real, active men, as they are conditioned by a definite development of their productive forces and of the intercourse corresponding to these, up to its furthest forms. Consciousness can never be anything else than conscious existence, and the existence of men is their actual life-process. If in all ideology men and their circumstances appear upside-down as in a *camera obscura*,[3] this phenomenon arises just as much from their historical life-process as the inversion of objects on the retina does from their physical life-process.

In direct contrast to German philosophy[4] which descends from heaven to earth, here we ascend from earth to heaven. That is to say, we do not set out from what men say, imagine, conceive, nor from men as narrated, thought of, imagined, conceived, in order to arrive at men in the flesh. We set out from real, active men, and on the basis of their real life-process we demonstrate the development of the ideological reflexes and echoes of this life-process. The phantoms formed in the human brain are also, necessarily, sublimates of their material life-process, which is empirically verifiable and bound to material premises. Morality, religion, metaphysics, all the rest of ideology and their corresponding forms of consciousness, thus no longer retain the semblance of independence. They have no history, no development; but men, developing their material production and their material intercourse, alter, along with this their real existence, their thinking and the products of their thinking. Life is not determined by consciousness, but consciousness by life. In the first method of approach the starting-point is consciousness taken as the living individual; in the second method, which conforms to real life, it is the real living individuals themselves, and consciousness is considered solely as *their* consciousness.

This method of approach is not devoid of premises. It starts out from the real premises and does not abandon them for a moment. Its premises are men, not in any fantastic isolation and rigidity, but in their actual, empirically perceptible process of development under definite conditions. As soon as this active life-process is described, history ceases to be a collection of dead facts as it is with the empiricists[5] (themselves still abstract), or an imagined activity of imagined subjects, as with the idealists.

Where speculation ends—in real life—there real, positive science begins: the representation of the practical activity, of the practical process of development of men. Empty talk about consciousness ceases, and real knowledge has to take its place.

* * *

1845–46 1932

3. Literally, "dark chamber" (Latin): an apparatus invented in the 17th century consisting of a darkened box with an aperture (usually a lens) through which an image is projected (inverted) on the opposite wall.

4. That is, idealism, which holds that reality and knowledge derive not from perceptions but from ideas or the workings of the human mind or spirit; idealists include IMMANUEL KANT (1724–1804) and GEORG WILHELM FRIEDRICH HEGEL (1770–1831).

5. Those who believe that experiences, especially of the senses, are the only sources of knowledge; for example, DAVID HUME (1711–1776).

From The Communist Manifesto[1]

A spectre is haunting Europe—the spectre of Communism. All the Powers of old Europe have entered into a holy alliance to exorcise this spectre: Pope and Czar, Metternich and Guizot,[2] French Radicals and German police-spies.

Where is the party in opposition that has not been decried as Communistic by its opponents in power? Where the Opposition that has not hurled back the branding reproach of Communism, against the more advanced opposition parties, as well as against its reactionary adversaries?

Two things result from this fact.

I. Communism is already acknowledged by all European Powers to be itself a Power.

II. It is high time that Communists should openly, in the face of the whole world, publish their views, their aims, their tendencies, and meet this nursery tale of the Spectre of Communism with a Manifesto of the party itself.

To this end, Communists of various nationalities have assembled in London,[3] and sketched the following Manifesto, to be published in the English, French, German, Italian, Flemish and Danish languages.

I. Bourgeois and Proletarians[4]

The history of all hitherto existing society is the history of class struggles.

Freeman and slave, patrician and plebeian, lord and serf, guild-master[5] and journeyman,[6] in a word, oppressor and oppressed, stood in constant opposition to one another, carried on an uninterrupted, now hidden, now open fight, a fight that each time ended either in a revolutionary re-constitution of society at large, or in the common ruin of the contending classes.

In the earlier epochs of history, we find almost everywhere a complicated arrangement of society into various orders, a manifold gradation of social rank. In ancient Rome we have patricians, knights, plebeians, slaves; in the Middle Ages, feudal lords, vassals, guild-masters, journeymen, apprentices, serfs; in almost all of these classes, again, subordinate gradations.

The modern bourgeois society that has sprouted from the ruins of feudal society has not done away with class antagonisms. It has but established new classes, new conditions of oppression, new forms of struggle in place of the old ones.

Our epoch, the epoch of the bourgeoisie, possesses, however, this distinctive feature: it has simplified the class antagonisms: Society as a whole

1. Originally titled *Manifesto of the Communist Party*. This English text was edited by Engels.
2. François Pierre Guillaume Guizot (1787–1874), French statesman and historian who supported the idea of a constitutional monarchy. Klemens Wenzel, Fürst (Prince) von Metternich (1773–1859), Austrian statesman and foreign minister, who worked to suppress nationalist and popular constitutional movements.
3. Members of the Communist League (an international association made up mostly of German emigrés) met in November 1847; they commissioned the writing of the *Manifesto*.
4. By bourgeoisie is meant the class of modern Capitalists, owners of the means of social production and employers of wage-labour. By proletariat, the class of modern wage-labourers who, having no means of production of their own, are reduced to selling their labour-power in order to live [Engels's note].
5. Guild-master, that is, a full member of a guild, a master within, not a head of a guild [Engels's note].
6. A skilled artisan, not yet a full member of a guild, who works for master artisans rather than for himself.

is more and more splitting up into two great hostile camps, into two great classes directly facing each other: Bourgeoisie and Proletariat.

From the serfs of the Middle Ages sprang the chartered burghers[7] of the earliest towns. From these burgesses[8] the first elements of the bourgeoisie were developed.

The discovery of America, the rounding of the Cape,[9] opened up fresh ground for the rising bourgeoisie. The East-Indian and Chinese markets, the colonisation of America, trade with the colonies, the increase in the means of exchange and in commodities generally, gave to commerce, to navigation, to industry, an impulse never before known, and thereby, to the revolutionary element in the tottering feudal society, a rapid development.

The feudal system of industry, under which industrial production was monopolised by closed guilds, now no longer sufficed for the growing wants of the new markets. The manufacturing system took its place. The guild-masters were pushed on one side by the manufacturing middle class; division of labour between the different corporate guilds vanished in the face of division of labour in each single workshop.

Meantime the markets kept ever growing, the demand ever rising. Even manufacture no longer sufficed. Thereupon, steam and machinery revolutionised industrial production. The place of manufacture was taken by the giant, Modern Industry, the place of the industrial middle class, by industrial millionaires, the leaders of whole industrial armies, the modern bourgeois.

Modern industry has established the world-market, for which the discovery of America paved the way. This market has given an immense development to commerce, to navigation, to communication by land. This development has, in its turn, reacted on the extension of industry; and in proportion as industry, commerce, navigation, railways extended, in the same proportion the bourgeoisie developed, increased its capital, and pushed into the background every class handed down from the Middle Ages.

We see, therefore, how the modern bourgeoisie is itself the product of a long course of development, of a series of revolutions in the modes of production and of exchange.

Each step in the development of the bourgeoisie was accompanied by a corresponding political advance of that class. An oppressed class under the sway of the feudal nobility, an armed and self-governing association in the medieval commune;[1] here independent urban republic (as in Italy and Germany), there taxable "third estate"[2] of the monarchy (as in France), afterwards, in the period of manufacture proper, serving either the semi-feudal or the absolute monarchy as a counterpoise against the nobility, and, in fact, corner-stone of the great monarchies in general, the bourgeoisie has at last, since the establishment of Modern Industry and of the world-market, conquered for itself, in the modern representative State, exclusive political sway. The executive of the modern State is but a committee for managing the common affairs of the whole bourgeoisie.

7. Privileged middle class.
8. Citizens.
9. The Cape of Good Hope, at the southern tip of Africa.
1. This was the name given their urban communities by the townsmen of Italy and France, after they had purchased or wrested their initial rights of self-government from their feudal lords [Engels's note].
2. The common people in France (the first estate or political order was the clergy, the second the nobility).

The bourgeoisie, historically, has played a most revolutionary part.

The bourgeoisie, wherever it has got the upper hand, has put an end to all feudal, patriarchal, idyllic relations. It has pitilessly torn asunder the motley feudal ties that bound man to his "natural superiors," and has left remaining no other nexus between man and man than naked self-interest, than callous "cash payment." It has drowned the most heavenly ecstasies of religious fervour, of chivalrous enthusiasm, of philistine[3] sentimentalism, in the icy water of egotistical calculation. It has resolved personal worth into exchange value, and in place of the numberless indefeasible chartered freedoms, has set up that single, unconscionable freedom—Free Trade. In one word, for exploitation, veiled by religious and political illusions, it has substituted naked, shameless, direct, brutal exploitation.

The bourgeoisie has stripped of its halo every occupation hitherto honoured and looked up to with reverent awe. It has converted the physician, the lawyer, the priest, the poet, the man of science, into its paid wage-labourers.

The bourgeoisie has torn away from the family its sentimental veil, and has reduced the family relation to a mere money relation.

The bourgeoisie has disclosed how it came to pass that the brutal display of vigour in the Middle Ages, which Reactionists[4] so much admire, found its fitting complement in the most slothful indolence. It has been the first to show what man's activity can bring about. It has accomplished wonders far surpassing Egyptian pyramids, Roman aqueducts, and Gothic cathedrals; it has conducted expeditions that put in the shade all former Exoduses of nations and crusades.

The bourgeoisie cannot exist without constantly revolutionising the instruments of production, and thereby the relations of production, and with them the whole relations of society. Conservation of the old modes of production in unaltered form, was, on the contrary, the first condition of existence for all earlier industrial classes. Constant revolutionising of production, uninterrupted disturbance of all social conditions, everlasting uncertainty and agitation distinguish the bourgeois epoch from all earlier ones. All fixed, fast-frozen relations, with their train of ancient and venerable prejudices and opinions, are swept away, all new-formed ones become antiquated before they can ossify. All that is solid melts into air, all that is holy is profaned, and man is at last compelled to face with sober senses, his real conditions of life, and his relations with his kind.

The need of a constantly expanding market for its products chases the bourgeoisie over the whole surface of the globe. It must nestle everywhere, settle everywhere, establish connexions everywhere.

The bourgeoisie has through its exploitation of the world-market given a cosmopolitan character to production and consumption in every country. To the great chagrin of Reactionists, it has drawn from under the feet of industry the national ground on which it stood. All old-established national industries have been destroyed or are daily being destroyed. They are dislodged by new industries, whose introduction becomes a life and death question for all civilised nations, by industries that no longer work up indigenous raw

3. Materialist middle-class; the term also is used by MATTHEW ARNOLD, "The Function of Criticism at the Present Time" (1864; see below).

4. Reactionaries.

material, but raw material drawn from the remotest zones; industries whose products are consumed, not only at home, but in every quarter of the globe. In place of the old wants, satisfied by the productions of the country, we find new wants, requiring for their satisfaction the products of distant lands and climes. In place of the old local and national seclusion and self-sufficiency, we have intercourse in every direction, universal inter-dependence of nations. And as in material, so also in intellectual production. The intellectual creations of individual nations become common property. National one-sidedness and narrow-mindedness become more and more impossible, and from the numerous national and local literatures, there arises a world literature.

The bourgeoisie, by the rapid improvement of all instruments of production, by the immensely facilitated means of communication, draws all, even the most barbarian, nations into civilisation. The cheap prices of its commodities are the heavy artillery with which it batters down all Chinese walls,[5] with which it forces the barbarians' intensely obstinate hatred of foreigners to capitulate.[6] It compels all nations, on pain of extinction, to adopt the bourgeois mode of production; it compels them to introduce what it calls civilisation into their midst, i.e., to become bourgeois themselves. In one word, it creates a world after its own image.

The bourgeoisie has subjected the country to the rule of the towns. It has created enormous cities, has greatly increased the urban population as compared with the rural, and has thus rescued a considerable part of the population from the idiocy of rural life. Just as it has made the country dependent on the towns, so it has made barbarian and semi-barbarian countries dependent on the civilised ones, nations of peasants on nations of bourgeois, the East on the West.

The bourgeoisie keeps more and more doing away with the scattered state of the population, of the means of production, and of property. It has agglomerated population, centralised means of production, and has concentrated property in a few hands. The necessary consequence of this was political centralisation. Independent, or but loosely connected provinces, with separate interests, laws, governments and systems of taxation, became lumped together into one nation, with one government, one code of laws, one national class-interest, one frontier and one customs-tariff.

The bourgeoisie, during its rule of scarce one hundred years, has created more massive and more colossal productive forces than have all preceding generations together. Subjection of Nature's forces to man, machinery, application of chemistry to industry and agriculture, steam-navigation, railways, electric telegraphs, clearing of whole continents for cultivation, canalisation of rivers, whole populations conjured out of the ground—what earlier century had even a presentiment that such productive forces slumbered in the lap of social labour?

* * *

1848, 1888

5. That is, barriers that separate two or more groups, usually as a means of restricting the flow of information, goods, and people (an allusion to the Great Wall of China).

6. China unsuccessfully fought the Opium Wars (1839–42, 1856–60) to prevent the expansion of Western trade.

From Grundrisse[1]

* * *

In the case of the arts, it is well known that certain periods of their flowering are out of all proportion to the general development of society, hence also to the material foundation, the skeletal structure as it were, of its organization. For example, the Greeks compared to the moderns or also Shakespeare. It is even recognized that certain forms of art, e.g. the epic, can no longer be produced in their world epoch-making, classical stature as soon as the production of art, as such, begins; that is, that certain significant forms within the realm of the arts are possible only at an undeveloped stage of artistic development. If this is the case with the relation between different kinds of art within the realm of the arts, it is already less puzzling that it is the case in the relation of the entire realm to the general development of society. The difficulty consists only in the general formulation of these contradictions. As soon as they have been specified, they are already clarified.

Let us take e.g. the relation of Greek art and then of Shakespeare to the present time. It is well known that Greek mythology is not only the arsenal of Greek art but also its foundation. Is the view of nature and of social relations on which the Greek imagination and hence Greek [mythology] is based possible with self-acting mule spindles[2] and railways and locomotives and electrical telegraphs? What chance has Vulcan against Roberts & Co., Jupiter against the lightning rod and Hermes against the Credit Mobilier?[3] All mythology overcomes and dominates and shapes the forces of nature in the imagination and by the imagination; it therefore vanishes with the advent of real mastery over them. What becomes of Fama[4] alongside Printing House Square? Greek art presupposes Greek mythology, i.e. nature and the social forms already reworked in an unconsciously artistic way by the popular imagination. This is its material. Not any mythology whatever, i.e. not an arbitrarily chosen unconsciously artistic reworking of nature (here meaning everything objective, hence including society). Egyptian mythology could never have been the foundation or the womb of Greek art. But, in any case, a *mythology*. Hence, in no way a social development which excludes all mythological, all mythologizing relations to nature; which therefore demands of the artist an imagination not dependent on mythology.

From another side, is Achilles[5] possible with powder and lead? Or the *Iliad* with the printing press, not to mention the printing machine? Do not the song and the saga and the muse necessarily come to an end with the printer's bar,[6] hence do not the necessary conditions of epic poetry vanish?

1. Translated by Martin Nicolaus, who sometimes includes clarifying words in brackets: the title, usually left untranslated, means "outlines" or "foundations."
2. Machines used in spinning thread, invented in the late 18th century.
3. A major investment bank in France during the Second Empire (1852–70), against which Marx pits Hermes, Greek god of commerce and invention. The other two (Roman) gods are similarly paired: Vulcan, god of metalworking, with a commercial firm and Jupiter, supreme god and wielder of the thunderbolt, with a lightning rod.
4. Rumor (Latin), a Roman personification; she repeated whatever she heard until everyone knew it.
5. The greatest of the Greek warriors at Troy, and the focus of Homer's *Iliad* (ca. 8th c. B.C.E.).
6. Lever used to screw down the flat plate of a manual printing press (the German word used here, *Preßbengel*, can also mean printing in general). "The muse": goddess presiding over the arts and intellectual pursuits, traditionally invoked by epic poets as an aid to memory.

But the difficulty lies not in understanding that the Greek arts and epic are bound up with certain forms of social development. The difficulty is that they still afford us artistic pleasure and that in a certain respect they count as a norm and as an unattainable model.

A man cannot become a child again, or he becomes childish. But does he not find joy in the child's naiveté, and must he himself not strive to reproduce its truth at a higher stage? Does not the true character of each epoch come alive in the nature of its children? Why should not the historic childhood of humanity, its most beautiful unfolding, as a stage never to return, exercise an eternal charm? There are unruly children and precocious children. Many of the old peoples belong in this category. The Greeks were normal children. The charm of their art for us is not in contradiction to the undeveloped stage of society on which it grew. [It] is its result, rather, and is inextricably bound up, rather, with the fact that the unripe social conditions under which it arose, and could alone arise, can never return.

1857–58 1939–42

From Preface to *A Contribution to the Critique of Political Economy*[1]

* * *

The first work which I undertook for a solution of the doubts which assailed me was a critical review of the Hegelian philosophy of right, a work the introduction to which appeared in 1844 in the *Deutsch-Französische Jahrbücher*,[2] published in Paris. My investigation led to the result that legal relations as well as forms of state are to be grasped neither from themselves nor from the so-called general development of the human mind, but rather have their roots in the material conditions of life, the sum total of which Hegel, following the example of the Englishmen and Frenchmen of the eighteenth century, combines under the name of "civil society," that, however, the anatomy of civil society is to be sought in political economy. The investigation of the latter, which I began in Paris, I continued in Brussels, whither I had emigrated in consequence of an expulsion order of M. Guizot.[3] The general result at which I arrived and which, once won, served as a guiding thread for my studies, can be briefly formulated as follows: In the social production of their life, men enter into definite relations that are indispensable and independent of their will, relations of production which correspond to a definite stage of development of their material productive forces. The sum total of these relations of production constitutes the economic structure of society, the real foundation, on which rises a legal and political superstructure and to which correspond definite forms of social consciousness. The mode of production of material life conditions the social, political and intellectual life process in

1. Translated by Robert C. Tucker.

2. *German-French Yearbook*. The German philosopher Georg Wilhelm Friedrich Hegel (1770–1831) described his political philosophy in the *Philosophy of Right* (1821); Marx's essay was "Contribution to the Critique of Hegel's Philosophy of Right."

3. François Pierre Guillaume Guizot (1787–1874), French statesman and historian who supported the idea of a constitutional monarchy; he was the chief power in the government between 1840 and 1848.

general. It is not the consciousness of men that determines their being, but, on the contrary, their social being that determines their consciousness. At a certain stage of their development, the material productive forces of society come in conflict with the existing relations of production, or—what is but a legal expression for the same thing—with the property relations within which they have been at work hitherto. From forms of development of the productive forces these relations turn into their fetters. Then begins an epoch of social revolution. With the change of the economic foundation the entire immense superstructure is more or less rapidly transformed. In considering such transformations a distinction should always be made between the material transformation of the economic conditions of production, which can be determined with the precision of natural science, and the legal, political, religious, aesthetic or philosophic—in short, ideological forms in which men become conscious of this conflict and fight it out. Just as our opinion of an individual is not based on what he thinks of himself, so can we not judge of such a period of transformation by its own consciousness; on the contrary, this consciousness must be explained rather from the contradictions of material life, from the existing conflict between the social productive forces and the relations of production. No social order ever perishes before all the productive forces for which there is room in it have developed; and new, higher relations of production never appear before the material conditions of their existence have matured in the womb of the old society itself. Therefore mankind always sets itself only such tasks as it can solve; since, looking at the matter more closely, it will always be found that the task itself arises only when the material conditions for its solution already exist or are at least in the process of formation. In broad outlines Asiatic, ancient, feudal, and modern bourgeois modes of production can be designated as progressive epochs in the economic formation of society. The bourgeois relations of production are the last antagonistic form of the social process of production—antagonistic not in the sense of individual antagonism, but of one arising from the social conditions of life of the individuals; at the same time the productive forces developing in the womb of bourgeois society create the material conditions for the solution of that antagonism.[4] This social formation brings, therefore, the prehistory of human society to a close.

* * *

1859

From Capital, Volume 1[1]

From *Chapter 1. Commodities*

SECTION 4. THE FETISHISM OF COMMODITIES AND THE SECRET THEREOF

A commodity appears, at first sight, a very trivial thing, and easily understood. Its analysis shows that it is, in reality, a very queer thing, abounding

4. That is, socialism—the final "mode of production," which is in the process of emerging through the class struggle of the bourgeoisie and proletarians.

1. Translated by Samuel Moore and Edward Aveling, and edited by Engels.

in metaphysical subtleties and theological niceties. So far as it is a value in use, there is nothing mysterious about it, whether we consider it from the point of view that by its properties it is capable of satisfying human wants, or from the point that those properties are the product of human labour. It is as clear as noon-day, that man, by his industry, changes the forms of the materials furnished by Nature, in such a way as to make them useful to him. The form of wood, for instance, is altered, by making a table out of it. Yet, for all that, the table continues to be that common, every-day thing, wood. But, so soon as it steps forth as a commodity, it is changed into something transcendent. It not only stands with its feet on the ground, but, in relation to all other commodities, it stands on its head, and evolves out of its wooden brain grotesque ideas, far more wonderful than "table-turning" ever was.

The mystical character of commodities does not originate, therefore, in their use-value. Just as little does it proceed from the nature of the determining factors of value. For, in the first place, however varied the useful kinds of labour, or productive activities, may be, it is a physiological fact, that they are functions of the human organism, and that each such function, whatever may be its nature or form, is essentially the expenditure of human brain, nerves, muscles, &c. Secondly, with regard to that which forms the groundwork for the quantitative determination of value, namely, the duration of that expenditure, or the quantity of labour, it is quite clear that there is a palpable difference between its quantity and quality. In all states of society, the labour-time that it costs to produce the means of subsistence, must necessarily be an object of interest to mankind, though not of equal interest in different stages of development. And lastly, from the moment that men in any way work for one another, their labour assumes a social form.

Whence, then, arises the enigmatical character of the product of labour, so soon as it assumes the form of commodities? Clearly from this form itself. The equality of all sorts of human labour is expressed objectively by their products all being equally values; the measure of the expenditure of labour-power by the duration of that expenditure, takes the form of the quantity of value of the products of labour; and finally, the mutual relations of the producers, within which the social character of their labour affirms itself, take the form of a social relation between the products.

A commodity is therefore a mysterious thing, simply because in it the social character of men's labour appears to them as an objective character stamped upon the product of that labour; because the relation of the producers to the sum total of their own labour is presented to them as a social relation, existing not between themselves, but between the products of their labour. This is the reason why the products of labour become commodities, social things whose qualities are at the same time perceptible and imperceptible by the senses. In the same way the light from an object is perceived by us not as the subjective excitation of our optic nerve, but as the objective form of something outside the eye itself. But, in the act of seeing, there is at all events, an actual passage of light from one thing to another, from the external object to the eye. There is a physical relation between physical things. But it is different with commodities. There, the existence of the things *quâ*[2] commodities, and the value-relation between the products of

2. As (originally Latin).

labour which stamps them as commodities, have absolutely no connexion with their physical properties and with the material relations arising therefrom. There it is a definite social relation between men, that assumes, in their eyes, the fantastic form of a relation between things. In order, therefore, to find an analogy, we must have recourse to the mist-enveloped regions of the religious world. In that world the productions of the human brain appear as independent beings endowed with life, and entering into relation both with one another and the human race. So it is in the world of commodities with the products of men's hands. This I call the Fetishism which attaches itself to the products of labour,[3] so soon as they are produced as commodities, and which is therefore inseparable from the production of commodities.

This Fetishism of commodities has its origin, as the foregoing analysis has already shown, in the peculiar social character of the labour that produces them.

As a general rule, articles of utility become commodities, only because they are products of the labour of private individuals or groups of individuals who carry on their work independently of each other. The sum total of the labour of all these private individuals forms the aggregate labour of society. Since the producers do not come into social contact with each other until they exchange their products, the specific social character of each producer's labour does not show itself except in the act of exchange. In other words, the labour of the individual asserts itself as a part of the labour of society, only by means of the relations which the act of exchange establishes directly between the products, and indirectly, through them, between the producers. To the latter, therefore, the relations connecting the labour of one individual with that of the rest appear, not as direct social relations between individuals at work, but as what they really are, material relations between persons and social relations between things. It is only by being exchanged that the products of labour acquire, as values, one uniform social status, distinct from their varied forms of existence as objects of utility. This division of a product into a useful thing and a value becomes practically important, only when exchange has acquired such an extension that useful articles are produced for the purpose of being exchanged, and their character as values has therefore to be taken into account, beforehand, during production. From this moment the labour of the individual producer acquires socially a two-fold character. On the one hand, it must, as a definite useful kind of labour, satisfy a definite social want, and thus hold its place as part and parcel of the collective labour of all, as a branch of a social division of labour that has sprung up spontaneously. On the other hand, it can satisfy the manifold wants of the individual producer himself, only in so far as the mutual exchangeability of all kinds of useful private labour is an established social fact, and therefore the private useful labour of each producer ranks on an equality with that of all others. The equalisation of the most different kinds of labour can be the result only of an abstraction from their inequalities, or of reducing them to their common denominator, viz.,[4]

3. By analogy with religious fetishism, the attribution of magical or divine power to objects. Similarly, according to Marx, we impute to commodities a life of their own (and a seemingly inherent value). We treat as relations between people what are in fact relations between commodities and people, thereby attributing human powers to things.

4. Namely, that is to say (from medieval Latin *videlicet*).

expenditure of human labour-power or human labour in the abstract. The two-fold social character of the labour of the individual appears to him, when reflected in his brain, only under those forms which are impressed upon that labour in every-day practice by the exchange of products. In this way, the character that his own labour possesses of being socially useful takes the form of the condition, that the product must be not only useful, but useful for others, and the social character that his particular labour has of being the equal of all other particular kinds of labour, takes the form that all the physically different articles that are the products of labour, have one common quality, viz., that of having value.

Hence, when we bring the products of our labour into relation with each other as values, it is not because we see in these articles the material receptacles of homogeneous human labour. Quite the contrary: whenever, by an exchange, we equate as values our different products, by that very act, we also equate, as human labour, the different kinds of labour expended upon them. We are not aware of this, nevertheless we do it. Value, therefore, does not stalk about with a label describing what it is. It is value, rather, that converts every product into a social hieroglyphic. Later on, we try to decipher the hieroglyphic, to get behind the secret of our own social products; for to stamp an object of utility as a value, is just as much a social product as language. The recent scientific discovery, that the products of labour, so far as they are values, are but material expressions of the human labour spent in their production, marks, indeed, an epoch in the history of the development of the human race, but, by no means, dissipates the mist through which the social character of labour appears to us to be an objective character of the products themselves. The fact, that in the particular form of production with which we are dealing, viz., the production of commodities, the specific social character of private labour carried on independently, consists in the equality of every kind of that labour, by virtue of its being human labour, which character, therefore, assumes in the product the form of value—this fact appears to the producers, notwithstanding the discovery above referred to, to be just as real and final, as the fact, that, after the discovery by science of the component gases of air, the atmosphere itself remained unaltered.

What, first of all, practically concerns producers when they make in exchange, is the question, how much of some other product they get for their own? in what proportions the products are exchangeable? When these proportions have, by custom, attained a certain stability, they appear to result from the nature of the products, so that, for instance, one ton of iron and two ounces of gold appear as naturally to be of equal value as a pound of gold and a pound of iron in spite of their different physical and chemical qualities appear to be of equal weight. The character of having value, when once impressed upon products, obtains fixity only by reason of their acting and re-acting upon each other as quantities of value. These quantities vary continually, independently of the will, foresight and action of the producers. To them, their own social action takes the form of the action of objects, which rule the producers instead of being ruled by them. It requires a fully developed production of commodities before, from accumulated experience alone, the scientific conviction springs up, that all the different kinds of private labour, which are carried on independently of each other, and yet as spontaneously developed branches of the social division of labour, are continually being reduced to the quantitative proportions in which society requires them. And why? Because, in the midst of all the accidental and ever fluctuating exchange-relations between the products, the labour-time socially necessary for their production forcibly asserts itself like an over-riding law of Nature. The law of gravity thus asserts itself when a house falls about our ears. The determination of the magnitude of value by labour-time is therefore a secret, hidden under the apparent fluctuations in the relative values of commodities. Its discovery, while removing all appearance of mere accidentality from the determination of the magnitude of the values of products, yet in no way alters the mode in which that determination takes place.

Man's reflections on the forms of social life, and consequently, also, his scientific analysis of those forms, take a course directly opposite to that of their actual historical development. He begins, post festum,[5] with the results of the process of development ready to hand before him. The characters that stamp products as commodities, and whose establishment is a necessary preliminary to the circulation of commodities, have already acquired the stability of natural, self-understood forms of social life, before man seeks to decipher, not their historical character, for in his eyes they are immutable, but their meaning. Consequently it was the analysis of the prices of commodities that alone led to the determination of the magnitude of value, and it was the common expression of all commodities in money that alone led to the establishment of their characters as values. It is, however, just this ultimate money-form of the world of commodities that actually conceals, instead of disclosing, the social character of private labour, and the social relations between the individual producers. When I state that coats or boots stand in a relation to linen, because it is the universal incarnation of abstract human labour, the absurdity of the statement is self-evident. Nevertheless, when the producers of coats and boots compare those articles with linen, or, what is the same thing, with gold or silver, as the universal equivalent, they express the relation between their own private labour and the collective labour of society in the same absurd form.

The categories of bourgeois economy consist of such like forms. They are forms of thought expressing with social validity the conditions and relations of a definite, historically determined mode of production, viz., the production of commodities. The whole mystery of commodities, all the magic and necromancy that surrounds the products of labour as long as they take the form of commodities, vanishes therefore, so soon as we come to other forms of production.

Since Robinson Crusoe's[6] experiences are a favourite theme with political economists, let us take a look at him on his island. Moderate though he be, yet some few wants he has to satisfy, and must therefore do a little useful work of various sorts, such as making tools and furniture, taming goats, fishing and hunting. Of his prayers and the like we take no account, since they are a source of pleasure to him, and he looks upon them as so much recreation. In spite of the variety of his work, he knows that his labour, whatever

5. After the feast (Latin); after the fact, too late.
6. The hero and title character of Daniel Defoe's 1719–20 novel, an English sailor shipwrecked for 24 years on a small tropical island. He is discussed by some political economists and philosophers—including Adam Smith (1723–1790) and Jean-Jacques Rousseau (1712–1778)—who base their analyses of production on the solitary independent worker.

its form, is but the activity of one and the same Robinson, and consequently, that it consists of nothing but different modes of human labour. Necessity itself compels him to apportion his time accurately between his different kinds of work. Whether one kind occupies a greater space in his general activity than another, depends on the difficulties, greater or less as the case may be, to be overcome in attaining the useful effect aimed at. This our friend Robinson soon learns by experience, and having rescued a watch, ledger, and pen and ink from the wreck, commences, like a true-born Briton, to keep a set of books. His stock-book contains a list of the objects of utility that belong to him, of the operations necessary for their production; and lastly, of the labour-time that definite quantities of those objects have, on an average, cost him. All the relations between Robinson and the objects that form this wealth of his own creation, are here so simple and clear as to be intelligible without exertion, even to Mr. Sedley Taylor.[7] And yet those relations contain all that is essential to the determination of value.

Let us now transport ourselves from Robinson's island bathed in light to the European middle ages shrouded in darkness. Here, instead of the independent man, we find everyone dependent, serfs and lords, vassals and suzerains, laymen and clergy. Personal dependence here characterises the social relations of production just as much as it does the other spheres of life organised on the basis of that production. But for the very reason that personal dependence forms the ground-work of society, there is no necessity for labour and its products to assume a fantastic form different from their reality. They take the shape, in the transactions of society, of services in kind and payments in kind. Here the particular and natural form of labour, and not, as in a society based on production of commodities, its general abstract form is the immediate social form of labour. Compulsory labour is just as properly measured by time, as commodity-producing labour, but every serf knows that what he expends in the service of his lord, is a definite quantity of his own personal labour-power. The tithe to be rendered to the priest is more matter of fact than his blessing. No matter, then, what we may think of the parts played by the different classes of people themselves in this society, the social relations between individuals in the performance of their labour, appear at all events as their own mutual personal relations, and are not disguised under the shape of social relations between the products of labour.

For an example of labour in common or directly associated labour, we have no occasion to go back to that spontaneously developed form which we find on the threshold of the history of all civilised races. We have one close at hand in the patriarchal industries of a peasant family, that produces corn, cattle, yarn, linen, and clothing for home use. These different articles are, as regards the family, so many products of its labour, but as between themselves, they are not commodities. The different kinds of labour, such as tillage, cattle tending, spinning, weaving and making clothes, which result in the various products, are in themselves, and such as they are, direct social functions, because functions of the family, which, just as much as a society based on the production of commodities, possesses a spontaneously developed system of division of labour. The distribution of the work within the family, and the regulation of

7. A Fellow of Trinity College, Cambridge (1834–1920), who wrote both about musical sounds and harmony and about the relationship between capital and labor.

the labour-time of the several members, depend as well upon differences of age and sex as upon natural conditions varying with the seasons. The labour-power of each individual, by its very nature, operates in this case merely as a definite portion of the whole labour-power of the family, and therefore, the measure of the expenditure of individual labour-power by its duration, appears here by its very nature as a social character of their labour.

Let us now picture to ourselves, by way of change, a community of free individuals, carrying on their work with the means of production in common, in which the labour-power of all the different individuals is consciously applied as the combined labour-power of the community. All the characteristics of Robinson's labour are here repeated, but with this difference, that they are social, instead of individual. Everything produced by him was exclusively the result of his own personal labour, and therefore simply an object of use for himself. The total product of our community is a social product. One portion serves as fresh means of production and remains social. But another portion is consumed by the members as means of subsistence. A distribution of this portion amongst them is consequently necessary. The mode of this distribution will vary with the productive organisation of the community, and the degree of historical development attained by the producers. We will assume, but merely for the sake of a parallel with the production of commodities, that the share of each individual producer in the means of subsistence is determined by his labour-time. Labour-time would, in that case, play a double part. Its apportionment in accordance with a definite social plan maintains the proper proportion between the different kinds of work to be done and the various wants of the community. On the other hand, it also serves as a measure of the portion of the common labour borne by each individual, and of his share in the part of the total product destined for individual consumption. The social relations of the individual producers, with regard both to their labour and to its products, are in this case perfectly simple and intelligible, and that with regard not only to production but also to distribution.

The religious world is but the reflex of the real world. And for a society based upon the production of commodities, in which the producers in general enter into social relations with one another by treating their products as commodities and values, whereby they reduce their individual private labour to the standard of homogeneous human labour—for such a society, Christianity with its *cultus*[8] of abstract man, more especially in its bourgeois developments, Protestantism, Deism,[9] &c., is the most fitting form of religion. In the ancient Asiatic and other ancient modes of production, we find that the conversion of products into commodities, and therefore the conversion of men into producers of commodities, holds a subordinate place, which, however, increases in importance as the primitive communities approach nearer and nearer to their dissolution. Trading nations, properly so called, exist in the ancient world only in its interstices, like the gods of Epicurus in the Intermundia,[1] or like Jews in the pores of Polish society. Those ancient social

8. Care of; adoration, worship (Latin).

9. Belief in a supreme being as the source of existence that rejects the supernatural doctrines of Christianity and the influence or revelation of God in the universe, stressing instead the importance of reason and ethical conduct.

1. The spaces between the worlds (Latin). Epicurus (341–270 B.C.E.), Greek philosopher who held that the gods had nothing to do with human affairs.

organisms of production are, as compared with bourgeois society, extremely simple and transparent. But they are founded either on the immature development of man individually, who has not yet severed the umbilical cord that unites him with his fellowmen in a primitive tribal community, or upon direct relations of subjection. They can arise and exist only when the development of the productive power of labour has not risen beyond a low stage, and when, therefore, the social relations within the sphere of material life, between man and man, and between man and Nature, are correspondingly narrow. This narrowness is reflected in the ancient worship of Nature, and in the other elements of the popular religions. The religious reflex of the real world can, in any case, only then finally vanish, when the practical relations of every-day life offer to man none but perfectly intelligible and reasonable relations with regard to his fellowmen and to Nature.

The life-process of society, which is based on the process of material production, does not strip off its mystical veil until it is treated as production by freely associated men, and is consciously regulated by them in accordance with a settled plan. This, however, demands for society a certain material ground-work or set of conditions of existence which in their turn are the spontaneous product of a long and painful process of development.

Political Economy has indeed analysed, however incompletely, value and its magnitude, and has discovered what lies beneath these forms. But it has never once asked the question why labour is represented by the value of its product and labour-time by the magnitude of that value. These formulæ, which bear it stamped upon them in unmistakeable letters that they belong to a state of society, in which the process of production has the mastery over man, instead of being controlled by him, such formulæ appear to the bourgeois intellect to be as much a self-evident necessity imposed by Nature as productive labour itself. Hence forms of social production that preceded the bourgeois form, are treated by the bourgeoisie in much the same way as the Fathers of the Church[2] treated pre-Christian religions.

To what extent some economists are misled by the Fetishism inherent in commodities, or by the objective appearance of the social characteristics of labour, is shown, amongst other ways, by the dull and tedious quarrel over the part played by Nature in the formation of exchange-value. Since exchange-value is a definite social manner of expressing the amount of labour bestowed upon object, Nature has no more to do with it, than it has in fixing the course of exchange.

The mode of production in which the product takes the form of a commodity, or is produced directly for exchange, is the most general and most embryonic form of bourgeois production. It therefore makes its appearance at an early date in history, though not in the same predominating and characteristic manner as now-a-days. Hence its Fetish character is comparatively easy to be seen through. But when we come to more concrete forms, even this appearance of simplicity vanishes. Whence arose the illusions of the monetary system? To it gold and silver, when serving as money, did not represent a social relation between producers but were natural objects with strange social properties. And modern economy, which looks down with such disdain on the monetary system, does not its superstition come out as

2. Early Christian writers who established Christian doctrine before the 8th century.

clear as noon-day, whenever it treats of capital? How long is it since economy discarded the physiocratic illusion, that rents grow out of the soil and not out of society?[3]

But not to anticipate, we will content ourselves with yet another example relating to the commodity-form. Could commodities themselves speak, they would say: Our use-value may be a thing that interests men. It is no part of us as objects. What, however, does belong to us as objects, is our value. Our natural intercourse as commodities proves it. In the eyes of each other we are nothing but exchange-values. Now listen how those commodities speak through the mouth of the economist. "Value"—(*i.e.*, exchange-value) "is a property of things, riches"—(*i.e.*, use-value) "of man. Value, in this sense, necessarily implies exchanges, riches do not." "Riches" (use-value) "are the attribute of men, value is the attribute of commodities. A man or a community is rich, a pearl or a diamond is valuable. . . . A pearl or a diamond is valuable" as a pearl or diamond. So far no chemist has ever discovered exchange-value either in a pearl or a diamond. The economic discoverers of this chemical element, who by-the-by lay special claim to critical acumen, find however that the use-value of objects belongs to them independently of their material properties, while their value, on the other hand, forms a part of them as objects. What confirms them in this view, is the peculiar circumstance that the use-value of objects is realised without exchange, by means of a direct relation between the objects and man, while, on the other hand, their value is realised only by exchange, that is, by means of a social process. Who fails here to call to mind our good friend, Dogberry, who informs neighbour Seacoal, that, "To be a well-favoured man is the gift of fortune; but reading and writing comes by Nature."[4]

From *Chapter 10. The Working-Day*

SECTION 5. THE STRUGGLE FOR A NORMAL WORKING-DAY. COMPULSORY LAWS FOR THE EXTENSION OF THE WORKING-DAY FROM THE MIDDLE OF THE 14TH TO THE END OF THE 17TH CENTURY

"What is a working-day? What is the length of time during which capital may consume the labour-power whose daily value it buys? How far may the working-day be extended beyond the working-time necessary for the reproduction of labour-power itself?" It has been seen that to these questions capital replies: the working-day contains the full 24 hours, with the deduction of the few hours of repose without which labour-power absolutely refuses its services again. Hence it is self-evident that the labourer is nothing else, his whole life through, than labour-power, that therefore all his disposable time is by nature and law labour-time, to be devoted to the self-expansion of capital. Time for education, for intellectual development, for the fulfilling of social functions and for social intercourse, for the free-play of his bodily and mental activity, even the rest time of Sunday (and that in a country of Sabbatarians!)—moonshine![5] But in its blind unrestrainable passion, its

3. The Physiocrats, late 18th-century French economists who were proponents of free trade, believed that agriculture is the source of all wealth.

4. Shakespeare, *Much Ado about Nothing* (ca. 1598), 3.3.13–14 (slightly misquoted). Dogberry is a comic character, the commander of the watch; Seacoal is one of the watchman.

5. Nonsense, foolishness. Sabbatarians: those who favor strict observance of the Sabbath.

were-wolf[6] hunger for surplus-labour, capital oversteps not only the moral, but even the merely physical maximum bounds of the working-day. It usurps the time for growth, development, and healthy maintenance of the body. It steals the time required for the consumption of fresh air and sunlight. It higgles[7] over a meal-time, incorporating it where possible with the process of production itself, so that food is given to the labourer as to a mere means of production, as coal is supplied to the boiler, grease and oil to the machinery. It reduces the sound sleep needed for the restoration, reparation, refreshment of the bodily powers to just so many hours of torpor as the revival of an organism, absolutely exhausted, renders essential. It is not the normal maintenance of the labour-power which is to determine the limits of the working-day; it is the greatest possible daily expenditure of labour-power, no matter how diseased, compulsory, and painful it may be, which is to determine the limits of the labourers' period of repose. Capital cares nothing for the length of life of labour-power. All that concerns it is simply and solely the maximum of labour-power, that can be rendered fluent in a working-day. It attains this end by shortening the extent of the labourer's life, as a greedy farmer snatches increased produce from the soil by robbing it of its fertility.

The capitalistic mode of production (essentially the production of surplus-value,[8] the absorption of surplus-labour), produces thus, with the extension of the working-day, not only the deterioration of human labour-power by robbing it of its normal, moral and physical, conditions of development and function. It produces also the premature exhaustion and death of this labour-power itself. It extends the labourer's time of production during a given period by shortening his actual life-time.

But the value of the labour-power includes the value of the commodities necessary for the reproduction of the worker, or for the keeping up of the working-class. If then the unnatural extension of the working-day, that capital necessarily strives after in its unmeasured passion for self-expansion, shortens the length of life of the individual labourer, and therefore the duration of his labour-power, the forces used up have to be replaced at a more rapid rate and the sum of the expenses for the reproduction of labour-power will be greater; just as in a machine the part of its value to be reproduced every day is greater the more rapidly the machine is worn out. It would seem therefore that the interest of capital itself points in the direction of a normal working-day.

The slave-owner buys his labourer as he buys his horse. If he loses his slave, he loses capital that can only be restored by new outlay in the slave-mart. But "the rice-grounds of Georgia, or the swamps of the Mississippi may be fatally injurious to the human constitution; but the waste of human life which the cultivation of these districts necessitates, is not so great that it cannot be repaired from the teeming preserves of Virginia and Kentucky. Considerations of economy, moreover, which, under a natural system, afford some security for human treatment by identifying the master's interest with the slave's preservation, when once trading in slaves is practised, become reasons

6. That is, ravenous (like the folkloric human able to transform into a wolf).
7. Haggles.
8. The difference between the amount of capital needed to produce something and the amount of capital that product is worth; it is created from labor power.

for racking to the uttermost the toil of the slave; for, when his place can at once be supplied from foreign preserves, the duration of his life becomes a matter of less moment than its productiveness while it lasts. It is accordingly a maxim of slave management, in slave-importing countries, that the most effective economy is that which takes out of the human chattel in the shortest space of time the utmost amount of exertion it is capable of putting forth. It is in tropical culture, where annual profits often equal the whole capital of plantations, that negro life is most recklessly sacrificed. It is the agriculture of the West Indies, which has been for centuries prolific of fabulous wealth, that has engulfed millions of the African race. It is in Cuba, at this day, whose revenues are reckoned by millions, and whose planters are princes, that we see in the servile class, the coarsest fare, the most exhausting and unremitting toil, and even the absolute destruction of a portion of its numbers every year."[9]

Mutato nomine de te fabula narratur.[1] For slave-trade read labour-market, for Kentucky and Virginia, Ireland and the agricultural districts of England, Scotland, and Wales, for Africa, Germany. We heard how over-work thinned the ranks of the bakers in London. Nevertheless, the London labour-market is always over-stocked with German and other candidates for death in the bakeries. Pottery, as we saw, is one of the shortest-lived industries. Is there any want therefore of potters? Josiah Wedgwood,[2] the inventor of modern pottery, himself originally a common workman, said in 1785 before the House of Commons that the whole trade employed from 15,000 to 20,000 people. In the year 1861 the population alone of the town centres of this industry in Great Britain numbered 101,302. "The cotton trade has existed for ninety years . . . It has existed for three generations of the English race, and I believe I may safely say that during that period it has destroyed nine generations of factory operatives."[3] * * *

What experience shows to the capitalist generally is a constant excess of population, *i.e.*, an excess in relation to the momentary requirements of surplus-labour-absorbing capital, although this excess is made up of generations of human beings stunted, short-lived, swiftly replacing each other, plucked, so to say, before maturity. And, indeed, experience shows to the intelligent observer with what swiftness and grip the capitalist mode of production, dating, historically speaking, only from yesterday, has seized the vital power of the people by the very root—shows how the degeneration of the industrial population is only retarded by the constant absorption of primitive and physically uncorrupted elements from the country—shows how even the country labourers, in spite of fresh air and the principle of natural selection, that works so powerfully amongst them, and only permits the survival of the strongest, are already beginning to die off. Capital that has such good reasons for denying the sufferings of the legions of workers that surround it, is in practice moved as much and as little by the sight of the coming degradation and final depopulation of the human race, as by the probable fall of the earth into the sun. In every stock-jobbing swindle[4] every one knows

9. Quoted from J. E. Cairnes, *The Slave Power* (London, 1862).
1. Once the name has been changed, the story is told about you (Latin); from HORACE (65–8 B.C.E.), *Satires* 1.1.69–70.
2. Noted English potter (1730–1795).
3. Quoted from a speech delivered in the House of Commons, April 27, 1863. The following ellipsis is the translators'.
4. That is, dishonest stock speculation.

that some time or other the crash must come, but every one hopes that it may fall on the head of his neighbour, after he himself has caught the shower of gold and placed it in safety. *Après moi le déluge!*[5] is the watchword of every capitalist and of every capitalist nation. Hence Capital is reckless of the health or length of life of the labourer, unless under compulsion from society. To the out-cry as to the physical and mental degradation, the premature death, the torture of over-work, it answers: Ought these to trouble us since they increase our profits? But looking at things as a whole, all this does not, indeed, depend on the good or ill will of the individual capitalist. Free competition brings out the inherent laws of capitalist production, in the shape of external coercive laws having power over every individual capitalist.

The establishment of a normal working-day is the result of centuries of struggle between capitalist and labourer. The history of this struggle shows two opposed tendencies. Compare, *e.g.*, the English factory legislation of our time with the English Labour Statutes from the 14th century to well into the middle of the 18th. Whilst the modern Factory Acts[6] compulsorily shortened the working-day, the earlier statutes tried to lengthen it by compulsion. Of course the pretensions of capital in embryo—when, beginning to grow, it secures the right of absorbing a *quantum sufficit*[7] of surplus-labour, not merely by the force of economic relations, but by the help of the State—appear very modest when put face to face with the concessions that, growling and struggling, it has to make in its adult condition. It takes centuries ere the "free" labourer, thanks to the development of capitalistic production, agrees, *i.e.*, is compelled by social conditions, to sell the whole of his active life, his very capacity for work, for the price of the necessaries of life, his birthright for a mess of pottage.[8] Hence it is natural that the lengthening of the work-day, which capital, from the middle of the 14th to the end of the 17th century, tries to impose by State-measures on adult labourers, approximately coincides with the shortening of the working-day which, in the second half of the 19th century, has here and there been effected by the State to prevent the coining of children's blood into capital. That which to-day, *e.g.*, in the State of Massachusetts, until recently the freest State of the North-American Republic, has been proclaimed as the statutory limit of the labour of children under 12,[9] was in England, even in the middle of the 17th century, the normal working-day of able-bodied artisans, robust labourers, athletic blacksmiths.

* * *

1867

5. After me the flood (French); an old French proverb, often attributed to Louis XV or his mistress, Madame de Pompadour, after the 1757 defeat of the French and Austrian armies in the battle of Rossbach.

6. Series of measures, passed beginning in 1819, intended to improve working conditions (particularly for children and women workers).

7. Sufficient quantity (Latin).

8. As the hungry Esau sold his birthright to his brother Jacob; Genesis 25.29–34.

9. That is, a 10-hour day (the law passed in 1842).

From Letter from Friedrich Engels to Joseph Bloch[1]

London, September 21–22, 1890

According to the materialist conception of history, the *ultimately* determining element in history is the production and reproduction of real life. More than this neither Marx nor I have ever asserted. Hence if somebody twists this into saying that the economic element is the *only* determining one, he transforms that proposition into a meaningless, abstract, senseless phrase. The economic situation is the basis, but the various elements of the superstructure: political forms of the class struggle and its results, to wit: constitutions established by the victorious class after a successful battle, etc., juridical forms, and then even the reflexes of all these actual struggles in the brains of the participants, political, juristic, philosophical theories, religious views and their further development into systems of dogmas, also exercise their influence upon the course of the historical struggles and in many cases preponderate in determining their *form*. There is an interaction of all these elements in which, amid all the endless host of accidents (that is, of things and events, whose inner connection is so remote or so impossible of proof that we can regard it as non-existent, as negligible) the economic movement finally asserts itself as necessary. Otherwise the application of the theory to any period of history one chose would be easier than the solution of a simple equation of the first degree.

We make our history ourselves, but, in the first place, under very definite assumptions and conditions. Among these the economic ones are ultimately decisive. But the political ones, etc., and indeed even the traditions which haunt human minds also play a part, although not the decisive one. The Prussian state also arose and developed from historical, ultimately economic causes. But it could scarcely be maintained without pedantry that among the many small states of North Germany, Brandenburg[2] was specifically determined by economic necessity to become the great power embodying the economic, linguistic and, after the Reformation, also the religious difference between North and South, and not by other elements as well (above all by its entanglement with Poland, owing to the possession of Prussia, and hence with international political relations—which were indeed also decisive in the formation of the Austrian dynastic power). Without making oneself ridiculous it would be a difficult thing to explain in terms of economics the existence of every small state in Germany, past and present, or the origin of the High German consonant shifts,[3] which widened the geographical wall of partition, formed by the mountains from the Sudetic range to the Taunus,[4] to the extent of a regular fissure across all Germany.

1. A socialist (1871–1936), who in the 1890s was a student at the University of Berlin. The translator is not named.
2. Region that became the core of the kingdom of Prussia (1701–1871) and of the German Empire (1871–1918).
3. Linguistic changes (ca. 500–700 C.E.) that distinguish the German of central and southern Germany (High German, the official dialect) from the speech of northern Germany (Low German); for example, *hopen* (to hope) becomes in High German *hoffen*, and *Plante* (plant) becomes *Pflanze*.
4. A mountain range in southwest central Germany. "The Sudetic range": the Sudetes, mountains between the Czech Republic and Poland.

In the second place, however, history is made in such a way that the final result always arises from conflicts between many individual wills, of which each again has been made what it is by a host of particular conditions of life. Thus there are innumerable intersecting forces, an infinite series of parallelograms of forces which give rise to one resultant—the historical event. This may again itself be viewed as the product of a power which works as a whole, *unconsciously* and without volition. For what each individual wills is obstructed by everyone else, and what emerges is something that no one willed. Thus past history proceeds in the manner of a natural process and is essentially subject to the same laws of motion. But from the fact that individual wills—of which each desires what he is impelled to by his physical constitution and external, in the last resort economic, circumstances (either his own personal circumstances or those of society in general)—do not attain what they want, but are merged into a collective mean, a common resultant, it must not be concluded that their value is equal to zero. On the contrary, each contributes to the resultant and is to this degree involved in it.

I would furthermore ask you to study this theory from its original sources and not at second-hand; it is really much easier. Marx hardly wrote anything in which it did not play a part. But especially *The Eighteenth Brumaire of Louis Bonaparte* is a most excellent example of its application. There are also many allusions in *Capital*.[5] Then may I also direct you to my writings: *Herr Eugen Dühring's Revolution in Science* and *Ludwig Feuerbach and the End of Classical German Philosophy*,[6] in which I have given the most detailed account of historical materialism which, as far as I know, exists.

Marx and I are ourselves partly to blame for the fact that the younger people sometimes lay more stress on the economic side than is due to it. We had to emphasise the main principle *vis-à-vis* our adversaries, who denied it, and we had not always the time, the place or the opportunity to allow the other elements involved in the interaction to come into their rights. But when it was a case of presenting a section of history, that is, of a practical application, it was a different matter and there no error was possible. Unfortunately, however, it happens only too often that people think they have fully understood a new theory and can apply it without more ado from the moment they have mastered its main principles, and even those not always correctly. And I cannot exempt many of the more recent "Marxists" from this reproach, for the most amazing rubbish has been produced in this quarter, too.

* * *

1890

5. Vol. 1 was published in 1867, vols. 2 and 3 in 1893 and 1894; *The Eighteenth Brumaire* first appeared in 1852.

6. Published in 1886; *Dühring's Revolution in Science*, now known as *Anti-Dühring*, was published in 1877–78.

MATTHEW ARNOLD
1822–1888

In an assessment published in the 1970s, the literary scholar and essayist Lionel Trilling concluded that Matthew Arnold is "virtually the founding father of modern criticism in the English-speaking world." Citing our first selection, "The Function of Criticism at the Present Time" (1865), Trilling quoted Arnold's famous injunction that the critic should strive to "see the object as in itself it really is" and his celebrated definition of criticism as the "disinterested endeavour to learn and propagate the best that is known and thought in the world." These authoritative statements, Trilling maintained, gave later scholars and teachers their inspiration and interpretive mission.

Arnold provided literary criticism with an important social function and paved the way for its institutionalization in the academy. He regarded the writing and reading of literature as urgent activities in the world, insisting "that poetry is at bottom a criticism of life; that the greatness of a poet lies in his powerful and beautiful application of ideas to life,—to the question: How to live." Serious criticism, he believed, was responsible for generating and maintaining the context of ideas and high standards that the production of literature required. Even more: criticism, for Arnold, meant an engagement with history, education, politics, religion, philosophy, and other subjects and concerns; literature is vitally connected to society and culture.

Arnold continues today to represent an ideal of literary and cultural humanism that many critics honor. But this same ideal is one that radical critics and contemporary literary theorists have sought to complicate or undermine. As the scholar Joseph Carroll has noted, Arnold's key term "disinterestedness" is "now the most violently disputed word in the Arnoldian lexicon," and many theorists from the 1970s to the present have launched their proposals by taking issue with Arnold's and his followers' account of the critic's role and procedures. For example, STANLEY FISH's reader-response criticism denies the possibility of "disinterested" objective perception, and the Marxist critic TERRY EAGLETON emphasizes Arnold's alignment with state power and the privileged classes in his stress on "timeless truths."

Arnold excelled as a critic and polemicist, and he frequently took delight in the public controversies that his books and articles kindled and in the charges hurled against him. Arnold was also a poet, an educator, and an advocate for civility and moderation who followed in the footsteps of his eminent father—Thomas Arnold (1795–1842), a religious leader, historian, and, from 1828 to 1841, the influential, reform-minded headmaster of Rugby, a venerable boarding school for boys. At Rugby, Thomas Arnold added the study of French, German, and mathematics to the traditional classical curriculum and gave new emphasis to history and geography. He resolutely campaigned for Christianity, patriotism, self-reliance, loyalty, duty, and public service, and he won great renown for his commitment to them in education.

Educated at Rugby and Oxford University, Matthew Arnold at first concentrated more on his social life (he was something of a dandy) than on his studies. His poetry—most of which he wrote during the 1840s and 1850s—left him unsatisfied, yet it eloquently expresses the self-doubt, intellectual unease, and emotional hesitancy felt by midcentury intellectuals, when Charles Darwin's theories of evolution and the skeptical inquiry into the historical status and transmission of biblical texts (the "higher criticism") were calling the time-honored principles of Christian faith into question. Arnold's first two books were *The Strayed Reveller, and Other Poems* (1849) and *Empedocles on Etna, and Other Poems* (1852). In his preface to his 1853 collection, *Poems: A New Edition*—his first piece of published prose—Arnold articulated what he conceded was missing from his own verse: "the spirit of the great classical works," "their intense significance, their noble simplicity, and their calm pathos" that create "unity and profoundness of moral impression." He felt that this failure to evoke the best in European moral value was widespread in modern literature.

In 1851 Arnold received an appointment as an inspector of schools, and this demanding work involved much tedious discussion with teachers and administrators and painstaking reviews of students' examinations and papers. It also required extensive travel in England and research trips abroad in 1859 and 1865, which led to three books on European (particularly French) systems of education. Though it was wearying, Arnold took pride in his work and did not retire until 1883; he viewed the schools as the crucial site for "civilising the next generation of the lower classes, who, as things are going, will have most of the political power of the country in their hands." Clearly, much more than literary interpretation was at stake. In his duties as an inspector, he saw the privations that workers and their families suffered, and he was dedicated to the task of social and cultural progress, identifying himself as a "Liberal of the future."

Arnold was named Professor of Poetry at Oxford University in 1857, a position he held until 1867. Because this appointment did not oblige him to teach or supervise students or to be in residence, he was able both to remain in his government post and to gain notice as a prolific social, cultural, and literary critic. His major prose works are *Essays in Criticism, First Series* (1865), *Essays in Criticism, Second Series* (1888), and *Culture and Anarchy* (1869), which examines the condition of England as represented by the three groups Arnold nicknamed the Barbarians (the aristocracy), the Philistines (the middle classes), and the Populace (the working classes). He also wrote extensively on religion, including *Literature and Dogma* (1873), which, he said, was the "most important" of all his prose works, the one most capable "of being useful." Examining the shaken doctrines and tenets of orthodox creeds and churches, it made a forthright case for a literary response and approach to the Scriptures that would treasure their enduring moral truths. *Literature and Dogma* sold 100,000 copies, far more than any of his other books.

Arnold stated in *Culture and Anarchy* that he wanted culture to heighten among the English "the impulse to the development of the whole man, to connecting and harmonizing all parts of him, perfecting all, leaving none to take their chance." Though these sentiments were presented as possessing a timeless validity, Arnold voiced them at a moment in English history when "anarchy"—social unrest and rioting—had erupted in the streets and revolution seemed a real possibility. The Reform Act of 1832 had increased the number of voters by 50 percent, but the working class and the poor remained without the vote. The defeat of an effort to extend eligibility to their ranks in 1866 brought down the Liberal government and spurred mass protests and violent demonstrations across the country. The Reform Act of 1867, passed in the midst of this social and political upheaval, added 938,000 voters and thereby doubled the size of the electorate.

Who shall inherit England? This question, which Trilling called central to a major tradition of English novelists from Charles Dickens (1812–1870) to E. M. Forster (1879–1970), was raised as well by intellectuals of the nineteenth century (such as Thomas Carlyle and John Ruskin) and twentieth century (such as T. S. ELIOT and D. H. Lawrence) in their works of cultural criticism. Not only *who* shall inherit England, but what kinds of power could they be trusted with? What forms of education should they receive? For Arnold in particular, the answers to these interconnected questions could be found in many literary sources—some in the distant past, others closer to his own era. He counseled moral betterment and spiritual renewal, achieved through the appreciative reading of the best literature. The best persons would be critics—poised, balanced, and reflective; they would be foes of fanaticism, zealotry, and political enthusiasm, and they would be aspirants to "perfection" (a term Arnold fastened on in both *Essays in Criticism* and *Culture and Anarchy*). Such arguments echo those of literary and philosophical precursors and contemporaries. In *The Defence of Poesy* (1595; see above), for example, SIR PHILIP SIDNEY had affirmed that "the final end" of learning "is to lead and draw us to as high a perfection as our degenerate souls, made worse by their clayey lodgings, can be capable of." In "The Poet" (1844; see above), RALPH WALDO EMERSON, whose writings Arnold knew well, celebrated the poet as "representative of man, in virtue of being the largest power to receive and impart."

Because Arnold is mainly interested in the personality and moral tone of the author, not in the resources of language or the unfolding meanings of literary works themselves, he does not devote much attention to specific texts; an exception is his series of lectures *On Translating Homer*, published in 1861. Lines that he does quote typically function for him as "touchstones," those "specimens of poetry of the high, the very highest quality" that "save us from fallacious estimates of value"—and that seem to beg the very question of "greatness" that they are meant to answer. Arnold assumed that his readers would know these authors and texts and their contexts, and that the "touchstones" would be recognized by all as profound and memorable. Yet he himself had minimal sympathy for (or understanding of) English writers of the eighteenth and nineteenth centuries. Moreover, Arnold mentioned fiction only briefly and not very perceptively. Unlike, for example, HENRY JAMES, he showed little interest in music, sculpture, painting, or the theater.

These faults do not diminish the power with which Arnold defined the "function of criticism" for the Victorian and modern periods. Wholeheartedly defending literature against its enemies and detractors, whose emphasis on science, moneymaking, and commercial prosperity had led them to regard poetry as merely a pleasant pastime, he argued that it equipped men and women to perceive authentic value in the workings of the society and culture around them.

Criticism is not, ultimately, something one does; it gestures toward who one is. The same is true of "culture," as Arnold presents it in *Culture and Anarchy* (excerpted below). Culture is "a study of perfection," an "*internal* condition"; it mandates a sharp yet supple movement of mind, a vigilant guard against an excess of commitment to a single point of view, and a refusal to accept the alluring power of extreme, polarizing judgments. Unlike later critics influenced by anthropology, Arnold does not view culture as designating the distinctive whole way of life of a people or a period. Nor would he agree with such critics as ANTONIO GRAMSCI, STUART HALL, and EDWARD W. SAID, who characterize culture as often an instrument of social and political control and conquest. For Arnold, culture is selective and harmonious, not conflictual. Criticism and culture loom large because of their beneficent effects on the individual, as they impel sustained acts of reflection and prevent persons from falling into complacency and "self-satisfaction."

Arnold defines criticism as involving flexibility, openness to new experiences, and curiosity (a word he explores in both "The Function of Criticism" and *Culture and Anarchy*). He insists, too, on the "free play" of mind—a phrase that poststructuralist theorists such as JACQUES DERRIDA would define far more radically and subversively, without Arnold's belief in a stable textual object that provides a center around which analysis and reflection occur. Arnold tethers criticism to a rigorous duty; criticism, he explains, "tends to *establish* an order of ideas" and seeks to "make the best ideas *prevail*." As his choice of verbs indicates, criticism is challenging work; the campaign must be waged, in a phrase used in "The Function of Criticism," with "inflexible honesty." Arnold firmly believes that some ideas are right and others wrong: he is no relativist. Nor is he a revolutionary, but rather a careful, cautious, deliberate reformer, wary of the ways in which the impulse for change can run wild and become destructive. A good literary critic is, inevitably for Arnold, a good critic in general: a person of culture embarked on a steady, steadfast inquiry into self and society. For all of his witty turns of phrase, topical references and allusions, and stylistic clarity and poise, Arnold is at heart a writer who realized, as he acknowledged in a letter in 1863, that his arguments would make "a good many people uncomfortable."

"The Function of Criticism at the Present Time" Keywords: The Canon/Tradition, Defense of Criticism, Ideology, Literary History, Nationhood, Religion
Culture and Anarchy **Keywords:** The Canon/Tradition, Defense of Criticism, Ethics, Ideology, Literary History, Modernity, Nationhood, Religion

The Function of Criticism at the Present Time[1]

Many objections have been made to a proposition which, in some remarks of mine on translating Homer,[2] I ventured to put forth; a proposition about criticism, and its importance at the present day. I said: 'Of the literature of France and Germany, as of the intellect of Europe in general, the main effort, for now many years, has been a critical effort; the endeavour, in all branches of knowledge, theology, philosophy, history, art, science, to see the object as in itself it really is.' I added, that owing to the operation in English literature of certain causes, 'almost the last thing for which one would come to English literature is just that very thing which now Europe most desires,—criticism'; and that the power and value of English literature was thereby impaired. More than one rejoinder declared that the importance I here assigned to criticism was excessive, and asserted the inherent superiority of the creative effort of the human spirit over its critical effort. And the other day, having been led by a Mr. Shairp's excellent notice of Wordsworth[3] to turn again to his biography, I found, in the words of this great man, whom I, for one, must always listen to with the profoundest respect, a sentence passed on the critic's business, which seems to justify every possible disparagement of it. Wordsworth says in one of his letters:—

'The writers in these publications' (the Reviews), 'while they prosecute their inglorious employment, can not be supposed to be in a state of mind very favourable for being affected by the finer influences of a thing so pure as genuine poetry.'

And a trustworthy reporter[4] of his conversation quotes a more elaborate judgment to the same effect:—

'Wordsworth holds the critical power very low, infinitely lower than the inventive; and he said to-day that if the quantity of time consumed in writing critiques on the works of others were given to original composition, of

1. First delivered as a lecture at Oxford University, on October 29, 1864, and published in the *National Review* in November 1864, with the title given in the plural, "Functions." Arnold altered the title for the book version (1865) and added several footnotes. The text reprinted here is that of the 1875 third edition, the last one that Arnold prepared.
2. See Lecture II of *On Translating Homer* (1861). The Greek *Iliad* and *Odyssey* attributed to Homer (ca. 8th c. B.C.E.) were a standard part of English elite education.
3. I cannot help thinking that a practice, common in England during the last century, and still followed in France, of printing a notice of this kind,—a notice by a competent critic,—to serve as an introduction to an eminent author's works, might be revived among us with advantage. To introduce all succeeding editions of Wordsworth, Mr. Shairp's notice might, it seems to me, excellently serve; it is written from the point of view of an admirer, nay, of a disciple, and that is right; but then the disciple must be also, as in this case he is, a critic, a man of letters, not, as too often happens, some relation or friend with no qualification for his task except affection for his author [Arnold's note]. John Campbell Shairp (1819–1885) was a friend of Arnold's at Balliol College, Oxford; the "notice" (in which Arnold is praised) is "Wordsworth: The Man and the Poet," *North British Review* 41 (August 1864): 1–54. WILLIAM WORDSWORTH (1770–1850) is the preeminent English Romantic poet.
4. Christopher Wordsworth, *Memoirs of William Wordsworth* (1851).

whatever kind it might be, it would be much better employed; it would make a man find out sooner his own level, and it would do infinitely less mischief. A false or malicious criticism may do much injury to the minds of others, a stupid invention, either in prose or verse, is quite harmless.'

It is almost too much to expect of poor human nature, that a man capable of producing some effect in one line of literature, should, for the greater good of society, voluntarily doom himself to impotence and obscurity in another. Still less is this to be expected from men addicted to the composition of the 'false or malicious criticism' of which Wordsworth speaks. However, everybody would admit that a false or malicious criticism had better never have been written. Everybody, too, would be willing to admit, as a general proposition, that the critical faculty is lower than the inventive. But is it true that criticism is really, in itself, a baneful and injurious employment; is it true that all time given to writing critiques on the works of others would be much better employed if it were given to original composition, of whatever kind this may be? Is it true that Johnson had better have gone on producing more *Irenes*[5] instead of writing his *Lives of the Poets*; nay, is it certain that Wordsworth himself was better employed in making his Ecclesiastical Sonnets than when he made his celebrated Preface,[6] so full of criticism, and criticism of the works of others? Wordsworth was himself a great critic, and it is to be sincerely regretted that he has not left us more criticism; Goethe[7] was one of the greatest of critics, and we may sincerely congratulate ourselves that he has left us so much criticism. Without wasting time over the exaggeration which Wordsworth's judgment on criticism clearly contains, or over an attempt to trace the causes,—not difficult, I think, to be traced,[8]—which may have led Wordsworth to this exaggeration, a critic may with advantage seize an occasion for trying his own conscience, and for asking himself of what real service at any given moment the practice of criticism either is or may be made to his own mind and spirit, and to the minds and spirits of others.

The critical power is of lower rank than the creative. True; but in assenting to this proposition, one or two things are to be kept in mind. It is undeniable that the exercise of a creative power, that a free creative activity, is the highest function of man; it is proved to be so by man's finding in it his true happiness. But it is undeniable, also, that men may have the sense of exercising this free creative activity in other ways than in producing great works of literature or art; if it were not so, all but a very few men would be shut out from the true happiness of all men. They may have it in well-doing, they may have it in learning, they may have it in criticising. This is one thing to be kept in mind. Another is, that the exercise of the creative power in the production of great works of literature or art, however high this exercise of it may rank, is not at all epochs and under all conditions possible; and that therefore labour may be vainly spent in attempting it, which might with

5. *Irene* (1749), an unsuccessful neoclassical tragedy by SAMUEL JOHNSON (1709–1784), whose *Lives of the Poets* (1779–81) was a considerable critical achievement.

6. The Preface to *Lyrical Ballads* (1800, 1802; see above). The 132 "Ecclesiastical Sonnets" (1821–22), which recount the history of the Church of England, are not considered among Wordsworth's major works.

7. Johann Wolfgang von Goethe (1749–1832), German poet, dramatist, novelist, and scientist.

8. That is, to hostile reviews of Wordsworth's poetry.

more fruit be used in preparing for it, in rendering it possible. This creative power works with elements, with materials; what if it has not those materials, those elements, ready for its use? In that case it must surely wait till they are ready. Now, in literature,—I will limit myself to literature, for it is about literature that the question arises,—the elements with which the creative power works are ideas; the best ideas on every matter which literature touches, current at the time. At any rate we may lay it down as certain that in modern literature no manifestation of the creative power not working with these can be very important or fruitful. And I say *current* at the time, not merely accessible at the time; for creative literary genius does not principally show itself in discovering new ideas, that is rather the business of the philosopher. The grand work of literary genius is a work of synthesis and exposition, not of analysis and discovery; its gift lies in the faculty of being happily inspired by a certain intellectual and spiritual atmosphere, by a certain order of ideas, when it finds itself in them; of dealing divinely with these ideas, presenting them in the most effective and attractive combinations,—making beautiful works with them, in short. But it must have the atmosphere, it must find itself amidst the order of ideas, in order to work freely; and these it is not so easy to command. This is why great creative epochs in literature are so rare, this is why there is so much that is unsatisfactory in the productions of many men of real genius; because, for the creation of a master-work of literature two powers must concur, the power of the man and the power of the moment, and the man is not enough without the moment;[9] the creative power has, for its happy exercise, appointed elements, and those elements are not in its own control.

Nay, they are more within the control of the critical power. It is the business of the critical power, as I said in the words already quoted, 'in all branches of knowledge, theology, philosophy, history, art, science, to see the object as in itself it really is.' Thus it tends, at last, to make an intellectual situation of which the creative power can profitably avail itself. It tends to establish an order of ideas, if not absolutely true, yet true by comparison with that which it displaces; to make the best ideas prevail. Presently these new ideas reach society, the touch of truth is the touch of life, and there is a stir and growth everywhere; out of this stir and growth come the creative epochs of literature.

Or, to narrow our range, and quit these considerations of the general march of genius and of society,—considerations which are apt to become too abstract and impalpable,—every one can see that a poet, for instance, ought to know life and the world before dealing with them in poetry; and life and the world being in modern times very complex things, the creation of a modern poet, to be worth much, implies a great critical effort behind it; else it must be a comparatively poor, barren, and short-lived affair. This is why Byron's[1] poetry had so little endurance in it, and Goethe's so much; both Byron and Goethe had a great productive power, but Goethe's was nourished by a great critical effort providing the true materials for it, and Byron's was not; Goethe knew life and the world, the poet's necessary sub-

9. A reference to Hippolyte Taine's *History of English Literature* (3 vols., 1863–64); in the introduction, the French critic and philosopher (1828–1893) describes the impact of heredity, environment, and history ("la race, le milieu, le moment").

1. George Gordon, Lord Byron (1788–1824), English Romantic poet.

jects, much more comprehensively and thoroughly than Byron. He knew a great deal more of them, and he knew them much more as they really are.

It has long seemed to me that the burst of creative activity in our literature, through the first quarter of this century, had about it in fact something premature; and that from this cause its productions are doomed, most of them, in spite of the sanguine hopes which accompanied and do still accompany them, to prove hardly more lasting than the productions of far less splendid epochs. And this prematureness comes from its having proceeded without having its proper data, without sufficient materials to work with. In other words, the English poetry of the first quarter of this century, with plenty of energy, plenty of creative force, did not know enough. This makes Byron so empty of matter, Shelley[2] so incoherent, Wordsworth even, profound as he is, yet so wanting in completeness and variety. Wordsworth cared little for books, and disparaged Goethe. I admire Wordsworth, as he is, so much that I cannot wish him different; and it is vain, no doubt, to imagine such a man different from what he is, to suppose that he *could* have been different. But surely the one thing wanting to make Wordsworth an even greater poet than he is,—his thought richer, and his influence of wider application,—was that he should have read more books, among them, no doubt, those of that Goethe whom he disparaged without reading him.

But to speak of books and reading may easily lead to a misunderstanding here. It was not really books and reading that lacked to our poetry at this epoch; Shelley had plenty of reading, Coleridge[3] had immense reading. Pindar and Sophocles[4]—as we all say so glibly, and often with so little discernment of the real import of what we are saying—had not many books; Shakespeare was no deep reader. True; but in the Greece of Pindar and Sophocles, in the England of Shakespeare, the poet lived in a current of ideas in the highest degree animating and nourishing to the creative power; society was, in the fullest measure, permeated by fresh thought, intelligent and alive. And this state of things is the true basis for the creative power's exercise, in this it finds its data, its materials, truly ready for its hand; all the books and reading in the world are only valuable as they are helps to this. Even when this does not actually exist, books and reading may enable a man to construct a kind of semblance of it in his own mind, a world of knowledge and intelligence in which he may live and work. This is by no means an equivalent to the artist for the nationally diffused life and thought of the epochs of Sophocles or Shakespeare; but, besides that it may be a means of preparation for such epochs, it does really constitute, if many share in it, a quickening and sustaining atmosphere of great value. Such an atmosphere the many-sided learning and the long and widely-combined critical effort of Germany formed for Goethe, when he lived and worked. There was no national glow of life and thought there as in the Athens of Pericles or the England of Elizabeth.[5] That was the poet's weakness. But there was a sort of

2. PERCY BYSSHE SHELLEY (1792–1822), English poet.
3. SAMUEL TAYLOR COLERIDGE (1772–1834), English poet and critic, whose wide reading in German Romantic philosophers led to his introducing many of their ideas to English readers.
4. Greek tragedian (ca. 496–406 B.C.E.). Pindar (ca. 518–438 B.C.E.), Greek lyric poet.
5. Elizabeth I (1533–1603; reigned 1558–1603). Pericles (ca. 495–429 B.C.E.), Athenian statesman, military leader, and supporter of the arts. He was the most influential man in Athens during the city's Golden Age.

equivalent for it in the complete culture and unfettered thinking of a large body of Germans. That was his strength. In the England of the first quarter of this century there was neither a national glow of life and thought, such as we had in the age of Elizabeth, nor yet a culture and a force of learning and criticism such as were to be found in Germany. Therefore the creative power of poetry wanted,[6] for success in the highest sense, materials and a basis; a thorough interpretation of the world was necessarily denied to it.

At first sight it seems strange that out of the immense stir of the French Revolution and its age should not have come a crop of works of genius equal to that which came out of the stir of the great productive time of Greece, or out of that of the Renascence, with its powerful episode the Reformation.[7] But the truth is that the stir of the French Revolution took a character which essentially distinguished it from such movements as these. These were, in the main, disinterestedly intellectual and spiritual movements; movements in which the human spirit looked for its satisfaction in itself and in the increased play of its own activity. The French Revolution took a political, practical character. The movement which went on in France under the old *régime*, from 1700 to 1789, was far more really akin than that of the Revolution itself to the movement of the Renascence; the France of Voltaire and Rousseau[8] told far more powerfully upon the mind of Europe than the France of the Revolution. Goethe reproached this last expressly with having 'thrown quiet culture back.'[9] Nay, and the true key to how much in our Byron, even in our Wordsworth, is this!—that they had their source in a great movement of feeling, not in a great movement of mind. The French Revolution, however,—that object of so much blind hatred,—found undoubtedly its motive-power in the intelligence of men, and not in their practical sense; this is what distinguishes it from the English Revolution of Charles the First's[1] time. This is what makes it a more spiritual event than our Revolution, an event of much more powerful and worldwide interest, though practically less successful; it appeals to an order of ideas which are universal, certain, permanent. 1789 asked of a thing, Is it rational? 1642 asked of a thing, Is it legal? or, when it went furthest, Is it according to conscience? This is the English fashion, a fashion to be treated, within its own sphere, with the highest respect; for its success, within its own sphere, has been prodigious. But what is law in one place is not law in another; what is law here to-day is not law even here to-morrow; and as for conscience, what is binding on one man's conscience is not binding on another's. The old woman who threw her stool at the head of the surpliced minister in St. Giles's Church at Edinburgh[2] obeyed an impulse to which millions of the human

6. Lacked.
7. The 16th-century movement in western Europe that aimed at reforming some doctrines and practices of the Roman Catholic Church and resulted in the establishment of the Protestant churches. Renascence: that is, the Renaissance, the great revival of art, literature, and learning in Europe that began in the 14th century and extended to the 17th century, marking the transition from the medieval to the modern world.
8. Jean-Jacques Rousseau (1712–1778), Swiss-born French political theorist and philosopher. Voltaire: pen name of François-Marie Arouet (1694–1778), French poet, dramatist, historian, and satirist.
9. In "The Four Seasons: Autumn" (1800).
1. King of England (1600–1649, reigned 1625–49). His conflicts with Parliament led to civil war, which began in 1642 and ended in his defeat and execution.
2. A riot broke out in July 1637 in St. Giles' Cathedral in protest against a new Anglican liturgy written by Archbishop Laud. It was said to have begun when a Presbyterian woman in Edinburgh, Scotland, named Jenny Geddes threw her stool at the dean giving the service and accused him of saying Mass.

race may be permitted to remain strangers. But the prescriptions of reason are absolute, unchanging, of universal validity; *to count by tens is the easiest way of counting*—that is a proposition of which every one, from here to the Antipodes,[3] feels the force; at least I should say so if we did not live in a country where it is not impossible that any morning we may find a letter in the *Times* declaring that a decimal coinage is an absurdity.[4] That a whole nation should have been penetrated with an enthusiasm for pure reason, and with an ardent zeal for making its prescriptions triumph, is a very remarkable thing, when we consider how little of mind, or anything so worthy and quickening as mind, comes into the motives which alone, in general, impel great masses of men. In spite of the extravagant direction given to this enthusiasm, in spite of the crimes and follies in which it lost itself, the French Revolution derives from the force, truth, and universality of the ideas which it took for its law, and from the passion with which it could inspire a multitude for these ideas, a unique and still living power; it is—it will probably long remain—the greatest, the most animating event in history. And as no sincere passion for the things of the mind, even though it turn out in many respects an unfortunate passion, is ever quite thrown away and quite barren of good, France has reaped from hers one fruit—the natural and legitimate fruit, though not precisely the grand fruit she expected: she is the country in Europe where *the people* is most alive.

But the mania for giving an immediate political and practical application to all these fine ideas of the reason was fatal. Here an Englishman is in his element: on this theme we can all go on for hours. And all we are in the habit of saying on it has undoubtedly a great deal of truth. Ideas cannot be too much prized in and for themselves, cannot be too much lived with; but to transport them abruptly into the world of politics and practice, violently to revolutionise this world to their bidding,—that is quite another thing. There is the world of ideas and there is the world of practice; the French are often for suppressing the one and the English the other; but neither is to be suppressed. A member of the House of Commons said to me the other day: 'That a thing is an anomaly, I consider to be no objection to it whatever.' I venture to think he was wrong; that a thing is an anomaly *is* an objection to it, but absolutely and in the sphere of ideas: it is not necessarily, under such and such circumstances, or at such and such a moment, an objection to it in the sphere of politics and practice. Joubert[5] has said beautifully: 'C'est la force et le droit qui règlent toutes choses dans le monde; la force en attendant le droit.' (Force and right are the governors of this world; force till right is ready.) *Force till right is ready*; and till right is ready, force, the existing order of things, is justified, is the legitimate ruler. But right is something moral, and implies inward recognition, free assent of the will; we are not ready for right,—*right*, so far as we are concerned, *is not ready*,—until we have attained this sense of seeing it and willing it. The way in which for us it may change and transform force, the existing order of

3. The parts of the earth diametrically opposite the speaker (thus often used of Australia and New Zealand, from the reference point of England).

4. Letters in the London *Times* in 1863 debated whether England should change its system of weights and measures to the metric system (itself an outgrowth of the French Revolution).

5. Joseph Joubert (1754–1824), French writer and moralist, known for his essays, maxims, and letters.

things, and become, in its turn, the legitimate ruler of the world, should depend on the way in which, when our times comes, we see it and will it. Therefore for other people enamoured of their own newly discerned right, to attempt to impose it upon us as ours, and violently to substitute their right for our force, is an act of tyranny, and to be resisted. It sets at nought the second great half of our maxim, *force till right is ready*. This was the grand error of the French Revolution; and its movement of ideas, by quitting the intellectual sphere and rushing furiously into the political sphere, ran, indeed, a prodigious and memorable course, but produced no such intellectual fruit as the movement of ideas of the Renascence, and created, in opposition to itself, what I may call an *epoch of concentration*. The great force of that epoch of concentration was England; and the great voice of the epoch of concentration was Burke.[6] It is the fashion to treat Burke's writings on the French Revolution as superannuated and conquered by the event; as the eloquent but unphilosophical tirades of bigotry and prejudice. I will not deny that they are often disfigured by the violence and passion of the moment, and that in some directions Burke's view was bounded, and his observation therefore at fault. But on the whole, and for those who can make the needful corrections, what distinguishes these writings is their profound, permanent, fruitful, philosophical truth. They contain the true philosophy of an epoch of concentration, dissipate the heavy atmosphere which its own nature is apt to engender round it, and make its resistance rational instead of mechanical.

But Burke is so great because, almost alone in England, he brings thought to bear upon politics, he saturates politics with thought. It is his accident[7] that his ideas were at the service of an epoch of concentration, not of an epoch of expansion; it is his characteristic that he so lived by ideas, and had such a source of them welling up within him, that he could float even an epoch of concentration and English Tory politics with them. It does not hurt him that Dr. Price[8] and the Liberals were enraged with him; it does not even hurt him that George the Third and the Tories[9] were enchanted with him. His greatness is that he lived in a world which neither English Liberalism nor English Toryism is apt to enter;—the world of ideas, not the world of catchwords and party habits. So far is it from being really true of him that he 'to party gave up what was meant for mankind,'[1] that at the very end of his fierce struggle with the French Revolution, after all his invectives against its false pretensions, hollowness, and madness, with his sincere conviction of its mischievousness, he can close a memorandum on the best means of combating it, some of the last pages he ever wrote,[2]—the *Thoughts on French Affairs*, in December 1791,—with these striking words:—

'The evil is stated, in my opinion, as it exists. The remedy must be where power, wisdom, and information, I hope, are more united with good inten-

6. EDMUND BURKE (1729–1797), statesman and author of *Reflections on the French Revolution* (1790).
7. Fortune.
8. Richard Price (1723–1791), Welsh dissenting minister, moral philosopher, supporter of the American and French Revolutions, and one of Burke's opponents.
9. Members of the political party in Great Britain that, in the late 18th and early 19th century, favored royal authority, the interest of the country gentry, and the preservation of the existing social and political order; it was succeeded by the Conservative Party.
1. An observation about "good Edmund" Burke in Oliver Goldsmith's poem "Retaliation" (1774), line 32.
2. R. H. Super, the modern editor of Arnold's prose works, notes that in fact Burke continued to write until his death in 1797.

tions than they can be with me. I have done with this subject, I believe, for ever. It has given me many anxious moments for the last two years. *If a great change is to be made in human affairs, the minds of men will be fitted to it; the general opinions and feelings will draw that way. Every fear, every hope will forward it; and then they who persist in opposing this mighty current in human affairs, will appear rather to resist the decrees of Providence itself, than the mere designs of men. They will not be resolute and firm, but perverse and obstinate.*'

That return of Burke upon himself has always seemed to me one of the finest things in English literature, or indeed in any literature. That is what I call living by ideas: when one side of a question has long had your earnest support, when all your feelings are engaged, when you hear all round you no language but one, when your party talks this language like a steam-engine and can imagine no other,—still to be able to think, still to be irresistibly carried, if so it be, by the current of thought to the opposite side of the question, and, like Balaam,[3] to be unable to speak anything *but what the Lord has put in your mouth.* I know nothing more striking, and I must add that I know nothing more un-English.

For the Englishman in general is like my friend the Member of Parliament, and believes, point-blank, that for a thing to be an anomaly is absolutely no objection to it whatever. He is like the Lord Auckland[4] of Burke's day, who, in a memorandum on the French Revolution, talks of 'certain miscreants, assuming the name of philosophers, who have presumed themselves capable of establishing a new system of society.' The Englishman has been called a political animal, and he values what is political and practical so much that ideas easily become objects of dislike in his eyes, and thinkers 'miscreants,' because ideas and thinkers have rashly meddled with politics and practice. This would be all very well if the dislike and neglect confined themselves to ideas transported out of their own sphere, and meddling rashly with practice; but they are inevitably extended to ideas as such, and to the whole life of intelligence; practice is everything, a free play of the mind is nothing. The notion of the free play of the mind upon all subjects being a pleasure in itself, being an object of desire, being an essential provider of elements without which a nation's spirit, whatever compensations it may have for them, must, in the long run, die of inanition, hardly enters into an Englishman's thoughts. It is noticeable that the word *curiosity*, which in other languages is used in a good sense, to mean, as a high and fine quality of man's nature, just this disinterested love of a free play of the mind on all subjects, for its own sake,—it is noticeable, I say, that this word has in our language no sense of the kind, no sense but a rather bad and disparaging one. But criticism, real criticism, is essentially the exercise of this very quality. It obeys an instinct prompting it to try to know the best that is known and thought in the world, irrespectively of practice, politics, and everything of the kind; and to value knowledge and thought as they approach this best, without the intrusion of any other considerations whatever. This is an instinct for which there is, I think, little original sympathy in the practical English nature, and what there was of it

3. Despite being sent by his king to curse the Israelites, Balaam blessed them, speaking "the word that God putteth in [his] mouth" (Numbers 22.38).

4. William Eden, first Baron Auckland (1744–1814), statesman and diplomat.

has undergone a long benumbing period of blight and suppression in the epoch of concentration which followed the French Revolution.

But epochs of concentration cannot well endure for ever; epochs of expansion, in the due course of things, follow them. Such an epoch of expansion seems to be opening in this country. In the first place all danger of a hostile forcible pressure of foreign ideas upon our practice has long disappeared; like the traveller in the fable, therefore, we begin to wear our cloak a little more loosely.[5] Then, with a long peace, the ideas of Europe steal gradually and amicably in, and mingle, though in infinitesimally small quantities at a time, with our own notions. Then, too, in spite of all that is said about the absorbing and brutalising influence of our passionate material progress, it seems to me indisputable that this progress is likely, though not certain, to lead in the end to an apparition[6] of intellectual life; and that man, after he has made himself perfectly comfortable and has now to determine what to do with himself next, may begin to remember that he has a mind, and that the mind may be made the source of great pleasure. I grant it is mainly the privilege of faith, at present, to discern this end to our railways, our business, and our fortune-making; but we shall see if, here as elsewhere, faith is not in the end the true prophet. Our ease, our travelling, and our unbounded liberty to hold just as hard and securely as we please to the practice to which our notions have given birth, all tend to beget an inclination to deal a little more freely with these notions themselves, to canvass them a little, to penetrate a little into their real nature. Flutterings of curiosity, in the foreign sense of the word, appear amongst us, and it is in these that criticism must look to find its account. Criticism first; a time of true creative activity, perhaps,—which, as I have said, must inevitably be preceded amongst us by a time of criticism,—hereafter, when criticism has done its work.

It is of the last importance that English criticism should clearly discern what rule for its course, in order to avail itself of the field now opening to it, and to produce fruit for the future, it ought to take. The rule may be summed up in one word,—*disinterestedness*.[7] And how is criticism to show disinterestedness? By keeping aloof from what is called 'the practical view of things'; by resolutely following the law of its own nature, which is to be a free play of the mind on all subjects which it touches. By steadily refusing to lend itself to any of those ulterior, political, practical considerations about ideas, which plenty of people will be sure to attach to them, which perhaps ought often to be attached to them, which in this country at any rate are certain to be attached to them quite sufficiently, but which criticism has really nothing to do with. Its business is, as I have said, simply to know the best that is known and thought in the world, and by in its turn making this known, to create a current of true and fresh ideas. Its business is to do this with inflexible honesty, with due ability; but its business is to do no more, and to leave alone all questions of practical consequences and applications, questions which will never fail to have due prominence given to them. Else criticism, besides being really false to its own nature, merely continues in the old rut which it has hitherto followed in this country, and

5. In Aesop's fable of the wind and the sun, the two have a contest (which the sun wins) to see which can first make a traveler remove his cloak.

6. An appearance before the world.

7. Objectivity, independence of judgment.

will certainly miss the chance now given to it. For what is at present the bane of criticism in this country? It is that practical considerations cling to it and stifle it. It subserves interests not its own. Our organs of criticism are organs of men and parties having practical ends to serve, and with them those practical ends are the first thing and the play of mind the second; so much play of mind as is compatible with the prosecution of those practical ends is all that is wanted. An organ like the *Revue des Deux Mondes*,[8] having for its main function to understand and utter the best that is known and thought in the world, existing, it may be said, as just an organ for a free play of the mind, we have not. But we have the *Edinburgh Review*, existing as an organ of the old Whigs,[9] and for as much play of the mind as may suit its being that; we have the *Quarterly Review*, existing as an organ of the Tories, and for as much play of mind as may suit its being that; we have the *British Quarterly Review*, existing as an organ of the political Dissenters,[1] and for as much play of mind as may suit its being that; we have the *Times*, existing as an organ of the common, satisfied, well-to-do Englishman, and for as much play of mind as may suit its being that. And so on through all the various fractions, political and religious, of our society; every fraction has, as such, its organ of criticism, but the notion of combining all fractions in the common pleasure of a free disinterested play of mind meets with no favour. Directly this play of mind wants to have more scope, and to forget the pressure of practical considerations a little, it is checked, it is made to feel the chain. We saw this the other day in the extinction, so much to be regretted, of the *Home and Foreign Review*.[2] Perhaps in no organ of criticism in this country was there so much knowledge, so much play of mind; but these could not save it. The *Dublin Review* subordinates play of mind to the practical business of English and Irish Catholicism, and lives. It must needs be that men should act in sects and parties, that each of these sects and parties should have its organ, and should make this organ subserve the interests of its action; but it would be well, too, that there should be a criticism, not the minister of these interests, not their enemy, but absolutely and entirely independent of them. No other criticism will ever attain any real authority or make any real way towards its end,—the creating a current of true and fresh ideas.

It is because criticism has so little kept in the pure intellectual sphere, has so little detached itself from practice, has been so directly polemical and controversial, that it has so ill accomplished, in this country, its best spiritual work; which is to keep man from a self-satisfaction which is retarding and vulgarising, to lead him towards perfection, by making his mind dwell upon what is excellent in itself, and the absolute beauty and fitness of things. A polemical practical criticism makes men blind even to the ideal imperfection of their practice, makes them willingly assert its ideal perfection, in order the better to secure it against attack; and clearly this is nar-

8. A highly respected and widely read French bimonthly review of culture, the arts, politics, and economics (begun in 1829).
9. Members of the political party in Great Britain that, in the late 18th and early 19th century, was associated with parliamentary authority, with the interests of industrialists, and with reform; it was succeeded by the Liberal Party.
1. English Protestants who do not conform to the practices of the established Church of England; in the 19th century, they became associated with political liberalism and reform.
2. Liberal Catholic quarterly in London (1862–64).

rowing and baneful for them. If they were reassured on the practical side, speculative considerations of ideal perfection they might be brought to entertain, and their spiritual horizon would thus gradually widen. Sir Charles Adderley[3] says to the Warwickshire farmers:—

'Talk of the improvement of breed! Why, the race we ourselves represent, the men and women, the old Anglo-Saxon race, are the best breed in the whole world. . . . The absence of a too enervating climate, too unclouded skies, and a too luxurious nature, has produced so vigorous a race of people, and has rendered us so superior to all the world.'

Mr. Roebuck[4] to the Sheffield cutlers:—

'I look around me and ask what is the state of England? Is not property safe? Is not every man able to say what he likes? Can you not walk from one end of England to the other in perfect security? I ask you whether, the world over or in past history, there is anything like it? Nothing. I pray that our unrivalled happiness may last.'

Now obviously there is a peril for poor human nature in words and thoughts of such exuberant self-satisfaction, until we find ourselves safe in the streets of the Celestial City.

> Das wenige verschwindet leicht dem Blicke,
> Der vorwärts sieht, wie viel noch übrig bleibt—

says Goethe;[5] 'the little that is done seems nothing when we look forward and see how much we have yet to do.' Clearly this is a better line of reflection for weak humanity, so long as it remains on this earthly field of labour and trial.

But neither Sir Charles Adderley nor Mr. Roebuck is by nature inaccessible to considerations of this sort. They only lose sight of them owing to the controversial life we all lead, and the practical form which all speculation takes with us. They have in view opponents whose aim is not ideal, but practical; and in their zeal to uphold their own practice against these innovators, they go so far as even to attribute to this practice an ideal perfection. Somebody has been wanting to introduce a six-pound franchise, or to abolish church-rates,[6] or to collect agricultural statistics by force, or to diminish local self-government. How natural, in reply to such proposals, very likely improper or ill-timed, to go a little beyond the mark, and to say stoutly, 'Such a race of people as we stand, so superior to all the world! The old Anglo-Saxon race, the best breed in the whole world! I pray that our unrivalled happiness may last! I ask you whether, the world over or in past history, there is anything like it?' And so long as criticism answers this dithyramb[7] by insisting that the old Anglo-Saxon race would be still more superior to all others if it had no church-rates, or that our unrivalled happiness would last yet longer with a six-pound franchise, so long will the strain, 'The best breed in the whole world!' swell louder and louder, everything ideal and refining will be lost out of sight, and both the assailed and their critics will remain in

3. Conservative member of Parliament (1814–1905), wealthy holder of a large estate in Warwickshire (in central England).
4. John Arthur Roebuck (1801–1879), radical member of Parliament.
5. *Iphigenia in Tauris* (1787), 1.2.91–92.
6. Taxes legally imposed by the Church of England. "Six-pound franchise": a proposal by radicals to extend the vote to anyone who owned land or buildings worth £6 annual rent (not £10, as set in 1832).
7. That is, statement of impassioned praise (in classical Greece, a wild choral hymn in honor of Dionysus).

a sphere, to say the truth, perfectly unvital, a sphere in which spiritual progression is impossible. But let criticism leave church-rates and the franchise alone, and in the most candid spirit, without a single lurking thought of practical innovation, confront with our dithyramb this paragraph on which I stumbled in a newspaper immediately after reading Mr. Roebuck:—

'A shocking child murder has just been committed at Nottingham. A girl named Wragg[8] left the workhouse there on Saturday morning with her young illegitimate child. The child was soon afterwards found dead on Mapperly Hills, having been strangled. Wragg is in custody.'

Nothing but that; but, in juxtaposition with the absolute eulogies of Sir Charles Adderley and Mr. Roebuck, how eloquent, how suggestive are those few lines! 'Our old Anglo-Saxon breed, the best in the whole world!'—how much that is harsh and ill-favoured there is in this best! *Wragg!* If we are to talk of ideal perfection, of 'the best in the whole world,' has any one reflected what a touch of grossness in our race, what an original shortcoming in the more delicate spiritual perceptions, is shown by the natural growth amongst us of such hideous names,—Higginbottom, Stiggins, Bugg! In Ionia and Attica[9] they were luckier in this respect than 'the best race in the world'; by the Ilissus[1] there was no Wragg, poor thing! And 'our unrivalled happiness';—what an element of grimness, bareness, and hideousness mixes with it and blurs it; the workhouse, the dismal Mapperly Hills,[2]—how dismal those who have seen them will remember;—the gloom, the smoke, the cold, the strangled illegitimate child! 'I ask you whether, the world over or in past history, there is anything like it?' Perhaps not, one is inclined to answer; but at any rate, in that case, the world is very much to be pitied. And the final touch,—short, bleak, and inhuman: *Wragg is in custody.* The sex lost in the confusion of our unrivalled happiness; or (shall I say?) the superfluous Christian name lopped off by the straightforward vigour of our old Anglo-Saxon breed! There is profit for the spirit in such contrasts as this; criticism serves the cause of perfection by establishing them. By eluding sterile conflict, by refusing to remain in the sphere where alone narrow and relative conceptions have any worth and validity, criticism may diminish its momentary importance, but only in this way has it a chance of gaining admittance for those wider and more perfect conceptions to which all its duty is really owed. Mr. Roebuck will have a poor opinion of an adversary who replies to his defiant songs of triumph only by murmuring under his breath, *Wragg is in custody*; but in no other way will these songs of triumph be induced gradually to moderate themselves, to get rid of what in them is excessive and offensive, and to fall into a softer and truer key.

It will be said that it is a very subtle and indirect action which I am thus prescribing for criticism, and that, by embracing in this manner the Indian virtue of detachment[3] and abandoning the sphere of practical life, it condemns itself to a slow and obscure work. Slow and obscure it may be, but it is the only proper work of criticism. The mass of mankind will never have any ardent zeal for seeing things as they are; very inadequate ideas will always

8. Elizabeth Wragg; this crime was committed on September 10, 1864.
9. District of Greece that includes Athens. Ionia: area of the west coast of Asia Minor (where Homer is thought to have lived).
1. River south of Athens.
2. An area in Nottingham, in central England, that was the site of large brickworks.
3. The ideal of detaching oneself from worldly activity, here associated with Hinduism.

satisfy them.[4] On these inadequate ideas reposes, and must repose, the general practice of the world. That is as much as saying that whoever sets himself to see things as they are will find himself one of a very small circle; but it is only by this small circle resolutely doing its own work that adequate ideas will ever get current at all. The rush and roar of practical life will always have a dizzying and attracting effect upon the most collected spectator, and tend to draw him into its vortex; most of all will this be the case where that life is so powerful as it is in England. But it is only by remaining collected, and refusing to lend himself to the point of view of the practical man, that the critic can do the practical man any service; and it is only by the greatest sincerity in pursuing his own course, and by at last convincing even the practical man of his sincerity, that he can escape misunderstandings which perpetually threaten him.

For the practical man is not apt for fine distinctions, and yet in these distinctions, truth and the highest culture greatly find their account. But it is not easy to lead a practical man,—unless you reassure him as to your practical intentions, you have no chance of leading him,—to see that a thing which he has always been used to look at from one side only, which he greatly values, and which, looked at from that side, quite deserves, perhaps, all the prizing and admiring which he bestows upon it,—that this thing, looked at from another side, may appear much less beneficent and beautiful, and yet retain all its claims to our practical allegiance. Where shall we find language innocent enough, how shall we make the spotless purity of our intentions evident enough, to enable us to say to the political Englishman that the British Constitution itself, which, seen from the practical side, looks such a magnificent organ of progress and virtue, seen from the speculative side,—with its compromises, its love of facts, its horror of theory, its studied avoidance of clear thoughts,—that, seen from this side, our august Constitution sometimes looks,—forgive me, shade of Lord Somers![5]—a colossal machine for the manufacture of Philistines?[6] How is Cobbett[7] to say this and not be misunderstood, blackened as he is with the smoke of a lifelong conflict in the field of political practice? how is Mr. Carlyle[8] to say it and not be misunderstood, after his furious raid into this field with his *Latter-day Pamphlets*? how is Mr. Ruskin,[9] after his pugnacious political economy? I say, the critic must keep out of the region of immediate practice in the political, social, humanitarian sphere, if he wants to make a beginning for that more free speculative treatment of things, which may perhaps one day make its benefits felt even in this sphere, but in a natural and thence irresistible manner.

Do what he will, however, the critic will still remain exposed to frequent misunderstandings, and nowhere so much as in this country. For here people are particularly indisposed even to comprehend that without this

4. Arnold takes the terms "adequate" and "inadequate" from the *Ethics* (1677) of the Dutch philosopher BARUCH SPINOZA.
5. John Somers (1651–1716), English constitutional lawyer and statesman.
6. The materialist middle classes (a name taken from a biblical people that waged war against the Israelites).
7. William Cobbett (1762–1835), English radical journalist and reformer.
8. Thomas Carlyle (1795–1881), Scottish-born essayist and historian; he expressed bitter antidemocratic views in *Latter-Day Pamphlets* (1850).
9. John Ruskin (1819–1900), art critic and social critic. In *Unto This Last* (1860–62), he challenged the business and industrial practices and the materialism of the age.

free disinterested treatment of things, truth and the highest culture are out of the question. So immersed are they in practical life, so accustomed to take all their notions from this life and its processes, that they are apt to think that truth and culture themselves can be reached by the process of this life, and that it is an impertinent singularity to think of reaching them in any other. 'We are all *terræ filii*,'[1] cries their eloquent advocate; 'all Philistines together. Away with the notion of proceeding by any other course than the course dear to the Philistines; let us have a social movement, let us organise and combine a party to pursue truth and new thought, let us call it *the liberal party*, and let us all stick to each other, and back each other up. Let us have no nonsense about independent criticism, and intellectual delicacy, and the few and the many. Don't let us trouble ourselves about foreign thought; we shall invent the whole thing for ourselves as we go along. If one of us speaks well, applaud him; if one of us speaks ill, applaud him too; we are all in the same movement, we are all liberals, we are all in pursuit of truth.' In this way the pursuit of truth becomes really a social, practical, pleasurable affair, almost requiring a chairman, a secretary, and advertisements; with the excitement of an occasional scandal, with a little resistance to give the happy sense of difficulty overcome; but, in general, plenty of bustle and very little thought. To act is so easy, as Goethe says; to think is so hard![2] It is true that the critic has many temptations to go with the stream, to make one of the party movement, one of these *terræ filii*; it seems ungracious to refuse to be a *terræ filius*, when so many excellent people are; but the critic's duty is to refuse, or, if resistance is vain, at least to cry with Obermann: *Périssons en résistant*.[3]

How serious a matter it is to try and resist, I had ample opportunity of experiencing when I ventured some time ago to criticise the celebrated first volume of Bishop Colenso.[4] The echoes of the storm which was then raised I still, from time to time, hear grumbling round me. That storm arose out of a misunderstanding almost inevitable. It is a result of no little culture to attain to a clear perception that science and religion are two wholly different things. The multitude will for ever confuse them, but happily that is of no great real importance, for while the multitude imagines itself to live by its false science, it does really live by its true religion. Dr. Colenso, however, in his first volume did all he could to strengthen the confusion,[5] and to

1. Sons of the earth (Latin); that is, men of the soil.

2. A reference to Goethe's novel *Wilhelm Meister's Apprenticeship* (1795–96).

3. Let us die resisting (French). Quoted from *Obermann* (1804), a Romantic epistolary novel by Etienne de Sénancour.

4. So sincere is my dislike to all personal attack and controversy, that I abstain from reprinting, at this distance of time from the occasion which called them forth, the essays in which I criticised Dr. Colenso's book; I feel bound, however, after all that has passed, to make here a final declaration of my sincere impenitence for having published them. Nay, I cannot forbear repeating yet once more, for his benefit and that of his readers, this sentence from my original remarks upon him: *There is truth of science and truth of religion; truth of science does not become truth of religion till it is made religious.* And I will add: Let us have all the science there is from the men of science; from the men of religion let us have religion [Arnold's note]. John William Colenso (1814–1883), bishop of Natal in South Africa, whose controversial studies disputed orthodox theology and the historical accuracy of biblical texts. In "The Bishop and the Philosopher" (*Macmillan's Magazine*, January 1863), Arnold sharply criticized Colenso's scholarship and failure to address true spiritual needs.

5. It has been said I make it "a crime against literary criticism and the higher culture to attempt to inform the ignorant." Need I point out that the ignorant are not informed by being confirmed in a confusion? [Arnold's note]. Quoted from the jurist and essayist Fitzjames Stephen (1829–1894) in "Mr. Matthew Arnold and His Countrymen," *Saturday Review*, December 3, 1864.

make it dangerous. He did this with the best intentions, I freely admit, and with the most candid ignorance that this was the natural effect of what he was doing; but, says Joubert, 'Ignorance, which in matters of morals extenuates the crime, is itself, in intellectual matters, a crime of the first order.' I criticised Bishop Colenso's speculative confusion. Immediately there was a cry raised: 'What is this? here is a liberal attacking a liberal. Do not you belong to the movement? are not you a friend of truth? Is not Bishop Colenso in pursuit of truth? then speak with proper respect of his book. Dr. Stanley[6] is another friend of truth, and you speak with proper respect of his book; why make these invidious differences? both books are excellent, admirable, liberal; Bishop Colenso's perhaps the most so, because it is the boldest, and will have the best practical consequences for the liberal cause. Do you want to encourage to the attack of a brother liberal his, and your, and our implacable enemies, the *Church and State Review* or the *Record*,—the High Church rhinoceros and the Evangelical hyæna? Be silent, therefore; or rather speak, speak as loud as ever you can! and go into ecstasies over the eighty and odd pigeons.'[7]

But criticism cannot follow this coarse and indiscriminate method. It is unfortunately possible for a man in pursuit of truth to write a book which reposes upon a false conception. Even the practical consequences of a book are to genuine criticism no recommendation of it, if the book is, in the highest sense, blundering. I see that a lady[8] who herself, too, is in pursuit of truth, and who writes with great ability, but a little too much, perhaps, under the influence of the practical spirit of the English liberal movement, classes Bishop Colenso's book and M. Renan's[9] together, in her survey of the religious state of Europe, as facts of the same order, works, both of them, of 'great importance'; 'great ability, power, and skill'; Bishop Colenso's, perhaps, the most powerful; at least, Miss Cobbe gives special expression to her gratitude that to Bishop Colenso 'has been given the strength to grasp, and the courage to teach, truths of such deep import.' In the same way, more than one popular writer has compared him to Luther.[1] Now it is just this kind of false estimate which the critical spirit is, it seems to me, bound to resist. It is really the strongest possible proof of the low ebb at which, in England, the critical spirit is, that while the critical hit in the religious literature of Germany is Dr. Strauss's book,[2] in that of France M. Renan's book, the book of Bishop Colenso is the critical hit in the religious literature of England. Bishop Colenso's book reposes on a total misconception of the essential elements of the religious problem, as that problem is now presented for solution. To criticism, therefore, which seeks to have the best that is known and thought on this problem, it is, however well meant, of no importance whatever. M. Renan's book attempts a new synthesis of the elements furnished to us by the Four Gospels. It attempts, in my opinion, a synthesis, perhaps

6. Arthur Penrhyn Stanley (1815–1881), English biographer of Thomas Arnold, an ecclesiastical historian and advocate of religious toleration.
7. Colenso used mathematics to cast doubt on the historical validity of certain passages in Leviticus and Numbers.
8. Frances Power Cobbe (1822–1908), Irish social worker and author of books on reform, women's rights, and religion. Her "survey" is *Broken Lights* (1864).
9. Ernest Renan (1823–1892), French critic, historian, Orientalist, and author of *The Life of Jesus* (1863).
1. Martin Luther (1483–1546), German religious reformer and founder of the Reformation.
2. *The Life of Jesus* (1835–36), by the German theologian David Friedrich Strauss (1808–1874).

premature, perhaps impossible, certainly not successful. Up to the present time, at any rate, we must acquiesce in Fleury's sentence on such recastings of the Gospel-story: *Quiconque s'imagine la pouvoir mieux écrire, ne l'entend pas.*[3] M. Renan had himself passed by anticipation a like sentence on his own work, when he said: 'If a new presentation of the character of Jesus were offered to me, I would not have it; its very clearness would be, in my opinion, the best proof of its insufficiency.' His friends may with perfect justice rejoin that at the sight of the Holy Land, and of the actual scene of the Gospel-story, all the current of M. Renan's thoughts may have naturally changed, and a new casting of that story irresistibly suggested itself to him; and that this is just a case for applying Cicero's maxim: Change of mind is not inconsistency—*nemo doctus unquam mutationem consilii inconstantiam dixit esse.*[4] Nevertheless, for criticism, M. Renan's first thought must still be the truer one, as long as his new casting so fails more fully to commend itself, more fully (to use Coleridge's happy phrase about the Bible) to *find* us.[5] Still M. Renan's attempt is, for criticism, of the most real interest and importance, since, with all its difficulty, a fresh synthesis of the New Testament *data*,—not a making war on them, in Voltaire's fashion,[6] not a leaving them out of mind, in the world's fashion, but the putting a new construction upon them, the taking them from under the old, traditional, conventional point of view and placing them under a new one,—is the very essence of the religious problem, as now presented; and only by efforts in this direction can it receive a solution.

Again, in the same spirit in which she judges Bishop Colenso, Miss Cobbe, like so many earnest liberals of our practical race, both here and in America, herself sets vigorously about a positive reconstruction of religion, about making a religion of the future out of hand, or at least setting about making it. We must not rest, she and they are always thinking and saying, in negative criticism, we must be creative and constructive; hence we have such works as her recent *Religious Duty*,[7] and works still more considerable, perhaps by others, which will be in every one's mind. These works often have much ability; they often spring out of sincere convictions, and a sincere wish to do good; and they sometimes, perhaps, do good. Their fault is (if I may be permitted to say so) one which they have in common with the British College of Health, in the New Road. Every one knows the British College of Health; it is that building with the lion and the statue of the Goddess Hygeia[8] before it; at least I am sure about the lion, though I am not absolutely certain about the Goddess Hygeia. This building does credit, perhaps, to the resources of Dr. Morrison[9] and his disciples; but it falls a good deal short of one's idea of what a British College of Health ought to be. In England, where we hate public interference and love individual enterprise, we have a

3. Whoever imagines he can write it better does not understand it (French). From the *Histoire ecclésiastique* (1691–1720), by the French historian and teacher Claude Fleury (1640–1723).
4. No educated man has ever said that a change of opinion is inconsistency (Latin). From *Letters to Atticus*, no. 16, by the Roman orator and statesman Cicero (106–43 B.C.E.).
5. See Coleridge's *Confessions of an Inquiring Spirit* (1840): "In the Bible there is more that *finds* me than I have experienced in all other books put together."
6. Voltaire's works include a number of attacks on Catholic doctrine and religious intolerance.
7. Published in 1864.
8. Greek deity personifying health.
9. James Morrison (1770–1840), merchant and vendor, described himself as "the Hygeist"; in 1828 he founded the British College of Health, from which he distributed his cure-all patent medicine.

whole crop of places like the British College of Health; the grand name without the grand thing. Unluckily, creditable to individual enterprise as they are, they tend to impair our taste by making us forget what more grandiose, noble, or beautiful character properly belongs to a public institution. The same may be said of the religions of the future of Miss Cobbe and others. Creditable, like the British College of Health, to the resources of their authors, they yet tend to make us forget what more grandiose, noble, or beautiful character properly belongs to religious constructions. The historic religions, with all their faults, have had this; it certainly belongs to the religious sentiment, when it truly flowers, to have this; and we impoverish our spirit if we allow a religion of the future without it. What then is the duty of criticism here? To take the practical point of view, to applaud the liberal movement and all its works,—its New Road religions of the future into the bargain,—for their general utility's sake? By no means; but to be perpetually dissatisfied with these works, while they perpetually fall short of a high and perfect ideal.

For criticism, these are elementary laws; but they never can be popular, and in this country they have been very little followed, and one meets with immense obstacles in following them. That is a reason for asserting them again and again. Criticism must maintain its independence of the practical spirit and its aim. Even with well-meant efforts of the practical spirit it must express dissatisfaction, if in the sphere of the ideal they seem impoverishing and limiting. It must not hurry on to the goal because of its practical importance. It must be patient, and know how to wait; and flexible, and know how to attach itself to things and how to withdraw from them. It must be apt to study and praise elements that for the fulness of spiritual perfection are wanted, even though they belong to a power which in the practical sphere may be maleficent. It must be apt to discern the spiritual shortcomings or illusions of powers that in the practical sphere may be beneficent. And this without any notion of favouring or injuring, in the practical sphere, one power or the other; without any notion of playing off, in this sphere, one power against the other. When one looks, for instance, at the English Divorce Court,—an institution which perhaps has its practical conveniences, but which in the ideal sphere is so hideous; an institution which neither makes divorce impossible nor makes it decent, which allows a man to get rid of his wife, or a wife of her husband, but makes them drag one another first, for the public edification, through a mire of unutterable infamy,—when one looks at this charming institution, I say, with its crowded trials, its newspaper reports, and its money compensations, this institution in which the gross unregenerate British Philistine has indeed stamped an image of himself,—one may be permitted to find the marriage theory of Catholicism[1] refreshing and elevating. Or when Protestantism, in virtue of its supposed rational and intellectual origin, gives the law to criticism too magisterially, criticism may and must remind it that its pretensions, in this respect, are illusive and do it harm; that the Reformation was a moral rather than an intellectual event; that Luther's theory of grace no more exactly reflects the mind of the spirit than Bossuet's[2] philosophy of

1. That is, that in Christian marriage, once consummated, there can never be an absolute divorce.
2. Jacques Bénigne Bossuet (1627–1704), French bishop and moralist; he maintained that Providence guided history in order to establish Christianity and, especially, the Catholic Church.

history reflects it; and that there is no more antecedent probability of the Bishop of Durham's stock of ideas being agreeable to perfect reason than of Pope Pius the Ninth's.[3] But criticism will not on that account forget the achievements of Protestantism in the practical and moral sphere; nor that, even in the intellectual sphere, Protestantism, though in a blind and stumbling manner, carried forward the Renascence, while Catholicism threw itself violently across its path.

I lately heard a man of thought and energy contrasting the want of ardor and movement which he now found amongst young men in this country with what he remembered in his own youth, twenty years ago. 'What reformers we were then!' he exclaimed; 'what a zeal we had! how we canvassed every institution in Church and State, and were prepared to remodel them all on first principles!' He was inclined to regret, as a spiritual flagging, the lull which he saw. I am disposed rather to regard it as a pause in which the turn to a new mode of spiritual progress is being accomplished. Everything was long seen, by the young and ardent amongst us, in inseparable connection with politics and practical life. We have pretty well exhausted the benefits of seeing things in this connection, we have got all that can be got by so seeing them. Let us try a more disinterested mode of seeing them; let us betake ourselves more to the serener life of the mind and spirit. This life, too, may have its excesses and dangers; but they are not for us at present. Let us think of quietly enlarging our stock of true and fresh ideas, and not, as soon as we get an idea or half an idea, be running out with it into the street, and trying to make it rule there. Our ideas will, in the end, shape the world all the better for maturing a little. Perhaps in fifty years' time it will in the English House of Commons be an objection to an institution that it is an anomaly, and my friend the Member of Parliament will shudder in his grave. But let us in the meanwhile rather endeavour that in twenty years' time it may, in English literature, be an objection to a proposition that it is absurd. That will be a change so vast, that the imagination almost fails to grasp it. *Ab integro sæclorum nascitur ordo*.[4]

If I have insisted so much on the course which criticism must take where politics and religion are concerned, it is because, where these burning matters are in question, it is most likely to go astray. I have wished, above all, to insist on the attitude which criticism should adopt toward things in general; on its right tone and temper of mind. But then comes another question as to the subject-matter which literary criticism should most seek. Here, in general, its course is determined for it by the idea which is the law of its being; the idea of a disinterested endeavour to learn and propagate the best that is known and thought in the world, and thus to establish a current of fresh and true ideas. By the very nature of things, as England is not all the world, much of the best that is known and thought in the world cannot be of English growth, must be foreign; by the nature of things, again, it is just this that we are least likely to know, while English thought is streaming in upon us from all sides, and takes excellent care that we shall not be ignorant of its existence. The English critic of literature, therefore, must dwell much on foreign

3. Pius IX (1792–1878), pope from 1846 to 1878, was criticized for his conservative views. Bishop of Durham: Charles Thomas Baring (1807–1879).
4. From the renewal of the generations a [great] order is born (Latin). From Virgil, *Eclogue* 4.5 (ca. 37 B.C.E.). This poem was sometimes interpreted by Christians as predicting the birth of the Messiah.

thought, and with particular heed on any part of it, which, while significant and fruitful in itself, is for any reason specially likely to escape him. Again, judging is often spoken of as the critic's one business, and so in some sense it is; but the judgment which almost insensibly forms itself in a fair and clear mind, along with fresh knowledge, is the valuable one; and thus knowledge, and ever fresh knowledge, must be the critic's great concern for himself. And it is by communicating fresh knowledge, and letting his own judgment pass along with it,—but insensibly, and in the second place, not the first, as a sort of companion and clue, not as an abstract lawgiver,—that the critic will generally do most good to his readers. Sometimes, no doubt, for the sake of establishing an author's place in literature, and his relation to a central standard (and if this is not done, how are we to get at our *best in the world*?), criticism may have to deal with a subject-matter so familiar that fresh knowledge is out of the question, and then it must be all judgment; an enunciation and detailed application of principles. Here the great safeguard is never to let oneself become abstract, always to retain an intimate and lively consciousness of the truth of what one is saying, and, the moment this fails us, to be sure that something is wrong. Still, under all circumstances, this mere judgment and application of principles is, in itself, not the most satisfactory work to the critic; like mathematics, it is tautological, and cannot well give us, like fresh learning, the sense of creative activity.

But stop, some one will say; all this talk is of no practical use to us whatever; this criticism of yours is not what we have in our minds when we speak of criticism; when we speak of critics and criticism, we mean critics and criticism of the current English literature of the day; when you offer to tell criticism its function, it is to this criticism that we expect you to address yourself. I am sorry for it, for I am afraid I must disappoint these expectations. I am bound by my own definition of criticism: *a disinterested endeavour to learn and propagate the best that is known and thought in the world.* How much of current English literature comes into this 'best that is known and thought in the world'? Not very much, I fear; certainly less, at this moment, than of the current literature of France or Germany. Well, then, am I to alter my definition of criticism, in order to meet the requirements of a number of practising English critics, who, after all, are free in their choice of a business? That would be making criticism lend itself just to one of those alien practical considerations, which, I have said, are so fatal to it. One may say, indeed, to those who have to deal with the mass—so much better disregarded—of current English literature, that they may at all events endeavour, in dealing with this, to try it, so far as they can, by the standard of the best that is known and thought in the world; one may say, that to get anywhere near this standard, every critic should try and possess one great literature, at least, besides his own; and the more unlike his own, the better. But, after all, the criticism I am really concerned with,—the criticism which alone can much help us for the future, the criticism which, throughout Europe, is at the present day meant, when so much stress is laid on the importance of criticism and the critical spirit,—is a criticism which regards Europe as being, for intellectual and spiritual purposes, one great confederation, bound to a joint action and working to a common result; and whose members have, for their proper outfit, a knowledge of Greek, Roman, and Eastern antiquity, and of one another. Special, local, and temporary advantages being put out of account, that modern nation will in the intellectual and spiritual sphere make most progress, which most thoroughly carries out this programme. And what is that but saying that we too, all of us, as individuals, the more thoroughly we carry it out, shall make the more progress?

There is so much inviting us!—what are we to take? what will nourish us in growth towards perfection? That is the question which, with the immense field of life and of literature lying before him, the critic has to answer; for himself first, and afterwards for others. In this idea of the critic's business the essays brought together in the following pages[5] have had their origin; in this idea, widely different as are their subjects, they have, perhaps, their unity.

I conclude with what I said at the beginning: to have the sense of creative activity is the great happiness and the great proof of being alive, and it is not denied to criticism to have it; but then criticism must be sincere, simple, flexible, ardent, ever widening its knowledge. Then it may have, in no contemptible measure, a joyful sense of creative activity; a sense which a man of insight and conscience will prefer to what he might derive from a poor, starved, fragmentary, inadequate creation. And at some epochs no other creation is possible.

Still, in full measure, the sense of creative activity belongs only to genuine creation; in literature we must never forget that. But what true man of letters ever can forget it? It is no such common matter for a gifted nature to come into possession of a current of true and living ideas, and to produce amidst the inspiration of them, that we are likely to underrate it. The epochs of Æschylus[6] and Shakespeare make us feel their pre-eminence. In an epoch like those is, no doubt, the true life of literature; there is the promised land, towards which criticism can only beckon. That promised land it will not be ours to enter, and we shall die in the wilderness:[7] but to have desired to enter it, to have saluted it from afar, is already, perhaps, the best distinction among contemporaries; it will certainly be the best title to esteem with posterity.

1864, 1875

From Culture and Anarchy

From *Chapter 1. Sweetness and Light*[1]

The disparagers of culture make its motive curiosity; sometimes, indeed, they make its motive mere exclusiveness and vanity. The culture which is supposed to plume itself on a smattering of Greek and Latin is a culture which is begotten by nothing so intellectual as curiosity; it is valued either out of sheer vanity and ignorance or else as an engine of social and class

5. In the book *Essays in Criticism*; this essay was the first in the volume.
6. Greek tragedian (525–456 B.C.E.).
7. Like Moses, who viewed the Promised Land but did not live to enter it. See Deuteronomy 32.48–52, 34.1–4.
1. First delivered, with the title "Culture and Its Enemies," as Arnold's final lecture as Professor of Poetry at Oxford University, June 7, 1867, and published in the *Cornhill Magazine* in July. It appeared as chapter 1 of *Culture and Anarchy* in 1869. The text reprinted here is that of the 1882 third edition, the last that Arnold himself prepared.

distinction, separating its holder, like a badge or title, from other people who have not got it. No serious man would call this *culture*, or attach any value to it, as culture, at all. To find the real ground for the very different estimate which serious people will set upon culture, we must find some motive for culture in the terms of which may lie a real ambiguity; and such a motive the word *curiosity* gives us.

I have before now pointed out[2] that we English do not, like the foreigners, use this word in a good sense as well as in a bad sense. With us the word is always used in a somewhat disapproving sense. A liberal and intelligent eagerness about the things of the mind may be meant by a foreigner when he speaks of curiosity, but with us the word always conveys a certain notion of frivolous and unedifying activity. In the *Quarterly Review*, some little time ago, was an estimate of the celebrated French critic, M. Sainte-Beuve,[3] and a very inadequate estimate it in my judgment was. And its inadequacy consisted chiefly in this: that in our English way it left out of sight the double sense really involved in the word *curiosity*, thinking enough was said to stamp M. Sainte-Beuve with blame if it was said that he was impelled in his operations as a critic by curiosity, and omitting either to perceive that M. Sainte-Beuve himself, and many other people with him, would consider that this was praiseworthy and not blameworthy, or to point out why it ought really to be accounted worthy of blame and not of praise. For as there is a curiosity about intellectual matters which is futile, and merely a disease, so there is certainly a curiosity,—a desire after the things of the mind simply for their own sakes and for the pleasure of seeing them as they are,—which is, in an intelligent being, natural and laudable. Nay, and the very desire to see things as they are implies a balance and regulation of mind which is not often attained without fruitful effort, and which is the very opposite of the blind and diseased impulse of mind which is what we mean to blame when we blame curiosity. Montesquieu[4] says: 'The first motive which ought to impel us to study is the desire to augment the excellence of our nature, and to render an intelligent being yet more intelligent.' This is the true ground to assign for the genuine scientific passion, however manifested, and for culture, viewed simply as a fruit of this passion; and it is a worthy ground, even though we let the term *curiosity* stand to describe it.

But there is of culture another view, in which not solely the scientific passion, the sheer desire to see things as they are, natural and proper in an intelligent being, appears as the ground of it. There is a view in which all the love of our neighbour, the impulses towards action, help, and beneficence, the desire for removing human error, clearing human confusion, and diminishing human misery, the noble aspiration to leave the world better and happier than we found it,—motives eminently such as are called social,—come in as part of the grounds of culture, and the main and pre-eminent part. Culture is then properly described not as having its origin in curiosity, but as having its origin in the love of perfection; it is *a study of perfection*. It moves

2. In "The Function of Criticism at the Present Time" (1864; see above).

3. Charles Augustin Sainte-Beuve (1804–1869), French literary critic. In the review mentioned (*Quarterly Review* 119 [January 1866]: 80–108), the author identifies Arnold as Sainte-Beuve's disciple and states that the *Essays in Criticism* are "graceful but perfectly unsatisfactory."

4. Charles de Secondat Montesquieu (1689–1755), French philosopher and legal and political theorist. Arnold quotes his "Discourse on the Motives That Ought to Encourage Us to the Sciences" (1725).

by the force, not merely or primarily of the scientific passion for pure knowledge, but also of the moral and social passion for doing good. As, in the first view of it, we took for its worthy motto Montesquieu's words: 'To render an intelligent being yet more intelligent!' so, in the second view of it, there is no better motto which it can have than these words of Bishop Wilson:[5] 'To make reason and the will of God prevail!'

Only, whereas the passion for doing good is apt to be overhasty in determining what reason and the will of God say, because its turn is for acting rather than thinking and it wants to be beginning to act; and whereas it is apt to take its own conceptions, which proceed from its own state of development and share in all the imperfections and immaturities of this, for a basis of action; what distinguishes culture is, that it is possessed by the scientific passion as well as by the passion of doing good; that it demands worthy notions of reason and the will of God, and does not readily suffer its own crude conceptions to substitute themselves for them. And knowing that no action or institution can be salutary and stable which is not based on reason and the will of God, it is not so bent on acting and instituting, even with the great aim of diminishing human error and misery ever before its thoughts, but that it can remember that acting and instituting are of little use, unless we know how and what we ought to act and to institute.

This culture is more interesting and more far-reaching than that other, which is founded solely on the scientific passion for knowing. But it needs times of faith and ardour, times when the intellectual horizon is opening and widening all round us, to flourish in. And is not the close and bounded intellectual horizon within which we have long lived and moved now lifting up, and are not new lights finding free passage to shine in upon us? For a long time there was no passage for them to make their way in upon us, and then it was of no use to think of adapting the world's action to them. Where was the hope of making reason and the will of God prevail among people who had a routine which they had christened reason and the will of God, in which they were inextricably bound, and beyond which they had no power of looking? But now the iron force of adhesion to the old routine,—social, political, religious,—has wonderfully yielded; the iron force of exclusion of all which is new has wonderfully yielded. The danger now is, not that people should obstinately refuse to allow anything but their old routine to pass for reason and the will of God, but either that they should allow some novelty or other to pass for these too easily, or else that they should underrate the importance of them altogether, and think it enough to follow action for its own sake, without troubling themselves to make reason and the will of God prevail therein. Now, then, is the moment for culture to be of service, culture which believes in making reason and the will of God prevail, believes in perfection, is the study and pursuit of perfection, and is no longer debarred, by a rigid invincible exclusion of whatever is new, from getting acceptance for its ideas, simply because they are new.

The moment this view of culture is seized, the moment it is regarded not solely as the endeavour to see things as they are, to draw towards a knowledge of the universal order which seems to be intended and aimed at in the world,

5. Thomas Wilson (1663–1755), English churchman and author of devotional works. Arnold is condensing a passage from Wilson's *Maxims* (first published in 1781).

and which it is a man's happiness to go along with or his misery to go counter to,—to learn, in short, the will of God,—the moment, I say, culture is considered not merely as the endeavour to *see* and *learn* this, but as the endeavour, also, to make it *prevail*, the moral, social, and beneficent character of culture becomes manifest. The mere endeavour to see and learn the truth for our own personal satisfaction is indeed a commencement for making it prevail, a preparing the way for this, which always serves this, and is wrongly, therefore, stamped with blame absolutely in itself and not only in its caricature and degeneration. But perhaps it has got stamped with blame, and disparaged with the dubious title of curiosity, because in comparison with this wider endeavour of such great and plain utility it looks selfish, petty, and unprofitable.

And religion, the greatest and most important of the efforts by which the human race has manifested its impulse to perfect itself,—religion, that voice of the deepest human experience,—does not only enjoin and sanction the aim which is the great aim of culture, the aim of setting ourselves to ascertain what perfection is and to make it prevail; but also, in determining generally in what human perfection consists, religion comes to a conclusion identical with that which culture,—culture seeking the determination of this question through *all* the voices of human experience which have been heard upon it, of art, science, poetry, philosophy, history, as well as of religion, in order to give a greater fulness and certainty to its solution,—likewise reaches. Religion says: *The kingdom of God is within you*;[6] and culture, in like manner, places human perfection in an *internal* condition, in the growth and predominance of our humanity proper, as distinguished from our animality. It places it in the ever-increasing efficacy and in the general harmonious expansion of those gifts of thought and feeling, which make the peculiar dignity, wealth, and happiness of human nature. As I have said on a former occasion:[7] 'It is in making endless additions to itself, in the endless expansion of its powers, in endless growth in wisdom and beauty, that the spirit of the human race finds its ideal. To reach this ideal, culture is an indispensable aid, and that is the true value of culture.' Not a having and a resting, but a growing and a becoming, is the character of perfection as culture conceives it; and here, too, it coincides with religion.

And because men are all members of one great whole, and the sympathy which is in human nature will not allow one member to be indifferent to the rest or to have a perfect welfare independent of the rest, the expansion of our humanity, to suit the idea of perfection which culture forms, must be a *general* expansion. Perfection, as culture conceives it, is not possible while the individual remains isolated. The individual is required, under pain of being stunted and enfeebled in his own development if he disobeys, to carry others along with him in his march towards perfection, to be continually doing all he can to enlarge and increase the volume of the human stream sweeping thitherward. And here, once more, culture lays on us the same obligation as religion, which says, as Bishop Wilson has admirably put it, that 'to promote the kingdom of God is to increase and hasten one's own happiness.'

But, finally, perfection,—as culture from a thorough disinterested study of human nature and human experience learns to conceive it,—is a harmonious expansion of *all* the powers which make the beauty and worth of

6. Luke 17.21.

7. In *A French Eton* (1864), chapter 3.

human nature, and is not consistent with the over-development of any one power at the expense of the rest. Here culture goes beyond religion, as religion is generally conceived by us.

If culture, then, is a study of perfection, and of harmonious perfection, general perfection, and perfection which consists in becoming something rather than in having something, in an inward condition of the mind and spirit, not in an outward set of circumstances,—it is clear that culture, instead of being the frivolous and useless thing which Mr. Bright, and Mr. Frederic Harrison,[8] and many other Liberals are apt to call it, has a very important function to fulfil for mankind. And this function is particularly important in our modern world, of which the whole civilisation is, to a much greater degree than the civilisation of Greece and Rome, mechanical and external, and tends constantly to become more so. But above all in our own country has culture a weighty part to perform, because here that mechanical character, which civilisation tends to take everywhere, is shown in the most eminent degree. Indeed nearly all the characters of perfection, as culture teaches us to fix them, meet in this country with some powerful tendency which thwarts them and sets them at defiance. The idea of perfection as an *inward* condition of the mind and spirit is at variance with the mechanical and material civilisation in esteem with us, and nowhere, as I have said, so much in esteem as with us. The idea of perfection as a *general* expansion of the human family is at variance with our strong individualism, our hatred of all limits to the unrestrained swing of the individual's personality, our maxim of 'every man for himself.' Above all, the idea of perfection as a *harmonious* expansion of human nature is at variance with our want of flexibility, with our inaptitude for seeing more than one side of a thing, with our intense energetic absorption in the particular pursuit we happen to be following. So culture has a rough task to achieve in this country. Its preachers have, and are likely long to have, a hard time of it, and they will much oftener be regarded, for a great while to come, as elegant or spurious Jeremiahs[9] than as friends and benefactors. That, however, will not prevent their doing in the end good service if they persevere. And, meanwhile, the mode of action they have to pursue, and the sort of habits they must fight against, ought to be made quite clear for every one to see, who may be willing to look at the matter attentively and dispassionately.

Faith in machinery is, I said, our besetting danger; often in machinery most absurdly disproportioned to the end which this machinery, if it is to do any good at all, is to serve; but always in machinery, as if it had a value in and for itself.[1] What is freedom but machinery? what is population but machinery? what is coal but machinery? what are railroads but machinery? what is wealth but machinery? what are, even, religious organisations but machinery? Now almost every voice in England is accustomed to speak of these things as if they were precious ends in themselves, and therefore had some of the characters of perfection indisputably joined to them. I have before now

8. English jurist and philosopher (1831–1923), and critic of Arnold's cultural views. John Bright (1811–1889), English political reformer, orator, and member of Parliament.
9. That is, speakers who complain, lament, or condemn at length, like the biblical prophet.
1. In "Signs of the Times" (1829), the Scottish-born author Thomas Carlyle had stated that it was now "the Mechanical Age. It is the Age of Machinery, in every outward and inward sense of that word."

noticed Mr. Roebuck's[2] stock argument for proving the greatness and happiness of England as she is, and for quite stopping the mouths of all gainsayers. Mr. Roebuck is never weary of reiterating this argument of his, so I do not know why I should be weary of noticing it. 'May not every man in England say what he likes?'—Mr. Roebuck perpetually asks; and that, he thinks, is quite sufficient, and when every man may say what he likes, our aspirations ought to be satisfied. But the aspirations of culture, which is the study of perfection, are not satisfied, unless what men say, when they may say what they like, is worth saying,—has good in it, and more good than bad. In the same way the *Times*, replying to some foreign strictures on the dress, looks, and behaviour of the English abroad, urges that the English ideal is that every one should be free to do and to look just as he likes. But culture indefatigably tries, not to make what each raw person may like the rule by which he fashions himself; but to draw ever nearer to a sense of what is indeed beautiful, graceful, and becoming, and to get the raw person to like that.

And in the same way with respect to railroads and coal. Every one must have observed the strange language current during the late discussions as to the possible failure of our supplies of coal. Our coal, thousands of people were saying, is the real basis of our national greatness; if our coal runs short, there is an end of the greatness of England. But what *is* greatness?—culture makes us ask. Greatness is a spiritual condition worthy to excite love, interest, and admiration; and the outward proof of possessing greatness is that we excite love, interest, and admiration. If England were swallowed up by the sea to-morrow, which of the two, a hundred years hence, would most excite the love, interest, and admiration of mankind,—would most, therefore, show the evidences of having possessed greatness,—the England of the last twenty years, or the England of Elizabeth,[3] of a time of splendid spiritual effort, but when our coal, and our industrial operations depending on coal, were very little developed? Well, then, what an unsound habit of mind it must be which makes us talk of things like coal or iron as constituting the greatness of England, and how salutary a friend is culture, bent on seeing things as they are, and thus dissipating delusions of this kind and fixing standards of perfection that are real!

Wealth, again, that end to which our prodigious works for material advantage are directed,—the commonest of commonplaces tells us how men are always apt to regard wealth as a precious end in itself; and certainly they have never been so apt thus to regard it as they are in England at the present time. Never did people believe anything more firmly than nine Englishmen out of ten at the present day believe that our greatness and welfare are proved by our being so very rich. Now, the use of culture is that it helps us, by means of its spiritual standard of perfection, to regard wealth as but machinery, and not only to say as a matter of words that we regard wealth as but machinery, but really to perceive and feel that it is so. If it were not for this purging effect wrought upon our minds by culture, the whole world, the future as well as the present, would inevitably belong to the Philistines.[4] The people who believe most that most greatness and welfare are proved by

2. John Arthur Roebuck (1801–1879), radical member of Parliament. "Before now": see "The Function of Criticism at the Present Time."
3. Elizabeth I (1533–1603; reigned 1558–1603).
4. The materialist middle classes (a name taken from a biblical people that waged war against the Israelites).

our being very rich, and who most give their lives and thoughts to becoming rich, are just the very people whom we call Philistines. Culture says: 'Consider these people, then, their way of life, their habits, their manners, the very tones of their voice; look at them attentively; observe the literature they read, the things which give them pleasure, the words which come forth out of their mouths, the thoughts which make the furniture of their minds: would any amount of wealth be worth having with the condition that one was to become just like these people by having it?' And thus culture begets a dissatisfaction which is of the highest possible value in stemming the common tide of men's thoughts in a wealthy and industrial community, and which saves the future, as one may hope, from being vulgarised, even if it cannot save the present.

Population, again, and bodily health and vigour, are things which are nowhere treated in such an unintelligent, misleading, exaggerated way as in England. Both are really machinery; yet how many people all around us do we see rest in them and fail to look beyond them! Why, one has heard people, fresh from reading certain articles of the *Times* on the Registrar-General's returns of marriages and births in this country,[5] who would talk of our large English families in quite a solemn strain, as if they had something in itself beautiful, elevating, and meritorious in them; as if the British Philistine would have only to present himself before the Great Judge with his twelve children, in order to be received among the sheep[6] as a matter of right!

But bodily health and vigour, it may be said, are not to be classed with wealth and population as mere machinery; they have a more real and essential value. True; but only as they are more intimately connected with a perfect spiritual condition than wealth or population are. The moment we disjoin them from the idea of a perfect spiritual condition, and pursue them, as we do pursue them, for their own sake and as ends in themselves, our worship of them becomes as mere worship of machinery, as our worship of wealth or population, and as unintelligent and vulgarising a worship as that is. Every one with anything like an adequate idea of human perfection has distinctly marked this subordination to higher and spiritual ends of the cultivation of bodily vigour and activity. 'Bodily exercise profiteth little; but godliness is profitable unto all things,' says the author of the Epistle to Timothy.[7] And the utilitarian Franklin[8] says as explicitly:—'Eat and drink such an exact quantity as suits the constitution of thy body, *in reference to the services of the mind*.' But the point of view of culture, keeping the mark of human perfection simply and broadly in view, and not assigning to this perfection, as religion or utilitarianism assigns to it, a special and limited character, this point of view, I say, of culture is best given by these words of Epictetus:[9]—'It is a sign of *ἀφυΐα*,' says he,—that is, of a nature not finely tempered,—'to give yourselves for instance, a great fuss about exercise, a great fuss about eating, a great fuss about drinking, a great fuss about walking, a great fuss about riding. All these things ought to be done merely by the way: the formation of the spirit and character must be our real concern.' This is admirable; and, indeed, the Greek word *εὐφυΐα*, a finely tempered nature, gives exactly the notion of perfection

5. "When Marriages are many and Deaths are few it is certain that the people are doing well" (London *Times*, February 3, 1866).
6. That is, the saved; see Matthew 25.31–46.
7. 1 Timothy 4.8.
8. Benjamin Franklin (1706–1790), American statesman, writer, and scientist. Arnold quotes Franklin's first recommendation in "Rules of Health," from *Poor Richard's Almanack* (1732–57).
9. Greek Stoic philosopher (ca. 55–ca. 135 C.E.), who taught in Rome, in *Enchiridion* 41.

as culture brings us to conceive it: a harmonious perfection, a perfection in which the characters of beauty and intelligence are both present, which unites 'the two noblest of things,'—as Swift,[1] who of one of the two, at any rate, had himself all too little, most happily calls them in his *Battle of the Books,*—'the two noblest of things, *sweetness and light.*' The εὐφυής[2] is the man who tends towards sweetness and light; the ἀφυής, on the other hand, is our Philistine. The immense spiritual significance of the Greeks is due to their having been inspired with this central and happy idea of the essential character of human perfection; and Mr. Bright's misconception of culture, as a smattering of Greek and Latin, comes itself, after all, from this wonderful significance of the Greeks having affected the very machinery of our education, and is in itself a kind of homage to it.

In thus making sweetness and light to be characters of perfection, culture is of like spirit with poetry, follows one law with poetry. Far more than on our freedom, our population, and our industrialism, many amongst us rely upon our religious organisations to save us. I have called religion a yet more important manifestation of human nature than poetry, because it has worked on a broader scale for perfection, and with greater masses of men. But the idea of beauty and of a human nature perfect on all its sides, which is the dominant idea of poetry, is a true and invaluable idea, though it has not yet had the success that the idea of conquering the obvious faults of our animality, and of a human nature perfect on the moral side,—which is the dominant idea of religion,—has been enabled to have; and it is destined, adding to itself the religious idea of a devout energy, to transform and govern the other.

The best art and poetry of the Greeks, in which religion and poetry are one, in which the idea of beauty and of a human nature perfect on all sides adds to itself a religious and devout energy, and works in the strength of that, is on this account of such surpassing interest and instructiveness for us, though it was,—as, having regard to the human race in general, and, indeed, having regard to the Greeks themselves, we must own,—a premature attempt, an attempt which for success needed the moral and religious fibre in humanity to be more braced and developed than it had yet been. But Greece did not err in having the idea of beauty, harmony, and complete human perfection, so present and paramount. It is impossible to have this idea too present and paramount; only, the moral fibre must be braced too. And we, because we have braced the moral fibre, are not on that account in the right way, if at the same time the idea of beauty, harmony, and complete human perfection, is wanting or misapprehended amongst us; and evidently it *is* wanting or misapprehended at present. And when we rely as we do on our religious organisations, which in themselves do not and cannot give us this idea, and think we have done enough if we make them spread and prevail, then, I say, we fall into our common fault of overvaluing machinery.

* * *

1867, 1882

1. Jonathan Swift (1667–1745), English satirist, poet, and clergyman. In *The Battle of the Books* (1704), he recounts why Aesop, judging a contest between the spider (here representing the moderns) and the bee (the ancients), decided in favor of the bee: "the difference is, that, instead of dirt and poison, we have rather chosen to fill our hives with honey and wax; thus furnishing mankind with the two noblest of things, which are sweetness and light." In the larger battle that Swift describes, the outcome is less certain.

2. That is, a well-tempered nature.

WALTER PATER
1839–1894

Contemporary critics and theorists have returned to Walter Pater's books and essays, reexamined them in relation to current interests in figurative language, creativity in criticism, and historical study, and dramatically raised his critical stock. Literary histories had often described Pater as a "minor" Victorian overshadowed by MATTHEW ARNOLD. An impressionist critic who coined the English phrase "art for art's sake" (which he later amended to "art for its own sake"), he sketched, it was said, the adventures of his soul among masterpieces. Now, however, Pater's conception of art and his exaltation of aesthetic experience have linked him with his contemporaries RALPH WALDO EMERSON and FRIEDRICH NIETZSCHE as a crucial writer for postmodern theory and criticism.

Pater's work has always been important for creative writers, including William Butler Yeats, who refashioned Pater's prose description of Leonardo da Vinci's *Mona Lisa* in *Studies in the History of the Renaissance* (1873) and made it the first "poem" in the *Oxford Book of Modern Verse* (1936). Pater has also inspired such twentieth-century theorists of literary and critical consciousness as Georges Poulet and (in his early writings) PAUL DE MAN. HAROLD BLOOM and J. Hillis Miller point to Pater as having enriched and supplemented the Romantic tradition in criticism inaugurated by SAMUEL TAYLOR COLERIDGE and refined by John Ruskin in *Modern Painters*, 1843–56, and *The Stones of Venice*, 1851–53.

Pater was born in the East End of London. His father, a surgeon, died in 1842, and he was raised in a household of women that included his mother, a grandmother, and an aunt. After attending King's School, Canterbury, he began his undergraduate career at Queen's College, Oxford University, where he wrote essays on Greek philosophy for the eminent scholar Benjamin Jowett. Pater received his degree in 1862 and the following year was elected to Old Mortality, a literary society at Oxford. He became a fellow of Oxford's Brasenose College in 1864, living there and, later, in London as a teacher, scholar, and critic.

During the summer of 1865, Pater made his first trip to Italy, traveling in the company of his pupil and close friend C. L. Shadwell, to whom he would dedicate *Studies in the History of the Renaissance*. The paintings he saw in Florence and other cities deeply moved him, giving him "a richer, more daring sense of life than any to be seen in Oxford." For Pater, the Italian Renaissance was not merely a historical period but a tremor in the heart that marked the consciousness of the person attuned to its splendors. To know the glorious works of Renaissance art was intensely, indeed erotically, to *feel* them, and this feeling was Pater's means of countering the dulling of sensation, the termination of feeling, the inevitability of death.

Pater's first essays were published anonymously in the late 1860s. A study of Coleridge in the *Westminster Review* (1866) suggests that Pater found a central theme early on: "Modern thought is distinguished from ancient by its cultivation of the 'relative' spirit in place of the 'absolute.' . . . To the modern spirit nothing is, or can be rightly known, except relatively and under certain conditions." Pater's first publication under his name was "Notes on Leonardo da Vinci" (1869). *Studies in the History of the Renaissance*, a collection of essays on writers and Italian painters (including Leonardo da Vinci and Sandro Botticelli), appeared four years later.

Pater's next book, the romance *Marius the Epicurean* (1885), describes the development of a young Roman in the time of Marcus Aurelius, the second-century C.E. Roman emperor and Stoic philosopher. He conceived it as the first of a three-part series—the second to be set in sixteenth-century France and the third in late eighteenth-century England—but the other volumes remained unwritten. Pater's later books include *Imaginary Portraits* (1887), *Appreciations, with an Essay on Style* (1889), and *Plato and Platonism* (1893). *Greek Studies* (1895) and an unfinished romance, *Gaston de Latour* (1896), were published posthumously. The three-volume theological project that Pater planned for his later years, which he seems to have envisioned as a response to Arnold's writings on religion and culture, was left undone.

Studies in the History of the Renaissance was a momentous text for a number of Pater's younger contemporaries, including OSCAR WILDE. Pater states that his primary concern is with Italy in the fifteenth century, but he deliberately defines the term *Renaissance* much more widely, describing it as an "outbreak of the human spirit" from the "limits which the religious system of the middle ages imposed on the heart and the imagination." Throughout the book, Pater emphasizes the precious, fine textures of art, but always with the implication that only persons of rich receptiveness, of exquisite and accurate perception, can wholly sense and appreciate its singularities. The reliance on austere discipline to achieve liberation—the free life that art renders possible—helps explain Pater's great appeal. By making a religion of art, a sacred duty of artistic creation and perception, Pater built the foundation for modern aestheticist rapture as well as for impressionist criticism.

Studies in the History of the Renaissance received mixed reviews. Some concurred with Pater, against Ruskin, in his esteem for the Renaissance. But others attacked Pater for advocating pleasure as the highest good and self-gratification as the best rule for the conduct of life. George Eliot in a letter called the book "quite poisonous in its false principles of criticism and false conceptions of life." Some accused Pater of projecting nineteenth-century modes of thinking onto the Renaissance. To defend himself against these charges of hedonism and ahistoricism, Pater changed the title of the second edition (1877) to *The Renaissance: Studies in Art and Poetry* and omitted the conclusion, which declared that nothing mattered more than the experience of brilliant moments (he restored it, in a slightly modified form, for the third and fourth editions). The damage had been done, however; in later years, he failed to win Oxford appointments he might otherwise have received.

In the preface, Pater sounds a concrete, pragmatic note. Impatient with the notion that critics should seek broad, general definitions of key terms, he declares that "Beauty, like all other qualities presented to human experience, is relative." Referring to the pleasure that we receive from "a picture, a landscape, a fair personality in life or in a book," Pater intimates that on one level at least there is no difference between life and art, nature and culture: each matters only insofar as it gives pleasure.

Pater at first seems directly to challenge Arnold's dictum that the critic must see the object as in itself it really is by adding a necessary "first step": "to know one's own impression as it really is, to discriminate it, to realise it distinctly." Yet their goal is the same; knowing the impression is the means through which one perceives how and why one is "deeply moved by the presence of beautiful objects." This response to art matters, according to Pater, because it frees each mind from being "a solitary prisoner [in] its own dream of a world." Even more important, it frees individuals from their bondage to routine and particularly to death. The love of art for its own sake is what makes us, while the response lasts, more alive than dead. Like other late nineteenth-century figures, Pater registers a heightened sense of fleeting beauty wherever it materializes, qualities also evident in so-called decadent literature and impressionist painting of the time.

Pater's view of criticism and art startled his contemporaries, because God is absent from it. Most of them saw death not as final but as the pathway to the highest form of life. Pater neither offers religious consolation nor invokes the moral earnestness and high seriousness of earlier Victorian writers, including Thomas Carlyle, Arnold, and Eliot. He seems unconcerned as well about social and political change: there is no higher purpose than seizing, desperately, each moment for whatever intensities it might supply. This is obviously the main limitation of his position, for the responsibility of the critic is maximizing his or her *pleasure*, not contributing to knowledge or to change in a body politic that in Pater's view can no more withstand decay and death than anything or anyone else.

***Studies in the History of the Renaissance* Keywords:** Aesthetics, Affect, The Body, Defense of Criticism, Identity, Literary History, Religion, Subjectivity

From Studies in the History of the Renaissance

Preface

Many attempts have been made by writers on art and poetry to define beauty in the abstract, to express it in the most general terms, to find some universal formula for it. The value of these attempts has most often been in the suggestive and penetrating things said by the way. Such discussions help us very little to enjoy what has been well done in art or poetry, to discriminate between what is more and what is less excellent in them, or to use words like beauty, excellence, art, poetry, with a more precise meaning than they would otherwise have. Beauty, like all other qualities presented to human experience, is relative; and the definition of it becomes unmeaning and useless in proportion to its abstractness. To define beauty, not in the most abstract but in the most concrete terms possible, to find, not its universal formula, but the formula which expresses most adequately this or that special manifestation of it, is the aim of the true student of æsthetics.

"To see the object as in itself it really is,"[1] has been justly said to be the aim of all true criticism whatever; and in æsthetic criticism the first step towards seeing one's object as it really is, is to know one's own impression as it really is, to discriminate it,[2] to realise it distinctly. The objects with which æsthetic criticism deals—music, poetry, artistic and accomplished forms of human life—are indeed receptacles of so many powers or forces: they possess, like the products of nature, so many virtues or qualities. What is this song or picture, this engaging personality presented in life or in a book, to *me*? What effect does it really produce on me? Does it give me pleasure? and if so, what sort or degree of pleasure? How is my nature modified by its presence, and under its influence? The answers to these questions are the original facts with which the æsthetic critic has to do; and, as in the study of light, of morals, of number, one must realise such primary data for one's self, or not at all. And he who experiences these impressions strongly, and drives directly at the discrimination and analysis of them, has no need to trouble himself with the abstract question what beauty is in itself, or what its exact relation to truth or experience—metaphysical questions, as unprofitable as metaphysical questions elsewhere. He may pass them all by as being, answerable or not, of no interest to him.

The æsthetic critic, then, regards all the objects with which he has to do, all works of art, and the fairer forms of nature and human life, as powers or forces producing pleasurable sensations, each of a more or less peculiar or

1. MATTHEW ARNOLD's phrase, which he used first in "On Translating Homer" (1862) and then in the opening paragraph of a more widely read essay, "The Function of Criticism at the Present Time" (1864; see above).

2. To perceive its distinguishing features.

unique kind. This influence he feels, and wishes to explain, by analysing and reducing it to its elements. To him, the picture, the landscape, the engaging personality in life or in a book, *La Gioconda*, the hills of Carrara, Pico of Mirandola,[3] are valuable for their virtues, as we say, in speaking of a herb, a wine, a gem; for the property each has of affecting one with a special, a unique, impression of pleasure. Our education becomes complete in proportion as our susceptibility to those impressions increases in depth and variety. And the function of the æsthetic critic is to distinguish, to analyse, and separate from its adjuncts, the virtue by which a picture, a landscape, a fair personality in life or in a book, produces this special impression of beauty or pleasure, to indicate what the source of that impression is, and under what conditions it is experienced. His end is reached when he has disengaged that virtue, and noted it, as a chemist notes some natural element, for himself and others; and the rule for those who would reach this end is stated with great exactness in the words of a recent critique of Sainte-Beuve:—*De se borner à connaître de près les belles choses, et à s'en nourrir en exquis amateurs, en humanistes accomplis.*[4]

What is important, then, is not that the critic should possess a correct abstract definition of beauty for the intellect, but a certain kind of temperament, the power of being deeply moved by the presence of beautiful objects. He will remember always that beauty exists in many forms. To him all periods, types, schools of taste, are in themselves equal. In all ages there have been some excellent workmen, and some excellent work done. The question he asks is always:—In whom did the stir, the genius, the sentiment of the period find itself? where was the receptacle of its refinement, its elevation, its taste? "The ages are all equal," says William Blake, "but genius is always above its age."[5]

Often it will require great nicety to disengage this virtue from the commoner elements with which it may be found in combination. Few artists, not Goethe or Byron[6] even, work quite cleanly, casting off all *débris*, and leaving us only what the heat of their imagination has wholly fused and transformed. Take, for instance, the writings of Wordsworth.[7] The heat of his genius, entering into the substance of his work, has crystallised a part, but only a part, of it; and in that great mass of verse there is much which might well be forgotten. But scattered up and down it, sometimes fusing and transforming entire compositions, like the Stanzas on *Resolution and Independence*, or the *Ode on the Recollections of Childhood*,[8] sometimes, as if at random, depositing a fine crystal here or there, in a matter it does not wholly search through and transmute, we trace the action of his unique, incommunicable

3. Giovanni Pico, count of Mirandola (1463–1494), an Italian humanist and Neoplatonist philosopher whom Pater examines in one of the chapters of *The Renaissance*. *La Gioconda*: Leonardo da Vinci's painting *Mona Lisa* (ca. 1504). Carrara: a region of Italy famous for its white marble.

4. One should limit oneself to knowing beautiful things intimately, and nourish oneself on them like exquisite amateurs, like accomplished humanists (French). Charles-Augustin Sainte-Beuve (1804–1869), an eminent French critic and journalist; he wrote this sentence in an 1867 essay on the French poet and humanist JOACHIM DU BELLAY (1522–1560). Pater devotes a later chapter of *Studies in the Renaissance* to du Bellay.

5. From annotations to volume 1 of *The Works of Sir Joshua Reynolds* made by the Romantic poet Blake (1757–1827).

6. George Gordon, Lord Byron (1788–1824), English Romantic poet. Johann Wolfgang von Goethe (1749–1832), German poet, dramatist, and novelist.

7. WILLIAM WORDSWORTH (1770–1850), the greatest of the English Romantic poets.

8. That is, "Ode: Intimations of Immortality from Recollections of Early Childhood" (1807). "Resolution and Independence" was also published in 1807.

faculty, that strange, mystical sense of a life in natural things, and of man's life as a part of nature, drawing strength and colour and character from local influences, from the hills and streams, and from natural sights and sounds. Well! that is the *virtue*, the active principle in Wordsworth's poetry; and then the function of the critic of Wordsworth is to follow up that active principle, to disengage it, to mark the degree in which it penetrates his verse.

The subjects of the following studies are taken from the history of the *Renaissance*, and touch what I think the chief points in that complex, many-sided movement. I have explained in the first of them what I understand by the word, giving it a much wider scope than was intended by those who originally used it to denote that revival of classical antiquity in the fifteenth century which was only one of many results of a general excitement and enlightening of the human mind, but of which the great aim and achievements of what, as Christian art, is often falsely opposed to the Renaissance, were another result. This outbreak of the human spirit may be traced far into the Middle Age itself, with its motives already clearly pronounced, the care for physical beauty, the worship of the body, the breaking down of those limits which the religious system of the Middle Age imposed on the heart and the imagination. I have taken as an example of this movement, this earlier Renaissance within the Middle Age itself, and as an expression of its qualities, two little compositions in early French; not because they constitute the best possible expression of them, but because they help the unity of my series, inasmuch as the Renaissance ends also in France, in French poetry, in a phase of which the writings of Joachim du Bellay are in many ways the most perfect illustration. The Renaissance, in truth, put forth in France an aftermath, a wonderful later growth, the products of which have to the full that subtle and delicate sweetness which belongs to a refined and comely decadence, as its earliest phases have the freshness which belongs to all periods of growth in art, the charm of *ascêsis*,[9] of the austere and serious girding of the loins in youth.

But it is in Italy, in the fifteenth century, that the interest of the Renaissance mainly lies,—in that solemn fifteenth century which can hardly be studied too much, not merely for its positive results in the things of the intellect and the imagination, its concrete works of art, its special and prominent personalities, with their profound æsthetic charm, but for its general spirit and character, for the ethical qualities of which it is a consummate type.

The various forms of intellectual activity which together make up the culture of an age, move for the most part from different starting-points, and by unconnected roads. As products of the same generation they partake indeed of a common character, and unconsciously illustrate each other; but of the producers themselves, each group is solitary, gaining what advantage or disadvantage there may be in intellectual isolation. Art and poetry, philosophy and the religious life, and that other life of refined pleasure and action in the conspicuous places of the world, are each of them confined to its own circle of ideas, and those who prosecute either of them are generally little curious of the thoughts of others. There come, however, from time to

9. Practice, training (Greek); but in his essay "Style," included in *Appreciations* (1889), Pater defines it as "self-restraint, a skillful economy of means."

time, eras of more favourable conditions, in which the thoughts of men draw nearer together than is their wont, and the many interests of the intellectual world combine in one complete type of general culture. The fifteenth century in Italy is one of these happier eras, and what is sometimes said of the age of Pericles is true of that of Lorenzo:[1]—it is an age productive in personalities, many-sided, centralised, complete. Here, artists and philosophers and those whom the action of the world has elevated and made keen, do not live in isolation, but breathe a common air, and catch light and heat from each other's thoughts. There is a spirit of general elevation and enlightenment in which all alike communicate. The unity of this spirit gives unity to all the various products of the Renaissance; and it is to this intimate alliance with mind, this participation in the best thoughts which that age produced, that the art of Italy in the fifteenth century owes much of its grave dignity and influence.

I have added an essay on Winckelmann,[2] as not incongruous with the studies which precede it, because Winckelmann, coming in the eighteenth century, really belongs in spirit to an earlier age. By his enthusiasm for the things of the intellect and the imagination for their own sake, by his Hellenism, his life-long struggle to attain to the Greek spirit, he is in sympathy with the humanists of a previous century. He is the last fruit of the Renaissance, and explains in a striking way its motive and tendencies.

Conclusion[3]

Λέγει που Ἡράκλειτος ὅτι πάντα χωρεῖ καὶ οὐδὲν μένει[4]

To regard all things and principles of things as inconstant modes or fashions has more and more become the tendency of modern thought. Let us begin with that which is without—our physical life. Fix upon it in one of its more exquisite intervals, the moment, for instance, of delicious recoil from the flood of water in summer heat. What is the whole physical life in that moment but a combination of natural elements to which science gives their names? But those elements, phosphorus and lime and delicate fibres, are present not in the human body alone: we detect them in places most remote from it. Our physical life is a perpetual motion of them—the passage of the blood, the waste and repairing of the lenses of the eye, the modification of the tissues of the brain under every ray of light and sound—processes which science reduces to simpler and more elementary forces. Like the elements of which we are composed, the action of these forces extends beyond us: it rusts iron and ripens corn.[5] Far out on every side of us those elements are

1. Lorenzo de Medici (1449–1492), ruler of and patron of the arts in Florence, and himself a poet. Pericles (ca. 495–429 B.C.E.), Athenian statesman and patron of the arts and architecture.

2. Johann Joachim Winckelmann (1717–1768), German classical archaeologist and art historian.

3. This brief "Conclusion" was omitted in the second edition of this book, as I conceived it might possibly mislead some of those young men into whose hands it might fall. On the whole, I have thought it best to reprint it here, with some slight changes which bring it closer to my original meaning. I have dealt more fully in *Marius the Epicurean* with the thoughts suggested by it [Pater's note]. *Marius the Epicurean* (1885), philosophical novel set in 2d-century C.E. Rome.

4. Somewhere Heraclitus says that all things are in motion and nothing is lasting (Greek); in *Plato and Platonism* (1893), Pater translated the end of the epigraph, "All things give way: nothing remaineth." Heraclitus (active ca. 500 B.C.E), pre-Socratic Greek philosopher.

5. That is, wheat.

broadcast, driven in many currents; and birth and gesture and death and the springing of violets from the grave[6] are but a few out of ten thousand resultant combinations. That clear, perpetual outline of face and limb is but an image of ours, under which we group them—a design in a web, the actual threads of which pass out beyond it. This at least of flame-like our life has, that it is but the concurrence, renewed from moment to moment, of forces parting sooner or later on their ways.

Or if we begin with the inward world of thought and feeling, the whirlpool is still more rapid, the flame more eager and devouring. There it is no longer the gradual darkening of the eye, the gradual fading of colour from the wall—movements of the shore-side, where the water flows down indeed, though in apparent rest—but the race of the midstream, a drift of momentary acts of sight and passion and thought. At first sight experience seems to bury us under a flood of external objects, pressing upon us with a sharp and importunate reality, calling us out of ourselves in a thousand forms of action. But when reflexion begins to play upon those objects they are dissipated under its influence; the cohesive force seems suspended like some trick of magic; each object is loosed into a group of impressions—colour, odour, texture—in the mind of the observer. And if we continue to dwell in thought on this world, not of objects in the solidity with which language invests them, but of impressions, unstable, flickering, inconsistent, which burn and are extinguished with our consciousness of them, it contracts still further: the whole scope of observation is dwarfed into the narrow chamber of the individual mind. Experience, already reduced to a group of impressions, is ringed round for each one of us by that thick wall of personality through which no real voice has ever pierced on its way to us, or from us to that which we can only conjecture to be without. Every one of those impressions is the impression of the individual in his isolation, each mind keeping as a solitary prisoner its own dream of a world. Analysis goes a step further still, and assures us that those impressions of the individual mind to which, for each one of us, experience dwindles down, are in perpetual flight; that each of them is limited by time, and that as time is infinitely divisible, each of them is infinitely divisible also; all that is actual in it being a single moment, gone while we try to apprehend it, of which it may ever be more truly said that it has ceased to be than that it is. To such a tremulous wisp constantly re-forming itself on the stream, to a single sharp impression, with a sense in it, a relic more or less fleeting, of such moments gone by, what is real in our life fines itself down. It is with this movement, with the passage and dissolution of impressions, images, sensations, that analysis leaves off—that continual vanishing away, that strange, perpetual, weaving and unweaving of ourselves.

Philosophiren, says Novalis, *ist dephlegmatisiren, vivificiren.*[7] The service of philosophy, of speculative culture, towards the human spirit, is to rouse, to startle it to a life of constant and eager observation. Every moment some form grows perfect in hand or face; some tone on the hills or the sea is choicer than the rest; some mood of passion or insight or intellectual excitement is

6. An echo of Laertes's words at the grave of Ophelia, *Hamlet* (ca. 1600), 5.1.222–23: "And from her fair and unpolluted flesh / May violets spring."

7. To philosophize is to cast away inertia, to bring oneself to life (German). Novalis: the pen name of Baron Friedrich von Hardenberg (1772–1801), German Romantic poet and novelist; "Fragmente II" from his *Hymns to the Night* (1800) is quoted here.

irresistibly real and attractive to us,—for that moment only. Not the fruit of experience, but experience itself, is the end. A counted number of pulses only is given to us of a variegated, dramatic life. How may we see in them all that is to be seen in them by the finest senses? How shall we pass most swiftly from point to point, and be present always at the focus where the greatest number of vital forces unite in their purest energy?

To burn always with this hard, gem-like flame, to maintain this ecstasy, is success in life. In a sense it might even be said that our failure is to form habits: for, after all, habit is relative to a stereotyped world, and meantime it is only the roughness of the eye that makes any two persons, things, situations, seem alike. While all melts under our feet, we may well grasp at any exquisite passion, or any contribution to knowledge that seems by a lifted horizon to set the spirit free for a moment, or any stirring of the senses, strange dyes, strange colours, and curious odours, or work of the artist's hands, or the face of one's friend. Not to discriminate every moment some passionate attitude in those about us, and in the very brilliancy of their gifts some tragic dividing of forces on their ways, is, on this short day of frost and sun, to sleep before evening. With this sense of the splendour of our experience and of its awful brevity, gathering all we are into one desperate effort to see and touch, we shall hardly have time to make theories about the things we see and touch. What we have to do is to be for ever curiously testing new opinions and courting new impressions, never acquiescing in a facile orthodoxy, of Comte, or of Hegel,[8] or of our own. Philosophical theories or ideas, as points of view, instruments of criticism, may help us to gather up what might otherwise pass unregarded by us. "Philosophy is the microscope of thought."[9] The theory or idea or system which requires of us the sacrifice of any part of this experience, in consideration of some interest into which we cannot enter, or some abstract theory we have not identified with ourselves, or of what is only conventional, has no real claim upon us.

One of the most beautiful passages of Rousseau[1] is that in the sixth book of the *Confessions*, where he describes the awakening in him of the literary sense. An undefinable taint of death had clung always about him, and now in early manhood he believed himself smitten by mortal disease. He asked himself how he might make as much as possible of the interval that remained; and he was not biassed by anything in his previous life when he decided that it must be by intellectual excitement, which he found just then in the clear, fresh writings of Voltaire.[2] Well! we are all *condamnés*, as Victor Hugo says: we are all under sentence of death but with a sort of indefinite reprieve—*les hommes sont tous condamnés à mort avec des sursis indéfinis*:[3] we have an interval, and then our place knows us no more. Some spend this interval in listlessness, some in high passions, the wisest, at least among "the children of this world,"[4] in art and song. For our one chance

8. GEORG WILHELM FRIEDRICH HEGEL (1770–1831), German idealist philosopher. Auguste Comte (1798–1857), French positivist philosopher.

9. From *Les Misérables* (1862) by Victor Hugo (1802–1885), the leader of the Romantic movement in France.

1. Jean-Jacques Rousseau (1712–1778), Swiss-born French philosopher and political theorist; his *Confessions* were published in 12 books (1781, 1788).

2. The scholar Donald L. Hill has pointed out that Rousseau, in his *Confessions*, nowhere mentions reading the French Enlightenment philosopher and writer Voltaire (François-Marie Arouet, 1694–1778).

3. Men are all condemned to death with indefinite reprieves (French). From Hugo, *The Last Day of a Condemned Person* (1832).

4. Luke 16.8.

lies in expanding that interval, in getting as many pulsations as possible into the given time. Great passions may give us this quickened sense of life, ecstasy and sorrow of love, the various forms of enthusiastic activity, disinterested or otherwise, which come naturally to many of us. Only be sure it is passion—that it does yield you this fruit of a quickened, multiplied consciousness. Of such wisdom, the poetic passion, the desire of beauty, the love of art for its own sake, has most. For art comes to you proposing frankly to give nothing but the highest quality to your moments as they pass, and simply for those moments' sake.

1873, 1893

HENRY JAMES
1843–1916

Born in New York City, Henry James typically is placed in anthologies of American literature, but he was in truth a cosmopolitan novelist and critic who sought to make his mark on the American, English, and European literary scenes. "We can deal freely with forms of civilization not our own," he affirmed in a letter in 1867, "can pick and choose and assimilate and in short (aesthetically) claim our property wherever we find it." He wished to bring about "a vast intellectual fusion and synthesis of the various National tendencies of the world"; his concern with the complex challenges and rewards of the "art of fiction" was general, not limited to American fiction alone.

Henry James Sr., a religious philosopher and visionary, believed that his five children should be educated with as few restrictions as possible; hence he had taken them to Europe in 1855 for a three-year acquisition of a "sensuous education." Theaters, art galleries, museums, monuments, and landscapes were his favored sites for learning. Among the gifted members of this family was William James, Henry's elder brother, a professor of philosophy and then psychology at Harvard whose influential books include *The Varieties of Religious Experience* (1902) and *Pragmatism* (1907). During the late 1860s and early 1870s, Henry James lived abroad much of the time; in 1876 he decided to reside in London and frequently visit the Continent, especially Rome and Paris.

James was an explorer of, and mediator between, cultures. One of his best early stories, "A Passionate Pilgrim" (1871), deals with the social and cultural challenges faced by an American visitor to Europe. He developed this theme of cultural interanimation and difference in his travel writings, such as *Transatlantic Sketches* (1875), and in a series of novels and novellas that includes *Roderick Hudson* (1876), *The American* (1877), *The Europeans* (1878), *Daisy Miller* (1879), *An International Episode* (1879), and *The Portrait of a Lady* (1881). "I aspire to write in such a way," James declared, "that it would be impossible to an outsider to say whether I am at a given moment an American writing about England or an Englishman writing about America. . . . And so far from being ashamed of such an ambiguity I should be exceedingly proud of it, for it would be highly civilised."

As his work of the 1870s and early 1880s attests, James was already an accomplished author when our selection, "The Art of Fiction"—his credo as a novelist—was published in London in September 1884. A month after the essay appeared,

James lamented in a letter to the critic and biographer T. S. Perry that "my poor article has not attracted the smallest attention here & I haven't heard, or seen, an allusion to it." But soon critics and reviewers, especially in England, began to refer and reply to the piece. In subsequent decades, as James's own reputation rose, "The Art of Fiction" gained prominence as an inquiry into, and defense of, the novelist's craft. A century later, the scholar James E. Miller Jr. judged it "perhaps the most popular and surely the most influential brief statement of fictional theory ever made."

British and American novelists before James, including Henry Fielding, Jane Austen, Sir Walter Scott, and Nathaniel Hawthorne, had commented on the nature of the novel and its relationship to the romance. Beginning in the mid-eighteenth century with SAMUEL JOHNSON, critics had considered the status and structure of "fiction" as a narrative form. Book-length studies included Clara Reeve's *Progress of Romance* (1785) and John Dunlop's massive two-volume survey, *The History of Fiction* (1816). By 1884 countless essays and reviews in Victorian periodicals had debated plot, character, design and unity, morality in fiction, and many other topics in analyses written by such eminent novelists as George Eliot and by such noteworthy critics as G. H. Lewes and Leslie Stephen.

James added to his own rich experience as a writer the decades of development that the novel had undergone by the 1880s. He profited from extensive reading and close personal contact with the best writers of the day (among them William Dean Howells, Gustave Flaubert, Guy de Maupassant, Émile Zola, and Ivan Turgenev). As an active essayist and reviewer since the 1860s for the *Nation*, the *North American Review*, and the *Atlantic Monthly*, James was defining his own artistic identity and measuring himself alongside national and international competition. His critical books of this period include *French Poets and Novelists* (1878) and *Hawthorne* (1879), and he examined fiction with a keen awareness of his own practice.

Taking as his point of departure an 1884 lecture by the popular novelist, historian, and philanthropist Walter Besant and borrowing its title, James insisted that the novelist be allowed to pursue artistic experiments freely. He told his friend Robert Louis Stevenson that "The Art of Fiction" was "simply a plea for liberty," which for him signified the writer's choice of subject and right both to experiment and to dissent from conventional standards and opinions. In one of the ironies that makes James so intriguing, he was a very *interested* critic, not an objective one. Even when he focuses on authors whom he genuinely admires, such as Honoré de Balzac, Turgenev, and George Eliot, he cannot quite bring himself to respond to (let alone accept) them on their own terms—though his theory implies that he should. Here, as elsewhere in his critical writings, his allegiance to his own artistic aims and methods prevented James from engaging writers impartially and with full understanding; his assessments of Charles Dickens, Walt Whitman, Charles Baudelaire, and Fyodor Dostoyevsky, among others, suffer from his impatience with their often controversial subjects and innovations in form. James's criticisms thus sometimes tell us less about the shortcomings of the work discussed than about the tensions between his theory and practice.

Like MATTHEW ARNOLD in "The Function of Criticism at the Present Time" (1864; see above), James in "The Art of Fiction" maintains that criticism prepares and enhances the context for creative writing. In an essay about Arnold published in the same year as "The Art of Fiction," James describes the good novel (it "emits its light and stimulates our desire for perfection") in a manner very close to Arnold's definition of "the pursuit of perfection" as "the pursuit of sweetness and light" in *Culture and Anarchy* (1869; see above). James's tone is forthright, optimistic, and celebratory of the power of the literary imagination. "The Art of Fiction" is a controlled, resonant rearticulation of the tributes to the imagination voiced decades earlier by WILLIAM WORDSWORTH, SAMUEL TAYLOR COLERIDGE, PERCY BYSSHE SHELLEY, and RALPH WALDO EMERSON on behalf of the poet. James is often identified as a literary realist and early modernist—Ezra Pound and T. S. ELIOT esteemed him highly. But the roots of his creative and critical practice lie in Romanticism's organic conception of literary form, and in its exalted view of the literary vocation. The writer, James remarked, is an alchemist who "renews something like the old dream of the secret of life."

These connections are important to bear in mind when reading James's essay. "The Art of Fiction" often has been interpreted in isolation, with little note of its affinities to other critical and theoretical texts that preceded it. Sometimes it has been treated exclusively within the canon of James's own creative and critical writings, as a prelude both to his dense, difficult final three novels, *The Wings of the Dove* (1902), *The Ambassadors* (1903), and *The Golden Bowl* (1904), and to the later prefaces—a "comprehensive manual" for "aspirants" to the profession—that he composed for the twenty-six-volume New York Edition of his novels and stories (1907–09, 1917). Such intensively "Jamesian" readings value "The Art of Fiction" as a formative text in James's own career: it shows him, like Wordsworth and Coleridge, establishing the terms through which his own work should be understood and appraised. But if we locate the essay solely within James's corpus, we are prevented from understanding how this piece (and others he produced) contributes to his significance in the general history of narrative theory.

James's concern for taste, judgment, and discrimination glances backward to the eighteenth-century writers DAVID HUME and EDMUND BURKE. When he hails the novel as "a personal, a direct impression of life," he more immediately echoes the heightened phrasing that WALTER PATER had employed in *Studies in the History of the Renaissance* (1873; see above). His account of the novel as an "organism" not only reinforces the account of "organic form" delineated by Coleridge in the *Biographia Literaria* but also anticipates the elaborations of this same idea in the writings of JOHN CROWE RANSOM, CLEANTH BROOKS, and other New Critics of the 1930s and 1940s.

"The Art of Fiction" is a subtle verbal performance; playful, witty, and ironic, it is both generous and tough-minded toward James's target-of-opportunity Walter Besant. Reading James profitably means paying close attention to his metaphors (e.g., the "huge spider-web" of experience) and analogies (e.g., between the novel and the picture). It means being alert as well to the illuminations provided by James's handling of specific words, as when he reiterates the "torment" of the writer. There are also key moments when James invites readers to reflect on the implications of his claims. In perhaps the most elusive of these, he asserts that "the deepest quality of a work of art will always be the quality of the mind of the producer." James realized the demands inherent in such a claim: How will we know, in the case of each novel, when we have made contact with the mind of its producer? How can we determine that mind's special quality? But his chosen criterion highlights the intimate relationship between writer and reader that the cosmopolitan James always looked for, and that he called on readers of "The Art of Fiction" to share.

"The Art of Fiction" Keywords: Authorship, Defense of Criticism, Formalism, Narrative Theory, The Novel, Realism

The Art of Fiction

I should not have affixed so comprehensive a title to these few remarks, necessarily wanting in any completeness upon a subject the full consideration of which would carry us far, did I not seem to discover a pretext for my temerity in the interesting pamphlet lately published under this name by Mr. Walter Besant.[1] Mr. Besant's lecture at the Royal Institution—the original form of his pamphlet—appears to indicate that many persons are interested in the art of fiction, and are not indifferent to such remarks, as those who practise it may attempt to make about it. I am therefore anxious not to lose the benefit of this favourable association, and to edge in a few words under cover of the attention which Mr. Besant is sure to have excited. There is something very encouraging in his having put into form certain of his ideas on the mystery of story-telling.

It is a proof of life and curiosity—curiosity on the part of the brotherhood of novelists as well as on the part of their readers. Only a short time ago it might have been supposed that the English novel was not what the French call *discutable*.[2] It had no air of having a theory, a conviction, a consciousness of itself behind it—of being the expression of an artistic faith, the result of choice and comparison. I do not say it was necessarily the worse for that: it would take much more courage than I possess to intimate that the form of the novel as Dickens and Thackeray[3] (for instance) saw it had any taint of incompleteness. It was, however, *naïf* (if I may help myself out with another French word); and evidently if it be destined to suffer in any way for having lost its *naïveté* it has now an idea of making sure of the corresponding advantages. During the period I have alluded to there was a comfortable, good-humoured feeling abroad that a novel is a novel, as a pudding is a pudding, and that our only business with it could be to swallow it. But within a year or two, for some reason or other, there have been signs of returning animation—the era of discussion would appear to have been to a certain extent opened. Art lives upon discussion, upon experiment, upon curiosity, upon variety of attempt, upon the exchange of views and the comparison of standpoints; and there is a presumption that those times when no one has anything particular to say about it, and has no reason to give for practice or preference, though they may be times of honour, are not times of development—are times, possibly even, a little of dulness. The successful application of any art is a delightful spectacle, but the theory too is interesting; and though there is a great deal of the latter without the former I suspect there has never been a genuine success that has not had a latent core of conviction. Discussion, suggestion, formulation, these things are fertilising when they are frank and sincere. Mr. Besant has set an excellent example in saying what he thinks, for his part, about the way in which fiction should be written, as well as about the way in which it should be published; for his view of the "art," carried on into an appendix, covers that too. Other labourers in the same field will doubtless take up the argument, they will give it the light of their experience, and the effect will surely be to make our interest in the novel a little more what it had for some time threatened to fail to be—a serious, active, inquiring interest, under protection of which this delightful study may, in moments of confidence, venture to say a little more what it thinks of itself.

It must take itself seriously for the public to take it so. The old superstition about fiction being "wicked" has doubtless died out in England; but the

1. English novelist, historian, and critic (1836–1901). "Temerity": excessive confidence or boldness, audacity.
2. Discussable, debatable (French).
3. William Thackeray (1811–1863), English novelist and satirist. Charles Dickens (1812–1870), most popular 19th-century English novelist.

spirit of it lingers in a certain oblique regard directed toward any story which does not more or less admit that it is only a joke. Even the most jocular novel feels in some degree the weight of the proscription that was formerly directed against literary levity: the jocularity does not always succeed in passing for orthodoxy. It is still expected, though perhaps people are ashamed to say it, that a production which is after all only a "make believe" (for what else is a "story"?) shall be in some degree apologetic—shall renounce the pretension of attempting really to represent life. This, of course, any sensible, wide-awake story declines to do, for it quickly perceives that the tolerance granted to it on such a condition is only an attempt to stifle it disguised in the form of generosity. The old evangelical hostility to the novel, which was as explicit as it was narrow, and which regarded it as little less favourable to our immortal part than a stage-play, was in reality far less insulting. The only reason for the existence of a novel is that it does attempt to represent life.[4] When it relinquishes this attempt, the same attempt that we see on the canvas of the painter, it will have arrived at a very strange pass. It is not expected of the picture that it will make itself humble in order to be forgiven; and the analogy between the art of the painter and the art of the novelist is, so far as I am able to see, complete. Their inspiration is the same, their process (allowing for the different quality of the vehicle), is the same, their success is the same. They may learn from each other, they may explain and sustain each other. Their cause is the same, and the honour of one is the honour of another. The Mahometans[5] think a picture an unholy thing, but it is a long time since any Christian did, and it is therefore the more odd that in the Christian mind the traces (dissimulated though they may be) of a suspicion of the sister art should linger to this day. The only effectual way to lay it to rest is to emphasise the analogy to which I just alluded—to insist on the fact that as the picture is reality, so the novel is history. That is the only general description (which does it justice) that we may give of the novel. But history also is allowed to represent life; it is not, any more than painting, expected to apologise. The subject-matter of fiction is stored up likewise in documents and records, and if it will not give itself away, as they say in California, it must speak with assurance, with the tone of the historian. Certain accomplished novelists have a habit of giving themselves away which must often bring tears to the eyes of people who take their fiction seriously. I was lately struck, in reading over many pages of Anthony Trollope,[6] with his want of discretion in this particular. In a digression, a parenthesis or an aside, he concedes to the reader that he and this trusting friend are only "making believe." He admits that the events he narrates have not really happened, and that he can give his narrative any turn the reader may like best. Such a betrayal of a sacred office seems to me, I confess, a terrible crime; it is what I mean by the attitude of apology, and it shocks me every whit as much in Trollope as it would have shocked me in Gibbon or Macaulay.[7] It implies that

4. In the first version of the essay, James wrote "*does* compete with life." Robert Louis Stevenson criticized the use of the word "compete" in his reply to James, "A Humble Remonstrance," in the December 1884 issue of *Longman's*.

5. Muslims (i.e., followers of Muhammad, or Mahomet). Islam generally prohibits representational art.

6. Prolific English novelist (1815–1882).

7. Thomas Babington Macaulay (1800–1859), English historian, essayist, and statesman. Edward Gibbon (1737–1794), English historian, author of *The History of the Decline and Fall of the Roman Empire* (6 vols., 1776–88).

the novelist is less occupied in looking for the truth (the truth, of course I mean, that he assumes, the premises that we must grant him, whatever they may be), than the historian, and in doing so it deprives him at a stroke of all his standing-room. To represent and illustrate the past, the actions of men, is the task of either writer, and the only difference that I can see is, in proportion as he succeeds, to the honour of the novelist, consisting as it does in his having more difficulty in collecting his evidence, which is so far from being purely literary.[8] It seems to me to give him a great character, the fact that he has at once so much in common with the philosopher and the painter; this double analogy is a magnificent heritage.

It is of all this evidently that Mr. Besant is full when he insists upon the fact that fiction is one of the *fine* arts, deserving in its turn of all the honours and emoluments that have hitherto been reserved for the successful profession of music, poetry, painting, architecture. It is impossible to insist too much on so important a truth, and the place that Mr. Besant demands for the work of the novelist may be represented, a trifle less abstractly, by saying that he demands not only that it shall be reputed artistic, but that it shall be reputed very artistic indeed. It is excellent that he should have struck this note, for his doing so indicates that there was need of it, that his proposition may be to many people a novelty. One rubs one's eyes at the thought; but the rest of Mr. Besant's essay confirms the revelation. I suspect in truth that it would be possible to confirm it still further, and that one would not be far wrong in saying that in addition to the people to whom it has never occurred that a novel ought to be artistic, there are a great many others who, if this principle were urged upon them, would be filled with an indefinable mistrust. They would find it difficult to explain their repugnance, but it would operate strongly to put them on their guard. "Art," in our Protestant communities, where so many things have got so strangely twisted about, is supposed in certain circles to have some vaguely injurious effect upon those who make it an important consideration, who let it weigh in the balance. It is assumed to be opposed in some mysterious manner to morality, to amusement, to instruction. When it is embodied in the work of the painter (the sculptor is another affair!) you know what it is: it stands there before you, in the honesty of pink and green and a gilt frame; you can see the worst of it at a glance, and you can be on your guard. But when it is introduced into literature it becomes more insidious—there is danger of its hurting you before you know it. Literature should be either instructive or amusing, and there is in many minds an impression that these artistic preoccupations, the search for form, contribute to neither end, interfere indeed with both. They are too frivolous to be edifying, and too serious to be diverting; and they are moreover priggish and paradoxical and superfluous. That, I think, represents the manner in which the latent thought of many people who read novels as an exercise in skipping would explain itself if it were to become articulate. They would argue, of course, that a novel ought to be "good," but they would interpret this term in a fashion of their own, which indeed would vary considerably from one critic to another. One would say that being good means representing virtuous and aspiring characters, placed in prominent positions;

8. On somewhat different grounds, ARISTOTLE argues in *Poetics* 9 (see above) that poetry is more philosophical and more worthwhile than history.

another would say that it depends on a "happy ending," on a distribution at the last of prizes, pensions, husbands, wives, babies, millions, appended paragraphs, and cheerful remarks. Another still would say that it means being full of incident and movement, so that we shall wish to jump ahead, to see who was the mysterious stranger, and if the stolen will was ever found, and shall not be distracted from this pleasure by any tiresome analysis or "description." But they would all agree that the "artistic" idea would spoil some of their fun. One would hold it accountable for all the description, another would see it revealed in the absence of sympathy. Its hostility to a happy ending would be evident, and it might even in some cases render any ending at all impossible. The "ending" of a novel is, for many persons, like that of a good dinner, a course of dessert and ices, and the artist in fiction is regarded as a sort of meddlesome doctor who forbids agreeable aftertastes. It is therefore true that this conception of Mr. Besant's of the novel as a superior form encounters not only a negative but a positive indifference. It matters little that as a work of art it should really be as little or as much of its essence to supply happy endings, sympathetic characters, and an objective tone, as if it were a work of mechanics: the association of ideas, however incongruous, might easily be too much for it if an eloquent voice were not sometimes raised to call attention to the fact that it is at once as free and as serious a branch of literature as any other.

Certainly this might sometimes be doubted in presence of the enormous number of works of fiction that appeal to the credulity of our generation, for it might easily seem that there could be no great character in a commodity so quickly and easily produced. It must be admitted that good novels are much compromised by bad ones, and that the field at large suffers discredit from overcrowding. I think, however, that this injury is only superficial, and that the superabundance of written fiction proves nothing against the principle itself. It has been vulgarised, like all other kinds of literature, like everything else to-day, and it has proved more than some kinds accessible to vulgarisation. But there is as much difference as there ever was between a good novel and a bad one: the bad is swept with all the daubed canvases and spoiled marble into some unvisited limbo, or infinite rubbish-yard beneath the back-windows of the world, and the good subsists and emits its light and stimulates our desire for perfection. As I shall take the liberty of making but a single criticism of Mr. Besant, whose tone is so full of the love of his art, I may as well have done with it at once. He seems to me to mistake in attempting to say so definitely beforehand what sort of an affair the good novel will be. To indicate the danger of such an error as that has been the purpose of these few pages; to suggest that certain traditions on the subject, applied *a priori*, have already had much to answer for, and that the good health of an art which undertakes so immediately to reproduce life must demand that it be perfectly free. It lives upon exercise, and the very meaning of exercise is freedom. The only obligation to which in advance we may hold a novel, without incurring the accusation of being arbitrary, is that it be interesting. That general responsibility rests upon it, but it is the only one I can think of. The ways in which it is at liberty to accomplish this result (of interesting us) strike me as innumerable, and such as can only suffer from being marked out or fenced in by prescription. They are as various as the temperament of man, and they are successful in proportion as they reveal a particular mind, different from others. A novel is in its broadest definition a personal, a direct impression of life: that, to begin with, constitutes its value, which is greater or less according to the intensity of the impression. But there will be no intensity at all, and therefore no value, unless there is freedom to feel and say. The tracing of a line to be followed, of a tone to be taken, of a form to be filled out, is a limitation of that freedom and a suppression of the very thing that we are most curious about. The form, it seems to me, is to be appreciated after the fact: then the author's choice has been made, his standard has been indicated; then we can follow lines and directions and compare tones and resemblances. Then in a word we can enjoy one of the most charming of pleasures, we can estimate quality, we can apply the test of execution. The execution belongs to the author alone; it is what is most personal to him, and we measure him by that. The advantage, the luxury, as well as the torment and responsibility of the novelist, is that there is no limit to what he may attempt as an executant—no limit to his possible experiments, efforts, discoveries, successes. Here it is especially that he works, step by step, like his brother of the brush, of whom we may always say that he has painted his picture in a manner best known to himself. His manner is his secret, not necessarily a jealous one. He cannot disclose it as a general thing if he would; he would be at a loss to teach it to others. I say this with a due recollection of having insisted on the community of method of the artist who paints a picture and the artist who writes a novel. The painter *is* able to teach the rudiments of his practice, and it is possible, from the study of good work (granted the aptitude), both to learn how to paint and to learn how to write. Yet it remains true, without injury to the *rapprochement*,[9] that the literary artist would be obliged to say to his pupil much more than the other, "Ah, well, you must do it as you can!" It is a question of degree, a matter of delicacy. If there are exact sciences, there are also exact arts, and the grammar of painting is so much more definite that it makes the difference.

I ought to add, however, that if Mr. Besant says at the beginning of his essay that the "laws of fiction may be laid down and taught with as much precision and exactness as the laws of harmony, perspective, and proportion," he mitigates what might appear to be an extravagance by applying his remark to "general" laws, and by expressing most of these rules in a manner with which it would certainly be unaccommodating to disagree. That the novelist must write from his experience, that his "characters must be real and such as might be met with in actual life;" that "a young lady brought up in a quiet country village should avoid descriptions of garrison life," and "a writer whose friends and personal experiences belong to the lower middle-class should carefully avoid introducing his characters into society;" that one should enter one's notes in a common-place book; that one's figures should be clear in outline; that making them clear by some trick of speech or of carriage is a bad method, and "describing them at length" is a worse one: that English Fiction should have a "conscious moral purpose;" that "it is almost impossible to estimate too highly the value of careful workmanship—that is, of style;" that "the most important point of all is the story," that "the story is everything":

9. The bringing together (French); that is, of painting and novel writing.

these are principles with most of which it is surely impossible not to sympathise. That remark about the lower middle-class writer and his knowing his place is perhaps rather chilling; but for the rest I should find it difficult to dissent from any one of these recommendations. At the same time, I should find it difficult positively to assent to them, with the exception, perhaps, of the injunction as to entering one's notes in a common-place book. They scarcely seem to me to have the quality that Mr. Besant attributes to the rules of the novelist—the "precision and exactness" of "the laws of harmony, perspective, and proportion." They are suggestive, they are even inspiring, but they are not exact, though they are doubtless as much so as the case admits of: which is a proof of that liberty of interpretation for which I just contended. For the value of these different injunctions—so beautiful and so vague—is wholly in the meaning one attaches to them. The characters, the situation, which strike one as real will be those that touch and interest one most, but the measure of reality is very difficult to fix. The reality of Don Quixote or of Mr. Micawber[1] is a very delicate shade; it is a reality so coloured by the author's vision that, vivid as it may be, one would hesitate to propose it as a model: one would expose one's self to some very embarrassing questions on the part of a pupil. It goes without saying that you will not write a good novel unless you possess the sense of reality; but it will be difficult to give you a recipe for calling that sense into being. Humanity is immense, and reality has a myriad forms; the most one can affirm is that some of the flowers of fiction have the odour of it, and others have not; as for telling you in advance how your nosegay should be composed, that is another affair. It is equally excellent and inconclusive to say that one must write from experience; to our supposititious aspirant such a declaration might savor of mockery. What kind of experience is intended, and where does it begin and end? Experience is never limited, and it is never complete; it is an immense sensibility, a kind of huge spider-web of the finest silken threads suspended in the chamber of consciousness, and catching every airborne particle in its tissue. It is the very atmosphere of the mind; and when the mind is imaginative—much more when it happens to be that of a man of genius—it takes to itself the faintest hints of life, it converts the very pulses of the air into revelations. The young lady living in a village has only to be a damsel upon whom nothing is lost to make it quite unfair (as it seems to me) to declare to her that she shall have nothing to say about the military. Greater miracles have been seen than that, imagination assisting, she should speak the truth about some of these gentlemen. I remember an English novelist, a woman of genius,[2] telling me that she was much commended for the impression she had managed to give in one of her tales of the nature and way of life of the French Protestant youth. She had been asked where she learned so much about this recondite being, she had been congratulated on her peculiar opportunities. These opportunities consisted in her having once, in Paris, as she ascended a staircase, passed an open door where, in the household of a *pasteur*,[3] some of the young Protestants were seated at table

1. Character in *David Copperfield* (1849–50), by Dickens. Don Quixote: title character of the novel (1605, 1615), by Miguel de Cervantes (1547–1616).
2. Identified by James's biographer Leon Edel as Anne Thackeray, Lady Ritchie (1837–1919), the daughter of William Thackeray and the author of *The Story of Elizabeth* (1862–63), to which James seems to be alluding.
3. Protestant minister, pastor (French).

round a finished meal. The glimpse made a picture; it lasted only a moment, but that moment was experience. She had got her direct personal impression, and she turned out her type. She knew what youth was, and what Protestantism; she also had the advantage of having seen what it was to be French, so that she converted these ideas into a concrete image and produced a reality. Above all, however, she was blessed with the faculty which when you give it an inch takes an ell, and which for the artist is a much greater source of strength than any accident of residence or of place in the social scale. The power to guess the unseen from the seen, to trace the implication of things, to judge the whole piece by the pattern, the condition of feeling life in general so completely that you are well on your way to knowing any particular corner of it—this cluster of gifts may almost be said to constitute experience, and they occur in country and in town, and in the most differing stages of education. If experience consists of impressions, it may be said that impressions *are* experience, just as (have we not seen it?) they are the very air we breathe. Therefore, if I should certainly say to a novice, "Write from experience and experience only," I should feel that this was rather a tantalising monition if I were not careful immediately to add, "Try to be one of the people on whom nothing is lost!"

I am far from intending by this to minimise the importance of exactness—of truth of detail. One can speak best from one's own taste, and I may therefore venture to say that the air of reality (solidity of specification) seems to me to be the supreme virtue of a novel—the merit on which all its other merits (including that conscious moral purpose of which Mr. Besant speaks) helplessly and submissively depend. If it be not there they are all as nothing, and if these be there, they owe their effect to the success with which the author has produced the illusion of life. The cultivation of this success, the study of this exquisite process, form, to my taste, the beginning and the end of the art of the novelist. They are his inspiration, his despair, his reward, his torment, his delight. It is here in very truth that he competes with life; it is here that he competes with his brother the painter in *his* attempt to render the look of things, the look that conveys their meaning, to catch the colour, the relief, the expression, the surface, the substance of the human spectacle. It is in regard to this that Mr. Besant is well inspired when he bids him take notes. He cannot possibly take too many, he cannot possibly take enough. All life solicits him, and to "render" the simplest surface, to produce the most momentary illusion, is a very complicated business. His case would be easier, and the rule would be more exact, if Mr. Besant had been able to tell him what notes to take. But this, I fear, he can never learn in any manual; it is the business of his life. He has to take a great many in order to select a few, he has to work them up as he can, and even the guides and philosophers who might have most to say to him must leave him alone when it comes to the application of precepts, as we leave the painter in communion with his palette. That his characters "must be clear in outline," as Mr. Besant says—he feels that down to his boots; but how he shall make them so is a secret between his good angel and himself. It would be absurdly simple if he could be taught that a great deal of "description" would make them so, or that on the contrary the absence of description and the cultivation of dialogue, or the absence of dialogue and the multiplication of "incident," would rescue him from his difficulties. Nothing, for instance, is more possible than that he be of a turn of mind for which this odd, literal opposition of description and dialogue, incident and description, has little meaning and light. People often talk of these things as if they had a kind of internecine[4] distinctness, instead of melting into each other at every breath, and being intimately associated parts of one general effort of expression. I cannot imagine composition existing in a series of blocks, nor conceive, in any novel worth discussing at all, of a passage of description that is not in its intention narrative, a passage of dialogue that is not in its intention descriptive, a touch of truth of any sort that does not partake of the nature of incident, or an incident that derives its interest from any other source than the general and only source of the success of a work of art—that of being illustrative. A novel is a living thing, all one and continuous, like any other organism, and in proportion as it lives will it be found, I think, that in each of the parts there is something of each of the other parts. The critic who over the close texture of a finished work shall pretend to trace a geography of items will mark some frontiers as artificial, I fear, as any that have been known to history. There is an old-fashioned distinction between the novel of character and the novel of incident which must have cost many a smile to the intending fabulist who was keen about his work. It appears to me as little to the point as the equally celebrated distinction between the novel and the romance—to answer as little to any reality. There are bad novels and good novels, as there are bad pictures and good pictures; but that is the only distinction in which I see any meaning, and I can as little imagine speaking of a novel of character as I can imagine speaking of a picture of character. When one says picture one says of character, when one says novel one says of incident, and the terms may be transposed at will. What is character but the determination of incident? What is incident but the illustration of character? What is either a picture or a novel that is *not* of character? What else do we seek in it and find in it? It is an incident for a woman to stand up with her hand resting on a table and look out at you in a certain way; or if it be not an incident I think it will be hard to say what it is. At the same time it is an expression of character. If you say you don't see it (character in *that—allons donc!*[5]), this is exactly what the artist who has reasons of his own for thinking he *does* see it undertakes to show you. When a young man makes up his mind that he has not faith enough after all to enter the church as he intended, that is an incident, though you may not hurry to the end of the chapter to see whether perhaps he doesn't change once more. I do not say that these are extraordinary or startling incidents. I do not pretend to estimate the degree of interest proceeding from them, for this will depend upon the skill of the painter. It sounds almost puerile to say that some incidents are intrinsically much more important than others, and I need not take this precaution after having professed my sympathy for the major ones in remarking that the only classification of the novel that I can understand is into that which has life and that which has it not.

The novel and the romance, the novel of incident and that of character—these clumsy separations appear to me to have been made by critics and readers for their own convenience, and to help them out of some of their

4. Relating to conflict or struggle within a group; mutually destructive.

5. Come now, that's nonsense (French).

occasional queer predicaments, but to have little reality or interest for the producer, from whose point of view it is of course that we are attempting to consider the art of fiction. The case is the same with another shadowy category which Mr. Besant apparently is disposed to set up—that of the "modern English novel"; unless indeed it be that in this matter he has fallen into an accidental confusion of stand-points. It is not quite clear whether he intends the remarks in which he alludes to it to be didactic or historical. It is as difficult to suppose a person intending to write a modern English as to suppose him writing an ancient English novel: that is a label which begs the question. One writes the novel, one paints the picture, of one's language and of one's time, and calling it modern English will not, alas! make the difficult task any easier. No more, unfortunately, will calling this or that work of one's fellow-artist a romance—unless it be, of course, simply for the pleasantness of the thing, as for instance when Hawthorne gave this heading to his story of *Blithedale*.[6] The French, who have brought the theory of fiction to remarkable completeness, have but one name for the novel, and have not attempted smaller things in it, that I can see, for that. I can think of no obligation to which the "romancer" would not be held equally with the novelist; the standard of execution is equally high for each. Of course it is of execution that we are talking—that being the only point of a novel that is open to contention. This is perhaps too often lost sight of, only to produce interminable confusions and cross-purposes. We must grant the artist his subject, his idea, his *donnée*:[7] our criticism is applied only to what he makes of it. Naturally I do not mean that we are bound to like it or find it interesting: in case we do not our course is perfectly simple—to let it alone. We may believe that of a certain idea even the most sincere novelist can make nothing at all, and the event may perfectly justify our belief; but the failure will have been a failure to execute, and it is in the execution that the fatal weakness is recorded. If we pretend to respect the artist at all, we must allow him his freedom of choice, in the face, in particular cases, of innumerable presumptions that the choice will not fructify. Art derives a considerable part of its beneficial exercise from flying in the face of presumptions, and some of the most interesting experiments of which it is capable are hidden in the bosom of common things. Gustave Flaubert has written a story about the devotion of a servant-girl to a parrot,[8] and the production, highly finished as it is, cannot on the whole be called a success. We are perfectly free to find it flat, but I think it might have been interesting; and I, for my part, am extremely glad he should have written it; it is a contribution to our knowledge of what can be done—or what cannot. Ivan Turgénieff has written a tale about a deaf and dumb serf and a lap-dog,[9] and the thing is touching, loving, a little masterpiece. He struck the note of life where Gustave Flaubert missed it—he flew in the face of a presumption and achieved a victory.

Nothing, of course, will ever take the place of the good old fashion of "liking" a work of art or not liking it: the most improved criticism will not abolish that primitive, that ultimate test. I mention this to guard myself from the

6. *The Blithedale Romance* (1852), by Nathaniel Hawthorne (1804–1864). This American writer's clearest statement of the distinction he saw between novel and romance appears in his preface to *The House of Seven Gables* (1851).
7. That which is given, starting point (French).
8. "A Simple Soul" (1877), by the French author Flaubert (1821–1880).
9. "Mumu" (1856), by the Russian author Turgenev (1818–1883).

accusation of intimating that the idea, the subject, of a novel or a picture, does not matter. It matters, to my sense, in the highest degree, and if I might put up a prayer it would be that artists should select none but the richest. Some, as I have already hastened to admit, are much more remunerative than others, and it would be a world happily arranged in which persons intending to treat them should be exempt from confusions and mistakes. This fortunate condition will arrive only, I fear, on the same day that critics become purged from error. Meanwhile, I repeat, we do not judge the artist with fairness unless we say to him, "Oh, I grant you your starting-point, because if I did not I should seem to prescribe to you, and heaven forbid I should take that responsibility. If I pretend to tell you what you must not take, you will call upon me to tell you then what you must take; in which case I shall be prettily caught. Moreover, it isn't till I have accepted your data that I can begin to measure you. I have the standard, the pitch; I have no right to tamper with your flute and then criticise your music. Of course I may not care for your idea at all; I may think it silly, or stale, or unclean; in which case I wash my hands of you altogether. I may content myself with believing that you will not have succeeded in being interesting, but I shall, of course, not attempt to demonstrate it, and you will be as indifferent to me as I am to you. I needn't remind you that there are all sorts of tastes: who can know it better? Some people, for excellent reasons, don't like to read about carpenters; others, for reasons even better, don't like to read about courtesans. Many object to Americans. Others (I believe they are mainly editors and publishers) won't look at Italians. Some readers don't like quiet subjects; others don't like bustling ones. Some enjoy a complete illusion, others the consciousness of large concessions. They choose their novels accordingly, and if they don't care about your idea they won't, *a fortiori*,[1] care about your treatment."

So that it comes back very quickly, as I have said, to the liking: in spite of M. Zola,[2] who reasons less powerfully than he represents, and who will not reconcile himself to this absoluteness of taste, thinking that there are certain things that people ought to like, and that they can be made to like. I am quite at a loss to imagine anything (at any rate in this matter of fiction) that people *ought* to like or to dislike. Selection will be sure to take care of itself, for it has a constant motive behind it. That motive is simply experience. As people feel life, so they will feel the art that is most closely related to it. This closeness of relation is what we should never forget in talking of the effort of the novel. Many people speak of it as a factitious, artificial form, a product of ingenuity, the business of which is to alter and arrange the things that surround us, to translate them into conventional, traditional moulds. This, however, is a view of the matter which carries us but a very short way, condemns the art to an eternal repetition of a few familiar *clichés*, cuts short its development, and leads us straight up to a dead wall. Catching the very note and trick, the strange irregular rhythm of life, that is the attempt whose strenuous force keeps Fiction upon her feet. In proportion as in what she offers us we see life *without* rearrangement do we feel that we are touching the

1. For a still stronger reason; all the more (New Latin).
2. Émile Zola (1840–1902), French novelist, critic, and theorist of the naturalist movement in literature. James finds Zola's theory less impressive than his practice.

truth; in proportion as we see it *with* rearrangement do we feel that we are being put off with a substitute, a compromise and convention. It is not uncommon to hear an extraordinary assurance of remark in regard to this matter of rearranging, which is often spoken of as if it were the last word of art. Mr. Besant seems to me in danger of falling into the great error with his rather unguarded talk about "selection." Art is essentially selection, but it is a selection whose main care is to be typical, to be inclusive. For many people art means rose-coloured window-panes, and selection means picking a bouquet for Mrs. Grundy.[3] They will tell you glibly that artistic considerations have nothing to do with the disagreeable, with the ugly; they will rattle off shallow commonplaces about the province of art and the limits of art till you are moved to some wonder in return as to the province and the limits of ignorance. It appears to me that no one can ever have made a seriously artistic attempt without becoming conscious of an immense increase—a kind of revelation—of freedom. One perceives in that case—by the light of a heavenly ray—that the province of art is all life, all feeling, all observation, all vision. As Mr. Besant so justly intimates, it is all experience. That is a sufficient answer to those who maintain that it must not touch the sad things of life, who stick into its divine unconscious bosom little prohibitory inscriptions on the end of sticks, such as we see in public gardens—"It is forbidden to walk on the grass; it is forbidden to touch the flowers; it is not allowed to introduce dogs or to remain after dark; it is requested to keep to the right." The young aspirant in the line of fiction whom we continue to imagine will do nothing without taste, for in that case his freedom would be of little use to him; but the first advantage of his taste will be to reveal to him the absurdity of the little sticks and tickets. If he have taste, I must add, of course he will have ingenuity, and my disrespectful reference to that quality just now was not meant to imply that it is useless in fiction. But it is only a secondary aid; the first is a capacity for receiving straight impressions.

Mr. Besant has some remarks on the question of "the story" which I shall not attempt to criticise, though they seem to me to contain a singular ambiguity, because I do not think I understand them. I cannot see what is meant by talking as if there were a part of a novel which is the story and part of it which for mystical reasons is not—unless indeed the distinction be made in a sense in which it is difficult to suppose that any one should attempt to convey anything. "The story," if it represents anything, represents the subject, the idea, the *donnée* of the novel; and there is surely no "school"—Mr. Besant speaks of a school—which urges that a novel should be all treatment and no subject. There must assuredly be something to treat; every school is intimately conscious of that. This sense of the story being the idea, the starting-point, of the novel, is the only one that I see in which it can be spoken of as something different from its organic whole; and since in proportion as the work is successful the idea permeates and penetrates it, informs and animates it, so that every word and every punctuation-point contribute directly to the expression, in that proportion do we lose our sense of the story being a blade which may be drawn more or less out of its sheath. The story and the novel, the idea and the form, are the needle and thread,

3. The unseen arbiter of taste and morals in the play *Speed the Plough* (1798), by the English playwright Thomas Morton—a symbol of moral rigidity.

and I never heard of a guild of tailors who recommended the use of the thread without the needle, or the needle without the thread. Mr. Besant is not the only critic who may be observed to have spoken as if there were certain things in life which constitute stories, and certain others which do not. I find the same odd implication in an entertaining article[4] in the *Pall Mall Gazette*, devoted, as it happens, to Mr. Besant's lecture. "The story is the thing!" says this graceful writer, as if with a tone of opposition to some other idea. I should think it was, as every painter who, as the time for "sending in" his picture[5] looms in the distance, finds himself still in quest of a subject—as every belated artist not fixed about his theme will heartily agree. There are some subjects which speak to us and others which do not, but he would be a clever man who should undertake to give a rule—an index expurgatorius[6]—by which the story and the no-story should be known apart. It is impossible (to me at least) to imagine any such rule which shall not be altogether arbitrary. The writer in the *Pall Mall* opposes the delightful (as I suppose) novel of *Margot la Balafrée* to certain tales in which "Bostonian nymphs" appear to have "rejected English dukes for psychological reasons."[7] I am not acquainted with the romance just designated, and can scarcely forgive the *Pall Mall* critic for not mentioning the name of the author, but the title appears to refer to a lady who may have received a scar in some heroic adventure. I am inconsolable at not being acquainted with this episode, but am utterly at a loss to see why it is a story when the rejection (or acceptance) of a duke is not, and why a reason, psychological or other, is not a subject when a cicatrix[8] is. They are all particles of the multitudinous life with which the novel deals, and surely no dogma which pretends to make it lawful to touch the one and unlawful to touch the other will stand for a moment on its feet. It is the special picture that must stand or fall, according as it seem to possess truth or to lack it. Mr. Besant does not, to my sense, light up the subject by intimating that a story must, under penalty of not being a story, consist of "adventures." Why of adventures more than of green spectacles?[9] He mentions a category of impossible things, and among them he places "fiction without adventure." Why without adventure, more than without matrimony, or celibacy, or parturition, or cholera, or hydropathy, or Jansenism?[1] This seems to me to bring the novel back to the hapless little *rôle* of being an artificial, ingenious thing—bring it down from its large, free character of an immense and exquisite correspondence with life. And what *is* adventure, when it comes to that, and by what sign is the listening pupil to recognise it? It is an adventure—an immense one—for me to write this little article; and for a Bostonian nymph to reject an English duke is an adventure only less stirring, I should say, than for an English duke to be rejected by a Bostonian

4. "The Art of Fiction," *Pall Mall Gazette*, April 30, 1884, by the Scottish critic and journalist Andrew Lang.
5. That is, the time he sends it off to an exhibit at the Royal Academy.
6. Rule for justifying (James's Latin coinage).
7. In James's *International Episode* (1879) (the writer may also have had in mind *The Portrait of a Lady*, 1881). *Margot: Margot the Scarred Woman* (1884), by the French romantic novelist Fortuné du Boisgobey.
8. A scar left when new tissue forms over a sore or wound.
9. An allusion to an episode in Oliver Goldsmith's *Vicar of Wakefield* (1766), in which a son spends the money from the sale of the family colt on a gross of green spectacles.
1. A Roman Catholic religious movement, condemned as heresy, that emphasized predestination and the importance of personal holiness; it grew out of the writings of the Dutch theologian Cornelis Jansen (1585–1638).

nymph. I see dramas within dramas in that, and innumerable points of view. A psychological reason is, to my imagination, an object adorably pictorial; to catch the tint of its complexion—I feel as if that idea might inspire one to Titianesque[2] efforts. There are few things more exciting to me, in short, than a psychological reason, and yet, I protest, the novel seems to me the most magnificent form of art. I have just been reading, at the same time, the delightful story of *Treasure Island*, by Mr. Robert Louis Stevenson and, in a manner less consecutive, the last tale from M. Edmond de Goncourt, which is entitled *Chérie*.[3] One of these works treats of murders, mysteries, islands of dreadful renown, hairbreadth escapes, miraculous coincidences and buried doubloons. The other treats of a little French girl who lived in a fine house in Paris, and died of wounded sensibility because no one would marry her. I call *Treasure Island* delightful, because it appears to me to have succeeded wonderfully in what it attempts; and I venture to bestow no epithet upon *Chérie*, which strikes me as having failed deplorably in what it attempts—that is in tracing the development of the moral consciousness of a child. But one of these productions strikes me as exactly as much of a novel as the other, and as having a "story" quite as much. The moral consciousness of a child is as much a part of life as the islands of the Spanish Main, and the one sort of geography seems to me to have those "surprises" of which Mr. Besant speaks quite as much as the other. For myself (since it comes back in the last resort, as I say, to the preference of the individual), the picture of the child's experience has the advantage that I can at successive steps (an immense luxury, near to the "sensual pleasure" of which Mr. Besant's critic in the *Pall Mall* speaks) say Yes or No, as it may be, to what the artist puts before me. I have been a child in fact, but I have been on a quest for a buried treasure only in supposition, and it is a simple accident that with M. de Goncourt I should have for the most part to say No. With George Eliot,[4] when she painted that country with a far other intelligence, I always said Yes.

The most interesting part of Mr. Besant's lecture is unfortunately the briefest passage—his very cursory allusion to the "conscious moral purpose" of the novel. Here again it is not very clear whether he be recording a fact or laying down a principle; it is a great pity that in the latter case he should not have developed his idea. This branch of the subject is of immense importance, and Mr. Besant's few words point to considerations of the widest reach, not to be lightly disposed of. He will have treated the art of fiction but superficially who is not prepared to go every inch of the way that these considerations will carry him. It is for this reason that at the beginning of these remarks I was careful to notify the reader that my reflections on so large a theme have no pretension to be exhaustive. Like Mr. Besant, I have left the question of the morality of the novel till the last, and at the last I find I have used up my space. It is a question surrounded with difficulties, as witness the very first that meets us, in the form of a definite question, on the threshold. Vagueness, in such a discussion, is fatal, and what is the meaning of

2. That is, characteristic of the Venetian painter Titian (Tiziano Vecellio, ca. 1488–1576), especially famous for his use of color.
3. A psychological study of a young woman (1884), by Goncourt (1822–1896). *Treasure Island*, by Stevenson (1850–1894), was published in 1883.
4. English novelist (1819–1880). George Eliot depicted "that country" of a child's consciousness in *The Mill on the Floss* (1860) and *Silas Marner* (1861).

your morality and your conscious moral purpose? Will you not define your terms and explain how (a novel being a picture) a picture can be either moral or immoral? You wish to paint a moral picture or carve a moral statue: will you not tell us how you would set about it? We are discussing the Art of Fiction; questions of art are questions (in the widest sense) of execution; questions of morality are quite another affair, and will you not let us see how it is that you find it so easy to mix them up? These things are so clear to Mr. Besant that he has deduced from them a law which he sees embodied in English Fiction, and which is "a truly admirable thing and a great cause for congratulation." It is a great cause for congratulation indeed when such thorny problems become as smooth as silk. I may add that in so far as Mr. Besant perceives that in point of fact English Fiction has addressed itself preponderantly to these delicate questions he will appear to many people to have made a vain discovery. They will have been positively struck, on the contrary, with the moral timidity of the usual English novelist; with his (or with her) aversion to face the difficulties with which on every side the treatment of reality bristles. He is apt to be extremely shy (whereas the picture that Mr. Besant draws is a picture of boldness), and the sign of his work, for the most part, is a cautious silence on certain subjects. In the English novel (by which of course I mean the American as well), more than in any other, there is a traditional difference between that which people know and that which they agree to admit that they know, that which they see and that which they speak of, that which they feel to be a part of life and that which they allow to enter into literature. There is the great difference, in short, between what they talk of in conversation and what they talk of in print. The essence of moral energy is to survey the whole field, and I should directly reverse Mr. Besant's remark and say not that the English novel has a purpose, but that it has a diffidence. To what degree a purpose in a work of art is a source of corruption I shall not attempt to inquire; the one that seems to me least dangerous is the purpose of making a perfect work. As for our novel, I may say lastly on this score that as we find it in England to-day it strikes me as addressed in a large degree to "young people," and that this in itself constitutes a presumption that it will be rather shy. There are certain things which it is generally agreed not to discuss, not even to mention, before young people. That is very well, but the absence of discussion is not a symptom of the moral passion. The purpose of the English novel—"a truly admirable thing, and a great cause for congratulation"—strikes me therefore as rather negative.

There is one point at which the moral sense and the artistic sense lie very near together; that is in the light of the very obvious truth that the deepest quality of a work of art will always be the quality of the mind of the producer. In proportion as that intelligence is fine will the novel, the picture, the statue partake of the substance of beauty and truth. To be constituted of such elements is, to my vision, to have purpose enough. No good novel will ever proceed from a superficial mind; that seems to me an axiom which, for the artist in fiction, will cover all needful moral ground: if the youthful aspirant take it to heart it will illuminate for him many of the mysteries of "purpose." There are many other useful things that might be said to him, but I have come to the end of my article, and can only touch them as I pass. The critic in the *Pall Mall Gazette*, whom I have already quoted, draws attention to the danger, in speaking of the art of fiction, of generalising. The danger that he has in mind is rather, I imagine, that of particularising, for there are some comprehensive remarks which, in addition to those embodied in Mr. Besant's suggestive lecture, might without fear of misleading him be addressed to the ingenuous student. I should remind him first of the magnificence of the form that is open to him, which offers to sight so few restrictions and such innumerable opportunities. The other arts, in comparison, appear confined and hampered; the various conditions under which they are exercised are so rigid and definite. But the only condition that I can think of attaching to the composition of the novel is, as I have already said, that it be sincere. This freedom is a splendid privilege, and the first lesson of the young novelist is to learn to be worthy of it. "Enjoy it as it deserves," I should say to him; "take possession of it, explore it to its utmost extent, publish it, rejoice in it. All life belongs to you, and do not listen either to those who would shut you up into corners of it and tell you that it is only here and there that art inhabits, or to those who would persuade you that this heavenly messenger wings her way outside of life altogether, breathing a superfine air, and turning away her head from the truth of things. There is no impression of life, no manner of seeing it and feeling it, to which the plan of the novelist may not offer a place; you have only to remember that talents so dissimilar as those of Alexandre Dumas and Jane Austen,[5] Charles Dickens and Gustave Flaubert have worked in this field with equal glory. Do not think too much about optimism and pessimism; try and catch the colour of life itself. In France to-day we see a prodigious effort (that of Emile Zola, to whose solid and serious work no explorer of the capacity of the novel can allude without respect), we see an extraordinary effort vitiated by a spirit of pessimism on a narrow basis. M. Zola is magnificent, but he strikes an English reader as ignorant; he has an air of working in the dark; if he had as much light as energy, his results would be of the highest value. As for the aberrations of a shallow optimism, the ground (of English fiction especially) is strewn with their brittle particles as with broken glass. If you must indulge in conclusions, let them have the taste of a wide knowledge. Remember that your first duty is to be as complete as possible—to make as perfect a work. Be generous and delicate and pursue the prize."

1884, 1888

5. English novelist (1775–1817). Dumas (1802–1870), French dramatist and novelist whose works include *The Three Musketeers* (1844).

FRIEDRICH NIETZSCHE
1844–1900

Friedrich Nietzsche is the wild man, the self-proclaimed anti-Christ, of Western thought. A brilliant polemicist, he champions energy over reason and art over science while contemptuous of the quiet, "timid" virtues of domesticity, democracy, and peace. His extravagances not only remind us of modernism's persistent desire to shock the staid middle classes but also recall the many twentieth-century figures—from W. B. Yeats and Ezra Pound to MARTIN HEIDEGGER and PAUL DE MAN—whose genius is inextricably mixed with dubious political views. But Nietzsche, an inveterate foe of Christianity and of Platonic philosophy, is absolutely central to modern and postmodern attempts to rethink the Western tradition's most fundamental assumptions.

Nietzsche was born in Röcken, a small village in Prussian Saxony. He was the son and grandson (on both sides of the family) of Lutheran ministers. His father died when he was four and his younger brother died the next year, leaving him the only male in a household with five women. Nietzsche's subsequent infatuations with the work of the German philosopher Arthur Schopenhauer (1788–1860) and with the work, theories, and wife of the German composer Richard Wagner (1813–1883), followed by his equally violent rejections of the two men, are sometimes explained in terms of "surrogate father figures" and oedipal rebellion. Certainly, Wagner and his wife Cosima dominated Nietzsche's life in the early 1870s. Having received his doctorate at the University of Leipzig, Nietzsche was appointed professor of philology at the University of Basel in Switzerland in 1869. He met Wagner and Cosima von Bülow in late 1868, and his first book, *The Birth of Tragedy* (1872), combines a new theory of Greek tragedy with an extended argument that Wagner's work constitutes a German rebirth of that ancient form. By 1876, however, Nietzsche had broken completely with Wagner, repelled by Wagner's turn to Christianity and his increasing anti-Semitism. That same year, ill health forced Nietzsche to stop teaching. In 1879 he officially resigned his university post, receiving a small disability pension. He spent the next ten years writing the books that present his ambitious attempt to overthrow Christianity and post-Socratic philosophy through a radical "revaluation of all values." The last ten years of Nietzsche's life were lost to incoherent madness. After a mental breakdown in 1889, he returned to Röcken to live with his mother; when she died, in 1897, he came under the care of his sister Elisabeth, which continued until his death.

Even before Nietzsche's death, his sister wrote a biography to publicize his work, and she published her own editions of his writings. She stressed those elements that accorded with her own anti-Semitic and pro-Aryan views and is often blamed for the Nazis' later appropriation of Nietzsche as a philosopher sympathetic to their policies. But blaming his sister does not absolve Nietzsche. Some aspects of his thought chime with National Socialism, while others contradict it. Those who read and interpret Nietzsche's challenging work must grapple with his relation to the Nazis, just as they must take into account his tremendous influence on modernism, existentialism, and poststructuralism.

Our selections from *The Birth of Tragedy* show how Nietzsche returns to Greek thought before Plato to discover the artistic form and worldview that he prefers to the Platonic and Christian traditions. (MATTHEW ARNOLD in the nineteenth century and MARTIN HEIDEGGER and ERICH AUERBACH in the twentieth also return to the pre-Socratic Greeks for principles to counter modernity.) Nietzsche's mantra in this text is that "only as an aesthetic phenomenon do existence and the world appear justified!" This formula draws on the root meaning of *aesthetics* as "pertaining to sense perception." Nietzsche says that life is worthwhile only if we experience strong feelings or sensations. As WALTER PATER, who was writing at almost exactly the same time, would put it, the quality and intensity of our sensations indicates the quality of our lives. And for Nietzsche, as for Pater, the step from the "aesthetic" as sensation to the "aesthetic" as art is a short one. Art is the realm of heightened sensation. But whereas Pater stresses the experience of the spectator, Nietzsche focuses on the exuberant joy felt by the artist/creator in the struggle to bend recalcitrant materials to his or her will.

Nietzsche thus appears to promote heroic individualism and transcendent genius. He has often been read this way, not least by countless modernist artists, who also responded to his diatribes against the conformist "herds" that try to curb the strong, amoral artist. Much in Nietzsche celebrates the "will" of the "overman" (superman) and denigrates everything (from conventional morality to democracy) that would make the genius answerable to any authority outside of his self. "His" is used advisedly—Nietzsche often contrasts this individual's manly strength to the effeminate weakness of lesser souls.

Yet to read Nietzsche as a philosopher of heroic individualism is to miss much. Human suffering figures largely in Nietzsche's thought; the individual is subjected to a world that precedes and is more powerful than the self. Greek tragedy, in Nietzsche's view, grants us a glimpse of a "primordial unity" that predates individuation (which Nietzsche associates with comedy). He takes seriously the claim that Greek tragedy originated in choral songs performed at a festival of Dionysus and that Aeschylus introduced the first individualized characters.

Such individuation, Nietzsche argues in *The Birth of Tragedy*, is necessary for artistic expression, artistic form. (In his later work, he often claims that "the subject" is a grammatical form that we consistently mistake for a metaphysical entity.) The chaos of Dionysian nondifferentiation (intimated by music) can be rendered intelligible or expressible only by the "calm" Apollonian "semblance" (conveyed by words and images). But the glory of Greek tragedy is that it does not take Apollonian semblance for truth—or, at least, not for the entire truth. Prometheus becomes Nietzsche's primary example of the need to establish an existence apart from the primordial unity. But Prometheus "must suffer for the fact of [his] individuation." And Nietzsche insists that it is the sufferings of Dionysus himself, whose repeated deaths and rebirths enact the "end of individuation," that are represented in every tragedy. The "primal contradiction hidden within the things of this world" is that while humans can experience energy, will, and sensation only as individuals, the process of individuation separates them from the universe. Thus suffering is inevitable; the essence of the tragic view is to affirm that suffering, to glory in the active wrongdoing by which the hero offends the way things are, and to say, as Nietzsche imagines Aeschylus saying: "All that exists is just and unjust and is equally justified in both respects."

Tragedy can exist only so long as we recognize, accept, and affirm the irresolvable contradiction between our hopes and how the world is. Once we believe that suffering is not inevitable, tragedy dies: we begin to demand justice from our gods, and life is justified not as an aesthetic phenomenon but rather because justice is finally done. In the comic ending, the good are rewarded, the bad punished, and human desires and worldly facts are aligned. In *The Birth of Tragedy*, Nietzsche blames Euripides and Socrates for the death of the tragic worldview in ancient Athenian society. Euripides effects a reconciliation with the gods in many of his plays, thus assuring the audience that all can be made right in this world. Socrates, and then PLATO, suggests that reason can lead humans to ascertain the truths of the universe to which they can conform.

Later in his career Nietzsche attacked Christianity for its essentially comic vision. We get hints of that critique here when he contrasts the Semitic notion of "sin" to the Aryan notion of "wrongdoing." This passage, with its oppositions of Aryan and Semite, masculine and feminine, points to problematic features in

Nietzsche's work (as does his lyric call for a rebirth of the German spirit). Nietzsche highlights our admiration of the tragic hero, who often (as in Oedipus's case) could not have avoided wrongdoing. The notion of "sin," however, indicates both that one is free to act and that acting differently would have been better, would (it is strongly implied) not have led to suffering. Nietzsche urges us to have the strength to love life even though suffering is inevitable. Indeed, he suggests that we are most alive when we suffer, because that is when we are feeling most intensely. The murdered and resurrected god whose myth embodies this worldview is the tragic Dionysus, not the comic Christ.

This mixture of nobility and masochism, of rebellion (against Plato and Christianity) and submission (to Dionysus), proved heady stuff to many modernists. Of course, other factors—ranging from SIGMUND FREUD's use of the Oedipal myth to the slaughter of a generation in World War I—also shaped the modernist fascination with tragedy and pre-Socratic Greece. But Nietzsche is central to attempts during the previous and present centuries to find imaginative and historical alternatives to both the Christian worldview and to the narrative of Western progress and enlightenment. That such attempts come from both the political left and the right indicates the complexity of the Western heritage and of Nietzsche's engagement with it.

Our second selection, the essay "On Truth and Lying in a Non-Moral Sense" (written 1873), was not published during Nietzsche's lifetime. It articulates a number of Nietzsche's major themes and became a favorite reference point for poststructuralists such as JACQUES DERRIDA and Paul de Man during the 1970s. Nietzsche's target here is nothing less than the epistemological foundations of Western philosophy. From Plato on, Western philosophy has been committed (with a few exceptions) to ascertaining the fixed and solid truth that exists independently of human minds. Nietzsche simply denies that we can ever know anything except through the lens of human perception. We cannot put that lens aside in order to judge which perceptions accurately portray the world and which do not. Given this impossibility, why are humans committed to the search for "truth"? Because, Nietzsche answers, truth is a useful illusion, one that serves a fundamental drive to survive. Nietzsche's explanation here is recognizably Darwinian. Behaviors that sustain life will be adopted by the species as a whole. Truth is a comfortable lie; it suggests that "the world [is] something which is similar in kind to humanity," and it boosts self-confidence, the untroubled conviction of being right. While Nietzsche is scornful of this smug "anthropomorphism," he does underline its utility.

The essay's account of language's role in human cognition has been especially influential among literary theorists. Nietzsche accepts that the outer world impinges on the human perceiver, but we translate that experience into human terms by naming it. This "first metaphor" introduces an unbridgeable gap, which leads Nietzsche to conclude that "subject and object" are "absolutely different spheres." Nor do the nonrepresentational additions ("supplements") supplied by language stop there. We also use the same name to designate separate experiences of nerve stimulation. We call today's "leaf" by the same word used to label yesterday's. This substitution of one "concept" in the place of multiple experiences is the "second metaphor" that Nietzsche identifies—and his account of how concepts erase awareness of differences would later echo throughout poststructuralism. "Every concept," he writes, "comes into being by making equivalent that which is non-equivalent[,] . . . by forgetting those features which differentiate one thing from another."

Once Nietzsche pulls the veil of illusion from our eyes and shows that truth is a "mobile army of metaphors, metonymies, anthropomorphisms," what next? One possible response is stoicism, described in the essay's last paragraph. Alone in an alien world, humans could just endure, preserving a "dignified equilibrium" in the face of everything to which life subjects them. More extreme is the "nihilistic" denial of this world as "fallen" or "evil," a position that Nietzsche associates with Christianity. Against stoicism and nihilism, Nietzsche calls on humans to forcefully and joyfully step into the vacuum created by the death of truth, of God, and of the other metaphysical guarantees on which the West has traditionally relied. We must learn not just to accept but to proudly affirm that "humanity" is a "mighty architectural genius who succeeds in erecting the infinitely complicated cathedral of concepts on moving foundations, or even, one might say, on flowing water." Nietzsche celebrates the creativity and the will that builds a world for humans to inhabit—and he takes the artist as his prime example of an individual responding joyfully to the challenge of shedding the illusion of truth.

For the modernists of the early twentieth century, Nietzsche was often more an attitude, a stance, than a philosopher. A few powerful phrases—"the death of God," "overman," "will to power," "herd morality," and "beyond good and evil"—suggested his blasphemous demystification of progressive, "enlightened" values. Nietzsche's aestheticism, his disdain of reason, and his lyrical style led many readers to see his work as existing somewhere between poetry and philosophy. But his work has received much more extensive scholarly and philosophical analysis after 1945. His critiques of truth, of substance, and of the self, along with his accounts of language and the formation of moral codes, were all taken extremely seriously, despite their summary dismissal by some intellectuals. Perhaps debates about Nietzsche's politics have been especially fierce because his views have often been adopted—and not just by poststructuralists.

For literary critics, Nietzsche's methods may be as important as any view he holds. Famously described by the French philosopher Paul Ricoeur (1913–2005) as, in company with KARL MARX and Freud, a founder of the "hermeneutics of suspicion," Nietzsche teaches us not to take any pronouncement at face value. If we want to understand the meaning of a term, we must discover its "genealogy"—the way the term has been deployed in specific circumstances to achieve specific results. (MICHEL FOUCAULT later explicitly adopted this Nietzschean method in his studies of the prison and of sexuality.) From the perspective of Nietzschean genealogy, terms are tools and weapons in the continual struggles and conflicts that characterize human interactions with the world and with each other. Nietzsche's own effort to alter our understanding of tragedy is concerned less with determining the "truth" of tragedy than with revising the dominant worldviews that his readers have inherited from Christianity and Western philosophy. The success of that attempt stands apart from whatever virtues his genealogical method possesses—but those to whom the method appeals have usually been sympathetic to the message.

***The Birth of Tragedy* Keywords:** Aesthetics, The Canon/Tradition, Drama, Literary History, Philology, Religion
"On Truth and Lying in a Non-Moral Sense" Keywords: Deconstruction, Interpretation Theory, Language, Poststructuralism, Representation, Rhetoric

From The Birth of Tragedy[1]

1

We shall have gained much for the science of aesthetics when we have come to realize, not just through logical insight but also with the certainty of something directly apprehended (*Anschauung*), that the continuous evolution of art is bound up with the duality of the *Apolline* and the *Dionysiac* in much the

1. Translated by Ronald Speirs. Except as indicated, all subsequent notes are the translator's; in the text, he occasionally retains the original German in parentheses. The full title is *The Birth of Tragedy from the Spirit of Music*.

same way as reproduction depends on there being two sexes which co-exist in a state of perpetual conflict interrupted only occasionally by periods of reconciliation. We have borrowed these names from the Greeks who reveal the profound mysteries of their view of art to those with insight, not in concepts, admittedly, but through the penetratingly vivid figures of their gods. Their two deities of art, Apollo and Dionysos,[2] provide the starting-point for our recognition that there exists in the world of the Greeks an enormous opposition, both in origin and goals, between the Apolline art of the image-maker or sculptor (*Bildner*) and the imageless art of music, which is that of Dionysos. These two very different drives (*Triebe*) exist side by side, mostly in open conflict, stimulating and provoking (*reizen*) one another to give birth to ever-new, more vigorous offspring in whom they perpetuate the conflict inherent in the opposition between them, an opposition only apparently bridged by the common term 'art'—until eventually, by a metaphysical miracle of the Hellenic 'Will', they appear paired and, in this pairing, finally engender a work of art which is Dionysiac and Apolline in equal measure: Attic tragedy.[3]

In order to gain a closer understanding of these two drives, let us think of them in the first place as the separate art-worlds of *dream* and *intoxication* (*Rausch*). Between these two physiological phenomena an opposition can be observed which corresponds to that between the Apolline and the Dionysiac. As Lucretius[4] envisages it, it was in dream that the magnificent figures of the gods first appeared before the souls of men; in dream the great image-maker saw the delightfully proportioned bodies of super-human beings; and the Hellenic poet, if asked about the secrets of poetic procreation, would likewise have reminded us of dream and would have given an account much like that given by Hans Sachs in the *Meistersinger*:

> My friend, it is the poet's task
> To mark his dreams, their meaning ask.
> Trust me, the truest phantom man doth know
> Hath meaning only dreams may show:
> The arts of verse and poetry
> Tell nought but dreaming's prophecy.[5]

Every human being is fully an artist when creating the worlds of dream, and the lovely semblance of dream is the precondition of all the arts of image-making, including, as we shall see, an important half of poetry. We take pleasure in dreaming, understanding its figures without mediation; all forms speak to us; nothing is indifferent or unnecessary. Yet even while this dream-reality is most alive, we nevertheless retain a pervasive sense that it is *semblance*; at least this is my experience, and I could adduce a good deal of evidence and the statements of poets to attest to the frequency, indeed

2. Greek god of wine, the object of frenzied cult worship (somewhat muted in its official forms). Apollo: Greek god of music, prophecy, and medicine, associated with the higher developments of civilization; as Phoebus Apollo, he is god of light [editor's note].
3. Plays performed at the festival of Dionysus in Athens during the 5th century B.C.E. [editor's note].
4. Roman poet and philosopher (ca. 94–55 B.C.E.); see *De Rerum Natura* (*On the Nature of Things*) 5.1169–82 [editor's note].
5. Wagner, *Die Meistersinger*, Act III, sc. 2. [Richard Wagner (1813–1883), German composer whose music and aesthetic theories greatly influenced Nietzsche's argument in *The Birth of Tragedy*. Hans Sachs (1494–1576), German poet and dramatist who has a major role in Wagner's 1868 opera—editor's note.]

normality, of my experience. Philosophical natures even have a presentiment that hidden beneath the reality in which we live and have our being there also lies a second, quite different reality; in other words, this reality too is a semblance. Indeed Schopenhauer actually states that the mark of a person's capacity for philosophy is the gift for feeling occasionally as if people and all things were mere phantoms or dream-images.[6] A person with artistic sensibility relates to the reality of dream in the same way as a philosopher relates to the reality of existence: he attends to it closely and with pleasure, using these images to interpret life, and practising for life with the help of these events. Not that it is only the pleasant and friendly images which give him this feeling of complete intelligibility; he also sees passing before him things which are grave, gloomy, sad, dark, sudden blocks, teasings of chance, anxious expectations, in short the entire 'Divine Comedy'[7] of life, including the Inferno, but not like some mere shadow-play—for he, too, lives in these scenes and shares in the suffering—and yet never without that fleeting sense of its character as semblance. Perhaps others will recall, as I do, shouting out, sometimes successfully, words of encouragement in the midst of the perils and terrors of a dream: 'It is a dream! I will dream on!' I have even heard of people who were capable of continuing the causality of one and the same dream through three and more successive nights. All of these facts are clear evidence that our innermost being, the deep ground (*Untergrund*) common to all our lives, experiences the state of dreaming with profound pleasure (*Lust*) and joyous necessity.

The Greeks also expressed the joyous necessity of dream-experience in their Apollo: as the god of all image-making energies, Apollo is also the god of prophecy. According to the etymological root of his name, he is 'the luminous one' (*der Scheinende*), the god of light; as such, he also governs the lovely semblance produced by the inner world of fantasy. The higher truth, the perfection of these dream-states in contrast to the only partially intelligible reality of the daylight world, together with the profound consciousness of the helping and healing powers of nature in sleep and dream, is simultaneously the symbolic analogue of the ability to prophesy and indeed of all the arts through which life is made possible and worth living. But the image of Apollo must also contain that delicate line which the dream-image may not overstep if its effect is not to become pathological, so that, in the worst case, the semblance would deceive us as if it were crude reality; his image (*Bild*) must include that measured limitation (*maßvolle Begrenzung*), that freedom from wilder impulses, that wise calm of the image-making god. In accordance with his origin, his eye must be 'sun-like'; even when its gaze is angry and shows displeasure, it exhibits the consecrated quality of lovely semblance. Thus, in an eccentric sense, one could apply to Apollo what Schopenhauer says about human beings trapped in the veil of maya:

> Just as the boatman sits in his small boat, trusting his frail craft in a stormy sea that is boundless in every direction, rising and falling with the howling, mountainous waves, so in the midst of a world full of

6. *Aus Schopenhauers handschriftlichem Nachlass*, ed. J. Frauenstädt (Leipzig 1874), p. 295. [Arthur Schopenhauer (1788–1860), German philosopher, a major influence on Nietzsche—editor's note.]

7. Epic poem by the Italian poet DANTE ALIGHIERI (1265–1321); in the first part, *Inferno*, the poet narrates a passage through hell [editor's note].

> suffering and misery the individual man calmly sits, supported by and trusting in the *principium individuationis*[8] [. . .] (*World as Will and Representation*, I, p. 416)

Indeed one could say that Apollo is the most sublime expression of imperturbable trust in this principle and of the calm sitting-there of the person trapped within it; one might even describe Apollo as the magnificent divine image (*Götterbild*) of the *principium individuationis*, whose gestures and gaze speak to us of all the intense pleasure, wisdom and beauty of 'semblance'.

In the same passage Schopenhauer has described for us the enormous *horror* which seizes people when they suddenly become confused and lose faith in the cognitive forms of the phenomenal world because the principle of sufficient reason, in one or other of its modes, appears to sustain an exception. If we add to this horror the blissful ecstasy which arises from the innermost ground of man, indeed of nature itself, whenever this breakdown of the *principium individuationis* occurs, we catch a glimpse of the essence of the *Dionysiac*, which is best conveyed by the analogy of *intoxication*. These Dionysiac stirrings, which, as they grow in intensity, cause subjectivity to vanish to the point of complete self-forgetting, awaken either under the influence of narcotic drink, of which all human beings and peoples who are close to the origin of things speak in their hymns, or at the approach of spring when the whole of nature is pervaded by lust for life. In the German Middle Ages, too, ever-growing throngs roamed from place to place, impelled by the same Dionysiac power, singing and dancing as they went; in these St John's and St Vitus' dancers we recognize the Bacchic choruses of the Greeks, with their pre-history in Asia Minor, extending to Babylon and the orgiastic Sacaea.[9] There are those who, whether from lack of experience or from dullness of spirit, turn away in scorn or pity from such phenomena, regarding them as 'popular diseases' while believing in their own good health; of course, these poor creatures have not the slightest inkling of how spectral and deathly pale their 'health' seems when the glowing life of Dionysiac enthusiasts storms past them.

Not only is the bond between human beings renewed by the magic of the Dionysiac, but nature, alienated, inimical, or subjugated, celebrates once more her festival of reconciliation with her lost son, humankind. Freely the earth offers up her gifts, and the beasts of prey from mountain and desert approach in peace. The chariot of Dionysos is laden with flowers and wreaths; beneath its yoke stride panther and tiger. If one were to transform Beethoven's jubilant 'Hymn to Joy'[1] into a painting and place no constraints on one's imagination as the millions sink into the dust, shivering in awe, then one could begin to approach the Dionysiac. Now the slave is a freeman, now all the rigid, hostile barriers, which necessity, caprice, or 'impudent fashion'[2] have established between human beings, break asunder. Now, hearing this

8. Principle of individuation (Latin). For Schopenhauer, the mind can apprehend the world only by dividing it up into individual things; this process produces an erroneous vision of reality, which he calls "the veil of maya" [editor's note].

9. A festival of the winter solstice. Nietzsche links together a number of ecstatic celebrations [editor's note].

1. Beethoven used a version of Schiller's ode *To Joy* for the choral finale of his Ninth Symphony. [Ludwig van Beethoven (1770–1827), German composer. FRIEDRICH VON SCHILLER (1759–1805), German poet and playwright—editor's note.]

2. Quotation from Schiller's *To Joy*.

gospel of universal harmony, each person feels himself to be not simply united, reconciled or merged with his neighbour, but quite literally one with him, as if the veil of maya had been torn apart, so that mere shreds of it flutter before the mysterious primordial unity (*das Ur-Eine*). Singing and dancing, man expresses his sense of belonging to a higher community; he has forgotten how to walk and talk and is on the brink of flying and dancing, up and away into the air above. His gestures speak of his enchantment. Just as the animals now talk and the earth gives milk and honey,[3] there now sounds out from within man something supernatural: he feels himself to be a god, he himself now moves in such ecstasy and sublimity as once he saw the gods move in his dreams. Man is no longer an artist, he has become a work of art: all nature's artistic power reveals itself here, amidst shivers of intoxication, to the highest, most blissful satisfaction of the primordial unity. Here man, the noblest clay, the most precious marble, is kneaded and carved and, to the accompaniment of the chisel-blows of the Dionysiac world-artist, the call of the Eleusinian Mysteries rings out: 'Fall ye to the ground, ye millions? Feelst thou thy Creator, world?'[4]

* * *

9

Everything that rises to the surface in dialogue, the Apolline part of Greek tragedy, appears simple, transparent, beautiful. In this sense the dialogue is a copy of the Hellene, whose nature is expressed in dance, because in dance the greatest strength is still only potential, although it is betrayed by the suppleness and luxuriance of movement. Thus the language of Sophocles'[5] heroes surprises us by its Apolline definiteness and clarity, so that we feel as if we are looking straight into the innermost ground of its being, and are somewhat astonished that the road to this ground is so short. But if we once divert our gaze from the character of the hero as it rises to the surface and becomes visible—fundamentally, it is no more than an image of light (*Lichtbild*) projected on to a dark wall, i.e. appearance (*Erscheinung*) through and through—if, rather, we penetrate to the myth which projects itself in these bright reflections, we suddenly experience a phenomenon which inverts a familiar optical one. When we turn away blinded after a strenuous attempt to look directly at the sun, we have dark, coloured patches before our eyes, as if their purpose were to heal them; conversely, those appearances of the Sophoclean hero in images of light, in other words, the Apolline quality of the mask, are the necessary result of gazing into the inner, terrible depths of nature—radiant patches, as it were, to heal a gaze seared by gruesome night. Only in this sense may we believe that we have grasped the serious and significant concept of 'Greek serenity' (*Heiterkeit*) correctly; admittedly, wherever one looks at present one comes across a misunderstood notion of this as 'cheerfulness', something identified with a condition of unendangered ease and comfort.

3. Conflation of Euripides' *Bacchae* lines 142 and 708–11 with Exodus 3.8. [Euripides (ca. 485–ca. 406 B.C.E.), the last of the three great Attic tragedians; Nietzsche associates him with the decline of tragedy. The Bacchae of the play are the frenzied women who follow Dionysus—editor's note.]
4. Schiller's *To Joy*, lines 33–34. [Eleusinian Mysteries: the most famous of the secret Greek cults, which were connected with Demeter (goddess of the fruits of the earth) and Dionysus. Eleusis was an important town in southwest Attica—editor's note.]
5. Greek tragedian (ca. 496–406 B.C.E.) [editor's note].

The most suffering figure of the Greek stage, the unfortunate *Oedipus*,[6] was understood by Sophocles as the noble human being who is destined for error and misery despite his wisdom, but who in the end, through his enormous suffering, exerts on the world around him a magical, beneficent force which remains effective even after his death. The noble human being does not sin, so this profound poet wants to tell us; every law, all natural order, indeed the moral world, may be destroyed by his actions, yet by these very actions a higher, magical circle of effects is drawn which found a new world on the ruins of the old one that has been overthrown. This is what the poet, inasmuch as he is also a religious thinker, wishes to tell us; as a poet he first shows us a wonderfully tied trial-knot which the judge slowly undoes, strand by strand, to bring great harm upon himself; the genuinely Hellenic delight in this dialectical solution is so great that an air of sovereign serenity pervades the whole work, blunting all the sharp, horrifying preconditions of that trial. We encounter this same serenity in *Oedipus at Colonus*, but here it is elevated into infinite transfiguration; in this play the old man, stricken with an excess of suffering, and exposed, purely as a *suffering being*, to all that affects him, is contrasted with the unearthly serenity which comes down from the sphere of the gods as a sign to us that in his purely passive behaviour the hero achieves the highest form of activity, which has consequences reaching far beyond his own life, whereas all his conscious words and actions in his life hitherto have merely led to his passivity. Thus the trial-knot of the story of Oedipus, which strikes the mortal eye as inextricably tangled, is slowly unravelled—and we are overcome by the most profound human delight at this matching piece of divine dialectic. If our explanation has done justice to the poet, the question remains whether the content of the myth has been exhausted thereby; at this point it becomes plain that the poet's whole interpretation of the story is nothing other than one of those images of light held out to us by healing nature after we have gazed into the abyss. Oedipus, murderer of his father, husband of his mother, Oedipus the solver of the Sphinx's riddle! What does this trinity of fateful deeds tell us? There is an ancient popular belief, particularly in Persia, that a wise magician can only be born out of incest; the riddle-solving Oedipus who woos his mother immediately leads us to interpret this as meaning that some enormous offence against nature (such as incest in this case) must first have occurred to supply the cause whenever prophetic and magical energies break the spell of present and future, the rigid law of individuation, and indeed the actual magic of nature. How else could nature be forced to reveal its secrets, other than by victorious resistance to her, i.e. by some unnatural event? I see this insight expressed in that terrible trinity of Oedipus' fates: the same man who solves the riddle of nature—that of the double-natured[7] sphinx—must also destroy the most sacred orders of nature by murdering his father and becoming his mother's husband. Wisdom, the

6. The hero of *Oedipus Rex* (ca. 430 B.C.E.), who unknowingly kills his father, the king of Thebes, and then marries his mother, becoming king in turn; when he discovers the truth, he blinds himself and is banished. In *Oedipus at Colonus* (produced posthumously), the ruler of Thebes unsuccessfully attempts to persuade Oedipus, now a dying old man, to return so that after his death he will benefit and not curse the city (Greek heroes were thought to exert power even when dead) [editor's note].

7. Having the face of a woman and the body of a lion [editor's note].

myth seems to whisper to us, and Dionysiac wisdom in particular, is an unnatural abomination: whoever plunges nature into the abyss of destruction by what he knows must in turn experience the dissolution of nature in his own person. 'The sharp point of wisdom turns against the wise man; wisdom is an offence against nature': such are the terrible words the myth calls out to us. But, like a shaft of sunlight, the Hellenic poet touches the sublime and terrible Memnon's Column of myth[8] so that it suddenly begins to sound—in Sophoclean melodies!

I shall now contrast the glory of passivity with the glory of activity which shines around the *Prometheus* of Aeschylus.[9] What the thinker Aeschylus had to tell us here, but what his symbolic poetic image only hints at, has been revealed to us by the youthful Goethe in the reckless words of his Prometheus:

> Here I sit, forming men
> In my own image,
> A race to be like me,
> To suffer and to weep,
> To know delight and joy
> And heed you not,
> Like me![1]

Raising himself to Titanic heights, man fights for and achieves his own culture, and he compels the gods to ally themselves with him because, in his very own wisdom, he holds existence and its limits in his hands. But the most wonderful thing in that poem about Prometheus (which, in terms of its basic thought, is the true hymn of impiety) is its profound, Aeschylean tendency to *justice*: the limitless suffering of the bold 'individual' on the one hand, and the extreme plight of the gods, indeed a premonition of the twilight of the gods, on the other; the power of both these worlds of suffering to enforce reconciliation, metaphysical oneness—all this recalls in the strongest possible way the centre and principal tenet of the Aeschylean view of the world, which sees *moira*,[2] as eternal justice, throned above gods and men. If the boldness of Aeschylus in placing the world of the Olympians on his scales of justice seems astonishing, we must remember that the deep-thinking Greek had an unshakably firm foundation for metaphysical thought in his Mysteries, so that all attacks of scepticism could be discharged on the Olympians. The Greek artist in particular had an obscure feeling that he and these gods were mutually dependent, a feeling symbolized precisely in Aeschylus' Prometheus. The Titanic artist found within himself the defiant belief that he could create human beings and destroy the Olympian gods at least, and that his higher wisdom enabled him to do so, for which, admittedly, he was forced to do penance by suffering eternally. The magnificent

8. The remnants of a monumental statue in Egypt were said to produce a musical tone when illuminated by the rays of the rising sun.
9. Greek tragedian (525–456 B.C.E.), generally credited with giving Attic drama its traditional form. *Prometheus Bound* depicts Prometheus, a Titan (pre-Olympian god) punished by Zeus, the supreme god who has overthrown the Titans, for giving fire to humans. Prometheus is chained to a rock in the mountains, where daily a vulture tears out his liver. According to some stories, Prometheus created humans out of mud [editor's note].
1. Goethe, *Prometheus*, lines 51 ff. [Johann Wolfgang von Goethe (1749–1832), German poet, playwright, and novelist; Nietzsche quotes the final stanza of his 1773 poem—editor's note.]
2. Fate or destiny (Greek) [editor's note].

'ability' (*Können*) of the great genius, for which even eternal suffering is too small a price to pay, the bitter pride of the *artist*: this is the content and the soul of Aeschylus' play, whereas Sophocles, in his *Oedipus*, begins the prelude to the victory-hymn of the *saint*. But even Aeschylus' interpretation of the myth does not plumb its astonishing, terrible depths; rather, the artist's delight in Becoming, the serenity of artistic creation in defiance of all catastrophes, is merely a bright image of clouds and sky reflected in a dark sea of sadness. Originally, the legend of Prometheus belonged to the entire community of Aryan peoples[3] and documented their talent for the profound and the tragic; indeed, it is not unlikely that this myth is as significant for the Aryan character as the myth of the Fall is for the Semitic character, and that the relationship between the two myths is like that between brother and sister. The myth of Prometheus presupposes the unbounded value which naive humanity placed on *fire* as the true palladium[4] of every rising culture; but it struck those contemplative original men as a crime, a theft perpetrated on divine nature, to believe that man commanded fire freely, rather than receiving it as a gift from heaven, as a bolt of lightning which could start a blaze, or as the warming fire of the sun. Thus the very first philosophical problem presents a painful, irresolvable conflict between god and man, and pushes it like a mighty block of rock up against the threshold of every culture. Humanity achieves the best and highest of which it is capable by committing an offence and must in turn accept the consequences of this, namely the whole flood of suffering and tribulations which the offended heavenly powers *must* in turn visit upon the human race as it strives nobly towards higher things: a bitter thought, but one which, thanks to the *dignity* it accords to the offence, contrasts strangely with the Semitic myth of the Fall, where the origin of evil was seen to lie in curiosity, mendacious pretence, openness to seduction, lasciviousness, in short: in a whole series of predominantly feminine attributes. What distinguishes the Aryan conception is the sublime view that *active sin* is the true Promethean virtue; thereby we have also found the ethical foundation of pessimistic tragedy, its *justification* of the evil in human life, both in the sense of human guilt and in the sense of the suffering brought about by it. The curse in the nature of things, which the reflective Aryan is not inclined simply to explain away, the contradiction at the heart of the world, presents itself to him as a mixture of different worlds, e.g. a divine and a human one, each of which, taken individually, is in the right, but which, as one world existing alongside another, must suffer for the fact of its individuation. The heroic urge of the individual to reach out towards the general, the attempt to cross the fixed boundaries of individuation, and the desire to become the *one* world-being itself, all this leads him to suffer in his own person the primal contradiction hidden within the things of this world, i.e. he commits a great wrong and suffers. Thus great wrongdoing is understood as masculine by the Aryans, but as feminine by the Semites,[5]

3. Speakers of Indo-European, the prehistoric language whose descendents include Greek, German, English, and Hindi; here they are contrasted with speakers of Semitic languages, such as those who wrote Genesis in Hebrew [editor's note].

4. Here simply: "prized possession." [Specifically, in Greek mythology, the Palladium was a statue of the goddess Pallas Athena, whose presence at Troy supposedly kept the city safe—editor's note.]

5. The noun translated as "wrongdoing" (*der Frevel*) has masculine gender in German; "sin" (*die Sünde*) has feminine.

just as the original wrong was committed by a man and the original sin by a woman. These, incidentally, are the words of the warlocks' chorus:

> So what, if women on the whole
> Take many steps to reach the goal?
> Let them run as fast as they dare,
> With one good jump a man gets there.[6]

Anyone who understands the innermost kernel of the legend of Prometheus—namely that wrongdoing is of necessity imposed on the titanically striving individual—is bound also to sense the un-Apolline quality of this pessimistic view of things, for it is the will of Apollo to bring rest and calm to individual beings precisely by drawing boundaries between them, and by reminding them constantly, with his demands for self-knowledge and measure, that these are the most sacred laws in the world. But lest this Apolline tendency should cause form to freeze into Egyptian stiffness and coldness, lest the attempt to prescribe the course and extent of each individual wave should cause the movement of the whole lake to die away, the flood-tide of the Dionysiac would destroy periodically all the small circles in which the one-sidedly Apolline will attempted to confine Hellenic life. That sudden swell of the Dionysiac tide then lifts the separate little waves of individuals on to its back, just as the Titan Atlas,[7] brother of Prometheus, lifted up the earth. This Titanic urge to become, as it were, the Atlas of all single beings, and to carry them on a broad back higher and higher, further and further, is the common feature shared by the Promethean and the Dionysiac. In this respect the Prometheus of Aeschylus is a Dionysiac mask, whereas the aforementioned deep strain of justice in Aeschylus reveals to those with eyes to see his paternal descent from Apollo, the god of individuation and of the boundaries of justice. The double essence of Aeschylus' Prometheus, his simultaneously Apolline and Dionysiac nature, could therefore be expressed like this: 'All that exists is just and unjust and is equally justified in both respects.'

That is your world. That you call a world.[8]

10

It is a matter of indisputable historical record that the only subject-matter of Greek tragedy, in its earliest form, was the sufferings of Dionysos, and that for a long time the only hero present on the stage was, accordingly, Dionysos. But one may also say with equal certainty that, right down to Euripides, Dionysos never ceased to be the tragic hero, and that all the famous figures of the Greek stage, Prometheus, Oedipus etc., are merely masks of that original hero, Dionysos. The fact that there is a deity behind all these masks is one of the essential reasons for the 'ideal' quality of those famous figures which has prompted so much astonishment. Someone or other (I do not know who) once remarked that all individuals, as individuals, are comic, and therefore un-tragic; from which one could conclude that

6. Goethe, *Faust* [1808], I, 3982 ff.
7. In Greek myth, punished for warring against the Olympian gods by having to bear the world upon his shoulders [editor's note].
8. Goethe, *Faust*, I, 409.

the Greeks were quite *incapable* of tolerating any individuals on the tragic stage. And indeed this does appear to have been their feeling, just as the reason for the Platonic distinction between, and deprecation of, the 'idea' as opposed to the 'idol',[9] or copied image, lay deep within the Hellenic character. Using Plato's terminology, one would have to say something like this about the tragic figures of the Hellenic stage: the one, truly real Dionysos manifests himself in a multiplicity of figures, in the mask of a fighting hero and, as it were, entangled in the net of the individual will. In the way that he now speaks and acts, the god who appears resembles an erring, striving, suffering individual; and the fact that he *appears* at all with such epic definiteness and clarity, is the effect of Apollo, the interpreter of dreams, who interprets to the chorus its Dionysiac condition by means of this symbolic appearance. In truth, however, this hero is the suffering Dionysos of the Mysteries, the god who experiences the sufferings of individuation in his own person, of whom wonderful myths recount that he was torn to pieces by the Titans when he was a boy and is now venerated in this condition as Zagreus;[1] at the same time, it is indicated that his being torn into pieces, the genuinely Dionysiac *suffering*, is like a transformation into air, water, earth, and fire, so that we are to regard the state of individuation as the source and primal cause of all suffering, as something inherently to be rejected. From the smile of that Dionysos the Olympian gods were born, from his tears human beings. In this existence as a dismembered god, Dionysos has a double nature; he is both cruel, savage demon and mild, gentle ruler. But what the epopts[2] hoped for was the rebirth of Dionysos, which we must now understand, by premonition, as the end of individuation; the epopts' roaring song of jubilation rang out to greet this third Dionysos. Only in the hope of this is there a gleam of joy on the countenance of a world torn apart and shattered into individuals; myth symbolizes this in the image of Demeter, sunk in eternal mourning, who knows no *happiness* until she is told that she can give birth to Dionysos *again*. In the views described here we already have all the constituent elements of a profound and pessimistic way of looking at the world and thus, at the same time, of *the doctrine of the Mysteries taught by tragedy*: the fundamental recognition that everything which exists is a unity; the view that individuation is the primal source of all evil; and art as the joyous hope that the spell of individuation can be broken, a premonition of unity restored.

* * *

24

* * *

At this point we need to take a bold run-up and vault into a metaphysics of art, as I repeat my earlier sentence that only as an aesthetic phenomenon

9. That is, an *eikōn*, or "likeness," which PLATO (ca. 427–ca. 347 B.C.E.) sees as necessarily inferior to the Form or Idea (*idea*) of which it can be only an imperfect representation and through which it participates in what is truly real [editor's note].

1. A myth to the effect that Dionysos, under the name "Zagreus," is torn apart and then reassembled occurs in some late Hellenistic sources. Whether this is a survival of an older (perhaps secret) doctrine about Dionysos, as Nietzsche assumes, or a late innovative embellishment of earlier tradition is, given the state of our knowledge, undecidable. [In this version, Dionysus is the son of Demeter; in most myths, he is said to be the son of a mortal woman, Semele, and Zeus—editor's note.]

2. Devoted followers who have "seen" their god.

do existence and the world appear justified; which means that tragic myth in particular must convince us that even the ugly and disharmonious is an artistic game which the Will, in the eternal fullness of its delight, plays with itself. Yet this difficult, primal phenomenon of Dionysiac art can be grasped in a uniquely intelligible and direct way in the wonderful significance of *musical dissonance*; as indeed music generally is the only thing which, when set alongside the world, can illustrate what is meant by the justification of the world as an aesthetic phenomenon. The pleasure engendered by the tragic myth comes from the same homeland as our pleasurable sensation of dissonance in music. The Dionysiac, with the primal pleasure it perceives even in pain, is the common womb from which both music and the tragic myth are born.

Could it not be that, with the assistance of musical dissonance, we have eased significantly the difficult problem of the effect of tragedy? After all, we do now understand the meaning of our desire to look, and yet to long to go beyond looking when we are watching tragedy; when applied to our response to the artistic use of dissonance, this state of mind would have to be described in similar terms: we want to listen, but at the same time we long to go beyond listening. That striving towards infinity, that wing-beat of longing even as we feel supreme delight in a clearly perceived reality, these things indicate that in both these states of mind we are to recognize a Dionysiac phenomenon, one which reveals to us the playful construction and demolition of the world of individuality as an outpouring of primal pleasure and delight, a process quite similar to Heraclitus the Obscure's comparison of the force that shapes the world to a playing child who sets down stones here, there, and the next place, and who builds up piles of sand only to knock them down again.[3]

Thus, in order to judge the Dionysiac capacity of a people correctly, it is necessary for us to consider the evidence not simply of their music but also of their tragic myth. Given the intimate relationship between music and myth, one would expect that the atrophy of the one would be connected to the degeneration and depravation of the other, if indeed it is true that any weakening of myth generally expresses a waning of the capacity for the Dionysiac. One only needs to glance at the development of the German character to be left in no doubt on both counts: we saw that the nature of Socratic optimism,[4] something which is as unartistic as it is parasitic on life, was revealed in equal measure both in opera and in the abstract character of our mythless existence, in an art which had sunk to the level of mere entertainment as much as in a life guided by concepts. We took some comfort, however, from certain signs that, despite all this, the German spirit has remained whole, in magnificent health, depth, and Dionysiac strength, resting and dreaming in an inaccessible abyss like a knight who has sunk into slumber; now the Dionysiac song rises from this abyss to tell us that, at this very moment, this German knight still dreams his ancient Dionysiac myth in blissfully grave visions. Let no one believe that the German spirit has lost its mythical home for ever, if it can still understand so clearly the voices of the

3. Heraclitus, fragment 52. [Heraclitus (active ca. 500 B.C.E), pre-Socratic Greek philosopher—editor's note.]

4. In sections that we have omitted, Nietzsche portrays the Greek philosopher Socrates (469–399 B.C.E.) as opposed to Dionysus and an ally of Euripides [editor's note].

birds which tell of its homeland. One day it will find itself awake, with all the morning freshness that comes from a vast sleep; then it will slay dragons, destroy the treacherous dwarfs, and awaken Brünnhilde—and not even Wotan's spear itself will be able to bar its path![5]

My friends, you who believe in the music of Dionysos, you also know what tragedy means for us. In it we have the tragic myth, reborn from music—and in this you may hope for all things and forget that which is most painful! But for all of us the most painful thing is that long period of indignity when the German genius lived in the service of treacherous dwarfs, estranged from hearth and home. You understand what my words mean—just as you will also understand, finally, my hopes.

25

Music and tragic myth both express, in the same way, the Dionysiac capacity of a people, and they cannot be separated from one another. Both originate in an artistic realm which lies beyond the Apolline; both transfigure a region where dissonance and the terrible image of the world fade away in chords of delight; both play with the goad of disinclination, trusting to their immeasurably powerful arts of magic; both justify by their play the existence of even the 'worst of all worlds'. Here the Dionysiac shows itself, in comparison with the Apolline, to be the eternal and original power of art which summons the entire world of appearances into existence, in the midst of which a new, transfiguring semblance is needed to hold fast within life the animated world of individuation. If you could imagine dissonance assuming human form—and what else is man?—this dissonance would need, to be able to live, a magnificent illusion which would spread a veil of beauty over its own nature. This is the true artistic aim of Apollo, in whose name we gather together all those countless illusions of beautiful semblance which, at every moment, make existence at all worth living at every moment and thereby urge us on to experience the next.

At the same time, only as much of that foundation of all existence, that Dionysiac underground of the world, can be permitted to enter an individual's consciousness as can be overcome, in its turn, by the Apolline power of transfiguration, so that both of these artistic drives are required to unfold their energies in strict, reciprocal proportion, according to the law of eternal justice. Where the Dionysiac powers rise up with such unbounded vigour as we are seeing at present, Apollo, too, must already have descended amongst us, concealed in a cloud, and his most abundant effects of beauty will surely be seen by a generation which comes after us.

That there is a need for this effect is a feeling which each of us would grasp intuitively, if he were ever to feel himself translated, even just in dream, back into the life of an ancient Hellene. As he wandered beneath rows of high, Ionic columns, gazing upwards to a horizon cut off by pure and noble lines, seeing beside him reflections of his own, transfigured form in luminous marble, surrounded by human beings who walk solemnly or move delicately,

5. In Wagner's opera *Siegfried* (1876) the hero slays a dragon (really the giant Fafner), kills the dwarf Mime, and awakens the heroine Brünnhilde despite the efforts of Wotan, chief of the gods, to block him [editor's note].

with harmonious sounds and a rhythmical language of gestures—would such a person, with all this beauty streaming in on him from all sides, not be bound to call out, as he raised a hand to Apollo: 'Blessed people of Hellas! How great must Dionysos be amongst you, if the God of Delos considers such acts of magic are needed to heal your dithyrambic[6] madness!' It is likely, however, that an aged Athenian would reply to a visitor in this mood, looking up at him with the sublime eye of Aeschylus: 'But say also this, curious stranger: how much did this people have to suffer in order that it might become so beautiful! But now follow me to the tragedy and sacrifice along with me in the temple of both deities!'

1872

On Truth and Lying in a Non-Moral Sense[1]

1

In some remote corner of the universe, flickering in the light of the countless solar systems into which it had been poured, there was once a planet on which clever animals invented cognition. It was the most arrogant and most mendacious minute in the 'history of the world'; but a minute was all it was. After nature had drawn just a few more breaths the planet froze and the clever animals had to die. Someone could invent a fable like this and yet they would still not have given a satisfactory illustration of just how pitiful, how insubstantial and transitory, how purposeless and arbitrary the human intellect looks within nature; there were eternities during which it did not exist; and when it has disappeared again, nothing will have happened. For this intellect has no further mission that might extend beyond the bounds of human life. Rather, the intellect is human, and only its own possessor and progenitor regards it with such pathos, as if it housed the axis around which the entire world revolved. But if we could communicate with a midge we would hear that it too floats through the air with the very same pathos, feeling that it too contains within itself the flying centre of this world. There is nothing in nature so despicable and mean that would not immediately swell up like a balloon from just one little puff of that force of cognition; and just as every bearer of burdens wants to be admired, so the proudest man of all, the philosopher, wants to see, on all sides, the eyes of the universe trained, as through telescopes, on his thoughts and deeds.

It is odd that the intellect can produce this effect, since it is nothing other than an aid supplied to the most unfortunate, most delicate and most transient of beings so as to detain them for a minute within existence; otherwise, without this supplement, they would have every reason to flee existence as quickly as did Lessing's infant son.[2] The arrogance inherent in cognition

6. Manifest in dithyrambs, choral poems originally sung in honor of Dionysus and later associated with highly excited music and impassioned language. Delos: Greek island in the Cyclades, site of an important oracle of Apollo [editor's note].

1. Translated by Ronald Speirs. Except as indicated, all notes are the translator's.

2. Lessing's first and only son died immediately after birth, followed soon after by his mother. This drew from Lessing the comment: "Was it good sense that they had to pull him into the world with iron tongs, or that he noticed the filth

and feeling casts a blinding fog over the eyes and senses of human beings, and because it contains within itself the most flattering evaluation of cognition it deceives them about the value of existence. Its most general effect is deception—but each of its separate effects also has something of the same character.

As a means for the preservation of the individual, the intellect shows its greatest strengths in dissimulation, since this is the means to preserve those weaker, less robust individuals who, by nature, are denied horns or the sharp fangs of a beast of prey with which to wage the struggle for existence. This art of dissimulation reaches its peak in humankind, where deception, flattery, lying and cheating, speaking behind the backs of others, keeping up appearances,[3] living in borrowed finery, wearing masks, the drapery of convention, play-acting for the benefit of others and oneself—in short, the constant fluttering of human beings around the one flame of vanity is so much the rule and the law that there is virtually nothing which defies understanding so much as the fact that an honest and pure drive towards truth should ever have emerged in them. They are deeply immersed in illusions and dream-images; their eyes merely glide across the surface of things and see 'forms'; nowhere does their perception lead into truth; instead it is content to receive stimuli and, as it were, to play with its fingers on the back of things. What is more, human beings allow themselves to be lied to in dreams every night of their lives, without their moral sense ever seeking to prevent this happening, whereas it is said that some people have even eliminated snoring by willpower. What do human beings really know about themselves? Are they even capable of perceiving themselves in their entirety just once, stretched out as in an illuminated glass case? Does nature not remain silent about almost everything, even about our bodies, banishing and enclosing us within a proud, illusory consciousness, far away from the twists and turns of the bowels, the rapid flow of the blood stream and the complicated tremblings of the nerve-fibres? Nature has thrown away the key, and woe betide fateful curiosity should it ever succeed in peering through a crack in the chamber of consciousness, out and down into the depths, and thus gain an intimation of the fact that humanity, in the indifference of its ignorance, rests on the pitiless, the greedy, the insatiable, the murderous—clinging in dreams, as it were, to the back of a tiger. Given this constellation, where on earth can the drive to truth possibly have come from?

Insofar as the individual wishes to preserve himself in relation to other individuals, in the state of nature he mostly used his intellect for concealment and dissimulation; however, because necessity and boredom also lead men to want to live in societies and herds, they need a peace treaty, and so they endeavour to eliminate from their world at least the crudest forms of the *bellum omnium contra omnes.*[4] In the wake of this peace treaty, however,

---

so quickly? Was it not good sense that he took the first opportunity to leave it again?" (Letter to Eschenburg, 10 January 1778). [GOTTHOLD EPHRAIM LESSING (1729–1781), German dramatist and critic—editor's note.]

3. The verb Nietzsche uses is *repräsentieren.* This means keeping up a show in public, representing one's family, country, or social group before the eyes of the world.

4. War of all against all (Latin): phrase associated with Thomas Hobbes' description of the state of nature before the institution of political authority (*cf.* Hobbes, *De cive* I.12 and *Leviathan*, chapter XIII). [Hobbes (1588–1679), English political philosopher—editor's note.]

comes something which looks like the first step towards the acquisition of that mysterious drive for truth. For that which is to count as 'truth' from this point onwards now becomes fixed, i.e. a way of designating things is invented which has the same validity and force everywhere, and the legislation of language also produces the first laws of truth, for the contrast between truth and lying comes into existence here for the first time: the liar uses the valid tokens of designation—words—to make the unreal appear to be real; he says, for example, 'I am rich', whereas the correct designation for his condition would be, precisely, 'poor'. He misuses the established conventions by arbitrarily switching or even inverting the names for things. If he does this in a manner that is selfish and otherwise harmful, society will no longer trust him and therefore exclude him from its ranks. Human beings do not so much flee from being tricked as from being harmed by being tricked. Even on this level they do not hate deception but rather the damaging, inimical consequences of certain species of deception. Truth, too, is only desired by human beings in a similarly limited sense. They desire the pleasant, life-preserving consequences of truth; they are indifferent to pure knowledge if it has no consequences, but they are actually hostile towards truths which may be harmful and destructive. And, besides, what is the status of those conventions of language? Are they perhaps products of knowledge, of the sense of truth? Is there a perfect match between things and their designations? Is language the full and adequate expression of all realities?

Only through forgetfulness could human beings ever entertain the illusion that they possess truth to the degree described above. If they will not content themselves with truth in the form of tautology, i.e. with empty husks, they will for ever exchange illusions for truth. What is a word? The copy of a nervous stimulation in sounds. To infer from the fact of the nervous stimulation that there exists a cause outside us is already the result of applying the principle of sufficient reason wrongly. If truth alone had been decisive in the genesis of language, if the viewpoint of certainty had been decisive in creating designations, how could we possibly be permitted to say, 'The stone is hard', as if 'hard' were something known to us in some other way, and not merely as an entirely subjective stimulus? We divide things up by gender, describing a tree as masculine and a plant as feminine[5]—how arbitrary these translations are! How far they have flown beyond the canon of certainty! We speak of a snake; the designation captures only its twisting movements and thus could equally well apply to a worm. How arbitrarily these borders are drawn, how one-sided the preference for this or that property of a thing! When different languages are set alongside one another it becomes clear that, where words are concerned, what matters is never truth, never the full and adequate expression;[6] otherwise there would not be so many languages. The 'thing-in-itself'[7] (which would be, precisely, pure truth, truth without consequences) is impossible for even the creator of language to grasp, and indeed this is not at all desir-

5. "Tree" is masculine in German (*der Baum*) and "plant" (*die Pflanze*) is feminine.
6. Nietzsche uses the term *adäquat*, which indicates that the meaning of something is fully conveyed by a word or expression; English "adequate" alone does not convey this sense completely.
7. Term used by the German philosopher Immanuel Kant (1724–1804) for the real object independent of our awareness of it. Kant argues that such categories as time and space, mentioned later by Nietzsche, are part of our own form of thought, not of what we observe [editor's note].

able. He designates only the relations of things to human beings, and in order to express them he avails himself of the boldest metaphors. The stimulation of a nerve is first translated into an image: first metaphor! The image is then imitated by a sound: second metaphor! And each time there is a complete leap from one sphere into the heart of another, new sphere. One can conceive of a profoundly deaf human being who has never experienced sound or music; just as such a person will gaze in astonishment at the Chladnian sound-figures in sand,[8] find their cause in the vibration of a string, and swear that he must now know what men call sound—this is precisely what happens to all of us with language. We believe that when we speak of trees, colours, snow, and flowers, we have knowledge of the things themselves, and yet we possess only metaphors of things which in no way correspond to the original entities. Just as the musical sound appears as a figure in the sand, so the mysterious 'X' of the thing-in-itself appears first as a nervous stimulus, then as an image, and finally as an articulated sound. At all events, things do not proceed logically when language comes into being, and the entire material in and with which the man of truth, the researcher, the philosopher, works and builds, stems, if not from cloud-cuckoo land, then certainly not from the essence of things.

Let us consider in particular how concepts are formed; each word immediately becomes a concept, not by virtue of the fact that it is intended to serve as a memory (say) of the unique, utterly individualized, primary experience to which it owes its existence, but because at the same time it must fit countless other, more or less similar cases, i.e. cases which, strictly speaking, are never equivalent, and thus nothing other than non-equivalent cases. Every concept comes into being by making equivalent that which is non-equivalent. Just as it is certain that no leaf is ever exactly the same as any other leaf, it is equally certain that the concept 'leaf' is formed by dropping these individual differences arbitrarily, by forgetting those features which differentiate one thing from another, so that the concept then gives rise to the notion that something other than leaves exists in nature, something which would be 'leaf', a primal form, say, from which all leaves were woven, drawn, delineated, dyed, curled, painted—but by a clumsy pair of hands, so that no single example turned out to be a faithful, correct, and reliable copy of the primal form. We call a man honest; we ask, 'Why did he act so honestly today?' Our answer is usually: 'Because of his honesty.' Honesty!—yet again, this means that the leaf is the cause of the leaves. We have no knowledge of an essential quality which might be called honesty, but we do know of numerous individualized and hence non-equivalent actions which we equate with each other by omitting what is unlike, and which we now designate as honest actions; finally we formulate from them a *qualitas occulta*[9] with the name 'honesty'.

Like form, a concept is produced by overlooking what is individual and real, whereas nature knows neither forms nor concepts and hence no species, but only an 'X' which is inaccessible to us and indefinable by us.

8. The vibration of a string can create figures in the sand (in an appropriately constructed sandbox) which give a visual representation of that which the human ear perceives as a tone. The term comes from the name of the [German] physicist Ernst Chladni [1756–1827], whose experiments demonstrated the effect.

9. Hidden property (Latin).

For the opposition we make between individual and species is also anthropomorphic and does not stem from the essence of things, although we equally do not dare to say that it does *not* correspond to the essence of things, since that would be a dogmatic assertion and, as such, just as incapable of being proved as its opposite.

What, then, is truth? A mobile army of metaphors, metonymies, anthropomorphisms, in short a sum of human relations which have been subjected to poetic and rhetorical intensification, translation, and decoration, and which, after they have been in use for a long time, strike a people as firmly established, canonical, and binding; truths are illusions of which we have forgotten that they are illusions, metaphors which have become worn by frequent use and have lost all sensuous vigour, coins which, having lost their stamp, are now regarded as metal and no longer as coins. Yet we still do not know where the drive to truth comes from, for so far we have only heard about the obligation to be truthful which society imposes in order to exist, i.e. the obligation to use the customary metaphors, or, to put it in moral terms, the obligation to lie in accordance with firmly established convention, to lie *en masse* and in a style that is binding for all. Now, it is true that human beings forget that this is how things are; thus they lie unconsciously in the way we have described, and in accordance with centuries-old habits—and precisely *because of this unconsciousness*, precisely because of this forgetting, they arrive at the feeling of truth. The feeling that one is obliged to describe one thing as red, another as cold, and a third as dumb, prompts a moral impulse which pertains to truth; from its opposite, the liar whom no one trusts and all exclude, human beings demonstrate to themselves just how honourable, confidence-inspiring and useful truth is. As creatures of *reason*, human beings now make their actions subject to the rule of abstractions; they no longer tolerate being swept away by sudden impressions and sensuous perceptions; they now generalize all these impressions first, turning them into cooler, less colourful concepts in order to harness the vehicle of their lives and actions to them. Everything which distinguishes human beings from animals depends on this ability to sublimate sensuous metaphors into a schema, in other words, to dissolve an image into a concept. This is because something becomes possible in the realm of these schemata which could never be achieved in the realm of those sensuous first impressions, namely the construction of a pyramidal order based on castes and degrees, the creation of a new world of laws, privileges, subordinations, definitions of borders, which now confronts the other, sensuously perceived world as something firmer, more general, more familiar, more human, and hence as something regulatory and imperative. Whereas every metaphor standing for a sensuous perception is individual and unique and is therefore always able to escape classification, the great edifice of concepts exhibits the rigid regularity of a Roman *columbarium*,[1] while logic breathes out that air of severity and coolness which is peculiar to mathematics. Anyone who has been touched by that cool breath will scarcely believe that concepts too, which are as bony and eight-cornered as a dice and just as capable of being shifted around, are only the left-over *residue of a metaphor*, and that the

1. Originally a dovecote, then a catacomb with niches at regular intervals for urns containing the ashes of the dead.

illusion produced by the artistic translation of a nervous stimulus into images is, if not the mother, then at least the grandmother of each and every concept. Within this conceptual game of dice, however, 'truth' means using each die in accordance with its designation, counting its spots precisely, forming correct classifications, and never offending against the order of castes nor against the sequence of classes of rank. Just as the Romans and the Etruscans divided up the sky with rigid mathematical lines and confined a god in a space which they had thus delimited as in a *templum*,[2] all peoples have just such a mathematically divided firmament of concepts above them, and they understand the demand of truth to mean that the god of every concept is to be sought only in *his* sphere. Here one can certainly admire humanity as a mighty architectural genius who succeeds in erecting the infinitely complicated cathedral of concepts on moving foundations, or even, one might say, on flowing water; admittedly, in order to rest on such foundations, it has to be like a thing constructed from cobwebs, so delicate that it can be carried off on the waves and yet so firm as not to be blown apart by the wind. By these standards the human being is an architectural genius who is far superior to the bee; the latter builds with wax which she gathers from nature, whereas the human being builds with the far more delicate material of concepts which he must first manufacture from himself. In this he is to be much admired—but just not for his impulse to truth, to the pure cognition of things. If someone hides something behind a bush, looks for it in the same place and then finds it there, his seeking and finding is nothing much to boast about; but this is exactly how things are as far as the seeking and finding of 'truth' within the territory of reason is concerned. If I create the definition of a mammal and then, having inspected a camel, declare, 'Behold, a mammal', then a truth has certainly been brought to light, but it is of limited value, by which I mean that it is anthropomorphic through and through and contains not a single point which could be said to be 'true in itself', really and in a generally valid sense, regardless of mankind. Anyone who researches for truths of that kind is basically only seeking the metamorphosis of the world in human beings; he strives for an understanding of the world as something which is similar in kind to humanity, and what he gains by his efforts is at best a feeling of assimilation. Rather as the astrologer studies the stars in the service of human beings and in relation to humanity's happiness and suffering, this type of researcher regards the whole world as linked to humankind, as the infinitely refracted echo of an original sound, that of humanity, and as the multiple copy of a single, original image, that of humanity. His procedure is to measure all things against man, and in doing so he takes as his point of departure the erroneous belief that he has these things directly before him, as pure objects. Thus, forgetting that the original metaphors of perception were indeed metaphors, he takes them for the things themselves.

Only by forgetting this primitive world of metaphor, only by virtue of the fact that a mass of images, which originally flowed in a hot, liquid stream from the primal power of the human imagination, has become hard and rigid, only because of the invincible faith that *this* sun, *this* window, this table is a truth in itself—in short only because man forgets himself as a

2. Literally, a space marked out; the space of the heavens; sanctuary, temple (Latin) [editor's note].

subject, and indeed as *an artistically creative* subject, does he live with some degree of peace, security, and consistency; if he could escape for just a moment from the prison walls of this faith, it would mean the end of his 'consciousness of self'.[3] He even has to make an effort to admit to himself that insects or birds perceive a quite different world from that of human beings, and that the question as to which of these two perceptions of the world is the more correct is quite meaningless, since this would require them to be measured by the criterion of the *correct perception*, i.e. by a *non-existent* criterion. But generally it seems to me that the correct perception—which would mean the full and adequate expression of an object in the subject—is something contradictory and impossible; for between two absolutely different spheres, such as subject and object are, there is no causality, no correctness, no expression, but at most an *aesthetic* way of relating, by which I mean an allusive transference, a stammering translation into a quite different language. For which purpose a middle sphere and mediating force is certainly required which can freely invent and freely create poetry. The word appearance (*Erscheinung*) contains many seductions, and for this reason I avoid using it as far as possible; for it is not true that the essence of things appears in the empirical world. A painter who has no hands and who wished to express in song the image hovering before him will still reveal more through this substitution of one sphere for another than the empirical world betrays of the essence of things. Even the relation of a nervous stimulus to the image produced thereby is inherently not a necessary relationship; but when that same image has been produced millions of times and has been passed down through many generations of humanity, indeed eventually appears in the whole of humanity as a consequence of the same occasion, it finally acquires the same significance for all human beings, as if it were the only necessary image and as if that relation of the original nervous stimulus to the image produced were a relation of strict causality—in exactly the same way as a dream, if repeated eternally, would be felt and judged entirely as reality. But the fact that a metaphor becomes hard and rigid is absolutely no guarantee of the necessity and exclusive justification of that metaphor.

Anyone who is at home in such considerations will certainly have felt a deep mistrust of this kind of idealism when once he has become clearly convinced of the eternal consistency, ubiquitousness and infallibility of the laws of nature; he will then conclude that everything, as far as we can penetrate, whether to the heights of the telescopic world or the depths of the microscopic world, is so sure, so elaborated, so endless, so much in conformity to laws, and so free of lacunae, that science will be able to mine these shafts successfully for ever, and that everything found there will be in agreement and without self-contradiction. How little all of this resembles a product of the imagination, for if it were such a thing, the illusion and the unreality would be bound to be detectable somewhere. The first thing to be said against this view is this: if each of us still had a different kind of sensuous perception, if we ourselves could only perceive things as, variously, a bird, a worm, or a plant does, or if one of us were to see a stimulus as red, a second person were to see the same stimulus as blue, while a third were even to

3. The word Nietzsche uses here—*Selbstbewußtsein*—could also mean "self-confidence."

hear it as a sound, nobody would ever speak of nature as something conforming to laws; rather they would take it to be nothing other than a highly subjective formation. Consequently, what is a law of nature for us at all? It is not known to us in itself but only in its effects, i.e. in its relations to other laws of nature which are in turn known to us only as relations. Thus, all these relations refer only to one another, and they are utterly incomprehensible to us in their essential nature; the only things we really know about them are things which we bring to bear on them: time and space, in other words, relations of succession and number. But everything which is wonderful and which elicits our astonishment at precisely these laws of nature, everything which demands explanation of us and could seduce us into being suspicious of idealism, is attributable precisely and exclusively to the rigour and universal validity of the representations of time and space. But these we produce within ourselves and from ourselves with the same necessity as a spider spins; if we are forced to comprehend all things under these forms alone, then it is no longer wonderful that what we comprehend in all these things is actually nothing other than these very forms; for all of them must exhibit the laws of number, and number is precisely that which is most astonishing about things. All the conformity to laws which we find so imposing in the orbits of the stars and chemical processes is basically identical with those qualities which we ourselves bring to bear on things, so that what we find imposing is our own activity. Of course the consequence of this is that the artistic production of metaphor, with which every sensation begins within us, already presupposes those forms, and is thus executed in them; only from the stability of these original forms can one explain how it is possible for an edifice of concepts to be constituted in its turn from the metaphors themselves. For this conceptual edifice is an imitation of the relations of time, space, and number on the foundations of metaphor.

2

Originally, as we have seen, it is *language* which works on building the edifice of concepts; later it is *science*. Just as the bee simultaneously builds the cells of its comb and fills them with honey, so science works unceasingly at that great *columbarium* of concepts, the burial site of perceptions, builds ever-new, ever-higher tiers, supports, cleans, renews the old cells, and strives above all to fill that framework which towers up to vast heights, and to fit into it in an orderly way the whole empirical world, i.e. the anthropomorphic world. If even the man of action binds his life to reason and its concepts, so as not to be swept away and lose himself, the researcher builds his hut close by the tower of science so that he can lend a hand with the building and find protection for himself beneath its already existing bulwarks. And he has need of protection, for there exist fearful powers which constantly press in on him and which confront scientific truth with 'truths' of quite another kind, on shields emblazoned with the most multifarious emblems.

That drive to form metaphors, that fundamental human drive which cannot be left out of consideration for even a second without also leaving out human beings themselves, is in truth not defeated, indeed hardly even tamed, by the process whereby a regular and rigid new world is built from its own sublimated products—concepts—in order to imprison it in a fortress.

The drive seeks out a channel and a new area for its activity, and finds it in myth and in art generally. It constantly confuses the cells and the classifications of concepts by setting up new translations, metaphors, metonymies; it constantly manifests the desire to shape the given world of the waking human being in ways which are just as multiform, irregular, inconsequential, incoherent, charming and ever-new, as things are in the world of dream. Actually the waking human being is only clear about the fact that he is awake thanks to the rigid and regular web of concepts, and for that reason he sometimes comes to believe that he is dreaming if once that web of concepts is torn apart by art. Pascal is right to maintain that if the same dream were to come to us every night we would occupy ourselves with it just as much as we do with the things we see every day: 'If an artisan could be sure to dream each night for a full twelve hours that he was a king,' says Pascal, 'I believe he would be just as happy as a king who dreamt for twelve hours each night that he was an artisan.'[4] Thanks to the constantly effective miracle assumed by myth, the waking day of a people who are stimulated by myth, as the ancient Greeks were, does indeed resemble dream more than it does the day of a thinker whose mind has been sobered by science. If, one day, any tree may speak as a nymph, or if a god can carry off virgins in the guise of a bull, if the goddess Athene herself is suddenly seen riding on a beautiful chariot in the company of Pisistratus through the market-places of Athens[5]—and that was what the honest Athenian believed—then anything is possible at any time, as it is in dream, and the whole of nature cavorts around men as if it were just a masquerade of the gods who are merely having fun by deceiving men in every shape and form.

But human beings themselves have an unconquerable urge to let themselves be deceived, and they are as if enchanted with happiness when the bard recites epic fairy-tales as if they were true, or when the actor in a play acts the king more regally than reality shows him to be. The intellect, that master of pretence, is free and absolved of its usual slavery for as long as it can deceive without *doing harm*, and it celebrates its Saturnalian festivals[6] when it does so; at no time is it richer, more luxuriant, more proud, skilful, and bold. Full of creative contentment, it jumbles up metaphors and shifts the boundary stones of abstraction, describing a river, for example, as a moving road that carries men to destinations to which they normally walk. The intellect has now cast off the mark of servitude; whereas it normally labours, with dull-spirited industry, to show to some poor individual who lusts after life the road and the tools he needs, and rides out in search of spoils and booty for its master, here the intellect has become the master itself and is permitted to wipe the expression of neediness from its face. Whatever the intellect now does, all of it, compared with what it did before, bears the mark of pretence, just as what it did before bore the mark of distortion. It

4. *Pensées* VI.386. [Blaise Pascal (1623–1662), French mathematician, theologian, and philosopher—editor's note.]
5. Herodotus 1.60. [The Greek historian (ca. 484–ca. 425 B.C.E.) describes in the passage cited a ruse of the Athenian ruler Pisistratus (d. 527 B.C.E.) after he was forced out of the city in 566: he dressed a tall, handsome woman in armor and led the people to believe that Athena, goddess of war and wisdom and the patron of Athens, was herself restoring him to power. "The guise of a bull": Zeus, the Greek king of the gods, took the form of a bull when he abducted Europa, a Phoenician princess—editor's note.]
6. Roman holidays at the winter solstice during which no business was conducted, slaves were temporarily freed, and the normal rules of propriety were suspended [editor's note].

copies human life, but it takes it to be something good and appears to be fairly content with it. That vast assembly of beams and boards to which needy man clings, thereby saving himself on his journey through life, is used by the liberated intellect as a mere climbing frame and plaything on which to perform its most reckless tricks; and when it smashes this framework, jumbles it up and ironically re-assembles it, pairing the most unlike things and dividing those things which are closest to one another, it reveals the fact that it does not require those makeshift aids of neediness, and that it is now guided, not by concepts but by intuitions. No regular way leads from these intuitions into the land of the ghostly schemata and abstractions; words are not made for them; man is struck dumb when he sees them, or he will speak only in forbidden metaphors and unheard-of combinations of concepts so that, by at least demolishing and deriding the old conceptual barriers, he may do creative justice to the impression made on him by the mighty, present intuition.

There are epochs in which the man of reason and the man of intuition stand side by side, the one fearful of intuition, the other filled with scorn for abstraction, the latter as unreasonable as the former is unartistic. They both desire to rule over life; the one by his knowledge of how to cope with the chief calamities of life by providing for the future, by prudence and regularity, the other by being an 'exuberant hero'[7] who does not see those calamities and who only acknowledges life as real when it is disguised as beauty and appearance. Where the man of intuition, as was once the case in ancient Greece, wields his weapons more mightily and victoriously than his contrary, a culture can take shape, given favourable conditions, and the rule of art over life can become established; all the expressions of a life lived thus are accompanied by pretence, by the denial of neediness, by the radiance of metaphorical visions, and indeed generally by the immediacy of deception. Neither the house, nor the gait, nor the clothing, nor the pitcher of clay gives any hint that these things were invented by neediness; it seems as if all of them were intended to express sublime happiness and Olympian[8] cloudlessness and, as it were, a playing with earnest things. Whereas the man who is guided by concepts and abstractions only succeeds thereby in warding off misfortune, is unable to compel the abstractions themselves to yield him happiness, and strives merely to be as free as possible of pain, the man of intuition, standing in the midst of a culture, reaps directly from his intuitions not just protection from harm but also a constant stream of brightness, a lightening of the spirit, redemption, and release. Of course, *when* he suffers, he suffers more severely; indeed he suffers more frequently because he does not know how to learn from experience and keeps on falling into the very same trap time after time. When he is suffering he is just as unreasonable as he is when happy, he shouts out loudly and knows no solace. How differently the same misfortune is endured by the stoic who has learned from experience and who governs himself by means of concepts! This man, who otherwise seeks only honesty, truth, freedom from illusions, and

7. Phrase used to describe Siegfried in Wagner's *Götterdämmerung* (Act III). [Richard Wagner (1813–1883), German composer who was Nietzsche's friend and mentor until their falling out in 1876. *Götterdämmerung*, the conclusion of Wagner's *Ring* cycle, was first produced in 1876—editor's note.]

8. That is, characteristic of Mount Olympus, the home of the Greek gods [editor's note].

protection from the onslaughts of things which might distract him, now performs, in the midst of misfortune, a masterpiece of pretence, just as the other did in the midst of happiness: he does not wear a twitching, mobile, human face, but rather a mask, as it were, with its features in dignified equilibrium; he does not shout, nor does he even change his tone of voice. If a veritable storm-cloud empties itself on his head, he wraps himself in his cloak and slowly walks away from under it.

1873 | 1903

OSCAR WILDE
1854–1900

Oscar Wilde is known for his epigrammatic wit, dazzling skills in conversation, and scandalous homosexual behavior, which in 1895 led to his trial and imprisonment for sodomy. But Wilde was more than a brilliant—and tragic—cultural personality. He was a gifted, wonderfully entertaining, and disquieting writer, the author of an impressive body of work that includes the superb comedy *The Importance of Being Earnest*, the haunting novel *The Picture of Dorian Gray*, and sharp, suggestive critical essays.

Wilde was born in Dublin, Ireland. His father was a surgeon and respected author; his mother also wrote both verse and prose. Educated in classics at Trinity College, Dublin, Wilde won a fellowship to Magdalen College, Oxford University. There he was influenced by the eminent art historian John Ruskin, WALTER PATER, and the Pre-Raphaelite brotherhood of English poets and painters. The young Wilde began to lead his life as if it were a work of art, to be crafted, cultivated, and made to sparkle. Defying orthodoxy and social convention, he was flamboyant and theatrical.

In 1881, at his own expense, Wilde published his first book, *Poems*, a promising but derivative volume that reflects the influence of Wilde's reading of John Keats (1795–1821), Algernon Swinburne (1837–1909), Pater, and the Pre-Raphaelites. In the following year, Wilde toured and lectured in the United States. It is said that on his arrival in New York City, when asked by customs officials if he had anything to declare, he replied, "Only my genius." Wilde was by now a leader of the aesthetic movement, which rallied around the dictum of "art for art's sake." His deliberate eccentricity and exuberant self-regard drew ridicule in the weekly comic periodical *Punch*, and he was parodied as Bunthorne in Gilbert and Sullivan's 1881 operetta *Patience*.

Though Wilde had (in the words of one recent scholar) "flirted" with homosexuality for a number of years, he married Constance Lloyd, daughter of a prominent Irish barrister, in 1884. For his two sons Wilde wrote stories—inspired by the Danish writer Hans Christian Andersen—included in *The Happy Prince and Other Tales* (1888) and *A House of Pomegranates* (1892). He also wrote reviews for the *Pall Mall Gazette* and, from 1887 to 1889, served as the editor of *Woman's World*, a popular periodical to which Constance also contributed articles on politics and women's issues.

In the early 1890s, Wilde hit his stride. *The Picture of Dorian Gray* appeared first in *Lippincott's Magazine* in 1890; the book, revised and expanded by six chapters, was published in 1891. It recounts the story of a beautiful young man who seems not to age but whose portrait becomes aged and ugly over time, the sign of his own corruption. In *Intentions* (1891), an important collection of essays, Wilde presented his audacious views on literature, art, and criticism; and in *Collected Poems* (1892), he gathered his verse. Wilde had hoped to center his literary career in poetry, but his greatest success was as a comic and satiric dramatist. His plays include *Lady Windemere's Fan* (1892); *A Woman of No Importance* (1893); *An Ideal Husband* (1895); and, above all, *The Importance of Being Earnest* (1895), which describes the courtships and betrothals of two young men-about-town who are leading double lives. Wilde also wrote the historical tragedies *The Duchess of Padua* (1892) and *Salomé* (1893); the latter, about the woman who danced before Herod and afterward demanded the head of John the Baptist, was written in French and then published in an English translation (1894) that included eerie, erotic illustrations by Aubrey Beardsley.

Wilde's pleasure in titillating and unnerving his audiences and readers resulted in many striking witticisms, such as Cecily's reproach in *The Importance of Being Earnest*: "I hope you have not been leading a double life, pretending to be wicked and being really good all the time. That would be hypocrisy." Yet in his own way, Wilde was deeply serious and morally earnest. A critic of middle-class Philistine smugness and moral complacency, he too wanted greater opportunity—though more than MATTHEW ARNOLD would have accepted—for freedom of expression and dissent, for the right to contest the status quo.

In one of his lectures in America, Wilde had declared, "To disagree with three fourths of all England on all points of view is one of the first elements of sanity." But in 1895 Wilde discovered that social and moral convention could be relentlessly punitive. When the marquess of Queensberry, the father of Wilde's lover, Lord Alfred Douglas, left a card at his club addressed "To Oscar Wilde, posing as a sodomite," Wilde unsuccessfully sued for libel—and then was himself arrested for violating the law forbidding "indecencies between grown-up men, in public or private." Wilde was found guilty and sentenced to two years' imprisonment at hard labor.

After his release in May 1897, Wilde—separated from his wife and children, broken, bankrupt, and disgraced—left for France, calling himself "Sebastian Melmoth" ("Sebastian" after the Christian martyred by arrows in early fourth-century Rome, and "Melmoth" after the doomed hero of Charles Maturin's 1820 Gothic novel *Melmoth the Wanderer*). Wilde spent the rest of his life as an exile in Europe, recovering enough focus as a writer to tell of his painful prison experiences in *The Ballad of Reading Gaol* (1898). He died in Paris in November 1900, having remarked, "If I were to survive into the twentieth century, it would be more than the English people could bear." *De Profundis* ("out of the depths," the first two words of the Latin version of Psalm 130), both a book-length letter of reproach to Lord Alfred and a personal testament, was published in 1905. His self-judgment in this text is unsparing, as he declares: "Terrible as was what the world did to me, what I did to myself was far more terrible still."

In the preface to *The Picture of Dorian Gray*, our first selection, Wilde sketches his position on art and morality in a sequence of aphorisms. Authentic artists, says Wilde, concern themselves with style and form, with the adroit handling of the artistic medium and the shaping of beautiful works. Morality, he explains, is not a matter of an artist's or a writer's message; it instead rests in how well he or she has executed an aesthetic task. Wilde revises Arnold's statement that critics should be devoted to the best that has been thought and said by maintaining that the best is the most beautiful, whose nature is ultimately formal and stylistic rather than ethical. Wilde provokes us by concluding, "All art is quite useless."

Our next selection is an excerpt from the final part of Wilde's "The Decay of Lying: An Observation," which he completed in December 1888. It was published in the January 1889 issue of the journal *The Nineteenth Century*, and Wilde then revised and expanded it for his collection *Intentions*. Showing his mastery of the "dialogue" form, Wilde presents two characters, Vivian and Cyril, in conversation in the library of a country house in Nottinghamshire. Vivian has written an essay titled "The Decay of Lying: A Protest," which he reads aloud to, and explicates for, Cyril—Wilde named the characters after his own sons Cyril (born in 1885) and Vivian (born in 1886). Wilde here deftly explores a two-part antirealist claim: "Art never expresses anything but itself" and "Life imitates Art far more than Art imitates Life."

As Wilde's biographer Richard Ellman has noted, Wilde mocks "conventional theories of sincerity and verisimilitude" and proposes instead an aesthetic based on "lies and masks." Ellman makes the astute point that Wilde avoids the term "imagination" because it connotes a Romantic flow or outpouring from within; he prefers the deliberately disquieting term "lying," with its implication of a self-aware desire to mislead and deceive. Writers do not tell the truth, but rather are engaged in doing the opposite. Furthermore, they do not reflect or take expression from the era in which they live but instead give shape to the era: Art gives character and meaning to Life.

From one perspective, Wilde's goal in "The Decay of Lying" is a familiar one; like HORACE, SIR PHILIP SIDNEY, and others from the classical period to the Renaissance, he seeks to entertain and instruct readers. He revels in paradox and exaggeration; he enjoys clever turns of phrase and reversing conventional judgments and assumptions; and he is fond of sequences of wit and irony. Throughout it is a bright, amusing performance.

But at the same time, the ideas that Wilde holds up for inspection are highly subversive, indeed outrageous. "The Decay of Lying," as Ellman has observed, presents the writer-artist as "a sacred malefactor," a liar, a nontruth teller who is not bound by any taken-for-granted norms of good and evil. In a sense, Wilde is reaching back to PLATO, who denounced fiction for its falsehood—the claim that Wilde comes forward to embrace and rejoice in. Both exhilarating and unnerving, Wilde's cleverly articulated conception of art gives supreme power to writers, critics, and playwrights: it is for him a manifesto and an act of self-expression. Just as much or more, however, what Wilde offers to his readers is a provocative pose that impels them to ask whether there is a significant difference between telling the truth and lying.

In "The Critic as Artist" (1890, 1891), a brisk, pointed dialogue on the nature of, and relationship between, the arts and criticism, Wilde expands on and develops the claims he advanced in the preface to *Dorian Gray* and in "The Decay of Lying." His mouthpiece Gilbert not only celebrates criticism in its own right but asserts and praises its superiority over so-called creative or primary literary and artistic work. Throughout, Wilde emphasizes and honors style, form, and self-conscious craft; in an anti-Romantic thrust, he devalues inspiration. He is antihistorical as well, opposed to history because of (and here he echoes RALPH WALDO EMERSON) the constraints that it imposes on individual expression.

"The details of history," according to Gilbert in part 1, "are always wearisome." Criticism "is more fascinating than history," for it "is concerned simply with oneself": it is a type of autobiography and impressionism. As Gilbert's comments on Ruskin and Pater indicate, for Wilde it does not matter whether the creative critic is faithful to the work of art: accurate statements about an aesthetic object or the artist's intentions count less than the critical essay's status as an independent work of art. In part 2, Wilde qualifies and complicates this position; for example, in his references to Shakespeare he concedes that historical study is important after all. But he continues to stress that "the highest Criticism, being the purest form of personal impression, is, in its way, more creative than creation."

Wilde is not an especially original thinker. He draws on nineteenth-century French and English authors, including the poet-critic Théophile Gautier, the novelist Joris-Karl Huysman, the poet Charles Baudelaire, and Pater. The concept of "art for art's sake" was in fact proposed by Gautier, in the preface to *Mademoiselle de Maupin*

(1835), where he affirmed: "Les choses sont belles en proportion inverse de leur utilité" (Things are beautiful in inverse proportion to their usefulness). Sometimes Wilde's cool, canny ironies can feel predictable, produced on cue and according to formula. There is a measure of truth to the complaint of the American cultural critic H. L. Mencken (1880–1956) that in his endless flaunting of paradoxes, Wilde can be as insufferable as an overpious preacher.

On the other hand, Wilde's epigrams and arguments at their best are compelling, and in recent years his life has drawn equal interest. Literary critics and theorists and scholars in gender and gay and lesbian studies have since the 1980s devoted many books and essays to Wilde's writings and extraordinary and aggrieved life. Even earlier, critics including NORTHROP FRYE and HAROLD BLOOM praised him extravagantly; Frye, in *Creation and Recreation* (1980), portrayed Wilde as a theorist of the imagination equal in significance to the revolutionary painter and poet William Blake (1757–1827). Like Blake, and like the later Romantics PERCY BYSSHE SHELLEY and Emerson, Wilde contends that great writers and artists give structure to life through the power of their enlightened vision. For him the terms and values of art themselves constitute life. Nature, Wilde maintained, "is our creation. . . . Things are because we see them." The result of critical inquiry is not truth, but an interpretation—or rather a series of misinterpretations, of misreadings, since we do not (and never will) possess an objectively known reality with which we could appraise and firmly decide among conflicting views.

This line of argument gives us a Wilde akin less to Pater than to the German philosopher FRIEDRICH NIETZSCHE, the Nietzsche of *The Will to Power* (1901) in particular: "It is our needs that interpret the world; our drives and their For and Against. Every drive is a kind of lust to rule; each one has its perspective that it would like to compel all the other drives to accept as a norm." Wilde lacks this tone of grim intensity, but his elegantly articulated ideas imply the consequences that Nietzsche and later authors have expressed.

"Preface to *The Picture of Dorian Gray*" Keywords: Aesthetics, Authorship, Defense of Criticism, Ethics
"The Decay of Lying: An Observation" Keywords: Aesthetics, Authorship, Realism, Representation
"The Critic as Artist" Keywords: Aesthetics, Authorship, The Canon/Tradition, Defense of Criticism, Ethics, Interpretation Theory, Literary History, Representation, Subjectivity

Preface to *The Picture of Dorian Gray*

The artist is the creator of beautiful things.

To reveal art and conceal the artist is art's aim.

The critic is he who can translate into another manner or a new material his impression of beautiful things.

The highest as the lowest form of criticism is a mode of autobiography.

Those who find ugly meanings in beautiful things are corrupt without being charming. This is a fault.

Those who find beautiful meanings in beautiful things are the cultivated. For these there is hope.

They are the elect to whom beautiful things mean only Beauty.

There is no such thing as a moral or an immoral book.

Books are well written, or badly written. That is all.

The nineteenth century dislike of Realism is the rage of Caliban seeing his own face in a glass.[1]

The nineteenth century dislike of Romanticism is the rage of Caliban not seeing his own face in a glass.

The moral life of man forms part of the subject-matter of the artist, but the morality of art consists in the perfect use of an imperfect medium.

No artist desires to prove anything. Even things that are true can be proved.

No artist has ethical sympathies. An ethical sympathy in an artist is an unpardonable mannerism of style.

No artist is ever morbid. The artist can express everything.

Thought and language are to the artist instruments of an art.

Vice and virtue are to the artist materials for an art.

From the point of view of form, the type of all the arts is the art of the musician. From the point of view of feeling, the actor's craft is the type.

All art is at once surface and symbol.

Those who go beneath the surface do so at their peril.

Those who read the symbol do so at their peril.

It is the spectator, and not life, that art really mirrors.

Diversity of opinion about a work of art shows that the work is new, complex, and vital.

When critics disagree the artist is in accord with himself.

We can forgive a man for making a useful thing as long as he does not admire it. The only excuse for making a useless thing is that one admires it intensely.

All art is quite useless.

1891

From The Decay of Lying: An Observation

* * *

Cyril. * * * But even admitting this strange imitative instinct in Life and Nature, surely you would acknowledge that Art expresses the temper of its age, the spirit of its time, the moral and social conditions that surround it, and under whose influence it is produced.

Vivian. Certainly not! Art never expresses anything but itself. This is the principle of my new æsthetics; and it is this, more than that vital connection between form and substance, on which Mr Pater[1] dwells, that makes music the type of all the arts. Of course, nations and individuals, with that healthy natural vanity which is the secret of existence, are always under the impression that it is of them that the Muses are talking, always trying to find in the calm dignity of imaginative art some mirror of their own turbid[2] passions, always forgetting that the singer of life is not Apollo, but Marsyas.[3]

1. Mirror. Caliban: half-human slave of Prospero in Shakespeare's play *The Tempest* (1611).

1. Walter Pater (1839–1834), English essayist and art critic. The reference is to "The School of Giorgione," included in *The Renaissance: Studies in Art and Poetry* (2d ed., 1877), where Pater explores "a certain interpenetration of the matter or subject of a work of art with the form of it" in painting, music, and poetry. The Italian painter Giorgione (1478–1510) was an early master of the Venetian school.

2. Not clear or transparent; confused, muddled.

3. In Greek mythology, a flute player who challenged Apollo, god of music and poetry, to a musical contest, judged by the Muses (the 9 daughters of Memory who presided over the arts and all intellectual pursuits); after he lost, Apollo flayed him alive for his presumption.

Remote from reality, and with her eyes turned away from the shadows of the cave,[4] Art reveals her own perfection, and the wondering crowd that watches the opening of the marvellous, many-petalled rose[5] fancies that it is its own history that is being told to it, its own spirit that is finding expression in a new form. But it is not so. The highest art rejects the burden of the human spirit, and gains more from a new medium or a fresh material than she does from any enthusiasm for art, or from any lofty passion, or from any great awakening of the human consciousness. She develops purely on her own lines. She is not symbolic of any age. It is the ages that are her symbols.

Even those who hold that Art is representative of time and place and people, cannot help admitting that the more imitative an art is, the less it represents to us the spirit of its age. The evil faces of the Roman emperors look out at us from the foul porphyry and spotted jasper[6] in which the realistic artists of the day delighted to work, and we fancy that in those cruel lips and heavy sensual jaws we can find the secret of the ruin of the Empire. But it was not so. The vices of Tiberius[7] could not destroy that supreme civilization, any more than the virtues of the Antonines[8] could save it. It fell for other, for less interesting reasons. The sibyls and prophets of the Sistine[9] may indeed serve to interpret for some that new birth of the emancipated spirit that we call the Renaissance; but what do the drunken boors and brawling peasants of Dutch art tell us about the great soul of Holland? The more abstract, the more ideal an art is, the more it reveals to us the temper of its age. If we wish to understand a nation by means of its art, let us look at its architecture or its music.

Cyril. I quite agree with you there. The spirit of an age may be best expressed in the abstract ideal arts, for the spirit itself is abstract and ideal. Upon the other hand, for the visible aspect of an age, for its look, as the phrase goes, we must of course go to the arts of imitation.

Vivian. I don't think so. After all, what the imitative arts really give us are merely the various styles of particular artists, or of certain schools of artists. Surely you don't imagine that the people of the Middle Ages bore any resemblance at all to the figures on mediæval stained glass, or in mediæval stone and wood carving, or on mediæval metal-work, or tapestries, or illuminated MSS.[1] They were probably very ordinary-looking people, with nothing grotesque, or remarkable, or fantastic in their appearance. The Middle Ages, as we know them in art, are simply a definite form of style, and there is no reason at all why an artist with this style should not be produced in the nineteenth century. No great artist ever sees things as they really are. If he did, he would cease to be an artist. Take an example from our own day. I know that

4. PLATO (ca. 427–ca. 347 B.C.E.), in *Republic* 7.514a–518b, compares the human condition to that of prisoners in a cave, able to see only shadows cast by representations of things (and thus at a double remove from reality).

5. See DANTE (1265–1321), *Paradiso* 31: the sacred host in Heaven appears in the form of a white rose.

6. A variety of quartz, usually colored red. "Porphyry": a reddish-purplish rock. Wilde is referring here to stoneware and sculpture made from these materials.

7. The second Roman emperor (42 B.C.E.–37 C.E.; emperor 14–37 C.E.) accused by ancient historians of cruelty, perversion, and vice.

8. The collective name of 4 Roman emperors of the 2d century C.E.; the first, Antoninus Pius (86–161; emperor, 138–161), was known for his beneficence and enjoyed a peaceful reign.

9. The Sistine Chapel in Rome, whose ceiling was painted by Michelangelo Buonarroti between 1508 and 1512. "Sibyls": female prophets.

1. Manuscripts.

you are fond of Japanese things.[2] Now, do you really imagine that the Japanese people, as they are presented to us in art, have any existence? If you do, you have never understood Japanese art at all. The Japanese people are the deliberate self-conscious creation of certain individual artists. If you set a picture by Hokusai, or Hokkei,[3] or any of the great native painters, beside a real Japanese gentleman or lady, you will see that there is not the slightest resemblance between them. The actual people who live in Japan are not unlike the general run of English people; that is to say, they are extremely commonplace, and have nothing curious or extraordinary about them. In fact the whole of Japan is a pure invention. There is no such country, there are no such people. One of our most charming painters[4] went recently to the Land of the Chrysanthemum in the foolish hope of seeing the Japanese. All he saw, all he had the chance of painting, were a few lanterns and some fans. He was quite unable to discover the inhabitants, as his delightful exhibition at Messrs Dowdeswell's Gallery showed only too well. He did not know that the Japanese people are, as I have said, simply a mode of style, an exquisite fancy of art. And so, if you desire to see a Japanese effect, you will not behave like a tourist and go to Tokio. On the contrary, you will stay at home, and steep yourself in the work of certain Japanese artists, and then, when you have absorbed the spirit of their style, and caught their imaginative manner of vision, you will go some afternoon and sit in the Park or stroll down Piccadilly,[5] and if you cannot see an absolutely Japanese effect there, you will not see it anywhere. Or, to return again to the past, take as another instance the ancient Greeks. Do you think that Greek art ever tells us what the Greek people were like? Do you believe that the Athenian women were like the stately dignified figures of the Parthenon frieze,[6] or like those marvellous goddesses who sat in the triangular pediments of the same building? If you judge from the art, they certainly were so. But read an authority, like Aristophanes[7] for instance. You will find that the Athenian ladies laced tightly, wore high-heeled shoes, dyed their hair yellow, painted and rouged their faces, and were exactly like any silly fashionable or fallen creature of our own day. The fact is that we look back on the ages entirely through the medium of Art, and Art, very fortunately, has never once told us the truth.

Cyril. But modern portraits by English painters, what of them? Surely they are like the people they pretend to represent?

Vivian. Quite so. They are so like them that a hundred years from now no one will believe in them. The only portraits in which one believes are portraits where there is very little of the sitter, and a very great deal of the artist. Holbein's[8] drawings of the men and women of his time impress us with a

2. Japanese art, especially woodblock prints, influenced many Western artists in the late 19th century and became highly fashionable in England.
3. Totoya (Katsushika) Hokkei (1780–1850), Japanese printmaker, a student of the artist Katsushika Hokusai (1760–1849), who is remembered for his historical scenes and landscapes.
4. Mortimer Menpes (1859–1938), an Australian-born painter who was one of the first to study Japanese art in Japan; he exhibited his work at the Dowdeswell Gallery in London in April–May 1888.
5. A major shopping street in central London. The Park: Hyde Park, popular for fashionable promenades.
6. The continuous band of low-relief sculpture, depicting a religious procession, that adorned the outside of the Parthenon, the temple of Athena (built 447–432 B.C.E.) on the Acropolis of Athens; in 1816 almost half of the 525-foot frieze was bought by London's British Museum.
7. Greek comic playwright (ca. 450–ca. 385 B.C.E.).
8. Hans Holbein the Younger (1497?–1553), German portrait artist and printmaker.

sense of their absolute reality. But this is simply because Holbein compelled life to accept his conditions, to restrain itself within his limitations, to reproduce his type, and to appear as he wished it to appear. It is style that makes us believe in a thing—nothing but style. Most of our modern portrait painters are doomed to absolute oblivion. They never paint what they see. They paint what the public sees, and the public never sees anything.

* * *

Cyril. * * * But in order to avoid making any error I want you to tell me briefly the doctrines of the new Æsthetics.

Vivian. Briefly, then, they are these. Art never expresses anything but itself. It has an independent life, just as Thought has, and develops purely on its own lines. It is not necessarily realistic in an age of realism, nor spiritual in an age of faith. So far from being the creation of its time, it is usually in direct opposition to it, and the only history that it preserves for us is the history of its own progress. Sometimes it returns upon its footsteps, and revives some antique form, as happened in the archaistic movement of late Greek Art, and in the pre-Raphaelite movement[9] of our own day. At other times it entirely anticipates its age, and produces in one century work that it takes another century to understand, to appreciate, and to enjoy. In no case does it reproduce its age. To pass from the art of a time to the time itself is the great mistake that all historians commit.

The second doctrine is this. All bad art comes from returning to Life and Nature, and elevating them into ideals. Life and Nature may sometimes be used as part of Art's rough material, but before they are of any real service to art they must be translated into artistic conventions. The moment Art surrenders its imaginative medium it surrenders everything. As a method Realism is a complete failure, and the two things that every artist should avoid are modernity of form and modernity of subject-matter. To us, who live in the nineteenth century, any century is a suitable subject for art except our own. The only beautiful things are the things that do not concern us. It is, to have the pleasure of quoting myself,[1] exactly because Hecuba is nothing to us that her sorrows are so suitable a motive for a tragedy. Besides, it is only the modern that ever becomes old-fashioned. M. Zola sits down to give us a picture of the Second Empire.[2] Who cares for the Second Empire now? It is out of date. Life goes faster than Realism, but Romanticism is always in front of Life.

The third doctrine is that Life imitates Art far more than Art imitates Life. This results not merely from Life's imitative instinct, but from the fact that the self-conscious aim of Life is to find expression, and that Art offers it certain beautiful forms through which it may realize that energy. It is a theory that has never been put forward before, but it is extremely fruitful,

9. A "brotherhood" founded in 1848 by English poets and painters who rejected Victorian materialism and neoclassical conventions of academic art, focusing instead on the medieval world and imitating Italian painters prior to Raphael (Raffaelo Sanzio, 1483–1520). "Archaistic": imitating earlier archaic art (ca. 660–480 B.C.E.), especially sculpture, as produced in the 4th century B.C.E.

1. Wilde repeats the following phrase from an earlier passage not included in our selection. The reference is to *Hamlet* (ca. 1600)—"What's Hecuba to him, or he to Hecuba, / That he should weep for her?" (2.2.536–37)—Hamlet's response to an actor's impassioned sympathy for the suffering of a mythical figure, the Trojan queen Hecuba.

2. The imperial Bonapartist regime (1852–70) of Napoleon III. Émile Zola (1840–1902), French novelist whose naturalist works described the corruption and decadence of the Second Empire in realistic detail.

and throws an entirely new light upon the history of Art. It follows, as a corollary from this, that external Nature also imitates Art. The only effects that she can show us are effects that we have already seen through poetry, or in paintings. This is the secret of Nature's charm, as well as the explanation of Nature's weakness. The final revelation is that Lying, the telling of beautiful untrue things, is the proper aim of Art. But of this I think I have spoken at sufficient length. And now let us go out on the terrace, where 'droops the milk-white peacock like a ghost', while the evening star 'washes the dusk with silver'.[3] At twilight nature becomes a wonderfully suggestive effect, and is not without loveliness, though perhaps its chief use is to illustrate quotations from the poets. Come! We have talked long enough.

1891

From The Critic as Artist[1]

From *Part 1*

* * *

Ernest. * * * I am quite ready to admit that I was wrong in what I said about the Greeks. They were, as you have pointed out, a nation of art critics. I acknowledge it, and I feel a little sorry for them. For the creative faculty is higher than the critical. There is really no comparison between them.

Gilbert. The antithesis between them is entirely arbitrary. Without the critical faculty, there is no artistic creation at all worthy of the name. You spoke a little while ago of that fine spirit of choice and delicate instinct of selection by which the artist realises life for us, and gives to it a momentary perfection. Well, that spirit of choice, that subtle tact of omission, is really the critical faculty in one of its most characteristic moods, and no one who does not possess this critical faculty can create anything at all in art. Arnold's definition of literature as a criticism of life,[2] was not very felicitous in form, but it showed how keenly he recognised the importance of the critical element in all creative work.

Ernest. I should have said that great artists worked unconsciously, that they were "wiser than they knew," as, I think, Emerson remarks somewhere.[3]

Gilbert. It is really not so, Ernest. All fine imaginative work is self-conscious and deliberate. No poet sings because he must sing. At least, no great poet does. A great poet sings because he chooses to sing. It is so now, and it has always been so. We are sometimes apt to think that the voices that sounded at the dawn of poetry were simpler, fresher, and more natural than ours, and

3. Wilde quotes first "Now Sleeps the Crimson Petal, Now the White," a lyric from *The Princess* (1847), by Alfred, Lord Tennyson, and then the poem "To the Evening Star" (1783), by William Blake.

1. Originally titled "The True Function and Value of Criticism, with Some Remarks on the Importance of Doing Nothing." For his book *Intentions* (1891), Wilde retitled and revised the text.

2. Often in "The Critic as Artist," Wilde alludes or responds directly to MATTHEW ARNOLD'S views on literature and criticism in *Essays in Criticism: First Series* (1865), in particular "The Function of Criticism at the Present Time" (see above).

3. See "The Over-Soul" and "Compensation," both in *Essays: First Series* (1841), by RALPH WALDO EMERSON (1803–1882).

that the world which the early poets looked at, and through which they walked, had a kind of poetical quality of its own, and almost without changing could pass into song. The snow lies thick now upon Olympus, and its steep, scarped sides are bleak and barren, but once, we fancy, the white feet of the Muses brushed the dew from the anemones in the morning, and at evening came Apollo[4] to sing to the shepherds in the vale. But in this we are merely lending to other ages what we desire, or think we desire, for our own. Our historical sense is at fault. Every century that produces poetry is, so far, an artificial century, and the work that seems to us to be the most natural and simple product of its time is always the result of the most self-conscious effort. Believe me, Ernest, there is no fine art without self-consciousness, and self-consciousness and the critical spirit are one.

Ernest. I see what you mean, and there is much in it. But surely you would admit that the great poems of the early world, the primitive, anonymous collective poems, were the result of the imagination of races, rather than of the imagination of individuals?

Gilbert. Not when they became poetry. Not when they received a beautiful form. For there is no art where there is no style, and no style where there is no unity, and unity is of the individual. No doubt Homer had old ballads and stories to deal with, as Shakespeare had chronicles and plays and novels from which to work, but they were merely his rough material. He took them and shaped them into song. They became his, because he made them lovely. They were built out of music,

> And so not built at all,
> And therefore built for ever.[5]

The longer one studies life and literature, the more strongly one feels that behind everything that is wonderful stands the individual, and that it is not the moment that makes the man, but the man who creates the age. Indeed, I am inclined to think that each myth and legend that seems to us to spring out of the wonder, or terror, or fancy of tribe and nation, was in its origin the invention of one single mind. The curiously limited number of the myths seems to me to point to this conclusion. But we must not go off into questions of comparative mythology. We must keep to criticism. And what I want to point out is this. An age that has no criticism is either an age in which art is immobile, hieratic,[6] and confined to the reproduction of formal types, or an age that possesses no art at all. There have been critical ages that have not been creative, in the ordinary sense of the word, ages in which the spirit of man has sought to set in order the treasures of his treasure-house, to separate the gold from the silver, and the silver from the lead, to count over the jewels, and to give names to the pearls. But there has never been a creative age that has not been critical also. For it is the critical faculty that invents fresh forms. The tendency of creation is to repeat itself. It is to the critical instinct that we owe each new school that springs up, each new

4. The Greek god of prophecy, music, and poetry. Olympus: mountain range in northern Greece and home of the Greek gods. Muses: in Greek mythology, the 9 daughters of memory; they presided over the arts and sciences.
5. Slightly misquoting Alfred, Lord Tennyson, *Idylls of the King* (1859–85), "Gareth and Lynette," lines 272–74.
6. Pertaining to the priesthood; here a reference to certain styles in art in which the representations or methods are fixed by religious tradition.

mould that art finds ready to its hand. There is really not a single form that art now uses that does not come to us from the critical spirit of Alexandria,[7] where these forms were either stereotyped,[8] or invented, or made perfect. I say Alexandria, not merely because it was there that the Greek spirit became most self-conscious, and indeed ultimately expired in scepticism and theology, but because it was to that city, and not to Athens, that Rome turned for her models, and it was through the survival, such as it was, of the Latin language that culture lived at all. When, at the Renaissance, Greek literature dawned upon Europe, the soil had been in some measure prepared for it. But to get rid of the details of history, which are always wearisome, and usually inaccurate, let us say generally that the forms of art have been due to the Greek critical spirit. To it we owe the epic, the lyric, the entire drama in every one of its developments, including burlesque, the idyll, the romantic novel, the novel of adventure, the essay, the dialogue, the oration, the lecture, for which perhaps we should not forgive them, and the epigram, in all the wide meaning of that word. In fact, we owe it everything, except the sonnet, to which, however, some curious parallels of thought movement may be traced in the Anthology,[9] American journalism, to which no parallel can be found anywhere, and the ballad in sham Scotch dialect, which one of our most industrious writers[1] has recently proposed should be made the basis for a final and unanimous effort on the part of our second-rate poets to make themselves really romantic. Each new school, as it appears, cries out against criticism, but it is to the critical faculty in man that it owes its origin. The mere creative instinct does not innovate, but reproduces.

Ernest. You have been talking of criticism as an essential part of the creative spirit, and I now fully accept your theory. But what of criticism outside creation? I have a foolish habit of reading periodicals, and it seems to me that most modern criticism is perfectly valueless.

Gilbert. So is most modern creative work, also. Mediocrity weighing mediocrity in the balance, and incompetence applauding its brother—that is the spectacle which the artistic activity of England affords us from time to time. And yet, I feel I am a little unfair in this matter. As a rule, the critics—I speak, of course, of the higher class, of those, in fact, who write for the sixpenny papers—are far more cultured than the people whose work they are called upon to review. This is, indeed, only what one would expect, for criticism demands infinitely more cultivation than creation does.

Ernest. Really?

Gilbert. Certainly. Anybody can write a three-volumed novel.[2] It merely requires a complete ignorance of both life and literature. The difficulty that I should fancy the reviewer feels is the difficulty of sustaining any standard. Where there is no style a standard must be impossible. The poor reviewers are apparently reduced to be the reporters of the police court of literature, the chroniclers of the doings of the habitual criminals of art. It is sometimes

7. City and major seaport in northern Egypt. Founded by Alexander the Great after he conquered Egypt in 331 B.C.E., it was the center of Hellenistic commerce and learning, with a great university and two royal libraries.
8. Fixed in unchanging form.
9. The Greek or Palatine Anthology, a collection of Greek epigrams (some from as early as the 7th c. B.C.E.) compiled ca. 980 C.E.
1. William Sharp (1855–1905), Scottish writer whose works (written under the name Fiona Macleod) include mystic Celtic tales and romances of peasant life.
2. Standard length of Victorian novels.

said of them that they do not read all through the works they are called upon to criticise. They do not. Or at least they should not. If they did so, they would become confirmed misanthropes; or, if I may borrow a phrase from one of the pretty Newnham graduates, confirmed womanthropes[3] for the rest of their lives. Nor is it necessary. To know the vintage and quality of a wine one need not drink the whole cask. It must be perfectly easy in half an hour to say whether a book is worth anything or worth nothing. Ten minutes are really sufficient, if one has the instinct for form. Who wants to wade through a dull volume? One tastes it, and that is quite enough—more than enough, I should imagine. I am aware that there are many honest workers in painting as well as in literature who object to criticism entirely. They are quite right. Their work stands in no intellectual relation to their age. It brings us no new element of pleasure. It suggests no fresh departure of thought, or passion, or beauty. It should not be spoken of. It should be left to the oblivion that it deserves.

Ernest. But, my dear fellow—excuse me for interrupting you—you seem to me to be allowing your passion for criticism to lead you a great deal too far. For, after all, even you must admit that it is much more difficult to do a thing than to talk about it.

Gilbert. More difficult to do a thing than to talk about it? Not at all. That is a gross popular error. It is very much more difficult to talk about a thing than to do it. In the sphere of actual life that is, of course, obvious. Anybody can make history. Only a great man can write it. There is no mode of action, no form of emotion, that we do not share with the lower animals. It is only by language that we rise above them, or above each other—by language, which is the parent, and not the child, of thought. Action, indeed, is always easy, and when presented to us in its most aggravated, because most continuous form, which I take to be that of real industry, becomes simply the refuge of people who have nothing whatsoever to do. No, Ernest, don't talk about action. It is a blind thing, dependent on external influences, and moved by an impulse of whose nature it is unconscious. It is a thing incomplete in its essence, because limited by accident, and ignorant of its direction, being always at variance with its aim. Its basis is the lack of imagination. It is the last resource of those who know not how to dream.

Ernest. Gilbert, you treat the world as if it were a crystal ball. You hold it in your hand, and reverse it to please a wilful fancy. You do nothing but rewrite history.

Gilbert. The one duty we owe to history is to rewrite it. That is not the least of the tasks in store for the critical spirit. When we have fully discovered the scientific laws that govern life we shall realise that the one person who has more illusions than the dreamer is the man of action. He, indeed, knows neither the origin of his deeds nor their results. From the field in which he thought that he had sown thorns we have gathered our vintage, and the fig-tree that he planted for our pleasure is as barren as the thistle, and more bitter.[4] It is because Humanity has never known where it was going that it has been able to find its way.

3. A nonsensical coinage meaning "woman-haters." Newnham: the second of the colleges for women in Cambridge (founded in 1871; women initially did not follow the university curriculum and were not granted Cambridge degrees for another half century).

4. See Matthew 7.16: "Do men gather grapes of thorns, or figs of thistles?"

Ernest. You think, then, that in the sphere of action a conscious aim is a delusion?

Gilbert. It is worse than a delusion. If we lived long enough to see the results of our actions, it may be that those who call themselves good would be sickened with a dull remorse, and those whom the world calls evil stirred by a noble joy. Each little thing that we do passes into the great machine of life, which may grind our virtues to powder and make them worthless, or transform our sins into elements of a new civilisation, more marvellous and more splendid than any that has gone before. * * *

Ernest. * * * But, surely, the higher you place the creative artist, the lower must the critic rank.

Gilbert. Why so?

Ernest. Because the best that he can give us will be but an echo of rich music, a dim shadow of clear-outlined form. It may, indeed, be that life is chaos, as you tell me that it is; that its martyrdoms are mean and its heroisms ignoble; and that it is the function of Literature to create, from the rough material of actual existence, a new world that will be more marvellous, more enduring, and more true than the world that common eyes look upon, and through which common natures seek to realise their perfection. But surely, if this new world has been made by the spirit and touch of a great artist, it will be a thing so complete and perfect that there will be nothing left for the critic to do. I quite understand now, and indeed admit most readily, that it is far more difficult to talk about a thing than to do it. But it seems to me that this sound and sensible maxim, which is really extremely soothing to one's feelings, and should be adopted as its motto by every Academy of Literature all over the world, applies only to the relations that exist between Art and Life, and not to any relations that there may be between Art and Criticism.

Gilbert. But, surely, Criticism is itself an art. And just as artistic creation implies the working of the critical faculty, and, indeed, without it cannot be said to exist at all, so Criticism is really creative in the highest sense of the word. Criticism is, in fact, both creative and independent.

Ernest. Independent?

Gilbert. Yes; independent. Criticism is no more to be judged by any low standard of imitation or resemblance than is the work of poet or sculptor. The critic occupies the same relation to the work of art that he criticises as the artist does to the visible world of form and colour, or the unseen world of passion and of thought. He does not even require for the perfection of his art the finest materials. Anything will serve his purpose. And just as out of the sordid and sentimental amours of the silly wife of a small country doctor in the squalid village of Yonville-l'Abbaye, near Rouen, Gustave Flaubert[5] was able to create a classic, and make a masterpiece of style, so from subjects of little or of no importance, such as the pictures in this year's Royal Academy, or in any year's Royal Academy, for that matter, Mr. Lewis Morris's poems, M. Ohnet's novels, or the plays of Mr. Henry Arthur Jones,[6] the true critic can, if it be his pleasure so to direct or waste his faculty of contemplation, produce work that will be flawless in beauty and instinct with

5. French novelist (1821–1880); the "amours" are treated in *Madame Bovary* (1856).

6. English dramatist (1851–1929). Morris (1833–1907), Welsh poet, essayist, and barrister. Georges Ohnet (1848–1918), French novelist and dramatist.

intellectual subtlety. Why not? Dulness is always an irresistible temptation for brilliancy, and stupidity is the permanent *Bestia Trionfans*[7] that calls wisdom from its cave. To an artist so creative as the critic, what does subject-matter signify? No more and no less than it does to the novelist and the painter. Like them, he can find his motives everywhere. Treatment is the test. There is nothing that has not in it suggestion or challenge.

Ernest. But is Criticism really a creative art?

Gilbert. Why should it not be? It works with materials, and puts them into a form that is at once new and delightful. What more can one say of poetry? Indeed, I would call criticism a creation within a creation. For just as the great artists, from Homer and Æschylus, down to Shakespeare and Keats,[8] did not go directly to life for their subject-matter, but sought for it in myth, and legend, and ancient tale, so the critic deals with materials that others have, as it were, purified for him, and to which imaginative form and colour have been already added. Nay, more, I would say that the highest Criticism, being the purest form of personal impression, is, in its way, more creative than creation, as it has least reference to any standard external to itself, and is, in fact, its own reason for existing, and, as the Greeks would put it, in itself, and to itself, an end. Certainly, it is never trammelled by any shackles of verisimilitude. No ignoble considerations of probability, that cowardly concession to the tedious repetitions of domestic or public life, affect it ever. One may appeal from fiction unto fact. But from the soul there is no appeal.

Ernest. From the soul?

Gilbert. Yes, from the soul. That is what the highest Criticism really is, the record of one's own soul. It is more fascinating than history, as it is concerned simply with oneself. It is more delightful than philosophy, as its subject is concrete and not abstract, real and not vague. It is the only civilised form of autobiography, as it deals not with the events, but with the thoughts of one's life; not with life's physical accidents of deed or circumstance, but with the spiritual moods and imaginative passions of the mind. I am always amused by the silly vanity of those writers and artists of our day who seem to imagine that the primary function of the critic is to chatter about their second-rate work. The best that one can say of most modern creative art is that it is just a little less vulgar than reality, and so the critic, with his fine sense of distinction and sure instinct of delicate refinement, will prefer to look into the silver mirror or through the woven veil, and will turn his eyes away from the chaos and clamour of actual existence, though the mirror be tarnished and the veil be torn. His sole aim is to chronicle his own impressions. It is for him that pictures are painted, books written, and marble hewn into form.

Ernest. I seem to have heard another theory of Criticism.

Gilbert. Yes: it has been said by one whose gracious memory we all revere, and the music of whose pipe once lured Proserpina from her Sicilian fields, and made those white feet stir, and not in vain, the Cumnor cowslips, that

7. Triumphant Beast (Italian); the reference is to *Spaccio della bestia Trionfante* (1584, *Expulsion of the Triumphant Beast*), a philosophical allegory by the Italian scientist and philosopher Giordano Bruno (1548–1600).

8. John Keats (1795–1821), English Romantic poet; roughly 2 centuries separated his works from those of Shakespeare, and the tragedies of Aeschylus (525–456 B.C.E.) from the epics of Homer.

the proper aim of Criticism is to see the object as in itself it really is.[9] But this is a very serious error, and takes no cognisance of Criticism's most perfect form, which is in its essence purely subjective, and seeks to reveal its own secret and not the secret of another. For the highest Criticism deals with art not as expressive, but as impressive, purely.

Ernest. But is that really so?

Gilbert. Of course it is. Who cares whether Mr. Ruskin's views on Turner[1] are sound or not? What does it matter? That mighty and majestic prose of his, so fervid and so fiery-coloured in its noble eloquence, so rich in its elaborate, symphonic music, so sure and certain, at its best, in subtle choice of word and epithet, is at least as great a work of art as any of those wonderful sunsets that bleach or rot on their corrupted canvases in England's Gallery;[2] greater, indeed, one is apt to think at times, not merely because its equal beauty is more enduring, but on account of the fuller variety of its appeal, soul speaking to soul in those long-cadenced lines, not through form and colour alone, though through these, indeed, completely and without loss, but with intellectual and emotional utterance, with lofty passion and with loftier thought, with imaginative insight, and with poetic aim; greater, I always think, even as Literature is the greater art. Who, again, cares whether Mr. Pater has put into the portrait of Monna Lisa[3] something that Lionardo never dreamed of? The painter may have been merely the slave of an archaic smile, as some have fancied, but whenever I pass into the cool galleries of the Palace of the Louvre, and stand before that strange figure "set in its marble chair in that cirque of fantastic rocks, as in some faint light under sea," I murmur to myself, "She is older than the rocks among which she sits; like the vampire, she has been dead many times, and learned the secrets of the grave; and has been a diver in deep seas, and keeps their fallen day about her; and trafficked for strange webs with Eastern merchants; and, as Leda, was the mother of Helen of Troy, and, as St. Anne, the mother of Mary; and all this has been to her but as the sound of lyres and flutes, and lives only in the delicacy with which it has moulded the changing lineaments, and tinged the eyelids and the hands." And I say to my friend, "The presence that thus so strangely rose beside the waters is expressive of what in the ways of a thousand years man had come to desire"; and he answers me, "Hers is the head upon which all 'the ends of the world are come,' and the eyelids are a little weary."

And so the picture becomes more wonderful to us than it really is, and reveals to us a secret of which, in truth, it knows nothing, and the music of the mystical prose is as sweet in our ears as was that flute-player's music that lent to the lips of La Gioconda[4] those subtle and poisonous curves. Do you ask me what Lionardo would have said had any one told him of this picture that "all the thoughts and experience of the world had etched and moulded there in that which they had of power to refine and make expressive the outward

9. Matthew Arnold defines the "aim of criticism" in "The Function of Criticism at the Present Time." In his poem "Thyrsis" (1866), Arnold says that he would supplicate Proserpina, the Roman goddess of fertility and queen of the underworld, "in vain"; for while she knows Sicily well, she does not know the "Cumnor cowslips," near Oxford.

1. The painter J. M. W. Turner (1775–1851), passionately defended by the English writer, reformer, and art critic John Ruskin (1819–1900).

2. The National Gallery, in London.

3. In the essay on Leonardo da Vinci (1452–1519) included in *Studies in the History of the Renaissance* (1873), by Walter Pater (1839–1894); Gilbert then quotes Pater.

4. The subject of Leonardo's painting (ca. 1504) was the wife of Francesco del Gioconda; thus, the *Mona Lisa* is sometimes referred to as *La Gioconda*.

form, the animalism of Greece, the lust of Rome, the reverie of the Middle Age with its spiritual ambition and imaginative loves, the return of the Pagan world, the sins of the Borgias?"[5] He would probably have answered that he had contemplated none of these things, but had concerned himself simply with certain arrangements of lines and masses, and with new and curious colour-harmonies of blue and green. And it is for this very reason that the criticism which I have quoted is criticism of the highest kind. It treats the work of art simply as a starting-point for a new creation. It does not confine itself—let us at least suppose so for the moment—to discovering the real intention of the artist and accepting that as final. And in this it is right, for the meaning of any beautiful created thing is, at least, as much in the soul of him who looks at it as it was in his soul who wrought it. Nay, it is rather the beholder who lends to the beautiful thing its myriad meanings, and makes it marvellous for us, and sets it in some new relation to the age, so that it becomes a vital portion of our lives, and a symbol of what we pray for, or perhaps of what, having prayed for, we fear that we may receive. The longer I study, Ernest, the more clearly I see that the beauty of the visible arts is, as the beauty of music, impressive primarily, and that it may be marred, and indeed often is so, by any excess of intellectual intention on the part of the artist. For when the work is finished it has, as it were, an independent life of its own, and may deliver a message far other than that which was put into its lips to say. Sometimes, when I listen to the overture of *Tannhäuser*,[6] I seem indeed to see that comely knight treading delicately on the flower-strewn grass, and to hear the voice of Venus calling to him from the caverned hill. But at other times it speaks to me of a thousand different things, of myself, it may be, and my own life, or of the lives of others whom one has loved and grown weary of loving, or of the passions that man has known, or of the passions that man has not known, and so has sought for. To-night it may fill one with that *ΕΡΩΣ ΤΩΝ ΑΔΥΝΑΤΩΝ*, that *Amour de l'Impossible*,[7] which falls like a madness on many who think they live securely and out of reach of harm, so that they sicken suddenly with the poison of unlimited desire, and, in the infinite pursuit of what they may not obtain, grow faint and swoon or stumble. To-morrow, like the music of which Aristotle and Plato tell us, the noble Dorian music[8] of the Greek, it may perform the office of a physician, and give us an anodyne against pain, and heal the spirit that is wounded, and "bring the soul into harmony with all right things." And what is true about music is true about all the arts. Beauty has as many meanings as man has moods. Beauty is the symbol of symbols. Beauty reveals everything, because it expresses nothing. When it shows us itself it shows us the whole fiery-coloured world.

Ernest. But is such work as you have talked about really criticism?

Gilbert. It is the highest Criticism, for it criticises not merely the individual work of art, but Beauty itself, and fills with wonder a form which the artist may have left void, or not understood, or understood incompletely.

5. An Italian family, influential from the 14th to the 16th century, that included religious, military, and political leaders and patrons of the arts; they were notorious for their ruthlessness and greed.

6. An 1845 opera by the German composer Richard Wagner (1813–1883), which describes the legendary relationship between the 14th-century German poet of the title and Venus, Roman goddess of love.

7. The Greek and French phrases both mean "love of the impossible."

8. Restrained and simple music associated with the Dorians, the last of the northern invaders of Greece (ca. 11th c. B.C.E.). On the Greek philosophers PLATO (ca. 427–ca. 347 B.C.E.) and ARISTOTLE (384–322 B.C.E.), see above.

Ernest. The highest Criticism, then, is more creative than creation, and the primary aim of the critic is to see the object as in itself it really is not; that is your theory, I believe?

Gilbert. Yes, that is my theory. To the critic the work of art is simply a suggestion for a new work of his own, that need not necessarily bear any obvious resemblance to the thing it criticises. The one characteristic of a beautiful form is that one can put into it whatever one wishes, and see in it whatever one chooses to see; and the Beauty, that gives to creation its universal and æsthetic element, makes the critic a creator in his turn, and whispers of a thousand different things which were not present in the mind of him who carved the statue or painted the panel or graved the gem.

It is sometimes said by those who understand neither the nature of the highest Criticism nor the charm of the highest Art, that the pictures that the critic loves most to write about are those that belong to the anecdotage of painting, and that deal with scenes taken out of literature or history. But this is not so. Indeed, pictures of this kind are far too intelligible. As a class, they rank with illustrations, and, even considered from this point of view, are failures, as they do not stir the imagination, but set definite bounds to it. For the domain of the painter is, as I suggested before, widely different from that of the poet. To the latter belongs life in its full and absolute entirety; not merely the beauty that men look at, but the beauty that men listen to also; not merely the momentary grace of form or the transient gladness of colour, but the whole sphere of feeling, the perfect cycle of thought. The painter is so far limited that it is only through the mask of the body that he can show us the mystery of the soul; only through conventional images that he can handle ideas; only through its physical equivalents that he can deal with psychology. And how inadequately does he do it then, asking us to accept the torn turban of the Moor for the noble rage of Othello, or a dotard in a storm for the wild madness of Lear! Yet it seems as if nothing could stop him. Most of our elderly English painters spend their wicked and wasted lives in poaching upon the domain of the poets, marring their motives by clumsy treatment, and striving to render, by visible form or colour, the marvel of what is invisible, the splendour of what is not seen. Their pictures are, as a natural consequence, insufferably tedious. They have degraded the visible arts into the obvious arts, and the one thing not worth looking at is the obvious. I do not say that poet and painter may not treat of the same subject. They have always done so, and will always do so. But while the poet can be pictorial or not, as he chooses, the painter must be pictorial always. For a painter is limited, not to what he sees in nature, but to what upon canvas may be seen.

And so, my dear Ernest, pictures of this kind will not really fascinate the critic. He will turn from them to such works as make him brood and dream and fancy, to works that possess the subtle quality of suggestion, and seem to tell one that even from them there is an escape into a wider world. It is sometimes said that the tragedy of an artist's life is that he cannot realise his ideal. But the true tragedy that dogs the steps of most artists is that they realise their ideal too absolutely. For, when the ideal is realised, it is robbed of its wonder and its mystery, and becomes simply a new starting point for an ideal that is other than itself. This is the reason why music is the perfect type of art. Music can never reveal its ultimate secret. This, also, is the explanation of the value of limitations in art. The sculptor gladly surrenders imitative colour, and the painter the actual dimensions of form, because by such renunciations they are able to avoid too definite a presentation of the Real, which would be mere imitation, and too definite a realisation of the Ideal, which would be too purely intellectual. It is through its very incompleteness that Art becomes complete in beauty, and so addresses itself, not to the faculty of recognition nor to the faculty of reason, but to the æsthetic sense alone, which, while accepting both reason and recognition as stages of apprehension, subordinates them both to a pure synthetic impression of the work of art as a whole, and, taking whatever alien emotional elements the work may possess, uses their very complexity as a means by which a richer unity may be added to the ultimate impression itself. You see, then, how it is that the æsthetic critic rejects those obvious modes of art that have but one message to deliver, and having delivered it becomes dumb and sterile, and seeks rather for such modes as suggest reverie and mood, and by their imaginative beauty make all interpretations true and no interpretation final. Some resemblance, no doubt, the creative work of the critic will have to the work that has stirred him to creation, but it will be such resemblance as exists, not between Nature and the mirror that the painter of landscape or figure may be supposed to hold up to her, but between Nature and the work of the decorative artist. Just as on the flowerless carpets of Persia, tulip and rose blossom indeed, and are lovely to look on, though they are not reproduced in visible shape or line; just as the pearl and purple of the sea-shell is echoed in the church of St. Mark at Venice; just as the vaulted ceiling of the wondrous chapel of Ravenna[9] is made gorgeous by the gold and green and sapphire of the peacock's tail, though the birds of Juno[1] fly not across it; so the critic reproduces the work that he criticises in a mode that is never imitative, and part of whose charm may really consist in the rejection of resemblance, and shows us in this way not merely the meaning but also the mystery of Beauty, and, by transforming each art into literature, solves once for all the problem of Art's unity.

* * *

From *Part 2*

* * *

Ernest. * * * You have told me that the highest criticism deals with art, not as expressive, but as impressive purely, and is, consequently, both creative and independent; is, in fact, an art by itself, occupying the same relation to creative work that creative work does to the visible world of form and colour, or the unseen world of passion and of thought. Well, now tell me, will not the critic be sometimes a real interpreter?

Gilbert. Yes; the critic will be an interpreter, if he chooses. He can pass from his sympathetic impression of the work of art as a whole, to an analysis or exposition of the work itself, and in this lower sphere, as I hold it to be, there are many delightful things to be said and done. Yet his object will not always be to explain the work of art. He may seek rather to deepen its mystery, to

9. City in north central Italy, known for its Roman and Byzantine buildings, tombs (including that of the poet DANTE ALIGHIERI), and mosaics.

1. That is, peacocks (associated with Juno, the queen of the Roman gods).

raise round it, and round its maker, that mist of wonder which is dear to both gods and worshippers alike. Ordinary people are "terribly at ease in Zion."[2] They propose to walk arm in arm with the poets, and have a glib, ignorant way of saying, "Why should we read what is written about Shakespeare and Milton? We can read the plays and the poems. That is enough." But an appreciation of Milton is, as the late Rector of Lincoln[3] remarked once, the reward of consummate scholarship. And he who desires to understand Shakespeare truly must understand the relations in which Shakespeare stood to the Renaissance and the Reformation, to the age of Elizabeth and the age of James;[4] he must be familiar with the history of the struggle for supremacy between the old classical forms and the new spirit of romance, between the school of Sidney, and Daniel, and Jonson, and the school of Marlowe[5] and Marlowe's greater son; he must know the materials that were at Shakespeare's disposal, and the method in which he used them, and the conditions of theatric presentation in the sixteenth and seventeenth centuries, their limitations and their opportunities for freedom, and the literary criticism of Shakespeare's day, its aims and modes and canons; he must study the English language in its progress, and blank or rhymed verse in its various developments; he must study the Greek drama, and the connection between the art of the creator of the Agamemnon[6] and the art of the creator of Macbeth; in a word, he must be able to bind Elizabethan London to the Athens of Pericles,[7] and to learn Shakespeare's true position in the history of European drama and the drama of the world. The critic will certainly be an interpreter, but he will not treat Art as a riddling Sphinx, whose shallow secret may be guessed and revealed by one whose feet are wounded and who knows not his name.[8] Rather, he will look upon Art as a goddess whose mystery it is his province to intensify, and whose majesty his privilege to make more marvellous in the eyes of men.

And here, Ernest, this strange thing happens. The critic will, indeed, be an interpreter, but he will not be an interpreter in the sense of one who simply repeats in another form a message that has been put into his lips to say. For, just as it is only by contact with the art of foreign nations that the art of a country gains that individual and separate life that we call nationality, so, by curious inversion, it is only by intensifying his own personality that the critic can interpret the personality and work of others, and the more strongly this personality enters into the interpretation the more real the interpretation becomes, the more satisfying, the more convincing, and the more true.

Ernest. I would have said that personality would have been a disturbing element.

2. In a passage in *Culture and Anarchy* (1868, 1869), Matthew Arnold quotes a remark by the Scottish-born essayist and historian Thomas Carlyle (1795–1881) on the difference between Hellenism and Hebraism: "Socrates is terribly at ease in Zion."

3. Mark Pattison (1813–1884), English scholar whose works include a book on John Milton (1879); he was elected rector of Lincoln College, Oxford University, in 1861.

4. James I (1566–1625) reigned 1603–25, after the death of Elizabeth I.

5. Christopher Marlowe (1564–1593), English poet and dramatist. SIR PHILIP SIDNEY (1554–1586), English poet, politician, and soldier. Samuel Daniel (1562–1619), English poet and historian. Ben Jonson (1572–1637), English poet and dramatist.

6. *Agamemnon* (458 B.C.E.) is the first play in the *Oresteia* trilogy of Aeschylus.

7. Great Athenian statesman, military leader, and famous patron of the arts (ca. 495–429 B.C.E.).

8. The parents of Oedipus (literally, "swollen foot") left their newborn son—his feet pierced and bound together—on a mountainside to die. He grew up to solve the Sphinx's riddle and fulfill the prophecy they had hoped to avert by his death (that he would kill his father). His story is told in the *Iliad* and in many Greek dramas, most notably Sophocles' *Oedipus Rex* (ca. 430 B.C.E.).

Gilbert. No; it is an element of revelation. If you wish to understand others you must intensify your own individualism.

Ernest. What, then, is the result?

Gilbert. I will tell you, and perhaps I can tell you best by definite example. It seems to me that, while the literary critic stands, of course, first, as having the wider range, and larger vision, and nobler material, each of the arts has a critic, as it were, assigned to it. The actor is a critic of the drama. He shows the poet's work under new conditions, and by a method special to himself. He takes the written word, and action, gesture, and voice become the media of revelation. The singer, or the player on lute and viol, is the critic of music. The etcher of a picture robs the painting of its fair colours, but shows us by the use of a new material its true colour-quality, its tones and values, and the relations of its masses, and so is, in his way, a critic of it, for the critic is he who exhibits to us a work of art in a form different from that of the work itself, and the employment of a new material is a critical as well as a creative element. Sculpture, too, has its critic, who may be either the carver of a gem, as he was in Greek days, or some painter like Mantegna,[9] who sought to reproduce on canvas the beauty of plastic line and the symphonic dignity of processional bas-relief. And in the case of all these creative critics of art it is evident that personality is an absolute essential for any real interpretation. When Rubinstein plays to us the *Sonata Appassionata*[1] of Beethoven, he gives us not merely Beethoven, but also himself, and so gives us Beethoven absolutely—Beethoven reinterpreted through a rich artistic nature, and made vivid and wonderful to us by a new and intense personality. When a great actor plays Shakespeare we have the same experience. His own individuality becomes a vital part of the interpretation. People sometimes say that actors give us their own Hamlets, and not Shakespeare's; and this fallacy—for it is a fallacy—is, I regret to say, repeated by that charming and graceful writer who has lately deserted the turmoil of literature for the peace of the House of Commons—I mean the author of *Obiter Dicta*.[2] In point of fact, there is no such thing as Shakespeare's Hamlet. If Hamlet has something of the definiteness of a work of art, he has also all the obscurity that belongs to life. There are as many Hamlets as there are melancholies.

Ernest. As many Hamlets as there are melancholies?

Gilbert. Yes: and as art springs from personality, so it is only to personality that it can be revealed, and from the meeting of the two comes right interpretative criticism.

Ernest. The critic, then, considered as the interpreter, will give no less than he receives, and lend as much as he borrows?

Gilbert. He will be always showing us the work of art in some new relation to our age. He will always be reminding us that great works of art are living things—are, in fact, the only things that live. So much, indeed, will he feel this, that I am certain that, as civilisation progresses and we become more highly organised, the elect spirits of each age, the critical and cultured spirits, will grow less and less interested in actual life, and *will seek to gain*

9. Andrea Mantegna (1431–1506), northern Italian painter and engraver, known for his mastery of perspective and compositional techniques.
1. Piano Sonata in F Minor, opus 57 (1805), by Ludwig van Beethoven (1770–1827). Anton Rubinstein (1829–1894), famous Russian pianist.
2. Augustine Birrell (1850–1933), English writer and politician; *Obiter Dicta* was published in 3 vols. (1884, 1887, 1924).

their impressions almost entirely from what Art has touched. For Life is terribly deficient in form. Its catastrophes happen in the wrong way and to the wrong people. There is a grotesque horror about its comedies, and its tragedies seem to culminate in farce. One is always wounded when one approaches it. Things last either too long, or not long enough.

* * *

Ernest. But where in this is the function of the critical spirit?

Gilbert. The culture that this transmission of racial experiences[3] makes possible can be made perfect by the critical spirit alone, and indeed may be said to be one with it. For who is the true critic but he who bears within himself the dreams, and ideas, and feelings of myriad generations, and to whom no form of thought is alien, no emotional impulse obscure? And who the true man of culture, if not he who by fine scholarship and fastidious rejection has made instinct self-conscious and intelligent, and can separate the work that has distinction from the work that has it not, and so by contact and comparison makes himself master of the secrets of style and school, and understands their meanings, and listens to their voices, and develops that spirit of disinterested curiosity which is the real root, as it is the real flower, of the intellectual life, and thus attains to intellectual clarity; and, having learned "the best that is known and thought in the world," lives it—is not fanciful to say so—with those who are the Immortals?

Yes, Ernest: the contemplative life, the life that has for its aim not *doing* but *being*, and not *being* merely, but *becoming*—that is what the critical spirit can give us. The gods live thus: either brooding over their own perfection, as Aristotle tells us, or, as Epicurus[4] fancied, watching with the calm eyes of the spectator the tragi-comedy of the world that they have made. We, too, might live like them, and set ourselves to witness with appropriate emotions the varied scenes that man and nature afford. We might make ourselves spiritual by detaching ourselves from action, and become perfect by the rejection of energy. It has often seemed to me that Browning[5] felt something of this. Shakespeare hurls Hamlet into active life, and makes him realise his mission by effort. Browning might have given us a Hamlet who would have realised his mission by thought. Incident and event were to him unreal or unmeaning. He made the soul the protagonist of life's tragedy, and looked on action as the one undramatic element of a play. To us, at any rate, the *ΒΙΟΣ ΘΕΩΡΗΤΙΚΟΣ*[6] is the true ideal. From the high tower of Thought we can look out at the world. Calm, and self-centred, and complete, the æsthetic critic contemplates life, and no arrow drawn at a venture can pierce between the joints of his harness. He at least is safe. He has discovered how to live.

Is such a mode of life immoral? Yes: all the arts are immoral, except those baser forms of sensual or didactic art that seek to excite to action of evil or of good. For action of every kind belongs to the sphere of ethics. The aim of art is simply to create a mood. Is such a mode of life unpractical? Ah! it is not so

3. That is, the experiences of a tribe, nation, or people, regarded as forming a distinct ethnic stock or group.

4. Greek philosopher (341–270 B.C.E.), whose teachings emphasize gaining happiness through self-restraint, moderation, and detachment. Aristotle: see *Metaphysics* 12.7, 9.

5. Robert Browning (1812–1889), English poet.

6. *Bios theōrētikos*: contemplative life (Greek).

easy to be unpractical as the ignorant Philistine[7] imagines. It were well for England if it were so. There is no country in the world so much in need of unpractical people as this country of ours. With us, Thought is degraded by its constant association with practice. Who that moves in the stress and turmoil of actual existence, noisy politician, or brawling social reformer, or poor, narrow-minded priest, blinded by the sufferings of that unimportant section of the community among whom he has cast his lot, can seriously claim to be able to form a disinterested intellectual judgment about any one thing? Each of the professions means a prejudice. The necessity for a career forces every one to take sides. We live in the age of the overworked, and the under-educated; the age in which people are so industrious that they become absolutely stupid. And, harsh though it may sound, I cannot help saying that such people deserve their doom. The sure way of knowing nothing about life is to try to make oneself useful.

Ernest. A charming doctrine, Gilbert.

Gilbert. I am not sure about that, but it has at least the minor merit of being true.

* * *

1890, 1891

7. A member of a biblical people who waged war against the Israelites. Matthew Arnold applies the name in *Culture and Anarchy* to the complacent materialist middle classes, indifferent or antagonistic to artistic and cultural values.

SIGMUND FREUD
1856–1939

It is hard to imagine the twentieth century without Sigmund Freud. Along with Charles Darwin (1809–1882), KARL MARX (1818–1883), and Albert Einstein (1879–1955), he helped revolutionize the modern Western conception of human life and its place in the universe. For Freud, human reason was not master in its own house but a precarious defense mechanism struggling against, and often motivated by, unconscious desires and forces. His theory and practice of psychoanalysis have changed the way people think about themselves today, whether they are aware of it or not. At the same time, psychoanalysis has been controversial from the beginning because, unlike experimental science, it cannot be adequately tested, falsified, or objectified. It aims higher than—or falls short of—objective verifiability because it is a study of the very limits of objectivity itself. The impossibility of separating psychoanalysis from the biography of its founder has been used to discredit it, but in fact Freud's writings signal a significant change in the relation between autobiography and thought. They make visible in new ways the narrative challenges involved in telling the story of a life—one's own in particular. Freud's attention to language may help explain why his writings have grown in importance for literary scholars at the same time that they are increasingly criticized for diverging from the protocols of science. Yet perhaps it is also in large part because his writings exist at the limits of *both* literature and science that Freud continues to fascinate us.

Freud was born in Moravia (in what is now the Czech Republic), the first of seven children, to poor Jewish parents. His young mother, Amalia, was his father Jacob's third wife. The Freuds moved to Vienna in 1860, where Sigmund obtained all his education (with the exception of a few months in Paris). Although psychoanalysis today is associated with the "talking cure" and the theory of infantile sexuality, Freud began his career as a clinical neurologist, obtaining his medical degree in 1881. He entered the University of Vienna in 1873, at a time when Jews, who had moved to liberal Vienna in sizable numbers, were already being scapegoated for Austria's economic problems. Freud, in his *Autobiographical Study* (1925), attributed his independence of mind to his position just outside the "compact majority" (Henrik Ibsen's phrase) of German gentile culture, which he nevertheless also shared. When Nazi Germany annexed Austria in 1938, Freud left Vienna reluctantly and under duress. In his lifetime, social liberalism had given way to the most virulent anti-Semitism—a sad confirmation of his warning against taking any notion of the progress of civilization for granted.

While working to obtain his medical degree, Freud was distracted by his broad interests in research. Among other subjects, he became fascinated by the account given by the respected physician Josef Breuer of the treatment of a particularly intelligent hysterical patient. "Anna O." invented the term "talking cure"; she is often considered the first patient of psychoanalysis, although Freud himself never treated her. Fifteen years later, Freud and Breuer would write *Studies on Hysteria* (1895) about this and later cases. In the meantime Freud met Martha Bernays, the woman he hoped would become his wife, and went to Paris. Too poor to marry, he progressed in his profession by getting a small grant to work at the famous Salpêtrière mental hospital under the supervision of the medical showman and great specialist in hysteria Jean-Martin Charcot. In 1886 he returned to Vienna, opened his medical practice, and married Martha; they had six children (three girls and three boys). From 1891 onward, the Freuds lived at Berggasse 19, where Sigmund set up his famous consulting room.

In the years leading up to his groundbreaking *Interpretation of Dreams* (1900), Freud began a formative and intellectually wide-ranging correspondence with Wilhelm Fliess, an ear, nose, and throat specialist from Berlin. In his practice, Freud gradually abandoned the hypnotic treatments for hysteria recommended by Charcot, substituting instead a form of dialogue between patient and doctor. At first convinced that many of his patients had suffered sexual abuse (or "seduction") by their fathers in childhood, he later came to realize that some of his patients' tales of sexual events were fantasies. The death in 1896 of Freud's own father perhaps increased his unwillingness to believe in paternal guilt. What he called the "abandonment of the seduction theory" has become controversial in recent decades (largely because of Jeffrey Moussaieff Masson's 1984 book, *The Assault on Truth: Freud's Suppression of the Seduction Theory*), criticized as an abandonment of the realities of childhood sexual abuse. But the shift was not first and foremost a denial of the reality of incest; Freud saw in fantasies of incest a psychic reality, and an infantile sexuality, that had to be taken seriously in itself. In his move from realities of fact to realities of fantasy, however, Freud changed the sex of the representative subject: in his new theory of unconscious desire (the "Oedipus complex"), he substituted the desiring son for the abused daughter, the desirable mother for the guilty father. The father, in his account, was no longer a lawbreaker but a lawgiver: the enforcer of the law prohibiting incest between the son and the mother.

In order to gather evidence of the existence of unconscious forces at work in everyday life, Freud turned to psychological phenomena that were at once recognized and disregarded. His first three books—*The Interpretation of Dreams, The Psychopathology of Everyday Life* (published in a journal in 1901 and as a book in 1904), and *Jokes and Their Relation to the Unconscious* (1905)—lay out the analytical strategies that would inform the better-known *Three Essays in the Theory of*

Sexuality (1905). His theory would have been impossible without the meticulous study of the discredited forms of knowledge revealed by dreams, slips of the tongue, memory lapses, and jokes.

Freud continued seeing patients and published several extensive and now famous case studies—*Fragment of an Analysis of a Case of Hysteria* (better known as "Dora," 1905), "Analysis of a Phobia in a Five-Year-Old Boy" ("Little Hans," 1909), "Notes Upon a Case of Obsessional Neurosis" ("Rat Man," 1909), "Psycho-Analytic Notes on an Autobiographical Account of a Case of Paranoia" ("Schreber," 1911), and *From the History of an Infantile Neurosis* ("Wolf Man," written 1914 and published 1918). Each attempts to come to terms with a difficult psychoanalytic but also *narrative* challenge: for example, Dora left treatment before Freud was finished with her, and his later footnotes allude to oversights in his understanding; Wolf Man's childhood neurosis could be analyzed only through the screen of adult constructions; and Schreber was analyzed not as Freud's patient but as the author of an autobiography. Freud's case histories offer a fascinating hybrid of certainty, doubt, and inner debate.

In addition to his research and his practice, Freud, at the suggestion of a disciple, founded the Psychological Wednesday Society (later transformed into the Vienna Psychoanalytic Society) in 1902. He traveled to the United States in 1909 to lecture and receive an honorary degree from Clark University in Worcester, Massachusetts, accompanied by his younger colleagues Carl G. Jung and Sandor Ferenczi (his lectures were subsequently published as *Five Lectures on Psychoanalysis*, 1910). The tensions—theoretical, personal, and institutional—between Freud and Jung were already growing; by the end of 1912, the two had essentially stopped speaking to each other. Freud took his revenge on his wayward disciples in his polemical "History of the Psycho-Analytic Movement" (1914). He also published a new series of lectures and a number of papers on psychoanalytic technique.

When World War I began Freud's three sons volunteered for the army, but he grew more and more critical of war as a solution to human problems. (Later, at the request of the League of Nations, Freud would collaborate with Albert Einstein in writing *Why War?* [1933].) The war deeply affected his thought, already in a new phase with the publication of his celebrated essay on narcissism in 1914. Traumatic neuroses seemed to put in question the dominance in psychic life of the "pleasure principle" that he had posited as the motive force of dreams. Even children's games sometimes seemed to give greater weight to the process of repetition itself than to the pleasurable thing repeated. It was at this time that Freud wrote his essay "The 'Uncanny'" (1919) and the longer *Beyond the Pleasure Principle* (1920). A sense of strangeness, of genuinely enigmatic forces, pervades his theory of the "death instinct" and the "repetition compulsion." But perhaps this strangeness was also a way of reconnecting with the strangeness of his original discoveries, which had grown quite familiar. The theoretical gains from this period are formulated in *The Ego and the Id* (1923). (The famous Latin names for the almost allegorical parts of the self—ego, id, superego—were bestowed by translators; Freud himself used German terms meaning "I," "it," and "over-I.")

In the 1920s Freud wrote about larger cultural forces and structures (*Group Psychology and the Analysis of the Ego*, 1921; *The Future of an Illusion*, 1927; and *Civilization and Its Discontents*, 1929), provided major reformulations of his theory, and turned his attention to the problem of sexual difference. His paper "Some Psychical Consequences of the Anatomical Distinction between the Sexes" (1925) began to explore the question of "castration" in a new way. When children observe that some people have penises and others do not, he asserted, they assume that everyone must at first have had one, and that in some people it had been cut off. This encounter with the fact of difference is more satisfying to the little boy than to the little girl. But the "psychic consequences" are far-reaching: the boy takes seriously the father's threat of castration as the punishment for incest, thus experiencing "castration anxiety," while the girl tries to deal with her "inferiority," thus feeling "penis envy." In later essays—especially "Female Sexuality" (1931) and "Femininity" (1932)—Freud attempted to make sense of the desires his theory allotted to women. Feminists have treated his theories with ambivalence: on the one hand, he had the merit of describing human sexuality as a *question*, not a *given*; on the other hand, his phrase "anatomy is destiny" seems in the final analysis to uphold the sexual certainties he himself questioned.

The lectures Freud wrote that include "Femininity" were never meant to be delivered; a series of operations for mouth cancer (beginning in 1923) had left him unable to perform in public. The political situation was also worrisome: Adolf Hitler had been appointed chancellor of Germany, and the Nazi Party was in control. Freud's books were among those burned in Berlin. His last book, *Moses and Monotheism*, was not completed until his own "exodus" to England in 1938. In London in 1939, his cancer worsening, Freud officially closed his practice; and, just after the Germans invaded Poland and after France and Britain declared war on Germany, Freud asked his physician to give him a lethal dose of morphine. He died in September of that year.

How did Freud practice interpretation, then, and how did his theory transform it? Although the details of each individual dream are particular to the dreamer, there are, says Freud, some dreams that occur widely and point to the existence of universal desires. Incest and its prohibition—the universal break between nature and culture, according to anthropologists—form the core of Freud's theory of unconscious desire. In our first selection from *The Interpretation of Dreams*, he turns to the same literary text as ARISTOTLE for a version of the fundamental human plot: Sophocles' *Oedipus Rex*. Warned by an oracle that he will kill his father and marry his mother, Oedipus leaves home in order to escape his fate, only to kill a man and marry a woman who turn out to be the very biological parents who had abandoned him as an infant in order to thwart the same oracle. Literature thus exists for Freud as a form of evidence: the play's centuries-long hold over the attention of viewers must correspond to its depiction of something universally fascinating and repressed. The truth told by the oracle corresponds to unconscious desire, fulfilling itself despite—or perhaps because of—every conscious effort to escape it. The plot of Sophocles' play also furnishes a parallel to the plot of an analysis: a patient's resistance to unconscious knowledge is like Oedipus's reluctance to learn his true identity. Freud goes on to discuss the relation between *Oedipus Rex* and Shakespeare's *Hamlet*—both in terms of the incest taboo. In answer to the question "Why does Hamlet delay his revenge for his father's death?" Freud replies, "Because his uncle has only carried out a murder that he himself wanted to accomplish." In a few short pages, Freud thus revolutionized the reading of two major canonical texts of Western culture and placed the world of the imagination at the center of human subjectivity.

Freud's attention to new modes of meaning has been immensely suggestive for literary studies. While the relation between literature and dreams has often been noted, as in the ancient work of Macrobius (b. ca. 360 C.E.), Freud pursues the connection beyond the realm of general symbolism to lay out a kind of rhetoric of everyday dreams. In our second selection, on the dream-work, he writes that dreams are not nonsensical but meaningful. They are composites made out of the residues of individual lives chosen by the unconscious to represent the fulfilment of a wish: no simple "key" can decode them. Only the dreamer can provide a set of associations to illuminate the "dream-thoughts" behind the dream. Beneath the composite surface, which functions like a puzzle, lies the wish, the puzzle's solution. The dream-thoughts function like a "latent content" behind the "manifest content" of the dream.

Distortion and disguise fill dreams—or literary texts—because the unconscious wish is in some way unacceptable and must evade censorship. Dreams have three main sources of unavoidable distortion, he argues: condensation, displacement, and the needs of representation. These unconscious "primary processes" are also subject to "secondary revision," the editing to which a dream is subject if the dreamer tries to remember it on awakening. Freud's description of the four rhetorical operations ("distortions") performed by dreams has been productively extended to literary texts: while the role of secondary revision there is stronger and more complex, literary texts may provide access to forces that are not directly accessible in other ways.

Freud often uses literary texts to illustrate or confirm his theory. His reading of a 1903 novella by Wilhelm Jensen (*Delusion and Dream in Wilhelm Jensen's "Gradiva,"* 1907) aims to ratify his theory of dreams; "Creative Writers and Daydreaming" (1908) expands on his description of fantasy life; in "The Theme of the Three Caskets" (1913), he turns again to Shakespeare; and in numerous other short essays and notes Freud focuses directly on literature or art. But some of the most explicit literary demonstrations function as "secondary revisions" of the theory itself, eliding the role of literature in *forming* central concepts (the Oedipus complex, narcissism, etc.). For Freud, it is always as if a bourgeois drama is playing on the conscious stage of the psyche, while a Greek tragedy is going on somewhere else.

Freud's celebrated essay "The 'Uncanny,'" our second selection, offers both a literary application and a new theoretical direction. It contains an extensive analysis of E. T. A. Hoffmann's short story "The Sandman" (1816), in which a young man, Nathaniel, traumatized by the mysterious death of his father, falls in love with a wooden doll, Olympia, in preference to his flesh-and-blood sweetheart. Freud argues that what is uncanny about the story is related not to intellectual uncertainty about whether the doll is alive (as an article by Ernst Jentsch had speculated), but to anxiety about the cause of Nathaniel's father's death. When Nathaniel encounters Coppola, an optician, he thinks he recognizes Coppelius, a lawyer, whom he believes to have caused his father's death and who is conflated in his mind with the Sandman—a storybook figure who takes the eyes of little children who won't go to bed. These threats to the eyes are connected in Freud's mind to the castration complex (Oedipus had blinded himself on learning that he had fulfilled the prophecy). The uncanny return of these figures (the Sandman, Coppelius, Coppola) is also related to Freud's new sense of the "repetition compulsion." Dolls and inanimate objects, which for Freud are not uncanny in the story, nevertheless return to haunt the essay's discussion of "the omnipotence of thoughts" and of the supposedly surmounted childhood belief in animism.

Freud begins his discussion with the characteristics of the word *uncanny*, extensively documented through citations from a dictionary. The German *unheimlich* (unhomelike, uncanny) turns out to share a meaning with its apparent opposite. *Heimlich* (homey, familiar) can also mean "concealed, secret," and thus the opposite of the familiar and open. This process of estrangement of the familiar (of the "home") is exactly the same as the process of repression. The fear of being buried alive, for example, is a distorted desire to return to the mother's womb—the "home" of all humanity. The German term gives a clue to a process that psychoanalysis tries to understand more generally. Freud expresses astonishment that other languages lack the equivalent of what in German is such a handy word. But if all languages had the same process in the same place, that process would become a theme, a topic, and thus belong to conscious, rather than unconscious, knowledge.

The essay also addresses "aesthetics" more generally, as its first sentence announces. Indeed, it investigates what analyses of the "beautiful" and the "sublime" leave out: the disturbing, the unsettling, the uncomfortable. Freud's essay itself is far from beautiful: it wanders from topic to topic, it quotes others at great length, it places major points in footnotes, and, in general, it seems sewn together from mismatched parts. Hence, we have edited an already poorly sutured text. Yet "The 'Uncanny'" offers the reader an opportunity to follow the *process*, and not just the *result*, of Freud's thinking. Indeed, that the essay lacks "organic" form, so that readers tend to get lost in it, contributes powerfully to its own uncanny effect. In recent years, partly as a result of Freud's essay, critics have devoted increasing attention to the Gothic in literature and to elements Freud associates with the uncanny—unexpected doubles, severed limbs, bodies buried alive, the return of the dead, magical thinking. Freud's reading of Hoffmann's story allows him to touch many theoretical bases that he, unlike many others, feels comfortable with—unacceptable authorial desires, castration anxieties, homosexual fantasies. But Freud's essay itself also makes readable the persistence of questions he dismisses, and it vividly reveals, in its wandering way, his fascination with what is escaping his grasp.

Freud's short essay titled "Fetishism" (1927), our final selection, builds on his analysis of the consequences of sexual difference. Certain men, he claims, cannot accept the evidence that the woman (the mother) doesn't have a penis. In order to fall in love with women and not become homosexual, they choose as a substitute some object that will continue to support the sexual interest they originally had in the missing maternal penis. The logic of fetishism thus involves both perceiving and denying the evidence of maternal "castration." In a very different way, the same logic of denial and displacement underlies Karl Marx's theory of "the fetishism of the commodity" (*Capital*, vol. 1, 1867; see above). There, the commodity itself appears to contain the value that is really produced by the processes of labor invisible behind it. Here, the substitute (foot, velvet, hair, etc.) appears to function like a sexual organ. In both cases there is a "gleam" around the fetish that attracts desire (sexual or commercial), as if the fetish actually contained the values that it represents.

Freud's analyses have had a fundamental impact on what we now understand as literary theory, influencing virtually every twentieth-century critic. On the one hand, Freud's radical new view of subjectivity has deeply affected the analysis of characters, authors, and readers, enabling a new understanding of split, hidden, or contradictory desires and intentions. On the other hand, for Freud literature is not just an illustration but also a source and authority for understanding those desires and intentions in the first place.

Perhaps more profoundly, Freud changed the nature of attentiveness itself. It was in listening to patients differently that Freud discovered the unconscious—a force of otherness as powerful as, but in no way equivalent to, a god. Inside every person, he said, there was *something* transmitting scrambled messages in a cryptic language, trying to break through the conscious surface of life. The "other" was in ourselves—indeed, it *was* ourselves. Despite the limitations of Freud's middle-class Viennese patriarchal assumptions, his conception of a human subjectivity fundamentally at odds with itself opened up possibilities he never dreamed of. Each person's life was documented in more than one way: official personal history (conscious remembrance and self-image) and unofficial personal history (the record of changes, traumas, desires, anxieties, and associations that might never have been conscious). Unconscious history contained impossible or forbidden wishes, repressed from the official record or simply outgrown—wishes that remained active in the unconscious and sought expression in dreams, mistakes, jokes, myths, and other discredited or discounted forms of communication. Psychoanalysis is the name for the theory and practice of their interpretation, and literary theory continues to derive inspiration from the psychoanalytic engagement with the most canonical as well as the most uncanonical of texts.

***The Interpretation of Dreams* Keywords:** Drama, Interpretation Theory, Narrative Theory, Poetry, Psychoanalysis, Rhetoric, Sexuality
"The 'Uncanny'" Keywords: Aesthetics, Language, Psychoanalysis, Representation
"Fetishism" Keywords: The Body, Gender, Identity, Psychoanalysis, Sexuality, Subjectivity

From The Interpretation of Dreams[1]

From *Chapter V. The Material and Sources of Dreams*

* * *

[THE OEDIPUS COMPLEX]

In my experience, which is already extensive, the chief part in the mental lives of all children who later become psychoneurotics is played by their parents. Being in love with the one parent and hating the other are among the essential constituents of the stock of psychical impulses which is formed at that time and which is of such importance in determining the symptoms of the later neurosis. It is not my belief, however, that psychoneurotics differ sharply in this respect from other human beings who remain normal—that they are able, that is, to create something absolutely new and peculiar to themselves. It is far more probable—and this is confirmed by occasional observations on normal children—that they are only distinguished by exhibiting on a magnified scale feelings of love and hatred to their parents which occur less obviously and less intensely in the minds of most children.

This discovery is confirmed by a legend that has come down to us from classical antiquity: a legend whose profound and universal power to move can only be understood if the hypothesis I have put forward in regard to the psychology of children has an equally universal validity. What I have in mind is the legend of King Oedipus and Sophocles'[2] drama which bears his name.

Oedipus, son of Laïus, King of Thebes, and of Jocasta, was exposed as an infant because an oracle had warned Laïus that the still unborn child would be his father's murderer. The child was rescued, and grew up as a prince in an alien court, until, in doubts as to his origin, he too questioned the oracle and was warned to avoid his home since he was destined to murder his father and take his mother in marriage. On the road leading away from what he believed was his home, he met King Laïus and slew him in a sudden quarrel. He came next to Thebes and solved the riddle set him by the Sphinx[3] who barred his way. Out of gratitude the Thebans made him their king and gave him Jocasta's hand in marriage. He reigned long in peace and honour, and she who, unknown to him, was his mother bore him two sons and two daughters. Then at last a plague broke out and the Thebans made enquiry once more of the oracle. It is at this point that Sophocles' tragedy opens. The messengers bring back the reply that the plague will cease when the murderer of Laïus has been driven from the land.

> But he, where is he? Where shall now be read
> The fading record of this ancient guilt?[4]

The action of the play consists in nothing other than the process of revealing, with cunning delays and ever-mounting excitement—a process that can

1. Translated by James Strachey. This standard edition incorporates later revisions made by Freud.
2. Greek tragic dramatist (ca. 496–406 B.C.E.), author of *Oedipus Rex* (ca. 430).
3. A monster with a woman's face, lion's body, and bird's wings who killed travelers who could not answer her riddle; when Oedipus solved it, she killed herself.
4. Lewis Campbell's translation (1883), lines 108–9 [translator's note].

be likened to the work of a psychoanalysis—that Oedipus himself is the murderer of Laïus, but further that he is the son of the murdered man and of Jocasta. Appalled at the abomination which he has unwittingly perpetrated, Oedipus blinds himself and forsakes his home. The oracle has been fulfilled.

Oedipus Rex is what is known as a tragedy of destiny. Its tragic effect is said to lie in the contrast between the supreme will of the gods and the vain attempts of mankind to escape the evil that threatens them. The lesson which, it is said, the deeply moved spectator should learn from the tragedy is submission to the divine will and realization of his own impotence. Modern dramatists have accordingly tried to achieve a similar tragic effect by weaving the same contrast into a plot invented by themselves. But the spectators have looked on unmoved while a curse or an oracle was fulfilled in spite of all the efforts of some innocent man: later tragedies of destiny have failed in their effect.

If *Oedipus Rex* moves a modern audience no less than it did the contemporary Greek one, the explanation can only be that its effect does not lie in the contrast between destiny and human will, but is to be looked for in the particular nature of the material on which that contrast is exemplified. There must be something which makes a voice within us ready to recognize the compelling force of destiny in the *Oedipus*, while we can dismiss as merely arbitrary such dispositions as are laid down in [Grillparzer's] *Die Ahnfrau*[5] or other modern tragedies of destiny. And a factor of this kind is in fact involved in the story of King Oedipus. His destiny moves us only because it might have been ours—because the oracle laid the same curse upon us before our birth as upon him. It is the fate of all of us, perhaps, to direct our first sexual impulse towards our mother and our first hatred and our first murderous wish against our father. Our dreams convince us that that is so. King Oedipus, who slew his father Laïus and married his mother Jocasta, merely shows us the fulfilment of our own childhood wishes. But, more fortunate than he, we have meanwhile succeeded, in so far as we have not become psychoneurotics, in detaching our sexual impulses from our mothers and in forgetting our jealousy of our fathers. Here is one in whom these primaeval wishes of our childhood have been fulfilled, and we shrink back from him with the whole force of the repression by which those wishes have since that time been held down within us. While the poet, as he unravels the past, brings to light the guilt of Oedipus, he is at the same time compelling us to recognize our own inner minds, in which those same impulses, though suppressed, are still to be found. The contrast with which the closing Chorus leaves us confronted—

> . . . Fix on Oedipus your eyes,
> Who resolved the dark enigma, noblest champion and most wise.
> Like a star his envied fortune mounted beaming far and wide:
> Now he sinks in seas of anguish, whelmed beneath a raging tide . . .[6]

—strikes as a warning at ourselves and our pride, at us who since our childhood have grown so wise and so mighty in our own eyes. Like Oedipus, we

5. *The Ancestress* (1817), by the Austrian dramatist Franz Grillparzer. The play's protagonist unknowingly falls in love with his sister and kills his father.

6. Campbell's translation, lines 1524–27 [translator's note].

live in ignorance of these wishes, repugnant to morality, which have been forced upon us by Nature, and after their revelation we may all of us well seek to close our eyes to the scenes of our childhood.[7]

There is an unmistakable indication in the text of Sophocles' tragedy itself that the legend of Oedipus sprang from some primaeval dream-material which had as its content the distressing disturbance of a child's relation to his parents owing to the first stirrings of sexuality. At a point when Oedipus, though he is not yet enlightened, has begun to feel troubled by his recollection of the oracle, Jocasta consoles him by referring to a dream which many people dream, though, as she thinks, it has no meaning:

Many a man ere now in dreams hath lain
With her who bare him. He hath least annoy
Who with such omens troubleth not his mind.[8]

To-day, just as then, many men dream of having sexual relations with their mothers, and speak of the fact with indignation and astonishment. It is clearly the key to the tragedy and the complement to the dream of the dreamer's father being dead. The story of Oedipus is the reaction of the imagination to these two typical dreams. And just as these dreams, when dreamt by adults, are accompanied by feelings of repulsion, so too the legend must include horror and self-punishment. Its further modification originates once again in a misconceived secondary revision of the material, which has sought to exploit it for theological purposes. (Cf. the dream-material in dreams of exhibiting [discussed earlier].) The attempt to harmonize divine omnipotence with human responsibility must naturally fail in connection with this subject-matter just as with any other.

Another of the great creations of tragic poetry, Shakespeare's *Hamlet*, has its roots in the same soil as *Oedipus Rex*. But the changed treatment of the same material reveals the whole difference in the mental life of these two widely separated epochs of civilization: the secular advance of repression in the emotional life of mankind. In the *Oedipus* the child's wishful phantasy that underlies it is brought into the open and realized as it would be in a dream. In *Hamlet* it remains repressed; and—just as in the case of a neurosis—we only learn of its existence from its inhibiting consequences. Strangely enough, the overwhelming effect produced by the more modern

7. [*Footnote added* 1914:] None of the findings of psycho-analytic research has provoked such embittered denials, such fierce opposition—or such amusing contortions—on the part of critics as this indication of the childhood impulses towards incest which persist in the unconscious. An attempt has even been made recently to make out, in the face of all experience, that the incest should only be taken as "symbolic."—Ferenczi ("The Symbolic Representation of the Pleasure and Reality Principles in the Oedipus Myth," 1912) has proposed an ingenious "over-interpretation" of the Oedipus myth, based on a passage in one of Schopenhauer's letters.—[*Added* 1919:] Later studies have shown that the "Oedipus complex," which was touched upon for the first time in the above paragraphs in the *Interpretation of Dreams*, throws a light of undreamt-of importance on the history of the human race and the evolution of religion and morality. (See my *Totem and Taboo*, 1912–13 [Essay IV].) [Freud's note].—[Actually the gist of this discussion of the Oedipus complex and of the *Oedipus Rex*, as well as of what follows on the subject of *Hamlet*, had already been put forward by Freud in a letter to Fliess as early as October 15, 1897. A still earlier hint at the discovery of the Oedipus complex was included in a letter of May 31, 1897.—The actual term "Oedipus complex" seems to have been first used by Freud in his published writings in the first of his "Contributions to the Psychology of Love" (1910)—translator's note.] Some of Freud's later footnotes are omitted.

8. Campbell's translation, lines 982–84 [translator's note].

tragedy has turned out to be compatible with the fact that people have remained completely in the dark as to the hero's character. The play is built up on Hamlet's hesitations over fulfilling the task of revenge that is assigned to him; but its text offers no reasons or motives for these hesitations and an immense variety of attempts at interpreting them have failed to produce a result. According to the view which was originated by Goethe[9] and is still the prevailing one to-day, Hamlet represents the type of man whose power of direct action is paralysed by an excessive development of his intellect. (He is 'sicklied o'er with the pale cast of thought'.)[1] According to another view, the dramatist has tried to portray a pathologically irresolute character which might be classed as neurasthenic. The plot of the drama shows us, however, that Hamlet is far from being represented as a person incapable of taking any action. We see him doing so on two occasions: first in a sudden outburst of temper, when he runs his sword through the eavesdropper behind the arras, and secondly in a premeditated and even crafty fashion, when, with all the callousness of a Renaissance prince, he sends the two courtiers to the death that had been planned for himself. What is it, then, that inhibits him in fulfilling the task set him by his father's ghost? The answer, once again, is that it is the peculiar nature of the task. Hamlet is able to do anything—except take vengeance on the man who did away with his father and took that father's place with his mother, the man who shows him the repressed wishes of his own childhood realized. Thus the loathing which should drive him on to revenge is replaced in him by self-reproaches, by scruples of conscience, which remind him that he himself is literally no better than the sinner whom he is to punish. Here I have translated into conscious terms what was bound to remain unconscious in Hamlet's mind; and if anyone is inclined to call him a hysteric, I can only accept the fact as one that is implied by my interpretation. The distaste for sexuality expressed by Hamlet in his conversation with Ophelia fits in very well with this: the same distaste which was destined to take possession of the poet's mind more and more during the years that followed, and which reached its extreme expression in *Timon of Athens*. For it can of course only be the poet's own mind which confronts us in Hamlet. I observe in a book on Shakespeare by Georg Brandes[2] (1896) a statement that *Hamlet* was written immediately after the death of Shakespeare's father (in 1601), that is, under the immediate impact of his bereavement and, as we may well assume, while his childhood feelings about his father had been freshly revived. It is known, too, that Shakespeare's own son who died at an early age bore the name of 'Hamnet', which is identical with 'Hamlet'. Just as *Hamlet* deals with the relation of a son to his parents, so *Macbeth* (written at approximately the same period) is concerned with the subject of childlessness. But just as all neurotic symptoms, and, for that matter, dreams, are capable of being 'over-interpreted' and indeed need to be, if they are to be fully understood, so all genuinely creative writings are the product of more than a single motive and more than a single impulse in the poet's mind, and are open to more than a single interpretation. In

9. Johann Wolfgang von Goethe (1749–1832), German poet, playwright, and novelist.
1. *Hamlet* (ca. 1600), 3.1.87.
2. Danish critic and scholar (1842–1927); his *William Shakespeare* (1895–96) was translated into German in 1896.

what I have written I have only attempted to interpret the deepest layer of impulses in the mind of the creative writer.[3]

* * *

From *Chapter VI. The Dream-Work*

Every attempt that has hitherto been made to solve the problem of dreams has dealt directly with their *manifest* content as it is presented in our memory. All such attempts have endeavoured to arrive at an interpretation of dreams from their manifest content or (if no interpretation was attempted) to form a judgement as to their nature on the basis of that same manifest content. We are alone in taking something else into account. We have introduced a new class of psychical material between the manifest content of dreams and the conclusions of our enquiry: namely, their *latent* content, or (as we say) the 'dream-thoughts', arrived at by means of our procedure. It is from these dream-thoughts and not from a dream's manifest content that we disentangle its meaning. We are thus presented with a new task which had no previous existence: the task, that is, of investigating the relations between the manifest content of dreams and the latent dream-thoughts, and of tracing out the processes by which the latter have been changed into the former.

The dream-thoughts and the dream-content are presented to us like two versions of the same subject-matter in two different languages. Or, more properly, the dream-content seems like a transcript of the dream-thoughts into another mode of expression, whose characters and syntactic laws it is our business to discover by comparing the original and the translation. The dream-thoughts are immediately comprehensible, as soon as we have learnt them. The dream-content, on the other hand, is expressed as it were in a pictographic script, the characters of which have to be transposed individually into the language of the dream-thoughts. If we attempted to read these characters according to their pictorial value instead of according to their symbolic relation, we should clearly be led into error. Suppose I have a picture-puzzle, a rebus, in front of me. It depicts a house with a boat on its roof, a single letter of the alphabet, the figure of a running man whose head has been conjured away, and so on. Now I might be misled into raising objections and declaring that the picture as a whole and its component parts are nonsensical. A boat has no business to be on the roof of a house, and a headless man cannot run. Moreover, the man is bigger than the house; and if the whole picture is intended to represent a landscape, letters of the alphabet are out of place in it since such objects do not occur in nature. But obviously we can only form a proper judgement of the rebus if we put aside criticisms such as these of the whole composition and its parts and if, instead, we try to replace each separate element by a syllable or word that can be represented by that element in some way or other. The words which are put together in this way are no longer nonsensical but may form a poetical phrase of the greatest beauty and significance. A dream is a picture-puzzle of this sort and

3. [*Footnote added* 1919:] The above indications of a psycho-analytic explanation of *Hamlet* have since been amplified by Ernest Jones and defended against the alternative views put forward in the literature of the subject. (See Jones, *Hamlet and Oedipus*, 1910 [and, in a completer form, 1949].)—[*Added* 1930:] Incidentally, I have in the meantime ceased to believe that the author of Shakespeare's works was the man from Stratford [Freud's note].

our predecessors in the field of dream-interpretation have made the mistake of treating the rebus as a pictorial composition: and as such it has seemed to them nonsensical and worthless.

(A). THE WORK OF CONDENSATION

The first thing that becomes clear to anyone who compares the dream-content with the dream-thoughts is that a work of *condensation* on a large scale has been carried out. Dreams are brief, meagre and laconic in comparison with the range and wealth of the dream-thoughts. If a dream is written out it may perhaps fill half a page. The analysis setting out the dream-thoughts underlying it may occupy six, eight or a dozen times as much space. This relation varies with different dreams; but so far as my experience goes its direction never varies. As a rule one underestimates the amount of compression that has taken place, since one is inclined to regard the dream-thoughts that have been brought to light as the complete material, whereas if the work of interpretation is carried further it may reveal still more thoughts concealed behind the dream. I have already had occasion to point out that it is in fact never possible to be sure that a dream has been completely interpreted. Even if the solution seems satisfactory and without gaps, the possibility always remains that the dream may have yet another meaning. Strictly speaking, then, it is impossible to determine the amount of condensation.

* * *

(B). THE WORK OF DISPLACEMENT

* * *

Among the thoughts that analysis brings to light are many which are relatively remote from the kernel of the dream and which look like artificial interpolations made for some particular purpose. That purpose is easy to divine. It is precisely *they* that constitute a connection, often a forced and far-fetched one, between the dream-content and the dream-thoughts; and if these elements were weeded out of the analysis the result would often be that the component parts of the dream-content would be left not only without overdetermination[4] but without any satisfactory determination at all. We shall be led to conclude that the multiple determination which decides what shall be included in a dream is not always a primary factor in dream-construction but is often the secondary product of a psychical force which is still unknown to us. Nevertheless multiple determination must be of importance in choosing what particular elements shall enter a dream, since we can see that a considerable expenditure of effort is used to bring it about in cases where it does not arise from the dream-material unassisted.

It thus seems plausible to suppose that in the dream-work a psychical force is operating which on the one hand strips the elements which have a high psychical value of their intensity, and on the other hand, *by means of overdetermination*, creates from elements of low psychical value new values, which afterwards find their way into the dream-content. If that is so, *a trans-*

4. That is, multiple causal factors (a model for causality implying a network rather than the simply linear).

ference[5] *and displacement of psychical intensities* occurs in the process of dream-formation, and it is as a result of these that the difference between the text of the dream-content and that of the dream-thoughts comes about. The process which we are here presuming is nothing less than the essential portion of the dream-work; and it deserves to be described as 'dream-displacement'. Dream-displacement and dream-condensation are the two governing factors to whose activity we may in essence ascribe the form assumed by dreams.

Nor do I think we shall have any difficulty in recognizing the psychical force which manifests itself in the facts of dream-displacement. The consequence of the displacement is that the dream-content no longer resembles the core of the dream-thoughts and that the dream gives no more than a distortion of the dream-wish which exists in the unconscious. But we are already familiar with dream-distortion. We traced it back to the censorship which is exercised by one psychical agency in the mind over another. Dream-displacement is one of the chief methods by which that distortion is achieved. *Is fecit cui profuit.*[6] We may assume, then, that dream-displacement comes about through the influence of the same censorship—that is, the censorship of endopsychic defence.

The question of the interplay of these factors—of displacement, condensation and overdetermination—in the construction of dreams, and the question which is a dominant factor and which a subordinate one—all of this we shall leave aside for later investigation. But we can state provisionally a second condition which must be satisfied by those elements of the dream-thoughts which make their way into the dream: *they must escape the censorship imposed by resistance.* And henceforward in interpreting dreams we shall take dream-displacement into account as an undeniable fact.

(C). THE MEANS OF REPRESENTATION IN DREAMS

In the process of transforming the latent thoughts into the manifest content of a dream we have found two factors at work: dream-condensation and dream-displacement. As we continue our investigation we shall, in addition to these, come across two further determinants which exercise an undoubted influence on the choice of the material which is to find access to the dream.

* * *

We are here interested only in the essential dream-thoughts. These usually emerge as a complex of thoughts and memories of the most intricate possible structure, with all the attributes of the trains of thought familiar to us in waking life. They are not infrequently trains of thought starting out from more than one centre, though having points of contact. Each train of thought is almost invariably accompanied by its contradictory counterpart, linked with it by antithetical association.

5. A term that in psychoanalysis later comes to signify a displacement of psychical intensities from a person in the past to a person in the present (especially to the analyst, in the course of a treatment).

6. The old legal tag: "He did the deed who gained by it" [(Latin); translator's note].

The different portions of this complicated structure stand, of course, in the most manifold logical relations to one another. They can represent foreground and background, digressions and illustrations, conditions, chains of evidence and counter-arguments. When the whole mass of these dream-thoughts is brought under the pressure of the dream-work, and its elements are turned about, broken into fragments and jammed together—almost like pack-ice—the question arises of what happens to the logical connections which have hitherto formed its framework. What representation do dreams provide for 'if', 'because', 'just as', 'although', 'either—or', and all the other conjunctions without which we cannot understand sentences or speeches?

In the first resort our answer must be that dreams have no means at their disposal for representing these logical relations between the dream-thoughts. For the most part dreams disregard all these conjunctions, and it is only the substantive content of the dream-thoughts that they take over and manipulate. The restoration of the connections which the dream-work has destroyed is a task which has to be performed by the interpretative process.

The incapacity of dreams to express these things must lie in the nature of the psychical material out of which dreams are made. The plastic arts of painting and sculpture labour, indeed, under a similar limitation as compared with poetry, which can make use of speech; and here once again the reason for their incapacity lies in the nature of the material which these two forms of art manipulate in their effort to express something. Before painting became acquainted with the laws of expression by which it is governed, it made attempts to get over this handicap. In ancient paintings small labels were hung from the mouths of the persons represented, containing in written characters the speeches which the artist despaired of representing pictorially.

At this point an objection may perhaps be raised in dispute of the idea that dreams are unable to represent logical relations. For there are dreams in which the most complicated intellectual operations take place, statements are contradicted or confirmed, ridiculed or compared, just as they are in waking thought. But here again appearances are deceitful. If we go into the interpretation of dreams such as these, we find that the whole of this *is part of the material of the dream-thoughts and is not a representation of intellectual work performed during the dream itself.* What is reproduced by the ostensible thinking in the dream is the *subject-matter* of the dream-thoughts and not the *mutual relations between them*, the assertion of which constitutes thinking. I shall bring forward some instances of this. But the easiest point to establish in this connection is that all spoken sentences which occur in dreams and are specifically described as such are unmodified or slightly modified reproductions of speeches which are also to be found among the recollections in the material of the dream-thoughts. A speech of this kind is often no more than an allusion to some event included among the dream-thoughts, and the meaning of the dream may be a totally different one.

* * *

What means does the dream-work possess for indicating these relations in the dream-thoughts which it is so hard to represent? I will attempt to enumerate them one by one.

In the first place, dreams take into account in a general way the connection which undeniably exists between all the portions of the dream-thoughts by combining the whole material into a single situation or event. They reproduce *logical connection* by *simultaneity in time*. Here they are acting like the painter who, in a picture of the School of Athens or of Parnassus,[7] represents in one group all the philosophers or all the poets. It is true that they were never in fact assembled in a single hall or on a single mountain-top; but they certainly form a group in the conceptual sense.

Dreams carry this method of reproduction down to details. Whenever they show us two elements close together, this guarantees that there is some specially intimate connection between what correspond to them among the dream-thoughts. In the same way, in our system of writing, '*ab*' means that the two letters are to be pronounced in a single syllable. If a gap is left between the '*a*' and the '*b*', it means that the '*a*' is the last letter of one word and the '*b*' is the first of the next one. So, too, collocations in dreams do not consist of any chance, disconnected portions of the dream-material, but of portions which are fairly closely connected in the dream-thoughts as well.

For representing *causal relations* dreams have two procedures which are in essence the same. Suppose the dream-thoughts run like this: 'Since this was so and so, such and such was bound to happen.' Then the commoner method of representation would be to introduce the dependent clause as an introductory dream and to add the principal clause as the main dream. If I have interpreted aright, the temporal sequence may be reversed. But the more extensive part of the dream always corresponds to the principal clause.

* * *

The alternative 'either–or' cannot be expressed in dreams in any way whatever. Both of the alternatives are usually inserted in the text of the dream as though they were equally valid. The dream of Irma's injection contains a classic instance of this.[8] Its latent thoughts clearly ran: 'I am not responsible for the persistence of Irma's pains; the responsibility lies *either* in her recalcitrance to accepting my solution, *or* in the unfavourable sexual conditions under which she lives and which I cannot alter, *or* in the fact that her pains are not hysterical at all but of an organic nature.' The dream, on the other hand, fulfilled *all* of these possibilities (which were almost mutually exclusive), and did not hesitate to add a fourth solution, based on the dream-wish. After interpreting the dream, I proceeded to insert the 'either–or' into the context of the dream-thoughts.

If, however, in reproducing a dream, its narrator feels inclined to make use of an 'either–or'—e.g. 'it was either a garden or a sitting-room'—what was present in the dream-thoughts was not an alternative but an 'and', a simple addition. An 'either–or' is mostly used to describe a dream-element that has a quality of vagueness—which, however, is capable of being resolved. In such cases the rule for interpretation is: treat the two apparent alternatives as of equal validity and link them together with an 'and'.

7. A mountain in Greece sacred to Apollo and the Muses and hence the region of poetry. The School of Athens: Raphael's famous fresco of this title (1509–11) depicts philosophers of very different times as if they were contemporaries.

8. Freud has previously described a dream in which he tells a patient, Irma, "If you still get pains, it's really only your fault"; it is that dream that Freud calls "the specimen dream of psychoanalysis."

For instance, on one occasion a friend of mine was stopping in Italy and I had been without his address for a considerable time. I then had a dream of receiving a telegram containing this address. I saw it printed in blue on the telegraph form. The first word was vague:

> '*Via*', perhaps
> or '*Villa*'
> or possibly even ('*Casa*') } ; the second was clear: '*Secerno*'.

The second word sounded like some Italian name and reminded me of discussions I had had with my friend on the subject of etymology. It also expressed my anger with him for having kept his address *secret* from me for so long.[9] On the other hand, each of the three alternatives for the first word turned out on analysis to be an independent and equally valid starting-point for a chain of thoughts.[1]

During the night before my father's funeral I had a dream of a printed notice, placard or poster—rather like the notices forbidding one to smoke in railway waiting-rooms—on which appeared either

'You are requested to close the eyes'
or, 'You are requested to close an eye'.

I usually write this in the form:

'You are requested to close the / an eye(s).'

Each of these two versions had a meaning of its own and led in a different direction when the dream was interpreted. I had chosen the simplest possible ritual for the funeral, for I knew my father's own views on such ceremonies. But some other members of the family were not sympathetic to such puritanical simplicity and thought we should be disgraced in the eyes of those who attended the funeral. Hence one of the versions: 'You are requested to close an eye', i.e. to 'wink at' or 'overlook'. Here it is particularly easy to see the meaning of the vagueness expressed by the 'either–or'. The dream-work failed to establish a unified wording for the dream-thoughts which could at the same time be ambiguous, and the two main lines of thought consequently began to diverge even in the manifest content of the dream.[2]

In a few instances the difficulty of representing an alternative is got over by dividing the dream into two pieces of equal length.

The way in which dreams treat the category of contraries and contradictories is highly remarkable. It is simply disregarded. 'No' seems not to exist so far as dreams are concerned. They show a particular preference for com-

9. The Italian word meaning "secret" is *segreto*; the verb *secernere* means "to secrete," in the sense of giving off a secretion.

1. This dream will be found described in greater detail in Freud's letter to [Wilhelm] Fliess (the friend in question) of April 28, 1897 [translator's note].

2. This dream is reported by Freud in a letter to Fliess of November 2, 1896. It is there stated to have occurred during the night *after* the funeral. In its first wording the dream referred to closing the dead man's eyes as a filial duty [translator's note].

bining contraries into a unity or for representing them as one and the same thing. Dreams feel themselves at liberty, moreover, to represent any element by its wishful contrary; so that there is no way of deciding at a first glance whether any element that admits of a contrary is present in the dream-thoughts as a positive or as a negative.[3]

* * *

1900, 1929

From The "Uncanny"[1]

I

It is only rarely that a psycho-analyst feels impelled to investigate the subject of aesthetics, even when aesthetics is understood to mean not merely the theory of beauty but the theory of the qualities of feeling. He works in other strata of mental life and has little to do with the subdued emotional impulses which, inhibited in their aims and dependent on a host of concurrent factors, usually furnish the material for the study of aesthetics. But it does occasionally happen that he has to interest himself in some particular province of that subject; and this province usually proves to be a rather remote one, and one which has been neglected in the specialist literature of aesthetics.

The subject of the 'uncanny'[2] is a province of this kind. It is undoubtedly related to what is frightening—to what arouses dread and horror; equally certainly, too, the word is not always used in a clearly definable sense, so that it tends to coincide with what excites fear in general. Yet we may expect that a special core of feeling is present which justifies the use of a special conceptual term. One is curious to know what this common core is which allows us to distinguish as 'uncanny' certain things which lie within the field of what is frightening.

As good as nothing is to be found upon this subject in comprehensive treatises on aesthetics, which in general prefer to concern themselves with what is beautiful, attractive and sublime—that is, with feelings of a positive nature—and with the circumstances and the objects that call them forth, rather than with the opposite feelings of repulsion and distress. I know of only one attempt in medico-psychological literature, a fertile but not exhaustive paper by Jentsch (1906).[3] But I must confess that I have not made a very

3. [*Footnote added* 1911:] I was astonished to learn from a pamphlet by K. Abel, *The Antithetical Meaning of Primal Words* (1884) (cf. my review of it, 1910)—and the fact has been confirmed by other philologists—that the most ancient languages behave exactly like dreams in this respect. In the first instance they have only a single word to describe the two contraries at the extreme ends of a series of qualities or activities (e.g., "strong-weak," "old-young," "far-near," "bind-sever"); they only form distinct terms for the two contraries by a secondary process of making small modifications in the common word. Abel demonstrates this particularly from Ancient Egyptian; but he shows that there are distinct traces of the same course of development in the Semitic and Indo-Germanic languages as well [Freud's note].

1. Translated by Alix Strachey, who sometimes adds a word or phrase in square brackets in the text for clarification.

2. The German word, translated throughout this paper by the English "uncanny," is *unheimlich*, literally "unhomely." The English term is not, of course, an exact equivalent of the German one [translator's note].

3. "On the Psychology of the Uncanny," by the German psychologist Ernst Jentsch (1867–1919).

thorough examination of the literature, especially the foreign literature, relating to this present modest contribution of mine, for reasons which, as may easily be guessed, lie in the times in which we live;[4] so that my paper is presented to the reader without any claim to priority.

In his study of the 'uncanny' Jentsch quite rightly lays stress on the obstacle presented by the fact that people vary so very greatly in their sensitivity to this quality of feeling. The writer of the present contribution, indeed, must himself plead guilty to a special obtuseness in the matter, where extreme delicacy of perception would be more in place. It is long since he has experienced or heard of anything which has given him an uncanny impression, and he must start by translating himself into that state of feeling, by awakening in himself the possibility of experiencing it. Still, such difficulties make themselves powerfully felt in many other branches of aesthetics; we need not on that account despair of finding instances in which the quality in question will be unhesitatingly recognized by most people.

Two courses are open to us at the outset. Either we can find out what meaning has come to be attached to the word 'uncanny' in the course of its history; or we can collect all those properties of persons, things, sense-impressions, experiences and situations which arouse in us the feeling of uncanniness, and then infer the unknown nature of the uncanny from what all these examples have in common. I will say at once that both courses lead to the same result: the uncanny is that class of the frightening which leads back to what is known of old and long familiar. How this is possible, in what circumstances the familiar can become uncanny and frightening, I shall show in what follows. Let me also add that my investigation was actually begun by collecting a number of individual cases, and was only later confirmed by an examination of linguistic usage. In this discussion, however, I shall follow the reverse course.

The German word '*unheimlich*' is obviously the opposite of '*heimlich*' [homely], '*heimisch*' ['native']—the opposite of what is familiar; and we are tempted to conclude that what is 'uncanny' is frightening precisely because it is *not* known and familiar. Naturally not everything that is new and unfamiliar is frightening, however; the relation is not capable of inversion. We can only say that what is novel can easily become frightening and uncanny; some new things are frightening but not by any means all. Something has to be added to what is novel and unfamiliar in order to make it uncanny.

On the whole, Jentsch did not get beyond this relation of the uncanny to the novel and unfamiliar. He ascribes the essential factor in the production of the feeling of uncanniness to intellectual uncertainty; so that the uncanny would always, as it were, be something one does not know one's way about in. The better oriented in his environment a person is, the less readily will he get the impression of something uncanny in regard to the objects and events in it.

It is not difficult to see that this definition is incomplete, and we will therefore try to proceed beyond the equation 'uncanny' = 'unfamiliar'. We will first turn to other languages. But the dictionaries that we consult tell us nothing new, perhaps only because we ourselves speak a language that is

4. An allusion to the First World War only just concluded [translator's note].

foreign. Indeed, we get an impression that many languages are without a word for this particular shade of what is frightening.

* * *

Let us therefore return to the German language. In Daniel Sanders's *Wörterbuch der Deutschen Sprache* (1860, 1:729), the following entry, which I here reproduce in full, is to be found under the word '*heimlich*'. I have laid stress on one or two passages by italicizing them.

Heimlich, adj., subst. *Heimlichkeit* (pl. *Heimlichkeiten*): I. Also *heimelich, heimelig*, belonging to the house, not strange, familiar, tame, intimate, friendly, etc.

(*a*) (Obsolete) belonging to the house or the family, or regarded as so belonging (cf. Latin *familiaris*, familiar): *Die Heimlichen*, the members of the household; *Der heimliche Rat* (Gen. xli, 45; 2 Sam. xxiii. 23; 1 Chron. xii. 25; Wisd. viii. 4), now more usually *Geheimer Rat* [Privy Councillor].

(*b*) Of animals: tame, companionable to man. As opposed to wild, e.g. 'Animals which are neither wild nor *heimlich*', etc. 'Wild animals . . . that are trained to be *heimlich* and accustomed to men.' 'If these young creatures are brought up from early days among men they become quite *heimlich*, friendly' etc.—So also: 'It (the lamb) is so *heimlich* and eats out of my hand.' 'Nevertheless, the stork is a beautiful, *heimelich* bird.'

(*c*) Intimate, friendly, comfortable; the enjoyment of quiet content, etc., arousing a sense of agreeable restfulness and security as in one within the four walls of his house. 'Is it still *heimlich* to you in your country where strangers are felling your woods?' 'She did not feel too *heimlich* with him.' 'Along a high, *heimlich*, shady path . . . , beside a purling, gushing and babbling woodland brook.' 'To destroy the *Heimlichkeit* of the home.' 'I could not readily find another spot so intimate and *heimlich* as this.' 'We pictured it so comfortable, so nice, so cosy and *heimlich*.' * * * 'You go to sleep there so soft and warm, so wonderfully *heim'lig*.'—*This form of the word deserves to become general in order to protect this perfectly good sense of the word from becoming obsolete through an easy confusion with II* [see below]. Cf: '"*The Zecks* [a family name] *are all 'heimlich'.*" (in sense II) "'*Heimlich*'? . . . *What do you understand by 'heimlich'?" "Well, . . . they are like a buried spring or a dried-up pond. One cannot walk over it without always having the feeling that water might come up there again." "Oh, we call it 'unheimlich'; you call it 'heimlich'. Well, what makes you think that there is something secret and untrustworthy about this family?"*' (Gutzkow).[5]

(*d*) Especially in Silesia: gay, cheerful; also of the weather.

II. Concealed, kept from sight, so that others do not get to know of or about it, withheld from others. To do something *heimlich*, i.e. behind someone's back; to steal away *heimlich; heimlich* meetings and appointments; to look on with *heimlich* pleasure at someone's discomfiture; to sigh or weep *heimlich*; to behave *heimlich*, as though there was something to conceal; *heimlich* love-affair, love, sin; *heimlich* places (which good manners oblige us to conceal) (1 Sam. v. 6). 'The *heimlich* chamber' (privy) (2 Kings x. 27). Also, 'the *heimlich* chair'. 'To throw into pits or *Heimlichkeiten*'.—'Led the

5. Karl Gutzkow (1811–1878), German novelist and dramatist.

steeds *heimlich* before Laomedon.'—'As secretive, *heimlich*, deceitful and malicious towards cruel masters . . . as frank, open, sympathetic and helpful towards a friend in misfortune.' 'You have still to learn what is *heimlich* holiest to me.' 'The *heimlich* art' (magic). * * *

For compounds see above, Ic. Note especially the negative '*un-*': eerie, weird, arousing gruesome fear: 'Seeming quite *unheimlich* and ghostly to him.' 'The *unheimlich*, fearful hours of night.' 'I had already long since felt an *unheimlich*, even gruesome feeling.' 'Now I am beginning to have an *unheimlich* feeling.' . . . 'Feels an *unheimlich* horror.' '*Unheimlich* and motionless like a stone image.' 'The *unheimlich* mist called hill-fog.' 'These pale youths are *unheimlich* and are brewing heaven knows what mischief.' '"*Unheimlich" is the name for everything that ought to have remained . . . secret and hidden but has come to light*' (Schelling).[6]—'To veil the divine, to surround it with a certain *Unheimlichkeit*.'—*Unheimlich* is not often used as opposite to meaning II (above).

What interests us most in this long extract is to find that among its different shades of meaning the word '*heimlich*' exhibits one which is identical with its opposite, '*unheimlich*'. What is *heimlich* thus comes to be *unheimlich*. (Cf. the quotation from Gutzkow: 'We call it "*unheimlich*"; you call it "*heimlich*".') In general we are reminded that the word '*heimlich*' is not unambiguous, but belongs to two sets of ideas, which, without being contradictory, are yet very different: on the one hand it means what is familiar and agreeable, and on the other, what is concealed and kept out of sight.[7] '*Unheimlich*' is customarily used, we are told, as the contrary only of the first signification of '*heimlich*', and not of the second. Sanders tells us nothing concerning a possible genetic connection between these two meanings of *heimlich*. On the other hand, we notice that Schelling says something which throws quite a new light on the concept of the *Unheimlich*, for which we were certainly not prepared. According to him, everything is *unheimlich* that ought to have remained secret and hidden but has come to light.

Some of the doubts that have thus arisen are removed if we consult Grimm's dictionary. (1877, 4.2:873ff.)

We read:

Heimlich; adj. and adv. *vernaculus, occultus*; MHG. heimelîch, heimlîch.

(P. 874.) In a slightly different sense: 'I feel *heimlich*, well, free from fear.' . . .

[3] (*b*) *Heimlich* is also used of a place free from ghostly influences . . . familiar, friendly, intimate.

(P. 875: *β*) Familiar, amicable, unreserved.

4. *From the idea of 'homelike', 'belonging to the house', the further idea is developed of something withdrawn from the eyes of strangers, something concealed, secret; and this idea is expanded in many ways* . . .

* * *

6. Friedrich von Schelling (1775–1854), German philosopher; quoted from *Philosophy of Mythology* (published 1856).

7. According to the *Oxford English Dictionary*, a similar ambiguity attaches to the English "canny," which may mean not only "cosy" but also "endowed with occult or magical powers" [translator's note].

9. The notion of something hidden and dangerous, which is expressed in the last paragraph, is still further developed, so that 'heimlich' comes to have the meaning usually ascribed to 'unheimlich'. Thus: 'At times I feel like a man who walks in the night and believes in ghosts; every corner is heimlich and full of terrors for him'. (Klinger,[8] Theater, 3:298.)

Thus *heimlich* is a word the meaning of which develops in the direction of ambivalence, until it finally coincides with its opposite, *unheimlich. Unheimlich* is in some way or other a sub-species of *heimlich*. Let us bear this discovery in mind, though we cannot yet rightly understand it, alongside of Schelling's definition of the *Unheimlich*. If we go on to examine individual instances of uncanniness, these hints will become intelligible to us.

II

When we proceed to review the things, persons, impressions, events and situations which are able to arouse in us a feeling of the uncanny in a particularly forcible and definite form, the first requirement is obviously to select a suitable example to start on. Jentsch has taken as a very good instance 'doubts whether an apparently animate being is really alive; or conversely, whether a lifeless object might not be in fact animate'; and he refers in this connection to the impression made by waxwork figures, ingeniously constructed dolls and automata. To these he adds the uncanny effect of epileptic fits, and of manifestations of insanity, because these excite in the spectator the impression of automatic, mechanical processes at work behind the ordinary appearance of mental activity. Without entirely accepting this author's view, we will take it as a starting-point for our own investigation because in what follows he reminds us of a writer who has succeeded in producing uncanny effects better than anyone else.

Jentsch writes: 'In telling a story, one of the most successful devices for easily creating uncanny effects is to leave the reader in uncertainty whether a particular figure in the story is a human being or an automaton, and to do it in such a way that his attention is not focused directly upon his uncertainty, so that he may not be led to go into the matter and clear it up immediately. That, as we have said, would quickly dissipate the peculiar emotional effect of the thing. E. T. A. Hoffmann[9] has repeatedly employed this psychological artifice with success in his fantastic narratives.'

This observation, undoubtedly a correct one, refers primarily to the story of 'The Sand-Man' in Hoffmann's *Nachtstücken*,[1] which contains the original of Olympia, the doll that appears in the first act of Offenbach's opera, *Tales of Hoffmann*.[2] But I cannot think—and I hope most readers of the story will agree with me—that the theme of the doll Olympia, who is to all appearances a living being, is by any means the only, or indeed the most important, element that must be held responsible for the quite unparalleled atmosphere of

8. Friedrich von Klinger (1752–1831), German dramatist and novelist.
9. German author of fantastic and often humorous tales (1776–1822).
1. *Night Pieces* (1816–17); "The Sandman" was published in vol. 1 (1816).
2. An 1881 opera based on three tales by Hoffmann, by Jacques Offenbach (1819–1880), a German-born French composer of many light operas.

uncanniness evoked by the story. Nor is this atmosphere heightened by the fact that the author himself treats the episode of Olympia with a faint touch of satire and uses it to poke fun at the young man's idealization of his mistress. The main theme of the story is, on the contrary, something different, something which gives it its name, and which is always re-introduced at critical moments: it is the theme of the 'Sand-Man' who tears out children's eyes.

This fantastic tale opens with the childhood recollections of the student Nathaniel. In spite of his present happiness, he cannot banish the memories associated with the mysterious and terrifying death of his beloved father. On certain evenings his mother used to send the children to bed early, warning them that 'the Sand-Man was coming'; and, sure enough, Nathaniel would not fail to hear the heavy tread of a visitor, with whom his father would then be occupied for the evening. When questioned about the Sand-Man, his mother, it is true, denied that such a person existed except as a figure of speech; but his nurse could give him more definite information: 'He's a wicked man who comes when children won't go to bed, and throws handfuls of sand in their eyes so that they jump out of their heads all bleeding. Then he puts the eyes in a sack and carries them off to the half-moon to feed his children. They sit up there in their nest, and their beaks are hooked like owls' beaks, and they use them to peck up naughty boys' and girls' eyes with.'

Although little Nathaniel was sensible and old enough not to credit the figure of the Sand-Man with such gruesome attributes, yet the dread of him became fixed in his heart. He determined to find out what the Sand-Man looked like; and one evening, when the Sand-Man was expected again, he hid in his father's study. He recognized the visitor as the lawyer Coppelius, a repulsive person whom the children were frightened of when he occasionally came to a meal; and he now identified this Coppelius with the dreaded Sand-Man. As regards the rest of the scene, Hoffmann already leaves us in doubt whether what we are witnessing is the first delirium of the panic-stricken boy, or a succession of events which are to be regarded in the story as being real. His father and the guest are at work at a brazier with glowing flames. The little eavesdropper hears Coppelius call out: 'Eyes here! Eyes here!' and betrays himself by screaming aloud. Coppelius seizes him and is on the point of dropping bits of red-hot coal from the fire into his eyes, and then of throwing them into the brazier, but his father begs him off and saves his eyes. After this the boy falls into a deep swoon; and a long illness brings his experience to an end. Those who decide in favour of the rationalistic interpretation of the Sand-Man will not fail to recognize in the child's phantasy the persisting influence of his nurse's story. The bits of sand that are to be thrown into the child's eyes turn into bits of red-hot coal from the flames; and in both cases they are intended to make his eyes jump out. In the course of another visit of the Sand-Man's, a year later, his father is killed in his study by an explosion. The lawyer Coppelius disappears from the place without leaving a trace behind.

Nathaniel, now a student, believes that he has recognized this phantom of horror from his childhood in an itinerant optician, an Italian called Giuseppe Coppola, who at his university town, offers him weather-glasses for sale. When Nathaniel refuses, the man goes on: 'Not weather-glasses? not weather-glasses? also got fine eyes, fine eyes!' The student's terror is allayed when he finds that the proffered eyes are only harmless spectacles, and he buys a pocket spy-glass from Coppola. With its aid he looks across into Professor Spalanzani's house opposite and there spies Spalanzani's beautiful, but strangely silent and motionless daughter, Olympia. He soon falls in love with her so violently that, because of her, he quite forgets the clever and sensible girl to whom he is betrothed. But Olympia is an automaton whose clock-work has been made by Spalanzani, and whose eyes have been put in by Coppola, the Sand-Man. The student surprises the two Masters quarrelling over their handiwork. The optician carries off the wooden eyeless doll; and the mechanician, Spalanzani, picks up Olympia's bleeding eyes from the ground and throws them at Nathaniel's breast, saying that Coppola had stolen them from the student. Nathaniel succumbs to a fresh attack of madness, and in his delirium his recollection of his father's death is mingled with this new experience. 'Hurry up! hurry up! ring of fire!' he cries. 'Spin about, ring of fire—Hurrah! Hurry up, wooden doll! lovely wooden doll, spin about—.' He then falls upon the professor, Olympia's 'father', and tries to strangle him.

Rallying from a long and serious illness, Nathaniel seems at last to have recovered. He intends to marry his betrothed, with whom he has become reconciled. One day he and she are walking through the city market-place, over which the high tower of the Town Hall throws its huge shadow. On the girl's suggestion, they climb the tower, leaving her brother, who is walking with them, down below. From the top, Clara's attention is drawn to a curious object moving along the street. Nathaniel looks at this thing through Coppola's spy-glass, which he finds in his pocket, and falls into a new attack of madness. Shouting 'Spin about, wooden doll!' he tries to throw the girl into the gulf below. Her brother, brought to her side by her cries, rescues her and hastens down with her to safety. On the tower above, the madman rushes round, shrieking 'Ring of fire, spin about!'—and we know the origin of the words. Among the people who begin to gather below there comes forward the figure of the lawyer Coppelius, who has suddenly returned. We may suppose that it was his approach, seen through the spy-glass, which threw Nathaniel into his fit of madness. As the onlookers prepare to go up and overpower the madman, Coppelius laughs and says: 'Wait a bit; he'll come down of himself.' Nathaniel suddenly stands still, catches sight of Coppelius, and with a wild shriek 'Yes! "Fine eyes—fine eyes"!' flings himself over the parapet. While he lies on the paving-stones with a shattered skull the Sand-Man vanishes in the throng.

This short summary leaves no doubt, I think, that the feeling of something uncanny is directly attached to the figure of the Sand-Man, that is, to the idea of being robbed of one's eyes, and that Jentsch's point of an intellectual uncertainty has nothing to do with the effect. Uncertainty whether an object is living or inanimate, which admittedly applied to the doll Olympia, is quite irrelevant in connection with this other, more striking instance of uncanniness. It is true that the writer creates a kind of uncertainty in us in the beginning by not letting us know, no doubt purposely, whether he is taking us into the real world or into a purely fantastic one of his own creation. He has, of course, a right to do either; and if he chooses to stage his action in a world peopled with spirits, demons and ghosts, as Shakespeare does in *Hamlet*, in *Macbeth* and, in a different sense, in *The Tempest* and *A Midsummer-Night's Dream*, we must bow to his decision and treat his setting as though it were real for as long as we put ourselves into his hands.

But this uncertainty disappears in the course of Hoffmann's story, and we perceive that he intends to make us, too, look through the demon optician's spectacles or spy-glass—perhaps, indeed, that the author in his very own person once peered through such an instrument. For the conclusion of the story makes it quite clear that Coppola the optician really *is* the lawyer Coppelius[3] and also, therefore, the Sand-Man.

There is no question therefore, of any intellectual uncertainty here: we know now that we are not supposed to be looking on at the products of a madman's imagination, behind which we, with the superiority of rational minds, are able to detect the sober truth; and yet this knowledge does not lessen the impression of uncanniness in the least degree. The theory of intellectual uncertainty is thus incapable of explaining that impression.

We know from psycho-analytic experience, however, that the fear of damaging or losing one's eyes is a terrible one in children. Many adults retain their apprehensiveness in this respect, and no physical injury is so much dreaded by them as an injury to the eye. We are accustomed to say, too, that we will treasure a thing as the apple of our eye. A study of dreams, phantasies and myths has taught us that anxiety about one's eyes, the fear of going blind, is often enough a substitute for the dread of being castrated. The self-blinding of the mythical criminal, Oedipus,[4] was simply a mitigated form of the punishment of castration—the only punishment that was adequate for him by the *lex talionis*.[5] We may try on rationalistic grounds to deny that fears about the eye are derived from the fear of castration, and may argue that it is very natural that so precious an organ as the eye should be guarded by a proportionate dread. Indeed, we might go further and say that the fear of castration itself contains no other significance and no deeper secret than a justifiable dread of this rational kind. But this view does not account adequately for the substitutive relation between the eye and the male organ which is seen to exist in dreams and myths and phantasies; nor can it dispel the impression that the threat of being castrated in especial excites a peculiarly violent and obscure emotion, and that this emotion is what first gives the idea of losing other organs its intense colouring. All further doubts are removed when we learn the details of their 'castration complex' from the analysis of neurotic patients, and realize its immense importance in their mental life.

Moreover, I would not recommend any opponent of the psycho-analytic view to select this particular story of the Sand-Man with which to support his argument that anxiety about the eyes has nothing to do with the castration complex. For why does Hoffmann bring the anxiety about eyes into such intimate connection with the father's death? And why does the Sand-Man always appear as a disturber of love? He separates the unfortunate Nathaniel from his betrothed and from her brother, his best friend; he destroys the second object of his love, Olympia, the lovely doll; and he drives him into suicide at the moment when he has won back his Clara and is about to be happily

3. Frau Dr. Rank has pointed out the association of the name with *coppella* = crucible, connecting it with the chemical operations that caused the father's death; and also with *coppo* = eye-socket [Freud's note]. Tola Rank (1895–1967), Polish-born wife of Freud's longtime colleague Otto Rank; she also became a member of the Vienna Psychoanalytical Society.

4. Oedipus, a favorite subject of Greek tragedy and vase painting, was king of Thebes; he blinded himself when he realized that he had killed his father and married his mother.

5. Law of retaliation in kind (Latin).

united to her. Elements in the story like these, and many others, seem arbitrary and meaningless so long as we deny all connection between fears about the eye and castration; but they become intelligible as soon as we replace the Sand-Man by the dreaded father at whose hands castration is expected.[6]

We shall venture, therefore, to refer the uncanny effect of the Sand-Man to the anxiety belonging to the castration complex of childhood. But having reached the idea that we can make an infantile factor such as this responsible for feelings of uncanniness, we are encouraged to see whether we can apply it to other instances of the uncanny. We find in the story of the Sand-Man the other theme on which Jentsch lays stress, of a doll which appears to be alive. Jentsch believes that a particularly favourable condition for awakening uncanny feelings is created when there is intellectual uncertainty whether an object is alive or not, and when an inanimate object becomes too much like an animate one. Now, dolls are of course rather closely connected with childhood life. We remember that in their early games children do not distinguish at all sharply between living and inanimate objects, and that they are especially fond of treating their dolls like live people. In fact, I have occasionally heard a woman patient declare that even at the age of eight she had still been convinced that her dolls would be certain to come to life if she were to look at them in a particular, extremely concentrated, way. So that here, too, it is not difficult to discover a factor from childhood. But, curiously enough, while the Sand-Man story deals with the arousing of an early childhood fear, the idea of a 'living doll' excites no fear at all; children have no fear of their dolls coming to life, they may even desire it. The source of

6. In fact, Hoffmann's imaginative treatment of his material has not made such wild confusion of its elements that we cannot reconstruct their original arrangement. In the story of Nathaniel's childhood, the figures of his father and Coppelius represent the two opposites into which the father-imago is split by his ambivalence; whereas the one threatens to blind him—that is, to castrate him,—the other, the "good" father, intercedes for his sight. The part of the complex which is most strongly repressed, the death-wish against the "bad" father, finds expression in the death of the "good" father, and Coppelius is made answerable for it. This pair of fathers is represented later, in his student days, by Professor Spalanzani and Coppola the optician. The Professor is in himself a member of the father-series, and Coppola is recognized as identical with Coppelius the lawyer. Just as they used before to work together over the secret brazier, so now they have jointly created the doll Olympia; the Professor is even called the father of Olympia. This double occurrence of activity in common betrays them as divisions of the father-imago: both the mechanician and the optician were the father of Nathaniel (and of Olympia as well). In the frightening scene in childhood, Coppelius, after sparing Nathaniel's eyes, had screwed off his arms and legs as an experiment; that is, he had worked on him as a mechanician would on a doll. This singular feature, which seems quite outside the picture of the Sand-Man, introduces a new castration equivalent; but it also points to the inner identity of Coppelius with his later counterpart, Spalanzani the mechanician, and prepares us for the interpretation of Olympia. This automatic doll can be nothing else than a materialization of Nathaniel's feminine attitude towards his father in his infancy. Her fathers, Spalanzani and Coppola, are, after all, nothing but new editions, reincarnations of Nathaniel's pair of fathers. Spalanzani's otherwise incomprehensible statement that the optician has stolen Nathaniel's eyes, so as to set them in the doll, now becomes significant as supplying evidence of the identity of Olympia and Nathaniel. Olympia is, as it were, a dissociated complex of Nathaniel's which confronts him as a person, and Nathaniel's enslavement to this complex is expressed in his senseless obsessive love for Olympia. We may with justice call love of this kind narcissistic, and we can understand why someone who has fallen victim to it should relinquish the real, external object of his love. The psychological truth of the situation in which the young man, fixated upon his father by his castration complex, becomes incapable of loving a woman, is amply proved by numerous analyses of patients whose story, though less fantastic, is hardly less tragic than that of the student Nathaniel.

Hoffmann was the child of an unhappy marriage. When he was three years old, his father left his small family, and was never united to them again. According to Grisebach, in his biographical introduction to Hoffmann's works, the writer's relation to his father was always a most sensitive subject with him [Freud's note]. Eduard Grisebach (1845–1906), German diplomat, editor, and literary historian; his edition of Hoffmann's *Complete Works* was published in 1905.

uncanny feelings would not, therefore, be an infantile fear in this case, but rather an infantile wish or even merely an infantile belief. There seems to be a contradiction here; but perhaps it is only a complication, which may be helpful to us later on.

* * *

At this point I will put forward two considerations which, I think, contain the gist of this short study. In the first place, if psycho-analytic theory is correct in maintaining that every affect belonging to an emotional impulse, whatever its kind, is transformed, if it is repressed, into anxiety, then among instances of frightening things there must be one class in which the frightening element can be shown to be something repressed which *recurs*. This class of frightening things would then constitute the uncanny; and it must be a matter of indifference whether what is uncanny was itself originally frightening or whether it carried some *other* affect. In the second place, if this is indeed the secret nature of the uncanny, we can understand why linguistic usage has extended *das Heimliche* ['homely'] into its opposite, *das Unheimliche*; for this uncanny is in reality nothing new or alien, but something which is familiar and old-established in the mind and which has become alienated from it only through the process of repression. This reference to the factor of repression enables us, furthermore, to understand Schelling's definition of the uncanny as something which ought to have remained hidden but has come to light.

It only remains for us to test our new hypothesis on one or two more examples of the uncanny.

Many people experience the feeling in the highest degree in relation to death and dead bodies, to the return of the dead, and to spirits and ghosts. As we have seen some languages in use to-day can only render the German expression 'an *unheimlich* house' by 'a *haunted* house'. We might indeed have begun our investigation with this example, perhaps the most striking of all, of something uncanny, but we refrained from doing so because the uncanny in it is too much intermixed with what is purely gruesome and is in part overlaid by it. There is scarcely any other matter, however, upon which our thoughts and feelings have changed so little since the very earliest times, and in which discarded forms have been so completely preserved under a thin disguise, as our relation to death. Two things account for our conservatism: the strength of our original emotional reaction to death and the insufficiency of our scientific knowledge about it. Biology has not yet been able to decide whether death is the inevitable fate of every living being or whether it is only a regular but yet perhaps avoidable event in life. It is true that the statement 'All men are mortal' is paraded in text-books of logic as an example of a general proposition; but no human being really grasps it, and our unconscious has as little use now as it ever had for the idea of its own mortality. Religions continue to dispute the importance of the undeniable fact of individual death and to postulate a life after death; civil governments still believe that they cannot maintain moral order among the living if they do not uphold the prospect of a better life hereafter as a recompense for mundane existence. In our great cities, placards announce lectures that undertake to tell us how to get into touch with the souls of the departed; and it cannot be denied that not a few of the most able and penetrating minds among our men of science have come to the conclusion, especially towards the close of their own lives, that a contact of this kind is not impossible. Since almost all of us still think as savages do on this topic, it is no matter for surprise that the primitive fear of the dead is still so strong within us and always ready to come to the surface on any provocation. Most likely our fear still implies the old belief that the dead man becomes the enemy of his survivor and seeks to carry him off to share his new life with him. Considering our unchanged attitude towards death, we might rather enquire what has become of the repression, which is the necessary condition of a primitive feeling recurring in the shape of something uncanny. But repression is there, too. All supposedly educated people have ceased to believe officially that the dead can become visible as spirits, and have made any such appearances dependent on improbable and remote conditions; their emotional attitude towards their dead, moreover, once a highly ambiguous and ambivalent one, has been toned down in the higher strata of the mind into an unambiguous feeling of piety.

We have now only a few remarks to add—for animism, magic and sorcery, the omnipotence of thoughts, man's attitude to death, involuntary repetition and the castration complex comprise practically all the factors which turn something frightening into something uncanny.

We can also speak of a living person as uncanny, and we do so when we ascribe evil intentions to him. But that is not all; in addition to this we must feel that his intentions to harm us are going to be carried out with the help of special powers. A good instance of this is the *'Gettatore'*,[7] that uncanny figure of Romanic superstition which Schaeffer,[8] with intuitive poetic feeling and profound psycho-analytic understanding, has transformed into a sympathetic character in his *Josef Montfort*. But the question of these secret powers brings us back again to the realm of animism. It was the pious Gretchen's intuition that Mephistopheles possessed secret powers of this kind that made him so uncanny to her.

> Sie fühlt dass ich ganz sicher ein Genie,
> Vielleicht sogar der Teufel bin.[9]

The uncanny effect of epilepsy and of madness has the same origin. The layman sees in them the working of forces hitherto unsuspected in his fellow-men, but at the same time he is dimly aware of them in remote corners of his own being. The Middle Ages quite consistently ascribed all such maladies to the influence of demons, and in this their psychology was almost correct. Indeed, I should not be surprised to hear that psycho-analysis, which is concerned with laying bare these hidden forces, has itself become uncanny to many people for that very reason. In one case, after I had succeeded—though none too rapidly—in effecting a cure in a girl who had been an invalid for many years, I myself heard this view expressed by the patient's mother long after her recovery.

7. Literally "thrower" (of bad luck), or "one who casts" (the evil eye) [translator's note].
8. Albrecht Schaeffer (1885–1950), who published the novel *Josef Montfort* in 1918.
9. "She feels that surely I'm a genius now,— Perhaps the very Devil indeed!" Goethe, *Faust*, Part I [1808], scene 16; Bayard Taylor's translation [1870–71; translator's note]. Johann Wolfgang von Goethe (1749–1832), German poet, playwright, and dramatist. Mephistopheles is the spirit to whom the old Faust promises his soul; Gretchen is the young girl whom Faust, made young again, falls in love with and seduces.

Dismembered limbs, a severed head, a hand cut off at the wrist, as in a fairy tale of Hauff's,[1] feet which dance by themselves, as in the book by Schaeffer which I mentioned above—all these have something peculiarly uncanny about them, especially when, as in the last instance, they prove capable of independent activity in addition. As we already know, this kind of uncanniness springs from its proximity to the castration complex. To some people the idea of being buried alive by mistake is the most uncanny thing of all. And yet psycho-analysis has taught us that this terrifying phantasy is only a transformation of another phantasy which had originally nothing terrifying about it at all, but was qualified by a certain lasciviousness—the phantasy, I mean, of intra-uterine existence.

There is one more point of general application which I should like to add, though, strictly speaking, it has been included in what has already been said about animism and modes of working of the mental apparatus that have been surmounted; for I think it deserves special emphasis. This is that an uncanny effect is often and easily produced when the distinction between imagination and reality is effaced, as when something that we have hitherto regarded as imaginary appears before us in reality, or when a symbol takes over the full functions of the thing it symbolizes, and so on. It is this factor which contributes not a little to the uncanny effect attaching to magical practices. The infantile element in this, which also dominates the minds of neurotics, is the over-accentuation of psychical reality in comparison with material reality—a feature closely allied to the belief in the omnipotence of thoughts. In the middle of the isolation of war-time a number of the English *Strand Magazine* fell into my hands; and, among other somewhat redundant matter, I read a story about a young married couple who move into a furnished house in which there is a curiously shaped table with carvings of crocodiles on it. Towards evening an intolerable and very specific smell begins to pervade the house; they stumble over something in the dark; they seem to see a vague form gliding over the stairs—in short, we are given to understand that the presence of the table causes ghostly crocodiles to haunt the place, or that the wooden monsters come to life in the dark, or something of the sort. It was a naïve enough story, but the uncanny feeling it produced was quite remarkable.

To conclude this collection of examples, which is certainly not complete, I will relate an instance taken from psycho-analytic experience; if it does not rest upon mere coincidence, it furnishes a beautiful confirmation of our theory of the uncanny. It often happens that neurotic men declare that they feel there is something uncanny about the female genital organs. This *unheimlich* place, however, is the entrance to the former *Heim* [home] of all human beings, to the place where each one of us lived once upon a time and in the beginning. There is a joking saying that 'Love is home-sickness'; and whenever a man dreams of a place or a country and says to himself, while he is still dreaming: 'this place is familiar to me, I've been here before', we may interpret the place as being his mother's genitals or her body. In this case too, then, the *unheimlich* is what was once *heimisch*, familiar; the prefix '*un*' ['un-'] is the token of repression.

1. *Die Geschichte von der abgehauenen Hand* (The Story of the Severed Hand) [translator's note]. Wilhelm Hauff (1802–1827), German novelist.

III

In the course of this discussion the reader will have felt certain doubts arising in his mind; and he must now have an opportunity of collecting them and bringing them forward.

It may be true that the uncanny [*unheimlich*] is something which is secretly familiar [*heimlich-heimisch*], which has undergone repression and then returned from it, and that everything that is uncanny fulfils this condition. But the selection of material on this basis does not enable us to solve the problem of the uncanny. For our proposition is clearly not convertible. Not everything that fulfils this condition—not everything that recalls repressed desires and surmounted modes of thinking belonging to the prehistory of the individual and of the race—is on that account uncanny.

Nor shall we conceal the fact that for almost every example adduced in support of our hypothesis one may be found which rebuts it. The story of the severed hand in Hauff's fairy tale certainly has an uncanny effect, and we have traced that effect back to the castration complex; but most readers will probably agree with me in judging that no trace of uncanniness is provoked by Herodotus's story of the treasure of Rhampsinitus,[2] in which the master-thief, whom the princess tries to hold fast by the hand, leaves his brother's severed hand behind with her instead. Again, the prompt fulfilment of the wishes of Polycrates[3] undoubtedly affects us in the same uncanny way as it did the king of Egypt; yet our own fairy stories are crammed with instantaneous wish-fulfilments which produce no uncanny effect whatever. In the story of 'The Three Wishes', the woman is tempted by the savoury smell of a sausage to wish that she might have one too, and in an instant it lies on a plate before her. In his annoyance at her hastiness her husband wishes it may hang on her nose. And there it is, dangling from her nose. All this is very striking but not in the least uncanny. Fairy tales quite frankly adopt the animistic standpoint of the omnipotence of thoughts and wishes, and yet I cannot think of any genuine fairy story which has anything uncanny about it. We have heard that it is in the highest degree uncanny when an inanimate object—a picture or a doll—comes to life; nevertheless in Hans Andersen's[4] stories the household utensils, furniture and tin soldiers are alive, yet nothing could well be more remote from the uncanny. And we should hardly call it uncanny when Pygmalion's beautiful statue comes to life.[5]

Apparent death and the re-animation of the dead have been represented as most uncanny themes. But things of this sort too are very common in fairy stories. Who would be so bold as to call it uncanny, for instance, when Snow-White opens her eyes once more?[6] And the resuscitation of the dead in accounts of miracles, as in the New Testament, elicits feelings quite unrelated to the uncanny. Then, too, the theme that achieves such an indubitably uncanny effect, the unintended recurrence of the same thing, serves other

2. See Herodotus (Greek historian, ca. 484–ca. 425 B.C.E.) 2.121. Rhampsinitus was the king of Egypt.
3. Freud discussed the story (told in Herodotus 3.40–43) of the uncannily lucky Polycrates, king of Samos, in a passage omitted from our selection.
4. Hans Christian Andersen (1805–1875), Danish writer best known for his fairy tales.
5. In *Metamorphoses* (ca. 10 C.E.), 10.243–97, the Roman poet Ovid tells the story of the sculptor Pygmalion, who fell in love with his own creation.
6. Snow White, believed dead, comes back to life when the poisoned apple is dislodged from her throat.

and quite different purposes in another class of cases. We have already come across one example in which it is employed to call up a feeling of the comic;[7] and we could multiply instances of this kind. Or again, it works as a means of emphasis, and so on. And once more: what is the origin of the uncanny effect of silence, darkness and solitude? Do not these factors point to the part played by danger in the genesis of what is uncanny, notwithstanding that in children these same factors are the most frequent determinants of the expression of fear [rather than of the uncanny]? And are we after all justified in entirely ignoring intellectual uncertainty as a factor, seeing that we have admitted its importance in relation to death?

It is evident therefore, that we must be prepared to admit that there are other elements besides those which we have so far laid down as determining the production of uncanny feelings. We might say that these preliminary results have satisfied *psycho-analytic* interest in the problem of the uncanny, and that what remains probably calls for an *aesthetic* enquiry. But that would be to open the door to doubts about what exactly is the value of our general contention that the uncanny proceeds from something familiar which has been repressed.

We have noticed one point which may help us to resolve these uncertainties: nearly all the instances that contradict our hypothesis are taken from the realm of fiction, of imaginative writing. This suggests that we should differentiate between the uncanny that we actually experience and the uncanny that we merely picture or read about.

What is *experienced* as uncanny is much more simply conditioned but comprises far fewer instances. We shall find, I think, that it fits in perfectly with our attempt at a solution, and can be traced back without exception to something familiar that has been repressed. But here, too, we must make a certain important and psychologically significant differentiation in our material, which is best illustrated by turning to suitable examples.

Let us take the uncanny associated with the omnipotence of thoughts, with the prompt fulfilment of wishes, with secret injurious powers and with the return of the dead. The condition under which the feeling of uncanniness arises here is unmistakable. We—or our primitive forefathers—once believed that these possibilities were realities, and were convinced that they actually happened. Nowadays we no longer believe in them, we have *surmounted* these modes of thought; but we do not feel quite sure of our new beliefs, and the old ones still exist within us ready to seize upon any confirmation. As soon as something *actually happens* in our lives which seems to confirm the old, discarded beliefs we get a feeling of the uncanny; it is as though we were making a judgement something like this: 'So, after all, it is *true* that one can kill a person by the mere wish!' or, 'So the dead *do* live on and appear on the scene of their former activities!' and so on. Conversely, anyone who has completely and finally rid himself of animistic beliefs will be insensible to this type of the uncanny. The most remarkable coincidences of wish and fulfilment, the most mysterious repetition of similar experiences in a particular place or on a particular date, the most deceptive sights and suspicious noises—none of these things will disconcert him or raise the kind of fear which can be described as

7. That is, in Mark Twain's *A Tramp Abroad* (1880), mentioned in a passage omitted from our selection.

'a fear of something uncanny'. The whole thing is purely an affair of 'reality-testing', a question of the material reality of the phenomena.[8]

The state of affairs is different when the uncanny proceeds from repressed infantile complexes, from the castration complex, womb-phantasies, etc.; but experiences which arouse this kind of uncanny feeling are not of very frequent occurrence in real life. The uncanny which proceeds from actual experience belongs for the most part to the first group [the group dealt with in the previous paragraph]. Nevertheless the distinction between the two is theoretically very important. Where the uncanny comes from infantile complexes the question of material reality does not arise; its place is taken by psychical reality. What is involved is an actual repression of some content of thought and a return of this repressed content, not a cessation of *belief in the reality* of such a content. We might say that in the one case what had been repressed is a particular ideational content, and in the other the belief in its (material) reality. But this last phrase no doubt extends the term 'repression' beyond its legitimate meaning. It would be more correct to take into account a psychological distinction which can be detected here, and to say that the animistic beliefs of civilized people are in a state of having been (to a greater or lesser extent) *surmounted* [rather than repressed]. Our conclusion could then be stated thus: an uncanny experience occurs either when infantile complexes which have been repressed are once more revived by some impression, or when primitive beliefs which have been surmounted seem once more to be confirmed. Finally, we must not let our predilection for smooth solutions and lucid exposition blind us to the fact that these two classes of uncanny experience are not always sharply distinguishable. When we consider that primitive beliefs are most intimately connected with infantile complexes, and are, in fact, based on them, we shall not be greatly astonished to find that the distinction is often a hazy one.

The uncanny as it is depicted in *literature*, in stories and imaginative productions, merits in truth a separate discussion. Above all, it is a much more fertile province than the uncanny in real life, for it contains the whole of the latter and something more besides, something that cannot be found in real life. The contrast between what has been repressed and what has been surmounted cannot be transposed on to the uncanny in fiction without profound modification; for the realm of phantasy depends for its effect on the fact that its content is not submitted to reality-testing. The somewhat paradoxical

8. Since the uncanny effect of a "double" also belongs to this same group it is interesting to observe what the effect is of meeting one's own image unbidden and unexpected. Ernst Mach has related two such observations in his *Analyse der Empfindungen* (1900 [*Analysis of Sensations*]). On the first occasion he was not a little startled when he realized that the face before him was his own. The second time he formed a very unfavorable opinion about the supposed stranger who had entered the omnibus, and thought "What a shabby-looking school-master that man is who is getting in!"—I can report a similar adventure. I was sitting alone in my *wagon-lit* compartment when a more than usually violent jolt of the train swung back the door of the adjoining washing-cabinet, and an elderly gentleman in a dressing-gown and a travelling cap came in. I assumed that in leaving the washing-cabinet, which lay between the two compartments, he had taken the wrong direction and come into my cabinet by mistake. Jumping up with the intention of putting him right, I at once realized to my dismay that the intruder was nothing but my own reflection in the looking-glass on the open door. I can still recollect that I thoroughly disliked his appearance. Instead, therefore, of being *frightened* by our doubles, both Mach and I simply failed to recognize them as such. Is it not possible, though, that our dislike of them was a vestigial trace of the archaic reaction which feels the "double" to be something uncanny? [Freud's note]. Mach (1838–1916), Austrian physicist and philosopher. *Wagon-lit*: sleeping car (French).

result is that *in the first place a great deal that is not uncanny in fiction would be so if it happened in real life; and in the second place that there are many more means of creating uncanny effects in fiction than there are in real life.*

The imaginative writer has this licence among many others, that he can select his world of representation so that it either coincides with the realities we are familiar with or departs from them in what particulars he pleases. We accept his ruling in every case. In fairy tales, for instance, the world of reality is left behind from the very start, and the animistic system of beliefs is frankly adopted. Wish-fulfilments, secret powers, omnipotence of thoughts, animation of inanimate objects, all the elements so common in fairy stories, can exert no uncanny influence here; for, as we have learnt, that feeling cannot arise unless there is a conflict of judgement as to whether things which have been 'surmounted' and are regarded as incredible may not, after all, be possible; and this problem is eliminated from the outset by the postulates of the world of fairy tales. Thus we see that fairy stories, which have furnished us with most of the contradictions to our hypothesis of the uncanny, confirm the first part of our proposition—that in the realm of fiction many things are not uncanny which would be so if they happened in real life. In the case of these stories there are other contributory factors, which we shall briefly touch upon later.

The creative writer can also choose a setting which though less imaginary than the world of fairy tales, does yet differ from the real world by admitting superior spiritual beings such as daemonic spirits or ghosts of the dead. So long as they remain within their setting of poetic reality, such figures lose any uncanniness which they might possess. The souls in Dante's *Inferno*, or the supernatural apparitions in Shakespeare's *Hamlet, Macbeth* or *Julius Caesar*, may be gloomy and terrible enough, but they are no more really uncanny than Homer's jovial world of gods.[9] We adapt our judgement to the imaginary reality imposed on us by the writer, and regard souls, spirits and ghosts as though their existence had the same validity as our own has in material reality. In this case too we avoid all trace of the uncanny.

The situation is altered as soon as the writer pretends to move in the world of common reality. In this case he accepts as well all the conditions operating to produce uncanny feelings in real life; and everything that would have an uncanny effect in reality has it in his story. But in this case he can even increase his effect and multiply it far beyond what could happen in reality, by bringing about events which never or very rarely happen in fact. In doing this he is in a sense betraying us to the superstitiousness which we have ostensibly surmounted; he deceives us by promising to give us the sober truth, and then after all overstepping it. We react to his inventions as we would have reacted to real experiences; by the time we have seen through his trick it is already too late and the author has achieved his object. But it must be added that his success is not unalloyed. We retain a feeling of dissatisfaction, a kind of grudge against the attempted deceit. I have noticed this particularly after reading Schnitzler's *Die Weissagung* [*The Prophecy*][1] and similar sto-

9. Freud names writers from a range of cultures and times: DANTE ALIGHIERI (1265–1321) visits the dead in hell in *Inferno*, the first volume of his *Divine Comedy*; in the tragedies of William Shakespeare (1564–1616) named here, ghosts appear; and in Homer's *Iliad* and *Odyssey* (ca. 8th c. B.C.E.), the gods play active roles.

1. A short story (1905) by the Austrian playwright and novelist Arthur Schnitzler (1862–1931).

ries which flirt with the supernatural. However, the writer has one more means which he can use in order to avoid our recalcitrance and at the same time to improve his chances of success. He can keep us in the dark for a long time about the precise nature of the presuppositions on which the world he writes about is based, or he can cunningly and ingeniously avoid any definite information on the point to the last. Speaking generally, however, we find a confirmation of the second part of our proposition—that fiction presents more opportunities for creating uncanny feelings than are possible in real life.

Strictly speaking, all these complications relate only to that class of the uncanny which proceeds from forms of thought that have been surmounted. The class which proceeds from repressed complexes is more resistant and remains as powerful in fiction as in real experience, subject to one exception. The uncanny belonging to the first class—that proceeding from forms of thought that have been surmounted—retains its character not only in experience but in fiction as well, so long as the setting is one of material reality; but where it is given an arbitrary and artificial setting in fiction, it is apt to lose that character.

We have clearly not exhausted the possibilities of poetic licence and the privileges enjoyed by story-writers in evoking or in excluding an uncanny feeling. In the main we adopt an unvarying passive attitude towards real experience and are subject to the influence of our physical environment. But the story-teller has a *peculiarly* directive power over us; by means of the moods he can put us into, he is able to guide the current of our emotions, to dam it up in one direction and make it flow in another, and he often obtains a great variety of effects from the same material. All this is nothing new, and has doubtless long since been fully taken into account by students of aesthetics. We have drifted into this field of research half involuntarily, through the temptation to explain certain instances which contradicted our theory of the causes of the uncanny. Accordingly we will now return to the examination of a few of those instances.

We have already asked why it is that the severed hand in the story of the treasure of Rhampsinitus has no uncanny effect in the way that the severed hand has in Hauff's story. The question seems to have gained in importance now that we have recognized that the class of the uncanny which proceeds from repressed complexes is the more resistant of the two. The answer is easy. In the Herodotus story our thoughts are concentrated much more on the superior cunning of the master-thief than on the feelings of the princess. The princess may very well have had an uncanny feeling, indeed she very probably fell into a swoon; but *we* have no such sensations, for we put ourselves in the thief's place, not in hers. In Nestroy's farce, *Der Zerrissene* [*The Torn Man*],[2] another means is used to avoid any impression of the uncanny in the scene in which the fleeing man, convinced that he is a murderer, lifts up one trapdoor after another and each time sees what he takes to be the ghost of his victim rising up out of it. He calls out in despair, 'But I've only killed *one* man. Why this ghastly multiplication?' We know what went before this scene and do not share his error, so what must be uncanny to him has an irresistibly comic effect on us. Even a 'real' ghost, as in Oscar Wilde's

2. An 1845 production by the Austrian playwright Johann Nestroy (1801–1862).

Canterville Ghost,[3] loses all power of at least arousing *gruesome* feelings in us as soon as the author begins to amuse himself by being ironical about it and allows liberties to be taken with it. Thus we see how independent emotional effects can be of the actual subject-matter in the world of fiction. In fairy stories feelings of fear—including therefore uncanny feelings—are ruled out altogether. We understand this, and that is why we ignore any opportunities we find in them for developing such feelings.

Concerning the factors of silence, solitude and darkness, we can only say that they are actually elements in the production of the infantile anxiety from which the majority of human beings have never become quite free. This problem has been discussed from a psycho-analytic point of view elsewhere.

1919

Fetishism[1]

In the last few years I have had an opportunity of studying analytically a number of men whose object-choice was dominated by a fetish. There is no need to expect that these people came to analysis on account of their fetish. For though no doubt a fetish is recognized by its adherents as an abnormality, it is seldom felt by them as the symptom of an ailment accompanied by suffering. Usually they are quite satisfied with it, or even praise the way in which it eases their erotic life. As a rule, therefore, the fetish made its appearance in analysis as a subsidiary finding.

For obvious reasons the details of these cases must be withheld from publication; I cannot, therefore, show in what way accidental circumstances have contributed to the choice of a fetish. The most extraordinary case seemed to me to be one in which a young man had exalted a certain sort of 'shine on the nose' into a fetishistic precondition. The surprising explanation of this was that the patient had been brought up in an English nursery but had later come to Germany, where he forgot his mother-tongue almost completely. The fetish, which originated from his earliest childhood, had to be understood in English, not German. The 'shine on the nose' [in German *'Glanz auf der Nase'*]—was in reality a *'glance'* at the nose'. The nose was thus the fetish, which, incidentally, he endowed at will with the luminous shine which was not perceptible to others.

In every instance, the meaning and the purpose of the fetish turned out, in analysis, to be the same. It revealed itself so naturally and seemed to me so compelling that I am prepared to expect the same solution in all cases of fetishism. When now I announce that the fetish is a substitute for the penis, I shall certainly create disappointment; so I hasten to add that it is not a substitute for any chance penis, but for a particular and quite special penis that had been extremely important in early childhood but had later been lost. That is to say, it should normally have been given up, but the fetish is precisely designed to preserve it from extinction. To put it more

3. A short story (1887) by the Irish-born writer WILDE (1854–1900).

1. Translated by Joan Rivière, who sometimes adds a word or phrase in square brackets in the text for clarification.

plainly: the fetish is a substitute for the woman's (the mother's) penis that the little boy once believed in and—for reasons familiar to us—does not want to give up.[2]

What happened, therefore, was that the boy refused to take cognizance of the fact of his having perceived that a woman does not possess a penis. No, that could not be true: for if a woman had been castrated, then his own possession of a penis was in danger; and against that there rose in rebellion the portion of his narcissism which Nature has, as a precaution, attached to that particular organ. In later life a grown man may perhaps experience a similar panic when the cry goes up that Throne and Altar are in danger, and similar illogical consequences will ensue. If I am not mistaken, Laforgue would say in this case that the boy 'scotomizes' his perception of the woman's lack of a penis.[3] A new technical term is justified when it describes a new fact or emphasizes it. This is not so here. The oldest word in our psycho-analytic terminology, 'repression', already relates to this pathological process. If we wanted to differentiate more sharply between the vicissitude of the *idea* as distinct from that of the *affect* and reserve the word *'Verdrängung'* ['repression'] for the affect, then the correct German word for the vicissitude of the idea would be *'Verleugnung'* ['disavowal']. 'Scotomization' seems to me particularly unsuitable, for it suggests that the perception is entirely wiped out, so that the result is the same as when a visual impression falls on the blind spot in the retina. In the situation we are considering, on the contrary, we see that the perception has persisted, and that a very energetic action has been undertaken to maintain the disavowal. It is not true that, after the child has made his observation of the woman, he has preserved unaltered his belief that women have a phallus. He has retained that belief, but he has also given it up. In the conflict between the weight of the unwelcome perception and the force of his counter-wish, a compromise has been reached, as is only possible under the dominance of the unconscious laws of thought—the primary processes. Yes, in his mind the woman *has* got a penis, in spite of everything; but this penis is no longer the same as it was before. Something else has taken its place, has been appointed its substitute, as it were, and now inherits the interest which was formerly directed to its predecessor. But this interest suffers an extraordinary increase as well, because the horror of castration has set up a memorial to itself in the creation of this substitute. Furthermore, an aversion, which is never absent in any fetishist, to the real female genitals remains a *stigma indelebile*[4] of the repression that has taken place. We can now see what the fetish achieves and what it is that maintains it. It remains a token of triumph over the threat of castration and a protection against it. It also saves the fetishist from becoming a homosexual, by endowing women with the characteristic which makes them tolerable as sexual objects. In later

2. This interpretation was made as early as 1910, in my study on Leonardo da Vinci [*Leonardo da Vinci and a Memory of His Childhood*], without any reasons being given for it [Freud's note].

3. I correct myself, however, by adding that I have the best reasons for supposing that Laforgue would not say anything of the sort. It is clear from his own remarks [in "Repression and Scotomization," 1926] that "scotomization" is a term which derives from descriptions of dementia praecox [schizophrenia], which does not arise from a carrying-over of psycho-analytic concepts to the psychoses and which has no application to developmental processes or to the formation of neuroses. In his exposition in the text of his paper, the author has been at pains to make this incompatibility clear [Freud's note]. René Laforgue (1894–1962), French psychoanalyst. "Scotomize": to form a mental blind spot about.

4. Indelible mark (Latin).

life, the fetishist feels that he enjoys yet another advantage from his substitute for a genital. The meaning of the fetish is not known to other people, so the fetish is not withheld from him: it is easily accessible and he can readily obtain the sexual satisfaction attached to it. What other men have to woo and make exertions for can be had by the fetishist with no trouble at all.

Probably no male human being is spared the fright of castration at the sight of a female genital. Why some people become homosexual as a consequence of that impression, while others fend it off by creating a fetish, and the great majority surmount it, we are frankly not able to explain. It is possible that, among all the factors at work, we do not yet know those which are decisive for the rare pathological results. We must be content if we can explain what has happened, and may for the present leave on one side the task of explaining why something has *not* happened.

One would expect that the organs or objects chosen as substitutes for the absent female phallus would be such as appear as symbols of the penis in other connections as well. This may happen often enough, but is certainly not a deciding factor. It seems rather that when the fetish is instituted some process occurs which reminds one of the stopping of memory in traumatic amnesia. As in this latter case, the subject's interest comes to a halt halfway, as it were; it is as though the last impression before the uncanny and traumatic one is retained as a fetish. Thus the foot or shoe owes its preference as a fetish—or a part of it—to the circumstance that the inquisitive boy peered at the woman's genitals from below, from her legs up; fur and velvet—as has long been suspected—are a fixation of the sight of the pubic hair, which should have been followed by the longed-for sight of the female member; pieces of underclothing, which are so often chosen as a fetish, crystallize the moment of undressing, the last moment in which the woman could still be regarded as phallic. But I do not maintain that it is invariably possible to discover with certainty how the fetish was determined.

An investigation of fetishism is strongly recommended to anyone who still doubts the existence of the castration complex or who can still believe that fright at the sight of the female genital has some other ground—for instance, that it is derived from a supposed recollection of the trauma of birth.[5]

For me, the explanation of fetishism had another point of theoretical interest as well. Recently, along quite speculative lines, I arrived at the proposition that the essential difference between neurosis and psychosis was that in the former the ego, in the service of reality, suppresses a piece of the id,[6] whereas in a psychosis it lets itself be induced by the id to detach itself from a piece of reality. I returned to this theme once again later on.[7] But soon after this I had reason to regret that I had ventured so far. In the analysis of two young men I learned that each—one when he was two years old and the other when he was ten—had failed to take cognizance of the death of his beloved father—had 'scotomized' it—and yet neither of them

5. This argument was made by the Austrian psychotherapist Otto Rank in *The Trauma of Birth* (1924).

6. The unconscious (literally, "it"). In the Standard Edition, Freud's German terms *das Ich* ("the I," or "ego," referring to the conscious self) and *das Es* ("the it") are rendered in Latin, as is *das Uber-Ich* (the superego), the internalized voice of conscience and judgment directed toward the ego.

7. "Neurosis and Psychosis" (1924) and "The Loss of Reality in Neurosis and Psychosis" (1924) [Freud's note].

had developed a psychosis. Thus a piece of reality which was undoubtedly important had been disavowed by the ego, just as the unwelcome fact of women's castration is disavowed in fetishists. I also began to suspect that similar occurrences in childhood are by no means rare, and I believed that I had been guilty of an error in my characterization of neurosis and psychosis. It is true that there was one way out of the difficulty. My formula needed only to hold good where there was a higher degree of differentiation in the psychical apparatus; things might be permissible to a child which would entail severe injury to an adult.

But further research led to another solution of the contradiction. It turned out that the two young men had no more 'scotomized' their father's death than a fetishist does the castration of women. It was only one current in their mental life that had not recognized their father's death; there was another current which took full account of that fact. The attitude which fitted in with the wish and the attitude which fitted in with reality existed side by side. In one of my two cases this split had formed the basis of a moderately severe obsessional neurosis. The patient oscillated in every situation in life between two assumptions: the one, that his father was still alive and was hindering his activities; the other, opposite one, that he was entitled to regard himself as his father's successor. I may thus keep to the expectation that in a psychosis the one current—that which fitted in with reality—would have in fact been absent.

Returning to my description of fetishism, I may say that there are many and weighty additional proofs of the divided attitude of fetishists to the question of the castration of women. In very subtle instances both the disavowal and the affirmation of the castration have found their way into the construction of the fetish itself. This was so in the case of a man whose fetish was an athletic support-belt which could also be worn as bathing drawers. This piece of clothing covered up the genitals entirely and concealed the distinction between them. Analysis showed that it signified that women were castrated and that they were not castrated; and it also allowed of the hypothesis that men were castrated, for all these possibilities could equally well be concealed under the belt—the earliest rudiment of which in his childhood had been the fig-leaf on a statue. A fetish of this sort, doubly derived from contrary ideas, is of course especially durable. In other instances the divided attitude shows itself in what the fetishist does with his fetish, whether in reality or in his imagination. To point out that he reveres his fetish is not the whole story; in many cases he treats it in a way which is obviously equivalent to a representation of castration. This happens particularly if he has developed a strong identification with his father and plays the part of the latter; for it is to him that as a child he ascribed the woman's castration. Affection and hostility in the treatment of the fetish—which run parallel with the disavowal and the acknowledgment of castration—are mixed in unequal proportions in different cases, so that the one or the other is more clearly recognizable. We seem here to approach an understanding, even if a distant one, of the behaviour of the *'coupeur de nattes'*.[8] In him the need to carry out the castration which he disavows has come to the front. His action contains in itself the two mutually

8. A pervert who enjoys cutting off the hair of females [translator's note].

incompatible assertions: 'the woman has still got a penis' and 'my father has castrated the woman'. Another variant, which is also a parallel to fetishism in social psychology, might be seen in the Chinese custom of mutilating the female foot[9] and then revering it like a fetish after it has been mutilated. It seems as though the Chinese male wants to thank the woman for having submitted to being castrated.

In conclusion we may say that the normal prototype of fetishes is a man's penis, just as the normal prototype of inferior organs is a woman's real small penis, the clitoris.[1]

1927

9. Through footbinding, practiced from the 10th into the 20th century.

1. This is an allusion to Alfred Adler's insistence on "organ-inferiority" as the basis of all neuroses [translator's note]. Adler (1870–1937), Austrian psychiatrist who broke with Freud to form his own school of psychoanalysis in 1911.

FERDINAND DE SAUSSURE
1857–1913

Ferdinand de Saussure gave birth to structuralism by means of a book he never wrote. The *Course in General Linguistics*, based on student notes, was compiled by colleagues in 1916 after Saussure's death. Always described as being born into a "Swiss family distinguished for its intellectual achievements," Saussure, it seems, had no biography apart from the universities in which he studied or taught and the books he failed to write. In fact, Saussure's untimely death at age fifty-six is considered one of the few notable facts about him. Yet this man without a life came to be known as "the father of modern linguistics," and his intellectual progeny affected mid-twentieth-century thought in a wide variety of fields. After Saussure, the very idea of what it meant to study language was transformed.

In the late eighteenth century, the European study of languages had been revolutionized by the encounter with Sanskrit (brought about by the British colonization of India). Comparison between Sanskrit, Greek, and Latin suggested a common ancestor behind all three, which scholars dubbed Proto-Indo-European. Comparative philologists sought to map languages as comparative anatomists had mapped organisms. But the generation of Saussure's teachers, the Neogrammarians, had begun to explore the rules of affinity and transformation in a more truly historical way. Saussure studied historical linguistics with some of them at the University of Leipzig, where he published his only book, *Mémoire sur le système primitif des voyelles dans les langues indo-européennes* (*Memoir on the Primitive System of Vowels in Indo-European Languages*) in 1878, while he was still a graduate student. His precocity was recognized by scholars in the field, and his purely theoretical description of an unknown vowel was later confirmed by studies of the Hittite language.

After spending a year studying in Berlin and receiving his doctorate from the University of Leipzig in 1880, he became a senior lecturer at the École des Hautes Études (School for Advanced Study) in Paris, where he began by teaching Gothic and Old High German, later adding Sanskrit (which he had studied since 1874), Latin, Persian, and Lithuanian. In 1891 he accepted a professorship at the University of Geneva, teaching there for the rest of his life. It was in 1906 that, after the death of a colleague, he was asked to add "general linguistics" to his teaching in historical and comparative linguistics.

In a letter written in 1894 to fellow linguist Antoine Meillet, Saussure outlined his dissatisfaction with linguistic theory as he knew it:

> For a long time I have been above all preoccupied with the logical classification of linguistic facts and with the classification of the points of view from which we treat them; and I am more and more aware of the immense amount of work that would be required to show the linguist *what he is doing*. . . . The utter inadequacy of current terminology, the need to reform it and, in order to do that, to demonstrate what sort of object language is, continually spoil my pleasure in philology, though I have no dearer wish than not to be made to think about the nature of language in general.

Seldom has the condition for a real theoretical breakthrough been described so movingly. Saussure had taken "current terminology" to the point where it began to raise questions it could not answer. The need to study "the nature of language in general" was lived as a spoiled pleasure in philology.

As Saussure's originality increased, his scholarly productivity slowed. Searching for the best approach, he taught general linguistics in three different ways. Not only did he not write up his course, but he did not even keep his lecture notes, starting afresh each time. After his death, his young colleagues found themselves fabricating a synthesis of three fragmentary sets of student notes, with the result that the Saussure who is the author of the *Course in General Linguistics* is a function of the edited text, not its origin. Yet that was the Saussure who changed intellectual history.

What was Saussure's new theory of language? The diversity of languages, often thought to indicate a falling away from one original language (as in the story of Babel), indicated to Saussure not a story but a principle: the principle of the "arbitrary" (purely conventional) nature of the sign. Since there are thousands of human languages, the relation between words and things cannot be based on natural resemblances. For example, no inherent affinity or motivation leads people to call an avian creature *bird* or *oiseau*. Not only that, Saussure went on, but *language is not a nomenclature*. Rather than the world consisting of things that need names (the Adamic conception), each language brings into being, by describing, a world that it then knows as external. To be sure, the external world exists—but its reality remains quite nebulous until language articulates it. The way lines divide concepts and phrases, the way even concrete items are viewed, is specific to each language; each covers all that needs to be said, but in its different way.

Saussure's own theory illustrates this point: his terms *langage, langue*, and *parole* have never been satisfactorily translated into English. *Le langage* (in English, "language") is a general human faculty, that which enables us to speak of "body language" or "the language of fashion." *La langue*, which in English is also called "language," is the name for specific languages (*la langue anglaise*, the English language); but it is also the most general term for language itself, the term Saussure uses to name the object of linguistics. *La langue* in this sense does not exist: it is a theoretical object abstracted from the structures of specific languages. *La parole* (speech) is what Saussure calls "the executive side": the concrete utterances that constitute all acts of language. These individual utterances are excluded from his theory of language insofar as they only "execute" possibilities that exist in language already, or depart from it for creative purposes without fundamentally changing it. But where Saussure uses three terms for these distinctions, English possesses only two.

Language, for Saussure, is a structured system of conventional signs, studied in their internal complexity as if frozen in time (synchronically) rather than as changing over time (diachronically). Saussure saw the study of language as eventually forming part of a larger science of signs in culture, which he called *semiology*, a field that later scholars (see ROLAND BARTHES) went on to develop. The atom of language is the sign, which is functionally split into two parts: a *signifier* (sound-image) and a *signified* (concept), brought inseparably together like the two sides of a sheet of paper. The relation between the signifier and the signified is "arbitrary," not "motivated" (by natural resemblance), even in cases of onomatopoiea (words that sound like what they mean). The word *arbitrary* means not that individual speakers can just make language up, but precisely that they can't: the sign is a convention that has to be learned and is not subject to individual will. The point is not that languages do not change (they are changing all the time), but that the changes themselves follow paths that have more to do with the overall structure of the language than with any intentional intervention by its speakers.

Though the signifier and the signified seem to function together as a unit to produce signification, each has *value* only by virtue of the ways in which it differs from other terms. Here, the chain of signifiers and the chain of signifieds diverge. A signifier differs from other signifiers while its signified distinguishes itself from other signifieds, and the networks of connection and distinction are not parallel, as Saussure's misleading diagram of the two realms might suggest. Saussure's distinction between "signification" and "value" is similar to KARL MARX's distinction between "use value" and "exchange value": the first appears tied to the characteristics of the object or term, whereas the second is entirely a function of the system of exchange or of language. Saussure goes so far as to say that *everything* in language is relational: "in language there are only differences. Even more important: a difference generally implies positive terms between which the difference is set up; but in language there are only differences *without positive terms*" (Saussure's emphasis). In other words, neither ideas nor sounds exist prior to their combination. This description of a difference that does not depend on the prior existence of knowable entities is one of Saussure's most radical declarations.

Jokes often play on the purely differential aspect of language. A homeowner answering the phone and hearing that "The viper is coming" might feel fear, but when the voice on the line explains that "he's coming to vipe your vindows," what had initially been a serpent becomes a benign household maintenance worker. A foreign accent changes the sounds in a language without changing the system of differences. The sound *v* takes on the differential role of *w* in this joke as soon as it becomes clear *to what* it is being opposed.

Nevertheless, once combined, the signifier and signified do become a unit, an *articulus* in a system of articulations. The articulations are positive facts—the only kind of facts language possesses, since, as Saussure stresses, *language is a form and not a substance*. Once the differential structure has severed any natural connection between language and things, the sign becomes a building block of a system of oppositions: singular, plural; past, present, future; voiced, unvoiced; masculine, feminine. Saussure's favorite metaphor for the kind of structure he has in mind is chess: a rule-bound system of oppositions and differences that governs a closed but infinite set of operations.

In Saussure's conception of language, the sign is not only arbitrary but also linear (he thus uses a spatial term for what is in fact temporal, the succession of signs as they unfold in time during speech). Signs are combined like links in a chain to form the line of language according to two relations: the *syntagmatic* (all units present in their articulation) and the *associative* (all related units present in the mind but absent from the actual sequence). This distinction, later called *syntagmatic* and *paradigmatic*, would form an important part of ROMAN JAKOBSON's theory of metaphor and metonymy (see below). For Saussure, some syntagmatic relations beyond mere grammatical rules count as *language* rather than *speech*. Far from being freely chosen by each speaker, they constitute the "idioms" that a newcomer must master in order to "know" a language.

At the end of his life, Saussure was working on another project in which he had even less confidence than in his theory of general linguistics. According to notebooks published by Jean Starobinski starting in 1964 and eventually collected as *Les Mots sous les mots* (1971; trans. 1979, *Words upon Words*), Saussure was fascinated by the idea that within the verses written by certain Latin poets, deliberately concealed anagrams of proper names could be detected. Thus, a hidden poetics of names generated textual patterns that appeared to be dictated by the surface meanings of the words used as "carriers" for the letters. But Saussure could never be sure of what he found, and the notebooks remained hidden away. To compound the difficulty, the anagram project entailed a displacement of a major principle of the *Course*: while the *Course* treated the signifier-signified relation as a unit, the anagrams implied that signifiers and signifieds could function separately, that a signifier could serve more than one function, and that the signifier could take the lead in the organization of a text. These implications, which Saussure viewed with incredulity, had a profound impact on later textual theory.

Saussure's work provided the groundwork for both structuralism and poststructuralism. It was part of the larger "linguistic turn" in twentieth-century philosophy, history, anthropology, psychoanalysis, and literary studies. CLAUDE LÉVI-STRAUSS, for example, studied myths and kinship systems within different cultures as a system of signs to be interpreted. Roland Barthes explored the semiology of fashion, advertising, travel, and many other cultural phenomena. JACQUES DERRIDA, while critiquing Saussure's privileging of spoken language (Saussure called writing secondary, pathological, even monstrous with respect to the speech it records), nevertheless took up many aspects of Saussure's system of differences into what he called *différance*. LOUIS ALTHUSSER understood, on the basis of what Saussure says about language as a system, that economic and social structures, too, possess structural (rather than transitive) causality. And finally, JACQUES LACAN used Saussure to reformulate SIGMUND FREUD in linguistic terms, while JULIA KRISTEVA developed a theory of the anagrammatical nature of literature.

Of course, the very things that made Saussure's thought so revealing and influential also led to the most serious objections. By focusing on the relation between signifier and signified, he gained insight into linguistic structure yet eliminated the world. "Bracketing the referent"—that is, leaving out the third dimension of the sign, that to which it refers—has been criticized by those, like TERRY EAGLETON, who find it impossible to speak of language without speaking of reference, things, history. After all, they argue, language is not chess. How can it be studied apart from the world to which it refers? How can reference not have a role in structure? In addition, language is neither unified nor closed, as deconstructors and poststructuralists were quick to point out. Even if it is frozen in time, conflict remains unresolved and essential within the system. And the later postmodern critique of the "universal subject" has emphasized that speakers are placed in very different positions within language by class, gender, race, geography, and so on. In our "viper" joke, for example, a small linguistic difference points to a whole system of class, property, ethnicity, and, varying with the gender of the homeowner, sexual politics—including an echo of the story of Adam, Eve, and the serpent.

Despite these criticisms, the *Course in General Linguistics* opened up as never before the question of the role of signs in culture and the role of language in the mind. As Jonathan Culler put it in *Ferdinand de Saussure* (1986), "What the study of language reveals about mind is not a set of primitive conceptions or natural ideas but the general structuring and differentiating operations by which things are made to signify."

***Course in General Linguistics* Keywords:** Language, Semiotics, Structuralism

From Course in General Linguistics[1]

From *Introduction*

FROM CHAPTER III. THE OBJECT OF LINGUISTICS

2. *Place of Language in the Facts of Speech*

* * *

To summarize, these are the characteristics of language:

(1) Language is a well-defined object in the heterogeneous mass of speech facts. It can be localized in the limited segment of the speaking-circuit where an auditory image becomes associated with a concept. It is the social side of speech, outside the individual who can never create nor modify it by himself; it exists only by virtue of a sort of contract signed by the members of a community. Moreover, the individual must always serve an apprenticeship in order to learn the functioning of language; a child assimilates it only gradually. It is such a distinct thing that a man deprived of the use of speaking retains it provided that he understands the vocal signs that he hears.

(2) Language, unlike speaking, is something that we can study separately. Although dead languages are no longer spoken, we can easily assimilate their linguistic organisms. We can dispense with the other elements of speech; indeed, the science of language is possible only if the other elements are excluded.

(3) Whereas speech is heterogeneous, language, as defined, is homogeneous. It is a system of signs in which the only essential thing is the union of meanings and sound-images, and in which both parts of the sign are psychological.

(4) Language is concrete, no less so than speaking; and this is a help in our study of it. Linguistic signs, though basically psychological, are not abstractions; associations which bear the stamp of collective approval—and which added together constitute language—are realities that have their seat in the brain. Besides, linguistic signs are tangible; it is possible to reduce them to conventional written symbols, whereas it would be impossible to provide detailed photographs of acts of speaking [*actes de parole*]; the pronunciation of even the smallest word represents an infinite number of muscular movements that could be identified and put into graphic form only with great difficulty. In language, on the contrary, there is only the sound-image, and the latter can be translated into a fixed visual image. For if we disregard the vast number of movements necessary for the realization of sound-images in speaking, we see that each sound-image is nothing more than the sum of a limited number of elements or phonemes[2] that can in turn be called up by a corresponding number of written symbols. The very possibility of putting the things that relate to language into graphic form allows dictionaries and grammars to represent it accurately, for language is a storehouse of sound-images, and writing is the tangible form of those images.

1. Edited by Charles Bally and Albert Sechehaye in collaboration with Albert Riedlinger; translated by Wade Baskin, who occasionally includes the French in square brackets.
2. The smallest distinctive unit of sound in a spoken language.

3. *Place of Language in Human Facts: Semiology*

The foregoing characteristics of language reveal an even more important characteristic. Language, once its boundaries have been marked off within the speech data, can be classified among human phenomena, whereas speech cannot.

We have just seen that language is a social institution; but several features set it apart from other political, legal, etc. institutions. We must call in a new type of facts in order to illuminate the special nature of language.

Language is a system of signs that express ideas, and is therefore comparable to a system of writing, the alphabet of deaf-mutes, symbolic rites, polite formulas, military signals, etc. But it is the most important of all these systems.

A science that studies the life of signs within society is conceivable; it would be a part of social psychology and consequently of general psychology; I shall call it *semiology* (from Greek *sēmeîon* 'sign'). Semiology would show what constitutes signs, what laws govern them. Since the science does not yet exist, no one can say what it would be; but it has a right to existence, a place staked out in advance. Linguistics is only a part of the general science of semiology; the laws discovered by semiology will be applicable to linguistics, and the latter will circumscribe a well-defined area within the mass of anthropological facts.

To determine the exact place of semiology is the task of the psychologist. The task of the linguist is to find out what makes language a special system within the mass of semiological data. This issue will be taken up again later; here I wish merely to call attention to one thing: if I have succeeded in assigning linguistics a place among the sciences, it is because I have related it to semiology.

Why has semiology not yet been recognized as an independent science with its own object like all the other sciences? Linguists have been going around in circles: language, better than anything else, offers a basis for understanding the semiological problem; but language must, to put it correctly, be studied in itself; heretofore language has almost always been studied in connection with something else, from other viewpoints.

There is first of all the superficial notion of the general public: people see nothing more than a name-giving system in language, thereby prohibiting any research into its true nature.

Then there is the viewpoint of the psychologist, who studies the sign-mechanism in the individual; this is the easiest method, but it does not lead beyond individual execution and does not reach the sign, which is social.

Or even when signs are studied from a social viewpoint, only the traits that attach language to the other social institutions—those that are more or less voluntary—are emphasized; as a result, the goal is by-passed and the specific characteristics of semiological systems in general and of language in particular are completely ignored. For the distinguishing characteristic of the sign—but the one that is least apparent at first sight—is that in some way it always eludes the individual or social will.

In short, the characteristic that distinguishes semiological systems from all other institutions shows up clearly only in language where it manifests itself in the things which are studied least, and the necessity or specific value of a semiological science is therefore not clearly recognized. But to me the language problem is mainly semiological, and all developments derive their significance from that important fact. If we are to discover the true nature of language we must learn what it has in common with all other semiological systems; linguistic forces that seem very important at first glance (e.g., the role of the vocal apparatus) will receive only secondary consideration if they serve only to set language apart from the other systems. This procedure will do more than to clarify the linguistic problem. By studying rites, customs, etc. as signs, I believe that we shall throw new light on the facts and point up the need for including them in a science of semiology and explaining them by its laws.

From *Part One. General Principles*

CHAPTER I. NATURE OF THE LINGUISTIC SIGN

1. *Sign, Signified, Signifier*

Some people regard language, when reduced to its elements, as a naming-process only—a list of words, each corresponding to the thing that it names. For example:[3]

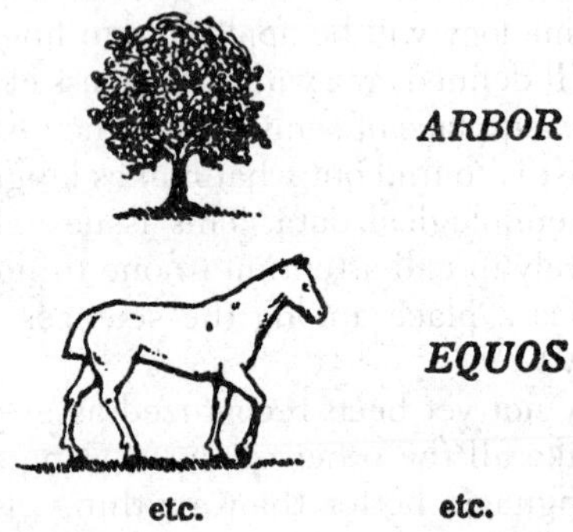

This conception is open to criticism at several points. It assumes that ready-made ideas exist before words (on this point, see below); it does not tell us whether a name is vocal or psychological in nature (*arbor*, for instance, can be considered from either viewpoint); finally, it lets us assume that the linking of a name and a thing is a very simple operation—an assumption that is anything but true. But this rather naive approach can bring us near the truth by showing us that the linguistic unit is a double entity, one formed by the associating of two terms.

We have seen in considering the speaking-circuit that both terms involved in the linguistic sign are psychological and are united in the brain by an associative bond. This point must be emphasized.

The linguistic sign unites, not a thing and a name, but a concept and a sound-image.[4] The latter is not the material sound, a purely physical thing, but the psychological imprint of the sound, the impression that it makes on

3. In the figure, tree and horse (the more usual base form is *equus*), respectively (Latin).

4. The term sound-image may seem to be too restricted inasmuch as beside the representation of the sounds of a word there is also that of its articulation, the muscular image of the phonational act. But for F. de Saussure language is essentially a depository, a thing received from without. The sound-image is par excellence the natural representation of the word as a fact of potential language, outside any actual use of it in speaking. The motor side is thus implied or, in any event, occupies only a subordinate role with respect to the sound-image [Bally, Sechehaye, and Riedlinger's note].

our senses. The sound-image is sensory, and if I happen to call it "material," it is only in that sense, and by way of opposing it to the other term of the association, the concept, which is generally more abstract.

The psychological character of our sound-images becomes apparent when we observe our own speech. Without moving our lips or tongue, we can talk to ourselves or recite mentally a selection of verse. Because we regard the words of our language as sound-images, we must avoid speaking of the "phonemes" that make up the words. This term, which suggests vocal activity, is applicable to the spoken word only, to the realization of the inner image in discourse. We can avoid that misunderstanding by speaking of the *sounds* and *syllables* of a word provided we remember that the names refer to the sound-image.

The linguistic sign is then a two-sided psychological entity that can be represented by the drawing:

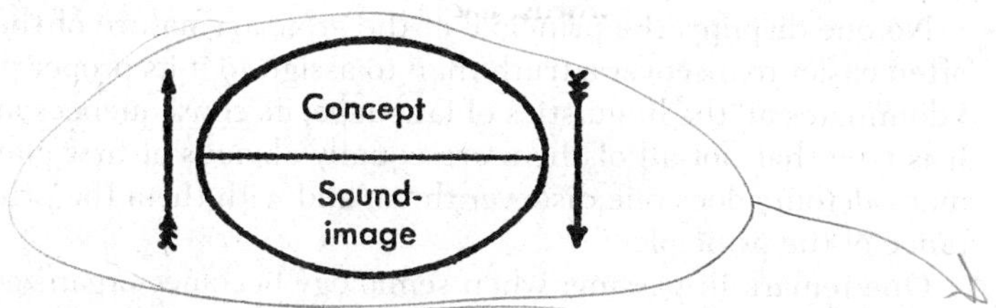

The two elements are intimately united, and each recalls the other. Whether we try to find the meaning of the Latin word *arbor* or the word that Latin uses to designate the concept "tree," it is clear that only the associations sanctioned by that language appear to us to conform to reality, and we disregard whatever others might be imagined.

Our definition of the linguistic sign poses an important question of terminology. I call the combination of a concept and a sound-image a *sign*, but in current usage the term generally designates only a sound-image, a word, for example (*arbor*, etc.). One tends to forget that *arbor* is called a sign only because it carries the concept "tree," with the result that the idea of the sensory part implies the idea of the whole.

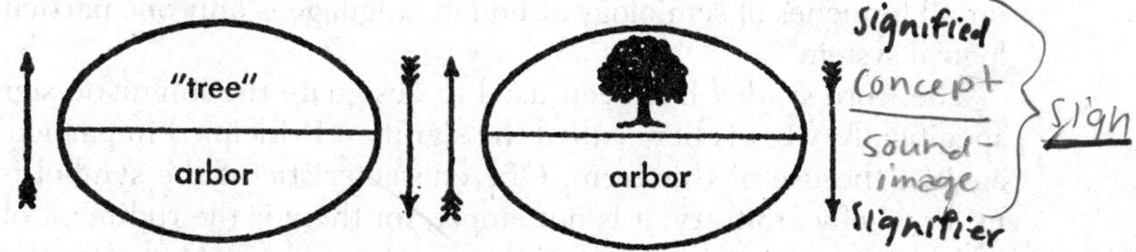

Ambiguity would disappear if the three notions involved here were designated by three names, each suggesting and opposing the others. I propose to retain the word *sign* [*signe*] to designate the whole and to replace *concept* and *sound-image* respectively by *signified* [*signifié*] and *signifier* [*signifiant*]; the last two terms have the advantage of indicating the opposition that separates them from each other and from the whole of which they are parts. As regards *sign*, if I am satisfied with it, this is simply because I do not know of any word to replace it, the ordinary language suggesting no other.

The linguistic sign, as defined, has two primordial characteristics. In enunciating them I am also positing the basic principles of any study of this type.

2. *Principle I: The Arbitrary Nature of the Sign*

The bond between the signifier and the signified is arbitrary. Since I mean by sign the whole that results from the associating of the signifier with the signified, I can simply say: *the linguistic sign is arbitrary.*

The idea of "sister" is not linked by any inner relationship to the succession of sounds *s-ö-r* which serves as its signifier in French; that it could be represented equally by just any other sequence is proved by differences among languages and by the very existence of different languages: the signified "ox" has as its signifier *b-ö-f* on one side of the border and *o-k-s* (*Ochs*) on the other.[5]

No one disputes the principle of the arbitrary nature of the sign, but it is often easier to discover a truth than to assign to it its proper place. Principle I dominates all the linguistics of language; its consequences are numberless. It is true that not all of them are equally obvious at first glance; only after many detours does one discover them, and with them the primordial importance of the principle.

One remark in passing: when semiology becomes organized as a science, the question will arise whether or not it properly includes modes of expression based on completely natural signs, such as pantomime. Supposing that the new science welcomes them, its main concern will still be the whole group of systems grounded on the arbitrariness of the sign. In fact, every means of expression used in society is based, in principle, on collective behavior or—what amounts to the same thing—on convention. Polite formulas, for instance, though often imbued with a certain natural expressiveness (as in the case of a Chinese who greets his emperor by bowing down to the ground nine times), are nonetheless fixed by rule; it is this rule and not the intrinsic value of the gestures that obliges one to use them. Signs that are wholly arbitrary realize better than the others the ideal of the semiological process; that is why language, the most complex and universal of all systems of expression, is also the most characteristic; in this sense linguistics can become the master-pattern for all branches of semiology although language is only one particular semiological system.

The word *symbol* has been used to designate the linguistic sign, or more specifically, what is here called the signifier. Principle I in particular weighs against the use of this term. One characteristic of the symbol is that it is never wholly arbitrary; it is not empty, for there is the rudiment of a natural bond between the signifier and the signified. The symbol of justice, a pair of scales, could not be replaced by just any other symbol, such as a chariot.

The word *arbitrary* also calls for comment. The term should not imply that the choice of the signifier is left entirely to the speaker (we shall see below that the individual does not have the power to change a sign in any way once it has become established in the linguistic community); I mean that it is unmotivated, i.e. arbitrary in that it actually has no natural connection with the signified.

5. That is, in Germany.

In concluding let us consider two objections that might be raised to the establishment of Principle I:

(1) *Onomatopoeia* might be used to prove that the choice of the signifier is not always arbitrary. But onomatopoeic formations are never organic elements of a linguistic system. Besides, their number is much smaller than is generally supposed. Words like French *fouet* 'whip' or *glas* 'knell' may strike certain ears with suggestive sonority, but to see that they have not always had this property we need only examine their Latin forms (*fouet* is derived from *fāgus* 'beech-tree,' *glas* from *classicum* 'sound of a trumpet'). The quality of their present sounds, or rather the quality that is attributed to them, is a fortuitous result of phonetic evolution.

As for authentic onomatopoeic words (e.g. *glug-glug, tick-tock*, etc.), not only are they limited in number, but also they are chosen somewhat arbitrarily, for they are only approximate and more or less conventional imitations of certain sounds (cf. English *bow-wow* and French *ouaoua*). In addition, once these words have been introduced into the language, they are to a certain extent subjected to the same evolution—phonetic, morphological, etc.—that other words undergo (cf. *pigeon*, ultimately from Vulgar Latin *pīpiō*, derived in turn from an onomatopoeic formation): obvious proof that they lose something of their original character in order to assume that of the linguistic sign in general, which is unmotivated.

(2) *Interjections*, closely related to onomatopoeia, can be attacked on the same grounds and come no closer to refuting our thesis. One is tempted to see in them spontaneous expressions of reality dictated, so to speak, by natural forces. But for most interjections we can show that there is no fixed bond between their signified and their signifier. We need only compare two languages on this point to see how much such expressions differ from one language to the next (e.g. the English equivalent of French *aïe!* is *ouch!*). We know, moreover, that many interjections were once words with specific meanings (cf. French *diable!*[6] 'darn!' *mordieu!* 'golly!' from *mort Dieu* 'God's death,' etc.).

Onomatopoeic formations and interjections are of secondary importance, and their symbolic origin is in part open to dispute.

3. *Principle II: The Linear Nature of the Signifier*

The signifier, being auditory, is unfolded solely in time from which it gets the following characteristics: (a) it represents a span, and (b) the span is measurable in a single dimension; it is a line.

While Principle II is obvious, apparently linguists have always neglected to state it, doubtless because they found it too simple; nevertheless, it is fundamental, and its consequences are incalculable. Its importance equals that of Principle I; the whole mechanism of language depends upon it. In contrast to visual signifiers (nautical signals, etc.) which can offer simultaneous groupings in several dimensions, auditory signifiers have at their command only the dimension of time. Their elements are presented in succession; they form a chain. This feature becomes readily apparent when they are represented in writing and the spatial line of graphic marks is substituted for succession in time.

6. Literally, "devil."

Sometimes the linear nature of the signifier is not obvious. When I accent a syllable, for instance, it seems that I am concentrating more than one significant element on the same point. But this is an illusion; the syllable and its accent constitute only one phonational act. There is no duality within the act but only different oppositions to what precedes and what follows.

From *Part Two. Synchronic Linguistics*

CHAPTER IV. LINGUISTIC VALUE

1. *Language as Organized Thought Coupled with Sound*

To prove that language is only a system of pure values, it is enough to consider the two elements involved in its functioning: ideas and sounds.

Psychologically our thought—apart from its expression in words—is only a shapeless and indistinct mass. Philosophers and linguists have always agreed in recognizing that without the help of signs we would be unable to make a clear-cut, consistent distinction between two ideas. Without language, thought is a vague, uncharted nebula. There are no pre-existing ideas, and nothing is distinct before the appearance of language.

Against the floating realm of thought, would sounds by themselves yield predelimited entities? No more so than ideas. Phonic substance is neither more fixed nor more rigid than thought; it is not a mold into which thought must of necessity fit but a plastic substance divided in turn into distinct parts to furnish the signifiers needed by thought. The linguistic fact can therefore be pictured in its totality—i.e. language—as a series of contiguous subdivisions marked off on both the indefinite plane of jumbled ideas (*A*) and the equally vague plane of sounds (*B*). The following diagram gives a rough idea of it:

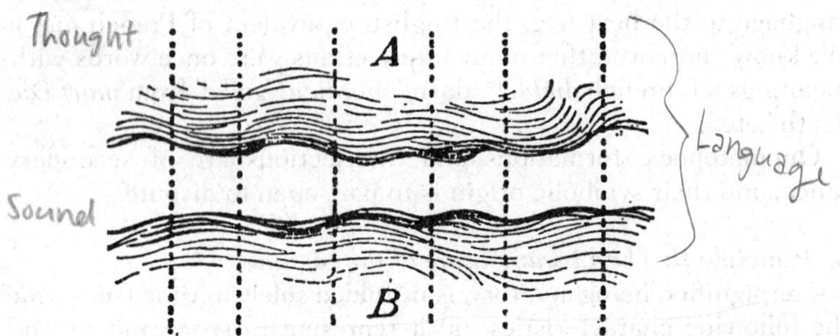

The characteristic role of language with respect to thought is not to create a material phonic means for expressing ideas but to serve as a link between thought and sound, under conditions that of necessity bring about the reciprocal delimitations of units. Thought, chaotic by nature, has to become ordered in the process of its decomposition. Neither are thoughts given material form nor are sounds transformed into mental entities; the somewhat mysterious fact is rather that "thought-sound" implies division, and that language works out its units while taking shape between two shapeless masses. Visualize the air in contact with a sheet of water; if the atmospheric pressure changes, the surface of the water will be broken up into a series of divisions, waves; the waves resemble the union or coupling of thought with phonic substance.

Language might be called the domain of articulations, using the word as it was defined earlier. Each linguistic term is a member, an *articulus* in which an idea is fixed in a sound and a sound becomes the sign of an idea.

Language can also be compared with a sheet of paper:[7] thought is the front and the sound the back; one cannot cut the front without cutting the back at the same time; likewise in language, one can neither divide sound from thought nor thought from sound; the division could be accomplished only abstractedly, and the result would be either pure psychology or pure phonology.

Linguistics then works in the borderland where the elements of sound and thought combine; *their combination produces a form, not a substance*.

These views give a better understanding of what was said before about the arbitrariness of signs. Not only are the two domains that are linked by the linguistic fact shapeless and confused, but the choice of a given slice of sound to name a given idea is completely arbitrary. If this were not true, the notion of value would be compromised, for it would include an externally imposed element. But actually values remain entirely relative, and that is why the bond between the sound and the idea is radically arbitrary.

The arbitrary nature of the sign explains in turn why the social fact alone can create a linguistic system. The community is necessary if values that owe their existence solely to usage and general acceptance are to be set up; by himself the individual is incapable of fixing a single value.

In addition, the idea of value, as defined, shows that to consider a term as simply the union of a certain sound with a certain concept is grossly misleading. To define it in this way would isolate the term from its system; it would mean assuming that one can start from the terms and construct the system by adding them together when, on the contrary, it is from the interdependent whole that one must start and through analysis obtain its elements.

To develop this thesis, we shall study value successively from the viewpoint of the signified or concept (Section 2), the signifier (Section 3), and the complete sign (Section 4).

Being unable to seize the concrete entities or units of language directly, we shall work with words. While the word does not conform exactly to the definition of the linguistic unit, it at least bears a rough resemblance to the unit and has the advantage of being concrete; consequently, we shall use words as specimens equivalent to real terms in a synchronic system, and the principles that we evolve with respect to words will be valid for entities in general.

2. *Linguistic Value from a Conceptual Viewpoint*

When we speak of the value of a word, we generally think first of its property of standing for an idea, and this is in fact one side of linguistic value. But if this is true, how does *value* differ from *signification*? Might the two words be synonyms? I think not, although it is easy to confuse them, since the confusion results not so much from their similarity as from the subtlety of the distinction that they mark.

From a conceptual viewpoint, value is doubtless one element in signification, and it is difficult to see how signification can be dependent upon value

7. The French expression *une feuille de papier* literally means "a *leaf* of paper."

and still be distinct from it. But we must clear up the issue or risk reducing language to a simple naming-process.

Let us first take signification as it is generally understood. As the arrows in the drawing show, it is only the counterpart of the sound-image. Everything that occurs concerns only the sound-image and the concept when we look upon the word as independent and self-contained.

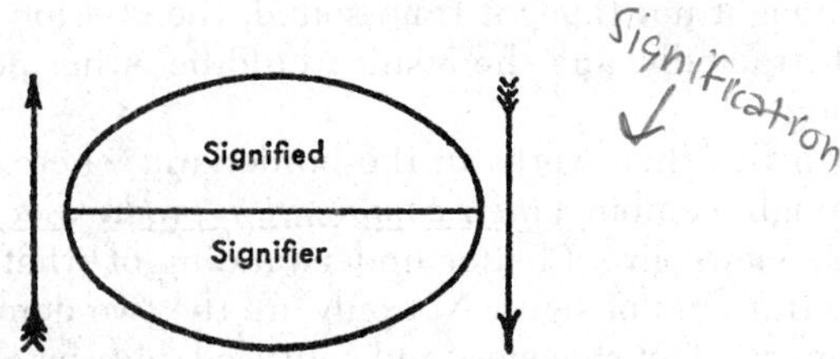

But here is the paradox: on the one hand the concept seems to be the counterpart of the sound-image, and on the other hand the sign itself is in turn the counterpart of the other signs of language.

Language is a system of interdependent terms in which the value of each term results solely from the simultaneous presence of the others, as in the diagram:

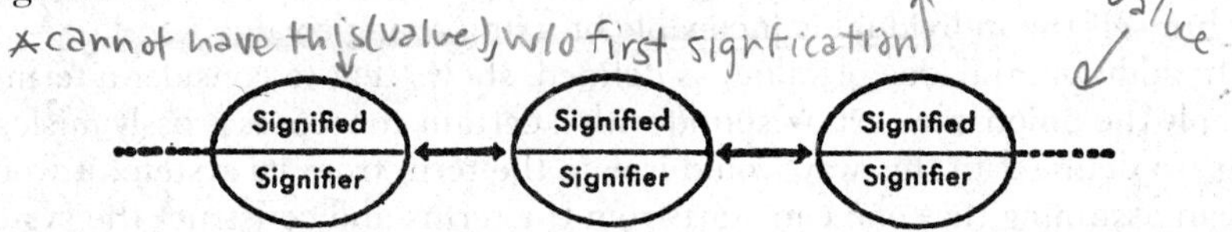

How, then, can value be confused with signification, i.e. the counterpart of the sound-image? It seems impossible to liken the relations represented here by horizontal arrows to those represented above by vertical arrows. Putting it another way—and again taking up the example of the sheet of paper that is cut in two—it is clear that the observable relation between the different pieces A, B, C, D, etc. is distinct from the relation between the front and back of the same piece as in A / A', B / B', etc.

To resolve the issue, let us observe from the outset that even outside language all values are apparently governed by the same paradoxical principle. They are always composed:

(1) of a *dissimilar* thing that can be *exchanged* for the thing of which the value is to be determined; and

(2) of *similar* things that can be *compared* with the thing of which the value is to be determined.

Both factors are necessary for the existence of a value. To determine what a five-franc piece is worth one must therefore know: (1) that it can be exchanged for a fixed quantity of a different thing, e.g. bread; and (2) that it can be compared with a similar value of the same system, e.g. a one-franc piece, or with coins of another system (a dollar, etc.). In the same way a word can be exchanged for something dissimilar, an idea; besides, it can be compared with something of the same nature, another word. Its value is therefore not fixed so long as one simply states that it can be "exchanged" for a given concept, i.e. that it has this or that signification: one must also compare it with similar values, with other words that stand in opposition to it. Its content is really fixed only by the concurrence of everything that exists outside it. Being part of a system, it is endowed not only with a signification but also and especially with a value, and this is something quite different.

A few examples will show clearly that this is true. Modern French *mouton* can have the same signification as English *sheep* but not the same value, and this for several reasons, particularly because in speaking of a piece of meat ready to be served on the table, English uses *mutton* and not *sheep*. The difference in value between *sheep* and *mouton* is due to the fact that *sheep* has beside it a second term while the French word does not.

Within the same language, all words used to express related ideas limit each other reciprocally; synonyms like French *redouter* 'dread,' *craindre* 'fear,' and *avoir peur* 'be afraid' have value only through their opposition: if *redouter* did not exist, all its content would go to its competitors. Conversely, some words are enriched through contact with others: e.g. the new element introduced in *décrépit* (un vieillard *décrépit*) results from the co-existence of *décrépi* (un mur *décrépi*).[8] [The value of just any term is accordingly determined by its environment; it is impossible to fix even the value of the word signifying "sun" without first considering its surroundings: in some languages it is not possible to say "sit in the *sun*."]

Everything said about words applies to any term of language, e.g. to grammatical entities. The value of a French plural does not coincide with that of a Sanskrit plural even though their signification is usually identical; Sanskrit has three numbers instead of two (*my eyes, my ears, my arms, my legs,* etc. are dual[9]); it would be wrong to attribute the same value to the plural in Sanskrit and in French; its value clearly depends on what is outside and around it.

If words stood for pre-existing concepts, they would all have exact equivalents in meaning from one language to the next; but this is not true. French uses *louer (une maison)* 'let (a house)' indifferently to mean both "pay for" and "receive payment for," whereas German uses two words, *mieten* and *vermieten*; there is obviously no exact correspondence of values. The German verbs *schätzen* and *urteilen*[1] share a number of significations, but that correspondence does not hold at several points.

Inflection offers some particularly striking examples. Distinctions of time, which are so familiar to us, are unknown in certain languages. Hebrew does not recognize even the fundamental distinctions between the past, present, and future. Proto-Germanic has no special form for the future; to say that the future is expressed by the present is wrong, for the value of the present is not the same in Germanic as in languages that have a future along with the present. The Slavic languages regularly single out two aspects of the verb: the perfective represents action as a point, complete in its totality; the imperfective represents it as taking place, and on the line of time. The categories are difficult for a Frenchman to understand, for they are unknown in French; if they were predetermined, this would not be true. Instead of pre-existing ideas then, we find in all the foregoing examples *values* emanating from the system. When they are said to correspond to concepts, it is

8. The words translated as "decrepit" in "a decrepit old man" and "a decrepit wall" come from two different sources: *décrépit* is derived from the Latin *dēcrepitus*, *décrépi* from *crispus*.

9. A special form applied to 2 of something.

1. "To value, assess" and "to judge," respectively.

understood that the concepts are purely differential and defined not by their positive content but negatively by their relations with the other terms of the system. Their most precise characteristic is in being what the others are not.

Now the real interpretation of the diagram of the signal becomes apparent. Thus

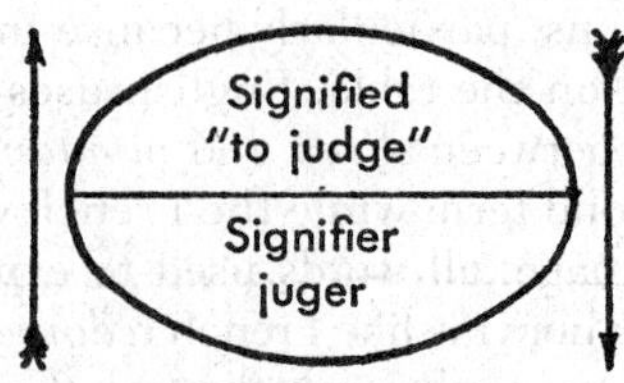

means that in French the concept "to judge" is linked to the sound-image *juger*; in short, it symbolizes signification. But it is quite clear that initially the concept is nothing, that is only a value determined by its relations with other similar values, and that without them the signification would not exist. If I state simply that a word signifies something when I have in mind the associating of a sound-image with a concept, I am making a statement that may suggest what actually happens, but by no means am I expressing the linguistic fact in its essence and fullness.

3. *Linguistic Value from a Material Viewpoint*

The conceptual side of value is made up solely of relations and differences with respect to the other terms of language, and the same can be said of its material side. The important thing in the word is not the sound alone but the phonic differences that make it possible to distinguish this word from all others, for differences carry signification.

This may seem surprising, but how indeed could the reverse be possible? Since one vocal image is no better suited than the next for what it is commissioned to express, it is evident, even *a priori*, that a segment of language can never in the final analysis be based on anything except its noncoincidence with the rest. *Arbitrary* and *differential* are two correlative qualities.

The alteration of linguistic signs clearly illustrates this. It is precisely because the terms *a* and *b* as such are radically incapable of reaching the level of consciousness—one is always conscious of only the *a* / *b* difference—that each term is free to change according to laws that are unrelated to its signifying function. No positive sign characterizes the genitive plural in Czech *žen;* still the two forms *žena: žen* function as well as the earlier forms *žena: ženъ; žen* has value only because it is different.

Here is another example that shows even more clearly the systematic role of phonic differences: in Greek, *éphēn* is an imperfect and *éstēn* an aorist[2] although both words are formed in the same way; the first belongs to the system of the present indicative of *phēmī* 'I say,' whereas there is no present **stēmi*; now it is precisely the relation *phēmī: éphēn* that corresponds to the relation between the

2. "Imperfect" and "aorist" are two past tenses of Greek verbs (representing an incomplete or continuing action and the simple occurrence of an action, respectively).

present and the imperfect (cf. *déiknūmi: edéiknūn*,[3] etc.). Signs function, then, not through their intrinsic value but through their relative position.

In addition, it is impossible for sound alone, a material element, to belong to language. It is only a secondary thing, substance to be put to use. All our conventional values have the characteristic of not being confused with the tangible element which supports them. For instance, it is not the metal in a piece of money that fixes its value. A coin nominally worth five francs may contain less than half its worth of silver. Its value will vary according to the amount stamped upon it and according to its use inside or outside a political boundary. This is even more true of the linguistic signifier, which is not phonic but incorporeal—constituted not by its material substance but by the differences that separate its sound-image from all others.

The foregoing principle is so basic that it applies to all the material elements of language, including phonemes. Every language forms its words on the basis of a system of sonorous elements, each element being a clearly delimited unit and one of a fixed number of units. Phonemes are characterized not, as one might think, by their own positive quality but simply by the fact that they are distinct. Phonemes are above all else opposing, relative, and negative entities.

Proof of this is the latitude that speakers have between points of convergence in the pronunciation of distinct sounds. In French, for instance, general use of a dorsal *r* does not prevent many speakers from using a tongue-tip trill; language is not in the least disturbed by it; language requires only that the sound be different and not, as one might imagine, that it have an invariable quality. I can even pronounce the French *r* like German *ch* in *Bach, doch*, etc., but in German I could not use *r* instead of *ch*, for German gives recognition to both elements and must keep them apart. Similarly, in Russian there is no latitude for *t* in the direction of *t'* (palatalized *t*), for the result would be the confusing of two sounds differentiated by the language (cf. *govorit'* 'speak' and *goverit* 'he speaks'), but more freedom may be taken with respect to *th* (aspirated *t*) since this sound does not figure in the Russian system of phonemes.

Since an identical state of affairs is observable in writing, another system of signs, we shall use writing to draw some comparisons that will clarify the whole issue. In fact:

(1) The signs used in writing are arbitrary; there is no connection, for example, between the letter *t* and the sound that it designates.

(2) The value of letters is purely negative and differential. The same person can write *t*, for instance, in different ways:

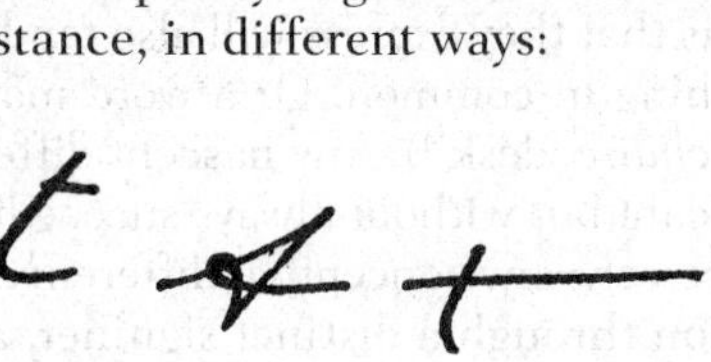

The only requirement is that the sign for *t* not be confused in his script with the signs used for *l, d*, etc.

3. The present and imperfect, respectively, of the Greek verb "to show" (all the forms in this paragraph are 1st-person singular).

(3) Values in writing function only through reciprocal opposition within a fixed system that consists of a set number of letters. This third characteristic, though not identical to the second, is closely related to it, for both depend on the first. Since the graphic sign is arbitrary, its form matters little or rather matters only within the limitations imposed by the system.

(4) The means by which the sign is produced is completely unimportant, for it does not affect the system (this also follows from characteristic 1). Whether I make the letters in white or black, raised or engraved, with pen or chisel—all this is of no importance with respect to their signification.

4. *The Sign Considered in Its Totality*

Everything that has been said up to this point boils down to this: in language there are only differences. Even more important: a difference generally implies positive terms between which the difference is set up; but in language there are only differences *without positive terms*. Whether we take the signified or the signifier, language has neither ideas nor sounds that existed before the linguistic system, but only conceptual and phonic differences that have issued from the system. The idea or phonic substance that a sign contains is of less importance than the other signs that surround it. Proof of this is that the value of a term may be modified without either its meaning or its sound being affected, solely because a neighboring term has been modified.

But the statement that everything in language is negative is true only if the signified and the signifier are considered separately; when we consider the sign in its totality, we have something that is positive in its own class. A linguistic system is a series of differences of sound combined with a series of differences of ideas; but the pairing of a certain number of acoustical signs with as many cuts made from the mass of thought engenders a system of values; and this system serves as the effective link between the phonic and psychological elements within each sign. Although both the signified and the signifier are purely differential and negative when considered separately, their combination is a positive fact; it is even the sole type of facts that language has, for maintaining the parallelism between the two classes of differences is the distinctive function of the linguistic institution.

Certain diachronic facts are typical in this respect. Take the countless instances where alteration of the signifier occasions a conceptual change and where it is obvious that the sum of the ideas distinguished corresponds in principle to the sum of the distinctive signs. When two words are confused through phonetic alteration (e.g. French *décrépit* from *dēcrepitus* and *décrépi* from *crispus*), the ideas that they express will also tend to become confused if only they have something in common. Or a word may have different forms (cf. *chaise* 'chair' and *chaire* 'desk'[4]). Any nascent difference will tend invariably to become significant but without always succeeding or being successful on the first trial. Conversely, any conceptual difference perceived by the mind seeks to find expression through a distinct signifier, and two ideas that are no longer distinct in the mind tend to merge into the same signifier.

When we compare signs—positive terms—with each other, we can no longer speak of difference; the expression would not be fitting, for it applies only to the comparing of two sound-images, e.g. *father* and *mother*, or two

4. Both words derive from the Old French *chaiere*.

ideas, e.g. the idea "father" and the idea "mother"; two signs, each having a signified and signifier, are not different but only distinct. Between them there is only *opposition*. The entire mechanism of language, with which we shall be concerned later, is based on oppositions of this kind and on the phonic and conceptual differences that they imply.

What is true of value is true also of the unit. A unit is a segment of the spoken chain that corresponds to a certain concept; both are by nature purely differential.

Applied to units, the principle of differentiation can be stated in this way: *the characteristics of the unit blend with the unit itself.* In language, as in any semiological system, whatever distinguishes one sign from the others constitutes it. Difference makes character just as it makes value and the unit.

Another rather paradoxical consequence of the same principle is this: in the last analysis what is commonly referred to as a "grammatical fact" fits the definition of the unit, for it always expresses an opposition of terms; it differs only in that the opposition is particularly significant (e.g. the formation of German plurals of the type *Nacht: Nächte*). Each term present in the grammatical fact (the singular without umlaut or final *e* in opposition to the plural with umlaut and *–e*) consists of the interplay of a number of oppositions within the system. When isolated, neither *Nacht* nor *Nächte* is anything: thus everything is opposition. Putting it another way, the *Nacht: Nächte* relation can be expressed by an algebraic formula *a / b* in which *a* and *b* are not simple terms but result from a set of relations. Language, in a manner of speaking, is a type of algebra consisting solely of complex terms. Some of its oppositions are more significant than others; but units and grammatical facts are only different names for designating diverse aspects of the same general fact: the functioning of linguistic oppositions. This statement is so true that we might very well approach the problem of units by starting from grammatical facts. Taking an opposition like *Nacht: Nächte*, we might ask what are the units involved in it. Are they only the two words, the whole series of similar words, *a* and *ä*, or all singulars and plurals, etc.?

Units and grammatical facts would not be confused if linguistic signs were made up of something besides differences. But language being what it is, we shall find nothing simple in it regardless of our approach; everywhere and always there is the same complex equilibrium of terms that mutually condition each other. Putting it another way, *language is a form and not a substance*. This truth could not be overstressed, for all the mistakes in our terminology, all our incorrect ways of naming things that pertain to language, stem from the involuntary supposition that the linguistic phenomenon must have substance.

CHAPTER V. SYNTAGMATIC AND ASSOCIATIVE RELATIONS

1. *Definitions*

In a language-state everything is based on relations. How do they function?

Relations and differences between linguistic terms fall into two distinct groups, each of which generates a certain class of values. The opposition between the two classes gives a better understanding of the nature of each class. They correspond to two forms of our mental activity, both indispensable to the life of language.

In discourse, on the one hand, words acquire relations based on the linear nature of language because they are chained together. This rules out the possibility of pronouncing two elements simultaneously. The elements are arranged in sequence on the chain of speaking. Combinations supported by linearity are *syntagms.*[5] The syntagm is always composed of two or more consecutive units (e.g. French *re-lire* 're-read,' *contre tous* 'against everyone,' *la vie humaine* 'human life,' *Dieu est bon* 'God is good,' *s'il fait beau temps, nous sortirons* 'if the weather is nice, we'll go out,' etc.). In the syntagm a term acquires its value only because it stands in opposition to everything that precedes or follows it, or to both.

Outside discourse, on the other hand, words acquire relations of a different kind. Those that have something in common are associated in the memory, resulting in groups marked by diverse relations. For instance, the French word *enseignement* 'teaching' will unconsciously call to mind a host of other words (*enseigner* 'teach,' *renseigner* 'acquaint,' etc.; or, *armement* 'armament,' *changement* 'amendment,' etc.; or *éducation* 'education,' *apprentissage* 'apprenticeship,' etc.). All those words are related in some way.

We see that the co-ordinations formed outside discourse differ strikingly from those formed inside discourse. Those formed outside discourse are not supported by linearity. Their seat is in the brain; they are a part of the inner storehouse that makes up the language of each speaker. They are *associative relations.*

The syntagmatic relation is *in praesentia.*[6] It is based on two or more terms that occur in an effective series. Against this, the associative relation unites terms *in absentia* in a potential mnemonic series.

From the associative and syntagmatic viewpoint a linguistic unit is like a fixed part of a building, e.g. a column. On the one hand, the column has a certain relation to the architrave that it supports; the arrangement of the two units in space suggests the syntagmatic relation. On the other hand, if the column is Doric, it suggests a mental comparison of this style with others (Ionic, Corinthian, etc.) although none of these elements is present in space: the relation is associative.

Each of the two classes of co-ordination calls for some specific remarks.

2. *Syntagmatic Relations*

The examples have already indicated that the notion of syntagm applies not only to words but to groups of words, to complex units of all lengths and types (compounds, derivatives, phrases, whole sentences).

It is not enough to consider the relation that ties together the different parts of syntagms (e.g. French *contre* 'against' and *tous* 'everyone' in *contre tous, contre* and *maître* 'master' in *contremaître* 'foreman'); one must also bear in mind the relation that links the whole to its parts (e.g. *contre tous* in opposition on the one hand to *contre* and on the other *tous*, or *contremaître* in opposition to *contre* and *maître*).

5. It is scarcely necessary to point out that the study of *syntagms* is not to be confused with syntax. Syntax is only one part of the study of syntagms [Bally, Sechehaye, and Riedlinger's note].

6. Present (Latin).

An objection might be raised at this point. The sentence is the ideal type of syntagm. But it belongs to speaking, not to language.[7] Does it not follow that the syntagm belongs to speaking? I do not think so. Speaking is characterized by freedom of combinations; one must therefore ask whether or not all syntagms are equally free.

It is obvious from the first that many expressions belong to language. These are the pat phrases in which any change is prohibited by usage, even if we can single out their meaningful elements (cf. *à quoi bon?* 'what's the use?' *allons donc!* 'nonsense!'). The same is true, though to a lesser degree, of expressions like *prendre la mouche*[8] 'take offense easily,' *forcer la main à quelqu'un* 'force someone's hand,' *rompre une lance* 'break a lance,' or even *avoir mal* (*à la tête*, etc.) 'have (a headache, etc.),' *à force de* (*soins*, etc.) 'by dint of (care, etc.),' *que vous en semble?* 'how do you feel about it?' *pas n'est besoin de . . .* 'there's no need for . . . ,' etc., which are characterized by peculiarities of signification or syntax. These idiomatic twists cannot be improvised; they are furnished by tradition. There are also words which, while lending themselves perfectly to analysis, are characterized by some morphological anomaly that is kept solely by dint of usage (cf. *difficulté* 'difficulty' beside *facilité* 'facility,' etc., and *mourrai* '[I] shall die' beside *dormirai* '[I] shall sleep').[9]

There are further proofs. To language rather than to speaking belong the syntagmatic types that are built upon regular forms. Indeed, since there is nothing abstract in language, the types exist only if language has registered a sufficient number of specimens. When a word like *indécorable*[1] arises in speaking, its appearance supposes a fixed type, and this type is in turn possible only through remembrance of a sufficient number of similar words belonging to language (*impardonable* 'unpardonable,' *intolérable* 'intolerable,' *infatigable* 'indefatigable,' etc.). Exactly the same is true of sentences and groups of words built upon regular patterns. Combinations like *la terre tourne* 'the world turns,' *que vous dit-il?* 'what does he say to you?' etc. correspond to general types that are in turn supported in the language by concrete remembrances.

But we must realize that in the syntagm there is no clear-cut boundary between the language fact, which is a sign of collective usage, and the fact that belongs to speaking and depends on individual freedom. In a great number of instances it is hard to class a combination of units because both forces have combined in producing it, and they have combined in indeterminable proportions.

3. *Associative Relations*

Mental association creates other groups besides those based on the comparing of terms that have something in common; through its grasp of the nature of the relations that bind the terms together, the mind creates as many associative series as there are diverse relations. For instance, in *enseignement* 'teaching,' *enseigner* 'teach,' *enseignons* '(we) teach,' etc., one element, the radical, is common to every term; the same word may occur in a

7. That is, it belongs to *la parole*, not to *la langue*, in Saussure's terms.
8. Literally, "lay hold of the fly."
9. The anomaly of the double *r* in the future forms of certain verbs in French may be compared to irregular plurals like *oxen* in English [translator's note].
1. That is, a word coined by analogy.

different series formed around another common element, the suffix (cf. *enseignement, armement, changement,* etc.); or the association may spring from the analogy of the concepts signified (*enseignement, instruction, apprentissage, éducation,* etc.); or again, simply from the similarity of the sound-images (e.g. *enseignement* and *justement* 'precisely'). Thus there is at times a double similarity of meaning and form, at times similarity only of form or of meaning. A word can always evoke everything that can be associated with it in one way or another.

Whereas a syntagm immediately suggests an order of succession and a fixed number of elements, terms in an associative family occur neither in fixed numbers nor in a definite order. If we associate *painful, delightful, frightful,* etc. we are unable to predict the number of words that the memory will suggest or the order in which they will appear. A particular word is like the center of a constellation; it is the point of convergence of an indefinite number of co-ordinated terms.

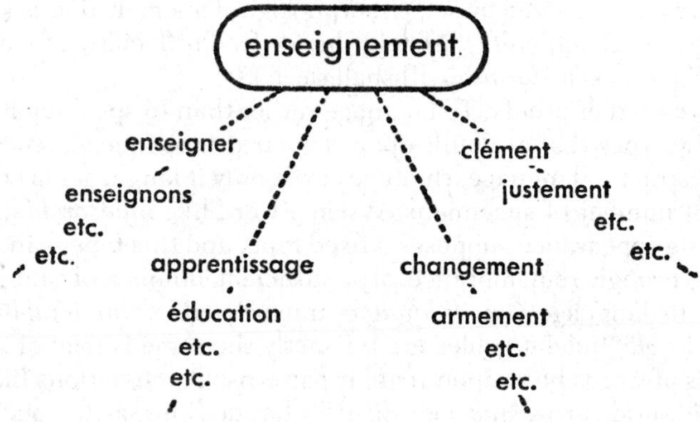

But of the two characteristics of the associative series—indeterminate order and indefinite number—only the first can always be verified; the second may fail to meet the test. This happens in the case of inflectional paradigms, which are typical of associative groupings. Latin *dominus, dominī, dominō,* etc. is obviously an associative group formed around a common element, the noun theme *domin–*, but the series is not indefinite as in the case of *enseignement, changement,* etc.; the number of cases is definite. Against this, the words have no fixed order of succession, and it is by a purely arbitrary act that the grammarian groups them in one way rather than in another; in the mind of speakers the nominative case is by no means the first one in the declension,[2] and the order in which terms are called depends on circumstances.

1906–13 1916

2. In standard grammars of inflected languages such as Greek and Latin, tables illustrating the case endings of each declension, or class of nouns or adjectives sharing the same forms, always begin with the nominative case (i.e., the form of the subject).

W. E. B. DU BOIS
1868–1963

W. E. B. Du Bois excelled in many disciplines and creative endeavors, from sociology to social commentary to poetry. He was one of the most accomplished scholar-activists and public intellectuals in American history, and his extraordinary life spanned ninety-five years. Born, raised, and educated in the latter decades of the nineteenth century, Du Bois was a Romantic visionary and Victorian professional writer who decades later grappled with the political tensions of the cold war. He was also an African American radical, a Pan-African leader, and eventually a defiant Marxist revolutionary.

William Edward Burghardt Du Bois was born in Great Barrington, a small town in western Massachusetts with few African American residents. Raised by his mother and her relatives, in his youth he became a lover of books, and he began writing early. Before even graduating from high school in 1885, Du Bois served as a correspondent for newspapers in Massachusetts and New York City.

As he explains in his *Autobiography* (published in 1968, five years after his death), Du Bois then "went South," to "the South of slavery, rebellion, and black folk," earning his B.A. at Fisk University, in Nashville, Tennessee, in 1888. Both as a student and as a teacher in rural schools during the summers, he came into contact with many African African families and communities, later recalling: "Into this world I leapt with enthusiasm. A new loyalty and allegiance replaced my Americanism: henceforward I was a Negro."

Du Bois next attended Harvard University, receiving a second B.A. in 1890 and doing graduate work (M.A., 1891; Ph.D., 1895). He also studied at the University of Berlin (1892–94), where he "began to see the race problem in America, the problem of the peoples of Africa and Asia, and the political development of Europe as one."

In the 1890s there were few professional careers open to African Americans. Du Bois taught and did research, eventually joining the faculty of Atlanta University, in Georgia, where he instructed its African American student body in economics, history, and sociology (1897–1910, 1933–44).

Du Bois's first book, based on his dissertation, was *The Suppression of the African Slave Trade to the United States of America, 1638–1870* (1896). He was a serious and well-trained scholar. But his belief in the transformative power of social scientific knowledge was shattered by the virulent racism of turn-of-the-century America, when segregation laws proliferated and anti-black terror and lynching intensified.

By 1900 Du Bois had already begun to project his vision of race relations outward from America's shores, becoming active in Pan-African organizations and congresses. In his major work *The Souls of Black Folk* (1903), he not only examines the history of slavery and segregation in the United States but also emphasizes, more generally, that "the problem of the Twentieth Century is the problem of the color line." Still, his focus is American; *The Souls of Black Folk* includes essays, sketches, and stories on African American politics, history, education, music, and culture. In the excerpt below, Du Bois speaks evocatively of "the veil" that separates blacks from whites, and he describes the "double consciousness" that defines African American identity: "One ever feels his twoness—an American, a Negro; two souls, two thoughts, two unreconciled strivings; two warring ideals in one dark body, whose dogged strength alone keeps it from being torn asunder." *The Souls of Black Folk* is the foremost work in the African American literary canon—"the pre-eminent text," the scholar Eric J. Sundquist has said, "of African American cultural consciousness."

Ernest Hemingway famously referred to Twain's *Adventures of Huckleberry Finn* (1884) as the book from which "all modern American literature" derived, and many African American critics, writers, and intellectuals have echoed his claim to stress the similar importance for the African American tradition of *The Souls of Black Folk*, with its multiple forms of style and registers of voice, its array of topics, and above all its brooding emphasis on the African American's "double consciousness." Du Bois was not the first to use this striking phrase. It appears, for example, in RALPH WALDO EMERSON's essay "The Transcendentalist" (1843), where it evokes the challenge faced by a person who experiences "moments of illumination" that he or she cannot reconcile with the trivial facts and mean demands of daily life. It was used too in other texts and fields of discourse in the nineteenth century: for instance, in *The Principles of Psychology* (1890) by William James, one of Du Bois's most important teachers during his period of undergraduate and undergraduate study at Harvard. Du Bois's seminal contribution was to apply this term to the conflicted self-definition of himself and his people, at once both American and African. In a sense his intention throughout *The Souls of Black Folk* was to take account of, subject to critique, and move through and beyond the decision made in 1896 by the U.S. Supreme Court in *Plessy v. Ferguson*, which affirmed the constitutionality of state laws requiring racial segregation in public facilities under the doctrine of "separate but equal." Du Bois sought to recontextualize the dominant terms of his era for racial classification and forthrightly shift them from black and white to African and American.

Du Bois sees "double consciousness" as a source of pain and anguish: there are two souls, thoughts, and strivings at war with one another. But he stresses that African Americans' special strength is that they have endured amid suffering and have not been "torn asunder." The story of African Americans, according to Du Bois, is sorrow laden yet also inspirational, for there is always among them the urge to express a better self and bring a message of hope to the United States and the world. Du Bois does not underplay the brutalities of racism, but it is crucial for him that African Americans have never succumbed to the limitations that America has imposed on them: they are consoled and empowered by their religious commitment and vision. "For Du Bois," Dickson Bruce has noted (in "W. E. B. Du Bois and the Idea of Double Consciousness," 1992), "the essence of a distinctive African consciousness was its spirituality, a spirituality based in Africa but revealed among African Americans in their folklore, their history of patient suffering and their faith." In *The Souls of Black Folk*, Du Bois is at once a fierce, unrelenting critic of racist oppression, a fervent advocate of racial uplift, and a visionary dedicated to the goal of individual and national integration.

It is a tribute to the eloquence and power of Du Bois's writing, and especially to his concept of double consciousness, that nearly as many African American thinkers have criticized him as have praised him for his claims in this foundational text. The journalist George Schuyler, for example, declared in "The Negro-Art Hokum" (1926) that "aside from his color, which ranges from the very dark brown to pink, your American Negro is just plain American"; and the writer Jean Toomer maintained in "What I Believe" (1929) that the only race that really exists and that we should affirm is "the human race"—"we all belong to it." In "How It Feels to Be Colored Me" (1928), ZORA NEALE HURSTON insisted, in contrast to the mournful timbre in which Du Bois sometimes spoke and wrote: "I am not tragically colored. There is no great sorrow dammed up in my soul, nor lurking behind my eyes. I do not mind at all." The educator and sociologist C. Eric Lincoln, the novelist and essayist Ishmael Reed, and the Pan-African/Afrocentric scholar Molefi Kete Asante, among others, also have objected to Du Bois's term, calling attention to its status as a rhetorical construct (rather than a fact of nature) and to the narrowness that in their view results from such a stark binary opposition.

Whatever its limitations, *The Souls of Black Folk*, bearing witness throughout to Du Bois's double consciousness, has been and will remain an inevitable point of departure, discussion, and debate for creative and critical work in African American literature and culture. The book is of great historical importance, as Du Bois's biographer David Levering Lewis has stressed: "For the first time in the brutal, mocked, patronized, and embattled history of Negro life on the North American continent, there was now a revelation of the race's social and psychological realities and prospects of such lyricism, lucidity, and humanity as to leave its mark on a white America guilty of evasion, obfuscation, and hypocrisy." It is also perpetually modern and contemporary, for its central term "double consciousness" remains an essential concept for the exploration of African American identity.

Du Bois was perhaps best known in the early 1900s for his opposition to Booker T. Washington (1856–1915), the founder of Tuskegee Institute in Alabama and the leading spokesman on the national scene for African Americans; Du Bois argued in *The Souls of Black Folk* and elsewhere that Washington had been chosen for this position because he presented the accommodationist message that whites wanted to hear. Du Bois was far more militant; not satisfied with limited economic progress, he insisted on social and political rights, access to higher education, and the development of an elite African American intellectual and professional class (the "talented tenth").

Du Bois's opposition to Washington led him in 1905 to take a central role in the Niagara Movement for full rights for African Americans. He became editor of *Horizon: A Journal of the Color Line* (1907–10); he helped found the National Association for the Advancement of Colored People (NAACP) in 1909 and served as its director of publications and research; and he expanded his role in the international Pan-African movement. He was actively publishing books and articles, too, as a social critic and theorist, creative writer, and historian.

From 1910 to 1934 Du Bois was the editor of the NAACP's monthly magazine, *The Crisis*; by 1919 it reached an audience of 100,000 readers. He was an important influence on the writers and artists of the Harlem Renaissance and the "New Negro" movement of the 1920s. In the pages of *The Crisis*, he repeatedly urged readers to see "Beauty in Black," an imperative that a dazzling array of African American authors and artists sought to fulfill.

These diversely gifted men and women—LANGSTON HUGHES, Jean Toomer, Zora Neale Hurston, Duke Ellington, and many others—were forming the intellectual vanguard for which Du Bois had called. But because their emphasis was cultural rather than political, he had a mixed response to them. Du Bois welcomed their innovative creative work, but he regretted the dependence of African American authors, artists, and musicians on white patrons and audiences. While he called for greater openness and honesty about sexual themes, he was also quick to criticize some African American writers (for example, the poet and novelist Claude McKay) for reinforcing white stereotypes of black sexual behavior.

The Depression of the 1930s hit African Americans hard and provoked Du Bois to call for "voluntary segregation," which, he maintained, would lead to economic self-sufficiency, solidarity, and self-advancement in a country that was not seeking to reach the goal of racial integration. Because of his separatist views, Du Bois was forced out of the NAACP in 1934.

From the 1930s until his death in 1963, Du Bois remained an activist and a prolific author. His books include the epic historical study *Black Reconstruction in America, 1860–1880* (1935); *Dusk of Dawn* (1940), which he described as "the autobiography of a concept of race"; and *Color and Democracy: Colonies and Peace* (1945), one of many writings of the 1940s and 1950s that challenged imperialism and made the case for African independence. Such pioneering, uncompromising work made him highly respected on the international scene. But together with his ever-deepening interest in Communism and admiration of the Soviet Union, it brought Du Bois under suspicion in the United States. In 1951 he was placed on trial for being an "unregistered foreign agent"; though he was acquitted, his passport was revoked from 1952 to 1958. Embittered by this treatment, in 1961 Du Bois joined the Communist Party, renounced his U.S. citizenship, and took up residence in Ghana. There, at work on a multivolume *Encyclopedia Africana*, he died in Accra, two years later.

Du Bois's writings in literary criticism and theory from the decades after *The Souls of Black Folk* blend genteel Victorianism, literary realism and naturalism, and radical politics. As our second selection, "Criteria of Negro Art" (1926), indicates, Du Bois believed that "all Art is propaganda and ever must be." In this address he tells African American writers and artists to strive for Truth and Beauty. He also stresses the marketplace conditions, and the racism, that block and undercut African American literary and cultural achievement, and he insists on the need for art to function as agitation, protest, and racial propaganda. Underlying his argument is the problem that confronts literary intellectuals who maintain strong political views: how to resolve the dual demands of art and politics. Du Bois affirms that the central duty of African American writers and artists is to advance the cause of the race; at the same time, he insists that they express the truth about African American life. But someone looking ahead several decades to reader-response theory (see, for example, STANLEY FISH and WOLFGANG ISER) might nonetheless propose that Du Bois's real concern is as much with a work's reception as with its production: How does the work of art affect the general American perception of African Americans? What will be the impact of the text on the social and political attitudes of readers?

The weakness in Du Bois's position lies in his extreme demand that art must be used for propaganda and for nothing else. No doubt he believes that the needs of his people mandate this requirement. Yet in "Criteria of Negro Art" it clashes with his earlier evocation of the splendid beauty of Cologne's cathedral and the Venus de Milo, which he seems to value for their own sake rather than for any propagandistic service they did or might perform. Du Bois's vision is inclusive, and challengingly so: he links the cathedral and the famous Greek statue with a village in West Africa and a Negro song or spiritual. But he appears not to recognize the reductive nature of his fiery dismissal: "I do not care a damn for any art that is not used for propaganda."

Du Bois is one voice in a complex, ongoing African American debate. His address can be placed alongside and measured against the literary critical ideas that Zora Neale Hurston and Richard Wright articulate, and to which other twentieth-century authors—notably James Baldwin, Ralph Ellison, Amiri Baraka, and TONI MORRISON—contributed. All, in their writings, have acknowledged Du Bois's majestic stature as an intellectual and cultural critic and historian. But all of them are also primarily creative writers—Du Bois was not—and they call for and exemplify forms of freedom in artistic expression that for political reasons he could not wholly share.

***The Souls of Black Folk* Keywords:** Identity, Nationhood, Race and Ethnicity Studies, Subjectivity
"Criteria of Negro Art" Keywords: Aesthetics, Authorship, Identity, Nationhood, Race and Ethnicity Studies, Representation

From The Souls of Black Folk[1]

From *Chapter I. Of Our Spiritual Strivings*

O water, voice of my heart, crying in the sand,
All night long crying with a mournful cry,
As I lie and listen, and cannot understand
The voice of my heart in my side or the voice of the sea,
O water, crying for rest, is it I, is it I?
All night long the water is crying to me.

Unresting water, there shall never be rest
Till the last moon droop and the last tide fail,
And the fire of the end begin to burn in the west;
And the heart shall be weary and wonder and cry like the sea,
All life long crying without avail,
As the water all night long is crying to me.

—Arthur Symons[2]

Between me and the other world[3] there is ever an unasked question: unasked by some through feelings of delicacy; by others through the difficulty of rightly framing it. All, nevertheless, flutter round it. They approach me in a half-hesitant sort of way, eye me curiously or compassionately, and then, instead of saying directly, How does it feel to be a problem? They say, I know an excellent colored man in my town; or, I fought at Mechanicsville;[4] or, Do not these Southern outrages make your blood boil? At these I smile, or am interested, or reduce the boiling to a simmer, as the occasion may require. To the real question, How does it feel to be a problem? I answer seldom a word.

And yet, being a problem is a strange experience,—peculiar even for one who has never been anything else, save perhaps in babyhood and in Europe. It is in the early days of rollicking boyhood that the revelation first bursts upon one, all in a day, as it were. I remember well when the shadow swept across me. I was a little thing, away up in the hills of New England, where the dark Housatonic winds between Hoosac and Taghkanic[5] to the sea. In a wee wooden schoolhouse, something put it into the boys' and girls' heads

1. Du Bois based these pages in *The Souls of Black Folk* on an essay titled "Strivings of the Negro People," which he published in the *Atlantic Monthly* 80 (August 1897): 194–97.

2. English poet, critic, and editor (1865–1945); his poem is titled "The Crying of Water" (1902). The music below is the opening bars of "Nobody Knows the Trouble I've Seen," a well-known spiritual first published as "Nobody Knows the Trouble I've Had" in *Slave Songs of the United States*, edited by William Francis Allen, Charles Pickard Ware, and Lucy McKim Garrison (1867). Each essay in DuBois's book begins with an epigraph, followed by a musical bar from a "sorrow song" or slave spiritual.

3. That is, the white world.

4. A town near Richmond, Virginia; the site of an 1862 Civil War battle (which the Confederate Army lost).

5. A river and two ranges of hills in the Berkshires, close to Du Bois's childhood home in western Massachusetts. The "Taghkanic" is better known as the Taconic.

to buy gorgeous visiting-cards—ten cents a package—and exchange.[6] The exchange was merry, till one girl, a tall newcomer, refused my card,—refused it peremptorily, with a glance. Then it dawned upon me with a certain suddenness that I was different from the others; or like, mayhap, in heart and life and longing, but shut out from their world by a vast veil. I had thereafter no desire to tear down that veil, to creep through; I held all beyond it in common contempt, and lived above it in a region of blue sky and great wandering shadows. That sky was bluest when I could beat my mates at examination-time, or beat them at a foot-race, or even beat their stringy heads. Alas, with the years all this fine contempt began to fade; for the worlds I longed for, and all their dazzling opportunities, were theirs, not mine. But they should not keep these prizes, I said; some, all, I would wrest from them. Just how I would do it I could never decide: by reading law, by healing the sick, by telling the wonderful tales that swam in my head,—some way. With other black boys the strife was not so fiercely sunny: their youth shrunk into tasteless sycophancy, or into silent hatred of the pale world about them and mocking distrust of everything white; or wasted itself in a bitter cry, Why did God make me an outcast and a stranger in mine own house?[7] The shades of the prison-house[8] closed round about us all: walls strait and stubborn to the whitest, but relentlessly narrow, tall, and unscalable to sons of night who must plod darkly on in resignation, or beat unavailing palms against the stone, or steadily, half hopelessly, watch the streak of blue above.

After the Egyptian and Indian, the Greek and Roman, the Teuton and Mongolian,[9] the Negro is a sort of seventh son, born with a veil,[1] and gifted with second-sight in this American world,—a world which yields him no true self-consciousness, but only lets him see himself through the revelation of the other world. It is a peculiar sensation, this double-consciousness, this sense of always looking at one's self through the eyes of others, of measuring one's soul by the tape of a world that looks on in amused contempt and pity. One ever feels his two-ness,—an American, a Negro; two souls, two thoughts, two unreconciled strivings; two warring ideals in one dark body, whose dogged strength alone keeps it from being torn asunder.

The history of the American Negro is the history of this strife,—this longing to attain self-conscious manhood, to merge his double self into a better and truer self. In this merging he wishes neither of the older selves to be lost. He would not Africanize America, for America has too much to teach the world and Africa. He would not bleach his Negro soul in a flood of white Americanism, for he knows that Negro blood has a message for the world. He simply wishes to make it possible for a man to be both a Negro and an American, without being cursed and spit upon by his fellows, without having the doors of Opportunity closed roughly in his face.

* * *

1903

6. Visiting cards were an important part of middle-class American and European social etiquette in the 19th century, with elaborate rules for their use and exchange.
7. See Exodus 2.22; Psalm 69.8.
8. An echo of WILLIAM WORDSWORTH, "Ode: Intimations of Immortality" (1807), lines 67–68.
9. A member of a tribal people of Central Asia. "Teuton": one of the Germanic peoples of Scandinavia and northern Germany.
1. In European folklore, babies born with their heads covered by a caul ("veil"), or membrane that is part of the amniotic sac, have psychic powers; seventh sons who have no sisters born in between are believed to be similarly gifted.

Criteria of Negro Art

So many persons have asked for the complete text of the address delivered by Dr. Du Bois at the Chicago Conference of the National Association for the Advancement of Colored People that we are publishing the address here.[1]

I do not doubt but there are some in this audience who are a little disturbed at the subject of this meeting, and particularly at the subject I have chosen. Such people are thinking something like this: "How is it that an organization like this, a group of radicals trying to bring new things into the world, a fighting organization which has come up out of the blood and dust of battle, struggling for the right of black men to be ordinary human beings—how is it that an organization of this kind can turn aside to talk about Art? After all, what have we who are slaves and black to do with Art?"

Or perhaps there are others who feel a certain relief and are saying, "After all it is rather satisfactory after all this talk about rights and fighting to sit and dream of something which leaves a nice taste in the mouth."

Let me tell you that neither of these groups is right. The thing we are talking about tonight is part of the great fight we are carrying on and it represents a forward and an upward look—a pushing onward. You and I have been breasting hills; we have been climbing upward; there has been progress and we can see it day by day looking back along blood-filled paths. But as you go through the valleys and over the foothills, so long as you are climbing, the direction,—north, south, east or west,—is of less importance. But when gradually the vista widens and you begin to see the world at your feet and the far horizon, then it is time to know more precisely whither you are going and what you really want.

What do we want? What is the thing we are after? As it was phrased last night it had a certain truth: We want to be Americans, full-fledged Americans, with all the rights of other American citizens. But is that all? Do we want simply to be Americans? Once in a while through all of us there flashes some clairvoyance, some clear idea, of what America really is. We who are dark can see America in a way that white Americans can not. And seeing our country thus, are we satisfied with its present goals and ideals?

In the high school where I studied we learned most of Scott's "Lady of the Lake"[2] by heart. In after life once it was my privilege to see the lake. It was Sunday. It was quiet. You could glimpse the deer wandering in unbroken forests; you could hear the soft ripple of romance on the waters. Around me fell the cadence of that poetry of my youth. I fell asleep full of the enchantment of the Scottish border. A new day broke and with it came a sudden rush of excursionists. They were mostly Americans and they were loud and strident. They poured upon the little pleasure boat,—men with their hats a little on one side and drooping cigars in the wet corners of their mouths; women who shared their conversation with the world. They all tried to get everywhere first. They pushed other people out of the way. They made all sorts of incoherent noises and gestures so that the quiet home folk and the visitors from other lands silently and half-wonderingly gave way before

1. *The Crisis*; the address was delivered in 1926.
2. A poem in 6 cantos about early 16th-century knights and ladies (1810), by Sir Walter Scott (1771–1832).

them. They struck a note not evil but wrong. They carried, perhaps, a sense of strength and accomplishment, but their hearts had no conception of the beauty which pervaded this holy place.

If you tonight suddenly should become full-fledged Americans; if your color faded, or the color line here in Chicago was miraculously forgotten; suppose, too, you became at the same time rich and powerful:—what is it that you would want? What would you immediately seek? Would you buy the most powerful of motor cars and outrace Cook County?[3] Would you buy the most elaborate estate on the North Shore? Would you be a Rotarian or a Lion or a What-not of the very last degree?[4] Would you wear the most striking clothes, give the richest dinners and buy the longest press notices?

Even as you visualize such ideals you know in your hearts that these are not the things you really want. You realize this sooner than the average white American because, pushed aside as we have been in America, there has come to us not only a certain distaste for the tawdry and flamboyant but a vision of what the world could be if it were really a beautiful world; if we had the true spirit; if we had the Seeing Eye, the Cunning Hand, the Feeling Heart; if we had, to be sure, not perfect happiness, but plenty of good hard work, the inevitable suffering that always comes with life; sacrifice and waiting, all that—but, nevertheless, lived in a world where men know, where men create, where they realize themselves and where they enjoy life. It is that sort of a world we want to create for ourselves and for all America.

After all, who shall describe Beauty? What is it? I remember tonight four beautiful things: The Cathedral at Cologne,[5] a forest in stone, set in light and changing shadow, echoing with sunlight and solemn song; a village of the Veys[6] in West Africa, a little thing of mauve and purple quiet, lying content and shining in the sun; a black and velvet room where on a throne rests, in old and yellowing marble; the broken curves of the Venus of Milo;[7] a single phrase of music in the Southern South—utter melody, haunting and appealing, suddenly arising out of night and eternity, beneath the moon.

Such is Beauty. Its variety is infinite, its possibility is endless. In normal life all may have it and have it yet again. The world is full of it; and yet today the mass of human beings are choked away from it, and their lives distorted and made ugly. This is not only wrong, it is silly. Who shall right this well-nigh universal failing? Who shall let this world be beautiful? Who shall restore to men the glory of sunsets and the peace of quiet sleep?

We black folk may help for we have within us as a race new stirrings, stirrings of the beginning of a new appreciation of joy, of a new desire to create, of a new will to be; as though in this morning of group life we had awakened from some sleep that at once dimly mourns the past and dreams a splendid future; and there has come the conviction that the Youth that is here today, the Negro Youth, is a different kind of Youth, because in some new way it bears this mighty prophecy on its breast, with a new realization of itself, with new determination for all mankind.

3. County in which Chicago is located.
4. The Rotary and Lions clubs are national service organizations; Freemasons, a fraternal organization with many members in the United States and abroad, are described as achieving certain degrees.
5. Magnificent Gothic cathedral in Cologne, Germany, begun in 1248 and consecrated in 1322.
6. One of the Mandingo peoples of Senegal, West Africa.
7. Famous classical statue of Aphrodite, Greek goddess of love (2d c. B.C.E. copy of a 4th c. original), now armless.

What has this Beauty to do with the world? What has Beauty to do with Truth and Goodness—with the facts of the world and the right actions of men? "Nothing," the artists rush to answer. They may be right. I am but an humble disciple of art and cannot presume to say. I am one who tells the truth and exposes evil and seeks with Beauty and for Beauty to set the world right. That somehow, somewhere eternal and perfect Beauty sits above Truth and Right I can conceive, but here and now and in the world in which I work they are for me unseparated and inseparable.

This is brought to us peculiarly when as artists we face our own past as a people. There has come to us—and it has come especially through the man we are going to honor tonight[8]—a realization of that past, of which for long years we have been ashamed, for which we have apologized. We thought nothing could come out of that past which we wanted to remember; which we wanted to hand down to our children. Suddenly, this same past is taking on form, color and reality, and in a half shamefaced way we are beginning to be proud of it. We are remembering that the romance of the world did not die and lie forgotten in the Middle Age; that if you want romance to deal with you must have it here and now and in your own hands.

I once knew a man and woman. They had two children, a daughter who was white and a daughter who was brown; the daughter who was white married a white man; and when her wedding was preparing the daughter who was brown prepared to go and celebrate. But the mother said, "No!" and the brown daughter went into her room and turned on the gas and died. Do you want Greek tragedy swifter than that?

Or again, here is a little Southern Town and you are in the public square. On one side of the square is the office of a colored lawyer and on all the other sides are men who do not like colored lawyers. A white woman goes into the black man's office and points to the white-filled square and says, "I want five hundred dollars now and if I do not get it I am going to scream."

Have you heard the story of the conquest of German East Africa?[9] Listen to the untold tale: There were 40,000 black men and 4,000 white men who talked German. There were 20,000 black men and 12,000 white men who talked English. There were 10,000 black men and 400 white men who talked French. In Africa then where the Mountains of the Moon raised their white and snow-capped heads into the mouth of the tropic sun, where Nile and Congo rise and the Great Lakes swim, these men fought; they struggled on mountain, hill and valley, in river, lake and swamp, until in masses they sickened, crawled and died; until the 4,000 white Germans had become mostly bleached bones; until nearly all the 12,000 white Englishmen had returned to South Africa, and the 400 Frenchmen to Belgium and Heaven; all except a mere handful of the white men died; but thousands of black men from East, West and South Africa, from Nigeria and the Valley of the Nile, and from the West Indies still struggled, fought and died. For four years they fought and won and lost German East Africa; and all you hear about it is that England and Belgium conquered German Africa for the allies!

8. Carter G. Woodson (1875–1950), to whom the NAACP in 1926 awarded the Spingarn Medal for African American achievement, was an African American educator and historian who in 1916 founded the *Journal of Negro History*.

9. Du Bois recounts events of World War I.

Such is the true and stirring stuff of which Romance is born and from this stuff come the stirrings of men who are beginning to remember that this kind of material is theirs; and this vital life of their own kind is beckoning them on.

The question comes next as to the interpretation of these new stirrings, of this new spirit: Of what is the colored artist capable? We have had on the part of both colored and white people singular unanimity of judgment in the past. Colored people have said: "This work must be inferior because it comes from colored people." White people have said: "It is inferior because it is done by colored people." But today there is coming to both the realization that the work of the black man is not always inferior. Interesting stories come to us. A professor in the University of Chicago read to a class that had studied literature a passage of poetry and asked them to guess the author. They guessed a goodly company from Shelley and Robert Browning down to Tennyson and Masefield. The author was Countée Cullen.[1] Or again the English critic John Drinkwater[2] went down to a Southern seminary, one of the sort which "finishes" young white women of the South. The students sat with their wooden faces while he tried to get some response out of them. Finally he said, "Name me some of your Southern poets." They hesitate. He said finally, "I'll start out with your best: Paul Laurence Dunbar"![3]

With the growing recognition of Negro artists in spite of the severe handicaps, one comforting thing is occurring to both white and black. They are whispering, "Here is a way out. Here is the real solution of the color problem. The recognition accorded Cullen, Hughes, Fauset, White[4] and others shows there is no real color line. Keep quiet! Don't complain! Work! All will be well!"

I will not say that already this chorus amounts to a conspiracy. Perhaps I am naturally too suspicious. But I will say that there are today a surprising number of white people who are getting great satisfaction out of these younger Negro writers because they think it is going to stop agitation of the Negro question. They say, "What is the use of your fighting and complaining; do the great thing and the reward is there." And many colored people are all too eager to follow this advice; especially those who are weary of the eternal struggle along the color line, who are afraid to fight and to whom the money of philanthropists and the alluring publicity are subtle and deadly bribes. They say, "What is the use of fighting? Why not show simply what we deserve and let the reward come to us?"

And it is right here that the National Association for the Advancement of Colored People comes upon the field, comes with its great call to a new battle, a new fight and new things to fight before the old things are wholly won; and to say that the Beauty of Truth and Freedom which shall some day be our heritage and the heritage of all civilized men is not in our hands yet and that we ourselves must not fail to realize.

1. African American poet (1903–1946); his first book, *Color* (1925), used forms such as the sonnet. Du Bois locates him in the company of the English poets PERCY BYSSHE SHELLEY (1792–1822), Robert Browning (1812–1889), Alfred, Lord Tennyson (1809–1892), and John Masefield (1878–1967).
2. English poet, dramatist, and critic (1882–1937).
3. African American short story writer and poet (1872–1906).
4. Walter White (1893–1955), NAACP leader and novelist. LANGSTON HUGHES (1902–1967), poet, fiction writer, and playwright. Jessie Redmon Fauset (ca. 1884–1961), novelist and editor.

There is in New York tonight a black woman molding clay by herself in a little bare room, because there is not a single school of sculpture in New York where she is welcome. Surely there are doors she might burst through, but when God makes a sculpture He does not always make the pushing sort of person who beats his way through doors thrust in his face. This girl is working her hands off to get out of this country so that she can get some sort of training.

There was Richard Brown.[5] If he had been white he would have been alive today instead of dead of neglect. Many helped him when he asked but he was not the kind of boy that always asks. He was simply one who made colors sing.

There is a colored woman in Chicago who is a great musician. She thought she would like to study at Fontainbleau this summer where Walter Damrosch[6] and a score of leaders of Art have an American school of music. But the application blank of this school says: "I am a white American and I apply for admission to the school."

We can go on the stage; we can be just as funny as white Americans wish us to be; we can play all the sordid parts that America likes to assign to Negroes; but for any thing else there is still small place for us.

And so I might go on. But let me sum up with this: Suppose the only Negro who survived some centuries hence was the Negro painted by white Americans in the novels and essays they have written. What would people in a hundred years say of black Americans? Now turn it around. Suppose you were to write a story and put in it the kind of people you know and like and imagine. You might get it published and you might not. And the "might not" is still far bigger than the "might." The white publishers catering to white folk would say, "It is not interesting"—to white folk, naturally not. They want Uncle Toms, Topsies,[7] good "darkies" and clowns. I have in my office a story with all the earmarks of truth. A young man says that he started out to write and had his stories accepted. Then he began to write about the things he knew best about, that is, about his own people. He submitted a story to a magazine which said, "We are sorry, but we cannot take it." "I sat down and revised my story, changing the color of the characters and the locale and sent it under an assumed name with a change of address and it was accepted by the same magazine that had refused it, the editor promising to take anything else I might send in providing it was good enough."

We have, to be sure, a few recognized and successful Negro artists; but they are not all those fit to survive or even a good minority. They are but the remnants of that ability and genius among us whom the accidents of education and opportunity have raised on the tidal waves of chance. We black folk are not altogether peculiar in this. After all, in the world at large, it is only the accident, the remnant, that gets the chance to make the most of itself; but if this is true of the white world it is infinitely more true of the colored world. It is not simply the great clear tenor of Roland Hayes[8] that opened the ears of America. We have had many voices of all kinds as fine as his and

5. An African American artist (d. 1917).
6. German American conductor and composer (1862–1950). Fontainbleau: a French resort.
7. Uncle Tom and Topsy are African American characters, a saintly and an impish slave, respectively, in Harriet Beecher Stowe's novel *Uncle Tom's Cabin* (1852).
8. African American singer of classical works and spirituals (1887–1976), the son of former slaves.

America was and is as deaf as she was for years to him. Then a foreign land heard Hayes and put its imprint on him and immediately America with all its imitative snobbery woke up. We approved Hayes because London, Paris and Berlin approved him and not simply because he was a great singer.

Thus it is the bounden duty of black America to begin this great work of the creation of Beauty, of the preservation of Beauty, of the realization of Beauty, and we must use in this work all the methods that men have used before. And what have been the tools of the artists in times gone by? First of all, he has used the Truth—not for the sake of truth, not as a scientist seeking truth, but as one upon whom Truth eternally thrusts itself as the highest handmaid of imagination, as the one great vehicle of universal understanding. Again artists have used Goodness—goodness in all its aspects of justice, honor and right—not for sake of an ethical sanction but as the one true method of gaining sympathy and human interest.

The apostle of Beauty thus becomes the apostle of Truth and Right not by choice but by inner and outer compulsion. Free he is but his freedom is ever bounded by Truth and Justice; and slavery only dogs him when he is denied the right to tell the Truth or recognize an ideal of Justice.

Thus all Art is propaganda and ever must be, despite the wailing of the purists. I stand in utter shamelessness and say that whatever art I have for writing has been used always for propaganda for gaining the right of black folk to love and enjoy. I do not care a damn for any art that is not used for propaganda. But I do care when propaganda is confined to one side while the other is stripped and silent.

In New York we have two plays: "White Cargo" and "Congo."[9] In "White Cargo" there is a fallen woman. She is black. In "Congo" the fallen woman is white. In "White Cargo" the black woman goes down further and further and in "Congo" the white woman begins with degradation but in the end is one of the angels of the Lord.

You know the current magazine story: A young white man goes down to Central America and the most beautiful colored woman there falls in love with him. She crawls across the whole isthmus to get to him. The white man says nobly, "No." He goes back to his white sweetheart in New York.

In such cases, it is not the positive propaganda of people who believe white blood divine, infallible and holy to which I object. It is the denial of a similar right of propaganda to those who believe black blood human, lovable and inspired with new ideals for the world. White artists themselves suffer from this narrowing of their field. They cry for freedom in dealing with Negroes because they have so little freedom in dealing with whites. DuBose Heyward writes "Porgy"[1] and writes beautifully of the black Charleston underworld. But why does he do this? Because he cannot do a similar thing for the white people of Charleston, or they would drum him out of town. The only chance he had to tell the truth of pitiful human degradation was to tell it of colored people. I should not be surprised if Octavus Roy Cohen[2] had approached the *Saturday Evening Post* and asked permission to write

9. *Kongo* (1926), by Kilbourn Gordon and Chester DeVonde. *White Cargo*: *White Cargo: A Play of the Primitive* (1925), by Leon Gordon.

1. The 1925 novel by Heyward (1885–1940) that was the basis for the later opera *Porgy and Bess* (1935).

2. South Carolina playwright, novelist, short story writer, and humorist (1891–1959).

about a different kind of colored folk than the monstrosities he has created: but if he has, the *Post* has replied. "No. You are getting paid to write about the kind of colored people you are writing about."

In other words, the white public today demands from its artists, literary and pictorial, racial pre-judgment which deliberately distorts Truth and Justice, as far as colored races are concerned, and it will pay for no other.

On the other hand, the young and slowly growing black public still wants its prophets almost equally unfree. We are bound by all sorts of customs that have come down as second-hand soul clothes of white patrons. We are ashamed of sex and we lower our eyes when people will talk of it. Our religion holds us in superstition. Our worst side has been so shamelessly emphasized that we are denying we have or ever had a worst side. In all sorts of ways we are hemmed in and our new young artists have to fight their way to freedom.

The ultimate judge has got to be you and you have got to build yourselves up into that wide judgment, that catholicity of temper[3] which is going to enable the artist to have his widest chance for freedom. We can afford the Truth. White folk today cannot. As it is now we are handing everything over to a white jury. If a colored man wants to publish a book, he has got to get a white publisher and a white newspaper to say it is great; and then you and I say so. We must come to the place where the work of art when it appears is reviewed and acclaimed by our own free and unfettered judgment. And we are going to have a real and valuable and eternal judgment only as we make ourselves free of mind, proud of body and just of soul to all men.

And then do you know what will be said? It is already saying. Just as soon as true Art emerges; just as soon as the black artist appears, someone touches the race on the shoulder and says, "He did that because he was an American, not because he was a Negro; he was born here; he was trained here; he is not a Negro—what is a Negro anyhow? He is just human; it is the kind of thing you ought to expect."

I do not doubt that the ultimate art coming from black folk is going to be just as beautiful, and beautiful largely in the same ways, as the art that comes from white folk, or yellow, or red; but the point today is that until the art of the black folk compels recognition they will not be rated as human. And when through art they compel recognition then let the world discover if it will that their art is as new as it is old and as old as new.

I had a classmate once who did three beautiful things and died. One of them was a story of a folk who found fire and then went wandering in the gloom of night seeking again the stars they had once known and lost; suddenly out of blackness they looked up and there loomed the heavens; and what was it that they said? They raised a mighty cry: "It is the stars, it is the ancient stars, it is the young and everlasting stars!"

1926

3. Range of disposition.

VIRGINIA WOOLF
1882–1941

Invited to address the topic of "women and fiction" at Cambridge University's Newnham and Girton Colleges in October of 1928, Virginia Woolf presented two lectures that would later become, after considerable expansion and revision, her celebrated book *A Room of One's Own* (1929). Working at the intersection of modernism and feminism, both of which she stood for, Woolf analyzed the differences between women as *objects* of representation and women as *authors* of representation, and invited her audience to think about "the books that are not there." In the process, she opened up the entire territory of modern feminist criticism.

Woolf was a member of a highly literate and artistic family. Born Adeline Virginia Stephen, she was the daughter of Leslie Stephen, a distinguished Victorian literary figure, and Julia Jackson Duckworth Stephen, a beauty who had once frequented pre-Raphaelite circles. It was the second marriage for both. The resultant blended family included three Duckworths (George, Stella, and Gerald), one Stephen from the first marriage (Laura, mentally incapacitated and later institutionalized), and four new Stephens (Vanessa, Thoby, Virginia, and Adrian). Leslie Stephen lived in a world of letters: his first wife was the daughter of novelist William Makepeace Thackeray; he possessed a large library (in which Virginia got her education); he published several books of philosophy and literary history; and he became, partly for financial reasons, the first editor of the multivolume *Dictionary of National Biography* in 1882, the year of Virginia's birth. The Stephen family was organized in a typically Victorian way, the father occupying himself with money and intellectual matters and the mother attending to the emotional and social needs of her husband and eight children.

Her mother's death in 1895 was for thirteen-year-old Virginia a terrible loss. When Sir Leslie died nine years later, twenty-two-year-old Virginia felt an intense though ambivalent liberation, and began to write. The Stephen children moved across London to Gordon Square, Bloomsbury, where they were surrounded by Thoby's Cambridge friends, many of whom had been members of a college group known as the Apostles, and who later would become well known: Lytton Strachey, a biographer and historian; John Maynard Keynes, an economist; Clive Bell, a critic of art and literature; and Leonard Woolf, a writer of novels and political science.

In 1906, however, the circle was devastated by the unexpected loss of its connecting link: Thoby Stephen died of typhoid fever. Two days after Thoby's death, Vanessa agreed to marry Clive Bell. Virginia and her remaining brother, Adrian, moved to 29 Fitzroy Square (London), where Virginia began working on a novel. She had also begun to publish reviews for money and do some (unpaid) teaching in a working-class college. When she inherited £2,500 from an aunt, she acquired an important economic safety net.

In 1912 Virginia married Leonard Woolf, who had just returned from serving as an administrator in Ceylon (now Sri Lanka). They shared many intellectual interests and both felt themselves to be outsiders within their social circle. In response to Virginia's periodic nervous breakdowns, Leonard was both attentive and controlling: she relied on, and raged against, his prescriptions. In the 1920s, Virginia had an affair with Victoria ("Vita") Sackville-West, a fellow writer, who was married to Harold Nicolson, a diplomat. The relationship coincided with a period of great productivity and originality in Woolf's writing.

In 1917 Leonard had had the inspired idea of buying a printing press, originally to provide a therapeutic hobby. The Hogarth Press, born of a machine small enough to fit on a kitchen table, soon became an important disseminator of modernist texts. It published brightly covered books, often designed by Vanessa Bell or Roger Fry, and launched T. S. Eliot's *Waste Land* (1922); fiction by Maksim Gorky, E. M. Forster, and Katherine Mansfield; all the works of Virginia Woolf, beginning with *Jacob's Room* (1922); and the complete twenty-four-volume translation of the works of SIGMUND FREUD. The "Woolves," as their friends called them, had found their outlet.

Starting with *The Voyage Out*, her first novel (1915), Woolf wrote a great deal. Her novels experiment increasingly with form and style: *Mrs. Dalloway* (1925), her fourth, is set, like James Joyce's *Ulysses* in Dublin, in a single day in London, pairing the war and the drawing room; *To the Lighthouse* (1927) is a radical rethinking of what a novel can do, a fictional biography of her parents relying on a stream of consciousness narrative. Her later novels take diverse approaches to expanding the form, and she published three very different "biographies," including *Orlando* (1928, a novel celebrating her relationship with Vita), whose three-hundred-year-old protagonist changes sex in midlife, and *Flush* (1933), about the life of Elizabeth Barrett Browning's spaniel. Woolf also wrote more than four volumes' worth of essays and short fiction and two groundbreaking feminist works: *A Room of One's Own* and *Three Guineas* (1938).

Her productivity was all the more remarkable in that it was often punctuated by nervous illnesses and by treatments, of dubious effectiveness, that required her to stop writing. In 1941, with the voices in her head becoming more insistent and the war in Europe ever more threatening (she and Leonard, who was Jewish, had made provisions to kill themselves in the event of a Nazi invasion), she drowned herself.

People attempting to explain the sources of Woolf's creativity have written a great deal on several topics: her sexuality, her class position, and her madness. Much has been said about her sexuality: she had too much of it or too little; her androgyny obscured her bisexuality, or vice versa; she idealized motherhood, or feared it, or resented Leonard, who was afraid of inherited insanity, for deciding that they shouldn't have children; and so on. Evidence for these arguments comes, of course, from her writing itself; their contradictions indicate her success in finding textual forms—in her diaries and letters, her fiction and essays—that would allow all these forces to do battle.

Both of her feminist treatises link women and money. As one of the "daughters of educated men" (as she puts it in *Three Guineas*), she belonged to a culturally, if not economically, privileged class. In *A Room of One's Own* she argues that women need £500 a year (an amount somewhere between subsistence and comfort), and in *Three Guineas*—a meditation on the ties between war and patriarchal values—she responds to a solicitation to sign a petition and contribute money to a society for the prevention of war. On the one hand, the link she makes between freedom and property can be critiqued from a Marxist perspective; on the other, society's denial of women's independent rights over property marks a resistance to women's freedom. It is clear that Woolf is breaking a gender taboo, rather than merely claiming a class privilege, by going into the economic details of women's lives.

Woolf has also been seen as a representative of the sexual sea change that came after, and out of, the Victorian era. She grew up, like many others, in a world of exaggerated gender roles, secret transgressions, and repressive silence about sexual matters (she was apparently abused in childhood by her two stepbrothers). The Bloomsbury group, in contrast, broke gender taboos spectacularly—almost all of them had relations with both sexes, and they sometimes lived with the people they were *not* sleeping with. Nevertheless, even in liberated Bloomsbury, female creativity could still be categorized as "madness" whenever it became too hard to handle (this is the premise behind *The Madwoman in the Attic*, the influential 1979 study by SANDRA M. GILBERT and SUSAN GUBAR). The line between psychopathology and impeded gifts is very hard to draw, as Woolf makes clear in her parable of Shakespeare's sister.

Our selection contains three celebrated moments from *A Room of One's Own*, which we have labeled "Shakespeare's Sister," "Chloe Liked Olivia," and "Androgyny." What would have happened, Woolf asks in the first, if Shakespeare had had a sister as gifted as himself? She would have lacked even the education *he* had, she answers. Shakespeare's sister would have been excluded from the Renaissance stage (on which all the parts were played by males); she would probably have found herself with child by some man who had taken pity on her; and, crazed by her gifts and her prospects, she would probably have ended up committing suicide. Judith Shakespeare thus represents one kind of "book that isn't there."

A second kind of missing book may be lurking behind the cover of the fictitious novel Woolf is about to open in our second section, Mary Carmichael's *Life's Adventure*. "Chloe liked Olivia," she reads, and looks about her to make sure the room contains only women. By wondering whether "that red curtain over there" conceals the figure of Sir Chartres Biron—the magistrate presiding at that very moment over the censorship trial of Radclyffe Hall's lesbian novel *The Well of Loneliness* (1928)—Woolf implies that one of the things that keeps women unfree is the law's policing of the relations women can have with women. Women in literature have almost always been imagined as *only* sexual, she argues, and usually only in their relations or non-relations to men, leaving no dealings with each other but as rivals ("Cleopatra did not like Octavia"). But, Woolf exclaims, how small a part of any woman's life is the part seen by the other sex and in relation to the other sex! Women as authors now have the opportunity to depict "that vast chamber where nobody has yet been."

Woolf's idealization of authorial "androgyny" in our third passage would seem to fly in the face of her descriptions earlier in the essay of male and female sentences or male and female plots. How can she argue both that the exclusion of women from the canon has made a difference and that great authors are androgynous? Two clarifications need to be made. First, the "woman" in Shakespeare's brain is not the same as the "women" who did not write in history. But second, the women entering literature do more than fill up an absence. If the greatest authors used both "sides" of their brain, the new authors must do so as well. Her warning that "consciousness of sex" destroys literature can be interpreted as both feminist and antifeminist. Writing with "unconsciousness of sex" may very well be taken as "indifference to sex"—often seen as a modernist privileging of style over politics. Yet this unconsciousness does not preclude gender difference, mandating simply that the gender differences that inform good writing not become *conscious*. If women were free to write, would they not open a window on a world of experiences that have remained invisible, even to themselves? A world too quickly dismissed or devalued, a world that would *require* different sentences? Woolf presents *men*, not women, as having become overly conscious of their sex as a result of feminism. In arguing for a new writerly androgyny, Woolf comes close to what HÉLÈNE CIXOUS later calls "the other bisexuality."

A Room of One's Own is one of the most imitated titles ever devised. Written during the trial of Radclyffe Hall's lesbian novel and published during the same month as the stock market crash of 1929, *A Room of One's Own* marks an upheaval more subtle, yet in some ways as profound, as these. The time was right for it: the book was so successful that the proceeds enabled Virginia Woolf to add a room of her own onto her house in Sussex.

A *Room of One's Own* Keywords: Authorship, Feminist Criticism, Gender, Literary History, Modernity, Queer Theory, Women's Literature

From A Room of One's Own

* * *

[SHAKESPEARE'S SISTER]

Let me imagine, since facts are so hard to come by, what would have happened had Shakespeare had a wonderfully gifted sister, called Judith, let us say. Shakespeare himself went, very probably—his mother was an heiress—to the grammar school, where he may have learnt Latin—Ovid, Virgil and Horace[1]—and the elements of grammar and logic. He was, it is well known, a wild boy who poached rabbits, perhaps shot a deer, and had, rather sooner than he should have done, to marry a woman in the neighborhood, who bore him a child rather quicker than was right. That escapade sent him to seek his fortune in London. He had, it seemed, a taste for the theatre; he began by holding horses at the stage door. Very soon he got work in the theatre, became a successful actor, and lived at the hub of the universe, meeting everybody, knowing everybody, practising his art on the boards, exercising his wits in the streets, and even getting access to the palace of the queen. Meanwhile his extraordinarily gifted sister, let us suppose, remained at home. She was as adventurous, as imaginative, as agog to see the world as he was. But she was not sent to school. She had no chance of learning grammar and logic, let alone of reading Horace and Virgil. She picked up a book now and then, one of her brother's perhaps, and read a few pages. But then her parents came in and told her to mend the stockings or mind the stew and not moon about with books and papers. They would have spoken sharply but kindly, for they were substantial people who knew the conditions of life for a woman and loved their daughter—indeed, more likely than not she was the apple of her father's eye. Perhaps she scribbled some pages up in an apple loft on the sly, but was careful to hide them or set fire to them. Soon, however, before she was out of her teens, she was to be betrothed to the son of a neighboring wool-stapler. She cried out that marriage was hateful to her, and for that she was severely beaten by her father. Then he ceased to scold her. He begged her instead not to hurt him, not to shame him in this matter of her marriage. He would give her a chain of beads or a fine petticoat, he said; and there were tears in his eyes. How could she disobey him? How could she break his heart? The force of her own gift alone drove her to it. She made up a small parcel of her belongings, let herself down by a rope one summer's night and took the road to London. She was not seventeen. The birds that sang in the hedge were not more musical than she was. She had the quickest fancy, a gift like her brother's, for the tune of words. Like him, she had a taste for the theatre. She stood at the stage door; she wanted to act, she said. Men laughed in her face. The manager—a fat, loose-lipped man—guffawed. He bellowed something about poodles dancing and women acting—no woman, he said, could possibly be an actress.[2] He hinted—you can imagine what. She could get no training in her craft. Could she even seek her dinner in a tavern or roam

1. The three Roman poets—Ovid (43 B.C.E.–17 C.E.), Virgil (70–19 B.C.E.), and HORACE (65–8 B.C.E.)—were standard authors studied by boys in schools from the Renaissance on.

2. In the Elizabethan theater, women's roles were played by boys.

the streets at midnight? Yet her genius was for fiction and lusted to feed abundantly upon the lives of men and women and the study of their ways. At last—for she was very young, oddly like Shakespeare the poet in her face, with the same grey eyes and rounded brows—at last Nick Greene[3] the actor-manager took pity on her; she found herself with child by that gentleman and so—who shall measure the heat and violence of the poet's heart when caught and tangled in a woman's body?—killed herself one winter's night and lies buried at some cross-roads where the omnibuses now stop outside the Elephant and Castle.[4]

That, more or less, is how the story would run, I think, if a woman in Shakespeare's day had had Shakespeare's genius. But for my part, I agree with the deceased bishop,[5] if such he was—it is unthinkable that any woman in Shakespeare's day should have had Shakespeare's genius. For genius like Shakespeare's is not born among labouring, uneducated, servile people. It was not born in England among the Saxons and the Britons. It is not born today among the working classes. How, then, could it have been born among women whose work began, according to Professor Trevelyan,[6] almost before they were out of the nursery, who were forced to it by their parents and held to it by all the power of law and custom? Yet genius of a sort must have existed among women as it must have existed among the working classes. Now and again an Emily Brontë or a Robert Burns[7] blazes out and proves its presence. But certainly it never got itself on to paper. When, however, one reads of a witch being ducked, of a woman possessed by devils, of a wise woman selling herbs, or even of a very remarkable man who had a mother, then I think we are on the track of a lost novelist, a suppressed poet, of some mute and inglorious Jane Austen,[8] some Emily Brontë who dashed her brains out on the moor or mopped and mowed about the highways crazed with the torture that her gift had put her to. Indeed, I would venture to guess that Anon, who wrote so many poems without signing them, was often a woman. It was a woman Edward Fitzgerald,[9] I think, suggested who made the ballads and the folk-songs, crooning them to her children, beguiling her spinning with them, or the length of the winter's night.

This may be true or it may be false—who can say?—but what is true in it, so it seemed to me, reviewing the story of Shakespeare's sister as I had made it, is that any woman born with a great gift in the sixteenth century would certainly have gone crazed, shot herself, or ended her days in some lonely cottage outside the village, half witch, half wizard, feared and mocked at. For it needs little skill in psychology to be sure that a highly gifted girl who had tried to use her gift for poetry would have been so thwarted and hindered

3. Possibly modeled on Robert Greene (1558–1592), a dramatist whose 1592 pamphlet contains the first literary reference to Shakespeare (an attack).

4. Suicides were often buried at crossroads to prevent their spirits from returning. The Elephant and Castle was a famous tavern, bombed during World War II, that stood at one of the busiest intersections in London.

5. An "old gentleman" who earlier in the essay is said to have "declared that it was impossible for any woman past, present, or to come, to have the genius of Shakespeare."

6. George Macaulay Trevelyan (1876–1962), English historian; Woolf has already referred to his *History of England* (1926).

7. Scottish poet (1759–1796). Brontë (1818–1848), English novelist and poet.

8. Probably the most canonical of English women novelists (1775–1817); the phrase "some mute and inglorious Jane Austen" echoes "some mute inglorious Milton," in Thomas Gray's "Elegy Written in a Country Churchyard" (1751).

9. English scholar and poet (1809–1883), who anonymously translated *The Rubáiyát of Omar Khayyam* (1859).

by other people, so tortured and pulled asunder by her own contrary instincts, that she must have lost her health and sanity to a certainty.

* * *

[CHLOE LIKED OLIVIA]

I am almost sure, I said to myself, that Mary Carmichael[1] is playing a trick on us. For I feel as one feels on a switchback railway when the car, instead of sinking, as one has been led to expect, swerves up again. Mary is tampering with the expected sequence. First she broke the sentence; now she has broken the sequence. Very well, she has every right to do both these things if she does them not for the sake of breaking, but for the sake of creating. Which of the two it is I cannot be sure until she has faced herself with a situation. I will give her every liberty, I said, to choose what that situation shall be; she shall make it of tin cans and old kettles if she likes; but she must convince me that she believes it to be a situation; and then when she has made it she must face it. She must jump. And, determined to do my duty by her as reader if she would do her duty by me as writer, I turned the page and read . . . I am sorry to break off so abruptly. Are there no men present? Do you promise me that behind that red curtain over there the figure of Sir Chartres Biron[2] is not concealed? We are all women, you assure me? Then I may tell you that the very next words I read were these—"Chloe liked Olivia . . ." Do not start. Do not blush. Let us admit in the privacy of our own society that these things sometimes happen. Sometimes women do like women.

"Chloe liked Olivia," I read. And then it struck me how immense a change was there. Chloe liked Olivia perhaps for the first time in literature. Cleopatra did not like Octavia.[3] And how completely *Antony and Cleopatra* would have been altered had she done so! As it is, I thought, letting my mind, I am afraid, wander a little from *Life's Adventure*, the whole thing is simplified, conventionalised, if one dared say it, absurdly. Cleopatra's only feeling about Octavia is one of jealousy. Is she taller than I am? How does she do her hair? The play, perhaps, required no more. But how interesting it would have been if the relationship between the two women had been more complicated. All these relationships between women, I thought, rapidly recalling the splendid gallery of fictitious women, are too simple. So much has been left out, unattempted. And I tried to remember any case in the course of my reading where two women are represented as friends. There is an attempt at it in *Diana of the Crossways*.[4] They are confidantes, of course, in Racine[5] and the Greek tragedies. They are now and then mothers and daughters. But almost without exception they are shown in their relation to men. It was strange to think that all the great women of fiction were, until Jane Austen's day, not only seen by the other sex, but seen only in relation

1. Woolf's name for a fictitious contemporary author of a novel, *Life's Adventure*, which bears a resemblance to the novel published by Mary Stopes (under the name Mary Carmichael) titled *Love's Creation* (1928).
2. The magistrate (1863–1940) presiding over the trial that was to ban Radclyffe Hall's *Well of Loneliness* (1928) for depicting lesbianism.
3. In Shakespeare's *Antony and Cleopatra* (1606–07), Antony loves Cleopatra but marries Octavia to cement a political alliance; Cleopatra interrogates a messenger about Octavia's height, voice, gait, and hair color (3.3).
4. An 1885 novel by George Meredith, who had been a friend of Woolf's father.
5. Jean Racine (1639–1699), French dramatist.

to the other sex. And how small a part of a woman's life is that; and how little can a man know even of that when he observes it through the black or rosy spectacles which sex puts upon his nose. Hence, perhaps, the peculiar nature of woman in fiction; the astonishing extremes of her beauty and horror; her alternations between heavenly goodness and hellish depravity—for so a lover would see her as his love rose or sank, was prosperous or unhappy. This is not so true of the nineteenth-century novelists, of course. Woman becomes much more various and complicated there. Indeed it was the desire to write about women perhaps that led men by degrees to abandon the poetic drama which, with its violence, could make so little use of them, and to devise the novel as a more fitting receptacle. Even so it remains obvious, even in the writing of Proust,[6] that a man is terribly hampered and partial in his knowledge of women, as a woman in her knowledge of men.

Also, I continued, looking down at the page again, it is becoming evident that women, like men, have other interests besides the perennial interests of domesticity. "Chloe liked Olivia. They shared a laboratory together. . . ." I read on and discovered that these two young women were engaged in mincing liver, which is, it seems, a cure for pernicious anaemia: although one of them was married and had—I think I am right in stating—two small children. Now all that, of course, has had to be left out, and thus the splendid portrait of the fictitious woman is much too simple and much too monotonous. Suppose, for instance, that men were only represented in literature as the lovers of women, and were never the friends of men, soldiers, thinkers, dreamers; how few parts in the plays of Shakespeare could be allotted to them; how literature would suffer! We might perhaps have most of Othello; and a good deal of Antony; but no Caesar, no Brutus, no Hamlet, no Lear, no Jaques[7]—literature would be incredibly impoverished, as indeed literature is impoverished beyond our counting by the doors that have been shut upon women. Married against their will, kept in one room, and to one occupation, how could a dramatist give a full or interesting or truthful account of them? Love was the only possible interpreter. The poet was forced to be passionate or bitter, unless indeed he chose to "hate women," which meant more often than not that he was unattractive to them.

Now if Chloe likes Olivia and they share a laboratory, which of itself will make their friendship more varied and lasting because it will be less personal; if Mary Carmichael knows how to write, and I was beginning to enjoy some quality in her style; if she has a room to herself, of which I am not quite sure; if she has five hundred a year of her own—but that remains to be proved—then I think that something of great importance has happened.

For if Chloe likes Olivia and Mary Carmichael knows how to express it she will light a torch in that vast chamber where nobody has yet been. It is all half lights and profound shadows like those serpentine caves where one goes with a candle peering up and down, not knowing where one is stepping. And I began to read the book again, and read how Chloe watched Olivia put a jar on a shelf and say how it was time to go home to her children. That is a sight that

6. Marcel Proust (1871–1922), French novelist, whose multivolume *À la recherche du temps perdu* (1913–27, *In Search of Lost Time*) Woolf read with great appreciation.

7. All characters in Shakespeare's plays, from *Othello, Antony and Cleopatra, Julius Caesar, Hamlet, King Lear,* and *As You Like It.*

has never been seen since the world began, I exclaimed. And I watched too, very curiously. For I wanted to see how Mary Carmichael set to work to catch those unrecorded gestures, those unsaid or half-said words, which form themselves, no more palpably than the shadows of moths on the ceiling, when women are alone, unlit by the capricious and coloured light of the other sex. She will need to hold her breath, I said, reading on, if she is to do it; for women are so suspicious of any interest that has not some obvious motive behind it, so terribly accustomed to concealment and suppression, that they are off at the flicker of an eye turned observingly in their direction. The only way for you to do it, I thought, addressing Mary Carmichael as if she were there, would be to talk of something else, looking steadily out of the window, and thus note, not with a pencil in a notebook, but in the shortest of shorthand, in words that are hardly syllabled yet, what happens when Olivia—this organism that has been under the shadow of the rock these million years—feels the light fall on it, and sees coming her way a piece of strange food—knowledge, adventure, art. And she reaches out for it, I thought, again raising my eyes from the page, and has to devise some entirely new combination of her resources, so highly developed for other purposes, so as to absorb the new into the old without disturbing the infinitely intricate and elaborate balance of the whole.

* * *

[ANDROGYNY]

But the sight of the two people getting into the taxi and the satisfaction it gave me made me also ask whether there are two sexes in the mind corresponding to the two sexes in the body, and whether they also require to be united in order to get complete satisfaction and happiness. And I went on amateurishly to sketch a plan of the soul so that in each of us two powers preside, one male, one female; and in the man's brain, the man predominates over the woman, and in the woman's brain, the woman predominates over the man. The normal and comfortable state of being is that when the two live in harmony together, spiritually cooperating. If one is a man, still the woman part of the brain must have effect; and a woman also must have intercourse with the man in her. Coleridge[8] perhaps meant this when he said that a great mind is androgynous. It is when this fusion takes place that the mind is fully fertilised and uses all its faculties. Perhaps a mind that is purely masculine cannot create, any more than a mind that is purely feminine, I thought. But it would be well to test what one meant by man-womanly, and conversely by woman-manly, by pausing and looking at a book or two.

Coleridge certainly did not mean, when he said that a great mind is androgynous, that it is a mind that has any special sympathy with women; a mind that takes up their cause or devotes itself to their interpretation. Perhaps the androgynous mind is less apt to make these distinctions than the single-sexed mind. He meant, perhaps, that the androgynous mind is resonant and porous; that it transmits emotion without impediment; that it is naturally creative, incandescent and undivided. In fact one goes back to

8. SAMUEL TAYLOR COLERIDGE (1772–1834), English Romantic poet and critic; see *Table Talk*, September 1, 1832.

Shakespeare's mind as the type of the androgynous, of the man-womanly mind, though it would be impossible to say what Shakespeare thought of women. And if it be true that it is one of the tokens of the fully developed mind that it does not think specially or separately of sex, how much harder it is to attain that condition now than ever before. Here I came to the books by living writers, and there paused and wondered if this fact were not at the root of something that had long puzzled me. No age can ever have been as stridently sex-conscious as our own; those innumerable books by men about women in the British Museum[9] are a proof of it. The Suffrage campaign[1] was no doubt to blame. It must have roused in men an extraordinary desire for self-assertion; it must have made them lay an emphasis upon their own sex and its characteristics which they would not have troubled to think about had they not been challenged. And when one is challenged, even by a few women in black bonnets, one retaliates, if one has never been challenged before, rather excessively. That perhaps accounts for some of the characteristics that I remember to have found here, I thought, taking down a new novel by Mr. A, who is in the prime of life and very well thought of, apparently, by the reviewers. I opened it. Indeed, it was delightful to read a man's writing again. It was so direct, so straightforward after the writing of women. It indicated such freedom of mind, such liberty of person, such confidence in himself. One had a sense of physical well-being in the presence of this well-nourished, well-educated, free mind, which had never been thwarted or opposed, but had had full liberty from birth to stretch itself in whatever way it liked. All this was admirable. But after reading a chapter or two a shadow seemed to lie across the page. It was a straight dark bar, a shadow shaped something like the letter "I." One began dodging this way and that to catch a glimpse of the landscape behind it. Whether that was indeed a tree or a woman walking[2] I was not quite sure. Back one was always hailed to the letter "I." One began to be tired of "I." Not but what this "I" was a most respectable "I"; honest and logical; as hard as a nut, and polished for centuries by good teaching and good feeding. I respect and admire that "I" from the bottom of my heart. But—here I turned a page or two, looking for something or other—the worst of it is that in the shadow of the letter "I" all is shapeless as mist. Is that a tree? No, it is a woman. But . . . she has not a bone in her body, I thought, watching Phoebe, for that was her name, coming across the beach. Then Alan got up and the shadow of Alan at once obliterated Phoebe. For Alan had views and Phoebe was quenched in the flood of his views. And then Alan, I thought, has passions; and here I turned page after page very fast, feeling that the crisis was approaching, and so it was. It took place on the beach under the sun. It was done very openly. It was done very vigorously. Nothing could have been more indecent. But . . . I had said "but" too often.[3] One cannot go on saying "but." One must finish the sentence somehow, I rebuked myself. Shall I finish it, "But—I am bored!" But why was I bored? Partly because of the dominance of the letter "I" and the aridity, which, like the giant beech tree, it casts within its shade. Nothing will grow

9. That is, in the Reading Room of the British Museum (in Bloomsbury), where Woolf did her research.

1. The movement to obtain the vote for women succeeded in England in 1918.

2. Possibly an allusion to Mark 8.24: "I see men as trees, walking."

3. The first word of *A Room of One's Own* is "But."

there. And partly for some more obscure reason. There seemed to be some obstacle, some impediment of Mr. A's mind which blocked the fountain of creative energy and shored it within narrow limits. And remembering the lunch party at Oxbridge, and the cigarette ash and the Manx cat and Tennyson and Christina Rossetti[4] all in a bunch, it seemed possible that the impediment lay there. As he no longer hums under his breath, "There has fallen a splendid tear from the passion-flower at the gate," when Phoebe crosses the beach, and she no longer replies, "My heart is like a singing bird whose nest is in a water'd shoot," when Alan approaches what can he do? Being honest as the day and logical as the sun, there is only one thing he can do. And that he does, to do him justice, over and over (I said, turning the pages) and over again. And that, I added, aware of the awful nature of the confession, seems somehow dull. Shakespeare's indecency uproots a thousand other things in one's mind, and is far from being dull. But Shakespeare does it for pleasure; Mr. A, as the nurses say, does it on purpose. He does it in protest. He is protesting against the equality of the other sex by asserting his own superiority. He is therefore impeded and inhibited and self-conscious as Shakespeare might have been if he too had known Miss Clough and Miss Davies.[5] Doubtless Elizabethan literature would have been very different from what it is if the woman's movement had begun in the sixteenth century and not in the nineteenth.

What, then, it amounts to, if this theory of the two sides of the mind holds good, is that virility has now become self-conscious—men, that is to say, are now writing only with the male side of their brains. It is a mistake for a woman to read them, for she will inevitably look for something that she will not find. It is the power of suggestion that one most misses, I thought, taking Mr. B the critic in my hand and reading, very carefully and very dutifully, his remarks upon the art of poetry. Very able they were, acute and full of learning; but the trouble was, that his feelings no longer communicated; his mind seemed separated into different chambers; not a sound carried from one to the other. Thus, when one takes a sentence of Mr. B into the mind it falls plump to the ground—dead; but when one takes a sentence of Coleridge into the mind, it explodes and gives birth to all kinds of other ideas, and that is the only sort of writing of which one can say that it has the secret of perpetual life.

But whatever the reason may be, it is a fact that one must deplore. For it means—here I had come to rows of books by Mr. Galsworthy and Mr. Kipling[6]—that some of the finest works of our greatest living writers fall upon deaf ears. Do what she will a woman cannot find in them that fountain of perpetual life which the critics assure her is there. It is not only that

4. In the book's first chapter, Woolf discusses the missing tails of Manx cats along with the poems (quoted here) "Maud" (1855) by Alfred, Lord Tennyson (1809–1892), and "A Birthday" (1862), by Christina Rossetti (1830–1894), which represent what men and women, respectively, hummed at garden parties before the war. "Oxbridge": an invented place, blending Oxford and Cambridge Universities.

5. Anne Jemima Clough (1820–1892) and Emily Davies (1830–1921), leaders in the movement to promote women's education. Clough was the first principal of Newnham Hall, the first institution for women at Cambridge University; Davies helped found and was the first mistress of Girton College, the second such institution at Cambridge.

6. Rudyard Kipling (1865–1936), English poet and novelist. John Galsworthy (1867–1933), English novelist and playwright. Jolyon, mentioned below, is a character in his *Forsyte Saga* (1906–22).

they celebrate male virtues, enforce male values and describe the world of men; it is that the emotion with which these books are permeated is to a woman incomprehensible. It is coming, it is gathering, it is about to burst on one's head, one begins saying long before the end. That picture will fall on old Jolyon's head; he will die of the shock; the old clerk will speak over him two or three obituary words; and all the swans on the Thames will simultaneously burst out singing. But one will rush away before that happens and hide in the gooseberry bushes, for the emotion which is so deep, so subtle, so symbolical to a man moves a woman to wonder. So with Mr. Kipling's officers who turn their backs; and his Sowers who sow the Seed; and his Men who are alone with their Works; and the Flag—one blushes at all these capital letters as if one had been caught eavesdropping at some purely masculine orgy. The fact is that neither Mr. Galsworthy nor Mr. Kipling has a spark of the woman in him. Thus all their qualities seem to a woman, if one may generalise, crude and immature. They lack suggestive power. And when a book lacks suggestive power, however hard it hits the surface of the mind it cannot penetrate within.

And in that restless mood in which one takes books out and puts them back again without looking at them I began to envisage an age to come of pure, of self-assertive virility, such as the letters of professors (take Sir Walter Raleigh's[7] letters, for instance) seem to forebode, and the rulers of Italy have already brought into being. For one can hardly fail to be impressed in Rome by the sense of unmitigated masculinity; and whatever the value of unmitigated masculinity upon the state, one may question the effect of it upon the art of poetry. At any rate, according to the newspapers, there is a certain anxiety about fiction in Italy. There has been a meeting of academicians whose object it is "to develop the Italian novel." "Men famous by birth, or in finance, industry or the Fascist corporations" came together the other day and discussed the matter, and a telegram was sent to the Duce[8] expressing the hope "that the Fascist era would soon give birth to a poet worthy of it." We may all join in that pious hope, but it is doubtful whether poetry can come out of an incubator. Poetry ought to have a mother as well as a father. The Fascist poem, one may fear, will be a horrid little abortion such as one sees in a glass jar in the museum of some county town. Such monsters never live long, it is said; one has never seen a prodigy of that sort cropping grass in a field. Two heads on one body do not make for length of life.

However, the blame for all this, if one is anxious to lay blame, rests no more upon one sex than upon the other. All seducers and reformers are responsible, Lady Bessborough when she lied to Lord Granville; Miss Davies when she told the truth to Mr. Greg.[9] All who have brought about a state of sex-consciousness are to blame, and it is they who drive me, when I want to stretch my faculties on a book, to seek it in that happy age, before Miss Davies and Miss Clough were born, when the writer used both sides of his mind equally. One must turn back to Shakespeare then, for Shakespeare

7. English essayist and critic (1861–1922), the first professor of English literature at Oxford; his letters were published in 1926.
8. Benito Mussolini (1883–1945), Italian dictator.
9. Probably the English essayist William Rathbone Greg (1809–1891), who in a text of 1862 asked, "Why Are Women Redundant?" Lady Bessborough (1761–1821) is Henrietta, countess of Bessborough, the lover of Lord Granville Leveson-Gower (1773–1846).

was androgynous; and so was Keats and Sterne and Cowper and Lamb and Coleridge. Shelley perhaps was sexless. Milton and Ben Jonson had a dash too much of the male in them. So had Wordsworth and Tolstoi.[1] In our time Proust was wholly androgynous, if not perhaps a little too much of a woman. But that failing is too rare for one to complain of it, since without some mixture of the kind the intellect seems to predominate and the other faculties of the mind harden and become barren. However, I consoled myself with the reflection that this is perhaps a passing phase; much of what I have said in obedience to my promise to give you the course of my thoughts will seem out of date; much of what flames in my eyes will seem dubious to you who have not yet come of age.

Even so, the very first sentence that I would write here, I said, crossing over to the writing-table and taking up the page headed Women and Fiction, is that it is fatal for any one who writes to think of their sex. It is fatal to be a man or woman pure and simple; one must be woman-manly or man-womanly. It is fatal for a woman to lay the least stress on any grievance; to plead even with justice any cause; in any way to speak consciously as a woman. And fatal is no figure of speech; for anything written with that conscious bias is doomed to death. It ceases to be fertilised. Brilliant and effective, powerful and masterly, as it may appear for a day or two, it must wither at nightfall; it cannot grow in the minds of others. Some collaboration has to take place in the mind between the woman and the man before the act of creation can be accomplished. Some marriage of opposites has to be consummated. The whole of the mind must lie wide open if we are to get the sense that the writer is communicating his experience with perfect fullness. There must be freedom and there must be peace. Not a wheel must grate, not a light glimmer. The curtains must be close drawn. The writer, I thought, once his experience is over, must lie back and let his mind celebrate its nuptials in darkness. He must not look or question what is being done. Rather, he must pluck the petals from a rose or watch the swans float calmly down the river. And I saw again the current which took the boat and the undergraduate and the dead leaves; and the taxi took the man and the woman,[2] I thought, seeing them come together across the street, and the current swept them away, I thought, hearing far off the roar of London's traffic, into that tremendous stream.

* * *

1929

1. All canonical authors, in varying degrees: John Keats (1795–1821), English poet; Laurence Sterne (1713–1768), English novelist; William Cowper (1731–1800), English poet; Charles Lamb (1775–1834), English essayist and critic; PERCY BYSSHE SHELLEY (1792–1822), English poet; John Milton (1608–1674), English poet; Ben Jonson (1572–1637), English poet and playwright; WILLIAM WORDSWORTH (1770–1850), English poet; and Leo Tolstoy (1828–1910), Russian novelist and moral philosopher.
2. Scenes described earlier in the book.

GYÖRGY LUKÁCS
1885–1971

The Marxist philosopher and aesthetician György Lukács played a fundamental role in the early development of Marxist literary and cultural theory. His original analysis of the commodity form in *History and Class Consciousness* (1923) continues to influence Marxist cultural theory, especially in the wide-ranging work of FREDRIC JAMESON. In the area of aesthetics, Lukács remains influential as well, not only because of his participation in the so-called realism debate of the 1930s, which involved such Marxist luminaries as THEODOR ADORNO, WALTER BENJAMIN, and Bertolt Brecht, but also because of his sophisticated historical approach to literature, best exemplified in *The Historical Novel* (1937).

Growing out of eighteenth-century realism, the historical novel in the early nineteenth century is, for Lukács, the product of the broad European social transformation initiated by the French Revolution and Napoleonic wars. The mass experience of history and the consolidation of nationalist sensibilities throughout Europe constitute the preconditions for the emergence of a new type of realist writing most notably exemplified by the works of Sir Walter Scott (1771–1832) and others such as Alessandro Manzoni (1785–1873), Aleksandr Pushkin (1799–1837), and Honoré de Balzac (1799–1850). According to Lukács, the historical novel of this time presents an expansive picture (the concrete totality) of society, including the class factions and struggles shaping it. History is no longer a mere element of decor or a pure object of abstraction as in Romantic and earlier literature: it is now a process assuming artistic form that shapes the past to comprehend the present and to sketch possible futures. To this aesthetic and political cause, Lukács devoted much of his professional life, securing his reputation as the most passionate defender of literary realism and critic of modernistic experimental work during the mid-twentieth century.

Born to an affluent Jewish family in Budapest, György Lukács displayed at an early age a repugnance for his parents' middle-class values. His father, József Lowinger, was the director of the Hungarian General Credit Bank, a leading financial institution of Austria-Hungary; Lowinger changed his last name to Lukács in 1890 to reflect his assimilation to Hungarian culture. Lukács's mother, Adél Wertheimer, derived her ancestry from one of the oldest and wealthiest Jewish families in eastern Europe. In his youth Lukács embraced the fin de siècle attitudes inspired by the nineteenth-century writers Søren Kierkegaard, FRIEDRICH NIETZSCHE, and Fyodor Dostoyevsky, among others. His intellectual interests eventually took him to Germany, where he studied under the sociologists Georg Simmel and Max Weber. Characterized by an anguished Romanticism, this initial phase of Lukács's career is reflected in his two early works, *Soul and Form* (1911) and *The Theory of the Novel* (1916), both published in German under the German version of his name, Georg Lukács. With its typology of forms indebted to G. W. F. HEGEL, the latter work became influential in large part because it interestingly historicized the novel; but Lukács later renounced it for developing a bleak view of the novel as fragmentary and ironic.

The barbarism of World War I, the promise of the Russian Revolution of 1917, and the subsequent demise of the Austro-Hungarian Empire precipitated Lukács's conversion to Marxism in 1918. He was a deeply committed communist, but he often ran into trouble with the Communist Party. He found his *History and Class Consciousness*, for example, censured by the Comintern Congress in Moscow. In this crucial work, which later became an important text for the student uprisings of the 1960s, Lukács addressed the widespread sense of fragmentation and alienation under capitalism, out of which emerged his conception of "reification"—the sense of objectification experienced by individuals who are subordinated to the rationalizing processes of commodity production and reduced to the status of things. He achieved an original synthesis of MARX's theory of commodity fetishism, Weber's concept of rationalization, and Hegel's philosophy of the dialectic. However, the Comintern objected to the unorthodox Hegelian (idealist) emphasis on the consciousness of the proletariat, thus setting the stage for Lukács's "autocriticisms," or public recantations of his own published writings.

From the 1930s onward, Lukács directed considerable effort toward the construction and defense of a Marxist realist aesthetic conceived in materialist terms and opposed to the idealist tradition from FRIEDRICH VON SCHILLER (1759–1805) to Arthur Schopenhauer (1788–1860). However, during Joseph Stalin's consolidation of power in the 1930s and up to the "thaw" of the 1950s, Lukács sometimes employed a coded language to express his unorthodox opinions on realism, because the theory and practice of literature in the Soviet Union had been increasingly regulated by the policy of Proletkult, the Bolshevik Party Central Committee, and the All Russian Association of Proletarian Writers (RAPP)—all of which endorsed the view that writers must serve the interests of the party. The result was a growing intolerance that prompted the exile of such figures as the revolutionary and cultural theorist Leon Trotsky and the noted Russian formalist ROMAN JAKOBSON. At issue was the theory of "socialist realism," which was devised by Maksim Gorky in consultation with Stalin, promulgated by A. A. Zhdanov, and sanctioned by the Congress of Soviet Writers in 1934. In theory, socialist realism insisted that realistic novels must be overtly didactic, serving the interests of socialism and the working class. Trotsky thought such a definition of realism was too narrow, and Lukács himself would have nothing to do with it because he opposed overt didacticism and admired such European novelists as Sir Walter Scott, Honoré de Balzac, and Thomas Mann (1875–1955), classifying them as "critical realists." After Stalin's death in 1953, Lukács was able to work more openly, summing up his views in *Die Eigenart des Ästhetischen* (1963, *The Specificity of the Aesthetic*).

In our selection from the first chapter of *The Historical Novel*, "The Classical Form of the Historical Novel," Lukács offers an orthodox Marxist analysis of the underlying socioeconomic and political conditions governing the rise of the historical novel in early nineteenth-century Europe. The emergence of bourgeois society and the simultaneous awakening of national sensibility during the Enlightenment entail, in Lukács's view, a decisive shift in the understanding of social existence from feudal absolutist inertia to modern democratic progress linked with increasing industrialization, urbanization, and capitalism. In the wake of the widespread revolutionary and independence movements triggered by the French Revolution and Napoleonic wars, broad segments of the European population begin to experience a growing sense of historical awareness. As modern warfare is integrated into society in the form of large national armies drawn from the population and shaped by political propaganda, people see their lives for the first time as historically embedded in a changing reality that is self-created rather than pregiven. Later FRANTZ FANON would confirm the role of war in the development of nation-states while similarly highlighting the internal tensions of class struggle, and BENEDICT ANDERSON would add spreading literacy as a key factor in the creation of nation-states and national consciousness during the nineteenth century.

The historical novel, according to Lukács, is a major catalyst of national cohesion and class consciousness. At its best, as exemplified by the novels of Sir Walter Scott, it reflects the totality of social relationships by creating "types" or representative characters. Unlike some Romantic literature, which offers reactionary descriptions of the past, abstract and idealistic, realist historical accounts are rooted in the concrete socioeconomic conditions of the present and are committed to the objective depiction of the socially formative forces in history. Lukács faults Romanticism for overlooking popular life as it superficially derives the spirit of an age from biographies of leading historical figures. At the same time, he praises Scott for placing at the center of his epic-scale narratives prosaic, mediocre heroes, who engage in dialogue and typify social trends while displaying the political potential of the masses. Lukács here distinguishes between the complex reality depicted in Scott's novels and the author's own conservative political views, as he will later do with other novelists like Balzac. Unlike socialist realism, the historical novel in Lukács's handling is not a programmed genre directed by a political party. Like seismographs, the great historical realists register present social tremors and often those to come through instinct. For Lukács, historical realism constitutes an aesthetic vanguard of works whose portrayals anticipate where social developments are headed.

Moreover, historical realism is distinguished by Lukács not only from reactionary Romanticism but also from expressionism and other modernist artistic movements such as symbolism and surrealism, all of which regressively emphasize subjectivity, alienation, and fragmentation. In texts such as "Realism in the Balance" (1938), Lukács faults modernism, especially expressionism, for being content merely to depict immediate sense impressions and fragmentary subjective states, as demonstrated by its practitioners' preference for montage. In "juxtaposing heterogeneous, unrelated pieces of reality torn from their context," expressionism attends only to the uncomprehended surfaces and appearances of things, producing opaque, chaotic, and plotless works. It thus abandons the goal of mirroring objective reality and its underlying socioeconomic laws, becoming instead a passive depiction of the alienation of people under capitalism. More important, by universalizing alienation (rather than seeing it as an effect of capitalism), the movement provides no basis for progressive politics.

Lukács also distinguishes realism from other ostensibly realistic movements such as naturalism and impressionism, both of which focus on immediate and random sense perceptions. In his opinion, the entire historical progression of modern literary periods—naturalism, impressionism, symbolism, expressionism, and surrealism—marks an increasing dissolution of the objectivity of classic early nineteenth-century realism, as represented by Scott's and Balzac's fiction, which occupies the opposite end of the spectrum from James Joyce's decadent modernist fiction. The historical basis for this undermining of classic realism is fully developed in Lukács's *The Historical Novel*. His great hope is that twentieth-century realists like Thomas Mann can stem the tide of this reactionary process by providing the basis for a truly accessible popular literature attuned to objectivity and adaptable to leftist political coalitions and popular fronts.

Lukács's advocacy of realism came under immediate and persistent criticism. Perhaps best known is that of Bertolt Brecht, who accuses Lukács of inadvertently lapsing into formalism by privileging the form of an outdated nineteenth-century genre above all others. More severe are the criticisms directed at Lukács's central conceptions of totality and typicality. With the advent of postmodernism, totalizing theories in general have come under attack; for instance, the leading philosopher of the postmodern, JEAN-FRANÇOIS LYOTARD, famously urged his readers to "wage a war on totality" and to critique "grand narratives" that purport to explain everything within a single theoretical framework. Moreover, in light of the postmodern questioning of historical objectivity, exemplified by the work of HAYDEN WHITE, Lukács's theory of history can seem one-dimensional. In spite of all this, Lukács's work has made important contributions to contemporary debates; his influence is clear in the roles that reification, realism, and periodization play in the work of Fredric Jameson, the most important American theorist of postmodernism. Lukács's historical account of the gradual and complex rise of the modern middle class (the European nationalist bourgeoisies portrayed by leading realists) is stunning in its breadth and detail.

The Historical Novel **Keywords:** Ideology, Literary History, Marxism, Modernity, Nationhood, The Novel, Realism

From The Historical Novel[1]

From *Chapter One. The Classical Form of the Historical Novel*

1. SOCIAL AND HISTORICAL CONDITIONS FOR THE RISE OF THE HISTORICAL NOVEL

The historical novel arose at the beginning of the nineteenth century at about the time of Napoleon's[2] collapse (Scott's *Waverley*[3] appeared in 1814). Of course, novels with historical themes are to be found in the seventeenth and eighteenth centuries, too, and, should one feel inclined, one can treat medieval adaptations of classical history or myth as "precursors" of the historical novel and indeed go back still further to China or India. But one will find nothing here that sheds any real light on the phenomenon of the historical novel. The so-called historical novels of the seventeenth century (Scudéry, Calpranède,[4] etc.) are historical only as regards their purely external choice of theme and costume. Not only the psychology of the characters, but the manners depicted are entirely those of the writer's own day. And in the most famous "historical novel" of the eighteenth century, Walpole's *Castle of Otranto*,[5] history is likewise treated as mere costumery: it is only the curiosities and oddities of the *milieu* that matter, not an artistically faithful image of a concrete historical epoch. What is lacking in the so-called historical novel before Sir Walter Scott is precisely the specifically historical, that is, derivation of the individuality of characters from the historical peculiarity of their age. The great critic Boileau,[6] who judged the historical novels of his contemporaries with much scepticism, insisted only that characters should be socially and psychologically true, demanding that a ruler make love differently from a shepherd, and so on. The question of historical truth in the artistic reflection of reality still lies beyond his horizon.

However, even the great realistic social novel of the eighteenth century, which in its portrayal of contemporary morals and psychology, accomplished a revolutionary breakthrough to reality for world literature is not concerned to show its characters as belonging to any concrete time. The contemporary world is portrayed with unusual plasticity and truth-to-life, but is accepted naïvely as something given: whence and how it has developed have not yet become problems for the writer. This abstractness in the portrayal of historical time also affects the portrayal of historical place. Thus Lesage[7] is able to transfer his highly truthful pictures of the France of his day to Spain and still feel quite at ease. Similarly, Swift, Voltaire and even

1. Translated by Hannah and Stanley Mitchell.
2. Napoléon Bonaparte (1769–1821), French military and political leader who attempted to create a European empire.
3. The first in a long series of some two dozen books that would come to be called the Waverly Novels, by the Scottish historical novelist and poet Sir Walter Scott (1771–1832).
4. Gautier de Costes, seigneur de la Calprenède (ca. 1610–63), French novelist and dramatist. Madeleine de Scudéry (1607–1701), French writer.
5. The pioneering Gothic novel (1764) by the English man of letters Horace Walpole (1717–1797).
6. Nicolas Boileau (1636–1711), French poet and critic.
7. Alain-René Lesage (1668–1747), French novelist and playwright.

Diderot[8] set their satirical novels in a "never and nowhere" which nevertheless faithfully reflects the essential characteristics of contemporary England and France. These writers, then, grasp the salient features of their world with a bold and penetrating realism. But they do not see the specific qualities of their own age historically.

This basic attitude remains essentially unchanged despite the fact that realism continues to bring out the specific features of the present with ever greater artistic power. Think of novels like *Moll Flanders, Tom Jones,*[9] etc. Their broad, realistic portrayal of the present takes in here and there important events of contemporary history which it links with the fortunes of the characters. In this way, particularly in Smollett[1] and Fielding, time and place of action acquire much greater concreteness than was customary in the earlier period of the social novel or in most contemporary French writing. Fielding indeed is to some extent aware of this development, this increasing concreteness of the novel in its grasp of the historical peculiarity of characters and events. His definition of himself as a writer is that of an historian of bourgeois society.[2]

Altogether, when analyzing the prehistory of the historical novel, one must break with the Romantic-reactionary legend which denies to the Enlightenment any sense or understanding of history and attributes the invention of historical sense to the opponents of the French Revolution, Burke, de Maistre,[3] etc. One need only think of the extraordinary historical achievements of Montesquieu, Voltaire, Gibbon,[4] etc., in order to cut this legend down to size.

What matters for us, however, is to concretize the particular character of this sense of history both before and after the French Revolution in order to see clearly what was the social and ideological basis from which the historical novel was able to emerge. And here we must stress that the history writing of the Enlightenment was, in its main trend, an ideological preparation for the French Revolution. The often superb historical construction, with its discovery of numerous new facts and connections, serves to demonstrate the necessity for transforming the "unreasonable" society of feudal absolutism; and the lessons of history provide the principles with whose help a "reasonable" society, a "reasonable" state may be created. For this reason the classical world[5] is central to both the historical theory and the practice of the Enlightenment. To ascertain the causes of the greatness and decline of the classical states is one of the most important theoretical preliminaries for the future transformation of society.

This applies above all to France, the spiritual leader during the period of militant Enlightenment. The position in England is somewhat different.

8. Denis Diderot (1713–1784), French philosopher and writer. Jonathan Swift (1667–1745), Anglo-Irish satirist, poet, and cleric. Voltaire: pen name of François-Marie Arouet (1694–1778), French Enlightenment essayist and philosopher.
9. A comic novel (1749), by the English playwright and novelist Henry Fielding (1707–1754). *Moll Flanders* (1772), a novel by the English novelist and journalist Daniel Defoe (ca. 1660–1731).
1. Tobias George Smollett (1721–1771), Scottish author, best known for his picaresque novels.
2. That is, postfeudal middle-class society.
3. Joseph-Marie, comte de Maistre (1753–1821), a French-speaking Savoyard diplomat and writer. EDMUND BURKE (1729–1797), Anglo-Irish statesman, political theorist, and philosopher. Both were conservatives who strongly opposed the aims of the French Revolution (1789–99).
4. Edward Gibbon (1737–1794), English historian and member of Parliament. Charles-Louis de Secondat, baron de La Brède et de Montesquieu (1689–1755), French Enlightenment social commentator and political theorist.
5. That is, the civilizations of ancient Greece and Rome (ca. 5th c. B.C.E.–ca. 5th c. C.E.).

Economically, eighteenth century England indeed finds itself in the midst of the greatest transformation, the creation of the economic and social preconditions for the Industrial Revolution. Politically, however, England is already a post-revolutionary country.[6] Thus where it is a question of mastering bourgeois society theoretically and subjecting it to criticism, of working out the principles of political economy, history is grasped as history more concretely than in France. But where it is a question of conscious and consistent application of such specifically historical viewpoints, they occupy an episodic position in the development as a whole. The really dominating economic theorist towards the end of the eighteenth century is Adam Smith.[7] James Steuart,[8] who posed the problem of capitalist economy far more historically and who investigated the process by which capital came into being, was soon forgotten. Marx[9] characterizes the difference between these two important economists in the following way: Steuart's "contribution to the concept of capital is to have shown how the process of separation takes place between the conditions of production, as the property of definite classes, and labour-power. He gives a great deal of attention to this *process of the birth* of capital—*without as yet directly comprehending it as such* (my italics G.L.), although he sees it as the condition of large-scale industry. He examines the process particularly in agriculture; and he correctly presents manufacturing industry proper as dependent on this prior process of separation in agriculture. In Adam Smith's works this process of separation is assumed as already completed." This unawareness of the significance of the historical sense already present in practice, of the possibility of generalizing the historical peculiarity of the immediate present, which had been correctly observed by instinct, characterizes the position which the great social novel of England occupies in the development of our problem. It drew the attention of writers to the concrete (i.e. historical) significance of time and place, to social conditions and so on, it created the realistic, literary means of expression for portraying this spatio-temporal (i.e. historical) character of people and circumstances. But this, as in the economics of Steuart, was a product of realistic instinct and did not amount to a clear understanding of history as a process, of history as the concrete precondition of the present.

It is only during the last phase of the Enlightenment that the problem of the artistic reflection of past ages emerges as a central problem of literature. This occurs in Germany. Initially, it is true, the ideology of the German Enlightenment follows in the wake of that of France and England: the great achievements of Winckelmann and Lessing[1] do not in the main diverge from the general trend of the Enlightenment. Lessing, whose important contributions to the clarification of the problem of historical drama we shall discuss at length later, still defines the relationship of writer to history entirely in

6. During the English Civil War (1642–49), royal forces were defeated by a parliamentary army, the monarchy and the House of Lords were temporarily abolished, the king was executed for treason, and a republican Commonwealth was established.

7. Scottish moral philosopher and pioneering political economist (1723–1790); his major work was *The Wealth of Nations* (1776).

8. Scottish lawyer and economist (1713–1780).

9. KARL MARX (1818–1883), German philosopher, political economist, and revolutionary; Lukács quotes from Marx's *Capital*, vol. 4 (1905), which discusses Steuart's *Inquiry into the Principles of Political Oeconomy* (1767).

1. GOTTHOLD EPHRAIM LESSING (1729–1781), German philosopher, dramatist, and art critic. Johann Joachim Winckelmann (1717–1768), German art historian and archaeologist.

the spirit of Enlightenment philosophy. He maintains that for the great dramatist history is no more than a "repertory" of names.

But soon after Lessing, in the *Sturm und Drang*,[2] the problem of the artistic mastery of history already appears as a conscious one. Goethe's *Götz von Berlichingen*[3] not only ushers in a new flowering of historical drama, but has a direct and powerful influence on the rise of the historical novel in the work of Sir Walter Scott. This conscious growth of historicism, which receives its first theoretical expression in the writings of Herder,[4] has its roots in the special position of Germany, in the discrepancy between Germany's economic and political backwardness and the ideology of the German Enlighteners, who, standing on the shoulders of their English and French predecessors, developed the ideas of the Enlightenment to a higher level. As a result not only do the general contradictions underlying the whole ideology of the Enlightenment appear more sharply there than in France, but the specific contrast between these ideas and German reality is thrust vigorously into the foreground.

In England and France, the economic, political and ideological preparation and completion of the bourgeois revolution and the setting-up of a national state are one and the same process. So that in looking to the past, however intense the bourgeois-revolutionary patriotism and however important the works it produces (Voltaire's *Henriade*[5]), the chief concern is inevitably the Enlightenment critique of the "unreasonable". Not so in Germany. Here revolutionary patriotism comes up against national division, against the political and economic fragmentation[6] of a country which imports its cultural and ideological means of expression from France. For everything that was produced in the small German courts in the way of culture and particularly in the way of pseudo-culture was nothing more than a slavish imitation of the French court. Thus the small courts constitute not only a political obstacle to German unity, but also an ideological hindrance to the development of a culture stemming from the needs of German middle-class life. The German form of Enlightenment necessarily engages in sharp polemic with this French culture; and it preserves this note of revolutionary patriotism even where the real content of the ideological battle is simply the conflict between different stages in the development of the Enlightenment (Lessing's struggle against Voltaire).

The inevitable result of this situation is to turn to German history. Partly it is the reawakening of past national greatness which gives strength to hopes of national rebirth. It is a requirement of the struggle for this national greatness that the historical causes for the decline, the disintegration of Germany should be explored and artistically portrayed. As a result, in Germany, which in the preceding centuries had been no more than an object of historical changes, art becomes historical earlier and more radically than in the economically and politically more advanced countries of the West.

2. Storm and Stress (German), a movement in German literature and music (late 1760s–early 1780s) characterized by a focus on subjectivity and extremes of emotion.
3. *Götz of Berlichingen with the Iron Hand* (1773), a drama by the German poet, dramatist, novelist, and scientist Johann Wolfgang von Goethe (1749–1832).
4. Johann Gottfried von Herder (1744–1803), German philosopher, poet, and literary critic.
5. An epic poem on Henry IV of France (1723).
6. Germany's 25 states were not unified until 1871.

It was the French Revolution, the revolutionary wars and the rise and fall of Napoleon,[7] which for the first time made history a *mass experience,* and moreover on a European scale. During the decades between 1789 and 1814 each nation of Europe underwent more upheavals than they had previously experienced in centuries. And the quick succession of these upheavals gives them a qualitatively distinct character, it makes their historical character far more visible than would be the case in isolated, individual instances: the masses no longer have the impression of a "natural occurrence". One need only read over Heine's reminiscences of his youth in *Buch le Grand,*[8] to quote just one example, where it is vividly shown how the rapid change of governments affected Heine as a boy. Now if experiences such as these are linked with the knowledge that similar upheavals are taking place all over the world, this must enormously strengthen the feeling first that there is such a thing as history, that it is an uninterrupted process of changes and finally that it has a direct effect upon the life of every individual.

This change from quantity into quality appears, too, in the differences of these wars from all preceding ones. The wars of absolute states in the pre-Revolutionary period were waged by small professional armies. They were conducted so as to isolate the army as sharply as possible from the civilian population, supplies from depots, fear of desertion, etc. Not for nothing did Frederick II[9] of Prussia declare that war should be waged in such a manner that the civilian population simply would not notice it. "To keep the peace is the first duty of the citizen" was the motto of the wars of absolutism.

This changes at one stroke with the French Revolution. In its defensive struggle against the coalition of absolute monarchies, the French Republic was compelled to create mass armies. The qualitative difference between mercenary and mass armies is precisely a question of their relations with the mass of the population. If in place of the recruitment or pressing into professional service of small contingents of the declassed, a mass army is to be created, then the content and purpose of the war must be made clear to the masses by means of propaganda. This happens not only in France itself during the defence of the Revolution and the later offensive wars. The other states, too, if they transfer to mass armies, are compelled to resort to the same means. (Think of the part played by German literature and philosophy in this propaganda after the battle of Jena.[1]) Such propaganda cannot possibly, however, restrict itself to the individual, isolated war. It has to reveal the social content, the historical presuppositions and circumstances of the struggle, to connect up the war with the entire life and possibilities of the nation's development. It is sufficient to point to the importance of the defence of Revolutionary achievements in France and to the connection between the creation of a mass army and political and social reforms in Germany and in other countries.

The inner life of a nation is linked with the modern mass army in a way it could not have been with the absolutist armies of the earlier period. In France the estate barrier[2] between nobleman, officer and common soldier

7. The dominant figure in continental Europe between 1799 and 1815.
8. *Ideas: The Book of Le Grand* (1827), a prose work by the German Romantic poet, journalist, and essayist Heinrich Heine (1797–1856).
9. King of Prussia (1712–1786; reigned 1740–86).
1. City in east-central Germany; in this battle, in 1806, the forces of Napoleon I defeated those of Frederick William III of Prussia.
2. That is, the division of classes; before the Revolution, the French legislative assembly represented the three estates: the clergy, nobles, and commons.

disappears: the highest positions in the army are open to all and it is well known that this barrier fell as a direct result of the Revolution. And even in those countries fighting against the Revolution, estate barriers were inevitably breached to some extent. One need only read the writings of Gneisenau[3] to see how clearly these reforms were connected with the new historical situation created by the French Revolution. Further, the war inevitably destroyed the former separation of army from people. It is impossible to maintain mass armies on a depot basis. Since they have to maintain themselves by requisition they inevitably come into direct and permanent contact with the people of the country where the war is being waged. Of course, this contact very often consists of robbery and plunder. But not always. And it must not be forgotten that the wars of the Revolution and, to some extent, those of Napoleon were waged as conscious propaganda wars.

Finally, the enormous quantitative expansion of war plays a qualitatively new role, bringing with it an extraordinary broadening of horizons. Whereas the wars fought by the mercenary armies of absolutism consisted mostly of tiny manoeuvres around fortresses etc., now the whole of Europe becomes a war arena. French peasants fight first in Egypt, then in Italy, again in Russia; German and Italian auxiliary troops take part in the Russian campaign; German and Russian troops occupy Paris after Napoleon's defeat, and so forth. What previously was experienced only by isolated and mostly adventurous-minded individuals, namely an acquaintance with Europe or at least certain parts of it, becomes in this period the mass experience of hundreds of thousands, of millions.

Hence the concrete possibilities for men to comprehend their own existence as something historically conditioned, for them to see in history something which deeply affects their daily lives and immediately concerns them. There is no point in dealing here with the social transformations in France itself. It is quite obvious the extent to which the economic and cultural life of the entire nation was disrupted by the huge, rapidly successive changes of the period. It should be mentioned, however, that the Revolutionary armies and later those of Napoleon, too, did liquidate, completely or partially, the remnants of feudalism in many of the places they conquered, as for example in the Rhineland and Northern Italy. The social and cultural contrast between the Rhineland and the rest of Germany, still very noticeable at the time of the '48 Revolution,[4] is a legacy handed down from the Napoleonic era, and the broad masses were conscious of the connection between these social changes and the French Revolution. To mention once again some of the literary reflexes: besides Heine's remembrances of his youth, it is most instructive to read the first chapters of Stendhal's *La Chartreuse de Parme*[5] to see what a lasting impression was evoked by French rule in Northern Italy.

It is in the nature of a bourgeois revolution that, if seriously carried through to its conclusion, the national idea becomes the property of the broadest masses. In France it was only as a result of the Revolution and Napoleonic rule[6] that a feeling of nationhood became the experience and property of the

3. August Neidhardt von Gneisenau (1760–1831), Prussian field marshal who helped reform the Prussian army after its defeat at Jena.

4. A series of political uprisings in France, the German states, the Hapsburg states, and Italy in 1848.

5. *The Charterhouse of Parma* (1839), by Stendhal, pen name of French writer Henri-Marie Beyle (1784–1842).

6. The rule of Napoléon I (1799–1815).

peasantry, the lower strata of the petty bourgeoisie and so on. For the first time they experienced France as their own country, as their self-created motherland.

But the awakening of national sensibility and with it a feeling and understanding for national history occurs not only in France. The Napoleonic wars everywhere evoked a wave of national feeling, of national resistance to the Napoleonic conquests, an experience of enthusiasm for national independence. To be sure, these movements are mostly, as Marx says, a compound of "regeneration and reaction,"[7] as in Spain, Germany etc. In Poland, on the other hand, the struggle for independence, the flare-up of national feeling is essentially progressive. But whatever the proportions of "regeneration and reaction" in individual national movements, it is clear that these movements—real mass movements—inevitably conveyed a sense and experience of history to broad masses. The appeal to national independence and national character is necessarily connected with a re-awakening of national history, with memories of the past, of past greatness, of moments of national dishonour, whether this results in a progressive or reactionary ideology.

Thus in this mass experience of history the national element is linked on the one hand with problems of social transformation; and on the other, more and more people become aware of the connection between national and world history. This increasing consciousness of the historical character of development begins to influence judgments on economic conditions and class struggle. In the eighteenth century it was only the odd critic of nascent capitalism, the wit and paradox-monger, who compared the exploitation of workers by Capital with forms of exploitation in earlier periods in order to expose Capitalism as the more inhumane form (Linguet[8]). In the ideological struggle against the French Revolution a similar comparison, admittedly shallow in economic terms and reactionary in tendency, between society before and after the Revolution or, on a wider scale, between Capitalism and Feudalism becomes the war-cry of Legitimist Romanticism.[9] The inhumanity of Capitalism, the chaos of competition, the destruction of the small by the big, the debasement of culture by the transformation of all things into commodities—all this is contrasted, in a manner generally reactionary in tendency, with the social idyll of the Middle Ages, seen as a period of peaceful co-operation among all classes, an age of the organic growth of culture. But if mostly a reactionary tendency prevails in these polemical writings, it should not be forgotten that it was in this period that the notion of Capitalism as a definite, historical era of human development first arose, and this occurred not in the works of the great theorists of Capitalism, but in those of their enemies. It suffices to mention Sismondi[1] here, who despite theoretical confusion over fundamental questions, raised certain individual historical problems of economic development with great clarity. One has only to think of his dictum that while in antiquity the

7. From Marx, "Revolutionary Spain" (1854).
8. Simon-Nicolas-Henri Linguet (1736–1794), French journalist and lawyer.
9. Legitimists were French Royalists—those who believe in or advocate rule by hereditary right.
1. Jean Charles Léonard Sismondi (1773–1842), Swiss economist and historian. For his dictum, cited by Marx both in vol. 1 of *Capital* (1867) and in the preface to the 2d ed. of *The Eighteenth Brumaire* of Louis Bonaparte (1869), see vol. 1 of *Studies in the Social Sciences* (1836).

proletariat lived at the expense of society, in modern times it is society which lives at the expense of the proletariat.

It is already clear from these remarks that the tendencies towards a conscious historicism reach their peak after the fall of Napoleon, at the time of the Restoration and the Holy Alliance.[2] Admittedly, the spirit of historicism which at first prevails and gains official status is reactionary and by its nature pseudo-historical. The historical interpretation, publicist writings and *belles lettres* of Legitimism develop the historical spirit in radical opposition to the Enlightenment and the ideas of the French Revolution. The ideal of Legitimism is to return to pre-Revolutionary conditions, that is, to eradicate from history the greatest historical events of the epoch.

According to this interpretation history is a silent, imperceptible, natural, "organic" growth, that is, a development of society which is basically stagnation, which alters nothing in the time-honoured, legitimate institutions of society and, above all, alters nothing consciously. Man's activity in history is ruled out completely. The German historical school of law even denies nations the right to make new laws for themselves, it prefers to leave the old motley feudal laws of custom to their "organic growth".

Thus under the banner of historicism and of a struggle against the "abstract, unhistorical" spirit of the Enlightenment, there arises a pseudo-historicism, an ideology of immobility, of return to the Middle Ages. In the interests of these reactionary political aims, historical development is ruthlessly distorted. And the inner falsity of the reactionary ideology is intensified by the fact that the Restoration in France is compelled for economic reasons to come to terms socially with the Capitalism which has grown up in the meantime, indeed even to seek its partial support, economically and politically. (The situation of the reactionary governments in Prussia, Austria etc. is similar.) These then are the foundations on which history is to be written afresh. Chateaubriand[3] tries hard to revise classical history in order to depreciate historically the old revolutionary ideal of the Jacobin[4] and Napoleonic period. He and other pseudo-historians of reaction furnish a falsely idyllic picture of the unsurpassed, harmonious society of the Middle Ages. This historical interpretation of the Middle Ages determines the portrayal of feudal times in the Romantic novel of the Restoration.

Despite this ideological mediocrity of Legitimist pseudo-historicism, it exerts an extraordinarily powerful influence. Admittedly distorted and mendacious, it is nevertheless an historically necessary expression of the great period of transformation which sets in with the French Revolution. And the new stage of development, which begins precisely with the Restoration, compels the defenders of human progress to forge for themselves a new ideological armour. We have seen with what undaunted vigour the Enlightenment fought the historical legitimacy and continuity of feudal survivals. Similarly, we have seen how post-Revolutionary Legitimism regarded

2. A somewhat vague agreement, initially signed in 1815 by the rulers of Russia, Austria, and Prussia, that was intended to reestablish order in Europe after the fall of Napoléon. Restoration: in French history, the restoration (1814–30) of the Bourbon dynasty after Napoléon.

3. François-Auguste-René de Chateaubriand (1768–1848), French writer, politician, and diplomat.

4. That is, the Reign of Terror (1793–94), a period marked by mass executions of "enemies of the revolution"; it was spearheaded by members of the Jacobin Club (1789–94), the largest and most powerful political club of the French Revolution.

precisely their conservation as the content of history. The defenders of progress after the French Revolution had necessarily to reach a conception which would prove the *historical necessity* of the latter, furnish evidence that it constituted a peak in a long and gradual historical development and not a sudden eclipse of human consciousness, not a Cuvier-like "natural catastrophe" in human history,[5] and that this was the only course open to the future development of mankind.

This, however, means a big change of outlook in the interpretation of human progress in comparison with the Enlightenment. Progress is no longer seen as an essentially unhistorical struggle between humanist reason and feudal-absolutist unreason. According to the new interpretation the reasonableness of human progress develops ever increasingly out of the inner conflict of social forces in history itself; according to this interpretation history itself is the bearer and realizer of human progress. The most important thing here is the increasing historical awareness of the decisive role played in human progress by the struggle of classes in history. The new spirit of historical writing, which is most clearly visible in the important French historians of the Restoration period, concentrates precisely on this question: on showing historically how modern bourgeois society arose out of the class struggles between nobility and bourgeoisie, out of class struggles which raged throughout the entire "idyllic Middle Ages" and whose last decisive stage was the great French Revolution. These ideas produce the first attempt at a rational periodization of history, an attempt to comprehend the historical nature and origins of the present rationally and scientifically. The first large-scale attempt at such a periodization had already been undertaken by Condorcet[6] in the middle of the French Revolution, in his historico-philosophical major work. These ideas are further developed and scientifically enlarged in the Restoration period. Indeed, in the works of the great Utopians[7] the periodization of history already transcends the horizon of bourgeois society. And if this transition, this step beyond Capitalism follows fantastic paths, its critical-historical basis is nonetheless linked—especially in the case of Fourier[8]—with a devastating critique of the contradictions of bourgeois society. In Fourier, despite the fantastic nature of his ideas about Socialism and of the ways to Socialism, the picture of Capitalism is shown with such overwhelming clarity in all its contradiction that the idea of the transitory nature of this society appears tangibly and plastically before us.

This new phase in the ideological defence of human progress found its philosophical expression in Hegel.[9] As we have seen, the central historical question was to demonstrate the necessity of the French Revolution, to show that revolution and historical development are not opposed to one another, as the apologists of feudal Legitimism maintained. The philosophy of Hegel

5. A cataclysmic event of the kind that—according to advocates of catastrophism, such as the French naturalist Georges Cuvier (1769–1832)—explained geological features and the extinction of species.

6. Jean-Antoine-Nicolas de Caritat, marquis de Condorcet (1743–1794), French philosopher, mathematician, and early political scientist; his "major work" was *Sketch for a Historical Picture of the Progress of the Human Mind* (1795).

7. Proponents of utopian socialism, the dominant branch of socialism in the first quarter of the 19th century.

8. Charles Fourier (1772–1837), French utopian social philosopher.

9. GEORG WILHELM FRIEDRICH HEGEL (1770–1831), German philosopher.

provides the philosophic basis for this conception of history. Hegel's discovery of the universal law of transformation of quantity into quality is, seen historically, a philosophic methodology for the idea that revolutions constitute necessary, organic components of evolution and that without such a "nodal line of proportions"[1] true evolution is impossible in reality and unthinkable philosophically.

On this basis, the Enlightenment conception of man is philosophically cancelled, preserved and raised to a higher level (*aufgehoben*).[2] The greatest obstacle to an understanding of history lay in the Enlightenment's conception of man's unalterable nature. Thus, any change in the course of history had meant, in extreme cases, merely a change of costume and, in general, merely the moral ups and down of the same man. Hegelian philosophy draws all the inferences from the new progressive historicism. It sees man as a product of himself and of his own activity in history. And even if this historical process seems to stand idealistically upon its head, even if the bearer of the process is mystified into a "world spirit", Hegel nevertheless sees this world spirit as embodying the dialectics of historical development. "Thus the spirit opposes itself (i.e. in history G.L.) and has to overcome itself, as the really hostile obstacle to its own purpose: the evolution . . . in the spirit . . . is a hard, unceasing struggle against itself. What the spirit desires is to realize its own idea, yet it conceals this idea from itself, is proud and full of self-enjoyment in this alienation of its own self . . . With the spiritual form it is different (from what it is in nature G.L.); here the change takes place not merely on the surface, but in the idea. It is the idea itself which is corrected."[3] Hegel gives an apt description here—admittedly in an idealist and abstract fashion—of the ideological change which has occurred in his age. The thought of the earlier period oscillated antinomously between a fatalistic law-conforming conception of all social occurrence and an over-estimation of the possibilities of conscious intervention in social development. But on both sides of the antinomy[4] the principles were considered to be "supra-historical", stemming from the "eternal" nature of "reason". Hegel, however, sees a process in history, a process propelled, on the one hand, by the inner motive forces of history and which, on the other, extends its influence to all the phenomena of human life, including thought. He sees the total life of humanity as a great historical process.

Thus there arose, in both a concrete historical as well as philosophic manner, a new humanism, a new concept of progress. A humanism which wished to preserve the achievements of the French Revolution as the imperishable basis of future human development, which regarded the French Revolution (and revolutions in history altogether) as an indispensable component of human progress. Of course, this new historical humanism was itself a child of its age and unable to transcend the limits of that age—except in a fantastical form, as was the case with the great Utopians. The important bourgeois humanists of this period find themselves in a paradoxical situation: while they comprehend the necessity of revolutions in the

1. A phrase from Hegel's *Science of Logic* (1812–16).
2. A technical term from Hegelian dialectics, usually translated "sublation": the process by which a thesis, though canceled by its antithesis, is partially preserved in a higher synthesis.
3. From Hegel, *Lectures on the Philosophy of History* (1837).
4. Mutual incompatibility of two terms.

past and see in them the foundation for all that is reasonable and worthy of affirmation in the present, nevertheless they interpret future development in terms of a henceforth peaceful evolution on the basis of these achievements. As M. Lifschitz very rightly shows in his article on Hegel's aesthetics,[5] they seek the positive things in the new world order created by the French Revolution and do not consider any new revolution to be necessary for the final realization of these positive things.

This conception of the last great intellectual and artistic period of bourgeois humanism has nothing to do with the barren and shallow apologia of capitalism which sets in later (and to some extent simultaneously). It is founded upon a ruthlessly truthful investigation and disclosure of all the contradictions of progress. There is no criticism of the present from which it will shrink. And even if it cannot consciously transcend the spiritual horizon of its time, yet the constantly oppressive sense of the contradictions of its own historical situation casts a profound shadow over the whole historical conception. This feeling that—contrary to the consciously philosophic and historical conception which proclaims unceasing and peaceful progress—one is experiencing a last brief, irretrievable intellectual prime of humanity manifests itself in the greatest representatives of this period in very different ways, in keeping with the unconscious character of this feeling. Yet for the same reason the emotional accent is very similar. Think of the old Goethe's theory of "abnegation", of Hegel's "Owl of Minerva" which takes flight only at dusk, of Balzac's[6] sense of universal doom, etc. It was the 1848 Revolution which for the first time placed before the surviving representatives of this epoch the choice of either recognizing the perspective held out by the new period in human development and of affirming it, even if with a tragic cleavage of spirit, like Heine, or of sinking into the position of apologists for declining capitalism, as Marx, immediately after the 1848 Revolution, critically demonstrated in the case of such important figures as Guizot and Carlyle.[7]

2. SIR WALTER SCOTT

Such was the historical basis upon which Sir Walter Scott's historical novel arose. But one must never think of this relationship in terms of the idealist "history of the spirit" (*Geistesgeschichte*). In the latter we should find shrewd hypotheses to show the devious routes by which Hegelian ideas, for example, found their way to Scott; and some forgotten writer would be discovered who contained the common source of Scott's and Hegel's historicism. It is certain that Scott had no knowledge of Hegel's philosophy and had he come across it would probably not have understood a word. The new historical conception of the great historians of the Restoration actually makes its appearance later than the works of Scott and some of its problems are influenced by them. The fashionable philosophic-cum-philologic hunting down

5. "Hegel's Aesthetics and Dialectical Materialism," written in 1931, on the centennial anniversary of Hegel's death, by the Russian philosopher and art historian Mikhail Lifschitz (1905–1983).
6. Honoré de Balzac (1799–1850), French novelist and playwright. Hegel wrote of the "Owl of Minerva" (the Roman goddess of wisdom) in the preface to *Philosophy of Right* (1821).
7. Thomas Carlyle (1795–1881), Scottish essayist, satirist, and historian. François Pierre Guillaume Guizot (1787–1874), French historian, orator, and statesman.

of individual "influences" is no more fruitful for the writing of history than the old philological hunting down of the effects of individual writers on one another. With Scott, in particular, it was the fashion to quote a long list of second and third-rate writers (Radcliffe,[8] etc.), who were supposed to be important literary forerunners of his. All of which brings us not a jot nearer to understanding what was *new* in Scott's art, that is in his historical novel.

We have attempted to outline the general framework of those economic and political transformations which occurred throughout Europe as a result of the French Revolution; in the preceding remarks we briefly sketched the latter's ideological consequences. These events, this transformation of men's existence and consciousness throughout Europe form the economic and ideological basis for Scott's historical novel. Biographical evidence of the individual instances which enabled Scott to become aware of these trends offers nothing of importance to the real history of the rise of the historical novel. The less so, as Scott ranks among those great writers whose depth is manifest mainly in their work, a depth which they often do not understand themselves, because it has sprung from a truly realistic mastery of their material in conflict with their personal views and prejudices.

Scott's historical novel is the direct continuation of the great realistic social novel of the eighteenth century. Scott's studies on eighteenth century writers, on the whole not very penetrating theoretically, reveal an intensive knowledge and detailed study of this literature. Yet his work, in comparison with theirs, signifies something entirely new. His great contemporaries clearly recognized this new quality. Pushkin[9] writes of him: . . . "The influence of Walter Scott can be felt in every province of the literature of his age. The new school of French historians formed itself under the influence of the Scottish novelist. He showed them entirely new sources which had so far remained unknown despite the existence of the historical drama of Shakespeare[1] and Goethe . . ." And Balzac, in his criticism of Stendhal's *La Chartreuse de Parme,* emphasizes the new artistic features which Scott's novel introduced into epic literature: the broad delineation of manners and circumstances attendant upon events, the dramatic character of action and, in close connection with this, the new and important role of dialogue in the novel.

It is no accident that this new type of novel arose in England. We have already mentioned, in dealing with the literature of the eighteenth century, important realistic features in the English novel of this period, and we described them as necessary consequences of the post-revolutionary character of England's development at the time, in contrast to France and Germany. Now, in a period when the whole of Europe, including its progressive classes and their ideologists, are swayed (temporarily) by a post-revolutionary ideology, these features in England must stand out with more than usual distinctness. For England has now once more become the model land of development for the majority of continental ideologists, though of course in a different sense from that of the eighteenth century. Then, the fact that bourgeois freedoms had actually been realized, served as an example to the

8. Ann Radcliffe (1764–1823), English author who was a pioneer of the Gothic novel.

9. Aleksandr Sergeyevich Pushkin (1799–1837), Russian Romantic poet.

1. Many of the plays of William Shakespeare (1564–1616) treat history (especially English history).

Continental Enlighteners. Now, in the eyes of the historical ideologists of progress, England appears as the classic example of historical development in their sense. The fact that England had fought out its bourgeois revolution in the seventeenth century[2] and had from then on experienced a peaceful, upward development, lasting over centuries, on the basis of the Revolution's achievements, showed England to be the practical, model example for the new style of historical interpretation. The "Glorious Revolution" of 1688,[3] likewise, inevitably presented itself as an ideal to the bourgeois ideologists who were combating the Restoration in the name of progress.

On the other hand, however, honest writers, keenly observant of the real facts of social development, like Scott, were made to see that this peaceful development was peaceful only as the ideal of an historical conception, only from the bird's-eye view of a philosophy of history. The organic character of English development is a resultant made up of the components of ceaseless class struggles and their bloody resolution in great or small, successful or abortive uprisings. The enormous political and social transformations of the preceding decades awoke in England, too, the feeling for history, the awareness of historical development.

* * *

1937

2. That is, during the English Civil War.
3. The almost bloodless ouster of the Catholic king James II; he was replaced by William III and Mary II, who were made joint rulers in a newly defined constitutional monarchy that decisively shifted power to Parliament.

T. S. ELIOT
1888–1965

T. S. Eliot is the central Anglo-American poet and critic of the twentieth century. He is the author of the most influential poem, *The Waste Land* (1922), and the most authoritative literary essays and reviews. In the history of literary theory and criticism, Eliot belongs—with SAMUEL JOHNSON, SAMUEL TAYLOR COLERIDGE, and MATTHEW ARNOLD—among the poet-critics who have defined the critical standards of an era, recast the literary tradition, and established key terms for analysis and evaluation. So immense was Eliot's authority that the poet Dylan Thomas referred to him as "the Pope" and the critic Delmore Schwartz dubbed him a "literary dictator."

Thomas Stearns Eliot was born in St. Louis, Missouri, the seventh and youngest child of Henry Ware Eliot, a businessman, and Charlotte Stearns Eliot, an amateur poet and volunteer social worker. From 1898 to 1905, Eliot attended Smith Academy in St. Louis, a preparatory school where his studies included Greek and Latin, rhetoric, French, and German, and during 1905–06 he was a student at Milton Academy, in Milton, Massachusetts. In 1906 he entered Harvard University, receiving his bachelor's degree in 1909 and his master's in 1910.

At Harvard, Eliot became interested in philosophy and comparative literature—DANTE's *Divine Comedy* was a sublime discovery for him. Important influences on his intellectual development include the philosopher, poet, and humanist George Santayana (1863–1952), from whom Eliot took a course on modern philosophy, and the literary scholar Irving Babbitt (1865–1933), a relentless foe of Romanticism, with whom Eliot studied nineteenth-century French literary criticism. A strong influence on his early verse was the theory of the dynamic flux and movement of consciousness propounded by the French philosopher Henri Bergson (1859–1941). But for Eliot's poetry and criticism, the crucial experience of his Harvard years was his reading in December 1908 of Arthur Symons's *The Symbolist Movement in Literature* (1899), which introduced French symbolist poetry to English and American readers. Eliot was busy writing verse himself, publishing some of it in *The Harvard Advocate*; between 1909 and 1911, he worked on two of his best poems, "Portrait of a Lady" and "The Love Song of J. Alfred Prufrock," drawing on the style of irony and symbolism he had encountered in the nineteenth-century French poets—especially Charles Baudelaire, Arthur Rimbaud, and Jules Laforgue—whom Symons quoted and discussed.

Eliot was a self-made modernist; as his friend Ezra Pound later said, Eliot had "trained himself *and* modernized himself *on his own*." In his introduction to Pound's *Selected Poems* (1928), Eliot made much the same point: "the form in which I began to write, in 1908 or 1909, was directly drawn from the study of Laforgue together with the later Elizabethan drama; and I do not know anyone who started from exactly that point." He read widely, modifying (and sometimes parodying) the verbal techniques of other poets.

After a year at the Sorbonne in Paris, Eliot returned to Harvard to pursue graduate work and serve as a teaching assistant. For his dissertation topic, he focused on the writings of the British idealist philosopher F. H. Bradley, the author of *Appearance and Reality* (1893). His research led him to the University of Marburg in Germany, in the summer of 1914; but as the threat of world war loomed, he relocated to Merton College, Oxford. He was to settle in England permanently.

In September 1914 Eliot met Pound, who quickly became his adviser, editor, and literary agent. "The Love Song of J. Alfred Prufrock" was published in *Poetry* magazine in June 1915; in the following month, Eliot married Vivien (sometimes Vivienne) Haigh-Wood. The marriage proved unhappy and, as Vivien's mental and physical illnesses deepened in the 1920s and 1930s, it was harrowing for both of them. His despair is reflected in the torment, bitterness, and isolation expressed in much of his poetry. "No artist produces great art," Eliot claimed, "by a deliberate attempt to express his personality. He expresses his personality indirectly through concentrating upon a task which is a task in the same sense as the making of an efficient engine or the turning of a jug or a table-leg" (*Selected Essays, 1917–1932*). Eliot's work is itself impersonal and objective; it is filled—especially the poetry—with masks, role-playing, and multiple voices. Yet it is saturated everywhere, too, with displaced personal pain, regret, sexual desire, and emotional and spiritual yearning.

For two years Eliot taught in grammar schools, gave lectures on literature, and wrote dense, technical articles and reviews on philosophy. In March 1917, tired of makeshift teaching, he took a job at Lloyd's Bank in London. He held this position for the next eight years, while laboring on his poetry—his first volume, *Prufrock and Other Observations*, appeared in 1917—and on literary criticism, publishing essays and book reviews in the *Times Literary Supplement* and other leading periodicals. A number are included in *The Sacred Wood* (1920), a landmark collection of criticism and theory.

Work and worry brought Eliot near a nervous breakdown, and to recuperate he went first to Margate, in southeast England, and then to a sanatorium in Lausanne, Switzerland, where he worked on the draft of a long poem he had started years earlier. In Paris, on his way back to London, he showed the draft to Ezra Pound, who edited it skillfully and turned it (in Eliot's words) from "a jumble of good and bad passages into a poem"—*The Waste Land*. Allusive, experimental, and technically daring, showily learned and archly witty, *The Waste Land* is a primary text of literary modernism. The poem was published in *The Criterion*—a new literary and cultural quarterly edited by Eliot—in October 1922. For many writers, critics, intellectuals, and general readers, *The Waste Land* evoked the waste and sterility of a Western world ravaged by the horrors of World War I, which had brought carnage on an unprecedented scale: more than 8.5 million soldiers and 13 million civilians had died. *The Waste Land* is not a poem about the war, but the war's trauma informs it from beginning to end.

Eliot was a literary and cultural force throughout the 1920s and 1930s. As editor of the quarterly *The Criterion* until the journal's demise in 1939, he published leading English modernists (including VIRGINIA WOOLF and James Joyce) and was the first to publish in English such significant European writers as Jean Cocteau and Marcel Proust. In 1925 Eliot accepted a position in the London firm of Faber and Gwyer (later, Faber and Faber), which became a leading publisher of poets from Ezra Pound to Sylvia Plath. He began writing plays in the 1930s, with *Murder in the Cathedral* (1935), and he enjoyed considerable popular success with his dramas of the 1950s, including *The Cocktail Party* (1950).

In 1927 Eliot became a British citizen and joined the Church of England; in the following year, he announced in *For Lancelot Andrewes*, a collection of critical essays, that he was "classicist in literature, royalist in politics, and Anglo-Catholic in religion." Eliot was conservative, even reactionary, and sometimes he drifted close to fascism and into racism and anti-Semitism. In his social and cultural writings and in much of his literary criticism of the 1930s and 1940s, Eliot is austere and sometimes censorious in attitude and pontificating in tone. From 1932 to 1933, he held the Charles Eliot Norton Professorship of Poetry at Harvard, where he delivered the lectures that became *The Use of Poetry and the Use of Criticism* (1933). Much of his late cultural criticism, gloomily resentful and hectoring, is today unread, but it does not diminish the force and influence of the best of Eliot's poetry and literary criticism. In 1948 he was awarded the Order of Merit by King George VI and the Nobel Prize in Literature.

Our first selection, "Tradition and the Individual Talent" (1919), begins: "In English writing we seldom speak of tradition." The poise and authority of Eliot's critical voice, backed up by his masterful performances as a poet, soon made "tradition" a key topic for poets, critics, intellectuals, and teachers of literature in the academy. Two of the canonical texts of modern Anglo-American literary criticism, F. R. LEAVIS's *Revaluation: Tradition and Development in English Poetry* (1936) and CLEANTH BROOKS's *Modern Poetry and the Tradition* (1939), were expansions of Eliot's ideas about tradition, and many other books (and countless syllabi) were similarly based on the terms that he had articulated.

For Eliot, each poem exists within the tradition from which it takes shape and which it, in turn, redefines. Thus tradition is both something to which the poet must be "faithful" and something that he or she actively makes: novelty emerges out of being steeped in tradition. Some later critics, such as HAROLD BLOOM, have characterized Eliot as a "weak" poet-critic because of the priority that he assigns to tradition, but in doing so they overlook the extent to which the poet challenges and revises the tradition to which he or she defers: "What happens when a new work of art is created," he says, "is something that happens simultaneously to all the works of art that preceded it." Eliot has also been criticized for picturing tradition as variously a "simultaneous order," a "living whole," an "ideal order," and the "mind of Europe," thereby idealizing its conflicts, contradictions, and omissions.

"The Metaphysical Poets" (1921) is another central work in the history of modern criticism. Almost as soon as it appeared, the difficult seventeenth-century metaphysical poets—John Donne, Andrew Marvell, and their contemporaries, whom Eliot described as "more often named than read, and more often read than profitably studied"—became models of good poetry. Eliot's essay is condensed in its argument, highly suggestive, and extraordinarily ambitious. In it he deploys the evaluative terms that in the eighteenth century Samuel Johnson had used against the metaphysical poets ("the most heterogeneous ideas are yoked by violence together") to elevate the poets whom his eminent precursor had assailed, insisting that modern poetry *must* be difficult. He packs "The Metaphysical Poets" with unelaborated argument and assertion, stressing in particular the seventeenth century's disastrous "dissociation of sensibility" into "thought" and "feeling." In the process, he illustrates how "tradition" is made, is *forced*, into the form that later generations of writers require. Many of Eliot's readers took his generalizations as literal truths, and even skeptics, such as the English critic Frank Kermode (see *The Romantic Image*, 1957), judged that refuting Eliot demanded full-scale scholarly and critical demonstration.

Eliot liked being a troublemaker, saying outrageous things from on high and often not quite clarifying whether he meant them seriously. In "Hamlet and His Problems" (1920), for instance, Eliot presents his brilliant theory of the "objective correlative": "The only way of expressing emotion in the form of art is by finding an 'objective correlative'; in other words, a set of objects, a situation, a chain of events which shall be the formula for that particular emotion; such that, when the external facts, which must terminate in sensory experience, are given, the emotion is immediately evoked." Eliot uses *Hamlet* as a test case, surprisingly labeling the play an "artistic failure" precisely because in it the "emotions" that Shakespeare evokes are "in excess" of the facts of the story, the dramatic action. It is a perverse judgment, in which Eliot may not have believed, but which he uttered with such assurance that it is still cited and debated.

Eliot was adept at formulating the nature and function of literary criticism, and the New Critics (such as JOHN CROWE RANSOM and Brooks) invoked his critical practice as a model. He described criticism as "the disinterested exercise of intelligence . . . the elucidation of works of art and the correction of taste . . . the common pursuit of true judgment," and the New Critics followed his injunction to center arguments in formalist analysis of specific passages and poems. "Comparison and analysis," Eliot said, "are the chief tools of the critic," enabling a precise perception of literary effects, relationships, and values. By the 1950s, Eliot was lamenting the rise of copiously detailed interpretation of texts—which he called "lemon-squeezing"—but more than anyone else he had launched the new movement. "Honest criticism and sensitive appreciation are directed not upon the poet but upon the poetry," Eliot states in section II of "Tradition and the Individual Talent." In such sentences, we can see the origins of the New Criticism, with its abiding concern for the words on the page—in R. P. Blackmur's formulation, "the words and the motions of the words . . . all the technical devices of literature."

For many critics in the 1970s and after, Eliot—Anglican, conservative, New Critical formalist—has been the archenemy. Bloom, for example, has derided Eliot's poetry and criticism and sought to revitalize the Romantic tradition that Eliot had shunned. Explicitly or implicitly, many others arguing for the inclusion of women and minority writers within the literary canon have attacked his judgments about literary and cultural tradition. Eliot's and the New Critics' "tradition," they maintain, is narrow and elitist, enshrining a limited range of authors and presenting to students a partial, misleading literary history.

While these critics have exposed Eliot's failings, they have not lessened his importance. Now that the critical sifting has been done, it may be possible to return to Eliot in order to see anew, and appreciate again, the scale of his accomplishments in poetry and prose. Literary modernism is unimaginable without Eliot, and the best of his work has remained extraordinarily influential.

"Tradition and the Individual Talent" Keywords: Authorship, The Canon/Tradition, Literary History, Modernity, Poetry
"The Metaphysical Poets" Keywords: Authorship, The Canon/Tradition, Formalism, Language, Literary History, Poetry

Tradition and the Individual Talent

I

In English writing we seldom speak of tradition, though we occasionally apply its name in deploring its absence. We cannot refer to 'the tradition' or to 'a tradition'; at most, we employ the adjective in saying that the poetry of So-and-so is 'traditional' or even 'too traditional'. Seldom, perhaps, does the word appear except in a phrase of censure. If otherwise, it is vaguely approbative, with the implication, as to the work approved, of some pleasing archaeological reconstruction. You can hardly make the word agreeable to English ears without this comfortable reference to the reassuring science of archaeology.

Certainly the word is not likely to appear in our appreciations of living or dead writers. Every nation, every race, has not only its own creative, but its own critical turn of mind; and is even more oblivious of the shortcomings and limitations of its critical habits than of those of its creative genius. We know, or think we know, from the enormous mass of critical writing that has appeared in the French language the critical method or habit of the French; we only conclude (we are such unconscious people) that the French are 'more critical' than we, and sometimes even plume ourselves a little with the fact, as if the French were the less spontaneous. Perhaps they are; but we might remind ourselves that criticism is as inevitable as breathing, and that we should be none the worse for articulating what passes in our minds when we read a book and feel an emotion about it, for criticizing our own minds in their work of criticism. One of the facts that might come to light in this process is our tendency to insist, when we praise a poet, upon those aspects of his work in which he least resembles anyone else. In these aspects or parts of his work we pretend to find what is individual, what is the peculiar essence of the man. We dwell with satisfaction upon the poet's difference from his predecessors, especially his immediate predecessors; we endeavour to find something that can be isolated in order to be enjoyed. Whereas if we approach a poet without this prejudice we shall often find that not only the best, but the most individual parts of his work may be those in which the dead poets, his ancestors, assert their immortality most vigorously. And I do not mean the impressionable period of adolescence, but the period of full maturity.

Yet if the only form of tradition, of handing down, consisted in following the ways of the immediate generation before us in a blind or timid adherence to its successes, 'tradition' should positively be discouraged. We have seen many such simple currents soon lost in the sand; and novelty is better than repetition. Tradition is a matter of much wider significance. It cannot be inherited, and if you want it you must obtain it by great labour. It involves, in the first place, the historical sense, which we may call nearly indispensable to anyone who would continue to be a poet beyond his twenty-fifth year; and the historical sense involves a perception, not only of the pastness of the past, but of its presence; the historical sense compels a man to write not merely with his own generation in his bones, but with a feeling that the whole of the literature of Europe from Homer and within it the whole of the literature of his own country has a simultaneous existence and composes a simultaneous order. This historical sense, which is a sense of the timeless as well as of the temporal and of the timeless and of the temporal together, is what makes a writer traditional. And it is at the same time what makes a writer most acutely conscious of his place in time, of his own contemporaneity.

No poet, no artist of any art, has his complete meaning alone. His significance, his appreciation is the appreciation of his relation to the dead poets and artists. You cannot value him alone; you must set him, for contrast and comparison, among the dead. I mean this as a principle of aesthetic, not merely historical, criticism. The necessity that he shall conform, that he shall cohere, is not onesided; what happens when a new work of art is created is something that happens simultaneously to all the works of art which preceded it. The existing monuments form an ideal order among themselves, which is modified by the introduction of the new (the really new) work of art among them. The existing order is complete before the new work arrives; for order to persist after the supervention of novelty, the *whole* existing order must be, if ever so slightly, altered; and so the relations, proportions, values of each work of art toward the whole are readjusted; and this is conformity between the old and the new. Whoever has approved this idea of order, of the form of European, of English literature will not find it preposterous that the past should be altered by the present as much as the present is directed by the past. And the poet who is aware of this will be aware of great difficulties and responsibilities.

In a peculiar sense he will be aware also that he must inevitably be judged by the standards of the past. I say judged, not amputated, by them; not judged to be as good as, or worse or better than, the dead; and certainly not judged by the canons of dead critics. It is a judgment, a comparison, in which two things are measured by each other. To conform merely would be for the new work not really to conform at all; it would not be new, and would therefore not be a work of art. And we do not quite say that the new is more valuable because it fits in; but its fitting in is a test of its value—a test, it is true, which can only be slowly and cautiously applied, for we are none of us infallible judges of conformity. We say: it appears to conform, and is perhaps individual, or it appears individual, and may conform; but we are hardly likely to find that it is one and not the other.

To proceed to a more intelligible exposition of the relation of the poet to the past: he can neither take the past as a lump, an indiscriminate bolus,[1] nor can he form himself wholly on one or two private admirations, nor can he form himself wholly upon one preferred period. The first course is inadmissible, the second is an important experience of youth, and the third is a pleasant and highly desirable supplement. The poet must be very conscious of the main current, which does not at all flow invariably through the most distinguished reputations. He must be quite aware of the obvious fact that art never improves, but that the material of art is never quite the same. He must be aware that the mind of Europe—the mind of his own country—a mind which he learns in time to be much more important than his own private mind—is a mind which changes, and that this change is a development which abandons nothing *en route*, which does not superannuate either Shakespeare,

1. A rounded mass of material.

or Homer, or the rock drawing of the Magdalenian draughtsmen.[2] That this development, refinement perhaps, complication certainly, is not, from the point of view of the artist, any improvement. Perhaps not even an improvement from the point of view of the psychologist or not to the extent which we imagine; perhaps only in the end based upon a complication in economics and machinery. But the difference between the present and the past is that the conscious present is an awareness of the past in a way and to an extent which the past's awareness of itself cannot show.

Someone said: 'The dead writers are remote from us because we *know* so much more than they did'. Precisely, and they are that which we know.

I am alive to a usual objection to what is clearly part of my programme for the *métier*[3] of poetry. The objection is that the doctrine requires a ridiculous amount of erudition (pedantry), a claim which can be rejected by appeal to the lives of poets in any pantheon. It will even be affirmed that much learning deadens or perverts poetic sensibility. While, however, we persist in believing that a poet ought to know as much as will not encroach upon his necessary receptivity and necessary laziness, it is not desirable to confine knowledge to whatever can be put into a useful shape for examinations, drawing-rooms, or the still more pretentious modes of publicity. Some can absorb knowledge, the more tardy must sweat for it. Shakespeare acquired more essential history from Plutarch[4] than most men could from the whole British Museum. What is to be insisted upon is that the poet must develop or procure the consciousness of the past and that he should continue to develop this consciousness throughout his career.

What happens is a continual surrender of himself as he is at the moment to something which is more valuable. The progress of an artist is a continual self-sacrifice, a continual extinction of personality.

There remains to define this process of depersonalization and its relation to the sense of tradition. It is in this depersonalization that art may be said to approach the condition of science. I therefore invite you to consider, as a suggestive analogy, the action which takes place when a bit of finely filiated platinum is introduced into a chamber containing oxygen and sulphur dioxide.

II

Honest criticism and sensitive appreciation is directed not upon the poet but upon the poetry. If we attend to the confused cries of the newspaper critics and the susurrus[5] of popular repetition that follows, we shall hear the names of poets in great numbers; if we seek not Blue-book knowledge[6] but the enjoyment of poetry, and ask for a poem, we shall seldom find it. I have tried to point out the importance of the relation of the poem to other poems by other authors, and suggested the conception of poetry as a living whole of all the poetry that has ever been written. The other aspect of this Impersonal theory of poetry is

2. Artists of the late Paleolithic period who created the cave paintings discovered at La Madeleine, France. The epic poems attributed to Homer were composed ca. 8th century B.C.E.
3. Trade, vocation; a line of activity in which one excels (originally French).
4. Greek philosopher and biographer (ca. 50–ca. 120 C.E.); his *Lives* of important Greeks and Romans provided Shakespeare with source material for his Roman plays.
5. Whispering, murmuring.
6. That is, the ability to name-drop, gleaned from the social register (or "blue book"). Also, a report on knowledge or an examination written in a blue notebook.

the relation of the poem to its author. And I hinted, by an analogy, that the mind of the mature poet differs from that of the immature one not precisely in any valuation of 'personality', not being necessarily more interesting, or having 'more to say', but rather by being a more finely perfected medium in which special, or very varied, feelings are at liberty to enter into new combinations.

The analogy was that of the catalyst. When the two gases previously mentioned are mixed in the presence of a filament of platinum, they form sulphurous acid. This combination takes place only if the platinum is present; nevertheless the newly formed acid contains no trace of platinum, and the platinum itself is apparently unaffected: has remained inert, neutral, and unchanged.[7] The mind of the poet is the shred of platinum. It may partly or exclusively operate upon the experience of the man himself; but, *the more perfect the artist, the more completely separate in him will be the man who suffers and the mind which creates*; the more perfectly will the mind digest and transmute the passions which are its material.

The experience, you will notice, the elements which enter the presence of the transforming catalyst, are of two kinds: emotions and feelings. The effect of a work of art upon the person who enjoys it is an experience different in kind from any experience not of art. It may be formed out of one emotion, or may be a combination of several; and various feelings, inhering for the writer in particular words or phrases or images, may be added to compose the final result. Or great poetry may be made without the direct use of any emotion whatever: composed out of feelings solely. Canto XV of the *Inferno* (Brunetto Latini)[8] is a working up of the emotion evident in the situation; but the effect, though single as that of any work of art, is obtained by considerable complexity of detail. The last quatrain gives an image, a feeling attaching to an image, which 'came',[9] which did not develop simply out of what precedes, but which was probably in suspension in the poet's mind until the proper combination arrived for it to add itself to. The poet's mind is in fact a receptacle for seizing and storing up numberless feelings, phrases, images, which remain there until all the particles which can unite to form a new compound are present together.

If you compare several representative passages of the greatest poetry you see how great is the variety of types of combination, and also how completely any semi-ethical criterion of 'sublimity' misses the mark.[1] For it is not the 'greatness', the intensity, of the emotions, the components, but the intensity of the artistic process, the pressure, so to speak, under which the fusion takes place, that counts. The episode of Paolo and Francesca[2] employs a definite emotion, but the intensity of the poetry is something quite different from whatever intensity in the supposed experience it may give the impression of. It is no more intense, furthermore, than Canto XXVI, the voyage of

7. In *The Use of Poetry and the Use of Criticism* (1933), Eliot cites with approval an observation in an 1817 letter by the Romantic poet John Keats: "Men of Genius are great as certain etherial Chemicals operating on the Mass of neutral intellect—but they have not any individuality, any determined Character."

8. During his journey through hell in the *Inferno* (1321), DANTE ALIGHIERI meets his former master Brunetto Latini, whom he still admires, confined in the seventh circle (for committing sodomy).

9. Dante likens Latini to the winner of the annual footrace in Verona.

1. Eliot is seeking to distinguish his notion of the sublime not only from that of LONGINUS and EDMUND BURKE, who stressed "greatness," but also from that of MATTHEW ARNOLD, who had argued that the sublime effects of the highest poetry could and should function as a form of (or even a substitute for) religion.

2. Illicit lovers, who were murdered by Francesca's husband; Dante meets them in the second circle of hell (*Inferno* 6.38–142).

Ulysses,[3] which has not the direct dependence upon an emotion. Great variety is possible in the process of transmutation of emotion: the murder of Agamemnon,[4] or the agony of Othello, gives an artistic effect apparently closer to a possible original than the scenes from Dante. In the *Agamemnon*, the artistic emotion approximates to the emotion of an actual spectator; in *Othello* to the emotion of the protagonist himself. But the difference between art and the event is always absolute; the combination which is the murder of Agamemnon is probably as complex as that which is the voyage of Ulysses. In either case there has been a fusion of elements. The ode of Keats[5] contains a number of feelings which have nothing particular to do with the nightingale, but which the nightingale, partly perhaps because of its attractive name, and partly because of its reputation, served to bring together.

The point of view which I am struggling to attack is perhaps related to the metaphysical theory of the substantial unity of the soul: for my meaning is, that the poet has, not a 'personality' to express, but a particular medium, which is only a medium and not a personality, in which impressions and experiences combine in peculiar and unexpected ways. Impressions and experiences which are important for the man may take no place in the poetry, and those which become important in the poetry may play quite a negligible part in the man, the personality.

I will quote a passage which is unfamiliar enough to be regarded with fresh attention in the light—or darkness—of these observations:

And now methinks I could e'en chide myself
For doating on her beauty, though her death
Shall be revenged after no common action.
Does the silkworm expend her yellow labours
For thee? For thee does she undo herself?
Are lordships sold to maintain ladyships
For the poor benefit of a bewildering minute?
Why does yon fellow falsify highways,
And put his life between the judge's lips,
To refine such a thing—keeps horse and men
To beat their valours for her? . . .[6]

In this passage (as is evident if it is taken in its context) there is a combination of positive and negative emotions: an intensely strong attraction toward beauty and an equally intense fascination by the ugliness which is contrasted with it and which destroys it. This balance of contrasted emotion is in the dramatic situation to which the speech is pertinent, but that situation alone is inadequate to it. This is, so to speak, the structural emotion, provided by the drama. But the whole effect, the dominant tone, is due to the fact that a number of floating feelings, having an affinity to this emotion by no means superficially evident, have combined with it to give us a new art emotion.

3. Ulysses, suffering in hell for his false counsel, describes to Dante the voyage—after his return to Ithaca—that ended in his death.
4. The story of the Greek warrior king Agamemnon, murdered by his wife Clytemnestra, is told by the tragedian Aeschylus in *Agamemnon* (458 B.C.E.). Shakespeare's *Othello* was written in 1603–04.
5. "Ode to a Nightingale" (1819), by John Keats (1795–1821).
6. From *The Revenger's Tragedy*, 3.5.67–78, published anonymously in 1607. When Eliot was writing, the play was attributed to Cyril Tourneur (ca. 1575–1626), but most scholars now believe that the author is Thomas Middleton (1580–1627).

It is not in his personal emotions, the emotions provoked by particular events in his life, that the poet is in any way remarkable or interesting. His particular emotions may be simple, or crude, or flat. The emotion in his poetry will be a very complex thing, but not with the complexity of the emotions of people who have very complex or unusual emotions in life. One error, in fact, of eccentricity in poetry is to seek for new human emotions to express; and in this search for novelty in the wrong place it discovers the perverse. The business of the poet is not to find new emotions, but to use the ordinary ones and, in working them up into poetry, to express feelings which are not in actual emotions at all. And emotions which he has never experienced will serve his turn as well as those familiar to him. Consequently, we must believe that 'emotion recollected in tranquillity'[7] is an inexact formula. For it is neither emotion, nor recollection, nor, without distortion of meaning, tranquillity. It is a concentration, and a new thing resulting from the concentration, of a very great number of experiences which to the practical and active person would not seem to be experiences at all; it is a concentration which does not happen consciously or of deliberation. These experiences are not 'recollected', and they finally unite in an atmosphere which is 'tranquil' only in that it is a passive attending upon the event. Of course this is not quite the whole story. There is a great deal, in the writing of poetry, which must be conscious and deliberate. In fact, the bad poet is usually unconscious where he ought to be conscious, and conscious where he ought to be unconscious. Both errors tend to make him 'personal'. Poetry is not a turning loose of emotion, but an escape from emotion; it is not the expression of personality, but an escape from personality. But, of course, only those who have personality and emotions know what it means to want to escape from these things.

III

ὁ δὲ νοῦς ἴσως θειότερόν τι καί ἀπαθές ἐστιν.[8]

This essay proposes to halt at the frontier of metaphysics or mysticism, and confine itself to such practical conclusions as can be applied by the responsible person interested in poetry. To divert interest from the poet to the poetry is a laudable aim: for it would conduce to a juster estimation of actual poetry, good and bad. There are many people who appreciate the expression of sincere emotion in verse, and there is a smaller number of people who can appreciate technical excellence. But very few know when there is an expression of *significant* emotion, emotion which has its life in the poem and not in the history of the poet. The emotion of art is impersonal. And the poet cannot reach this impersonality without surrendering himself wholly to the work to be done. And he is not likely to know what is to be done unless he lives in what is not merely the present, but the present moment of the past, unless he is conscious, not of what is dead, but of what is already living.

1919

7. Quoted from WILLIAM WORDSWORTH, Preface to *Lyrical Ballads* (1800; see above).
8. The mind is doubtless something more divine and unaffected (Greek). From ARISTOTLE, *De Anima* (*On the Soul*), 1.4, 408b.

The Metaphysical Poets

By collecting these poems from the work of a generation more often named than read, and more often read than profitably studied, Professor Grierson has rendered a service of some importance.[1] Certainly the reader will meet with many poems already preserved in other anthologies, at the same time that he discovers poems such as those of Aurelian Townshend or Lord Herbert of Cherbury here included. But the function of such an anthology as this is neither that of Professor Saintsbury's admirable edition of Caroline poets[2] nor that of the *Oxford Book of English Verse*. Mr. Grierson's book is in itself a piece of criticism, and a provocation of criticism; and we think that he was right in including so many poems of Donne, elsewhere (though not in many editions) accessible, as documents in the case of 'metaphysical poetry'.[3] The phrase has long done duty as a term of abuse, or as the label of a quaint and pleasant taste. The question is to what extent the so-called metaphysicals formed a school (in our own time we should say a 'movement'), and how far this so-called school or movement is a digression from the main current.

Not only is it extremely difficult to define metaphysical poetry, but difficult to decide what poets practise it and in which of their verses. The poetry of Donne (to whom Marvell and Bishop King[4] are sometimes nearer than any of the other authors) is late Elizabethan, its feeling often very close to that of Chapman. The 'courtly' poetry is derivative from Jonson, who borrowed liberally from the Latin; it expires in the next century with the sentiment and witticism of Prior.[5] There is finally the devotional verse of Herbert, Vaughan, and Crashaw (echoed long after by Christina Rossetti and Francis Thompson);[6] Crashaw, sometimes more profound and less sectarian than the others, has a quality which returns through the Elizabethan period to the early Italians. It is difficult to find any precise use of metaphor, simile, or other conceit, which is common to all the poets and at the same time important enough as an element of style to isolate these poets as a group. Donne, and often Cowley,[7] employ a device which is sometimes considered characteristically 'metaphysical'; the elaboration (contrasted with the condensation) of a figure of speech to the furthest stage to which ingenuity can carry it. Thus Cowley develops the commonplace comparison of the world to a chess-board through long stanzas (*To Destiny*), and Donne, with more grace, in *A Valediction*,[8] the comparison of two lovers to a pair of compasses. But elsewhere we find, instead of the mere explication of the

1. Eliot is reviewing the groundbreaking collection *Metaphysical Lyrics and Poems of the Seventeenth Century: Donne to Butler* (1921), ed. Herbert J. C. Grierson (1866–1960).
2. *Minor Poets of the Caroline Period* (1905–21), 3 vols., ed. George Saintsbury (1845–1933). The Caroline poets, such as Richard Lovelace and Thomas Carew, wrote during the reign of Charles I (1625–49), the Caroline Age (the Latin version of Charles is "Carolus").
3. For the term, see SAMUEL JOHNSON, *Life of Cowley* (1783; above). John Donne (1572–1631), English poet, prose writer, and clergyman.
4. Henry King (1592–1669), English poet and Anglican bishop. Andrew Marvell (1621–1678), English poet and satirist.
5. Matthew Prior (1664–1721), English poet, epigrammatist, and diplomat. George Chapman (ca. 1559–1634), English poet, scholar, and playwright. Ben Jonson (1572–1637), English poet and playwright.
6. English poet (1859–1907), as are all those named here: George Herbert (1593–1633), the Welsh-born Henry Vaughan (1622–1695), Richard Crashaw (1612–1649), and Rossetti (1830–1894).
7. Abraham Cowley (1618–1667), English poet and essayist.
8. Donne, "A Valediction: Forbidding Mourning" (1633). Grierson gives the title of Cowley's poem as "Destinie."

content of a comparison, a development by rapid association of thought which requires considerable agility on the part of the reader.

> *On a round ball*
> *A workeman that hath copies by, can lay*
> *An Europe, Afrique, and an Asia,*
> *And quickly make that, which was nothing,* All,
> *So doth each teare,*
> *Which thee doth weare,*
> *A globe, yea world by that impression grow,*
> *Till thy tears mixt with mine doe overflow*
> *This world, by waters sent from thee, my heaven dissolved so.*[9]

Here we find at least two connexions which are not implicit in the first figure, but are forced upon it by the poet: from the geographer's globe to the tear, and the tear to the deluge. On the other hand, some of Donne's most successful and characteristic effects are secured by brief words and sudden contrasts:

> *A bracelet of bright hair about the bone,*[1]

where the most powerful effect is produced by the sudden contrast of associations of 'bright hair' and of 'bone'. This telescoping of images and multiplied associations is characteristic of the phrase of some of the dramatists of the period which Donne knew: not to mention Shakespeare, it is frequent in Middleton, Webster, and Tourneur,[2] and is one of the sources of the vitality of their language.

Johnson, who employed the term 'metaphysical poets', apparently having Donne, Cleveland, and Cowley chiefly in mind, remarks of them that 'the most heterogeneous ideas are yoked by violence together'.[3] The force of this impeachment lies in the failure of the conjunction, the fact that often the ideas are yoked but not united; and if we are to judge of styles of poetry by their abuse, enough examples may be found in Cleveland to justify Johnson's condemnation. But a degree of heterogeneity of material compelled into unity by the operation of the poet's mind is omnipresent in poetry. We need not select for illustration such a line as:

> *Notre âme est un trois-mâts cherchant son Icarie;*[4]

we may find it in some of the best lines of Johnson himself (*The Vanity of Human Wishes*):

> *His fate was destined to a barren strand,*
> *A petty fortress, and a dubious hand;*
> *He left a name at which the world grew pale,*
> *To point a moral, or adorn a tale.*[5]

9. Donne, "A Valediction: Of Weeping" (1633), lines 10–18.
1. Donne, "The Relic" (1633), line 6.
2. All English dramatists: Thomas Middleton (1580–1627), John Webster (ca. 1580–ca. 1634), and Cyril Tourneur (ca. 1575–1626).
3. Johnson, *Life of Cowley*. John Cleveland (1613–1658), English poet and satirist.
4. Our soul is a three-masted ship searching for her Icarie (French). From "Le Voyage" (1861), by Charles Baudelaire (1821–1867). Icarie: a utopia described in the French socialist Étienne Cabet's novel *Voyage en Icarie* (1840).
5. Johnson, "The Vanity of Human Wishes" (1749), lines 219–22, slightly misquoted ("fate" should be "fall").

where the effect is due to a contrast of ideas, different in degree but the same in principle, as that which Johnson mildly reprehended. And in one of the finest poems of the age (a poem which could not have been written in any other age), the *Exequy* of Bishop King, the extended comparison is used with perfect success: the idea and the simile become one, in the passage in which the Bishop illustrates his impatience to see his dead wife, under the figure of a journey:

Stay for me there; I will not faile
To meet thee in that hollow Vale.
And think not much of my delay;
I am already on the way,
And follow thee with all the speed
Desire can make, or sorrows breed.
Each minute is a short degree,
And ev'ry houre a step towards thee.
At night when I betake to rest,
Next morn I rise nearer my West
Of life, almost by eight houres sail,
Than when sleep breath'd his drowsy gale. . . .
But heark! My Pulse, like as a soft Drum
Beats my approach, tells Thee *I come;*
And slow howere my marches be,
I shall at last sit down by Thee.[6]

(In the last few lines there is that effect of terror which is several times attained by one of Bishop King's admirers, Edgar Poe.[7]) Again, we may justly take these quatrains from Lord Herbert's Ode,[8] stanzas which would, we think, be immediately pronounced to be of the metaphysical school:

So when from hence we shall be gone,
   And be no more, nor you, nor I,
   As one another's mystery,
Each shall be both, yet both but one.

This said, in her up-lifted face,
   Her eyes, which did that beauty crown,
   Were like two starrs, that having faln down,
Look up again to find their place:

While such a moveless silent peace
   Did seize on their becalmed sense,
   One would have thought some influence
Their ravished spirits did possess.

There is nothing in these lines (with the possible exception of the stars, a simile not at once grasped, but lovely and justified) which fits Johnson's general observations on the metaphysical poets in his essay on Cowley. A good

6. King, "The Exequy" (1657), lines 89–114.
7. EDGAR ALLAN POE (1809–1849), American poet, critic, and short story writer.
8. "An Ode upon a Question Moved, Whether Love Should Continue Forever?" by Lord Herbert of Cherbury (1583–1648). Eliot quotes lines 129–40.

deal resides in the richness of association which is at the same time borrowed from and given to the word 'becalmed'; but the meaning is clear, the language simple and elegant. It is to be observed that the language of these poets is as a rule simple and pure; in the verse of George Herbert this simplicity is carried as far as it can go—a simplicity emulated without success by numerous modern poets. The *structure* of the sentences, on the other hand, is sometimes far from simple, but this is not a vice; it is a fidelity to thought and feeling. The effect, at its best, is far less artificial than that of an ode by Gray.[9] And as this fidelity induces variety of thought and feeling, so it induces variety of music. We doubt whether, in the eighteenth century, could be found two poems in nominally the same metre, so dissimilar as Marvell's *Coy Mistress* and Crashaw's *Saint Teresa*;[1] the one producing an effect of great speed by the use of short syllables, and the other an ecclesiastical solemnity by the use of long ones:

Love, thou art absolute sole lord
Of life and death.

If so shrewd and sensitive (though so limited) a critic as Johnson failed to define metaphysical poetry by its faults, it is worth while to inquire whether we may not have more success by adopting the opposite method: by assuming that the poets of the seventeenth century (up to the Revolution[2])were the direct and normal development of the precedent age; and, without prejudicing their case by the adjective 'metaphysical', consider whether their virtue was not something permanently valuable, which subsequently disappeared, but ought not to have disappeared. Johnson has hit, perhaps by accident, on one of their peculiarities, when he observes that 'their attempts were always analytic'; he would not agree that, after the dissociation, they put the material together again in a new unity.

It is certain that the dramatic verse of the later Elizabethan and early Jacobean poets expresses a degree of development of sensibility which is not found in any of the prose, good as it often is. If we except Marlowe, a man of prodigious intelligence, these dramatists were directly or indirectly (it is at least a tenable theory) affected by Montaigne.[3] Even if we except also Jonson and Chapman, these two were notably erudite, and were notably men who incorporated their erudition into their sensibility: their mode of feeling was directly and freshly altered by their reading and thought. In Chapman especially there is a direct sensuous apprehension of thought, or a recreation of thought into feeling, which is exactly what we find in Donne:

in this one thing, all the discipline
Of manners and of manhood is contained;
A man to join himself with th' Universe

9. Thomas Gray (1716–1771), "Elegy Written in a Country Churchyard" (1751), a poem of mourning and reflection.
1. Crashaw, "A Hymn to the Name and Honor of the Admirable Saint Teresa" (1652); Eliot quotes its opening lines. Marvell, "To His Coy Mistress" (1681).
2. Either the Glorious Revolution of 1688, when James II was replaced by William and Mary, or the English Civil War, which climaxed in the execution of Charles I in 1649; scholars disagree on Eliot's reference.
3. Michel de Montaigne (1533–1592), French moralist and essayist. Christopher Marlowe (1564–1593), English dramatist and poet.

In his main sway, and make in all things fit
One with that All, and go on, round as it;
Not plucking from the whole his wretched part,
And into straits, or into nought revert,
Wishing the complete Universe might be
Subject to such a rag of it as he;
But to consider great Necessity.[4]

We compare this with some modern passage:

No, when the fight begins within himself,
A man's worth something. God stoops o'er his head,
Satan looks up between his feet—both tug—
He's left, himself, i' the middle; the soul wakes
And grows. Prolong that battle through his life![5]

It is perhaps somewhat less fair, though very tempting (as both poets are concerned with the perpetuation of love by offspring), to compare with the stanzas already quoted from Lord Herbert's Ode the following from Tennyson:

One walked between his wife and child,
With measured footfall firm and mild,
And now and then he gravely smiled.
The prudent partner of his blood
Leaned on him, faithful, gentle, good,
Wearing the rose of womanhood.
And in their double love secure,
The little maiden walked demure,
Pacing with downward eyelids pure.
These three made unity so sweet,
My frozen heart began to beat,
Remembering its ancient heat.[6]

The difference is not a simple difference of degree between poets. It is something which had happened to the mind of England between the time of Donne or Lord Herbert of Cherbury and the time of Tennyson and Browning; it is the difference between the intellectual poet and the reflective poet. Tennyson and Browning are poets, and they think; but they do not feel their thought as immediately as the odour of a rose. A thought to Donne was an experience; it modified his sensibility. When a poet's mind is perfectly equipped for its work, it is constantly amalgamating disparate experience; the ordinary man's experience is chaotic, irregular, fragmentary. The latter falls in love, or reads Spinoza,[7] and these two experiences have nothing to do with each other, or with the noise of the typewriter or

4. Chapman, *The Revenge of Bussy d'Ambois* (ca. 1613), 4.1.137–46.
5. "Bishop Blougram's Apology" (1855), lines 693–97, by Robert Browning (1812–1889).
6. "The Two Voices" (1832), lines 412–23, by Alfred, Lord Tennyson (1809–1892).
7. BARUCH SPINOZA (1632–1677), Dutch philosopher and theologian, whose major work is *Ethics* (1677).

the smell of cooking; in the mind of the poet these experiences are always forming new wholes.[8]

We may express the difference by the following theory: The poets of the seventeenth century, the successors of the dramatists of the sixteenth, possessed a mechanism of sensibility which could devour any kind of experience. They are simple, artificial, difficult, or fantastic, as their predecessors were; no less nor more than Dante, Guido Cavalcanti, Guinicelli, or Cino.[9] In the seventeenth century a dissociation of sensibility set in, from which we have never recovered; and this dissociation, as is natural, was aggravated by the influence of the two most powerful poets of the century, Milton and Dryden.[1] Each of these men performed certain poetic functions so magnificently well that the magnitude of the effect concealed the absence of others. The language went on and in some respects improved; the best verse of Collins, Gray, Johnson, and even Goldsmith[2] satisfies some of our fastidious demands better than that of Donne or Marvell or King. But while the language became more refined, the feeling became more crude. The feeling, the sensibility, expressed in the *Country Churchyard* (to say nothing of Tennyson and Browning) is cruder than that in the *Coy Mistress*.

The second effect of the influence of Milton and Dryden followed from the first, and was therefore slow in manifestation. The sentimental age began early in the eighteenth century, and continued. The poets revolted against the ratiocinative,[3] the descriptive; they thought and felt by fits, unbalanced; they reflected. In one or two passages of Shelley's *Triumph of Life*, in the second *Hyperion*,[4] there are traces of a struggle toward unification of sensibility. But Keats and Shelley died, and Tennyson and Browning ruminated.

After this brief exposition of a theory—too brief, perhaps, to carry conviction—we may ask, what would have been the fate of the 'metaphysical' had the current of poetry descended in a direct line from them, as it descended in a direct line to them? They would not, certainly, be classified as metaphysical. The possible interests of a poet are unlimited; the more intelligent he is the better; the more intelligent he is the more likely that he will have interests: our only condition is that he turn them into poetry, and not merely meditate on them poetically. A philosophical theory which has entered into poetry is established, for its truth or falsity in one sense ceases to matter, and its truth in another sense is proved. The poets in question have, like other poets, various faults. But they were, at best, engaged in the task of trying to find the verbal equivalent for states of mind and feeling. And this means both that they

8. Compare SAMUEL TAYLOR COLERIDGE, *Biographia Literaria* (1817; see above), chap. 14: "[The poet] diffuses a tone and spirit of unity, that blends, and (as it were) *fuses*, each into each, by that synthetic and magical power, to which we have exclusively appropriated the name of imagination."

9. Italian poets (roughly contemporary) known for their *dolce stil nuovo* (sweet new style): DANTE ALIGHIERI (1265–1321), Guido Cavalcanti (1250–1300), Guido Guinicelli (1220–1276), and Cino da Pistoia (1270–1336).

1. JOHN DRYDEN (1631–1700), English poet, dramatist, and critic. John Milton (1608–1674), English writer of poetry and prose, and author of *Paradise Lost* (1667).

2. Oliver Goldsmith (1731–1774), Irish-born English poet, playwright, and novelist. William Collins (1721–1759), English poet.

3. Relating to the process of logical reasoning.

4. "Hyperion, a fragment" and "The Fall of Hyperion" (written 1818–19), fragments of epic poems by John Keats (1795–1821). "The Triumph of Life" (written in 1822), an unfinished visionary poem by PERCY BYSSHE SHELLEY (1792–1822).

are more mature, and that they wear better, than later poets of certainly not less literary ability.

It is not a permanent necessity that poets should be interested in philosophy, or in any other subject. We can only say that it appears likely that poets in our civilization, as it exists at present, must be *difficult*. Our civilization comprehends great variety and complexity, and this variety and complexity, playing upon a refined sensibility, must produce various and complex results. The poet must become more and more comprehensive, more allusive, more indirect, in order to force, to dislocate if necessary, language into his meaning. (A brilliant and extreme statement of this view, with which it is not requisite to associate oneself, is that of M. Jean Epstein, *La Poésie d' aujourd-hui.*[5]) Hence we get something which looks very much like the conceit—we get, in fact, a method curiously similar to that of the 'metaphysical poets', similar also in its use of obscure words and of simple phrasing.

O géraniums diaphanes, guerroyeurs sortilèges,
Sacrilèges monomanes!
Emballages, dévergondages, douches! O pressoirs
Des vendanges des grands soirs!
Layettes aux abois,
Thyrses au fond des bois!
Transfusions, représailles,
Relevailles, compresses et l' éternal potion,
Angélus! n' en pouvoir plus
De débâcles nuptiales! de débâcles nuptiales![6]

The same poet could write also simply:

Elle est bien loin, elle pleure,
Le grand vent se lamente aussi . . .[7]

Jules Laforgue, and Tristan Corbière[8] in many of his poems, are nearer to the 'school of Donne' than any modern English poet. But poets more classical than they have the same essential quality of transmuting ideas into sensations, of transforming an observation into a state of mind.

Pour l' enfant, amoureux de cartes et d' estampes,
L' univers est égal à son vaste appétit.
Ah, que le monde est grand à la clarté des lampes!
Aux yeux du souvenir que le monde est petit![9]

5. *The Poetry of Today* (French), published in 1921. Epstein (1897–1953), French filmmaker, film theorist, literary critic, and novelist.

6. O translucent geraniums, warring wizardry, / Monomaniac impieties! / Enwrappings, licentiousness, showers! O winepresses / Of grape harvestings on great evenings! / Layettes at bay, / Thrysis deep in the woods! / Transfusion, repayings, / Churchings, compresses and the eternal potion, / *Angelus*! can't bear any more / Those bursting nuptials! Bursting nuptials! (French; trans. June Guicharnaud). From *Derniers vers X* (1890, *Last Poems*), by the French symbolist poet Jules Laforgue (1860–1887).

7. She is far away, she weeps / The great wind also mourns (French). From Laforgue, *Derniers vers XI*, "Sur une défunte" ("On a Dead Woman").

8. French symbolist poet (1845–1875).

9. For the child in love with maps and prints, the universe matches his vast appetite. Ah, how big the world is, in the lamplight; but how small, viewed through the eyes of memory (French; trans. Francis Scarfe). From Baudelaire, "Le Voyage."

In French literature the great master of the seventeenth century—Racine[1]—and the great master of the nineteenth—Baudelaire—are in some ways more like each other than they are like anyone else. The greatest two masters of diction are also the greatest two psychologists, the most curious explorers of the soul. It is interesting to speculate whether it is not a misfortune that two of the greatest masters of diction in our language, Milton and Dryden, triumph with a dazzling disregard of the soul. If we continued to produce Miltons and Drydens it might not so much matter, but as things are it is a pity that English poetry has remained so incomplete. Those who object to the 'artificiality' of Milton or Dryden sometimes tell us to 'look into our hearts and write'.[2] But that is not looking deep enough; Racine or Donne looked into a good deal more than the heart. One must look into the cerebral cortex, the nervous system, and the digestive tracts.

May we not conclude, then, that Donne, Crashaw, Vaughan, Herbert and Lord Herbert, Marvell, King, Cowley at his best, are in the direct current of English poetry, and that their faults should be reprimanded by this standard rather than coddled by antiquarian affection? They have been enough praised in terms which are implicit limitations because they are 'metaphysical' or 'witty', 'quaint' or 'obscure,' though at their best they have not these attributes more than other serious poets. On the other hand, we must not reject the criticism of Johnson (a dangerous person to disagree with) without having mastered it, without having assimilated the Johnsonian canons of taste. In reading the celebrated passage in his essay on Cowley we must remember that by wit he clearly means something more serious than we usually mean to-day; in his criticism of their versification we must remember in what a narrow discipline he was trained, but also how well trained; we must remember that Johnson tortures chiefly the chief offenders, Cowley and Cleveland. It would be a fruitful work, and one requiring a substantial book, to break up the classification of Johnson (for there has been none since) and exhibit these poets in all their difference of kind and of degree, from the massive music of Donne to the faint, pleasing tinkle of Aurelian Townshend[3]—whose *Dialogue between a Pilgrim and Time* is one of the few regrettable omissions from the excellent anthology of Professor Grierson.

1921

1. Jean Racine (1639–1699), French playwright.
2. A slight recasting of the final words of the first sonnet in the sonnet sequence *Astrophil and Stella* (1591), by SIR PHILIP SIDNEY.
3. Poet and writer of court masques (ca. 1583–1643).

JOHN CROWE RANSOM
1888–1974

The poet, critic, and editor John Crowe Ransom is perhaps the central figure in the institutionalization of the New Criticism, the formalist theory and practice that dominated U.S. teaching and literary criticism in the mid–twentieth century. Through his essays on literary theory, his important work as an editor of the prestigious journal the *Kenyon Review*, and his friendships with many noteworthy authors and critics, Ransom was able to gain a wide and respectful hearing for his and the other New Critics' literary views and values. By the 1950s, the New Critical focus on "the text itself" had become the basic method of literary criticism and of college and university pedagogy.

Ransom was born in Pulaski, Tennessee, the son of a Methodist minister. He was a brilliant student at Bowen School (a private academy) and then at Vanderbilt University in Nashville, where he received rigorous training in the classics. He studied Greek and Roman literature and history at Christ Church, Oxford University, on a Rhodes Scholarship from 1910 to 1913, and in 1914 joined the faculty of Vanderbilt's English Department. He became the leader of Nashville's literary and cultural community, which in the 1920s and 1930s included the poets Allen Tate and Donald Davidson, the poet, novelist, and critic Robert Penn Warren, and the critic CLEANTH BROOKS.

In the early 1920s Ransom was one of the Fugitive poets, a group that came together in Nashville as "fugitives" both from preachy, sentimental nineteenth-century verse and from contemporary verse that struck them as far removed from the Southern regionalist values they embraced. They focused on the language, forms, and techniques of poetry and published in the bimonthly the *Fugitive* (1922–25); many of Ransom's best poems as well as a number of his critical essays appeared in this journal. Later in the decade, Ransom played a prominent role in the Agrarian movement; he contributed both the introduction and a chapter to the Agrarian manifesto *I'll Take My Stand* (1930), a spirited attack on science and industrialization and a defense of Southern tradition and an agricultural economy.

During the Agrarian phase of his career, Ransom wrote many essays on social and cultural criticism, including "The South—Old or New?" (1928), "The Aesthetics of Regionalism" (1934), and "What Does the South Want?" (1936). But the Agrarian cause never won widespread support among Southerners, and by the late 1930s, Ransom was himself shifting away from sociocultural commentary. In 1937 he left Vanderbilt for a position in the English Department at Kenyon College in Ohio, a move that coincided with his sharp turn toward literary criticism and the reforms needed to give it precision and clarity as an autonomous academic discipline. In a 1937 letter to Allen Tate, Ransom noted that the new journal he hoped to launch at Kenyon should "stick to literature entirely. . . . In the severe field of letters there is vocation enough for us: in criticism, in poetry, in fiction."

For two decades, beginning in 1939, Ransom edited the *Kenyon Review*; this journal, which became one of the best U.S. literary quarterlies, was among his greatest achievements. Moreover, his distinguished reputation as an editor as well as a poet and critic enabled him to gain much institutional support for his ideas and programs. During the late 1940s, the Rockefeller Foundation provided funds for a series of *Kenyon Review* Fellows (scholars) and for the Kenyon School of English, which had on its faculty important intellectuals, creative writers, and critics—among the first (in 1948) were Eric Bentley, Cleanth Brooks, and William Empson. The *Kenyon Review* also offered fellowships each year to a poet, a writer of fiction, and a critic; prominent recipients included Flannery O'Connor, Howard Nemerov, and

Irving Howe. The New Criticism was not simply a body of theory and practice but a network of programs, journals, and institutions, and Ransom was involved in nearly all of them.

Our selection from *The World's Body*, "Criticism, Inc." (1938), is, as its title suggests, Ransom's attempt to define the business of criticism—what it is not and what it should be. He lists a number of false or misleading types of current criticism—including the "ethical" approach of the New Humanism and Marxism—but he focuses on the teaching of literature in universities by literary historians and scholars who stress backgrounds, sources, and influences rather than the poems themselves. Historical study, he contends, dominates at the expense of a truly "critical" approach, preventing students from acquiring the skills needed for them to understand the "technical effects" of literary works. As a result, they cannot respond in a direct, rigorous way to contemporary literature or, for that matter, to any poem placed before them.

Ransom urges teachers and students to concentrate on "technical studies of poetry." By this, he means studies of imagery, metaphor, and meter—the stylistic devices through which the poet differentiates the language of his or her text from that of prose. Ransom calls for a revitalized department of English that will make literary history, scholarship, and linguistics secondary to criticism. In his view, criticism must be rescued from book reviewers and amateurs who focus on feelings, not the artistic object itself, and reduce texts to paraphrases with a moral message. Advocating disciplinary coherence and integrity, Ransom is a harbinger of the professionalization of literary analysis that characterized mid- and late twentieth-century U.S. literary culture.

These arguments had great appeal to many teachers and students, and Ransom's approach was so helpful for readers grappling with exacting modern poets that its limits were overlooked at first. By defining the work of literary studies, he supplied a clear procedure: the teacher-critic should concentrate on the text itself and not be distracted by nonliterary contexts and issues. But Ransom and the other New Critics, opponents pointed out, excluded too much; in giving literary studies a disciplinary identity, they failed to clarify how it could engage with social, cultural, and historical issues in a meaningful way. In a sense Ransom allowed the opposition to dictate the terms of his own approach—literary criticism is defined against, not in *relation* to, other fields, subjects, and disciplines. But why should the analysis of specific literary texts require the exclusion of other kinds of analytical work? Ransom defined the enterprise of "Criticism, Inc." with brilliant precision but narrowly, as though the forms of social and cultural critique he had embarked on in his Agrarian writing were wholly incompatible with literary criticism.

To be sure, in stressing that critics should explore how the poem "removes itself from history" Ransom had a specific target: the practice of making history rather than the poem the object of attention in the classroom. Neither he nor the other New Critics asserted that history was irrelevant, or that teachers and students should ignore everything except "the words on the page"; they assumed that teachers would be well-trained and knowledgeable about much more, as they were themselves. Those in the first generation of New Critics were later dismayed at the reductive, mechanical criticism and teaching practiced in their name.

As the New Criticism came under widespread attack in the 1960s and 1970s, it lost the authority it had enjoyed when Ransom, Warren, and Brooks first promoted it. Its emphasis on the text in and for itself seemed far removed from the crises and social movements—civil rights, antiwar, and women's—that were tearing American society apart. The New Critical canon was too limited (male and white) to prove acceptable to feminists, African American critics, and other theorists. In addition, by the 1970s poststructuralists were arguing that the New Critical distinction between what was inside and outside the text could not be maintained: thus the discrete poetic text that was to be the basis of literary studies seemed no longer to exist. Soon, from another direction, New Historicist scholars began to recuperate and renovate historical analysis; by demonstrating that close reading could be extended to all kinds of texts and documents, they made possible a richer, more diverse approach to history than that found in the earlier literary historians whom Ransom, Brooks, and the others had displaced.

A crucial tenet of the New Critical program survives: the emphasis on "close reading," the central focus of the new business for literary studies that Ransom advocates in "Criticism, Inc." In this respect, the New Criticism has not so much faded as become the foundation that modern approaches build upon.

"Criticism, Inc." Keywords: Defense of Criticism, Ethics, Formalism, Institutional Studies, Interpretation Theory, Poetry

Criticism, Inc.

It is strange, but nobody seems to have told us what exactly is the proper business of criticism. There are many critics who might tell us, but for the most part they are amateurs. So have the critics nearly always been amateurs; including the best ones. They have not been trained to criticism so much as they have simply undertaken a job for which no specific qualifications were required. It is far too likely that what they call criticism when they produce it is not the real thing.

There are three sorts of trained performers who would appear to have some of the competence that the critic needs. The first is the artist himself. He should know good art when he sees it; but his understanding is intuitive rather than dialectical—he cannot very well explain his theory of the thing. It is true that literary artists, with their command of language, are better critics of their own art than are other artists; probably the best critics of poetry we can now have are the poets. But one can well imagine that any artist's commentary on the art-work is valuable in the degree that he sticks to its technical effects, which he knows minutely, and about which he can certainly talk if he will.

The second is the philosopher, who should know all about the function of the fine arts. But the philosopher is apt to see a lot of wood and no trees, for his theory is very general and his acquaintance with the particular works of art is not persistent and intimate, especially his acquaintance with their technical effects. Or at least I suppose so, for philosophers have not proved that they can write close criticism by writing it; and I have the feeling that even their handsome generalizations are open to suspicion as being grounded more on other generalizations, those which form their prior philosophical stock, than on acute study of particulars.

The third is the university teacher of literature, who is styled professor, and who should be the very professional we need to take charge of the critical activity. He is hardly inferior as critic to the philosopher, and perhaps not on the whole to the poet, but he is a greater disappointment because we have the right to expect more of him. Professors of literature are learned but not critical men. The professional morale of this part of the university staff is evidently low. It is as if, with conscious or unconscious cunning, they had appropriated every avenue of escape from their responsibility which was decent and official; so that it is easy for one of them without public reproach to spend a lifetime in compiling the data of literature and yet rarely or never commit himself to a literary judgment.

Nevertheless it is from the professors of literature, in this country the professors of English for the most part, that I should hope eventually for the erection of intelligent standards of criticism. It is their business.

Criticism must become more scientific, or precise and systematic, and this means that it must be developed by the collective and sustained effort of learned persons—which means that its proper seat is in the universities.

Scientific: but I do not think we need be afraid that criticism, trying to be a sort of science, will inevitably fail and give up in despair, or else fail without realizing it and enjoy some hollow and pretentious career. It will never be a very exact science, or even a nearly exact one. But neither will psychology, if that term continues to refer to psychic rather than physical phenomena; nor will sociology, as Pareto,[1] quite contrary to his intention, appears to have furnished us with evidence for believing; nor even will economics. It does not matter whether we call them sciences or just systematic studies; the total effort of each to be effective must be consolidated and kept going. The studies which I have mentioned have immeasurably improved in understanding since they were taken over by the universities, and the same career looks possible for criticism.

Rather than occasional criticism by amateurs, I should think the whole enterprise might be seriously taken in hand by professionals. Perhaps I use a distasteful figure, but I have the idea that what we need is Criticism, Inc., or Criticism, Ltd.

The principal resistance to such an idea will come from the present incumbents of the professorial chairs. But its adoption must come from them too. The idea of course is not a private one of my own. If it should be adopted before long, the credit would probably belong to Professor Ronald S. Crane,[2] of the University of Chicago, more than to any other man. He is the first of the great professors to have advocated it as a major policy for departments of English. It is possible that he will have made some important academic history.

2

Professor Crane published recently a paper of great note in academic circles, on the reform of the courses in English. It appeared in *The English Journal*, under the title: "History Versus Criticism in the University Study of Literature." He argues there that historical scholarship has been overplayed heavily in English studies, in disregard of the law of diminishing returns, and that the emphasis must now be shifted to the critical.

To me this means, simply: the students of the future must be permitted to study literature, and not merely about literature. But I think this is what the good students have always wanted to do. The wonder is that they have

1. Vilfredo Pareto (1848–1923), French-born Italian economist and sociologist.
2. The leader (1886–1967) of the Chicago School of neo-Aristotelian criticism, whose views were influenced by, and defined in part in contrast to, the restructuring of the undergraduate curriculum of the University of Chicago in the 1930s, to a focus on interdisciplinary studies and "Great Books." He published "History Versus Criticism" (discussed below) in 1935.

allowed themselves so long to be denied. But they have not always been amiable about it, and the whole affair presents much comic history.

At the University of Chicago, I believe that Professor Crane, with some others, is putting the revolution into effect in his own teaching, though for the time being perhaps with a limited programme, mainly the application of Aristotle's critical views.[3] (My information is not at all exact.) The university is an opulent one, not too old to experience waves of reformational zeal, uninhibited as yet by bad traditions. Its department of English has sponsored plenty of old-line scholarship, but this is not the first time it has gone in for criticism. If the department should now systematically and intelligently build up a general school of literary criticism, I believe it would score a triumph that would be, by academic standards, spectacular. I mean that the alive and brilliant young English scholars all over the country would be saying they wanted to go there to do their work. That would place a new distinction upon the university, and it would eventually and profoundly modify the practices of many other institutions. It would be worth even more than Professor Crane's careful presentation of the theory.

This is not the first time that English professors have tilted against the historians, or "scholars," in the dull sense which that word has acquired. They did not score heavily, at those other times. Probably they were themselves not too well versed in the historical studies, so that it could be said with honest concern that they scarcely had the credentials to judge of such matters. At the same time they may have been too unproductive critically to offer a glowing alternative.

The most important recent diversion from the orthodox course of literary studies was that undertaken by the New Humanists.[4] I regret to think that it was not the kind of diversion which I am advocating; nor the kind approved by Professor Crane, who comments briefly against it. Unquestionably the Humanists did divert, and the refreshment was grateful to anybody who felt resentful for having his literary predilections ignored under the schedule of historical learning. But in the long run the diversion proved to be nearly as unliterary as the round of studies from which it took off at a tangent. No picnic ideas were behind it.

The New Humanists were, and are, moralists; more accurately, historians and advocates of a certain moral system. Criticism is the attempt to define and enjoy the æsthetic or characteristic values of literature, but I suppose the Humanists would shudder at "æsthetic" as hard as ordinary historical scholars do. Did an official Humanist ever make any official play with the term? I do not remember it. The term "art" is slightly more ambiguous, and they have availed themselves of that; with centuries of loose usage behind it, art connotes, for those who like, high seriousness, and high seriousness connotes moral self-consciousness, and an inner check, and finally either Plato[5] or Aristotle.

3. For the *Poetics* of ARISTOTLE (384–322 B.C.E), see above.

4. Members of an early 20th-century critical movement in the United States that attacked the decadence of modern life and the immorality of contemporary literature, condemning the influence of Romanticism and appealing for classical values. The leaders of New Humanism were Paul Elmer More (1864–1937), a critic, editor, and lecturer at Princeton University, and Irving Babbitt (1865–1933), professor of Romance languages at Harvard University.

5. For the views of PLATO (ca. 427–ca. 347 B.C.E), see above.

Mr. Babbitt consistently played on the terms classical and romantic. They mean any of several things each, so that unquestionably Mr. Babbitt could make war on romanticism for purely moral reasons; and his preoccupation was ethical, not æsthetic. It is perfectly legitimate for the moralist to attack romantic literature if he can make out his case; for example, on the ground that it deals with emotions rather than principles, or the ground that its author discloses himself as flabby, intemperate, escapist, unphilosophical, or simply adolescent. The moral objection is probably valid; a romantic period testifies to a large-scale failure of adaptation, and defense of that failure to adapt, to the social and political environment; unless, if the Humanists will consent, it sometimes testifies to the failure of society and state to sympathize with the needs of the individual. But this is certainly not the charge that Mr. T. S. Eliot, a literary critic, brings against romanticism.[6] His, if I am not mistaken, is æsthetic, though he may not ever care to define it very sharply. In other words, the literary critic also has something to say about romanticism, and it might come to something like this: that romantic literature is imperfect in objectivity, or "æsthetic distance,"[7] and that out of this imperfection comes its weakness of structure; that the romantic poet does not quite realize the æsthetic attitude, and is not the pure artist. Or it might come to something else. It would be quite premature to say that when a moralist is obliged to disapprove a work the literary critic must disapprove it too.

Following the excitement produced by the Humanist diversion, there is now one due to the Leftists, or Proletarians,[8] who are also diversionists. Their diversion is likewise moral. It is just as proper for them to ferret out class-consciousness in literature, and to make literature serve the cause of loving-comradeship, as it is for the Humanists to censure romanticism and to use the topic, and the literary exhibit, as the occasion of reviving the Aristotelian moral canon. I mean that these are procedures of the same sort. Debate could never occur between a Humanist and a Leftist on æsthetic grounds, for they are equally intent on ethical values. But the debate on ethical grounds would be very spirited, and it might create such a stir in a department conducting English studies that the conventional scholars there would find themselves slipping, and their pupils deriving from literature new and seductive excitements which would entice them away from their scheduled English exercises.

On the whole, however, the moralists, distinguished as they may be, are like those who have quarrelled with the ordinary historical studies on purer or more aesthetic grounds: they have not occupied in English studies the positions of professional importance. In a department of English, as in any other going business, the proprietary interest becomes vested, and in old and reputable departments the vestees have uniformly been gentlemen who have gone through the historical mill. Their laborious Ph.D.'s and historical publications are their patents.[9] Naturally, quite spontaneously, they would

6. At Harvard, Eliot (1888–1965) was taught by Babbitt, who reinforced Eliot's own anti-Romantic tendencies.
7. The detachment from, or nonidentification with, the characters or circumstances of a work of art that permits judgments based on aesthetic rather than extra-aesthetic criteria.
8. Marxist critics who emphasized the class struggle between workers (proletarians) and owners, and the problems of poverty and racism.
9. Documents conferring privilege.

tend to perpetuate a system in which the power and the glory belonged to them. But English scholars in this country can rarely have better credentials than those which Professor Crane has earned in his extensive field, the eighteenth century. It is this which makes his disaffection significant.

It is really atrocious policy for a department to abdicate its own self-respecting identity. The department of English is charged with the understanding and the communication of literature, an art, yet it has usually forgotten to inquire into the peculiar constitution and structure of its product. English might almost as well announce that it does not regard itself as entirely autonomous, but as a branch of the department of history, with the option of declaring itself occasionally a branch of the department of ethics. It is true that the historical and the ethical studies will cluster round objects which for some reason are called artistic objects. But the thing itself the professors do not have to contemplate; and only last spring the head of English studies in a graduate school fabulously equipped made the following impromptu disclaimer to a victim who felt aggrieved at having his own studies forced in the usual direction: "This is a place for exact scholarship, and you want to do criticism. Well, we don't allow criticism here, because that is something which anybody can do."

But one should never speak impromptu in one's professional capacity. This speech may have betrayed a fluttery private apprehension which should not have been made public: that you can never be critical and be exact at the same time, that history is firmer ground than æsthetics, and that, to tell the truth, criticism is a painful job for the sort of mind that wants to be very sure about things. Not in that temper did Aristotle labor towards a critique in at least one branch of letters; nor in that temper are strong young minds everywhere trying to sharpen their critical apparatus into precision tools, in this decade as never before.

It is not anybody who can do criticism. And for an example, the more eminent (as historical scholar) the professor of English, the less apt he is to be able to write decent criticism, unless it is about another professor's work of historical scholarship, in which case it is not literary criticism. The professor may not be without æsthetic judgments respecting an old work, especially if it is "in his period," since it must often have been judged by authorities whom he respects. Confronted with a new work, I am afraid it is very rare that he finds anything particular to say. Contemporary criticism is not at all in the hands of those who direct the English studies. Contemporary literature, which is almost obliged to receive critical study if it receives any at all, since it is hardly capable of the usual historical commentary, is barely officialized as a proper field for serious study.

Here is contemporary literature, waiting for its criticism; where are the professors of literature? They are watering their own gardens; elucidating the literary histories of their respective periods. So are their favorite pupils. The persons who save the occasion, and rescue contemporary literature from the humiliation of having to go without a criticism, are the men who had to leave the university before their time because they felt themselves being warped into mere historians; or those who finished the courses and took their punishment but were tough, and did not let it engross them and spoil them. They are home-made critics. Naturally they are not too wise, these amateurs who furnish our reviews and critical studies. But when they distinguish themselves, the universities which they attended can hardly claim more than a trifling share of the honor.

It is not so in economics, chemistry, sociology, theology, and architecture. In these branches it is taken for granted that criticism of the performance is the prerogative of the men who have had formal training in its theory and technique. The historical method is useful, and may be applied readily to any human performance whatever. But the exercise does not become an obsession with the university men working in the other branches; only the literary scholars wish to convert themselves into pure historians. This has gone far to nullify the usefulness of a departmental personnel larger, possibly, than any other, and of the lavish endowment behind it.

3

Presumably the departments of English exist in order to communicate the understanding of the literary art. That will include both criticism and also whatever may be meant by "appreciation." This latter term seems to stand for the kind of understanding that is had intuitively, without benefit of instruction, by merely being constrained to spend time in the presence of the literary product. It is true that some of the best work now being done in departments is by the men who do little more than read well aloud, enforcing a private act of appreciation upon the students. One remembers how good a service that may be, thinking perhaps of Professor Copeland of Harvard, or Dean Cross at Greeley Teachers College.[1] And there are men who try to get at the same thing in another way, which they would claim is surer: by requiring a great deal of memory work, in order to enforce familiarity with fine poetry. These might defend their strategy by saying that at any rate the work they required was not as vain as the historical rigmarole which the scholars made their pupils recite, if the objective was really literary understanding and not external information. But it would be a misuse of terms to employ the word instruction for the offices either of the professors who read aloud or of those who require the memory work. The professors so engaged are properly curators, and the museum of which they have the care is furnished with the cherished literary masterpieces, just as another museum might be filled with paintings. They conduct their squads from one work to another, making appropriate pauses or reverent gestures, but their own obvious regard for the masterpieces is somewhat contagious, and contemplation is induced. Naturally they are grateful to the efficient staff of colleagues in the background who have framed the masterpieces, hung them in the proper schools and in the chronological order, and prepared the booklet of information about the artists and the occasions. The colleagues in their turn probably feel quite happy over this division of labor, thinking that they have done the really productive work, and that it is appropriate now if less able men should undertake a little salesmanship.

Behind appreciation, which is private, and criticism, which is public and negotiable, and represents the last stage of English studies, is historical

1. "Dean Cross" is Neal Cross, who taught in the English department at Greeley Teachers College (now the University of Northern Colorado) from 1941 to 1979. Charles Townsend Copeland (1860–1952), member of the English department at Harvard.

scholarship. It is indispensable. But it is instrumental and cannot be the end itself. In this respect historical studies have the same standing as linguistic studies: language and history are aids.

On behalf of the historical studies. Without them what could we make of Chaucer, for instance? I cite the familiar locus of the "hard" scholarship, the center of any program of advanced studies in English which intends to initiate the student heroically, and once for all, into the historical discipline. Chaucer writes allegories for historians to decipher, he looks out upon institutions and customs unfamiliar to us.[2] Behind him are many writers in various tongues from whom he borrows both forms and materials. His thought bears constant reference to classical and mediæval philosophies and sciences which have passed from our effective knowledge. An immense labor of historical adaptation is necessary before our minds are ready to make the æsthetic approach to Chaucer.

Or to any author out of our own age. The mind with which we enter into an old work is not the mind with which we make our living, or enter into a contemporary work. It is under sharp restraints, and it is quite differently furnished. Out of our actual contemporary mind we have to cancel a great deal that has come there under modern conditions but was not in the earlier mind at all. This is a technique on the negative side, a technique of suspension; difficult for practical persons, literal scientists, and aggressive moderns who take pride in the "truth" or the "progress" which enlightened man, so well represented in their own instance, has won. Then, on the positive side, we must supply the mind with the precise beliefs and ways of thought it had in that former age, with the specific content in which history instructs us; this is a technique of make-believe. The whole act of historical adaptation, through such techniques, is a marvellous feat of flexibility. Certainly it is a thing hard enough to justify university instruction. But it is not sufficient for an English program.

The achievement of modern historical scholarship in the field of English literature has been, in the aggregate, prodigious; it should be very proud. A good impression of the volume of historical learning now available for the students of English may be quickly had from inspecting a few chapters of the Cambridge History,[3] with the bibliographies. Or, better, from inspecting one of a large number of works which have come in since the Cambridge History: the handbooks, which tell all about the authors, such as Chaucer, Shakespeare, Milton, and carry voluminous bibliographies; or the period books, which tell a good deal about whole periods of literature.

There is one sense in which it may be justly said that we can never have too much scholarship. We cannot have too much of it if the critical intelligence functions, and has the authority to direct it. There is hardly a critical problem which does not require some arduous exercises in fact-finding, but each problem is quite specific about the kind of facts it wants. Mountains of facts may have been found already, but often they have been found for no purpose at all except the purpose of piling up into a big exhibit, to offer intoxicating delights to the academic population.

2. Chaucer's allegories include the dream-poems *The Book of the Duchess* (ca. 1369) and *The House of Fame* (ca. 1374–85).

3. *The Cambridge History of English Literature* (14 vols., 1907–17); and *The Cambridge History of American Literature* (4 vols., 1917–21).

To those who are æsthetically minded among students, the rewards of many a historical labor will have to be disproportionately slight. The official Chaucer course is probably over ninety-five per cent historical and linguistic, and less than five per cent aesthetic or critical. A thing of beauty is a joy forever.[4] But it is not improved because the student has had to tie his tongue before it. It is an artistic object, with a heroic human labor behind it, and on these terms it calls for public discussion. The dialectical possibilities are limitless, and when we begin to realize them we are engaged in criticism.

4

What is criticism? Easier to ask, What is criticism not? It is an act now notoriously arbitrary and undefined. We feel certain that the critical act is not one of those which the professors of literature habitually perform, and cause their students to perform. And it is our melancholy impression that it is not often cleanly performed in those loose compositions, by writers of perfectly indeterminate qualifications, that appear in print as reviews of books.

Professor Crane excludes from criticism works of historical scholarship and of Neo-Humanism, but more exclusions are possible than that. I should wish to exclude:

1. Personal registrations, which are declarations of the effect of the art-work upon the critic as reader. The first law to be prescribed to criticism, if we may assume such authority, is that it shall be objective, shall cite the nature of the object rather than its effects upon the subject. Therefore it is hardly criticism to assert that the proper literary work is one that we can read twice; or one that causes in us some remarkable physiological effect, such as oblivion of the outer world, the flowing of tears, visceral or laryngeal[5] sensations, and such like; or one that induces perfect illusion, or brings us into a spiritual ecstasy; or even one that produces a catharsis of our emotions. Aristotle concerned himself with this last in making up his definition of tragedy[6]—though he did not fail to make some acute analyses of the objective features of the work also. I have read that some modern Broadway producers of comedy require a reliable person to seat himself in a trial audience and count the laughs; their method of testing is not so subtle as Aristotle's, but both are concerned with the effects. Such concern seems to reflect the view that art comes into being because the artist, or the employer behind him, has designs upon the public, whether high moral designs or box-office ones. It is an odious view in either case, because it denies the autonomy of the artist as one who interests himself in the artistic object in his own right, and likewise the autonomy of the work itself as existing for its own sake. (We may define a chemical as something which can effect a certain cure, but that is not its meaning to the chemist; and we may define toys, if we are weary parents, as things which keep our children quiet, but that is not what they are to engineers.) Furthermore, we must regard as uncritical the use of an extensive vocabulary which ascribes to the object properties really discovered in the subject, as: *moving, exciting, entertaining, pitiful; great*, if I am not

4. John Keats, *Endymion* (1818), 1.1.

5. Of the internal organs or of the larynx (which contains the vocal cords).

6. See *Poetics* 6, 1449b.

mistaken, and *admirable*, on a slightly different ground; and, in strictness, *beautiful* itself.

2. Synopsis and paraphrase. The high-school classes and the women's clubs delight in these procedures, which are easiest of all the systematic exercises possible in the discussion of literary objects. I do not mean that the critic never uses them in his analysis of fiction and poetry, but he does not consider plot or story as identical with the real content. Plot is an abstract from content.

3. Historical studies. These have a very wide range, and include studies of the general literary background; author's biography, of course with special reference to autobiographical evidences in the work itself; bibliographical items; the citation of literary originals and analogues, and therefore what, in general, is called comparative literature. Nothing can be more stimulating to critical analysis than comparative literature. But it may be conducted only superficially, if the comparisons are perfunctory and mechanical, or if the scholar is content with merely making the parallel citations.

4. Linguistic studies. Under this head come those studies which define the meaning of unusual words and idioms, including the foreign and archaic ones, and identify the allusions. The total benefit of linguistics for criticism would be the assurance that the latter was based on perfect logical understanding of the content, or "interpretation." Acquaintance with all the languages and literatures in the world would not necessarily produce a critic, though it might save one from damaging errors.

5. Moral studies. The moral standard applied is the one appropriate to the reviewer; it may be the Christian ethic, or the Aristotelian one, or the new proletarian gospel. But the moral content is not the whole content, which should never be relinquished.

6. Any other special studies which deal with some abstract or prose content taken out of the work. Nearly all departments of knowledge may conceivably find their own materials in literature, and take them out. Studies have been made of Chaucer's command of mediæval sciences, of Spenser's view of the Irish question, of Shakespeare's understanding of the law, of Milton's geography, of Hardy's place-names.[7] The critic may well inform himself of these materials as possessed by the artist, but his business as critic is to discuss the literary assimilation of them.

5

With or without such useful exercises as these, probably assuming that the intelligent reader has made them for himself, comes the critical act itself.

Mr. Austin Warren,[8] whose writings I admire, is evidently devoted to the academic development of the critical project. Yet he must be a fair representative of what a good deal of academic opinion would be when he sees no reason why criticism should set up its own house, and try to dissociate itself from historical and other scholarly studies; why not let all sorts of studies, including the critical ones, flourish together in the same act of

7. Much of the fiction of Thomas Hardy (1840–1928) is set in "Wessex," a thinly fictionalized version of his native Dorsetshire. "The Irish question": The status of the Irish within the British Empire. The poet Edmund Spenser (1552–1599) wrote a defense of the current repressive policy, *A View of the Present State of Ireland* (1596).

8. American teacher and critic (1899–1986).

sustained attention, or the same scheduled "course"? But so they are supposed to do at present; and I would only ask him whether he considers that criticism prospers under this arrangement. It has always had the chance to go ahead in the hands of the professors of literature, and it has not gone ahead. A change of policy suggests itself. Strategy requires now, I should think, that criticism receive its own charter of rights and function independently. If he fears for its foundations in scholarship, the scholars will always be on hand to reprove it when it tries to function on an unsound scholarship.

I do not suppose the reviewing of books can be reformed in the sense of being turned into pure criticism. The motives of the reviewers are as much mixed as the performance, and indeed they condition the mixed performance. The reviewer has a job of presentation and interpretation as well as criticism. The most we can ask of him is that he know when the criticism begins, and that he make it as clean and definitive as his business permits. To what authority may he turn?

I know of no authority. For the present each critic must be his own authority. But I know of one large class of studies which is certainly critical, and necessary, and I can suggest another sort of study for the critic's consideration if he is really ambitious.

Studies in the technique of the art belong to criticism certainly. They cannot belong anywhere else, because the technique is not peculiar to any prose materials discoverable in the work of art, nor to anything else but the unique form of that art. A very large volume of studies is indicated by this classification. They would be technical studies of poetry, for instance, the art I am specifically discussing, if they treated its metric; its inversions, solecisms,[9] lapses from the prose norm of language, and from close prose logic; its tropes;[1] its fictions, or inventions, by which it secures "æsthetic distance" and removes itself from history; or any other devices, on the general understanding that any systematic usage which does not hold good for prose is a poetic device.

A device with a purpose: the superior critic is not content with the compilation of the separate devices; they suggest to him a much more general question. The critic speculates on why poetry, through its devices, is at such pains to dissociate itself from prose at all, and what it is trying to represent that cannot be represented by prose.

I intrude here with an idea of my own, which may serve as a starting point of discussion. Poetry distinguishes itself from prose on the technical side by the devices which are, precisely, its means of escaping from prose. Something is continually being killed by prose which the poet wants to preserve. But this must be put philosophically. (Philosophy sounds hard, but it deals with natural and fundamental forms of experience.)

The critic should regard the poem as nothing short of a desperate ontological or metaphysical manœuvre. The poet himself, in the agony of composition, has something like this sense of his labors. The poet perpetuates in his poem an order of existence which in actual life is constantly crumbling beneath his touch. His poem celebrates the object which is real, individual,

9. Ungrammatical combinations, minor errors.

1. Figures of speech.

and qualitatively infinite. He knows that his practical interests will reduce this living object to a mere utility, and that his sciences will disintegrate it for their convenience into their respective abstracts. The poet wishes to defend his object's existence against its enemies, and the critic wishes to know what he is doing, and how. The critic should find in the poem a total poetic or individual object which tends to be universalized, but is not permitted to suffer this fate. His identification of the poetic object is in terms of the universal or commonplace object to which it tends, and of the tissue, or totality of connotation, which holds it secure. How does he make out the universal object? It is the prose object, which any forthright prosy reader can discover to him by an immediate paraphrase; it is a kind of story, character, thing, scene, or moral principle. And where is the tissue that keeps it from coming out of the poetic object? That is, for the laws of the prose logic, its superfluity; and I think I would even say, its irrelevance.

A poet is said to be distinguishable in terms of his style. It is a comprehensive word, and probably means: the general character of his irrelevances, or tissues. All his technical devices contribute to it, elaborating or individualizing the universal, the core-object; likewise all his material detail. For each poem even, ideally, there is distinguishable a logical object or universal, but at the same time a tissue of irrelevance from which it does not really emerge. The critic has to take the poem apart, or analyze it, for the sake of uncovering these features. With all the finesse possible, it is rude and patchy business by comparison with the living integrity of the poem. But without it there could hardly be much understanding of the value of poetry, or of the natural history behind any adult poem.

The language I have used may sound too formidable, but I seem to find that a profound criticism generally works by some such considerations. However the critic may spell them, the two terms are in his mind: the prose core to which he can violently reduce the total object, and the differentia, residue, or tissue, which keeps the object poetical or entire. The character of the poem resides for the good critic in its way of exhibiting the residuary quality. The character of the poet is defined by the kind of prose object to which his interest evidently attaches, plus his way of involving it firmly in the residuary tissue. And doubtless, incidentally, the wise critic can often read behind the poet's public character his private history as a man with a weakness for lapsing into some special form of prosy or scientific bondage.

Similar considerations hold, I think, for the critique of fiction, or of the non-literary arts. I remark this for the benefit of philosophers who believe, with propriety, that the arts are fundamentally one. But I would prefer to leave the documentation to those who are better qualified.

1938

MARTIN HEIDEGGER
1889–1976

One of the most influential philosophers of the twentieth century, Martin Heidegger spent much of his long career preoccupied by the age-old philosophical question of the meaning of "being." He made his reputation with the publication of his magnum opus, *Being and Time* (1927, *Sein und Zeit*), a groundbreaking amalgam and extension of the phenomenology of Edmund Husserl (1859–1938) and the hermeneutics of Wilhelm Dilthey (1833–1911) that analyzes "what we really mean by the word 'being.'" His later philosophical reflections on Being, the writings that are most relevant for literary theorists and critics, are bound up inextricably with the experience and the analysis of poetry and language. For the later Heidegger, language and poetry are not simply devices employed to describe an already existing world. Instead, "language is the house of Being," and poetry is the means by which humankind creates worlds.

Heidegger was born to a poor Catholic family in the small town of Messkirch, Germany. His education at the high schools in Konstanz and Freiburg was largely a preparation for the priesthood. While at Freiburg, he first became interested in philosophy following his reading of Franz Brentano's *On the Various Meanings of Being according to Aristotle* (1862) and Carl Braig's *On Being: An Outline of Ontology* (1896). He left high school in 1909 to become a Jesuit novice, but he was discharged within a month, most likely because he felt a lack of vocation for the priesthood. He instead entered Freiburg University, where he studied theology and scholastic philosophy. In 1911 a spiritual crisis prompted Heidegger to discontinue his training in theology and concentrate on philosophy. He was particularly influenced by Edmund Husserl's *Logical Investigations* (1900), a treatise that attempted a systematic inquiry into consciousness (what its author called "phenomenology"). In timely fashion, Heidegger completed his dissertation, *The Theory of the Judgment in Psychologism* (1913), and his habilitation thesis, *Duns Scotus's Theory of Categories and Meaning* (1915).

In 1919 Heidegger further distanced himself from Catholicism by officially announcing his breach with its theological system. Following World War I, he became a lecturer at Freiburg and an assistant to Husserl. He soon began to acquire a reputation as a brilliant teacher for his lectures on ARISTOTLE, St. Paul, ST. AUGUSTINE, and phenomenology. In 1923 he became an associate professor at Marburg University, where he lectured on Greek, medieval, and German idealist philosophy. The year after the publication of his celebrated *Being and Time,* he succeeded Husserl at Freiburg.

In the early 1930s Heidegger developed sympathy for the Nazi cause, joining the National Socialist German Workers' Party in 1933, shortly after he was elected rector of Freiburg University. Understandably, this aspect of his career is extremely controversial. It is complicated by Heidegger's refusal following World War II to discuss his involvement with the Nazis. He did permit an interview on the subject in the 1960s, subsequently titled "Only a God Can Save Us Now," but on the condition that it not appear during his lifetime; it was published in 1976.

Heidegger's early work significantly broadened the field of hermeneutics, the theory and art of interpretation. Whereas FRIEDRICH SCHLEIERMACHER (1768–1834) and Dilthey conceived of hermeneutics as the objective exegesis of a specific text or utterance, Heidegger proposed that hermeneutics was central to understanding in general, linking traditional modes of textual interpretation to phenomenology's focus on the contents of consciousness. In effect, he connected the apprehension of Being and the dynamics of language as co-constituents.

Through the 1930s Heidegger turned his attention more and more to the subject of art: one central outcome was his long lecture "The Origin of the Work of Art" (1935)—a main text for the later Heidegger. This development is commonly referred to as the "turn" (*Kehre*), because Heidegger became less concerned with the everyday human existence discussed in his *Being and Time* and increasingly preoccupied with the examination of language and poetry. Another distinguishing trait of the turn is that Heidegger changed his analytical discourse to a poetic prose style attentive to the multiple meanings of words. His late prose became performative: it followed the paths of thinking, including its false twists and turns, and broke down the traditional distinction between poetry and philosophy. Some of the major poets who figure prominently in his late lectures are the Germans Friedrich Hölderlin (1770–1843), Stefan George (1868–1933), and Rainer Maria Rilke (1875–1926) plus the Austrian Georg Trakl (1887–1914).

Our selection, "Language" (1950), is a work of Heidegger's later years. In it he propounds his celebrated view that "language speaks man." Language brings man and his world into conscious existence; it is inaugural speaking in that it grants an abode or a dwelling for the being of mortals in the larger context of what Heidegger cryptically calls the "fourfold world" (comprising earth, sky, divinities, and mortals). In this account, language is neither mimetic nor expressive: it does not represent an external reality, nor does it express a preexisting feeling or thought. Language shapes consciousness and perception, calling things into being; it does not merely designate or label objects. In poetry, Heidegger argues, the essence of language is manifested with particular clarity, since poetry is less concerned with communication and expression than with imaginative creation.

In our selection, Heidegger presents a now famous explication of Georg Trakl's poem "A Winter Evening." As a poetic or imaginative act, Trakl's poem, he argues, founds and fashions a world. It bids things to appear *as* things; things as things are constituted in language and thus revealed and made near. But for Heidegger, as he notes while discussing the last stanza of the poem, a "dif-ference" between thing and world subsists. This dif-ference is a fundamental threshold where the gathering of things and world in stillness happens. Poetry allows for meditation on the dif-ference, and thus it distinguishes itself from the worn-out instrumental language of everyday speech. This phenomenological account of language as inaugural and performative prefigures later poststructuralist accounts of textuality and discourse developed by PAUL DE MAN, JACQUES DERRIDA, and other admirers of Heidegger.

Heidegger has often been criticized for his views, especially for his mysticism and his quietism, both of which suggest that he never abandoned his youthful religious sensibilities. His late poetic style, moreover, has been criticized as repetitive and obscure, a form of smoke and mirrors. His focus on poetry as pure speech ignores the sociological or "dialogical" dimensions of discourse depicted, most famously, by his contemporary MIKHAIL BAKHTIN. But the major criticism of Heidegger is that he involved himself with the Nazi Party and remained publicly silent about it for the remainder of his life, raising the issue of whether his vast corpus of writings reflects Nazi ideology or sensibility. Some critics separate his philosophy from his politics yet others see the two as fundamentally related. While it is unlikely that this debate will be resolved to everyone's satisfaction, all acknowledge that Heidegger has had a tremendous influence on philosophy, particularly in Europe, as exemplified powerfully in the existentialism of Jean-Paul Sartre, the phenomenological hermeneutics of Hans-Georg Gadamer, and the deconstructive philosophy of Jacques Derrida. In this context, Heidegger is widely believed to be the most important Continental philosopher of the twentieth century.

"Language" Keywords: Hermeneutics, Language, Phenomenology, Poetry

Language[1]

Man speaks. We speak when we are awake and we speak in our dreams. We are always speaking, even when we do not utter a single word aloud, but merely listen or read, and even when we are not particularly listening or speaking but are attending to some work or taking a rest. We are continually speaking in one way or another. We speak because speaking is natural to us. It does not first arise out of some special volition. Man is said to have language by nature. It is held that man, in distinction from plant and animal, is the living being capable of speech. This statement does not mean only that, along with other faculties, man also possesses the faculty of speech. It means to say that only speech enables man to be the living being he is as man. It is as one who speaks that man is—man. These are Wilhelm von Humboldt's[2] words. Yet it remains to consider what it is to be called—man.

In any case, language belongs to the closest neighborhood of man's being. We encounter language everywhere. Hence it cannot surprise us that as soon as man looks thoughtfully about himself at what is, he quickly hits upon language too, so as to define it by a standard reference to its overt aspects. Reflection tries to obtain an idea of what language is universally. The universal that holds for each thing is called its essence or nature. To represent universally what holds universally is, according to prevalent views, the basic feature of thought. To deal with language thoughtfully would thus mean to give an idea of the nature of language and to distinguish this idea properly from other ideas. This lecture,[3] too, seems to attempt something of that kind. However, the title of the lecture is not "On the Nature of Language." It is only "Language." "Only," we say, and yet we are clearly placing a far more presumptuous title at the head of our project than if we were to rest content with just making a few remarks about language. Still, to talk about language is presumably even worse than to write about silence. We do not wish to assault language in order to force it into the grip of ideas already fixed beforehand. We do not wish to reduce the nature of language to a concept, so that this concept may provide a generally useful view of language that will lay to rest all further notions about it.

To discuss language, to place it, means to bring to its place of being not so much language as ourselves: our own gathering into the appropriation.[4]

We would reflect on language itself, and on language only. Language itself is—language and nothing else besides. Language itself is language. The understanding that is schooled in logic, thinking of everything in terms of calculation and hence usually overbearing, calls this proposition an empty tautology. Merely to say the identical thing twice—language is language—how is that supposed to get us anywhere? But we do not want to get anywhere. We would like only, for once, to get to just where we are already.

1. Translated by Albert Hofstadter.
2. German philologist and diplomat (1767–1835).
3. "Language" is a revised version of Heidegger's lecture notes.
4. A complicated and elusive term in Heidegger's thought: the "appropriation" (*Ereignis*) refers to the original appearance and nature of being in language. The perceptible traits or qualities proper to the various things of the world are manifested, made present, and brought into their own being solely through the inaugural granting of language. Human beings dwell in this appropriation, perceiving only what language founds; thus, they do not speak language but are spoken by it.

This is why we ponder the question, "What about language itself?" This is why we ask, "In what way does language occur as language?" We answer: *Language speaks*. Is this, seriously, an answer? Presumably—that is, when it becomes clear what speaking is.

To reflect on language thus demands that we enter into the speaking of language in order to take up our stay with language, i.e., within *its* speaking, not within our own. Only in that way do we arrive at the region within which it may happen—or also fail to happen—that language will call to us from there and grant us its nature. We leave the speaking to language. We do not wish to ground language in something else that is not language itself, nor do we wish to explain other things by means of language.

On the tenth of August, 1784, Hamann wrote to Herder[5] (*Hamanns Schriften*, ed. Roth, VII, pp. 151f.):

> If I were as eloquent as Demosthenes[6] I would yet have to do nothing more than repeat a single word three times: reason is language, *logos*.[7] I gnaw at this marrow-bone and will gnaw myself to death over it. There still remains a darkness, always, over this depth for me; I am still waiting for an apocalyptic angel with a key to this abyss.

For Hamann, this abyss consists in the fact that reason is language. Hamann returns to language in his attempt to say what reason is. His glance, aimed at reason, falls into the depths of an abyss. Does this abyss consist only in the fact that reason resides in language, or is language itself the abyss? We speak of an abyss where the ground falls away and a ground is lacking to us, where we seek the ground and set out to arrive at a ground, to get to the bottom of something. But we do not ask now what reason may be; here we reflect immediately on language and take as our main clue the curious statement, "Language is language." This statement does not lead us to something else in which language is grounded. Nor does it say anything about whether language itself may be a ground for something else. The sentence, "Language is language," leaves us to hover over an abyss as long as we endure what it says.

Language is—language, speech. Language speaks. If we let ourselves fall into the abyss denoted by this sentence, we do not go tumbling into emptiness. We fall upward, to a height. Its loftiness opens up a depth. The two span a realm in which we would like to become at home, so as to find a residence, a dwelling place for the life of man.

To reflect on language means—to reach the speaking of language in such a way that this speaking takes place as that which grants an abode for the being of mortals.

What does it mean to speak? The current view declares that speech is the activation of the organs for sounding and hearing. Speech is the audible expression and communication of human feelings. These feelings are accompanied by thoughts. In such a characterization of language three points are taken for granted:

5. Johann Gottfried von Herder (1744–1803), German philosopher, theologian, and critic. Johann Georg Hamann (1730–1788), German philosopher and theologian. [From Johann Georg Hamann, *Schriften*, edited by F. Roth and G. A. Wiener, 8 parts (Berlin: G. Reimer, 1821)—translator's note.]

6. Athenian orator and statesman (384–322 B.C.E.), generally held to be the greatest Greek orator.

7. Word, speech, discourse, reason (Greek).

First and foremost, speaking is expression. The idea of speech as an utterance is the most common. It already presupposes the idea of something internal that utters or externalizes itself. If we take language to be utterance, we give an external, surface notion of it at the very moment when we explain it by recourse to something internal.

Secondly, speech is regarded as an activity of man. Accordingly we have to say that man speaks, and that he always speaks some language. Hence we cannot say, "Language speaks." For this would be to say: "It is language that first brings man about, brings him into existence." Understood in this way, man would be bespoken by language.

Finally, human expression is always a presentation and representation of the real and the unreal.

It has long been known that the characteristics we have advanced do not suffice to circumscribe the nature of language. But when we understand the nature of language in terms of expression, we give it a more comprehensive definition by incorporating expression, as one among many activities, into the total economy of those achievements by which man makes himself.

As against the identification of speech as a merely human performance, others stress that the word of language is of divine origin. According to the opening of the Prologue of the Gospel of St. John, in the beginning the Word was with God.[8] The attempt is made not only to free the question of origin from the fetters of a rational-logical explanation, but also to set aside the limits of a merely logical description of language. In opposition to the exclusive characterization of word-meanings as concepts, the figurative and symbolical character of language is pushed into the foreground. Biology and philosophical anthropology, sociology and psychopathology, theology and poetics are all then called upon to describe and explain linguistic phenomena more comprehensively.

In the meantime, all statements are referred in advance to the traditionally standard way in which language appears. The already fixed view of the whole nature of language is thus consolidated. This is how the idea of language in grammar and logic, philosophy of language and linguistics, has remained the same for two and a half millennia, although knowledge about language has progressively increased and changed. This fact could even be adduced as evidence for the unshakable correctness of the leading ideas about language. No one would dare to declare incorrect, let alone reject as useless, the identification of language as audible utterance of inner emotions, as human activity, as a representation by image and by concept. The view of language thus put forth is correct, for it conforms to what an investigation of linguistic phenomena can make out in them at any time. And all *questions* associated with the description and explanation of linguistic phenomena also move within the precincts of this correctness.

We still give too little consideration, however, to the singular role of these correct ideas about language. They hold sway, as if unshakable, over the whole field of the varied scientific perspectives on language. They have their roots in an ancient tradition. Yet they ignore completely the oldest natural cast of language. Thus, despite their antiquity and despite their comprehensibility, they never bring us to language as language.

8. John 1.1: "In the beginning was the Word, and the Word was with God, and the Word was God."

Language speaks. What about its speaking? Where do we encounter such speaking? Most likely, to be sure, in what is spoken. For here speech has come to completion in what is spoken. The speaking does not cease in what is spoken. Speaking is kept safe in what is spoken. In what is spoken, speaking gathers the ways in which it persists as well as that which persists by it—its persistence, its presencing. But most often, and too often, we encounter what is spoken only as the residue of a speaking long past.

If we must, therefore, seek the speaking of language in what is spoken, we shall do well to find something that is spoken purely rather than to pick just any spoken material at random. What is spoken purely is that in which the completion of the speaking that is proper to what is spoken is, in its turn, an original. What is spoken purely is the poem. For the moment, we must let this statement stand as a bare assertion. We may do so, if we succeed in hearing in a poem something that is spoken purely. But what poem shall speak to us? Here we have only one choice, but one that is secured against mere caprice. By what? By what is already told us as the presencing element in language, if we follow in thought the speaking *of language*. Because of this bond between what we think and what we are told by language we choose, as something spoken purely, a poem which more readily than others can help us in our first steps to discover what is binding in that bond. We listen to what is spoken. The poem bears the title:

A Winter Evening

Window with falling snow is arrayed,
Long tolls the vesper bell,
The house is provided well,
The table is for many laid.

Wandering ones, more than a few,
Come to the door on darksome courses.
Golden blooms the tree of graces
Drawing up the earth's cool dew.

Wanderer quietly steps within;
Pain has turned the threshold to stone.
There lie, in limpid brightness shown,
Upon the table bread and wine.

The two last verses of the second stanza and the third stanza read in the first version (Letter to Karl Kraus,[9] December 13, 1913):

Love's tender power, full of graces,
Binds up his wounds anew.

O! man's naked hurt condign.
Wrestler with angels mutely held,
Craves, by holy pain compelled,
Silently God's bread and wine.

9. Austrian poet, critic, and journalist (1874–1936).

(Cf. the new Swiss edition of the poems of G. Trakl edited by Kurt Horwitz, 1946.)[1]

The poem was written by Georg Trakl. Who the author is remains unimportant here, as with every other masterful poem. The mastery consists precisely in this, that the poem can deny the poet's person and name.

The poem is made up of three stanzas. Their meter and rhyme pattern can be defined accurately according to the schemes of metrics and poetics. The poem's content is comprehensible. There is not a single word which, taken by itself, would be unfamiliar or unclear. To be sure, a few of the verses sound strange, like the third and fourth in the second stanza:

> Golden blooms the tree of graces
> Drawing up the earth's cool dew.

Similarly, the second verse of the third stanza is startling:

> Pain has turned the threshold to stone.

But the verses here singled out also manifest a particular beauty of imagery. This beauty heightens the charm of the poem and strengthens its aesthetic perfection as an artistic structure.

The poem describes a winter evening. The first stanza describes what is happening outside: snowfall, and the ringing of the vesper bell. The things outside touch the things inside the human homestead. The snow falls on the window. The ringing of the bell enters into every house. Within, everything is well provided and the table set.

The second stanza raises a contrast. While many are at home within the house and at the table, not a few wander homeless on darksome paths. And yet such—possibly evil—roads sometimes lead to the door of the sheltering house. To be sure, this fact is not presented expressly. Instead, the poem names the tree of graces.

The third stanza bids the wanderer enter from the dark outdoors into the brightness within. The houses of the many and the tables of their daily meals have become house of God and altar.

The content of the poem might be dissected even more distinctly, its form outlined even more precisely, but in such operations we would still remain confined by the notion of language that has prevailed for thousands of years. According to this idea language is the expression, produced by men, of their feelings and the world view that guides them. Can the spell this idea has cast over language be broken? Why should it be broken? In its essence, language is neither expression nor an activity of man. Language speaks. We are now seeking the speaking of language in the poem. Accordingly, what we seek lies in the poetry of the spoken word.

The poem's title is "A Winter Evening." We expect from it the description of a winter evening as it actually is. But the poem does not picture a winter evening occurring somewhere, sometime. It neither merely describes a winter evening that is already there, nor does it attempt to produce the sem-

1. Georg Trakl, *Die Dichtungen. Gesamtausgabe mit einem Anhang: Zeugnisse und Erinnerungen*, ed. Kurt Horwitz (Zurich: Arche Verlag, 1946). This poem, "Ein Winterabend," may also be found in *Die Dichtungen*, 11th ed. (Salzburg: Otto Müller, 1938), p. 124. The letter to Karl Kraus may be found in *Erinnerung an Georg Trakl: Zeugnisse und Briefe* (Salzburg: Otto Müller, 1959), pp. 172–73 [translator's note]. Trakl (1887–1914), Austrian expressionist poet.

blance, leave the impression, of a winter evening's presence where there is no such winter evening. Naturally not, it will be replied. Everyone knows that a poem is an invention. It is imaginative even where it seems to be descriptive. In his fictive act the poet pictures to himself something that could be present in its presence. The poem, as composed, images what is thus fashioned for our own act of imaging. In the poem's speaking the poetic imagination gives itself utterance. What is spoken in the poem is what the poet enunciates out of himself. What is thus spoken out, speaks by enunciating its content. The language of the poem is a manifold enunciating. Language proves incontestably to be expression. But this conclusion is in conflict with the proposition "Language speaks," assuming that speaking, in its essential nature, is not an expressing.

Even when we understand what is spoken in the poem in terms of poetic composition, it seems to us, as if under some compulsion, always and only to be an expressed utterance. Language is expression. Why do we not reconcile ourselves to this fact? Because the correctness and currency of this view of language are insufficient to serve as a basis for an account of the nature of language. How shall we gauge this inadequacy? Must we not be bound by a different standard before we can gauge anything in that manner? Of course. That standard reveals itself in the proposition, "Language speaks." Up to this point this guiding proposition has had merely the function of warding off the ingrained habit of disposing of speech by throwing it at once among the phenomena of expression instead of thinking it in its own terms. The poem cited has been chosen because, in a way not further explicable, it demonstrates a peculiar fitness to provide some fruitful hints for our attempt to discuss language.

Language *speaks*. This means at the same time and before all else: *language* speaks. Language? And not man? What our guiding proposition demands of us now—is it not even worse than before? Are we, in addition to everything else, also going to deny now that man is the being who speaks? Not at all. We deny this no more than we deny the possibility of classifying linguistic phenomena under the heading of "expression." But we ask, "How does man speak?" We ask, "What is it to speak?"

Window with falling snow is arrayed
Long tolls the vesper bell.

This speaking names the snow that soundlessly strikes the window late in the waning day, while the vesper bell rings. In such a snowfall, everything lasting lasts longer. Therefore the vesper bell, which daily rings for a strictly fixed time, tolls long. The speaking names the winter evening time. What is this naming? Does it merely deck out the imaginable familiar objects and events—snow, bell, window, falling, ringing—with words of a language? No. This naming does not hand out titles, it does not apply terms, but it calls into the word. The naming calls. Calling brings closer what it calls. However this bringing closer does not fetch what is called only in order to set it down in closest proximity to what is present, to find a place for it there. The call does indeed call. Thus it brings the presence of what was previously uncalled into a nearness. But the call, in calling it here, has already called out to what it calls. Where to? Into the distance in which what is called remains, still absent.

The calling here calls into a nearness. But even so the call does not wrest what it calls away from the remoteness, in which it is kept by the calling there. The calling calls into itself and therefore always here and there—here into presence, there into absence. Snowfall and tolling of vesper bell are spoken to us here and now in the poem. They are present in the call. Yet they in no way fall among the things present here and now in this lecture hall. Which presence is higher, that of these present things or the presence of what is called?

The house is provided well,
The table is for many laid.

The two verses speak like plain statements, as though they were noting something present. The emphatic "is" sounds that way. Nevertheless it speaks in the mode of calling. The verses bring the well-provided house and the ready table into that presence that is turned toward something absent.

What does the first stanza call? It calls things, bids them come. Where? Not to be present among things present; it does not bid the table named in the poem to be present here among the rows of seats where you are sitting. The place of arrival which is also called in the calling is a presence sheltered in absence. The naming call bids things to come into such an arrival. Bidding is inviting. It invites things in, so that they may bear upon men as things. The snowfall brings men under the sky that is darkening into night. The tolling of the evening bell brings them, as mortals, before the divine. House and table join mortals to the earth. The things that were named, thus called, gather to themselves sky and earth, mortals and divinities. The four are united primally in being toward one another, a fourfold. The things let the fourfold of the four stay with them. This gathering, assembling, letting-stay is the thinging of things. The unitary fourfold of sky and earth, mortals and divinities, which is stayed in the thinging of things, we call—the world. In the naming, the things named are called into their thinging. Thinging, they unfold world, in which things abide and so are the abiding ones. By thinging, things carry out world. Our old language calls such carrying *bern, bären*—Old High German *beran*—to bear; hence the words *gebaren*, to carry, gestate, give birth, and *Gebärde*, bearing, gesture. Thinging, things are things. Thinging, they gesture—gestate—world.

The first stanza calls things into their thinging, bids them come. The bidding that calls things calls them here, invites them, and at the same time calls out to the things, commending them to the world out of which they appear. Hence the first stanza names not only things. It simultaneously names world. It calls the "many" who belong as mortals to the world's fourfold. Things be-thing—i.e., condition—mortals. This now means: things, each in its time, literally visit mortals with a world. The first stanza speaks by bidding the things to come.

The second stanza speaks in a different way. To be sure, it too bids to come. But its calling begins as it calls and names mortals:

Wandering ones, more than a few . . .

Not all mortals are called, not the many of the first stanza, but only "more than a few"—those who wander on dark courses. These mortals are capable of dying as the wandering toward death. In death the supreme concealed-ness of Being crystallizes. Death has already overtaken every dying. Those "wayfarers" must first wander their way to house and table through the darkness of their courses; they must do so not only and not even primarily for themselves, but for the many, because the many think that if they only install themselves in houses and sit at tables, they are already bethinged, conditioned, by things and have arrived at dwelling.

The second stanza begins by calling more than a few of the mortals. Although mortals belong to the world's fourfold along with the divinities, with earth and sky, the first two verses of the second stanza do not expressly call the world. Rather, very much like the first stanza but in a different sequence, they at the same time name things—the door, the dark paths. It is the two remaining verses that expressly name the world. Suddenly they name something wholly different:

> Golden blooms the tree of graces
> Drawing up the earth's cool dew.

The tree roots soundly in the earth. Thus it is sound and flourishes into a blooming that opens itself to heaven's blessing. The tree's towering has been called. It spans both the ecstasy of flowering and the soberness of the nourishing sap. The earth's abated growth and the sky's open bounty belong together. The poem names the tree of graces. Its sound blossoming harbors the fruit that falls to us unearned—holy, saving, loving toward mortals. In the golden-blossoming tree there prevail earth and sky, divinities and mortals. Their unitary fourfold is the world. The word "world" is now no longer used in the metaphysical sense. It designates neither the universe of nature and history in its secular representation nor the theologically conceived creation (*mundus*), nor does it mean simply the whole of entities present (*kosmos*).[2]

The third and fourth lines of the second stanza call the tree of graces. They expressly bid the world to come. They call the world-fourfold here, and thus call world to the things.

The two lines start with the word "golden." So that we may hear more clearly this word and what it calls, let us recollect a poem of Pindar's:[3] *Isthmians* V. At the beginning of this ode the poet calls gold *periosion panton*, that which above all shines through everything, *panta*, shines through each thing present all around. The splendor of gold keeps and holds everything present in the unconcealedness of its appearing.

As the calling that names things calls here and there, so the saying that names the world calls into itself, calling here and there. It entrusts world to the things and simultaneously keeps the things in the splendor of world. The world grants to things their presence. Things bear world. World grants things.

The speaking of the first two stanzas speaks by bidding things to come to world, and world to things. The two modes of bidding are different but not separated. But neither are they merely coupled together. For world and things do not subsist alongside one another. They penetrate each other. Thus the two traverse a middle. In it, they are at one. Thus at one they are intimate.

2. Both *mundus* (Latin) and *kosmos* (Greek) mean "world," in the different senses that Heidegger gives.

3. Greek lyric poet (ca. 518–438 B.C.E.), known for his elaborate victory odes. In fact, the word *panton* is not used at the beginning of the poem cited.

The middle of the two is intimacy—in Latin, *inter*. The corresponding German word is *unter*, the English *inter-*. The intimacy of world and thing is not a fusion. Intimacy obtains only where the intimate—world and thing—divides itself cleanly and remains separated. In the midst of the two, in the between of world and thing, in their *inter*, division prevails: a *dif-ference*.

The intimacy of world and thing is present in the separation of the between; it is present in the dif-ference. The word dif-ference is now removed from its usual and customary usage. What it now names is not a generic concept for various kinds of differences. It exists only as this single difference. It is unique. Of itself, it holds apart the middle in and through which world and things are at one with each other. The intimacy of the dif-ference is the unifying element of the *diaphora*, the carrying out that carries through. The dif-ference carries out world in its worlding, carries out things in their thinging. Thus carrying them out, it carries them toward one another. The dif-ference does not mediate after the fact by connecting world and things through a middle added on to them. Being the middle, it first determines world and things in their presence, i.e., in their being toward one another, whose unity it carries out.

The word consequently no longer means a distinction established between objects only by our representations. Nor is it merely a relation obtaining between world and thing, so that a representation coming upon it can establish it. The dif-ference is not abstracted from world and thing as their relationship after the fact. The dif-ference for world and thing *disclosingly appropriates* things into bearing a world; it *disclosingly appropriates* world into the granting of things.

The dif-ference is neither distinction nor relation. The dif-ference is, at most, dimension for world and thing. But in this case "dimension" also no longer means a precinct already present independently in which this or that comes to settle. The dif-ference is *the* dimension, insofar as it measures out, apportions, world and thing, each to its own. Its allotment of them first opens up the separateness and towardness of world and thing. Such an opening up is the way in which the dif-ference here spans the two. The dif-ference, as the middle for world and things, metes out the measure of their presence. In the bidding that calls thing and world, what is really called is: the dif-ference.

The first stanza of the poem bids the things to come which, thinging, bear world. The second stanza bids that world to come which, worlding, grants things. The third stanza bids the middle for world and things to come: the carrying out of the intimacy. On this account the third stanza begins with an emphatic calling:

Wanderer quietly steps within.

Where to? The verse does not say. Instead, it calls the entering wanderer into the stillness. This stillness ministers over the doorway. Suddenly and strangely the call sounds:

Pain has turned the threshold to stone.

This verse speaks all by itself in what is spoken in the whole poem. It names pain. What pain? The verse says merely "pain." Whence and in what way is pain called?

Pain has turned the threshold to stone.

"Turned . . . to stone"—these are the only words in the poem that speak in the past tense. Even so, they do not name something gone by, something no longer present. They name something that persists and that has already persisted. It is only in turning to stone that the threshold presences at all.

The threshold is the ground-beam that bears the doorway as a whole. It sustains the middle in which the two, the outside and the inside, penetrate each other. The threshold bears the between. What goes out and goes in, in the between, is joined in the between's dependability. The dependability of the middle must never yield either way. The settling of the between needs something that can endure, and is in this sense hard. The threshold, as the settlement of the between, is hard because pain has petrified it. But the pain that became appropriated to stone did not harden into the threshold in order to congeal there. The pain presences unflagging in the threshold, as pain.

But what is pain? Pain rends. It is the rift. But it does not tear apart into dispersive fragments. Pain indeed tears asunder, it separates, yet so that at the same time it draws everything to itself, gathers it to itself. Its rending, as a separating that gathers, is at the same time that drawing which, like the pen-drawing of a plan or sketch, draws and joins together what is held apart in separation. Pain is the joining agent in the rending that divides and gathers. Pain is the joining of the rift. The joining is the threshold. It settles the between, the middle of the two that are separated in it. Pain joins the rift of the dif-ference. Pain is the dif-ference itself.

Pain has turned the threshold to stone.

The verse calls the dif-ference, but it neither thinks it specifically nor does it call its nature by this name. The verse calls the separation of the between, the gathering middle, in whose intimacy the bearing of things and the granting of world pervade one another.

Then would the intimacy of the dif-ference for world and thing be pain? Certainly. But we should not imagine pain anthropologically as a sensation that makes us feel afflicted. We should not think of the intimacy psychologically as the sort in which sentimentality makes a nest for itself.

Pain has turned the threshold to stone.

Pain has already fitted the threshold into its bearing. The dif-ference presences already as the collected presence, from which the carrying out of world and thing appropriatingly takes place. How so?

There lie, in limpid brightness shown,
Upon the table bread and wine.

Where does the pure brightness shine? On the threshold, in the settling of the pain. The rift of the dif-ference makes the limpid brightness shine. Its luminous joining decides the brightening of the world into its own. The rift of the dif-ference expropriates the world into its worlding, which grants things. By the brightening of the world in their golden gleam, bread and wine at the same time attain to their own gleaming. The nobly named things are lustrous in the simplicity of their thinging. Bread and wine are the fruits of heaven and earth, gifts from the divinities to mortals. Bread and wine gather these four to themselves from the simple unity of their fourfoldness. The things that are called bread and wine are simple things because their bearing of world is fulfilled, without intermediary, by the favor of the world. Such things have their sufficiency in letting the world's fourfold stay with them. The pure limpid brightness of world and the simple gleaming of things go through their between, the dif-ference.

The third stanza calls world and things into the middle of their intimacy. The seam that binds their being toward one another is pain.

Only the third stanza gathers the bidding of things and the bidding of world. For the third stanza calls primally out of the simplicity of the intimate bidding which calls the dif-ference by leaving it unspoken. The primal calling, which bids the intimacy of world and thing to come, is the authentic bidding. This bidding is the nature of speaking. Speaking occurs in what is spoken in the poem. It is the speaking of language. Language speaks. It speaks by bidding the bidden, thing-world and world-thing, to come to the between of the dif-ference. What is so bidden is commanded to arrive from out of the dif-ference into the dif-ference. Here we are thinking of the old sense of command, which we recognize still in the phrase, "Commit thy way unto the Lord."[4] The bidding of language commits the bidden thus to the bidding of the dif-ference. The dif-ference lets the thinging of the thing rest in the worlding of the world. The dif-ference expropriates the thing into the repose of the fourfold. Such expropriation does not diminish the thing. Only so is the thing exalted into its own, so that it stays world. To keep in repose is to still. The dif-ference stills the thing, as thing, into the world.

Such stilling, however, takes place only in such a way that at the same time the world's fourfold fulfills the bearing of the thing, in that the stilling grants to the thing the sufficiency of staying world. The dif-ference stills in a twofold manner. It stills by letting things rest in the world's favor. It stills by letting the world suffice itself in the thing. In the double stilling of the dif-ference there takes place: stillness.

What is stillness? It is in no way merely the soundless. In soundlessness there persists merely a lack of the motion of entoning, sounding. But the motionless is neither limited to sounding by being its suspension, nor is it itself already something genuinely tranquil. The motionless always remains, as it were, merely the other side of that which rests. The motionless itself still rests on rest. But rest has its being in the fact that it stills. As the stilling of stillness, rest, conceived strictly, is always more in motion than all motion and always more restlessly active than any agitation.

The dif-ference stills particularly in two ways: it stills the things in thinging and the world in worlding. Thus stilled, thing and world never escape from the dif-ference. Rather, they rescue it in the stilling, where the dif-ference is itself the stillness.

In stilling things and world into their own, the dif-ference calls world and thing into the middle of their intimacy. The dif-ference is the bidder. The dif-ference gathers the two out of itself as it calls them into the rift that is the dif-ference itself. This gathering calling is the pealing. In it there occurs something different from a mere excitation and spreading of sound.

4. Psalm 37.5.

When the dif-ference gathers world and things into the simple onefold of the pain of intimacy, it bids the two to come into their very nature. The dif-ference is the command out of which every bidding itself is first called, so that each may follow the command. The command of the dif-ference has ever already gathered all bidding within itself. The calling, gathered together with itself, which gathers to itself in the calling, is the pealing as the peal.

The calling of the dif-ference is the double stilling. The gathered bidding, the command, in the form of which the dif-ference calls world and things, is the peal of stillness. Language speaks in that the command of the dif-ference calls world and things into the simple onefold of their intimacy.

Language speaks as the peal of stillness. Stillness stills by the carrying out, the bearing and enduring, of world and things in their presence. The carrying out of world and thing in the manner of stilling is the appropriative taking place of the dif-ference. Language, the peal of stillness, is, inasmuch as the dif-ference takes place. Language goes on as the taking place or occurring of the dif-ference for world and things.

The peal of stillness is not anything human. But on the contrary, the human is indeed in its nature given to speech—it is linguistic. The word "linguistic" as it is here used means: having taken place out of the speaking of language. What has thus taken place, human being, has been brought into its own by language, so that it remains given over or appropriated to the nature of language, the peal of stillness. Such an appropriating takes place in that the very *nature*, the *presencing*, of language *needs and uses* the speaking of mortals in order to sound as the peal of stillness for the hearing of mortals. Only as men belong within the peal of stillness are mortals able to speak in *their own* way in sounds.

Mortal speech is a calling that names, a bidding which, out of the simple onefold of the difference, bids thing and world to come. What is purely bidden in mortal speech is what is spoken in the poem. Poetry proper is never merely a higher mode (*melos*)[5] of everyday language. It is rather the reverse: everyday language is a forgotten and therefore used-up poem, from which there hardly resounds a call any longer.

The opposite of what is purely spoken, the opposite of the poem, is not prose. Pure prose is never "prosaic." It is as poetic and hence as rare as poetry.

If attention is fastened exclusively on human speech, if human speech is taken simply to be the voicing of the inner man, if speech so conceived is regarded as language itself, then the nature of language can never appear as anything but an expression and an activity of man. But human speech, as the speech of mortals, is not self-subsistent. The speech of mortals rests in its relation to the speaking of language.

At the proper time it becomes unavoidable to think of how mortal speech and its utterance take place in the speaking of language as the peal of the stillness of the dif-ference. Any uttering, whether in speech or writing, breaks the stillness. On what does the peal of stillness break? How does the broken stillness come to sound in words? How does the broken stillness shape the mortal speech that sounds in verses and sentences?

5. A song, tune, or melody considered apart from rhythm (Greek).

Assuming that thinking will succeed one day in answering these questions, it must be careful not to regard utterance, let alone expression, as the decisive element of human speech.

The structure of human speech can only be the manner (*melos*) in which the speaking of language, the peal of the stillness of the dif-ference, appropriates mortals by the command of the dif-ference.

The way in which mortals, called out of the dif-ference into the difference, speak on their own part, is: by responding. Mortal speech must first of all have listened to the command, in the form of which the stillness of the dif-ference calls world and things into the rift of its onefold simplicity. Every word of mortal speech speaks out of such a listening, and as such a listening.

Mortals speak insofar as they listen. They heed the bidding call of the stillness of the dif-ference even when they do not know that call. Their listening draws from the command of the dif-ference what it brings out as sounding word. This speaking that listens and accepts is responding.

Nevertheless by receiving what it says from the command of the dif-ference, mortal speech has already, in its own way, followed the call. Response, as receptive listening, is at the same time a recognition that makes due acknowledgment. Mortals speak by responding to language in a twofold way, receiving and replying. The mortal word speaks by cor-responding in a multiple sense.

Every authentic hearing holds back with its own saying. For hearing keeps to itself in the listening by which it remains appropriated to the peal of stillness. All responding is attuned to this restraint that reserves itself. For this reason such reserve must be concerned to be ready, in the mode of listening, for the command of the dif-ference. But the reserve must take care not just to hear the peal of stillness afterward, but to hear it even beforehand, and thus as it were to anticipate its command.

This anticipating while holding back determines the manner in which mortals respond to the dif-ference. In this way mortals live in the speaking of language.

Language speaks. Its speaking bids the dif-ference to come which expropriates world and things into the simple onefold of their intimacy.

Language speaks.

Man speaks in that he responds to language. This responding is a hearing. It hears because it listens to the command of stillness.

It is not a matter here of stating a new view of language. What is important is learning to live in the speaking of language. To do so, we need to examine constantly whether and to what extent we are capable of what genuinely belongs to responding: anticipation in reserve. For:

> Man speaks only as he responds to language.
> Language speaks.
> Its speaking speaks for us in what has been spoken:

A Winter Evening

> Window with falling snow is arrayed.
> Long tolls the vesper bell,
> The house is provided well,
> The table is for many laid.

Wandering ones, more than a few,
Come to the door on darksome courses.
Golden blooms the tree of graces
Drawing up the earth's cool dew.

Wanderer quietly steps within;
Pain has turned the threshold to stone.
There lie, in limpid brightness shown,
Upon the table bread and wine.

1950

ANTONIO GRAMSCI
1891–1937

A Marxist martyr, determined to balance "pessimism of the intellect" with "optimism of the will," Antonio Gramsci is central to cultural studies and to all attempts to locate the roles that literature and culture play in the establishment, maintenance, and contestation of political power. Caught between the Russian Revolution, which he hoped to see reenacted in Italy, and the rise to power instead of the Fascist Party led by Benito Mussolini, Gramsci's failed political efforts motivated his revisionist Marxism, which emphasized the way cultural activities interact with both the economy and the state to forge the "manufactured consent" he calls "hegemony."

Gramsci was born on the impoverished and marginalized island of Sardinia into the family of a minor government official. His schooling was interrupted at age twelve, when he was forced to begin working sixty-hour weeks to help support his family after his father's imprisonment for fraud (the conviction may have been politically motivated). An early childhood bout with tuberculosis left Gramsci deformed (he described himself as a hunchback) and stunted (four feet, ten inches tall). Having won a modest scholarship, he left Sardinia in 1911 to attend the University of Turin. The site of Fiat's factories, Turin was a major industrial city of Italy and home to a strong socialist movement among the factory workers. By 1914 Gramsci was a committed socialist, and in December 1916 he became an editor of the official Socialist Party newspaper. For the next six years, he worked as a political journalist and editor for various leftist publications.

An enthusiastic champion of the Russian Revolution, Gramsci had reason to believe that Italy's socialist revolution would not be far behind. In response to a company lockout, Fiat workers occupied the factories and produced cars on their own in September 1920, while the Socialist Party's various trade unions had over two million members that same year. But membership quickly declined as Mussolini's Fascist movement grew. Fascism's nationalist trumpeting of the glories of empire and of Italy's Roman past swept away concerns about its use of a militaristic state to keep workers and other potential dissidents under strict control. As popular support for Fascism mounted, leftist groups fought among themselves over how to respond. In 1921 Gramsci was one of the leading figures in the formation of the Communist Party of Italy.

Like other European Communist parties, the Italian one looked to Moscow for financial and intellectual sustenance. While Gramsci spent the bulk of 1922 and 1923 in Russia, the newly installed Fascist government in Italy issued a warrant for his arrest. Elected to Parliament on the Communist ticket in 1924, Gramsci returned to take his seat, protected from prosecution by parliamentary immunity. Mussolini announced a one-party state the following year, and Gramsci was placed under police surveillance. The leaders of the Communist Party, including Gramsci, were arrested in November 1926 and were tried together in June 1928. Gramsci was sentenced to twenty years in prison. Released from prison because of ill health in April 1937, he died less than two weeks after gaining his freedom.

For four years (1929–33) in prison, before his health collapsed, Gramsci was allowed to write. The result was the four volumes of the *Quaderni del carcere* (*The Prison Notebooks*), on which most of Gramsci's reputation as a social and cultural theorist is based and from which "The Formation of the Intellectuals" is taken.

Gramsci is one of the major figures of Western Marxism, a term that covers the work of twentieth-century German, French, British, and Italian leftist intellectuals. One abiding concern of these theorists is why the working-class revolution predicted by KARL MARX did not occur in Western Europe. An orthodox Soviet reading of Marx, promulgated and enforced by the Russian Bolsheviks, claimed that both political action and intellectual beliefs derive from economic interest. Since capitalism is against the economic interest of the workers, and since the workers are much more numerous than their employers, a proletarian revolution should be both inevitable and successful. But Western Marxists recognized that many workers were indifferent or even hostile to workers' movements and socialism, and that many workers supported fascist parties, even when they seemed obvious enemies of workers' interests. Significantly, Western Marxists proposed that economic interests are only part of the story when one considers the beliefs, values, commitments, and aspirations that motivate action; cultural factors are also crucial. It is this attention to how culture influences attitudes and actions that has made Western Marxism important for literary and cultural studies.

Gramsci's immediate concern was the Left's failure to win the hearts and minds of the Italian people, who supported the Fascists instead. Vladimir Lenin had already theorized that the workers' revolution could not happen spontaneously; revolution could succeed only if a dedicated cadre of revolutionaries stirred the workers to action and organized those actions once they occurred. This vanguard is the "party" for Lenin; its necessity justified the leadership role taken by the Bolsheviks in a supposedly egalitarian revolution. Subsequent writers have seen Lenin's justification of "the dictatorship of the party" as the first step toward the betrayal of Marxism that led to the tyranny in Soviet Russia between 1919 and 1989.

Gramsci's meditations on intellectuals subtly contest Lenin's writings on the role of the party. He wants to consider how the intellectual can be effective, especially in moving people to action. (Similar worries still bedevil literary intellectuals who espouse political causes.) Gramsci identifies two types of intellectuals. Traditional intellectuals are the administrators and apologists for existing social and cultural institutions, such as schools, various religious denominations, corporations, the military, the press, political bureaucracies, and the judicial system. Writers, artists, and philosophers are traditional intellectuals insofar as they work within formal institutions. In contrast, organic intellectuals rise out of membership in social groups (or classes) that have an antagonistic relationship to established institutions and official power. They "articulate" those groups' needs and aspirations, which have frequently gone unexpressed. The organic intellectual does not simply parrot preexisting group beliefs or demands but brings to the level of public speech what has not been officially recognized. While a given group does have certain tendencies, the process of articulation itself will shape it, giving it new identities and commitments—new ways of understanding itself and its desires.

For Gramsci, the traditional Marxist notion of "class" is too inert if it leads us to believe that workers, by virtue of their social position, always belong to the same class and possess the same attitudes and interests. The phrase "historic bloc"—Gramsci's own coinage—expresses his sense that social groups are dynamically created in specific historical moments, or so-called conjunctures. Any bloc's ability to intervene effectively in social arrangements depends on the relative strength of other blocs in a social field marked by conflict and continual jockeying for advantage. Intellectuals play a key role in the ongoing formation and re-formation of historic blocs.

The emphasis on intellectuals, articulation, and the formation of a historic bloc culminates in the concept of "hegemony," which substantially revises standard Marxist theories of "ideology." There are two notions of ideology found in Marx's *German Ideology* (written 1845–46; see above): the first holds that a person's beliefs and values are a reflection of that person's economic interests (though often not recognized as such); the second maintains that the leading ideas of the ruling class will be the ruling ideas of the age. In both cases, ideology mirrors economic interest, though in complex ways. Hegemony, like the historic bloc, aims to make this static Marxist concept dynamic. Gramsci argues elsewhere that a stable state never rules by force alone but relies on a combination of coercion and consent. Dominance is secure only if a majority voluntarily complies with the law. Any group that aspires to rule must work to gain the people's consent, and this work must be done before any directly revolutionary effort to seize and hold on to "material force." The effort to win consent—an effort that is ongoing and never entirely successful (force will be needed against some recalcitrant citizens)—is the attempt to gain hegemony, the dominant position in a given society. Hegemony is "manufactured consent," created through the articulation of intellectuals in a public sphere in which contending articulations are also voiced.

Gramsci's dynamic model has been especially crucial for later British Marxists and for the version of cultural studies that comes from Britain. Leading figures in cultural studies such as STUART HALL and DICK HEBDIGE use the concept of hegemony to move away from the class-based politics of the Labour Party; they embrace instead a cultural politics that emphasizes the need of intellectuals to contest power in multiple ways and to engage issues of race, gender, and identity. The most frequent criticisms of Gramsci also resurface in evaluations of British cultural studies. Orthodox Marxists worry that concentrating on cultural influences on behavior will cause material and economic factors to slide from view. For those outside the Marxist tradition, the focus on intellectuals seems potentially antidemocratic, while the stress on gaining power within a conflicted social field often moves issues of ethics and justice to the margins. Despite such criticisms, Gramsci's focus on the cultural work that intellectuals do, joined with his revision of key Marxist concepts, ensures his continuing influence within cultural studies.

"The Formation of the Intellectuals" Keywords: Cultural Studies, Hegemony, Ideology, Marxism

The Formation of the Intellectuals[1]

Are intellectuals an autonomous and independent social group, or does every social group have its own particular specialised category of intellectuals? The problem is a complex one, because of the variety of forms assumed to date by the real historical process of formation of the different categories of intellectuals.

1. Translated by Quintin Hoare and Geoffrey Nowell Smith, who occasionally retain the original Italian in brackets.

The most important of these forms are two:

1. Every social group, coming into existence on the original terrain of an essential function in the world of economic production, creates together with itself, organically, one or more strata of intellectuals which give it homogeneity and an awareness of its own function not only in the economic but also in the social and political fields. The capitalist entrepreneur creates alongside himself the industrial technician, the specialist in political economy, the organisers of a new culture, of a new legal system, etc. It should be noted that the entrepreneur himself represents a higher level of social elaboration, already characterised by a certain directive [*dirigente*] and technical (i.e. intellectual) capacity: he must have a certain technical capacity, not only in the limited sphere of his activity and initiative but in other spheres as well, at least in those which are closest to economic production. He must be an organiser of masses of men; he must be an organiser of the "confidence" of investors in his business, of the customers for his product, etc.

If not all entrepreneurs, at least an *élite* amongst them must have the capacity to be an organiser of society in general, including all its complex organism of services, right up to the state organism, because of the need to create the conditions most favourable to the expansion of their own class; or at the least they must possess the capacity to choose the deputies (specialised employees) to whom to entrust this activity of organising the general system of relationships external to the business itself. It can be observed that the "organic" intellectuals which every new class creates alongside itself and elaborates in the course of its development, are for the most part "specialisations" of partial aspects of the primitive activity of the new social type which the new class has brought into prominence.[2]

Even feudal lords were possessors of a particular technical capacity, military capacity, and it is precisely from the moment at which the aristocracy loses its monopoly of technico-military capacity that the crisis of feudalism begins. But the formation of intellectuals in the feudal world and in the preceding classical world is a question to be examined separately: this formation and elaboration follows ways and means which must be studied concretely. Thus it is to be noted that the mass of the peasantry, although it performs an essential function in the world of production, does not elaborate its own "organic" intellectuals, nor does it "assimilate" any stratum of "traditional" intellectuals, although it is from the peasantry that other social groups draw many of their intellectuals and a high proportion of traditional intellectuals are of peasant origin.

2. However, every "essential" social group which emerges into history out of the preceding economic structure, and as an expression of a development of this structure, has found (at least in all of history up to the present) categories of intellectuals already in existence and which seemed indeed to represent an historical continuity uninterrupted even by the most complicated and radical changes in political and social forms.

2. [Gaetano] Mosca's *Elementi di Scienza Politica* [*Elements of Political Science*] (new expanded edition, 1923) is worth looking at in this connection. Mosca's so-called "political class" is nothing other than the intellectual category of the dominant social group. Mosca's concept of "political class" can be connected with Pareto's concept of the *élite*, which is another attempt to interpret the historical phenomena of the intellectuals and their function in the life of the state and of society [Gramsci's note]. Vilfredo Pareto (1848–1923), Italian economist and sociologist.

The most typical of these categories of intellectuals is that of the ecclesiastics, who for a long time (for a whole phase of history, which is partly characterised by this very monopoly) held a monopoly of a number of important services: religious ideology, that is the philosophy and science of the age, together with schools, education, morality, justice, charity, good works, etc. The category of ecclesiastics can be considered the category of intellectuals organically bound to the landed aristocracy. It had equal status juridically with the aristocracy, with which it shared the exercise of feudal ownership of land, and the use of state privileges connected with property.[3] But the monopoly held by the ecclesiastics in the superstructural field[4] was not exercised without a struggle or without limitations, and hence there took place the birth, in various forms (to be gone into and studied concretely), of other categories, favoured and enabled to expand by the growing strength of the central power of the monarch, right up to absolutism. Thus we find the formation of the *noblesse de robe*,[5] with its own privileges, a stratum of administrators, etc., scholars and scientists, theorists, non-ecclesiastical philosophers, etc.

Since these various categories of traditional intellectuals experience through an "*esprit de corps*" their uninterrupted historical continuity and their special qualification, they thus put themselves forward as autonomous and independent of the dominant social group. This self-assessment is not without consequences in the ideological and political field, consequences of wide-ranging import. The whole of idealist philosophy[6] can easily be connected with this position assumed by the social complex of intellectuals and can be defined as the expression of that social utopia by which the intellectuals think of themselves as "independent", autonomous, endowed with a character of their own, etc.

One should note however that if the Pope and the leading hierarchy of the Church consider themselves more linked to Christ and to the apostles than they are to senators Agnelli and Benni, the same does not hold for Gentile and Croce,[7] for example: Croce in particular feels himself closely linked to Aristotle and Plato,[8] but he does not conceal, on the other hand, his links with senators Agnelli and Benni, and it is precisely here that one can discern the most significant character of Croce's philosophy.

3. For one category of these intellectuals, possibly the most important after the ecclesiastical for its prestige and the social function it performed in primitive societies, the category of *medical men* in the wide sense, that is all those who "struggle" or seem to struggle against death and disease, compare the *Storia della medicina* [1927, *A History of Medicine*] of Arturo Castiglioni. Note that there has been a connection between religion and medicine, and in certain areas there still is: hospitals in the hands of religious orders for certain organisational functions, apart from the fact that wherever the doctor appears, so does the priest (exorcism, various forms of assistance, etc.). Many great religious figures were and are conceived of as great "healers": the idea of miracles, up to the resurrection of the dead. Even in the case of kings the belief long survived that they could heal with the laying on of hands, etc. [Gramsci's note].

4. From this has come the general sense of "intellectual" or "specialist" of the word *chierico* (clerk, cleric) in many languages of romance origin or heavily influenced, through church Latin, by the romance languages, together with its correlative *laico* (lay, layman) in the sense of profane, non-specialist [Gramsci's note].

5. Nobility of the robe or gown (French); Gramsci refers to judges and lawyers.

6. A philosophy that posits the existence of ideas, motives, and actions separate from their material, economic origins and their consequences.

7. Benedetto Croce (1866–1952), the major liberal, idealist philosopher of Italy; a staunch opponent of fascism, his international fame protected him. Giovanni Agnelli (1866–1945), founder of Fiat and an Italian senator. Antonio Benni (1880–1945), industrialist turned politician, later a Fascist minister. Giovanni Gentile (1874–1944), Sicilian philosopher, early ally of Croce, and later Fascist minister of education. Gramsci's point is that Croce, despite his idealism and antifascism, understands the realities of political and economic power, taking care to maintain good relations with his friends in high places.

8. For the Greek philosophers ARISTOTLE (384–322 B.C.E.) and PLATO (ca. 427–ca. 347 B.C.E.), see above.

What are the "maximum" limits of acceptance of the term "intellectual"? Can one find a unitary criterion to characterise equally all the diverse and disparate activities of intellectuals and to distinguish these at the same time and in an essential way from the activities of other social groupings? The most widespread error of method seems to me that of having looked for this criterion of distinction in the intrinsic nature of intellectual activities, rather than in the ensemble of the system of relations in which these activities (and therefore the intellectual groups who personify them) have their place within the general complex of social relations. Indeed the worker or proletarian, for example, is not specifically characterised by his manual or instrumental work, but by performing this work in specific conditions and in specific social relations (apart from the consideration that purely physical labour does not exist and that even Taylor's[9] phrase of "trained gorilla" is a metaphor to indicate a limit in a certain direction: in any physical work, even the most degraded and mechanical, there exists a minimum of technical qualification, that is, a minimum of creative intellectual activity). And we have already observed that the entrepreneur, by virtue of his very function, must have to some degree a certain number of qualifications of an intellectual nature although his part in society is determined not by these, but by the general social relations which specifically characterise the position of the entrepreneur within industry.

All men are intellectuals, one could therefore say: but not all men have in society the function of intellectuals.[1]

When one distinguishes between intellectuals and non-intellectuals, one is referring in reality only to the immediate social function of the professional category of the intellectuals, that is, one has in mind the direction in which their specific professional activity is weighted, whether towards intellectual elaboration or towards muscular-nervous effort. This means that, although one can speak of intellectuals, one cannot speak of non-intellectuals, because non-intellectuals do not exist. But even the relationship between efforts of intellectual-cerebral elaboration and muscular-nervous effort is not always the same, so that there are varying degrees of specific intellectual activity. There is no human activity from which every form of intellectual participation can be excluded: *homo faber* cannot be separated from *homo sapiens*.[2] Each man, finally, outside his professional activity, carries on some form of intellectual activity, that is, he is a "philosopher", an artist, a man of taste, he participates in a particular conception of the world, has a conscious line of moral conduct, and therefore contributes to sustain a conception of the world or to modify it, that is, to bring into being new modes of thought.

The problem of creating a new stratum of intellectuals consists therefore in the critical elaboration of the intellectual activity that exists in everyone at a certain degree of development, modifying its relationship with the muscular-nervous effort towards a new equilibrium, and ensuring that the

9. Frederick Taylor (1856–1915), American efficiency expert who greatly influenced the organization of factory work. In *The Principles of Scientific Management* (1911), he declared that he believed an intelligent gorilla could be trained to handle pig iron more efficiently than any man.

1. Thus, because it can happen that everyone at some time fries a couple of eggs or sews up a tear in a jacket, we do not necessarily say that everyone is a cook or a tailor [Gramsci's note].

2. Literally, "man the thinker" (Latin). *Homo faber*: man the maker (Latin).

muscular-nervous effort itself, in so far as it is an element of a general practical activity, which is perpetually innovating the physical and social world, becomes the foundation of a new and integral conception of the world. The traditional and vulgarised type of the intellectual is given by the man of letters, the philosopher, the artist. Therefore journalists, who claim to be men of letters, philosophers, artists, also regard themselves as the "true" intellectuals. In the modern world, technical education, closely bound to industrial labour even at the most primitive and unqualified level, must form the basis of the new type of intellectual.

On this basis the weekly *Ordine Nuovo*[3] worked to develop certain forms of new intellectualism and to determine its new concepts, and this was not the least of the reasons for its success, since such a conception corresponded to latent aspirations and conformed to the development of the real forms of life. The mode of being of the new intellectual can no longer consist in eloquence, which is an exterior and momentary mover of feelings and passions, but in active participation in practical life, as constructor, organiser, "permanent persuader" and not just a simple orator (but superior at the same time to the abstract mathematical spirit); from technique-as-work one proceeds to technique-as-science and to the humanistic conception of history, without which one remains "specialised" and does not become "directive" (specialised and political).

Thus there are historically formed specialised categories for the exercise of the intellectual function. They are formed in connection with all social groups, but especially in connection with the more important, and they undergo more extensive and complex elaboration in connection with the dominant social group. One of the most important characteristics of any group that is developing towards dominance is its struggle to assimilate and to conquer "ideologically" the traditional intellectuals, but this assimilation and conquest is made quicker and more efficacious the more the group in question succeeds in simultaneously elaborating its own organic intellectuals.

The enormous development of activity and organisation of education in the broad sense in the societies that emerged from the medieval world is an index of the importance assumed in the modern world by intellectual functions and categories. Parallel with the attempt to deepen and to broaden the "intellectuality" of each individual, there has also been an attempt to multiply and narrow the various specialisations. This can be seen from educational institutions at all levels, up to and including the organisms that exist to promote so-called "high culture" in all fields of science and technology.

School is the instrument through which intellectuals of various levels are elaborated. The complexity of the intellectual function in different states can be measured objectively by the number and gradation of specialised schools: the more extensive the "area" covered by education and the more numerous the "vertical" "levels" of schooling, the more complex is the cultural world, the civilisation, of a particular state. A point of comparison can be found in the sphere of industrial technology: the industrialisation of a country can be measured by how well equipped it is in the production of

3. *New Order*, a socialist magazine edited by Gramsci in 1919–20.

machines with which to produce machines, and in the manufacture of ever more accurate instruments for making both machines and further instruments for making machines, etc. The country which is best equipped in the construction of instruments for experimental scientific laboratories and in the construction of instruments with which to test the first instruments, can be regarded as the most complex in the technical-industrial field, with the highest level of civilisation, etc. The same applies to the preparation of intellectuals and to the schools dedicated to this preparation; schools and institutes of high culture can be assimilated to each other. In this field also, quantity cannot be separated from quality. To the most refined technical-cultural specialisation there cannot but correspond the maximum possible diffusion of primary education and the maximum care taken to expand the middle grades numerically as much as possible. Naturally this need to provide the widest base possible for the selection and elaboration of the top intellectual qualifications—i.e. to give a democratic structure to high culture and top-level technology—is not without its disadvantages: it creates the possibility of vast crises of unemployment for the middle intellectual strata, and in all modern societies this actually takes place.

It is worth noting that the elaboration of intellectual strata in concrete reality does not take place on the terrain of abstract democracy but in accordance with very concrete traditional historical processes. Strata have grown up which traditionally "produce" intellectuals and these strata coincide with those which have specialised in "saving", i.e. the petty and middle landed bourgeoisie and certain strata of the petty and middle urban bourgeoisie. The varying distribution of different types of school (classical and professional) over the "economic" territory and the varying aspirations of different categories within these strata determine, or give form to, the production of various branches of intellectual specialisation. Thus in Italy the rural bourgeoisie produces in particular state functionaries and professional people, whereas the urban bourgeoisie produces technicians for industry. Consequently it is largely northern Italy which produces technicians and the South which produces functionaries and professional men.

The relationship between the intellectuals and the world of production is not as direct as it is with the fundamental social groups but is, in varying degrees, "mediated" by the whole fabric of society and by the complex of superstructures, of which the intellectuals are, precisely, the "functionaries". It should be possible both to measure the "organic quality" [*organicità*] of the various intellectual strata and their degree of connection with a fundamental social group, and to establish a gradation of their functions and of the superstructures from the bottom to the top (from the structural base upwards). What we can do, for the moment, is to fix two major superstructural "levels": the one that can be called "civil society", that is the ensemble of organisms commonly called "private", and that of "political society" or "the State". These two levels correspond on the one hand to the function of "hegemony" which the dominant group exercises throughout society and on the other hand to that of "direct domination" or command exercised through the State and "juridical" government. The functions in question are precisely organisational and connective. The intellectuals are the dominant group's "deputies" exercising the subaltern functions of social hegemony and political government. These comprise:

1. The "spontaneous" consent given by the great masses of the population to the general direction imposed on social life by the dominant fundamental group; this consent is "historically" caused by the prestige (and consequent confidence) which the dominant group enjoys because of its position and function in the world of production.

2. The apparatus of state coercive power which "legally" enforces discipline on those groups who do not "consent" either actively or passively. This apparatus is, however, constituted for the whole of society in anticipation of moments of crisis of command and direction when spontaneous consent has failed.

This way of posing the problem has as a result a considerable extension of the concept of intellectual, but it is the only way which enables one to reach a concrete approximation of reality. It also clashes with preconceptions of caste. The function of organising social hegemony and state domination certainly gives rise to a particular division of labour and therefore to a whole hierarchy of qualifications in some of which there is no apparent attribution of directive or organisational functions. For example, in the apparatus of social and state direction there exist a whole series of jobs of a manual and instrumental character (non-executive work, agents rather than officials or functionaries). It is obvious that such a distinction has to be made just as it is obvious that other distinctions have to be made as well. Indeed, intellectual activity must also be distinguished in terms of its intrinsic characteristics, according to levels which in moments of extreme opposition represent a real qualitative difference—at the highest level would be the creators of the various sciences, philosophy, art, etc., at the lowest the most humble "administrators" and divulgators of pre-existing, traditional, accumulated intellectual wealth.[4]

In the modern world the category of intellectuals, understood in this sense, has undergone an unprecedented expansion. The democratic-bureaucratic system has given rise to a great mass of functions which are not all justified by the social necessities of production, though they are justified by the political necessities of the dominant fundamental group. Hence Loria's[5] conception of the unproductive "worker" (but unproductive in relation to whom and to what mode of production?), a conception which could in part be justified if one takes account of the fact that these masses exploit their position to take for themselves a large cut out of the national income. Mass formation has standardised individuals both psychologically and in terms of individual qualification and has produced the same phenomena as with other standardised masses: competition which makes necessary organisations for the defence of professions, unemployment, over-production in the schools, emigration, etc.

1929–33 1948–51

4. Here again military organisation offers a model of complex gradations between subaltern officers, senior officers and general staff, not to mention the NCOs, whose importance is greater than is generally admitted. It is worth observing that all these parts feel a solidarity and indeed it is the lower strata that display the most blatant *esprit de corps*, from which they derive a certain "conceit" which is apt to lay them open to jokes and witticisms [Gramsci's note].

5. Achille Loria (1857–1943), Italian economic theorist.

ZORA NEALE HURSTON
1891–1960

Zora Neale Hurston's *Their Eyes Were Watching God* (1937) is said to be the most frequently taught text in U.S. colleges and universities, but few readers have paid attention to the rich body of her work—including other novels, stories, and cultural criticism. Hurston identified herself as a "literary anthropologist," a phrase that reflects her training in anthropology at Columbia University, her deep and abiding interest in folklore, and her commitment to the creative power of the literary imagination.

Born near Tuskegee, Alabama, Hurston grew up in Eatonville, Florida, the first incorporated, self-governing black township in the United States, where her father, a Baptist minister, served three terms as mayor. Her childhood experiences played a central role in the development of the characters and themes of her literary work. As Hurston's novels and her autobiography *Dust Tracks on a Road* (1942) attest, she felt an intimate bond to the customs, beliefs, and forms of speech of the African American community. Hurston studied between 1918 and 1924 at Howard University in Washington, D.C. Encouraged by Alain Locke, one of her teachers and a distinguished African American intellectual, she first submitted a story to the journal *Opportunity*, where it was published in December 1924. Hurston also contributed the story "Spunk" to Locke's groundbreaking collection *The New Negro* (1925).

In 1925 Hurston traveled to New York City, where she soon became one of the leading lights of the Harlem Renaissance, known both for her plays and stories and for her oral performances of black folklore and folktales. Helped by white patrons, she was able to attend Barnard College, studying with the eminent anthropologist Franz Boas, a professor at Columbia; she graduated in 1928. Her research in the South and in the Caribbean formed the basis of her landmark collection of African American folklore, *Mules and Men* (1935), which was followed by a second compilation, *Tell My Horse* (1938).

While undertaking ethnographic study in Haiti, Hurston completed *Their Eyes Were Watching God*. She had published one novel already—*Jonah's Gourd Vine* (1934), which focuses on a Baptist minister—and other novels would follow, including *Moses, Man of the Mountain* (1939), her retelling of the Exodus story. But *Their Eyes Were Watching God* is her masterpiece, an evocative, often painful, but ultimately celebratory account of its black heroine's quest for emotional and sexual fulfillment and personal freedom.

Hurston's defense of the language she uses in *Their Eyes Were Watching God*, "Characteristics of Negro Expression" (1934), had appeared three years earlier. In that essay, our first selection, she describes the rich, flexible resources of African American dialect and folk expression. Her subject is language in the broadest sense—including gestures and forms of music and dance—but she dwells particularly on African American speech, which had so often been mocked and ridiculed, misinterpreted and devalued. "Negro dialect" was suppressed by schools and attacked by contemporary critics of language and culture such as H. L. Mencken. Hurston praises and celebrates the linguistic prowess and cultural greatness of her people, even as she also points to (and calls attention to the flaws in) efforts by white artists to adapt distinctively African American styles and expressions in language and, especially, in music and dance.

Hurston's career peaked in the 1930s. Her later novels were less successful, and other writings were left unfinished. She had come under attack by some black writers, such as Richard Wright and Ralph Ellison, who blasted *Their Eyes Were Watch-*

ing God as a "minstrel novel" and her writing as "calculated burlesque"; moreover, the benefits she saw in a black-run community like Eatonville made her suspicious of demands for integration, a view that set her outside the African American intellectual mainstream in the 1950s. During the final decade of her life, she worked as a cleaning woman and at other menial jobs. She died in poverty, forgotten, with none of her books in print. In the early 1970s, the African American novelist Alice Walker wrote movingly of locating the approximate site of Hurston's unmarked grave; Walker's essays, particularly her comments on *Their Eyes Were Watching God*, were instrumental in reviving Hurston's reputation.

In her last novel, *Seraph on the Suwanee* (1948), Hurston focused on a white woman, a shift implying a view of artistic freedom that our second selection, "What White Publishers Won't Print" (1950), makes explicit. Though her emphasis is on the need for publishers, theater producers, editors, and audiences to accept a more honest and nuanced treatment of black and other minority characters, she argues here against any restrictions on subject matter. For Hurston, it is crucial that writers and readers strive to break through racial and ethnic stereotypes, even when readers find the new kinds of characters and themes unfamiliar and disorienting. She stresses, on the one hand, that the consciousness of black people is different (and not captured by the reductive, distorted versions in popular thought and in past and present literature). But on the other hand, she contends that all individuals have much in common: "Minorities," she explains, are "just like everybody else."

Though set in a specific political context, when cold war tensions seemed to make imperative a national unity that appeared to be unattainable without better understanding of racial and ethnic minorities, "What White Publishers Won't Print" is in large part a lively adaptation of an oft-repeated (and historically very important) argument. In the nineteenth century, Frederick Douglass and other African American abolitionists argued that black men and women, slave and free alike, must be portrayed and understood as authentic individuals; many twentieth-century black writers and critics, including Wright, Ellison, W. E. B. DU BOIS, LANGSTON HUGHES, and James Baldwin, similarly attacked stereotyping and argued for artistic freedom. Hurston's call for literary works about average and well-to-do African Americans is both a plea for realism and a criticism of the typical depiction of "Negro" characters as quaint or exceptional.

But Hurston's essay also bears witness to her ongoing literary, critical, and cultural disputes with her peers. In her judgment, because of their emphasis on politics they misleadingly represent black experience as primarily defined by white racism, from which there is no escape. Hurston stresses that the search for freedom is profoundly personal and cannot be captured by the category of race alone. As "What White Publishers Won't Print" reveals, Hurston insists that the independence to explore the inner lives of her characters, white as well as black, is essential both sociopolitically and artistically.

"Characteristics of Negro Expression" Keywords: Aesthetics, Identity, Language, Popular Culture, Race and Ethnicity Studies, Religion, Vernacular Language
"What White Publishers Won't Print" Keywords: Literary History, Nationhood, Print Culture, Race and Ethnicity Studies, Representation

Characteristics of Negro Expression

Drama

The Negro's universal mimicry is not so much a thing in itself as an evidence of something that permeates his entire self. And that thing is drama.

His very words are action words. His interpretation of the English language is in terms of pictures. One act described in terms of another. Hence the rich metaphor and simile.

The metaphor is of course very primitive. It is easier to illustrate than it is to explain because action came before speech. Let us make a parallel. Language is like money. In primitive communities actual goods, however bulky, are bartered for what one wants. This finally evolves into coin, the coin being not real wealth but a symbol of wealth. Still later even coin is abandoned for legal tender, and still later for checks in certain usages.

Every phase of Negro life is highly dramatized. No matter how joyful or how sad the case there is sufficient poise for drama. Everything is acted out. Unconsciously for the most part of course. There is an impromptu ceremony always ready for every hour of life. No little moment passes unadorned.

Now the people with highly developed languages have words for detached ideas. That is legal tender. "That-which-we-squat-on" has become "chair." "Groan-causer" has evolved into "spear," and so on. Some individuals even conceive of the equivalent of check words, like "ideation" and "pleonastic." Perhaps we might say that *Paradise Lost* and *Sartor Resartus*[1] are written in check words.

The primitive man exchanges descriptive words. His terms are all close-fitting. Frequently the Negro, even with detached words in his vocabulary—not evolved in him but transplanted on his tongue by contact—must add action to it to make it do. So we have "chop-axe," "sitting-chair," "cook-pot" and the like because the speaker has in his mind the picture of the object in use. Action. Everything illustrated. So we can say the white man thinks in a written language and the Negro thinks in hieroglyphics.

A bit of Negro drama familiar to all is the frequent meeting of two opponents who threaten to do atrocious murder one upon the other.

Who has not observed a robust young Negro chap posing upon a street corner, possessed of nothing but his clothing, his strength and his youth? Does he bear himself like a pauper? No, Louis XIV[2] could be no more insolent in his assurance. His eyes say plainly "Female, halt!" His posture exults "Ah, female, I am the eternal male, the giver of life. Behold in my hot flesh all the delights of this world. Salute me, I am strength." All this with a languid posture, there is no mistaking his meaning.

A Negro girl strolls past the corner lounger. Her whole body panging and posing. A slight shoulder movement that calls attention to her bust, that is all of a dare. A hippy undulation below the waist that is a sheaf of promises tied with conscious power. She is acting out "I'm a darned sweet woman and you know it."

1. A dense philosophical satire (1833) by the Scottish-born historian and essayist Thomas Carlyle. *Paradise Lost* (1667), epic poem by John Milton.

2. King of France (1638–1715); his reign (1673–1715) was a flowering of French art, literature, and extravagant style.

These little plays by strolling players are acted out daily in a dozen streets in a thousand cities, and no one ever mistakes the meaning.

Will to Adorn

The will to adorn is the second most notable characteristic in Negro expression. Perhaps his idea of ornament does not attempt to meet conventional standards, but it satisfies the soul of its creator.

In this respect the American Negro has done wonders to the English language. It has often been stated by etymologists that the Negro has introduced no African words to the language. This is true, but it is equally true that he has made over a great part of the tongue to his liking and has had his revision accepted by the ruling class. No one listening to a Southern white man talk could deny this. Not only has he softened and toned down strongly consonanted words like "aren't" to "aint" and the like, he has made new force words out of old feeble elements. Examples of this are "ham-shanked," "battle-hammed," "double-teen," "bodaciously," "muffle-jawed."

But the Negro's greatest contribution to the language is: (1) the use of metaphor and simile; (2) the use of the double descriptive; (3) the use of verbal nouns.

1. Metaphor and Simile
One at a time, like lawyers going to heaven.
You sho is propaganda.
Sobbing hearted.
I'll beat you till: (*a*) rope like okra, (*b*) slack like lime, (*c*) smell like onions.
Fatal for naked.
Kyting[3] along.
That's a lynch.
That's a rope.
Cloakers—deceivers.
Regular as pig-tracks.
Mule blood—black molasses.
Syndicating—gossiping.
Flambeaux—cheap café (lighted by flambeaux).
To put yo'self on de ladder.

2. The Double Descriptive
High-tall.
Little-tee-ninchy (tiny).
Low-down.
Top-superior.
Sham-polish.
Lady-people.
Kill-dead.
Hot-boiling.
Chop-axe.

3. Hurrying.

Sitting-chairs.
De watch wall.
Speedy-hurry.
More great and more better.

3. Verbal Nouns
She features somebody I know.
Funeralize.
Sense me into it.
Puts the shamery on him.
'Taint everybody you kin confidence.
I wouldn't friend with her.
Jooking—playing piano or guitar as it is done in Jook-houses (houses of ill-fame).
Uglying away.
I wouldn't scorn my name all up on you.
Bookooing (beaucoup) around—showing off.

Nouns from Verbs
Won't stand a broke.
She won't take a listen.
He won't stand straightening.
That is such a compliment.
That's a lynch.

The stark, trimmed phrases of the Occident seem too bare for the voluptuous child of the sun, hence the adornment. It arises out of the same impulse as the wearing of jewelry and the making of sculpture—the urge to adorn.

On the walls of the homes of the average Negro one always finds a glut of gaudy calendars, wall pockets and advertising lithographs. The sophisticated white man or Negro would tolerate none of these, even if they bore a likeness to the Mona Lisa.[4] No commercial art for decoration. Nor the calendar nor the advertisement spoils the picture for this lowly man. He sees the beauty in spite of the declaration of the Portland Cement Works or the butcher's announcement. I saw in Mobile a room in which there was an overstuffed mohair living-room suite, an imitation mahogany bed and chifforobe, a console victrola.[5] The walls were gaily papered with Sunday supplements of the *Mobile Register.* There were seven calendars and three wall pockets. One of them was decorated with a lace doily. The mantel-shelf was covered with a scarf of deep homemade lace, looped up with a huge bow of pink crepe paper. Over the door was a huge lithograph showing the Treaty of Versailles[6] being signed with a Waterman fountain pen.

It was grotesque, yes. But it indicated the desire for beauty. And decorating a decoration, as in the case of the doily on the gaudy wall pocket, did not seem out of place to the hostess. The feeling back of such an act is that there can never be enough of beauty, let alone too much. Perhaps she is right. We each have our standards of art, and thus are we all interested parties and so unfit to pass judgment upon the art concepts of others.

4. Painting (ca. 1504) by Leonardo da Vinci.
5. Brand of phonograph.
6. Peace treaty of 1919 that formally ended World War I.

Whatever the Negro does of his own volition he embellishes. His religious service is for the greater part excellent prose poetry. Both prayers and sermons are tooled and polished until they are true works of art. The supplication is forgotten in the frenzy of creation. The prayer of the white man is considered humorous in its bleakness. The beauty of the Old Testament does not exceed that of a Negro prayer.

Angularity

After adornment the next most striking manifestation of the Negro is Angularity. Everything that he touches becomes angular. In all African sculpture and doctrine of any sort we find the same thing.

Anyone watching Negro dancers will be struck by the same phenomenon. Every posture is another angle. Pleasing, yes. But an effect achieved by the very means which an European strives to avoid.

The pictures on the walls are hung at deep angles. Furniture is always set at an angle. I have instances of a piece of furniture in the *middle* of a wall being set with one end nearer the wall than the other to avoid the simple straight line.

Asymmetry

Asymmetry is a definite feature of Negro art. I have no samples of true Negro painting unless we count the African shields, but the sculpture and carvings are full of this beauty and lack of symmetry.

It is present in the literature, both prose and verse. I offer an example of this quality in verse from Langston Hughes:[7]

> I ain't gonna mistreat ma good gal any more,
> I'm just gonna kill her next time she makes me sore.
>
> I treats her kind but she don't do me right,
> She fights and quarrels most ever' night.
>
> I can't have no woman's got such low-down ways
> Cause de blue gum woman aint de style now'days.
>
> I brought her from the South and she's goin on back,
> Else I'll use her head for a carpet track.

It is the lack of symmetry which makes Negro dancing so difficult for white dancers to learn. The abrupt and unexpected changes. The frequent change of key and time are evidences of this quality in music. (Note the St. Louis Blues.)[8]

The dancing of the justly famous Bo-Jangles and Snake Hips[9] are excellent examples.

7. African American poet (1902–1967; see below); the poem is "Evil Woman" (1927).
8. Song written in 1914 by W. C. Handy, performed most notably by the blues singer Bessie Smith, and often called the most popular blues song ever written.
9. Nicknames of, respectively, the African American dancers Bill Robinson (1878–1949) and Earl Tucker (1905–1937).

The presence of rhythm and lack of symmetry are paradoxical, but there they are. Both are present to a marked degree. There is always rhythm, but it is the rhythm of segments. Each unit has a rhythm of its own, but when the whole is assembled it is lacking in symmetry. But easily workable to a Negro who is accustomed to the break in going from one part to another, so that he adjusts himself to the new tempo.

Dancing

Negro dancing is dynamic suggestion. No matter how violent it may appear to the beholder, every posture gives the impression that the dancer will do much more. For example, the performer flexes one knee sharply, assumes a ferocious face mask, thrusts the upper part of the body forward with clenched fists, elbows taut as in hard running or grasping a thrusting blade. That is all. But the spectator himself adds the picture of ferocious assault, hears the drums and finds himself keeping time with the music and tensing himself for the struggle. It is compelling insinuation. That is the very reason the spectator is held so rapt. He is participating in the performance himself—carrying out the suggestions of the performer.

The difference in the two arts is: the white dancer attempts to express fully; the Negro is restrained, but succeeds in gripping the beholder by forcing him to finish the action the performer suggests. Since no art ever can express all the variations conceivable, the Negro must be considered the greater artist, his dancing is realistic suggestion, and that is about all a great artist can do.

Negro Folklore

Negro folklore is not a thing of the past. It is still in the making. Its great variety shows the adaptability of the black man: nothing is too old or too new, domestic or foreign, high or low, for his use. God and the Devil are paired, and are treated no more reverently than Rockefeller and Ford.[1] Both of these men are prominent in folklore, Ford being particularly strong, and they talk and act like good-natured stevedores or mill-hands. Ole Massa is sometimes a smart man and often a fool. The automobile is ranged alongside of the oxcart. The angels and the apostles walk and talk like section hands.[2] And through it all walks Jack, the greatest culture hero of the South; Jack beats them all—even the Devil, who is often smarter than God.

Culture Heroes

The Devil is next after Jack as a culture hero. He can outsmart everyone but Jack. God is absolutely no match for him. He is good-natured and full of humor. The sort of person one may count on to help out in any difficulty.

Peter the Apostle is the third in importance. One need not look far for the explanation. The Negro is not a Christian really. The primitive gods are not deities of too subtle inner reflection; they are hardworking bodies who serve

1. Henry Ford (1863–1947), American automobile manufacturer and pioneer of the assembly line. John D. Rockefeller (1839–1937), U.S. oil magnate and philanthropist of enormous wealth.
2. Laborers in work gangs assigned to a section of a railroad.

their devotees just as laboriously as the suppliant serves them. Gods of physical violence, stopping at nothing to serve their followers. Now of all the apostles Peter is the most active. When the other ten fell back trembling in the garden, Peter wielded the blade on the posse.[3] Peter first and foremost in all action. The gods of no peoples have been philosophic until the people themselves have approached that state.

The rabbit, the bear, the lion, the buzzard, the fox are culture heroes from the animal world. The rabbit is far in the lead of all the others and is blood brother to Jack. In short, the trickster-hero of West Africa has been transplanted to America.

John Henry[4] is a culture hero in song, but no more so than Stacker Lee, Smokey Joe or Bad Lazarus. There are many, many Negroes who have never heard of any of the song heroes, but none who do not know John (Jack) and the rabbit.

EXAMPLES OF FOLKLORE AND THE MODERN CULTURE HERO

Why de Porpoise's Tail Is On Crosswise

Now, I want to tell you 'bout de porpoise. God had done made de world and everything. He set de moon and de stars in de sky. He got de fishes of de sea, and de fowls of de air completed.

He made de sun and hung it up. Then He made a nice gold track for it to run on. Then He said, "Now, Sun, I got everything made but Time. That's up to you. I want you to start out and go round de world on dis track just as fast as you kin make it. And de time it takes you to go and come, I'm going to call day and night." De Sun went zoonin' on cross de elements. Now, de porpoise was hanging round there and heard God what he tole de Sun, so he decided he'd take dat trip round de world hisself. He looked up and saw de Sun kytin' along, so he lit out too, him and dat Sun!

So de porpoise beat de Sun round de world by one hour and three minutes. So God said, "Aw naw, this aint gointer do! I didn't mean for nothin' to be faster than de Sun!" So God run dat porpoise for three days before he run him down and caught him, and took his tail off and put it on crossways to slow him up. Still he's de fastest thing in de water. And dat's why de porpoise got his tail on crossways.

Rockefeller and Ford

Once John D. Rockefeller and Henry Ford was woofing at each other. Rockefeller told Henry Ford he could build a solid gold road round the world. Henry Ford told him if he would he would look at it and see if he liked it, and if he did he would buy it and put one of his tin lizzies[5] on it.

3. See John 18.10–11: Peter draws a sword and cuts off the ear of a servant who is among those coming to seize Jesus.

4. Legendary and prodigiously strong black hero of American tall tales and ballads, and by far the best known of the "song heroes" named here (though in the 1930s the black bandleader Cab Calloway recorded songs featuring Stacker Lee and Smokey Joe).

5. Model T Fords (the first mass-produced car).

Originality

It has been said so often that the Negro is lacking in originality that it has almost become a gospel. Outward signs seem to bear this out. But if one looks closely its falsity is immediately evident.

It is obvious that to get back to original sources is much too difficult for any group to claim very much as a certainty. What we really mean by originality is the modification of ideas. The most ardent admirer of the great Shakespeare cannot claim first source even for him. It is his treatment of the borrowed material.

So if we look at it squarely, the Negro is a very original being. While he lives and moves in the midst of a white civilization, everything that he touches is reinterpreted for his own use. He has modified the language, mode of food preparation, practice of medicine, and most certainly the religion of his new country, just as he adapted to suit himself the Sheik haircut made famous by Rudolph Valentino.[6]

Everyone is familiar with the Negro's modification of the whites' musical instruments, so that his interpretation has been adopted by the white man himself and then reinterpreted. In so many words, Paul Whiteman[7] is giving an imitation of a Negro orchestra making use of white-invented musical instruments in a Negro way. Thus has arisen a new art in the civilized world, and thus has our so-called civilization come. The exchange and re-exchange of ideas between groups.

Imitation

The Negro, the world over, is famous as a mimic. But this in no way damages his standing as an original. Mimicry is an art in itself. If it is not, then all art must fall by the same blow that strikes it down. When sculpture, painting, acting, dancing, literature neither reflect nor suggest anything in nature or human experience we turn away with a dull wonder in our hearts at why the thing was done. Moreover, the contention that the Negro imitates from a feeling of inferiority is incorrect. He mimics for the love of it. The group of Negroes who slavishly imitate is small. The average Negro glories in his ways. The highly educated Negro the same. The self-despisement lies in a middle class who scorns to do or be anything Negro. "That's just like a Nigger" is the most terrible rebuke one can lay upon this kind. He wears drab clothing, sits through a boresome church service, pretends to have no interest in the community, holds beauty contests, and otherwise apes all the mediocrities of the white brother. The truly cultured Negro scorns him, and the Negro "farthest down" is too busy "spreading his junk" in his own way to see or care. He likes his own things best. Even the group who are not Negroes but belong to the "sixth race,"[8] buy such records as "Shake dat thing" and "Tight lak dat." They really enjoy hearing a good bible-beater preach, but wild horses could drag no such admission from them. Their ready-made expression is: "We done got away from all that now." Some refuse to countenance Negro music on the

6. Italian-born American actor (1895–1926), a star of silent films, including *The Sheik* (1921).
7. American conductor (1890–1967).
8. A new and higher race that will evolve in the Americas from a great amalgamation of all the current races of the earth, according to the teachings of theosophy, a system of mystic and occult speculation popular in the late 19th and early 20th century.

grounds that it is niggerism, and for that reason should be done away with. Roland Hayes[9] was thoroughly denounced for singing spirituals until he was accepted by white audiences. Langston Hughes is not considered a poet by this group because he writes of the man in the ditch, who is more numerous and real among us than any other.

But, this group aside, let us say that the art of mimicry is better developed in the Negro than in other racial groups. He does it as the mockingbird does it, for the love of it, and not because he wishes to be like the one imitated. I saw a group of small Negro boys imitating a cat defecating and the subsequent toilet of the cat. It was very realistic, and they enjoyed it as much as if they had been imitating a coronation ceremony. The dances are full of imitations of various animals. The buzzard lope, walking the dog, the pig's hind legs, holding the mule, elephant squat, pigeon's wing, falling off the log, seabord (imitation of an engine starting), and the like.

It is said that Negroes keep nothing secret, that they have no reserve. This ought not to seem strange when one considers that we are an outdoor people accustomed to communal life. Add this to all-permeating drama and you have the explanation.

There is no privacy in an African village. Loves, fights, possessions are, to misquote Woodrow Wilson, "Open disagreements openly arrived at."[1] The community is given the benefit of a good fight as well as a good wedding. An audience is a necessary part of any drama. We merely go with nature rather than against it.

Discord is more natural than accord. If we accept the doctrine of the survival of the fittest there are more fighting honors than there are honors for other achievements. Humanity places premiums on all things necessary to its well-being, and a valiant and good fighter is valuable in any community. So why hide the light under a bushel? Moreover, intimidation is a recognized part of warfare the world over, and threats certainly must be listed under that head. So that a great threatener must certainly be considered an aid to the fighting machine. So then if a man or woman is a facile hurler of threats why should he or she not show their wares to the community? Hence the holding of all quarrels and fights in the open. One relieves one's pent-up anger and at the same time earns laurels in intimidation. Besides, one does the community a service. There is nothing so exhilarating as watching well-matched opponents go into action. The entire world likes action, for that matter. Hence prize-fighters become millionaires.

Likewise lovemaking is a biological necessity the world over and an art among Negroes. So that a man or woman who is proficient sees no reason why the fact should not be moot.[2] He swaggers. She struts hippily about. Songs are built on the power to charm beneath the bedclothes. Here again we have individuals striving to excel in what the community considers an art. Then if all of his world is seeking a great lover, why should he not speak right out loud?

It is all in a viewpoint. Lovemaking and fighting in all their branches are high arts, other things are arts among other groups where they brag about

9. American tenor (1887–1977).
1. In an address to Congress on January 8, 1918, President Wilson (1856–1924; 28th U.S. president, 1913–21) spoke of "Open covenants of peace, openly arrived at."
2. Brought up.

their proficiency just as brazenly as we do about these things that others consider matters for conversation behind closed doors. At any rate, the white man is despised by Negroes as a very poor fighter individually, and a very poor lover. One Negro, speaking of white men, said, "White folks is alright when dey gits in de bank and on de law bench, but dey sho' kin lie about wimmen folks."

I pressed him to explain. "Well you see, white mens makes out they marries wimmen to look at they eyes, and they know they gits em for just what us gits em for. 'Nother thing, white mens say they goes clear round de world and wins all de wimmen folks way from they men folks. Dat's a lie too. They don't win nothin, they buys em. Now de way I figgers it, if a woman don't want me enough to be wid me, 'thout[3] I got to pay her, she kin rock right on, but these here white men don't know what to do wid a woman when they gits her—dat's how come they gives they wimmen so much. They got to. Us wimmen works jus as hard as us does an come home an sleep wid us every night. They own wouldn't do it and its de mens fault. Dese white men done fooled theyself bout dese wimmen.

"Now me, I keeps me some wimmens all de time. Dat's whut dey wuz put here for—us mens to use. Dat's right now, Miss. Y'all wuz put here so us mens could have some pleasure. Course I don't run round like heap uh men folks. But if my ole lady go way from me and stay more'n two weeks, I got to git me somebody, aint I?"

The Jook

Jook is the word for a Negro pleasure house. It may mean a bawdy house. It may mean the house set apart on public works where the men and women dance, drink and gamble. Often it is a combination of all these.

In past generations the music was furnished by "boxes," another word for guitars. One guitar was enough for a dance; to have two was considered excellent. Where two were playing one man played the lead and the other seconded him. The first player was "picking" and the second was "framming," that is, playing chords while the lead carried the melody by dexterous finger work. Sometimes a third player was added, and he played a tom-tom effect on the low strings. Believe it or not, this is excellent dance music.

Pianos soon came to take the place of the boxes, and now player-pianos and victrolas are in all of the Jooks.

Musically speaking, the Jook is the most important place in America. For in its smelly, shoddy confines has been born the secular music known as blues, and on blues has been founded jazz. The singing and playing in the true Negro style is called "jooking."

The songs grow by incremental repetition as they travel from mouth to mouth and from Jook to Jook for years before they reach outside ears. Hence the great variety of subject-matter in each song.

The Negro dances circulated over the world were also conceived inside the Jooks. They too make the round of Jooks and public works before going into the outside world.

3. Without, unless.

In this respect it is interesting to mention the Black Bottom. I have read several false accounts of its origin and name. One writer claimed that it got its name from the black sticky mud on the bottom of the Mississippi river. Other equally absurd statements gummed the press. Now the dance really originated in the Jook section of Nashville, Tennessee, around Fourth Avenue. This is a tough neighborhood known as Black Bottom—hence the name.

The Charleston is perhaps forty years old, and was danced up and down the Atlantic seaboard from North Carolina to Key West, Florida.

The Negro social dance is slow and sensuous. The idea in the Jook is to gain sensation, and not so much exercise. So that just enough foot movement is added to keep the dancers on the floor. A tremendous sex stimulation is gained from this. But who is trying to avoid it? The man, the woman, the time and the place have met. Rather, little intimate names are indulged in to heap fire on fire.

These too have spread to all the world.

The Negro theatre, as built up by the Negro, is based on Jook situations, with women, gambling, fighting, drinking. Shows like "Dixie to Broadway"[4] are only Negro in cast, and could just as well have come from pre-Soviet Russia.

Another interesting thing—Negro shows before being tampered with did not specialize in octoroon chorus girls. The girl who could hoist a Jook song from her belly and lam it against the front door of the theatre was the lead, even if she were as black as the hinges of hell. The question was "Can she jook?" She must also have a good belly wobble, and her hips must, to quote a popular work song, "Shake like jelly all over and be so broad, Lawd, Lawd, and be so broad." So that the bleached chorus is the result of a white demand and not the Negro's.

The woman in the Jook may be nappy headed and black, but if she is a good lover she gets there just the same. A favorite Jook song of the past has this to say:

Singer: It aint good looks dat takes you through dis world.
Audience: What is it, good mama?
Singer: Elgin movements[5] in your hips
Twenty years guarantee.

And it always brought down the house too.

Oh de white gal rides in a Cadillac,
De yaller[6] gal rides de same,
Black gal rides in a rusty Ford
But she gits dere just de same.

The sort of woman her men idealize is the type that is put forth in the theatre. The art-creating Negro prefers a not too thin woman who can shake like jelly all over as she dances and sings, and that is the type he put forth on the stage. She has been banished by the white producer and the Negro who takes his cue from the white.

4. A revue that opened on Broadway in 1924 featuring black performers, with music written by the black composer Will Vodery.

5. That is, the smooth movements of an Elgin watch.

6. Yellow (that is, mulatto).

Of course a black woman is never the wife of the upper class Negro in the North. This state of affairs does not obtain in the South, however. I have noted numerous cases where the wife was considerably darker than the husband. People of some substance, too.

This scornful attitude towards black women receives mouth sanction by the mud-sills.[7]

Even on the works and in the Jooks the black man sings disparagingly of black women. They say that she is evil. That she sleeps with her fists doubled up and ready for action. All over they are making a little drama of waking up a yaller wife and a black one.

A man is lying beside his yaller wife and wakes her up. She says to him, "Darling, do you know what I was dreaming when you woke me up?" He says, "No honey, what was you dreaming?" She says, "I dreamt I had done cooked you a big, fine dinner and we was setting down to eat out de same plate and I was setting on yo' lap jus huggin you and kissin you and you was so sweet."

Wake up a black woman, and before you kin git any sense into her she be done up and lammed you over the head four or five times. When you git her quiet she'll say, "Nigger, know whut I was dreamin when you woke me up?"

You say, "No honey, what was you dreamin?" She says, "I dreamt you shook yo' rusty fist under my nose and I split yo' head open wid a axe."

But in spite of disparaging fictitious drama, in real life the black girl is drawing on his account at the commissary. Down in the Cypress Swamp[8] as he swings his axe he chants:

Dat ole black gal, she keep on grumblin,
New pair shoes, new pair shoes,
I'm goint to buy her shoes and stockings
Slippers too, slippers too.

Then adds aside: "Blacker de berry, sweeter de juice."

To be sure the black gal is still in power, men are still cutting and shooting their way to her pillow. To the queen of the Jook!

Speaking of the influence of the Jook, I noted that Mae West[9] in "Sex" had much more flavor of the turpentine quarters[1] than she did of the white bawd. I know that the piece she played on the piano is a very old Jook composition. "Honey let yo' drawers hang low" had been played and sung in every Jook in the South for at least thirty-five years. It has always puzzled me why she thought it likely to be played in a Canadian bawdy house.

Speaking of the use of Negro material by white performers, it is astonishing that so many are trying it, and I have never seen one yet entirely realistic. They often have all the elements of the song, dance, or expression, but they are misplaced or distorted by the accent falling on the wrong element. Every one seems to think that the Negro is easily imitated when nothing is further from the truth. Without exception I wonder why the blackface comedians *are* blackface; it is a puzzle—good comedians, but darn poor niggers. Gershwin[2]

7. Those at the bottom of the social scale.
8. In southern Florida.
9. American actress (1892–1980), who began in burlesque and continued to specialize in double entendre in films; she wrote as well as starred in the 1926 play *Sex*.
1. The housing (usually shanties) for black workers who collected tree sap to be processed into turpentine.
2. George Gershwin (1898–1937), American composer who wrote both Broadway musicals and concert works that incorporated jazz elements, including *Rhapsody in Blue* (1924).

and the other "Negro" rhapsodists come under this same axe. Just about as Negro as caviar or Ann Pennington's[3] athletic Black Bottom. When the Negroes who knew the Black Bottom in its cradle saw the Broadway version they asked each other, "Is you learnt dat new Black Bottom yet?" Proof that it was not *their* dance.

And God only knows what the world has suffered from the white damsels who try to sing Blues.

The Negroes themselves have sinned also in this respect. In spite of the goings up and down on the earth, from the original Fisk Jubilee Singers[4] down to the present, there has been no genuine presentation of Negro songs to white audiences. The spirituals that have been sung around the world are Negroid to be sure, but so full of musicians' tricks that Negro congregations are highly entertained when they hear their old songs so changed. They never use the new style songs, and these are never heard unless perchance some daughter or son has been off to college and returns with one of the old songs with its face lifted, so to speak.

I am of the opinion that this trick style of delivery was originated by the Fisk Singers; Tuskegee and Hampton[5] followed suit and have helped spread this misconception of Negro spirituals. This Glee Club style has gone on so long and become so fixed among concert singers that it is considered quite authentic. But I say again, that not one concert singer in the world is singing the songs as the Negro song-makers sing them.

If anyone wishes to prove the truth of this let him step into some unfashionable Negro church and hear for himself.

To those who want to institute the Negro theatre, let me say it is already established. It is lacking in wealth, so it is not seen in the high places. A creature with a white head and Negro feet struts the Metropolitan boards. The real Negro theatre is in the Jooks and the cabarets. Self-conscious individuals may turn away the eye and say, "Let us search elsewhere for our dramatic art." Let 'em search. They certainly won't find it. Butter Beans and Susie,[6] Bo-Jangles and Snake Hips are the only performers of the real Negro school it has ever been my pleasure to behold in New York.

Dialect

If we are to believe the majority of writers of Negro dialect and the burnt-cork artists,[7] Negro speech is a weird thing, full of "ams" and "Ises." Fortunately we don't have to believe them. We may go directly to the Negro and let him speak for himself.

I know that I run the risk of being damned as an infidel for declaring that nowhere can be found the Negro who asks "am it?" nor yet his brother who announces "Ise uh gwinter." He exists only for a certain type of writers and performers.

3. American dancer and actress (1893–1971).

4. An ensemble formed in 1871 at Fisk University, a historically black institution that opened in 1866 in Nashville, Tennessee; it toured the United States and Europe to raise money for the school (the ensemble still exists).

5. Two schools begun as industrial training institutes, in Tuskegee, Alabama (founded 1881), and in Hampton, Virginia (founded 1868), respectively; both are now universities.

6. Married African American vaudeville entertainers, Jodie "Butterbeans" Edwards (1895–1967) and Susie Hawthorne (ca. 1896–1963), who toured together for almost 50 years.

7. That is, white performers who act in blackface, a form popularized in the 19th century that lasted into the 1950s.

Very few Negroes, educated or not, use a clear clipped "I." It verges more or less upon "Ah." I think the lip form is responsible for this to a great extent. By experiment the reader will find that a sharp "I" is very much easier with a thin taut lip than with a full soft lip. Like tightening violin strings.

If one listens closely one will note too that a word is slurred in one position in the sentence but clearly pronounced in another. This is particularly true of the pronouns. A pronoun as a subject is likely to be clearly enunciated, but slurred as an object. For example: "You better not let me ketch yuh."

There is a tendency in some localities to add the "h" to "it" and pronounce it "hit." Probably a vestige of old English. In some localities "if" is "ef."

In storytelling "so" is universally the connective. It is used even as an introductory word, at the very beginning of a story. In religious expression "and" is used. The trend in stories is to state conclusions; in religion, to enumerate.

I am mentioning only the most general rules in dialect because there are so many quirks that belong only to certain localities that nothing less than a volume would be adequate.

> Now He told me, He said: "You got the three witnesses. One is water, one is spirit, and one is blood. And these three correspond with the three in heben—Father, Son, and Holy Ghost."
>
> Now I ast Him about this lyin in sin and He give me a handful of seeds and He tole me to sow 'em in a bed and He tole me: "I want you to watch them seeds." The seeds come up about in places and He said: "Those seeds that come up, they died in the heart of the earth and quickened and come up and brought forth fruit. But those seeds that didn't come up, they died in the heart of the earth and rottened.
>
> "And a soul that dies and quickens through my spirit they will live forever, but those that dont never pray, they are lost forever."

(Rev. Jessie Jefferson.)[8]

1934

What White Publishers Won't Print

I have been amazed by the Anglo-Saxon's lack of curiosity about the internal lives and emotions of the Negroes, and for that matter, any non-Anglo-Saxon peoples within our borders, above the class of unskilled labor.

This lack of interest is much more important than it seems at first glance. It is even more important at this time than it was in the past. The internal affairs of the nation have bearings on the international stress and strain,[1] and this gap in the national literature now has tremendous weight in world affairs. National coherence and solidarity is implicit in a thorough understanding of the various groups within a nation, and this lack of knowledge about the internal emotions and behavior of the minorities cannot fail to bar

8. A local minister whom Hurston had observed.
1. The cold war—the post–World War II rivalry between the United States and the Soviet Union.

our understanding. Man, like all the other animals, fears and is repelled by that which he does not understand, and mere difference is apt to connote something malign.

The fact that there is no demand for incisive and full-dress stories around Negroes above the servant class is indicative of something of vast importance to this nation. This blank is NOT filled by the fiction built around upperclass Negroes exploiting the race problem. Rather, it tends to point it up. A college-bred Negro still is not a person like other folks, but an interesting problem, more or less. It calls to mind a story of slavery time. In this story, a master with more intellectual curiosity than usual, set out to see how much he could teach a particularly bright slave of his. When he had gotten him up to higher mathematics and to be a fluent reader of Latin, he called in a neighbor to show off his brilliant slave, and to argue that Negroes had brains just like the slave-owners had, and given the same opportunities, would turn out the same.

The visiting master of slaves looked and listened, tried to trap the literate slave in Algebra and Latin, and failing to do so in both, turned to his neighbor and said:

"Yes, he certainly knows his higher mathematics, and he can read Latin better than many white men I know, but I cannot bring myself to believe that he understands a thing that he is doing. It is all an aping of our culture. All on the outside. You are crazy if you think that it has changed him inside in the least. Turn him loose, and he will revert at once to the jungle. He is still a savage, and no amount of translating Virgil and Ovid[2] is going to change him. In fact, all you have done is to turn a useful savage into a dangerous beast."

That was in slavery time, yes, and we have come a long, long way since then, but the troubling thing is that there are still too many who refuse to believe in the ingestion and digestion of western culture as yet. Hence the lack of literature about the higher emotions and love life of upperclass Negroes and the minorities in general.

Publishers and producers are cool to the idea. Now, do not leap to the conclusion that editors and producers constitute a special class of unbelievers. That is far from true. Publishing houses and theatrical promoters are in business to make money. They will sponsor anything that they believe will sell. They shy away from romantic stories about Negroes and Jews because they feel that they know the public indifference to such works, unless the story or play involves racial tension. It can then be offered as a study in Sociology, with the romantic side subdued. They know the skepticism in general about the complicated emotions in the minorities. The average American just cannot conceive of it, and would be apt to reject the notion, and publishers and producers take the stand that they are not in business to educate, but to make money. Sympathetic as they might be, they cannot afford to be crusaders.

In proof of this, you can note various publishers and producers edging forward a little, and ready to go even further when the trial balloons show that the public is ready for it. This public lack of interest is the nut of the matter.

The question naturally arises as to the why of this indifference, not to say skepticism, to the internal life of educated minorities.

2. Roman poets: the *Aeneid* of Virgil (70–19 B.C.E.) and stories from the *Metamorphoses* of Ovid (43 B.C.E.–17 C.E.) were staples of the schoolroom for centuries.

The answer lies in what we may call THE AMERICAN MUSEUM OF UNNATURAL HISTORY.[3] This is an intangible built on folk belief. It is assumed that all non-Anglo-Saxons are uncomplicated stereotypes. Everybody knows all about them. They are lay figures mounted in the museum where all may take them in at a glance. They are made of bent wires without insides at all. So how could anybody write a book about the nonexistent?

The American Indian is a contraption of copper wires in an eternal war-bonnet, with no equipment for laughter, expressionless face and that says "How" when spoken to. His only activity is treachery leading to massacres. Who is so dumb as not to know all about Indians, even if they have never seen one, nor talked with anyone who ever knew one?

The American Negro exhibit is a group of two. Both of these mechanical toys are built so that their feet eternally shuffle, and their eyes pop and roll. Shuffling feet and those popping, rolling eyes denote the Negro, and no characterization is genuine without this monotony. One is seated on a stump picking away on his banjo and singing and laughing. The other is a most amoral character before a sharecropper's shack mumbling about injustice. Doing this makes him out to be a Negro "intellectual." It is as simple as all that.

The whole museum is dedicated to the convenient "typical." In there is the "typical" Oriental, Jew, Yankee, Westerner, Southerner, Latin, and even out-of-favor Nordics like the German. The Englishman "I say old chappie," and the gesticulating Frenchman. The least observant American can know them all at a glance. However, the public willingly accepts the untypical in Nordics, but feels cheated if the untypical is portrayed in others. The author of *Scarlet Sister Mary*[4] complained to me that her neighbors objected to her book on the grounds that she had the characters thinking, "and everybody know that Nigras don't think."

But for the national welfare, it is urgent to realize that the minorities do think, and think about something other than the race problem. That they are very human and internally, according to natural endowment, are just like everybody else. So long as this is not conceived, there must remain that feeling of unsurmountable difference, and difference to the average man means something bad. If people were made right, they would be just like him.

The trouble with the purely problem arguments is that they leave too much unknown. Argue all you will or may about injustice, but as long as the majority cannot conceive of a Negro or a Jew feeling and reacting inside just as they do, the majority will keep right on believing that people who do not look like them cannot possibly feel as they do, and conform to the established pattern. It is well known that there must be a body of waived matter, let us say, things accepted and taken for granted by all in a community before there can be that commonality of feeling. The usual phrase is having things in common. Until this is thoroughly established in respect to Negroes in America, as well as of other minorities, it will remain impossible for the majority to conceive of a Negro experiencing a deep and abiding love and not just the passion of sex. That a great mass of Negroes can be stirred by the pageants of Spring and

3. New York City's American Museum of Natural History opened in 1877; among its exhibits were dioramas of "primitive" life similar to those mockingly suggested by Hurston.

4. The Southern writer Julia Peterkin (1880–1961), whose fiction focused on the Gullahs of coastal South Carolina; this novel was published in 1928.

Fall; the extravaganza of summer, and the majesty of winter. That they can and do experience discovery of the numerous subtle faces as a foundation for a great and selfless love, and the diverse nuances that go to destroy that love as with others. As it is now, this capacity, this evidence of high and complicated emotions, is ruled out. Hence the lack of interest in a romance uncomplicated by the race struggle has so little appeal.

This insistence on defeat in a story where upperclass Negroes are portrayed perhaps says something from the subconscious of the majority. Involved in western culture, the hero or the heroine, or both, must appear frustrated and go down to defeat, somehow. Our literature reeks with it. Is it the same as saying, "You can translate Virgil, and fumble with the differential calculus, but can you really comprehend it? Can you cope with our subtleties?"

That brings us to the folklore of "reversion to type." This curious doctrine has such wide acceptance that it is tragic. One has only to examine the huge literature on it to be convinced. No matter how high we may *seem* to climb, put us under strain and we revert to type, that is, to the bush. Under a superficial layer of western culture, the jungle drums throb in our veins.

This ridiculous notion makes it possible for that majority who accept it to conceive of even a man like the suave and scholarly Dr. Charles S. Johnson[5] to hide a black cat's bone on his person, and indulge in a midnight voodoo ceremony, complete with leopard skin and drums, if threatened with the loss of the presidency of Fisk University, or the love of his wife. "Under the skin . . . better to deal with them in business, etc., but otherwise keep them at a safe distance and under control. I tell you, Carl Van Vechten,[6] think as you like, but they are just not like us."

The extent and extravagance of this notion reaches the ultimate in nonsense in the widespread belief that the Chinese have bizarre genitals, because of that eye-fold that makes their eyes seem to slant. In spite of the fact that no biology has ever mentioned any such difference in reproductive organs makes no matter. Millions of people believe it. "Did you know that a Chinese has . . ." Consequently, their quiet contemplative manner is interpreted as a sign of slyness and a treacherous inclination.

But the opening wedge for better understanding has been thrust into the crack. Though many Negroes denounced Carl Van Vechten's *Nigger Heaven* because of the title, and without ever reading it, the book, written in the deepest sincerity, revealed Negroes of wealth and culture to the white public. It created curiosity even when it aroused skepticism. It made folks want to know. Worth Tuttle Hedden's *The Other Room*[7] has definitely widened the opening. Neither of these well-written works take a romance of upperclass Negro life as the central theme, but the atmosphere and the background is there. These works should be followed up by some incisive and intimate stories from the inside.

The realistic story around a Negro insurance official, dentist, general practitioner, undertaker and the like would be most revealing. Thinly disguised

5. African American sociologist and educator (1893–1956), president of Fisk University from 1946 to 1956.

6. White American critic and novelist (1880–1964), whose works include *Nigger Heaven* (1926), a novel about Harlem life.

7. Prize-winning novel published in 1947; Hedden (1896–1985), a white woman, was a champion of rights for blacks and women.

fiction around the well known Negro names is not the answer, either. The "exceptional" as well as the Ol' Man Rivers[8] has been exploited all out of context already. Everybody is already resigned to the "exceptional" Negro, and willing to be entertained by the "quaint." To grasp the penetration of western civilization in a minority, it is necessary to know how the average behaves and lives. Books that deal with people like in Sinclair Lewis' *Main Street*[9] is the necessary metier. For various reasons, the average, struggling, nonmorbid Negro is the best-kept secret in America. His revelation to the public is the thing needed to do away with that feeling of difference which inspires fear, and which ever expresses itself in dislike.

It is inevitable that this knowledge will destroy many illusions and romantic traditions which America probably likes to have around. But then, we have no record of anybody sinking into a lingering death on finding out that there was no Santa Claus. The old world will take it in its stride. The realization that Negroes are no better nor no worse, and at times just as boring as everybody else, will hardly kill off the population of the nation.

Outside of racial attitudes, there is still another reason why this literature should exist. Literature and other arts are supposed to hold up the mirror to nature.[1] With only the fractional "exceptional" and the "quaint" portrayed, a true picture of Negro life in America cannot be. A great principle of national art has been violated.

These are the things that publishers and producers, as the accredited representatives of the American people, have not as yet taken into consideration sufficiently. Let there be light![2]

1950

8. "Ol' Man River" is the title of a song sung by a black dockworker in the American musical *Show Boat* (1927), written by Jerome Kern and Oscar Hammerstein II.

9. Satiric 1920 novel about small-town America by Lewis (1885–1961).

1. In Shakespeare's *Hamlet* (ca. 1600), Hamlet urges the players "to hold as 'twere the mirror up to nature" (3.2.20).

2. Genesis 1.3.

ERICH AUERBACH
1892–1957

A founder of modern academic comparative literature, Erich Auerbach is one of a number of brilliant European philologists who, displaced by the rise of fascism and World War II, settled in the United States during the 1930s and 1940s and who, during the 1950s, helped make Romance philology—a European discipline that studies cultures through historical analyses of their languages—a vital alternative to the New Criticism that was then dominating the study of literature in the United States. Auerbach's monumental study, *Mimesis: The Representation of Reality in Western Literature* (1946), was perhaps his attempt to salvage European humanism from fascism. "The challenge," he wrote to a student in 1938, "is not to grasp and digest all the evil that's happening—that's not too difficult—but much more to find a point of departure [*Ausgangspunkt*] for those historical forces that can be set against it." The work for which he is best remembered was written in Istanbul, where he had fled Nazi persecution, without access to libraries, books, journals, or even reliable critical editions of the literary texts discussed. In his epilogue, he speculates that his distance from the specialized libraries of Europe may have enabled him to write the book.

Auerbach was born in Berlin to a middle-class Jewish family. He attended the prestigious Französisches Gymnasium and universities in Berlin, Freiburg, and Munich before receiving a degree in law from the University of Heidelberg in 1913. After serving in the German army during World War I, he abandoned law to pursue studies in Romance languages; he received his doctorate from the University of Greifswald in 1921. From 1923 to 1929 he was on the staff of the Prussian State Library in Berlin, a position that enabled him to research and publish two books—a German translation of GIAMBATTISTA VICO's *New Science* (1926) and a book on DANTE, *Dante: Poet of the Secular World* (1929). In 1929 he succeeded Leo Spitzer as chair of Romance philology at the University of Marburg, remaining there until 1935, when the Nazis stripped him of his post. In 1936 Auerbach emigrated to Turkey, where he took on the task of creating a modernized European literature curriculum at the State University of Istanbul, staying until 1947. In 1947 he emigrated again, this time to the United States, where he taught at Pennsylvania State University and later became affiliated with the Institute for Advanced Studies at Princeton University. In 1950 he moved to Yale University, where in 1956 he was appointed Sterling Professor of Romance Philology. He died the following year. Auerbach's *Mimesis* stands among the highest achievements of literary philology, a discipline that counts Vico, FRIEDRICH SCHLEIERMACHER, and FRIEDRICH NIETZSCHE as its most illustrious forerunners, and EDWARD W. SAID and FREDRIC JAMESON as its most esteemed contemporary heirs.

In the epilogue to *Mimesis*, Auerbach notes that the starting point for his study of literary representations of reality was PLATO's discussion of mimesis—representation—in book 10 of the *Republic*. However, he approaches the perennial problem of literature's vexed relationships with truth and reality not, as Plato does, from a philosophical perspective but from the perspective of historical linguistics and literary stylistics. For Auerbach, mimesis does not primarily concern the faithfulness of correspondence between a particular text and something we might call "reality"; it is instead a matter of style—and the history of style—that, he argues, offers insight into characteristically Western means of perceiving and forming reality. His book provides a crucial link between classical notions of mimesis, which persisted through the end of the Enlightenment, and modern theorists' renewed interest in representation and its dynamics.

Our selection, "Odysseus' Scar," the first chapter of *Mimesis*, provides a memorable example of Auerbach's method of "partial investigation," which relies on minute contextualized observations of particular texts. Unlike New Critical close reading, which focuses on individual literary style divorced from cultural contexts, Auerbach's philological close reading scrutinizes and compares the dynamics of *cultural* styles. The essay begins with a reading of the scene near the end of Homer's *Odyssey* in which the hero, Odysseus, having returned to Ithaca after twenty years' absence, is recognized by the old housekeeper Euryclea from a scar on his thigh. Comparing Homer's narrative style in this scene with the Old Testament narrative of the sacrifice of Isaac, Auerbach describes two distinct styles of *realism*—two means of representing or inscribing "reality"—which we might call the Hellenistic and the Hebraic. Even though Odysseus's scar represents a focal point in the story—a point at which both past and present come together—no such temporal perspective emerges in Homer's narrative, Auerbach argues. Everything in Homer's style is presented as foreground: that is, as a local and temporal present that is absolute. All phenomena, including psychological processes, are fully externalized, fully visible, fixed in their temporal and spatial relationship. Homer's realism presents a uniformly illuminated and uniformly objective present. As a result, his narrative can be analyzed but not interpreted. The biblical style in the story of Abraham's sacrifice of Isaac presents a very different sort of realism—one fraught with background, in which temporal and spatial markers are mostly missing or symbolic, in which psychological motivation is complex but absent. Such a narrative style demands investigation and interpretation. Along the way Auerbach provocatively contrasts Greek and Hebrew syntax, social class, patriarchy, and preferred genres. While Auerbach depicts European literature as alternating between these two styles of realism, it is the latter, with its openness to ambiguity, contradiction, and plurality of meaning and reference, that most interests him.

Even as Auerbach's fascination with ambiguity in and interpretation of biblical narrative provides a bridge between nineteenth-century historicism and more recent New Historicism, it also displays his difference from contemporary historians, whose treatments of history are more open and relativistic. For Auerbach, the potential for indeterminacy in biblical realism is held in check by the process of figural interpretation—a process he describes in his famous essay "Figura" (1938) as establishing "a connection between two events or persons in such a way that the first signifies not only itself but also the second, while the second involves or fulfils the first." In a figural view of history, two events separated by historical time (for example, the sacrifice of Isaac and the crucifixion of Jesus) are connected by one figure; and the consciousness of their connection is, as Auerbach puts it, "a spiritual act." Auerbach's historicism, which he employs while analyzing modernist as well as ancient literature, is closer to that of medieval allegorical thinkers like Dante than to that articulated by contemporary historicist theory. The indeterminacy of historical interpretation often highlighted by contemporary theorists of history is for him delimited by the unifying process of figuration.

Auerbach's critics have maintained that the theoretical underpinnings of his historicism are indebted to an outdated medieval worldview, that he minimizes politics and economics, that he advocates a mystical humanism at odds with his radically relativist framework, and that his reluctance to propose universal laws of history clashes with his desire to describe the figural truth of history. But the sheer force of his original readings of an impressive range of European texts has inspired critics as different as NORTHROP FRYE, Fredric Jameson, and Edward W. Said, all of whom have found much of interest in his methods and wide-ranging claims.

***Mimesis: The Representation of Reality in Western Literature* Keywords:** The Canon/Tradition, Epic, Globalization, Language, Literary History, Narrative Theory, Philology, Realism, Representation

From Mimesis: The Representation of Reality in Western Literature[1]

Chapter 1. Odysseus' Scar

Readers of the *Odyssey*[2] will remember the well-prepared and touching scene in book 19, when Odysseus has at last come home, the scene in which the old housekeeper Euryclea, who had been his nurse, recognizes him by a scar on his thigh. The stranger has won Penelope's[3] good will; at his request she tells the housekeeper to wash his feet, which, in all old stories, is the

1. Translated by Willard R. Trask.
2. Greek epic attributed to Homer (ca. 8th c. B.C.E.); its hero is Odysseus.
3. Odysseus's faithful wife; during his long absence, many suitors urge her to marry again.

first duty of hospitality toward a tired traveler. Euryclea busies herself fetching water and mixing cold with hot, meanwhile speaking sadly of her absent master, who is probably of the same age as the guest, and who perhaps, like the guest, is even now wandering somewhere, a stranger; and she remarks how astonishingly like him the guest looks. Meanwhile Odysseus, remembering his scar, moves back out of the light; he knows that, despite his efforts to hide his identity, Euryclea will now recognize him, but he wants at least to keep Penelope in ignorance. No sooner has the old woman touched the scar than, in her joyous surprise, she lets Odysseus' foot drop into the basin; the water spills over, she is about to cry out her joy; Odysseus restrains her with whispered threats and endearments; she recovers herself and conceals her emotion. Penelope, whose attention Athena's[4] foresight had diverted from the incident, has observed nothing.

All this is scrupulously externalized and narrated in leisurely fashion. The two women express their feelings in copious direct discourse. Feelings though they are, with only a slight admixture of the most general considerations upon human destiny, the syntactical connection between part and part is perfectly clear, no contour is blurred. There is also room and time for orderly, perfectly well-articulated, uniformly illuminated descriptions of implements, ministrations, and gestures; even in the dramatic moment of recognition, Homer does not omit to tell the reader that it is with his right hand that Odysseus takes the old woman by the throat to keep her from speaking, at the same time that he draws her closer to him with his left. Clearly outlined, brightly and uniformly illuminated, men and things stand out in a realm where everything is visible; and not less clear—wholly expressed, orderly even in their ardor—are the feelings and thoughts of the persons involved.

In my account of the incident I have so far passed over a whole series of verses which interrupt it in the middle. There are more than seventy of these verses—while to the incident itself some forty are devoted before the interruption and some forty after it. The interruption, which comes just at the point when the housekeeper recognizes the scar—that is, at the moment of crisis—describes the origin of the scar, a hunting accident which occurred in Odysseus' boyhood, at a boar hunt, during the time of his visit to his grandfather Autolycus. This first affords an opportunity to inform the reader about Autolycus, his house, the precise degree of the kinship, his character, and, no less exhaustively than touchingly, his behavior after the birth of his grandson; then follows the visit of Odysseus, now grown to be a youth; the exchange of greetings, the banquet with which he is welcomed, sleep and waking, the early start for the hunt, the tracking of the beast, the struggle, Odysseus' being wounded by the boar's tusk, his recovery, his return to Ithaca, his parents' anxious questions—all is narrated, again with such a complete externalization of all the elements of the story and of their interconnections as to leave nothing in obscurity. Not until then does the narrator return to Penelope's chamber, not until then, the digression having run its course, does Euryclea, who had recognized the scar before the digression began, let Odysseus' foot fall back into the basin.

The first thought of a modern reader—that this is a device to increase suspense—is, if not wholly wrong, at least not the essential explanation of this

4. Greek goddess of wisdom, who favors the wily Odysseus.

Homeric procedure. For the element of suspense is very slight in the Homeric poems; nothing in their entire style is calculated to keep the reader or hearer breathless. The digressions are not meant to keep the reader in suspense, but rather to relax the tension. And this frequently occurs, as in the passage before us. The broadly narrated, charming, and subtly fashioned story of the hunt, with all its elegance and self-sufficiency, its wealth of idyllic pictures, seeks to win the reader over wholly to itself as long as he is hearing it, to make him forget what had just taken place during the foot-washing. But an episode that will increase suspense by retarding the action must be so constructed that it will not fill the present entirely, will not put the crisis, whose resolution is being awaited, entirely out of the reader's mind, and thereby destroy the mood of suspense; the crisis and the suspense must continue, must remain vibrant in the background. But Homer—and to this we shall have to return later—knows no background. What he narrates is for the time being the only present, and fills both the stage and the reader's mind completely. So it is with the passage before us. When the young Euryclea (vv. 401ff.) sets the infant Odysseus on his grandfather Autolycus' lap after the banquet, the aged Euryclea, who a few lines earlier had touched the wanderer's foot, has entirely vanished from the stage and from the reader's mind.

Goethe and Schiller,[5] who, though not referring to this particular episode, exchanged letters in April 1797 on the subject of "the retarding element" in the Homeric poems in general, put it in direct opposition to the element of suspense—the latter word is not used, but is clearly implied when the "retarding" procedure is opposed, as something proper to epic, to tragic procedure (letters of April 19, 21, and 22). The "retarding element," the "going back and forth" by means of episodes, seems to me, too, in the Homeric poems, to be opposed to any tensional and suspensive striving toward a goal, and doubtless Schiller is right in regard to Homer when he says that what he gives us is "simply the quiet existence and operation of things in accordance with their natures"; Homer's goal is "already present in every point of his progress." But both Schiller and Goethe raise Homer's procedure to the level of a law for epic poetry in general, and Schiller's words quoted above are meant to be universally binding upon the epic poet, in contradistinction from the tragic. Yet in both modern and ancient times, there are important epic works which are composed throughout with no "retarding element" in this sense but, on the contrary, with suspense throughout, and which perpetually "rob us of our emotional freedom"—which power Schiller will grant only to the tragic poet. And besides it seems to me undemonstrable and improbable that this procedure of Homeric poetry was directed by aesthetic considerations or even by an aesthetic feeling of the sort postulated by Goethe and Schiller. The effect, to be sure, is precisely that which they describe, and is, furthermore, the actual source of the conception of epic which they themselves hold, and with them all writers decisively influenced by classical antiquity. But the true cause of the impression of "retardation" appears to me to lie elsewhere—namely, in the need of the Homeric style to leave nothing which it mentions half in darkness and unexternalized.

5. Friedrich von Schiller (1759–1803), German poet, philosopher, dramatist, and historian. Johann Wolfgang von Goethe (1749–1832), German poet, playwright, and novelist.

The excursus upon the origin of Odysseus' scar is not basically different from the many passages in which a newly introduced character, or even a newly appearing object or implement, though it be in the thick of a battle, is described as to its nature and origin; or in which, upon the appearance of a god, we are told where he last was, what he was doing there, and by what road he reached the scene; indeed, even the Homeric epithets[6] seem to me in the final analysis to be traceable to the same need for an externalization of phenomena in terms perceptible to the senses. Here is the scar, which comes up in the course of the narrative; and Homer's feeling simply will not permit him to see it appear out of the darkness of an unilluminated past; it must be set in full light, and with it a portion of the hero's boyhood—just as, in the *Iliad*, when the first ship is already burning and the Myrmidons[7] finally arm that they may hasten to help, there is still time not only for the wonderful simile of the wolf, not only for the order of the Myrmidon host, but also for a detailed account of the ancestry of several subordinate leaders (16, vv. 155ff.). To be sure, the aesthetic effect thus produced was soon noticed and thereafter consciously sought; but the more original cause must have lain in the basic impulse of the Homeric style: to represent phenomena in a fully externalized form, visible and palpable in all their parts, and completely fixed in their spatial and temporal relations. Nor do psychological processes receive any other treatment: here too nothing must remain hidden and unexpressed. With the utmost fullness, with an orderliness which even passion does not disturb, Homer's personages vent their inmost hearts in speech; what they do not say to others, they speak in their own minds, so that the reader is informed of it. Much that is terrible takes place in the Homeric poems, but it seldom takes place wordlessly: Polyphemus talks to Odysseus; Odysseus talks to the suitors when he begins to kill them; Hector[8] and Achilles talk at length, before battle and after; and no speech is so filled with anger or scorn that the particles[9] which express logical and grammatical connections are lacking or out of place. This last observation is true, of course, not only of speeches but of the presentation in general. The separate elements of a phenomenon are most clearly placed in relation to one another; a large number of conjunctions, adverbs, particles, and other syntactical tools, all clearly circumscribed and delicately differentiated in meaning, delimit persons, things, and portions of incidents in respect to one another, and at the same time bring them together in a continuous and ever flexible connection; like the separate phenomena themselves, their relationships—their temporal, local, causal, final, consecutive, comparative, concessive, antithetical, and conditional limitations—are brought to light in perfect fullness; so that a continuous rhythmic procession of phenomena passes by, and never is there a form left fragmentary or half-illuminated, never a lacuna, never a gap, never a glimpse of unplumbed depths.

6. Word (often compound adjectives) repeatedly used to describe people or things in Homer's epics (e.g., "wine-dark sea").
7. The host of warriors under the command of Achilles, the greatest fighter among the Greeks, during the Trojan War. The events of the *Iliad*, an epic also ascribed to Homer, precede those of the *Odyssey*, and the poem appears to have been composed first.
8. Trojan hero, killed by the Greek Achilles in the *Iliad*. Polyphemus: the Cyclops Odysseus encounters and blinds during his return home from Troy in the *Odyssey*.
9. Words expressing modes of thought or moods (used frequently in classical Greek).

And this procession of phenomena takes place in the foreground—that is, in a local and temporal present which is absolute. One might think that the many interpolations, the frequent moving back and forth, would create a sort of perspective in time and place; but the Homeric style never gives any such impression. The way in which any impression of perspective is avoided can be clearly observed in the procedure for introducing episodes, a syntactical construction with which every reader of Homer is familiar; it is used in the passage we are considering, but can also be found in cases when the episodes are much shorter. To the word scar (v. 393) there is first attached a relative clause ("which once long ago a boar . . ."), which enlarges into a voluminous syntactical parenthesis; into this an independent sentence unexpectedly intrudes (v. 396: "A god himself gave him . . ."), which quietly disentangles itself from syntactical subordination, until, with verse 399, an equally free syntactical treatment of the new content begins a new present which continues unchallenged until, with verse 467 ("The old woman now touched it . . ."), the scene which had been broken off is resumed. To be sure, in the case of such long episodes as the one we are considering, a purely syntactical connection with the principal theme would hardly have been possible; but a connection with it through perspective would have been all the easier had the content been arranged with that end in view; if, that is, the entire story of the scar had been presented as a recollection which awakens in Odysseus' mind at this particular moment. It would have been perfectly easy to do; the story of the scar had only to be inserted two verses earlier, at the first mention of the word scar, where the motifs "Odysseus" and "recollection" were already at hand. But any such subjectivistic-perspectivistic procedure, creating a foreground and background, resulting in the present lying open to the depths of the past, is entirely foreign to the Homeric style; the Homeric style knows only a foreground, only a uniformly illuminated, uniformly objective present. And so the excursus does not begin until two lines later, when Euryclea has discovered the scar—the possibility for a perspectivistic connection no longer exists, and the story of the wound becomes an independent and exclusive present.

The genius of the Homeric style becomes even more apparent when it is compared with an equally ancient and equally epic style from a different world of forms. I shall attempt this comparison with the account of the sacrifice of Isaac, a homogeneous narrative produced by the so-called Elohist.[1] The King James version[2] translates the opening as follows (Genesis 22:1): "And it came to pass after these things, that God did tempt Abraham, and said to him, Abraham! and he said, Behold, here I am." Even this opening startles us when we come to it from Homer. Where are the two speakers? We are not told. The reader, however, knows that they are not normally to be found together in one place on earth, that one of them, God, in order to speak to Abraham, must come from somewhere, must enter the earthly realm from some unknown heights or depths. Whence does he come, whence does he call to Abraham? We are not told. He does not come, like Zeus or Poseidon,

1. Author of one of the common collections of oral traditions (ca. 9th c. B.C.E.) that served as a source for the Hebrew scriptures, distinguished by referring to God as *Elohim* instead of *Yahweh* in stories set before the time of Moses. Isaac: the son of Abraham, the founder of the Jewish people.

2. An English translation of the Bible (1611) commissioned during the reign of James I (1603–25) to be the official version used by the Church of England; its use became widespread in all Protestant churches and it had enormous influence on literature written in English.

from the Aethiopians,[3] where he has been enjoying a sacrificial feast. Nor are we told anything of his reasons for tempting Abraham so terribly. He has not, like Zeus, discussed them in set speeches with other gods gathered in council; nor have the deliberations in his own heart been presented to us; unexpected and mysterious, he enters the scene from some unknown height or depth and calls: Abraham! It will at once be said that this is to be explained by the particular concept of God which the Jews held and which was wholly different from that of the Greeks. True enough—but this constitutes no objection. For how is the Jewish concept of God to be explained? Even their earlier God of the desert was not fixed in form and content, and was alone; his lack of form, his lack of local habitation, his singleness, was in the end not only maintained but developed even further in competition with the comparatively far more manifest gods of the surrounding Near Eastern world. The concept of God held by the Jews is less a cause than a symptom of their manner of comprehending and representing things.

This becomes still clearer if we now turn to the other person in the dialogue, to Abraham. Where is he? We do not know. He says, indeed: Here I am—but the Hebrew word means only something like "behold me," and in any case is not meant to indicate the actual place where Abraham is, but a moral position in respect to God, who has called to him—Here am I awaiting thy command. Where he is actually, whether in Beersheba[4] or elsewhere, whether indoors or in the open air, is not stated; it does not interest the narrator, the reader is not informed; and what Abraham was doing when God called to him is left in the same obscurity. To realize the difference, consider Hermes' visit to Calypso,[5] for example, where command, journey, arrival and reception of the visitor, situation and occupation of the person visited, are set forth in many verses; and even on occasions when gods appear suddenly and briefly, whether to help one of their favorites or to deceive or destroy some mortal whom they hate, their bodily forms, and usually the manner of their coming and going, are given in detail. Here, however, God appears without bodily form (yet he "appears"), coming from some unspecified place—we only hear his voice, and that utters nothing but a name, a name without an adjective, without a descriptive epithet for the person spoken to, such as is the rule in every Homeric address; and of Abraham too nothing is made perceptible except the words in which he answers God: *Hinne-ni*, Behold me here—with which, to be sure, a most touching gesture expressive of obedience and readiness is suggested, but it is left to the reader to visualize it. Moreover the two speakers are not on the same level: if we conceive of Abraham in the foreground, where it might be possible to picture him as prostrate or kneeling or bowing with outspread arms or gazing upward, God is not there too: Abraham's words and gestures are directed toward the depths of the picture or upward, but in any case the undetermined, dark place from which the voice comes to him is not in the foreground.

After this opening, God gives his command,[6] and the story itself begins: everyone knows it; it unrolls with no episodes in a few independent sentences

3. That is, Ethiopia. Zeus: chief god of the Greeks. Poseidon: Greek god of the sea (at the beginning of *Odyssey* 1, he is described as feasting among the Ethiopians).
4. The southernmost city of Old Testament Israel.
5. In the *Odyssey*, the nymph who detained Odysseus for 7 years until Zeus—his orders carried by Hermes, the messenger god—commanded her to release the hero.
6. That is, to offer Isaac as a burnt offering (Genesis 22.2).

whose syntactical connection is of the most rudimentary sort. In this atmosphere it is unthinkable that an implement, a landscape through which the travelers passed, the serving-men, or the ass, should be described, that their origin or descent or material or appearance or usefulness should be set forth in terms of praise; they do not even admit an adjective: they are serving-men, ass, wood, and knife, and nothing else, without an epithet; they are there to serve the end which God has commanded; what in other respects they were, are, or will be, remains in darkness. A journey is made, because God has designated the place where the sacrifice is to be performed; but we are told nothing about the journey except that it took three days, and even that we are told in a mysterious way: Abraham and his followers rose "early in the morning" and "went unto" the place of which God had told him; on the third day he lifted up his eyes and saw the place from afar. That gesture is the only gesture, is indeed the only occurrence during the whole journey, of which we are told; and though its motivation lies in the fact that the place is elevated, its uniqueness still heightens the impression that the journey took place through a vacuum; it is as if, while he traveled on, Abraham had looked neither to the right nor to the left, had suppressed any sign of life in his followers and himself save only their footfalls.

Thus the journey is like a silent progress through the indeterminate and the contingent, a holding of the breath, a process which has no present, which is inserted, like a blank duration, between what has passed and what lies ahead, and which yet is measured: three days! Three such days positively demand the symbolic interpretation which they later received. They began "early in the morning." But at what time on the third day did Abraham lift up his eyes and see his goal? The text says nothing on the subject. Obviously not "late in the evening," for it seems that there was still time enough to climb the mountain and make the sacrifice. So "early in the morning" is given, not as an indication of time, but for the sake of its ethical significance; it is intended to express the resolution, the promptness, the punctual obedience of the sorely tried Abraham. Bitter to him is the early morning in which he saddles his ass, calls his serving-men and his son Isaac, and sets out; but he obeys, he walks on until the third day, then lifts up his eyes and sees the place. Whence he comes, we do not know, but the goal is clearly stated: Jeruel[7] in the land of Moriah. What place this is meant to indicate is not clear—"Moriah" especially may be a later correction of some other word. But in any case the goal was given, and in any case it is a matter of some sacred spot which was to receive a particular consecration by being connected with Abraham's sacrifice. Just as little as "early in the morning" serves as a temporal indication does "Jeruel in the land of Moriah" serve as a geographical indication; and in both cases alike, the complementary indication is not given, for we know as little of the hour at which Abraham lifted up his eyes as we do of the place from which he set forth—Jeruel is significant not so much as the goal of an earthly journey, in its geographical relation to other places, as through its special election, through its relation to God, who designated it as the scene of the act, and therefore it must be named.

7. The place-name appears only in 2 Chronicles 20.16 as the site of a battle. It is not mentioned in Genesis. It is possible Auerbach has in mind the name that Abraham subsequently gives to the mountain on which the sacrifice takes place, Jehovahjireh (in Hebrew, "the Lord will see"; Genesis 22.14).

In the narrative itself, a third chief character appears: Isaac. While God and Abraham, the serving-men, the ass, and the implements are simply named, without mention of any qualities or any other sort of definition, Isaac once receives an appositive; God says, "Take Isaac, thine only son, whom thou lovest." But this is not a characterization of Isaac as a person, apart from his relation to his father and apart from the story; he may be handsome or ugly, intelligent or stupid, tall or short, pleasant or unpleasant—we are not told. Only what we need to know about him as a personage in the action, here and now, is illuminated, so that it may become apparent how terrible Abraham's temptation is, and that God is fully aware of it. By this example of the contrary, we see the significance of the descriptive adjectives and digressions of the Homeric poems; with their indications of the earlier and as it were absolute existence of the persons described, they prevent the reader from concentrating exclusively on a present crisis; even when the most terrible things are occurring, they prevent the establishment of an overwhelming suspense. But here, in the story of Abraham's sacrifice, the overwhelming suspense is present; what Schiller makes the goal of the tragic poet—to rob us of our emotional freedom, to turn our intellectual and spiritual powers (Schiller says "our activity") in one direction, to concentrate them there[8]—is effected in this Biblical narrative, which certainly deserves the epithet epic.

We find the same contrast if we compare the two uses of direct discourse. The personages speak in the Bible story too; but their speech does not serve, as does speech in Homer, to manifest, to externalize thoughts—on the contrary, it serves to indicate thoughts which remain unexpressed. God gives his command in direct discourse, but he leaves his motives and his purpose unexpressed; Abraham, receiving the command, says nothing and does what he has been told to do. The conversation between Abraham and Isaac on the way to the place of sacrifice is only an interruption of the heavy silence and makes it all the more burdensome. The two of them, Isaac carrying the wood and Abraham with fire and a knife, "went together." Hesitantly, Isaac ventures to ask about the ram, and Abraham gives the well-known answer.[9] Then the text repeats: "So they went both of them together." Everything remains unexpressed.

It would be difficult, then, to imagine styles more contrasted than those of these two equally ancient and equally epic texts. On the one hand, externalized, uniformly illuminated phenomena, at a definite time and in a definite place, connected together without lacunae in a perpetual foreground; thoughts and feeling completely expressed; events taking place in leisurely fashion and with very little of suspense. On the other hand, the externalization of only so much of the phenomena as is necessary for the purpose of the narrative, all else left in obscurity; the decisive points of the narrative alone are emphasized, what lies between is nonexistent; time and place are undefined and call for interpretation; thoughts and feeling remain unexpressed, are only suggested by the silence and the fragmentary speeches; the whole, permeated with the most unrelieved suspense and directed toward a single goal (and to that extent far more of a unity), remains mysterious and "fraught with background."

8. See Schiller's "On Tragic Art" (1792) and "On the Pleasure We Derive from Tragic Representation" (1792) for statements on tragedy.

9. "My son, God will provide himself a lamb for a burnt offering" (Genesis 22.8).

I will discuss this term in some detail, lest it be misunderstood. I said above that the Homeric style was "of the foreground" because, despite much going back and forth, it yet causes what is momentarily being narrated to give the impression that it is the only present, pure and without perspective. A consideration of the Elohistic text teaches us that our term is capable of a broader and deeper application. It shows that even the separate personages can be represented as possessing "background"; God is always so represented in the Bible, for he is not comprehensible in his presence, as is Zeus; it is always only "something" of him that appears, he always extends into depths. But even the human beings in the Biblical stories have greater depths of time, fate, and consciousness than do the human beings in Homer; although they are nearly always caught up in an event engaging all their faculties, they are not so entirely immersed in its present that they do not remain continually conscious of what has happened to them earlier and elsewhere; their thoughts and feelings have more layers, are more entangled. Abraham's actions are explained not only by what is happening to him at the moment, nor yet only by his character (as Achilles' actions by his courage and his pride, and Odysseus' by his versatility and foresightedness), but by his previous history; he remembers, he is constantly conscious of, what God has promised him and what God has already accomplished for him—his soul is torn between desperate rebellion and hopeful expectation; his silent obedience is multilayered, has background. Such a problematic psychological situation as this is impossible for any of the Homeric heroes, whose destiny is clearly defined and who wake every morning as if it were the first day of their lives: their emotions, though strong, are simple and find expression instantly.

How fraught with background, in comparison, are characters like Saul and David![1] How entangled and stratified are such human relations as those between David and Absalom, between David and Joab![2] Any such "background" quality of the psychological situation as that which the story of Absalom's death and its sequel (II Samuel 18 and 19, by the so-called Jahvist[3]) rather suggests than expresses, is unthinkable in Homer. Here we are confronted not merely with the psychological processes of characters whose depth of background is veritably abysmal, but with a purely geographical background too. For David is absent from the battlefield; but the influence of his will and his feelings continues to operate, they affect even Joab in his rebellion and disregard for the consequences of his actions; in the magnificent scene with the two messengers,[4] both the physical and psychological background is fully manifest, though the latter is never expressed. With this, compare, for example, how Achilles, who sends Patroclus[5] first to scout and then into battle, loses almost all "presentness" so long as he is not physically present. But the most important thing is the "multilayeredness" of the individual character; this is hardly to be met with in Homer, or at

1. King of ancient Israel (d. ca. 970 B.C.E.); he succeeded Saul, the first king, who at one point out of jealousy sought to kill him (see 1 Samuel).

2. King David's nephew; disobeying the king's orders, Joab killed David's son Absalom, who was leading a revolt against him. As he was dying, David cursed Joab (2 Samuel 15–18; 1 Kings 2.5–6).

3. The conjectured author of the earliest oral tradition that was a source for the Hebrew scriptures; throughout it, God is called *Yahweh*.

4. From the first messenger, David learns that his forces have won; from the second, that Absalom is dead (2 Samuel 18.28–33).

5. In the *Iliad*, Achilles' closest friend; anger and grief at his death (at the hands of Hector) draw Achilles back into battle.

most in the form of a conscious hesitation between two possible courses of action; otherwise, in Homer, the complexity of the psychological life is shown only in the succession and alternation of emotions; whereas the Jewish writers are able to express the simultaneous existence of various layers of consciousness and the conflict between them.

The Homeric poems, then, though their intellectual, linguistic, and above all syntactical culture appears to be so much more highly developed, are yet comparatively simple in their picture of human beings; and no less so in their relation to the real life which they describe in general. Delight in physical existence is everything to them, and their highest aim is to make that delight perceptible to us. Between battles and passions, adventures and perils, they show us hunts, banquets, palaces and shepherds' cots,[6] athletic contests and washing days—in order that we may see the heroes in their ordinary life, and seeing them so, may take pleasure in their manner of enjoying their savory present, a present which sends strong roots down into social usages, landscape, and daily life. And thus they bewitch us and ingratiate themselves to us until we live with them in the reality of their lives; so long as we are reading or hearing the poems, it does not matter whether we know that all this is only legend, "make-believe." The oft-repeated reproach that Homer is a liar takes nothing from his effectiveness, he does not need to base his story on historical reality, his reality is powerful enough in itself; it ensnares us, weaving its web around us, and that suffices him. And this "real" world into which we are lured, exists for itself, contains nothing but itself; the Homeric poems conceal nothing, they contain no teaching and no secret second meaning. Homer can be analyzed, as we have essayed to do here, but he cannot be interpreted. Later allegorizing trends have tried their arts of interpretation upon him, but to no avail. He resists any such treatment; the interpretations are forced and foreign, they do not crystallize into a unified doctrine. The general considerations which occasionally occur (in our episode, for example, v. 360: that in misfortune men age quickly) reveal a calm acceptance of the basic facts of human existence, but with no compulsion to brood over them, still less any passionate impulse either to rebel against them or to embrace them in an ecstasy of submission.

It is all very different in the Biblical stories. Their aim is not to bewitch the senses, and if nevertheless they produce lively sensory effects, it is only because the moral, religious, and psychological phenomena which are their sole concern are made concrete in the sensible matter of life. But their religious intent involves an absolute claim to historical truth. The story of Abraham and Isaac is not better established than the story of Odysseus, Penelope, and Euryclea; both are legendary. But the Biblical narrator, the Elohist, had to believe in the objective truth of the story of Abraham's sacrifice—the existence of the sacred ordinances of life rested upon the truth of this and similar stories. He had to believe in it passionately; or else (as many rationalistic interpreters believed and perhaps still believe) he had to be a conscious liar—no harmless liar like Homer, who lied to give pleasure, but a political liar with a definite end in view, lying in the interest of a claim to absolute authority.

6. Cottages.

To me, the rationalistic interpretation seems psychologically absurd; but even if we take it into consideration, the relation of the Elohist to the truth of his story still remains a far more passionate and definite one than is Homer's relation. The Biblical narrator was obliged to write exactly what his belief in the truth of the tradition (or, from the rationalistic standpoint, his interest in the truth of it) demanded of him—in either case, his freedom in creative or representative imagination was severely limited; his activity was perforce reduced to composing an effective version of the pious tradition. What he produced, then, was not primarily oriented toward "realism" (if he succeeded in being realistic, it was merely a means, not an end); it was oriented toward truth. Woe to the man who did not believe it! One can perfectly well entertain historical doubts on the subject of the Trojan War or of Odysseus' wanderings, and still, when reading Homer, feel precisely the effects he sought to produce; but without believing in Abraham's sacrifice, it is impossible to put the narrative of it to the use for which it was written. Indeed, we must go even further. The Bible's claim to truth is not only far more urgent than Homer's, it is tyrannical—it excludes all other claims. The world of the Scripture stories is not satisfied with claiming to be a historically true reality—it insists that it is the only real world, is destined for autocracy. All other scenes, issues, and ordinances have no right to appear independently of it, and it is promised that all of them, the history of all mankind, will be given their due place within its frame, will be subordinated to it. The Scripture stories do not, like Homer's, court our favor, they do not flatter us that they may please us and enchant us—they seek to subject us, and if we refuse to be subjected we are rebels.

Let no one object that this goes too far, that not the stories, but the religious doctrine, raises the claim to absolute authority; because the stories are not, like Homer's, simply narrated "reality." Doctrine and promise are incarnate in them and inseparable from them; for that very reason they are fraught with "background" and mysterious, containing a second, concealed meaning. In the story of Isaac, it is not only God's intervention at the beginning and the end, but even the factual and psychological elements which come between, that are mysterious, merely touched upon, fraught with background; and therefore they require subtle investigation and interpretation, they demand them. Since so much in the story is dark and incomplete, and since the reader knows that God is a hidden God, his effort to interpret it constantly finds something new to feed upon. Doctrine and the search for enlightenment are inextricably connected with the physical side of the narrative—the latter being more than simple "reality"; indeed they are in constant danger of losing their own reality, as very soon happened when interpretation reached such proportions that the real vanished.

If the text of the Biblical narrative, then, is so greatly in need of interpretation on the basis of its own content, its claim to absolute authority forces it still further in the same direction. Far from seeking, like Homer, merely to make us forget our own reality for a few hours, it seeks to overcome our reality: we are to fit our own life into its world, feel ourselves to be elements in its structure of universal history. This becomes increasingly difficult the further our historical environment is removed from that of the Biblical books; and if these nevertheless maintain their claim to absolute authority, it is inevitable that they themselves be adapted through interpretative transformation. This was for a long time comparatively easy; as late as the European Middle Ages it was possible to represent Biblical events as ordinary phenomena of contemporary life, the methods of interpretation themselves forming the basis for such a treatment. But when, through too great a change in environment and through the awakening of a critical consciousness, this becomes impossible, the Biblical claim to absolute authority is jeopardized; the method of interpretation is scorned and rejected, the Biblical stories become ancient legends, and the doctrine they had contained, now dissevered from them, becomes a disembodied image.

As a result of this claim to absolute authority, the method of interpretation spread to traditions other than the Jewish. The Homeric poems present a definite complex of events whose boundaries in space and time are clearly delimited; before it, beside it, and after it, other complexes of events, which do not depend upon it, can be conceived without conflict and without difficulty. The Old Testament, on the other hand, presents universal history: it begins with the beginning of time, with the creation of the world, and will end with the Last Days, the fulfilling of the Covenant, with which the world will come to an end. Everything else that happens in the world can only be conceived as an element in this sequence; into it everything that is known about the world, or at least everything that touches upon the history of the Jews, must be fitted as an ingredient of the divine plan; and as this too became possible only by interpreting the new material as it poured in, the need for interpretation reaches out beyond the original Jewish-Israelitish realm of reality—for example to Assyrian, Babylonian, Persian, and Roman history; interpretation in a determined direction becomes a general method of comprehending reality; the new and strange world which now comes into view and which, in the form in which it presents itself, proves to be wholly unutilizable within the Jewish religious frame, must be so interpreted that it can find a place there. But this process nearly always also reacts upon the frame, which requires enlarging and modifying. The most striking piece of interpretation of this sort occurred in the first century of the Christian era, in consequence of Paul's mission to the Gentiles: Paul and the Church Fathers[7] reinterpreted the entire Jewish tradition as a succession of figures prognosticating the appearance of Christ, and assigned the Roman Empire its proper place in the divine plan of salvation. Thus while, on the one hand, the reality of the Old Testament presents itself as complete truth with a claim to sole authority, on the other hand that very claim forces it to a constant interpretative change in its own content; for millennia it undergoes an incessant and active development with the life of man in Europe.

The claim of the Old Testament stories to represent universal history, their insistent relation—a relation constantly redefined by conflicts—to a single and hidden God, who yet shows himself and who guides universal history by promise and exaction, gives these stories an entirely different perspective from any the Homeric poems can possess. As a composition, the Old Testament is incomparably less unified than the Homeric poems, it is more obviously pieced together—but the various components all belong to one concept

7. Early writers and teachers of the Christian Church (1st–6th c.), including ST. AUGUSTINE (354–430). St. Paul (d. ca. 67 C.E.), Roman Jew whose conversion to Christianity is recorded in Acts of the New Testament; he went on three missionary journeys in Asia Minor and Greece.

of universal history and its interpretation. If certain elements survived which did not immediately fit in, interpretation took care of them; and so the reader is at every moment aware of the universal religio-historical perspective which gives the individual stories their general meaning and purpose. The greater the separateness and horizontal disconnection of the stories and groups of stories in relation to one another, compared with the *Iliad* and the *Odyssey*, the stronger is their general vertical connection, which holds them all together and which is entirely lacking in Homer. Each of the great figures of the Old Testament, from Adam to the prophets, embodies a moment of this vertical connection. God chose and formed these men to the end of embodying his essence and will—yet choice and formation do not coincide, for the latter proceeds gradually, historically, during the earthly life of him upon whom the choice has fallen. How the process is accomplished, what terrible trials such a formation inflicts, can be seen from our story of Abraham's sacrifice. Herein lies the reason why the great figures of the Old Testament are so much more fully developed, so much more fraught with their own biographical past, so much more distinct as individuals, than are the Homeric heroes. Achilles and Odysseus are splendidly described in many well-ordered words, epithets cling to them, their emotions are constantly displayed in their words and deeds—but they have no development, and their life-histories are clearly set forth once and for all. So little are the Homeric heroes presented as developing or having developed, that most of them—Nestor, Agamemnon,[8] Achilles—appear to be of an age fixed from the very first. Even Odysseus, in whose case the long lapse of time and the many events which occurred offer so much opportunity for biographical development, shows almost nothing of it. Odysseus on his return is exactly the same as he was when he left Ithaca two decades earlier. But what a road, what a fate, lie between the Jacob[9] who cheated his father out of his blessing and the old man whose favorite son has been torn to pieces by a wild beast!—between David the harp player, persecuted by his lord's jealousy, and the old king, surrounded by violent intrigues, whom Abishag the Shunnamite warmed in his bed, and he knew her not![1] The old man, of whom we know how he has become what he is, is more of an individual than the young man; for it is only during the course of an eventful life that men are differentiated into full individuality; and it is this history of a personality which the Old Testament presents to us as the formation undergone by those whom God has chosen to be examples. Fraught with their development, sometimes even aged to the verge of dissolution, they show a distinct stamp of individuality entirely foreign to the Homeric heroes. Time can touch the latter only outwardly, and even that change is brought to our observation as little as possible; whereas the stern hand of God is ever upon the Old Testament figures; he has not only made them once and for all and chosen them, but he continues to work upon them, bends them and kneads them, and, without destroying them in essence, produces from them forms which their youth gave no grounds for anticipating. The objection

8. King of Mycenae, and leader of the Greeks in the Trojan War. Nestor: king of Pylos, and the eldest of the Greek warriors in the *Iliad*.

9. Younger son of Isaac, who deceived his blind father to cheat his elder brother Esau out of the firstborn's birthright (Genesis 27). Jacob's own sons would trick him into believing that his favorite, their brother Joseph, had been killed by "an evil beast" (37.33).

1. That is, he did not have sexual relations with the young virgin from Shunem brought to warm him (1 Kings 1.1–3).

that the biographical element of the Old Testament often springs from the combination of several legendary personages does not apply; for this combination is a part of the development of the text. And how much wider is the pendulum swing of their lives than that of the Homeric heroes! For they are bearers of the divine will, and yet they are fallible, subject to misfortune and humiliation—and in the midst of misfortune and in their humiliation their acts and words reveal the transcendent majesty of God. There is hardly one of them who does not, like Adam, undergo the deepest humiliation—and hardly one who is not deemed worthy of God's personal intervention and personal inspiration. Humiliation and elevation go far deeper and far higher than in Homer, and they belong basically together. The poor beggar Odysseus is only masquerading, but Adam is really cast down, Jacob really a refugee, Joseph[2] really in the pit and then a slave to be bought and sold. But their greatness, rising out of humiliation, is almost superhuman and an image of God's greatness. The reader clearly feels how the extent of the pendulum's swing is connected with the intensity of the personal history—precisely the most extreme circumstances, in which we are immeasurably forsaken and in despair, or immeasurably joyous and exalted, give us, if we survive them, a personal stamp which is recognized as the product of a rich existence, a rich development. And very often, indeed generally, this element of development gives the Old Testament stories a historical character, even when the subject is purely legendary and traditional.

Homer remains within the legendary with all his material, whereas the material of the Old Testament comes closer and closer to history as the narrative proceeds; in the stories of David the historical report predominates. Here too, much that is legendary still remains, as for example the story of David and Goliath;[3] but much—and the most essential—consists in things which the narrators knew from their own experience or from firsthand testimony. Now the difference between legend and history is in most cases easily perceived by a reasonably experienced reader. It is a difficult matter, requiring careful historical and philological training, to distinguish the true from the synthetic or the biased in a historical presentation; but it is easy to separate the historical from the legendary in general. Their structure is different. Even where the legendary does not immediately betray itself by elements of the miraculous, by the repetition of well-known standard motives, typical patterns and themes, through neglect of clear details of time and place, and the like, it is generally quickly recognizable by its composition. It runs far too smoothly. All cross-currents, all friction, all that is casual, secondary to the main events and themes, everything unresolved, truncated, and uncertain, which confuses the clear progress of the action and the simple orientation of the actors, has disappeared. The historical event which we witness, or learn from the testimony of those who witnessed it, runs much more variously, contradictorily, and confusedly; not until it has produced results in a definite domain are we able, with their help, to classify it to a certain extent; and how often the order to which we think we have attained becomes doubtful again,

2. Youngest son of Jacob and Rachel, sold by his elder brothers into slavery in Egypt (Genesis 37). Adam is "cast down" by his expulsion from Eden and by his need to labor (Genesis 3.17–24), and Jacob, after fleeing from the anger of his brother Esau, stays away for years.

3. Philistine giant killed by David (1 Samuel 17).

how often we ask ourselves if the data before us have not led us to a far too simple classification of the original events! Legend arranges its material in a simple and straightforward way; it detaches it from its contemporary historical context, so that the latter will not confuse it; it knows only clearly outlined men who act from few and simple motives and the continuity of whose feelings and actions remains uninterrupted. In the legends of martyrs, for example, a stiff-necked and fanatical persecutor stands over against an equally stiff-necked and fanatical victim; and a situation so complicated—that is to say, so real and historical—as that in which the "persecutor" Pliny finds himself in his celebrated letter to Trajan on the subject of the Christians,[4] is unfit for legend. And that is still a comparatively simple case. Let the reader think of the history which we are ourselves witnessing; anyone who, for example, evaluates the behavior of individual men and groups of men at the time of the rise of National Socialism[5] in Germany, or the behavior of individual peoples and states before and during the last war,[6] will feel how difficult it is to represent historical themes in general, and how unfit they are for legend; the historical comprises a great number of contradictory motives in each individual, a hesitation and ambiguous groping on the part of groups; only seldom (as in the last war) does a more or less plain situation, comparatively simple to describe, arise, and even such a situation is subject to division below the surface, is indeed almost constantly in danger of losing its simplicity; and the motives of all the interested parties are so complex that the slogans of propaganda can be composed only through the crudest simplification—with the result that friend and foe alike can often employ the same ones. To write history is so difficult that most historians are forced to make concessions to the technique of legend.

It is clear that a large part of the life of David as given in the Bible contains history and not legend. In Absalom's rebellion, for example, or in the scenes from David's last days, the contradictions and crossing of motives both in individuals and in the general action have become so concrete that it is impossible to doubt the historicity of the information conveyed. Now the men who composed the historical parts are often the same who edited the older legends too; their peculiar religious concept of man in history, which we have attempted to describe above, in no way led them to a legendary simplification of events; and so it is only natural that, in the legendary passages of the Old Testament, historical structure is frequently discernible—of course, not in the sense that the traditions are examined as to their credibility according to the methods of scientific criticism; but simply to the extent that the tendency to a smoothing down and harmonizing of events, to a simplification of motives, to a static definition of characters which avoids conflict, vacillation, and development, such as are natural to legendary structure, does not predominate in the Old Testament world of legend. Abraham, Jacob, or even Moses[7] produces a more concrete, direct, and historical impression than the figures of the Homeric world—not because they are better described in terms of sense

4. As Roman governor of Bithynia (111–ca. 112 C.E.), Pliny the Younger (ca. 61–ca. 112) sent a letter to the emperor Trajan (53–117; emperor 98–117) to inquire about his policy of prosecuting Christians.
5. That is, Nazism, the doctrines of the National Socialist German Workers' Party (founded 1919), led from 1920 to 1945 by Adolph Hitler.
6. That is, World War I.
7. Biblical lawgiver and prophet who led the exodus from Egypt.

(the contrary is the case) but because the confused, contradictory multiplicity of events, the psychological and factual cross-purposes, which true history reveals, have not disappeared in the representation but still remain clearly perceptible. In the stories of David, the legendary, which only later scientific criticism makes recognizable as such, imperceptibly passes into the historical; and even in the legendary, the problem of the classification and interpretation of human history is already passionately apprehended—a problem which later shatters the framework of historical composition and completely overruns it with prophecy; thus the Old Testament, in so far as it is concerned with human events, ranges through all three domains: legend, historical reporting, and interpretative historical theology.

Connected with the matters just discussed is the fact that the Greek text seems more limited and more static in respect to the circle of personages involved in the action and to their political activity. In the recognition scene with which we began, there appears, aside from Odysseus and Penelope, the housekeeper Euryclea, a slave whom Odysseus' father Laertes had bought long before. She, like the swineherd Eumaeus, has spent her life in the service of Laertes' family; like Eumaeus, she is closely connected with their fate, she loves them and shares their interests and feelings. But she has no life of her own, no feelings of her own; she has only the life and feelings of her master. Eumaeus too, though he still remembers that he was born a freeman and indeed of a noble house (he was stolen as a boy), has, not only in fact but also in his own feeling, no longer a life of his own, he is entirely involved in the life of his masters. Yet these two characters are the only ones whom Homer brings to life who do not belong to the ruling class. Thus we become conscious of the fact that in the Homeric poems life is enacted only among the ruling class—others appear only in the role of servants to that class. The ruling class is still so strongly patriarchal, and still itself so involved in the daily activities of domestic life, that one is sometimes likely to forget their rank. But they are unmistakably a sort of feudal aristocracy, whose men divide their lives between war, hunting, marketplace councils, and feasting, while the women supervise the maids in the house. As a social picture, this world is completely stable; wars take place only between different groups of the ruling class; nothing ever pushes up from below. In the early stories of the Old Testament the patriarchal condition is dominant too, but since the people involved are individual nomadic or half-nomadic tribal leaders, the social picture gives a much less stable impression; class distinctions are not felt. As soon as the people completely emerges—that is, after the exodus from Egypt—its activity is always discernible, it is often in ferment, it frequently intervenes in events not only as a whole but also in separate groups and through the medium of separate individuals who come forward; the origins of prophecy seem to lie in the irrepressible politico-religious spontaneity of the people. We receive the impression that the movements emerging from the depths of the people of Israel-Judah must have been of a wholly different nature from those even of the later ancient democracies—of a different nature and far more elemental.

With the more profound historicity and the more profound social activity of the Old Testament text, there is connected yet another important distinction from Homer: namely, that a different conception of the elevated style and of the sublime is to be found here. Homer, of course, is not afraid to let the realism of daily life enter into the sublime and tragic; our episode of the scar is an example, we see how the quietly depicted, domestic scene of the foot-washing is incorporated into the pathetic and sublime action of Odysseus' homecoming. From the rule of the separation of styles which was later almost universally accepted and which specified that the realistic depiction of daily life was incompatible with the sublime and had a place only in comedy or, carefully stylized, in idyl[8]—from any such rule Homer is still far removed. And yet he is closer to it than is the Old Testament. For the great and sublime events in the Homeric poems take place far more exclusively and unmistakably among the members of a ruling class; and these are far more untouched in their heroic elevation than are the Old Testament figures, who can fall much lower in dignity (consider, for example, Adam, Noah, David, Job[9]); and finally, domestic realism, the representation of daily life, remains in Homer in the peaceful realm of the idyllic, whereas, from the very first, in the Old Testament stories, the sublime, tragic, and problematic take shape precisely in the domestic and commonplace: scenes such as those between Cain and Abel, between Noah and his sons,[1] between Abraham, Sarah, and Hagar, between Rebekah,[2] Jacob, and Esau, and so on, are inconceivable in the Homeric style. The entirely different ways of developing conflicts are enough to account for this. In the Old Testament stories the peace of daily life in the house, in the fields, and among the flocks, is undermined by jealousy over election and the promise of a blessing, and complications arise which would be utterly incomprehensible to the Homeric heroes. The latter must have palpable and clearly expressible reasons for their conflicts and enmities, and these work themselves out in free battles; whereas, with the former, the perpetually smouldering jealousy and the connection between the domestic and the spiritual, between the paternal blessing and the divine blessing, lead to daily life being permeated with the stuff of conflict, often with poison. The sublime influence of God here reaches so deeply into the everyday that the two realms of the sublime and the everyday are not only actually unseparated but basically inseparable.

We have compared these two texts, and, with them, the two kinds of style they embody, in order to reach a starting point for an investigation into the literary representation of reality in European culture. The two styles, in their opposition, represent basic types: on the one hand fully externalized description, uniform illumination, uninterrupted connection, free expression, all events in the foreground, displaying unmistakable meanings, few elements of historical development and of psychological perspective; on the other hand, certain parts brought into high relief, others left obscure, abruptness, suggestive influence of the unexpressed, "background" quality,

8. A poem (usually short) that presents simple scenes of pastoral or rustic life.
9. A just and upright man who is brought low to test his faith in God, as described in the book of Job. Noah: the biblical builder of the ark who later became drunk on his own wine (see the following note).
1. While Noah was drunk, his son Canaan saw his nakedness and told his brothers, who, without looking, covered their father; for this, Noah cursed Canaan (Genesis 9.20–27). Cain and Abel: sons of Adam and Eve; because Cain was jealous that Abel's offerings to God were preferred, he killed his younger brother (Genesis 4.1–8).
2. Wife of Isaac; she helped Jacob scheme against Esau. Sarah: Abraham's wife; at her urging, her Egyptian servant Hagar bore Abraham a son, Ishmael, but after Sarah bore Isaac, Hagar and her son were sent into the wilderness (Genesis 16, 21.1–21).

multiplicity of meanings and the need for interpretation, universal-historical claims, development of the concept of the historically becoming, and preoccupation with the problematic.

Homer's realism is, of course, not to be equated with classical-antique realism in general; for the separation of styles, which did not develop until later, permitted no such leisurely and externalized description of everyday happenings; in tragedy[3] especially there was no room for it; furthermore, Greek culture very soon encountered the phenomena of historical becoming and of the "multilayeredness" of the human problem, and dealt with them in its fashion; in Roman realism, finally, new and native concepts are added. We shall go into these later changes in the antique representation of reality when the occasion arises; on the whole, despite them, the basic tendencies of the Homeric style, which we have attempted to work out, remained effective and determinant down into late antiquity.

Since we are using the two styles, the Homeric and the Old Testament, as starting points, we have taken them as finished products, as they appear in the texts; we have disregarded everything that pertains to their origins, and thus have left untouched the question whether their peculiarities were theirs from the beginning or are to be referred wholly or in part to foreign influences. Within the limits of our purpose, a consideration of this question is not necessary; for it is in their full development, which they reached in early times, that the two styles exercised their determining influence upon the representation of reality in European literature.

1946

3. A form that developed after the *Iliad* and *Odyssey* were composed.

WALTER BENJAMIN
1892–1940

"It has always been one of the primary tasks of art to create a demand whose hour of full satisfaction has not yet come," remarks Walter Benjamin in his celebrated essay "The Work of Art in the Age of Its Technological Reproducibility" (1936–39). The same could be said of Benjamin's criticism itself. During his lifetime, he was considered, by a small coterie of admirers such as the philosopher THEODOR ADORNO, one of the most original and promising writers on literature, language, and aesthetics of his generation; but at the time of his premature death fleeing the Nazis in 1940, his name had passed into obscurity both within and outside Germany. The publication in 1955 of a collection of his works in a German edition sponsored by Adorno spurred renewed attention, and since the 1970s Benjamin has become one of the most highly esteemed critics of the twentieth century; he is seen as an innovator in diverse fields, including Marxist literary criticism, deconstruction, historiography, and media studies. A broad speculative account of the interaction of industrial production and modern aesthetics, "The Work of Art in the Age of Its Technological Reproducibility" has had particular influence in contemporary film and visual studies and is considered a fundamental work of cultural studies.

Born in Berlin into a wealthy Jewish family, Benjamin was first educated by private tutors, later attending boarding school and the University of Freiburg. He continued his studies in Berlin and Munich, but settled in Berne, Switzerland, in 1917 to avoid being drafted into the German army in World War I. In 1919 he received his doctorate from the university there; his thesis, *The Concept of Criticism in German Romanticism*, was published the following year. Returning to Berlin in 1920, he wrote essays and newspaper articles as he worked on a translation of the important nineteenth-century French poet Charles Baudelaire, building a significant reputation as a cultural critic. Under financial pressure from his father, who wanted him to take a position in a bank, Benjamin considered starting a used book business but finally decided to pursue an academic career. To complete an additional requirement for a teaching post in the German university system, he wrote a second dissertation in 1925, *The Origins of German Tragic Drama* (1928; trans. 1977); however, it was rejected because of its density and difficulty. One examiner commented that it was an "incomprehensible morass" (another examiner who criticized the submission was MAX HORKHEIMER, later an associate of Benjamin's).

Thus thwarted, Benjamin became an independent scholar, writing articles for leading German periodicals, translating, and conducting research for an ambitious but never-completed historical work on nineteenth-century Paris later known as the *Arcades Project* (trans. 1999). During the twenties and thirties, he traveled across Europe; in a visit to Moscow (1926–27), he observed firsthand the achievements and limitations of the Bolshevik Revolution. Though his friend Gershom Scholem, the Jewish mystical thinker, urged him to emigrate to Palestine, Benjamin remained in Germany, participating in the German Communist Party (as his brother had done). Initially attracted to Marxism in the 1920s on reading GYÖRGY LUKÁCS's *History and Class Consciousness* (1923) and influenced by his friendship during the 1930s with the German Marxist writer Bertolt Brecht, Benjamin adopted increasingly left-wing political positions and showed the influence of Marxism in his writings on culture.

Exiled in Paris after the Nazi takeover in Germany in 1933, Benjamin lived a lonely and, as the threat of war approached, increasingly desperate existence. He struggled to support himself by writing while pursuing research for his *Arcades Project*, one small section of which, "On Some Motifs in Baudelaire" (1939), appeared in the journal of the Institute for Social Research at the University of Frankfurt. But Benjamin's methods and political orientation were increasingly at loggerheads with those of the institute—members of the Frankfurt School were turning away from the traditional paths of Marxism—and he became distant from his friend Adorno, as correspondence from the 1930s reveals. After the German invasion of France in 1940, Benjamin attempted to escape to Spain, intending to emigrate from there to the United States. Stopped at the border in the Pyrenees and fearful that he would be sent back to France to face internment in a concentration camp, Benjamin committed suicide.

Though many of his larger projects remained unfinished at the time of his death, and his essays were often composed under financial and emotional duress, Benjamin's work encompasses a rich and heterogeneous range: autobiographical writings and familiar essays on topics including his travels to Moscow, his experiments with hashish, and his love of book collecting; dense theoretical considerations of allegory and language, such as *Origins of German Tragic Drama* and "The Task of the Translator" (1923), which speculates on how translation offers fragments of a "pure language"; translations into German of Baudelaire and the modern French novelist Marcel Proust; literary criticism introducing contemporary authors such as Franz Kafka to general audiences; aphoristic considerations of the philosophy of history; and avowedly Marxist examinations of the role of art in modern society, such as "The Author as Producer" (1934) and "The Work of Art in the Age of Its Technological Reproducibility." Academically trained but denied an academic career, Benjamin represents a crossover figure in literary theory, resembling the mid-twentieth-century American literary and social critic Edmund Wilson in the range of his writing and cultural concerns, as well as the more academic Adorno in his philosophical sophistication.

Among the texts that Benjamin published under the auspices of the Frankfurt Institute, none has become more famous than "The Work of Art in the Age of Its Technological Reproducibility." It introduces his seminal concept of "aura"—the unique quality traditionally attributed to an artwork, giving it a special status equivalent to that of a sacred object in religious ritual. Investigating the perennial theoretical problem of the relation of aesthetics to social history, Benjamin argues that the status of the artwork is not timeless: it changed with the advent of capitalist mass production, which dispelled its unique aura and revered standing by devaluing the concept of the "original." Taking photography and film as his prime examples, he speculates that social transformations induced by technological changes in production alter aesthetic perception itself. He contrasts painting—a topic of comparison made familiar in aesthetics by GOTTHOLD EPHRAIM LESSING (1729–1781)—with film, noting that the stream of images in film promotes a "deepening of apperception" and that the close-up, among other techniques, "furthers insight into the necessities governing our lives." These are benefits of the reproducibility of art.

Though many view Benjamin as a mystical thinker, he does not express nostalgia for a time when the artwork possessed an "aura"; indeed, he denounces theories that assert an auratic or ritualistic power of film, branding them politically and aesthetically regressive. In contrast to painting or orchestral music, film has revolutionary potential because it abolishes authenticity and aura and enjoins the participation of the audience. Echoing Brecht on the "alienation effects" achieved by actors and staging in experimental theater, Benjamin maintains that the very process through which a movie is constructed—shot by shot, as the editor sutures together sequences filmed at different times—prevents audience members from unconsciously empathizing or identifying with any actor, thereby provoking them to thought and perhaps to action.

Nonetheless, Benjamin recognizes that any art form can be turned to reactionary purposes, and that the apparatus or technology of film does not guarantee a singular political outcome. He thus dispels the utopian belief that technology necessarily generates beneficial changes (a belief sometimes expressed today in rhapsodic pronouncements on the Internet). Mindful of the uses that fascists had made of film—notably Leni Riefenstahl's *Triumph of the Will* (1934), an infamous celebration of Nazi ideology—Benjamin sternly rebukes the aestheticization of politics, by which sheer technical brilliance and beauty mask the representation of a pernicious political program. Instead of offering a fascination with aesthetic qualities, communism positively "politicizes art" by foregrounding political action in the work and compelling the audience to reflect on the problems it raises. As is often the case with Benjamin, "The Work of Art in the Age of Its Technological Reproducibility" is less an authoritative statement of general aesthetic principles than a sequence of striking observations and an injunction for future work.

Some critics have stressed Benjamin's trajectory from the philosophical idealism of his early writings on language, aesthetics, and philosophy to his more explicitly Marxist later writings, but the very range of his work—on language, allegory, translation theory, historiography, aesthetics, film, and the philosophy of technology—has sometimes led commentators to shape Benjamin's work according to their own tastes. Beginning with his lifelong friend, Gershom Scholem, one prominent strand of readings foregrounds Benjamin's more philosophical works, seeing them as an expression of Jewish mysticism. Such readings downplay his mature works of the 1930s, viewing them as a misguided infatuation with the Marxist Brecht. Deconstructive critics, notably PAUL DE MAN and Geoffrey Hartman, draw on Benjamin's writings on allegory and language, claiming him as a precursor of deconstruction in his focus on the problematics of language. Marxists like TERRY EAGLETON have stressed his exemplary role as a revolutionary critic, though one with messianic leanings. Despite the legendary obscurity of his prose style and his use of idioms derived from mysticism and German idealist philosophy (especially in his earlier writings), Benjamin persistently calls attention in his later work to the influence of the means of production on culture; he commands the revolutionary intellectual to assume an attitude that would transform him "from a supplier of the productive apparatus into an engineer who sees it as his task to adapt this apparatus to the purposes of proletarian revolution" ("The Author as Producer").

"The Work of Art in the Age of Its Technological Reproducibility" Keywords: Aesthetics, Cultural Studies, Marxism, Media, Modernity, Popular Culture, Religion

The Work of Art in the Age of Its Technological Reproducibility[1]

> Our fine arts were developed, their types and uses were established, in times very different from the present, by men whose power of action upon things was insignificant in comparison with ours. But the amazing growth of our techniques, the adaptability and precision they have attained, the ideas and habits they are creating, make it a certainty that profound changes are impending in the ancient craft of the Beautiful. In all the arts, there is a physical component which can no longer be considered or treated as it used to be, which cannot remain unaffected by our modern knowledge and power. For the last twenty years, neither matter nor space nor time has been what it was from time immemorial. We must expect great innovations to transform the entire technique of the arts, thereby affecting artistic invention itself and perhaps even bringing about an amazing change in our very notion of art.
>
> —Paul Valéry,[2] *Pièces sur l'art* ("La conquête de l'ubiquité")

Introduction

When Marx undertook his analysis of the capitalist mode of production, this mode was in its infancy.[3] Marx adopted an approach which gave his investigations prognostic value. Going back to the basic conditions of capitalist production, he presented them in a way which showed what could be expected of capitalism in the future. What could be expected, it emerged, was not only an increasingly harsh exploitation of the proletariat but, ultimately, the creation of conditions which would make it possible for capitalism to abolish itself.

Since the transformation of the superstructure proceeds far more slowly than that of the base, it has taken more than half a century for the change

1. Translated by Harry Zohn and Edmund Jephcott.
2. A leading French poet and essayist (1871–1945); the quote is taken from "The Conquest of Ubiquity," an essay published in *Pieces on Art* (3d ed., 1936).
3. The German philosopher KARL MARX (1818–1883) divided human history into seven modes of production, the most recent being feudalism and capitalism; he undertook his analyses only a short time after the capitalist industrial revolution had taken hold in England. Marx argued that capitalism's economic base (the mode of production, or "substructure") determines all noneconomic aspects of life ("superstructure").

in the conditions of production to be manifested in all areas of culture. How this process has affected culture can only now be assessed, and these assessments must meet certain prognostic requirements. They do not, however, call for theses on the art of the proletariat after its seizure of power, and still less for any on the art of the classless society. They call for theses defining the tendencies of the development of art under the present conditions of production. The dialectic of these conditions of production is evident in the superstructure, no less than in the economy. Theses defining the developmental tendencies of art can therefore contribute to the political struggle in ways that it would be a mistake to underestimate. They neutralize a number of traditional concepts—such as creativity and genius, eternal value and mystery—which, used in an uncontrolled way (and controlling them is difficult today), allow factual material to be manipulated in the interests of fascism. *In what follows, the concepts which are introduced into the theory of art differ from those now current in that they are completely useless for the purposes of fascism. On the other hand, they are useful for the formulation of revolutionary demands in the politics of art.*

I

In principle, the work of art has always been reproducible. Objects made by humans could always be copied by humans. Replicas were made by pupils in practicing for their craft, by masters in disseminating their works, and, finally, by third parties in pursuit of profit. But the technological reproduction of artworks is something new. Having appeared intermittently in history, at widely spaced intervals, it is now being adopted with ever-increasing intensity. The Greeks had only two ways of technologically reproducing works of art: casting and stamping. Bronzes, terracottas, and coins were the only artworks they could produce in large numbers. All others were unique and could not be technologically reproduced. Graphic art was first made technologically reproducible by the woodcut, long before written language became reproducible by movable type. The enormous changes brought about in literature by movable type, the technological reproducibility of writing, are well known. But they are only a special case, though an important one, of the phenomenon considered here from the perspective of world history. In the course of the Middle Ages the woodcut was supplemented by engraving and etching, and at the beginning of the nineteenth century by lithography.

Lithography marked a fundamentally new stage in the technology of reproduction. This much more direct process—distinguished by the fact that the drawing is traced on a stone, rather than incised on a block of wood or etched on a copper plate—first made it possible for graphic art to market its products not only in large numbers, as previously, but in daily changing variations. Lithography enabled graphic art to provide an illustrated accompaniment to everyday life. It began to keep pace with movable-type printing. But only a few decades after the invention of lithography, graphic art was surpassed by photography. For the first time, photography freed the hand from the most important artistic tasks in the process of pictorial reproduction—tasks that now devolved solely upon the eye looking into a lens. And since the eye perceives more swiftly than the hand can draw, the process of pictorial reproduction was enormously accelerated, so that it could now keep pace with speech. A cinematographer shooting a scene in the studio captures the images at the speed of an actor's speech. Just as the illustrated newspaper virtually lay hidden within lithography, so the sound film was latent in photography. The technological reproduction of sound was tackled at the end of the last century. These convergent endeavors made it possible to conceive of the situation that Paul Valéry describes in this sentence: "Just as water, gas, and electricity are brought into our houses from far off to satisfy our needs with minimal effort, so we shall be supplied with visual or auditory images, which will appear and disappear at a simple movement of the hand, hardly more than a sign."[4] *Around 1900, technological reproduction not only had reached a standard that permitted it to reproduce all known works of art, profoundly modifying their effect, but it also had captured a place of its own among the artistic processes.* In gauging this standard, we would do well to study the impact which its two different manifestations—the reproduction of artworks and the art of film—are having on art in its traditional form.

II

In even the most perfect reproduction, *one* thing is lacking: the here and now of the work of art—its unique existence in a particular place. It is this unique existence—and nothing else—that bears the mark of the history to which the work has been subject. This history includes changes to the physical structure of the work over time, together with any changes in ownership.[5] Traces of the former can be detected only by chemical or physical analyses (which cannot be performed on a reproduction), while changes of ownership are part of a tradition which can be traced only from the standpoint of the original in its present location.

The here and now of the original underlies the concept of its authenticity. Chemical analyses of the patina of a bronze can help to establish its authenticity, just as the proof that a given manuscript of the Middle Ages came from an archive of the fifteenth century helps to establish its authenticity. *The whole sphere of authenticity eludes technological—and, of course, not only technological—reproducibility.*[6] But whereas the authentic work retains its full authority in the face of a reproduction made by hand, which it generally brands a forgery, this is not the case with technological reproduction. The reason is twofold. First, technological reproduction is more independent of the original than is manual reproduction. For example, in photography it can bring out aspects of the original that are accessible only to the lens (which is adjustable and can easily change viewpoint) but not to

4. Valéry, *Pièces sur l'art* (Paris), p. 105 [Benjamin's note]. Some of the author's notes have been edited, and some omitted.

5. Of course, the history of a work of art encompasses more than this. The history of the "Mona Lisa," for instance, encompasses the kind and number of its copies made in the 17th, 18th, and 19th centuries [Benjamin's note]. *Mona Lisa* (ca. 1504), painting by Leonardo da Vinci.

6. Precisely because authenticity is not reproducible, the intensive penetration of certain (technological) processes of reproduction was instrumental in differentiating and gradating authenticity. To develop such differentiations was an important function of the trade in works of art. Such trade had a manifest interest in distinguishing among various prints of a woodblock engraving (those before and those after inscription), of a copperplate engraving, and so on. The invention of the woodcut may be said to have struck at the root of the quality of authenticity even before its late flowering. To be sure, a medieval picture of the Madonna at the time it was created could not yet be said to be "authentic." It became "authentic" only during the succeeding centuries, and perhaps most strikingly so during the 19th [Benjamin's note].

the human eye; or it can use certain processes, such as enlargement or slow motion, to record images which escape natural optics altogether. This is the first reason. Second, technological reproduction can place the copy of the original in situations which the original itself cannot attain. Above all, it enables the original to meet the recipient halfway, whether in the form of a photograph or in that of a gramophone record. The cathedral leaves its site to be received in the studio of an art lover; the choral work performed in an auditorium or in the open air is enjoyed in a private room.

The situations into which the product of technological reproduction can be brought may leave the artwork's other properties untouched, but they certainly devalue the here and now of the artwork. And although this can apply not only to art but (say) to a landscape moving past the spectator in a film, in the work of art this process touches on a highly sensitive core, more vulnerable than that of any natural object. That core is its authenticity. The authenticity of a thing is the quintessence of all that is transmissible in it from its origin on, ranging from its physical duration to the historical testimony relating to it. Since the historical testimony is founded on the physical duration, the former, too, is jeopardized by reproduction, in which the physical duration plays no part. And what is really jeopardized when the historical testimony is affected is the authority of the object.[7]

One might encompass the eliminated element within the concept of the aura, and go on to say: what withers in the age of the technological reproducibility of the work of art is the latter's aura. The process is symptomatic; its significance extends far beyond the realm of art. *It might be stated as a general formula that the technology of reproduction detaches the reproduced object from the sphere of tradition. By replicating the work many times over, it substitutes a mass existence for a unique existence. And in permitting the reproduction to reach the recipient in his or her own situation, it actualizes that which is reproduced.* These two processes lead to a massive upheaval in the domain of objects handed down from the past—a shattering of tradition which is the reverse side of the present crisis and renewal of humanity. Both processes are intimately related to the mass movements of our day. Their most powerful agent is film. The social significance of film, even—and especially—in its most positive form, is inconceivable without its destructive, cathartic[8] side: the liquidation of the value of tradition in the cultural heritage. This phenomenon is most apparent in the great historical films. It is assimilating ever more advanced positions in its spread. When Abel Gance fervently proclaimed in 1927, "Shakespeare, Rembrandt, Beethoven will make films. . . . All legends, all mythologies, and all myths, all the founders of religions, indeed, all religions, . . . await their celluloid resurrection, and the heroes are pressing at the gates," he was inviting the reader, no doubt unawares, to witness a comprehensive liquidation.[9]

7. The poorest provincial staging of Goethe's *Faust* is superior to a film of *Faust* in that, ideally, it competes with the first performance at Weimar [Benjamin's note]. *Faust* (1808, 1832), a drama by the German Romantic writer Johann Wolfgang von Goethe (1749–1832), who lived for most of his life in Weimar.

8. Purgative. Benjamin here invokes a sense very different from the traditional literary meaning of catharsis, a term applied by ARISTOTLE (384–322 B.C.E.) in the *Poetics* (see above) to the emotional release experienced by an audience watching a tragedy.

9. Abel Gance, "Le Temps de l'image est venu!" ["It Is Time for the Image!" (French)], in *L'Art cinématographique*, vol. 2 (Paris, 1927), pp. 94–95 [Benjamin's note]. Gance (1889–1981), French silent film director. Rembrandt van Rijn (1606–1669), Dutch painter and etcher. Ludwig van Beethoven (1770–1827), German composer.

III

Just as the entire mode of existence of human collectives changes over long historical periods, so too does their mode of perception. The way in which human perception is organized—the medium in which it occurs—is conditioned not only by nature but by history. The era of the migration of peoples, an era which saw the rise of the late-Roman art industry and the Vienna Genesis, developed not only an art different from that of antiquity but also a different perception. The scholars of the Viennese school Riegl and Wickhoff,[1] resisting the weight of the classical tradition beneath which this art had been buried, were the first to think of using such art to draw conclusions about the organization of perception at the time the art was produced. However far-reaching their insight, it was limited by the fact that these scholars were content to highlight the formal signature which characterized perception in late-Roman times. They did not attempt to show the social upheavals manifested in these changes of perception—and perhaps could not have hoped to do so at that time. Today, the conditions for an analogous insight are more favorable. And if changes in the medium of present-day perception can be understood as a decay of the aura, it is possible to demonstrate the social determinants of that decay.

The concept of the aura which was proposed above with reference to historical objects can be usefully illustrated with reference to an aura of natural objects. We define the aura of the latter as the unique apparition of a distance, however near it may be. To follow with the eye—while resting on a summer afternoon—a mountain range on the horizon or a branch that casts its shadow on the beholder is to breathe the aura of those mountains, of that branch. In the light of this description, we can readily grasp the social basis of the aura's present decay. It rests on two circumstances, both linked to the increasing significance of the masses in contemporary life. Namely: *the desire of the present-day masses to "get closer" to things spatially and humanly, and their equally passionate concern for overcoming each thing's uniqueness by assimilating it as a reproduction.*[2] Every day the urge grows stronger to get hold of an object at close range in an image, or better, in a facsimile, a reproduction. And the reproduction as offered by illustrated magazines and newsreels, differs unmistakably from the image. Uniqueness and permanence are as closely entwined in the latter as are transitoriness and repeatability in the former. The stripping of the veil from the object, the destruction of the aura, is the signature of a perception whose "sense for sameness in the world"[3] has so increased that, by means of reproduction, it extracts sameness even from what is unique. Thus is manifested in the field of perception what in the theoretical sphere is noticeable in the increasing significance of statis-

1. Alois Riegl (1858–1905) and Franz Wickhoff (1853–1909), Austrian art historians who studied the inception (hence "genesis") of European art in Vienna in the Middle Ages, an inception influenced by earlier Roman art.
2. Getting closer (in terms of human interest) to the masses may involve having one's social function removed from the field of vision. Nothing guarantees that a portraitist of today, when painting a famous surgeon at the breakfast table with his family, depicts his social function more precisely than a painter of the seventeenth century who showed the viewer doctors representing their profession, as Rembrandt did in his "Anatomy Lesson" [Benjamin's note]. *Anatomy Lesson of Dr. Tulp*, a group portrait, was painted in 1632.
3. Quoted from *Exotische Novellen* (1919, *Exotic Novella*), by the Danish writer Johannes V. Jensen.

tics. The alignment of reality with the masses and of the masses with reality is a process of immeasurable importance for both thinking and perception.

IV

The uniqueness of the work of art is identical to its embeddedness in the context of tradition. Of course, this tradition itself is thoroughly alive and extremely changeable. An ancient statute of Venus,[4] for instance, existed in a traditional context for the Greeks (who made it an object of worship) that was different from the context in which it existed for medieval clerics (who viewed it as a sinister idol). But what was equally evident to both was its uniqueness—that is, its aura. Originally, the embeddedness of an artwork in the context of tradition found expression in a cult. As we know, the earliest artworks originated in the service of rituals—first magical, then religious. And it is highly significant that the artwork's auratic mode of existence is never entirely severed from its ritual function.[5] In other words: *the unique value of the "authentic" work of art has its basis in ritual, the source of its original use value.* This ritualistic basis, however mediated it may be, is still recognizable as secularized ritual in even the most profane forms of the cult of beauty.[6] The secular worship of beauty, which developed during the Renaissance and prevailed for three centuries, clearly displayed that ritualistic basis in its subsequent decline and in the first severe crisis which befell it. For when, with the advent of the first truly revolutionary means of reproduction (namely, photography, which emerged at the same time as socialism), art felt the approach of that crisis which a century later has become unmistakable, it reacted with the doctrine of *l'art pour l'art*[7]—that is, with a theology of art. This in turn gave rise to a negative theology, in the form of an idea of "pure" art, which rejects not only any social function but any definition in terms of a representational content. (In poetry, Mallarmé[8] was the first to adopt this standpoint.)

No investigation of the work of art in the age of its technological reproducibility can overlook these connections. They lead to crucial insight: for the first time in world history, technological reproducibility emancipates the work of art from its parasitic subservience to ritual. To an ever-increasing degree, the work reproduced becomes the reproduction of a work designed for reproducibility.[9] From a photographic plate, for example, one can make

4. Roman goddess of love, identified with the Greek Aphrodite.
5. The definition of the aura as the "unique apparition of a distance, however near it may be," represents nothing more than a formulation of the cult value of the work of art in categories of spatiotemporal perception. Distance is the opposite of nearness. The *essentially* distant is the unapproachable. Unapproachability is, indeed, a primary quality of the cult image; true to its nature, the cult image remains "distant, however near it may be." The nearness which one may gain from its substance does not impair the distance it retains in its apparition [Benjamin's note].
6. To the extent that the cult value of a painting is secularized, the impressions of its fundamental uniqueness become less distinct. In the viewer's imagination, the uniqueness of the phenomena holding sway in the cult image is more and more displaced by the empirical uniqueness of the artist or of his creative achievement. To be sure, never completely so—the concept of authenticity always transcends that of proper attribution. (This is particularly apparent in the collector, who always displays some traits of the fetishist and who, through his possession of the artwork, shares in its cultic power.) Nevertheless, the concept of authenticity still functions as a determining factor in the evaluation of art; as art becomes secularized, authenticity displaces the cult value of the work [Benjamin's note].
7. Art for art's sake (French), a 19th-century aesthetic doctrine; see WALTER PATER, above.
8. Stéphane Mallarmé (1842–1898), French poet.
9. In film, the technological reproducibility of the product is not an externally imposed condition of its mass dissemination, as it is, say, in literature or painting. *The technological reproducibility of films*

any number of prints; to ask for the "authentic" print makes no sense. *But as soon as the criterion of authenticity ceases to be applied to artistic production, the whole social function of art is revolutionized. Instead of being founded on ritual, it is based on a different practice: politics.*

V

The reception of works of art varies in character, but in general two polar types stand out: one accentuates the artwork's cult value; the other, its exhibition value. Artistic production begins with figures in the service of a cult. One may assume that it was more important for these figures to be present than to be seen. The elk depicted by Stone Age man on the walls of his cave is an instrument of magic. He exhibits it to his fellow men, to be sure, but in the main it is meant for the spirits. Cult value as such tends today, it would seem, to keep the artwork out of sight: certain statues of gods are accessible only to the priest in the cella[1]; certain images of the Madonna remain covered nearly all year round; certain sculptures on medieval cathedrals are not visible to the viewer at ground level. *With the emancipation of specific artistic practices from the service of ritual, the opportunities for exhibiting their products increase.* It is easier to exhibit a portrait bust that can be sent here and there than to exhibit the statue of a divinity that has a fixed place in the interior of a temple. A panel painting can be exhibited more easily than the mosaic or fresco which preceded it. And although a Mass may have been no less suited to public presentation than a symphony, the symphony came into being at a time when the possibility of such presentation promised to be greater.

The scope for exhibiting the work of art has increased so enormously with the various methods of technologically reproducing it that, as happened in prehistoric times, a quantitative shift between the two poles of the artwork has led to a qualitative transformation in its nature. Just as the work of art in prehistoric times, through the absolute emphasis placed on its cult value, became first and foremost an instrument of magic which only later came to be recognized as a work of art, so today, through the absolute emphasis placed on its exhibition value, the work of art becomes a construct with quite new functions. Among these, the one we are conscious of—the artistic function—may subsequently be seen as incidental.[2] This much is

is based directly on the technology of their production. This not only makes possible the mass dissemination of films in the most direct way, but actually enforces it. It does so because the process of producing a film is so costly that an individual who could afford to buy a painting, for example, could not afford to buy a [master print of a] film. It was calculated in 1927 that, in order to make a profit, a major film needed to reach an audience of 9 million. Of course, the advent of sound film initially caused a movement in the opposite direction: its audience was restricted by language boundaries. And that coincided with the emphasis placed on national interests by fascism. But it is less important to note this setback (which in any case was mitigated by dubbing) than to observe its connection with fascism. The simultaneity of the two phenomena results from the economic crisis. The same disorders which led, in the world at large, to an attempt to maintain existing property relations by brute force induced film capital, under the threat of crisis, to speed up the development of sound film. Its introduction brought temporary relief, not only because sound film attracted the masses back into the cinema but because it consolidated new capital from the electrical industry with that of film. Thus, considered from the outside, sound film promoted national interests; but seen from the inside, it helped internationalize film production even more than before [Benjamin's note].

1. Small room (Latin); specifically, a priest's cell.

2. Bertolt Brecht, on a different level, engaged in analogous reflections: "If the concept of 'work of art' can no longer be applied to the thing that emerges once the work is transformed into a com-

certain: today, photography and film are the most serviceable vehicles of this new understanding.

VI

In photography, exhibition value begins to drive back cult value on all fronts. But cult value does not give way without resistance. It falls back to a last entrenchment: the human countenance. It is no accident that the portrait is central to early photography. In the cult of remembrance of dead or absent loved ones, the cult value of the image finds its last refuge. In the fleeting expression of a human face, the aura beckons from early photographs for the last time. This is what gives them their melancholy and incomparable beauty. But as the human being withdraws from the photographic image, exhibition value for the first time shows its superiority to cult value. To have given this development its local habitation constitutes the unique significance of Atget,[3] who, around 1900, took photographs of deserted Paris streets. It has justly been said that he photographed them like scenes of crimes. A crime scene, too, is deserted; it is photographed for the purpose of establishing evidence. With Atget, photographic records begin to be evidence in the historical trial. This constitutes their hidden political significance. They demand a specific kind of reception. Free-floating contemplation is no longer appropriate to them. They unsettle the viewer; he feels challenged to find a particular way to approach them. At the same time, illustrated magazines begin to put up signposts for him—whether these are right or wrong is irrelevant. For the first time, captions become obligatory. And it is clear that they have a character altogether different from the titles of paintings. The directives given by captions to those looking at images in illustrated magazines soon become even more precise and commanding in films, where the way each single image is understood appears prescribed by the sequence of all the preceding images.

VII

The nineteenth-century dispute over the relative artistic merits of painting and photography seems misguided and confused today. But this does not diminish its importance, and may even underscore it. The dispute was in fact an expression of a world-historical upheaval whose true nature was concealed from both parties. Insofar as the age of technological reproducibility separated art from its basis in cult, all semblance of art's autonomy disappeared forever. But the resulting change in the function of art lay beyond the horizon of the nineteenth century. And even the twentieth, which saw the development of film, was slow to perceive it.

---

modity, we have to eliminate this concept with due caution but without fear, lest we liquidate the function of the very thing as well. For it has to go through this phase unswervingly; there is no viable detour from the straight path. Rather, what happens here with the work of art will change it fundamentally, will erase its past to such an extent that—should the old concept be taken up again (and it will be; why not?)—it will no longer evoke any memory of the thing it once designated." Brecht, *Versuche* [*Experiments*], 8–10 (Berlin, 1931), pp. 301–2 [Benjamin's note]. Brecht (1898–1956), German playwright and influential Marxist friend of Benjamin.

3. Eugène Atget (1857–1927), French photographer.

Though commentators had earlier expended much fruitless ingenuity on the question of whether photography was an art—without asking the more fundamental question of whether the invention of photography had not transformed the entire character of art—film theorists quickly adopted the same ill-considered standpoint. But the difficulties which photography caused for traditional aesthetics were child's play compared to those presented by film. Hence the obtuse and hyperbolic character of early film theory. Abel Gance, for instance, compares film to hieroglyphs: "By a remarkable regression, we are transported back to the expressive level of the Egyptians. . . . Pictorial language has not matured, because our eyes are not yet adapted to it. There is not yet enough respect, not enough *cult*, for what it expresses."[4] Or, in the words of Séverin-Mars: "What other art has been granted a dream . . . at once more poetic and more real? Seen in this light, film might represent an incomparable means of expression, and only the noblest minds should move within its atmosphere, in the most perfect and mysterious moments of their lives."[5] Alexander Arnoux, for his part, concludes a fantasy about the silent film with the question: "Do not all the bold descriptions we have given amount to a definition of prayer?"[6] It is instructive to see how the desire to annex film to "art" impels these theoreticians to attribute elements of cult to film—with a striking lack of discretion. Yet when these speculations were published, works like *A Woman of Paris* and *The Gold Rush*[7] had already appeared. This did not deter Abel Gance from making the comparison with hieroglyphs, while Séverin-Mars speaks of film as one might speak of paintings by Fra Angelico.[8] It is revealing that even today especially reactionary authors look in the same direction for the significance of film—finding, if not actually a sacred significance, then at least a supernatural one. In connection with Max Reinhardt's film version of *A Midsummer Night's Dream,* Werfel[9] comments that it was undoubtedly the sterile copying of the external world—with its streets, interiors, railroad stations, restaurants, automobiles, and beaches—that had prevented film up to now from ascending to the realm of art. "Film has not yet realized its true purpose, its real possibilities. . . . These consist in its unique ability to use natural means to give incomparably convincing expression to the fairylike, the marvelous, the supernatural."[1]

VIII

The artistic performance of a stage actor is directly presented to the public by the actor in person; that of a screen actor, however, is presented through a camera, with two consequences. The recording apparatus that brings the film actor's performance to the public need not respect the performance as

4. Gance, p. 101 [Benjamin's note].
5. Quoted in Gance, p. 100 [Benjamin's note]. Séverin-Mars (Armand Jean de Malasayade, 1873–1921), French writer and actor who appeared in three of Gance's films.
6. Alexandre Arnoux, *Cinéma* (Paris, 1929), p. 28 [Benjamin's note]. Arnoux (1884–1973), French playwright.
7. Two American silent films (1923, 1925) written and directed by the English actor and director Charlie Chaplin (1889–1977).
8. Florentine painter (Giovanni da Fiesole, ca. 1400–1455), a monk whose works often have religious subjects.
9. Franz Werfel (1890–1945), Austrian poet, playwright, and novelist. Reinhardt (1873–1943), Austrian-born actor and producer of theater and film; his version of Shakespeare's *A Midsummer Night's Dream* (ca. 1595) was released in 1935.
1. Franz Werfel, "Ein Sommernachtstraum: Ein Film von Shakespeare und Reinhardt" ["A Midsummer Night's Dream: A Film by Shakespeare and Reinhardt"], *Neues Wiener Journal*, cited in *Lu*, Nov. 15, 1935 [Benjamin's note].

an integral whole. Guided by the cameraman, the camera continually changes its position with respect to the performance. The sequence of positional views which the editor composes from the material supplied him constitutes the completed film. It comprises a certain number of movements, of various kinds and duration, which must be apprehended as such through the camera, not to mention special camera angles, close-ups, and so on. Hence, the performance of the actor is subjected to a series of optical tests. This is the first consequence of the fact that the actor's performance is presented by means of a camera. The second consequence is that the film actor lacks the opportunity of the stage actor to adjust to the audience during his performance, since he does not present his performance to the audience in person. This permits the audience to take the position of a critic, without experiencing any personal contact with the actor. *The audience's empathy with the actor is really an empathy with the camera. Consequently, the audience takes the position of the camera; its approach is that of testing.*[2] This is not an approach compatible with cult value.

IX

In the case of film, the fact that the actor represents someone else before the audience matters much less than the fact that he represents himself before the apparatus. One of the first to sense this transformation of the actor by the test performance was Pirandello.[3] That his remarks on the subject in his novel *Si gira* are confined to the negative aspects of this change, and to silent film only, does little to diminish their relevance. For in this respect, the sound film changed nothing essential. What matters is that the actor is performing for a piece of equipment—or, in the case of sound film, for two pieces of equipment. "The film actor," Pirandello writes, "feels as if exiled. Exiled not only from the stage but from his own person. With a vague unease, he senses an inexplicable void, stemming from the fact that his body has lost its substance, that he has been volatilized, stripped of his reality, his life, his voice, the noises he makes when moving about, and has been turned into a mute image that flickers for a moment on the screen, then vanishes into silence. . . . The little apparatus will play with his shadow before the audience, and he himself must be content to play before the apparatus." The situation can also be characterized as follows: for the first time—and this is the effect of film—the human being is placed in a position where he must operate with his whole living person, while forgoing its aura. For the aura is bound to his presence in the here and now. There is no facsimile of the aura. The aura surrounding Macbeth[4] on the stage cannot be divorced from the aura which, for the living spectators, surrounds the actor who plays him. What distinguishes the shot in the film studio, however,

2. The expansion of the field of the testable which the film apparatus brings about for the actor corresponds to the extraordinary expansion of the field of the testable brought about for the individual through economic conditions. Thus, vocational aptitude tests become constantly more important. What matters in these tests are segmental performances of the individual. The final cut of a film and the vocational aptitude test are both taken before a panel of experts. The director in the studio occupies a position identical to that of the examiner during aptitude tests [Benjamin's note].

3. Luigi Pirandello (1867–1936), Italian dramatist and novelist; his novel *Si Gira* (1915) was translated as *Shoot!* in 1926.

4. Title character of Shakespeare's play (1606).

is that the camera is substituted for the audience. As a result, the aura surrounding the actor is dispelled—and, with it, the aura of the figure he portrays.

It is not surprising that it should be a dramatist such as Pirandello who, in reflecting on the special character of film acting, inadvertently touches on the crisis now affecting the theater. Indeed, nothing contrasts more starkly with a work of art completely subject to (or, like film, founded in) technological reproduction than a stage play. Any thorough consideration will confirm this. Expert observers have long recognized that, in film, "the best effects are almost always achieved by 'acting' as little as possible. . . . The development," according to Rudolf Arnheim, writing in 1932, has been toward "using the actor as one of the 'props,' chosen for his typicalness and . . . introduced in the proper context."[5] Closely bound up with this development is something else. *The stage actor identifies himself with a role. The film actor very often is denied this opportunity.* His performance is by no means a unified whole, but is assembled from many individual performances. Apart from incidental concerns about studio rental, availability of other actors, scenery, and so on, there are elementary necessities of the machinery that split the actor's performance into a series of episodes capable of being assembled. In particular, lighting and its installation require the representation of an action—which on the screen appears as a swift, unified sequence—to be filmed in a series of separate takes, which may be spread over hours in the studio. Not to mention the more obvious effects of montage. A leap from a window, for example, can be shot in the studio as a leap from a scaffold, while the ensuing fall may be filmed weeks later at an outdoor location. And far more paradoxical cases can easily be imagined. Let us assume that an actor is supposed to be startled by a knock at the door. If his reaction is not satisfactory, the director can resort to an expedient: he could have a shot fired without warning behind the actor's back on some other occasion when he happens to be in the studio. The actor's frightened reaction at that moment could be recorded and then edited into the film. Nothing shows more graphically that art has escaped the realm of "beautiful semblance," which for so long was regarded as the only sphere in which it could thrive.

X

The film actor's feeling of estrangement in the face of the apparatus, as Pirandello describes this experience, is basically of the same kind as the estrangement felt before one's appearance in a mirror. But now the mirror image has become detachable from the person mirrored, and is transportable. And where is it transported? To a site in front of the public.[6] The

5. Rudolf Arnheim, *Film als Kunst* [*Film as Art*] (Berlin, 1932), pp. 176–77. If the actor thus becomes a prop, the prop, in its turn, not infrequently functions as an actor. At any rate, it is not unusual for films to allocate a role to a prop. [For example,] a clock that is running will always be a disturbance on the stage, where it cannot be permitted its role of measuring time. Even in a naturalistic play, real-life time would conflict with theatrical time. In view of this, it is very revealing that film—where appropriate—can readily make use of time as measured by a clock. This feature, more than many others, makes it clear that—circumstances permitting—each and every prop in a film may assume decisive functions [Benjamin's note]. Arnheim (1904–2007), German-born writer on art and visual thinking.

6. The change noted here in the mode of exhibition—a change brought about by reproduction technology—is also noticeable in politics.

screen actor never for a moment ceases to be aware of this. *While he stands before the apparatus, the screen actor knows that in the end he is confronting the public, the consumers who constitute the market.* This market, where he offers not only his labor but his entire self, his heart and soul, is beyond his reach. During the shooting, he has as little contact with it as would any article being made in a factory. This may contribute to that oppression, that new anxiety which, according to Pirandello, grips the actor before the camera. Film responds to the shriveling of the aura by artificially building up the "personality" outside the studio. The cult of the movie star, fostered by the money of the film industry, preserves that magic of the personality which has long been no more than the putrid magic of its own commodity character. So long as moviemakers' capital sets the fashion, as a rule the only revolutionary merit that can be ascribed to today's cinema is the promotion of a revolutionary criticism of traditional concepts of art. We do not deny that in some cases today's films can also foster revolutionary criticism of social conditions, even of property relations. But the present study is no more specifically concerned with this than is western European film production.

It is inherent in the technology of film, as of sports, that everyone who witnesses these performances does so as a quasi-expert. This is obvious to anyone who has listened to a group of newspaper boys leaning on their bicycles and discussing the outcome of a bicycle race. It is no accident that newspaper publishers arrange races for their delivery boys. These arouse great interest among the participants, for the winner has a chance to rise from delivery boy to professional racer. Similarly, the newsreel offers everyone the chance to rise from passer-by to movie extra. In this way, a person might even see himself becoming part of a work of art: think of Vertov's *Three Songs of Lenin* or Ivens' *Borinage.*[7] *Any person today can lay claim to being filmed.* This claim can best be clarified by considering the historical situation of literature today.

For centuries it was in the nature of literature that a small number of writers confronted many thousands of readers. This began a change toward the end of the past century. With the growth and extension of the press, which constantly made new political, religious, scientific, professional, and local journals available to readers, an increasing number of readers—in isolated cases, at first—turned into writers. It began with the space set aside for "letters to the editor" in the daily press, and has now reached a point where there is hardly a European engaged in the work process who could not, in

---

The present crisis of the bourgeois democracies involves a crisis in the conditions governing the public presentation of leaders. Democracies exhibit the leader directly, in person, before elected representatives. The parliament is his public. But innovations in recording equipment now enable the speaker to be heard by an unlimited number of people while he is speaking, and to be seen by an unlimited number shortly afterward. This means that priority is given to presenting the politician before the recording equipment. Parliaments are becoming depopulated at the same time as theaters. Radio and film are changing not only the function of the professional actor but, equally, the function of those who, like the leaders, present themselves before these media. The direction of this change is the same for the film actor and for the leader, regardless of their different tasks. It tends toward the exhibition of controllable, transferable skills under certain social conditions. This results in a new form of selection—selection before an apparatus—from which the star and the dictator emerge as victors [Benjamin's note].

7. A 1933 film directed by the Dutch director Joris Ivens (1898–1989). Dziga Vertov (1896–1954), early Russian film director; *Three Songs about Lenin* appeared in 1934.

principle, find an opportunity to publish somewhere or other an account of a work experience, a complaint, a report, or something of the kind. Thus, the distinction between author and public is about to lose its axiomatic character. The difference becomes functional; it may vary from case to case. At any moment, the reader is ready to become a writer. As an expert—which he has had to become in any case in a highly specialized work process, even if only in some minor capacity—the reader gains access to authorship. In the Soviet Union, work itself is given a voice. And the ability to describe a job in words now forms part of the expertise needed to carry it out. Literary competence is no longer founded on specialized higher education but on polytechnic training, and thus is common property.[8]

All this can readily be applied to film, where shifts that in literature took place over centuries have occurred in a decade. In cinematic practice—above all, in Russia—this shift has already been partly realized. Some of the actors taking part in Russian films are not actors in our sense but people who portray *themselves*—and primarily in their own work process. In western Europe today, the capitalist exploitation of film obstructs the human being's legitimate claim to being reproduced. Under these circumstances, the film industry has an overriding interest in stimulating the involvement of the masses through illusionary displays and ambiguous speculations.

XI

The shooting of a film, especially a sound film, offers a hitherto unimaginable spectacle. It presents a process in which it is impossible to assign to the spectator a single viewpoint which would exclude from his or her field of vision the equipment not directly involved in the action being filmed—the camera, the lighting units, the technical crew, and so forth (unless the alignment of the spectator's pupil coincided with that of the camera). This circumstance, more than any other, makes any resemblance between a scene

8. The privileged character of the respective techniques is lost. Aldous Huxley writes: "Advances in technology have led . . . to vulgarity. . . . Process reproduction and the rotary press have made possible the indefinite multiplication of writing and pictures. Universal education and relatively high wages have created an enormous public who know how to read and can afford to buy reading and pictorial matter. A great industry has been called into existence in order to supply these commodities. Now, artistic talent is a very rare phenomenon; whence it follows . . . that, at every epoch and in all countries, most art has been bad. But the proportion of trash in the total artistic output is greater now than at any other period. That it must be so is a matter of simple arithmetic. The population of Western Europe has a little more than doubled during the last century. But the amount of reading—and seeing—matter has increased, I should imagine, at least twenty and possibly fifty or even a hundred times. If there were n men of talent in a population of x millions, there will presumably be 2n men of talent among 2x millions. The situation may be summed up thus. For every page of print and pictures published a century ago, twenty or perhaps even a hundred pages are published today. But for every man of talent then living, there are now only two men of talent. It may be of course that, thanks to universal education, many potential talents which in the past would have been stillborn are now enabled to realize themselves. Let us assume, then, that there are now three or even four men of talent to every one of earlier times. It still remains true to say that the consumption of reading—and seeing—matter has far outstripped the natural production of gifted writers and draftsmen. It is the same with hearing-matter. Prosperity, the gramophone and the radio have created an audience of hearers who consume an amount of hearing-matter that has increased out of all proportion to the increase of population and the consequent natural increase of talented musicians. It follows from all this that in all the arts the output of trash is both absolutely and relatively greater than it was in the past; and that it must remain greater for just so long as the world continues to consume the present inordinate quantities of reading-matter, seeing-matter, and hearing-matter" (Aldous Huxley, *Beyond the Mexique Bay: A Traveller's Journal*, 1934 [reprint, London, 1949, pp. 274ff.]). This mode of observation is obviously not progressive [Benjamin's note]. Huxley (1894–1963), English novelist and essayist.

in a film studio and one onstage superficial and irrelevant. In principle, the theater includes a position from which the action on the stage cannot easily be detected as an illusion. There is no such position where a film is being shot. The illusory nature of film is of the second degree; it is the result of editing. That is to say: *In the film studio the apparatus has penetrated so deeply into reality that a pure view of that reality, free of the foreign body of equipment, is the result of a special procedure, namely, the shooting by the specially adjusted photographic device and the assembly of that shot with others of the same kind.* The equipment-free aspect of reality has here become the height of artifice, and the vision of immediate reality the Blue Flower in the land of technology.[9]

This state of affairs, which contrasts so sharply with that which obtains in the theater, can be compared even more instructively to the situation in painting. Here we have to pose the question: How does the camera operator compare with the painter? In answer to this, it will be helpful to consider the concept of the operator as it is familiar to us from surgery. The surgeon represents the polar opposite of the magician. The attitude of the magician, who heals a sick person by a laying-on of hands, differs from that of the surgeon, who makes an intervention in the patient. The magician maintains the natural distance between himself and the person treated; more precisely, he reduces it slightly by laying on his hands, but increases it greatly by his authority. The surgeon does exactly the reverse; he greatly diminishes the distance from the patient by penetrating the patient's body, and increases it only slightly by the caution with which his hand moves among the organs. In short: unlike the magician (traces of whom are still found in the medical practitioner), the surgeon abstains at the decisive moment from confronting his patient person to person; instead, he penetrates the patient by operating.— Magician is to surgeon as painter is to cinematographer. The painter maintains in his work a natural distance from reality, whereas the cinematographer penetrates deeply into its tissue. The images obtained by each differ enormously. The painter's is a total image, whereas that of the cinematographer is piecemeal, its manifold parts being assembled according to a new law. *Hence, the presentation of reality in film is incomparably the more significant for people of today, since it provides the equipment-free aspect of reality they are entitled to demand from a work of art, and does so precisely on the basis of the most intensive interpenetration of reality with equipment.*

XII

The technological reproducibility of the artwork changes the relation of the masses to art. The extremely backward attitude toward a Picasso[1] painting changes into a highly progressive reaction to a Chaplin film. The progressive reaction is characterized by an immediate, intimate fusion of pleasure—pleasure in seeing and experiencing—with an attitude of expert appraisal. Such a fusion is an important social index. As is clearly seen in the case of

9. An allusion to *Heinrich von Ofterdingen* (1802), an unfinished novel by the German Romantic writer Novalis (Friedrich Freiherr von Hardenberg, 1772–1801), in which a medieval poet searches for a blue flower that bears the face of his beloved.

1. Pablo Picasso (1881–1973), Spanish-born painter who was a pioneer of modern art.

painting, the more reduced the social impact of an art form, the more widely criticism and enjoyment of it diverge in the public. The conventional is uncritically enjoyed, while the truly new is criticized with aversion. With regard to the cinema, the critical and uncritical attitudes of the public coincide. The decisive reason for this is that nowhere more than in the cinema are the reactions of individuals, which together make up the massive reaction of the audience, determined by the imminent concentration of reactions into a mass. No sooner are these reactions manifest than they regulate one another. Again, the comparison with painting is fruitful. A painting has always exerted a claim to be viewed primarily by a single person or by a few. The simultaneous viewing of paintings by a large audience, as happened in the nineteenth century, is an early symptom of the crisis in painting, a crisis triggered not only by photography but, in a relatively independent way, by the artwork's claim to the attention of the masses.

Painting, by its nature, cannot provide an object of simultaneous collective reception, as architecture has always been able to do, as the epic poem could do at one time, and as film is able to do today. And although direct conclusions about the social role of painting cannot be drawn from this fact alone, it does have a strongly adverse effect whenever painting is led by special circumstances, as if against its nature, to confront the masses directly. In the churches and monasteries of the Middle Ages, and at the princely courts up to about the end of the eighteenth century, the collective reception of paintings took place not simultaneously but in a manifoldly graduated and hierarchically mediated way. If that has changed, the change testifies to the special conflict in which painting has become enmeshed by the technological reproducibility of the image. And while efforts have been made to present paintings to the masses in galleries and salons, this mode of reception gives the masses no means of organizing and regulating their response. Thus, the same public which reacts progressively to a slapstick comedy inevitably displays a backward attitude toward Surrealism.[2]

XIII

Film can be characterized not only in terms of man's presentation of himself to the camera but also in terms of his representation of his environment by means of this apparatus. A glance at occupational psychology illustrates the testing capacity of the equipment. Psychoanalysis illustrates it in a different perspective. In fact, film has enriched our field of perception with methods that can be illustrated by those of Freudian theory. Fifty years ago, a slip of the tongue passed more or less unnoticed. Only exceptionally may such a slip have opened a perspective on depths in a conversation which had seemed to be proceeding on a superficial plane. Since the publication of *On the Psychopathology of Everyday Life*,[3] things have changed. This book isolated and made analyzable things which had previously floated unnoticed on the broad stream of perception. A similar deepening of appreciation through-

2. An experimental literary and political movement founded in France in 1924; its members sought to express subconscious thought and feeling.

3. An early work (1904) of SIGMUND FREUD (1856–1939), the Austrian founder of psychoanalysis, that discusses how what has come to be called a "Freudian slip" reveals unconscious feelings.

out the entire spectrum of optical—and now also auditory—impressions has been accomplished by film. One is merely stating the obverse of this fact when one says that actions shown in a movie can be analyzed much more precisely and from more points of view than those presented in a painting or on the stage. In contrast to what obtains in painting, filmed action lends itself more readily to analysis because it delineates situations far more precisely. In contrast to what obtains on the stage, filmed action lends itself more readily to analysis because it can be isolated more easily. This circumstance derives its prime importance from the fact that it tends to foster the interpenetration of art and science. Actually, if we think of a filmed action as neatly delineated within a particular situation—like a flexed muscle in a body—it is difficult to say which is more fascinating, its artistic value or its value for science. *Demonstrating that the artistic uses of photography are identical to its scientific uses—these two dimensions having usually been separated until now—will be one of the revolutionary functions of film.*[4]

On the one hand, film furthers insight into the necessities governing our lives by its use of close-ups, by its accentuation of hidden details in familiar objects, and by its exploration of commonplace milieux through the ingenious guidance of the camera; on the other hand, it manages to assure us of a vast and unsuspected field of action. Our bars and city streets, our offices and furnished rooms, our railroad stations and our factories seemed to close relentlessly around us. Then came film and exploded this prison-world with the dynamite of the split second,[5] so that now we can set off calmly on journeys of adventure among its far-flung debris. With the close-up, space expands; with slow motion, movement is extended. And just as enlargement not merely clarifies what we see indistinctly "in any case," but brings to light entirely new structures of matter, slow motion not only reveals familiar aspects of movements, but discloses quite unknown aspects within them—aspects "which do not appear as the retarding of natural movements but have a curious gliding, floating character of their own."[6] Clearly, it is another nature which speaks to the camera as compared to the eye. "Other" above all in the sense that a space informed by human consciousness gives way to a space informed by the unconscious. Whereas it is a commonplace that, for example, we have some idea what is involved in the act of walking (if only in general terms), we have no idea at all what happens during the split second when a person actually takes a step. We are familiar with the movement of picking up a cigarette lighter or a spoon, but know almost nothing of what really goes on between hand and metal, and still less how this varies with different moods. This is where the camera comes into play, with all its resources for swooping and rising, disrupting and isolating, stretching or compressing a sequence, enlarging or reducing an object. It is through the camera that we first discover the optical unconscious, just as we discover the instinctual unconscious through psychoanalysis.

4. Renaissance painting offers a revealing analogy to this situation. The incomparable development of this art and its significance depended not least on the integration of various new sciences, or at least various new scientific data. Renaissance painting made use of anatomy and perspective, of mathematics, meteorology, and chromatology [Benjamin's note].

5. The viewing time of the individual frames of a film.

6. Arnheim, p. 138 [Benjamin's note].

XIV

It has always been one of the primary tasks of art to create a demand whose hour of full satisfaction has not yet come.[7] The history of every art form has critical periods in which the particular form strains after effects which can be easily achieved only with a changed technical standard—that is to say, in a new art form. The excesses and crudities of art which thus result, particularly in periods of so-called decadence, actually emerge from the core of its richest historical energies. In recent years, Dadaism has abounded in such barbarisms. Only now is its impulse recognizable: *Dadaism attempted to produce with the means of painting (or literature) the effects which the public today seeks in film.*

Every fundamentally new, pioneering creation of demand will overshoot its target. Dadaism did so to the extent that it sacrificed the market values so characteristic of film in favor of more significant aspirations—of which, to be sure, it was unaware in the form described here. The Dadaists attached much less importance to the commercial usefulness of their artworks than to the uselessness of those works as objects of contemplative immersion. They sought to achieve this uselessness not least by thorough degradation of their material. Their poems are "word-salad"[8] containing obscene expressions and every imaginable kind of linguistic refuse. It is not otherwise with their paintings, on which they mounted buttons or train tickets. What they achieved by such means was a ruthless annihilation of the aura in every object they produced, which they branded as a reproduction through the very means of production. Before a painting by Arp or a poem by August Stramm, it is impossible to take time for concentration and evaluation, as one can before a painting by Derain or a poem by Rilke.[9] Contemplative immersion—

7. "The artwork," writes André Breton, "has value only insofar as it is alive to reverberations of the future." And indeed every highly developed art form stands at the intersection of three lines of development. First, technology is working toward a particular form of art. Before film appeared, there were little books of photos that could be made to flit past the viewer under the pressure of the thumb, presenting a boxing match or a tennis match; then there were coin-operated peepboxes in bazaars, with image sequences kept in motion by the turning of a handle. Second, traditional art forms, at certain stages in their development, strain laboriously for effects which later are effortlessly achieved by new art forms. Before film became established, Dadaists' performances sought to stir in their audience reactions which Chaplin then elicited more naturally. Third, apparently insignificant social changes often foster a change in reception which benefits only the new art form. Before film had started to create its public, images (which were no longer motionless) were received by an assembled audience in the *Kaiserpanorama*. Here the audience faced a screen into which stereoscopes were fitted, one for each spectator. In front of these stereoscopes single images automatically appeared, remained briefly in view, and then gave way to others. Edison still had to work with similar means when he presented the first film strip—before the movie screen and projection were known; a small audience gazed into an apparatus in which a sequence of images was shown. Incidentally, the institution of the *Kaiserpanorama* very clearly manifests a dialectic of development. Shortly before film turned the viewing of images into a collective activity, image viewing by the individual, through the stereoscopes of these soon outmoded establishments, was briefly intensified, as it had been once before in the isolated contemplation of the divine image by the priest in the cella [Benjamin's note]. Dadaists: members of a literary and artistic movement, founded in 1916, that stressed irrationality and anarchy and mocked normal aesthetic conventions. Breton (1896–1966), French artist and writer who broke with Dadaism in 1921 and founded surrealism in 1924. Thomas Alva Edison (1847–1931), American inventor, holder of patents for the microphone (1877), the phonograph (1878), the incandescent lamp (1879), and the Kinetoscope (1889), the single-view machine described by Benjamin; he also experimented with synchronizing motion pictures and sound.

8. Incoherent speech or writing made up of real and invented words.

9. Rainer Maria Rilke (1875–1926), Austrian poet. Jean Arp (1887–1966), French sculptor, one of the founders of Dadaism. Stramm (1874–1915), German poet. André Derain (1880–1954), French painter.

which, as the bourgeoisie degenerated, became a breeding ground for asocial behavior—is here opposed by distraction as a variant of social behavior. Dadaist manifestations actually guaranteed a quite vehement distraction by making artworks the center of scandal. One requirement was paramount: to outrage the public.

From an alluring visual composition or an enchanting fabric of sound, the Dadaists turned the artwork into a missile. It jolted the viewer, taking on a tactile quality. It thereby fostered the demand for film, since the distracting element in film is also primarily tactile, being based on successive changes of scene and focus which have a percussive effect on the spectator. Let us compare the screen on which a film unfolds with the canvas of a painting. The painting invites the viewer to contemplation; before it, he can give himself up to his train of associations. Before a film image, he cannot do so. No sooner has he seen it than it has already changed. It cannot be fixed on. Duhamel, who detests the cinema and knows nothing of its significance, though he does know something about its structure, describes the situation as follows: "I can no longer think what I want to think. My thoughts have been replaced by moving images."[1] Indeed, the train of associations in the person contemplating these images is immediately interrupted by new images. This constitutes the shock effect of film, which, like all shock effects, seeks to induce heightened attention.[2] *By means of its technological structure, film has freed the physical shock effect—which Dadaism had kept wrapped, as it were, inside the moral shock effect—from this wrapping.*[3]

XV

The masses are a matrix from which all customary behavior toward works of art is today emerging newborn. Quantity has been transformed into quality: *the greatly increased mass of participants has produced a different kind of participation.* The fact that the new mode of participation first appeared in a disreputable form should not mislead the observer. Yet some people have launched spirited attacks against precisely this superficial aspect of the matter. Among these critics, Duhamel has expressed himself most radically. What he objects to most is the kind of participation which the movie elicits from the masses. Duhamel calls the movie "a pastime for helots, a diversion for uneducated, wretched, worn-out creatures who are consumed by their

1. Georges Duhamel, *Scènes de la vie future* [*Scenes from Future Life*], 2d ed. (Paris, 1930), p. 52 [Benjamin's note]. Duhamel (1884–1966), French novelist and poet.

2. Film is the art form corresponding to the increased threat to life that faces people today. Humanity's need to expose itself to shock effects represents an adaptation to the dangers threatening it. Film corresponds to profound changes in the apparatus of apperception—changes that are experienced on the scale of private existence by each passerby in big-city traffic, and on a historical scale by every present-day citizen [Benjamin's note].

3. Film proves useful in illuminating Cubism and Futurism, as well as Dadaism. Both appear as deficient attempts on the part of art to take into account the pervasive interpenetration of reality by the apparatus. Unlike film, these schools did not try to use the apparatus as such for the artistic representation of reality, but aimed at a sort of alloy of represented reality and represented apparatus. In Cubism, a premonition of the structure of this apparatus, which is based on optics, plays a dominant part; in Futurism, it is the premonition of the effects of the apparatus—effects which are brought out by the rapid coursing of the band of film [Benjamin's note]. A movement beginning in the early 1900s, cubism reacted against sentimental and realistic painting, using primarily abstract form; a radical movement in art and literature, futurism glorified speed, war, and machinery, as well as advocated rebellion.

worries . . . , a spectacle which requires no concentration and presupposes no intelligence . . . , which kindles no light in the heart and awakens no hope other than the ridiculous one of someday becoming a 'star' in Los Angeles."[4] Clearly, this is in essence the ancient lament that the masses seek distraction, whereas art demands concentration from the spectator. That is a commonplace. The question remains whether it provides a basis for the analysis of film. This calls for closer examination. Distraction and concentration form an antithesis, which may be formulated as follows. A person who concentrates before a work of art is absorbed by it; he enters into the work, just as, according to legend, a Chinese painter entered his completed painting while beholding it. By contrast, the distracted masses absorb the work of art into themselves. This is most obvious with regard to buildings. Architecture has always offered the prototype of an artwork that is received in a state of distraction and through the collective. The laws of architecture's reception are highly instructive.

Buildings have accompanied human existence since primeval times. Many art forms have come into being and passed away. Tragedy begins with the Greeks, is extinguished along with them, and is revived centuries later, though only according to its "rules."[5] The epic, which originates in the early days of peoples, dies out in Europe at the end of the Renaissance. Panel painting is a creation of the Middle Ages, and nothing guarantees its uninterrupted existence. But the human need for shelter is permanent. Architecture has never had fallow periods. Its history is longer than that of any other art, and its effect ought to be recognized in any attempt to account for the relationship of the masses to the work of art. Buildings are received in a twofold manner: by use and by perception. Or, better: tactilely and optically. Such reception cannot be understood in terms of the concentrated attention of a traveler before a famous building. On the tactile side, there is no counterpart to what contemplation is on the optical side. Tactile reception comes about not so much by way of attention as by way of habit. The latter largely determines even the optical reception of architecture, which spontaneously takes the form of casual noticing, rather than attentive observation. Under certain circumstances, this form of reception shaped by architecture acquires canonical value. *For the tasks which face the human apparatus of perception at historical turning points cannot be performed solely by optical means—that is, by way of contemplation. They are mastered gradually—taking their cue from tactile reception—through habit.*

Even the distracted person can form habits. What is more, the ability to master certain tasks in a state of distraction proves that their performance has become habitual. The sort of distraction that is provided by art represents a covert measure of the extent to which it has become possible to perform new tasks of apperception. Since, moreover, individuals are tempted to evade such tasks, art will tackle the most difficult and most important tasks wherever it is able to mobilize the masses. It does so currently in film. *Reception in distraction—the sort of reception which is increasingly noticeable in*

4. Duhamel, p. 58 [Benjamin's note].

5. Tragedy developed from Greek religious festivals of Dionysus; Aristotle described the genre in his *Poetics,* but its "rules" were laid down by neoclassical critics and playwrights of the 17th and 18th centuries (e.g., see PIERRE CORNEILLE, above).

all areas of art and is a symptom of profound changes in apperception—finds in film its true training ground. Film, by virtue of its shock effects, is predisposed to this form of reception. It makes cult value recede into the background, not only because it encourages an evaluating attitude in the audience but also because, at the movies, the evaluating attitude requires no attention. The audience is an examiner, but a distracted one.

Epilogue

The increasing proletarianization of modern man and the increasing formation of masses are two sides of the same process. Fascism attempts to organize the newly proletarianized masses while leaving intact the property relations which they strive to abolish. It sees its salvation in granting expression to the masses—but on no account granting them rights.[6] The masses have a right to changed property relations; fascism seeks to give them *expression* in keeping these relations unchanged. *The logical outcome of fascism is an aestheticizing of political life.* The violation of the masses, whom fascism, with its *Führer*[7] cult, forces to their knees, has its counterpart in the violation of an apparatus which is pressed into serving the production of ritual values.

All efforts to aestheticize politics culminate in one point. That one point is war. War, and only war, makes it possible to set a goal for mass movements on the grandest scale while preserving traditional property relations. That is how the situation presents itself in political terms. In technological terms it can be formulated as follows: only war makes it possible to mobilize all of today's technological resources while maintaining property relations. It goes without saying that the fascist glorification of war does not make use of *these* arguments. Nevertheless, a glance at such glorification is instructive. In Marinetti's manifesto for the colonial war in Ethiopia, we read:

> For twenty-seven years we Futurists have rebelled against the idea that war is anti-aesthetic. . . . We therefore state: . . . War is beautiful because—thanks to its gas masks, its terrifying megaphones, its flame throwers, and light tanks—it establishes man's dominion over the subjugated machine. War is beautiful because it inaugurates the dreamed-of metallization of the human body. War is beautiful because it enriches a flowering meadow with the fiery orchids of machine-guns. War is beautiful because it combines gunfire, barrages, cease-fires, scents, and the fragrance of putrefaction into a symphony. War is beautiful

6. A technological factor is important here, especially with regard to the newsreel, whose significance for propaganda purposes can hardly be overstated. *Mass reproduction is especially favored by the reproduction of the masses.* In great ceremonial processions, giant rallies, and mass sporting events, and in war, all of which are now fed into the camera, the masses come face to face with themselves. This process, whose significance need not be emphasized, is closely bound up with the development of reproduction and recording technologies. In general, mass movements are more clearly apprehended by the camera than by the eye. A bird's-eye view best captures assemblies of hundreds of thousands. And even when this perspective is no less accessible to the human eye than to the camera, the image formed by the eye cannot be enlarged in the same way as a photograph. This is to say that mass movements, including war, are a form of human behavior especially suited to the camera [Benjamin's note].

7. Leader (German), the title assumed by Adolf Hitler.

> because it creates new architectures, like those of armored tanks, geometric squadrons of aircraft, spirals of smoke from burning villages, and much more. . . . Poets and artists of Futurism, . . . remember these principles of an aesthetic of war, that they may illuminate . . . your struggles for a new poetry and a new sculpture![8]

This manifesto has the merit of clarity. The question it poses deserves to be taken up by the dialectician. To him, the aesthetic of modern warfare appears as follows: if the natural use of productive forces is impeded by the property system, then the increase in technological means, in speed, in sources of energy will press toward an unnatural use. This is found in war, and the destruction caused by war furnishes proof that society was not mature enough to make technology its organ, that technology was not sufficiently developed to master the elemental forces of society. The most horrifying features of imperialist war are determined by the discrepancy between the enormous means of production and their inadequate use in the process of production (in other words, by unemployment and the lack of markets). *Imperialist war is an uprising on the part of technology, which demands repayment in "human material" for the natural material society has denied it.* Instead of draining rivers, society directs a human stream into a bed of trenches; instead of dropping seeds from airplanes, it drops incendiary bombs over cities; and in gas warfare it has found a new means of abolishing the aura.

"Fiat ars—pereat mundus,"[9] says fascism, expecting from war, as Marinetti admits, the artistic gratification of a sense perception altered by technology. This is evidently the consummation of *l'art pour l'art.* Humankind, which once, in Homer,[1] was an object of contemplation for the Olympian gods, has now become one for itself. Its self-alienation has reached the point where it can experience its own annihilation as a supreme aesthetic pleasure. *Such is the aestheticizing of politics, as practiced by fascism. Communism replies by politicizing art.*

1936–39 1936, 1955

8. Likely cited from a French newspaper, one of several manifestos issued by Filippo Tommaso Marinetti (1876–1944), Italian poet and novelist who in 1909 founded futurism; for a time, the movement was endorsed by Italian Fascists. "The Colonial War in Ethiopia": an ambiguously worded 1889 treaty led Italy to claim Ethiopia as its protectorate; the war of 1895–96 forced Italy to recognize Ethiopia's independence, but in 1935 Italy invaded the country.

9. Let art be made, let the world perish (Latin).

1. Greek poet credited with authoring the *Iliad* and the *Odyssey* (ca. 8th c. B.C.E.).

MIKHAIL M. BAKHTIN
1895–1975

Proclaimed by TZVETAN TODOROV as perhaps the greatest twentieth-century theorist of literature, M. M. Bakhtin, since his discovery in the 1970s, has been acclaimed by literary critics across a wide theoretical and political spectrum. He has been called a formalist, a Marxist, a Christian humanist, a conservative, and a radical; because his work intersects in eccentric ways with so many of the critical orthodoxies of contemporary literary criticism, it resists easy classification.

Almost everything about Bakhtin's life and writing is colored by the fact that his greatest period of productivity coincided with the Russian Revolution, the ensuing civil war (1918–21), and the repressive Soviet regime under Joseph Stalin. Lacking Communist Party credentials, he labored most of his adult life in obscurity, a circumstance that probably saved his life at a time when his close—and better connected—friends were disappearing into death camps. The circumstances of Bakhtin's life make it sometimes difficult to verify the authorship and chronology of his writings. Certain works written during his youth in the 1920s were not published until late in his life or after his death, and controversies continue over three disputed books from the 1920s that appeared under the names of his colleagues Valentin Vološinov and Pavel Medvedev, held by some to be the works of Bakhtin himself. Yet these difficulties in separating Bakhtin's voice from those of others are of a piece with his own philosophical beliefs about the dialogic nature of language. As he wrote in a note that was later published in his *Speech Genres and Other Late Essays*, "Quests for my own words are quests for a word that is not my own."

Born in the Russian town of Orel, Bakhtin grew up in Vilnius and later Odessa. He earned a degree in classics and philology from the University of Petrograd in 1918. Working as a schoolteacher in Nevel in western Russia during the civil war between the Red Army and the anti-Bolshevist White armies, he first met the group of intellectuals who would become part of his circle and within whose wide-ranging discussions Bakhtin would formulate the critical concepts that were to dominate his thinking for the rest of his life. In 1920 Bakhtin settled in Vitebsk, where his circle, which by now included Vološinov and Medvedev, continued to meet. In 1924 Bakhtin moved back to Petrograd (or St. Petersburg), now renamed Leningrad; there in January 1929 he was arrested and imprisoned for alleged antigovernment activity and the Socratic crime of "corrupting the young." In prison he suffered from health problems caused by chronic osteomyelitis, a painful inflammation of the bone marrow. He was sentenced to ten years in a labor camp, but on the intervention of friends, the sentence was commuted to six years' internal exile in Kazakhstan. In 1936, his exile over, he taught at Mordovia Pedagogical Institute in Saransk until new purges forced him to resign. He moved to a small town outside of Moscow where his worsening osteomyelitis led to the amputation of his right leg. After that surgery, Bakhtin had difficulty finding permanent employment, though he occasionally delivered lectures at the Gorky Institute of World Literature.

In the 1930s and 1940s Bakhtin began to write a dissertation on the French writer François Rabelais (1490–1553), as well as a book on novels that chronicle the main character's maturation and education (the bildungsroman). World War II interrupted his work on the dissertation and the planned book on the bildungsroman; only fragments of this book survive. Following the war, Bakhtin was allowed to return to his university position in Saransk, and to his unfinished dissertation on Rabelais. Although he was finally granted the doctoral degree, he could not publish his dissertation; it remained unread until it was discovered in the Gorky Institute's archives by graduate students in the early 1960s. After Stalin's death in 1953, Bakhtin's scholarly fortunes began to rise even as his health began to decline. In addition to osteomyelitis, he also suffered from emphysema caused by his heavy smoking. By the time of his death from complications of emphysema, he had become something of a cult figure in Russia. In the 1970s his reputation spread to Paris through the work of Eastern European émigrés such as JULIA KRISTEVA and Tzvetan Todorov; from there in the 1980s it reached North America and England, where his work had significant impact.

Bakhtin's earliest writings, in such essays as "Towards a Philosophy of the Act" (1919, published 1986) and "Author and Hero in Aesthetic Activity" (1919, published 1975), are densely philosophical and heavily indebted to IMMANUEL KANT (1724–1804). Although these lengthy essays exhibit a keen interest in phenomenology and the intersubjective nature of language, the publications of the Bakhtin Circle from the late 1920s defined the problems of language that would occupy Bakhtin for the rest of his life. In 1926 Vološinov published *Freudianism: A Marxist Critique*, and Medvedev followed in 1928 with *The Formal Method in Literary Scholarship*. In 1929 Vološinov's *Marxism and the Philosophy of Language* appeared and also Bakhtin's *Problems of Dostoevsky's Poetics*, the only book to be published under his own name before Stalin's death. Critics wary of Marxism have attempted to distance Bakhtin from the work of his circle, arguing that he did not share the Communist sympathies of Vološinov and Medvedev (both members of the Communist Party; both disappeared during the political purges of the 1930s). But regardless of whether Bakhtin actually wrote the books ascribed to his two colleagues, as some have claimed, the influences among the members of the circle were undoubtedly strong and indelible. Bakhtin's words became inextricably and dialogically intertwined with those of his collaborators, whose thought influenced the key concepts he later developed in his celebrated writings on the novel, just as his thought undoubtedly influenced theirs.

Bakhtin's theory of the novel relies on three key concepts. The *carnivalesque*—an idea first introduced in *Rabelais and His World* (written in the 1930s and 1940s, published 1965)—is Bakhtin's term for those forms of unofficial culture (the early novel among them) that resist official culture, political oppression, and totalitarian order through laughter, parody, and "grotesque realism." In "Forms of Time and Chronotope in the Novel" (1937–38), he develops the influential term *chronotope* to describe the intrinsic connectedness of time and space and their central role in constituting literary genres. Finally and most significantly, the *dialogism* of language, the "intense interanimation and struggle between one's own and another's word," would come to dominate Bakhtin's thinking about language after 1926. This concept of the multivoiced nature of discourse received its fullest treatment in "Discourse in the Novel" (1934–35), a key text for narrative, linguistic, and literary theory, from which we have taken our selection.

Bakhtin here addresses the limitations for literary studies of the abstract and formal analyses of literary technique widespread among critics during the interwar period. Traditional linguistics, stylistics, and literary theory—including the theory of the Russian formalists, represented by critics like Boris Eichenbaum—as well as contemporary Marxist philosophy of language (see Leon Trotsky, for instance) and the new structural linguistics indebted to FERDINAND DE SAUSSURE, all fail to articulate an adequate account of the novel because they have not pursued a properly "sociological stylistics." The philosophy of language on which these inadequate critical methods are based posits, on the one hand, a unitary system of language—a system of more or less absolute norms that govern speech—and, on the other hand, an individual who is seen as the controlling "author" of discourse. Bakhtin calls such a view of language "monologic," and he argues that it is alien to the dynamics of the novel because it describes not real, living language but an abstraction created through self-conscious deliberation about language and cut off from the daily ideological activities of social life. Living language exhibits *heteroglossia*, the term Bakhtin famously uses to describe the "internal stratification" of language: the interplay among its social dialects, class dialects, professional jargons, languages of generations and age groups and of passing fads, "languages that serve the specific sociopolitical purposes of the day, even of the hour." Heteroglossia, which Bakhtin hails as the characteristic stylistic feature of the novel, celebrates not, as structuralism does, the systematic nature of language but the multiplicity of all those "centrifugal" forces at work in language, the variety of social speech types, and the diversity of voices interacting with one another.

Central to Bakhtin's theory of the novel is his belief that language is fundamentally dialogic. "Discourse in the Novel" offers his most elaborate analysis of "dialogism" and its relationship to style in the novel. Between any word and its object, between any word and its speaking subject, between any word and its active respondent(s), Bakhtin argues, there exists "an elastic environment of other, alien words about the same object"; and this "dialogically agitated and tension-filled environment of alien words, value judgments and accents" that weaves in and out of discourse in complex patterns finds its most artistic expression in the novel. Bakhtin celebrates the dialogics of the novel while criticizing the monologism of poetry, which characteristically aims for a unified and pure discourse. Although conflict, contradiction, and doubt may be present in the subject matter of poetry, they do not, according to Bakhtin, enter into the language of the poem itself, as they consistently do in the novel.

Bakhtin's theories can sometimes appear confusing and vague because his critical terminology often seems at once evaluative and descriptive; he regularly establishes his critical vocabulary by defining certain terms positively against related terms given negative valences. Thus the novel is opposed to poetry, the carnivalesque to official discourse, the dialogic to the monologic. These judgments have posed problems for critics who value those genres that Bakhtin most frequently derogates as monologic, especially poetry, the epic, and drama. Other critics object that it is not clear to what degree Bakhtin espouses a mimetic theory of literature, insofar as language for him seems less to represent or reflect reality than to refract and rework it.

Nevertheless, Bakhtin's work has been much admired and extended by scholars in many fields. Those in cultural studies have found two major contributions particularly useful. First, Bakhtin focuses on "language" as the utterances of speaking subjects: that is, as spoken "discourse" and not the impersonal, prevocal signifiers or rhetorical tropes posited by the influential structuralist and poststructuralist traditions. Second, he insists that discourse unfolds in a heteroglot, dialogic force field of conflicting interests and ideologies—with literary language being only one of many discursive strata and itself divided by generic, stylistic, professional, and other special features. These Bakhtinian views, widely advocated by cultural studies scholars, promote a complex sociopoetics suited to a contemporary globalized world of diverse peoples, languages, and cultural forms.

"Discourse in the Novel" Keywords: Ideology, Language, Literary History, The Novel, Vernacular Language

From Discourse in the Novel[1]

The principal idea of this essay is that the study of verbal art can and must overcome the divorce between an abstract "formal" approach and an equally abstract "ideological" approach. Form and content in discourse are one, once we understand that verbal discourse is a social phenomenon—social throughout its entire range and in each and every of its factors, from the sound image to the furthest reaches of abstract meaning.

1. Translated by Caryl Emerson and Michael Holquist, who occasionally retain the original Russian words or add information in brackets.

It is this idea that has motivated our emphasis on "the stylistics of genre." The separation of style and language from the question of genre has been largely responsible for a situation in which only individual and period-bound overtones of a style are the privileged subjects of study, while its basic social tone is ignored. The great historical destinies of genres are overshadowed by the petty vicissitudes of stylistic modifications, which in their turn are linked with individual artists and artistic movements. For this reason, stylistics has been deprived of an authentic philosophical and sociological approach to its problems; it has become bogged down in stylistic trivia; it is not able to sense behind the individual and period-bound shifts the great and anonymous destinies of artistic discourse itself. More often than not, stylistics defines itself as a stylistics of "private craftsmanship" and ignores the social life of discourse outside the artist's study, discourse in the open spaces of public squares, streets, cities and villages, of social groups, generations and epochs. Stylistics is concerned not with living discourse but with a histological specimen made from it, with abstract linguistic discourse in the service of an artist's individual creative powers. But these individual and tendentious overtones of style, cut off from the fundamentally social modes in which discourse lives, inevitably come across as flat and abstract in such a formulation and cannot therefore be studied in organic unity with a work's semantic components.

Modern Stylistics & the Novel

Before the twentieth century, problems associated with a stylistics of the novel had not been precisely formulated—such a formulation could only have resulted from a recognition of the stylistic uniqueness of novelistic (artistic-prose) discourse.

For a long time treatment of the novel was limited to little more than abstract ideological examination and publicistic commentary. Concrete questions of stylistics were either not treated at all or treated in passing and in an arbitrary way: the discourse of artistic prose was either understood as being poetic in the narrow sense, and had the categories of traditional stylistics (based on the study of tropes) uncritically applied to it, or else such questions were limited to empty, evaluative terms for the characterization of language, such as "expressiveness," "imagery," "force," "clarity" and so on—without providing these concepts with any stylistic significance, however vague and tentative.

Toward the end of the last century, as a counterweight to this abstract ideological way of viewing things, interest began to grow in the concrete problems of artistic craftsmanship in prose, in the problems of novel and short-story technique. However, in questions of stylistics the situation did not change in the slightest; attention was concentrated almost exclusively on problems of composition (in the broad sense of the word). But, as before, the peculiarities of the stylistic life of discourse in the novel (and in the short story as well) lacked an approach that was both principled and at the same time concrete (one is impossible without the other); the same arbitrary judgmental observations about language—in the spirit of traditional stylistics—continued to reign supreme, and they totally overlooked the authentic nature of artistic prose.

There is a highly characteristic and widespread point of view that sees novelistic discourse as an extra-artistic medium, a discourse that is not worked into any special or unique style. After failure to find in novelistic discourse a purely poetic formulation ("poetic" in the narrow sense) as was expected, prose discourse is denied any artistic value at all; it is the same as practical speech for everyday life, or speech for scientific purposes, an artistically neutral means of communication.[2]

Such a point of view frees one from the necessity of undertaking stylistic analyses of the novel; it in fact gets rid of the very problem of a stylistics of the novel, permitting one to limit oneself to purely thematic analyses of it.

It was, however, precisely in the 1920s that this situation changed: the novelistic prose word began to win a place for itself in stylistics. On the one hand there appeared a series of concrete stylistic analyses of novelistic prose; on the other hand, systematic attempts were made to recognize and define the stylistic uniqueness of artistic prose as distinct from poetry.

But it was precisely these concrete analyses and these attempts at a principled approach that made patently obvious the fact that all the categories of traditional stylistics—in fact the very concept of a *poetic* artistic discourse, which lies at the heart of such categories—were not applicable to novelistic discourse. Novelistic discourse proved to be the acid test for this whole way of conceiving style, exposing the narrowness of this type of thinking and its inadequacy in all areas of discourse's artistic life.

All attempts at concrete stylistic analysis of novelistic prose either strayed into linguistic descriptions of the language of a given novelist or else limited themselves to those separate, isolated stylistic elements of the novel that were includable (or gave the appearance of being includable) in the traditional categories of stylistics. In both instances the stylistic whole of the novel and of novelistic discourse eluded the investigator.

The novel as a whole is a phenomenon multiform in style and variform in speech and voice. In it the investigator is confronted with several heterogeneous stylistic unities, often located on different linguistic levels and subject to different stylistic controls.

We list below the basic types of compositional-stylistic unities into which the novelistic whole usually breaks down:

(1) Direct authorial literary-artistic narration (in all its diverse variants);
(2) Stylization of the various forms of oral everyday narration (*skaz*);[3]

2. As recently as the 1920s, V. M. Žirmunskij [important fellow traveler of the Formalists (translators' note)] was writing: "When lyrical poetry appears to be authentically a work of *verbal art*, due to its choice and combination of words (on semantic as well as sound levels) all of which are completely subordinated to the aesthetic project, Tolstoy's novel, by contrast, which is free in its verbal composition, does not use words as an artistically significant element of interaction but as a neutral medium or as a system of significations subordinated (as happens in practical speech) to the communicative function, directing our attention to thematic aspects quite abstracted from purely verbal considerations. We cannot call such a *literary work* a work of *verbal art* or, in any case, not in the sense that the term is used for lyrical poetry" ["On the Problem of the Formal Method," in an anthology of his articles, *Problems of a Theory of Literature* (Leningrad, 1928, p. 173); Russian edition: "K voprosu o 'formal' nom metode'," in *Voprosy teorii literatury* (L., 1928) (trans.)] [Bakhtin's note]. Leo Tolstoy (1828–1910), Russian novelist and moral philosopher.

3. This term has no precise equivalent in English; *skaz* is a technique or mode of narration that imitates the oral speech or "yarn" of an individualized narrator, as in Mark Twain's "Celebrated Jumping Frog of Calaveras County" (1865). *Skaz* was the subject of much Russian formalist criticism.

(3) Stylization of the various forms of semiliterary (written) everyday narration (the letter, the diary, etc.);
(4) Various forms of literary but extra-artistic authorial speech (moral, philosophical or scientific statements, oratory, ethnographic descriptions, memoranda and so forth);
(5) The stylistically individualized speech of characters.

These heterogeneous stylistic unities, upon entering the novel, combine to form a structured artistic system, and are subordinated to the higher stylistic unity of the work as a whole, a unity that cannot be identified with any single one of the unities subordinated to it.

The stylistic uniqueness of the novel as a genre consists precisely in the combination of these subordinated, yet still relatively autonomous, unities (even at times comprised of different languages) into the higher unity of the work as a whole: the style of a novel is to be found in the combination of its styles; the language of a novel is the system of its "languages." Each separate element of a novel's language is determined first of all by one such subordinated stylistic unity into which it enters directly—be it the stylistically individualized speech of a character, the down-to-earth voice of a narrator in *skaz*, a letter or whatever. The linguistic and stylistic profile of a given element (lexical, semantic, syntactic) is shaped by that subordinated unity to which it is most immediately proximate. At the same time this element, together with its most immediate unity, figures into the style of the whole, itself supports the accent of the whole and participates in the process whereby the unified meaning of the whole is structured and revealed.

The novel can be defined as a diversity of social speech types (sometimes even diversity of languages) and a diversity of individual voices, artistically organized. The internal stratification of any single national language into social dialects, characteristic group behavior, professional jargons, generic languages, languages of generations and age groups, tendentious languages, languages of the authorities, of various circles and of passing fashions, languages that serve the specific sociopolitical purposes of the day, even of the hour (each day has its own slogan, its own vocabulary, its own emphases)—this internal stratification present in every language at any given moment of its historical existence is the indispensable prerequisite for the novel as a genre. The novel orchestrates all its themes, the totality of the world of objects and ideas depicted and expressed in it, by means of the social diversity of speech types [*raznorečie*] and by the differing individual voices that flourish under such conditions. Authorial speech, the speeches of narrators, inserted genres, the speech of characters are merely those fundamental compositional unities with whose help heteroglossia [*raznorečie*] can enter the novel; each of them permits a multiplicity of social voices and a wide variety of their links and interrelationships (always more or less dialogized). These distinctive links and interrelationships between utterances and languages, this movement of the theme through different languages and speech types, its dispersion into the rivulets and droplets of social heteroglossia, its dialogization—this is the basic distinguishing feature of the stylistics of the novel.

Such a combining of languages and styles into a higher unity is unknown to traditional stylistics; it has no method for approaching the distinctive social dialogue among languages that is present in the novel. Thus stylistic analysis is not oriented toward the novel as a whole, but only toward one or another of its subordinated stylistic unities. The traditional scholar bypasses the basic distinctive feature of the novel as a genre; he substitutes for it another object of study, and instead of novelistic style he actually analyzes something completely different. He transposes a symphonic (orchestrated) theme on to the piano keyboard.

We notice two such types of substitutions: in the first type, an analysis of novelistic style is replaced by a description of the language of a given novelist (or at best of the "languages" of a given novel); in the second type, one of the subordinated styles is isolated and analyzed as if it were the style of the whole.

In the first type, style is cut off from considerations of genre, and from the work as such, and regarded as a phenomenon of language itself: the unity of style in a given work is transformed either into the unity of an individual language ("individual dialect"), or into the unity of an individual speech (*parole*). It is precisely the individuality of the speaking subject that is recognized to be that style-generating factor transforming a phenomenon of language and linguistics into a stylistic unity.

We have no need to follow where such an analysis of novelistic style leads, whether to a disclosing of the novelist's individual dialect (that is, his vocabulary, his syntax) or to a disclosing of the distinctive features of the work taken as a "complete speech act," an "utterance." Equally in both cases, style is understood in the spirit of Saussure:[4] as an individualization of the general language (in the sense of a system of general language norms). Stylistics is transformed either into a curious kind of linguistics treating individual languages, or into a linguistics of the utterance.

In accordance with the point of view selected, the unity of a style thus presupposes on the one hand a unity of language (in the sense of a system of general normative forms) and on the other hand the unity of an individual person realizing himself in this language.

Both these conditions are in fact obligatory in the majority of verse-based poetic genres, but even in these genres they far from exhaust or define the style of the work. The most precise and complete description of the individual language and speech of a poet—even if this description does choose to treat the expressiveness of language and speech elements—does not add up to a stylistic analysis of the work, inasmuch as these elements relate to a system of language or to a system of speech, that is, to various linguistic unities and not to the system of the artistic work, which is governed by a completely different system of rules than those that govern the linguistic systems of language and of speech.

But—we repeat—in the majority of poetic genres, the unity of the language system and the unity (and uniqueness) of the poet's individuality as reflected in his language and speech, which is directly realized in this unity, are indispensable prerequisites of poetic style. The novel, however, not only does not require these conditions but (as we have said) even makes of the internal stratification of language, of its social heteroglossia and the variety of individual voices in it, the prerequisite for authentic novelistic prose.

4. Specifically, the emphasis by the Swiss linguist FERDINAND DE SAUSSURE (1857–1913) on *langue* (a language system) and *parole* (individual speech).

Thus the substitution of the individualized language of the novelist (to the extent that one can recover this language from the "speech" and "language" systems of the novel) for the style of the novel itself is doubly imprecise: it distorts the very essence of a stylistics of the novel. Such substitution inevitably leads to the selection from the novel of only those elements that can be fitted within the frame of a single language system and that express, directly and without mediation, an authorial individuality in language. The whole of the novel and the specific tasks involved in constructing this whole out of heteroglot, multi-voiced, multi-styled and often multi-languaged elements remain outside the boundaries of such a study.

Such is the first type of substitution for the proper object of study in the stylistic analysis of the novel. We will not delve further into the diverse variations of this type, which are determined by the different ways in which such concepts as "the speech whole," "the system of language," "the individuality of the author's language and speech" are understood, and by a difference in the very way in which the relationship between style and language is conceived (and also the relationship between stylistics and linguistics). In all possible variants on this type of analysis, which acknowledge only one single language and a single authorial individuality expressing itself directly in that language, the stylistic nature of the novel slips hopelessly away from the investigator.

The second type of substitution is characterized not by an orientation toward the language of the author, but rather toward the style of the novel itself—although style thus understood is narrowed down to mean the style of merely one out of the several subordinated unities (which are relatively autonomous) within the novel.

In the majority of cases the style of the novel is subsumed under the concept of "epic style," and the appropriate categories of traditional stylistics are applied to it. In such circumstances only those elements of epic representation (those occurring predominantly in direct authorial speech) are isolated from the novel for consideration. The profound difference between novelistic and purely epic modes of expression is ignored. Differences between the novel and the epic are usually perceived on the level of composition and thematics alone.

In other instances, different aspects of novelistic style are selected out as most characteristic of one or another concrete literary work. Thus the narrational aspect can be considered from the point of view not of its objective descriptive mode, but of its subjective expression mode (expressiveness). One might select elements of vernacular extraliterary narration (*skaz*) or those aspects that provide the information necessary to further the plot (as one might do, for example, in analyzing an adventure novel).[5] And it is possible, finally, to select those purely dramatic elements of the novel that lower the narrational aspect to the level of a commentary on the dialogues of the novel's characters. But the system of languages in drama is organized on completely different principles, and therefore its languages sound utterly different than do the languages of the novel. In drama there is no all-

5. Artistic prose style has been studied in Russia by the Formalists largely on these two last levels, that is, either *skaz* (Eichenbaum) or plot-informational aspects (Shklovsky) were studied as most characteristic of literary prose [Bakhtin's note]. Boris Eichenbaum (1886–1959), Russian formalist critic. Viktor Shklovsky (1893–1984), Russian formalist writer and critic.

encompassing language that addresses itself dialogically to separate languages, there is no second all-encompassing plotless (nondramatic) dialogue outside that of the (nondramatic) plot.

All these types of analysis are inadequate to the style not only of the novelistic whole but even of that element isolated as fundamental for a given novel—inasmuch as that element, removed from its interaction with others, changes its stylistic meaning and ceases to be that which it in fact had been in the novel.

The current state of questions posed by a stylistics of the novel reveals, fully and clearly, that all the categories and methods of traditional stylistics remain incapable of dealing effectively with the artistic uniqueness of discourse in the novel, or with the specific life that discourse leads in the novel. "Poetic language," "individuality of language," "image," "symbol," "epic style" and other general categories worked out and applied by stylistics, as well as the entire set of concrete stylistic devices subsumed by these categories (no matter how differently understood by individual critics), are all equally oriented toward the single-languaged and single-styled genres, toward the poetic genres in the narrow sense of the word. Their connection with this exclusive orientation explains a number of the particular features and limitations of traditional stylistic categories. All these categories, and the very philosophical conception of poetic discourse in which they are grounded, are too narrow and cramped, and cannot accommodate the artistic prose of novelistic discourse.

Thus stylistics and the philosophy of discourse indeed confront a dilemma: either to acknowledge the novel (and consequently all artistic prose tending in that direction) an unartistic or quasi-artistic genre, or to radically reconsider that conception of poetic discourse in which traditional stylistics is grounded and which determines all its categories.

This dilemma, however, is by no means universally recognized. Most scholars are not inclined to undertake a radical revision of the fundamental philosophical conception of poetic discourse. Many do not even see or recognize the philosophical roots of the stylistics (and linguistics) in which they work, and shy away from any fundamental philosophical issues. They utterly fail to see behind their isolated and fragmented stylistic observations and linguistic descriptions any theoretical problems posed by novelistic discourse. Others—more principled—make a case for consistent individualism in their understanding of language and style. First and foremost they seek in the stylistic phenomenon a direct and unmediated expression of authorial individuality, and such an understanding of the problem is least likely of all to encourage a reconsideration of basic stylistic categories in the proper direction.

However, there is another solution of our dilemma that does take basic concepts into account: one need only consider oft-neglected rhetoric, which for centuries has included artistic prose in its purview. Once we have restored rhetoric to all its ancient rights, we may adhere to the old concept of poetic discourse, relegating to "rhetorical forms" everything in novelistic prose that does not fit the Procrustean bed of traditional stylistic categories.[6]

6. Such a solution to the problem was especially tempting to adherents of the formal method in poetics: in fact, the re-establishment of rhetoric, with all its rights, greatly strengthens the Formalist position. Formalist rhetoric is a necessary addition to Formalist poetics. Our Formalists were being completely consistent when they spoke of the necessity of reviving rhetoric alongside poetics (on this, see B. M. Eichenbaum, *Literature* [*Literatura*; Leningrad, 1927], pp. 147–48) [Bakhtin's note].

Gustav Shpet,[7] in his time, proposed such a solution to the dilemma, with all due rigorousness and consistency. He utterly excluded artistic prose and its ultimate realization—the novel—from the realm of poetry, and assigned it to the category of purely rhetorical forms.[8]

Here is what Shpet says about the novel: "The recognition that contemporary forms of moral propaganda—i.e., the *novel*—do not spring from *poetic creativity* but are purely rhetorical compositions, is an admission, and a conception, that apparently cannot arise without immediately confronting a formidable obstacle in the form of the universal recognition, despite everything, that the novel *does* have a certain aesthetic value."[9]

Shpet utterly denies the novel any aesthetic significance. The novel is an extra-artistic rhetorical genre, "the contemporary form of moral propaganda"; artistic discourse is exclusively poetic discourse (in the sense we have indicated above).

Viktor Vinogradov[1] adopted an analogous point of view in his book *On Artistic Prose*, assigning the problem of artistic prose to rhetoric. While agreeing with Shpet's basic philosophical definitions of the "poetic" and the "rhetorical," Vinogradov was, however, not so paradoxically consistent: he considered the novel a syncretic, mixed form ("a hybrid formation") and admitted that it contained, along with rhetorical elements, some purely poetic ones.[2]

The point of view that completely excludes novelistic prose, as a rhetorical formation, from the realm of poetry—a point of view that is basically false—does nevertheless have a certain indisputable merit. There resides in it an acknowledgment in principle and in substance of the inadequacy of all contemporary stylistics, along with its philosophical and linguistic base, when it comes to defining the specific distinctive features of novelistic prose. And what is more, the very reliance on rhetorical forms has a great heuristic significance. Once rhetorical discourse is brought into the study with all its living diversity, it cannot fail to have a deeply revolutionizing influence on linguistics and on the philosophy of language. It is precisely those aspects of any discourse (the internally dialogic quality of discourse, and the phenomena related to it), not yet sufficiently taken into account and fathomed in all the enormous weight they carry in the life of language, that are revealed with great external precision in rhetorical forms, provided a correct and unprejudiced approach to those forms is used. Such is the general methodological and heuristic significance of rhetorical forms for linguistics and for the philosophy of language.

The special significance of rhetorical forms for understanding the novel is equally great. The novel, and artistic prose in general, has the closest gene-

7. Gustav Shpet (1879–1937), outstanding representative of the neo-Kantian and (especially) Husserlian traditions in Russia; as professor at the University of Moscow for many years he influenced many (among others, the young Roman Jakobson) [translators' note]. IMMANUEL KANT (1724–1804), German idealist philosopher. Edmund Husserl (1859–1938), German phenomenologist. JAKOBSON (1896–1982), Russian-born literary theorist and linguist.

8. Originally in his *Aesthetic Fragments* [*Estetičeskie fragmenty*]; in a more complete aspect in the book *The Inner Form of the Word* [*Vnutrennjaja forma slova*] (M., 1927) [Bakhtin's note].

9. *Vnutrennjaja forma slova*, p. 215 [Bakhtin's note].

1. Viktor Vinogradov (1895–1969), outstanding linguist and student of style in literature, a friendly critic of the Formalists, and an important theorist in his own right (especially his work on *skaz* technique) [translators' note].

2. V. V. Vinogradov, *On Artistic Prose* [*O xudožestvennom proze*], Moscow-Leningrad, 1930, pp. 75–106 [Bakhtin's note].

tic, family relationship to rhetorical forms. And throughout the entire development of the novel, its intimate interaction (both peaceful and hostile) with living rhetorical genres (journalistic, moral, philosophical and others) has never ceased; this interaction was perhaps no less intense than was the novel's interaction with the artistic genres (epic, dramatic, lyric). But in this uninterrupted interrelationship, novelistic discourse preserved its own qualitative uniqueness and was never reducible to rhetorical discourse.

The novel is an artistic genre. Novelistic discourse is poetic discourse, but one that does not fit within the frame provided by the concept of poetic discourse as it now exists. This concept has certain underlying presuppositions that limit it. The very concept—in the course of its historical formulation from Aristotle[3] to the present day—has been oriented toward the specific "official" genres and connected with specific historical tendencies in verbal ideological life. Thus a whole series of phenomena remained beyond its conceptual horizon.

Philosophy of language, linguistics and stylistics [i.e., such as they have come down to us] have all postulated a simple and unmediated relation of speaker to his unitary and singular "own" language, and have postulated as well a simple realization of this language in the monologic utterance of the individual. Such disciplines actually know only two poles in the life of language, between which are located all the linguistic and stylistic phenomena they know: on the one hand, the system of a *unitary language,* and on the other the *individual* speaking in this language.

Various schools of thought in the philosophy of language, in linguistics and in stylistics have, in different periods (and always in close connection with the diverse concrete poetic and ideological styles of a given epoch), introduced into such concepts as "system of language," "monologic utterance," "the speaking *individuum,*" various differing nuances of meaning, but their basic content remains unchanged. This basic content is conditioned by the specific sociohistorical destinies of European languages and by the destinies of ideological discourse, and by those particular historical tasks that ideological discourse has fulfilled in specific social spheres and at specific stages in its own historical development.

These tasks and destinies of discourse conditioned specific verbal-ideological movements, as well as various specific genres of ideological discourse, and ultimately the specific philosophical concept of discourse itself—in particular, the concept of poetic discourse, which had been at the heart of all concepts of style.

The strength and at the same time the limitations of such basic stylistic categories become apparent when such categories are seen as conditioned by specific historical destinies and by the task that an ideological discourse assumes. These categories arose from and were shaped by the historically *aktuell*[4] forces at work in the verbal-ideological evolution of specific social groups; they comprised the theoretical expression of actualizing forces that were in the process of creating a life for language.

These forces are *the forces that serve to unify and centralize the verbal-ideological world.*

3. The Greek philosopher (384–322 B.C.E.) discusses poetic discourse in his *Poetics* (see above).

4. Topical, of pressing current importance (German).

Unitary language constitutes the theoretical expression of the historical processes of linguistic unification and centralization, an expression of the centripetal forces of language. A unitary language is not something given [*dan*] but is always in essence posited [*zadan*]—and at every moment of its linguistic life it is opposed to the realities of heteroglossia. But at the same time it makes its real presence felt as a force for overcoming this heteroglossia, imposing specific limits to it, guaranteeing a certain maximum of mutual understanding and crystalizing into a real, although still relative, unity—the unity of the reigning conversational (everyday) and literary language, "correct language."

A common unitary language is a system of linguistic norms. But these norms do not constitute an abstract imperative; they are rather the generative forces of linguistic life, forces that struggle to overcome the heteroglossia of language, forces that unite and centralize verbal-ideological thought, creating within a heteroglot national language the firm, stable linguistic nucleus of an officially recognized literary language, or else defending an already formed language from the pressure of growing heteroglossia.

What we have in mind here is not an abstract linguistic minimum of a common language, in the sense of a system of elementary forms (linguistic symbols) guaranteeing a *minimum* level of comprehension in practical communication. We are taking language not as a system of abstract grammatical categories, but rather language conceived as ideologically saturated, language as a world view, even as a concrete opinion, insuring a *maximum* of mutual understanding in all spheres of ideological life. Thus a unitary language gives expression to forces working toward concrete verbal and ideological unification and centralization, which develop in vital connection with the processes of sociopolitical and cultural centralization.

Aristotelian poetics, the poetics of Augustine, the poetics of the medieval church, of "the one language of truth," the Cartesian poetics of neoclassicism, the abstract grammatical universalism of Leibniz (the idea of a "universal grammar"), Humboldt's[5] insistence on the concrete—all these, whatever their differences in nuance, give expression to the same centripetal forces in sociolinguistic and ideological life; they serve one and the same project of centralizing and unifying the European languages. The victory of one reigning language (dialect) over the others, the supplanting of languages, their enslavement, the process of illuminating them with the True Word, the incorporation of barbarians and lower social strata into a unitary language of culture and truth, the canonization of ideological systems, philology with its methods of studying and teaching dead languages, languages that were by that very fact "unities," Indo-European linguistics with its focus of attention, directed away from language plurality to a single proto-language—all this determined the content and power of the category of "unitary language" in linguistic and stylistic thought, and determined its creative, style-shaping role in the majority of the poetic genres that coalesced in the channel formed by those same centripetal forces of verbal-ideological life.

5. Wilhelm Freiherr von Humboldt (1767–1835), German humanist writer and philologist. AUGUSTINE (354–430), early Christian philosopher and theologian; on his poetics, see above. "The poetics of the medieval church": see Hugh of St. Victor (ca. 1097–1141). "The Cartesian poetics of neoclassicism": on these dualistic (from the French philosopher René Descartes, 1596–1650) poetics, see PIERRE CORNEILLE (1606–1684). Gottfried Wilhelm von Leibniz (1646–1716), German philosopher and mathematician.

But the centripetal forces of the life of language, embodied in a "unitary language," operate in the midst of heteroglossia. At any given moment of its evolution, language is stratified not only into linguistic dialects in the strict sense of the word (according to formal linguistic markers, especially phonetic), but also—and for us this is the essential point—into languages that are socio-ideological: languages of social groups, "professional" and "generic" languages, languages of generations and so forth. From this point of view, literary language itself is only one of these heteroglot languages—and in its turn is also stratified into languages (generic, period-bound and others). And this stratification and heteroglossia, once realized, is not only a static invariant of linguistic life, but also what insures its dynamics: stratification and heteroglossia widen and deepen as long as language is alive and developing. Alongside the centripetal forces, the centrifugal forces of language carry on their uninterrupted work; alongside verbal-ideological centralization and unification, the uninterrupted processes of decentralization and disunification go forward.

Every concrete utterance of a speaking subject serves as a point where centrifugal as well as centripetal forces are brought to bear. The processes of centralization and decentralization, of unification and disunification, intersect in the utterance; the utterance not only answers the requirements of its own language as an individualized embodiment of a speech act, but it answers the requirements of heteroglossia as well; it is in fact an active participant in such speech diversity. And this active participation of every utterance in living heteroglossia determines the linguistic profile and style of the utterance to no less a degree than its inclusion in any normative-centralizing system of a unitary language.

Every utterance participates in the "unitary language" (in its centripetal forces and tendencies) and at the same time partakes of social and historical heteroglossia (the centrifugal, stratifying forces).

Such is the fleeting language of a day, of an epoch, a social group, a genre, a school and so forth. It is possible to give a concrete and detailed analysis of any utterance, once having exposed it as a contradiction-ridden, tension-filled unity of two embattled tendencies in the life of language.

The authentic environment of an utterance, the environment in which it lives and takes shape, is dialogized heteroglossia, anonymous and social as language, but simultaneously concrete, filled with specific content and accented as an individual utterance.

At the time when major divisions of the poetic genres were developing under the influence of the unifying, centralizing, centripetal forces of verbal-ideological life, the novel—and those artistic-prose genres that gravitate toward it—was being historically shaped by the current of decentralizing, centrifugal forces. At the time when poetry was accomplishing the task of cultural, national and political centralization of the verbal-ideological world in the higher official socio-ideological levels, on the lower levels, on the stages of local fairs and at buffoon spectacles, the heteroglossia of the clown sounded forth, ridiculing all "languages" and dialects; there developed the literature of the *fabliaux* and *Schwänke*[6] of street songs,

6. Medieval comic folktales (German). *Fabliaux*: medieval short tales in verse (French).

folksayings, anecdotes, where there was no language-center at all, where there was to be found a lively play with the "languages" of poets, scholars, monks, knights and others, where all "languages" were masks and where no language could claim to be an authentic, incontestable face.

Heteroglossia, as organized in these low genres, was not merely heteroglossia vis-à-vis the accepted literary language (in all its various generic expressions), that is, vis-à-vis the linguistic center of the verbal-ideological life of the nation and the epoch, but was a heteroglossia consciously opposed to this literary language. It was parodic, and aimed sharply and polemically against the official languages of its given time. It was heteroglossia that had been dialogized.

Linguistics, stylistics and the philosophy of language that were born and shaped by the current of centralizing tendencies in the life of language have ignored this dialogized heteroglossia, in which is embodied the centrifugal forces in the life of language. For this very reason they could make no provision for the dialogic nature of language, which was a struggle among socio-linguistic points of view, not an intra-language struggle between individual wills or logical contradictions. Moreover, even intra-language dialogue (dramatic, rhetorical, cognitive or merely casual) has hardly been studied linguistically or stylistically up to the present day. One might even say outright that the dialogic aspect of discourse and all the phenomena connected with it have remained to the present moment beyond the ken of linguistics.

Stylistics has been likewise completely deaf to dialogue. A literary work has been conceived by stylistics as if it were a hermetic and self-sufficient whole, one whose elements constitute a closed system presuming nothing beyond themselves, no other utterances. The system comprising an artistic work was thought to be analogous with the system of a language, a system that could not stand in a dialogic interrelationship with other languages. From the point of view of stylistics, the artistic work as a whole—whatever that whole might be—is a self-sufficient and closed authorial monologue, one that presumes only passive listeners beyond its own boundaries. Should we imagine the work as a rejoinder in a given dialogue, whose style is determined by its interrelationship with other rejoinders in the same dialogue (in the totality of the conversation)—then traditional stylistics does not offer an adequate means for approaching such a dialogized style. The sharpest and externally most marked manifestations of this stylistic category—the polemical style, the parodic, the ironic—are usually classified as rhetorical and not as poetic phenomena. Stylistics locks every stylistic phenomenon into the monologic context of a given self-sufficient and hermetic utterance, imprisoning it, as it were, in the dungeon of a single context; it is not able to exchange messages with other utterances; it is not able to realize its own stylistic implications in a relationship with them; it is obliged to exhaust itself in its own single hermetic context.

Linguistics, stylistics and the philosophy of language—as forces in the service of the great centralizing tendencies of European verbal-ideological life—have sought first and foremost for *unity* in diversity. This exclusive "orientation toward unity" in the present and past life of languages has concentrated the attention of philosophical and linguistic thought on the firmest, most stable, least changeable and most mono-semic aspects of discourse—on the *phonetic* aspects first of all—that are furthest removed from the changing socio-semantic spheres of discourse. Real ideologically saturated "language consciousness," one that participates in actual heteroglossia and multi-languagedness, has remained outside its field of vision. It is precisely this orientation toward unity that has compelled scholars to ignore all the verbal genres (quotidian, rhetorical, artistic-prose) that were the carriers of the decentralizing tendencies in the life of language, or that were in any case too fundamentally implicated in heteroglossia. The expression of this hetero- as well as polyglot consciousness in the specific forms and phenomena of verbal life remained utterly without determinative influence on linguistics and stylistic thought.

Therefore proper theoretical recognition and illumination could not be found for the specific feel for language and discourse that one gets in stylizations, in *skaz*, in parodies and in various forms of verbal masquerade, "not talking straight," and in the more complex artistic forms for the organization of contradiction, forms that orchestrate their themes by means of languages—in all characteristic and profound models of novelistic prose, in Grimmelshausen, Cervantes, Rabelais, Fielding, Smollett, Sterne[7] and others.

The problem of stylistics for the novel inevitably leads to the necessity of engaging a series of fundamental questions concerning the philosophy of discourse, questions connected with those aspects in the life of discourse that have had no light cast on them by linguistic and stylistic thought—that is, we must deal with the life and behavior of discourse in a contradictory and multi-languaged world.

Discourse in Poetry and Discourse in the Novel

For the philosophy of language, for linguistics and for stylistics structured on their base, a whole series of phenomena have therefore remained almost entirely beyond the realm of consideration: these include the specific phenomena that are present in discourse and that are determined by its dialogic orientation, first, amid others' utterances inside a *single* language (the primordial dialogism of discourse), amid other "social languages" within a single *national* language and finally amid different national languages within the same *culture*, that is, the same socio-ideological conceptual horizon.[8]

In recent decades, it is true, these phenomena have begun to attract the attention of scholars in language and stylistics, but their fundamental and wide-ranging significance in all spheres of the life of discourse is still far from acknowledged.

The dialogic orientation of a word among other words (of all kinds and degrees of otherness) creates new and significant artistic potential in discourse, creates the potential for a distinctive art of prose, which has found its fullest and deepest expression in the novel.

7. All important early novelists—German: Hans Jakob Christoffel von Grimmelshausen (ca. 1621–1676); Spanish: Miguel de Cervantes (1547–1616); French: François Rabelais (ca. 1490–ca. 1533); and English: Henry Fielding (1707–1754), (Scottish-born) Tobias Smollett (1721–1771), and Laurence Sterne (1713–1768).

8. Linguistics acknowledges only a mechanical reciprocal influencing and intermixing of languages (that is, one that is unconscious and determined by social conditions) which is reflected in abstract linguistic elements (phonetic and morphological) [Bakhtin's note].

We will focus our attention here on various forms and degrees of dialogic orientation in discourse, and on the special potential for a distinctive prose-art.

As treated by traditional stylistic thought, the word acknowledges only itself (that is, only its own context), its own object, its own direct expression and its own unitary and singular language. It acknowledges another word, one lying outside its own context, only as the neutral word of language, as the word of no one in particular, as simply the potential for speech. The direct word, as traditional stylistics understands it, encounters in its orientation toward the object only the resistance of the object itself (the impossibility of its being exhausted by a word, the impossibility of saying it all), but it does not encounter in its path toward the object the fundamental and richly varied opposition of another's word. No one hinders this word, no one argues with it.

But no living word relates to its object in a *singular* way: between the word and its object, between the word and the speaking subject, there exists an elastic environment of other, alien words about the same object, the same theme, and this is an environment that it is often difficult to penetrate. It is precisely in the process of living interaction with this specific environment that the word may be individualized and given stylistic shape.

Indeed, any concrete discourse (utterance) finds the object at which it was directed already as it were overlain with qualifications, open to dispute, charged with value, already enveloped in an obscuring mist—or, on the contrary, by the "light" of alien words that have already been spoken about it. It is entangled, shot through with shared thoughts, points of view, alien value judgments and accents. The word, directed toward its object, enters a dialogically agitated and tension-filled environment of alien words, value judgments and accents, weaves in and out of complex interrelationships, merges with some, recoils from others, intersects with yet a third group: and all this may crucially shape discourse, may leave a trace in all its semantic layers, may complicate its expression and influence its entire stylistic profile.

The living utterance, having taken meaning and shape at a particular historical moment in a socially specific environment, cannot fail to brush up against thousands of living dialogic threads, woven by socio-ideological consciousness around the given object of an utterance; it cannot fail to become an active participant in social dialogue. After all, the utterance arises out of this dialogue as a continuation of it and as a rejoinder to it—it does not approach the object from the sidelines.

The way in which the word conceptualizes its object is a complex act—all objects, open to dispute and overlain as they are with qualifications, are from one side highlighted while from the other side dimmed by heteroglot social opinion, by an alien word about them.[9] And into this complex play of light

9. Highly significant in this respect is the struggle that must be undertaken in such movements as Rousseauism, Naturalism, Impressionism, Acmeism, Dadaism, Surrealism and analogous schools with the "qualified" nature of the object (a struggle occasioned by the idea of a return to primordial consciousness, to original consciousness, to the object itself in itself, to pure perception and so forth) [Bakhtin's note]. Acmeism: a movement of early 20th-century Russian poets who reacted against what they saw as the vagueness of symbolism, stressing form, poetic craft, and concrete representation.

and shadow the word enters—it becomes saturated with this play, and must determine within it the boundaries of its own semantic and stylistic contours. The way in which the word conceives its object is complicated by a dialogic interaction within the object between various aspects of its socio-verbal intelligibility. And an artistic representation, an "image" of the object, may be penetrated by this dialogic play of verbal intentions that meet and are interwoven in it; such an image need not stifle these forces, but on the contrary may activate and organize them. If we imagine the *intention* of such a word, that is, its *directionality toward the object*, in the form of a ray of light, then the living and unrepealable play of colors and light on the facets of the image that it constructs can be explained as the spectral dispersion of the ray-word, not within the object itself (as would be the case in the play of an image-as-trope, in poetic speech taken in the narrow sense, in an "autotelic word"), but rather as its spectral dispersion in an atmosphere filled with the alien words, value judgments and accents through which the ray passes on its way toward the object; the social atmosphere of the word, the atmosphere that surrounds the object, makes the facets of the image sparkle.

The word, breaking through to its own meaning and its own expression across an environment full of alien words and variously evaluating accents, harmonizing with some of the elements in this environment and striking a dissonance with others, is able, in this dialogized process, to shape its own stylistic profile and tone.

Such is the *image in artistic prose* and the image of *novelistic prose* in particular. In the atmosphere of the novel, the direct and unmediated intention of a word presents itself as something impermissably naive, something in fact impossible, for naiveté itself, under authentic novelistic conditions, takes on the nature of an internal polemic and is consequently dialogized (in, for example, the work of the Sentimentalists, in Chateaubriand[1] and in Tostoy). Such a dialogized image can occur in all the poetic genres as well, even in the lyric (to be sure, without setting the tone).[2] But such an image can fully unfold, achieve full complexity and depth and at the same time artistic closure, only under the conditions present in the genre of the novel.

In the poetic image narrowly conceived (in the image-as-trope), all activity—the dynamics of the image-as-word—is completely exhausted by the play between the word (with all its aspects) and the object (in all its aspects). The word plunges into the inexhaustible wealth and contradictory multiplicity of the object itself, with its "virginal," still "unuttered" nature; therefore it presumes nothing beyond the borders of its own context (except, of course, what can be found in the treasure-house of language itself). The word forgets that its object has its own history of contradictory acts of verbal recognition, as well as that heteroglossia that is always present in such acts of recognition.

For the writer of artistic prose, on the contrary, the object reveals first of all precisely the socially heteroglot multiplicity of its names, definitions and value judgments. Instead of the virginal fullness and inexhaustibility of

1. François-Auguste-René, vicomte de Chateaubriand (1768–1848), French novelist.

2. The Horatian lyric, Villon, Heine, Laforgue, Annenskij and others—despite the fact that these are extremely varied instances [Bakhtin's note]. All lyric poets: HORACE (65–8 B.C.E.), Roman; François Villon (1431–ca.1463), French; Heinrich Heine (1797–1856), German; Jules Laforgue (1860–1887), French; and Innokenty Annenskij (1855–1909), Russian.

the object itself, the prose writer confronts a multitude of routes, roads and paths that have been laid down in the object by social consciousness. Along with the internal contradictions inside the object itself, the prose writer witnesses as well the unfolding of social heteroglossia *surrounding* the object, the Tower-of-Babel mixing of languages[3] that goes on around any object; the dialectics of the object are interwoven with the social dialogue surrounding it. For the prose writer, the object is a focal point for heteroglot voices among which his own voice must also sound; these voices create the background necessary for his own voice, outside of which his artistic prose nuances cannot be perceived, and without which they "do not sound."

The prose artist elevates the social heteroglossia surrounding objects into an image that has finished contours, an image completely shot through with dialogized overtones; he creates artistically calculated nuances on all the fundamental voices and tones of this heteroglossia. But as we have already said, every extra-artistic prose discourse—in any of its forms, quotidian, rhetorical, scholarly—cannot fail to be oriented toward the "already uttered," the "already known," the "common opinion" and so forth. The dialogic orientation of discourse is a phenomenon that is, of course, a property of *any* discourse. It is the natural orientation of any living discourse. On all its various routes toward the object, in all its directions, the word encounters an alien word and cannot help encountering it in a living, tension-filled interaction. Only the mythical Adam, who approached a virginal and as yet verbally unqualified world with the first word, could really have escaped from start to finish this dialogic inter-orientation with the alien word that occurs in the object. Concrete historical human discourse does not have this privilege: it can deviate from such inter-orientation only on a conditional basis and only to a certain degree.

It is all the more remarkable that linguistics and the philosophy of discourse have been primarily oriented precisely toward this artificial, preconditioned status of the word, a word excised from dialogue and taken for the norm (although the primacy of dialogue over monologue is frequently proclaimed). Dialogue is studied merely as a compositional form in the structuring of speech, but the internal dialogism of the word (which occurs in a monologic utterance as well as in a rejoinder), the dialogism that penetrates its entire structure, all its semantic and expressive layers, is almost entirely ignored. But it is precisely this internal dialogism of the word, which does not assume any external compositional forms of dialogue, that cannot be isolated as an independent act, separate from the word's ability to form a concept [*koncipirovanie*] of its object—it is precisely this internal dialogism that has such enormous power to shape style. The internal dialogism of the word finds expression in a series of peculiar features in semantics, syntax and stylistics that have remained up to the present time completely unstudied by linguistics and stylistics (nor, what is more, have the peculiar semantic features of ordinary dialogue been studied).

The word is born in a dialogue as a living rejoinder within it; the word is shaped in dialogic interaction with an alien word that is already in the object. A word forms a concept of its own object in a dialogic way.

3. See Genesis 11.1–9.

But this does not exhaust the internal dialogism of the word. It encounters an alien word not only in the object itself: every word is directed toward an *answer* and cannot escape the profound influence of the answering word that it anticipates.

The word in living conversation is directly, blatantly, oriented toward a future answer-word: it provokes an answer, anticipates it and structures itself in the answer's direction. Forming itself in an atmosphere of the already spoken, the word is at the same time determined by that which has not yet been said but which is needed and in fact anticipated by the answering word. Such is the situation in any living dialogue.

All rhetorical forms, monologic in their compositional structure, are oriented toward the listener and his answer. This orientation toward the listener is usually considered the basic constitutive feature of rhetorical discourse.[4] It is highly significant for rhetoric that this relationship toward the concrete listener, taking him into account, is a relationship that enters into the very internal construction of rhetorical discourse. This orientation toward an answer is open, blatant and concrete.

This open orientation toward the listener and his answer in everyday dialogue and in rhetorical forms has attracted the attention of linguists. But even where this has been the case, linguists have by and large gotten no further than the compositional forms by which the listener is taken into account; they have not sought influence springing from more profound meaning and style. They have taken into consideration only those aspects of style determined by demands for comprehensibility and clarity—that is, precisely those aspects that are deprived of any internal dialogism, that take the listener for a person who passively understands but not for one who actively answers and reacts.

The listener and his response are regularly taken into account when it comes to everyday dialogue and rhetoric, but every other sort of discourse as well is oriented toward an understanding that is "responsive"—although this orientation is not particularized in an independent act and is not compositionally marked. Responsive understanding is a fundamental force, one that participates in the formulation of discourse, and it is moreover an *active* understanding, one that discourse senses as resistance or support enriching the discourse.

Linguistics and the philosophy of language acknowledge only a passive understanding of discourse, and moreover this takes place by and large on the level of common language, that is, it is an understanding of an utterance's *neutral signification* and not its *actual meaning*.

The linguistic significance of a given utterance is understood against the background of language, while its actual meaning is understood against the background of other concrete utterances on the same theme, a background made up of contradictory opinions, points of view and value judgments—that is, precisely that background that, as we see, complicates the path of any word toward its object. Only now this contradictory environment of alien words is present to the speaker not in the object, but rather in the consciousness of the listener, as his apperceptive background, pregnant with responses

4. Cf. V. Vinogradov's book *On Artistic Prose*, the chapter "Rhetoric and Poetics," pp. 75ff., where definitions taken from the older rhetorics are introduced [Bakhtin's note].

and objections. And every utterance is oriented toward this apperceptive background of understanding, which is not a linguistic background but rather one composed of specific objects and emotional expressions. There occurs a new encounter between the utterance and an alien word, which makes itself felt as a new and unique influence on its style.

A passive understanding of linguistic meaning is no understanding at all, it is only the abstract aspect of meaning. But even a more concrete *passive* understanding of the meaning of the utterance, an understanding of the speaker's intention insofar as that understanding remains purely passive, purely receptive, contributes nothing new to the word under consideration, only mirroring it, seeking, at its most ambitious, merely the full reproduction of that which is already given in the word—even such an understanding never goes beyond the boundaries of the word's context and in no way enriches the word. Therefore, insofar as the speaker operates with such a passive understanding, nothing new can be introduced into his discourse; there can be no new aspects in his discourse relating to concrete objects and emotional expressions. Indeed the purely negative demands, such as could only emerge from a passive understanding (for instance, a need for greater clarity, more persuasiveness, more vividness and so forth), leave the speaker in his own personal context, within his own boundaries; such negative demands are completely immanent in the speaker's own discourse and do not go beyond his semantic or expressive self-sufficiency.

In the actual life of speech, every concrete act of understanding is active: it assimilates the word to be understood into its own conceptual system filled with specific objects and emotional expressions, and is indissolubly merged with the response, with a motivated agreement or disagreement. To some extent, primacy belongs to the response, as the activating principle: it creates the ground for understanding, it prepares the ground for an active and engaged understanding. Understanding comes to fruition only in the response. Understanding and response are dialectically merged and mutually condition each other; one is impossible without the other.

Thus an active understanding, one that assimilates the word under consideration into a new conceptual system, that of the one striving to understand, establishes a series of complex interrelationships, consonances and dissonances with the word and enriches it with new elements. It is precisely such an understanding that the speaker counts on. Therefore his orientation toward the listener is an orientation toward a specific conceptual horizon, toward the specific world of the listener; it introduces totally new elements into his discourse; it is in this way, after all, that various different points of view, conceptual horizons, systems for providing expressive accents, various social "languages" come to interact with one another. The speaker strives to get a reading on his own word, and on his own conceptual system that determines this word, within the alien conceptual system of the understanding receiver; he enters into dialogical relationships with certain aspects of this system. The speaker breaks through the alien conceptual horizon of the listener, constructs his own utterance on alien territory, against his, the listener's, apperceptive background.

This new form of internal dialogism of the word is different from that form determined by an encounter with an alien word within the object itself: here it is not the object that serves as the arena for the encounter, but rather the subjective belief system of the listener. Thus this dialogism bears a more subjective, psychological and (frequently) random character, sometimes crassly accommodating, sometimes provocatively polemical. Very often, especially in the rhetorical forms, this orientation toward the listener and the related internal dialogism of the word may simply overshadow the object: the strong point of any concrete listener becomes a self-sufficient focus of attention, and one that interferes with the word's creative work on its referent.

Although they differ in their essentials and give rise to varying stylistic effects in discourse, the dialogic relationship toward an alien word within the object and the relationship toward an alien word in the anticipated answer of the listener can, nevertheless, be very tightly interwoven with each other, becoming almost indistinguishable during stylistic analysis.

Thus, discourse in Tolstoy is characterized by a sharp internal dialogism, and this discourse is moreover dialogized in the belief system of the reader—whose peculiar semantic and expressive characteristics Tolstoy acutely senses—as well as in the object. These two lines of dialogization (having in most cases polemical overtones) are tightly interwoven in his style: even in the most "lyrical" expressions and the most "epic" descriptions, Tolstoy's discourse harmonizes and disharmonizes (more often disharmonizes) with various aspects of the heteroglot socio-verbal consciousness ensnaring the object, while at the same time polemically invading the reader's belief and evaluative system, striving to stun and destroy the apperceptive background of the reader's active understanding. In this respect Tolstoy is an heir of the eighteenth century, especially of Rousseau.[5] This propagandizing impulse sometimes leads to a narrowing-down of heteroglot social consciousness (against which Tolstoy polemicizes) to the consciousness of his immediate contemporary, a contemporary of the day and not of the epoch; what follows from this is a radical concretization of dialogization (almost always undertaken in the service of a polemic). For this reason Tolstoy's dialogization, no matter how acutely we sense it in the expressive profile of his style, sometimes requires special historical or literary commentary: we are not sure with *what* precisely a given tone is in harmony or disharmony, for this dissonance or consonance has entered into the positive project of creating a style.[6] It is true that such extreme concreteness (which approaches at time the feuilleton[7]) is present only in those secondary aspects, the overtones of internal dialogization in Tolstoy's discourse.

In those examples of the internal dialogization of discourse that we have chosen (the internal, as contrasted with the external, compositionally marked, dialogue) the relationship to the alien word, to an alien utterance enters into the positing of the style. Style organically contains within itself indices that reach outside itself, a correspondence of its own elements and the elements of an alien context. The internal politics of style (how the elements are put together) is determined by its external politics (its relationship to alien discourse). Discourse lives, as it were, on the boundary between its own context and another, alien, context.

5. Jean-Jacques Rousseau (1712–1778), Swiss-born French philosopher and author.
6. Cf. B. M. Eichenbaum's book *Lev Tolstoj*, book I (Leningrad, 1928), which contains much relevant material; for example, an explication of the topical context of "Family Happiness" [Bakhtin's note]. Tolstoy famously observed in *Anna Karenina* (1875–77) that "Happy families are all alike; every unhappy family is unhappy in its own way."
7. Light, popular piece of newspaper writing.

In any actual dialogue the rejoinder also leads such a double life: it is structured and conceptualized in the context of the dialogue as a whole, which consists of its own utterances ("own" from the point of view of the speaker) and of alien utterances (those of the partner). One cannot excise the rejoinder from this combined context made up of one's own words and the words of another without losing its sense and tone. It is an organic part of a heteroglot unity.

The phenomenon of internal dialogization, as we have said, is present to a greater or lesser extent in all realms of the life of the word. But if in extra-artistic prose (everyday, rhetorical, scholarly) dialogization usually stands apart, crystallizes into a special kind of act of its own and runs its course in ordinary dialogue or in other, compositionally clearly marked forms for mixing and polemicizing with the discourse of another—then in *artistic* prose, and especially in the novel, this dialogization penetrates from within the very way in which the word conceives its object and its means for expressing itself, reformulating the semantics and syntactical structure of discourse. Here dialogic inter-orientation becomes, as it were, an event of discourse itself, animating from within and dramatizing discourse in all aspects.

In the majority of poetic genres (poetic in the narrow sense), as we have said, the internal dialogization of discourse is not put to artistic use, it does not enter into the work's "aesthetic object," and is artificially extinguished in poetic discourse. In the novel, however, this internal dialogization becomes one of the most fundamental aspects of prose style and undergoes a specific artistic elaboration.

But internal dialogization can become such a crucial force for creating form only where individual differences and contradictions are enriched by social heteroglossia, where dialogic reverberations do not sound in the semantic heights of discourse (as happens in the rhetorical genres) but penetrate the deep strata of discourse, dialogize language itself and the world view a particular language has (the internal form of discourse)—where the dialogue of voices arises directly out of a social dialogue of "languages," where an alien utterance begins to sound like a socially alien language, where the orientation of the word among alien utterances changes into an orientation of a word among socially alien languages within the boundaries of one and the same national language.

In genres that are poetic in the narrow sense, the natural dialogization of the word is not put to artistic use, the word is sufficient unto itself and does not presume alien utterances beyond its own boundaries. Poetic style is by convention suspended from any mutual interaction with alien discourse, any allusion to alien discourse.

Any way whatever of alluding to alien languages, to the possibility of another vocabulary, another semantics, other syntactic forms and so forth, to the possibility of other linguistic points of view, is equally foreign to poetic style. It follows that any sense of the boundedness, the historicity, the social determination and specificity of one's own language is alien to poetic style, and therefore a critical qualified relationship to one's own language (as merely one of many languages in a heteroglot world) is foreign to poetic style—as is a related phenomenon, the incomplete commitment of oneself, of one's full meaning, to a given language.

Of course this relationship and the relationship to his own language (in greater or lesser degree) could never be foreign to a historically existent poet, as a human being surrounded by living hetero- and polyglossia; but this relationship could not find a place in the *poetic style* of his work without destroying that style, without transposing it into a prosaic key and in the process turning the poet into a writer of prose.

In poetic genres, artistic consciousness—understood as a unity of all the author's semantic and expressive intentions—fully realizes itself within its own language; in them alone is such consciousness fully immanent, expressing itself in it directly and without mediation, without conditions and without distance. The language of the poet is *his* language, he is utterly immersed in it, inseparable from it, he makes use of each form, each word, each expression according to its unmediated power to assign meaning (as it were, "without quotation marks"), that is, as a pure and direct expression of his own intention. No matter what "agonies of the word" the poet endured in the process of creation, in the finished work language is an obedient organ, fully adequate to the author's intention.

The language in a poetic work realizes itself as something about which there can be no doubt, something that cannot be disputed, something all-encompassing. Everything that the poet sees, understands and thinks, he does through the eyes of a given language, in its inner forms, and there is nothing that might require, for its expression, the help of any other or alien language. The language of the poetic genre is a unitary and singular Ptolemaic world[8] outside of which nothing else exists and nothing else is needed. The concept of many worlds of language, all equal in their ability to conceptualize and to be expressive, is organically denied to poetic style.

The world of poetry, no matter how many contradictions and insoluble conflicts the poet develops within it, is always illumined by one unitary and indisputable discourse. Contradictions, conflicts and doubts remain in the object, in thoughts, in living experiences—in short, in the subject matter—but they do not enter into the language itself. In poetry, even discourse about doubts must be cast in a discourse that cannot be doubted.

To take responsibility for the language of the work as a whole at all of its points as *its* language, to assume a full solidarity with each of the work's aspects, tones, nuances—such is the fundamental prerequisite for poetic style; style so conceived is fully adequate to a single language and a single linguistic consciousness. The poet is not able to oppose his own poetic consciousness, his own intentions to the language that he uses, for he is completely within it and therefore cannot turn it into an object to be perceived, reflected upon or related to. Language is present to him only from inside, in the work it does to effect its intention, and not from outside, in its objective specificity and boundedness. Within the limits of poetic style, direct unconditional intentionality, language at its full weight and the objective display of language (as a socially and historically limited linguistic reality) are all simultaneous, but incompatible. The unity and singularity of language are the indispensable prerequisites for a realization of the direct (but not objectively

8. That is, the stationary center of the universe. In the system of the universe postulated by Ptolemy (active 127–148 C.E.), the Alexandrian astronomer, mathematician, and geographer, the sun, planets, and stars revolve around the earth.

typifying) intentional individuality of poetic style and of its monologic steadfastness.

This does not mean, of course, that heteroglossia or even a foreign language is completely shut out of a poetic work. To be sure, such possibilities are limited: a certain latitude for heteroglossia exists only in the "low" poetic genres—in the satiric and comic genres and others. Nevertheless, heteroglossia (other socio-ideological languages) can be introduced into purely poetic genres, primarily in the speeches of characters. But in such a context it is objective. It appears, in essence, as a *thing*, it does not lie on the *same* plane with the real language of the work: it is the depicted gesture of one of the characters and does not appear as an aspect of the word doing the depicting. Elements of heteroglossia enter here not in the capacity of another language carrying its own particular points of view, about which one can say things not expressible in one's own language, but rather in the capacity of a depicted thing. Even when speaking of alien things, the poet speaks in his own language. To shed light on an alien world, he never resorts to an alien language, even though it might in fact be more adequate to that world. Whereas the writer of prose, by contrast—as we shall see—attempts to talk about even his *own* world in an alien language (for example, in the nonliterary language of the teller of tales, or the representative of a specific socio-ideological group); he often measures his own world by alien linguistic standards.

As a consequence of the prerequisites mentioned above, the language of poetic genres, when they approach their stylistic limit,[9] often becomes authoritarian, dogmatic and conservative, sealing itself off from the influence of extraliterary social dialects. Therefore such ideas as a special "poetic language," a "language of the gods," a "priestly language of poetry" and so forth could flourish on poetic soil. It is noteworthy that the poet, should he not accept the given literary language, will sooner resort to the artificial creation of a new language specifically for poetry than he will to the exploitation of actual available social dialects. Social languages are filled with specific objects, typical, socially localized and limited, while the artificially created language of poetry must be a directly intentional language, unitary and singular. Thus, when Russian prose writers at the beginning of the twentieth century began to show a profound interest in dialects and *skaz*, the Symbolists (Bal'mont, V. Ivanov) and later the Futurists dreamed of creating a special "language of poetry," and even made experiments directed toward creating such a language (those of V. Khlebnikov).[1]

The idea of a special unitary and singular language of poetry is a typical utopian philosopheme[2] of poetic discourse: it is grounded in the actual conditions and demands of poetic style, which is always a style adequately serviced

9. It goes without saying that we continually advance as typical the extreme to which poetic genres aspire; in concrete examples of poetic works it is possible to find features fundamental to prose, and numerous hybrids of various generic types exist. These are especially widespread in periods of shift in literary poetic languages [Bakhtin's note].

1. Velimir Khlebnikov (1885–1922), Russian experimental poet and playwright. Konstantin Bal'mont (1867–1943), Russian symbolist poet. Vyacheslav Ivanov (1866–1949), Russian poet and philologist. Symbolism, a poetic movement that began in France in the last third of the 19th century, emphasized the evocation of subjective emotion, via symbol and metaphor, rather than objective description. Futurism, a revolutionary movement in art and literature begun in Italy in 1909, stressed speed, modernity, and rebellion; it quickly found adherents in Russia.

2. Basic unit or element of philosophy.

by one directly intentional language from whose point of view other languages (conversational, business and prose languages, among others) are perceived as objects that are in no way its equal.[3] The idea of a "poetic language" is yet another expression of that same Ptolemaic conception of the linguistic and stylistic world.

Language—like the living concrete environment in which the consciousness of the verbal artist lives—is never unitary. It is unitary only as an abstract grammatical system of normative forms, taken in isolation from the concrete, ideological conceptualizations that fill it, and in isolation from the uninterrupted process of historical becoming that is a characteristic of all living language. Actual social life and historical becoming create within an abstractly unitary national language a multitude of concrete worlds, a multitude of bounded verbal-ideological and social belief systems; within these various systems (identical in the abstract) are elements of language filled with various semantic and axiological content and each with its own different sound.

Literary language—both spoken and written—although it is unitary not only in its shared, abstract, linguistic markers but also in its forms for conceptualizing these abstract markers, is itself stratified and heteroglot in its aspect as an expressive system, that is, in the forms that carry its meanings.

This stratification is accomplished first of all by the specific organisms called *genres*. Certain features of language (lexicological, semantic, syntactic) will knit together with the intentional aim, and with the overall accentual system inherent in one or another genre: oratorical, publicistic, newspaper and journalistic genres, the genres of low literature (penny dreadfuls, for instance) or, finally, the various genres of high literature. Certain features of language take on the specific flavor of a given genre: they knit together with specific points of view, specific approaches, forms of thinking, nuances and accents characteristic of the given genre.

In addition, there is interwoven with this generic stratification of language a *professional* stratification of language, in the broad sense of the term "professional": the language of the lawyer, the doctor, the businessman, the politician, the public education teacher and so forth, and these sometimes coincide with, and sometimes depart from, the stratification into genres. It goes without saying that these languages differ from each other not only in their vocabularies; they involve specific forms for manifesting intentions, forms for making conceptualization and evaluation concrete. And even the very language of the writer (the poet or novelist) can be taken as a professional jargon on a par with professional jargons.

What is important to us here is the intentional dimensions, that is, the denotative and expressive dimension of the "shared" language's stratification. It is in fact not the neutral linguistic components of language being stratified and differentiated, but rather a situation in which the intentional possibilities of language are being expropriated: these possibilities are realized in specific directions, filled with specific content, they are made concrete, particular, and are permeated with concrete value judgments; they knit together with specific objects and with the belief systems of certain

3. Such was the point of view taken by Latin toward national languages in the Middle Ages [Bakhtin's note].

genres of expression and points of view peculiar to particular professions. Within these points of view, that is, for the speakers of the language themselves, these generic languages and professional jargons are directly intentional—they denote and express directly and fully, and are capable of expressing themselves without mediation; but outside, that is, for those not participating in the given purview, these languages may be treated as objects, as typifactions, as local color. For such outsiders, the intentions permeating these languages become *things*, limited in their meaning and expression; they attract to, or excise from, such language a particular word—making it difficult for the word to be utilized in a directly intentional way, without any qualifications.

But the situation is far from exhausted by the generic and professional stratification of the common literary language. Although at its very core literary language is frequently socially homogeneous, as the oral and written language of a dominant social group, there is nevertheless always present, even here, a certain degree of social differentiation, a social stratification, that in other eras can become extremely acute. Social stratification may here and there coincide with generic and professional stratification, but in essence it is, of course, a thing completely autonomous and peculiar to itself.

Social stratification is also and primarily determined by differences between the forms used to convey meaning and between the expressive planes of various belief systems—that is, stratification expresses itself in typical differences in ways used to conceptualize and accentuate elements of language, and stratification may not violate the abstractly linguistic dialectological unity of the shared literary language.

What is more, all socially significant world views have the capacity to exploit the intentional possibilities of language through the medium of their specific concrete instancing. Various tendencies (artistic and otherwise), circles, journals, particular newspapers, even particular significant artistic works and individual persons are all capable of stratifying language, in proportion to their social significance; they are capable of attracting its words and forms into their orbit by means of their own characteristic intentions and accents, and in so doing to a certain extent alienating these words and forms from other tendencies, parties, artistic works and persons.

Every socially significant verbal performance has the ability—sometimes for a long period of time, and for a wide circle of persons—to infect with its own intention certain aspects of language that had been affected by its semantic and expressive impulse, imposing on them specific semantic nuances and specific axiological overtones; thus, it can create slogan-words, curse-words, praise-words and so forth.

In any given historical moment of verbal-ideological life, each generation at each social level has its own language; moreover, every age group has as a matter of fact its own language, its own vocabulary, its own particular accentual system that, in their turn, vary depending on social level, academic institution (the language of the cadet, the high school student, the trade school student are all different languages) and other stratifying factors. All this is brought about by socially typifying languages, no matter how narrow the social circle in which they are spoken. It is even possible to have a family jargon define the societal limits of a language, as, for instance, the jargon of the Irtenevs[4] in Tolstoy, with its special vocabulary and unique accentual system.

And finally, at any given moment, languages of various epochs and periods of socio-ideological life cohabit with one another. Even languages of the day exist: one could say that today's and yesterday's socio-ideological and political "day" do not, in a certain sense, share the same language; every day represents another socio-ideological semantic "state of affairs," another vocabulary, another accentual system, with its own slogans, its own ways of assigning blame and praise. Poetry depersonalizes "days" in language, while prose, as we shall see, often deliberately intensifies difference between them, gives them embodied representation and dialogically opposes them to one another in unresolvable dialogues.

Thus at any given moment of its historical existence, language is heteroglot from top to bottom: it represents the co-existence of socio-ideological contradictions between the present and the past, between differing epochs of the past, between different socio-ideological groups in the present, between tendencies, schools, circles and so forth, all given a bodily form. These "languages" of heteroglossia intersect each other in a variety of ways, forming new socially typifying "languages."

Each of these "languages" of heteroglossia requires a methodology very different from the others; each is grounded in a completely different principle for marking differences and for establishing units (for some this principle is functional, in others it is the principle of theme and content, in yet others it is, properly speaking, a socio-dialectological principle). Therefore languages do not *exclude* each other, but rather intersect with each other in many different ways (the Ukrainian language, the language of the epic poem, of early Symbolism, of the student, of a particular generation of children, of the run-of-the-mill intellectual, of the Nietzschean[5] and so on). It might even seem that the very word "language" loses all meaning in this process—for apparently there is no single plane on which all these "languages" might be juxtaposed to one another.

In actual fact, however, there does exist a common plane that methodologically justifies our juxtaposing them: all languages of heteroglossia, whatever the principle underlying them and making each unique, are specific points of view on the world, forms for conceptualizing the world in words, specific world views, each characterized by its own objects, meanings and values. As such they all may be juxtaposed to one another, mutually supplement one another, contradict one another and be interrelated dialogically. As such they encounter one another and co-exist in the consciousness of real people—first and foremost, in the creative consciousness of people who write novels. As such, these languages live a real life, they struggle and evolve in an environment of social heteroglossia. Therefore they are all able to enter into the unitary plane of the novel, which can unite in itself parodic stylizations of generic languages, various forms of stylizations and illustrations of professional and period-bound languages, the languages of particular generations, of social dialects and others (as occurs, for example, in the English comic novel). They may all be drawn in by the novelist for the

4. Family in Tolstoy's short story "The Devil" (1911).

5. Follower of FRIEDRICH NIETZSCHE (1844–1900), German philologist and philosopher.

orchestration of his themes and for the refracted (indirect) expression of his intentions and values.

This is why we constantly put forward the referential and expressive—that is, intentional—factors as the force that stratifies and differentiates the common literary language, and not the linguistic markers (lexical coloration, semantic overtones, etc.) of generic languages, professional jargons and so forth—markers that are, so to speak, the sclerotic deposits of an intentional process, signs left behind on the path of the real living project of an intention, of the particular way it imparts meaning to general linguistic norms. These external markers, linguistically observable and fixable, cannot in themselves be understood or studied without understanding the specific conceptualization they have been given by an intention.

Discourse lives, as it were, beyond itself, in a living impulse [*napravlennost'*] toward the object; if we detach ourselves completely from this impulse all we have left is the naked corpse of the word, from which we can learn nothing at all about the social situation or the fate of a given word in life. *To study the word as such, ignoring the impulse that reaches out beyond it, is just as senseless as to study psychological experience outside the context of that real life toward which it was directed and by which it is determined.*

By stressing the intentional dimension of stratification in literary language, we are able, as has been said, to locate in a single series such methodologically heterogeneous phenomena as professional and social dialects, world views and individual artistic works, for in their intentional dimension one finds that common plane on which they can all be juxtaposed, and juxtaposed dialogically. The whole matter consists in the fact that there may be, between "languages," highly specific dialogic relations; no matter how these languages are conceived, they may all be taken as particular points of view on the world. However varied the social forces doing the work of stratification—a profession, a genre, a particular tendency, an individual personality—the work itself everywhere comes down to the (relatively) protracted and socially meaningful (collective) saturation of language with specific (and consequently limiting) intentions and accents. The longer this stratifying saturation goes on, the broader the social circle encompassed by it and consequently the more substantial the social force bringing about such a stratification of language, then the more sharply focused and stable will be those traces, the linguistic changes in the language markers (linguistic symbols), that are left behind in language as a result of this social force's activity—from stable (and consequently social) semantic nuances to authentic dialectological markers (phonetic, morphological and others), which permit us to speak of particular social dialects.

As a result of the work done by all these stratifying forces in language, there are no "neutral" words and forms—words and forms that can belong to "no one"; language has been completely taken over, shot through with intentions and accents. For any individual consciousness living in it, language is not an abstract system of normative forms but rather a concrete heteroglot conception of the world. All words have the "taste" of a profession, a genre, a tendency, a party, a particular work, a particular person, a generation, an age group, the day and hour. Each word tastes of the context and contexts in which it has lived its socially charged life; all words and forms are populated by intentions. Contextual overtones (generic, tendentious, individualistic) are inevitable in the word.

As a living, socio-ideological concrete thing, as heteroglot opinion, language, for the individual consciousness, lies on the borderline between oneself and the other. The word in language is half someone else's. It becomes "one's own" only when the speaker populates it with his own intention, his own accent, when he appropriates the word, adapting it to his own semantic and expressive intention. Prior to this moment of appropriation, the word does not exist in a neutral and impersonal language (it is not, after all, out of a dictionary that the speaker gets his words!), but rather it exists in other people's mouths, in other people's contexts, serving other people's intentions: it is from there that one must take the word, and make it one's own. And not all words for just anyone submit equally easily to this appropriation, to this seizure and transformation into private property: many words stubbornly resist, others remain alien, sound foreign in the mouth of the one who appropriated them and who now speaks them; they cannot be assimilated into his context and fall out of it; it is as if they put themselves in quotation marks against the will of the speaker. Language is not a neutral medium that passes freely and easily into the private property of the speaker's intentions; it is populated—overpopulated—with the intentions of others. Expropriating it, forcing it to submit to one's own intentions and accents, is a difficult and complicated process.

We have so far proceeded on the assumption of the abstract-linguistic (dialectological) unity of literary language. But even a literary language is anything but a closed dialect. Within the scope of literary language itself there is already a more or less sharply defined boundary between everyday-conversational language and written language. Distinctions between genres frequently coincide with dialectological distinctions (for example, the high—Church Slavonic[6]—and the low—conversational—genres of the eighteenth century); finally, certain dialects may be legitimized in literature and thus to a certain extent be appropriated by literary language.

As they enter literature and are appropriated to literary language, dialects in this new context lose, of course, the quality of closed socio-linguistic systems; they are deformed and in fact cease to be that which they had been simply as dialects. On the other hand, these dialects, on entering the literary language and preserving within it their own dialectological elasticity, their other-languagedness, have the effect of deforming the literary language; it, too, ceases to be that which it had been, a closed socio-linguistic system. Literary language is a highly distinctive phenomenon, as is the linguistic consciousness of the educated person who is its agent; within it, intentional diversity of speech [*raznorečivost'*] (which is present in every living dialect as a closed system) is transformed into diversity of language [*raznojazyčie*]; what results is not a single language but a dialogue of languages.

The national literary language of a people with a highly developed art of prose, especially if it is novelistic prose with a rich and tension-filled verbal-ideological history, is in fact an organized microcosm that reflects

6. The South Slavic language used in the standard 9th-century translation of the Bible done by the brothers Sts. Cyril (827–869) and Methodius (826–885) and still used as a liturgical language by all Slavic Orthodox Christian Churches.

the macrocosm not only of national heteroglossia, but of European heteroglossia as well. The unity of a literary language is not a unity of a single, closed language system, but is rather a highly specific unity of several "languages" that have established contact and mutual recognition with each other (merely one of which is poetic language in the narrow sense). Precisely this constitutes the peculiar nature of the methodological problem in literary language.

Concrete socio-ideological language consciousness, as it becomes creative—that is, as it becomes active as literature—discovers itself already surrounded by heteroglossia and not at all a single, unitary language, inviolable and indisputable. The actively literary linguistic consciousness at all times and everywhere (that is, in all epochs of literature historically available to us) comes upon "languages," and not language. Consciousness finds itself inevitably facing the necessity of *having to choose a language*. With each literary-verbal performance, consciousness must actively orient itself amidst heteroglossia, it must move in and occupy a position for itself within it, it chooses, in other words, a "language." Only by remaining in a closed environment, one without writing or thought, completely off the maps of socio-ideological becoming, could a man fail to sense this activity of selecting a language and rest assured in the inviolability of his own language, the conviction that his language is predetermined.

Even such a man, however, deals not in fact with a single language, but with languages—except that the place occupied by each of these languages is fixed and indisputable, the movement from one to the other is predetermined and not a thought process; it is as if these languages were in different chambers. They do not collide with each other in his consciousness, there is no attempt to coordinate them, to look at one of these languages through the eyes of another language.

Thus an illiterate peasant, miles away from any urban center, naively immersed in an unmoving and for him unshakable everyday world, nevertheless lived in several language systems: he prayed to God in one language (Church Slavonic), sang songs in another, spoke to his family in a third and, when he began to dictate petitions to the local authorities through a scribe, he tried speaking yet a fourth language (the official-literate language, "paper" language). All these are *different languages*, even from the point of view of abstract socio-dialectological markers. But these languages were not dialogically coordinated in the linguistic consciousness of the peasant; he passed from one to the other without thinking, automatically: each was indisputably in its own place, and the place of each was indisputable. He was not yet able to regard one language (and the verbal world corresponding to it) through the eyes of another language (that is, the language of everyday life and the everyday world with the language of prayer or song, or vice versa).[7]

As soon as a critical interanimation of languages began to occur in the consciousness of our peasant, as soon as it became clear that these were not only various different languages but even internally variegated languages, that the ideological systems and approaches to the world that were indissolubly connected with these languages contradicted each other and

7. We are of course deliberately simplifying: the real-life peasant could and did do this to a certain extent [Bakhtin's note].

in no way could live in peace and quiet with one another—then the inviolability and predetermined quality of these languages came to an end, and the necessity of actively choosing one's orientation among them began.

The language and world of prayer, the language and world of song, the language and world of labor and everyday life, the specific language and world of local authorities, the new language and world of the workers freshly immigrated to the city—all these languages and worlds sooner or later emerged from a state of peaceful and moribund equilibrium and revealed the speech diversity in each.

Of course the actively literary linguistic consciousness comes upon an even more varied and profound heteroglossia within literary language itself, as well as outside it. Any fundamental study of the stylistic life of the word must begin with this basic fact. The nature of the heteroglossia encountered and the means by which one orients oneself in it determine the concrete stylistic life that the word will lead.

The poet is a poet insofar as he accepts the idea of a unitary and singular language and a unitary, monologically sealed-off utterance. These ideas are immanent in the poetic genres with which he works. In a condition of actual contradiction, these are what determine the means of orientation open to the poet. The poet must assume a complete single-personed hegemony over his own language, he must assume equal responsibility for each one of its aspects and subordinate them to his own, and only his own, intentions. Each word must express the poet's *meaning* directly and without mediation; there must be no distance between the poet and his word. The meaning must emerge from language as a single intentional whole: none of its stratification, its speech diversity, to say nothing of its language diversity, may be reflected in any fundamental way in his poetic work.

To achieve this, the poet strips the word of others' intentions, he uses only such words and forms (and only in such a way) that they lose their link with concrete intentional levels of language and their connection with specific contexts. Behind the words of a poetic work one should not sense any typical or reified images of genres (except for the given poetic genre), nor professions, tendencies, directions (except the direction chosen by the poet himself), nor world views (except for the unitary and singular world view of the poet himself), nor typical and individual images of speaking persons, their speech mannerisms or typical intonations. *Everything that enters the work must immerse itself in Lethe,*[8] *and forget its previous life in any other contexts: language may remember only its life in poetic contexts (in such contexts, however, even concrete reminiscences are possible).*

Of course there always exists a limited sphere of more or less concrete contexts, and a connection with them must be deliberately evidenced in poetic discourse. But these contexts are purely semantic and, so to speak, accented in the abstract; in their linguistic dimension they are impersonal or at least no particularly concrete linguistic specificity is sensed behind them, no particular manner of speech and so forth, no socially typical linguistic face (the possible personality of the narrator) need peek out from behind them. Everywhere there is only one face—the linguistic face of the author,

8. A mythological river through the Greek underworld, Hades (literally, "Forgetfulness"; Greek). All who drink from it lose their memory.

answering for every word as if it were his own. No matter how multiple and varied these semantic and accentual threads, associations, pointers, hints, correlations that emerge from every poetic word, one language, one conceptual horizon, is sufficient to them all; there is no need of heteroglot social contexts. What is more, the very movement of the poetic symbol (for example, the unfolding of a metaphor) presumes precisely this unity of language, an unmediated correspondence with its object. Social diversity of speech, were it to arise in the work and stratify its language, would make impossible both the normal development and the activity of symbols within it.

The very rhythm of poetic genres does not promote any appreciable degree of stratification. *Rhythm, by creating an unmediated involvement between every aspect of the accentual system of the whole* (via the most immediate rhythmic unities), destroys in embryo those social worlds of speech and of persons that are potentially embedded in the word: in any case, rhythm puts definite limits on them, does not let them unfold or materialize. Rhythm serves to strengthen and concentrate even further the unity and hermetic quality of the surface of poetic style, and of the unitary language that this style posits.

As a result of this work—stripping all aspects of language of the intentions and accents of other people, destroying all traces of social heteroglossia and diversity of language—a tension-filled unity of language is achieved in the poetic work. This unity may be naive, and present only in those extremely rare epochs of poetry, when poetry had not yet exceeded the limits of a closed, unitary, undifferentiated social circle whose language and ideology were not yet stratified. More often than not, we experience a profound and conscious tension through which the unitary poetic language of a work rises from the heteroglot and language-diverse chaos of the literary language contemporary to it.

This is how the poet proceeds. The novelist working in prose (and almost any prose writer) takes a completely different path. He welcomes the heteroglossia and language diversity of the literary and extraliterary language into his own work not only not weakening them but even intensifying them (for he interacts with their particular self-consciousness). It is in fact out of this stratification of language, its speech diversity and even language diversity, that he constructs his style, while at the same time he maintains the unity of his own creative personality and the unity (although it is, to be sure, unity of another order) of his own style.

The prose writer does not purge words of intentions and tones that are alien to him, he does not destroy the seeds of social heteroglossia embedded in words, he does not eliminate those language characterizations and speech mannerisms (potential narrator-personalities) glimmering behind the words and forms, each at a different distance from the ultimate semantic nucleus of his work, that is, the center of his own personal intentions.

The language of the prose writer deploys itself according to degrees of greater or lesser proximity to the author and to his ultimate semantic instantiation: certain aspects of language directly and unmediatedly express (as in poetry) the semantic and expressive intentions of the author, others refract these intentions; the writer of prose does not meld completely with any of these words, but rather accents each of them in a particular way—humorously, ironically, parodically and so forth;[9] yet another group may stand even further from the author's ultimate semantic instantiation, still more thoroughly refracting his intentions; and there are, finally, those words that are completely denied any authorial intentions: the author does not express *himself* in them (as the author of the word)—rather, he *exhibits* them as a unique speech-thing, they function for him as something completely reified. Therefore the stratification of language—generic, professional, social in the narrow sense, that of particular world views, particular tendencies, particular individuals, the social speech diversity and language-diversity (dialects) of language—upon entering the novel establishs its own special order within it, and becomes a unique artistic system, which orchestrates the intentional theme of the author.

Thus a prose writer can distance himself from the language of his own work, while at the same time distancing himself, in varying degrees, from the different layers and aspects of the work. He can make use of language without wholly giving himself up to it, he may treat it as semi-alien or completely alien to himself, while compelling language ultimately to serve all his own intentions. The author does not speak in a given language (from which he distances himself to a greater or lesser degree), but he speaks, as it were, *through* language, a language that has somehow more or less materialized, become objectivized, that he merely ventriloquates.

The prose writer as a novelist does not strip away the intentions of others from the heteroglot language of his works, he does not violate those socio-ideological cultural horizons (big and little worlds) that open up behind heteroglot languages—rather, he welcomes them into his work. The prose writer makes use of words that are already populated with the social intentions of others and compels them to serve his own new intentions, to serve a second master. Therefore the intentions of the prose writer are refracted, and refracted at *different angles*, depending on the degree to which the refracted, heteroglot languages he deals with are socio-ideologically alien, already embodied and already objectivized.

The orientation of the word amid the utterances and languages of others, and all the specific phenomena connected with this orientation, takes on *artistic* significance in novel style. Diversity of voices and heteroglossia enter the novel and organize themselves within it into a structured artistic system. This constitutes the distinguishing feature of the novel as a genre.

Any stylistics capable of dealing with the distinctiveness of the novel as a genre must be a *sociological stylistics*. The internal social dialogism of novelistic discourse requires the concrete social context of discourse to be exposed, to be revealed as the force that determines its entire stylistic structure, its "form" and its "content," determining it not from without, but from within; for indeed, social dialogue reverberates in all aspects of discourse, in those relating to "content" as well as the "formal" aspects themselves.

The development of the novel is a function of the deepening of dialogic essence, its increased scope and greater precision. Fewer and fewer neutral, hard elements ("rock bottom truths") remain that are not drawn into

9. That is to say, the words are not his if we understand them as direct words, but they are his as things that are being transmitted ironically, exhibited and so forth, that is, as words that are understood from the distances appropriate to humor, irony, parody, etc. [Bakhtin's note].

dialogue. Dialogue moves into the deepest molecular and, ultimately, subatomic levels.

Of course, even the poetic word is social, but poetic forms reflect lengthier social processes, i.e., those tendencies in social life requiring centuries to unfold. The novelistic word, however, registers with extreme subtlety the tiniest shifts and oscillations of the social atmosphere; it does so, moreover, while registering it as a whole, in all of its aspects.

When heteroglossia enters the novel it becomes subject to an artistic reworking. The social and historical voices populating language, all its words and all its forms, which provide language with its particular concrete conceptualizations, are organized in the novel into a structured stylistic system that expresses the differentiated socio-ideological position of the author amid the heteroglossia of his epoch.

* * *

1934–35

MAX HORKHEIMER 1895–1973 THEODOR W. ADORNO 1903–1969

In a celebrated aphorism, the German philosopher and social critic Theodor Wiesengrund Adorno proclaimed that "To write poetry after Auschwitz is barbaric." This terse and austere statement encapsulates Adorno's bitterly melancholic understanding of modern art and society, which he often expressed in his highly influential writings on music, sociology, and aesthetics. For Adorno, as for some other members of the celebrated Institute for Social Research, the production of consumable, stylized mass art is complicit with a disinterested view of society that permits social atrocities such as Nazi concentration camps and genocide to go unchecked. The production of such art is also complicit with what Adorno and his fellow German social critic Max Horkheimer called the "culture industry," meaning the constellation of entertainment businesses that produce film, television, radio, magazines, and popular music—all phenomena created by mass technology in which the lines between art, advertising, and propaganda blur. In this world of manipulation and carefree amusement, mass art serves the status quo. As Adorno would assert on many occasions, the only legitimate form of art that can do some justice to the immense suffering in the world is the autonomous art of modernism, which, through its apparent detachment from reality, critiques the world as it is, holding up the promise of a better future.

Adorno was born in Frankfurt am Main to a wealthy and assimilated Jewish wine merchant, Oskar Wiesengrund, and his Catholic wife, Maria Calvelli-Adorno, whose last name Adorno may have assumed because he flirted with embracing his mother's faith. An important influence on Adorno's intellectual development was his training in music, particularly because in the 1920s it enabled him to meet and study with famous Viennese expressionist composers, such as Arnold Schoenberg and his disciples Alban Berg and Anton Webern. The atonal compositions of Schoenberg inspired Adorno, providing him with models for the unsystematic methodology of his critical work in philosophy, sociology, and aesthetics and for what art in the modern world should be. Another formative contemporary influence on Adorno was the noted film critic and social theorist Siegfried Kracauer, who introduced him to earlier German philosophy. As an anti-idealist who would become well-known for his groundbreaking sociological analyses of popular culture, Kracauer taught Adorno how to read the works of IMMANUEL KANT as symptomatic historical and social documents, which is how Adorno would later read mass art and the autonomous artworks of modernism.

At the University of Frankfurt in the 1920s, Kracauer introduced Adorno to WALTER BENJAMIN, who was also interested in sociological analyses of contemporary culture. Adorno was particularly taken with Benjamin's *Origin of German Tragic Drama* (1928), whose reflections on antisystematic philosophy helped Adorno develop his "atonal" philosophy, which, as he would explain in his *Negative Dialectics* (1966), avoids fixed concepts, much as modernist autonomous art shuns any kind of didactic or affirmative statements. With the help of Benjamin and Kracauer, Adorno's circle of associates later widened to include Ernst Bloch, whom Adorno regarded as the leading philosopher of expressionism, and Bertolt Brecht, the foremost Marxist dramatist. During this time Adorno began studying various materialist approaches to culture, falling under the influence of unorthodox Marxian texts such as Bloch's *Spirit of Utopia* (1918) and GYÖRGY LUKÁCS's *History and Class Consciousness* (1922). Bloch's utopian notion of art influenced Adorno's understanding of autonomous art, and Lukács's conception of reification informed his theory of the "mass deception" wrought by the modern culture industry.

At the University of Frankfurt, Adorno also met Max Horkheimer, a member of the now famous interdisciplinary Institute for Social Research (the so-called Frankfurt School), which was founded in 1924 and concerned initially with Marxist political economy, labor-movement history, and MARX-ENGELS scholarship. Born near Stuttgart to an upwardly mobile Jewish family, the young Horkheimer resisted his father's plans for him to run the family textile business because he could not accept the exploitation of labor on which it was based. After World War I, Horkheimer began his studies in Munich and then moved to the University of Frankfurt, which offered an exciting environment for those interested in social philosophy. He studied with the neo-Kantian philosopher Hans Cornelius, submitted his *Habilitationsschrift* (dissertation) in 1925, and became a regular lecturer in the history of philosophy. Like Adorno, Horkheimer moved away from idealist philosophy and its unhistorical approaches to Marxist materialist views. When Horkheimer assumed the directorship of the institute in 1930, he shifted its focus to cultural studies and so-called Critical Theory, a term he coined for the emerging mode of theoretical and empirical social analyses of modern culture typical of Adorno, Herbert Marcuse, and other members of the Frankfurt School.

Through his relationship with Horkheimer, Adorno would publish in the institute's journal, become a member in 1938, and ultimately succeed Horkheimer as director in 1964. Even more important, in the mid-1930s Horkheimer invited Adorno to America to do sociological work for the institute, which had been forced to relocate after being closed by the Nazis in 1933. Adorno himself had been denied the right to teach at the university level because he was Jewish. Consequently, in 1938 Adorno accepted Horkheimer's invitation and moved to New York and then, in 1941, to Los Angeles. There Adorno and Horkheimer collaborated on *Dialectic of Enlightenment* (1947), their major critique of modern culture, in which they interrogate the notion that the Western world has been progressing since the Enlightenment. In this dense polemical work, they claim that the modern West has not fulfilled the utopian promise of the Enlightenment, becoming instead a rationalized, administered world that dominates individuals through instrumental reason, monopoly capitalism, and political totalitarianism.

Appearing as a long chapter in Adorno and Horkheimer's *Dialectic of Enlightenment*, "The Culture Industry: Enlightenment as Mass Deception" argues that the administered modern world is sustained in part by technologically reproduced mass art. In contrast to Benjamin, who on occasion was optimistic about the emancipatory potential of mass art, Adorno and Horkheimer contend that the culture industry serves the totalitarian impulses of modern capitalist society, not least because the interests of leading broadcasting firms, publishing companies, and motion picture studios are economically interwoven with those of all other capitalist industries. In its attempt to produce and reproduce the social relations of a homogenized society, the culture industry contributes to the liquidation of the individual and the maintenance of the status quo. It transforms art into commodities and people into complacent consumers, depicting a "realistic" world that is really no more than a combination of stereotypes, advertising, and propaganda.

The culture industry, moreover, helps create a state of mind in which people's desires for pleasure and happiness are activated but deferred in endless entertainment. It inculcates resignation, habituating consumers to the everyday drudgery of the modern world. It does not "sublimate" the desire for happiness by providing compensatory entertainment for the life of regimentation but instead "represses" the desire for happiness, depicting the modern world in a degraded tragedy of "realistic" characters who accept the inexorable order of things. In this way the culture industry manages the psyche of its consumers, a line of thought that weds Marxian and Freudian insights—a combination often first credited to the Frankfurt School.

After World War II, Adorno and Horkheimer returned to Germany and reestablished the Institute for Social Research at the University of Frankfurt, where they also assumed professorships. Horkheimer eventually became rector of the university, serving from 1951 to 1953. During the 1960s, as he completed *Negative Dialectics* and addressed timely sociological issues, Adorno worked on a monumental and never-completed study, *Aesthetic Theory*, which was posthumously published in 1970. In numerous writings published before his death, Adorno propounded his views on the autonomous art of modernism, praising such writers as Samuel Beckett and Franz Kafka, whose difficult works he viewed as specific responses to the historical and social conditions of modernity. For Adorno, modern art resists the self-evidence of empirical reality, lends suffering a voice, and acknowledges a better future to come. In the 1960s Adorno saw his Marxist utopian position on art and his melancholic "mandarin" view of mass culture criticized by German student activists who demonstrated against him, questioned his Marxist credentials, and charged him with political quietism. While his work on the culture industry accurately portrays tendencies present in mid-twentieth-century Western societies, many later theorists would find it losing some of its point as social disaggregation and niche marketing came to characterize mass societies. But even so, Adorno still serves as a forerunner for critics concerned with the politics of popular culture and the prospects for cultural studies.

Dialectic of Enlightenment **Keywords:** Aesthetics, Affect, Cultural Studies, Ideology, Marxism, Media, Popular Culture

From Dialectic of Enlightenment[1]

From *The Culture Industry: Enlightenment as Mass Deception*

The sociological view that the loss of support from objective religion and the disintegration of the last precapitalist residues, in conjunction with technical and social differentiation and specialization, have given rise to cultural chaos is refuted by daily experience. Culture today is infecting everything with sameness. Film, radio, and magazines form a system. Each branch of culture is unanimous within itself and all are unanimous together. Even the aesthetic manifestations of political opposites proclaim the same inflexible rhythm. The decorative administrative and exhibition buildings of industry differ little between authoritarian and other countries. The bright monumental structures shooting up on all sides show off the systematic ingenuity of the state-spanning combines, toward which the unfettered entrepreneurial system, whose monuments are the dismal residential and commercial blocks in the surrounding areas of desolate cities, was already swiftly advancing. The older buildings around the concrete centers already look like slums, and the new bungalows on the outskirts, like the flimsy structures at international trade fairs, sing the praises of technical progress while inviting their users to throw them away after short use like tin cans. But the town-planning projects, which are supposed to perpetuate individuals as autonomous units in hygienic small apartments, subjugate them only more completely to their adversary, the total power of capital. Just as the occupants of city centers are uniformly summoned there for purposes of work and leisure, as producers and consumers, so the living cells crystallize into homogenous, well-organized complexes. The conspicuous unity of macrocosm and microcosm confronts human beings with a model of their culture: the false identity of universal and particular. All mass culture under monopoly is identical, and the contours of its skeleton, the conceptual armature fabricated by monopoly, are beginning to stand out. Those in charge no longer take much trouble to conceal the structure, the power of which increases the more bluntly its existence is admitted. Films and radio no longer need to present themselves as art. The truth that they are nothing but business is used as an ideology to legitimize the trash they intentionally produce. They call themselves industries, and the published figures for their directors' incomes quell any doubts about the social necessity of their finished products.

Interested parties like to explain the culture industry in technological terms. Its millions of participants, they argue, demand reproduction processes which inevitably lead to the use of standard products to meet the same needs at countless locations. The technical antithesis between few production centers and widely dispersed reception necessitates organization and planning by those in control. The standardized forms, it is claimed, were originally derived from the needs of the consumers: that is why they are accepted with so little resistance. In reality, a cycle of manipulation and retroactive need is unifying the system ever more tightly. What is not mentioned is that the basis on which technology is gaining power over society is the power of those whose economic position in society is strongest. Technical

1. Translated by Edmund Jephcott.

rationality today is the rationality of domination. It is the compulsive character of a society alienated from itself. Automobiles, bombs, and films hold the totality together until their leveling element demonstrates its power against the very system of injustice it served. For the present the technology of the culture industry confines itself to standardization and mass production and sacrifices what once distinguished the logic of the work from that of society. These adverse effects, however, should not be attributed to the internal laws of technology itself but to its function within the economy today. Any need which might escape the central control is repressed by that of individual consciousness. The step from telephone to radio has clearly distinguished the roles. The former liberally permitted the participant to play the role of subject. The latter democratically makes everyone equally into listeners, in order to expose them in authoritarian fashion to the same programs put out by different stations. No mechanism of reply has been developed, and private transmissions are condemned to unfreedom. They confine themselves to the apocryphal sphere of "amateurs," who, in any case, are organized from above. Any trace of spontaneity in the audience of the official radio is steered and absorbed into a selection of specializations by talent-spotters, performance competitions, and sponsored events of every kind. The talents belong to the operation long before they are put on show; otherwise they would not conform so eagerly. The mentality of the public, which allegedly and actually favors the system of the culture industry, is a part of the system, not an excuse for it. If a branch of art follows the same recipe as one far removed from it in terms of its medium and subject matter, if the dramatic denouement in radio "soap operas" is used as an instructive example of how to solve technical difficulties—which are mastered no less in "jam sessions" than at the highest levels of jazz—or if a movement from Beethoven is loosely "adapted" in the same way as a Tolstoy[2] novel is adapted for film, the pretext of meeting the public's spontaneous wishes is mere hot air. An explanation in terms of the specific interests of the technical apparatus and its personnel would be closer to the truth, provided that apparatus were understood in all its details as a part of the economic mechanism of selection. Added to this is the agreement, or at least the common determination, of the executive powers to produce or let pass nothing which does not conform to their tables, to their concept of the consumer, or, above all, to themselves.

If the objective social tendency of this age is incarnated in the obscure subjective intentions of board chairmen, this is primarily the case in the most powerful sectors of industry: steel, petroleum, electricity, chemicals. Compared to them the culture monopolies are weak and dependent. They have to keep in with the true wielders of power, to ensure that their sphere of mass society, the specific product of which still has too much of cozy liberalism and Jewish intellectualism about it, is not subjected to a series of purges. The dependence of the most powerful broadcasting company on the electrical industry, or of film on the banks, characterizes the whole sphere, the individual sectors of which are themselves economically intertwined. Everything is so tightly clustered that the concentration of intellect

2. Leo Tolstoy (1828–1910), Russian author; by 1947, there were more than a dozen films based on his novels *Anna Karenina* (1875–77) and *Resurrection* (1899) alone. Ludwig van Beethoven (1770–1827), German composer.

reaches a level where it overflows the demarcations between company names and technical sectors. The relentless unity of the culture industry bears witness to the emergent unity of politics. Sharp distinctions like those between A and B films, or between short stories published in magazines in different price segments, do not so much reflect real differences as assist in the classification, organization, and identification of consumers. Something is provided for everyone so that no one can escape; differences are hammered home and propagated. The hierarchy of serial qualities purveyed to the public serves only to quantify it more completely. Everyone is supposed to behave spontaneously according to a "level" determined by indices and to select the category of mass product manufactured for their type. On the charts of research organizations, indistinguishable from those of political propaganda, consumers are divided up as statistical material into red, green, and blue areas according to income group.

The schematic nature of this procedure is evident from the fact that the mechanically differentiated products are ultimately all the same. That the difference between the models of Chrysler and General Motors is fundamentally illusory is known by any child, who is fascinated by that very difference. The advantages and disadvantages debated by enthusiasts serve only to perpetuate the appearance of competition and choice. It is no different with the offerings of Warner Brothers and Metro Goldwyn Mayer. But the differences, even between the more expensive and cheaper products from the same firm, are shrinking—in cars to the different number of cylinders, engine capacity, and details of the gadgets, and in films to the different number of stars, the expense lavished on technology, labor and costumes, or the use of the latest psychological formulae. The unified standard of value consists in the level of conspicuous production, the amount of investment put on show. The budgeted differences of value in the culture industry have nothing to do with actual differences, with the meaning of the product itself. The technical media, too, are being engulfed by an insatiable uniformity. Television aims at a synthesis of radio and film, delayed only for as long as the interested parties cannot agree. Such a synthesis, with its unlimited possibilities, promises to intensify the impoverishment of the aesthetic material so radically that the identity of all industrial cultural products, still scantily disguised today, will triumph openly tomorrow in a mocking fulfillment of Wagner's[3] dream of the total art work. The accord between word, image, and music is achieved so much more perfectly than in *Tristan* because the sensuous elements, which compliantly document only the surface of social reality, are produced in principle within the same technical work process, the unity of which they express as their true content. This work process integrates all the elements of production, from the original concept of the novel, shaped by its sidelong glance at film, to the last sound effect. It is the triumph of invested capital. To impress the omnipotence of capital on the hearts of expropriated job candidates as the power of their true master is the purpose of all films, regardless of the plot selected by the production directors.

* * *

3. Richard Wagner (1813–1883), German composer who promoted the ideal of a "total artwork" (*Gesamtkunstwerk*). His operas include *Tristan und Isolde* (1859).

The whole world is passed through the filter of the culture industry. The familiar experience of the moviegoer, who perceives the street outside as a continuation of the film he has just left, because the film seeks strictly to reproduce the world of everyday perception, has become the guideline of production. The more densely and completely its techniques duplicate empirical objects, the more easily it creates the illusion that the world outside is a seamless extension of the one which has been revealed in the cinema. Since the abrupt introduction of the sound film, mechanical duplication has become entirely subservient to this objective. According to this tendency, life is to be made indistinguishable from the sound film. Far more strongly than the theatre of illusion, film denies its audience any dimension in which they might roam freely in imagination—contained by the film's framework but unsupervised by its precise actualities—without losing the thread; thus it trains those exposed to it to identify film directly with reality. The withering of imagination and spontaneity in the consumer of culture today need not be traced back to psychological mechanisms. The products themselves, especially the most characteristic, the sound film, cripple those faculties through their objective makeup. They are so constructed that their adequate comprehension requires a quick, observant, knowledgeable cast of mind but positively debars the spectator from thinking, if he is not to miss the fleeting facts. This kind of alertness is so ingrained that it does not even need to be activated in particular cases, while still repressing the powers of imagination. Anyone who is so absorbed by the world of the film, by gesture, image, and word, that he or she is unable to supply that which would have made it a world in the first place, does not need to be entirely transfixed by the special operations of the machinery at the moment of the performance. The required qualities of attention have become so familiar from other films and other culture products already known to him or her that they appear automatically. The power of industrial society is imprinted on people once and for all. The products of the culture industry are such that they can be alertly consumed even in a state of distraction. But each one is a model of the gigantic economic machinery, which, from the first, keeps everyone on their toes, both at work and in the leisure time which resembles it. In any sound film or any radio broadcast something is discernible which cannot be attributed as a social effect to any one of them, but to all together. Each single manifestation of the culture industry inescapably reproduces human beings as what the whole has made them. And all its agents, from the producer to the women's organizations, are on the alert to ensure that the simple reproduction of mind does not lead on to the expansion of mind.

The complaints of art historians and cultural attorneys over the exhaustion of the energy which created artistic style in the West are frighteningly unfounded. The routine translation of everything, even of what has not yet been thought, into the schema of mechanical reproducibility goes beyond the rigor and scope of any true style—the concept with which culture lovers idealize the precapitalist past as an organic era. No Palestrina[4] could have eliminated the unprepared or unresolved dissonance more puristically than the jazz arranger excludes any phrase which does not exactly fit the

4. Giovanni Pierluigi da Palestrina (1525–1594), Italian composer.

jargon. If he jazzes up Mozart, he changes the music not only where it is too difficult or serious but also where the melody is merely harmonized differently, indeed, more simply, than is usual today. No medieval patron of architecture can have scrutinized the subjects of church windows and sculptures more suspiciously than the studio hierarchies examine a plot by Balzac or Victor Hugo[5] before it receives the imprimatur of feasibility. No cathedral chapter could have assigned the grimaces and torments of the damned to their proper places in the order of divine love more scrupulously than production managers decide the position of the torture of the hero or the raised hem of the leading lady's dress within the litany of the big film. The explicit and implicit, exoteric and esoteric catalog of what is forbidden and what is tolerated is so extensive that it not only defines the area left free but wholly controls it. Even the most minor details are modeled according to this lexicon. Like its adversary, avant-garde art, the culture industry defines its own language positively, by means of prohibitions applied to its syntax and vocabulary. The permanent compulsion to produce new effects which yet remain bound to the old schema, becoming additional rules, merely increases the power of the tradition which the individual effect seeks to escape. Every phenomenon is by now so thoroughly imprinted by the schema that nothing can occur that does not bear in advance the trace of the jargon, that is not seen at first glance to be approved.

* * *

Nevertheless, this caricature of style reveals something about the genuine style of the past. The concept of a genuine style becomes transparent in the culture industry as the aesthetic equivalent of power. The notion of style as a merely aesthetic regularity is a retrospective fantasy of Romanticism. The unity of style not only of the Christian Middle Ages but of the Renaissance expresses the different structures of social coercion in those periods, not the obscure experience of the subjects, in which the universal was locked away. The great artists were never those whose works embodied style in its least fractured, most perfect form but those who adopted style as a rigor to set against the chaotic expression of suffering, as a negative truth. In the style of these works expression took on the strength without which existence is dissipated unheard. Even works which are called classical, like the music of Mozart, contain objective tendencies which resist the style they incarnate. Up to Schönberg and Picasso,[6] great artists have been mistrustful of style, which at decisive points has guided them less than the logic of the subject matter. What the Expressionists and Dadaists attacked in their polemics,[7] the untruth of style as such, triumphs today in the vocal jargon of the crooner, in the adept grace of the film star, and even in the mastery of the photographic shot of a farm laborer's hovel. In every work of art, style is a promise. In being absorbed through style into the dominant

5. Victor Hugo (1802–1885), French poet and novelist. Honoré de Balzac (1799–1850), French novelist.

6. Pablo Picasso (1881–1975), Spanish-born Cubist painter. Arnold Schoenberg (1874–1951), Austrian composer known for his expressionistic atonal or serial compositions (see following note).

7. Expressionism is an artistic movement that went beyond impressionism by magnifying dark inner experiences. Dadaism, a precursor to surrealism, is an artistic movement that protested the insanity of World War I by demolishing the tenets of art, philosophy, and logic.

form of universality, into the current musical, pictorial, or verbal idiom, what is expressed seeks to be reconciled with the idea of the true universal. This promise of the work of art to create truth by impressing its unique contours on the socially transmitted forms is as necessary as it is hypocritical. By claiming to anticipate fulfillment through their aesthetic derivatives, it posits the real forms of the existing order as absolute. To this extent the claims of art are always also ideology. Yet it is only in its struggle with tradition, a struggle precipitated in style, that art can find expression for suffering. The moment in the work of art by which it transcends reality cannot, indeed, be severed from style; that moment, however, does not consist in achieved harmony, in the questionable unity of form and content, inner and outer, individual and society, but in those traits in which the discrepancy emerges, in the necessary failure of the passionate striving for identity. Instead of exposing itself to this failure, in which the style of the great work of art has always negated itself, the inferior work has relied on its similarity to others, the surrogate of identity. The culture industry has finally posited this imitation as absolute. Being nothing other than style, it divulges style's secret: obedience to the social hierarchy. Aesthetic barbarism today is accomplishing what has threatened intellectual formations since they were brought together as culture and neutralized. To speak about culture always went against the grain of culture. The general designation "culture" already contains, virtually, the process of identifying, cataloging, and classifying which imports culture into the realm of administration. Only what has been industrialized, rigorously subsumed, is fully adequate to this concept of culture. Only by subordinating all branches of intellectual production equally to the single purpose of imposing on the senses of human beings, from the time they leave the factory in the evening to the time they clock on in the morning, the imprint of the work routine which they must sustain throughout the day, does this culture mockingly fulfill the notion of a unified culture which the philosophers of the individual personality held out against mass culture.

* * *

Nevertheless, the culture industry remains the entertainment business. Its control of consumers is mediated by entertainment, and its hold will not be broken by outright dictate but by the hostility inherent in the principle of entertainment to anything which is more than itself. Since the tendencies of the culture industry are turned into the flesh and blood of the public by the social process as a whole, those tendencies are reinforced by the survival of the market in the industry. Demand has not yet been replaced by simple obedience. The major reorganization of the film industry shortly before the First World War, the material precondition for its expansion, was a deliberate adaptation to needs of the public registered at the ticket office, which were hardly thought worthy of consideration in the pioneering days of the screen. That view is still held by the captains of the film industry, who accept only more or less phenomenal box-office success as evidence and prudently ignore the counterevidence, truth. Their ideology is business. In this they are right to the extent that the power of the culture industry lies in its unity with fabricated need and not in simple antithesis to it—or even in the antithesis between omnipotence and powerlessness. Entertainment is the prolongation of work under late capitalism. It is sought by those who want to escape the mechanized labor process so that they can cope with it again. At the same time, however, mechanization has such power over leisure and its happiness, determines so thoroughly the fabrication of entertainment commodities, that the off-duty worker can experience nothing but after-images of the work process itself. The ostensible content is merely a faded foreground; what is imprinted is the automated sequence of standardized tasks. The only escape from the work process in factory and office is through adaptation to it in leisure time. This is the incurable sickness of all entertainment. Amusement congeals into boredom, since, to be amusement, it must cost no effort and therefore moves strictly along the well-worn grooves of association. The spectator must need no thoughts of his own: the product prescribes each reaction, not through any actual coherence—which collapses once exposed to thought—but through signals. Any logical connection presupposing mental capacity is scrupulously avoided. Developments are to emerge from the directly preceding situation, not from the idea of the whole. There is no plot which could withstand the screenwriters' eagerness to extract the maximum effect from the individual scene. Finally, even the schematic formula seems dangerous, since it provides some coherence of meaning, however meager, when only meaninglessness is acceptable. Often the plot is willfully denied the development called for by characters and theme under the old schema. Instead, the next step is determined by what the writers take to be their most effective idea. Obtusely ingenious surprises disrupt the plot. The product's tendency to fall back perniciously on the pure nonsense which, as buffoonery and clowning, was a legitimate part of popular art up to Chaplin and the Marx brothers,[8] emerges most strikingly in the less sophisticated genres. Whereas the films of Greer Garson and Bette Davis[9] can still derive some claim to a coherent plot from the unity of the socio-psychological case represented, the tendency to subvert meaning has taken over completely in the text of novelty songs, suspense films, and cartoons. The idea itself, like objects in comic and horror films, is massacred and mutilated. Novelty songs have always lived on contempt for meaning, which, as both ancestors and descendants of psychoanalysis, they reduce to the monotony of sexual symbolism. In crime and adventure films the spectators are begrudged even the opportunity to witness the resolution. Even in non-ironic examples of the genre they must make do with the mere horror of situations connected in only the most perfunctory way.

* * *

* * * This makes it doubtful whether the culture industry even still fulfils its self-proclaimed function of distraction. If the majority of radio stations and cinemas were shut down, consumers probably would not feel too much deprived. In stepping from the street into the cinema, they no longer enter the world of dream in any case, and once the use of these institutions was no longer made obligatory by their mere existence, the urge to use them

8. American comic actors: Chico (Leonard) (1887–1961), Harpo (Adolph) (1888–1964), Groucho (Julius Henry) (1890–1977), Gummo (Milton) (1893–1977), and Zeppo (Herbert) (1901–1979). Charlie (Sir Charles Spencer) Chaplin (1889–1977), English comic actor and producer.

9. American actor (1908–1989). Garson (1904–1996), English actor. Both are best known for Hollywood roles that are dramatic, not comic.

might not be so overwhelming. Shutting them down in this way would not be reactionary machine-wrecking. Those who suffered would not be the film enthusiasts but those who always pay the penalty in any case, the ones who had lagged behind. For the housewife, despite the films which are supposed to integrate her still further, the dark of the cinema grants a refuge in which she can spend a few unsupervised hours, just as once, when there were still dwellings and evening repose, she could sit gazing out of the window. The unemployed of the great centers find freshness in summer and warmth in winter in these places of regulated temperature. Apart from that, and even by the measure of the existing order, the bloated entertainment apparatus does not make life more worthy of human beings. The idea of "exploiting" the given technical possibilities, of fully utilizing the capacities for aesthetic mass consumption, is part of an economic system which refuses to utilize capacities when it is a question of abolishing hunger.

The culture industry endlessly cheats its consumers out of what it endlessly promises. The promissory note of pleasure issued by plot and packaging is indefinitely prolonged: the promise, which actually comprises the entire show, disdainfully intimates that there is nothing more to come, that the diner must be satisfied with reading the menu. The desire inflamed by the glossy names and images is served up finally with a celebration of the daily round it sought to escape. Of course, genuine works of art were not sexual exhibitions either. But by presenting denial as negative, they reversed, as it were, the debasement of the drive and rescued by mediation what had been denied. That is the secret of aesthetic sublimation: to present fulfillment in its brokenness. The culture industry does not sublimate: it suppresses. By constantly exhibiting the object of desire, the breasts beneath the sweater, the naked torso of the sporting hero, it merely goads the unsublimated anticipation of pleasure, which through the habit of denial has long since been mutilated as masochism. There is no erotic situation in which innuendo and incitement are not accompanied by the clear notification that things will never go so far. The Hays Office merely confirms the ritual which the culture industry has staged in any case: that of Tantalus.[1] Works of art are ascetic and shameless; the culture industry is pornographic and prudish. It reduces love to romance. And, once reduced, much is permitted, even libertinage as a marketable specialty, purveyed by quota with the trade description "daring." The mass production of sexuality automatically brings about its repression. Because of his ubiquity, the film star with whom one is supposed to fall in love is, from the start, a copy of himself. Every tenor now sounds like a Caruso[2] record, and the natural faces of Texas girls already resemble those of the established models by which they would be typecast in Hollywood. The mechanical reproduction of beauty—which, admittedly, is made only more inescapable by the reactionary culture zealots with their methodical idolization of individuality—no longer leaves any room for the unconscious idolatry with which the experience of beauty has always been linked. The triumph over beauty is completed by humor, the malicious pleasure elicited by any

1. A Greek mythological figure whose punishment in Hades is always to have food and drink just out of his reach. Hays Office: unofficial name of the Motion Picture Producers and Distributors of America, founded in 1922 by Will Hays to monitor the film industry (precursor to the Production Code Administration, founded in 1934).

2. Enrico Caruso (1873–1921), popular Italian opera tenor.

successful deprivation. There is laughter because there is nothing to laugh about. Laughter, whether reconciled or terrible, always accompanies the moment when a fear is ended. It indicates a release, whether from physical danger or from the grip of logic. Reconciled laughter resounds with the echo of escape from power, wrong laughter copes with fear by defecting to the agencies which inspire it. It echoes the inescapability of power. Fun is a medicinal bath which the entertainment industry never ceases to prescribe. It makes laughter the instrument for cheating happiness. To moments of happiness laughter is foreign; only operettas, and now films, present sex amid peals of merriment. But Baudelaire is as humorless as Hölderlin.[3] In wrong society laughter is a sickness infecting happiness and drawing it into society's worthless totality. Laughter about something is always laughter at it, and the vital force which, according to Bergson,[4] bursts through rigidity in laughter is, in truth, the irruption of barbarity, the self-assertion which, in convivial settings, dares to celebrate its liberation from scruple. The collective of those who laugh parodies humanity. They are monads, each abandoning himself to the pleasure—at the expense of all others and with the majority in support—of being ready to shrink from nothing. Their harmony presents a caricature of solidarity. What is infernal about wrong laughter is that it compellingly parodies what is best, reconciliation. Joy, however, is austere: *res severa verum gaudium*.[5] The ideology of monasteries, that it is not asceticism but the sexual act which marks the renunciation of attainable bliss, is negatively confirmed by the gravity of the lover who presciently pins his whole life to the fleeting moment. The culture industry replaces pain, which is present in ecstasy no less than in asceticism, with jovial denial. Its supreme law is that its consumers shall at no price be given what they desire: and in that very deprivation they must take their laughing satisfaction. In each performance of the culture industry the permanent denial imposed by civilization is once more inflicted on and unmistakably demonstrated to its victims. To offer them something and to withhold it is one and the same. That is what the erotic commotion achieves. Just because it can never take place, everything revolves around the coitus. In film, to allow an illicit relationship without due punishment of the culprits is even more strictly tabooed than it is for the future son-in-law of a millionaire to be active in the workers' movement. Unlike that of the liberal era, industrial no less than nationalist culture can permit itself to inveigh against capitalism, but not to renounce the threat of castration. This threat constitutes its essence. It outlasts the organized relaxation of morals toward the wearers of uniforms, first in the jaunty films produced for them and then in reality. What is decisive today is no longer Puritanism, though it still asserts itself in the form of women's organizations, but the necessity, inherent in the system, of never releasing its grip on the consumer, of not for a moment allowing him or her to suspect that resistance is possible. This principle requires that while all needs should be presented to individuals as capable of fulfillment by the culture industry, they should be so set up in advance that individuals experience themselves through their

3. Friedrich Hölderlin (1770–1843), German poet and translator. Charles Baudelaire (1821–1867), French poet, critic, and forerunner of modernism.
4. Henri Bergson (1859–1941), French philosopher, author of *Laughter: An Essay on the Meaning of the Comic* (1900). "Vital impulse" (*élan vital*) is a key phrase in his writing.
5. True joy is a serious thing (Latin). From Seneca the Younger (ca. 4 B.C.E.–65 C.E.), *Moral Epistles* 3.23.

needs only as eternal consumers, as the culture industry's object. Not only does it persuade them that its fraud is satisfaction; it also gives them to understand that they must make do with what is offered, whatever it may be. The flight from the everyday world, promised by the culture industry in all its branches, is much like the abduction of the daughter in the American cartoon: the father is holding the ladder in the dark. The culture industry presents that same everyday world as paradise. Escape, like elopement, is destined from the first to lead back to its starting point. Entertainment fosters the resignation which seeks to forget itself in entertainment.

* * *

The more strongly the culture industry entrenches itself, the more it can do as it chooses with the needs of consumers—producing, controlling, disciplining them; even withdrawing amusement altogether: here, no limits are set to cultural progress. But the tendency is immanent in the principle of entertainment itself, as a principle of bourgeois enlightenment. If the need for entertainment was largely created by industry, which recommended the work to the masses through its subject matter, the oleograph[6] through the delicate morsel it portrayed and, conversely, the pudding mix through the image of a pudding, entertainment has always borne the trace of commercial brashness, of sales talk, the voice of the fairground huckster. But the original affinity between business and entertainment reveals itself in the meaning of entertainment itself: as society's apologia.[7] To be entertained means to be in agreement. Entertainment makes itself possible only by insulating itself from the totality of the social process, making itself stupid and perversely renouncing from the first the inescapable claim of any work, even the most trivial: in its restrictedness to reflect the whole. Amusement always means putting things out of mind, forgetting suffering, even when it is on display. At its root is powerlessness. It is indeed escape, but not, as it claims, escape from bad reality but from the last thought of resisting that reality. The liberation which amusement promises is from thinking as negation. The shamelessness of the rhetorical question "What do people want?" lies in the fact that it appeals to the very people as thinking subjects whose subjectivity it specifically seeks to annul. Even on those occasions when the public rebels against the pleasure industry it displays the feebleness systematically instilled in it by that industry. Nevertheless, it has become increasingly difficult to keep the public in submission. The advance of stupidity must not lag behind the simultaneous advance of intelligence. In the age of statistics the masses are too astute to identify with the millionaire on the screen and too obtuse to deviate even minutely from the law of large numbers. Ideology hides itself in probability calculations. Fortune will not smile on all—just on the one who draws the winning ticket or, rather, the one designated to do so by a higher power—usually the entertainment industry itself, which presents itself as ceaselessly in search of talent. Those discovered by the talent scouts and then built up by the studios are ideal types of the new, dependent middle classes. The female starlet is supposed to symbolize the secretary, though in a way which makes her

6. A chromolithograph printed on cloth to imitate an oil painting.

7. Defense.

seem predestined, unlike the real secretary, to wear the flowing evening gown. Thus she apprises the female spectator not only of the possibility that she, too, might appear on the screen but still more insistently of the distance between them. Only one can draw the winning lot, only one is prominent, and even though all have mathematically the same chance, it is so minimal for each individual that it is best to write it off at once and rejoice in the good fortune of someone else, who might just as well be oneself but never is. Where the culture industry still invites naïve identification, it immediately denies it. It is no longer possible to lose oneself in others. Once, film spectators saw their own wedding in that of others. Now the happy couple on the screen are specimens of the same species as everyone in the audience, but the sameness posits the insuperable separation of its human elements. The perfected similarity is the absolute difference. The identity of the species prohibits that of the individual cases. The culture industry has sardonically realized man's species being. Everyone amounts only to those qualities by which he or she can replace everyone else: all are fungible, mere specimens. As individuals they are absolutely replaceable, pure nothingness, and are made aware of this as soon as time deprives them of their sameness. This changes the inner composition of the religion of success, which they are sternly required to uphold. The path *per aspera ad astra*,[8] which presupposes need and effort, is increasingly replaced by the prize. The element of blindness in the routine decision as to which song is to be a hit, which extra a heroine, is celebrated by ideology. Films emphasize chance. By imposing an essential sameness on their characters, with the exception of the villain, to the point of excluding any faces which do not conform—for example, those which, like Garbo's,[9] do not look as if they would welcome the greeting "Hello, sister"—the ideology does, it is true, make life initially easier for the spectators. They are assured that they do not need to be in any way other than they are and that they can succeed just as well without having to perform tasks of which they know themselves incapable. But at the same time they are given the hint that effort would not help them in any case, because even bourgeois success no longer has any connection to the calculable effect of their own work. They take the hint. Fundamentally, everyone recognizes chance, by which someone is sometimes lucky, as the other side of planning. Just because society's energies have developed so far on the side of rationality that anyone might become an engineer or a manager, the choice of who is to receive from society the investment and confidence to be trained for such functions becomes entirely irrational. Chance and planning become identical since, given the sameness of people, the fortune or misfortune of the individual, right up to the top, loses all economic importance. Chance itself is planned; not in the sense that it will affect this or that particular individual but in that people believe in its control. For the planners it serves as an alibi, giving the impression that the web of transactions and measures into which life has been transformed still leaves room for spontaneous, immediate relationships between human beings. Such freedom is symbolized in the various media of the culture industry by the arbitrary selection of average cases. In the detailed reports on the modestly

8. Through adversities to the stars (Latin).
9. Greta Garbo (born Greta Gustafsson, 1905–1990), famously reclusive Swedish-born American film star.

luxurious pleasure trip organized by the magazine for the lucky competition winner—preferably a shorthand typist who probably won through contacts with local powers-that-be—the powerlessness of everyone is reflected. So much are the masses mere material that those in control can raise one of them up to their heaven and cast him or her out again: let them go hang with their justice and their labor. Industry is interested in human beings only as its customers and employees and has in fact reduced humanity as a whole, like each of its elements, to this exhaustive formula. Depending on which aspect happens to be paramount at the time, ideology stresses plan or chance, technology or life, civilization or nature. As employees people are reminded of the rational organization and must fit into it as common sense requires. As customers they are regaled, whether on the screen or in the press, with human interest stories demonstrating freedom of choice and the charm of not belonging to the system. In both cases they remain objects.

The less the culture industry has to promise and the less it can offer a meaningful explanation of life, the emptier the ideology it disseminates necessarily becomes. Even the abstract ideals of the harmony and benevolence of society are too concrete in the age of the universal advertisement. Abstractions in particular are identified as publicity devices. Language which appeals to mere truth only arouses impatience to get down to the real business behind it. Words which are not a means seem meaningless, the others seem to be fiction, untruth. Value judgments are perceived either as advertisements or as mere charter. The noncommittal vagueness of the resulting ideology does not make it more transparent, or weaker. Its very vagueness, the quasiscientific reluctance to be pinned down to anything which cannot be verified, functions as an instrument of control. Ideology becomes the emphatic and systematic proclamation of what is. Through its inherent tendency to adopt the tone of the factual report, the culture industry makes itself the irrefutable prophet of the existing order.

* * *

The emphasis on the heart of gold is society's way of admitting the suffering it creates: everyone knows that they are helpless within the system, and ideology must take account of this. Far from merely concealing the suffering under the cloak of improvised comradeship, the culture industry stakes its company pride on looking it manfully in the eye and acknowledging it with unflinching composure. This posture of steadfast endurance justifies the world which that posture makes necessary. Such is the world—so hard, yet therefore so wonderful, so healthy. The lie does not shrink back even from tragedy. Just as totalitarian society does not abolish the suffering of its members, but registers and plans it, mass culture does the same with tragedy. Hence the persistent borrowings from art. Art supplies the tragic substance which pure entertainment cannot provide on its own yet which it needs if it is to adhere to its principle of meticulously duplicating appearance. Tragedy, included in society's calculations and affirmed as a moment of the world, becomes a blessing. It deflects the charge that truth is glossed over, whereas in fact it is appropriated with cynical regret. It imparts an element of interest to the insipidity of censored happiness and makes that interest manageable. To the consumer who has seen culturally better days it offers the surrogate of long-abolished depth, and to regular moviegoers the veneer of culture they need for purposes of prestige. To all it grants the solace that human fate in its strength and authenticity is possible even now and its unflinching depiction inescapable. The unbroken surface of existence, in the duplication of which ideology consists solely today, appears all the more splendid, glorious, and imposing the more it is imbued with necessary suffering. It takes on the aspect of fate. Tragedy is leveled down to the threat to destroy anyone who does not conform, whereas its paradoxical meaning once lay in hopeless resistance to mythical threat. Tragic fate becomes the just punishment into which bourgeois aesthetics has always longed to transform it. The morality of mass culture has come down to it from yesterday's children's books. In the first-class production the villain is dressed up as the hysteric who, in a study of ostensibly clinical exactitude, seeks to trick her more realistic rival out of her life's happiness and who herself suffers a quite untheatrical death. To be sure, only at the top are things managed as scientifically as this. Further down, the resources are scarcer. There tragedy has its teeth drawn without social psychology. Just as any honest Hungarian-Viennese operetta must have its tragic finale in the second act, leaving nothing for the third but the righting of misunderstandings, mass culture gives tragedy permanent employment as routine. The obvious existence of a formula is enough in itself to allay the concern that tragedy might still be untamed. The housewife's description of the recipe for drama as "getting into trouble and out again" encompasses the whole of mass culture from the weak-minded women's serial to its highest productions. Even the worst outcome, which once had better intentions, still confirms the established order and corrupts tragedy, whether because the irregular lover pays for her brief happiness with death or because the sad end in the picture makes the indestructibility of actual life shine all the more brightly. Tragic cinema is becoming truly a house of moral correction. The masses, demoralized by existence under the pressure of the system and manifesting civilization only as compulsively rehearsed behavior in which rage and rebelliousness everywhere show through, are to be kept in order by the spectacle of implacable life and the exemplary conduct of those it crushes. Culture has always contributed to the subduing of revolutionary as well as of barbaric instincts. Industrial culture does something more. It inculcates the conditions on which implacable life is allowed to be lived at all. Individuals must use their general satiety as a motive for abandoning themselves to the collective power of which they are sated. The permanently hopeless situations which grind down filmgoers in daily life are transformed by their reproduction, in some unknown way, into a promise that they may continue to exist. One needs only to become aware of one's nullity, to subscribe to one's own defeat, and one is already a party to it. Society is made up of the desperate and thus falls prey to rackets. In a few of the most significant German novels of the prefascistic era, such as *Berlin Alexanderplatz* and *Kleiner Mann, was nun?*,[1] this tendency was as vividly evident as in the mediocre film and in the procedures of jazz. Fundamentally, they all present the self-mockery of man. The possibility of becoming an economic subject, an entrepreneur, a proprietor, is entirely liquidated. Right down to

1. *Little Man, What Now?* (1932), by Hans Fallada (pseudonym of Rudolf Ditzen, 1893–1947). *Berlin Alexanderplatz*, by Alfred Döblin (1878–1957), was published in 1929; its main character is Franz Biberkopf (mentioned below).

the small grocery, the independent firm on the running and inheriting of which the bourgeois family and the position of its head were founded, has fallen into hopeless dependence. All have become employees, and in the civilization of employees the dignity of the father, dubious in any case, ceases to be. The behavior of the individual toward the racket, whether commercial, professional, or political, both before and after admittance to it; the gestures of the leader before the masses, of the lover before the woman he woos, are taking on peculiarly masochistic traits. The attitude all are forced to adopt in order to demonstrate ever again their moral fitness for this society is reminiscent of that of boys during admission to a tribe; circling under the blows of the priest, they wear stereotypical smiles. Existence in late capitalism is a permanent rite of initiation. Everyone must show that they identify wholeheartedly with the power which beats them. This is inherent in the principle of syncopation in jazz, which mocks the act of stumbling while elevating it to the norm. The eunuch-like voice of the radio crooner, the handsome suitor of the heiress, who falls into the swimming pool wearing his tuxedo, are models for those who want to make themselves into that to which the system breaks them. Everyone can be like the omnipotent society, everyone can be happy if only they hand themselves over to it body and soul and relinquish their claim to happiness. In their weakness society recognizes its own strength and passes some of it back to them. Their lack of resistance certifies them as reliable customers. Thus is tragedy abolished. Once, the antithesis between individual and society made up its substance. Tragedy glorified "courage and freedom of feeling in face of a mighty foe, sublime adversity, a problem which awakened dread."[2] Today tragedy has been dissipated in the void of the false identity of society and subject, the horror of which is still just fleetingly visible in the vacuous semblance of the tragic. But the miracle of integration, the permanent benevolence of those in command, who admit the unresisting subject while he chokes down his unruliness—all this signifies fascism. Fascism lurks in the humaneness with which Döblin allows his protagonist Biberkopf to find refuge, no less than in films with a social slant. The ability to slip through, to survive one's own ruin, which has superseded tragedy, is ingrained in the new generation; its members are capable of any work, since the work process allows them to become attached to none. One is reminded of the sad pliability of the soldier returning home, unaffected by the war, of the casual laborer who finally joins the clandestine groups and the paramilitary organizations. The liquidation of tragedy confirms the abolition of the individual.

It is not only the standardized mode of production of the culture industry which makes the individual illusory in its products. Individuals are tolerated only as far as their wholehearted identity with the universal is beyond question. From the standardized improvisation in jazz to the original film personality who must have a lock of hair straying over her eyes so that she can be recognized as such, pseudoindividuality reigns. The individual trait is reduced to the ability of the universal so completely to mold the accidental that it can be recognized as accidental. The sulky taciturnity or the ele-

2. Nietzsche, *Götzendämmerung* [1888, *Twilight of the Idols*], *Werke*, vol. VIII, p. 136 [Horkheimer and Adorno's note]. FRIEDRICH NIETZSCHE (1844–1900), German philosopher.

gant walk of the individual who happens to be on show is serially produced like the Yale locks which differ by fractions of a millimeter. The peculiarity of the self is a socially conditioned monopoly commodity misrepresented as natural. It is reduced to the moustache, the French accent, the deep voice of the prostitute, the "Lubitsch touch"[3]—like a fingerprint on the otherwise uniform identity cards to which the lives and faces of all individuals, from the film star to the convict, have been reduced by the power of the universal. Pseudoindividuality is a precondition for apprehending and detoxifying tragedy: only because individuals are none but mere intersections of universal tendencies is it possible to reabsorb them smoothly into the universal. Mass culture thereby reveals the fictitious quality which has characterized the individual throughout the bourgeois era and is wrong only in priding itself on this murky harmony between universal and particular. The principle of individuality was contradictory from the outset. First, no individuation was ever really achieved. The class-determined form of self-preservation maintained everyone at the level of mere species being. Every bourgeois character expressed the same thing, even and especially when deviating from it: the harshness of competitive society. The individual, on whom society was supported, itself bore society's taint; in the individual's apparent freedom he was the product of society's economic and social apparatus. Power has always invoked the existing power relationships when seeking the approval of those subjected to power. At the same time, the advance of bourgeois society has promoted the development of the individual. Against the will of those controlling it, technology has changed human beings from children into persons. But all such progress of individuation has been at the expense of the individuality in whose name it took place, leaving behind nothing except individuals' determination to pursue their own purposes alone. The citizens whose lives are split between business and private life, their private life between ostentation and intimacy, their intimacy between the sullen community of marriage and the bitter solace of being entirely alone, at odds with themselves and with everyone, are virtually already Nazis, who are at once enthusiastic and fed up, or the city dwellers of today, who can imagine friendship only as "social contact" between the inwardly unconnected. The culture industry can only manipulate individuality so successfully because the fractured nature of society has always been reproduced within it. In the ready-made faces of film heroes and private persons fabricated according to magazine-cover stereotypes, a semblance of individuality—in which no one believes in any case—is fading, and the love for such hero-models is nourished by the secret satisfaction that the effort of individuation is at last being replaced by the admittedly more breathless one of imitation. The hope that the contradictory, disintegrating person could not survive for generations, that the psychological fracture within it must split the system itself, and that human beings might refuse to tolerate the mendacious substitution of the stereotype for the individual—that hope is vain. The unity of the personality has been recognized as illusory since Shakespeare's Hamlet.[4] In the synthetically manufactured

3. Ernst Lubitsch (1892–1947) was a German-American film director whose widely imitated style ("the Lubitsch touch") brought European elegance and irony to Hollywood cinema from the 1920s to the 1940s.

4. *Hamlet* was first staged ca. 1600.

physiognomies of today the fact that the concept of human life ever existed is already forgotten. For centuries society has prepared for Victor Mature and Mickey Rooney.[5] They come to fulfill the very individuality they destroy.

The heroizing of the average forms part of the cult of cheapness. The highest-paid stars resemble advertisements for unnamed merchandise. Not for nothing are they often chosen from the ranks of commercial models. The dominant taste derives its ideal from the advertisement, from commodified beauty. Socrates' dictum that beauty is the useful[6] has at last been ironically fulfilled. The cinema publicizes the cultural conglomerate as a totality, while the radio advertises individually the products for whose sake the cultural system exists. For a few coins you can see the film which cost millions, for even less you can buy the chewing gum behind which stand the entire riches of the world, and the sales of which increase those riches still further. Through universal suffrage the vast funding of armies is generally known and approved, if *in absentia*, while prostitution behind the lines is not permitted. The best orchestras in the world, which are none, are delivered free of charge to the home. All this mockingly resembles the land of milk and honey[7] as the national community apes the human one. Something is served up for everyone. A provincial visitor's comment on the old Berlin Metropoltheater that "it is remarkable what can be done for the money" has long since been adopted by the culture industry and elevated to the substance of production itself. Not only is a production always accompanied by triumphant celebration that it has been possible at all, but to a large extent it is that triumph itself. To put on a show means to show everyone what one has and can do. The show is still a fairground, but one incurably infected by culture. Just as people lured by the fairground crier overcame their disappointment inside the booths with a brave smile, since they expected it in any case, the moviegoer remains tolerantly loyal to the institution. But the cheapness of mass-produced luxury articles and its complement, universal fraud, are changing the commodity character of art itself. That character is not new: it is the fact that art now dutifully admits to being a commodity, abjures its autonomy and proudly takes its place among consumer goods, that has the charm of novelty. Art was only ever able to exist as a separate sphere in its bourgeois form. Even its freedom, as negation of the social utility which is establishing itself through the market, is essentially conditioned by the commodity economy. Pure works of art, which negated the commodity character of society by simply following their own inherent laws, were at the same time always commodities. To the extent that, up to the eighteenth century, artists were protected from the market by patronage, they were subject to the patrons and their purposes instead. The purposelessness of the great modern work of art is sustained by the anonymity of the market. The latter's demands are so diversely mediated that the artist is exempted from any particular claim, although only to a certain degree, since his autonomy, being merely tolerated, has been attended throughout bourgeois history by a moment of untruth, which has

5. Mature (1913–1999) and Rooney (1920–2014), American actors.

6. See PLATO, *Hippias Major* 295c–e; as usual in Plato's dialogues, the Greek philosopher Socrates (469–399 B.C.E.) is the primary speaker.

7. That is, the promised land; see, e.g., Exodus 3.8, Numbers 14.8.

culminated now in the social liquidation of art. The mortally sick Beethoven, who flung away a novel by Walter Scott[8] with the cry: "The fellow writes for money," while himself proving an extremely experienced and tenacious businessman in commercializing the last quartets—works representing the most extreme repudiation of the market—offers the most grandiose example of the unity of the opposites of market and autonomy in bourgeois art. The artists who succumb to ideology are precisely those who conceal this contradiction instead of assimilating it into the consciousness of their own production, as Beethoven did: he improvised on "Rage over a Lost Penny" and derived the metaphysical injunction "It must be," which seeks aesthetically to annul the world's compulsion by taking that burden onto itself, from his housekeeper's demand for her monthly wages. The principle of idealist aesthetics, purposiveness without purpose,[9] reverses the schema socially adopted by bourgeois art: purposelessness for purposes dictated by the market. In the demand for entertainment and relaxation, purpose has finally consumed the realm of the purposeless. But as the demand for the marketability of art becomes total, a shift in the inner economic composition of cultural commodities is becoming apparent. For the use which is made of the work of art in antagonistic society is largely that of confirming the very existence of the useless, which art's total subsumption under usefulness has abolished. In adapting itself entirely to need, the work of art defrauds human beings in advance of the liberation from the principle of utility which it is supposed to bring about. What might be called use value in the reception of cultural assets is being replaced by exchange value; enjoyment is giving way to being there and being in the know, connoisseurship by enhanced prestige. The consumer becomes the ideology of the amusement industry, whose institutions he or she cannot escape. One has to have seen Mrs. Miniver,[1] just as one must subscribe to *Life* and *Time*. Everything is perceived only from the point of view that it can serve as something else, however vaguely that other thing might be envisaged. Everything has value only in so far as it can be exchanged, not in so far as it is something in itself. For consumers the use value of art, its essence, is a fetish, and the fetish—the social valuation which they mistake for the merit of works of art—becomes its only use value, the only quality they enjoy. In this way the commodity character of art disintegrates just as it is fully realized. Art becomes a species of commodity, worked up and adapted to industrial production, saleable and exchangeable; but art as the species of commodity which exists in order to be sold yet not for sale becomes something hypocritically unsaleable as soon as the business transaction is no longer merely its intention but its sole principle. The Toscanini performance on the radio[2] is, in a sense, unsaleable. One listens to it for nothing, and each note of the symphony is accompanied, as it were, by the sublime advertisement that the symphony is not being interrupted by advertisements—"This concert is brought to you as a public service." The

8. Scottish poet and novelist (1771–1832), forced by financial difficulties late in his life to undertake much hack work. Wealthy aristocrats paid for a number of Beethoven's late quartets, which he also offered to music publishers for a sizable fee.

9. IMMANUEL KANT's terminology in his *Critique of Judgment* (1790; see above).

1. The heroine of a 1942 movie of the same name, played by Greer Garson.

2. The great Italian conductor Arturo Toscanini (1867–1957) led the National Broadcasting Company Symphony Orchestra, which was organized specifically for him, in a notable series of radio broadcasts from 1937 to 1954.

deception takes place indirectly *via* the profit of all the united automobile and soap manufacturers, on whose payments the stations survive, and, of course, *via* the increased sales of the electrical industry as the producer of the receiver sets.

* * *

1947

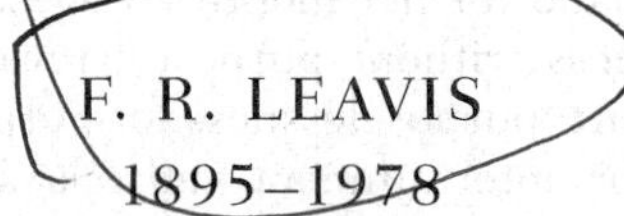

F. R. LEAVIS
1895–1978

By sheer strength of conviction and will, Frank Raymond Leavis became a major arbiter of British literary taste and values for four decades during the mid-twentieth century. Leavis was an indefatigable proselytizer. As a teacher at Cambridge University and as editor of the influential literary journal *Scrutiny*, he preached his vitalist doctrine and championed the writers he loved: Jane Austen, George Eliot, Gerard Manley Hopkins, and D. H. Lawrence.

Born and raised in Cambridge, Leavis, a conscientious objector, served in the ambulance corps on the Western Front during World War I. He returned to the university after the war, earning his graduate degree in 1924. In 1929, he married Queenie Dorothy Roth, whose Jewish parents disowned her for marrying the Anglo-Irish Leavis. Together, as a couple and as critics (at times, coauthors), the two took on the literary and academic establishment. Surprisingly, Leavis did not publish his first book, *New Bearings in English Poetry* (1932), until he was thirty-seven years old. In that year, he joined the editorial staff of a new journal, *Scrutiny*, which he soon was running and financing himself. Until its demise in 1954, *Scrutiny* maintained a remarkable unity of tone and outlook, spreading the Leavisite outlook even more effectively than did the editor's own books. Leavis demanded unquestioning fealty; by the time the journal folded, he had quarreled with most of his contributors. His sense of embattlement was hardly assuaged by his failure to gain a full-time position at Cambridge until 1947, when he was fifty-two. In 1962, his attack on C. P. Snow's notion of the "two cultures" (science and the arts) made Leavis a public figure beyond the confines of the university, and during the remainder of his life he increasingly was called upon to comment on cultural and educational issues on radio and TV and in the popular press.

Our selection from the opening of *The Great Tradition* (1948), Leavis's most influential work, exhibits his sensibility, his style, and his contradictions. Leavis staunchly rejects modernist aestheticism, with its separation and elevation of form over content. Formal excellence is important, Leavis concedes, but what ultimately distinguishes greatness is "a kind of reverent openness before life, and a marked moral intensity." Ideally, form and content work together organically, but for Leavis it is content that dictates form, not the other way around. Leavis's general outlook is best characterized as vitalist. Art must be alive, and it has life only when the content addresses central and abiding human concerns. Criticism, likewise, must be about life, not about art alone.

Impatient with a pristine literary formalism that stands "away from life as from a leprosy," Leavis implicitly repudiates the fastidious close readings of Anglo-American New Criticism and ignores the dictum that an author must always be carefully distinguished from her textual persona. The great authors teach us about life, revealing their own convictions, and criticism should encapsulate those lessons. Wearing his moral and didactic purposes on his sleeve, Leavis can appear simultaneously political and naive. Certainly his work—along with that of his English contemporaries C. S. Lewis, William Empson, and Christopher Caudwell—ensured that British literary criticism never aspired to the kinds of technical methodologies, studied apoliticism, or deadpan explication that marked much American New Criticism after World War II.

Leavis's politics are complicated. In an American context, he would probably qualify as a populist with an authoritarian streak. In England, "Tory radical" best captures his outlook. He staunchly abhors the mechanization of modern life that he associates with industrial capitalism and the bureaucratic modern state, and he retains a strong faith in the common sense of the English people. But all his images of desirable community lie in the past, in the ideal world of the rural village where an enlightened noble patriarch deserves and gets the allegiance of the people. In other words, Leavis's critique of modernity is "radical," but his yearning for a hierarchical social order is conservative ("Tory").

Thus in our selection we find Leavis fighting against the "high" modernist contempt for novels with moral or political agendas, but exhibiting a T. S. ELIOT–like need to distinguish "great" works from lesser ones. On the one hand, Leavis dislikes intensely what he deems the modernist disdain (as represented by Gustave Flaubert, James Joyce, and Lytton Strachey) for ordinary human aspirations and ambitions. On the other hand, Leavis battles the would-be levelers who offer Walter Scott, Anthony Trollope, or Charlotte Brontë as novelists equal with Jane Austen, George Eliot, or HENRY JAMES. Standards must be maintained. The critic must discern true greatness and instruct the people to pay such greatness due reverence. Otherwise, we will wallow in an anarchic lack of differentiation, mistakenly rating the "minor" novelist Charlotte Yonge as highly as a recognized master like Joseph Conrad.

Leavis adapts T. S. Eliot's "Tradition and the Individual Talent" (1919; see above) for his own purposes, which are mostly didactic. Tradition is found in only the greatest writers, and it is transmuted and passed on by other great writers. To designate "the great tradition" is to identify those texts in which the formal possibilities of a genre are most fully utilized in service of moral insights. Life is too short to waste reading second-rate books, Leavis tells us. The moral genius of the tradition is embodied in its great literature.

A common objection to Leavis argues that there are various ways to designate the tradition of the English novel. Feminist critics such as SANDRA M. GILBERT and SUSAN GUBAR make a compelling case for a tradition formed from the novels written by women. Leavis's famous banishment of Charles Dickens from the great tradition demonstrates that constructions of the tradition are contestable. (Leavis tacitly withdrew his objections to Dickens, though without explaining why or how his opinion had changed, when he later coauthored with Queenie a study of Dickens.) Magisterial pronouncements from a critic who assumes the self-appointed role of distinguishing the great from the not-so-great can go only so far. Monolithic standards and once-for-all inclusions and exclusions will likely cheat us of the pleasures and insights a broader vision would afford.

Leavis plays out a dilemma of authority that has bedeviled many literary intellectuals since at least MATTHEW ARNOLD. If we want to entertain visions that run counter to dominant forms of modern life, literature does offer a rich repository of alternatives to prevailing assumptions. But how can these neglected visions gain authority or indeed any purchase in the mainstream, which ignores literary insights at no apparent cost? Richard Hoggart and RAYMOND WILLIAMS, the leftist founders of cultural studies, were directly influenced by Leavis—and they too look to literature and other cultural forms to find resources to battle the dominance of commercial culture. But LEO STRAUSS and HAROLD BLOOM, who embody an elitist attitude toward culture as the preserve of the select few, are also Leavis's heirs, drawing on a quite different strain in his work. The choice seems stark: either the critic, like Williams, places his faith in the people and strives to keep alive the alternative visions to which the people eventually will turn. Or the critic, like Bloom or Strauss, becomes a lonely voice in the wilderness, bemoaning the general benightedness of the culture—a benightedness that he and a few others have managed to escape. The only consolation for this critic is to spend his time in the library in communion with the great writers, who are largely ignored and unread by the populace at large. While Leavis's own work fluctuates between these two positions, his pervasive personal sense of embattlement weights the role of solitary teller of the truth over the voice of a residual common sense.

The Great Tradition: George Eliot, Henry James, Joseph Conrad **Keywords:** The Canon/Tradition, Cultural Studies, Ethics, Modernity, The Novel, Realism

From The Great Tradition: George Eliot, Henry James, Joseph Conrad

From *1. The Great Tradition*

"... not dogmatically but deliberately ..."

—Johnson,[1] *Preface to Shakespeare*

The great English novelists are Jane Austen, George Eliot, Henry James and Joseph Conrad[2]—to stop for the moment at that comparatively safe point in history. Since Jane Austen, for special reasons, needs to be studied at considerable length, I confine myself in this book to the last three. Critics have found me narrow, and I have no doubt that my opening proposition, whatever I may say to explain and justify it, will be adduced in reinforcement of their strictures. It passes as fact (in spite of the printed evidence) that I pronounce Milton negligible, dismiss 'the Romantics', and hold that, since Donne, there is no poet we need bother about except Hopkins and Eliot.[3] The view, I suppose, will be as confidently attributed to me that, except Jane Austen, George Eliot, James and Conrad, there are no novelists in English worth reading.

The only way to escape misrepresentation is never to commit oneself to any critical judgment that makes an impact—that is, never to *say* anything. I still, however, think that the best way to promote profitable discussion is to be as clear as possible with oneself about what one sees and judges, to try and establish the essential discriminations in the given field of interest, and to state them as clearly as one can (for disagreement, if necessary). And it seems to me that in the field of fiction some challenging discriminations are very much called for; the field is so large and offers such insidious temp-

1. SAMUEL JOHNSON (1709–1784), English critic, essayist, and lexicographer; for this quotation from his preface to *Shakespeare* (1765), see p. 405, above.

2. Leavis lists the novelists chronologically: Austen (1775–1817); Eliot (pen name of Marian Evans, 1819–1880); JAMES (1843–1916), who was American-born; and Conrad (1857–1924), who was Polish-born.

3. T. S. ELIOT (1888–1965), American-born English poet. The other three poets—John Milton (1608–1674), John Donne (1572–1631), and Gerard Manley Hopkins (1844–1889)—are all English.

tations to complacent confusions of judgment and to critical indolence. It is of the field of fiction belonging to Literature that I am thinking, and I am thinking in particular of the present vogue of the Victorian age. Trollope, Charlotte Yonge, Mrs. Gaskell, Wilkie Collins, Charles Reade, Charles and Henry Kingsley, Marryat, Shorthouse[4]—one after another the minor novelists of that period are being commended to our attention, written up, and publicized by broadcast, and there is a marked tendency to suggest that they not only have various kinds of interest to offer but that they are living classics. (Are not they all in the literary histories?) There are Jane Austen, Mrs. Gaskell, Scott, 'the Brontës', Dickens, Thackeray,[5] George Eliot, Trollope and so on, all, one gathers, classical novelists.

It is necessary to insist, then, that there are important distinctions to be made, and that far from all of the names in the literary histories really belong to the realm of significant creative achievement. And as a recall to a due sense of differences it is well to start by distinguishing the few really great—the major novelists who count in the same way as the major poets, in the sense that they not only change the possibilities of the art for practitioners and readers, but that they are significant in terms of the human awareness they promote; awareness of the possibilities of life.[6]

To insist on the pre-eminent few in this way is not to be indifferent to tradition; on the contrary, it is the way towards understanding what tradition is. 'Tradition', of course, is a term with many forces—and often very little at all. There is a habit nowadays of suggesting that there is a tradition of 'the English Novel', and that all that can be said of the tradition (that being its peculiarity) is that 'the English Novel' can be anything you like. To distinguish the major novelists in the spirit proposed is to form a more useful idea of tradition (and to recognize that the conventionally established view of the past of English fiction needs to be drastically revised). It is in terms of the major novelists, those significant in the way suggested, that tradition, in any serious sense, has its significance.

4. The novelist who has not been revived is Disraeli. Yet, though he is not one of the great novelists, he is so alive and intelligent as to deserve permanent currency, at any rate in the trilogy *Coningsby* (1844), *Sybil* (1845) and *Tancred* (1847): his own interests as expressed in these books—the interests of a supremely intelligent politician who has a sociologist's understanding of civilization and its movement in his time—are so mature [Leavis's note; some of Leavis's notes have been edited and others omitted]. Benjamin Disraeli (1804–1881), more successful as a Conservative politician (twice prime minister). Leavis lists the other novelists roughly in order of decreasing reputation: Anthony Trollope (1815–1882), Yonge (1823–1901), Elizabeth Gaskell (1810–1865), Collins (1824–1889), Reade (1814–1884), Charles Kingsley (1819–1875), Henry Kingsley (1830–1876), Frederick Marryat (1792–1848), and Joseph Henry Shorthouse (1834–1903).

5. William Makepeace Thackeray (1811–1863), English novelist. Sir Walter Scott (1771–1832), Emily Brontë (1818–1848), Charlotte Brontë (1816–1855), and Charles Dickens (1812–1870), all English novelists.

6. Characteristic of the confusion I am contending against is the fashion (for which the responsibility seems to go back to VIRGINIA WOOLF and Mr. E. M. Forster) of talking of *Moll Flanders* as a "great novel." Defoe was a remarkable writer, but all that need be said about him as a novelist was said by Leslie Stephen in *Hours in a Library* (First Series). He made no pretension to practice the novelist's art, and matters little as an influence. * * * Associated with this use of Defoe is the use that was made in much the same *milieu* of Sterne, in whose irresponsible (and nasty) trifling, regarded as in some way extraordinarily significant and mature, was found a sanction for attributing value to other trifling. * * * [Leavis's note]. Daniel Defoe (1660–1731) is often credited with writing the first English novels, *Robinson Crusoe* (1719) and *Moll Flanders* (1722). The novelists and critics WOOLF (1882–1941) and Forster (1879–1970) belonged to the same artistic circle, the Bloomsbury group. Stephen (1832–1904), Woolf's father, was a Victorian man of letters. The works of the Irish-born Laurence Sterne (1713–1768) include *Tristram Shandy* (1759–67), a satirical novel that pioneers many of the techniques found in 20th-century experimental fiction.

To be important historically is not, of course, to be necessarily one of the significant few. Fielding[7] deserves the place of importance given him in the literary histories, but he hasn't the kind of classical distinction we are also invited to credit him with. He is important not because he leads to Mr. J. B. Priestley[8] but because he leads to Jane Austen, to appreciate whose distinction is to feel that life isn't long enough to permit of one's giving much time to Fielding or any to Mr. Priestley.

Fielding made Jane Austen possible by opening the central tradition of English fiction. In fact, to say that the English novel began with him is as reasonable as such propositions ever are. He completed the work begun by *The Tatler* and *The Spectator*,[9] in the pages of which we see the drama turning into the novel—that this development should occur by way of journalism being in the natural course of things. To the art of presenting character and *mœurs*[1] learnt in that school (he himself, before he became a novelist, was both playwright and periodical essayist) he joined a narrative habit the nature of which is sufficiently indicated by his own phrase, 'comic epic in prose'.[2] That the eighteenth century, which hadn't much lively reading to choose from, but had much leisure, should have found *Tom Jones* exhilarating is not surprising; nor is it that Scott and Coleridge[3] should have been able to give that work superlative praise. Standards are formed in comparison, and what opportunities had they for that? But the conventional talk about the 'perfect construction' of *Tom Jones* (the late Hugh Walpole[4] brought it out triumphantly and you may hear it in almost any course of lectures on 'the English Novel') is absurd. There can't be subtlety of organization without richer matter to organize, and subtler interests, than Fielding has to offer. He is credited with range and variety and it is true that some episodes take place in the country and some in Town, some in the churchyard and some in the inn, some on the high-road and some in the bed-chamber, and so on. But we haven't to read a very large proportion of *Tom Jones* in order to discover the limits of the essential interests it has to offer us. Fielding's attitudes, and his concern with human nature, are simple, and not such as to produce an effect of anything but monotony (on a mind, that is, demanding more than external action) when exhibited at the length of an 'epic in prose'. What he *can* do appears to best advantage in *Joseph Andrews*. *Jonathan Wild*, with its famous irony, seems to me mere hobbledehoydom[5] (much as one applauds the determination to explode the gangster-hero), and by *Amelia* Fielding has gone soft.

We all know that if we want a more inward interest it is to Richardson[6] we must go. And there is more to be said for Johnson's preference, and his

7. Henry Fielding (1707–1754), English author whose novels include *Joseph Andrews* (1742), *Jonathan Wild* (1743), *Tom Jones* (1749), and *Amelia* (1751).
8. English novelist and playwright (1894–1984).
9. Two periodicals (published 1709–11, 1711–14, respectively) written by Richard Steele and JOSEPH ADDISON, often in the form of gossipy letters from made-up correspondents.
1. Manners, customs (French).
2. In his preface to *Joseph Andrews*, Fielding claims that the work is a new kind of writing: "a comic epic poem in prose."
3. SAMUEL TAYLOR COLERIDGE (1772–1834), English poet and literary critic.
4. English novelist and man of letters (1884–1941).
5. That is, adolescent, callow.
6. Samuel Richardson (1689–1761), English novelist of epistolary novels, including *Pamela* (1740)—satirized by Fielding's *Joseph Andrews*—and *Clarissa* (1748–49). Johnson famously preferred Richardson's "characters of nature" to the "characters of manners" of Fielding, whom he called "a barren rascal," declaring that "there is more knowledge of the heart in one letter of Richardson's, than in all *Tom Jones*" (James Boswell, *Life of Johnson* [1791], Spring 1768; Monday, 6 April 1772).

emphatic way of expressing it at Fielding's expense, than is generally recognized. Richardson's strength in the analysis of emotional and moral states is in any case a matter of common acceptance; and *Clarissa* is a really impressive work. But it's no use pretending that Richardson can ever be made a current classic again. The substance of interest that he too has to offer is in its own way extremely limited in range and variety, and the demand he makes on the reader's time is in proportion—and absolutely—so immense as to be found, in general, prohibitive (though I don't know that I wouldn't sooner read through again *Clarissa* than *A la recherche du temps perdu*[7]). But we can understand well enough why his reputation and influence should have been so great throughout Europe; and his immediately relevant historical importance is plain: he too is a major fact in the background of Jane Austen.

The social gap between them was too wide, however, for his work to be usable by her directly: the more he tries to deal with ladies and gentlemen, the more immitigably vulgar he is. It was Fanny Burney[8] who, by transposing him into educated life, made it possible for Jane Austen to absorb what he had to teach her. Here we have one of the important lines of English literary history—Richardson–Fanny Burney–Jane Austen. It is important because Jane Austen is one of the truly great writers, and herself a major fact in the background of other great writers. Not that Fanny Burney is the only other novelist who counts in her formation; she read all there was to read, and took all that was useful to her—which wasn't only lessons.[9] In fact, Jane Austen, in her indebtedness to others, provides an exceptionally illuminating study of the nature of originality, and she exemplifies beautifully the relations of 'the individual talent' to tradition. If the influences bearing on her hadn't comprised something fairly to be called tradition she couldn't have found herself and her true direction; but her relation to tradition is a creative one. She not only makes tradition for those coming after, but her achievement has for us a retroactive effect: as we look back beyond her we see in what goes before, and see because of her, potentialities and significances brought out in such a way that, for us, she creates the tradition we see leading down to her. Her work, like the work of all great creative writers, gives a meaning to the past.

* * *

The great novelists in that tradition are all very much concerned with 'form'; they are all very original technically, having turned their genius to the working out of their own appropriate methods and procedures. But the peculiar quality of their preoccupation with 'form' may be brought out by a contrasting reference to Flaubert.[1] Reviewing Thomas Mann's *Der Tod in Venedig*, D. H. Lawrence[2] adduces Flaubert as figuring to the world the

7. *In Search of Lost Time* (7 vols., 1913–27), by Marcel Proust (first translated from the French as *The Remembrance of Things Past*). *Clarissa*, one of the longest novels in English, is about three-quarters its length.
8. English writer (1752–1840), best-known for *Evelina* (1778), a novel of manners.
9. For the relation of Jane Austen to other writers see the essay by Q. D. Leavis, *A Critical Theory of Jane Austen's Writings*, in *Scrutiny*, vol. X, no. 1 [Leavis's note].
1. Gustave Flaubert (1821–1880), French novelist who was a pioneer of realism.
2. English novelist and poet (1885–1930); his comments on *Death in Venice* (1912), a short novel by the German author Mann (1875–1955), appeared in "German Books: Thomas Mann," *Blue Review* 1 (July 1913).

'will of the writer to be greater than and undisputed lord over the stuff he writes'. This attitude in art, as Lawrence points out, is indicative of an attitude in life—or towards life. Flaubert, he comments, 'stood away from life as from a leprosy'. For the later Aesthetic writers, who, in general, represent in a weak kind of way the attitude that Flaubert maintained with a perverse heroism, 'form' and 'style' are ends to be sought for themselves, and the chief preoccupation is with elaborating a beautiful style to apply to the chosen subject. There is George Moore,[3] who in the best circles, I gather (from a distance), is still held to be among the very greatest masters of prose, though—I give my own limited experience for what it is worth—it is very hard to find an admirer who, being pressed, will lay his hand on his heart and swear he has read one of the 'beautiful' novels through. 'The novelist's problem is to evolve an orderly composition which is also a convincing picture of life'—this is the way an admirer of George Moore sees it. Lord David Cecil,[4] attributing this way to Jane Austen, and crediting her with a superiority over George Eliot in 'satisfying the rival claims of life and art', explains this superiority, we gather, by a freedom from moral preoccupations that he supposes her to enjoy. (George Eliot, he tells us, was a Puritan, and earnestly bent on instruction.)

As a matter of fact, when we examine the formal perfection of *Emma*,[5] we find that it can be appreciated only in terms of the moral preoccupations that characterize the novelist's peculiar interest in life. Those who suppose it to be an 'aesthetic matter', a beauty of 'composition' that is combined, miraculously, with 'truth to life', can give no adequate reason for the view that *Emma* is a great novel, and no intelligent account of its perfection of form. It is in the same way true of the other great English novelists that their interest in their art gives them the opposite of an affinity with Pater[6] and George Moore; it is, brought to an intense focus, an unusually developed interest in life. For, far from having anything of Flaubert's disgust or disdain or boredom, they are all distinguished by a vital capacity for experience, a kind of reverent openness before life, and a marked moral intensity.

It might be commented that what I have said of Jane Austen and her successors is only what can be said of any novelist of unqualified greatness. That is true. But there *is*—and this is the point—an English tradition, and these great classics of English fiction belong to it; a tradition that, in the talk about 'creating characters' and 'creating worlds', and the appreciation of Trollope and Mrs. Gaskell and Thackeray and Meredith and Hardy[7] and Virginia Woolf, appears to go unrecognized. It is not merely that we have no Flaubert (and I hope I haven't seemed to suggest that a Flaubert is no more worth having than a George Moore). Positively, there is a continuity from Jane Austen. It is not for nothing that George Eliot admired her work profoundly, and wrote one of the earliest appreciations of it to be published.[8] The writer whose intellectual weight and moral earnestness strike

3. Irish novelist and man of letters (1852–1933).
4. English literary critic and biographer (1902–1986). The quotation is from his *Early Victorian Novelists: Essays in Revaluation* (1934).
5. Published in 1816, and often paired with *Pride and Prejudice* (1813) as the best of Austen's novels.
6. WALTER PATER (1839–1894), English aestheticist literary and art critic.
7. Thomas Hardy (1840–1928), English novelist and poet. George Meredith (1828–1909), English novelist and poet.
8. This appreciation, "The Novels of Jane Austen" (1859), was actually written by George Henry Lewes, who lived with Eliot from 1854 until his death in 1878.

some critics as her handicap certainly saw in Jane Austen something more than an ideal contemporary of Lytton Strachey.[9]

* * *

Henry James also was a great admirer of Jane Austen, and in his case too there is that obvious aspect of influence which can be brought out by quotation. And there is for him George Eliot as well, coming between. In seeing him in an English tradition I am not slighting the fact of his American origin; an origin that doesn't make him less of an English novelist, of the great tradition, than Conrad later. That he was an American is a fact of the first importance for the critic, as Mr. Yvor Winters brings out admirably in his book, *Maule's Curse*.[1] Mr. Winters discusses him as a product of the New England ethos in its last phase, when a habit of moral strenuousness remained after dogmatic Puritanism had evaporated and the vestigial moral code was evaporating too. This throws a good deal of light on the elusiveness that attends James's peculiar ethical sensibility. We have, characteristically, in reading him, a sense that important choices are in question and that our finest discrimination is being challenged, while at the same time we can't easily produce for discussion any issues that have moral substance to correspond.

It seems relevant also to note that James was actually a New Yorker. In any case, he belonged by birth and upbringing to that refined civilization of the old European America which we have learnt from Mrs. Wharton[2] to associate with New York. His bent was to find a field for his ethical sensibility in the appreciative study of such a civilization—the 'civilization' in question being a matter of personal relations between members of a mature and sophisticated Society. It is doubtful whether at any time in any place he could have found what would have satisfied his implicit demand: the actual fine art of civilized social intercourse that would have justified the flattering intensity of expectation he brought to it in the form of his curiously transposed and subtilized ethical sensibility.

History, it is plain, was already leaving him *déraciné*[3] in his own country, so that it is absurd to censure him, as some American critics have done, for pulling up his roots. He could hardly become deeply rooted elsewhere, but the congenial soil and climate were in Europe rather than in the country of his birth. There is still some idealizing charm about his English country-house in *The Portrait of a Lady*,[4] but that book is one of the classics of the language, and we can't simply regret the conditions that produced something so finely imagined. It is what *The Egoist*[5] is supposed to be. Compare the two books, and the greatness of Henry James as intellectual poet-novelist of 'high civilization' comes out in a way that, even for the most innocently deferential reader, should dispose of Meredith's pretensions for ever. James's wit is real and always natural, his poetry intelligent as well as

9. English biographer and man of letters (1880–1932). Leavis implicitly contrasts Strachey's snide portraits of 19th-century luminaries in *Eminent Victorians* (1918) with the more positive satire in Austen's novels.
1. New Directions, Norfolk, Conn. (1938) [Leavis's note]. Winters (1900–1968), American poet and literary critic.
2. Edith Wharton (1862–1937), American novelist.
3. Uprooted; an uprooted person (French).
4. Novel published in 1880–81.
5. Comic novel (1879) by Meredith.

truly rich, and there is nothing bogus, cheap or vulgar about his idealizations: certain human potentialities are nobly celebrated.

That he is a novelist who has closely studied his fellow-craftsmen is plain—and got from them more than lessons in the craft. It is plain, for instance, in *The Portrait of a Lady* that he sees England through literature. We know that he turned an attentive professional eye on the French masters. He has (in his early mature work) an easy and well-bred technical sophistication, a freedom from any marks of provinciality, and a quiet air of knowing his way about the world that distinguish him from among his contemporaries in the language. If from the English point of view he is unmistakably an American, he is also very much a European.

* * *

His own problem was to justify in terms of an intense interest in sophisticated 'civilization' his New England ethical sensibility. The author who offered a congenial study would have to be very different from Flaubert. It was, as a matter of fact, a very English novelist, the living representative of the great tradition—a writer as unlike Flaubert as George Eliot.

* * *

To say this is to have the confident wisdom of hindsight, for it can be shown, with a conclusiveness rarely possible in these matters, that James did actually go to school to George Eliot.

That is a fair way of putting the significance of the relation between *The Portrait of a Lady* and *Daniel Deronda*[6] that I discuss in my examination of the latter book. That relation demonstrated, nothing more is needed in order to establish the general relation I posit between the two novelists. James's distinctive bent proclaims itself uncompromisingly in what he does with *Daniel Deronda* (on the good part of which—I call it *Gwendolen Harleth*[7]—*The Portrait of a Lady* is a variation; for the plain fact I point out amounts to that). The moral substance of George Eliot's theme is subtilized into something going with the value James sets on 'high civilization'; her study of conscience has disappeared. A charming and intelligent girl, determined to live 'finely', confidently exercises her 'free ethical sensibility' (Mr. Winters' phrase) and discovers that she is capable of disastrous misvaluation (which is not surprising, seeing not only how inexperienced she is, but how much an affair of inexplicitnesses, overtones and fine shades is the world of discourse she moves in). It is a tragedy in which, for her, neither remorse is involved, nor, in the ordinary sense, the painful growth of conscience, though no doubt her 'ethical sensibility' matures.

Along the line revealed by the contrast between the two novels James develops an art so unlike George Eliot's that, but for the fact (which seems to have escaped notice) of the relation of *The Portrait of a Lady* to *Daniel Deronda*, it would, argument being necessary, have been difficult to argue at all convincingly that there was the significant relation between the novelists. And I had better insist that I am not concerned to establish *indebtedness*. What I have in mind is the fact of the great tradition and the apartness

6. Novel (1876) by George Eliot.
7. A major character in *Daniel Deronda*, whose story—more conventional than that of Deronda—is preferred by many readers.

of the two great novelists above the ruck of Gaskells and Trollopes and Merediths. Of the earlier novelists it was George Eliot alone (if we except the minor relevance of Jane Austen) whose work had a direct and significant bearing on his own problem. It had this bearing because she *was* a great novelist, and because in her maturest work she handled with unprecedented subtlety and refinement the personal relations of sophisticated characters exhibiting the 'civilization' of the 'best society', and used, in so doing, an original psychological notation corresponding to the fineness of her psychological and moral insight. Her moral seriousness was for James very far from a disqualification; it qualified her for a kind of influence that neither Flaubert nor the admired Turgènev[8] could have.

* * *

When we come to Conrad we can't, by way of insisting that he is indeed significantly 'in' the tradition—in and of it, neatly and conclusively relate him to any one English novelist. Rather, we have to stress his foreignness—that he was a Pole, whose first other language was French. I remember remarking to André Chevrillon[9] how surprising a choice it was on Conrad's part to write in English, especially seeing he was so clearly a student of the French masters. And I remember the reply, to the effect that it wasn't at all surprising, since Conrad's work couldn't have been written in French. M. Chevrillon, with the authority of a perfect bilingual, went on to explain in terms of the characteristics of the two languages why it had to be English. Conrad's themes and interests demanded the concreteness and action—the dramatic energy—of English. We might go further and say that Conrad chose to write his novels in English for the reasons that led him to become a British Master Mariner.

I am not, in making this point, concurring in the emphasis generally laid on the Prose Laureate of the Merchant Service. What needs to be stressed is the great novelist. Conrad's great novels, if they deal with the sea at all, deal with it only incidentally. But the Merchant Service is for him both a spiritual fact and a spiritual symbol, and the interests that made it so for him control and animate his art everywhere. Here, then, we have a master of the English language, who chose it for its distinctive qualities and because of the moral tradition associated with it, and whose concern with art—he being like Jane Austen and George Eliot and Henry James an innovator in 'form' and method—is the servant of a profoundly serious interest in life. To justify our speaking of such a novelist as in the tradition, that represented by those three, we are not called on to establish particular relations with any one of them. Like James, he brought a great deal from outside, but it was of the utmost importance to him that he found a serious art of fiction there in English, and that there *were*, in English, great novelists to study. He drew from English literature what he needed, and learnt in that peculiar way of genius which is so different from imitation. And for us, who have *him* as well as the others, there he is, unquestionably a constitutive part of the tradition, belonging in the full sense.

8. Ivan Turgenev (1818–1883), a Russian novelist admired by Henry James.

9. French writer (1864–1957).

As being technically sophisticated he may be supposed to have found fortifying stimulus in James, whom he is quite unlike (though James, in his old age, was able to take a connoisseur's interest in *Chance*[1] and appreciate with a professional eye the sophistication of the 'doing'). But actually, the one influence at all obvious is that of a writer at the other end of the scale from sophistication, Dickens. As I point out in my discussion of him, Conrad is in certain respects so like Dickens that it is difficult to say for just how much influence Dickens counts. He is undoubtedly there in the London of *The Secret Agent*,[2] though—except for the unfortunate *macabre* of the cab-journey, and one or two local mannerisms—he has been transmuted into Conrad. This co-presence of obvious influence with assimilation suggests that Dickens may have counted for more in Conrad's mature art (we don't find much to suggest Dickens in the early adjectival phase) than seems at first probable: it suggests that Dickens may have encouraged the development in Conrad's art of that extraordinary energy of vision and registration in which they are akin. ('When people say that Dickens exaggerates', says Mr. Santayana;[3] 'it seems to me that they can have no eyes and no ears. They probably have only *notions* of what things and people are; they accept them conventionally, at their diplomatic value.') We may reasonably, too, in the same way see some Dickensian influence, closely related and of the same order, in Conrad's use of melodrama, or what would have been melodrama in Dickens; for in Conrad the end is a total significance of a profoundly serious kind.

The reason for not including Dickens in the line of great novelists is implicit in this last phrase. The kind of greatness in question has been sufficiently defined. That Dickens was a great genius and is permanently among the classics is certain. But the genius was that of a great entertainer, and he had for the most part no profounder responsibility as a creative artist than this description suggests. Praising him magnificently in a very fine critique,[4] Mr. Santayana, in concluding, says: 'In every English-speaking home, in the four quarters of the globe, parents and children would do well to read Dickens aloud of a winter's evening.' This note is right and significant. The adult mind doesn't as a rule find in Dickens a challenge to an unusual and sustained seriousness. I can think of only one of his books in which his distinctive creative genius is controlled throughout to a unifying and organizing significance, and that is *Hard Times*,[5] which seems, because of its unusualness and comparatively small scale, to have escaped recognition for the great thing it is. Conrad's views on it, supposing it to have caught his attention, would have been interesting; he was qualified to have written an apt appreciation.

It has a kind of perfection as a work of art that we don't associate with Dickens—a perfection that is one with the sustained and complete seriousness for which among his productions it is unique. Though in length it makes a good-sized modern novel, it is on a small scale for Dickens: it leaves no room for the usual repetitive overdoing and loose inclusiveness. It is plain that he felt no temptation to these, he was too urgently possessed by

1. Novel (1912) by Conrad.
2. Novel (1907) by Conrad.
3. George Santayana (1863–1952), Spanish-born American philosopher and man of letters.
4. See *Soliloquies in England* [(1922); Leavis's note]. The essay quoted is "Dickens" (1921).
5. Novel published in 1854.

his themes; the themes were too rich, too tightly knit in their variety and too commanding, Certain key characteristics of Victorian civilization had clearly come home to him with overwhelming force, embodied in concrete manifestations that suggested to him connexions and significances he had never realized so fully before. The fable is perfect; the symbolic and representative values are inevitable, and, sufficiently plain at once, yield fresh subtleties as the action develops naturally in its convincing historical way.

* * *

Though the greatness of *Hard Times* passed unnoticed, Dickens couldn't fail to have a wide influence. We have remarked his presence in *The Secret Agent*. It is there again, in a minor way, in George Eliot, in some of her less felicitous characterization; and it is there in Henry James, most patently, perhaps, in *The Princess Casamassima*, but most importantly in *Roderick Hudson*.[6] It is there once more, and even more interestingly, in D. H. Lawrence, in *The Lost Girl*.[7] The ironic humour, and the presentation in general, in the first part of that book bear a clear relation to the Dickensian, but are incomparably more mature and belong to a total serious significance.

* * *

To come back to Conrad and his major quality: he is one of those creative geniuses whose distinction is manifested in their being peculiarly alive in their time—peculiarly alive *to* it; not 'in the vanguard' in the manner of Shaw and Wells and Aldous Huxley,[8] but sensitive to the stresses of the changing spiritual climate as they begin to be registered by the most conscious. His interest in the tradition of the Merchant Service as a constructive triumph of the human spirit is correlative with his intense consciousness of the dependence, not only of the distinctive humanities at all levels, but of sanity itself and our sense of a normal outer world, on an analogous creative collaboration. His Robinson Crusoe[9] cannot bear a few days alone on his island, and blows out his brains. We are a long way from Jane Austen, for whom the problem was not to rescue the highly conscious individual from his isolation, but much the contrary. Conrad, of course, was a *déraciné*, which no doubt counts for a good deal in the intensity with which he renders his favourite theme of isolation. But then a state of something like deracination is common to-day among those to whom the question of who the great novelists are is likely to matter. Conrad is representative in the way genius is, which is not the way of those writers in whom journalist-critics acclaim the Zeitgeist. (It is relevant to note here that in the early hey-day of Wells and Shaw Conrad wrote *Nostromo*[1]—a great creative masterpiece which, among other things, is essentially an implicit comment on their preoccupations, made from a very much profounder level of preoccupation than theirs. And it is also relevant to venture that in Mr. Arthur Koestler's[2] very distinguished novel, *Darkness at Noon*, we have the work of

6. Novels published in 1886 and 1875, respectively.
7. Novel published in 1920.
8. English novelist and critic (1894–1963). George Bernard Shaw (1856–1950), Irish playwright and critic. H. G. Wells (1866–1946), English novelist and sociologist.
9. The hero of Defoe's novel, shipwrecked for 28 years and alone for all but the last 3 or 4 years.
1. Novel published in 1904.
2. Hungarian-born British novelist and journalist (1905–1983); *Darkness at Noon* (1940) is his best-known work.

a writer—also, we note, not born to the language—who knows and admires Conrad, especially the Conrad of *Nostromo* and *Under Western Eyes*.[3]

* * *

Is there no name later than Conrad's to be included in the great tradition? There is, I am convinced, one: D. H. Lawrence. Lawrence, in the English language, was the great genius of our time (I mean the age, or climatic phase, following Conrad's). It would be difficult to separate the novelist off for consideration, but it was in the novel that he committed himself to the hardest and most sustained creative labour, and he was, as a novelist, the representative of vital and significant development. He might, he has shown conclusively, have gone on writing novels with the kind of 'character creation' and psychology that the conventional cultivated reader immediately appreciates—novels that demanded no unfamiliar effort of approach. He might—if his genius had let him. In nothing is the genius more manifest than in the way in which, after the great success—and *succès d'estime*—of *Sons and Lovers*[4] he gives up that mode and devotes himself to the exhausting toil of working out the new things, the developments, that as the highly conscious and intelligent servant of life he saw to be necessary. Writing to Edward Garnett[5] of the work that was to become *Women in Love* he says: 'It is *very* different from *Sons and Lovers*: written in another language almost. I shall be sorry if you don't like it, but am prepared. I shan't write in the same manner as *Sons and Lovers* again, I think—in that hard, violent style full of sensation and presentation.'[6]

* * *

It is a spirit that, for all the unlikeness, relates Lawrence closely to George Eliot. He writes, again, to Edward Garnett:[7]

> 'You see—you tell me I am half a Frenchman and one-eighth a Cockney. But that isn't it. I have very often the vulgarity and disagreeableness of the common people, as you say Cockney, and I may be a Frenchman. But primarily I am a passionately religious man, and my novels must be written from the depth of my religious experience. That I must keep to, because I can only work like that. And my Cockneyism and commonness are only when the deep feeling doesn't find its way out, and a sort of jeer comes instead, and sentimentality and purplism. But you should see the religious, earnest, suffering man in me first, and then the flippant or common things after. Mrs. Garnett says I have no true nobility—with all my cleverness and charm. But that is not true. It is there, in spite of all the littlenesses and commonnesses.'

It is this spirit, by virtue of which he can truly say that what he writes must be written from the depth of his religious experience, that makes him, in my opinion, so much more significant in relation to the past and future, so much more truly creative as a technical inventor, an innovator, a master

3. Novel published in 1911.
4. Novel published in 1913. *Succès d'estime*: a critical (but not commercial) success (French).
5. English man of letters (1868–1937). Lawrence finished the first version of *Women in Love* (1920) in 1916.
6. *The Letters of D. H. Lawrence* (1932), p. 172 [Leavis's note].
7. *Letters*, p. 190 [Leavis's note].

of language, than James Joyce.[8] I know that Mr. T. S. Eliot has found in Joyce's work something that recommends Joyce to him as positively religious in tendency (see *After Strange Gods*[9]). But it seems plain to me that there is no organic principle determining, informing, and controlling into a vital whole, the elaborate analogical structure, the extraordinary variety of technical devices, the attempts at an exhaustive rendering of consciousness, for which *Ulysses* is remarkable, and which got it accepted by a cosmopolitan literary world as a new start. It is rather, I think, a dead end, or at least a pointer to disintegration—a view strengthened by Joyce's own development (for I think it significant and appropriate that *Work in Progress—Finnegans Wake*, as it became—should have engaged the interest of the inventor of Basic English[1]).

It is true that we can point to the influence of Joyce in a line of writers to which there is no parallel issuing from Lawrence. But I find here further confirmation of my view. For I think that in these writers, in whom a regrettable (if minor) strain of Mr. Eliot's influence seems to me to join with that of Joyce, we have, in so far as we have anything significant, the wrong kind of reaction against liberal idealism. I have in mind writers in whom Mr. Eliot has expressed an interest in strongly favourable terms: Djuna Barnes of *Nightwood*, Henry Miller, Lawrence Durrell[2] of *The Black Book*. In these writers—at any rate in the last two (and the first seems to me insignificant)—the spirit of what we are offered affects me as being essentially a desire, in Laurentian phrase, to 'do dirt' on life. It seems to me important that one should, in all modesty, bear one's witness in these matters. 'One must speak for life and growth, amid all this mass of destruction and disintegration.'[3] This is Lawrence, and it is the spirit of all his work. It is the spirit of the originality that gives his novels their disconcerting quality, and gives them the significance of works of genius.

* * *

I have, then, given my hostages. What I think and judge I have stated as responsibly and clearly as I can. Jane Austen, George Eliot, Henry James, Conrad, and D. H. Lawrence: the great tradition of the English novel is *there*.

1948

8. Irish novelist (1882–1941), generally viewed as one of the great innovators of 20th-century English prose; his works include *Ulysses* (1922) and *Finnegans Wake* (1939).
9. *After Strange Gods: A Primer of Modern Heresy* (1934), a series of lectures delivered at the University of Virginia (1933).
1. C. K. Ogden (1889–1957), English writer and linguist; he developed a simplified form of English to be used as an international language.
2. English author (1912–1990); his novel *The Black Book* was published in 1938. Miller (1891–1980), American novelist. Barnes (1892–1982), American writer; her novel *Nightwood* was published in 1936.
3. *The Letters of D. H. Lawrence*, p. 256 [Leavis's note].

ROMAN JAKOBSON
1896–1982

Roman Jakobson's role in literary theory arises out of his use of two highly suggestive sets of paired terms: "linguistics and poetics" and "metaphor and metonymy." These terms, and the thoughts behind them, profoundly shaped the structuralist movement in anthropology, philosophy, and psychoanalysis as well as literary studies, especially in France after World War II. But this groundbreaking theorist chose to characterize himself as a "Russian philologist," the phrase inscribed on his tombstone. He was a linguist who could lecture in six languages ("unfortunately, all of them Russian," joked his colleagues, referring to his pronounced accent). A large proportion of his many publications addressed minute topics in phonology, Slavic languages and literatures, and folklore. Yet that technical linguistic work grounded bold speculations about human linguistic behavior that opened up new channels for research in a number of different fields.

Born in Moscow, Jakobson entered the Lazarev Institute of Oriental Languages there in his early teens; he went on to study linguistics, literature, and folklore at Moscow University, where in 1915 he co-founded the Moscow Linguistic Circle. In this period of ferment just before the Russian Revolution, he wrote poetry and moved in avant-garde circles; like his friend the poet Vladimir Mayakovsky and others, he thought that a social revolution should include a revolution in artistic forms. At St. Petersburg University, where he studied in 1917, he worked with Victor Shklovsky and Boris Eichenbaum in the Society for the Study of Poetic Language, a group that has come to be known as the "Russian formalists."

In 1920 Jakobson moved to Prague, where he studied linguistics and Old Czech literature; in 1926 he co-founded the Prague Linguistic Circle, which included Jan Mukařovský. The work of FERDINAND DE SAUSSURE (1857–1913) was central to the group, though Jakobson moved beyond the Swiss linguist in 1927 when he realized that the Saussurean dichotomy between linguistic synchrony (a cross section of language at a given time) and diachrony (a transverse section *through* time) was too absolute: languages could be studied structurally as they changed over time. His work on poetic language also questioned the two founding Saussurean principles of language, the arbitrariness and the linearity of the sign. Nevertheless, his disagreements with Saussure helped shape his thought.

In 1938, when the Nazis invaded Czechoslovakia, Jakobson fled to Denmark, then Norway, then Sweden, before settling in the United States in 1941. He taught at the École Libre des Hautes Études (Free School of Advanced Study) in New York, where in 1942 he met CLAUDE LÉVI-STRAUSS, who had fled France; the two began attending each other's lectures. In 1943 Jakobson co-founded the Linguistic Circle of New York; he taught at Columbia University until 1949, then moved to Harvard University, where he taught first Slavic languages and literatures and then linguistics. From 1957 onward, he held a concurrent professorship at the Massachusetts Institute of Technology. He became emeritus in 1967 but never retired; he was writing letters from his hospital bed as he lay dying.

As a linguist, Jakobson clarified many important concepts. Phonemes or morphemes, for example, were once thought to be the smallest units of language, but Jakobson showed them to comprise bundles of "distinctive features" that themselves were formed by binary oppositions: voiced / unvoiced, consonant / vowel, singular / plural, and so on. Furthermore, his analysis of the tendency of binary oppositions to fall into "marked / unmarked" pairs prepared the way for later ideological analyses of structures and norms—where the "unmarked" (often the male, white, Christian, heterosexual point of view) goes unexamined, functioning as the standard against which "differences" are defined.

As a reader of poetry, Jakobson pursued two kinds of analysis that are not often found together. By studying "the poetry of grammar and the grammar of poetry," he scrutinized linguistic patterns that contribute to the overall poetic effect but normally escape the notice of readers—leading many critics to protest that those patterns could not have been intended by the poet. At the same time, he was fascinated by the difficulty of separating a poet's life and work, not because the life explained the work but because the life was largely structured like another work. Jakobson was similar to but profoundly different from his contemporaries, the American New Critics, in several ways. Both opposed "vulgar biographism" and the "intentional fallacy" (see WILLIAM K. WIMSATT JR. and MONROE C. BEARDSLEY, below), but Jakobson analyzed the myth of the poet as a function of cultural history, whereas the New Critics tuned their readings to a sense of the individual. Both Jakobson and the New Critics read texts closely, but the New Critics tended to frame interpretation within a working sense of imagination and mind, whereas Jakobson subjected the largest and the smallest patterns to linguistic and cultural analysis, without regard for individual craft. It was not that Jakobson did not believe in the unity of the human imagination, but precisely that he believed in it so much that he thought he was in no danger of departing from it. Jakobson welcomed the contributions of science to the work of literary studies, while the New Critics were trying to defend "humanistic" values *against* the spread of scientific "professionalism."

In his broad position paper "Linguistics and Poetics" (our first selection)—his concluding statement to a 1958 conference on style, published as *Style in Language* (ed. Thomas Sebeok, 1960)—Jakobson argues that what he calls the "poetic function" is at work in all verbal communication. The other five major functions of language are the *emotive* (focused on the speaker), the *conative* (focused on the addressee), the *phatic* (focused on the channel of communication), the *metalingual* (focused on explanations of the code itself), and the *referential* (focused on the context).

In defining the poetic function, Jakobson cites approvingly the French poet Paul Valéry (1871–1945), who called poetry a "sustained hesitation between the sound and the sense." He connects verbal art to the palpability (sound, sight) of signs. The poetic function consists of making connections *within the utterance* among the properties of the words, images, and sounds in a message, using those connections ("equivalences") to generate the linguistic sequence itself. Meter, rhyme, imagery, and generic conventions are not *subsequent* to the poetic function: they *are* the poetic function. Drawing on a mathematical sense of mapping ("projecting") one function upon another, he declares that "the poetic function projects the principle of equivalence from the axis of selection into the axis of combination." What does this formula mean? While ordinary speakers select one of the terms they perceive as equivalent in order to convey a message, the poet combines what is perceived as equivalent. Poetry seeks to *maximize* redundancy; ordinary communication seeks to *minimize* it.

Careful to distinguish between evaluation and analytical description, Jakobson discusses *the poetic function* rather than *poetry*. His remarks about the self-reflections and sounds in the 1950s political slogan "I like Ike" is a classic analysis of the poetic function without claiming to be an analysis of poetry. In showing how the slogan verbally embodies "the loving subject enveloped by the beloved object," he suggests the multiple uses to which the poetic function is put in everyday life, while noting that poetry employs all the "everyday" functions, too.

Literary scholars unwilling to separate function from evaluation have protested that Jakobson's definition fails to do justice to poetry, which depends on values of meaning and creativity. Jakobson claimed that the extent to which effects of meaning and creativity could be subject to linguistic analysis could not be known in advance. This did not keep critics from charging Jakobson with annexing poetics to linguistics. It was sometimes pointed out that the poets who best illustrate Jakobson's definition are not always those most esteemed in literary history. Here, as so often, EDGAR ALLAN POE—loved by the French, often dismissed by the Americans—stands as a test case, perhaps suggesting a parallel to Jakobson's impact on literary studies in France and in the United States. But in the final analysis, Jakobson does not, after all, claim to define poetry. He is more interested in how the poetic function accounts for broad linguistic behavior and effectiveness both within and outside any poetic canon. For this reason, he writes about Baudelaire, Shakespeare, Pushkin, Yeats, Blake, and Hopkins with the same curiosity he applies to the linguistic mechanisms of slogans, folklore, and everyday speech.

Jakobson's distinction between metaphor and metonymy in "Two Aspects of Language and Two Types of Aphasic Disturbances" (1956; our second selection) became for him—and many others following him—a key to language itself. Derived from studies of aphasia (inability to speak), Jakobson detected two primordial principles of language use: similarity and contiguity (i.e., resemblance and nearness). In the vast array of normal verbal behavior, both operate at once. But in the early stages of language learning by children, in the late stages of language loss by aphasics (who can either provide a synonym for a word or construct a sentence around it, but not both), and to some extent in literary forms like Romanticism or realism, the outline of the two distinct principles becomes visible. Jakobson chooses to call these *metaphor* and *metonymy*, using the names of two rhetorical figures that had not previously been set in opposition.

Metaphor, which has often stood as the general name for all figures and has long been the object of philosophical and rhetorical analyses, stands in Jakobson's essay as the name for any two terms related by similarity (synonymy, analogy, comparison, even antithesis, with or without the word *like*). The opposing term, *metonymy*, has historically generated far less commentary. It is usually defined as the substitution of symbol for thing symbolized ("the throne is in danger" for "the king is in danger"), maker for thing made ("I drive a Ford" or "I read Shakespeare"), container for contained ("drink the whole glass"), part for whole ("all hands on deck"), and so on. In each case, the association is *not* based on similarity; thus all are relations of contiguity. Contiguity is observed not just in the connections among the meanings of terms but also in the very fact of sequence, syntactically relating all terms that are present in a sentence. In Jakobson's scheme there are ultimately not two principles but four: similarity, contiguity, substitution, and combination. And all verbal behavior can be analyzed along these lines. JACQUES LACAN, building on SIGMUND FREUD's opposition between "condensation" and "displacement" in the rhetoric of dreams, sees in the relation between metaphor and metonymy the general psychoanalytic laws governing symptom and desire. Other figures who see tropology as foundational to cognition and discourse include GIAMBATTISTA VICO, PAUL DE MAN, and HAYDEN WHITE.

Jakobson was criticized for the same reasons he was praised. He was less interested in where to stop than in where to go, and his bold and painstaking writings opened up many domains of study in linguistics, poetics, folklore, and in the relations among them; but the gap between his microanalyses and his broad generalizations left much room for quibbles. He was fond of loosely paraphrasing the Roman playwright Terence: "Linguista sum; linguistici nihil a me alienum esse puto"—"I am a linguist; I consider nothing linguistic to be alien to me." (Terence's original formulation was "Homo [a human] sum; humani nil a me alienum puto.") In Jakobson's work, "linguistic" often became synonymous with Terence's "human."

"Linguistics and Poetics" Keywords: Language, Literary History, Narrative Theory, Philology, Poetry, Semiotics, Structuralism, Vernacular Language
"Two Aspects of Language and Two Types of Aphasic Disturbances" Keywords: Language, Literary History, Poetry, Realism, Rhetoric, Semiotics

From Linguistics and Poetics

* * *

I have been asked for summary remarks about poetics in its relation to linguistics. Poetics deals primarily with the question, "What makes a verbal message a work of art?" Because the main subject of poetics is the *differentia specifica*[1] of verbal art in relation to other arts and in relation to other kinds of verbal behavior, poetics is entitled to the leading place in literary studies. Poetics deals with problems of verbal structure, just as the analysis of painting is concerned with pictorial structure. Since linguistics is the global science of verbal structure, poetics may be regarded as an integral part of linguistics.

Arguments against such a claim must be thoroughly discussed. It is evident that many devices studied by poetics are not confined to verbal art. We can refer to the possibility of transporting *Wuthering Heights*[2] into a motion picture, medieval legends into frescoes and miniatures, or *L'Aprés-midi d'un faune*[3] into music, ballet, and graphic art. However ludicrous the idea of the *Iliad* and *Odyssey* in comics may seem,[4] certain structural features of their plot are preserved despite the disappearance of their verbal shape. The question of whether W. B. Yeats was right in affirming that William Blake was "the one perfectly fit illustrator for the *Inferno* and the *Purgatorio*"[5] is a proof that different arts are comparable. The problems of the baroque or any other historical style transgress the frame of a single art. When handling the surrealistic metaphor, we could hardly pass by Max Ernst's pictures or Luis Buñuel's films, *The Andalusian Dog* and *The Golden Age*.[6] In short, many poetic features belong not only to the science of language but to the whole theory of signs, that is, to general semiotics.[7] This statement, however, is valid not only for verbal art but also for all varieties of language, since language shares many properties with certain other systems of signs or even with all of them (pansemiotic features).

Likewise, a second objection contains nothing that would be specific for literature: the question of relations between the word and the world concerns not only verbal art but actually all kinds of discourse. Linguistics is likely to explore all possible problems of relation between discourse and the "universe of discourse": what of this universe is verbalized by a given discourse and how it is verbalized. The truth values, however, as far as they are—to say with the logicians—"extra-linguistic entities," obviously exceed the bounds of poetics and of linguistics in general.

1. Specific difference (Latin).
2. An 1847 novel by Emily Brontë; the best-known film version was directed by William Wyler (1939).
3. *The Afternoon of a Faun* (1876), a poem by Stéphane Mallarmé; it was set to music by Claude Debussy (1894), and choreographed and danced by Vaslav Nijinsky for Sergei Diaghilev's Ballets Russes (1912). Its original edition was illustrated by Édouard Manet.
4. Homer's epic poems (ca. 8th c. B.C.E.) were among the many literary works presented as comics in the American "Classics Illustrated" series (1940s–60s).
5. *Inferno* and *Purgatorio* are two of the three books of DANTE ALIGHIERI's *Divine Comedy* (1321). Yeats (1865–1939), Irish poet and dramatist; the quotation is from "William Blake and His Illustrations to *The Divine Comedy*" (1897). Blake (1757–1827), English poet and engraver.
6. Films (1928 and 1930, respectively) on which the Spanish-born filmmaker Buñuel (1900–1983) collaborated with the surrealist painter Salvador Dali (1904–1989). Ernst (1891–1976), German-born French painter.
7. *Semiotics*, a term derived from the work of the American philosopher C. S. Peirce (1839–1914), and *semiology*, from that of the Swiss linguist FERDINAND DE SAUSSURE (1857–1913), both name the general theory of signs.

Sometimes we hear that poetics in contradistinction to linguistics, is concerned with evaluation. This separation of the two fields from each other is based on a current but erroneous interpretation of the contrast between the structure of poetry and other types of verbal structure: the latter are said to be opposed by their "casual," designless nature to the "noncasual," purposeful character of poetic language. In point of fact, any verbal behavior is goal-directed, but the aims are different and the conformity of the means used to the effect aimed at is a problem that evermore preoccupies inquirers into the diverse kinds of verbal communication. There is a close correspondence, much closer than critics believe, between the question of linguistic phenomena expanding in space and time and the spatial and temporal spread of literary models. Even such discontinuous expansion as the resurrection of neglected or forgotten poets—for instance, the posthumous discovery and subsequent canonization of Emily Dickinson (d. 1886) and Gerard Manley Hopkins (d. 1889), the tardy fame of Lautréamont (d. 1870) among surrealist poets, and the salient influence of the hitherto ignored Cyprian Norwid (d. 1883) on Polish modern poetry—finds a parallel in the history of standard languages that tend to revive outdated models, sometimes long forgotten, as was the case in literary Czech, which toward the beginning of the nineteenth century leaned toward sixteenth-century models.

Unfortunately, the terminological confusion of "literary studies" with "criticism" tempts the student of literature to replace the description of the intrinsic values of a literary work with a subjective, censorious verdict. The label "literary critic" applied to an investigator of literature is as erroneous as "grammatical (or lexical) critic" would be applied to a linguist. Syntactic and morphologic[8] research cannot be supplanted by a normative grammar, and likewise no manifesto, foisting a critic's own tastes and opinions on creative literature, can serve as a substitute for an objective scholarly analysis of verbal art. This statement should not be mistaken for the quietist principle of laissez faire; any verbal culture involves programmatic, planning, normative endeavors. Yet why is a clear-cut discrimination made between pure and applied linguistics or between phonetics and orthoepy,[9] but not between literary studies and criticism?

Literary studies, with poetics as their focal point, consist like linguistics of two sets of problems: synchrony and diachrony.[1] The synchronic description envisages not only the literary production of any given stage but also that part of the literary tradition which for the stage in question has remained vital or has been revived. Thus, for instance, Shakespeare, on the one hand, and Donne, Marvell, Keats, and Emily Dickinson, on the other, are experienced by the present English poetic world, whereas the works of James Thomson and Longfellow,[2] for the time being, do not belong to viable artistic values. The selection of classics and their reinterpretation by a novel

8. Pertaining to the forms taken by words in usage (conjugations, tenses, declensions, etc.). "Syntactic": pertaining to the structure of phrases and sentences.
9. The study of correct pronunciation. "Phonetics": the study of the sounds of language.
1. Change in a system over time. "Synchrony": the relations of parts within a system arrested in time.
2. Jakobson contrasts the now highly regarded English poets John Donne (1562–1631), Andrew Marvell (1621–1678), John Keats (1795–1821), and the American Dickinson (who all, unlike Shakespeare, received relatively little attention in their lifetimes) to the once popular but now critically scorned Scottish-born English poet Thomson (1700–1748) and American poet Henry Wadsworth Longfellow (1807–1882).

trend is a substantial problem of synchronic literary studies. Synchronic poetics, like synchronic linguistics, is not to be confused with statics; any stage discriminates between more conservative and more innovative forms. Any contemporary stage is experienced in its temporal dynamics, and, on the other hand, the historical approach both in poetics and in linguistics is concerned not only with changes but also with continuous, enduring, static factors. A thoroughly comprehensive historical poetics or history of language is a superstructure to be built on a series of successive synchronic descriptions.

Insistence on keeping poetics apart from linguistics is warranted only when the field of linguistics appears to be illicitly restricted, for example, when the sentence is viewed by some linguists as the highest analyzable construction, or when the scope of linguistics is confined to grammar alone or uniquely to nonsemantic questions of external form or to the inventory of denotative devices with no reference to free variations. Voegelin has clearly pointed out the two most important and related problems that face structural linguistics, namely, a revision of "the monolithic hypothesis about language" and a concern with "the interdependence of diverse structures within one language."[3] No doubt, for any speech community, for any speaker, there exists a unity of language, but this over-all code represents a system of interconnected subcodes; every language encompasses several concurrent patterns, each characterized by different functions.

Obviously we must agree with Sapir that, on the whole, "ideation reigns supreme in language,"[4] but this supremacy does not authorize linguistics to disregard the "secondary factors." The emotive elements of speech, which, as Joos is prone to believe, cannot be described "with a finite number of absolute categories," are classified by him "as nonlinguistic elements of the real world." Hence, "for us they remain vague, protean, fluctuating phenomena," he concludes, "which we refuse to tolerate in our science."[5] Joos is indeed a brilliant expert in reduction experiments, and his emphatic demand for the "expulsion" of emotive elements "from linguistic science" is a radical experiment in reduction—*reductio ad absurdum*.

Language must be investigated in all the variety of its functions. Before discussing the poetic function we must define its place among the other functions of language. An outline of these functions demands a concise survey of the constitutive factors in any speech event, in any act of verbal communication. The ADDRESSER sends a MESSAGE to the ADDRESSEE. To be operative the message requires a CONTEXT referred to (the "referent" in another, somewhat ambiguous, nomenclature), graspable by the addressee, and either verbal or capable of being verbalized; a CODE fully, or at least partially, common to the addresser and addressee (or in other words, to the encoder and decoder of the message); and, finally, a CONTACT, a physical channel and psychological connection between the addresser and the addressee, enabling both of them to enter and stay in communication. All

3. Charles F. Voegelin, "Casual and Noncasual Utterances within Unified Structures," in *Style in Language*, ed. Thomas Sebeok (Cambridge, Mass., 1960), p. 57 [Jakobson's note]. Voegelin (1908–1986), American anthropologist and linguist.

4. Edward Sapir, *Language* (New York, 1921), p. 40 [Jakobson's note]. Sapir (1884–1939), German-born American linguist.

5. Martin Joos, "Description of Language Design," *Journal of the Acoustical Society of America* 22 (1950): 701–8 [Jakobson's note]. Joos (1907–1978), American linguist.

these factors inalienably involved in verbal communication may be schematized as follows:

CONTEXT

ADDRESSER MESSAGE ADDRESSEE

CONTACT

CODE

Each of these six factors determines a different function of language. Although we distinguish six basic aspects of language, we could, however, hardly find verbal messages that would fulfill only one function. The diversity lies not in a monopoly of some one of these several functions but in a different hierarchical order of functions. The verbal structure of a message depends primarily on the predominant function. But even though a set (*Einstellung*) toward the referent, an orientation toward the context—briefly, the so-called REFERENTIAL, "denotative," "cognitive" function—is the leading task of numerous messages, the accessory participation of the other functions in such messages must be taken into account by the observant linguist.

The so-called EMOTIVE or "expressive" function, focused on the addresser, aims a direct expression of the speaker's attitude toward what he is speaking about. It tends to produce an impression of a certain emotion, whether true or feigned; therefore, the term "emotive," launched and advocated by Marty,[6] has proved to be preferable to "emotional." The purely emotive stratum in language is presented by the interjections. They differ from the means of referential language both by their sound pattern (peculiar sound sequences or even sounds elsewhere unusual) and by their syntactic role (they are not components but equivalents of sentences). "*Tut! Tut!* said McGinty": the complete utterance of Conan Doyle's[7] character consists of two suction clicks. The emotive function, laid bare in the interjections, flavors to some extent all our utterances, on their phonic, grammatical, and lexical level. If we analyze language from the standpoint of the information it carries, we cannot restrict the notion of information to the cognitive aspect of language. A man, using expressive features to indicate his angry or ironic attitude, conveys ostensible information, and evidently this verbal behavior cannot be likened to such nonsemiotic, nutritive activities as "eating grapefruit" (despite Chatman's bold simile).[8] The difference between [bɪg] and the emphatic prolongation of the vowel [bɪ:g] is a conventional, coded linguistic feature like the difference between the short and long vowel in such Czech pairs as [vi] "you" and [vi:] "knows," but in the latter pair the differential information is phonemic and in the former emotive. As long as we are interested in phonemic invariants, the English /i/ and /i:/ appear to be mere variants of one and the same phoneme, but if we are concerned with emotive units, the relation between the invariants and variants is reversed: length and shortness are invariants imple-

6. Anton Marty, *Untersuchungen zur Grundlegung der allgemeinen Grammatik und Sprachphilosophie*, I (Halle, 1908) [Jakobson's note]. Marty (1847–1914), Austrian linguist.

7. Sir Arthur Conan Doyle (1859–1930), English novelist, best known for his tales featuring Sherlock Holmes; the quotation is from *The Valley of Fear* (1915).

8. Seymour Chatman (1928–2015) was another American participant in the *Style* conference. No reference to grapefruit occurs in his paper, which discusses the metrical contrasts between the poets John Donne and ALEXANDER POPE. Perhaps there was some connection between "segmental sound" and grapefruit segments.

mented by variable phonemes. Saporta's surmise that emotive difference is a nonlinguistic feature, "attributable to the delivery of the message and not to the message,"[9] arbitrarily reduces the informational capacity of messages.

A former actor of Stanislavskij's[1] Moscow Theater told me how at his audition he was asked by the famous director to make forty different messages from the phrase *Segodnja večerom* (This evening), by diversifying its expressive tint. He made a list of some forty emotional situations, then emitted the given phrase in accordance with each of these situations, which his audience had to recognize only from the changes in the sound shape of the same two words. For our research work in the description and analysis of contemporary Standard Russian (under the auspices of the Rockefeller Foundation) this actor was asked to repeat Stanislavskij's test. He wrote down some fifty situations framing the same elliptic sentence and made of it fifty corresponding messages for a tape recording. Most of the messages were correctly and circumstantially decoded by Moscovite listeners. May I add that all such emotive cues easily undergo linguistic analysis.

Orientation toward the addressee, the CONATIVE function, finds its purest grammatical expression in the vocative and imperative, which syntactically, morphologically, and often even phonemically deviate from other nominal and verbal categories. The imperative sentences cardinally differ from declarative sentences: the latter are and the former are not liable to a truth test. When in O'Neill's[2] play *The Fountain*, Nano "(in a fierce tone of command)" says "Drink!"—the imperative cannot be challenged by the question "is it true or not?" which may be, however, perfectly well asked after such sentences as "one drank," "one will drink," "one would drink." In contradistinction to the imperative sentences, the declarative sentences are convertible into interrogative sentences: "did one drink?," "will one drink?," "would one drink?"

The traditional model of language as elucidated particularly by Bühler[3] was confined to these three functions—emotive, conative, and referential—and the three apexes of this model—the first person of the addresser, the second person of the addressee, and the "third person" properly (someone or something spoken of). Certain additional verbal functions can be easily inferred from this triadic model. Thus the magic, incantatory function is chiefly some kind of conversion of an absent or inanimate "third person" into an addressee of a conative message. "May this sty dry up, *tfu, tfu, tfu, tfu*" (Lithuanian spell).[4] "Water, queen river, daybreak! Send grief beyond the blue sea, to the sea bottom, like a gray stone never to rise from the sea bottom, may grief never come to burden the light heart of God's servant, may grief be removed and sink away" (North Russian incantation).[5] "Sun, stand thou still upon Gibeon; and thou, Moon, in the valley of Aj-a-lon. And the sun stood still, and the moon stayed" (Joshua 10.12). We observe,

9. Sol Saporta, "The Application of Linguistics to the Study of Poetic Language," in *Style in Language*, p. 88 [Jakobson's note]. Saporta (1925–2008), American linguist.
1. Konstantin Stanislavsky (1863–1938), Russian actor and director of the Moscow Art Theater; he developed what became known in the United States as "method acting."
2. Eugene O'Neill (1888–1953), American playwright; *The Fountain* was staged in 1925.
3. Karl Bühler, "Die Axiomatik der Sprachwissenschaft," *Kant-Studien* (Berlin) 38 (1933): 19–20 [Jakobson's note]. Bühler (1879–1963), German psychologist.
4. V. J. Mansikka, *Litauische Zaubersprüche* (*Folklore Fellows Communications*) 87 (1929): 69 [Jakobson's note].
5. P. N. Rybnikov, *Pesni* (Moscow, 1910), III, 217–18 [Jakobson's note].

however, three further constitutive factors of verbal communication and three corresponding functions of language.

There are messages primarily serving to establish, to prolong, or to discontinue communication, to check whether the channel works ("Hello, do you hear me?"), to attract the attention of the interlocutor or to confirm his continued attention ("Are you listening?" or in Shakespearean diction, "Lend me your ears!"[6]—and on the other end of the wire "Um-hum!"). This set for contact, or in Malinowski's terms PHATIC function,[7] may be displayed by a profuse exchange of ritualized formulas, by entire dialogues with the mere purport of prolonging communication. Dorothy Parker[8] caught eloquent examples: "'Well!' the young man said. 'Well!' she said. 'Well, here we are,' he said. 'Here we are,' she said, 'Aren't we?' 'I should say we were,' he said, 'Eeyop! Here we are.' 'Well!' she said. 'Well!' he said, 'well.'" The endeavor to start and sustain communication is typical of talking birds; thus the phatic function of language is the only one they share with human beings. It is also the first verbal function acquired by infants; they are prone to communicate before being able to send or receive informative communication.

A distinction has been made in modern logic between two levels of language: "object language" speaking of objects and "metalanguage" speaking of language.[9] But metalanguage is not only a necessary scientific tool utilized by logicians and linguists; it plays also an important role in our everyday language. Like Molière's Jourdain[1] who used prose without knowing it, we practice metalanguage without realizing the metalingual character of our operations. Whenever the addresser and/or the addressee need to check up whether they use the same code, speech is focused on the code: it performs a METALINGUAL (i.e., glossing) function. "I don't follow you—what do you mean?" asks the addressee, or in Shakespearean diction, "What is't thou say'st?"[2] And the addresser in anticipation of such recapturing question inquires: "Do you know what I mean?" Imagine such an exasperating dialogue: "The sophomore was plucked." "But what is *plucked?*" "*Plucked* means the same as *flunked*." "And *flunked?*" "*To be flunked is to fail an exam.*" "And what is *sophomore*?" persists the interrogator innocent of school vocabulary. "A *sophomore* is (or means) a *second-year student*." All these equational sentences convey information merely about the lexical code of English; their function is strictly metalingual. Any process of language learning, in particular child acquisition of the mother tongue, makes wide use of such metalingual operations; and aphasia may often be defined as a loss of ability for metalingual operations.

I have brought up all the six factors involved in verbal communication except the message itself. The set (*Einstellung*) toward the message as

6. See Shakespeare, *Julius Caesar* (1599), 3.2.70.
7. Bronislaw Malinowski, "The Problem of Meaning in Primitive Languages," in *The Meaning of Meaning*, ed. C. K. Ogden and I. A. Richards, 9th ed. (New York, 1953), pp. 296–336 [Jakobson's note]. Malinowski (1884–1942), Polish-born American anthropologist.
8. American writer of light verse and short stories (1893–1967); the quoted dialogue is from the story "Here We Are" (1931).
9. Term introduced by Alfred Tarski, *Pojeçie prawdy w jezykach nauk dedukcyjnych* (Warsaw, 1933), and "Der Wahrheitsbegriff in den formalisierten Sprachen," *Studia Philosophica* I (1936) [Jakobson's note].
1. M. Jourdain is the protagonist of *Le Bourgeois gentilhomme* (1670, *The Would-be Gentleman*), a play by Molière (pen name of Jean-Baptiste Poquelin, 1622–1673); he is surprised to learn that he has been speaking prose all his life without knowing it.
2. See Shakespeare, *Antony and Cleopatra* (1606–07), 5.1.2; *King Lear* (1605), 5.3.246.

such, focus on the message for its own sake, is the POETIC function of language. This function cannot be productively studied out of touch with the general problems of language, and, on the other hand, the scrutiny of language requires a thorough consideration of its poetic function. Any attempt to reduce the sphere of the poetic function to poetry or to confine poetry to the poetic function would be a delusive oversimplification. The poetic function is not the sole function of verbal art but only its dominant, determining function, whereas in all other verbal activities it acts as a subsidiary, accessory constituent. This function, by promoting the palpability of signs, deepens the fundamental dichotomy of signs and objects. Hence, when dealing with the poetic function, linguistics cannot limit itself to the field of poetry.

"Why do you always say *Joan and Margery*, yet never *Margery and Joan?* Do you prefer Joan to her twin sister?" "Not at all, it just sounds smoother." In a sequence of two coordinate names, so far as no problems of rank interfere, the precedence of the shorter name suits the speaker, unaccountably for him, as a well-ordered shape for the message.

A girl used to talk about "the horrible Harry." "Why horrible?" "Because I hate him." "But why not *dreadful, terrible, frightful, disgusting?*" "I don't know why, but *horrible* fits him better." Without realizing it, she clung to the poetic device of paronomasia.[3]

The political slogan "I like Ike" /ay layk ayk/,[4] succinctly structured, consists of three monosyllables and counts three diphthongs /ay/, each of them symmetrically followed by one consonantal phoneme, / .. l .. k .. k /. The makeup of the three words presents a variation: no consonantal phonemes in the first word, two around the diphthong in the second, and one final consonant in the third. A similar dominant nucleus /ay/ was noticed by Hymes in some of the sonnets of Keats.[5] Both cola[6] of the trisyllabic formula "I like / Ike" rhyme with each other, and the second of the two rhyming words is fully included in the first one (echo rhyme), /layk/ — /ayk/, a paronomastic image of a feeling which totally envelops its object. Both cola alliterate with each other, and the first of the two alliterating words is included in the second: /ay/ — /ayk/, a paronomastic image of the loving subject enveloped by the beloved object. The secondary, poetic function of this campaign slogan reinforces its impressiveness and efficacy.

As I said, the linguistic study of the poetic function must overstep the limits of poetry, and, on the other hand, the linguistic scrutiny of poetry cannot limit itself to the poetic function. The particularities of diverse poetic genres imply a differently ranked participation of the other verbal functions along with the dominant poetic function. Epic poetry, focused on the third person, strongly involves the referential function of language; the lyric, oriented toward the first person, is intimately linked with the emotive function; poetry of the second person is imbued with the conative function and is either supplicatory or exhortative, depending on whether the first person is subordinated to the second one or the second to the first.

3. A play on words that sound alike.
4. The 1952 campaign slogan of Dwight D. Eisenhower (U.S. president, 1953–61).
5. Dell H. Hymes, "Phonological Aspects of Style: Some English Sonnets," in *Style in Language*, pp. 123–26 [Jakobson's note]. Hymes (1927–2009), American anthropologist and linguist.
6. Sections of a sentence or rhythmical period (the plural of *colon*).

Now that our cursory description of the six basic functions of verbal communication is more or less complete, we may complement our scheme of the fundamental factors with a corresponding scheme of the functions:

	REFERENTIAL	
EMOTIVE	POETIC	CONATIVE
	PHATIC	
	METALINGUAL	

What is the empirical linguistic criterion of the poetic function? In particular, what is the indispensable feature inherent in any piece of poetry? To answer this question we must recall the two basic modes of arrangement used in verbal behavior, *selection* and *combination*. If "child" is the topic of the message, the speaker selects one among the extant, more or less similar nouns like child, kid, youngster, tot, all of them equivalent in a certain respect, and then, to comment on this topic, he may select one of the semantically cognate verbs—sleeps, dozes, nods, naps. Both chosen words combine in the speech chain. The selection is produced on the basis of equivalence, similarity and dissimilarity, synonymy and antonymy, while the combination, the build-up of the sequence, is based on contiguity. *The poetic function projects the principle of equivalence from the axis of selection into the axis of combination.* Equivalence is promoted to the constitutive device of the sequence. In poetry one syllable is equalized with any other syllable of the same sequence; word stress is assumed to equal word stress, as unstress equals unstress; prosodic long is matched with long, and short with short; word boundary equals word boundary, no boundary equals no boundary; syntactic pause equals syntactic pause, no pause equals no pause. Syllables are converted into units of measure, and so are morae[7] or stresses.

It may be objected that metalanguage also makes a sequential use of equivalent units when combining synonymic expressions into an equational sentence: A=A ("*Mare is the female of the horse*"). Poetry and metalanguage, however, are in diametrical opposition to each other: in metalanguage the sequence is used to build an equation, whereas in poetry the equation is used to build a sequence.

* * *

1960

From Two Aspects of Language and Two Types of Aphasic Disturbances

V. The Metaphoric and Metonymic Poles

The varieties of aphasia[1] are numerous and diverse, but all of them lie between the two polar types just described. Every form of aphasic disturbance consists in some impairment, more or less severe, of the faculty either

7. Short (unstressed) syllables.

1. Loss of the ability to use or understand speech.

for selection and substitution or for combination and contexture. The former affliction involves a deterioration of metalinguistic operations, while the latter damages the capacity for maintaining the hierarchy of linguistic units. The relation of similarity is suppressed in the former, the relation of contiguity in the latter type of aphasia. Metaphor is alien to the similarity disorder, and metonymy to the contiguity disorder.

The development of a discourse may take place along two different semantic lines: one topic may lead to another either through their similarity or through their contiguity. The metaphoric way would be the most appropriate term for the first case and the metonymic way for the second, since they find their most condensed expression in metaphor and metonymy respectively. In aphasia one or the other of these two processes is restricted or totally blocked—an effect which makes the study of aphasia particularly illuminating for the linguist. In normal verbal behavior both processes are continually operative, but careful observation will reveal that under the influence of a cultural pattern, personality, and verbal style, preference is given to one of the two processes over the other.

In a well-known psychological test, children are confronted with some noun and told to utter the first verbal response that comes into their heads. In this experiment two opposite linguistic predilections are invariably exhibited: the response is intended either as a substitute for or as a complement to the stimulus. In the latter case the stimulus and the response together form a proper syntactic construction, most usually a sentence. These two types of reaction have been labeled *substitutive* and *predicative*.

To the stimulus *hut* one response was *burnt out*; another *is a poor little house*. Both reactions are predicative; but the first creates a purely narrative context, while in the second there is a double connection with the subject *hut*: on the one hand, a positional (namely, syntactic) contiguity and, on the other, a semantic similarity.

The same stimulus produced the following substitutive reactions: the tautology *hut*; the synonyms *cabin* and *hovel*; the antonym *palace*; and the metaphors *den* and *burrow*. The capacity of two words to replace one another is an instance of positional similarity, and, in addition, all these responses are linked to the stimulus by semantic similarity (or contrast). Metonymical responses to the same stimulus, such as *thatch, litter,* or *poverty,* combine and contrast the positional similarity with semantic contiguity.

In manipulating these two kinds of connection (similarity and contiguity) in both their aspects (positional and semantic)—selecting, combining, and ranking them—an individual exhibits his personal style, his verbal predilections and preferences.

In verbal art the interaction of these two elements is especially pronounced. Rich material for the study of this relationship is to be found in verse patterns which require a compulsory *parallelism* between adjacent lines, for example in biblical poetry or in the Finnic and, to some extent, the Russian oral traditions. This provides an objective criterion of what in the given speech community acts as a correspondence. Since on any verbal level—morphemic, lexical, syntactic, and phraseological[2]—either of these

2. That is, pertaining respectively to the smallest meaningful sound, to individual words, to the structure of phrases and sentences, and to the organization of phrases into larger elements.

two relations (similarity and contiguity) can appear—and each in either of two aspects, an impressive range of possible configurations is created. Either of the two gravitational poles may prevail. In Russian lyrical songs, for example, metaphoric constructions predominate, while in the heroic epics the metonymic way is preponderant.

In poetry there are various motives which determine the choice between these alternants. The primacy of the metaphoric process in the literary schools of Romanticism and Symbolism has been repeatedly acknowledged, but it is still insufficiently realized that it is the predominance of metonymy which underlies and actually predetermines the so-called Realist trend, which belongs to an intermediary stage between the decline of Romanticism and the rise of Symbolism and is opposed to both. Following the path of contiguous relationships, the Realist author metonymically digresses from the plot to the atmosphere and from the characters to the setting in space and time. He is fond of synecdochic details. In the scene of Anna Karenina's suicide Tolstoj's[3] artistic attention is focused on the heroine's handbag; and in *War and Peace* the synecdoches "hair on the upper lip" and "bare shoulders" are used by the same writer to stand for the female characters to whom these features belong.

The alternative predominance of one or the other of these two processes is by no means confined to verbal art. The same oscillation occurs in sign systems other than language. A salient example from the history of painting is the manifestly metonymical orientation of Cubism, where the object is transformed into a set of synecdoches; the Surrealist painters[4] responded with a patently metaphorical attitude. Ever since the productions of D. W. Griffith,[5] the art of the cinema, with its highly developed capacity for changing the angle, perspective, and focus of shots, has broken with the tradition of the theater and ranged an unprecedented variety of synecdochic close-ups and metonymic set-ups in general. In such motion pictures as those of Charlie Chaplin and Eisenstein,[6] these devices in turn were overlaid by a novel, metaphoric montage with its lap dissolves—the filmic similes.

The bipolar structure of language (or other semiotic systems) and, in aphasia, the fixation on one of these poles to the exclusion of the other require systematic comparative study. The retention of either of these alternatives in the two types of aphasia must be confronted with the predominance of the same pole in certain styles, personal habits, current fashions, etc. A careful analysis and comparison of these phenomena with the whole syndrome of the corresponding type of aphasia is an imperative task for joint research by experts in psychopathology, psychology, linguistics, poetics, and semiotics, the general science of signs. The dichotomy discussed

3. Leo Tolstoy (1828–1910), Russian novelist and moral philosopher; his works include *Anna Karenina* (1873–76) and *War and Peace* (1864–69).
4. Members of an experimental literary and artistic movement founded in France in 1924; inspired in part by SIGMUND FREUD (1856–1939), surrealists sought to express subconscious thought and feeling. Cubism: early 20th-century art movement that attempted to present objects from all points of view.
5. American film director and producer (1875–1948), a pioneer in motion pictures.
6. Cf. his striking essay "Dickens, Griffith, and We": Sergej Eisenstein, *Izbrannye stat'i* [*Selected Articles*] (Moscow, 1950) [Jakobson's note]. Chaplin (1889–1977), English actor and film director. Eisenstein (1898–1948), Russian film director, an early innovator in cinematic technique.

here appears to be of primal significance and consequence for all verbal behavior and for human behavior in general.[7]

To indicate the possibilities of the projected comparative research, I choose an example from a Russian folktale which employs parallelism as a comic device: "Thomas is a bachelor; Jeremiah is unmarried" (*Fomá xólost; Erjóma neženát*). Here the predicates in the two parallel clauses are associated by similarity: they are in fact synonymous. The subjects of both clauses are masculine proper names and hence morphologically similar, while on the other hand they denote two contiguous heroes of the same tale, created to perform identical actions and thus to justify the use of synonymous pairs of predicates. A somewhat modified version of the same construction occurs in a familiar wedding song in which each of the wedding guests is addressed in turn by his first name and patronymic: "Gleb is a bachelor; Ivanovič is unmarried." While both predicates here are again synonyms, the relationship between the two subjects is changed: both are proper names denoting the same man and are normally used contiguously as a mode of polite address.

In the quotation from the folktale, the two parallel clauses refer to two separate facts, the marital status of Thomas and the similar status of Jeremiah. In the verse from the wedding song, however, the two clauses are synonymous: they redundantly reiterate the celibacy of the same hero, splitting him into two verbal hypostases.[8]

The Russian novelist Gleb Ivanovič Uspenskij (1840–1902) in the last years of his life suffered from a mental illness involving a speech disorder. His first name and patronymic, *Gleb Ivanovič,* traditionally combined in polite intercourse, for him split into two distinct names designating two separate beings: Gleb was endowed with all his virtues, while Ivanovič, the name relating a son to his father, became the incarnation of all Uspenskij's vices. The linguistic aspect of this split personality is the patient's inability to use two symbols for the same thing, and it is thus a similarity disorder. Since the similarity disorder is bound up with the metonymical bent, an examination of the literary manner Uspenskij had employed as a young writer takes on particular interest. And the study of Anatolij Kamegulov, who analyzed Uspenskij's style, bears out our theoretical expectations. He shows that Uspenskij had a particular penchant for metonymy, and especially for synecdoche, and that he carried it so far that "the reader is crushed by the multiplicity of detail unloaded on him in a limited verbal space, and is physically unable to grasp the whole, so that the portrait is often lost."[9]

7. For the psychological and sociological aspects of this dichotomy, see Gregory Bateson's views on progressional and selective integration and Talcott Parsons on the conjunction-disjunction dichotomy in child development: J. Ruesch and G. Bateson, *Communication, the Social Matrix of Psychiatry* (New York, 1951); T. Parsons and R. F. Bales, *Family Socialization and Interaction Process* (Glencoe, Ill., 1955) [Jakobson's note].

8. Concepts to which real identity is attributed.

9. A. Kamegulov, *Stil' Gleba Uspenskogo* (Leningrad, 1930), pp. 65, 145. One of such disintegrated portraits cited in the monograph: "From underneath an ancient straw cap, with a black spot on its visor, peeked two braids resembling the tusks of a wild boar; a chin, grown fat and pendulous, had spread definitively over the greasy collar of the calico dicky and lay in a thick layer on the coarse collar of the canvas coat, firmly buttoned at the neck. From underneath this coat to the eyes of the observer protruded massive hands with a ring which had eaten into the fat finger, a cane with a copper top, a significant bulge of the stomach, and the presence of very broad pants, almost of a muslin quality, in the wide bottoms of which hid the toes of the boots" [Jakobson's note].

To be sure, the metonymical style in Uspenskij is obviously prompted by the prevailing literary canon of his time, late nineteenth-century "realism"; but the personal stamp of Gleb Invanovič made his pen particularly suitable for this artistic trend in its extreme manifestations and finally left its mark upon the verbal aspect of his mental illness.

A competition between both devices, metonymic and metaphoric, is manifest in any symbolic process, be it intrapersonal or social. Thus in an inquiry into the structure of dreams, the decisive question is whether the symbols and the temporal sequences used are based on contiguity (Freud's metonymic "displacement" and synecdochic "condensation")[1] or on similarity (Freud's "identification and symbolism"). The principles underlying magic rites have been resolved by Frazer[2] into two types: charms based on the law of similarity and those founded on association by contiguity. The first of these two great branches of sympathetic magic has been called "homoeopathic" or "imitative," and the second, "contagious" magic.[3] This bipartition is indeed illuminating. Nonetheless, for the most part, the question of the two poles is still neglected, despite its wide scope and importance for the study of any symbolic behavior, especially verbal, and of its impairments. What is the main reason for this neglect?

Similarity in meaning connects the symbols of a metalanguage with the symbols of the language referred to. Similarity connects a metaphorical term with the term for which it is substituted. Consequently, when constructing a metalanguage to interpret tropes, the researcher possesses more homogeneous means to handle metaphor, whereas metonymy, based on a different principle, easily defies interpretation. Therefore nothing comparable to the rich literature on metaphor can be cited for the theory of metonymy. For the same reason, it is generally realized that Romanticism is closely linked with metaphor, whereas the equally intimate ties of Realism with metonymy usually remain unnoticed. Not only the tool of the observer but also the object of observation are responsible for the preponderance of metaphor over metonymy in scholarship. Since poetry is focused upon the sign, and pragmatical prose primarily upon the referent, tropes and figures were studied mainly as poetic devices. The principle of similarity underlies poetry; the metrical parallelism of lines or the phonic equivalence of rhyming words prompts the question of semantic similarity and contrast; there exist, for instance, grammatical and antigrammatical but never agrammatical rhymes. Prose, on the contrary, is forwarded essentially by contiguity. Thus for poetry, metaphor—and for prose, metonymy—is the line of least resistance and consequently the study of poetical tropes is directed chiefly toward metaphor. The actual bipolarity has been artificially replaced in these studies by an amputated, unipolar scheme which, strikingly enough, coincides with one of the two aphasic patterns, namely with the contiguity disorder.

1956

1. Sigmund Freud uses these terms in his analysis of the dream-work in *Interpretation of Dreams* (1900; see above).

2. James George Frazer (1854–1941), Scottish anthropologist and folklorist.

3. James G. Frazer, *The Golden Bough: A Study in Magic and Religion*, 3d ed. (Vienna, 1950), part I, chap. 3 [Jakobson's note].

FRIEDRICH A. HAYEK
1899–1992

As the intellectual godfather of neoliberalism, the political economist Friedrich A. Hayek fought tirelessly for the supremacy of the market in Western liberal democracies and against what he deemed socialism's dire threat to individual freedom. Hayek was a skilled polemicist and tireless organizer as well as an original thinker. He almost single-handedly created the "Chicago school" of economic thought after World War II. His work and that of the Chicago "boys" (as they are sometimes called) directly influenced both the Thatcherite revolution in 1980s Britain and the heavy-handed tactics employed by the International Monetary Fund between 1970 and 2000 to move Latin American and Eastern European economies away from protectionist and social welfare policies and toward "liberalization."

Hayek was born in Vienna, Austria, to an academically inclined family. He served in the Austrian artillery on the Italian front during World War I. After the war, he returned to Vienna to complete his education, studying with the economist Ludwig von Mises. Hayek spent the 1923–24 academic year at New York University. Upon returning to Vienna, Hayek and Mises worked together to found the "Austrian school" of economics, shaped by Mises's influential arguments against the possible success of planned economies. In 1931, Hayek was invited to spend a year as a visiting professor at the London School of Economics, then assumed a permanent post in 1932. All of his subsequent work was written in English, and he became a British citizen in 1938. In 1944, alarmed by the leftward turn of British politics (which brought the Labour Party to power in 1945), Hayek published his most famous and influential work, *The Road to Serfdom*. He argues that any form of socialism that involves state regulation or control of the economy must both lead to a drastic loss of liberty and prove economically disastrous. In 1947, Hayek formed the Mont Pelerin Society to help promulgate his free market ideas, and he accepted a teaching position at the University of Chicago in 1950. Among his most important American disciples, both based in Chicago, were Milton Friedman and Gary Becker. Hayek moved back to Europe permanently in 1962, teaching first at the University of Freiburg in Germany and then, following his retirement, as honorary professor at the University of Salzburg in his native Austria. He was awarded the Nobel Memorial Prize in Economics in 1974.

Our selection highlights two of Hayek's foundational positions: the identification of liberty as the primary, perhaps the only, political good, and the hostility to any notion of "social justice" tied to ideas of equal access to economic goods. Hayek insists that material equality cannot be achieved except at the intolerably high price of extensive governmental coercion. Like most postmodern thinkers, he understands differences among individual human subjects as inevitable and irreducible. He argues that the most benefit to any given society will result from letting those differences flourish. If individuals are free to develop their own talents and pursue their own interests, then society will be prosperous and stable. This argument constitutes Hayek's "liberalism"—his continuity with the work of Adam Smith (1723–1790) and John Stuart Mill (1806–1873). From Mill, we get the insistence that the raison d'être of government is to protect individual freedom; from Smith comes the notion that the untrammeled pursuit of individual interest redounds to the general benefit of all.

But Hayek, unlike Smith and Mill, has to deal with the leftist critique (first found in KARL MARX) that the freedoms offered by liberalism are only nominal, not substantial. For example, having the liberty to develop talents is worthless if one does not have enough to eat. Economic necessity often denies individuals the opportunity to choose their professions or even the ability to avoid taking work that is hazardous to their health. Proponents of regulation are quick to point out the various coercions characteristic of nineteenth-century capitalism—child labor, subsistence wages, and long working hours in unsanitary conditions, as well as the periodic depressions that brought massive unemployment—that made government regulation of the economy and government provision of basic "safety net" benefits (social security, unemployment insurance, workmen's compensation, minimum wage laws) standard practice in twentieth-century Western societies. Neoliberalism is the name for the attempt, which has gathered political momentum since 1970, to roll back those government programs in order to return to a more fully laissez-faire economy, as DAVID HARVEY details below. Hayek explains why citizens would not be much worse off in a neoliberal regime than they are in the post–World War II welfare state.

His explanation is rather surprising because it only partly aligns with the ideas of the politicians who have claimed him as their inspiration. Basically, Hayek asserts that markets, through a kind of "crowd wisdom," provide knowledge about society's needs along with incentives to meet those needs. In other words, the process of supply and demand, which is registered by fluctuations in prices, indicates desires; producers can then make money by working to service those desires. No individual or institution can access that knowledge. The attempt to control or command social production will necessarily lead to inefficiencies as too many unneeded things and too few needed things are produced. This epistemological argument is Hayek's most important contribution to political economy. It is the basis for Margaret Thatcher's famous assertion that "there is no alternative": the market is the one and only way to meet society's needs. For that reason, everything from health care to the supply of water to cities should be handed over to the market. Neoliberalism advocates the "privatization" of state-run services like the National Health Service in Britain or the public transportation and public schools in the United States. In our selection Hayek argues that distorting the market in order to increase economic equality will only hamper the production of goods and, thus, make everyone poorer. As he puts it elsewhere, "social justice is a mirage," because all attempts to achieve it will only lessen economic well-being while also severely hampering liberty.

Hayek, however, takes his epistemological argument in a surprising direction. He tells us that justice is a moral term that points to our desire to reward merit and punish those who lack it. But we cannot know merit. It is a hidden, subjective thing. Only value is apparent, where "value" means the price set by the market for a particular good. Consumers pay for a commodity because it answers to a need or a desire. They have no interest in whether the person who made that commodity was a good person who worked hard or a talented ne'er-do-well. In short, Hayek acknowledges that the market is unjust; its results do not align in any predictable way with merit. There is no meritocracy, if the measure of merit remains people's incomes or wealth. Furthermore, if we as a society decide that we want to provide health insurance to everyone, as Hayek suggests in *The Road to Serfdom*, we should do so. He simply states that such a decision has nothing to do with justice (the motive is more like charity) and, most importantly, that no citizen (as a matter of justice) is "entitled" to health care. The moral issues of justice and the functioning of markets have nothing to do with one another.

Hayek does, however, believe that justice requires what we today call "equal opportunity." He always called himself a "liberal," because he was a firm adherent of equality before the law. The law should treat everyone equally—and the inevitable result, he claims, is that people's different abilities will gain them unequal economic outcomes. But that stance leads him to struggle with the issue of the extent to which those different outcomes are the result of different starting places. Today, a person born in America to a prosperous family has immensely better chances in life than someone born to an impoverished family in rural India. Even within the

United States, how is the law treating everyone equally if one child goes to an underfunded public school while another attends a much better one? In our selection, Hayek addresses the objection that differential access to education undercuts the notion that individual differences are the cause of unequal outcomes. His response is to argue that all societies depend on their best and brightest, on their elites, to produce the innovations that most benefit all members of those societies. Therefore, we should not do anything that curtails the production of elites. And he accuses those who wish to level the playing field of being motivated by envy, not by a sense of justice.

The stringent amoralism of Hayek's view of the market complicates efforts to place him on the political spectrum. Those who label themselves neoliberals (especially in Europe) generally take this amoral position, simply calling on society to face up to the grim realities of the market, which at least gives us freedom even as its whims create winners and losers. But in the United States especially, conservatives (who tend to extol the free market) are much more moralistic, more likely to seek stricter government control of individual behavior (e.g., sexuality, drugs, immigration) and to see success in the market as proof of virtue. In other words, such conservative politicians believe fervently in meritocracy, which is why they can see the poor as deserving their destitution. As a matter of justice, the lazy and unproductive should suffer.

Criticisms of Hayek usually begin from his refusal to consider trade-offs. For him, every single instance of government regulation places us on the road to serfdom. But it is hardly obvious that child labor laws are an outrageous limitation on freedom—or that the limitation they represent is not far outweighed by the benefits. His addiction to either/or dichotomies similarly gets him into trouble when he discusses education. Inherited advantages clearly give some people access to a better education than others enjoy—a disparity that suggests some need for state action to right the balance, if everyone is to have equality of opportunity. But Hayek does not support any such action. Liberty as an absolute value, never to be limited in relation to other goods, produces an unjust (by Hayek's own admission) market-driven world that does not seem very attractive to critics of the market. The political dividing line is drawn, in many contemporary debates, between those who wish to mobilize political or state power to temper market outcomes and those who agree with Hayek that all interference in market processes not only hampers economic productivity but jeopardizes freedom.

***The Constitution of Liberty* Keywords:** Ethics, Globalization, Institutional Studies, Marxism, Postmodernity

From The Constitution of Liberty

Chapter 6. Equality, Value, and Merit

> I have no respect for the passion for equality, which seems to me merely idealizing envy.
>
> —Oliver Wendell Holmes Jr.[1]

1. The great aim of the struggle for liberty has been equality before the law. This equality under the rules which the state enforces may be supplemented by a similar equality of the rules that men voluntarily obey in their

1. The quotation is taken from *The Holmes–Laski Letters*, ed. Mark DeWolfe Howe (Cambridge, Mass.: Harvard University Press, 1953), 2:942. Holmes (1841–1935), American legal historian and Supreme Court justice. Except as indicated, all subsequent notes are Hayek's; some of his notes have been edited.

relations with one another. This extension of the principle of equality to the rules of moral and social conduct is the chief expression of what is commonly called the democratic spirit—and probably that aspect of it that does most to make inoffensive the inequalities that liberty necessarily produces.

Equality of the general rules of law and conduct, however, is the only kind of equality conducive to liberty and the only equality which we can secure without destroying liberty. Not only has liberty nothing to do with any other sort of equality, but it is even bound to produce inequality in many respects.[2] This is the necessary result and part of the justification of individual liberty: if the result of individual liberty did not demonstrate that some manners of living are more successful than others, much of the case for it would vanish.

It is neither because it assumes that people are in fact equal nor because it attempts to make them equal that the argument for liberty demands that government treat them equally. This argument not only recognizes that individuals are very different but in a great measure rests on that assumption. It insists that these individual differences provide no justification for government to treat them differently. And it objects to the differences in treatment by the state that would be necessary if persons who are in fact very different were to be assured equal positions in life.

Modern advocates of a more far-reaching material equality usually deny that their demands are based on any assumption of the factual equality of all men.[3] It is nevertheless still widely believed that this is the main justification for such demands. Nothing, however, is more damaging to the demand for equal treatment than to base it on so obviously untrue an assumption as that of the factual equality of all men. To rest the case for equal treatment of national or racial minorities on the assertion that they do not differ from other men is implicitly to admit that factual inequality would justify unequal treatment; and the proof that some differences do, in fact, exist would not be long in forthcoming. It is of the essence of the demand for equality before the law that people should be treated alike in spite of the fact that they are different.

2. The boundless variety of human nature—the wide range of differences in individual capacities and potentialities—is one of the most distinctive facts about the human species. Its evolution has made it probably the most variable among all kinds of creatures. It has been well said that "biology, with variability as its cornerstone, confers on every human individual a unique set of attributes which give him a dignity he could not otherwise possess. Every newborn baby is an unknown quantity so far as potentialities are concerned because there are many thousands of unknown interrelated genes and gene patterns which contribute to his makeup. As a result of nature and nurture the newborn infant may become one of the greatest men or women ever to have lived. In every case he or she has the making of a distinctive individual. . . . If the differences are not very important, then freedom is not very important and the idea of individual worth is not very

2. Hayek's note here quotes the German legal scholar Gerhard Leibholz (1901–1982): "Freedom necessarily creates inequality and equality necessarily creates unfreedom" [editor's note].

3. See, e.g., Richard Henry Tawney, *Equality* (London: Allen and Unwin, 1929), pp. 47–70. [Tawney (1880–1962), English economic historian and Christian socialist—editor's note.]

important."[4] The writer justly adds that the widely held uniformity theory of human nature, "which on the surface appears to accord with democracy . . . would in time undermine the very basic ideals of freedom and individual worth and render life as we know it meaningless."[5]

It has been the fashion in modern times to minimize the importance of congenital differences between men and to ascribe all the important differences to the influence of environment.[6] However important the latter may be, we must not overlook the fact that individuals are very different from the outset. The importance of individual differences would hardly be less if all people were brought up in very similar environments. As a statement of fact, it just is not true that "all men are born equal." We may continue to use this hallowed phrase to express the ideal that legally and morally all men ought to be treated alike. But if we want to understand what this ideal of equality can or should mean, the first requirement is that we free ourselves from the belief in factual equality.

From the fact that people are very different it follows that, if we treat them equally, the result must be inequality in their actual position,[7] and that the only way to place them in an equal position would be to treat them differently. Equality before the law and material equality are therefore not only different but are in conflict with each other; and we can achieve either the one or the other, but not both at the same time. The equality before the law which freedom requires leads to material inequality. Our argument will be that, though where the state must use coercion for other reasons, it should treat all people alike, the desire of making people more alike in their condition cannot be accepted in a free society as a justification for further and discriminatory coercion.

We do not object to equality as such. It merely happens to be the case that a demand for equality is the professed motive of most of those who desire to impose upon society a preconceived pattern of distribution. Our objection is against all attempts to impress upon society a deliberately chosen pattern of distribution, whether it be an order of equality or of inequality. We shall indeed see that many of those who demand an extension of equality do not really demand equality but a distribution that conforms more closely to human conceptions of individual merit and that their desires are as irreconcilable with freedom as the more strictly egalitarian demands.

If one objects to the use of coercion in order to bring about a more even or a more just distribution, this does not mean that one does not regard these as desirable. But if we wish to preserve a free society, it is essential that we recognize that the desirability of a particular object is not sufficient justification for the use of coercion. One may well feel attracted to a community in which there are no extreme contrasts between rich and poor and may welcome the fact that the general increase in wealth seems gradually to reduce those

4. Roger John Williams, *Free and Unequal: The Biological Basis of Individual Liberty* (Austin: University of Texas Press, 1953), pp. 23, 70. [Williams (1893–1988), American biochemist—editor's note.]

5. Williams, *Free and Unequal*, p. 152.

6. See the description of this fashionable view in Horace Meyer Kallen's article "Behaviorism," in *Encyclopedia of the Social Sciences*, ed. Edwin R. A. Seligman and Alvin Johnson (New York: Macmillan, 1930), 2:498: "At birth human infants, regardless of their heredity, are as equal as Fords."

7. Cf. Plato, *Laws* 7.757a: "To unequals equals become unequal." [PLATO (ca. 427–ca. 347 B.C.E.), Greek philosopher—editor's note.]

differences. I fully share these feelings and certainly regard the degree of social equality that the United States has achieved as wholly admirable.

There also seems no reason why these widely felt preferences should not guide policy in some respects. Wherever there is a legitimate need for government action and we have to choose between different methods of satisfying such a need, those that incidentally also reduce inequality may well be preferable. If, for example, in the law of intestate succession one kind of provision will be more conducive to equality than another, this may be a strong argument in its favor. It is a different matter, however, if it is demanded that, in order to produce substantive equality, we should abandon the basic postulate of a free society, namely, the limitation of all coercion by equal law. Against this we shall hold that economic inequality is not one of the evils which justify our resorting to discriminatory coercion or privilege as a remedy.

3. Our contention rests on two basic propositions which probably need only be stated to win fairly general assent. The first of them is an expression of the belief in a certain similarity of all human beings: it is the proposition that no man or group of men possesses the capacity to determine conclusively the potentialities of other human beings and that we should certainly never trust anyone invariably to exercise such a capacity. However great the differences between men may be, we have no ground for believing that they will ever be so great as to enable one man's mind in a particular instance to comprehend fully all that another responsible man's mind is capable of.

The second basic proposition is that the acquisition by any member of the community of additional capacities to do things which may be valuable must always be regarded as a gain for that community. It is true that particular people may be worse off because of the superior ability of some new competitor in their field; but any such additional ability in the community is likely to benefit the majority. This implies that the desirability of increasing the abilities and opportunities of any individual does not depend on whether the same can also be done for the others—provided, of course, that others are not thereby deprived of the opportunity of acquiring the same or other abilities which might have been accessible to them had they not been secured by that individual.

Egalitarians generally regard differently those differences in individual capacities which are inborn and those which are due to the influences of environment, or those which are the result of "nature" and those which are the result of "nurture." Neither, be it said at once, has anything to do with moral merit.[8] Though either may greatly affect the value which an individual has for his fellows, no more credit belongs to him for having been born with desirable qualities than for having grown up under favorable circumstances. The distinction between the two is important only because the former advantages are due to circumstances clearly beyond human control, while the latter are due to factors which we might be able to alter. The important question is whether there is a case for so changing our institutions as to eliminate as much as possible those advantages due to environment. Are we to agree that "all inequalities that rest on birth and inherited

8. Cf. Frank Hyneman Knight, *Freedom and Reform: Essays in Economics and Social Philosophy* (New York: Harper and Brothers, 1947), p. 151: "There is no visible reason why anyone is more or less entitled to the earnings of inherited personal capacities than to those of inherited property in any other form."

property ought to be abolished and none remain unless it is an effect of superior talent and industry?"[9]

The fact that certain advantages rest on human arrangements does not necessarily mean that we could provide the same advantages for all or that, if they are given to some, somebody else is thereby deprived of them. The most important factors to be considered in this connection are the family, inheritance, and education, and it is against the inequality which they produce that criticism is mainly directed. They are, however, not the only important factors of environment. Geographic conditions such as climate and landscape, not to speak of local and sectional differences in cultural and moral traditions, are scarcely less important. We can, however, consider here only the three factors whose effects are most commonly impugned.

So far as the family is concerned, there exists a curious contrast between the esteem most people profess for the institution and their dislike of the fact that being born into a particular family should confer on a person special advantages. It seems to be widely believed that, while useful qualities which a person acquires because of his native gifts under conditions which are the same for all are socially beneficial, the same qualities become somehow undesirable if they are the result of environmental advantages not available to others. Yet it is difficult to see why the same useful quality which is welcomed when it is the result of a person's natural endowment should be less valuable when it is the product of such circumstances as intelligent parents or a good home.

The value which most people attach to the institution of the family rests on the belief that, as a rule, parents can do more to prepare their children for a satisfactory life than anyone else. This means not only that the benefits which particular people derive from their family environment will be different but also that these benefits may operate cumulatively through several generations. What reason can there be for believing that a desirable quality in a person is less valuable to society if it has been the result of family background than if it has not? There is, indeed, good reason to think that there are some socially valuable qualities which will be rarely acquired in a single generation but which will generally be formed only by the continuous efforts of two or three. This means simply that there are parts of the cultural heritage of a society that are more effectively transmitted through the family.[1] Granted this, it would be unreasonable to deny that a society is likely to get a better elite if ascent is not limited to one generation, if individuals are not deliberately made to start from the same level, and if children are not deprived of the chance to benefit from the better education and material environment which their parents may be able to provide. To admit this is merely to recognize that belonging to a particular family is part of the individual personality, that society is

9. This is the position of Richard Henry Tawney as summarized by John Petrov Plamenatz, "Equality of Opportunity," in *Aspects of Human Equality: Fifteenth Symposium*, ed. Lyman Bryson (New York: distributed by Harper, 1956), p. 100.

1. See William Graham Sumner, *Andrew Jackson* (Boston: Houghton Mifflin, 1899), pp. 24–45: "True honor, truthfulness, suppression of individual personal feelings, self-control and courtesy are inculcated best, if not exclusively, by the constant precept and example, in earliest childhood of high-bred parents and relatives. There is nothing on earth which it costs more labor to produce than a high-bred man. It is also indispensable that home discipline and training ingrain into the character of men the most solid and valuable elements and that, without such training, more civilization means better food and clothes rather than better men." [Sumner (1840–1910), American economist and influential sociologist whose views were libertarian, social Darwinist, and anti-imperialist—editor's note.]

made up as much of families as of individuals, and that the transmission of the heritage of civilization within the family is as important a tool in man's striving toward better things as is the heredity of beneficial physical attributes.

4. Many people who agree that the family is desirable as an instrument for the transmission of morals, tastes, and knowledge still question the desirability of the transmission of material property. Yet there can be little doubt that, in order that the former may be possible, some continuity of standards, of the external forms of life, is essential, and that this will be achieved only if it is possible to transmit not only immaterial but also material advantages. There is, of course, neither greater merit nor any greater injustice involved in some people being born to wealthy parents than there is in others being born to kind or intelligent parents. The fact is that it is no less of an advantage to the community if at least some children can start with the advantages which at any given time only wealthy homes can offer than if some children inherit great intelligence or are taught better morals at home.

We are not concerned here with the chief argument for private inheritance, namely, that it seems essential as a means to preserve the dispersal in the control of capital and as an inducement for its accumulation. Rather, our concern here is whether the fact that it confers unmerited benefits on some is a valid argument against the institution. It is unquestionably one of the institutional causes of inequality. In the present context we need not inquire whether liberty demands unlimited freedom of bequest. Our problem here is merely whether people ought to be free to pass on to children or others such material possessions as will cause substantial inequality.

Once we agree that it is desirable to harness the natural instincts of parents to equip the new generation as well as they can, there seems no sensible ground for limiting this to non-material benefits. The family's function of passing on standards and traditions is closely tied up with the possibility of transmitting material goods. And it is difficult to see how it would serve the true interest of society to limit the gain in material conditions to one generation.

There is also another consideration which, though it may appear somewhat cynical, strongly suggests that if we wish to make the best use of the natural partiality of parents for their children, we ought not to preclude the transmission of property. It seems certain that among the many ways in which those who have gained power and influence might provide for their children, the bequest of a fortune is socially by far the cheapest. Without this outlet, these men would look for other ways of providing for their children, such as placing them in positions which might bring them the income and the prestige that a fortune would have done; and this would cause a waste of resources and an injustice much greater than is caused by the inheritance of property. Such is the case with all societies in which inheritance of property does not exist, including the Communist. Those who dislike the inequalities caused by inheritance should therefore recognize that, men being what they are, it is the least of evils, even from their point of view.

5. Though inheritance used to be the most widely criticized source of inequality, it is today probably no longer so. Egalitarian agitation now tends

to concentrate on the unequal advantages due to differences in education. There is a growing tendency to express the desire to secure equality of conditions in the claim that the best education we have learned to provide for some should be made gratuitously available for all and that, if this is not possible, one should not be allowed to get a better education than the rest merely because one's parents are able to pay for it, but only those and all those who can pass a uniform test of ability should be admitted to the benefits of the limited resources of higher education.

The problem of educational policy raises too many issues to allow of their being discussed incidentally under the general heading of equality. We shall have to devote a separate chapter to them at the end of this book. For the present we shall only point out that enforced equality in this field can hardly avoid preventing some from getting the education they otherwise might. Whatever we might do, there is no way of preventing those advantages which only some can have, and which it is desirable that some should have, from going to people who neither individually merit them nor will make as good a use of them as some other person might have done. Such a problem cannot be satisfactorily solved by the exclusive and coercive powers of the state.

It is instructive at this point to glance briefly at the change that the ideal of equality has undergone in this field in modern times. A hundred years ago, at the height of the classical liberal movement, the demand was generally expressed by the phrase *la carrière ouverte aux talents.*[2] It was a demand that all man-made obstacles to the rise of some should be removed, that all privileges of individuals should be abolished, and that what the state contributed to the chance of improving one's conditions should be the same for all. That so long as people were different and grew up in different families this could not assure an equal start was fairly generally accepted. It was understood that the duty of government was not to ensure that everybody had the same prospect of reaching a given position but merely to make available to all on equal terms those facilities which in their nature depended on government action. That the results were bound to be different, not only because the individuals were different, but also because only a small part of the relevant circumstances depended on government action, was taken for granted.

This conception that all should be allowed to try has been largely replaced by the altogether different conception that all must be assured an equal start and the same prospects. This means little less than that the government, instead of providing the same circumstances for all, should aim at controlling all conditions relevant to a particular individual's prospects and so adjust them to his capacities as to assure him of the same prospects as everybody else. Such deliberate adaptation of opportunities to individual aims and capacities would, of course, be the opposite of freedom. Nor could it be justified as a means of making the best use of all available knowledge except on the assumption that government knows best how individual capacities can be used.

When we inquire into the justification of these demands, we find that they rest on the discontent that the success of some people often produces in those that are less successful, or, to put it bluntly, on envy. The modern

2. The career open to the talents (French), a phrase attributed to Napoleon (1769–1821), emperor of the French, and associated with the rise of the middle class following the French Revolution [editor's note].

tendency to gratify this passion and to disguise it in the respectable garment of social justice is developing into a serious threat to freedom. Recently an attempt was made to base these demands on the argument that it ought to be the aim of politics to remove all sources of discontent.[3] This would, of course, necessarily mean that it is the responsibility of government to see that nobody is healthier or possesses a happier temperament, a better-suited spouse or more prospering children, than anybody else. If really all unfulfilled desires have a claim on the community, individual responsibility is at an end. However human, envy is certainly not one of the sources of discontent that a free society can eliminate. It is probably one of the essential conditions for the preservation of such a society that we do not countenance envy, not sanction its demands by camouflaging it as social justice, but treat it, in the words of John Stuart Mill, as "that most anti-social and odious of all passions."[4]

6. While most of the strictly egalitarian demands are based on nothing better than envy, we must recognize that much that on the surface appears as a demand for greater equality is in fact a demand for a juster distribution of the good things of this world and springs therefore from much more creditable motives. Most people will object not to the bare fact of inequality but to the fact that the differences in reward do not correspond to any recognizable differences in the merits of those who receive them. The answer commonly given to this is that a free society on the whole achieves this kind of justice.[5] This, however, is an indefensible contention if by justice is meant proportionality of reward to moral merit. Any attempt to found the case for freedom on this argument is very damaging to it, since it concedes that material rewards ought to be made to correspond to recognizable merit and then opposes the conclusion that most people will draw from this by an assertion which is untrue. The proper answer is that in a free system it is neither desirable nor practicable that material rewards should be made generally to correspond to what men recognize as merit and that it is an essential characteristic of a free society that an individual's position should not necessarily depend on the views that his fellows hold about the merit he has acquired.

This contention may appear at first so strange and even shocking that I will ask the reader to suspend judgment until I have further explained the distinc-

3. Charles Anthony Raven Crosland, *The Future of Socialism* (London: Jonathan Cape, 1956), p. 205. [Crosland (1918–1977), British Labour Party politician—editor's note.]

4. John Stuart Mill, "On Liberty" [1859], in *On Liberty and Considerations on Representative Government*, ed. Ronald Buchanan McCallum (Oxford: Blackwell, 1946), p. 70. [Mill (1806–1873), English philosopher and economist—editor's note.]

5. Cf. Walter Bryce Gallie, "Liberal Morality and Socialist Morality," in *Philosophy, Politics, and Society*, ed. Peter Laslett (Oxford: Blackwell, 1956), pp. 123–35. The author represents it as the essence of "liberal morality" that it claims that rewards are equal to merit in a free society. This was the position of some nineteenth-century liberals which often weakened their argument. A characteristic example is William Graham Sumner, *What Social Classes Owe to Each Other* (New York: Harper and Brothers, 1883), p. 164. Sumner argued that if all "have equal chances so far as chances are provided or limited by society," this will "produce inequal results—that is, results which shall be proportioned to the merits of individuals." This is true only if "merit" is used in the sense in which we have used "value," without any moral connotation, but certainly not if it is meant to suggest proportionality to any endeavor to do the good or right thing, or to any subjective effort to conform to an ideal standard. But, as we shall presently see, Mr. Gallie is right that, in the Aristotelian terms he uses, liberalism aims at commutative justice and socialism at distributive justice. But, like most socialists, he does not see that distributive justice is irreconcilable with freedom in the choice of one's activities: it is the justice of a hierarchic organization, not of a free society. ["Commutative justice" refers to the determinate rules governing the relation of one individual to another (e.g., criminal laws or laws enforcing contracts), while "distributive justice" refers to the broader and less exact question of what a community (whether figured as state, society, church, or family) owes to its members—editor's note.]

tion between value and merit.[6] The difficulty in making the point clear is due to the fact that the term "merit," which is the only one available to describe what I mean, is also used in a wider and vaguer sense. It will be used here exclusively to describe the attributes of conduct that make it deserving of praise, that is, the moral character of the action and not the value of the achievement.[7]

As we have seen throughout our discussion, the value that the performance or capacity of a person has to his fellows has no necessary connection with its ascertainable merit in this sense. The inborn as well as the acquired gifts of a person clearly have a value to his fellows which does not depend on any credit due to him for possessing them. There is little a man can do to alter the fact that his special talents are very common or exceedingly rare. A good mind or a fine voice, a beautiful face or a skilful hand, and a ready wit or an attractive personality are in a large measure as independent of a person's efforts as the opportunities or the experiences he has had. In all these instances the value which a person's capacities or services have for us and for which he is recompensed has little relation to anything that we can call moral merit or deserts. Our problem is whether it is desirable that people should enjoy advantages in proportion to the benefits which their fellows derive from their activities or whether the distribution of these advantages should be based on other men's views of their merits.

Reward according to merit must in practice mean reward according to assessable merit, merit that other people can recognize and agree upon and not merit merely in the sight of some higher power. Assessable merit in this sense presupposes that we can ascertain that a man has done what some accepted rule of conduct demanded of him and that this has cost him some pain and effort. Whether this has been the case cannot be judged by the result: merit is not a matter of the objective outcome but of subjective effort. The attempt to achieve a valuable result may be highly meritorious but a complete failure, and full success may be entirely the result of accident and thus without merit. If we know that a man has done his best, we will often wish to see him rewarded irrespective of the result; and if we know that a most valuable achievement is almost entirely due to luck or favorable circumstances, we will give little credit to the author.

We may wish that we were able to draw this distinction in every instance. In fact, we can do so only rarely with any degree of assurance. It is possible only where we possess all the knowledge which was at the disposal of the

6. Although I believe that this distinction between merit and value is the same as that which Aristotle and Thomas Aquinas had in mind when they distinguished "distributive justice" from "commutative justice," I prefer not to tie up the discussion with the difficulties and confusions which in the course of time have become associated with these traditional concepts. That what we call here "reward according to merit" corresponds to the Aristotelian distributive justice seems clear. The difficult concept is "commutative justice," and to speak of justice in this sense seems always to cause a little confusion. [ARISTOTLE (384–322 B.C.E.), Greek philosopher. THOMAS AQUINAS (1225–1274), Italian-born medieval theologian and philosopher—editor's note.]

7. The terminological difficulties arise from the fact that we use the word merit also in an objective sense and will speak of the "merit" of an idea, a book, or a picture, irrespective of the merit acquired by the person who has created them. Sometimes the word is also used to describe what we regard as the "true" value of some achievement as distinguished from its market value. Yet even a human achievement which has the greatest value or merit in this sense is not necessarily proof of moral merit on the part of him to whom it is due. It seems that our use has the sanction of the philosophical tradition. Cf., for instance, David Hume, *A Treatise of Human Nature* [1739], ed. Thomas Hill Green and Thomas Hill Gross (London: Longmans, Green, 1880), [bk. 3, pt. 2, sec. 1,] 2:252: "The external performance has no merit. We must look within to find the moral quality. . . . The ultimate object of our praise and approbation is the motive that produced them." [HUME (1711–1776), Scottish philosopher—editor's note.]

acting person, including a knowledge of his skill and confidence, his state of mind and his feelings, his capacity for attention, his energy and persistence, etc. The possibility of a true judgment of merit thus depends on the presence of precisely those conditions whose general absence is the main argument for liberty. It is because we want people to use knowledge which we do not possess that we let them decide for themselves. But insofar as we want them to be free to use capacities and knowledge of facts which we do not have, we are not in a position to judge the merit of their achievements. To decide on merit presupposes that we can judge whether people have made such use of their opportunities as they ought to have made and how much effort of will or self-denial this has cost them; it presupposes also that we can distinguish between that part of their achievement which is due to circumstances within their control and that part which is not.

7. The incompatibility of reward according to merit with freedom to choose one's pursuit is most evident in those areas where the uncertainty of the outcome is particularly great and our individual estimates of the chances of various kinds of effort very different.[8] In those speculative efforts which we call "research" or "exploration," or in economic activities which we commonly describe as "speculation," we cannot expect to attract those best qualified for them unless we give the successful ones all the credit or gain, though many others may have striven as meritoriously. For the same reason that nobody can know beforehand who will be the successful ones, nobody can say who has earned greater merit. It would clearly not serve our purpose if we let all who have honestly striven share in the prize. Moreover, to do so would make it necessary that somebody have the right to decide who is to be allowed to strive for it. If in their pursuit of uncertain goals people are to use their own knowledge and capacities, they must be guided, not by what other people think they ought to do, but by the value others attach to the result at which they aim.

What is so obviously true about those undertakings which we commonly regard as risky is scarcely less true of any chosen object we decide to pursue. Any such decision is beset with uncertainty, and if the choice is to be as wise as it is humanly possible to make it, the alternative results anticipated must be labeled according to their value. If the remuneration did not correspond to the value that the product of a man's efforts has for his fellows, he would have no basis for deciding whether the pursuit of a given object is worth the effort and risk. He would necessarily have to be told what to do, and some other person's estimate of what was the best use of his capacities would have to determine both his duties and his remuneration.[9]

8. Cf. the important essay by Armen Albert Alchian, "Uncertainty, Evolution, and Economic Theory," *Journal of Political Economy* 58 (1950): 211–21, esp. 213–14, sec. 2, headed "Success Is Based on Results, Not Motivation."

9. It is often maintained that justice requires that remuneration be proportional to the unpleasantness of the job and that for this reason the street cleaner or the sewage worker ought to be paid more than the doctor or office worker. This, indeed, would seem to be the consequence of the principle of remuneration according to merit (or "distributive justice"). In a market such a result would come about only if all people were equally skillful in all jobs so that those who could earn as much as others in the more pleasant occupations would have to be paid more to undertake the distasteful ones. In the actual world those unpleasant jobs provide those whose usefulness in the more attractive jobs is small an opportunity to earn more than they could elsewhere. That persons who have little to offer their fellows should be able to earn an income similar to that of the rest only at a much greater sacrifice is inevitable in any arrangement under which the individual is allowed to choose his own sphere of usefulness.

The fact is, of course, that we do not wish people to earn a maximum of merit but to achieve a maximum of usefulness at a minimum of pain and sacrifice and therefore a minimum of merit. Not only would it be impossible for us to reward all merit justly, but it would not even be desirable that people should aim chiefly at earning a maximum of merit. Any attempt to induce them to do this would necessarily result in people being rewarded differently for the same service. And it is only the value of the result that we can judge with any degree of confidence, not the different degrees of effort and care that it has cost different people to achieve it.

The prizes that a free society offers for the result serve to tell those who strive for them how much effort they are worth. However, the same prizes will go to all those who produce the same result, regardless of effort. What is true here of the remuneration for the same services rendered by different people is even more true of the relative remuneration for different services requiring different gifts and capacities: they will have little relation to merit. The market will generally offer for services of any kind the value they will have for those who benefit from them; but it will rarely be known whether it was necessary to offer so much in order to obtain these services, and often, no doubt, the community could have had them for much less. The pianist who was reported not long ago to have said that he would perform even if he had to pay for the privilege probably described the position of many who earn large incomes from activities which are also their chief pleasure.

8. Though most people regard as very natural the claim that nobody should be rewarded more than he deserves for his pain and effort, it is nevertheless based on a colossal presumption. It presumes that we are able to judge in every individual instance how well people use the different opportunities and talents given to them and how meritorious their achievements are in the light of all the circumstances which have made them possible. It presumes that some human beings are in a position to determine conclusively what a person is worth and are entitled to determine what he may achieve. It presumes, then, what the argument for liberty specifically rejects: that we can and do know all that guides a person's action.

A society in which the position of the individuals was made to correspond to human ideas of moral merit would therefore be the exact opposite of a free society. It would be a society in which people were rewarded for duty performed instead of for success, in which every move of every individual was guided by what other people thought he ought to do, and in which the individual was thus relieved of the responsibility and the risk of decision. But if nobody's knowledge is sufficient to guide all human action, there is also no human being who is competent to reward all efforts according to merit.

In our individual conduct we generally act on the assumption that it is the value of a person's performance and not his merit that determines our obligation to him. Whatever may be true in more intimate relations, in the ordinary business of life we do not feel that, because a man has rendered us a service at a great sacrifice, our debt to him is determined by this, so long as we could have had the same service provided with ease by somebody else. In our dealings with other men we feel that we are doing justice if we recompense value rendered with equal value, without inquiring what it might have cost the particular individual to supply us with these services.

What determines our responsibility is the advantage we derive from what others offer us, not their merit in providing it. We also expect in our dealings with others to be remunerated not according to our subjective merit but according to what our services are worth to them. Indeed, so long as we think in terms of our relations to particular people, we are generally quite aware that the mark of the free man is to be dependent for his livelihood not on other people's views of his merit but solely on what he has to offer them. It is only when we think of our position or our income as determined by "society" as a whole that we demand reward according to merit.

Though moral value or merit is a species of value, not all value is moral value, and most of our judgments of value are not moral judgments. That this must be so in a free society is a point of cardinal importance; and the failure to distinguish between value and merit has been the source of serious confusion. We do not necessarily admire all activities whose product we value; and in most instances where we value what we get, we are in no position to assess the merit of those who have provided it for us. If a man's ability in a given field is more valuable after thirty years' work than it was earlier, this is independent of whether these thirty years were most profitable and enjoyable or whether they were a time of unceasing sacrifice and worry. If the pursuit of a hobby produces a special skill or an accidental invention turns out to be extremely useful to others, the fact that there is little merit in it does not make it any less valuable than if the result had been produced by painful effort.

This difference between value and merit is not peculiar to any one type of society—it would exist anywhere. We might, of course, attempt to make rewards correspond to merit instead of value, but we are not likely to succeed in this. In attempting it, we would destroy the incentives which enable people to decide for themselves what they should do. Moreover, it is more than doubtful whether even a fairly successful attempt to make rewards correspond to merit would produce a more attractive or even a tolerable social order. A society in which it was generally presumed that a high income was proof of merit and a low income of the lack of it, in which it was universally believed that position and remuneration corresponded to merit, in which there was no other road to success than the approval of one's conduct by the majority of one's fellows, would probably be much more unbearable to the unsuccessful ones than one in which it was frankly recognized that there was no necessary connection between merit and success.[1]

It would probably contribute more to human happiness if, instead of trying to make remuneration correspond to merit, we made clearer how uncertain is the connection between value and merit. We are probably all much too ready to ascribe personal merit where there is, in fact, only superior value. The possession by an individual or a group of a superior civilization or education certainly represents an important value and constitutes an

1. Cf. Crosland, *The Future of Socialism*, p. 235: "Even if all the failures could be convinced that they had an equal chance, their discontent would still not be assuaged; indeed it might actually be intensified. When opportunities are known to be unequal, and the selection clearly biased towards wealth or lineage, people can comfort themselves for failure by saying that they never had a proper chance—the system was unfair, the scales too heavily weighted against them. But if the selection is obviously by merit, this source of comfort disappears, and failure induces a total sense of inferiority, with no excuse or consolation; and this, by a natural quirk of human nature, actually increases the envy and resentment at the success of others."

asset for the community to which they belong; but it usually constitutes little merit. Popularity and esteem do not depend more on merit than does financial success. It is, in fact, largely because we are so used to assuming an often non-existent merit wherever we find value that we balk when, in particular instances, the discrepancy is too large to be ignored.

There is every reason why we ought to endeavor to honor special merit where it has gone without adequate reward. But the problem of rewarding action of outstanding merit which we wish to be widely known as an example is different from that of the incentives on which the ordinary functioning of society rests. A free society produces institutions in which, for those who prefer it, a man's advancement depends on the judgment of some superior or of the majority of his fellows. Indeed, as organizations grow larger and more complex, the task of ascertaining the individual's contribution will become more difficult; and it will become increasingly necessary that, for many, merit in the eyes of the managers rather than the ascertainable value of the contribution should determine the rewards. So long as this does not produce a situation in which a single comprehensive scale of merit is imposed upon the whole society, so long as a multiplicity of organizations compete with one another in offering different prospects, this is not merely compatible with freedom but extends the range of choice open to the individual.

9. Justice, like liberty and coercion, is a concept which, for the sake of clarity, ought to be confined to the deliberate treatment of men by other men. It is an aspect of the intentional determination of those conditions of people's lives that are subject to such control. Insofar as we want the efforts of individuals to be guided by their own views about prospects and chances, the results of the individual's efforts are necessarily unpredictable, and the question as to whether the resulting distribution of incomes is just has no meaning.[2] Justice does require that those conditions of people's lives that are determined by government be provided equally for all. But equality of those conditions must lead to inequality of results. Neither the equal provision of particular public facilities nor the equal treatment of different partners in our voluntary dealings with one another will secure reward that is proportional to merit. Reward for merit is reward for obeying the wishes of others in what we do, not compensation for the benefits we have conferred upon them by doing what we thought best.

It is, in fact, one of the objections against attempts by government to fix income scales that the state must attempt to be just in all it does. Once the principle of reward according to merit is accepted as the just foundation for the distribution of incomes, justice would require that all who desire it should be rewarded according to that principle. Soon it would also be demanded that the same principle be applied to all and that incomes not in proportion to recognizable merit not be tolerated. Even an attempt merely to distinguish between those incomes or gains which are "earned" and those which are not will set up a principle which the state will have to try

2. See the interesting discussion in Robin George Collingwood, "Economics as a Philosophical Science," *International Journal of Ethics* 36 (1926), who concludes (p. 174): "A just price, a just wage, a just rate of interest, is a contradiction in terms. The question what a person ought to get in return for his goods and labor is a question absolutely devoid of meaning. The only valid questions are what he *can* get in return for his goods or labor, and whether he ought to sell them at all." [Collingwood (1889–1943), English historian and philosopher—editor's note.]

to apply but cannot in fact apply generally.[3] And every such attempt at deliberate control of some remunerations is bound to create further demands for new controls. The principle of distributive justice, once introduced, would not be fulfilled until the whole of society was organized in accordance with it. This would produce a kind of society which in all essential respects would be the opposite of a free society—a society in which authority decided what the individual was to do and how he was to do it.

10. In conclusion we must briefly look at another argument on which the demands for a more equal distribution are frequently based, though it is rarely explicitly stated. This is the contention that membership in a particular community or nation entitles the individual to a particular material standard that is determined by the general wealth of the group to which he belongs. This demand is in curious conflict with the desire to base distribution on personal merit. There is clearly no merit in being born into a particular community, and no argument of justice can be based on the accident of a particular individual's being born in one place rather than another. A relatively wealthy community in fact regularly confers advantages on its poorest members unknown to those born in poor communities. In a wealthy community the only justification its members can have for insisting on further advantages is that there is much private wealth that the government can confiscate and redistribute and that men who constantly see such wealth being enjoyed by others will have a stronger desire for it than those who know of it only abstractly, if at all.

There is no obvious reason why the joint efforts of the members of any group to ensure the maintenance of law and order and to organize the provision of certain services should give the members a claim to a particular share in the wealth of this group. Such claims would be especially difficult to defend where those who advanced them were unwilling to concede the same rights to those who did not belong to the same nation or community. The recognition of such claims on a national scale would in fact only create a new kind of collective (but not less exclusive) property right in the resources of the nation that could not be justified on the same grounds as individual property. Few people would be prepared to recognize the justice of these demands on a world scale. And the bare fact that within a given nation the majority had the actual power to enforce such demands, while in the world as a whole it did not yet have it, would hardly make them more just.

There are good reasons why we should endeavor to use whatever political organization we have at our disposal to make provision for the weak or infirm or for the victims of unforeseeable disaster. It may well be true that the most effective method of providing against certain risks common to all citizens of a state is to give every citizen protection against those risks. The level on which such provisions against common risks can be made will necessarily depend on the general wealth of the community.

3. It is, of course, possible to give the distinction between "earned" and "unearned" incomes, gains, or increments a fairly precise legal meaning, but it then rapidly ceases to correspond to the moral distinction which provides its justification. Any serious attempt to apply the moral distinction in practice soon meets the same insuperable difficulties in any attempt to assess subjective merit. How little these difficulties are generally understood by philosophers (except in rare instances, as that quoted in the preceding note) is well illustrated by a discussion in Lizzie Susan Stebbing, *Thinking to Some Purpose* (Harmondsworth, UK: Penguin, 1939), p. 184, in which, as an illustration of a distinction which is clear but not sharp, she chooses that between "legitimate" and "excess" profits and asserts: "The distinction is clear between 'excess profits' (or 'profiteering') and 'legitimate profits,' although it is not a sharp distinction."

It is an entirely different matter, however, to suggest that those who are poor, merely in the sense that there are those in the same community who are richer, are entitled to a share in the wealth of the latter or that being born into a group that has reached a particular level of civilization and comfort confers a title to a share in all its benefits. The fact that all citizens have an interest in the common provision of some services is no justification for anyone's claiming as a right a share in all the benefits. It may set a standard for what some ought to be willing to give, but not for what anyone can demand.

National groups will become more and more exclusive as the acceptance of this view that we have been contending against spreads. Rather than admit people to the advantages that living in their country offers, a nation will prefer to keep them out altogether; for, once admitted, they will soon claim as a right a particular share in its wealth. The conception that citizenship or even residence in a country confers a claim to a particular standard of living is becoming a serious source of international friction. And since the only justification for applying the principle within a given country is that its government has the power to enforce it, we must not be surprised if we find the same principle being applied by force on an international scale. Once the right of the majority to the benefits that minorities enjoy is recognized on a national scale, there is no reason why this should stop at the boundaries of the existing states.

1960

LEO STRAUSS
1899–1973

Leo Strauss is one of the most interesting, complex, and controversial American philosophers and intellectuals of the mid-twentieth century. He wrote many important books and essays on major thinkers and topics in classical political philosophy; he developed and practiced a compelling theory of close reading and textual interpretation; and, through his seminars and lectures at the University of Chicago and elsewhere, he exercised a charismatic influence on many students who went on to prominent careers inside and outside the academy.

One of his best-known students, Allan Bloom, who wrote the best-seller *The Closing of the American Mind* (1987), observed that "those of us who knew him saw in him such a power of mind, such a unity and purpose of life, such a rare mixture of the human elements resulting in a harmonious expression of the virtues, moral and intellectual, that our account of him is likely to evoke disbelief or ridicule from those who have never experienced a man of this quality." Harry Jaffa, who over the span of seven years took nineteen courses with Strauss and who later became a renowned scholar of Abraham Lincoln's political thought, said that in a course taught by Strauss, "you felt that you had Plato or Aristotle or Cicero or Hobbes as your personal tutor. . . . Reading great books with Strauss was never an end in itself, but part of the larger quest—the unfinished and unfinishable quest, for the crucial truth about the highest things."

Leo Strauss was born in 1899 in the town of Kirchhain in central Germany. Raised in what he termed "a conservative, even orthodox Jewish home," by age seventeen he was a fervent believer in Zionism, the movement begun in 1897 to establish a Jewish nation in Palestine. Strauss attended the gymnasium (an advanced secondary school) in nearby Marburg, completing his studies in spring 1917; after serving in the German army from July 1917 through World War I's end in 1918, he pursued further academic work at the University of Hamburg, receiving his Ph.D. under the direction of the German-Jewish philosopher Ernst Cassirer in 1921. Strauss then did a postgraduate year at the University of Freiburg in southwest Germany, where his instructors included Edmund Husserl and MARTIN HEIDEGGER and where the students in Heidegger's circle included Hans-George Gadamer and HANNAH ARENDT. Soon thereafter, Strauss met the Jewish scholar and philosopher Franz Rosenzweig, and in his early work he focused on Jewish themes and topics; he was a researcher for the Academy for the Science of Judaism in Berlin from 1925 to 1932. Strauss's first book, written in German and published in 1930, was a study of the seventeenth-century Dutch philosopher BARUCH SPINOZA, whose radical theological views had led to his censure by and expulsion from Amsterdam's Jewish community at age twenty-three.

In 1932–34, Strauss was a Rockefeller fellow and researcher in France and England. In June 1933, while in Paris, he married Mirjam Bernsohn, a widow with a young son; in 1946 they would adopt the daughter of Strauss's deceased sister Bettina. Among Strauss's intellectual connections during this period of his life were the German political theorist and jurist Carl Schmitt (who later became notorious as the legal philosopher of the Nazi movement), the German-born Israeli philosopher and historian Gershom Scholem, and the cultural critic and theorist WALTER BENJAMIN. But as the power and popularity of National Socialism rose under the leadership of Hitler, who put an end to parliamentary democracy shortly after becoming chancellor in January 1933, Strauss concluded that it was too dangerous for a Jewish philosopher to return to Germany. (Indeed, in 1942 all of his relatives still living in Germany were sent to a concentration camp, where they died.) No permanent academic position was available for him in England, so when his research fellowship at Cambridge University ended in 1937, he left for New York City. After spending a year at Columbia University as a research fellow, he joined the faculty of New York's New School for Social Research, teaching political philosophy from 1938 to 1949; he became a U.S. citizen in 1944. During this time, Strauss published on Xenophon, PLATO, and classical philosophy. He also wrote on Jewish and Islamic thinkers, including the twelfth-century Jewish philosopher and rabbinic scholar MAIMONIDES, whose *Guide for the Perplexed* (1190) sought to reconcile Talmudic scripture with the philosophy of ARISTOTLE.

Strauss's first book written in English, *On Tyranny: An Interpretation of Xenophon's "Hiero"* (1948), was an eighty-page close commentary on a minor work by the ancient Greek historian. In this dialogue, Hiero, tyrant of Syracuse, and the lyric poet Simonides discuss legitimate and illegitimate rule, government by fear and coercion, and the prospects for human happiness. The contemporary context for Strauss's book was charged, but he focused—as he did in most of his writings—on detailed exegesis of the text. Despite gesturing toward the "modern tyrannies," as he called them, of Hitler's Germany and Stalin's Soviet Union in his introduction, Strauss nowhere in the text or notes refers to the dictators by name. In the 1950s he did express his understanding of tyranny in the period during and after the war more openly in his response to an essay on his book by Alexandre Kojève, France's leading HEGEL scholar, and in letters that the two exchanged. Strauss wrote and taught about political issues, but he was by vocation and training an interpreter of texts, not a cultural critic or historian or journalist. His aim in the seminar room and in publications, he often said, was to understand writers and philosophers as they understood themselves.

In 1949, Strauss moved to the University of Chicago, where he remained until 1968. During this phase of his career, he became widely known through two books, *Persecution and the Art of Writing* (1952) and *Natural Right and History* (1953). Many other books and essays followed, which often took the form of lengthy, rigorous textual explication. Strauss's final years were spent at Claremont Men's College in California and at St. John's College in Annapolis, Maryland, where—fittingly for Strauss—the curriculum is based on the study of the "great books," the classic texts in all fields of the Western tradition.

For Strauss, philosophy was even more than a subject or a discipline—it was a way of life, of being in the world, and he was especially attracted to Plato and to the figure of Socrates. Strauss acknowledged the virtues and strengths of modern liberal democracy; he was writing while witnessing the murderous rise of fascism, Nazism, and Stalinism. But he was ambivalent about aspects of life and work in modern democracies, including mass education, which, in his view, overemphasized career training and moneymaking at the expense of philosophical inquiry and reflection. Strauss valued the idea and ideal of higher education for all, yet at the same time he was skeptical of it, for in his judgment it did not promote the study of the best that has been thought and said and did not foster excellence. Strauss believed that liberalism and mass culture leveled downward, thereby reducing commitment to the highest aspirations and to permanent truths. His student Allan Bloom noted that Strauss in his work as a scholar and teacher "was dedicated to intransigent seriousness as opposed to popularization."

In his writing and teaching, Strauss approached texts meticulously and from a perspective that captivated many students and readers even as it baffled, and sometimes angered, many others, who found his claims unconvincing. Strauss emphasizes—as his central interpretive principle—that most of the great philosophers wrote in the midst of censorship and persecution, with free speech restricted or denied; they therefore were obliged to present truth indirectly, implicitly, through metaphor, parable, allusion, story, and myth. In addition, they often had to express their views in a deliberately obscure or flawed form: they trusted that readers—more specifically, an elite readership possessing deep knowledge—would perceive that the writer-philosopher in fact believed the opposite of what he stated. The great thinkers of the past, says Strauss, could have written plainly and simply, yet often in their work they chose not to, for by doing so they would have placed themselves in peril. When we read the texts of classical and political philosophy, we therefore must be attentive to the meanings between the lines, and give a special notice to passages that are abstruse, evasive, puzzling, ambiguous, for there the writer may be conveying to us his most important teaching.

This, for Strauss, is "esoteric writing," intended for or likely to be understood by only a small number of people with specialized knowledge or interest. For readers in general, the writer of a philosophical text presents an "exoteric" political or religious argument that accords in large measure with religious or political orthodoxy. Subtle, perceptive readers will sense and see that this same text presents esoterically, in concealed form, a private unorthodox teaching. The text is not what it seems or what most readers take it to be. It must be this way, Strauss maintains, not only because of the perils of censorship and persecution (suffered by Socrates and Spinoza, among others) but also because the writers themselves realize that to be socially and politically responsible they must, in the short term, preserve the stability of the regime. Though political philosophers raise challenging questions and make provocative arguments, they do not want to incite disorder, chaos, or even revolution. Doing philosophy hence is very demanding and perhaps paradoxical, for both writers and readers. Philosophy is not for everyone, as its practitioners must exercise extreme concentration and discipline as they, in effect, write two texts simultaneously, ensuring that one is properly interpreted by the few, highly trained readers capable of absorbing its lessons.

Strauss describes this approach to textual interpretation in essays, most notably "Persecution and the Art of Writing" (1941), and in his seminars. Such interpretive work is intricate and dense, and even devoted so-called Straussians differ about his views. Some have maintained that Strauss surely must have sought in his own work to practice the esoteric writing that he described in the texts of the great philosophers—placing his real meanings not on the surface but between the lines, visible only to highly attentive and aware readers.

Strauss was critical of historicism and relativism, which for him convey the erroneous belief that truth is conditional (i.e., dependent on context, time, and place) and that all value judgments are subjective. In *Natural Right and History,* he says that people in the United States have become too complacent and tolerant, unable or unwilling to speak on behalf of truth: "The majority among the learned who still adhere to the principles of the Declaration of Independence interpret these principles not as expressions of natural right but as an ideal, if not as an ideology or a myth." So absorbed have people become in the pursuit of material well-being and prosperity that they have forgotten what the permanent values are; as a result, they cannot argue for the superiority of the principles upon which the nation was founded and which they profess to believe. The way is open, says Strauss, for rule by force: might makes right. He stresses that our easy affirmations of freedom and tolerance can and will lead to indifference, cynicism, nihilism—the unprincipled notion that one regime, culture, or civilization is as good as any other.

Strauss's commitment to the permanent truths of justice and freedom have prompted some left and liberal critics to link him to the contemporary American neoconservative movement and some of its leading figures, such as William J. Bennett, Irving Kristol, William Kristol, Robert Kagan, and Norman Podhoretz, and to advocates of an aggressive American foreign policy. Writers, intellectuals, and policy makers on the right are said to have taken to heart Strauss's critique of relativism, interpreting him as offering philosophical sanction and support for the claim that government leaders have the right, the duty, to wage relentless war against international enemies, terrorists, and nihilists and, if necessary for that end, to mislead and deceive the public. But while it is true that Plato speaks of the philosopher-king, and Machiavelli of the philosopher as an adviser to the prince, Strauss was not a political figure and he did not take part in political activity. He focused on textual commentary and pedagogy—when asked what he taught, he replied, "Old books"—and he should not be held responsible for the abuses and misuses of his interpretive work. As Gregory Bruce Smith has noted: "When one looks at Strauss's own large and complicated corpus, one primarily sees a great number of novel thought experiments. One sees a questioning of accepted orthodoxies and a desire to try to approach the phenomena of human existence afresh. . . . Philosophic questioning manifests itself in a refusal either to be dogmatic or to give in to a skepticism that is dogmatically relativist."

Our selection below, "What Is Liberal Education?," is a concise introduction to Strauss's views and values as a philosopher and teacher. Originally delivered in 1959 at the tenth annual graduation exercises of the University of Chicago's Basic Program of Liberal Education for Adults, it was printed by the University of Chicago Press and reprinted first in C. Scott Fletcher's collection *Education for Public Responsibility* (1961) and later in Strauss's *Liberalism Ancient and Modern* (1968), the source of our text. When first encountered, "What Is Liberal Education?" might seem familiar—yet another call for the study of the great books. In this respect it could bring to mind the Harvard Classics (1909), a fifty-one-volume collection of major works from world literature, compiled and edited by Harvard University president Charles W. Eliot and William A. Neilson, a professor of English. Even more strongly, it seems to resonate with curricular reforms in the 1920s and later—most notably at Columbia University and the University of Chicago—led by University of Chicago president Robert M. Hutchins, the American philosopher and educator Mortimer Adler, the literature professor John Erskine, and others. Troubled by the increasing specialization they perceived in the kinds of courses taken by students, these reformers countered by stressing a common core of great books: a liberal arts education in Western culture's central texts, particularly but not exclusively in philosophy and literature. For readers (and book buyers) outside the academy, Hutchins and Adler also prepared *Great Books of the Western World*, published in 1952 as a fifty-four-volume set and expanded to sixty volumes in 1990. The authors in the 1952 edition range from Homer to FREUD, and among the figures in between are Aeschylus, Sophocles, Euripides, Plato, Aristotle, DANTE, Shakespeare, Descartes, KANT, HEGEL, Melville, and Darwin. What Strauss counsels in "What Is Liberal Education?" both does and does not align with these curricular innovations and publications.

Strauss, too, emphasizes "the great books" and "the greatest minds." But with the exception of Socrates, Plato, and Aristotle, who are touched on or alluded to briefly, he does not list names or titles. He acknowledges that his emphasis is on Western culture—seemingly leaving him open to the charge frequently made against great books programs, then and now, that they undervalue women, minority, and non-Western authors. But he does not present an argument for Western primacy, saying only that we cannot deal, for example, with works from India or China because we do not know the languages. Nor does Strauss make clear what the relationship is between liberal education and democracy. Is he recommending that everybody in a democracy should receive a liberal education? Or does he believe that such an education should be reserved only for a select group who can truly profit from it? In a key passage, he notes: "Liberal education is the necessary endeavor to found an aristocracy within democratic mass society. Liberal education reminds those members of a mass democracy who have ears to hear, of human greatness." Strauss does not speak about visual art and music and the many forms through which the arts are widely experienced. He is silent as well about the significance of liberal education for the challenges and demands of work, family, and social and political activity.

Another limitation of the essay is its too-condensed reference to evil. "All evils are in a sense necessary," Strauss says, "if there is to be understanding." We should "accept all evils which befall us and which may well break our hearts in the spirit of good citizens of the city of God." But are there evils that members of a society should oppose and fight against, in a spirit of resistance rather than acceptance? This question becomes all the more pertinent when we recognize that not all citizens define themselves within a religious framework, in relation to "the city of God." In other writings, Strauss deals more directly with the problem of evil; for example, in *The City and Man* (1962), he states: "No bloody or unbloody change of society can eradicate the evil in man: as long as there will be men, there will be malice, envy and hatred, and hence there cannot be a society which does not have to employ coercive restraint." Here, Strauss's claim is that evil is inherent in the human condition, which leads him to insist, in a disquieting phrase, on the necessity for a "coercive restraint" that he neither elaborates on nor justifies.

Strauss could have been more explicit in "What Is Liberal Education?" but his intention here, as in his work in general, is to prompt and provoke questions. This is, after all, a curious choice of topic for a graduation address. Someone reading the essay without knowing its original context might have guessed that Strauss had delivered it to students just beginning their college careers. Who are "the greatest minds"? Strauss could identify them, for as he indicates they are relatively few in number; he even says that in our time there might not be a single one. However, he does not identify them, because—we can read this between the lines, esoterically—he believes that we should already know the names; if we do not, then we are obliged to ask why we do not—and, furthermore, to ask what it means for liberal education and for culture that we are uncertain (or at odds) about who the great authors, the greatest minds, are. Strauss also dismisses "mass culture"; if we think better of it than he does, then it is up to us to make a strong case for it. "The dignity of the mind," the "experience in things beautiful": if these phrases seem vague and superficial to us, perhaps the fault is in us, because we do not possess the insight and understanding to know their full and deep meanings. Strauss's title is a question, and he points to an answer to it and expects one from us. This is the same question—abiding and permanent—that many theorists and critics address explicitly or implicitly in their work.

"What Is Liberal Education?" Keywords: The Canon/Tradition, Defense of Criticism, Institutional Studies, Interpretation Theory, Print Culture

What Is Liberal Education?

Liberal education is education in culture or toward culture. The finished product of a liberal education is a cultured human being. "Culture" (*cultura*) means primarily agriculture: the cultivation of the soil and its products, taking care of the soil, improving the soil in accordance with its nature. "Culture" means derivatively and today chiefly the cultivation of the mind, the taking care and improving of the native faculties of the mind in accordance with the nature of the mind. Just as the soil needs cultivators of the soil, the mind needs teachers. But teachers are not as easy to come by as farmers. The teachers themselves are pupils and must be pupils. But there cannot be an infinite regress: ultimately there must be teachers who are not in turn pupils. Those teachers who are not in turn pupils are the great minds or, in order to avoid any ambiguity in a matter of such importance, the greatest minds. Such men are extremely rare. We are not likely to meet any of them in any classroom. We are not likely to meet any of them anywhere. It is a piece of good luck if there is a single one alive in one's time. For all practical purposes, pupils, of whatever degree of proficiency, have access to the teachers who are not in turn pupils, to the greatest minds, only through the great books. Liberal education will then consist in studying with the proper care the great books which the greatest minds have left behind—a study in which the more experienced pupils assist the less experienced pupils, including the beginners.

This is not an easy task, as would appear if we were to consider the formula which I have just mentioned. That formula requires a long commentary. Many lives have been spent and may still be spent in writing such commentaries. For instance, what is meant by the remark that the great books should be studied "with the proper care"? At present I mention only one difficulty which is obvious to everyone among you: the greatest minds do not all tell us the same things regarding the most important themes; the community of the greatest minds is rent by discord and even by various kinds of discord. Whatever further consequences this may entail, it certainly entails the consequence that liberal education cannot be simply indoctrination. I mention yet another difficulty. "Liberal education is education in culture." In what culture? Our answer is: culture in the sense of the Western tradition. Yet Western culture is only one among many cultures. By limiting ourselves to Western culture, do we not condemn liberal education to a kind of parochialism, and is not parochialism incompatible with the liberalism, the generosity, the openmindedness, of liberal education? Our notion of liberal education does not seem to fit an age which is aware of the fact that there is not *the* culture of *the* human mind, but a variety of cultures. Obviously, culture if susceptible of being used in the plural is not quite the same thing as culture which is a *singulare tantum*,[1] which can be used only in the singular. Culture is now no longer, as people say, an absolute, but has become relative. It is not easy to say what culture susceptible of being used in the plural means. As a consequence of this obscurity people have suggested, explicitly or implicitly, that culture is any pattern of conduct common to any human group. Hence we do not hesitate to speak of the culture of suburbia or of the cultures of juvenile gangs, both nondelinquent and delinquent. In other words, every human being outside of lunatic asylums is a cultured human being, for he participates in a culture. At the frontiers of research there arises the question as to whether there are not cultures also of inmates of lunatic asylums. If we contrast the present-day usage of "culture" with the original meaning, it is as if someone would say that the cultivation of a garden may consist of the garden's being littered with empty tin cans and whisky bottles and used papers of various descriptions thrown around the garden at random. Having arrived at this point, we realize that we have lost our way somehow. Let us then make a fresh start by raising the question: what can liberal education mean here and now?

Liberal education is literate education of a certain kind: some sort of education in letters or through letters. There is no need to make a case for literacy; every voter knows that modern democracy stands or falls by literacy. In order to understand this need we must reflect on modern democracy. What is modern democracy? It was once said that democracy is the regime that stands or falls by virtue: a democracy is a regime in which all or most adults are men of virtue, and since virtue seems to require wisdom, a regime in which all or most adults are virtuous and wise, or the society in which all or most adults have developed their reason to a high degree, or *the* rational society. Democracy, in a word, is meant to be an aristocracy which has broadened into a universal aristocracy. Prior to the emergence of modern democracy some doubts were felt whether democracy thus understood is possible. As one of the two greatest minds among the theorists of democracy put it, "If there were a people consisting of gods, it would rule itself democratically. A government of such perfection is not suitable for human beings."[2] This still and small voice has by now become a high-powered loudspeaker.

There exists a whole science—the science which I among thousands profess to teach, political science—which so to speak has no other theme than the contrast between the original conception of democracy, or what one may call the ideal of democracy, and democracy as it is. According to an extreme view, which is the predominant view in the profession, the ideal of

1. Singular only (Latin), a grammatical term.
2. From *The Social Contract* (1762), 3.4, by the Swiss-born French philosopher and political theorist Jean-Jacques Rousseau (1712–1778).

democracy was a sheer delusion, and the only thing which matters is the behavior of democracies and the behavior of men in democracies. Modern democracy, so far from being universal aristocracy, would be mass rule were it not for the fact that the mass cannot rule, but is ruled by elites, that is, groupings of men who for whatever reason are on top or have a fair chance to arrive at the top; one of the most important virtues required for the smooth working of democracy, as far as the mass is concerned, is said to be electoral apathy, viz., lack of public spirit; not indeed the salt of the earth,[3] but the salt of modern democracy are those citizens who read nothing except the sports page and the comic section. Democracy is then not indeed mass rule, but mass culture. A mass culture is a culture which can be appropriated by the meanest capacities without any intellectual and moral effort whatsoever and at a very low monetary price. But even a mass culture and precisely a mass culture requires a constant supply of what are called new ideas, which are the products of what are called creative minds: even singing commercials lose their appeal if they are not varied from time to time. But democracy, even if it is only regarded as the hard shell which protects the soft mass culture, requires in the long run qualities of an entirely different kind: qualities of dedication, of concentration, of breadth, and of depth. Thus we understand most easily what liberal education means here and now. Liberal education is the counterpoison to mass culture, to the corroding effects of mass culture, to its inherent tendency to produce nothing but "specialists without spirit or vision and voluptuaries without heart."[4] Liberal education is the ladder by which we try to ascend from mass democracy to democracy as originally meant. Liberal education is the necessary endeavor to found an aristocracy within democratic mass society. Liberal education reminds those members of a mass democracy who have ears to hear, of human greatness.

Someone might say that this notion of liberal education is merely political, that it dogmatically assumes the goodness of modern democracy. Can we not turn our backs on modern society? Can we not return to nature, to the life of preliterate tribes? Are we not crushed, nauseated, degraded by the mass of printed material, the graveyards of so many beautiful and majestic forests? It is not sufficient to say that this is mere romanticism, that we today cannot return to nature: may not coming generations, after a man-wrought cataclysm, be compelled to live in illiterate tribes? Will our thoughts concerning thermonuclear wars not be affected by such prospects? Certain it is that the horrors of mass culture (which include guided tours to integer[5] nature) render intelligible the longing for a return to nature. An illiterate society at its best is a society ruled by age-old ancestral custom which it traces to original founders, gods, or sons of gods or pupils of gods; since there are no letters in such a society, the late heirs cannot be in direct contact with the original founders; they cannot know whether the fathers or grandfathers have not deviated from what the original founders meant, or have not defaced the divine message by merely human additions or subtractions; hence an illiterate society cannot consistently act on its principle that the best is the oldest. Only letters which have come down

3. Matthew 5.13; that is, people of great worth and reliability.
4. From Max Weber, *The Protestant Ethic and the Spirit of Capitalism* (1904–05; trans. 1930), chap. 5.
5. Untouched, whole.

from the founders can make it possible for the founders to speak directly to the latest heirs. It is then self-contradictory to wish to return to illiteracy. We are compelled to live with books. But life is too short to live with any but the greatest books. In this respect as well as in some others, we do well to take as our model that one among the greatest minds who because of his common sense is *the* mediator between us and the greatest minds. Socrates[6] never wrote a book, but he read books. Let me quote a statement of Socrates which says almost everything that has to be said on our subject, with the noble simplicity and quiet greatness of the ancients. "Just as others are pleased by a good horse or dog or bird, I myself am pleased to an even higher degree by good friends. . . . And the treasures of the wise men of old which they left behind by writing them in books, I unfold and go through them together with my friends, and if we see something good, we pick it out and regard it as a great gain if we thus become useful to one another." The man who reports this utterance adds the remark: "When I heard this, it seemed to me both that Socrates was blessed and that he was leading those listening to him toward perfect gentlemanship."[7] This report is defective since it does not tell us anything as to what Socrates did regarding those passages in the books of the wise men of old of which he did not know whether they were good. From another report we learn that Euripides once gave Socrates the writing of Heraclitus[8] and then asked him for his opinion about that writing. Socrates said: "What I have understood is great and noble; I believe this is also true of what I have not understood; but one surely needs for understanding that writing some special sort of a diver."[9]

Education to perfect gentlemanship, to human excellence, liberal education consists in reminding oneself of human excellence, of human greatness. In what way, by what means does liberal education remind us of human greatness? We cannot think highly enough of what liberal education is meant to be. We have heard Plato's suggestion that education in the highest sense is philosophy.[1] Philosophy is quest for wisdom or quest for knowledge regarding the most important, the highest, or the most comprehensive things; such knowledge, he suggested, is virtue and is happiness. But wisdom is inaccessible to man, and hence virtue and happiness will always be imperfect. In spite of this, the philosopher, who, as such, is not simply wise, is declared to be the only true king;[2] he is declared to possess all the excellences of which man's mind is capable, to the highest degree. From this we must draw the conclusion that we cannot be philosophers—that we cannot acquire the highest form of education. We must not be deceived by the fact that we meet many people who say that they are philosophers. For those people employ a loose expression which is perhaps necessitated by administrative convenience. Often they mean merely that they are members of philosophy departments. And it is as absurd to expect members of philosophy departments to be philosophers as it is to expect members of

6. Greek philosopher (469–399 B.C.E.), who is the main speaker in most of the dialogues of his student PLATO (ca. 427–ca. 347 B.C.E.).

7. Quoted by the Greek historian Xenophon (ca. 428/27–ca. 354 B.C.E.), one of Socrates' students, in *Memorabilia* 1.6.14.

8. Pre-Socratic Greek philosopher (active ca. 500 B.C.E.), whose writings exist only in fragments. Euripides (ca. 485–ca. 406 B.C.E.), Greek tragedian.

9. This story is told in Diogenes Laertius (ca. early 3d c. C.E.), *Lives and Opinions of Eminent Philosophers* 2.5.22.

1. See, for example, Socrates' description of education and knowledge of "the good" in *Republic* 6.492a–7.520a.

2. See *Republic* 5.473c–d.

art departments to be artists. We cannot be philosophers, but we can love philosophy; we can try to philosophize. This philosophizing consists at any rate primarily and in a way chiefly in listening to the conversation between the great philosophers or, more generally and more cautiously, between the greatest minds, and therefore in studying the great books. The greatest minds to whom we ought to listen are by no means exclusively the greatest minds of the West. It is merely an unfortunate necessity which prevents us from listening to the greatest minds of India and of China: we do not understand their languages, and we cannot learn all languages.

To repeat: liberal education consists in listening to the conversation among the greatest minds. But here we are confronted with the overwhelming difficulty that this conversation does not take place without our help—that in fact we must bring about that conversation. The greatest minds utter monologues. We must transform their monologues into a dialogue, their "side by side" into a "together." The greatest minds utter monologues even when they write dialogues. When we look at the Platonic dialogues, we observe that there is never a dialogue among minds of the highest order: all Platonic dialogues are dialogues between a superior man and men inferior to him. Plato apparently felt that one could not write a dialogue between two men of the highest order. We must then do something which the greatest minds were unable to do. Let us face this difficulty—a difficulty so great that it seems to condemn liberal education as an absurdity. Since the greatest minds contradict one another regarding the most important matters, they compel us to judge of their monologues; we cannot take on trust what any one of them says. On the other hand, we cannot but notice that we are not competent to be judges.

This state of things is concealed from us by a number of facile delusions. We somehow believe that our point of view is superior, higher than those of the greatest minds—either because our point of view is that of our time, and our time, being later than the time of the greatest minds, can be presumed to be superior to their times; or else because we believe that each of the greatest minds was right from his point of view but not, as he claims, simply right: we know that there cannot be *the* simply true substantive view, but only a simply true formal view; that formal view consists in the insight that every comprehensive view is relative to a specific perspective, or that all comprehensive views are mutually exclusive and none can be simply true. The facile delusions which conceal from us our true situation all amount to this: that we are, or can be, wiser than the wisest men of the past. We are thus induced to play the part, not of attentive and docile listeners, but of impresarios or lion-tamers. Yet we must face our awesome situation, created by the necessity that we try to be more than attentive and docile listeners, namely, judges, and yet we are not competent to be judges. As it seems to me, the cause of this situation is that we have lost all simply authoritative traditions in which we could trust, the *nomos*[3] which gave us authoritative guidance, because our immediate teachers and teachers' teachers believed in the possibility of a simply rational society. Each of us here is compelled to find his bearings by his own powers, however defective they may be.

3. Law, custom (Greek).

We have no comfort other than that inherent in this activity. Philosophy, we have learned, must be on its guard against the wish to be edifying—philosophy can only be intrinsically edifying. We cannot exert our understanding without from time to time understanding something of importance; and this act of understanding may be accompanied by the awareness of our understanding, by the understanding of understanding, by *noesis noeseos*,[4] and this is so high, so pure, so noble an experience that Aristotle could ascribe it to his God.[5] This experience is entirely independent of whether what we understand primarily is pleasing or displeasing, fair or ugly. It leads us to realize that all evils are in a sense necessary if there is to be understanding. It enables us to accept all evils which befall us and which may well break our hearts in the spirit of good citizens of the city of God.[6] By becoming aware of the dignity of the mind, we realize the true ground of the dignity of man and therewith the goodness of the world, whether we understand it as created or as uncreated, which is the home of man because it is the home of the human mind.

Liberal education, which consists in the constant intercourse with the greatest minds, is a training in the highest form of modesty, not to say of humility. It is at the same time a training in boldness: it demands from us the complete break with the noise, the rush, the thoughtlessness, the cheapness of the Vanity Fair[7] of the intellectuals as well as of their enemies. It demands from us the boldness implied in the resolve to regard the accepted views as mere opinions, or to regard the average opinions as extreme opinions which are at least as likely to be wrong as the most strange or the least popular opinions. Liberal education is liberation from vulgarity. The Greeks had a beautiful word for "vulgarity"; they called it *apeirokalia*, lack of experience in things beautiful. Liberal education supplies us with experience in things beautiful.

1959

4. Thought of thought (Greek).
5. See *Metaphysics* 12.9, 1074a. For the Greek philosopher ARISTOTLE (384–322 B.C.E.), see above.
6. An allusion to *The City of God* (413–426/27), by Saint AUGUSTINE: it describes two societies that are in contention with one another, that of the elect ("The City of God"), or the faithful, and that of the damned ("The City of Man"), or the unbelievers.
7. A place of frivolity and idle amusement, as described in John Bunyan's allegory *The Pilgrim's Progress* (1678).

JACQUES LACAN
1901–1981

Difficult, polemical, and ironic, organized in sometimes baffling ways, and dotted with strange syntax, foreign words, wordplay, obscure allusions, personality, and mathematical formulas, Jacques Lacan's writings genuinely stretch the reader's resources. He writes psychoanalytic theory as if it were poetry, philosophy, and symbolic logic. In writing, Lacan says that he tries "to leave the reader no other way out than the way in, which I prefer to be difficult." The reader cannot simply pick up a "meaning" and carry it away. And that is the point. It is not the fact of difficulty, but the experience and path of difficulty that are significant. Lacan demystifies as a fantasy of omniscience the objective, impersonal, external position often associated with science and theory. But to analyze the consequences of *wanting it anyway* is at the heart of Lacanian psychoanalysis. Insofar as most psychoanalytic theory is today Lacanian or post-Lacanian, there is no way around Jacques Lacan, the French Freud.

Lacan is known for his larger-than-life persona, but his description of his career sounds distinctly unrevolutionary: it consists of a return to the discoveries of his predecessor. For more than thirty years, Lacan analyzed a single case: the writings of SIGMUND FREUD. Thus, what was revolutionary in his work was a reading—a reading that, he claimed, returned to what was radical about "the Freudian discovery" (which he always refers to in the singular). Lacan's return and its radicality were made possible by the development in his lifetime of modern linguistics: Lacan read Freud through the theories of FERDINAND DE SAUSSURE and ROMAN JAKOBSON, and, in the process, they all were changed. Like CLAUDE LÉVI-STRAUSS (by whose work he was also influenced), he found that the structuralist models opened up by Saussure made possible a sea change in theoretical thinking.

Born to middle-class Parisian Catholic parents who named him Jacques-Marie, he was the first of four children (the second child did not survive). His father worked for a soap and oil manufacturer. While Jacques renounced religion and dropped the "-Marie" from his name, his brother Marc-François entered a monastery. Though the celibacy of one brother was more than counterbalanced by the active sexual life of the other, it can be argued that both remained profoundly marked by the church.

In the 1920s Lacan studied medicine in Paris, beginning clinical training in psychiatry (which requires a medical degree) in 1927. Interested in paranoia (delusions of persecution) and erotomania (delusions of love), he connected his work with surrealism, particularly with that of the Spanish painter Salvador Dali, a contemporary whose theory of "paranoid criticism" resonated strongly with Lacan's research. In 1932 Lacan published his doctoral dissertation, *On Paranoiac Psychosis in Its Relations with the Personality*, and sent a copy to Freud. Although Freud lived another seven years and passed through Paris when escaping Nazi-occupied Austria in 1938, the two men never met. Freud acknowledged receipt of the thesis by postcard.

Lacan married Marie-Louise Blondin in 1934 (one month before the birth of their child) and pursued his training analysis with Rudolph Loewenstein, who later became, after emigrating to the United States, one of the founders of American "ego psychology," which was often a target of Lacan's critique. Like others of his generation, he was deeply affected by a famous series of lectures given on G. W. F. HEGEL by Alexandre Kojève in the 1930s. Lacan was particularly inspired by Kojève's interpretation of the Master-Slave dialectic and of the dynamics of recognition. But he was also struck by Kojève's ability to revolutionize a text by reading it against its critical reception. His reading of Freud would do nothing less. And for twenty years Lacan's weekly seminars played, for the next generation of French intellectuals, the role that Kojève's lectures had played for his.

In 1938 Lacan became a member of the Société Psychanalytique de Paris (SPP), the official French branch of the International Psychoanalytical Association (IPA) founded by Freud in 1910. During World War II, the SPP was forced to suspend its operations. Lacan's personal life was also in flux; the birth in 1941 of Judith Bataille, Lacan's daughter with Sylvia Bataille (the estranged wife of the celebrated critic and novelist Georges Bataille; their separation was not made public until the end of the war), led Marie-Louise to seek a divorce. In 1953 Lacan became president of the SPP and married Sylvia.

Relations between the Freudian establishment and Lacan were always fraught. The prominent psychoanalyst Marie Bonaparte, who had apparently had an affair with Lacan's analyst, was particularly suspicious of him. His practice of seeing patients for variable lengths of time (the so-called short sessions) rather than for the prescribed fifty minutes led the commission on instruction to demand that he regularize his practice. He never did so. His intuitive brilliance as a clinician was often incompatible with institutional rules and safeguards, yet his charismatic personality seemed to call for new institutions. He resigned from the SPP and joined the newer Société Française de Psychanalyse (SFP)—which, upon being told in 1963 that it could join the IPA if Lacan were not included, tried to ban his teaching and his practice. This episode is what Lacan called his "excommunication." Unwilling to conform to the existing rules and excluded from the official organizations, Lacan decided to set up on his own. He founded L'École Freudienne de Paris (the Freudian School of Paris), and with the support of LOUIS ALTHUSSER he moved his weekly seminar, which had been held at the Sainte-Anne hospital, to the prestigious École Normale.

In 1966 Lacan published a legendary 900-page collection of his essays and conference papers titled *Écrits* (*Writings*). Despite its difficulty, the book was a sensation. Crowds began filling his weekly seminar. Along with other French thinkers, Lacan spoke that same year at Johns Hopkins University at a conference—"The Languages of Criticism and the Sciences of Man"—that launched structuralism and poststructuralism in the United States. And together with Althusser, JACQUES DERRIDA, JULIA KRISTEVA, HÉLÈNE CIXOUS, and many others, Lacan became very closely associated with the intellectual ferment that helped lead to the student demonstrations in May 1968 in Paris. Indeed, some of his students became so disruptive that the director of the École Normale made it known to Lacan that he would have to seek another venue. In 1969 he began holding his seminars at the Faculté de Droit (Law School). Meanwhile, at the just-opened branch of the University of Paris at Vincennes, the first university department of psychoanalysis in France was created by people sympathetic to Lacan. Among them was Jacques-Alain Miller, a student of Althusser who later became important as Lacan's editor and son-in-law.

In 1975 Lacan visited the United States again, lecturing at Yale University and MIT. But controversy raged at the École Freudienne de Paris over two developments: the influence of Miller (who was not a medical doctor and preferred Lacan-the-logician to Lacan-the-clinician) and the new pedagogical procedure (called "la passe") that Lacan had introduced into his school to certify those who would receive the title "Analyste de l'École" (Analyst of the Freudian School). The controversy became so fierce that in 1980, the aging Lacan announced the closing of the school he had founded (and, in effect, his own impending death), saying, "Je dissous . . ." (I dissolve). But many members of the Freudian School felt the school was not his to dissolve. As he created a new school ("La Cause Freudienne"), they fought the legality of his dissolution of the old one, but lost. He died of cancer a little more than a year later.

Lacan published only one "book"—his 1932 dissertation; *Écrits* was a collection of assorted papers. But his name is attached to the many articles he published in the numerous journals of the Freudian School, and transcripts of all twenty-six of his annual book-length seminars were and still are being edited and published by Jacques-Alain Miller. His speaking style resembled writing in its "poetic" richness and its need for active listening, but he did not consider his *Écrits* to be quite worthy of their name ("writings"). He jokingly referred to publication as poubellication (*poubelle* means "wastebasket").

The most influential seminar from the literary point of view is his 1955 seminar on EDGAR ALLAN POE's "Purloined Letter" (1844); parts were published as the opening texts in the French *Écrits*, but they are not included in the much shorter English translation of the book. (The entire seminar was published in English in 1988 as *The Ego in Freud's Theory and in the Technique of Psychoanalysis*.) In his "Seminar on 'The Purloined Letter'" Lacan shows how a text can be read even when a major piece of information is not disclosed, a lesson important for psychoanalysis. The *path* of the desired or feared letter in Poe's story does not depend on knowledge of its contents; and the behavior of those who seek it creates a story around their presumptions about the contents, whether or not the letter is ever opened. In this seminar, Lacan is commenting on Freud's concept of the "repetition compulsion," which he translates as "repetition automatism." The story is composed of two different scenes in which the same letter is stolen: the two scenes are repetitions of each other with the set roles being played by different characters. Like the lights on a news strip showing streaming headlines (the analogy is Lacan's), the individual characters are like the light bulbs that go on and off according to the structure being repeated, and not according to their individual volition or characteristics. The repetition is *unconscious*. For Lacan, in other words, Poe's story illustrates the fact that the letter's position among the characters, and not the psychology of the individuals, determines what each will do: "Their displacement is determined by the place which a pure signifier—the purloined letter—comes to occupy." Lacan calls this mechanism "symbolic determination." Like a "free cell" in the solitaire of that name (included in the software of many computers) that allows the other cards to be moved, the "pure" signifier functions as the point of articulation whether or not anything is known about it. Although the story's reader never gains access to the text of the letter, the story's characters do read it; like the analyst, the reader has to understand the functioning of the repetition without necessarily knowing its content.

For Lacan, there are three "orders" or "dimensions" in the psyche: the "Symbolic," the "Imaginary," and the "Real." They are all equally important to the formation of subjectivity. The Real is the easiest to define and the hardest to talk about. In fact, it *can't* be talked about; any such discussion is "impossible." The moment it becomes an object of discourse, it ceases to be the "Real" because it becomes real *for someone* and becomes the "truth." "We are used to the real. The truth we repress," writes Lacan late in his essay "The Agency of the Letter in the Unconscious." "The truth is always disturbing." The "Real" is also defined by Lacan as "that to which the fact that I'm thinking about it doesn't matter." But what is disturbing can be disturbing only *for someone*. The Real can thus only be studied in its effects on the other two dimensions, the Imaginary and the Symbolic.

The Imaginary originates in the human being's fascination with form. The fundamental role of form for the human being is described in Lacan's essay "The Mirror Stage as Formative of the Function of the I" (1949; the concept was introduced in a 1936 lecture), our first selection. The essay describes the founding moment of the Imaginary: the infant's recognition of its image in the mirror. The baby forgets how weak it is and identifies jubilantly with the wholeness of a reflected form. The human self thus comes into being through a fundamentally *aesthetic* recognition. The self-image that causes identification and recognition is a *fiction* "over there," dictating the efforts of the subject ("I") toward a totality and autonomy it can never attain. Through an external medium (a mirror), the child's fragmented body is made whole: the newly fashioned specular "I" precedes the social "I." SLAVOJ ŽIŽEK extends Lacan's concepts of the Imaginary, Real, and Symbolic, especially in his analyses of popular culture.

The relation between the self and its image constitutes the "Imaginary" dimension—so named not because it is unreal, but because it involves an image. The Symbolic, in contrast, is the dimension of symbolization into which the human being's body, to the extent that he or she begins to *speak*, must translate itself. The Symbolic is the dimension of articulation, not equivalent to pointing or naming. Like algebra, the "Symbolic" is a structure of *relations* rather than *things*. (These terms can be confusing; for example, so-called phallic symbols would belong in the Imaginary, not the Symbolic, dimension.)

"The Agency of the Letter in the Unconscious" (1957), from which our second selection is drawn, develops some aspects of the "symbolic" structure of the psyche. It is one of Lacan's most explicit structuralist attempts to bring Freud and Saussure together. The unconscious, for Lacan, is not a hidden reservoir of repressed desires but rather a form of rhetorical energy designed both to disguise and to express those desires, which exist for psychoanalysis only in their effects. "The unconscious is structured like a language," he famously claims. This means not that the unconscious *is* language, but that the unconscious is *like* a language—a foreign language. In other words, the unconscious is *structured*, not amorphous, and it *speaks* rhetorically through the dreams, mistakes, and symptoms of the subject. In the case of psychoanalytic symptoms, it is the body itself that provides the raw material that the unconscious uses to express itself and that the analyst, like a literary critic, must "read."

Saussure's influential model of the linguistic sign has two parts: the sign is composed of a *signifier* and a *signified*. In his example, a drawing of a tree functions as the signified (concept-image), while the spoken word "tree" functions as the signifier (sound-image). By playing with the notion of the tree in Western theory and poetry, Lacan makes it clear that even this representative of "nature" is really a form of "culture." Saussure's model of the sign has three implications that Lacan wants to challenge: that a sign is the representation of a thing, that signs function individually, and that the line that separates signifier from signified is only an abstract function of the diagram (see chapter 1 of Saussure's *Course in General Linguistics*, above). Lacan's countermodel of the sign—or rather, of the signifying chain—consists of two doors; one is labeled "ladies" and the other "gentlemen." The sign can no longer be considered a picture of a thing (since the doors are identical, except for their labels, and resemble neither men nor women). Rather, the sign is a structure into which the reader has to fit his or her body. The signs tell the reader where to "go": they instate the law of sexual difference but do not explain it. They also create a difference where none existed before; the doors are the same, but "ladies" and "gentlemen" are henceforth different. The line in the diagram plays the role of censor merely by dividing one sex from the other. Lacan rewrites Saussure's model of the sign as S/*s*. The "signifier" (S) marks the spot where the "signified" (*s*) has been struck by the bar of repression, which is indistinguishable from the structuring function of civilization. Signs thus systematically and unconsciously constitute all social codes, conventions, and prohibitions. We are constituted and acculturated by signs. Even before we begin to speak, we are already being spoken.

Language, in Lacan's analysis, operates on us as much as we operate on it. We follow the signs. Language speaks us. But in the process, we become split between a conscious self and an unconscious self that we repress, deny, and repeat. Given the power of the unconscious, Lacan rewrites the celebrated self-identity of Descartes's "I think, therefore I am" as enigmatic self-estrangement: "I think where I am not, therefore I am where I do not think." In attempting to describe the rhetoric of this self-estrangement, Lacan aligns Roman Jakobson's linguistic studies of metaphor and metonymy with Freud's distinction (in *The Interpretation of Dreams*, 1900) between condensation and displacement in the dream-work of the unconscious. Because an unconscious wish is, in Freud's model, unacceptable or forbidden, it must get around the censorship of consciousness if it is to express itself. It does so either by choosing a stand-in ("one word for another"= metaphor) or by sliding along and selecting adjacent signifiers ("word-to-word"= metonymy). In "The Agency of the Letter," Lacan thus extends the theories of Saussure and Jakobson in the direction of Freud's implicit rhetoric of unconscious processes, while at the same time drawing on modern linguistics to precisely formulate that which, in Freud, remains largely intuitive.

"The Signification of the Phallus" (1958), our final selection, is one of the most condensed, contested, suggestive, and misunderstood of Lacan's essays. It is about castration—a concept that never fails to be considered scandalous. Why, he asks, did Freud need the concept of castration at all? Women are not castrated men, are they? Little boys don't really believe their fathers will castrate them, do they? It's ridiculous to think that Mommy once had a penis and lost it, isn't it? How could a theory so manifestly absurd and disprovable have been taken seriously? The outrageousness of these infantile sexual theories is of course the point. The human being comes into sexuality epistemologically unprepared. But why did Freud imagine that *these* were the theories that came most readily to mind to stanch the wound created by the discovery that not everyone resembles me, and that *that* has something to do with sexuality?

Lacan tackles these questions in several ways. His originality lies in the connections he makes between the functioning of language and the functioning of desire. As soon as man begins to speak (there is no getting away from the masculine universal in Lacan), he must launder everything important or even routine about his bodily life through linguistic structures that don't exactly correspond to biological requirements. Lacan defines desire as what is left of absolute demand when all possible satisfaction of needs has been subtracted from it. In other words, desire is what by definition remains unsatisfiable.

Linguistic structures preexist the subject and are not created by him. Lacan calls "the Other" "the very locus evoked by the recourse to speech." (The *other* designates a mirror image, a counterpart or competitor, another person; the *Other*, capitalized, designates the Symbolic dimension itself insofar as the subject has to relate to it.) The very fact of speaking routes everything through the Other. The intuition that somehow one has lost direct connection with the body—that something about the body is missing—is itself a first definition of the concept of castration. This lost object that is defined retrospectively is also called, in Lacan's terms, *objet petit a* (a phrase that should be translated "object little o," since the *a* is from *autre*, "other"). The lost object is one that the subject never had, the loss brought into being by symbolization itself.

But if that were all, then everyone would be in exactly the same position with respect to the unattainability of naturalness. There would be no sexual asymmetry. Sexual difference would disappear. Thus, what Lacan has to add to this "universal" castration is a *specific* castration caused by the encounter with sexual difference. The castration that counts is the symbolic castration of the mother—the mother as not-all (not all there is for the child, not a total body form, not entirely focused on the child without other relationships). At this point, in other writings, Lacan describes the function of the father as both the instatement of language ("le nom du père"—the name of the father) and the prohibition of incest ("le non du père"—the "no" of the father).

The phallus that is determining in the phallic stage of human development is thus the one that has never existed. The "something missing" cannot be anything real: it can be generated only by the fact of structure itself. It is missing without ever having been there. It is an interpretation, a theory, a comparison, not a thing. The linguistic counterpart of the missing thing is an extra signifier whose only function is to be the name of the missing thing. There is no signified, but the signifier names the fact of signification—the fact that sexual difference is an interpretation—as such. For Lacan, the phallus is the name for that signifier.

In his seminar *Feminine Sexuality* (1972–73), Lacan goes so far as to claim that "there is no sexual relation." If there were a sexual relation, that would imply that the sexes are complementary, that they fit together to make a whole. But (according to Lacan and, he claims, all of literature), they don't. Women's pleasure is supplementary, not complementary, to a sexual universe that revolves around the position of the one, the phallus, the center. The wholeness and completion that is desired in the sexual relation is precisely what would make it impossible, deadly. When Lacan says that woman does not exist, he is referring to "woman" as a fantasy of complementarity. If "woman" existed, women could not. To account for the existence of women as something that does not merely confirm the preeminence of the phallic signifier,

Lacan adds "God" to the couple. God is the third who keeps "two" from collapsing into "one." The point is not that Lacan "believes" in God, but that the position God occupies in the structure (that of the Other) cannot disappear. For that reason, Lacan focuses on the writings of mystics: Saint John of the Cross, Hadewijch d'Anvers, Saint Teresa—and Jacques Lacan.

It is easy to see why Lacan has been both useful for and anathema to feminists. On the one hand, his theory is useful because it is not in any simple way essentialist: "men" and "women" are not essences or biological givens but rather positions in a structure. On the other hand, his theory is "phallocentric" in the very terms he uses to displace phallocentrism. He writes as if the ménage à trois implied in every relationship consisted of the phallus, the not-all, and God. Like Freud's theory, Lacan's theory takes patriarchy as a given. Whether his writing constitutes a defense or simply an analysis of that given is open to interpretation. The writings of the French feminists Luce Irigaray and Hélène Cixous, in particular, are attempts to give voice, figure, and flesh to alternative versions of sexuality starting from the feminine, not the phallic, perspective without falling into essentialist thinking themselves.

Any analysis, whether clinical or scholarly, implies what Lacan memorably calls "the subject presumed to know." The knowledge sought is presumed to exist somewhere. That fantasy of a knower "out there" is what we have to be cured of. But it is therefore ironic that no one performs the role of that knower better than Lacan. One can only conclude that the demystifier of the "subject presumed to know" is the most powerful of its incarnations. This is an observation with which PLATO's Socrates, who "knew nothing but the fact that he was ignorant," would agree.

"The Mirror Stage as Formative of the Function of the I as Revealed in Psychoanalytic Experience" Keywords: The Body, Identity, Psychoanalysis, Representation, Subjectivity
"The Agency of the Letter in the Unconscious" Keywords: Language, Literary History, Psychoanalysis, Representation, Rhetoric, Structuralism, Subjectivity
"The Signification of the Phallus" Keywords: The Body, Gender, Identity, Language, Psychoanalysis, Queer Theory, Sexuality, Subjectivity

The Mirror Stage as Formative of the Function of the I as Revealed in Psychoanalytic Experience[1]

The conception of the mirror stage that I introduced at our last congress, thirteen years ago, has since become more or less established in the practice of the French group.[2] However, I think it worthwhile to bring it again to your attention, especially today, for the light it sheds on the formation of the *I* as we experience it in psychoanalysis. It is an experience that leads us to oppose any philosophy directly issuing from the *Cogito*.[3]

Some of you may recall that this conception originated in a feature of human behaviour illuminated by a fact of comparative psychology. The child, at an age when he is for a time, however short, outdone by the chim-

1. Translated by Alan Sheridan, who occasionally includes the original French in parentheses.
2. That is, the Psychoanalytical Society of Paris, the official French branch of the International Psychoanalytical Association.
3. I think (Latin), a reference to the philosophy of René Descartes (1596–1650), which was founded on the statement "I think, therefore I am" (*cogito ergo sum*)—that is, the occurrence of thought guarantees the existence of the thinker. Here, it implies that thinking can perfectly coincide with being and is the basis for human reality.

panzee in instrumental intelligence, can nevertheless already recognize as such his own image in a mirror. This recognition is indicated in the illuminative mimicry of the *Aha-Erlebnis*, which Köhler[4] sees as the expression of situational apperception, an essential stage of the act of intelligence.

This act, far from exhausting itself, as in the case of the monkey, once the image has been mastered and found empty, immediately rebounds in the case of the child in a series of gestures in which he experiences in play the relation between the movements assumed in the image and the reflected environment, and between this virtual complex and the reality it reduplicates—the child's own body, and the persons and things, around him.

This event can take place, as we have known since Baldwin,[5] from the age of six months, and its repetition has often made me reflect upon the startling spectacle of the infant in front of the mirror. Unable as yet to walk, or even to stand up, and held tightly as he is by some support, human or artificial (what, in France, we call a '*trotte-bébé*'[6]), he nevertheless overcomes, in a flutter of jubilant activity, the obstructions of his support and, fixing his attitude in a slightly leaning-forward position, in order to hold it in his gaze, brings back an instantaneous aspect of the image.

For me, this activity retains the meaning I have given it up to the age of eighteen months. This meaning discloses a libidinal dynamism, which has hitherto remained problematic, as well as an ontological structure of the human world that accords with my reflections on paranoiac knowledge.[7]

We have only to understand the mirror stage *as an identification*, in the full sense that analysis gives to the term: namely, the transformation that takes place in the subject when he assumes an image—whose predestination to this phase-effect is sufficiently indicated by the use, in analytic theory, of the ancient term *imago*.[8]

This jubilant assumption of his specular image by the child at the *infans*[9] stage, still sunk in his motor incapacity and nursling dependence, would seem to exhibit in an exemplary situation the symbolic matrix in which the *I* is precipitated in a primordial form, before it is objectified in the dialectic of identification with the other, and before language restores to it, in the universal, its function as subject.

This form would have to be called the Ideal-I,[1] if we wished to incorporate it into our usual register, in the sense that it will also be the source of secondary identifications, under which term I would place the functions of libidinal normalization. But the important point is that this form situates the agency of the ego, before its social determination, in a fictional direction, which will always remain irreducible for the individual alone, or rather, which will only rejoin the coming-into-being (*le devenir*) of the subject asymptotically,[2] whatever the success of the dialectical syntheses by which he must resolve as *I* his discordance with his own reality.

4. Wolfgang Köhler (1887–1967), German cofounder of Gestalt psychology. *Aha-Erlebnis*: aha experience (German).
5. James Baldwin (1861–1934), American developmental psychologist.
6. Baby trotter (French); that is, a walker.
7. According to Lacan, knowledge itself is structured like paranoia, in that it projects a coherence onto the world that may not be there.
8. Likeness, statue (Latin).
9. Incapable of speech (Latin).
1. Throughout this article I leave in its peculiarity the translation I have adopted for Freud's *Ideal-Ich* [i.e., "je-idéal"] without further comment, other than to say that I have not maintained it since [Lacan's note].
2. Coming ever closer but never reaching.

The fact is that the total form of the body by which the subject anticipates in a mirage the maturation of his power is given to him only as *Gestalt*,[3] that is to say, in an exteriority in which this form is certainly more constituent than constituted, but in which it appears to him above all in a contrasting size (*un relief de stature*) that fixes it and in a symmetry that inverts it, in contrast with the turbulent movements that the subject feels are animating him. Thus, this *Gestalt*—whose pregnancy should be regarded as bound up with the species, though its motor style remains scarcely recognizable—by these two aspects of its appearance, symbolizes the mental permanence of the *I*, at the same time as it prefigures its alienating destination; it is still pregnant with the correspondences that unite the *I* with the statue in which man projects himself, with the phantoms that dominate him, or with the automaton in which, in an ambiguous relation, the world of his own making tends to find completion.

Indeed, for the *imagos*—whose veiled faces it is our privilege to see in outline in our daily experience and in the penumbra of symbolic efficacity[4]—the mirror-image would seem to be the threshold of the visible world, if we go by the mirror disposition that the *imago of one's own body* presents in hallucinations or dreams, whether it concerns its individual features, or even its infirmities, or its object-projections; or if we observe the role of the mirror apparatus in the appearances of the *double*, in which psychical realities, however heterogeneous, are manifested.

That a *Gestalt* should be capable of formative effects in the organism is attested by a piece of biological experimentation that is itself so alien to the idea of psychical causality that it cannot bring itself to formulate its results in these terms. It nevertheless recognizes that it is a necessary condition for the maturation of the gonad of the female pigeon that it should see another member of its species, of either sex; so sufficient in itself is this condition that the desired effect may be obtained merely by placing the individual within reach of the field of reflection of a mirror. Similarly, in the case of the migratory locust, the transition within a generation from the solitary to the gregarious form can be obtained by exposing the individual, at a certain stage, to the exclusively visual action of a similar image, provided it is animated by movements of a style sufficiently close to that characteristic of the species. Such facts are inscribed in an order of homeomorphic identification that would itself fall within the larger question of the meaning of beauty as both formative and erogenic.[5]

But the facts of mimicry are no less instructive when conceived as cases of heteromorphic identification, in as much as they raise the problem of the signification of space for the living organism—psychological concepts hardly seem less appropriate for shedding light on these matters than ridiculous attempts to reduce them to the supposedly supreme law of adaptation. We have only to recall how Roger Caillois[6] (who was then very young, and still fresh from his breach with the sociological school in which he was trained) illuminated the subject by using the term '*legendary psychasthenia*'[7] to

3. Form, pattern, whole (German).
4. Cf. Claude Lévi-Strauss [1908–2009], *Structural Anthropology* [1958], chapter 10 [Lacan's note].
5. Giving rise to sexual desire. "Homeomorphic": having the same form (as opposed to "heteromorphic," differing from the usual form).
6. French philosopher and critic (1913–1978), who when young was a surrealist.
7. A term once used for general neuroses.

classify morphological mimicry as an obsession with space in its derealizing effect.

I have myself shown in the social dialectic that structures human knowledge as paranoiac[8] why human knowledge has greater autonomy than animal knowledge in relation to the field of force of desire, but also why human knowledge is determined in that 'little reality' (*ce peu de réalité*), which the Surrealists,[9] in their restless way, saw as its limitation. These reflections lead me to recognize in the spatial captation manifested in the mirror-stage, even before the social dialectic, the effect in man of an organic insufficiency in his natural reality—in so far as any meaning can be given to the word 'nature'.

I am led, therefore, to regard the function of the mirror-stage as a particular case of the function of the *imago*, which is to establish a relation between the organism and its reality—or, as they say, between the *Innenwelt* and the *Umwelt*.[1]

In man, however, this relation to nature is altered by a certain dehiscence at the heart of the organism, a primordial Discord betrayed by the signs of uneasiness and motor unco-ordination of the neo-natal months. The objective notion of the anatomical incompleteness of the pyramidal system[2] and likewise the presence of certain humoral residues of the maternal organism confirm the view I have formulated as the fact of a real *specific prematurity of birth* in man.

It is worth noting, incidentally, that this is a fact recognized as such by embryologists, by the term *foetalization*, which determines the prevalence of the so-called superior apparatus of the neurax,[3] and especially of the cortex, which psycho-surgical operations lead us to regard as the intra-organic mirror.

This development is experienced as a temporal dialectic that decisively projects the formation of the individual into history. The *mirror stage* is a drama whose internal thrust is precipitated from insufficiency to anticipation—and which manufactures for the subject, caught up in the lure of spatial identification, the succession of phantasies that extends from a fragmented body-image to a form of its totality that I shall call orthopaedic[4]—and, lastly, to the assumption of the armour of an alienating identity, which will mark with its rigid structure the subject's entire mental development. Thus, to break out of the circle of the *Innenwelt* into the *Umwelt* generates the inexhaustible quadrature[5] of the ego's verifications.

This fragmented body—which term I have also introduced into our system of theoretical references—usually manifests itself in dreams when the movement of the analysis encounters a certain level of aggressive disintegration in the individual. It then appears in the form of disjointed limbs, or of those organs represented in exoscopy, growing wings and taking up arms

8. Cf. "Aggressivity in Psychoanalysis," in *Écrits* [Lacan's note]. "The social dialectic": human interactions.
9. Members of an experimental literary and artistic movement founded in France in 1924; inspired in part by SIGMUND FREUD, surrealists sought to express subconscious thought and feeling.
1. The inner world and the outer world (German).
2. Part of the central nervous system that links the brain and spinal cord and controls voluntary movement.
3. Neuraxis, or central nervous system.
4. Relating to correct child rearing (Lacan is drawing on the core meanings of the word's Greek roots).
5. An allusion to "squaring the circle," or constructing a square whose area is equal to that of a given circle (an impossible task if, following the dictates of classical geometry, one uses only a straightedge and a compass).

for intestinal persecutions—the very same that the visionary Hieronymus Bosch[6] has fixed, for all time, in painting, in their ascent from the fifteenth century to the imaginary zenith of modern man. But this form is even tangibly revealed at the organic level, in the lines of 'fragilization' that define the anatomy of phantasy, as exhibited in the schizoid and spasmodic symptoms of hysteria.

Correlatively, the formation of the *I* is symbolized in dreams by a fortress, or a stadium—its inner arena and enclosure, surrounded by marshes and rubbish-tips,[7] dividing it into two opposed fields of contest where the subject flounders in quest of the lofty, remote inner castle whose form (sometimes juxtaposed in the same scenario) symbolizes the id in a quite startling way. Similarly, on the mental plane, we find realized the structures of fortified works, the metaphor of which arises spontaneously, as if issuing from the symptoms themselves, to designate the mechanisms of obsessional neurosis—inversion, isolation, reduplication, cancellation and displacement.

But if we were to build on these subjective givens alone—however little we free them from the condition of experience that makes us see them as partaking of the nature of a linguistic technique—our theoretical attempts would remain exposed to the charge of projecting themselves into the unthinkable of an absolute subject. This is why I have sought in the present hypothesis, grounded in a conjunction of objective data, the guiding grid for a *method of symbolic reduction*.[8]

It establishes in the *defences of the ego* a genetic order, in accordance with the wish formulated by Miss Anna Freud,[9] in the first part of her great work, and situates (as against a frequently expressed prejudice) hysterical repression and its returns at a more archaic stage than obsessional inversion and its isolating processes, and the latter in turn as preliminary to paranoic alienation, which dates from the deflection of the specular *I* into the social *I*.

This moment in which the mirror-stage comes to an end inaugurates, by the identification with the *imago* of the counterpart and the drama of primordial jealousy (so well brought out by the school of Charlotte Bühler in the phenomenon of infantile *transitivism*[1]), the dialectic that will henceforth link the *I* to socially elaborated situations.

It is this moment that decisively tips the whole of human knowledge into mediatization through the desire of the other, constitutes its objects in an abstract equivalence by the co-operation of others, and turns the I into that apparatus for which every instinctual thrust constitutes a danger, even though it should correspond to a natural maturation—the very normalization of this maturation being henceforth dependent, in man, on a cultural mediation as exemplified, in the case of the sexual object, by the Oedipus complex.[2]

6. Dutch painter (ca. 1450–1516), best known for his detailed depictions of grotesque, fantastic creatures. "Exoscopy": a view from outside.
7. Garbage dumps.
8. A method derived from the phenomenologists' practice of "bracketing" or isolating the experience being described.
9. Austrian-born English psychoanalyst (1895–1982), Freud's daughter; her "great work" is *The Ego and the Mechanisms of Defense* (1936).
1. Aggressive mimicry. Bühler (1893–1974), German child psychologist.
2. The universal internalization of the prohibited desire for one's mother and the love-hate relation to one's father posited by Freud. Lacan's point is that human desire is not natural: it is shaped by fictions and prohibitions.

In the light of this conception, the term primary narcissism,[3] by which analytic doctrine designates the libidinal investment characteristic of that moment, reveals in those who invented it the most profound awareness of semantic latencies. But it also throws light on the dynamic opposition between this libido[4] and the sexual libido, which the first analysts tried to define when they invoked destructive and, indeed, death instincts, in order to explain the evident connection between the narcissistic libido and the alienating function of the *I*, the aggressivity it releases in any relation to the other, even in a relation involving the most Samaritan of aid.[5]

In fact, they were encountering that *existential negativity* whose reality is so vigorously proclaimed by the contemporary philosophy of being and nothingness.[6]

But unfortunately that philosophy grasps negativity only within the limits of a self-sufficiency of consciousness, which, as one of its premises links to the *méconnaissances*[7] that constitute the ego, the illusion of autonomy to which it entrusts itself. This flight of fancy, for all that it draws, to an unusual extent, on borrowings from psychoanalytic experience culminates in the pretention of providing an existential psychoanalysis.

At the culmination of the historical effort of a society to refuse to recognize that it has any function other than the utilitarian one, and in the anxiety of the individual confronting the 'concentrational'[8] form of the social bond that seems to arise to crown this effort, existentialism must be judged by the explanations it gives of the subjective impasses that have indeed resulted from it; a freedom that is never more authentic than when it is within the walls of a prison; a demand for commitment, expressing the impotence of a pure consciousness to master any situation; a voyeuristic-sadistic idealization of the sexual relation; a personality that realizes itself only in suicide; a consciousness of the other than can be satisfied only by Hegelian murder.[9]

These propositions are opposed by all our experience, in so far as it teaches us not to regard the ego as centred on the *perception-consciousness system*, or as organized by the 'reality principle'—a principle that is the expression of a scientific prejudice most hostile to the dialectic of knowledge. Our experience shows that we should start instead from the *function of méconnaissance* that characterizes the ego in all its structures, so markedly articulated by Miss Anna Freud. For, if the *Verneinung*[1] represents the patent form of that function, its effects will, for the most part, remain latent, so long as they are not illuminated by some light reflected on to the level of fatality, which is where the id manifests itself.

We can thus understand the inertia characteristic of the formations of the *I*, and find there the most extensive definition of neurosis—just as the captation[2] of the subject by the situation gives us the most general formula

3. Self-preservation.
4. Desire (Latin), a Freudian term.
5. That is, generous and altruistic help; for the parable of the good Samaritan, see Luke 10.30–37.
6. That is, by Jean-Paul Sartre (1905–1980), author of *Being and Nothingness* (1943); the French philosopher argued that humans have no essence before they act and thus shape themselves through their autonomous choices.
7. Misrecognitions (French).
8. "*Concentrationnaire*," an adjective coined after World War II (this article was written in 1949) to describe the life of the concentration camp. In the hands of certain writers it became, by extension, applicable to many aspects of "modern" life [translator's note].
9. An allusion to the Master-Slave dialectic (see above) described by GEORG WILHELM FRIEDRICH HEGEL (1770–1831), German idealist philosopher.
1. Denial (German).
2. Seizure.

for madness, not only the madness that lies behind the walls of asylums, but also the madness that deafens the world with its sound and fury.

The sufferings of neurosis and psychosis are for us a schooling in the passions of the soul, just as the beam of the psychoanalytic scales, when we calculate the tilt of its threat to entire communities, provides us with an indication of the deadening of the passions in society.

At this junction of nature and culture, so persistently examined by modern anthropology, psychoanalysis alone recognizes this knot of imaginary servitude that love must always undo again, or sever.

For such a task, we place no trust in altruistic feeling, we who lay bare the aggressivity that underlies the activity of the philanthropist, the idealist, the pedagogue, and even the reformer.

In the recourse of subject to subject that we preserve, psychoanalysis may accompany the patient to the ecstatic limit of the *'Thou art that,'* in which is revealed to him the cipher of his mortal destiny, but it is not in our mere power as practitioners to bring him to that point where the real journey begins.

1949

From The Agency of the Letter in the Unconscious[1]

* * *

As my title suggests, beyond this 'speech', what the psychoanalytic experience discovers in the unconscious is the whole structure of language. Thus from the outset I have alerted informed minds to the extent to which the notion that the unconscious is merely the seat of the instincts will have to be rethought.

But how are we to take this 'letter' here? Quite simply, literally.[2]

By 'letter' I designate that material support that concrete discourse borrows from language.

This simple definition assumes that language is not to be confused with the various psychical and somatic functions that serve it in the speaking subject—primarily because language and its structure exist prior to the moment at which each subject at a certain point in his mental development makes his entry into it.

Let us note, then, that aphasias,[3] although caused by purely anatomical lesions in the cerebral apparatus that supplies the mental centre for these functions, prove, on the whole, to distribute their deficits between the two sides of the signifying effect of what we call here 'the letter' in the creation of signification.[4] A point that will be clarified later.

1. Translated by Alan Sheridan, who occasionally includes the original French in parentheses.
2. "*À la lettre*" [translator's note].
3. Speech losses.
4. This aspect of aphasia, so useful in overthrowing the concept of "psychological function," which only obscures every aspect of the question, becomes quite clear in the purely linguistic analysis of the two major forms of aphasia worked out by one of the leaders of modern linguistics, Roman Jakobson. See the most accessible of his works, the *Fundamentals of Language* (with Morris Halle, Gravenhage: Mouton, 1956), part II, chapters 1 to 4 [Lacan's note]. JAKOBSON (1896–1982), Russian-born American linguist.

Thus the subject, too, if he can appear to be the slave of language is all the more so of a discourse in the universal movement in which his place is already inscribed at birth, if only by virtue of his proper name.

Reference to the experience of the community, or to the substance of this discourse, settles nothing. For this experience assumes its essential dimension in the tradition that this discourse itself establishes. This tradition, long before the drama of history is inscribed in it, lays down the elementary structures of culture. And these very structures reveal an ordering of possible exchanges which, even if unconscious, is inconceivable outside the permutations authorized by language.

With the result that the ethnographic duality of nature and culture is giving way to a ternary conception of the human condition—nature, society, and culture—the last term of which could well be reduced to language, or that which essentially distinguishes human society from natural societies.

But I shall not make of this distinction either a point or a point of departure, leaving to its own obscurity the question of the original relations between the signifier and labour. I shall be content, for my little jab at the general function of *praxis* in the genesis of history, to point out that the very society that wished to restore, along with the privileges of the producer, the causal hierarchy of the relations between production and the ideological superstructure to their full political rights, has none the less failed to give birth to an esperanto in which the relations of language to socialist realities would have rendered any literary formalism radically impossible.[5]

For my part, I shall trust only those assumptions that have already proven their value by virtue of the fact that language through them has attained the status of an object of scientific investigation.

For it is by virtue of this fact that linguistics[6] is seen to occupy the key position in this domain, and the reclassification of the sciences and a regrouping of them around it signals, as is usually the case, a revolution in knowledge; only the necessities of communication made me inscribe it at the head of this volume under the title 'the sciences of man'[7]—despite the confusion that is thereby covered over.

To pinpoint the emergence of linguistic science we may say that, as in the case of all sciences in the modern sense, it is contained in the constitutive moment of an algorithm that is its foundation. This algorithm is the following:

$$\frac{S}{s}$$

which is read as: the signifier over the signified, 'over' corresponding to the bar separating the two stages.

5. We may recall that the discussion of the need for a new language in communist society did in fact take place, and Stalin, much to the relief of those who adhered to his philosophy, put an end to it with the following formulation: language is not a superstructure [Lacan's note]. "Superstructure": the term used by KARL MARX (1818–1883) to designate the political, legal, social, and cultural forms of a society, which are based on its economic structure. Joseph Stalin (1879–1953), leader of the U.S.S.R. (1924–53). "Esperanto": artificial universal language.

6. By "linguistics" I mean the study of existing languages (*langues*) in their structure and in the laws revealed therein; this excludes any theory of abstract codes sometimes included under the heading of communication theory, as well as the theory, originating in the physical sciences, called information theory, or any semiology more or less hypothetically generalized [Lacan's note]. *Langue*, language in its totality, is distinct from *parole*, language as actually spoken by an individual.

7. *Psychanalyse et sciences de l'homme* [Lacan's note]. Lacan is stressing the changes that the scientific study of language has brought about in the very notion of a "human science."

This sign should be attributed to Ferdinand de Saussure,[8] although it is not found in exactly this form in any of the numerous schemas, which none the less express it, to be found in the printed version of his lectures of the years 1906–7, 1908–9, and 1910–11, which the piety of a group of his disciples caused to be published under the title, *Cours de linguistique générale*, a work of prime importance for the transmission of a teaching worthy of the name, that is, that one can come to terms with only in its own terms.

That is why it is legitimate for us to give him credit for the formulation S/*s* by which, in spite of the differences among schools, the beginning of modern linguistics can be recognized.

The thematics of this science is henceforth suspended, in effect, at the primordial position of the signifier and the signified as being distinct orders separated initially by a barrier resisting signification. And that is what was to make possible an exact study of the connections proper to the signifier, and of the extent of their function in the genesis of the signified.

For this primordial distinction goes well beyond the discussion concerning the arbitrariness of the sign, as it has been elaborated since the earliest reflections of the ancients, and even beyond the impasse which, through the same period, has been encountered in every discussion of the bi-univocal correspondence between the word and the thing, if only in the mere act of naming. All this, of course, is quite contrary to the appearances suggested by the importance often imputed to the role of the index finger pointing to an object in the learning process of the *infans*[9] subject learning his mother tongue, or the use in foreign language teaching of so-called 'concrete' methods.

One cannot go further along this line of thought than to demonstrate that no signification can be sustained other than by reference to another signification:[1] in its extreme form this amounts to the proposition that there is no language (*langue*) in existence for which there is any question of its inability to cover the whole field of the signified, it being an effect of its existence as a language (*langue*) that it necessarily answers all needs. If we try to grasp in language the constitution of the object, we cannot fail to notice that this constitution is to be found only at the level of concept, a very different thing from a simple nominative, and that the thing, when reduced to the noun, breaks up into the double, divergent beam of the 'cause' (*causa*)[2] in which it has taken shelter in the French word *chose*, and the nothing (*rien*) to which it has abandoned its Latin dress (*rem*).

These considerations, important as their existence is for the philosopher, turn us away from the locus in which language questions us as to its very nature. And we will fail to pursue the question further as long as we cling to the illusion that the signifier answers to the function of representing the signified, or better, that the signifier has to answer for its existence in the name of any signification whatever.

For even reduced to this latter formulation, the heresy is the same—the heresy that leads logical positivism in search of the 'meaning of

8. Swiss linguist (1857–1913; see above); he described and named the two parts of a linguistic sign, the *signified* (the concept or meaning) and the *signifier* (the sound that conveys the concept or meaning). His *Course in General Linguistics* was published in 1916.

9. Incapable of speech (Latin).

1. Cf. the *De Magistro* of St. Augustine, especially the chapter "De significatione locutionis" which I analyzed in my seminar of June 23, 1954 [Lacan's note]. AUGUSTINE (354–430), early Christian philosopher and theologian.

2. Latin, as is *rem* (thing), below.

meaning',[3] as its objective is called in the language of its devotees. As a result, we can observe that even a text highly charged with meaning can be reduced, through this sort of analysis, to insignificant bagatelles, all that survives being mathematical algorithms that are, of course, without any meaning.[4]

To return to our formula S/s: if we could infer nothing from it but the notion of the parallelism of its upper and lower terms, each one taken in its globality, it would remain the enigmatic sign of a total mystery. Which of course is not the case.

In order to grasp its function I shall begin by reproducing the classic, yet faulty illustration (see below) by which its usage is normally introduced, and one can see how it opens the way to the kind of error referred to above.

TREE

In my lecture, I replaced this illustration with another, which has no greater claim to correctness than that it has been transplanted into that incongruous dimension that the psychoanalyst has not yet altogether renounced because of his quite justified feeling that his conformism takes its value entirely from it. Here is the other diagram:

LADIES GENTLEMEN

where we see that, without greatly extending the scope of the signifier concerned in the experiment, that is, by doubling a noun through the mere juxtaposition of two terms whose complementary meanings ought appar-

3. English in the original [translator's note]. *The Meaning of Meaning* was a 1923 work by Charles K. Ogden and I. A. Richards, English linguists who viewed the study of literature as an objective, scientific discipline.

4. So Mr. I. A. Richards, author of a work precisely in accord with such an objective, has in another work shown us its application. He took for his purposes a page from Mong-tse (Mencius, to the Jesuits) and called the piece, *Mencius on the Mind* [1932]. The guarantees of the purity of the experiment are nothing to the luxury of the approaches. And our expert on the traditional Canon that contains the text is found right on the spot in Peking where our demonstration-model mangle has been transported regardless of cost.

But we shall be no less transported, if less expensively, to see a bronze that gives out bell-tones at the slightest contact with thought, transformed into a rag to wipe the blackboard of the most dismaying British psychologism. And not without eventually being identified with the meninx of the author himself—all that remains of him or his object after having exhausted the meaning of the latter and the good sense of the former [Lacan's note]. "Meninx": a membrane around the brain.

ently to reinforce each other, a surprise is produced by an unexpected precipitation of an unexpected meaning: the image of twin doors symbolizing, through the solitary confinement offered Western Man for the satisfaction of his natural needs away from home, the imperative that he seems to share with the great majority of primitive communities by which his public life is subjected to the laws of urinary segregation.[5]

It is not only with the idea of silencing the nominalist debate[6] with a low blow that I use this example, but rather to show how in fact the signifier enters the signified, namely, in a form which, not being immaterial, raises the question of its place in reality. For the blinking gaze of a short sighted person might be justified in wondering whether this was indeed the signifier as he peered closely at the little enamel signs that bore it, a signifier whose signified would in this call receive its final honours from the double and solemn procession from the upper nave.

But no contrived example can be as telling as the actual experience of truth. So I am happy to have invented the above, since it awoke in the person whose word I most trust a memory of childhood, which having thus happily come to my attention is best placed here.

A train arrives at a station. A little boy and a little girl, brother and sister, are seated in a compartment face to face next to the window through which the buildings along the station platform can be seen passing as the train pulls to a stop. 'Look', says the brother, 'we're at Ladies!'; 'Idiot!' replies his sister, 'Can't you see we're at Gentlemen'.

Besides the fact that the rails in this story materialize the bar in the Saussurian algorithm (and in a form designed to suggest that its resistance may be other than dialectical), we should add that only someone who didn't have his eyes in front of the holes (it's the appropriate image here) could possibly confuse the place of the signifier and the signified in this story, or not see from what radiating centre the signifier sends forth its light into the shadow of incomplete significations.

For this signifier will now carry a purely animal Dissension, destined for the usual oblivion of natural mists, to the unbridled power of ideological warfare, relentless for families, a torment to the Gods. For these children, Ladies and Gentlemen will be henceforth two countries towards which each of their souls will strive on divergent wings, and between which a truce will be the more impossible since they are actually the same country and neither can compromise on its own superiority without detracting from the glory of the other.

But enough. It is beginning to sound like the history of France. Which it is more human, as it ought to be, to evoke here than that of England, destined to tumble from the Large to the Small End of Dean Swift's egg.[7]

5. Lacan has transformed Saussure's model of the sign (in which the signified can still be understood to be a representation of a tree; see *Course in General Linguistics*, above) into a structure in which the representative function of the sign is less important than its law-giving function. In Saussure, the reader's body is not implicated; in Lacan, the sign exists to tell the reader where to "go." The two doors are identical, but the subject confronting them must conform to the law of "urinary segregation" (i.e., sexual difference) if he or she wishes to find bodily relief.

6. The debate that tries to determine which came first, words or things.

7. In *Gulliver's Travels* (1726), by the Irish-born English satirist and clergyman Jonathan Swift (1667–1745), the narrator visits an empire convulsed by civil war over the question of which end of an egg to eat from.

It remains to be conceived what steps, what corridor, the S of the signifier, visible here in the plurals[8] in which it focuses its welcome beyond the window, must take in order to rest its elbows on the ventilators through which, like warm and cold air, indignation and scorn come hissing out below.

One thing is certain: if the algorithm S/s with its bar is appropriate, access from one to the other cannot in any case have a signification. For in so far as it is itself only pure function of the signifier, the algorithm can reveal only the structure of a signifier in this transfer.

Now the structure of the signifier is, as it is commonly said of language itself, that it should be articulated.

This means that no matter where one starts to designate their reciprocal encroachments and increasing inclusions, these units are subjected to the double condition of being reducible to ultimate differential elements and of combining them according to the laws of a closed order.[9]

These elements, one of the decisive discoveries of linguistics, are *phonemes*; but we must not expect to find any *phonetic* constancy in the modulatory variability to which this term applies, but rather the synchronic[1] system of differential couplings necessary for the discernment of sounds in a given language. Through this, one sees that an essential element of the spoken word itself was predestined to flow into the mobile characters which, in a jumble of lower-case Didots or Garamonds,[2] render validly present what we call the 'letter', namely, the essentially localized structure of the signifier.

With the second property of the signifier, that of combining according to the laws of a closed order, is affirmed the necessity of the topological substratum of which the term I ordinarily use, namely, the signifying chain, gives an approximate idea: rings of a necklace that is a ring in another necklace made of rings.

Such are the structural conditions that define grammar as the order of constitutive encroachments of the signifier up to the level of the unit immediately superior to the sentence, and lexicology as the order of constitutive inclusions of the signifier to the level of the verbal locution.

In examining the limits by which these two exercises in the understanding of linguistic usage are determined, it is easy to see that only the correlations between signifier and signifier provide the standard for all research into signification, as is indicated by the notion of 'usage' of a taxeme or semanteme,[3] which in fact refers to the context just above that of the units concerned.

But it is not because the undertakings of grammar and lexicology are exhausted within certain limits that we must think that beyond those limits signification reigns supreme. That would be an error.

For the signifier, by its very nature, always anticipates meaning by unfolding its dimension before it. As is seen at the level of the sentence when it is interrupted before the significant term: 'I shall never . . .', 'All the same it

8. Not, unfortunately, the case in the English here—the plural of "gentleman" being indicated other than by the addition of an "s" [translator's note].

9. In structural linguistics these conditions are often termed the paradigmatic relationship, which obtains between items that can be substituted for one another in a given context (e.g., two adverbs) and the syntagmatic relationship, which obtains between linguistic items that combine to form a meaningful whole (e.g., the words in a given sentence).

1. At a single point in time (as opposed to the *diachronic*, which pertains to the development of a phenomenon over time).

2. Names of different type-faces [translator's note].

3. An irreducible unit of meaning. "Taxeme": a minimal linguistic feature (pitch, order, etc.) that differentiates two otherwise identical utterances.

is . . .', 'And yet there may be . . .'. Such sentences are not without meaning, a meaning all the more oppressive in that it is content to make us wait for it.[4]

But the phenomenon is no different which by the mere recoil of a 'but' brings to the light, comely as the Shulamite, honest as the dew, the negress adorned for the wedding and the poor woman ready for the auction-block.[5]

From which we can say that it is in the chain of the signifier that the meaning 'insists'[6] but that none of its elements 'consists' in the signification of which it is at the moment capable.

We are forced, then, to accept the notion of an incessant sliding of the signified under the signifier—which Ferdinand de Saussure illustrates with an image resembling the wavy lines of the upper and lower Waters in miniatures from manuscripts of *Genesis*; a double flux marked by fine streaks of rain, vertical dotted lines supposedly confining segments of correspondence.

All our experience runs counter to this linearity, which made me speak once, in one of my seminars on psychosis, of something more like 'anchoring points' ('*points de capiton*')[7] as a schema for taking into account the dominance of the letter in the dramatic transformation that dialogue can effect in the subject.

The linearity that Saussure holds to be constitutive of the chain of discourse, in conformity with its emission by a single voice and with its horizontal position in our writing—if this linearity is necessary, in fact, it is not sufficient. It applies to the chain of discourse only in the direction in which it is orientated in time, being taken as a signifying factor in all languages in which 'Peter hits Paul' reverses its time when the terms are inverted.

But one has only to listen to poetry, which Saussure was no doubt in the habit of doing,[8] for a polyphony to be heard, for it to become clear that all discourse is aligned along the several staves of a score.

There is in effect no signifying chain that does not have, as if attached to the punctuation of each of its units, a whole articulation of relevant contexts suspended 'vertically', as it were, from that point.

Let us take our word 'tree' again, this time not as an isolated noun, but at the point of one of these punctuations, and see how it crosses the bar of the Saussurian algorithm. (The anagram of '*arbre*' and '*barre*'[9] should be noted.)

For even broken down into the double spectre of its vowels and consonants, it can still call up with the robur[1] and the plane tree the significations it takes on, in the context of our flora, of strength and majesty. Drawing on all the symbolic contexts suggested in the Hebrew of the Bible, it erects on a barren hill the shadow of the cross. Then reduces to the capital Y, the sign of

4. To which verbal hallucination, when it takes this form, opens a communicating door with the Freudian structure of psychosis—a door until now unnoticed (cf. "On a Question Preliminary to Any Possible Treatment of Psychosis," *Écrits*) [Lacan's note].

5. The allusions are to the "I am black, but comely . . ." of the *Song of Solomon* [1.5], and to the 19th-century cliché of the "poor, but honest" woman [translator's note].

6. The word "insists"—like the French word *instance* (translated as "agency") in the title of the essay—emphasizes location ("in-") and law ("legal instance") rather than content, stressing the links in articulation rather than the meaning of any one term.

7. The image is that of an upholster's button.

8. The publication by Jean Starobinski, in *Le Mercure de France* (February 1964) of Saussure's notes on anagrams and their hypogrammatical use, from the Saturnine verses to the writings of Cicero, provides the corroboration that I then lacked [Lacan's note, added 1966]. "Saturnine verses": poetry in the Saturnian meter used by some early Latin writers (3d c. B.C.E.). Cicero (106–43 B.C.E.), Roman orator, philosopher, and undistinguished poet.

9. Tree and bar (French). Lacan goes on to explore the ways in which the "tree" has been fundamental to Western thought.

1. Oak (Latin).

dichotomy which, except for the illustration used by heraldry, would owe nothing to the tree however genealogical we may think it. Circulatory tree, tree of life of the cerebellum, tree of Saturn, tree of Diana,[2] crystals formed in a tree struck by lightning, is it your figure that traces our destiny for us in the tortoise-shell cracked by the fire, or your lightning that causes that slow shift in the axis of being to surge up from an unnamable night into the *Ενπάντα*[3] of language:

> *No! says the Tree, it says No! in the shower of sparks*
> *Of its superb head*

lines that require the harmonics of the tree just as much as their continuation:

> *Which the storm treats as universally*
> *As it does a blade of grass.*[4]

For this modern verse is ordered according to the same law of the parallelism of the signifier that creates the harmony governing the primitive Slavic epic or the most refined Chinese poetry.

As is seen in the fact that the tree and the blade of grass are chosen from the same mode of the existent in order for the signs of contradiction—saying 'No!' and 'treat as'—to affect them, and also so as to bring about, through the categorical contrast of the particularity of 'superb' with the 'universally' that reduces it, in the condensation of the 'head' (*tête*) and the 'storm' (*tempête*), the indiscernible shower of sparks of the eternal instant.

But this whole signifier can only operate, it may be said, if it is present in the subject. It is this objection that I answer by supposing that it has passed over to the level of the signified.

For what is important is not that the subject know anything whatsoever. (If LADIES and GENTLEMEN were written in a language unknown to the little boy and girl, their quarrel would simply be the more exclusively a quarrel over words, but no less ready to take on signification.)

What this structure of the signifying chain discloses is the possibility I have, precisely in so far as I have this language in common with other subjects, that is to say, in so far as it exists as a language, to use it in order to signify *something quite other* than what it says. This function of speech is more worth pointing out than that of 'disguising the thought' (more often than not indefinable) of the subject; it is no less than the function of indicating the place of this subject in the search for the true.

I have only to plant my tree in a locution; climb the tree, even project on to it the cunning illumination a descriptive context gives to a word; raise it (*arborer*) so as not to let myself be imprisoned in some sort of *communiqué* of the facts, however official, and if I know the truth, make it heard, in spite of all the *between-the-lines* censures by the only signifier my acrobatics through the branches of the tree can constitute, provocative to the point of

2. Diana, Roman goddess of the hunt, and Saturn, the Roman god of agriculture, both had tree cults associated with them. In addition, the "tree" shape of a stag's antlers might also be associated with Diana.

3. All one (Greek).

4. *Non! dit l'Arbre, il dit: Non! dans l'étincellement / De sa tête superbe / Que la tempête traite universellement / Comme elle fait une herbe.* (Paul Valéry, "Au Platane," *Les Charmes* [1922]) [Lacan's note].

burlesque, or perceptible only to the practised eye, according to whether I wish to be heard by the mob or by the few.

The properly signifying function thus depicted in language has a name. We learned this name in some grammar of our childhood, on the last page, where the shade of Quintilian,[5] relegated to some phantom chapter concerning 'final considerations on style', seemed suddenly to speed up his voice in an attempt to get in all he had to say before the end.

It is among the figures of style, or tropes—from which the verb 'to find' (*trouver*) comes to us—that this name is found. This name is *metonymy*.[6]

I shall refer only to the example given there: 'thirty sails'. For the disquietude I felt over the fact that the word 'ship', concealed in this expression, seemed, by taking on its figurative sense, through the endless repetition of the same old example, only to increase its presence, obscured (*voilait*) not so much those illustrious sails (*voiles*)[7] as the definition they were supposed to illustrate.

The part taken for the whole, we said to ourselves, and if the thing is to be taken seriously, we are left with very little idea of the importance of this fleet, which 'thirty sails' is precisely supposed to give us: for each ship to have just one sail is in fact the least likely possibility.

By which we see that the connexion between ship and sail is nowhere but in the signifier, and that it is in the *word-to-word* connexion that metonymy is based.[8]

I shall designate as metonymy, then, the one side (*versant*) of the effective field constituted by the signifier, so that meaning can emerge there.

The other side is *metaphor*.[9] Let us immediately find an illustration; Quillet's[1] dictionary seemed an appropriate place to find a sample that would not seem to be chosen for my own purposes, and I didn't have to go any further than the well known line of Victor Hugo:

His sheaf was neither miserly nor spiteful . . .[2]

under which aspect I presented metaphor in my seminar on the psychoses.

It should be said that modern poetry and especially the Surrealist school[3] have taken us a long way in this direction by showing that any conjunction of two signifiers would be equally sufficient to constitute a metaphor, except for the additional requirement of the greatest possible disparity of the images

5. Roman rhetorician (ca. 30/35–ca. 100 C.E.).
6. The substitution of one word for another dissociated with it in any way *except* resemblance (i.e., except as metaphor): part for whole ("thirty sails"), material for thing made ("a glass"), author's name for text ("Lacan"), and so on.
7. The French word *voile* has two meanings and two genders: *la voile* is a veil, while *le voile* is a sail. Playing on this ambiguity, Lacan shows that if "thirty sails" is a metonym for "thirty ships," that connection exists by linguistic convention rather than in reality.
8. I pay homage here to the works of Roman Jakobson—to which I owe much of this formulation; works to which a psychoanalyst can constantly refer in order to structure his own experience, and which render superfluous the "personal communications" of which I could boast as much as the next fellow [Lacan's note].
9. The substitution of one word for another associated by resemblance ("my love is a rose"). In "Two Aspects of Language and Two Types of Aphasic Disturbances" (1956; see above), Jakobson contrasts the two figures.
1. Aristide Quillet (1880–1955), publisher of a French dictionary.
2. "Sa gerbe n'était pas avare ni haineuse," a line from "Booz endormi" [translator's note], by Hugo (1802–1885), French Romantic poet, playwright, and novelist. "Booz endormi," from Hugo's *La Légende des siècles* (1859), is a retelling of the book of Ruth.
3. An experimental literary and artistic movement founded in France in 1924; surrealists sought to express subconscious thought and feeling, and believed that the incongruous juxtapositions created by automatic writing and painting revealed inner truths.

signified, needed for the production of the poetic spark, or in other words for metaphoric creation to take place.

* * *

For in the analysis of dreams, Freud intends only to give us the laws of the unconscious in their most general extension.[4] One of the reasons why dreams were most propitious for this demonstration is exactly, Freud tells us, that they reveal the same laws whether in the normal person or in the neurotic.

But in either case, the efficacy of the unconscious does not cease in the waking state. The psychoanalytic experience does nothing other than establish that the unconscious leaves none of our actions outside its field. The presence of the unconscious in the psychological order, in other words in the relation-functions of the individual, should, however, be more precisely defined: it is not coextensive with that order, for we know that if unconscious motivation is manifest in conscious psychical effects, as well as in unconscious ones, conversely it is only elementary to recall to mind that a large number of psychical effects that are quite legitimately designated as unconscious, in the sense of excluding the characteristic of consciousness, are nonetheless without any relation whatever to the unconscious in the Freudian sense. So it is only by an abuse of the term that unconscious in that sense is confused with psychical, and that one may thus designate as psychical what is in fact an effect of the unconscious, as on the somatic for instance.

It is a matter, therefore, of defining the topography of this unconscious. I say that it is the very topography defined by the algorithm:

$$\frac{S}{s}$$

What we have been able to develop concerning the effects of the signifier on the signified suggests its transformation into:[5]

$$f(S)\frac{I}{s}$$

We have shown the effects not only of the elements of the horizontal signifying chain, but also of its vertical dependencies in the signified, divided into two fundamental structures called metonymy and metaphor. We can symbolize them by, first:[6]

$$f(S \ldots S')S \cong S(-)s$$

that is to say, the metonymic structure, indicating that it is the connexion between signifier and signifier that permits the elision in which the signifier installs the lack-of-being in the object relation, using the value of 'reference back' possessed by signification in order to invest it with the desire aimed at the very lack it supports. The sign – placed between ( ) represents here the maintenance of the bar – which, in the original algorithm, marked

4. On SIGMUND FREUD (1856–1939), the Austrian founder of psychoanalysis, see above; *The Interpretation of Dreams* (1900) was his seminal work.
5. According to the equation, the function of the signifier is in inverse relation to (depends on the repression of) the signified.
6. According to the equation, the metonymic connection ("signifying chain") among signifiers depends on maintaining the bar of repression.

the irreducibility in which, in the relations between signifier and signified, the resistance of signification is constituted.[7]

Secondly,[8]

$$f\left(\frac{S'}{S}\right)S \cong S(+)s$$

the metaphoric structure indicating that it is in the substitution of signifier for signifier that an effect of signification is produced that is creative or poetic, in other words, which is the advent of the signification in question.[9] The sign + between ( ) represents here the crossing of the bar – and the constitutive value of this crossing for the emergence of signification.

This crossing expresses the condition of passage of the signifier into the signified that I pointed out above, although provisionally confusing it with the place of the subject.

It is the function of the subject, thus introduced, that we must now turn to since it lies at the crucial point of our problem.

'I think, therefore I am' (*cogito ergo sum*)[1] is not merely the formula in which is constituted, with the historical high point of reflection on the conditions of science, the link between the transparency of the transcendental subject and his existential affirmation.

Perhaps I am only object and mechanism (and so nothing more than phenomenon), but assuredly in so far as I think so, I am—absolutely. No doubt philosophers have brought important corrections to this formulation, notably that in that which thinks (*cogitans*), I can never constitute myself as anything but object (*cogitatum*). Nonetheless it remains true that by way of this extreme purification of the transcendental subject,[2] my existential link to its project seems irrefutable, at least in its present form, and that: *'cogito ergo sum' ubi cogito, ibi sum*,[3] overcomes this objection.

Of course, this limits me to being there in my being only in so far as I think that I am in my thought; just how far I actually think this concerns only myself and if I say it, interests no one.[4]

Yet to elude this problem on the pretext of its philosophical pretensions is simply to admit one's inhibition. For the notion of subject is indispensable even to the operation of a science such as strategy (in the modern sense) whose calculations exclude all 'subjectivism'.

It is also to deny oneself access to what might be called the Freudian universe—in the way that we speak of the Copernican universe.[5] It was in

7. The sign ≅ here designates congruence [Lacan's note].

8. According to the equation, the metaphoric connection "crosses over"—it breaks through the bar between the unconscious signified and the signifying chain.

9. S' designating here the term productive of the signifying effect (or significance); one can see that the term is latent in metonymy, patent in metaphor [Lacan's note].

1. The Latin is the foundational statement of the French philosopher René Descartes (1596–1650), who relied on this certainty of existence to deduce other truths. Lacan will subtly critique American "ego psychology" for modeling the psyche on this attempt to make "thinking" coincide with "being," or to make the unconscious more like consciousness.

2. That is, the subject abstractly considered, outside of any experience.

3. Where I think, there I am (Latin).

4. It is quite otherwise if by posing a question such as "Why philosophers?" I become more candid than nature, for then I am asking not only the question that philosophers have been asking themselves for all time, but also the one in which they are perhaps most interested [Lacan's note].

5. That is, the universe at whose center was the sun, as the Polish astronomer Nicolaus Copernicus (1473–1543) suggested, and not the earth, as the Egyptian astronomer Ptolemy (active 127–148 C.E.) had believed. Freud compares his discoveries to a Copernican revolution in his *Introductory Lectures on Psychoanalysis* (1917).

fact the so-called Copernican revolution to which Freud himself compared his discovery, emphasizing that it was once again a question of the place man assigns to himself at the centre of a universe.

Is the place that I occupy as the subject of a signifier concentric or excentric, in relation to the place I occupy as subject of the signified?—that is the question.

It is not a question of knowing whether I speak of myself in a way that conforms to what I am, but rather of knowing whether I am the same as that of which I speak. And it is not at all inappropriate to use the word 'thought' here. For Freud uses the term to designate the elements involved in the unconscious, that is the signifying mechanisms that we now recognize as being there.

It is nonetheless true that the philosophical *cogito* is at the centre of the mirage that renders modern man so sure of being himself even in his uncertainties about himself, and even in the mistrust he has learned to practise against the traps of self-love.

Furthermore, if, turning the weapon of metonymy against the nostalgia that it serves, I refuse to seek any meaning beyond tautology, if in the name of 'war is war' and 'a penny's a penny' I decide to be only what I am, how even here can I elude the obvious fact that I am in that very act?

And it is no less true if I take myself to the other, metaphoric pole of the signifying quest, and if I dedicate myself to becoming what I am, to coming into being, I cannot doubt that even if I lose myself in the process, I am in that process.

Now it is on these very points, where evidence will be subverted by the empirical, that the trick of the Freudian conversion lies.

This signifying game between metonymy and metaphor, up to and including the active edge that splits my desire between a refusal of the signifier and a lack of being, and links my fate to the question of my destiny, this game, in all its inexorable subtlety, is played until the match is called,[6] there where I am not, because I cannot situate myself there.

That is to say, what is needed is more than these words with which, for a brief moment I disconcerted my audience: I think where I am not, therefore I am where I do not think. Words that render sensible to an ear properly attuned with what elusive ambiguity[7] the ring of meaning flees from our grasp along the verbal thread.

What one ought to say is: I am not wherever I am the plaything of my thought; I think of what I am where I do not think to think.

This two-sided mystery is linked to the fact that the truth can be evoked only in that dimension of alibi in which all 'realism' in creative works takes its virtue from metonymy; it is likewise linked to this other fact that we accede to meaning only through the double twist of metaphor when we have the one and only key: the S and the *s* of the Saussurian algorithm are not on the same level, and man only deludes himself when he believes his true place is at their axis, which is nowhere.

6. That is, until I die.

7. "*Ambiguité de furet*"—literally, "ferret-like ambiguity." This is one of a number of references in Lacan to the game "hunt-the-slipper" (*jeu du furet*) [translator's note]. The wordplay depends on the name of the game (literally, "game of the ferret"), not the animal. "Hunt-the-slipper" is also known as "button, button, who's got the button."

Was nowhere, that is, until Freud discovered it; for if what Freud discovered isn't that, it isn't anything.

* * *

1957

The Signification of the Phallus[1]

The following is the original, unaltered text of a lecture that I delivered in German on 9 May, 1958, at the Max-Planck Institute, Munich, where Professor Paul Matussek had invited me to speak.

If one has any notion of the state of mind then prevalent in even the least unaware circles, one will appreciate the effect that my use of such terms as, for example, 'the other scene', which I was the first to extract from Freud's work, must have had.

If 'deferred action' (*Nachtrag*), to rescue another of these terms from the facility into which they have since fallen, renders this effort impracticable, it should be known that they were unheard of at that time.

We know that the unconscious castration complex[2] has the function of a knot:

(1) in the dynamic structuring of symptoms in the analytic sense of the term, that is to say, in that which is analysable in the neuroses, perversions, and psychoses;

(2) in a regulation of the development that gives its *ratio* to this first role: namely, the installation in the subject of an unconscious position without which he would be unable to identify himself with the ideal type of his sex, or to respond without grave risk to the needs of his partner in the sexual relation, or even to accept in a satisfactory way the needs of the child who may be produced by this relation.

There is an antinomy, here, that is internal to the assumption by man (*Mensch*)[3] of his sex: why must he assume the attributes of that sex only through a threat—the threat, indeed, of their privation? In 'Civilization and its Discontents' Freud, as we know, went so far as to suggest a disturbance of human sexuality, not of a contingent, but of an essential kind, and one of his last articles concerns the irreducibility in any finite (*endliche*) analysis of the sequellae[4] resulting from the castration complex in the masculine unconscious and from *penisneid*[5] in the unconscious of women.

1. Translated by Alan Sheridan, who occasionally includes the original French or German in parentheses.
2. A more general understanding of the castration complex theorized by SIGMUND FREUD. For Freud, "castration anxiety" was the fear of every male child that his desire to sleep with his mother would lead to his castration by his father (see *Three Essays on the Theory of Sexuality*, 1905).
3. A human being of either sex (German).
4. Secondary consequences. *Civilization and Its Discontents* was published in 1930.
5. Penis envy (German).

This is not the only aporia,[6] but it is the first that the Freudian experience and the metapsychology that resulted from it introduced into our experience of man. It is insoluble by any reduction to biological givens: the very necessity of the myth subjacent to the structuring of the Oedipus complex[7] demonstrates this sufficiently.

It would be mere trickery to invoke in this case some hereditary amnesic trait, not only because such a trait is in itself debatable, but because it leaves the problem unsolved: namely, what is the link between the murder of the father and the pact of the primordial law, if it is included in that law that castration should be the punishment for incest?

It is only on the basis of the clinical facts that any discussion can be fruitful. These facts reveal a relation of the subject to the phallus that is established without regard to the anatomical difference of the sexes, and which, by this very fact, makes any interpretation of this relation especially difficult in the case of women. This problem may be treated under the following four headings:

(1) from this 'why', the little girl considers herself, if only momentarily, as castrated, in the sense of deprived of the phallus, by someone, in the first instance by her mother, an important point, and then by her father, but in such a way that one must recognize in it a transference in the analytic sense of the term;
(2) from this 'why', in a more primordial sense, the mother is considered, by both sexes, as possessing the phallus, as the phallic mother;
(3) from this 'why', correlatively, the signification of castration in fact takes on its (clinically manifest) full weight as far as the formation of symptoms is concerned, only on the basis of its discovery as castration of the mother;
(4) these three problems lead, finally, to the question of the reason, in development, for the phallic stage.[8] We know that in this term Freud specifies the first genital maturation: on the one hand, it would seem to be characterized by the imaginary dominance of the phallic attribute and by masturbatory *jouissance*[9] and, on the other, it localizes this *jouissance* for the woman in the clitoris, which is thus raised to the function of the phallus. It therefore seems to exclude in both sexes, until the end of this stage, that is, to the decline of the Oedipal stage, all instinctual mapping of the vagina as locus of genital penetration.

This ignorance is suspiciously like *méconnaissance*[1] in the technical sense of the term—all the more so in that it is sometimes quite false. Does this not bear out the fable in which Longus[2] shows us the initiation of Daphnis and Chloe subordinated to the explanations of an old woman?

Thus certain authors have been led to regard the phallic stage as the effect of a repression, and the function assumed in it by the phallic object as a

6. Difficulty, logical impasse (a term often used in deconstructive criticism to indicate the point in a text where inherent contradictions render interpretation undecidable).
7. The universal internalization by the male child of the prohibited desire for his mother and the love-hate relation to his father, as posited by Freud.
8. According to Freud, the stages through which the child passes are the oral, anal, phallic, and (if the Oedipal complex is successfully resolved) genital (i.e., mature sexuality).
9. Orgasm (French).
1. Misrecognition; misprision (French).
2. Greek author (dates highly uncertain; 2d–6th c. C.E.) credited with writing the first pastoral prose romance, *Daphnis and Chloë*, which tells of two foundlings brought up by shepherds who meet in childhood and gradually fall in love.

symptom. The difficulty begins when one asks, *what* symptom? Phobia, says one, perversion, says another, both, says a third. It seems in the last case that nothing more can be said: not that interesting transmutations of the object of a phobia into a fetish do not occur, but if they are interesting it is precisely on account of the difference of their place in the structure. It would be pointless to demand of these authors that they formulate this difference from the perspectives currently in favour, that is to say, in terms of the object relation. Indeed, there is no other reference on the subject than the approximate notion of part-object, which—unfortunately, in view of the convenient uses to which it is being put in our time, has never been subjected to criticism since Karl Abraham[3] introduced it.

The fact remains that the now abandoned discussion of the phallic stage, to be found in the surviving texts of the years 1928–32, is refreshing for the example it sets us of a *devotion to doctrine*—to which the degradation of psychoanalysis consequent on its *American transplantation* adds a note of nostalgia.

Merely to summarize the debate would be to distort the authentic diversity of the positions taken up by a Helene Deutsch, a Karen Horney, and an Ernest Jones,[4] to mention only the most eminent.

The series of three articles devoted by Jones to the subject are especially fruitful—if only for the development of the notion of *aphanisis*, a term that he himself had coined.[5] For, in positing so correctly the problem of the relation between castration and desire, he demonstrates his inability to recognize what he nevertheless grasped so clearly that the term that earlier provided us with the key to it seems to emerge from his very failure.

Particularly amusing is the way in which he manages to extract from a letter by Freud himself a position that is strictly contrary to it: an excellent model in a difficult *genre*.

Yet the matter refuses to rest there, Jones appearing to contradict his own case for a re-establishment of the equality of natural rights (does he not win the day with the Biblical 'God created them man and woman' with which his plea concludes?). In fact, what has he gained in normalizing the function of the phallus as a part-object if he has to invoke its presence in the mother's body as an internal object, which term is a function of the phantasies revealed by Melanie Klein,[6] and if he cannot separate himself from Klein's view that these phantasies originate as far back as in early childhood, during Oedipal formation?

It might be a good idea to re-examine the question by asking what could have necessitated for Freud the evident paradox of his position. For one has to admit that he was better guided than anyone in his recognition of the order of unconscious phenomena, of which he was the inventor, and that,

3. German psychoanalyst (1877–1925), who focused on child sexual development. "Part-object": the tendency of a child to relate to parts rather than to complete objects (e.g., to the breast rather than the mother).

4. All early psychoanalysts: Deutsch (1884–1982), a Polish-born American who wrote on the psychology of women; Horney (1885–1952), a German-born American who rejected the notion of penis envy; and Jones (1879–1958), a British champion of psychoanalysis who wrote the first definitive biography of Freud (3 vols., 1953–57).

5. *Aphanisis*, the disappearance of sexual desire. This Greek term was introduced into psychoanalysis by Jones in "Early Development of Female Sexuality" (1927), in *Papers on Psycho-analysis*, 5th ed. (London, 1950). For Jones, the fear of aphanisis exists, in both boys and girls, at a deeper level than the castration complex [translator's note].

6. Austrian-born English psychoanalyst (1882–1960), particularly interested in early mother-child relations.

failing an adequate articulation of the nature of these phenomena, his followers were doomed to lose their way to a greater or lesser degree.

It is on the basis of the following bet—which I lay down as the principle of a commentary of Freud's work that I have pursued during the past seven years—that I have been led to certain results: essentially, to promulgate as necessary to any articulation of analytic phenomena the notion of the signifier, as opposed to that of the signified, in modern linguistic analysis.[7] Freud could not take this notion, which postdates him, into account, but I would claim that Freud's discovery stands out precisely because, although it set out from a domain in which one could not expect to recognize its reign, it could not fail to anticipate its formulas. Conversely, it is Freud's discovery that gives to the signifier / signified opposition the full extent of its implications: namely, that the signifier has an active function in determining certain effects in which the signifiable appears as submitting to its mark, by becoming through that passion the signified.

This passion of the signifier now becomes a new dimension of the human condition in that it is not only man who speaks, but that in man and through man *it* speaks (*ça parle*), that his nature is woven by effects in which is to be found the structure of language, of which he becomes the material, and that therefore there resounds in him, beyond what could be conceived of by a psychology of ideas, the relation of speech.

In this sense one can say that the consequences of the discovery of the unconscious have not yet been so much as glimpsed in theory, although its effects have been felt in praxis to a greater degree than perhaps we are aware of, if only in the form of effects of retreat.

It should be made clear that this advocacy of man's relation to the signifier as such has nothing to do with a 'culturalist' position in the ordinary sense of the term, the position in which Karen Horney, for example, was anticipated in the dispute concerning the phallus by a position described by Freud himself as a feminist one. It is not a question of the relation between man and language as a social phenomenon, there being no question even of something resembling the ideological psychogenesis with which we are familiar, and which is not superseded by peremptory recourse to the quite metaphysical notion, which lurks beneath its question-begging appeal to the concrete, conveyed so pitifully by the term 'affect'.

It is a question of rediscovering in the laws that govern that other scene (*ein andere Schauplatz*),[8] which Freud, on the subject of dreams, designates as being that of the unconscious, the effects that are discovered at the level of the chain of materially unstable elements that constitutes language: effects determined by the double play of combination and substitution in the signifier, according to the two aspects that generate the signified, metonymy and metaphor; determining effects for the institution of the subject. From this test, a *topology*, in the mathematical sense of the term,[9] appears, without

7. The sign was divided into *signified* (the meaning conveyed) and *signifier* (the symbol or sound that conveys that meaning) by the Swiss linguist FERDINAND DE SAUSSURE (1857–1913).

8. Another theater (German). Freud, in *The Interpretation of Dreams*, uses this metaphor to refer to conscious and unconscious processes. Lacan extends this "topological" model of psychic location, suggesting that while a bourgeois drama may be playing on the main stage, a Greek tragedy is being performed somewhere else.

9. That is, the study of a figure's properties that are unchanged by such deformations as stretching.

which one soon realizes that is impossible simply to note the structure of a symptom in the analytic sense of the term.

It speaks in the Other, I say, designating by the Other the very locus evoked by the recourse to speech in any relation in which the Other intervenes. If *it* speaks in the Other, whether or not the subject hears it with his ear, it is because it is there that the subject, by means of a logic anterior to any awakening of the signified, finds its signifying place. The discovery of what it articulates in that place, that is to say, in the unconscious, enables us to grasp at the price of what splitting (*Spaltung*) it has thus been constituted.[1]

The phallus reveals its function here. In Freudian doctrine, the phallus is not a phantasy, if by that we mean an imaginary effect. Nor is it as such an object (part-, internal, good, bad, etc.) in the sense that this term tends to accentuate the reality pertaining in a relation. It is even less the organ, penis or clitoris, that it symbolizes. And it is not without reason that Freud used the reference to the simulacrum that it represented for the Ancients.

For the phallus is a signifier, a signifier whose function, in the intra-subjective economy of the analysis, lifts the veil perhaps from the function it performed in the mysteries. For it is the signifier intended to designate as a whole the effects of the signified,[2] in that the signifier conditions them by its presence as a signifier.

Let us now examine the effects of this presence. In the first instance, they proceed from a deviation of man's needs from the fact that he speaks, in the sense that in so far as his needs are subjected to demand, they return to him alienated. This is not the effect of his real dependence (one should not expect to find here the parasitic conception represented by the notion of dependence in the theory of neurosis), but rather the turning into signifying form as such, from the fact that it is from the locus of the Other that its message is emitted.

That which is thus alienated in needs constitutes an *Urverdrängung* (primal repression), an inability, it is supposed, to be articulated in demand, but it re-appears in something it gives rise to that presents itself in man as desire (*das Begehren*). The phenomenology that emerges from analytic experience is certainly of a kind to demonstrate in desire the paradoxical, deviant, erratic, eccentric, even scandalous character by which it is distinguished from need. This fact has been too often affirmed not to have been always obvious to moralists worthy of the name. The Freudianism of earlier days seemed to owe its status to this fact. Paradoxically, however, psychoanalysis is to be found at the head of an ever-present obscurantism that is still more boring when it denies the fact in an ideal of theoretical and practical reduction of desire to need.

This is why we must articulate this status here, beginning with *demand*, whose proper characteristics are eluded in the notion of frustration (which Freud never used).

1. In other words, the subject is "split" by language: even the most nonverbal of needs are formulated through the "elsewhere" that the system of language constitutes.

2. Lacan writes that the phallic signifier designates as a whole "les effets DE signifié" ("signified-effects," like "sound effects" or "special effects"), not "les effets DU signifié," which would imply that the signified functions as a knowable cause.

Demand in itself bears on something other than the satisfactions it calls for. It is demand of a presence or of an absence—which is what is manifested in the primordial relation to the mother, pregnant with that Other to be situated *within* the needs that it can satisfy. Demand constitutes the Other as already possessing the 'privilege' of satisfying needs, that it is to say, the power of depriving them of that alone by which they are satisfied. This privilege of the Other thus outlines the radical form of the gift of that which the Other does not have, namely, its love.

In this way, demand annuls (*aufhebt*) the particularity of everything that can be granted by transmuting it into a proof of love, and the very satisfactions that it obtains for need are reduced (*sich erniedrigt*) to the level of being no more than the crushing of the demand for love (all of which is perfectly apparent in the psychology of child-rearing, to which our analyst-nurses are so attached).

It is necessary, then, that the particularity thus abolished should reappear *beyond* demand. It does, in fact, reappear there, but preserving the structure contained in the unconditional element of the demand for love. By a reversal that is not simply a negation of the negation, the power of pure loss emerges from the residue of an obliteration. For the unconditional element of demand, desire substitutes the 'absolute' condition: this condition unties the knot of that element in the proof of love that is resistant to the satisfaction of a need. Thus desire is neither the appetite for satisfaction, nor the demand for love, but the difference that results from the subtraction of the first from the second, the phenomenon of their splitting (*Spaltung*).

One can see how the sexual relation occupies this closed field of desire, in which it will play out its fate. This is because it is the field made for the production of the enigma that this relation arouses in the subject by doubly 'signifying' it to him: the return of the demand that it gives rise to, as a demand on the subject of the need—an ambiguity made present on to the Other in question in the proof of love demanded. The gap in this enigma betrays what determines it, namely, to put it in the simplest possible way, that for both partners in the relation, both the subject and the Other, it is not enough to be subjects of need, or objects of love, but that they must stand for the cause of desire.

This truth lies at the heart of all the distortions that have appeared in the field of psychoanalysis on the subject of the sexual life. It also constitutes the condition of the happiness of the subject: and to disguise the gap it creates by leaving it to the virtue of the 'genital' to resolve it through the maturation of tenderness (that is to say, solely by recourse to the Other as reality), however well intentioned, is fraudulent nonetheless. It has to be said here that the French analysts, with their hypocritical notion of genital oblativity,[3] opened the way to the moralizing tendency, which, to the accompaniment of its Salvationist choirs, is now to be found everywhere.

In any case, man cannot aim at being whole (the 'total personality' is another of the deviant premises of modern psychotherapy), while ever the play of displacement and condensation to which he is doomed in the exercise of his functions marks his relation as a subject to the signifier.

3. A mature form of love in which it is the person as a whole, and not what he or she can give, that is loved.

The phallus is the privileged signifier of that mark in which the role of the logos[4] is joined with the advent of desire.

It can be said that this signifier is chosen because it is the most tangible element in the real of sexual copulation, and also the most symbolic in the literal (typographical) sense of the term, since it is equivalent there to the (logical) copula. It might also be said that, by virtue of its turgidity, it is the image of the vital flow as it is transmitted in generation.

All these propositions merely conceal the fact that it can play its role only when veiled, that is to say, as itself a sign of the latency with which any signifiable is struck, when it is raised (*aufgehoben*) to the function of signifier.

The phallus is the signifier of this *Aufhebung*[5] itself, which it inaugurates (initiates) by its disappearance. That is why the demon of *Αἰδως* (*Scham*, shame) arises at the very moment when, in the ancient mysteries, the phallus is unveiled (cf. the famous painting in the Villa di Pompei[6]).

It then becomes the bar which, at the hands of this demon, strikes the signified,[7] marking it as the bastard offspring of this signifying concatenation.

Thus a condition of complementarity is produced in the establishment of the subject by the signifier—which explains the *Spaltung* in the subject and the movement of intervention in which that 'splitting' is completed.

Namely:

(1) that the subject designates his being only by barring everything he signifies, as it appears in the fact that he wants to be loved for himself, a mirage that cannot be dismissed as merely grammatical (since it abolishes discourse);

(2) that the living part of that being in the *urverdrängt* (primally repressed) finds its signifier by receiving the mark of the *Verdrängung* (repression) of the phallus (by virtue of which the unconscious is language).

The phallus as signifier gives the ratio of desire (in the sense in which the term is used in music in the 'mean and extreme ratio' of harmonic division).

I shall also be using the phallus as an algorithm, so if I am to help you to grasp this use of the term I shall have to rely on the echoes of the experience that we share—otherwise, my account of the problem could go on indefinitely.

The fact that the phallus is a signifier means that it is in the place of the Other that the subject has access to it. But since this signifier is only veiled, as ratio of the Other's desire, it is this desire of the Other as such that the subject must recognize, that is to say, the other in so far as he is himself a subject divided by the signifying *Spaltung*.

The emergences that appear in psychological genesis confirm this signifying function of the phallus.

4. Word, speech (Greek).

5. Raising, abolition (German), a term taken from the German philosopher GEORG WILHELM FRIEDRICH HEGEL (1770–1831). The verb *aufheben*, which means "to annul," "to preserve," and "to raise," is often translated "to sublate."

6. In the entrance hall of Pompeii's House of the Vettii is a fresco of the fertility god Priapus weighing his enormous phallus.

7. On this "bar," see Lacan's "Agency of the Letter in the Unconscious" (1957; above).

Thus, to begin with, the Kleinian fact that the child apprehends from the outset that the mother 'contains' the phallus may be formulated more correctly.

But it is in the dialectic[8] of the demand for love and the test of desire that development is ordered.

The demand for love can only suffer from a desire whose signifier is alien to it. If the desire of the mother *is* the phallus, the child wishes to be the phallus in order to satisfy that desire. Thus the division immanent in desire is already felt to be experienced in the desire of the Other, in that it is already opposed to the fact that the subject is content to present to the Other what in reality he may *have* that corresponds to this phallus, for what he has is worth no more than what he does not have, as far as his demand for love is concerned because that demand requires that he be the phallus.

Clinical experience has shown us that this test of the desire of the Other is decisive not in the sense that the subject learns by it whether or not he has a real phallus, but in the sense that he learns that the mother does not have it. This is the moment of the experience without which no symptomatic consequence (phobia) or structural consequence (*Penisneid*) relating to the castration complex can take effect. Here is signed the conjunction of desire, in that the phallic signifier is its mark, with the threat or nostalgia of lacking it.

Of course, its future depends on the law introduced by the father into this sequence.

But one may, simply by reference to the function of the phallus, indicate the structures that will govern the relations between the sexes.

Let us say that these relations will turn around a 'to be' and a 'to have', which, by referring to a signifier, the phallus, have the opposed effect, on the one hand, of giving reality to the subject in this signifier, and, on the other, of derealizing the relations to be signified.

This is brought about by the intervention of a 'to seem' that replaces the 'to have', in order to protect it on the one side, and to mask its lack in the other, and which has the effect of projecting in their entirety the ideal or typical manifestations of the behaviour of each sex, including the act of copulation itself, into the comedy.

These ideals take on new vigour from the demand that they are capable of satisfying, which is always a demand for love, with its complement of the reduction of desire to demand.

Paradoxical as this formulation may seem, I am saying that it is in order to be the phallus, that is to say, the signifier of the desire of the Other, that a woman will reject an essential part of femininity, namely, all her attributes in the masquerade.[9] It is for that which she is not that she wishes to be desired as well as loved. But she finds the signifier of her own desire in the body of him to whom she addresses her demand for love. Perhaps it should not be forgotten that the organ that assumes this signifying function takes on the value of a fetish. But the result for the woman remains that an experience of love, which, as such (cf. above), deprives her ideally of that which the object gives, and a desire which finds its signifier in this object, converge on

8. Reciprocal interaction.
9. An allusion to Joan Riviere's famous 1929 essay, "Womanliness as a Masquerade."

the same object. That is why one can observe that a lack in the satisfaction proper to sexual need, in other words, frigidity, is relatively well tolerated in women, whereas the *Verdrängung* (repression) inherent in desire is less present in women than in men.

In the case of men, on the other hand, the dialectic of demand and desire engenders the effects—and one must once more admire the sureness with which Freud situated them at the precise articulations on which they depended—of a specific depreciation (*Erniedrigung*) of love.

If, in effect, the man finds satisfaction for his demand for love in the relation with the woman, in as much as the signifier of the phallus constitutes her as giving in love what she does not have—conversely, his own desire for the phallus will make its signifier emerge in its persistent divergence towards 'another woman' who may signify this phallus in various ways, either as a virgin or as a prostitute. There results from this a centrifugal tendency of the genital drive in love life, which makes impotence much more difficult to bear for him, while the *Verdrängung* inherent in desire is more important.

Yet it should not be thought that the sort of infidelity that would appear to be constitutive of the male function is proper to it. For if one looks more closely, the same redoubling is to be found in the woman, except that the Other of Love as such, that is to say, in so far as he is deprived of what he gives, finds it difficult to see himself in the retreat in which he is substituted for the being of the very man whose attributes she cherishes.

One might add here that male homosexuality, in accordance with the phallic mark that constitutes desire, is constituted on the side of desire, while female homosexuality, on the other hand, as observation shows, is orientated on a disappointment that reinforces the side of the demand for love. These remarks should really be examined in greater detail, from the point of view of a return to the function of the mask in so far as it dominates the identifications in which refusals of demand are resolved.

The fact that femininity finds its refuge in this mask, by virtue of the fact of the *Verdrängung* inherent in the phallic mark of desire, has the curious consequence of making virile display in the human being itself seem feminine.

Correlatively, one can glimpse the reason for a characteristic that had never before been elucidated, and which shows once again the depth of Freud's intuition: namely, why he advances the view that there is only one *libido*,[1] his text showing that he conceives it as masculine in nature. The function of the phallic signifier touches here on its most profound relation: that in which the Ancients embodied the Νοῦς and the Λογὸς.[2]

1958

1. Desire (Latin).

2. "Mind" and "Word" (Greek).

LANGSTON HUGHES
1902–1967

The most celebrated African American writer of the first half of the twentieth century, Langston Hughes was a poet, playwright, and fiction writer who also worked tirelessly to promote black literature and, more generally, the status of black people in American society. Associated with the Harlem Renaissance, Hughes was interested in the relation of literature to the other arts; but he was particularly concerned with bridging the gap between "high" culture and the life of his people.

Hughes was born in Missouri and spent an impoverished childhood living with various relatives after his father, discouraged by American racism, moved to Mexico shortly after his birth. His mother was a Langston, born of a family that had played a prominent role in the fight against slavery. Among Hughes's Langston relatives were a veteran of John Brown's famous raid on Harpers Ferry in 1859 and a congressman from Virginia during the Reconstruction years. Hughes's life stabilized on joining his remarried mother in Cleveland when he was thirteen. After a successful four years at an integrated high school, he went to Columbia University for a year (1921–22) but dropped out.

Over the next four years, Hughes traveled widely, held a number of menial jobs, and published poetry in the journals that constituted the literary portion of the Harlem Renaissance—the outpouring of work in all the arts by young blacks during the 1920s and early 1930s. Hughes's work was included in Alain Locke's famous anthology *The New Negro* (1925), which announced the movement, and Hughes knew—and collaborated with—almost all the major figures of the Harlem Renaissance, though he did not himself spend much time in New York during the 1920s. His first book of poems, *Weary Blues*, was published in 1926, the same year he wrote the essay "The Negro Artist and the Racial Mountain" and enrolled in Lincoln University, the all-male black college in southeastern Pennsylvania from which he received his B.A.

During the 1930s Hughes was desperately poor, living on funds provided by patrons or on the earnings he could garner from poetry readings. Increasingly involved in radical causes, he wrote plays in support of the Scottsboro Boys (nine young black men from Alabama accused of raping two white women), spent almost a year in Russia, and served as a war correspondent during the Spanish Civil War. After World War II he taught at various universities, was called before the House Un-American Activities Committee as a suspected Communist, and lived to champion some of the young writers of the 1960s Black Arts Movement. Whether or not Hughes was a homosexual is a matter of dispute among scholars; not surprisingly, given the times and his position as a prominent representative of his race, Hughes was secretive about his sexual desires and experiences. Hughes's poetry remains his claim to fame since his death, but growing attention has been paid by critics to his fiction (both novels and short stories), plays, and nonfiction prose, which includes many essays of social advocacy and extensive travel writings in addition to his autobiographies.

His biographer Arnold Rampersad calls our selection, "The Negro Artist and the Racial Mountain" (1926), the "finest essay of Hughes's life." It was written for the *Nation* as a solicited response to an essay by George Schuyler called "The Negro-Art Hokum," which argued that the idea of a separate black American culture and aesthetic was untenable. Hughes's reply succinctly captures the varied pressures under which the African American artist labors. First and foremost, perhaps, is the problem of a heterogeneous audience. The Negro (to use Hughes's term) poet knows that both black and white people are potential readers of his work. Yet those two audiences have very different expectations and demands. To complicate matters even further, Hughes's ever-present sensitivity to class deprives him of any simple image of the black audience. "High-toned" blacks are mostly terrified by the artist, afraid that he will endanger their desperate hold on respectability. "O, be respectable, write about nice people, show how good we are," Hughes imagines them saying. The "low-down folks," on the other hand, "are not ashamed of [the artist]—if they know he exists at all." Whereas "the better class Negro would tell the artist what to do, the people at least let him alone." But it's hardly a happy situation for the writer caught between an anxious and an unaware black audience.

Meanwhile, "'Be stereotyped, don't go too far, don't shatter our illusions about you, don't amuse us too seriously. We will pay you,' say the whites." The Negro writer can win acclaim and fortune in the white world so long as he does nothing to disturb the whites' comfort, their conviction that they are good, enlightened people. The temptations created by these constraints are obvious. Just as the modernist artist often set out deliberately to shock and outrage the bourgeoisie, so the black artist will be tempted merely to shake the patronizing white audience out of its complacency.

Hughes intimates, without quite saying it directly, that the best work will please neither the black nor the white audience. (His example is Jean Toomer's *Cane*.) And like many modernists, he believes that such problems are best solved by developing an indifference to all audiences—by cultivating an art that is true to itself: "We younger Negro artists who create now intend to express our individual dark-skinned selves without fear or shame." Bravely and defiantly, Hughes proclaims that it "doesn't matter" if neither white nor colored audiences "are pleased" by this work. "Free within ourselves" and building "our temples for tomorrow," the younger artists are already creating "an honest American Negro literature."

Out of what material is that literature created? Here Hughes raises another recurring problem for African American writers. Despite his line about expressing "our individual dark-skinned selves," Hughes actually looks toward the collective experience of the black folk as the "great field of unused material ready for his art." Anticipating the black power movement of the 1960s, Hughes responds to America's persistent racism by insisting that "'I am a Negro—and beautiful.'" The black artist should "interest himself in interpreting the beauty of his own people." Hence the essay's essential move: the repudiation of a black middle and upper class that has alienated itself from the black folk; Hughes will celebrate the common people. The problem, of course, is that Hughes himself is not of the folk, and to "interpret" their "beauty" is not identical with "expressing" his own "dark-skinned" individuality. There is a sizable gap between the "they" who "furnish a wealth of colorful, distinctive material for any artist" and the artist who belongs more obviously with the classes Hughes wishes to repudiate.

Hughes strives to find a meeting place in African American music, especially jazz (but also the blues): "Jazz to me is one of the inherent expressions of Negro life in America." Music provides an entry point to the "Negro soul," offering themes to which "the Negro artist can give his racial individuality." Hughes hopes that jazz's merger of the folk and the artist can be reproduced in the other arts: theater, painting, dance. He believes that a "racial art" is already evident in the literature of the Harlem Renaissance.

Writing in 1926, Hughes is uneasy about "the present vogue in things Negro," and he is scathing in his 1940 autobiography about the whites who poured into Harlem in the 1920s to listen to black music in clubs (like the famous Cotton Club) that excluded black patrons and black employees (with the sole exception of the musicians). He knows that black artists want their voices to be heard and that they are, like all artists, hungry for acclaim as well as for an audience. But he worries about the price paid for gaining the attention of whites. The perils facing the black artist are so many—from self-loathing to currying the favor of whites to providing a safe window on the exotic world of the racial other—that success depends on an honesty and fearlessness that are almost too much to ask. But these very difficulties point to another source of material for the African American artist, for "when he chooses to touch on the relations between Negroes and whites in this country with their innumerable overtones and undertones, . . . there is an inexhaustible supply of themes at hand." In calling on the African American artist to affirm his race, to cut loose from white standards and white ideals of high culture, and to explore the experience of the black folk and the realities of racism, Hughes enunciates a program for and vision of black literature that is taken up again during the civil rights and black power movements of the mid-1950s to the early 1970s.

"The Negro Artist and the Racial Mountain" Keywords: Aesthetics, Identity, Popular Culture, Race and Ethnicity Studies, Vernacular Language

The Negro Artist and the Racial Mountain

One of the most promising of the young Negro poets[1] said to me once, "I want to be a poet—not a Negro poet," meaning, I believe, "I want to write like a white poet"; meaning subconsciously, "I would like to be a white poet"; meaning behind that, "I would like to be white." And I was sorry the young man said that, for no great poet has ever been afraid of being himself. And I doubted then that, with his desire to run away spiritually from his race, this boy would ever be a great poet. But this is the mountain standing in the way of any true Negro art in America—this urge within the race toward whiteness, the desire to pour racial individuality into the mold of American standardization, and to be as little Negro and as much American as possible.

But let us look at the immediate background of this young poet. His family is of what I suppose one would call the Negro middle class: people who are by no means rich yet never uncomfortable nor hungry—smug, contented, respectable folk, members of the Baptist church. The father goes to work every morning. He is a chief steward at a large white club. The mother sometimes does fancy sewing or supervises parties for the rich families of the town. The children go to a mixed school. In the home they read white papers and magazines. And the mother often says "Don't be like niggers" when the children are bad. A frequent phrase from the father is, "Look how well a white man does things." And so the word white comes to be unconsciously a symbol of all the virtues. It holds for the children beauty, morality, and money. The whisper of "I want to be white" runs silently through their minds. This young poet's home is, I believe, a fairly typical home of the colored middle class. One sees immediately how difficult it would be for an artist born in such a home to interest himself in interpreting the beauty of his own people. He is never taught to see that beauty. He is taught rather not to see it, or if he does, to be ashamed of it when it is not according to Caucasian patterns.

For racial culture the home of a self-styled "high-class" Negro has nothing better to offer. Instead there will perhaps be more aping of things white

1. According to Hughes's biographer Arnold Rampersad, this is almost certainly Countee Cullen (1903–1946), one of the African American poets associated with the Harlem Renaissance.

than in a less cultured or less wealthy home. The father is perhaps a doctor, lawyer, landowner, or politician. The mother may be a social worker, or a teacher, or she may do nothing and have a maid. Father is often dark but he has usually married the lightest woman he could find. The family attend a fashionable church where few really colored faces are to be found. And they themselves draw a color line. In the North they go to white theaters and white movies. And in the South they have at least two cars and a house "like white folks." Nordic manners, Nordic faces, Nordic hair, Nordic art (if any), and an Episcopal heaven. A very high mountain indeed for the would-be racial artist to climb in order to discover himself and his people.

But then there are the low-down folks, the so-called common element, and they are the majority—may the Lord be praised! The people who have their nip of gin on Saturday nights and are not too important to themselves or the community, or too well fed, or too learned to watch the lazy world go round. They live on Seventh Street in Washington or State Street in Chicago and they do not particularly care whether they are like white folks or anybody else. Their joy runs, bang! into ecstasy. Their religion soars to a shout. Work maybe a little today, rest a little tomorrow. Play awhile. Sing awhile. O, let's dance! These common people are not afraid of spirituals, as for a long time their more intellectual brethren were, and jazz is their child. They furnish a wealth of colorful, distinctive material for any artist because they still hold their own individuality in the face of American standardizations. And perhaps these common people will give to the world its truly great Negro artist, the one who is not afraid to be himself. Whereas the better-class Negro would tell the artist what to do, the people at least let him alone when he does appear. And they are not ashamed of him—if they know he exists at all. And they accept what beauty is their own without question.

Certainly there is, for the American Negro artist who can escape the restrictions the more advanced among his own group would put upon him, a great field of unused material ready for his art. Without going outside his race, and even among the better classes with their "white" culture and conscious American manners, but still Negro enough to be different, there is sufficient matter to furnish a black artist with a lifetime of creative work. And when he chooses to touch on the relations between Negroes and whites in this country with their innumerable overtones and undertones, surely, and especially for literature and the drama, there is an inexhaustible supply of themes at hand. To these the Negro artist can give his racial individuality, his heritage of rhythm and warmth, and his incongruous humor that so often, as in the Blues, becomes ironic laughter mixed with tears. But let us look again at the mountain.

A prominent Negro clubwoman in Philadelphia paid eleven dollars to hear Raquel Meller[2] sing Andalusian popular songs. But she told me a few weeks before she would not think of going to hear "that woman," Clara Smith,[3] a great black artist, sing Negro folksongs. And many an upper-class Negro church, even now, would not dream of employing a spiritual in its services.

2. Spanish singer (1888–1962) who made her highly successful New York debut in the spring of 1926 (with the New York Philharmonic). Andalusia is a region of Spain; Meller would introduce her Spanish songs by telling little stories about the folkways of the different regions from which they came.

3. African American blues singer (1894–1935) who performed regularly in Harlem throughout the 1920s.

The drab melodies in white folks' hymnbooks are much to be preferred. "We want to worship the Lord correctly and quietly. We don't believe in 'shouting.' Let's be dull like the Nordics," they say, in effect.

The road for the serious black artist, then, who would produce a racial art is most certainly rocky and the mountain is high. Until recently he received almost no encouragement for his work from either white or colored people. The fine novels of Chesnutt[4] go out of print with neither race noticing their passing. The quaint charm and humor of Dunbar's[5] dialect verse brought to him, in his day, largely the same kind of encouragement one would give a side-show freak (A colored man writing poetry! How odd!) or a clown (How amusing!).

The present vogue in things Negro, although it may do as much harm as good for the budding colored artist, has at least done this: it has brought him forcibly to the attention of his own people among whom for so long, unless the other race had noticed him beforehand, he was a prophet with little honor. I understand that Charles Gilpin[6] acted for years in Negro theaters without any special acclaim from his own, but when Broadway gave him eight curtain calls, Negroes, too, began to beat a tin pan in his honor. I know a young colored writer, a manual worker by day, who had been writing well for the colored magazines for some years, but it was not until he recently broke into the white publications and his first book was accepted by a prominent New York publisher that the "best" Negroes in his city took the trouble to discover that he lived there. Then almost immediately they decided to give a grand dinner for him. But the society ladies were careful to whisper to his mother that perhaps she'd better not come. They were not sure she would have an evening gown.

The Negro artist works against an undertow of sharp criticism and misunderstanding from his own group and unintentional bribes from the whites. "O, be respectable, write about nice people, show how good we are," say the Negroes. "Be stereotyped, don't go too far, don't shatter our illusions about you, don't amuse us too seriously. We will pay you," say the whites. Both would have told Jean Toomer[7] not to write "Cane." The colored people did not praise it. The white people did not buy it. Most of the colored people who did read "Cane" hate it. They are afraid of it. Although the critics gave it good reviews the public remained indifferent. Yet (excepting the work of Du Bois)[8] "Cane" contains the finest prose written by a Negro in America. And like the singing of Robeson,[9] it is truly racial.

But in spite of the Nordicized Negro intelligentsia and the desires of some white editors we have an honest American Negro literature already with us. Now I await the rise of the Negro theater. Our folk music, having achieved world-wide fame, offers itself to the genius of the great individual American Negro composer who is to come. And within the next decade I expect to see the work of a growing school of colored artists who paint and model the

4. Charles Chesnutt (1858–1932), African American novelist who lived in Cleveland and published most of his work between 1890 and 1910.

5. Paul Laurence Dunbar (1872–1906), African American poet who died young of tuberculosis. He was a major influence on Hughes.

6. African American actor and theater manager (1878–1930). He played the title role in Eugene O'Neill's *Emperor Jones* in 1920, the first black actor to play the lead in a Broadway production. His all-black Lafayette stock company was based in Harlem.

7. African American writer (1894–1967). His book *Cane* (1923), a formally experimental mixture of poetry and prose, was a major landmark in the Harlem Renaissance.

8. W. E. B. DU BOIS (1868–1963), African American historian, sociologist, political activist, and author; the foremost black intellectual and academic of the first half of the twentieth century.

9. Paul Robeson (1898–1976), African American stage actor, singer, and political activist.

beauty of dark faces and create with new technique the expressions of their own soul-world. And the Negro dancers who will dance like flame and the singers who will continue to carry our songs to all who listen—they will be with us in even greater numbers tomorrow.

Most of my own poems are racial in theme and treatment, derived from the life I know. In many of them I try to grasp and hold some of the meanings and rhythms of jazz. I am sincere as I know how to be in these poems and yet after every reading I answer questions like these from my own people: Do you think Negroes should always write about Negroes? I wish you wouldn't read some of your poems to white folks. How do you find anything interesting in a place like a cabaret? Why do you write about black people? You aren't black. What makes you do so many jazz poems?

But jazz to me is one of the inherent expressions of Negro life in America: the eternal tom-tom beating in the Negro soul—the tom-tom of revolt against weariness in a white world, a world of subway trains, and work, work, work; the tom-tom of joy and laughter, and pain swallowed in a smile. Yet the Philadelphia clubwoman is ashamed to say that her race created it and she does not like me to write about it. The old subconscious "white is best" runs through her mind. Years of study under white teachers, a lifetime of white books, pictures, and papers, and white manners, morals, and Puritan standards made her dislike the spirituals. And now she turns up her nose at jazz and all its manifestations—likewise almost everything else distinctly racial. She doesn't care for the Winold Reiss[1] portraits of Negroes because they are "too Negro." She does not want a true picture of herself from anybody. She wants the artist to flatter her, to make the white world believe that all Negroes are as smug and as near white in soul as she wants to be. But, to my mind, it is the duty of the younger Negro artist, if he accepts any duties at all from outsiders, to change through the force of his art that old whispering "I want to be white," hidden in the aspirations of his people, to "Why should I want to be white? I am a Negro—and beautiful!"

So I am ashamed for the black poet who says, "I want to be a poet, not a Negro poet," as though his own racial world were not as interesting as any other world. I am ashamed, too, for the colored artist who runs from the painting of Negro faces to the painting of sunsets after the manner of the academicians because he fears the strange un-whiteness of his own features. An artist must be free to choose what he does, certainly, but he must also never be afraid to do what he might choose.

Let the blare of Negro jazz bands and the bellowing voice of Bessie Smith[2] singing Blues penetrate the closed ears of the colored near-intellectuals until they listen and perhaps understand. Let Paul Robeson singing Water Boy, and Rudolph Fisher[3] writing about the streets of Harlem, and Jean Toomer holding the heart of Georgia in his hands, and Aaron Douglas[4] drawing strange black fantasies cause the smug Negro middle class to turn from their

1. German-born painter (1886–1953), best known for his portraits of Native Americans and African Americans. He contributed most of the illustrations to Alain Locke's pathbreaking anthology *The New Negro* (1925).
2. African American singer (ca. 1894–1937), known as "the Empress of the Blues."
3. African American short story writer and physician (1897–1934), associated with the Harlem Renaissance.
4. African American artist and educator (1899–1979), the most significant visual artist of the Harlem Renaissance. Douglas studied with Winold Reiss, and his work was included in Locke's *New Negro*.

white, respectable, ordinary books and papers to catch a glimmer of their own beauty. We younger Negro artists who create now intend to express our individual dark-skinned selves without fear or shame. If white people are pleased we are glad. If they are not, it doesn't matter. We know we are beautiful. And ugly too. The tom-tom cries and the tom-tom laughs. If colored people are pleased we are glad. If they are not, their displeasure doesn't matter either. We build our temples for tomorrow, strong as we know how, and we stand on top of the mountain, free within ourselves.

1926

LIONEL TRILLING
1905–1975

Lionel Trilling was a contemporary of the major theorists and practitioners of the New Criticism, including Robert Penn Warren, CLEANTH BROOKS, and WILLIAM K. WIMSATT JR. His first book, a study of the English poet-critic MATTHEW ARNOLD, was published in 1939, a year after Brooks and Warren's influential textbook of New Critical interpretation, *Understanding Poetry.* But in his teaching and writing, Trilling did not emphasize the explication of poems and other literary texts. While literature was his central field of interest, he was fundamentally an eloquent and wide-ranging cultural critic, not a close reader. In Trilling's view, the New Criticism excluded too much. It was narrowly academic, not historical, not worldly. Attentive to social and cultural issues, Trilling crafted and cultivated an identity for himself as an articulate generalist and elegant stylist whose essays—the essay became his preferred form—treated topics and themes in literature and criticism that led him toward general reflections on politics, education, psychoanalysis, and more.

For example, in his best-known book, *The Liberal Imagination*, an essay collection published in 1950, Trilling wrote literary criticism about American and English authors—Sherwood Anderson, HENRY JAMES, Mark Twain, Rudyard Kipling, WILLIAM WORDSWORTH, and F. Scott Fitzgerald. He also examined the Roman historian Tacitus, SIGMUND FREUD, and the sex researcher Alfred Kinsey, and he explored still other social, cultural, and historical topics in "Reality in America," "The Function of the Little Magazine," "Art and Neurosis," "The Sense of the Past," "Manners, Morals, and the Novel," "Art and Fortune," and "The Meaning of a Literary Idea."

The Liberal Imagination was an extraordinary success, selling more than 70,000 copies in hardcover and more than 100,000 in paperback. This book and Trilling's other written work, his position at Columbia, and his network of friendships and connections with New York writers and critics, editors, and publishers transformed him by the mid-1950s into an exemplary public intellectual—in the words of the scholar John Rodden, "America's first academic celebrity in the humanities."

Lionel Trilling was born in New York City on July 4, 1905, the son of eastern European Jews: David W. Trilling, first a tailor and then a maker of men's fur-lined coats, and Fannie Cohen, who had been born and educated in London. Trilling recalled that when he was a child, his mother read to him from the works of English writers such as Dickens and Kipling, and throughout his career he felt a special affinity with the English literary canon and culture. Trilling attended grammar school and high school in New York City and did his undergraduate and graduate work at Columbia (B.A., 1925; M.A., 1926; Ph.D., 1938).

In 1927, while a graduate student at Columbia, Trilling met Diana Rubin, another native New Yorker; her parents were Jewish immigrants from Poland, and in 1924 she had graduated from Radcliffe College, a women's liberal arts college that functioned as a female coordinate institution for the all-male Harvard College. They married in 1929, and, as Diana Trilling later observed, "with marriage I had entered Lionel's world. It was with his friends that I chiefly associated. They were not easy companions, these intellectuals. They were overbearing and arrogant, excessively competitive; they lacked magnanimity and often they lacked common courtesy. Ours was a cruelly judgmental society, often malicious and riddled with envy." The dynamic, intense, and demanding world of the New York Intellectuals that she describes has been much chronicled, teeming with literary and political rivalry and argument and with powerful, often brilliantly incisive and polemical writing. Among this loosely connected group in the 1930s and early 1940s, and affiliated with the journal *Partisan Review,* were the literary critic Philip Rahv, the art critics Clement Greenberg and Harold Rosenberg, the essayist and novelist Mary McCarthy, and the editor and cultural critic Dwight Macdonald; later participants in this heady New York City–based milieu were the critics Irving Howe, Alfred Kazin, and SUSAN SONTAG.

Dedicated to modernism in the arts and hostile to Soviet Communism, the New York Intellectuals sought, in Howe's formulation, "the union of politics and culture, with the politics radical and the culture cosmopolitan." These men and women, it has been said, very much resembled a family—because they fought with one another all the time. Sometimes, they are labeled (as they called themselves) a "herd of independent minds." What they had in common, as again Howe has remarked, was a commitment to an advanced alliance of "critical consciousness and political conscience." Diana Trilling, combative and contentious in her prose like many of her fellow New York Intellectuals, herself became an astute reviewer and a critic about literature, culture, and politics; a number of her essays are collected in *Claremont Essays* (1964), *We Must March My Darlings: A Critical Decade* (1977), and *Reviewing the Forties* (1978). She is the author as well of *The Beginning of the Journey: The Marriage of Diana and Lionel Trilling* (1993), a compelling and, in its revelations about Lionel Trilling's bouts of depression and alcoholism, unsettling memoir.

Trilling lived and worked in the midst of this intellectual scene in New York City, but without being confrontational. His concern was with ideas, not with names, personalities, or partisan disputes about literary and political positions. In his introduction to *The Portable Matthew Arnold* (1949), Trilling's summary of Arnold's style captures his sense of his own role: "He spoke of literature as one who loved it and lived in it; but he spoke too as one who knew the world and lived in the world and believed that literature was connected in a complex multitude of ways with actual practical life." Trilling's writing is suggestive, rather elusive, tending toward the philosophical; it is highly generalized, detached yet brooding and troubled in tone, and perhaps above all complicated. According to his colleague Jacques Barzun, Trilling typically replied to ideas and arguments expressed by others by saying, "It's complicated. . . . It's much more complicated. . . . It's very complicated." When the sociologist Richard Sennett said to Trilling, "You have no position; you are always in between," he answered, "Between is the only honest place to be."

Trilling taught first at the University of Wisconsin (1926–27), and then at Hunter College in New York City (1927–30). In 1931, he began teaching at Columbia, where he remained for the rest of his career. Trilling's first decade at Columbia was difficult for him because, as a Jew, he was regarded with suspicion and even hostility by some of his colleagues, who did not believe he could ever be wholly at one with Anglo-Saxon cultural values and with the great authors and Christian contexts of

English literature. From 1923 to 1931, Trilling had been a contributor to, and editorial assistant for, *The Menorah Journal*, a Jewish leftist periodical edited by Elliot Cohen that, on the one hand, was attached to Jewish culture but, on the other hand, aspired to bring about the full involvement of Jews in American intellectual life.

Through his work for *The Menorah Journal*, Trilling said that he and other Jewish writers found they could "define ourselves and our society; we could discover who we were and who we wished to be." Yet in the 1930s and later, he also insisted, "I do not think of myself as a Jewish writer," despite his uneasy situation at Columbia, where "my appointment to an instructorship was pretty openly regarded as an experiment and for some time my career in the College was conditioned by my being Jewish."

In 1936, Trilling nearly lost his job, after being told that as "a Freudian, a Marxist, and a Jew, I would be more comfortable teaching somewhere else"; he fought to stay on and prevailed. Following the publication of his dissertation on Matthew Arnold, in 1939 he became the first Jewish tenured English professor at Columbia, even as he was cautioned by his adviser not to use his own success "as a wedge to open the English department to more Jews." His second book, published in 1943, was a study of the English novelist E. M. Forster. Meanwhile, Trilling was writing essays and reviews for *Partisan Review*, the *Nation*, and the *New Republic*, establishing his reputation as a critic and a man of letters among readers outside the academy.

The great irony of Trilling's career is that this eminent critic desired above all to be a writer of fiction. He wrote a number of short stories in the 1940s, the most famous of which, "Of This Time, Of That Place," was published in *Partisan Review* in January–February 1943. He also published a novel, *The Middle of the Journey* (1947), which locates its characters in the midst of Cold War politics. In particular, the novel criticizes the tendency among liberals to retain a sentimental, corrupting attachment to the Soviet Union, excusing or not wanting to face the hideous cruelty and mass murder perpetuated by Stalin's regime. *The Middle of the Journey* is a meditative, absorbing novel but not really a vital one: it came across to readers in the late 1940s (as it does today) as a skillful seminar-like study of political ideas, populated with characters who represent positions that Trilling aligned against one another, as if in a debate. He never gave up his interest in the writing of fiction, and his papers include an unfinished second novel. But the critical response to *The Middle of the Journey* impelled Trilling to concentrate on a career as a critic. With the publication of *The Liberal Imagination*, he became a distinguished and honored presence, the foremost intellectual of the early Cold War era.

In the early 1950s, Trilling was elected to the American Academy of Arts and Letters, and he took part in literary and cultural programs sponsored by the Ford Foundation and the U.S. State Department. In 1955 he gave the prestigious Freud Anniversary Lecture to the New York Psychoanalytic Society, and in 1962 he prepared an abridgment of Ernest Jones's *The Life and Work of Sigmund Freud* (3 vols., 1953–57). Trilling also served during the 1950s as an editorial adviser for book clubs, writing short essays about the biographies, literary studies, and other books that these subscription services offered. He edited textbooks, including *The Experience of Literature: A Reader with Commentaries* (1967) and *Literary Criticism: An Introductory Reader* (1970), and co-edited the volumes on Victorian prose and poetry and on Romantic poetry and prose in *The Oxford Anthology of English Literature* (1973). In 1970, he was appointed university professor, the highest honor awarded to a faculty member at Columbia, and around the same time he lectured at Harvard (1969–70)—delivering lectures that formed the basis of his book *Sincerity and Authenticity* (1972)—and at Oxford (1972–73).

In his novel, in his essays of the 1940s, and in *The Liberal Imagination*, Trilling presented himself as a liberal critic of liberalism—a term that for him has a massive reach and inclusiveness, including communists, socialists, sympathizers with the Soviet Union, progressives, and (it seems) Democratic Party members. For Trilling, being liberal, or liberal minded, should mean openness, balance, nuance, the acceptance of multiple points of view and complexity—virtues and values that, in his judgment, liberalism had lost, in its politically and morally dangerous commitment to the making of a better society whatever the social and personal costs. For Trilling, the truly "liberal imagination" is a tragic one that acknowledges the risks and perils of liberal and radical ideas and projects for social change.

Trilling was highly respected for his resistance to liberalism, insistence on complexity, and dialectical turn of mind. But he also came in for sharp criticism. In *A Margin of Hope* (1982), Irving Howe recalled that the "most subtle and perhaps most influential mind in the culture of the fifties was that of Lionel Trilling"; but he stressed too that some liberal critics and intellectuals "felt that his work had come to serve as a high-toned justification for the increasingly accommodating moods of American intellectuals. . . . To a generation that in its youth had been persuaded, even coerced, to believe that action in the public world was a moral necessity, Trilling's critique of 'the liberal imagination' eased a turning away from all politics, whether liberal, radical, or conservative." In an essay published in the *Sewanee Review* in 1963, Joseph Frank made this point forcefully, declaring that "from a critic of the liberal imagination, Mr. Trilling has evolved into one of the least belligerent and most persuasive spokesmen of the conservative imagination."

One of Trilling's literary heroes was the Romantic poet John Keats, about whom he said: "Keats believed that life was given for him to find the right use of it, that it was a kind of continuous magical confrontation requiring to be met with the right answer. He believed that this answer was to be derived from intuition, courage, and the accumulation of experience. It was not, of course, to be a formula of any kind, not a piece of rationality, but rather a way of being and of acting." In his literary and cultural criticism, Trilling sought to counter formulaic thinking and taken-for-granted views about authors, texts, and positions, and for many years he was a beloved teacher and lecturer at Columbia. Among his students who went on to great success are the poets Allen Ginsberg, John Hollander, and Richard Howard and the critics Steven Marcus, Louis Menand, and Leon Wieseltier. Like the readers of Trilling's books, students were struck by his combination of passion for the life of the mind and cool contemplativeness—his care and his balance in judgment, forthright but measured, sage and shrewd.

With some extravagance, the scholar Peter Glassman remembered the impact of Trilling's lectures: "He referred occasionally to his notes, read frequently from each of the volumes he'd placed on his desk, and in his protracted extemporaneous discourse created exquisite prose. . . . He wanted us to consider how radically the imaginative arts, literature in particular, celebrate, institutionalize, and yet subvert the authority of civilization." This gets at one of the most important features of Trilling's work—one that the selection below, "On the Teaching of Modern Literature," dramatizes: the ambivalent power of literature, and the limits of this power.

In *The Liberal Imagination*, Trilling says that "literature is the human activity that takes the fullest and most precise account of variousness, possibility, complexity, and difficulty." "The most effective agent of the moral imagination," he contends, "has been the novel of the last two hundred years. . . . Its greatness and its practical usefulness lay in its unremitting work of involving the reader himself in the moral life, inviting him to put his own motives under examination, suggesting that reality is not as his conventional education has led him to see it." But in *Beyond Culture: Essays on Literature and Learning* (1965), a later collection of essays, Trilling emphasizes "that art does not always tell the truth and does not always point out the right way, that it can even generate falsehood and habituate us to it." Great literature, then, instructs us yet may also mislead us. It can be a force both for illumination and for falsehood and self-deception.

In addition to *The Liberal Imagination*, Trilling gathered essays, reviews, and lectures in a number of other collections. In *The Opposing Self: Nine Essays in Criticism* (1955), his essays on Keats, Henry James, and George Orwell are especially keen and imply a closeness of Trilling himself to the writers he describes. The essays in *A Gathering of Fugitives* (1956) are also stimulating and cover a wide range of authors, critics, and topics—he is insightful on Edmund Wilson, F. R. LEAVIS, and Edith Wharton. In *Beyond Culture*, Trilling surveys the life and work of Jane Austen, Nathaniel Hawthorne, Freud, and Isaac Babel, and he explores other topics in literary study and the humanities. *The Last Decade: Essays and Reviews, 1965–1975*, edited by Diana Trilling (1979), brings together pieces from the final ten years of Trilling's life, including important statements on Joyce, Austen, and Freud; a reflection on modern art; and a memoir of Trilling's relationship with Whittaker Chambers, an acquaintance as an undergraduate at Columbia, who testified to a U.S. Senate committee that his former friend Alger Hiss had been a member of the Communist Party and had given government documents to the Soviet Union. Chambers was the basis for the character Gifford Maxim in *The Middle of the Journey* and became a prominent anticommunist during the cold war.

Other key late essays by Trilling include "What Is Criticism?" (1970), which served as the introduction to his edited collection, *Literary Criticism: An Introductory Reader*; "Mind in the Modern World" (1972), delivered as the first Thomas Jefferson Lecture sponsored by the Humanities of the National Endowment for the Humanities; "Art, Will, and Necessity" (1973), a lecture presented at Cambridge University; and "The Uncertain Future of the Humanistic Educational Ideal" (1974), a paper delivered at a conference at the Aspen Institute for Humanistic Studies.

"On the Teaching of Modern Literature" is one of Trilling's most rewarding essays. First published as "On the Modern Element in Modern Literature" in *Partisan Review* 28.1 (January–February 1961), it was reprinted with the current title as the first essay in *Beyond Culture*. This essay is still pertinent to contemporary debate and discussion about the power of literature and the institutionalization of literature and criticism in colleges and universities, where teachers and students often interpret and write about modern texts that present unsparing, sometimes nihilistic critiques of family, community, society, work, education—everything that in day-to-day life we consider most important and believe we should cherish. What does it mean, for example, for a student to write his or her term paper about the grim narratives of Joseph Conrad, the bleak stories of Franz Kafka, the radically erotic novels of D. H. Lawrence? Trilling makes vividly clear how much these literary works shock and alarm him, yet at the same time he says he finds as a teacher that his students at Columbia are, it seems, comfortable and at ease with these texts and their themes of madness, despair, and alienation from middle-class society.

One of the limitations of Trilling's essay is that he defines modernism in relation to a limited range of major texts. Sir James Frazer, Freud, NIETZSCHE: these authors and others whom Trilling highlights are essential figures for an understanding of modernism, but there are no women or minority authors here. Trilling says little about poetry, nor does he make any reference to American literature or more generally to modernism in the arts, nationally and internationally. RAYMOND WILLIAMS, commenting in the *Manchester Guardian* (April 1966) on Trilling's essay, gets at this point when he notes with some severity that Trilling's canon seemed "curiously dated and fixed" and that other approaches to modernism could emerge from the consideration of different texts. Trilling likely would acknowledge that his canon and conception of modernism are partial and slanted—not inaccurate, but testifying to his own preoccupations, in particular to the hostility of certain leading modern writers, in a variety of fields, to civilization and culture.

Trilling's tone is at moments condescending toward his students. Were they really so untroubled by the readings he assigned? Indeed, some of these students, including Morris Dickstein in his memoir *Why Not Say What Happened: A Sentimental Education* (2015), recall having been more contentious in the classroom and more provoked by the authors and texts than Trilling suggests. But it is important to see Trilling's essay not as a sociological or historical report but rather as a form of intensely personal reflection. The essay is about the movements and ambivalences of Trilling's mind as he ponders the literature he most cares about, his vocation as teacher, and the career he has chosen.

Trilling's essay is itself a literary performance, an eloquent and complex one about his relation to literature, literary criticism, modernism, and higher education, especially the enthronement—which means the transformation, but which may entail the devaluation—of great and classic texts from the late nineteenth century into the early and mid-twentieth century as they became objects of study. During the 1930s, it seemed far from probable that Trilling, a Jew interested in Freud and MARX, would make a career for himself at Columbia. Two decades later, he was a major critic and public intellectual, giving courses on modern literature to hundreds of students in large lecture halls. There is something grand, but also something sobering, in Trilling's self-representation in this essay and in much of his writing in the aftermath of his great success in 1950 with *The Liberal Imagination*.

Trilling's essay was published during a decade that saw the rise of the civil rights movement, antiwar protests, and feminism. We now study, live, and work in a society far removed from the 1960s. Our vision of modernism is more capacious than Trilling's, and the academic study of literature today includes voices, texts, points of view, topics, theories, and media that extend beyond anything that Trilling imagined or ever would support. Yet in its central themes, "On the Teaching of Modern Literature" is acute and timely. Trilling urges that we confront vital questions: What is the ethical power of literature? What is its impact on each of us? Where do we stand in relation to it? New Critical close reading—dominant in the academy when Trilling was writing—is all well and good, but literature in its essence demands a deeply personal engagement by the reader.

"On the Teaching of Modern Literature" Keywords: The Canon/Tradition, Defense of Criticism, Ethics, Institutional Studies, Literary History, Modernity, Psychoanalysis

On the Teaching of Modern Literature

I propose to consider here a particular theme of modern literature which appears so frequently and with so much authority that it may be said to constitute one of the shaping and controlling ideas of our epoch. I can identify it by calling it the disenchantment of our culture with culture itself—it seems to me that the characteristic element of modern literature, or at least of the most highly developed modern literature, is the bitter line of hostility to civilization which runs through it. It happens that my present awareness of this theme is involved in a personal experience, and I am impelled to speak of it not abstractly but with the husks of the experience clinging untidily to it. I shall go so far in doing this as to describe the actual circumstances in which the experience took place. These circumstances are pedagogic—they consist of some problems in teaching modern literature to undergraduates and my attempt to solve these problems. I know that pedagogy is a depressing subject to all persons of sensibility, and yet I shall not apologize for touching upon it because the emphasis upon the teaching of literature and especially of modern literature is in itself one of the most salient and significant manifestations of the culture of our time. Indeed, if, having in mind Matthew Arnold's lecture, "On the Modern Element in Literature,"[1] we are on the hunt for *the* modern element in modern literature, we might want to find it in the susceptibility of modern literature to being made into an academic subject.

For some years I have taught the course in modern literature in Columbia College. I did not undertake it without misgiving and I have never taught it with an undivided mind. My doubts do not refer to the value of the literature itself, only to the educational propriety of its being studied in college. These doubts persist even though I wholly understand that the relation of our collegiate education to modernity is no longer an open question. The unargued assumption of most curriculums is that the real subject of all study is the modern world; that the justification of all study is its immediate and presumably practical relevance to modernity; that the true purpose of all study is to lead the young person to be at home in, and in control of, the modern world. There is really no way of quarreling with the assumption or with what follows upon it, the instituting of courses of which the substance is chiefly contemporary or at least makes ultimate reference to what is contemporary.

It might be asked why anyone should *want* to quarrel with the assumption. To that question I can return only a defensive, eccentric, self-depreciatory answer. It is this: that to some of us who teach and who think of our students as the creators of the intellectual life of the future, there comes a kind of despair. It does not come because our students fail to respond to ideas, rather because they respond to ideas with a happy vagueness, a delighted glibness, a joyous sense of power in the use of received or receivable generalizations, a grateful wonder at how easy it is to formulate and judge, at how little resistance language offers to their intentions. When that despair strikes us, we are tempted to give up the usual and accredited ways of evaluating education, and instead of prizing responsiveness and aptitude, to set store by some sign of personal character in our students, some token of individual will. We think of this as taking the form of resistance and imperviousness, of personal density or gravity, of some power of supposing that ideas are real, a power which will lead a young man to say what Goethe[2] thought was the modern thing to say, "But is this really true—is it true for *me*?" And to say this not in the facile way, not following the progressive educational prescription to "think for yourself," which means to think in the progressive pieties rather than in the conservative pieties (if any of the latter do still exist), but to say it from his sense of himself as a person rather than as a bundle of attitudes and responses which are all alert to please the teacher and the progressive community.

We can't do anything about the quality of personal being of our students, but we are led to think about the cultural analogue of a personal character that is grave, dense, and resistant—we are led to think about the past. Perhaps the protagonist of Thomas Mann's[3] story, "Disorder and Early Sorrow"

1. Delivered by the English poet, essayist, and social critic ARNOLD (1822–1888) in 1857 as his inaugural lecture as Oxford Professor of Poetry.
2. Johann Wolfgang von Goethe (1749–1832), German poet, playwright, novelist, philosopher, and scientist.
3. German novelist and essayist (1875–1955); his novella *Disorder and Early Sorrow* (1925), which deals with the themes of economic struggle, social and cultural decline, and generational conflict, tells the story of the Cornelius family from the point of view of Abel Cornelius, a middle-aged university professor.

comes to mind, that sad Professor Cornelius with his intense and ambivalent sense of history. For Professor Cornelius, who is a historian, the past is dead, is death itself, but for that very reason it is the source of order, value, piety, and even love. If we think about education in the dark light of the despair I have described, we wonder if perhaps there is not to be found in the past that quiet place at which a young man might stand for a few years, at least a little beyond the competing attitudes and generalizations of the present, at least a little beyond the contemporary problems which he is told he can master only by means of attitudes and generalizations, that quiet place in which he can be silent, in which he can *know* something—in what year the Parthenon was begun, the order of battle at Trafalgar, how Linear B was deciphered:[4] almost anything at all that has nothing to do with the talkative and attitudinizing present, anything at all but variations on the accepted formulations about *anxiety*, and *urban society*, and *alienation*, and *Gemeinschaft* and *Gesellschaft*,[5] all the matter of the academic disciplines which are founded upon the modern self-consciousness and the modern self-pity. The modern self-pity is certainly not without its justification; but, if the circumstances that engender it are ever to be overcome, we must sometimes wonder whether this work can be done by minds which are taught in youth to accept these sad conditions of ours as the only right objects of contemplation. And quite apart from any practical consequences, one thinks of the simple aesthetic personal pleasure of having to do with young minds, and maturing minds, which are free of cant, which are, to quote an old poet, "fierce, moody, patient, venturous, modest, shy."[6]

This line of argument I have called eccentric and maybe it ought to be called obscurantist and reactionary. Whatever it is called, it is not likely to impress a Committee on the Curriculum. It was, I think, more or less the line of argument of my department in Columbia College, when, up to a few years ago, it would decide, whenever the question came up, not to carry its courses beyond the late nineteenth century. But our rationale could not stand against the representations which a group of students made to our Dean and which he communicated to us. The students wanted a course in modern literature—very likely, in the way of students, they said that it was a scandal that no such course was being offered in the College. There was no argument that could stand against this expressed desire: we could only capitulate, and then, with pretty good grace, muster the arguments that justified our doing so. Was not the twentieth century more than half over? Was it not nearly fifty years since Eliot wrote "Portrait of a Lady"?[7] George Meredith[8] had not died until 1909, and even the oldest among us had read

4. All matters of fact: the Parthenon, the temple of Athena on the Acropolis in Athens, was built in 447 to 432 B.C.E.; the battle fought off Cape Trafalgar on the southwest coast of Spain, on October 21, 1805, was a decisive victory by a British fleet of 33 ships over 18 French and 15 Spanish ships; and Linear B, a syllabic script used ca. 1400 to 1200 B.C.E. in Crete and continental Greece, in 1952 was identified as an archaic form of Greek and deciphered by the English cryptographer Michael Ventris using statistical analysis.

5. Two ideal types of social organization, based respectively on social relations between individuals (close personal and family ties, community) and on impersonal ties (contracts or duty to a society or organization). These terms, borrowed from the original German, derive from the categories first articulated in *Gemeinschaft und Gesellschaft* (1887, 2d ed. 1912; *Community and Civil Society*), by the German philosopher and sociologist Ferdinand Tönnies; they were also used by Max Weber in *Economy and Society* (1921).

6. Quoted from *The Prelude* (1850), 5.417, by the English Romantic poet WILLIAM WORDSWORTH (1770–1850).

7. A poem (1915) by the Anglo-American poet and critic T. S. ELIOT (1888–1965).

8. English novelist and poet (1828–1909).

one of his novels in a college course—many American universities had been quick to bring into their purview the literature of the later nineteenth century, and even the early twentieth century; there was a strong supporting tradition for our capitulation. Had not Yeats[9] been Matthew Arnold's contemporary for twenty-three years?

Our resistance to the idea of the course had never been based on an adverse judgment of the literature itself. We are a department not only of English but of comparative literature, and if the whole of modern literature is surveyed, it could be said—and we were willing to say it—that no literature of the past surpassed the literature of our time in power and magnificence. Then too, it is a difficult literature, and it is difficult not merely as defenders of modern poetry say that all literature is difficult. We nowadays believe that Keats[1] is a very difficult poet, but his earlier readers did not. We now see the depths and subtleties of Dickens,[2] but his contemporary readers found him as simply available as a plate of oysters on the half shell. Modern literature, however, shows its difficulties at first blush; they are literal as well as doctrinal difficulties—if our students were to know their modern literary heritage, surely they needed all the help that a teacher can give?

These made cogent reasons for our decision to establish, at long last, the course in modern literature. They also made a ground for our display of a certain mean-spirited, last-ditch vindictiveness. I recall that we said something like, "Very well, if they want the modern, let them have it—let them have it, as Henry James[3] says, full in the face. We shall give the course, but we shall give it on the highest level, and if they think, as students do, that the modern will naturally meet them in a genial way, let them have their gay and easy time with Yeats and Eliot, with Joyce and Proust and Kafka, with Lawrence, Mann and Gide."[4]

Eventually the course fell to me to give. I approached it with an uneasiness which has not diminished with the passage of time—it has, I think, even increased. It arises, this uneasiness, from my personal relation with the works that form the substance of the course. Almost all of them have been involved with me for a long time—I invert the natural order not out of lack of modesty but taking the cue of W. H. Auden's remark that a real book reads us.[5] I have been read by Eliot's poems and by *Ulysses* and by *Remembrance of Things Past* and by *The Castle* for a good many years now, since early youth. Some of these books at first rejected me; I bored them. But as I grew older and they knew me better, they came to have more sympathy with me and to understand my hidden meanings. Their nature is such that our relationship has been very intimate. No literature has ever been so shockingly personal as that of our time—it asks every question that is forbidden in polite society. It asks us if we are content with our marriages,

9. William Butler Yeats (1865–1939), Irish poet and playwright.
1. John Keats (1795–1821), English Romantic poet.
2. Charles Dickens (1812–1870), the most popular English novelist of his time.
3. American writer of fiction and nonfiction (1843–1916; see above); he uses the phrase "full in the face" in a number of stories and novels, including *The American* (1877) and "The Figure in the Carpet" (1896).
4. Major modern writers of different nationalities: James Joyce (1882–1941), Irish author of *Ulysses* (1922); Marcel Proust (1871–1922), French author of *À la recherche du temps perdu* (7 vols., 1913–27; first translated as *Remembrance of Things Past*); Franz Kafka (1883–1924), Czech-born writer of German fiction, including *The Castle* (1926); D. H. Lawrence (1885–1930), English; and André Gide (1869–1951), French.
5. This remark (or "A real book is not one that we read, but one that reads us") has not been found in any of the works by the English poet and critic Auden (1907–1973).

with our family lives, with our professional lives, with our friends. It is all very well for me to describe my course in the College catalogue as "paying particular attention to the role of the writer as a critic of his culture"—this is sheer evasion: the questions asked by our literature are not about our culture but about ourselves. It asks us if we are content with ourselves, if we are saved or damned—more than with anything else, our literature is concerned with salvation. No literature has ever been so intensely spiritual as ours. I do not venture to call it actually religious, but certainly it has the special intensity of concern with the spiritual life which Hegel[6] noted when he spoke of the great modern phenomenon of the secularization of spirituality.

I do not know how other teachers deal with this extravagant personal force of modern literature, but for me it makes difficulty. Nowadays the teaching of literature inclines to a considerable technicality, but when the teacher has said all that can be said about formal matters, about verse-patterns, metrics, prose conventions, irony, tension, etc., he must confront the necessity of bearing personal testimony. He must use whatever authority he may possess to say whether or not a work is true, and if not, why not; and if so, why so. He can do this only at considerable cost to his privacy. How does one say that Lawrence is right in his great rage against the modern emotions, against the modern sense of life and ways of being, unless one speaks from the intimacies of one's own feelings, and one's own sense of life, and one's own wished-for way of being? How, except with the implication of personal judgment, does one say to students that Gide is perfectly accurate in his representation of the awful boredom and slow corruption of respectable life? Then probably one rushes in to say that this doesn't of itself justify homosexuality and the desertion of one's dying wife, certainly not.[7] But then again, having paid one's *devoirs*[8] to morality, how does one rescue from morality Gide's essential point about the supreme rights of the individual person, and without making it merely historical, academic?

My first response to the necessity of dealing with matters of this kind was resentment of the personal discomfort it caused me. These are subjects we usually deal with either quite unconsciously or in the privacy of our own conscious minds, and if we now and then disclose our thoughts about them, it is to friends of equal age and especial closeness. Or if we touch upon them publicly, we do so in the relative abstractness and anonymity of print. To stand up in one's own person and to speak of them in one's own voice to an audience which each year grows younger as one grows older—that is not easy, and probably it is not decent.

And then, leaving aside the personal considerations, or taking them merely as an indication of something wrong with the situation, can we not say that, when modern literature is brought into the classroom, the subject being taught is betrayed by the pedagogy of the subject? We have to ask ourselves whether in our day too much does not come within the purview of the academy. More and more, as the universities liberalize themselves, and turn their beneficent imperialistic gaze upon what is called Life Itself, the feeling grows among our educated classes that little can be experienced unless it is validated by some established intellectual discipline, with the

6. GEORG WILHELM FRIEDRICH HEGEL (1770–1831), German Idealist philosopher.

7. An allusion to the plot of Gide's novel *The Immoralist* (1902).

8. Duties, respects (French).

result that experience loses much of its personal immediacy for us and becomes part of an accredited societal activity. This is not entirely true and I don't want to play the boring academic game of pretending that it is entirely true, that the university mind wilts and withers whatever it touches. I must believe, and I do believe, that the university study of art is capable of confronting the power of a work of art fully and courageously. I even believe that it can discover and disclose power where it has not been felt before. But the university study of art achieves this end chiefly with works of art of an older period. Time has the effect of seeming to quiet the work of art, domesticating it and making it into a classic, which is often another way of saying that it is an object of merely habitual regard. University study of the right sort can reverse this process and restore to the old work its freshness and force—can, indeed, disclose unguessed-at power. But with the works of art of our own present age, university study tends to accelerate the process by which the radical and subversive work becomes the classic work, and university study does this in the degree that it is vivacious and responsive and what is called non-academic. In one of his poems Yeats mocks the literary scholars, "the bald heads forgetful of their sins," "the old, learned, respectable bald heads,"[9] who edit the poems of the fierce and passionate young men.

> Lord, what would they say
> Did their Catullus[1] walk this way?

Yeats, of course, is thinking of his own future fate, and no doubt there is all the radical and comical discrepancy that he sees between the poet's passions and the scholars' close-eyed concentration on the text. Yet for my part, when I think of Catullus, I am moved to praise the tact of all those old heads, from Heinsius and Bentley to Munro and Postgate,[2] who worked on Codex C and Codex O and drew conclusions from them about the lost Codex V—for doing only this and for not trying to realize and demonstrate the true intensity and the true quality and the true cultural meaning of Catullus's passion and managing to bring it somehow into eventual accord with their respectability and baldness. Nowadays we who deal with books in universities live in fear that the World, which we imagine to be a vital, palpitating, passionate, reality-loving World, will think of us as old, respectable, and bald, and we see to it that in our dealings with Yeats (to take him as the example) his wild cry of rage and sexuality is heard by our students and quite thoroughly understood by them as—what is it that we eventually call it?—*a significant expression of our culture*. The exasperation of Lawrence and the subversiveness of Gide, by the time we have dealt with them boldly and straightforwardly, are notable instances of the *alienation of modern man as exemplified by the artist.* "Compare Yeats, Gide, Lawrence, and Eliot in the use which they make of the theme of sexuality to criticize the deficiencies of modern culture. Support your statement by specific references to the work of each author. [Time: one hour.]" And the distressing

9. Slightly misquoted from "The Scholars" (1919); the couplet below is the poem's conclusion.
1. Roman poet (ca. 84–ca. 54 B.C.E.), known particularly for his love poems.
2. All classical scholars who published editions of Catullus: the Dutch Nicolaas Heinsius the Elder (1620–1681) and the British Richard Bentley (1662–1742), Hugh Andrew Johnstone Munro (1819–1885), and John Percival Postgate (1853–1926). The main book manuscripts (codices) for Catullus are codex Sangermanensis (G), in Paris, and codex Oxoniensis (O), at Oxford, both derived from the codex Veronensis (V), preserved at Verona but now lost.

thing about our examination questions is that they are not ridiculous, they make perfectly good sense—such good sense that the young person who answers them can never again know the force and terror of what has been communicated to him by the works he is being examined on.

Very likely it was with the thought of saving myself from the necessity of speaking personally and my students from having to betray the full harsh meaning of a great literature that I first taught my course in as *literary* a way as possible. A couple of decades ago the discovery was made that a literary work is a structure of words: this doesn't seem a surprising thing to have learned except for its polemical tendency, which is to urge us to minimize the amount of attention we give to the poet's social and personal will, to what he wants to happen outside the poem as a result of the poem; it urges us to fix our minds on what is going on inside the poem. For me this polemical tendency has been of the greatest usefulness, for it has corrected my inclination to pay attention chiefly to what the poet *wants*. For two or three years I directed my efforts toward dealing with the matter of the course chiefly as structures of words, in a formal way, with due attention paid to the literal difficulty which marked so many of the works. But it went against the grain. It went against my personal grain. It went against the grain of the classroom situation, for formal analysis is best carried on by question-and-answer, which needs small groups, and the registration for the course in modern literature in any college is sure to be large. And it went against the grain of the authors themselves—structures of words they may indeed have created, but these structures were not pyramids or triumphal arches, they were manifestly contrived to be not static and commemorative but mobile and aggressive, and one does not describe a quinquereme[3] or a howitzer or a tank without estimating how much damage it can do.

Eventually I had to decide that there was only one way to give the course, which was to give it without strategies and without conscious caution. It was not honorable, either to the students or to the authors, to conceal or disguise my relation to the literature, my commitment to it, my fear of it, my ambivalence toward it. The literature had to be dealt with in the terms it announced for itself. As for the students, I have never given assent to the modern saw about "teaching students, not subjects"—I have always thought it right to teach subjects, believing that if one gives his first loyalty to the subject, the student is best instructed. So I resolved to give the course with no considerations in mind except my own interests. And since my own interests lead me to see literary situations as cultural situations, and cultural situations as great elaborate fights about moral issues, and moral issues as having something to do with gratuitously chosen images of personal being, and images of personal being as having something to do with literary style, I felt free to begin with what for me was a first concern, the animus of the author, the objects of his will, the things he wants or wants to have happen.

My cultural and non-literary method led me to decide that I would begin the course with a statement of certain themes or issues that might especially engage our attention. I even went so far in non-literariness as to think that my purposes would best be served if I could contrive a "background"

3. An ancient warship, used by the Romans and Hellenistic Greeks, with oarsmen arranged in groups of five (perhaps stacked in a vertical group of two or three banks of oars on each side).

for the works we would read—I wanted to propose a history for the themes or issues that I hoped to discover. I did not intend that this history should be either very extensive or very precise. I wanted merely to encourage a *sense* of a history, some general intuition of a past, in students who, as it seems to me, have not been provided with any such thing by their education and who are on the whole glad to be without it. And because there is as yet no adequate general work of history of the culture of the last two hundred years, I asked myself what books of the age just preceding ours had most influenced our literature, or, since I was far less concerned with showing influence than with discerning a tendency, what older books might seem to fall into a line the direction of which pointed to our own literature and thus might serve as a prolegomenon to the course.

It was virtually inevitable that the first work that should have sprung to mind was Sir James Frazer's *The Golden Bough*,[4] not, of course, the whole of it, but certain chapters, those that deal with Osiris, Attis, and Adonis.[5] Anyone who thinks about modern literature in a systematic way takes for granted the great part played in it by myth, and especially by those examples of myth which tell about gods dying and being reborn—the imagination of death and rebirth, reiterated in the ancient world in innumerable variations that are yet always the same, captivated the literary mind at the very moment when, as all accounts of the modern age agree, the most massive and compelling of all the stories of resurrection had lost much of its hold upon the world.

Perhaps no book has had so decisive an effect upon modern literature as Frazer's. It was beautifully to my purpose that it had first been published ten years before the twentieth century began. Yet forty-three years later, in 1933, Frazer delivered a lecture,[6] very eloquent, in which he bade the world be of good hope in the face of the threat to the human mind that was being offered by the Nazi power. He was still alive in 1941. Yet he had been born in 1854, three years before Matthew Arnold gave the lecture "On the Modern Element in Literature." Here, surely, was history, here was the past I wanted, beautifully connected with our present. Frazer was wholly a man of the nineteenth century, and the more so because the eighteenth century was so congenial to him—the lecture of 1933 in which he predicted the Nazi defeat had as its subject Condorcet's *Progress of the Human Mind;* when he took time from his anthropological studies to deal with literature, he prepared editions of Addison's essays and Cowper's letters.[7] He had the old lost belief in the virtue and power of rationality. He loved and counted on order, decorum, and good sense. This great historian of the primitive

4. A study of comparative religion (2 vols., 1890; enlarged ed., 12 vols., 1911–15), in which the Scottish anthropologist Frazer (1854–1941) proposed an evolutionary theory of the development of human thought from the magical to the religious to the scientific.

5. Frazer argued that the figures of Adonis (in Greek mythology, a beautiful youth beloved by both Aphrodite and Persephone and killed by a boar), Osiris (the Egyptian consort and brother of Isis, and god of the underworld after he was slain by Seth), and Attis (in Asia Minor, the youthful consort of the Great Mother Cybele who castrated himself and died) were all associated with resurrection and represented the yearly decay and revival of life, especially of vegetation in the spring.

6. "Condorcet on the Progress of the Human Mind," the Zaharoff Lecture at the University of Oxford. Nicolas de Caritat, marquis de Condorcet (1743–1794), French philosopher, mathematician, and political scientist; he wrote *Outlines of a Historical View of the Progress of the Human Mind* (1795) in 1794 while he was in hiding during the French Revolution.

7. William Cowper (1731–1800), English poet. JOSEPH ADDISON (1672–1719), English writer and Whig politician.

imagination was in the dominant intellectual tradition of the West which, since the days of the pre-Socratics,[8] has condemned the ways of thought that we call primitive.

It can be said of Frazer that in his conscious intention he was a perfect representative of what Arnold meant when he spoke of a modern age. And perhaps nothing could make clearer how the conditions of life and literature have changed in a hundred years than to note the difference between the way in which Arnold defines the modern element in literature and the way in which we must define it.

Arnold used the word *modern* in a wholly honorific sense. So much so that he seems to dismiss all temporal idea from the word and makes it signify certain timeless intellectual and civic virtues—his lecture, indeed, was about the modern element in the ancient literatures. A society, he said, is a modern society when it maintains a condition of repose, confidence, free activity of the mind, and the tolerance of divergent views. A society is modern when it affords sufficient material well-being for the conveniences of life and the development of taste. And, finally, a society is modern when its members are intellectually mature, by which Arnold means that they are willing to judge by reason, to observe facts in a critical spirit, and to search for the law of things. By this definition Periclean Athens is for Arnold a modern age, Elizabethan England is not; Thucydides is a modern historian, Sir Walter Raleigh is not.[9]

I shall not go into further details of Arnold's definition or description of the modern.[1] I have said enough, I think, to suggest what Arnold was up to, what he wanted to see realized as the desideratum[2] of his own society, what ideal he wanted the works of intellect and imagination of his own time to advance. And at what a distance his ideal of the modern puts him from our present sense of modernity, from our modern literature! To anyone conditioned by our modern literature, Arnold's ideal of order, convenience, decorum, and rationality might well seem to reduce itself to the small advantages and excessive limitations of the middle-class life of a few prosperous nations of the nineteenth century. Arnold's historic sense presented to his mind the long, bitter, bloody past of Europe, and he seized passionately upon the hope of true civilization at last achieved. But the historic sense of our literature has in mind a long excess of civilization to which may be ascribed the bitterness and bloodiness both of the past and of the present and of which the peaceful aspects are to be thought of as mainly contemptible—its order achieved at the cost of extravagant personal repression, either that of coer-

8. The Greek speculative philosophers, most born before the philosopher Socrates (469–399 B.C.E.), who attempted to find rational explanations for natural phenomena. Among the best known are Parmenides (b. ca. 515 B.C.E.), Heraclitus (active ca. 500 B.C.E.), and Pythagoras (6th c. B.C.E.).

9. Raleigh (1554–1618), an English explorer, courtier, and writer, was a favorite of Queen Elizabeth (1533–1603; reigned 1558–1603). The Greek historian Thucydides (ca. 455–ca. 400 B.C.E.) wrote extensively in his *History of the Peloponnesian War* about Pericles (ca. 495–429 B.C.E.), the Athenian statesman, military leader, and supporter of the arts who was the most influential man in Athens during the city's golden age.

1. I leave out of my summary account the two supreme virtues that Arnold ascribes to the most successful examples of a "modern" literature. One is the power of effecting an "intellectual deliverance," by which Arnold means leading men to comprehend the "vast multitude of facts" which make up "a copious and complex present, and behind it a copious and complex past." The other is "adequacy," the ability to represent the complex high human development of a modern age "in its completest and most harmonious" aspect, doing so with "the charm of that noble serenity which always accompanies true insight" [Trilling's note].

2. Something desired or needed.

cion or that of acquiescence; its repose otiose; its tolerance either flaccid or capricious; its material comfort corrupt and corrupting; its taste a manifestation either of timidity or of pride; its rationality attained only at the price of energy and passion.

For the understanding of this radical change of opinion nothing is more illuminating than to be aware of the doubleness of mind of the author of *The Golden Bough*. I have said that Frazer in his conscious mind and in his first intention exemplifies all that Arnold means by the modern. He often speaks quite harshly of the irrationality and the orgiastic excesses of the primitive religions he describes, and even Christianity comes under his criticism both because it stands in the way of rational thought and because it can draw men away from intelligent participation in the life of society. But Frazer had more than one intention, and he had an unconscious as well as a conscious mind. If he deplores the primitive imagination, he also does not fail to show it as wonderful and beautiful. It is the rare reader of *The Golden Bough* who finds the ancient beliefs and rituals wholly alien to him. It is to be expected that Frazer's adduction of the many pagan analogues to the Christian mythos will be thought by Christian readers to have an adverse effect on faith, it was undoubtedly Frazer's purpose that it should, yet many readers will feel that Frazer makes all faith and ritual indigenous to humanity, virtually biological; they feel, as De Quincey[3] put it, that not to be at least a *little* superstitious is to lack generosity of mind. Scientific though his purpose was, Frazer had the effect of validating those old modes of experiencing the world which modern men, beginning with the Romantics, have sought to revive in order to escape from positivism and common sense.

The direction of the imagination upon great and mysterious objects of worship is not the only means men use to liberate themselves from the bondage of quotidian fact, and although Frazer can scarcely be held accountable for the ever-growing modern attraction to the extreme mental states—to rapture, ecstasy, and transcendence, which are achieved by drugs, trance, music and dance, orgy, and the derangement of personality—yet he did provide a bridge to the understanding and acceptance of these states, he proposed to us the idea that the desire for them and the use of them for heuristic purposes is a common and acceptable manifestation of human nature.

This one element of Frazer's masterpiece could scarcely fail to suggest the next of my prolegomenal[4] works. It is worth remarking that its author was in his own way as great a classical scholar as Frazer himself—Nietzsche[5] was Professor of Classical Philology at the University of Basel when, at the age of twenty-seven, he published his essay *The Birth of Tragedy*. After the appearance of this stunningly brilliant account of Greek civilization, of which Socrates is not the hero but the villain,[6] what can possibly be left to us of that rational and ordered Greece, that modern, that eighteenth-century,

3. Thomas De Quincey (1785–1859), English essayist and critic.
4. Preliminary, introductory.
5. FRIEDRICH NIETZSCHE (1844–1900), German philosopher; in *The Birth of Tragedy* (1872; excerpted above), he argues that Greek tragedy reflects a struggle between two elements, one identified with Dionysus, the god of fertility and wine who was later associated with wild and ecstatic religious rites (i.e., enthusiasm, frenzy, chaos), and the other identified with Apollo, the god of the sun, healing, prophecy, and poetry (i.e., measure, reason, calm, harmony).
6. Socrates appears as the hero of Western rationalism mainly through his depiction in the dialogues written by PLATO (ca. 427–ca. 347 B.C.E.), his student.

Athens that Arnold so entirely relied on as the standard for judging all civilizations? Professor Kaufmann[7] is right when he warns us against supposing that Nietzsche exalts Dionysus over Apollo and tells us that Nietzsche "emphasizes the Dionysiac only because he feels that the Apollonian genius of the Greeks cannot be fully understood apart from it." But no one reading Nietzsche's essay for the first time is likely to heed this warning. What will reach him before due caution intervenes, before he becomes aware of the portentous dialectic between Dionysus and Apollo, is the excitement of suddenly being liberated from Aristotle,[8] the joy of finding himself acceding to the author's statement that "art rather than ethics constitutes the essential metaphysical activity of man," that tragedy has its source in the Dionysiac rapture, "whose closest analogy is furnished by physical intoxication," and that this rapture, in which "the individual forgets himself completely," was in itself no metaphysical state but an orgiastic display of lust and cruelty, "of sexual promiscuity overriding every form of tribal law." This sadic[9] and masochistic frenzy, Nietzsche is at pains to insist, needs the taming hand of Apollo before it can become tragedy, but it is the primal stuff of the great art, and to the modern experience of tragedy this explanation seems far more pertinent than Aristotle's, with its eagerness to forget its origin in its achievement of a state of noble imperturbability.

Of supreme importance in itself, Nietzsche's essay had for me the added pedagogic advantage of allowing me to establish a historical line back to William Blake.[1] Nothing is more characteristic of modern literature than its discovery and canonization of the primal, non-ethical energies, and the historical point could be made the better by remarking the correspondence of thought of two men of different nations and separated from each other by a good many decades, for Nietzsche's Dionysian orgy and Blake's Hell are much the same thing.

Whether or not Joseph Conrad[2] read either Blake or Nietzsche I do not know, but his *Heart of Darkness* follows in their line. This very great work has never lacked for the admiration it deserves, and it has been given a kind of canonical place in the legend of modern literature by Eliot's having it so clearly in mind when he wrote *The Waste Land* and his having taken from it the epigraph to "The Hollow Men."[3] But no one, to my knowledge, has ever confronted in an explicit way its strange and terrible message of ambivalence toward the life of civilization. Consider that its protagonist, Kurtz, is a progressive and a liberal and that he is the highly respected representative of a society which would have us believe it is benign, although in fact it is vicious. Consider too that he is a practitioner of several arts, a painter, a writer, a musician, and into the bargain a political orator. He is at once the most idealistic and the most practically successful of all the agents of the

7. Walter A. Kaufmann (1921–1980), German-born American philosopher and renowned scholar and translator of Nietzsche. The quotation is from *Nietzsche: Philosopher, Psychologist, Antichrist* (1950).
8. Greek philosopher and scientist (384–322 B.C.E.), one of the great systematizers of Western intellectual history. His *Poetics* (see above) is one of the most influential accounts of Greek tragedy.
9. Sadistic.
1. English artist and Romantic poet (1757–1827), whose works include monumental "prophetic" poems that present his own mythology. In *The Marriage of Heaven and Hell* (1790–93), a prose work, he appears to favor Hell and the Devil.
2. Polish-born British novelist (1857–1924); his novella *Heart of Darkness* (1899) is a nightmarish exploration of the themes of imperialism, racism, and obsession.
3. The first epigraph of this 1925 poem by Eliot is "Mistah Kurtz—he dead." *The Waste Land* (1922), Eliot's most important poem, is a key text of modernism.

Belgian exploitation of the Congo.[4] Everybody knows the truth about him which Marlow[5] discovers—that Kurtz's success is the result of a terrible ascendancy he has gained over the natives of his distant station, an ascendancy which is derived from his presumed magical or divine powers, that he has exercised his rule with an extreme of cruelty, that he has given himself to unnamable acts of lust. This is the world of the darker pages of *The Golden Bough.* It is one of the great points of Conrad's story that Marlow speaks of the primitive life of the jungle not as being noble or charming or even free but as being base and sordid—and for *that* reason compelling: he himself feels quite overtly its dreadful attraction. It is to this devilish baseness that Kurtz has yielded himself, and yet Marlow, although he does indeed treat him with hostile irony, does not find it possible to suppose that Kurtz is anything but a hero of the spirit. For me it is still ambiguous whether Kurtz's famous deathbed cry, "The horror! The horror!" refers to the approach of death or to his experience of savage life. Whichever it is, to Marlow the fact that Kurtz could utter this cry at the point of death, while Marlow himself, when death threatens him, can know it only as a weary grayness, marks the difference between the ordinary man and a hero of the spirit. Is this not the essence of the modern belief about the nature of the artist, the man who goes down into that hell which is the historical beginning of the human soul, a beginning not outgrown but established in humanity as we know it now, preferring the reality of this hell to the bland lies of the civilization that has overlaid it?

This idea is proposed again in the somewhat less powerful but still very moving work with which I followed *Heart of Darkness*, Thomas Mann's *Death in Venice.*[6] I wanted this story not so much for its account of an extravagantly Apollonian personality surrendering to forces that, in his Apollonian character, he thought shameful—although this was certainly to my purpose—but rather for Aschenbach's fevered dreams of the erotic past, and in particular that dream of the goat-orgy which Mann, being the kind of writer he is, having the kind of relation to Nietzsche he had, might well have written to serve as an illustration of what *The Birth of Tragedy* means by religious frenzy, the more so, of course, because Mann chooses that particular orgiastic ritual, the killing and eating of the goat, from which tragedy is traditionally said to have been derived.[7]

A notable element of this story in which the birth of tragedy plays an important part is that the degradation and downfall of that protagonist is not represented as tragic in the usual sense of the word—that is, it is not represented as a great deplorable event. It is a commonplace of modern literary thought that the tragic mode is not available even to the gravest and noblest of our writers. I am not sure that this is the deprivation that some people think it to be and a mark of our spiritual inferiority. But if we ask why it has come about, one reason may be that we have learned to think our

4. The Congo Free State, coextensive with the modern Democratic Republic of the Congo, was privately owned by Europeans and ruled with notorious brutality by King Leopold II of Belgium from 1885 to 1908.
5. The narrator of *Heart of Darkness*.
6. A 1912 novella by the German novelist and essayist Mann (1875–1955). Its main character is Gustav von Aschenbach, a famous author who is disciplined and ascetic but becomes obsessed with a beautiful Polish boy, Tadzio, whom he encounters in a Venetian hotel.
7. The traditional etymology of the Greek word *tragōidia* is "goat song," and the earliest Greek tragedies are associated with the festival of Dionysus.

way back through tragedy to the primal stuff out of which tragedy arose. If we consider the primitive forbidden ways of conduct which traditionally in tragedy led to punishment by death, we think of them as being the path to reality and truth, to an ultimate self-realization. We have always wondered if tragedy itself may not have been saying just this in a deeply hidden way, drawing us to think of the hero's sin and death as somehow conferring justification, even salvation of a sort—no doubt this is what Nietzsche had in mind when he said that "tragedy denies ethics."[8] What tragedy once seemed to hint, our literature now is willing to say quite explicitly. If Mann's Aschenbach dies at the height of his intellectual and artistic powers, overcome by a passion that his ethical reason condemns, we do not take this to be a defeat, rather a kind of terrible rebirth; at his latter end the artist knows a reality that he had until now refused to admit to consciousness.

Thoughts like these suggested that another of Nietzsche's works, *The Genealogy of Morals*,[9] might be in point. It proposes a view of society which is consonant with the belief that art and not ethics constitutes the essential metaphysical activity of man and with the validation and ratification of the primitive energies. Nietzsche's theory of the social order dismisses all ethical impulse from its origins—the basis of society is to be found in the rationalization of cruelty: as simple as that. Nietzsche has no ultimate Utopian intention in saying this, no hope of revising the essence of the social order, although he does believe that its pain can be mitigated. He represents cruelty as a social necessity, for only by its exercise could men ever have been induced to develop a continuity of will: nothing else than cruel pain could have created in mankind that memory of intention which makes society possible. The method of cynicism which Nietzsche pursued—let us be clear that it is a method and not an attitude—goes so far as to describe punishment in terms of the pleasure derived from the exercise of cruelty: "Compensation," he says, "consists in a legal warrant entitling one man to exercise his cruelty on another."[1] There follows that most remarkable passage in which Nietzsche describes the process whereby the individual turns the cruelty of punishment against himself and creates the bad conscience and the consciousness of guilt which manifests itself as a pervasive anxiety. Nietzsche's complexity of mind is beyond all comparison, for in this book which is dedicated to the liberation of the conscience, Nietzsche makes his defense of the bad conscience as a decisive force in the interests of culture. It is much the same line of argument that he takes when, having attacked the Jewish morality and the priestly existence in the name of the health of the spirit, he reminds us that only by his sickness does man become interesting.

From *The Genealogy of Morals* to Freud's *Civilization and Its Discontents*[2] is but a step, and some might think that, for pedagogic purposes, the step is so small as to make the second book supererogatory. But although Freud's view of society and culture has indeed a very close affinity to Nietzsche's, Freud does add certain considerations which are essential to our sense of the modern disposition.

8. A Nietzschean sentiment, though this precise phrase has not been found in any specific work by Nietzsche.
9. Published in 1887.
1. Nietzsche, *The Genealogy of Morals: An Attack*, in *The Birth of Tragedy and The Genealogy of Morals*, trans. Francis Golffing (New York: Anchor Doubleday, 1956), p. 197.
2. Published in 1929, by the Austrian neurologist and founder of psychoanalysis SIGMUND FREUD (1856–1939).

For one thing, he puts to us the question of whether or not we want to *accept* civilization. It is not the first time that the paradox of civilization has been present to the mind of civilized people, the sense that civilization makes men behave worse and suffer more than does some less developed state of human existence. But hitherto all such ideas were formulated in a moralizing way—civilization was represented as being "corrupt," a divagation from a state of innocence. Freud had no illusions about a primitive innocence, he conceived no practicable alternative to civilization. In consequence, there was a unique force to the question he asked: whether we wished to accept civilization, with all its contradictions, with all its pains—pains, for "discontents" does not accurately describe what Freud has in mind. He had his own answer to the question—his tragic, or stoic, sense of life dictated it: we do well to accept it, although we also do well to cast a cold eye on the fate that makes it our better part to accept it. Like Nietzsche, Freud thought that life was justified by our heroic response to its challenge.

But the question Freud posed has not been set aside or closed up by the answer that he himself gave to it. His answer, like Nietzsche's, is essentially in the line of traditional humanism—we can see this in the sternness with which he charges women not to interfere with men in the discharge of their cultural duty, not to claim men for love and the family to the detriment of their free activity in the world. But just here lies the matter of Freud's question that the world more and more believes Freud himself did not answer. The pain that civilization inflicts is that of the instinctual renunciation that civilization demands, and it would seem that fewer and fewer people wish to say with Freud that the loss of instinctual gratification, emotional freedom, or love, is compensated for either by the security of civilized life or by the stern pleasures of the masculine moral character.

With Freud's essay I brought to a close my list of prolegomenal books for the first term of the course. I shall not do much more than mention the books with which I introduced the second term, but I should like to do at least that. I began with *Rameau's Nephew*,[3] thinking that the peculiar moral authority which Diderot assigns to the envious, untalented, unregenerate protagonist was peculiarly relevant to the line taken by the ethical explora-

tions of modern literature. Nothing is more characteristic of the literature of our time than the replacement of the hero by what has come to be called the anti-hero, in whose indifference to or hatred of ethical nobility there is presumed to lie a special authenticity. Diderot is quite overt about this—he himself in his public character is the deuteragonist,[4] the "honest consciousness," as Hegel calls him,[5] and he takes delight in the discomfiture of the decent, dull person he is by the Nephew's nihilistic mind.

It seemed to me too that there was particular usefulness in the circumstance that this anti-hero should avow so openly his *envy*, which Tocqueville[6] has called the ruling emotion of democracy, and that, although he envied

3. A novel by the French man of letters and philosopher Denis Diderot (1713–1784), completed in 1774 but first published in a German translation in 1805. The book is a lively, witty philosophical conversation between Lui ("Him," Rameau's nephew) and Moi ("Me," Diderot).

4. In ancient Greek tragedy, the actor playing the second most important figure; the most important is the protagonist.

5. Hegel alludes to the book in *Phänomenologie des Geistes* (1807, *Phenomenology of Spirit* or *Mind*), VI.B.I.a.

6. Alexis de Tocqueville (1805–1859), French politician, political scientist, and historian; he called envy the "democratic sentiment" in *Democracy in America* (4 vols., 1835–40), part 1, chap. 13.

anyone at all who had access to the creature-comforts and the social status which he lacked, what chiefly animated him was envy of men of genius. Ours is the first cultural epoch in which many men aspire to high achievement in the arts and, in their frustration, form a dispossessed class which cuts across the conventional class lines, making a proletariat of the spirit.

Although *Rameau's Nephew* was not published until fairly late in the century, it was known in manuscript by Goethe and Hegel: it suited the temper and won the admiration of Marx[7] and Freud for reasons that are obvious. And there is ground for supposing that it was known to Dostoevski, whose *Notes from Underground*[8] is a restatement of the essential idea of Diderot's dialogue in terms both more extreme and less genial. The Nephew is still on the defensive—he is naughtily telling secrets about the nature of man and society. But Dostoevski's underground man shouts aloud his envy and hatred and carries the ark of his self-hatred and alienation into a remorseless battle with what he calls "the good and the beautiful," mounting an attack upon every belief not merely of bourgeois society but of the whole humanist tradition. The inclusion of *Notes from Underground* among my prolegomenal books constituted something of a pedagogic risk, for if I wished to emphasize the subversive tendency of modern literature, here was a work which made all subsequent subversion seem like affirmation, so radical and so brilliant was its negation of our traditional pieties and its affirmation of our new pieties.

I hesitated in compunction before following *Notes from Underground* with Tolstoi's *Death of Ivan Ilyitch*,[9] which so ruthlessly and with such dreadful force destroys the citadel of the commonplace life in which we all believe we can take refuge from ourselves and our fate. But I did assign it and then two of Pirandello's[1] plays which, in the atmosphere of the sordidness of the commonplace life, undermine all the certitudes of the commonplace, common-sense mind.

From time to time I have raised with myself the question of whether my choice of these prolegomenal works was not extravagant, quite excessively tendentious. I have never been able to believe that it is. And if these works do indeed serve to indicate in an accurate way the nature of modern literature, a teacher might find it worth asking how his students respond to the strong dose.

One response I have already described—the readiness of the students to engage in the process that we might call the socialization of the anti-social, or the acculturation of the anti-cultural, or the legitimization of the subversive. When the term-essays come in, it is plain to me that almost none of the students have been taken aback by what they have read: they have wholly contained the attack. The chief exceptions are the few who simply do not comprehend, although they may be awed by, the categories of our discourse. In their papers, like poor hunted creatures in a Kafka story, they take refuge first in misunderstood large phrases, then in bad grammar, then in general incoherence. After my pedagogical exasperation has run its course, I find

7. KARL MARX (1818–1883), German philosopher and revolutionary; in a letter to FRIEDRICH ENGELS of April 15, 1869, he calls *Rameau's Nephew* a "unique masterpiece."

8. *Notes from Underground* (1864), a novella by the Russian writer Fyodor Dostoyevsky (1821–1881).

9. *The Death of Ivan Ilyich* (1886), a novella by the Russian writer Leo Tolstoy (1828–1910).

1. Luigi Pirandello (1867–1936), prolific Italian playwright and novelist, often seen as a forerunner of the theater of the absurd.

that I am sometimes moved to give them a queer respect, as if they had stood up and said what in fact they don't have the wit to stand up and say: "Why do you harry us? Leave us alone. We are not Modern Man. We are the Old People. Ours is the Old Faith. We serve the little Old Gods, the gods of the copybook maxims, the small, dark, somewhat powerful deities of lawyers, doctors, engineers, accountants. With them is neither sensibility nor *angst*. With them is no disgust—it is they, indeed, who make ready the way for 'the good and the beautiful' about which low-minded doubts have been raised in this course, that 'good and beautiful' which we do not possess and don't want to possess but which we know justifies our lives. Leave us alone and let us worship our gods in the way they approve, in peace and unawareness." Crass, but—to use that interesting modern word which we have learned from the curators of museums—authentic. The rest, the minds that give me the A papers and the B papers and even the C+ papers, move through the terrors and mysteries of modern literature like so many Parsifals,[2] asking no questions at the behest of wonder and fear. Or like so many seminarists[3] who have been systematically instructed in the constitution of Hell and the ways to damnation. Or like so many *readers*, entertained by moral horror stories. I asked them to look into the Abyss, and, both dutifully and gladly, they have looked into the Abyss, and the Abyss has greeted them with the grave courtesy of all objects of serious study, saying: "Interesting, am I not? And *exciting*, if you consider how deep I am and what dread beasts lie at my bottom. Have it well in mind that a knowledge of me contributes materially to your being whole, or well-rounded, men."

In my distress over the outrage I have conspired to perpetrate upon a great literature, I wonder if perhaps I have not been reading these papers too literally. After all, a term-essay is not a diary of the soul, it is not an occasion for telling the truth. What my students might reveal of their true feelings to a younger teacher they will not reveal to me; they will give me what they conceive to be the proper response to the official version of terror I have given them. I bring to mind their faces, which are not necessarily the faces of the authors of these unperturbed papers, nor are they, not yet, the faces of fathers of families, or of theatergoers, or of buyers of modern paintings: not yet. I must think it possible that in ways and to a degree which they keep secret they have responded directly and personally to what they have read.

And if they have? And if they have, am I the more content?

What form would I want their response to take? It is a teacher's question that I am asking, not a critic's. We have decided in recent years to think of the critic and the teacher of literature as one and the same, and no doubt it is both possible and useful to do so. But there are some points at which the functions of the two do not coincide, or can be made to coincide only with great difficulty. Of criticism we have been told, by Arnold, that "it must be apt to study and praise elements that for fullness of spiritual perfection are wanted even though they belong to a power which in the practical sphere may be maleficent."[4] But teaching, or at least undergraduate teaching, is not

2. In the medieval story of Perceval or Parzival, which is the basis of the opera *Parsifal* (1882) by the German composer Richard Wagner, the hero—a naive youth who becomes a knight of King Arthur's Round Table—initially is punished for his failure to ask the essential question of the keeper of the Holy Grail (the legendary cup used by Jesus at the Last Supper and used to catch his blood while he was on the cross).

3. Seminarians.

4. From "The Function of Criticism at the Present Time" (1864; see above).

given the same licensed mandate—cannot be given it because the teacher's audience, which stands before his very eyes, as the critic's audience does not, asks questions about "the practical sphere," as the critic's audience does not. For instance, on the very day that I write this, when I had said to my class all I could think of to say about *The Magic Mountain*[5] and invited questions and comments, one student asked. "How would you generalize the idea of the educative value of illness, so that it would be applicable not only to a particular individual, Hans Castorp, but to young people at large?" It makes us smile, but it was asked in all seriousness, and it is serious in its substance, and it had to be answered seriously, in part by the reflection that this idea, like so many ideas encountered in the books of the course, had to be thought of as having reference only to the private life; that it touched the public life only in some indirect or tangential way; that it really ought to be encountered in solitude, even in secrecy, since to talk about it in public and in our academic setting was to seem to propose for it a public practicality and thus to distort its meaning. To this another student replied; he said that, despite the public ritual of the classroom, each student inevitably experienced the books in privacy and found their meaning in reference to his own life. True enough, but the teacher sees the several privacies coming together to make a group, and they propose—no doubt the more because they come together every Monday, Wednesday, and Friday at a particular hour—the idea of a community, that is to say, "the practical sphere."

This being so, the teacher cannot escape the awareness of certain circumstances which the critic, who writes for an ideal, uncircumstanced reader, has no need to take into account. The teacher considers, for example, the social situation of his students—they are not of patrician origin, they do not come from homes in which stubbornness, pride, and conscious habit prevail, nor are they born into a culture marked by these traits, a culture in which other interesting and valuable things compete with and resist ideas; they come, mostly, from "good homes" in which authority and valuation are weak or at least not very salient and bold, so that ideas have for them, at their present stage of development, a peculiar power and preciousness. And in this connection the teacher will have in mind the special prestige that our culture, in its upper reaches, gives to art, and to the ideas that art proposes—the agreement, ever growing in assertiveness, that art yields more truth than any other intellectual activity. In this culture what a shock it is to encounter Santayana's[6] acerb skepticism about art, or Keats's remark, which the critics and scholars never take notice of, presumably because they suppose it to be an aberration, that poetry is "not so fine a thing as philosophy—For the same reason that an eagle is not so fine a thing as a truth."[7] For many students no ideas that they will encounter in any college discipline will equal in force and sanction the ideas conveyed to them by modern literature.

The author of *The Magic Mountain* once said that all his work could be understood as an effort to free himself from the middle class,[8] and this, of

5. Thomas Mann's celebrated 1924 bildungsroman (novel of moral and psychological education); Castorp, its main character, spends 7 years in a tuberculosis sanitarium in the Swiss mountains.

6. George Santayana (1863–1952), Spanish-born American philosopher, essayist, poet, and novelist; though he celebrated the power of art, he was highly skeptical of the idea that it might rest on some transcendent inspiration.

7. Quoted from Keats's letter dated February 19, 1819, to his younger brother George Keats and George's wife, Georgiana.

8. This statement attributed to Mann has not been found in any of his writings.

course, will serve to describe the chief intention of all modern literature. And the means of freedom which Mann prescribes (the characteristic irony notwithstanding) is the means of freedom which in effect all of modern literature prescribes. It is, in the words of Clavdia Chauchat, *"se perdre et même . . . se laisser dépérír,"*[9] and thus to name the means is to make plain that the end is not merely freedom from the middle class but freedom from society itself. I venture to say that the idea of losing oneself up to the point of self-destruction, of surrendering oneself to experience without regard to self-interest or conventional morality, of escaping wholly from the societal bonds, is an "element" somewhere in the mind of every modern person who dares to think of what Arnold in his unaffected Victorian way called "the fulness of spiritual perfection."[1] But the teacher who undertakes to present modern literature to his students may not allow that idea to remain in the *somewhere* of his mind; he must take it from the place where it exists habitual and unrealized and put it in the conscious forefront of his thought. And if he is committed to an admiration of modern literature, he must also be committed to this chief idea of modern literature. I press the logic of the situation not in order to question the legitimacy of the commitment, or even the propriety of expressing the commitment in the college classroom (although it does seem odd!), but to confront those of us who do teach modern literature with the striking actuality of our enterprise.

1961, 1965

9. "To lose oneself and likewise . . . to let oneself be ruined" (French). Chauchat (in French, literally "Hot Cat") is Castorp's romantic interest in *The Magic Mountain*.

1. Quoted from "The Function of Criticism at the Present Time."

HANNAH ARENDT

1906–1975

The life and work of the political theorist Hannah Arendt have been equally controversial and inspirational. Especially after the attacks of 9/11, her reflections on human rights, statelessness, evil, and particularly the nature of the political have become central to discussions of terrorism and the varied responses to it. She contended that violence renders political relationships impossible, even as she examined the various forms of violence perpetrated by state and nonstate agents. Arendt was also a strong critic of commercial culture, and our selections from her work highlight her insistence that politics is not primarily about economic well-being. Thus, her work is often enlisted in critiques of neoliberalism and in defenses of the humanities against utilitarian understandings of education's value.

Raised in Konigsberg (the Prussian birthplace of KANT) in a prosperous and well-assimilated Jewish family, Arendt was a sickly child whose father died when she was seven. At sixteen Arendt began classes at the University of Berlin to complete her secondary schooling; two years later she started her university education at Marburg, specifically to study with MARTIN HEIDEGGER. By the end of her first year, she was having an affair with him. In part because of the complications of this relationship (he was thirty-five, married, and controlling), a year after it began Arendt left

Marburg for Heidelberg, where she completed her dissertation under the direction of Karl Jaspers in 1929. She then moved to Berlin, where she worked on her habilitation thesis—the second thesis required in Germany to obtain an academic position—and married Günther Stern, a leftist whom she had met in Heidegger's lectures. When the Nazis came to power in 1933, she was arrested and detained for a week because of her communist connections; after being released, she immediately left for Paris, where Stern had already fled. But their marriage fell apart, and he went on to America in 1936. In Paris's German ex-pat community Arendt met WALTER BENJAMIN and Heinrich Blücher, whom she married in 1940. Separately held in internment camps in 1941 as "enemy aliens," after several weeks Arendt and Blücher both escaped, reunited, and, with the help of Stern, managed to get papers to leave Marseilles for the United States via Portugal. They reached New York in May 1941.

The thirty-five-year-old Arendt set about learning English and became involved with Jewish émigré groups based in New York. By 1944, she was working for Schocken Books (where she oversaw the first publication in English of Kafka's and Benjamin's work) and publishing essays in *Partisan Review*, a leftist quarterly literary magazine. Her first book, the masterpiece *The Origins of Totalitarianism* (1951), offers a detailed historical and theoretical explanation for the deadly regimes of Hitler and Stalin. Arendt was associated with the New York Intellectuals, a group of liberal and leftist writers who during the cold war were critical of the United States but extremely hostile to the Soviet Union. Between 1955 and her death, Arendt wrote a series of works in political theory, most notably *The Human Condition* (1958). She also wrote about current affairs in popular venues, including the *New Yorker*, *New York Times*, and *New York Review of Books*. She taught at Princeton University, at the University of Chicago from 1963 to 1967, and at the New School for Social Research from 1967 to 1975.

In 1960, Arendt persuaded the *New Yorker* to send her to Jerusalem to cover the trial of Adolph Eichmann, who had been seized in Argentina by Israeli agents for his war crimes—he had been the Nazi functionary in charge of transporting Europe's Jews to the death camps. Eichmann presented himself merely as a bureaucrat, and Arendt's published report, with its famous phrase "the banality of evil," sparked a firestorm. Many readers, Jews and non-Jews alike, saw it as an attack on Israel, whitewashing Nazi crimes while appearing to blame Jewish victims (especially their community leaders) for the horrors of the Holocaust. The posthumous revelation of Arendt's affair with Heidegger, who in 1933 joined the Nazi Party, together with her making several visits to him in the 1950s and corresponding with him until her death, added fuel to the claim that she was a "self-hating Jew." Arendt did criticize Heidegger's infamous support of the Nazis in several essays, but she seemed to have mostly forgiven him for his political sins. The controversy lives on, as Jewish writers such as JUDITH BUTLER and Corey Robin have gone to Arendt's work when voicing their own objections to policies pursued by the state of Israel.

Arendt's distinctive understanding of the political rests on a three-part distinction between labor, work, and (especially) action. Labor is the effort required to produce the necessities of life. Arendt's hostility to both Marxism and capitalism is rooted in their reduction of life to labor. Inspired by the Greeks, especially ARISTOTLE, Arendt insists that life is meaningful only when humans *work* to produce things of lasting value (things that persist, as opposed to the necessities of life that are consumed) and *act*. Our selection from *The Human Condition* presents her theory of action, which is the centerpiece of her political philosophy. Crucially, action produces nothing, even as it is the highest expression of human freedom. In action is revealed the actor's identity—an identity that was unknown to the agent and to others prior to the performed action. Arendt's notion of action is thus recognizably performative (to use a term from J. L. AUSTIN's contemporaneous work, of which she appears to have been unaware). An equally crucial point is that action occurs in public, in the intersubjective space where the "I" appears in front of others. That space *is* the political for Arendt: action's performative nature creates both the agent's identity and the *polis* (political community). The political disappears unless public action is ongoing, as action creates and sustains "the web of relationships" that is the stuff of politics.

This understanding of politics is radically nonutilitarian. Politics is not about the distribution of resources (whether those resources consist of power, wealth, or status). Rather, politics is about freedom and meaning—an emphasis that suggests Arendt's affinity with the existentialism of Heidegger. Arendt's "action" is free because it is divorced from having to provide the necessities of life, and meaningful because it enables the agent to discover "who" she is—and to discover "who" these others she lives with are. The "joy" of politics, Arendt tells us at the end of our second selection, comes from "inserting ourselves into the world by word and deed, thus acquiring and sustaining our personal identity and beginning something entirely new." Action as self-creation requires others even as it introduces something new—this unique self—into the world.

Especially important to literary theorists has been Arendt's connection of action to speech and storytelling. In JULIA KRISTEVA's words, Arendt shows us "we must tell the story of our life before we can ascribe a meaning to it." Mute action is without meaning, partly because the meaning of actions is not under the control of the agent. Instead, it is in the intersubjectively produced story of deeds that their meaning unfolds. Elsewhere in her work, Arendt laments that the possibility of this intersubjective relationship, dependent on the existence of a public sphere that is nonutilitarian, has diminished in modernity, which relentlessly focuses on the production of items for exchange, the accumulation of wealth, and the consumption of commodities. In *The Human Condition* she stresses the inability of any single agent to make or control the story that action tells. The notion of "an invisible actor behind the scenes" who dictates what occurs in the public space of appearances has haunted Western thought since PLATO, she tells us, but should be rejected. Action unfolds without guarantees; its consequences and meanings will develop in ways we cannot predict or control. That is why Aristotle was correct to identify "action" as the key component of tragedy and why "theater is the political art par excellence." In front of others, the risk-laden drama of one's identity unfolds in a space of exhilarating yet terrifying freedom.

Our second selection, from the essay "Truth and Politics" (1968), touches again on Arendt's emphasis on storytelling as the site of meaning. However, meaning is distinct from truth. Meaning attends to the significance we as humans attach to our actions and existence, whereas truth refers to the basic conditions of existence within which our actions and our efforts to attain meaning take place. Arendt was led to this account of truth because of the many falsehoods that she felt pervaded the attacks on her report of the Eichmann trial. Her attempt to define and defend truth enriches her understanding of the political. Arendt famously—and influentially—argues that truth is irrelevant, even dangerous, in the political sphere. In that sphere, citizens argue about *things*, often about the best course of action for the collective to undertake. In those arguments, every citizen's opinion is entitled to be heard. (Arendt's valorization of "opinion" as the stuff of politics is a deliberate repudiation of the Platonic attempt to banish opinion from the ideal republic in favor of the philosopher's truths.) And the things we argue about have no right or wrong answer. Should my town build a bridge over the nearby river? Since we cannot know consequences in advance, arguments for and against building it are equally worth hearing. When as a group we come to a decision, we are making only an educated guess about those future consequences. For that reason, those who vote on the other side from me must be recognized. We disagree, but neither of us has access to an unequivocal truth about this matter we are debating. In that debate, I am also revealing who I am and realizing what is most meaningful to me through my interaction with others. So it is meaning, not truth, that is political.

Truth, Arendt says, compels—and that is why it has no place in the political, which deals with uncertain matters open to debate. But that does not mean truth is irrelevant. Quite the contrary. Rather, she argues, truth should be established apart from the political sphere. In our selection, she sees the judiciary, the university, and the press as three places for the discovery of truth. In a court, the trial should decide if the person actually committed the deed of which he or she is accused; at a university, scholars should "find out, stand guard over, and interpret factual truth"; and journalists should give us the truth about what our politicians, those engaged in business, and other public actors are doing. The political debates Arendt so cherishes are impossible, she declares, unless grounded on truth. We can legitimately argue about the causes of World War I and the question of who was to blame, but such an argument is impossible if one party to the dispute denies that Germany invaded Belgium in August 1914. Arendt's position here is, in part, a passionate defense of academic freedom, and it resonates with the later work of MARTHA NUSSBAUM. If a polity allows political ideology to override the disinterested, impartial pursuit of the truth, then it abandons any footing in reality.

Arendt wants to maintain both the purity of a political sphere separated from all questions of interest and the clarity of a truth separated from the taint of disputable opinion, though her success in doing so may be limited. Even so, her passionate commitment to nonutilitarian values, her attention to the centrality of storytelling and meaning as human concerns, and her attempt to balance truth and opinion in ways that leave space open for reasonable political debate have inspired defenders of the humanities as they struggle to articulate how there is more to life than evidence-based science and economic productivity.

***The Human Condition* Keywords:** Authorship, Drama, Identity, Language, Narrative Theory
"Truth and Politics" Keywords: Defense of Criticism, Interpretation Theory, Narrative Theory, Rhetoric

From The Human Condition

From 24. *The Disclosure of the Agent in Speech and Action*

* * *

Action and speech are so closely related because the primordial and specifically human act must at the same time contain the answer to the question asked of every newcomer: "Who are you?" This disclosure of who somebody is, is implicit in both his words and his deeds; yet obviously the affinity between speech and revelation is much closer than that between action and revelation, just as the affinity between action and beginning is closer than that between speech and beginning, although many, and even most acts, are performed in the manner of speech. Without the accompaniment of speech, at any rate, action would not only lose its revelatory character, but, and by the same token, it would lose its subject, as it were; not acting men but performing robots would achieve what, humanly speaking, would remain incomprehensible. Speechless action would no longer be action because there would no longer be an actor, and the actor, the doer of deeds, is possible only if he is at the same time the speaker of words. The action he begins is humanly disclosed by the word, and though his deed can be perceived in its brute physical appearance without verbal accompaniment, it becomes relevant only through the spoken word in which he identifies himself as the actor, announcing what he does, has done, and intends to do.

No other human performance requires speech to the same extent as action. In all other performances speech plays a subordinate role, as a means of communication or a mere accompaniment to something that could also be achieved in silence. It is true that speech is extremely useful as a means of communication and information, but as such it could be replaced by a sign language, which then might prove to be even more useful and expedient to convey certain meanings, as in mathematics and other scientific disciplines or in certain forms of teamwork. Thus, it is also true that man's capacity to act, and especially to act in concert, is extremely useful for purposes of self-defense or pursuit of interests; but if nothing more were at stake here than to use action as a means to an end, it is obvious that the same end could be much more easily attained in mute violence, so that action seems a not very efficient substitute for violence, just as speech, from the viewpoint of sheer utility, seems an awkward substitute for sign language.

In acting and speaking, men show who they are, reveal actively their unique personal identities and thus make their appearance in the human world, while their physical identities appear without any activity of their own in the unique shape of the body and sound of the voice. This disclosure of "who" in contradistinction to "what" somebody is—his qualities, gifts, talents, and shortcomings, which he may display or hide—is implicit in everything somebody says and does. It can be hidden only in complete silence and perfect passivity, but its disclosure can almost never be achieved as a willful purpose, as though one possessed and could dispose of this "who" in the same manner he has and can dispose of his qualities. On the contrary, it is more than likely that the "who," which appears so clearly and unmistakably to others, remains hidden from the person himself, like the *daimōn*[1] in Greek religion which accompanies each man throughout his life, always looking over his shoulder from behind and thus visible only to those he encounters.

This revelatory quality of speech and action comes to the fore where people are *with* others and neither for nor against them—that is, in sheer human togetherness. Although nobody knows whom he reveals when he discloses himself in deed or word, he must be willing to risk the disclosure, and this neither the doer of good works, who must be without self and preserve complete anonymity, nor the criminal, who must hide himself from others, can take upon themselves. Both are lonely figures, the one being for, the other against, all men; they, therefore, remain outside the pale of human intercourse and are, politically, marginal figures who usually enter the historical scene in times of corruption, disintegration, and political bankruptcy. Because of its inherent tendency to disclose the agent together with the act, action needs for its full appearance the shining brightness we once called glory, and which is possible only in the public realm.

Without the disclosure of the agent in the act, action loses its specific character and becomes one form of achievement among others. It is then

1. Divine power, especially a power controlling the destiny of an individual.

indeed no less a means to an end than making is a means to produce an object. This happens whenever human togetherness is lost, that is, when people are only for or against other people, as for instance in modern warfare, where men go into action and use means of violence in order to achieve certain objectives for their own side and against the enemy. In these instances, which of course have always existed, speech becomes indeed "mere talk," simply one more means toward the end, whether it serves to deceive the enemy or to dazzle everybody with propaganda; here words reveal nothing, disclosure comes only from the deed itself, and this achievement, like all other achievements, cannot disclose the "who," the unique and distinct identity of the agent.

In these instances action has lost the quality through which it transcends mere productive activity, which, from the humble making of use objects to the inspired creation of art works, has no more meaning than is revealed in the finished product and does not intend to show more than is plainly visible at the end of the production process. Action without a name, a "who" attached to it, is meaningless, whereas an art work retains its relevance whether or not we know the master's name. The monuments to the "Unknown Soldier" after World War I bear testimony to the then still existing need for glorification, for finding a "who," an identifiable somebody whom four years of mass slaughter should have revealed. The frustration of this wish and the unwillingness to resign oneself to the brutal fact that the agent of the war was actually nobody inspired the erection of the monuments to the "unknown," to all those whom the war had failed to make known and had robbed thereby, not of their achievement, but of their human dignity.[2]

25. *The Web of Relationships and the Enacted Stories*

The manifestation of who the speaker and doer unexchangeably is, though it is plainly visible, retains a curious intangibility that confounds all efforts toward unequivocal verbal expression. The moment we want to say *who* somebody is, our very vocabulary leads us astray into saying *what* he is; we get entangled in a description of qualities he necessarily shares with others like him; we begin to describe a type or a "character" in the old meaning of the word, with the result that his specific uniqueness escapes us.

This frustration has the closest affinity with the well-known philosophic impossibility to arrive at a definition of man, all definitions being determinations or interpretations of *what* man is, of qualities, therefore, which he could possibly share with other living beings, whereas his specific difference would be found in a determination of what kind of a "who" he is. Yet apart from this philosophic perplexity, the impossibility, as it were, to solidify in words the living essence of the person as it shows itself in the flux of action and speech, has great bearing upon the whole realm of human affairs, where we exist primarily as acting and speaking beings. It excludes in principle our ever being able to handle these affairs as we handle things whose nature is at our disposal because we can name them. The point is

2. William Faulkner's *A Fable* (1954) surpasses almost all of World War I literature in perceptiveness and clarity because its hero is the Unknown Soldier [Arendt's note].

that the manifestation of the "who" comes to pass in the same manner as the notoriously unreliable manifestations of ancient oracles, which, according to Heraclitus, "neither reveal nor hide in words, but give manifest signs."[3] This is a basic factor in the equally notorious uncertainty not only of all political matters, but of all affairs that go on between men directly, without the intermediary, stabilizing, and solidifying influence of things.[4]

This is only the first of many frustrations by which action, and consequently the togetherness and intercourse of men, are ridden. It is perhaps the most fundamental of those we shall deal with, in so far as it does not rise out of comparisons with more reliable and productive activities, such as fabrication or contemplation or cognition or even labor, but indicates something that frustrates action in terms of its own purposes. What is at stake is the revelatory character without which action and speech would lose all human relevance.

Action and speech go on between men, as they are directed toward them, and they retain their agent-revealing capacity even if their content is exclusively "objective," concerned with the matters of the world of things in which men move, which physically lies between them and out of which arise their specific, objective, worldly interests. These interests constitute, in the word's most literal significance, something which *inter-est*, which lies between people and therefore can relate and bind them together. Most action and speech is concerned with this in-between, which varies with each group of people, so that most words and deeds are *about* some worldly objective reality in addition to being a disclosure of the acting and speaking agent. Since this disclosure of the subject is an integral part of all, even the most "objective" intercourse, the physical, worldly in-between along with its interests is overlaid and, as it were, overgrown with an altogether different in-between which consists of deeds and words and owes its origin exclusively to men's acting and speaking directly *to* one another. This second, subjective in-between is not tangible, since there are no tangible objects into which it could solidify; the process of acting and speaking can leave behind no such results and end products. But for all its intangibility, this in-between is no less real than the world of things we visibly have in common. We call this reality the "web" of human relationships, indicating by the metaphor its somewhat intangible quality.

To be sure, this web is no less bound to the objective world of things than speech is to the existence of a living body, but the relationship is not like that of a façade or, in Marxian terminology, of an essentially superfluous superstructure[5] affixed to the useful structure of the building itself. The basic error of all materialism in politics—and this materialism is not Marxian

3. *Oute legei oute kryptei alla semainei* (Diels, *Fragmente der Vorsokratiker* [4th ed., 1922], frag. B93) [Arendt's note]. Heraclitus (active ca. 500 B.C.E.), Greek philosopher whose work has survived only in fragments quoted by later authors.

4. Socrates used the same word as Heraclitus, *semainein* ("to show and give signs"), for the manifestation of his *daimonion* [literally, "divine something"] (Xenophon *Memorabilia* 1.1.2, 4). If we are to trust Xenophon, Socrates likened his *daimonion* to the oracles and insisted that both should be used only for human affairs, where nothing is certain, and not for problems of the arts and crafts, where everything is predictable (ibid. 7–9) [Arendt's note]. Socrates (469–399 B.C.E.), Greek philosopher who speaks of his *daimonion* at the trial that condemns him to death; the most familiar account is in *Apology* 38d, by Socrates' student PLATO (ca. 427–ca. 347 B.C.E.). Xenophon (ca. 428/27–ca. 354 B.C.E.), Greek historian and student of Socrates.

5. In Marxist thought, the elements of society—language, literature, political institutions, legal statutes—that emanate from the material "base" of production and the relations of production.

and not even modern in origin, but as old as our history of political theory—is to overlook the inevitability with which men disclose themselves as subjects, as distinct and unique persons, even when they wholly concentrate upon reaching an altogether worldly, material object. To dispense with this disclosure, if indeed it could ever be done, would mean to transform men into something they are not; to deny, on the other hand, that this disclosure is real and has consequences of its own is simply unrealistic.

The realm of human affairs, strictly speaking, consists of the web of human relationships which exists wherever men live together. The disclosure of the "who" through speech, and the setting of a new beginning through action, always fall into an already existing web where their immediate consequences can be felt. Together they start a new process which eventually emerges as the unique life story of the newcomer, affecting uniquely the life stories of all those with whom he comes into contact. It is because of this already existing web of human relationships, with its innumerable, conflicting wills and intentions, that action almost never achieves its purpose; but it is also because of this medium, in which action alone is real, that it "produces" stories with or without intention as naturally as fabrication produces tangible things.[6] These stories may then be recorded in documents and monuments, they may be visible in use objects or art works, they may be told and retold and worked into all kinds of material. They themselves, in their living reality, are of an altogether different nature than these reifications. They tell us more about their subjects, the "hero" in the center of each story, than any product of human hands ever tells us about the master who produced it, and yet they are not products, properly speaking. Although everybody started his life by inserting himself into the human world through action and speech, nobody is the author or producer of his own life story. In other words, the stories, the results of action and speech, reveal an agent, but this agent is not an author or producer. Somebody began it and is its subject in the twofold sense of the word, namely, its actor and sufferer, but nobody is its author.

That every individual life between birth and death can eventually be told as a story with beginning and end is the prepolitical and prehistorical condition of history, the great story without beginning and end. But the reason why each human life tells its story and why history ultimately becomes the storybook of mankind, with many actors and speakers and yet without any tangible authors, is that both are the outcome of action. For the great unknown in history, that has baffled the philosophy of history in the modern age, arises not only when one considers history as a whole and finds that its subject, mankind, is an abstraction which never can become an active agent; the same unknown has baffled political philosophy from its beginning in antiquity and contributed to the general contempt in which philosophers since Plato have held the realm of human affairs. The perplexity is that in any series of events that together form a story with a unique meaning we can at best isolate the agent who set the whole process into motion; and although

6. In Arendt, "labor" is the effort required to produce the necessities of life (food, shelter, clothing) that are consumed and thus must be produced again. "Work" produces material objects that are not consumed by use, but that often last longer than the worker's lifetime. "Action," unlike labor and work, is nonmaterial.

this agent frequently remains the subject, the "hero" of the story, we never can point unequivocally to him as the author of its eventual outcome.

It is for this reason that Plato thought that human affairs (*ta tōn anthrōpōn pragmata*), the outcome of action (*praxis*), should not be treated with great seriousness; the actions of men appear like the gestures of puppets led by an invisible hand behind the scene, so that man seems to be a kind of plaything of a god.[7] It is noteworthy that Plato, who had no inkling of the modern concept of history, should have been the first to invent the metaphor of an actor behind the scenes who, behind the backs of acting men, pulls the strings and is responsible for the story. The Platonic god is but a symbol for the fact that real stories, in distinction from those we invent, have no author; as such, he is the true forerunner of Providence, the "invisible hand," Nature, the "world spirit," class interest,[8] and the like, with which Christian and modern philosophers of history tried to solve the perplexing problem that although history owes its existence to men, it is still obviously not "made" by them. (Nothing in fact indicates more clearly the political nature of history—its being a story of action and deeds rather than of trends and forces or ideas—than the introduction of an invisible actor behind the scenes whom we find in all philosophies of history, which for this reason alone can be recognized as political philosophies in disguise. By the same token, the simple fact that Adam Smith needed an "invisible hand" to guide economic dealings on the exchange market shows plainly that more than sheer economic activity is involved in exchange and that "economic man," when he makes his appearance on the market, is an acting being and neither exclusively a producer nor a trader and barterer.)

The invisible actor behind the scenes is an invention arising from a mental perplexity but corresponding to no real experience. Through it, the story resulting from action is misconstrued as a fictional story, where indeed an author pulls the strings and directs the play. The fictional story reveals a maker just as every work of art clearly indicates that it was made by somebody; this does not belong to the character of the story itself but only to the mode in which it came into existence. The distinction between a real and a fictional story is precisely that the latter was "made up" and the former not made at all. The real story in which we are engaged as long as we live has no visible or invisible maker because it is not made. The only "somebody" it reveals is its hero, and it is the only medium in which the originally intangible manifestation of a uniquely distinct "who" can become tangible *ex post facto*[9] through action and speech. *Who* somebody is or was we can know only by knowing the story of which he is himself the hero—his biography, in other words; everything else we know of him, including the work he may have produced and left behind, tells us only *what* he is or was. Thus, although we know much less of Socrates, who did not write a single line and left no work behind, than of Plato or Aristotle,[1] we know

7. *Laws* 803 and 644 [Arendt's note]. *Ta tōn anthrōpōn pragmata*: literally, "practical matters related to humans" (Greek).
8. All nonhuman powers used to explain the source of events and the outcomes of human actions in different explanatory systems: Providence in much Protestant thought, the "invisible hand" in *The Wealth of Nations* (1776) by the Scottish philosopher Adam Smith (1723–1790), Nature in modern science, the "world spirit" in the writing of GEORG WILHELM FRIEDRICH HEGEL (1770–1831), and class interest in the works of KARL MARX (1818–1883).
9. After the fact (Latin).
1. Greek philosopher (384–322 B.C.E.); see above.

much better and more intimately who he was, because we know his story, than we know who Aristotle was, about whose opinions we are so much better informed.

The hero the story discloses needs no heroic qualities; the word "hero" originally, that is, in Homer, was no more than a name given each free man who participated in the Trojan enterprise[2] and about whom a story could be told. The connotation of courage, which we now feel to be an indispensable quality of the hero, is in fact already present in a willingness to act and speak at all, to insert one's self into the world and begin a story of one's own. And this courage is not necessarily or even primarily related to a willingness to suffer the consequences; courage and even boldness are already present in leaving one's private hiding place and showing who one is, in disclosing and exposing one's self. The extent of this original courage, without which action and speech and therefore, according to the Greeks, freedom, would not be possible at all, is not less great and may even be greater if the "hero" happens to be a coward.

The specific content as well as the general meaning of action and speech may take various forms of reification in art works which glorify a deed or an accomplishment and, by transformation and condensation, show some extraordinary event in its full significance. However, the specific revelatory quality of action and speech, the implicit manifestation of the agent and speaker, is so indissolubly tied to the living flux of acting and speaking that it can be represented and "reified" only through a kind of repetition, the imitation or *mimēsis*,[3] which according to Aristotle prevails in all arts but is actually appropriate only to the *drama*, whose very name (from the Greek verb *dran*, "to act") indicates that play-acting actually is an imitation of acting.[4] But the imitative element lies not only in the art of the actor, but, as Aristotle rightly claims, in the making or writing of the play, at least to the extent that the drama comes fully to life only when it is enacted in the theater. Only the actors and speakers who re-enact the story's plot can convey the full meaning, not so much of the story itself, but of the "heroes" who reveal themselves in it.[5] In terms of Greek tragedy, this would mean that the story's direct as well as its universal meaning is revealed by the chorus, which does not imitate[6] and whose comments are pure poetry, whereas the intangible identities of the agents in the story, since they escape all generalization and therefore all reification, can be conveyed only through an imitation of their acting. This is also why the theater is the political art par

2. In Homer, the word *hērōs* has certainly a connotation of distinction, but of no other than every free man was capable. Nowhere does it appear in the later meaning of "half-god," which perhaps arose out of a deification of the ancient epic heroes [Arendt's note]. Homer (ca. 8th c. B.C.E.), Greek epic poet to whom the *Iliad* (the story of "the Trojan enterprise"—the Trojan War) and the *Odyssey* are attributed.

3. Imitation or representation (Greek): a key term in Plato's work and especially in Aristotle's *Poetics* (see above), where art is seen as a *mimēsis* of reality.

4. Aristotle already mentions that the word *drama* was chosen because *drōntes* ("acting people") are imitated (*Poetics* 1448a28). From the treatise itself, it is obvious that Aristotle's model for "imitation" in art is taken from the drama, and the generalization of the concept to make it applicable to all arts seems rather awkward [Arendt's note].

5. Aristotle therefore usually speaks not of an imitation of action (*praxis*) but of the agents (*prattontes*) (see *Poetics* 1448a1 ff., 1448b25, 1449b24 ff.). He is not consistent, however, in this use (cf. 1451a29, 1447a28). The decisive point is that tragedy does not deal with the qualities of men, their *poiotēs*, but with whatever happened with respect to them, with their actions and life and good or ill fortune (1450a15–18). The content of tragedy, therefore, is not what we would call character but action or the plot [Arendt's note].

6. That the chorus "imitates less" is mentioned in the Ps. Aristotelian *Problemata* (918b28) [Arendt's note]. The Pseudo-Aristotelian *Problems* is a compilation of perhaps the 5th or 6th century C.E.

excellence; only there is the political sphere of human life transposed into art. By the same token, it is the only art whose sole subject is man in his relationship to others.

1958

From Truth and Politics

* * *

In conclusion, I return to the questions I raised at the beginning of these reflections. Truth, though powerless and always defeated in a head-on clash with the powers that be, possesses a strength of its own: whatever those in power may contrive, they are unable to discover or invent a viable substitute for it. Persuasion and violence can destroy truth, but they cannot replace it. And this applies to rational or religious truth just as it applies, more obviously, to factual truth. To look upon politics from the perspective of truth, as I have done here, means to take one's stand outside the political realm. This standpoint is the standpoint of the truthteller, who forfeits his position—and, with it, the validity of what he has to say—if he tries to interfere directly in human affairs and to speak the language of persuasion or of violence. It is to this position and its significance for the political realm that we must now turn our attention.

The standpoint outside the political realm—outside the community to which we belong and the company of our peers—is clearly characterized as one of the various modes of being alone. Outstanding among the existential modes of truthtelling are the solitude of the philosopher, the isolation of the scientist and the artist, the impartiality of the historian and the judge, and the independence of the fact-finder, the witness, and the reporter. (This impartiality differs from that of the qualified, representative opinion, mentioned earlier, in that it is not acquired inside the political realm but is inherent in the position of the outsider required for such occupations.) These modes of being alone differ in many respects, but they have in common that as long as any one of them lasts, no political commitment, no adherence to a cause, is possible. They are, of course, common to all men; they are modes of human existence as such. Only when one of them is adopted as a way of life—and even then life is never lived in complete solitude or isolation or independence—is it likely to conflict with the demands of the political.

It is quite natural that we become aware of the non-political and, potentially, even anti-political nature of truth—*Fiat veritas, et pereat mundus*[1]—only in the event of conflict, and I have stressed up to now this side of the matter. But this cannot possibly tell the whole story. It leaves out of account certain public institutions, established and supported by the powers that be, in which, contrary to all political rules, truth and truthfulness have always constituted the highest criteria of speech and endeavor. Among these we find notably the judiciary, which either as a branch of government

1. Let truth be served, though the world perish (Latin). By replacing *justitia* with *veritas*, Arendt alters a famous Latin phrase that means "Let justice be done, though the world perish"—the motto of the Holy Roman emperor Ferdinand I (1503–1564; emperor 1558–64).

or as direct administration of justice is carefully protected against social and political power, as well as all institutions of higher learning, to which the state entrusts the education of its future citizens. To the extent that the Academe remembers its ancient origins, it must know that it was founded by the polis's most determined and most influential opponent. To be sure, Plato's[2] dream did not come true: the Academe never became a countersociety, and nowhere do we hear of any attempt by the universities at seizing power. But what Plato never dreamed of did come true: The political realm recognized that it needed an institution outside the power struggle in addition to the impartiality required in the administration of justice; for whether these places of higher learning are in private or in public hands is of no great importance; not only their integrity but their very existence depends upon the good will of the government anyway. Very unwelcome truths have emerged from the universities, and very unwelcome judgments have been handed down from the bench time and again; and these institutions, like other refuges of truth, have remained exposed to all the dangers arising from social and political power. Yet the chances for truth to prevail in public are, of course, greatly improved by the mere existence of such places and by the organization of independent, supposedly disinterested scholars associated with them. And it can hardly be denied that, at least in constitutionally ruled countries, the political realm has recognized, even in the event of conflict, that it has a stake in the existence of men and institutions over which it has no power.

This authentically political significance of the Academe is today easily overlooked because of the prominence of its professional schools and the evolution of its natural-science divisions, where, unexpectedly, pure research has yielded so many decisive results that have proved vital to the country at large. No one can possibly gainsay the social and technical usefulness of the universities, but this importance is not political. The historical sciences and the humanities, which are supposed to find out, stand guard over, and interpret factual truth and human documents, are politically of greater relevance. The telling of factual truth comprehends much more than the daily information supplied by journalists, though without them we should never find our bearings in an ever-changing world and, in the most literal sense, would never know where we are. This is, of course, of the most immediate political importance; but if the press should ever really become the "fourth branch of government," it would have to be protected against government power and social pressure even more carefully than the judiciary is. For this very important political function of supplying information is exercised from outside the political realm, strictly speaking; no action and no decision are, or should be, involved.

Reality is different from, and more than, the totality of facts and events, which, anyhow, is unascertainable. Who says what is—λέγει τὰ ἐόντα[3]—always tells a story, and in this story the particular facts lose their contingency and acquire some humanly comprehensible meaning. It is perfectly

2. Greek philosopher (ca. 427–ca. 347 B.C.E.; see above); the words *academe* and *academy* derive from the name of the school that he founded on the outskirts of Athens, which in turn took its name from a nearby park, the Academy (*Akadēmeia*).

3. Says the things that are (Greek). This echoes Hesiod (active ca. 700 B.C.E.), *Theogony* 38 (from his invocation to the Muses, the 9 daughters of Memory who preside over the arts and all intellectual pursuits).

true that "all sorrows can be borne if you put them into a story or tell a story about them," in the words of Isak Dinesen,[4] who not only was one of the great storytellers of our time but also—and she was almost unique in this respect—knew what she was doing. She could have added that joy and bliss, too, become bearable and meaningful for men only when they can talk about them and tell them as a story. To the extent that the teller of factual truth is also a storyteller, he brings about that "reconciliation with reality" which Hegel,[5] the philosopher of history *par excellence*, understood as the ultimate goal of all philosophical thought, and which, indeed, has been the secret motor of all historiography that transcends mere learnedness. The transformation of the given raw material of sheer happenings which the historian, like the fiction writer (a good novel is by no means a simple concoction or a figment of pure fantasy), must effect is closely akin to the poet's transfiguration of moods or movements of the heart—the transfiguration of grief into lamentations or of jubilation into praise. We may see, with Aristotle,[6] in the poet's political function the operation of a catharsis, a cleansing or purging of all emotions that could prevent men from acting. The political function of the storyteller—historian or novelist—is to teach acceptance of things as they are. Out of this acceptance, which can also be called truthfulness, arises the faculty of judgment—that, again in Isak Dinesen's words, "at the end we shall be privileged to view, and review, it—and that is what is named the day of judgment."[7]

There is no doubt that all these politically relevant functions are performed from outside the political realm. They require non-commitment and impartiality, freedom from self-interest in thought and judgment. The disinterested pursuit of truth has a long history; its origin, characteristically, precedes all our theoretical and scientific traditions, including our tradition of philosophical and political thought. I think it can be traced to the moment when Homer chose to sing the deeds of the Trojans no less than those of the Achaeans, and to praise the glory of Hector, the foe and the defeated man, no less than the glory of Achilles, the hero of his kinfolk.[8] This had happened nowhere before; no other civilization, however splendid, had been able to look with equal eyes upon friend and foe, upon success and defeat—which since Homer have not been recognized as ultimate standards of men's judgment, even though they are ultimates for the destinies of men's lives. Homeric impartiality echoes throughout Greek history, and it inspired the first great teller of factual truth, who became the father of history: Herodotus[9] tells us in the very first sentences of his stories that he set out to prevent "the great and wondrous deeds of the Greeks *and* the barbarians from losing their due meed of glory." This is the root of all

4. Pen name of Karen Blixen (1885–1962), Danish writer who wrote in Danish, French, and English. She is quoted from an interview by Bent Mohn published in the *New York Times Book Review*, November 3, 1957; Arendt uses the same quotation as an epigraph to chapter 5 in *The Human Condition* (1958; see above).

5. GEORG WILHELM FRIEDRICH HEGEL (1770–1831), German philosopher. The phrase "reconciliation with reality," often used in discussions of Hegel, appears in *Elements of the Philosophy of Right* (1821).

6. Greek philosopher (384–322 B.C.E.); on catharsis, see *Poetics* 1449b, above.

7. Quoted from "The Day of Judgment" (1957); "it" refers to "the story."

8. That is, the Greeks; Achilles is the mightiest of their warriors, as Hector is the mightiest of the Trojans. Their deeds in the Trojan War are sung in the *Iliad*, attributed to the Greek epic poet Homer (ca. 8th c. B.C.E.).

9. The earliest great Greek historian (ca. 484–ca. 425 B.C.E.); the quotation is from the first sentence of his *History*.

so-called objectivity—this curious passion, unknown outside Western civilization, for intellectual integrity at any price. Without it no science would ever have come into being.

Since I have dealt here with politics from the perspective of truth, and hence from a viewpoint outside the political realm, I have failed to mention even in passing the greatness and the dignity of what goes on inside it. I have spoken as though the political realm were no more than a battlefield of partial, conflicting interests, where nothing counted but pleasure and profit, partisanship, and the lust for dominion. In short, I have dealt with politics as though I, too, believed that all public affairs were ruled by interest and power, that there would be no political realm at all if we were not bound to take care of life's necessities. The reason for this deformation is that factual truth clashes with the political only on this lowest level of human affairs, just as Plato's philosophical truth clashed with the political on the considerably higher level of opinion and agreement. From this perspective, we remain unaware of the actual content of political life—of the joy and the gratification that arise out of being in company with our peers, out of acting together and appearing in public, out of inserting ourselves into the world by word and deed, thus acquiring and sustaining our personal identity and beginning something entirely new. However, what I meant to show here is that this whole sphere, its greatness notwithstanding, is limited—that it does not encompass the whole of man's and the world's existence. It is limited by those things which men cannot change at will. And it is only by respecting its own borders that this realm, where we are free to act and to change, can remain intact, preserving its integrity and keeping its promises. Conceptually, we may call truth what we cannot change; metaphorically, it is the ground on which we stand and the sky that stretches above us.

1967, 1968

CLEANTH BROOKS
1906–1994

The reputation of Cleanth Brooks suffered during the 1970s and 1980s when his books and essays were repeatedly cited to illustrate the flaws of the American New Criticism. Brooks, it was said, isolated literary criticism by limiting it to intensive analysis of the text itself, ignored history, failed to consider writings by women and minorities, and disabled any and all attempts to relate literary study to political, social, and cultural issues and debates. But while there are shortcomings to Brooks's work, his criticism is more interesting and complex than the standard accounts suggest. He is an incisive interpreter of literary texts and an adept theorist whose turns and twists of argument anticipated the theories later deployed against him.

Brooks was born in Murray, Kentucky, one of six children of a Methodist minister. He attended McTyeire School, a private classical academy in Tennessee, and received his B.A. from Vanderbilt in 1928 and his M.A. from Tulane University in 1929. He next studied as a Rhodes Scholar at Exeter College at Oxford, returning to the United States in 1932 to begin his teaching career at Louisiana State University in Baton Rouge.

While at Oxford, Brooks became good friends with Robert Penn Warren, another Vanderbilt graduate and Rhodes Scholar; when Warren joined LSU's English department in 1934, the two of them started to work together on criticism and pedagogy. Disturbed by the inability of their students to interpret literary works, Brooks and Warren prepared a booklet designed to teach the skills of close reading by providing examples. Their desire to improve literary study in the classroom led to Brooks and Warren's influential, best-selling textbooks: *An Approach to Literature* (1936), *Understanding Poetry* (1938), *Understanding Fiction* (1943), *Modern Rhetoric* (1949), and, with Robert Heilman, *Understanding Drama* (1945).

From 1935 to 1942, Brooks and Warren co-edited the *Southern Review*, making it one of the foremost journals of its era. They published not only critical essays but also creative writing by Eudora Welty, Katherine Anne Porter, and others. In the first year alone, the authors appearing in the *Southern Review* included JOHN CROWE RANSOM, Allen Tate, Wallace Stevens, Kenneth Burke, R. P. Blackmur, Randall Jarrell, Ford Madox Ford, and Yvor Winters—leading poets and critics of the time. In 1947 Brooks left LSU for a professorship at Yale University (Warren later followed), where he taught until retiring in 1975. He researched, wrote, and published many essays and books on modern fiction and literary criticism, as well as editing textbooks.

Brooks's two most important critical books, *Modern Poetry and the Tradition* (1939) and *The Well Wrought Urn: Studies in the Structure of Poetry* (1947), focus on poetry, and he extended and reinforced their arguments in essays, reviews, and lectures. For example, with J. E. Hardy, he edited and wrote detailed commentary for *Poems of Mr. John Milton* (1951), showing that Milton's verse, which T. S. ELIOT had attacked as numbing and monolithic, could be appreciated as subtle and complex.

In a retrospective 1989 essay on his teacher and friend John Crowe Ransom, Brooks said that as a student he had read the Southern Agrarian manifesto of 1930, *I'll Take My Stand*, "over and over": "I tried my best to assimilate the whole position, philosophical and political. I learned a great deal from my intensive study." But in his own work he never argued on behalf of conservative Southern traditions, values, and beliefs as specifically and as forcefully as did Ransom, Warren, and Tate. For him the lesson put forward by the Agrarians was a general and unobjectionable one: "They asked that we consider what the good life is or ought to be."

Brooks was above all a literary critic and theorist. He said that his interest in "close reading" was kindled in his school days when he studied the classical languages—"my prep school discipline in reading Latin and Greek." He noted too that he was affected by the approach to literature and criticism taken by his teachers and friends at Vanderbilt, especially the poets, "who were talking about the making of poems." Like many young literary critics in the 1930s, Brooks rebelled against the emphasis in graduate studies on "historical and biographical" information and protested the lack of attention to "the interior life of the poem." At Oxford he encountered the English theorist and critic I. A. Richards's books *The Principles of Literary Criticism* (1924) and *Practical Criticism* (1929). Brooks did not accept everything he found in Richards's work—in particular, he disapproved of its "psychological terminology" and "confident positivism"—but as he read and reread *Principles* ("perhaps a dozen times" the first year he encountered it) and *Practical Criticism*, he borrowed terms (such as *tone*, *irony*, and *attitude*) and developed Richards's guidelines for examining the poem itself into his own intrinsic (or formalist) criticism.

For Brooks, criticism means scrutinizing technical elements, textual patterns, and incongruities in texts; as he indicates at the outset of *The Well Wrought Urn*, the critic should always begin "by making the closest examination of what the poem says as a poem." Genuine literary criticism is neither biographical nor historical, a matter of sources-and-influences and background information. Nor is it subjective, the record of a reader's impressions as he or she reacts to a literary work. Illustrating the conclusions that WILLIAM K. WIMSATT JR. and MONROE C. BEARDSLEY presented in "The Intentional Fallacy" (1946; see below) and "The Affective Fallacy" (1949), Brooks shows how literary study deals not with the author, the reader, or the historical context but instead with the specific text at hand.

In one sense Brooks seeks to make literary criticism more like a science—rigorous, precise, intensive, analytical. But like other formalist critics, he insists that literature and science use language in very different ways. Science is referential, abstract, and denotative, whereas literature is nonreferential, concrete, and connotative. "The tendency of science," he states in *The Well Wrought Urn*, "is necessarily to stabilize terms, to freeze them into strict denotations; the poet's tendency is by contrast disruptive. The terms are continually modifying each other, and thus violating their dictionary meanings."

In the chapter we reprint below, "The Heresy of Paraphrase," Brooks emphasizes that it is not the purpose of a poem to produce a statement, a proposition, a didactic lesson, or message. Through irony, paradox, ambiguity, and other rhetorical and poetic devices of his or her art, the poet works constantly to resist any reduction of the poem to a paraphrasable core, favoring the presentation of conflicting facets of theme and patterns of resolved stresses. For Brooks, all poetry exhibits "irony," by which he means pervasive incongruity.

His focus on the text has led Brooks's critics to accuse him of narrowing the field of literary criticism and pedagogy by brushing aside biographical and historical contexts. Many later theorists, including EDWARD W. SAID and STEPHEN J. GREENBLATT, have called attention to the antihistorical thrust of the New Criticism and sought to connect literary criticism with new forms of ideological critique and historical inquiry. But this complaint about Brooks and the New Critics is in fact an old one: it was made from the beginning of the New Critical movement, both by traditional literary scholars and by public intellectuals and writers. Because Brooks did more than anyone else to articulate and codify the principles of Anglo-American New Criticism and demonstrate how they applied to a wide range of texts, he became a prime target for opponents of the approach.

Already in 1942, the American writer and essayist Alfred Kazin was attacking the New Critics for making "a fetish of form." Philip Rahv, who was, like Kazin, a critic and intellectual on the political left, also objected to the restricted nature of the New Critical approach: "Their attachment to the text is what is appealing about the 'new critics'; what is unappealing is their neglect of context." Rahv indicted the New Critics for "a narrow textual-formalistic approach which cannot account for change and movement in literature and which systematically eliminates ideas from criticism." Throughout his career, Brooks insisted that these charges were inaccurate and unfair. He claimed that he was not ignoring biography and history, but that as a literary critic he was intent on exploring the attitudes toward history that an author expressed in the language of the text itself. For Brooks the text possesses organic unity. A poem by Donne or Marvell does not depend for its success on outside knowledge that we bring to it; it is richly ambiguous yet harmoniously orchestrated, coherent in its own special aesthetic terms.

Brooks's close readings, while illuminating, do run the risk of always coming to more or less the same conclusion. Each poem that he examines, from whatever period, receives the same kind of inspection of its images, metaphors, tones of voice; each is valued or reproved for its handling of irony and paradox in the labor of controlling incongruities. In a 1948 essay, the scholar-theorist R. S. Crane faulted Brooks for "critical monism," remarking that all of the texts from the Renaissance through the modern period treated in *The Well Wrought Urn* end up seeming like seventeenth-century lyrics. Brooks from the outset pretty much conceded this point; as he notes in "The Heresy of Paraphrase," he is undertaking in his book an analytical experiment—reading eighteenth- and nineteenth-century poems "as one has learned to read Donne and the moderns." While acknowledging the historical differences among the poems, he intends to show that there are common elements in their use and organization of language.

The terms and emphases that shape Brooks's argument about how poetry operates are an uneasy mix. On the one hand, he refers to the warping, resisting, and violating of meaning (for example, "the resistance which any good poem sets up against all attempts to paraphrase it"). On the other hand, taking his cue from SAMUEL TAYLOR COLERIDGE and I. A. Richards, he speaks of harmony, balance, order, unity. Perhaps these impulses are not contradictory; Brooks would likely say that the poem can contain a "tension" among its paradoxical meanings while maintaining its coherence. But later theorists exploited an opening in Brooks's position. If there is a warping or resisting of meaning, how intense and deep is it? Can one claim that irony empowers the poem to achieve unity, or is irony the dimension of literary language that undermines and forestalls unity?

In the work of poststructuralists such as PAUL DE MAN and JACQUES DERRIDA, it is precisely the competing, conflicting, indeed warring relationship among the words in the text that keeps it from the self-contained equilibrium that Brooks celebrates. Where he sees in the poem's "essential structure" a "pattern of resolutions and balances and harmonizations," the deconstructionist critic, in the words of his younger Yale colleague J. Hillis Miller, seeks "the thread in the text in question which will unravel it all."

Such an approach, in Brooks's mind, was gravely mistaken, and in his final years he sharply criticized Miller, STANLEY FISH, HAROLD BLOOM, and other advocates of deconstruction and reader-response theory. In Brooks's view, poststructuralist theory denied the authority of the work of art and invited subjectivism and relativism, as each critic played with the text's language unmindful of aesthetic relevance and formal design. The irony is that the newer critics had been trained as New Critics themselves: they seized on and reframed the insights and arguments that Brooks had advanced, and were closer to him in their conception of literature and criticism than perhaps they realized. In 1975, Brooks's Yale colleague Paul de Man affirmed in "Semiology and Rhetoric" (see below): "A literary text simultaneously asserts and denies the authority of its own rhetorical mode." He found radical instability where Brooks perceived harmony and balance, but the special sense of the paradoxical workings of literary language is one that these critics share. Brooks and de Man, New Criticism and deconstruction, are very different from one another, yet not so different after all.

***The Well Wrought Urn* Keywords:** Aesthetics, Defense of Criticism, Formalism, Interpretation Theory, Poetry

From The Well Wrought Urn

Chapter 11. The Heresy of Paraphrase

The ten poems[1] that have been discussed were not selected because they happened to express a common theme or to display some particular style or to share a special set of symbols. It has proved, as a matter of fact, somewhat surprising to see how many items they do have in common: the light symbolism as used in "L'Allegro-Il Penseroso" and in the "Intimations" ode, for example; or, death as a sexual metaphor in "The Canonization" and in *The Rape of the Lock*; or the similarity of problem and theme in the "Intimations" ode and "Among School Children."

On reflection, however, it would probably warrant more surprise if these ten poems did not have much in common. For they are all poems which most of us will feel are close to the central stream of the tradition. Indeed, if there is any doubt on this point, it will have to do with only the first and last members of the series[2]—poems whose relation to the tradition I shall, for reasons to be given a little later, be glad to waive. The others, it will be granted, are surely in the main stream of the tradition.

As a matter of fact, a number of the poems discussed in this book were not chosen by me but were chosen for me. But having written on these, I found that by adding a few poems I could construct a chronological series which (though it makes no pretension to being exhaustive of periods or types) would not leave seriously unrepresented any important period since Shakespeare. In filling the gaps I tried to select poems which had been held in favor in their own day and which most critics still admire. There were, for example, to be no "metaphysical" poems[3] beyond the first exhibit and no "modern" ones other than the last. But the intervening poems were to be read as one has learned to read Donne and the moderns. One was to attempt to see, in terms of this approach, what the masterpieces had in common rather than to see how the poems of different historical periods differed—and in particular to see whether they had anything in common with the "metaphysicals" and with the moderns.

The reader will by this time have made up his mind as to whether the readings are adequate. (I use the word advisedly, for the readings do not pretend to be exhaustive, and certainly it is highly unlikely that they are not in error in one detail or another.) If the reader feels that they are seriously inadequate, then the case has been judged; for the generalizations that follow will be thoroughly vitiated by the inept handling of the particular cases on which they depend.

If, however, the reader does feel them to be adequate, it ought to be readily apparent that the common goodness which the poems share will have to

1. *The Well Wrought Urn* contains sequential analyses of ten works: John Donne, "The Canonization" (1633); William Shakespeare, *Macbeth* (ca. 1606); John Milton, "L'Allegro" and "Il Penseroso" (1632); Robert Herrick, "Corinna's Going A-Maying" (1648); ALEXANDER POPE, *The Rape of the Lock* (1714); Thomas Gray, "Elegy Written in a Country Churchyard" (1751); WILLIAM WORDSWORTH, "Ode: Intimations of Immortality from Recollections of Early Childhood" (1807); John Keats, "Ode on a Grecian Urn" (1819); Alfred, Lord Tennyson, "Tears, Idle Tears" (1847); and William Butler Yeats, "Among School Children" (1927).

2. That is, the poems by Donne and Yeats.

3. The metaphysical poetry of the early 17th century (including that of Donne) is characterized by complex extended metaphors, unusual imagery, irregular meter, and highly condensed meanings.

be stated, not in terms of "content" or "subject matter" in the usual sense in which we use these terms, but rather in terms of structure. The "content" of the poems is various, and if we attempt to find one *quality* of content which is shared by all the poems—a "poetic" subject matter or diction or imagery—we shall find that we have merely confused the issues. For what is it to be poetic? Is the schoolroom of Yeats's poem poetic or unpoetic? Is Shakespeare's "new-borne babe / Striding the blast" poetic whereas the idiot of his "Life is a tale tolde by an idiot"[4] is unpoetic? If Herrick's "budding boy or girl" is poetic, then why is not that monstrosity of the newspaper's society page, the "society bud,"[5] poetic too?

To say this is not, of course, to say that all materials have precisely the same potentialities (as if the various pigments on the palette had the same potentialities, any one of them suiting the given picture as well as another). But what has been said, on the other hand, requires to be said: for, if we are to proceed at all, we must draw a sharp distinction between the attractiveness or beauty of any particular item taken as such and the "beauty" of the poem considered as a whole. The latter is the effect of a total pattern, and of a kind of pattern which can incorporate within itself items intrinsically beautiful or ugly, attractive or repulsive. Unless one asserts the primacy of the pattern, a poem becomes merely a bouquet of intrinsically beautiful items.

But though it is in terms of structure that we must describe poetry, the term "structure" is certainly not altogether satisfactory as a term. One means by it something far more internal than the metrical pattern, say, or than the sequence of images. The structure meant is certainly not "form" in the conventional sense in which we think of form as a kind of envelope which "contains" the "content." The structure obviously is everywhere conditioned by the nature of the material which goes into the poem. The nature of the material sets the problem to be solved, and the solution is the ordering of the material.

Pope's *Rape of the Lock* will illustrate: the structure is not the heroic couplet[6] as such, or the canto arrangement; for, important as is Pope's use of the couplet as one means by which he secures the total effect, the heroic couplet can be used—has been used many times—as an instrument in securing very different effects. The structure of the poem, furthermore, is not that of the mock-epic convention, though here, since the term "mock-epic" has implications of attitude, we approach a little nearer to the kind of structure of which we speak.

The structure meant is a structure of meanings, evaluations, and interpretations; and the principle of unity which informs it seems to be one of balancing and harmonizing connotations, attitudes, and meanings. But even here one needs to make important qualifications: the principle is not one which involves the arrangement of the various elements into homogeneous groupings, pairing like with like. It unites the like with the unlike. It does not unite them, however, by the simple process of allowing one connotation to cancel out another nor does it reduce the contradictory attitudes to harmony by a process of subtraction. The unity is not a unity of the sort to be achieved by the reduction and simplification appropriate to an algebraic formula. It is a

4. *Macbeth* 1.7.21–22 and (slightly misquoted) 5.5.25–26.
5. A facetious term for a young, unmarried woman.
6. A rhymed couplet in iambic pentameter (called "heroic" because of its use in English epic poetry).

positive unity, not a negative; it represents not a residue but an achieved harmony.

The attempt to deal with a structure such as this may account for the frequent occurrence in the preceding chapters of such terms as "ambiguity," "paradox," "complex of attitudes," and—most frequent of all, and perhaps most annoying to the reader—"irony." I hasten to add that I hold no brief for these terms as such. Perhaps they are inadequate. Perhaps they are misleading. It is to be hoped in that case that we can eventually improve upon them. But adequate terms—whatever those terms may turn out to be—will certainly have to be terms which do justice to the special kind of structure which seems to emerge as the common structure of poems so diverse on other counts as are *The Rape of the Lock* and "Tears, Idle Tears."

The conventional terms are much worse than inadequate: they are positively misleading in their implication that the poem constitutes a "statement" of some sort, the statement being true or false, and expressed more or less clearly or eloquently or beautifully; for it is from this formula that most of the common heresies about poetry derive. The formula begins by introducing a dualism which thenceforward is rarely overcome, and which at best can be overcome only by the most elaborate and clumsy qualifications. Where it is not overcome, it leaves the critic lodged upon one or the other of the horns of a dilemma: the critic is forced to judge the poem by its political or scientific or philosophical truth; or, he is forced to judge the poem by its form as conceived externally and detached from human experience. Mr. Alfred Kazin,[7] for example, to take an instance from a recent and popular book, accuses the "new formalists"—his choice of that epithet is revealing—of accepting the latter horn of the dilemma because he notices that they have refused the former. In other words, since they refuse to rank poems by their messages, he assumes that they are compelled to rank them by their formal embellishments.

The omnipresence of this dilemma, a false dilemma, I believe, will also account for the fact that so much has been made in the preceding chapters of the resistance which any good poem sets up against all attempts to paraphrase it. The point is surely not that we cannot describe adequately enough for many purposes what the poem in general is "about" and what the general effect of the poem is: *The Rape of the Lock* is about the foibles of an eighteenth-century belle. The effect of "Corinna's going a-Maying" is one of gaiety tempered by the poignance of the fleetingness of youth. We can very properly use paraphrases as pointers and as shorthand references provided that we know what we are doing. But it is highly important that we know what we are doing and that we see plainly that the paraphrase is not the real core of meaning which constitutes the essence of the poem.

For the imagery and the rhythm are not merely the instruments by which this fancied core-of-meaning-which-can-be-expressed-in-a-paraphrase is directly rendered. Even in the simplest poem their mediation is not positive and direct. Indeed, whatever statement we may seize upon as incorporating the "meaning" of the poem, immediately the imagery and the rhythm seem to set up tensions with it, warping and twisting it, qualifying and revising

7. American critic (1915–1998); his book is *On Native Grounds: An Interpretation of Modern American Prose Literature* (1942).

it. This is true of Wordsworth's "Ode" no less than of Donne's "Canonization." To illustrate: if we say that the "Ode" celebrates the spontaneous "naturalness" of the child, there is the poem itself to indicate that Nature has a more sinister aspect—that the process by which the poetic lamb becomes the dirty old sheep or the child racing over the meadows becomes the balding philosopher is a process that is thoroughly "natural." Or, if we say that the thesis of the "Ode" is that the child brings into the natural world a supernatural glory which acquaintance with the world eventually and inevitably quenches in the light of common day, there is the last stanza and the drastic qualifications which it asserts: it is significant that the thoughts that lie too deep for tears are mentioned in this sunset stanza of the "Ode" and that they are thoughts, not of the child, but of the man.

We have precisely the same problem if we make our example *The Rape of the Lock*. Does the poet assert that Belinda is a goddess? Or does he say that she is a brainless chit? Whichever alternative we take, there are elaborate qualifications to be made. Moreover, if the simple propositions offered seem in their forthright simplicity to make too easy the victory of the poem over any possible statement of its meaning, then let the reader try to formulate a proposition that will say what the poem "says." As his proposition approaches adequacy, he will find, not only that it has increased greatly in length, but that it has begun to fill itself up with reservations and qualifications—and most significant of all—the formulator will find that he has himself begun to fall back upon metaphors of his own in his attempt to indicate what the poem "says." In sum, his proposition, as it approaches adequacy, ceases to be a proposition.

Consider one more case, "Corinna's going a-Maying." Is the doctrine preached to Corinna throughout the first four stanzas true? Or is it damnably false? Or is it a "harmlesse follie"? Here perhaps we shall be tempted to take the last option as the saving mean—what the poem really *says*—and my account of the poem at the end of the third chapter is perhaps susceptible of this interpretation—or misinterpretation. If so, it is high time to clear the matter up. For we mistake matters grossly if we take the poem to be playing with opposed extremes, only to point the golden mean in a doctrine which, at the end, will correct the falsehood of extremes. The reconcilement of opposites which the poet characteristically makes is not that of a prudent splitting of the difference between antithetical overemphases.

It is not so in Wordsworth's poem nor in Keats's nor in Pope's. It is not so even in this poem of Herrick's. For though the poem reflects, if we read it carefully, the primacy of the Christian mores, the pressure exerted throughout the poem is upon the pagan appeal; and the poem ends, significantly, with a reiteration of the appeal to Corinna to go a-Maying, an appeal which, if qualified by the Christian view, still, in a sense, has been deepened and made more urgent by that very qualification. The imagery of loss and decay, it must be remembered, comes in this last stanza after the admission that the May-day rites[8] are not a real religion but a "harmless follie."

If we are to get all these qualifications into our formulation of what the poem says—and they are relevant—then, our formulation of the "statement" made by Herrick's poem will turn out to be quite as difficult as that

8. The traditional celebration of spring on May 1, including setting up and dancing around a maypole, crowning a May queen, and other amusements.

of Pope's mock-epic. The truth of the matter is that all such formulations lead away from the center of the poem—not toward it; that the "prose-sense" of the poem is not a rack on which the stuff of the poem is hung; that it does not represent the "inner" structure or the "essential" structure or the "real" structure of the poem. We may use—and in many connections must use—such formulations as more or less convenient ways of referring to parts of the poem. But such formulations are scaffoldings which we may properly for certain purposes throw about the building: we must not mistake them for the internal and essential structure of the building itself.

Indeed, one may sum up by saying that most of the distempers of criticism come about from yielding to the temptation to take certain remarks which we make *about* the poem—statements about what it says or about what truth it gives or about what formulations it illustrates—for the essential core of the poem itself. As W. M. Urban puts it in his *Language and Reality*:[9] "The general principle of the inseparability of intuition and expression holds with special force for the aesthetic intuition. Here it means that form and content, or content and medium, are inseparable. The artist does not first intuit his object and then find the appropriate medium. It is rather in and through his medium that he intuits the object." So much for the process of composition. As for the critical process: "To pass from the intuitible to the nonintuitible is to negate the function and meaning of the symbol." For it "is precisely because the more universal and ideal relations cannot be adequately expressed directly that they are indirectly expressed by means of the more intuitible." The most obvious examples of such error (and for that reason those which are really least dangerous) are those theories which frankly treat the poem as propaganda. The most subtle (and the most stubbornly rooted in the ambiguities of language) are those which, beginning with the "paraphrasable" elements of the poem, refer the other elements of the poem finally to some role subordinate to the paraphrasable elements. (The relation between all the elements must surely be an organic one—there can be no question about that. There is, however, a very serious question as to whether the paraphrasable elements have primacy.)

Mr. Winters'[1] position will furnish perhaps the most respectable example of the paraphrastic heresy. He assigns primacy to the "rational meaning" of the poem. "The relationship, in the poem, between rational statement and feeling," he remarks in his latest book, "is thus seen to be that of motive to emotion." He goes on to illustrate his point by a brief and excellent analysis of the following lines from Browning:

So wore night; the East was gray,
White the broad-faced hemlock flowers. . . .[2]

"The verb *wore*," he continues, "means literally that the night passed, but it carries with it connotations of exhaustion and attrition which belong to the condition of the protagonist; and grayness is a color which we associate with such a condition. If we change the phrase to read: 'Thus night passed,' we

9. *Language and Reality: The Philosophy of Language and the Principles of Symbolism* (1939), by the American philosopher of language Wilbur Marshall Urban (1873–1952).
1. The American poet and critic Yvor Winters (1900–1968). The "latest book" from which Brooks quotes is *In Defense of Reason* (1947)—specifically, an essay reprinted from *Anatomy of Nonsense* (1943).
2. "A Serenade at the Villa" (1855), by the English poet Robert Browning (1812–1889).

shall have the same rational meaning, and a meter quite as respectable, but no trace of the power of the line: the connotation of *wore* will be lost, and the connotation of *gray* will remain in a state of ineffective potentiality."

But the word *wore* does not mean *literally* "that the night passed," it means literally "that the night *wore*"—whatever *wore* may mean, and as Winters' own admirable analysis indicates, *wore* "means," whether *rationally* or *irrationally*, a great deal. Furthermore, "So wore night" and "Thus night passed" can be said to have "the same rational meaning" only if we equate "rational meaning" with the meaning of a loose paraphrase. And can a loose paraphrase be said to be the "motive to emotion"? Can it be said to "generate" the feelings in question? (Or, would Mr. Winters not have us equate "rational statement" and "rational meaning"?)

Much more is at stake here than any quibble. In view of the store which Winters sets by rationality and of his penchant for poems which make their evaluations overtly, and in view of his frequent blindness to those poems which do not—in view of these considerations, it is important to see that what "So wore night" and "Thus night passed" have in common as their "rational meaning" is not the "rational meaning" of each but the lowest common denominator of both. To refer the structure of the poem to what is finally a paraphrase of the poem is to refer it to something outside the poem.

To repeat, most of our difficulties in criticism are rooted in the heresy of paraphrase. If we allow ourselves to be misled by it, we distort the relation of the poem to its "truth," we raise the problem of belief in a vicious and crippling form, we split the poem between its "form" and its "content"—we bring the statement to be conveyed into an unreal competition with science or philosophy or theology. In short, we put our questions about the poem in a form calculated to produce the battles of the last twenty-five years over the "use of poetry."[3]

If we allow ourselves to be misled by the heresy of paraphrase, we run the risk of doing even more violence to the internal order of the poem itself. By taking the paraphrase as our point of stance, we misconceive the function of metaphor and meter. We demand logical coherences where they are sometimes irrelevant, and we fail frequently to see imaginative coherences on levels where they are highly relevant. Some of the implications of the paraphrastic heresy are so stubborn and so involved that I have thought best to relegate them to an appendix.[4] There the reader who is interested may find further discussion of the problem and, I could hope, answers to certain misapprehensions of the positive theory to be adumbrated here.

But what would be a positive theory? We tend to embrace the doctrine of a logical structure the more readily because, to many of us, the failure to do so seems to leave the meaning of the poem hopelessly up in the air. The alternative position will appear to us to lack even the relative stability of an Ivory Tower: it is rather commitment to a free balloon. For, to deny the possibility of pinning down what the poem "says" to some "statement" will seem to assert that the poem really says nothing. And to point out what has been suggested in earlier chapters and brought to a head in this one, namely, that one can never measure a poem against the scientific or philosophical yard-

3. I do not, of course, intend to minimize the fact that some of these battles have been highly profitable, or to imply that the foregoing paragraphs could have been written except for the illumination shed by the discussions of the last 25 years [Brooks's note].

4. In an appendix, Brooks discusses literary history, value judgments, and critical relativism.

stick for the reason that the poem, when laid along the yardstick, is never the "full poem" but an abstraction from the poem—such an argument will seem to such readers a piece of barren logic-chopping—a transparent dodge.

Considerations of strategy then, if nothing more, dictate some positive account of what a poem is and does. And some positive account can be given, though I cannot promise to do more than suggest what a poem is, nor will my terms turn out to be anything more than metaphors.[5]

The essential structure of a poem (as distinguished from the rational or logical structure of the "statement" which we abstract from it) resembles that of architecture or painting: it is a pattern of resolved stresses. Or, to move closer still to poetry by considering the temporal arts, the structure of a poem resembles that of a ballet or musical composition. It is a pattern of resolutions and balances and harmonizations, developed through a temporal scheme.[6]

Or, to move still closer to poetry, the structure of a poem resembles that of a play. This last example, of course, risks introducing once more the distracting element, since drama, like poetry, makes use of words. Yet, on the whole, most of us are less inclined to force the concept of "statement" on drama than on a lyric poem; for the very nature of drama is that of something "acted out"—something which arrives at its conclusion through conflict—something which builds conflict into its very being. The dynamic nature of drama, in short, allows us to regard it as *an action* rather than as a formula for action or as a statement about action. For this reason, therefore, perhaps the most helpful analogy by which to suggest the structure of poetry is that of the drama, and for many readers at least, the least confusing way in which to approach a poem is to think of it as a drama.

The general point, of course, is not that either poetry or drama makes no use of ideas, or that either is "merely emotional"—whatever *that* is—or that there is not the closest and most important relationship between the intellectual materials which they absorb into their structure and other elements in the structure. The relationship between the intellectual and the nonintellectual elements in a poem is actually far more intimate than the conventional accounts would represent it to be: the relationship is not that of an idea "wrapped in emotion" or a "prose-sense decorated by sensuous imagery."

5. For those who cannot be content with metaphors (or with the particular metaphors which I can give) I recommend René Wellek's excellent "The Mode of Existence of a Literary Work of Art" (*Southern Review*, spring, 1942). I shall not try to reproduce here as a handy, thumb-nail definition his account of a poem as "a stratified system of norms," for the definition would be relatively meaningless without the further definitions which he assigns to the individual terms which he uses. I have made no special use of his terms in this chapter, but I believe that the generalizations about poetry outlined here can be thoroughly accommodated to the position which his essay sets forth [Brooks's note]. Wellek (1903–1995), Austrian-born New Critic and historian of criticism.

6. In recent numbers of *Accent*, two critics for whose work I have high regard have emphasized the dynamic character of poetry. Kenneth Burke argues that if we are to consider a poem as a poem, we must consider it as a "mode of action." R. P. Blackmur asks us to think of it as gesture, "the outward and dramatic play of inward and imagined meaning." I do not mean to commit either of these critics to my own interpretation of dramatic or symbolic action; and I have, on my own part, several rather important reservations with respect to Mr. Burke's position. But there are certainly large areas of agreement among our positions. The reader might also compare the account of poetic structure given in this chapter with the following passage from Susanne Langer's *Philosophy in a New Key* [1942]: ". . . though the *material* of poetry is verbal, its import is not the literal assertion made in the words, but *the way the assertion is made,* and this involves the sound, the tempo, the aura of associations of the words, the long or short sequences of ideas, the wealth or poverty of transient imagery that contains them, the sudden arrest of fantasy by pure fact, or of familiar fact by sudden fantasy, the suspense of literal meaning by a sustained ambiguity resolved in a long-awaited key-word, and the unifying, all-embracing artifice of rhythm" [Brooks's note]. Burke (1897–1993), American critic and philosopher. Blackmur (1904–1965), American critic and poet. Langer (1895–1985), American philosopher and aesthetician.

The dimension in which the poem moves is not one which excludes ideas, but one which does include attitudes. The dimension includes ideas, to be sure; we can always abstract an "idea" from a poem—even from the simplest poem—even from a lyric so simple and unintellectual as

Western wind, when wilt thou blow
That the small rain down can rain?
Christ, that my love were in my arms
And I in my bed again![7]

But the idea which we abstract—assuming that we can all agree on what that idea is—will always be *abstracted*: it will always be the projection of a plane along a line or the projection of a cone upon a plane.

If this last analogy proves to be more confusing than illuminating, let us return to the analogy with drama. We have argued that any proposition asserted in a poem is not to be taken in abstraction but is justified, in terms of the poem, if it is justified at all, not by virtue of its scientific or historical or philosophical truth, but is justified in terms of a principle analogous to that of dramatic propriety. Thus, the proposition that "Beauty is truth, truth beauty"[8] is given its precise meaning and significance by its relation to the total context of the poem.

This principle is easy enough to see when the proposition is asserted overtly in the poem—that is, when it constitutes a specific detail of the poem. But the reader may well ask: is it not possible to frame a proposition, a statement, which will adequately represent the total meaning of the poem; that is, is it not possible to elaborate a summarizing proposition which will "say," briefly and in the form of a proposition, what the poem "says" as a poem, a proposition which will say it fully and will say it exactly, no more and no less? Could not the poet, if he had chosen, have framed such a proposition? Cannot we as readers and critics frame such a proposition?

The answer must be that the poet himself obviously did not—else he would not have had to write his poem. We as readers can attempt to frame such a proposition in our effort to understand the poem; it may well help toward an understanding. Certainly, the efforts to arrive at such propositions can do no harm *if we do not mistake them for the inner core of the poem*—if we do not mistake them for "what the poem *really* says." For, if we take one of them to represent the essential poem, we have to disregard the qualifications exerted by the total context as of no account, or else we have assumed that we can reproduce the effect of the total context in a condensed prose statement.[9]

7. Anonymous 15th-century lyric.

8. From the next-to-last line of Keats's "Ode on a Grecian Urn."

9. We may, it is true, be able to adumbrate what the poem says if we allow ourselves enough words, and if we make enough reservations and qualifications, thus attempting to come nearer to the meaning of the poem by successive approximations and refinements, gradually encompassing the meaning and pointing to the area in which it lies rather than realizing it. The earlier chapters of this book, if they are successful, are obviously illustrations of this process. But such adumbrations will lack, not only the tension—the dramatic force—of the poem; they will be at best crude approximations of the poem. Moreover—and this is the crucial point—they will be compelled to resort to the methods of the poem—analogy, metaphor, symbol, etc.—in order to secure even this near an approximation.

Urban's comment upon this problem is interesting: he says that if we expand the symbol, "we lose the 'sense' or value of the symbol *as symbol*. The solution . . . seems to me to lie in an adequate theory of interpretation of the symbol. It does not consist in substituting *literal* for symbol sentences, in other words substituting 'blunt' truth for symbolic truth, but rather in deepening and enriching the meaning of the symbol" [Brooks's note].

But to deny that the coherence of a poem is reflected in a logical paraphrase of its "real meaning" is not, of course, to deny coherence to poetry; it is rather to assert that its coherence is to be sought elsewhere. The characteristic unity of a poem (even of those poems which may accidentally possess a logical unity as well as this poetic unity) lies in the unification of attitudes into a hierarchy subordinated to a total and governing attitude. In the unified poem, the poet has "come to terms" with his experience. The poem does not merely eventuate in a logical conclusion. The conclusion of the poem is the working out of the various tensions—set up by whatever means—by propositions, metaphors, symbols. The unity is achieved by a dramatic process, not a logical; it represents an equilibrium of forces, not a formula. It is "proved" as a dramatic conclusion is proved: by its ability to resolve the conflicts which have been accepted as the *données*[1] of the drama.

Thus, it is easy to see why the relation of each item to the whole context is crucial, and why the effective and essential structure of the poem has to do with the complex of attitudes achieved. A scientific proposition can stand alone. If it is true, it is true. But the expression of an attitude, apart from the occasion which generates it and the situation which it encompasses, is meaningless. For example, the last two lines of the "Intimations" ode,

To me the meanest flower that blows can give
Thoughts that do often lie too deep for tears,

when taken in isolation—I do not mean quoted in isolation by one who is even vaguely acquainted with the context—makes a statement which is sentimental if taken in reference to the speaker, and one which is patent nonsense if taken with a general reference. The man in the street (of whom the average college freshman is a good enough replica) knows that the meanest flower that grows does not give *him* thoughts that lie too deep for tears: and, if he thinks about the matter at all, he is inclined to feel that the person who can make such an assertion is a very fuzzy sentimentalist.

We have already seen the ease with which the statement "Beauty is truth, truth beauty" becomes detached from its context, even in the hands of able critics; and we have seen the misconceptions that ensue when this detachment occurs. To take one more instance: the last stanza of Herrick's "Corinna," taken in isolation, would probably not impress the average reader as sentimental nonsense. Yet it would suffer quite as much by isolation from its context as would the lines from Keats's "Ode." For, as mere statement, it would become something flat and obvious—of course our lives are short! And the conclusion from the fact would turn into an obvious truism for the convinced pagan, and, for the convinced Christian, equally obvious, though damnable, nonsense.

Perhaps this is why the poet, to people interested in hard-and-fast generalizations, must always seem to be continually engaged in blurring out distinctions, effecting compromises, or, at the best, coming to his conclusions only after provoking and unnecessary delays. But this last position is merely another variant of the paraphrastic heresy: to assume it is to misconceive the end of poetry—to take its meanderings as negative, or to excuse them (with the comfortable assurance that the curved line is the line of beauty)

1. Basic facts or assumptions (French).

because we can conceive the purpose of a poem to be only the production, in the end, of a proposition—of a statement.

But the meanderings of a good poem (they are meanderings only from the standpoint of the prose paraphrase of the poem) are not negative, and they do not have to be excused; and most of all, we need to see what their positive function is; for unless we can assign them a positive function, we shall find it difficult to explain why one divergence from "the prose line of the argument" is not as good as another. The truth is that the apparent irrelevancies which metrical pattern and metaphor introduce do become relevant when we realize that they function in a good poem to modify, qualify, and develop the total attitude which we are to take in coming to terms with the total situation.

If the last sentence seems to take a dangerous turn toward some special "use of poetry"—some therapeutic value for the sake of which poetry is to be cultivated—I can only say that I have in mind no special ills which poetry is to cure. Uses for poetry are always to be found, and doubtless will continue to be found. But my discussion of the structure of poetry is not being conditioned at this point by some new and special role which I expect poetry to assume in the future or some new function to which I would assign it. The structure described—a structure of "gestures" or attitudes—seems to me to describe the essential structure of both the *Odyssey* and *The Waste Land*.[2] It seems to be the kind of structure which the ten poems considered in this book possess in common.

If the structure of poetry is a structure of the order described, that fact may explain (if not justify) the frequency with which I have had to have recourse, in the foregoing chapters, to terms like "irony" and "paradox." By using the term irony, one risks, of course, making the poem seem arch and self-conscious, since irony, for most readers of poetry, is associated with satire, *vers de société*,[3] and other "intellectual" poetries. Yet, the necessity for some such term ought to be apparent; and irony is the most general term that we have for the kind of qualification which the various elements in a context receive from the context. This kind of qualification, as we have seen, is of tremendous importance in any poem. Moreover, irony is our most general term for indicating that recognition of incongruities—which, again, pervades all poetry to a degree far beyond what our conventional criticism has been heretofore willing to allow.

Irony in this general sense, then, is to be found in Tennyson's "Tears, Idle Tears" as well as in Donne's "Canonization." We have, of course, been taught to expect to find irony in Pope's *Rape of the Lock*, but there is a profound irony in Keats's "Ode on a Grecian Urn"; and there is irony of a very powerful sort in Wordsworth's "Intimations" ode. For the thrusts and pressures exerted by the various symbols in this poem are not avoided by the poet: they are taken into account and played, one against the other. Indeed, the symbols—from a scientific point of view—are used perversely: it is the child who is the best philosopher; it is from a kind of darkness—from something that is "shadowy"—that the light proceeds; growth into manhood is viewed, not as an extrication from, but as an incarceration within, a prison.

2. The modernist poem (1922) by T. S. Eliot (1888–1965), usually not seen as structured like Homer's Greek epic (8th c. B.C.E.).

3. Verse of society (French); that is, verse that wittily treats topics favored by polite society.

There should be no mystery as to why this must be so. The terms of science are abstract symbols which do not change under the pressure of the context. They are pure (or aspire to be pure) denotations; they are defined in advance. They are not to be warped into new meanings. But where is the dictionary which contains the terms of a poem? It is a truism that the poet is continually forced to remake language. As Eliot has put it, his task is to "dislocate language into meaning."[4] And, from the standpoint of a scientific vocabulary, this is precisely what he performs: for, rationally considered, the ideal language would contain one term for each meaning, and the relation between term and meaning would be constant. But the word, as the poet uses it, has to be conceived of, not as a discrete particle of meaning, but as a potential of meaning, a nexus[5] or cluster of meanings.

What is true of the poet's language in detail is true of the larger wholes of poetry. And therefore, if we persist in approaching the poem as primarily a rational statement, we ought not to be surprised if the statement seems to be presented to us always in the ironic mode. When we consider the statement immersed in the poem, it presents itself to us, like the stick immersed in the pool of water, warped and bent. Indeed, whatever the statement, it will always show itself as deflected away from a positive, straightforward formulation.

It may seem perverse, however, to maintain, in the face of our revived interest in Donne, that the essential structure of poetry is not logical. For Donne has been appealed to of late as the great master of metaphor who imposes a clean logic on his images beside which the ordering of the images in Shakespeare's sonnets is fumbling and loose. It is perfectly true that Donne makes a great show of logic; but two matters need to be observed. In the first place, the elaborated and "logical" figure is not Donne's only figure or even his staple one. "Telescoped" figures like "Made one anothers hermitage" are to be found much more frequently than the celebrated comparison of the souls of the lovers to the legs of a pair of compasses. In the second place, where Donne uses "logic," he regularly uses it to justify illogical positions. He employs it to overthrow a conventional position or to "prove" an essentially illogical one.

Logic, as Donne uses it, is nearly always an ironic logic to state the claims of an idea or attitude which we have agreed, with our everyday logic, is false. This is not to say, certainly, that Donne is not justified in using his logic so, or that the best of his poems are not "proved" in the only senses in which poems can be proved.

But the proof is not a logical proof. "The Canonization" will scarcely prove to the hard-boiled naturalist that the lovers, by giving up the world, actually attain a better world. Nor will the argument advanced in the poem convince the dogmatic Christian that Donne's lovers are really saints.

In using logic, Donne as a poet is fighting the devil with fire. To adopt Robert Penn Warren's[6] metaphor (which, though I lift it somewhat scandalously out of another context, will apply to this one): "The poet, somewhat less spectacularly [than the saint], proves his vision by submitting it to the fires of irony—to the drama of the structure—in the hope that the fires will

4. From T. S. Eliot's essay "The Metaphysical Poets" (1921; see above).
5. Connected series or group; center or focus.
6. Poet, novelist, and critic (1905–1989); co-editor with Brooks of *Understanding Poetry* (1938). The quotation is from Warren's essay "Pure and Impure Poetry" (1943).

refine it. In other words, the poet wishes to indicate that his vision has been earned, that it can survive reference to the complexities and contradictions of experience."

The same principle that inspires the presence of irony in so many of our great poems also accounts for the fact that so many of them seem to be built around paradoxes. Here again the conventional associations of the term may prejudice the reader just as the mention of Donne may prejudice him. For Donne, as one type of reader knows all too well, was of that group of poets who wished to impress their audience with their cleverness. All of us are familiar with the censure passed upon Donne and his followers by Dr. Johnson,[7] and a great many of us still retain it as our own, softening only the rigor of it and the thoroughness of its application, but not giving it up as a principle.

Yet there are better reasons than that of rhetorical vain-glory that have induced poet after poet to choose ambiguity and paradox rather than plain, discursive simplicity. It is not enough for the poet to analyse his experience as the scientist does, breaking it up into parts, distinguishing part from part, classifying the various parts. His task is finally to unify experience. He must return to us the unity of the experience itself as man knows it in his own experience. The poem, if it be a true poem, is a simulacrum[8] of reality—in this sense, at least, it is an "imitation"—by *being* an experience rather than any mere statement about experience or any mere abstraction from experience.

Tennyson cannot be content with *saying* that in memory the poet seems both dead *and* alive; he must dramatize its life-in-death for us, and his dramatization involves, necessarily, ironic shock and wonder. The dramatization demands that the antithetical aspects of memory be coalesced into one entity which—if we take it on the level of statement—is a paradox, the assertion of the union of opposites. Keats's Urn must express a life which is above life and its vicissitudes, but it must also bear witness to the fact that its life is not life at all but is a kind of death. To put it in other terms, the Urn must, in its role as historian, assert that myth is truer than history. Donne's lovers must reject the world in order to possess the world.

Or, to take one further instance: Wordsworth's light must serve as the common symbol for aspects of man's vision which seem mutually incompatible—intuition and analytic reason. Wordsworth's poem, as a matter of fact, typifies beautifully the poet's characteristic problem itself. For even this poem, which testifies so heavily to the way in which the world is split up and parceled out under the growing light of reason, cannot rest in this fact as its own mode of perception, and still be a poem. Even after the worst has been said about man's multiple vision, the poet must somehow prove that the child is father to the man, that the dawn light is still somehow the same light as the evening light.

If the poet, then, must perforce dramatize the oneness of the experience, even though paying tribute to its diversity, then his use of paradox and ambiguity is seen as necessary. He is not simply trying to spice up, with a superficially exciting or mystifying rhetoric, the old stale stockpot (though doubtless this will be what the inferior poet does generally and what the real poet

7. SAMUEL JOHNSON (1709–1784), English critic, lexicographer, and poet. See his comments on metaphysical poetry in *Life of Cowley* (1783; above).

8. Image or representation.

does in his lapses). He is rather giving us an insight which preserves the unity of experience and which, at its higher and more serious levels, triumphs over the apparently contradictory and conflicting elements of experience by unifying them into a new pattern.

Wordsworth's "Intimations" ode, then, is not only a poem, but, among other things, a parable about poetry. Keats's "Ode on a Grecian Urn" is quite obviously such a parable. And, indeed, most of the poems which we have discussed in this study may be taken as such parables.

In one sense, Pope's treatment of Belinda raises all the characteristic problems of poetry. For Pope, in dealing with his "goddess," must face the claims of naturalism and of common sense which would deny divinity to her. Unless he faces them, he is merely a sentimentalist. He must do an even harder thing: he must transcend the conventional and polite attributions of divinity which would be made to her as an acknowledged belle. Otherwise, he is merely trivial and obvious. He must "prove" her divinity against the common-sense denial (the brutal denial) and against the conventional assertion (the polite denial). The poetry must be wrested from the context: Belinda's lock, which is what the rude young man wants and which Belinda rather prudishly defends and which the naturalist asserts is only animal and which displays in its curled care the style of a particular era of history, must be given a place of permanence among the stars.

1947

WILLIAM K. WIMSATT JR. 1907–1975 / MONROE C. BEARDSLEY 1915–1985

"The Intentional Fallacy" (1946) and "The Affective Fallacy" (1949), coauthored by William K. Wimsatt Jr. and Monroe C. Beardsley, are two of the most important position papers in the history of twentieth-century criticism. Neither presents an argument that is wholly original, but each codifies a crucial tenet of New Critical formalist orthodoxy. In "The Intentional Fallacy," our selection below, Wimsatt and Beardsley argue that we cannot use the author's intention, even when we possess information about it, to judge a literary work; the work is a public utterance, not a private one that depends for its meaning on the intent or design of its author. In the later piece, "The Affective Fallacy," Wimsatt and Beardsley emphasize that the meaning of a literary work is not equivalent to its effects, especially its emotional impact, on the reader. Both of these positions are connected to Wimsatt and Beardsley's formalist view that analysis must center on the text itself: the critic's task is to examine its linguistic structure and its aesthetic unity as an autonomous object.

Wimsatt, born in Washington, D.C., attended Georgetown University and Yale University, where he received his Ph.D. In 1939 he became a member of Yale's English department, and he soon won wide acclaim for his work in eighteenth-century studies and in literary theory and criticism. Beardsley, a native of Connecticut, received his B.A. and Ph.D. from Yale University, and held a position in the philosophy department there before moving on to Mount Holyoke College in 1944. He later taught at Swarthmore College and at Temple University, focusing on aesthetics and literary criticism.

In their critique of intention, Wimsatt and Beardsley take aim at the Romantic idea of poetry as the expression of a writer's soul or personality. Influenced by T. S. ELIOT, as well as by JOHN CROWE RANSOM, CLEANTH BROOKS, and other New Critics, Wimsatt and Beardsley define poetry as an impersonal art: what matters is the text itself. They also challenge literary historians who, according to Wimsatt and Beardsley, mistakenly believe that when evaluating a poem, one must know its biographical and historical origins. For Wimsatt and Beardsley, one must attend only to the organization of the words on the page and the coherence that the words do or do not possess. As they affirm near the beginning of the essay, "the poem itself shows what [the poet] is trying to do. And if the poet did not succeed, then the poem is not adequate evidence, and the critic must go outside the poem—for evidence of an intention that did not become effective in the poem."

"The Intentional Fallacy" is a powerful polemic, but somewhat confused, as critics have pointed out. How convincing, for example, is the distinction that its authors draw between the inside and the outside of a text? They insist a poem is a public utterance and hence cannot depend for its success on personal or private knowledge about the author, whether deliberately revealed or unearthed by literary historians and biographers. But one could reply that what an author says and the information that a scholar brings forward are public as well. It is precisely the idea that a text has discrete inside and outside meanings that clearly separate into the private and public that Kenneth Burke, HAROLD BLOOM, and SANDRA M. GILBERT and SUSAN GUBAR, among others, have in their different ways disputed. For the purposes of their polemic, Wimsatt and Beardsley's distinction is effective, but it has not held up under attack.

As is true of many New Critical precepts, one of the appeals of "the intentional fallacy" is pedagogical. A teacher and students can concentrate on the text at hand without feeling that interpretive work needs the support of information about the author and the historical period when the text was composed. Wimsatt and Beardsley have a convenient rule of thumb: if information about the author or period is relevant, it will be *in* the poem; if it is not realized in the poem already, then it is not relevant. Thus they regard as extraneous all reference to psychology, social history, and anthropology, disciplines focused on *extrinsic* rather than *intrinsic* matters—a key distinction for New Critics. Yet their claim creates pedagogical problems of its own, as E. D. Hirsch noted in *Validity in Interpretation* (1967) and *The Aims of Interpretation* (1976). Once we set aside the author's intention, Hirsch maintains, we have no way to determine which reading of a poem is correct. The words on the page, he argues, can sustain interpretations that conflict with one another, and the only principled way to resolve such disagreements is by recourse to the author's "original meaning."

Such foregrounding of authorial intention might seem to be common sense, but poets and novelists as well as critics have denied that the author is the best authority on the meaning of his or her work. T. S. Eliot, the most influential poet-critic of the twentieth century, remarks in *The Use of Poetry and the Use of Criticism* (1933) that "What a poem means is as much what it means to others as what it means to the author; and indeed, in the course of time a poet may become merely a reader in respect to his own works, forgetting his original meaning—or without forgetting, merely changing." Earlier, in *Studies in Classic American Literature* (1923), D. H. Lawrence set out this maxim: "Never trust the artist. Trust the tale. The proper function of a critic is to save the tale from the artist who created it." Wimsatt and Beardsley would accept these claims only insofar as they reaffirm the primacy of the text. For them, the text shapes and controls what we say about it. Meaning is in the text, not in the intention of the author and, as "The Affective Fallacy" suggests, not in the reader, either.

In "The Affective Fallacy," Wimsatt and Beardsley contend that what the poem *is* is one thing (and the important thing), and what it *does* is another: it should be judged on the basis of itself, not according to its effects. For these theorists, the affective fallacy is "a special case of epistemological skepticism"; it derives "the standard of criticism from the psychological effects of the poem and ends in impressionism and relativism." While not forbidding discussion of emotion or feeling, they seek instead to keep all lines of inquiry connected to the "text": that is, to the elements of the poem that account for the effects that it creates. They distinguish between "classical objectivity" and "romantic reader psychology," and accent the former.

For Wimsatt and Beardsley, the authority is the poem. Only by keeping our focus on the text can we guard against the dangers of impressionism, subjectivism, and relativism—a vital concern for scholars and teachers intent on giving legitimacy to "English" as an academic field of study and source of scientific knowledge. This position reaches back at least as far as MATTHEW ARNOLD, who in "The Study of Poetry" (1880) warned against the "personal fallacy," by which we judge poetry "on grounds personal to ourselves." Paradoxically, however, many of the same critics who in the nineteenth and twentieth centuries highlighted the priority of the text also spoke about the creative or constructive role played by the reader. I. A. Richards, for example, in "The Interactions of Words" (1942) maintained: "Understanding is not a preparation for reading the poem. It is itself the poem. And it is a constructive, hazardous, free creative process, a process of conception through which a new being is growing in the mind."

During the late 1960s and 1970s, a new movement in criticism, reader-response theory, drew on the insights about the reading process that Richards and others had advanced or implied in formulating their text-centered approaches. One of its most important members, STANLEY FISH, explicitly invoked Wimsatt and Beardsley's arguments in his essay "Literature in the Reader" (1970). For Fish, criticism should be concerned with the "analysis of the developing responses of the reader in relation to the words as they succeed one another in time."

Other critics and theorists during this same period challenged and complicated Wimsatt and Beardsley's conception—in effect, a diminution—of the author. For example, MICHEL FOUCAULT and STEPHEN J. GREENBLATT are as much opposed to the Romantic conception of the author as were Wimsatt and Beardsley. But for them the author, reimagined and reconfigured, is nonetheless a focal point for literary investigation and analysis. Thus in "What Is an Author?" (1969; see below), Foucault considers not the author as such but rather the historical "author-function," a "mode of existence, circulation, and functioning of certain discourses within a society." For Wimsatt and Beardsley, and for those they influenced, this position, and reader-response criticism as well, takes us too far afield from the specific text, the self-contained poem. Studying literature, in a disciplined way, means directly examining literary artifacts, not authors or readers or social contexts.

"The Intentional Fallacy" and "The Affective Fallacy" are important historically as documents in the theory and practice of New Criticism, the major mode of American academic criticism during the mid-twentieth century. They remain pertinent to debates today about interpretation and judgment. Where do we locate the authority or control for textual meaning? in the poem itself? in the author? or in the reader? How do we define these terms, and what is their relationship to one another? Can we make a distinction between the inside and the outside of a text, between intrinsic and extrinsic criticism? What is the nature of the knowledge that literary study gives us? These are permanent questions in the field of literary theory and criticism, and Wimsatt and Beardsley raised them as vividly as anyone has done.

"The Intentional Fallacy" Keywords: Authorship, Defense of Criticism, Formalism, Interpretation Theory, Poetry, Subjectivity

The Intentional Fallacy

He owns with toil he wrote the following scenes;
But, if they're naught, ne'er spare him for his pains:
Damn him the more; have no commiseration
For dullness on mature deliberation.
—William Congreve, Prologue to
The Way of the World[1]

The claim of the author's "intention" upon the critic's judgment has been challenged in a number of recent discussions, notably in the debate entitled *The Personal Heresy*, between Professors Lewis and Tillyard,[2] and at least implicitly in periodical essays like those in the "Symposiums" of 1940 in the *Southern* and *Kenyon Reviews*.[3] But it seems doubtful if this claim and most of its romantic corollaries are as yet subject to any widespread questioning. The present writers, in a short article entitled "Intention" for a *Dictionary*[4] of literary criticism, raised the issue but were unable to pursue its implications at any length. We argued that the design or intention of the author is neither available nor desirable as a standard for judging the success of a work of literary art, and it seems to us that this is a principle which goes deep into some differences in the history of critical attitudes. It is a principle which accepted or rejected points to the polar opposites of classical "imitation" and romantic expression. It entails many specific truths about inspiration, authenticity, biography, literary history and scholarship, and about some trends of contemporary poetry, especially its allusiveness. There is hardly a problem of literary criticism in which the critic's approach will not be qualified by his view of "intention."

"Intention," as we shall use the term, corresponds to *what he intended* in a formula which more or less explicitly has had wide acceptance. "In order to judge the poet's performance, we must know *what he intended*." Intention is design or plan in the author's mind. Intention has obvious affinities for the author's attitude toward his work, the way he felt, what made him write.

We begin our discussion with a series of propositions summarized and abstracted to a degree where they seem to us axiomatic, if not truistic.

1. A poem does not come into existence by accident. The words of a poem, as Professor Stoll[5] has remarked, come out of a head, not out of a hat. Yet to insist on the designing intellect as a *cause* of a poem is not to grant the design or intention as a *standard*.

2. One must ask how a critic expects to get an answer to the question about intention. How is he to find out what the poet tried to do? If the poet succeeded in doing it, then the poem itself shows what he was trying to do.

1. Restoration comedy (1700) by the English dramatist and poet Congreve (1670–1729).
2. *The Personal Heresy: A Controversy* (1939), by the English literary scholar E. M. W. Tillyard (1889–1962) and the Irish-born literary scholar and novelist C. S. Lewis (1898–1963).
3. Cf. Louis Teeter, "Scholarship and the Art of Criticism," *ELH* 5 (Sept. 1938), 173–94; René Wellek, review of Geoffrey Tillotson's *Essays in Criticism and Research, Modern Philology* 41 (May 1944), 262; G. Wilson Knight, *Shakespeare and Tolstoy*, English Association Pamphlet no. 88 (April 1934), p. 10; Bernard C. Heyl, *New Bearings in Esthetics and Art Criticism* (New Haven, 1943), pp. 66, 113, 149 [Wimsatt and Beardsley's note].
4. *Dictionary of World Literature*, ed. Joseph T. Shipley (New York, 1943), pp. 326–39 [Wimsatt and Beardsley's note].
5. E. E. Stoll (1874–1959), literary critic whose works focused primarily on drama (especially Shakespeare).

And if the poet did not succeed, then the poem is not adequate evidence, and the critic must go outside the poem—for evidence of an intention that did not become effective in the poem. "Only one *caveat* must be borne in mind," says an eminent intentionalist[6] in a moment when his theory repudiates itself; "the poet's aim must be judged at the moment of the creative act, that is to say, by the art of the poem itself."

3. Judging a poem is like judging a pudding or a machine. One demands that it work. It is only because an artifact works that we infer the intention of an artificer. "A poem should not mean but be."[7] A poem can *be* only through its *meaning*—since its medium is words—yet it *is*, simply *is*, in the sense that we have no excuse for inquiring what part is intended or meant.[8] Poetry is a feat of style by which a complex of meaning is handled all at once. Poetry succeeds because all or most of what is said or implied is relevant; what is irrelevant has been excluded, like lumps from pudding and "bugs" from machinery. In this respect poetry differs from practical messages, which are successful if and only if we correctly infer the intention. They are more abstract than poetry.

4. The meaning of a poem may certainly be a personal one, in the sense that a poem expresses a personality or state of soul rather than a physical object like an apple. But even a short lyric poem is dramatic, the response of a speaker (no matter how abstractly conceived) to a situation (no matter how universalized). We ought to impute the thoughts and attitudes of the poem immediately to the dramatic *speaker*, and if to the author at all, only by a biographical act of inference.

5. If there is any sense in which an author, by revision, has better achieved his original intention, it is only the very abstract, tautological, sense that he intended to write a better work and now has done it. (In this sense every author's intention is the same.) His former specific intention was not his intention. "He's the man we were in search of, that's true," says Hardy's rustic constable, "and yet he's not the man we were in search of. For the man we were in search of was not the man we wanted."[9]

"Is not a critic," asks Professor Stoll, ". . . a judge, who does not explore his own consciousness, but determines the author's meaning or intention, as if the poem were a will, a contract, or the constitution? The poem is not the critic's own."[1] He has diagnosed very accurately two forms of irresponsibility, one which he prefers. Our view is yet different. The poem is not the critic's own and not the author's (it is detached from the author at birth and goes about the world beyond his power to intend about it or control it). The

6. J. E. Spingarn, "The New Criticism," in *Criticism in America* (New York, 1924), pp. 24–25 [Wimsatt and Beardsley's note]. *Caveat*: let a person beware (Latin); that is, a warning or proviso.

7. From "Ars Poetica" (1926), by the American poet Archibald MacLeish (1892–1982).

8. As critics and teachers constantly do. "We have here a deliberate blurring. . . ." "Should this be regarded as ironic or unplanned?" ". . . is the literal meaning intended . . . ?" ". . . a paradox of religious faith which is intended to exult. . . ." "It seems to me that Herbert intends. . . ." These examples are chosen from three pages of an issue of *The Explicator* (Fredericksburg, Va.), 2, no. 1 (Oct. 1943). Authors often judge their own works in the same way. See *This Is My Best*, ed. Whit Burnett (New York, 1942), e.g., pp. 539–40 [Wimsatt and Beardsley's note].

9. A close relative of the intentional fallacy is that of talking about "means" and "end" in poetry instead of "part" and "whole." We have treated this relation concisely in our dictionary article [Wimsatt and Beardsley's note]. The quotation is from "The Three Strangers" (1883), by the English writer Thomas Hardy (1840–1928).

1. E. E. Stoll, "*The Tempest*," *PMLA* 47 (Sept. 1932), 703 [Wimsatt and Beardsley's note].

poem belongs to the public. It is embodied in language, the peculiar possession of the public, and it is about the human being, an object of public knowledge. What is said about the poem is subject to the same scrutiny as any statement in linguistics or in the general science of psychology or morals. Mr. Richards[2] has aptly called the poem a *class*—"a class of experiences which do not differ in any character more than a certain amount . . . from a standard experience." And he adds, "We may take as this standard experience the relevant experience of the poet when contemplating the completed composition." Professor Wellek[3] in a fine essay on the problem has preferred to call the poem "a system of norms," "extracted from every individual experience," and he objects to Mr. Richards' deference to the poet as reader. We side with Professor Wellek in not wishing to make the poet (outside the poem) an authority.

A critic of our *Dictionary* article, Mr. Ananda K. Coomaraswamy, has argued[4] that there are two kinds of enquiry about a work of art: (1) whether the artist achieved his intentions; (2) whether the work of art "ought ever to have been undertaken at all" and so "whether it is worth preserving." Number (2), Mr. Coomaraswamy maintains, is not "criticism of any work of art *qua* work of art," but is rather moral criticism; number (1) is artistic criticism. But we maintain that (2) need not be moral criticism: that there is another way of deciding whether works of art are worth preserving and whether, in a sense, they "ought" to have been undertaken, and this is the way of objective criticism of works of art as such, the way which enables us to distinguish between a skilful murder and a skilful poem. A skilful murder is an example which Mr. Coomaraswamy uses, and in his system the difference between the murder and the poem is simply a "moral" one, not an "artistic" one, since each if carried out according to plan is "artistically" successful. We maintain that (2) is an enquiry of more worth than (1), and since (2), and not (1), is capable of distinguishing poetry from murder, the name "artistic criticism" is properly given to (2).

II

It is not so much an empirical as an analytic judgment, not a historical statement, but a definition, to say that the intentional fallacy is a romantic one. When a rhetorician, presumably of the first century A.D., writes: "Sublimity is the echo of a great soul," or tells us that "Homer enters into the sublime actions of his heroes" and "shares the full inspiration of the combat," we shall not be surprised to find this rhetorician considered as a distant harbinger of romanticism and greeted in the warmest terms by so romantic a critic as Saintsbury.[5] One may wish to argue whether Longinus should be called romantic,[6] but there can hardly be a doubt that in one important way he is.

2. I. A. Richards (1893–1979), English literary theorist. His *Principles of Literary Criticism* (1925) is quoted here.
3. René Wellek (1903–1995), Austrian-born American literary theorist and scholar; the "fine essay" is "The Mode of Existence of a Literary Work of Art," *Southern Review* 7 (spring 1942), 735–54.
4. Ananda K. Coomaraswamy, "Intention," *American Bookman* 1 (winter 1944), 41–48 [Wimsatt and Beardsley's note].
5. George Saintsbury (1845–1933), English scholar and critic, whose works include *A History of Criticism and Literary Taste in Europe from the Earliest Texts to the Present Day* (3 vols., 1900–05).
6. For the relation of Longinus to modern romanticism, see R. S. Crane, review of Samuel Monk's *The Sublime, Philological Quarterly* 15 (April 1936), 165–66 [Wimsatt and Beardsley's note]. On the Greek rhetorician LONGINUS, see above.

Goethe's[7] three questions for "constructive criticism" are "What did the author set out to do? Was his plan reasonable and sensible, and how far did he succeed in carrying it out?" If one leaves out the middle question, one has in effect the system of Croce[8]—the culmination and crowning philosophic expression of romanticism. The beautiful is the successful intuition-expression, and the ugly is the unsuccessful; the intuition or private part of art is *the* aesthetic fact, and the medium or public part is not the subject of aesthetic at all. Yet aesthetic reproduction takes place only "if all the other conditions remain equal."

> Oil-paintings grow dark, frescoes fade, statues lose noses . . . the text of a poem is corrupted by bad copyists or bad printing.
>
> The Madonna of Cimabue is still in the Church of Santa Maria Novella; but does she speak to the visitor of to-day as to the Florentines of the thirteenth century?
>
> *Historical interpretation* labours . . . to reintegrate in us the psychological conditions which have changed in the course of history. It . . . enables us to see a work of art (a physical object) as its *author saw it* in the moment of production.[9]

The first italics are Croce's, the second ours. The upshot of Croce's system is an ambiguous emphasis on history. With such passages as a point of departure a critic may write a close analysis of the meaning or "spirit" of a play of Shakespeare or Corneille[1]—a process that involves close historical study but remains aesthetic criticism—or he may write sociology, biography, or other kinds of non-aesthetic history. The Crocean system seems to have given more of a boost to the latter way of writing.

"What has the poet tried to do," asks Spingarn in his 1910 Columbia Lecture from which we have already quoted, "and how has he fulfilled his intention?" The place to look for "insuperable" ugliness, says Bosanquet, in his third *Lecture* of 1914, is the "region of insincere and affected art."[2] The seepage of the theory into a non-philosophic place may be seen in such a book as Marguerite Wilkinson's inspirational *New Voices*,[3] about the poetry of 1919 to 1931—where symbols "as old as the ages . . . retain their strength and freshness" through "Realization." We close this section with two examples from quarters where one might least expect a taint of the Crocean. Mr. I. A. Richards' fourfold distinction of meaning into "sense," "feeling," "tone," "intention" has been probably the most influential statement of intentionalism in the past fifteen years, though it contains a hint of self-repudiation: "This function [intention]," says Mr. Richards, "is not on all

7. Johann Wolfgang von Goethe (1749–1832), German poet, playwright, and novelist.

8. Benedetto Croce (1866–1952), Italian literary critic, and philosopher; Wimsatt and Beardsley quote his *Aesthetics as Science of Expression and General Linguistic* (1909).

9. It is true that Croce himself in his *Ariosto, Shakespeare, and Corneille*, trans. Douglas Ainslie (London, 1920), chap. 7, "The Practical Personality and the Poetical Personality," and in his *Defence of Poetry*, trans. E. F. Carritt (Oxford, 1933), p. 24, has delivered a telling attack on intentionalism, but the prevailing drift of such passages in the *Aesthetics* as we quote is in the opposite direction [Wimsatt and Beardsley's note].

1. PIERRE CORNEILLE (1606–1684), French dramatist.

2. From *Three Lectures on Aesthetics* (1915) by the English philosopher Bernard Bosanquet (1848–1923).

3. *New Voices: An Introduction to Contemporary Poetry* (1919; rev. ed., 1923), by the Canadian-born poet Wilkinson (1883–1928).

fours with the others."[4] In an essay on "Three Types of Poetry" Mr. Allen Tate[5] writes as follows:

> We must understand that the lines
>
> Life like a dome of many-colored glass
> Stains the white radiance of eternity
>
> are not poetry; they express the *frustrated will* trying to compete with science. The *will* asserts a rhetorical proposition about the whole of life, but the *imagination* has not seized upon the materials of the poem and made them into a whole. Shelley's simile is imposed upon the material from above; it does not grow out of the material.

The last sentence contains a promise of objective analysis which is not fulfilled. The reason why the essay relies so heavily throughout on the terms "will" and "imagination" is that Mr. Tate is accusing the romantic poets of a kind of insincerity (romanticism in reverse) and at the same time is trying to describe something mysterious and perhaps indescribable, an "imaginative whole of life," a "wholeness of vision at a particular moment of experience," something which "yields us the quality of the experience." If a poet had a toothache at the moment of conceiving a poem, that would be part of the experience, but Mr. Tate of course does not mean anything like that. He is thinking about some kind of "whole" which in this essay at least he does not describe, but which doubtless it is the prime need of criticism to describe—in terms that may be publicly tested.

III

> I went to the poets; tragic, dithyrambic, and all sorts. . . . I took them some of the most elaborate passages in their own writings, and asked what was the meaning of them. . . . Will you believe me? . . . there is hardly a person present who would not have talked better about their poetry than they did themselves. Then I knew that not by wisdom do poets write poetry, but by a sort of genius and inspiration.[6]

That reiterated mistrust of the poets which we hear from Socrates may have been part of a rigorously ascetic view in which we hardly wish to participate, yet Plato's Socrates saw a truth about the poetic mind which the world no longer commonly sees—so much criticism, and that the most inspirational and most affectionately remembered, has proceeded from the poets themselves.

Certainly the poets have had something to say that the analyst and professor could not say; their message has been more exciting: that poetry should come as naturally as leaves to a tree, that poetry is the lava of the imagination, or that it is emotion recollected in tranquillity.[7] But it is necessary that we realize the character and authority of such testimony. There is

4. Richards, *Practical Criticism* (1929), part 3, chapter 1.

5. American poet and critic (1899–1979). In the passage that follows, Tate quotes from PERCY BYSSHE SHELLEY's pastoral elegy "Adonais" (1821).

6. From PLATO (ca. 427–ca. 347 B.C.E.), *Apology* 22a–c. The speaker is the Greek philosopher Socrates (469–399 B.C.E.).

7. The conceptions of poetry articulated by the Romantic poets John Keats (1795–1821), George Gordon, Lord Byron (1788–1824), and WILLIAM WORDSWORTH (1770–1850), respectively.

only a fine shade between those romantic expressions and a kind of earnest advice that authors often give. Thus Edward Young, Carlyle, Walter Pater:[8]

> I know two golden rules from *ethics*, which are no less golden in *Composition*, than in life. 1. *Know thyself*; 2dly, *Reverence thyself*.
>
> This is the grand secret for finding readers and retaining them: let him who would move and convince others, be first moved and convinced himself. Horace's rule, *Si vis me flere*,[9] is applicable in a wider sense than the literal one. To every poet, to every writer, we might say: Be true, if you would be believed.
>
> Truth! there can be no merit, no craft at all, without that. And further, all beauty is in the long run only *fineness* of truth, or what we call expression, the finer accommodation of speech to that vision within.

And Housman's little handbook[1] to the poetic mind yields the following illustration:

> Having drunk a pint of beer at luncheon—beer is a sedative to the brain, and my afternoons are the least intellectual portion of my life—I would go out for a walk of two or three hours. As I went along, thinking of nothing in particular, only looking at things around me and following the progress of the seasons, there would flow into my mind, with sudden and unaccountable emotion, sometimes a line or two of verse, sometimes a whole stanza at once. . . .

This is the logical terminus of the series already quoted. Here is a confession of how poems were written which would do as a definition of poetry just as well as "emotion recollected in tranquility"—and which the young poet might equally well take to heart as a practical rule. Drink a pint of beer, relax, go walking, think on nothing in particular, look at things, surrender yourself to yourself, search for the truth in your own soul, listen to the sound of your own inside voice, discover and express the *vraie vérité*.[2]

It is probably true that all this is excellent advice for poets. The young imagination fired by Wordsworth and Carlyle is probably closer to the verge of producing a poem than the mind of the student who has been sobered by Aristotle[3] or Richards. The art of inspiring poets, or at least of inciting something like poetry in young persons, has probably gone further in our day than ever before. Books of creative writing such as those issued from the Lincoln School are interesting evidence of what a child can do if taught how to manage himself honestly.[4] All this, however, would appear to belong to an art separate from criticism, or to a discipline which one might call the

8. English critic and essayist (1839–1894; see above); his quotation is from "Style" (1888). Young (1683–1765), English poet; his quotation is from *Conjectures on Original Composition* (1759). Thomas Carlyle (1795–1881), Scottish-born historian and essayist; his quotation is from "Burns" (1828).
9. If you want me to cry [mourn first yourself] (Latin). From HORACE (65–8 B.C.E.), *Ars Poetica*, line 102 (see above).
1. *The Name and Nature of Poetry* (1933), by the English poet and classical scholar A. E. Housman (1859–1936).
2. True truth (French).
3. That is, by the *Poetics* (see above) of ARISTOTLE (384–322 B.C.E.).
4. See Hugh Mearns, *Creative Youth* (Garden City, 1925), esp. pp. 10, 27–29. The technique of inspiring poems keeps pace today with a parallel analysis of the process of inspiration in successful artists. See Rosamond E. M. Harding, *An Anatomy of Inspiration* (Cambridge, 1940); Julius Portnoy, *A Psychology of Art Creation* (Philadelphia, 1942) [Wimsatt and Beardsley's note]. Lincoln School: an experimental school affiliated with Teachers College of Columbia University.

psychology of composition, valid and useful, an individual and private culture, yoga, or system of self-development which the young poet would do well to notice, but different from the public science of evaluating poems.

Coleridge and Arnold[5] were better critics than most poets have been, and if the critical tendency dried up the poetry in Arnold and perhaps in Coleridge, it is not inconsistent with our argument, which is that judgment of poems is different from the art of producing them. Coleridge has given us the classic "anodyne" story, and tells what he can about the genesis of a poem[6] which he calls a "psychological curiosity," but his definitions of poetry and of the poetic quality "imagination" are to be found elsewhere and in quite other terms.

The day may arrive when the psychology of composition is unified with the science of objective evaluation, but so far they are separate. It would be convenient if the passwords of the intentional school, "sincerity," "fidelity," "spontaneity," "authenticity," "genuineness," "originality," could be equated with terms of analysis such as "integrity," "relevance," "unity," "function"; with "maturity," "subtlety," and "adequacy," and other more precise axiological terms—in short, if "expression" always meant aesthetic communication. But this is not so.

"Aesthetic" art, says Professor Curt Ducasse, an ingenious theorist of expression, is the conscious objectification of feelings, in which an intrinsic part is the critical moment. The artist corrects the objectification when it is not adequate, but this may mean that the earlier attempt was not successful in objectifying the self, or "it may also mean that it was a successful objectification of a self which, when it confronted us clearly, we disowned and repudiated in favor of another."[7] What is the standard by which we disown or accept the self? Professor Ducasse does not say. Whatever it may be, however, this standard is an element in the definition of art which will not reduce to terms of objectification. The evaluation of the work of art remains public; the work is measured against something outside the author.

IV

There is criticism of poetry and there is, as we have seen, author psychology, which when applied to the present or future takes the form of inspirational promotion; but author psychology can be historical too, and then we have literary biography, a legitimate and attractive study in itself, one approach, as Mr. Tillyard would argue, to personality, the poem being only a parallel approach. Certainly it need not be with a derogatory purpose that one points out personal studies, as distinct from poetic studies, in the realm of literary scholarship. Yet there is danger of confusing personal and poetic studies; and there is the fault of writing the personal as if it were poetic.

There is a difference between internal and external evidence for the meaning of a poem. And the paradox is only verbal and superficial that what is (1) internal is also public: it is discovered through the semantics and syntax of a poem, through our habitual knowledge of the language, through grammars,

5. Matthew Arnold (1822–1888), English critic and poet. Samuel Taylor Coleridge (1772–1834), English poet and critic.

6. "Kubla Khan" (written 1797; pub. 1816); Coleridge's general account of poetry and the imagination is found in *Biographia Literaria* (1817; see above). "Anodyne": serving to alleviate pain.

7. Curt Ducasse, *The Philosophy of Art* (New York, 1929), p. 116 [Wimsatt and Beardsley's note]. Ducasse (1881–1969), French-born American philosopher.

dictionaries, and all the literature which is the source of dictionaries, in general through all that makes a language and culture; while what is (2) external is private or idiosyncratic; not a part of the work as a linguistic fact: it consists of revelations (in journals, for example, or letters or reported conversations) about how or why the poet wrote the poem—to what lady, while sitting on what lawn, or at the death of what friend or brother. There is (3) an intermediate kind of evidence about the character of the author or about private or semi-private meanings attached to words or topics by an author or by a coterie of which he is a member. The meaning of words is the history of words, and the biography of an author, his use of a word, and the associations which the word had for *him*, are part of the word's history and meaning.[8] But the three types of evidence, especially (2) and (3), shade into one another so subtly that it is not always easy to draw a line between examples, and hence arises the difficulty for criticism. The use of biographical evidence need not involve intentionalism, because while it may be evidence of what the author intended, it may also be evidence of the meaning of his words and the dramatic character of his utterance. On the other hand, it may not be all this. And a critic who is concerned with evidence of type (1) and moderately with that of type (3) will in the long run produce a different sort of comment from that of the critic who is concerned with type (2) and with (3) where it shades into (2).

The whole glittering parade of Professor Lowes' *Road to Xanadu*,[9] for instance, runs along the border between types (2) and (3) or boldly traverses the romantic region of (2). "'Kubla Khan'," says Professor Lowes, "is the fabric of a vision, but every image that rose up in its weaving had passed that way before. And it would seem that there is nothing haphazard or fortuitous in their return." This is not quite clear—not even when Professor Lowes explains that there were clusters of associations, like hooked atoms, which were drawn into complex relation with other clusters in the deep well of Coleridge's memory, and which then coalesced and issued forth as poems. If there was nothing "haphazard or fortuitous" in the way the images returned to the surface, that may mean (1) that Coleridge could not produce what he did not have, that he was limited in his creation by what he had read or otherwise experienced, or (2) that having received certain clusters of associations, he was bound to return them in just the way he did, and that the value of the poem may be described in terms of the experiences on which he had to draw. The latter pair of propositions (a sort of Hartleyan associationism[1] which Coleridge himself repudiated in the *Biographia*) may not be assented to. There were certainly other combinations, other poems, worse or better, that might have been written by men who had read Bartram and Purchas and Bruce and Milton.[2] And this will be true no matter how many times

8. And the history of words *after* a poem is written may contribute meanings which if relevant to the original pattern should not be ruled out by a scruple about intention. Cf. C. S. Lewis and E. M. W. Tillyard, *The Personal Heresy* (Oxford, 1939), p. 16; Teeter, loc cit., pp. 183, 192; review of Tillotson's *Essays*, *TLS* 41 (April 1942), 174 [Wimsatt and Beardsley's note].

9. An exhaustive examination (1927; rev. ed., 1930) of the sources of Coleridge's poems "The Rime of the Ancient Mariner" and "Kubla Khan," by the literary historian John Livingston Lowes (1867–1945).

1. Characteristic of David Hartley (1705–1757), English philosopher and physician; his *Observations on Man: His Frame, His Duty, and His Expectations* (1749) links mental phenomena to the associations of simple sensation.

2. The English poet John Milton (1608–1674) is an anomaly in this list, whose other members are the American naturalist and traveler William Bartram (1739–1823), author of *Travels through North and South Carolina* (1791); the English compiler of travel books Samuel Purchas (ca. 1577–1626); and the Scottish traveler and author James Bruce (1730–1794).

we are able to add to the brilliant complex of Coleridge's reading. In certain flourishes (such as the sentence we have quoted) and in chapter headings like "The Shaping Spirit," "The Magical Synthesis," "Imagination Creatrix," it may be that Professor Lowes pretends to say more about the actual poems than he does. There is a certain deceptive variation in these fancy chapter titles; one expects to pass on to a new stage in the argument, and one finds—more and more sources, more about "the streamy nature of association."[3]

"Wohin der Weg?" quotes Professor Lowes for the motto of his book. "Kein Weg! Ins Unbetretene."[4] Precisely because the way is *unbetreten*, we should say, it leads away from the poem. Bartram's *Travels* contains a good deal of the history of certain words and romantic Floridian conceptions that appear in "Kubla Khan." And a good deal of that history has passed and was then passing into the very stuff of our language. Perhaps a person who has read Bartram appreciates the poem more than one who has not. Or, by looking up the vocabulary of "Kubla Khan" in the *Oxford English Dictionary*, or by reading some of the other books there quoted, a person may know the poem better. But it would seem to pertain little to the poem to know that *Coleridge* had read Bartram. There is a gross body of life, of sensory and mental experience, which lies behind and in some sense causes every poem, but can never be and need not be known in the verbal and hence intellectual composition which is the poem. For all the objects of our manifold experience, especially for the intellectual objects, for every unity, there is an action of the mind which cuts off roots, melts away context—or indeed we should never have objects or ideas or anything to talk about.

It is probable that there is nothing in Professor Lowes' vast book which could detract from anyone's appreciation of either *The Ancient Mariner* or *Kubla Khan*. We next present a case where preoccupation with evidence of type (3) has gone so far as to distort a critic's view of a poem (yet a case not so obvious as those that abound in our critical journals).

In a well-known poem by John Donne appears the following quatrain:

> Moving of th' earth brings harmes and feares,
>   Men reckon what it did and meant,
> But trepidation of the spheares,
>   Though greater farre, is innocent.[5]

A recent critic in an elaborate treatment of Donne's learning has written of this quatrain as follows:

> . . . he touches the emotional pulse of the situation by a skillful allusion to the new and the old astronomy. . . . Of the new astronomy, the "moving of the earth" is the most radical principle; of the old, the "trepidation of the spheres" is the motion of the greatest complexity. . . . As the poem is a valediction forbidding mourning, the poet must exhort his love to quietness and calm upon his departure; and for this purpose the figure based

3. Chapters 8, "The Pattern," and 16, "The Known and Familiar Landscape," will be found of most help to the student of the poem. For an extreme example of intentionalist criticism, see Kenneth Burke's analysis of *The Ancient Mariner* in *The Philosophy of Literary Form* (Baton Rouge, 1941), pp. 22–23, 93–102. Mr. Burke must be credited with realizing very clearly what he is up to [Wimsatt and Beardsley's note]. Burke (1897–1993), American critic.

4. Where is the way? No way! It is untrodden (German). From Goethe's *Faust* (1808, 1832).

5. "A Valediction: Forbidding Mourning" (1633), lines 9–12, by the English poet Donne (1572–1631).

> upon the latter motion (trepidation), long absorbed into the traditional astronomy, fittingly suggests the tension of the moment without arousing the "harmes and feares" implicit in the figure of the moving earth.[6]

The argument is plausible and rests on a well-substantiated thesis that Donne was deeply interested in the new astronomy and its repercussions in the theological realm. In various works Donne shows his familiarity with Kepler's *De Stella Nova*, with Galileo's *Siderius Nuncius*, with William Gilbert's *De Magnete*, and with Clavius's commentary on the *De Sphaera* of Sacrobosco.[7] He refers to the new science in his Sermon at Paul's Cross and in a letter to Sir Henry Goodyer.[8] In *The First Anniversary* he says the "new philosophy calls all in doubt." In the *Elegy on Prince Henry* he says that the "least moving of the center" makes "the world to shake."

It is difficult to answer argument like this, and impossible to answer it with evidence of like nature. There is no reason why Donne might not have written a stanza in which the two kinds of celestial motion stood for two sorts of emotion at parting. And if we become full of astronomical ideas and see Donne only against the background of the new science, we may believe that he did. But the text itself remains to be dealt with, the analyzable vehicle of a complicated metaphor. And one may observe: (1) that the movement of the earth according to the Copernican theory[9] is a celestial motion, smooth and regular, and while it might cause religious or philosophic fears, it could not be associated with the crudity and earthiness of the kind of commotion which the speaker in the poem wishes to discourage; (2) that there is another moving of the earth, an earthquake, which has just these qualities and is to be associated with the tear-floods and sigh-tempests of the second stanza of the poem; (3) that "trepidation" is an appropriate opposite of earthquake, because each is a shaking or vibratory motion; and "trepidation of the spheres" is "greater far" than an earthquake, but not much greater (if two such motions can be compared as to greatness) than the annual motion of the earth; (4) that reckoning what it "did and meant" shows that the event has passed, like an earthquake, not like the incessant celestial movement of the earth. Perhaps a knowledge of Donne's interest in the new science may add another shade of meaning, an overtone to the stanza in question, though to say even this runs against the words. To make the geocentric and heliocentric antithesis the core of the metaphor is to disregard the English language, to prefer private evidence to public, external to internal.

V

If the distinction between kinds of evidence has implications for the historical critic, it has them no less for the contemporary poet and his critic. Or, since every rule for a poet is but another side of a judgment by a critic,

6. Charles M. Coffin, *John Donne and the New Philosophy* (New York, 1927), pp. 97–98 [Wimsatt and Beardsley's note].

7. All works of science, by Johannes Kepler (1571–1630), German astronomer and mathematician; Galileo (1564–1642), Italian astronomer and physicist; Gilbert (1544–1603), English court physician who studied electricity and magnetism; and Johannes de Sacrobosco (or John Holywood or Halifax), English mathematician (mid-13th c.), whose commentators include the Italian mathematician Christopher Clavius (16th c.).

8. Goodyer (1571–1628), a friend of Donne's and an occasional poet himself.

9. That is, the heliocentric theory of the Polish astronomer Nicolaus Copernicus (1473–1543), that the sun is the center of the universe; it replaced the geocentric theory of the Greek astronomer Ptolemy (active 127–148 C.E.), according to which all heavenly bodies revolve around the earth.

and since the past is the realm of the scholar and critic, and the future and present that of the poet and the critical leaders of taste, we may say that the problems arising in literary scholarship from the intentional fallacy are matched by others which arise in the world of progressive experiment.

The question of "allusiveness," for example, as acutely posed by the poetry of Eliot, is certainly one where a false judgment is likely to involve the intentional fallacy. The frequency and depth of literary allusion in the poetry of Eliot and others has driven so many in pursuit of full meanings to the *Golden Bough*[1] and the Elizabethan drama that it has become a kind of commonplace to suppose that we do not know what a poet means unless we have traced him in his reading—a supposition redolent with intentional implications. The stand taken by Mr. F. O. Matthiessen[2] is a sound one and partially forestalls the difficulty.

> If one reads these lines with an attentive ear and is sensitive to their sudden shifts in movement, the contrast between the actual Thames and the idealized vision of it during an age before it flowed through a megalopolis is sharply conveyed by that movement itself, whether or not one recognizes the refrain to be from Spenser.[3]

Eliot's allusions work when we know them—and to a great extent even when we do not know them, through their suggestive power.

But sometimes we find allusions supported by notes, and it is a very nice question whether the notes function more as guides to send us where we may be educated, or more as indications in themselves about the character of the allusions. "Nearly everything of importance . . . that is apposite to an appreciation of 'The Waste Land'," writes Mr. Matthiessen of Miss Weston's book,[4] "has been incorporated into the structure of the poem itself, or into Eliot's Notes." And with such an admission it may begin to appear that it would not much matter if Eliot invented his sources (as Sir Walter Scott[5] invented chapter epigraphs from "old plays" and "anonymous" authors, or as Coleridge wrote marginal glosses for "The Ancient Mariner"). Allusions to Dante, Webster, Marvell, or Baudelaire,[6] doubtless gain something because these writers existed, but it is doubtful whether the same can be said for an allusion to an obscure Elizabethan:

> The sound of horns and motors, which shall bring
> Sweeney to Mrs. Porter in the spring.[7]

"Cf. Day, *Parliament of Bees*:" says Eliot,

> When of a sudden, listening, you shall hear,
> A noise of horns and hunting, which shall bring

1. *The Golden Bough: A Study in Magic and Religion* (12 vols., 1890–1915), by J. G. Frazer; alluded to in *The Waste Land* (1922) by T. S. ELIOT (1888–1965).
2. American literary critic (1902–1950); the quotation is from *The Achievement of T. S. Eliot: An Essay on the Nature of Poetry* (1935).
3. Edmund Spenser (1552–1599), English poet. In "The Fire Sermon," part 3 of *The Waste Land*, Eliot quotes and cites Spenser's "Prothalamion" (1596).
4. *From Ritual to Romance* (1920), by Jessie Weston (1850–1928).
5. Scottish poet and novelist (1771–1832).
6. Charles Baudelaire (1821–1867), French writer, translator, and critic. DANTE ALIGHIERI (1265–1321), Italian poet. John Webster (ca. 1580–ca. 1634), English playwright. Andrew Marvell (1621–1678), English metaphysical poet.
7. From "The Fire Sermon." The "obscure Elizabethan" is John Day (1574–ca. 1640), whose *Parliament of Bees* is an allegorical masque.

> Actaeon to Diana[8] in the spring,
> Where all shall see her naked skin. . . .

The irony is completed by the quotation itself; had Eliot, as is quite conceivable, composed these lines to furnish his own background, there would be no loss of validity. The conviction may grow as one reads Eliot's next note: "I do not know the origin of the ballad from which these lines are taken: it was reported to me from Sydney, Australia." The important word in this note—on Mrs. Porter and her daughter who washed their feet in soda water—is "ballad." And if one should feel from the lines themselves their "ballad" quality, there would be little need for the note. Ultimately, the inquiry must focus on the integrity of such notes as part of the poem, for where they constitute special information about the meaning of phrases in the poem, they ought to be subject to the same scrutiny as any of the other words in which it is written. Mr. Matthiessen believes the notes were the price Eliot "had to pay in order to avoid what he would have considered muffling the energy of his poem by extended connecting links in the text itself." But it may be questioned whether the notes and the need for them are not equally muffling. The omission from poems of the explanatory stratum on which is built the dramatic or poetic stuff is a dangerous responsibility. Mr. F. W. Bateson has plausibly argued[9] that Tennyson's "The Sailor Boy" would be better if half the stanzas were omitted, and the best versions of ballads like "Sir Patrick Spens"[1] owe their power to the very audacity with which the minstrel has taken for granted the story upon which he comments. What then if a poet finds he cannot take so much for granted in a more recondite context and rather than write informatively, supplies notes? It can be said in favor of this plan that at least the notes do not pretend to be dramatic, as they would if written in verse. On the other hand, the notes may look like unassimilated material lying loose beside the poem, necessary for the meaning of the verbal symbol, but not integrated, so that the symbol stands incomplete.

We mean to suggest by the above analysis that whereas notes tend to seem to justify themselves as external indexes to the author's *intention*, yet they ought to be judged like any other parts of a composition (verbal arrangement special to a particular context), and when so judged their reality as parts of the poem or their imaginative integration with the rest of the poem, may come into question. Mr. Matthiessen, for instance, sees that Eliot's titles for poems and his epigraphs are informative apparatus, like the notes. But while he is worried by some of the notes and thinks that Eliot "appears to be mocking himself for writing the note at the same time that he wants to convey something by it," Mr. Matthiessen believes that the "device" of epigraphs "is not at all open to the objection of not being sufficiently structural." "The *intention*," he says, "is to enable the poet to secure a condensed expression in the poem itself." "In each case the epigraph is *designed* to form an integral part of the effect of the poem." And Eliot himself, in his notes, has justified his poetic practice in terms of intention.

8. The Roman name of Artemis, the Greek goddess of the hunt; after the hunter Actaeon by chance saw her bathing, she turned him into a stag and he was torn apart by his own dogs.
9. In *English Poetry and the English Language: An Experiment in Literary History* (1934), by the English academic Bateson (1901–1978).
1. An early Scottish ballad. "The Sailor Boy" (1861), a 6-stanza poem by Alfred, Lord Tennyson (1809–1892).

> The Hanged Man, a member of the traditional pack, fits my purpose in two ways: because he is associated in my mind with the Hanged God of Frazer, and because I associate him with the hooded figure in the passage of the disciples to Emmaus in Part V. . . . The man with Three Staves (an authentic member of the Tarot pack) I associate, quite arbitrarily, with the Fisher King himself.

And perhaps he is to be taken more seriously here, when off guard in a note, than when in his Norton Lectures[2] he comments on the difficulty of saying what a poem means and adds playfully that he thinks of prefixing to a second edition of *Ash Wednesday* some lines from *Don Juan*:[3]

> I don't pretend that I quite understand
> My own meaning when I would be *very* fine;
> But the fact is that I have nothing planned
> Unless it were to be a moment merry.

If Eliot and other contemporary poets have any characteristic fault, it may be in *planning* too much.[4]

Allusiveness in poetry is one of several critical issues by which we have illustrated the more abstract issue of intentionalism, but it may be for today the most important illustration. As a poetic practice allusiveness would appear to be in some recent poems an extreme corollary of the romantic intentionalist assumption, and as a critical issue it challenges and brings to light in a special way the basic premise of intentionalism. The following instance from the poetry of Eliot may serve to epitomize the practical implications of what we have been saying. In Eliot's "Love Song of J. Alfred Prufrock," towards the end, occurs the line: "I have heard the mermaids singing, each to each," and this bears a certain resemblance to a line in a Song[5] by John Donne, "Teach me to heare Mermaides singing," so that for the reader acquainted to a certain degree with Donne's poetry, the critical question arises: Is Eliot's line an allusion to Donne's? Is Prufrock thinking about Donne? Is Eliot thinking about Donne? We suggest that there are two radically different ways of looking for an answer to this question. There is (1) the way of poetic analysis and exegesis, which inquires whether it makes any sense if Eliot-Prufrock *is* thinking about Donne. In an earlier part of the poem, when Prufrock asks, "Would it have been worth while, . . . To have squeezed the universe into a ball," his words take half their sadness and irony from certain energetic and passionate lines of Marvell's "To His Coy Mistress."[6] But the exegetical inquirer may wonder whether mermaids considered as "strange sights" (to hear them is in Donne's poem analogous to getting with child a mandrake root) have much to do with Prufrock's mermaids, which seem to be symbols of romance and dynamism, and which incidentally

2. Delivered at Harvard University in the winter of 1932–33; Eliot later published them as *The Use of Poetry and the Use of Criticism* (1933).
3. A mock epic (1819–24) by Lord Byron; the lines quoted are from canto 4, stanza 5. Eliot published *Ash Wednesday* in 1930.
4. In his critical writings Eliot has expressed the right view of author psychology. See *The Use of Poetry and the Use of Criticism* (Cambridge, 1933), p. 139, and "Tradition and the Individual Talent" in *Selected Essays* (New York, 1932), though his record is not entirely consistent. See *A Choice of Kipling's Verse* (London, 1941), pp. 10–11, 20–21 [Wimsatt and Beardsley's note]. For "Tradition and the Individual Talent," see above.
5. "Go and catch a falling star" (1633). "Prufrock" was published in 1915.
6. "To His Coy Mistress" (1651), lines 41–42: "Let us roll our strength and all / Our sweetness up into one ball."

have literary authentication, if they need it, in a line of a sonnet by Gérard de Nerval.[7] This method of inquiry may lead to the conclusion that the given resemblance between Eliot and Donne is without significance and is better not thought of, or the method may have the disadvantage of providing no certain conclusion. Nevertheless, we submit that this is the true and objective way of criticism, as contrasted to what the very uncertainty of exegesis might tempt a second kind of critic to undertake: (2) the way of biographical or genetic inquiry, in which, taking advantage of the fact that Eliot is still alive, and in the spirit of a man who would settle a bet, the critic writes to Eliot and asks what he meant, or if he had Donne in mind. We shall not here weigh the probabilities—whether Eliot would answer that he meant nothing at all, had nothing at all in mind—a sufficiently good answer to such a question—or in an unguarded moment might furnish a clear and, within its limit, irrefutable answer. Our point is that such an answer to such an inquiry would have nothing to do with the poem "Prufrock"; it would not be a critical inquiry. Critical inquiries, unlike bets, are not settled in this way. Critical inquiries are not settled by consulting the oracle.

1946

7. French symbolist poet (1808–1855); the sonnet is in *The Chimeras* (1854).

SIMONE DE BEAUVOIR
1908–1986

Written in the absence of any organized feminist movement, Simone de Beauvoir's classic manifesto, *The Second Sex* (1949), provided the theoretical basis for the emergence in the 1960s and 1970s of feminist activism in both Europe and North America. Though her significant contributions to existentialist philosophy have often been overshadowed by the fame of her lifelong associate and lover, the philosopher Jean-Paul Sartre, Beauvoir's importance for feminist theory is indisputable. With her famous remark that "One is not born, but rather becomes, a woman," which opens the second volume of *The Second Sex* (the original French text was published separately in two volumes issued months apart), Beauvoir inaugurated the social constructionist critique of essentialism that occupied feminist literary theory starting in the 1980s. While her uncompromising rejection of any notion of a female nature or essence finds echoes in the writing of later feminist theorists such as JULIA KRISTEVA, MONIQUE WITTIG, and JUDITH BUTLER, *The Second Sex* has left its mark on virtually every aspect of the contemporary women's movement.

Born Simone Lucie Ernestine Marie Bertrande de Beauvoir in Paris, Beauvoir grew up the elder of two daughters in a comfortable middle-class family. Educated in a conservative Catholic girls' preparatory school, she attended various institutions of higher learning, successfully pursuing *licenses* (equivalent to a master's degree) in literature, philosophy, and mathematics. Among the first generation of women to be educated in the elite universities that had once been all-male preserves, Beauvoir graduated in 1929 from the Sorbonne with a degree in philosophy, having written a thesis on Leibniz. While a student she met Sartre, who was studying philosophy at the École Normale Supérieure, and began a friendship with the philosopher most closely associated with existentialism; other fellow students included the phenomenologist Maurice Merleau-Ponty, the anthropologist CLAUDE LÉVI-STRAUSS, and the French theologian and mystic Simone Weil. Beauvoir was only the ninth woman and the youngest student ever to pass the rigorous *agrégation* in philosophy (a competitive national exam for students who want to become tenured *lycée* professors), taking second place to Sartre (who had failed the first time). After completing her degree, she taught at various *lycées* in Marseilles, Rouen, and Paris from 1931 to 1943, when her contract was suspended after she was accused of sleeping with a student. Although she was reinstated after the war, she never taught again; for the rest of her life she supported herself by her writing.

The variety of Beauvoir's writing over the next half century is impressive. In 1945 she and Sartre, along with Merleau-Ponty, founded *Les Temps Modernes*, a monthly magazine devoted to politics and literature. Between 1943 and 1968, Beauvoir wrote six novels, winning the Prix Goncourt in 1954 for *Les Mandarins* (1954), a fictionalized account of postwar leftist intellectuals and their attempts to give up their "mandarin" (educated elite) status and engage in political activism. This novel includes characters who resemble Beauvoir, Sartre, the French writer Albert Camus, and the American novelist Nelson Algren, with whom Beauvoir had a relationship for nearly fifteen years. During this time, she also wrote four books on philosophy—including *The Ethics of Ambiguity* (1947), which importantly articulates an ethics for Sartrean existentialism—and a number of essays, some of them book-length, the best known of which is *The Second Sex*. In addition to novels, philosophy, and feminist critique, Beauvoir wrote at least six volumes of autobiography between 1958 and 1972, creating a detailed portrait of French intellectual life from the 1930s to the 1970s. Beauvoir addressed the issue of aging in *A Very Easy Death* (1964, *Une Mort très douce*), on her mother's death in a hospital; *Old Age* (1970, *La Viellesse*), a reflection on society's indifference to the elderly; and, in 1981, in *Adieux: A Farewell to Sartre*, a account of Sartre's last years. During the 1970s, Beauvoir was very active in feminist politics, in 1979 joining the editorial collective Questions Féministes.

The Second Sex is a wide-ranging, multidisciplinary essay that draws on and critiques history, biology, anthropology, literature, psychoanalysis, Marxism, and existentialist philosophy as means of understanding the lived experiences of women. Beauvoir argues that throughout history, women have been reduced to objects for men. Because men have imagined women as the "Other," women have been denied subjectivity. In this claim, Beauvoir echoes VIRGINIA WOOLF's statement in *A Room of One's Own* (1929) that women serve "as looking-glasses possessing the magic and delicious power of reflecting the figure of man at twice its natural size." While Beauvoir's argument that in patriarchal cultures man is the norm and woman the deviation has become a commonplace of feminist theory, in 1949 it was revolutionary. *The Second Sex* shows how these fundamental assumptions dominate social, political, and cultural life and how women have internalized this ideology, so that they live in a constant state of "inauthenticity." In existentialist terms, patriarchy constructs woman as immanence (as stagnation and immersion in nature) and man as transcendence (as continually striving for freedom and authenticity), thereby impeding women's struggle to achieve existential freedom and autonomous subjectivity.

To illustrate her theoretical insights, *The Second Sex* employs a number of different perspectives. In the first part Beauvoir examines woman "objectively"—that is, as object of analysis—through a series of cultural lenses, including biology, psychoanalysis, Marxism, history, literature, and myth. At the same time she critiques each of these cultural lenses. In the second part she examines women "subjectively" from the perspective of their own lived experience, showing the processes through which women internalize the ideologies of otherness that relegate them to immanence and to the position of being man's Other.

Our selection is the last in a series of three chapters on myths about women, asking what significance they have in "daily life." What is the relationship between the myth of the Eternal Feminine and the lived experience of actual women? True to her roots in existentialism, Beauvoir argues that "essence does not precede existence"; that is, a human being is neither more nor less than the sum total of her or his acts. The myth of the Eternal Feminine, however, takes the values, beliefs, practices, and institutions that constitute women's experience and projects them into the realm of Platonic Forms as timeless and unchanging essences. The myth becomes the only reality; against it, "the contrary facts of experience are impotent." Woman is defined as the absolute Other of man and denied any subjectivity.

Moreover, the various and invariably partial myths about femininity—each claiming to be a totalizing explanation—are contradictory, leading to the biggest myth of all: that women are mysterious, beyond the comprehension of men, an explanation that Beauvoir argues "flatters laziness and vanity at once." In fact, Beauvoir contends, in recognizing that all human beings have within them the potential for both transcendence and immanence, men would lose an attractive relationship that benefits them. Patriarchy relies on the myth of woman's essential immanence and her otherness in constructing male subjectivity.

As this summary suggests, the primary influence on *The Second Sex* is Sartrean existentialism. However, the extent of Beauvoir's debt to Sartre has been somewhat exaggerated and her own philosophical contributions to existentialism obscured. In particular, she rejects Sartre's alienating view of freedom, preferring instead to see authentic relationships as involving reciprocity between subjects, "the mutual recognition of free beings who confirm one another's freedom." In addition, she more quickly understood and developed the notion that the body is situated in culture and history, an idea that makes possible a more nuanced analysis of oppression and political activism. Because of her close association with Sartre, readers have also tended to overlook the other influences on *The Second Sex*, including phenomenology, Marxism, and psychoanalysis.

Our selection, which heavily influenced Kate Millett's 1970 feminist classic, *Sexual Politics*, illustrates what feminists in the 1960s and 1970s found most appealing in *The Second Sex*: its complete blurring of fictional and autobiographical ways of knowing the world and gaining a voice as a woman. Throughout *The Second Sex*, Beauvoir refuses to distinguish between literary accounts, anecdotes, and what might be taken as more "expert" discourses about women such as psychoanalysis and biology, a technique central to her project of tearing down (de-essentializing) patriarchal myths. This strategy empowered second-wave feminists to construct new discourses about women to counter those from which women's voices had largely been excluded.

Although *The Second Sex* has been an enormously influential text for feminist literary theory (even if its influence has often been tacit rather than explicit), it has not been without its critics, most of whom point to a masculinist bias in the text (seen as a result of Sartre's influence). Beauvoir, critics argue, tends to define what men do as transcendent and what women do—childbearing, motherhood, housework—as necessarily immanent. Economic independence is seen as the cornerstone of women's liberation, while both marriage and motherhood are disparaged as inauthentic choices. As Kristeva points out in "Women's Time" (1979), Beauvoir is unable to imagine that motherhood might be an active and authentic choice—even a form of transcendence. Beauvoir also tends to generalize from her specific observations of white, middle-class, and well-educated European women to universal claims about all women. Despite these criticisms, *The Second Sex*, revolutionary in its own time, offers a powerful analysis of the status of women and remains a foundational text for feminist theory.

***The Second Sex* Keywords:** The Body, Ethics, Feminist Theory, Gender, Institutional Studies, Phenomenology, Popular Culture, Sexuality, Subjectivity

From The Second Sex[1]

From *Volume I: Facts and Myths*

FROM PART THREE: MYTHS

Chapter 3

The myth of woman plays a significant role in literature; but what is its importance in everyday life? To what extent does it affect individual social customs and behavior? To reply to this question, we will need to specify the relation of this myth to reality.

There are different kinds of myths. This one, sublimating an immutable aspect of the human condition—that is, the "division" of humanity into two categories of individuals—is a static myth; it projects into a Platonic heaven[2] a reality grasped through experience or conceptualized from experience; for fact, value, significance, notion, and empirical law, it substitutes a transcendent Idea, timeless, immutable, and necessary. This idea escapes all contention because it is situated beyond the given; it is endowed with an absolute truth. Thus, to the dispersed, contingent, and multiple existence of *women*, mythic thinking opposes the Eternal Feminine, unique and fixed; if the definition given is contradicted by the behavior of real flesh-and-blood women, it is women who are wrong: it is said not that Femininity is [not] an entity but that women are not feminine. Experiential denials cannot do anything against myth. Though in a way, its source is in experience. It is thus true that woman is other than man, and this alterity is concretely felt in desire, embrace, and love; but the real relation is one of reciprocity; as such, it gives rise to authentic dramas: through eroticism, love, friendship, and their alternatives of disappointment, hatred, and rivalry, the relation is a struggle of consciousnesses, each of which wants to be essential, it is the recognition of freedoms that confirm each other, it is the undefined passage from enmity to complicity. To posit the Woman is to posit the absolute Other, without reciprocity, refusing, against experience, that she could be a subject, a peer.

In concrete reality, women manifest themselves in many different ways; but each of the myths built around woman tries to summarize her as a whole; each is supposed to be unique; the consequence of this is a multiplicity of incompatible myths, and men are perplexed before the strange inconsistencies of the idea of Femininity; as every woman enters into many of these archetypes, each of which claims to incarnate its Truth alone, men also find the same old confusion before their companions as did the Sophists,[3] who had difficulty understanding how a person could be light and dark at the same time. The transition to the absolute shows up in social representations: relations are quickly fixed in classes, and roles in types, just as, for the childlike mentality, relations are fixed in things. For example, patriarchal society, focused on preserving the patrimony, necessarily implies, in addition to individuals who hold and transmit goods, the existence of men and women who

1. Translated by Constance Borde and Sheila Malovany-Chevallier.

2. That is, the realm of Forms or Ideas, transcendent entities in whose reality existing things (their imperfect representations) participate; on the Greek philosopher PLATO (ca. 427–ca. 347 B.C.E.), see above.

3. Itinerant professional teachers of philosophy and especially rhetoric in 5th-century B.C.E. Greece (see GORGIAS, above).

wrest them from their owners and circulate them; men—adventurers, crooks, thieves, speculators—are generally repudiated by the group; women using their sexual attraction can lure young people and even family men into dissipating their patrimony, all within the law; they appropriate men's fortunes or seize their inheritance; this role being considered bad, women who play it are called "bad women." But in other families—those of their fathers, brothers, husbands, or lovers—they can in fact seem like guardian angels; the courtesan who swindles rich financiers is a patroness of painters and writers. The ambiguity of personalities like Aspasia and Mme de Pompadour[4] is easy to understand as a concrete experience. But if woman is posited as the Praying Mantis, the Mandrake, or the Demon, then the mind reels to discover in her the Muse, the Goddess Mother, and Beatrice[5] as well.

As group representation and social types are generally defined by pairs of opposite terms, ambivalence will appear to be an intrinsic property of the Eternal Feminine. The saintly mother has its correlation in the cruel stepmother, the angelic young girl has the perverse virgin: so Mother will be said sometimes to equal Life and sometimes Death, and every virgin is either a pure spirit or flesh possessed by the devil.

It is obviously not reality that dictates to society or individuals their choices between the two opposing principles of unification; in every period, in every case, society and individual decide according to their needs. Very often they project the values and institutions to which they adhere onto the myth they adopt. Thus paternalism that calls for woman to stay at home defines her as sentiment, interiority, and immanence; in fact, every existent is simultaneously immanence and transcendence;[6] when he is offered no goal, or is prevented from reaching any goal, or denied the victory of it, his transcendence falls uselessly into the past, that is, it falls into immanence; this is the lot assigned to women in patriarchy; but this is in no way a vocation, any more than slavery is the slave's vocation. The development of this mythology is all too clear in Auguste Comte.[7] To identify Woman with Altruism is to guarantee man absolute rights to her devotion; it is to impose on women a categorical must-be.

The myth must not be confused with the grasp of a signification; signification is immanent in the object; it is revealed to consciousness in a living experience, whereas the myth is a transcendent Idea that escapes any act of consciousness. When Michel Leiris[8] in *L'âge d'homme* (*Manhood*) describes

4. Jeanne-Antoinette Poisson, marquise de Pompadour (1721–1764), influential mistress (from 1745 on) of the French king Louis XV and a notable patron of literature and the arts. Aspasia: mistress of the 5th-century B.C.E. Athenian statesman Pericles, a woman of considerable learning.

5. Beatrice Portinari, the daughter of a noble Florentine family, who died at the age of 24 in 1290; she provided the inspiration for much of DANTE's poetry, especially his masterpiece, *The Divine Comedy* (1321). Praying Mantis: in the first paragraph of *The Second Sex*, Beauvoir writes of "the female praying mantis and the spider, gorged on love, crushing their partners and devouring them up." Mandrake: a plant long used as both a narcotic and an aphrodisiac. Muse: in Greek mythology, one of the 9 daughters of Memory who preside over the arts and all intellectual pursuits. Goddess Mother: any of a variety of feminine deities and maternal symbols of creativity, birth, fertility, sexual union, nurturing, and the cycle of growth. The term also has been applied to figures as diverse as the so-called Stone Age Venuses and the Virgin Mary.

6. All terms associated with existential philosophy. The *existent* is the subject of existentialism, the human actor whose subjectivity is shaped through human activity. Activity that achieves liberty is a mode of *transcendence*; without it, there is only *immanence*, stagnation and subjugation to given conditions.

7. French philosopher (1798–1857), known as the founder of sociology and of positivism; he idealized the role of women in society.

8. French writer (1901–1990), a pioneer in modern confessional literature and a noted anthropologist, poet, and art critic. His *L'âge d'homme* (1939, *Manhood: A Journey from Childhood into the Fierce Order of Virility*) was autobiographical.

his vision of female organs, he provides significations and does not develop a myth. Wonder at the feminine body and disgust for menstrual blood are apprehensions of a concrete reality. There is nothing mythical in the experience of discovering the voluptuous qualities of feminine flesh, and expressing these qualities by comparisons to flowers or pebbles does not turn them into myth. But to say that Woman is Flesh, to say that Flesh is Night and Death, or that she is the splendor of the cosmos, is to leave terrestrial truth behind and spin off into an empty sky. After all, man is also flesh for woman; and woman is other than a carnal object; and for each person and in each experience the flesh takes on singular significations. It is likewise perfectly true that woman—like man—is a being rooted in nature; she is more enslaved to the species than the male is, her animality is more manifest; but in her as in him, the given is taken on by existence; she also belongs to the human realm. Assimilating her with Nature is simply a prejudice.

Few myths have been more advantageous to the ruling master caste than this one: it justifies all its privileges and even authorizes taking advantage of them. Men do not have to care about alleviating the suffering and burdens that are physiologically women's lot since they are "intended by Nature"; they take this as a pretext to increase the misery of the woman's condition—for example, by denying woman the right to sexual pleasure, or making her work like a beast of burden.[9]

Of all these myths, none is more anchored in masculine hearts than the feminine "mystery." It has numerous advantages. And first it allows an easy explanation for anything that is inexplicable; the man who does not "understand" a woman is happy to replace his subjective deficiency with an objective resistance; instead of admitting his ignorance, he recognizes the presence of a mystery exterior to himself: here is an excuse that flatters his laziness and vanity at the same time. An infatuated heart thus avoids many disappointments: if the loved one's behavior is capricious, her remarks stupid, the mystery serves as an excuse. And thanks to the mystery, this negative relation that seemed to Kierkegaard[1] infinitely preferable to positive possession is perpetuated; faced with a living enigma, man remains alone: alone with his dreams, hopes, fears, love, vanity; this subjective game that can range from vice to mystical ecstasy is for many a more attractive experience than an authentic relation with a human being. Upon what bases does such a profitable illusion rest?

Surely, in a way, woman is mysterious, "mysterious like everyone," according to Maeterlinck.[2] Each one is subject only for himself; each one can grasp only his own self in his immanence; from this point of view, the other is always mystery. In men's view, the opacity of the for-itself[3] is more fla-

9. Cf. Balzac: *Physiology of Marriage* [1830]: "Do not trouble yourself in any way about her murmurings, her cries, her pains; nature has made her for your use, made her to bear all: the children, the worries, the blows, and the sorrows of man. But do not accuse us of harshness. In the codes of all the so-called civilised nations, man has written the laws which rule the destiny of woman beneath this blood inscription: *Vae victis!* Woe to the vanquished" [Beauvoir's note]. Honoré de Balzac (1799–1850), French novelist renowned for fictions of French middle-class society.

1. Søren Kierkegaard (1813–1855), Danish philosopher and religious thinker, a forerunner of existentialism.

2. Maurice Maeterlinck (1862–1949), Belgian poet, dramatist, and essayist, whose antinaturalist plays were precursors of the theater of the absurd.

3. The *pour-soi* (being-for-itself), an existentialist term that contrasts human consciousness with the being-in-itself (*en-soi*) of those creatures that lack consciousness.

grant in the feminine other; they are unable to penetrate her unique experience by any effect of sympathy; they are condemned to ignorance about the quality of woman's sexual pleasure, the discomforts of menstruation, and the pains of childbirth. The truth is that mystery is reciprocal: as another, and as a masculine other, there is also a presence closed on itself and impenetrable to woman in the heart of every man; she is without knowledge of male eroticism. But according to a universal rule already mentioned, the categories in which men think the world are constituted from *their point of view as absolutes:* they fail to understand reciprocity here as everywhere. As she is mystery for man, woman is regarded as mystery in herself.

It is true that her situation especially disposes her to be seen in this image. Her physiological destiny is very complex; she herself endures it as a foreign story; her body is not for her a clear expression of herself; she feels alienated from it; the link that for every individual joins physiological to psychic life—in other words, the relation between the facticity of an individual and the freedom that assumes it—is the most difficult enigma brought about by the human condition: for woman, this enigma is posed in the most disturbing way.

But what is called mystery is not the subjective solitude of consciousness, or the secret of organic life. The word's true meaning is found at the level of communication: it cannot be reduced to pure silence, to obscurity, to absence; it implies an emerging presence that fails to appear. To say that woman is mystery is to say not that she is silent but that her language is not heard; she is there, but hidden beneath veils; she exists beyond these uncertain appearances. Who is she? An angel, a demon, an inspiration, an actress? One supposes that either there are answers impossible to uncover or none is adequate because a fundamental ambiguity affects the feminine being; in her heart she is indefinable for herself: a sphinx.[4]

The fact is, deciding *who* she *is* would be quite awkward for her; the question has no answer; but it is not that the hidden truth is too fluctuating to be circumscribed; in this area there is no truth. An existent *is* nothing other than what he does; the possible does not exceed the real, essence does not precede existence: in his pure subjectivity, the human being *is nothing.* He is measured by his acts. It can be said that a peasant woman is a good or bad worker, that an actress has or does not have talent: but if a woman is considered in her immanent presence, absolutely nothing can be said about that, she is outside of the realm of qualification. Now, in amorous or conjugal relations and in all relations where woman is the vassal, the Other, she is grasped in her immanence. It is striking that the woman friend, colleague, or associate is without mystery; on the other hand, if the vassal is male and if, in front of an older and richer man or woman, a young man, for example, appears as the inessential object, he also is surrounded in mystery. And this uncovers for us an infrastructure of feminine mystery that is economic. A sentiment cannot *be* something, either. "In the domain of feeling, what is real is indistinguishable from what is imaginary," writes Gide.[5]

4. That is, an enigma; in Greek mythology, the sphinx was a monster with a woman's face, a lion's body, and a bird's wings whose riddle was finally answered by Oedipus.

5. André Gide (1869–1951), major French literary figure of the first half of the 20th century. Beauvoir quotes from chapter 8 of *Les Faux-Monnayeurs* (1925, *The Counterfeiters*).

"And it is sufficient to imagine one loves, in order to love, so it is sufficient to say to oneself that when one loves one imagines one loves, in order to love a little less." There is no discriminating between the imaginary and the real except through behavior. As man holds a privileged place in this world, he is the one who is able actively to display his love; very often he keeps the woman, or at least he helps her out; in marrying her, he gives her social status; he gives her gifts; his economic and social independence permits his endeavors and innovations: separated from Mme de Villeparisis, M. de Norpois[6] takes twenty-four-hour trips to be with her; very often he is busy and she is idle: he *gives* her the time he spends with her; she takes it: with pleasure, passion, or simply for entertainment? Does she accept these benefits out of love or out of one interest? Does she love husband or marriage? Of course, even the proof man gives is ambiguous: Is such a gift given out of love or pity? But while normally woman finds numerous advantages in commerce with man, commerce with woman is profitable to man only inasmuch as he loves her. Thus, the degree of his attachment to her can be roughly estimated by his general attitude, while woman barely has the means to sound out her own heart; according to her moods she will take different points of view about her own feelings, and as long as she submits to them passively, no interpretation will be truer than another. In the very rare cases where it is she who holds the economic and social privileges, the mystery is reversed: this proves that it is not linked to *this* sex rather than to the other but to a situation. For many women, the roads to transcendence are blocked: because they *do* nothing, they do not make themselves *be* anything; they wonder indefinitely what they *could have* become, which leads them to wonder what they *are:* it is a useless questioning; if man fails to find that secret essence, it is simply because it does not exist. Kept at the margins of the world, woman cannot be defined objectively through this world, and her mystery conceals nothing but emptiness.

Furthermore, like all oppressed people, woman deliberately dissimulates her objective image; slave, servant, indigent, all those who depend upon a master's whims[7] have learned to present him with an immutable smile or an enigmatic impassivity; they carefully hide their real feelings and behavior. Woman is also taught from adolescence to lie to men, to outsmart, to sidestep them. She approaches them with artificial expressions; she is prudent, hypocritical, playacting.

But feminine Mystery as recognized by mythical thinking is a more profound reality. In fact, it is immediately implied in the mythology of the absolute Other. If one grants that the inessential consciousness is also a transparent subjectivity, capable of carrying out the cogito,[8] one grants that it is truly sovereign and reverts to the essential; for all reciprocity to seem impossible, it is necessary that the Other be another for itself, that its very subjectivity be affected by alterity; this consciousness, which would be alienated as consciousness, in its pure immanent presence, would obviously

6. Two characters in Marcel Proust's 7-volume novel, *À la recherche du temps perdu* (1913–27, *In Search of Lost Time* [first translated into English as *Remembrance of Things Past*]).

7. An allusion to the famous Master-Slave dialectic of GEORG WILHELM FRIEDRICH HEGEL (1770–1831), described in his *Phenomenology of Spirit* (1807; see above).

8. I think (Latin); an allusion to the French philosopher René Descartes (1596–1650), whose most fundamental proposition was "cogito, ergo sum" (I think, therefore I am).

be a Mystery; it would be a Mystery in itself because it would be it for itself; it would be absolute Mystery. It is thus that, beyond the secrecy their dissimulation creates, there is a mystery of the Black, of the Yellow, insofar as they are considered absolutely as the inessential Other. It must be noted that the American citizen who deeply confounds the average European is nonetheless not considered "mysterious": one more modestly claims not to understand him; likewise, woman does not always "understand" man, but there is no masculine mystery; the fact is that rich America and the male are on the side of the Master, and Mystery belongs to the slave.

Of course, one can only dream about the positive reality of the Mystery in the twilight of bad faith;[9] like certain marginal hallucinations, it dissolves once one tries to pin it down. Literature always fails to depict "mysterious" women; they can only appear at the beginning of a novel as strange and enigmatic; but unless the story remains unfinished, they give up their secret in the end and become consistent and translucent characters. The heroes in Peter Cheyney's[1] books, for example, never cease to be amazed by women's unpredictable caprices; one can never guess how they will behave, they confound all calculations; in truth, as soon as the workings of their actions are exposed to the reader, they are seen as very simple mechanisms: this one is a spy or that one a thief; however clever the intrigue, there is always a key, and it could not be otherwise, even if the author had all the talent, all the imagination possible. Mystery is never more than a mirage; it vanishes as soon as one tries to approach it.

Thus we see that myths are explained in large part by the use man makes of them. The myth of the woman is a luxury. It can appear only if man escapes the imperious influence of his needs; the more relations are lived concretely, the less idealized they are. The fellah in ancient Egypt, the bedouin[2] peasant, the medieval artisan, and the worker of today, in their work needs and their poverty, have relations with the particular woman who is their companion that are too basic for them to embellish her with an auspicious or fatal aura. Eras and social classes that had the leisure to daydream were the ones who created the black-and-white statues of femininity. But luxury also has its usefulness; these dreams were imperiously guided by interest. Yes, most myths have their roots in man's spontaneous attitude to his own existence and the world that invests it: but the move to surpass experience toward the transcendent Idea was deliberately effected by patriarchal society for the end of self-justification; through myths, this society imposed its laws and customs on individuals in an imagistic and sensible way; it is in a mythical form that the group imperative insinuated itself into each consciousness. By way of religions, traditions, language, tales, songs, and film, myths penetrate even into the existence of those most harshly subjected to material realities. Everyone can draw on myth to sublimate his own modest experiences: betrayed by a woman he loves, one man calls her a slut; another is obsessed by his own virile impotence: this woman is a praying mantis; yet another takes pleasure in his wife's company: here we

9. An existentialist term referring to the effort to avoid the responsibility of one's own freedom by denying its full extent.
1. English writer of detective fiction (1896–1951).

2. Arabic-speaking pastoral nomad of the Middle East and North Africa. "Fellah": agricultural laborer (Arabic), as opposed to a nomadic desert dweller.

have Harmony, Repose, Mother Earth. The taste for eternity at bargain prices and for a handy, pocket-sized absolute, seen in most men, is satisfied by myths. The least emotion, a small disagreement, become the reflection of a timeless Idea; this illusion comfortably flatters one's vanity.

The myth is one of those traps of false objectivity into which the spirit of seriousness falls headlong. It is once again a matter of replacing lived experience and the free judgments of experience it requires by a static idol. The myth of Woman substitutes for an authentic relationship with an autonomous existent the immobile contemplation of a mirage. "Mirage! Mirage! Kill them since we cannot seize them; or else reassure them, instruct them, help them give up their taste for jewelry, make them real equal companions, our intimate friends, associates in the here and now, dress them differently, cut their hair, tell them everything," cried Laforgue.[3] Man would have nothing to lose, quite the contrary, if he stopped disguising woman as a symbol. Dreams, when collective and controlled—clichés—are so poor and monotonous compared to living reality: for the real dreamer, for the poet, living reality is a far more generous resource than a worn-our fantasy. The times when women were the most sincerely cherished were not courtly feudal ones, nor the gallant nineteenth century; they were the times—the eighteenth century, for example—when men regarded women as their peers; this is when women looked truly romantic: only read *Les liaisons dangereuses* (*Dangerous Liaisons*), *Le rouge et le noir* (*The Red and the Black*), or *A Farewell to Arms* to realize this. Laclos' heroines like Stendhal's and Hemingway's[4] are without mystery: and they are no less engaging for it. To recognize a human being in a woman is not to impoverish man's experience: that experience would lose none of its diversity, its richness, or its intensity if it was taken on in its intersubjectivity; to reject myths is not to destroy all dramatic relations between the sexes, it is not to deny the significations authentically revealed to man through feminine reality; it is not to eliminate poetry, love, adventure, happiness, and dreams: it is only to ask that behavior, feelings, and passion be grounded in truth.[5]

"Woman is lost. Where are the women? Today's women are not women"; we have seen what these mysterious slogans mean. In the eyes of men—and of the legions of women who see through these eyes—it is not enough to have a woman's body or to take on the female function as lover and mother to be a "real woman"; it is possible for the subject to claim autonomy through sexuality and maternity; the "real woman" is one who accepts herself as Other. The duplicitous attitude of men today creates a painful split for women; they accept, for the most part, that woman be a peer, an equal; and yet they continue to oblige her to remain the inessential; for her, these two destinies are not reconcilable; she hesitates between them without being

3. Jules Laforgue (1860–1887), French symbolist poet. Here and in note 5 below, Beauvoir quotes from his essay "Sur la femme" ("On Woman"), in *Melanges Posthumes* (1903).

4. The authors of the three novels named: the French Pierre Choderlos de Laclos (1741–1803) wrote *Dangerous Liaisons* (1782); the French Stendhal, pen name of Henri-Marie Beyle (1783–1842), wrote *The Red and the Black* (1830); and the American Ernest Hemingway (1899–1961) wrote *A Farewell to Arms* (1929).

5. Laforgue goes on to say about woman: "Since she has been left in slavery, idleness, without arms other than her sex, she has overdeveloped it and has become the Feminine . . . we have permitted her to overdevelop; she is here on the earth for us. . . . Well, that is all wrong . . . we have played doll with the woman until now. This has gone on too long!" [Beauvoir's note].

exactly suited to either, and that is the source of her lack of balance. For man, there is no hiatus between public and private life: the more he asserts his grasp on the world through action and work, the more virile he looks; human and vital characteristics are merged in him; but women's own successes are in contradiction with her femininity since the "real woman" is required to make herself object, to be the Other. It is very possible that on this point even men's sensibility and sexuality are changing. A new aesthetic has already been born. Although the fashion for flat chests and narrow hips—the boyish woman—only lasted a short while, the opulent ideal of past centuries has nevertheless not returned. The feminine body is expected to be flesh, but discreetly so; it must be slim and not burdened with fat; toned, supple, robust, it has to suggest transcendence; it is preferred tanned, having been bared to a universal sun like a worker's torso, not white like a hothouse plant. Woman's clothes, in becoming more practical, have not made her look asexual: on the contrary, short skirts have shown off her legs and thighs more than before. There is no reason for work to deprive her of her erotic appeal. To see woman as both a social person and carnal prey can be disturbing: in a recent series of drawings by Peynet,[6] there is a young fiancé deserting his fiancée because he was seduced by the pretty mayoress about to celebrate the marriage; that a woman could hold a "man's office" and still be desirable has long been a subject of more or less dirty jokes; little by little, scandal and irony have lost their bite and a new form of eroticism seems to be coming about: perhaps it will produce new myths.

What is certain is that today it is very difficult for women to assume both their status of autonomous individual and their feminine destiny; here is the source of the awkwardness and discomfort that sometimes leads them to be considered "a lost sex." And without doubt it is more comfortable to endure blind bondage than to work for one's liberation; the dead, too, are better suited to the earth than the living. In any case, turning back is no more possible than desirable. What must be hoped is that men will assume, without reserve, the situation being created; only then can women experience it without being torn. Then will Laforgue's wish be fulfilled: "O young women, when will you be our brothers, our closest brothers without ulterior motives of exploitation? When will we give to each other a true handshake?" Then "Melusina, no longer under the burden of the fate unleashed on her by man alone, Melusina rescued," will find "her human base."[7] Then will she fully be a human being, "when woman's infinite servitude is broken, when she lives for herself and by herself, man—abominable until now—giving her her freedom."[8]

1949

6. November 1948 [Beauvoir's note]. Raymond Peynet (1909–1999), French graphic artist and designer.
7. Breton, *Arcanum 17* [Beauvoir's note]. André Breton (1896–1966), French surrealist poet, essayist, critic, and editor. In the legends of Brittany, Melusina was part sea serpent and part woman.
8. Rimbaud, to Paul Demeny, May 15, 1871 [Beauvoir's note]. Arthur Rimbaud (1854–1891), French symbolist poet. Demeny (1844–1918), French poet.

CLAUDE LÉVI-STRAUSS
1908–2009

The French anthropologist Claude Lévi-Strauss is most famous for his role in the cross-disciplinary phenomenon known as "structuralism" that came to prominence in the late 1950s and reached its peak of popularity in the late 1960s. Taking inspiration from FERDINAND DE SAUSSURE (1857–1913), who had defined language as a system of signs and linguistics as a branch of semiology (the larger science of all signs), Lévi-Strauss argued that the objects of social anthropology—cultural phenomena such as kinship systems and rituals—consist of communications, not just functions. Focusing both on the role of unconscious structures in western European cultural practices and on the meaningful order informing what had appeared to earlier Western observers as the purely irrational or instinct-driven customs of so-called primitive peoples, he simultaneously proclaimed the death of the Enlightenment concept of "Man" and posited a kind of universal mind. Reframing anthropology as a study of Culture rather than cultures, Lévi-Strauss underscored the discipline's implications for history, politics, art, literature, economics, and philosophy, dramatically transforming anthropology's profile in the academy. Within the discipline many scholars contested the empirical validity of his analyses of kinship, totemism, and myth and accused Lévi-Strauss of engaging in a kind of metaphysical colonization. Nevertheless, his adoption of linguistic metaphors and methods and his acute self-consciousness about the role of the ethnographer have had a lasting impact on the practice of anthropology proper and on the humanities and social sciences more generally. Though the structuralist method that Lévi-Strauss pioneered has been superseded, the analogy he proposed—that cultural phenomena constitute exchanges of messages and that cultural codes may be analyzed as languages—remains a tacit working assumption of many forms of cultural theory.

While Lévi-Strauss may be the best-known and most broadly influential anthropologist of the twentieth century, he never received formal academic training in the study of other cultures (ethnology). Born in Brussels, son of a painter and grandson of a rabbi, he grew up primarily in Paris. Having pursued studies in philosophy and law and passed the prestigious *agrégation* exam in philosophy in 1931 (along with fellow students Maurice Merleau-Ponty and SIMONE DE BEAUVOIR), he went on to spend a couple of years teaching philosophy in provincial secondary schools; but he soon became disaffected with that discipline. Evincing a bias that JACQUES DERRIDA was later to remark on, he complained of philosophy that "the signifier did not relate to any signified; there was no referent" (*Tristes Tropiques*, 1955). Yet more empirically oriented anthropologists reproached Lévi-Strauss for failing to leave philosophy far enough behind. While his criticisms of philosophy seem implicitly to extol the virtues of firsthand observation, Lévi-Strauss later claimed to have "realized early on that [he] was a library man, not a fieldworker," and he suggested that "fieldwork is a kind of 'women's work'" for which he had "neither the interest nor the patience" (Eribon, *Conversations*, 1988). Indeed, he was to spend relatively little time among the people whose cultures he studied, instead drawing heavily on others' ethnographic data.

Lévi-Strauss conducted the fieldwork on which much of his later work was based between 1935 and 1938, during breaks from teaching sociology at the newly created University of São Paulo in Brazil. *Tristes Tropiques*, from which our selection is taken, was written almost twenty years later; it is among other things an autobiographical account of his expeditions into the Brazilian interior, where he sojourned among the Bororo, Caduveo, Nambikwara, and Tupi-Kawahib peoples. Lévi-Strauss returned to France in 1939 but the following year was dismissed from his teaching post: the racial laws of the Vichy government of occupied France decreed him ineligible to teach because he was a Jew. In 1941, with the help of an aunt living in the United States and a Rockefeller Foundation program to assist European scientists and scholars threatened by World War II, he was able to obtain an exit visa to travel to New York, where he was offered a position at the New School for Social Research.

In New York Lévi-Strauss met the Russian ROMAN JAKOBSON and attended his lectures on linguistics. This encounter affected him as a "revelation": "Jakobson revealed to me the existence of a body of doctrine that had already been formed within a discipline, linguistics, with which I was unacquainted" (Eribon, *Conversations*). Jakobson was elaborating Saussurean linguistics, with its proposition that language does not consist of positive terms with meaning in and of themselves, but instead is a system of relations in which each term is defined by its difference from other terms. Suggesting that "the kinship system is a language," Lévi-Strauss proposed adapting the methods of structural linguistics to the analysis of kinship and other cultural phenomena. He pursued this semiological project in his doctoral thesis at the Sorbonne, published as *The Elementary Structures of Kinship* (1949). In his view, the prohibition of incest, which seems to be a universal rule in human society, is designed not to ward off biological or psychological damage but to make women available for "trade" by men of their group with men of other groups. Extending the argument of Marcel Mauss, who in *The Gift* (1925) had emphasized the symbolic rather than the economic value of gifts exchanged, Lévi-Strauss suggests that gift giving in general and wife trafficking in particular are above all modes of communication. In other words, women and other gifts are traded as words are exchanged in conversation; the fact that in matrimonial exchange "the mediating factor . . . should be the *women of the group*, who are *circulated* between clans, lineages, or families, in place of the *words of the group*, which are *circulated* between individuals, does not at all change the fact that the essential aspect of the phenomenon is identical in both cases" (*Structural Anthropology*, 1958).

As the feminist theorists Teresa de Lauretis and GAYLE RUBIN have observed, this way of reading kinship systems excludes women from the role of cultural *agents*, treating them only as cultural *objects*. In addition, Lévi-Strauss's account of the origin of culture through the exchange of female "valuables *par excellence*" puts the symbolization and subordination of women at the root of culture. Theorists of gender and sexuality have found the critique of Lévi-Strauss's blind spot a useful starting point in challenging the naturalization of gender hierarchy.

The interest of literary theorists was initially attracted by Lévi-Strauss's work in mythology. His writings about myth were first published in book form in the manifesto-like *Structural Anthropology* and later in a four-volume collection, *Mythologiques* (1964–71). These and later writings focus not on what myths *mean*, but on what they *do*. What they do, he argues, is to make a story out of fundamental and irresolvable human contradictions or enigmas (for example, the differences between humans and animals, life and death, one and two). They layer many different versions of the same contradiction on top of each other, so that in essence a myth is "three-dimensional," not linear. It might be useful here to compare the structural analysis of myth by Lévi-Strauss to the "morphological" study of folktales by the Russian formalist Vladimir Propp (1895–1970), since both kinds of analysis influenced structuralism. Propp studied a large number of Russian folktales and found that despite their differences, they all made use of a small number of functions (hero, helper, villain, test, prohibition, etc.) arranged in a predictable order. Narrative order was a function of unfolding linear time: the narrative had a beginning, a middle, and an end. For Lévi-Strauss, in contrast, the linear (or diachronic) ordering of a myth is less important than the systematic (or synchronic) pattern of repetitions, which can exist in different versions or different arrangements without disturbing the mythic system (he foresaw how useful computer analysis would be to this kind of study). In a famous essay, first published in English in 1955, titled "The Structural Study of Myth," Lévi-Strauss applied his method to the myth of Oedipus. Myths make order out of the simultaneity of conflicting theories: they narrate over, without resolving, a cultural contradiction.

The essay was published in the same year as his influential book *Tristes Tropiques*, a year that marked a turning point for Lévi-Strauss. After two failed attempts to be appointed to France's prestigious Collège de France, in 1959 he was appointed to the first chair in social anthropology; in 1973 he was elected to the French Academy. Lévi-Strauss, who had always considered himself an outsider, had become the consummate insider.

Written twenty years after the fieldwork on which it is based, *Tristes Tropiques* was an instant sensation and Lévi-Strauss became a best-selling author. It was first published in English in 1961 as *A World on the Wane* (with several chapters omitted); the book appeared in a more complete translation that dates from 1973 and leaves the title in French (literally, "sad tropics"). *Tristes Tropiques* began as a novel, became an autobiography, and ended up an account of an exoticized journey just like those Lévi-Strauss feared it would resemble. The book's first sentence is "I hate travelling and explorers." Praised as a masterpiece by such leading critics as SUSAN SONTAG and George Steiner, loved and hated by a generation of anthropologists, and made into an opera in 1996 with libretto by the French feminist Catherine Clément and music by Georges Aperghis, *Tristes Tropiques* is a unique and symptomatic book. The sadness of its title comes from the unbearable loss of all societies previously uncontaminated by Western intrusions. But the desire to find and document such societies is a form of the very same evil that has already violated them: "Not content with having eliminated savage life, and unaware even of having done so, it [the Western public] feels the need feverishly to appease the nostalgic cannibalism of history with the shadows of those that history has already destroyed." Lamenting the blindness of the West, Lévi-Strauss also personifies it—an irony he recognizes.

Our selection from the work, "A Writing Lesson," shows Lévi-Strauss in all of his dimensions. Constantly baffled, lost, and nervous, yet confident in the intuitions of his own mind, he narrates a succession of encounters with the Nambikwara societies he tries to understand. His skill as a narrator is to make the reader feel that a great deal is not being understood and, at the same time, that all of human life is at stake. Something of the fictional power of writing is unmasked when Lévi-Strauss's wife contracts an eye disease and has to be evacuated. This is the only mention of her presence. The "eye disease" affects Lévi-Strauss's own narrative eye, previously so solitary and single: it reveals that Lévi-Strauss is not a lone fieldworker but part of a group of Westerners that had remained invisible. The chapter thus illustrates the manipulations of writing that it discusses in its central passages.

When an unpopular chief pretends to his people that he knows how to write, Lévi-Strauss launches into a famous meditation on the role of writing in world history. His theory of writing (discussed by Derrida in his poststructuralist *Of Grammatology*) can be usefully compared to PLATO's censorious myth of writing in the *Phaedrus* (see above; see also Derrida's comments on Plato in *Dissemination*). Writing, concludes Lévi-Strauss, is a technology for mass exploitation, a point MICHEL FOUCAULT would develop in his *Discipline and Punish* (1975). But the apparent anti-Western animus in Lévi-Strauss's remarks depends on a concept of societies without writing, an idealization of innocence lost, that is tied to an entirely Western fantasy he both attacks and prolongs: the fantasy of the noble savage.

It is tempting to apply Lévi-Strauss's theory of myths to his own multilayered writing in *Tristes Tropiques*, as Clifford Geertz (in *Works and Lives*, 1988) and Cleo McNelly (in "Natives, Women, and Claude Lévi-Strauss," 1975), in different ways, have done. What is the contradiction that Lévi-Strauss himself is covering over? One answer is suggested by his publication of "The Structural Study of Myth" at the same time as *Tristes Tropiques*. While *Tristes Tropiques* expresses the pain and mourns the destructive impact of Western civilization on non-Western people, the study of myth sees the different moments of human history as structurally simultaneous. On the one hand, this allows for a cultural relativism that enables Lévi-Strauss to contest any narrative of "progress," with its concomitant belief in the superiority of the modern. But on the other hand, it makes the destruction of "primitive" societies *total* so as to internalize the lost object. In seeing "neolithic" structures as located *within* modern civilization, he is papering over loss (and also survival) through incorporation. It is no longer necessary to mourn, because in a sense nothing is lost: the "savage" is internalized in the deep structures of "all" thought. Yet such structural consolation remains haunted by the history and remainders it represses. In *Tristes Tropiques*, Lévi-Strauss gives voice to that haunting.

***Tristes Tropiques* Keywords:** Aesthetics, Authorship, Cultural Studies, Language, Modernity, Postcolonial Theory, Structuralism

From Tristes Tropiques[1]

Chapter 28. A Writing Lesson

I was keen to find out, at least indirectly, the approximate size of the Nambikwara[2] population. In 1915, Rondon[3] had suggested a figure of twenty thousand, which was probably too high an estimate; but at that time, each group comprised several hundred members, and, according to information I had picked up along the line, there had since been a rapid decline. Thirty years ago, the known fraction of the Sabané[4] group comprised more than a thousand individuals; when the group visited the telegraph station at Campos Novos[5] in 1928, a hundred and twenty-seven men were counted in addition to women and children. However, in 1929 an influenza epidemic broke out when the group was camping in a locality known as Espirro. The illness developed into a form of pulmonary oedema[6] and, within forty-eight hours, three hundred natives had died. The group broke up, leaving the sick and the dying behind. Of the thousand Sabané who were once known to exist, there remained in 1938 only nineteen men with their women and children. These figures are perhaps to be explained, not only by the epidemic, but also by the fact that, a few years before, the Sabané had started a war against some of their eastern neighbours. But a large group, which had settled not far from Tres Buritis,[7] was wiped out by a flu epidemic in 1927, with the exception of six or seven individuals, of whom only three were still alive in 1938. The Tarundé[8] group, which was once one of the largest, numbered only twelve men (plus the women and children) in 1936; of these twelve men four survived in 1939.

Now, there were perhaps no more than two thousand natives scattered across the area. A systematic census was out of the question, because of the

1. Translated by John and Doreen Weightman.
2. A tribe of hunter-gatherers who live scattered in villages, primarily in Amazon rain forests in central Brazil.
3. Cândido Mariano da Silva Rondon (1865–1958), a Brazilian army engineer who "discovered" the Nambikwara in 1907 when he entered their territory to supervise construction of a telegraph line.
4. A language of the Nambikwara linguistic family; also, the subgroup of Nambikwara who speak this dialect.
5. A Brazilian settlement that was established on the telegraph line built through the Nambikwara territory.
6. That is, edema: accumulation of fluids.
7. Another Brazilian settlement built on the telegraph line.
8. A subgroup of the Nambikwara tribe (later anthropologists found no trace of this name).

permanent hostility shown by certain groups and the fact that all groups were on the move during the nomadic period. But I tried to persuade my Utiarity[9] friends to take me to their village, after organizing some kind of meeting there with other groups to whom they were related either by kinship or marriage; in this way I would be able to gauge the size of a contemporary gathering and compare it in this respect with those previously observed. I promised to bring presents and to engage in barter. The chief of the group was rather reluctant to comply with my request: he was not sure of his guests, and if my companions and myself were to disappear in an area where no white men had set foot since the murder of the seven telegraph employees in 1925, the precarious peace which had prevailed since then might well be endangered for some time to come.

He finally agreed on condition that we reduced the size of our expedition, taking only four oxen to carry the presents. Even so, it would be impossible to follow the usual tracks along the valley bottoms where the vegetation was too dense for the animals to get through. We would have to go across the plateaux following a route specially worked out for the occasion.

In retrospect, this journey, which was an extremely hazardous one, seems to me now to have been like some grotesque interlude. We had hardly left Juruena[1] when my Brazilian companion noticed that the women and children were not with us: we were accompanied only by the men, armed with bows and arrows. In travel books, such circumstances mean that an attack is imminent. So we moved ahead with mixed feelings, checking the position of our Smith-and-Wesson revolvers (our men pronounced the name as 'Cemite Vechetone') and our rifles from time to time. Our fears proved groundless: about midday we caught up with the rest of the group, whom the chief had taken the precaution of sending off the previous evening, knowing that our mules would advance more quickly than the basket-carrying women, whose pace was further slowed down by the children.

A little later, however, the Indians lost their way: the new route was not as straightforward as they had imagined. Towards evening we had to stop in the bush; we had been told that there would be game to shoot; the natives were relying on our rifles and had brought nothing with them; we only had emergency provisions, which could not possibly be shared out among everybody. A herd of deer grazing around a water-hole fled at our approach. The next morning, there was widespread discontent, openly directed against the chief who was held responsible for a plan he and I had devised together. Instead of setting out on a hunting or collecting expedition, all the natives decided to lie down under the shelters, leaving the chief to discover the solution to the problem. He disappeared along with one of his wives; towards evening we saw them both return, their heavy baskets full of the grasshoppers they had spent the entire day collecting. Although crushed grasshopper is considered rather poor fare, the natives all ate heartily and recovered their spirits. We set off again the following morning.

At last we reached the appointed meeting-place. It was a sandy terrace overlooking a stream lined with trees, between which lay half-hidden native gardens. Groups arrived intermittently. Towards evening, there were seventy-

9. The site of another telegraph station in Nambikwara territory.

1. The site of a telegraph station on the edge of Nambikwara territory.

five persons representing seventeen families, all grouped together under thirteen shelters hardly more substantial than those to be found in native camps. It was explained to me that, during the rainy season, all these people would be housed in five round huts built to last for some months. Several of the natives appeared never to have seen a white man before and their surly attitude and the chief's edginess suggested that he had persuaded them to come rather against their will. We did not feel safe, nor did the Indians. The night promised to be cold, and as there were no trees on the terrace, we had to lie down like the Nambikwara on the bare earth. Nobody slept: the hours were spent keeping a close but polite watch on each other.

It would have been unwise to prolong such a dangerous situation, so I urged the chief to proceed without further delay to the exchange of gifts. It was at this point that there occurred an extraordinary incident that I can only explain by going back a little. It is unnecessary to point out that the Nambikwara have no written language, but they do not know how to draw either, apart from making a few dotted lines or zigzags on their gourds. Nevertheless, as I had done among the Caduveo[2] I handed out sheets of paper and pencils. At first they did nothing with them, then one day I saw that they were all busy drawing wavy, horizontal lines. I wondered what they were trying to do, then it was suddenly borne upon me that they were writing or, to be more accurate, were trying to use their pencils in the same way as I did mine, which was the only way they could conceive of, because I had not yet tried to amuse them with my drawings. The majority did this and no more, but the chief had further ambitions. No doubt he was the only one who had grasped the purpose of writing. So he asked me for a writing-pad, and when we both had one, and were working together, if I asked for information on a given point, he did not supply it verbally but drew wavy lines on his paper and presented them to me, as if I could read his reply. He was half taken in by his own make-believe; each time he completed a line, he examined it anxiously as if expecting the meaning to leap from the page, and the same look of disappointment came over his face. But he never admitted this, and there was a tacit understanding between us to the effect that his unintelligible scribbling had a meaning which I pretended to decipher; his verbal commentary followed almost at once, relieving me of the need to ask for explanations.

As soon as he had got the company together, he took from a basket a piece of paper covered with wavy lines and made a show of reading it, pretending to hesitate as he checked on it the list of objects I was to give in exchange for the presents offered me: so-and-so was to have a chopper in exchange for a bow and arrows, someone else beads in exchange for his necklaces . . . This farce went on for two hours. Was he perhaps hoping to delude himself? More probably he wanted to astonish his companions, to convince them that he was acting as an intermediary agent for the exchange of the goods, that he was in alliance with the white man and shared his secrets. We were eager to be off, since the most dangerous point would obviously be reached when all the marvels I had brought had been transferred to native hands. So I did not try to explore the matter further, and we began the return journey with the Indians still acting as our guides.

2. Another tribe living in Brazil.

The abortive meeting and the piece of humbug of which I had unwittingly been the cause had created an atmosphere of irritation; to make matters worse, my mule had ulcers in its mouth which were causing it pain. It either rushed impatiently ahead or came to a sudden stop; the two of us fell out. Suddenly, before I realized what was happening, I found myself alone in the bush, with no idea which way to go.

Travel books tell us that the thing to do is attract the attention of the main party by firing a shot. I got down from my mount and fired. No response. At the second shot I seemed to hear a reply. I fired a third, the only effect of which was to frighten the mule; it trotted off and stopped some distance away.

I systematically divested myself of my weapons and photographic equipment and laid them all at the foot of a tree, carefully noting its position. Then I ran off to recapture my mule, which I had glimpsed in the distance, seemingly in docile mood. It waited till I got near, then fled just as I was about to seize the reins, repeating this little game several times and leading me further and further on. In despair I took a leap and hung on to its tail with both hands. Surprised at this unwonted procedure, it made no further attempt to escape from me. I climbed back into the saddle and tried to return to collect my equipment, but we had wandered round so much that I was unable to find it.

Disheartened by the loss, I then decided to try and rejoin the caravan. Neither the mule nor I knew which way it had gone. Either I would decide on one direction which the mule was reluctant to follow, or I would let it have its head, and it would start going round in circles. The sun was sinking towards the horizon, I had lost my weapons and at any moment I expected to be pierced by a shower of arrows. I might not be the first person to have entered that hostile area, but my predecessors had not returned, and, irrespective of myself, my mule would be a most desirable prey for people whose food supplies were scanty. While turning these sombre thoughts over and over in my mind, I waited for the sun to set, my plan being to start a bush fire, since at least I had some matches. Just when I was about to do this, I heard voices: two Nambikwara had turned back as soon as my absence was noticed and had been following my trail since midday; for them, finding my equipment was child's play. They led me back through the darkness to the encampment, where the others were waiting.

Being still perturbed by this stupid incident, I slept badly and whiled away the sleepless hours by thinking over the episode of the exchange of gifts. Writing had, on that occasion, made its appearance among the Nambikwara but not, as one might have imagined, as a result of long and laborious training. It had been borrowed as a symbol, and for a sociological rather than an intellectual purpose, while its reality remained unknown. It had not been a question of acquiring knowledge, of remembering or understanding, but rather of increasing the authority and prestige of one individual—or function—at the expense of others. A native still living in the Stone Age had guessed that this great means towards understanding, even if he was unable to understand it, could be made to serve other purposes. After all, for thousands of years, writing has existed as an institution—and such is still the case today in a large part of the world—in societies the majority of whose members have never learnt to handle it. The inhabitants of the villages

I stayed in in the Chittagong hills in eastern Pakistan were illiterate, but each village had its scribe who acted on behalf of individuals or of the community as a whole. All the villagers know about writing, and make use of it if the need arises, but they do so from the outside, as if it were a foreign mediatory agent that they communicate with by oral methods. The scribe is rarely a functionary or employee of the group: his knowledge is accompanied by power, with the result that the same individual is often both scribe and money-lender; not just because he needs to be able to read and write to carry on his business, but because he thus happens to be, on two different counts, someone who *has a hold* over others.

Writing is a strange invention. One might suppose that its emergence could not fail to bring about profound changes in the conditions of human existence, and that these transformations must of necessity be of an intellectual nature. The possession of writing vastly increases man's ability to preserve knowledge. It can be thought of as an artificial memory, the development of which ought to lead to a clearer awareness of the past, and hence to a greater ability to organize both the present and the future. After eliminating all other criteria which have been put forward to distinguish between barbarism and civilization, it is tempting to retain this one at least: there are peoples with, or without, writing; the former are able to store up their past achievements and to move with ever-increasing rapidity towards the goal they have set themselves, whereas the latter, being incapable of remembering the past beyond the narrow margin of individual memory, seem bound to remain imprisoned in a fluctuating history which will always lack both a beginning and any lasting awareness of an aim.

Yet nothing we know about writing and the part it has played in man's evolution justifies this view. One of the most creative periods in the history of mankind occurred during the early stages of the neolithic age, which was responsible for agriculture, the domestication of animals and various arts and crafts. This stage could only have been reached if, for thousands of years, small communities had been observing, experimenting and handing on their findings. This great development was carried out with an accuracy and a continuity which are proved by its success, although writing was still unknown at the time. If writing was invented between 4000 and 3000 B.C., it must be looked upon as an already remote (and no doubt indirect) result of the neolithic revolution, but certainly not as the necessary precondition for it. If we ask ourselves what great innovation writing was linked to, there is little we can suggest on the technical level, apart from architecture. But Egyptian and Sumerian architecture was not superior to the achievements of certain American peoples who knew nothing of writing in the pre-Columbian period. Conversely, from the invention of writing right up to the birth of modern science, the world lived through some five thousand years when knowledge fluctuated more than it increased. It has often been pointed out that the way of life of a Greek or Roman citizen was not so very different from that of an eighteenth-century middle-class European. During the neolithic age, mankind made gigantic strides without the help of writing; with writing, the historic civilizations of the West stagnated for a long time. It would no doubt be difficult to imagine the expansion of science in the nineteenth and twentieth centuries without writing. But, although a necessary precondition, it is certainly not enough to explain the expansion.

To establish a correlation between the emergence of writing and certain characteristic features of civilization, we must look in a quite different direction. The only phenomenon with which writing has always been concomitant is the creation of cities and empires, that is, the integration of large numbers of individuals into a political system, and their grading into castes or classes. Such, at any rate, is the typical pattern of development to be observed from Egypt to China, at the time when writing first emerged: it seems to have favoured the exploitation of human beings rather than their enlightenment. This exploitation, which made it possible to assemble thousands of workers and force them to carry our exhausting tasks, is a much more likely explanation of the birth of architecture than the direct link referred to above. My hypothesis, if correct, would oblige us to recognize the fact that the primary function of written communication is to facilitate slavery. The use of writing for disinterested purposes, and as a source of intellectual and aesthetic pleasure, is a secondary result, and more often than not it may even be turned into a means of strengthening, justifying or concealing the other.

There are, nevertheless, exceptions to the rule: there were native empires in Africa which grouped together several hundreds of thousands of subjects; millions lived under the Inca empire in pre-Columbian America. But in both continents such attempts at empire building did not produce lasting results. We know that the Inca empire was established around the twelfth century: Pizarro's[3] soldiers would not have conquered it so easily, three centuries later, had they not found it in a state of advanced decay. Although we know little about ancient African history, we can sense that the situation must have been similar: great political groupings came into being and then vanished again within the space of a few decades. It is possible, then, that these examples confirm the hypothesis, instead of contradicting it. Although writing may not have been enough to consolidate knowledge, it was perhaps indispensable for the strengthening of dominion. If we look at the situation nearer home, we see that the systematic development of compulsory education in the European countries goes hand in hand with the extension of military service and proletarianization. The fight against illiteracy is therefore connected with an increase in governmental authority over the citizens. Everyone must be able to read, so that the government can say: Ignorance of the law is no excuse.

The process has moved from the national to the international level, thanks to a kind of complicity that has grown up between newly created states—which find themselves facing problems which we had to cope with a hundred or two hundred years ago—and an international society of privileged countries worried by the possibility of its stability being threatened by the reactions of peoples insufficiently trained in the use of the written word to think in slogans that can be modified at will or to be an easy prey to suggestion. Through gaining access to the knowledge stored in libraries, these peoples have also become vulnerable to the still greater proportion of lies propagated in printed documents. No doubt, there can be no turning back now. But in my Nambikwara village, the insubordinate characters were the most sensible. The villagers who withdrew their allegiance to their chief after he had

3. Francisco Pizarro (ca. 1475–1541), a Spanish explorer and colonizer who conquered the Inca empire in western South America.

tried to exploit a feature of civilization (after my visit he was abandoned by most of his people) felt in some obscure way that writing and deceit had penetrated simultaneously into their midst. They went off into a more remote area of the bush to allow themselves a period of respite. Yet at the same time I could not help admiring their chief's genius in instantly recognizing that writing could increase his authority, thus grasping the basis of the institution without knowing how to use it. At the same time, the episode drew my attention to another aspect of Nambikwara life: the political relationships between individuals and groups. I was soon to be able to observe them more directly.

While we were still at Utiarity, an epidemic of putrid ophthalmia had broken out among the natives. The infection, which was gonorrheal in origin, spread to the whole community, causing terrible pain and temporary blindness which could become permanent. For several days the group was completely paralysed. The natives treated the infection with water in which a certain kind of bark had been allowed to soak and which they injected into the eye by means of a leaf rolled into a cornet shape. The disease spread to our group: the first person to catch it was my wife who had taken part in all my expeditions so far, her speciality being the study of material culture and skills; the infection was so serious that she had to be evacuated. Then it affected most of the men, as well as my Brazilian companion. Soon the expedition was brought to a halt; I left the main body to rest, with our doctor to give them such treatment as they needed, and with two men and a few beasts I headed for Campos Novos, near which post several bands of natives had been reported. I spent a fortnight there in semi-idleness, gathering barely ripe fruit in an orchard which had reverted to the wild state: there were guavas, the bitter taste and gritty texture of which always fall far short of their aroma, and caju, as brilliantly coloured as parrots, which contain an acid and strongly flavoured juice in the spongy cells of their coarse pulp. To get meat for our meals we had only to go a few hundred metres from the camp at dawn to a copse regularly visited by wood-pigeons, which were easy to shoot. It was at Campos Novos that I met with two groups, whom the expectation of my presents had lured down from the north.

These two groups were as ill-disposed towards each other as they both were towards me. From the start, they did not so much ask for my presents as demand to be given them. During the first few days, only one group was present, as well as a native from Utiarity who had gone on ahead of me. I think perhaps he was showing too great an interest in a young woman belonging to his hosts' group, since relations between the strangers and their visitor became strained almost at once and he started coming to my encampment in search of a more friendly atmosphere; he also shared my meals. This fact was noticed and one day while he was out hunting I received a visit from four natives forming a kind of delegation. In threatening tones, they urged me to put poison in my guest's food; they had, in fact, brought the necessary preparation along with them, a grey powder packed in four little tubes tied together with thread. It was a very awkward situation: if I refused outright, I might well be attacked by the group, whose hostile intentions called for a prudent response. I therefore thought it better to exaggerate my ignorance of the language, and I pretended to understand nothing at all. After several attempts, during which I was told over and over again that my protégé was *kakoré*, that is, very wicked, and should be got rid of as soon as possible, the delegation withdrew with many expressions of displeasure. I warned the interested party, who at once disappeared; I did not see him again until I returned to the area several months later.

Fortunately, the second group arrived the next day, thus providing the first with a different object on which to vent their animosity. The meeting took place at my encampment which was both neutral territory and the goal of these various journeyings. Consequently, I had a good view of the proceedings. The men had come alone; and almost immediately a lengthy conversation began between their respective chiefs. It might be more accurately termed a series of alternating monologues, uttered in plaintive, nasal tones which I had never heard before. 'We are extremely annoyed. You are our enemies!' moaned one group, whereupon the others replied more or less, 'We are not annoyed. We are your brothers. We are friends—friends! We can get along together! etc.' Once this exchange of provocations and protestations was over, a communal camp was set up next to mine. After a few songs and dances, during which each group ran down its own performance by comparing it with that of its opponents ('The Taimaindé are good singers! We are poor singers!'), the quarrel was resumed, and before long the tension heightened. The night had only just begun when the mixture of songs and arguments produced a most extraordinary din, the meaning of which I failed to grasp. Threatening gestures were made, and sometimes scuffles broke out, and other natives intervened as peacemakers. All the threatening gestures centred round the sexual organs. A Nambikwara Indian expresses dislike by grasping his penis in both hands and pointing it towards his opponent. This gesture is followed by an assault on that person, the aim being to pull off the tuft of *buriti* straw attached to the front of the belt above the genitals. These 'are hidden by the straw', and 'the object of the fight is to pull off the straw.' The action is purely symbolical, because the genital covering of the male is made of such flimsy material and is so insubstantial that it neither affords protection nor conceals the organs. Attempts are also made to seize the opponent's bow and arrows and to put them beyond his reach. Throughout these actions, the natives remain extremely tense, as if they were in a state of violent and pent-up anger. The scuffles may sometimes degenerate into a free-for-all, but on this occasion the fighting subsided at dawn. Still in the same stare of visible irritation and with gestures that were anything but gentle, the two sets of opponents then set about examining each other, fingering their ear-pendants, cotton bracelets and little feather ornaments, and muttering a series of rapid comments, such as 'Give it . . . give it . . . see, that's pretty,' while the owner would protest, 'It's ugly . . . old, . . . damaged!'

This 'reconciliatory inspection' marked the end of the quarrel, and initiated another kind of relationship between the groups: commercial exchanges. Rudimentary the material culture of the Nambikwara may be, but the crafts and produce of each group are highly prized by the others. The eastern Nambikwara need pottery and seeds; those from the north consider that their more southerly neighbours make particularly delicate necklaces. It follows that when a meeting between two groups is conducted peacefully, it leads to a reciprocal exchange of gifts; strife is replaced by barter.

Actually, it was difficult to believe that an exchange of gifts was in progress; the morning after the quarrel, each man went about his usual business and the objects or produce were passed from one to another without the giver calling attention to the fact that he was handing over a gift, and without the receiver paying any heed to his new acquisition. The items thus exchanged included raw cotton and balls of thread; lumps of wax or resin; urucu[4] paste; shells, ear-drops, bracelets and necklaces; tobacco and seeds, feathers and bamboo laths to be made into arrow heads; bundles of palm fibres, porcupine quills; whole pots or fragments of pottery and gourds. This mysterious exchange of goods went on for half a day, after which the groups took leave of each other and went their separate ways.

The Nambikwara rely, then, on the generosity of the other side. It simply does not occur to them to evaluate, argue, bargain, demand or take back. I offered a native a machete as payment for taking a message to a neighbouring group. On his return, I omitted to hand over the agreed reward immediately, thinking that he would come to fetch it. He did not do so, and the next day I could not find him; he had departed in a rage, so his companions told me, and I never saw him again. I had to ask another native to accept the present on his behalf. This being so, it is hardly surprising that, when the exchanges are over, one group should go off dissatisfied with its share, and (taking stock of its acquisitions and remembering its own gifts) should build up feelings of resentment which become increasingly aggressive. Very often these feelings are enough to start a war; of course, there are other causes, such as the need to commit, or avenge, a murder or the kidnapping of a woman; however, it does not seem that a group feels collectively bound to exact reprisals for some injury done to one of its members. Nevertheless, because of the hostility between the groups, such pretexts are often willingly accepted, especially if a particular group feels itself to be strong. The proposal is presented by a warrior who expounds his grievances in the same tone and style as is used for the inter-group speeches: 'Hallo! Come here! Come along! I am angry! very angry! arrows! big arrows!'

Clad in special finery, consisting of tufts of *buriti* straw daubed with red and helmets made from jaguar hides, the men assemble under the leadership of their chief and dance. A divinatory rite has to be performed: the chief, or the shaman in those groups which have one, hides an arrow somewhere in the bush. A search is made for it the following day. If it is stained with blood, war is decided upon; if not, the idea is dropped. Many expeditions begun in this way come to an end after a few kilometres' march. The excitement and enthusiasm abate, and the warriors return home. But some expeditions are carried through and may result in bloodshed. The Nambikwara attack at dawn and arrange their ambush by posting themselves at intervals in the bush. The signal for the attack is passed from man to man by means of the whistle which each carries slung around his neck. This consists of two bamboo tubes bound together with thread, and its sound approximates to the cricket's chirp; no doubt this is why its name is the same as that of the insect. The war arrows are identical to those normally used for hunting large animals, except that their spear-shaped tip is given a serrated edge. Arrows dipped in curare poison, which are commonly employed for hunting, are never used, because an opponent hit by one would be able to remove it before the poison had time to spread through his body.

1955

4. A tropical shrub (*Bixa orellana*), from whose seeds a red dye can be extracted.

J. L. AUSTIN
1911–1960

The work of the Oxford University philosopher John Langshaw Austin (along with that of the Cambridge-based Ludwig Wittgenstein) broke the stranglehold of logical positivism on Anglo-American philosophy in the 1950s. Championing the virtues of "ordinary language" against the idealized and purified language that logical positivism tried to create, Austin stressed varieties of linguistic utterance that do not simply use names to refer to existing objects. His account of "performatives"—that is, words that are used to do things—has been especially influential for the understanding of literary language and, more recently, of the social processes through which identity is created and cultural values transmitted.

Although he published only seven essays during his lifetime, Austin was a legendary figure at Oxford University and in the philosophy departments of Harvard University and the University of California at Berkeley, where he lectured in the late 1950s. Austin was born in Lancaster, England, but spent his childhood in Scotland, where his father was a schoolmaster. After studying at Oxford, he joined the faculty there, briefly at All Soul's College, then from 1935 on at Magdalen College. He worked for the British Intelligence Corps during World War II and played a large role in coordinating intelligence for the Allied invasion of France on D-day (June 6, 1944). He ended the war a lieutenant colonel, decorated by both France and the United States, as well as receiving the Order of the British Empire from the British government. Returning to Oxford in 1948, Austin presided over a generation of philosophers noted for their fierce intelligence and even fiercer subjection of one another's work to careful scrutiny. Austin's ability to find the holes in others' arguments made him feared as well as admired, while his own lectures and (few) published essays were models of clarity and logic. His was not a style of work likely to lead to prolific publication, but philosophers on both sides of the Atlantic came to believe something must be right if Austin could be convinced of its validity. Austin's early death in 1960 left his major projects unfinished, but two books—*Sense and Sensibilia* and *How to Do Things with Words*—were assembled posthumously from his lecture notes.

The logical positivism of Bertrand Russell, the early Wittgenstein, and the "Vienna Circle" (many of whom, notably Rudolph Carnap and Otto Neurath, joined American university faculties after fleeing the Nazis) reigned supreme in Anglo-American philosophy from the 1930s into the 1970s. But as early as 1937, Wittgenstein was radically rethinking his earlier position (in work not published until after his death in 1951), and Austin was leading a parallel attack at Oxford.

The three cornerstones of logical positivism were an epistemology based on sense data as the only source of certain knowledge, an account of linguistic meaning that tied a word's meaning to its reference to (or correspondence with) a perceivable fact in the world, and an insistence that knowledge claims and linguistic uses that did not meet these stringent criteria were "nonsense." Thus, famously, the positivists saw ethical judgments of right and wrong as emotive statements that presented personal preferences or recommendations for action in the guise of statements of fact. A. J. Ayer codified the positivist position in his widely read *Language, Truth, and Logic* (1936). Significantly, positivists recognized that everyday language was full of uses they deemed "nonsense." Their interest was directed, therefore, toward creating a rigorous language that, once purified of nonsense, would be adequate for the needs (as they understood them) of an epistemologically sound modern science. But, as critics soon pointed out, the positivists' own account of what was nonsense and what was certain knowledge was based not on sense data but on a normative understanding of what counts as true.

In *Sense and Sensibilia*, Austin dismantles the logical positivists' account of perception in order to undermine their model of knowledge. When he turns his attention to language, Austin champions "ordinary language" against the purified language the positivists try to create. He starts from a faith in the usages and distinctions found in the languages we already possess. His working principle is that such usages and distinctions probably make sense precisely because people have maintained them. We would not continue to use an expression like "saving for a rainy day" or make a distinction between "an accident" and "a mistake" unless such expressions and distinctions fit our experiences and served to clarify them. The philosopher should work from ordinary language, striving to make explicit the claims about the world and the social relations that such language already contains.

Austin is sometimes castigated as conservative, as accepting the world as given. And, certainly, he is suspicious of an intellectual arrogance that regards common sense and daily practice as most likely faulty. But the clarity that philosophy can bring to prevailing habits of speech and daily practice does not necessarily reinforce such habits and practices; it may stir efforts at reform.

Austin is a pluralist. In examining ordinary language, he sees that we use words for many different purposes. The logical positivists were fixated on reference—the use of words to pick out and designate some thing in the world. They believed that meaning resided in correspondence between word and world. Where such correspondence was absent, so was meaning. Austin recognizes referential utterances ("statements, reports or descriptions") as one kind of meaningful speech but chastises logical positivism for failing to notice, or for denigrating when noticing, other kinds, including greetings, apologies, imperatives, pleas, curses, exclamations, and counterconditionals ("if I were king, I would . . .").

In considering this range, Austin attempts in our selection, "Performative Utterances," to make a basic distinction. There are "statements," which refer to an already existing state of affairs "out there" and are "true" or "false" depending on whether the words fit the facts. And there are "performatives," which do not refer to an existing state of affairs but which, instead, bring a state of affairs into existence by being uttered. Performatives are speech acts, cases in which saying something counts as an action: they serve to alter the world, to bring something new into existence, or to modify, create, or establish a certain relationship between people. "[P]erformative utterances are not true or false, then"; rather, Austin deems them "felicitous" when they succeed in establishing the state of affairs they strive to create. He is interested in outlining the conditions that must be fulfilled for a performative to be felicitous.

For starters, Austin realizes (as did FERDINAND DE SAUSSURE and Wittgenstein) that individual utterances rely heavily on "background conditions" in order to make sense. Among these conditions are a whole set of "conventions," as well as the context in which an utterance is made. Austin points out that many conventions are, in fact, institutional, understanding "institutions" as formal organizations of authority. Performative speech acts such as a judge's sentencing of a criminal or a minister's "I now pronounce you man and wife" succeed only when uttered by a person with the appropriate authority.

Austin also considers noninstitutional causes of infelicity—insincerity, misunderstanding, and nonseriousness. When discussing these sources of "unhappy" utterances and returning to questions of truth and falsehood, Austin finds himself increasingly unable to sort out the different uses of language into separate bins. He cannot maintain the firm line between statements and performatives. If I say "with a stern look, he opened the debate," am I being merely descriptive, or does my use of the adjective "stern" create a view of events for my auditors? In addition, the verb "opened" is a "dead metaphor"; that is, a word designating physical action ("opening") is used to describe a different action. In other words, Austin runs into the kinds of difficulties FRIEDRICH NIETZSCHE describes in the essay "On Truth and Lying in a Non-Moral Sense" (1873; see above), difficulties that led Nietzsche eventually to claim that "there are no facts, only interpretations."

Austin does not phrase the problem in Nietzschean terms. But he does recognize that we seldom speak purely descriptively; we are always doing other things—even when we say "the chair is blue." We have a reason to say "the chair is blue," and that reason is almost always a desire to sway our auditor in some way or another. Austin's essay on performatives thus leads him to recognize the *rhetorical* element in most utterances. We say things in particular contexts to certain others with the aim of influencing their opinions, attitudes, beliefs, and so on. For this reason, Austin concludes the essay with the suggestion that utterances have "force" as well as "meaning"; he uses "force" to designate their impact on listeners, an impact that the speaker can try but cannot always manage to control. And he also concludes that we need to "loosen up" the dichotomy "true/false" so we can more subtly appraise the complex relation between facts and utterances.

Austin's notion of performatives entered literary theory through the JACQUES DERRIDA–John Searle debate of the 1970s. Derrida found Austin's work suggestive but castigated the British philosopher for trying to exclude "non-serious" utterances (a category that included statements made in poems) from consideration. The American philosopher Searle had studied under Austin at Oxford and he defended Austin against what he saw as Derrida's misunderstandings. The pyrotechnics of the debate—which cemented the hostility between Anglo-American philosophers and "French theory"—obscured the fact that Derrida actually wanted to endorse the general notion of performatives, even though he criticized some of Austin's ways of characterizing them. JUDITH BUTLER and EVE KOSOFSKY SEDGWICK in the 1990s recuperated the notion of the performative for literary and cultural theorists by stressing the extent to which gender (and other) identities are produced through performances of the ritualized practices of daily life. Joining Derrida's emphasis on "iteration" (repetition) with Austin's insistence that language is productive, Butler and Sedgwick show how prevailing social scripts (ideology) acquire reality for individuals through being performed.

"Performative Utterances" Keywords: Institutional Studies, Language, Rhetoric, Semiotics, Vernacular Language

Performative Utterances

I

You are more than entitled not to know what the word 'performative' means. It is a new word and an ugly word, and perhaps it does not mean anything very much. But at any rate there is one thing in its favour, it is not a profound word. I remember once when I had been talking on this subject that somebody afterwards said: 'You know, I haven't the least idea what he means, unless it could be that he simply means what he says'. Well, that is what I should like to mean.

Let us consider first how this affair arises. We have not got to go very far back in the history of philosophy to find philosophers assuming more or less as a matter of course that the sole business, the sole interesting business, of any utterance—that is, of anything we say—is to be true or at least false. Of course they had always known that there are other kinds of things which we say—things like imperatives, the expressions of wishes, and exclamations—some of which had even been classified by grammarians, though it wasn't perhaps too easy to tell always which was which. But still philosophers have assumed that the only things that they are interested in are utterances which report facts or which describe situations truly or falsely. In recent times this kind of approach has been questioned—in two stages, I think. First of all people began to say: 'Well, if these things are true or false it ought to be possible to decide which they are, and if we can't decide which they are they aren't any good but are, in short, nonsense'. And this new approach did a great deal of good; a great many things which probably are nonsense were found to be such. It is not the case, I think, that all kinds of nonsense have been adequately classified yet, and perhaps some things have been dismissed as nonsense which really are not; but still this movement, the verification movement, was, in its way, excellent.

However, we then come to the second stage. After all, we set some limits to the amount of nonsense that we talk, or at least the amount of nonsense that we are prepared to admit we talk; and so people began to ask whether after all some of those things which, treated as statements, were in danger of being dismissed as nonsense did after all really set out to be statements at all. Mightn't they perhaps be intended not to report facts but to influence people in this way or that, or to let off steam in this way or that? Or perhaps at any rate some elements in these utterances performed such functions, or, for example, drew attention in some way (without actually reporting it) to some important feature of the circumstances in which the utterance was being made. On these lines people have now adopted a new slogan, the slogan of the 'different uses of language'. The old approach, the old statemental approach, is sometimes called even a fallacy, the descriptive fallacy.

Certainly there are a great many uses of language. It's rather a pity that people are apt to invoke a new use of language whenever they feel so inclined, to help them out of this, that, or the other well-known philosophical tangle; we need more of a framework in which to discuss these uses of language; and also I think we should not despair too easily and talk, as people are apt to do, about the *infinite* uses of language. Philosophers will do this when they have listed as many, let us say, as seventeen; but even if there were something like ten thousand uses of language, surely we could list them all in time. This, after all, is no larger than the number of species of beetle that entomologists have taken the pains to list. But whatever the defects of either of these movements—the 'verification' movement or the 'use of language' movement—at any rate they have effected, nobody could deny, a great revolution in philosophy and, many would say, the most salutary in its history. (Not, if you come to think of it, a very immodest claim.)

Now it is one such sort of use of language that I want to examine here. I want to discuss a kind of utterance which looks like a statement and grammatically, I suppose, would be classed as a statement, which is not nonsensical, and yet is not true or false. These are not going to be utterances which contain curious verbs like 'could' or 'might', or curious words like 'good', which many philosophers regard nowadays simply as danger signals. They will be perfectly straightforward utterances, with ordinary verbs in the first person singular present indicative active, and yet we shall see at once that they couldn't possibly be true or false. Furthermore, if a person makes an utterance of this sort we should say that he is *doing* something rather than merely *saying* something. This may sound a little odd, but the examples I shall give will in fact not be odd at all, and may even seem decidedly dull. Here are three or four. Suppose, for example, that in the course of a marriage ceremony I say, as people will, 'I do'—(sc.[1] take this woman to be my lawful wedded wife). Or again, suppose that I tread on your toe and say 'I apologize'. Or again, suppose that I have the bottle of champagne in my hand and say 'I name this ship the *Queen Elizabeth*'. Or suppose I say 'I bet you sixpence it will rain tomorrow'. In all these cases it would be absurd to regard the thing that I say as a report of the performance of the action which is undoubtedly done—the action of betting, or christening, or apologizing. We should say rather that, in saying what I do, I actually perform that action. When I say 'I name this ship the *Queen Elizabeth*' I do not describe the christening ceremony, I actually perform the christening; and when I say 'I do' (sc. take this woman to be my lawful wedded wife), I am not reporting on a marriage, I am indulging in it.

Now these kinds of utterance are the ones that we call *performative* utterances. This is rather an ugly word, and a new word, but there seems to be no word already in existence to do the job. The nearest approach that I can think of is the word 'operative', as used by lawyers. Lawyers when talking about legal instruments will distinguish between the preamble, which recites the circumstances in which a transaction is effected, and on the other hand the operative part—the part of it which actually performs the legal act which it is the purpose of the instrument to perform. So the word 'operative' is very near to what we want. 'I give and bequeath my watch to my brother' would be an operative clause and is a performative utterance. However, the word 'operative' has other uses, and it seems preferable to have a word specially designed for the use we want.

Now at this point one might protest, perhaps even with some alarm, that I seem to be suggesting that marrying is simply saying a few words, that just saying a few words *is* marrying. Well, that certainly is not the case. The words have to be said in the appropriate circumstances, and this is a matter that will come up again later. But the one thing we must not suppose is that what is needed in addition to the saying of the words in such cases is the performance of some internal spiritual act, of which the words then are to be the report. It's very easy to slip into this view at least in difficult, portentous cases, though perhaps not so easy in simple cases like apologizing. In the case of promising—for example, 'I promise to be there tomorrow'—it's very easy to think that the utterance is simply the outward and visible (that is, verbal) sign of the performance of some inward spiritual act of promising, and this view has certainly been expressed in many classic places. There is the case of Euripides' Hippolytus,[2] who said 'My tongue swore to, but my heart did not'—perhaps it should be 'mind' or 'spirit' rather than 'heart', but at any rate some kind of backstage artiste. Now it is clear from this sort of example that, if we slip into thinking that such utterances are reports, true or false, of the performance of inward and spiritual acts, we open a loop-hole to perjurers and welshers and bigamists and so on, so that there are disadvantages in being excessively solemn in this way. It is better, perhaps, to stick to the old saying that our word is our bond.

However, although these utterances do not themselves report facts and are not themselves true or false, saying these things does very often *imply* that certain things are true and not false, in some sense at least of that rather

1. Scilicet; namely.
2. *Hippolytus* (428 B.C.E.), line 612, by the Greek playwright Euripides (ca. 485–ca. 406 B.C.E.). The Greek word here translated "heart" is *phrēn*, which can also mean "mind" or "understanding."

woolly word 'imply'. For example, when I say 'I do take this woman to be my lawful wedded wife', or some other formula in the marriage ceremony, I do imply that I'm not already married, with wife living, sane, undivorced, and the rest of it. But still it is very important to realize that to imply that something or other is true, is not at all the same as saying something which is true itself.

These performative utterances are not true or false, then. But they do suffer from certain disabilities of their own. They can fail to come off in special ways, and that is what I want to consider next. The various ways in which a performative utterance may be unsatisfactory we call, for the sake of a name, the infelicities; and an infelicity arises—that is to say, the utterance is unhappy—if certain rules, transparently simple rules, are broken. I will mention some of these rules and then give examples of some infringements.

First of all, it is obvious that the conventional procedure which by our utterance we are purporting to use must actually exist. In the examples given here this procedure will be a verbal one, a verbal procedure for marrying or giving or whatever it may be; but it should be borne in mind that there are many non-verbal procedures by which we can perform exactly the same acts as we perform by these verbal means. It's worth remembering too that a great many of the things we do are at least in part of this conventional kind. Philosophers at least are too apt to assume that an action is always in the last resort the making of a physical movement, whereas it's usually, at least in part, a matter of convention.

The first rule is, then, that the convention invoked must exist and be accepted. And the second rule, also a very obvious one, is that the circumstances in which we purport to invoke this procedure must be appropriate for its invocation. If this is not observed, then the act that we purport to perform would not come off—it will be, one might say, a misfire. This will also be the case if, for example, we do not carry through the procedure—whatever it may be—correctly and completely, without a flaw and without a hitch. If any of these rules are not observed, we say that the act which we purported to perform is void, without effect. If, for example, the purported act was an act of marrying, then we should say that we 'went through a form' of marriage, but we did not actually succeed in marrying.

Here are some examples of this kind of misfire. Suppose that, living in a country like our own, we wish to divorce our wife. We may try standing her in front of us squarely in the room and saying, in a voice loud enough for all to hear, 'I divorce you'. Now this procedure is not accepted. We shall not thereby have succeeded in divorcing our wife, at least in this country and others like it. This is a case where the convention, we should say, does not exist or is not accepted. Again, suppose that, picking sides at a children's party, I say 'I pick George'. But George turns red in the face and says 'Not playing'. In that case I plainly, for some reason or another, have not picked George—whether because there is no convention that you can pick people who aren't playing, or because George in the circumstances is an inappropriate object for the procedure of picking. Or consider the case in which I say 'I appoint you Consul', and it turns out that you have been appointed already—or perhaps it may even transpire that you are a horse;[3] here again

3. A reference to an anecdote about the Roman emperor known as Caligula (Gaius Caesar Germanicus, 12–41 C.E.), who was said to have wished to make his favorite horse consul.

we have the infelicity of inappropriate circumstances, inappropriate objects, or what not. Examples of flaws and hitches are perhaps scarcely necessary—one party in the marriage ceremony says 'I will', the other says 'I won't'; I say 'I bet sixpence', but nobody says 'Done', nobody takes up the offer. In all these and other such cases, the act which we purport to perform, or set out to perform, is not achieved.

But there is another and a rather different way in which this kind of utterance may go wrong. A good many of these verbal procedures are designed for use by people who hold certain beliefs or have certain feelings or intentions. And if you use one of these formulae when you do not have the requisite thoughts or feelings or intentions then there is an abuse of the procedure, there is insincerity. Take, for example, the expression, 'I congratulate you'. This is designed for use by people who are glad that the person addressed has achieved a certain feat, believe that he was personally responsible for the success, and so on. If I say 'I congratulate you' when I'm not pleased or when I don't believe that the credit was yours, then there is insincerity. Likewise if I say I promise to do something, without having the least intention of doing it or without believing it feasible. In these cases there is something wrong certainly, but it is not like a misfire. We should not say that I didn't in fact promise, but rather that I did promise but promised insincerely; I did congratulate you but the congratulations were hollow. And there may be an infelicity of a somewhat similar kind when the performative utterance commits the speaker to future conduct of a certain description and then in the future he does not in fact behave in the expected way. This is very obvious, of course, if I promise to do something and then break my promise, but there are many kinds of commitment of a rather less tangible form than that in the case of promising. For instance, I may say 'I welcome you', bidding you welcome to my home or wherever it may be, but then I proceed to treat you as though you were exceedingly unwelcome. In this case the procedure of saying 'I welcome you' has been abused in a way rather different from that of simple insincerity.

Now we might ask whether this list of infelicities is complete, whether the kinds of infelicity are mutually exclusive, and so forth. Well, it is not complete, and they are not mutually exclusive; they never are. Suppose that you are just about to name the ship, you have been appointed to name it, and you are just about to bang the bottle against the stem; but at that very moment some low type comes up, snatches the bottle out of your hand, breaks it on the stem, shouts out 'I name this ship the *Generalissimo Stalin*', and then for good measure kicks away the chocks. Well, we agree of course on several things. We agree that the ship certainly isn't now named the *Generalissimo Stalin*, and we agree that it's an infernal shame and so on and so forth. But we may not agree as to how we should classify the particular infelicity in this case. We might say that here is a case of a perfectly legitimate and agreed procedure which, however, has been invoked in the wrong circumstances, namely by the wrong person, this low type instead of the person appointed to do it. But on the other hand we might look at it differently and say that this is a case where the procedure has not as a whole been gone through correctly, because part of the procedure for naming a ship is that you should first of all get yourself appointed as the person to do the naming and that's what this fellow did not do. Thus the way we should classify infelicities in different cases will be perhaps rather a difficult matter, and may even in the last resort be a bit arbitrary. But of course lawyers, who have to deal very much with this kind of thing, have invented all kinds of technical terms and have made numerous rules about different kinds of cases, which enable them to classify fairly rapidly what in particular is wrong in any given case.

As for whether this list is complete, it certainly is not. One further way in which things may go wrong is, for example, through what in general may be called misunderstanding. You may not hear what I say, or you may understand me to refer to something different from what I intended to refer to, and so on. And apart from further additions which we might make to the list, there is the general over-riding consideration that, as we are performing an act when we issue these performative utterances, we may of course be doing so under duress or in some other circumstances which make us not entirely responsible for doing what we are doing. That would certainly be an unhappiness of a kind—any kind of non-responsibility might be called an unhappiness; but of course it is a quite different kind of thing from what we have been talking about. And I might mention that, quite differently again, we could be issuing any of these utterances, as we can issue an utterance of any kind whatsoever, in the course, for example, of acting a play or making a joke or writing a poem—in which case of course it would not be seriously meant and we shall not be able to say that we seriously performed the act concerned. If the poet says 'Go and catch a falling star'[4] or whatever it may be, he doesn't seriously issue an order. Considerations of this kind apply to any utterance at all, not merely to performatives.

That, then, is perhaps enough to be going on with. We have discussed the performative utterance and its infelicities. That equips us, we may suppose, with two shining new tools to crack the crib of reality maybe. It also equips us—it always does—with two shining new skids under our metaphysical feet. The question is how we use them.

II

So far we have been going firmly ahead, feeling the firm ground of prejudice glide away beneath our feet which is always rather exhilarating, but what next? You will be waiting for the bit when we bog down, the bit where we take it all back, and sure enough that's going to come but it will take time. First of all let us ask a rather simple question. How can we be sure, how can we tell, whether any utterance is to be classed as a performative or not? Surely, we feel, we ought to be able to do that. And we should obviously very much like to be able to say that there is a grammatical criterion for this, some grammatical means of deciding whether an utterance is performative. All the examples I have given hitherto do in fact have the same grammatical form; they all of them begin with the verb in the first person singular present indicative active—not just any kind of verb of course, but still they all are in fact of that form. Furthermore, with these verbs that I have used there is a typical asymmetry between the use of this person and tense of the verb and the use of the same verb in other persons and other tenses, and this asymmetry is rather an important clue.

4. The first line of an untitled poem (1633) by John Donne.

For example, when we say 'I promise that . . .', the case is very different from when we say 'He promises that . . .', or in the past tense 'I promised that . . .'. For when we say 'I promise that . . .' we do perform an act of promising—we give a promise. What we do *not* do is to report on somebody's performing an act of promising—in particular, we do not report on somebody's use of the expression 'I promise'. We actually do use it and do the promising. But if I say 'He promises', or in the past tense 'I promised', I precisely do report on an act of promising, that is to say an act of using this formula 'I promise'—I report on a present act of promising by him, or on a past act of my own. There is thus a clear difference between our first person singular present indicative active, and other persons and tenses. This is brought out by the typical incident of little Willie whose uncle says he'll give him half-a-crown[5] if he promises never to smoke till he's 55. Little Willie's anxious parent will say 'Of course he promises, don't you, Willie?' giving him a nudge, and little Willie just doesn't vouchsafe. The point here is that he must do the promising himself by saying 'I promise', and his parent is going too fast in saying he promises.

That, then, is a bit of a test for whether an utterance is performative or not, but it would not do to suppose that every performative utterance has to take this standard form. There is at least one other standard form, every bit as common as this one, where the verb is in the passive voice and in the second or third person, not in the first. The sort of case I mean is that of a notice inscribed 'Passengers are warned to cross the line by the bridge only', or of a document reading 'You are hereby authorized' to do so-and-so. These are undoubtedly performative, and in fact a signature is often required in order to show who it is that is doing the act of warning, or authorizing, or whatever it may be. Very typical of this kind of performative—especially liable to occur in written documents of course—is that the little word 'hereby' either actually occurs or might naturally be inserted.

Unfortunately, however, we still can't possibly suggest that every utterance which is to be classed as a performative has to take one or another of these two, as we might call them, standard forms. After all it would be a very typical performative utterance to say 'I order you to shut the door'. This satisfies all the criteria. It is performing the act of ordering you to shut the door, and it is not true or false. But in the appropriate circumstances surely we could perform exactly the same act by simply saying 'Shut the door', in the imperative. Or again, suppose that somebody sticks up a notice 'This bull is dangerous', or simply 'Dangerous bull', or simply 'Bull'. Does this necessarily differ from sticking up a notice, appropriately signed, saying 'You are hereby warned that this bull is dangerous'? It seems that the simple notice 'Bull' can do just the same job as the more elaborate formula. Of course the difference is that if we just stick up 'Bull' it would not be quite clear that it is a warning; it might be there just for interest or information, like 'Wallaby' on the cage at the zoo, or 'Ancient Monument'. No doubt we should know from the nature of the case that it was a warning, but it would not be explicit.

Well, in view of this break-down of grammatical criteria, what we should like to suppose—and there is a good deal in this—is that any utterance which

5. Under the old U.K. system of money, a crown was worth 5 shillings; little Willie is given the equivalent of about a half-dollar.

is performative could be reduced or expanded or analysed into one of these two standard forms beginning 'I . . .' so and so or beginning 'You (or he) hereby . . .' so and so. If there was any justification for this hope, as to some extent there is, then we might hope to make a list of all the verbs which can appear in these standard forms, and then we might classify the kinds of acts that can be performed by performative utterances. We might do this with the aid of a dictionary, using such a test as that already mentioned—whether there is the characteristic asymmetry between the first person singular present indicative active and the other persons and tenses—in order to decide whether a verb is to go into our list or not. Now if we make such a list of verbs we do in fact find that they fall into certain fairly well-marked classes. There is the class of cases where we deliver verdicts and make estimates and appraisals of various kinds. There is the class where we give undertakings, commit ourselves in various ways by saying something. There is the class where by saying something we exercise various rights and powers, such as appointing and voting and so on. And there are one or two other fairly well-marked classes.

Suppose this task accomplished. Then we could call these verbs in our list explicit performative verbs, and any utterance that was reduced to one or the other of our standard forms we could call an explicit performative utterance. 'I order you to shut the door' would be an explicit performative utterance, whereas 'Shut the door' would not—that is simply a 'primary' performative utterance or whatever we like to call it. In using the imperative we may be ordering you to shut the door, but it just isn't made clear whether we are ordering you or entreating you or imploring you or beseeching you or inciting you or tempting you, or one or another of many other subtly different acts which, in an unsophisticated primitive language, are very likely not yet discriminated. But we need not over-estimate the unsophistication of primitive languages. There are a great many devices that can be used for making clear, even at the primitive level, what act it is we are performing when we say something—the tone of voice, cadence, gesture—and above all we can rely upon the nature of the circumstances, the context in which the utterance is issued. This very often makes it quite unmistakable whether it is an order that is being given or whether, say, I am simply urging you or entreating you. We may, for instance, say something like this: 'Coming from him I was bound to take it as an order'. Still, in spite of all these devices, there is an unfortunate amount of ambiguity and lack of discrimination in default of our explicit performative verbs. If I say something like 'I shall be there', it may not be certain whether it is a promise, or an expression of intention, or perhaps even a forecast of my future behaviour, of what is going to happen to me; and it may matter a good deal, at least in developed societies, precisely which of these things it is. And that is why the explicit performative verb is evolved—to make clear exactly which it is, how far it commits me and in what way, and so forth.

This is just one way in which language develops in tune with the society of which it is the language. The social habits of the society may considerably affect the question of which performative verbs are evolved and which, sometimes for rather irrelevant reasons, are not. For example, if I say 'You are a poltroon', it might be that I am censuring you or it might be that I am insulting you. Now since apparently society approves of censuring or reprimanding, we have here evolved a formula 'I reprimand you', or 'I censure you', which enables us expeditiously to get this desirable business over. But on the other hand, since apparently we don't approve of insulting, we have not evolved a simple formula 'I insult you', which might have done just as well.

By means of these explicit performative verbs and some other devices, then, we make explicit what precise act it is that we are performing when we issue our utterance. But here I would like to put in a word of warning. We must distinguish between the function of making explicit what act it is we are performing, and the quite different matter of *stating* what act it is we are performing. In issuing an explicit performative utterance we are not stating what act it is, we are showing or making explicit what act it is. We can draw a helpful parallel here with another case in which the act, the conventional act that we perform, is not a speech-act but a physical performance. Suppose I appear before you one day and bow deeply from the waist. Well, this is ambiguous. I may be simply observing the local flora, tying my shoe-lace, something of that kind; on the other hand, conceivably I might be doing obeisance to you. Well, to clear up this ambiguity we have some device such as raising the hat, saying 'Salaam',[6] or something of that kind, to make it quite plain that the act being performed is the conventional one of doing obeisance rather than some other act. Now nobody would want to say that lifting your hat was stating that you were performing an act of obeisance; it certainly is not, but it does make it quite plain that you are. And so in the same way to say 'I warn you that . . .' or 'I order you to . . .' or 'I promise that . . .' is not to state that you are doing something, but makes it plain that you are—it does constitute your verbal performance, a performance of a particular kind.

So far we have been going along as though there was a quite clear difference between our performative utterances and what we have contrasted them with, statements or reports or descriptions. But now we begin to find that this distinction is not as clear as it might be. It's now that we begin to sink in a little. In the first place, of course, we may feel doubts as to how widely our performatives extend. If we think up some odd kinds of expression we use in odd cases, we might very well wonder whether or not they satisfy our rather vague criteria for being performative utterances. Suppose, for example, somebody says 'Hurrah'. Well, not true or false; he is performing the act of cheering. Does that make it a performative utterance in our sense or not? Or suppose he says 'Damn'; he is performing the act of swearing, and it is not true or false. Does that make it performative? We feel that in a way it does and yet it's rather different. Again, consider cases of 'suiting the action to the words'; these too may make us wonder whether perhaps the utterance should be classed as performative. Or sometimes, if somebody says 'I am sorry', we wonder whether this is just the same as 'I apologize'—in which case of course we have said it's a performative utterance—or whether perhaps it's to be taken as a description, true or false, of the state of his feelings. If he had said 'I feel perfectly awful about it', then we should think it must be meant to be a description of the state of his feelings. If he had said 'I apologize', we should feel this was clearly a performative utterance, going through the ritual of apologizing. But if he says 'I am sorry' there is an unfortunate hovering between the two. This phenomenon is quite common.

6. Literally, "peace" (Arabic); a greeting sometimes spoken while making a ceremonial bow.

We often find cases in which there is an obvious pure performative utterance and obvious other utterances connected with it which are not performative but descriptive, but on the other hand a good many in between where we're not quite sure which they are. On some occasions of course they are obviously used the one way, on some occasions the other way, but on some occasions they seem positively to revel in ambiguity.

Again, consider the case of the umpire when he says 'Out' or 'Over',[7] or the jury's utterance when they say that they find the prisoner guilty. Of course, we say, these are cases of giving verdicts, performing the act of appraising and so forth, but still in a way they have some connexion with the facts. They seem to have something like the duty to be true or false, and seem not to be so very remote from statements. If the umpire says 'Over', this surely has at least something to do with six balls in fact having been delivered rather than seven, and so on. In fact in general we may remind ourselves that 'I state that . . .' does not look so very different from 'I warn you that . . .' or 'I promise to . . .'. It makes clear surely that the act that we are performing is an act of stating, and so functions just like 'I warn' or 'I order'. So isn't 'I state that . . .' a performative utterance? But then one may feel that utterances beginning 'I state that . . .' do have to be true or false, that they *are* statements.

Considerations of this sort, then, may well make us feel pretty unhappy. If we look back for a moment at our contrast between statements and performative utterances, we realize that we were taking statements very much on trust from, as we said, the traditional treatment. Statements, we had it, were to be true or false; performative utterances on the other hand were to be felicitous or infelicitous. They were the doing of something, whereas for all we said making statements was not doing something. Now this contrast surely, if we look back at it, is unsatisfactory. Of course statements are liable to be assessed in this matter of their correspondence or failure to correspond with the facts, that is, being true or false. But they are also liable to infelicity every bit as much as are performative utterances. In fact some troubles that have arisen in the study of statements recently can be shown to be simply troubles of infelicity. For example, it has been pointed out that there is something very odd about saying something like this: 'The cat is on the mat but I don't believe it is'. Now this is an outrageous thing to say, but it is not self-contradictory. There is no reason why the cat shouldn't be on the mat without my believing that it is. So how are we to classify what's wrong with this peculiar statement? If we remember now the doctrine of infelicity we shall see that the person who makes this remark about the cat is in much the same position as somebody who says something like this: 'I promise that I shall be there, but I haven't the least intention of being there'. Once again you can of course perfectly well promise to be there without having the least intention of being there, but there is something outrageous about saying it, about actually avowing the insincerity of the promise you give. In the same way there is insincerity in the case of the person who says 'The cat is on the mat but I don't believe it is', and he is actually avowing that insincerity—which makes a peculiar kind of nonsense.

A second case that has come to light is the one about John's children—the case where somebody is supposed to say 'All John's children are bald but John

7. Umpire's calls in cricket.

hasn't got any children'.[8] Or perhaps somebody says 'All John's children are bald', when as a matter of fact—he doesn't say so—John has no children. Now those who study statements have worried about this; ought they to say that the statement 'All John's children are bald' is meaningless in this case? Well, if it is, it is not a bit like a great many other more standard kinds of meaninglessness; and we see, if we look back at our list of infelicities, that what is going wrong here is much the same as what goes wrong in, say, the case of a contract for the sale of a piece of land when the piece of land referred to does not exist. Now what we say in the case of this sale of land, which of course would be effected by a performative utterance, is that the sale is void—void for lack of reference or ambiguity of reference; and so we can see that the statement about all John's children is likewise void for lack of reference. And if the man actually says that John has no children in the same breath as saying they're all bald, he is making the same kind of outrageous utterance as the man who says 'The cat is on the mat and I don't believe it is', or the man who says 'I promise to but I don't intend to'.

In this way, then, ills that have been found to afflict statements can be precisely paralleled with ills that are characteristic of performative utterances. And after all when we state something or describe something or report something, we do perform an act which is every bit as much an act as an act of ordering or warning. There seems no good reason why stating should be given a specially unique position. Of course philosophers have been wont to talk as though you or I or anybody could just go round stating anything about anything and that would be perfectly in order, only there's just a little question: is it true or false? But besides the little question, is it true or false, there is surely the question: *is* it in order? Can you go round just making statements about anything? Suppose for example you say to me 'I'm feeling pretty mouldy this morning'. Well, I say to you 'You're not'; and you say 'What the devil do you mean, I'm not?' I say 'Oh nothing—I'm just stating you're not, is it true or false?' And you say 'Wait a bit about whether it's true or false, the question is what did you mean by making statements about somebody else's feelings? I told you I'm feeling pretty mouldy. You're just not in a position to say, to state that I'm not'. This brings out that you can't just make statements about other people's feelings (though you can make guesses if you like); and there are very many things which, having no knowledge of, not being in a position to pronounce about, you just can't state. What we need to do for the case of stating, and by the same token describing and reporting, is to take them a bit off their pedestal, to realize that they are speech-acts no less than all these other speech-acts that we have been mentioning and talking about as performative.

Then let us look for a moment at our original contrast between the performative and the statement from the other side. In handling performatives we have been putting it all the time as though the only thing that a performative utterance had to do was to be felicitous, to come off, not to be a misfire, not to be an abuse. Yes, but that's not the end of the matter. At least in the case of many utterances which, on what we have said, we should have to class as performative—cases where we say 'I warn you to . . .', 'I advise you to . . .'

8. A reference to a famous example in "On Denoting" (1905) by Bertrand Russell, one of the earliest of the logical positivists: "The present king of France is bald." (France had no king.)

and so on—there will be other questions besides simply: was it in order, was it all right, as a piece of advice or a warning, did it come off? After that surely there will be the question: was it good or sound advice? Was it a justified warning? Or in the case, let us say, of a verdict or an estimate: was it a good estimate, or a sound verdict? And these are questions that can only be decided by considering how the content of the verdict or estimate is related in some way to fact, or to evidence available about the facts. This is to say that we do require to assess at least a great many performative utterances in a general dimension of correspondence with fact. It may still be said, of course, that this does not make them *very* like statements because still they are not true or false, and that's a little black and white speciality that distinguishes statements as a class apart. But actually—though it would take too long to go on about this—the more you think about truth and falsity the more you find that very few statements that we ever utter are just true or just false. Usually there is the question are they fair or are they not fair, are they adequate or not adequate, are they exaggerated or not exaggerated? Are they too rough, or are they perfectly precise, accurate, and so on? 'True' and 'false' are just general labels for a whole dimension of different appraisals which have something or other to do with the relation between what we say and the facts. If, then, we loosen up our ideas of truth and falsity we shall see that statements, when assessed in relation to the facts, are not so very different after all from pieces of advice, warnings, verdicts, and so on.

We see then that stating something is performing an act just as much as is giving an order or giving a warning; and we see, on the other hand, that, when we give an order or a warning or a piece of advice, there is a question about how this is related to fact which is not perhaps so very different from the kind of question that arises when we discuss how a statement is related to fact. Well, this seems to mean that in its original form our distinction between the performative and the statement is considerably weakened, and indeed breaks down. I will just make a suggestion as to how to handle this matter. We need to go very much farther back, to consider all the ways and senses in which saying anything at all is doing this or that—because of course it is always doing a good many different things. And one thing that emerges when we do do this is that, besides the question that has been very much studied in the past as to what a certain utterance *means*, there is a further question distinct from this as to what was the *force*, as we may call it, of the utterance. We may be quite clear what 'Shut the door' means, but not yet at all clear on the further point as to whether as uttered at a certain time it was an order, an entreaty or whatnot. What we need besides the old doctrine about meanings is a new doctrine about all the possible forces of utterances, towards the discovery of which our proposed list of explicit performative verbs would be a very great help; and then, going on from there, an investigation of the various terms of appraisal that we use in discussing speech-acts of this, that, or the other precise kind—orders, warnings, and the like.

The notions that we have considered then, are the performative, the infelicity, the explicit performative, and lastly, rather hurriedly, the notion of the forces of utterances. I dare say that all this seems a little unremunerative, a little complicated. Well, I suppose in some ways it is unremunerative, and I suppose it ought to be remunerative. At least, though, I think that if we pay attention to these matters we can clear up some mistakes in philosophy; and after all philosophy is used as a scapegoat, it parades mistakes which are really the mistakes of everybody. We might even clear up some mistakes in grammar, which perhaps is a little more respectable.

And is it complicated? Well, it is complicated a bit; but life and truth and things do tend to be complicated. It's not things, it's philosophers that are simple. You will have heard it said, I expect, that over-simplification is the occupational disease of philosophers, and in a way one might agree with that. But for a sneaking suspicion that it's their occupation.

1956 1961

NORTHROP FRYE
1912–1991

By the mid-1950s, the New Critical "close reading" of texts had become the dominant theory and practice of literary criticism in the North American academy (see JOHN CROWE RANSOM and CLEANTH BROOKS). Its reign was not uncontested; some scholars argued that this critical approach failed to consider historical and biographical contexts, and the "Chicago School" led by R. S. Crane maintained that the New Criticism emphasized irony and metaphor in all texts at the expense of crucial distinctions among the literary genres. But it was not until the late 1950s, with the publication of Northrop Frye's *Anatomy of Criticism* (1957), that the New Criticism was comprehensively challenged by a fully defined alternative.

In the *Anatomy of Criticism*, Frye pointedly contrasted his archetypal or myth criticism with the "rhetorical analysis of the new critics":

> The further back we go, the more conscious we are of the organizing design. At a great distance from, say, a Madonna, we can see nothing but the archetype of the Madonna, a large centripetal blue mass with a contrasting point of interest at its center. In the criticism of literature, too, we often have to "stand back" from the poem to see its archetypal organization.

Frye thus took issue with the critical orthodoxy of his own day, even as his approach looked forward to the structuralist poetics and analysis of narrative that theorists such as TZVETAN TODOROV, ROLAND BARTHES, and HAYDEN WHITE would articulate in the 1960s and 1970s.

A Canadian born in southern Quebec province, Frye attended the University of Toronto, studied theology at Emmanuel College in Toronto, was ordained in the United Church of Canada in 1936, and then did postgraduate work at Merton College, Oxford University. He began his academic career at Victoria College, University of Toronto, in 1939, and later held administrative positions both in the English department and in the college. He was keenly interested in Canadian literature, culture, and education, but his influence as a literary critic, theorist, and educator extended worldwide. He lectured and taught at many colleges and universities in the United States, England, and elsewhere, winning numerous awards and prizes for his scholarship and criticism.

Frye's first book was *Fearful Symmetry: A Study of William Blake* (1947), an influential examination of Blake's symbolism. Here, Frye describes the imagination as the "creative force in the mind" from which "everything that we call culture and civilization" derives: "it is the power of transforming a sub-human physical world into a world with a human shape and meaning." The next important work, *Anatomy of Criticism*, articulated the role of archetypal symbols, myths, and generic conventions in creating literary meaning.

The word "archetype" derives from the Greek *archetypon*, which means "beginning pattern"; as developed by Frye within the field of literary criticism, it refers to a recurrent image, character, plot, theme, or pattern that, through its repetitions in many works across the centuries, takes on a universal quality. Frye drew from many sources, including the Bible, Blake's prophetic books, and (from the early twentieth century) the German historicist writer Oswald Spengler, SIGMUND FREUD, the Scottish folklorist and anthropologist J. G. Frazer, and the classical scholar Gilbert Murray. But perhaps the main source for Frye was the psychologist Carl Jung—his account of the "collective unconscious." Part of what makes us human, according to Jung, is an "unconscious" inhabited by shared memories, desires, impulses, images, ideas—in a word, archetypes—distinct from the personal unconscious that each of us acquires from our individual experiences.

Frye objected to being called a "Jungian critic," however. As he explains in *Anatomy of Criticism*, the literary critic should be "concerned only with ritual or dream patterns which are actually in what he is studying, however they got there." Throughout his career, he continued to focus on and define the repeating images that are structural "building blocks" of literature. It was, he later observed, "a vision of literature as forming a total schematic order" (*Spiritus Mundi*, 1976).

This conception of literature as constituting a total order or universe explains why Frye's work has intrigued and inspired theorists interested in intertextuality—the ways in which one text leads to, evokes, is made from, and is intersected by others. The French feminist theorist JULIA KRISTEVA, for example, described reading *Fearful Symmetry* in the late 1960s as a "revelation" in its insertion of the poetic text into Western literary tradition. Through *Anatomy of Criticism*, she adds, we can begin to grasp the "extraordinary polysemy [i.e., the coexistence of many possible meanings for a word or phrase] of literary art and take up the challenge it permanently poses."

Frye's work has been widely discussed and admired but also sharply criticized. Often, in reply, Frye embraces the charges made against him. He cheerfully admits his refusal to judge differences between good and bad literary works, even though this position puts him at odds with many of the major critics of the English and American traditions. Marxist and leftist critics have stated that Frye strips away the historical and political meanings from texts; in the words of TERRY EAGLETON, Frye's "formalism" is "even more full-blooded than that of New Criticism. The New Critic allowed that literature was in some significant sense cognitive, yielding a sort of knowledge of the world; Frye insists that literature is an 'autonomous verbal structure' quite cut off from any reference beyond itself." But for Frye this is hardly a failing, for he is determined to understand literature in its own terms, "opposed to any construct—Marxist, Freudian, Thomist [i.e., based on the thought of the thirteenth-century scholastic philosopher and theologian THOMAS AQUINAS], or whatever—that is going to annex literature and simply explain literature in its own terminology" ("Freedom and Concern," 1985).

In our selection, "The Archetypes of Literature" (1951), Frye sketches an early version of his approach. He argues that literature teachers must not confuse literature with criticism: we cannot in our classrooms "teach literature"; rather, we teach the criticism of literature. If teachers aim as they should to make criticism a "systematic structure of knowledge," then they will need to shed their mistaken ideas and habitual practices. For Frye, a common mistake is the assumption that criticism is the making of value judgments; these, he says, amount to no more than exercises in the history of taste. Other mistakes include the intensive analysis of specific texts (disconnected "close readings" do not lead us toward the goal of a unified and coherent field of scientific study) and a focus on conventional literary history (periods such as Gothic and baroque are cultural rather than truly literary categories).

In defining genuine criticism, Frye shows that it is connected to but different from philosophy, theology, history, and the social sciences, meriting autonomy as a rigorous and comprehensive professional university discipline. He finds the work of cultural anthropologists particularly valuable in his search for a "co-ordinating principle," and from Frazer, Jung, and others he develops his theory of "archetypes," such as the quest of the hero. Knowledge of the archetypes enables us to perceive the shared myths that literary works rely on and explore: through this awareness we can glimpse the underlying *structure* of the structures of all works.

Like Jung, Frye uses terms with a looseness that can make his writing both suggestive and exasperating. Sometimes he refers to archetype as different from myth; sometimes he states that the archetype is itself a myth, like the quest. While his theory, supported by a rich and wide range of reading, allows him to make connections between many texts, he rarely if ever attends to the text's language. We could also point out that Frye's canon, while capacious, is not capacious enough: few women and minorities figure in it. In this respect Frye is no different from most other critics and theorists of his generation, but his theory could be said to have a built-in answer to the charge: the nature of archetypes ensures that they also structure the literature he himself fails to discuss, and thus in a sense he has included it after all.

Frye is an extraordinary synthesizer, whose system building is matched in early to mid-twentieth-century literary criticism and theory only by the very different system building of I. A. Richards and Kenneth Burke. At a certain point, however, the categories, patterns, classifications, lists, and charts in Frye's major theoretical works threaten to become formulaic, as perhaps happens at the close of the selection below. Many texts are briefly touched on and connections among them made, but none of them is really brought into focus. Curiously enough, Frye now often seems most rewarding less for his bold vision of literature as a whole than for the essays on specific texts that he did produce. When he writes about Milton's elegy "Lycidas" (in *Fables of Identity*) or *Hamlet* (in *Northrop Frye on Shakespeare*), he demonstrates a subtle, sensitive, compelling feeling for the text in its own right—the text as related to countless other texts but a discrete literary experience nonetheless. Frye's work as a practical critic departs on occasion from the tenets of his theory, and is arguably the better for it.

"The Archetypes of Literature" Keywords: The Canon/Tradition, Defense of Criticism, Interpretation Theory, Literary History, Narrative Theory, Religion, Structuralism

The Archetypes of Literature[1]

Every organized body of knowledge can be learned progressively; and experience shows that there is also something progressive about the learning of literature. Our opening sentence has already got us into a semantic difficulty. Physics is an organized body of knowledge about nature, and a student of it says that he is learning physics, not that he is learning nature. Art, like nature, is the subject of a systematic study, and has to be distinguished from the study itself, which is criticism. It is therefore impossible to "learn literature": one learns about it in a certain way, but what one learns, transitively, is the criticism of literature. Similarly, the difficulty often felt in "teaching literature" arises from the fact that it cannot be done: the criticism of litera-

1. First published in the *Kenyon Review* series "My Credo."

ture is all that can be directly taught. So while no one expects literature itself to behave like a science, there is surely no reason why criticism, as a systematic and organized study, should not be, at least partly, a science. Not a "pure" or "exact" science, perhaps, but these phrases form part of a 19th Century cosmology which is no longer with us. Criticism deals with the arts and may well be something of an art itself, but it does not follow that it must be unsystematic. If it is to be related to the sciences too, it does not follow that it must be deprived of the graces of culture.

Certainly criticism as we find it in learned journals and scholarly monographs has every characteristic of a science. Evidence is examined scientifically; previous authorities are used scientifically; fields are investigated scientifically; texts are edited scientifically. Prosody is scientific in structure; so is phonetics; so is philology. And yet in studying this kind of critical science the student becomes aware of a centrifugal movement carrying him away from literature. He finds that literature is the central division of the "humanities," flanked on one side by history and on the other by philosophy. Criticism so far ranks only as a subdivision of literature; and hence, for the systematic mental organization of the subject, the student has to turn to the conceptual framework of the historian for events, and to that of the philosopher for ideas. Even the more centrally placed critical sciences, such as textual editing, seem to be part of a "background" that recedes into history or some other non-literary field. The thought suggests itself that the ancillary critical disciplines may be related to a central expanding pattern of systematic comprehension which has not yet been established, but which, if it were established, would prevent them from being centrifugal. If such a pattern exists, then criticism would be to art what philosophy is to wisdom and history to action.

Most of the central area of criticism is at present, and doubtless always will be, the area of commentary. But the commentators have little sense, unlike the researchers, of being contained within some sort of scientific discipline: they are chiefly engaged, in the words of the gospel hymn, in brightening the corner where they are. If we attempt to get a more comprehensive idea of what criticism is about, we find ourselves wandering over quaking bogs of generalities, judicious pronouncements of value, reflective comments, perorations to works of research, and other consequences of taking the large view. But this part of the critical field is so full of pseudo-propositions, sonorous nonsense that contains no truth and no falsehood, that it obviously exists only because criticism, like nature, prefers a waste space to an empty one.

The term "pseudo-proposition" may imply some sort of logical positivist[2] attitude on my own part. But I would not confuse the significant proposition with the factual one; nor should I consider it advisable to muddle the study of literature with a schizophrenic dichotomy between subjective-emotional and objective-descriptive aspects of meaning, considering that in order to produce any literary meaning at all one has to ignore this dichotomy. I say only that the principles by which one can distinguish a significant from a meaningless statement in criticism are not clearly defined. Our first step, therefore, is to recognize and get rid of meaningless criticism: that is, talking

2. Characteristic of the philosophy that views all knowledge as deriving from empirical experience and logical reasoning; any statement that cannot be proved true or false is nonsense (i.e., a "pseudo-proposition").

about literature in a way that cannot help to build up a systematic structure of knowledge. Casual value-judgments belong not to criticism but to the history of taste, and reflect, at best, only the social and psychological compulsions which prompted their utterance. All judgments in which the values are not based on literary experience but are sentimental or derived from religious or political prejudice may be regarded as casual. Sentimental judgments are usually based either on non-existent categories or antitheses ("Shakespeare studied life, Milton books") or on a visceral reaction to the writer's personality. The literary chit-chat which makes the reputations of poets boom and crash in an imaginary stock exchange is pseudo-criticism. That wealthy investor Mr. Eliot, after dumping Milton on the market, is now buying him again; Donne has probably reached his peak and will begin to taper off; Tennyson may be in for a slight flutter but the Shelley stocks are still bearish.[3] This sort of thing cannot be part of any systematic study, for a systematic study can only progress: whatever dithers or vacillates or reacts is merely leisure-class conversation.

We next meet a more serious group of critics who say: the foreground of criticism is the impact of literature on the reader. Let us, then, keep the study of literature centripetal, and base the learning process on a structural analysis of the literary work itself. The texture of any great work of art is complex and ambiguous, and in unravelling the complexities we may take in as much history and philosophy as we please, if the subject of our study remains at the center. If it does not, we may find that in our anxiety to write about literature we have forgotten how to read it.

The only weakness in this approach is that it is conceived primarily as the antithesis of centrifugal or "background" criticism, and so lands us in a somewhat unreal dilemma, like the conflict of internal and external relations in philosophy. Antitheses are usually resolved, not by picking one side and refuting the other, or by making eclectic choices between them, but by trying to get past the antithetical way of stating the problem. It is right that the first effort of critical apprehension should take the form of a rhetorical or structural analysis of a work of art. But a purely structural approach has the same limitation in criticism that it has in biology. In itself it is simply a discrete series of analyses based on the mere existence of the literary structure, without developing any explanation of how the structure came to be what it was and what its nearest relatives are. Structural analysis brings rhetoric back to criticism, but we need a new poetics as well, and the attempt to construct a new poetics out of rhetoric alone can hardly avoid a mere complication of rhetorical terms into a sterile jargon. I suggest that what is at present missing from literary criticism is a co-ordinating principle, a central hypothesis which, like the theory of evolution in biology, will see the phenomena it deals with as parts of a whole. Such a principle, though it would retain the centripetal perspective of structural analysis, would try to give the same perspective to other kinds of criticism too.

The first postulate of this hypothesis is the same as that of any science: the assumption of total coherence. The assumption refers to the science, not to what it deals with. A belief in an order of nature is an inference from the

3. Frye is referring to the evaluations of poets that the poet and critic T. S. ELIOT (1888–1965) made, and that others—for example, the English critic F. R. LEAVIS (1895–1978) and the American Yvor Winters (1900–1968)—subsequently reinforced, modified, or disputed.

intelligibility of the natural sciences; and if the natural sciences ever completely demonstrated the order of nature they would presumably exhaust their subject. Criticism, as a science, is totally intelligible; literature, as the subject of a science, is, so far as we know, an inexhaustible source of new critical discoveries, and would be even if new works of literature ceased to be written. If so, then the search for a limiting principle in literature in order to discourage the development of criticism is mistaken. The assertion that the critic should not look for more in a poem than the poet may safely be assumed to have been conscious of putting there is a common form of what may be called the fallacy of premature teleology.[4] It corresponds to the assertion that a natural phenomenon is as it is because Providence in its inscrutable wisdom made it so.

Simple as the assumption appears, it takes a long time for a science to discover that it is in fact a totally intelligible body of knowledge. Until it makes this discovery it has not been born as an individual science, but remains an embryo within the body of some other subject. The birth of physics from "natural philosophy" and of sociology from "moral philosophy" will illustrate the process. It is also very approximately true that the modern sciences have developed in the order of their closeness to mathematics. Thus physics and astronomy assumed their modern form in the Renaissance, chemistry in the 18th Century, biology in the 19th, and the social sciences in the 20th. If systematic criticism, then, is developing only in our day, the fact is at least not an anachronism.

We are now looking for classifying principles lying in an area between two points that we have fixed. The first of these is the preliminary effort of criticism, the structural analysis of the work of art. The second is the assumption that there is such a subject as criticism, and that it makes, or could make, complete sense. We may next proceed inductively from structural analysis, associating the data we collect and trying to see larger patterns in them. Or we may proceed deductively, with the consequences that follow from postulating the unity of criticism. It is clear, of course, that neither procedure will work indefinitely without correction from the other. Pure induction will get us lost in haphazard guessing; pure deduction will lead to inflexible and over-simplified pigeon-holing. Let us now attempt a few tentative steps in each direction, beginning with the inductive one.

II

The unity of a work of art, the basis of structural analysis, has not been produced solely by the unconditioned will of the artist, for the artist is only its efficient cause: it has form, and consequently a formal cause.[5] The fact that revision is possible, that the poet makes changes not because he likes them better but because they are better, means that poems, like poets, are born and not made. The poet's task is to deliver the poem in as uninjured a state as possible, and if the poem is alive, it is equally anxious to be rid of

4. That is, the assumption that everything is directed toward a particular end or shaped by a specific purpose.

5. Terms borrowed from the Greek philosopher ARISTOTLE (384–322 B.C.E.), who argued that there were four types of cause or explanation: material (what a thing is made from), formal (a thing's shape or definition), efficient (the primary source of change in a thing), and final (the end or goal for which a thing is done).

him, and screams to be cut loose from his private memories and associations, his desire for self-expression, and all the other navel-strings and feeding tubes of his ego. The critic takes over where the poet leaves off, and criticism can hardly do without a kind of literary psychology connecting the poet with the poem. Part of this may be a psychological study of the poet, though this is useful chiefly in analysing the failures in his expression, the things in him which are still attached to his work. More important is the fact that every poet has his private mythology, his own spectroscopic band or peculiar formation of symbols, of much of which he is quite unconscious. In works with characters of their own, such as dramas and novels, the same psychological analysis may be extended to the interplay of characters, though of course literary psychology would analyse the behavior of such characters only in relation to literary convention.

There is still before us the problem of the formal cause of the poem, a problem deeply involved with the question of genres. We cannot say much about genres, for criticism does not know much about them. A good many critical efforts to grapple with such words as "novel" or "epic" are chiefly interesting as examples of the psychology of rumor. Two conceptions of the genre, however, are obviously fallacious, and as they are opposite extremes, the truth must lie somewhere between them. One is the pseudo-Platonic conception of genres as existing prior to and independently of creation,[6] which confuses them with mere conventions of form like the sonnet. The other is that pseudo-biological conception of them as evolving species which turns up in so many surveys of the "development" of this or that form.

We next inquire for the origin of the genre, and turn first of all to the social conditions and cultural demands which produced it—in other words to the material cause of the work of art. This leads us into literary history, which differs from ordinary history in that its containing categories, "Gothic," "Baroque," "Romantic," and the like are cultural categories, of little use to the ordinary historian. Most literary history does not get as far as these categories, but even so we know more about it than about most kinds of critical scholarship. The historian treats literature and philosophy historically; the philosopher treats history and literature philosophically; and the so-called "history of ideas" approach marks the beginning of an attempt to treat history and philosophy from the point of view of an autonomous criticism.

But still we feel that there is something missing. We say that every poet has his own peculiar formation of images. But when so many poets use so many of the same images, surely there are much bigger critical problems involved than biographical ones. As Mr. Auden's brilliant essay *The Enchafèd Flood*[7] shows, an important symbol like the sea cannot remain within the poetry of Shelley or Keats or Coleridge:[8] it is bound to expand over many poets into an archetypal symbol of literature. And if the genre has a historical origin, why does the genre of drama emerge from medieval religion in a way so strikingly similar to the way it emerged from Greek religion centuries before? This is

6. According to the Greek philosopher PLATO (ca. 427–ca. 347 B.C.E.), all phenomena derive from a realm of perfect and immutable transcendent Forms or Ideas.

7. A set of lectures published by the poet and critic W. H. Auden (1907–1973) in 1950.

8. Three English Romantic poets: PERCY BYSSHE SHELLEY (1792–1822), John Keats (1795–1821), and SAMUEL TAYLOR COLERIDGE (1772–1834).

a problem of structure rather than origin, and suggests that there may be archetypes of genres as well as of images.

It is clear that criticism cannot be systematic unless there is a quality in literature which enables it to be so, an order of words corresponding to the order of nature in the natural sciences. An archetype should be not only a unifying category of criticism, but itself a part of a total form, and it leads us at once to the question of what sort of total form criticism can see in literature. Our survey of critical techniques has taken us as far as literary history. Total literary history moves from the primitive to the sophisticated, and here we glimpse the possibility of seeing literature as a complication of a relatively restricted and simple group of formulas that can be studied in primitive culture. If so, then the search for archetypes is a kind of literary anthropology, concerned with the way that literature is informed by pre-literary categories such as ritual, myth and folk tale. We next realize that the relation between these categories and literature is by no means purely one of descent, as we find them reappearing in the greatest classics—in fact there seems to be a general tendency on the part of great classics to revert to them. This coincides with a feeling that we have all had: that the study of mediocre works of art, however energetic, obstinately remains a random and peripheral form of critical experience, whereas the profound masterpiece seems to draw us to a point at which we can see an enormous number of converging patterns of significance. Here we begin to wonder if we cannot see literature, not only as complicating itself in time, but as spread out in conceptual space from some unseen center.

This inductive movement towards the archetype is a process of backing up, as it were, from structural analysis, as we back up from a painting if we want to see composition instead of brushwork. In the foreground of the grave-digger scene in *Hamlet*, for instance, is an intricate verbal texture, ranging from the puns of the first clown to the *danse macabre*[9] of the Yorick soliloquy, which we study in the printed text. One step back, and we are in the Wilson Knight and Spurgeon group of critics,[1] listening to the steady rain of images of corruption and decay. Here too, as the sense of the place of this scene in the whole play begins to dawn on us, we are in the network of psychological relationships which were the main interest of Bradley.[2] But after all, we say, we are forgetting the genre: *Hamlet* is a play, and an Elizabethan play. So we take another step back into the Stoll and Shaw[3] group and see the scene conventionally as part of its dramatic context. One step more, and we can begin to glimpse the archetype of the scene, as the hero's *Liebestod*[4] and first unequivocal declaration of his love, his struggle with Laertes and the sealing of his own fate, and the sudden sobering of his mood that marks the transition to the final scene, all take shape around a leap into and return from the grave that has so weirdly yawned open on the stage.

At each stage of understanding this scene we are dependent on a certain kind of scholarly organization. We need first an editor to clean up the text

9. Dance of death (French). See *Hamlet* (ca. 1600), 5.1.
1. Critics who call attention to Shakespeare's patterns of imagery and symbolism, led by Caroline Spurgeon (1869–1941) and G. Wilson Knight (1897–1985).
2. A. C. Bradley (1851–1935); his *Shakespearean Tragedy* (1904) provided a detailed study of "character."
3. The playwright and critic George Bernard Shaw (1856–1950). E. E. Stoll (1874–1959), critic who focused in his scholarship on the relationship of Shakespeare's plays to the dramatic conventions of the Elizabethan and Jacobean age.
4. Literally, "death of love" (German); the *Liebestod* is specifically an operatic aria or duet on the suicide of lovers and, more generally, the thematic linking of love and death.

for us, then the rhetorician and philologist, then the literary psychologist. We cannot study the genre without the help of the literary social historian, the literary philosopher and the student of the "history of ideas," and for the archetype we need a literary anthropologist. But now that we have got our central pattern of criticism established, all these interests are seen as converging on literary criticism instead of receding from it into psychology and history and the rest. In particular, the literary anthropologist who chases the source of the Hamlet legend from the pre-Shakespeare play to Saxo,[5] and from Saxo to nature-myths, is not running away from Shakespeare: he is drawing closer to the archetypal form which Shakespeare recreated. A minor result of our new perspective is that contradictions among critics, and assertions that this and not that critical approach is the right one, show a remarkable tendency to dissolve into unreality. Let us now see what we can get from the deductive end.

III

Some arts move in time, like music; others are presented in space, like painting. In both cases the organizing principle is recurrence, which is called rhythm when it is temporal and pattern when it is spatial. Thus we speak of the rhythm of music and the pattern of painting; but later, to show off our sophistication, we may begin to speak of the rhythm of painting and the pattern of music. In other words, all arts may be conceived both temporally and spatially. The score of a musical composition may be studied all at once; a picture may be seen as the track of an intricate dance of the eye. Literature seems to be intermediate between music and painting: its words form rhythms which approach a musical sequence of sounds at one of its boundaries, and form patterns which approach the hieroglyphic or pictorial image at the other. The attempts to get as near to these boundaries as possible form the main body of what is called experimental writing. We may call the rhythm of literature the narrative, and the pattern, the simultaneous mental grasp of the verbal structure, the meaning or significance. We hear or listen to a narrative, but when we grasp a writer's total pattern we "see" what he means.

The criticism of literature is much more hampered by the representational fallacy than even the criticism of painting. That is why we are apt to think of narrative as a sequential representation of events in an outside "life," and of meaning as a reflection of some external "idea." Properly used as critical terms, an author's narrative is his linear movement; his meaning is the integrity of his completed form. Similarly an image is not merely a verbal replica of an external object, but any unit of a verbal structure seen as part of a total pattern or rhythm. Even the letters an author spells his words with form part of his imagery, though only in special cases (such as alliteration) would they call for critical notice. Narrative and meaning thus become respectively, to borrow musical terms, the melodic and harmonic contexts of the imagery.

5. Saxo Grammaticus (12th–13th c.), Danish historian whose *Gesta Danorum* (*Deeds of the Danes*) includes the Hamlet story.

Rhythm, or recurrent movement, is deeply founded on the natural cycle, and everything in nature that we think of as having some analogy with works of art, like the flower or the bird's song, grows out of a profound synchronization between an organism and the rhythms of its environment, especially that of the solar year. With animals some expressions of synchronization, like the mating dances of birds, could almost be called rituals. But in human life a ritual seems to be something of a voluntary effort (hence the magical element in it) to recapture a lost rapport with the natural cycle. A farmer must harvest his crop at a certain time of year, but because this is involuntary, harvesting itself is not precisely a ritual. It is the deliberate expression of a will to synchronize human and natural energies at that time which produces the harvest songs, harvest sacrifices and harvest folk customs that we call rituals. In ritual, then, we may find the origin of narrative, a ritual being a temporal sequence of acts in which the conscious meaning or significance is latent: it can be seen by an observer, but is largely concealed from the participators themselves. The pull of ritual is toward pure narrative, which, if there could be such a thing, would be automatic and unconscious repetition. We should notice too the regular tendency of ritual to become encyclopedic. All the important recurrences in nature, the day, the phases of the moon, the seasons and solstices of the year, the crises of existence from birth to death, get rituals attached to them, and most of the higher religions are equipped with a definitive total body of rituals suggestive, if we may put it so, of the entire range of potentially significant actions in human life.

Patterns of imagery, on the other hand, or fragments of significance, are oracular in origin, and derive from the epiphanic moment, the flash of instantaneous comprehension with no direct reference to time, the importance of which is indicated by Cassirer in *Myth and Language*.[6] By the time we get them, in the form of proverbs, riddles, commandments and etiological folk tales, there is already a considerable element of narrative in them. They too are encyclopedic in tendency, building up a total structure of significance, or doctrine, from random and empiric fragments. And just as pure narrative would be unconscious act, so pure significance would be an incommunicable state of consciousness, for communication begins by constructing narrative.

The myth is the central informing power that gives archetypal significance to the ritual and archetypal narrative to the oracle. Hence the myth *is* the archetype, though it might be convenient to say myth only when referring to narrative, and archetype when speaking of significance. In the solar cycle of the day, the seasonal cycle of the year, and the organic cycle of human life, there is a single pattern of significance, out of which myth constructs a central narrative around a figure who is partly the sun, partly vegetative fertility and partly a god or archetypal human being. The crucial importance of this myth has been forced on literary critics by Jung and Frazer[7] in particular, but the several books now available on it are not always

6. Properly, *Language and Myth* (1925), by the German philosopher and historian of ideas Ernst Cassirer (1874–1945).

7. Sir James George Frazer (1854–1941), Scottish anthropologist and folklorist, whose *The Golden Bough* (12 vols., 1890–1915) is largely concerned with the fertility figure. Carl Gustav Jung (1875–1961), Swiss psychiatrist and theorist of archetypes.

systematic in their approach, for which reason I supply the following table of its phases:

1.

The dawn, spring and birth phase. Myths of the birth of the hero, of revival and resurrection, of creation and (because the four phases are a cycle) of the defeat of the powers of darkness, winter and death. Subordinate characters: the father and the mother. The archetype of romance and of most dithyrambic and rhapsodic poetry.

2.

The zenith, summer, and marriage or triumph phase. Myths of apotheosis, of the sacred marriage, and of entering into Paradise. Subordinate characters: the companion and the bride. The archetype of comedy, pastoral and idyll.

3.

The sunset, autumn and death phase. Myths of fall, of the dying god, of violent death and sacrifice and of the isolation of the hero. Subordinate characters: the traitor and that siren. The archetype of tragedy and elegy.

4.

The darkness, winter and dissolution phase. Myths of the triumph of these powers; myths of floods and the return of chaos, of the defeat of the hero, and Götterdämmerung[8] myths. Subordinate characters: the ogre and the witch. The archetype of satire (see, for instance, the conclusion of *The Dunciad*[9]).

The quest of the hero also tends to assimilate the oracular and random verbal structures, as we can see when we watch the chaos of local legends that results from prophetic epiphanies consolidating into a narrative mythology of departmental gods. In most of the higher religions this in turn has become the same central quest-myth that emerges from ritual, as the Messiah myth became the narrative structure of the oracles of Judaism. A local flood may beget a folk tale by accident, but a comparison of flood stories will show how quickly such tales become examples of the myth of dissolution. Finally, the tendency of both ritual and epiphany to become encyclopedic is realized in the definitive body of myth which constitutes the sacred scriptures of religions. These sacred scriptures are consequently the first documents that the literary critic has to study to gain a comprehensive view of his subject. After he has understood their structure, then he can descend from archetypes to genres, and see how the drama emerges from the ritual side of myth and lyric from the epiphanic or fragmented side, while the epic carries on the central encyclopedic structure.

8. Literally, "the twilight of the gods" (German), and the title of an opera (1876) by the German composer Richard Wagner. More generally, the term refers to catastrophic collapse into violence and disorder.

9. Mock-heroic satire (1728–43) by ALEXANDER POPE.

Some words of caution and encouragement are necessary before literary criticism has clearly staked out its boundaries in these fields. It is part of the critic's business to show how all literary genres are derived from the quest-myth, but the derivation is a logical one within the science of criticism: the quest-myth will constitute the first chapter of whatever future handbooks of criticism may be written that will be based on enough organized critical knowledge to call themselves "introductions" or "outlines" and still be able to live up to their titles. It is only when we try to expound the derivation chronologically that we find ourselves writing pseudo-prehistorical fictions and theories of mythological contract. Again, because psychology and anthropology are more highly developed sciences, the critic who deals with this kind of material is bound to appear, for some time, a dilettante of those subjects. These two phases of criticism are largely undeveloped in comparison with literary history and rhetoric, the reason being the later development of the sciences they are related to. But the fascination which *The Golden Bough* and Jung's book on libido symbols[1] have for literary critics is not based on dilettantism, but on the fact that these books are primarily studies in literary criticism, and very important ones.

In any case the critic who is studying the principles of literary form has a quite different interest from the psychologist's concern with states of mind or the anthropologist's with social institutions. For instance: the mental response to narrative is mainly passive; to significance mainly active. From this fact Ruth Benedict's[2] *Patterns of Culture* develops a distinction between "Apollonian" cultures based on obedience to ritual and "Dionysiac" ones based on a tense exposure of the prophetic mind to epiphany. The critic would tend rather to note how popular literature which appeals to the inertia of the untrained mind puts a heavy emphasis on narrative values, whereas a sophisticated attempt to disrupt the connection between the poet and his environment produces the Rimbaud type of *illumination*, Joyce's solitary epiphanies, and Baudelaire's[3] conception of nature as a source of oracles. Also how literature, as it develops from the primitive to the self-conscious, shows a gradual shift of the poet's attention from narrative to significant values, this shift of attention being the basis of Schiller's distinction between naive and sentimental poetry.[4]

The relation of criticism to religion, when they deal with the same documents, is more complicated. In criticism, as in history, the divine is always treated as a human artifact. God for the critic, whether he finds him in *Paradise Lost*[5] or the Bible, is a character in a human story; and for the critic all epiphanies are explained, not in terms of the riddle of a possessing god or devil, but as mental phenomena closely associated in their origin with dreams. This once established, it is then necessary to say that nothing in criticism or art compels the critic to take the attitude of ordinary waking

1. *Transformations and Symbols of the Libido* (1912; trans. first as *Psychology of the Unconscious* and then as *Symbols of Transformation*).
2. American anthropologist (1887–1948); *Patterns of Culture* was published in 1934. On the opposition between Apollonian and Dionysian, see FRIEDRICH NIETZSCHE's *The Birth of Tragedy* (1872), above.
3. Charles Baudelaire (1821–1867), French symbolist poet. Arthur Rimbaud (1854–1891), French symbolist poet. James Joyce (1882–1941), Irish novelist who extended the term "epiphany" to refer to peak moments recorded in literature.
4. See *On Naive and Sentimental Poetry* (1795–96) by FRIEDRICH VON SCHILLER (1759–1805), German dramatist, poet, and historian.
5. Epic poem (1667) by John Milton (1608–1674).

consciousness towards the dream or the god. Art deals not with the real but with the conceivable; and criticism, though it will eventually have to have some theory of conceivability, can never be justified in trying to develop, much less assume, any theory of actuality. It is necessary to understand this before our next and final point can be made.

We have identified the central myth of literature, in its narrative aspect, with the quest-myth. Now if we wish to see this central myth as a pattern of meaning also, we have to start with the workings of the subconscious where the epiphany originates, in other words in the dream. The human cycle of waking and dreaming corresponds closely to the natural cycle of light and darkness, and it is perhaps in this correspondence that all imaginative life begins. The correspondence is largely an antithesis: it is in daylight that man is really in the power of darkness, a prey to frustration and weakness; it is in the darkness of nature that the "libido" or conquering heroic self awakes. Hence art, which Plato called a dream for awakened minds,[6] seems to have as its final cause the resolution of the antithesis, the mingling of the sun and the hero, the realizing of a world in which the inner desire and the outward circumstance coincide. This is the same goal, of course, that the attempt to combine human and natural power in ritual has. The social function of the arts, therefore, seems to be closely connected with visualizing the goal of work in human life. So in terms of significance, the central myth of art must be the vision of the end of social effort, the innocent world of fulfilled desires, the free human society. Once this is understood, the integral place of criticism among the other social sciences, in interpreting and systematizing the vision of the artist, will be easier to see. It is at this point that we can see how religious conceptions of the final cause of human effort are as relevant as any others to criticism.

The importance of the god or hero in the myth lies in the fact that such characters, who are conceived in human likeness and yet have more power over nature, gradually build up the vision of an omnipotent personal community beyond an indifferent nature. It is this community which the hero regularly enters in his apotheosis. The world of this apotheosis thus begins to pull away from the rotary cycle of the quest in which all triumph is temporary. Hence if we look at the quest-myth as a pattern of imagery, we see the hero's quest first of all in terms of its fulfillment. This gives us our central pattern of archetypal images, the vision of innocence which sees the world in terms of total human intelligibility. It corresponds to, and is usually found in the form of, the vision of the unfallen world or heaven in religion. We may call it the comic vision of life, in contrast to the tragic vision, which sees the quest only in the form of its ordained cycle.

We conclude with a second table of contents, in which we shall attempt to set forth the central pattern of the comic and tragic visions. One essential principle of archetypal criticism is that the individual and the universal forms of an image are identical, the reasons being too complicated for us just now. We proceed according to the general plan of the game of Twenty Questions, or, if we prefer, of the Great Chain of Being:[7]

6. See Plato, *Sophist* 266c.

7. The notion of the universe as a hierarchical order consisting of an enormous (or even infinite) number of links; Frye probably has in mind the American philosopher and intellectual historian Arthur O. Lovejoy's *The Great Chain of Being* (1936).

1.

In the comic vision the *human* world is a community, or a hero who represents the wish-fulfillment of the reader. The archetype of images of symposium, communion, order, friendship and love. In the tragic vision the human world is a tyranny or anarchy, or an individual or isolated man, the leader with his back to his followers, the bullying giant of romance, the deserted or betrayed hero. Marriage or some equivalent consummation belongs to the comic vision; the harlot, witch and other varieties of Jung's "terrible mother" belong to the tragic one. All divine, heroic, angelic or other superhuman communities follow the human pattern.

2.

In the comic vision the *animal* world is a community of domesticated animals, usually a flock of sheep, or a lamb, or one of the gentler birds, usually a dove. The archetype of pastoral images. In the tragic vision the animal world is seen in terms of beasts and birds of prey, wolves, vultures, serpents, dragons and the like.

3.

In the comic vision the *vegetable* world is a garden, grove or park, or a tree of life, or a rose or lotus. The archetype of Arcadian images, such as that of Marvell's green world or of Shakespeare's forest comedies.[8] In the tragic vision it is a sinister forest like the one in *Comus* or at the opening of the *Inferno*,[9] or a heath or wilderness, or a tree of death.

4.

In the comic vision the *mineral* world is a city, or one building or temple, or one stone, normally a glowing precious stone—in fact the whole comic series, especially the tree, can be conceived as luminous or fiery. The archetype of geometrical images: the "starlit dome"[1] belongs here. In the tragic vision the mineral world is seen in terms of deserts, rocks and ruins, or of sinister geometrical images like the cross.

5.

In the comic vision the *unformed* world is a river, traditionally fourfold, which influenced the Renaissance image of the temperate body with its four humors.[2] In the tragic vision this world usually becomes the sea, as the narrative myth of dissolution is so often a flood myth. The combination of the sea and beast images gives us the leviathan and similar water-monsters.

8. Shakespeare's forest (that is, pastoral) comedies include *As You Like It* (ca. 1599). For the "green world" of Andrew Marvell (1621–1678), English metaphysical poet, see especially "The Garden" (1681).
9. The first book of DANTE ALIGHIERI's *Divine Comedy* (1321). *Comus* (1634), a religious masque by Milton.
1. See, for example, Coleridge's poem "Kubla Khan" (written 1797; pub. 1816), which refers to Kubla Khan's "stately pleasure-dome."
2. The four fluids of the body—blood, phlegm, choler, and black bile—whose relative proportions were thought to determine a person's disposition and general health.

Obvious as this table looks, a great variety of poetic images and forms will be found to fit it. Yeats's "Sailing to Byzantium,"[3] to take a famous example of the comic vision at random, has the city, the tree, the bird, the community of sages, the geometrical gyre and the detachment from the cyclic world. It is, of course, only the general comic or tragic context that determines the interpretation of any symbol: this is obvious with relatively neutral archetypes like the island, which may be Prospero's island or Circe's.[4]

Our tables are, of course, not only elementary but grossly over-simplified, just as our inductive approach to the archetype was a mere hunch. The important point is not the deficiencies of either procedure, taken by itself, but the fact that, somewhere and somehow, the two are clearly going to meet in the middle. And if they do meet, the ground plan of a systematic and comprehensive development of criticism has been established.

1951

3. Poem (1927) by the Irish poet William Butler Yeats (1865–1939).

4. In Greek mythology, a sorceress who lived on the island of Acaea (where Odysseus and his men land in Homer's *Odyssey*). Prospero's island: the setting of Shakespeare's play *The Tempest* (1611).

ROLAND BARTHES
1915–1980

Generally considered one of the leading figures in French structuralism, Roland Barthes is, as Jonathan Culler puts it, "famous for contradictory reasons." On the one hand, there is the scientific Barthes: the one who sought a universal grammar of narrative in his influential essay "Introduction to the Structural Study of Narrative" (1966), or who explored FERDINAND DE SAUSSURE's notion of semiology—a broad science of signs in human culture, of which linguistics would provide a model—in such works as *Elements of Semiology* (1965) and *The Fashion System* (1967). But on the other hand, there is the hedonist and connoisseur: the Barthes who wrote playfully and allusively about pleasure in *The Pleasure of the Text* (1973) and in *A Lover's Discourse* (1977). Even his literary tastes seemed contradictory: he promoted avant-garde writers (Robbe-Grillet, Brecht, Sollers), but he also loved and wrote about the most traditional of French authors (La Bruyère, Racine, Chateaubriand, Balzac, Proust). And he who questioned the importance of the author was himself preeminently an author—indeed, the only author to have written his own volume in a series of "perennial masters" (*Roland Barthes by Roland Barthes*, 1975). A quintessential "man of letters" in the traditional sense, he was also a man of letters in an idiosyncratic, literal sense, organizing three of his books alphabetically so as to avoid thematic or logical organization, and highlighting the material form of letters in one of his book titles, *S/Z* (1970). He was less a path breaker than a habit breaker, resolutely committed to unlearning the routines of intelligibility, even those he himself had helped promote.

Roland Barthes was born in Cherbourg, France. His father, a naval officer, was killed a year later, and Barthes's mother moved to the paternal family home in Bayonne in southern France. The theorist of the death of the author thus grew up without a father, living with or near his mother until her death in 1977, three years before his own. In 1924 mother and son moved to Paris, where Barthes progressed to the *baccalauréat* in the Parisian schools and began studying for entrance into the prestigious École Normale, until his promising academic trajectory was interrupted by the first of several attacks of tuberculosis. Meanwhile, his mother's already strained relations with her Parisian family worsened in 1927 when she gave birth to an illegitimate child—Roland's half-brother, Michel Salzado. Although Barthes's grandparents were well-off, they refused Henriette Binger Barthes and her two sons any financial support, with the result that Henriette had to scrape by on what she earned as a bookbinder.

From 1934 to 1950 Barthes's life alternated between tuberculosis sanitoria (he was exempted from military duty and spent the years of the Occupation in a sanatorium in the Isère), academic institutions where he studied, and, when his health permitted, teaching jobs in Biarritz and abroad in Bucharest and Alexandria. Despite—or perhaps because of—his forced convalescences, he read avidly, founded a theatrical troupe, and began to write. From the first Barthes's writings reflect both his idiosyncratic creativity and his attunement to the intellectual milieu in which he found himself. His first book, *Writing Degree Zero* (1953), initially published as articles in Albert Camus's journal, *Combat*, analyzes the history of literary styles in terms derived from MARX and from Sartre. In this book Barthes looks at the relations between Literature with a capital *L* and the various modern forms of its demystification, from Stéphane Mallarmé's "vibratory near-disappearance" to Camus's "blank" style (the "zero degree" of the title).

A second, quite different, project Barthes undertook at the same time was an extensive study of the imagery used by the nineteenth-century historian Jules Michelet. Scribbling passages on index cards, Barthes organized Michelet's "imagination" in ways that did not correspond to the explicit intentions of his writing. Like the work of the phenomenological critics Jean-Pierre Richard and Georges Poulet, Barthes's analysis was a way of structuring Michelet's writing around its unconscious "obsessions." This research was published as a book titled *Michelet* (1954) in the same writers' series in which Barthes himself later appeared.

Barthes's third project in the mid-1950s, different yet again, was a series of short occasional pieces later published as *Mythologies* (1957). In these essays, of which we give one example, Barthes does a kind of Marxian semiology of mass culture and everyday life. His object is to show how mass culture is saturated with ideological propositions ("myths") presented as if they were natural and self-evident; the result in many ways anticipates what is today called "cultural studies." Barthes combines a sharp eye for the social life of signs with a subtle critique of the naturalizations of the ethnocentric, patriarchal, petit-bourgeois French worldview. Critical of the covert functions of *what-goes-without-saying*, Barthes nevertheless enjoys the exhibitions, advertisements, photographs, articles, films, wrestling matches, and commodities that provide the occasion for his little feats of writing.

As a researcher in Paris for ten years at the CNRS (National Center for Scientific Research), Barthes—like many others in Paris at that time, including CLAUDE LÉVI-STRAUSS in anthropology, JACQUES LACAN in psychoanalysis, and TZVETAN TODOROV and Gérard Genette in literary studies—continued his exploration of the possibilities of extending Saussure's synchronic linguistic analysis to larger cultural structures. In 1962 Barthes was appointed to a tenured post in "the sociology of signs, symbols, and representations" at the École des Hautes Études (School for Advanced Study), where his seminar became legendary. His book *On Racine* (1963) raised hackles in the traditional academic community for its concentration on the structures of Racine's *textual* world rather than his biographical or historical world. Raymond Picard, a Racine scholar at the Sorbonne, countered with *New Criticism or New Fraud?* (1965). Barthes responded to Picard by arguing that traditional critics' recourse to the values of clarity, nobility, and humanity, which they treat as neutral and self-evident, actually exerts a coercive, censoring force on other interpretive possibilities.

The Picard affair is the backdrop for one of Barthes's most notorious essays, "The Death of the Author." Written at the height of the antiestablishment uprisings of May 1968, it assails academic criticism's typical focus on "the man and his work" (which is in many ways the organizing principle of the present anthology). Indeed, Barthes was surprised to find himself caught in 1968 between generations: while he was attacking the generation of Picard, the students—brandishing the anti-structuralist slogan "Structures don't take to the streets!"—were rebelling against the generation of Barthes himself.

"The Death of the Author" begins with an example taken from Balzac's novella *Sarrasine*—the tale of a sculptor who falls in love with an Italian diva subsequently revealed to be not a woman but a castrato (*Sarrasine* was the text analyzed that year in his seminar, and Barthes went on to publish a full-length study of it in his book S/Z). Barthes focuses on a sentence in the text in which a series of exclamations about femininity cannot be clearly attributed to the conscious intentions of any one person, whether that be the author, the narrator, a character, or even "universal wisdom." Barthes argues that the effective, productive, and engaged reading of a text depends on the suspension of preconceived ideas about the character of the particular author—or even about human psychology in general. The text itself is feigning a set of assumptions it will subsequently reveal to be misguided. From the moment that writing detaches itself from an immediate context, "It is language which speaks, not the author." The author, the text, and the reader are each composed of a universe of quotations without origin or end. In its celebration of the birth of the reader, "The Death of the Author" explores the consequences of freeing the reading process from the constraints of fidelity to an origin, a unified meaning, an identity, or any other pregiven exterior or interior reality.

The publication of S/Z marks a turning point in Barthes's relation to structuralism. It is a multilevel analysis that refuses to structure the text otherwise than by cutting it into hundreds of little pieces of varying lengths (called *lexias*) and also by identifying five broad functions (called *codes*) at work in the text. Written as if it were meant to constitute a methodological examplar, it exaggerates the performance of methodology to such an extent that it becomes inimitable and perhaps parodic. When commentators look for a break between structuralism and poststructuralism, S/Z stands as a revealing hinge. In it Barthes pursues not so much a *critique* of structuralism (as does JACQUES DERRIDA, for example) as an *explosion* of it. The hints of larger structures at work are fragmentary and multiple, not sustained, and the theoretical comments are printed as digressions, numbering almost a hundred. Boredom with the structuralist project of reducing all narratives to a common grammar combines with delight in the foretaste of a multitude of grammars and rhetorics hinted at but not developed in S/Z.

Also originally published in 1968 was Barthes's seminal essay "The Reality Effect," translated and reprinted in *The Rustle of Language* (1986). For Barthes, a better understanding of narrative, character, and history requires structural analysis to engage seemingly inconsequential details. Barthes begins with two sentences: one from "A Simple Heart" (1877), by the realist writer Gustave Flaubert, and the other from the recounting of the execution of Charlotte Corday by Jules Michelet. He then launches into theorizing on the importance of what may appear "superfluous" or as "insignificant notations," which, in point of fact, actually reinforce literary and historical realism, as their representations themselves effect reality. Near the close of his essay, Barthes proposes a new verisimilitude and representation to replace the old classical realist concept. At issue is a contemporary linguistic turn in which the signifier (a word) replaces the referent (a thing): that is, language defers and supplants reality, thereby challenging the long-standing claim that literature represents reality. Reality is instead an effect of language.

Barthes's subsequent essay reprinted here, "From Work to Text" (1971), is one of the clearest available summaries (including the obligatory disavowal of such a summary) of the poststructuralist theory of the "text" as it was developed not only by Barthes but by all the writers associated with the vanguard journal *Tel Quel*, including Philippe Sollers, JULIA KRISTEVA, Derrida, and others. This description of "textuality" can be seen as one way of marking the transition between structuralism and poststructuralism. Whereas culture and language for Lévi-Strauss and Saussure were structured like a game (chess is the favorite example), the text is structured like *play*—children's play, musical performance, or the excess motion in a machine. But both structuralists and poststructuralists would contrast their analyses to the classical study of literary and other cultural objects ("work"). The *text* is a process; the *work* is a product. *Works* can be found on library shelves; *texts* are signifying fields into which one enters. (The development of the Internet has perhaps made this distinction seem less radical than it did in the 1970s.) Their point is not that literature can be divided into works and texts but that the reader can activate either the closure of the signified (the coherence of a meaning) or the "play" of the signifier (the dissemination and disruption of meanings). The text deserves no vital "respect"—it is not alive and can thus be "broken" or "manhandled" in ways that would violate organic forms. The death of the author turns out to be based not on a murder but on an elimination of the metaphor of life in the first place. The work is "consumed"; the text is "produced" (in *S/Z*, Barthes called these the *readerly* and the *writerly* aspects of a text). Barthes ends the essay by opening onto pleasure, a topic that would engage him more and more from then on.

In later writings (*The Empire of Signs*, 1970; *The Pleasure of the Text*, 1973; *Roland Barthes by Roland Barthes*, 1975; *Camera Lucida*, 1980; and the posthumously published *Incidents*, 1987), Roland Barthes seems to resurrect precisely the author he had killed off. But the contradiction is more apparent than real. While the disembodied, abstract author of the network of signs does indeed become an embodied and particular author, the body and biography are both seen as historical, and both are structured like a text. The author is still not an extratextual *identity* determining meaning. The body can be read like a text, just as the text can be read like a body. Gaps in meaning, like the gaps in a garment, are equivalent sites of pleasure. *Roland Barthes by Roland Barthes* does not create a person retrospectively but gives an alphabetically arranged mosaic of the preoccupations of someone who is just like a character in a novel. Indeed, in an interview Barthes called autobiography a "novel that dares not speak its name." He thus subtly alludes to Wildean homosexuality ("The Love That Dares Not Speak Its Name") in a context in which Barthes's own homosexuality is being, by that very expression, *detached* from any real person. This sophisticated relation to homosexuality (neither hidden nor claimed) is readable throughout Barthes's work.

In 1976 this critic of academic criticism was elected to the Chair in Literary Semiology at France's most prestigious institution, the Collège de France. In his inaugural lecture, published as *Leçon* (1978), he explains why he is an unlikely choice for such a post and then goes on to recapitulate many of his thoughts about semiology and literature. Barthes thus ended up as one of the most established of antiestablishment academics.

Barthes's last book published during his lifetime, *Camera Lucida*, is both a meditation on photography and an act of mourning for his mother. Whereas in *Mythologies* he had revealed the contrived nature of the "reality" inherent in the campaign photograph, in *Camera Lucida*, on the contrary, he finds something in a photograph, particularly a snapshot, that is real. Neither a rhetorical sleight-of-hand nor an arbitrary contrivance, the photograph has a way of telling us "This has been." Although Barthes was only sixty-four years old at the time of its publication, the book reads in many ways like a voice from beyond the grave. That same year Roland Barthes was hit by a laundry truck in the street; his injuries proved fatal.

Writing on the cusp of structuralism and poststructuralism, Barthes was a master of the provocative essay, weaving together science and pleasure, critique and eloquence, and never simply choosing between them. For him, specialized vocabularies were delicious in themselves, and ordinary language already multidimensional.

***Mythologies* Keywords:** Cultural Studies, Ideology, Institutional Studies, Media, Popular Culture, Print Culture, Representation, Semiotics
"The Death of the Author" Keywords: Authorship, Identity, Ideology, Language, Literary History, Modernity, Poststructuralism, Reception Theory
"The Reality Effect" Keywords: Aesthetics, Language, Literary History, Narrative Theory, Realism, Representation, Semiotics
"From Work to Text" Keywords: Authorship, The Canon/Tradition, Interpretation Theory, Language, Literary History, Poststructuralism, Reception Theory

From Mythologies[1]

Photography and Electoral Appeal

Some candidates for Parliament adorn their electoral prospectus with a portrait. This presupposes that photography has a power to convert which must be analysed. To start with, the effigy of a candidate establishes a personal link between him and the voters; the candidate does not only offer a programme for judgment, he suggests a physical climate, a set of daily choices expressed in a morphology, a way of dressing, a posture. Photography thus tends to restore the paternalistic nature of elections, whose elitist essence has been disrupted by proportional representation and the rule of parties (the Right seems to use it more than the Left). Inasmuch as photography is an ellipse[2] of language and a condensation of an 'ineffable' social whole, it constitutes an anti-intellectual weapon and tends to spirit away 'politics' (that is to say a body of problems and solutions) to the advantage of a 'manner of being', a socio-moral status. It is well known that this antithesis is one of the major myths of Poujadism (Poujade[3] on television saying: '*Look at me: I am like you*').

Electoral photography is therefore above all the acknowledgment of something deep and irrational co-extensive with politics. What is transmitted through the photograph of the candidate are not his plans, but his deep motives, all his family, mental, even erotic circumstances, all this style of life of which he is at once the product, the example and the bait. It is obvious that what most of our candidates offer us through their likeness is a type of social setting, the spectacular comfort of family, legal and religious norms, the suggestion of innately owning such items of bourgeois property as Sunday Mass, xenophobia, steak and chips, cuckold jokes, in short, what we call an ideology. Needless to say the use of electoral photography presupposes a kind of complicity: a photograph is a mirror, what we are asked to

1. Translated by Annette Lavers.
2. Ellipsis.
3. Pierre-Marie Poujade (1920–2003), French politician; leader of a right-wing movement in the 1950s.

read is the familiar, the known; it offers to the voter his own likeness, but clarified, exalted, superbly elevated into a type. This glorification is in fact the very definition of the photogenic: the voter is at once expressed and heroized, he is invited to elect himself, to weigh the mandate which he is about to give with a veritable physical transference: he is delegating his 'race'.

The types which are thus delegated are not very varied. First there is that which stands for social status, respectability, whether sanguine and well-fed (lists of 'National' parties), or genteel and insipid (lists of the M.R.P.[4]—the Christian Democrats). Then, the type of the intellectual (let it be repeated that we are dealing here with 'signified' types, not actual ones): whether sanctimonious like the candidate of centre right parties like the Rassemblement National, or 'searching' like that of the Communists. In the last two cases, the iconography is meant to signify the exceptional conjunction of thought and will, reflection and action: the slightly narrowed eyes allow a sharp look to filter through, which seems to find its strength in a beautiful inner dream without however ceasing to alight on real obstacles, as if the ideal candidate had in this case magnificently to unite social idealism with bourgeois empiricism. The last type is quite simply that of the 'good-looking chap', whose obvious credentials are his health and virility. Some candidates, incidentally, beautifully manage to win on both counts, appearing for instance as a handsome hero (in uniform) on one side of the handout, and as a mature and virile citizen on the other, displaying his little family. For in most cases, the morphological type is assisted by very obvious attributes: one candidate is surrounded by his kids (curled and dolled-up like all children photographed in France), another is a young parachutist with rolled-up sleeves, or an officer with his chest covered with decorations. Photography constitutes here a veritable blackmail by means of moral values: country, army, family, honour, reckless heroism.

The conventions of photography, moreover, are themselves replete with signs. A full-face photograph underlines the realistic outlook of the candidate, especially if he is provided with scrutinizing glasses. Everything there expresses penetration, gravity, frankness: the future deputy is looking squarely at the enemy, the obstacle, the 'problem'. A three-quarter face photograph, which is more common, suggests the tyranny of an ideal: the gaze is lost nobly in the future, it does not confront, it soars, and fertilizes some other domain, which is chastely left undefined. Almost all three-quarter face photos are ascensional, the face is lifted towards a supernatural light which draws it up and elevates it to the realm of a higher humanity; the candidate reaches the Olympus of elevated feelings, where all political contradictions are solved: peace and war in Algeria,[5] social progress and employers' profits, so-called 'free' religious schools and subsidies from the sugar-beet lobby, the Right and the Left (an opposition always 'superseded'!): all these coexist peacefully in this thoughtful gaze, nobly fixed on the hidden interests of Order.

1957

4. Mouvement Républicain Populaire (Republican Popular Movement; French).

5. The Algerian struggle for independence from France (1954–62).

The Death of the Author[1]

In his story *Sarrasine*[2] Balzac, describing a castrato disguised as a woman, writes the following sentence: '*This was woman herself, with her sudden fears, her irrational whims, her instinctive worries, her impetuous boldness, her fussings, and her delicious sensibility.*' Who is speaking thus? Is it the hero of the story bent on remaining ignorant of the castrato hidden beneath the woman? Is it Balzac the individual, furnished by his personal experience with a philosophy of Woman? Is it Balzac the author professing 'literary' ideas on femininity? Is it universal wisdom? Romantic psychology? We shall never know, for the good reason that writing is the destruction of every voice, of every point of origin. Writing is that neutral, composite, oblique space where our subject slips away, the negative where all identity is lost, starting with the very identity of the body writing.

No doubt it has always been that way. As soon as a fact is *narrated* no longer with a view to acting directly on reality but intransitively, that is to say, finally outside of any function other than that of the very practice of the symbol itself, this disconnection occurs, the voice loses its origin, the author enters into his own death, writing begins. The sense of this phenomenon, however, has varied; in ethnographic societies the responsibility for a narrative is never assumed by a person but by a mediator, shaman or relator whose 'performance'—the mastery of the narrative code—may possibly be admired but never his 'genius'. The author is a modern figure, a product of our society insofar as, emerging from the Middle Ages with English empiricism, French rationalism and the personal faith of the Reformation, it discovered the prestige of the individual, of, as it is more nobly put, the 'human person'. It is thus logical that in literature it should be this positivism, the epitome and culmination of capitalist ideology, which has attached the greatest importance to the 'person' of the author. The *author* still reigns in histories of literature, biographies of writers, interviews, magazines, as in the very consciousness of men of letters anxious to unite their person and their work through diaries and memoirs. The image of literature to be found in ordinary culture is tyrannically centred on the author, his person, his life, his tastes, his passions, while criticism still consists for the most part in saying that Baudelaire's work is the failure of Baudelaire the man, Van Gogh's his madness, Tchaikovsky's his vice.[3] The *explanation* of a work is always sought in the man or woman who produced it, as if it were always in the end, through the more or less transparent allegory of the fiction, the voice of a single person, the *author* 'confiding' in us.

Though the sway of the Author remains powerful (the new criticism[4] has often done no more than consolidate it), it goes without saying that certain

1. Translated by Stephen Heath.
2. Short novel (1830) by Honoré de Balzac (1799–1850), about which Barthes was in the process of writing (see S/Z, 1970).
3. Pyotr Tchaikovsky (1840–1893), Russian composer; his "vice" is presumably homosexuality. Charles Baudelaire (1821–1867), French poet. Vincent van Gogh (1853–1890), Dutch painter.
4. The "new criticism" in France at that time included structuralist, thematic, phenomenological, sociological, Marxist, and psychoanalytic criticism.

writers have long since attempted to loosen it. In France, Mallarmé[5] was doubtless the first to see and to foresee in its full extent the necessity to substitute language itself for the person who until then had been supposed to be its owner. For him, for us too, it is language which speaks, not the author; to write is, through a prerequisite impersonality (not at all to be confused with the castrating objectivity of the realist novelist), to reach that point where only language acts, 'performs', and not 'me'. Mallarmé's entire poetics consists in suppressing the author in the interests of writing (which is, as will be seen, to restore the place of the reader). Valéry,[6] encumbered by a psychology of the Ego, considerably diluted Mallarmé's theory but, his taste for classicism leading him to turn to the lessons of rhetoric, he never stopped calling into question and deriding the Author; he stressed the linguistic and, as it were, 'hazardous' nature of his activity, and throughout his prose works he militated in favour of the essentially verbal condition of literature, in the face of which all recourse to the writer's interiority seemed to him pure superstition. Proust[7] himself, despite the apparently psychological character of what are called his *analyses*, was visibly concerned with the task of inexorably blurring, by an extreme subtilization, the relation between the writer and his characters; by making of the narrator not he who has seen and felt nor even he who is writing, but he who *is going to write* (the young man in the novel—but, in fact, how old is he and who is he?—wants to write but cannot; the novel ends when writing at last becomes possible), Proust gave modern writing its epic. By a radical reversal, instead of putting his life into his novel, as is so often maintained, he made of his very life a work for which his own book was the model; so that it is clear to us that Charlus[8] does not imitate Montesquiou but that Montesquiou—in his anecdotal, historical reality—is no more than a secondary fragment, derived from Charlus. Lastly, to go no further than this prehistory of modernity, Surrealism, though unable to accord language a supreme place (language being system and the aim of the movement being, romantically, a direct subversion of codes—itself moreover illusory: a code cannot be destroyed, only 'played off'), contributed to the desacralization of the image of the Author by ceaselessly recommending the abrupt disappointment of expectations of meaning (the famous surrealist 'jolt'), by entrusting the hand with the task of writing as quickly as possible what the head itself is unaware of (automatic writing), by accepting the principle and the experience of several people writing together. Leaving aside literature itself (such distinctions really becoming invalid), linguistics has recently provided the destruction of the Author with a valuable analytical tool by showing that the whole of the enunciation is an empty process, functioning perfectly without there being any need for it to be filled with the person of the interlocutors. Linguistically, the author is never more than the instance writing, just as *I* is nothing other than the instance saying *I*: language knows a 'subject', not a 'person', and this subject, empty outside of the very enunciation which defines it, suffices to make language 'hold together', suffices, that is to say, to exhaust it.

5. Stéphane Mallarmé (1842–1898), French poet.
6. Paul Valéry (1871–1945), French poet and critic.
7. Marcel Proust (1871–1922), French novelist.
8. Le baron de Charlus, a character in Proust's *In Search of Lost Time* (7 vols., 1913–27), said to have been modeled on the aesthete Robert, comte de Montesquiou-Fézensac (1855–1921).

The removal of the Author (one could talk here with Brecht[9] of a veritable 'distancing', the Author diminishing like a figurine at the far end of the literary stage) is not merely an historical fact or an act of writing; it utterly transforms the modern text (or—which is the same thing—the text is henceforth made and read in such a way that at all its levels the author is absent). The temporality is different. The Author, when believed in, is always conceived of as the past of his own book: book and author stand automatically on a single line divided into a *before* and an *after*. The Author is thought to *nourish* the book, which is to say that he exists before it, thinks, suffers, lives for it, is in the same relation of antecedence to his work as a father to his child. In complete contrast, the modern scriptor is born simultaneously with the text, is in no way equipped with a being preceding or exceeding the writing, is not the subject with the book as predicate; there is no other time than that of the enunciation and every text is eternally written *here* and *now*. The fact is (or, it follows) that *writing* can no longer designate an operation of recording, notation, representation, 'depiction' (as the Classics would say); rather, it designates exactly what linguists, referring to Oxford philosophy,[1] call a performative, a rare verbal form (exclusively given in the first person and in the present tense) in which the enunciation has no other content (contains no other proposition) than the act by which it is uttered—something like the *I declare* of kings or the *I sing* of very ancient poets. Having buried the Author, the modern scriptor can thus no longer believe, as according to the pathetic view of his predecessors, that this hand is too slow for his thought or passion and that consequently, making a law of necessity, he must emphasize this delay and indefinitely 'polish' his form. For him, on the contrary, the hand, cut off from any voice, borne by a pure gesture of inscription (and not of expression), traces a field without origin—or which, at least, has no other origin than language itself, language which ceaselessly calls into question all origins.

We know now that a text is not a line of words releasing a single 'theological' meaning (the 'message' of the Author-God) but a multi-dimensional space in which a variety of writings, none of them original, blend and clash. The text is a tissue of quotations drawn from the innumerable centres of culture. Similar to Bouvard and Pécuchet,[2] those eternal copyists, at once sublime and comic and whose profound ridiculousness indicates precisely the truth of writing, the writer can only imitate a gesture that is always anterior, never original. His only power is to mix writings, to counter the ones with the others, in such a way as never to rest on any one of them. Did he wish to *express himself*, he ought at least to know that the inner 'thing' he thinks to 'translate' is itself only a ready-formed dictionary, its words only explainable through other words, and so on indefinitely; something experienced in exemplary fashion by the young Thomas de Quincey,[3] he who was so good at Greek that in order to translate absolutely modern ideas and images into that dead language, he had, so Baudelaire tells us (in *Paradis Artificiels*),[4] 'created for himself an unfailing dictionary, vastly more extensive and complex than those resulting

9. Bertolt Brecht (1898–1956), German poet and dramatist, whose "epic theater" was intended to distance and alienate the audience from traditional theatrical illusion.
1. That is, philosophy of language; see especially J. L. AUSTIN, *How to Do Things with Words* (1962).
2. The title characters in Gustave Flaubert's unfinished novel *Bouvard and Pécuchet* (1881), who leave their jobs as copyists and unsuccessfully attempt to master all knowledge.
3. English essayist and critic (1785–1859).
4. *Artificial Paradises* (1869).

from the ordinary patience of purely literary themes'. Succeeding the Author, the scriptor no longer bears within him passions, humours, feelings, impressions, but rather this immense dictionary from which he draws a writing that can know no halt: life never does more than imitate the book, and the book itself is only a tissue of signs, an imitation that is lost, infinitely deferred.

Once the Author is removed, the claim to decipher a text becomes quite futile. To give a text an Author is to impose a limit on that text, to furnish it with a final signified, to close the writing. Such a conception suits criticism very well, the latter then allotting itself the important task of discovering the Author (or its hypostases:[5] society, history, psyche, liberty) beneath the work: when the Author has been found, the text is 'explained'—victory to the critic. Hence there is no surprise in the fact that, historically, the reign of the Author has also been that of the Critic, nor again in the fact that criticism (be it new) is today undermined along with the Author. In the multiplicity of writing, everything is to be *disentangled*, nothing *deciphered*; the structure can be followed, 'run' (like the thread of a stocking) at every point and at every level, but there is nothing beneath: the space of writing is to be ranged over, not pierced; writing ceaselessly posits meaning ceaselessly to evaporate it, carrying out a systematic exemption of meaning. In precisely this way literature (it would be better from now on to say *writing*), by refusing to assign a 'secret', an ultimate meaning, to the text (and to the world as text), liberates what may be called an anti-theological activity, an activity that is truly revolutionary since to refuse to fix meaning is, in the end, to refuse God and his hypostases—reason, science, law.

Let us come back to the Balzac sentence. No one, no 'person', says it: its source, its voice, is not the true place of the writing, which is reading. Another—very precise—example will help to make this clear: recent research (J.-P. Vernant)[6] has demonstrated the constitutively ambiguous nature of Greek tragedy, its texts being woven from words with double meanings that each character understands unilaterally (this perpetual misunderstanding is exactly the 'tragic'); there is, however, someone who understands each word in its duplicity and who, in addition, hears the very deafness of the characters speaking in front of him—this someone being precisely the reader (or here, the listener). Thus is revealed the total existence of writing: a text is made of multiple writings, drawn from many cultures and entering into mutual relations of dialogue, parody, contestation, but there is one place where this multiplicity is focused and that place is the reader, not, as was hitherto said, the author. The reader is the space on which all the quotations that make up a writing are inscribed without any of them being lost; a text's unity lies not in its origin but in its destination. Yet this destination cannot any longer be personal: the reader is without history, biography, psychology; he is simply that *someone* who holds together in a single field all the traces by which the written text is constituted. Which is why it is derisory to condemn the new writing in the name of a humanism hypocritically turned champion of the reader's rights. Classic criticism has never paid any attention to the reader; for it, the writer is the only person in literature. We are now beginning to let ourselves

5. Stand-ins (the concrete forms of abstractions).

6. Cf. Jean-Pierre Vernant (with Pierre Vidal-Naquet), *Mythe et tragédie en Grèce ancienne* (Paris, 1972), esp. pp. 19–40, 99–131 [translator's note]. Vernant (1914–2007), French scholar of ancient Greece.

be fooled no longer by the arrogant antiphrastical[7] recriminations of good society in favour of the very thing it sets aside, ignores, smothers, or destroys; we know that to give writing its future, it is necessary to overthrow the myth: the birth of the reader must be at the cost of the death of the Author.

1968

The Reality Effect[1]

When Flaubert,[2] describing the room occupied by Mme Aubain, Félicité's employer, tells us that "an old piano supported, under a barometer, a pyramidal heap of boxes and cartons" ("A Simple Heart," from *Three Tales*); when Michelet,[3] recounting the death of Charlotte Corday[4] and reporting that, before the executioner's arrival, she was visited in prison by an artist who painted her portrait, includes the detail that "after an hour and a half, there was a gentle knock at a little door behind her" (*Histoire de France: La Révolution*)—these authors (among many others) are producing notations which structural analysis, concerned with identifying and systematizing the major articulations of narrative, usually and heretofore has left out, either because its inventory omits all details that are "superfluous" (in relation to structure) or because these same details are treated as "filling" (catalyses), assigned an indirect functional value insofar as, cumulatively, they constitute some index of character or atmosphere and so can ultimately be recuperated by structure.

It would seem, however, that if analysis seeks to be exhaustive (and what would any method be worth which did not account for the totality of its object, i.e., in this case, of the entire surface of the narrative fabric?), if it seeks to encompass the absolute detail, the indivisible unit, the fugitive transition, in order to assign them a place in the structure, it inevitably encounters notations which no function (not even the most indirect) can justify: such notations are scandalous (from the point of view of structure), or, what is even more disturbing, they seem to correspond to a kind of narrative *luxury*, lavish to the point of offering many "futile" details and thereby increasing the cost of narrative information. For if, in Flaubert's description, it is just possible to see in the notation of the piano an indication of its owner's bourgeois standing and in that of the cartons a sign of disorder and a kind of lapse in status likely to connote the atmosphere of the Aubain household, no purpose seems to justify reference to the barometer, an object neither incongruous nor significant, and therefore not participating, at first glance, in the order of the *notable*; and in Michelet's sentence, we have the same difficulty in accounting structurally for all the details: that the executioner came after the painter is all that is necessary to the account; how long the sitting lasted, the dimension and location of the door are useless (but the theme of the door, the softness of death's knock have an indisputable symbolic value). Even if they are not numerous, the "useless details"

7. Characterized by using a word to intend its opposite.

1. Translated by Richard Howard.

2. Gustave Flaubert (1821–1880), French author; Barthes refers here to a story published in 1877 and later to his masterpiece, the novel *Madame Bovary* (1856).

3. Jules Michelet (1798–1874), French historian best known for his monumental *History of France* (17 vols., 1833–67).

4. Marie-Anne Charlotte de Corday d'Armont (1768–1793), minor French aristocrat guillotined for assassinating Jean-Paul Marat, a journalist and leader of a radical faction in the French Revolution.

therefore seem inevitable: every narrative, at least every Western narrative of the ordinary sort nowadays, possesses a certain number.

Insignificant notation[5] (taking this word in its strong sense: apparently detached from the narrative's semiotic structure) is related to description, even if the object seems to be denoted only by a single word (in reality, the "pure" word does not exist: Flaubert's barometer is not cited in isolation; it is located, placed in a syntagm[6] at once referential and syntactic); thus is underlined the enigmatic character of all description, about which a word is necessary: the general structure of narrative, at least as it has been occasionally analyzed till now, appears as essentially *predictive*; schematizing to the extreme, and without taking into account numerous detours, delays, reversals, and disappointments which narrative institutionally imposes upon this schema, we can say that, at each articulation of the narrative syntagm, someone says to the hero (or to the reader, it does not matter which): if you act in this way, if you choose this alternative, this is what will happen (the *reported* character of these predictions does not call into question their practical nature). Description is entirely different: it has no predictive mark; "analogical," its structure is purely summatory and does not contain that trajectory of choices and alternatives which gives narration the appearance of a huge traffic-control center, furnished with a referential (and not merely discursive) temporality. This is an opposition which, anthropologically, has its importance: when, under the influence of von Frisch's[7] experiments, it was assumed that bees had a language, it had to be realized that, while these insects possessed a predictive system of dances (in order to collect their food), nothing in it approached a *description*. Thus, description appears as a kind of characteristic of the so-called higher languages, to the apparently paradoxical degree that it is justified by no finality of action or of communication. The singularity of description (or of the "useless detail") in narrative fabric, its isolated situation, designates a question which has the greatest importance for the structural analysis of narrative. This question is the following: Is everything in narrative significant, and if not, if insignificant stretches subsist in the narrative syntagm, what is ultimately, so to speak, the significance of this insignificance?

First of all, we must recall that Western culture, in one of its major currents, has certainly not left description outside meaning, and has furnished it with a finality quite "recognized" by the literary institution. This current is Rhetoric, and this finality is that of the "beautiful": description has long had an aesthetic function. Very early in antiquity, to the two expressly functional genres of discourse, legal and political, was added a third, the epideictic, a ceremonial discourse intended to excite the admiration of the audience (and no longer to persuade it); this discourse contained in germ—whatever the ritual rules of its use: eulogy or obituary—the very idea of an aesthetic finality of language; in the Alexandrian neo-rhetoric of the second century A.D., there was a craze for ecphrasis, the detachable set piece (thus having its end in itself, independent of any general function), whose object was to describe places, times, people, or works of art, a tradition which was maintained throughout the Middle Ages. As

5. In this brief account, we shall not give examples of "insignificant" notations, for the insignificant can be revealed only on the level of an immense structure: once cited, a notion is neither significant nor insignificant; it requires an already analyzed context [Barthes's note].

6. An element of discourse or narrative that is arranged with others in a linear sequence; the term is derived from the work of the Swiss linguist FERDINAND DE SAUSSURE (1857–1913).

7. Karl von Frisch (1886–1982), Austrian zoologist who studied communication among bees.

Curtius[8] has emphasized, description in this period is constrained by no realism; its truth is unimportant (or even its verisimilitude); there is no hesitation to put lions or olive trees in a northern country; only the constraint of the descriptive genre counts; plausibility is not referential here but openly discursive: it is the generic rules of discourse which lay down the law.

Moving ahead to Flaubert, we see that the aesthetic purpose of description is still very strong. In *Madame Bovary*, the description of Rouen (a real referent if ever there was one) is subject to the tyrannical constraints of what we must call aesthetic verisimilitude, as is attested by the corrections made in this passage in the course of six successive rewritings. Here we see, first of all, that the corrections do not in any way issue from a closer consideration of the model: Rouen, perceived by Flaubert, remains just the same, or more precisely, if it changes somewhat from one version to the next, it is solely because he finds it necessary to focus an image or avoid a phonic redundance condemned by the rules of *le beau style*,[9] or again to "arrange" a quite contingent felicity of expression;[1] next we see that the descriptive fabric, which at first glance seems to grant a major importance (by its dimension, by the concern for its detail) to the object *Rouen*, is in fact only a sort of setting meant to receive the jewels of a number of rare metaphors, the neutral, prosaic excipient which swathes the precious symbolic substance, as if, in Rouen, all that mattered were the figures of rhetoric to which the sight of the city lends itself—as if Rouen were notable only by its substitutions (*the masts like a forest of needles, the islands like huge motionless black fish, the clouds like aerial waves silently breaking against a cliff*); last, we see that the whole description is *constructed* so as to connect Rouen to a painting: it is a painted scene which the language takes up ("Thus, seen from above, the whole landscape had the motionless look of a painting"); the writer here fulfills Plato's[2] definition of the artist as a maker in the third degree, since he imitates what is already the simulation of an essence. Thus, although the description of Rouen is quite irrelevant to the narrative structure of *Madame Bovary* (we can attach it to no functional sequence nor to any characterial, atmospheric, or sapiential[3] signified), it is not in the least scandalous, it is justified, if not by the work's logic, at least by the laws of literature: its "meaning" exists, it depends on conformity not to the model but to the cultural rules of representation.

All the same, the aesthetic goal of Flaubertian description is thoroughly mixed with "realistic" imperatives, as if the referent's exactitude, superior or indifferent to any other function, governed and alone justified its description, or—in the case of descriptions reduced to a single word—its denotation: here aesthetic constraints are steeped—at least as an alibi—in referential constraints: it is likely that, if one came to Rouen in a diligence,[4] the view one would have coming down the slope leading to the town would not be "objectively" different from the panorama Flaubert describes. This mixture—this

8. Ernst Robert Curtius (1886–1956), German literary scholar and philologist.
9. The beautiful style (French).
1. A mechanism distinguished by Valéry, in *Littérature* [1929], commenting on Baudelaire's line "*La servante au grand Coeur . . .*": "This line *came* to Baudelaire . . . And Baudelaire continued. He buried the cook out on the lawn, which goes against the custom, but goes with the rhyme," etc. [Barthes's note]. Paul Valéry (1871–1945), French critic and poet. Charles Baudelaire (1821–1867), French poet; the line ("The kind-hearted servant . . .") begins one of the poems in his collection *Fleurs du Mal* (1861 ed., *Flowers of Evil*).
2. Greek philosopher (ca. 427–ca. 347 B.C.E.); he makes this argument about art simply imitating appearance in *Republic* 10.596–602 (see above).
3. Specific to wisdom.
4. A large public horse-drawn carriage, used in 18th- and 19th-century France.

interweaving—of constraints has a double advantage: on the one hand, aesthetic function, giving a meaning to "the fragment," halts what we might call the vertigo of notation; for once, discourse is no longer guided and limited by structural imperatives of the anecdote (functions and indices), nothing could indicate why we should halt the details of the description here and not there; if it were not subject to an aesthetic or rhetorical choice, any "view" would be inexhaustible by discourse: there would always be a corner, a detail, an inflection of space or color to report; on the other hand, by positing the referential as real, by pretending to follow it in a submissive fashion, realistic description avoids being reduced to fantasmatic activity (a precaution which was supposed necessary to the "objectivity" of the account); classical rhetoric had in a sense institutionalized the fantasmatic as a specific figure, *hypotyposis*, whose function was to "put things before the hearer's eyes," not in a neutral, constative manner, but by imparting to representation all the luster of desire (this was the vividly illuminated sector of discourse, with prismatic outlines: *illustris oratio*[5]); declaratively renouncing the constraints of the rhetorical code, realism must seek a new reason to describe.

The irreducible residues of functional analysis have this in common: they denote what is ordinarily called "concrete reality" (insignificant gestures, transitory attitudes, insignificant objects, redundant words). The pure and simple "representation" of the "real," the naked relation of "what is" (or has been) thus appears as a resistance to meaning; this resistance confirms the great mythic opposition of the *true-to-life* (the lifelike) and the *intelligible*; it suffices to recall that, in the ideology of our time, obsessive reference to the "concrete" (in what is rhetorically demanded of the human sciences, of literature, of behavior) is always brandished like a weapon against meaning, as if, by some statutory exclusion, what is alive cannot not signify—and vice versa. Resistance of the "real" (in its written form, of course) to structure is very limited in the fictive account, constructed by definition on a model which, for its main outlines, has no other constraints than those of intelligibility; but this same "reality" becomes the essential reference in historical narrative, which is supposed to report "what really happened": what does the non-functionality of a detail matter then, once it denotes "what took place"; "concrete reality" becomes the sufficient justification for speaking. History (historical discourse: *historia rerum gestarum*[6]) is in fact the model of those narratives which consent to fill in the interstices of their functions by structurally superfluous notations, and it is logical that literary realism should have been—give or take a few decades—contemporary with the regnum of "objective" history, to which must be added the contemporary development of techniques, of works, and institutions based on the incessant need to authenticate the "real": the photograph (immediate witness of "what was here"), reportage, exhibitions of ancient objects (the success of the Tutankhamen[7] show makes this quite clear), the tourism of monuments and historical sites. All this shows that the "real" is supposed to be self-sufficient, that it is strong enough to belie any notion of "function," that its "speech-act"[8] has no need to be integrated into a structure and that the *having-been-there* of things is a sufficient principle of speech.

5. Clear speech (Latin).
6. Narrative of things done (Latin).
7. King of Egypt (reigned 1333–1323 B.C.E.), 18th dynasty; artifacts from his largely intact tomb, discovered in 1922, were shown in several countries (including France) in a traveling exhibition from 1961 to 1967.
8. For the idea of a "speech-act," or performative (an utterance that does something), see especially the writings of the English philosopher J. L. AUSTIN (1911–1960).

Since antiquity, the "real" has been on History's side; but this was to help it oppose the "lifelike," the "plausible," to oppose the very order of narrative (of imitation or "poetry"). All classical culture lived for centuries on the notion that reality could in no way contaminate verisimilitude; first of all, because verisimilitude is never anything but *opinable*: it is entirely subject to (public) opinion; as Nicole[9] said: "One must not consider things as they are in themselves, nor as they are known to be by one who speaks or writes, but only in relation to what is known of them by those who read or hear"; then, because History was thought to be general, not particular (whence the propensity, in classical texts, to functionalize all details, to produce strong structures and to justify no notation by the mere guarantee of "reality"); finally, because, in verisimilitude, the contrary is never impossible, since notation rests on a majority, but not an absolute, opinion. The motto implicit on the threshold of all classical discourse (subject to the ancient idea of verisimilitude) is: *Esto* (*Let there be, suppose* . . .). "Real," fragmented, interstitial notation, the kind we are dealing with here, renounces this implicit introduction, and it is free of any such postulation that occurs in the structural fabric. Hence, there is a break between the ancient mode of verisimilitude and modern realism; but hence, too, a new verisimilitude is born, which is precisely *realism* (by which we mean any discourse which accepts "speech-acts" justified by their referent alone).

Semiotically, the "concrete detail" is constituted by the *direct* collusion of a referent and a signifier; the signified is expelled from the sign, and with it, of course, the possibility of developing a *form of the signified*, i.e., narrative structure itself. (Realistic literature is narrative, of course, but that is because its realism is only fragmentary, erratic, confined to "details," and because the most realistic narrative imaginable develops along unrealistic lines.) This is what we might call the *referential illusion*.[1] The truth of this illusion is this: eliminated from the realist speech-act as a signified of denotation, the "real" returns to it as a signified of connotation; for just when these details are reputed to *denote* the real directly, all that they do—without saying so—is *signify* it; Flaubert's barometer, Michelet's little door finally say nothing but this: *we are the real*; it is the category of "the real" (and not its contingent contents) which is then signified; in other words, the very absence of the signified, to the advantage of the referent alone, becomes the very signifier of realism: the *reality effect* is produced, the basis of that unavowed verisimilitude which forms the aesthetic of all the standard works of modernity.

This new verisimilitude is very different from the old one, for it is neither a respect for the "laws of the genre" nor even their mask, but proceeds from the intention to degrade the sign's tripartite nature[2] in order to make notation the pure encounter of an object and its expression. The disintegration of the sign—which seems indeed to be modernity's grand affair—is of course present in the realistic enterprise, but in a somewhat regressive manner, since it occurs in the name of a referential plenitude, whereas the goal today is to

9. Pierre Nicole (1625–1695), French theologian; Barthes quotes from his *Treatise on True and False Beauty* (1683).

1. An illusion clearly illustrated by the program Thiers assigned to the historian: "To be simply true, to be what things are and nothing more than that, and nothing except that" [Barthes's note]. Adolphe Thiers (1787–1877), French historian and the first president of the Third Republic (1871–73); the quotation is from vol. 12 of his *Histoire du Consulat et de l'Empire* (21 vols., 1845–62; *History of the Consulate and the Empire*).

2. That is, the sign's composition as signified (the concept conveyed), signifier (word or words conveying the concept), and referent (thing referred to).

empty the sign and infinitely to postpone its object so as to challenge, in a radical fashion, the age-old aesthetic of "representation."

1968

From Work to Text[1]

It is a fact that over the last few years a certain change has taken place (or is taking place) in our conception of language and, consequently, of the literary work which owes at least its phenomenal existence to this same language. The change is clearly connected with the current development of (amongst other disciplines) linguistics, anthropology, Marxism and psychoanalysis (the term 'connection' is used here in a deliberately neutral way: one does not decide a determination, be it multiple and dialectical). What is new and which affects the idea of the work comes not necessarily from the internal recasting of each of these disciplines, but rather from their encounter in relation to an object which traditionally is the province of none of them. It is indeed as though the *interdisciplinarity* which is today held up as a prime value in research cannot be accomplished by the simple confrontation of specialist branches of knowledge. Interdisciplinarity is not the calm of an easy security; it begins *effectively* (as opposed to the mere expression of a pious wish) when the solidarity of the old disciplines breaks down—perhaps even violently, via the jolts of fashion—in the interests of a new object and a new language neither of which has a place in the field of the sciences that were to be brought peacefully together, this unease in classification being precisely the point from which it is possible to diagnose a certain mutation. The mutation in which the idea of the work seems to be gripped must not, however, be over-estimated: it is more in the nature of an epistemological slide than of a real break. The break, as is frequently stressed, is seen to have taken place in the last century with the appearance of Marxism and Freudianism;[2] since then there has been no further break, so that in a way it can be said that for the last hundred years we have been living in repetition. What History, our History, allows us today is merely to slide, to vary, to exceed, to repudiate. Just as Einsteinian science[3] demands that *the relativity of the frames of reference* be included in the object studied, so the combined action of Marxism, Freudianism and structuralism demands, in literature, the relativization of the relations of writer, reader and observer (critic). Over against the traditional notion of the *work*, for long—and still—conceived of in a, so to speak, Newtonian way, there is now the requirement of a new object, obtained by the sliding or overturning of former categories. That object is the *Text*. I know the word is fashionable (I am myself often led to use it) and therefore regarded by some with suspicion, but that is exactly why I should like to remind myself of the principal propositions at the intersection of which I see the Text as standing. The word 'proposition' is to be understood more in a grammatical than in a logical sense: the following are

1. Translated by Stephen Heath.
2. On the economic and political theorist KARL MARX (1818–1883) and the founder of psychoanalysis SIGMUND FREUD (1856–1939), see above.
3. That is, the theory of special relativity developed by Albert Einstein (1879–1955), which explains what the mechanical worldview associated with Sir Isaac Newton (1642–1727) could not: the interactions of radiation and matter viewed from different inertial frames of reference.

not argumentations but enunciations, 'touches', approaches that consent to remain metaphorical. Here then are these propositions; they concern method, genres, signs, plurality, filiation, reading and pleasure.

1. The Text is not to be thought of as an object that can be computed. It would be futile to try to separate out materially works from texts. In particular, the tendency must be avoided to say that the work is classic, the text avant-garde; it is not a question of drawing up a crude honours list in the name of modernity and declaring certain literary productions 'in' and others 'out' by virtue of their chronological situation: there may be 'text' in a very ancient work, while many products of contemporary literature are in no way texts. The difference is this: the work is a fragment of substance, occupying a part of the space of books (in a library for example), the Text is a methodological field. The opposition may recall (without at all reproducing term for term) Lacan's[4] distinction between 'reality' and 'the real': the one is displayed, the other demonstrated; likewise, the work can be seen (in bookshops, in catalogues, in exam syllabuses), the text is a process of demonstration, speaks according to certain rules (or against certain rules); the work can be held in the hand, the text is held in language, only exists in the movement of a discourse (or rather, it is Text for the very reason that it knows itself as text); the Text is not the decomposition of the work, it is the work that is the imaginary tail of the Text; or again, *the Text is experienced only in an activity of production*. It follows that the Text cannot stop (for example on a library shelf); its constitutive movement is that of cutting across (in particular, it can cut across the work, several works).

2. In the same way, the Text does not stop at (good) Literature; it cannot be contained in a hierarchy, even in a simple division of genres. What constitutes the Text is, on the contrary (or precisely), its subversive force in respect of the old classifications. How do you classify a writer like Georges Bataille?[5] Novelist, poet, essayist, economist, philosopher, mystic? The answer is so difficult that the literary manuals generally prefer to forget about Bataille who, in fact, wrote texts, perhaps continuously one single text. If the Text poses problems of classification (which is furthermore one of its 'social' functions), this is because it always involves a certain experience of limits (to take up an expression from Philippe Sollers). Thibaudet[6] used already to talk—but in a very restricted sense—of limit-works (such as Chateaubriand's[7] *Vie de Rancé*, which does indeed come through to us today as a 'text'); the Text is that which goes to the limit of the rules of enunciation (rationality, readability, etc.). Nor is this a rhetorical idea, resorted to for some 'heroic' effect: the Text tries to place itself very exactly *behind* the limit of the *doxa*[8] (is not general opinion—constitutive of our democratic societies and powerfully aided by mass communications—defined by its limits, the energy with which it excludes, its *censorship*?). Taking the word literally, it may be said that the Text is always *paradoxical*.[9]

3. The Text can be approached, experienced, in reaction to the sign. The work closes on a signified.[1] There are two modes of signification which can

4. JACQUES LACAN (1901–1981), French psychoanalyst.
5. French writer (1897–1962).
6. Albert Thibaudet (1874–1936), French critic. Sollers (b. 1936), French writer.
7. François-René, vicomte de Chateaubriand (1768–1848), French writer and statesman. In 1980 a new edition of his *Life of Rancé* (1844) was published with a preface by Barthes.
8. Received opinion (Greek).
9. That is, contrary to received opinion.
1. The sign was divided into *signified* (the meaning conveyed) and *signifier* (the symbol or sound that conveys that meaning) by the Swiss linguist FERDINAND DE SAUSSURE (1857–1913).

be attributed to this signified: either it is claimed to be evident and the work is then the object of a literal science, of philology, or else it is considered to be secret, ultimate, something to be sought out, and the work then falls under the scope of a hermeneutics, of an interpretation (Marxist, psychoanalytic, thematic, etc.); in short, the work itself functions as a general sign and it is normal that it should represent an institutional category of the civilization of the Sign. The Text, on the contrary, practises the infinite deferment of the signified, is dilatory; its field is that of the signifier and the signifier must not be conceived of as 'the first stage of meaning', its material vestibule, but, in complete opposition to this, as its *deferred action*. Similarly, the *infinity* of the signifier refers not to some idea of the ineffable (the unnameable signified) but to that of a *playing*; the generation of the perpetual signifier (after the fashion of a perpetual calendar) in the field of the text (better, of which the text is the field) is realized not according to an organic progress of maturation or a hermeneutic course of deepening investigation, but, rather, according to a serial movement of disconnections, overlappings, variations. The logic regulating the Text is not comprehensive (define 'what the work means') but metonymic; the activity of associations, contiguities, carryings-over coincides with a liberation of symbolic energy (lacking it, man would die); the work—in the best of cases—is *moderately* symbolic (its symbolic runs out, comes to a halt); the Text is *radically* symbolic: *a work conceived, perceived and received in its integrally symbolic nature is a text*. Thus is the Text restored to language; like language, it is structured but off-centred, without closure (note, in reply to the contemptuous suspicion of the 'fashionable' sometimes directed at structuralism, that the epistemological privilege currently accorded to language stems precisely from the discovery there of a paradoxical idea of structure: a system with neither close nor centre).

4. The Text is plural. Which is not simply to say that it has several meanings, but that it accomplishes the very plural of meaning: an *irreducible* (and not merely an acceptable) plural. The Text is not a co-existence of meanings but a passage, an overcrossing; thus it answers not to an interpretation, even a liberal one, but to an explosion, a dissemination. The plural of the Text depends, that is, not on the ambiguity of its contents but on what might be called the *stereographic plurality* of its weave of signifiers (etymologically, the text is a tissue, a woven fabric). The reader of the Text may be compared to someone at a loose end (someone slackened off from any imaginary); this passably empty subject strolls—it is what happened to the author of these lines, then it was that he had a vivid idea of the Text—on the side of a valley, a *oued*[2] flowing down below (*oued* is there to bear witness to a certain feeling of unfamiliarity); what he perceives is multiple, irreducible, coming from a disconnected, heterogeneous variety of substances and perspectives: lights, colours, vegetation, heat, air, slender explosions of noises, scant cries of birds, children's voices from over on the other side, passages, gestures, clothes of inhabitants near or far away. All these *incidents* are half-identifiable: they come from codes which are known but their combination is unique, founds the stroll in a difference repeatable only as difference. So the Text: it can be it only in its difference (which does not mean its individuality), its reading is semelfactive[3] (this rendering illusory any inductive-deductive science of

2. Wadi (Arabic); a streambed that is usually dry, except during the rainy season.
3. A term from linguistics used to describe a verb form that expresses a single, noncontinuous, no repeating action.

texts—no 'grammar' of the text) and nevertheless woven entirely with citations, references, echoes, cultural languages (what language is not?), antecedent or contemporary, which cut across it through and through in a vast stereophony. The intertextual in which every text is held, it itself being the text-between of another text, is not to be confused with some origin of the text: to try to find the 'sources', the 'influences' of a work, is to fall in with the myth of filiation; the citations which go to make up a text are anonymous, untraceable, and yet *already read*: they are quotations without inverted commas. The work has nothing disturbing for any monistic philosophy (we know that there are opposing examples of these); for such a philosophy, plural is the Evil. Against the work, therefore, the text could well take as its motto the words of the man possessed by demons (*Mark* 5: 9): 'My name is Legion: for we are many.' The plural of demoniacal texture which opposes text to work can bring with it fundamental changes in reading, and precisely in areas where monologism appears to be the Law: certain of the 'texts' of Holy Scripture traditionally recuperated by theological monism (historical or anagogical) will perhaps offer themselves to a diffraction of meanings (finally, that is to say, to a materialist reading), while the Marxist interpretation of works, so far resolutely monistic, will be able to materialize itself more by pluralizing itself (if, however, the Marxist 'institutions' allow it).

5. The work is caught up in a process of filiation. Are postulated: a *determination* of the work by the world (by race, then by History), a *consecution* of works amongst themselves, and a *conformity* of the work to the author. The author is reputed the father and the owner of his work: literary science therefore teaches *respect* for the manuscript and the author's declared intentions, while society asserts the legality of the relation of author to work (the '*droit d'auteur*'[4] or 'copyright', in fact of recent date since it was only really legalized at the time of the French Revolution). As for the Text, it reads without the inscription of the Father. Here again, the metaphor of the Text separates from that of the work: the latter refers to the image of an *organism* which grows by vital expansion, by 'development' (a word which is significantly ambiguous, at once biological and rhetorical); the metaphor of the Text is that of the *network*; if the Text extends itself, it is as a result of a combinatory systematic (an image, moreover, close to current biological conceptions of the living being). Hence no vital 'respect' is due to the Text: it can be *broken* (which is just what the Middle Ages did with two nevertheless authoritative texts—Holy Scripture and Aristotle[5]); it can be read without the guarantee of its father, the restitution of the inter-text paradoxically abolishing any legacy. It is not that the Author may not 'come back' in the Text, in his text, but he then does so as a 'guest'. If he is a novelist, he is inscribed in the novel like one of his characters, figured in the carpet; no longer privileged, paternal, aletheological,[6] his inscription is ludic. He becomes, as it were, a paper-author: his life is no longer the origin of his fictions but a fiction contributing to his work; there is a reversion of the work on to the life (and no longer the contrary); it is the work of Proust, of Genet[7] which allows their lives to be read as a text. The word 'bio-graphy' re-acquires a strong, etymological sense,

4. Right of the author (French).

5. Greek philosopher (384–322 B.C.E.; see above), whose writings for centuries provided the main framework for Western thought.

6. A neologism—*alētheia* (Greek) = the self-presentation of Truth; *theological* = relating to the study of religious faith—meaning that the author's writing no longer operates in a theological realm of truth.

7. Jean Genet (1910–1986), French dramatist. Marcel Proust (1871–1922), French novelist.

at the same time as the sincerity of the enunciation—veritable 'cross' borne by literary morality—becomes a false problem: the *I* which writes the text, it too, is never more than a paper-*I*.

6. The work is normally the object of a consumption; no demagogy is intended here in referring to the so-called consumer culture but it has to be recognized that today it is the 'quality' of the work (which supposes finally an appreciation of 'taste') and not the operation of reading itself which can differentiate between books: structurally, there is no difference between 'cultured' reading and casual reading in trains. The Text (if only by its frequent 'unreadability') decants the work (the work permitting) from its consumption and gathers it up as play, activity, production, practice. This means that the Text requires that one try to abolish (or at the very least to diminish) the distance between writing and reading, in no way by intensifying the projection of the reader into the work but by joining them in a single signifying practice. The distance separating reading from writing is historical. In the times of the greatest social division (before the setting up of democratic cultures), reading and writing were equally privileges of class. Rhetoric, the great literary code of those times, taught one to *write* (even if what was then normally produced were speeches, not texts). Significantly, the coming of democracy reversed the word of command: what the (secondary) School prides itself on is teaching to *read* (well) and no longer to write (consciousness of the deficiency is becoming fashionable again today: the teacher is called upon to teach pupils to 'express themselves', which is a little like replacing a form of repression by a misconception). In fact, *reading*, in the sense of consuming, is far from *playing* with the text. 'Playing' must be understood here in all its polysemy: the text itself *plays* (like a door, like a machine with 'play') and the reader plays twice over, playing the Text as one plays a game, looking for a practice which re-produces it, but, in order that that practice not be reduced to a passive, inner *mimesis*[8] (the Text is precisely that which resists such a reduction), also playing the Text in the musical sense of the term. The history of music (as a practice, not as an 'art') does indeed parallel that of the Text fairly closely: there was a period when practising amateurs[9] were numerous (at least within the confines of a certain class) and 'playing' and 'listening' formed a scarcely differentiated activity; then two roles appeared in succession, first that of the performer, the interpreter to whom the bourgeois public (though still itself able to play a little—the whole history of the piano) delegated its playing, then that of the (passive) amateur, who listens to music without being able to play (the gramophone record takes the place of the piano). We know that today post-serial music[1] has radically altered the role of the 'interpreter', who is called on to be in some sort the co-author of the score, completing it rather than giving it 'expression'. The Text is very much a score of this new kind: it asks of the reader a practical collaboration. Which is an important change, for who executes the work? (Mallarmé[2] posed the question, wanting the audience to *produce* the book). Nowadays only the critic executes the work (accepting the play on words). The reduction of reading to a consumption is clearly responsible for the 'boredom' experienced by many in the face of the modern ('unreadable')

8. Representation, imitation (Greek).
9. Barthes was an avid amateur pianist.
1. Music that was a reaction against serialism, the total mathematization of all musical variables in the atonal compositions of Pierre Boulez (1925–2016) and others; in some cases the interpreter shapes a deliberately "open" work, still viewed as a network of variables.
2. Stéphane Mallarmé (1842–1898), French poet.

text, the avant-garde film or painting: to be bored means that one cannot produce the text, open it out, *set it going*.

7. This leads us to pose (to propose) a final approach to the Text, that of pleasure. I do not know whether there has ever been a hedonistic aesthetics (eudæmonist philosophies are themselves rare). Certainly there exists a pleasure of the work (of certain works); I can delight in reading and re-reading Proust, Flaubert, Balzac, even—why not?—Alexandre Dumas.[3] But this pleasure, no matter how keen and even when free from all prejudice, remains in part (unless by some exceptional critical effort) a pleasure of consumption; for if I can read these authors, I also know that I cannot *re-write* them (that it is impossible today to write 'like that') and this knowledge, depressing enough, suffices to cut me off from the production of these works, in the very moment their remoteness establishes my modernity (is not to be modern to know clearly what cannot be started over again?). As for the Text, it is bound to *jouissance*,[4] that is to a pleasure without separation. Order of the signifier, the Text participates in its own way in a social utopia; before History (supposing the latter does not opt for barbarism), the Text achieves, if not the transparence of social relations, that at least of language relations: the Text is that space where no language has a hold over any other, where languages circulate (keeping the circular sense of the term).

These few propositions, inevitably, do not constitute the articulations of a Theory of the Text and this is not simply the result of the failings of the person here presenting them (who in many respects has anyway done no more than pick up what is being developed round about him). It stems from the fact that a Theory of the Text cannot be satisfied by a metalinguistic exposition: the destruction of meta-language, or at least (since it may be necessary provisionally to resort to meta-language) its calling into doubt, is part of the theory itself: the discourse on the Text should itself be nothing other than text, research, textual activity, since the Text is that *social* space which leaves no language safe, outside, nor any subject of the enunciation in position as judge, master, analyst, confessor, decoder. The theory of the Text can coincide only with a practice of writing.

1971

3. Popular French novelist and dramatist (1802–1870). Gustave Flaubert (1821–1880) and Honoré de Balzac (1799–1850), French novelists.

4. In French, *jouissance* (the surprise of orgasm, bliss, ecstasy) is distinguished from *plaisir* (pleasure).

LOUIS ALTHUSSER
1918–1990

Louis Althusser exposed a ghost in the machine of capitalism: ideology. One of the most influential Marxist thinkers of the second half of the twentieth century, Althusser explained how capitalism perpetuated itself through "ideological state apparatuses." In Marxist thought, the concept of ideology was usually considered secondary, but Althusser placed it front and center. His landmark essay, "Ideology and Ideological State Apparatuses (Notes towards an Investigation)" (1970), our selection, analyzes how dominant social systems and institutions subtly mold human subjects through ideology, in turn reproducing the system. To traditional Marxist analysis Althusser grafted the methods of structuralism, developed by CLAUDE LÉVI-STRAUSS, and psychoanalysis, notably of JACQUES LACAN, to explain how people consented to a society in which many were oppressed.

Born in French-held Algeria, Louis Althusser was educated in Marseilles and in Lyons. In 1939 he was admitted to the prestigious École Normale Supérieure in Paris, but his academic career was delayed when he was drafted into the military during the early days of World War II. Captured in 1940 and held for five years in a German prisoner-of-war camp, he returned to the École Normale after the war, completing a master's thesis on the philosopher G. W. F. HEGEL (1770–1831) in 1948. He then joined the faculty at the school, also doing doctoral work under the supervision of the celebrated Hegelian philosopher Jean Hyppolite. His membership in the French Communist Party from 1948 on was also decisive for his future work. His relations with the Party hierarchy were never easy, and his writings were often attacked by official Communist philosophers—he was almost expelled in 1966 in a dispute over China's Cultural Revolution—but Althusser remained a lifelong member.

Publishing little beforehand, Althusser burst onto the intellectual world in the turbulent 1960s with a series of important texts, gathered in *For Marx* (1965; trans. 1969) and *Reading Capital* (coauthored with his student Étienne Balibar, 1968; trans. 1970). Both quickly captured the attention of French and later British intellectuals, changing the face of Western Marxist theory by shattering the pieties of Stalinist dogmatism and the newer Marxist humanism, which, influenced by Hegel and the twentieth-century philosophers GYÖRGY LUKÁCS and Jean-Paul Sartre, saw Marxism as an effort to recover an alienated humanity. Elevating the individual as its center of concern, humanism generally stresses human freedom and self-determination; in contrast, many structuralist thinkers argue that freedom of thought and action is limited by linguistic, psychological, or socioeconomic systems. Propounding an "antihumanism," Althusser emphasizes how societal structures determine lived experience. His critique of humanism continues to help shape postmodern and poststructuralist theory.

Following KARL MARX and FRIEDRICH ENGELS's central claim in *The Communist Manifesto* (1848; see above) that "the history of all hitherto existing society is the history of class struggles," Althusser held that the task of the philosopher was to "represent the class struggle in theory," taking the side of the oppressed in ongoing ideological struggles with representatives of the ruling class. His injunction inspired the participants in the May 1968 student and worker uprising in France; but Althusser himself was absent during the turbulent events of May, recuperating in a sanatorium from a recurrence of the clinical depression that had plagued him following his experiences in World War II. After recovering he embarked on an ambitious new theoretical project addressing two questions: how a society achieves stability over time by reproducing its dominant relations of production and what conditions make social revolution possible. "Ideology and Ideological State Apparatuses" stems from this larger project, which was never completed. Althusser would continue to teach and to write throughout the 1970s, but his illness worsened, and in 1980 he murdered his wife in a manic fit of rage. Declared mentally incompetent, he was sentenced to house arrest under psychiatric care and isolated from all but a few friends. At the time of his death a decade later, Althusser's reputation had reached a low point.

Althusser's major concepts—"ideological state apparatuses," "interpellation," "imaginary relations," and "overdetermination"—permeate the discourse of contemporary literary and cultural theory, and his theory of ideology has influenced virtually all subsequent serious work on the topic. The problem that Althusser sets out to solve in "Ideology and Ideological State Apparatuses"—to determine how a society reproduces its basic social relations, thereby ensuring its continuing existence—is a perennial one in social theory, raised as early as PLATO's *Republic* (ca. 373 B.C.E.). Plato thought that the key to sustaining a just state was controlling the education of its citizens, particularly its ruling class. Althusser concurs, while emphasizing that the dominant values in a society are for the most part endorsed by the majority of its members. Winning their endorsement is the work of ideology, and Althusser employs a structuralist account of the societal mechanisms that inculcate such consent, as well as a psychoanalytic account of how ideology makes individuals "subjects" of the dominant social order. Contrary to its colloquial sense, which suggests a set of ideas or beliefs that one chooses to espouse or reject, ideology for Althusser is not voluntary but the result of structural factors in society; he thus dispenses with the standard humanist notion of free will.

Althusser famously terms the societal mechanisms for creating pliant, obedient citizens who practice dominant values "ideological state apparatuses" (ISAs). Complex, numerous, and differing from one society to another, they are civil institutions that have legal standing (hence their designation as "state" apparatuses), including churches, schools, the family, courts, political parties, unions, the media, sports, and the arts. ISAs differ from "repressive state apparatuses" (RSAs), such as the police, the military, the prison system, and government, in several key ways: they are not unified, they operate primarily in the private sphere, and they attain their power not by means of explicit coercion or force but through implicit consent realized in accepted "practices." One tacitly learns the practice of obedience to authority, for example, in church, in school, at home, or on sports teams. As Althusser notes, a dominant social order would not survive if it relied only on force, and he traces the rising influence of schools as the dominant ISA in modern society. Schools have supplanted the church in this role, instilling in students the habits that will make them productive workers in modern capitalist societies, so that they show up at the factory or office day after day without question.

Althusser's theory revises the standard Marxist definition of ideology as "false consciousness," the explanation of why people willingly participate in the capitalist exploitation seen to undergird modern society. Many Marxists argue that we simply misunderstand what is really going on: believing that the economic system is fair and offers equal opportunity, rather than favoring those who control the means of production and capital, we identify with and emulate the owners and capitalists. Althusser retains the classical Marxist stress on economic causes, which he says are decisive "in the last instance," but his concept of the ISAs presents a fuller explanation of the diverse societal processes of ideology. It also allows for more complexity: ISAs operate with "relative autonomy," sometimes for different and contradictory ends (they are "overdetermined"). His theory thus has affinities with the thought a generation earlier of the Italian Marxist ANTONIO GRAMSCI, whose concept of hegemony explains the flexibility of social dominance and its operation through cultural institutions.

Althusser defines ideology as "the imaginary relationship of individuals to their real conditions of existence." It is here that he turns to a subtle psychoanalytic account, adopting Jacques Lacan's concepts of the imaginary, mirroring, and subject formation. Revising SIGMUND FREUD's concepts of the unconscious, ego, and superego, Lacan posits a three-part structure—the Imaginary, the Real, and the Symbolic—that forms the individual subject. The Imaginary constitutes the preverbal realm in which human beings exist from earliest years; it is not a false but a primordial structure of consciousness. For Althusser, ideology substitutes for the Imaginary, which one is "born into" and which, like the Freudian unconscious, deeply influences how one acts. But unlike Lacan, he sees an individual's subjectivity as generated through social forces. Using Lacan's ideas of mirroring and recognition, Althusser describes how ISAs "interpellate or hail individuals as subjects." A pivotal stage in character development for Lacan is "the mirror stage," when an infant recognizes him- or herself in a mirror. For Althusser, ideology works through our tacit recognition of being hailed, as when we turn around to answer the call, "Hey, you there!"

Provoking sharp reaction as well as a devoted following, Althusser's work has had wide-ranging influence. Some have found his reliance on a structural account of society too deterministic; others, most notably E. P. Thompson, the English historian usually considered a founding father of cultural studies, have criticized his lack of attention to empirical history. Despite Thompson's disavowal, Althusser's concept of ideology has been crucial to cultural studies, as recounted in STUART HALL's "Cultural Studies and Its Theoretical Legacies" (1992; see below) and as evidenced in DICK HEBDIGE's *Subculture: The Meaning of Style* (1979; see below). Althusser's concept of ideology has also been foundational for the leading contemporary Marxist literary critics in Britain and in America, TERRY EAGLETON and FREDRIC JAMESON. Eagleton's *Criticism and Ideology* (1976), for instance, draws heavily on Althusser, though focusing on how art produces ideology rather than how ideology informs art. Jameson's *The Political Unconscious: Narrative as a Socially Symbolic Act* (1981; see below), perhaps the most sustained consideration of the ideological implications of the modern novel, both elaborates on and critiques Althusser. Less faithfully, the French sociologist PIERRE BOURDIEU shows the influence of Althusser in his focus on education and its formative effect in producing social "distinction" and creating "cultural capital"; Bourdieu swerves, however, from traditional Marxist analyses by stressing the cultural over the economic. Although the breadth of his influence has dissipated some of the Marxist political charge of his social criticism, Althusser's theory of ideology remains a touchstone in contemporary criticism.

"Ideology and Ideological State Apparatuses" Keywords: Hegemony, Ideology, Marxism, Structuralism, Subjectivity

From Ideology and Ideological State Apparatuses (Notes towards an Investigation)[1]

From *On the Reproduction of the Conditions of Production*

* * *

As Marx said, every child knows that a social formation which did not reproduce the conditions of production at the same time as it produced would not last a year.[2] The ultimate condition of production is therefore the reproduction of the conditions of production. This may be 'simple' (reproducing exactly the previous conditions of production) or 'on an extended scale' (expanding them). Let us ignore this last distinction for the moment.

What, then, is *the reproduction of the conditions of production?*

* * *

To simplify my exposition, and assuming that every social formation arises from a dominant mode of production,[3] I can say that the process of production sets to work the existing productive forces in and under definite relations of production.

1. Translated by Ben Brewster, who sometimes retains the French word or phrase in parentheses. Some of the author's notes have been edited, and some omitted.
2. Marx to Kugelmann, July 11, 1868, *Selected Correspondence* (Moscow, 1955), p. 209 [Althusser's note]. KARL MARX (1818–1883), German social, economic, and political theorist.
3. Now capitalism, which superseded the feudal mode of production of the medieval period, and which will be supplanted, according to Marx, by socialism.

It follows that, in order to exist, every social formation must reproduce the conditions of its production at the same time as it produces, and in order to be able to produce. It must therefore reproduce:

1. the productive forces,
2. the existing relations of production.

* * *

REPRODUCTION OF LABOUR-POWER

* * *

How is the reproduction of labour power ensured?

It is ensured by giving labour power the material means with which to reproduce itself: by wages. Wages feature in the accounting of each enterprise, but as 'wage capital', not at all as a condition of the material reproduction of labour power.

However, that is in fact how it 'works', since wages represent only that part of the value produced by the expenditure of labour power which is indispensable for its reproduction: sc.[4] indispensable to the reconstitution of the labour power of the wage-earner (the wherewithal to pay for housing, food and clothing, in short to enable the wage-earner to present himself again at the factory gate the next day—and every further day God grants him); and we should add: indispensable for raising and educating the children in whom the proletarian reproduces himself (in n models where n = 0, 1, 2, etc. . . .) as labour power.

Remember that this quantity of value (wages) necessary for the reproduction of labour power is determined not by the needs of a 'biological' Guaranteed Minimum Wage (*Salaire Minimum Interprofessionnel Garanti*) alone, but by the needs of a historical minimum (Marx noted that English workers need beer while French proletarians need wine)—i.e. a historically variable minimum.

I should also like to point out that this minimum is doubly historical in that it is not defined by the historical needs of the working class 'recognized' by the capitalist class, but by the historical needs imposed by the proletarian class struggle (a double class struggle: against the lengthening of the working day and against the reduction of wages).

However, it is not enough to ensure for labour power the material conditions of its reproduction if it is to be reproduced as labour power. I have said that the available labour power must be 'competent', i.e. suitable to be set to work in the complex system of the process of production. The development of the productive forces and the type of unity historically constitutive of the productive forces at a given moment produce the result that the labour power has to be (diversely) skilled and therefore reproduced as such. Diversely: according to the requirements of the socio-technical division of labour, its different 'jobs' and 'posts'.

How is this reproduction of the (diversified) skills of labour power provided for in a capitalist regime? Here, unlike social formations characterized by slavery or serfdom, this reproduction of the skills of labour power tends (this is a tendential law) decreasingly to be provided for 'on the spot' (apprenticeship

4. Scilicet; namely.

within production itself), but is achieved more and more outside production: by the capitalist education system, and by other instances and institutions.

What do children learn at school? They go varying distances in their studies, but at any rate they learn to read, to write and to add—i.e. a number of techniques, and a number of other things as well, including elements (which may be rudimentary or on the contrary thoroughgoing) of 'scientific' or 'literary culture', which are directly useful in the different jobs in production (one instruction for manual workers, another for technicians, a third for engineers, a final one for higher management, etc.). Thus they learn 'know-how'.

But besides these techniques and knowledges, and in learning them, children at school also learn the 'rules' of good behaviour, i.e. the attitude that should be observed by every agent in the division of labour, according to the job he is 'destined' for: rules of morality, civic and professional conscience, which actually means rules of respect for the socio-technical division of labour and ultimately the rules of the order established by class domination. They also learn to 'speak proper French', to 'handle' the workers correctly, i.e. actually (for the future capitalists and their servants) to 'order them about' properly, i.e. (ideally) to 'speak to them' in the right way, etc.

To put this more scientifically, I shall say that the reproduction of labour power requires not only a reproduction of its skills, but also, at the same time, a reproduction of its submission to the rules of the established order, i.e. a reproduction of submission to the ruling ideology for the workers, and a reproduction of the ability to manipulate the ruling ideology correctly for the agents of exploitation and repression, so that they, too, will provide for the domination of the ruling class 'in words'.

In other words, the school (but also other State institutions like the Church, or other apparatuses like the Army) teaches 'know-how', but in forms which ensure *subjection to the ruling ideology* or the mastery of its 'practice'. All the agents of production, exploitation and repression, not to speak of the 'professionals of ideology' (Marx), must in one way or another be 'steeped' in this ideology in order to perform their tasks 'conscientiously'—the tasks of the exploited (the proletarians), of the exploiters (the capitalists), of the exploiters' auxiliaries (the managers), or of the high priests of the ruling ideology (its 'functionaries'), etc.

The reproduction of labour power thus reveals as its *sine qua non* not only the reproduction of its 'skills' but also the reproduction of its subjection to the ruling ideology or of the 'practice' of that ideology, with the proviso that it is not enough to say 'not only but also', for it is clear that *it is in the forms and under the forms of ideological subjection that provision is made for the reproduction of the skills of labour power.*

But this is to recognize the effective presence of a new reality: *ideology*.

* * *

From *Infrastructure and Superstructure*

On a number of occasions I have insisted on the revolutionary character of the Marxist conception of the 'social whole' insofar as it is distinct from the Hegelian[5] 'totality'. I said (and this thesis only repeats famous propositions of historical materialism) that Marx conceived the structure of every society as

5. Of GEORG FRIEDRICH WILHELM HEGEL (1770–1831), German idealist philosopher.

constituted by 'levels' or 'instances' articulated by a specific determination: the *infrastructure*, or economic base (the 'unity' of the productive forces and the relations of production) and the *superstructure*, which itself contains two 'levels' or 'instances': the politico-legal (law and the State) and ideology (the different ideologies, religious, ethical, legal, political, etc.).

Besides its theoretico-didactic interest (it reveals the difference between Marx and Hegel), this representation has the following crucial theoretical advantage: it makes it possible to inscribe in the theoretical apparatus of its essential concepts what I have called their *respective indices of effectivity*. What does this mean?

It is easy to see that this representation of the structure of every society as an edifice containing a base (infrastructure) on which are erected the two 'floors' of the superstructure, is a metaphor, to be quite precise, a spatial metaphor: the metaphor of a topography (*topique*).[6] Like every metaphor, this metaphor suggests something, makes something visible. What? Precisely this: that the upper floors could not 'stay up' (in the air) alone, if they did not rest precisely on their base.

Thus the object of the metaphor of the edifice is to represent above all the 'determination in the last instance' by the economic base. The effect of this spatial metaphor is to endow the base with an index of effectivity known by the famous terms: the determination in the last instance of what happens in the upper 'floors' (of the superstructure) by what happens in the economic base.

Given this index of effectivity 'in the last instance', the 'floors' of the superstructure are clearly endowed with different indices of effectivity. What kind of indices?

It is possible to say that the floors of the superstructure are not determinant in the last instance, but that they are determined by the effectivity of the base; that if they are determinant in their own (as yet undefined) ways, this is true only insofar as they are determined by the base.

Their index of effectivity (or determination), as determined by the determination in the last instance of the base, is thought by the Marxist tradition in two ways: (1) there is a 'relative autonomy' of the superstructure with respect to the base; (2) there is a 'reciprocal action' of the superstructure on the base.

We can therefore say that the great theoretical advantage of the Marxist topography, i.e. of the spatial metaphor of the edifice (base and superstructure) is simultaneously that it reveals that questions of determination (or of index of effectivity) are crucial; that it reveals that it is the base which in the last instance determines the whole edifice; and that, as a consequence, it obliges us to pose the theoretical problem of the types of 'derivatory' effectivity peculiar to the superstructure, i.e. it obliges us to think what the Marxist tradition calls conjointly the relative autonomy of the superstructure and the reciprocal action of the superstructure on the base.

* * *

I shall give a short analysis of Law, the State and Ideology *from this point of view*. And I shall reveal what happens both from the point of view of practice and production on the one hand, and from that of reproduction on the other.

6. *Topography* from the Greek *topos*: place. A topography represents in a definite space the respective *sites* occupied by several realities: thus the economic is *at the bottom* (the base), the superstructure *above it* [Althusser's note].

From *The State*

The Marxist tradition is strict, here: in the *Communist Manifesto* and the *Eighteenth Brumaire* (and in all the later classical texts, above all in Marx's writings on the Paris Commune and Lenin's[7] on *State and Revolution*), the State is explicitly conceived as a repressive apparatus. The State is a 'machine' of repression, which enables the ruling classes (in the nineteenth century the bourgeois class and the 'class' of big landowners) to ensure their domination over the working class, thus enabling the former to subject the latter to the process of surplus-value extortion (i.e. to capitalist exploitation).

The State is thus first of all what the Marxist classics have called *the State apparatus*. This term means: not only the specialized apparatus (in the narrow sense) whose existence and necessity I have recognized in relation to the requirements of legal practice, i.e. the police, the courts, the prisons; but also the army, which (the proletariat has paid for this experience with its blood) intervenes directly as a supplementary repressive force in the last instance, when the police and its specialized auxiliary corps are 'outrun by events'; and above this ensemble, the head of State, the government and the administration.

Presented in this form, the Marxist-Leninist 'theory' of the State has its finger on the essential point, and not for one moment can there be any question of rejecting the fact that this really is the essential point. The State apparatus, which defines the State as a force of repressive execution and intervention 'in the interests of the ruling classes' in the class struggle conducted by the bourgeoisie and its allies against the proletariat, is quite certainly the State, and quite certainly defines its basic 'function'.

* * *

THE ESSENTIALS OF THE MARXIST THEORY OF THE STATE

Let me first clarify one important point: the State (and its existence in its apparatus) has no meaning except as a function of *State power*. The whole of the political class struggle revolves around the State. By which I mean around the possession, i.e. the seizure and conservation of State power by a certain class or by an alliance between classes or class fractions. This first clarification obliges me to distinguish between State power (conservation of State power or seizure of State power), the objective of the political class struggle on the one hand, and the State apparatus on the other.

We know that the State apparatus may survive, as is proved by bourgeois 'revolutions' in nineteenth-century France (1830, 1848), by *coups d'état* (2 December, May 1958), by collapses of the State (the fall of the Empire in 1870, of the Third Republic in 1940), or by the political rise of the petty bourgeoisie (1890–95 in France), etc., without the State apparatus being affected or modified:[8] it may survive political events which affect the possession of State power.

7. V. I. Lenin (1870–1924), leader of the Russian Revolution of 1917 and author of many works on revolutionary politics, including *The State and Revolution: The Marxist Theory of the State and the Tasks of the Proletariat in the Revolution* (1917). Marx's famous *Communist Manifesto* (cowritten with FRIEDRICH ENGELS) dates from 1848, and his *Eighteenth Brumaire of Louis Bonaparte* from 1852. The latter, along with his *Class Stuggles in France, 1848–1850* (1850) and *The Civil War in France* (1871), deals with political struggles in France; the Paris Commune was a revolutionary government briefly established in Paris in the spring of 1871.

8. After the French Revolution (1789–99) and through the 19th century, France became a modern bureaucratic state dominated by the bourgeoisie (rather than a feudal aristocracy). Althusser refers to the overthrow of the restored Bourbon monarchy in 1830; the "February Revolution" of

Even after a social revolution like that of 1917,[9] a large part of the State apparatus survived after the seizure of State power by the alliance of the proletariat and the small peasantry: Lenin repeated the fact again and again.

It is possible to describe the distinction between State power and State apparatus as part of the 'Marxist theory' of the State, explicitly present since Marx's *Eighteenth Brumaire* and *Class Struggles in France*.

To summarize the 'Marxist theory of the State' on this point, it can be said that the Marxist classics have always claimed that (1) the State is the repressive State apparatus, (2) State power and State apparatus must be distinguished, (3) the objective of the class struggle concerns State power, and in consequence the use of the State apparatus by the classes (or alliance of classes or of fractions of classes) holding State power as a function of their class objectives, and (4) the proletariat must seize State power in order to destroy the existing bourgeois State apparatus and, in a first phase, replace it with a quite different, proletarian, State apparatus, then in later phases set in motion a radical process, that of the destruction of the State (the end of State power, the end of every State apparatus).

In this perspective, therefore, what I would propose to add to the 'Marxist theory' of the State is already there in so many words. But it seems to me that even with this supplement, this theory is still in part descriptive, although it does now contain complex and differential elements whose functioning and action cannot be understood without recourse to further supplementary theoretical development.

THE STATE IDEOLOGICAL APPARATUSES

* * *

In order to advance the theory of the State it is indispensable to take into account not only the distinction between *State power* and *State apparatus*, but also another reality which is clearly on the side of the (repressive) State apparatus, but must not be confused with it. I shall call this reality by its concept: *the ideological State apparatuses.*[1]

What are the ideological State apparatuses (ISAs)?

They must not be confused with the (repressive) State apparatus. Remember that in Marxist theory, the State Apparatus (SA) contains: the Government, the Administration, the Army, the Police, the Courts, the Prisons, etc., which constitute what I shall in future call the Repressive State Apparatus. Repressive suggests that the State Apparatus in question

1848 after which Napoleon III became president and in 1852 emperor, establishing the Second Empire, which fell in 1870; and the Paris Commune and the establishment of the Third Republic, which ended with the German Occupation of France in 1940. In 1958, during a political crisis caused by France's colonial war in Algeria, Charles de Gaulle (1890–1970), the leader of the French Resistance during World War II, became Prime Minister with broad powers and then president (1959–69) of the Fifth Republic.

9. That is, in Russia.

1. To my knowledge, Gramsci is the only one who went any distance in the road I am taking. He had the "remarkable" idea that the State could not be reduced to the (Repressive) State Apparatus, but included, as he put it, a certain number of institutions from "*civil society*": the Church, the Schools, the trade unions, etc. Unfortunately, Gramsci did not systematize his institutions, which remained in the state of acute but fragmentary notes (cf. Gramsci, *Selections from the Prison Notebooks* [International Publishers, 1971], pp. 12, 259, 260–63) [Althusser's note]. ANTONIO GRAMSCI (1891–1937), Italian Marxist philosopher.

'functions by violence'—at least ultimately (since repression, e.g. administrative repression, may take non-physical forms).

I shall call Ideological State Apparatuses a certain number of realities which present themselves to the immediate observer in the form of distinct and specialized institutions. I propose an empirical list of these which will obviously have to be examined in detail, tested, corrected and reorganized. With all the reservations implied by this requirement, we can for the moment regard the following institutions as Ideological State Apparatuses (the order in which I have listed them has no particular significance):

—the religious ISA (the system of the different Churches),
—the educational ISA (the system of the different public and private 'Schools'),
—the family ISA,[2]
—the legal ISA,[3]
—the political ISA (the political system, including the different Parties),
—the trade-union ISA,
—the communications ISA (press, radio and television, etc.),
—the cultural ISA (Literature, the Arts, sports, etc.).

I have said that the ISAs must not be confused with the (Repressive) State Apparatus. What constitutes the difference?

As a first moment, it is clear that while there is *one* (Repressive) State Apparatus, there is a *plurality* of Ideological State Apparatuses. Even presupposing that it exists, the unity that constitutes this plurality of ISAs as a body is not immediately visible.

As a second moment, it is clear that whereas the—unified—(Repressive) State Apparatus belongs entirely to the *public* domain, much the larger part of the Ideological State Apparatuses (in their apparent dispersion) are part, on the contrary, of the *private* domain. Churches, Parties, Trade Unions, families, some schools, most newspapers, cultural ventures, etc., etc., are private.

We can ignore the first observation for the moment. But someone is bound to question the second, asking me by what right I regard as Ideological *State* Apparatuses, institutions which for the most part do not possess public status, but are quite simply *private* institutions. As a conscious Marxist, Gramsci already forestalled this objection in one sentence. The distinction between the public and the private is a distinction internal to bourgeois law, and valid in the (subordinate) domains in which bourgeois law exercises its 'authority'. The domain of the State escapes it because the latter is 'above the law': the State, which is the State *of* the ruling class, is neither public nor private; on the contrary, it is the precondition for any distinction between public and private. The same thing can be said from the starting-point of our State Ideological Apparatuses. It is unimportant whether the institutions in which they are realized are 'public' or 'private'. What matters is how they function. Private institutions can perfectly well 'function' as Ideological State Apparatuses. A reasonably thorough analysis of any one of the ISAs proves it.

2. The family obviously has other "functions" than that of an ISA. It intervenes in the reproduction of labour power. In different modes of production it is the unit of production and/or the unit of consumption [Althusser's note].

3. The "Law" belongs both to the (Repressive) State Apparatus and to the system of the ISAs [Althusser's note].

But now for what is essential. What distinguishes the ISAs from the (Repressive) State Apparatus is the following basic difference: the Repressive State Apparatus functions 'by violence', whereas the Ideological State Apparatuses *function 'by ideology'*.

I can clarify matters by correcting this distinction. I shall say rather that every State Apparatus, whether Repressive or Ideological, 'functions' both by violence and ideology, but with one very important distinction which makes it imperative not to confuse the Ideological State Apparatus with the (Repressive) State Apparatus.

This is the fact that the (Repressive) State Apparatus functions massively and predominantly *by repression* (including physical repression), while functioning secondarily by ideology. (There is no such thing as a purely repressive apparatus.) For example, the Army and the Police also function by ideology both to ensure their own cohesion and reproduction, and in the 'values' they propound externally.

In the same way, but inversely, it is essential to say that for their part the Ideological State Apparatuses function massively and predominantly *by ideology*, but they also function secondarily by repression, even if ultimately, but only ultimately, this is very attenuated and concealed, even symbolic. (There is no such thing as a purely ideological apparatus.) Thus Schools and Churches use suitable methods of punishment, expulsion, selection, etc., to 'discipline' not only their shepherds, but also their flocks. The same is true of the Family. . . . The same is true of the cultural IS Apparatus (censorship, among other things), etc.

Is it necessary to add that this determination of the double 'functioning' (predominantly, secondarily) by repression and by ideology, according to whether it is a matter of the (Repressive) State Apparatus or the Ideological State Apparatus, makes it clear that very subtle explicit or tacit combinations may be woven from the interplay of the (Repressive) State Apparatus and the Ideological State Apparatuses? Everyday life provides us with innumerable examples of this, but they must be studied in detail if we are to go further than this mere observation.

Nevertheless, this remark leads us towards an understanding of what constitutes the unity of the apparently disparate body of the ISAs. If the ISAs 'function' massively and predominantly by ideology, what unifies their diversity is precisely this functioning, insofar as the ideology by which they function is always in fact unified, despite its diversity and its contradictions, *beneath the ruling ideology*, which is the ideology of 'the ruling class'. Given the fact that the 'ruling class' in principle holds State power (openly or more often by means of alliances between classes or class fractions), and therefore has at its disposal the (Repressive) State Apparatus, we can accept the fact that this same ruling class is active in the Ideological State Apparatuses insofar as it is ultimately the ruling ideology which is realized in the Ideological State Apparatuses, precisely in its contradictions. Of course, it is a quite different thing to act by laws and decrees in the (Repressive) State Apparatus and to 'act' through the intermediary of the ruling ideology in the Ideological State Apparatuses. We must go into the details of this difference—but it cannot mask the reality of a profound identity. To my knowledge, *no class can hold State power over a long period without at the same time exercising its hegemony over and in the State Ideological Appara-*

tuses. I only need one example and proof of this: Lenin's anguished concern to revolutionize the educational Ideological State Apparatus (among others), simply to make it possible for the Soviet proletariat, who had seized State power, to secure the future of the dictatorship of the proletariat and the transition of socialism.

This last comment puts us in a position to understand that the Ideological State Apparatuses may be not only the *stake*, but also the *site* of class struggle, and often of bitter forms of class struggle. The class (or class alliance) in power cannot lay down the law in the ISAs as easily as it can in the (repressive) State apparatus, not only because the former ruling classes are able to retain strong positions there for a long time, but also because the resistance of the exploited classes is able to find means and occasions to express itself there, either by the utilization of their contradictions, or by conquering combat positions in them in struggle.[4]

* * *

From *On the Reproduction of the Relations of Production*

I can now answer the central question which I have left in suspense for many long pages: *how is the reproduction of the relations of production secured?*

In the topographical language (Infrastructure, Superstructure), I can say: for the most part, it is secured by the legal-political and ideological superstructure.

But as I have argued that it is essential to go beyond this still descriptive language, I shall say: for the most part, it is secured by the exercise of State power in the State Apparatuses, on the one hand the (Repressive) State Apparatus, on the other the Ideological State Apparatuses.

What I have just said must also be taken into account, and it can be assembled in the form of the following three features:

1. All the State Apparatuses function both by repression and by ideology, with the difference that the (Repressive) State Apparatus functions massively and predominantly by repression, whereas the Ideological State Apparatuses function massively and predominantly by ideology.

2. Whereas the (Repressive) State Apparatus constitutes an organized whole whose different parts are centralized beneath a commanding unity, that of the politics of class struggle applied by the political representatives of the ruling classes in possession of State power, the Ideological State Apparatuses are multiple, distinct, 'relatively autonomous' and capable of providing an objective field to contradictions which express, in forms which

4. What I have said in these few brief words about the class struggle in the ISAs is obviously far from exhausting the question of the class struggle.

To approach this question, two principles must be borne in mind:

The first principle was formulated by Marx in the preface to *A Contribution to the Critique of Political Economy* [1859]: "In considering such transformations [a social revolution] a distinction should always be made between the material transformation of the economic conditions of production, which can be determined with the precision of natural science, and the legal, political, religious, aesthetic or philosophic—in short, ideological forms in which men become conscious of this conflict and fight it out." The class struggle is thus expressed and exercised in ideological forms, thus also in the ideological forms of the ISAs. But the class struggle *extends far beyond* these forms, and it is because it extends beyond them that the struggle of the exploited classes may also be exercised in the forms of the ISAs, and thus turn the weapon of ideology against the classes in power.

This is by virtue of the *second principle*: the class struggle extends beyond the ISAs because it is rooted elsewhere than in ideology, in the Infrastructure, in the relations of production, which are relations of exploitation and constitute the base for class relations [Althusser's note].

may be limited or extreme, the effects of the clashes between the capitalist class struggle and the proletarian class struggle, as well as their subordinate forms.

3. Whereas the unity of the (Repressive) State Apparatus is secured by its unified and centralized organization under the leadership of the representatives of the classes in power executing the politics of the class struggle of the classes in power, the unity of the different Ideological State Apparatuses is secured, usually in contradictory forms, by the ruling ideology, the ideology of the ruling class.

Taking these features into account, it is possible to represent the reproduction of the relations of production in the following way, according to a kind of 'division of labour'.

The role of the repressive State apparatus, insofar as it is a repressive apparatus, consists essentially in securing by force (physical or otherwise) the political conditions of the reproduction of relations of production which are in the last resort *relations of exploitation*. Not only does the State apparatus contribute generously to its own reproduction (the capitalist State contains political dynasties, military dynasties, etc.), but also and above all, the State apparatus secures by repression (from the most brutal physical force, via mere administrative commands and interdictions, to open and tacit censorship) the political conditions for the action of the Ideological State Apparatuses.

In fact, it is the latter which largely secure the reproduction specifically of the relations of production, behind a 'shield' provided by the repressive State apparatus. It is here that the role of the ruling ideology is heavily concentrated, the ideology of the ruling class, which holds State power. It is the intermediation of the ruling ideology that ensures a (sometimes teeth-gritting) 'harmony' between the repressive State apparatus and the Ideological State Apparatuses, and between the different State Ideological Apparatuses.

We are thus led to envisage the following hypothesis, as a function precisely of the diversity of ideological State Apparatuses in their single, because shared, role of the reproduction of the relations of production.

Indeed we have listed a relatively large number of ideological State apparatuses in contemporary capitalist social formations: the educational apparatus, the religious apparatus, the family apparatus, the political apparatus, the trade-union apparatus, the communications apparatus, the 'cultural' apparatus, etc.

But in the social formations of that mode of production characterized by 'serfdom' (usually called the feudal mode of production), we observe that although there is a single repressive State apparatus which, since the earliest known Ancient States, let alone the Absolute Monarchies, has been formally very similar to the one we know today, the number of Ideological State Apparatuses is smaller and their individual types are different. For example, we observe that during the Middle Ages, the Church (the religious ideological State apparatus) accumulated a number of functions which have today devolved on to several distinct ideological State apparatuses, new ones in relation to the past I am invoking, in particular educational and cultural functions. Alongside the Church there was the family Ideological State Apparatus, which played a considerable part, incommensurable with its role in capitalist social formations. Despite appearances, the Church and the Family were not the only Ideological State Apparatuses. There was also a political Ideological State Apparatus (the Estates General, the *Parlement*, the different political factions and Leagues, the ancestors of the modern political parties, and the whole political system of the free Communes and then of the *Villes*[5]). There was also a powerful 'proto-trade-union' Ideological State Apparatus, if I may venture such an anachronistic term (the powerful merchants' and bankers' guilds and the journeymen's associations, etc.). Publishing and Communications, even, saw an indisputable development, as did the theatre; initially both were integral parts of the Church, then they became more and more independent of it.

In the pre-capitalist historical period which I have examined extremely broadly, it is absolutely clear that *there was one dominant Ideological State Apparatus, the Church*, which concentrated within it not only religious functions, but also educational ones, and a large proportion of the functions of communications and 'culture'. It is no accident that all ideological struggle, from the sixteenth to the eighteenth century, starting with the first shocks of the Reformation, was *concentrated* in an anti-clerical and anti-religious struggle; rather this is a function precisely of the dominant position of the religious ideological State apparatus.

The foremost objective and achievement of the French Revolution was not just to transfer State power from the feudal aristocracy to the merchant-capitalist bourgeoisie, to break part of the former repressive State apparatus and replace it with a new one (e.g., the national popular Army)—but also to attack the number-one Ideological State Apparatus: the Church. Hence the civil constitution of the clergy, the confiscation of ecclesiastical wealth, and the creation of new ideological State apparatuses to replace the religious ideological State apparatus in its dominant role.

* * *

I believe that the ideological State apparatus which has been installed in the *dominant* position in mature capitalist social formations as a result of a violent political and ideological class struggle against the old dominant ideological State apparatus, is the *educational ideological apparatus*.

* * *

Why is the educational apparatus in fact the dominant ideological State apparatus in capitalist social formations, and how does it function?

For the moment it must suffice to say:

1. All ideological State apparatuses, whatever they are, contribute to the same result: the reproduction of the relations of production, i.e. of capitalist relations of exploitation.

2. Each of them contributes towards this single result in the way proper to it. The political apparatus by subjecting individuals to the political State ideology, the 'indirect' (parliamentary) or 'direct' (plebiscitary or fascist)

5. The *Villes*: a system instituted under Napoleon in 1799 that divided the country into districts administered by a central government. The Estates General: the three groups holding distinct political powers in France: the clergy, nobility, and commoners. When convened by Louis XVI to stave off social unrest in 1789, they instead created their own assembly, the *Parlement*, which was overthrown in 1792 during the French Revolution and replaced briefly by a radical commune.

'democratic' ideology. The communications apparatus by cramming every 'citizen' with daily doses of nationalism, chauvinism, liberalism, moralism, etc., by means of the press, the radio and television. The same goes for the cultural apparatus (the role of sport in chauvinism is of the first importance), etc. The religious apparatus by recalling in sermons and the other great ceremonies of Birth, Marriage and Death, that man is only ashes, unless he loves his neighbour to the extent of turning the other cheek to whoever strikes first. The family apparatus . . . but there is no need to go on.

3. This concert is dominated by a single score, occasionally disturbed by contradictions (those of the remnants of former ruling classes, those of the proletarians and their organizations): the score of the Ideology of the current ruling class which integrates into its music the great themes of the Humanism of the Great Forefathers,[6] who produced the Greek Miracle even before Christianity, and afterwards the Glory of Rome, the Eternal City, and the themes of Interest, particular and general, etc. nationalism, moralism and economism.

4. Nevertheless, in this concert, one ideological State apparatus certainly has the dominant role, although hardly anyone lends an ear to its music: it is so silent! This is the School.

It takes children from every class at infant-school age, and then for years, the years in which the child is most 'vulnerable', squeezed between the family State apparatus and the educational State apparatus, it drums into them, whether it uses new or old methods, a certain amount of 'know-how' wrapped in the ruling ideology (French, arithmetic, natural history, the sciences, literature) or simply the ruling ideology in its pure state (ethics, civic instruction, philosophy). Somewhere around the age of sixteen, a huge mass of children are ejected 'into production': these are the workers or small peasants. Another portion of scholastically adapted youth carries on: and, for better or worse, it goes somewhat further, until it falls by the wayside and fills the posts of small and middle technicians, white-collar workers, small and middle executives, petty bourgeois of all kinds. A last portion reaches the summit, either to fall into intellectual semi-employment, or to provide, as well as the 'intellectuals of the collective labourer', the agents of exploitation (capitalists, managers), the agents of repression (soldiers, policemen, politicians, administrators, etc.) and the professional ideologists (priests of all sorts, most of whom are convinced 'laymen').

Each mass ejected *en route* is practically provided with the ideology which suits the role it has to fulfil in class society: the role of the exploited (with a 'highly-developed' 'professional', 'ethical', 'civic', 'national' and a-political consciousness); the role of the agent of exploitation (ability to give the workers orders and speak to them: 'human relations'), of the agent of repression (ability to give orders and enforce obedience 'without discussion', or ability to manipulate the demagogy of a political leader's rhetoric), or of the professional ideologist (ability to treat consciousnesses with the respect, i.e. with the contempt, blackmail, and demagogy they deserve, adapted to the

6. That is, privileging the concept of "Man" and idealizing the achievements of the ancient Greeks as well as Christianity and the Catholic Church.

accents of Morality, of Virtue, of 'Transcendence', of the Nation, of France's World Role, etc.).

Of course, many of these contrasting Virtues (modesty, resignation, submissiveness on the one hand, cynicism, contempt, arrogance, confidence, self-importance, even smooth talk and cunning on the other) are also taught in the Family, in the Church, in the Army, in Good Books, in films and even in the football[7] stadium. But no other ideological State apparatus has the obligatory (and not least, free) audience of the totality of the children in the capitalist social formation, eight hours a day for five or six days out of seven.

But it is by an apprenticeship in a variety of know-how wrapped up in the massive inculcation of the ideology of the ruling class that the *relations of production* in a capitalist social formation, i.e. the relations of exploited to exploiters and exploiters to exploited, are largely reproduced. The mechanisms which produce this vital result for the capitalist regime are naturally covered up and concealed by a universally reigning ideology of the School, universally reigning because it is one of the essential forms of the ruling bourgeois ideology: an ideology which represents the School as a neutral environment purged of ideology (because it is . . . lay), where teachers respectful of the 'conscience' and 'freedom' of the children who are entrusted to them (in complete confidence) by their 'parents' (who are free, too, i.e. the owners of their children) open up for them the path to the freedom, morality and responsibility of adults by their own example, by knowledge, literature and their 'liberating' virtues.

I ask the pardon of those teachers who, in dreadful conditions, attempt to turn the few weapons they can find in the history and learning they 'teach' against the ideology, the system and the practices in which they are trapped. They are a kind of hero. But they are rare and how many (the majority) do not even begin to suspect the 'work' the system (which is bigger than they are and crushes them) forces them to do, or worse, put all their heart and ingenuity into performing it with the most advanced awareness (the famous new methods!). So little do they suspect it that their own devotion contributes to the maintenance and nourishment of this ideological representation of the School, which makes the School today as 'natural', indispensable-useful and even beneficial for our contemporaries as the Church was 'natural', indispensable and generous for our ancestors a few centuries ago.

In fact, the Church has been replaced today *in its role as the dominant Ideological State Apparatus* by the School. It is coupled with the Family just as the Church was once coupled with the Family. We can now claim that the unprecedentedly deep crisis which is now shaking the education system of so many States across the globe, often in conjunction with a crisis (already proclaimed in the *Communist Manifesto*) shaking the family system, takes on a political meaning, given that the School (and the School-Family couple) constitutes the dominant Ideological State Apparatus, the Apparatus playing a determinant part in the reproduction of the relations of production of a mode of production threatened in its existence by the world class struggle.

7. Soccer.

From *On Ideology*

When I put forward the concept of an Ideological State Apparatus, when I said that the ISAs 'function by ideology', I invoked a reality which needs a little discussion: ideology.

* * *

IDEOLOGY HAS NO HISTORY

One word first of all to expound the reason in principle which seems to me to found, or at least to justify, the project of a theory of ideology *in general*, and not a theory of particular ideolog*ies*, which, whatever their form (religious, ethical, legal, political), always express *class positions*.

It is quite obvious that it is necessary to proceed towards a theory of ideolog*ies* in the two respects I have just suggested. It will then be clear that a theory of ideolog*ies* depends in the last resort on the history of social formations, and thus of the modes of production combined in social formations, and of the class struggles which develop in them. In this sense it is clear that there can be no question of a theory of ideolog*ies in general*, since ideolog*ies* (defined in the double respect suggested above: regional and class) have a history, whose determination in the last instance is clearly situated outside ideologies alone, although it involves them.

On the contrary, if I am able to put forward the project of a theory of ideology *in general*, and if this theory really is one of the elements on which theories of ideolog*ies* depend, that entails an apparently paradoxical proposition which I shall express in the following terms: *ideology has no history*.

As we know, this formulation appears in so many words in a passage from *The German Ideology*.[8] Marx utters it with respect to metaphysics, which, he says, has no more history than ethics (meaning also the other forms of ideology).

In *The German Ideology*, this formulation appears in a plainly positivist[9] context. Ideology is conceived as a pure illusion, a pure dream, i.e. as nothingness. All its reality is external to it. Ideology is thus thought as an imaginary construction whose status is exactly like the theoretical status of the dream among writers before Freud.[1] For these writers, the dream was the purely imaginary, i.e. null, result of 'day's residues', presented in an arbitrary arrangement and order, sometimes even 'inverted', in other words, in 'disorder'. For them, the dream was the imaginary, it was empty, null and arbitrarily 'stuck together' (*bricolé*), once the eyes had closed, from the residues of the only full and positive reality, the reality of the day. This is

8. "The phantoms formed in the human brain are also, necessarily, sublimates of their material life-processes, which is empirically verifiable and bound to material premises. Morality, religion, metaphysics, all the rest of ideology and their corresponding forms of consciousness, thus no longer retain the semblance of independence. They have no history, no development; but men, developing their material production and their material intercourse, alter, along with their real existence, their thinking and the products of their thinking." *The German Ideology* (1846), in *The Marx-Engels Reader*, ed. Robert C. Tucker, 2d ed. (New York: Norton, 1978), pp. 154–55.

9. Taking knowledge and meaning to derive solely from what can be empirically observed.

1. SIGMUND FREUD (1856–1939), Austrian founder of psychoanalysis; *The Interpretation of Dreams* (1900) was his seminal work.

exactly the status of philosophy and ideology (since in this book philosophy is ideology *par excellence*) in *The German Ideology*.

Ideology, then, is for Marx an imaginary assemblage (*bricolage*),[2] a pure dream, empty and vain, constituted by the 'day's residues' from the only full and positive reality, that of the concrete history of concrete material individuals materially producing their existence. It is on this basis that ideology has no history in *The German Ideology*, since its history is outside it, where the only existing history is the history of concrete individuals, etc. In *The German Ideology*, the thesis that ideology has no history is therefore a purely negative thesis, since it means both:

1. ideology is nothing insofar as it is a pure dream (manufactured by who knows what power: if not by the alienation of the division of labour, but that, too, is a *negative* determination);
2. ideology has no history, which emphatically does not mean that there is no history in it (on the contrary, for it is merely the pale, empty and inverted reflection of real history) but that it has no history *of its own*.

Now, while the thesis I wish to defend formally speaking adopts the terms of *The German Ideology* ('ideology has no history'), it is radically different from the positivist and historicist thesis of *The German Ideology*.

For on the one hand, I think it is possible to hold that ideolog*ies have a history of their own* (although it is determined in the last instance by the class struggle); and on the other, I think it is possible to hold that ideology *in general has no history*, not in a negative sense (its history is external to it), but in an absolutely positive sense.

This sense is a positive one if it is true that the peculiarity of ideology is that it is endowed with a structure and a functioning such as to make it a non-historical reality, i.e. an *omni-historical* reality, in the sense in which that structure and functioning are immutable, present in the same form throughout what we can call history, in the sense in which the *Communist Manifesto* defines history as the history of class struggles, i.e. the history of class societies.

To give a theoretical reference-point here, I might say that, to return to our example of the dream, in its Freudian conception this time, our proposition: ideology has no history, can and must (and in a way which has absolutely nothing arbitrary about it, but, quite the reverse, is theoretically necessary, for there is an organic link between the two propositions) be related directly to Freud's proposition that the *unconscious is eternal*, i.e. that it has no history.

If eternal means, not transcendent to all (temporal) history, but omnipresent, trans-historical and therefore immutable in form throughout the extent of history, I shall adopt Freud's expression word for word, and write *ideology is eternal*, exactly like the unconscious. And I add that I find this comparison theoretically justified by the fact that the eternity of the unconscious is not unrelated to the eternity of ideology in general.

That is why I believe I am justified, hypothetically at least, in proposing a theory of ideology *in general*, in the sense that Freud presented a theory of the unconscious *in general*.

2. A term associated with the French anthropologist CLAUDE LÉVI-STRAUSS (1908–2009), who employed it to describe the patchwork of tools used in his structuralist methodology.

To simplify the phrase, it is convenient, taking into account what has been said about ideologies, to use the plain term ideology to designate ideology in general, which I have just said has no history, or, what comes to the same thing, is eternal, i.e. omnipresent in its immutable form throughout history (= the history of social formations containing social classes). For the moment I shall restrict myself to 'class societies' and their history.

IDEOLOGY IS A 'REPRESENTATION' OF THE IMAGINARY RELATIONSHIP OF INDIVIDUALS TO THEIR REAL CONDITIONS OF EXISTENCE

In order to approach my central thesis on the structure and functioning of ideology, I shall first present two theses, one negative, the other positive. The first concerns the object which is 'represented' in the imaginary form of ideology, the second concerns the materiality of ideology.

THESIS I: Ideology represents the imaginary relationship of individuals to their real conditions of existence.

We commonly call religious ideology, ethical ideology, legal ideology, political ideology, etc., so many 'world outlooks'. Of course, assuming that we do not live one of these ideologies as the truth (e.g. 'believe' in God, Duty, Justice, etc. . . .), we admit that the ideology we are discussing from a critical point of view, examining it as the ethnologist examines the myths of a 'primitive society', that these 'world outlooks' are largely imaginary, i.e. do not 'correspond to reality.'

However, while admitting that they do not correspond to reality, i.e. that they constitute an illusion, we admit that they do make allusion to reality, and that they need only be 'interpreted' to discover the reality of the world behind their imaginary representation of that world (ideology = *illusion/allusion*).

There are different types of interpretation, the most famous of which are the *mechanistic* type, current in the eighteenth century (God is the imaginary representation of the real King), and the '*hermeneutic*' interpretation, inaugurated by the earliest Church Fathers, and revived by Feuerbach and the theologico-philosophical school which descends from him, e.g. the theologian Barth[3] (to Feuerbach, for example, God is the essence of real Man). The essential point is that on condition that we interpret the imaginary transposition (and inversion) of ideology we arrive at the conclusion that in ideology 'men represent their real conditions of existence to themselves in an imaginary form'.

Unfortunately, this interpretation leaves one small problem unsettled: why do men 'need' this imaginary transposition of their real conditions of existence in order to 'represent to themselves' their real conditions of existence?

The first answer (that of the eighteenth century) proposes a simple solution: Priests or Despots are responsible. They 'forged' the Beautiful Lies so that, in the belief that they were obeying God, men would in fact obey the Priests and Despots, who are usually in alliance in their imposture, the

3. Karl Barth (1886–1968), Swiss theologian. Ludwig Feuerbach (1804–1872), German philosopher to whom Marx responded in "Theses on Feuerbach" (1845), *The German Ideology*, and *The Jewish Question* (1843).

Priests acting in the interests of the Despots or *vice versa*, according to the political positions of the 'theoreticians' concerned. There is therefore a cause for the imaginary transposition of the real conditions of existence: that cause is the existence of a small number of cynical men who base their domination and exploitation of the 'people' on a falsified representation of the world which they have imagined in order to enslave other minds by dominating their imaginations.

The second answer (that of Feuerbach, taken over word for word by Marx in his Early Works) is more 'profound', i.e. just as false. It, too, seeks and finds a cause for the imaginary transposition and distortion of men's real conditions of existence, in short, for the alienation in the imaginary of the representation of men's conditions of existence. This cause is no longer Priests or Despots, nor their active imagination and the passive imagination of their victims. This cause is the material alienation which reigns in the conditions of existence of men themselves. This is how, in *The Jewish Question* and elsewhere, Marx defends the Feuerbachian idea that men make themselves an alienated (= imaginary) representation of their conditions of existence because these conditions of existence are themselves alienating (in the *1844 Manuscripts*:[4] because these conditions are dominated by the essence of alienated society—*'alienated labour'*).

All these interpretations thus take literally the thesis which they presuppose, and on which they depend, i.e. that what is reflected in the imaginary representation of the world found in an ideology is the conditions of existence of men, i.e. their real world.

Now I can return to a thesis which I have already advanced: it is not their real conditions of existence, their real world, that 'men' 'represent to themselves' in ideology, but above all it is their relation to those conditions of existence which is represented to them there. It is this relation which is at the centre of every ideological, i.e. imaginary, representation of the real world. It is this relation that contains the 'cause' which has to explain the imaginary distortion of the ideological representation of the real world. Or rather, to leave aside the language of causality it is necessary to advance the thesis that it is the *imaginary nature of this relation* which underlies all the imaginary distortion that we can observe (if we do not live in its truth) in all ideology.

To speak in a Marxist language, if it is true that the representation of the real conditions of existence of the individuals occupying the posts of agents of production, exploitation, repression, ideologization and scientific practice, does in the last analysis arise from the relations of production, and from relations deriving from the relations of production, we can say the following: all ideology represents in its necessarily imaginary distortion not the existing relations of production (and the other relations that derive from them), but above all the (imaginary) relationship of individuals to the relations of production and the relations that derive from them. What is represented in ideology is therefore not the system of the real relations which govern the existence of individuals, but the imaginary relation of those individuals to the real relations in which they live.

4. Marx's *Economic and Philosophic Manuscripts of 1844* was not published until 1932.

If this is the case, the question of the 'cause' of the imaginary distortion of the real relations in ideology disappears and must be replaced by a different question: why is the representation given to individuals of their (individual) relation to the social relations which govern their conditions of existence and their collective and individual life necessarily an imaginary relation? And what is the nature of this imaginariness? Posed in this way, the question explodes the solution by a 'clique',[5] by a group of individuals (Priests or Despots) who are the authors of the great ideological mystification, just as it explodes the solution by the alienated character of the real world. We shall see why later in my exposition. For the moment I shall go no further.

THESIS II: Ideology has a material existence.

I have already touched on this thesis by saying that the 'ideas' or 'representations', etc., which seem to make up ideology do not have an ideal (*idéale* or *idéelle*)[6] or spiritual existence, but a material existence. I even suggested that the ideal (*idéale, idéelle*) and spiritual existence of 'ideas' arises exclusively in an ideology of the 'idea' and of ideology, and let me add, in an ideology of what seems to have 'founded' this conception since the emergence of the sciences, i.e. what the practicians of the sciences represent to themselves in their spontaneous ideology as 'ideas', true or false. Of course, presented in affirmative form, this thesis is unproven. I simply ask that the reader be favourably disposed towards it, say, in the name of materialism. A long series of arguments would be necessary to prove it.

This hypothetical thesis of the not spiritual but material existence of 'ideas' or other 'representations' is indeed necessary if we are to advance in our analysis of the nature of ideology. Or rather, it is merely useful to us in order the better to reveal what every at all serious analysis of any ideology will immediately and empirically show to every observer, however critical.

While discussing the ideological State apparatuses and their practices, I said that each of them was the realization of an ideology (the unity of these different regional ideologies—religious, ethical, legal, political, aesthetic, etc.—being assured by their subjection to the ruling ideology). I now return to this thesis: an ideology always exists in an apparatus, and its practice, or practices. This existence is material.

Of course, the material existence of the ideology in an apparatus and its practices does not have the same modality as the material existence of a paving-stone or a rifle. But, at the risk of being taken for a Neo-Aristotelian (NB Marx had a very high regard for Aristotle),[7] I shall say that 'matter is discussed in many senses', or rather that it exists in different modalities, all rooted in the last instance in 'physical' matter.

Having said this, let me move straight on and see what happens to the 'individuals' who live in ideology, i.e. in a determinate (religious, ethical, etc.) representation of the world whose imaginary distortion depends on their imaginary relation to their conditions of existence, in other words, in the last instance, to the relations of production and to class relations (ideology = an

5. I use this very modern term deliberately. For even in Communist circles, unfortunately, it is a commonplace to "explain" some political deviation by the action of a "clique" [Althusser's note].

6. Though the words sound similar in French, *idéale* means "ideal" and *idéelle* means "ideational" or "conceptual."

7. The Greek philosopher ARISTOTLE (384–322 B.C.E.) emphasized the direct observation of nature and insisted on rigorous scientific procedure.

imaginary relation to real relations). I shall say that this imaginary relation is itself endowed with a material existence.

Now I observe the following.

An individual believes in God, or Duty, or Justice, etc. This belief derives (for everyone, i.e. for all those who live in an ideological representation of ideology, which reduces ideology to ideas endowed by definition with a spiritual existence) from the ideas of the individual concerned, i.e. from him as a subject with a consciousness which contains the ideas of his belief. In this way, i.e. by means of the absolutely ideological 'conceptual' device (*dispositif*) thus set up (a subject endowed with a consciousness in which he freely forms or freely recognizes ideas in which he believes), the (material) attitude of the subject concerned naturally follows.

The individual in question behaves in such and such a way, adopts such and such a practical attitude, and, what is more, participates in certain regular practices which are those of the ideological apparatus on which 'depend' the ideas which he has in all consciousness freely chosen as a subject. If he believes in God, he goes to Church to attend Mass, kneels, prays, confesses, does penance (once it was material in the ordinary sense of the term) and naturally repents and so on. If he believes in Duty, he will have the corresponding attitudes, inscribed in ritual practices 'according to the correct principles'. If he believes in Justice, he will submit unconditionally to the rules of the Law, and may even protest when they are violated, sign petitions, take part in a demonstration, etc.

Throughout this schema we observe that the ideological representation of ideology is itself forced to recognize that every 'subject' endowed with a 'consciousness' and believing in the 'ideas' that his 'consciousness' inspires in him and freely accepts, must '*act* according to his ideas', must therefore inscribe his own ideas as a free subject in the actions of his material practice. If he does not do so, 'that is wicked'.

Indeed, if he does not do what he ought to do as a function of what he believes, it is because he does something else, which, still as a function of the same idealist scheme, implies that he has other ideas in his head as well as those he proclaims, and that he acts according to these other ideas, as a man who is either 'inconsistent' ('no one is willingly evil') or cynical, or perverse.

In every case, the ideology of ideology thus recognizes, despite its imaginary distortion, that the 'ideas' of a human subject exist in his actions, or ought to exist in his actions, and if that is not the case, it lends him other ideas corresponding to the actions (however perverse) that he does perform. This ideology talks of actions: I shall talk of actions inserted into *practices*. *And* I shall point out that these practices are governed by the *rituals* in which these practices are inscribed, within the *material existence of an ideological apparatus*, be it only a small part of that apparatus: a small mass in a small church, a funeral, a minor match at a sports' club, a school day, a political party meeting, etc.

Besides, we are indebted to Pascal's[8] defensive 'dialectic' for the wonderful formula which will enable us to invert the order of the notional

8. Blaise Pascal (1623–1662), French theologian and mathematician; he was influenced by the religious thinking of Bishop Cornelius Jansen (1585–1638), whose posthumously published writings fostered a movement condemned as heretical by the Roman Catholic Church.

schema of ideology. Pascal says more or less: 'Kneel down, move your lips in prayer, and you will believe.' He thus scandalously inverts the order of things, bringing, like Christ, not peace but strife, and in addition something hardly Christian (for woe to him who brings scandal into the world!)—scandal itself. A fortunate scandal which makes him stick with Jansenist defiance to a language that directly names the reality.

I will be allowed to leave Pascal to the arguments of his ideological struggle with the religious ideological State apparatus of his day. And I shall be expected to use a more directly Marxist vocabulary, if that is possible, for we are advancing in still poorly explored domains.

I shall therefore say that, where only a single subject (such and such an individual) is concerned, the existence of the ideas of his belief is material in that *his ideas are his material actions inserted into material practices governed by material rituals which are themselves defined by the material ideological apparatus from which derive the ideas of that subject*. Naturally, the four inscriptions of the adjective 'material' in my proposition must be affected by different modalities: the materialities of a displacement for going to mass, of kneeling down, of the gesture of the sign of the cross, or of the *mea culpa*, of a sentence, of a prayer, of an act of contrition, of a penitence, of a gaze, of a hand-shake, of an external verbal discourse or an 'internal' verbal discourse (consciousness), are not one and the same materiality. I shall leave on one side the problem of a theory of the differences between the modalities of materiality.

It remains that in this inverted presentation of things, we are not dealing with an 'inversion' at all, since it is clear that certain notions have purely and simply disappeared from our presentation, whereas others on the contrary survive, and new terms appear.

Disappeared: the term *ideas*.

Survive: the terms *subject, consciousness, belief, actions*.

Appear: the terms *practices, rituals, ideological apparatus*.

* * *

But this very presentation reveals that we have retained the following notions: subject, consciousness, belief, actions. From this series I shall immediately extract the decisive central term on which everything else depends: the notion of the *subject*.

And I shall immediately set down two conjoint theses:

1. there is no practice except by and in an ideology;
2. there is no ideology except by the subject and for subjects.

I can now come to my central thesis.

IDEOLOGY INTERPELLATES INDIVIDUALS AS SUBJECTS

This thesis is simply a matter of making my last proposition explicit: there is no ideology except by the subject and for subjects. Meaning, there is no ideology except for concrete subjects, and this destination for ideology is only made possible by the subject: meaning, *by the category of the subject* and its functioning.

By this I mean that, even if it only appears under this name (the subject) with the rise of bourgeois ideology, above all with the rise of legal ideology,[9] the category of the subject (which may function under other names: e.g., as the soul in Plato,[1] as God, etc.) is the constitutive category of all ideology, whatever its determination (regional or class) and whatever its historical date—since ideology has no history.

I say: the category of the subject is constitutive of all ideology, but at the same time and immediately I add that *the category of the subject is only constitutive of all ideology insofar as all ideology has the function (which defines it) of 'constituting' concrete individuals as subjects*. In the interaction of this double constitution exists the functioning of all ideology, ideology being nothing but its functioning in the material forms of existence of that functioning.

* * *

At work in this reaction is the ideological *recognition* function which is one of the two functions of ideology as such (its inverse being the function of *misrecognition—méconnaissance*).

To take a highly 'concrete' example, we all have friends who, when they knock on our door and we ask, through the door, the question 'Who's there?', answer (since 'it's obvious') 'It's me'. And we recognize that 'it is him', or 'her'. We open the door, and 'it's true, it really was she who was there'. To take another example, when we recognize somebody of our (previous) acquaintance ((*re*)-*connaissance*) in the street, we show him that we have recognized him (and have recognized that he has recognized us) by saying to him 'Hello, my friend', and shaking his hand (a material ritual practice of ideological recognition in everyday life—in France, at least; elsewhere, there are other rituals).

In this preliminary remark and these concrete illustrations, I only wish to point out that you and I are *always already* subjects, and as such constantly practice the rituals of ideological recognition, which guarantee for us that we are indeed concrete, individual, distinguishable and (naturally) irreplaceable subjects. The writing I am currently executing and the reading you are currently[2] performing are also in this respect rituals of ideological recognition, including the 'obviousness' with which the 'truth' or 'error' of my reflections may impose itself on you.

But to recognize that we are subjects and that we function in the practical rituals of the most elementary everyday life (the hand-shake, the fact of calling you by your name, the fact of knowing, even if I do not know what it is, that you 'have' a name of your own, which means that you are recognized as a unique subject, etc.)—this recognition only gives us the 'consciousness' of our incessant (eternal) practice of ideological recognition—its consciousness,

9. Which borrowed the legal category of "subject in law" to make an ideological notion: man is by nature a subject [Althusser's note].

1. In discussing the structure of the ideal city in his *Republic*, the Greek philosopher PLATO (ca. 427–ca. 347 B.C.E.) analyzed the structure of the inhabitants' souls.

2. NB: this double "currently" is one more proof of the fact that ideology is "eternal," since these two "currentlys" are separated by an indefinite interval; I am writing these lines on April 6, 1969, you may read them at any subsequent time [Althusser's note].

i.e. its *recognition*—but in no sense does it give us the (scientific) *knowledge* of the mechanism of this recognition. Now it is this knowledge that we have to reach, if you will, while speaking in ideology, and from within ideology we have to outline a discourse which tries to break with ideology, in order to dare to be the beginning of a scientific (i.e. subjectless) discourse on ideology.

Thus in order to represent why the category of the 'subject' is constitutive of ideology, which only exists by constituting concrete subjects as subjects, I shall employ a special mode of exposition: 'concrete' enough to be recognized, but abstract enough to be thinkable and thought, giving rise to a knowledge.

As a first formulation I shall say: *all ideology hails or interpellates concrete individuals as concrete subjects*, by the functioning of the category of the subject.

This is a proposition which entails that we distinguish for the moment between concrete individuals on the one hand and concrete subjects on the other, although at this level concrete subjects only exist insofar as they are supported by a concrete individual.

I shall then suggest that ideology 'acts' or 'functions' in such a way that it 'recruits' subjects among the individuals (it recruits them all), or 'transforms' the individuals into subjects (it transforms them all) by that very precise operation which I have called *interpellation* or hailing, and which can be imagined along the lines of the most commonplace everyday police (or other) hailing: 'Hey, you there!'[3]

Assuming that the theoretical scene I have imagined takes place in the street, the hailed individual will turn round. By this mere one-hundred-and-eighty-degree physical conversion, he becomes a *subject*. Why? Because he has recognized that the hail was 'really' addressed to him, and that 'it was *really him* who was hailed' (and not someone else). Experience shows that the practical telecommunication of hailings is such that they hardly ever miss their man: verbal call or whistle, the one hailed always recognizes that it is really him who is being hailed. And yet it is a strange phenomenon, and one which cannot be explained solely by 'guilt feelings', despite the large numbers who 'have something on their consciences'.

Naturally for the convenience and clarity of my little theoretical theatre I have had to present things in the form of a sequence, with a before and an after, and thus in the form of a temporal succession. There are individuals walking along. Somewhere (usually behind them) the hail rings out: 'Hey, you there!' One individual (nine times out of ten it is the right one) turns round, believing/suspecting/knowing that it is for him, i.e. recognizing that 'it really is he' who is meant by the hailing. But in reality these things happen without any succession. The existence of ideology and the hailing or interpellation of individuals as subjects are one and the same thing.

* * *

Thus ideology hails or interpellates individuals as subjects. As ideology is eternal, I must now suppress the temporal form in which I have presented the functioning of ideology, and say: ideology has always-already interpellated

3. Hailing as an everyday practice subject to a precise ritual takes a quite "special" form in the policeman's practice of "hailing" which concerns the hailing of "suspects" [Althusser's note].

individuals as subjects, which amounts to making it clear that individuals are always-already interpellated by ideology as subjects, which necessarily leads us to one last proposition: *individuals are always-already subjects*. Hence individuals are 'abstract' with respect to the subjects which they always-already are. This proposition might seem paradoxical.

That an individual is always-already a subject, even before he is born, is nevertheless the plain reality, accessible to everyone and not a paradox at all. Freud shows that individuals are always 'abstract' with respect to the subjects they always-already are, simply by noting the ideological ritual that surrounds the expectation of a 'birth', that 'happy event'. Everyone knows how much and in what way an unborn child is expected. Which amounts to saying, very prosaically, if we agree to drop the 'sentiments', i.e. the forms of family ideology (paternal/maternal/conjugal/fraternal) in which the unborn child is expected: it is certain in advance that it will bear its Father's Name, and will therefore have an identity and be irreplaceable. Before its birth, the child is therefore always-already a subject, appointed as a subject in and by the specific familial ideological configuration in which it is 'expected' once it has been conceived. I hardly need add that this familial ideological configuration is, in its uniqueness, highly structured, and that it is in this implacable and more or less 'pathological' (presupposing that any meaning can be assigned to that term) structure that the former subject-to-be will have to 'find' 'its' place, i.e. 'become' the sexual subject (boy or girl) which it already is in advance. It is clear that this ideological constraint and pre-appointment, and all the rituals of rearing and then education in the family, have some relationship with what Freud studied in the forms of the pre-genital and genital 'stages' of sexuality, i.e. in the 'grip' of what Freud registered by its effects as being the unconscious. But let us leave this point, too, on one side.

Let me go one step further. What I shall now turn my attention to is the way the 'actors' in this *mise en scène* of interpellation, and their respective roles, are reflected in the very structure of all ideology.

AN EXAMPLE: THE CHRISTIAN RELIGIOUS IDEOLOGY

As the formal structure of all ideology is always the same, I shall restrict my analysis to a single example, one accessible to everyone, that of religious ideology, with the proviso that the same demonstration can be produced for ethical, legal, political, aesthetic ideology, etc.

Let us therefore consider the Christian religious ideology. I shall use a rhetorical figure and 'make it speak', i.e. collect into a fictional discourse what it 'says' not only in its two Testaments, its Theologians, Sermons, but also in its practices, its rituals, its ceremonies and its sacraments. The Christian religious ideology says something like this:

It says: I address myself to you, a human individual called Peter (every individual is called by his name, in the passive sense, it is never he who provides his own name), in order to tell you that God exists and that you are answerable to Him. It adds: God addresses himself to you through my voice (Scripture having collected the Word of God, Tradition having transmitted it, Papal Infallibility fixing it for ever on 'nice' points). It says: this is who you are: you are Peter! This is your origin, you were created by God for all eternity, although you were born in the 1920th year of Our Lord! This is your place in the world! This is what you must do! By these means, if you observe the 'law of love' you will be saved, you, Peter, and will become part of the Glorious Body of Christ! Etc. . . .

Now this is quite a familiar and banal discourse, but at the same time quite a surprising one.

Surprising because if we consider that religious ideology is indeed addressed to individuals, in order to 'transform them into subjects', by interpellating the individual, Peter, in order to make him a subject, free to obey or disobey the appeal, i.e. God's commandments; if it calls these individuals by their names, thus recognizing that they are always-already interpellated as subjects with a personal identity (to the extent that Pascal's Christ says: 'It is for you that I have shed this drop of my blood!'); if it interpellates them in such a way that the subject responds: *'Yes, it really is me!'* if it obtains from them the *recognition* that they really do occupy the place it designates for them as theirs in the world, a fixed residence: 'It really is me, I am here, a worker, a boss or a soldier!' in this vale of tears; if it obtains from them the recognition of a destination (eternal life or damnation) according to the respect or contempt they show to 'God's Commandments', Law become Love;—if everything does happen in this way (in the practices of the well-known rituals of baptism, confirmation, communion, confession and extreme unction, etc. . . .), we should note that all this 'procedure' to set up Christian religious subjects is dominated by a strange phenomenon: the fact that there can only be such a multitude of possible religious subjects on the absolute condition that there is a Unique, Absolute, *Other Subject*, i.e. God.

It is convenient to designate this new and remarkable Subject by writing Subject with a capital S to distinguish it from ordinary subjects, with a small s.

It then emerges that the interpellation of individuals as subjects presupposes the 'existence' of a Unique and central Other Subject, in whose Name the religious ideology interpellates all individuals as subjects. All this is clearly written in what is rightly called the Scriptures. 'And it came to pass at that time that God the Lord (Yahweh) spoke to Moses in the cloud. And the Lord cried to Moses, "Moses!" And Moses replied "It is (really) I! I am Moses thy servant, speak and I shall listen!" And the Lord spoke to Moses and said to him, "*I am that I am*"'.[4]

God thus defines himself as the Subject *par excellence*, he who is through himself and for himself ('I am that I am'), and he who interpellates his subject, the individual subjected to him by his very interpellation, i.e. the individual named Moses. And Moses, interpellated-called by his Name, having recognized that it 'really' was he who was called by God, recognizes that he is a subject, a subject *of* God, a subject subjected to God, *a subject through the Subject and subjected to the Subject*. The proof: he obeys him, and makes his people obey God's Commandments.

God is thus the Subject, and Moses and the innumerable subjects of God's people, the Subject's interlocutors-interpellates: his *mirrors*, his *reflections*. Were not men made *in the image* of God? As all theological reflection proves,

4. See Exodus 3.4, 14 (spoken from a burning bush, not a cloud).

whereas He 'could' perfectly well have done without men, God needs them, the Subject needs the subjects, just as men need God, the subjects need the Subject. Better: God needs men, the great Subject needs subjects, even in the terrible inversion of his image in them (when the subjects wallow in debauchery, i.e. sin).

* * *

Let us decipher into theoretical language this wonderful necessity for the duplication of *the Subject into subjects* and of *the Subject itself into a subject-Subject*.

We observe that the structure of all ideology, interpellating individuals as subjects in the name of a Unique and Absolute Subject is *speculary*, i.e. a mirror-structure, and *doubly* speculary: this mirror duplication is constitutive of ideology and ensures its functioning. Which means that all ideology is *centred*, that the Absolute Subject occupies the unique place of the Centre, and interpellates around it the infinity of individuals into subjects in a double mirror-connexion such that it *subjects* the subjects to the Subject, while giving them in the Subject in which each subject can contemplate its own image (present and future) the *guarantee* that this really concerns them and Him, and that since everything takes place in the Family (the Holy Family: the Family is in essence Holy), 'God will *recognize* his own in it', i.e. those who have recognized God, and have recognized themselves in Him, will be saved.

Let me summarize what we have discovered about ideology in general.

The duplicate mirror-structure of ideology ensures simultaneously:

1. the interpellation of 'individuals' as subjects;
2. their subjection to the Subject;
3. the mutual recognition of subjects and Subject, the subjects' recognition of each other, and finally the subject's recognition of himself;
4. the absolute guarantee that everything really is so, and that on condition that the subjects recognize what they are and behave accordingly, everything will be all right: Amen—'*So be it*'.

Result: caught in this quadruple system of interpellation as subjects, of subjection to the Subject, of universal recognition and of absolute guarantee, the subjects 'work', they 'work by themselves' in the vast majority of cases, with the exception of the 'bad subjects' who on occasion provoke the intervention of one of the detachments of the (repressive) State apparatus. But the vast majority of (good) subjects work all right 'all by themselves', i.e. by ideology (whose concrete forms are realized in the Ideological State Apparatuses). They are inserted into practices governed by the rituals of the ISAs. They 'recognize' the existing state of affairs, that 'it really is true that it is so and not otherwise', and that they must be obedient to God, to their conscience, to the priest, to de Gaulle, to the boss, to the engineer, that thou shalt 'love thy neighbour as thyself', etc. Their concrete, material behaviour is simply the inscription in life of the admirable words of the prayer: '*Amen—So be it*'.

Yes, the subjects 'work by themselves'. The whole mystery of this effect lies in the first two moments of the quadruple system I have just discussed, or, if you prefer, in the ambiguity of the term *subject*. In the ordinary use of the term, subject in fact means: (1) a free subjectivity, a centre of initiatives, author of and responsible for its actions; (2) a subjected being, who submits to a higher authority, and is therefore stripped of all freedom except that of freely accepting his submission. This last note gives us the meaning of this ambiguity, which is merely a reflection of the effect which produces it: the individual *is interpellated as a (free) subject in order that he shall submit freely to the commandments of the Subject, i.e. in order that he shall (freely) accept his subjection*, i.e. in order that he shall make the gestures and actions of his subjection 'all by himself'. *There are no subjects except by and for their subjection*. That is why they 'work all by themselves'.

'*So be it!* . . .' This phrase which registers the effect to be obtained proves that it is not 'naturally' so ('naturally': outside the prayer, i.e. outside the ideological intervention). This phrase proves that it *has* to be so if things are to be what they must be, and let us let the words slip: if the reproduction of the relations of production is to be assured, even in the processes of production and circulation, every day, in the 'consciousness', i.e. in the attitudes of the individual-subjects occupying the posts which the socio-technical division of labour assigns to them in production, exploitation, repression, ideologization, scientific practice, etc. Indeed, what is really in question in this mechanism of the mirror recognition of the Subject and of the individuals interpellated as subjects, and of the guarantee given by the Subject to the subjects if they freely accept their subjection to the Subject's 'commandments'? The reality in question in this mechanism, the reality which is necessarily *ignored (méconnue)* in the very forms of recognition (ideology = misrecognition/ignorance) is indeed, in the last resort, the reproduction of the relations of production and of the relations deriving from them.

January–April 1969

P.S.

* * *

I have suggested that the ideologies were *realized* in institutions, in their rituals and their practices, in the ISAs. We have seen that on this basis they contribute to that form of class struggle, vital for the ruling class, the reproduction of the relations of production. But the point of view itself, however real, is still an abstract one.

In fact, the State and its Apparatuses only have meaning from the point of view of the class struggle, as an apparatus of class struggle ensuring class oppression and guaranteeing the conditions of exploitation and its reproduction. But there is no class struggle without antagonistic classes. Whoever says class struggle of the ruling class says resistance, revolt and class struggle of the ruled class.

* * *

It is only from the point of view of the classes, i.e. of the class struggle, that it is possible to explain the ideolog*ies* existing in a social formation. Not only is it from this starting-point that it is possible to explain the realization of the ruling ideology in the ISAs and of the forms of class struggle for which the ISAs are the seat and the stake. But it is also and above all from this starting-point that it is possible to understand the provenance of the ideologies which are realized in the ISAs and confront one another there. For if it is true that the ISAs represent the *form* in which the ideology of the ruling class must *necessarily* be realized, and the form in which the ideology of the ruled class must *necessarily* be measured and confronted, ideologies are not 'born' in the ISAs but from the social classes at grips in the class struggle: from their conditions of existence, their practices, their experience of the struggle, etc.

1970

PAUL DE MAN
1919–1983

Spurred by the expansion of research universities, American academic literary criticism flourished from the late 1960s through the 1980s. New ideas from Continental philosophy, linguistics, psychoanalysis, and criticism surged into its comparatively narrow confines, which had been dominated by the model of close reading practiced by New Critics like CLEANTH BROOKS. Central to these new and avowedly theoretical stances toward literature was the group of critics then at Yale University, including Paul de Man, HAROLD BLOOM, JACQUES DERRIDA, Geoffrey Hartman, J. Hillis Miller, Shoshana Felman, and de Man's student Barbara Johnson. Called the "Yale School," they revitalized—or, according to antagonists, ruined—American literary criticism by importing Continental theory and, to varying degrees, by espousing deconstruction. An erudite and wide-ranging critic of critics as well as a sophisticated reader of literary texts, de Man was the most influential literary theorist of the Yale School, and perhaps of his generation. Complementing Derrida's broader philosophical project, de Man promulgated deconstruction in literary criticism. His essay "Semiology and Rhetoric" (1973) programmatically outlines his model of deconstructive reading, arguing that rhetoric and figural language ultimately undermine determinate interpretation and that texts become allegories of their own interpretive difficulties.

De Man was a prominent academic figure in the United States in his later life, but his early life in Europe was marked by the experience of World War II, the decisive historical event of his generation. He was born and schooled in Antwerp, Belgium, where his father was a manufacturer of medical equipment and his uncle, Hendrik de Man, was a leading figure in the Socialist Party. In 1937 he entered the University of Brussels, first studying engineering and eventually taking degrees in chemistry (1940) and then philosophy (1942). While he was a student, Belgium was invaded by German forces, and it was under German military occupation from 1940 to 1944. De Man tried to flee to Spain in the summer of 1940 but was denied permission to immigrate; he returned to Belgium in the fall. During this period, he published journalism on literature and music; in 1939 he wrote for a democratic, antifascist student paper, and from 1940 to 1942 he regularly wrote for a Belgian newspaper, *Le Soir* (*The Evening*), then under German control.

After the war de Man tried his hand at publishing and translating, but in 1948 he emigrated to the United States, where he worked at Doubleday Bookstore in New York and was introduced to prominent New York intellectuals. With the help of the writer Mary McCarthy, in 1949 he took a job as an instructor of French at Bard College, and in 1951 he moved to Boston to teach at the Berlitz language school. In 1952 he entered the graduate program in comparative literature at Harvard University, attaining a prestigious appointment at the Harvard Society of Fellows (1955–58) and working with the New Critic Reuben Brower, for whom he was a teaching assistant. While a lecturer at Harvard, he received his M.A. in 1958 and his Ph.D. in 1960. Though he began his academic career relatively late in life, he quickly rose to prominence, teaching at Cornell University from 1960 to 1967, intermittently at the University of Zurich from 1963 to 1970, and at Johns Hopkins University from 1968 to 1970. In 1970 he moved to Yale University, where he was appointed Sterling Professor of Comparative Literature in 1979. In 1983, at the height of his influence, de Man died of cancer.

It was not until four years after his death that a Belgian researcher rediscovered his wartime journalism. Although most of it consisted of cerebral literary reviews, one article contained explicitly anti-Semitic statements, to the effect that European literature would not be diminished if there were no Jewish writers; a few other articles were also troubling. These writings were met with shock, for they suggested that de Man had been complicit with Nazi policies. Though de Man had been cleared of charges of collaboration by the Belgian postwar military prosecutor investigating those who had worked for *Le Soir*, his wartime writings became a focal point of debate thereafter, diminishing his influence in literary theory.

De Man was ever attuned to the figural contradictions of language, and his own career took many ironic turns. A debunker of the figure of personification in literary and critical language, he came for many to personify both deconstruction and literary theory. Despite eschewing personality in teaching—as he sternly remarks in "The Resistance to Theory" (1982), pedagogy is not show business—he had a large following of students and colleagues who carried out his line of deconstruction. While he was persistently skeptical that any method could yield determinable results, his manner of reading became a model for others' critical practice, fulfilling his prediction, in "Semiology and Rhetoric," that "The whole of literature would respond in similar fashion." And although he advocated the priority of linguistic indeterminacy in interpreting historical events, his work was put into question by the discovery of the historical fact of his wartime writings.

Trained both in the European tradition of philosophy, especially phenomenology, at Brussels and in the American New Criticism during his time at Harvard, de Man was well positioned to adapt the developing discourses of Continental theory to American literary criticism. He showed a consistent affinity with the New Critics in his assiduous practice of close reading. As he remarked in an interview, he worked not from larger ideas but "one inch over the text." He also shared the New Critics' disdain for paraphrase, which reductively glosses texts rather than teasing out their complications. However, de Man departed from the New Critics in several key ways: in denying the determinate meaning that they assumed, in stressing allegory as a primary literary mode, and in continually investigating the theoretical bases of reading.

A foundational statement of deconstructive literary analysis, "Semiology and Rhetoric" takes aim at the semiological approaches characteristic of French structuralism, which attempt to develop a grammar of literary structure on the scientific model of linguistics. Using William Butler Yeats's poem "Among School Children" (1927) as a test case, de Man shows how meaning cannot be determined by grammar but is exceeded by the figural properties of language. Focusing on the poem's famous last line, "How can we know the dancer from the dance?," he adduces two different readings, taking it first as a rhetorical question reinforcing the images of unity in the poem (the standard interpretation) and then as a serious question that culminates in an image of dramatic uncertainty rather than unity. These yield "two entirely coherent but entirely incompatible readings," and thus "the entire scheme set up by the first reading can be undermined, or deconstructed, in terms of the second." Bringing home his point about the limitations of structuralism as well as of hermeneutic approaches, de Man shows how the poem's rhetoric renders interpretation undecidable. He calls this the "rhetorization of grammar."

As a complement to this rhetorical move, de Man also analyzes what he calls the "grammatization of rhetoric." Taking an example from Marcel Proust's *In Search of Lost Time* (7 vols., 1913–27), de Man traces the sequence of figures in a passage describing the coolness of a room during summer, which seem necessarily linked and unified in "semi-automatic grammatical patterns." However, de Man argues that this link is deceptive and works only associatively, by contiguity; as he points out, a fly's buzz is no more necessarily connected to summer than the man Henry Ford is connected to an automobile. The figural nature of language again undoes the stable pattern that we assume to determine meaning. Although de Man claims that the indeterminacy generated by figuration applies to all linguistic acts, he specifies that it is explicitly foregrounded in literature. He thereby proposes one answer to the perennial question in literary theory of what distinguishes literature from other kinds of discourse, though he at the same time undercuts this distinction by analyzing how the literary occurs in presumably propositional discourses such as criticism and philosophy.

Generalizing from these examples, de Man finds that all literary texts become, in his trademark phrase, "allegories of reading," offering narratives of the problematic nature of language and interpretation. One of de Man's most influential moves was to reconsider the place of allegory, usually associated with schematic forms of medieval literature, notably in his important early essay "The Rhetoric of Temporality" (1969), as well as in his masterwork, *Allegories of Reading* (1979; "Semiology and Rhetoric" was reprinted as its introduction). De Man stresses that his allegorical rendering is not something overlaid on texts as a theoretical template; as he puts it, "The deconstruction is not something we have added to the text but it constituted the text in the first place." Likewise, one does not "deconstruct" texts; rather, one unravels the ways in which language deconstructs its own assertions, a distinction that suggests the impersonality of language and its operation, beyond human control. For de Man, the workings of language have priority over historical or other considerations; in another essay he makes the startling but consistent claim that "the bases for historical knowledge are not empirical facts but written texts, even if these texts masquerade in the guise of wars and revolutions."

De Man's work has drawn an unparalleled amount of criticism from both traditionalists and fellow theorists within the academy, as well as from those outside. Although he studied a wide range of canonical literary texts, his advocacy of theory led to the accusation that he was an enemy of literature. And despite being an inveterate close reader, he was charged with threatening the foundations of literary criticism because he radically questioned the possibility of meaning. Within the domain of theory, in perhaps the central struggle of the 1980s, de Man—and deconstruction—was pitted against leftist calls that attention be paid to history, society, and politics. The Marxist critic TERRY EAGLETON claimed that de Man had "given up the world entirely for the aporias and unthinkable paradoxes of a text," and that deconstruction was "politically quietistic"; the postcolonial critic EDWARD W. SAID charged that deconstruction, by its use of overspecialized "camouflaging jargons" that "obscure the social realities," detracted from the social role and mission of criticism. Analyzing de Man's own rhetoric, the critic Frank Lentricchia quipped that de Man's authoritative pronouncements about language seemed the orders of a Mafia boss, contradicting his own theory of indeterminacy. Although de Man's influence waned somewhat after the 1980s, in part because of the discovery of his wartime writings and in part because of the resurgence of historical methods, he remains a pivotal figure in the assimilation of Continental theory, especially deconstruction, to the North American scene.

***Allegories of Reading* Keywords:** Deconstruction, Interpretation Theory, Language, Poststructuralism, Rhetoric, Semiotics

From Allegories of Reading

Semiology and Rhetoric

To judge from various recent publications, the spirit of the times is not blowing in the direction of formalist and intrinsic criticism.[1] We may no longer be hearing too much about relevance but we keep hearing a great deal about reference, about the nonverbal "outside" to which language refers, by which it is conditioned and upon which it acts. The stress falls not so much on the fictional status of literature—a property now perhaps somewhat too easily taken for granted—but on the interplay between these fictions and categories that are said to partake of reality, such as the self, man, society, "the artist, his culture and the human community,"[2] as one critic puts it. Hence the emphasis on hybrid texts considered to be partly literary and partly referential, on popular fictions deliberately aimed towards social and psychological gratification, on literary autobiography as a key to the understanding of the self, and so on. We speak as if, with the problems of literary form resolved once and forever, and with the techniques of structural analysis refined to near-perfection, we could now move "beyond formalism" towards the questions that really interest us and reap, at last, the fruits of the ascetic concentration on techniques that prepared us for this decisive step. With the internal law and order of literature well policed, we can now confidently devote ourselves to the foreign affairs, the external politics of literature. Not only do we feel able to do so, but we owe it to ourselves to take this step: our moral conscience would not allow us to do otherwise. Behind the assurance that valid interpretation is possible, behind the recent interest in writing and reading as potentially effective public speech acts, stands a highly respectable moral imperative that strives to reconcile the internal, formal, private structures of literary language with their external, referential, and public effects.

I want, for the moment, to consider briefly this tendency in itself, as an undeniable and recurrent historical fact, without regard for its truth or falseness or for its value as desirable or pernicious. It is a fact that this sort of thing happens, again and again, in literary studies. On the one hand, literature cannot merely be received as a definite unit of referential meaning that can be decoded without leaving a residue. The code is unusually conspicuous, complex, and enigmatic; it attracts an inordinate amount of attention to itself, and this attention has to acquire the rigor of a method. The structural moment of concentration on the code for its own sake cannot be avoided, and literature necessarily breeds its own formalism. Technical innovations in the methodical study of literature only occur when this kind of attention predominates. It can legitimately be said, for example, that, from a technical point of view, very little has happened in American criticism since the innovative works of New Criticism. There certainly have been numerous excellent books of criticism since, but in none of them have the techniques of description and interpretation evolved beyond the techniques of close read-

1. The New Critical distinction between "intrinsic" and "extrinsic" criticism derives from the influential handbook *Theory of Literature* (1949), by René Wellek and Austin Warren; they opposed criticism limited to internal, "formal" features of a literary work to that focusing on external concerns such as the author, readers, or history.

2. Quoted from the preface to *Beyond Formalism: Literary Essays, 1958–1970* (1970), by Geoffrey Hartman, de Man's colleague at Yale University.

ing established in the thirties and the forties. Formalism, it seems, is an all-absorbing and tyrannical muse; the hope that one can be at the same time technically original and discursively eloquent is not borne out by the history of literary criticism.

On the other hand—and this is the real mystery—no literary formalism, no matter how accurate and enriching in its analytic powers, is ever allowed to come into being without seeming reductive. When form is considered to be the external trappings of literary meaning or content, it seems superficial and expendable. The development of intrinsic, formalist criticism in the twentieth century has changed this model: form is now a solipsistic category of self-reflection, and the referential meaning is said to be extrinsic. The polarities of inside and outside have been reversed, but they are still the same polarities that are at play: internal meaning has become outside reference, and the outer form has become the intrinsic structure. A new version of reductiveness at once follows this reversal: formalism nowadays is mostly described in an imagery of imprisonment and claustrophobia: the "prison house of language," "the impasse of formalist criticism,"[3] etc. Like the grandmother in Proust's novel[4] ceaselessly driving the young Marcel out into the garden, away from the unhealthy inwardness of his closeted reading, critics cry out for the fresh air of referential meaning. Thus, with the structure of the code so opaque, but the meaning so anxious to blot out the obstacle of form, no wonder that the reconciliation of form and meaning would be so attractive. The attraction of reconciliation is the elective breeding-ground of false models and metaphors; it accounts for the metaphorical model of literature as a kind of box that separates an inside from an outside, and the reader or critic as the person who opens the lid in order to release in the open what was secreted but inaccessible inside. It matters little whether we call the inside of the box the content or the form, the outside the meaning or the appearance. The recurrent debate opposing intrinsic to extrinsic criticism stands under the aegis of an inside/outside metaphor that is never being seriously questioned.

Metaphors are much more tenacious than facts, and I certainly don't expect to dislodge this age-old model in one short try. I merely wish to speculate on a different set of terms, perhaps less simple in their differential relationships than the strictly polar, binary opposition between inside and outside and therefore less likely to enter into the easy play of chiasmic[5] reversals. I derive these terms (which are as old as the hills) pragmatically from the observation of developments and debates in recent critical methodology.

One of the most controversial among these developments coincides with a new approach to poetics or, as it is called in Germany, poetology, as a branch of general semiotics. In France, a semiology of literature comes about as the outcome of the long-deferred but all the more explosive encounter of the nimble French literary mind with the category of form. Semiology, as opposed

3. The title of one of de Man's own essays published in French in 1956, later translated as "The Dead-End of Formalist Criticism," in his *Blindness and Insight* (2d ed., 1983). "The 'prison house'": an allusion to *The Prison-House of Language: A Critical Account of Structuralism and Russian Formalism* (1972), by the American Marxist critic FREDRIC JAMESON.

4. *À la recherche du temps perdu* (7 vols., 1913–27; *In Search of Lost Time*), by the French novelist Marcel Proust (1871–1924). De Man uses this work as an example throughout the essay; its main character is the semi-autobiographical Marcel.

5. Of chiasmus, a rhetorical device in which the elements of the second of two parallel syntactic structures are inverted (e.g., "renowned for conquest, and in counsel skilled").

to semantics, is the science or study of signs as signifiers; it does not ask what words mean but how they mean. Unlike American New Criticism, which derived the internalization of form from the practice of highly self-conscious modern writers, French semiology turned to linguistics for its model and adopted Saussure and Jakobson rather than Valéry[6] or Proust for its masters. By an awareness of the arbitrariness of the sign (Saussure) and of literature as an autotelic statement "focused on the way it is expressed" (Jakobson) the entire question of meaning can be bracketed, thus freeing the critical discourse from the debilitating burden of paraphrase. The demystifying power of semiology, within the context of French historical and thematic criticism, has been considerable. It demonstrated that the perception of the literary dimensions of language is largely obscured if one submits uncritically to the authority of reference. It also revealed how tenaciously this authority continues to assert itself in a variety of disguises, ranging from the crudest ideology to the most refined forms of aesthetic and ethical judgment. It especially explodes the myth of semantic correspondence between sign and referent, the wishful hope of having it both ways, of being, to paraphrase Marx in the *German Ideology*, a formalist critic in the morning and a communal moralist in the afternoon,[7] of serving both the technique of form and the substance of meaning. The results, in the practice of French criticism, have been as fruitful as they are irreversible. Perhaps for the first time since the late eighteenth century, French critics can come at least somewhat closer to the kind of linguistic awareness that never ceased to be operative in its poets and novelists and that forced all of them, including Sainte Beuve,[8] to write their main works "contre Sainte Beuve." The distance was never so considerable in England and the United States, which does not mean, however, that we may be able, in this country, to dispense altogether with some preventative semiological hygiene.

One of the most striking characteristics of literary semiology as it is practiced today, in France and elsewhere, is the use of grammatical (especially syntactical) structures conjointly with rhetorical structures, without apparent awareness of a possible discrepancy between them. In their literary analyses, Barthes, Genette, Todorov, Greimas,[9] and their disciples all simplify and regress from Jakobson in letting grammar and rhetoric function in perfect continuity, and in passing from grammatical to rhetorical structures without difficulty or interruption. Indeed, as the study of grammatical structures is refined in contemporary theories of generative, transformational, and distributive grammar, the study of tropes and of figures (which is how the term *rhetoric* is used here, and not in the derived sense of comment or of eloquence or persuasion) becomes a mere extension of grammatical models, a particular subset of syntactical relations. In the recent *Dictionnaire encyclopédique des*

6. Paul Valéry (1871–1945), major modern French poet and essayist. FERDINAND DE SAUSSURE (1857–1913), Swiss linguist, the founder of structuralism and semiology. ROMAN JAKOBSON (1896–1982), Russian-born American linguist, literary theorist, and semiologist.

7. In his *German Ideology* (1845–46), the German economic and political theorist KARL MARX (1818–1883) notes that the goal of communist society would be to remove alienating regulations of work, so that one could "hunt in the morning, fish in the afternoon . . . [and] criticize after dinner."

8. Charles-Augustin Sainte-Beuve (1804–1869), the leading 19th-century French literary critic and historian. *Contre Sainte-Beuve* (*Against Saint-Beuve*) is the title of a critical response by Proust (published 1954).

9. All French critics: ROLAND BARTHES (1915–1980), major structuralist and poststructuralist; Gérard Genette (b. 1930), French literary critic and author of *Figures III* (1972; trans. 1980 as *Narrative Discourse: An Essay in Method*), mentioned later; TZVETAN TODOROV (1939–2017), Bulgarian-born structuralist; and A. J. Greimas (1917–1992), Lithuanian-born semiologist.

sciences du langage,[1] Ducrot and Todorov write that rhetoric has always been satisfied with a paradigmatic view over words (words substituting for each other), without questioning their syntagmatic relationship (the contiguity of words to each other). There ought to be another perspective, complementary to the first, in which metaphor, for example, would not be defined as a substitution but as a particular type of combination. Research inspired by linguistics or, more narrowly, by syntactical studies, has begun to reveal this possibility—but it remains to be explored. Todorov, who calls one of his books a *Grammar of the Decameron*,[2] rightly thinks of his own work and that of his associates as first explorations in the elaboration of a systematic grammar of literary modes, genres, and also of literary figures. Perhaps the most perceptive work to come out of this school, Genette's studies of figural modes, can be shown to be assimilations of rhetorical transformations or combinations to syntactical, grammatical patterns. Thus a recent study, now printed in *Figures III* and entitled *Metaphor and Metonymy in Proust*, shows the combined presence, in a wide and astute selection of passages, of paradigmatic, metaphorical figures with syntagmatic, metonymic structures. The combination of both is treated descriptively and nondialectically without considering the possibility of logical tensions.

One can ask whether this reduction of figure to grammar is legitimate. The existence of grammatical structures, within and beyond the unit of the sentence, in literary texts is undeniable, and their description and classification are indispensable. The question remains if and how figures of rhetoric can be included in such a taxonomy. This question is at the core of the debate going on, in a wide variety of apparently unrelated forms, in contemporary poetics. But the historical picture of contemporary criticism is too confused to make the mapping out of such a topography a useful exercise. Not only are these questions mixed in and mixed up within particular groups or local trends, but they are often co-present, without apparent contradiction, within the work of a single author.

Neither is the theory of the question suitable for quick expository treatment. To distinguish the epistemology of grammar from the epistemology of rhetoric is a redoubtable task. On an entirely naïve level, we tend to conceive of grammatical systems as tending towards universality and as simply generative, i.e., as capable of deriving an infinity of versions from a single model (that may govern transformations as well as derivations) without the intervention of another model that would upset the first. We therefore think of the relationship between grammar and logic, the passage from grammar to propositions, as being relatively unproblematic: no true propositions are conceivable in the absence of grammatical consistency or of controlled deviation from a system of consistency no matter how complex. Grammar and logic stand to each other in a dyadic relationship of unsubverted support. In a logic of acts rather than of statements, as in Austin's[3] theory of speech acts, that has had such a

1. Published in 1972; translated as *Encyclopedic Dictionary of the Sciences of Language* (1979). Oswald Ducrot (b. 1930), French linguist. The distinction between *paradigmatic* and *syntagmatic* draws on Saussure.

2. *Grammaire du Décaméron* (1969). *The Decameron* (1348–53), a collection of 100 tales, is the best-known work of the Italian writer GIOVANNI BOCCACCIO.

3. J. L. AUSTIN (1911–1960), influential British philosopher of language, especially of speech acts (what we typically perform when we speak). He distinguishes between locutionary acts (saying something meaningful), illocutionary acts (saying something meaningful for some purpose), and perlocutionary acts (having an effect on those who hear what is said).

strong influence on recent American work in literary semiology, it is also possible to move between speech acts and grammar without difficulty. The performance of what is called illocutionary acts such as ordering, questioning, denying, assuming, etc., within the language is congruent with the grammatical structures of syntax in the corresponding imperative, interrogative, negative, optative sentences. "The rules for illocutionary acts," writes Richard Ohmann in a recent paper, "determine whether performance of a given act is well-executed, in just the same way as *grammatical* rules determine whether the product of a locutionary act—a sentence—is well formed. . . . But whereas the rules of grammar concern the relationships among sound, syntax, and meaning, the rules of illocutionary acts concern relationships among people."[4] And since rhetoric is then conceived exclusively as persuasion, as actual action upon others (and not as an intralinguistic figure or trope), the continuity between the illocutionary realm of grammar and the perlocutionary realm of rhetoric is self-evident. It becomes the basis for a new rhetoric that, exactly as is the case for Todorov and Genette, would also be a new grammar.

Without engaging the substance of the question, it can be pointed out, without having to go beyond recent and American examples, and without calling upon the strength of an age-old tradition, that the continuity here assumed between grammar and rhetoric is not borne out by theoretical and philosophical speculation. Kenneth Burke[5] mentions *deflection* (which he compares structurally to Freudian displacement), defined as "any slight bias or even unintended error," as the rhetorical basis of language, and deflection is then conceived as a dialectical subversion of the consistent link between sign and meaning that operates within grammatical patterns; hence Burke's well-known insistence on the distinction between grammar and rhetoric. Charles Sanders Peirce, who, with Nietzsche[6] and Saussure, laid the philosophical foundation for modern semiology, stressed the distinction between grammar and rhetoric in his celebrated and so suggestively unfathomable definition of the sign. He insists, as is well known, on the necessary presence of a third element, called the interpretant, within any relationship that the sign entertains with its object. The sign is to be interpreted if we are to understand the idea it is to convey, and this is so because the sign is not the thing but a meaning derived from the thing by a process here called representation that is not simply generative, i.e., dependent on a univocal origin. The interpretation of the sign is not, for Peirce, a meaning but another sign; it is a reading, not a decodage, and this reading has, in its turn, to be interpreted into another sign, and so on *ad infinitum*. Peirce calls this process by means of which "one sign gives birth to another" pure rhetoric, as distinguished from pure grammar, which postulates the possibility of unproblematic, dyadic meaning, and pure logic, which postulates the possibility of the universal truth of meanings. Only if the sign engendered meaning in the same way that the object engenders the sign, that is, by representation, would there be no need to distinguish between grammar and rhetoric.

4. "Speech, Literature, and the Space in Between," *New Literary History* 4 (autumn 1972): 50 [de Man's note]. OHMANN (b. 1931), American literary and cultural critic.

5. American rhetorician and literary critic (1897–1993); he drew on the work of the Austrian founder of psychoanalysis SIGMUND FREUD (1856–1939), among many others.

6. FRIEDRICH NIETZSCHE (1844–1900), German philosopher. Peirce (1839–1914), American pragmatist philosopher and linguist.

These remarks should indicate at least the existence and the difficulty of the question, a difficulty which puts its concise theoretical exposition beyond my powers. I must retreat therefore into a pragmatic discourse and try to illustrate the tension between grammar and rhetoric in a few specific textual examples. Let me begin by considering what is perhaps the most commonly known instance of an apparent symbiosis between a grammatical and a rhetorical structure, the so-called rhetorical question, in which the figure is conveyed directly by means of a syntactical device. I take the first example from the sub-literature of the mass media: asked by his wife whether he wants to have his bowling shoes laced over or laced under, Archie Bunker[7] answers with a question: "What's the difference?" Being a reader of sublime simplicity, his wife replies by patiently explaining the difference between lacing over and lacing under, whatever this may be, but provokes only ire. "What's the difference" did not ask for difference but means instead "I don't give a damn what the difference is." The same grammatical pattern engenders two meanings that are mutually exclusive: the literal meaning asks for the concept (difference) whose existence is denied by the figurative meaning. As long as we are talking about bowling shoes, the consequences are relatively trivial; Archie Bunker, who is a great believer in the authority of origins (as long, of course, as they are the right origins) muddles along in a world where literal and figurative meanings get in each other's way, though not without discomforts. But suppose that it is a *de*-bunker rather than a "Bunker," and a de-bunker of the arche (or origin), an archie De-bunker such as Nietzsche or Jacques Derrida[8] for instance, who asks the question "What is the Difference"—and we cannot even tell from his grammar whether he "really" wants to know "what" difference is or is just telling us that we shouldn't even try to find out. Confronted with the question of the difference between grammar and rhetoric, grammar allows us to ask the question, but the sentence by means of which we ask it may deny the very possibility of asking. For what is the use of asking, I ask, when we cannot even authoritatively decide whether a question asks or doesn't ask?

The point is as follows. A perfectly clear syntactical paradigm (the question) engenders a sentence that has at least two meanings, of which the one asserts and the other denies its own illocutionary mode. It is not so that there are simply two meanings, one literal and the other figural, and that we have to decide which one of these meanings is the right one in this particular situation. The confusion can only be cleared up by the intervention of an extra-textual intention, such as Archie Bunker putting his wife straight; but the very anger he displays is indicative of more than impatience; it reveals his despair when confronted with a structure of linguistic meaning that he cannot control and that holds the discouraging prospect of an infinity of similar future confusions, all of them potentially catastrophic in their consequences. Nor is this intervention really a part of the mini-text constituted by the figure which holds our attention only as long as it remains suspended and unresolved. I follow the usage of common speech in calling this semiological enigma "rhetorical." The grammatical model of the question becomes

7. The main character in the popular CBS television series *All in the Family* (1971–79), played by Carroll O'Connor; his wife, Edith, was played by Jean Stapleton.

8. Algerian-born French philosopher and progenitor of deconstruction (1930–2004; see below). "Arche" derives from the Greek *archē* (origin).

rhetorical not when we have, on the one hand, a literal meaning and on the other hand a figural meaning, but when it is impossible to decide by grammatical or other linguistic devices which of the two meanings (that can be entirely incompatible) prevails. Rhetoric radically suspends logic and opens up vertiginous possibilities of referential aberration. And although it would perhaps be somewhat more remote from common usage, I would not hesitate to equate the rhetorical, figural potentiality of language with literature itself. I could point to a great number of antecedents to this equation of literature with figure; the most recent reference would be to Monroe Beardsley's insistence in his contribution to the *Essays* to honor William Wimsatt, that literary language is characterized by being "distinctly above the norm in ratio of implicit [or, I would say rhetorical] to explicit meaning."[9]

Let me pursue the matter of the rhetorical question through one more example. Yeats's poem "Among School Children"[1] ends with the famous line: "How can we know the dancer from the dance?" Although there are some revealing inconsistencies within the commentaries, the line is usually interpreted as stating, with the increased emphasis of a rhetorical device, the potential unity between form and experience, between creator and creation. It could be said that it denies the discrepancy between the sign and the referent from which we started out. Many elements in the imagery and the dramatic development of the poem strengthen this traditional reading; without having to look any further than the immediately preceding lines, one finds powerful and consecrated images of the continuity from part to whole that makes synecdoche into the most seductive of metaphors: the organic beauty of the tree, stated in the parallel syntax of a similar rhetorical question, or the convergence, in the dance, of erotic desire with musical form:

> O chestnut-tree, great-rooted blossomer,
> Are you the leaf, the blossom or the bole?
> O body swayed to music, O brightening glance,
> How can we know the dancer from the dance?

A more extended reading, always assuming that the final line is to be read as a rhetorical question, reveals that the thematic and rhetorical grammar of the poem yields a consistent reading that extends from the first line to the last and that can account for all the details in the text. It is equally possible, however, to read the last line literally rather than figuratively, as asking with some urgency the question we asked earlier within the context of contemporary criticism: *not* that sign and referent are so exquisitely fitted to each other that all difference between them is at times blotted out but, rather, since the two essentially different elements, sign and meaning, are so intricately intertwined in the imagined "presence" that the poem addresses, how can we possibly make the distinctions that would shelter us from the error of identifying what cannot be identified? The clumsiness of the paraphrase reveals that it is not necessarily the literal reading which is simpler than the figurative one, as was the case in our first example; here, the figural reading,

9. "The Concept of Literature," in *Literary Theory and Structure: Essays in Honor of William K. Wimsatt*, ed. Frank Brady, John Palmer, and Martin Price (New Haven, 1973), p. 37 [de Man's note]. BEARDSLEY (1915–1985), American aesthetic philosopher and Wimsatt's collaborator. WIMSATT (1907–1975), American New Critic based at Yale.

1. First published in *The Dial* (1927), by William Butler Yeats (1865–1939), a leading modernist Irish poet and the subject of de Man's Ph.D. dissertation.

which assumes the question to be rhetorical, is perhaps naïve, whereas the literal reading leads to greater complication of theme and statement. For it turns out that the entire scheme set up by the first reading can be undermined, or deconstructed, in the terms of the second, in which the final line is read literally as meaning that, since the dancer and the dance are not the same, it might be useful, perhaps even desperately necessary—for the question can be given a ring of urgency, "Please tell me, how *can* I know the dancer from the dance"—to tell them apart. But this will replace the reading of each symbolic detail by a divergent interpretation. The oneness of trunk, leaf, and blossom, for example, that would have appealed to Goethe, would find itself replaced by the much less reassuring Tree of Life from the Mabinogion that appears in the poem "Vacillation," in which the fiery blossom and the earthly leaf are held together, as well as apart, by the crucified and castrated God Attis,[2] of whose body it can hardly be said that it is "not bruised to pleasure soul."[3] This hint should suffice to suggest that two entirely coherent but entirely incompatible readings can be made to hinge on one line, whose grammatical structure is devoid of ambiguity, but whose rhetorical mode turns the mood as well as the mode of the entire poem upside down. Neither can we say, as was already the case in the first example, that the poem simply has two meanings that exist side by side. The two readings have to engage each other in direct confrontation, for the one reading is precisely the error denounced by the other and has to be undone by it. Nor can we in any way make a valid decision as to which of the readings can be given priority over the other; none can exist in the other's absence. There can be no dance without a dancer, no sign without a referent. On the other hand, the authority of the meaning engendered by the grammatical structure is fully obscured by the duplicity of a figure that cries out for the differentiation that it conceals.

Yeats's poem is not explicitly "about" rhetorical questions but about images or metaphors, and about the possibility of convergence between experiences of consciousness such as memory or emotions—what the poem calls passion, piety, and affection—and entities accessible to the senses such as bodies, persons, or icons. We return to the inside/outside model from which we started out and which the poem puts into question by means of a syntactical device (the question) made to operate on a grammatical as well as on a rhetorical level. The couple grammar/rhetoric, certainly not a binary opposition since they in no way exclude each other, disrupts and confuses the neat antithesis of the inside/outside pattern. We can transfer this scheme to the act of reading and interpretation. By reading we get, as we say, *inside* a text that was first something alien to us and which we now make our own by an act of understanding. But this understanding becomes at once the representation of an extra-textual meaning; in Austin's terms, the illocutionary speech act becomes a perlocutionary actual act—in Frege's[4] terms, *Bedeutung*

2. Greek god of fertility and vegetation (though not crucified, in Greek versions of his myth). Johann Wolfgang von Goethe (1749–1832), German poet, playwright, and novelist, whose works (including writings in botany) reflected an interest in the organic, developing whole. The *Mabinogion* (comp. 14th c.), a collection of medieval Welsh prose tales. "Vacillation" (1932), a poem by Yeats.

3. Earlier in the final stanza of "Among School Children," Yeats wrote, "The body is not bruised to please the soul."

4. Gottlob Frege (1848–1925), German philosopher of language, logic, and mathematics, who distinguishes between a word's reference (in German, *Bedeutung*), or the object it represents, and its sense (*Sinn*), or the thought it expresses.

becomes *Sinn*. Our recurrent question is whether this transformation is semantically controlled along grammatical or along rhetorical lines. Does the metaphor of reading really unite outer meaning with inner understanding, action with reflection, into one single totality? The assertion is powerfully and suggestively made in a passage from Proust that describes the experience of reading as such a union. It describes the young Marcel, near the beginning of Combray,[5] hiding in the closed space of his room in order to read. The example differs from the earlier ones in that we are not dealing with a grammatical structure that also functions rhetorically but have instead the representation, the dramatization, in terms of the experience of a subject, of a rhetorical structure—just as, in many other passages, Proust dramatizes tropes by means of landscapes or descriptions of objects. The figure here dramatized is that of metaphor, an inside/outside correspondence as represented by the act of reading. The reading scene is the culmination of a series of actions taking place in enclosed spaces and leading up to the "dark coolness" of Marcel's room.

> I had stretched out on my bed, with a book, in my room which sheltered, tremblingly, its transparent and fragile coolness from the afternoon sun, behind the almost closed blinds through which a glimmer of daylight had nevertheless managed to push its yellow wings, remaining motionless between the wood and the glass, in a corner, poised like a butterfly. It was hardly light enough to read, and the sensation of the light's splendor was given me only by the noise of Camus[6] . . . hammering dusty crates; resounding in the sonorous atmosphere that is peculiar to hot weather, they seemed to spark off scarlet stars; and also by the flies executing their little concert, the chamber music of summer: evocative not in the manner of a human tune that, heard perchance during the summer, afterwards reminds you of it but connected to summer by a more necessary link: born from beautiful days, resurrecting only when they return, containing some of their essence, it does not only awaken their image in our memory; it guarantees their return, their actual, persistent, unmediated presence.
>
> The dark coolness of my room related to the full sunlight of the street as the shadow relates to the ray of light, that is to say it was just as luminous and it gave my imagination the total spectacle of the summer, whereas my senses, if I had been on a walk, could only have enjoyed it by fragments; it matched my repose which (thanks to the adventures told by my book and stirring my tranquility) supported, like the quiet of a motionless hand in the middle of a running brook the shock and the motion of a torrent of activity.[7]

For our present purpose, the most striking aspect of this passage is the juxtaposition of figural and metafigural language. It contains seductive metaphors that bring into play a variety of irresistible objects: chamber music, butterflies, stars, books, running brooks, etc., and it inscribes these objects within dazzling fire- and waterworks of figuration. But the passage also com-

5. The title of the second section of the first volume of Proust's *Recherche*; it is the name of the small town where Marcel spent his childhood holidays at his grandparents' house.

6. A servant.

7. *Swann's Way* [*Du côté de chez Swann*] (Paris: Pléiade, 1954), p. 83 [de Man's note and translation].

ments normatively on the best way to achieve such effects; in this sense, it is metafigural: it writes figuratively about figures. It contrasts two ways of evoking the natural experience of summer and unambiguously states its preference for one of these ways over the other: the "necessary link" that unites the buzzing of the flies to the summer makes it a much more effective symbol than the tune heard "perchance" during the summer. The preference is expressed by means of a distinction that corresponds to the difference between metaphor and metonymy, necessity and chance being a legitimate way to distinguish between analogy and contiguity. The inference of identity and totality that is constitutive of metaphor is lacking in the purely relational metonymic contact: an element of truth is involved in taking Achilles for a lion but none in taking Mr. Ford[8] for a motor car. The passage is *about* the aesthetic superiority of metaphor over metonymy, but this aesthetic claim is made by means of categories that are the ontological ground of the metaphysical system that allows for the aesthetic to come into being as a category. The metaphor for summer (in this case, the synesthesia[9] set off by the "chamber music" of the flies) guarantees a presence which, far from being contingent, is said to be essential, permanently recurrent and unmediated by linguistic representations or figurations. Finally, in the second part of the passage, the metaphor of presence not only appears as the ground of cognition but as the performance of an action, thus promising the reconciliation of the most disruptive of contradictions. By then, the investment in the power of metaphor is such that it may seem sacrilegious to put it in question.

Yet, it takes little perspicacity to show that the text does not practice what it preaches. A rhetorical reading of the passage reveals that the figural praxis and the metafigural theory do not converge and that the assertion of the mastery of metaphor over metonymy owes its persuasive power to the use of metonymic structures. I have carried out such an analysis in a somewhat more extended context;[1] at this point, we are more concerned with the results than with the procedure. For the metaphysical categories of presence, essence, action, truth, and beauty do not remain unaffected by such a reading. This would become clear from an inclusive reading of Proust's novel or would become even more explicit in a language-conscious philosopher such as Nietzsche who, as a philosopher, has to be concerned with the epistemological consequences of the kind of rhetorical seductions exemplified by the Proust passage. It can be shown that the systematic critique of the main categories of metaphysics undertaken by Nietzsche in his late work, the critique of the concepts of causality, of the subject, of identity, of referential and revealed truth, etc., occurs along the same pattern of deconstruction that was operative in Proust's text; and it can also be shown that this pattern exactly corresponds to Nietzsche's description, in texts that precede *The Will to Power*[2] by more than fifteen years, of the structure of the

8. Henry Ford (1863–1947), American innovator of mass production and founder of the Ford Motor Company. Achilles: the greatest of the Greek warriors who fought at Troy. De Man draws on Jakobson's seminal distinction of metaphor (the figurative relation between brave Achilles and a lion) and metonymy (the figurative relation between Ford and one of his cars).

9. Rhetorical figure in which one sense is represented in terms of another; for example, "a loud tie."

1. In a later chapter of *Allegories of Reading: Figural Language in Rousseau, Nietzsche, Rilke, and Proust* (1979); this essay was reprinted to serve as the book's introduction.

2. A late work, drawing on fragments from ca. 1888 (published posthumously in 1901). For the earlier works to which de Man refers, see especially "On Truth and Lying in a Non-Moral Sense" (1873; above).

main rhetorical tropes. The key to this critique of metaphysics, which is itself a recurrent gesture throughout the history of thought, is the rhetorical model of the trope or, if one prefers to call it that, literature. It turns out that in these innocent-looking didactic exercises we are in fact playing for very sizeable stakes.

It is therefore all the more necessary to know what is linguistically involved in a rhetorically conscious reading of the type here undertaken on a brief fragment from a novel and extended by Nietzsche to the entire text of post-Hellenic thought. Our first examples dealing with the rhetorical questions were rhetorizations of grammar, figures generated by syntactical paradigms, whereas the Proust example could be better described as a grammatization of rhetoric. By passing from a paradigmatic structure based on substitution, such as metaphor, to a syntagmatic structure based on contingent association such as metonymy, the mechanical, repetitive aspect of grammatical forms is shown to be operative in a passage that seemed at first sight to celebrate the self-willed and autonomous inventiveness of a subject. Figures are assumed to be inventions, the products of a highly particularized individual talent, whereas no one can claim credit for the programmed pattern of grammar. Yet, our reading of the Proust passage shows that precisely when the highest claims are being made for the unifying power of metaphor, these very images rely in fact on the deceptive use of semi-automatic grammatical patterns. The deconstruction of metaphor and of all rhetorical patterns such as mimesis, paronomasia,[3] or personification that use resemblance as a way to disguise differences, takes us back to the impersonal precision of grammar and of a semiology derived from grammatical patterns. Such a reading puts into question a whole series of concepts that underlie the value judgments of our critical discourse: the metaphors of primacy, of genetic history, and, most notably, of the autonomous power to will of the self.

There seems to be a difference, then, between what I called the rhetorization of grammar (as in the rhetorical question) and the grammatization of rhetoric, as in the readings of the type sketched out in the passage from Proust. The former end up in indetermination, in a suspended uncertainty that was unable to choose between two modes of reading, whereas the latter seems to reach a truth, albeit by the negative road of exposing an error, a false pretense. After the rhetorical reading of the Proust passage, we can no longer believe the assertion made in this passage about the intrinsic, metaphysical superiority of metaphor over metonymy. We seem to end up in a mood of negative assurance that is highly productive of critical discourse. The further text of Proust's novel, for example, responds perfectly to an extended application of this pattern: not only can similar gestures be repeated throughout the novel, at all the crucial articulations or all passages where large aesthetic and metaphysical claims are being made—the scenes of involuntary memory, the workshop of Elstir, the septette of Vinteuil,[4] the convergence of author and narrator at the end of the novel—but a vast thematic and semiotic network is revealed that structures the entire narrative and that remained invisible to a reader caught in naïve metaphorical mysti-

3. Wordplay, especially a pun.

4. Vinteuil, a composer, and Elstir, a painter, are characters in Proust's *Recherche*. "Septette": a septet, a musical composition for 7 performers.

fication. The whole of literature would respond in similar fashion, although the techniques and the patterns would have to vary considerably, of course, from author to author. But there is absolutely no reason why analyses of the kind here suggested for Proust would not be applicable, with proper modifications of technique, to Milton or to Dante or to Hölderlin.[5] This will in fact be the task of literary criticism in the coming years.

It would seem that we are saying that criticism is the deconstruction of literature, the reduction to the rigors of grammar of rhetorical mystifications. And if we hold up Nietzsche as the philosopher of such a critical deconstruction, then the literary critic would become the philosopher's ally in his struggle with the poets. Criticism and literature would separate around the epistemological axis that distinguishes grammar from rhetoric. It is easy enough to see that this apparent glorification of the critic-philosopher in the name of truth is in fact a glorification of the poet as the primary source of this truth; if truth is the recognition of the systematic character of a certain kind of error, then it would be fully dependent on the prior existence of this error. Philosophers of science like Bachelard or Wittgenstein[6] are notoriously dependent on the aberrations of the poets. We are back at our unanswered question: does the grammatization of rhetoric end up in negative certainty or does it, like the rhetorization of grammar, remain suspended in the ignorance of its own truth or falsehood?

Two concluding remarks should suffice to answer the question. First of all, it is not true that Proust's text can simply be reduced to the mystified assertion (the superiority of metaphor over metonymy) that our reading deconstructs. The reading is not "our" reading, since it uses only the linguistic elements provided by the text itself; the distinction between author and reader is one of the false distinctions that the reading makes evident. The deconstruction is not something we have added to the text but it constituted the text in the first place. A literary text simultaneously asserts and denies the authority of its own rhetorical mode, and by reading the text as we did we were only trying to come closer to being as rigorous a reader as the author had to be in order to write the sentence in the first place. Poetic writing is the most advanced and refined mode of deconstruction; it may differ from critical or discursive writing in the economy of its articulation, but not in kind.

But if we recognize the existence of such a moment as constitutive of all literary language, we have surreptitiously reintroduced the categories that this deconstruction was supposed to eliminate and that have merely been displaced. We have, for example, displaced the question of the self from the referent into the figure of the narrator, who then becomes the *signifé*[7] of the passage. It becomes again possible to ask such naïve questions as what Proust's, or Marcel's, motives may have been in thus manipulating language: was he fooling himself, or was he represented as fooling himself and fooling us into believing that fiction and action are as easy to unite, by reading, as the passage asserts? The pathos of the entire section, which would have been more noticeable if the quotation had been a little more extended, the

5. Friedrich Hölderlin (1770–1843), German Romantic poet. John Milton (1608–1674), English poet whose works include *Paradise Lost* (1667). DANTE ALIGHIERI (1265–1321), Italian poet, best known for the *Divine Comedy* (1321).

6. Ludwig Wittgenstein (1889–1951), Austrian-born philosopher. Gaston Bachelard (1884–1962), French philosopher.

7. Signified (French); a term used by Saussure, who divided the sign into the *signified* (the meaning conveyed) and *signifier* (the symbol or word that conveys that meaning).

constant vacillation of the narrator between guilt and well-being, invites such questions. They are absurd questions, of course, since the reconciliation of fact and fiction occurs itself as a mere assertion made in a text, and is thus productive of more text at the moment when it asserts its decision to escape from textual confinement. But even if we free ourselves of all false questions of intent and rightfully reduce the narrator to the status of a mere grammatical pronoun, without which the narrative could not come into being, this subject remains endowed with a function that is not grammatical but rhetorical, in that it gives voice, so to speak, to a grammatical syntagm. The term *voice*, even when used in a grammatical terminology as when we speak of the passive or interrogative voice, is, of course, a metaphor inferring by analogy the intent of the subject from the structure of the predicate. In the case of the deconstructive discourse that we call literary, or rhetorical, or poetic, this creates a distinctive complication illustrated by the Proust passage. The reading revealed a first paradox: the passage valorizes metaphor as being the "right" literary figure, but then proceeds to constitute itself by means of the epistemologically incompatible figure of metonymy. The critical discourse reveals the presence of this delusion and affirms it as the irreversible mode of its truth. It cannot pause there however. For if we then ask the obvious and simple next question, whether the rhetorical mode of the text in question is that of metaphor or metonymy, it is impossible to give an answer. Individual metaphors, such as the chiaroscuro effect or the butterfly, are shown to be subordinate figures in a general clause whose syntax is metonymic; from this point of view, it seems that the rhetoric is superseded by a grammar that deconstructs it. But this metonymic clause has as its subject a voice whose relationship to this clause is again metaphorical. The narrator who tells us about the impossibility of metaphor is himself, or itself, a metaphor, the metaphor of a grammatical syntagm whose meaning is the denial of metaphor stated, by antiphrasis,[8] as its priority. And this subject-metaphor is, in its turn, open to the kind of deconstruction to the second degree, the rhetorical deconstruction of psycholinguistics, in which the more advanced investigations of literature are presently engaged, against considerable resistance.

We end up therefore, in the case of the rhetorical grammatization of semiology, just as in the grammatical rhetorization of illocutionary phrases, in the same state of suspended ignorance. Any question about the rhetorical mode of a literary text is always a rhetorical question which does not even know whether it is really questioning. The resulting pathos is an anxiety (or bliss, depending on one's momentary mood or individual temperament) of ignorance, not an anxiety of reference—as becomes thematically clear in Proust's novel when reading is dramatized, in the relationship between Marcel and Albertine,[9] not as an emotive reaction to what language does, but as an emotive reaction to the impossibility of knowing what it might be up to. Literature as well as criticism—the difference between them being delusive—is condemned (or privileged) to be forever the most rigorous and, consequently, the most unreliable language in terms of which man names and transforms himself.

1973, 1979

8. Rhetorical device of using words in a sense opposite to their generally accepted meaning.

9. Marcel's love interest in the novel.

C. D. NARASIMHAIAH
1921–2005

Along with K. R. Srinivasa Iyengar, Closepet Dasappa Narasimhaiah helped create the field of Indian literatures in English in the twentieth century and pioneered its criticism. Largely rejecting Western approaches to Indian literatures written in English, he argued for the establishment of an Indian critical tradition relying on the centuries-old Sanskritist theories that locate the significance of a text in *rasa* (emotion and soul) and *dhvani* (meaning and suggestion). Narasimhaiah simultaneously promoted the ancient *rasa-dhvani* tradition of poetics and called for its modernization.

C. D. Narasimhaiah was born in Closepet, in the southern Indian state of Mysore (as was traditional, his first name indicated his birthplace), and lived virtually all of his life in Mysore. He studied at the University of Mysore and then at Cambridge University (1947–49); there he earned a degree in English and was strongly influenced by the major British literary critic F. R. LEAVIS, who taught at Downing College. In his book on Leavis, *Better Literary History and Better Literary Criticism* (1963), Narasimhaiah writes, "I hadn't heard of Dr. Leavis until 1947 when by a lucky chance I went on a scholarship to Cambridge to read for the English tripos [honors examination]. I went to Christ's [College]. But my other home was to be Downing." Narasimhaiah was drawn into the community of intellectuals associated with *Scrutiny*, a leading journal of literary criticism founded by Leavis. When Narasimhaiah returned to India, he taught at Maharajah's College in Mysore from 1950 to 1979. Later, he traveled widely and taught at Yale and the Universities of Wisconsin, Texas, and Hawaii in the United States; at the University of Leeds in the United Kingdom; and at Flinders University in Australia. His contribution to the study of Indian literatures in English and of British Commonwealth literatures lies not just in his works of literary criticism but also in the library and study center he founded, Dhvanyaloka—named after the celebrated Sanskrit treatise, which Narasimhaiah revered, and modeled on the famous Rockefeller Study Center at Bellagio, Italy. Its unique collection of Indian and Commonwealth literary materials is a magnet for scholars.

British merchants began trading in India early in the seventeenth century, and after the British Empire took control of the subcontinent in the eighteenth century the knowledge and use of English spread. When Thomas Babington Macaulay, in his "Minute on Indian Education" (1835) addressed to Parliament, argued that the "natives" should be instructed in English, he pointed out that many were already "quite competent to discuss political or scientific questions with fluency and precision in the English language." Raja Rammohun Roy (1772–1833), among others, was writing literary works in English; and in the 1870s two precocious sisters, both writers—Aru and Toru Dutt—attended the "Higher Lectures for women" at Cambridge. Rabindranath Tagore, the first Indian writer to achieve worldwide fame, won the 1913 Nobel Prize in Literature largely on the strength of English translations of his Bengali verses. Three great writers of Indian literature in English—R. K. Narayan, Raja Rao, and Mulk Raj Anand—began publishing fiction in the 1930s, and literature in English continued to flourish in India after it gained independence from the United Kingdom in 1947.

With the rise of English-language Indian literature came distinctive problems for critics. In his landmark work *Indian Writing in English* (1962; 3d ed., 1983), which surveys the literature from its beginnings, Srinivasa Iyengar asked pointedly:

> What critical criteria shall we apply? Should we judge it as English literature because it comes with an English skin . . . or shall we judge it as Indian literature because it is after all the creation of Indians? There is a continuous Western

> critical tradition from Aristotle to T. S. Eliot, and more particularly an English tradition from Sidney and Ben Jonson and Dryden to the mentors of our own day, Eliot, Richards and Leavis. Likewise there is an Indian critical tradition with the emphasis on *rasa* and *dhwani*, the *bhavas* and the *alankaras*, and in the line of law givers like Bharata, Bhatta Nayaka, Mamta, Anandavardhana and Abhinava Gupta have come modern thinkers like Tagore and Sri Aurobindo.

The Indian critical tradition goes back to Sanskrit texts written from before the Common Era through medieval times, especially during the ninth to the thirteenth centuries; works by such writers as Bharata (3d c. B.C.E.?), Anandavardhana (820–890 C.E), and Abhinavagupta (950–1020) were retrieved by Narasimhaiah as he developed an Indian poetics and literary criticism from indigenous sources.

In a groundbreaking collection of essays, *The Swan and the Eagle* (1969), Narasimhaiah addresses the issues involved in creating a genuine Indian literature and criticism written in English. He observes: "Now what holds writers so divergent as those whose work is examined here, together? First and foremost, their writing is the expression of a distinct, identifiable sensibility which is Indian, and the language, foreign in the sense that it is not picked up on the mother's lap but learnt assiduously by a most sensitive exposure to its practitioners in a wide-ranging variety of speech and writing in India and abroad." Narasimhaiah goes on to dismiss as futile and fatuous such questions as whether Indians can write in English or whether English has a future as a medium of creative activity in India. He seeks to prevent the early Indian writers—Sarojini Naidu, Toru Dutt, and Aurobindo Ghose, among others—from being labeled "exiles in their own country," and he is preoccupied with establishing writing in English that is both of high quality and innately Indian. He regards Western critical practice as an imposition and continuation of the yoke of imperialism.

Similar battles were being fought at the time over African postcolonial literatures in English. The Nigerian author CHINUA ACHEBE defended the English language against those questioning whether African writers could and should write in it: "If it failed to give them a song, it at least gave them a tongue for sighing." In 1976, in an essay provocatively titled "The Future of Indian Literature in English Is Pretty Dim," the Indian poet and critic Dom Moraes argued that standards in writing had fallen dramatically and blamed the lack of a "proper critic" (a phrase borrowed from Leavis). Narasimhaiah agreed that more and better criticism was needed: "I would like to think that responsible criticism might have made a tremendous difference to our literatures, and if it has not done so it may be that we have merely degenerated into cataloguing and classifying and wrangling over grammatical subtleties, allowing the song to slip through our fingers."

But what criteria would these better critics employ? An emphasis on "universal" or Western standards or on the general belletristic quality that English language novels and poetry were held to embody was fostering an imitative tradition, in which modern Indian poets attempted to write like T. S. ELIOT and novelists emulated James Joyce. Narasimhaiah entered the debate and declared that Indian writing should be measured by the yardsticks supplied by Sanskritist criticism, particularly *rasa* and *dhvani*. He advocated studying the *Indianness* of Indian literature.

In our selection, "Towards the Formulation of a Common Poetic for Indian Literatures Today," published as an appendix to a volume of conference proceedings, *A Common Poetic for Indian Literatures* (1984), Narasimhaiah lays out an account of critical principles that are both steeped in Sanskrit tradition and open to Western poetics. Although he presents this text as a consensus document arrived at by a small working group, its recommendations were clearly his own. The traditional purpose of Indian Literatures is enlightenment and detachment, rather than accurate representation or self-expression as in the West. The function of criticism is evaluation as well as education. Ideally, the Indian critic is educated and informed, aware of ancient and current Indian and Western traditions. The ideal reader is open and sympathetic, and more knowledgeable and experienced than less adept readers and enthusiasts. The *rasas*—that is, eight primary emotions and experiences that flow through aesthetic transactions (between author, text, and audience)—resonate simultaneously as felt meaning, implication, and suggestion (*dhvani*). The ancient Sanskrit word *dhvani* includes in its broad range of connotations metaphysical as well as linguistic and physiological dimensions of sound. We are born into sound; it works in and through us continuously in the form of energy and is also a bodily foundation of existence. Like the classic Western theory of literature as mimetic-didactic, over more than a millennium the *rasa-dhvani* poetics of India has received much commentary and become highly nuanced. But, argues Narasimhaiah, it needs further revision and explication to incorporate modern discoveries such as the operations of the unconscious, the dynamics of symbolization, and the techniques of poetic suggestion (e.g., showing, not telling; deliberately omitting material; using ambiguous language). Narasimhaiah sees India's *rasa-dhvani* theory factoring both the future and the past into its poetics.

This notion of Indianness and the Sanskritic tradition has been rejected by others—perhaps most notably by Salman Rushdie, arguably the leading figure in the explosion of Indian English-language literature (largely by diaspora writers) that began in the 1980s and has continued to be published in the United States and Britain. In the introduction to *Imaginary Homelands* (1991), Rushdie recalls attending a conference on Indian literatures in English in London as a young writer at which "one distinguished novelist began his contribution by reciting a Sanskrit *sloka*." Rushdie objects: "None of us had been raised in a Sanskritic tradition. We were all reasonably 'educated,' however; so what were we being told? Perhaps that we weren't really 'Indian?'" Although Rushdie is probably referring here not to Narasimhaiah but to Raja Rao (who often began his speeches with Sanskrit couplets), the two held similar positions. The greatest resistance to Narasimhaiah's emphasis on Indianness has come from younger Indian writers raised or born overseas who want to be measured either by postcolonial criteria or by "universal" criteria of criticism.

Postcolonial theory, which often engages with writings in English by Indians, likewise frequently ignores or challenges the importance of this literature's quintessential Indianness. Postcolonial critics such as GAYATRI CHAKRAVORTY SPIVAK and HOMI K. BHABHA have rejected the turn toward indigenous critical practices as nostalgia for lost origins, and they typically draw instead on the work of European theorists such as JACQUES DERRIDA and JACQUES LACAN. Not surprisingly, many in India criticize the use of European theories to gauge the success or failure of Indian literature as demonstrating a further colonization of the culture.

Younger Indian literary and social critics, particularly those who are non-Brahmin, often reject both "postcolonial" criticism and the earlier generation of critics such as Narasimhaiah for displaying excessive Western influence. While they praise Narasimhaiah for the recovery and resurgence of traditional Indian language theories, particularly Sanskrit ones, they criticize him for being "Brahmanical and feudal." One representative blog posting declares that the "exclusive use of Sanskrit higher learning was in many ways instrumental in consolidating the hegemony of the Brahmins over Hindu society."

The question of Indianness—its nature and degree—has not disappeared. It remains a defining issue in the criticism and reception of literature in English by still younger diasporic Indian writers such as Jhumpa Lahiri as well as in the reception of Bollywood films and other new Indian cultural productions targeted to an international market. Even as the world has become increasingly globalized, Indian critics and writers have turned to expressing themselves in uniquely Indian ways and demanding to be judged by Indian standards. Thus, Narasimhaiah's emphasis on Indian intellectual traditions and the Sanskritist tradition continues to be relevant.

"Towards the Formulation of a Common Poetic for Indian Literatures Today"
Keywords: Aesthetics, Affect, The Body, Defense of Criticism, Nationhood, Postcolonial Criticism and Theory, Tradition, Vernacular Language

Towards the Formulation of a Common Poetic for Indian Literatures Today

The need for a common Poetic for Indian Literatures today is part of a larger realization since Independence,[1] of the need to forge forward. On the one hand, thanks to a long period of colonial rule we tended to look up to Western models—first English, then European—for our writing and look at Western literature exclusively through Western eyes, both of which led to a complacency which made us dependent on Western critical criteria and even values in dealing with our own literatures[2] and inhibited exploration of viable Indian alternatives. On the other hand, it was argued, perhaps rightly, that despite spells of resurgence since the turn of the first Millennium A.C. life in India had decayed, creativity dried up and decadence had set in making our art and literature repetitive. Both colonial rule and centuries of decadence had resulted in our loss of touch with the vital past of India. Understandably, we began to convince ourselves that traditional Indian poetic was inadequate in responding to literatures of the present day while, strangely, this fear did not seem to extend to Aristotelian Poetics.[3]

Interestingly, this period began to witness scattered but serious attempts by notable Western intellectuals themselves (for instance Spengler[4] in his *Decline of the West*) to reassess the West thanks to a growing disenchantment with its world-view. Pointing to the staying power of Indian civilization Camus[5] had occasion to remark that 'a civilization can endure in so far as its unity and greatness . . . stem from a spiritual principle'. Which reminded an Indian of the admonition of Ananda Coomaraswamy[6] in his celebrated essay 'What Has India Contributed to Human Welfare?' 'Her great humiliation', said Coomaraswamy, 'would be to substitute a cosmopolitan veneer, for then indeed, she must come before the world empty-handed' and in answer to his own question 'What then can India give?' he said 'simply, her Indianness'. Aurobindo's *Future Poetry*,[7] a rare volume of criticism, lost in the limbo of the great unread, contained valuable pointers to a new poetic.

It is against this background that a Seminar was held in January 1984 at Dhvanyaloka,[8] Mysore to consider the possibility of reaching a consensus

1. Independence from the British Empire, which had ruled India from the 18th century until 1947.
2. That is, in the several dozen languages written and spoken in India (its constitution recognizes 15 regional languages).
3. For the *Poetics* of the Greek philosopher ARISTOTLE (384–322 B.C.E.), see above.
4. Oswald Spengler (1880–1936), German historian and philosopher; in *The Decline of the West* (1918–22), he argued that civilizations have life cycles and the West was in decline.
5. Albert Camus (1913–1960), Algerian-born French writer; the quotation is from his lecture "The New Mediterranean Culture" (1937).
6. Ceylonese art historian (1877–1947), first curator of Indian art at Boston's Museum of Fine Art; the essay quoted was published in 1915.
7. A volume on the theory of poetry (1953) by Sri Aurobindo (1872–1950), Indian nationalist and mystic.
8. The center for literary studies established in 1979 by Narasimhaiah, named after the treatise by the philosopher Anandavardhana (820–890 C.E.) that set forth the principle of *rasa* (soul or essence) and *dhvani* (meaning and suggestion).

on the 'Formulation of a Common Poetic for Indian Literatures Today'. At the end of the three-day discussions which involved participants representing different regions and languages a small working party was set up with a view to preparing a draft on the subject to serve as a basis for wider debate in the country. It was suggested that in constructing a critical framework attention should be paid to critical problems, critical positions or approaches, critical criteria and tools as constituting a minimal equipment for those wanting to engage themselves in the business of criticism.

When the working party met in June 1984, although one of the members had reservations on how such a poetic could be constructed or how rewarding the new poetic could be in practice, it was decided by consensus that in constructing a new poetic it was advisable to make use of an existing framework of poetic which will suit the genius of India and (i) preserve our link with Tradition and foster a sense of continuity; (ii) assimilate the best elements in Western criticism; and (iii) be capable of facilitating a completeness of response to current works of literature.

The group started its deliberations by asking some of the seminal questions and formulating tentative answers:

Who is a Poet?

Traditionally, a poet is a seer (the Latin *Vates*)—*not* enough for him to look *at* life but look *into* it and write. His equipment is threefold: *Pratibha* (imagination), *Vyutpatti* (acquired knowledge) and *Abhyasa* (practice).[9]

How does the poet create?

The Western view is Mimesis or Imitation of life, while the Indian is summed up in Bharata's term *Bhāvānukīrtana* (as opposed to *anukarana*).[1] The traditional Indian view that Literature is imaginative experience rendered in words, whether it be verse, prose or drama, can be recognised in the inclusive term *kāvya*.[2] And *Rasa* (sap, juice, taste, flavour, experience which is supreme, disinterested, impersonal), the animating principle underlying all art and literature, is its soul (not 'plot' as to Aristotle). Interestingly Susan Langer, probably echoing a verse in Mahabharata,[3] has affirmed that all the worldly pleasures and those promised in Heaven do not equal one tithe of what Rasa can offer.

While Rasa may be of different kinds Bharata recognized eight[4] (corroborated by the list of primary emotions offered by the American psychologist Mcdougall[5]) and subsequently *sānta* was added as the ninth rasa. According to Bharata, rasa is evoked by a conjunction or fusion of *bhāva*, state of mind, *vibhāva*, its objective equivalent, *anubhāva*, concretization and *Vyabhicāribhava* or *sancāribhāva*, fleeting states. (See Bharata's *Nātyasāstra* and

9. Terms in Sanskrit, the language of ancient India and of Hindu scriptures; it was used in literary texts until the 11th century C.E. (All subsequent translations in this essay are from Sanskrit.)

1. That is, the equivalent of mimesis; *bhāvānu kīrtana* corresponds to Aristotle's idea of catharsis. Bharata Muni (3d c. B.C.E.?), Indian sage to whom is attributed the treatise *Nātyasāstra* (*The Science of Dance*), which describes the eight *rasas* (emotions).

2. Poetry, poetics.

3. Classic Sanskrit epic and major text of Hinduism, probably begun ca. 8th century B.C.E and codified ca. 4th century C.E. Susanne Langer (1895–1985), American philosopher and aesthetician.

4. Roughly translated as erotic, comic, pathetic, furious, heroic, horrific, odious, and wondrous: the emotional states connected with moods and gestures that link the author, text, and audience. The ninth (*sānta*) is associated with peace or serenity.

5. William McDougall (1871–1938), British-born American social psychologist; a chapter in his *Introduction to Social Psychology* (1908) discusses principal instincts and primary emotions.

subsequent expositions by Kuntaka, Anandavardhana, Abhinavagupta and Kshemendra[6]).

While each critic that came after Bharata made his own approach, Indian critics never forgot the end in view, namely the evocation of Rasa.

What is the purpose of Literature?

Delight and Instruction have been said to be the ends of literature in the West.[7] In the Indian tradition, Literature has an immediate and an ultimate use: immediately, there is in the presence of a work of art a *prayōjana,* usefulness, such as sensitizing the mind, likened to cleansing of the dust-covered mirror and awakening, or unfolding, of the lotus of man's inner being; the ultimate use, *purushārtha* is in the nature of value which consists in cultivating an attitude so aptly described by Matthew Arnold[8] as the Indian virtue of detachment.

What is the Function of Criticism?

Obviously, the function of criticism is to help the reader to realize these two ends of literature by means of elucidation and evaluation of the work in front of him.

What should be the Indian critic's equipment and training?

Primarily, he should be a Sahrdaya, responsive reader, actively collaborating with the writer and seeking corroboration from his fellows in what T. S. Eliot[9] called "the common pursuit of true judgement." The critic of literature must have a keen sense of the Indian past—its essential continuity, despite its diversity in race, religion, language, philosophical outlook and its spirit of questioning. Since our concern is with Indian criticism it calls for a fair grounding in Indian Poetics as presented in the major critical texts, a familiarity with literary masterpieces in Sanskrit and Prakrit[1] as well as one's own language; an awareness of significant movements in contemporary Indian literatures; and an exposure to important Western critical approaches ranging from the Classical and Neo-classical to the Romantic and 20th century critical modes like New Criticism, Marxist, Anthropological, Psychological, Linguistic-Stylistic.

What does a critic look for in a work of art?

He should recognize: *rasagati,* the dynamic flow or enactment of rasa; how the world of dry fact is suffused with rasa as embodied in language; *Vyangya-camatkriti,* which roughly means *dhvani,* insight into unstated meaning and all it entails; *aucitya,* congruity or propriety; and generally an awareness of the quintessential experience of life—'the horror, the boredom and the glory of existence'[2]—and its concretization reminding one of Gerard Manley Hopkins's inscape and instress.[3]

6. Indian literary critics, philosophers, and sages: Kuntaka (950–1000 C.E.), whose *Vakroktijivita* presents a theory of figurative expression; Anandavardhana, author of the *Dhvanyaloka*; Abhinava Gupta (950–1020), whose *Locana* is a commentary on it; and Kshemendra (active ca. 1150), whose treatise on poetry is titled *Kavikanthabhana.*

7. See HORACE's declaration that "Poets aim either to do good or to give pleasure" (*Ars Poetica,* ca. 10 B.C.E.; see above).

8. English critic and poet (1822–1888); he discusses detachment (critical "disinterestedness") in "The Function of Criticism at the Present Time" (1864; see above).

9. American-born English poet and critic (1888–1965; see above); the quotation is from "The Function of Criticism" (1923).

1. Vernacular languages.

2. An echo of Eliot's claim that the poet should see "the boredom, the horror, and the glory" of the world (*The Use of Poetry and the Use of Criticism,* 1933).

3. The force manifest in nature, art, and self—like "inscape" (divine design), a term invented by Hopkins (1844–1889), English poet and Jesuit priest.

Critical Problems

Certain critical problems will arise when the Indian critic trained in Western criticism proceeds to apply these concepts in the judgement of his literatures. For instance, Western critics have often pointed out that Indian life and literature lack in the vision of Evil. The Indian world-view has not been preoccupied with Good and Evil, but rather with *Vidya* and *avidya*,[4] the door being ever open to the individual to pass from ignorance to knowledge, whereas the Christian view of Sin, Redemption, Grace points in a different direction. Hence, predictably, the absence of Tragedy in the Western sense of the term. It should however be possible for the Indian critic to redefine Tragedy in terms of *avidya-Kama-Karma*,[5] the egocentric predicament, the transcending[6] of which has been regarded as the supreme end of life. Art and literature are believed to aid in this process—art has been said to be the layman's *yoga*.[7]

Another problem before the Indian critic is the Western concern with the personality of the author *vis-à-vis* his art. The expression of personal emotion in art, except as transmuted into artistic terms, when it becomes impersonal, has not been of any interest to the Indian critic, because, traditionally, in India the individual artist has looked upon himself as *nimittamatra* or instrument, and many have preferred to remain anonymous, be it literature, architecture or sculpture.

This position is the opposite of Romantic poets who regarded poetry as expression of personal emotion. Consider in this connection T. S. Eliot's 'Tradition and the Individual Talent'[8] in which it is a writer's tradition which expresses itself in art and the individual talent is but a catalyst. In India however, the work of art was held to be the expression of an unseen power, be it God, the Muse of Poetry or the grace of an exalted preceptor. This holds good even in cases where a poet chooses to assert his poetic identity, as the work never became a vehicle for his personal concerns—his vocation called for a surrender to the work in front of him. In contemporary literature, however, not all writers seem to conform to this view of art.

The focus of Indian aesthetic discussion is on the affective process, the way a work of art affects the reader. The reader enters into a dialogue, *hrdayasamvāda*, with the work of art before him and as the engagement with the work advances by stages variously described as *ahlāda, rasōllāsa*,[9] *cittavistara*, it matures into an absorption, *tallinatha* in it: for the duration of this condition, the reader has achieved his detachment or release from his egocentric predicament. The greater the work of art, the stronger its power to return the reader to itself and promote endless chewing of the work in all its aspects, *akhandacarvana*. This approximates to 'close reading' in analysis which calls for what F. R. Leavis[1] describes as 'minute attention to particularities'.

4. Ignorance. *Vidya*: knowledge.
5. Ignorance—desire—action (akin to hubris); terms taken from the *Upanishads*, ancient Hindu scriptures.
6. Shakespeare's *King Lear* [1605] seems to fit into this view admirably as his other tragedies do not [Narasimhaiah's note].
7. Discipline or practice. The philosopher Patanjali (ca. 2d c. B.C.E.) compiled the *yoga sutras*, texts that taught exercises to promote mental and physical discipline.
8. For this essay (1919), see above.
9. One of the "perfections" of literature that translates into *bhavas*, or feelings. The other two terms refer to the thrill that a reader experiences upon reading.
1. English literary critic (1895–1978; see above), a major influence on Narsimhaiah.

Indian theory was able to organize in hierarchical order the various levels of aesthetic response ranging from that of the *Ācārya,* the most-practised reader and the *pandita,* the scholar to the *bhakta,* the devotee or the mere enthusiast, the *sādhārana jana,* the average reader and *alpabuddhi jana* the unintelligent reader.

The *Rasa-Dhvani* theory of Abhinavagupta formed on the basis of Bharata's concept of *rasa* and Anandavardhana's concept of *dhvani* (which for Coomaraswamy means not sound, but sounding, indicating a lasting resonance in the heart of the reader) established itself as the most comprehensive literary theory in Sanskrit, assimilating all the earlier schools such as *Alankāra, Riti, Guna,* and *Vakrōkti.*[2] Its dominance as a poetic was further reinforced by the works of Mammata, Jagannatha and Viswanatha.[3] Some of its principles have since found independent corroboration in other critical traditions, notably the American (i.e. Poe, Emerson, Whitman, the New Criticism[4]), the French (i.e. Baudelaire, Mallarmé, Valéry[5]) and the British (i.e. Eliot, Empson[6]). *Dhvani* or suggestion has in substance been upheld by 20th century literary theory and also by the general shift from statement to suggestion in European writing at the beginning of the century. By defining emotion in art as suggested or implied meaning and 'literariness' as suggestiveness, it has acquired great explanatory power capable of accounting for a wide range and variety of literary phenomena.

The *Rasa-Dhvani* theory needs, however, to be enlarged to incorporate the insights of subsequent aesthetic theories: (1) The symbol as a fountain of expanding meaning and as generative force in creative activity thus becomes an important principle to be added to the Rasa-Dhvani theory. (2) Modern psychology has shown that states of mind (*bhava-s*) are infinite in number, diversity, mutual overlap and wealth of nuance. (3) It has further pointed to the importance of the unconscious as the source of all creativity. Modernist writing has discovered many more new channels of suggestion—such as non-propositional imagery, indeterminate language with a wealth of associations and evocative power, or precise, delicate verbal effects generating specific meaning. (4) Post-modernist literature has demonstrated how suggestion can operate through brevity, omission, reticence. (5) Modern fiction has proved how 'showing' is superior to 'telling' or statement and how submerged levels of narration can develop beneath the surface action. (6) Above all, the Dhvani theory's view of literature as language generating meaning is shared by most twentieth-century literary theories (consider also Leavis's 'language creates what it conveys').

While the work of art provided for enactment of states of mind and the corresponding *rasa-s, Santa rasa*[7] came to be eventually credited with the highest form of literary experience. (Interestingly though, the *pradhāna* or dominant

2. The science of speech, or poetics (also written *vakrōti*). *Alankāra*: literary embellishment. *Riti*: practice. *Guna*: descriptor associated with five elements, senses, body parts, and psychological states of being.
3. Vishwanatha (ca. 1378–ca. 1467), critic and dramatist, best known for his *Sahityadarpana* (*The Mirror of Literature*). Mammta or Mammata (ca. 11th c.) and Jagannatha (1620–1660) were also literary critics and dramatists.
4. The dominant Anglo-American school of criticism in the mid-20th century (promoted by CLEANTH BROOKS, W. K. WIMSATT JR., and others), emphasizing close reading of the text as an autonomous whole. The poets and critics are EDGAR ALLAN POE (1809–1849), RALPH WALDO EMERSON (1803–1882), and Walt Whitman (1819–1892).
5. Poets and critics: Charles Baudelaire (1821–1867), Stéphane Mallarmé (1842–1898), and Paul Valéry (1871–1945).
6. Sir William Empson (1906–1984), poet and critic; his best-known work of criticism is *Seven Types of Ambiguity* (1930).
7. Satisfaction.

rasa of the Ramayana[8] is *Karuna* (the compassionate) while that of the Mahabharata is *santa* (the poise, caused by what Keats[9] calls the evaporation of opposites) both acknowledged to be great works of art.)

The *Rasa-Dhvani* theory is more widely known in Indian literatures than any other critical system and its concepts are in vogue in our arts and literatures. As an important component of our common cultural heritage, it has made its influence felt in our literatures in varying degrees. It is therefore more capable than any other existing theory of serving as the basis of a common poetic for Indian literatures.

It should be understood that whatever be the critical framework, it can't be said to inhibit the individual reader's response to the work before him. On the contrary, it is hoped the poetic will provide a framework within which the responsive reader will find signs and landmarks to aid his exploration, assessment and possibly disagreement, all of which can advance the cause of criticism.

In any case, what is offered here is not a readymade system with a prescriptiveness, but a tentative formulation designed to provoke thought and stimulate discussion, *samalocana.*

1984

8. The second great classic Sanskrit epic (probably composed 3d c. B.C.E.), the story of the adventures of Rama (an incarnation of the god Vishnu).

9. John Keats (1795–1821), English poet.

RAYMOND WILLIAMS

1921–1988

Raymond Williams was the leading literary intellectual in Britain in the later twentieth century. A prolific writer, he was a literary journalist and novelist; a prominent critic of drama, the novel, culture, and media; and one of the founding figures of cultural studies, media studies, and communications. He was also a committed socialist, known for articulating Marxism and its relevance to literary studies. In our selection, "Base and Superstructure in Marxist Cultural Theory" (1973), Williams revises the traditional Marxist conception of culture, promoting ANTONIO GRAMSCI's more flexible concept of hegemony and developing a three-part account of historical change that notes emergent and residual forms alongside dominant ones.

The son of a railway worker, Williams grew up in a small farming village, Pandy, in Wales. A sense of class and place informs all his work, most visibly his novels, which depict working-class life and politics in Wales. In 1939 he entered Cambridge University on a state scholarship, where he became acutely aware of class distinctions; he was politically active in the Socialist Club and, for a short time, the Communist Party. In 1941 he left to serve in an artillery division of the British Army during World War II. He returned to Cambridge after the war, taking a degree in English in 1945. By that time he was married, with one small child and another on the way; so instead of accepting a postgraduate fellowship, he began teaching evening classes at Oxford in drama and fiction. His experience in adult education and

his involvement with the Workers Educational Association helped convince him of the importance of literature's social and political contexts and of the need for a democratic, "permanent education." In 1961 he returned to Cambridge as a lecturer, and in 1974 a professorship of drama was created for him, a position he held until retiring in 1983. At Cambridge Williams not only wrote prolifically but taught a number of students—among them, STUART HALL and TERRY EAGLETON—who would themselves become important figures in literary and cultural studies.

Literary studies in England after World War II were dominated by "Cambridge English," strongly influenced by F. R. LEAVIS, a longtime professor at Cambridge and the editor of the leading critical journal of its day, *Scrutiny*. Extolling, in his famous phrase, "the Great Tradition," Leavis privileged literature above all other disciplines, as offering a special morally edifying force. In so doing, he followed MATTHEW ARNOLD, who in *Culture and Anarchy* (1869) claimed that the literary canon could provide a civilizing "sweetness and light" to society, in effect assuming the redemptive power previously enjoyed by religion. Williams's answer was *Culture and Society, 1780–1950* (1958), which argued that "a culture is not only a body of intellectual and imaginative works; it is also a whole way of life," and that to study literature, high or low, one must also study society.

"Base and Superstructure in Marxist Cultural Theory" addresses a central issue in social theory: determinism. In building his theory of capitalism, KARL MARX used a spatial metaphor to describe how society works: the economic means of production form the foundation or base of human life, and other elements, such as politics and culture, form a superstructure arising from it. Early interpreters tended to see this relation in a rigid way, with the base fully determining the superstructure, whereas later interpreters have seen the relation between the two as more interactive. In particular, Gramsci examined the fluid ways in which the ruling class effected its domination through the consent of most citizens rather than through force or strict controls. For Williams, following Gramsci, culture plays a key role in gaining consent.

One of Williams's innovations was to show how culture has varied roles that can change over time. In addition to the dominant culture, there are also, he famously argues, residual and emergent forms, which are sometimes tolerated and sometimes not. For instance, in the 1970s punk culture was emergent and posed an anarchic challenge to dominant culture. However, as DICK HEBDIGE (see below) has shown, punk eventually became incorporated into capitalism as a style option. Another useful distinction Williams makes is between alternative and truly oppositional culture. As a style, it is questionable that punk holds real oppositional value. To take another example, a person living on an organic farm might present an alternative to industrial farming but have little political effect, whereas a person who organizes a group against industrial farming has more oppositional force against the dominant order. This question of resistance—of whether personal choices, group protests, or mass organizations have political effect—is portrayed by Williams as the problem of "incorporation," and it has incited much debate in contemporary cultural studies.

Williams also addresses a perennial issue in aesthetic theory about the relation of art and society. Early twentieth-century Marxist theorists, especially those advocating socialist realism, held that art directly reflects its society. In contrast, late twentieth-century theorists focused on mediation and what LOUIS ALTHUSSER and others deemed the "relative autonomy" of art. While Williams believes that the ruling class and its interests mold society, he sees the relation between art and society as interactive: society can be influenced by culture just as culture can be influenced by society. For this reason he is critical of formalism, which fetishizes the artwork as an object rather than a practice. Williams called his approach "cultural materialism," a label that encompasses both the Marxist concern with the material bases of society and the fluid ways that culture shapes society.

Although Marxist and radical thought played a significant role in Anglo-American criticism during the 1930s, such approaches were largely shunned during the cold war, particularly in the United States. The New York Intellectuals, for instance, as the title of Irving Howe's *Politics and the Novel* (1957) suggests, were like Williams in joining the literary and the social; but they were avowedly anticommunist and anti-Marxist. It was not until the 1970s and 1980s, in part through Williams's influence and example, that Marxist and socialist ideas once again became accepted in literary studies.

Williams's work, as he remarks in *Culture and Society*, "has been classified under headings as various as cultural history, historical semantics, history of ideas, social criticism, literary history and sociology." While some critics complain about Williams's style, which can be murky and ponderous, his disciplinary boundary crossing made him a model for cultural studies. Conversely, his stress on the political significance of literary works was criticized by more traditional scholars for falling outside the purview of literary studies proper. In a career extending the traditional boundaries of literary studies, Williams exemplifies the possibilities for combining literary work with committed politics, and literary criticism with social criticism.

"Base and Superstructure in Marxist Cultural Theory" Keywords: Cultural Studies, Hegemony, Ideology, Marxism

Base and Superstructure in Marxist Cultural Theory

Any modern approach to a Marxist theory of culture must begin by considering the proposition of a determining base and a determined superstructure.[1] From a strictly theoretical point of view this is not, in fact, where we might choose to begin. It would be in many ways preferable if we could begin from a proposition which originally was equally central, equally authentic: namely the proposition that social being determines consciousness.[2] It is not that the two propositions necessarily deny each other or are in contradiction. But the proposition of base and superstructure, with its figurative element, with its suggestion of a fixed and definite spatial relationship, constitutes, at least in certain hands, a very specialized and at times unacceptable version of the other proposition. Yet in the transition from Marx to Marxism, and in the development of mainstream Marxism itself, the proposition of the determining base and the determined superstructure has been commonly held to be the key to Marxist cultural analysis.

It is important, as we try to analyse this proposition, to be aware that the term of relationship which is involved, that is to say 'determines', is of great linguistic and theoretical complexity. The language of determination and even more of determinism was inherited from idealist and especially theological accounts of the world and man. It is significant that it is in one of his familiar inversions, his contradictions of received propositions, that Marx

1. In Marxist theory, the economic mode of production forms the base of society, determining the "superstructure"—its legal, political, and cultural aspects. Marxist theory is inspired by KARL MARX (1818–1883), German social, political, and economic philosopher.

2. In *A Contribution to the Critique of Political Economy* (1859; see above), Marx notes that "It is not the consciousness of men that determines their being, but, on the contrary, their social being that determines their consciousness," and in *The German Ideology* (1845–46; see above), Marx and his frequent coauthor, FRIEDRICH ENGELS (1820–1895), declare that "Life is not determined by consciousness, but consciousness by life."

uses the word which becomes, in English translation, 'determines' (the usual but not invariable German word is *bestimmen*). He is opposing an ideology that had been insistent on the power of certain forces outside man, or, in its secular version, on an abstract determining consciousness. Marx's own proposition explicitly denies this, and puts the origin of determination in men's own activities. Nevertheless, the particular history and continuity of the term serves to remind us that there are, within ordinary use—and this is true of most of the major European languages—quite different possible meanings and implications of the word 'determine'. There is, on the one hand, from its theological inheritance, the notion of an external cause which totally predicts or prefigures, indeed totally controls a subsequent activity. But there is also, from the experience of social practice, a notion of determination as setting limits, exerting pressures.

Now there is clearly a difference between a process of setting limits and exerting pressures, whether by some external force or by the internal laws of a particular development, and that other process in which a subsequent content is essentially prefigured, predicted and controlled by a preexisting external force. Yet it is fair to say, looking at many applications of Marxist cultural analysis, that it is the second sense, the notion of prefiguration, prediction or control, which has often explicitly or implicitly been used.

Superstructure: Qualifications and Amendments

The term of relationship is then the first thing that we have to examine in this proposition, but we have to do this by going on to look at the related terms themselves. 'Superstructure' (*Überbau*) has had most attention. In common usage, after Marx, it acquired a main sense of a unitary 'area' within which all cultural and ideological activities could be placed. But already in Marx himself, in the later correspondence of Engels, and at many points in the subsequent Marxist tradition, qualifications were made about the determined character of certain superstructural activities. The first kind of qualification had to do with delays in time, with complications, and with certain indirect or relatively distant relationships. The simplest notion of a superstructure, which is still by no means entirely abandoned, had been the reflection, the imitation or the reproduction of the reality of the base in the superstructure in a more or less direct way. Positivist notions of reflection and reproduction of course directly supported this. But since in many real cultural activities this relationship cannot be found, or cannot be found without effort or even violence to the material or practice being studied, the notion was introduced of delays in time, the famous lags; of various technical complications; and of indirectness, in which certain kinds of activity in the cultural sphere—philosophy, for example—were situated at a greater distance from the primary economic activities. That was the first stage of qualification of the notion of superstructure: in effect, an operational qualification. The second stage was related but more fundamental, in that the process of the relationship itself was more substantially looked at. This was the kind of reconsideration which gave rise to the modern notion of 'mediation', in which something more than simple reflection or reproduction—indeed something radically different from either reflection or reproduction—actively occurs. In the later twentieth century there is the notion of 'homologous structures', where there may be no direct or easily apparent similarity, and certainly nothing like reflection or reproduction, between the superstructural process and the reality of the base, but in which there is an essential homology or correspondence of structures, which can be discovered by analysis. This is not the same notion as 'mediation', but it is the same kind of amendment in that the relationship between the base and the superstructure is not supposed to be direct, nor simply operationally subject to lags and complications and indirectnesses, but that of its nature it is not direct reproduction.

These qualifications and amendments are important. But it seems to me that what has not been looked at with equal care is the received notion of the 'base' (*Basis, Grundlage*). And indeed I would argue that the base is the more important concept to look at if we are to understand the realities of cultural process. In many uses of the proposition of base and superstructure, as a matter of verbal habit, 'the base' has come to be considered virtually as an object, or in less crude cases, it has been considered in essentially uniform and usually static ways. 'The base' is the real social existence of man. 'The base' is the real relations of production corresponding to a stage of development of the material productive forces. 'The base' is a mode of production at a particular stage of its development. We make and repeat propositions of this kind, but the usage is then very different from Marx's emphasis on productive activities, in particular structural relations, constituting the foundation of all other activities. For while a particular stage of the development of production can be discovered and made precise by analysis, it is never in practice either uniform or static. It is indeed one of the central propositions of Marx's sense of history that there are deep contradictions in the relationships of production and in the consequent social relationships. There is therefore the continual possibility of the dynamic variation of these forces. Moreover, when these forces are considered, as Marx always considers them, as the specific activities and relationships of real men, they mean something very much more active, more complicated and more contradictory than the developed metaphorical notion of 'the base' could possibly allow us to realize.

The Base and the Productive Forces

So we have to say that when we talk of 'the base', we are talking of a process and not a state. And we cannot ascribe to that process certain fixed properties for subsequent translation to the variable processes of the superstructure. Most people who have wanted to make the ordinary proposition more reasonable have concentrated on refining the notion of superstructure. But I would say that each term of the proposition has to be revalued in a particular direction. We have to revalue 'determination' towards the setting of limits and the exertion of pressure, and away from a predicted, prefigured and controlled content. We have to revalue 'superstructure' towards a related range of cultural practices, and away from a reflected, reproduced or specifically dependent content. And, crucially, we have to revalue 'the base' away from the notion of a fixed economic or technological abstraction, and towards the specific activities of men in real social and economic relationships, containing fundamental contradictions and variations and therefore always in a state of dynamic process.

It is worth observing one further implication behind the customary definitions. 'The base' has come to include, especially in certain twentieth-century developments, a strong and limiting sense of basic industry. The emphasis on heavy industry, even, has played a certain cultural role. And this raises a more general problem, for we find ourselves forced to look again at the ordinary notion of 'productive forces'. Clearly what we are examining in the base is primary productive forces. Yet some very crucial distinctions have to be made here. It is true that in his analysis of capitalist production Marx considered 'productive work' in a very particular and specialized sense corresponding to that mode of production. There is a difficult passage in the *Grundrisse*[3] in which he argues that while the man who makes a piano is a productive worker, there is a real question whether the man who distributes the piano is also a productive worker; but he probably is, since he contributes to the realization of surplus value. Yet when it comes to the man who plays the piano, whether to himself or to others, there is no question: he is not a productive worker at all. So piano-maker is base, but pianist superstructure. As a way of considering cultural activity, and incidentally the economics of modern cultural activity, this is very clearly a dead-end. But for any theoretical clarification it is crucial to recognize that Marx was there engaged in an analysis of a particular kind of production, that is capitalist commodity production. Within his analysis of this mode, he had to give to the notion of 'productive labour' and 'productive forces' a specialized sense of primary work on materials in a form which produced commodities. But this has narrowed remarkably, and in a cultural context very damagingly, from his more central notion of *productive forces*, in which, to give just brief reminders, the most important thing a worker ever produces is himself, himself in the fact of that kind of labour, or the broader historical emphasis of men producing themselves, themselves and their history. Now when we talk of the base, and of primary productive forces, it matters very much whether we are referring, as in one degenerate form of this proposition became habitual, to primary production within the terms of capitalist economic relationships, or to the primary production of society itself, and of men themselves, the material production and reproduction of real life. If we have the broad sense of productive forces, we look at the whole question of the base differently, and we are then less tempted to dismiss as superstructural, and in that sense as merely secondary, certain vital productive social forces, which are in the broad sense, from the beginning, basic.

Uses of Totality

Yet, because of the difficulties of the ordinary proposition of base and superstructure, there was an alternative and very important development, an emphasis primarily associated with Lukács,[4] on a social 'totality'. The totality of social practices was opposed to this layered notion of base and a consequent superstructure. This concept of a totality of practices is compatible with the notion of social being determining consciousness, but it does not

3. "Foundations" or "Outlines" (German); an uncompleted work by Marx (written 1857–58; see above).

4. György Lukács (1885–1971), Hungarian Marxist theorist.

necessarily interpret this process in terms of a base and a superstructure. Now the language of totality has become common, and it is indeed in many ways more acceptable than the notion of base and superstructure. But with one very important reservation. It is very easy for the notion of totality to empty of its essential content the original Marxist proposition. For if we come to say that society is composed of a large number of social practices which form a concrete social whole, and if we give to each practice a certain specific recognition, adding only that they interact, relate and combine in very complicated ways, we are at one level much more obviously talking about reality, but we are at another level withdrawing from the claim that there is any process of determination. And this I, for one, would be very unwilling to do. Indeed, the key question to ask about any notion of totality in cultural theory is this: whether the notion of totality includes the notion of intention.

If totality is simply concrete, if it is simply the recognition of a large variety of miscellaneous and contemporaneous practices, then it is essentially empty of any content that could be called Marxist. Intention, the notion of intention, restores the key question, or rather the key emphasis. For while it is true that any society is a complex whole of such practices, it is also true that any society has a specific organization, a specific structure, and that the principles of this organization and structure can be seen as directly related to certain social intentions, intentions by which we define the society, intentions which in all our experience have been the rule of a particular class. One of the unexpected consequences of the crudeness of the base/superstructure model has been the too easy acceptance of models which appear less crude—models of totality or of a complex whole—but which exclude the facts of social intention, the class character of a particular society and so on. And this reminds us of how much we lose if we abandon the superstructural emphasis altogether. Thus I have great difficulty in seeing processes of art and thought as superstructural in the sense of the formula as it is commonly used. But in many areas of social and political thought—certain kinds of ratifying theory, certain kinds of law, certain kinds of institution, which after all in Marx's original formulations were very much part of the superstructure—in all that kind of social apparatus, and in a decisive area of political and ideological activity and construction, if we fail to see a superstructural element we fail to recognize reality at all. These laws, constitutions, theories, ideologies, which are so often claimed as natural, or as having universal validity or significance, simply have to be seen as expressing and ratifying the domination of a particular class. Indeed the difficulty of revising the formula of base and superstructure has had much to do with the perception of many militants—who have to fight such institutions and notions as well as fighting economic battles—that if these institutions and their ideologies are not perceived as having that kind of dependent and ratifying relationship, if their claims to universal validity or legitimacy are not denied and fought, then the class character of the society can no longer be seen. And this has been the effect of some versions of totality as the description of cultural process. Indeed I think we can properly use the notion of totality only when we combine it with that other crucial Marxist concept of 'hegemony'.[5]

5. Key concept used by the Italian Marxist philosopher ANTONIO GRAMSCI (1891–1937) to describe the dynamics of domination by the ruling class.

The Complexity of Hegemony

It is Gramsci's great contribution to have emphasized hegemony, and also to have understood it at a depth which is, I think, rare. For hegemony supposes the existence of something which is truly total, which is not merely secondary or superstructural, like the weak sense of ideology, but which is lived at such a depth, which saturates the society to such an extent, and which, as Gramsci put it, even constitutes the substance and limit of common sense for most people under its sway, that it corresponds to the reality of social experience very much more clearly than any notions derived from the formula of base and superstructure. For if ideology were merely some abstract, imposed set of notions, if our social and political and cultural ideas and assumptions and habits were merely the result of specific manipulation, of a kind of overt training which might be simply ended or withdrawn, then the society would be very much easier to move and to change than in practice it has ever been or is. This notion of hegemony as deeply saturating the consciousness of a society seems to me to be fundamental. And hegemony has the advantage over general notions of totality, that it at the same time emphasizes the facts of domination.

Yet there are times when I hear discussions of hegemony and feel that it too, as a concept, is being dragged back to the relatively simple, uniform and static notion which 'superstructure' in ordinary use had become. Indeed I think that we have to give a very complex account of hegemony if we are talking about any real social formation. Above all we have to give an account which allows for its elements of real and constant change. We have to emphasize that hegemony is not singular; indeed that its own internal structures are highly complex, and have continually to be renewed, recreated and defended; and by the same token, that they can be continually challenged and in certain respects modified. That is why instead of speaking simply of 'the hegemony', 'a hegemony', I would propose a model which allows for this kind of variation and contradiction, its sets of alternatives and its processes of change.

For one thing that is evident in some of the best Marxist cultural analysis is that it is very much more at home in what one might call *epochal* questions than in what one has to call *historical* questions. That is to say, it is usually very much better at distinguishing the large features of different epochs of society, as commonly between feudal and bourgeois, than at distinguishing between different phases of bourgeois society, and different moments within these phases: that true historical process which demands a much greater precision and delicacy of analysis than the always striking epochal analysis which is concerned with main lineaments and features.

The theoretical model which I have been trying to work with is this. I would say first that in any society, in any particular period, there is a central system of practices, meanings and values, which we can properly call dominant and effective. This implies no presumption about its value. All I am saying is that it is central. Indeed I would call it a corporate system, but this might be confusing, since Gramsci uses 'corporate' to mean the subordinate as opposed to the general and dominant elements of hegemony. In any case what I have in mind is the central, effective and dominant system of meanings and values, which are not merely abstract but which are organized and lived. That is why hegemony is not to be understood at the level of mere opinion or mere manipulation. It is a whole body of practices and expectations; our assignments of energy, our ordinary understanding of the nature of man and of his world. It is a set of meanings and values which as they are experienced as practices appear as reciprocally confirming. It thus constitutes a sense of reality for most people in the society, a sense of absolute because experienced reality beyond which it is very difficult for most members of the society to move, in most areas of their lives. But this is not, except in the operation of a moment of abstract analysis, in any sense a static system. On the contrary we can only understand an effective and dominant culture if we understand the real social process on which it depends: I mean the process of incorporation. The modes of incorporation are of great social significance. The educational institutions are usually the main agencies of the transmission of an effective dominant culture, and this is now a major economic as well as a cultural activity; indeed it is both in the same moment. Moreover, at a philosophical level, at the true level of theory and at the level of the history of various practices, there is a process which I call the *selective tradition*: that which, within the terms of an effective dominant culture, is always passed off as '*the* tradition', '*the* significant past'. But always the selectivity is the point; the way in which from a whole possible area of past and present, certain meanings and practices are chosen for emphasis, certain other meanings and practices are neglected and excluded. Even more crucially, some of these meanings and practices are reinterpreted, diluted, or put into forms which support or at least do not contradict other elements within the effective dominant culture. The processes of education; the processes of a much wider social training within institutions like the family; the practical definitions and organization of work; the selective tradition at an intellectual and theoretical level: all these forces are involved in a continual making and remaking of an effective dominant culture, and on them, as experienced, as built into our living, its reality depends. If what we learn there were merely an imposed ideology, or if it were only the isolable meanings and practices of the ruling class, or of a section of the ruling class, which gets imposed on others, occupying merely the top of our minds, it would be—and one would be glad—a very much easier thing to overthrow.

It is not only the depths to which this process reaches, selecting and organizing and interpreting our experience. It is also that it is continually active and adjusting; it isn't just the past, the dry husks of ideology which we can more easily discard. And this can only be so, in a complex society, if it is something more substantial and more flexible than any abstract imposed ideology. Thus we have to recognize the alternative meanings and values, the alternative opinions and attitudes, even some alternative senses of the world, which can be accommodated and tolerated within a particular effective and dominant culture. This has been much under-emphasized in our notions of a superstructure, and even in some notions of hegemony. And the under-emphasis opens the way for retreat to an indifferent complexity. In the practice of politics, for example, there are certain truly incorporated modes of what are nevertheless, within those terms, real oppositions, that are felt and fought out. Their existence within the incorporation is recognizable by the fact that, whatever the degree of internal conflict or internal variation, they do not in practice go beyond the limits of the central effective and dominant definitions. This is true, for example, of the practice of parliamentary politics, though its internal oppositions are real. It is true about a whole range of practices and arguments, in any real society, which can by no means be reduced to an ideological cover, but which can nevertheless be properly analysed as in my sense corporate, if we find that, whatever the degree of internal controversy and variation, they do not in the end exceed the limits of the central corporate definitions.

But if we are to say this, we have to think again about the sources of that which is not corporate; of those practices, experiences, meanings, values which are not part of the effective dominant culture. We can express this in two ways. There is clearly something that we can call alternative to the effective dominant culture, and there is something else that we can call oppositional, in a true sense. The degree of existence of these alternative and oppositional forms is itself a matter of constant historical variation in real circumstances. In certain societies it is possible to find areas of social life in which quite real alternatives are at least left alone. (If they are made available, of course, they are part of the corporate organization.) The existence of the possibility of opposition, and of its articulation, its degree of openness, and so on, again depends on very precise social and political forces. The facts of alternative and oppositional forms of social life and culture, in relation to the effective and dominant culture, have then to be recognized as subject to historical variation, and as having sources which are very significant as a fact about the dominant culture itself.

Residual and Emergent Cultures

I have next to introduce a further distinction, between *residual* and *emergent* forms, both of alternative and of oppositional culture. By 'residual' I mean that some experiences, meanings and values, which cannot be verified or cannot be expressed in terms of the dominant culture, are nevertheless lived and practised on the basis of the residue—cultural as well as social—of some previous social formation. There is a real case of this in certain religious values, by contrast with the very evident incorporation of most religious meanings and values into the dominant system. The same is true, in a culture like Britain, of certain notions derived from a rural past, which have a very significant popularity. A residual culture is usually at some distance from the effective dominant culture, but one has to recognize that, in real cultural activities, it may get incorporated into it. This is because some part of it, some version of it—and especially if the residue is from some major area of the past—will in many cases have had to be incorporated if the effective dominant culture is to make sense in those areas. It is also because at certain points a dominant culture cannot allow too much of this kind of practice and experience outside itself, at least without risk. Thus the pressures are real, but certain genuinely residual meanings and practices in some important cases survive.

By 'emergent' I mean, first, that new meanings and values, new practices, new significances and experiences, are continually being created. But there is then a much earlier attempt to incorporate them, just because they are part—and yet not a defined part—of effective contemporary practice. Indeed it is significant in our own period how very early this attempt is, how alert the dominant culture now is to anything that can be seen as emergent. We have then to see, first, as it were a temporal relation between a dominant culture and on the one hand a residual and on the other hand an emergent culture. But we can only understand this if we can make distinctions, that usually require very precise analysis, between residual-incorporated and residual not incorporated, and between emergent-incorporated and emergent not incorporated. It is an important fact about any particular society, how far it reaches into the whole range of human practices and experiences in an attempt at incorporation. It may be true of some earlier phases of bourgeois society, for example, that there were some areas of experience which it was willing to dispense with, which it was prepared to assign as the sphere of private or artistic life, and as being no particular business of society or the state. This went along with certain kinds of political tolerance, even if the reality of that tolerance was malign neglect. But I am sure it is true of the society that has come into existence since the last war,[6] that progressively, because of developments in the social character of labour, in the social character of communications, and in the social character of decision, it extends much further than ever before in capitalist society into certain hitherto resigned areas of experience and practice and meaning. Thus the effective decision, as to whether a practice is alternative or oppositional, is often now made within a very much narrower scope. There is a simple theoretical distinction between alternative and oppositional, that is to say between someone who simply finds a different way to live and wishes to be left alone with it, and someone who finds a different way to live and wants to change the society in its light. This is usually the difference between individual and small-group solutions to social crisis and those solutions which properly belong to political and ultimately revolutionary practice. But it is often a very narrow line, in reality, between alternative and oppositional. A meaning or a practice may be tolerated as a deviation, and yet still be seen only as another particular way to live. But as the necessary area of effective dominance extends, the same meanings and practices can be seen by the dominant culture, not merely as disregarding or despising it, but as challenging it.

Now it is crucial to any Marxist theory of culture that it can give an adequate explanation of the sources of these practices and meanings. We can understand, from an ordinary historical approach, at least some of the sources of residual meanings and practices. These are the results of earlier social formations, in which certain real meanings and values were generated. In the subsequent default of a particular phase of a dominant culture, there is then a reaching back to those meanings and values which were created in real societies in the past, and which still seem to have some significance because they represent areas of human experience, aspiration and achievement, which the dominant culture under-values or opposes, or even cannot recognise. But our hardest task, theoretically, is to find a non-metaphysical and non-subjectivist explanation of emergent cultural practice. Moreover, part of our answer to this question bears on the process of persistence of residual practices.

6. That is, World War II, which was followed by far-reaching social reforms in Great Britain.

Class and Human Practice

We have indeed one source to hand from the central body of Marxist theory. We have the formation of a new class, the coming to consciousness of a new class. This remains, without doubt, quite centrally important. Of course, in itself, this process of formation complicates any simple model of base and superstructure. It also complicates some of the ordinary versions of hegemony, although it was Gramsci's whole purpose to see and to create by organization that hegemony of a proletarian kind which would be capable of challenging the bourgeois hegemony. We have then one central source of new practice, in the emergence of a new class. But we have also to recognize certain other kinds of source, and in cultural practice some of these are very important. I would say that we can recognize them on the basis of this proposition: that no mode of production, and therefore no dominant society or order of society, and therefore no dominant culture, in reality exhausts the full range of human practice, human energy, human intention (this range is not the inventory of some original 'human nature' but, on the contrary, is that extraordinary range of variations, both practised and imagined, of which human beings are and have shown themselves to be capable). Indeed it seems to me that this emphasis is not merely a negative proposition, allowing us to account for certain things which happen outside the dominant mode. On the contrary, it is a fact about the modes of domination that they select from and consequently exclude the full range of actual and possible human practice. The difficulties of human practice outside or against the dominant mode are, of course, real. It depends very much whether it is in an area in which the dominant class and the dominant culture have an interest and a stake. If the interest and the stake are explicit, many new practices will be reached for, and if possible incorporated, or else extirpated with extraordinary vigour. But in certain areas, there will be in certain periods practices and meanings which are not reached for. There will be areas of practice and meaning which, almost by definition from its own limited character, or in its profound deformation, the dominant culture is unable in any real terms to recognize. This gives us a bearing on the observable difference between, for example, the practices of a capitalist state and a state like the contemporary Soviet Union in relation to writers.[7] Since from the whole Marxist tradition literature was seen as an important activity, indeed a crucial activity, the Soviet state is very much sharper in investigating areas where different versions of practice, different meanings and values, are being attempted and expressed. In capitalist practice, if the thing is not making a profit, or if it is not being widely circulated, then it can for some time be overlooked, at least while it remains alternative. When it becomes oppositional in an explicit way, it does, of course, get approached or attacked.

I am saying then that in relation to the full range of human practice at any one time, the dominant mode is a conscious selection and organization. At least in its fully formed state it is conscious. But there are always sources of actual human practice which it neglects or excludes. And these can be different in quality from the developing and articulate interests of a rising class. They can include, for example, alternative perceptions of others, in immedi-

7. In the Soviet Union, the Union of Soviet Writers exercised control over what writers could publish.

ate personal relationships, or new perceptions of material and media, in art and science, and within certain limits these new perceptions can be practised. The relations between the two kinds of source—the emerging class and either the dominatively excluded or the more generally new practices—are by no means necessarily contradictory. At times they can be very close, and on the relations between them much in political practice depends. But culturally and as a matter of theory the areas can be seen as distinct.

Now if we go back to the cultural question in its most usual form—what are the relations between art and society, or literature and society?—in the light of the preceding discussion, we have to say first that there are no relations between literature and society in that abstracted way. The literature is there from the beginning as a practice in the society. Indeed until it and all other practices are present, the society cannot be seen as fully formed. A society is not fully available for analysis until each of its practices is included. But if we make that emphasis we must make a corresponding emphasis: that we cannot separate literature and art from other kinds of social practice, in such a way as to make them subject to quite special and distinct laws. They may have quite specific features as practices, but they cannot be separated from the general social process. Indeed one way of emphasizing this is to say, to insist, that literature is not restricted to operating in any one of the sectors I have been seeking to describe in this model. It would be easy to say, it is a familiar rhetoric, that literature operates in the emergent cultural sector, that it represents the new feelings, the new meanings, the new values. We might persuade ourselves of this theoretically, by abstract argument, but when we read much literature, over the whole range, without the sleight-of-hand of calling Literature only that which we have already selected as embodying certain meanings and values at a certain scale of intensity, we are bound to recognize that the act of writing, the practices of discourse in writing and speech, the making of novels and poems and plays and theories, all this activity takes place in all areas of the culture.

Literature appears by no means only in the emergent sector, which is always, in fact, quite rare. A great deal of writing is of a residual kind, and this has been deeply true of much English literature in the last half-century. Some of its fundamental meanings and values have belonged to the cultural achievements of long-past stages of society. So widespread is this fact, and the habits of mind it supports, that in many minds 'literature' and 'the past' acquire a certain identity, and it is then said that there is now no literature: all that glory is over. Yet most writing, in any period, including our own, is a form of contribution to the effective dominant culture. Indeed many of the specific qualities of literature—its capacity to embody and enact and perform certain meanings and values, or to create in single particular ways what would be otherwise merely general truths—enable it to fulfil this effective function with great power. To literature, of course, we must add the visual arts and music, and in our own society the powerful arts of film and of broadcasting. But the general theoretical point should be clear. If we are looking for the relations between literature and society, we cannot either separate out this one practice from a formed body of other practices, nor when we have identified a particular practice can we give it a uniform, static and ahistorical relation to some abstract social formation. The arts of writing and the arts of creation and performance, over their whole range, are parts of the cultural process in all the different ways, the different sectors, that I have been seeking to describe. They contribute to the effective dominant culture and are a central articulation of it. They embody residual meanings and values, not all of which are incorporated, though many are. They express also and significantly some emergent practices and meanings, yet some of these may eventually be incorporated, as they reach people and begin to move them. Thus it was very evident in the sixties, in some of the emergent arts of performance, that the dominant culture reached out to transform, or seek to transform, them. In this process, of course, the dominant culture itself changes, not in its central formation, but in many of its articulated features. But then in a modern society it must always change in this way, if it is to remain dominant, if it is still to be felt as in real ways central in all our many activities and interests.

Critical Theory as Consumption

What then are the implications of this general analysis for the analysis of particular works of art? This is the question towards which most discussion of cultural theory seems to be directed: the discovery of a method, perhaps even a methodology, through which particular works of art can be understood and described. I would not myself agree that this is the central use of cultural theory, but let us for a moment consider it. What seems to me very striking is that nearly all forms of contemporary critical theory are theories of *consumption*. That is to say, they are concerned with understanding an object in such a way that it can profitably or correctly be consumed. The earliest stage of consumption theory was the theory of 'taste', where the link between the practice and the theory was direct in the metaphor. From taste there came the more elevated notion of 'sensibility', in which it was the consumption by sensibility of elevated or insightful works that was held to be the essential practice of reading, and critical activity was then a function of this sensibility. There were then more developed theories, in the 1920s with I. A. Richards, and later in New Criticism,[8] in which the effects of consumption were studied directly. The language of the work of art as object then became more overt. 'What effect does this work ("the poem" as it was ordinarily described) have on me?' Or, 'what impact does it have on me?', as it was later to be put in a much wider area of communication studies. Naturally enough, the notion of the work of art as *object*, as *text*, as an isolated artefact, became central in all these later consumption theories. It was not only that the practices of *production* were then overlooked, though this fused with the notion that most important literature anyway was from the past. The real social conditions of production were in any case neglected because they were believed to be at best secondary. The true relationship was seen always as between the taste, the sensibility or the training of the reader and this isolated work, this object 'as in itself it really is', as most people came to put it. But the notion of the work of art as object had a further large theoretical effect. If you ask questions about the work of art seen

8. Major movement in Anglo-American literary criticism during the mid-20th century, promoted by CLEANTH BROOKS, W. K. WIMSATT JR., and others, that focused on close reading of the text as an autonomous whole. It was influenced by the "practical criticism" of the British critic I. A. Richards (1893–1979).

as object, they may include questions about the components of its production. Now, as it happened, there was a use of the formula of base and superstructure which was precisely in line with this. The components of a work of art were the real activities of the base, and you could study the object to discover these components. Sometimes you even studied the components and then projected the object. But in any case the relationship that was looked for was one between an object and its components. But this was not only true of Marxist suppositions of a base and a superstructure. It was true also of various kinds of psychological theory, whether in the form of archetypes, or the images of the collective unconscious, or the myths and symbols which were seen as the *components* of particular works of art. Or again there was biography, or psychobiography and its like, where the components were in the man's life and the work of art was an object in which components of this kind were discovered. Even in some of the more rigorous forms of New Criticism and of structuralist criticism, this essential procedure of regarding the work as an object which has to be reduced to its components, even if later it may be reconstituted, came to persist.

Objects and Practices

Now I think the true crisis in cultural theory, in our own time, is between this view of the work of art as object and the alternative view of art as a practice. Of course it is at once argued that the work of art *is* an object: that various works have survived from the past, particular sculptures, particular paintings, particular buildings, and these are objects. This is of course true, but the same way of thinking is applied to works which have no such singular existence. There is no *Hamlet*, no *Brothers Karamazov*, no *Wuthering Heights*, in the sense that there is a particular great painting. There is no *Fifth Symphony*,[9] there is no work in the whole area of music and dance and performance, which is an object in any way comparable to those works in the visual arts which have survived. And yet the habit of treating all such works as objects has persisted because this is a basic theoretical and practical presupposition. But in literature (especially in drama), in music and in a very wide area of the performing arts, what we permanently have are not objects but *notations*. These notations have then to be interpreted in an active way, according to the particular conventions. But indeed this is true over an even wider field. The relationship between the making of a work of art and its reception is always active, and subject to conventions, which in themselves are forms of (changing) social organization and relationship, and this is radically different from the production and consumption of an object. It is indeed an activity and a practice, and in its accessible forms, although it may in some arts have the character of a singular object, it is still only accessible through active perception and interpretation. This makes the case of notation, in arts like drama and literature and music, only a special case of a much wider truth. What this can show us here about the practice of analysis is that we have to break from the common procedure of isolating the object

9. Symphony (1804–08) by Ludwig van Beethoven; *Hamlet* (ca. 1600), tragedy by William Shakespeare; *Brothers Karamazov* (1878–80), novel by Fyodor Dostoyevsky; *Wuthering Heights* (1847), novel by Emily Brontë.

and then discovering its components. On the contrary we have to discover the nature of a practice and then its conditions.

Often these two procedures may in part resemble each other, but in many other cases they are of radically different kinds, and I would conclude with an observation on the way this distinction bears on the Marxist tradition of the relation between primary economic and social practices, and cultural practices. If we suppose that what is produced in cultural practice is a series of objects, we shall, as in most current forms of sociological-critical procedure, set about discovering their components. Within a Marxist emphasis these components will be from what we have been in the habit of calling the base. We then isolate certain features which we can so to say recognize *in component form*, or we ask what processes of transformation or mediation these components have gone through before they arrived in this accessible state.

But I am saying that we should look not for the components of a product but for the conditions of a practice. When we find ourselves looking at a particular work, or group of works, often realizing, as we do so, their essential community as well as their irreducible individuality, we should find ourselves attending first to the reality of their practice and the conditions of the practice as it was then executed. And from this I think we ask essentially different questions. Take for example the way in which an object—'a text'—is related to a genre, in orthodox criticism. We identify it by certain leading features, we then assign it to a larger category, the genre, and then we may find the components of the genre in a particular social history (although in some variants of criticism not even that is done, and the genre is supposed to be some permanent category of the mind).

It is not that way of proceeding that is now required. The recognition of the relation of a collective mode and an individual project—and these are the only categories that we can initially presume—is a recognition of related practices. That is to say, the irreducibly individual projects that particular works are, may come in experience and in analysis to show resemblances which allow us to group them into collective modes. These are by no means always genres. They may exist as resemblances within and across genres. They may be the practice of a group in a period, rather than the practice of a phase in a genre. But as we discover the nature of a particular practice, and the nature of the relation between an individual project and a collective mode, we find that we are analysing, as two forms of the same process, both its active composition and its conditions of composition, and in either direction this is a complex of extending active relationships. This means, of course, that we have no built-in procedure of the kind which is indicated by the fixed character of an object. We have the principles of the relations of practices, within a discoverably intentional organization, and we have the available hypotheses of dominant, residual and emergent. But what we are actively seeking is the true practice which has been alienated to an object, and the true conditions of practice—whether as literary conventions or as social relationships—which have been alienated to components or to mere background.

As a general proposition this is only an emphasis, but it seems to me to suggest at once the point of break and the point of departure, in practical and theoretical work, within an active and self-renewing Marxist cultural tradition.

1973, 1980

FRANTZ FANON
1925–1961

A leading third world intellectual whose work helped inspire the struggle against colonialism and ground theoretically the subsequent growth of postcolonial culture, Frantz Fanon was one of the most influential thinkers of the twentieth century. Though born in the French Antilles, he had particular impact in Africa, where his writings undergird the works of important anticolonial writers, such as Kenya's NGUGI WĂ THIONG'O and Senegal's Ousmane Sembène. During the 1950s and early 1960s, Fanon's various writings, especially *Les Damnés de la terre* (1961; trans. 1963, *The Wretched of the Earth*), elaborated with passion on the historical conditions of anticolonial struggle. Significantly, Fanon articulated the role to be played by intellectuals in this struggle, offering stern (and prescient, as it turned out) warnings of the difficulties that would face emerging African nations once independence had been won.

Born to a middle-class black family on the island of Martinique, then a French colony, Fanon grew up amid descendants of African slaves brought to the Caribbean to work on the island's sugar plantations. As a teenager, he became intellectually attuned to the problems of colonialism and racism. He was politically active, participating in the guerrilla struggle against the supporters of the pro-Nazi French Vichy government. After the Free French forces gained control of Martinique in 1943, Fanon volunteered to go to Europe to fight. He emerged a decorated war hero, and he stayed in France to complete his education and train as a psychiatrist in Paris and Lyons. There he found that his service to the French state made no difference to the whites around him, who regarded black French subjects like himself as the *Other*—as alien and inferior, yet frightening and dangerous. He came to understand that despite his intelligence, high level of education, and mastery of the French language, he was regarded not as a human being but as a specimen of an exotic and savage race, viewed through stereotypes developed over centuries of racial prejudice.

While in France, Fanon began his writing career, publishing his first book in 1952: *Peau noire, masques blancs* (trans. 1967, *Black Skin, White Masks*). This book includes the important chapter, and our first selection, "The Fact of Blackness" (in a later translation, "The Lived Experience of the Black Man"), which describes Fanon's growing awareness of racism in France. The work, personal and lyrical, shows the strong influence of Fanon's psychiatric training, as he concentrates primarily on the impact of racism and colonialism on the black and white psyches. It also engages in a critical dialogue with French Hegelian Marxism and existentialism, particularly that of Jean-Paul Sartre, and exhibits the influence of the *négritude* movement (which called in the 1940s and 1950s for a distinctive black cultural identity rather than complete assimilation into French culture). Indeed, one of the leaders of that movement, Aimé Césaire, had been Fanon's teacher and mentor back in Martinique and remained an important influence throughout his life. Fanon movingly describes, with anguish and anger, the various modes of accommodation and alienation that characterize black life in white societies. In particular, Fanon tells of his own struggle to make sense of the white world and to address it on its own rationalist terms, only to be rejected on the basis of his race and driven back by white prejudice to an antirational, primitivist stance. Then, realizing that such primitivism was taken by whites as simply verifying their own stereotypical attitudes toward blacks, Fanon began to explore the cultural achievements of African civilization, finally achieving a dialectical resolution between Western rationalism and Africanist primitivism. In the end, he finds black identity and strength not only in the long history of African civilizations but also in the radical black poetry of Césaire, Léopold Senghor, and David Diop, in addition to the novels of the African American writers Richard Wright and Chester Himes.

After completing his medical training, in 1953 Fanon was appointed chief of staff of the Blida-Joinville psychiatric hospital in Algeria, a French colony in North Africa. In 1954 the Algerians, led by the National Liberation Front (FLN), revolted against French rule, initiating a period of violent revolutionary struggle that would last until full Algerian independence was gained in 1962. Sympathetic to the revolution from its inception, Fanon resigned his medical post in 1956 to become the editor of the FLN newspaper. He remained involved in the revolution until his death from leukemia five years later, at the age of thirty-six.

Much of Fanon's writing of that period concentrated on the Algerian revolution, including the essays published in *L'An cinq de la révolution algérienne* (1959; trans. 1965, *A Dying Colonialism*). Other essays were posthumously collected and published in 1964 as *Pour la révolution africaine* (trans. 1976, *Toward the African Revolution*). The culmination of his work, however, was the publication of *The Wretched of the Earth*, just weeks before his death. This volume, which featured an impassioned introduction by Sartre, gained widespread recognition and solidified Fanon's reputation as a leading revolutionary thinker of the twentieth century.

Fanon displays a distinctive political vision, centrally informed by the European tradition of Marxist thought in a version heavily modified to reflect third world, anticolonial perspectives. For example, in his conviction that colonialism would be ended only through violent anticolonial struggle, Fanon was very much in accord with the Marxist view of capitalism's inevitable end. However, Fanon's reasons differed; in particular, he stressed that the anticolonial struggle would counteract the long-term psychological effects of the violence of colonialism itself. In addition, whereas Marx envisioned the European working class, or proletariat, as the crux of the revolution, Fanon felt that in Africa and other colonial regions, the revolution would have to be led by a coalition of peasants and social outcasts, the so-called lumpenproletariat in whom Marx saw little revolutionary potential in Europe.

Perhaps the most important aspect of Fanon's political thought was his insight into the complex interaction in the colonies between class and race. Though he was intensely aware of the centrality of racism to European colonialism, Fanon as a Marxist argued that social, economic, and political oppression in the third world was equally a matter of class. He makes this point most forcefully in his influential argument in *The Wretched of the Earth* that postcolonial African nations court disaster if they simply replace their white colonial bourgeois leaders with a black African postcolonial bourgeoisie, while leaving the basic class structure of the societies in place.

In the chapter "On National Culture," our second selection (excerpted), Fanon examines nationalism, exploring the role played by culture in the development of viable postcolonial identities for emergent African nations. Here he particularly concentrates on the importance of intellectuals as well as the arts in helping to develop cultural identities for emerging postcolonial nations. He urges African intellectuals to join actively in the anticolonial struggle and to place the building of new postcolonial national identities at the very center of their work. At the same time, he warns these intellectuals to remain aware that the new nation must exist within an international community. As they pursue national culture, they should draw their strength from the African masses but eschew isolationist or traditionalist solutions; they must maintain an understanding of and sense of connection to the outside world.

Fanon's work was an inspiration to the black power movement in the United States during the 1960s. At the same time, he was a key theoretical resource for the generation of intellectuals and writers who struggled to create viable postcolonial cultural identities in Africa and elsewhere. Fanon's work was especially important to a number of radical African novelists (including Ngugi and Sembène), and it continues to provide a central framework within which to interpret their work. Indeed, Fanon is arguably the most important theoretical gloss on the work of some contemporary African novelists, such as Ghana's Ayi Kwei Armah, Nigeria's Chimamanda Ngozi Adichie, Senegal's Ken Bugul, and Zimbabwe's Tsitsi Dangarembga, who have been deeply influenced by his ideas. Ngugi has been among the most explicit in pointing to the importance of Fanon to his work, declaring in *Decolonising the Mind* (1992) that it is "impossible to understand what informs African writing" without first reading two books: Lenin's *Imperialism: The Highest Stage of Capitalism* (1917) and Fanon's *Wretched of the Earth*.

During the closing decades of the twentieth century, Fanon's work was joined by that of a new wave of scholars, such as EDWARD W. SAID and HOMI K. BHABHA, who often drew on poststructuralist theorists in describing the postcolonial condition. Nevertheless, Fanon's logical but passionate arguments, rooted in Sartrean existentialism and a Marxist humanist engagement with the material world, have remained a strong force in postcolonial studies.

***Black Skin, White Masks* Keywords:** The Body, Identity, Literary History, Marxism, Phenomenology, Postcolonial Theory, Race and Ethnicity Studies, Representation, Subjectivity
***The Wretched of the Earth* Keywords:** Aesthetics, Authorship, Identity, Literary History, Marxism, Nationhood, Postcolonial Theory, Race and Ethnicity Studies, Representation

From Black Skin, White Masks[1]

From *The Fact of Blackness*

* * *

And then the occasion arose when I had to meet the white man's eyes. An unfamiliar weight burdened me. The real world challenged my claims. In the white world the man of color encounters difficulties in the development of his bodily schema. Consciousness of the body is solely a negating activity. It is a third-person consciousness.

* * *

* * * I had the feeling that I was repeating a cycle. My originality had been torn out of me. I wept a long time, and then I began to live again. But I was haunted by a galaxy of erosive stereotypes: the Negro's *sui generis* odor . . . the Negro's *sui generis* good nature . . . the Negro's *sui generis* gullibility. . . .

I had tried to flee myself through my kind, but the whites had thrown themselves on me and hamstrung me. I tested the limits of my essence; beyond all doubt there was not much of it left. It was here that I made my most remarkable discovery. Properly speaking, this discovery was a rediscovery.

I rummaged frenetically through all the antiquity of the black man. What I found there took away my breath. In his book *L'abolition de l'esclavage*

1. Translated by Charles Lam Markmann. The title of Fanon's chapter is "L'expérience vécue du Noir" (literally, "The Lived Experience of the Black").

Schoelcher[2] presented us with compelling arguments. Since then, Frobenius, Westermann, Delafosse[3]—all of them white—had joined the chorus: Ségou, Djenné,[4] cities of more than a hundred thousand people; accounts of learned blacks (doctors of theology who went to Mecca to interpret the Koran). All of that, exhumed from the past, spread with its insides out, made it possible for me to find a valid historic place. The white man was wrong, I was not a primitive, not even a half-man, I belonged to a race that had already been working in gold and silver two thousand years ago. And too there was something else, something else that the white man could not understand. Listen:

> What sort of men were these, then, who had been torn away from their families, their countries, their religions, with a savagery unparalleled in history?
>
> Gentle men, polite, considerate, unquestionably superior to those who tortured them—that collection of adventurers who slashed and violated and spat on Africa to make the stripping of her the easier.
>
> The men they took away knew how to build houses, govern empires, erect cities, cultivate fields, mine for metals, weave cotton, forge steel.
>
> Their religion had its own beauty, based on mystical connections with the founder of the city. Their customs were pleasing, built on unity, kindness, respect for age.
>
> No coercion, only mutual assistance, the joy of living, a free acceptance of discipline.
>
> Order—Earnestness—Poetry and Freedom.
>
> From the untroubled private citizen to the almost fabulous leader there was an unbroken chain of understanding and trust. No science? Indeed yes; but also, to protect them from fear, they possessed great myths in which the most subtle observation and the most daring imagination were balanced and blended. No art? They had their magnificent sculpture, in which human feeling erupted so unrestrained yet always followed the obsessive laws of rhythm in its organization of the major elements of a material called upon to capture, in order to redistribute, the most secret forces of the universe. . . .[5]

Monuments in the very heart of Africa? Schools? Hospitals? Not a single good burgher of the twentieth century, no Durand, no Smith, no Brown even suspects that such things existed in Africa before the Europeans came. . . .

But Schoelcher reminds us of their presence, discovered by Caillé, Mollien, the Cander brothers.[6] And, though he nowhere reminds us that when

2. Victor Schoelcher (1804–1893), French journalist and politician who worked to end slavery throughout the French colonies, writing the decree that abolished it in 1848; he published *The Abolition of Slavery* in 1840.

3. Maurice Delafosse (1870–1926), French ethnographer who worked in Africa in the colonial service. Leo Frobenius (1873–1938), German ethnographer and Africanist historian. Diedrich Westermann (1875–1956), German scholar of African languages and culture.

4. An ancient center for Islamic scholarship in southern Mali, first settled in 200 B.C.E. Ségou, in south-central Mali, established in the 11th century.

5. Aimé Césaire, Introduction to Victor Schoelcher, *Esclavage et colonisation* (Paris, Presses Universitaires de France, 1948), p. 7 [Fanon's note]. Césaire (1913–2008), French Martinican poet, author, and politician who coined the term *négritude* in his prose poem *Cahier d'un retour au pays natal* (1939, *Notebook of a Return to My Native Land*).

6. Césaire's error for "Lander brothers," the British explorers Richard (1804–1834) and John (1806–1839). René Caillié (1799–1838) and Gaspard-Théodore Mollien (1796–1872) were both French explorers of West Africa.

> the Portuguese landed on the banks of the Congo in 1498, they found a rich and flourishing state there and that the courtiers of Ambas[7] were dressed in robes of silk and brocade, at least he knows that Africa had brought itself up to a juridical concept of the state, and he is aware, living in the very flood of imperialism, that European civilization, after all, is only one more civilization among many—and not the most merciful.[8]

I put the white man back into his place; growing bolder, I jostled him and told him point-blank, "Get used to me, I am not getting used to anyone." I shouted my laughter to the stars. The white man, I could see, was resentful. His reaction time lagged interminably. . . . I had won. I was jubilant.

"Lay aside your history, your investigations of the past, and try to feel yourself into our rhythm. In a society such as ours, industrialized to the highest degree, dominated by scientism, there is no longer room for your sensitivity. One must be tough if one is to be allowed to live. What matters now is no longer playing the game of the world but subjugating it with integers and atoms. Oh, certainly, I will be told, now and then when we are worn out by our lives in big buildings, we will turn to you as we do to our children—to the innocent, the ingenuous, the spontaneous. We will turn to you as to the childhood of the world. You are so real in your life—so funny, that is. Let us run away for a little while from our ritualized, polite civilization and let us relax, bend to those heads, those adorably expressive faces. In a way, you reconcile us with ourselves."

Thus my unreason was countered with reason, my reason with "real reason." Every hand was a losing hand for me. I analyzed my heredity. I made a complete audit of my ailment. I wanted to be typically Negro—it was no longer possible. I wanted to be white—that was a joke. And, when I tried, on the level of ideas and intellectual activity, to reclaim my negritude, it was snatched away from me. Proof was presented that my effort was only a term in the dialectic:

> But there is something more important: The Negro, as we have said, creates an anti-racist racism for himself. In no sense does he wish to rule the world: He seeks the abolition of all ethnic privileges, wherever they come from; he asserts his solidarity with the oppressed of all colors. At once the subjective, existential, ethnic idea of *negritude* "passes," as Hegel[9] puts it, into the objective, positive, exact idea of *proletariat*. "For Césaire," Senghor[1] says, "the white man is the symbol of capital as the Negro is that of labor. . . . Beyond the black-skinned men of his race it is the battle of the world proletariat that is his song."
>
> That is easy to say, but less easy to think out. And undoubtedly it is no coincidence that the most ardent poets of negritude are at the same time militant Marxists.
>
> But that does not prevent the idea of race from mingling with that of class: The first is concrete and particular, the second is universal and

7. Ambas or Amboise, a coastal area of present-day Cameroon, in West Africa.
8. Césaire, Introduction to Schoelcher, *Esclavage et colonisation*, p. 8 [Fanon's note].
9. GEORG WILHELM FRIEDRICH HEGEL (1770–1831), German philosopher; his concept of the Master-Slave dialectic (see above) was derived from his studies of the Haitian Revolution (1794–1804).
1. Léopold Senghor (1906–2001), Senegalese poet, politician, and one of the founders of the *négritude* movement. In 1960 he would become the first black African elected president in independent Senegal.

> abstract; the one stems from what Jaspers[2] calls understanding and the other from intellection; the first is the result of a psychobiological syncretism and the second is a methodical construction based on experience. In fact, negritude appears as the minor term of a dialectical progression: The theoretical and practical assertion of the supremacy of the white man is its thesis; the position of negritude as an antithetical value is the moment of negativity. But this negative moment is insufficient by itself, and the Negroes who employ it know this very well; they know that it is intended to prepare the synthesis or realization of the human in a society without races. Thus negritude is the root of its own destruction, it is a transition and not a conclusion, a means and not an ultimate end.[3]

When I read that page, I felt that I had been robbed of my last change. I said to my friends, "The generation of the younger black poets has just suffered a blow that can never be forgiven." Help had been sought from a friend of the colored peoples, and that friend had found no better response than to point out the relativity of what they were doing. For once, that born Hegelian had forgotten that consciousness has to lose itself in the night of the absolute, the only condition to attain to consciousness of self. In opposition to rationalism, he summoned up the negative side, but he forgot that this negativity draws its worth from an almost substantive absoluteness. A consciousness committed to experience is ignorant, has to be ignorant, of the essences and the determinations of its being.

Orphée Noir is a date in the intellectualization of the *experience* of being black. And Sartre's mistake was not only to seek the source of the source but in a certain sense to block that source:

> Will the source of Poetry be dried up? Or will the great black flood, in spite of everything, color the sea into which it pours itself? It does not matter: Every age has its own poetry; in every age the circumstances of history choose a nation, a race, a class to take up the torch by creating situations that can be expressed or transcended only through Poetry; sometimes the poetic impulse coincides with the revolutionary impulse, and sometimes they take different courses. Today let us hail the turn of history that will make it possible for the black men to utter "the great Negro cry with a force that will shake the pillars of the world" (Césaire).[4]

And so it is not I who make a meaning for myself, but it is the meaning that was already there, pre-existing, waiting for me. It is not out of my bad nigger's misery, my bad nigger's teeth, my bad nigger's hunger that I will shape a torch with which to burn down the world, but it is the torch that was already there, waiting for that turn of history.

In terms of consciousness, the black consciousness is held out as an absolute density, as filled with itself, a stage preceding any invasion, any abolition

2. Karl Jaspers (1883–1969), German philosopher.
3. Jean-Paul Sartre, *Orphée Noir*, preface to *Anthologie de la nouvelle poésie nègre et malgache* (Paris, Presses Universitaires de France, 1948), pp. xl ff. [Fanon's note]. "Black Orpheus" was the preface by the French philosopher and novelist Sartre (1905–1980) to *Anthology of New Black and Malagasy Poetry*, edited by Léopold Senghor; it was the first collection of poetry by black French-speaking writers.
4. Ibid., p. xliv [Fanon's note]. The quotation is from Césaire's *Les Armes miraculeuses* (1948, *Miraculous Weapons*).

of the ego by desire. Jean-Paul Sartre, in this work, has destroyed black zeal. In opposition to historical becoming, there had always been the unforeseeable. I needed to lose myself completely in negritude. One day, perhaps, in the depths of that unhappy romanticism. . . .

In any case I *needed* not to know. This struggle, this new decline had to take on an aspect of completeness. Nothing is more unwelcome than the commonplace: "You'll change, my boy; I was like that too when I was young . . . you'll see, it will all pass."

The dialectic that brings necessity into the foundation of my freedom drives me out of myself. It shatters my unreflected position. Still in terms of consciousness, black consciousness is immanent in its own eyes. I am not a potentiality of something, I am wholly what I am. I do not have to look for the universal. No probability has any place inside me. My Negro consciousness does not hold itself out as a lack. It *is*. It is its own follower.

But, I will be told, your statements show a misreading of the processes of history. Listen then:

Africa I have kept your memory Africa
you are inside me
Like the splinter in the wound
like a guardian fetish in the center of the village
make me the stone in your sling
make my mouth the lips of your wound
make my knees the broken pillars of your abasement
AND YET
I want to be of your race alone
workers peasants of all lands . . .
. . . white worker in Detroit black peon in Alabama
uncountable nation in capitalist slavery
destiny ranges us shoulder to shoulder
repudiating the ancient maledictions of blood taboos
we roll away the ruins of our solitudes
If the flood is a frontier
we will strip the gully of its endless
covering flow
If the Sierra is a frontier
we will smash the jaws of the volcanoes
upholding the Cordilleras[5]
and the plain will be the parade ground of the dawn
where we regroup our forces sundered
by the deceits of our masters
As the contradiction among the features
creates the harmony of the face
we proclaim the oneness of the suffering
and the revolt
of all the peoples on all the face of the earth
  and we mix the mortar of the age of brotherhood
  out of the dust of idols.[6]

5. Mountain ranges (Spanish).
6. Jacques Roumain, "Bois-d'Ebène" ["Ebony Wood"], Prelude, in *Anthologie de la nouvelle poésie nègre et malgache*, p. 113 [Fanon's note]. Roumain (1907–1944), Haitian writer.

Exactly, we will reply, Negro experience is not a whole, for there is not merely *one* Negro, there are *Negroes*. What a difference, for instance, in this other poem:

The white man killed my father
Because my father was proud
The white man raped my mother
Because my mother was beautiful
The white man wore out my brother in the hot sun
of the roads
Because my brother was strong
Then the white man came to me
His hands red with blood
Spat his contempt into my black face
Out of his tyrant's voice:
"Hey boy, a basin, a towel, water."[7]

Or this other one:

My brother with teeth that glisten at the compliments
of hypocrites
My brother with gold-rimmed spectacles
Over eyes that turn blue at the sound of the Master's
voice
My poor brother in dinner jacket with its silk lapels
Clucking and whispering and strutting through the
drawing rooms of Condescension
How pathetic you are
The sun of your native country is nothing more now
than a shadow
On your composed civilized face
And your grandmother's hut
Brings blushes into cheeks made white by years of
abasement and *Mea culpa*
But when regurgitating the flood of lofty empty words
Like the load that presses on your shoulders
You walk again on the rough red earth of Africa
These words of anguish will state the rhythm of your
uneasy gait
I feel so alone, so alone here![8]

From time to time one would like to stop. To state reality is a wearing task. But, when one has taken it into one's head to try to express existence, one runs the risk of finding only the nonexistent. What is certain is that, at the very moment when I was trying to grasp my own being, Sartre, who remained The Other, gave me a name and thus shattered my last illusion. While I was saying to him:

My negritude is neither a tower nor a cathedral,
it thrusts into the red flesh of the sun,

7. David Diop, "Le temps du martyre" ["The Time of the Martyr"], in ibid., p. 174 [Fanon's note]. Diop (1927–1960), French-born West African poet.

8. David Diop, "Le Renégat" ["The Renegade"; Fanon's note].

> it thrusts into the burning flesh of the sky,
> it hollows through the dense dismay of its own pillar
> of patience . . .[9]

while I was shouting that, in the paroxysm of my being and my fury, he was reminding me that my blackness was only a minor term. In all truth, in all truth I tell you, my shoulders slipped out of the framework of the world, my feet could no longer feel the touch of the ground. Without a Negro past, without a Negro future, it was impossible for me to live my Negrohood. Not yet white, no longer wholly black, I was damned. Jean-Paul Sartre had forgotten that the Negro suffers in his body quite differently from the white man.[1] Between the white man and me the connection was irrevocably one of transcendence.[2]

But the constancy of my love had been forgotten. I defined myself as an absolute intensity of beginning. So I took up my negritude, and with tears in my eyes I put its machinery together again. What had been broken to pieces was rebuilt, reconstructed by the intuitive lianas[3] of my hands.

My cry grew more violent: I am a Negro, I am a Negro, I am a Negro. . . .

And there was my poor brother—living out his neurosis to the extreme and finding himself paralyzed:

> THE NEGRO: I can't, ma'am.
> LIZZIE: Why not?
> THE NEGRO: I can't shoot white folks.
> LIZZIE: Really! That would bother them, wouldn't it?
> THE NEGRO: They're white folks, ma'am.
> LIZZIE: So what? Maybe they got a right to bleed you like a pig just because they're white?
> THE NEGRO: But they're white folks.

A feeling of inferiority? No, a feeling of nonexistence. Sin is Negro as virtue is white. All those white men in a group, guns in their hands, cannot be wrong. I am guilty. I do not know of what, but I know that I am no good.

> THE NEGRO: That's how it goes, ma'am. That's how it always goes with white folks.
> LIZZIE: You too? You feel guilty?
> THE NEGRO: Yes, ma'am.[4]

It is Bigger Thomas—he is afraid, he is terribly afraid. He is afraid, but of what is he afraid? Of himself. No one knows yet who he is, but he knows

9. From Césaire, *Notebook of a Return to My Native Land.*

1. Though Sartre's speculations on the existence of The Other may be correct (to the extent, we must remember, to which *Being and Nothingness* describes an alienated consciousness), their application to a black consciousness proves fallacious. That is because the white man is not only The Other but also the master, whether real or imaginary [Fanon's note]. *Being and Nothingness: An Essay on Phenomenological Ontology* (1943) is Sartre's central work of philosophy.

2. In the sense in which the word is used by Jean Wahl in *Existence humaine et transcendence* [*Human Existence and Transcendence*] (Neuchâtel, La Baconnière, 1944) [Fanon's note]. Wahl (1888–1974), French philosopher.

3. Climbing vines (typically woody in rainforests).

4. Jean-Paul Sartre, *The Respectful Prostitute*, in *Three Plays* (New York, Knopf, 1949), pp. 189, 191. Originally, *La Putain respectueuse* (Paris, Gallimard, 1947). See also *Home of the Brave*, a film by Mark Robson [Fanon's note]. Robson (1913–1978), Canadian-born film director; the 1949 American film was based on a 1946 play by Arthur Laurent.

that fear will fill the world when the world finds out. And when the world knows, the world always expects something of the Negro. He is afraid lest the world know, he is afraid of the fear that the world would feel if the world knew. Like that old woman on her knees who begged me to tie her to her bed:

"I just know, Doctor: Any minute that thing will take hold of me."
"What thing?"
"The wanting to kill myself. Tie me down, I'm afraid."

In the end, Bigger Thomas acts. To put an end to his tension, he acts, he responds to the world's anticipation.[5]

So it is with the character in *If He Hollers Let Him Go*[6]—who does precisely what he did not want to do. That big blonde who was always in his way, weak, sensual, offered, open, fearing (desiring) rape, became his mistress in the end.

The Negro is a toy in the white man's hands; so, in order to shatter the hellish cycle, he explodes. I cannot go to a film without seeing myself. I wait for me. In the interval, just before the film starts, I wait for me. The people in the theater are watching me, examining me, waiting for me. A Negro groom is going to appear. My heart makes my head swim.

The crippled veteran of the Pacific war says to my brother, "Resign yourself to your color the way I got used to my stump; we're both victims."[7]

Nevertheless with all my strength I refuse to accept that amputation. I feel in myself a soul as immense as the world, truly a soul as deep as the deepest of rivers, my chest has the power to expand without limit. I am a master and I am advised to adopt the humility of the cripple. Yesterday, awakening to the world, I saw the sky turn upon itself utterly and wholly. I wanted to rise, but the disemboweled silence fell back upon me, its wings paralyzed. Without responsibility, straddling Nothingness and Infinity, I began to weep.

1952

5. Richard Wright, *Native Son* (New York, Harper, 1940) [Fanon's note]. Wright (1908–1960), African American author; Bigger Thomas is the novel's main character, and the action he takes is a murder.

6. By Chester Himes (Garden City, Doubleday, 1945) [Fanon's note]. Himes (1909–1984), African American author.

7. *Home of the Brave* [Fanon's note].

From The Wretched of the Earth[1]

From *On National Culture*

* * *

RECIPROCAL BASES OF NATIONAL CULTURE AND THE FIGHT FOR FREEDOM

Colonial domination, because it is total and tends to oversimplify, very soon manages to disrupt in spectacular fashion the cultural life of a conquered people. This cultural obliteration is made possible by the negation of national reality, by new legal relations introduced by the occupying power, by the banishment of the natives and their customs to outlying districts by colonial society, by expropriation, and by the systematic enslaving of men and women.

Three years ago at our first congress[2] I showed that, in the colonial situation, dynamism is replaced fairly quickly by a substantification of the attitudes of the colonizing power. The area of culture is then marked off by fences and signposts. These are in fact so many defense mechanisms of the most elementary type, comparable for more than one good reason to the simple instinct for preservation. The interest of this period for us is that the oppressor does not manage to convince himself of the objective nonexistence of the oppressed nation and its culture. Every effort is made to bring the colonized person to admit the inferiority of his culture which has been transformed into instinctive patterns of behavior, to recognize the unreality of his "nation," and, in the last extreme, the confused and imperfect character of his own biological structure.

Vis-à-vis this state of affairs, the native's reactions are not unanimous. While the mass of the people maintain intact traditions which are completely different from those of the colonial situation, and the artisanal style solidifies into a formalism which is more and more stereotyped, the intellectual throws himself in frenzied fashion into the frantic acquisition of the culture of the occupying power and takes every opportunity of unfavorably criticizing his own national culture, or else takes refuge in setting out and substantiating the claims of that culture in a way that is passionate but rapidly becomes unproductive.

The common nature of these two reactions lies in the fact that they both lead to impossible contradictions. Whether a turncoat or a substantialist, the native is ineffectual precisely because the analysis of the colonial situation is not carried out on strict lines. The colonial situation calls a halt to national culture in almost every field. Within the framework of colonial domination there is not and there will never be such phenomena as new cultural departures or changes in the national culture. Here and there valiant attempts are sometimes made to reanimate the cultural dynamic and to give fresh impulses to its themes, its forms, and its tonalities. The immediate, palpable, and obvious interest of such leaps ahead is nil. But if we follow up the consequences to the very end we see that preparations are

1. Translated by Constance Farrington.
2. The First Congress of Black Writers and Artists (this chapter is derived from an address delivered in 1959 at the Second Congress, in Rome).

being thus made to brush the cobwebs off national consciousness, to question oppression, and to open up the struggle for freedom.

A national culture under colonial domination is a contested culture whose destruction is sought in systematic fashion. It very quickly becomes a culture condemned to secrecy. This idea of a clandestine culture is immediately seen in the reactions of the occupying power which interprets attachment to traditions as faithfulness to the spirit of the nation and as a refusal to submit. This persistence in following forms of cultures which are already condemned to extinction is already a demonstration of nationality; but it is a demonstration which is a throwback to the laws of inertia. There is no taking of the offensive and no redefining of relationships. There is simply a concentration on a hard core of culture which is becoming more and more shrivelled up, inert, and empty.

By the time a century or two of exploitation has passed there comes about a veritable emaciation of the stock of national culture. It becomes a set of automatic habits, some traditions of dress, and a few broken-down institutions. Little movement can be discerned in such remnants of culture; there is no real creativity and no overflowing life. The poverty of the people, national oppression, and the inhibition of culture are one and the same thing. After a century of colonial domination we find a culture which is rigid in the extreme, or rather what we find are the dregs of culture, its mineral strata. The withering away of the reality of the nation and the death pangs of the national culture are linked to each other in mutual dependence. This is why it is of capital importance to follow the evolution of these relations during the struggle for national freedom. The negation of the native's culture, the contempt for any manifestation of culture whether active or emotional, and the placing outside the pale of all specialized branches of organization contribute to breed aggressive patterns of conduct in the native. But these patterns of conduct are of the reflexive type; they are poorly differentiated, anarchic, and ineffective. Colonial exploitation, poverty, and endemic famine drive the native more and more to open, organized revolt. The necessity for an open and decisive breach is formed progressively and imperceptibly, and comes to be felt by the great majority of the people. Those tensions which hitherto were non-existent come into being. International events, the collapse of whole sections of colonial empires and the contradictions inherent in the colonial system strengthen and uphold the native's combativity while promoting and giving support to national consciousness.

These new-found tensions which are present at all stages in the real nature of colonialism have their repercussions on the cultural plane. In literature, for example, there is relative overproduction. From being a reply on a minor scale to the dominating power, the literature produced by natives becomes differentiated and makes itself into a will to particularism. The intelligentsia, which during the period of repression was essentially a consuming public, now themselves become producers. This literature at first chooses to confine itself to the tragic and poetic style; but later on novels, short stories, and essays are attempted. It is as if a kind of internal organization or law of expression existed which wills that poetic expression become less frequent in proportion as the objectives and the methods of the struggle for liberation become more precise. Themes are completely altered; in fact, we find less and less of bitter, hopeless recrimination and less also of that violent, resounding, florid writing which on the whole serves to reassure the occupying power. The colonialists have in former times encouraged these modes of expression and made their existence possible. Stinging denunciations, the exposing of distressing conditions and passions which find their outlet in expression are in fact assimilated by the occupying power in a cathartic process. To aid such processes is in a certain sense to avoid their dramatization and to clear the atmosphere.

But such a situation can only be transitory. In fact, the progress of national consciousness among the people modifies and gives precision to the literary utterances of the native intellectual. The continued cohesion of the people constitutes for the intellectual an invitation to go further than his cry of protest. The lament first makes the indictment; and then it makes an appeal. In the period that follows, the words of command are heard. The crystallization of the national consciousness will both disrupt literary styles and themes, and also create a completely new public. While at the beginning the native intellectual used to produce his work to be read exclusively by the oppressor, whether with the intention of charming him or of denouncing him through ethnic or subjectivist means, now the native writer progressively takes on the habit of addressing his own people.

It is only from that moment that we can speak of a national literature. Here there is, at the level of literary creation, the taking up and clarification of themes which are typically nationalist. This may be properly called a literature of combat, in the sense that it calls on the whole people to fight for their existence as a nation. It is a literature of combat, because it molds the national consciousness, giving it form and contours and flinging open before it new and boundless horizons; it is a literature of combat because it assumes responsibility, and because it is the will to liberty expressed in terms of time and space.

On another level, the oral tradition—stories, epics, and songs of the people—which formerly were filed away as set pieces are now beginning to change. The storytellers who used to relate inert episodes now bring them alive and introduce into them modifications which are increasingly fundamental. There is a tendency to bring conflicts up to date and to modernize the kinds of struggle which the stories evoke, together with the names of heroes and the types of weapons. The method of allusion is more and more widely used. The formula "This all happened long ago" is substituted with that of "What we are going to speak of happened somewhere else, but it might well have happened here today, and it might happen tomorrow." The example of Algeria[3] is significant in this context. From 1952–53 on, the storytellers, who were before that time stereotyped and tedious to listen to, completely overturned their traditional methods of storytelling and the contents of their tales. Their public, which was formerly scattered, became compact. The epic, with its typified categories, reappeared; it became an authentic form of entertainment which took on once more a cultural value. Colonialism made no mistake when from 1955 on it proceeded to arrest these storytellers systematically.

The contact of the people with the new movement gives rise to a new rhythm of life and to forgotten muscular tensions, and develops the

3. Officially a part of France in North Africa; it began an armed revolt in 1954. Fanon actively participated in the revolution, which led to Algeria's independence from French rule in 1962.

imagination. Every time the storyteller relates a fresh episode to his public, he presides over a real invocation. The existence of a new type of man is revealed to the public. The present is no longer turned in upon itself but spread out for all to see. The storyteller once more gives free rein to his imagination; he makes innovations and he creates a work of art. It even happens that the characters, which are barely ready for such a transformation—highway robbers or more or less anti-social vagabonds—are taken up and remodeled. The emergence of the imagination and of the creative urge in the songs and epic stories of a colonized country is worth following. The storyteller replies to the expectant people by successive approximations, and makes his way, apparently alone but in fact helped on by his public, toward the seeking out of new patterns, that is to say national patterns. Comedy and farce disappear, or lose their attraction. As for dramatization, it is no longer placed on the plane of the troubled intellectual and his tormented conscience. By losing its characteristics of despair and revolt, the drama becomes part of the common lot of the people and forms part of an action in preparation or already in progress.

Where handicrafts are concerned, the forms of expression which formerly were the dregs of art, surviving as if in a daze, now begin to reach out. Woodwork, for example, which formerly turned out certain faces and attitudes by the million, begins to be differentiated. The inexpressive or overwrought mask comes to life and the arms tend to be raised from the body as if to sketch an action. Compositions containing two, three, or five figures appear. The traditional schools are led on to creative efforts by the rising avalanche of amateurs or of critics. This new vigor in this sector of cultural life very often passes unseen; and yet its contribution to the national effort is of capital importance. By carving figures and faces which are full of life, and by taking as his theme a group fixed on the same pedestal, the artist invites participation in an organized movement.

If we study the repercussions of the awakening of national consciousness in the domains of ceramics and pottery-making, the same observations may be drawn. Formalism is abandoned in the craftsman's work. Jugs, jars, and trays are modified, at first imperceptibly, then almost savagely. The colors, of which formerly there were but few and which obeyed the traditional rules of harmony, increase in number and are influenced by the repercussion of the rising revolution. Certain ochres and blues, which seemed forbidden to all eternity in a given cultural area, now assert themselves without giving rise to scandal. In the same way the stylization of the human face, which according to sociologists is typical of very clearly defined regions, becomes suddenly completely relative. The specialist coming from the home country and the ethnologist are quick to note these changes. On the whole such changes are condemned in the name of a rigid code of artistic style and of a cultural life which grows up at the heart of the colonial system. The colonialist specialists do not recognize these new forms and rush to the help of the traditions of the indigenous society. It is the colonialists who become the defenders of the native style. We remember perfectly, and the example took on a certain measure of importance since the real nature of colonialism was not involved, the reactions of the white jazz specialists when after the Second World War new styles such as the be-bop took definite shape. The fact is that in their eyes jazz should only be the despairing, broken-down nostalgia of an old Negro who is trapped between five glasses of whiskey, the curse of his race, and the racial hatred of the white men. As soon as the Negro comes to an understanding of himself, and understands the rest of the world differently, when he gives birth to hope and forces back the racist universe, it is clear that his trumpet sounds more clearly and his voice less hoarsely. The new fashions in jazz are not simply born of economic competition. We must without any doubt see in them one of the consequences of the defeat, slow but sure, of the southern world of the United States. And it is not utopian to suppose that in fifty years' time the type of jazz howl hiccuped by a poor misfortunate Negro will be upheld only by the whites who believe in it as an expression of negritude, and who are faithful to this arrested image of a type of relationship.

We might in the same way seek and find in dancing, singing, and traditional rites and ceremonies the same upward-springing trend, and make out the same changes and the same impatience in this field. Well before the political or fighting phase of the national movement, an attentive spectator can thus feel and see the manifestation of new vigor and feel the approaching conflict. He will note unusual forms of expression and themes which are fresh and imbued with a power which is no longer that of invocation but rather of the assembling of the people, a summoning together for a precise purpose. Everything works together to awaken the native's sensibility and to make unreal and inacceptable the contemplative attitude, or the acceptance of defeat. The native rebuilds his perceptions because he renews the purpose and dynamism of the craftsmen, of dancing and music, and of literature and the oral tradition. His world comes to lose its accursed character. The conditions necessary for the inevitable conflict are brought together.

We have noted the appearance of the movement in cultural forms and we have seen that this movement and these new forms are linked to the state of maturity of the national consciousness. Now, this movement tends more and more to express itself objectively, in institutions. From thence comes the need for a national existence, whatever the cost.

A frequent mistake, and one which is moreover hardly justifiable, is to try to find cultural expressions for and to give new values to native culture within the framework of colonial domination. This is why we arrive at a proposition which at first sight seems paradoxical: the fact that in a colonized country the most elementary, most savage, and the most undifferentiated nationalism is the most fervent and efficient means of defending national culture. For culture is first the expression of a nation, the expression of its preferences, of its taboos and of its patterns. It is at every stage of the whole of society that other taboos, values, and patterns are formed. A national culture is the sum total of all these appraisals; it is the result of internal and external tensions exerted over society as a whole and also at every level of that society. In the colonial situation, culture, which is doubly deprived of the support of the nation and of the state, falls away and dies. The condition for its existence is therefore national liberation and the renaissance of the state.

The nation is not only the condition of culture, its fruitfulness, its continuous renewal, and its deepening. It is also a necessity. It is the fight for national existence which sets culture moving and opens to it the doors of creation. Later on it is the nation which will ensure the conditions and framework necessary to culture. The nation gathers together the various indispensable elements necessary for the creation of a culture, those elements which alone can give it credibility, validity, life, and creative power. In the same way it is its national character that will make such a culture open to other cultures and which will enable it to influence and permeate other cultures. A non-existent culture can hardly be expected to have bearing on reality, or to influence reality. The first necessity is the re-establishment of the nation in order to give life to national culture in the strictly biological sense of the phrase.

Thus we have followed the breakup of the old strata of culture, a shattering which becomes increasingly fundamental; and we have noticed, on the eve of the decisive conflict for national freedom, the renewing of forms of expression and the rebirth of the imagination. There remains one essential question: what are the relations between the struggle—whether political or military—and culture? Is there a suspension of culture during the conflict? Is the national struggle an expression of a culture? Finally, ought one to say that the battle for freedom however fertile *a posteriori* with regard to culture is in itself a negation of culture? In short, is the struggle for liberation a cultural phenomenon or not?

We believe that the conscious and organized undertaking by a colonized people to re-establish the sovereignty of that nation constitutes the most complete and obvious cultural manifestation that exists. It is not alone the success of the struggle which afterward gives validity and vigor to culture; culture is not put into cold storage during the conflict. The struggle itself in its development and in its internal progression sends culture along different paths and traces out entirely new ones for it. The struggle for freedom does not give back to the national culture its former value and shapes; this struggle which aims at a fundamentally different set of relations between men cannot leave intact either the form or the content of the people's culture. After the conflict there is not only the disappearance of colonialism but also the disappearance of the colonized man.

This new humanity cannot do otherwise than define a new humanism both for itself and for others. It is prefigured in the objectives and methods of the conflict. A struggle which mobilizes all classes of the people and which expresses their aims and their impatience, which is not afraid to count almost exclusively on the people's support, will of necessity triumph. The value of this type of conflict is that it supplies the maximum of conditions necessary for the development and aims of culture. After national freedom has been obtained in these conditions, there is no such painful cultural indecision which is found in certain countries which are newly independent, because the nation by its manner of coming into being and in the terms of its existence exerts a fundamental influence over culture. A nation which is born of the people's concerted action and which embodies the real aspirations of the people while changing the state cannot exist save in the expression of exceptionally rich forms of culture.

The natives who are anxious for the culture of their country and who wish to give to it a universal dimension ought not therefore to place their confidence in the single principle of inevitable, undifferentiated independence written into the consciousness of the people in order to achieve their task. The liberation of the nation is one thing; the methods and popular content of the fight are another. It seems to us that the future of national culture and its riches are equally also part and parcel of the values which have ordained the struggle for freedom.

And now it is time to denounce certain pharisees. National claims, it is here and there stated, are a phase that humanity has left behind. It is the day of great concerted actions, and retarded nationalists ought in consequence to set their mistakes aright. We however consider that the mistake, which may have very serious consequences, lies in wishing to skip the national period. If culture is the expression of national consciousness, I will not hesitate to affirm that in the case with which we are dealing it is the national consciousness which is the most elaborate form of culture.

The consciousness of self is not the closing of a door to communication. Philosophic thought teaches us, on the contrary, that it is its guarantee. National consciousness, which is not nationalism, is the only thing that will give us an international dimension. This problem of national consciousness and of national culture takes on in Africa a special dimension. The birth of national consciousness in Africa has a strictly contemporaneous connection with the African consciousness. The responsibility of the African as regards national culture is also a responsibility with regard to African Negro culture. This joint responsibility is not the fact of a metaphysical principle but the awareness of a simple rule which wills that every independent nation in an Africa where colonialism is still entrenched is an encircled nation, a nation which is fragile and in permanent danger.

If man is known by his acts, then we will say that the most urgent thing today for the intellectual is to build up his nation. If this building up is true, that is to say if it interprets the manifest will of the people and reveals the eager African peoples, then the building of a nation is of necessity accompanied by the discovery and encouragement of universalizing values. Far from keeping aloof from other nations, therefore, it is national liberation which leads the nation to play its part on the stage of history. It is at the heart of national consciousness that international consciousness lives and grows. And this two-fold emerging is ultimately only the source of all culture.

1961

GILLES DELEUZE 1925–1995 / FÉLIX GUATTARI 1930–1992

Alternately hailed or dismissed in North America as the "enfants terribles" of poststructuralist philosophy and psychoanalysis following the publication of their *Anti-Oedipus: Capitalism and Schizophrenia* (1972), Gilles Deleuze and Félix Guattari are known for their antiestablishment thinking in many domains. Trained as a philosopher and a psychoanalyst, respectively, Deleuze and Guattari critique the patterns of knowledge that govern the disciplines in which they were schooled. In the process, they question the dominance of conceptual stability, organization, and unity as such. Their critique is well summed up in their pun on the word "General":

knowledge functions like an operation of conquest and mastery, driven by "generality" as if it were a military "General."

Born in Paris to a middle-class family, Deleuze was educated in the French university system and taught philosophy at the University of Paris at Vincennes (now St. Denis) from 1969 until his retirement in 1987. At the time of the 1968 student-worker revolts in France, Deleuze began to write books in his "own" voice, aiming to replace official philosophy with what he called "bastard" philosophy. Deleuze declared that his early writings, such as *Empiricism and Subjectivity: An Essay on Hume's Theory of Nature* (1953) and *Bergsonism* (1966), still too closely resembled those of an "academic bureaucrat." In his *Nietzsche and Philosophy* (1962) but especially in *Difference and Repetition* (1968), *The Logic of Sense* (1969), and *Spinoza: Practical Philosophy* (1970), Deleuze developed a new philosophy of becoming and exteriority—joining an orphan line of metaphysical thinkers that includes Lucretius, BARUCH SPINOZA, Gottfried Leibniz, DAVID HUME, FRIEDRICH NIETZSCHE, and Henri Bergson—that his work combines with various other strands of contemporary theory.

In the interdisciplinary mix of French philosophy and theory of the 1960s and 1970s, he came in contact with the person who would become his "intercessor" for many years, Félix Guattari, a practicing psychoanalyst and political activist. Guattari, usually said to be the more "delirious" of the two, was born in the Paris suburb of Colombes and had received an erratic education; never having earned any official degrees, he had worked since the mid-1950s at La Borde, a psychiatric hospital outside Paris known for innovative practices in group therapy. One of JACQUES LACAN's earliest trainees, Guattari quickly took leave of the master. Lacan, he felt, had transformed structural psychoanalysis into a religion devoted to cultivating and initiating followers. Guattari's antihierarchical and anarchic tendencies drew him into an alliance with Deleuze. Together they wrote the polemical *Anti-Oedipus*.

Described by MICHEL FOUCAULT as "an introduction to non-fascist living," *Anti-Oedipus* was an immediate sensation in France and soon thereafter in England, Canada, and the United States, where it became an academic bestseller when its translation appeared in 1983. It was hailed as a productive attack not only on state philosophy but also on the orthodox Marxism and institutional Freudianism that pervaded the postwar years. In the view of Deleuze and Guattari, psychoanalysis combines with capitalism to channel and control desire, not to liberate it. As a negative critique, the book is more interested in freeing the forces that have been constrained than in proposing alternatives.

After this moment of destruction, they experimented with a philosophy of becoming. In another of their books, *Kafka: Toward a Minor Literature* (1975; trans. 1986), from which we have taken our first selection, Deleuze and Guattari claim that Franz Kafka (1883–1924), although writing in a dominant language (German), introduces into it elements of his own Jewish, minoritarian culture. He thus recombines dominant ways of thinking with elements of a minority culture to produce something entirely different—a minor literature—thereby undermining power. But Deleuze and Guattari make clear that it does not suffice to *be* Jewish. One has to *become* Jewish—or minoritarian—in an ongoing way. The "outside" is never a *given*. Consider SIGMUND FREUD, whose own relation to dominant German culture was similar to Kafka's. Freud considered himself an observer whose distance from the "compact majority" enabled him to explore the hidden forces underlying the culture around him. Yet over time, according to Deleuze and Guattari, those explorations had become hardened into doctrine.

A Thousand Plateaus: Capitalism and Schizophrenia, the sequel to *Anti-Oedipus*, appeared in 1980. The least well received of their books, as Deleuze and Guattari proudly admitted, its project is very different from that of its predecessor. It is more a work of art, a positive exercise in the productive desire and affirmative "nomad" thought that *Anti-Oedipus* called for. The book's introductory chapter (or "plateau"), from which our second selection is taken, is titled "Rhizome" and is often cited as an exemplary text of postmodern philosophy.

Deleuze and Guattari claim that state philosophy as practiced in the academy is a form of the representational thought that has dominated the West since PLATO. Representation posits the self-identity of the thinking subject. The subject, the concepts, and the objects in the world are thus presumed to share a self-resemblance essential for maintaining their identity. Representational thought establishes a correspondence between two symmetrical domains. It is analogical: the success of a representation is derived from its accuracy, its closeness to an original, which nevertheless remains more "real." Deleuze and Guattari take the mimetic hierarchy described by Plato and turn it on its side. Whereas the traditional model for knowledge is drawn from plants with "roots" (the ground or origin that leads to the main growth through genealogy or evolution), Deleuze and Guattari draw their metaphor from fungal "rhizomes"—a network of threads that can send up new growths anywhere along their length, not subject to centralized control or structure. This logic (or rather, nonlogic) is exemplified by invasive species such as mushrooms and crabgrass that proliferate without a controlling structure. As Deleuze and Guattari suggest, the same antihierarchical perspective is what may have led Walt Whitman to choose *Leaves of Grass* (1855) as the title for his book of poems. They thus replace the rooted tree (the Western metaphor for knowledge par excellence) with the rhizome, conceived as an adventitious mode of thinking that grows between things and produces offshoots in unforeseen directions. It is striking that FERDINAND DE SAUSSURE (1857–1913) should choose "tree" as his example of a sign—his structural linguistics conform exactly to the static, binary logic that Deleuze and Guattari critique. (See also Lacan's tribute to the importance of the tree in Western culture, above.)

In their difficult yet rewarding texts, Deleuze and Guattari distinguish between the segment—that is, the official, "molar" line that occupies a given social or political position—and another, "molecular" line that begins to separate itself, and to disaggregate, from the first. Thus, for example, in *Anti-Oedipus* Deleuze and Guattari—both married—write: "We are heterosexuals statistically or in molar terms, but homosexuals personally, whether we know it or not, and finally transsexuals elementarily, molecularly." Sexuality for them is that experience of desire that breaks through any self-definition; requires a new, temporarily synthesized multiplicity; and yet does not provide a new identity. The de-Oedipalized body becomes a "Body without Organs," a "desiring-machine" not governed by "phases" of development and not organized into "bundles" or knowable "organs."

Rhizomatic thinking promotes becoming, not being. Deleuze and Guattari state—a statement for which they have been much criticized—that because of the special relation of women to the man-standard, all becomings (-child, -animal, -vegetal, -intense) begin with the "becoming-woman" of man. But the "becoming-woman" of man may involve the renunciation not only of sexuality as mastery but also of family trees as trees: "family trees" resemble trees only when the patriarchal name is followed, and when one particular generation or individual is the focus. A true map of all lines—male and female, legitimate and illegitimate—even in heterosexual reproduction would resemble a rhizome, not a tree. At the same time, the women who have been invisible in the family tree cannot simply become an alternative to it. Women, as well as homosexuals, Jews, and blacks, according to Deleuze and Guattari, must constantly reinvent themselves as "minoritarian" to avoid becoming a minority as a new state. This way of being in, and open to, the world is called "ethics" by Spinoza; Deleuze and Guattari call it pragmatics. And for them, books themselves are pragmatic assemblages or tool kits for becoming.

The rhizome replaces, or at least complements, history (the story people tell) with geography (the ground they inhabit). A "map," for Deleuze and Guattari, is a drawing that *is* and *transforms* the object it purportedly represents; a "tracing" merely tries to duplicate the object. Yet the rhizomatic process is not pure "dissemination": it is structured, but not organized, by moments of synthesis. Always in movement, a rhizome has neither beginning nor end. Influenced by theories of chaos and complexity, Deleuze and Guattari claim to study subjectivity where it emerges, society where it mutates, and the world where it is re-created. With the development of the Internet and virtual reality, we have already in some ways entered the rhizomatic structures they describe; but there is no guarantee that the logics they critique have therefore disappeared.

In literature, Deleuze and Guattari do not look for meaning. When reading Heinrich von Kleist (1777–1811) or Franz Kafka against alleged state writers such as Johann Wolfgang von Goethe (1749–1832), or when reading HENRY JAMES (1843–1916) or the twentieth-century writers F. Scott Fitzgerald, VIRGINIA WOOLF, or Nathalie Sarraute, they look for the lines of flight by means of which these writers detach themselves—and their texts—from an immobilizing order. In becoming, these writers "deterritorialize" themselves from and within official culture before "reterritorializing" themselves elsewhere.

From the early 1980s up to his death, Deleuze continued to emphasize the need to mesh aesthetics and philosophy. After *A Thousand Plateaus*, he studied the affective potential of color and line in *Francis Bacon: The Logic of Sensation* (1981); in that work he notes the Irish-born British painter's capacity to affect and to be affected by chromatic vibration. Architecture, logic, and aesthetics are examined as events in *The Fold: Leibniz and the Baroque* (1988), where Deleuze further writes about the world as a set of lines in relations of movement and rest. His two-volume analysis of cinema invents a taxonomy to replace the one underlying linguistic theories of film. The first volume, *The Movement-Image* (1983), projects the lexicon of classical cinema (close-up, medium shot, long shot) into a philosophical field that associates bodily sensation with mobility, whose effect constitutes cinematic events in the first fifty years of cinema's history. In the second, *The Time-Image* (1985), Deleuze analyzes the effect of duration, invention, and the absence of mimesis in films that follow the aftermath of World War II.

Concurrently, Félix Guattari also published on his own. Developing long-standing relations with radical Italian social groups, he collaborated with the philosopher and political activist ANTONIO NEGRI. It was, for him, a line of flight away from a fashionable intellectual lassitude reigning in France. He loathed postmodern melancholia, which he excoriated repeatedly. In *The Three Ecologies* (1989), one of his most forceful essays, Guattari mobilizes concepts developed elsewhere with Deleuze. Discussing the relations between thought and politics, he clarifies his theoretical and political stance on many contemporary issues, ranging from the exploitation of women to problems of the third world to racism and environmental degradation. He also reemphasizes the importance of literary texts and broaches the difference between militantism and artistic invention in what he calls the converging of aesthetics, ethics, and politics. The slim volume serves as an indication of how Guattari's thought evolved after texts like "Rhizome." Without reverting back to prestructuralism or to phenomenological analyses, Guattari pleaded for a philosophy of becoming (now renamed "ecosophy") in more openly existential terms.

Deleuze's *Negotiations* (1990) records a series of interviews from 1972 to 1990. Emphasis is placed on the urgency of practicing philosophy in view of the controlling discourses of power—namely, religion, capitalism, science, law, television, and public opinion. He too makes a case for philosophy as guerrilla warfare not just in the streets but within subjects themselves. In the same vein, Deleuze and Guattari wrote their last joint work, the compelling *What Is Philosophy?* (1991), which had an impact similar to that of *Anti-Oedipus*. They reiterate their belief in the continued importance of philosophy as a way of thinking and a mode of action. The inseparability of thought from context informs the hybrid nature of all national philosophical and literary traditions.

Affirmation and *action* were key words in the lexicon and the lives of Deleuze and Guattari. In addition to writing on literature and the arts, Guattari unsuccessfully ran for office in the French Green Party, shortly before his untimely death from a heart attack in 1992. In essays written for *Le Monde diplomatique* he stressed the necessity of restructuring social thought and action. In "The Exhausted," an afterword of sorts to Samuel Beckett's *Quad and Other Plays for Television* (1992), Deleuze reflects that the exhausted person—in contrast to the tired person—has exhausted all the possibilities. For the next three years, he nonetheless continued to teach and write while cancer ravaged his body. In 1995 he jumped to his death from the window of his Parisian apartment.

Kafka: Toward a Minor Literature **Keywords:** Language, Nationhood, Psychoanalysis, Race and Ethnicity Studies
A Thousand Plateaus: Capitalism and Schizophrenia **Keywords:** Aesthetics, Authorship, The Body, Poststructuralism, Representation

From Kafka: Toward a Minor Literature[1]

From *Chapter 3. What Is a Minor Literature?*

* * *

A minor literature doesn't come from a minor language; it is rather that which a minority constructs within a major language. But the first characteristic of minor literature in any case is that in it language is affected with a high coefficient of deterritorialization. In this sense, Kafka[2] marks the impasse that bars access to writing for the Jews of Prague and turns their literature into something impossible—the impossibility of not writing, the impossibility of writing in German, the impossibility of writing otherwise.[3] The impossibility of not writing because national consciousness, uncertain or oppressed, necessarily exists by means of literature ("The literary struggle has its real justification at the highest possible levels"). The impossibility of writing other than in German is for the Prague Jews the feeling of an irreducible distance from their primitive Czech territoriality. And the impossibility of writing in German is the deterritorialization of the German population itself, an oppressive minority that speaks a language cut off from the masses, like a "paper language" or an artificial language; this is all the more true for the Jews who are simultaneously a part of this minority and excluded from it, like "gypsies who have stolen a German child from its crib." In short, Prague German is a deterritorialized language, appropriate for strange and minor uses. (This can be compared in another context to what blacks in America today are able to do with the English language.)

The second characteristic of minor literatures is that everything in them is political. In major literatures, in contrast, the individual concern (familial, marital, and so on) joins with other no less individual concerns, the social milieu serving as a mere environment or a background; this is so much the

1. Translated by Dana Polan, who occasionally retains the original French in parentheses.
2. Franz Kafka (1883–1924), Jewish Austrian writer who lived much of his life in Prague and wrote in German; his work is here the focus of the process of "becoming-minor."
3. See letter to [Max] Brod, Kafka, *Letters*, June 1921, and commentaries in [Klaus] Wagenbach, *Franz Kafka: Années de jeunesse* [1958] [Deleuze and Guattari's note]. Some of the authors' notes have been omitted. Brod (1884–1968), a close friend and biographer of Kafka; he disobeyed the dying Kafka's request to destroy his papers.

case that none of these Oedipal intrigues are specifically indispensable or absolutely necessary but all become as one in a large space. Minor literature is completely different; its cramped space forces each individual intrigue to connect immediately to politics. The individual concern thus becomes all the more necessary, indispensable, magnified, because a whole other story is vibrating within it. In this way, the family triangle connects to other triangles—commercial, economic, bureaucratic, juridical—that determine its values. When Kafka indicates that one of the goals of a minor literature is the "purification of the conflict that opposes father and son and the possibility of discussing that conflict," it isn't a question of an Oedipal phantasm[4] but of a political program. "Even though something is often thought through calmly, one still does not reach the boundary where it connects up with similar things, one reaches the boundary soonest in politics, indeed, one even strives to see it before it is there, and often sees this limiting boundary everywhere. . . . What in great literature goes on down below, constituting a not indispensable cellar of the structure, here takes place in the full light of day, what is there a matter of passing interest for a few, here absorbs everyone no less than as a matter of life and death."[5]

The third characteristic of minor literature is that in it everything takes on a collective value. Indeed, precisely because talent isn't abundant in a minor literature, there are no possibilities for an individuated enunciation that would belong to this or that "master" and that could be separated from a collective enunciation. Indeed, scarcity of talent is in fact beneficial and allows the conception of something other than a literature of masters; what each author says individually already constitutes a common action, and what he or she says or does is necessarily political, even if others aren't in agreement. The political domain has contaminated every statement (*énoncé*).[6] But above all else, because collective or national consciousness is "often inactive in external life and always in the process of break-down," literature finds itself positively charged with the role and function of collective, and even revolutionary, enunciation. It is literature that produces an active solidarity in spite of skepticism; and if the writer is in the margins or completely outside his or her fragile community, this situation allows the writer all the more the possibility to express another possible community and to forge the means for another consciousness and another sensibility; just as the dog of "Investigations"[7] calls out in his solitude to *another science*. The literary machine thus becomes the relay for a revolutionary machine-to-come, not at all for ideological reasons but because the literary machine alone is determined to fill the conditions of a collective enunciation that is lacking elsewhere in this milieu: *literature is the people's concern*.[8] It is certainly in these terms that Kafka sees the problem. The message doesn't refer back to an enunciating subject who would be its cause, no more than to a subject of the statement (*sujet d'énoncé*) who would be its effect. Undoubtedly, for a while, Kafka thought according to these traditional categories of the two subjects, the author and the hero, the narrator and the

4. That is, the Oedipus complex—the desire of a young boy for his mother that makes him view his father as a competitor—described by Sigmund Freud (1856–1939).

5. Kafka, *Diaries*, December 25, 1911 [Deleuze and Guattari's note].

6. *Énoncé* (French) is the statement or content of an utterance; *énonciation* is the act of uttering it.

7. "Investigations of a Dog" is the title of a story by Kafka.

8. Kafka, *Diaries*, December 25, 1911: "[L]iterature is less a concern of literary history, than of the people" [Deleuze and Guattari's note].

character, the dreamer and the one dreamed of. But he will quickly reject the role of the narrator, just as he will refuse an author's or master's literature, despite his admiration for Goethe. Josephine the mouse[9] renounces the individual act of singing in order to melt into the collective enunciation of "the immense crowd of the heros of [her] people." A movement from the individuated animal to the pack or to a collective multiplicity—seven canine musicians. In "The Investigations of a Dog," the expressions of the solitary researcher tend toward the assemblage (*agencement*) of a collective enunciation of the canine species even if this collectivity is no longer or not yet given. There isn't a subject; *there are only collective assemblages of enunciation*, and literature expresses these acts insofar as they're not imposed from without and insofar as they exist only as diabolical powers to come or revolutionary forces to be constructed. Kafka's solitude opens him up to everything going on in history today. The letter K[1] no longer designates a narrator or a character but an assemblage that becomes all the more machine-like, an agent that becomes all the more collective because an individual is locked into it in his or her solitude (it is only in connection to a subject that something individual would be separable from the collective and would lead its own life).

The three characteristics of minor literature are the deterritorialization of language, the connection of the individual to a political immediacy, and the collective assemblage of enunciation. We might as well say that minor no longer designates specific literatures but the revolutionary conditions for every literature within the heart of what is called great (or established) literature. Even he who has the misfortune of being born in the country of a great literature must write in its language, just as a Czech Jew writes in German, or an Ouzbekian writes in Russian. Writing like a dog digging a hole, a rat digging its burrow.[2] And to do that, finding his own point of underdevelopment, his own *patois*, his own third world, his own desert. There has been much discussion of the questions "What is a marginal literature?" and "What is a popular literature, a proletarian literature?" The criteria are obviously difficult to establish if one doesn't start with a more objective concept—that of minor literature. Only the possibility of setting up a minor practice of major language from within allows one to define popular literature, marginal literature, and so on. Only in this way can literature really become a collective machine of expression and really be able to treat and develop its contents. Kafka emphatically declares that a minor literature is much more able to work over its material.[3] Why this machine of expression, and what is it? We know that it is in a relation of multiple deterritorializations with language; it is the situation of the Jews who have dropped the Czech language at the same time as the rural environment, but it is also the situation of the German language as a "paper language." Well, one can go even farther; one can push this movement of deterritorialization of expression even farther. But there are only two ways to do this. One way is to artificially enrich this German, to swell it up through all the resources of symbolism, of oneirism,

9. Title character in "Josephine the Singer, or the Mouse Folk," the last story written by Kafka. Johann Wolfgang von Goethe (1749–1832), magisterial German poet, playwright, and novelist.

1. The hero of *The Castle* (1926), a posthumously published unfinished novel by Kafka, is known only as K.; the hero of *The Trial* (1925), another posthumously published unfinished novel, is Joseph K.

2. "The Burrow" is a story by Kafka.

3. Kafka, *Diaries*, December 25, 1911: "A small nation's memory is not smaller than the memory of a large one and so can digest the existing material more thoroughly" [Deleuze and Guattari's note].

of esoteric sense, of a hidden signifier. This is the approach of the Prague school, Gustav Meyrink and many others, including Max Brod.[4] But this attempt implies a desperate attempt at symbolic reterritorialization, based in archetypes, Kabbala, and alchemy, that accentuates its break from the people and will find its political result only in Zionism and such things as the "dream of Zion."[5] Kafka will quickly choose the other way, or, rather, he will invent another way. He will opt for the German language of Prague as it is and in its very poverty. Go always farther in the direction of deterritorialization, to the point of sobriety. Since the language is arid, make it vibrate with a new intensity. Oppose a purely intensive usage of language to all symbolic or even significant or simply signifying usages of it. Arrive at a perfect and unformed expression, a materially intense expression. (For these two possible paths, couldn't we find the same alternatives, under other conditions, in Joyce and Beckett?[6] As Irishmen, both of them live within the genial conditions of a minor literature. That is the glory of this sort of minor literature—to be the revolutionary force for all literature. The utilization of English and of every language in Joyce. The utilization of English and French in Beckett. But the former never stops operating by exhilaration and overdetermination and brings about all sorts of worldwide reterritorializations. The other proceeds by dryness and sobriety, a willed poverty, pushing deterritorialization to such an extreme that nothing remains but intensities.)

How many people today live in a language that is not their own? Or no longer, or not yet, even know their own and know poorly the major language that they are forced to serve? This is the problem of immigrants, and especially of their children, the problem of minorities, the problem of a minor literature, but also a problem for all of us: how to tear a minor literature away from its own language, allowing it to challenge the language and making it follow a sober revolutionary path? How to become a nomad and an immigrant and a gypsy in relation to one's own language? Kafka answers: steal the baby from its crib, walk the tightrope.

* * *

1975

From A Thousand Plateaus: Capitalism and Schizophrenia[1]

From *Introduction: Rhizome*

The two of us wrote *Anti-Oedipus*[2] together. Since each of us was several, there was already quite a crowd. Here we have made use of everything that

4. See the excellent chapter "Prague at the Turn of the Century," in Wagenbach, *Franz Kafka*, on the situation of the German language in Czechoslovakia and on the Prague School [Deleuze and Guattari's note]. Meyrink (1868–1932), German author of occult fiction, including the novel *The Golem* (1915).

5. The Jewish homeland in Palestine, sought by Zionism and achieved in the establishment of the State of Israel in 1948. Kabbala: a system of Jewish mysticism, especially the esoteric theosophy of the 13th century and later (also spelled "Cabala").

6. Samuel Beckett (1906–1989), Irish-born novelist and playwright who published in both French and English. James Joyce (1882–1941), Irish writer whose fiction is extraordinarily innovative in technique and language. Both wrote outside Ireland.

1. Translated by Brian Massumi, who occasionally retains the original French in parentheses.

2. *Anti-Oedipus: Capitalism and Schizophrenia*, to which this work is a sequel, was published in French in 1972.

came within range, what was closest as well as farthest away. We have assigned clever pseudonyms to prevent recognition. Why have we kept our own names? Out of habit, purely out of habit. To make ourselves unrecognizable in turn. To render imperceptible, not ourselves, but what makes us act, feel, and think. Also because it's nice to talk like everybody else, to say the sun rises, when everybody knows it's only a manner of speaking. To reach, not the point where one no longer says I, but the point where it is no longer of any importance whether one says I. We are no longer ourselves. Each will know his own. We have been aided, inspired, multiplied.

A book has neither object nor subject; it is made of variously formed matters, and very different dates and speeds. To attribute the book to a subject is to overlook this working of matters, and the exteriority of their relations. It is to fabricate a beneficent God to explain geological movements. In a book, as in all things, there are lines of articulation or segmentarity, strata and territories; but also lines of flight, movements of deterritorialization and destratification. Comparative rates of flow on these lines produce phenomena of relative slowness and viscosity, or, on the contrary, of acceleration and rupture. All this, lines and measurable speeds, constitutes an *assemblage*. A book is an assemblage of this kind, and as such is unattributable. It is a multiplicity—but we don't know yet what the multiple entails when it is no longer attributed, that is, after it has been elevated to the status of a substantive. One side of a machinic assemblage faces the strata, which doubtless make it a kind of organism, or signifying totality, or determination attributable to a subject; it also has a side facing a *body without organs*,[3] which is continually dismantling the organism, causing asignifying particles or pure intensities to pass or circulate, and attributing to itself subjects that it leaves with nothing more than a name as the trace of an intensity. What is the body without organs of a book? There are several, depending on the nature of the lines considered, their particular grade or density, and the possibility of their converging on a "plane of consistency" assuring their selection. Here, as elsewhere, the units of measure are what is essential: *quantify writing*. There is no difference between what a book talks about and how it is made. Therefore a book also has no object. As an assemblage, a book has only itself, in connection with other assemblages and in relation to other bodies without organs. We will never ask what a book means, as signified or signifier;[4] we will not look for anything to understand in it. We will ask what it functions with, in connection with what other things it does or does not transmit intensities, in which other multiplicities its own are inserted and metamorphosed, and with what bodies without organs it makes its own converge. A book exists only through the outside and on the outside. A book itself is a little machine; what is the relation (also measurable) of this literary machine to a war machine, love machine, revolutionary machine, etc.—and an *abstract machine* that sweeps them along? We have been criticized for overquoting literary authors. But when one writes, the only question is which other machine the literary

3. A way of thinking about bodily experience as an interconnected system of flows and forces rather than a structure of organs. Also referred to as *BwO*, it highlights the difference between the unpredictable live body and the dissectable dead body and sees the body as a ceaseless "desiring-machine."

4. The terms come from the structural theory of language developed by FERDINAND DE SAUSSURE (1857–1913). The division of the "sign" into "signifier" (the material of the sign) and "signified" (the meaning of the sign) mirrors the division between matter and meaning that Deleuze and Guattari aim to displace here.

machine can be plugged into, must be plugged into in order to work. Kleist and a mad war machine, Kafka[5] and a most extraordinary bureaucratic machine . . . (What if one became animal or plant *through* literature, which certainly does not mean literarily? Is it not first through the voice that one becomes animal?) Literature is an assemblage. It has nothing to do with ideology. There is no ideology and never has been.

All we talk about are multiplicities, lines, strata and segmentarities, lines of flight and intensities, machinic assemblages and their various types, bodies without organs and their construction and selection, the plane of consistency, and in each case the units of measure. *Stratometers, deleometers,*[6] *BwO units of density, BwO units of convergence*: Not only do these constitute a quantification of writing, but they define writing as always the measure of something else. Writing has nothing to do with signifying. It has to do with surveying, mapping, even realms that are yet to come.

A first type of book is the root-book. The tree is already the image of the world, or the root the image of the world-tree. This is the classical book, as noble, signifying, and subjective organic interiority (the strata of the book). The book imitates the world, as art imitates nature: by procedures specific to it that accomplish what nature cannot or can no longer do. The law of the book is the law of reflection, the One that becomes two. How could the law of the book reside in nature, when it is what presides over the very division between world and book, nature and art? One becomes two: whenever we encounter this formula, even stated strategically by Mao[7] or understood in the most "dialectical" way possible, what we have before us is the most classical and well reflected, oldest, and weariest kind of thought. Nature doesn't work that way: in nature, roots are taproots with a more multiple, lateral, and circular system of ramification, rather than a dichotomous one. Thought lags behind nature. Even the book as a natural reality is a taproot, with its pivotal spine and surrounding leaves. But the book as a spiritual reality, the Tree or Root as an image, endlessly develops the law of the One that becomes two, then of the two that become four . . . Binary logic[8] is the spiritual reality of the root-tree. Even a discipline as "advanced" as linguistics retains the root-tree as its fundamental image, and thus remains wedded to classical reflection (for example, Chomsky[9] and his grammatical trees, which begin at a point S and proceed by dichotomy). This is as much as to say that this system of thought has never reached an understanding of multiplicity: in order to arrive at two following a spiritual method it must assume a strong principal unity. On the side of the object, it is no doubt possible, following the natural method, to go directly from One to three, four, or five, but only if

5. Franz Kafka (1883–1924), Austrian novelist and short story writer who lived much of his life in Prague; he memorably depicted the bureaucratic machine in his unfinished novel *The Castle* (1926). Heinrich von Kleist (1777–1811), German writer of plays and novellas; his play *Prince Friedrich von Homburg* (1811) is concerned with the "war machine."

6. Deleuze and Guattari's coinage: conversions into lines of death.

7. Mao Zedong (1893–1976), leader and principal Marxist theorist of China's communist revolution; the phrase "one becomes two" (applied to the birth of children) appears in his *Examples of Dialectics* (1959).

8. The logic of either/or, in which all values come in pairs of opposition.

9. Noam Chomsky (b. 1928), American linguist who devised transformational-generative grammar, which attempts to relate sentences with different structures and account for all the acceptable sentences of a language by differentiating between "deep structures" (innate and unconscious forms that ensure competence) and "surface structures" (the particular sentences into which the deep structures are transformed in performance).

there is a strong principal unity available, that of the pivotal taproot supporting the secondary roots. That doesn't get us very far. The binary logic of dichotomy has simply been replaced by biunivocal[1] relationships between successive circles. The pivotal taproot provides no better understanding of multiplicity than the dichotomous root. One operates in the object, the other in the subject. Binary logic and biunivocal relationships still dominate psychoanalysis (the tree of delusion in the Freudian interpretation of Schreber's[2] case), linguistics, structuralism, and even information science.

The radicle-system, or fascicular root,[3] is the second figure of the book, to which our modernity pays willing allegiance. This time, the principal root has aborted, or its tip has been destroyed; an immediate, indefinite multiplicity of secondary roots grafts onto it and undergoes a flourishing development. This time, natural reality is what aborts the principal root, but the root's unity subsists, as past or yet to come, as possible. We must ask if reflexive, spiritual reality does not compensate for this state of things by demanding an even more comprehensive secret unity, or a more extensive totality. Take William Burroughs's[4] cut-up method: the folding of one text onto another, which constitutes multiple and even adventitious roots (like a cutting), implies a supplementary dimension to that of the texts under consideration. In this supplementary dimension of folding, unity continues its spiritual labor. That is why the most resolutely fragmented work can also be presented as the Total Work or Magnum Opus.[5] Most modern methods for making series proliferate or a multiplicity grow are perfectly valid in one direction, for example, a linear direction, whereas a unity of totalization asserts itself even more firmly in another, circular or cyclic, dimension. Whenever a multiplicity is taken up in a structure, its growth is offset by a reduction in its laws of combination. The abortionists of unity are indeed angel makers, *doctores angelici*, because they affirm a properly angelic and superior unity. Joyce's[6] words, accurately described as having "multiple roots," shatter the linear unity of the word, even of language, only to posit a cyclic unity of the sentence, text, or knowledge. Nietzsche's[7] aphorisms shatter the linear unity of knowledge, only to invoke the cyclic unity of the eternal return, present as the nonknown in thought. This is as much as to say that the fascicular system does not really break with dualism, with the complementarity between a subject and an object, a natural reality and a spiritual reality: unity is consistently thwarted and obstructed in the object, while a new type of unity triumphs in the subject. The world has lost its pivot; the subject can no longer even dichotomize, but accedes to a higher unity, of ambivalence or overdetermination, in an always supplementary dimension to that of its object. The world has become

1. Turning to both sides, but only in a prescribed way.
2. Daniel Paul Schreber (1842–1911), German judge whose *Memoirs of My Nervous Illness* (1903) were analyzed by SIGMUND FREUD (1856–1939), Austrian founder of psychoanalysis, in an important 1911 study.
3. A small, secondary root (a *fascicle* is also a division of a book published in parts, and both words share their Latin root with *fascism*).
4. American writer of experimental novels (1914–1997); see "The Cut-Up Method of Brion Gysin" in *The Third Mind* (1978) by Burroughs and Gysin.
5. An allusion to the French poet Stéphane Mallarmé (1842–1898), who combined a notoriously fragmentary style with an alchemical dream of the Great Work.
6. James Joyce (1882–1941), Irish writer known for the innovations of technique and inventions of words in his fiction, especially in *Finnegans Wake* (1939), which ends in an unfinished sentence that is completed by the fragment with which the book begins. *Doctores angelici*: angelic teachers (Latin).
7. FRIEDRICH NIETZSCHE (1844–1900), German philosopher.

chaos, but the book remains the image of the world: radicle-chaosmos rather than root-cosmos. A strange mystification: a book all the more total for being fragmented. At any rate, what a vapid idea, the book as the image of the world. In truth, it is not enough to say, "Long live the multiple," difficult as it is to raise that cry. No typographical, lexical, or even syntactical cleverness is enough to make it heard. The multiple *must be made*, not by always adding a higher dimension, but rather in the simplest of ways, by dint of sobriety, with the number of dimensions one already has available—always $n - 1$ (the only way the one belongs to the multiple: always subtracted). Subtract the unique from the multiplicity to be constituted; write at $n - 1$ dimensions. A system of this kind could be called a rhizome. A rhizome as subterranean stem is absolutely different from roots and radicles. Bulbs and tubers are rhizomes. Plants with roots or radicles may be rhizomorphic in other respects altogether: the question is whether plant life in its specificity is not entirely rhizomatic. Even some animals are, in their pack form. Rats are rhizomes. Burrows are too, in all of their functions of shelter, supply, movement, evasion, and breakout. The rhizome itself assumes very diverse forms, from ramified surface extension in all directions to concretion into bulbs and tubers. When rats swarm over each other. The rhizome includes the best and the worst: potato and couchgrass, or the weed. Animal and plant, couchgrass is crabgrass.

* * *

Let us summarize the principal characteristics of a rhizome: unlike trees or their roots, the rhizome connects any point to any other point, and its traits are not necessarily linked to traits of the same nature; it brings into play very different regimes of signs, and even nonsign states. The rhizome is reducible neither to the One nor the multiple. It is not the One that becomes Two or even directly three, four, five, etc. It is not a multiple derived from the One, or to which One is added $(n + 1)$. It is composed not of units but of dimensions, or rather directions in motion. It has neither beginning nor end, but always a middle (*milieu*) from which it grows and which it overspills. It constitutes linear multiplicities with n dimensions having neither subject nor object, which can be laid out on a plane of consistency, and from which the One is always subtracted $(n - 1)$. When a multiplicity of this kind changes dimension, it necessarily changes in nature as well, undergoes a metamorphosis. Unlike a structure, which is defined by a set of points and positions, with binary relations between the points and biunivocal relationships between the positions, the rhizome is made only of lines: lines of segmentarity and stratification as its dimensions, and the line of flight or deterritorialization as the maximum dimension after which the multiplicity undergoes metamorphosis, changes in nature. These lines, or lineaments, should not be confused with lineages of the arborescent type, which are merely localizable linkages between points and positions. Unlike the tree, the rhizome is not the object of reproduction: neither external reproduction as image-tree nor internal reproduction as tree-structure. The rhizome is an antigenealogy. It is a short-term memory, or antimemory. The rhizome operates by variation, expansion, conquest, capture, offshoots. Unlike the graphic arts, drawing, or photography, unlike tracings, the rhizome pertains to a map that must be produced, constructed, a map that is always detachable, connectable, reversible, modifiable, and has multiple entryways and exits and its own lines of flight. It is tracings that must be put on the map, not the opposite. In contrast to centered (even polycentric) systems with hierarchical modes of communication and preestablished paths, the rhizome is an acentered, nonhierarchical, nonsignifying system without a General and without an organizing memory or central automaton, defined solely by a circulation of states. What is at question in the rhizome is a relation to sexuality—but also to the animal, the vegetal, the world, politics, the book, things natural and artificial—that is totally different from the arborescent relation: all manner of "becomings."

A plateau is always in the middle, not at the beginning or the end. A rhizome is made of plateaus. Gregory Bateson[8] uses the word "plateau" to designate something very special: a continuous, self-vibrating region of intensities whose development avoids any orientation toward a culmination point or external end. Bateson cites Balinese culture as an example: mother-child sexual games, and even quarrels among men, undergo this bizarre intensive stabilization. "Some sort of continuing plateau of intensity is substituted for [sexual] climax," war, or a culmination point. It is a regrettable characteristic of the Western mind to relate expressions and actions to exterior or transcendent ends, instead of evaluating them on a plane of consistency on the basis of their intrinsic value.[9] For example, a book composed of chapters has culmination and termination points. What takes place in a book composed instead of plateaus that communicate with one another across microfissures, as in a brain? We call a "plateau" any multiplicity connected to other multiplicities by superficial underground stems in such a way as to form or extend a rhizome. We are writing this book as a rhizome. It is composed of plateaus. We have given it a circular form, but only for laughs. Each morning we would wake up, and each of us would ask himself what plateau he was going to tackle, writing five lines here, ten there. We had hallucinatory experiences, we watched lines leave one plateau and proceed to another like columns of tiny ants. We made circles of convergence. Each plateau can be read starting anywhere and can be related to any other plateau. To attain the multiple, one must have a method that effectively constructs it; no typographical cleverness, no lexical agility, no blending or creation of words, no syntactical boldness, can substitute for it. In fact, these are more often than not merely mimetic procedures used to disseminate or disperse a unity that is retained in a different dimension for an image-book. Technonarcissism. Typographical, lexical, or syntactic creations are necessary only when they no longer belong to the form of expression of a hidden unity, becoming themselves dimensions of the multiplicity under consideration; we only know of rare successes in this.[1] We ourselves were unable to do it. We just used words that in turn function for us as plateaus. RHIZOMATICS = SCHIZOANALYSIS = STRATOANALYSIS = PRAGMATICS = MICROPOLITICS. These words are concepts, but concepts

8. English anthropologist, biologist, ethnologist, and philosopher (1904–1980).
9. Gregory Bateson, *Steps to an Ecology of Mind* (New York: Ballantine Books, 1972), p. 113. It will be noted that the word "plateau" is used in classical studies of bulbs, tubers, and rhizomes: see the entry for "Bulb" in M. H. Baillon, *Dictionnaire de botanique* [*Dictionary of Botany*] (Paris: Hachette, 1876–92) [Deleuze and Guattari's note].
1. For example, Joëlle de La Casinière, *Absolument nécessaire* [*Absolutely Necessary*]: *The Emergency Book* (Paris: Minuit, 1973), a truly nomadic book. In the same vein, see the research in progress at the Montfaucon Research Center [Deleuze and Guattari's note].

are lines, which is to say, number systems attached to a particular dimension of the multiplicities (strata, molecular chains, lines of flight or rupture, circles of convergence, etc.). Nowhere do we claim for our concepts the title of a science. We are no more familiar with scientificity than we are with ideology; all we know are assemblages. And the only assemblages are machinic assemblages of desire and collective assemblages of enunciation. No signifiance,[2] no subjectification: writing to the *n*th power (all individuated enunciation remains trapped within the dominant significations, all signifying desire is associated with dominated subjects). An assemblage, in its multiplicity, necessarily acts on semiotic flows, material flows, and social flows simultaneously (independently of any recapitulation that may be made of it in a scientific or theoretical corpus). There is no longer a tripartite division between a field of reality (the world) and a field of representation (the book) and a field of subjectivity (the author). Rather, an assemblage establishes connections between certain multiplicities drawn from each of these orders, so that a book has no sequel nor the world as its object nor one or several authors as its subject. In short, we think that one cannot write sufficiently in the name of an outside. The outside has no image, no signification, no subjectivity. The book as assemblage with the outside, against the book as image of the world. A rhizome-book, not a dichotomous, pivotal, or fascicular book. Never send down roots, or plant them, however difficult it may be to avoid reverting to the old procedures. "Those things which occur to me, occur to me not from the root up but rather only from somewhere about their middle. Let someone then attempt to seize them, let someone attempt to seize a blade of grass and hold fast to it when it begins to grow only from the middle."[3] Why is this so difficult? The question is directly one of perceptual semiotics. It's not easy to see things in the middle, rather than looking down on them from above or up at them from below, or from left to right or right to left: try it, you'll see that everything changes. It's not easy to see the grass in things and in words (similarly, Nietzsche said that an aphorism had to be "ruminated";[4] never is a plateau separable from the cows that populate it, which are also the clouds in the sky).

History is always written from the sedentary point of view and in the name of a unitary State apparatus, at least a possible one, even when the topic is nomads. What is lacking is a Nomadology, the opposite of a history. There are rare successes in this also, for example, on the subject of the Children's Crusades:[5] Marcel Schwob's book multiplies narratives like so many plateaus with variable numbers of dimensions. Then there is Andrzejewski's book, *Les portes du paradis* (The gates of paradise), composed of a single uninterrupted sentence; a flow of children; a flow of walking with pauses, straggling, and forward rushes; the semiotic flow of the confessions of all the children who go up to the old monk at the head of the procession to make their declarations; a flow of desire and sexuality, each child having left out of love and more or less directly led by the dark posthumous pederastic desire of the count of Vendôme; all this with circles of convergence. What is

2. A term that emphasizes the process of producing meaning (in contrast to *significance*, which emphasizes the result).

3. *The Diaries of Franz Kafka*, ed. Max Brod, trans. Joseph Kresh (New York: Schocken, 1948), p. 12 [Deleuze and Guattari's note].

4. See the final paragraph of Nietzsche's preface to *Genealogy of Morals* (1888).

5. The attempt of thousands of children to make their way to the Holy Land to reclaim it from the Muslims; the first group set out from Vendôme in the summer of 1212.

important is not whether the flows are "One or multiple"—we're past that point: there is a collective assemblage of enunciation, a machinic assemblage of desire, one inside the other and both plugged into an immense outside that is a multiplicity in any case. A more recent example is Armand Farrachi's book on the Fourth Crusade,[6] *La dislocation*, in which the sentences space themselves out and disperse, or else jostle together and coexist, and in which the letters, the typography begin to dance as the crusade grows more delirious.[7] These are models of nomadic and rhizomatic writing. Writing weds a war machine and lines of flight, abandoning the strata, segmentarities, sedentarity, the State apparatus. But why is a model still necessary? Aren't these books still "images" of the Crusades? Don't they still retain a unity, in Schwob's case a pivotal unity, in Farrachi's an aborted unity, and in the most beautiful example, *Les portes du paradis*, the unity of the funereal count? Is there a need for a more profound nomadism than that of the Crusades, a nomadism of true nomads, or of those who no longer even move or imitate anything? The nomadism of those who only assemble (*agencent*). How can the book find an adequate outside with which to assemble in heterogeneity, rather than a world to reproduce? The cultural book is necessarily a tracing: already a tracing of itself, a tracing of the previous book by the same author, a tracing of other books however different they may be, an endless tracing of established concepts and words, a tracing of the world present, past, and future. Even the anticultural book may still be burdened by too heavy a cultural load: but it will use it actively, for forgetting instead of remembering, for underdevelopment instead of progress toward development, in nomadism rather than sedentarity, to make a map instead of a tracing. RHIZOMATICS=POP ANALYSIS, even if the people have other things to do besides read it, even if the blocks of academic culture or pseudoscientificity in it are still too painful or ponderous. For science would go completely mad if left to its own devices. Look at mathematics: it's not a science, it's a monster slang, it's nomadic. Even in the realm of theory, especially in the realm of theory, any precarious and pragmatic framework is better than tracing concepts, with their breaks and progress changing nothing. Imperceptible rupture, not signifying break. The nomads invented a war machine in opposition to the State apparatus. History has never comprehended nomadism, the book has never comprehended the outside. The State as the model for the book and for thought has a long history: logos,[8] the philosopher-king, the transcendence of the Idea, the interiority of the concept, the republic of minds, the court of reason, the functionaries of thought, man as legislator and subject. The State's pretension to be a world order, and to root man. The war machine's relation to an outside is not another "model"; it is an assemblage that makes thought itself nomadic, and the book a working part in

6. One of 8 European military expeditions (1095–1291) intended to drive the Muslims from Jerusalem and other Christian holy sites; the Fourth Crusade was putatively targeted at Egypt (a center of Muslim power) but was diverted to conquer the Christian cities of Zara (in Hungary) and Constantinople, which was sacked in 1203.

7. Marcel Schwob, *The Children's Crusade*, trans. Henry Copley (Boston: Small, Maynard, 1898); Jerzy Andrzejewski, *Les Portes du paradis* [*The Gates of Paradise*] (Paris: Gallimard, 1949); Armand Farrachi, *La Dislocation* [*Dislocation*] (Paris: Stock, 1974). It was in the context of Schwob's book that Paul Alphandéry remarked that literature, in certain cases, could revitalize history and impose upon it "genuine research directions"; *La Chrétienté et l'idée de croisade* [*Christianity and the Idea of the Crusade*] (Paris: Albin Michel, 1959), vol. 2, p. 116 [Deleuze and Guattari's note].

8. Word, speech; discourse, reason (Greek); in the New Testament, logos is often identified with Christ.

every mobile machine, a stem for a rhizome (Kleist and Kafka against Goethe[9]).

Write to the *n*th power, the *n*–1 power, write with slogans: Make rhizomes, not roots, never plant! Don't sow, grow offshoots! Don't be one or multiple, be multiplicities! Run lines, never plot a point! Speed turns the point into a line![1] Be quick, even when standing still! Line of chance, line of hips, line of flight. Don't bring out the General in you! Don't have just ideas, just have an idea (Godard).[2] Have short-term ideas. Make maps, not photos or drawings. Be the Pink Panther and your loves will be like the wasp and the orchid, the cat and the baboon. As they say about old man river:

He don't plant 'tatos
Don't plant cotton
Them that plants them is soon forgotten
But old man river he just keeps rollin' along[3]

A rhizome has no beginning or end; it is always in the middle, between things, interbeing, *intermezzo*. The tree is filiation, but the rhizome is alliance, uniquely alliance. The tree imposes the verb "to be," but the fabric of the rhizome is the conjunction, "and . . . and . . . and . . ." This conjunction carries enough force to shake and uproot the verb "to be." Where are you going? Where are you coming from? What are you heading for?[4] These are totally useless questions. Making a clean slate, starting or beginning again from ground zero, seeking a beginning or a foundation—all imply a false conception of voyage and movement (a conception that is methodical, pedagogical, initiatory, symbolic . . .). But Kleist, Lenz, and Büchner[5] have another way of traveling and moving: proceeding from the middle, through the middle, coming and going rather than starting and finishing.[6] American literature, and already English literature, manifest this rhizomatic direction to an even greater extent; they know how to move between things, establish a logic of the AND, overthrow ontology, do away with foundations, nullify endings and beginnings. They know how to practice pragmatics. The middle is by no means an average; on the contrary, it is where things pick up speed. *Between* things does not designate a localizable relation going from one thing to the other and back again, but a perpendicular direction, a transversal movement that sweeps one *and* the other away, a stream without beginning or end that undermines its banks and picks up speed in the middle.

1980

9. Johann Wolfgang von Goethe (1749–1832), magisterial German poet, playwright, and novelist.
1. See Paul Virilio, "Véhiculaire," in *Nomades et vagabonds* [*Nomads and Vagabonds*], ed. Jacques Bergue (Paris: Union Générale d'Éditions, 1975), on the appearance of linearity and the disruption of perception by speed [Deleuze and Guattari's note].
2. Jean-Luc Godard (b. 1930), French filmmaker and screenwriter best known for his work of the 1950s and 1960s during the New Wave in France.
3. From "Ol' Man River," an imitation of a Negro spiritual composed by Jerome Kern with lyrics (here slightly misquoted) by Oscar Hammerstein for the musical *Show Boat* (1927).
4. Paul Gauguin (1848–1903), a French painter who became a "nomad" in Tahiti, gave one of his Tahitian paintings these three questions as a title.
5. Georg Büchner (1813–1837), German dramatist. Jakob Lenz (1751–1792), German poet.
6. See Jean-Christopher Bailly's description of movement in German Romanticism, in his introduction to *La Légende dispersée: Anthologie du romantisme allemand* [*The Dispersed Legend: An Anthology of German Romanticism*] (Paris: Union Générale d'Éditions, 1976), pp. 18ff. [Deleuze and Guattari's note].

JEAN-FRANÇOIS LYOTARD
1924–1998

Jean-François Lyotard was at the center of debates about postmodernism during the 1980s and 1990s. His celebrated announcement of the demise of "grand narratives" and of the "incommensurability" of local "language games" made his *Postmodern Condition* (1979; trans. 1984) the most succinct, accessible, and memorable manifesto of the postmodernist position. Lyotard, along with MICHEL FOUCAULT, was labeled a "young conservative" by the German philosopher JÜRGEN HABERMAS—and the battle was joined. The postmodernists contended that "general human emancipation" could not be gained through the universalist strategies characteristic of both liberalism (with its appeal to human rights) and communism (with its goal of a one-class society).

Born in Versailles, Lyotard received the equivalent of a master's degree in philosophy from the Sorbonne in 1949 and spent the 1950s teaching high school, including a two-year stint in Algeria. Following in the footsteps of the phenomenologist Maurice Merleau-Ponty (1908–1961), Lyotard attempts in his early work to reconcile Marxist politics and philosophy. Active in leftist agitation against the French colonial war in Algeria and in the student revolution of 1968, Lyotard, like many French intellectuals, was dismayed by the powerful French Communist Party's less than adequate responses to these two crises. Increasingly, Marxism appeared unable to understand or to support any political action that did not derive from the working class and address specifically economic grievances. Turning first to psychoanalysis (in *Des dispositifs pulsionnels*, 1973; and *Libidinal Economy*, 1974, trans. 1993) and then to the philosophy of Ludwig Wittgenstein (1889–1951) and IMMANUEL KANT (1724–1804), Lyotard tried to reevaluate the "emancipatory" narratives of Marxism and liberalism, and to consider new bases for aesthetic, moral, and political judgment as well as action. He taught philosophy at the University of Paris (1959–66), the University of Nanterre (1966–70), and the University of Paris VIII at Vincennes (1972–87) and held visiting positions at a number of American universities, most notably the University of California at Irvine. During the early 1980s, he was the first president of the prestigious but controversial International College of Philosophy in Paris, which he co-founded.

Our brief selection, "Defining the Postmodern" (1986), captures many of Lyotard's major themes. Modernism in the arts, he argues, partakes of the universal aims of modernity. Thus modernist architecture sought to make everything new, to transform the whole world, to effect a total revolution in how people live together by creating entirely new cities. But we have now—after Auschwitz and the Soviet gulags—come to recognize that such modern dreams of transforming humanity can be pursued only violently, and even then they will not succeed. Allegiance to one universal standard by which all are judged generates murderous hostility to the different, to whatever resists or simply does not desire to go along with the program. Modernist architects and city planners blithely razed old neighborhoods, confident that their plans for "urban renewal" would make for better lives. Instead, they created inhospitable concrete wastelands, unconnected to how people interact in lived space.

Postmodernism attempts to turn its back on this understanding of progress as the whole world marching in lockstep toward the same utopian future. Instead, Lyotard preaches an appreciation and respect for diversity, for local differences, for the plurality of ways in which humans choose to live. In *The Postmodern Condition*, he argues that there is no common measure by which such local differences (which, following Wittgenstein, he calls distinct "language games") can be compared. We cannot confidently declare one way of life or thought superior to another—one more progressive and modern, the other reactionary and residual. Such differences are "incommensurate," like those between apples and oranges. The use of "progress" as a yardstick has been discredited by the unintended side effects (such as ecological damage and weapons of mass destruction) of increasing scientific knowledge and technological innovation. We would do better if we stopped trying to force the world and its inhabitants into one mold and stopped trying to make history move in one direction.

At times, Lyotard recognizes that belief in progress, the notion that "development" is necessarily a good thing, is still very prevalent and must be combated. At other times, he writes as if a general loss of faith in progress has taken over, as if we are all already postmodern and thus skeptical of the "grand narratives" of modernization and its attendant emancipation of the poor, the ignorant, the oppressed, or whomever.

The debates generated by Lyotard's work certainly do not indicate that a postmodern vision prevails. The political objection voiced by Habermas and others focuses on the apparent passivity of Lyotard's position. If we have no way to judge different ways of life, then whatever exists must be tolerated. Moreover, this absence of standards also seems to leave us unable to imagine a future that we can claim would be better than the status quo. Lyotard addresses some of these concerns in *Just Gaming* (1984), in which he argues that violation of another's chosen way of life is a crime that can and should be halted by intervention (by the state or by other agencies). Thus, since the Nazis forcibly prevented people from living in their own chosen way, forceful intervention against the Nazis was justified.

In matters literary and artistic, Lyotard focuses on shifts in style and expression between modernism and postmodernism. Our selection highlights the extent to which he sees postmodernism in the arts manifesting the signs of what psychologists call post-traumatic stress disorder. The postmodern artist, he observes, is haunted by "the sanguinary last two centuries," the massive crimes against humanity and increasingly vicious wars since the French Revolution. The often-noted use in contemporary art of pastiche (the citation or quoting of various previous moments in art or literary history) is a Freudian "working through" of past material in an effort to break the spell of the traumatic past that paralyzes the present moment. "Postmodernism," as the name suggests, is perhaps not a period in its own right but instead is linked to the modernism it tries to shake. Having discovered that the modernist dream of utterly breaking with the past ensures "repeating" that past, postmodernist art strives instead to work through the tradition in order to overcome it.

Though Lyotard is not sure what lies on the other side of that overcoming, he is optimistic that ours is a healthy moment, implicitly critiquing FREDRIC JAMESON's association of postmodern art with schizophrenia, with the fragmentation of the self. For Lyotard, we would be schizophrenic only if we did not reflect on and recast the various fragments from the tradition. But we should not expect that all the incommensurate pieces of our world and of our selves will fit together neatly. Complexity, he insists, cannot be sidestepped by simple visions of right and wrong or by simple models of all-encompassing systems. And he wants an art that is attentive to complexity, that grapples with the multiple meanings of our past and the plural realities of our present.

In *The Postmodern Condition* and subsequent works (especially *Lessons on the Analytic of the Sublime*, 1991), Lyotard links postmodernist art with the sublime. (See above LONGINUS, JOSEPH ADDISON, EDMUND BURKE, and Kant for traditional accounts of this concept.) Art, Lyotard suggests, is one place where that which resists being fully captured within any existing signifying system can make its existence felt. To avoid modernity's persistent tendency to reduce everything back into known terms or (worse) to obliterate everything that resists such reduction, we must cultivate an appreciation of the sublime, of that which exceeds calculation and understanding. If postmodern art can foster such a sensibility, a future where difference exists and even flourishes just might be possible. Only such a future, Lyotard insists, can do justice to the complexity and variety of the world we inhabit.

"Defining the Postmodern" Keywords: Aesthetics, Deconstruction, Modernity, Postmodernity, Poststructuralism

Defining the Postmodern

I should like to make only a small number of observations, in order to point to—and not at all to resolve—some problems surrounding the term 'postmodern'. My aim is not to close the debate, but to open it, to allow it to develop by avoiding certain confusions and ambiguities, as far as this is possible.

There are many debates implied by, and implicated in, the term 'postmodern'. I will distinguish three of them.

First, the opposition between postmodernism and modernism, or the Modern Movement (1910–45), in architectural theory. According to Paolo Portoghesi[1] (*Dopo architettura moderna*), there is a rupture or break, and this break would be the abrogation of the hegemony of Euclidean geometry,[2] which was sublimated in the plastic poetry of the movement known as De Stijl,[3] for example. According to Victorio Grigotti,[4] another Italian architect, the difference between the two periods is characterized by what is possibly a more interesting fissure. There is no longer any close linkage between the architectural project and socio-historical progress in the realization of human emancipation on the larger scale. Postmodern architecture is condemned to generate a multiplicity of small transformations in the space it inherits, and to give up the project of a last rebuilding of the whole space occupied by humanity. In this sense, a perspective is opened in the larger landscape.

In this account there is no longer a horizon of universalization, of general emancipation before the eyes of postmodern man, or in particular, of the postmodern architect. The disappearance of this idea of progress within rationality and freedom would explain a certain tone, style or modus which are specific to postmodern architecture. I would say a sort of *bricolage*:[5] the high frequency of quotations of elements from previous styles or periods (classical or modern), giving up the consideration of environment, and so on.

Just a remark about this aspect. The 'post-', in the term 'postmodernist' is in this case to be understood in the sense of a simple succession, of a diachrony[6] of periods, each of them clearly identifiable. Something like a conversion, a new direction after the previous one. I should like to observe

1. Italian architect and critic (b. 1931), whose books *After Modern Architecture* (1981) and *Postmodern, the Architecture of the Post-Industrial Society* (1982) offer influential definitions of the distinction between modernist and postmodernist art.
2. Geometry based on ordinary 2- or 3-dimensional space. The reference here is apparently to modernist art's break with perspectival painting, which tries to represent spatial depth realistically on the canvas.
3. A movement of Dutch painters and architects formed in 1917; it called for purity of line and color in art, along with attention to technological progress in modern society.
4. Vittorio Gregotti (b. 1927).
5. Literally, "tinkering" (French). The anthropologist CLAUDE LÉVI-STRAUSS (1908–2009) uses the term to describe forms of thought or of work that combine elements taken from various sources.
6. Events strung out along a time line, as contrasted to synchrony (events happening at the same time); both terms are associated with structuralism.

that this idea of chronology is totally modern. It belongs to Christianity, Cartesianism, Jacobinism.[7] Since we are beginning something completely new, we have to re-set the hands of the clock at zero. The idea of modernity is closely bound up with this principle that it is possible and necessary to break with tradition and to begin a new way of living and thinking. Today we can presume that this 'breaking' is, rather, a manner of forgetting or repressing the past. That's to say of repeating it. Not overcoming it.

I would say that the quotation of elements of past architectures in the new one seems to me to be the same procedure as the use of remains coming from past life in the dream-work as described by Freud, in the *Interpretation of Dreams*.[8] This use of repetition or quotation, be it ironical or not, cynical or not, can be seen in the trends dominating contemporary painting, under the name of 'transavantgardism' (Achille Bonito Oliva) or under the name of neo-expressionism.[9] I'll come back to this question in my third point.

The second point. A second connotation of the term 'postmodern', and I admit that I am at least partly responsible for the misunderstanding associated with this meaning.

The general idea is a trivial one. One can note a sort of decay in the confidence placed by the two last centuries in the idea of progress. This idea of progress as possible, probable or necessary was rooted in the certainty that the development of the arts, technology, knowledge and liberty would be profitable to mankind as a whole. To be sure, the question of knowing which was the subject truly victimized by the lack of development—whether it was the poor, the worker, the illiterate—remained open during the 19th and 20th centuries. There were disputes, even wars, between liberals, conservatives and leftists over the very name of the subject we are to help to become emancipated. Nevertheless, all the parties concurred in the same belief that enterprises, discoveries and institutions are legitimate only insofar as they contribute to the emancipation of mankind.

After two centuries, we are more sensitive to signs that signify the contrary. Neither economic nor political liberalism, nor the various Marxisms, emerge from the sanguinary last two centuries free from the suspicion of crimes against mankind. We can list a series of proper names (names of places, persons and dates) capable of illustrating and founding our suspicion. Following Theodor Adorno,[1] I use the name of Auschwitz to point out the irrelevance of empirical matter, the stuff of recent past history, in terms of the modern claim to help mankind to emancipate itself. What kind of thought is able to sublate (*Aufheben*)[2] Auschwitz in a general (either empiri-

7. The philosophy of the most radical group during the French Revolution, the one most determined to make an entirely new world. "Cartesianism": the philosophy of René Descartes (1596–1650), which breaks from the past by starting from a radical doubting of all received truths.

8. Published in 1900 (see above) by SIGMUND FREUD (1856–1939), Austrian founder of psychoanalysis. Throughout this essay, Lyotard sees the work done by postmodern artists as analogous to the psychic memory work that Freud claimed was done in dreams or done by the patient in psychoanalytic therapy.

9. The name given to the work of Julian Schnabel, Anselm Kiefer, and other painters in the early 1980s who returned to earlier abstract and representational styles to "express" psychological and historical material. *Transavantgarde International* (1982), by the art critic Oliva (b. 1939), describes neo-expressionism as a break from the impersonal experimentation of the avant-gardes.

1. German philosopher and cultural critic (1903–1969). ADORNO famously declared that "To write poetry after Auschwitz"—the Nazis' largest concentration camp—"is barbaric."

2. A technical term from the philosophy of GEORG WILHELM FRIEDRICH HEGEL (1770–1831). In Hegel the thesis and its opposite, the antithesis, are "sublated" in the synthesis that joins them together. Here progress, the movement of humanity to its perfection, is met by an antithesis, the murderous acts of Auschwitz.

cal or speculative) process towards a universal emancipation? So there is a sort of sorrow in the *Zeitgeist*. This can express itself by reactive or reactionary attitudes or by utopias, but never by a positive orientation offering a new perspective.

The development of techno-sciences has become a means of increasing disease, not of fighting it. We can no longer call this development by the old name of progress. This development seems to be taking place by itself, by an autonomous force or 'motricity'.[3] It doesn't respond to a demand coming from human needs. On the contrary, human entities (individual or social) seem always to be destabilized by the results of this development. The intellectual results as much as the material ones. I would say that mankind is in the condition of running after the process of accumulating new objects of practice and thought. In my view it is a real and obscure question to determine the reason of this process of complexification. It's something like a destiny towards a more and more complex condition. Our demands for security, identity and happiness, coming from our condition as living beings and even social beings appear today irrelevant in the face of this sort of obligation to complexify, mediate, memorize and synthesize every object, and to change its scale. We are in this techno-scientific world like Gulliver:[4] sometimes too big, sometimes too small, never at the right scale. Consequently, the claim for simplicity, in general, appears today that of a barbarian.

From this point, it would be necessary to consider the division of mankind into two parts: one part confronted with the challenge of complexity; the other with the terrible ancient task of survival. This is a major aspect of the failure of the modern project (which was, in principle, valid for mankind as a whole).

The third argument is more complex, and I shall present it as briefly as possible. The question of postmodernity is also the question of the expressions of thought: art, literature, philosophy, politics. You know that in the field of art for example, and more especially the plastic arts, the dominant idea is that the big movement of avant-gardism is over. There seems to be general agreement about laughing at the avant-gardes,[5] considered as the expression of an obsolete modernity. I don't like the term avant-garde any more than anyone else, because of its military connotations. Nevertheless I would like to observe that the very process of avant-gardism in painting was in reality a long, obstinate and highly responsible investigation of the presuppositions implied in modernity. The right approach, in order to understand the work of painters from, say, Manet to Duchamp or Barnett Newman[6] is to compare their work with the anamnesis[7] which takes place in psychoanalytical therapy. Just as the patient elaborates his present trouble by freely associating the more imaginary, immaterial, irrelevant bits with past situations, so discovering hidden meanings of his life, we can consider the work of Cézanne,

3. Lyotard's coinage, conveying the sense that the motor of history, its movement, is now out of human control.
4. The narrator-hero of Jonathan Swift's *Gulliver's Travels* (1726), who visits both an island whose inhabitants are 6 inches tall and an island inhabited by giants.
5. What today are designated the modernist or historical avant-gardes were the self-organized and self-named "cutting-edge" movements such as surrealism, dadaism, futurism, and constructivism of the high modernist period (1914–30). The term originally meant the advance guard of an army.
6. American abstract expressionist painter (1905–1970). Édouard Manet (1832–1883), French artist sometimes called the first modern painter, a forerunner of the impressionists. Marcel Duchamp (1887–1968), French (later American) painter and conceptual artist, whose experiments foreshadowed much postmodern art.
7. Remembering.

Picasso, Delaunay, Kandinsky, Klee, Mondrian, Malevitch[8] and finally Duchamp as a working through—what Freud called *Durcharbeitung*[9]—operated by modernity on itself. If we give up this responsibility, it is certain that we are condemned to repeat, without any displacement, the modern neurosis, the Western schizophrenia, paranoia, and so on. This being granted, the 'post-' of postmodernity does not mean a process of coming back or flashing back, feeding back, but of *ana*-lysing, *ana*-mnesing, of reflecting.[1]

1986

8. All important modern artists: Paul Cézanne (1839–1906), French impressionist painter and forerunner of cubism; Pablo Picasso (1881–1973), Spanish painter who is the most celebrated modernist artist; Robert Delaunay (1885–1941), French modernist painter; Wassily Kandinsky (1866–1944), Russian abstract painter; Paul Klee (1879–1940), Swiss avant-garde painter; Piet Mondrian (1872–1944), Dutch abstract painter and member of De Stijl; Kazimir Malevich (1878–1935), Russian constructivist painter, active during the Russian Revolution and its immediate aftermath.

9. Working through (German), a technical term from Freudian theories of therapy. Only after "working through" various elements in the past not assimilated into self-understanding can the patient get rid of the symptomatic (and/or neurotic) behaviors that have grown out of the repression of the past.

1. *Ana-* literally means "again" or "back" (Greek).

MICHEL FOUCAULT
1926–1984

Michel Foucault is arguably the most influential European writer and thinker of the second half of the twentieth century. His unclassifiable work (is it history? philosophy? cultural theory?) is controversial and has attracted much criticism, but the questions he raised, the topics he addressed, and the positions he took have become central features of today's intellectual landscape. In literary studies, Foucault stands as a major source for poststructuralism, New Historicism, cultural studies, and queer theory, while also fueling the growing interest in literature and medicine, the examination of the institutional bases from which writers and critics operate, and the interest in processes of identity formation.

Foucault was born in Poitiers, France. His father was a doctor, and he (unlike his brother) went against the family's wishes that he study medicine; he eventually became a fierce critic of modern medical practices and institutions. Awkward, bookish, and brilliant, Foucault progressed easily through the elaborate French educational system, with its extremely competitive exams for gaining a place in the multitiered hierarchy. Foucault took his university degree at the nation's top university, the École Normale Supérieure, where he specialized in the philosophy of psychology.

Under the influence of his teacher LOUIS ALTHUSSER, Foucault joined the Communist Party in 1950, quitting three years later. He spent the 1950s teaching in France (briefly) and then abroad—in Sweden, Poland, and Germany. Returning to France in 1960, he defended the graduate thesis that became his first book, *Folie et deraison* (1961; an abridged edition was translated into English as *Madness and Civilization*). A major theme of this book and its follow-up, *The Birth of the Clinic* (1963), is an attack on the institutions and procedures characteristic of modern medicine. They inaugurate Foucault's lifelong preoccupation with the ways in which individuals are "administered" by the various bureaucratic institutions—hospitals, prisons, the military, schools—that increasingly render selves docile in the modern world.

Foucault's 1966 *Les Mots et les choses* (translated as *The Order of Things*) made his reputation. Recognizably a structuralist history, *The Order of Things* examines how the disciplines of economics, linguistics, and biology emerged, offering along the way a brilliant, if overly schematic, characterization of the three different "epistemes" (deep-rooted, unconscious structures for organizing knowledge) of the Middle Ages, the "classical period" (Foucault's term for the Enlightenment), and modernity. Foucault attempted to explicate and justify the methodology of *The Order of Things* in his next major book, *The Archaeology of Knowledge* (1969).

By 1969 Foucault's focus had shifted away from intellectual history and methodological meditations. The events of May 1968, when a student-led revolt almost toppled the French government before itself collapsing, together with his own involvement in student unrest in Tunisia (where he taught from 1966 to 1968), "radicalized" Foucault. He became politically active—and remained so to the end of his life. His book *Surveiller et punir: Naissance de la prison* (1975, *Discipline and Punish: The Birth of the Prison*) is a direct outgrowth of his work on prison reform. Foucault asks himself in the first chapter of the book why he has written a history of the prison: "Simply because I am interested in the past? No, if one means by that writing a history of the past in terms of the present. Yes, if one means writing the history of the present." He aims at describing the present through an analysis of the forces that created it, a historical and critical undertaking that he calls "genealogy" to mark its debt to the nineteenth-century philosopher FRIEDRICH NIETZSCHE. From the history of the prison, Foucault turned next to the history of sexuality. Three volumes of his work on that topic were published, although the entire project was incomplete when he died of complications from AIDS at the age of fifty-seven.

From 1970 on, Foucault spent longer and longer stints in North America as a lecturer or visiting professor at various universities—most notably at the University of California at Berkeley, where the New Historicists gathered around STEPHEN GREENBLATT brought Foucault-inspired work directly into literary studies. Tales of Foucault's experimentation with and explorations of drugs and sex were oral legend before being recorded in James Miller's notorious, yet mostly accurate, biography, *The Passion of Michel Foucault* (1993). The relevance of his personal life to the work is debatable, but Foucault's own growing interest in "the care of the self" in his later years suggests that separating private and public is no easy task.

Our selections present work particularly important to literary and cultural studies. The essay "What Is an Author?" (1969) directly questions some of the most fundamental assumptions of literary criticism. Foucault realizes that he had taken the author for granted in *The Order of Things*, and asks himself what it would mean to take seriously "the death of the author" (in ROLAND BARTHES's famous phrase). Foucault's approach to this question is characteristic of much of his work. We must consider, he says, what "functions" the category of "author" fulfills within the "discourse" the historian or critic deploys in the analysis of written texts. The concept *author*, he points out, is an organizing device, permitting us to group certain texts together. More crucially, the concept underwrites a number of interpretive conventions. We ascribe a certain unity and coherence to all the works written by a single author, or at least we feel that an author's drastic changes in style or opinion must be explained. And we assume, at the most fundamental level, that the author is the source of the text. Interpretation moves from the written text (which may be all we know of a writer) back toward the author, searching out an individual's biography, psychology, and intentions. The author thus functions both to organize the vast reservoir of materials that the past bequeaths us and to anchor a certain way of interpreting those materials.

Foucault's ultimate target here is "humanism," the postmedieval understanding of who and what individuals are. He highlights the historical contingency of the belief that we are "individuals" with unique natures, possessing coherent interior identities, motives, desires, and conscious intentions that cause our actions. Humanism claims for each individual the capacities that literary criticism ascribes to authors.

Significantly, the "author function" has not always been deemed necessary to the apprehension and interpretation of texts. Prior to 1500 anonymous texts were the norm. Even today the importance of authors varies from field to field. A contract has no author, nor does the average poster. We barely note the authors of most newspaper articles. Generally speaking, Foucault opines, emphasis on the author is a mark of prestige. "Discourse that possesses an author's name is not to be immediately consumed and forgotten. . . . Rather, its status and its manner of reception are regulated by the culture in which it circulates."

Foucault's essay, then, invites us to examine the ways in which literary criticism approaches its object—the text—and accords it the prestigious title of "literature" partly through the exaltation of the author (as talented, as worthy of honor and study). He also—and we see here his importance to New Historicism—shifts our focus away from the author and toward larger systematic social forces. What if the author is not the cause, the source, of the text? What if author and text are both effects? In that case, the critic's inquiries and scrutiny need to be directed toward their common cause, toward cultural conventions and their inclusions and exclusions, not confined to formal analyses of texts or psychological investigations of writers' lives.

Such questions reveal a persistent Foucauldian preoccupation: the social constitution of the "subject" (structuralism's preferred term for the self or the individual). In "What Is an Author?" he writes that "the subject should not be entirely abandoned. It should be reconsidered, not to restore the theme of an originating subject, but to seize its functions, its intervention in discourse, and its system of dependencies. . . . [W]e should ask: under what conditions and through what forms can an entity like the subject appear in the order of discourse; what position does it occupy; what functions does it exhibit; and what rules does it follow in each type of discourse?" Though antihumanistic "deconstruction of the self" is characteristic of French poststructuralism, Foucault insists on keeping the category of the *subject* as a means to study the historical discourses of power and knowledge that constitute it.

Foucault uses the term *subject* for two reasons. First, he is thinking of the grammatical subject, the subject of a sentence. Following the structuralists, he is influenced by the idea of a "subject position" that exists as a slot in syntax and is then occupied by different actual selves at different times. That selves assume the subject position only tentatively and temporarily is highlighted by grammatical "shifters," whose most dramatic example is the pronoun "I." When I use "I," it means me; when you use "I," it means you. I become "I," the first-person subject of the sentence, only when I am authorized to speak or when I seize that position. Shifters thus indicate that subject positions—created by language—preexist individual selves, and that power enables their use.

Second, Foucault draws on *subject* as a verb. Individuals get to occupy subject positions (the various roles existing within a discourse or an institution) only through a process in which they are "subjected" to power. Indeed, individuals are constituted by power as subjects prior to having any standing as individuals.

Foucault's work from 1969 to 1980 focuses on the processes through which subjects are produced. In his late work (1980–84) he writes of *selves*, using a term that might allow individuals an existence apart from their relations to a constituting power. But in the works of his middle period from which our selections are drawn, Foucault turns the usually celebratory narrative of the rise of the individual in modern Western societies on its head by connecting that rise with a tremendous decrease in freedom. Our selection "The Carceral" (the final section of *Discipline and Punish*) presents Foucault's sweeping, bleak, and all-too-convincing portrait of modern society since the 1740s as a series of increasingly prisonlike institutions that aim at "the accumulation and useful administration of men," rendered docile subjects by disciplinary power. The modern individual is produced by a power that individualizes precisely in order to better control. A panoptic (all-seeing) power keeps subjects under constant surveillance. (Foucault takes the term *panoptic* from the early nineteenth-century English reformer Jeremy Bentham, who designed a circular prison, the Panopticon, in which each inmate was always in view of a single guard in a central tower.)

Foucault argues that premodern power intervened in subjects' lives only intermittently. Unless they broke the law, most premodern persons lived in deep obscurity, unnoticed by various authorities. But modern societies intervene from day one to shape, train, and normalize individuals. Compulsory schooling, public health measures, passports, employment records, family counseling, and the like are all very recent social practices—none more than 250 years old. In each case, an institution molds behavior according to a norm, subordinates individuals to institutional demands, examines and watches over all subjects, and punishes deviants. Such a society, Foucault argues, not only needs prisons because it inevitably produces deviants but also is itself prisonlike, "carceral," from top to bottom. The institutions that administer individuals (schools, factories, the army) use the same strategies and techniques of control that prisons employ. The modern state focuses its energies on "governmentality"—that is, on rendering citizens governable.

Alongside this historical argument, Foucault developed—in both *Discipline and Punish* and *The History of Sexuality*, volume 1, *An Introduction* (1976)—an influential account of the interconnections between power, knowledge, and the subject. Two short phrases provide excellent points of entry to Foucault's revision of traditional notions of power. Famously, he writes that "power is exercised, rather than possessed," and he insists that power is not repressive but "productive."

Power in Foucault's account does not belong to anyone, nor does it all emanate from one specific location, such as the state. Rather, power is diffused throughout social institutions, as it is exercised by innumerable, replaceable functionaries. It operates through the daily disciplines and routines to which bodies are subjected. Thus, for example, the teacher exercises power over students, and schools have countless ways of governing students' behavior. But the teacher holds that power only as a function of his or her place in the institution, being subject as a teacher to various rules, incentives, and punishments. Both teacher and students are located (though differently) within the institution, and both go through their paces within a network that guides and oversees their conduct. Foucault stresses modern power's "microtechniques," its ubiquitous reinforcement of the norm at every step, its direct work upon "docile" bodies. Think of how much time is spent making schoolchildren sit still or develop the motor skills required for "good" handwriting. Foucault sees power as decentralized and depersonalized.

The insistence that "power is productive" underwrites Foucault's rejection of "the repressive hypothesis" in our selection from volume 1 of *The History of Sexuality*. Power is traditionally seen as repressing behaviors that it finds unproductive, threatening, or otherwise undesirable. For example, people have various sexual desires (to masturbate or to seek same-sex partners) that are deemed unacceptable, and social power is exerted to repress those desires and the behaviors that follow from them. Foucault argues, however, that modern power produces the very categories, desires, and actions it strives to regulate. Before an act is prohibited, it is not singled out as something separate and identifiable or perhaps even desirable. The enunciation of the category and the law both creates (identifies, designates) certain actions as crimes and affords them a heightened presence.

In keeping with his historical argument that modern power operates through continual classification, surveillance, and intervention, Foucault goes further, proposing that such power names actions as crimes and perversions precisely to increase its opportunities for intervention. This is why he insists that modern society "is in actual fact, and directly, perverse." It produces the very desires and behaviors it claims to abhor, relying largely on discourse. Power can operate physically on bodies, but discursively it carves up the world. Through language various bodies are assigned to various categories (race, gender, IQ, etc.), and various actions are designated in relation to norms as praiseworthy, deviant, punishable, or criminal. A whole new array of identifiable "perverse" sexualities were named in the nineteenth century. Discourse disposes: it puts everything in its place. Modern power penetrates everywhere, giving a specific name to every possible variant of human action so as to master the world and leave nothing unexamined, unknown, uncatalogued. The nineteenth century (with its supposedly repressed Victorians) began this "explosion of discourse," which in the field of sexuality produced extensive new vocabularies and categories for naming desires and actions that could then become subjected to medical, legal, and other institutional and state interventions.

Along with producing subjects, modern power produces sexual (and other) categories that structure the world in certain ways. Here *Discipline and Punish* and volume 1 of *The History of Sexuality* are in accord. (In the later two volumes of *The History of Sexuality*, partly in response to criticism, Foucault examines how selves might act to produce themselves.) Consider Foucault's comment (one of the founding remarks of queer theory) on the medical categorization of homosexuality in 1870: "Homosexuality appeared as one of the forms of sexuality when it was transposed from the practice of sodomy to a kind of interior androgyny, a hermaphrodism of the soul. The sodomite had been a temporary aberration; the homosexual now was a species." Power acts discursively to produce homosexuality when it separates out and labels as *homosexual* certain actions that had previously been included in the grab-bag term *sodomy* (which also included bestiality and some nonreproductive heterosexual acts). The new attempt to be more precise, more "scientific," in categorizing human sexual behavior itself requires that behavior to be scrutinized more carefully than ever before.

Foucault further argues that the way that the courts and sociologists treat criminals and the medical profession and psychologists view homosexuals indicates a dramatic shift in the very form of subjecthood. In modern society, actions begin to be taken as evidence of a deep-rooted and persistent identity. In the premodern world, in contrast, sodomy and other crimes were seen as temporary aberrations, single acts that carried no particular relation to the self who committed them; they certainly were not seen as demonstrating a sexual identity or a criminal nature. The label *sodomite* says nothing beyond pointing to the commission of particular acts. But the homosexual carries his homosexuality within himself at every moment; the act comes to determine identity. Foucault's argument is that through this connection of actions to "being," of what I do to what I am, modern power produces subjects who have identities, thereby enabling its grip on us. Subjects whose identities must be figured out through an interpretation of their actions become "both an object of analysis and a target of intervention."

Foucault is exposing—and questioning—our era's most fundamental assumptions about who and what individuals are. And he argues that these assumptions have been produced by and are the foundational principles of the "social sciences"—what the French call "the human sciences." It is no coincidence that the modern academic disciplines arise during the same period that sees the shift toward disciplinary power. The knowledge produced in psychology, sociology, anthropology, criminology, and medicine is itself an integral part of the discursive ordering and physical management wielded by modern power.

Power/knowledge is the term Foucault uses to indicate how the production of knowledge is wedded to productive power. Modern power requires increasingly narrow categories through which it analyzes, differentiates, identifies, and administers individuals. The human sciences not only provide tools for this sorting process but also legitimate the actions that follow it. The psychological exam, for example, tells us what needs to be done: is this murderer a criminal who must be sent to prison, or an insane person who must be sent to a hospital?

Clearly, power/knowledge undercuts any lofty humanistic narrative of "the life of the mind" or "the disinterested pursuit of knowledge." The intellectual comes to look like power's dupe, or perhaps a privileged insider to power's activities. The university, in particular, serves a dual function. As gatekeeper, it sorts students via grades, exams, course requirements, and so on, thereby limiting access to various cherished places in the social hierarchy, such as medical careers. At the same time the university undertakes funded research, thereby producing the knowledge through which populations are observed and managed.

Beginning in 2000, first in French and subsequently in English translation, Foucault's thirteen yearly lecture courses of the 1970s and 1980s at the Collège de France were published. The lectures cover a wide range of topics and have proved immensely generative as theorists engage with them. In particular, the lectures collected under the titles *"Society Must Be Defended," 1975–1976* (2003), *Security, Territory, Population, 1977–1978* (2007), and *The Birth of Biopolitics, 1978–1979* (2008) have spawned a growing literature on biopolitics. Although he did not live to fully develop the ideas first broached in these lectures, Foucault, in the selection from them presented here, clearly felt that his theory of disciplinary power needed to be supplemented with a notion of biopolitical power. In particular, he was interested in how modern Western societies after 1700 increasingly accorded to the state a responsibility to protect, and even to enhance, the "life" of its citizens. Most obviously, this responsibility justifies the kinds of public health actions (inoculations, maintenance of clean water supplies, testing of food products) we now take for granted. But a focus on life can also justify various defensive measures against criminals and terrorists or even against the kinds of welfare provisions offered to the poor and disabled.

Among the many vital questions raised by the notion of biopolitics, two have especially interested subsequent theorists such as GIORGIO AGAMBEN, JUDITH BUTLER, Roberto Esposito, and Wendy Brown. The first is sovereignty. As Foucault notes in our selection, biopolitics suggests a fundamental shift in how sovereignty is understood, even as conditions in a globalized world today appear to undermine national sovereignty. The response of many nation-states to the threat of terrorism and to the mass migration of refugees from war-torn countries to Europe and the United States has been to reinforce the nation's borders and the nation's sovereignty through "security" legislation. Crucial to the attempt to consider what sovereignty means today and how it is deployed is Foucault's notion that biopolitics is applied at the level of "populations," not individual bodies. Hence he tells us that his concept of disciplinary power does not on its own offer an adequate account of how power works in the modern era. We must also think about the forms of power that are justified by actuarial tables and other ways to calculate the "general welfare." And this issue brings the state back onstage after Foucault's theory of disciplinary power had seemed to diminish direct state power.

Second, the Foucault lectures have inspired a robust examination of the very concept of life. At a time when the mantle of the most important science has passed from physics to biology, it has become increasingly important both theoretically and practically to understand what we mean by life. Just think of debates over abortion or end-of-life issues, not to mention concerns regarding "quality of life." Questions of life are sites of political contestation and of state intervention. Biopower, as Foucault presents it, attends to all the techniques (at the level of the state or elsewhere) that aim to control or administer human beings "insofar as they are living beings. It is continuous, scientific, and it is the power to make live."

We can justly say that questions of power remain central to Foucault's work, even as his understandings of that complex term kept evolving. His bleak view of power's omnipresence has sparked the most intense criticisms of his work, and in his work of the 1980s he did soften some of his most extreme statements.

In our selection from *Discipline and Punish*, Foucault writes that "there is no outside." Nothing—whether selves, desires, or truth—is external to the productive power/knowledge that creates the categories by which something is apprehended and thought. Disciplinary power and biopower are so all-pervasive and triumphant that meaningful resistance and independent agency appear to be impossible. Foucault insisted repeatedly that there was resistance everywhere throughout the world created by power, but his logic necessitates the view that such resistance, like everything else, is an offshoot of power. As a result, many activities that may seem to oppose power are, a Foucauldian analysis shows, "complicitous" with it, reinforcing rather than contesting its reign. (Analysis of this sort, preoccupied with trying to differentiate the truly oppositional from the apparently oppositional, abound within New Historicism and cultural studies, while "the problem of agency" everywhere haunts contemporary theory.) Foucault struggled to find ways to get out from under the compelling logic of "there is no outside" without returning to naive appeals to "truth" or "selves" or "life" that exist independently of the discursive and social networks in which they appear. His efforts in that direction focused on "the care of the self" (in the final two volumes of *The History of Sexuality*) and are suggestive, but are not fully worked through. Similarly, the work on biopower points toward a political care of the populace, but seems on the whole more ominous than not. Since his death, individuals and whole populations (such as migrants) have continued to be incorporated into the bureaucratic slots of a "globalized" world of transnational corporations, nation-states, international organizations such as the United Nations and the International Monetary Fund, and the increasingly prominent nongovernmental organizations (NGOs) responsible for "humanitarian" work, making Foucault's accounts of a supervising, norm-enforcing, disciplinary power supplemented by a biopower that manages populations appear as pertinent as ever.

"What Is an Author?" Keywords: Authorship, The Canon/Tradition, Literary History, New Historicism, Poststructuralism, Subjectivity
***Discipline and Punish: The Birth of the Prison* Keywords:** The Body, Cultural Studies, Identity, Institutional Studies, Modernity, New Historicism, Poststructuralism, Subjectivity
***The History of Sexuality, Volume 1, An Introduction* Keywords:** The Body, Identity, New Historicism, Psychoanalysis, Queer Theory, Religion, Sexuality, Subjectivity
"Society Must Be Defended" Keywords: Institutional Studies, Modernity, Nationhood, Sexuality, Subjectivity

What Is an Author?[1]

In proposing this slightly odd question, I am conscious of the need for an explanation. To this day, the "author" remains an open question both with respect to its general function within discourse and in my own writings; that is, this question permits me to return to certain aspects of my own work which now appear ill-advised and misleading. In this regard, I wish to propose a necessary criticism and reevaluation.

For instance, my objective in *The Order of Things*[2] had been to analyse verbal clusters as discursive layers which fall outside the familiar categories of a book, a work, or an author. But while I considered "natural history," the "analysis of wealth," and "political economy" in general terms, I neglected a

1. Translated by Donald F. Bouchard and Sherry Simon.
2. Published in 1966 as *Les Mots et les choses*; in it, Foucault uncovered the epistemic assumptions of the "classical" (Enlightenment) and modern periods by examining the work of natural scientists, political economists, and linguists.

similar analysis of the author and his works; it is perhaps due to this omission that I employed the names of authors throughout this book in a naive and often crude fashion. I spoke of Buffon, Cuvier, Ricardo,[3] and others as well, but failed to realize that I had allowed their names to function ambiguously. This has proved an embarrassment to me in that my oversight has served to raise two pertinent objections.

It was argued that I had not properly described Buffon or his work and that my handling of Marx[4] was pitifully inadequate in terms of the totality of his thought. Although these objections were obviously justified, they ignored the task I had set myself: I had no intention of describing Buffon or Marx or of reproducing their statements or implicit meanings, but, simply stated, I wanted to locate the rules that formed a certain number of concepts and theoretical relationships in their works. In addition, it was argued that I had created monstrous families by bringing together names as disparate as Buffon and Linnaeus or in placing Cuvier next to Darwin[5] in defiance of the most readily observable family resemblances and natural ties. This objection also seems inappropriate since I had never tried to establish a genealogical table of exceptional individuals, nor was I concerned in forming an intellectual daguerreotype of the scholar or naturalist of the seventeenth and eighteenth century. In fact, I had no intention of forming any family, whether holy or perverse. On the contrary, I wanted to determine—a much more modest task—the functional conditions of specific discursive practices.

Then why did I use the names of authors in *The Order of Things*? Why not avoid their use altogether, or, short of that, why not define the manner in which they were used? These questions appear fully justified and I have tried to gauge their implications and consequences in a book that will appear shortly.[6] These questions have determined my effort to situate comprehensive discursive units, such as "natural history" or "political economy," and to establish the methods and instruments for delimiting, analyzing, and describing these unities. Nevertheless, as a privileged moment of individualization in the history of ideas, knowledge, and literature, or in the history of philosophy and science, the question of the author demands a more direct response. Even now, when we study the history of a concept, a literary genre, or a branch of philosophy, these concerns assume a relatively weak and secondary position in relation to the solid and fundamental role of an author and his works.

For the purposes of this paper, I will set aside a sociohistorical analysis of the author as an individual and the numerous questions that deserve attention in this context: how the author was individualized in a culture such as ours; the status we have given the author, for instance, when we began our research into authenticity and attribution; the systems of valorization in which he was included; or the moment when the stories of heroes gave way to an author's biography; the conditions that fostered the formulation of the fundamental critical category of "the man and his work." For the time being, I wish to restrict myself to the singular relationship that holds between an

3. David Ricardo (1772–1823), English economist. Georges-Louis Leclerc, comte de Buffon (1707–1788), French naturalist. Georges Cuvier (1769–1832), French anatomist.

4. KARL MARX (1818–1883), German social, political, and economic philosopher.

5. Charles Darwin (1809–1882), English naturalist and theorist of evolution. Carolus Linnaeus: Carl von Linné (1707–1778), Swedish botanist who devised the modern scientific nomenclature of living things.

6. *The Archaeology of Knowledge* (1969).

author and a text, the manner in which a text apparently points to this figure who is outside and precedes it.

Beckett supplies a direction: "What matter who's speaking, someone said, what matter who's speaking."[7] In an indifference such as this we must recognize one of the fundamental ethical principles of contemporary writing. It is not simply "ethical" because it characterizes our way of speaking and writing, but because it stands as an immanent rule, endlessly adopted and yet never fully applied. As a principle, it dominates writing as an ongoing practice and slights our customary attention to the finished product. For the sake of illustration, we need only consider two of its major themes. First, the writing of our day has freed itself from the necessity of "expression"; it only refers to itself, yet it is not restricted to the confines of interiority. On the contrary, we recognize it in its exterior deployment. This reversal transforms writing into an interplay of signs, regulated less by the content it signifies than by the very nature of the signifier. Moreover, it implies an action that is always testing the limits of its regularity, transgressing and reversing an order that it accepts and manipulates. Writing unfolds like a game that inevitably moves beyond its own rules and finally leaves them behind. Thus, the essential basis of this writing is not the exalted emotions related to the act of composition or the insertion of a subject into language. Rather, it is primarily concerned with creating an opening where the writing subject endlessly disappears.

The second theme is even more familiar: it is the kinship between writing and death. This relationship inverts the age-old conception of Greek narrative or epic, which was designed to guarantee the immortality of a hero. The hero accepted an early death because his life, consecrated and magnified by death, passed into immortality; and the narrative redeemed his acceptance of death. In a different sense, Arabic stories, and *The Arabian Nights* in particular, had as their motivation, their theme and pretext, this strategy for defeating death. Storytellers continued their narratives late into the night to forestall death and to delay the inevitable moment when everyone must fall silent. Scheherazade's story is a desperate inversion of murder; it is the effort, throughout all those nights, to exclude death from the circle of existence.[8] This conception of a spoken or written narrative as a protection against death has been transformed by our culture. Writing is now linked to sacrifice and to the sacrifice of life itself; it is a voluntary obliteration of the self that does not require representation in books because it takes place in the everyday existence of the writer. Where a work had the duty of creating immortality, it now attains the right to kill, to become the murderer of its author. Flaubert, Proust, and Kafka[9] are obvious examples of this reversal. In addition, we find the link between writing and death manifested in the total effacement of the individual characteristics of the writer; the quibbling and confrontations that a writer generates between himself and his text cancel out the signs of his particular individuality. If we wish to know the writer in our day, it will be through the singularity of his absence and in his link to

7. Samuel Beckett, *Texts for Nothing* (1974), p. 16 [translators' note]. Beckett (1906–1989), Irish-born novelist and playwright; he wrote in French.

8. Scheherazade, narrator of *The Arabian Nights* (a collection of traditional tales from several Middle Eastern cultures, codified ca. 1450), tells her stories to avoid the fate of the king's previous brides: execution on the morning after he marries them.

9. Franz Kafka (1883–1924), Austrian novelist, who lived much of his life in Prague. Gustave Flaubert (1821–1880), and Marcel Proust (1871–1922), French novelists.

death, which has transformed him into a victim of his own writing. While all of this is familiar in philosophy, as in literary criticism, I am not certain that the consequences derived from the disappearance or death of the author[1] have been fully explored or that the importance of this event has been appreciated. To be specific, it seems to me that the themes destined to replace the privileged position accorded the author have merely served to arrest the possibility of genuine change. Of these, I will examine two that seem particularly important.

To begin with, the thesis concerning a work. It has been understood that the task of criticism is not to reestablish the ties between an author and his work or to reconstitute an author's thought and experience through his works and, further, that criticism should concern itself with the structures of a work, its architectonic forms, which are studied for their intrinsic and internal relationships. Yet, what of a context that questions the concept of a work? What, in short, is the strange unit designated by the term, work? What is necessary to its composition, if a work is not something written by a person called an "author"? Difficulties arise on all sides if we raise the question in this way. If an individual is not an author, what are we to make of those things he has written or said, left among his papers or communicated to others? Is this not properly a work? What, for instance, were Sade's papers before he was consecrated as an author?[2] Little more, perhaps, than rolls of paper on which he endlessly unravelled his fantasies while in prison.

Assuming that we are dealing with an author, is everything he wrote and said, everything he left behind, to be included in his work? This problem is both theoretical and practical. If we wish to publish the complete works of Nietzsche,[3] for example, where do we draw the line? Certainly, everything must be published, but can we agree on what "everything" means? We will, of course, include everything that Nietzsche himself published, along with the drafts of his works, his plans for aphorisms, his marginal notations and corrections. But what if, in a notebook filled with aphorisms, we find a reference, a reminder of an appointment, an address, or a laundry bill, should this be included in his works? Why not? These practical considerations are endless once we consider how a work can be extracted from the millions of traces left by an individual after his death. Plainly, we lack a theory to encompass the questions generated by a work and the empirical activity of those who naively undertake the publication of the complete works of an author often suffers from the absence of this framework. Yet more questions arise. Can we say that *The Arabian Nights*, and *Stromates* of Clement of Alexandria, or the *Lives* of Diogenes Laertes[4] constitute works? Such questions only begin to suggest the range of our difficulties, and, if some have found it convenient to bypass the individuality of the writer or his status as an author to concentrate on a work, they have failed to appreciate the equally problematic nature of the word "work" and the unity it designates.

1. The phrase "death of the author" comes from the French literary critic ROLAND BARTHES (1915–1980).
2. The French author the marquis de Sade (1740–1814) began to write while in prison.
3. FRIEDRICH NIETZSCHE (1844–1900), the German philosopher, was insane the last ten years of his life and left many unpublished works, including wild jottings from his later years.
4. Greek scholar (ca. early 3d c. C.E.) whose *Lives* is a compilation of the lives and doctrines of the philosophers. Clement of Alexandria (ca. 150–ca. 215 C.E.), early church father and theologian; the *Stromates* (*Miscellanies*) is a collection of notes, full of digressions, on Christian philosophy.

Another thesis has detained us from taking full measure of the author's disappearance. It avoids confronting the specific event that makes it possible and, in subtle ways, continues to preserve the existence of the author. This is the notion of *écriture*.[5] Strictly speaking, it should allow us not only to circumvent references to an author, but to situate his recent absence. The conception of *écriture*, as currently employed, is concerned with neither the act of writing nor the indications, as symptoms or signs within a text, of an author's meaning; rather, it stands for a remarkably profound attempt to elaborate the conditions of any text, both the conditions of its spatial dispersion and its temporal deployment.

It appears, however, that this concept, as currently employed, has merely transposed the empirical characteristics of an author to a transcendental anonymity. The extremely visible signs of the author's empirical activity are effaced to allow the play, in parallel or opposition, of religious and critical modes of characterization. In granting a primordial status to writing, do we not, in effect, simply reinscribe in transcendental terms the theological affirmation of its sacred origin or a critical belief in its creative nature? To say that writing, in terms of the particular history it made possible, is subjected to forgetfulness and repression, is this not to reintroduce in transcendental terms the religious principle of hidden meanings (which require interpretation) and the critical assumption of implicit significations, silent purposes, and obscure contents (which give rise to commentary)?[6] Finally, is not the conception of writing as absence a transposition into transcendental terms of the religious belief in a fixed and continuous tradition or the aesthetic principle that proclaims the survival of the work as a kind of enigmatic supplement of the author beyond his own death?

This conception of *écriture* sustains the privileges of the author through the safeguard of the a priori;[7] the play of representations that formed a particular image of the author is extended within a gray neutrality. The disappearance of the author—since Mallarmé,[8] an event of our time—is held in check by the transcendental. Is it not necessary to draw a line between those who believe that we can continue to situate our present discontinuities within the historical and transcendental tradition of the nineteenth century and those who are making a great effort to liberate themselves, once and for all, from this conceptual framework?

It is obviously insufficient to repeat empty slogans: the author has disappeared; God and man died a common death. Rather, we should reexamine the empty space left by the author's disappearance; we should attentively observe, along its gaps and fault lines, its new demarcations, and the reapportionment of this void; we should await the fluid functions released by this disappearance. In this context we can briefly consider the problems that arise in the use of an author's name. What is the name of an author?

5. Written language or writing (French). In poststructuralist thought, especially that of Jacques Derrida (1930–2004), *écriture* designates that which is required for any particular speech act—whether spoken or written—to take place.
6. Here Foucault is criticizing the writings of Derrida.
7. That is, that which is derived from self-evident propositions (vs. from experience).
8. Stéphane Mallarmé (1842–1898), French symbolist poet; he was interested in writing techniques that diminished the author's role in the creation of the poem.

How does it function? Far from offering a solution, I will attempt to indicate some of the difficulties related to these questions.

The name of an author poses all the problems related to the category of the proper name. (Here, I am referring to the work of John Searle,[9] among others.) Obviously not a pure and simple reference, the proper name (and the author's name as well) has other than indicative functions. It is more than a gesture, a finger pointed at someone; it is, to a certain extent, the equivalent of a description. When we say "Aristotle,"[1] we are using a word that means one or a series of definite descriptions of the type: "the author of the *Analytics*," or "the founder of ontology," and so forth. Furthermore, a proper name has other functions than that of signification: when we discover that Rimbaud[2] has not written *La Chasse spirituelle*, we cannot maintain that the meaning of the proper name or this author's name has been altered. The proper name and the name of an author oscillate between the poles of description and designation,[3] and, granting that they are linked to what they name, they are not totally determined either by their descriptive or designative functions. Yet—and it is here that the specific difficulties attending an author's name appear—the link between a proper name and the individual being named and the link between an author's name and that which it names are not isomorphous and do not function in the same way; and these differences require clarification.

To learn, for example, that Pierre Dupont[4] does not have blue eyes, does not live in Paris, and is not a doctor does not invalidate the fact that the name, Pierre Dupont, continues to refer to the same person; there has been no modification of the designation that links the name to the person. With the name of an author, however, the problems are far more complex. The disclosure that Shakespeare was not born in the house that tourists now visit would not modify the functioning of the author's name, but, if it were proved that he had not written the sonnets that we attribute to him, this would constitute a significant change and affect the manner in which the author's name functions. Moreover, if we establish that Shakespeare wrote Bacon's *Organon* and that the same author was responsible for both the works of Shakespeare and those of Bacon, we would have introduced a third type of alteration which completely modifies the functioning of the author's name.[5] Consequently the name of an author is not precisely a proper name among others.

Many other factors sustain this paradoxical singularity of the name of an author. It is altogether different to maintain that Pierre Dupont does not exist and that Homer or Hermes Trismegistes[6] have never existed. While

9. See John Searle, *Speech Acts: An Essay in the Philosophy of Language* (1969), pp. 162–74 [translators' note]. Searle (b. 1932), American philosopher.
1. Greek philosopher (384–322 B.C.E; see above).
2. Arthur Rimbaud (1854–1891), French poet. The prose poem "La Chasse spirituelle" was published in 1949 as a recovered "lost" work by Rimbaud; its actual authors revealed the hoax shortly after publication.
3. In the philosophy of language, a *description* is a meaningful set of words that refers to a particular object. Hence, "the author of *Great Expectations*" describes "Charles Dickens." In contrast, the name "Charles Dickens" is a *designation* of the person who bears that name.
4. The French equivalent of "John Doe," a random designation of a living person.
5. Some people have argued that the plays of William Shakespeare (1564–1616) were actually written by the English philosopher Francis Bacon (1561–1626), whose *New Organon* (1620) is often cited as the founding text of the scientific method.
6. The god of letters, to whom 42 philosophico-religious works and books on alchemy and astrology, presumed to be the ancient wisdom of Egypt, were attributed. Homer is the traditional author of the *Iliad* and the *Odyssey* (ca. 8th c. B.C.E.); but the question of whether these two poems, originally transmitted orally, were the work of any single author remains open.

the first negation merely implies that there is no one by the name of Pierre Dupont, the second indicates that several individuals have been referred to by one name or that the real author possessed none of the traits traditionally associated with Homer or Hermes. Neither is it the same thing to say that Jacques Durand, not Pierre Dupont, is the real name of *X* and that Stendhal's name was Henri Beyle.[7] We could also examine the function and meaning of such statements as "Bourbaki is this or that person," and "Victor Eremita, Climacus, Anticlimacus, Frater Taciturnus, Constantin Constantius, all of these are Kierkegaard."[8]

These differences indicate that an author's name is not simply an element of speech (as a subject, a complement, or an element that could be replaced by a pronoun or other parts of speech). Its presence is functional in that it serves as a means of classification. A name can group together a number of texts and thus differentiate them from others. A name also establishes different forms of relationships among texts. Neither Hermes not Hippocrates existed in the sense that we can say Balzac[9] existed, but the fact that a number of texts were attached to a single name implies that relationships of homogeneity, filiation, reciprocal explanation, authentification, or of common utilization were established among them. Finally, the author's name characterizes a particular manner of existence of discourse. Discourse that possesses an author's name is not to be immediately consumed and forgotten; neither is it accorded the momentary attention given to ordinary, fleeting words. Rather, its status and its manner of reception are regulated by the culture in which it circulates.

We can conclude that, unlike a proper name, which moves from the interior of a discourse to the real person outside who produced it, the name of the author remains at the contours of texts—separating one from the other, defining their form, and characterizing their mode of existence. It points to the existence of certain groups of discourse and refers to the status of this discourse within a society and culture. The author's name is not a function of a man's civil status, nor is it fictional; it is situated in the breach, among the discontinuities, which gives rise to new groups of discourse and their singular mode of existence. Consequently, we can say that in our culture, the name of an author is a variable that accompanies only certain texts to the exclusion of others: a private letter may have a signatory, but it does not have an author; a contract can have an underwriter, but not an author; and, similarly, an anonymous poster attached to a wall may have a writer, but he cannot be an author. In this sense, the function of an author is to characterize the existence, circulation, and operation of certain discourses within a society.

In dealing with the "author" as a function of discourse, we must consider the characteristics of a discourse that support this use and determine its

7. The real name of the French novelist (1783–1842) who wrote under the pen name Stendhal.

8. Victor Eremita and the other names listed here were all pseudonyms used by the Danish philosopher Søren Kierkegaard (1813–1855) at various times during his career. Nicolas Bourbaki, the pseudonym shared by a group of 20th-century algebraists.

9. Honoré de Balzac (1799–1850), French novelist. Hippocrates (ca. 460–ca. 377 B.C.E.), Greek physician usually considered the father of medicine; though it is unlikely that he wrote any of the books attributed to him, Hippocrates did exist.

difference from other discourses. If we limit our remarks to only those books or texts with authors, we can isolate four different features.

First, they are objects of appropriation; the form of property they have become is of a particular type whose legal codification was accomplished some years ago. It is important to notice, as well, that its status as property is historically secondary to the penal code controlling its appropriation. Speeches and books were assigned real authors, other than mythical or important religious figures, only when the author became subject to punishment and to the extent that his discourse was considered transgressive. In our culture—undoubtedly in others as well—discourse was not originally a thing, a product, or a possession, but an action situated in a bipolar field of sacred and profane, lawful and unlawful, religious and blasphemous. It was a gesture charged with risks long before it became a possession caught in a circuit of property values. But it was at the moment when a system of ownership and strict copyright rules were established (toward the end of the eighteenth and beginning of the nineteenth century) that the transgressive properties always intrinsic to the act of writing became the forceful imperative of literature. It is as if the author, at the moment he was accepted into the social order of property which governs our culture, was compensating for his new status by reviving the older bipolar field of discourse in a systematic practice of transgression and by restoring the danger of writing which, on another side, had been conferred the benefits of property.

Secondly, the "author-function" is not universal or constant in all discourse. Even within our civilization, the same types of texts have not always required authors; there was a time when those texts which we now call "literary" (stories, folk tales, epics, and tragedies) were accepted, circulated, and valorized without any question about the identity of their author. Their anonymity was ignored because their real or supposed age was a sufficient guarantee of their authenticity. Texts, however, that we now call "scientific" (dealing with cosmology and the heavens, medicine or illness, the natural sciences or geography) were only considered truthful during the Middle Ages if the name of the author was indicated. Statements on the order of "Hippocrates said . . ." or "Pliny[1] tells us that . . ." were not merely formulas for an argument based on authority; they marked a proven discourse. In the seventeenth and eighteenth centuries, a totally new conception was developed when scientific texts were accepted on their own merits and positioned within an anonymous and coherent conceptual system of established truths and methods of verification. Authentification no longer required reference to the individual who had produced them; the role of the author disappeared as an index of truthfulness and, where it remained as an inventor's name, it was merely to denote a specific theorem or proposition, a strange effect, a property, a body, a group of elements, or pathological syndrome.

At the same time, however, "literary" discourse was acceptable only if it carried an author's name; every text of poetry or fiction was obliged to state its author and the date, place, and circumstance of its writing. The meaning and value attributed to the text depended on this information. If by accident or design a text was presented anonymously, every effort was made

1. Roman writer (23/24–79 C.E.); only his 37-book *Natural History* survives.

to locate its author. Literary anonymity was of interest only as a puzzle to be solved as, in our day, literary works are totally dominated by the sovereignty of the author. (Undoubtedly, these remarks are far too categorical. Criticism has been concerned for some time now with aspects of a text not fully dependent on the notion of an individual creator; studies of genre or the analysis of recurring textual motifs and their variations from a norm other than the author. Furthermore, where in mathematics the author has become little more than a handy reference for a particular theorem or group of propositions, the reference to an author in biology and medicine, or to the date of his research has a substantially different bearing. This latter reference, more than simply indicating the source of information, attests to the "reliability" of the evidence, since it entails an appreciation of the techniques and experimental materials available at a given time and in a particular laboratory.)

The third point concerning this "author-function" is that it is not formed spontaneously through the simple attribution of a discourse to an individual. It results from a complex operation whose purpose is to construct the rational entity we call an author. Undoubtedly, this construction is assigned a "realistic" dimension as we speak of an individual's "profundity" or "creative" power, his intentions or the original inspiration manifested in writing. Nevertheless, these aspects of an individual, which we designate as an author (or which comprise an individual as an author), are projections, in terms always more or less psychological, of our way of handling texts: in the comparisons we make, the traits we extract as pertinent, the continuities we assign, or the exclusions we practice. In addition, all these operations vary according to the period and the form of discourse concerned. A "philosopher" and a "poet" are not constructed in the same manner; and the author of an eighteenth-century novel was formed differently from the modern novelist. There are, nevertheless, transhistorical constants in the rules that govern the construction of an author.

In literary criticism, for example, the traditional methods for defining an author—or, rather, for determining the configuration of the author from existing texts—derive in large part from those used in the Christian tradition to authenticate (or to reject) the particular texts in its possession. Modern criticism, in its desire to "recover" the author from a work, employs devices strongly reminiscent of Christian exegesis when it wished to prove the value of a text by ascertaining the holiness of its author. In *De Viris Illustribus,* Saint Jerome[2] maintains that homonymy is not proof of the common authorship of several works, since many individuals could have the same name or someone could have perversely appropriated another's name. The name, as an individual mark, is not sufficient as it relates to a textual tradition. How, then, can several texts be attributed to an individual author? What norms, related to the function of the author, will disclose the involvement of several authors? According to Saint Jerome, there are four criteria: the texts that must be eliminated from the list of works attributed to a single author are those inferior to the others (thus, the author is defined as a standard level of quality); those whose ideas conflict with the doctrine

2. Church father and scholar (ca. 347–420), the first to translate the complete Bible into Latin. *De Viris Illustribus* (392–93, *Of Illustrious Men*) is a collection of 130 biographies of Christian writers.

expressed in the others (here the author is defined as a certain field of conceptual or theoretical coherence); those written in a different style and containing words and phrases not ordinarily found in the other works (the author is seen as a stylistic uniformity); and those referring to events or historical figures subsequent to the death of the author (the author is thus a definite historical figure in which a series of events converge). Although modern criticism does not appear to have these same suspicions concerning authentication, its strategies for defining the author present striking similarities. The author explains the presence of certain events within a text, as well as their transformations, distortions, and their various modifications (and this through an author's biography or by reference to his particular point of view, in the analysis of his social preferences and his position within a class or by delineating his fundamental objectives). The author also constitutes a principle of unity in writing where any unevenness of production is ascribed to changes caused by evolution, maturation, or outside influence. In addition, the author serves to neutralize the contradictions that are found in a series of texts. Governing this function is the belief that there must be—at a particular level of an author's thought, of his conscious or unconscious desire—a point where contradictions are resolved, where the incompatible elements can be shown to relate to one another or to cohere around a fundamental and originating contradiction. Finally, the author is a particular source of expression who, in more or less finished forms, is manifested equally well, and with similar validity, in a text, in letters, fragments, drafts, and so forth. Thus, even while Saint Jerome's four principles of authenticity might seem largely inadequate to modern critics, they, nevertheless, define the critical modalities now used to display the function of the author.

However, it would be false to consider the function of the author as a pure and simple reconstruction after the fact of a text given as passive material, since a text always bears a number of signs that refer to the author. Well known to grammarians, these textual signs are personal pronouns, adverbs of time and place, and the conjugation of verbs. But it is important to note that these elements have a different bearing on texts with an author and on those without one. In the latter, these "shifters"[3] refer to a real speaker and to an actual deictic situation, with certain exceptions such as the case of indirect speech in the first person. When discourse is linked to an author, however, the role of "shifters" is more complex and variable. It is well known that in a novel narrated in the first person, neither the first person pronoun, the present indicative tense, nor, for that matter, its signs of localization refer directly to the writer, either to the time when he wrote, or to the specific act of writing; rather, they stand for a "second self" whose similarity to the author is never fixed and undergoes considerable alteration within the course of a single book. It would be as false to seek the author in relation to the actual writer as to the fictional narrator; the "author-function" arises out of their scission—in the division and distance of the two. One might object that this phenomenon only applies to novels or poetry, to a context of "quasi-discourse," but, in fact, all discourse that supports this "author-function" is characterized by this plurality of egos. In a mathematical treatise, the ego who

Importance of tense.

3. Words whose referent changes according to the identity and context of the speaker, such as "I" (personal pronouns), "now" (adverbs of time), and "here" (adverbs of place)—that is, according to the "deictic situation."

indicates the circumstances of composition in the preface is not identical, either in terms of his position or his function, to the "I" who concludes a demonstration within the body of the text. The former implies a unique individual who, at a given time and place, succeeded in completing a project, whereas the latter indicates an instance and plan of demonstration that anyone could perform provided the same set of axioms, preliminary operations, and an identical set of symbols were used. It is also possible to locate a third ego: one who speaks of the goals of his investigation, the obstacles encountered, its results, and the problems yet to be solved and this "I" would function in a field of existing or future mathematical discourses. We are not dealing with a system of dependencies where a first and essential use of the "I" is reduplicated, as a kind of fiction, by the other two. On the contrary, the "author-function" in such discourses operates so as to effect the simultaneous dispersion of the three egos.

Further elaboration would, of course, disclose other characteristics of the "author-function," but I have limited myself to the four that seemed the most obvious and important. They can be summarized in the following manner: the "author-function" is tied to the legal and institutional systems that circumscribe, determine, and articulate the realm of discourses; it does not operate in a uniform manner in all discourses, at all times, and in any given culture; it is not defined by the spontaneous attribution of a text to its creator, but through a series of precise and complex procedures; it does not refer, purely and simply, to an actual individual insofar as it simultaneously gives rise to a variety of egos and to a series of subjective positions that individuals of any class may come to occupy.

I am aware that until now I have kept my subject within unjustifiable limits; I should also have spoken of the "author-function" in painting, music, technical fields, and so forth. Admitting that my analysis is restricted to the domain of discourse, it seems that I have given the term "author" an excessively narrow meaning. I have discussed the author only in the limited sense of a person to whom the production of a text, a book, or a work can be legitimately attributed. However, it is obvious that even within the realm of discourse a person can be the author of much more than a book—of a theory, for instance, of a tradition or a discipline within which new books and authors can proliferate. For convenience, we could say that such authors occupy a "transdiscursive" position.

Homer, Aristotle,[4] and the Church Fathers played this role, as did the first mathematicians and the originators of the Hippocratic tradition. This type of author is surely as old as our civilization. But I believe that the nineteenth century in Europe produced a singular type of author who should not be confused with "great" literary authors, or the authors of canonical religious texts, and the founders of sciences. Somewhat arbitrarily, we might call them "initiators of discursive practices."

The distinctive contribution of these authors is that they produced not only their own work, but the possibility and the rules of formation of other texts. In this sense, their role differs entirely from that of a novelist, for example, who is basically never more than the author of his own text.

4. Aristotle's encyclopedic writings enormously influenced medieval philosophy and science.

Freud[5] is not simply the author of *The Interpretation of Dreams* or of *Wit and its Relation to the Unconscious* and Marx is not simply the author of the *Communist Manifesto* or *Capital*: they both established the endless possibility of discourse. Obviously, an easy objection can be made. The author of a novel may be responsible for more than his own text; if he acquires some "importance" in the literary world, his influence can have significant ramifications. To take a very simple example, one could say that Ann Radcliffe[6] did not simply write *The Mysteries of Udolpho* and a few other novels, but also made possible the appearance of Gothic romances at the beginning of the nineteenth century. To this extent, her function as an author exceeds the limits of her work. However, this objection can be answered by the fact that the possibilities disclosed by the initiators of discursive practices (using the examples of Marx and Freud, whom I believe to be the first and the most important) are significantly different from those suggested by novelists. The novels of Ann Radcliffe put into circulation a certain number of resemblances and analogies patterned on her work—various characteristic signs, figures, relationships, and structures that could be integrated into other books. In short, to say that Ann Radcliffe created the Gothic Romance means that there are certain elements common to her works and to the nineteenth-century Gothic romance: the heroine ruined by her own innocence, the secret fortress that functions as a counter-city, the outlaw-hero who swears revenge on the world that has cursed him, etc. On the other hand, Marx and Freud, as "initiators of discursive practices," not only made possible a certain number of analogies that could be adopted by future texts, but, as importantly, they also made possible a certain number of differences. They cleared a space for the introduction of elements other than their own, which, nevertheless, remain within the field of discourse they initiated. In saying that Freud founded psychoanalysis, we do not simply mean that the concept of libido or the techniques of dream analysis reappear in the writings of Karl Abraham or Melanie Klein,[7] but that he made possible a certain number of differences with respect to his books, concepts, and hypotheses, which all arise out of psychoanalytic discourse.

Is this not the case, however, with the founder of any new science or of any author who successfully transforms an existing science? After all, Galileo[8] is indirectly responsible for the texts of those who mechanically applied the laws he formulated, in addition to having paved the way for the production of statements far different from his own. If Cuvier is the founder of biology and Saussure[9] of linguistics, it is not because they were imitated or that an organic concept or a theory of the sign was uncritically integrated into new texts, but because Cuvier, to a certain extent, made possible a theory of evolution diametrically opposed to his own system and because Saussure made possible a generative grammar radically different from his own structural analysis. Superficially, then, the initiation of discursive practices appears similar to the founding of any scientific endeavor, but I believe there is a fundamental difference.

5. SIGMUND FREUD (1856–1939), Austrian founder of psychoanalysis.
6. English novelist (1764–1823); her *Mysteries of Udolpho* (1794) was extremely popular.
7. Austrian-born English psychoanalyst (1882–1960). Abraham (1877–1925), German psychoanalyst.
8. Galileo Galilei (1564–1642), Italian astronomer and physicist who formulated 3 laws of motion.
9. FERDINAND DE SAUSSURE (1857–1913), Swiss linguist.

In a scientific program, the founding act is on an equal footing with its future transformations: it is merely one among the many modifications that it makes possible. This interdependence can take several forms. In the future development of a science, the founding act may appear as little more than a single instance of a more general phenomenon that has been discovered. It might be questioned, in retrospect, for being too intuitive or empirical and submitted to the rigors of new theoretical operations in order to situate it in a formal domain. Finally, it might be thought a hasty generalization whose validity should be restricted. In other words, the founding act of a science can always be rechanneled through the machinery of transformations it has instituted.

On the other hand, the initiation of a discursive practice is heterogeneous to its ulterior transformations. To extend psychoanalytic practice, as initiated by Freud, is not to presume a formal generality that was not claimed at the outset; it is to explore a number of possible applications. To limit it is to isolate in the original texts a small set of propositions or statements that are recognized as having an inaugurative value and that mark other Freudian concepts or theories as derivative. Finally, there are no "false" statements in the work of these initiators; those statements considered inessential or "prehistoric," in that they are associated with another discourse, are simply neglected in favor of the more pertinent aspects of the work. The initiation of a discursive practice, unlike the founding of a science, overshadows and is necessarily detached from its later developments and transformations. As a consequence, we define the theoretical validity of a statement with respect to the work of the initiator, whereas in the case of Galileo or Newton,[1] it is based on the structural and intrinsic norms established in cosmology or physics. Stated schematically, the work of these initiators is not situated in relation to a science or in the space it defines; rather, it is science or discursive practice that relate to their works as the primary points of reference.

In keeping with this distinction, we can understand why it is inevitable that practitioners of such discourses must "return to the origin." Here, as well, it is necessary to distinguish a "return" from scientific "rediscoveries" or "reactivations." "Rediscoveries" are the effects of analogy or isomorphism with current forms of knowledge that allow the perception of forgotten or obscured figures. For instance, Chomsky in his book on Cartesian grammar[2] "rediscovered" a form of knowledge that had been in use from Cordemoy to Humboldt.[3] It could only be understood from the perspective of generative grammar because this later manifestation held the key to its construction: in effect, a retrospective codification of an historical position. "Reactivation" refers to something quite different: the insertion of discourse into totally new domains of generalization, practice, and transformations. The history of mathematics abounds in examples of this phenomenon as the work of Michel Serres on mathematical anamnesis shows.[4]

1. Sir Isaac Newton (1642–1727), English physicist and mathematician.
2. Noam Chomsky, *Cartesian Linguistics* (1966) [translators' note]. Chomsky (b. 1928), American linguist.
3. Wilhelm von Humboldt (1767–1835), German statesman and philologist. Géraud de Cordemoy (1626–1684), French author of *A Philosophical Discourse Concerning Speech* (1668).
4. Michel Serres, *La Communication: Hermes I* (1968), pp. 78–112 [translators' note]. "Mathematical anamnesis": the "recollection" (in Greek, *anamnēsis*) of innate concepts, as demonstrated by PLATO (ca. 427–ca. 347 B.C.E.) in *Meno* 80a–86c. Serres (b. 1930), French philosopher.

The phrase, "return to," designates a movement with its proper specificity, which characterizes the initiation of discursive practices. If we return, it is because of a basic and constructive omission, an omission that is not the result of accident or incomprehension. In effect, the act of initiation is such, in its essence, that it is inevitably subjected to its own distortions; that which displays this act and derives from it is, at the same time, the root of its divergences and travesties. This nonaccidental omission must be regulated by precise operations that can be situated, analysed, and reduced in a return to the act of initiation. The barrier imposed by omission was not added from the outside; it arises from the discursive practice in question, which gives it its law. Both the cause of the barrier and the means for its removal, this omission—also responsible for the obstacles that prevent returning to the act of initiation—can only be resolved by a return. In addition, it is always a return to a text in itself, specifically, to a primary and unadorned text with particular attention to those things registered in the interstices of the text, its gaps and absences. We return to those empty spaces that have been masked by omission or concealed in a false and misleading plenitude. In these rediscoveries of an essential lack, we find the oscillation of two characteristic responses: "This point was made—you can't help seeing it if you know how to read"; or, inversely, "No, that point is not made in any of the printed words in the text, but it is expressed through the words, in their relationships and in the distance that separates them." It follows naturally that this return, which is a part of the discursive mechanism, constantly introduces modifications that would come to fix itself upon the primary discursivity and redouble it in the form of an ornament which, after all, is not essential. Rather, it is an effective and necessary means of transforming discursive practice. A study of Galileo's works could alter our knowledge of the history, but not the science, of mechanics; whereas, a re-examination of the books of Freud or Marx can transform our understanding of psychoanalysis or Marxism.

A last feature of these returns is that they tend to reinforce the enigmatic link between an author and his works. A text has an inaugurative value precisely because it is the work of a particular author, and our returns are conditioned by this knowledge. The rediscovery of an unknown text by Newton or Cantor[5] will not modify classical cosmology or group theory; at most, it will change our appreciation of their historical genesis. Bringing to light, however, *An Outline of Psychoanalysis*, to the extent that we recognize it as a book by Freud, can transform not only our historical knowledge, but the field of psychoanalytic theory—if only through a shift of accent or of the center of gravity. These returns, an important component of discursive practices, form a relationship between "fundamental" and mediate authors, which is not identical to that which links an ordinary text to its immediate author.

These remarks concerning the initiation of discursive practices have been extremely schematic, especially with regard to the opposition I have tried to trace between this initiation and the founding of sciences. The distinction between the two is not readily discernible; moreover, there is no proof that the two procedures are mutually exclusive. My only purpose in setting up

5. Georg Cantor (1845–1918), Russian-born German mathematician.

this opposition, however, was to show that the "author-function," sufficiently complex at the level of a book or a series of texts that bear a definite signature, has other determining factors when analysed in terms of larger entities—groups of works or entire disciplines.

Unfortunately, there is a decided absence of positive propositions in this essay, as it applies to analytic procedures or directions for future research, but I ought at least to give the reasons why I attach such importance to a continuation of this work. Developing a similar analysis could provide the basis for a typology of discourse. A typology of this sort cannot be adequately understood in relation to the grammatical features, formal structures, and objects of discourse, because there undoubtedly exist specific discursive properties or relationships that are irreducible to the rules of grammar and logic and to the laws that govern objects. These properties require investigation if we hope to distinguish the larger categories of discourse. The different forms of relationships (or nonrelationships) that an author can assume are evidently one of these discursive properties.

This form of investigation might also permit the introduction of an historical analysis of discourse. Perhaps the time has come to study not only the expressive value and formal transformations of discourse, but its mode of existence: the modifications and variations, within any culture, of modes of circulation, valorization, attribution, and appropriation. Partially at the expense of themes and concepts that an author places in his work, the "author-function" could also reveal the manner in which discourse is articulated on the basis of social relationships.

Is it not possible to reexamine, as a legitimate extension of this kind of analysis, the privileges of the subject? Clearly, in undertaking an internal and architectonic analysis of a work (whether it be a literary text, a philosophical system, or a scientific work) and in delimiting psychological and biographical references, suspicions arise concerning the absolute nature and creative role of the subject. But the subject should not be entirely abandoned. It should be reconsidered, not to restore the theme of an originating subject, but to seize its functions, its intervention in discourse, and its system of dependencies. We should suspend the typical questions: how does a free subject penetrate the density of things and endow them with meaning; how does it accomplish its design by animating the rules of discourse from within? Rather, we should ask: under what conditions and through what forms can an entity like the subject appear in the order of discourse; what position does it occupy; what functions does it exhibit; and what rules does it follow in each type of discourse? In short, the subject (and its substitutes) must be stripped of its creative role and analysed as a complex and variable function of discourse.

The author—or what I have called the "author-function"—is undoubtedly only one of the possible specifications of the subject and, considering past historical transformations, it appears that the form, the complexity, and even the existence of this function are far from immutable. We can easily imagine a culture where discourse would circulate without any need for an author. Discourses, whatever their status, form, or value, and regardless of our manner of handling them, would unfold in a pervasive anonymity. No longer the tiresome repetitions:

"Who is the real author?"
"Have we proof of his authenticity and originality?"
"What has he revealed of his most profound self in his language?"

New questions will be heard:

"What are the modes of existence of this discourse?"
"Where does it come from; how is it circulated; who controls it?"
"What placements are determined for possible subjects?"
"Who can fulfill these diverse functions of the subject?"

Behind all these questions we would hear little more than the murmur of indifference:

"What matter who's speaking?"

1969

From Discipline and Punish: The Birth of the Prison[1]

The Carceral

Were I to fix the date of completion of the carceral[2] system, I would choose not 1810 and the penal code, nor even 1844, when the law laying down the principle of cellular internment was passed; I might not even choose 1838, when books on prison reform by Charles Lucas, Moreau-Christophe and Faucher were published.[3] The date I would choose would be 22 January 1840, the date of the official opening of Mettray.[4] Or better still, perhaps, that glorious day, unremarked and unrecorded, when a child in Mettray remarked as he lay dying: 'What a pity I left the colony so soon'.[5] This marked the death of the first penitentiary saint. Many of the blessed no doubt went to join him, if the former inmates of the penal colonies are to be believed when, in singing the praises of the new punitive policies of the body, they remarked: 'We preferred the blows, but the cell suits us better'.

Why Mettray? Because it is the disciplinary form at its most extreme, the model in which are concentrated all the coercive technologies of behaviour. In it were to be found 'cloister, prison, school, regiment'. The small, highly hierarchized groups, into which the inmates were divided, followed simultaneously five models: that of the family (each group was a 'family' composed of 'brothers' and two 'elder brothers'); that of the army (each family, commanded by a head, was divided into two sections, each of which had a second in command; each inmate had a number and was taught basic military exercises; there was a cleanliness inspection every day, an inspection of clothing every week; a roll-call was taken three times a day); that of the

1. Translated by Alan Sheridan.
2. Related to the act of incarceration and to institutions that discipline the body, especially prisons.
3. Charles Lucas, *De la réforme des prisons* (1836); L. Moreau-Christophe, *De la mortalité et la folie dans le régime pénitentiaire* (1839); L. Faucher, *De la réforme des prisons* (1838) [Foucault's note].
4. French prison farm for juvenile criminals founded in 1840; it was widely imitated throughout Europe as a model of modern disciplinary techniques.
5. E. Ducpétiaux, *De la condition physique et morale des jeunes ouvriers* (1852), p. 383 [Foucault's note].

workshop, with supervisors and foremen, who were responsible for the regularity of the work and for the apprenticeship of the younger inmates; that of the school (an hour or an hour and a half of lessons every day; the teaching was given by the instructor and by the deputy-heads); lastly, the judicial model (each day 'justice' was meted out in the parlour: 'The least act of disobedience is punished and the best way of avoiding serious offences is to punish the most minor offences very severely: at Mettray, a useless word is punishable'; the principal punishment inflicted was confinement to one's cell; for 'isolation is the best means of acting on the moral nature of children; it is there above all that the voice of religion, even if it has never spoken to their hearts, recovers all its emotional power'[6]); the entire parapenal[7] institution, which is created in order not to be a prison, culminates in the cell, on the walls of which are written in black letters: 'God sees you'.

This superimposition of different models makes it possible to indicate, in its specific features, the function of 'training'. The chiefs and their deputies at Mettray had to be not exactly judges, or teachers, or foremen, or non-commissioned officers, or 'parents', but something of all these things in a quite specific mode of intervention. They were in a sense technicians of behaviour: engineers of conduct, orthopaedists[8] of individuality. Their task was to produce bodies that were both docile and capable; they supervised the nine or ten working hours of every day (whether in a workshop or in the fields); they directed the orderly movements of groups of inmates, physical exercises, military exercises, rising in the morning, going to bed at night, walks to the accompaniment of bugle and whistle; they taught gymnastics;[9] they checked cleanliness, supervised bathing. Training was accompanied by permanent observation; a body of knowledge was being constantly built up from the everyday behaviour of the inmates; it was organized as an instrument of perpetual assessment: 'On entering the colony, the child is subjected to a sort of interrogation as to his origins, the position of his family, the offence for which he was brought before the courts and all the other offences that make up his short and often very sad existence. This information is written down on a board on which everything concerning each inmate is noted in turn, his stay at the colony and the place to which he is sent when he leaves'.[1] The modelling of the body produces a knowledge of the individual, the apprenticeship of the techniques induces modes of behaviour and the acquisition of skills is inextricably linked with the establishment of power relations; strong, skilled agricultural workers are produced; in this very work, provided it is technically supervised, submissive subjects are produced and a dependable body of knowledge built up about them. This disciplinary technique exercised upon the body had a double effect: a 'soul' to be known and a subjection to be maintained. One result vindicated this work of training: in 1848, at a moment when 'the fever of revolution fired the imagination of all, when the schools at Angers, La

6. Ibid., p. 377 [Foucault's note].
7. Closely related to the penal.
8. Those who correct, or set straight, children.
9. "Anything that helps to tire the body helps to expel bad thoughts; so care is taken that games consist of violent exercise. At night, they fall asleep the moment they touch the pillow" (Ducpétiaux, *De la condition physique et morale*, pp. 375–76) [Foucault's note].
1. E. Ducpétiaux, *Des colonies agricoles* (1851), p. 61 [Foucault's note].

Flèche, Alfort, even the boarding schools, rose up in rebellion, the inmates of Mettray were calmer than ever'.[2]

Where Mettray was especially exemplary was in the specificity that it recognized in this operation of training. It was related to other forms of supervision, on which it was based: medicine, general education, religious direction. But it cannot be identified absolutely with them. Nor with administration in the strict sense. Heads or deputy-heads of 'families', monitors and foremen, had to live in close proximity to the inmates; their clothes were 'almost as humble' as those of the inmates themselves; they practically never left their side, observing them day and night; they constituted among them a network of permanent observation. And, in order to train them themselves, a specialized school had been organized in the colony. The essential element of its programme was to subject the future cadres to the same apprenticeships and to the same coercions as the inmates themselves: they were 'subjected as pupils to the discipline that, later, as instructors, they would themselves impose'. They were taught the art of power relations. It was the first training college in pure discipline: the 'penitentiary' was not simply a project that sought its justification in 'humanity' or its foundations in a 'science', but a technique that was learnt, transmitted and which obeyed general norms. The practice that normalized by compulsion the conduct of the undisciplined or dangerous could, in turn, by technical elaboration and rational reflection, be 'normalized'. The disciplinary technique became a 'discipline' which also had its school.

It so happens that historians of the human sciences date the birth of scientific psychology at this time: during these same years, it seems, Weber[3] was manipulating his little compass for the measurement of sensations. What took place at Mettray (and in other European countries sooner or later) was obviously of a quite different order. It was the emergence or rather the institutional specification, the baptism as it were, of a new type of supervision—both knowledge and power—over individuals who resisted disciplinary normalization. And yet, in the formation and growth of psychology, the appearance of these professionals of discipline, normality and subjection surely marks the beginning of a new stage. It will be said that the quantitative assessment of sensorial responses could at least derive authority from the prestige of the emerging science of physiology and that for this alone it deserves to feature in the history of the sciences. But the supervision of normality was firmly encased in a medicine or a psychiatry that provided it with a sort of 'scientificity'; it was supported by a judicial apparatus which, directly or indirectly, gave it legal justification. Thus, in the shelter of these two considerable protectors, and, indeed, acting as a link between them, or a place of exchange, a carefully worked out technique for the supervision of norms has continued to develop right up to the present day. The specific, institutional supports of these methods have proliferated since the founding of the small school at Mettray; their apparatuses have increased in quantity and scope; their auxiliary services have

2. G. Ferrus, *Des prisonniers* (1850) [Foucault's note]. The Revolution of 1848, against Louis-Philippe, established the short-lived Second Republic (1848–52).

3. Ernst Weber (1795–1878), German physiologist who devised a method of measuring the sensitivity of the skin.

increased, with hospitals, schools, public administrations and private enterprises; their agents have proliferated in number, in power, in technical qualification; the technicians of indiscipline have founded a family. In the normalization of the power of normalization, in the arrangement of a power-knowledge over individuals, Mettray and its school marked a new era.

But why choose this moment as the point of emergence of the formation of an art of punishing that is still more or less our own? Precisely because this choice is somewhat 'unjust'. Because it situates the 'end' of the process in the lower reaches of criminal law. Because Mettray was a prison, but not entirely; a prison in that it contained young delinquents condemned by the courts; and yet something else, too, because it also contained minors who had been charged, but acquitted under article 66 of the code,[4] and boarders held, as in the eighteenth century, as an alternative to paternal correction. Mettray, a punitive model, is at the limit of strict penality. It was the most famous of a whole series of institutions which, well beyond the frontiers of criminal law, constituted what one might call the carceral archipelago.[5]

Yet the general principles, the great codes and subsequent legislation were quite clear on the matter: no imprisonment 'outside the law', no detention that had not been decided by a qualified judicial institution, no more of those arbitrary and yet widespread confinements. Yet the very principle of extra-penal incarceration was in fact never abandoned. (A whole study remains to be done of the debates that took place during the Revolution[6] concerning family courts, paternal correction and the right of parents to lock up their children.) And, if the apparatus of the great classical form of confinement was partly (and only partly) dismantled, it was very soon reactivated, rearranged, developed in certain directions. But what is still more important is that it was homogenized, through the mediation of the prison, on the one hand with legal punishments and, on the other, with disciplinary mechanisms. The frontiers between confinement, judicial punishment and institutions of discipline, which were already blurred in the classical age,[7] tended to disappear and to constitute a great carceral continuum that diffused penitentiary techniques into the most innocent disciplines, transmitting disciplinary norms into the very heart of the penal system and placing over the slightest illegality, the smallest irregularity, deviation or anomaly, the threat of delinquency. A subtle, graduated carceral net, with compact institutions, but also separate and diffused methods, assumed responsibility for the arbitrary, widespread, badly integrated confinement of the classical age.

I shall not attempt here to reconstitute the whole network that formed first the immediate surroundings of the prison, then spread farther and farther outwards. However, a few references and dates should give some idea of the breadth and precocity of the phenomenon.

4. An article in the French Penal Code that condemned children for acting "sans discernement" (without discretion).

5. An allusion to *The Gulag Archipelago* (1973–75), by the Russian novelist Aleksandr Solzhenitsyn, which dramatized for the West the extensive chain of prison camps in the Soviet Union between 1918 and 1956.

6. That is, the French Revolution of 1789.

7. Foucault's term for (roughly) the period from 1650 to 1789.

There were agricultural sections in the *maisons centrales*[8] (the first example of which was Gaillon in 1824, followed later by Fontevrault, Les Douaires, Le Boulard); there were colonies for poor, abandoned vagrant children (Petit-Bourg[9] in 1840, Ostwald in 1842); there were almshouses for young female offenders who 'recoiled before the idea of entering a life of disorder', for 'poor innocent girls whose mothers' immorality has exposed to precocious perversity', or for poor girls found on the doorsteps of hospitals and lodging houses. There were penal colonies envisaged by the law of 1850: minors, acquitted or condemned, were to be sent to these colonies and 'brought up in common, under strict discipline, and trained in agricultural work and in the principal industries related to it'; later, they were to be joined by minors sentenced to hard labour for life and 'vicious and insubordinate wards of the Public Assistance'.[1] And, moving still farther away from penality in the strict sense, the carceral circles widen and the form of the prison slowly diminishes and finally disappears altogether: the institutions for abandoned or indigent children, the orphanages (like Neuhof or Mesnil-Firmin), the establishments for apprentices (like the Bethléem de Reims or the Maison de Nancy); still farther away the factory-convents, such as La Sauvagère, Tarare and Jujurieu (where the girl workers entered about the age of thirteen, lived confined for years and were allowed out only under surveillance, received instead of wages pledged payment, which could be increased by bonuses for zeal and good behaviour, which they could use only on leaving). And then, still farther, there was a whole series of mechanisms that did not adopt the 'compact' prison model, but used some of the carceral methods: charitable societies, moral improvement associations, organizations that handed out assistance and also practised surveillance, workers' estates and lodging houses—the most primitive of which still bear the all too visible marks of the penitentiary system.[2] And, lastly, this great carceral network reaches all the disciplinary mechanisms that function throughout society.

We have seen that, in penal justice, the prison transformed the punitive procedure into a penitentiary technique; the carceral archipelago transported this technique from the penal institution to the entire social body. With several important results.

1. This vast mechanism established a slow, continuous, imperceptible gradation that made it possible to pass naturally from disorder to offence and back from a transgression of the law to a slight departure from a rule, an average, a demand, a norm. In the classical period, despite a certain common reference to offence in general,[3] the order of the crime, the order of sin and

8. State prisons (French); the four named here began to use prisoners to do agricultural labor.

9. Town in Guadeloupe, a French colony in the Caribbean. The other places named are all in France.

1. On all these institutions, cf. H. Gaillac, *Les Maisons de correction* (1971) [Foucault's note].

2. Cf., for example, the following description of workers' accommodation built at Lille in the mid-19th century: 'Cleanliness is the order of the day. It is the heart of the regulations. There are a number of severe provisions against noise, drunkenness, disorders of all kinds. A serious offence brings expulsion. Brought back to regular habits of order and economy, the workers no longer desert the workshops on Mondays. . . . The children are better supervised and are no longer a cause of scandal. . . . Prizes are given for the upkeep of the dwellings, for good behavior, for signs of devotion and each year these prizes are competed for by a large number of competitors' (Houzé de l'Aulnay, *Des logements ouvriers à Lille* [1863], pp. 13–15) [Foucault's note]. "Estates": public housing projects.

3. Crime was explicitly defined by certain jurists such as P. F. Muyart de Vouglans, *Refutation du Traité des délits et des peines* (1767), p. 108, and *Les Lois criminelles en France* (1780), p. 3; and G. Rousseaud de la Combe, *Traité des matières criminelles* (1741), pp. 1–2 [Foucault's note].

the order of bad conduct remained separate in so far as they related to separate criteria and authorities (court, penitence, confinement). Incarceration with its mechanisms of surveillance and punishment functioned, on the contrary, according to a principle of relative continuity. The continuity of the institutions themselves, which were linked to one another (public assistance with the orphanage, the reformitory, the penitentiary, the disciplinary battalion, the prison; the school with the charitable society, the workshop, the almshouse, the penitentiary convent; the workers' estate with the hospital and the prison). A continuity of the punitive criteria and mechanisms, which on the basis of a mere deviation gradually strengthened the rules and increased the punishment. A continuous gradation of the established, specialized and competent authorities (in the order of knowledge and in the order of power) which, without resort to arbitrariness, but strictly according to the regulations, by means of observation and assessment hierarchized, differentiated, judged, punished and moved gradually from the correction of irregularities to the punishment of crime. The 'carceral' with its many diffuse or compact forms, its institutions of supervision or constraint, of discreet surveillance and insistent coercion, assured the communication of punishments according to quality and quantity; it connected in series or disposed according to subtle divisions the minor and the serious penalties, the mild and the strict forms of treatment, bad marks and light sentences. You will end up in the convict-ship, the slightest indiscipline seems to say; and the harshest of prisons says to the prisoners condemned to life: I shall note the slightest irregularity in your conduct. The generality of the punitive function that the eighteenth century sought in the 'ideological' technique of representations and signs now had as its support the extension, the material framework, complex, dispersed, but coherent, of the various carceral mechanisms. As a result, a certain significant generality moved between the least irregularity and the greatest crime; it was no longer the offence, the attack on the common interest, it was the departure from the norm, the anomaly; it was this that haunted the school, the court, the asylum or the prison. It generalized in the sphere of meaning the function that the carceral generalized in the sphere of tactics. Replacing the adversary of the sovereign, the social enemy was transformed into a deviant, who brought with him the multiple danger of disorder, crime and madness. The carceral network linked, through innumerable relations, the two long, multiple series of the punitive and the abnormal.

2. The carceral, with its far-reaching networks, allows the recruitment of major 'delinquents'. It organizes what might be called 'disciplinary careers' in which, through various exclusions and rejections, a whole process is set in motion. In the classical period, there opened up in the confines or interstices of society the confused, tolerant, and dangerous domain of the 'outlaw' or at least of that which eluded the direct hold of power: an uncertain space that was for criminality a training ground and a region of refuge; there poverty, unemployment, pursued innocence, cunning, the struggle against the powerful, the refusal of obligations and laws, and organized crime all came together as chance and fortune would dictate; it was the domain of adventure that Gil Blas, Sheppard or Mandrin,[4] each in his own

4. Louis Mandrin (1724–1755), French highwayman. Gil Blas: rogue hero and title character of a picaresque French novel (1715–35) by Alain René Lesage. Jack Sheppard (1702–1724), famous English robber, the subject of several popular 18th-century plays, ballads, and books.

way, inhabited. Through the play of disciplinary differentiations and divisions, the nineteenth century constructed rigorous channels which, within the system, inculcated docility and produced delinquency by the same mechanisms. There was a sort of disciplinary 'training', continuous and compelling, that had something of the pedagogical curriculum and something of the professional network. Careers emerged from it, as secure, as predictable, as those of public life: assistance associations, residential apprenticeships, penal colonies, disciplinary battalions, prisons, hospitals, almshouses. These networks were already well mapped out at the beginning of the nineteenth century: 'Our benevolent establishments present an admirably coordinated whole by means of which the indigent does not remain a moment without help from the cradle to the grave. Follow the course of the unfortunate man: you will see him born among foundlings; from there he passes to the nursery, then to an orphanage; at the age of six he goes off to primary school and later to adult schools. If he cannot work, he is placed on the list of the charity offices of his district, and if he falls ill he may choose between twelve hospitals . . . Lastly, when the poor Parisian reaches the end of his career, seven almshouses await his age and often their salubrious régime has prolonged his useless days well beyond those of the rich man'.[5]

The carceral network does not cast the unassimilable into a confused hell; there is no outside. It takes back with one hand what it seems to exclude with the other. It saves everything, including what it punishes. It is unwilling to waste even what it has decided to disqualify. In this panoptic[6] society of which incarceration is the omnipresent armature, the delinquent is not outside the law; he is, from the very outset, in the law, at the very heart of the law, or at least in the midst of those mechanisms that transfer the individual imperceptibly from discipline to the law, from deviation to offence. Although it is true that prison punishes delinquency, delinquency is for the most part produced in and by an incarceration which, ultimately, prison perpetuates in its turn. The prison is merely the natural consequence, no more than a higher degree, of that hierarchy laid down step by step. The delinquent is an institutional product. It is no use being surprised, therefore, that in a considerable proportion of cases the biography of convicts passes through all these mechanisms and establishments, whose purpose, it is widely believed, is to lead away from prison. That one should find in them what one might call the index of an irrepressibly delinquent 'character': the prisoner condemned to hard labour was meticulously produced by a childhood spent in a reformatory, according to the lines of force of the generalized carceral system. Conversely, the lyricism of marginality may find inspiration in the image of the 'outlaw', the great social nomad, who prowls on the confines of a docile, frightened order. But it is not on the fringes of society and through successive exiles that criminality is born, but by means of ever more closely placed insertions, under ever more insistent surveillance, by an accumulation of disciplinary coercion. In

5. Moreau de Jonnès, quoted in H. du Touquet, *De la condition des classes pauvres* (1846) [Foucault's note].

6. All-seeing. Jeremy Bentham (1748–1832), English philosopher and reformer, designed an ideal circular prison, which he called the Panopticon, in which the prisoners could be kept under constant surveillance by a single guard in a central tower. In an earlier section of *Discipline and Punish*, Foucault presents this prison as a model and summation of disciplinary power.

short, the carceral archipelago assures, in the depths of the social body, the formation of delinquency on the basis of subtle illegalities, the overlapping of the latter by the former and the establishment of a specified criminality.

3. But perhaps the most important effect of the carceral system and of its extension well beyond legal imprisonment is that it succeeds in making the power to punish natural and legitimate, in lowering at least the threshold of tolerance to penalty. It tends to efface what may be exorbitant in the exercise of punishment. It does this by playing the two registers in which it is deployed—the legal register of justice and the extra-legal register of discipline—against one another. In effect, the great continuity of the carceral system throughout the law and its sentences gives a sort of legal sanction to the disciplinary mechanisms, to the decisions and judgements that they enforce. Throughout this network, which comprises so many 'regional' institutions, relatively autonomous and independent, is transmitted, with the 'prison-form', the model of justice itself. The regulations of the disciplinary establishments may reproduce the law, the punishments imitate the verdicts and penalties, the surveillance repeat the police model; and, above all these multiple establishments, the prison, which in relation to them is a pure form, unadulterated and unmitigated, gives them a sort of official sanction. The carceral, with its long gradation stretching from the convict-ship or imprisonment with hard labour to diffuse, slight limitations, communicates a type of power that the law validates and that justice uses as its favourite weapon. How could the disciplines and the power that functions in them appear arbitrary, when they merely operate the mechanisms of justice itself, even with a view to mitigating their intensity? When, by generalizing its effects and transmitting it to every level, it makes it possible to avoid its full rigour? Carceral continuity and the fusion of the prison-form make it possible to legalize, or in any case to legitimate disciplinary power, which thus avoids any element of excess or abuse it may entail.

But, conversely, the carceral pyramid gives to the power to inflict legal punishment a context in which it appears to be free of all excess and all violence. In the subtle gradation of the apparatuses of discipline and of the successive 'embeddings' that they involve, the prison does not at all represent the unleashing of a different kind of power, but simply an additional degree in the intensity of a mechanism that has continued to operate since the earliest forms of legal punishment. Between the latest institution of 'rehabilitation', where one is taken in order to avoid prison, and the prison where one is sent after a definable offence, the difference is (and must be) scarcely perceptible. There is a strict economy that has the effect of rendering as discreet as possible the singular power to punish. There is nothing in it now that recalls the former excess of sovereign power when it revenged its authority on the tortured body of those about to be executed.[7] Prison continues, on those who are entrusted to it, a work begun elsewhere, which the whole of the society pursues on each individual through innumerable mechanisms of discipline. By means of a carceral continuum, the authority that sentences infiltrates all those other authorities that supervise, trans-

7. In earlier sections of *Discipline and Punish*, Foucault argues that autocratic power prior to 1789 operated directly and theatrically on an offender's body for a short time, as contrasted to the continuous discreet disciplinary work on bodies that is characteristic of modern carceral society.

form, correct, improve. It might even be said that nothing really distinguishes them any more except the singularly 'dangerous' character of the delinquents, the gravity of their departures from normal behaviour and the necessary solemnity of the ritual. But, in its function, the power to punish is not essentially different from that of curing or educating. It receives from them, and from their lesser, smaller task, a sanction from below; but one that is no less important for that, since it is the sanction of technique and rationality. The carceral 'naturalizes' the legal power to punish, as it 'legalizes' the technical power to discipline. In thus homogenizing them, effacing what may be violent in one and arbitrary in the other, attenuating the effects of revolt that they may both arouse, thus depriving excess in either of any purpose, circulating the same calculated, mechanical and discreet methods from one to the other, the carceral makes it possible to carry out that great 'economy' of power whose formula the eighteenth century had sought, when the problem of the accumulation and useful administration of men first emerged.

By operating at every level of the social body and by mingling ceaselessly the art of rectifying and the right to punish, the universality of the carceral lowers the level from which it becomes natural and acceptable to be punished. The question is often posed as to how, before and after the Revolution, a new foundation was given to the right to punish. And no doubt the answer is to be found in the theory of the contract.[8] But it is perhaps more important to ask the reverse question: how were people made to accept the power to punish, or quite simply, when punished, tolerate being so. The theory of the contract can only answer this question by the fiction of a juridical subject giving to others the power to exercise over him the right that he himself possesses over them. It is highly probable that the great carceral continuum, which provides a communication between the power of discipline and the power of the law, and extends without interruption from the smallest coercions to the longest penal detention, constituted the technical and real, immediately material counterpart of that chimerical granting of the right to punish.

4. With this new economy of power, the carceral system, which is its basic instrument, permitted the emergence of a new form of 'law': a mixture of legality and nature, prescription and constitution, the norm. This had a whole series of effects: the internal dislocation of the judicial power or at least of its functioning; an increasing difficulty in judging, as if one were ashamed to pass sentence; a furious desire on the part of the judges to judge, assess, diagnose, recognize the normal and abnormal and claim the honour of curing or rehabilitating. In view of this, it is useless to believe in the good or bad consciences of judges, or even of their unconscious. Their immense 'appetite for medicine' which is constantly manifested—from their appeal to psychiatric experts, to their attention to the chatter of criminology—expresses the major fact that the power they exercise has been 'denatured'; that it is at a certain level governed by laws; that at another, more fundamental level it functions as a normative power; it is the economy of power

8. The "social contract" theory expounded by the political philosophers Thomas Hobbes (1588–1679), John Locke (1632–1704), and Jean-Jacques Rousseau (1712–1778); it explains states' power over individuals by positing an original contract in which those individuals cede power to the state in return for protection.

that they exercise, and not that of their scruples or their humanism, that makes them pass 'therapeutic' sentences and recommend 'rehabilitating' periods of imprisonment. But, conversely, if the judges accept ever more reluctantly to condemn for the sake of condemning, the activity of judging has increased precisely to the extent that the normalizing power has spread. Borne along by the omnipresence of the mechanisms of discipline, basing itself on all the carceral apparatuses, it has become one of the major functions of our society. The judges of normality are present everywhere. We are in the society of the teacher-judge, the doctor-judge, the educator-judge, the 'social worker'-judge; it is on them that the universal reign of the normative is based; and each individual, wherever he may find himself, subjects to it his body, his gestures, his behaviour, his aptitudes, his achievements. The carceral network, in its compact or disseminated forms, with its systems of insertion, distribution, surveillance, observation, has been the greatest support, in modern society, of the normalizing power.

5. The carceral texture of society assures both the real capture of the body and its perpetual observation; it is, by its very nature, the apparatus of punishment that conforms most completely to the new economy of power and the instrument for the formation of knowledge that this very economy needs. Its panoptic functioning enables it to play this double role. By virtue of its methods of fixing, dividing, recording, it has been one of the simplest, crudest, also most concrete, but perhaps most indispensable conditions for the development of this immense activity of examination that has objectified human behaviour. If, after the age of 'inquisitorial' justice, we have entered the age of 'examinatory' justice,[9] if, in an even more general way, the method of examination has been able to spread so widely throughout society, and to give rise in part to the sciences of man, one of the great instruments for this has been the multiplicity and close overlapping of the various mechanisms of incarceration. I am not saying that the human sciences emerged from the prison. But, if they have been able to be formed and to produce so many profound changes in the episteme,[1] it is because they have been conveyed by a specific and new modality of power: a certain policy of the body, a certain way of rendering the group of men docile and useful. This policy required the involvement of definite relations of knowledge in relations of power; it called for a technique of overlapping subjection and objectification; it brought with it new procedures of individualization. The carceral network constituted one of the armatures of this power-knowledge that has made the human sciences historically possible. Knowable man (soul, individuality, consciousness, conduct, whatever it is called) is the object-effect of this analytical investment, of this domination-observation.

6. This no doubt explains the extreme solidity of the prison, that slight invention that was nevertheless decried from the outset. If it had been no more than an instrument of rejection or repression in the service of a state apparatus, it would have been easier to alter its more overt forms or to find a more acceptable substitute for it. But, rooted as it was in mechanisms and

9. Earlier in *Discipline and Punish*, Foucault discusses the development of examination techniques in churches, schools, hospitals, the military, and other institutions.

1. Foucault's term for the unconscious deep structure that undergirds a historical period's conscious beliefs and knowledge.

strategies of power, it could meet any attempt to transform it with a great force of inertia. One fact is characteristic: when it is a question of altering the system of imprisonment, opposition does not come from the judicial institutions alone; resistance is to be found not in the prison as penal sanction, but in the prison with all its determinations, links and extra-judicial results; in the prison as the relay in a general network of disciplines and surveillances; in the prison as it functions in a panoptic régime. This does not mean that it cannot be altered, nor that it is once and for all indispensable to our kind of society. One may, on the contrary, cite the two processes which, in the very continuity of the processes that make the prison function, are capable of exercising considerable restraint on its use and of transforming its internal functioning. And no doubt these processes have already begun to a large degree. The first is that which reduces the utility (or increases its inconveniences) of a delinquency accommodated as a specific illegality, locked up and supervised; thus the growth of great national or international illegalities directly linked to the political and economic apparatuses (financial illegalities, information services, arms and drugs trafficking, property speculation) makes it clear that the somewhat rustic and conspicuous work force of delinquency is proving ineffective; or again, on a smaller scale, as soon as the economic levy on sexual pleasure is carried out more efficiently by the sale of contraceptives, or obliquely through publications, films or shows, the archaic hierarchy of prostitution loses much of its former usefulness. The second process is the growth of the disciplinary networks, the multiplication of their exchanges with the penal apparatus, the ever more important powers that are given them, the ever more massive transference to them of judicial functions; now, as medicine, psychology, education, public assistance, 'social work' assume an ever greater share of the powers of supervision and assessment, the penal apparatus will be able, in turn, to become medicalized, psychologized, educationalized; and by the same token that turning-point represented by the prison becomes less useful when, through the gap between its penitentiary discourse and its effect of consolidating delinquency, it articulates the penal power and the disciplinary power. In the midst of all these mechanisms of normalization, which are becoming ever more rigorous in their application, the specificity of the prison and its role as link are losing something of their purpose.

If there is an overall political issue around the prison, it is not therefore whether it is to be corrective or not; whether the judges, the psychiatrists or the sociologists are to exercise more power in it than the administrators or supervisors; it is not even whether we should have prison or something other than prison. At present, the problem lies rather in the steep rise in the use of these mechanisms of normalization and the wide-ranging powers which, through the proliferation of new disciplines, they bring with them.

In 1836, a correspondent wrote to *La Phalange*: 'Moralists, philosophers, legislators, flatterers of civilization, this is the plan of your Paris, neatly ordered and arranged, here is the improved plan in which all like things are gathered together. At the centre, and within a first enclosure: hospitals for all diseases, almshouses for all types of poverty, madhouses, prisons, convict-prisons for men, women and children. Around the first enclosure, barracks, courtrooms, police stations, houses for prison warders, scaffolds, houses for the executioner and his assistants. At the four corners, the Chamber of Deputies, the Chamber of Peers, the Institute and the Royal Palace. Outside, there are the various services that supply the central enclosure, commerce, with its swindlers and its bankruptcies; industry and its furious struggles; the press, with its sophisms; the gambling dens; prostitution, the people dying of hunger or wallowing in debauchery, always ready to lend an ear to the voice of the Genius of Revolutions; the heartless rich . . . Lastly the ruthless war of all against all'.[2]

I shall stop with this anonymous text. We are now far away from the country of tortures, dotted with wheels, gibbets, gallows, pillories; we are far, too, from that dream of the reformers, less than fifty years before: the city of punishments in which a thousand small theatres would have provided an endless multicoloured representation of justice in which the punishments, meticulously produced on decorative scaffolds, would have constituted the permanent festival of the penal code. The carceral city, with its imaginary 'geo-politics', is governed by quite different principles. The extract from *La Phalange* reminds us of some of the more important ones: that at the centre of this city, and as if to hold it in place, there is, not the 'centre of power', not a network of forces, but a multiple network of diverse elements—walls, space, institution, rules, discourse; that the model of the carceral city is not, therefore, the body of the king,[3] with the powers that emanate from it, nor the contractual meeting of wills from which a body that was both individual and collective was born, but a strategic distribution of elements of different natures and levels. That the prison is not the daughter of laws, codes or the judicial apparatus; that it is not subordinated to the court and the docile or clumsy instrument of the sentences that it hands out and of the results that it would like to achieve; that it is the court that is external and subordinate to the prison. That in the central position that it occupies, it is not alone, but linked to a whole series of 'carceral' mechanisms which seem distinct enough—since they are intended to alleviate pain, to cure, to comfort—but which all tend, like the prison, to exercise a power of normalization. That these mechanisms are applied not to transgressions against a 'central' law, but to the apparatus of production—'commerce' and 'industry'—to a whole multiplicity of illegalities, in all their diversity of nature and origin, their specific role in profit and the different ways in which they are dealt with by the punitive mechanisms. And that ultimately what presides over all these mechanisms is not the unitary functioning of an apparatus or an institution, but the necessity of combat and the rules of strategy. That, consequently, the notions of institutions of repression, rejection, exclusion, marginalization, are not adequate to describe, at the very centre of the carceral city, the formation of the insidious leniencies, unavowable petty cruelties, small acts of cunning, calculated methods, techniques, 'sciences' that permit the fabrication of the disciplinary individual. In this central and centralized humanity, the effect and instrument of complex power relations, bodies and forces subjected by multiple mechanisms of 'incarceration', objects for discourses

2. *La Phalange*, 10 August 1836 [Foucault's note]. "War of all against all": in *Leviathan* (1651), Hobbes described "the condition of man" as "a condition of war of everyone against everyone." *La Phalange* was a socialist journal.

3. The idea of modeling the city on the human body was common in the Renaissance (see especially the *Treatise* of Francesco di Giorgio, 1439–1501/2).

that are in themselves elements for this strategy, we must hear the distant roar of battle.

At this point I end a book that must serve as a historical background to various studies of the power of normalization and the formation of knowledge in modern society.

1975

From The History of Sexuality, Volume 1, An Introduction[1]

Part Two: The Repressive Hypothesis

CHAPTER 1.
THE INCITEMENT TO DISCOURSE

The seventeenth century, then, was the beginning of an age of repression emblematic of what we call the bourgeois societies, an age which perhaps we still have not completely left behind. Calling sex by its name thereafter became more difficult and more costly. As if in order to gain mastery over it in reality, it had first been necessary to subjugate it at the level of language, control its free circulation in speech, expunge it from the things that were said, and extinguish the words that rendered it too visibly present. And even these prohibitions, it seems, were afraid to name it. Without even having to pronounce the word, modern prudishness was able to ensure that one did not speak of sex, merely through the interplay of prohibitions that referred back to one another: instances of muteness which, by dint of saying nothing, imposed silence. Censorship.

Yet when one looks back over these last three centuries with their continual transformations, things appear in a very different light: around and apropos of sex, one sees a veritable discursive explosion. We must be clear on this point, however. It is quite possible that there was an expurgation—and a very rigorous one—of the authorized vocabulary. It may indeed be true that a whole rhetoric of allusion and metaphor was codified. Without question, new rules of propriety screened out some words: there was a policing of statements. A control over enunciations as well: where and when it was not possible to talk about such things became much more strictly defined; in which circumstances, among which speakers, and within which social relationships. Areas were thus established, if not of utter silence, at least of tact and discretion: between parents and children, for instance, or teachers and pupils, or masters and domestic servants. This almost certainly constituted a whole restrictive economy, one that was incorporated into that politics of language and speech—spontaneous on the one hand, concerted on the other—which accompanied the social redistributions of the classical period.[2]

At the level of discourses and their domains, however, practically the opposite phenomenon occurred. There was a steady proliferation of discourses concerned with sex—specific discourses, different from one another

1. Translated by Robert Hurley.
2. Foucault's term for (roughly) the period from 1650 to 1789.

both by their form and by their object: a discursive ferment that gathered momentum from the eighteenth century onward. Here I am thinking not so much of the probable increase in "illicit" discourses, that is, discourses of infraction that crudely named sex by way of insult or mockery of the new code of decency; the tightening up of the rules of decorum likely did produce, as a countereffect, a valorization and intensification of indecent speech. But more important was the multiplication of discourses concerning sex in the field of exercise of power itself: an institutional incitement to speak about it, and to do so more and more; a determination on the part of the agencies of power to hear it spoken about, and to cause *it* to speak through explicit articulation and endlessly accumulated detail.

Consider the evolution of the Catholic pastoral and the sacrament of penance after the Council of Trent.[3] Little by little, the nakedness of the questions formulated by the confession manuals of the Middle Ages, and a good number of those still in use in the seventeenth century, was veiled. One avoided entering into that degree of detail which some authors, such as Sanchez or Tamburini,[4] had for a long time believed indispensable for the confession to be complete: description of the respective positions of the partners, the postures assumed, gestures, places touched, caresses, the precise moment of pleasure—an entire painstaking review of the sexual act in its very unfolding. Discretion was advised, with increasing emphasis. The greatest reserve was counseled when dealing with sins against purity: "This matter is similar to pitch, for, however one might handle it, even to cast it far from oneself, it sticks nonetheless, and always soils."[5] And later, Alfonso de' Liguori prescribed starting—and possibly going no further, especially when dealing with children—with questions that were "roundabout and vague."[6]

But while the language may have been refined, the scope of the confession—the confession of the flesh—continually increased. This was partly because the Counter Reformation[7] busied itself with stepping up the rhythm of the yearly confession in the Catholic countries, and because it tried to impose meticulous rules of self-examination; but above all, because it attributed more and more importance in penance—and perhaps at the expense of some other sins—to all the insinuations of the flesh: thoughts, desires, voluptuous imaginings, delectations, combined movements of the body and the soul; henceforth all this had to enter, in detail, into the process of confession and guidance. According to the new pastoral, sex must not be named imprudently, but its aspects, its correlations, and its effects must be pursued down to their slenderest ramifications: a shadow in a daydream, an image too slowly dispelled, a badly exorcised complicity between the body's mechanics and the mind's complacency: everything had to be told. A twofold evolution tended to make the flesh into the root of all evil, shifting the most important moment of transgression from the act itself to the stirrings—so difficult to perceive and formulate—of desire. For this was

3. Series of meetings (1545–63) at which the Catholic hierarchy developed its response to the Protestant Reformation.
4. Tommaso Tamburini (1591–1675), Italian Jesuit theologian. Francisco Sanchez (ca. 1550–1623), Portuguese physician and philosopher.
5. Paolo Segneri, *L'Instruction du pénitent* (French translation 1695), p. 301 [Foucault's note]. Segneri (1624–1694), Italian Jesuit.
6. Alfonso de' Liguori, *La Pratique des confesseurs* (French translation 1854), p. 140 [Foucault's note]. Liguori (1696–1787), Italian prelate.
7. Effort (beginning with the Council of Trent) to secure the traditions of the Catholic Church against the innovations of the Protestant Reformation.

an evil that afflicted the whole man, and in the most secret of forms: "Examine diligently, therefore, all the faculties of your soul: memory, understanding, and will. Examine with precision all your senses as well. . . . Examine, moreover, all your thoughts, every word you speak, and all your actions. Examine even unto your dreams, to know if, once awakened, you did not give them your consent. And finally, do not think that in so sensitive and perilous a matter as this, there is anything trivial or insignificant."[8] Discourse, therefore, had to trace the meeting line of the body and the soul, following all its meanderings: beneath the surface of the sins, it would lay bare the unbroken nervure of the flesh. Under the authority of a language that had been carefully expurgated so that it was no longer directly named, sex was taken charge of, tracked down as it were, by a discourse that aimed to allow it no obscurity, no respite.

It was here, perhaps, that the injunction, so peculiar to the West, was laid down for the first time, in the form of a general constraint. I am not talking about the obligation to admit to violations of the laws of sex, as required by traditional penance; but of the nearly infinite task of telling—telling oneself and another, as often as possible, everything that might concern the interplay of innumerable pleasures, sensations, and thoughts which, through the body and the soul, had some affinity with sex. This scheme for transforming sex into discourse had been devised long before in an ascetic and monastic setting. The seventeenth century made it into a rule for everyone. It would seem in actual fact that it could scarcely have applied to any but a tiny elite; the great majority of the faithful who only went to confession on rare occasions in the course of the year escaped such complex prescriptions. But the important point no doubt is that this obligation was decreed, as an ideal at least, for every good Christian. An imperative was established: Not only will you confess to acts contravening the law, but you will seek to transform your desire, your every desire, into discourse. Insofar as possible, nothing was meant to elude this dictum, even if the words it employed had to be carefully neutralized. The Christian pastoral prescribed as a fundamental duty the task of passing everything having to do with sex through the endless mill of speech.[9] The forbidding of certain words, the decency of expressions, all the censorings of vocabulary, might well have been only secondary devices compared to that great subjugation: ways of rendering it morally acceptable and technically useful.

One could plot a line going straight from the seventeenth-century pastoral to what became its projection in literature, "scandalous" literature at that. "Tell everything," the directors would say time and again: "not only consummated acts, but sensual touchings, all impure gazes, all obscene remarks . . . all consenting thoughts."[1] Sade takes up the injunction in words that seem to have been retranscribed from the treatises of spirtual direction: "Your narrations must be decorated with the most numerous and searching details; the precise way and extent to which we may judge how the passion you

8. Segneri, *L'Instruction du pénitent*, pp. 301–2 [Foucault's note].

9. The reformed pastor also laid down rules, albeit in a more discreet way, for putting sex into discourse. This notion will be developed in the next volume, *The Body and the Flesh* [Foucault's note]. Foucault's plan later changed; the volumes he managed to complete deal instead with sexuality in the ancient world.

1. Alfonso de' Liguori, *Préceptes sur le sixième commandement* (French translation 1835), p. 5 [Foucault's note].

describe relates to human manners and man's character is determined by your willingness to disguise no circumstances; and what is more, the least circumstance is apt to have an immense influence upon the procuring of that kind of sensory irritation we expect from your stories."[2] And again at the end of the nineteenth century, the anonymous author of *My Secret Life* submitted to the same prescription; outwardly, at least, this man was doubtless a kind of traditional libertine; but he conceived the idea of complementing his life—which he had almost totally dedicated to sexual activity—with a scrupulous account of every one of its episodes. He sometimes excuses himself by stressing his concern to educate young people, this man who had eleven volumes published, in a printing of only a few copies, which were devoted to the least adventures, pleasures, and sensations of his sex. It is best to take him at his word when he lets into his text the voice of a pure imperative: "I recount the facts, just as they happened, insofar as I am able to recollect them; this is all that I can do"; "a secret life must not leave out anything; there is nothing to be ashamed of . . . one can never know too much concerning human nature."[3] The solitary author of *My Secret Life* often says, in order to justify his describing them, that his strangest practices undoubtedly were shared by thousands of men on the surface of the earth. But the guiding principle for the strangest of these practices, which was the fact of recounting them all, and in detail, from day to day, had been lodged in the heart of modern man for over two centuries. Rather than seeing in this singular man a courageous fugitive from a "Victorianism" that would have compelled him to silence, I am inclined to think that, in an epoch dominated by (highly prolix) directives enjoining discretion and modesty, he was the most direct and in a way the most naïve representative of a plurisecular injunction[4] to talk about sex. The historical accident would consist rather of the reticences of "Victorian puritanism"; at any rate, they were a digression, a refinement, a tactical diversion in the great process of transforming sex into discourse.

This nameless Englishman will serve better than his queen[5] as the central figure for a sexuality whose main features were already taking shape with the Christian pastoral. Doubtless, in contrast to the latter, for him it was a matter of augmenting the sensations he experienced with the details of what he said about them; like Sade, he wrote "for his pleasure alone," in the strongest sense of the expression; he carefully mixed the editing and rereading of his text with erotic scenes which those writer's activities repeated, prolonged, and stimulated. But after all, the Christian pastoral also sought to produce specific effects on desire, by the mere fact of transforming it—fully and deliberately—into discourse: effects of mastery and detachment, to be sure, but also an effect of spiritual reconversion, of turning back to God, a physical effect of blissful suffering from feeling in one's body the pangs of temptation and the love that resists it. This is the essential thing: that Western man has been drawn for three centuries to the task

2. Donatien-Alphonse de Sade, *The 120 Days of Sodom*, trans. Austryn Wainhouse and Richard Seaver (New York: Grove Press, 1966), p. 271 [Foucault's note (English edition supplied by translator)]. Marquis de Sade (1740–1814), French writer best known for his works of sexual fantasy.

3. Anonymous, *My Secret Life* (New York: Grove Press, 1966) [Foucault's note].

4. That is, an injunction from many parts of the secular (nonreligious) world.

5. Victoria (1819–1901), whose long reign (1837–1901) delimits the age that bears her name.

of telling everything concerning his sex; that since the classical age there has been a constant optimization and an increasing valorization of the discourse on sex; and that this carefully analytical discourse was meant to yield multiple effects of displacement, intensification, reorientation, and modification of desire itself. Not only were the boundaries of what one could say about sex enlarged, and men compelled to hear it said; but more important, discourse was connected to sex by a complex organization with varying effects, by a deployment that cannot be adequately explained merely by referring it to a law of prohibition. A censorship of sex? There was installed rather an apparatus for producing an ever greater quantity of discourse about sex, capable of functioning and taking effect in its very economy.

This technique might have remained tied to the destiny of Christian spirituality if it had not been supported and relayed by other mechanisms. In the first place, by a "public interest." Not a collective curiosity or sensibility; not a new mentality; but power mechanisms that functioned in such a way that discourse on sex—for reasons that will have to be examined—became essential. Toward the beginning of the eighteenth century, there emerged a political, economic, and technical incitement to talk about sex. And not so much in the form of a general theory of sexuality as in the form of analysis, stocktaking, classification, and specification, of quantitative or causal studies. This need to take sex "into account," to pronounce a discourse on sex that would not derive from morality alone but from rationality as well, was sufficiently new that at first it wondered at itself and sought apologies for its own existence. How could a discourse based on reason speak of *that?* "Rarely have philosophers directed a steady gaze to these objects situated between disgust and ridicule, where one must avoid both hypocrisy and scandal."[6] And nearly a century later, the medical establishment, which one might have expected to be less surprised by what it was about to formulate, still stumbled at the moment of speaking: "The darkness that envelops these facts, the shame and disgust they inspire, have always repelled the observer's gaze. . . . For a long time I hesitated to introduce the loathsome picture into this study."[7] What is essential is not in all these scruples, in the "moralism" they betray, or in the hypocrisy one can suspect them of, but in the recognized necessity of overcoming this hesitation. One had to speak of sex; one had to speak publicly and in a manner that was not determined by the division between licit and illicit, even if the speaker maintained the distinction for himself (which is what these solemn and preliminary declarations were intended to show): one had to speak of it as of a thing to be not simply condemned or tolerated but managed, inserted into systems of utility, regulated for the greater good of all, made to function according to an optimum. Sex was not something one simply judged; it was a thing one administered. It was in the nature of a public potential; it called for management procedures; it had to be taken charge of by analytical discourses. In the eighteenth century, sex became a "police" matter—in the full and strict sense given the term at the time: not the repression of disorder, but an ordered maximization of collective and individual forces: "We must con-

6. Condorcet, cited by Jean-Louis Flandrin, *Familles: Parenté, maison, sexualité dans l'ancienne société* (Paris: Hachette, 1976) [Foucault's note]. Marquis de Condorcet (1743–1794), French mathematician and philosopher.

7. Auguste Tardieu, *Étude médico-légale sur les attentats aux moeurs* (1857), p. 114 [Foucault's note].

solidate and augment, through the wisdom of its regulations, the internal power of the state; and since this power consists not only in the Republic in general, and in each of the members who constitute it, but also in the faculties and talents of those belonging to it, it follows that the police must concern themselves with these means and make them serve the public welfare. And they can only obtain this result through the knowledge they have of those different assets."[8] A policing of sex: that is, not the rigor of a taboo, but the necessity of regulating sex through useful and public discourses.

A few examples will suffice. One of the great innovations in the techniques of power in the eighteenth century was the emergence of "population" as an economic and political problem: population as wealth, population as manpower or labor capacity, population balanced between its own growth and the resources it commanded. Governments perceived that they were not dealing simply with subjects, or even with a "people," but with a "population," with its specific phenomena and its peculiar variables: birth and death rates, life expectancy, fertility, state of health, frequency of illnesses, patterns of diet and habitation. All these variables were situated at the point where the characteristic movements of life and the specific effects of institutions intersected: "States are not populated in accordance with the natural progression of propagation, but by virtue of their industry, their products, and their different institutions. . . . Men multiply like the yields from the ground and in proportion to the advantages and resources they find in their labors."[9] At the heart of this economic and political problem of population was sex: it was necessary to analyze the birthrate, the age of marriage, the legitimate and illegitimate births, the precocity and frequency of sexual relations, the ways of making them fertile or sterile, the effects of unmarried life or of the prohibitions, the impact of contraceptive practices—of those notorious "deadly secrets" which demographers on the eve of the Revolution knew were already familiar to the inhabitants of the countryside.

Of course, it had long been asserted that a country had to be populated if it hoped to be rich and powerful; but this was the first time that a society had affirmed, in a constant way, that its future and its fortune were tied not only to the number and the uprightness of its citizens, to their marriage rules and family organization, but to the manner in which each individual made use of his sex. Things went from ritual lamenting over the unfruitful debauchery of the rich, bachelors, and libertines to a discourse in which the sexual conduct of the population was taken both as an object of analysis and as a target of intervention; there was a progression from the crudely populationist arguments of the mercantilist epoch to the much more subtle and calculated attempts at regulation that tended to favor or discourage—according to the objectives and exigencies of the moment—an increasing birthrate. Through the political economy of population there was formed a whole grid of observations regarding sex. There emerged the analysis of the modes of sexual conduct, their determinations and their effects, at the boundary line of the biological and the economic domains. There also

8. Johann von Justi, *Éléments généraux de police* (French translation 1769), p. 20 [Foucault's note].

9. Claude-Jacques Herbert, *Essai sur la police générale des grains* (1753), pp. 320–21 [Foucault's note].

appeared those systematic campaigns which, going beyond the traditional means—moral and religious exhortations, fiscal measures—tried to transform the sexual conduct of couples into a concerted economic and political behavior. In time these new measures would become anchorage points for the different varieties of racism of the nineteenth and twentieth centuries. It was essential that the state know what was happening with its citizens' sex, and the use they made of it, but also that each individual be capable of controlling the use he made of it. Between the state and the individual, sex became an issue, and a public issue no less; a whole web of discourses, special knowledges, analyses, and injunctions settled upon it.

The situation was similar in the case of children's sex. It is often said that the classical period consigned it to an obscurity from which it scarcely emerged before the *Three Essays* or the beneficent anxieties of Little Hans.[1] It is true that a longstanding "freedom" of language between children and adults, or pupils and teachers, may have disappeared. No seventeenth-century pedagogue would have publicly advised his disciple, as did Erasmus[2] in his *Dialogues*, on the choice of a good prostitute. And the boisterous laughter that had accompanied the precocious sexuality of children for so long—and in all social classes, it seems—was gradually stifled. But this was not a plain and simple imposition of silence. Rather, it was a new regime of discourses. Not any less was said about it; on the contrary. But things were said in a different way; it was different people who said them, from different points of view, and in order to obtain different results. Silence itself—the things one declines to say, or is forbidden to name, the discretion that is required between different speakers—is less the absolute limit of discourse, the other side from which it is separated by a strict boundary, than an element that functions alongside the things said, with them and in relation to them within over-all strategies. There is no binary division to be made between what one says and what one does not say; we must try to determine the different ways of not saying such things, how those who can and those who cannot speak of them are distributed, which type of discourse is authorized, or which form of discretion is required in either case. There is not one but many silences, and they are an integral part of the strategies that underlie and permeate discourses.

Take the secondary schools of the eighteenth century, for example. On the whole, one can have the impression that sex was hardly spoken of at all in these institutions. But one only has to glance over the architectural layout, the rules of discipline, and their whole internal organization: the question of sex was a constant preoccupation. The builders considered it explicitly. The organizers took it permanently into account. All who held a measure of authority were placed in a state of perpetual alert, which the fixtures, the precautions taken, the interplay of punishments and responsibilities, never ceased to reiterate. The space for classes, the shape of the tables, the planning of the recreation lessons, the distribution of the dormitories (with or without partitions, with or without curtains), the rules for monitoring bedtime and sleep periods—all this referred, in the most prolix manner, to

1. SIGMUND FREUD's *Three Essays on Sexuality* was published in 1905; his case study of Little Hans, titled "Analysis of a Phobia of a Five-Year-Old Boy," dates from 1909.

2. Dutch humanist scholar (1466–1536); his *Dialogues* (1518) covers a wide variety of topics.

the sexuality of children.[3] What one might call the internal discourse of the institution—the one it employed to address itself, and which circulated among those who made it function—was largely based on the assumption that this sexuality existed, that it was precocious, active, and ever present. But this was not all: the sex of the schoolboy became in the course of the eighteenth century—and quite apart from that of adolescents in general—a public problem. Doctors counseled the directors and professors of educational establishments, but they also gave their opinions to families; educators designed projects which they submitted to the authorities; schoolmasters turned to students, made recommendations to them, and drafted for their benefit books of exhortation, full of moral and medical examples. Around the schoolboy and his sex there proliferated a whole literature of precepts, opinions, observations, medical advice, clinical cases, outlines for reform, and plans for ideal institutions. With Basedow[4] and the German "philanthropic" movement, this transformation of adolescent sex into discourse grew to considerable dimensions. Salzmann[5] even organized an experimental school which owed its exceptional character to a supervision and education of sex so well thought out that youth's universal sin would never need to be practiced there. And with all these measures taken, the child was not to be simply the mute and unconscious object of attentions prearranged between adults only; a certain reasonable, limited, canonical, and truthful discourse on sex was prescribed for him—a kind of discursive orthopedics.[6] The great festival organized at the Philanthropinum in May of 1776 can serve as a vignette in this regard. Taking the form of an examination, mixed with floral games, the awarding of prizes, and a board of review, this was the first solemn communion of adolescent sex and reasonable discourse. In order to show the success of the sex education given the students, Basedow had invited all the dignitaries that Germany could muster (Goethe[7] was one of the few to decline the invitation). Before the assembled public, one of the professors, a certain Wolke, asked the students selected questions concerning the mysteries of sex, birth, and procreation. He had them comment on engravings that depicted a pregnant woman, a couple, and a cradle. The replies were enlightened, offered without shame or embarrassment. No unseemly laughter intervened to disturb them—except from the very ranks of an adult audience more childish than the children themselves, and whom Wolke severely reprimanded. At the end, they all applauded these cherub-faced boys who, in front of adults, had skillfully woven the garlands of discourse and sex.[8]

3. *Règlement de police pour les lycées* (1809),
art. 67: "There shall always be, during class and study hours, an instructor watching the exterior, so as to prevent students who have gone out to relieve themselves from stopping and congregating.
art. 68: "After the evening prayer, the students will be conducted back to the dormitory, where the schoolmasters will put them to bed at once.
art. 69: "The masters will not retire except after having made certain that every student is in bed.
art. 70: "The beds shall be separated by partitions two meters in height. The dormitories shall be illuminated during the night" [Foucault's note].

4. Johann Basedow (1724–1790), German teacher and educational reformer; his model school was the Philanthropinum, at Dessau.

5. Christian Salzmann (1744–1811), German educator.

6. Discourse that corrects children.

7. Johann Wolfgang von Goethe (1749–1832), German poet, dramatist, and novelist.

8. Johann Gottlieb Schummel, *Fritzens Reise nach Dessau* (1776), cited by Auguste Pinloche, *La Réforme de l'éducation en Allemagne au XVIIIe siècle* (1889), pp. 125–29 [Foucault's note].

It would be less than exact to say that the pedagogical institution has imposed a ponderous silence on the sex of children and adolescents. On the contrary, since the eighteenth century it has multiplied the forms of discourse on the subject; it has established various points of implantation for sex; it has coded contents and qualified speakers. Speaking about children's sex, inducing educators, physicians, administrators, and parents to speak of it, or speaking to them about it, causing children themselves to talk about it, and enclosing them in a web of discourses which sometimes address them, sometimes speak about them, or impose canonical bits of knowledge on them, or use them as a basis for constructing a science that is beyond their grasp—all this together enables us to link an intensification of the intervention of power to a multiplication of discourse. The sex of children and adolescents has become, since the eighteenth century, an important area of contention around which innumerable institutional devices and discursive strategies have been deployed. It may well be true that adults and children themselves were deprived of a certain way of speaking about sex, a mode that was disallowed as being too direct, crude, or coarse. But this was only the counterpart of other discourses, and perhaps the condition necessary in order for them to function, discourses that were interlocking, hierarchized, and all highly articulated around a cluster of power relations.

One could mention many other centers which in the eighteenth or nineteenth century began to produce discourses on sex. First there was medicine, via the "nervous disorders"; next psychiatry, when it set out to discover the etiology of mental illnesses, focusing its gaze first on "excess," then onanism, then frustration, then "frauds against procreation," but especially when it annexed the whole of the sexual perversions as its own province; criminal justice, too, which had long been concerned with sexuality, particularly in the form of "heinous" crimes and crimes against nature, but which, toward the middle of the nineteenth century, broadened its jurisdiction to include petty offenses, minor indecencies, insignificant perversions; and lastly, all those social controls, cropping up at the end of the last century, which screened the sexuality of couples, parents and children, dangerous and endangered adolescents—undertaking to protect, separate, and forewarn, signaling perils everywhere, awakening people's attention, calling for diagnoses, piling up reports, organizing therapies. These sites radiated discourses aimed at sex, intensifying people's awareness of it as a constant danger, and this in turn created a further incentive to talk about it.

One day in 1867, a farm hand from the village of Lapcourt, who was somewhat simple-minded, employed here then there, depending on the season, living hand-to-mouth from a little charity or in exchange for the worst sort of labor, sleeping in barns and stables, was turned in to the authorities. At the border of a field, he had obtained a few caresses from a little girl, just as he had done before and seen done by the village urchins round about him; for, at the edge of the wood, or in the ditch by the road leading to Saint-Nicolas, they would play the familiar game called "curdled milk."[9] So he was pointed out by the girl's parents to the mayor of the village, reported by the mayor to the gendarmes, led by the gendarmes to the judge, who indicted him and

9. She masturbated him.

turned him over first to a doctor, then to two other experts who not only wrote their report but also had it published.[1] What is the significant thing about this story? The pettiness of it all; the fact that this everyday occurrence in the life of village sexuality, these inconsequential bucolic pleasures, could become, from a certain time, the object not only of a collective intolerance but of a judicial action, a medical intervention, a careful clinical examination, and an entire theoretical elaboration. The thing to note is that they went so far as to measure the brainpan, study the facial bone structure, and inspect for possible signs of degenerescence the anatomy of this personage who up to that moment had been an integral part of village life; that they made him talk; that they questioned him concerning his thoughts, inclinations, habits, sensations, and opinions. And then, acquitting him of any crime, they decided finally to make him into a pure object of medicine and knowledge—an object to be shut away till the end of his life in the hospital at Maréville, but also one to be made known to the world of learning through a detailed analysis. One can be fairly certain that during this same period the Lapcourt schoolmaster was instructing the little villagers to mind their language and not to talk about all these things aloud. But this was undoubtedly one of the conditions enabling the institutions of knowledge and power to overlay this everyday bit of theater with their solemn discourse. So it was that our society—and it was doubtless the first in history to take such measures—assembled around these timeless gestures, these barely furtive pleasures between simple-minded adults and alert children, a whole machinery for speechifying, analyzing, and investigating.

Between the licentious Englishman, who earnestly recorded for his own purposes the singular episodes of his secret life, and his contemporary, this village halfwit who would give a few pennies to the little girls for favors the older ones refused him, there was without doubt a profound connection: in any case, from one extreme to the other, sex became something to say, and to say exhaustively in accordance with deployments that were varied, but all, in their own way, compelling. Whether in the form of a subtle confession in confidence or an authoritarian interrogation, sex—be it refined or rustic—had to be put into words. A great polymorphous injunction bound the Englishman and the poor Lorrainese peasant alike. As history would have it, the latter was named Jouy.[2]

Since the eighteenth century, sex has not ceased to provoke a kind of generalized discursive erethism.[3] And these discourses on sex did not multiply apart from or against power, but in the very space and as the means of its exercise. Incitements to speak were orchestrated from all quarters, apparatuses everywhere for listening and recording, procedures for observing, questioning, and formulating. Sex was driven out of hiding and constrained to lead a discursive existence. From the singular imperialism that compels everyone to transform their sexuality into a perpetual discourse, to the manifold mechanisms which, in the areas of economy, pedagogy, medicine, and justice, incite, extract, distribute, and institutionalize the sexual discourse,

1. H. Bonnet and J. Bulard, *Rapport médico-légal sur l'état mental de Ch.-J. Jouy*, January 4, 1868 [Foucault's note].

2. Jouy sounds like the past participle of *jouir*, the French verb meaning to enjoy, to delight in (something), but also to have an orgasm, to come [translator's note].

3. Abnormal irritability or responsiveness to stimulation.

an immense verbosity is what our civilization has required and organized. Surely no other type of society has ever accumulated—and in such a relatively short span of time—a similar quantity of discourses concerned with sex. It may well be that we talk about sex more than anything else; we set our minds to the task; we convince ourselves that we have never said enough on the subject, that, through inertia or submissiveness, we conceal from ourselves the blinding evidence, and that what is essential always eludes us, so that we must always start out once again in search of it. It is possible that where sex is concerned, the most long-winded, the most impatient of societies is our own.

But as this first overview shows, we are dealing less with *a* discourse on sex than with a multiplicity of discourses produced by a whole series of mechanisms operating in different institutions. The Middle Ages had organized around the theme of the flesh and the practice of penance a discourse that was markedly unitary. In the course of recent centuries, this relative uniformity was broken apart, scattered, and multiplied in an explosion of distinct discursivities which took form in demography, biology, medicine, psychiatry, psychology, ethics, pedagogy, and political criticism. More precisely, the secure bond that held together the moral theology of concupiscence and the obligation of confession (equivalent to the theoretical discourse on sex and its first-person formulation) was, if not broken, at least loosened and diversified: between the objectification of sex in rational discourses, and the movement by which each individual was set to the task of recounting his own sex, there has occurred, since the eighteenth century, a whole series of tensions, conflicts, efforts at adjustment, and attempts at retranscription. So it is not simply in terms of a continual extension that we must speak of this discursive growth; it should be seen rather as a dispersion of centers from which discourses emanated, a diversification of their forms, and the complex deployment of the network connecting them. Rather than the uniform concern to hide sex, rather than a general prudishness of language, what distinguishes these last three centuries is the variety, the wide dispersion of devices that were invented for speaking about it, for having it be spoken about, for inducing it to speak of itself, for listening, recording, transcribing, and redistributing what is said about it: around sex, a whole network of varying, specific, and coercive transpositions into discourse. Rather than a massive censorship, beginning with the verbal proprieties imposed by the Age of Reason, what was involved was regulated and polymorphous incitement to discourse.

The objection will doubtless be raised that if so many stimulations and constraining mechanisms were necessary in order to speak of sex, this was because there reigned over everyone a certain fundamental prohibition; only definite necessities—economic pressures, political requirements—were able to lift this prohibition and open a few approaches to the discourse on sex, but these were limited and carefully coded; so much talk about sex, so many insistent devices contrived for causing it to be talked about—but under strict conditions: does this not prove that it was an object of secrecy, and more important, that there is still an attempt to keep it that way? But this often-stated theme, that sex is outside of discourse and that only the removing of an obstacle, the breaking of a secret, can clear the way leading to it, is precisely what needs to be examined. Does it not partake of the injunction by which discourse is provoked? Is it not with the aim of inciting people to speak of sex that it is made to mirror, at the outer limit of every actual discourse, something akin to a secret whose discovery is imperative, a thing abusively reduced to silence, and at the same time difficult and necessary, dangerous and precious to divulge? We must not forget that by making sex into that which, above all else, had to be confessed, the Christian pastoral always presented it as the disquieting enigma: not a thing which stubbornly shows itself, but one which always hides, the insidious presence that speaks in a voice so muted and often disguised that one risks remaining deaf to it. Doubtless the secret does not reside in that basic reality in relation to which all the incitements to speak of sex are situated—whether they try to force the secret, or whether in some obscure way they reinforce it by the manner in which they speak of it. It is a question rather of a theme that forms part of the very mechanics of these incitements: a way of giving shape to the requirement to speak about the matter, a fable that is indispensable to the endlessly proliferating economy of the discourse on sex. What is peculiar to modern societies, in fact, is not that they consigned sex to a shadow existence, but that they dedicated themselves to speaking of it *ad infinitum*, while exploiting it as *the* secret.

CHAPTER 2.
THE PERVERSE IMPLANTATION

A possible objection: it would be a mistake to see in this proliferation of discourses merely a quantitative phenomenon, something like a pure increase, as if what was said in them were immaterial, as if the fact of speaking about sex were of itself more important than the forms of imperatives that were imposed on it by speaking about it. For was this transformation of sex into discourse not governed by the endeavor to expel from reality the forms of sexuality that were not amenable to the strict economy of reproduction: to say no to unproductive activities, to banish casual pleasures, to reduce or exclude practices whose object was not procreation? Through the various discourses, legal sanctions against minor perversions were multiplied; sexual irregularity was annexed to mental illness; from childhood to old age, a norm of sexual development was defined and all the possible deviations were carefully described; pedagogical controls and medical treatments were organized; around the least fantasies, moralists, but especially doctors, brandished the whole emphatic vocabulary of abomination. Were these anything more than means employed to absorb, for the benefit of a genitally centered sexuality, all the fruitless pleasures? All this garrulous attention which has us in a stew over sexuality, is it not motivated by one basic concern: to ensure population, to reproduce labor capacity, to perpetuate the form of social relations: in short, to constitute a sexuality that is economically useful and politically conservative?[4]

I still do not know whether this is the ultimate objective. But this much is certain: reduction has not been the means employed for trying to achieve it. The nineteenth century and our own have been rather the age of multiplication: a dispersion of sexualities, a strengthening of their disparate forms, a multiple implantation of "perversions." Our epoch has initiated sexual heterogeneities.

4. This paragraph encapsulates the received view against which Foucault will argue.

Up to the end of the eighteenth century, three major explicit codes—apart from the customary regularities and constraints of opinion—governed sexual practices: canonical law, the Christian pastoral, and civil law. They determined, each in its own way, the division between licit and illicit. They were all centered on matrimonial relations: the marital obligation, the ability to fulfill it, the manner in which one complied with it, the requirements and violences that accompanied it, the useless or unwarranted caresses for which it was a pretext, its fecundity or the way one went about making it sterile, the moments when one demanded it (dangerous periods of pregnancy or breast-feeding, forbidden times of Lent or abstinence), its frequency or infrequency, and so on. It was this domain that was especially saturated with prescriptions. The sex of husband and wife was beset by rules and recommendations. The marriage relation was the most intense focus of constraints; it was spoken of more than anything else; more than any other relation, it was required to give a detailed accounting of itself. It was under constant surveillance: if it was found to be lacking, it had to come forward and plead its case before a witness. The "rest" remained a good deal more confused: one only has to think of the uncertain status of "sodomy," or the indifference regarding the sexuality of children.

Moreover, these different codes did not make a clear distinction between violations of the rules of marriage and deviations with respect to genitality. Breaking the rules of marriage or seeking strange pleasures brought an equal measure of condemnation. On the list of grave sins, and separated only by their relative importance, there appeared debauchery (extramarital relations), adultery, rape, spiritual or carnal incest, but also sodomy, or the mutual "caress." As to the courts, they could condemn homosexuality as well as infidelity, marriage without parental consent, or bestiality. What was taken into account in the civil and religious jurisdictions alike was a general unlawfulness. Doubtless acts "contrary to nature" were stamped as especially abominable, but they were perceived simply as an extreme form of acts "against the law"; they were infringements of decrees which were just as sacred as those of marriage, and which had been established for governing the order of things and the plan of beings. Prohibitions bearing on sex were essentially of a juridical nature. The "nature" on which they were based was still a kind of law. For a long time hermaphrodites were criminals, or crime's offspring, since their anatomical disposition, their very being, confounded the law that distinguished the sexes and prescribed their union.

The discursive explosion of the eighteenth and nineteenth centuries caused this system centered on legitimate alliance to undergo two modifications. First, a centrifugal movement with respect to heterosexual monogamy. Of course, the array of practices and pleasures continued to be referred to it as their internal standard; but it was spoken of less and less, or in any case with a growing moderation. Efforts to find out its secrets were abandoned; nothing further was demanded of it than to define itself from day to day. The legitimate couple, with its regular sexuality, had a right to more discretion. It tended to function as a norm, one that was stricter, perhaps, but quieter. On the other hand, what came under scrutiny was the sexuality of children, mad men and women, and criminals; the sensuality of those who did not like the opposite sex; reveries, obsessions, petty manias, or great transports of rage. It was time for all these figures, scarcely noticed in the past, to step forward and speak, to make the difficult confession of what they were. No doubt they were condemned all the same; but they were listened to; and if regular sexuality happened to be questioned once again, it was through a reflux movement, originating in these peripheral sexualities.

Whence the setting apart of the "unnatural" as a specific dimension in the field of sexuality. This kind of activity assumed an autonomy with regard to the other condemned forms such as adultery or rape (and the latter were condemned less and less): to marry a close relative or practice sodomy, to seduce a nun or engage in sadism, to deceive one's wife or violate cadavers, became things that were essentially different. The area covered by the Sixth Commandment[5] began to fragment. Similarly, in the civil order, the confused category of "debauchery," which for more than a century had been one of the most frequent reasons for administrative confinement, came apart. From the debris, there appeared on the one hand infractions against the legislation (or morality) pertaining to marriage and the family, and on the other, offenses against the regularity of a natural function (offenses which, it must be added, the law was apt to punish). Here we have a likely reason, among others, for the prestige of Don Juan,[6] which three centuries have not erased. Underneath the great violator of the rules of marriage—stealer of wives, seducer of virgins, the shame of families, and an insult to husbands and fathers—another personage can be glimpsed: the individual driven, in spite of himself, by the somber madness of sex. Underneath the libertine, the pervert. He deliberately breaks the law, but at the same time, something like a nature gone awry transports him far from all nature; his death is the moment when the supernatural return of the crime and its retribution thwarts the flight into counternature. There were two great systems conceived by the West for governing sex: the law of marriage and the order of desires—and the life of Don Juan overturned them both. We shall leave it to psychoanalysts to speculate whether he was homosexual, narcissistic, or impotent.

Although not without delay and equivocation, the natural laws of matrimony and the immanent rules of sexuality began to be recorded on two separate registers. There emerged a world of perversion which partook of that of legal or moral infraction, yet was not simply a variety of the latter. An entire sub-race race was born, different—despite certain kinship ties—from the libertines of the past. From the end of the eighteenth century to our own, they circulated through the pores of society; they were always hounded, but not always by laws; were often locked up, but not always in prisons; were sick perhaps, but scandalous, dangerous victims, prey to a strange evil that also bore the name of vice and sometimes crime. They were children wise beyond their years, precocious little girls, ambiguous schoolboys, dubious servants and educators, cruel or maniacal husbands, solitary collectors, ramblers with bizarre impulses; they haunted the houses of correction, the penal colonies, the tribunals, and the asylums; they carried their infamy to the doctors and their sickness to the judges. This was the numberless family of perverts who were on friendly terms with delinquents and akin to madmen. In the course of the century they successively bore

5. "Thou shalt not commit adultery" (Exodus 20.14).

6. Legendary libertine, whose story is variously told in Molière's play (1665), Mozart's opera (1787), Byron's poem (1819–24), and elsewhere.

the stamp of "moral folly," "genital neurosis," "aberration of the genetic instinct," "degenerescence," or "physical imbalance."

What does the appearance of all these peripheral sexualities signify? Is the fact that they could appear in broad daylight a sign that the code had become more lax? Or does the fact that they were given so much attention testify to a stricter regime and to its concern to bring them under close supervision? In terms of repression, things are unclear. There was permissiveness, if one bears in mind that the severity of the codes relating to sexual offenses diminished considerably in the nineteenth century and that law itself often deferred to medicine. But an additional ruse of severity, if one thinks of all the agencies of control and all the mechanisms of surveillance that were put into operation by pedagogy or therapeutics. It may be the case that the intervention of the Church in conjugal sexuality and its rejection of "frauds" against procreation had lost much of their insistence over the previous two hundred years. But medicine made a forceful entry into the pleasures of the couple: it created an entire organic, functional, or mental pathology arising out of "incomplete" sexual practices; it carefully classified all forms of related pleasures; it incorporated them into the notions of "development" and instinctual "disturbances"; and it undertook to manage them.

Perhaps the point to consider is not the level of indulgence or the quantity of repression but the form of power that was exercised. When this whole thicket of disparate sexualities was labeled, as if to disentangle them from one another, was the object to exclude them from reality? It appears, in fact, that the function of the power exerted in this instance was not that of interdiction, and that it involved four operations quite different from simple prohibition.

1. Take the ancient prohibitions of consanguine marriages (as numerous and complex as they were) or the condemnation of adultery, with its inevitable frequency of occurrence; or on the other hand, the recent controls through which, since the nineteenth century, the sexuality of children has been subordinated and their "solitary habits" interfered with. It is clear that we are not dealing with one and the same power mechanism. Not only because in the one case it is a question of law and penality, and in the other, medicine and regimentation; but also because the tactics employed is not the same. On the surface, what appears in both cases is an effort at elimination that was always destined to fail and always constrained to begin again. But the prohibition of "incests" attempted to reach its objective through an asymptotic decrease in the thing it condemned, whereas the control of infantile sexuality hoped to reach it through a simultaneous propagation of its own power and of the object on which it was brought to bear. It proceeded in accordance with a twofold increase extended indefinitely. Educators and doctors combatted children's onanism like an epidemic that needed to be eradicated. What this actually entailed, throughout this whole secular campaign that mobilized the adult world around the sex of children, was using these tenuous pleasures as a prop, constituting them as secrets (that is, forcing them into hiding so as to make possible their discovery), tracing them back to their source, tracking them from their origins to their effects, searching out everything that might cause them or simply enable them to exist. Wherever there was the chance they might appear, devices of surveillance were installed; traps were laid for compelling admissions; inexhaustible

and corrective discourses were imposed; parents and teachers were alerted, and left with the suspicion that all children were guilty, and with the fear of being themselves at fault if their suspicions were not sufficiently strong; they were kept in readiness in the face of this recurrent danger; their conduct was prescribed and their pedagogy recodified; an entire medico-sexual regime took hold of the family milieu. The child's "vice" was not so much an enemy as a support; it may have been designated as the evil to be eliminated, but the extraordinary effort that went into the task that was bound to fail leads one to suspect that what was demanded of it was to persevere, to proliferate to the limits of the visible and the invisible, rather than to disappear for good. Always relying on this support, power advanced, multiplied its relays and its effects, while its target expanded, subdivided, and branched out, penetrating further into reality at the same pace. In appearance, we are dealing with a barrier system; but in fact, all around the child, indefinite *lines of penetration* were disposed.

2. This new persecution of the peripheral sexualities entailed an *incorporation of perversions* and a new *specification of individuals*. As defined by the ancient civil or canonical codes, sodomy was a category of forbidden acts; their perpetrator was nothing more than the juridical subject of them. The nineteenth-century homosexual became a personage, a past, a case history, and a childhood, in addition to being a type of life, a life form, and a morphology, with an indiscreet anatomy and possibly a mysterious physiology. Nothing that went into his total composition was unaffected by his sexuality. It was everywhere present in him: at the root of all his actions because it was their insidious and indefinitely active principle; written immodestly on his face and body because it was a secret that always gave itself away. It was consubstantial with him, less as a habitual sin than as a singular nature. We must not forget that the psychological, psychiatric, medical category of homosexuality was constituted from the moment it was characterized—Westphal's famous article of 1870[7] on "contrary sexual sensations" can stand as its date of birth—less by a type of sexual relations than by a certain quality of sexual sensibility, a certain way of inverting the masculine and the feminine in oneself. Homosexuality appeared as one of the forms of sexuality when it was transposed from the practice of sodomy onto a kind of interior androgyny, a hermaphrodism of the soul. The sodomite had been a temporary aberration; the homosexual was now a species.

So too were all those minor perverts whom nineteenth-century psychiatrists entomologized by giving them strange baptismal names: there were Krafft-Ebing's zoophiles and zooerasts, Rohleder's auto-monosexualists; and later, mixoscopophiles, gynecomasts, presbyophiles, sexoesthetic inverts, and dyspareunist women.[8] These fine names for heresies referred to a nature that

7. Carl Westphal, *Archiv für Neurologie*, 1870 [Foucault's note]. Westphal (1833–1890), German neurologist.

8. The scientists named are Richard Krafft-Ebing (1840–1902), a German psychiatrist best known for his study of sexual abnormalities, and Hermann Rohleder (1866–1938), a German physician who wrote extensively on sexual behavior. They and other psychiatrists labeled people who desire sexual contact with animals (zoophiles, zooerasts), people who masturbate but have no sexual contact with other people (auto-monosexualists), people who get sexual pleasure from viewing pictures of animals or humans having sexual intercourse (mixoscopophiles), men with enlarged breasts (gynecomasts), people who are sexually attracted to old men (presbyophiles), homosexuals who idealize the young male body (sexoesthetic inverts), and women for whom sexual intercourse is painful (dyspareunist women).

was overlooked by the law, but not so neglectful of itself that it did not go on producing more species, even where there was no order to fit them into. The machinery of power that focused on this whole alien strain did not aim to suppress it, but rather to give it an analytical, visible, and permanent reality: it was implanted in bodies, slipped in beneath modes of conduct, made into a principle of classification and intelligibility, established as a *raison d'être* and a natural order of disorder. Not the exclusion of these thousand aberrant sexualities, but the specification, the regional solidification of each one of them. The strategy behind this dissemination was to strew reality with them and incorporate them into the individual.

3. More than the old taboos, this form of power demanded constant, attentive, and curious presences for its exercise; it presupposed proximities; it proceeded through examination and insistent observation; it required an exchange of discourses, through questions that extorted admissions, and confidences that went beyond the questions that were asked. It implied a physical proximity and an interplay of intense sensations. The medicalization of the sexually peculiar was both the effect and the instrument of this. Imbedded in bodies, becoming deeply characteristic of individuals, the oddities of sex relied on a technology of health and pathology. And conversely, since sexuality was a medical and medicalizable object, one had to try and detect it—as a lesion, a dysfunction, or a symptom—in the depths of the organism, or on the surface of the skin, or among all the signs of behavior. The power which thus took charge of sexuality set about contacting bodies, caressing them with its eyes, intensifying areas, electrifying surfaces, dramatizing troubled moments. It wrapped the sexual body in its embrace. There was undoubtedly an increase in effectiveness and an extension of the domain controlled; but also a sensualization of power and a gain of pleasure. This produced a twofold effect: an impetus was given to power through its very exercise; an emotion rewarded the overseeing control and carried it further; the intensity of the confession renewed the questioner's curiosity; the pleasure discovered fed back to the power that encircled it. But so many pressing questions singularized the pleasures felt by the one who had to reply. They were fixed by a gaze, isolated and animated by the attention they received. Power operated as a mechanism of attraction; it drew out those peculiarities over which it kept watch. Pleasure spread to the power that harried it; power anchored the pleasure it uncovered.

The medical examination, the psychiatric investigation, the pedagogical report, and family controls may have the over-all and apparent objective of saying no to all wayward or unproductive sexualities, but the fact is that they function as mechanisms with a double impetus: pleasure and power. The pleasure that comes of exercising a power that questions, monitors, watches, spies, searches out, palpates, brings to light; and on the other hand, the pleasure that kindles at having to evade this power, flee from it, fool it, or travesty it. The power that lets itself be invaded by the pleasure it is pursuing; and opposite it, power asserting itself in the pleasure of showing off, scandalizing, or resisting. Capture and seduction, confrontation and mutual reinforcement: parents and children, adults and adolescents, educator and students, doctors and patients, the psychiatrist with his hysteric and his perverts, all have played this game continually since the nineteenth century. These attractions, these evasions, these circular incitements have traced around bodies and sexes, not boundaries not to be crossed, but *perpetual spirals of power and pleasure*.

4. Whence those *devices of sexual saturation* so characteristic of the space and the social rituals of the nineteenth century. People often say that modern society has attempted to reduce sexuality to the couple—the heterosexual and, insofar as possible, legitimate couple. There are equal grounds for saying that it has, if not created, at least outfitted and made to proliferate, groups with multiple elements and a circulating sexuality: a distribution of points of power, hierarchized and placed opposite to one another; "pursued" pleasures, that is, both sought after and searched out; compartmental sexualities that are tolerated or encouraged; proximities that serve as surveillance procedures, and function as mechanisms of intensification; contacts that operate as inductors. This is the way things worked in the case of the family, or rather the household, with parents, children, and in some instances, servants. Was the nineteenth-century family really a monogamic and conjugal cell? Perhaps to a certain extent. But it was also a network of pleasures and powers linked together at multiple points and according to transformable relationships. The separation of grown-ups and children, the polarity established between the parents' bedroom and that of the children (it became routine in the course of the century when working-class housing construction was undertaken), the relative segregation of boys and girls, the strict instructions as to the care of nursing infants (maternal breast-feeding, hygiene), the attention focused on infantile sexuality, the supposed dangers of masturbation, the importance attached to puberty, the methods of surveillance suggested to parents, the exhortations, secrets, and fears, the presence—both valued and feared—of servants: all this made the family, even when brought down to its smallest dimensions, a complicated network, saturated with multiple, fragmentary, and mobile sexualities. To reduce them to the conjugal relationship, and then to project the latter, in the form of a forbidden desire, onto the children, cannot account for this apparatus which, in relation to these sexualities, was less a principle of inhibition than an inciting and multiplying mechanism.[9] Educational or psychiatric institutions, with their large populations, their hierarchies, their spatial arrangements, their surveillance systems, constituted, alongside the family, another way of distributing the interplay of powers and pleasures; but they too delineated areas of extreme sexual saturation, with privileged spaces or rituals such as the classroom, the dormitory, the visit, and the consultation. The forms of a nonconjugal, nonmonogamous sexuality were drawn there and established.

Nineteenth-century "bourgeois" society—and it is doubtless still with us—was a society of blatant and fragmented perversion. And this was not by way of hypocrisy, for nothing was more manifest and more prolix, or more manifestly taken over by discourses and institutions. Not because, having tried to erect too rigid or too general a barrier against sexuality, society succeeded only in giving rise to a whole perverse outbreak and a long pathology of the sexual instinct. At issue, rather, is the type of power it brought to bear on the body and on sex. In point of fact, this power had neither the form of the law, nor the effects of the taboo. On the contrary, it acted by multiplication of singular sexualities. It did not set boundaries for sexuality; it extended

9. An oblique critique of Freud's concept of the Oedipus complex.

the various forms of sexuality, pursuing them according to lines of indefinite penetration. It did not exclude sexuality, but included it in the body as a mode of specification of individuals. It did not seek to avoid it; it attracted its varieties by means of spirals in which pleasure and power reinforced one another. It did not set up a barrier; it provided places of maximum saturation. It produced and determined the sexual mosaic. Modern society is perverse, not in spite of its puritanism or as if from a backlash provoked by its hypocrisy; it is in actual fact, and directly, perverse.

In actual fact. The manifold sexualities—those which appear with the different ages (sexualities of the infant or the child), those which become fixated on particular tastes or practices (the sexuality of the invert, the gerontophile,[1] the fetishist), those which, in a diffuse manner, invest relationships (the sexuality of doctor and patient, teacher and student, psychiatrist and mental patient), those which haunt spaces (the sexuality of the home, the school, the prison)—all form the correlate of exact procedures of power. We must not imagine that all these things that were formerly tolerated attracted notice and received a pejorative designation when the time came to give a regulative role to the one type of sexuality that was capable of reproducing labor power and the form of the family. These polymorphous conducts were actually extracted from people's bodies and from their pleasures; or rather, they were solidified in them; they were drawn out, revealed, isolated, intensified, incorporated, by multifarious power devices. The growth of perversions is not a moralizing theme that obsessed the scrupulous minds of the Victorians. It is the real product of the encroachment of a type of power on bodies and their pleasures. It is possible that the West has not been capable of inventing any new pleasures, and it has doubtless not discovered any original vices. But it has defined new rules for the game of powers and pleasures. The frozen countenance of the perversions is a fixture of this game.

Directly. This implantation of multiple perversions is not a mockery of sexuality taking revenge on a power that has thrust on it an excessively repressive law. Neither are we dealing with paradoxical forms of pleasure that turn back on power and invest it in the form of a "pleasure to be endured." The implantation of perversions is an instrument-effect: it is through the isolation, intensification, and consolidation of peripheral sexualities that the relations of power to sex and pleasure branched out and multiplied, measured the body, and penetrated modes of conduct. And accompanying this encroachment of powers, scattered sexualities rigidified, became stuck to an age, a place, a type of practice. A proliferation of sexualities through the extension of power; an optimization of the power to which each of these local sexualities gave a surface of intervention: this concatenation, particularly since the nineteenth century, has been ensured and relayed by the countless economic interests which, with the help of medicine, psychiatry, prostitution, and pornography, have tapped into both this analytical multiplication of pleasure and this optimization of the power that controls it. Pleasure and power do not cancel or turn back against one another; they seek out, overlap, and reinforce one another. They are linked together by complex mechanisms and devices of excitation and incitement.

1. Lover of the old.

We must therefore abandon the hypothesis that modern industrial societies ushered in an age of increased sexual repression. We have not only witnessed a visible explosion of unorthodox sexualities; but—and this is the important point—a deployment quite different from the law, even if it is locally dependent on procedures of prohibition, has ensured, through a network of interconnecting mechanisms, the proliferation of specific pleasures and the multiplication of disparate sexualities. It is said that no society has been more prudish; never have the agencies of power taken such care to feign ignorance of the thing they prohibited, as if they were determined to have nothing to do with it. But it is the opposite that has become apparent, at least after a general review of the facts: never have there existed more centers of power; never more attention manifested and verbalized; never more circular contacts and linkages; never more sites where the intensity of pleasures and the persistency of power catch hold, only to spread elsewhere.

1976

From "Society Must Be Defended"[1]

From *Chapter 11. 17 March 1976*

[BIOPOWER]

* * *

It seems to me that one of the basic phenomena of the nineteenth century was what might be called power's hold over life. What I mean is the acquisition of power over man insofar as man is a living being, that the biological came under State control, that there was at least a certain tendency that leads to what might be termed State control of the biological. And I think that in order to understand what was going on, it helps if we refer to what used to be the classical theory of sovereignty, which ultimately provided us with the backdrop to—a picture of—all these analyses of war, races, and so on. You know that in the classical theory of sovereignty, the right of life and death was one of sovereignty's basic attributes. Now the right of life and death is a strange right. Even at the theoretical level, it is a strange right. What does having the right of life and death actually mean? In one sense, to say that the sovereign has a right of life and death means that he can, basically, either have people put to death or let them live, or in any case that life and death are not natural or immediate phenomena which are primal or radical, and which fall outside the field of power. If we take the argument a little further, or to the point where it becomes paradoxical, it means that in terms of his relationship with the sovereign, the subject is, by rights, neither dead nor alive. From the point of view of life and death, the subject is neutral, and it is thanks to the sovereign that the subject has the right to be alive or, possibly, the right to be dead. In any case, the lives and deaths of subjects become rights only as a result of the will of the sovereign. That is, if you like, the theoretical paradox. And it is of course a theoretical paradox that must have as its corollary a sort of practi-

1. Translated by David Macey.

cal disequilibrium. What does the right of life and death actually mean? Obviously not that the sovereign can grant life in the same way that he can inflict death. The right of life and death is always exercised in an unbalanced way: the balance is always tipped in favor of death. Sovereign power's effect on life is exercised only when the sovereign can kill. The very essence of the right of life and death is actually the right to kill: it is at the moment when the sovereign can kill that he exercises his right over life. It is essentially the right of the sword. So there is no real symmetry in the right over life and death. It is not the right to put people to death or to grant them life. Nor is it the right to allow people to live or to leave them to die. It is the right to take life or let live. And this obviously introduces a startling dissymmetry.

And I think that one of the greatest transformations political right underwent in the nineteenth century was precisely that, I wouldn't say exactly that sovereignty's old right—to take life or let live—was replaced, but it came to be complemented by a new right which does not erase the old right but which does penetrate it, permeate it. This is the right, or rather precisely the opposite right. It is the power to "make" live and "let" die. The right of sovereignty was the right to take life or let live. And then this new right is established: the right to make live and to let die.

This transformation obviously did not occur all at once. We can trace it in the theory of right (but here, I will be extraordinarily rapid). The jurists of the seventeenth and especially the eighteenth century were, you see, already asking this question about the right of life and death. The jurists ask: When we enter into a contract, what are individuals doing at the level of the social contract,[2] when they come together to constitute a sovereign, to delegate absolute power over them to a sovereign? They do so because they are forced to by some threat or by need. They therefore do so in order to protect their lives. It is in order to live that they constitute a sovereign. To the extent that this is the case, can life actually become one of the rights of the sovereign? Isn't life the foundation of the sovereign's right, and can the sovereign actually demand that his subjects grant him the right to exercise the power of life and death over them, or in other words, simply the power to kill them? Mustn't life remain outside the contract to the extent that it was the first, initial, and foundational reason for the contract itself? All this is a debate within political philosophy that we can leave on one side, but it clearly demonstrates how the problem of life began to be problematized in the field of political thought, of the analysis of political power. I would in fact like to trace the transformation not at the level of political theory, but rather at the level of the mechanisms, techniques, and technologies of power. And this brings us back to something familiar: in the seventeenth and eighteenth centuries, we saw the emergence of techniques of power that were essentially centered on the body, on the individual body. They included all devices that were used to ensure the spatial distribution of individual bodies (their separation, their alignment, their serialization, and their surveillance) and the organization, around those individuals, of a whole field of visibility. They were also techniques that could be used to take control over bodies. Attempts were made to increase their productive force through exercise,

2. For "social contract" theory, see the political philosophers Thomas Hobbes (1588–1679), John Locke (1632–1704), and Jean-Jacques Rousseau (1712–1778).

drill, and so on. They were also techniques for rationalizing and strictly economizing on a power that had to be used in the least costly way possible, thanks to a whole system of surveillance, hierarchies, inspections, bookkeeping, and reports—all the technology that can be described as the disciplinary technology of labor. It was established at the end of the seventeenth century, and in the course of the eighteenth.[3]

Now I think we see something new emerging in the second half of the eighteenth century: a new technology of power, but this time it is not disciplinary. This technology of power does not exclude the former, does not exclude disciplinary technology, but it does dovetail into it, integrate it, modify it to some extent, and above all, use it by sort of infiltrating it, embedding itself in existing disciplinary techniques. This new technique does not simply do away with the disciplinary technique, because it exists at a different level, on a different scale, and because it has a different bearing area, and makes use of very different instruments.

Unlike discipline, which is addressed to bodies, the new nondisciplinary power is applied not to man-as-body but to the living man, to man-as-living-being; ultimately, if you like, to man-as-species. To be more specific, I would say that discipline tries to rule a multiplicity of men to the extent that their multiplicity can and must be dissolved into individual bodies that can be kept under surveillance, trained, used, and, if need be, punished. And that the new technology that is being established is addressed to a multiplicity of men, not to the extent that they are nothing more than their individual bodies, but to the extent that they form, on the contrary, a global mass that is affected by overall processes characteristic of birth, death, production, illness, and so on. So after a first seizure of power over the body in an individualizing mode, we have a second seizure of power that is not individualizing but, if you like, massifying, that is directed not at man-as-body but at man-as-species. After the anatomo-politics of the human body established in the course of the eighteenth century, we have, at the end of that century, the emergence of something that is no longer an anatomo-politics of the human body, but what I would call a "biopolitics" of the human race.

What does this new technology of power, this biopolitics, this biopower that is beginning to establish itself, involve? I told you very briefly a moment ago; a set of processes such as the ratio of births to deaths, the rate of reproduction, the fertility of a population, and so on. It is these processes—the birth rate, the mortality rate, longevity, and so on—together with a whole series of related economic and political problems (which I will not come back to for the moment) which, in the second half of the eighteenth century, become biopolitics' first objects of knowledge and the targets it seeks to control. It is at any rate at this moment that the first demographers begin to measure these phenomena in statistical terms. They begin to observe the more or less spontaneous, more or less compulsory techniques that the population actually used to control the birth rate; in a word, if you like, to identify the phenomena of birth-control practices in the eighteenth century. We also see the beginnings of a natalist policy, plans to intervene in all phe-

3. On the question of disciplinary technology, see *Discipline and Punish* [1975; translator's note]. Disciplinary technologies are practices focused on the body such as surveillance, drills, uniforms, and posture.

nomena relating to the birth rate. This biopolitics is not concerned with fertility alone. It also deals with the problem of morbidity, but not simply, as had previously been the case, at the level of the famous epidemics, the threat of which had haunted political powers ever since the early Middle Ages (these famous epidemics were temporary disasters that caused multiple deaths, times when everyone seemed to be in danger of imminent death).[4] At the end of the eighteenth century, it was not epidemics that were the issue, but something else—what might broadly be called endemics, or in other words, the form, nature, extension, duration, and intensity of the illnesses prevalent in a population. These were illnesses that were difficult to eradicate and that were not regarded as epidemics that caused more frequent deaths, but as permanent factors which—and that is how they were dealt with—sapped the population's strength, shortened the working week, wasted energy, and cost money, both because they led to a fall in production and because treating them was expensive. In a word, illness as phenomena affecting a population. Death was no longer something that suddenly swooped down on life—as in an epidemic. Death was now something permanent, something that slips into life, perpetually gnaws at it, diminishes it and weakens it.

These are the phenomena that begin to be taken into account at the end of the eighteenth century, and they result in the development of a medicine whose main function will now be public hygiene, with institutions to coordinate medical care, centralize information, and normalize knowledge. And which also takes the form of campaigns to teach hygiene and to medicalize the population. So, problems of reproduction, the birth rate, and the problem of the mortality rate too. Biopolitics' other field of intervention will be a set of phenomena some of which are universal, and some of which are accidental but which can never be completely eradicated, even if they are accidental. They have similar effects in that they incapacitate individuals, put them out of the circuit or neutralize them. This is the problem, and it will become very important in the early nineteenth century (the time of industrialization), of old age, of individuals who, because of their age, fall out of the field of capacity, of activity. The field of biopolitics also includes accidents, infirmities, and various anomalies. And it is in order to deal with these phenomena that this biopolitics will establish not only charitable institutions (which had been in existence for a very long time), but also much more subtle mechanisms that were much more economically rational than an indiscriminate charity which was at once widespread and patchy, and which was essentially under church control. We see the introduction of more subtle, more rational mechanisms: insurance, individual and collective savings, safety measures, and so on.[5]

Biopolitics' last domain is, finally—I am enumerating the main ones, or at least those that appeared in the late eighteenth and early nineteenth centuries; many others would appear later—control over relations between the human race, or human beings insofar as they are a species, insofar as they are living beings, and their environment, the milieu in which they live. This includes the direct effects of the geographical, climatic, or hydrographic

4. Many of these epidemics were caused by plague; the most famous, the Black Death (1347–51), killed up to one-third of Europe's population. Other epidemic diseases include typhus and cholera.

5. On all these questions, see *Psychiatric Power: Lectures at the Collège de France, 1973–1974* [translator's note].

environment: the problem, for instance, of swamps, and of epidemics linked to the existence of swamps throughout the first half of the nineteenth century. And also the problem of the environment to the extent that it is not a natural environment, that it has been created by the population and therefore has effects on that population. This is, essentially, the urban problem. I am simply pointing out some of biopolitics' starting points, some of its practices, and the first of its domains of intervention, knowledge, and power: biopolitics will derive its knowledge from, and define its power's field of intervention in terms of, the birth rate, the mortality rate, various biological disabilities, and the effects of the environment.

In all this, a number of things are, I think, important. The first appears to be this: the appearance of a new element—I almost said a new character—of which both the theory of right and disciplinary practice knew nothing. The theory of right basically knew only the individual and society: the contracting individual and the social body constituted by the voluntary or implicit contract among individuals. Disciplines, for their part, dealt with individuals and their bodies in practical terms. What we are dealing with in this new technology of power is not exactly society (or at least not the social body, as defined by the jurists), nor is it the individual-as-body. It is a new body, a multiple body, a body with so many heads that, while they might not be infinite in number, cannot necessarily be counted. Biopolitics deals with the population, with the population as political problem, as a problem that is at once scientific and political, as a biological problem and as power's problem. And I think that biopolitics emerges at this time.

Second, the other important thing—quite aside from the appearance of the "population" element itself—is the nature of the phenomena that are taken into consideration. You can see that they are collective phenomena which have their economic and political effects, and that they become pertinent only at the mass level. They are phenomena that are aleatory and unpredictable when taken in themselves or individually, but which, at the collective level, display constants that are easy, or at least possible, to establish. And they are, finally, phenomena that occur over a period of time, which have to be studied over a certain period of time; they are serial phenomena. The phenomena addressed by biopolitics are, essentially, aleatory events that occur within a population that exists over a period of time.

On this basis—and this is, I think, the third important point—this technology of power, this biopolitics, will introduce mechanisms with a certain number of functions that are very different from the functions of disciplinary mechanisms. The mechanisms introduced by biopolitics include forecasts, statistical estimates, and overall measures. And their purpose is not to modify any given phenomenon as such, or to modify a given individual insofar as he is an individual, but, essentially, to intervene at the level at which these general phenomena are determined, to intervene at the level of their generality. The mortality rate has to be modified or lowered; life expectancy has to be increased; the birth rate has to be stimulated. And most important of all, regulatory mechanisms must be established to establish an equilibrium, maintain an average, establish a sort of homeostasis, and compensate for variations within this general population and its aleatory field. In a word, security mechanisms have to be installed around the random element inherent in a population of living beings so as to optimize a state of life. Like disciplinary mechanisms, these mechanisms are designed to maximize and extract forces, but they work in very different ways. Unlike disciplines, they no longer train individuals by working at the level of the body itself. There is absolutely no question relating to an individual body, in the way that discipline does. It is therefore not a matter of taking the individual at the level of individuality but, on the contrary, of using overall mechanisms and acting in such a way as to achieve overall states of equilibration or regularity; it is, in a word, a matter of taking control of life and the biological processes of man-as-species and of ensuring that they are not disciplined, but regularized.[6]

Beneath that great absolute power, beneath the dramatic and somber absolute power that was the power of sovereignty, and which consisted in the power to take life, we now have the emergence, with this technology of biopower, of this technology of power over "the" population as such, over men insofar as they are living beings. It is continuous, scientific, and it is the power to make live. Sovereignty took life and let live. And now we have the emergence of a power that I would call the power of regularization, and it, in contrast, consists in making live and letting die.

I think that we can see a concrete manifestation of this power in the famous gradual disqualification of death, which sociologists and historians have discussed so often. Everyone knows, thanks in particular to a certain number of recent studies, that the great public ritualization of death gradually began to disappear, or at least to fade away, in the late eighteenth century and that it is still doing so today. So much so that death—which has ceased to be one of those spectacular ceremonies in which individuals, the family, the group, and practically the whole of society took part—has become, in contrast, something to be hidden away. It has become the most private and shameful thing of all (and ultimately, it is now not so much sex as death that is the object of a taboo). Now I think that the reason why death had become something to be hidden away is not that anxiety has somehow been displaced or that repressive mechanisms have been modified. What once (and until the end of the eighteenth century) made death so spectacular and ritualized it so much was the fact that it was a manifestation of a transition from one power to another. Death was the moment when we made the transition from one power—that of the sovereign of this world—to another—that of the sovereign of the next world. We went from one court of law to another, from a civil or public right over life and death, to a right to either eternal life or eternal damnation. A transition from one power to another. Death also meant the transmission of the power of the dying, and that power was transmitted to those who survived him: last words, last recommendations, last wills and testaments, and so on. All these phenomena of power were ritualized.

Now that power is decreasingly the power of the right to take life, and increasingly the right to intervene to make live, or once power begins to intervene mainly at this level in order to improve life by eliminating accidents, the random element, and deficiencies, death becomes, insofar as it is the end of life, the term, the limit, or the end of power too. Death is outside

6. Foucault comes back to all these disciplines, especially in the lectures from the Collège de France of 1977–1978, *Security, Territory, and Population*, and of 1978–1979, *The Birth of Biopolitics* [translator's note].

the power relationship. Death is beyond the reach of power, and power has a grip on it only in general, overall, or statistical terms. Power has no control over death, but it can control mortality. And to that extent, it is only natural that death should now be privatized, and should become the most private thing of all. In the right of sovereignty, death was the moment of the most obvious and most spectacular manifestation of the absolute power of the sovereign; death now becomes, in contrast, the moment when the individual escapes all power, falls back on himself and retreats, so to speak, into his own privacy. Power no longer recognizes death. Power literally ignores death.

To symbolize all this, let's take, if you will, the death of Franco,[7] which is after all a very, very interesting event. It is very interesting because of the symbolic values it brings into play, because the man who died had, as you know, exercised the sovereign right of life and death with great savagery, was the bloodiest of all the dictators, wielded an absolute right of life and death for forty years, and at the moment when he himself was dying, he entered this sort of new field of power over life which consists not only in managing life, but in keeping individuals alive after they are dead. And thanks to a power that is not simply scientific prowess, but the actual exercise of the political biopower established in the eighteenth century, we have become so good at keeping people alive that we've succeeded in keeping them alive when, in biological terms, they should have been dead long ago. And so the man who had exercised the absolute power of life and death over hundreds of thousands of people fell under the influence of a power that managed life so well, that took so little heed of death, and he didn't even realize that he was dead and was being kept alive after his death. I think that this minor but joyous event symbolizes the clash between two systems of power: that of sovereignty over death, and that of the regularization of life.

I would now like to go back to comparing the regulatory technology of life and the disciplinary technology of the body I was telling you about a moment ago. From the eighteenth century onward (or at least the end of the eighteenth century onward) we have, then, two technologies of power which were established at different times and which were superimposed. One technique is disciplinary; it centers on the body, produces individualizing effects, and manipulates the body as a source of forces that have to be rendered both useful and docile. And we also have a second technology which is centered not upon the body but upon life: a technology which brings together the mass effects characteristic of a population, which tries to control the series of random events that can occur in a living mass, a technology which tries to predict the probability of those events (by modifying it, if necessary), or at least to compensate for their effects. This is a technology which aims to establish a sort of homeostasis, not by training individuals, but by achieving an overall equilibrium that protects the security of the whole from internal dangers. So, a technology of drilling, as opposed to, as distinct from, a technology of security; a disciplinary technology, as distinct from a reassuring or regulatory technology. Both technologies are obviously technologies of the body, but

7. Francisco Franco (1892–1975), leader of the rightist military forces that overthrew the Republic in the Spanish Civil War (1936–39) and military dictator of Spain from 1939 until his death. Foucault is referring to Franco's protracted final illness, which ended only when his family ordered doctors to turn off the life support.

one is a technology in which the body is individualized as an organism endowed with capacities, while the other is a technology in which bodies are replaced by general biological processes.

One might say this: It is as though power, which used to have sovereignty as its modality or organizing schema, found itself unable to govern the economic and political body of a society that was undergoing both a demographic explosion and industrialization. So much so that far too many things were escaping the old mechanism of the power of sovereignty, both at the top and at the bottom, both at the level of detail and at the mass level. A first adjustment was made to take care of the details. Discipline had meant adjusting power mechanisms to the individual body by using surveillance and training. That, of course, was the easier and more convenient thing to adjust. That is why it was the first to be introduced—as early as the seventeenth century, or the beginning of the eighteenth—at a local level, in intuitive, empirical, and fragmented forms, and in the restricted framework of institutions such as schools, hospitals, barracks, workshops, and so on. And then at the end of the eighteenth century, you have a second adjustment; the mechanisms are adjusted to phenomena of population, to the biological or biosociological processes characteristic of human masses. This adjustment was obviously much more difficult to make because it implied complex systems of coordination and centralization.

So we have two series: the body-organism-discipline-institutions series, and the population-biological processes-regulatory mechanisms-State.[8] An organic institutional set, or the organo-discipline of the institution, if you like, and, on the other hand, a biological and Statist set, or bioregulation by the State. I am not trying to introduce a complete dichotomy between State and institution, because disciplines in fact always tend to escape the institutional or local framework in which they are trapped. What is more, they easily take on a Statist dimension in apparatuses such as the police, for example, which is both a disciplinary apparatus and a State apparatus (which just goes to prove that discipline is not always institutional). In similar fashion, the great overall regulations that proliferated throughout the nineteenth century are, obviously enough, found at the State level, but they are also found at the sub-State level, in a whole series of sub-State institutions such as medical institutions, welfare funds, insurance, and so on. That is the first remark I would like to make.

What is more, the two sets of mechanisms—one disciplinary and the other regulatory—do not exist at the same level. Which means of course that they are not mutually exclusive and can be articulated with each other. To take one or two examples. Take, if you like, the example of the town or, more specifically, the rationally planned layout of the model town, the artificial town, the town of utopian reality that was not only dreamed of but actually built in the nineteenth century. What were working-class housing estates, as they existed in the nineteenth century? One can easily see how the very grid pattern, the very layout, of the estate articulated, in a sort of perpendicular way, the disciplinary mechanisms that controlled the body, or bodies, by localizing familes (one to a house) and individuals (one to a

8. The manuscript has "assuring" in place of "regulatory" [translator's note].

room). The layout, the fact that individuals were made visible, and the normalization of behavior meant that a sort of spontaneous policing or control was carried out by the spatial layout of the town itself. It is easy to identify a whole series of disciplinary mechanisms in the working-class estate. And then you have a whole series of mechanisms which are, by contrast, regulatory mechanisms, which apply to the population as such and which allow, which encourage patterns of saving related to housing, to the renting of accommodations and, in some cases, their purchase. Health-insurance systems, old-age pensions; rules on hygiene that guarantee the optimal longevity of the population; the pressures that the very organization of the town brings to bear on sexuality and therefore procreation; child care, education, et cetera, so you have [certain] disciplinary measures and [certain] regulatory mechanisms.[9]

Take the very different—though it is not altogether that different—take a different axis, something like sexuality. Basically, why did sexuality become a field of vital strategic importance in the nineteenth century? I think that sexuality was important for a whole host of reasons, and for these reasons in particular. On the one hand, sexuality, being an eminently corporeal mode of behavior, is a matter for individualizing disciplinary controls that take the form of permanent surveillance (and the famous controls that were, from the late eighteenth to the twentieth century, placed both at home and at school on children who masturbated represent precisely this aspect of the disciplinary control of sexuality). But because it also has procreative effects, sexuality is also inscribed, takes effect, in broad biological processes that concern not the bodies of individuals but the element, the multiple unity of the population. Sexuality exists at the point where body and population meet. And so it is a matter for discipline, but also a matter for regularization.

It is, I think, the privileged position it occupies between organism and population, between the body and general phenomena, that explains the extreme emphasis placed upon sexuality in the nineteenth century. Hence too the medical idea that when it is undisciplined and irregular, sexuality also has effects at two levels. At the level of the body, of the undisciplined body that is immediately sanctioned by all the individual diseases that the sexual debauchee brings down upon himself. A child who masturbates too much will be a lifelong invalid: disciplinary sanction at the level of the body. But at the same time, debauched, perverted sexuality has effects at the level of the population, as anyone who has been sexually debauched is assumed to have a heredity. Their descendants also will be affected for generations, unto the seventh generation and unto the seventh of the seventh and so on. This is the theory of degeneracy:[1] given that it is the source of individual diseases and that it is the nucleus of degeneracy, sexuality represents the precise point where the disciplinary and the regulatory, the body

9. The bracketed words are in Foucault's lecture notes, though he did not speak them when giving the lecture.

1. Foucault refers here to the theory elaborated in mid-nineteenth-century France by certain alienists. [. . .] This theory of degeneracy, which is based upon a principle that a so-called hereditary trait can be transmitted, was the kernel of the medical knowledge about madness and abnormality in the second half of the nineteenth century. It was quickly adopted by forensic medicine, and it had a considerable effect on eugenicist doctrines and practices, and was not without its influence on a whole literature, a whole criminology, and a whole anthropology [translator's note].

and the population, are articulated. Given these conditions, you can understand how and why a technical knowledge such as medicine, or rather the combination of medicine and hygiene, is in the nineteenth century, if not the most important element, an element of considerable importance because of the link it establishes between scientific knowledge of both biological and organic processes (or in other words, the population and the body), and because, at the same time, medicine becomes a political intervention-technique with specific power-effects. Medicine is a power-knowledge that can be applied to both the body and the population, both the organism and biological processes, and it will therefore have both disciplinary effects and regulatory effects.

In more general terms still, we can say that there is one element that will circulate between the disciplinary and the regulatory, which will also be applied to body and population alike, which will make it possible to control both the disciplinary order of the body and the aleatory events that occur in the biological multiplicity. The element that circulates between the two is the norm. The norm is something that can be applied to both a body one wishes to discipline and a population one wishes to regularize. The normalizing society is therefore not, under these conditions, a sort of generalized disciplinary society whose disciplinary institutions have swarmed and finally taken over everything—that, I think, is no more than a first and inadequate interpretation of a normalizing society. The normalizing society is a society in which the norm of discipline and the norm of regulation intersect along an orthogonal articulation. To say that power took possession of life in the nineteenth century, or to say that power at least takes life under its care in the nineteenth century, is to say that it has, thanks to the play of technologies of discipline on the one hand and technologies of regulation on the other, succeeded in covering the whole surface that lies between the organic and the biological, between body and population.

We are, then, in a power that has taken control of both the body and life or that has, if you like, taken control of life in general—with the body as one pole and the population as the other. We can therefore immediately identify the paradoxes that appear at the points where the exercise of this biopower reaches its limits. The paradoxes become apparent if we look, on the one hand, at atomic power, which is not simply the power to kill, in accordance with the rights that are granted to any sovereign, millions and hundreds of millions of people (after all, that is traditional). The workings of contemporary political power are such that atomic power represents a paradox that is difficult, if not impossible, to get around. The power to manufacture and use the atom bomb represents the deployment of a sovereign power that kills, but it is also the power to kill life itself. So the power that is being exercised in this atomic power is exercised in such a way that it is capable of suppressing life itself. And, therefore, to suppress itself insofar as it is the power that guarantees life. Either it is sovereign and uses the atom bomb, and therefore cannot be power, biopower, or the power to guarantee life, as it has been ever since the nineteenth century. Or, at the opposite extreme, you no longer have a sovereign right that is in excess of biopower, but a biopower that is in excess of sovereign right. This excess of biopower appears when it becomes technologically and politically possible for man not only to manage life but to make it proliferate, to create living matter, to build the monster, and, ultimately, to build viruses that cannot be controlled and that are universally destructive. This formidable extension of biopower, unlike what I was just saying about atomic power, will put it beyond all human sovereignty.

You must excuse this long digression into biopower, but I think that it does provide us with a basic argument that will allow us to get back to the problem I was trying to raise.

If it is true that the power of sovereignty is increasingly on the retreat and that disciplinary or regulatory disciplinary power is on the advance, how will the power to kill and the function of murder operate in this technology of power, which takes life as both its object and its objective? How can a power such as this kill, if it is true that its basic function is to improve life, to prolong its duration, to improve its chances, to avoid accidents, and to compensate for failings? How, under these conditions, is it possible for a political power to kill, to call for deaths, to demand deaths, to give the order to kill, and to expose not only its enemies but its own citizens to the risk of death? Given that this power's objective is essentially to make live, how can it let die? How can the power of death, the function of death, be exercised in a political system centered upon biopower?

1976

WOLFGANG ISER
1926–2007

Against a narrow focus on "the text itself," theorists in the 1970s turned to consider the role of the reader. Alongside French poststructuralist approaches that asserted, in ROLAND BARTHES's phrase, the "writerly" nature of reading and psychoanalytic views that studied the psychology of reading, the German "Constance School" was most prominent in advocating the investigation of *Rezeptionsästhetik*, or "the aesthetics of reception." Wolfgang Iser was a leading member of the Constance School, and he focused particularly on the way in which texts are actively constructed by individual readers through the phenomenology of the reading process.

Born in Germany and trained as an undergraduate at the University of Leipzig and the University of Tubingen, Iser earned his Ph.D. in 1950 from the University of Heidelberg, where he studied with the philosopher Hans-Georg Gadamer. Thereafter, Iser held a series of appointments in English literature at the Universities of Glasgow, Heidelberg, Würzburg, and Cologne, settling finally in 1967 in Germany at the newly founded University of Constance as a professor of English and comparative literature. He technically retired from Constance in 1991, but he remained active there until his death. Iser's arrival at Constance, where he joined a research group that included the reader-response theorist Hans Robert Jauss, proved especially fruitful for the development of his theories of reader response. Iser also held an appointment as professor of English at the University of California at Irvine from 1978 to 2005.

The Constance School draws on the philosophical tradition of aesthetics inaugurated in eighteenth-century German philosophy by Alexander Baumgarten, IMMANUEL

KANT, and FRIEDRICH VON SCHILLER, and it focuses on the affective as well as the formal dimensions of art. The work of the Constance School has also been influenced by philosophical considerations of hermeneutics, or the theory of interpretation, developed by FRIEDRICH SCHLEIERMACHER (1768–1834), MARTIN HEIDEGGER (1889–1976), and others. In particular, Iser's work draws on the hermeneutic philosophy of Gadamer and the phenomenological literary theory of Roman Ingarden (1893–1970), which examines the processes of cognition through which we understand literary works.

Iser's early work includes two scholarly studies of English literature, but it was not until his inaugural lecture at Constance in 1970, "The Affective Structure of the Text," that he articulated his theory of the interactive nature of the reading experience. This was followed by two influential books, *The Implied Reader: Patterns of Communication in Prose Fiction from Bunyan to Beckett* (1972; trans. 1974) and *The Act of Reading: A Theory of Aesthetic Response* (1976; trans. 1978). In the former, Iser holds that literary texts provide the foundation for their interpretation, but they also imply the action of the reader. Reading is not passive but a process of discovery; a reader questions, negates, and revises the expectations that the text establishes, filling in what Iser calls "blanks" or "gaps" in the text and continually modifying his or her interpretation. In *The Act of Reading*, Iser argues that texts provide "sets of instructions" or a "repertoire" that the reader must assemble, so that interpretation depends on both the text and response, producing what he calls "the virtual text."

Iser's version of reader response differs from that of Jauss, who deals with the historical reception of a literary work and how it tempers our expectations and therefore influences our interpretation. We never see a text on its own, but always in the context of its reception by others. Iser focuses on the individual interactive process—the phenomenology or cognition—of reading, rather than the larger literary-historical concerns that Jauss describes. Iser's investigation of response also differs from that of STANLEY FISH, an early advocate of response criticism in the United States, who locates the meaning of literary texts in the protocols of the interpretive communities to which readers belong rather than in the interaction of text and reader.

Reader-response criticism takes particular aim at the once-dominant dictates of the New Criticism, codified in W. K. WIMSATT JR. and MONROE BEARDSLEY's "Affective Fallacy" (1949), which dismisses considerations of the reader as "a confusion between the poem and its results." Iser carves out a compromise position between such formalist theories of literature that assume a stable object of study (witness the titles of the best-known books of the New Criticism, CLEANTH BROOKS's *Well Wrought Urn* and Wimsatt's *Verbal Icon*) and more radical reader-based approaches, such as Fish's. Iser carefully qualifies his position, insisting that a theory of response, "if it is to carry any weight at all, must have its foundations in literary texts." A text functions in much the same way as a script does for a play. A script guides a performance, but performers enact it in different ways at different times.

Some critics of reader-response criticism charge that it promotes radical relativism and indeterminacy, leaving meaning to the subjective whim of each individual reader, with no objective or secure basis for literary interpretation. Further, there might be an infinite number of possible readings for every text—as many as there are readers. Iser's analyses of literature do not subscribe to these views. His concept of a textual "repertoire" acknowledges the formal dimensions of literary works and their determinate role in producing the "virtual text."

Our selection, "Interaction between Text and Reader" (1980), summarizes the theoretical argument offered in *The Act of Reading*. Iser stresses that interpretation is neither objective nor subjective, but always a result of the dynamic interaction of text and reader. The structure of the literary text guides the reader, but the reader continually modifies her or his viewpoint, connecting new segments of the text and filling in the "gaps" of what the text does not mention. Meaning is constantly revised in a process that Iser compares to a feedback loop in communication theory, resembling what philosophers call "the hermeneutic circle."

As Stanley Fish remarks in an essay titled "Why No One Is Afraid of Wolfgang Iser," despite the sometimes contentious debates in contemporary literary theory, there has been relatively little disagreement with Iser's work. This results, in part, from Iser's middle-ground position between formalism and certain poststructuralist approaches that argue for the ultimate indeterminacy of interpretation. Fish also argues that Iser's terms are vague and contradictory; for instance, to postulate the existence of gaps, one must assume that there are definite givens, and Fish questions whether one can determine the difference between the two. Other criticism has been voiced by those advocating the study of the social dimensions of literature, such as the Marxist critic TERRY EAGLETON, who notes that by solely concentrating on the "aesthetic aspects" of texts, Iser ignores their social and historical dimensions. Nonetheless, Iser has influenced those focusing on the actual processes of reading, particularly those exploring new cognitive approaches to literature and those concerned with pedagogy.

"Interaction between Text and Reader" Keywords: Aesthetics, Affect, Hermeneutics, Phenomenology, Reception Theory

Interaction between Text and Reader

Central to the reading of every literary work is the interaction between its structure and its recipient. This is why the phenomenological theory of art[1] has emphatically drawn attention to the fact that the study of a literary work should concern not only the actual text but also, and in equal measure, the actions involved in responding to that text. The text itself simply offers "schematized aspects"[2] through which the aesthetic object of the work can be produced.

From this we may conclude that the literary work has two poles, which we might call the artistic and the aesthetic: the artistic pole is the author's text, and the aesthetic is the realization accomplished by the reader. In view of this polarity, it is clear that the work itself cannot be identical with the text or with its actualization but must be situated somewhere between the two. It must inevitably be virtual in character, as it cannot be reduced to the reality of the text or to the subjectivity of the reader, and it is from this virtuality that it derives its dynamism. As the reader passes through the various perspectives offered by the text, and relates the different views and patterns to one another, he sets the work in motion, and so sets himself in motion, too.

If the virtual position of the work is between text and reader, its actualization is clearly the result of an interaction between the two, and so exclusive concentration on either the author's techniques or the reader's psychology will tell us little about the reading process itself. This is not to deny the vital importance of each of the two poles—it is simply that if one loses sight of

1. Phenomenological theories of philosophy focus on human consciousness and perception, particularly the interrelation between the perceiving subject and the perceived object (here, audience and work).

2. See Roman Ingarden, *The Literary Work of Art*, trans. George G. Grabowicz (Evanston, Ill., 1973), pp. 276 ff. [Iser's note]. (Some of Iser's notes have been omitted, and some have been edited.) Ingarden (1893–1970), Polish theorist of literary cognition.

the relationship, one loses sight of the virtual work. Despite its uses, separate analysis would only be conclusive if the relationship were that of transmitter and receiver, for this would presuppose a common code, ensuring accurate communication since the message would only be traveling one way. In literary works, however, the message is transmitted in two ways, in that the reader "receives" it by composing it. There is no common code—at best one could say that a common code may arise in the course of the process. Starting out from this assumption, we must search for structures that will enable us to describe basic conditions of interaction, for only then shall we be able to gain some insight into the potential effects inherent in the work.

It is difficult to describe this interaction, not least because literary criticism has very little to go on in the way of guidelines, and, of course, the two partners in the communication process, namely, the text and the reader, are far easier to analyze than is the event that takes place between them. However, there are discernible conditions that govern interaction generally, and some of these will certainly apply to the special reader-text relationship. The differences and similarities may become clear if we briefly examine types of interaction that have emerged from psychoanalytical research into the structure of communication. The findings of the *Tavistock School*[3] will serve us as a model in order to move the problem into focus.

In assessing interpersonal relationships R. D. Laing writes: "I may not actually be able to see myself as others see me, but I am constantly supposing them to be seeing me in particular ways, and I am constantly acting in the light of the actual or supposed attitudes, opinions, needs, and so on the other has in respect of me."[4] Now, the views that others have of me cannot be called "pure" perception; they are the result of interpretation. And this need for interpretation arises from the structure of interpersonal experience. We have experience of one another insofar as we know one another's conduct; but we have no experience of how others experience us.

In his book, *The Politics of Experience*, Laing pursues this line of thought by saying: "*your experience of me is invisible to me and my experience of you is invisible to you.* I cannot experience your experience. You cannot experience my experience. We are both invisible men. All men are invisible to one another. Experience is man's invisibility to man."[5] It is this invisibility, however, that forms the basis of interpersonal relations—a basis which Laing calls "no-thing." "That which is really 'between' cannot be named by any things that come between. The between is itself no-thing."[6] In all our interpersonal relations we build upon this "no-thing," for we react as if we knew how our partners experienced us; we continually form views of their views, and then act as if our views of their views were realities. Contact therefore depends upon our continually filling in a central gap in our experience. Thus, dyadic[7] and dynamic interaction comes about only because we are unable to experience how we experience one another, which in turn proves to be a propellant to interaction. Out of this fact arises the basic need for interpretation, which regulates the

3. A British school of psychology, prominent in the 1960s and 1970s, focused on interpersonal relations; its most prominent member was R. D. Laing (1927–1989), a Scottish psychiatrist.
4. R. D. Laing, H. Phillipson, and A. R. Lee, *Interpersonal Perception: A Theory and a Method of Research* (New York, 1966), p. 4 [Iser's note].
5. R. D. Laing, *The Politics of Experience* (Harmondsworth, 1968), p. 16. Laing's italics [Iser's note].
6. Ibid., p. 34 [Iser's note].
7. Involving two entities.

whole process of interaction. As we cannot perceive without preconception, each percept, in turn, only makes sense to us if it is processed, for pure perception is quite impossible. Hence dyadic interaction is not given by nature but arises out of an interpretative activity, which will contain a view of others and, unavoidably, an image of ourselves.

An obvious and major difference between reading and all forms of social interaction is the fact that with reading there is no *face-to-face-situation*.[8] A text cannot adapt itself to each reader it comes into contact with. The partners in dyadic interaction can ask each other questions in order to ascertain how far their images have bridged the gap of the inexperienceability of one another's experiences. The reader, however, can never learn from the text how accurate or inaccurate are his views of it. Furthermore, dyadic interaction serves specific purposes, so that the interaction always has a regulative context, which often serves as a *tertium comparationis*.[9] There is no such frame of reference governing the text-reader relationship; on the contrary, the codes which might regulate this interaction are fragmented in the text, and must first be reassembled or, in most cases, restructured before any frame of reference *can* be established. Here, then, in conditions and intention, we find two basic differences between the text-reader relationship and the dyadic interaction between social partners.

Now, it is the very lack of ascertainability and defined intention that brings about the text-reader interaction, and here there is a vital link with dyadic interaction. Social communication, as we have seen, arises out of the fact that people cannot experience how others experience them, and not out of the common situation or out of the conventions that join both partners together. The situations and conventions regulate the manner in which gaps are filled, but the gaps in turn arise out of the inexperienceability and, consequently, function as a basic inducement to communication. Similarly, it is the gaps, the fundamental asymmetry between text and reader, that give rise to communication in the reading process; the lack of a common situation and a common frame of reference corresponds to the "no-thing," which brings about the interaction between persons. Asymmetry and the "no-thing" are all different forms of an indeterminate, constitutive blank, which underlies all processes of interaction. With dyadic interaction, the imbalance is removed by the establishment of pragmatic connections resulting in an action, which is why the preconditions are always clearly defined in relation to situations and common frames of reference. The imbalance between text and reader, however, is undefined, and it is this very indeterminacy that increases the variety of communication possible.

Now, if communication between text and reader is to be successful, clearly the reader's activity must also be controlled in some way by the text. The control cannot be as specific as in a *face-to-face-situation*, equally it cannot be as determinate as a social code, which regulates social interaction. However, the guiding devices operative in the reading process have to initiate communication and to control it. This control cannot be understood as a tangible entity occurring independently of the process of communication.

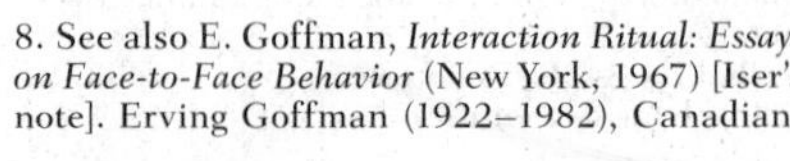

8. See also E. Goffman, *Interaction Ritual: Essays on Face-to-Face Behavior* (New York, 1967) [Iser's note]. Erving Goffman (1922–1982), Canadian-born American sociologist.

9. Third point of comparison (Latin).

Athough exercised *by* the text, it is not in the text. This is well illustrated by a comment Virginia Woolf made on the novels of Jane Austen:[1]

> Jane Austen is thus a mistress of much deeper emotion than appears upon the surface. She stimulates us to supply what is not there. What she offers is, apparently, a trifle, yet is composed of something that expands in the reader's mind and endows with the most enduring form of life scenes which are outwardly trivial. Always the stress is laid upon character. . . . The turns and twists of the dialogue keep us on the tenterhooks of suspense. Our attention is half upon the present moment, half upon the future. . . . Here, indeed, in this unfinished and in the main inferior story, are all the elements of Jane Austen's greatness.[2]

What is missing from the apparently trivial scenes, the gaps arising out of the dialogue—this is what stimulates the reader into filling the blanks with projections. He is drawn into the events and made to supply what is meant from what is not said. What is said only appears to take on significance as a reference to what is not said; it is the implications and not the statements that give shape and weight to the meaning. But as the unsaid comes to life in the reader's imagination, so the said "expands" to take on greater significance than might have been supposed: even trivial scenes can seem surprisingly profound. The "enduring form of life" which Virginia Woolf speaks of is not manifested on the printed page; it is a product arising out of the interaction between text and reader.

Communication in literature, then, is a process set in motion and regulated, not by a given code, but by a mutually restrictive and magnifying interaction between the explicit and the implicit, between revelation and concealment. What is concealed spurs the reader into action, but this action is also controlled by what is revealed; the explicit in its turn is transformed when the implicit has been brought to light. Whenever the reader bridges the gaps, communication begins. The gaps function as a kind of pivot on which the whole text-reader relationship revolves. Hence, the structured blanks of the text stimulate the process of ideation to be performed by the reader on terms set by the text. There is, however, another place in the textual system where text and reader converge, and that is marked by the various types of negation which arise in the course of the reading. Blanks and negations both control the process of communication in their own different ways: the blanks leave open the connection between textual perspectives, and so spur the reader into coordinating these perspectives and patterns—in other words, they induce the reader to perform basic operations *within* the text. The various types of negation invoke familiar and determinate elements or knowledge only to cancel them out. What is cancelled, however, remains in view, and thus brings about modifications in the reader's attitude toward what is familiar or determinate—in other words, he is guided to adopt a position in *relation* to the text.

In order to spotlight the communication process we shall confine our consideration to how the blanks trigger off and simultaneously control the reader's activity. Blanks indicate that the different segments and patterns

1. English novelist (1775–1817). WOOLF (1882–1941), English novelist and essayist.

2. Virginia Woolf, *The Common Reader, First Series* (London, 1957), p. 174 [Iser's note].

of the text are to be connected even though the text itself does not say so. They are the unseen joints of the text, and as they mark off schemata and textual perspectives from one another, they simultaneously prompt acts of ideation on the reader's part. Consequently when the schemata and perspectives have been linked together, the blanks "disappear."

If we are to grasp the unseen structure that regulates but does not formulate the connection or even the meaning, we must bear in mind the various forms in which the textual segments are presented to the reader's viewpoint in the reading process. Their most elementary form is to be seen on the level of the story. The threads of the plot are suddenly broken off, or continued in unexpected directions. One narrative section centers on a particular character and is then continued by the abrupt introduction of new characters. These sudden changes are often denoted by new chapters and so are clearly distinguished; the object of this distinction, however, is not separation so much as a tacit invitation to find the missing link. Furthermore, in each articulated reading moment, only segments of textual perspectives are present to the reader's wandering viewpoint.

In order to become fully aware of the implication, we must bear in mind that a narrative text, for instance, is composed of a variety of perspectives, which outline the author's view and also provide access to what the reader is meant to visualize. As a rule, there are four main perspectives in narration: those of the narrator, the characters, the plot, and the fictitious reader.[3] Although these may differ in order of importance, none of them on its own is identical to the meaning of the text, which is to be brought about by their constant intertwining through the reader in the reading process. An increase in the number of blanks is bound to occur through the frequent subdivisions of each of the textual perspectives; thus the narrator's perspective is often split into that of the implied author's set against that of the author as narrator. The hero's perspective may be set against that of the minor characters. The fictitious reader's perspective may be divided between the explicit position ascribed to him and the implicit attitude he must adopt to that position.

As the reader's wandering viewpoint travels between all these segments, its constant switching during the time flow of reading intertwines them, thus bringing forth a network of perspectives, within which each perspective opens a view not only of others, but also of the intended imaginary object. Hence no single textual perspective can be equated with this imaginary object, of which it forms only one aspect. The object itself is a product of interconnection, the structuring of which is to a great extent regulated and controlled by blanks.

In order to explain this operation, we shall first give a schematic description of how the blanks function, and then we shall try to illustrate this function with an example. In the time flow of reading, segments of the various perspectives move into focus and are set off against preceding segments. Thus the segments of characters, narrator, plot, and fictitious reader perspectives are not only marshaled into a graduated sequence but are also transformed into reciprocal reflectors. The blank as an empty space between segments enables them to be joined together, thus constituting a field of vision for the wandering viewpoint. A referential field is always

3. The reader addressed in a text, as distinct from the actual reader.

formed when there are at least two positions related to and influencing one another—it is the minimal organizational unit in all processes of comprehension,[4] and it is also the basic organizational unit of the wandering viewpoint.

The first structural quality of the blank, then, is that it makes possible the organization of a referential field of interacting textual segments projecting themselves one upon another. Now, the segments present in the field are structurally of equal value, and the fact that they are brought together highlights their affinities and their differences. This relationship gives rise to a tension that has to be resolved, for, as Arnheim has observed in a more general context: "It is one of the functions of the third dimension to come to the rescue when things get uncomfortable in the second."[5] The third dimension comes about when the segments of the referential field are given a common framework, which allows the reader to relate affinities and differences and so to grasp the patterns underlying the connections. But this framework is also a blank, which requires an act of ideation in order to be filled. It is as if the blank in the field of the reader's viewpoint had changed its position. It began as the empty space between perspective segments, indicating their connectability, and so organizing them into projections of reciprocal influence. But with the establishment of this connectability the blank, as the unformulated framework of these interacting segments, now enables the reader to produce a determinate relationship between them. We may infer already from this change in position that the blank exercises significant control over all the operations that occur within the referential field of the wandering viewpoint.

Now we come to the third and most decisive function of the blank. Once the segments have been connected and a determinate relationship established, a referential field is formed which constitutes a particular reading moment, and which in turn has a discernible structure. The grouping of segments within the referential field comes about, as we have seen, by making the viewpoint switch between the perspective segments. The segment on which the viewpoint focuses in each particular moment becomes the theme. The theme of one moment becomes the background against which the next segment takes on its actuality, and so on. Whenever a segment becomes a theme, the previous one must lose its thematic relevance[6] and be turned into a marginal, thematically vacant position, which can be and usually is occupied by the reader so that he may focus on the new thematic segment.

In this connection it might be more appropriate to designate the marginal or horizontal position as a vacancy and not as a blank; blanks refer to suspended connectability in the text, vacancies refer to nonthematic segments within the referential field of the wandering viewpoint. Vacancies, then, are important guiding devices for building up the aesthetic object, because they condition the reader's view of the new theme, which in turn conditions his view of previous themes. These modifications, however, are not formulated in the text—they are to be implemented by the reader's ide-

4. See Aron Gurwitsch, *The Field of Consciousness* (Pittsburgh, 1964), pp. 309–75 [Iser's note].

5. Rudolf Arnheim, *Toward a Psychology of Art* (Berkeley, 1967), p. 239 [Iser's note]. Arnheim (1904–2007), a German-born theorist of perception in art and film.

6. For a discussion of the problem of changing relevance and abandoned thematic relevance, see Alfred Schütz, *Reflections on the Problem of Relevance*, ed. Richard M. Zaner (New Haven, 1970) [Iser's note].

ational activity. And so these vacancies enable the reader to combine segments into a field by reciprocal modification, to form positions from those fields, and then to adapt each position to its successor and predecessors in a process that ultimately transforms the textual perspectives, through a whole range of alternating themes and background relationships, into the aesthetic object of the text.

Let us turn now to an example in order to illustrate the operations sparked off and governed by the vacancies in the referential field of the wandering viewpoint. For this reason we shall have a brief look at Fielding's[7] *Tom Jones* and again, in particular, at the characters' perspective: that of the hero and that of the minor characters. Fielding's aim of depicting human nature is fulfilled by way of a repertoire that incorporates the prevailing norms of eighteenth-century thought systems and social systems and represents them as governing the conduct of the most important characters. In general, these norms are arranged in more or less explicitly contrasting patterns; Allworthy (*benevolence*) is set against Squire Western (*ruling passion*); the same applies to the two pedagogues, Square (*the eternal fitness of things*) and Thwackum (*the human mind as a sink of iniquity*), who in turn are also contrasted with Allworthy and so forth.

Thus in the individual situations, the hero is linked up with the norms of latitudinarian morality, orthodox theology, deistic philosophy,[8] eighteenth-century anthropology, and eighteenth-century aristocracy. Contrasts and discrepancies within the perspective of the characters give rise to the missing links, which enable the hero and the norms to shed light upon one another, and through which the individual situations may combine into a referential field. The hero's conduct cannot be subsumed under the norms, and through the sequence of situations the norms shrink to a reified manifestation of human nature. This, however, is already an observation which the reader must make for himself, because such syntheses are rarely given in the text, even though they are prefigured in the theme-and-background structure. The discrepancies continually arising between the perspectives of hero and minor characters bring about a series of changing positions, with each theme losing its relevance but remaining in the background to influence and condition its successor. Whenever the hero violates the norms—as he does most of the time—the resultant situation may be judged in one or two different ways: either the norm appears as a drastic reduction of human nature, in which case we view the theme from the standpoint of the hero, or the violation shows the imperfections of human nature, in which case it is the norm that conditions our view.

In both cases, we have the same structure of interacting positions being transformed into a determinate meaning. For those characters that represent a norm—in particular Allworthy, Squire Western, Square, and Thwackum—human nature is defined in terms of one principle, so that all those possibilities which are not in harmony with the principle are given a negative slant. But when the negated possibilities exert their influence upon the course of

7. Henry Fielding (1707–1754), English novelist and playwright; *Tom Jones* was published in 1749.
8. Belief in a supreme being as the source of existence of the universe that rejects the supernatural doctrines of Christianity and the influence or revelation of God in the events of the universe, stressing instead the importance of reason and ethical conduct. "Latitudinarian morality": tolerating free thought or a range of opinion, especially on religious questions.

events, and so show up the limitations of the principle concerned, the norms begin to appear in a different light. The apparently negative aspects of human nature fight back, as it were, against the principle itself and cast doubt upon it in proportion to its limitations.

In this way, the negation of other possibilities by the norm in question gives rise to a virtual diversification of human nature, which takes on a definite form to the extent that the norm is revealed as a restriction on human nature. The reader's attention is now fixed, not upon what the norms represent, but upon what their representation excludes, and so the aesthetic object—which is the whole spectrum of human nature—begins to arise out of what is adumbrated by the negated possibilities. In this way, the function of the norms themselves has changed: they no longer represent the social regulators prevalent in the thought systems of the eighteenth century, but instead they indicate the amount of human experience which they suppress because, as rigid principles, they cannot tolerate any modifications.

Transformations of this kind take place whenever the norms are the foregrounded theme and the perspective of the hero remains the background conditioning the reader's viewpoint. But whenever the hero becomes the theme, and the norms of the minor characters shape the viewpoint, his well-intentioned spontaneity turns into the depravity of an impulsive nature. Thus the position of the hero is also transformed, for it is no longer the standpoint from which we are to judge the norms; instead we see that even the best of intentions may come to nought if they are not guided by *circumspection*, and spontaneity must be controlled by *prudence*[9] if it is to allow a possibility of self-preservation.

The transformations brought about by the theme-and-background interaction are closely connected with the changing position of the vacancy within the referential field. Once a theme has been grasped, conditioned by the marginal position of the preceding segment, a feedback is bound to occur, thus retroactively modifying the shaping influence of the reader's viewpoint. This reciprocal transformation is hermeneutic by nature,[1] even though we may not be aware of the processes of interpretation resulting from the switching and reciprocal conditioning of our viewpoints. In this sense, the vacancy transforms the referential field of the moving viewpoint into a self-regulating structure, which proves to be one of the most important links in the interaction between text and reader, and which prevents the reciprocal transformation of textual segments from being arbitrary.

To sum up, then, the blank in the fictional text induces and guides the reader's constitutive activity. As a suspension of connectability between textual perspective and perspective segments, it marks the need for an equivalence, thus transforming the segments into reciprocal projections, which in turn organize the reader's wandering viewpoint as a referential field. The tension that occurs within the field between heterogeneous perspective segments is resolved by the theme-and-background structure, which makes

9. See Henry Fielding, *Tom Jones*, III.7 and XVIII, Chapter the Last (London, 1962), pp. 92, 427 [Iser's note].

1. Hermeneutics is the theory of interpretation; Iser is alluding to what is called the "hermeneutic circle," a model which holds that meaning is not straightforward but continually modified by feedback.

the viewpoint focus on one segment as the theme, to be grasped from the thematically vacant position now occupied by the reader as his standpoint. Thematically vacant positions remain present in the background against which new themes occur; they condition and influence those themes and are also retroactively influenced by them, for as each theme recedes into the background of its successor, the vacancy shifts, allowing for a reciprocal transformation to take place. As the vacancy is structured by the sequence of positions in the time flow of reading, the reader's viewpoint cannot proceed arbitrarily; the thematically vacant position always acts as the angle from which a selective interpretation is to be made.

Two points need to be emphasized: (1) we have described the structure of the blank in an abstract, somewhat idealized way in order to explain the pivot on which the interaction between text and reader turns; (2) the blank has different structural qualities, which appear to dovetail. The reader fills in the blank in the text, thereby bringing about a referential field; the blank arising in turn out of the referential field is filled in by way of the theme-and-background structure; and the vacancy arising from juxtaposed themes and backgrounds is occupied by the reader's standpoint, from which the various reciprocal transformations lead to the emergence of the aesthetic object. The structural qualities outlined make the blank shift, so that the changing positions of the empty space mark out a definite need for determination, which the constitutive activity of the reader is to fulfill. In this sense, the shifting blank maps out the path along which the wandering viewpoint is to travel, guided by the self-regulatory sequence in which the structural qualities of the blank interlock.

Now we are in a position to qualify more precisely what is actually meant by reader participation in the text. If the blank is largely responsible for the activities described, then participation means that the reader is not simply called upon to "internalize" the positions given in the text, but he is induced to make them act upon and so transform each other, as a result of which the aesthetic object begins to emerge. The structure of the blank organizes this participation, revealing simultaneously the intimate connection between this structure and the reading subject. This interconnection completely conforms to a remark made by Piaget: "In a word, the subject is there and alive, because the basic quality of each structure is the structuring process itself."[2] The blank in the fictional text appears to be a paradigmatic structure; its function consists in initiating structured operations in the reader, the execution of which transmits the reciprocal interaction of textual positions into consciousness. The shifting blank is responsible for a sequence of colliding images, which condition each other in the time flow of reading. The discarded image imprints itself on its successor, even though the latter is meant to resolve the deficiencies of the former. In this respect the images hang together in a sequence, and it is by this sequence that the meaning of the text comes alive in the reader's imagination.

1980

2. Jean Piaget, *Structuralism*, trans. Chaninah Maschler (New York, 1970), p. 140 [Iser's note]. Piaget (1896–1980), Swiss psychologist who applied structuralist methods in psychology.

HAYDEN WHITE
1928–2018

A historian by training, Hayden White was a central figure in literary debates about the nature of history since the 1970s. At the same time literary critics like STEPHEN GREENBLATT began to turn to history to explain the formal structures of literary texts, White was investigating the formal literary structures of history, beginning with his celebrated 1973 book *Metahistory: The Historical Imagination of Nineteenth-Century Europe*, which outlines an ambitious structuralist scheme for describing a "poetics of history." Drawing on NORTHROP FRYE's *Anatomy of Criticism* (1957) to describe the underlying "deep structure" of historical narratives, this project brings together historiography and literary criticism in a broad reflection on narrative and its relation to culture. "To raise the question of the nature of narrative," White writes in *The Content of the Form: Narrative Discourse and Historical Representation* (1987), "is to invite reflection on the very nature of culture and, possibly, even on the nature of humanity itself. So natural is the impulse to narrative, so inevitable is the form of narrative for any report on the way things really happened, that narrativity could appear problematical only in a culture in which it was absent—or, as in some domains of contemporary Western intellectual and artistic culture, programmatically refused." Reacting against the tendency of history as a discipline to seek its models in the sciences, White contends that the literary dimension of history cannot be dismissed as mere decoration; rather, historians deploy the traditional devices of narrative to make sense of raw data, to organize and give meaning to their accounts of the past. Bringing the tools of the literary critic to bear on historical writing, White's analyses are powerful extensions of narrative theory for students and scholars of literature interested in understanding the nature and mechanisms of history as discourse.

White was born in Martin, Tennessee. After attending Wayne State University he did his graduate work in history at the University of Michigan, earning an M.A. in 1952 and a Ph.D. in 1956. He taught first as an instructor at Wayne State (1955–58), then in 1958 was appointed to the history faculty at the University of Rochester, where he served as head of the department from 1962 to 1964. He subsequently taught history at the University of California at Los Angeles (1968–73), served as the director of the Center for Humanities at Wesleyan University in Connecticut (1973–77), and in 1978 became a professor in the History of Consciousness program at the University of California at Santa Cruz. After formally retiring in 1994, he was the Bonsall Professor of Comparative Literature at Stanford University until his death in 2018.

White, who began his career as a historian of the medieval church and turned to nineteenth-century thought in the 1960s, was always eclectic in his scholarly interests. With the publication of *Metahistory*, however, his scholarship became explicitly engaged in literary and theoretical issues, as he responded to critics from the disciplines of both history and literature. His book *Tropics of Discourse: Essays in Cultural Criticism* (1978), from which our selection is taken, examines the structuring role of plots and tropes (figures of speech) in the discourse of history. *The Content of Form* explores the contemporary interplay between narrative theory and history in the work of both historians such as MICHEL FOUCAULT and literary theorists such as FREDRIC JAMESON and Paul Ricoeur. And in *Figural Realism: Studies in the Mimesis Effect* (1999), White takes on mimesis—the representation of reality—in history, an issue that has concerned literary critics from PLATO to ERICH AUERBACH (see *Mimesis: The Representation of Reality in Western Literature*, 1946).

Hayden White was in the vanguard of the movement among historians, starting in the 1980s, that has come to be known as the "new cultural history." Historians associated with the movement, such as Lynn Hunt, Thomas Laqueur, and, in France, Roger Chartier, began to question the methods and goals of history in general, many turning to literary techniques and approaches to develop new materials and methods of analysis. The influences on this group of historians are varied. They include cultural Marxist approaches developed in the 1960s by British scholars such as E. P. Thompson and RAYMOND WILLIAMS, as well as the French Annales school, founded in the late 1920s by the historians Marc Bloch and Lucien Febvre. The new cultural history has also been strongly influenced by the work of Foucault, by literary theorists such as JACQUES DERRIDA and MIKHAIL BAKHTIN, and, of course, by White himself. Many of the historians associated with the new cultural history have ties with literary practitioners of the New Historicism and cultural studies.

"The Historical Text as Literary Artifact," our selection, provides an accessible and engaging synopsis of White's main arguments in *Metahistory*, beginning with his definition of metahistory as the attempt to "get behind or beneath the presuppositions which sustain a given type of inquiry [in this case historical inquiry]." A key assumption that, according to White, has sustained historical inquiry is the belief that history (judged by its correspondence to reality) and literature (judged as fiction) are two distinct, diametrically opposed, activities, a presupposition shared by practitioners in both disciplines. On the contrary, White argues, because history, like literature, is a verbal structure and the historian, first and foremost, is a writer, the tools that have served literary critics, the tools that compose the linguistic and rhetorical structures of a text, serve the historian as well. The language in which history is written cannot be dismissed as window dressing, as most historians are tempted to do. Language in history is never merely a means to an end; it is neither transparent nor neutral, nor does it disappear to allow the pure truth of history to emerge. In White's view, historical narratives are verbal fictions with invented contexts. He goes beyond Auerbach, arguing that history, because of its claims to represent reality adequately, is the form best suited for a study of the style of narrative "realism."

Histories gain their explanatory power by processing data into stories. Those stories take their shape from what White calls "emplotment," the process through which the facts contained in "chronicles" are encoded as components of plots. Plots are not immanent in events themselves but exist in the minds of historians, who rarely reflect on them. No historical event can itself constitute a story, tragic or ironic: it can be presented as such only from a particular historian's narrative point of view. The event emerges as a plotted story, which takes on meaning when it is combined with other elements in the limited number of generic plot structures by which a series of events can be constituted. Following Northrop Frye's archetypal analysis, White identifies four possible emplotments: tragic, comic, romantic, and ironic. These generic deep-plot structures are shared between historians and their audiences by virtue of their participation in a common culture.

The kind of emplotment historians will employ to give meaning to a series of events, White argues, is determined by the dominant figurative mode of the language they use to describe these events and story elements. Drawing on the eighteenth-century philosopher GIAMBATTISTA VICO and the twentieth-century critic Kenneth Burke, White identifies four master tropes or modes of figurative representation—metaphor, metonymy, synecdoche, and irony—which correspond to the four types of emplotment. For White, the differences between contending histories of, say, the French Revolution cannot be resolved by recourse to the facts, because the facts—and, more important, the relationships among those facts—do not inhere in the events themselves, but instead are constituted by historians in the linguistic and literary structures they use to identify and describe the events they study. Tropes are ineradicable from discourse, as are plots. Thus history evokes reality: it does not reproduce or represent it.

This analysis of historical narrative makes special sense in the context of the structuralism of the 1970s, when it first caught public attention. Although White does not draw directly on the terminology of structural linguistics, his debts to such modern structuralists as CLAUDE LÉVI-STRAUSS, ROMAN JAKOBSON, and the linguist Noam Chomsky are clear. And his adaptation of Frye's archetypal criticism is structuralist both in its basic argument that history uses a few "deep structures" to generate its "surface structures" and in its broad contention that historians have mistakenly focused their attention only on the surface, while ignoring the underlying deep structures that produce those narratives.

Historians have objected to White's narrowing of history to language, while more poststructuralist-minded literary critics have taken issue with White's structuralist reductionism (only four master plots and tropes). Some critics argue that Frye's archetypal approach to narrative, which White relies on, is too simple, forcing all narratives willy-nilly into abstract and timeless structures without regard to how they might function in particular cultural contexts. Others contend that unlike most structuralists, White imagines plot as a quintessential expression of the historian's personal style and self. Despite these objections, White's skillful dismantling of the opposition between history and literature has paved the way for many productive studies in both fields. Once historians and literary critics no longer believe that history gives its readers a privileged access to the real or the truth, they turn to investigating the grounds of history—its nature and forms, its uses and abuses—as well as its links to other fields of knowledge and to ideologies.

"The Historical Text as Literary Artifact" Keywords: Narrative Theory, New Historicism, Realism, Representation, Rhetoric, Semiotics, Structuralism

The Historical Text as Literary Artifact[1]

One of the ways that a scholarly field takes stock of itself is by considering its history. Yet it is difficult to get an objective history of a scholarly discipline, because if the historian is himself a practitioner of it, he is likely to be a devotee of one or another of its sects and hence biased; and if he is not a practitioner, he is unlikely to have the expertise necessary to distinguish between the significant and the insignificant events of the field's development. One might think that these difficulties would not arise in the field of history itself, but they do and not only for the reasons mentioned above. In order to write the history of any given scholarly discipline or even of a science, one must be prepared to ask questions *about* it of a sort that do not have to be asked in the practice *of* it. One must try to get behind or beneath the presuppositions which sustain a given type of inquiry and ask the questions that can be begged[2] in its practice in the interest of determining why this type of inquiry has been designed to solve the problems it characteristically tries to solve. This is what metahistory seeks to do. It addresses itself to such questions as, What is the structure of a peculiarly *historical* consciousness?

1. This essay is a revised version of a lecture given before the Comparative Literature Colloquium of Yale University on 24 January, 1974. In it I have tried to elaborate some of the themes that I originally discussed in an article, "The Structure of Historical Narrative," *Clio* 1 (1972): 5–20. I have also drawn upon the materials of my book *Metahistory: The Historical Imagination in Nineteenth-Century Europe* (Baltimore, 1973), especially the introduction, entitled "The Poetics of History" [White's note].

2. That is, questions that are wrongly assumed to be settled.

What is the epistemological status of historical *explanations*, as compared with other kinds of explanations that might be offered to account for the materials with which historians ordinarily deal? What are the possible *forms* of historical representation and what are their bases? What authority can historical accounts claim as contributions to a secured knowledge of reality in general and to the human sciences in particular?

Now, many of these questions have been dealt with quite competently over the last quarter-century by philosophers concerned to define history's relationships to other disciplines, especially the physical and social sciences, and by historians interested in assessing the success of their discipline in mapping the past and determining the relationship of the past to the present. But there is one problem that neither philosophers nor historians have looked at very seriously and to which literary theorists have given only passing attention. This question has to do with the status of the historical narrative, considered purely as a verbal artifact purporting to be a model of structures and processes long past and therefore not subject to either experimental or observational controls. This is not to say that historians and philosophers of history have failed to take notice of the essentially provisional and contingent nature of historical representations and of their susceptibility to infinite revision in the light of new evidence or more sophisticated conceptualization of problems. One of the marks of a good professional historian is the consistency with which he reminds his readers of the purely provisional nature of his characterizations of events, agents, and agencies found in the always incomplete historical record. Nor is it to say that literary theorists have *never* studied the structure of historical narratives. But in general there has been a reluctance to consider historical narratives as what they most manifestly are: verbal fictions, the contents of which are as much *invented* as *found* and the forms of which have more in common with their counterparts in literature than they have with those in the sciences.

Now, it is obvious that this conflation of mythic and historical consciousness will offend some historians and disturb those literary theorists whose conception of literature presupposes a radical opposition of history to fiction or of fact to fancy. As Northrop Frye has remarked, "In a sense the historical is the opposite of the mythical, and to tell the historian that what gives shape to his book is a myth would sound to him vaguely insulting."[3] Yet Frye himself grants that "when a historian's scheme gets to a certain point of comprehensiveness it becomes mythical in shape, and so approaches the poetic in its structure." He even speaks of different kinds of historical myths: Romantic myths "based on a quest or pilgrimage to a City of God or classless society"; Comic "myths of progress through evolution or revolution"; Tragic myths of "decline and fall, like the works of Gibbon and Spengler"; and Ironic "myths of recurrence or casual catastrophe." But Frye appears to believe that these myths are operative only in such victims of what might be called the "poetic fallacy" as Hegel, Marx, Nietzsche, Spengler, Toynbee, and Sartre[4]—

3. From *Anatomy of Criticism* (1957); White also cites "New Directions from Old," in *Fables of Identity* (1963), by FRYE (1912–1991), Canadian literary critic.

4. French philosopher (1905–1980). Edward Gibbon (1737–1794), English historian, author of *The History of the Decline and Fall of the Roman Empire* (1776–87). Oswald Spengler (1880–1936), German philosopher of history, author of *The Decline of the West* (1918–22). GEORG WILHELM FRIEDRICH HEGEL (1770–1831), German philosopher, author of *The Philosophy of History* (1837). KARL MARX (1818–1883), political and economic theorist whose philosophy of communism draws on Hegel. FRIEDRICH NIETZSCHE (1844–1900), German philosopher. Arnold Toynbee (1889–1975), English historian, author of the 12-volume *Study of History* (1936–61).

historians whose fascination with the "constructive" capacity of human thought has deadened their responsibility to the "found" data. "The historian works inductively," he says, "collecting his facts and trying to avoid any informing patterns except those he sees, or is honestly convinced he sees, in the facts themselves." He does not work "from" a "unifying form," as the poet does, but "toward" it; and it therefore follows that the historian, like any writer of discursive prose, is to be judged "by the truth of what he says, or by the adequacy of his verbal reproduction of his external model," whether that external model be the actions of past men or the historian's own thought about such actions.

What Frye says is true enough as a statement of the *ideal* that has inspired historical writing since the time of the Greeks, but that ideal presupposes an opposition between myth and history that is as problematical as it is venerable. It serves Frye's purposes very well, since it permits him to locate the specifically "fictive" in the space between the two concepts of the "mythic" and the "historical." As readers of Frye's *Anatomy of Criticism* will remember, Frye conceives fictions to consist in part of sublimates of archetypal myth-structures. These structures have been displaced to the interior of verbal artifacts in such a way as to serve as their latent meanings. The fundamental meanings of all fictions, their thematic content, consist, in Frye's view, of the "pre-generic plot-structures" or *mythoi* derived from the corpora of Classical and Judaeo-Christian religious literature. According to this theory, we understand *why* a particular story has "turned out" as it has when we have identified the archetypal myth, or pregeneric plot structure, of which the story is an exemplification. And we see the "point" of a story when we have identified its theme (Frye's translation of *dianoia*[5]), which makes of it a "parable or illustrative fable." "Every work of literature," Frye insists, "has both a fictional and a thematic aspect," but as we move from "fictional projection" toward the overt articulation of theme, the writing tends to take on the aspect of "direct address, or straight discursive writing and cease[s] to be literature." And in Frye's view, as we have seen, history (or at least "proper history") belongs to the category of "discursive writing," so that when the fictional element—or mythic plot structure—is *obviously* present in it, it ceases to be history altogether and becomes a bastard genre, product of an unholy, though not unnatural, union between history and poetry.

Yet, I would argue, histories gain part of their explanatory effect by their success in making stories out of *mere* chronicles; and stories in turn are made out of chronicles by an operation which I have elsewhere called "emplotment." And by emplotment I mean simply the encodation of the facts contained in the chronicle as components of specific *kinds* of plot structures, in precisely the way that Frye has suggested is the case with "fictions" in general.

The late R. G. Collingwood[6] insisted that the historian was above all a story teller and suggested that historical sensibility was manifested in the capacity to make a plausible story out of a congeries of "facts" which, in their unprocessed form, made no sense at all. In their efforts to make sense of the historical record, which is fragmentary and always incomplete, historians have to make use of what Collingwood called "the constructive imagination,"

5. Thought (Greek).
6. English historian (1889–1943), author of *The Idea of History* (1946).

which told the historian—as it tells the competent detective—what "must have been the case" given the available evidence and the formal properties it displayed to the consciousness capable of putting the right question to it. This constructive imagination functions in much the same way that Kant[7] supposed the *a priori* imagination functions when it tells us that even though we cannot perceive both sides of a tabletop simultaneously, we can be certain it has *two* sides if it has one, because the very concept of *one side* entails at least *one other.* Collingwood suggested that historians come to their evidence endowed with a sense of the *possible* forms that different kinds of recognizably human situations *can* take. He called this sense the nose for the "story" contained in the evidence or for the "true" story that was buried in or hidden behind the "apparent" story. And he concluded that historians provide plausible explanations for bodies of historical evidence when they succeed in discovering the story or complex of stories implicitly contained within them.

What Collingwood failed to see was that no given set of casually recorded historical events can in itself constitute a story; the most it might offer to the historian are story *elements*. The events are *made* into a story by the suppression or subordination of certain of them and the highlighting of others, by characterization, motific repetition, variation of tone and point of view, alternative descriptive strategies, and the like—in short, all of the techniques that we would normally expect to find in the emplotment of a novel or a play. For example, no historical event is *intrinsically tragic*; it can only be conceived as such from a particular point of view or from within the context of a structured set of events of which it is an element enjoying a privileged place. For in history what is tragic from one perspective is comic from another, just as in society what appears to be tragic from the standpoint of one class may be, as Marx purported to show of the 18th Brumaire of Louis Buonaparte,[8] only a farce from that of another class. Considered as potential elements of a story, historical events are value-neutral. Whether they find their place finally in a story that is tragic, comic, romantic, or ironic—to use Frye's categories—depends upon the historian's decision to *con*figure them according to the imperatives of one plot structure or mythos rather than another. The same set of events can serve as components of a story that is tragic *or* comic, as the case may be, depending on the historian's choice of the plot structure that he considers most appropriate for ordering events of that kind so as to make them into a comprehensible story.

This suggests that what the historian brings to his consideration of the historical record is a notion of the *types* of configurations of events that can be recognized as stories by the audience for which he is writing. True, he can misfire. I do not suppose that anyone would accept the emplotment of the life of President Kennedy as comedy, but whether it ought to be emplotted romantically, tragically, or satirically is an open question. The important point is that most historical sequences can be emplotted in a number of different ways, so as to provide different interpretations of those events and to endow them with different meanings. Thus, for example, what Michelet

7. IMMANUEL KANT (1724–1804), German philosopher. He distinguished between knowledge deduced from self-evident propositions (a priori) and knowledge deduced from empirical observation (a posteriori).

8. Marx, *The Eighteenth Brumaire of Louis Bonaparte* (1852).

in his great history of the French Revolution construed as a drama of Romantic transcendence, his contemporary Tocqueville[9] emplotted as an ironic Tragedy. Neither can be said to have had more knowledge of the "facts" contained in the record; they simply had different notions of the kind of story that best fitted the facts they knew. Nor should it be thought that they told different stories of the Revolution because they had discovered different *kinds* of facts, political on the one hand, social on the other. They sought out different kinds of facts because they had different kinds of stories to tell. But why did these alternative, not to say mutually exclusive, representations of what was substantially the same set of events appear equally plausible to their respective audiences? Simply because the historians shared with their audiences certain preconceptions about how the Revolution might be emplotted, in response to imperatives that were generally extra historical, ideological, aesthetic, or mythical.

Collingwood once remarked that you could never explicate a tragedy to anyone who was not already acquainted with the kinds of situations that are regarded as "tragic" in our culture. Anyone who has taught or taken one of those omnibus courses usually entitled Western Civilization or Introduction to the Classics of Western Literature will know what Collingwood had in mind. Unless you have some idea of the generic attributes of tragic, comic, romantic, or ironic situations, you will be unable to recognize them as such when you come upon them in a literary text. But historical situations do not have built into them intrinsic meanings in the way that literary texts do. Historical situations are not *inherently* tragic, comic, or romantic. They may all be inherently ironic, but they need not be emplotted that way. All the historian needs to do to transform a tragic into a comic situation is to shift his point of view or change the scope of his perceptions. Anyway, we only think of situations as tragic or comic because these concepts are part of our generally cultural and specifically literary heritage. *How* a given historical situation is to be configured depends on the historian's subtlety in matching up a specific plot structure with the set of historical events that he wishes to endow with a meaning of a particular kind. This is essentially a literary, that is to say fiction-making, operation. And to call it that in no way detracts from the status of historical narratives as providing a kind of knowledge. For not only are the pregeneric plot structures by which sets of events can be constituted as stories of a particular kind limited in number, as Frye and other archetypal critics suggest; but the encodation of events in terms of such plot structures is one of the ways that a culture has of making sense of both personal and public pasts.

We can make sense of sets of events in a number of different ways. One of the ways is to subsume the events under the causal laws which may have governed their concatenation in order to produce the particular configuration that the events appear to assume when considered as "effects" of mechanical forces. This is the way of scientific explanation. Another way we make sense of a set of events which appears strange, enigmatic, or mysterious in its immediate manifestations is to encode the set in terms of culturally provided categories, such as metaphysical concepts, religious beliefs, or story

9. Alexis de Tocqueville (1805–1859), French historian and author of *The Old Régime and the French Revolution* (1856). Jules Michelet (1798–1874), French historian, author of a 7-volume history of the French Revolution (1847–53).

forms. The effect of such encodations is to familiarize the unfamiliar; and in general this is the way of historiography, whose "data" are always immediately strange, not to say exotic, simply by virtue of their distance from us in time and their origin in a way of life different from our own.

The historian shares with his audience *general notions* of the *forms* that significant human situations *must* take by virtue of his participation in the specific processes of sense-making which identify him as a member of one cultural endowment rather than another. In the process of studying a given complex of events, he begins to perceive the *possible* story form that such events *may* figure. In his narrative account of how this set of events took on the shape which he perceives to inhere within it, he emplots his account as a story of a particular kind. The reader, in the process of following the historian's account of those events, gradually comes to realize that the story he is reading is of one kind rather than another: romance, tragedy, comedy, satire, epic, or what have you. And when he has perceived the class or type to which the story that he is reading belongs, he experiences the effect of having the events in the story explained to him. He has at this point not only successfully *followed* the story; he has grasped the point of it, *understood* it, as well. The original strangeness, mystery, or exoticism of the events is dispelled, and they take on a familiar aspect, not in their details, but in their functions as elements of a familiar kind of configuration. They are rendered comprehensible by being subsumed under the categories of the plot structure in which they are encoded as a story of a particular kind. They are familiarized, not only because the reader now has more *information* about the events, but also because he has been shown how the data conform to an *icon* of a comprehensible finished process, a plot structure with which he is familiar as a part of his cultural endowment.

This is not unlike what happens, or is supposed to happen, in psychotherapy. The sets of events in the patient's past which are the presumed cause of his distress, manifested in the neurotic syndrome, have been defamiliarized, rendered strange, mysterious, and threatening and have assumed a meaning that he can neither accept nor effectively reject. It is not that the patient does not *know* what those events were, does not know the facts; for if he did not in some sense know the facts, he would be unable to recognize them and repress them whenever they arise in his consciousness. On the contrary, he knows them all too well. He knows them so well, in fact, that he lives with them constantly and in such a way as to make it impossible for him to see any other facts except through the coloration that the set of events in question gives to his perception of the world. We might say that, according to the theory of psychoanalysis, the patient has overemplotted these events, has charged them with a meaning so intense that, whether real or merely imagined, they continue to shape both his perceptions and his responses to the world long after they should have become "past history." The therapist's problem, then, is not to hold up before the patient the "real facts" of the matter, the "truth" as against the "fantasy" that obsesses him. Nor is it to give him a short course in psychoanalytical theory by which to enlighten him as to the true nature of his distress by cataloguing it as a manifestation of some "complex." This is what the analyst might do in relating the patient's case to a third party, and especially to another analyst. But psychoanalytic theory recognizes that the patient will resist both of these tactics in the same way that he resists the intrusion into consciousness of the traumatized memory traces in the *form* that he obsessively remembers them. The problem is to get the patient to "reemplot" his whole life history in such a way as to change the *meaning* of those events for him and their *significance* for the economy of the whole set of events that make up his life. As thus envisaged, the therapeutic process is an exercise in the refamiliarization of events that have been defamiliarized, rendered alienated from the patient's life-history, by virtue of their overdetermination as causal forces. And we might say that the events are detraumatized by being removed from the plot structure in which they have a dominant place and inserted in another in which they have a subordinate or simply ordinary function as elements of a life shared with all other men.

Now, I am not interested in forcing the analogy between psychotherapy and historiography; I use the example merely to illustrate a point about the fictive component in historical narratives. Historians seek to refamiliarize us with events which have been forgotten through either accident, neglect, or repression. Moreover, the greatest historians have always dealt with those events in the histories of their cultures which are "traumatic" in nature and the meaning of which is either problematical or overdetermined in the significance that they still have for current life, events such as revolutions, civil wars, large-scale processes such as industrialization and urbanization, or institutions which have lost their original function in a society but continue to play an important role on the current social scene. In looking at the ways in which such structures took shape or evolved, historians *re*familiarize them, not only by providing more information about them, but also by showing how their developments conformed to one or another of the story types that we conventionally invoke to make sense of our own life-histories.

Now, if any of this is plausible as a characterization of the explanatory effect of historical narrative, it tells us something important about the *mimetic* aspect of historical narratives.[1] It is generally maintained—as Frye said—that a history is a verbal model of a set of events external to the mind of the historian. But it is wrong to think of a history as a model similar to a scale model of an airplane or ship, a map, or a photograph. For we can check the adequacy of this latter kind of model by going and looking at the original and, by applying the necessary rules of translation, seeing in what respect the model has actually succeeded in reproducing aspects of the original. But historical structures and processes are not like these originals; we cannot go and look at them in order to see if the historian has adequately reproduced them in his narrative. Nor should we want to, even if we could; for after all it was the very strangeness of the original as it appeared in the documents that inspired the historian's efforts to make a model of it in the first place. If the historian only did that for us, we should be in the same situation as the patient whose analyst merely told him, on the basis of interviews with his parents, siblings, and childhood friends, what the "true facts" of the patient's early life were. We would have no reason to think that anything at all had been *explained* to us.

This is what leads me to think that historical narratives are not only models of past events and processes, but also metaphorical statements which suggest a relation of similitude between such events and processes and the

1. White explores in history the same problem of mimesis that PLATO explored in poetry in *Republic* 10 (ca. 373 B.C.E.; see above).

story types that we conventionally use to endow the events of our lives with culturally sanctioned meanings. Viewed in a purely formal way, a historical narrative is not only a *reproduction* of the events reported in it, but also a *complex of symbols* which gives us directions for finding an *icon* of the structure of those events in our literary tradition.

I am here, of course, invoking the distinctions between sign, symbol, and icon which C. S. Peirce[2] developed in his philosophy of language. I think that these distinctions will help us to understand what is fictive in all putatively realistic representations of the world and what is realistic in all manifestly fictive ones. They help us, in short, to answer the question, What are historical representations *representations of?* It seems to me that we must say of histories what Frye seems to think is true only of poetry or philosophies of history, namely that, considered as a system of signs, the historical narrative points in two directions simultaneously: *toward* the events described in the narrative and *toward* the story type or mythos which the historian has chosen to serve as the icon of the structure of the events. The narrative itself is not the icon; what it does is *describe* events in the historical record in such a way as to inform the reader *what to take as an icon* of the events so as to render them "familiar" to him. The historical narrative thus mediates between the events reported in it on the one side and pregeneric plot structures conventionally used in our culture to endow unfamiliar events and situation with meanings on the other.

The evasion of the implications of the fictive nature of historical narrative is in part a consequence of the utility of the concept "history" for the definition of other types of discourse. "History" can be set over against "science" by virtue of its want of conceptual rigor and failure to produce the kinds of universal laws that the sciences characteristically seek to produce. Similarly, "history" can be set over against "literature" by virtue of its interest in the "actual" rather than the "possible," which is supposedly the object of representation of "literary" works. Thus, within a long and distinguished critical tradition that has sought to determine what is "real" and what is "imagined" in the novel, history has served as a kind of archetype of the "realistic" pole of representation. I am thinking of Frye, Auerbach, Booth, Scholes and Kellogg,[3] and others. Nor is it unusual for literary theorists, when they are speaking about the "context" of a literary work, to suppose that this context—the "historical milieu"—has a concreteness and an accessibility that the work itself can never have, as if it were easier to perceive the reality of a past world put together from a thousand historical documents than it is to probe the depths of a single literary work that is present to the critic studying it. But the presumed concreteness and accessibility of historical milieux, these contexts of the texts that literary scholars study, are themselves products of the fictive capability of the historians who have studied those contexts. The historical documents are not less opaque than the texts studied by the literary critic. Nor

2. Charles Sanders Peirce (1839–1914), American philosopher generally credited, along with FERDINAND DE SAUSSURE (1857–1913), with the founding of semiotics, the modern science that studies all types of sign systems. An icon is a sign in which the signifier (the sound or symbol that conveys meaning) resembles or imitates the signified (the meaning conveyed); a symbol is a sign in which the relationship between the two is purely conventional.

3. All those named are authors of key texts of narrative theory. ERICH AUERBACH (1892–1957), German literary critic and author of *Mimesis: The Representation of Reality in Western Literature* (1946); Wayne Booth (1921–2005), American literary critic and author of *The Rhetoric of Fiction* (1961); and Robert Scholes (1929–2016) and Robert Kellogg (1928–2004), American coauthors of *The Nature of Narrative* (1966).

is the world those documents figure more accessible. The one is no more "given" than the other. In fact, the opaqueness of the world figured in historical documents is, if anything, increased by the production of historical narratives. Each new historical work only adds to the number of possible texts that have to be interpreted if a full and accurate picture of a given historical milieu is to be faithfully drawn. The relationship between the past to be analyzed and historical works produced by analysis of the documents is paradoxical; the *more* we know about the past, the more difficult it is to generalize about it.

But if the increase in our knowledge of the past makes it more difficult to generalize about it, it should make it easier for us to generalize about the forms in which that knowledge is transmitted to us. Our knowledge of the past may increase incrementally, but our understanding of it does not. Nor does our understanding of the past progress by the kind of revolutionary breakthroughs that we associate with the development of the physical sciences.[4] Like literature, history progresses by the production of classics, the nature of which is such that they cannot be disconfirmed or negated, in the way that the principal conceptual schemata of the sciences are. And it is their nondisconfirmability that testifies to the essentially *literary* nature of historical classics. There is something in a historical masterpiece that cannot be negated, and this nonnegatable element is its form, the form which is its fiction.

It is frequently forgotten or, when remembered, denied that no given set of events attested by the historical record comprises a *story* manifestly finished and complete. This is as true as the events that comprise the life of an individual as it is of an institution, a nation, or a whole people. We do not *live* stories, even if we give our lives meaning by retrospectively casting them in the form of stories. And so too with nations or whole cultures. In an essay on the "mythical" nature of historiography, Lévi-Strauss[5] remarks on the astonishment that a visitor from another planet would feel if confronted by the thousands of histories written about the French Revolution. For in those works, the "authors do not always make use of the same incidents; when they do, the incidents are revealed in different lights. And yet these are variations which have to do with the same country, the same period, and the same events—events whose reality is scattered across every level of a multilayered structure." He goes on to suggest that the criterion of validity by which historical accounts might be assessed cannot depend on their "elements"—that is to say—their putative factual content. On the contrary, he notes, "pursued in isolation, each element shows itself to be beyond grasp. But certain of them derive consistency from the fact that they can be integrated into a system whose terms are more or less credible when set against the overall coherence of the series." But his "coherence of the series" cannot be the coherence of the *chronological* series, that sequence of "facts" organized into the temporal order of their original occurrence. For the "chronicle" of events, out of which the historian fashions his story of "what really happened," already comes preencoded. There are "hot" and "cold" chronologies, chronologies in which more or fewer dates appear to demand inclusion in a full chronicle of

4. White may be alluding to Thomas Kuhn's celebrated *Structure of Scientific Revolutions* (1962), which characterizes scientific progress as a sequence of abrupt revolutions that overturn existing paradigms, rendering them obsolete.

5. CLAUDE LÉVI-STRAUSS (1908–2009), French anthropologist whose work was influential in the development of structuralism. White cites Lévi-Strauss's *Savage Mind* (1966) and his "Overture to *Le Cru et le cuit*," published in *Structuralism* (ed. Jacques Ehrmann, 1966).

what happened. Moreover, the dates themselves come to us already grouped into classes of dates, classes which are constitutive of putative domains of the historical field, domains which appear as problems for the historian to solve if he is to give a full and culturally responsible account of the past.

All this suggests to Lévi-Strauss that, when it is a matter of working up a comprehensive account of the various domains of the historical record in the form of a story, the "alleged historical continuities" that the historian purports to find in the record are "secured only by dint of fraudulent outlines" imposed by the historian on the record. These "fraudulent outlines" are, in his view, a product of "abstraction" and a means of escape from the "threat of an infinite regress" that always lurks at the interior of every complex set of historical "facts." We can construct a comprehensible story of the past, Lévi-Strauss insists, only by a decision to "give up" one or more of the domains of facts offering themselves for inclusion in our accounts. Our *explanations* of historical structures and processes are thus determined more by what we leave out of our representations than by what we put in. For it is in this brutal capacity to exclude certain facts in the interest of constituting others as components of comprehensible stories that the historian displays his tact as well as his understanding. The "overall coherence" of any given "series" of historical facts is the coherence of story, but this coherence is achieved only by a tailoring of the "facts" to the requirements of the story form. And thus Lévi-Strauss concludes: "In spite of worthy and indispensable efforts to bring another moment in history alive and to possess it, a clairvoyant history should admit that it never completely escapes from the nature of myth."

It is this mediative function that permits us to speak of a historical narrative as an extended metaphor. As a symbolic structure, the historical narrative does not *reproduce* the events it describes; it tells us in what direction to think about the events and charges our thought about the events with different emotional valences. The historical narrative does not *image* the things it indicates; it *calls to mind* images of the things it indicates, in the same way that a metaphor does. When a given concourse of events is emplotted as a "tragedy," this simply means that the historian has so described the events as to *remind us* of that form of fiction which we associate with the concept "tragic." Properly understood, histories ought never to be read as unambiguous signs of the events they report, but rather as symbolic structures, extended metaphors, that "liken" the events reported in them to some form with which we have already become familiar in our literary culture.

Perhaps I should indicate briefly what is meant by the *symbolic* and *iconic* aspects of a metaphor. The hackneyed phrase "My love, a rose" is not, obviously, intended to be understood as suggesting that the loved one is *actually* a rose. It is not even meant to suggest that the loved one has the specific attributes of a rose—that is to say, that the loved one is red, yellow, orange, or black, is a plant, has thorns, needs sunlight, should be sprayed regularly with insecticides, and so on. It is meant to be understood as indicating that the beloved shares the *qualities* which the rose has come to *symbolize* in the customary linguistic usages of Western culture. That is to say, considered as a message, the metaphor gives directions for finding an entity that will evoke the images associated *with loved ones and roses alike* in our culture. The metaphor does not *image* the thing it seeks to characterize, *it gives directions* for finding the set of images that are intended to be associated with that thing. It functions as a symbol, rather than as a sign: which is to say that it does not give us either a *description* or an *icon* of the thing it represents, but *tells us* what images to look for in our culturally encoded experience in order to determine how we *should feel* about the thing represented.

So too for historical narratives. They succeed in endowing sets of past events with meanings, over and above whatever comprehension they provide by appeal to putative causal laws, by exploiting the metaphorical similarities between sets of real events and the conventional structures of our fictions. By the very constitution of a set of events in such a way as to make a comprehensible story out of them, the historian charges those events with the symbolic significance of a comprehensible plot structure. Historians may not like to think of their works as translations of fact into fictions; but this is one of the effects of their works. By suggesting alternative emplotments of a given sequence of historical events, historians provide events with all of the possible meanings with which the literary art of their culture is capable of endowing them. The real dispute between the proper historian and the philosopher of history has to do with the latter's insistence that events can be emplotted in one and only one story form. History-writing thrives on the discovery of all the possible plot structures that might be invoked to endow sets of events with different meanings. And our understanding of the past increases precisely in the degree to which we succeed in determining how far that past conforms to the strategies of sense-making that are contained in their purest forms in literary art.

Conceiving historical narratives in this way may give us some insight into the crisis in historical thinking which has been under way since the beginning of our century. Let us imagine that the problem of the historian is to make sense of a hypothetical *set* of events by arranging them in a *series* that is at once chronologically *and* syntactically structured, in the way that any discourse from a sentence all the way up to a novel is structured. We can see immediately that the imperatives of chronological arrangement of the events constituting the set must exist in tension with the imperatives of the syntactical strategies alluded to, whether the latter are conceived as those of logic (the syllogism) or those of narrative (the plot structure).

Thus, we have a set of events

(1) *a, b, c, d, e, ... , n,*

ordered chronologically but requiring description and characterization as elements of plot or argument by which to give them meaning. Now, the series can be emplotted in a number of different ways and thereby endowed with different meanings without violating the imperatives of the chronological arrangement at all. We may briefly characterize some of these emplotments in the following ways:

(2) A, *b, c, d, e, ... , n*

(3) *a*, B, *c, d, e, ... , n*

(4) *a, b*, C, *d, e, ... , n*

(5) *a, b, c*, D, *e, ... , n*

And so on.

The capitalized letters indicate the privileged status given to certain events or sets of events in the series by which they are endowed with explanatory force, either as causes explaining the structure of the whole series or as symbols of the plot structure of the series considered as a story of a specific kind. We might say that any history which endows any putatively original event (*a*) with the status of a decisive factor (*A*) in the structuration of the whole series of events following after it is "deterministic." The emplotments of the history of "society" by Rousseau in his *Second Discourse*, Marx in the *Manifesto*, and Freud in *Totem and Taboo* would fall into this category.[6] So too, any history which endows the last event in the series (*e*), whether real or only speculatively projected, with the force of full explanatory power (*E*) is of the type of all eschatological or apocalyptical histories. St. Augustine's *City of God* and the various versions of the Joachite notion[7] of the advent of a millennium, Hegel's *Philosophy of History*, and, in general, all Idealist histories are of this sort. In between we would have the various forms of historiography which appeal to plot structures of a distinctively "fictional" sort (Romance, Comedy, Tragedy, and Satire) by which to endow the series with a perceivable form and a conceivable "meaning."

If the series were simply recorded in the order in which the events originally occurred, under the assumption that the ordering of the events in their temporal sequence itself provided a kind of explanation of why they occurred when and where they did, we would have the pure form of the *chronicle*. This would be a "naive" form of chronicle, however, inasmuch as the categories of time and space alone served as the informing interpretative principles. Over against the naive form of chronicle we could postulate as a logical possibility its "sentimental" counterpart,[8] the ironic denial that historical series have any kind of larger significance or describe any imaginable plot structure or indeed can even be construed as a story with a discernible beginning, middle, and end. We could conceive such accounts of history as intending to serve as antidotes to their false or overemplotted counterparts (nos. 2, 3, 4, and 5 above) and could represent them as an ironic return to mere chronicle as constituting the only sense which any cognitively responsible history could take. We could characterize such histories thus:

(6) "*a*, *b*, *c*, *d*, *e* . . . . , *n*"

with the quotation marks indicating the conscious interpretation of the events as having nothing other than seriality as their meaning.

This schema is of course highly abstract and does not do justice to the possible mixtures of and variations within the types that it is meant to distinguish. But it helps us, I think, to conceive how events might be emplotted in different ways without violating the imperatives of the chronological order of the events (however they are construed) so as to yield alternative, mutually

6. SIGMUND FREUD (1856–1939), Austrian founder of psychoanalysis; *Totem and Taboo* was published in 1918. Jean-Jacques Rousseau (1712–1778), Swiss-born French philosopher and political theorist; his "second" discourse is the *Discourse on the Origin and Bases of Inequality among Men* (1754). Marx and FRIEDRICH ENGELS's *Communist Manifesto* appeared as a pamphlet in 1848.

7. Taken from Joachim of Fiore (1135–1202), an Italian monk who propounded a millenarian theory of history between 1190 and 1195. AUGUSTINE (354–430), early Christian philosopher and theologian.

8. For the opposition of "naive" and "sentimental," see FRIEDRICH VON SCHILLER, *On Naive and Sentimental Poetry* (1795–96).

exclusive, and yet, equally plausible interpretations of the set. I have tried to show in *Metahistory* how such mixtures and variations occur in the writings of the master historians of the nineteenth century; and I have suggested in that book that classic historical accounts always represent attempts both to emplot the historical series adequately and implicitly to come to terms with other plausible emplotments. It is this dialectical tension between two or more possible emplotments that signals the elements of critical self-consciousness present in any historian of recognizably classical stature.

Histories, then, are not only about events but also about the possible sets of relationships that those events can be demonstrated to figure. These sets of relationships are not, however, immanent in the events themselves; they exist only in the mind of the historian reflecting on them. Here they are present as the modes of relationships conceptualized in the myth, fable, and folklore, scientific knowledge, religion, and literary art, of the historian's own culture. But more importantly, they are, I suggest, immanent in the very language which the historian must use to *describe* events prior to a scientific analysis of them or a fictional emplotment of them. For if the historian's aim is to familiarize us with the unfamiliar, he must use figurative, rather than technical, language. Technical languages are familiarizing only *to* those who have been indoctrinated in their uses and only *of* those sets of events which the practitioners of a discipline have agreed to describe in a uniform terminology. History possesses no such generally accepted technical terminology and in fact no agreement on what kind of events make up its specific subject matter. The historian's characteristic instrument of encodation, communication, and exchange is ordinary educated speech. This implies that the only instruments that he has for endowing his data with meaning, of rendering the strange familiar, and of rendering the mysterious past comprehensible, are the techniques of *figurative* language. All historical narratives presuppose figurative characterizations of the events they purport to represent and explain. And this means that historical narratives, considered purely as verbal artifacts, can be characterized by the mode of figurative discourse in which they are cast.

If this is the case, then it may well be that the kind of emplotment that the historian decides to use to give meaning to a set of historical events is dictated by the dominant figurative mode of the language he has used to *describe* the elements of his account *prior* to his composition of a narrative. Geoffrey Hartman[9] once remarked in my hearing, at a conference on literary history, that he was not sure that he knew what historians of literature might want to do, but he did know that to write a history meant to place an event within a context, by relating it as a part to some conceivable whole. He went on to suggest that as far as he knew, there were only two ways of relating parts to wholes, by metonymy and by synecdoche.[1] Having been engaged for some time in the study of the thought of Giambattista Vico,[2] I was much taken with this thought, because it conformed to Vico's

9. American literary critic and theorist (1929–2016).
1. A figure of speech in which a part is used for the whole (e.g., "all *hands* on deck") or the whole for a part (e.g., "*England* won the World Cup"). "Metonymy": a figure of speech in which one word or phrase is substituted for another with which it is closely associated (e.g., *the stage* meaning "the theater").
2. Italian philosopher and historian (1668–1744), author of *New Science* (1725; see above).

notion that the "logic" of all "poetic wisdom" was contained in the relationships which language itself provided in the four principal modes of figurative representation: metaphor, metonymy, synecdoche, and irony. My own hunch—and it is a hunch which I find confirmed in Hegel's reflections on the nature of nonscientific discourse—is that in any field of study which, like history, has not yet become disciplinized to the point of constructing a formal terminological system for describing its objects, in the way that physics and chemistry have, it is the types of figurative discourse that dictate the fundamental forms of the data to be studied. This means that the *shape* of the *relationships* which will appear to be inherent in the objects inhabiting the field will in reality have been imposed on the field by the investigator in the very *act of identifying and describing* the objects that he finds there. The implication is that historians *constitute* their subjects as possible objects of narrative representation by the very language they use to *describe* them. And if this is the case, it means that the different kinds of historical interpretations that we have of the same set of events, such as the French Revolution as interpreted by Michelet, Tocqueville, Taine,[3] and others, are little more than projections of the linguistic protocols that these historians used to *pre*-figure that set of events prior to writing their narratives of it. It is only a hypothesis, but it seems possible that the conviction of the historian that he has "found" the form of his narrative in the events themselves, rather than imposed it upon them, in the way the poet does, is a result of a certain lack of linguistic self-consciousness which obscures the extent to which descriptions of events *already* constitute interpretations of their nature. As thus envisaged, the difference between Michelet's and Tocqueville's accounts of the Revolution does not reside only in the fact that the former emplotted his story in the modality of a Romance and the latter his in the modality of Tragedy; it resides as well in the tropological mode—metaphorical and metonymic, respectively—with each brought to his apprehension of the facts as they appeared in the documents.

I do not have the space to try to demonstrate the plausibility of this hypothesis, which is the informing principle of my book *Metahistory*. But I hope that this essay may serve to suggest an approach to the study of such discursive prose forms as historiography, an approach that is as old as the study of rhetoric and as new as modern linguistics. Such a study would proceed along the lines laid out by Roman Jakobson[4] in a paper entitled "Linguistics and Poetics," in which he characterized the difference between Romantic poetry and the various forms of nineteenth-century Realistic prose as residing in the essentially metaphorical nature of the former and the essentially metonymical nature of the latter. I think that this characterization of the difference between poetry and prose is too narrow, because it presupposes that complex macrostructural narratives such as the novel are little more than projections of the "selective" (i.e., phonemic) axis of all speech acts. Poetry, and especially Romantic poetry, is then characterized by Jakobson as a projection of the "combinatory" (i.e., morphemic) axis of

3. Hippolyte-Adolphe Taine (1828–1893), French literary and art critic, philosopher, and historian who analyzed art and literature as products of race, environment, and epoch.

4. Russian-born American linguist (1896–1982); for "Linguistics and Poetics" (1960), see above.

language. Such a binary theory pushes the analyst toward a dualistic opposition between poetry and prose which appears to rule out the possibility of a metonymical poetry and a metaphorical prose. But the fruitfulness of Jakobson's theory lies in its suggestion that the various forms of both poetry and prose, all of which have their counterparts in narrative in general and therefore in historiography too, can be characterized in terms of the dominant trope which serves as the paradigm, provided by language itself, of all significant relationships conceived to exist in the world by anyone wishing to represent those relationships in language.

Narrative, or the syntagmatic dispersion of events across a temporal series presented as a prose discourse,[5] in such a way as to display their progressive elaboration as a comprehensible form, would represent the "inward turn" that discourse takes when it tries to *show* the reader the true form of things existing behind a merely apparent formlessness. Narrative *style*, in history as well as in the novel, would then be construed as the modality of the movement from a representation of some original state of affairs to some subsequent state. The primary *meaning* of a narrative would then consist of the destructuration of a set of events (real or imagined) originally encoded in one tropological mode and the progressive restructuration of the set in another tropological mode. As thus envisaged, narrative would be a process of decodation and recodation in which an original perception is clarified by being cast in a figurative mode different from that in which it has come encoded by convention, authority, or custom. And the explanatory force of the narrative would then depend on the contrast between the original encodation and the later one.

For example, let us suppose that a set of experiences comes to us as a grotesque, i.e., as unclassified and unclassifiable. Our problem is to identify the modality of the relationships that bind the discernible elements of the formless totality together in such a way as to make of it a whole of some sort. If we stress the similarities among the elements, we are working in the mode of metaphor; if we stress the differences among them, we are working in the mode of metonymy. Of course, in order to make sense of any set of experiences, we must obviously identify both the parts of a thing that appear to make it up and the nature of the shared aspects of the parts that make them identifiable as a totality. This implies that all original characterizations of anything must utilize *both* metaphor and metonymy in order to "fix" it as something about which we can meaningfully discourse.

In the case of historiography, the attempts of commentators to make sense of the French Revolution are instructive. Burke[6] decodes the events of the Revolution which his contemporaries experience as a grotesque by recoding it in the mode of irony; Michelet recodes these events in the mode of synecdoche; Tocqueville recodes them in the mode of metonymy. In each case, however, the movement from code to recode is narratively described, i.e., laid out on a time-line in such a way as to make the interpretation of the events that made up the "Revolution" a kind of drama that we can recognize as Satirical, Romantic, and Tragic, respectively. This drama can be followed

5. In linguistics, *syntagmatic* designates the relationship between items that combine to form a meaningful whole (e.g., the words in a sentence); by extension, the term here refers to the relationships between events in a narrative, their sequence.

6. EDMUND BURKE (1729–1797), English author of *Reflections on the Revolution in France* (1790).

by the reader of the narrative in such a way as to be experienced as a progressive revelation of what the *true* nature of the events consists of. The revelation is not experienced, however, as a restructuring of perception so much as an illumination of a field of occurrence. But actually what has happened is that a set of events originally encoded in one way is simply being decoded by being recoded in another. The events themselves are not substantially changed from one account to another. That is to say, the data that are to be analyzed are not significantly different in the different accounts. What is different are the modalities of their relationships. These modalities, in turn, although they *may* appear to the reader to be based on different theories of the nature of society, politics, and history, ultimately have their origin in the figurative characterizations of the whole set of events as representing wholes of fundamentally different sorts. It is for this reason that, when it is a matter of setting different interpretations of the same set of historical phenomena over against one another in an attempt to decide which is the best or most convincing, we are often driven to confusion or ambiguity. This is not to say that we cannot distinguish between good and bad historiography, since we can always fall back on such criteria as responsibility to the rules of evidence, the relative fullness of narrative detail, logical consistency, and the like to determine this issue. But it is to say that the effort to distinguish between good and bad interpretations of a historical event such as the Revolution is not as easy as it might at first appear when it is a matter of dealing with alternative interpretations produced by historians of relatively equal learning and conceptual sophistication. After all, a great historical classic cannot be disconfirmed or nullified either by the discovery of some new datum that might call a specific explanation of some element of the whole account into question or by the generation of new methods of analysis which permit us to deal with questions that earlier historians might not have taken under consideration. And it is precisely because great historical classics, such as works by Gibbon, Michelet, Thucydides, Mommsen, Ranke, Burckhardt, Bancroft,[7] and so on, cannot be definitely disconfirmed that we must look to the specifically literary aspects of their work as crucial, and not merely subsidiary, elements in their historiographical technique.

What all this points to is the necessity of revising the distinction conventionally drawn between poetic and prose discourse in discussion of such narrative forms as historiography and recognizing that the distinction, as old as Aristotle,[8] between history and poetry obscures as much as it illuminates about both. If there is an element of the historical in all poetry, there is an element of poetry in every historical account of the world. And this because in our account of the historical world we are dependent, in ways perhaps that we are not in the natural sciences, on the techniques of *figurative language*

7. All prominent historians: Thucydides (ca. 455–ca. 400 B.C.E.), Greek author of *The History of the Peloponnesian Wars*; Theodor Mommsen (1817–1903), German classical scholar and author of *The History of Rome* (1854–55), who received the 1902 Nobel Prize in Literature; Leopold von Ranke (1795–1886), German founder of the modern school of history that championed objectivity based on source materials rather than on legend and tradition; Jakob Burckhardt (1818–1897), Swiss historian of art and culture, author of *The Civilization of the Renaissance in Italy* (1860); and George Bancroft (1800–1891), U.S. statesman and author of a 10-volume *History of the United States* (1837–74).

8. See ARISTOTLE (384–322 B.C.E.), *Poetics* 9, 1451b: "The difference [between history and poetry] is that the former relates things that have happened, the latter things that may happen. For this reason poetry is more philosophical and more serious than history; poetry tends to speak of universals, history of particulars."

both for our *characterization* of the objects of our narrative representations and for the *strategies* by which to constitute narrative accounts of the transformations of those objects in time. And this because history has no stipulatable subject matter uniquely its own; it is always written as part of a contest between contending poetic figurations of what the past *might* consist of.

The older distinction between fiction and history, in which fiction is conceived as the representation of the imaginable and history as the representation of the actual, must give place to the recognition that we can only know the *actual* by contrasting it with or likening it to the *imaginable*. As thus conceived, historical narratives are complex structures in which a world of experience is imagined to exist under at least two modes, one of which is encoded as "real," the other of which is "revealed" to have been illusory in the course of the narrative. Of course, it is a fiction of the historian that the various states of affairs which he constitutes as the beginning, the middle, and the end of a course of development are all "actual" or "real" and that he has merely recorded "what happened" in the transition from the inaugural to the terminal phase. But both the beginning state of affairs and the ending one are inevitably poetic constructions, and as such, dependent upon the modality of the figurative language used to give them the aspect of coherence. This implies that all narrative is not simply a recording of "what happened" in the transition from one state of affairs to another, but a progressive *redescription* of sets of events in such a way as to dismantle a structure encoded in one verbal mode in the beginning so as to justify a recoding of it in another mode at the end. This is what the "middle" of all narratives consist of.

All of this is highly schematic, and I know that this insistence on the fictive element in all historical narratives is certain to arouse the ire of historians who believe that they are doing something fundamentally different from the novelist, by virtue of the fact that they deal with "real," while the novelist deals with "imagined," events. But neither the form nor the explanatory power of narrative derives from the different contents it is presumed to be able to accommodate. In point of fact, history—the real world as it evolves in time—is made sense of in the same way that the poet or novelist tries to make sense of it, i.e., by endowing what originally appears to be problematical and mysterious with the aspect of a recognizable, because it is a familiar, form. It does not matter whether the world is conceived to be real or only imagined; the manner of making sense of it is the same.

So too, to say that we make sense of the real world by imposing upon it the formal coherency that we customarily associate with the products of writers of fiction in no way detracts from the status as knowledge which we ascribe to historiography. It would only detract from it if we were to believe that literature did not teach us anything about reality, but was a product of an imagination which was not of this world but of some other, inhuman one. In my view, we experience the "fictionalization" of history as an "explanation" for the same reason that we experience great fiction as an illumination of a world that we inhabit along with the author. In both we recognize the forms by which consciousness both constitutes and colonizes the world it seeks to inhabit comfortably.

Finally, it may be observed that if historians were to recognize the fictive element in their narratives, this would not mean the degradation of historiography to the status of ideology or propaganda. In fact, this recognition would serve as a potent antidote to the tendency of historians to become captive of ideological preconceptions which they do not recognize as such but honor as the "correct" perception of "the way things *really* are." By drawing historiography nearer to its origins in literary sensibility, we should be able to identify the ideological, because it is the fictive, element in our own discourse. We are always able to see the fictive element in those historians with whose interpretations of a given set of events we disagree; we seldom perceive that element in our own prose. So, too, if we recognized the literary or fictive element in every historical account, we would be able to move the teaching of historiography onto a higher level of self-consciousness than it currently occupies.

What teacher has not lamented his inability to give instruction to apprentices in the *writing* of history? What graduate student of history has not despaired at trying to comprehend and imitate the model which his instructors *appear* to honor but the principles of which remain uncharted? If we recognize that there is a fictive element in all historical narrative, we would find in the theory of language and narrative itself the basis for a more subtle presentation of what historiography consists of than that which simply tells the student to go and "find out the facts" and write them up in such a way as to tell "what really happened."

In my view, history as a discipline is in bad shape today because it has lost sight of its origins in the literary imagination. In the interest of *appearing* scientific and objective, it has repressed and denied to itself its own greatest source of strength and renewal. By drawing historiography back once more to an intimate connection with its literary basis, we should not only be putting ourselves on guard against *merely* ideological distortions; we should be by way of arriving at that "theory" of history without which it cannot pass for a "discipline" at all.

1978

JEAN BAUDRILLARD
1929–2007

A prophet crying out in the wilderness of postmodernity, the sociologist Jean Baudrillard made dramatic pronouncements that hit a nerve in the 1980s and 1990s, especially in the international art world. The urge to define our "postmodern condition" has perhaps faded, but the basic tenets of Baudrillard's critique still speak directly to the phenomena of global financial speculation, ever-increasing tourism, and the frenzied stimulation of consumer desire through the media. The obliteration of nature by culture, particularly the replacement of the real by signs, is Baudrillard's great theme. Paradoxically enough, the accuracy of his analysis, its correspondence to what is happening in the contemporary world, secures him a hearing even from those who find his style cryptic and his claims about media simulation of reality hyperbolic.

The son of civil servants and the grandson of peasants, Baudrillard shares the formative experiences of others among his generation of French intellectuals:

coming to age in the aftermath of the German Occupation during World War II, when Jean-Paul Sartre's existential Marxism dominated French thought; political radicalization in response to French colonial wars in Indochina and Algeria during the 1950s; opposition to the American war in Vietnam; and involvement, as a young professor, in the "events" of 1968, when French student protesters brought the nation to a standstill for the month of May.

Baudrillard earned his graduate degree in sociology in 1966, and in 1968 he was teaching at Nanterre, one of the new universities at the center of the students' movement. Before getting his degree, he wrote about and translated German literature; he was deeply influenced by the Frankfurt School social theorists MAX HORKHEIMER and THEODOR ADORNO and by the semiotic criticism of ROLAND BARTHES. In the late 1960s he was affiliated with the "Situationists," an international anarchist group that combined Marxist analysis with innovative critiques of consumer society and bourgeois values. After the collapse of the student movement, Baudrillard, like other members of his generation, began to consider what went wrong, starting with his critiques of Marxism (most notably in his *Mirror of Production*, 1973; trans. 1983) and moving toward the issues of media simulation and the hyperreality of consumer society taken up in our selection from *Simulations* (1981; trans. 1983). After becoming a minor cult figure in the 1980s, Baudrillard in 1987 resigned his post at Nanterre and published increasingly experimental texts that abandon consecutive argumentation for impressionistic collages of travel narrative, autobiographical material, social critique, and theoretical musings.

The key to Baudrillard's thought is his reversal of the commonsense understanding of the relation of culture to nature, of sign to thing signified. Conventional thought holds that nature (both human and nonhuman, such as trees, weather, ecological systems, the law of gravity) precedes culture (the human-made), which is built on top of it. Similarly, we think of a thing as existing in the world, and then of a word being invented and used to designate that thing. At times, Baudrillard implies that this commonsense view accurately describes how things used to be, at some unspecified time in the past. In our selection, he speaks of four "successive phases of the image [the sign]."

Baudrillard argues that signs have now taken priority over the things signified. In fact, things have just about disappeared altogether. He links this development to the "death of God" (an event famously heralded in the nineteenth century by FRIEDRICH NIETZSCHE), to the devastation of natural environments, and to Western imperial destruction of all "primitive," non-Western, nonmetropolitan "others." Something has changed in the human relation to the nonhuman that plays itself out in a deadly hostility to all things different. It is, Baudrillard makes clear, a change for the worse, and all attempts to turn back the clock only accelerate the triumph of the sign. We are left yearning for the things we have killed, and "nostalgia assumes its full meaning" as we create ever more signs to simulate those lost things. This is "the vengeance of the dead," who haunt us in their absence.

To designate this new function of signs, Baudrillard chooses the term *simulacrum*, a word that denotes representation but also carries the sense of a counterfeit, sham, or fake. Simulacra seem to have referents (real phenomena they refer to), but they are merely pretend representations that mark the absence, not the existence, of the objects they purport to represent. Baudrillard blames two distinct but related culprits for this change: contemporary consumer culture and imperialistic Western science and philosophy.

In consumer society, natural needs or desires have been buried under, if not totally eliminated by, desires stimulated by cultural discourses (advertising, media, and the rest), which tell us what we want. We are so precoded, so filled from the very start with the images of what we desire, that we process our relation to the world completely through those images. Furthermore, capitalist production in our time proceeds by first creating a demand through marketing and then producing the product to meet that demand. There are no longer natural needs that human work strives to satisfy. Rather, there are culturally produced "hyperreal" needs that are generated to provide work and profits. The world is remade in the image of our desires. The signs (the images of what we want) exist before we create the thing to which the sign refers. Thus, for example, sexual desire is no longer a response to a person whom we meet and know face-to-face. Rather, sexual desire is stimulated by images promulgated by the media, and we strive to remake our bodies to fit those images. The "hyperreality" of the model overwhelms the reality of the people we actually live among. Consumer society provides a "precession of simulacra," a parade of images that project a life that consumers are encouraged to try to live.

The second part of Baudrillard's argument—his view of Western thought and Western science—explains how things lose their reality in the final phase, the phase of the simulacrum. His account here parallels visions of the West found earlier in Nietzsche and later in JACQUES DERRIDA, MICHEL FOUCAULT, and other poststructuralist thinkers. The West, with its compulsions to explore and to know the whole globe, is driven to *name* and to explain each thing it encounters. The name, our knowledge, replaces the thing. For the difference and otherness of the thing, we substitute the signs that translate, account for, and tame it within our own signifying system. This is why Baudrillard insists that signs murder. The ethnologist (the anthropologist) erases the very people being studied by embalming them in his or her categories, replacing their reality with an explanatory, scholarly account. Having killed the real thing by reducing it to scientific terms, the anthropologist provides an embalmed simulation of that thing for display in the natural history museum. Western science, especially since the Enlightenment, has increasingly translated all otherness into its own terms, making it safe for subsequent touristlike encounters with the packaged exotic. We get simulated otherness; the real thing has evaporated.

In claiming that "we all become living specimens under the spectral light of ethnology," Baudrillard suggests that we all live our lives as if within quotation marks, as if playing a part in a movie. The student who is starting college, for example, has so many images of college students (from movies or TV) in mind that his or her way of being a student will inevitably be patterned in response to those preexisting images. The patterning may come from an attempt to resist the stereotype, to play against expectations, but the priority of the image still prevails. As "authentic" experience becomes ever harder to conceive, simulation, willed or not, rules the day.

We sense this loss of the real, according to Baudrillard; and our search for authenticity, often subconscious, has become ever more panicky as a result. He interprets Disneyland as an elaborately artificial land created precisely to convince us that our "real" lives are real. Caught up in the "precession of simulacra" that kills everything real and replaces it with fabricated models, we feel that something is wrong; but we have no satisfactory strategies for overturning the growing dominance of images and signs.

In many ways, Baudrillard's work echoes Horkheimer and Adorno's earlier critique of the culture industry. Like them, he often comes across as a European intellectual appalled by American mass culture, extravagantly pessimistic and overgeneralizing. Los Angeles for these critics stands for a dystopian future whose worst feature is that its inhabitants apparently like it. The passivity of (post)modern consumers in Baudrillard's work leaves little space for hope. Only his apocalyptic rhetoric, with its hints of coming implosions, offers any prospect of change.

Critiques of Baudrillard's work since the 1980s have emerged largely from cultural studies, with its attention to the creative and progressive uses to which resisting audiences put the materials offered to them by the various media. In describing how we as social agents live out prescripted patterns, Baudrillard misses the playful and parodic resignifications emphasized by performative accounts of action like JUDITH BUTLER's. But the power of his work—and its influence—rests in its one-sidedness, the energy with which he presents his vision of a globalized economy of simulacra, of signs gone mad as they dictate all of our lives and obliterate anything that stands outside of them.

"The Precession of Simulacra" Keywords: Aesthetics, Media, Postmodernity, Poststructuralism, Representation, Semiotics

From The Precession of Simulacra[1]

> The simulacrum is never that which conceals the truth—it is the truth which conceals that there is none.
> The simulacrum is true.
>
> *Ecclesiastes*[2]

If we were able to take as the finest allegory of simulation the Borges tale[3] where the cartographers of the Empire draw up a map so detailed that it ends up exactly covering the territory (but where the decline of the Empire sees this map become frayed and finally ruined, a few shreds still discernible in the deserts—the metaphysical beauty of this ruined abstraction, bearing witness to an Imperial pride and rotting like a carcass, returning to the substance of the soil, rather as an aging double ends up being confused with the real thing)—then this fable has come full circle for us, and now has nothing but the discrete charm of second-order simulacra.[4]

Abstraction today is no longer that of the map, the double, the mirror or the concept. Simulation is no longer that of a territory, a referential being or a substance. It is the generation by models of a real without origin or reality: a hyperreal. The territory no longer precedes the map, nor survives it. Henceforth, it is the map that precedes the territory—**PRECESSION OF SIMULACRA**—it is the map that engenders the territory and if we were to revive the fable today, it would be the territory whose shreds are slowly rotting across the map. It is the real, and not the map, whose vestiges subsist here and there, in the deserts which are no longer those of the Empire, but our own. *The desert of the real itself.*

In fact, even inverted, the fable is useless. Perhaps only the allegory of the Empire remains. For it is with the same Imperialism that present-day simulators try to make the real, all the real, coincide with their simulation models. But it is no longer a question of either maps or territory. Something has disappeared: the sovereign difference between them that was the abstraction's charm. For it is the difference which forms the poetry of the map and the charm of the territory, the magic of the concept and the charm of the real. This representational imaginary, which both culminates in and is engulfed by the cartographer's mad project of an ideal coextensivity between the map and the territory, disappears with simulation—whose operation is nuclear and genetic, and no longer specular and discursive. With it goes all of metaphysics.[5] No more mirror of being and appearances, of the real and

1. Translated by Paul Foss and Paul Patton.
2. Baudrillard's epigraph does not appear in Ecclesiastes.
3. "On Exactitude in Science" (1960), by Jorge Luis Borges (1899–1986), Argentinian short story writer and poet.
4. Cf. J. Baudrillard, *Symbolic Exchange and Death* (1976) [Baudrillard's note].
5. The branch of philosophy that deals with the ultimate structures or substance of the real. With the replacement of the real by the sign, there would be nothing left for metaphysics to ponder.

its concept. No more imaginary coextensivity: rather, genetic miniaturisation is the dimension of simulation. The real is produced from miniaturised units, from matrices, memory banks and command models—and with these it can be reproduced an indefinite number of times. It no longer has to be rational, since it is no longer measured against some ideal or negative instance. It is nothing more than operational. In fact, since it is no longer enveloped by an imaginary, it is no longer real at all. It is a hyperreal, the product of an irradiating synthesis of combinatory models in a hyperspace without atmosphere.

In this passage to a space whose curvature is no longer that of the real, nor of truth, the age of simulation thus begins with a liquidation of all referentials—worse: by their artificial resurrection in systems of signs, a more ductile material than meaning, in that it lends itself to all systems of equivalence, all binary oppositions and all combinatory algebra. It is no longer a question of imitation, nor of reduplication, nor even of parody. It is rather a question of substituting signs of the real for the real itself, that is, an operation to deter every real process by its operational double, a metastable, programmatic, perfect descriptive machine which provides all the signs of the real and short-circuits all its vicissitudes. Never again will the real have to be produced—this is the vital function of the model in a system of death, or rather of anticipated resurrection which no longer leaves any chance even in the event of death. A hyperreal henceforth sheltered from the imaginary, and from any distinction between the real and the imaginary, leaving room only for the orbital recurrence of models and the simulated generation of difference.

The Divine Irreference of Images

To dissimulate is to feign not to have what one has. To simulate is to feign to have what one hasn't. One implies a presence, the other an absence. But the matter is more complicated, since to simulate is not simply to feign: "Someone who feigns an illness can simply go to bed and make believe he is ill. Some who simulates an illness produces in himself some of the symptoms." (Littre)[6] Thus, feigning or dissimulating leaves the reality principle intact: the difference is always clear, it is only masked; whereas simulation threatens the difference between "true" and "false", between "real" and "imaginary". Since the simulator produces "true" symptoms, is he ill or not? He cannot be treated objectively either as ill, or as not-ill. Psychology and medicine stop at this point, before a thereafter undiscoverable truth of the illness. For if any symptom can be "produced", and can no longer be accepted as a fact of nature, then every illness may be considered as simulatable and simulated, and medicine loses its meaning since it only knows how to treat "true" illnesses by their objective causes. Psychosomatics[7] evolves in a dubious way on the edge of the illness principle. As for psychoanalysis, it transfers the symptom from the organic to the unconscious order: once again, the latter is held to be true, more true than the former—but why should

6. Maximilien-Paul-Émile Littré (1801–1881), French lexicographer and translator of Hippocrates. Baudrillard takes this definition from Littré's dictionary.

7. Bodily symptoms caused by mental or emotional disturbance; these interest Baudrillard as an example of how ideas or images produce a physical reality.

simulation stop at the portals of the unconscious? Why couldn't the "work" of the unconscious be "produced" in the same way as any other symptom in classical medicine? Dreams already are.[8]

The alienist,[9] of course, claims that "for each form of the mental alienation there is a particular order in the succession of symptoms, of which the simulator is unaware and in the absence of which the alienist is unlikely to be deceived." This (which dates from 1865) in order to save at all cost the truth principle, and to escape the spectre raised by simulation—namely that truth, reference and objective causes have ceased to exist. What can medicine do with something which floats on either side of illness, on either side of health, or with the reduplication of illness in a discourse that is no longer true or false? What can psychoanalysis do with the reduplication of the discourse of the unconscious in a discourse of simulation that can never be unmasked, since it isn't false either?[1]

What can the army do with simulators? Traditionally, following a direct principle of identification, it unmasks and punishes them. Today, it can reform an excellent simulator as though he were equivalent to a "real" homosexual, heart-case or lunatic. Even military psychology retreats from the Cartesian clarities[2] and hesitates to draw the distinction between true and false, between the "produced" symptom and the authentic symptom. "If he acts crazy so well, then he must be mad." Nor is it mistaken: in the sense that all lunatics are simulators, and this lack of distinction is the worst form of subversion. Against it classical reason armed itself with all its categories. But it is this today which again outflanks them, submerging the truth principle.

Outside of medicine and the army, favored terrains of simulation, the affair goes back to religion and the simulacrum of divinity: "I forbad any simulacrum in the temples because the divinity that breathes life into nature cannot be represented." Indeed it can. But what becomes of the divinity when it reveals itself in icons, when it is multiplied in simulacra? Does it remain the supreme authority, simply incarnated in images as a visible theology? Or is it volatilized into simulacra which alone deploy their pomp and power of fascination—the visible machinery of icons being substituted for the pure and intelligible Idea of God? This is precisely what was feared by the Iconoclasts, whose millennial quarrel is still with us today.[3] Their rage to destroy images rose precisely because they sensed this omnipotence of simulacra, this facility they have of effacing God from the consciousness of men, and the overwhelming, destructive truth which they suggest: that ultimately there has never been any God, that only the simulacrum exists, indeed that God himself has only ever been his own simulacrum. Had they

8. That is, patients in therapy have dreams that fit their therapist's style of interpretation, "produced" in response to the therapist's prompting rather than reflective of some "truth" or "reality."
9. Psychologist (a 19th-century term).
1. And which is not susceptible to resolution in transference. It is the entanglement of these two discourses which makes psychoanalysis interminable [Baudrillard's note]. SIGMUND FREUD (1856–1939), the Austrian founder of psychoanalysis, wrote that therapy, strictly speaking, was "interminable," but that it should end when the "transference"—which involves the patient's repetition of his or her basic problems in the relationship developed with the therapist—was complete and understood by the patient. The therapist uses this repetition as a way of enlightening the patient about the more general patterns of his or her life.
2. The French philosopher René Descartes (1596–1650) proposed a method for discerning "clear" and hence "certain" ideas.
3. Cf. M. Perniola, "Icones, Visions, Simulacres," *Traverses* / *10*, p. 39 [Baudrillard's note].

been able to believe that images only occulted or masked the Platonic Idea[4] of God, there would have been no reason to destroy them. One can live with the idea of a distorted truth. But their metaphysical despair came from the idea that the images concealed nothing at all, and that in fact they were not images, such as the original model would have made them, but actually perfect simulacra forever radiant with their own fascination. But this death of the divine referential has to be exorcised at all cost.

It can be seen that the iconoclasts, who are often accused of despising and denying images, were in fact the ones who accorded them their actual worth, unlike the iconolaters, who saw in them only reflections and were content to venerate God at one remove. But the converse can also be said, namely that the iconolaters were the most modern and adventurous minds, since underneath the idea of the apparition of God in the mirror of images, they already enacted his death and his disappearance in the epiphany of his representations (which they perhaps knew no longer represented anything, and that they were purely a game, but that this was precisely the greatest game—knowing also that it is dangerous to unmask images, since they dissimulate the fact that there is nothing behind them).

This was the approach of the Jesuits,[5] who based their politics on the virtual disappearance of God and on the worldly and spectacular manipulation of consciences—the evanescence of God in the epiphany of power—the end of transcendence, which no longer serves as alibi for a strategy completely free of influences and signs. Behind the baroque of images hides the grey eminence of politics.

Thus perhaps at stake has always been the murderous capacity of images, murderers of the real, murderers of their own model as the Byzantine icons could murder the divine identity.[6] To this murderous capacity is opposed the dialectical capacity of representations as a visible and intelligible mediation of the Real. All of Western faith and good faith was engaged in this wager on representation: that a sign could refer to the depth of meaning, that a sign could *exchange* for meaning and that something could guarantee this exchange—God, of course. But what if God himself can be simulated, that is to say, reduced to the signs which attest his existence? Then the whole system becomes weightless, it is no longer anything but a gigantic simulacrum—not unreal, but a simulacrum, never again exchanging for what is real, but exchanging in itself, in an uninterrupted circuit without reference or circumference.

So it is with simulation, insofar as it is opposed to representation. The latter starts from the principle that the sign and the real are equivalent (even if this equivalence is utopian, it is a fundamental axiom). Conversely, simulation starts from the *utopia* of this principle of equivalence, *from the radical negation of the sign as value*, from the sign as reversion and death sentence of every reference. Whereas representation tries to absorb simula-

4. That is, a perfect, immutable, transcendent Form or Idea in whose reality particular phenomena imperfectly participate, as described in the writings of PLATO (ca. 427–ca. 347 B.C.E.).

5. Members of a Roman Catholic religious order founded in response to the Protestant Reformation, who have long had a reputation for being manipulative and unscrupulous in promoting Catholicism over Protestantism.

6. The Byzantine empire, the eastern half of the Roman Empire, was the home of the Greek Orthodox Church, whose lavish icons have been seen by Western commentators, depending on their own attitude toward images of the divine, as examples either of pagan idolatry or of beautiful religious art.

tion by interpreting it as false representation, simulation envelops the whole edifice of representation as itself a simulacrum.

This would be the successive phases of the image:

—it is the reflection of a basic reality

—it masks and perverts a basic reality

—it masks the *absence* of a basic reality

—it bears no relation to any reality whatever: it is its own pure simulacrum.

In the first case, the image is a *good* appearance—the representation is of the order of sacrament. In the second, it is an *evil* appearance—of the order of malefice.[7] In the third, it *plays at being* an appearance—it is of the order of sorcery. In the fourth, it is no longer in the order of appearance at all, but of simulation.

The transition from signs which dissimulate something to signs which dissimulate that there is nothing, marks the decisive turning point. The first implies a theology of truth and secrecy (to which the notion of ideology still belongs). The second inaugurates an age of simulacra and stimulation, in which there is no longer any God to recognise his own, nor any last judgement to separate true from false, the real from its artificial resurrection, since everything is already dead and risen in advance.

When the real is no longer what it used to be, nostalgia assumes its full meaning. There is a proliferation of myths of origin and signs of reality; of second-hand truth, objectivity and authenticity. There is an escalation of the true, of the lived experience; a resurrection of the figurative where the object and substance have disappeared. And there is a panic-stricken production of the real and the referential, above and parallel to the panic of material production: this is how simulation appears in the phase that concerns us—a strategy of the real, neo-real and hyperreal whose universal double is a strategy of deterrence.

Rameses, or Rose-Coloured Resurrection

Ethnology almost met a paradoxical death that day in 1971 when the Philippino government decided to return the few dozen Tasaday[8] discovered deep in the jungle, where they had lived for eight centuries undisturbed by the rest of mankind, to their primitive state, out of reach of colonists, tourists and ethnologists. This was at the initiative of the anthropologists themselves, who saw the natives decompose immediately on contact, like a mummy in the open air.

For ethnology to live, its object must die. But the latter revenges itself by dying for having been "discovered," and defies by its death the science that wants to take hold of it.

Doesn't every science live on this paradoxical slope to which it is doomed by the evanescence of its object in the very process of its apprehension, and by the pitiless reversal this dead object exerts on it? Like Orpheus it always turns around too soon, and its object, like Eurydice, falls back into Hades.[9]

7. An evil deed.

8. A small group of people "discovered" in 1971 living in the highland rain forest in the Philippines; they were acclaimed as an example of a "primitive" tribe untouched by modern life. (By the mid-1980s, many anthropologists were convinced that the whole episode was a hoax perpetrated by the Philippine government. Opinion remains divided about the "authenticity" of the Tasaday.)

9. In Greek mythology, the poet-singer Orpheus wins back his dead wife, Eurydice, from the underworld—on the condition (which he does not keep) that he not look back at her until they are on the earth's surface.

It was against this hades of paradox that the ethnologists wanted to protect themselves by cordoning off the Tasaday with virgin forest. Nobody now will touch it: the vein is closed down, like a mine. Science loses a precious capital, but the object will be safe—lost to science, but intact in its "virginity". It isn't a question of sacrifice (science never sacrifices itself: it is always murderous), but of the simulated sacrifice of its object in order to save its reality principle. The Tasaday, frozen in their natural element, provide a perfect alibi, an eternal guarantee. At this point begins a persistent anti-ethnology to which Jaulin, Castaneda and Clastres[1] variously belong. In any case, the logical evolution of a science is to distance itself ever further from its object until it dispenses with it entirely: its autonomy evermore fantastical in reaching its pure form.

The Indian thereby driven back into the ghetto, into the glass coffin of virgin forest, becomes the simulation model for all conceivable Indians *before ethnology*. The latter thus allows itself the luxury of being incarnate beyond itself, in the "brute" reality of these Indians it has entirely reinvented—Savages who are indebted to ethnology for still being Savages: what a turn of events, what a triumph for this science which seemed dedicated to their destruction!

Of course, these particular Savages are posthumous: frozen, cryogenised, sterilised, protected *to death*, they have become referential simulacra, and the science itself a pure simulation. Same thing at Creusot[2] where, in the form of an "open" museum exhibition, they have "museumised" on the spot, as historical witnesses to their period, entire working class quarters, living metallurgical zones, a complete culture including men, women and children and their gestures, languages and habits—living beings fossilised as in a snap shot. The museum, instead of being circumscribed in a geometrical location, is now everywhere, like a dimension of life itself. Thus ethnology, now freed from its object, will no longer be circumscribed as an objective science but is applied to all living things and becomes invisible, like an omnipresent fourth dimension, that of the simulacrum. *We are all Tasaday*, or Indians who have once more become "what they used to be", or at least that which ethnology has made them—simulacra Indians who proclaim at last the universal truth of ethnology.

We all become living specimens under the spectral light of ethnology, or of anti-ethnology which is only the pure form of triumphal ethnology, under the sign of dead differences, and of the resurrection of differences. It is thus extremely naive to look for ethnology among the Savages or in some Third World—it is here, everywhere, in the metropolis, among the whites, in a world completely catalogued and analysed and then *artificially revived as though real*, in a world of simulation: of the hallucination of truth, of blackmail by the real, of the murder and historical (hysterical) retrospection of every symbolic form—a murder whose first victims were, noblesse oblige, the Savages, but which for a long time now has been extended to all Western societies.

1. Three revisionist anthropologists of the 1960s and 1970s, especially interested in Native American peoples and their suffering at the hands of the West: the French Robert Jaulin (1928–1996), Mexican American Carlos Castaneda (1925–1998), and French Pierre Clastres (1934–1977).

2. A town in the Burgundy region of central France and home of the historic Schneider iron and steel mills, founded in 1837. In response to the mill's economic troubles and to the decline of coal mining in the region, the town established a museum in the Schneider family mansion, where it stages the work that it once did in earnest.

But at the same moment ethnology gives up its final and only lesson, the secret which kills it (and which the savages understood much better): the vengeance of the dead.

The confinement of the scientific object is the same as that of the insane and the dead. And just as the whole of society is hopelessly contaminated by that mirror of madness it has held out for itself, so science can only die contaminated by the death of the object which is its inverse mirror. It is science which ostensibly masters the object, but it is the latter which deeply invests the former, following an unconscious reversion, giving only dead and circular replies to a dead and circular interrogation.

Nothing changes when society breaks the mirror of madness (abolishes asylums, gives speech back to the mad, etc.) nor when science seems to break the mirror of its objectivity (effacing itself before its object, as Castaneda does, etc.) and to bow down before "differences." Confinement is succeeded by an apparatus which assumes a countless and endlessly diffractable, multipliable form. As fast as ethnology in its classical institution collapses, it survives in an anti-ethnology whose task is to reinject fictional difference and Savagery everywhere, in order to conceal the fact that it is this world, our own, which in its way has become savage again, that is to say devastated by difference and death.

It is in this way, under the pretext of saving the original, that the caves of Lascaux[3] have been forbidden to visitors and an exact replica constructed 500 metres away, so that everyone can see them (you glance through a peephole at the real grotto and then visit the reconstituted whole). It is possible that the very memory of the original caves will fade in the mind of future generations, but from now on there is no longer any difference: the duplication is sufficient to render both artificial.

In the same way the whole of science and technology were recently mobilised to save the mummy of Rameses II, after it had been left to deteriorate in the basement of a museum.[4] The West was panic-stricken at the thought of not being able to save what the symbolic order had been able to preserve for 40 centuries, but away from the light and gaze of onlookers. Rameses means nothing to us: only the mummy is of inestimable worth since it is what guarantees that accumulation means something. Our entire linear and accumulative culture would collapse if we could not stockpile the past in plain view. To this end the pharaohs must be brought out of their tombs, and the mummies out of their silence. To this end they must be exhumed and given military honors. They are prey to both science and the worms. Only absolute secrecy ensured their potency throughout the millennia—their mastery over putrefaction, which signified a mastery over the total cycle of exchange with death. *We* know better than to use our science for the *reparation* of the mummy, that is, to restore a *visible* order, whereas embalming was a mythical labor aimed at immortalising a *hidden* dimension.

We need a visible past, a visible continuum, a visible myth of origin to reassure us as to our ends, since ultimately we have never believed in them.

3. Site in southern France of cave paintings from the Upper Paleolithic period.

4. In 1977, at the instigation of a French archaeologist, the mummy of Rameses II (Egyptian pharaoh, ca. 1303–1213 B.C.E.) was brought from Cairo to Paris for restoration. French scientists declared it cured of all infection and "immunized" for the future after repairing some tissues and sterilizing them with gamma radiation.

Whence that historic scene of the mummy's reception at Orly airport.[5] All because Rameses was a great despot and military figure? Certainly: but above all because the order which our culture dreams of, behind that defunct power it seeks to annex, could have had nothing to do with it, and it dreams thus because it has exterminated this order by exhuming it *as if it were our own past.*

We are fascinated by Rameses as Renaissance Christians were by the American Indians: those (human?) beings who had never known the word of Christ. Thus, at the beginning of colonisation, there was a moment of stupor and amazement before the very possibility of escaping the universal law of the Gospel. There were two possible responses: either to admit that this law was not universal, or to exterminate the Indians so as to remove the evidence. In general, it was enough to convert them, or even simply to discover them, to ensure their slow extermination.

Thus it would have been enough to exhume Rameses to ensure his extermination by museumification. For mummies do not decay because of worms: they die from being transplanted from a prolonged symbolic order, which is master over death and putrescence, on to an order of history, science and museums—our own, which is no longer master over anything, since it only knows how to condemn its predecessors to death and putrescence and their subsequent resuscitation by science. An irreparable violence towards all secrets, the violence of a civilisation without secrets. The hatred by an entire civilization for its own foundations.

And just as with ethnology playing at surrendering its object the better to establish itself in its pure form, so museumification is only one more turn in the spiral of artificiality. Witness the cloister of St-Michel de Cuxa, which is going to be repatriated at great expense from the Cloisters in New York to be reinstalled on "its original site".[6] And everyone is supposed to applaud this restitution (as with the "experimental campaign to win back the sidewalks" on the Champs-Elysees![7]). However, if the exportation of the cornices was in effect an arbitrary act, and if the Cloisters of New York are really an artificial mosaic of all cultures (according to a logic of the capitalist centralisation of value), then reimportation to the original location is even more artificial: it is a total simulacrum that links up with "reality" by a complete circumvolution.

The cloister should have stayed in New York in its simulated environment, which at least would have fooled no one. Repatriation is only a supplementary subterfuge, in order to make out as though nothing had happened and to indulge in a retrospective hallucination.

In the same way Americans flatter themselves they brought the number of Indians back to what it was before their conquest. Everything is obliterated only to begin again. They even flatter themselves they went one better, by surpassing the original figure. This is presented as proof of the superiority of civilisation: it produces more Indians than they were capable of themselves. By a sinister mockery, this overproduction is yet again a way of destroying

5. One of two main airports serving Paris.
6. A 9th-century Benedictine monastery located in the northeast Pyrenees in France. (This cloister has not in fact been removed from the Cloisters, a New York City museum that contains medieval ecclesiastic architecture taken from Europe.)
7. Broad avenue in Paris.

them: for Indian culture, like all tribal culture, rests on the limitation of the group and prohibiting any of its "unrestricted" growth, as can be seen in case of Ishi.[8] Demographic "promotion", therefore, is just one more step towards symbolic extermination.

We too live in a universe everywhere strangely similar to the original—here things are duplicated by their own scenario. But this double does not mean, as in folklore, the imminence of death—they are already purged of death, and are even better than in life; more smiling, more authentic, in light of their model, like the faces in funeral parlors.

Hyperreal and Imaginary

Disneyland is a perfect model of all the entangled orders of simulation. To begin with it is a play of illusions and phantasms: Pirates, the Frontier, Future World, etc. This imaginary world is supposed to be what makes the operation successful. But what draws the crowds is undoubtedly much more the social microcosm, the miniaturised and *religious* revelling in real America, in its delights and drawbacks. You park outside, queue up inside, and are totally abandoned at the exit. In this imaginary world the only phantasmagoria is in the inherent warmth and affection of the crowd, and in that sufficiently excessive number of gadgets used there to specifically maintain the multitudinous affect. The contrast with the absolute solitude of the parking lot—a veritable concentration camp—is total. Or rather: inside, a whole range of gadgets magnetise the crowd into direct flows—outside, solitude is directed onto a single gadget: the automobile. By an extraordinary coincidence (one that undoubtedly belongs to the peculiar enchantment of this universe), this deep-frozen infantile world happens to have been conceived and realised by a man who is himself now cryogenised: Walt Disney,[9] who awaits his resurrection at minus 180 degrees centigrade.

The objective profile of America, then, may be traced throughout Disneyland, even down to the morphology of individuals and the crowd. All its values are exalted here, in miniature and comic strip form. Embalmed and pacified. Whence the possibility of an ideological analysis of Disneyland (L. Marin[1] does it well in *Utopies, jeux d'espaces*): digest of the American way of life, panegyric to American values, idealised transposition of a contradictory reality. To be sure. But this conceals something else, and that "ideological" blanket exactly serves to cover over a *third-order simulation*: Disneyland is there to conceal the fact that it is the "real" country, all of "real" America, which *is* Disneyland (just as prisons are there to conceal the fact that it is the social in its entirety, in its banal omnipresence, which is carceral[2]). Disneyland is presented as imaginary in order to make us believe that the rest is real, when in fact all of Los Angeles and the America

8. The last surviving member of the Yahi (d. 1916), a Native American tribe of northern California. "Discovered" in 1911 and famed as "the last Stone Age man," Ishi lived his last five years at the University of California's Museum of Anthropology in Berkeley.

9. The cartoonist and film producer (1901–1966), who opened Disneyland in 1955. Disney is widely (though mistakenly) believed to have had his body cryogenically preserved upon death.

1. Louis Marin (1931–1992), French cultural historian and semiotician, who writes about Disneyland in *Utopics: Spatial Play* (1973).

2. Relating to prisons and imprisonment and incarceration. In his book about prisons, *Discipline and Punish* (1975; see above), MICHEL FOUCAULT claimed that modern society was increasingly "carceral."

surrounding it are no longer real, but of the order of the hyperreal and of simulation. It is no longer a question of a false representation of reality (ideology), but of concealing the fact that the real is no longer real, and thus of saving the reality principle.

The Disneyland imaginary is neither true nor false; it is a deterrence machine set up in order to rejuvenate in reverse the fiction of the real. Whence the debility, the infantile degeneration of this imaginary. It is meant to be an infantile world, in order to make us believe that the adults are elsewhere, in the "real" world, and to conceal the fact that real childishness is everywhere, particularly amongst those adults who go there to act the child in order to foster illusions as to their real childishness.

Moreover, Disneyland is not the only one. Enchanted Village, Magic Mountain, Marine World: Los Angeles is encircled by these "imaginary stations" which feed reality, reality-energy, to a town whose mystery is precisely that it is nothing more than a network of endless, unreal circulation—a town of fabulous proportions, but without space or dimensions. As much as electrical and nuclear power stations, as much as film studios, this town, which is nothing more than an immense script and a perpetual motion picture, needs this old imaginary made up of childhood signals and faked phantasms for its sympathetic nervous system.

* * *

1981

JÜRGEN HABERMAS
b. 1929

Committed to completing what he calls "the unfinished project of modernity," Jürgen Habermas is the most important liberal political philosopher and public intellectual of post–World War II Germany. Although steeped in the Marxist tradition of the University of Frankfurt, Habermas nonetheless champions the civil liberties and formal equality before the law associated with constitutional democracy. In particular, he sees the Federal Republic of West Germany, formed after the war, as proof that constitutional representative government serves as a necessary, although not always sufficient, bulwark against the abuses of state power characteristic of the Nazis and, later, of East Germany's Democratic Republic. Habermas recognizes that liberal democracies have been less successful when addressing questions of economic justice and equality, but he argues that the welfare state or what some Europeans call "social democracy" has a better track record in promoting and spreading prosperity than socialism or other alternatives. His political views led him to argue vehemently against the critique of modernity developed by French poststructuralist writers such as MICHEL FOUCAULT, JACQUES DERRIDA, and JEAN-FRANÇOIS LYOTARD. The postmodernism debates initiated in the 1970s often center on Habermas's attempt to defend Enlightenment ideals (most fully articulated in the work of IMMANUEL KANT) of universal reason, rights, and justice against the critiques of the poststructuralists. In the first years of the twenty-first century, however, Derrida and

Habermas found common ground in their joint effort to articulate a "European" ethos against the United States and Britain's military response to the terrorist attacks of 9/11.

Born in Düsseldorf in 1929, Habermas was just young enough to avoid service in Adolf Hitler's army. He recalls the Nuremburg trials of the Nazi war criminals as the formative historical event of his youth, and he insists that Germany must always keep in mind the lessons of its militaristic, totalitarian, and genocidal past. As a public intellectual, Habermas has commented on just about every important event of the past fifty years, including strongly opposing (at the outset) the reunification of Germany after 1989 and arguing vehemently against the so-called new historians who tried to mitigate views of Nazi crimes by comparing them to Joseph Stalin's murders in Russia. As a student, Habermas worked for and with THEODOR ADORNO at the Frankfurt Institute for Social Research, and he eventually directed the Frankfurt Institute himself for ten years (1983–93) after an earlier stint as director of the Max Planck Institute. Since his retirement from Frankfurt in 1993, Habermas has taught at several American universities and maintained an active presence as a scholar and a public intellectual.

Habermas's early work, especially *Knowledge and Human Interests* (1968), reveals a Marxist concern with domination, class struggle, and emancipation. His liberalism retains a Marxist tint, notably in his refusal to consider the economic sphere a "private" domain off-limits to state action and in his focus on illegitimate power inequities. But his battle with poststructuralism and, in particular, his defense of a normative ideal of "communicative reason" shape his later work more than does Marxism. Fundamentally, Habermas remains committed to Kant's desire to identify universal norms that underlie all claims to legitimate authority. Yet even in his early work, Habermas had a more historical understanding than Kant of how those norms emerge and of the specific social conditions needed for their efficacy. Since the 1980s, he has consistently moved away from "transcendental" arguments that ground reason or norms in the necessary conditions of communication or of thought. Instead, his work has become more "pragmatic" (to use a term from linguistics)—that is, more reliant on the intersubjective processes of communication in specific settings as the means through which norms are produced, revised, and enforced. Thus, he has become more interested in laws as they are politically established in specific societies and less interested in "reason," especially in its universal form.

Habermas's first book, *The Structural Transformation of the Public Sphere* (1962), already indicates the interest in civil society, civil liberties, and public communication that marks his endorsement of "the project of modernity" in his later debate with the postmodernists. Modernity, for Habermas, is largely a product of the Enlightenment dream of a free and just society guided by the light of reason. Western societies have not realized that dream, but it provides the standards by which they can measure their failings and thus strive for improvement. Of course, modernity is also a product of the economic arrangements of capitalism, of technological advances, and of the formation of nation-states grounded in ethnic and racial nationalisms. Habermas exhibits his Marxist training in his understanding of society as the product of conflicting forces and in his concern about the various forms of domination (economic, political, and bureaucratic) that threaten the possibility of a free and just society. But he firmly believes that we can criticize domination only from a standpoint that legitimizes political and social arrangements in terms of their rationality and their normative commitment to equality.

Poststructuralists argue that *reason* is an exclusionary term, used to denigrate or silence unwelcome opinions. The other side is always "irrational." In particular, nonprivileged social groups such as women, the poor, children, racial and ethnic others, and the disabled are consistently portrayed as unreasonable. Thus, the "universality" that purports to treat all people equally becomes a double bind: because the standards of "reason" are deemed universally applicable (and everywhere the same), whole social groups are marginalized (or worse) for supposedly failing to meet those standards. Moreover, the instrumental reason associated with the economic and scientific practices that prevail in "modern" societies has produced nuclear weapons, environmental degradation, and the merciless bureaucracies that Foucault so memorably describes in *Discipline and Punish* (1975). It is far from obvious that modernity has increased the freedom or improved the quality of life of most of the world's inhabitants. To many poststructuralists, in light of this history of oppression and destruction the unconditional celebration of reason appears naive at best, and complicit with those ill effects at worst.

Habermas disagrees. He admits that universal rights have been honored more in the breach than in the observance, but he still thinks that reason, suitably revised, can serve as the ideal against which actual practice can be judged. Only the existence of such a norm, he insists, frees us from a political world in which might makes right. And he argues that Foucault (in particular) assumes this very norm even as he attacks reason, since it is the failure of reason in practice to be universal that incites Foucault's ire.

Habermas identifies the norm as "the ideal speech situation," on which depends the very possibility of what he calls "communicative action." He argues that we can derive an effective rational and universal norm if we examine the conditions required for successful communication. This focus on pragmatics makes Habermas especially interesting for literary theorists. He contends that people would not be able to understand one another or to coordinate their activities together without some fundamental agreements embedded in the speech situation.

In our first selection, "The Public Sphere" (1964), Habermas summarizes his influential historical account of the genesis of the Enlightenment ideal of reason. Before the formation of the bourgeoisie (men who command considerable wealth not based on owning land), power and rights in Europe were divided up among the monarch, the nobility (the "first estate"), and the clergy (the "second estate"); members of the populace as a whole (the "third estate") were passive subjects. King, nobility, and clergy continually jockeyed for advantage in the medieval social order, each drawing power from the allegiance of different segments of the nation's population, as the balance tilted first one way, then another.

The bourgeoisie, however, gained social but not political power by accumulating "private" wealth—that is, wealth unconnected with the political power that comes from holding legitimate and actual sway over other people. Within the old order (often called the *ancien régime*), the bourgeoisie had no way to translate its growing economic and social power into political power. So this new class needed to change the whole order. (Habermas is offering his own answer here to the question "What caused the French Revolution?") One key issue is whether the bourgeoisie's revolution can benefit the nonbourgeois members of the third estate. Habermas believes that the values associated with the new public sphere are at least potentially liberating for all, even if in fact the poor, the uneducated, and various stigmatized groups have not enjoyed the fruits of that transformation.

The crucial change began with the transformation of the public sphere, the creation of "civil society" in its modern form. Unlike the court, the aristocratic estate, the cathedral, the family home, or the place of business, civil society features the congregation of private persons who are not acting in any official capacity when they get together, who do not know each other intimately, and who gather primarily to talk and exchange opinions. Habermas has in mind not just the face-to-face exchanges of the salon and the coffeehouse but also the explosion of newspapers and other written expressions of opinion during the eighteenth century. As Terry Eagleton puts it in his Habermasian *The Function of Criticism* (1984): "Modern criticism was born of a struggle against the absolutist state." Post-Renaissance literary criticism is one important form of the publicly enunciated opinions that mark the emergence of the bourgeoisie from the "private" realm onto the public stage of politics. This claim that the eighteenth century saw the creation of a new "public," one that developed a sense of its own identity through the emergence of a print culture that mediated its interactions, is later deployed by BENEDICT ANDERSON to explain the rise of nationalism during that same time period.

For Habermas, as he explains in *The Structural Transformation of the Public Sphere*, Enlightenment "standards of 'reason' and the forms of the 'law'" emerge from this explosion of speech aimed at persuading others. He is not claiming here (as at times he appears to do) that some agreement about these standards has been reached. Rather, the point is that the very grounds of legitimacy have shifted. Increasingly, governments must account for their actions in the court of public opinion, and they will win the case only if they can convince significant portions of the population that those actions are "reasonable" and "legal." Appeals to traditional authority or to absolutist imposition will no longer do. The bourgeoisie triumphs over the monarchy, nobility, and clergy because "public opinion" becomes powerful (although not all-powerful), and the transformation of the public sphere is an essential precondition for that victory.

Habermas ends his encyclopedia article by briefly considering how the public sphere in the twentieth century differs from its eighteenth-century ancestor. In mass democracies, he worries, face-to-face interactions in public spaces are no longer common: they have been replaced by the circulation of ideas and images in the mass media. The centralized and corporate control of the media threatens a free, open, and fully diverse exchange of ideas and information. Against this threat, he does find hope in the rights and freedoms guaranteed in democracies. But he argues that those benefits can be maintained only if various social groups organize themselves politically and work ceaselessly to make the state deliver on its promises.

This theme of bringing pressure to bear so that ideals of democracy and freedom can be realized returns in our second selection, "Modernity—An Incomplete Project" (1980), which sharply delineates his differences with the postmodernists. Habermas argues that the Enlightenment project of basing authority on reason has gone awry because the specialized discourses of economics, of bureaucratic administration, of technological knowledge, and of art have become separated from the "life-world" of everyday moral and practical decisions. As science, economics, government, and art become increasingly autonomous and professionalized, they grow distant from the needs of the people. Thus, the criticism of modernity and its experts launched by traditional conservatives, neoconservatives, and "young conservative" poststructuralists is understandable, even justified. But Habermas strongly urges that we not condemn modernity altogether. Instead of rejecting Enlightenment ideals of equality and civil liberties and their extension to all, we must strive to fully reintegrate the discourses of modern science, art, and politics with the everyday perspectives of a life-world in which people seek a decent life for themselves and their loved ones. The prestige of Enlightenment ideals gives people in post-Enlightenment societies a lever with which to move their less-than-perfect societies toward a better future.

Habermas reads modernism in the arts as a failed attempt to rectify on a cultural level "the differentiation of science, morality and art . . . from the hermeneutics of everyday communication" that is characteristic of social modernization. He scorns neoconservative attempts to blame the arts for the erosion of tradition caused by capitalist transformations. But he sees modernist art, even the radical "surrealist attempt to blow up the autarkical sphere of art and to force a reconciliation of art and life," as incapable of reversing the alienations of modernity, because it is confined to "a single cultural sphere." Remedying the ills of modernity requires a more holistic analysis and action on a wider social terrain. Habermas admits that "the chances for this today are not very good." But he points out that "young conservative" poststructuralists are beholden to a modernity they claim to despise, because they launch their critique from a distanced aesthetic space. They rely on that distance for their antimodernism, not realizing that such distance is quintessentially modern and is in fact what is most wrong with modernity. In short, Habermas (once again displaying his Marxist roots) insists that only a holistic approach can ensure political effectiveness. At the same time, he believes that liberal constitutional guarantees offer the best bulwark against oppression by accumulated economic or state power.

It would be hard to overestimate the impact of Habermas's characterization of the poststructuralists as "young conservatives" or of his description of a surprising "alliance of postmodernists with premodernists" linked by their shared hostility to modernity. The argument over the political significance of poststructuralism has been fierce—and inconclusive. Like the contemporaneous debate between Anglo-American and French feminisms, the battle is between two visions of social transformation, both of which are left of center. At issue is the extent to which the very terms by which political emancipation has been understood since the Enlightenment are themselves a hindrance to liberation. "Modernity—An Incomplete Project" has been a major rallying point for artists and critics who believe that liberal ideals of universal right, equal protection under the law, and economic justice are norms that should be protected from critique and norms to which our societies should be held answerable.

Not a single thing Habermas has argued has gone uncontested, from his historical claims about the eighteenth century to his various accounts of speech pragmatics to his arguments about the necessity of rational norms and of completing the project of modernity. Critics have questioned the possibility of isolating universal norms of "communicative reason" or of other liberal ideals from the vastly different situations in which they are embedded. Similarly, the existence of many different public spheres—with distinctive conventions, protocols, and histories of censorship, media development, and cultural or national identity formation—makes generalizations about the "ideal speech situation" suspect. In short, norms appear more context-sensitive and potentially oppressive than Habermas allows. Partly in response to such criticisms, Habermas's own work has continued to evolve, moving from a focus on communicative reason in the early 1980s to issues of "discourse ethics" in the late 1980s, questions of law and democracy in the 1990s, and questions of the pressures of nationalism, religion, terrorism, and immigration in his twenty-first-century work.

"The Public Sphere: An Encyclopedia Article" Keywords: Enlightenment Theory, Marxism, Modernity, Print Culture
"Modernity—An Incomplete Project" Keywords: Aesthetics, Enlightenment Theory, Modernity, Postmodernity

The Public Sphere: An Encyclopedia Article[1]

1. *The Concept*. By "the public sphere" we mean first of all a realm of our social life in which something approaching public opinion can be formed. Access is guaranteed to all citizens. A portion of the public sphere comes into being in every conversation in which private individuals assemble to form a public body.[2] They then behave neither like business or professional people transacting private affairs, nor like members of a constitutional order subject to the legal constraints of a state bureaucracy. Citizens behave as a

1. Edited by Peter Uwe Hohendahl, and translated by Sara Lennox and Frank Lennox, who sometimes include the original German in parentheses.
2. Habermas' concept of the public sphere is not to be equated with that of "the public," i.e. of the individuals who assemble. His concept is directed instead at the institution, which to be sure only assumes concrete form through the participation of people. It cannot, however, be characterized simply as a crowd [Hohendahl's note].

public body when they confer in an unrestricted fashion—that is, with the guarantee of freedom of assembly and association and the freedom to express and publish their opinions—about matters of general interest. In a large public body this kind of communication requires specific means for transmitting information and influencing those who receive it. Today newspapers and magazines, radio and television are the media of the public sphere. We speak of the political public sphere in contrast, for instance, to the literary one, when public discussion deals with objects connected to the activity of the state. Although state authority is so to speak the executor of the political public sphere, it is not a part of it.[3] To be sure, state authority is usually considered "public" authority, but it derives its task of caring for the well-being of all citizens primarily from this aspect of the public sphere. Only when the exercise of political control is effectively subordinated to the democratic demand that information be accessible to the public, does the political public sphere win an institutionalized influence over the government through the instrument of law-making bodies. The expression "public opinion" refers to the tasks of criticism and control which a public body of citizens informally—and, in periodic elections, formally as well—practices *vis-à-vis* the ruling structure organized in the form of a state. Regulations demanding that certain proceedings be public (*Publizitätsvorschriften*), for example those providing for open court hearings, are also related to this function of public opinion. The public sphere as a sphere which mediates between society and state, in which the public organizes itself as the bearer of public opinion, accords with the principle of the public sphere[4]—that principle of public information which once had to be fought for against the arcane policies of monarchies and which since that time has made possible the democratic control of state activities.

It is no coincidence that these concepts of the public sphere and public opinion arose for the first time only in the eighteenth century. They acquire their specific meaning from a concrete historical situation. It was at that time that the distinction of "opinion" from "opinion publique" and "public opinion" came about. Though mere opinions (cultural assumptions, normative attitudes, collective prejudices and values) seem to persist unchanged in their natural form as a kind of sediment of history, public opinion can by definition only come into existence when a reasoning public is presupposed. Public discussions about the exercise of political power which are both critical in intent and institutionally guaranteed have not always existed—they grew out of a specific phase of bourgeois society and could enter into the order of the bourgeois constitutional state only as a result of a particular constellation of interests.

2. *History.* There is no indication European society of the high middle ages possessed a public sphere as a unique realm distinct from the private

3. The state and the public sphere do not overlap, as one might suppose from casual language use. Rather they confront one another as opponents. Habermas designates that sphere as public which antiquity understood to be private, i.e. the sphere of non-governmental opinion making [Hohendahl's note].

4. The principle of the public sphere could still be distinguished from an institution which is demonstrable in social history. Habermas thus would mean a model of norms and modes of behavior by means of which the very functioning of public opinion can be guaranteed for the first time. These norms and modes of behavior include: (a) general accessibility; (b) elimination of all privileges and (c) discovery of general norms and rational legitimations [Hohendahl's note].

sphere. Nevertheless, it was not coincidental that during that period symbols of sovereignty, for instance the princely seal, were deemed "public." At that time there existed a public representation of power. The status of the feudal lord, at whatever level of the feudal pyramid, was oblivious to the categories "public" and "private," but the holder of the position represented it publicly: he showed himself, presented himself as the embodiment of an ever present "higher" power. The concept of this representation has been maintained up to the most recent constitutional history. Regardless of the degree to which it has loosed itself from the old base, the authority of political power today still demands a representation at the highest level by a head of state. Such elements, however, derive from a pre-bourgeois social structure. Representation in the sense of a bourgeois public sphere,[5] for instance the representation of the nation or of particular mandates, has nothing to do with the medieval representative public sphere—a public sphere directly linked to the concrete existence of a ruler. As long as the prince and the estates of the realm still "are" the land, instead of merely functioning as deputies for it, they are able to "re-present"; they represent their power "before" the people, instead of for the people.

The feudal authorities (church, princes and nobility), to which the representative public sphere was first linked, disintegrated during a long process of polarization. By the end of the eighteenth century they had broken apart into private elements on the one hand, and into public on the other. The position of the church changed with the reformation:[6] the link to divine authority which the church represented, that is, religion, became a private matter. So-called religious freedom came to insure what was historically the first area of private autonomy. The church itself continued its existence as one public and legal body among others. The corresponding polarization within princely authority was visibly manifested in the separation of the public budget from the private household expenses of a ruler. The institutions of public authority, along with the bureaucracy and the military, and in part also with the legal institutions, asserted their independence from the privatized sphere of the princely court. Finally, the feudal estates[7] were transformed as well: the nobility became the organs of public authority, parliament and the legal institutions; while those occupied in trades and professions, insofar as they had already established urban corporations and territorial organizations, developed into a sphere of bourgeois society which would stand apart from the state as a genuine area of private autonomy.

The representative public sphere yielded to that new sphere of "public authority" which came into being with national and territorial states. Continuous state activity (permanent administration, standing army) now corresponded to the permanence of the relationships which with the stock exchange and the press had developed within the exchange of commodities and information. Public authority consolidated into a concrete opposition

5. The expression "represent" is used in a very specific sense in the following section, namely to "present oneself." The important thing to understand is that the medieval public sphere, if it even deserves this designation, is tied to the *personal*. The feudal lord and estates create the public sphere by means of their very presence [Hohendahl's note].

6. The religious movement to reform the Catholic Church, initiated by Martin Luther in 1517, that led to the establishment of Protestant churches in Europe.

7. That is, classes. Before the Revolution of 1789, the French legislative assembly represented the three estates: nobility, clergy, and commons.

for those who were merely subject to it and who at first found only a negative definition of themselves within it. These were the "private individuals" who were excluded from public authority because they held no office. "Public" no longer referred to the "representative" court of a prince endowed with authority, but rather to an institution regulated according to competence, to an apparatus endowed with a monopoly on the legal exertion of authority. Private individuals subsumed in the state at whom public authority was directed now made up the public body.

Society, now a private realm occupying a position in opposition to the state, stood on the one hand as if in clear contrast to the state. On the other hand, that society had become a concern of public interest to the degree that the reproduction of life in the wake of the developing market economy had grown beyond the bounds of private domestic authority. *The bourgeois public sphere* could be understood as the sphere of private individuals assembled into a public body, which almost immediately laid claim to the officially regulated "intellectual newspapers" for use against the public authority itself. In those newspapers, and in moralistic and critical journals, they debated that public authority on the general rules of social intercourse in their fundamentally privatized yet publically relevant sphere of labor and commodity exchange.

3. *The Liberal Model of the Public Sphere.* The medium of this debate—public discussion—was unique and without historical precedent. Hitherto the estates had negotiated agreements with their princes, settling their claims to power from case to case. This development took a different course in England, where the parliament limited royal power,[8] than it did on the continent, where the monarchies mediatized the estates. The third estate then broke with this form of power arrangement since it could no longer establish itself as a ruling group. A division of power by means of the delineation of the rights of the nobility was no longer possible within an exchange economy—private authority over capitalist property is, after all, unpolitical. Bourgeois individuals are private individuals. As such, they do not "rule." Their claims to power *vis-à-vis* public authority were thus directed not against the concentration of power, which was to be "shared." Instead, their ideas infiltrated the very principle on which the existing power is based. To the principle of the existing power, the bourgeois public opposed the principle of supervision—that very principle which demands that proceedings be made public (*Publizität*). The principle of supervision is thus a means of transforming the nature of power, not merely one basis of legitimation exchanged for another.

In the first modern constitutions the catalogues of fundamental rights were a perfect image of the liberal model of the public sphere: they guaranteed the society as a sphere of private autonomy and the restriction of public authority to a few functions. Between these two spheres, the constitutions further insured the existence of a realm of private individuals assembled into a public body who as citizens transmit the needs of bourgeois society to the state, in order, ideally, to transform political into "rational" authority within the medium of this public sphere. The general interest, which was the measure of such a rationality, was then guaranteed, according to the

8. The provisions of the 1689 Bill of Rights, which declared William of Orange and his wife, Mary, joint sovereigns of Great Britain, also gave Parliament political supremacy.

presuppositions of a society of free commodity exchange, when the activities of private individuals in the marketplace were freed from social compulsion and from political pressure in the public sphere.

At the same time, daily political newspapers assumed an important role. In the second half of the eighteenth century literary journalism created serious competition for the earlier news sheets which were mere compilations of notices. Karl Bücher[9] characterized this great development as follows: "Newspapers changed from mere institutions for the publication of news into bearers and leaders of public opinion—weapons of party politics. This transformed the newspaper business. A new element emerged between the gathering and the publication of news: the editorial staff. But for the newspaper publisher it meant that he changed from a vendor of recent news to a dealer in public opinion." The publishers insured the newspapers a commercial basis, yet without commercializing them as such. The press remained an institution of the public itself, effective in the manner of a mediator and intensifier of public discussion, no longer a mere organ for the spreading of news but not yet the medium of a consumer culture.

This type of journalism can be observed above all during periods of revolution when newspapers of the smallest political groups and organizations spring up, for instance in Paris in 1789. Even in the Paris of 1848[1] every halfway eminent politician organized his club, every other his journal: 450 clubs and over 200 journals were established there between February and May alone. Until the permanent legalization of a politically functional public sphere, the appearance of a political newspaper meant joining the struggle for freedom and public opinion, and thus for the public sphere as a principle. Only with the establishment of the bourgeois constitutional state was the intellectual press relieved of the pressure of its convictions. Since then it has been able to abandon its polemical position and take advantage of the earning possibilities of a commercial undertaking. In England, France, and the United States the transformation from a journalism of conviction to one of commerce began in the 1830s at approximately the same time. In the transition from the literary journalism of private individuals to the public services of the mass media the public sphere was transformed by the influx of private interests, which received special prominence in the mass media.

4. *The Public Sphere in the Social Welfare State Mass Democracy.* Although the liberal model of the public sphere is still instructive today with respect to the normative claim that information be accessible to the public,[2] it cannot be applied to the actual conditions of an industrially advanced mass democracy organized in the form of the social welfare state. In part the liberal model had always included ideological components, but it is also in part true that the social pre-conditions, to which the ideological elements could at one time at least be linked, had been fundamentally transformed. The very forms in which the public sphere manifested itself, to which supporters of the liberal model could appeal for evidence, began to change with the Chartist move-

9. German economist (1847–1930), founder of an institute for "newspaper science."

1. The year of a revolution (begun in February) that ended the reign of Louis-Philippe, king of the French. The French Revolution began in 1789.

2. Here it should be understood that Habermas considers the principle behind the bourgeois public sphere as indispensable but not its historical form [Hohendahl's note].

ment in England[3] and the February revolution in France. Because of the diffusion of press and propaganda, the public body expanded beyond the bounds of the bourgeoisie. The public body lost not only its social exclusivity; it lost in addition the coherence created by bourgeois social institutions and a relatively high standard of education. Conflicts hitherto restricted to the private sphere now intrude into the public sphere. Group needs which can expect no satisfaction from a self-regulating market now tend towards a regulation by the state. The public sphere, which must now mediate these demands, becomes a field for the competition of interests, competitions which assume the form of violent conflict. Laws which obviously have come about under the "pressure of the street" can scarcely still be understood as arising from the consensus of private individuals engaged in public discussion. They correspond in a more or less unconcealed manner to the compromise of conflicting private interests. Social organizations which deal with the state act in the political public sphere, whether through the agency of political parties or directly in connection with the public administration. With the interweaving of the public and private realm, not only do the political authorities assume certain functions in the sphere of commodity exchange and social labor, but conversely social powers now assume political functions. This leads to a kind of "refeudalization" of the public sphere. Large organizations strive for political compromises with the state and with each other, excluding the public sphere whenever possible. But at the same time the large organizations must assure themselves of at least plebiscitary support from the mass of the population through an apparent display of openness (*demonstrative Publizität*).[4]

The political public sphere of the social welfare state is characterized by a peculiar weakening of its critical functions. At one time the process of making proceedings public (*Publizität*) was intended to subject persons or affairs to public reason, and to make political decisions subject to appeal before the court of public opinion. But often enough today the process of making public simply serves the arcane policies of special interests; in the form of "publicity" it wins public prestige for people or affairs, thus making them worthy of acclamation in a climate of non-public opinion. The very words "public relations work" (*Öffentlichkeitserbeit*) betray the fact that a public sphere must first be arduously constructed case by case, a public sphere which earlier grew out of the social structure. Even the central relationship of the public, the parties and the parliament is affected by this change in function.

Yet this trend towards the weakening of the public sphere as a principle is opposed by the extension of fundamental rights in the social welfare state. The demand that information be accessible to the public is extended from organs of the state to all organizations dealing with the state. To the degree that this is realized, a public body of organized private individuals would take the place of the now-defunct public body of private individuals who relate individually to each other. Only these organized individuals could participate effectively in the process of public communication; only they could

3. A working-class movement (1838–48) that took its name from a petition, the People's Charter, calling for such reforms as universal male suffrage.

4. One must distinguish between Habermas' concept of "making proceedings public" (*Publizität*) and the "public sphere" (*Öffentlichkeit*). The term *Publizität* describes the degree of public effect generated by a public act. Thus a situation can arise in which the form of public opinion making is maintained, while the substance of the public sphere has long ago been undermined [Hohendahl's note].

use the channels of the public sphere which exist within parties and associations and the process of making proceedings public (*Publizität*) which was established to facilitate the dealings of organizations with the state. Political compromises would have to be legitimized through this process of public communication. The idea of the public sphere, preserved in the social welfare state mass democracy, an idea which calls for a rationalization of power through the medium of public discussion among private individuals, threatens to disintegrate with the structural transformation of the public sphere itself. It could only be realized today, on an altered basis, as a rational reorganization of social and political power under the mutual control of rival organizations committed to the public sphere in their internal structure as well as in their relations with the state and each other.

1964

Modernity—An Incomplete Project[1]

In 1980, architects were admitted to the Biennial in Venice,[2] following painters and filmmakers. The note sounded at this first Architecture Biennial was one of disappointment. I would describe it by saying that those who exhibited in Venice formed an avant-garde of reversed fronts. I mean that they sacrificed the tradition of modernity in order to make room for a new historicism. Upon this occasion, a critic of the German newspaper, *Frankfurter Allgemeine Zeitung*, advanced a thesis whose significance reaches beyond this particular event; it is a diagnosis of our times: "Postmodernity definitely presents itself as Antimodernity." This statement describes an emotional current of our times which has penetrated all spheres of intellectual life. It has placed on the agenda theories of postenlightenment, postmodernity, even of posthistory.

From history we know the phrase, "The Ancients and the Moderns." Let me begin by defining these concepts. The term "modern" has a long history, one which has been investigated by Hans Robert Jauss.[3] The word "modern" in its Latin form "modernus" was used for the first time in the late 5th century in order to distinguish the present, which had become officially Christian, from the Roman and pagan past. With varying content, the term "modern" again and again expresses the consciousness of an epoch that relates itself to the past of antiquity, in order to view itself as the result of a transition from the old to the new.

Some writers restrict this concept of "modernity" to the Renaissance, but this is historically too narrow. People considered themselves modern during the period of Charles the Great in the 12th century, as well as in France of the late 17th century at the time of the famous "Querelle des

1. Translated by Seyla Benhabib [and edited by Hal Foster]. This essay was originally delivered as a talk in September 1980 when Habermas was awarded the THEODOR W. ADORNO prize by the city of Frankfurt. It was subsequently delivered as a James Lecture of the New York Institute for the Humanities at New York University in March 1981 [Foster's note].

2. A prestigious international exhibition of contemporary art, held every two years.

3. German literary historian and critic (1921–1997). See his *Aesthetic Standards and Historical Reflection in the "Quarrel of the Ancients and the Moderns"* (1964).

Anciens et des Modernes."[4] That is to say, the term "modern" appeared and reappeared exactly during those periods in Europe when the consciousness of a new epoch formed itself through a renewed relationship to the ancients—whenever, moreover, antiquity was considered a model to be recovered through some kind of imitation.

The spell which the classics of the ancient world cast upon the spirit of later times was first dissolved with the ideals of the French Enlightenment. Specifically, the idea of being "modern" by looking back to the ancients changed with the belief, inspired by modern science, in the infinite progress of knowledge and in the infinite advance towards social and moral betterment. Another form of modernist consciousness was formed in the wake of this change. The romantic modernist sought to oppose the antique ideals of the classicists; he looked for a new historical epoch and found it in the idealized Middle Ages. However, this new ideal age, established early in the 19th century, did not remain a fixed ideal. In the course of the 19th century, there emerged out of this romantic spirit that radicalized consciousness of modernity which freed itself from all specific historical ties. This most recent modernism simply makes an abstract opposition between tradition and the present; and we are, in a way, still the contemporaries of that kind of aesthetic modernity which first appeared in the midst of the 19th century. Since then, the distinguishing mark of works which count as modern is "the new" which will be overcome and made obsolete through the novelty of the next style. But, while that which is merely "stylish" will soon become outmoded, that which is modern preserves a secret tie to the classical. Of course, whatever can survive time has always been considered to be a classic. But the emphatically modern document no longer borrows this power of being a classic from the authority of a past epoch; instead, a modern work becomes a classic because it has once been authentically modern. Our sense of modernity creates its own self-enclosed canons of being classic. In this sense we speak, e.g., in view of the history of modern art, of classical modernity. The relation between "modern" and "classical" has definitely lost a fixed historical reference.

The Discipline of Aesthetic Modernity

The spirit and discipline of aesthetic modernity assumed clear contours in the work of Baudelaire.[5] Modernity then unfolded in various avant-garde movements and finally reached its climax in the Café Voltaire of the dadaists and in surrealism.[6] Aesthetic modernity is characterized by attitudes which find a common focus in a changed consciousness of time. This time consciousness expresses itself through metaphors of the vanguard and the avant-garde. The avant-garde understands itself as invading unknown territory, exposing itself to the dangers of sudden, shocking encounters, conquering an as yet unoccupied future. The avant-garde must find a direction in a landscape into which no one seems to have yet ventured.

4. Quarrel of the Ancients and the Moderns (French), a literary dispute between those arguing for strict adherence to classical (Greek and Latin) models and defenders of modern (contemporary) works. "Charles the Great" may refer to Charlemagne (742–814), though Habermas places him in the wrong century, perhaps intentionally.

5. Charles Baudelaire (1821–1867), French poet and critic.

6. An artistic movement, founded in 1924, that grew directly out of dadaism, which began during World War I; both reacted against logic and both intended to revolutionize art and society. Café Voltaire: meeting place (1915–17) in Zurich, Switzerland, of a group of artists identified with dadaism.

But these forward gropings, this anticipation of an undefined future and the cult of the new mean in fact the exaltation of the present. The new time consciousness, which enters philosophy in the writings of Bergson,[7] does more than express the experience of mobility in society, of acceleration in history, of discontinuity in everyday life. The new value placed on the transitory, the elusive and the ephemeral, the very celebration of dynamism, discloses a longing for an undefiled, immaculate and stable present.

This explains the rather abstract language in which the modernist temper has spoken of the "past." Individual epochs lose their distinct forces. Historical memory is replaced by the heroic affinity of the present with the extremes of history—a sense of time wherein decadence immediately recognizes itself in the barbaric, the wild and the primitive. We observe the anarchistic intention of blowing up the continuum of history, and we can account for it in terms of the subversive force of this new aesthetic consciousness. Modernity revolts against the normalizing functions of tradition; modernity lives on the experience of rebelling against all that is normative. This revolt is one way to neutralize the standards of both morality and utility. This aesthetic consciousness continuously stages a dialectical play between secrecy and public scandal; it is addicted to a fascination with that horror which accompanies the act of profaning, and yet is always in flight from the trivial results of profanation.

On the other hand, the time consciousness articulated in avant-garde art is not simply ahistorical; it is directed against what might be called a false normativity in history. The modern, avant-garde spirit has sought to use the past in a different way; it disposes those pasts which have been made available by the objectifying scholarship of historicism, but it opposes at the same time a neutralized history which is locked up in the museum of historicism.

Drawing upon the spirit of surrealism, Walter Benjamin[8] constructs the relationship of modernity to history in what I would call a posthistoricist attitude. He reminds us of the self-understanding of the French Revolution: "The Revolution cited ancient Rome, just as fashion cites an antiquated dress. Fashion has a scent for what is current, whenever this moves within the thicket of what was once." This is Benjamin's concept of the *Jetztzeit*,[9] of the present as a moment of revelation; a time in which splinters of a messianic presence are enmeshed. In this sense, for Robespierre, the antique Rome was a past laden with momentary revelations.[1]

Now, this spirit of aesthetic modernity has recently begun to age. It has been recited once more in the 1960s; after the 1970s, however, we must admit to ourselves that this modernism arouses a much fainter response today than it did fifteen years ago. Octavio Paz,[2] a fellow-traveller of modernity, noted already in the middle of the 1960s that "the avant-garde of 1967 repeats the deeds and gestures of those of 1917. We are experiencing the end of the idea of modern art." The work of Peter Bürger has since taught us to speak of "post-avant-garde" art; this term is chosen to indicate the failure of

7. Henri Bergson (1859–1941), French philosopher who emphasized the notion of lived time (vs. clock or mechanistic time).
8. German writer of literary and cultural criticism (1892–1940; see above).
9. Present time (German).
1. See Benjamin, "Theses on the Philosophy of History," *Illuminations*, trans. Harry Zohn (New York: Schocken, 1969), p. 21 [Foster's note]. Maximilien Robespierre (1758–1794), leader of the Jacobins, the most radical party of the French Revolution.
2. Mexican poet (1914–1998).

the surrealist rebellion.[3] But what is the meaning of this failure? Does it signal a farewell to modernity? Thinking more generally, does the existence of a post-avant-garde mean there is a transition to that broader phenomenon called postmodernity?

This is in fact how Daniel Bell,[4] the most brilliant of the American neoconservatives, interprets matters. In his book, *The Cultural Contradictions of Capitalism*, Bell argues that the crises of the developed societies of the West are to be traced back to a split between culture and society. Modernist culture has come to penetrate the values of everyday life; the life-world[5] is infected by modernism. Because of the forces of modernism, the principle of unlimited self-realization, the demand for authentic self-experience and the subjectivism of a hyperstimulated sensitivity have come to be dominant. This temperament unleashes hedonistic motives irreconcilable with the discipline of professional life in society, Bell says. Moreover, modernist culture is altogether incompatible with the moral basis of a purposive, rational conduct of life. In this manner, Bell places the burden of responsibility for the dissolution of the Protestant ethic (a phenomenon which had already disturbed Max Weber[6]) on the "adversary culture." Culture in its modern form stirs up hatred against the conventions and virtues of everyday life, which has become rationalized under the pressures of economic and administrative imperatives.

I would call your attention to a complex wrinkle in this view. The impulse of modernity, we are told on the other hand, is exhausted; anyone who considers himself avant-garde can read his own death warrant. Although the avant-garde is still considered to be expanding, it is supposedly no longer creative. Modernism is dominant but dead. For the neoconservative the question then arises: how can norms arise in society which will limit libertinism, reestablish the ethic of discipline and work? What new norms will put a brake on the levelling caused by the social welfare state so that the virtues of individual competition for achievement can again dominate? Bell sees a religious revival to be the only solution. Religious faith tied to a faith in tradition will provide individuals with clearly defined identities and existential security.

Cultural Modernity and Societal Modernization

One can certainly not conjure up by magic the compelling beliefs which command authority. Analyses like Bell's, therefore, only result in an attitude which is spreading in Germany no less than in the States: an intellectual and political confrontation with the carriers of cultural modernity. I cite Peter Steinfels, an observer of the new style which the neoconservatives have imposed upon the intellectual scene in the 1970s:

3. For Paz on the avant-garde see in particular *Children of the Mire: Modern Poetry from Romanticism to the Avant-Garde* (1974), pp. 148–64. For Bürger see *Theory of the Avant-Garde* (1983) [Foster's note]. Bürger (1936–2017), German literary critic.

4. American sociologist (1919–2011); *The Cultural Contradictions of Capitalism* was published in 1976.

5. Ordinary, daily lived experience: Habermas uses the term to distinguish everyday life from the specialized "systems" of knowledge and procedure that have emerged in complex, modern societies.

6. German sociologist (1864–1920); his best-known work is *The Protestant Ethic and the Spirit of Capitalism* (1905).

> The struggle takes the form of exposing every manifestation of what could be considered an oppositionist mentality and tracing its "logic" so as to link it to various forms of extremism: drawing the connection between modernism and nihilism . . . between government regulation and totalitarianism, between criticism of arms expenditures and subservience to communism, between Women's liberation or homosexual rights and the destruction of the family . . . between the Left generally and terrorism, anti-semitism, and fascism . . .[7]

The *ad hominem* approach and the bitterness of these intellectual accusations have also been trumpeted loudly in Germany. They should not be explained so much in terms of the psychology of neoconservative writers; rather, they are rooted in the analytical weaknesses of neoconservative doctrine itself.

Neoconservatism shifts onto cultural modernism the uncomfortable burdens of a more or less successful capitalist modernization of the economy and society. The neoconservative doctrine blurs the relationship between the welcomed process of societal modernization on the one hand, and the lamented cultural development on the other. The neoconservative does not uncover the economic and social causes for the altered attitudes towards work, consumption, achievement and leisure. Consequently, he attributes all of the following—hedonism, the lack of social identification, the lack of obedience, narcissism, the withdrawal from status and achievement competition—to the domain of "culture." In fact, however, culture is intervening in the creation of all these problems in only a very indirect and mediated fashion.

In the neoconservative view, those intellectuals who still feel themselves committed to the project of modernity are then presented as taking the place of those unanalyzed causes. The mood which feeds neoconservatism today in no way originates from discontent about the antinomian consequences[8] of a culture breaking from the museums into the stream of ordinary life. This discontent has not been called into life by modernist intellectuals. It is rooted in deep-seated reactions against the process of *societal* modernization. Under the pressures of the dynamics of economic growth and the organizational accomplishments of the state, this social modernization penetrates deeper and deeper into previous forms of human existence. I would describe this subordination of the life-worlds under the system's imperatives as a matter of disturbing the communicative infrastructure of everyday life.

Thus, for example, neopopulist protests only express in pointed fashion a widespread fear regarding the destruction of the urban and natural environment and of forms of human sociability. There is a certain irony about these protests in terms of neoconservatism. The tasks of passing on a cultural tradition, of social integration and of socialization require adherence to what I call communicative rationality. But the occasions for protest and discontent originate precisely when spheres of communicative action, centered on the reproduction and transmission of values and norms, are penetrated by a form of modernization guided by standards of economic and administra-

7. Peter Steinfels, *The Neoconservatives* (1979), p. 65 [Foster's note]. Steinfels (b. 1941), American editor and journalist.

8. That is, the resulting rejection of socially established norms and morality.

tive rationality—in other words, by standards of rationalization quite different from those of communicative rationality on which those spheres depend. But neoconservative doctrines turn our attention precisely away from such societal processes: they project the causes, which they do not bring to light, onto the plane of a subversive culture and its advocates.

To be sure, cultural modernity generates its own aporias[9] as well. Independently from the consequences of *societal* modernization and within the perspective of *cultural* development itself, there originate motives for doubting the project of modernity. Having dealt with a feeble kind of criticism of modernity—that of neoconservatism—let me now move our discussion of modernity and its discontents into a different domain that touches on these aporias of cultural modernity—issues that often serve only as a pretense for those positions which either call for a postmodernity, recommend a return to some form of premodernity, or throw modernity radically overboard.

The Project of Enlightenment

The idea of modernity is intimately tied to the development of European art, but what I call "the project of modernity" comes only into focus when we dispense with the usual concentration upon art. Let me start a different analysis by recalling an idea from Max Weber. He characterized cultural modernity as the separation of the substantive reason expressed in religion and metaphysics into three autonomous spheres. They are: science, morality and art. These came to be differentiated because the unified world-views of religion and metaphysics fell apart. Since the 18th century, the problems inherited from these older world-views could be arranged so as to fall under specific aspects of validity: truth, normative rightness, authenticity and beauty. They could then be handled as questions of knowledge, or of justice and morality, or of taste. Scientific discourse, theories of morality, jurisprudence, and the production and criticism of art could in turn be institutionalized. Each domain of culture could be made to correspond to cultural professions in which problems could be dealt with as the concern of special experts. This professionalized treatment of the cultural tradition brings to the fore the intrinsic structures of each of the three dimensions of culture. There appear the structures of cognitive-instrumental, of moral-practical and of aesthetic-expressive rationality, each of these under the control of specialists who seem more adept at being logical in these particular ways than other people are. As a result, the distance grows between the culture of the experts and that of the larger public. What accrues to culture through specialized treatment and reflection does not immediately and necessarily become the property of everyday praxis. With cultural rationalization of this sort, the threat increases that the life-world, whose traditional substance has already been devalued, will become more and more impoverished.

The project of modernity formulated in the 18th century by the philosophers of the Enlightenment consisted in their efforts to develop objective science, universal morality and law, and autonomous art according to their inner logic. At the same time, this project intended to release the cognitive

9. Difficulties, logical impasses (a term often used in deconstructive criticism to indicate the point in a text where inherent contradictions render interpretation undecidable).

potentials of each of these domains from their esoteric forms. The Enlightenment philosophers wanted to utilize this accumulation of specialized culture for the enrichment of everyday life—that is to say, for the rational organization of everyday social life.

Enlightenment thinkers of the cast of mind of Condorcet[1] still had the extravagant expectation that the arts and sciences would promote not only the control of natural forces but also understanding of the world and of the self, moral progress, the justice of institutions and even the happiness of human beings. The 20th century has shattered this optimism. The differentiation of science, morality and art has come to mean the autonomy of the segments treated by the specialist and their separation from the hermeneutics of everyday communication. This splitting off is the problem that has given rise to efforts to "negate" the culture of expertise. But the problem won't go away: should we try to hold on to the *intentions* of the Enlightenment, feeble as they may be, or should we declare the entire project of modernity a lost cause? I now want to return to the problem of artistic culture, having explained why, historically, aesthetic modernity is only a part of cultural modernity in general.

The False Programs of the Negation of Culture

Greatly oversimplifying, I would say that in the history of modern art one can detect a trend towards ever greater autonomy in the definition and practice of art. The category of "beauty" and the domain of beautiful objects were first constituted in the Renaissance. In the course of the 18th century, literature, the fine arts and music were institutionalized as activities independent from sacred and courtly life. Finally, around the middle of the 19th century an aestheticist conception of art emerged, which encouraged the artist to produce his work according to the distinct consciousness of art for art's sake. The autonomy of the aesthetic sphere could then become a deliberate project: the talented artist could lend authentic expression to those experiences he had in encountering his own de-centered subjectivity, detached from the constraints of routinized cognition and everyday action.

In the mid-19th century, in painting and literature, a movement began which Octavio Paz finds epitomized already in the art criticism of Baudelaire. Color, lines, sounds and movement ceased to serve primarily the cause of representation; the media of expression and the techniques of production themselves became the aesthetic object. Theodor W. Adorno[2] could therefore begin his *Aesthetic Theory* with the following sentence: "It is now taken for granted that nothing which concerns art can be taken for granted any more: neither art itself, nor art in its relationship to the whole, nor even the right of art to exist." And this is what surrealism then denied: *das Existenzrecht der Kunst als Kunst.*[3] To be sure, surrealism would not have challenged the right of art to exist, if modern art no longer had advanced a promise of happiness concerning its own relationship "to the whole" of life. For

1. Marie-Jean-Antoine-Nicolas de Caritat, marquis de Condorcet (1743–1794), French Enlightenment mathematician and philosopher who believed in the ultimate perfectability of men and women; he died during the revolutionary Reign of Terror.
2. German philosopher and social critic (1903–1969; see above); *Aesthetic Theory* was published in 1970.
3. The right of art to exist as art (German).

Schiller,[4] such a promise was delivered by aesthetic intuition, but not fulfilled by it. Schiller's *Letters on the Aesthetic Education of Man* speaks to us of a utopia reaching beyond art itself. But by the time of Baudelaire, who repeated this *promesse de bonheur*[5] via art, the utopia of reconciliation with society had gone sour. A relation of opposites had come into being; art had become a critical mirror, showing the irreconcilable nature of the aesthetic and the social worlds. This modernist transformation was all the more painfully realized, the more art alienated itself from life and withdrew into the untouchableness of complete autonomy. Out of such emotional currents finally gathered those explosive energies which unloaded in the surrealist attempt to blow up the autarkical sphere of art and to force a reconciliation of art and life.

But all those attempts to level art and life, fiction and praxis, appearance and reality to one plane; the attempts to remove the distinction between artifact and object of use, between conscious staging and spontaneous excitement; the attempts to declare everything to be art and everyone to be an artist, to retract all criteria and to equate aesthetic judgment with the expression of subjective experiences—all these undertakings have proved themselves to be sort of nonsense experiments. These experiments have served to bring back to life, and to illuminate all the more glaringly, exactly those structures of art which they were meant to dissolve. They gave a new legitimacy, as ends in themselves, to appearance as the medium of fiction, to the transcendence of the artwork over society, to the concentrated and planned character of artistic production as well as to the special cognitive status of judgments of taste. The radical attempt to negate art has ended up ironically by giving due exactly to these categories through which Enlightenment aesthetics had circumscribed its object domain. The surrealists waged the most extreme warfare, but two mistakes in particular destroyed their revolt. First, when the containers of an autonomously developed cultural sphere are shattered, the contents get dispersed. Nothing remains from a desublimated meaning or a destructured form; an emancipatory effect does not follow.

Their second mistake has more important consequences. In everyday communication, cognitive meanings, moral expectations, subjective expressions and evaluations must relate to one another. Communication processes need a cultural tradition covering all spheres—cognitive, moral-practical and expressive. A rationalized everyday life, therefore, could hardly be saved from cultural impoverishment through breaking open a single cultural sphere—art—and so providing access to just one of the specialized knowledge complexes. The surrealist revolt would have replaced only one abstraction.

In the spheres of theoretical knowledge and morality, there are parallels to this failed attempt of what we might call the false negation of culture. Only they are less pronounced. Since the days of the Young Hegelians,[6] there has been talk about the negation of philosophy. Since Marx,[7] the question of the relationship of theory and practice has been posed. However, Marxist intellectuals joined a social movement; and only at its peripheries were there sectarian attempts to carry out a program of the negation of philosophy similar

4. FRIEDRICH VON SCHILLER (1759–1805), German poet, dramatist, and historian; for his *Letters* (1795), see above.
5. Promise of happiness or fulfillment (French).
6. Followers of the German idealist philosopher GEORG WILHELM FRIEDRICH HEGEL (1770–1831) in Germany in the first half of the 19th century.
7. KARL MARX (1818–1883), German social, economic, and political philosopher and revolutionary.

to the surrealist program to negate art. A parallel to the surrealist mistakes becomes visible in these programs when one observes the consequences of dogmatism and of moral rigorism.

A reified[8] everyday praxis can be cured only by creating unconstrained interaction of the cognitive with the moral-practical and the aesthetic-expressive elements. Reification cannot be overcome by forcing just one of those highly stylized cultural spheres to open up and become more accessible. Instead, we see under certain circumstances a relationship emerge between terroristic activities and the over-extension of any one of these spheres into other domains: examples would be tendencies to aestheticize politics, or to replace politics by moral rigorism or to submit it to the dogmatism of a doctrine. These phenomena should not lead us, however, into denouncing the intentions of the surviving Enlightenment tradition as intentions rooted in a "terroristic reason." Those who lump together the very project of modernity with the state of consciousness and the spectacular action of the individual terrorist are no less short-sighted than those who would claim that the incomparably more persistent and extensive bureaucratic terror practiced in the dark, in the cellars of the military and secret police, and in camps and institutions, is the *raison d'être* of the modern state, only because this kind of administrative terror makes use of the coercive means of modern bureaucracies.

Alternatives

I think that instead of giving up modernity and its project as a lost cause, we should learn from the mistakes of those extravagant programs which have tried to negate modernity. Perhaps the types of reception of art may offer an example which at least indicates the direction of a way out.

Bourgeois art had two expectations at once from its audience. On the one hand, the layman who enjoyed art should educate himself to become an expert. On the other hand, he should also behave as a competent consumer who uses art and relates aesthetic experiences to his own life problems. This second, and seemingly harmless, manner of experiencing art has lost its radical implications exactly because it had a confused relation to the attitude of being expert and professional.

To be sure, artistic production would dry up, if it were not carried out in the form of a specialized treatment of autonomous problems and if it were to cease to be the concern of experts who do not pay so much attention to exoteric questions. Both artists and critics accept thereby the fact that such problems fall under the spell of what I earlier called the "inner logic" of a cultural domain. But this sharp delineation, this exclusive concentration on one aspect of validity alone and the exclusion of aspects of truth and justice, break down as soon as aesthetic experience is drawn into an individual life history and is absorbed into ordinary life. The reception of art by the layman, or by the "everyday expert," goes in a rather different direction than the reception of art by the professional critic.

Albrecht Wellmer[9] has drawn my attention to one way that an aesthetic experience which is not framed around the experts' critical judgments of

8. Ossified.

9. German philosopher (b. 1933).

taste can have its significance altered: as soon as such an experience is used to illuminate a life-historical situation and is related to life problems, it enters into a language game which is no longer that of the aesthetic critic. The aesthetic experience then not only renews the interpretation of our needs in whose light we perceive the world. It permeates as well our cognitive significations and our normative expectations and changes the manner in which all these moments refer to one another. Let me give an example of this process.

This manner of receiving and relating to art is suggested in the first volume of the work *The Aesthetics of Resistance* by the German-Swedish writer Peter Weiss. Weiss describes the process of reappropriating art by presenting a group of politically motivated, knowledge-hungry workers in 1937 in Berlin.[1] These were young people who, through an evening high-school education, acquired the intellectual means to fathom the general and social history of European art. Out of the resilient edifice of this objective mind, embodied in works of art which they saw again and again in the museums in Berlin, they started removing their own chips of stone, which they gathered together and reassembled in the context of their own milieu. This milieu was far removed from that of traditional education as well as from the then existing regime. These young workers went back and forth between the edifice of European art and their own milieu until they were able to illuminate both.

In examples like this which illustrate the reappropriation of the expert's culture from the standpoint of the life-world, we can discern an element which does justice to the intentions of the hopeless surrealist revolts, perhaps even more to Brecht's[2] and Benjamin's interests in how art works, which having lost their aura,[3] could yet be received in illuminating ways. In sum, the project of modernity has not yet been fulfilled. And the reception of art is only one of at least three of its aspects. The project aims at a differentiated relinking of modern culture with an everyday praxis that still depends on vital heritages, but would be impoverished through mere traditionalism. This new connection, however, can only be established under the condition that societal modernization will also be steered in a different direction. The life-world has to become able to develop institutions out of itself which set limits to the internal dynamics and imperatives of an almost autonomous economic system and its administrative complements.

If I am not mistaken, the chances for this today are not very good. More or less in the entire Western world a climate has developed that furthers capitalist modernization processes as well as trends critical of cultural modernism. The disillusionment with the very failures of those programs that called for the negation of art and philosophy has come to serve as a pretense for conservative positions. Let me briefly distinguish the antimodernism of the "young conservatives" from the premodernism of the "old conservatives" and from the postmodernism of the neoconservatives.

The "young conservatives" recapitulate the basic experience of aesthetic modernity. They claim as their own the revelations of a decentered

1. The reference is to the novel *Die Ästhetik des Widerstands* (3 vols., 1975–81) by the author [1916–1982] perhaps best known in the United States for his 1965 play *Marat/Sade*. The work of art "reappropriated" by the workers is the Pergamon altar, emblem of power, classicism, and rationality [Foster's note].

2. Bertolt Brecht (1898–1956), German Marxist playwright.

3. On the "aura" of the artwork, see Benjamin, "The Work of Art in the Age of Its Technological Reproducibility" (written 1936–39; see above).

subjectivity, emancipated from the imperatives of work and usefulness, and with this experience they step outside the modern world. On the basis of modernistic attitudes they justify an irreconcilable antimodernism. They remove into the sphere of the far-away and the archaic the spontaneous powers of imagination, self-experience and emotion. To instrumental reason they juxtapose in Manichean fashion[4] a principle only accessible through evocation, be it the will to power or sovereignty, Being or the Dionysiac force[5] of the poetical. In France this line leads from Georges Bataille via Michel Foucault to Jacques Derrida.[6]

The "old conservatives" do not allow themselves to be contaminated by cultural modernism. They observe the decline of substantive reason, the differentiation of science, morality and art, the modern world view and its merely procedural rationality, with sadness and recommend a withdrawal to a position *anterior* to modernity. Neo-Aristotelianism, in particular, enjoys a certain success today. In view of the problematic of ecology, it allows itself to call for a cosmological ethic. (As belonging to this school, which originates with Leo Strauss, one can count the interesting works of Hans Jonas and Robert Spaemann.)[7]

Finally, the neoconservatives welcome the development of modern science, as long as this only goes beyond its sphere to carry forward technical progress, capitalist growth and rational administration. Moreover, they recommend a politics of defusing the explosive content of cultural modernity. According to one thesis, science, when properly understood, has become irrevocably meaningless for the orientation of the life-world. A further thesis is that politics must be kept as far aloof as possible from the demands of moral-practical justification. And a third thesis asserts the pure immanence of art, disputes that it has a utopian content, and points to its illusory character in order to limit the aesthetic experience to privacy. (One could name here the early Wittgenstein, Carl Schmitt of the middle period, and Gottfried Benn[8] of the late period.) But with the decisive confinement of science, morality and art to autonomous spheres separated from the life-world and administered by experts, what remains from the project of cultural modernity is only what we would have if we were to give up the project of modernity altogether. As a replacement one points to traditions which, however, are held to be immune to demands of (normative) justification and validation.

This typology is like any other, of course, a simplification, but it may not prove totally useless for the analysis of contemporary intellectual and political confrontations. I fear that the ideas of antimodernity, together with an

4. That is, as a polar opposite (like the followers of Manichaeism, a religion founded in the 3d c. C.E., who saw the world as divided between two opposed forces—good and evil, spirit and matter, etc.).

5. A reference to *The Birth of Tragedy* (1872; see above) by FRIEDRICH NIETZSCHE, who saw in Greek culture a dynamic tension between the gods Apollo (representing form and reason) and Dionysus (representing frenzy and emotion). He also championed the idea of "the will to power."

6. All important French writers: Bataille (1897–1962), cultural critic and novelist; FOUCAULT (1926–1984), poststructuralist philosopher and historian of ideas; and DERRIDA (1930–2004), deconstructionist philosopher and critic.

7. All philosophers: STRAUSS (1899–1973), German-born American political philosopher; Jonas (1903–1993), German-born American moral philosopher; and Spaemann (b. 1927), German moral philosopher. Any philosopher who adapts the thought of ARISTOTLE (384–322 B.C.E.) to his or her own times may be called a "neo-Aristotelian"; Strauss argued in particular for the superiority of Aristotle's political science to the behavioralist approach dominant in the United States in the mid-20th century.

8. German poet (1886–1956). Ludwig Wittgenstein (1889–1951), Austrian-born English philosopher. Schmitt (1888–1985), German political philosopher.

additional touch of premodernity, are becoming popular in the circles of alternative culture. When one observes the transformations of consciousness within political parties in Germany, a new ideological shift (*Tendenzwende*) becomes visible. And this is the alliance of postmodernists with premodernists. It seems to me that there is no party in particular that monopolizes the abuse of intellectuals and the position of neoconservatism. I therefore have good reason to be thankful for the liberal spirit in which the city of Frankfurt offers me a prize bearing the name of Theodor Adorno, a most significant son of this city, who as philosopher and writer has stamped the image of the intellectual in our country in incomparable fashion, who, even more, has become the very image of emulation for the intellectual.

1980

ADRIENNE RICH
1929–2012

One of the most celebrated poets of her generation, Adrienne Rich was a major voice in American feminism during the latter half of the twentieth century. In her nonfiction prose and in her poetry, she explored the ways in which patriarchal society oppresses women and the ways in which women have responded to that oppression. While her analysis of "compulsory heterosexuality" may prove her most lasting contribution to social theory, Rich's contributions to feminist thought covered a wide range of topics, from the silencing of women's voices to the history of childbirth and motherhood. Like SUSAN BORDO, Rich linked patriarchal oppression to power exerted directly (and often violently) on women's bodies. But her concern with the psychic and social underpinnings of sexual identity also links Rich's work to the queer theory of JUDITH BUTLER and EVE KOSOFSKY SEDGWICK.

Born and raised in a Jewish family in Baltimore, Rich was chosen by the poet W. H. Auden as a winner of the prestigious Yale Younger Poets Award at the age of twenty-two, the year she graduated from Radcliffe College. She traveled in Europe in 1952–53 on a Guggenheim Fellowship. On her return, she married Alfred Conrad, an economist who taught at Harvard University. Between 1955 and 1976, she raised three sons while continuing to publish poetry. When the family moved to New York City in 1966, she began teaching at Columbia University and the City College of New York.

Rich became increasingly identified with the women's movement throughout the 1970s, composing poetry with feminist themes but also writing prose. She published essays and an important historical, theoretical, and first-person study of motherhood, *Of Woman Born: Motherhood as Experience and Institution* (1976). During this decade, *Diving into the Wreck* (1973) won the National Book Award for poetry, solidifying her status as a major literary figure.

By the mid-1970s Rich was openly lesbian, and in her poetry and prose she was exploring all aspects of what she calls in our selection "lesbian experience." Her work in the 1980s and 1990s, while still exploring feminist and lesbian themes, also included new attempts to connect to her Jewishness, her family (especially her father), and the poetic tradition. Rich was a visiting professor at Cornell University from 1981 to 1987, and she taught at Stanford University from 1987 to 1997. Rich received many honorary doctorates and literary prizes, but such awards do not convey how revered a figure she was. An inspiration especially for lesbian women and feminists, Rich was admired almost universally for her strength of character, staunch integrity, and immense talents as a poet and a writer.

The essay "Compulsory Heterosexuality and Lesbian Existence" (1980) has been widely influential. When it first appeared, it marked (along with several roughly contemporaneous works, many of them cited in Rich's first footnote) the end of "sisterhood" feminism—the assumption that all women were "sisters" in their shared oppression. Rich highlights the presence of both lesbians and heterosexual women in the feminist movement and calls on feminism to acknowledge its fear of lesbians. Because those hostile to feminism often dismiss it as the complaints of a small group of lesbians, many 1970s feminists went out of their way to prove their heterosexuality. Lesbians and the whole topic of lesbian experience became practically taboo within the movement (except in its more radical separatist branches, which the mainstream also held at a distance). Thus Rich's essay, along with the feminist work of women of color and of working-class women, challenged a feminism that purported to speak for all women yet assumed the viewpoint of a heterosexual, middle-class white woman. Much of the feminist work of the 1980s was devoted to considering the ramifications of these differences (of race, class, and sexual orientation) for the category "woman" and to attending to how such differences would strengthen or weaken feminist activism.

Rich's main purpose, however, was not so much to introduce or explore difference as to consider the extent to which heterosexual desire and identity are fundamental to women's oppression. Heterosexuality, she argued, is not natural but social, and it should be analyzed as we would any social institution. Similar arguments are advanced by the lesbian theorists MONIQUE WITTIG and Bonnie Zimmerman. How is heterosexuality established and maintained? What groups resist it? What alternatives must be suppressed for it to prevail? Who benefits from and who is harmed by this institution's dominance? What forms of enforcement underwrite that dominance? Rich argued that heterosexuality is compulsory because only partners of the opposite sex are deemed appropriate, all same-sex desire must be denied or indulged in secret, and various kinds of same-sex bonding (including friendships) are viewed with suspicion. Compulsory heterosexuality functions to ensure that women are sexually accessible to men, with consent or choice on the women's part neither legally nor practically taken into account. In sum, compulsory heterosexuality is an institution that punishes those who are not heterosexual and systematically ensures the power of men over women.

Because compulsory sexuality is central to creating and preserving the inequality between men and women, Rich argued that "the issue feminists have to address is not simple 'gender inequality' nor the domination of culture by males nor mere 'taboos against homosexuality,' but the enforcement of heterosexuality for women as a means of assuring male right of physical, economic, and emotional access." Feminism cannot truly comprehend the sources and system of inequality if it does not analyze the institution of compulsory heterosexuality. In the years since Rich published her essay, feminists have actively investigated the topics suggested by this charge.

Three topics in Rich's essay have been especially important for feminist literary theory: sexualized relations of power within institutions, lesbian experience, and questions of sexual identity. To begin with, Rich argued that women do not simply face the trials and tribulations experienced by all subordinates in hierarchical institutions; they must also present themselves as "attractive" according to dominant standards of heterosexual desirability and be concerned with sexuality in the appropriate ways (e.g., be flirtatious within the proper bounds, be supportive of male superiors). Such expectations, rarely conscious, even more rarely explicit, permeate public male-female relationships. They form part of a larger unwritten set of rules about the relative positions of men and women in society.

Second, *lesbian experience*—and its corollary term, the *lesbian continuum*—challenges the notion that women "need" men by calling attention to all the ways in which women interact with one another, all the activities central to their lives, that do not involve connection to a man. Rich wanted to highlight both how hostile to and threatened by women's independent action patriarchal society is *and* the prevalence of such action despite the price (sometimes very high) paid for it. The lesbian continuum encompasses a wide variety of relationships between and among women, ranging from "the sharing of a rich inner life, the bonding against male tyranny, [to] the giving and receiving of practical and political support." By desexualizing the term *lesbian*, Rich called our attention to the variety of bonds formed between women and to the various functions those bonds play in women's lives.

Finally, Rich's essay looks forward to the queer theory of the 1990s by asking a crucial question: How is sexual identity formed? Through what processes of psychic identification does a self form heterosexual and/or homosexual desires? While Rich was more suspicious of psychoanalytic understandings of these processes than are many subsequent queer theorists (such as Butler), she fully recognized that the "law of compulsory heterosexuality" plays a crucial role in the formation of selves, even as she noted that the early bond of the girl baby with her mother works against the injunction to be heterosexual. In addition, the notion of the lesbian continuum recognizes that sexuality comes in many forms and results in many different behaviors—a variety badly captured by the simple dichotomy homosexual/heterosexual.

Rich came very close here to queer theory's later interest in examples that confound received categories, that challenge the terms by which we make the world and our experiences intelligible. However, she was impatient with the poststructuralist and French psychoanalytic theory that stands behind much queer theory; in articulating similar concepts, she used her own idiom. Throughout her career, an uneasy truce prevailed between Rich and most theoretically minded American feminists, with both sides carefully avoiding direct attacks on the other. Desire, as Rich discovered in her own life, is neither unitary nor fixed once for all. Women especially suffer in a heterosexual regime that ignores the fluidity of desire in favor of channeling that desire toward heterosexual unions in which the needs of the male are primary.

"Compulsory Heterosexuality and Lesbian Existence" Keywords: The Body, Feminist Theory, Gender, Institutional Studies, Queer Theory, Sexuality, Women's Literature

From Compulsory Heterosexuality and Lesbian Existence[1]

Foreword (1983)

I want to say a little about the way "Compulsory Heterosexuality" was originally conceived and the context in which we are now living. It was written in part to challenge the erasure of lesbian existence from so much of scholarly feminist literature, an erasure which I felt (and feel) to be not just anti-lesbian, but anti-feminist in its consequences, and to distort the experience of heterosexual women as well. It was not written to widen divisions but to encourage heterosexual feminists to examine heterosexuality as a political

1. This essay was first published in *Signs: Journal of Women in Culture and Society* (1980). The shorter version printed here originally appeared in *Adrienne Rich's Poetry and Prose*, edited by Barbara Charlesworth Gelpi and Albert Gelpi (1993); the asterisks mark their deletions.

institution which disempowers women—and to change it. I also hoped that other lesbians would feel the depth and breadth of woman identification and woman bonding that has run like a continuous though stifled theme through the heterosexual experience, and that this would become increasingly a politically activating impulse, not simply a validation of personal lives. I wanted the essay to suggest new kinds of criticism, to incite new questions in classrooms and academic journals, and to sketch, at least, some bridge over the gap between *lesbian* and *feminist*. I wanted, at the very least, for feminists to find it less possible to read, write, or teach from a perspective of unexamined heterocentricity.

Within the three years since I wrote "Compulsory Heterosexuality"—with this energy of hope and desire—the pressures to conform in a society increasingly conservative in mood have become more intense. The New Right's[2] messages to women have been, precisely, that we are the emotional and sexual property of men, and that the autonomy and equality of women threaten family, religion, and state. The institutions by which women have traditionally been controlled—patriarchal motherhood, economic exploitation, the nuclear family, compulsory heterosexuality—are being strengthened by legislation, religious fiat, media imagery, and efforts at censorship. In a worsening economy, the single mother trying to support her children confronts the feminization of poverty which Joyce Miller of the National Coalition of Labor Union Women has named one of the major issues of the 1980s. The lesbian, unless in disguise, faces discrimination in hiring and harassment and violence in the street. Even within feminist-inspired institutions such as battered-women's shelters and Women's Studies programs, open lesbians are fired and others warned to stay in the closet. The retreat into sameness—assimilation for those who can manage it—is the most passive and debilitating of responses to political repression, economic insecurity, and a renewed open season on difference.

I want to note that documentation of male violence against women—within the home especially—has been accumulating rapidly in this period. At the same time, in the realm of literature which depicts woman bonding and woman identification as essential for female survival, a steady stream of writing and criticism has been coming from women of color in general and lesbians of color in particular—the latter group being even more profoundly erased in academic feminist scholarship by the double bias of racism and homophobia.[3]

2. Social or cultural conservatives who stress so-called moral and "family" values, and who are often self-identified Christians. They played a large role in the U.S. election of President Ronald Reagan in 1980.

3. See, for example, Paula Gunn Allen, *The Sacred Hoop: Recovering the Feminine in American Indian Traditions* (Boston: Beacon, 1986); Beth Brant, ed., *A Gathering of Spirit: Writing and Art by North American Indian Women* (Montpelier, Vt.: Sinister Wisdom Books, 1984); Gloria Anzaldúa and Cherríe Moraga, eds., *This Bridge Called My Back: Writings by Radical Women of Color* (Watertown, Mass.: Persephone, 1981; distributed by Kitchen Table/Women of Color Press, Albany, N.Y.); J. R. Roberts, *Black Lesbians: An Annotated Bibliography* (Tallahassee, Fla.: Naiad, 1981); Barbara Smith, ed., *Home Girls: A Black Feminist Anthology* (Albany, N.Y.: Kitchen Table/Women of Color Press, 1984). As Lorraine Bethel and Barbara Smith pointed out in *Conditions* 5: *The Black Women's Issue* (1980), a great deal of fiction by Black women depicts primary relationships between women. I would like to cite here the work of Ama Ata Aidoo, Toni Cade Bambara, Buchi Emecheta, Bessie Head, Zora Neale Hurston, Alice Walker. Donna Allegra, Red Jordan Arobateau, Audre Lorde, Ann Allen Shockley, among others, who write directly as Black lesbians. For fiction by other lesbians of color, see Elly Bulkin, ed., *Lesbian Fiction: An Anthology* (Watertown, Mass.: Persephone, 1981).

There has recently been an intensified debate on female sexuality among feminists and lesbians, with lines often furiously and bitterly drawn, with *sadomasochism* and *pornography* as key words which are variously defined according to who is talking.[4] The depth of women's rage and fear regarding sexuality and its relation to power and pain is real, even when the dialogue sounds simplistic, self-righteous, or like parallel monologues.

Because of all these developments, there are parts of this essay that I would word differently, qualify, or expand if I were writing it today. But I continue to think that heterosexual feminists will draw political strength for change from taking a critical stance toward the ideology which *demands* heterosexuality, and that lesbians cannot assume that we are untouched by that ideology and the institutions founded upon it. There is nothing about such a critique that requires us to think of ourselves as victims, as having been brainwashed or totally powerless. Coercion and compulsion are among the conditions in which women have learned to recognize our strength. Resistance is a major theme in this essay and in the study of women's lives, if we know what we are looking for.

I

> Biologically men have only one innate orientation—a sexual one that draws them to women,—while women have two innate orientations, sexual toward men and reproductive toward their young.[5]

> I was a woman terribly vulnerable, critical, using femaleness as a sort of standard or yardstick to measure and discard men. Yes—something like that. I was an Anna who invited defeat from men without ever being conscious of it. (But I am conscious of it. And being conscious of it means I shall leave it all behind me and become—but what?) I was stuck fast in an emotion common to women of our time, that can turn them bitter, or Lesbian, or solitary. Yes, that Anna during that time was . . .
>
> [Another blank line across the page:][6]

The bias of compulsory heterosexuality, through which lesbian experience is perceived on a scale ranging from deviant to abhorrent or simply rendered invisible, could be illustrated from many texts other than the two just preceding. The assumption made by Rossi, that women are "innately" sexually

See also, for accounts of contemporary Jewish-lesbian existence, Evelyn Torton Beck, ed., *Nice Jewish Girls: A Lesbian Anthology* (Watertown, Mass.: Persephone, 1982; distributed by Crossing Press, Trumansburg, N.Y.); Alice Bloch, *Lifetime Guarantee* (Watertown, Mass.: Persephone, 1982); and Melanie Kaye-Kantrowitz and Irena Klepfisz, eds., *The Tribe of Dina: A Jewish Women's Anthology* (Montpelier, Vt.: Sinister Wisdom Books, 1986).

The earliest formulation that I know of heterosexuality as an institution was in the lesbian-feminist paper *The Furies*, founded in 1971. For a collection of articles from that paper, see Nancy Myron and Charlotte Bunch, eds., *Lesbianism and the Women's Movement* (Oakland, Calif.: Diana Press, 1975; distributed by Crossing Press, Trumansburg, N.Y.) [Rich's note].

4. The so-called sex wars within feminism—with the status of sadomasochism a key issue as feminists argued about pornography—flared in the wake of an academic conference, "Toward a Politics of Sexuality," held at Barnard College in April 1982.

5. Alice Rossi, "Children and Work in the Lives of Women," paper delivered at the University of Arizona, Tucson, February 1976 [Rich's note].

6. Doris Lessing, *The Golden Notebook* (1962; reprint, New York: Bantam, 1977), p. 480 [Rich's note].

oriented only toward men, and that made by Lessing, that the lesbian is simply acting out of her bitterness toward men, are by no means theirs alone; these assumptions are widely current in literature and in the social sciences.

I am concerned here with two other matters as well: first, how and why women's choice of women as passionate comrades, life partners, co-workers, lovers, community has been crushed, invalidated, forced into hiding and disguise; and second, the virtual or total neglect of lesbian existence in a wide range of writings, including feminist scholarship. Obviously there is a connection here. I believe that much feminist theory and criticism is stranded on this shoal.

My organizing impulse is the belief that it is not enough for feminist thought that specifically lesbian texts exist. Any theory or cultural/political creation that treats lesbian existence as a marginal or less "natural" phenomenon, as mere "sexual preference," or as the mirror image of either heterosexual or male homosexual relations is profoundly weakened thereby, whatever its other contributions. Feminist theory can no longer afford merely to voice a toleration of "lesbianism" as an "alternative life style" or make token allusion to lesbians. A feminist critique of compulsory heterosexual orientation for women is long overdue. In this exploratory paper, I shall try to show why.

* * *

II

If women are the earliest sources of emotional caring and physical nurture for both female and male children, it would seem logical, from a feminist perspective at least, to pose the following questions: whether the search for love and tenderness in both sexes does not originally lead toward women; *why in fact women would ever redirect that search*; why species survival, the means of impregnation, and emotional/erotic relationships should ever have become so rigidly identified with each other; and why such violent strictures should be found necessary to enforce women's total emotional, erotic loyalty and subservience to men. I doubt that enough feminist scholars and theorists have taken the pains to acknowledge the societal forces which wrench women's emotional and erotic energies away from themselves and other women and from woman-identified values. These forces, as I shall try to show, range from literal physical enslavement to the disguising and distorting of possible options.

I do not assume that mothering by women is a "sufficient cause" of lesbian existence. But the issue of mothering by women has been much in the air of late, usually accompanied by the view that increased parenting by men would minimize antagonism between the sexes and equalize the sexual imbalance of power of males over females. These discussions are carried on without reference to compulsory heterosexuality as a phenomenon, let alone as an ideology. I do not wish to psychologize here, but rather to identify sources of male power. I believe large numbers of men could, in fact, undertake child care on a large scale without radically altering the balance of male power in a male-identified society.

In her essay "The Origin of the Family," Kathleen Gough lists eight characteristics of male power in archaic and contemporary societies which I would like to use as a framework: "men's ability to deny women sexuality or to force it upon them; to command or exploit their labor to control their produce; to control or rob them of their children; to confine them physically and prevent their movements; to use them as objects in male transactions; to cramp their creativeness; or to withhold from them large areas of the society's knowledge and cultural attainments."[7] (Gough does not perceive these power characteristics as specifically enforcing heterosexuality, only as producing sexual inequality.) Below, Gough's words appear in italics; the elaboration of each of her categories, in brackets, is my own.

Characteristics of male power include *the power of men*

1. *to deny women* [their own] *sexuality*—[by means of clitoridectomy and infibulation;[8] chastity belts; punishment, including death, for female adultery; punishment, including death, for lesbian sexuality; psychoanalytic denial of the clitoris;[9] strictures against masturbation; denial of maternal and postmenopausal sensuality; unnecessary hysterectomy; pseudolesbian images in the media and literature; closing of archives and destruction of documents relating to lesbian existence]
2. *or to force it* [male sexuality] *upon them*—[by means of rape (including marital rape) and wife beating; father-daughter, brother-sister incest; the socialization of women to feel that male sexual "drive" amounts to a right;[1] idealization of heterosexual romance in art, literature, the media, advertising, etc.; child marriage; arranged marriage; prostitution; the harem; psychoanalytic doctrines of frigidity and vaginal orgasm;[2] pornographic depictions of women responding pleasurably to sexual violence and humiliation (a subliminal message being that sadistic heterosexuality is more "normal" than sensuality between women)]
3. *to command or exploit their labor to control their produce*—[by means of the institutions of marriage and motherhood as unpaid production; the horizontal segregation of women in paid employment;[3] the decoy of the upwardly mobile token woman; male control of abortion, contraception, sterilization, and childbirth; pimping; female infanticide, which robs mothers of daughters and contributes to generalized devaluation of women]
4. *to control or rob them of their children*—[by means of father right and "legal kidnapping";[4] enforced sterilization, systematized infanticide;

7. Kathleen Gough, "The Origin of the Family," in *Toward an Anthropology of Women*, ed. Rayna Reiter (New York: Monthly Review Press, 1975), pp. 60–70 [Rich's note].

8. The stitching together of the vulva after a clitoridectomy, leaving a small opening for the passage of urine and menstrual blood. "Clitoridectomy": usually the removal of the clitoris occurs in the context of a cultural rite of passage to womanhood, but at times such surgery has been recommended to curb sexual desire.

9. The persistent medical claim, prior to the 1970s, that women's sexual pleasure derived from stimulation of the clitoris is not a "true" orgasm.

1. Kathleen Barry, *Female Sexual Slavery* (Englewood Cliffs, N.J.: Prentice-Hall, 1979), pp. 216–19 [Rich's note].

2. The notion that orgasm is achieved through vaginal stimulation (not the case for most women).

3. That is, at the lowest levels of wage labor.

4. Anna Demeter, *Legal Kidnapping* (Boston: Beacon, 1979), pp. xx, 126–28 [Rich's note]. Traditionally, fathers have sole rights to their children; and even when mothers win custody, the courts have often maintained the father's right of access to children despite a history of abuse or of financial or emotional neglect. Denied access by mothers, fathers have sometimes resorted to kidnappings, later upheld by the courts as legal.

seizure of children from lesbian mothers by the courts; the malpractice of male obstetrics; use of the mother as "token torturer"[5] in genital mutilation or in binding the daughter's feet (or mind) to fit her for marriage]

5. *to confine them physically and prevent their movement*—[by means of rape as terrorism, keeping women off the streets; purdah; foot binding; atrophying of women's athletic capabilities; high heels and "feminine" dress codes in fashions; the veil;[6] sexual harassment on the streets; horizontal segregation of women in employment; prescriptions for "full-time" mothering at home; enforced economic dependence of wives]
6. *to use them as objects in male transactions*—[use of women as "gifts"; bride price; pimping; arranged marriage; use of women as entertainers to facilitate male deals—e.g., wife-hostess, cocktail waitress required to dress for male sexual titillation, call girls, "bunnies," geisha, *kisaeng*[7] prostitutes, secretaries]
7. *to cramp their creativeness*—[witch persecutions as campaigns against midwives and female healers, and as pogrom against independent, "unassimilated" women;[8] definition of male pursuits as more valuable than female within any culture, so that cultural values become the embodiment of male subjectivity; restriction of female self-fulfillment to marriage and motherhood; sexual exploitation of women by male artists and teachers; the social and economic disruption of women's creative aspirations;[9] erasure of female tradition][1]
8. *to withhold from them large areas of the society's knowledge and cultural attainments*—[by means of noneducation of females; the "Great Silence" regarding women and particularly lesbian existence in history and culture;[2] sex-role tracking which deflects women from science, technology, and other "masculine" pursuits; male social/professional bonding which excludes women; discrimination against women in the professions]

These are some of the methods by which male power is manifested and maintained. Looking at the schema, what surely impresses itself is the fact that we are confronting not a simple maintenance of inequality and property possession, but a pervasive cluster of forces, ranging from physical brutality to control of consciousness, which suggests that an enormous potential counterforce is having to be restrained.

5. Mary Daly, *Gyn/Ecology: The Metaethics of Radical Feminism* (Boston: Beacon, 1978), pp. 139–41, 163–65 [Rich's note]. The practice of foot-binding among upper-class women in pre-Communist China was largely aimed at male sexual gratification.
6. Muslim women often wear a veil or *hijab* (sometimes covering their entire body); to "take the veil" in Western countries is to become a nun and traditionally to retire to a convent.
7. Appropriated (Korean); that is, women forced into prostitution. "Bunnies": women working at Playboy Clubs (a chain, 1960–91).
8. Barbara Ehrenreich and Deirdre English, *Witches, Midwives, and Nurses: A History of Women Healers* (Old Westbury, N.Y.: Feminist Press, 1973); Andrea Dworkin, *Woman Hating* (New York: Dutton, 1974), pp. 118–54; Daly, pp. 178–222 [Rich's note].
9. See VIRGINIA WOOLF, *A Room of One's Own* (London: Hogarth, 1929), and *id., Three Guineas* (New York: Harcourt Brace, [1938] 1966); Tillie Olsen, *Silences* (Boston: Delacorte, 1978); Michelle Cliff, "The Resonance of Interruption," *Chrysalis: A Magazine of Women's Culture* 8 (1979): 29–37 [Rich's note]. For *A Room of One's Own*, see above.
1. Mary Daly, *Beyond God the Father* (Boston: Beacon, 1973), pp. 347–51; Olsen, pp. 22–46 [Rich's note].
2. Daly, *Beyond God the Father*, p. 93 [Rich's note].

Some of the forms by which male power manifests itself are more easily recognizable as enforcing heterosexuality on women than are others. Yet each one I have listed adds to the cluster of forces within which women have been convinced that marriage and sexual orientation toward men are inevitable—even if unsatisfying or oppressive—components of their lives. The chastity belt; child marriage; erasure of lesbian existence (except as exotic and perverse) in art, literature, film; idealization of heterosexual romance and marriage—these are some fairly obvious forms of compulsion, the first two exemplifying physical force, the second two control of consciousness. While clitoridectomy has been assailed by feminists as a form of woman torture,[3] Kathleen Barry first pointed out that it is not simply a way of turning the young girl into a "marriageable" woman through brutal surgery. It intends that women in the intimate proximity of polygynous marriage will not form sexual relationships with each other, that—from a male, genital-fetishist[4] perspective—female erotic connections, even in a sex-segregated situation, will be literally excised.[5]

The function of pornography as an influence on consciousness is a major public issue of our time, when a multibillion-dollar industry has the power to disseminate increasingly sadistic, women-degrading visual images. But even so-called soft-core pornography and advertising depict women as objects of sexual appetite devoid of emotional context, without individual meaning or personality—essentially as a sexual commodity to be consumed by males. (So-called lesbian pornography, created for the male voyeuristic eye, is equally devoid of emotional context or individual personality.) The most pernicious message relayed by pornography is that women are natural sexual prey to men and love it, that sexuality and violence are congruent, and that for women sex is essentially masochistic, humiliation pleasurable, physical abuse erotic. But along with this message comes another, not always recognized: that enforced submission and the use of cruelty, if played out in heterosexual pairing, is sexually "normal," while sensuality between women, including erotic mutuality and respect, is "queer," "sick," and either pornographic in itself or not very exciting compared with the sexuality of whips and bondage.[6] Pornography does not simply create a climate in which sex and violence are interchangeable; *it widens the range of behavior considered acceptable from men in heterosexual intercourse*—behavior which reiteratively strips women of their autonomy, dignity, and sexual potential, including the potential of loving and being loved by women in mutuality and integrity.

In her brilliant study *Sexual Harassment of Working Women: A Case of Sex Discrimination*, Catharine A. MacKinnon delineates the intersection of compulsory heterosexuality and economics. Under capitalism, women are horizontally segregated by gender and occupy a structurally inferior position

3. Fran P. Hosken, "The Violence of Power: Genital Mutilation of Females," *Heresies: A Feminist Journal of Art and Politics* 6 (1979): 28–35; Diana Russell and Nicole Van de Ven, eds., *Proceedings of the Informational Tribunal of Crimes Against Women* (Millbrae, Calif.: Les Femmes, 1976), pp. 194–95. See especially "Circumcision of Girls," in Nawal El Saadawi, *The Hidden Face of Eve: Women in the Arab World* (Boston: Beacon, 1982), pp. 33–43 [Rich's note].

4. In the psychoanalytic theory of SIGMUND FREUD, mature sexuality is "genitally organized," while the fetishist takes an object or a nongenital part of the body as the site for a habitual erotic response or fixation. Rich is suggesting instead that male sexuality, fixated on the genitals, is itself fetishistic.

5. Barry, pp. 163–64 [Rich's note].

6. The issue of "lesbian sadomasochism" needs to be examined in terms of dominant cultures' teachings about the relation of sex and violence. I believe this to be another example of the "double life" of women [Rich's note].

in the workplace. This is hardly news, but MacKinnon raises the question why, even if capitalism "requires some collection of individuals to occupy low-status, low-paying positions . . . such persons must be biologically female," and goes on to point out that "the fact that male employers often do not hire qualified women, *even when they could pay them less than men* suggests that more than the profit motive is implicated" [emphasis added].[7] She cites a wealth of material documenting the fact that women are not only segregated in low-paying service jobs (as secretaries, domestics, nurses, typists, telephone operators, child-care workers, waitresses), but that "sexualization of the woman" is part of the job. Central and intrinsic to the economic realities of women's lives is the requirement that women will "market sexual attractiveness to men, who tend to hold the economic power and position to enforce their predilections." And MacKinnon documents that "sexual harassment perpetuates the interlocked structure by which women have been kept sexually in thrall to men at the bottom of the labor market. Two forces of American society converge: men's control over women's sexuality and capital's control over employees' work lives."[8] Thus, women in the workplace are at the mercy of sex as power in a vicious circle. Economically disadvantaged, women—whether waitresses or professors—endure sexual harassment to keep their jobs and learn to behave in a complaisantly and ingratiatingly heterosexual manner because they discover this is their true qualification for employment, whatever the job description. And, MacKinnon notes, the woman who too decisively resists sexual overtures in the workplace is accused of being "dried up" and sexless, or lesbian. This raises a specific difference between the experiences of lesbians and homosexual men. A lesbian, closeted on her job because of heterosexist prejudice, is not simply forced into denying the truth of her outside relationships or private life. Her job depends on her pretending to be not merely heterosexual, but a heterosexual *woman* in terms of dressing and playing the feminine, deferential role required of "real" women.

MacKinnon raises radical questions as to the qualitative differences between sexual harassment, rape, and ordinary heterosexual intercourse. ("As one accused rapist put it, he hadn't used 'any more force than is usual for males during the preliminaries.'") She criticizes Susan Brownmiller[9] for separating rape from the mainstream of daily life and for her unexamined premise that "rape is violence, intercourse is sexuality," removing rape from the sexual sphere altogether. Most crucially she argues that "taking rape from the realm of 'the sexual,' placing it in the realm of 'the violent,' allows one to be against it without raising any questions about the extent to which the institution of heterosexuality has defined force as a normal part of 'the preliminaries.'"[1] "Never is it asked whether, under conditions of male supremacy, the notion of 'consent' has any meaning."[2]

The fact is that the workplace, among other social institutions, is a place where women have learned to accept male violation of their psychic and

7. Catharine A. MacKinnon, *Sexual Harassment of Working Women: A Case of Sexual Discrimination* (New Haven: Yale University Press, 1979), pp. 15–16 [Rich's note].
8. Ibid., p. 174 [Rich's note].
9. Susan Brownmiller, *Against Our Will: Men, Women, and Rape* (New York: Simon and Schuster, 1975) [Rich's note].
1. MacKinnon, p. 219. Susan Schecter writes: "The push for heterosexual union at whatever cost is so intense that . . . it has become a cultural force of its own that creates battering. The ideology of romantic love and its jealous possession of the partner as property provide the masquerade for what can become severe abuse." (*Aegis: Magazine on Ending Violence against Women* [July–August, 1979]: 50–51) [Rich's note].
2. MacKinnon, p. 298 [Rich's note].

physical boundaries as the price of survival; where women have been educated—no less than by romantic literature or by pornography—to perceive themselves as sexual prey. A woman seeking to escape such casual violations along with economic disadvantage may well turn to marriage as a form of hoped-for protection, while bringing into marriage neither social nor economic power, thus entering that institution also from a disadvantaged position. MacKinnon finally asks:

> What if inequality is built into the social conceptions of male and female sexuality, of masculinity and femininity, of sexiness and heterosexual attractiveness? Incidents of sexual harassment suggest that male sexual desire itself may be aroused by female vulnerability. . . . Men feel they can take advantage, so they want to, so they do. Examination of sexual harassment, precisely because the episodes appear commonplace, forces one to confront the fact that sexual intercourse normally occurs between economic (as well as physical) unequals . . . the apparent legal requirement that violations of women's sexuality appear out of the ordinary before they will be punished helps prevent women from defining the ordinary conditions of their own consent.[3]

Given the nature and extent of heterosexual pressures—the daily "eroticization of women's subordination," as MacKinnon phrases it[4]—I question the more or less psychoanalytic perspective (suggested by such writers as Karen Horney, H. R. Hayes, Wolfgang Lederer, and, most recently, Dorothy Dinnerstein)[5] that the male need to control women sexually results from some primal male "fear of women" and of women's sexual insatiability. It seems more probable that men really fear not that they will have women's sexual appetites forced on them or that women want to smother and devour them, but that women could be indifferent to them altogether, that men could be allowed sexual and emotional—therefore economic—access to women *only* on women's terms, otherwise being left on the periphery of the matrix.

The means of assuring male sexual access to women have recently received searching investigation by Kathleen Barry.[6] She documents extensive and appalling evidence for the existence, on a very large scale, of international female slavery, the institution once known as "white slavery" but which in fact has involved, and at this very moment involves, women of every race and class. In the theoretical analysis derived from her research, Barry makes the connection between all enforced conditions under which women live subject to men: prostitution, marital rape, father-daughter and brother-sister incest, wife beating, pornography, bride price, the selling of daughters, purdah, and genital mutilation. She sees the rape paradigm—where the victim of sexual assault is held responsible for her own victimization—as leading to

3. Ibid., p. 220 [Rich's note].
4. Ibid., p. 221 [Rich's note].
5. Dinnerstein's *The Mermaid and the Minotaur* (1976) focuses on women's child-bearing and child-caring capacities and argues that a more balanced involvement of the male and female parents in child-rearing will greatly improve relations between the sexes. In *Feminine Psychology* (1967), Horney rejects the Freudian notion of "penis envy," arguing that men are afraid of women because of women's procreative abilities. Hayes's *The Dangerous Sex: The Myth of the Feminine* (1964) and Lederer's *The Fear of Women* (1968) make similar arguments.
6. Barry, op. cit. [Rich's note]. [A.R., 1986: See also Kathleen Barry, Charlotte Bunch, and Shirley Castley, eds., *International Feminism: Networking against Female Sexual Slavery* (New York: International Women's Tribune Center, 1984).]

the rationalization and acceptance of other forms of enslavement where the woman is presumed to have "chosen" her fate, to embrace it passively, or to have courted it perversely through rash or unchaste behavior. On the contrary, Barry maintains, "female sexual slavery is present in ALL situations where women or girls cannot change the conditions of their existence; where regardless of how they got into those conditions, e.g., social pressure, economic hardship, misplaced trust or the longing for affection, they cannot get out; and where they are subject to sexual violence and exploitation."[7] She provides a spectrum of concrete examples, not only as to the existence of a widespread international traffic in women, but also as to how this operates—whether in the form of a "Minnesota pipeline" funneling blonde, blue-eyed midwestern runaways to Times Square, or the purchasing of young women out of rural poverty in Latin America or Southeast Asia, or the providing of *maisons d'abattage*[8] for migrant workers in the eighteenth arrondissement of Paris. Instead of "blaming the victim" or trying to diagnose her presumed pathology, Barry turns her floodlights on the pathology of sex colonization itself, the ideology of "cultural sadism" represented by the pornography industry and by the overall identification of women primarily as "sexual beings whose responsibility is the sexual service of men."[9]

Barry delineates what she names a "sexual domination perspective" through whose lens sexual abuse and terrorism of women by men has been rendered almost invisible by treating it as natural and inevitable. From its point of view, women are expendable as long as the sexual and emotional needs of the male can be satisfied. To replace this perspective of domination with a universal standard of basic freedom for women from gender-specific violence, from constraints on movement, and from male right of sexual and emotional access is the political purpose of her book. Like Mary Daly in *Gyn/Ecology*, Barry rejects structuralist and other cultural-relativist rationalizations[1] for sexual torture and anti-woman violence. In her opening chapter, she asks of her readers that they refuse all handy escapes into ignorance and denial. "The only way we can come out of hiding, break through our paralyzing defenses, is to know it all—the full extent of sexual violence and domination of women. . . . In *knowing*, in facing directly, we can learn to chart our course out of this oppression, by envisioning and creating a world which will preclude sexual slavery."[2]

"Until we name the practice, give conceptual definition and form to it, illustrate its life over time and in space, those who are its most obvious victims will also not be able to name it or define their experience."

But women are all, in different ways and to different degrees, its victims; and part of the problem with naming and conceptualizing female sexual slavery is, as Barry clearly sees, compulsory heterosexuality.[3] Compulsory heterosexuality simplifies the task of the procurer and pimp in worldwide

7. Barry, p. 33 [Rich's note].
8. Houses for beating or battering (French). The 18th arrondissement is a district where many Algerians and other North African immigrants to France live.
9. Barry, p. 103 [Rich's note].
1. Structural anthropology in most cases tries to be value-neutral, simply describing the practices and structures of various cultures, without claiming any one culture is superior to another or morally reprehensible in some way.
2. Barry, p. 5 [Rich's note].
3. Ibid., p. 100 [Rich's note].
[A.R., 1986: This statement has been taken as claiming that "all women are victims" purely and simply, or that "all heterosexuality equals sexual slavery." I would say, rather, that all women are affected, though differently, by dehumanizing attitudes and practices directed at women as a group.]

prostitution rings and "eros centers," while, in the privacy of the hon leads the daughter to "accept" incest/rape by her father, the mother to deny that it is happening, the battered wife to stay on with an abusive husband. "Befriending or love" is a major tactic of the procurer, whose job it is to turn the runaway or the confused young girl over to the pimp for seasoning. The ideology of heterosexual romance, beamed at her from childhood out of fairy tales, television, films, advertising, popular songs, wedding pageantry, is a tool ready to the procurer's hand and one which he does not hesitate to use, as Barry documents. Early female indoctrination in "love" as an emotion may be largely a Western concept; but a more universal ideology concerns the primacy and uncontrollability of a male sexual drive. This is one of many insights offered by Barry's work:

> As sexual power is learned by adolescent boys through the social experience of their sex drive, so do girls learn that the locus of sexual power is male. Given the importance placed on the male sex drive in the socialization of girls as well as boys, early adolescence is probably the first significant phase of male identification in a girl's life and development. . . . As a young girl becomes aware of her own increasing sexual feelings . . . she turns away from her heretofore primary relationships with girlfriends. As they become secondary to her, recede in importance in her life, her own identity also assumes a secondary role and she grows into male identification.[4]

We still need to ask why some women never, even temporarily, turn away from "heretofore primary relationships" with other females. And why does male identification—the casting of one's social, political, and intellectual allegiances with men—exist among lifelong sexual lesbians? Barry's hypothesis throws us among new questions, but it clarifies the diversity of forms in which compulsory heterosexuality presents itself. In the mystique of the overpowering, all-conquering male sex drive, the penis-with-a-life-of-its-own, is rooted the law of male sex right to women, which justifies prostitution as a universal cultural assumption on the one hand, while defending sexual slavery within the family on the basis of "family privacy and cultural uniqueness" on the other.[5] The adolescent male sex drive, which, as both young women and men are taught, once triggered cannot take responsibility for itself or take no for an answer, becomes, according to Barry, the norm and rationale for adult male sexual behavior: a condition of *arrested sexual development*. Women learn to accept as natural the inevitability of this "drive" because they receive it as dogma. Hence, marital rape; hence, the Japanese wife resignedly packing her husband's suitcase for a weekend in the *kisaeng* brothels of Taiwan; hence, the psychological as well as economic imbalance of power between husband and wife, male employer and female worker, father and daughter, male professor and female student.

The effect of male identification means

> internalizing the values of the colonizer and actively participating in carrying out the colonization of one's self and one's sex. . . . Male identification is the act whereby women place men above women, including

4. Ibid., p. 218 [Rich's note].

5. Ibid., p. 140 [Rich's note].

> themselves, in credibility, status, and importance in most situations, regardless of the comparative quality the women may bring to the situation. . . . Interaction with women is seen as a lesser form of relating on every level.[6]

What deserves further exploration is the doublethink many women engage in and from which no woman is permanently and utterly free: However woman-to-woman relationships, female support networks, a female and feminist value system are relied on and cherished, indoctrination in male credibility and status can still create synapses in thought, denial of feeling, wishful thinking, a profound sexual and intellectual confusion.[7] I quote here from a letter I received the day I was writing this passage: "I have had very bad relationships with men—I am now in the midst of a very painful separation. I am trying to find my strength through women—without my friends, I could not survive." How many times a day do women speak words like these or think them or write them, and how often does the synapse reassert itself?

Barry summarizes her findings:

> Considering the arrested sexual development that is understood to be normal in the male population, and considering the numbers of men who are pimps, procurers, members of slavery gangs, corrupt officials participating in this traffic, owners, operators, employees of brothels and lodging and entertainment facilities, pornography purveyors, associated with prostitution, wife beaters, child molesters, incest perpetrators, johns (tricks) and rapists, one cannot but be momentarily stunned by the enormous male population engaging in female sexual slavery. The huge number of men engaged in these practices should be cause for declaration of an international emergency, a crisis in sexual violence. But what should be cause for alarm is instead accepted as normal sexual intercourse.[8]

Susan Cavin, in a rich and provocative, if highly speculative, dissertation, suggests that patriarchy becomes possible when the original female band, which includes children but ejects adolescent males, becomes invaded and outnumbered by males; that not patriarchal marriage, but the rape of the mother by the son, becomes the first act of male domination. The entering wedge, or leverage, which allows this to happen is not just a simple change in sex ratios; it is also the mother-child bond, manipulated by adolescent males in order to remain within the matrix past the age of exclusion. Maternal affection is used to establish male right of sexual access, which, however, must ever after be held by force (or through control of consciousness) since the original deep adult bonding is that of woman for woman.[9] I find this hypothesis extremely suggestive, since one form of false consciousness

6. Ibid., p. 172 [Rich's note].

7. Elsewhere I have suggested that male identification has been a powerful source of white women's racism and that it has often been women already seen as "disloyal" to male codes and systems who have actively battled against it (Adrienne Rich, "Disloyal to Civilization: Feminism, Racism, Gynephobia," in *On Lies, Secrets, and Silence: Selected Prose, 1966–1978* [New York: W. W. Norton, 1979]) [Rich's note].

8. Barry, p. 220 [Rich's note].

9. Susan Cavin, "Lesbian Origins" (Ph.D. diss., Rutgers University, 1978), unpublished, chap. 6 [Rich's note]. [A.R., 1986: This dissertation was recently published as *Lesbian Origins* (San Francisco: Ism Press, 1986).]

which serves compulsory heterosexuality is the maintenance of a mother-son relationship between women and men, including the demand that women provide maternal solace, nonjudgmental nurturing, and compassion for their harassers, rapists, and batterers (as well as for men who passively vampirize them).

But whatever its origins, when we look hard and clearly at the extent and elaboration of measures designed to keep women within a male sexual purlieu, it becomes an inescapable question whether the issue feminists have to address is not simple "gender inequality" nor the domination of culture by males nor mere "taboos against homosexuality," but the enforcement of heterosexuality for women as a means of assuring male right of physical, economic, and emotional access.[1] One of many means of enforcement is, of course, the rendering invisible of the lesbian possibility, an engulfed continent which rises fragmentedly into view from time to time only to become submerged again. Feminist research and theory that contribute to lesbian invisibility or marginality are actually working against the liberation and empowerment of women as a group.[2] The assumption that "most women are innately heterosexual" stands as a theoretical and political stumbling block for feminism. It remains a tenable assumption partly because lesbian existence has been written out of history or catalogued under disease, partly because it has been treated as exceptional rather than intrinsic, partly because to acknowledge that for women heterosexuality may not be a "preference" at all but something that has had to be imposed, managed, organized, propagandized, and maintained by force is an immense step to take if you consider yourself freely and "innately" heterosexual. Yet the failure to examine heterosexuality as an institution is like failing to admit that the economic system called capitalism or the caste system of racism is maintained by a variety of forces, including both physical violence and false consciousness.[3] To take the step of questioning heterosexuality as a "preference" or "choice" for women—and to do the intellectual and emotional work that follows—will call for a special quality of courage in heterosexually identified feminists, but I think the rewards will be great: a freeing-up of thinking, the exploring of new paths, the shattering of another great silence, new clarity in personal relationships.

1. For my perception of heterosexuality as an economic institution I am indebted to Lisa Leghorn and Katherine Parker, who allowed me to read the unpublished manuscript of their book *Woman's Worth: Sexual Economics and the World of Women* (London and Boston: Routledge and Kegan Paul, 1981) [Rich's note].

2. I would suggest that lesbian existence has been most recognized and tolerated where it has resembled a "deviant" version of heterosexuality—e.g., where lesbians have, like Stein and Toklas, played heterosexual roles (or seemed to in public) and have been chiefly identified with male culture. See also Claude E. Schaeffer, "The Kuterai Female Berdache: Courier, Guide, Prophetess and Warrior," *Ethnohistory* 12, no. 3 (summer 1965): 193–236. (Berdache: "an individual of a definite physiological sex [m. or f.] who assumes the role and status of the opposite sex and who is viewed by the community as being of one sex physiologically but as having assumed the role and status of the opposite sex" [Schaeffer, p. 231].) Lesbian existence has also been relegated to an upper-class phenomenon, an elite decadence (as in the fascination with Paris salon lesbians such as Renée Vivien and Natalie Clifford Barney), to the obscuring of such "common women" as Judy Grahn depicts in her *The Work of a Common Woman* (Oakland, Calif.: Diana Press, 1978) and *True to Life Adventure Stories* (Oakland, Calif.: Diana Press, 1978) [Rich's note]. Stein and Toklas: the American writer Gertrude Stein (1874–1946) lived from 1909 on with Alice B. Toklas (1877–1967), who in many respects acted like the "wife" of a "genius."

3. A Marxist term referring to an individual's tendency to view reality in ways congruent with the interests of the dominant orthodoxy rather than in ways that reflect his or her own class interest.

III

I have chosen to use the terms *lesbian existence* and *lesbian continuum* because the word *lesbianism* has a clinical and limiting ring. *Lesbian existence* suggests both the fact of the historical presence of lesbians and our continuing creation of the meaning of that existence. I mean the term *lesbian continuum* to include a range—through each woman's life and throughout history—of woman-identified experience, not simply the fact that a woman has had or consciously desired genital sexual experience with another woman. If we expand it to embrace many more forms of primary intensity between and among women, including the sharing of a rich inner life, the bonding against male tyranny, the giving and receiving of practical and political support, if we can also hear it in such associations as *marriage resistance* and the "haggard" behavior identified by Mary Daly (obsolete meanings: "intractable," "willful," "wanton," and "unchaste," "a woman reluctant to yield to wooing"),[4] we begin to grasp breadths of female history and psychology which have lain out of reach as a consequence of limited, mostly clinical, definitions of *lesbianism*.

Lesbian existence comprises both the breaking of a taboo and the rejection of a compulsory way of life. It is also a direct or indirect attack on male right of access to women. But it is more than these, although we may first begin to perceive it as a form of naysaying to patriarchy, an act of resistance. It has, of course, included isolation, self-hatred, breakdown, alcoholism, suicide, and intrawoman violence; we romanticize at our peril what it means to love and act against the grain, and under heavy penalties; and lesbian existence has been lived (unlike, say, Jewish or Catholic existence) without access to any knowledge of a tradition, a continuity, a social underpinning. The destruction of records and memorabilia and letters documenting the realities of lesbian existence must be taken very seriously as a means of keeping heterosexuality compulsory for women, since what has been kept from our knowledge is joy, sensuality, courage, and community, as well as guilt, self-betrayal, and pain.[5]

Lesbians have historically been deprived of a political existence through "inclusion" as female versions of male homosexuality. To equate lesbian existence with male homosexuality because each is stigmatized is to erase female reality once again. Part of the history of lesbian existence is, obviously, to be found where lesbians, lacking a coherent female community, have shared a kind of social life and common cause with homosexual men. But there are differences: women's lack of economic and cultural privilege relative to men; qualitative differences in female and male relationships—for example, the patterns of anonymous sex among male homosexuals, and the pronounced ageism in male homosexual standards of sexual attractiveness. I perceive the lesbian experience as being, like motherhood, a profoundly *female* experience, with particular oppressions, meanings, and potentialities we cannot comprehend as long as we simply bracket it with other sexually stigmatized

4. Daly, *Gyn/Ecology*, p. 15 [Rich's note].

5. "In a hostile world in which women are not supposed to survive except in relation with and in service to men, entire communities of women are simply erased. History tends to bury what it seeks to reject" (Blanche W. Cook, "'Women Alone Stir My Imagination': Lesbianism and the Cultural Tradition," *Signs: Journal of Women in Culture and Society* 4, no. 4 [summer 1979]: 719–20). The Lesbian Herstory Archives in New York City is one attempt to preserve contemporary documents on lesbian existence—a project of enormous value and meaning, working against the continuing censorship and obliteration of relationships, networks, communities in other archives and elsewhere in the culture [Rich's note].

existences. Just as the term *parenting* serves to conceal the particular and significant reality of being a parent who is actually a mother, the term *gay* may serve the purpose of blurring the very outlines we need to discern, which are of crucial value for feminism and for the freedom of women as a group.[6]

As the term *lesbian* has been held to limiting, clinical associations in its patriarchal definition, female friendship and comradeship have been set apart from the erotic, thus limiting the erotic itself. But as we deepen and broaden the range of what we define as lesbian existence, as we delineate a lesbian continuum, we begin to discover the erotic in female terms: as that which is unconfined to any single part of the body or solely to the body itself; as an energy not only diffuse but, as Audre Lorde has described it, omnipresent in "the sharing of joy, whether physical, emotional, psychic," and in the sharing of work; as the empowering joy which "makes us less willing to accept powerlessness, or those other supplied states of being which are not native to me, such as resignation, despair, self-effacement, depression, self-denial."[7] In another context, writing of women and work, I quoted the autobiographical passage in which the poet H.D. described how her friend Bryher[8] supported her in persisting with the visionary experience which was to shape her mature work:

> I knew that this experience, this writing-on-the-wall before me, could not be shared with anyone except the girl who stood so bravely there beside me. This girl said without hesitation, "Go on." It was she really who had the detachment and integrity of the Pythoness of Delphi. But it was I, battered and dissociated . . . who was seeing the pictures, and who was reading the writing or granted the inner vision. Or perhaps, in some sense, we were "seeing" it together, for without her, admittedly, I could not have gone on.[9]

If we consider the possibility that all women—from the infant suckling at her mother's breast, to the grown woman experiencing orgasmic sensations while suckling her own child, perhaps recalling her mother's milk smell in her own, to two women, like Virginia Woolf's Chloe and Olivia, who share a laboratory,[1] to the woman dying at ninety, touched and handled by women—exist on a lesbian continuum, we can see ourselves as moving in and out of this continuum, whether we identify ourselves as lesbian or not.

We can then connect aspects of woman identification as diverse as the impudent, intimate girl friendships of eight or nine year olds and the banding together of those women of the twelfth and fifteenth centuries known as Beguines who "shared houses, rented to one another, bequeathed houses to their room-mates . . . in cheap subdivided houses in the artisans' area of town," who "practiced Christian virtue on their own, dressing and living simply and not associating with men," who earned their livings as spinsters, bak-

6. [A.R., 1986: The shared historical and spiritual "crossover" functions of lesbians and gay men in cultures past and present are traced by Judy Grahn in *Another Mother Tongue: Gay Words, Gay Worlds* (Boston: Beacon Press, 1984). I now think we have much to learn both from the uniquely female aspects of lesbian existence and from the complex "gay" identity we share with gay men.]
7. Audre Lorde, "Uses of the Erotic: The Erotic as Power," in *Sister Outsider* (Trumansburg, N.Y.: Crossing Press, 1984) [Rich's note].
8. English writer, born Winifred Ellerman (1894–1983), who lived with H.D. (Hilda Doolittle, 1886–1961) for much of the 1920s to 1940s; a wealthy woman, she supported the American poet financially as well as emotionally.
9. Adrienne Rich, "Conditions for Work: The Common World of Women," in *On Lies, Secrets, and Silence*, p. 209; H.D., *Tribute to Freud* (Oxford: Carcanet, 1971), pp. 50–54 [Rich's note]. Pythoness of Delphi: oracular priestess of the Greek god Apollo.
1. Woolf, *A Room of One's Own*, p. 126 [Rich's note].

ers, nurses, or ran schools for young girls, and who managed—until the Church forced them to disperse—to live independent both of marriage and of conventual restrictions.[2] It allows us to connect these women with the more celebrated "Lesbians" of the women's school around Sappho[3] of the seventh century B.C., with the secret sororities and economic networks reported among African women, and with the Chinese marriage-resistance sisterhoods—communities of women who refused marriage or who, if married, often refused to consummate their marriages and soon left their husbands, the only women in China who were not footbound and who, Agnes Smedley[4] tells us, welcomed the births of daughters and organized successful women's strikes in the silk mills.[5] It allows us to connect and compare disparate individual instances of marriage resistance: for example, the strategies available to Emily Dickinson, a nineteenth-century white woman genius, with the strategies available to Zora Neale Hurston, a twentieth-century Black woman genius. Dickinson never married, had tenuous intellectual friendships with men, lived self-convented in her genteel father's house in Amherst, and wrote a lifetime of passionate letters to her sister-in-law Sue Gilbert and a smaller group of such letters to her friend Kate Scott Anthon. Hurston married twice but soon left each husband, scrambled her way from Florida to Harlem to Columbia University to Haiti and finally back to Florida, moved in and out of white patronage and poverty, professional success, and failure; her survival relationships were all with women, beginning with her mother. Both of these women in their vastly different circumstances were marriage resisters, committed to their own work and selfhood, and were later characterized as "apolitical." Both were drawn to men of intellectual quality; for both of them women provided the ongoing fascination and sustenance of life.

If we think of heterosexuality as *the* natural emotional and sexual inclination for women, lives such as these are seen as deviant, as pathological, or as emotionally and sensually deprived. Or, in more recent and permissive jargon, they are banalized as "life styles." And the work of such women, whether merely the daily work of individual or collective survival and resistance or the work of the writer, the activist, the reformer, the anthropologist, or the artist—the work of self-creation—is undervalued, or seen as the bitter fruit of "penis envy" or the sublimation of repressed eroticism or the meaningless rant of a "man-hater." But when we turn the lens of vision and consider the degree to which and the methods whereby heterosexual "preference" has actually been imposed on women, not only can we understand differently the meaning of individual lives and work, but we can begin to recognize a central fact of women's history: that women have always resisted male tyr-

2. Gracia Clark, "The Beguines: A Mediaeval Women's Community," *Quest: A Feminist Quarterly* 1, no. 4 (1975): 73–80 [Rich's note].

3. Greek lyric poet (b. ca. 612 B.C.E.) who lived on the island of Lesbos. Because some of Sappho's poems express love for women, both *lesbian* and *sapphic* are used to refer to female homosexuality. (The tradition that she had a "school" is not reliable.)

4. American journalist (1892–1950), who spent much time in and wrote about China.

5. See Denise Paulmé, ed., *Women of Tropical Africa* (Berkeley: University of California Press, 1963), pp. 7, 266–67. Some of these sororities are described as "a kind of defensive syndicate against the male element," their aims being "to offer concerted resistance to an oppressive patriarchate," "independence in relation to one's husband and with regard to motherhood, mutual aid, satisfaction of personal revenge." See also Audre Lorde, "Scratching the Surface: Some Notes on Barriers to Women and Loving," in *Sister Outsider*, pp. 45–52; Marjorie Topley, "Marriage Resistance in Rural Kwangtung," in *Women in Chinese Society*, ed. M. Wolf and R. Witke (Stanford, Calif.: Stanford University Press, 1978), pp. 67–89; Agnes Smedley, *Portraits of Chinese Women in Revolution*, ed. J. MacKinnon and S. MacKinnon (Old Westbury, N.Y.: Feminist Press, 1976), pp. 103–10 [Rich's note].

anny. A feminism of action, often though not always without a theory, has constantly re-emerged in every culture and in every period. We can then begin to study women's struggle against powerlessness, women's radical rebellion, not just in male-defined "concrete revolutionary situations"[6] but in all the situations male ideologies have not perceived as revolutionary—for example, the refusal of some women to produce children, aided at great risk by other women;[7] the refusal to produce a higher standard of living and leisure for men (Leghorn and Parker show how both are part of women's unacknowledged, unpaid, and ununionized economic contribution). We can no longer have patience with Dinnerstein's view that women have simply collaborated with men in the "sexual arrangements" of history. We begin to observe behavior, both in history and in individual biography, that has hitherto been invisible or misnamed, behavior which often constitutes, given the limits of the counterforce exerted in a given time and place, radical rebellion. And we can connect these rebellions and the necessity for them with the physical passion of woman for woman which is central to lesbian existence: the erotic sensuality which has been, precisely, the most violently erased fact of female experience.

* * *

IV

Woman identification is a source of energy, a potential springhead of female power, curtailed and contained under the institution of heterosexuality. The denial of reality and visibility to women's passion for women, women's choice of women as allies, life companions, and community, the forcing of such relationships into dissimulation and their disintegration under intense pressure have meant an incalculable loss to the power of all women *to change the social relations of the sexes, to liberate ourselves and each other.* The lie of compulsory female heterosexuality today afflicts not just feminist scholarship, but every profession, every reference work, every curriculum, every organizing attempt, every relationship or conversation over which it hovers. It creates, specifically, a profound falseness, hypocrisy, and hysteria in the heterosexual dialogue, for every heterosexual relationship is lived in the queasy strobe light of that lie. However we choose to identify ourselves, however we find ourselves labeled, it flickers across and distorts our lives.[8]

The lie keeps numberless women psychologically trapped, trying to fit mind, spirit, and sexuality into a prescribed script because they cannot look beyond the parameters of the acceptable. It pulls on the energy of such women even as it drains the energy of "closeted" lesbians—the energy exhausted in the double life. The lesbian trapped in the "closet," the woman imprisoned in prescriptive ideas of the "normal" share the pain of blocked options, broken connections, lost access to self-definition freely and powerfully assumed.

The lie is many-layered. In Western tradition, one layer—the romantic—asserts that women are inevitably, even if rashly and tragically, drawn to men;

6. See Rosalind Petchesky, "Dissolving the Hyphen: A Report on Marxist-Feminist Groups 1–5," in *Capitalist Patriarchy and the Case for Socialist Feminism*, ed. Zillah Eisenstein (New York: Monthly Review Press, 1979), p. 387 [Rich's note].

7. [A.R., 1986: See Angela Davis, *Women, Race, and Class* (New York: Random House, 1981), p. 102; Orlando Patterson, *Slavery and Social Death: A Comparative Study* (Cambridge: Harvard University Press, 1982), p. 133.]

8. See Russell and Van de Ven, p. 40: "Few heterosexual women realize their lack of free choice about their sexuality, and few realize how and why compulsory heterosexuality is also a crime against them" [Rich's note].

that even when that attraction is suicidal (e.g., *Tristan and Isolde*, Kate Chopin's *The Awakening*),[9] it is still an organic imperative. In the tradition of the social sciences it asserts that primary love between the sexes is "normal"; that women *need* men as social and economic protectors, for adult sexuality, and for psychological completion; that the heterosexually constituted family is the basic social unit; that women who do not attach their primary intensity to men must be, in functional terms, condemned to an even more devastating outsiderhood than their outsiderhood as women. Small wonder that lesbians are reported to be a more hidden population than male homosexuals. The Black lesbian-feminist critic Lorraine Bethel, writing on Zora Neale Hurston, remarks that for a Black woman—already twice an outsider—to choose to assume still another "hated identity" is problematic indeed. Yet the lesbian continuum has been a life line for Black women both in Africa and the United States.

> Black women have a long tradition of bonding together . . . in a Black/ women's community that has been a source of vital survival information, psychic and emotional support for us. We have a distinct Black woman-identified folk culture based on our experiences as Black women in this society; symbols, language and modes of expression that are specific to the realities of our lives. . . . Because Black women were rarely among those Blacks and females who gained access to literary and other acknowledged forms of artistic expression, this Black female bonding and Black woman-identification has often been hidden and unrecorded except in the individual lives of Black women through our own memories of our particular Black female tradition.[1]

Another layer of the lie is the frequently encountered implication that women turn to women out of hatred for men. Profound skepticism, caution, and righteous paranoia about men may indeed be part of any healthy woman's response to the misogyny of male-dominated culture, to the forms assumed by "normal" male sexuality, and to *the failure even of "sensitive" or "political" men to perceive or find these troubling*. Lesbian existence is also represented as mere refuge from male abuses, rather than as an electric and empowering charge between women. One of the most frequently quoted literary passages on lesbian relationship is that in which Colette's[2] Renée, in *The Vagabond*, describes "the melancholy and touching image of two weak creatures who have perhaps found shelter in each other's arms, there to sleep and weep, safe from man who is often cruel, and there to taste *better than any pleasure, the bitter happiness of feeling themselves akin, frail and forgotten* [emphasis added]."[3] Colette is often con-

9. *The Awakening* (1899), by the American fiction writer Chopin (1851–1904), records the heroine's sexual awakening through an adulterous liaison and ends with her suicide. *Tristan and Isolde*: the 1859 opera by Richard Wagner, with its celebratory mingling of love and death, retells the medieval legend of a doomed adulterous love.

1. Lorraine Bethel, "'This Infinity of Conscious Pain': Zora Neale Hurston and the Black Female Literary Tradition," in *All the Women Are White, All the Blacks Are Men, But Some of Us Are Brave*, ed. Gloria T. Hull, Patricia Bell Scott, and Barbara Smith (Old Westbury, N.Y.: Feminist Press, 1982), pp. 176–88 [Rich's note].

2. Pen name of Sidonie Gabrielle Claudine Colette (1873–1954), prolific French novelist; *The Vagabond* was published in 1910.

3. Dorothy Dinnerstein, the most recent writer to quote this passage, adds ominously: "But what has to be added to her account is that these 'women enlaced' are sheltering each other not just from what men want to do to them, but also from what they want to do to each other" (Dinnerstein, *The Mermaid and the Minotaur: Sexual Arrangements and the Human Malaise* [New York: Harper and Row, 1976], p. 103). The fact is, however, that woman-to-woman violence is a minute grain in the universe of male-against-female violence perpetuated and rationalized in every social institution [Rich's note].

sidered a lesbian writer. Her popular reputation has, I think, much to do with the fact that she writes about lesbian existence as if for a male audience; her earliest "lesbian" novels, the Claudine series, were written under compulsion for her husband and published under both their names. At all events, except for her writings on her mother, Colette is a less reliable source on the lesbian continuum than, I would think, Charlotte Brontë,[4] who understood that while women may, indeed must, be one another's allies, mentors, and comforters in the female struggle for survival, there is quite extraneous delight in each other's company and attraction to each others' minds and character, which attend a recognition of each others' strengths.

By the same token, we can say that there is a *nascent* feminist political content in the act of choosing a woman lover or life partner in the face of institutionalized heterosexuality.[5] But for lesbian existence to realize this political content in an ultimately liberating form, the erotic choice must deepen and expand into conscious woman identification—into lesbian feminism.

The work that lies ahead, of unearthing and describing what I call here "lesbian existence," is potentially liberating for all women. It is work that must assuredly move beyond the limits of white and middle-class Western Women's Studies to examine women's lives, work, and groupings within every racial, ethnic, and political structure. There are differences, moreover, between "lesbian existence" and the "lesbian continuum," differences we can discern even in the movement of our own lives. The lesbian continuum, I suggest, needs delineation in light of the "double life" of women, not only women self-described as heterosexual but also of self-described lesbians. We need a far more exhaustive account of the forms the double life has assumed. Historians need to ask at every point how heterosexuality as institution has been organized and maintained through the female wage scale, the enforcement of middle-class women's "leisure," the glamorization of so-called sexual liberation, the withholding of education from women, the imagery of "high art" and popular culture, the mystification of the "personal" sphere, and much else. We need an economics which comprehends the institution of heterosexuality, with its doubled workload for women and its sexual divisions of labor, as the most idealized of economic relations.

The question inevitably will arise: Are we then to condemn all heterosexual relationships, including those which are least oppressive? I believe this question, though often heartfelt, is the wrong question here. We have been stalled in a maze of false dichotomies which prevents our apprehending the institution as a whole: "good" versus "bad" marriages; "marriage for love" versus arranged marriage; "liberated" sex versus prostitution; heterosexual intercourse versus rape; *Liebesschmerz*[6] versus humiliation and dependency. Within the institution exist, of course, qualitative differences of experience; but the absence of choice remains the great unacknowledged reality, and in the absence of choice, women will remain dependent upon the chance or luck of particular relationships and will have no collective power to determine the meaning and place of sexuality in their lives. As we address the institution itself, moreover, we begin to perceive a history of female resistance which has never fully understood itself because it has been so fragmented, miscalled,

4. English novelist (1816–1855).
5. Conversation with Blanche W. Cook, New York City, March 1979 [Rich's note].
6. The sorrow or pain of love (German).

erased. It will require a courageous grasp of the politics and economics, as well as the cultural propaganda, of heterosexuality to carry us beyond individual cases or diversified group situations into the complex kind of overview needed to undo the power men everywhere wield over women, power which has become a model for every other form of exploitation and illegitimate control.

1980, 1986

CHINUA ACHEBE
1930–2013

In the wake of global realignments after World War II, many African, Asian, and other countries sought political independence from European colonial rule. The struggle for cultural recognition was an important part of this political process, and the 1960s and 1970s witnessed a profusion of writing from formerly colonial cultures. Arguably the most prominent African writer of his generation, Chinua Achebe brought to the English-speaking world highly regarded novelistic portraits of Nigeria. Alongside his fiction, he also published influential criticism exposing colonialist biases in English fiction and criticism and arguing for an indigenous African literature. Indicting the view of Africa in Joseph Conrad's classic *Heart of Darkness* (1902) as a reflection of European racist assumptions of the "darkness" or inferiority of Africans, Achebe's "An Image of Africa: Racism in Conrad's *Heart of Darkness*" (1977) is a touchstone of anticolonialist—or what has come to be called postcolonial—criticism.

Born in the village of Ogidi in eastern Nigeria, Achebe experienced the world of colonialism firsthand. Nigeria was a construction of European colonial powers; its disparate African tribes and territories were placed under British control from 1906 until 1960, when it achieved independence. His father was a churchman in an evangelical Protestant mission, but as a boy Achebe was also exposed to traditional Igbo culture. He was selected to attend a prestigious colonial secondary school, the Government College at Umuahia, and in 1948 went on to receive his undergraduate training at the newly formed University College in Ibadan, then an affiliate of the University of London. After graduating in 1953, he worked as a producer for the Nigerian Broadcasting Company, later founding and directing the Voice of Nigeria from 1961 to 1966.

Achebe caught the attention of the literary world with the publication of his first novel, *Things Fall Apart* (1958). Depicting traditional Igbo culture and its clash with European culture, it has been an international success, translated into nearly fifty languages and selling millions of copies. Achebe became a senior research fellow at the University of Nigeria in 1967, a professor of English in 1976, and professor emeritus in 1985. He taught at various U.S. schools, including the University of Massachusetts, the University of Virginia, UCLA, and Bard College, and he won numerous prizes and honors. He was also actively involved in publishing ventures to promote African writing; most notably, from 1962 through 1987 he was founding editor of the British publisher Heinemann's African Writers Series, which has issued several hundred titles. In addition, Achebe was an outspoken public figure, especially during the Nigerian Civil War (1967–70), when he supported the independence of Biafra from the Nigerian federation.

Achebe's fiction and criticism present, as one African critic notes, "exemplary texts of nationalist contestation of colonialist myths and distortions of Africans and Africa." Achebe himself, in his influential essay "Colonialist Criticism" (1975), shows how colonialist biases permeate even sophisticated critical commentary on fiction representing Africa. This is the theme of "An Image of Africa," our selection, in which Achebe argues that Conrad's *Heart of Darkness*, however critical of the European imperialist mission, presents Africans as savage, subhuman, and incapable of speech. While allowing for the novel's artistry, he unequivocally condemns this view as "offensive and deplorable." Significantly, he focuses much of his attack not on Conrad but on the critical position of Conrad's text in the Western canon as a masterpiece, a position largely forgiving of or blind to its racism. Thus its critical reception—up to the present day—unthinkingly perpetuates racist stereotypes.

Although focused on the racism inherent in the specific case of *Heart of Darkness*, Achebe's argument broaches large theoretical debates about the canon and about the moral and social values of art. It poses a difficult question: how should we respond to classic works that exhibit racist or other condemnable views? Achebe answers with an emphatic ethical judgment. In dismissing the aestheticist view that art is solely for art's sake or that we should merely appreciate and analyze the aesthetic or linguistic skill of a work, Achebe presupposes a social theory of art, holding that art reflects and propagates social views and values. He does not fully justify this position in "An Image of Africa," but in a central early statement of his views, "The Novelist as Teacher" (1965), he underscores literature's pedagogical mission and its ethical and political responsibilities.

Since its publication, "An Image of Africa" has set the terms of debate about one of the most read and taught books in the English curriculum. Some scholars maintain that Conrad disdainfully opposes European imperialism, which was at its height in 1900, and exhibits sympathy for the plight of Africans. Others argue that *Heart of Darkness* represents not a real Africa but an allegory of an individual psychological descent or of a decontextualized battle between good and evil. Critics heeding Achebe's angry battle cry find texts such as *Heart of Darkness* irretrievably flawed in their racism and limited in that they depict Africa only through Western eyes. More moderate historicist critics have tried to mend fences; while agreeing that *Heart of Darkness* exhibits racist views, they point out that it represents relatively progressive views for its time and conclude that Conrad is not particularly blameworthy, noting that any condemnation would be unfairly based on anachronistic criteria.

Beyond its impact on Conrad criticism, Achebe's denunciation of Conrad assumed a larger significance in the so-called culture wars of the 1980s and 1990s. Traditionalists have taken it as a prime example of "political correctness," an attempt to impose moralistic and political standards on classic works of literature. They claim that canonical works exhibit high aesthetic value, proven by the test of time, and thus should be esteemed. On the other side, a range of theorists—postcolonial, African American, feminist, queer, and so on—contest a literary canon that carries racist, orientalist, sexist, homophobic, and other negative values. This debate seems intractable, in part because both groups argue at cross-purposes; it is doubtful that a traditionalist critic would advocate racism, or that a progressive critic would dispense with aesthetic appreciation. Rather, their disagreement rests on their differing theories of art: traditionalist critics claim priority for formal aesthetic properties, while progressive critics claim priority for art's social—or in Achebe's terms, pedagogical—value.

Along with the Kenyan novelist and critic NGUGI WĂ THIONG'O and others, Achebe called for representations of imperialism to shift from European perspectives to the perspectives of those colonized. As he remarked in a 1989 interview, "The moment I realized in reading *Heart of Darkness* that I was not supposed to be part of Marlow's crew sailing down the Congo to a bend in the river, but I was one of those on the shore, jumping and clapping and making faces and so on, then I realized that was not me, and that that story had to be told again." This call, advocating a distinctive indigenous voice to represent its own experience, has been influential for the developing field of postcolonial studies, as well as for African American literature and criticism. Achebe's analysis of the West's imagination of Africa as a negative projection of itself draws on the psychoanalytic model of colonialism proposed by FRANTZ FANON, which argues that European depictions of colonies as the "Other" are symptomatic of the West's own cultural neuroses. This analysis of the literary and cultural representation of non-Western cultures has received its fullest treatment in the work of EDWARD W. SAID, who labels Western projections onto the Eastern Other "Orientalism" (see below). In "An Image of Africa," Achebe simply calls it racism.

"An Image of Africa: Racism in Conrad's *Heart of Darkness*" Keywords: The Canon/Tradition, Ethics, The Novel, Postcolonial Criticism, Race and Ethnicity Studies, Representation

An Image of Africa: Racism in Conrad's *Heart of Darkness*[1]

In the fall of 1974 I was walking one day from the English Department at the University of Massachusetts to a parking lot. It was a fine autumn morning such as encouraged friendliness to passing strangers. Brisk youngsters were hurrying in all directions, many of them obviously freshmen in their first flush of enthusiasm. An older man going the same way as I turned and remarked to me how very young they came these days. I agreed. Then he asked me if I was a student too. I said no, I was a teacher. What did I teach? African literature. Now that was funny, he said, because he knew a fellow who taught the same thing, or perhaps it was African *history*, in a certain community college not far from here. It always surprised him, he went on to say, because he never had thought of Africa as having that kind of stuff, you know. By this time I was walking much faster. "Oh well," I heard him say finally, behind me: "I guess I have to take your course to find out."

A few weeks later I received two very touching letters from high school children in Yonkers, New York, who—bless their teacher—had just read *Things Fall Apart*.[2] One of them was particularly happy to learn about the customs and superstitions of an African tribe.

I propose to draw from these rather trivial encounters rather heavy conclusions which at first sight might seem somewhat out of proportion to them. But only, I hope, at first sight.

The young fellow from Yonkers, perhaps partly on account of his age, but I believe also for much deeper and more serious reasons, is obviously unaware that the life of his own tribesmen in Yonkers, New York, is full of odd customs and superstitions and, like everybody else in his culture, imagines that he needs a trip to Africa to encounter those things.

The other person being fully my own age could not be excused on the grounds of his years. Ignorance might be a more likely reason; but here again I believe that something more wilful than a mere lack of information was at

1. This is an amended version of the second Chancellor's Lecture at the University of Massachusetts, Amherst, February 1975 [Achebe's note].

2. Achebe's first and best-known novel (published 1958); it depicts a traditional Nigerian society from an African rather than European perspective.

work. For did not that erudite British historian and Regius Professor at Oxford, Hugh Trevor-Roper,[3] also pronounce that African history did not exist?

If there is something in these utterances more than youthful inexperience, more than a lack of factual knowledge, what is it? Quite simply it is the desire—one might indeed say the need—in Western psychology to set Africa up as a foil to Europe, as a place of negations at once remote and vaguely familiar, in comparison with which Europe's own state of spiritual grace will be manifest.

This need is not new; which should relieve us all of considerable responsibility and perhaps make us even willing to look at this phenomenon dispassionately. I have neither the wish nor the competence to embark on the exercise with the tools of the social and biological sciences but do so more simply in the manner of a novelist responding to one famous book of European fiction: Joseph Conrad's *Heart of Darkness*,[4] which better than any other work that I know displays that Western desire and need which I have just referred to. Of course there are whole libraries of books devoted to the same purpose but most of them are so obvious and so crude that few people worry about them today. Conrad, on the other hand, is undoubtedly one of the great stylists of modern fiction and a good story-teller into the bargain. His contribution therefore falls automatically into a different class—permanent literature—read and taught and constantly evaluated by serious academics. *Heart of Darkness* is indeed so secure today that a leading Conrad scholar has numbered it "among the half-dozen greatest short novels in the English language."[5] I will return to this critical opinion in due course because it may seriously modify my earlier suppositions about who may or may not be guilty in some of the matters I will now raise.

Heart of Darkness projects the image of Africa as "the other world," the antithesis of Europe and therefore of civilization, a place where man's vaunted intelligence and refinement are finally mocked by triumphant bestiality. The book opens on the River Thames, tranquil, resting peacefully "at the decline of day after ages of good service done to the race that peopled its banks."[6] But the actual story will take place on the River Congo, the very antithesis of the Thames. The River Congo is quite decidedly not a River Emeritus. It has rendered no service and enjoys no old-age pension. We are told that "going up that river was like travelling back to the earliest beginning of the world."

Is Conrad saying then that these two rivers are very different, one good, the other bad? Yes, but that is not the real point. It is not the differentness that worries Conrad but the lurking hint of kinship, of common ancestry. For the Thames too "has been one of the dark places of the earth." It conquered its darkness, of course, and is now in daylight and at peace. But if it were to visit its primordial relative, the Congo, it would run the terrible risk of hearing grotesque echoes of its own forgotten darkness, and falling victim to an avenging recrudescence of the mindless frenzy of the first beginnings.

3. English historian (1914–2003) known for his studies of World War II and the Elizabethan period; Regius Professor of Modern History (1957–80). He made this comment in a lecture delivered in 1963, reprinted in *The Rise of Christian Europe* (1965).

4. The best-known work (1902) of Conrad (1857–1924), the Polish-born English novelist. In it, a ship captain named Marlow retells his journey down the Congo River on behalf of a Belgian company in search of their chief ivory agent, Kurtz.

5. Albert J. Guerard, introduction to *Heart of Darkness and the Secret Sharer*, by Joseph Conrad (New York: New American Library, 1950), p. 9 [Achebe's note].

6. Conrad, p. 66 [Achebe's note].

These suggestive echoes comprise Conrad's famed evocation of the African atmosphere in *Heart of Darkness*. In the final consideration, his method amounts to no more than a steady, ponderous, fake-ritualistic repetition of two antithetical sentences, one about silence and the other about frenzy. We can inspect samples of this on pages 103 and 105 of the New American Library edition: (a) "It was the stillness of an implacable force brooding over an inscrutable intention" and (b) "The steamer toiled along slowly on the edge of a black and incomprehensible frenzy." Of course, there is a judicious change of adjective from time to time, so that instead of "inscrutable," for example, you might have "unspeakable," even plain "mysterious," etc., etc.

The eagle-eyed English critic F. R. Leavis[7] drew attention long ago to Conrad's "adjectival insistence upon inexpressible and incomprehensive mystery." That insistence must not be dismissed lightly, as many Conrad critics have tended to do, as a mere stylistic flaw; for it raises serious questions of artistic good faith. When a writer while pretending to record scenes, incidents, and their impact is in reality engaged in inducing hypnotic stupor in his readers through a bombardment of emotive words and other forms of trickery, much more has to be at stake than stylistic felicity. Generally, normal readers are well armed to detect and resist such underhand activity. But Conrad chose his subject well—one which was guaranteed not to put him in conflict with the psychological predisposition of his readers or raise the need for him to contend with their resistance. He chose the role of purveyor of comforting myths.

The most interesting and revealing passages in *Heart of Darkness* are, however, about people. I must crave the indulgence of my reader to quote almost a whole page from about the middle of the story when representatives of Europe in a steamer going down the Congo encounter the denizens of Africa:

> We were wanderers on a prehistoric earth, on an earth that wore the aspect of an unknown planet. We could have fancied ourselves the first of men taking possession of an accursed inheritance, to be subdued at the cost of profound anguish and of excessive toil. But suddenly, as we struggled round a bend, there would be a glimpse of rush walls, of peaked grass-roofs, a burst of yells, a whirl of black limbs, a mass of hands clapping, of feet stamping, of bodies swaying, of eyes rolling, under the droop of heavy and motionless foliage. The steamer toiled along slowly on the edge of the black and incomprehensible frenzy. The prehistoric man was cursing us, praying to us, welcoming us—who could tell? We were cut off from the comprehension of our surroundings; we glided past like phantoms, wondering and secretly appalled, as sane men would be before an enthusiastic outbreak in a madhouse. We could not understand because we were too far and could not remember because we were travelling in the night of first ages, of those ages that are gone, leaving hardly a sign—and no memories.
>
> The earth seemed unearthly. We are accustomed to look upon the shackled form of a conquered monster, but there—there you could look

7. Influential modern literary critic (1895–1978; see above); the following quotation is from *The Great Tradition: George Eliot, Henry James, and Joseph Conrad* (1948; reprint, New York: New York University Press, 1960), p. 177.

> at a thing monstrous and free. It was unearthly, and the men were—No, they were not inhuman. Well, you know, that was the worst of it—this suspicion of their not being inhuman. It would come slowly to one. They howled and leaped, and spun, and made horrid faces; but what thrilled you was just the thought of their humanity—like yours—the thought of your remote kinship with this wild and passionate uproar. Ugly. Yes, it was ugly enough; but if you were man enough you would admit to yourself that there was in you just the faintest trace of a response to the terrible frankness of that noise, a dim suspicion of there being a meaning in it which you—you so remote from the night of first ages—could comprehend.[8]

Herein lies the meaning of *Heart of Darkness* and the fascination it holds over the Western mind: "What thrilled you was just the thought of their humanity—like yours . . . Ugly."

Having shown us Africa in the mass, Conrad then zeros in, half a page later, on a specific example, giving us one of his rare descriptions of an African who is not just limbs or rolling eyes:

> And between whiles I had to look after the savage who was fireman. He was an improved specimen; he could fire up a vertical boiler. He was there below me, and, upon my word, to look at him was as edifying as seeing a dog in a parody of breeches and a feather hat, walking on his hind legs.[9] A few months of training had done for that really fine chap. He squinted at the steam gauge and at the water gauge with an evident effort of intrepidity—and he had filed his teeth, too, the poor devil, and the wool of his pate shaved into queer patterns, and three ornamental scars on each of his cheeks. He ought to have been clapping his hands and stamping his feet on the bank, instead of which he was hard at work, a thrall to strange witchcraft, full of improving knowledge.[1]

As everybody knows, Conrad is a romantic on the side. He might not exactly admire savages clapping their hands and stamping their feet but they have at least the merit of being in their place, unlike this dog in a parody of breeches. For Conrad, things being in their place is of the utmost importance.

"Fine fellows—cannibals—in their place," he tells us pointedly. Tragedy begins when things leave their accustomed place, like Europe leaving its safe stronghold between the policeman and the baker to take a peep into the heart of darkness.

Before the story takes us into the Congo basin proper we are given this nice little vignette as an example of things in their place:

> Now and then a boat from the shore gave one a momentary contact with reality. It was paddled by black fellows. You could see from afar the white of their eyeballs glistening. They shouted, sang; their bodies streamed with perspiration; they had faces like grotesque masks—these chaps; but they had bone, muscle, a wild vitality, an intense energy of

8. Conrad, pp. 105–6 [Achebe's note].
9. An allusion to a famous remark of SAMUEL JOHNSON (1709–1784), who described a woman's preaching as "like a dog's walking on his hinder legs. It is not done well; but you are surprised to find it done at all" (quoted by James Boswell in his *Life of Johnson*, 1791).
1. Conrad, p. 106 [Achebe's note].

> movement, that was as natural and true as the surf along their coast. They wanted no excuse for being there. They were a great comfort to look at.[2]

Towards the end of the story Conrad lavishes a whole page quite unexpectedly on an African woman who has obviously been some kind of mistress to Mr. Kurtz and now presides (if I may be permitted a little liberty) like a formidable mystery over the inexorable imminence of his departure:

> She was savage and superb, wild-eyed and magnificent. . . . She stood looking at us without a stir and like the wilderness itself, with an air of brooding over an inscrutable purpose.[3]

This Amazon is drawn in considerable detail, albeit of a predictable nature, for two reasons. First, she is in her place and so can win Conrad's special brand of approval; and second, she fulfils a structural requirement of the story; a savage counterpart to the refined, European woman who will step forth to end the story:

> She came forward, all in black with a pale head, floating toward me in the dusk. She was in mourning. . . . She took both my hands in hers and murmured, "I had heard you were coming" . . . She had a mature capacity for fidelity, for belief, for suffering.[4]

The difference in the attitude of the novelist to these two women is conveyed in too many direct and subtle ways to need elaboration. But perhaps the most significant difference is the one implied in the author's bestowal of human expression to the one and the withholding of it from the other. It is clearly not part of Conrad's purpose to confer language on the "rudimentary souls" of Africa. In place of speech they made "a violent babble of uncouth sounds." They "exchanged short grunting phrases" even among themselves. But most of the time they were too busy with their frenzy. There are two occasions in the book, however, when Conrad departs somewhat from his practice and confers speech, even English speech, on the savages. The first occurs when cannibalism gets the better of them:

> "Catch 'im," he snapped, with a bloodshot widening of his eyes and a flash of sharp white teeth—"catch 'im. Give 'im to us." "To you, eh?" I asked; "what would you do with them?" "Eat 'im!" he said curtly.[5]

The other occasion was the famous announcement: "Mistah Kurtz—he dead."[6]

At first sight these instances might be mistaken for unexpected acts of generosity from Conrad. In reality they constitute some of his best assaults. In the case of the cannibals the incomprehensible grunts that had thus far served them for speech suddenly proved inadequate for Conrad's purpose of letting the European glimpse the unspeakable craving in their hearts. Weighing the necessity for consistency in the portrayal of the dumb brutes against the sensational advantages of securing their conviction by clear, unambiguous evidence issuing out of their own mouths, Conrad chose the

2. Ibid., p. 78 [Achebe's note].
3. Ibid., pp. 136–37.
4. Ibid., p. 153.
5. Ibid., p. 111.
6. Ibid., p. 148.

latter. As for the announcement of Mr. Kurtz's death by the "insolent black head in the doorway," what better or more appropriate *finis* could be written to the horror story of that wayward child of civilization who willfully had given his soul to the powers of darkness and "taken a high seat amongst the devils of the land" than the proclamation of his physical death by the forces he had joined?

It might be contended, of course, that the attitude to the African in *Heart of Darkness* is not Conrad's but that of his fictional narrator, Marlow, and that far from endorsing it Conrad might indeed be holding it up to irony and criticism. Certainly, Conrad appears to go to considerable pains to set up layers of insulation between himself and the moral universe of his story. He has, for example, a narrator behind a narrator. The primary narrator is Marlow, but his account is given to us through the filter of a second, shadowy person. But if Conrad's intention is to draw a cordon sanitaire between himself and the moral and psychological *malaise* of his narrator, his care seems to me totally wasted because he neglects to hint, clearly and adequately, at an alternative frame of reference by which we may judge the actions and opinions of his characters. It would not have been beyond Conrad's power to make that provision if he had thought it necessary. Conrad seems to me to approve of Marlow, with only minor reservations—a fact reinforced by the similarities between their two careers.

Marlow comes through to us not only as a witness of truth, but one holding those advanced and humane views appropriate to the English liberal tradition which required all Englishmen of decency to be deeply shocked by atrocities in Bulgaria or the Congo of King Leopold[7] of the Belgians or wherever.

Thus, Marlow is able to toss out such bleeding-heart sentiments as these:

> They were all dying slowly—it was very clear. They were not enemies, they were not criminals, they were nothing earthly now—nothing but black shadows of disease and starvation, lying confusedly in the greenish gloom. Brought from all the recesses of the coast in all the legality of time contracts, lost in uncongenial surroundings, fed on unfamiliar food, they sickened, became inefficient, and were then allowed to crawl away and rest.[8]

The kind of liberalism espoused here by Marlow/Conrad touched all the best minds of the age in England, Europe and America. It took different forms in the minds of different people but almost always managed to sidestep the ultimate question of equality between white people and black people. That extraordinary missionary Albert Schweitzer,[9] who sacrificed brilliant careers in music and theology in Europe for a life of service to Africans in much the same area as Conrad writes about, epitomizes the ambivalence. In a comment which has often been quoted Schweitzer says: "The African is

7. Leopold II (1835–1909; reigned 1865–1909), an ardent imperialist advocating the colonial development of the Congo region, which was then the private holding of a group of investors headed by Leopold and later (1908–60) a colonial possession of Belgium. "Atrocities in Bulgaria": after an unsuccessful Bulgarian rebellion against Turkish rule, in 1876 the Ottomans massacred some 30,000 Bulgarian men, women, and children.

8. Conrad, p. 82 [Achebe's note].

9. Alsatian theologian, philosopher, and physician (1875–1965), who in 1913 founded a hospital in Lambaréné, a city in the Gabon province of French Equatorial Africa. In 1952 he was awarded the Nobel Peace Prize for his humanitarian efforts in Africa.

indeed my brother but my junior brother." And so he proceeded to build a hospital appropriate to the needs of junior brothers with standards of hygiene reminiscent of medical practice in the days before the germ theory of disease came into being. Naturally he became a sensation in Europe and America. Pilgrims flocked, and I believed still flock even after he has passed on, to witness the prodigious miracle in Lambaréné, on the edge of the primeval forest.

Conrad's liberalism would not take him quite as far as Schweitzer's, though. He would not use the word "brother" however qualified; the farthest he would go was "kinship." When Marlow's African helmsman falls down with a spear in his heart he gives his white master one final disquieting look:

> And the intimate profundity of that look he gave me when he received his hurt remains to this day in my memory—like a claim of distant kinship affirmed in a supreme moment.[1]

It is important to note that Conrad, careful as ever with his words, is concerned not so much about "distant kinship" as about someone *laying a claim* on it. The black man lays a claim on the white man which is well-nigh intolerable. It is the laying of this claim which frightens and at the same time fascinates Conrad, "the thought of their humanity—like yours . . . Ugly."

The point of my observations should be quite clear by now, namely that Joseph Conrad was a thoroughgoing racist. That this simple truth is glossed over in criticisms of his work is due to the fact that white racism against Africa is such a normal way of thinking that its manifestations go completely unremarked. Students of *Heart of Darkness* will often tell you that Conrad is concerned not so much with Africa as with the deterioration of one European mind caused by solitude and sickness. They will point out to you that Conrad is, if anything, less charitable to the Europeans in the story than he is to the natives, that the point of the story is to ridicule Europe's civilizing mission in Africa. A Conrad student informed me in Scotland that Africa is merely a setting for the disintegration of the mind of Mr. Kurtz.

Which is partly the point. Africa as setting and backdrop which eliminates the African as human factor. Africa as a metaphysical battlefield devoid of all recognizable humanity, into which the wandering European enters at his peril. Can nobody see the preposterous and perverse arrogance in thus reducing Africa to the role of props for the break-up of one petty European mind? But that is not even the point. The real question is the dehumanization of Africa and Africans which this age-long attitude has fostered and continues to foster in the world. And the question is whether a novel which celebrates this dehumanization, which depersonalizes a portion of the human race, can be called a great work of art. My answer is: No, it cannot. I do not doubt Conrad's great talents. Even *Heart of Darkness* has its memorably good passages and moments:

> The reaches opened before us and closed behind, as if the forest had stepped leisurely across the water to bar the way for our return.[2]

Its exploration of the minds of the European characters is often penetrating and full of insight. But all that has been more than fully discussed in the last fifty years. His obvious racism has, however, not been addressed. And it is high time it was!

1. Conrad, p. 124 [Achebe's note].

2. Ibid., pp. 104–5.

Conrad was born in 1857, the very year in which the first Anglican missionaries were arriving among my own people in Nigeria. It was certainly not his fault that he lived his life at a time when the reputation of the black man was at a particularly low level. But even after due allowances have been made for all the influences of contemporary prejudice on his sensibility, there remains still in Conrad's attitude a residue of antipathy to black people which his peculiar psychology alone can explain. His own account of his first encounter with a black man is very revealing:

> A certain enormous buck nigger encountered in Haiti fixed my conception of blind, furious, unreasoning rage, as manifested in the human animal to the end of my days. Of the nigger I used to dream for years afterwards.[3]

Certainly Conrad had a problem with niggers. His inordinate love of that word itself should be of interest to psychoanalysts. Sometimes his fixation on blackness is equally interesting, as when he gives us this brief description: "A black figure stood up, strode on long black legs, waving long black arms"[4]—as though we might expect a black figure striding along on black legs to wave white arms! But so unrelenting is Conrad's obsession.

As a matter of interest, Conrad gives us in *A Personal Record* what amounts to a companion piece to the buck nigger of Haiti. At the age of sixteen Conrad encountered his first Englishman in Europe. He calls him "my unforgettable Englishman" and describes him in the following manner:

> [his] calves exposed to the public gaze . . . dazzled the beholder by the splendour of their marble-like condition and their rich tone of young ivory . . . The light of a headlong, exalted satisfaction with the world of men . . . illumined his face . . . and triumphant eyes. In passing he cast a glance of kindly curiosity and a friendly gleam of big, sound, shiny teeth . . . his white calves twinkled sturdily.[5]

Irrational love and irrational hate jostling together in the heart of that talented, tormented man. But whereas irrational love may at worst engender foolish acts of indiscretion, irrational hate can endanger the life of the community. Naturally, Conrad is a dream for psychoanalytic critics. Perhaps the most detailed study of him in this direction is by Bernard C. Meyer, M.D. In his lengthy book, Dr. Meyer follows every conceivable lead (and sometimes inconceivable ones) to explain Conrad. As an example, he gives us long disquisitions on the significance of hair and hair-cutting in Conrad. And yet not even one word is spared for his attitude to black people. Not even the discussion of Conrad's antisemitism was enough to spark off in Dr. Meyer's mind those other dark and explosive thoughts. Which only leads one to surmise that Western psychoanalysts must regard the kind of racism displayed by Conrad as absolutely normal despite the profoundly important work done by Frantz Fanon[6] in the psychiatric hospitals of French Algeria.

3. Qtd. in Jonah Raskin, *The Mythology of Imperialism* (New York: Random House, 1971), p. 143 [Achebe's note].
4. Conrad, p. 142 [Achebe's note].
5. Qtd. in Bernard C. Meyer, *Joseph Conrad: A Psychoanalytic Biography* (Princeton: Princeton University Press, 1967), p. 30 [Achebe's note]. Meyer (1910–1988), an American psychiatrist as well as a psychoanalytic literary critic.
6. Black West Indian psychoanalyst and social critic (1925–1961; see above), who was an influential proponent of the national liberation of colonial peoples.

Whatever Conrad's problems were, you might say he is now safely dead. Quite true. Unfortunately, his heart of darkness plagues us still. Which is why an offensive and deplorable book can be described by a serious scholar as "among the half-dozen greatest short novels in the English language." And why it is today perhaps the most commonly prescribed novel in twentieth-century literature courses in English departments of American universities.

There are two probable grounds on which what I have said so far may be contested. The first is that it is no concern of fiction to please people about whom it is written. I will go along with that. But I am not talking about pleasing people. I am talking about a book which parades in the most vulgar fashion prejudices and insults from which a section of mankind has suffered untold agonies and atrocities in the past and continues to do so in many ways and many places today. I am talking about a story in which the very humanity of black people is called in question.

Secondly, I may be challenged on the grounds of actuality. Conrad, after all, did sail down the Congo in 1890 when my own father was still a babe in arms. How could I stand up more than fifty years after his death and purport to contradict him? My answer is that as a sensible man I will not accept just any traveller's tales solely on the grounds that I have not made the journey myself. I will not trust the evidence even of a man's very eyes when I suspect them to be as jaundiced as Conrad's. And we also happen to know that Conrad was, in the words of his biographer, Bernard C. Meyer, "notoriously inaccurate in the rendering of his own history."[7]

But more important by far is the abundant testimony about Conrad's savages which we could gather if we were so inclined from other sources and which might lead us to think that these people must have had other occupations besides merging into the evil forest or materializing out of it simply to plague Marlow and his dispirited band. For as it happened, soon after Conrad had written his book an event of far greater consequence was taking place in the art world of Europe. This is how Frank Willett, a British art historian, describes it:

> Gauguin had gone to Tahiti, the most extravagant individual act of turning to a non-European culture in the decades immediately before and after 1900, when European artists were avid for new artistic experiences, but it was only about 1904–5 that African art began to make its distinctive impact. One piece is still identifiable; it is a mask that had been given to Maurice Vlaminck in 1905. He records that Derain was "speechless" and "stunned" when he saw it, bought it from Vlaminck and in turn showed it to Picasso and Matisse, who were also greatly affected by it. Ambroise Vollard then borrowed it and had it cast in bronze . . . The revolution of twentieth century art was under way![8]

The mask in question was made by other savages living just north of Conrad's River Congo. They have a name too: the Fang people, and are without a doubt among the world's greatest masters of the sculptured form. The event

7. Meyer, p. 30 [Achebe's note].

8. Frank Willett, *African Art* (New York: Praeger, 1971), pp. 35–36 [Achebe's note]. Willett (1925–2006), English art historian who focused on works from Africa. Willett names the important French modern painters Paul Gauguin (1848–1903), Maurice de Vlaminck (1876–1958), André Derain (1880–1954), and Henri Matisse (1869–1954), as well as the great Spanish modernist Pablo Picasso (1881–1973). Vollard (1867–1939) was an influential French art dealer and publisher who supported modern art.

Frank Willett is referring to marked the beginning of cubism and the infusion of new life into European art that had run completely out of strength.

The point of all this is to suggest that Conrad's picture of the peoples of the Congo seems grossly inadequate even at the height of their subjection to the ravages of King Leopold's International Association for the Civilization of Central Africa.[9]

Travellers with closed minds can tell us little except about themselves. But even those not blinkered, like Conrad, with xenophobia, can be astonishingly blind. Let me digress a little here. One of the greatest and most intrepid travellers of all time, Marco Polo, journeyed to the Far East from the Mediterranean in the thirteenth century and spent twenty years in the court of Kublai Khan[1] in China. On his return to Venice he set down in his book entitled *Description of the World* his impressions of the peoples and places and customs he had seen. But there were at least two extraordinary omissions in his account. He said nothing about the art of printing, unknown as yet in Europe but in full flower in China. He either did not notice it at all or, if he did, failed to see what use Europe could possibly have for it. Whatever the reason, Europe had to wait another hundred years for Gutenberg.[2] But even more spectacular was Marco Polo's omission of any reference to the Great Wall of China, nearly four thousand miles long and already more than one thousand years old at the time of his visit. Again, he may not have seen it; but the Great Wall of China is the only structure built by man which is visible from the moon![3] Indeed, travellers can be blind.

As I said earlier Conrad did not originate the image of Africa which we find in his book. It was and is the dominant image of Africa in the Western imagination and Conrad merely brought the peculiar gifts of his own mind to bear on it. For reasons which can certainly use close psychological inquiry, the West seems to suffer deep anxieties about the precariousness of its civilization and to have a need for constant reassurance by comparison with Africa. If Europe, advancing in civilization, could cast a backward glance periodically at Africa trapped in primordial barbarity it could say with faith and feeling: There go I but for the grace of God. Africa is to Europe as the picture is to Dorian Gray[4]—a carrier on to whom the master unloads his physical and moral deformities so that he may go forward, erect and immaculate. Consequently, Africa is something to be avoided just as the picture has to be hidden away to safeguard the man's jeopardous integrity. Keep away from Africa, or else! Mr. Kurtz of *Heart of Darkness* should have heeded that warning and the prowling horror in his heart would have kept its place, chained to its lair. But he foolishly exposed himself to the wild irresistible allure of the jungle and lo! the darkness found him out.

In my original conception of this essay I had thought to conclude it nicely on an appropriately positive note in which I would suggest from my privileged position in African and Western cultures some advantages the West might

9. An international group of explorers, geographers, and scientists, founded by Leopold II; it was first convened in Brussels in 1876.

1. Great Mongol ruler and emperor of China (1215–1294). Polo (1254–1324), Venetian merchant and traveler who is said to have spent years in the Khan's service; his writings about the court and Asia made him famous.

2. Johannes Gutenberg (ca. 1397–1468), the German printer credited with inventing movable type, which revolutionized book production.

3. This often-repeated claim is not true (no structure is visible).

4. The title character of *The Picture of Dorian Gray* (1890), by the Irish author OSCAR WILDE; he does not age while his portrait changes, reflecting his moral disintegration.

derive from Africa once it rid its mind of old prejudices and began to look at Africa not through a haze of distortions and cheap mystifications but quite simply as a continent of people—not angels, but not rudimentary souls either—just people, often highly gifted people and often strikingly successful in their enterprise with life and society. But as I thought more about the stereotype image, about its grip and pervasiveness, about the wilful tenacity with which the West holds it to its heart; when I thought of the West's television and cinema and newspapers, about books read in its schools and out of school, of churches preaching to empty pews about the need to send help to the heathen in Africa, I realized that no easy optimism was possible. And there was in any case something totally wrong in offering bribes to the West in return for its good opinion of Africa. Ultimately the abandonment of unwholesome thoughts must be its own and only reward. Although I have used the word "wilful" a few times here to characterize the West's view of Africa, it may well be that what is happening at this stage is more akin to reflex action than calculated malice. Which does not make the situation more but less hopeful.

The *Christian Science Monitor*, a paper more enlightened than most, once carried an interesting article written by its Education Editor on the serious psychological and learning problems faced by little children who speak one language at home and then go to school where something else is spoken. It was a wide-ranging article taking in Spanish-speaking children in America, the children of migrant Italian workers in Germany, the quadrilingual phenomenon in Malaysia and so on. And all this while the article speaks unequivocally about language. But then out of the blue sky comes this:

> In London there is an enormous immigration of children who speak Indian or Nigerian dialects, or some other native language.[5]

I believe that the introduction of "dialects," which is technically erroneous in the context, is almost a reflex action caused by an instinctive desire of the writer to downgrade the discussion to the level of Africa and India. And this is quite comparable to Conrad's withholding of language from his rudimentary souls. Language is too grand for these chaps; let's give them dialects!

In all this business a lot of violence is inevitably done not only to the image of despised peoples but even to words, the very tools of possible redress. Look at the phrase "native language" in the *Christian Science Monitor* excerpt. Surely the only *native* language possible in London is Cockney English. But our writer means something else—something appropriate to the sounds Indians and Africans make!

Although the work of redressing which needs to be done may appear too daunting, I believe it is not one day too soon to begin. Conrad saw and condemned the evil of imperial exploitation but was strangely unaware of the racism on which it sharpened its iron tooth. But the victims of racist slander who for centuries have had to live with the inhumanity it makes them heir to have always known better than any casual visitor, even when he comes loaded with the gifts of a Conrad.

1975 1977

5. *Christian Science Monitor*, November 25, 1974, p. 11 [Achebe's note].

ADŪNĪS
b. ca. 1930

Adūnīs is the pen name of ʿAlī Ahmad Saʿīd, a Syrian-born poet and critic who has Lebanese citizenship. Like many of his fellow countrymen and -women, he is not certain of his birthdate, but it is usually placed around 1930. The story has it that as a young boy, he sent a poem to a local newspaper. After it was rejected because of his age, he adopted the name of the traditional mythic figure Adonis (Adūnīs in Arabic) and submitted another poem, which was immediately published. He then went back to the newspaper and introduced himself as Adūnīs, whereupon his reputation was established. That reputation has continued to grow throughout his long career as a poet and literary-cultural scholar. He has produced not only books on literary history and criticism but also poetic manifestos and anthologies devoted to the Arabic poetic heritage. He is widely recognized as the Arab world's most significant advocate and practitioner of "modernizing" poetry.

In pursuing this combination of roles, Adūnīs self-consciously continues a longstanding tradition in Arabic literature. Abū Tammām (ca. 804–ca. 845), one of the greatest poets of the early Islamic era (which begins in 622 C.E.), was among many who compiled anthologies of his predecessors' poetry. Ibn al-Muʿtazz (861–908), a member of the Abbasid family of caliphs, who headed the Islamic community for a single day in Baghdad before being assassinated, not only was a renowned poet but also composed one of the pioneering studies of poetic devices in Arabic, the *Kitāb al-badīʿ* (*Book of Tropes*). Like his predecessors, then, Adūnīs is both a *shāʿir* (poet; literally, "someone possessed of inner vision") and an *adīb* (literary scholar), an acute thinker concerned with both the present and the past of his own literary culture. In his case, it is difficult, if not impossible, to separate the poet and creative writer from the analyst of the Arabic cultural tradition in general and its poetic heritage in particular.

As historian and critic, Adūnīs surveys the heritage of his predecessors over fifteen centuries with the eye and mind of a contemporary poet, one who is actively engaged in reformulating the past in light of the cultural and political trends of the present. It was OSCAR WILDE who, in one of his more serious moments, declared, "The one duty we owe to history is to rewrite it." In 1964 Adūnīs edited a pathbreaking three-volume anthology of premodern Arabic poetry, *Dīwān al-shiʿr al-ʿArabī* (*Collection of Arabic Poetry*), applying to the entire tradition many of his own developing critical principles regarding the nature and function of poetry and poetics. The results were startling and controversial: while almost all the great poets were included, a number of new names were added and some prominent figures omitted. His experience in compiling this collection probably led Adūnīs to the subject of his doctoral dissertation, written for St. Joseph's University in Beirut, which was published (also in three volumes) as *Al-Thābit wa-al-mutahawwil* (1974, *The Static and Dynamic*). As the title implies, this detailed study of the entire premodern tradition of Arabic poetry emphasizes the ongoing cultural tension between tradition and change. It foregrounds the tendency of Arabic poetry to focus on past models of excellence rather than value the promise of the new. Here again, Adūnīs uses his own modernizing perspective to recast how the tradition developed. Adopting the notion of "ruptures" from the contemporary French critical tradition, he identifies particular moments during the centuries of Arabic poetic production when a poet broke radically with the received tradition and moved in a new direction.

Within the classical tradition, Adūnīs singles out Abū Tammām for successfully challenging norms of reception and evaluation and transforming the functions of the poetic image. Abū Tammām had been roundly condemned by his contemporaries for the "obscurity" and complexity of his images and frequent rhetorical tricks. His defender ʿAbd al-Qāhir al-Jurjānī (ca. 1008–1078), the great critic who restored him to a central position within the history of Arabic poetry, is likewise crucial in Adūnīs's account of change in Arabic poetry and poetics. Though Adūnīs does not question the traditional ranking of al-Mutanabbī (915–965) as the greatest Arab poet of the classical era, he sees the role of Abū Tammām as pivotal—without someone to create poetic ruptures, the static (*thābit*) would always tend to prevail over the dynamic (*mutahawwil*), especially when writings are judged by a steadfastly conservative community of critics. Adūnīs, the modern poet, argues that it is the poet's function to decide on the poem's form, which emerges naturally from its content; the function of criticism, in turn, is to analyze what the poet has produced, not to use old formulas to dictate what the poet ought to produce. Other poets whose works he sees as leading to similar ruptures include the Lebanese American Jubrān Khalīl Jubrān (1883–1931), usually known in the Western world as Kahlil Gibran, and Adūnīs himself. At the conclusion of one of Adūnīs's most memorable poems, "Qabr min Ajl Nyū-Yūrk" (1971, "A Grave for New York"), these two poets find themselves surveying the Arab world and the United States. Once again in Adūnīs, the roles of poet and critic intertwine while remaining distinct.

In 1975 Adūnīs left his adopted homeland of Lebanon, where civil war had erupted (and would devastate the country until 1990), and he took up residence in Paris. He had long been influenced by French culture and poetry, particularly that of St. John Perse, pseudonym of Alexis Léger (1887–1975). There he formed a close friendship with the French poet and essayist Yves Bonnefoy, who was appointed a professor at the prestigious Collège de France in Paris in 1981. At Bonnefoy's suggestion Adūnīs was invited in 1984 to give a series of lectures on Arabic poetry and poetics, which were delivered in French though originally written in Arabic. It is from the English translation of the Arabic version (*An Introduction to Arab Poetics*, 1985) that our selections are taken.

Orality and modernity, the concerns of the two chapters excerpted here, are the main focus of almost everything Adūnīs has written as poet and critic. From its earliest beginnings, Arabic poetry has been a social and cultural event—above all, a public performance. Though the spread of print culture has made the creations of both premodern and modern Arab poets available to a wider public, almost every poem is first performed in front of a group of listeners. Poets have traditionally been and still often are important public figures, and the community often turns first to poetry, especially in times of celebration or crisis. When the late Palestinian poet Mahmūd Darwīsh came to Morocco in 2000 to hold a reading, the venue had to be changed to a soccer stadium, where 24,000 attended. Any Arab poet would agree with the observation of the American poet Stanley Kunitz: "The page . . . is a cold bed." Videos of poets vying to outdo one another in Lebanese *zajal*, a semi-improvised form that has flourished for centuries, can now be found online. Orality—broadly conceived to include the body, voice, gesture, rhythmic language, and living soul of the poet and audience—has always been and remains a crucial feature of the Arabic poetic tradition, and it is Adūnīs's first topic.

In both selections Adūnīs, the modern and modernist poet, is determined to use his analyses to show how the contemporary tradition of Arabic poetry is linked to the literary heritage of the past. In the first chapter his emphasis on the role of orality immediately introduces questions of audience, performance, conventions, and modes of evaluation. Adūnīs is judiciously reviving connections that were deemphasized as the culture shifted from sole reliance on oral transmission and memorization toward use of the written word and record, a process aided by the arrival of paper in the Muslim world in the second half of the ninth century. Still, the tradition of audience participation in and criticism of public recitations stretches from at least the seventh century, when—according to the earliest records—poets judged each other's performances at tribal gatherings and festivals, until today, as listeners frequently call for favored lines of poetry to be repeated and audibly condemn or suggest improvements for lines they dislike. But even as Adūnīs celebrates orality and poetic song, he notes problems associated with the codification of the tradition.

In chapter 1 Adūnīs refers to several of the key debates that were critical to the development of a classical tradition of Arabic poetry. In its early decades, Islam moved out of the Arabian Peninsula, with its twin holy cities of Mecca and Medina, and came into contact with other regions and peoples; cultural and literary traditions and values inevitably clashed. Especially productive was the friction with Persia (modern Iran), conquered in the mid-seventh century, which had its own language and established literary tradition against which the Arabic poets defined themselves. For example, the perceived urbanity of the Persians was confronted by the desert-based tribal values of the peninsular Muslims, leading to some poetry that drew on nostalgia and other poetry that satirized it in the increasingly multicultural milieu of the caliph's court (located first in Damascus and then, after 762, in Baghdad). As Islam spread geographically and the central authority of the caliph in Baghdad gradually broke down, numerous other power centers emerged, such as Cairo in Egypt, Fez in Morocco, Cordoba in Spain (which the Arabs called "Al-Andalus"), Rayy in Persia, and Basra in Mesopotamia (modern Iraq).

These cultural centers began to foster the development of a wide variety of scholarly disciplines, including philology, lexicography, prosody, and literary theory and criticism, and specialists on the poetic tradition started to organize and evaluate an enormous body of odes created during the pre-Islamic era. Rules were laid down for meter, rhyme, and diction. During this time, a major distinction was drawn between "natural" poetry and poets (Arabic *matbūʿ*), associated with traditional values of the desert, and the "artificial" poetry (*masnūʿ*) of the city and court. As these intellectual communities expanded and grew more sophisticated, Adūnīs notes, the critics became more powerful than the poets on whom they were commenting. He laments the result—namely, "absolute criteria," based on oral poetry, that dictate how the modern Arab poet writes and a set of aesthetic principles that foster retrospection and imitation. Stasis thus threatens to prevail over the dynamic development of poetics.

In chapter 4, from which we draw our second selection, Adūnīs discusses the concept of modernity, pointing out that there have been modernities in every era. Each "present," including our own, has identified itself as modern by distinguishing itself from a particular past. For example, the one-day caliph, Ibn al-Muʿtazz, in a study of poetry by many of his own ninth-century contemporaries called them "modernist poets" (*shuʿarāʾ muhdathūn*). Adopting a similarly historical approach, Adūnīs begins by identifying those parameters that he believes have colored the discussion of the modern within Arab Islamic culture. He again returns to Islam's early days, when the emerging community of Muslim intellectuals established a notion of religious orthodoxy supported by specific texts. Like many other scholars, Adūnīs sees the dominance of that orthodoxy and of the institutions upholding it, coupled with an extreme reverence for the past and everything ancient, as explaining why change itself and the advocacy of the new and modern were often equated with heresy.

He has continued to critique religious orthodoxy as a trend in Islamic culture dangerous to creativity and true authenticity. As a result, in the past four decades Adūnīs has faced increasing hostility from various groups advocating a religious solution to Arab society's various ills. In a more productive vein, this tension has also led Adūnīs to thoughtfully engage with the Qur'an as a creative artist, helping him to gain the profound insights he incorporates into his critical work *Al-Nass al-Qur'āniyya wa-āfaq al-kitāba* (1993, *The Qur'anic Text and the Horizons of Writing*), where he speaks movingly of the Qur'an as both an inspiration for and limit on the language of anyone who writes in Arabic.

As early as his *Al-Thābit*, Adūnīs proposed that the retreat from modernity was a series of "falls" of Islamic centers (most prominently, the fall of Baghdad to the

Mongols in 1258), which led to the modern being identified with the (usually Western) other. In chapter 4, after providing this historical background, Adūnīs concentrates on a more recent period—the past two centuries, known in Arabic as the *nahḍa*. The usual translation of the term, "renaissance" (literally, it means "process of rising up" or "revival"), is problematic, for its causes and characteristics are entirely different from those of the European Renaissance. Its two opposing currents have been, on the one hand, the revival of the past and its cultural heritage (*ihyā*ʾ) and, on the other, renewed contacts with Europeans, as a wave of colonization that began in the nineteenth century brought their cultures to the Arabic-speaking region and drew Arabic speakers to Europe for their education (a process termed in Arabic *iqtibās*, "borrowing").

While the dominance of Western technology and culture is largely responsible for the identification of literary modernity with the West, Adūnīs also points to indigenous obstacles to the development of an Arabic poetics of modernity, notably deference to religious authority and confusion about the nature of the Arabic language itself. To these should be added the attitude of the community of intellectuals, who so strongly favored the literary production of the earliest centuries of Islam that they dismissed as "a period of decadence" the years from about 1150 to 1850.

Adūnīs next considers modernity in the contemporary Middle East much more broadly. In assessing the relative influences of the two cultures, that are everywhere vaguely termed the "East" and the "West," Adūnīs shuns the simplistic ideology behind such labels as "clash of civilizations," focusing instead on some of the major underlying factors that shape cultural contacts and confrontations in the political and social spheres, both regionally and globally. The opposition between the two, he notes, has been political and ideological rather than "intellectual or poetic," and Western technological superiority has led to the judgment that the East's cultures and regions are "backward." But the emphasis on technology is wrong: scientific progress, Adūnīs argues, must not be confused with human progress, and "the Westerner who lives surrounded by computers and exposed to the latest in space travel is not necessarily more advanced in any profound sense than the Arab peasant living among trees and cattle." It is rather in culture, and specifically in poetry, that the distinctive qualities of a people are to be located and cherished.

Adūnīs's complex, multifaceted exploration of modernity can be dizzying and dense. He makes use of the inventive metaphorical poetry of Abū Tammām; the innovative ideas of another early poet, Abū Nuwās (ca. 750–ca. 813); the mystical writings of al-Niffarī (d. ca. 965); and the critical theories of ʿAbd al-Qāhir al-Jurjānī—all prominent figures writing from the eighth to the eleventh centuries—as he traces the birth of modernity in Arabic to a new urban culture in ancient times, as well as to interactions with and assimilations of Persian, Greek, Indian, and other cultures. Later crucial confrontations with the West include not just nineteenth- and twentieth-century imperialism and colonialism—with the mixed blessings of science, technology, and consumer culture—but also the illuminating and influential avant-garde writings of European poets such as Charles Baudelaire and Stéphane Mallarmé. In Adūnīs's view, all these vectors of modernity, internal and external, ancient and modern, oppose past-oriented authoritarian orthodoxies, conformisms, and traditionalisms, which are invariably rooted in scriptural fundamentalism. Modernity is associated with life-affirming innovation, freedom of thought, transgression, and heresy—both inside and outside Arab culture.

At the same time, the mechanical aspect of European-American modernity can be both superficial and destructive, a point also made by MAX HORKHEIMER and THEODOR W. ADORNO in their critique of modern culture. Scientific reason has no use for the past. Consumerism fills the present of global culture with material plenty, but is ephemeral and ultimately hollow. As both JÜRGEN HABERMAS and FREDRIC JAMESON note, vanguardist modernism puts a premium on new artistic styles and rapid change, without connection to the genuine sources of life. Speaking very personally as a contemporary Arab poet, Adūnīs recounts his own lifelong search for fulfilling and sustaining sources of meaning that embraced the past—legends, mystical imagery, and magical elements of the literary tradition. In restoring and revaluing these materials that some condemned as heretical, he places a premium on open horizons, a better life, a truer form of progress, and, above all, a more authentic modernity rooted in tradition.

In his later poetry and criticism, Adūnīs more systematically explores several of what MICHEL FOUCAULT would surely have termed "subjugated knowledges" within the Islamic tradition, most notably through the lens of Sufism (Islamic mysticism). This inward turn has led him increasingly to examine the interconnections of Self and Other through the mediation of language. The result of these meditations is displayed most clearly in his volume *Al-Sūfiyya wa-al-sūrīyāliyya* (1995; trans. 2005 as *Sufism and Surrealism*). Since, in Arabic, language always has a religious dimension conditioned by its use in the Qur'an, Adūnīs has found himself assailed by Islamists who claim monopoly over linguistic interpretation and meaning. Adūnīs maintains instead that the human use of language has a nostalgic quality, at once precluding a (false) assertion of unitary discourse by the human subject and lending a heroic quality to the search for such unity.

More recently, Adūnīs initially supported the uprisings in Egypt and Tunisia in 2011, seemingly reflecting his lifelong commitment to the positive power of spontaneous, individual change. When the protests spread to his homeland of Syria, however, he came to publicly fault both the government and the opposition for their respective positions. He accused President Assad of betraying the principles of his own secular Ba'th party, which had originally supported democracy and dialogue (power sharing) among the different religions and ethnic groups that formed the Syrian polity. With equal harshness, he criticized the opposition groups for not separating religion from politics, and for concentrating solely on the seizure of power. He was in turn attacked by many intellectuals, both younger and of his own generation, for being an elitist, a modernist thinker out of touch with the present situation, who relied too heavily on religion and the abandonment of secular ideals to explain the conflict. Yet his reiterated pessimism about the possibility that a political transition alone might bring lasting change accords well with his focus in his later critical writing on the individual and the self, sometimes to the detriment of the social and communal.

Yet again, Adūnīs's opinions leave him open to the charge of being a modernizer, a revisionist, a cosmopolitan, and a mystic. Yet his lifelong commitment to the tradition of Arabic poetics and poetry, including its earliest oral manifestations in the pre-Islamic period, underscores the complexity of his views on modernization. Insofar as the past is a malleable construct, always viewed from a present perspective, it is subject to revision by scholars, Adūnīs among them. With his wide-ranging focus on the pan-Arab tradition, he minimizes national and sectarian differences among Arabic-speaking peoples; to preserve that tradition, he promotes the use of modern standard Arabic rather than regional dialects, despite his emphasis on distinctive modernities. Adūnīs is a mystic, anchoring poetry in spiritual energy; but like the Sufi mystics known as the whirling dervishes, he recognizes the importance of the body (especially voice and gesture). Were he forced to choose between the static and the dynamic, Adūnīs would unquestionably opt for the latter, ensuring the continuous modernization of Arabic poetry and its tradition. For him the modern remains committed to the perfectible future.

***An Introduction to Arab Poetics* Keywords:** Globalization, Language, Modernity, Poetry, Race and Ethnicity Studies, Religion, Rhetoric, Subjectivity, Tradition

From An Introduction to Arab Poetics[1]

From *Chapter 1.* *Poetics and Orality in the Jāhiliyya*[2]

I use the term orality here in three senses: first, to mean that Arabic poetry at the time of the *Jāhiliyya* (the pre-Islamic era in Arabia[3]) was rooted in the oral and developed within an audio-vocal culture; second, to indicate that this poetry did not come down to us in written form but was 'anthologized' in the memory and preserved through oral transmission; and finally, to investigate the characteristics of this orality in poetry and assess the extent of its influence on written Arabic poetry in succeeding periods, in particular on its aesthetics.

Pre-Islamic poetry was born as song;[4] it developed as something heard and not read, sung and not written. The voice in this poetry was the breath of life — 'body music'. It was both speech and something which went beyond speech. It conveyed speech and also that which written speech in particular is incapable of conveying. This is an indication of the richness and complexity of the relationship between the voice and speech, and between the poet and his voice; it is the relationship between the individuality of the poet and the physical actuality of the voice, both of which are hard to define. When we hear speech in the form of a song, we do not hear the individual words but the being uttering them: we hear what goes beyond the body towards the expanses of the soul. The signifier[5] is no longer an isolated word, but a word bound to a voice, a music-word, a song-word. It is not merely an indication of a certain meaning, but an energy replete with signs, the self transformed into speech-song, life in the form of language. From this comes the profound congruence between the vocal and acoustic values of speech and the emotional and affective content of pre-Islamic poetry.

To start with, orality implies listening, for the voice appeals to the ear first of all. Orality therefore had its own art of poetic expression which lay not in what was said, but in how it was said. This was particularly important because, on the whole, the pre-Islamic poet spoke of what his listeners already knew: their customs and traditions, wars and heroic exploits, victories and defeats. Thus the poet's individuality manifested itself in his manner of expression: the more inventive this was, the more he was admired for his originality. It was his duty to give to the collective, to the everyday moral and ethical existence of the group, a unique image of itself in a unique poetic language. In doing this, the poet was not expressing himself as much as he was expressing the group, or rather he expressed himself only through expressing the group. He was their singing witness, and therefore we should

1. Translated by Catherine Cobham, who occasionally retains the original Arabic in parentheses.
2. Period of ignorance (Arabic); the era preceding the revelation of the Qur'an to the Prophet Muhammad (ca. 610 C.E.) and the subsequent establishment of Islam.
3. The Arabian Peninsula (today comprising Bahrain, Saudi Arabia, Kuwait, Qatar, Oman, the United Arab Emirates, and Yemen), the birthplace of the Arabic language.
4. Arabic poetry was frequently performed with some kind of musical accompaniment; the most famous collection of early Arabic poetry is titled *Kitāb al-Aghānī* (*The Book of Songs*).
5. The symbol or sound that conveys meaning (a term introduced into linguistics by FERDINAND DE SAUSSURE, 1857–1913).

not be surprised at this paradox in pre-Islamic poetry: unity of content and diversity of expression.

Let us say that recitation and memory did the work of a book in the dissemination and preservation of pre-Islamic poetry.

If we go back to the root of the word 'song' (*nashīd*) in Arabic, we see that it means the voice, the raising of the voice and the recited poetry itself. Two basic principles of pre-Islamic poetry were that it should be recited aloud and that the poet himself should recite his own poem: as al-Jāḥiẓ[6] (775–868) says, a poem sounds better from the mouth of its composer. The Arabs of the pre-Islamic period considered the recitation of poetry as a talent in itself, distinct from that of composition; obviously it was of considerable importance in drawing an audience and impressing them enough to hold them there—especially so since, at the time, listening was essential to the comprehension of words and to musical ecstasy (*ṭarab*[7]). For, in the words of Ibn Khaldūn[8] (1332–1406), 'Hearing is father to the linguistic faculties.' From this perspective, the better the recitation, the more profound the effect of the poetry.

Recitation of poetry is a form of song. The Arab literary tradition is full of signs confirming this. The poets who recite their work are often compared to singing birds and their verses to birdsong. 'Song is the leading-rein of poetry,' according to a well-known expression, while Ḥasan Ibn Thābit[9] (d. 674), 'the poet of the Prophet', has an equally famous verse:

Sing in every poem you compose
That song is poetry's domain.

Examples like these show the organic link that existed between poetry and song in the pre-Islamic period. This explains the significance of the claim that the Arabs 'measure poetry by song' or that 'Song is the measure for poetry.' The critic Ibn Rashīq[1] maintains that song was at the origin of rhyme and metre, and that 'Metres are the foundations of melodies, and poems set the standards for stringed instruments.'

Kitāb al-Aghānī (The Book of Songs) by Abu'l-Faraj al-Iṣfaḥānī[2] (897–967), which consists of twenty-one volumes and took fifty years to compile, is the most striking proof that poetry in the pre-Islamic period was synonymous with recitation and song.

Ibn Khaldūn writes:

> In the early period singing was a part of the art of literature, because it depended on poetry, being the setting of poetry to music. The literary

6. One of the greatest scholars and prose stylists of his era. His writings and collections on a wide variety of topics include *Kitāb al-Bayān wa-al-Tabyīn* (*Book on Clarity and Clarification*), one of the earliest works of literary criticism and theory in Arabic.
7. Literally, "heightened emotion" (of sadness or joy).
8. Great historian and historiographer, born in Tunis. In *Al-Muqaddima* (*Introduction*), he outlined a scientific view of history and developed a theory of the cyclical nature of civilization.
9. A convert to Islam and one of the best poets of his time, he recited many famous odes in praise of Muhammad, who rewarded him generously.
1. The compiler (d. 1046) of a major anthology of critical writing, *Al-'Umdah fī mahāsin al-shi'r wa-adabihi wa-naqdihi* (*The Pillar Regarding Poetry's Embellishments, Proper Usage, and Criticism*).
2. Iranian scholar; his *Kitāb al-Aghānī* was the most famous collection of early Arabic poetry and its musical accompaniment.

> and intellectual elite of the Abbasid state[3] occupied themselves with it, intent on acquiring a knowledge of the styles and genres of poetry.

Elsewhere he defines the craft of song as 'the setting of poems to music by dividing the sounds into regular intervals'.

The actual performance of poetry had its own rules in the pre-Islamic period which survived into later ages. Some poets, for example, recited standing up, while others proudly refused to recite unless they were seated. Some would gesture using their hands or their whole bodies, like the poetess al-Khansā'[4] (sixth–seventh century) who, it is said, rocked and swayed, and looked down at herself in a trance. Thus in orality there is a 'meeting in action' of voice, body, word and gesture.

* * *

It is important to note that the Arabs codified poetic orality, giving its conventions and practices systematic formulations, in the early years of the interaction between Arab-Islamic and other cultures, in particular Greek, Persian and Indian. The aim of this was to affirm, preserve and put into practice the rhetorical and musical specificity of the craft of Arabic poetry, thereby asserting its individual identity and that of the Arab poet. This eager pursuit of distinctiveness and specificity lay at the root of Arab intellectual activity during this period of social and cultural mingling between the Arabs and other peoples, especially in Basra (Iraq), the cultural capital, 'mediator to the earth and heart of the world', as an Arab historian has described it. Solecisms and mispronunciations had become widespread in the language. The Persians had introduced Persian words and some rules of grammar, as well as popularizing their music. Ṭaha Ḥusayn[5] (1889–1973) characterizes the cultural situation at the time as a mixture of:

> pure Arab culture based on the Qur'ān[6] and related religious sciences, and poetry and the lexical and grammatical issues which it raised; Greek culture based on medicine and philosophy; and an oriental culture stemming originally from the Persians, the Indians and the Semitic peoples in Iraq.

In this climate the rules of language were laid down for fear that solecisms and corruptions would creep into the Qur'ān and the *ḥadīths*.[7] Poetic metres were fixed to preserve the rhythms of poetry and to distinguish them from Greek, Syriac, Persian and Indian metres and rhythms, and rules for the composition, appreciation and transmission of poetry were laid down.

* * *

[I will now discuss] the relationship between poetic orality and the act of listening. Because of this relationship, poetry criticism revolved around the

3. The second dynasty of Muslim caliphs; the Abbasids ousted the Umayyads in 750 C.E. and established a new capital city in Baghdad in 762.
4. The nickname (literally, "Snub-Nosed") of Tumaydir bint 'Amr, renowned for her elegies for her brothers who died in tribal conflicts.
5. Scholar, novelist, literary critic, and historian, and a major figure in the Egyptian modernist movement.
6. The sacred text of Islam, which Muslims believe is the word of God revealed to Muhammad through the mediation of the angel Jibrīl (Gabriel).
7. Reports (Arabic); specifically, accounts of what the Prophet Muhammad said and did during his lifetime, which were collected and codified after his death. They are second only to the Qur'an in authority.

principle of listening and the link between the poetry and the audience. The poet of the *Jāhiliyya* did not create poetry for himself but for others, for those who listened to him in order to be moved by him. Poetic talent was judged by the poet's ability to invent something which would leave its mark on the listener's soul. The poet's basic preoccupation was therefore that his poem must correspond to what was in his listener's soul, because his eloquence was evaluated in terms of how much the listener understood of what he said. However, what was in the listener's soul was a part of the common code, and his comprehension merely reflected the prevailing common taste. So the merit of the poetry did not lie in what the poet affirmed, but rather in 'the manner of affirmation', as al-Jurjānī[8] (d. 1078) puts it, and the effect this had on the listener.

The poetry was therefore judged according to how far it could arouse *ṭarab*, a state of musical delight or ecstasy, and the poetics was founded on what could be called an aesthetics of listening and delight. This was then transformed by political exploitation and the general ideology into a sort of aesthetics of information, so that poetry became a variety of declamatory speech able to affect people in its own particular manner, through panegyric or satire, enticement or intimidation.

At the semantic level, this aesthetics of listening required the poet to avoid 'remote allusions, abstruse tales and ambiguous suggestions' and 'to aim at the opposite of these'. It also required him 'to use metaphors which were close to reality, not remote from it', because poetic speech should be 'based on what is useful, whether metaphoric or literal'.

These beliefs regarding the nature of poetry were what brought about the separation of poetry from thought. Al-Jāḥiẓ goes so far as to assert that poetry is the antithesis of thought because, according to him, eloquence in poetry is that which can be understood without recourse to thought and requires no interpretation.

This separation of poetry from thought reinforced the aesthetics of pre-Islamic orality as against an aesthetics of writing and confirmed a prejudice in favour of pure bedouinism[9] as opposed to the ignoble ways of the town. It also implanted in people's minds a particular image of poetry as something to be recited aloud or sung. Perhaps this explains the importance attached by the critics to the concept of 'naturalness' (*badāha*) in poetry, a concept which was synonymous with spontaneity and instinct, and antithetical to refinement of technique (*taḥbīr*) and artificiality. Abū Sulayman al-Manṭiq[1] (d. 985) defines *badāha* as 'a spiritual energy in a human temperament'.

* * *

This is what is embodied in the following characterization of eloquence (*faṣāḥa*): 'The pure bedouin Arabs are the essence of perfect eloquence,'[2] and in the characterization of naturalness (*badāha*) as 'what differentiates the

8. 'Abd al-Qāhir al-Jurjānī, one of the Arabic literary tradition's most illustrious critics; he pioneered the analysis of the psychological impact of the poetic image.
9. The life of nomadic desert dwellers. The different value systems of the Bedouins and of town dwellers are a focus of the historical writings of Ibn Khaldūn.
1. Prominent Baghdadi philosopher and historian of Greek and Islamic philosophy; Manṭiqī (Logician) is a nickname.
2. This and the following quotations in this paragraph are from al-Jāḥiẓ, *Book on Clarity and Clarification*.

Arabs from other peoples in eloquent expression'. It is the antithesis of an embellished style (*taḥbīr*), that is a style involving careful study and intellectual activity. *Taḥbīr* is an attribute of post-classical poetry[3] and urban culture, the product of self-conscious technique, while *badāha* and natural aptitude are properties of bedouin poetry. These concepts led to a formulation of artistic standards in poetry, summed up by al-Jāḥiẓ as follows: 'The best kind of discourse is that whose meaning is present in the literal meaning of the words.'

Various normative values resulted from these ideas, including the belief that different meanings require different metres, so that the poet should choose a metre appropriate to the meaning he wishes to express. This in turn led to the belief that there is a definite link between the nature of meanings and the nature of poetic rhythms. Serious or impassioned content requires long metres; subtle, gentle, jesting or dancing content requires short, light metres; and the names of the metres are derived from their characteristics, for example: *al-ṭawīl*, 'the long'; *al-khafīf*, 'the light'.

Rhyme, which always had to be present with metre in the contemporary definition of poetry, must have an agreeable ring and a sweet tunefulness. The poet must avoid any transgression against musicality, in particular rhyming with words which are composed of unmusical letters such as *thā*ʾ, *khā*ʾ, *shīn*, *ṣād*, *ḍād*, *ṭā*ʾ, *dhā*ʾ, *ghayn*, *dhāl*, *wāw*, *zay*. The beginning of the poem must be beautiful. If the beginning is ugly, the listener will be repelled. If beautiful, he will be drawn into it and delighted by it and listen with interest to what follows.

From the above it is clear that the view of poetry in Arab-Islamic society, particularly in the early years, was dictated by pre-Islamic orality. The poem was perceived as call and response, the dialectic of a mutual invitation between the poet and the group; it was as if the aim of the poet in composing his poem, and that of the group or tribe in listening to it, coincided by prior agreement. In this situation there was no difference between poetry and life: life was poetry and poetry life, and so the structure of the poem corresponded to the movement involved in the act of communication as well as to its effectiveness and its ultimate intention. Rhythm is the basis of pre-Islamic poetical speech because it is a living energy binding the self to the other. It is the pulse of the living being, bringing together the movements of body and soul.

Rhyme was the basic element which distinguished pre-Islamic Arabic poetry from the poetry of other peoples. Neither in Aramaic, Syriac, Hebrew or Greek was it considered an essential feature of poetry in the way it was for the Arabs. Because of this, the ancient Arab critics maintained that the structure of pre-Islamic prosody[4] was not an imitation of that of any other nation but was exclusive to the Arabs. They considered that it had passed through several stages, beginning with the chant of the camel-driver to his beasts, made up of words and sounds which seemed to follow rhythmic patterns, and with the chants and cries of war, and culminating in the musical

3. That is, poetry after ca. 1150 C.E.
4. The analysis of lines of poetry according to their rhythmic structure.

units called *tafāʿīl*.[5] Particular care was taken with rhyme because it was the repository of the meaning, and because it was the natural sound which took the place in the verse of the gesture accompanying the speaker's words.

* * *

I have discussed the theory of pre-Islamic poetic orality in a simplified and descriptive way. Whatever the critical discourse concerning it, pre-Islamic poetry is clearly our earliest poetry: here the foundations were laid for Arabic speech to confront life and for the Arab to confront himself and the other for the first time. It was not only a conscious application of speech, but also a conscious participation in the act of existence. Our awareness of history is expressed for the first time in this poetry, and a large part of the Arab group unconsciousness is stored there. When we read it today we are reminded of our earliest voice and we hear how the sounds of the language embraced history and mankind. It is the first artistic embodiment of the language which we use to express who we are and to open up pathways into the darkness of the unknown. As such it is not only our first memory but the first wellspring of our imagination.

Today, however, we are confronting a crisis in our relationship with this poetry, caused by the very interpretation and theorization of it which I have just discussed. This critical discourse, having defined the characteristics of pre-Islamic poetry as oral poetry, then transformed them into absolute criteria for written poetics: henceforth poetry was only to be considered as poetry if its metres followed the rules of oral poetry, as laid down by al-Khalīl.[6] These rules prevailed, drawing the dividing line between poetry and non-poetry. The climate of rule-making and intellectualization, generated by the climate of ideological struggle between the Arabs and other peoples in the seventh to the tenth centuries, helped these rules to become firmly established. Thus, instead of metre being considered as a regulating device for reciting and singing in a particular type of speech, it came to be viewed as the essence of all poetical speech. As a result, the written poetic text was viewed by the critics as if it were an oral text, in so far as all that writing demands—contemplation, exploration, abstruseness, thought itself—was banished from the domain of poetry. In other words, although oral and written poetry involve two different physical activities, the same critical standards were applied to both. Thus the critical discourse which pre-Islamic poetry generated in the past, and continues to generate, is the very thing which obscures that poetry from us.

* * *

5. The individual metrical units that combine to form a complete line of poetry.
6. It is said that al-Khalīl discussed many subjects: song and rhythm, theology and dialectics, chess and backgammon among others. "He had a knowledge of melody and the distribution of sounds which led him to become a pioneer in the study of prosody. . . . He also wrote a book about song and rhythm and called it *Tarākib al-aswāt* (*The Structures of Sounds*)." For this and other information. see Mahdī al-Makhzūmī's study of al-Khalīl [Adūnīs's note]. Al-Khalīl ibn Ahmad (ca. 718–ca. 791), a philologist who compiled the first Arabic dictionary and devised a system for the metrical analysis of Arabic poetry. Al-Makhzūmī's study is *Al-Khalīl ibn Ahmad: Aʿmāluhu wa-Manhajuhu* (1960).

From *Chapter 4.* *Poetics and Modernity*

We will only be able to reach a proper understanding of the poetics of Arab modernity by viewing it in its social, cultural and political context. Its development in the eighth century was bound up with the revolutionary movements demanding equality, justice and an end to discrimination between Muslims on grounds of race or colour.[7] It was also closely connected with the intellectual movements engaged in a re-evaluation of traditional ideas and beliefs, especially in the area of religion.

The dominant view held that the state was founded on a vision or message which was Islam. On the one hand, this state was constituted as a caliphate,[8] in which the designated successor not only followed on from his predecessor but preserved the heritage and conformed to it in both theory and practice; on the other hand, it was a state formed of a single community, meaning that unanimity of opinion was an essential requirement. Politics and thought were religious; religion was one and permitted no divergence.

This explains why for the most part those in power fought against these revolutionary and intellectual movements. Politically, they were considered as a rebellion against religion because they attacked the caliphate, which represented religious authority. From an intellectual and philosophical point of view, their adherents were seen as heretics and apostates, either for restricting the role of religion in the teaching of virtue, or for denying the role of revelation in knowledge and saying that knowledge and truth were the business of reason. The authorities viewed the mystical elements in these movements as constituting an attack on the law and practice of Islam; this was because they made a distinction between 'the evident' (*al-ẓāhir*) and 'the hidden' (*al-bāṭin*), or between 'the law' and 'the truth', asserting that knowledge and truth come from 'the hidden', hence the possibility of achieving a kind of unity or union between God and existence and between God and man.

To put it another way, those in power designated everyone who did not think according to the culture of the caliphate as 'the people of innovation' (*ahl al-iḥdāth*), excluding them with this indictment of heresy from their Islamic affiliation. This explains how the terms *iḥdāth* (innovation) and *muḥdath* (modern, new), used to characterize the poetry which violated the ancient poetic principles, came originally from the religious lexicon. Consequently we can see that the modern in poetry appeared to the ruling establishment as a political or intellectual attack on the culture of the regime and a rejection of the idealized standards of the ancient, and how, therefore, in Arab life the poetic has always been mixed up with the political and the religious, and indeed continues to be so.

7. The expansion of Islam outside the Arabian Peninsula led to confrontations between the Arab Muslims and numerous non-Arab peoples—in both Asia and Africa—many of whom became Muslim. The arguments of these revolutionary movements resonated in the emerging fields of "Islamic studies"—philology, grammar, history, Qur'anic commentary, text criticism, and so on—which reflected the increasingly multicultural nature of the Muslim community as well as its contacts with other cultures.

8. A state whose temporal and spiritual leader is the *khalīfa*, the "successor" (Arabic) of the Prophet Muhammad.

The problematic of poetic modernity (*ḥadātha*) in Arab society goes beyond poetry in the narrow sense and is indicative of a general cultural crisis, which is in some sense a crisis of identity. This is linked both to an internal power struggle which has many different aspects and operates on various levels, and to an external conflict against foreign powers. It would appear that the return to the ancient has been more eagerly pursued whenever the internal conflict has intensified or the danger from outside has grown more acute. In Arab society today[9] we find a powerful extension of this historical phenomenon which confirms our observation.

Perhaps this helps to explain why the current of modernity in Arab society sometimes flows strongly (as was the case in the eighth, ninth and tenth centuries) and at other times abates and recedes (as it did in the following centuries), according to whether the double-sided conflict, internal and external, is at a high or low point. It may also explain why modernity has tended to be a force which rejects, questions and provokes without entering in any conscious, radical way into the structure of the Arab mind or into Arab life as a whole. Perhaps, finally, it may go some way to explaining the dominance of the traditionalist mentality in Arab life and in Arabic poetry and thought.

The retreat of Arab society from the ways opened up by modernity began with the fall of Baghdad in 1258.[1] With the Crusades came a complete halt, prolonged by the period of Ottoman domination.[2]

From the beginning of the nineteenth century to the middle of the twentieth—the time of Western colonialism and of contact with its culture and its modernity, the period known as the *nahḍa*[3] (renaissance, a name which merits a detailed study in itself)—the question of modernity was revived and the debate resumed over the issues which it provoked. Opinions were divided into two general tendencies: the traditionalist/conformist (*uṣūlī*) tendency, which considered religion and the Arab linguistic sciences as its main base; and the transgressing/non-conformist (*tajāwuzī*) tendency, which saw its base, by contrast, as lying in European secularism.

It is the first philosophy that has prevailed, especially at the level of the establishment, encouraged by economic, social and political conditions, both internal and external. According to this interpretation, the ancient—be it in religion, poetry or language—is the ideal of true and definitive knowledge. This implies that the future is contained within it: nobody who is a product of this culture is permitted to imagine the possibility of truths or knowledge being developed which would transcend this ancient ideal. According to this theory, modernity—as established in poetry by Abū Nuwās and Abū Tammām,[4] in thought by Ibn al-Rāwandī (d. 910), al-Rāzī (d. 1210) and Jābir Ibn

9. That is, 1984, when Adūnīs originally delivered the lectures that became this book.
1. The sack of the city by a Mongol army, which executed the caliph; this conventionally marks the end of the "classical" period in Islamic history.
2. The Ottoman Empire (1299–1923), which began in modern-day Turkey, gained control of much of North Africa, southeastern Europe, and the Middle East (including Baghdad) by the mid-16th century, and from 1517 onward its sultan claimed succession to the caliphate. Crusades: the series of campaigns (1095–1291) mounted by European Christians against the Muslims to gain possession of the Holy Land.
3. Revival (Arabic).
4. Arab poet (ca. 804–ca. 845), much criticized by his contemporaries for linguistic complexity but later appreciated by Adūnīs and others as a major catalyst in the development of Arabic poetry. Abū Nuwās (ca. 750–ca. 813), renowned Arab poet best known for celebrating wine and both male and female beauty.

Hayyān (d. 815),[5] and in the nature of visionary experience by the mystics, and which assumes the emergence of new truths about man and the world—is not only a criticism of the ancient but a refutation of it.

In other words, to believe in the pronouncements of modernity is to believe in things that have not been known before. Seen in this light, the new reveals a certain failing or lack in the old. Modernity therefore constitutes an attack on the fundamentals. On this basis we can understand the connection made between innovation in poetry, which violates the ancient, and heresy, and also why words like *ḥadīth* (modern) and *iḥdāth* (innovation), originally religious terms, could be carried over into the domain of poetry.

This traditionalist culture is embodied in the uninterrupted practice of an epistemological method which sees truth as existing in the text, not in experience or reality; this truth is given definitively and finally and there is no other. The role of thought is to explain and teach, proceeding from a belief in this truth, and not to search and question in order to arrive at new, conflicting truths.

It was therefore natural that this culture should reject a theory that was fundamentally opposed to it, especially those aspects of it which might have led people to doubt its religious vision and its cultural and intellectual apparatus.

Because of the dominance of this 'fundamentalist' knowledge at the level of the establishment and those in power, the Arabs find themselves—in spite of all the changes of the past fourteen centuries—moving on a stage where history is repeating itself with just one objective: the continual actualization of the past.

The reason this approach has gained in ascendancy is because 'modern' Arab thought has not confronted it in an analytical and critical manner and dismantled it completely. Perhaps it has not dared to, or perhaps it has preferred to work some kind of magic to make it vanish into thin air, which has quickly had the opposite effect. This may go some way towards explaining why 'modern' Arab thinkers have adapted to the shock of modernization from the West by treating modernity primarily as a technological achievement. For this reason modernity in Arab society has continued to be something imported from abroad, a modernity which adopts the new things but not the intellectual attitude and method which produced them, whereas true modernity is a way of seeing before it is production.

From an artistic and poetical point of view the dominance of traditionalist or fundamentalist culture led to a return to the values of pre-Islamic orality. Most of the poetry written after the so-called Arab renaissance (*nahḍa*), by such poets as al-Bārūdī (1838–1904), Shawqī (1882–1932)[6] and their contemporaries, was no more than a ritual consolidation of this return.

5. All Arab philosophers: Ibn al-Rāwandī, a controversial figure whose critical writings on religion (especially on the veracity of prophets, including Muhammad) led to charges of heresy; Fakhr al-Dīn al-Rāzī, a theologian and wide-ranging scholar who wrote one of the major commentaries on the Qur'an; and Ibn Hayyān, an astrologer, alchemist, and court physician whose writings influenced later alchemists.

6. Two Egyptian poets: Mahmud Sami al-Bārūdī, a nationalist who spent 17 years in exile after participating in an unsuccessful revolt against British rule and who wrote poetry on classical models, and Aḥmad Shawqī (1868–1932), the most significant figure in the neoclassical movement in Arabic poetry and a pioneer of Arabic poetical drama.

The poets who opposed the ancient, claiming to be modernizers, did not turn to Arab modernity as manifested in the poetry of Abū Nuwās and Abū Tammām or the mystic writings, nor did they refer to the theorization of the new poetic language carried out by al-Jurjānī. Instead, they began to imitate modern Western poetry.

Thus the crisis of modernity appeared at its most complex during the *nahḍa*, a period which created a split in Arab life, both theoretically and practically. On the one hand, it was a revival of forms of expression developed in past ages to respond to present problems and experiences, which was also a resuscitation of old ways of feeling and thinking and methods of approach. It therefore helped to establish these forms as absolute inviolable principles, to be eternally perpetuated as the single true poetry. The result was that the Arab personality, as expressed through this poetry, appeared to be a bundle of self-delusions, and Arab time to stand outside time. On the other hand, at the level of practical politics and daily life, the age of the *nahḍa* was set in motion in a state of almost complete dependency on the West.

In this way the period laid the foundations of a double dependency: a dependency on the past, to compensate for the lack of creative activity by remembering and reviving; and a dependency on the European-American West, to compensate for the failure to invent and innovate by intellectual and technical adaptation and borrowing. The present reality is that the prevailing Arab culture derives from the past in most of its theoretical aspects, the religious in particular, while its technique comes mainly from the West.

In both cases there is an obliteration of personality; in both cases, a borrowed mind, a borrowed life. This culture teaches not only the consumption of things but also the consumption of human beings.

Since the 1950s the cultural background of Arab poets and critics has derived from two divergent traditions: that of the self (ancient, traditionalist) and that of the other (modern, European-American). These two traditions blur or blot out the values of modernity and creativity in the Arab literary heritage. The first does so on the pretext of a return to original sources; the second does so perhaps out of ignorance, or is so dazzled by the other that it cannot perceive its own particular nature, and what distinguishes it from the other.

I should acknowledge here that I was one of those who were captivated by Western culture. Some of us, however, went beyond that stage, armed with a changed awareness and new concepts which enabled us to reread our heritage with new eyes and to realize our own cultural independence. I must also admit that I did not discover this modernity in Arabic poetry from within the prevailing Arab cultural order and its systems of knowledge. It was reading Baudelaire[7] which changed my understanding of Abū Nuwās and revealed his particular poetical quality and modernity, and Mallarmé's[8] work which explained to me the mysteries of Abū Tammām's poetic language and the modern dimension in it. My reading of Rimbaud, Nerval and Breton[9] led me

7. Charles Baudelaire (1821–1867), French poet, critic, and translator.
8. Stéphane Mallarmé (1842–1898), French symbolist poet who focused on the role of sound in his poetry and critical writings.
9. All French poets: Arthur Rimbaud (1854–1891), whose hallucinatory prose-poems greatly influenced the symbolists; Gérard de Nerval (pen name of Gérard Larunie, 1808–1855), whose dream images in his poetry and prose made him a precursor of surrealists and symbolists; and André Breton (1896–1966), a theorist of dadaism and surrealism.

to discover the poetry of the mystic writers in all its uniqueness and splendour, and the new French criticism gave me an indication of the newness of al-Jurjānī's critical vision.

I find no paradox in declaring that it was recent Western modernity which led me to discover our own, older, modernity outside our 'modern' politico-cultural system established on a Western model.

The problem here is that the modern Arab poet sees himself in fundamental conflict both with the culture of the dominant political system, which reclaims the roots in a traditionalist manner, and with the images of Western culture as adapted and popularized by this system. The system separates us from our Arab modernity, from what is richest and most profound in our heritage. It is in collusion with the prevailing traditionalist tendencies and also with the cultural structures which came into existence in the climate of colonialism, imposing this relationship with the technical and consumerist forms of Western achievement upon us.

The most disturbing aspect of the problem is that the modern Arab poet lives in a state of 'double siege' imposed upon him by the culture of dependency on the one hand, and the culture based on a foetal relationship with the traditionalist past on the other.

What makes this aspect of the problem more serious is the position of the Arabic language itself. The Arab has grown up in a culture which views language as his speaking image, and himself as its feeling, thinking reflection. It is a union of reason and sentiment, the chief symbol and assurance of Arab identity. It is as if language 'created' the Arabs, through instinct in the *Jāhiliyya*, revelation in the prophecy, and reason in Islam; as if originally in the Arab consciousness language was the Supreme Being itself, and its science the science of this Being. From the 'materialness' of this created language the rhythm of existence explodes and its essence pours forth. In this context we can understand the significance of the case endings (*i'rāb*):[1] they represent the purest principle of language, the sign of unity between the static and the moving, the spoken word and the breath. If language is the rhythmic musical form of nature, then this form only reaches a proper state of wholeness and unity with inflexion.

Language, viewed from this perspective, is not a tool for communicating a detached meaning. It is meaning itself because it is thought. Indeed, it precedes thought and is succeeded by knowledge. This implies that the criterion of meaning was contained in language itself, and was defined by the rules of language.

The problem here is that this language which is regarded in theory as the essence of Arabness appears in practice to be an amorphous heap of words, which some use imperfectly, others abandon in favour of a dialect or foreign tongue and few know how to use creatively. It is like a huge storehouse which people enter, acknowledging their need for it, only to escape from it on some pretext or other. A gap exists between the language and those who speak it. What was once an end is now only a means. How can there be any

1. In many languages, the grammatical relationship between words in a sentence (e.g., a verb's subject and object) is indicated by their different inflections, or cases. Because in Arabic the different cases are marked by different vowels, those collecting or analyzing Arabic poetry have always focused on the musical (and therefore emotional) impact of vowel sounds in performance.

accommodation between a past which made language the essence of the human being, and a present which sees it only as an instrument and does not hesitate to call for its structure to be modified and for dialects to take its place?[2] If we remember its relation to the sacred, and more precisely to the Qur'ān, can we not see in the current ignorance surrounding its usage or in the call for it to be modified by dialectal structures which separate it from the sacred, a sort of declaration of a changed awareness and identity?

The problematic of modernity at the present time thus becomes clearer at the level of language. What was the first sign of the presence of the Arabs and their creativity is being corrupted and degraded. The Arab of today is in the process of forgetting the fundamental element through which he knew existence, and which established his presence in history. He has lost the sense of language, as defined by Ibn Khaldūn, and appears ignorant of what has given him his identity, or of who he is.

In the light of these considerations it would appear that modernity is the problem of Arab thought in its dialogues with itself and with the history of knowledge in the Arab tradition. If we are to treat the problem of modernity, we must first re-examine the structures of Arab thought. To question modernity, Arab thought must question itself. Arab modernity can be studied only within the perspective of Arab thought, on the level of principles and actual historical developments, within the framework of its specific assumptions, using its epistemological tools and in the context of the issues which gave rise to the phenomenon and have resulted from it. To study it from a Western perspective would be to distort it and distance oneself from the real issues.

Having acknowledged this, however, we come up against a crisis which, because it has gone on for so long, has become almost a natural phenomenon. I would formulate this crisis as follows: there is a desire in Arab society to separate religion from any form of authority, but there is a contrasting eagerness on the part of the authorities to see religion as one of the foundations of Arab life, its most nearly perfect system, inasmuch as it is divinely revealed, and therefore the key element in guaranteeing the security and stability of the political regime. For this reason politics and religion are bound together in an almost organic relationship. Thus it is easy to understand why the freedom to ask questions, especially on strictly religious matters, under a regime which relies for its existence on this link, is almost non-existent. In practice politics becomes a sort of submission (*islām*) and an act of faith in the existing regime; anything else is tantamount to rebellion and blasphemy.

This crisis is made more problematic because many of the so-called modern intellectual tendencies striving to separate religion from political power are based on a closed intellectual structure which refuses to accept divine religion but puts another positivist 'religion' in its place.

2. Arabic today exists in a wide variety of regional dialects (usually but not always mutually comprehensible), which traditionally were thought unsuitable for literary expression; in a "standard" form, which has more cultural prestige and is used in writing across the Arabic-speaking world; and in the sacred text of the Qur'an, whose language Islamic tradition views as inimitable. For centuries, these distinctions have shaped attitudes and fueled debate about the nature of literacy, the status of the intellectual, the appropriate means for expression in writing and in the theater, and the role of language in propagating religious values.

This crisis constitutes the nucleus around which the dominant structure of thought in Arab society is formed. Both the elements of it which are related to the politico-cultural order and those which characterize the opposition are firmly anchored in the belief that truth is given *a priori* in a text-source which is perfect and definitive. This article of faith, religious or ideological, serves as the all-inclusive founder text; the existing regime, together with its supposed alternative—the opposition which is eager to replace it—is the power which watches over it. Culture is the text which transmits and interprets. Poetry preaches and teaches or instructs and delights. Knowledge is no more than a mirror image of the truths in the all-inclusive founder text.

The flaw is not in the text but in the human being who does not understand it properly or deviates from it. This text contains truth and knowledge. Because it is unique the truth must be unique, because it is its truth, and the same goes for the knowledge. Therefore it is a text which is equated with power. According to this view, truth is always to be found at the heart of power, never outside it. Al-Māwardī[3] (d. 1058), writing in the eleventh century, comments that when a religion loses its authority, its truth is erased. Truth and power form a unity so the division or alteration of power is a division or alteration of truth, which threatens not only truth or power but the Islamic community (*umma*) itself.

This being the case, it is natural that in the eyes of its adherents this text should be absolute, irreplaceable and not open to criticism. The past is defined according to the time when the text came into existence. It is the crucible where all times meet. It is not measured in time, but is itself the measure of time. Decadence lies in distance from this text, failure to adopt it, or deviation from the path traced by it. The *nahḍa* was not an awakening but a return to the past and a firmer attachment to the text. Did not a renaissance in Arab thought, ancient and modern, always represent a return to the prophetic text, the text of the leader and teacher?

This completes the picture of the blockade imposed on us by this crisis: prevailing Arab thought with its two strands, the 'ancient' and the 'modern', is radically opposed to modernity. It is through this crisis-ridden structure of thought that our 'modern' connection with the West and its modernity has been achieved. This has led us to concoct an illusory, specious modernity which is embodied on the practical, day-to-day level in the importation of modern manufactured goods of every kind, and on the level of poetry in plagiarizing forms of expression from languages whose particular genius is intrinsically different from that of Arabic. Thus the intellectual principles which gave birth to modernity are lost to us, their substance wiped out: the unbridled commitment to discovering the mysteries of nature and the unknown aspects of being in deed and word, not for the sake of any return to the past, but to find out more, to proceed, searching and questioning, towards a horizon open to infinity.

The technical, mechanical aspect of modernity is turning our lives into a desert of imported goods and consumption, eating away at us from within and distracting us from thinking about our own distinctive powers of inven-

3. A Muslim judge, ambassador, and scholar of law and ethics (972–1058). In *Al-Ahkām al-Sultāniyya* (*The Rules of Governance*), he lays out principles for the proper exercise of authority and political power by Muslim rulers.

tion. In literature, and in poetry in particular, it generates superficial, naive conceptualizations that interpret modernity simply as a way of arranging and combining words, a mirror held up to everyday life, or an attempt to catch the spray as it flies off the rolling waves of time.

This superficial modernity which is predominant in our societies, engendered partly by a fear of confronting the true state of Arab culture and partly by an understanding which stops at appearances, gives rise to many illusions. I will limit myself to discussing those which act as obstacles to the development of modern poetry.

The first is temporality. There are those who see modernity as the quality of being directly connected with and alive to the present moment. To seize the movement of change in this moment is proof of modernity. It is obvious that these people view time as a series of regular uninterrupted leaps forward, so that what happens today is necessarily an advance on what happened yesterday, and what happens tomorrow is an advance on both. The mistake of this tendency is to turn poetry into a style, ignoring the essential point that the most modern poetry goes beyond the present moment, or goes against it. Poetry does not acquire its modernity merely from being current. Modernity is a characteristic latent in the actual structure of the poetic language.

The second illusion is the desire to be different from the ancient at all costs. Those who adhere to this belief think that merely to be different from what has gone before is proof of modernity. This is an instrumental point of view which turns creativity into a game of opposites, like the doctrine of temporality. One sets 'ancient' time against 'new' time, the other the 'ancient' text against the 'new' text. Thus innovation in poetry resembles waves on the surface of the water, vanishing one after another, despite the fact that a brief glance at the poetry of Abū Nuwās or al-Niffarī,[4] for example, reveals it as more modern than much of the 'counter-poetry' of poets who are alive today.

The third illusion is identification. The West is supposedly the source of modernity. There is no modernity outside Western poetry and its standards: to be modern it is necessary to identify with Western poetry. From this there arises an illusion about norms where standards of modernity in the West, springing from a specific language and experience, become the standards for a language and experience of a different nature. This amounts to looting at a personal, linguistic and poetic level, and is the way to complete alienation.

The fourth illusion is a technical one concerning prose as a poetic form. There are those who believe that simply to write in prose, because it is different from the old metric writing and conforms to models of poetic prose in the West, is a way in to modernity. Some go so far as to say that all metric writing is derivative and old-fashioned and all free verse is innovatory and modernist. This is the reverse of the traditionalist concept that metre in itself is poetry, and prose of whatever kind is the antithesis of poetry. The emphasis is placed not on the substance of poetry but on its external form. Neither metre nor free verse is enough in itself to ensure that the final product will be poetry. We all know verse which has metre and rhyme but is nothing to do with poetry, and supposedly poetic contemporary free verse which is similarly devoid of poetry.

4. An Iraqi mystic (d. ca. 965), whose ecstatic writings concerning the transcendent state are praised by Adūnīs.

The fifth illusion concerns content. Those who subscribe to this illusion believe that every poetic text which treats contemporary issues is necessarily modern, a claim which does not stand up to examination for a poet can treat these themes according to his intellectual understanding of them, while his artistic approach and manner of expression remain traditional. This is a fault which is all too evident in modern Arabic poetry; from the Iraqis, al-Ruṣāfī (1875–1945) and al-Zahāwī (1863–1936),[5] and the Egyptians, Ḥāfiz Ibrāhīm[6] (1872–1932) and Aḥmad Shawqī, up to the present, there are numerous examples, as there are in the work of all those poets who express their 'modern' ideological beliefs in their poetry.

The poetics of modernity in Arabic was born within a three-stranded movement: there was the urban-sedentary dimension with its own values and symbols (as opposed to the desert and bedouin life), given unique expression and anchored firmly in the literary consciousness by the poetry of Abū Nuwās; the linguistic-metaphoric dimension or the rhetoric of metaphor (as opposed to what may be called 'the rhetoric of reality' of pre-Islamic poetry), expressed for posterity in the poetry of Abū Tammām and the mystic poets;[7] and finally the dimension of interaction and assimilation with non-Arab cultures.

This modernity thus progressed beyond the normative and instead of referring to past authorities began to assert its uniqueness and individuality. It started to innovate, continually renewing the image of things and man's relationship to them, as well as ways of using language and styles of poetic writing. I would stress again that we must place some of the mystics, especially al-Niffarī and Abū Hayyān al-Tawḥīdī[8] (d. 1010), firmly at the heart of this modernist movement, and help rescue them from neglect or oblivion and restore to them the consideration they deserve.

This modernist poetry aroused a storm of criticism amounting in some cases to outright rejection, which was instigated by members of the traditionalist establishment culture and other patrons of the old. The reasons for this criticism can be summarized as follows: the poetry was seen as an attack on the values of the ancient and authentic, and it was this which led to Abū Nuwās being accused of belonging to the Persian-inspired, anti-Arab *Shuʿūbīyya* movement;[9] it was also seen as an attack on the authentic in poetic expression, held to exist in its exemplary form in ancient poetry, which was why Abū Tammām was said to have 'corrupted Arabic poetry'.[1]

Thus modernity in Arabic poetry had its origins in a climate which brought together two independent elements: awareness of the new urban culture which developed in Baghdad in the eighth century, and a new use of the language to embrace this awareness and express it in poetry. It developed in

5. Both neoclassical poets who portrayed social changes and symptoms of modernization in traditionally structured poems.
6. Neoclassical nationalist poet, who wrote odes denouncing the British occupation of Egypt and thus was known as the "poet of the Nile."
7. As mystical movements (Sufism) began to emerge in the Muslim community in the 8th century, a number of devotees expressed their quest for the transcendent by using the conventions and forms of Arabic poetry (particularly those of love and wine poetry).
8. Writer of belletristic philosophical works and compiler of several well-known collections of anecdotes.
9. A movement that began in the 8th century; with the spread of Islam beyond the Arabian Peninsula, scholars and authors associated with it claimed that within Islam the non-Arabs were equal to the Arabs (and some argued for the superiority of Persian culture). In Arabic, *shuʿūbīyya* denotes non-Arab Muslims.
1. What needs to be investigated is the fact that the same two "charges" are being leveled at modernity in Arabic poetry today, but with far greater ferocity [Adūnīs's note].

a spirit of opposition to the ancient, at the same time interacting with non-Arab currents. The whole thrust of Arab civilization testifies to this, for it is a synthesis of the pre-Islamic period and Islam, from whence it derives its origins and heritage, and of other cultures—Persian, Greek and Indian—through adoption and interaction, permeated by the most ancient elements deposited in the historical memory: Sumerian, Babylonian, Aramaean and Syriac.

The effectiveness of Arab creativity at this time demonstrates that no culture exists in isolation from other cultures—they give and take from each other; they influence and are influenced. It also shows that the first condition for this process of interaction is that it should be characterized by creativity and particularity at the same time. This combination carried Arab-Islamic civilization at its most mature to the West by way of Andalusia.[2]

The historical context outlined above demands a re-examination of the course of modernity and the problems it has encountered in its present stage. Such a re-examination must start from an awareness of past events with all their religious, social, political and cultural complexities. This is the only proper way of opening up horizons for understanding the self and the other, allowing us to have a new vision of ourselves and the world, and showing the path we should take in order to build the future. Without this, modernity in Arab society will always be a commodity imported in some underhand way. The society itself will remain a carriage rumbling and swaying along in the wake of the train of Western hegemony, lost between a blind acceptance which robs it of its identity, and an equally blind adherence to the traditionalist past, which robs it of its inventive spirit and prevents it from being a presence in the living reality.

Consciousness of the self forces us to acknowledge that our ancestors' many and varied achievements are not enough in themselves to answer our present problems or lead us to discover a new epistemology. This does not imply a denial of their achievements or their role in the historical process of the production of knowledge. Rather, we should acknowledge that we are confronting issues of which they were unaware; we are therefore bound to approach them in different ways, especially in an age which has witnessed such a tremendous explosion of knowledge. To continue to operate using the old forms of knowledge and within the old boundaries, using the old methods of approach, is to abandon knowledge in its present state, and therefore to abandon knowledge itself.

Continuing in the old ways does not necessarily mean preserving our heritage or holding on to our authenticity. Authenticity is not a fixed point in the past to which we must return in order to establish our identity. It is rather a constant capacity for movement and for going beyond existing limits towards a world which, while assimilating the past and its knowledge, looks ahead to a better future.

What we should take hold of and imitate is the flame of questioning which animated our ancestors, so that we can complement their work with a new vision and new approaches to knowledge. This requires us to dissect their

2. That is, al-Andalus, the Arabic name of the southern portion of the Iberian Peninsula (most of modern Spain and Portugal), ruled by Arab and North African Muslims from 711 to 1492.

views and intellectual achievements and assimilate them critically so that the new develops out of the old but at the same time is something completely different. This is the only way of ensuring a profound and constructive continuity between the old and the new.

Consciousness of the other assumes a realization on our part that the opposition between the Arab-Islamic East and the European-American West is not of an intellectual or poetic nature, but is political and ideological, originally a result of Western imperialism. This is why when we reject the West we should not reject it as a whole, but only this ideological aspect of it. Similarly when we reject the automated nature of its technology, this does not mean that we reject technology absolutely or the intellectual principles which led to its invention, but only the way the West uses it and imposes it upon us, in an attempt to buy us and turn us into mere consumers and our countries into market-places. We can learn from the creative energy of the West and its intellectual inventions and construct a dialogue with them, as the West itself did in the past with the products of our civilization. In this way our awareness of the other implies that its achievement is not all devoid of value. There is much in it which we can benefit from, not only in understanding our particular problems, but also in the production of knowledge.

Without such an awareness our political and ideological opposition to the West risks becoming an opposition to its culture and civilization. The desire to consolidate this latter form of opposition, whether it comes from the West or the Arabs, and is deliberate or involuntary, reveals another desire—that of asserting the notion of 'Western superiority', thereby perpetuating the false dualism of the civilized West and the backward East. I say false dualism because it is conceived on the basis of superficial criteria—the criteria of the mechanical and the technical—whereas there no longer exists a 'West' and an 'East', each forming a self-contained conceptual unity. The West contains many 'Wests' more decadent than any Arab decadence, and the Arab East has many 'Easts' more advanced than the most advanced of these Wests.

Seen from this perspective, the world today lives in the climate of a single universal civilization, but one which has its own specificities, obvious or hidden, that depend on the level of creative presence in the various peoples. This suggests that modernity is also a climate of universal forms and ideas and not a state specific to one people. If there is a disparity between the West and the Arab world in the practice of modernity, it is a quantitative disparity of the first order, generated by science in the narrow sense of the word. The level of scientific development is the main characteristic of modernity in the West and the factor which distinguishes it from the East. Modern Western science constitutes a complete epistemological break with the old world, especially with its religious and metaphysical dimensions. It is the area where thought advances unimpeded, more advanced today than yesterday, tomorrow than today. The truths it offers are not like those of philosophy or the arts. They are truths which everyone must of necessity accept, because they are proven in theory and practice.

Science, as a system of knowledge, is constantly self-critical. It moves beyond existing frontiers, does not know words like stasis or retreat, and represents continuous progress because it never ceases to question and search.

The need to transcend the past, or erase it, is therefore self-evident in scientific procedure. The past is error, and authority is sought not from what is past but from what is to come. Western science, with its intuitions and practical results, is the most revolutionary development in the history of mankind.

What does this scientific revolution contain, from a theoretical point of view, of particular relevance for us Arabs? I will try to summarize this in the following four points.

First, science changes human consciousness, engendering in it a new acceptance of astonishing facts which cannot be refuted because of the influence of scientific methodology and the idea that progress is natural and inevitable.

Second, scientific inquiry knows no restrictions or obstacles and refuses to accept any area as inaccessible to it. Scientific research is carried on regardless of the implications for ideas, morals, traditions or other aspects of life.

Third, science completely changes the way in which the past is viewed. In its eyes the past is not only error but also ignorance. Whatever parts of it will not stand up to scientific investigation are rejected as worthless.

Fourth, science makes people open to the idea of a future radically different from anything they have known before, and therefore ready to accept the ending of the past. However hard a person tries to reject science, on either a rhetorical or a technical level, he is doomed to failure. Today scientific invention and discovery are the most important signs of power and superiority. Mechanized industry is spreading to take its place alongside the most deeply rooted traditions and in the most backward societies. Scientific and technical progress are universal realities which cannot be ignored or avoided. They have gradually come to occupy a place in our ideas and awareness, to invade our lives and announce the collapse of the ancient world.

The Arabs have been much influenced by the scientific perspective and the cultural changes brought about by it. To be more precise, I should say that we have been affected in our intellectual awareness and our conscious minds, while our unconscious continues to teem with other things which have escaped the boundaries of scientific rationalism. We continue to come up against this paradox, to which I have already referred: why does Arab society rush to avail itself of the technical achievements of science, and reject its intellectual principles?

Scientific awareness created anxiety and insecurity in us, whereas our unconscious gave us certainty and reassurance. We considered science as a gain at the level of external progress, but a loss in terms of progress in the internal world of intimate human affairs; our consciousness of science therefore thrust us forcefully towards the future, while in our hearts we followed an ill-defined path back to some notion of the past where human warmth was more in evidence.

In this climate (and I will confine myself now to talking only about what happened in modernist poetry) we began to pose our artistic questions in relation to science. For example, what does progress mean in poetry? Nothing. The idea of progress is fundamental to science but quite separate from artistic creativity. Thus we found something which was incompatible with science as progress but was not an irrelevance. We began to deduce that scientific progress was not synonymous with progress as a whole and was therefore not to be used as a norm. Another sort of progress exists on a different level nearer to man and more expressive of the inwardness of his being.

We began to see that the aesthetics of the age we were living in was founded upon and motivated by an idea of resistance to the merely mechanical and technical side of science. This resistance saw a modernity of greater humanity and stature in certain elements of the past. Because the applications of technology were relatively homogeneous, they led to a uniformity and sameness which gave life itself a mechanical dimension. Poetry, on the other hand, affirmed difference, giving movement, ebullience and variation to life.

Thus we were split in two, our rational consciousness on the side of science and the future, and our hearts on the side of art and the past. It was as if we were reviving what science had neglected, disregarded or tried to kill off, and this split in us reflected the conflict between freedom and necessity, in this case represented by art and science.

From the perspective of this conflict, I started to see (I speak here only of my own experience and what I say does not necessarily apply to other writers) something inimical to the spirit of poetry in every move to make poetic creation subject to a rationalist scientific precept: one that seemed to say, the future before all else. I began to search for alternative forms which, while not rejecting the notion of the future, did not put an absolute ban on the past. They were forms which, on the contrary, embraced the past in some way: legend, mysticism, magical and non-rational elements of the literary tradition, the mysterious regions of the human soul. I used them to move away from the cold rationalism of science, in my efforts to reveal truths which are more sublime and concern humanity in a more profound way than scientific truths. This return to older sources was not passé, as some commentators described it. It was an attempt to reflect upon and comprehend human existence as a whole, beginning deep down where the reality of this existence was least cluttered by extraneous factors and man lived directly with the land and talked to it in a language which operated at the level of sensation and physical contact, inarticulate cries, instinct and sex. Such a way of proceeding is obviously the opposite of the rational, direct, clear approach, plunging deep into the obscure and terrifying areas which escape the grip of science and rationalism, but where great creation has its beginnings, suspended over the abyss of the undefined and the limitless.

It was therefore a rediscovery, or an attempt to create a starting-point from which to investigate the possibilities for a new direction in human affairs. I saw in legend especially something which afforded me this timeless perspective from which to view the human condition and strengthened my feeling of being one with mankind—a constant present. Through using legends, I was able to witness and journey among the earliest visions conjured up by the human imagination, the earliest motivating forces of behaviour, the first questions and the first inventions.

Thus I began to follow a path which was the opposite both of the scientific path, in the purely technical sense, and of the rationalism on which science is based, or which it gives rise to. Progress began to take on a different meaning in my mind. I gradually became aware that the essence of progress is human, that it is qualitative not quantitative, and that the Westerner who lives surrounded by computers and exposed to the latest in space travel is not necessarily more advanced in any profound sense than the Arab peasant living among trees and cattle.

As a result I came to believe that the progress of a society is not represented merely by economic and social renewal, but more fundamentally by the liberation of man himself, and the liberation of the suppressed elements beneath and beyond the socio-economic structure, in such a way that human beings at their freest and most responsive become both the pivot and the goal.

Technology and rationalism, and, let us say, modernism, have placed human beings within a closed 'mechanical' system. This leads them to focus on their immediate material existence, where all their powers are directed towards dominance in the external world, involving the control and exploitation of the other. It disregards their intimate natures, their passions, needs and desires, and betrays them while declaring that it alone is faithful to them.

The human being is a sublime creature, and there is nothing for him in this modernist technology except the materialism of an attachment to manufactured things, and to quantity. Technology does not cover the whole of existence; it only responds to the needs of an insignificant part of it. Moreover, man is not defined by quantity.

I saw poetry increasingly as the most important means available to humanity of breaking the hold of modern technology and its instrumental rationalism. If technology is the relationship which human beings have established with nature, through scientific rationality, then poetry is the relationship which one human being establishes with the individual essence of another, through nature. When there is no poetry in a period of history, there is no true human dimension. Poetry, according to this definition, is more than a means or a tool, like technology: it is rather, like language itself, an innate quality. It is not a stage in the history of human consciousness but a constituent of this consciousness.

I came to believe that modern technology, with its mechanical, repetitive reliability, had deprived nature of its significance for us and was now robbing the future itself of meaning. The future was no longer that unknown quantity, anticipated with hope and joy, but had begun to appear like a past which we mechanically relived. As a result some forms of the ancient appeared strange and fascinating, compared to the monotonously recurrent forms of modern technology, and the past, especially aspects of it which were officially suppressed or not widely known about, seemed magical and unfamiliar. I felt that we were in deep need of something that went beyond the technological in the direction of those areas which have been more or less obliterated from human memory, and towards the invisible which, however doggedly we try to unveil it and however deeply we penetrate it, remains invisible. Poetry keeps human beings open to the invisible, the hidden, the infinite unknown, always on the threshold of what is to come; at this point, which is both in time and outside time, poetry becomes a bridge joining what a man was, what he is here and now, and what he will be tomorrow in an all-inclusive movement which goes beyond the mechanical, blind indifference of technical progress and embraces the changing unknown.

* * *

1985

HAROLD BLOOM
b. 1930

Cantankerous rebel and staunch traditionalist, Harold Bloom embodies the tensions he depicts between tradition and innovation. The tradition of great writers is both a blessing and a curse, Bloom tells us. But most of all, it is an inescapable fact. Bloom thus finds himself fighting on two major fronts, seeking to deny tame visions of what the tradition offers *and* to shore up the primacy of the "strong" poets against those who wish to dismantle or stand aside from the tradition. This double fight has made Bloom that oddity more common in England than North America: a conservative rebel, addicted to sweeping condemnations of those who challenge the canon while carrying on his own revisionary battle with the received order.

The burden of Bloom's argument is that we are belated sons who will never be as great as our fathers, but it is death for us to admit that we are inferior. Bloom's basic model is SIGMUND FREUD's oedipal conflict between sons and fathers—a masculinist paradigm that requires the use of the male pronoun throughout this headnote. There is no denying Bloom's originality or his learning. His vision of our necessarily ambivalent relation to literary ancestors—"the anxiety of influence"—has itself been very influential, while his broad historical generalizations and strong judgments can be counted on to stimulate debate.

Educated at Cornell and Yale Universities, Bloom has taught at Yale and New York University since receiving his Ph.D. in 1955. He grew up in a Yiddish-speaking family in the Bronx and learned to read English (at the age of six) before he spoke it. Bloom received a MacArthur Foundation "genius" award in 1985. Like earlier critics such as SAMUEL TAYLOR COLERIDGE, Bloom quotes from memory the various poets he cites in his work, disdaining footnotes. In the 1970s, Bloom was sometimes associated with the so-called Yale School, which included PAUL DE MAN, J. Hillis Miller, Geoffrey Hartman, and Barbara Johnson, and was instrumental in bringing French literary theory to North American literature departments. But Bloom's hostility toward theory's skeptical relation to the Western literary and philosophical traditions was already evident by the late 1970s, when he seceded from Yale's English department by having himself named a University Professor. Of de Man, Bloom has said, "We were great friends, but we disagreed about everything."

After the productive decade of 1972 to 1982, in which Bloom developed his distinctive theory of poetic influence and deployed it in works on various English and American poets, he devoted the next ten years to massive editing projects (with more than 200 volumes of literary criticism edited for Chelsea House alone). Starting in the mid-1990s (even as his editing work continued), Bloom began writing for more general audiences, with works on how to read poetry, on Christianity, and on Shakespeare among other topics. His allegiance to the cult of genius and to the transcendentally great masterpiece, along with his antipathy to ideological criticism, made him a prominent critic of "cultural studies" and of critics interested in literature by women and people of color. In *The Western Canon* (1994), for example, he attacks the revisionist work on the literary canon performed by members of what he calls "the school of resentment" (all those who question the assumed greatness of received masterpieces).

For Bloom as for the Romantic poet William Blake, one of his heroes, energy is the only life; and both poetry and criticism for him are matters of life and death. In our selection from *The Anxiety of Influence* (1973), Bloom describes the "strong" poet as engaged in a "fight to the end" against both nature and previous poets. "Every poet begins . . . by rebelling more strongly against the consciousness of death's necessity than all other men and women do." In his impossible quest to achieve immortality, the strong poet strives to replace nature with art and previous poems with his own work, thereby declaring himself self-created and the master of his own fate.

But a basic oedipal ambivalence complicates the "ephebe's" (newcomer's) relation to his forebears. Even as a poet's world and aims are shaped by the words of the precursors he most admires, the project of self-creation requires the denial of all influence, a "misprision" (misunderstanding) of his actual sources. So too each child enters a world he did not create, is named by others (usually his parents), and is initiated into his culture's traditions. We are all "belated," arriving late into a cultural landscape already created by others, and given a preexisting language to express our selves. Most people fit themselves into typical roles, using common idioms; many try to make the world better fit their needs. But the "strong poet" attains a heightened individuality through a radical re-vision of tradition.

The striving for originality necessarily involves aggression, but this struggle with the past is disguised in what Bloom labeled "six revisionary ratios." Each represents a strategy enabling the latecomer to revise the previous poet while either denying influence or professing reverence. If the newcomer only faithfully repeated the words of the past, he would never attain selfhood or originality. Thus, "to imagine [a poem and a self] is to misinterpret, which makes all poems antithetical to their precursors." Every poem rewrites earlier poems; every poem is an interpretation. Only misinterpretation of precursors affords the poet his own voice, his own distinctive existence.

In *The Anxiety of Influence*'s "Manifesto for Antithetical Criticism," Bloom denies any categorical distinction between what poets do and what critics of poetry do: "Poets' misinterpretations or poems are more drastic than critics' misinterpretations or criticism, but there is only a difference in degree and not at all in kind." In other words, Bloom asserts that every critical act alters the text it interprets even when insisting on its faithfulness or accuracy. It is primarily this connection of criticism to misreading that prompted the association of Bloom with deconstructive theory. But while poststructuralists reject the humanist self, Bloom's version of "intertextuality" is placed in service of the psychological struggle to achieve selfhood. Bloom obviously admires those "strong" writers who most fully gain individuality, and he clearly aspires to write a strong, creative criticism that will overcome and outdo his own precursors, especially RALPH WALDO EMERSON, Kenneth Burke, and NORTHROP FRYE.

Bloom's psychoanalytic model, like Freud's, stresses competition, aggression, and self-assertion in ways that seem stereotypically male. From a feminist perspective, SANDRA M. GILBERT and SUSAN GUBAR stress more collaborative, nurturing, and cooperative relationships between writers and their precursors, between individuals and the tradition. Other critics have denied the unity that Bloom claims for the tradition (he makes Shakespeare and Milton the origin of all subsequent English poetry, Emerson and Whitman of American), pointing instead to the hybridity and pluralism of cultural life and arguing that poets are in dialogue with a wide variety of materials, both verbal and nonverbal. Finally, Bloom's work suffers from the ahistoricism of Freud's Oedipus complex, which is presented as (but not proved to be) true for all families at all times and in all places.

In response, Bloom insists that the tradition is so fully written into us that we delude ourselves if we think we can evade it. We must "consciously know" and accept that we are "latecomers." To gain access to images and ideas that we do not immediately recognize as our own, we need "antithetical texts"—which, paradoxically, are precisely the great works that constitute the Western tradition and us (*Paradise Lost* is Bloom's favorite example). That tradition is both endlessly conflicted and remarkably unitary. It continually produces a "we" that is mostly stable and similar, with the occasional genius possessing distinctive strength and individuality—recognized only in contrast to other voices in the tradition.

Bloom sees all poets as seeking "divination," or to be counted among the immortals. His view of readers (and their reasons for reading) is similarly narrow: they are all would-be poets, locked in the revisionary struggle with previous writers and striving for greatness.

This reverence for greatness shapes Bloom's style of argumentation. Greatness is conferred and confirmed by Time, transcending the nattering of literary critics. (In our selection, Bloom casually asserts the futility of all the existing types of criticism in one quick sentence.) But because it can be obscured in a particular era, it needs a spokesman (to tell us, for example, that T. S. ELIOT and Robert Lowell are negligible poets). Greatness for Bloom is both nowhere, off in misty Platonic regions of the transcendent, or embodied in Bloom, the one critic faithful to the long view amid "dying generations at their song" who perversely insist on wasting their time with lesser talents. Either way, the authority of greatness is beyond the reach of mere argument and brooks no disagreement.

***The Anxiety of Influence* Keywords:** Authorship, The Canon/Tradition, Interpretation Theory, Literary History, Modernity, Poetry, Psychoanalysis

From The Anxiety of Influence

Introduction. A Meditation upon Priority, and a Synopsis

This short book offers a theory of poetry by way of a description of poetic influence, or the story of intra-poetic relationships. One aim of this theory is corrective: to de-idealize our accepted accounts of how one poet helps to form another. Another aim, also corrective, is to try to provide a poetics that will foster a more adequate practical criticism.

Poetic history, in this book's argument, is held to be indistinguishable from poetic influence, since strong poets make that history by misreading one another, so as to clear imaginative space for themselves.

My concern is only with strong poets, major figures with the persistence to wrestle with their strong precursors, even to the death. Weaker talents idealize; figures of capable imagination[1] appropriate for themselves. But nothing is got for nothing, and self-appropriation involves the immense anxieties of indebtedness, for what strong maker desires the realization that he has failed to create himself? Oscar Wilde,[2] who knew he had failed as a poet because he lacked strength to overcome his anxiety of influence, knew also the darker truths concerning influence. *The Ballad of Reading Gaol* becomes an embarrassment to read, directly one recognizes that every lustre it exhibits is reflected from *The Rime of the Ancient Mariner*;[3] and Wilde's lyrics anthologize the whole of English High Romanticism. Knowing this, and armed with his customary intelligence, Wilde bitterly remarks in *The Portrait of Mr. W. H.* that: "Influence is simply a transference of personality, a mode of giving away what is most precious to one's self, and its exercise produces a sense, and, it may be, a reality of loss. Every disciple takes away something from his master." This is the

1. A phrase from the poem "Mrs. Alfred Uruguay" (1940) by Wallace Stevens (1879–1955), whom Bloom considers the greatest American poet of the twentieth century.
2. Irish-born playwright and critic (1854–1900; see above). His works mentioned by Bloom are *The Ballad of Reading Gaol* (1898), a poem on his experiences in prison; *The Portrait of Mr. W. H.* (1889), an essay on Shakespeare's sonnets; and *The Picture of Dorian Gray* (1890), a novel.
3. A 1798 poem by SAMUEL TAYLOR COLERIDGE (1772–1834), English Romantic poet and critic.

anxiety of influencing, yet no reversal in this area is a true reversal. Two years later, Wilde refined this bitterness in one of Lord Henry Wotton's elegant observations in *The Picture of Dorian Gray*, where he tells Dorian that all influence is immoral:

> Because to influence a person is to give him one's own soul. He does not think his natural thoughts, or burn with his natural passions. His virtues are not real to him. His sins, if there are such things as sins, are borrowed. He becomes an echo of someone else's music, an actor of a part that has not been written for him.

To apply Lord Henry's insight to Wilde, we need only read Wilde's review of Pater's[4] *Appreciations*, with its splendidly self-deceptive closing observation that Pater "has escaped disciples." Every major aesthetic consciousness seems peculiarly more gifted at denying obligation as the hungry generations go on treading one another down. Stevens, a stronger heir of Pater than even Wilde was, is revealingly vehement in his letters:

> While, of course, I come down from the past, the past is my own and not something marked Coleridge, Wordsworth,[5] etc. I know of no one who has been particularly important to me. My reality-imagination complex is entirely my own even though I see it in others.

He might have said: "particularly because I see it in others," but poetic influence was hardly a subject where Stevens' insights could center. Towards the end, his denials became rather violent, and oddly humored. Writing to the poet Richard Eberhart,[6] he extends a sympathy all the stronger for being self-sympathy:

> I sympathize with your denial of any influence on my part. This sort of thing always jars me because, in my own case, I am not conscious of having been influenced by anybody and have purposely held off from reading highly mannered people like Eliot and Pound[7] so that I should not absorb anything, even unconsciously. But there is a kind of critic who spends his time dissecting what he reads for echoes, imitations, influences, as if no one was ever simply himself but is always compounded of a lot of other people. As for W. Blake,[8] I think that this means Wilhelm Blake.

This view, that poetic influence scarcely exists, except in furiously active pedants, is itself an illustration of one way in which poetic influence is a variety of melancholy or an anxiety-principle. Stevens was, as he insisted, a highly individual poet, as much an American original as Whitman or Dickinson, or his own contemporaries: Pound, Williams, Moore.[9] But poetic influence need not make poets less original; as often it makes them more original, though not therefore necessarily better. The profundities of poetic influence cannot be reduced to source-study, to the history of ideas, to the

4. WALTER PATER (1839–1894), English critic who was one of Wilde's teachers at Oxford University; *Appreciations* (1889) is a collection of critical essays.
5. WILLIAM WORDSWORTH (1770–1850), English Romantic poet.
6. American poet and critic (1904–2005).
7. Ezra Pound (1885–1972), American poet and critic. T. S. ELIOT (1888–1965), American-born English poet and critic.
8. William Blake (1757–1827), Romantic poet, mystic, and artist.
9. Bloom names first 19th- and then 20th-century American poets: Walt Whitman (1819–1892), Emily Dickinson (1830–1886), William Carlos Williams (1883–1963), and Marianne Moore (1887–1972).

patterning of images. Poetic influence, or as I shall more frequently term it, poetic misprision,[1] is necessarily the study of the life-cycle of the poet-as-poet. When such study considers the context in which that life-cycle is enacted, it will be compelled to examine simultaneously the relations between poets as cases akin to what Freud called the family romance,[2] and as chapters in the history of modern revisionism, "modern" meaning here post-Enlightenment. The modern poet, as W. J. Bate[3] shows in *The Burden of the Past and the English Poet,* is the inheritor of a melancholy engendered in the mind of the Enlightenment by its skepticism of its own double heritage of imaginative wealth, from the ancients and from the Renaissance masters. In this book I largely neglect the area Bate has explored with great skill, in order to center upon intra-poetic relationships as parallels of family romance. Though I employ these parallels, I do so as a deliberate revisionist of some of the Freudian emphases.

Nietzsche[4] and Freud are, so far as I can tell, the prime influences upon the theory of influence presented in this book. Nietzsche is the prophet of the antithetical, and his *Genealogy of Morals* is the profoundest study available to me of the revisionary and ascetic strains in the aesthetic temperament. Freud's investigations of the mechanisms of defense and their ambivalent functionings provide the clearest analogues I have found for the revisionary ratios[5] that govern intra-poetic relations. Yet, the theory of influence expounded here is un-Nietzschean in its deliberate literalism, and in its Viconian[6] insistence that priority in divination is crucial for every strong poet, lest he dwindle merely into a latecomer. My theory rejects also the qualified Freudian optimism that happy substitution is possible, that a second chance can save us from the repetitive quest for our earliest attachments. Poets as poets cannot accept substitutions, and fight to the end to have their initial chance alone. Both Nietzsche and Freud underestimated poets and poetry, yet each yielded more power to phantasmagoria[7] than it truly possesses. They too, despite their moral realism, over-idealized the imagination. Nietzsche's disciple, Yeats, and Freud's disciple, Otto Rank,[8] show a greater awareness of the artist's fight against art, and of the relation of this struggle to the artist's antithetical battle against nature.

Freud recognized sublimation as the highest human achievement, a recognition that allies him to Plato[9] and to the entire moral traditions of both Judaism and Christianity. Freudian sublimation involves the yielding-up of more primordial for more refined modes of pleasure, which is to exalt the second chance above the first. Freud's poem, in the view of this book, is not severe enough, unlike the severe poems written by the creative lives of the strong poets. To equate emotional maturation with the discovery of acceptable sub-

1. Error, misinterpretation.
2. The son's sexual desire for his mother and aggression toward his father, according to SIGMUND FREUD (1856–1939), the Austrian founder of psychoanalysis; a term also applied to the child's fantasy that these are not his true parents.
3. Walter Jackson Bate (1918–1999), American literary critic whose 1970 book traces the role of influence in English poetry.
4. FRIEDRICH NIETZSCHE (1844–1900), German philosopher; *On the Genealogy of Morals* was published in 1887.
5. Relationships.
6. Like GIAMBATTISTA VICO (1668–1744), the Italian historian and philosopher who claimed that the first language was poetry and was of divine origin.
7. The fantasies and illusions produced by the mind.
8. Austrian psychoanalyst (1884–1939). William Butler Yeats (1865–1939), Irish poet.
9. Greek philosopher (ca. 427–ca. 347 B.C.E.; see above).

stitutes may be pragmatic wisdom, particularly in the realm of Eros, but this is not the wisdom of the strong poets. The surrendered dream is not merely a phantasmagoria of endless gratification, but is the greatest of all human illusions, the vision of immortality. If Wordsworth's *Ode: Intimations of Immortality from Recollections of Early Childhood* possessed only the wisdom found also in Freud, then we could cease calling it "the Great Ode."[1] Wordsworth too saw repetition or second chance as essential for development, and his ode admits that we can redirect our needs by substitution or sublimation. But the ode plangently also awakens into failure, and into the creative mind's protest against time's tyranny. A Wordsworthian critic, even one as loyal to Wordsworth as Geoffrey Hartman,[2] can insist upon clearly distinguishing between *priority*, as a concept from the natural order, and *authority*, from the spiritual order, but Wordsworth's ode declines to make this distinction. "By seeking to overcome priority," Hartman wisely says, "art fights nature on nature's own ground, and is bound to lose." The argument of this book is that strong poets are condemned to just this unwisdom; Wordsworth's Great Ode fights nature on nature's own ground, and suffers a great defeat, even as it retains its greater dream. That dream, in Wordsworth's ode, is shadowed by the anxiety of influence, due to the greatness of the precursor-poem, Milton's[3] *Lycidas*, where the human refusal wholly to sublimate is even more rugged, despite the ostensible yielding to Christian teachings of sublimation.

For every poet begins (however "unconsciously") by rebelling more strongly against the consciousness of death's necessity than all other men and women do. The young citizen of poetry, or ephebe[4] as Athens would have called him, is already the anti-natural or antithetical man, and from his start as a poet he quests for an impossible object, as his precursor quested before him. That this quest encompasses necessarily the diminishment of poetry seems to me an inevitable realization, one that accurate literary history must sustain. The great poets of the English Renaissance are not matched by their Enlightened descendants, and the whole tradition of the post-Enlightenment, which is Romanticism, shows a further decline in its Modernist and post-Modernist heirs. The death of poetry will not be hastened by any reader's broodings, yet it seems just to assume that poetry in our tradition, when it dies, will be self-slain, murdered by its own past strength. An implied anguish throughout this book is that Romanticism, for all its glories, may have been a vast visionary tragedy, the self-baffled enterprise not of Prometheus but of blinded Oedipus, who did not know that the Sphinx was his Muse.[5]

Oedipus, blind, was on the path to oracular godhood, and the strong poets have followed him by transforming their blindness towards their precursors into the revisionary insights of their own work. The six revisionary move-

1. Wordworth's so-called "Intimations Ode" (1807) traces the decline of human creativity from childhood (when we still have "intimations" of our divine origin) to adulthood.
2. American literary critic (1929–2016), a colleague of Bloom's at Yale University; his books include *Wordsworth's Poetry, 1787–1814* (1964).
3. John Milton (1608–1674), English poet; *Lycidas* (1637) is an elegy for a college classmate.
4. A young man (from *ephēbos*, Greek); here, more particularly, an initiate or trainee. Wallace Stevens uses the term in "Notes toward a Supreme Fiction" (1947).
5. That is, source of inspiration. Prometheus: the Titan punished for stealing fire from the gods and giving it to humans (by some accounts, he was their creator); he was a favorite figure of Romantic poets. Oedipus: in Greek mythology, the tragic hero whose correct answer to the riddle of the Sphinx—a monster with a woman's face and lion's body—led to his becoming king of Thebes and to his self-blinding after he realized he had unknowingly married his own mother and earlier killed his father, King Laius, in a fight at a crossroads.

ments that I will trace in the strong poet's life-cycle could as well be more, and could take quite different names than those I have employed. I have kept them to six, because these seem to be minimal and essential to my understanding of how one poet deviates from another. The names, though arbitrary, carry on from various traditions that have been central in Western imaginative life, and I hope can be useful.

The greatest poet in our language is excluded from the argument of this book for several reasons. One is necessarily historical; Shakespeare[6] belongs to the giant age before the flood, before the anxiety of influence became central to poetic consciousness. Another has to do with the contrast between dramatic and lyric form. As poetry has become more subjective, the shadow cast by the precursors has become more dominant. The main cause, though, is that Shakespeare's prime precursor was Marlowe,[7] a poet very much smaller than his inheritor. Milton, with all his strength, yet had to struggle, subtly and crucially, with a major precursor in Spenser,[8] and this struggle both formed and malformed Milton. Coleridge, ephebe of Milton and later of Wordsworth, would have been glad to find his Marlowe in Cowper (or in the much weaker Bowles),[9] but influence cannot be willed. Shakespeare is the largest instance in the language of a phenomenon that stands outside the concern of this book: the absolute absorption of the precursor. Battle between strong equals, father and son as mighty opposites, Laius and Oedipus at the crossroads; only this is my subject here, though some of the fathers, as will be seen, are composite figures. That even the strongest poets are subject to influences not poetical is obvious even to me, but again my concern is only with *the poet in a poet*, or the aboriginal poetic self.

A change like the one I propose in our ideas of influence should help us read more accurately any group of past poets who were contemporary with one another. To give one example, as misinterpreters of Keats,[1] *in their poems*, the Victorian disciples of Keats most notably include Tennyson, Arnold, Hopkins, and Rossetti.[2] That Tennyson triumphed in his long, hidden contest with Keats, no one can assert absolutely, but his clear superiority over Arnold, Hopkins, and Rossetti is due to his relative victory or at least holding of his own in contrast to their partial defeats. Arnold's elegiac poetry uneasily blends Keatsian style with anti-Romantic sentiment, while Hopkins' strained intensities and convolutions of diction and Rossetti's densely inlaid art are also at variance with the burdens they seek to alleviate in their own poetic selves. Similarly, in our time we need to look again at Pound's unending match with Browning;[3] as at Stevens' long and largely hidden civil war with the major poets of English and American Romanticism—Wordsworth, Keats, Shelley, Emerson,[4] and Whitman. As with the Victorian Keatsians, these are instances among many, if a more accurate story is to be told about poetic history.

6. William Shakespeare (1564–1616), English poet and playwright, wrote before the Enlightenment.
7. Christopher Marlowe (1564–1593), English poet and playwright.
8. Edmund Spenser (1552–1599), English poet.
9. William Lisle Bowles (1762–1850), English poet, critic, and priest. William Cowper (1731–1800), English poet.
1. John Keats (1795–1821), English Romantic poet.
2. All English poets: Alfred, Lord Tennyson (1809–1892); MATTHEW ARNOLD (1822–1888); Gerard Manley Hopkins (1844–1889); and Dante Gabriel Rossetti (1828–1882).
3. Robert Browning (1812–1889), English Victorian poet.
4. RALPH WALDO EMERSON (1803–1882), American essayist and poet. PERCY BYSSHE SHELLEY (1792–1822), English Romantic poet.

This book's main purpose is necessarily to present one reader's critical vision, in the context both of the criticism and poetry of his own generation, where their current crises most touch him, and in the context of his own anxieties of influence. In the contemporary poems that most move me, like the *Corsons Inlet* and *Saliences* of A. R. Ammons and the *Fragment* and *Soonest Mended* of John Ashbery,[5] I can recognize a strength that battles against the death of poetry, yet also the exhaustions of being a latecomer. Similarly, in the contemporary criticism that clarifies for me my own evasions, in books like *Allegory* by Angus Fletcher, *Beyond Formalism* by Geoffrey Hartman, and *Blindness and Insight* by Paul de Man,[6] I am made aware of the mind's effort to overcome the impasse of Formalist criticism, the barren moralizing that Archetypal criticism has come to be, and the anti-humanistic plain dreariness of all those developments in European criticism[7] that have yet to demonstrate that they can aid in reading any one poem by any poet whatsoever. My Interchapter,[8] proposing a more antithetical practical criticism than any we now have, is my response in this area of the contemporary.

A theory of poetry that presents itself as a severe poem, reliant upon aphorism, apothegm, and a quite personal (though thoroughly traditional) mythic pattern, still may be judged, and may ask to be judged, as argument. Everything that makes up this book—parables, definitions, the working-through of the revisionary ratios as mechanisms of defense—intends to be part of a unified meditation on the melancholy of the creative mind's desperate insistence upon priority. Vico, who read all creation as a severe poem, understood that priority in the natural order and authority in the spiritual order had been one and had to remain one, *for poets*, because only this harshness constituted Poetic Wisdom. Vico reduced both natural priority and spiritual authority to property, a Hermetic reduction that I recognize as the *Ananke*,[9] the dreadful necessity still governing the Western imagination.

Valentinus,[1] second-century Gnostic speculator, came out of Alexandria to teach the Pleroma, the Fullness of thirty Aeons, manifold of Divinity: "It was a great marvel that they were in the Father without knowing Him." To search for where you already are is the most benighted of quests, and the most fated. Each strong poet's Muse, his Sophia,[2] leaps as far out and down as can be, in a solipsistic passion of quest. Valentinus posited a Limit, at which quest ends, but no quest ends, if its context is Unconditioned Mind, the cosmos of the greatest post-Miltonic poets. The Sophia of Valentinus recovered, wed again within the Pleroma, and only her Passion or Dark Intention was separated

5. Ammons (1926–2001) and Ashbery (1927–2017) are American poets.
6. Belgian-born American literary theorist and critic (1919–1983; see above), author of *Blindness and Insight: Essays into the Rhetoric of Contemporary Criticism* (1971). Fletcher (1930–2016), American literary critic, author of *Allegory: The Theory of a Symbolic Mode* (1964). *Beyond Formalism: Literary Essays, 1958–1970* was published in 1970.
7. Structuralist and poststructuralist criticism, which began to influence North American critics in the 1960s and 1970s; it is "anti-humanist" in ignoring the individual. "Formalist criticism": criticism focusing on the literary work itself, primarily practiced by New Critics, who stressed "close reading" (e.g., Bloom's Yale colleagues CLEANTH BROOKS and WILLIAM K. WIMSATT JR.). "Archetypal criticism": criticism focusing on mythological patterns in texts (most prominently, the work of NORTHROP FRYE).
8. "A Manifesto for Antithetical Criticism" (see below), which appears between chapters 3 and 4 of Bloom's 6-chapter book.
9. Necessity (Greek). "Hermetic": occult; specifically, of or relating to the Gnostic writings or teachings attibuted to Hermes Trismegistus. Gnosticism, an early Christian heresy, radically rejected the visible world and especially the body as evil; Gnostic rituals emphasized ways to access the hidden knowledge of the spirit.
1. Best known of the Gnostic teachers (d. ca. 160 C.E.).
2. Wisdom (Greek); this personification (usually as the supreme female principle) played an important role in most Gnostic systems.

out into our world, beyond the Limit. Into this Passion, the Dark Intention that Valentinus called "strengthless and female fruit," the ephebe must fall. If he emerges from it, however crippled and blinded, he will be among the strong poets.

SYNOPSIS: SIX REVISIONARY RATIOS

1. *Clinamen*, which is poetic misreading or misprision proper; I take the word from Lucretius,[3] where it means a "swerve" of the atoms so as to make change possible in the universe. A poet swerves away from his precursor, by so reading his precursor's poem as to execute a *clinamen* in relation to it. This appears as a corrective movement in his own poem, which implies that the precursor poem went accurately up to a certain point, but then should have swerved, precisely in the direction that the new poem moves.

2. *Tessera*, which is completion and antithesis; I take the word not from mosaic-making, where it is still used, but from the ancient mystery cults, where it meant a token of recognition, the fragment say of a small pot which with the other fragments would re-constitute the vessel. A poet antithetically "completes" his precursor, by so reading the parent-poem as to retain its terms but to mean them in another sense, as though the precursor had failed to go far enough.

3. *Kenosis*, which is a breaking-device similar to the defense mechanisms our psyches employ against repetition compulsions; *kenosis* then is a movement towards discontinuity with the precursor. I take the word from St. Paul,[4] where it means the humbling or emptying-out of Jesus by himself, when he accepts reduction from divine to human status. The later poet, apparently emptying himself of his own afflatus, his imaginative godhood, seems to humble himself as though he were ceasing to be a poet, but this ebbing is so performed in relation to a precursor's poem-of-ebbing that the precursor is emptied out also, and so the later poem of deflation is not as absolute as it seems.

4. *Daemonization*, or a movement towards a personalized Counter-Sublime, in reaction to the precursor's Sublime; I take the term from general Neo-Platonic usage,[5] where an intermediary being, neither divine nor human, enters into the adept to aid him. The later poet opens himself to what he believes to be a power in the parent-poem that does not belong to the parent proper, but to a range of being just beyond that precursor. He does this, in his poem, by so stationing its relation to the parent-poem as to generalize away the uniqueness of the earlier work.

5. *Askesis*, or a movement of self-purgation which intends the attainment of a state of solitude; I take the term, general as it is, particularly from the practice of pre-Socratic shamans like Empedocles.[6] The later poet does not, as in *kenosis*, undergo a revisionary movement of emptying, but of curtailing; he yields up part of his own human and imaginative endowment, so as to separate himself from others, including the precursor, and he does this in his poem by so stationing it in regard to the parent-poem as to make that poem undergo an *askesis* too; the precursor's endowment is also truncated.

3. Roman poet and Epicurean philosopher (ca. 94–55 B.C.E.); see *On the Nature of Things* 2.292.
4. Early Christian leader and writer (d. ca. 67 C.E.); see Philippians 2.6–7.
5. On Neoplatonic thought, see Plotinus (ca. 204/5–270 C.E.), who sought ways to move through matter toward an apprehension of spirit.
6. Greek philosopher and poet (ca. 493–ca. 433 B.C.E.).

6. *Apophrades*, or the return of the dead; I take the word from the Athenian dismal or unlucky days upon which the dead returned to reinhabit the houses in which they had lived. The later poet, in his own final phase, already burdened by an imaginative solitude that is almost a solipsism, holds his own poem so open again to the precursor's work that at first we might believe the wheel has come full circle, and that we are back in the later poet's flooded apprenticeship, before his strength began to assert itself in the revisionary ratios. But the poem is now *held* open to the precursor, where once it *was* open, and the uncanny effect is that the new poem's achievement makes it seem to us, not as though the precursor were writing it, but as though the later poet himself had written the precursor's characteristic work.

Interchapter. A Manifesto for Antithetical Criticism

If to imagine is to misinterpret, which makes all poems antithetical to their precursors, then to imagine after a poet is to learn his own metaphors for his acts of reading. Criticism then necessarily becomes antithetical also, a series of swerves after unique acts of creative misunderstanding.

The first swerve is to learn to read a great precursor poet as his greater descendants compelled themselves to read him.

The second is to read the descendants as if we were their disciples, and so compel ourselves to learn where we must revise them if we are to be found by our own work, and claimed by the living of our own lives.

Neither of these quests is yet Antithetical Criticism.

That begins when we measure the first *clinamen* against the second. Finding just what the accent of deviation is, we proceed to apply it as corrective to the reading of the first but not the second poet or group of poets. To practice Antithetical Criticism on the more recent poet or poets becomes possible only when they have found disciples not ourselves. But these can be critics, and not poets.

It can be objected against this theory that we never read a poet as poet, but only read one poet in another poet, or even into another poet. Our answer is manifold: we deny that there is, was or ever can be a poet as poet—to a reader. Just as we can never embrace (sexually or otherwise) a single person, but embrace the whole of her or his family romance, so we can never read a poet without reading the whole of his or her family romance as poet. The issue is reduction and how best to avoid it. Rhetorical, Aristotelian, phenomenological, and structuralist criticisms[7] all reduce, whether to images, ideas, given things, or phonemes. Moral and other blatant philosophical or psychological criticisms all reduce to rival conceptualizations. We reduce—if at all—to another poem. The meaning of a poem can only be another poem. This is not a tautology, not even a deep tautology, since the two poems are not the same poem, any more than two lives can be the same life. The issue is true history or rather the true use of it, rather than the abuse of it, both in Nietzsche's sense. True poetic history is the story of how poets as poets have suffered

7. Again, Bloom lists the types of criticism prevalent in 1973. Rhetorical criticism considers the relation of text to audience (e.g., see Kenneth Burke). Aristotelian criticism combines interest in genre with a focus on rhetoric (associated with the University of Chicago). Phenomenological criticism highlights the experience of the reader (e.g., see WOLFGANG ISER). Structuralist criticism identifies the general patterns underlying the surface words of the text; it derives from the structuralist linguistics of FERDINAND DE SAUSSURE (1857–1913).

other poets, just as any true biography is the story of how anyone suffered his own family—or his own displacement of family into lovers and friends.

Summary—Every poem is a misinterpretation of a parent poem. A poem is not an overcoming of anxiety, but is that anxiety. Poets' misinterpretations or poems are more drastic than critics' misinterpretations or criticism, but this is only a difference in degree and not at all in kind. There are no interpretations but only misinterpretations, and so all criticism is prose poetry.

Critics are more or less valuable than other critics only (precisely) as poets are more or less valuable than other poets. For just as a poet must be found by the opening in a precursor poet, so must the critic. The difference is that a critic has more parents. His precursors are poets and critics. But—in truth—so are a poet's precursors, often and more often as history lengthens.

Poetry is the anxiety of influence, is misprision, is a disciplined perverseness. Poetry is misunderstanding, misinterpretation, misalliance.

Poetry (Romance) is Family Romance. Poetry is the enchantment of incest, disciplined by resistance to that enchantment.

Influence is *Influenza*—an astral disease.[8]

If influence were health, who could write a poem? Health is stasis.

Schizophrenia is bad poetry, for the schizophrenic has lost the strength of perverse, wilful, misprision.

Poetry is thus both contraction and expansion; for all the ratios of revision are contracting movements, yet making is an expansive one. Good poetry is a dialectic of revisionary movement (contraction) and freshening outward-going-ness.

The best critics of our time remain Empson and Wilson Knight,[9] for they have misinterpreted more antithetically than all others.

When we say that the meaning of a poem can only be another poem, we may mean a range of poems:

The precursor poem or poems.
The poem we write as our reading.
A rival poem, son or grandson of the same precursor.
A poem that never got written—that is—the poem that should have been written by the poet in question.
A composite poem, made up of these in some combination.

A poem is a poet's melancholy at his lack of priority. The failure to have begotten oneself is not the cause of the poem, for poems arise out of the illusion of freedom, out of a sense of priority being possible. But the poem—unlike the mind in creation—is a made thing, and as such is an achieved anxiety.

How do we understand an anxiety? By ourselves being anxious. Every deep reader is an Idiot Questioner. He asks, "Who wrote my poem?" Hence Emerson's insistence that: "In every work of genius we recognize our own rejected thoughts—they come back to us with a certain alienated majesty."[1]

Criticism is the discourse of the deep tautology—of the solipsist who knows that what he means is right, and yet that what he says is wrong. Criticism is the art of knowing the hidden roads that go from poem to poem.

1973

8. Epidemics (such as those associated with influenza) were once thought to be influenced by the stars.

9. William Empson (1906–1984) and George Wilson Knight (1897–1985), English literary critics.

1. Emerson, "Self-Reliance" (1841).

PIERRE BOURDIEU
1930–2002

The French sociologist Pierre Bourdieu demonstrates that the aesthetic is a historically produced category. The qualities of artworks, the aims of creative artists, and the taste exhibited by various audiences derive from a social "field" in which agents maneuver for status and power. His influential book *Distinction: A Social Critique of the Judgement of Taste* (1979) is nothing less than an attempt to rewrite IMMANUEL KANT's landmark *Critique of Judgment* (1790). Bourdieu challenges Kant's claim that our judgments about art are disinterested, arguing instead that cultivated sensibilities both derive from and produce a "cultural capital" that is tied to economic and social advantages. In *The Rules of Art: Genesis and Structure of the Literary Field* (1992), which focuses mainly on the producers, in contrast to the consumers, of art, Bourdieu traces the historical rise of the modern notion of aesthetic autonomy. Literary theorists have found Bourdieu's work congenial to their own questioning of aesthetic theories that make art a realm entirely separate from worldly ambitions and consumer culture.

Bourdieu comes from the provincial petit bourgeoisie (lower middle class); he was born in the village of Denguin, in the Pyrénées district of southwestern France, where his father was the village postmaster. At home his family spoke Gascon, an ancient peasant language, rather than French. A star rugby player in school, he was also a scholarship student, eventually receiving his degree in philosophy from the École Normale Superiéure, perhaps the most elite university in France. (JACQUES DERRIDA was a classmate.) After a year teaching high school, Bourdieu was drafted into the army and served for two years in Algeria during the bloody and controversial war between the Algerians seeking their independence and the French colonizers. Bourdieu stayed in Algeria after his army stint, eventually writing two books during the 1950s that he hoped would "highlight the plight of the Algerian people and, also, that of the French settlers. . . . I was appalled by the gap between the views of French intellectuals about this war and how it should be brought to an end, and my own experiences." Returning to France in 1960, Bourdieu began to study anthropology and sociology, and in 1964 he joined the faculty of the École Practique des Hautes Études (School for Advanced Studies). In 1981 Bourdieu was appointed to the prestigious chair of sociology at the Collège de France, a position he held until his death. In his later works, Bourdieu became a prominent public intellectual in fierce opposition to the advances of neoliberalism.

Our first selection captures Bourdieu's antagonistic response to Kant's *Critique of Judgment*, the founding text of modern aestheticism. For Bourdieu, aesthetic judgment (the ability to distinguish between good and bad art, to appreciate the truly fine as opposed to the vulgar) is a sorting process through which modern societies both produce and legitimate economic and status inequalities. The concepts central to Kant's work—disinterestedness, taste, and autonomy—point toward an effort to shelter art and its reception from worldly concerns. Many theories of art since Kant have repeated this attempt to secure art's purity, to insist that the essence of the artwork's value lies in qualities completely separable from any popular or commercial success the artist might achieve by producing the work, or from any pleasure or social prestige the audience might gain by consuming the work. "Disinterestedness"—especially prominent in Kant and MATTHEW ARNOLD, but found throughout the modern tradition—insists that art is adulterated if mundane purposes influence either artist or audience. Only aesthetic concerns (defined circularly as concerns having to do only with art) are legitimate; otherwise, the artist is corrupted by material considerations and the audience's judgments of artistic value are clouded by nonaesthetic aims. Art is to exist in its own autonomous realm.

Bourdieu argues that aesthetic disinterestedness and autonomy are historically formed class-based notions impossible to achieve. All acts of aesthetic production and consumption, like all other human actions, take place within social fields. Most importantly, their performance has consequences for the agents' social standing. Modern societies, Bourdieu claims, contain two distinct systems of social hierarchization that operate side by side. One is economic; in it, position and power are determined by financial capital (money, property, and other such resources). Another, whose logic he seeks to describe, is cultural; in it, status is determined by how much "cultural capital" one possesses. We might think of certain newly rich working- or middle-class business moguls who, for all their economic power, will always be deemed "vulgar." No amount of money can buy them respect from the cultural elites.

Bourdieu argues that cultural capital is central to the cultural elite's self-understanding and to the general willingness of society to grant it authority and prestige. Although this elite is produced, the process of its production is obscured so that its existence is accepted without question. Particularly mystified is the marker of the cultural elite: "taste" is regarded as a "natural" endowment. That taste (as displayed through the judgment of artworks) is notoriously difficult to define and to impart to others had already been made clear in the earlier works of EDMUND BURKE and DAVID HUME. But we do speak of "acquired tastes," and Bourdieu is determined to show quite specifically how taste is acquired, how it is socially produced in connection with very concrete material goals, and how spectators and readers respond in coded, habitual ways.

Setting aside those who inherit significant economic capital, we can make a rough distinction between those who do physical labor and those who do some kind of mental work to command a salary. Bourdieu favors calling the latter "intellectuals," and he memorably designates this group "the dominated faction of the dominant class" because they remain dependent on economic capital for their salaries. However, intellectuals possess (and fiercely defend) a semiautonomous source of social prestige and power: "cultural capital," which stems from their family backgrounds, their educational training, their postgraduate degrees, and their displayed taste for "high culture." In *Distinction* Bourdieu further divides the cultural elite into subspecies marked by linguistic, literary, musical, artistic, and scientific expertise. He provides a series of elaborate tables and graphs, based on extensive survey research, that correlate class standing with taste in music, literature, furniture, food, sports, TV shows, movies, and beauty products. People both demonstrate and create their social position through the tastes revealed by what they consume.

The vast differences in wages and employment opportunities in modern societies are justified as meritocratic, the rise to the top of the best and the brightest. Bourdieu aims to explode the myth of merit. The two great predictors of success in contemporary society are the socioeconomic status of one's parents and one's success in school. There is not a level playing field, Bourdieu insists. But taste, an acquired "cultural competence," is used to disguise this fact. "Taste classifies, and it classifies the classifier," Bourdieu writes, by which he means that merit and status accrue to those who have the right tastes—and that their having those tastes circularly proves the legitimacy of their claim to various economic and social privileges.

Aestheticism thus both mystifies taste and makes its possession prestigious. Bourdieu's argument is complex because aestheticism paradoxically turns the economic and material worlds upside down. "The progress of the literary field toward autonomy is marked by the fact that . . . the hierarchy among genres (and authors) . . . is almost exactly the inverse of the hierarchy according to commercial success." Taste is revealed through an (acquired) appreciation for everything that is nonmaterial: mind over body, intellectual over sensual, muted over gaudy, austere over pleasurable, nonpopular over commercial, and, crucially, form over content, "the mode of representation over the object of representation." Prestigious taste's pursuit of nonutilitarian disinterestedness and purity leads it to shun everything that might appeal to "lower," popular appetites. The role of taste in securing concrete economic advantages is thus masked by taste's attachment to artworks and genres esteemed precisely for their apparent unconcern for commercial success. The rarity of taste is ensured because it works against nature; it depends on "sublimating primary needs and impulses."

Since taste functions to make social "distinctions" (hence the title of Bourdieu's most famous book), intellectuals are driven by the desire to stay ahead of the crowd by displaying their appreciation for works often unknown or distasteful to the many. The shifts in reputation of various artists and various artworks can be traced back to the efforts of different groups or individuals to gain a leg up in the continual jockeying for position, prestige, and status. Modern culture's preference for the immaterial and the pure is encoded in the aesthetic ideology, and it helps explain why mental labor is so much more highly paid than the physical labor that is often more difficult, more dangerous, and arguably more necessary. Cultural capital—acquired through schooling and family upbringing, and maintained through a hierarchization of tastes and pleasures—plays an important role in securing the privileges of the upper classes in modern societies.

In our second selection (from *Rules of Art*), Bourdieu indicates how bringing the concept of a "social field" to bear on the question of artistic production changes our understanding of art. Crucially, a field—like the aesthetic—emerges historically and is dynamic over time. Various forces contend within the field of modern art: artists, critics, patrons, gallery owners, and audiences among them. Artists, critics, and experts strive to establish their authority over the field, demonstrating their ability to define what counts as a work of art or not, and what counts as a superb work instead of a mundane or bad one. They try to shape an audience who will appreciate and value art. That effort involves such cultural institutions as schools, museums, galleries, and the press, each of which acquires some power to label and consecrate certain works as masterpieces, to declare some works inferior, to dismiss some as obsolete. For Bourdieu, the whole process is relentlessly hierarchical; the social field is a site of endless struggle for prestige and success.

Crucially, these dynamic struggles are played out against the backdrop of *habitus*, a term that Bourdieu appropriates from medieval readers of ARISTOTLE by way of the French anthropologist Marcel Mauss (1872–1950). Acquired through early socialization, habitus designates dispositions to act, think, perceive, and feel in certain ways and not others. Habitus is nondiscursive knowledge about how to act within a certain field, neither wholly unconscious nor involuntary. The routinized behaviors that habitus generates are "second nature" and difficult (although not impossible) to change. Different groups and classes are marked by their distinctive habitus—and a whole society may contain several competing or conflicting sets of dispositions.

The Rules of Art provides a historical account of how the habitus of modern aestheticism and its hierarchy of genres were created. The pure gaze of the modern art lover derives from the Renaissance cult of the artist-god, the Romantic sacralization of art, and the Victorian era's celebration of charismatic aesthetic critics such as WALTER PATER and OSCAR WILDE. The dispositions (coded as "talents" and "taste") required to produce and appreciate fine art are available only to a privileged few. A network of institutions reinforces the instruction in aesthetic distinctions that begins in the family and in school. Salons, academies, museums, institutes for arts and humanities, and galleries display works of art and elicit the proper stances toward them, as they are revered, acclaimed, or rejected. A host of experts—curators, reviewers, art historians, literary critics and the like—police the boundaries of the field, determining both what genres and what people are deemed worthy of admittance. Rooted in the minutiae of everyday life, in the taken-for-granted understandings of what art is and how it should be experienced, the aesthetic habitus clearly distinguishes the leisured and educated classes from a working class made to feel its inferiority.

A major objection to Bourdieu's work—as to much materialist work—is that he is "reductionist," oversimplifying a complex phenomenon by taking part of the picture to be the whole. Few would deny that issues of social prestige and status influence judgments of artworks, but we might argue that a variety of desires and motives enter into our responses to art. We regularly distinguish the art snob from someone who values a work apart from the social standing that such appreciation affords. In addition, many people cling to frowned-on pleasures and tastes in defiance of the social costs. A different objection is that while Bourdieu's picture of idealist aestheticism and artistic autonomy applies to high modernism, it has much less relevance now that clear markers between high and low have dissolved. In the more mixed forms characteristic of postmodernist art, bodily pleasures are not outlawed and outright commercial ambitions on the part of artists do not lead to immediate condemnation by the elites. Surprisingly, in the last decade of his life, Bourdieu began to defend the autonomy of aesthetic, educational, literary, and scientific fields against what he deemed the threatening encroachments of the economic and political. Like THEODOR W. ADORNO, Bourdieu came to believe that such autonomy offered a crucial resource for independent thinking and critique in a world where globalized capital and mass media were swallowing up everything. As a champion of freedom, he wrote passionately against the growth of censorship in the name of religious or nationalist values and against increased demands that artistic and scientific work yield demonstrable profits.

Distinction: A Social Critique of the Judgement of Taste **Keywords:** Aesthetics, The Canon/Tradition, Cultural Studies, Ideology, Popular Culture, Reception Theory
The Rules of Art: Genesis and Structure of the Literary Field **Keywords:** Aesthetics, Authorship, Cultural Studies, Institutional Studies, Literary History

From Distinction: A Social Critique of the Judgement of Taste[1]

Introduction

> You said it, my good knight! There ought to be laws to protect the body of acquired knowledge.
>
> Take one of our good pupils, for example: modest and diligent, from his earliest grammar classes he's kept a little notebook full of phrases.
>
> After hanging on the lips of his teachers for twenty years, he's managed to build up an intellectual stock in trade; doesn't it belong to him as if it were a house, or money?
>
> —Paul Claudel,[2] *Le soulier de satin,* Day III, Scene ii

There is an economy of cultural goods, but it has a specific logic. Sociology endeavors to establish the conditions in which the consumers of cultural goods, and their taste for them, are produced, and at the same time to describe the different ways of appropriating such of these objects as are regarded at a particular moment as works of art, and the social conditions of the constitution of the mode of appropriation that is considered legitimate. But one cannot fully understand cultural practices unless 'culture', in the restricted,

1. Translated by Richard Nice, who occasionally retains the original French in parentheses.
2. French poet (1868–1955); the final version of his play *The Satin Slipper* was published in 1928–29.

normative sense of ordinary usage, is brought back into 'culture' in the anthropological sense, and the elaborated taste for the most refined objects is reconnected with the elementary taste for the flavors of food.

Whereas the ideology of charisma regards taste in legitimate culture as a gift of nature, scientific observation shows that cultural needs are the product of upbringing and education: surveys establish that all cultural practices (museum visits, concert-going, reading etc.), and preferences in literature, painting or music, are closely linked to educational level (measured by qualifications or length of schooling) and secondarily to social origin.[3] The relative weight of home background and of formal education (the effectiveness and duration of which are closely dependent on social origin) varies according to the extent to which the different cultural practices are recognized and taught by the educational system, and the influence of social origin is strongest—other things being equal—in 'extra-curricular' and avant-garde culture. To the socially recognized hierarchy of the arts, and within each of them, of genres, schools or periods, corresponds a social hierarchy of the consumers. This predisposes tastes to function as markers of 'class'. The manner in which culture has been acquired lives on in the manner of using it: the importance attached to manners can be understood once it is seen that it is these imponderables of practice which distinguish the different—and ranked—modes of culture acquisition, early or late, domestic or scholastic, and the classes of individuals which they characterize (such as 'pedants' and *mondains*[4]). Culture also has its titles of nobility—awarded by the educational system—and its pedigrees, measured by seniority in admission to the nobility.

The definition of cultural nobility is the stake in a struggle which has gone on unceasingly, from the seventeenth century to the present day, between groups differing in their ideas of culture and of the legitimate relation to culture and to works of art, and therefore differing in the conditions of acquisition of which these dispositions are the product.[5] Even in the classroom, the dominant definition of the legitimate way of appropriating culture and works of art favours those who have had early access to legitimate culture, in a cultured household, outside of scholastic disciplines, since even within the educational system it devalues scholarly knowledge and interpretation as 'scholastic' or even 'pedantic' in favour of direct experience and simple delight.

The logic of what is sometimes called, in typically 'pedantic' language, the 'reading' of a work of art, offers an objective basis for this opposition. Consumption is, in this case, a stage in a process of communication, that is, an act of deciphering, decoding, which presupposes practical or explicit mastery of a cipher or code. In a sense, one can say that the capacity to see (*voir*) is a function of the knowledge (*savoir*), or concepts, that is, the words, that are available to name visible things, and which are, as it were, programmes for perception. A work of art has meaning and interest only for someone who

3. Bourdieu et al., *Photography: A Middle-brow Art* (1996); P. Bourdieu and A. Darbel, *The Love of Art: European Art Museums and Their Public* (1991) [Bourdieu's note].

4. Sophisticated, fashionable people (French).

5. The word *disposition* seems particularly suited to express what is covered by the concept of habitus (defined as a system of dispositions)—used later in this chapter. It expresses first the *result of an organizing action*, with a meaning close to that of words such as structure; it also designates a way of being, a habitual state (especially of the body) and, in particular, a *predisposition, tendency, propensity* or *inclination*. P. Bourdieu, *Outline of a Theory of Practice* (1977), p. 214, n. 1 [Bourdieu's note].

possesses the cultural competence, that is, the code, into which it is encoded. The conscious or unconscious implementation of explicit or implicit schemes of perception and appreciation which constitutes pictorial or musical culture is the hidden condition for recognizing the styles characteristic of a period, a school or an author, and, more generally, for the familiarity with the internal logic of works that aesthetic enjoyment presupposes. A beholder who lacks the specific code feels lost in a chaos of sounds and rhythms, colours and lines, without rhyme or reason. Not having learnt to adopt the adequate disposition, he stops short at what Erwin Panofsky[6] calls the 'sensible properties', perceiving a skin as downy or lace-work as delicate, or at the emotional resonances aroused by these properties, referring to 'austere' colours or a 'joyful' melody. He cannot move from the 'primary stratum of the meaning we can grasp on the basis of our ordinary experience' to the 'stratum of secondary meanings', i.e., the 'level of the meaning of what is signified', unless he possesses the concepts which go beyond the sensible properties and which identify the specifically stylistic properties of the work.[7] Thus the encounter with a work of art is not 'love at first sight' as is generally supposed, and the act of empathy, *Einfühlung*,[8] which is the art-lover's pleasure, presupposes an act of cognition, a decoding operation, which implies the implementation of a cognitive acquirement, a cultural code.[9]

This typically intellectualist theory of artistic perception directly contradicts the experience of the art-lovers closest to the legitimate definition; acquisition of legitimate culture by insensible familiarization within the family circle tends to favour an enchanted experience of culture which implies forgetting the acquisition.[1] The 'eye' is a product of history reproduced by education. This is true of the mode of artistic perception now accepted as legitimate, that is, the aesthetic disposition, the capacity to consider in and for themselves, as form rather than function, not only the works designated for such apprehension, i.e., legitimate works of art, but everything in the world, including cultural objects which are not yet consecrated—such as, at one time, primitive arts, or, nowadays, popular photography or kitsch—and natural objects. The 'pure' gaze is a historical invention linked to the emergence of an autonomous field of artistic production, that is, a field capable of imposing its own norms on both the production and the consumption of its products.[2] An art which, like all Post-Impressionist painting,[3] is the product

6. German-born American art historian and theorist (1892–1968).
7. E. Panofsky, "Iconography and Iconology: An Introduction to the Study of Renaissance Art," *Meaning in the Visual Arts* (1955), p. 28 [Bourdieu's note].
8. Empathy (German).
9. It will be seen that this internalized code called culture functions as cultural capital owing to the fact that, being unequally distributed, it secures profits of distinction [Bourdieu's note].
1. The sense of familiarity in no way excludes the ethnocentric misunderstanding which results from applying the wrong code. Thus, Michael Baxandall's work in historical ethnology enables us to measure all that separates the perceptual schemes that now tend to be applied to Quattrocento [15th-c. Italian] paintings and those which their immediate addressees applied. The "moral and spiritual eye" of Quattrocento man, that is, the set of cognitive and evaluative dispositions which were the basis of his perception of the world and his perception of pictorial representation of the world, differs radically from the "pure" gaze (purified, first of all, from all reference to economic value) with which the modern cultivated spectator looks at works of art.* * * M. Baxandall, *Painting and Experience in Fifteenth-Century Italy: A Primer in the Social History of Pictorial Style* (1972) [Bourdieu's note].
2. See P. Bourdieu, "The Market of Symbolic Goods" and "Outline of a Sociological Theory of Art Perception" in *The Field of Cultural Production* (1993) [Bourdieu's note].
3. Styles developed in the last two decades of the 19th century, especially by Paul Cézanne (1839–1906), Paul Gauguin (1848–1903), and Vincent van Gogh (1853–1890).

of an artistic intention which asserts the primacy of the mode of representation over the object of representation demands categorically an attention to form which previous art only demanded conditionally.

The pure intention of the artist is that of a producer who aims to be autonomous, that is, entirely the master of his product, who tends to reject not only the 'programmes' imposed a priori by scholars and scribes, but also—following the old hierarchy of doing and saying—the interpretations superimposed a posteriori on his work. The production of an 'open work', intrinsically and deliberately polysemic,[4] can thus be understood as the final stage in the conquest of artistic autonomy by poets and, following in their footsteps, by painters, who had long been reliant on writers and their work of 'showing' and 'illustrating'. To assert the autonomy of production is to give primacy to that of which the artist is master, i.e., form, manner, style, rather than the 'subject', the external referent, which involves subordination to functions—even if only the most elementary one, that of representing, signifying, saying something. It also means a refusal to recognize any necessity other than that inscribed in the specific tradition of the artistic discipline in question: the shift from an art which imitates nature to an art which imitates art, deriving from its own history the exclusive source of its experiments and even of its breaks with tradition. An art which ever increasingly contains reference to its own history demands to be perceived historically; it asks to be referred not to an external referent, the represented or designated 'reality', but to the universe of past and present works of art. Like artistic production, in that it is generated in a field, aesthetic perception is necessarily historical, inasmuch as it is differential, relational, attentive to the deviations (*écarts*) which make styles. Like the so-called naive painter who, operating outside the field and its specific traditions, remains external to the history of the art, the 'naive' spectator cannot attain a specific grasp of works of art which only have meaning—or value—in relation to the specific history of an artistic tradition. The aesthetic disposition demanded by the products of a highly autonomous field of production is inseparable from a specific cultural competence. This historical culture functions as a principle of pertinence which enables one to identify, among the elements offered to the gaze, all the distinctive features and only these, by referring them, consciously or unconsciously, to the universe of possible alternatives. This mastery is, for the most part, acquired simply by contact with works of art—that is, through an implicit learning analogous to that which makes it possible to recognize familiar faces without explicit rules or criteria—and it generally remains at a practical level; it is what makes it possible to identify styles, i.e., modes of expression characteristic of a period, a civilization or a school, without having to distinguish clearly, or state explicitly, the features which constitute their originality. Everything seems to suggest that even among professional valuers, the criteria which define the stylistic properties of the 'typical works' on which all their judgments are based usually remain implicit.

The pure gaze implies a break with the ordinary attitude towards the world, which, given the conditions in which it is performed, is also a social separation. Ortega y Gasset[5] can be believed when he attributes to modern art a

4. Having many meanings.
5. José Ortega y Gassett (1883–1955), Spanish philosopher and social critic.

systematic refusal of all that is 'human', i.e., generic, common—as opposed to distinctive, or distinguished—namely, the passions, emotions and feelings which 'ordinary' people invest in their 'ordinary' lives. It is as if the 'popular aesthetic' (the quotation marks are there to indicate that this is an aesthetic 'in itself' not 'for itself'[6]) were based on the affirmation of the continuity between art and life, which implies the subordination of form to function. This is seen clearly in the case of the novel and especially the theatre, where the working-class audience refuses any sort of formal experimentation and all the effects which, by introducing a distance from the accepted conventions (as regards scenery, plot etc.), tend to distance the spectator, preventing him from getting involved and fully identifying with the characters (I am thinking of Brechtian 'alienation' or the disruption of plot in the *nouveau roman*[7]). In contrast to the detachment and disinterestedness which aesthetic theory regards as the only way of recognizing the work of art for what it is, i.e., autonomous, *selbständig*,[8] the 'popular aesthetic' ignores or refuses the refusal of 'facile' involvement and 'vulgar' enjoyment, a refusal which is the basis of the taste for formal experiment. And popular judgments of paintings or photographs spring from an 'aesthetic' (in fact it is an ethos) which is the exact opposite of the Kantian aesthetic.[9] Whereas, in order to grasp the specificity of the aesthetic judgment, Kant strove to distinguish that which pleases from that which gratifies and, more generally, to distinguish disinterestedness, the sole guarantor of the specifically aesthetic quality of contemplation, from the interest of reason which defines the Good, working-class people expect every image to explicitly perform a function, if only that of a sign, and their judgements make reference, often explicitly, to the norms of morality or agreeableness. Whether rejecting or praising, their appreciation always has an ethical basis.

Popular taste applies the schemes of the ethos, which pertain in the ordinary circumstances of life, to legitimate works of art, and so performs a systematic reduction of the things of art to the things of life. The very seriousness (or naivety) which this taste invests in fictions and representations demonstrates a contrario[1] that pure taste performs a suspension of 'naive' involvement which is one dimension of a 'quasi-ludic' relationship with the necessities of the world. Intellectuals could be said to believe in the representation—literature, theatre, painting—more than in the things represented, whereas the people chiefly expect representations and the conventions which govern them to allow them to believe 'naively' in the things represented. The pure aesthetic is rooted in an ethic, or rather, an ethos of elective distance from the necessities of the natural and social world, which may take the form of moral agnosticism (visible when ethical transgression becomes an artistic

6. Terms derived from GEORG WILHELM FRIEDRICH HEGEL's "Master-Slave dialectic" in *Phenomenology of Spirit* (1807; see above). The "in itself" exists passively as a material embodiment of an entity, while the "for itself" self-consciously shapes its identity as a particular kind of entity.
7. New novel (French). The "new novel" of Alain Robbe-Grillet (1922–2008) and other French novelists of the 1950s and 1960s disoriented readers by using narrative techniques that made time, place, and narrative point of view difficult to discern. "Brechtian 'alienation'": the German playwright Bertolt Brecht (1898–1956) advocated a political theater that prevented audiences from "identifying" with the characters or taking the events on stage as real, favoring instead a method that "alienated" or distanced spectators from what they were viewing.
8. Self-standing, self-sufficient (German).
9. The highly influential view of art and its appreciation put forward by the German philosopher IMMANUEL KANT (1724–1804) in his *Critique of Judgment* (1790; see above).
1. By way of contrast (Italian).

parti pris[2]) or of an aestheticism which presents the aesthetic disposition as a universally valid principle and takes the bourgeois denial of the social world to its limit. The detachment of the pure gaze cannot be dissociated from a general disposition towards the world which is the paradoxical product of conditioning by negative economic necessities—a life of ease—that tends to induce an active distance from necessity.

Although art obviously offers the greatest scope to the aesthetic disposition, there is no area of practice in which the aim of purifying, refining and sublimating primary needs and impulses cannot assert itself, no area in which the stylization of life, that is, the primacy of forms over function, of manner over matter, does not produce the same effects. And nothing is more distinctive, more distinguished, than the capacity to confer aesthetic status on objects that are banal or even 'common' (because the 'common' people make them their own, especially for aesthetic purposes), or the ability to apply the principles of a 'pure' aesthetic to the most everyday choices of everyday life, e.g., in cooking, clothing or decoration, completely reversing the popular disposition which annexes aesthetics to ethics.

In fact, through the economic and social conditions which they presuppose, the different ways of relating to realities and fictions, of believing in fictions and the realities they simulate, with more or less distance and detachment, are very closely linked to the different possible positions in social space and, consequently, bound up with the systems of dispositions (habitus)[3] characteristic of the different classes and class fractions. Taste classifies, and it classifies the classifier. Social subjects, classified by their classifications, distinguish themselves by the distinctions they make, between the beautiful and the ugly, the distinguished and the vulgar, in which their position in the objective classifications is expressed or betrayed. And statistical analysis does indeed show that oppositions similar in structure to those found in cultural practices also appear in eating habits. The antithesis between quantity and quality, substance and form, corresponds to the opposition—linked to different distances from necessity—between the taste of necessity, which favours the most 'filling' and most economical foods, and the taste of liberty—or luxury—which shifts the emphasis to the manner (of presenting, serving, eating, etc.) and tends to use stylized forms to deny function.

The science of taste and of cultural consumption begins with a transgression that is in no way aesthetic: it has to abolish the sacred frontier which makes legitimate culture a separate universe, in order to discover the intelligible relations which unite apparently incommensurable 'choices', such as preferences in music and food, painting and sport, literature and hairstyle. This barbarous reintegration of aesthetic consumption into the world of ordinary consumption abolishes the opposition, which has been the basis of high aesthetic since Kant, between the 'taste of sense' and the 'taste of reflection', and between facile pleasure, pleasure reduced to a pleasure of the senses,

2. A preconceived opinion, or bias; a position (French).

3. A key term in Bourdieu's work, defined elsewhere by him as "a system of acquired dispositions functioning on the practical level as categories of perception and assessment . . . as well as being the organizing principles of action." In other words, habitus names the cultural categories through which individuals process the world along with the bodily habits that characterize their interactions with things external to the body.

and pure pleasure, pleasure purified of pleasure, which is predisposed to become a symbol of moral excellence and a measure of the capacity for sublimation which defines the truly human man. The culture which results from this magical division is sacred. Cultural consecration does indeed confer on the objects, persons and situations it touches, a sort of ontological promotion akin to a transubstantiation. Proof enough of this is found in the two following quotations, which might almost have been written for the delight of the sociologist:

'What struck me most is this: nothing could be obscene on the stage of our premier theatre, and the ballerinas of the Opera, even as naked dancers, sylphs, sprites or Bacchae, retain an inviolable purity.'[4]

'There are obscene postures: the simulated intercourse which offends the eye. Clearly, it is impossible to approve, although the interpolation of such gestures in dance routines does give them a symbolic and aesthetic quality which is absent from the intimate scenes the cinema daily flaunts before its spectators' eyes . . . As for the nude scene, what can one say, except that it is brief and theatrically not very effective? I will not say it is chaste or innocent, for nothing commercial can be so described. Let us say it is not shocking, and that the chief objection is that it serves as a box-office gimmick. . . . In *Hair*, the nakedness fails to be symbolic.'[5]

The denial of lower, coarse, vulgar, venal, servile—in a word, natural—enjoyment, which constitutes the sacred sphere of culture, implies an affirmation of the superiority of those who can be satisfied with the sublimated, refined, disinterested, gratuitous, distinguished pleasures forever closed to the profane. That is why art and cultural consumption are predisposed, consciously and deliberately or not, to fulfil a social function of legitimating social differences.

1979

From The Rules of Art: Genesis and Structure of the Literary Field[1]

From *Part I. Three States of the Field*

FROM CHAPTER 2. THE EMERGENCE OF A DUALIST STRUCTURE

The Particularities of Genres

The progress of the literary field towards autonomy is marked by the fact that, at the end of the nineteenth century, the hierarchy among genres (and authors) according to specific criteria of peer judgement is almost exactly the inverse of the hierarchy according to commercial success. This is different from what was to be observed in the seventeenth century, when the

4. O. Merlin, "Mlle. Thibon dans la vision de Marguerite," *Le Monde*, 9 December 1965 [Bourdieu's note]. Bacchae: in the classical world, the frenzied female worshippers of Dionysus or Bacchus.

5. F. Chenique, "*Hair* est-il immoral?" *Le Monde*, 28 January 1970 [Bourdieu's note]. The anti–Vietnam War rock musical *Hair* (1967), by Gerome Ragni, James Rado, and Galt MacDermot, was a long-running Broadway hit.

1. Translated by Susan Emanuel.

two hierarchies were almost merged, with those most consecrated among people of letters, especially poets and scientists, being the best provided with pensions and profits.[2]

From the economic point of view, the hierarchy is simple, and relatively constant, despite conjunctural fluctuations. At the summit stands the theatre, providing large and immediate profits for a very small number of authors in return for a relatively small cultural investment. At the bottom of the hierarchy, there is poetry which, with very few exceptions (such as some successes in verse theatre), procures extremely small profits for a small number of producers. Situated in an intermediate position, the novel can assure large profits to a relatively large number of authors, but only so long as it extends its public well beyond the literary world itself (to which poetry is confined) and beyond the bourgeois world (as is the case for theatre), that is, to the petite-bourgeoisie or even, especially by the intermediary of municipal libraries, as far as to the 'labour aristocracy'.

From the point of view of the criteria of appreciation that dominate inside the field, things are less simple. Nevertheless, we see by a number of indices that, under the Second Empire,[3] the summit of the hierarchy is occupied by poetry. Consecrated as the art *par excellence* by the romantic tradition, it retains all its prestige; despite fluctuations—with the decline of Romanticism, never totally equalled by Théophile Gautier or Parnassus, and with the rise of the enigmatic and sulphurous figure of Baudelaire[4]—it continues to attract a large number of writers, even if it is almost totally devoid of a market: most poetic works reach at most a few hundred readers. At the opposite end, the theatre—with its direct exposure to the immediate sanction of the bourgeois public, its values and orthodoxies—procures, besides money, the institutionalized consecration of the academies and official honours. As for the novel, situated in a central position between the two poles of the literary space, it presents the largest dispersion from the viewpoint of symbolic status: even though it has acquired its marks of nobility, at least within the field, and even beyond it, with Stendhal and Balzac and especially Flaubert,[5] it remains associated with the image of mercantile literature, tied to journalism by the *feuilleton* (serial).[6] It acquires considerable weight in the literary field when with Zola[7] it achieves the success of exceptional sales (hence very substantial earnings that allow it to break free from the press and the serial), reaching a much wider public than any other mode of expression, but without letting go of specific requirements regarding form (it will even manage to

2. Cf. A. Viala, *Naissance de l'écrivain* (Paris: Minuit, 1984). One must be careful of reading clues of a sort of absolute beginning into the first signs of the institutionalization of the personage of the writer, such as the appearance of specific apparatuses of consecration. In effect, for a long time this process remains ambiguous, even contradictory, to the extent that artists must pay with a statutory dependence on the state for the recognition and official status that it accords them. And it is only at the end of the 19th century that the system of characteristics constitutive of an autonomous field is found assembled together (without ever excluding completely the possibility of regressions to heteronomy, such as the one starting today, thanks to new forms of patronage, public or private, and because of the encroachment of journalism) [Bourdieu's note].

3. The period when France was ruled by Napoléon III (1852–70).

4. Charles Baudelaire (1821–1867), French poet. Gautier (1811–1872), French writer and aesthete. Parnassus: a short-lived (1866–76) movement in French poetry, influenced by Gautier's call for an "art for art's sake."

5. The three most celebrated French novelists of the 19th century: Stendhal (pen name of Henri-Marie Beyle, 1783–1842), Honoré de Balzac (1799–1850), and Gustave Flaubert (1821–1880).

6. That is, a story published in installments.

7. Émile Zola (1840–1902), French naturalist novelist and critic.

obtain through the society novel a bourgeois consecration until then reserved to the theatre).

One can assess the chiasmatic[8] structure of this space, in which the hierarchy according to commercial profit (theatre, novel, poetry) coexists with an inverted hierarchy according to prestige (poetry, novel, theatre), by a *simple model* taking account of two principles of differentiation. On the one hand, the different genres, considered as economic enterprises, are distinguished in three respects: firstly, as a function of the price of the product or the act of symbolic consumption, relatively high in the case of theatre or the concert, low in the case of the book, the musical score or the museum or gallery visit (with the unit cost of a painting putting pictorial production in a completely separate situation); secondly, as a function of the numbers and the social qualities of the consumers, hence of the size of the economic but also symbolic profits (linked to the social standing of the public) assured by these enterprises; thirdly, as a function of the length of the production cycle, and in particular how quickly profits, material as much as symbolic, are obtained and for how long they are guaranteed.

On the other hand, to the extent that the field progressively gains in autonomy and imposes its own logic, these genres also grow more distinct from each other, and more clearly so, according to the degree of intrinsically symbolic credit they possess and confer, this tending to vary in inverse relation to economic profit. In effect, the credit attached to any cultural practice tends to decrease with the numbers and especially the social spread of the audience, because the value of the credit of recognition ensured by consumption decreases when the specific competence recognized in the consumer decreases (and even tends to change sign when it descends below a certain threshold).

This model takes account of the major oppositions among genres, but also the more subtle differences observed inside the same genre, as it does of the diverse forms that the consecration accorded to genres or authors may assume. It is in effect the social quality of the audience (measured principally by its volume) and the symbolic profit it assures which determine the specific hierarchy established among works and authors within each genre, with the hierarchized categories detected there corresponding rather closely to the social hierarchy of the respective audiences. This can be clearly seen in the case of theatre, with the opposition between classical theatre, boulevard theatre,[9] vaudeville and cabaret, or more sharply still in the case of the novel, where the hierarchy of specialties—the society novel that will become the psychological novel, the naturalist novel, the novel of manners, the regionalist novel, the popular novel—corresponds quite directly with the social hierarchy of the readerships concerned, and also, rather closely, with the hierarchy of the social universes represented in them, and even with the hierarchy of authors according to social origin and sex.

It also allows us to understand similarities and differences between the novel and the theatre. Boulevard theatre, able to provide established authors with considerable economic profits thanks to repeated performances of the same work before a limited and bourgeois public, brings to authors, almost

8. That is, inverted (inversion is the main feature of the rhetorical figure called chiasmus).

9. That is, the melodramas and murder stories that appealed to a bourgeois audience and dominated the Paris stage during the Second Empire.

all of them from the bourgeoisie, one form of social respectability, that consecrated by the Académie.[1] The very particular social characteristics of playwrights result from the fact that they are the product of a two-stage selection: the theatres being very few and their directors having an interest in keeping plays on the bill for as long as possible, the authors must first face a terrible competition for their work to be staged, and there the major trump is the social capital of relationships within the theatrical milieu; they must then face the competition for an audience, and there there is the factor (besides mastery of the tricks of the trade, itself also linked to familiarity with the world of the theatre) of closeness to the values of the audience, largely bourgeois and Parisian, and hence more 'distinguished' socially than culturally.

In contrast, the novelists cannot realize profits equal to those of playwrights unless they reach a 'broad audience' [*le grand public*], which means, as the pejorative connotations of the expression indicate, exposing oneself to the discredit attached to commercial success. Thus it is that Zola, whose novels met the most compromising success, no doubt owes his escape from the social destiny marked out for him by his large print runs and his vulgar subjects in part to the conversion of the 'commercial', negative and 'vulgar' into the 'popular', charged with all the positive prestiges of political progressivism—a conversion made possible by the role of social prophet that was vested in him at the heart of the field and which was acknowledged well beyond it with the help of militant devotion (and also, but much later, of professional progressivism).[2]

* * *

From *Part III. To Understand Understanding*

FROM CHAPTER 1. THE HISTORICAL GENESIS OF THE PURE AESTHETIC

Analysis of Essence and Illusion of the Absolute

* * *

Although it appears to itself like a gift of nature, the eye of the nineteenth-century art-lover is the product of history. From the angle of phylogenesis,[3] the pure gaze capable of apprehending the work of art as it demands to be apprehended (in itself and for itself, as form and not as function) is inseparable from the appearance of producers motivated by a pure artistic intention, itself indissociable from the emergence of an autonomous artistic field capable of posing and imposing its own goals in the face of external demands; and it is also inseparable from the corresponding appearance of a population of 'amateurs' or 'connoisseurs' capable of applying to the works thus produced the 'pure' gaze which they call for. And from the angle of ontogenesis,[4] it is

1. The Académie française (French Academy), a learned society established in 1635 that serves as the authority on the French language and on literary matters.

2. If, Courbet apart, painters have rarely invoked populist justification, it is perhaps because they are not confronted by the problem of mass diffusion since their products are unique and of a relatively high unit price, and since the only success they can know is worldly success, close in its social effects to success in the theatre [Bourdieu's note]. Gustave Courbet (1819–1877), French realist painter.

3. The history or course of development of a kind of organism.

4. The course of development of an individual organism.

associated with very particular conditions of training, such as the precocious frequenting of museums and the prolonged exposure to school teaching and especially to the *skholè*[5] as a form of leisure, and the distance with respect to the constraints and urgencies of necessity which such training presupposes. This means, it must be said in passing, that an analysis of essence which passes these conditions over in silence tacitly elevates into a universal norm of all practice claiming to be aesthetic these particular properties of an experience which is in fact the product of privilege.

What the ahistorical analysis of the work of art and of aesthetic experience really describes is an *institution* which, as such, enjoys a kind of twofold existence, in things and in minds. In things, it exists in the form of an artistic field, a relatively autonomous social universe which is the result of a slow process of emergence. In minds, it exists in the form of dispositions which invent themselves through the very movement of self-invention of the field to which they are adjusted. When things and dispositions are directly in accord with each other, meaning when the eye is the product of the field to which it relates, then everything appears to be immediately endowed with meaning and value. This is so clearly the case that in order for a totally extraordinary question to be posed about the foundation of the meaning and value of the work of art, something usually taken for granted by all those who swim like fish in the water of the cultural world, an experience has to arise which a cultivated person finds totally exceptional—even though it is, on the contrary, totally ordinary, as empirical observation shows,[6] for those who have not had the occasion or the chance to acquire the dispositions objectively required by the work of art. An example is Arthur Danto's visit to the exhibition of Warhol's Brillo boxes at the Stable Gallery,[7] when he discovered the arbitrary (*ex instituto*, as Leibniz[8] would have said) character of the imposition of value carried out by the field through exhibition in a place both consecrated and capable of consecrating.[9]

The experience of the work of art as immediately endowed with meaning and value is an effect of the harmony between the two aspects of the same historical institution, the cultivated *habitus*[1] and the artistic field, which mutually ground each other. Given that the work of art does not exist as such, meaning as an object symbolically endowed with meaning and value,

5. Leisure; discussion, lecture; school (Greek).

6. On the confusion besetting the most culturally deprived museum visitors for lack of a minimal mastery of the instruments of perception and appreciation, and in particular of reference points such as names of genres, schools, epochs, artists, etc., see P. Bourdieu and A. Darbel, with D. Schnapper, *Love of Art: European Art Museums and Their Public*, trans. D. Caroline Beattie and Nick Merriman (Stanford: Stanford University Press, 1990), and P. Bourdieu, "Outline of a Sociological Theory of Art Perception," in *The Field of Cultural Production*, ed. Randal Johnson (Cambridge: Polity, 1992) [Bourdieu's note].

7. Site in New York City of the first solo exhibition by the American pop artist Andy Warhol (1928–1987), including his large-scale reproductions of such commercial products as Brillo boxes and Campbell Soup cans. Danto (1924–2013), American philosopher and art critic.

8. Gottfried Wilhelm Leibniz (1646–1716), German rationalist philosopher; he described the meaning of words as *ex instituto* (literally, "according to custom"; Latin).

9. And if one wants to exhaust the analysis of the social conditions of the possibility of this extraordinary experience, one must add further the prophetic intervention of the artist (in these circumstances, Marcel Duchamp) who was the first to expose the effect of the aesthetic institution of the museum and the artists, in his case by exhibiting a urinal or a bottle rack [Bourdieu's note]. Duchamp (1887–1968), French avant-garde artist, famous for his "ready-mades"—found objects, such as the urinal that he displayed unchanged and titled *Fountain*.

1. The system of durable dispositions and beliefs that underlies a given culture, acquired by individual members through socialization (a key term throughout Bourdieu's writings).

unless it is apprehended by spectators possessing the aesthetic disposition and competence which it tacitly requires, one could say that it is the eye of the aesthete which constitutes the work of art—but only if one immediately remembers that it can only do so to the extent that it is itself the product of a long collective history, that is, of the progressive invention of the 'connoisseur', and of a long individual history, that is, of prolonged exposure to the work of art. This relation of circular causality, that of belief and the sacred, characterizes any institution which can only function if it is established simultaneously within the objectivity of a social game and within dispositions ready to enter into the game and participate in it. Museums could say at their gates—but they do not need to, since it so goes without saying—'Let no one enter here unless they are lovers of art.' The game makes up the *illusio*,[2] the investment in the game by the informed player who, possessing a sense of the game because made by the game, plays the game, and thereby makes it exist.

It is clear that one does not need to choose between, on the one hand, the subjectivism of theories of the 'aesthetic consciousness' which reduce the aesthetic quality of a natural thing or a human work to a simple correlate of a purely contemplative attitude of consciousness, neither theoretical nor practical, and on the other hand an ontology of the work of art such as that proposed by Gadamer in *Truth and Method*.[3] Questions of the meaning and value of the work of art, like the question of the specificity of aesthetic judgement, can only find solutions in a social history of the field, linked to a sociology of the conditions of the constitution of the particular disposition which the field calls for in each of its states.

Historical Anamnesis[4] *and the Return of the Repressed*

What makes a work of art a work of art and not a mundane thing or a simple utensil? What makes an artist an artist, as opposed to a craftsman or a Sunday painter? What makes a urinal or a bottle rack that is exhibited in a museum into a work of art? Is it the fact that it is signed by Duchamp, a recognized artist (and recognized first and foremost *as* an artist) and not by a wine merchant or a plumber? But is that not simply replacing the work-of-art-as-fetish with the 'fetish of the name of the master' of which Benjamin[5] spoke? Who, in other words, has created the 'creator' as a recognized producer of fetishes? And what confers its magic efficacy on his name, whose celebrity is the measure of his pretension to exist as an artist? What makes the affixing of his name, like the label of a famous designer, multiply the value of the object (which helps to raise the stakes in attribution disputes and to establish the power of experts)? Where does the ultimate principle reside of the effect of nomination or of theory (a particularly appropriate word since it is a matter of seeing, *theorein*,[6] and of giving to be seen)—that ultimate

2. Illusion (Latin).
3. The major work on hermeneutics (1960) by the German philosopher Hans-Georg Gadamer (1900–2002).
4. Recollection—according to the Greek philosopher PLATO, the process by which the soul recalls ideas present in it before birth.
5. WALTER BENJAMIN (1892–1940), German literary and cultural theorist; the reference is to his "Eduard Fuchs: Collector and Historian" (1937). "Fetish": an inanimate object to which special powers are attributed; in the psychoanalytic theory of SIGMUND FREUD, an object or body part to which special sexual significance becomes attached.
6. To look at, to contemplate or consider (Greek); the root of the English word *theory*.

principle which, by introducing difference, division and separation, produces the sacred?

Such questions are analogous in type to those raised by Mauss[7] in his *Theory of Magic*, when he pondered on the principle of magic's effectiveness and found himself moving back from the instruments employed by the sorcerer to the sorcerer himself, and from there to the belief of his clients, and little by little back to the whole social universe amidst which magic is evolved and practised. But in the infinite regress towards the primary cause and the ultimate foundation of the work of art's value, one must stop somewhere. And in order to explain this sort of miracle of transubstantiation[8] which is the source of the work of art's existence—and which, though commonly forgotten, is brutally recalled through moves à la Duchamp—one must replace the ontological question[9] with the historical question of the genesis of the universe in which the value of the work of art is ceaselessly produced and reproduced in a veritable continuous creation—that is, the artistic field.

The analysis of essence merely records the outcome of the analysis which history itself has performed objectively through the process of autonomization of the field and through the progressive invention by agents (artists, critics, historians, curators, experts, etc.) of techniques and concepts (genres, mannerisms, periods, styles, etc.) which are characteristic of this universe. The science of works will not free itself completely from an 'essentialist' vision unless it successfully carries out a historical analysis of the genesis of those central figures in the artistic game, the artist and the expert, and of the dispositions they put to work in the production and reception of works of art. Notions which have become obvious and banal such as those of the artist or 'creator', like the very words which designate and constitute them, are the products of a long historical process.

This is often forgotten by art historians themselves when they ponder the emergence of the artist in the modern sense of the term, still without avoiding completely the trap of 'essentialist thought' inscribed in the use (always haunted by anachronism) of historically invented, and therefore dated, words. Unable to question everything implicitly involved in the modern notion of the artist, and in particular the professional ideology of the uncreated 'creator' which evolved throughout the nineteenth century, they stop at the apparent object, meaning the artist (or, elsewhere, the writer, the philosopher, the scholar), instead of constructing and analysing the field of production of which the artist, socially instituted as a 'creator', is the product. They do not see that the ritual inquiry concerning the place and time of the appearance of the figure of the artist (as opposed to the craftsman) in fact leads back to the question of the economic and social conditions of the gradual constitution of an artistic field capable of grounding belief in the quasi-magical powers attributed to the artist.

It is not merely a matter of exorcizing the 'fetish of the name of the master' by a simple sacrilegious and slightly childish inversion—whether one wishes it or not, the name of the master is indeed a fetish. Rather, it is a matter of

7. Marcel Mauss (1872–1950), French anthropologist; author of *The Gift* (1925) and *A General Theory of Magic* (1904).

8. Transformation into another substance; in Roman Catholic and Eastern Orthodox rites, the change of the eucharistic bread and wine into the body and blood of Christ.

9. A question related to the nature of being or the unchanging essence of a thing.

describing the gradual emergence of the entire set of social mechanisms which make possible the figure of the artist as producer of that fetish which is the work of art—in other words, the constitution of the artistic field (in which analysts and art historians themselves are included) as the locus where belief in the value of art—and in that power to create value which belongs to the artist—is constantly produced and reproduced. This leads to surveying not only the indices of the artist's autonomy (such as those revealed through the analysis of contracts, like the appearance of the signature, affirmations of the artist's specific competence, recourse in cases of dispute to arbitration by peers, etc.), but also the indices of the field's autonomy, such as the emergence of a set of specific institutions which are required for the functioning of the economy of cultural goods—places of exhibition (galleries, museums, etc.), institutions of consecration (academies, salons, etc.), institutions for the reproduction of producers (art schools, etc.), and specialized agents (dealers, critics, art historians, collectors, etc.), endowed with the *dispositions* objectively required by the field and with *specific categories of perception and appreciation* which are irreducible to those in common use and which are capable of imposing a specific measure on the value of artists and their products.

As long as painting is measured by surface covered or by length of labour, or by the quantity and price of the raw materials used (gold or ultramarine paints), the artist-painter is not radically different from a house painter. This is why, among all the inventions which accompany the emergence of the field of production, one of the most important is undoubtedly the elaboration of a properly artistic language: first a way of naming painters and of speaking about them and about the nature and the mode of remunerating their work, and through this elaborating an autonomous definition of properly artistic value, irreducible as such to strictly economic value; and also, in the same way, a way of speaking about painting itself, using appropriate words, often pairs of adjectives, which enable one to talk about the specificity of pictorial technique, the *manifattura*,[1] even the particular manner of a painter, which it helps to make exist socially by naming it. By the same logic, the discourse of celebration, especially the biography, plays a determining role, probably less by what it says about painters and their work than by the fact of establishing the painter as a memorable figure, one worthy of a historical account, like a statesman or poet (we know that the ennobling comparison—*ut pictura poesis*[2]—contributes (at least for a while, until it becomes a hindrance) to the affirmation of the irreducibility of pictorial art).

A genetic sociology[3] should also include in its model the action of producers themselves, their claim to the right to be the sole judges of pictorial production, to make their own criteria for the perception and appreciation of their products. It should take into account the effect exercised on them and on the image they have of themselves and their production (and thereby, the effect exercised on their actual production) by the images of painters and their production which comes back to them from other agents engaged in the field—other artists but also critics, clients, patrons, collectors, etc.

1. The process of making or manufacturing (Italian).
2. Poetry is like painting (Latin); HORACE, *Ars Poetica* (ca. 10 B.C.E.; see above), line 361.
3. A systematic study that explains objects, agents, and behavior in terms of their origin and development within a social field.

(One may assume, for example, that the interest which certain collectors started to take in sketches and cartoons from the quattrocento[4] on could only have helped to exalt the impression the artist had of his own dignity.)

The history of the specific institutions which are indispensable to artistic production should be backed up with a history of the institutions which are indispensable to consumption; and hence to the production of consumers and in particular, of *taste*,[5] as disposition and as competence. The inclination of the 'expert' to consecrate a part of his or her time to the contemplation of works of art for the sole purpose of the pleasure to be enjoyed from them cannot become an essential dimension of the lifestyle of the gentleman or the aristocrat (increasingly identified, at least in England and France, with the person of taste) without the whole collective labour necessary to produce the instruments of the cult of the work of art: one thinks of notions such as 'good taste', undergoing constant elaboration, or of designations like *virtuoso*, borrowed from the Italian, or *connoisseur*, taken from the French, characterizing and producing figures in seventeenth- and eighteenth-century England who are able to boast an art of living freed from the utilitarian and basely material ends to which 'vulgar' people sacrifice themselves. But one must also take into account practices as highly ritualized as the 'Grand Tour', a cultural pilgrimage lasting several years and culminating in a visit to Italy and Rome, which constitutes the almost obligatory crowning achievement of their studies for the children of the great aristocracy of England and elsewhere; we must consider as well the institutions offering, usually for payment, cultural products to a broader and broader public, the specialized periodical publications, magazines and works of criticism, literary and artistic newspapers and weeklies, private galleries (gradually converted into museums), annual exhibitions, guidebooks aimed at visitors to the painting and sculpture collections of aristocratic palaces or museums, public concerts and so forth.

Besides the fact they foster the growth of a *public* for cultural works, which is thereby given the means (and required) to acquire a cultivated disposition, *public* institutions like museums, which have no other purpose than to offer for contemplation works often produced with quite other destinations in mind (such as religious paintings, dance or ceremonial music, etc.), have the effect of bringing about a social rupture which, by tearing works out of their original context, strips them of their diverse religious or political functions and thus reduces them, by a sort of active *épochè*,[6] to their properly artistic function. The museum, as it isolates and separates (*frames apart*), is undoubtedly the site *par excellence* of that act of *constitution*, continually repeated with the untiring constancy of things, through which both the status of the sacred conferred on works of art and the sacralizing disposition they call for are affirmed and continually reproduced.[7] The experience of the pictorial work as

4. The 15th century, as a period of Italian literature and art. "Cartoons": drawings made in preparation for a painting
5. A key term—especially for DAVID HUME and IMMANUEL KANT—in the establishment of aesthetics and literary theory as distinct fields of inquiry during the 18th century.
6. Suspension (Greek); a term used by the German philosopher Edmund Husserl (1859–1938) and other phenomenologists to refer to the "bracketing" of historical and natural assumptions and knowledge undertaken before the analysis of an object or phenomenon itself.
7. This rapid and at best schematic sketch of what might make up a social history of the aesthetic disposition with respect to painting relies in part on the observations of M. H. Abrams, *Doing Things with Texts* (New York: Norton, 1989), esp. pp. 135–38, and also on those of W. E. Houghton Jr., "The English *Virtuoso* in the Seventeenth Century," *Journal of the History of Ideas* 3 (1942): 51–73 and 190–219 [Bourdieu's note].

it has been asserted by this site in its exclusive devotion to pure contemplation tends to become the norm for the experience of all objects belonging to the very category which has been constituted by the fact of their being exhibited.

Everything inclines us to think that the history of aesthetic theory and of the philosophy of art is closely linked (without being its direct reflection, since it, too, develops in a field) to the history of the institutions suited to fostering access to pure delectation and disinterested contemplation, such as museums or those practical manuals of visual gymnastics called tourist guides or writings on art (among which must be included innumerable travel writings). In fact, it is clear that the theoretical writings which the history of traditional philosophy treats as contributions to the knowledge of the object are also (and more especially) contributions to the *social construction of the very reality* of this object, and hence of the theoretical and practical conditions of its existence (the same thing may be said about treatises on political theory by Machiavelli, Bodin or Montesquieu[8]).

It would be necessary to rewrite the history of pure aesthetics *from this perspective*, showing, for example, how professional philosophers have imported into the domain of art certain concepts originally developed in the *theological* tradition, especially a conception of the artist as a 'creator' endowed with an almost divine faculty called 'imagination' and capable of producing a 'second nature', a 'second world', *sui generis* and autonomous; how Alexandre Baumgarten,[9] in his *Philosophical Reflections on Poetry* of 1735, transposed into the aesthetic order a Leibnizian cosmogony[1] according to which God, in the creation of the best of all possible worlds, chose ours among an infinity of worlds, all formed of compossible[2] elements and governed by specific internal laws, making of the poet a creator and of the poem a world subject to its own laws, whose truth does not reside in its correspondence with the real, but in its internal coherence; how Karl Philipp Moritz[3] tried to prove that the work of art is a microcosm whose beauty 'has no need of being useful' because it has 'within itself the purpose of its existence'; how, following another theoretical line (which must also be considered in its social dimension, by situating each thinker in his field), the idea that supreme good consists of the contemplation of the Beautiful (with its different theoretical foundations, Platonic and Plotinian,[4] but also Leibnizian) was developed by different writers, and in particular Shaftesbury,[5] Karl Philipp Moritz and Kant (who adopts[6] the viewpoint of the receiver rather than the producer of the work of art, meaning the stance of contemplation), and then Schiller, Schlegel, Schopenhauer[7] and many others; and how this predominantly German philosophical tradition was connected through the intermediary of

8. French political philosopher (1689–1755). Niccolò Machiavelli (1469–1527), Italian political philosopher. Jean Bodin (1530–1596), French jurist and political philosopher.
9. German philosopher (1714–1762), founder of aesthetics as a distinct field within European philosophy.
1. Theory of the origin of the universe.
2. Possible in coexistence with something else.
3. German author and critic (1756–1793).
4. Derived from the theories of the Greek Neoplatonic philosopher Plotinus (ca. 204/5–270); like Plato, he located the Beautiful (together with reality and truth) in a transcendental spiritual realm.
5. Anthony Ashley Cooper, 3d earl of Shaftesbury (1671–1713), English philosopher. He viewed the sympathy that beauty awakens in us as central to ethics.
6. In *Critique of Judgment* (1790; see above), the most important text in modern aesthetics.
7. Arthur Schopenhauer (1788–1860), German philosopher who saw art as expressing mysteries and paradoxes that eluded philosophy. FRIEDRICH SCHILLER (1759–1805), German poet and philosopher. Friedrich Schlegel (1772–1829), German Romantic essayist and critic.

Victor Cousin[8] with French writers of art for art's sake, especially Baudelaire or Flaubert, who reinvented in their own fashion the theory of the 'creator', of the 'other world' and of pure contemplation.[9]

It would be necessary also to reveal in each case, as I have tried to do with respect to Kant, the indices of a social relation which is always implicated in the relationship to the work of art (for example in pairs of adjectives such as pure and impure, intelligible and sensory, refined and vulgar, etc.), and to put this hidden but fundamental relationship in turn into relation with the position and trajectory of the author in the field (philosophical, artistic, etc.) and in social space. This genealogy, which would probably rather irksomely record returns and repetitions which are linked, often in an indiscernible manner, to conscious or unconscious borrowings or to reinventions, would constitute the surest and most radical exploration of that unconscious which all cultivated people, because they have it in common, are ready to uphold as a universal (a priori) form of knowledge.

* * *

1992

8. French philosopher (1792–1867).
9. A deeper view of this history of aesthetic theory is to be found in M. H. Abrams, *Doing Things with Texts*, especially in the chapter entitled "From Addison to Kant: Modern Aesthetics and the Exemplary Art," pp. 159–87 [Bourdieu's note].

JACQUES DERRIDA
1930–2004

The name of the French philosopher Jacques Derrida has become synonymous with deconstruction, a French word (*déconstruction*) he revived but did not invent. Often described as a "method" of "analysis," a "type" of "critique," an "act" of "reading," or a "way" of "writing," deconstruction as a broad phenomenon has become all of those things. But in the writings of Derrida, the words here set in quotation marks are themselves the starting points of a deconstructive reading, not simply its description. Derridean deconstruction thus makes use of—and *at the same time* puts in question (at once uses, puts "under erasure," and does not erase)—the toolbox of classical Western philosophy. Those words that make up that toolbox have all functioned as philosophical terms, and Derrida, as a historian of philosophy, reads them as such. All the gestures of certainty that allow philosophers to say *what something is*, especially when that something is itself an intellectual operation ("concept," "method," "structure," "system," "deconstruction"), become objects of particular critical attention for Derridean deconstruction.

What has been seen—both positively and negatively—as revolutionary about Derrida's work for both philosophy and literary studies is the particular way he attends to language. Not only do the key terms as *terms* belong to a linguistic, and not some purely mental, domain, but that domain or object of inquiry *from the beginning* contains multiple languages. It cannot be traced back to one original language, "full presence," or "living present" that would function as the origin or the end of the multiplicity of languages. The biblical story of the tower of Babel, which recounts humanity's loss of an original universal language, is a powerful myth, but the need for such a myth is not evidence for its validity. Existing languages constantly try, and constantly fail, to present the "truth" or "Being" that is assumed to be behind or beyond language. Derrida thus investigates questions of *translation* that are at the very heart of what other philosophers have called "truth." As he wrote to Toshiko Izutsu, his Japanese translator, "the question of deconstruction is also through and through *the* question of translation." Since we have been conditioned to think of translation as a secondary activity that presupposes a primary text, this reversal—as what we have conceived of as primary simply disappears—changes everything. Language is not merely a vehicle for something that preexists it.

Born in Algeria to French-speaking Jewish parents, Derrida began life in an environment that was both multilingual and culturally complex. Like other Algerian Jews, he experienced firsthand the shifting borderlines of Frenchness: he was excluded from school as non-French during the Vichy government's collaboration with the Nazis in World War II, but in the following decade he was considered *too* French by the Arab and Berber population during the war for Algerian independence from France. He was the third of five children (four boys, one girl); the second and fourth sons died in infancy, the former just before his birth. In his autobiographical meditation called *Circumfessions* (1991)—which is, among other things, a sustained engagement with the *Confessions* of AUGUSTINE, another North African by birth—Derrida writes about the ghosts of his two dead brothers and about the unremembered circumcision that marks his Jewishness, knowing perfectly well that some readers will draw connections between his life and his work. But he leaves it to them to speculate whether certain preoccupations (with ghosts, substitutes, bodily inscriptions, the mobile border between the inside and the outside) are causes or effects of his writing. In any event, he explores precisely the relationship between "life" and "writing."

The pull between literature and philosophy that characterizes Derrida's work was there from the beginning: in high school in Algiers, he imagined writing and teaching literature and, after passing the *baccalauréat* in 1948, he enrolled in the two-year program preparatory to entering one of the prestigious French Grandes Écoles. While reading, he began to be "awed" by philosophers (especially by Søren Kierkegaard and MARTIN HEIDEGGER); he took his first trip to Paris and there enrolled at the famous Lycée Louis-le-Grand. After a difficult period in which he suffered health problems, writer's block, examination failures, and depression, in 1952 he was admitted to the prestigious École Normale Supérieure. In 1956 he passed the *agrégation* (a highly competitive nationwide exam that guarantees successful candidates a teaching job for life). A grant from Harvard University enabled him to work in Cambridge on what in 1962 became his first book: a translation from German of, and a long introduction to, "Questions as to the Origin of Geometry" by the phenomenologist Edmund Husserl (1859–1938). While at Harvard, he also read the works of James Joyce and, in June 1957, married Marguerite Aucouturier (with whom he would have two sons).

During the Algerian War, Derrida was expected to perform his obligatory military service, a requirement he satisfied by spending more than two years in Algeria as a civilian teacher of French and English. Although he condemned French colonialism, he hoped his parents would be able to remain in an independent Algeria; when that proved to be impossible, his whole family moved to Nice, in the south of France.

After several teaching jobs in *lycées* and at the Sorbonne, Derrida was invited in 1965 to become a *maître-assistant* at the École Normale Supérieure, where he taught the history of philosophy for twenty years, and where his seminars became legendary. In 1966, along with a number of other French intellectuals—notably ROLAND BARTHES, JACQUES LACAN, Georges Poulet, and Lucien Goldmann—he spoke at a landmark conference, "The Languages of Criticism and the Sciences of Man," at Johns Hopkins University. That conference helped shape how structuralism and poststructuralism began to influence literary studies in the United States. Derrida's own talk, an extension but also a critique of structuralism titled "Structure, Sign, and Play in the Discourse of the Human Sciences," was fundamental in articulating what was later seen as the "break" between the two schools.

In 1967 Derrida published his first three books: *La Voix et le phénomène* (*Speech and Phenomena*), a critique of Husserl's concept of the sign; *De la grammatologie* (*Of Grammatology*), an introduction to the necessity and impossibility of a science of writing; and *L'Écriture et la différence* (*Writing and Difference*), a collection of essays on authors that include MICHEL FOUCAULT (1926–1984), SIGMUND FREUD (1856–1939), G. W. F. HEGEL (1770–1831), and Emmanuel Lévinas (1906–1995). He was involved in yet ambivalent about the forces mobilized in the French strikes of May 1968, but his philosophy was crucial to the intellectual upheavals that took place at that time. Derrida published three more books in 1972: *La Dissémination* (*Dissemination*), a collection of four long essays, from which our selection titled "Plato's Pharmacy" is taken; *Marges de la philosophie* (*Margins of Philosophy*), another collection of essays; and *Positions*, the texts of three interviews (the first of many he granted over the years). These early books are touchstones for deconstructive literary criticism; many others followed.

In 1975 Derrida was invited to teach a few weeks a year at Yale University, where he was soon considered a member of the so-called Yale School (along with PAUL DE MAN, J. Hillis Miller, Geoffrey Hartman, and HAROLD BLOOM). From then on, his career was split between two countries, as his role became embattled and marginalized in France and increasingly active and important in the United States. In 1980 he submitted his published works as a *thèse d'état* (advanced doctoral thesis). In 1983 he was elected to the École des Hautes Études en Sciences Sociales (the School for Advanced Study in the Social Sciences). In addition, he regularly offered seminars at several universities in the United States—most notably, at the University of California at Irvine. Derrida died of cancer in Paris at the age of seventy-four.

Derrida is first and foremost an extraordinary critical reader. Whether he reads writings by philosophers or poets, autobiographers or anthropologists, linguists or psychoanalysts, he pulls out the threads that give the texts coherence and, at the same time, unravel them. His use of the figure of the *web* (well before the existence of but anticipating the World Wide Web) unpacks the appearance of unity presented by a book to reveal an articulation of conflicting messages woven together within it. Yet both forces—the unifying and unraveling—operate in what Derrida calls a "text." If PLATO's written "dialogues" mark the beginning of the "age of writing," the writings of Derrida, perhaps, signal its end.

Philosophy, like literature, is the study of things that can matter only to creatures that possess language, even—or especially—when they are attempting to get "beyond" it. That "beyond" is what philosophy calls "metaphysics." Instead of simply getting rid of metaphysics, as American neopragmatists like Richard Rorty try to do, Derrida analyzes the metaphysical residues that cling to the very gesture of going beyond metaphysics, whether it is made in philosophical language, literary language, or the language of everyday life. In a much-misunderstood sentence from *Of Grammatology* ("The Exorbitant. Question of Method"), Derrida makes the claim that "il n'y a pas de hors-texte," a phrase sometimes translated, not incorrectly, as "there is nothing outside the text." But this translation maintains the inside/outside opposition that the statement in fact aims to overturn. The text is *already* an attempt to include its own outside. There is no outside of *that*.

Though Derrida is known for his neologisms, the terms most closely associated with him are almost never his invention. He instead finds them already in the works he is reading, where they draw his attention by articulating the text in some way that has generally been overlooked. Take, for example, the word *supplément*, which in French means both "substitute" and "addition": in the late eighteenth-century *Confessions* of Jean-Jacques Rousseau, it is used consciously in only one of its senses at a time, but it necessarily always carries in it the other, thereby drawing together some threads in the text in ways that Rousseau seems not to have intended. As Derrida explains, "the reading must always aim at a certain relationship, unperceived by the writer, between what he commands and what he does not command of the patterns of the language that he uses. The relationship is not a certain quantitative distribution of shadow and light, of weakness or of force, but a signifying structure that critical reading should *produce*."

Derrida is famous for producing such critical readings, which have come to be called "deconstructions." His readings go beyond the mere accuracy of "doubling commentary" ("this indispensable guardrail has always only *protected*, it has never *opened*, a reading"), but they nevertheless remain "intrinsic" to the text. Instead of rushing to expound the text's presumed content, meaning, or referent, they try to remain at the point and within the logic that renders the leap to an outside so tempting. Instead of choosing *between* incompatible or contradictory readings, Derrida attempts to understand the double binds and tensions that are articulated in the text. Rousseau, standing between the Enlightenment and Romanticism, is a figure whose writings are symptomatic of the fissures in the logocentric system that he both reproduces and resists.

In order to see a relationship in a particular language between patterns one commands and patterns one does not command, Derrida works within the space between the *signified* (what is meant) and the *signifier* (the vehicle for conveying that meaning). The noncoincidence of the two sides of the sign can never be overcome: indeed, we detect a signified when a signifier doesn't quite coincide with it. The signifier, for Derrida, thus functions as a "trace" that gives the impression that a signified was prior to it, even though the only evidence for that signified is the trace itself.

The Swiss linguist FERDINAND DE SAUSSURE, who split the sign into signifier and signified, revolutionized the understanding of language by seeing it as a system (internally as well as externally articulated) and not as a nomenclature (a simple aggregation of names). According to Saussure, language does not arise cumulatively from either things or ideas but instead produces things or ideas out of a structure of differences. "Language is a system of differences," he says in *Course in General Linguistics* (1916), "*without positive terms.*" Derrida takes this concept of difference from Saussure and adds to it the dimension of temporality that Saussure's static (or synchronic) structure does not allow. In doing so, Derrida uncovers a significant contradiction in Saussure: although Saussure *thinks* he can eliminate writing as secondary and keep speech as essential, he treats language as fixed in time and thus as if it were a dead language—a language that we can only know *in writing*.

To mark the combination of such synchronic and diachronic differences, Derrida juxtaposes two grammatical extensions of the verb *différer* (translated into English by two different verbs, "to differ" and "to defer"): *différence*, a noun that implies synchronic comparison, and *différance*, a noun of identical pronunciation that invokes a *process*—the temporal process of deferring or postponing. The structure of language in real time—always changing, and always changing in more than one way—involves both of these senses. But, ironically, a difference (between "e" and "a") meant to be perceived only in writing has become, in English, recognizable in speech: "Derridean *différance*" (pronounced with the French nasal found in "*Vive la différence!*") does not escape the privileging of voice that it was designed to counteract.

Derrida makes the counterintuitive claim that writing is more fundamental than speech. This has often been misunderstood or taken literally. It is as though Derrida is not aware of the fact that babies learn to speak before they learn to write, or that some societies have oral cultures on which writing (Western and imperialistic) has been imposed. Indeed, critics say, hasn't the existence of a written tradition been used to demonstrate Western culture's superiority, and hasn't orality been dismissed as primitive? Why does Derrida say that "Western metaphysics" privileges speech—Logos—and represses writing? Isn't the case just the opposite?

Yes and no. Western culture has always been able to have it both ways, starting with Plato, who condemned writing *in writing* in his *Phaedrus* (ca. 370 B.C.E.; see above). Our selection from *Dissemination*—excerpts from "Plato's Pharmacy"—offers an analysis of that phenomenon. In his writing, Plato idealized speech as the living emanation of the word, as if it erased the gap between signifier and signified. This idealization of the *logos* (speech, presence, truth, reason) requires that it belong not to any actual language but only to God. And, paradoxically, such an idea of speech is *claimed only in writing*—a writing that pretends it doesn't exist, or is simply a tool that effaces itself in the final moment of truth. This pretence is what Derrida calls "the repression of writing."

In *Phaedrus*, Plato repeats an ancient story of the origin and judgment of writing. The inventor of writing, Theuth, presents it to King Thamus of Egypt as a remedy for forgetfulness. The king rejects his invention on the grounds that it will *induce* forgetfulness, not remedy the condition. The word that they use for writing, *pharmakon* (drug), means "remedy" as well as "poison." Though translators of Plato have chosen one rendering or the other, according to the context, the word contains both meanings; its translations thus dismember it into a *subsequent* either/or structure. Derrida here analyzes the crucial role of translation in the reception of the dialogues of Plato, in the nature of "Platonism," and indeed in the history of philosophy itself.

Derrida shows how the effort to fit everything into binary oppositions (speech and writing, good and bad, true and false, philosophy and literature, etc.) depends on a distinguishability that does not exist within the word *pharmakon*. The translations suggest that it names one side or the other of an existing polarity, but the word is the *medium* and not a result of the split into either/or. A logic prior to that split, however, is almost impossible to think. It risks seeming like sophistry—and after Plato, the distinction between philosophy and sophistry becomes the either/or split on which all the others (and philosophy itself) depend. The distinction Plato makes between sophistry and philosophy *is* philosophy, argues Derrida; philosophy is not merely one counterbalancing term (as Plato, but perhaps not Plato's *text*, seems to believe). Derrida reads Plato's *Phaedrus* as outlining the paradoxical logic of that claim.

In focusing on words—*supplément* in Rousseau, *pharmakon* in Plato (even the word *déconstruction* was originally chosen to translate Heidegger's *Destruktion*, bringing out the sense of "taking apart" rather than "blowing up")—Derrida does not fashion a theoretical metalanguage of concepts designed to support discriminations and generalizations. Each word is found in a text, not made to account for it or for other texts. Such terms are useful because they enable a rereading of the text in which they occur. Derrida is at pains not to separate out a set of terms and define them as "theory," aiming instead to read each new text and find *its* "exorbitant" terms. What these "undecidables" (as Derrida sometimes calls them) have in common is their displacement of what is normally taken for granted as the ground rules for a reading. In that sense, the logics they make visible and functional are generalizable—but they are not logics, if logic is understood as something separable from the text and generalizable apart from it. They are threads *in* it.

It came as a surprise when, late in his career, Derrida published *Specters of Marx: The State of Debt, the Work of Mourning, and the New International* (1993; trans. 1994). Here was Derrida addressing at length and at last political philosophy—and KARL MARX at that. Why the 1990s? Why Marx? The occasion was an American colloquium held in 1993 titled "Whither Marxism?" Derrida was the main invited speaker. With the collapse of the Union of Soviet Socialist Republics in the early

1990s, communism appeared to be dead and Marxism finished. The United States was the sole remaining superpower: capitalism was triumphant. In 1990 President George H. W. Bush foresaw the emergence of a new world order. The American political philosopher Francis Fukuyama captured the jubilant mood of the times in his best-selling book, *The End of History and the Last Man* (1992). In a well-known passage from the third chapter of *Specters of Marx*, excerpted here, Derrida outlines ten plagues of the new global disorder set against the blinkered celebratory claims of Bush and Fukuyama. Significantly, he quotes Marx's own statement, "I am not a Marxist." He thereby makes the point that although "Marxism" has hardened into a philosophy, a dogma, a program, a theory, Marx's heterogeneous works are filled with many other spirits, especially those of critique, historical change, and revolution. Prompted by the famous opening line of Marx and ENGELS's *The Communist Manifesto* (1848), "A specter is haunting Europe—the specter of communism," Derrida isolates many spirits (alternately ghosts or specters) in the texts of Marx. He wittily invokes Shakespeare's *Hamlet* to illustrate the dynamics of haunting as revealed by the play's father-ghost. Derrida's main point is that the world is not done with Marx's critiques of global capitalism. He recalls a similar attempt at exorcism of Marx during the 1950s. For Derrida, hegemonic political orders are always haunted by past and future specters such as suffering multitudes, militant organized workers, and revolutionaries seeking economic, political, or racial justice. The *specter* is another Derridean undecidable. "Injunctions of Marx" is Derrida's explicit call for a return to Marx in theory and in practice, and "Wears and Tears" enumerates the reasons why such a return is urgent.

In another of his late works, *The Animal That Therefore I Am* (2006; trans. 2008), Derrida memorably interrogates the binary opposition characteristic of the Western tradition from Plato to Lacan that not only separates man and animal, simply and firmly, but also denies human animality. Furthermore, it improbably casts animals as incapable of responding and of suffering. During the past two centuries, notes Derrida, the exploitation of animals has increased exponentially, engendering violence and torture on a mass industrial scale. Meanwhile we humans refuse to acknowledge the subjection of animals and wage a war on compassion and pity. We repress our links and commonalities with animals such as our shared finitude and mortality. The term "animal" itself, argues Derrida, reduces all animals from protozoa to dolphins to one category, obliterating innumerable and abyssal differences among critters (to use DONNA HARAWAY's alternative term). What Derrida's late works, including *Specters of Marx* and *The Animal That Therefore I Am*, have in common is a new turn to pressing contemporary social, political, and ethical issues, framed characteristically in terms of questionable philosophical concerns and values that lead back to the foundations of Western culture.

Dissemination **Keywords:** Authorship, The Canon/Tradition, Classical Theory, Deconstruction, Language, Print Culture, Rhetoric
Specters of Marx **Keywords:** Deconstruction, Globalization, Hegemony, Marxism, Media, Postmodernity
The Animal That Therefore I Am **Keywords:** The Canon/Tradition, Deconstruction, Ethics, Language, Modernity

From Dissemination[1]

From *Plato's Pharmacy*

A text is not a text unless it hides from the first comer, from the first glance, the law of its composition and the rules of its game. A text remains, moreover, forever imperceptible. Its law and its rules are not, however, harbored in the inaccessibility of a secret; it is simply that they can never be booked, in the *present*, into anything that could rigorously be called a perception.

And hence, perpetually and essentially, they run the risk of being definitively lost. Who will ever know of such disappearances?

The dissimulation of the woven texture can in any case take centuries to undo its web: a web that envelops a web, undoing the web for centuries; reconstituting it too as an organism, indefinitely regenerating its own tissue behind the cutting trace, the decision of each reading. There is always a surprise in store for the anatomy or physiology of any criticism[2] that might think it has mastered the game, surveyed all the threads at once, deluding itself, too, in wanting to look at the text without touching it, without laying a hand on the "object," without risking—which is the only chance of entering into the game, by getting a few fingers caught—the addition of some new thread. Adding, here, is nothing other than giving to read. One must manage to think this out: that it is not a question of embroidering upon a text, unless one considers that to know how to embroider still means to have the ability to follow the given thread. That is, if you follow me, the hidden thread. If reading and writing are one, as is easily thought these days, if reading *is* writing, this oneness designates neither undifferentiated (con)fusion nor identity at perfect rest; the *is* that couples reading with writing must rip apart.

One must then, in a single gesture, but doubled, read and write. And that person would have understood nothing of the game who, at this [*du coup*][3] would feel himself authorized merely to add on; that is, to add any old thing. He would add nothing: the seam wouldn't hold. Reciprocally, he who through "methodological prudence," "norms of objectivity," or "safeguards of knowledge" would refrain from committing anything of himself, would not read at all. The same foolishness, the same sterility, obtains in the "not serious" as in the "serious." The reading or writing supplement must be rigorously prescribed, but by the necessities of a *game*, by the logic of *play*, signs to which the system of all textual powers must be accorded and attuned.

I

To a considerable degree, we have already said all we *meant to say*. Our lexicon at any rate is not far from being exhausted. With the exception of this or that supplement, our questions will have nothing more to name but the texture of the text, reading and writing, mastery and play, the paradoxes of supplementarity, and the graphic relations between the living and the dead: within the textual, the textile, and the histological. We will keep within the

1. Translated by Barbara Johnson, who occasionally retains the original French in brackets.
2. Perhaps a reference to *Anatomy of Criticism* (1957), the best-known book by the Canadian critic NORTHROP FRYE.
3. At this blow (French).

limits of this *tissue*; between the metaphor of the *histos*[4] and the question of the *histos* of metaphor.

Since we have already said everything, the reader must bear with us if we continue on awhile. If we extend ourselves by force of play. If we then *write* a bit: on Plato,[5] who already said in the *Phaedrus* that writing can only repeat (itself), that it "always signifies (*sēmainei*) the same" and that it is a "game" (*paidia*).

FROM 1. PHARMACIA

* * *

This brief evocation of Pharmacia at the beginning of the *Phaedrus*—is it an accident? An hors d'œuvre? A fountain, "perhaps with curative powers," notes Robin,[6] was dedicated to Pharmacia near the Ilissus. Let us in any case retain this: that a little spot, a little stitch or mesh (*macula*[7]) woven into the back of the canvas, marks out for the entire dialogue the scene where that *virgin* was cast into the abyss, surprised by death *while playing with Pharmacia*. Pharmacia (*Pharmakeia*) is also a common noun signifying the administration of the *pharmakon*, the drug: the medicine and/or poison. "Poisoning" was not the least usual meaning of "pharmacia." Antiphon[8] has left us the logogram of an "accusation of poisoning against a mother-in-law" (*Pharmakeias kata tēs mētryias*). Through her games, Pharmacia has dragged down to death a virginal purity and an unpenetrated interior.

Only a little further on, Socrates compares the written texts Phaedrus has brought along to a drug (*pharmakon*). This *pharmakon*, this "medicine," this philter, which acts as both remedy and poison, already introduces itself into the body of the discourse with all its ambivalence. This charm, this spellbinding virtue, this power of fascination, can be—alternately or simultaneously—beneficent or maleficent. The *pharmakon* would be a *substance*—with all that that word can connote in terms of matter with occult virtues, cryptic depths refusing to submit their ambivalence to analysis, already paving the way for alchemy—if we didn't have eventually to come to recognize it as antisubstance itself: that which resists any philosopheme,[9] indefinitely exceeding its bounds as nonidentity, nonessence, nonsubstance; granting philosophy by that very fact the inexhaustible adversity of what funds it and the infinite absence of what founds it.

Operating through seduction, the *pharmakon* makes one stray from one's general, natural, habitual paths and laws. Here, it takes Socrates out of his proper place and off his customary track. The latter had always kept him inside the city. The leaves of writing act as a *pharmakon* to push or attract out of the city the one who never wanted to get out, even at the end, to escape the

4. "*Histos: anything set upright*, hence: I. *mast*. II. *beam* of a loom, which stood upright, instead of lying hoizontal as in our looms (except in the weaving methods used by the Gobelins and in India), to which the threads of the warp are attached, hence: 1. *loom*; 2. *the warp fixed to the loom*, hence, *the woof*; 3. *woven cloth, piece of canvas*; 4. by anal. *spider web*; or *honeycomb of bees*. III. *rod, wand, stick*. IV. by anal. *shinbone, leg*" [Derrida's note]. Derrida defines the word as used in classical Greek; in modern medicine, it refers to tissues (e.g., "histology"). Some of the author's notes are omitted.

5. Greek philosopher (ca. 427–ca. 347 B.C.E.; see above), many of whose dialogues are referred to by Derrida. He here quotes *Phaedrus* 275d, 276d (see above). The main speaker, as in most of the dialogues, is the Greek philosopher Socrates (469–399 B.C.E.), Plato's teacher.

6. Léon Robin (1866–1947), French translator of the *Phaedrus*.

7. Spot, stain (Latin).

8. Greek orator (ca. 480–411 B.C.E.).

9. Constituent element of philosophy.

hemlock.[1] They take him out of himself and draw him onto a path that is properly an *exodus*:[2]

> *Phaedrus:* Anyone would take you, as you say, for a foreigner being shown the country by a guide, and not a native—you never leave town to cross the frontier nor even, I believe, so much as set foot outside the walls.
>
> *Socrates:* You must forgive me, dear friend; I'm a lover of learning, and trees and open country won't teach me anything, whereas men in the town do. Yet you seem to have discovered a drug[3] for getting me out (*dokeis moi tēs emēs exodou to pharmakon hēurēkenai*). A hungry animal can be driven by dangling a carrot or a bit of greenstuff in front of it; similarly if you proffer me speeches bound in books (*en bibliois*) I don't doubt you can cart me all round Attica, and anywhere else you please. Anyhow, now that we've got here I propose for the time being to lie down, and you can choose whatever posture you think most convenient for reading, and proceed. (230*d–e*)[4]

It is at this point, when Socrates has finally stretched out on the ground and Phaedrus has taken the most comfortable position for handling the text or, if you will, the *pharmakon*, that the discussion actually gets off the ground. A spoken speech—whether by Lysias[5] or by Phaedrus in person—a speech proffered *in the present, in the presence* of Socrates, would not have had the same effect. Only the *logoi en bibliois*, only words that are deferred, reserved, enveloped, rolled up, words that force one to wait for them in the form and under cover of a solid object, letting themselves be desired for the space of a walk, only hidden letters can thus get Socrates moving. If a speech could be purely present, unveiled, naked, offered up in person in its truth, without the detours of a signifier foreign to it, if at the limit an undeferred *logos*[6] were possible, it would not seduce anyone. It would not draw Socrates, as if under the effects of a *pharmakon*, out of his way. Let us get ahead of ourselves. Already: writing, the *pharmakon*, the going or leading astray.

In our discussion of this text we have been using an authoritative French translation of Plato, the one published by Guillaume Budé. In the case of the *Phaedrus*, the translation is by Léon Robin. We will continue to refer to it, inserting the Greek text in parentheses, however, whenever it seems opportune or pertinent to our point. Hence, for example, the word *pharmakon*. In this way we hope to display in the most striking manner the regular, ordered polysemy[7] that has, through skewing, indetermination, or overdetermination, but without mistranslation, permitted the rendering of the same word by "remedy," "recipe," "poison," "drug," "philter," etc. It will also be seen to

1. The poison drunk by Socrates after an Athenian court condemned him to death for impiety and corrupting the youth.
2. A way out (Greek).
3. Translated by others as "recipe" and "remedy" [translator's note, edited].
4. As a rule, translations of Plato are taken from *The Collected Dialogues of Plato*, ed. Edith Hamilton and Huntington Cairns, Bollingen Series 71 (Princeton: Princeton University Press, 1961), supplemented by other renderings. In addition, I have occasionally modified the wording or word order of the Platonic texts in order to bring them into line with the parenthetical Greek inserts. Some minor adjustments have also been made when it seemed necessary to achieve a closer parallel to the French version with which Derrida is working [translator's note, edited].
5. Greek speechwriter (ca. 459–ca. 380 B.C.E.), who taught rhetoric and was one of the masters of classical oratory.
6. Word, speech, story, reason (Greek).
7. Possession of multiple meanings.

what extent the malleable unity of this concept, or rather its rules and the strange logic that links it with its signifier,[8] has been dispersed, masked, obliterated, and rendered almost unreadable not only by the imprudence or empiricism of the translators, but first and foremost by the redoubtable, irreducible difficulty of translation. It is a difficulty inherent in its very principle, situated less in the passage from one language to another, from one philosophical language to another, than already, as we shall see, in the tradition between Greek and Greek; a violent difficulty in the transference of a nonphilosopheme into a philosopheme. With this problem of translation we will thus be dealing with nothing less than the problem of the very passage into philosophy.

The *biblia* that will draw Socrates out of his reserve and out of the space in which he is wont to learn, to teach, to speak, to dialogue—the sheltered enclosure of the city—these *biblia* contain a text written by "the ablest writer of our day" (*deinotatos ōn nun graphein*). His name is Lysias. Phaedrus is keeping the text or, if you will, the *pharmakon*, hidden under his cloak. He needs it because he has not learned the speech by heart. This point is important for what follows, the problem of writing being closely linked to the problem of "knowing by heart." Before Socrates had stretched out on the ground and invited Phaedrus to take the most comfortable position, the latter had offered to reconstitute, without the help of the text, the reasoning, argument, and design of Lysias' speech, its *dianoia*. Socrates stops him short: "Very well, my dear fellow, but you must first show me what it is that you have in your left hand under your cloak, for I surmise that it is the actual discourse (*ton logon auton*)" (228*d*). Between the invitation and the start of the reading, while the *pharmakon* is wandering about under Phaedrus' cloak, there occurs the evocation of Pharmacia and the send-off of myths.

Is it after all by chance or by harmonics[9] that, even before the overt presentation of writing as a *pharmakon* arises in the middle of the myth of Theuth, the connection between *biblia* and *pharmaka* should already be mentioned in a malevolent or suspicious vein? As opposed to the true practice of medicine, founded on science, we find indeed, listed in a single stroke, empirical practice, treatments based on recipes learned by heart, mere bookish knowledge, and the blind usage of drugs. All that, we are told, springs out of *mania*: "I expect they would say, 'the man is mad; he thinks he has made himself a doctor by picking up something out of a book (*ek bibliou*), or coming across a couple of ordinary drugs (*pharmakiois*), without any real knowledge of medicine'" (268*c*).

This association between writing and the *pharmakon* still seems external; it could be judged artificial or purely coincidental. But the intention and intonation are recognizably the same: one and the same suspicion envelops in a single embrace the book and the drug, writing and whatever works in an occult, ambiguous manner open to empiricism and chance, governed by the ways of magic and not the laws of necessity. Books, the dead and rigid knowledge shut up in *biblia*, piles of histories, nomenclatures, recipes and formulas learned by heart, all this is as foreign to living knowledge and dialectics as the *pharmakon* is to medical science. And myth to true knowledge. In dealing with Plato,

8. The symbol or sound that conveys meaning (the signified), a term introduced by the Swiss linguist FERDINAND DE SAUSSURE (1857–1913).
9. Design, rhythm.

who knew so well on occasion how to treat myth in its archeo-logical or paleological capacity, one can glimpse the immensity and difficulty of this last opposition. The extent of the difficulty is marked out—this is, among a hundred others, the example that retains us here—in that the truth—the original truth—about writing as a *pharmakon* will at first be left up to a myth. The myth of Theuth, to which we now turn.

Up to this point in the dialogue, one can say that the *pharmakon* and the grapheme[1] have been beckoning to each other from afar, indirectly sending back to each other, and, as if by chance, appearing and disappearing together on the same line, for yet uncertain reasons, with an effectiveness that is quite discrete and perhaps after all unintentional. But in order to lift this doubt and on the supposition that the categories of the voluntary and the involuntary still have some absolute pertinence in a reading—which we don't for a minute believe, at least not on the textual level on which we are now advancing—let us proceed to the last phase of the dialogue, to the point where Theuth appears on the scene.

This time it is without indirection, without hidden mediation, without secret argumentation, that writing is proposed, presented, and asserted as a *pharmakon* (274*e*).

In a certain sense, one can see how this section could have been set apart as an appendix, a superadded supplement. And despite all that calls for it in the preceding steps, it is true that Plato offers it somewhat as an amusement, an hors d'œuvre or rather a dessert. All the subjects of the dialogue, both themes and speakers, seem exhausted at the moment the supplement, writing, or the *pharmakon*, are introduced: "Then we may feel that we have said enough both about the art of speaking and about the lack of art (*to men tekhnēs te kai atekhnias logōn*)"[2] (274*b*). And yet it is at this moment of general exhaustion that the question of writing is set out.[3] And, as was foreshadowed earlier by the use of the word *aiskhron* (or the adverb *aiskhrōs*[4]), the question of writing opens as a question of morality. It is truly *morality* that is at stake, both in the sense of the opposition between good and evil, or good and bad, and in the sense of mores, public morals and social conventions. It is a question of knowing what is done and what is not done. This moral disquiet is in no way to be distinguished from questions of truth, memory, and dialectics.[5] This latter question, which will quickly be engaged as *the* question of writing, is closely associated with the morality theme, and indeed develops it by affinity of essence and not by superimposition. But within a debate rendered very real by the political development of the city, the propagation of

1. Constituent element of writing.
2. Here, when it is a question of *logos*, Robin translates *tekhnē* by "art." Later, in the course of the indictment, the same word, this time pertaining to writing, will be rendered by "technical knowledge" [*connaissance technique*] [Derrida's note].
3. While Saussure, in his *Course in General Linguistics* [1916], excludes or settles the question of writing in a sort of preliminary excursus or hors d'œuvre, the chapter Rousseau devotes to writing in the *Essay on the Origin of Languages* [written 1761; pub. 1781] is also presented, despite its actual importance, as a sort of somewhat contingent supplement, a makeup criterion, "another means of comparing languages and of judging their relative antiquity." The same operation is found in Hegel's *Encyclopedia* [1817]; cf. "Le Puits et la pyramide" (1968), in *Hegel et la pensée moderne* (Paris: Presses Universitaires de France, 1970, coll. "Epiméthée") [Derrida's note]. Translated by Alan Bass as "The Pit and the Pyramid: Introduction to Hegel's Semiology," in Derrida's *Margins of Philosophy* (Chicago: University of Chicago Press, 1982). Jean-Jacques Rousseau (1712–1778), Swiss-born French philosopher. GEORG WILHELM FRIEDRICH HEGEL (1770–1831), German idealist philosopher.
4. Shamefully (Greek).
5. The pursuit of truth, philosophy.

writing and the activity of the sophists and speechwriters, the primary accent is naturally placed upon political and social proprieties. The type of arbitration proposed by Socrates plays within the opposition between the values of seemliness and unseemliness (*euprepeia*/*aprepeia*): "But there remains the question of propriety and impropriety in writing, that is to say the conditions which make it proper or improper. Isn't that so?" (274*b*).

Is writing seemly? Does the writer cut a respectable figure? Is it proper to write? Is it done?

Of course not. But the answer is not so simple, and Socrates does not immediately offer it on his own account in a rational discourse or *logos*. He lets it be heard by delegating it to an *akoē*,[6] to a well-known rumor, to hearsay evidence, to a fable transmitted from ear to ear: "I can tell you what our forefathers have said about it, but the truth of it is only known by tradition. However, if we could discover that truth for ourselves, should we still be concerned with the fancies of mankind?" (274*c*).

The truth of writing, that is, as we shall see, (the) nontruth, cannot be discovered in ourselves by ourselves. And it is not the object of a science, only of a history that is recited, a fable that is repeated. The link between writing and myth becomes clearer, as does its opposition to knowledge, notably the knowledge one seeks in oneself, by oneself. And at the same time, through writing or through myth, the genealogical break and the estrangement from the origin are sounded. One should note most especially that what writing will later be accused of—repeating without knowing—here defines the very approach that leads to the statement and determination of its status. One thus begins by repeating without knowing—through a myth—the definition of writing, which is to repeat without knowing. This kinship of writing and myth, both of them distinguished from *logos* and dialectics, will only become more precise as the text concludes. Having just repeated without knowing that writing consists of repeating without knowing, Socrates goes on to base the demonstration of his indictment, of his *logos*, upon the premises of the *akoē*, upon structures that are readable through a fabulous genealogy of writing. As soon as the myth has struck the first blow, the *logos* of Socrates will demolish the accused.

FROM 2. THE FATHER OF LOGOS

The story begins like this:

> *Socrates:* Very well, I heard, then, that at Naucratis in Egypt there lived one of the old gods of that country, the one whose sacred bird is called the ibis; and the name of the divinity was Theuth. It was he who first invented numbers and calculation, geometry and astronomy, not to speak of draughts and dice, and above all writing (*grammata*). Now the King of all Egypt at that time was Thamus who lived in the great city of the upper region which the Greeks call the Egyptian Thebes; the god himself they call Ammon. Theuth came to him and exhibited his arts and declared that they ought to be imparted to the other Egyptians. And Thamus questioned him about the usefulness of each one; and as Theuth enumerated, the King blamed or

6. Something heard (Greek).

> praised what he thought were the good or bad points in the explanation. Now Thamus is said to have had a good deal to remark on both sides of the question about every single art (it would take too long to repeat it here); but when it came to writing, Theuth said, "This discipline (*to mathēma*), my King, will make the Egyptians wiser and will improve their memories (*sophōterous kai mnēmonikōterous*): my invention is a recipe (*pharmakon*) for both memory and wisdom." But the King said . . . etc. (274*c*–*e*)

Let us cut the King off here. He is faced with the *pharmakon*. His reply will be incisive.

Let us freeze the scene and the characters and take a look at them. Writing (or, if you will, the *pharmakon*) is thus presented to the King. Presented: like a kind of present offered up in homage by a vassal to his lord (Theuth is a demigod speaking to the king of the gods), but above all as a finished work submitted to his appreciation. And this work is itself an art, a capacity for work, a power of operation. This artefactum is an art. But the value of this gift is still uncertain. The value of writing—or of the *pharmakon*—has of course been spelled out to the King, but it is the King who will give it its value, who will set the price of what, in the act of receiving, he constitutes or institutes. The king or god (Thamus represents[7] Ammon, the king of the gods, the king of kings, the god of gods. Theuth says to him: *Ō basileu*[8]) is thus the other name for the origin of value. The value of writing will not be itself, writing will have no value, unless and to the extent that god-the-king approves of it. But god-the-king nonetheless experiences the *pharmakon* as a product, an *ergon,*[9] which is not his own, which comes to him from outside but also from below, and which awaits his condescending judgment in order to be consecrated in its being and value. God the king does not know how to write, but that ignorance or incapacity only testifies to his sovereign independence. He has no need to write. He speaks, he says, he dictates, and his word suffices. Whether a scribe from his secretarial staff then adds the supplement of a transcription or not, that consignment is always in essence secondary.

From this position, without rejecting the homage, the god-king will depreciate it, pointing out not only its uselessness but its menace and its mischief. Another way of not receiving the offering of writing. In so doing, god-the-king-that-speaks is acting like a father. The *pharmakon* is here presented to the father and is by him rejected, belittled, abandoned, disparaged. The father is always suspicious and watchful toward writing.

Even if we did not want to give in here to the easy passage uniting the figures of the king, the god, and the father, it would suffice to pay systematic attention—which to our knowledge has never been done—to the permanence of a Platonic schema that assigns the origin and power of speech, precisely of

7. For Plato, Thamus is doubtless another name for Ammon, whose figure (that of the sun king and of the father of the gods) we shall sketch out later for its own sake. On this question and the debate to which it has given rise, see P. Frutiger, *Les Mythes de Platon* [*The Myths of Plato*] (Paris: Alcan, 1930), p. 233 n. 2, and notably R. Eisler, "Platon und das ägyptische Alphabet" ["Plato and the Egyptian Alphabet"], *Archiv für Geschichte der Philosophie* (1922); Pauly-Wissowa, *Real-Encylopädie der classischen Altertumswissenschaft* (s.v. "Ammon"); Roscher, *Lexikon der griechischen und römischen Mythologie* (s.v. "Thamus") [Derrida's note].

8. O king (Greek).

9. Work (Greek).

logos, to the paternal position. Not that this happens especially and exclusively in Plato. Everyone knows this or can easily imagine it. But the fact that "Platonism," which sets up the whole of Western metaphysics in its conceptuality, should not escape the generality of this structural constraint, and even illustrates it with incomparable subtlety and force, stands out as all the more significant.

Not that logos *is* the father, either. But the origin of logos is *its father*. One could say anachronously that the "speaking subject" is the *father* of his speech. And one would quickly realize that this is no metaphor, at least not in the sense of any common, conventional effect of rhetoric. *Logos* is a son, then, a son that would be destroyed in his very *presence* without the present *attendance* of his father. His father who answers. His father who speaks for him and answers for him. Without his father, he would be nothing but, in fact, writing. At least that is what is said by the one who says: it is the father's thesis. The specificity of writing would thus be intimately bound to the absence of the father. Such an absence can of course exist along very diverse modalities, distinctly or confusedly, successively or simultaneously: to have lost one's father, through natural or violent death, through random violence or patricide; and then to solicit the aid and attendance, possible or impossible, of the paternal presence, to solicit it directly or to claim to be getting along without it, etc. The reader will have noted Socrates' insistence on the misery, whether pitiful or arrogant, of a *logos* committed to writing: ". . . It always needs its father to attend to it, being quite unable to defend itself or attend to its own needs" (275*e*).

This misery is ambiguous: it is the distress of the orphan, of course, who needs not only an attending presence but also a presence that will attend to its needs; but in pitying the orphan, one also makes an accusation against him, along with writing, for claiming to do away with the father, for achieving emancipation with complacent self-sufficiency. From the position of the holder of the scepter, the desire of writing is indicated, designated, and denounced as a desire for orphanhood and patricidal subversion. Isn't this *pharmakon* then a criminal thing, a poisoned present?[1]

The status of this orphan, whose welfare cannot be assured by any attendance or assistance, coincides with that of a *graphein*[2] which, being nobody's son at the instant it reaches inscription, scarcely remains a son at all and no longer *recognizes* its origins, whether legally or morally. In contrast to writing, living *logos* is alive in that it has a living father (whereas the orphan is already half dead), a father that is *present, standing* near it, behind it, within it, sustaining it with his rectitude, attending it in person in his own name. Living *logos*, for its part, recognizes its debt, lives off that recognition, and forbids itself, thinks it can forbid itself patricide. But prohibition and patricide, like the relations between speech and writing, are structures surprising enough to require us later on to articulate Plato's text between a patricide prohibited and a patricide proclaimed. The deferred murder of the father and rector.

The *Phaedrus* would already be sufficient to prove that the responsibility for *logos*, for its meaning and effects, goes to those who attend it, to those who are present with the presence of a father. These "metaphors" must be

1. A multilingual pun: in English, *gift* means "present"; in German, *Gift* means "poison."

2. To write; writing (Greek).

tirelessly questioned. Witness Socrates, addressing Eros:[3] "If in our former speech Phaedrus or I said anything harsh against you, blame Lysias, the father of the subject (*ton tou logou patera*)" (275*b*). *Logos*—"discourse"—has the meaning here of argument, line of reasoning, guiding thread animating the spoken discussion (the *Logos*). To translate it by "subject" [*sujet*], as Robin does, is not merely anachronistic. The whole intention and the organic unity of signification is destroyed. For only the "living" discourse, only a spoken word (and not a speech's theme, object, or subject) can have a father; and, according to a necessity that will not cease to become clearer to us from now on, the *logoi* are the children. Alive enough to protest on occasion and to let themselves be questioned; capable, too, in contrast to written things, of responding when their father is there. They are their father's responsible presence.

Some of them, for example, descend from Phaedrus, who is sometimes called upon to sustain them. Let us refer again to Robin, who translates *logos* this time not by "subject" but by "argument," and disrupts in a space of ten lines the play on the *tekhnē tōn logōn*.[4] (What is in question is the *tekhnē* the sophists and rhetors had or pretended to have at their disposal, which was at once an art and an instrument, a recipe, an occult but transmissible "treatise," etc. Socrates considers the then classical problem in terms of the opposition between persuasion [*peithō*] and truth [*alētheia*] [260*a*].)

> *Socrates:* I agree—if, that is, the arguments (*logoi*) that come forward to speak for oratory should give testimony that it is an art (*tekhnē*). Now I seem, as it were, to hear some arguments advancing to give their evidence that it tells lies, that it is not an art at all, but an artless routine. "Without a grip on truth," says the Spartan, "there can be no genuine art of speaking (*tou de legein*) either now or in the future."
>
> *Phaedrus:* Socrates, we need these arguments (*Toutōn dei tōn logōn, ō Sōkrates*). Bring the witnesses here and let's find out what they have to say and how they'll say it (*ti kai pōs legousin*).
>
> *Socrates:* Come here, then, noble brood (*gennaia*), and convince Phaedrus, father of such fine children (*kallipaida te Phaidron*), that if he doesn't give enough attention to philosophy, he will never become a competent speaker on any subject. Now let Phaedrus answer. (260*e*–261*a*)

It is again Phaedrus, but this time in the *Symposium*, who must speak first because he is both "head of the table" and "father of our subject" (*patēr tou logou*) (177*d*).

What we are provisionally and for the sake of convenience continuing to call a metaphor thus in any event belongs to a whole system. If *logos* has a father, if it is a *logos* only when attended by its father, this is because it is always a being (*on*) and even a certain species of being (the *Sophist*, 260*a*), more precisely a *living* being. *Logos* is a *zōon*. An animal that is born, grows, belongs to the *phusis*.[5] Linguistics, logic, dialectics, and zoology are all in the same camp.

3. The personification of love.
4. The art of the arguments (Greek).
5. Nature; natural world (Greek).

In describing *logos* as a *zōon*, Plato is following certain rhetors and sophists before him who, as a contrast to the cadaverous rigidity of writing, had held up the living spoken word, which infallibly conforms to the necessities of the situation at hand, to the expectations and demands of the interlocutors present, and which sniffs out the spots where it ought to produce itself, feigning to bend and adapt at the moment it is actually achieving maximum persuasiveness and control.[6]

Logos, a living, animate creature, is thus also an organism that has been engendered. An *organism*: a differentiated body *proper*, with a center and extremities, joints, a head, and feet. In order to be "proper," a written discourse *ought* to submit to the laws of life just as a living discourse does. Logographical necessity (*anangkē logographikē*) ought to be analogous to biological, or rather zoological, necessity. Otherwise, obviously, it would have neither head nor tail. Both *structure* and *constitution* are in question in the risk run by *logos* of losing through writing both its tail and its head:

> *Socrates:* And what about the rest? Don't you think the different parts of the speech (*ta tou logou*) are tossed in hit or miss? Or is there really a cogent reason for starting his second point in the second place? And is that the case with the rest of the speech? As for myself, in my ignorance, I thought that the writer boldly set down whatever happened to come into his head. Can you explain his arrangement of the topics in the order he has adopted as the result of some principle of composition, some logographic necessity?
>
> *Phaedrus:* It's very kind of you to think me capable of such an accurate insight into his methods.
>
> *Socrates:* But to this you will surely agree: every discourse (*logon*), like a living creature (*ōsper zōon*), should be so put together (*sunestanai*) that it has its own body and lacks neither head nor foot, middle nor extremities, all composed in such a way that they suit both each other and the whole. (264*b*–*c*)

The organism thus engendered must be well born, of noble blood: "*gennaia*," we recall, is what Socrates called the *logoi*, those "noble creatures." This implies that the organism, having been engendered, must have a beginning and an end. Here, Socrates' standards become precise and insistent: a speech must have a beginning and an end, it must begin with the beginning and end with the end: "It certainly seems as though Lysias, at least, was far from satisfying our demands: it's from the end, not the beginning, that he tries to swim (on his back!) upstream through the current of his discourse. He starts out with what the lover ought to say at the very end to his beloved!" (264*a*). The implications and consequences of such a norm are immense, but they are obvious enough for us not to have to belabor them. It follows that the spoken discourse behaves like someone attended in origin and present in

6. The association *logos-zōon* appears in the discourse of Isocrates, *Against the Sophists*, and in that of Alcidamas, *On the Sophists*. Cf. also W. Süss, who compares these two discourses line by line with the *Phaedrus*, in *Ethos: Studien zur älteren greichischen Rhetorik* (Leipzig, 1910), pp. 34ff., and A. Diès, "Philosophie et rhétorique," in *Autour de Platon* (Paris: Gabriel Beauchesne, 1927), 1:103 [Derrida's note]. Isocrates (436–338 B.C.E.), Athenian orator; a student of both GORGIAS and Socrates, he was an important teacher of rhetoric. Alcidamas (4th c. B.C.E.), rhetorician and sophist; he was chief among Gorgias's orthodox followers.

person. *Logos: "Sermo tanquam persona ipse loquens,"*[7] as one Platonic Lexicon puts it.[8] Like any person, the *logos-zōon* has a father.

But what is a father?

Should we consider this known, and with this term—the known—classify the other term within what one would hasten to classify as a metaphor? One would then say that the origin or cause of *logos* is being compared to what we know to be the cause of a living son, his father. One would understand or imagine the birth and development of *logos* from the standpoint of a domain foreign to it, the transmission of life or the generative relation. But the father is not the generator or procreator in any "real" sense prior to or outside all relation to language.[9] In what way, indeed, is the father/son relation distinguishable from a mere cause/effect or generator/engendered relation, if not by the instance of logos? Only a power of speech can have a father. The father is always father to a speaking/living being. In other words, it is precisely *logos* that enables us to perceive and investigate something like paternity. If there were a simple metaphor in the expression "father of logos," the first word, which seemed the more *familiar*, would nevertheless receive more meaning *from* the second than it would transmit *to* it. The first familiarity is always involved in a relation of cohabitation with *logos*. Living-beings, father and son, are announced to us and related to each other within the household of *logos*. From which one does not escape, in spite of appearances, when one is transported, by "metaphor,"[1] to a foreign territory where one meets fathers, sons, living creatures, all sorts of beings that come in handy for explaining to anyone that doesn't know, by comparison, what *logos*, that strange thing, is all about. Even though this hearth is the heart of all metaphoricity, "father of logos" is not a simple metaphor. To have simple metaphoricity, one would have to make the statement that some living creature incapable of language, if anyone still wished to believe in such a thing, has a father. One must thus proceed to undertake a general reversal of all metaphorical directions, no longer asking whether *logos* can have a father but understanding that what the father claims to be the father of cannot go without the essential possibility of *logos*.

A *logos indebted* to a father, what does that mean? At least how can it be read within the stratum of the Platonic text that interests us here?

The figure of the father, of course, is also that of the good (*agathon*). Logos *represents* what it is indebted to: the father who is also chief, capital, and good(s). Or rather *the* chief, *the* capital, *the* good(s). *Patēr* in Greek means all that at once. Neither translators nor commentators of Plato seem to have accounted for the play of these schemes. It is extremely difficult, we must recognize, to respect this play in a translation, and the fact can at least be explained in that no one has ever raised the question. Thus, at the point in the *Republic* where Socrates backs away from speaking of the good in itself

7. Talk, just as if a person himself [were] speaking (Latin).

8. Fr. Ast, *Lexique platonicien*. Cf. also B. Parain, *Essai sur le logos platonicien* (Paris: Gallimard, 1942), p. 211; and P. Louis, *Les Métaphores de Platon* (Paris: Les Belles Lettres, 1945), pp. 43–44 [Derrida's note].

9. Until the advent of DNA testing and surrogate mothering, only maternity was considered certain. Paternity was thus always dependent on language (the mother's word, the father's name).

1. *Metaphor* derives from the Greek verb that means "to bear or carry across" (i.e., "transport").

(VI, 506*e*), he immediately suggests replacing it with its *ekgonos*, its son, its offspring:

> . . . let us dismiss for the time being the nature of the good in itself, for to attain to my present surmise of that seems a pitch above the impulse that wings my flight today. But what seems to be the offspring (*ekgonos*) of the good and most nearly made in its likeness I am willing to speak if you too wish it, and otherwise to let the matter drop.
>
> Well, speak on, he said, for you will duly pay me the tale of the parent another time.
>
> I could wish, I said, that I were able to make and you to receive the payment, and not merely as now the interest (*tokous*). But at any rate receive this interest and the offspring of the good (*tokon te kai ekgonon autou tou agathou*).

Tokos, which is here associated with *ekgonos*, signifies production and the product, birth and the child, etc. This word functions with this meaning in the domains of agriculture, of kinship relations, and of fiduciary operations. None of these domains, as we shall see, lies outside the investment and possibility of a *logos*.

As product, the *tokos* is the child, the human or animal brood, as well as the fruits of the seed sown in the field, and the interest on a capital investment: it is a *return* or *revenue*. The distribution of all these meanings can be followed in Plato's text. The meaning of *patēr* is sometimes even inflected in the exclusive sense of financial capital. In the *Republic* itself, and not far from the passage we have just quoted. One of the drawbacks of democracy lies in the role that capital is often allowed to play in it: "But these money-makers with down-bent heads, pretending not even to see the poor, but inserting the sting of their money into any of the remainder who do not resist, and harvesting from them in interest as it were a manifold progeny of the parent sum (*tou patros ekgonous tokous pollaplasious*), foster the drone and pauper element in the state" (555*e*).

Now, about this father, this capital, this good, this origin of value and of appearing beings, it is not possible to speak simply or directly. First of all because it is no more possible to look them in the face than to stare at the sun. On the subject of this bedazzlement before the face of the sun, a rereading of the famous passage of the *Republic* (VII, 515c ff) is strongly recommended here.

Thus will Socrates evoke only the visible sun, the son that resembles the father, the *analogon*[2] of the intelligible sun: "It was the sun, then, that I meant when I spoke of that offspring of the Good (*ton tou agathou ekgonon*), which the Good has created in its own image (*hon tagathon egennēsen analogon heautōi*), and which stands in the visible world in the same relation to vision and visible things as that which the good itself bears in the intelligible world to intelligence and to intelligible objects" (508*c*).

How does *Logos* intercede in this *analogy* between the father and the son, the *nooumena* and the *horōmena*?[3]

The Good, in the visible-invisible figure of the father, the sun, or capital, is the origin of all *onta*,[4] responsible for their appearing and their coming

2. Analogue (Greek).
3. The intelligible and the visible (Plato's terms in *Republic* 508c).
4. Beings (Greek).

into *logos*, which both assembles and distinguishes them: "We predicate 'to be' of many beautiful things and many good things, saying of them severally that they *are*, and so define them in our speech (*einai phamen te kai diorizomen tōi logōi*)" (507*b*).

The good (father, sun, capital) is thus the hidden illuminating, blinding source of *logos*. And since one cannot speak of that which enables one to speak (being forbidden to speak of it or to speak to it face to face), one will speak only of that which speaks and of things that, with a single exception, one is constantly speaking of. And since an account or reason cannot be given of what *logos* (account or reason: *ratio*) is accountable or owing *to*, since the capital cannot be counted nor the chief looked in the eye, it will be necessary, by means of a discriminative, diacritical[5] operation, to count up the plurality of interests, returns, products, and offspring: "Well, speak on (*lege*), he said, for you will duly pay me the tale of the parent another time—I could wish, I said, that I were able to make and you to receive the payment, and not merely as now the interest. But at any rate receive this interest and the offspring of the good. Have a care, however, lest I deceive you unintentionally with a false reckoning (*ton logon*) of the interest (*tou tokou*)" (507*a*).

From the foregoing passage we should also retain the fact that, along with the account (*logos*) of the supplements (to the father-good-capital-origin, etc.), along with what comes above and beyond the One in the very movement through which it absents itself and becomes invisible, thus requiring that its place be supplied, along with differance[6] and diacriticity, Socrates introduces or discovers the ever open possibility of the *kibdēlon*, that which is falsified, adulterated, mendacious, deceptive, equivocal. Have a care, he says, lest I deceive you with a false reckoning of the interest (*kibdēlon apodidous ton logon tou tokou*). *Kibdēleuma* is fraudulent merchandise. The corresponding verb (*kibdēleuō*) signifies "to tamper with money or merchandise, and, by extension, to be of bad faith."

This recourse to *logos*, from fear of being blinded by any direct intuition of the face of the father, of good, of capital, of the origin of being in itself, of the form of forms, etc., this recourse to logos as that which *protects us from the sun*, protects us under it and from it, is proposed by Socrates elsewhere, in the *analogous* order of the sensible or the visible. We shall quote at length from that text. In addition to its intrinsic interest, the text, in its official Robin translation, manifests a series of slidings, as it were, that are highly significant.[7] The passage in question is the critique, in the *Phaedo*, of "physicalists":

> Socrates proceeded:—I thought that as I had failed in the contemplation of true existence (*ta onta*), I ought to be careful that I did not lose the eye of my soul; as people may injure their bodily eye by observing and gazing on the sun during an eclipse, unless they take the precaution of only looking at the image (*eikona*) reflected in the water, or in

5. Differentiating, separating.

6. Temporal and spatial differentiating or deferral. *Différance* is Derrida's grammatical invention; like *différence*, which sounds the same and refers to synchronic comparison, it derives from *différer*, which means both "to differ" and "to defer, postpone."

7. I am indebted to the friendship and alertness of Francine Markovits for having brought this to my attention. This text should of course be placed alongside those of books 6 and 7 of the *Republic* [Derrida's note].

> some analogous medium. So in my own case, I was afraid that my soul might be blinded altogether if I looked at things with my eyes or tried to apprehend them with the help of the senses. And I thought that I had better have recourse to the world of theory (*en logois*) and seek there the truth of things. . . . So, basing myself in each case on the idea (*logon*) that I judged to be the strongest . . . (99*d*–100*a*)

Logos is a thus a *resource*. One *must turn* to it, and not merely when the solar source is *present* and risks burning the eyes if stared at; one has also to turn away toward *logos* when the sun seems to withdraw during its eclipse. Dead, extinguished, or hidden, that star is more dangerous than ever.

We will let these yarns of suns and sons spin on for a while. Up to now we have only followed this line so as to move from *logos* to the father, so as to tie speech to the *kurios*, the master, the lord, another name given in the *Republic* to the good-sun-capital-father (508*a*). Later, within the same tissue, within the same texts, we will draw on other filial filaments, pull the same strings once more, and witness the weaving or unraveling of other designs.

* * *

FROM 4. THE PHARMAKON

Let us return to the text of Plato, assuming we have ever really left it.[8] The word *pharmakon* is caught in a chain of significations. The play of that chain seems systematic. But the system here is not, simply, that of the intentions of an author who goes by the name of Plato. The system is not primarily that of what someone *meant-to-say* [*un vouloir-dire*]. Finely regulated communications are established, through the play of language, among diverse functions of the word and, within it, among diverse strata or regions of culture.

* * *

We have just sketched out the correspondence between the figure of Theuth in Egyptian mythology and a certain organization of concepts, philosophemes, metaphors, and mythemes picked up from what is called the Platonic text. The word *pharmakon* has seemed to us extremely apt for the task of tying all the threads of this correspondence together. Let us now reread, in a rendering derived from Robin, this sentence from the *Phaedrus*: "Here, O King, says Theuth, is a discipline (*mathēma*) that will make the Egyptians wiser (*sophōterous*) and will improve their memories (*mnēmonikōterous*): both memory (*mnēmē*) and instruction (*sophia*) have found their remedy (*pharmakon*)."

The common translation of *pharmakon* by *remedy* [*remède*]—a beneficent drug—is not, of course, inaccurate. Not only can *pharmakon* really mean *remedy* and thus erase, on a certain surface of its functioning, the ambiguity of its meaning. But it is even quite obvious here, the stated intention of Theuth being precisely to stress the worth of his product, that he *turns* the word on its strange and invisible pivot, presenting it from a single one, the

8. In section 3 (omitted here), Derrida has outlined the genealogy of the myth of Theuth.

most reassuring, of its *poles*.[9] This medicine is beneficial; it repairs and produces, accumulates and remedies, increases knowledge and reduces forgetfulness. Its translation by "remedy" nonetheless erases, in going outside the Greek language, the other pole reserved in the word *pharmakon*. It cancels out the resources of ambiguity and makes more difficult, if not impossible, an understanding of the context. As opposed to "drug" or even "medicine," *remedy* says the transparent rationality of science, technique, and therapeutic causality, thus excluding from the text any leaning toward the magic virtues of a force whose effects are hard to master, a dynamics that constantly surprises the one who tries to manipulate it as master and as subject.

Now, *on the one hand*, Plato is bent on presenting writing as an occult, and therefore suspect, power. Just like painting, to which he will later compare it, and like optical illusions and the techniques of *mimēsis*[1] in general. His mistrust of the mantic and magic, of sorcerers and casters of spells, is well attested.[2] In the *Laws*, in particular, he reserves them terrible punishments. According to an operation we will have cause to remember later, he recommends that they be excluded—expelled or cut off—from the social arena. Expulsion and ostracism can even be accomplished at the same time, by keeping them in prison, where they would no longer be visited by free men but only by the slave that would bring them their food; then by depriving them of burial: "At death he shall be cast out beyond the borders without burial, and if any free citizen has a hand in his burial, he shall be liable to a prosecution for impiety at the suit of any who cares to take proceedings" (X, 909*b*–*c*).

On the other hand, the King's reply presupposes that the effectiveness of the *pharmakon* can be reversed: it can worsen the ill instead of remedy it. Or rather, the royal answer suggests that Theuth, by ruse and/or naïveté, has exhibited the reverse of the true effects of writing. In order to vaunt the worth of his invention, Theuth would thus have denatured the *pharmakon*, said the opposite (*tounantion*) of what writing is capable of. He has passed a poison off as a remedy. So that in translating *pharmakon* by *remedy*, what one respects is not what Theuth intended, nor even what Plato intended, but rather what the King says Theuth has said, effectively deluding either the King or himself. If Plato's text then goes on to give the King's pronouncement as the truth of Theuth's production and his speech as the truth of writing, then the translation *remedy* makes Theuth into a simpleton or a flimflam artist, *from the sun's point of view*. From that viewpoint, Theuth has no doubt played on the word, interrupting, for his own purposes, the communication between the two opposing values. But the King restores that communication, and the translation takes no account of this. And all the while the two interlocutors, whatever they do and whether or not they choose, remain within the unity of the same signifier. Their discourse plays within it, which is no longer the case in translation. *Remedy* is the rendition that, more than "medicine" or "drug" would have done, obliterates the virtual, dynamic references to the other uses of the same word in Greek. The effect of such a translation

9. Derrida is making a link between the tipping of the earth (on one of its poles) and the privileging of one side of a polarity.

1. Imitation, representation (Greek).

2. Cf. in particular *Republic* 2.364ff.; Letter 7, 333e. The problem is raised with copious and useful references in E. Moutsopoulos, *La Musique dans l'œuvre de Platon* [*Music in the Work of Plato*] (Paris: Presses Universitaires de France, 1959), pp. 13ff. [Derrida's note].

is most importantly to destroy what we will later call Plato's anagrammatic writing,[3] to destroy it by interrupting the relations interwoven among different functions of the same word in different places, relations that are virtually but necessarily "citational." When a word inscribes itself as the citation of another sense of the same word, when the textual center-stage of the word *pharmakon*, even while it means *remedy*, cites, re-cites, and makes legible that which *in the same word* signifies, in another spot and on a different level of the stage, *poison* (for example, since that is not the only other thing *pharmakon* means), the choice of only one of these renditions by the translator has as its first effect the neutralization of the citational play, of the "anagram," and, in the end, quite simply of the very textuality of the translated text. It could no doubt be shown, and we will try to do so when the time comes, that this blockage of the passage among opposing values is itself already an effect of "Platonism," the consequence of something already at work in the translated text, in the relation between "Plato" and his "language." There is no contradiction between this proposition and the preceding one. Textuality being constituted by differences and by differences from differences, it is by nature absolutely heterogeneous and is constantly composing with the forces that tend to annihilate it.

One must therefore accept, follow, and analyze the composition of these two forces or of these two gestures. That composition is even, in a certain sense, the single theme of this essay. On the one hand Plato decides in favor of a logic that does not tolerate such passages between opposing senses of the same word, all the more so since such a passage would reveal itself to be something quite different from simple confusion, alternation, or the dialectic of opposites. And yet, on the other hand, the *pharmakon*, if our reading confirms itself, constitutes the original medium of that decision, the element that precedes it, comprehends it, goes beyond it, can never be reduced to it, and is not separated from it by a single word (or signifying apparatus), operating within the Greek and Platonic text. All translations into languages that are the heirs and depositaries of Western metaphysics thus produce on the *pharmakon* an *effect of analysis* that violently destroys it, reduces it to one of its simple elements by interpreting it, paradoxically enough, in the light of the ulterior developments it itself has made possible. Such an interpretative translation is thus as violent as it is impotent: it destroys the *pharmakon* but at the same time forbids itself access to it, leaving it untouched in its reserve.

The translation by "remedy" can thus be neither accepted nor simply rejected. Even if one intended thereby to save the "rational" pole and the laudatory intention, the idea of the *correct* use of the *science* or *art* of medicine, one would still run every risk of being deceived by language. Writing is no more valuable, says Plato, as a remedy than as a poison. Even before Thamus has let fall his pejorative sentence, the remedy is disturbing in itself. One must indeed be aware of the fact that Plato is suspicious of the *pharmakon* in general, even in the case of drugs used exclusively for therapeutic ends, even when they are wielded with good intentions, and even when they are as such

3. Patterns formed by rearranging letters or words. Generalizing from writings (not published until in the 1960s) of Ferdinand de Saussure, who thought he found proper names "anagrammatically" encoded in Latin poetry, many scholars, Derrida included, saw all texts as potentially tissues of anagrams—relations that, regardless of the author's conscious intentions, might reveal something fundamental to writing.

effective. There is no such thing as a harmless remedy. The *pharmakon* can never be simply beneficial.

For two different reasons, and at two different depths. First of all because the beneficial essence or virtue of a *pharmakon* does not prevent it from hurting. The *Protagoras* classes the *pharmaka* among the things that can be both good (*agatha*) and painful (*aniara*) (354*a*). The *pharmakon* is always caught in the mixture (*summeikton*) mentioned in the *Philebus* (46*a*), examples of which are *hubris*, that violent, unbounded excess of pleasure that makes the profligate cry out like a madman (45*e*), and "relieving an itch by rubbing, and anything that can be treated by such a remedy (*ouk allēs deomena pharmaxeōs*)." This type of painful pleasure, linked as much to the malady as to its treatment, is a *pharmakon* in itself. It partakes of both good and ill, of the agreeable and the disagreeable. Or rather, it is within its mass that these oppositions are able to sketch themselves out.

Then again, more profoundly, even beyond the question of pain, the pharmaceutical remedy is essentially harmful because it is artificial. In this, Plato is following Greek tradition and, more precisely, the doctors of Cos.[4] The *pharmakon* goes against natural life: not only life unaffected by any illness, but even sick life, or rather the life of the sickness. For Plato believes in the natural life and normal development, so to speak, of disease. In the *Timaeus*, natural disease, like *logos* in the *Phaedrus*, is compared to a living organism which must be allowed to develop according to its own norms and forms, its specific rhythms and articulations. In disturbing the normal and natural progress of the illness, the *pharmakon* is thus the enemy of the living in general, whether healthy or sick. One must bear this in mind, and Plato invites us to do so, when writing is proposed as a *pharmakon*. Contrary to life, writing—or, if you will, the *pharmakon*—can only *displace* or even *aggravate* the ill. Such will be, in its logical outlines, the objection the king raises to writing: under pretext of supplementing memory, writing makes one even more forgetful; far from increasing knowledge, it diminishes it. Writing does not answer the needs of memory, it aims to the side, does not reinforce the *mnēmē*, but only *hypomnēsis*.[5]

* * *

Sophistics—the deployment of hypomnesia—as well as dialectics—the deployment of anamnesia[6]—both presuppose the possibility of repetition. But sophistics this time keeps to the other side, to the other face, as it were, of repetition. And of signification. What is repeated is the repeater, the imitator, the signifier, the representative, in the absence, as it happens, of *the thing itself*, which these appear to reedit, and without psychic or mnesic animation, without the living tension of dialectics. Writing would indeed be the signifier's capacity to repeat itself by itself, mechanically, without a living soul to sustain or attend it in its repetition, that is to say, without truth's *presenting itself* anywhere. Sophistics, hypomnesia, and writing would thus only be separated from philosophy, dialectics, anamnesis, and living speech by the

4. That is, the followers of Hippocrates (ca. 460–ca. 377 B.C.E.), the most celebrated physician in antiquity, who was born on the island of Cos.

5. A reminding (Greek).

6. Recollection. "Hypomnesia": remembrance via a reminder.

invisible, almost nonexistent, thickness of that *leaf* between the signifier and the signified.[7] The "leaf": a significant metaphor, we should note, or rather one taken from the signifier face of things, since the leaf with its recto and verso first appears as a surface and support for writing. But by the same token, doesn't the unity of this leaf, of the system of this difference between signified and signifier, also point to the inseparability of sophistics and philosophy? The difference between signifier and signified is no doubt the governing pattern within which Platonism institutes itself and determines its opposition to sophistics. In being inaugurated in this manner, philosophy and dialectics are determined in the act of determining their other.

This profound complicity in the break has a first consequence: the argumentation against writing in the *Phaedrus* is able to borrow all its resources from Isocrates or Alcidamas at the moment it turns their own weapons, "transposing" them,[8] against the sophists. Plato imitates the imitators in order to restore the truth of what they imitate: namely, truth itself. Indeed, only truth as the presence (*ousia*) of the present (*on*) is here discriminative. And its power to discriminate, which commands or, as you will, is commanded by the difference between signified and signifier, in any case remains systematically inseparable from that difference. And this discrimination itself becomes so subtle that eventually it separates nothing, in the final analysis, but the same from itself, from its perfect, almost indistinguishable double. This is a movement that produces itself entirely within the structure of ambiguity and reversibility of the *pharmakon*.

How indeed does the dialectician simulate him whom he denounces as a simulator, as the simulacrum-man? On the one hand, the sophists advised, as does Plato, the exercise of memory. But, as we have seen, it was in order to enable themselves to speak without knowing, to recite without judgment, without regard for truth, in order to give signs. Or rather in order to sell them. Through this economy of signs, the sophists are indisputably men of writing at the moment they are protesting they are not. But isn't Plato one, too, through a symmetrical effect of reversal? Not only because he is actually a writer (a banal argument we will specify later on) and cannot, whether *de facto* or *de jure*, explain what dialectics is without recourse to writing; not only because he judges that the repetition of the same is necessary in anamnesis; but also because he judges it indispensable as an inscription in the type. (It is notable that *tupos* applies with equal pertinence to the graphic impression and to the *eidos*[9] as model. Among many other examples, cf. *Republic*, 402*d*.) This necessity belongs to the order of the law and is posited by the *Laws*. In this instance, the immutable, petrified identity of writing is not simply added to the signified law or prescribed rule like a mute, stupid simulacrum: it assures the law's permanence and identity with the vigilance of a guardian.[1] As another sort of guardian of the laws, writing guarantees

7. In his *Course in General Linguistics* (see above), Saussure uses the image of a *leaf* to describe the relation between the signifier and the signified; sophistry and philosophy are as closely connected—and as far apart—as the signifier and the signified.

8. We are here using Auguste Diès's word, referring to his study of *La Transposition platonicienne*, more precisely to his first chapter, "La Transposition de la rhétorique," in *Autour de Platon*, 2:400 [Derrida's note].

9. Form, shape (Greek); in Plato, one of the perfect and immutable transcendent Forms that, imperfectly recollected, are the source of all knowledge (see, e.g., *Meno* 81d; *Phaedo* 75b–e).

1. "Guardian" (*phulax*) is what Plato calls the rulers of his ideal city in the *Republic*.

the means of returning at will, as often as necessary, to that ideal object called the law. We can thus scrutinize it, question it, consult it, make it talk, without altering its identity. All this, even in the same words (notably *boētheia*[2]), is the other side, exactly opposite, of Socrates' speech in the *Phaedrus.*

> *Clinias*: And, mark you, such argument will be a most valuable aid to intelligent legislation (*nomothesia*), because legal prescriptions (*prostagmata*), once put into writing (*en grammasi tethenta*), remain always on record, as though to challenge the question of all time to come. Hence we need feel no dismay if they should be difficult on a first hearing, since even the dull student may return to them for reiterated scrutiny. Nor does their length, provided they are beneficial, make it less irrational than it is impious, in my opinion at least, for any man to refuse such discourse his heartiest support (*to mē ou boēthein toutois tois logois*). (X, 891*a*. I am still quoting from an authorized translation,[3] including the Greek where pertinent, and leaving the reader to appreciate the usual effects of translation. On the relation between written and unwritten laws, see notably VII, 793*b*–*c*.)

The italicized Greek words amply demonstrate it: the *prostagmata* of the law can be *posited* only in writing (*en grammasi tethenta*). *Nomothesia* is engrammatical. The legislator is a writer. And the judge a reader. Let us skip to book XII: "He that would show himself a righteously equal judge must keep these matters before his eyes; he must procure books (*grammata*) on the subject, and must make them his study. There is, in truth, no study whatsoever so potent as this of law, if the law be what it should be, to make a better man of its student" (975*c*).

Inversely, symmetrically, the rhetors had not waited around for Plato in order to *translate writing into judgment*. For Isocrates, for Alcidamas, *logos* was also a living thing (*zōon*) whose vigor, richness, agility, and flexibility were limited and constrained by the cadaverous rigidity of the written sign. The type does not adapt to the changing givens of the present situation, to what is unique and irreplaceable about it each time, with all the subtlety required. While *presence* is the general form of what is, the *present*, for its part, is always different. But writing, in that it repeats itself and remains identical in the type, cannot flex itself in all senses, cannot bend with all the differences among presents, with all the variable, fluid, furtive necessities of psychagogy. He who speaks, in contrast, is not controlled by any preestablished pattern; he is better able to conduct his signs; he is there to accentuate them, inflect them, retain them, or set them loose according to the demands of the moment, the nature of the desired effect, the hold he has on the listener. In attending his signs in their operation, he who acts by vocal means penetrates more easily into the soul of his disciple, producing effects that are always unique, leading the disciple, as though lodged within him, to the intended goal. It is thus not its pernicious violence but its

2. Help, aid (Greek).
3. Derrida is quoting from Diès; I am quoting from A. E. Taylor. Interestingly, another of these "effects of translation" is precisely the difficulty involved in translating a discussion of effects of translation [translator's note].

breathless impotence that the sophists held against writing. In contrast to this blind servant with its haphazard, clumsy movements, the Attic school (Gorgias, Isocrates, Alcidamas) extolled the force of living *logos*, the great master, the great power: *logos dunastēs megas estin,*[4] says Gorgias in his *Encomium of Helen*. The dynasty of speech may be just as violent as that of writing, but its infiltration is more profound, more penetrating, more diverse, more assured. The only ones who take refuge in writing are those who are no better speakers than the man in the street. Alcidamas recalls this in his treatise "on those who write speeches" and "on the Sophists." Writing is considered a consolation, a compensation, a remedy for sickly speech.

Despite these similarities, the condemnation of writing is not engaged in the same way by the rhetors as it is in the *Phaedrus*. If the written word is scorned, it is not as a *pharmakon* coming to corrupt memory and truth. It is because *logos* is a more effective *pharmakon*. This is what Gorgias calls it. As a *pharmakon, logos* is at once good and bad; it is not at the outset governed exclusively by goodness or truth. It is only within this ambivalence and this mysterious indetermination of *logos*, and after these have been recognized, that Gorgias *determines* truth as a *world*, a structure or order, the counterpart (*kosmos*) of *logos*. In so doing he no doubt prefigures the Platonic gesture. But before such a determination, we are in the ambivalent, indeterminate space of the *pharmakon*, of that which in *logos* remains potency, potentiality, and is not yet the transparent language of knowledge. If one were justified in trying to capture it in categories that are subsequent to and dependent upon the history thus opened up, categories arising precisely *in the aftermath of decision*, one would have to speak of the "irrationality" of living *logos*, of its spellbinding powers of enchantment, mesmerizing fascination, and alchemical transformation, which make it kin to witchcraft and magic. Sorcery (*goēteia*), psychagogy, such are the "facts and acts" of speech, the most fearsome of *pharmaka*. In his *Encomium of Helen*, Gorgias used these very words to qualify the power of speech.

> Sacred incantations sung with words (*hai gar entheoi dia logōn epōidai*) are bearers of pleasure and banishers of pain, for, merging with opinion in the soul, the power of incantation is wont to beguile it (*ethelxe*) and persuade it and alter it by witchcraft (*goēteiai*). There have been discovered two arts of witchcraft and magic: one consists of errors of soul and the other of deceptions of opinion. . . . What cause then prevents the conclusion that Helen similarly, against her will, might have come under the influence (*humnos*) of speech, just as if ravished by the force of the mighty? . . . For speech constrained the soul, persuading it which it persuaded, both to believe the things said and to approve the things done. The persuader, like a constrainer, does the wrong and the persuaded, like the constrained, in speech is wrongly charged.[5]

4. *Logos* is a great lord (Greek). For the *Encomium* (ca. 400 B.C.E.), a defense of Helen of Troy (whose abduction from Greece by a Trojan prince led to the Trojan War), see above.

5. On this passage of the *Encomium*, on the relations of *thelgō* and *peithō*, of charm and persuasion, on their use in Homer, Aeschylus, and Plato, see Diès, pp. 116–17 [Derrida's note]. English translation by George Kennedy, in *The Older Sophists*, ed. R. K. Sprague (Columbia: University of South Carolina Press, 1972), pp. 50–54 [translator's note].

Persuasive eloquence (*peithō*) is the power to break in, to carry off, to seduce internally, to ravish invisibly. It is furtive force per se. But in showing that Helen gave in to the violence of speech (would she have yielded to a letter?), in disculpating[6] this victim, Gorgias indicts *logos* in its capacity to lie. "By introducing some reasoning (*logismon*) into speech (*tōi logōi*)," he wishes "to free the accused of blame and, having reproved her detractors as prevaricators and proved the truth, to free her from their ignorance."

But before being reined in and tamed by the *kosmos* and order of truth, *logos* is a wild creature, an ambiguous animality. Its magical "pharmaceutical" force derives from this ambivalence, which explains the disproportion between the strength of that force and the inconsiderable thing speech seems to be:

> But if it was speech which persuaded her and deceived her heart, not even to this is it difficult to make an answer and to banish blame as follows. Speech is a powerful lord, which by means of the finest and most invisible body effects the divinest words: it can stop fear and banish grief and create joy and nurture pity.

Such persuasion entering the soul through speech is indeed a *pharmakon*, and that is precisely what Gorgias calls it:

> The effect of speech (*tou logou dunamis*) upon the condition of the soul (*pros tēn tēs psuchēs taxin*) is comparable (*ton auton de logon*) to the power of drugs (*tōn pharmakōn taxis*) over the nature of bodies (*tēn tōn somatōn phusin*). For just as different drugs dispel different secretions from the body, and some bring an end to disease and others to life, so also in the case of speeches, some distress, others delight, some cause fear, others make the hearers bold, and some drug and bewitch the soul with a kind of evil persuasion (*tēn psuchēn epharmakeusan kai exegoēteusan*).

The reader will have paused to reflect that the relation (the analogy) between the *logos*/soul relation and the *pharmakon*/body relation is itself designated by the term *logos*. The name of the relation is the same as that of one of its terms. The *pharmakon* is *comprehended* in the structure of *logos*. This comprehension is an act of both *domination* and *decision*.

5. THE PHARMAKEUS

> For if there were nothing any more to hurt us, we should have no need whatever of any assistance. And thus you see it would then be made apparent that it was only on account of evil that we felt regard and affection for good (*tagathon*), as we considered good to be a medicine (*pharmakon*) for evil, and evil to be a disease. But where there is no disease, there is, we are aware, no need of medicine (*ouden dei pharmakou*). This, then, it appears, is the nature of good. . . .
>
> —Yes, he said, that would seem to be true.
>
> —*Lysis*, 220c–d

But if this is the case, and if *logos* is already a penetrating supplement, then isn't Socrates, "he who does not write," also a master of the *pharmakon*?

6. Clearing from blame.

And in that way isn't he the spitting image of a sophist? a *pharmakeus?* a magician? a sorcerer? even a poisoner? and even one of those impostors denounced by Gorgias? The threads of these complicities are almost impossible to disentangle.

Socrates in the dialogues of Plato often has the face of a *pharmakeus*. That is the name given by Diotima[7] to Eros. But behind the portrait of Eros, one cannot fail to recognize the features of Socrates, as though Diotima, in looking at him, were proposing to Socrates the portrait of Socrates (*Symposium*, 203*c, d, e*). Eros, who is neither rich, nor beautiful, nor delicate, spends his life philosophizing (*philosophōn dia pantos tou biou*); he is a fearsome sorcerer (*deinos goēs*), magician (*pharmakeus*), and sophist (*sophistēs*). A being that no "logic" can confine within a noncontradictory definition, an individual of the demonic species, neither god nor man, neither immortal nor mortal, neither living nor dead, he forms "the medium of the prophetic arts, of the priestly rites of sacrifice, initiation, and incantation, of divination and of sorcery (*thusias-teletas-epōidas-manteian*)" (202*e*).

In that same dialogue, Agathon accuses Socrates of trying to bewitch him, to cast a spell over him (*Pharmattein boulei me, ō Sōkrates*, 194*a*). The portrait of Eros by Diotima is placed between this exclamation and the portrait of Socrates by Alcibiades.[8]

Who reminds us that Socrates' brand of magic is worked through *logos* without the aid of any instrument, through the effects of a voice without accessories, without the flute of the satyr[9] Marsyas:

> And aren't you a piper as well? I should think you were—and a far more wonderful piper than Marsyas, who had only to put his flute to his lips to bewitch mankind. . . . His tunes will still have a magic power, and by virtue of their own divinity they will show which of us are fit subjects for divine initiation. Now the only difference, Socrates, between you and Marsyas is that you can get just the same effect without any instrument at all (*aneu organōn*)—with nothing but a few simple words (*psilois logois*[1]). . . ."(215*c–d*)

When confronted with this simple, organless voice, one cannot escape its penetration by stopping up one's ears, like Ulysses[2] trying to block out the Sirens (216*a*).

The Socratic *pharmakon* also acts like venom, like the bite of a poisonous snake (217–18). And Socrates' bite is worse than a snake's since its traces invade the soul. What Socrates' words and the viper's venom have in common, in any case, is their ability to penetrate and make off with the most

7. The woman who, in Plato's *Symposium*, gives Socrates instruction about love.
8. Athenian general and statesman (ca. 450–404 B.C.E), who praises Socrates at the end of the *Symposium*. Agathon (d. ca. 401 B.C.E.), Greek tragic poet; the *Symposium* represents a feast in honor of his victory (tragedies were presented in a competition, as part of a religious festival).
9. In Greek mythology, an attendant (often represented as part goat) of Dionysus, god of wine; Marsyas had such confidence in his flute playing that he challenged Apollo, god of music, to a musical contest (and was flayed alive when he lost).

1. "Bare, ungarnished voice, etc."; *psilos logos* also has the sense of abstract argument or simple affirmation without proof (cf. *Theaetetus* 165e) [Derrida's note].
2. Odysseus, Greek king of Ithaca, whose efforts to return home after the Trojan War are recounted in Homer's *Odyssey* (ca. 8th c. B.C.E.); he ordered his crew to fill their ears with wax and tie him to the mast of his ship so that he might safely hear the Sirens—mythical monsters, half woman and half bird, whose singing so entranced passing sailors that the listeners forgot to eat, and died (*Odyssey* 12.173–200).

concealed interiority of the body or soul. The demonic speech of this thaumaturge (en)trains the listener in dionysian frenzy[3] and philosophic *mania* (218*b*). And when they don't act like the venom of a snake, Socrates' pharmaceutical charms provoke a kind of *narcosis*, benumbing and paralyzing into aporia,[4] like the touch of a sting ray (*narkē*):

> *Meno*: Socrates, even before I met you they told me that in plain truth you are a perplexed man yourself and reduce others to perplexity. At this moment I feel you are exercising magic and witchcraft upon me and positively laying me under your spell until I am just a mass of helplessness (*goēteueis me kai pharmatteis kai atekhnōs ketepaideis, hōste meston aporias gegonenai*). If I may be flippant, I think that not only in outward appearance (*eidos*) but in other respects as well you are exactly like the flat stringray (*narkē*) that one meets in the sea. Whenever anyone comes into contact with it, it numbs him, and that is the sort of thing that you seem to be doing to me now. My mind and my lips are literally numb, and I have nothing to reply to you. . . . In my opinion you are well advised not to leave Athens and live abroad. If you behaved like this as a foreigner in another country, you would most likely be arrested as a wizard (*goēs*). (*Meno*, 80*a–b*)

Socrates arrested as a wizard (*goēs* or *pharmakeus*): that will have to wait.

What can be said about this *analogy* that ceaselessly refers the Socratic *pharmakon* to the sophistic *pharmakon* and, proportioning them to each other, makes us go back indefinitely from one to the other? How can they be distinguished?

Irony does not consist in the dissolution of a sophistic charm or in the dismantling of an occult substance or power through analysis and questioning. It does not consist in undoing the charlatanesque confidence of a *pharmakeus* from the vantage point of some obstinate instance of transparent reason or innocent *logos*. Socratic irony precipitates out one *pharmakon* by bringing it in contact with another *pharmakon*. Or rather, it reverses the *pharmakon*'s powers and turns *its* surface over[5]—thus taking effect, being recorded and dated, in the act of *classing* the *pharmakon*, through the fact that the *pharmakon* properly consists in a certain inconsistency, a certain impropriety, this nonidentity-with-itself always allowing it to be turned against itself.

What is at stake in this overturning is no less than science and death. Which are consigned to a single type in the structure of the *pharmakon*, the one and only name for that portion that must be awaited. And even, in Socrates' case, deserved.

3. The ecstatic enthusiasm of the worshippers of Dionysus; on the creative force of this frenzy (connected with music), see FRIEDRICH NIETZSCHE, *The Birth of Tragedy* (1872; above).

4. Difficulty, logical impasse (a term often used in deconstructive criticism to indicate the point in a text where inherent contradictions render interpretation undecidable).

5. Alternately and/or all at once, the Socratic *pharmakon* petrifies and vivifies, anesthetizes and sensitizes, appeases and anguishes. Socrates is a benumbing stingray but also an animal that needles: we recall the bee in the *Phaedo* (91c); later we will open the *Apology* at the point where Socrates compares himself precisely to a gadfly. This whole Socratic configuration thus composes a bestiary. Is it surprising that the demonic inscribes itself in a bestiary? It is on the basis of this zoopharmaceutical ambivalence and of that other Socratic *analogy* that the contours of the *anthrōpos* [human] are determined [Derrida's note].

II

* * *

FROM 9. PLAY: FROM THE PHARMAKON TO THE LETTER AND FROM BLINDNESS TO THE SUPPLEMENT

It has been thought that Plato simply condemned play. And by the same token the art of *mimēsis* which is only a type of play.[6] But in all questions involving play and its "opposite," the "logic" will necessarily be baffling. Play and art are lost by Plato as he saves them, and his logos is then subject to that untold constraint that can no longer even be called "logic." Plato does very well speak of play. He speaks in praise of it. But he praises play "in the best sense of the word," if this can be said without eliminating play beneath the reassuring silliness of such a precaution. The best sense of play is play that is supervised and contained within the safeguards of ethics and politics. This is play comprehended under the innocent, innocuous category of "fun." Amusement: however far off it may be, the common translation of *paidia* by *pastime* [*divertissement*] no doubt only helps consolidate the Platonic repression of play.

The opposition *spoudē/paidia*[7] will never be one of simple symmetry. *Either* play is *nothing* (and that is its only *chance*); either it can give place to no activity, to no discourse worthy of the name—that is, one charged with truth or at least with meaning—and then it is *alogos* or *atopos*.[8] *Or else* play begins to *be* something and its very presence lays it open to some sort of dialectical confiscation. It takes on meaning and works in the service of seriousness, truth and ontology. Only *logoi peri ontōn*[9] can be taken seriously. As soon as it comes into being and into language, play *erases itself as such*. Just as writing must erase itself as such before truth, etc. The point is that there *is* no *as such* where writing or play are concerned. Having no essence, introducing difference as the condition for the presence of essence, opening up the possibility of the double, the copy, the imitation, the simulacrum—the game and the *graphē*[1] are constantly disappearing as they go along. They cannot, in classical affirmation, be affirmed without being negated.

Plato thus plays at taking play seriously. That is what we earlier called the stunning hand Plato has dealt himself. Not only are his writings defined as games,[2] but human affairs in general do not in his eyes need to be taken seriously. One thinks of the famous passage in the *Laws*. Let us reread it despite its familiarity, so as to follow the theological assumption of play into games, the progressive neutralization of the *singularity* of play:

> To be sure, man's life is a business which does not deserve to be taken too seriously (*megalēs men spoudēs ouk axia*); yet we cannot help being in earnest with it, and there's the pity. Still, as we are here in this world, no doubt, for us the becoming thing is to show this earnestness in a suitable way (*hēmin summetron*). . . . I mean we should keep our seriousness

6. Cf. *Republic* 10.602a–b; *Statesman* 288c–d; *Sophist* 234b–c; *Laws* 2.667e–668a; *Epinomis* 975d, etc. [Derrida's note].
7. Seriousness/play (Greek).
8. Not *logos* or not *topos* (place).
9. Words about real things (Greek).
1. Writing; indictment (Greek).
2. Cf. *Parmenides* 137b; *Statesman* 268d; *Timaeus* 59c–d. On the context and historical background of this problematic of play, cf. notably P. M. Schuhl, *Platon et l'art de son temps* [*Plato and the Art of His Time*, 2d ed.] (Paris: Presses Universitaires de France, 1952), pp. 61–63 [Derrida's note].

> for serious things, and not waste it on trifles, and that, while God is the real goal of all beneficent serious endeavor (*makariou spoudēs*), man, as we said before,[3] has been constructed as a toy (*paignion*) for God, and this is, in fact, the finest thing about him. All of us, then, men and women alike, must fall in with our role and spend life in making our *play* as perfect as possible—to the complete inversion of current theory. . . . It is the current fancy that our serious work should be done for the sake of our play; thus it is held that war is serious work which ought to be well discharged for the sake of peace. But the truth is that in war we do not find, and we never shall find, either any real play or any real education worth the name, and *these* are the things I count supremely serious for such creatures as ourselves. Hence it is peace in which each of us should spend most of his life and spend it best. What, then, is our right course? We should pass our lives in the playing of games—*certain* games, that is, sacrifice, song, and dance—with the result of ability to gain heaven's grace, and to repel and vanquish an enemy when we have to fight him. . . . (803*b–e*)

Play is always lost when it seeks salvation in games. We have examined elsewhere, in "Rousseau's era,"[4] this disappearance of play into games. This (non)logic of play and of writing enables us to understand what has always been considered so baffling:[5] why Plato, while subordinating or condemning writing and play, should have written so much, presenting his writings, *from out of Socrates' death*, as games, *indicting* writing in writing, lodging against it that complaint (*graphē*) whose reverberations even today have not ceased to resound.

What law governs this "contradiction," this opposition to itself of what is said against writing, of a dictum that pronounces itself against itself as soon as it finds its way into writing, as soon as it writes down its self-identity and carries away what is proper to it *against* this ground of writing? This "contradiction," which is nothing other than the relation-to-self of diction as it opposes itself to scription, as it *chases* itself (away) in hunting down what is properly its *trap*—this contradiction is not contingent. In order to convince ourselves of this, it would already suffice to note that what seems to inaugurate itself in Western literature with Plato will not fail to re-edit itself at least in Rousseau, and then in Saussure. In these three cases, in these three "eras" of the repetition of Platonism, which give us a new thread to follow and other knots to recognize in the history of *philosophia* or the *epistēmē*,[6] the exclusion and the devaluation of writing must somehow, in their very affirmation, come to terms with:

3. Cf. *Laws* 1.644d–e: "Let us look at the whole matter in some such light as this. We may imagine that each of us living creatures is a puppet made by gods, possibly as a plaything (*hōs paignion*) or possibly with some more serious purpose (*hōs spoudēi tini*). That, indeed, is more than we can tell, but one thing is certain. These interior states are, so to say, the cords, or strings, by which we are worked; they are opposed to one another, and pull us with opposite tensions in the direction of opposite actions, and therein lies the division of virtue from vice. In fact, so says our argument (*logos*), a man must always yield to one of these tensions without resistance, but pull against all the other strings—must yield, that is, to that golden and hallowed drawing of judgments (*tēn tou logismou agōgēn khrusēn kai hieran*) which goes by the name of the public law of the city. The others are hard and ironlike, it soft, as befits gold, whereas they resemble very various substances." Let us henceforth keep hold of this rein called *khrusos* [gold] or *chrysology* [Derrida's note].

4. Cf. *Of Grammatology* [Derrida's note].

5. The principal references are collected in L. Robin's *La Théorie platonicienne de l'amour* [*The Platonic Theory of Love*], 2d ed. (Paris: Presses Universitaires de France, 1964), pp. 54–59 [Derrida's note].

6. Knowledge, professional skill, profession (Greek).

1. a generalized sort of writing and, along with it,
2. a "contradiction": the written proposal of logocentrism; the simultaneous affirmation of the being-outside of the outside and of its injurious intrusion into the inside;
3. the construction of a "literary" work. Before Saussure's *Anagrams*, there were Rousseau's; and Plato's work, outside and independent of its logocentric "content," which is then only one of its inscribed "functions," can be read in its anagrammatical texture.

Thus it is that the "linguistics" elaborated by Plato, Rousseau, and Saussure must both put writing out of the question and yet nevertheless borrow from it, for fundamental reasons, all its demonstrative and theoretical resources. As far as the Genevans[7] are concerned, we have tried to show this elsewhere. The case is at least equally clear for Plato.

* * *

Grammatical science is doubtless not in itself dialectics. Plato indeed explicitly subordinates the former to the latter (253*b*–*c*). And, to him, this distinction can be taken for granted; but what, in the final analysis, justifies it? Both are in a sense sciences of language. For dialectics is also the science that guides us "*dia tōn logōn*,"[8] on the voyage through discourses or arguments (253*b*). At this point, what distinguishes dialectics from grammar appears twofold: on the one hand, the linguistic units it is concerned with are larger than the word (*Cratylus*, 385*a*–393*d*); on the other, dialectics is always guided by an intention of *truth*. It can only be satisfied by the presence of the *eidos*, which is here both the signified and the referent: the thing itself. The distinction between grammar and dialectics can thus only in all rigor be established at the point where truth is fully present and fills the *logos*. * * * If truth is the presence of the *eidos*, it must always, on pain of mortal blinding by the sun's fires, come to terms with relation, nonpresence, and thus nontruth. It then follows that the absolute precondition for a rigorous difference between grammar and dialectics (or ontology) cannot in principle be fulfilled. Or at least, it can perhaps be fulfilled *at the root of the principle*, at the point of arche-being or arche-truth.[9] * * * Which means, by the very necessity of *logos*. And that is the difference that prevents there being *in fact* any difference between grammar and ontology.

But now, what *is* the impossibility of any truth or of any full presence of being, of any fully-being? Or inversely, since such truth would be death as the absolute form of blindness, what is death as truth? Not *what is?* since the form of that question is produced by the very thing it questions, but how is the impossible plenitude of any absolute presence of the *ontōs on*[1] written? How is it inscribed? How is the necessity of the multiplicity of genres and ideas, of relation and difference, prescribed? How is dialectics traced?

The absolute invisibility of the origin of the visible, of the good-sun-father-capital, the unattainment of presence or beingness in any form, the whole surplus Plato calls *epekeina tēs ousias* (beyond beingness or presence), gives

7. Rousseau and Saussure.
8. Through the words (Greek).
9. "Arche-" derives from the Greek *archē*, meaning "beginning, origin."
1. The really real (literally, the "beingly being"; Greek), a term applied by Plato to the Forms.

rise to a structure of replacements such that all presences will be supplements substituted for the absent origin, and all differences, within the system of presence, will be the irreducible effect of what remains *epekeina tēs ousias*.

Just as Socrates supplements and replaces the father, as we have seen, dialectics supplements and replaces the impossible *noēsis*,[2] the forbidden intuition of the face of the father (good-sun-capital). The withdrawal of that face both opens and limits the exercise of dialectics. It welds it irremediably to its "inferiors," the mimetic arts, play, grammar, writing, etc. The disappearance of that face is the movement of difference which violently opens writing or, if one prefers, which opens itself to writing and which writing opens for itself. All these "movements," in all these "senses," belong to the same "system." * * * This philosophical, dialectical mastery of the *pharmaka* that should be handed down from legitimate father to well-born son is constantly put in question by a family scene that constitutes and undermines at once the passage between the pharmacy and the house. "Platonism" is both the general *rehearsal* of this family scene and the most powerful effort to master it, to prevent anyone's ever hearing of it, to conceal it by drawing the curtains over the dawning of the West. How can we set off in search of a different guard, if the pharmaceutical "system" contains not only, in a single stranglehold, the scene in the *Phaedrus*, * * * and the dialectics, logic, and mythology of Plato, but also, it seems, certain non-Greek structures of mythology? And if it is not certain that there are such things as non-Greek "mythologies"—the opposition *mythos/logos* being only authorized *following* Plato—into what general, unnamable necessity are we thrown? In other words, what does Platonism signify as repetition?

To repeat: the disappearance of the good-father-capital-sun is thus the precondition of discourse, taken this time as a moment and not as a principle of *generalized* writing. That writing (is) *epekeina tēs ousias*. The disappearance of truth as presence, the withdrawal of the present origin of presence, is the condition of all (manifestation of) truth. Nontruth is the truth. Nonpresence is presence. Difference, the disappearance of any originary presence, is *at once* the condition of possibility *and* the condition of impossibility of truth. At once. "At once" means that the being-present (*on*) in its truth, in the presence of its identity and in the identity of its presence, *is doubled* as soon as it appears, as soon as it presents itself. *It appears, in its essence, as* the possibility of its own most proper non-truth, of its pseudo-truth reflected in the icon, the phantasm, or the simulacrum. What is is not what it is, identical and identical to itself, unique, unless it *adds to itself* the possibility of being *repeated* as such. And its identity is hollowed out by that addition, withdraws itself in the supplement that presents it.

The disappearance of the Face or the structure of repetition can thus no longer be dominated by the value of truth. On the contrary, the opposition between the true and the untrue is entirely comprehended, *inscribed*, within this structure or this generalized writing. The true and the untrue are both species of repetition. And there is no repetition possible without the *graphics of supplementarity*, which supplies, for the lack of a full unity, another unit that comes to relieve it, being enough the same and enough other so that it can replace by addition. Thus, on the one hand, repetition is that without

2. Intelligence, understanding (Greek).

which there would be no truth: the truth of being in the intelligible form of ideality discovers in the *eidos* that which can be repeated, being the same, the clear, the stable, the identifiable in its equality with itself. And only the *eidos* can give rise to repetition as anamnesis or maieutics,[3] dialectics or didactics. Here repetition gives itself out to be a repetition of life. Tautology is life only going out of itself to come home to itself. Keeping close to itself through *mnēmē, logos*, and *phōnē*.[4] But on the other hand, repetition is the very movement of non-truth: the presence of what is gets lost, disperses itself, multiplies itself through mimemes,[5] icons, phantasms, simulacra, etc. Through phenomena, already. And this type of repetition is the possibility of becoming-perceptible-to-the-senses: nonideality. This is on the side of non-philosophy, bad memory, hypomnesia, writing. Here, tautology is life going out of itself beyond return. Death rehearsal. Unreserved spending. The irreducible excess, through the play of the supplement, of any self-intimacy of the living, the good, the true.

These two types of repetition relate to each other according to the graphics of supplementarity. Which means that one can no more "separate" them from each other, think of either one apart from the other, "label" them, than one can in *the pharmacy* distinguish the medicine from the poison, the good from the evil, the true from the false, the inside from the outside, the vital from the mortal, the first from the second, etc. Conceived within this original reversibility, the *pharmakon* is the *same* precisely because it has no identity. And the same (is) as supplement. Or in differance. In writing.[6] If he had *meant* to say something, such would have been the speech of Theuth making of writing as a *pharmakon* a singular present to the King.

But Theuth, it should be noted, spoke not another word.

The great god's sentence went unanswered.

. . . .

After closing the pharmacy, Plato went to retire, to get out of the sun. He took a few steps in the darkness toward the back of his reserves, found himself leaning over the *pharmakon*, decided to analyze.

Within the thick, cloudy liquid, trembling deep inside the drug, the whole pharmacy stood reflected, repeating the abyss of the Platonic phantasm.

The analyst cocks his ears, tries to distinguish between two repetitions.

He would like to isolate the good from the bad, the true from the false.

He leans over further: they repeat each other.

Holding the *pharmakon* in one hand, the calamus[7] in the other, Plato mutters as he transcribes the play of formulas. In the enclosed space of the pharmacy, the reverberations of the monologue are immeasurably amplified. The walled-in voice strikes against the rafters, the words come apart, bits and pieces of sentences are separated, disarticulated parts begin to circulate through the corridors, become fixed for a round or two, translate each other,

3. The Socratic midwifery by means of which the student gives birth to the truth.
4. Sound of the voice (Greek).
5. Constituent elements of mimesis.
6. Derrida has here analyzed the inexorable logic (or rather, graphic)—and not just the contingent metaphoricity—that leads Socrates to call *logos* "writing in the soul." In Section 8 of Part II of "Plato's Pharmacy" ("The Heritage of the Pharmakon: Family Scene" [omitted here]), he quotes from *Phaedrus* Socrates' definition of the discourse of truth: "The sort that goes together with knowledge, and is *written in the soul of the learner*, that can defend itself, and knows to whom it should speak and to whom it should say nothing" (276a; emphasis added).
7. Reed, pen.

become rejoined, bounce off each other, contradict each other, make trouble, tell on each other, come back like answers, organize their exchanges, protect each other, institute an internal commerce, take themselves for a dialogue. Full of meaning. A whole story. An entire history. All of philosophy.

* * *

1972

From Specters of Marx[1]

From *Chapter 1. Injunctions of Marx*

* * *

The specters of Marx. Why this plural? Would there be more than one of them? *Plus d'un* [More than one/No more one]: this can mean a crowd, if not masses, the horde, or society, or else some population of ghosts with or without a people, some community with or without a leader—but also the *less than one* of pure and simple dispersion. Without any possible gathering together. Then, if the specter is always animated by a spirit, one wonders who would dare to speak of a spirit of Marx, or more serious still, of a spirit of Marxism. Not only in order to predict a future for them today, but to appeal even to their multiplicity, or more serious still, to their heterogeneity.

More than a year ago, I had chosen to name the "specters" by their name starting with the title of this opening lecture. "Specters of Marx," the common noun and the proper name had thus been printed, they were already on the poster when, very recently, I reread *The Manifesto of the Communist Party*.[2] I confess it to my shame: I had not done so for decades—and that must tell one something. I knew very well there was a ghost waiting there, and from the opening, from the raising of the curtain. Now, of course, I have just discovered, in truth I have just remembered what must have been haunting my memory: the *first noun* of the *Manifesto*, and this time in the singular, is "specter": "A specter is haunting Europe—the specter of communism."

* * *

It was thus a fault on my part to have put so far out of memory what was the most manifest thing about the *Manifesto*. What manifests itself in the first place is a specter, this first paternal character, as powerful as it is unreal, a hallucination or simulacrum that is virtually more actual than what is so blithely called a living presence. Upon rereading the *Manifesto* and a few other great works of Marx, I said to myself that I know of few texts in the philosophical tradition, perhaps none, whose lesson seemed more urgent *today*, provided that one take into account what Marx and Engels themselves say (for example, in Engels' "Preface" to the 1888 re-edition[3]) about their own possible "aging" and their intrinsically irreducible historicity.

1. Translated by Peggy Kamuf, who sometimes gives French words and alternative translations in brackets. *Specters of Marx* began as two lectures given by Derrida in 1993 at a colloquium, "Whither Marxism?" When he revised the lectures for publication, he added passages in brackets.

2. Published in 1848 by KARL MARX (1818–1883) and FRIEDRICH ENGELS (1820–1895). Derrida quotes the first sentence.

3. The first English translation.

What other thinker has ever issued a similar warning in such an explicit fashion? Who has ever called for the *transformation* to come of his own theses? Not only in view of some progressive enrichment of knowledge, which would change nothing in the order of a system, but so as to take into account there, another account, the effects of rupture and restructuration? And so as to incorporate in advance, beyond any possible programming, the unpredictability of new knowledge, new techniques, and new political givens? No text in the tradition seems as lucid concerning the way in which the political is becoming worldwide, concerning the irreducibility of the technical and the media in the current of the most thinking thought—and this goes beyond the railroad and the newspapers of the time whose powers were analyzed in such an incomparable way in the *Manifesto*. And few texts have shed so much light on law, international law, and nationalism.

It will always be a fault not to read and reread and discuss Marx—which is to say also a few others—and to go beyond scholarly "reading" or "discussion." It will be more and more a fault, a failing of theoretical, philosophical, political responsibility. When the dogma machine and the "Marxist" ideological apparatuses (States, parties, cells, unions, and other places of doctrinal production) are in the process of disappearing,[4] we no longer have any excuse, only alibis, for turning away from this responsibility. There will be no future without this. Not without Marx, no future without Marx, without the memory and the inheritance of Marx: in any case of a certain Marx, of his genius, of at least one of his spirits. For this will be our hypothesis or rather our bias: *there is more than one of them, there must be more than one of them.*

Nevertheless, among all the temptations I will have to resist today, there would be the temptation of memory: to recount what was for me, and for those of my *generation* who shared it during a whole lifetime, the experience of Marxism, the quasi-paternal figure of Marx, the way it fought in us with other filiations, the reading of texts and the interpretation of a world in which the Marxist inheritance was—and still remains, and so it will remain—absolutely and thoroughly determinate. One need not be a Marxist or a communist in order to accept this obvious fact. We all live in a world, some would say a culture, that still bears, at an incalculable depth, the mark of this inheritance, whether in a directly visible fashion or not.

* * *

Many young people today (of the type "readers-consumers of Fukuyama"[5] or of the type "Fukuyama" himself) probably no longer sufficiently realize it: the eschatological themes of the "end of history," of the "end of Marxism," of the "end of philosophy," of the "ends of man," of the "last man" and so forth were, in the '50s, that is, forty years ago, our daily bread. We had this bread of apocalypse in our mouths naturally, already, just as naturally as that which I nicknamed after the fact, in 1980, the "apocalyptic tone in philosophy."[6]

4. A reference to the dissolution of the Soviet Union, which began in 1989.

5. Francis Fukuyama (b. 1952), American philosopher and neoconservative political economist; his tract *The End of History and the Last Man* (1992) celebrated the triumph of capitalism over communism.

6. At a 1980 conference, Derrida delivered the paper "On a Newly Arisen Apocalyptic Tone in Philosophy"; its title alludes to an essay by IMMANUEL KANT, "On a Newly Arisen Superior Tone in Philosophy" (1796).

What was its consistency? What did it taste like? It was, *on the one hand*, the reading or analysis of those whom we could nickname the *classics of the end*. They formed the canon of the modern apocalypse (end of History, end of Man, end of Philosophy, Hegel, Marx, Nietzsche, Heidegger, with their Kojevian codicil and the codicils of Kojève[7] himself). It was, *on the other hand and indissociably*, what we had known or what some of us for quite some time no longer hid from concerning totalitarian terror in all the Eastern countries, all the socio-economic disasters of Soviet bureaucracy, the Stalinism of the past and the neo-Stalinism in process (roughly speaking, from the Moscow trials to the repression in Hungary,[8] to take only these minimal indices). Such was no doubt the element in which what is called deconstruction developed—and one can understand nothing of this period of deconstruction, notably in France, unless one takes this historical entanglement into account.

* * *

(* * * In order to try to remove what we are going to say from what risks happening, if we judge by the many signs, to Marx's work today, which is to say also to his injunction. What risks happening is that one will try to play Marx off against Marxism so as to neutralize, or at any rate muffle the political imperative in the untroubled exegesis of a classified work. One can sense a coming fashion or stylishness in this regard in the culture and more precisely in the university. And what is there to worry about here? Why fear what may also become a cushioning operation? This recent stereotype would be destined, whether one wishes it or not, to depoliticize profoundly the *Marxist reference*, to do its best, by putting on a tolerant face, to neutralize a potential force, first of all by enervating a *corpus*, by silencing in it the revolt [the *return* is acceptable provided that the *revolt*, which initially inspired uprising, indignation, insurrection, revolutionary momentum, does not come back]. People would be ready to accept the return of Marx or the return to Marx, on the condition that a silence is maintained about Marx's injunction not just to decipher but to act and to make the deciphering [the interpretation] into a transformation that "changes the world." In the name of an old concept of reading, such an ongoing neutralization would attempt to conjure away a danger: now that Marx is dead, and especially now that Marxism seems to be in rapid decomposition, some people seem to say, we are going to be able to concern ourselves with Marx without being bothered—by the Marxists and, why not, by Marx himself, that is, by a ghost that goes on speaking. We'll treat him calmly, objectively, without bias: according to the academic rules, in the University, in the library, in colloquia! We'll do it systematically, by respecting the norms of hermeneutical, philological, philosophical exegesis. If one listens closely, one already hears whispered: "Marx, you see, was despite everything a philosopher like any other; what is more [and one can say this now that so many Marxists have fallen silent], he was a *great-philosopher* who deserves to figure on the list of those works we assign for study and from

7. Alexandre Kojève (1902–1968), Russian-French philosopher famous for his influential 1930s lectures in Paris on the German philosopher G. W. F. HEGEL (1770–1831) and the end of history. FRIEDRICH NIETZSCHE (1844–1900) and MARTIN HEIDEGGER (1889–1976), German philosophers who addressed the end of man and end of philosophy.

8. The invasion of Hungary in 1956 by Soviet troops to suppress a short-lived anti-Communist revolution. "The Moscow trials": political purges (1936–38) that helped Joseph Stalin (1879–1953) consolidate his power in the Soviet Union; a score of potential rivals were accused of engaging in a treasonous plot, and many were executed.

which he has been banned for too long.[9] He doesn't belong to the communists, to the Marxists, to the parties, he ought to figure within our great canon of Western political philosophy. Return to Marx, let's finally read him as a great philosopher." We have heard this and we will hear it again.

It is something altogether other that I wish to attempt here as I turn or return to Marx. It is "something other" to the point that I will have occasion instead, and this will not be only for lack of time and space, to insist even more on what commands us today, without delay, to do everything we can so as to avoid the neutralizing anesthesia of a new theoreticism, and to prevent a philosophico-philological return to Marx from prevailing. Let us spell things out, let us insist: to do everything we can so that it does not *prevail*, but not to avoid its taking place, because it remains just as necessary. This will cause me, for the moment, to give priority to the political gesture I am making here, at the opening of a colloquium, and to leave more or less in the state of a program and of schematic indications the work of philosophical exegesis, and all the "scholarship" that this "position-taking," today, still requires.)

* * *

In proposing this title, *Specters of Marx*, I was initially thinking of all the forms of a certain haunting obsession that seems to me to organize the *dominant* influence on discourse today. At a time when a new world disorder[1] is attempting to install its neo-capitalism and neo-liberalism, no disavowal has managed to rid itself of all of Marx's ghosts. Hegemony still organizes the repression and thus the confirmation of a haunting. Haunting belongs to the structure of every hegemony.[2] But I did not have in mind first of all the exordium of the *Manifesto*. In an apparently different sense, Marx-Engels spoke there already, in 1847–48, of a specter and more precisely of the "specter of communism" (*das Gespenst des Kommunismus*). A terrifying specter for all the powers of old Europe (*alle Mächte des alten Europa*), but specter of a communism then *to come*. Of a communism, to be sure, already namable (and well before the League of the Just or the Communist League[3]), but still to come beyond its name. Already promised but only promised. A specter all the more terrifying, some will say. Yes, on the condition that one can never distinguish between the future-to-come and the coming-back of a specter. Let us not forget that, around 1848, the First International[4] had to remain quasi-secret. The specter was there (but what is the *being-there* of a specter? what is the mode of presence of a specter? that is the only question we would like to pose here). But that of which it was the specter, communism (*das Gespenst des Kommunismus*), was itself not there, by definition. It was dreaded as communism to come. It had already been announced, with this

9. This is perhaps a reference specifically to the "programmes d'agrégation," that is, to the list of works drawn up annually by the French university establishment for the competitive examination that qualifies the successful candidates for advanced teaching positions in each discipline [translator's note].

1. An allusion to the "new world order" invoked by President George H. W. Bush in his September 1990 speech to Congress at the beginning of the Gulf War (1990–91).

2. For a novel elaboration, in a "deconstructive" style, of the concept of *hegemony*, I refer to Ernesto Laclau and Chantal Mouffe, *Hegemony and Socialist Strategy: Toward a Radical Politics* (London: Verso, 1985) [Derrida's note].

3. The name taken in 1847 by the League of the Just (founded in 1836) following its reorganization; at its second congress, it commissioned Marx and Engels to write *The Manifesto*.

4. The International Workingmen's Association, founded in London in September 1864. Derrida mentions 1848 because it was a year of widespread revolutionary upheaval throughout Europe.

name, some time ago, but it was not yet *there*. It is only a specter, seemed to say these allies of old Europe so as to reassure themselves; let's hope that in the future it does not become an actual, effectively present, manifest, non-secret reality. The question old Europe was asking itself was already the question of the future, the question "whither?": "whither communism?" if not "whither Marxism?" Whether one takes it as asking about the future of communism or about communism in the future, this anguished question did not just seek to know how, in the future, communism would affect European history, but also, in a more muffled way, already whether there would still be any future and any history at all for Europe. In 1848, the Hegelian discourse on the end of history in absolute knowledge had already resounded throughout Europe and had rung a consonant note with many other knells [*glas*].[5] And communism was essentially distinguished from other labor movements by its *international* character. No organized political movement in the history of humanity had ever yet presented itself as *geo-political*, thereby inaugurating the space that is now ours and that today is reaching its limits, the limits of the earth and the limits of the political.

The representatives of these forces or all these powers (*alle Mächte*), namely the States, wanted to *reassure* themselves. They wanted to be sure. So they were sure, for there is no difference between "being sure" and "wanting to be sure." They were sure and certain that between a specter and an actually present reality, between a spirit and a *Wirklichkeit*,[6] the dividing line was assured. It *had* to be safely drawn. It *ought* to be assured. No, it *ought to have been* assured. The sureness of this certainity is something they shared, moreover, with *Marx himself*. (This is the whole story, and we are coming to it: Marx thought, to be sure, on his side, from the other side, that the dividing line between the ghost and actuality ought to be crossed, like utopia itself, by a realization, that is, by a revolution; but *he too* will have continued to believe, to try to believe in the existence of this dividing line as real limit and conceptual distinction. He too? No, someone in him. Who? The "Marxist" who will engender what for a long time is going to prevail under the name of "Marxism." And which was also haunted by what it attempted to foreclose.)

Today, almost a century and a half later, there are many who, throughout the world, seem just as worried by the specter of communism, just as convinced that what one is dealing with there is only a specter without body, without present reality, without actuality or effectivity, but this time it is supposed to be a past specter. It was only a specter, an illusion, a phantasm, or a ghost: that is what one hears everywhere today ("Horatio saies, 'tis but our Fantasie, / And will not let beleefe take hold of him"[7]). A still worried sigh of relief: let us make sure that in the future it does not come back! At bottom, the specter is the future, it is always to come, it presents itself only as that which could come or come back; in the future, said the powers of old Europe in the last century, it must not incarnate itself, either publicly or in secret. In the future, we hear everywhere today, it must not re-incarnate itself; it must not be allowed to come back since it is past.

* * *

5. An allusion to Derrida's book *Glas* (1974), which addresses Hegel at length.
6. Reality (German).
7. William Shakespeare, *Hamlet* (ca. 1600), 1.1.21–22; the guard is referring to a ghost that he has seen and whose existence Horatio doubts.

From *Chapter 3. Wears and Tears*

The time is out of joint.[8] The world is going badly. It is worn but its wear no longer counts.

* * *

The world is going badly, the picture is bleak, one could say almost black. Let us form an hypothesis. Suppose that, for lack of time (the spectacle or the tableau is always "for lack of time"), we propose simply to paint, like the Painter in *Timon of Athens.*[9] A black picture on a blackboard. Taxonomy or freeze-frame image. Title: "The time is out of joint" or "What is going so badly today in the world." We would leave this banal title in its neutral form so as to avoid speaking of crisis, a very insufficient concept, and so as to avoid deciding between the bad as suffering and the bad as wrong or as crime.

We would add to this title of a possible blackboard picture merely a few subtitles. What are they?

* * *

Under the heading of international or civil-international war, is it still necessary to point out the economic wars, national wars, wars among minorities, the unleashing of racisms and xenophobias, ethnic conflicts, conflicts of culture and religion that are tearing apart so-called democratic Europe and the world today? Entire regiments of ghosts have returned, armies from every age, camouflaged by the archaic symptoms of the paramilitary and of the postmodern excess of arms (information technology, panoptical[1] surveillance via satellite, nuclear threat, and so forth). Let us accelerate things. Beyond these two types of war (civil and international) whose dividing line cannot even be distinguished any longer, let us blacken still more the picture of this wearing down beyond wear. Let us name with a single trait that which could risk making the euphoria of liberal-democrat capitalism resemble the blindest and most delirious of hallucinations, or even an increasingly glaring hypocrisy in its formal or juridicist rhetoric of human rights. It will not be a matter of merely accumulating, as Fukuyama might say, "empirical evidence," it will not suffice to point one's finger at the mass of undeniable facts that this picture could describe or denounce. The question posed too briefly would not even be that of the analysis with which one would then have to proceed in all these directions, but of the *double interpretation*, the concurrent readings that the picture seems to call for and to oblige us to associate. If one were permitted to name these plagues of the "new world order" in a ten-word telegram, one might perhaps choose the following ten words.

1. Unemployment, that more or less well-calculated deregulation of a new market, new technologies, new worldwide competitiveness, would no doubt, like labor or production, deserve another name today. All the more so in that tele-work inscribes there a new set of givens that perturbs both the methods of traditional calculation and the conceptual opposition between work and

8. *Hamlet*, 1.5.189.
9. Play by Shakespeare (ca. 1607–08); Painter is a minor character who will paint whatever he can sell to a patron.
1. All-seeing; an allusion to MICHEL FOUCAULT's invocation in *Discipline and Punish* (1975; see above) of the Panopticon, a circular prison that enabled a single guard to keep all the inmates under surveillance, as a model and summation of disciplinary power.

non-work, activity, employment, and their contrary. This regular deregulation is at once mastered, calculated, "socialized" (that is, most often disavowed), and irreducible to prediction—like suffering itself, a suffering that suffers still more, and more obscurely, for having lost its habitual models and language once it no longer recognizes itself in the old word unemployment and in the scene that word named for so long. The function of social inactivity, of non-work or of underemployment is entering into a new era. It calls for another politics. And another concept. The "new unemployment" no more resembles unemployment, in the very forms of its experience and its calculation, than what in France is called the "new poverty"[2] resembles poverty.

2. The massive exclusion of homeless citizens from any participation in the democratic life of States, the expulsion or deportation of so many exiles, stateless persons, and immigrants from a so-called national territory already herald a new experience of frontiers and identity—whether national or civil.

3. The ruthless economic war among the countries of the European Community themselves, between them and the Eastern European countries, between Europe and the United States, and between Europe, the United States, and Japan. This war controls everything, beginning with the other wars, because it controls the practical interpretation and an inconsistent and unequal application of international law. There have been too many examples in the last decade or more.

4. The inability to master the contradictions in the concept, norms, and reality of the free market (the barriers of a protectionism and the interventionist bidding wars of capitalist States seeking to protect their nationals, or even Westerners or Europeans in general, from cheap labor, which often has no comparable social protection). How is one to save one's own interests in the global market while claiming to protect one's "social advantages" and so forth?

5. The aggravation of the foreign debt and other connected mechanisms are starving or driving to despair a large portion of humanity. They tend thus to exclude it simultaneously from the very market that this logic nevertheless seeks to extend. This type of contradiction works through many geopolitical fluctuations even when they appear to be dictated by the discourse of democratization or human rights.

6. The arms industry and trade (whether it be "conventional" arms or at the cutting edge of tele-technological sophistication) are inscribed in the normal regulation of the scientific research, economy, and socialization of labor in Western democracies. Short of an unimaginable revolution, they cannot be suspended or even cut back without running major risks, beginning with the worsening of the said unemployment. As for arms trafficking, to the (limited) degree that it can still be distinguished from "normal" commerce, it remains the largest in the world, larger than the drug traffic, from which it is not always dissociated.

7. The spread ("dissemination") of nuclear weapons, maintained by the very countries that say they want to protect themselves from it, is no longer even controllable, as was the case for a long time, by statist structures. It exceeds not only statist control but every declared market.

2. A term used in France, beginning in the early 1980s, to refer to the condition of the growing numbers of individuals who, for a variety of social and economic reasons, are only marginally employed.

8. Inter-ethnic wars (have there ever been another kind?) are proliferating, driven by an *archaic* phantasm and concept, by a *primitive conceptual phantasm* of community, the nation-State, sovereignty, borders, native soil and blood. Archaism is not a bad thing in itself, it doubtless keeps some irreducible resource. But how can one deny that this conceptual phantasm is, so to speak, made more outdated than ever, in the very *ontopology* it supposes, by tele-technic dis-location? (By *ontopology* we mean an axiomatics linking indissociably the ontological value of present-being [*on*][3] to its *situation*, to the stable and presentable determination of a locality, the *topos* of territory, native soil, city, body in general). For having spread in an unheard-of fashion, which is more and more differentiated and more and more accelerated (it is acceleration itself, beyond the norms of speed that have until now informed human culture), the process of dislocation is no less arch-originary, that is, just as "archaic" as the archaism that it has always dislodged. This process is, moreover, the positive condition of the stabilization that it constantly relaunches. All stability in a place being but a stabilization or a sedentarization, it will have to have been necessary that the local differ*a*nce,[4] the spacing of a displacement gives the movement its start. And gives place and gives rise [*donne lieu*]. All national rootedness, for example, is rooted first of all in the memory or the anxiety of a displaced—or displaceable—population. It is not only time that is "out of joint," but space, space in time, spacing.

9. How can one ignore the growing and undelimitable, that is, worldwide power of those super-efficient and properly capitalist phantom-States that are the mafia and the drug cartels on every continent, including in the former so-called socialist States of Eastern Europe? These phantom-States have infiltrated and banalized themselves everywhere, to the point that they can no longer be strictly identified. Nor even sometimes clearly dissociated from the processes of democratization (think—for example—of the schema, telegraphically simplified here, that would associate them with the history-of-a-Sicilian-mafia-harassed-by-the-fascism-of-the-Mussolinian-State-thus-intimately-and-symbiotically-allied-to-the-Allies-in-the-democratic-camp-on-both-sides-of-the-Atlantic-as-well-as-in-the-reconstruction-of-the-Italian-Christian-democratic-State-which-has-today-entered-into-a-new-configuration-of-capital,[5] about which the least one can say is that we will understand nothing of what is happening there if we do not take account of its genealogy). All these infiltrations are going through a "critical" phase, as one says, which is no doubt what allows us to talk about them or to begin their analysis. These phantom-States invade not only the socio-economic fabric, the general circulation of capital, but also statist or inter-statist institutions.

10. For above all, above all, one would have to analyze the present state of international law and of its institutions. Despite a fortunate perfectibility, despite an undeniable progress, these international institutions suffer from at least two limits. The first and most radical of the two stems from the fact that their norms, their charter, the definition of their mission depend on a certain historical culture. They cannot be dissociated from certain European

3. Being (Greek). Derrida's coinage blends "being" and "place" (*topos* in Greek).

4. Temporal and spatial differentiating or deferral. *Différance* is Derrida's coinage; like *différence*, which sounds the same and refers to synchronic comparison, it derives from *différer*, which means both "to differ" and "to defer, postpone."

5. The Christian Democratic Party, founded in 1944, was the dominant force in Italian politics until it disbanded in 1994. It was preceded by the dictatorship of Benito Mussolini (1883–1945), one of the founders of Italian fascism.

philosophical concepts, and notably from a concept of State or national sovereignty whose genealogical closure is more and more evident, not only in a theoretico-juridical or speculative fashion, but concretely, practically, and practically quotidian. Another limit is strictly linked to the first: This supposedly universal international law remains, in its application, largely dominated by particular nation-States. Almost always their techno-economic and military power prepares and applies, in other words, *carries* the decision. As one says in English, it *makes the decision*. Countless examples, recent or not so recent, would amply demonstrate this, whether it is a question of deliberations and resolutions of the United Nations or of the putting into practice or the "enforcement" of these decisions: the incoherence, discontinuity, inequality of States before the law, the hegemony of certain States over military power in the service of international law, this is what, year after year, day after day, we are forced to acknowledge.[6]

These facts do not suffice to disqualify international institutions. Justice demands, on the contrary, that one pay tribute to certain of those who are working within them in the direction of the perfectibility and emancipation of institutions that must never be renounced. However insufficient, confused, or equivocal such signs may still be, we should salute what is heralded today in the reflection on the right of interference or intervention in the name of what is obscurely and sometimes hypocritically called the *humanitarian*, thereby limiting the sovereignty of the State in certain conditions. Let us salute such signs even as one remains vigilantly on guard against the manipulations or appropriations to which these novelties can be subjected.

* * *

Which Marxist spirit, then? It is easy to imagine why we will not please the Marxists, and still less all the others, by insisting in this way on the *spirit of Marxism*, especially if we let it be understood that we intend to understand *spirits* in the plural and in the sense of specters, of untimely specters that one must not chase away but sort out, critique, keep close by, and allow to come back.

* * *

And if one interprets the gesture we are risking here as a belated-rallying-to-Marxism, then one would have to have misunderstood quite badly. It is true, however, that I would be today, here, now, less insensitive than ever to the appeal of the contretemps or of being out-of-step, as well as to the style of an untimeliness that is more manifest and more urgent than ever. Already I hear people saying: "You picked a good time to salute Marx!" Or else: "It's about time!" "Why so late?"[7] I believe in the political virtue of the contretemps.

6. To which one would have to add the economic dependency of the U.N., whether one is talking about its major interventions (political, socio-educational, cultural, or military) or simply its administrative management. Now, one must also acknowledge that the U.N. is going through a serious financial crisis. The largest States do not all pay their dues. Solution: a campaign to attract the support of private capital, constitution of "councils" (associations of the biggest leaders in industry, commerce, and finance) meant to support, on certain conditions, either spoken or unspoken, a politics of the U.N. that can go (often, here or there, here rather than there, precisely) in the direction of the interests of the market. One must underscore and reflect on the fact that principles that are today guiding international institutions often agree with such interests. Why, how, and within what limits do they do so? What do these limits signify? This is the only question we can pose here for the moment [Derrida's note].

7. From the 1960s to the 1980s, Derrida was often criticized for not addressing the work of Marx and for avoiding politics.

And if a contretemps does not have the good luck, a more or less calculated luck, to come *just in time*, then the inopportuneness of a strategy (political or other) may still *bear witness*, precisely [*justement*], to justice, bear witness, at least, to the justice which is demanded and about which we were saying a moment ago that it must be disadjusted, irreducible to exactness [*justesse*] and to law. But that is not the decisive motivation here and we need finally to break with the simplism of these slogans. What is certain is that I am not a Marxist, as someone said a long time ago, let us recall, in a witticism reported by Engels.[8] Must we still cite Marx as an authority in order to say "I am not a Marxist"? What is the distinguishing trait of a Marxist statement? And who can still say "I am a Marxist"?

To continue to take inspiration from a certain spirit of Marxism would be to keep faith with what has always made of Marxism in principle and first of all a *radical* critique, namely a procedure ready to undertake its self-critique. This critique *wants itself* to be in principle and explicitly open to its own transformation, re-evaluation, self-reinterpretation. Such a critical "wanting-itself" necessarily takes root, it is involved in a ground that it not yet critical, even if it is not, not yet, pre-critical. This latter spirit is more than a style, even though it is also a style. It is heir to a spirit of the Enlightenment which must not be renounced. We would distinguish this spirit from other spirits of Marxism, those that rivet it to the body of Marxist doctrine, to its supposed systemic, metaphysical, or ontological totality (notably to its "dialectical method" or to "dialectical materialism"[9]), to its fundamental concepts of labor, mode of production, social class, and consequently to the whole history of its apparatuses (projected or real: the Internationals of the labor movement, the dictatorship of the proletariat, the single party, the State, and finally the totalitarian monstrosity).

* * *

1993

From The Animal That Therefore I Am[1]

From *Chapter 1. The Animal That Therefore I Am (More to Follow)*

* * *

The animal, what a word!

The animal is a word, it is an appellation that men have instituted, a name they have given themselves the right and the authority to give to the living other.

8. On November 2–3, 1882, Engels wrote in a letter to the German socialist and politician Eduard Bernstein, "Now what is known as 'Marxism' in France is, indeed, an altogether peculiar product—so much so that Marx once said to Lafargue: '*Ce qu'il y a de certain c'est que moi, je ne suis pas Marxiste*' [If anything is certain, it is that I myself am not a Marxist]." He repeated the quip in a letter of August 5, 1890, to the German economist and socialist Conrad Schmidt.

9. The Marxist theory that stresses the material basis of reality, including human consciousness and cultural forms, and posits that change results from a struggle of contradictory forces.

1. Translated by David Wills, who occasionally retains the original French in brackets.

At the point at which we find ourselves, even before I get involved, or try to drag you after me[2] or in pursuit of me upon an itinerary that some of you will no doubt find tortuous, labyrinthine, even aberrant, leading us astray from lure to lure, I'll attempt the operation of disarmament that consists in *posing* what one could call some hypotheses in view of theses; posing them simply, naked, frontally, as directly as possible, *pose* them as I just said, by no means posing in the way one indulgently poses by looking at oneself in front of a spectator, a portraitist, or a camera, but "pose" in the sense of situating a series of "positions."

First hypothesis: for about two centuries, intensely and by means of an alarming rate of acceleration, for we no longer even have a clock or chronological measure of it, we, we who call ourselves men or humans, we who recognize ourselves in that name, have been involved in an unprecedented transformation. This mutation affects the experience of what we continue to call imperturbably, as if there were nothing to it, the animal and/or animals. I intend to stake a lot, or play a lot on the flexible slash of this *and/or*. This new situation can be determined only on the basis of what is most ancient. We shall have to move continuously along this coming and going between the oldest and what is coming, in the exchange among the new, the "again [*de nouveau*]," and the "anew [*à nouveau*]" of repetition. Far from appearing, simply, within what we continue to call the world, history, life, etc., this unheard-of relation to the animal or to animals is so new that it should oblige us to worry all those concepts, more than just problematize them. That is why I would hesitate to say that we are *living through* that (if one can still confidently call *life* the experience whose limits come to tremble at the bordercrossings between *bios* and *zoē*,[3] the biological, zoological, and anthropological, as between life and death, life and technology, life and history, etc.). I would therefore hesitate just as much to say that we are living through a historical turning point. The figure of the turning point implies a rupture or an instantaneous mutation whose model or figure remains genetic, biological, or zoological and which therefore remains, precisely, to be questioned. As for history, historicity, even historicity, those motifs belong precisely—as we shall see in detail—to *this* auto-definition, *this* auto-apprehension, *this* auto-situation of man or of the human *Dasein*[4] as regards what is living and animal life; they belong to this auto-biography of man, which I wish to call into question today.

Since all these words, in particular *history*, belong in a constitutive manner to the language, interests, and lures of this autobiography, we should not be overhasty in giving them credence or in confirming their pseudo-evidence. I shall therefore not be speaking of a historical turning point in order to name a transformation in progress, an alteration that is at the same time more serious and less recognizable than a historical turning point in the relation to the animal, in the being-with shared by the human and by what the human calls the animal: the *being* of what calls itself man or the *Dasein with* what he himself calls, or what we ourselves are calling, what we are still daring, provisionally, to name in general but in the singular, *the animal*. However one names or interprets this alteration, no one could deny that it has been accelerating,

2. *Vous entraîner à ma suite*: also "to train you to follow me" [translator's note].

3. Physical life and eternal life (Greek), terms found in the New Testament.

4. Existence (literally, "being there"; German), a term famously used by the German philosopher MARTIN HEIDEGGER.

intensifying, no longer knowing where it is going, for about two centuries, at an incalculable rate and level.

Given this indetermination, the fact that it is left hanging, why should I say, as I have more than once, "for about two centuries," as though such a point of reference were rigorously possible within a process that is no doubt as old as man, what he calls his world, his knowledge, his history, and his technology? Well, in order to recall, for convenience to begin with and without laying claim here to being at all exact, certain preexisting indices that allow us to understand and agree in saying "us" today. Limiting ourselves to the most imposing of these indices, we can refer to those that go well beyond the animal sacrifices of the Bible or of ancient Greece, well beyond the hecatombs (sacrifices of one hundred cattle, with all the metaphors that that expression has since been charged with), beyond the hunting, fishing, domestication, training, or traditional exploitation of animal energy (transport, plowing, draught animals, the horse, ox, reindeer, etc., and then the guard dog, small-scale butchering, and then experiments on animals, etc.). It is all too evident that in the course of the last two centuries these traditional forms of treatment of the animal have been turned upside down by the joint developments of zoological, ethological, biological, and genetic forms of *knowledge*, which remain inseparable from *techniques* of intervention *into* their object, from the transformation of the actual object, and from the milieu and world of their object, namely, the living animal. This has occurred by means of farming and regimentalization at a demographic level unknown in the past, by means of genetic experimentation, the industrialization of what can be called the production for consumption of animal meat, artificial insemination on a massive scale, more and more audacious manipulations of the genome, the reduction of the animal not only to production and overactive reproduction (hormones, genetic crossbreeding, cloning, etc.) of meat for consumption, but also of all sorts of other end products, and all of that in the service of a certain being and the putative human well-being of man.

All that is all too well known; we have no need to take it further. However one interprets it, whatever practical, technical, scientific, juridical, ethical, or political consequence one draws from it, no one can today deny this event—that is, the *unprecedented* proportions of this subjection of the animal. Such a subjection, whose history we are attempting to interpret, can be called violence in the most morally neutral sense of the term and even includes the interventionist violence that is practiced, as in some very minor and in no way dominant cases, let us never forget, in the service of or for the protection of the animal, but most often the human animal. Neither can one seriously deny the disavowal that this involves. No one can deny seriously any more, or for very long, that men do all they can in order to dissimulate this cruelty or to hide it from themselves; in order to organize on a global scale the forgetting or misunderstanding of this violence, which some would compare to the worst cases of genocide (there are also animal genocides: the number of species endangered because of man takes one's breath away). One should neither abuse the figure of genocide nor too quickly consider it explained away. It gets more complicated: the annihilation of certain species is indeed in process, but it is occurring through the organization and exploitation of an artificial, infernal, virtually interminable survival, in conditions that previous generations would have judged monstrous, outside of every presumed norm of a life proper to animals that are thus exterminated by means of their continued existence or even their overpopulation. As if, for example, instead of throwing a people into ovens and gas chambers (let's say Nazi) doctors and geneticists had decided to organize the overproduction and overgeneration of Jews, gypsies, and homosexuals by means of artificial insemination, so that, being continually more numerous and better fed, they could be destined in always increasing numbers for the same hell, that of the imposition of genetic experimentation, or extermination by gas or by fire. In the same abattoirs. I don't wish to abuse the ease with which one can overload with pathos the self-evidences I am drawing attention to here. Everybody knows what terrifying and intolerable pictures a realist painting could give to the industrial, mechanical, chemical, hormonal, and genetic violence to which man has been submitting animal life for the past two centuries. Everybody knows what the production, breeding, transport, and slaughter of these animals has become. Instead of thrusting these images in your faces or awakening them in your memory, something that would be both too easy and endless, let me simply say a word about this "pathos." If these images are "pathetic," if they evoke sympathy, it is also because they "pathetically" open the immense question of pathos and the pathological, precisely, that is, of suffering, pity, and compassion; and the place that has to be accorded to the interpretation of this compassion, to the sharing of this suffering among the living, to the law, ethics, and politics that must be brought to bear upon this experience of compassion. What has been happening for two centuries now involves a new experience of this compassion. In response to what is, for the moment, the irresistible but unacknowledged unleashing and the organized disavowal of this torture, voices are raised—minority, weak, marginal voices, little assured of their discourse, of their right to discourse, and of the enactment of their discourse within the law, as a declaration of rights—in order to protest, in order to appeal (we'll return to this) to what is still presented in such a problematic way as *animal rights*, in order to awaken us to our responsibilities and our obligations vis-à-vis the living in general, and precisely to this fundamental compassion that, were we to take it seriously, would have to change even the very cornerstone (and it is next to that cornerstone that I wish to do my business today) of the philosophical problematic of the animal.

It is in thinking of the source and ends of this compassion that about two centuries ago someone like Bentham,[5] as is well known, proposed changing the very form of the question regarding the animal that dominated discourse within the tradition, in the language both of its most refined philosophical argumentation and of everyday acceptation and common sense. Bentham said something like this: the question is not to know whether the animal can think, reason, or speak, etc., something we still pretend to be asking ourselves (from Aristotle to Descartes, from Descartes, especially, to Heidegger, Levinas, and Lacan,[6] and this question determines so many others concerning *power* or *capability* [pouvoirs] and *attributes* [avoirs]: being able, having the power or capability to give, to die, to bury one's dead,

5. Jeremy Bentham (1748–1832), English philosopher and social reformer, a founder of utilitarianism.

6. JACQUES LACAN (1901–1981), French psychoanalyst. ARISTOTLE (384–322 B.C.E.), Greek philosopher; René Descartes (1596–1650), French philosopher; Emmanuel Lévinas (1906–1995), Lithuanian-born French philosopher.

to dress, to work, to invent a technique, etc, a power that consists in having such and such a faculty, thus such and such a capability, as an essential attribute). Thus the question will not be to know whether animals are of the type *zōon logon echon*,[7] whether they *can* speak or reason thanks to that *capacity* or that *attribute* of the *logos*,[8] the *can-have* [pouvoir-avoir] of the *logos*, the aptitude for the *logos* (and logo-centrism is first of all a thesis regarding the animal, the animal deprived of the *logos*, deprived of the *can-have-the-logos*: this is the thesis, position, or presupposition maintained from Aristotle to Heidegger, from Descartes to Kant,[9] Levinas, and Lacan). The *first* and *decisive* question would rather be to know whether animals *can suffer*.

"Can they suffer?" asks Bentham, simply yet so profoundly.

Once its protocol is established, the form of this question changes everything. It no longer simply concerns the *logos*, the disposition and whole configuration of the *logos*, having it or not, nor does it concern, more radically, a *dynamis* or *hexis*,[1] this having or manner of being, this *habitus*[2] that one calls a faculty or "capability," this can-have or the power one possesses (as in the power to reason, to speak, and everything that that implies). The question is disturbed by a certain *passivity*. It bears witness, manifesting already, as question, the response that testifies to a sufferance, a passion, a not-being-able. The word *can* [pouvoir] changes sense and sign here once one asks, "Can they suffer?" Henceforth it wavers. What counts at the origin of such a question is not only the idea of what transitivity or activity (being able to speak, to reason, etc.) refer to; what counts is rather what impels it toward this self-contradiction, something we will later relate back to autobiography. "Can they suffer?" amounts to asking "Can they *not be able*?" And what of this inability [*impouvoir*]? What of the vulnerability felt on the basis of this inability? What is this nonpower at the heart of power? What is its quality or modality? How should one take it into account? What right should be accorded it? To what extent does it concern us? Being able to suffer is no longer a power; it is a possibility without power, a possibility of the impossible. Mortality resides there, as the most radical means of thinking the finitude that we share with animals, the mortality that belongs to the very finitude of life, to the experience of compassion, to the possibility of sharing the possibility of this nonpower, the possibility of this impossibility, the anguish of this vulnerability, and the vulnerability of this anguish.

With this question—"Can they suffer?"—we are not undermining the rock of indubitable certainty, the foundation of every assurance that one could, for example, look for in the *cogito*, in *Je pense donc je suis*.[3] But from another perspective altogether we are putting our trust in an instance that is just as radical, although essentially different: namely, what is undeniable. No one can deny the suffering, fear, or panic, the terror or fright that can seize certain animals and that we humans can witness. (Descartes himself, as we shall see, was not able to claim that animals were insensitive to suf-

7. Animal having reason (Greek). The classical definition of humans as "rational animals" is often attributed to Aristotle.
8. Logic, reason, word (Greek).
9. IMMANUEL KANT (1724–1804), German philosopher.
1. A disposition to behave in a certain way: a key term in the work of the French philosopher PIERRE BOURDIEU. *Dynamis*: potentiality, power (Greek).
2. Habit (Greek).
3. I think therefore I am (French). This famous foundational dictum of Descartes' *Discourse on Method* (1637) is better known in Latin: "cogito [I think], ergo sum."

fering.) Some will still try—this is something else we will come to—to contest the right to call that *suffering* or *anguish*, words or concepts that would still have to be reserved for man and for the *Dasein* in the freedom of its being-toward-death. We will have reason to problematize that discourse later. But for the moment let us note the following: the response to the question "Can they suffer?" leaves no room for doubt. In fact, it has never left any room for doubt; that is why the experience that we have of it is not even indubitable; it precedes the indubitable, it is older than it. No doubt either, then, of there being within us the possibility of giving vent to a surge of compassion, even if it is then misunderstood, repressed, or denied, held at bay. Before the *undeniability* of this response (yes, they suffer, like us who suffer for them and with them), before this response that precedes all other questions, both ground and cornerstone of the problematic shift. Perhaps it loses all security, but in any case it no longer rests on the old, supposedly natural (ground) or historic and *artifactual* (cornerstone) foundation. The two centuries I have been referring to somewhat casually in order to situate the present in terms of this tradition have been those of an unequal struggle, a war (whose inequality could one day be reversed) being waged between, on the one hand, those who violate not only animal life but even and also this sentiment of compassion, and, on the other hand, those who appeal for an irrefutable testimony to this pity.

War is waged over the matter of pity. This war is probably ageless but, and here is my hypothesis, it is passing through a critical phase. We are passing through that phase, and it passes through us. To think the war we find ourselves waging is not only a duty, a responsibility, an obligation, it is also a necessity, a constraint that, like it or not, directly or indirectly, no one can escape. Henceforth more than ever. And I say "to think" this war, because I believe it concerns what we call "thinking." The animal looks at us, and we are naked before it. Thinking perhaps begins there.

Here now, in view of another thesis, is the *second hypothesis* that I think must be deduced without hesitation. It concerns or puts into effect another logic of the limit. I would thus be tempted to inscribe the subject of this thesis in the series of three conferences that, beginning with The Ends of Man and followed by The Crossing of Borders,[4] have been devoted to a properly *transgressal* if not transgressive experience of *limitrophy*. Let's allow that word to have a both general and strict sense: what abuts onto limits but also what feeds, is fed, is cared for, raised, and trained, what is cultivated on the edges of a limit. In the semantics of *trephō*, *trophē*, or *trophos*,[5] we should be able to find everything we need to speak about what we should be speaking about in the course of these ten days devoted to the autobiographical animal: feeding, food, nursing, breeding, offspring, care and keeping of animals, training, upbringing, culture, living and allowing to live by giving to live, be fed, and grown, autobiographically. *Limitrophy* is therefore my subject. Not just because it will concern what sprouts or grows at the limit, around the limit, by maintaining the limit, but also what *feeds the limit*,

4. Three weeklong conferences focused on Derrida's work took place in France at Cerisy-la-Salle's International Cultural Center, in 1980, 1992, and 1997 (Autobiographical Animal).

5. I rear or nourish (originally but rarely, "I thicken or curdle"), food, or feeder (Greek).

generates it, raises it, and complicates it. Everything I'll say will consist, certainly not in effacing the limit, but in multiplying its figures, in complicating, thickening, delinearizing, folding, and dividing the line precisely by making it increase and multiply. Moreover, the supposed first or literal sense of *trephō* is just that: to transform by thickening, for example, in curdling milk. So it will in no way mean questioning, even in the slightest, the limit that we have had a stomachful of, the limit between Man with a capital *M* and Animal with a capital *A*. It will not be a matter of attacking frontally or antithetically the thesis of philosophical or common sense on which has been constructed the relation to the self, the presentation of self of human life, the autobiography of the human species, the whole history of the self that man recounts to himself, that is to say, the thesis of a limit as rupture or abyss between those who say "we men," "I, a human," and what this man among men who say "we," what he *calls* the animal or animals. I shan't for a single moment venture to contest that thesis, nor the rupture or abyss between this "I-we" and what we *call* animals. To suppose that I, or anyone else for that matter, could ignore that rupture, indeed that abyss, would mean first of all blinding oneself to so much contrary evidence; and, as far as my own modest case is concerned, it would mean forgetting all the signs that I have managed to give, tirelessly, of my attention to difference, to differences, to heterogeneities and abyssal ruptures as against the homogeneous and the continuous. I have thus never believed in some homogeneous continuity between what calls *itself* man and what *he* calls the animal. I am not about to begin to do so now. That would be worse than sleepwalking, it would simply be too asinine [*bête*]. To suppose such a stupid memory lapse or to take to task such a naive misapprehension of this abyssal rupture would mean, more seriously still, venturing to say almost anything at all for the cause, for whatever cause or interest that no longer had anything to do with what we claimed to want to talk about. When that cause or interest seeks to profit from what it simplistically suspects to be a biologistic continuism, whose sinister connotations we are well aware of, or more generally to profit from what is suspected as a geneticism that one might wish to associate with this scatterbrained accusation of continuism, at that point the undertaking becomes in any case so aberrant that it neither calls for nor, it seems to me, deserves any direct discussion on my part. Everything I have suggested so far and every argument I shall put forward today stands overwhelmingly in opposition to the blunt instrument that such an allegation represents.

There is no interest to be found in debating something like a discontinuity, rupture, or even abyss between those who call themselves men and what so-called men, those who name themselves men, call the animal. Everybody agrees on this; discussion is closed in advance; one would have to be more asinine than any beast [*plus bête que les bêtes*] to think otherwise. Even animals know that (ask Abraham's ass or ram[6] or the living beasts that Abel[7] offered to God: they know what is about to happen to them when men say "Here I am"[8] to God, then consent to sacrifice themselves, to sacrifice their

6. In Genesis 22, Abraham, the first of the Hebrew patriarchs, takes his ass along with his son, Isaac, when he follows God's instructions to sacrifice Isaac as a burnt offering; at the last minute, a ram is provided him to sacrifice instead.

7. The younger son of Adam and Eve, who offered God sacrifices from his flock (Genesis 4.4).

8. Abraham's response when hailed by God (Genesis 22.1) and by the angel of God (22.11), as well as by Isaac (22.7).

sacrifice, or to forgive themselves). The discussion is worth undertaking once it is a matter of determining the number, form, sense, or structure, the foliated consistency, of this abyssal limit, these edges, this plural and repeatedly folded frontier. The discussion becomes interesting once, instead of asking whether or not there is a limit that produces a discontinuity, one attempts to think what a limit becomes once it is abyssal, once the frontier no longer forms a single indivisible line but more than one internally divided line; once, as a result, it can no longer be traced, objectified, or counted as single and indivisible. What are the edges of a limit that grows and multiplies by feeding on an abyss? Here is my thesis in three versions:

1. This abyssal rupture doesn't describe two edges, a unilinear and indivisible line having two edges, Man and the Animal in general.

2. The multiple and heterogeneous border of this abyssal rupture has a history. Both macroscopic and microscopic and far from being closed, that history is now passing through the most unusual phase in which we now find ourselves, and for which we have no scale. Indeed, one can speak here of history, of a historic moment or phase, only from one of the supposed edges of the said rupture, the edge of an anthropo-centric subjectivity that is recounted or allows a history to be recounted about it, autobiographically, the history of its life, and that it therefore calls *History*.

3. Beyond the edge of the *so-called* human, beyond it but by no means on a single opposing side, rather than "The Animal" or "Animal Life" there is already a heterogeneous multiplicity of the living, or more precisely (since to say "the living" is already to say too much or not enough), a multiplicity of organizations of relations between living and dead, relations of organization or lack of organization among realms that are more and more difficult to dissociate by means of the figures of the organic and inorganic, of life and/or death. These relations are at once intertwined and abyssal, and they can never be totally objectified. They do not leave room for any simple exteriority of one term with respect to another. It follows that one will never have the right to take animals to be the species of a kind that would be named The Animal, or animal in general. Whenever "one" says "The Animal," each time a philosopher, or anyone else, says "The Animal" in the singular and without further ado, claiming thus to designate every living thing that is held not to be human (man as *rational animal*, man as political animal,[9] speaking animal, *zōon logon echon*, man who says "I" and takes himself to be the subject of a statement that he proffers on the subject of the said animal, etc.), well, each time the subject of that statement, this "one," this "I," does that he utters an *asinanity* [bêtise]. He avows without avowing it, he declares, just as a disease is declared by means of a symptom, he offers up for diagnosis the statement "I am uttering an *asinanity*." And this "I am uttering an *asinanity*" should confirm not only the animality that he is disavowing but his complicit, continued, and organized involvement in a veritable war of the species.

Such are my hypotheses in view of theses on the animal, on animals, on the words *animal* [animal] or *animals* [animaux].

Yes, animal, what a word!

Animal is a word that men have given themselves the right to give. These humans are found giving it to themselves, this word, but as if they had

9. In *Politics* 1, 1253a, Aristotle defines man as "by nature a political animal."

received it as an inheritance. They have given themselves the word in order to corral a large number of living beings within a single concept: "The Animal," they say. And they have given it to themselves, this word, at the same time according themselves, reserving for them, for humans, the right to the word, the naming noun [*nom*], the verb, the attribute, to a language of words, in short to the very thing that the others in question would be deprived of, those that are corralled within the grand territory of the beasts: The Animal. All the philosophers we will investigate (from Aristotle to Lacan, and including Descartes, Kant, Heidegger, and Levinas), all of them say the same thing: the animal is deprived of language. Or, more precisely, of response, of a response that could be precisely and rigorously distinguished from a reaction; of the right and power to "respond," and hence of so many other things that would be proper to man.

Men would be first and foremost those living creatures who have given themselves the word that enables them to speak of the animal with a single voice and to designate it as the single being that remains without a response, without a word with which to respond.

That wrong was committed long ago and with long-term consequences. It derives from this word, or rather it comes together in this word *animal*, which men have given themselves as at the origin of humanity, and which they have given themselves in order to be identified, in order to be recognized, with a view to being what they say they are, namely, men, capable of replying and responding in the name of men.

I would like to try to speak of a certain wrong or evil that derives from this word, to begin with, by stammering some chimerical aphorisms.

The animal that I am (following), does it speak?

That is an intact question, virginal, new, still to come, a completely naked question.

For language is like the rest—it is not enough to speak of it.

From the moment of this first question, one should be able to sniff the trace of the fact that this animal seems to speak French here, and is no less asinine for it. "The animal that I am (following), does it speak?" This address could be a feint, like the switch from "I" to "it." The question could be the ruse or stratagem of what English calls a rhetorical question, one whose response is already taken for granted. The question will shortly be very much that of the response, and no doubt I shall try to imply that one cannot treat the supposed animality of the animal without treating the question of the response, and of what *responding* means. And what *being erased*[1] means. As we shall see, even those who, from Descartes to Lacan, have conceded to the animal some aptitude for signs and for communication have always denied it the power to *respond*—to *pretend*, to *lie*, to *cover its tracks* or *erase* its own traces.

But whether it is fictive or not, when I ask, "The animal that I am, does it speak?" the question seems at that moment to be signed, to be sealed by someone.

What does it seal? What claim does it make? Pretense or not, what does it seem to translate?

What this animal is, what it will have been, what it would, would like to, or could be is perhaps what I am (following).

1. *S'effacer*: more literally, "erasing" or "effacing itself," "to erase itself" or "oneself" [translator's note].

But if I say that *I am (following) it* in French, in this and in no other language, that amounts less to claiming some national idiom than to recalling an irreducible ambiguity about which we shall have more to say: an animal's signature might yet be able to erase or cover its traces. Or allow it to be erased, rather, be unable to prevent its being erased. And this possibility, that of tracing, effacing, or scrambling its signature, allowing it to be lost, would then have considerable consequences. Having or not having traces at one's disposal so as to be able to dissimulate [*brouiller*] or erase them, in such a manner as, it is said, some (man, for example) can and some (the animal, for example, according to Lacan) cannot do, does not perhaps constitute a reliable alternative defining an indivisible limit. We will have reason to go back over these steps and tracks. The fact that a trace can always be erased, and forever, in no way means—and this is a critical difference—that someone, man *or* animal, I am emphasizing here, *can of his own accord* erase his traces.

It is a question of words, therefore. For I am not sure that what I am going to set about saying to you amounts to anything more ambitious than an exploration of language in the course of a sort of chimerical experimental exercise, or the testing of a testimony. Just to see. We can act as though I were simply trying to analyze a number of discursive modalities or usages—in order to put them to the test and to see, to keep an eye out for, what will come of it—that *they* (I insist on this "they"), what *humans* do with certain words, but also, and for some time yet, to track, to sniff, to trail, and to follow some of the reasons they adduce for the so confident usage they make, and which for the moment we are making together, of words such as, therefore, *animal* and *I*.

A critical uneasiness will persist, in fact, a bone of contention will be incessantly repeated throughout everything that I wish to develop. It would be aimed in the first place, once again, at the usage, in the singular, of a notion as general as "The Animal," as if all nonhuman living things could be grouped within the common sense of this "commonplace," the Animal, whatever the abyssal differences and structural limits that separate, in the very essence of their being, all "animals," a name that we would therefore be advised, to begin with, to keep within quotation marks. Confined within this catch all concept, within this vast encampment of the animal, in this general singular, within the strict enclosure of this definite article ("the Animal" and not "animals"), as in a virgin forest, a zoo, a hunting or fishing ground, a paddock or an abattoir, a space of domestication, are *all the living things* that man does not recognize as his fellows, his neighbors, or his brothers. And that is so in spite of the infinite space that separates the lizard from the dog, the protozoon from the dolphin, the shark from the lamb, the parrot from the chimpanzee, the camel from the eagle, the squirrel from the tiger, the elephant from the cat, the ant from the silkworm, or the hedgehog from the echidna. I interrupt my nomenclature and call Noah[2] to help insure that no one gets left on the ark.

* * *

2006

2. In Genesis 6–9, the Hebrew patriarch who, on God's instruction, collects pairs of every sort of animal and leads them, together with his own family, onto an ark so that they may be saved from the coming flood.

LI ZEHOU
b. 1930

Li Zehou is a galvanizing presence in contemporary Chinese academic circles. During China's New Era (1977–89), a period of openness and reform after the death of Mao Zedong, Li's writings on philosophy and aesthetics as well as his observations on Chinese culture and society captivated a generation of intellectuals. His works continue to be widely read by thinkers, scholars, and the common people. The nuanced and wide-ranging aesthetic theory that he developed merits attention, particularly for its original account of "primitive sedimentation."

Li Zehou was born in a city of Hunan, China, not far away from Mao's hometown. In his youth, an emotional crisis brought by his realization of the inevitability of death shifted his interest from a career in the sciences to the humanities. He became a student at Peking University from 1950 to 1954, majoring in philosophy. After graduation, he worked at the Institute of Philosophy of the Chinese Academy of Sciences. In the great debate on aesthetics that engrossed Chinese academia in 1956, he distinguished himself by offering his own ideas as he criticized those of leading Chinese philosophers and aestheticians. His career, like that of all Chinese intellectuals, became dormant during the social upheaval and political repression of the Cultural Revolution (1966–76). But he regained national prominence with the publication in 1979 of *A Collection of Essays on Aesthetics* and *Critique of Critical Philosophy: A Study of Kant.* For the next decade, a time of antitraditional "cultural fever" that ended in 1989 with the government's violent suppression of the Tiananmen Democratic Movement, Li Zehou was acknowledged as "the teacher of youth" and enjoyed among Chinese intellectuals a national reputation comparable to that of RAYMOND WILLIAMS in England and Jean-Paul Sartre in France. Although Li was not directly involved with the Democratic Movement, the authorities identified his writings as a source of inspiration for the demonstrators; he was placed under surveillance and his works were banned for a period. In 1991 he was allowed to leave the country and he emigrated to the United States, where he now resides. Li has held academic appointments at a number of institutions, including Colorado College, University of Michigan, University of Wisconsin, Swarthmore College, University of Colorado at Boulder, and University of Tübingen. He was elected to the Collège International de Philosophie in Paris in 1998.

Li constructs his philosophical and aesthetic system by fusing a variety of intellectual sources from both East and West: his work is rooted most deeply in the ideas of IMMANUEL KANT and KARL MARX (which he distinguishes from Marxism) and in traditional Chinese thought. He links Marx and Kant by offering new accounts of subjectivity, human knowledge, and aesthetics that entail reinterpreting the two thinkers in relation to traditional Chinese thought. Kant sees human knowledge as arising from the interaction of sensibility and understanding, which themselves exist a priori. While human sensibility shapes raw data and sensations according to the intuitions of time and space, the understanding at a higher level structures sensible experience according to categories such as plurality, unity, substance, causation, and so on. For Kant, we can never know "things in themselves" free from such framing. Li challenges this metaphysical view by turning to human history: "All a priori intuitions, concepts, and principles are the psychological forms of the 'sedimentation' (*jidian*) of the primary practice, which lasted millions of years. They are beyond the experience of any individual, group, or society, but not beyond the experience of humankind as a whole, not 'absolutely independent of all experience,' as Kant claimed."

Drawing on this view of history, Li develops a series of ideas, the most famous and original of which is his theory of "sedimentation" (or "cultural-psychological formation"). It reflects his efforts to give Kant's a priori subjectivity a Marxian materialistic foundation, shaped by the traditional Chinese belief that "the Way of Heaven" is the same as the "Way of Humans." Li emphasizes a dynamism extending in two directions: people humanize the natural world to make it a better place to live, and at the same time humanize their own physical and mental constitution, increasingly distancing themselves from animals. By combining Chinese and Western perspectives, Li complements Marx's vision of the "humanization of nature" with the "naturalization of humans," and Kant's transcendental rationality with a materialist "pragmatic rationality" based on the race's long experience and practice. In that experience, the arts play a key role.

Li's major contribution to aesthetic theory lies in his introduction of practice into the study of the essence of beauty. He argues that individuals are capable of aesthetic appreciation of nature because their practice as a group has changed the relationship between nature and humans, turning what used to be an opposing force into something that serves human needs. An inquiry into the essence of beauty should take into account not only the sensual, psychological, and cultural responses of individuals but also the material and social dimensions of collective creative practices, including the development over time of the sense of beauty. Li's dual emphasis on the universal and the historical gives rise to an intrinsic yet essential tension in what he calls his "philosophy of subjective practice," underlying sedimentation. He once explained why he proposed this idea: "To explore how the rational is manifested in the sensual, the social in the individual, the historical in the psychological, I created the term, 'sedimentation,' by which I mean the process in which the social, rational, and historical are accumulated and precipitated into the individual, sensual, and intuitional. This process is realized through the humanization of nature."

In the sphere of aesthetics, sedimentation refers to the historical formation of universalized artistic forms among human beings. In our selection, "The Stratification of Form and Primitive Sedimentation," a chapter of his popular work *Four Essays on Aesthetics: Toward a Global View* (1989), he expounds on the nature of sedimentation. This text calls to mind the work of such Western aestheticians as VICO, HUME, SCHILLER, HEGEL, PIERRE BOURDIEU, and Barbara Herrnstein Smith, while fusing Chinese and Western aesthetic theories into an apparently simple theory of art that becomes increasingly complex. After raising a few common questions concerning the nature, essence, and conditions of art, Li describes how objects and activities created for other purposes came to be art.

Li points out that ancient tools exhibit elements and patterns of beauty, particularly symmetry, proportion, balance, and rhythm. The human energy (*qi*) that goes into labor (their fabrication) emerges in beautiful forms. Aesthetic objects evoke a feeling for beauty as well as pleasure in their making. These feelings are neither logical nor philosophy-oriented phenomena, he emphasizes. Such material vehicles as the movements of dancers and the sounds of poetry arouse emotions that precede critical understanding. None of these primitive dimensions of beauty and art, argues Li, relieves artists of the need to learn their crafts and traditions. Nor do artworks transcend their milieus or historical styles: every object or work, no matter how much its utilitarian aspects might diminish over time, no matter how purely aesthetic it might be, always has "worldly emotions" sedimented in it. It retains a legacy of materialization, of labor, of sensation, as well as social history, history of psychology, and form. Significantly, Li's theory of sedimentation explicitly adds labor theory to the social psychology and history congealed in the aesthetic forms that constitute traditions in the arts.

Li directly asks "What are artworks?" Analyzing some art forms, he shows that their "formal structures, which were originally subordinate to practical utility, have become independent aesthetic objects, with their practical utility fading away." When such art objects come into being, they exert an influence on the human mind. Philosophically speaking, they are responsible historically for the aesthetic psychological construction that makes possible the development of the artistic faculty and the preservation of aesthetic legacies. Calling into question the popular view that art unites beholder and material vehicle, subject and object, Li argues that the primary factor in the aesthetic experience is the prior constitution of an aesthetic psychological formation. Such aesthetic experience attains an objective character through sedimentation. Li sees artworks as "simultaneously the material products of a certain society at a certain time and the corresponding products of a human mental construction." Here, he deviates from the usual sociological view of artworks as reflections of social forces and human relationships in society. He supports this historicist and psychological shift by analyzing the emergence of different literary genres through successive dynasties in ancient China. The various literary forms display "the isomorphic structure of the materialized states of mind of specific societies in specific times."

Li elaborates a theory of three stratifications of a work of art: form, image, and significance. These are related to three forms of sedimentation: primitive sedimentation, art sedimentation, and life sedimentation. Although his complete theory of stratification and sedimentation is his own and original, it draws its inspiration from Western thinkers such as Vico, Marx, SIGMUND FREUD, and Carl Jung, as he acknowledges. The three stratifications are, in the final analysis, "a representation of the theory of humanized nature, the humanization of senses, and the humanization of desires."

In our selection, Li focuses on the primary sedimentation: "primitive sedimentation," which corresponds to the stratification of form and the humanization of nature. It is through primitive sedimentation formed from the process of labor, he claims, that humans learned to recognize the beautiful. He further notes that the appeal of any artwork is dependent on its medium. To explore the appeal of certain ways of manipulating the "medium," Li uses the Chinese concept of *qi* (variously translated as "pneuma," "vital energy," or "material force"), which involves not only human physiology but also material media and formal structure. According to Li, "The presence, development, and transformation of the perceptual formal stratification of artworks are just the interfusion of a person's physiological, historical, and social functions that occur in sensation through sense organs." This formal stratification of artworks, which corresponds to the humanization of a person's senses and sensibility, has two aspects. The first involves the subjective efforts of both the creator's and beholder's body and mind, which approach, tally with, and form parallels or "isomorphic structures" with the dynamics of nature. Li calls this aspect "the naturalization of the human" apparent in such physical-spiritual activities as Chinese *qigong*, Taiji boxing, and other self-cultivation exercises, as well as in artworks. The second aspect entails stratifications that extend "to the ever-changing events, objects, and relationships that reflect the trends of different times and societies." These two aspects are intimately interrelated. Citing as an example the evolution of literary genres in traditional Chinese literature, Li maintains that "different historical periods exhibit different styles and forms [a]s the consequence of differing psychological demands, which in turn are affected by the social political life of the time." He concludes that primitive sedimentation, the humanization of nature, and the socialization of the individual's senses intermingle and interact in the production and reception of artworks. Throughout his discussion, he grounds the arts in the body and spirit (*qi*).

Li Zehou's aesthetic theory of primitive sedimentation is open to a number of criticisms. While it addresses the harmonies and agreements between artist and era, beholder and artwork, body/mind and society, it does not pay sufficient attention to dissonances, resistances, and disputes. Although this ambitious mimetic aesthetics is historically oriented, it risks both universalizing art and reducing it to reflective powers. The theory also casts the body, senses, feelings, and emotions as preceding thinking, logic, and imagination—as prerational—without arguing for the claim or dealing with their interrelationships. Nevertheless, by putting the body, labor, and *qi* at the heart of aesthetic theorizing, Li offers a unique as well as a broad and persuasive account of art production and reception. Stressing historical change, he avoids the eternalizing that is characteristic of much archetypal theory while maintaining that the arts are grounded in social psychology and history. A strong democratizing impulse accompanies the theory of primitive sedimentation, which operates as an equalizing force at micro levels of the human and social body. In Li's analysis, crafts as well as great works remain part of the realm of art practice and history.

Four Essays on Aesthetics: Toward a Global View **Keywords:** Aesthetics, Affect, The Body, Literary History, Marxism, Tradition

From Four Essays on Aesthetics: Toward a Global View[1]

Chapter 8. The Stratification of Form and Primitive Sedimentation

Contemporary aesthetics focuses on art and rarely pays attention to metaphysical issues such as the root (essence) of beauty. The aesthetic experience is tested and verified mainly through an analysis of art's principles and history, from individual psychological responses (aesthetic experience), and from public cultural studies. The public art world is the subject of the sociology of art, which may be a part of aesthetics but not the hard core. For me, these approaches ignore the real problems of aesthetics. However, there is still no common agreement about what art is and which works constitute art. At least we know that artworks are individual pieces of sculpture, painting, music, and other objects that we call art. We also know that many objects we call art—such as the Pyramids in Egypt, bronze vessels of the Yin and Zhou[2] dynasties in China, churches of the Middle Ages in Europe, the statues and mural paintings of Buddha in India and China, and the masks in Africa—were created for religious, ethical, political, or social purposes. Ancient articles of pottery and bronze that have been unearthed were designed for storing and cooking food, not for aesthetic appreciation. The mixture of exhibits in folk and art museums reveal that the line between art and craft is ambiguous.

The fact that the works of the modernist school appear in an infinite variety of fantastic forms expands the meaning of art. For example, one exhibit is a mass of earth and sand with something like shells scattered on it. Another is a frame of scrap iron tubing welded together with colorful light bulbs on it. When a button is pressed the lights flash, giving the impression of a street as one drives through it at night. Marcel Duchamp[3] made a urinal a work of art by placing it in an exhibition hall. Some individuals smeared themselves with greasepaint and stood in an exhibition hall claiming to be works of art. Such a variety of artistic activity makes it difficult to distinguish art from nonart.

"What are artworks?" is one question and another is, "Do we mean the same thing by art and aesthetic experience, and by artworks and aesthetic objects?"

1. Translated by Li and Jane Cauval (who collaborated to create a version that differs significantly from the Chinese original).
2. Ca. 1046–256 B.C.E. Yin dynasty: ca. 1600–1050 B.C.E. (also called Shang).
3. French artist (1887–1968), associated with dadaism and surrealism.

Whether they are historical relics or modern articles, whether they are churches or furniture, artworks on many occasions do not serve as aesthetic objects. They have other purposes such as buildings to live in or to hold religious services, or as objects in which to store food or to sit upon. Only when they serve as aesthetic objects, do they become artworks.

ARTWORKS EXIST ONLY WHEN THEY HAVE BECOME AESTHETIC OBJECTS

So how do objects made by humans, including both the practical and the so-called pure fine arts, come to be aesthetic objects? In seemingly pure appreciation, traces of the object's past utility are still sedimented. For example, we experience a sense of religious awe when we appreciate ancient temples and statues of gods. In fact, if artworks become pure beauty by losing their social functions, they become perfect decorations. To answer the question of what artworks are, I say that artworks appear and exist only when material objects made by a human being appeal to a person's aesthetic psychoemotional construction, that is, when these material forms turn into aesthetic objects.

When material objects, including temples, dramas, poetry, and prose, serve various practical or spiritual needs, exhorting people to do good or to develop interpersonal intercourse, patterns of formal experience are present. Even at this stage, the aesthetic, psychological-emotional construction begins to develop an independent function which differentiates it from other psychological constructions through a process of mutual action and reaction with them. Although drama originally was intended for recreation, propaganda, admonishment, or other practical purposes, the intensification of a person's fate strengthened by drama's formal structures can offer the person a sense of substantial experience and life impetus. These examples show that the formal structures, which were originally subordinate to practical utility, have become independent aesthetic objects, with their practical utility fading away. In this manner, the so-called pure artworks have come into being. Temples no longer serve merely as places of worship but also as beautiful architecture; paintings no longer serve simply to "perfect civilized teachings and help social relationships"[4] but also become pleasures in the mind and heart.

However, even these artworks as aesthetic objects retain daily, practical psychical functions. For example, the emotion of worshipping God can coexist with an aesthetic experience in Gothic churches. And the fervent will to fight and universal love all weave into the aesthetic experience of Beethoven's Ninth Symphony.[5] The same is true of comfortable houses, clothes, and furniture that give pleasure to the senses and mind. Even Bell's significant forms,[6] which have nothing to do with daily practice, and the unique aesthetic emotion of intellectual aristocrats lead people to a mysterious, religious experience.

4. Zhang Yanyuan's (815–875) *Lidai minghuaji* (*Record of Famous Painters of All the Dynasties*) (Taibei: Yiwen yinshuguan, 1965). English translation based on Susan Bush and Hsio-yen Shih, *Early Chinese Texts on Painting* (Cambridge: Harvard University Press, 1985), 49 [translators' note].
5. The Ninth Symphony (1817–23) of the German composer Ludwig van Beethoven (1770–1827) ends with a celebratory choral setting of FRIEDRICH SCHILLER's "Ode to Joy."
6. The idea that "Significant Form is the one quality common to all works of visual art," famously proposed in *Art* (1914) by the English art critic and aesthetician Clive Bell (1881–1964), was one of the starting points for Li Zehou's aesthetic inquiry.

There has never been truly *pure* art, only art permeated with more or less worldly emotions. The difference lies, more or less, in the ways of permeation, that is, the mathematical equation or double helix.[7] Calligraphy differs from film and clothes from poetry but from the viewpoint of aesthetics when these artworks serve as aesthetic objects, they differ only in their relation to the aesthetic psychological construction and in the different proportions and elements of the meta-equation.

In short, the aesthetic psychological construction is important to the humanization of a person's interior nature because artworks directly produce the aesthetic psychological construction, which in turn creates new artworks. With the interaction and growth between these two processes, art has become an independent cultural classification. Simultaneously, the aesthetic psychological construction has become an important form and aspect of human mentality, which distinguishes itself from the intellectual psychological construction and volitional psychological construction. Therefore, we may explore and grasp the definition of art only by examining the direct effect, influence, and constitution of this human psychological construction. It is only from this approach that we can reasonably distinguish art from nonart.

An object is an artwork if it can arouse emotions (e.g., sorrow or joy) merely through its formal structure rather than depending on certain sorrowful or joyful images. This independent force or character of the formal structure of an artwork arises from its correspondence to the aesthetic psychological construction that developed in a gradual process of mutual penetration. This means that the force of the formal structure acts on, influences, and constitutes the aesthetic psychological construction.

Therefore, art as the sum of various kinds of artworks signifies the historical constitution of the human aesthetic psychological construction. Just as primitive tools prove that early humans lived on the earth and founded the material life of later generations, so artworks prove that early humans had a spiritual life and founded the spiritual life of their descendants. The legacy of art is deeply sedimented in the human psychological construction, in which lies the value and significance of artistic works as a kind of symbolic production. This system of symbols constitutes and affirms the human psychological construction.

WHAT ARE ARTWORKS?

Now I will expand on my response to the question, "What are artworks?" First, artworks manifest themselves in media made by human beings. In the process of creation, artists direct their illusory world of images and emotions onto specific materials such as stone, bronze, canvas, paper, wood, and even their own bodies, turning them into material objects. It is [in] the process of materialization through continuous correction and alteration that the illusory world is realized and becomes a work of art. For the beholder, without material media, the images could not affect the human senses, convey their aesthetic significance, and influence generations of people. Without material media, there would be no works of art.

7. In geometry, a spiral consisting of two strands around the same axis (most familiar as the structure of DNA).

Second, artworks exist only when a person perceiving them has an aesthetic experience. Only when we experience an object aesthetically does it become an aesthetic object, a work of art. Therefore, objects are works of art, whether created for appreciation, practical purposes, or spiritual reasons, as long as they directly appeal to, excite, and arouse an aesthetic experience. Since works of art exist as aesthetic objects only when a person appreciates them, they have only an illusory existence, which differs from the real existence of the artistic media or artistic vehicles. The illusory existence depends both on what is offered objectively by the material and by what is offered by the beholder because the nature of a beholder's aesthetic experience is relative to the person's culture, social class, background, character, cultivation, ideals, and previous aesthetic experiences. Scholars often repeat Marx's comment about a "musical ear,"[8] which implies that things become artworks only when they enter into a person's aesthetic awareness. Various and complicated subjective conditions determine if an artistic product can be accepted as an aesthetic object. If a material vehicle, an artistic product, is a necessary condition, then the subjective aesthetic experience is the sufficient condition. Works of art, as aesthetic objects, unite these two conditions. This is the kind of unity between subject and object advocated by Zhu Guangqian,[9] which explains the essential character of art.

Now, I wish to turn to the question of beauty in art. The social objectivity of artistic beauty means that artworks, which combine subjective experience and material media, change as aesthetic objects as the media changes. Since the illusory world of artworks exists in the aesthetic experiences of individuals, their common acceptability is possible because of the constitution of the aesthetic psychological construction. Psychological construction occurs because the summation and generalization of various aesthetic experiences develop a substantial character, comparatively independent of any single aesthetic experience, and in this way attain an objective character through sedimentation. This process brings about the materialization of a common psychological construction in human beings. The beauty of art possesses an objective character. However, this social objectivity differs from the social objectivity of the root of beauty.

Therefore, the definition of a work of art must be left open. There are no set conventions or rules for art to follow because materials change and so do subjective experiences. Therefore, there is no use in seeking an eternal and unchangeable definition of art. Jan Mukarovsky[1] said, "Artistic works are expressed in the form of symbols in their internal structure, in their relation with reality and society, and with creators and receivers." He made a study of artwork in three contexts: their relationships to society, to creators and appreciators, and to different elements in the artwork itself. Studying an artwork from these three aspects gives us a rather complete method. Undoubtedly, we will discover many specific aesthetic and artistic laws if we regard art as a pluralistic phenomenon instead of searching for one definition for all art. We

8. Karl Marx, *Economic and Philosophic Manuscripts of 1844*. See Robert C. Tucker ed., *The Marx-Engels Reader* [2d ed. (New York: Norton, 1978)], 89 [translators' note]. KARL MARX (1818–1883), German social and political philosopher; in the passage cited, he argues that aesthetic gratification can occur only in the context of "humanized nature."

9. Western-educated Chinese aesthetician (1897–1986); as a young scholar, Li Zehou criticized his ideas.

1. Czech structuralist (1891–1975).

should study and examine art as an organic unity of various mutually interacting elements such as readers, writers, social circumstances, the formal structures of artworks (tone, rhythm, vocabulary, image, and so on), and analyze its history, individual works, artists, styles, and tastes. With the development of science, studies of art will become more scientific, formalized, and specialized.

SOCIOLOGY OF ART AS A STUDY OF AESTHETIC CONSCIOUSNESS

In mainland China, questions are raised about the sociology of art such as "Does the sociology of art belong to aesthetics, including theory, and history of art, and art criticism?" and if it does, "What are the characteristics of art sociology as a meaningful component of aesthetics?"

From the standpoint of philosophical aesthetics, which comprises the subjects of the humanization of nature, the constitution of a new sensuousness, and the psychological-emotional construction, the sociology of art in general focuses only on the external conditions and circumstances of aesthetic experience. However, if it views artworks, art history, and criticism as the presence, history, and appreciation of aesthetic objects, this new approach will keep the sociology of art interacting and collaborating with the study of aesthetic psychology.

Only when we actively appreciate artworks do we encounter the real presence of aesthetic objects, which are simultaneously the material products of a certain society at a certain time and the corresponding products of a human mental construction. Therefore, the study of artworks as aesthetic objects is actually the study of a materialized mental structure formed in a certain society and time. In fact, the human psychological-emotional construction manifests a history of taste. As a result, the sociology of art can be the study of an aesthetic consciousness presented in certain form. When the sociology of art treats aesthetic objects in this way, it differentiates itself from art theory in general. That is, given that aesthetic objects are related to a given state of mind, we can see that the study of the appearance, prevalence, and decline of a certain artwork, and the fashion, taste, and conception of art in a certain society and epoch is closely related to the aesthetic experiences and ideals of people at that time. In other words, the study of modern artworks (art criticism) and ancient artworks (art history) and the establishment of certain aesthetic principles (art theory) with aesthetic experience as an indispensable guide and starting point, will become a part of the sociology of art within the category of aesthetics.

Artworks are just the materialization and condensation of human aesthetic psychological processes. The externalized material formations, artworks, provide us with volumes of touchable works that reveal the psychology of the human inner world. Art is a brilliant mirror of the mind and soul.

The history of aesthetic objects is the history of human aesthetic psychological constructions; the objects manifest the history of cultures formed by humans and inherited generation after generation. The changes in style and attitudes toward the same artwork reflect the states of mind of people living in different times and societies. A specific social economy, politics, and culture determine and normalize the states of mind of its inhabitants.

Artworks reflecting many different states of mind have circulated widely for centuries. For instance, *shi* was popular in the Tang Dynasty, *ci* was in vogue in the Five Dynasties and the Song Dynasty,[2] and novels and dramas reached their climax in the middle of the Ming Dynasty.[3] All were the products of their times and were displaying the isomorphic structure of the materialized states of mind of specific societies in specific times.

Various art trends, such as the rational, romantic, and sentimental reflect the various projections and proportions of different aspects of a peoples' aesthetic psychology and display the history of the unceasing enrichment, renewal, expansion, and growth of the human psychological-emotional construction. The study of works of art as the materialized aesthetic experience reveals richer and more varied historical details than does a direct study of psychology. In addition, this new approach to the sociology of art will give impetus and stimulation to the entire discipline of psychology. The fusion and unity of the sociology of art and of the psychology of aesthetics will be the scientific realization of Marx's philosophical conviction that the formation of the human mind and senses was, and continues to be, a labor of world history, the humanization of nature. This will result in the fundamental principles of the philosophy of beauty, aesthetic psychology, and sociology of art forming an integral unity.

My discussion in this essay—developing from the root of beauty to the aesthetic experience and on to aesthetic objects—tries to reflect the general development of the logical and historical from the abstract to the concrete and from the simple to the complex in the field of beauty and art. I try to show that the root (essence) of beauty relates to the root (essence) of human beings and that the art constructions relate to the emotional constructions. In other words, the origin of beauty connects with the instrumental-social construction and the artwork connects with the psychological-emotional construction.

THREE STRATIFICATIONS OF A WORK OF ART

Now, I will consider the three stratifications of a work of art: form, image, and significance. The former two are analogous to sensation and desire. Of course, we cannot draw a hard and fast line between any of these stratifications because they mutually penetrate, blend, and overlap and often exist in the same aesthetic object. Furthermore, they also exist in very complicated and crisscross patterns. For example, the stratification of form that appeals to sensation in literary works is vague. A novel appears to us through paper and words but the sensations of a novel are not the sensations of the paper and printed characters; instead, they are manifested in an imaginative presentation. Even the stratification of significance cannot exist by itself because it exists only in the stratification of form-sensation and in the stratification of image-desire, while simultaneously transcending them.

2. *Shi* [in Chinese] means poetry in general, but here it refers to a special type of poetry with eight or four lines, each containing five or seven characters, with a strict tonal pattern and rhyme scheme. This type of poetry was highly developed in the Tang Dynasty (618–907), though its origin can be traced back to preceding times. *Ci* is a type of poetry with strict tonal patterns and rhyme schemes in fixed numbers of lines and words in accordance with the melody it is supposed to attune to. It originated in the Tang Dynasty and fully developed in the Song Dynasty (960–1297) [translators' note]. Five Dynasties: the period in Chinese history between the end of the Tang and beginning of the Song dynasty.

3. 1368–1644.

From the characteristics of these three stratifications, we see that they are nothing but a representation of the theory of humanized nature, the humanization of senses, and the humanization of desires. Nevertheless, I must ask, "Which came first, art or the sense of beauty?" This endless dispute remains unresolved. Some scholars, arguing that art came first, brought evidence from mural paintings in primitive caves. Others, arguing from the study of linear decorations on stone tools made by primitive man, insisted that aesthetic experience came first.

Although I take the latter stand, I do not base my arguments on the linear decorations found on articles such as baskets and early art works or from the geometrical lines that were abstracted from realistic images of animals. I believe, as I have said in parts 1 and 2,[4] the earliest aesthetic experiences arose from labor through making and using tools. Linear patterns followed certain orders and laws, such as repetition, overlapping, symmetry, and balance, and became recognized as beautiful because primitive humans experienced, familiarized themselves with, and grasped these orders of nature and laws of form through human productive activities. Primitive sedimentation was the most important process that directed these changes and made them follow certain laws.

PRIMITIVE SEDIMENTATION

What is primitive sedimentation? It is the most fundamental sedimentation, formed from the process of material labor. Through a long process of labor, primitive humans employed aspects of the natural order, such as rhythm and sequence, and, in doing so, brought objective regularity and subjective purposiveness into a new unity. This new unity brought forth the earliest forms of beauty and aesthetic experience. In other words, through labor humans endowed the material world with forms which, although originally found in nature itself, began to develop an independent nature through the application of humans' abstractive faculty. Through the process of social labor production humans created the forms of beauty.

The earliest awareness of beauty arose from the human subjective emotions and sensations, which corresponded to the objective forms of beauty. This correspondence is the product of sedimentation. As humans began to utilize the laws of nature to create objects of beauty, their own senses and emotions formed an isomorphic correspondence with these external objects. Animals also have isomorphic correspondence, but humans differ from animals because they developed theirs through the long process of tool-using productive activity and by imbuing it with sociality. These social activities greatly extended the structures of isomorphic correspondence, and it is these dynamic structures of correspondence that I call primitive sedimentation.

At first, humans produced very simple tools—such as stone artifacts and bows and arrows—to improve their chances of survival. As they were engaged in these activities of making and using tools, they began to comprehend, imagine, understand, and become sensitive to the orders of nature. When a human achieved certain goals in the process of laboring (reforming the objective world), the regularity and purposiveness of the process would unite with

4. That is, the first two parts of the book from which this selection is taken, *Four Essays on Aesthetics*.

the human sensuous construction (the activity of labor) to produce feelings of pleasure. It is the pleasure derived from this process that is the pleasure of the earliest aesthetic experience. Although there may have been vague understandings, imaginings and intentions in the experience, sensation dominated. I call this the prehistory of humans' spiritual world or the process of primitive sedimentation.

At this primitive stage of sedimentation, the aesthetic psychological construction of humans was being formed. It was during the primitive productive practice that humans first experienced aesthetic pleasure from sensing the unity of their internal mentality and the laws of the external world. Because of these earliest processes and pleasures, I conclude that the feeling for beauty arose before our awareness of art.

Does any primitive sedimentation remain in the aesthetic experience of people, now that the productive activities are so different from those of primitive times? Our understanding of natural laws is far greater than it was thousands of years ago and the relation between aesthetic experience and productive labor is more complex. However, the fundamental relations, such as balance, symmetry, proportion, and rhythm in works of art, remain, although the concrete forms and laws are much more complicated and varied than during prehistoric times. These relationships are still the products of the accumulations of primitive sedimentations, derived from the activities of social productive practice in daily life.

For example, there is an essential difference between a human's sense of space and time derived from today's practical activities and that of primitive human beings. Primitive humans in the remote past had a sense of space and time similar to and as vague as that of children today. Primitive humans imagined time to be an uninterrupted sheet of expansion. As society progressed, the primary divisions of time appeared. At first, people's sense of space and time focused on specific events and content. For example, time meant seasons and space meant the directions of east, west, south, and north with no abstract or general concept of time or space. The views of space and time during agricultural, industrial, and our current information societies differ greatly and each period exerted its influence on the form and content of art. The feeling for different rhythms manifests the differences. Obviously, the rhythm in an agricultural society differs from that of the present information society. An individual sensation does not constitute the real character of a person's sense of space and time because character reflects the practice in society. This is equally true of our other senses, which have become what they are because of primitive sedimentation and express themselves in the sensory stratification of artworks.

Why is it that the different peoples in different times produce different machinery and architecture? Why is it that the technological modeling and design patterns of ancient times are so elaborate and complicated, while those of modern times so lucid and succinct? It must be true that small-scale agricultural production and large-scale industrial production produce great differences in design. Why is it that the fast rhythms, streams of consciousness, and vast expanses of space and time, which often appear in contemporary movies, make one feel full of energy? It must be that fast rhythms in time and vast expanses of space express the advent of an age of outer space navigation and of an information society. All of the above belong to the category of primitive sedimentation in the sensory stratification of art forms, mainly the perceptual sedimentation of history and society in the external forms of art.

THE APPEAL OF AN ARTWORK IS DEPENDENT UPON ITS MEDIUM

Although critically important, primitive sedimentation is only one component of the formal stratification of artworks. The relationship of the object's medium to the psychological construction of the subject affects the appeal of artworks. For example, a statue made of black, rough bronze or the same figure made of white smooth marble will produce different impressions. The size of artworks is also important. When you enter a Christian cathedral, its high and broad interior will immediately give you a sense of awe. A small image of the Buddha does not convey Buddha's boundless supernatural power in the way a huge, golden statue does.

In literary works, the sound of the words and the rhythm of the sentences influence the quality of the aesthetic experience. Chinese poets pay special attention to the tones[5] of characters. Stories of Chinese poets reveal the difficulty of choosing between *nong* (dense) and *nao* (sprightly) to describe the sense of spring and between *tui* (push) and *qiao* (knock) to open the gate.[6] The connection between high pitch and brightness and between low pitch and darkness indicate a rich and complicated isomorphic correspondence between sensation and emotion, as well as among other elements of sensation aroused by artistic forms. Hence, Chinese poets and prose writers emphasize the importance of reading their works aloud for the rhythm, tempo, and melody, all of which are manifested in the sound of reading, the sensation.

Some examples from Chinese literature exhibit the kinds of formal stratification that appeal to readers' senses. There is the dignity of the five-regulated poetry (a form of poetry with eight lines, each consisting of five characters), the fluidity of seven-regulated poetry (a form of poetry with eight lines, each consisting of seven characters), the heaviness of four-line poetry, the grandiosity of ancient-style poetry (a form of poetry longer than the above-mentioned ones and with fewer restrictions), the symmetry of rhythmical prose with parallelism, the smoothness of prose without parallelism, the machismo of Han Yu's (768–824) prose, the gentleness of Ouyang Xiu's (1007–1072) prose, the terseness of Wang Anshi's (1021–1086) prose, and the

5. In all forms of the Chinese language, different tones distinguish words that are otherwise pronounced alike (e.g., Mandarin has four tones, including "high" and "falling").

6. Li refers to two poems. *Nong* and *nao* refers to Song Qi's (998–1061) poem *The Spring of the Jade Towel*, wherein is a famous line: "The sense of spring is sprightly on the pink twigs of apricot trees." *Nao* (sprightly), although an unusual word in this context because this word also means "noisy," is generally regarded by Chinese critics as much better than a common word, say, *nong* (dense). *Tui* and *qiao* refers to Jia Dao's (779–843) poem, *To Li Ningyou's House*, in which he wrote: "Birds are sleeping on trees by a pool, / A monk is knocking on the gate under the moon." A story in connection with these two lines is that when Jia Dao, a common scholar, was riding on a donkey, concentrating on these two lines, and hesitating between "knocking" and "pushing," he collided with the servants of a high-ranking official, Han Yu (768–824), who was also a great poet and writer. It was a big offense according to the law at that time, but, after inquiring the cause, Han did not punish Jia; on the contrary, he helped him to decide to use "knocking," and henceforth took Jia as a friend. The main reason is that both words (*nao, qiao*) are correct, but when the poem is read aloud the sounds and tones differ, and the one selected is connected with the appropriate sensation [translators' note].

boundless expansion of Su Shi's (1036–1101) prose.[7] Therefore, people experience the beautiful forms of literary works not through logical thinking but through sensation and through literary *qi* (vital force).[8] This force comes alive and apparent in the process of reading aloud literary works, because the addition of the auditory to the visual intensifies the experience. In the earliest stages of learning, Chinese painters and calligraphers emphasized the importance of imitating works of the masters because by doing so, students experience the feel of the brush strokes used by the master and directly familiarize themselves with the beautiful forms that are the sensory formal stratifications of art.

In traditional China, many branches of learning discussed the importance of *qi* in philosophy and in traditional Chinese medicine as well as in literature and art. It is very difficult to know whether *qi* is material or spiritual or both, but it is a life force that appeals to sensuousness. Cao Pi[9] (187–226) wrote:

> The main point of literary works is *qi*, which may be strong or feeble in a fixed mold and cannot be changed by human effort. Take playing wind instruments for an example: The rules of melody, tempo, and rhythm may be the same, but the exertion of *qi* [vital force, but also breath or wind] is different, and thus ingenuity or clumsiness is distinguished. Such *qi* cannot be handed down, even from father to son or from the elder to the younger.[1]

Qi refers to human physiology as well as to material stuff and structure. In literary works, it refers to morphology and syntax, including the literary *qi* of Han Yu, Ouyang Xiu, Wang Anshi, and Su Shi. However, a person's physiological force requires a human body for expression. *Qi* (its static state is called *shi* or impetus) comes from an artwork's formal structure, that is, its composition, lines, and proportion. The blank spaces in Chinese painting and emotional-function words in traditional Chinese prose directly influence a person's mind.[2] The influence of this *qi* is much more powerful than that which comes from its content. It arouses and excites a person's feelings, sensations, emotions, and vitality immediately without the mediation of understanding and imagination.

THE GENIUS OF ARTISTS LIES IN THE USE OF FORM

The genius of an artist lies in the creation of a brand new sensuous world by the formal stratification of art. As Goethe[3] put it, everybody can see the content of artworks, an understanding mind can comprehend their implied

7. Famous Chinese literary figures, each with a distinctive prose style.
8. Literally, *qi* means "air" or "breath." In Chinese philosophy, it refers to the vital energy or material force in both humans and the universe (much like the classical Greek idea of pneuma). In aesthetics, it refers to the totality of creative force evinced by an artist, manifested in a piece of artwork, and experienced by a beholder or reader.
9. Founding emperor of Wei dynasty (220–280) and an influential poet and critic. In his most famous critical writing, "A Discourse on Literature," Cao posited the aesthetic concept of *wenqi* (literary pneuma), which became a foundational idea in Chinese literary criticism and aesthetics.
1. Cao Pi, "A Discourse on Literature (*Lun Wen*)," in Stephen Owens, *An Anthology of Chinese Literature: Beginnings to 1911* (New York: Norton, 1996), 361 [translators' note].
2. In Chinese painting, blank space is often pregnant with implications. Similarly, function words express no explicit meaning but convey subtle emotions and sensibilities.
3. Johann Wolfgang von Goethe (1749–1832), German poet, dramatist, novelist, and scientist.

significance, but for most people, the form is a mystery. The emergence of outstanding artworks and innovation does not necessarily mean a breakthrough in content; it may arise from a variation in formal and sensuous stratification. This leads to a variation in aesthetic experience as well as in genuine artistic creation. Although the breakthrough or creation arises from the form, the artwork may still be permeated with rich and substantial social content. Rudolf Arnheim[4] emphasized that content expressed by sensuous form can produce an isomorphic structure corresponding to mental feeling and engendering moving force. In our daily life, putting the palms together signifies devotion, making a deep bow expresses respect, raising one's head or lowering it displays respectively arrogance or humility. People with different cultural backgrounds and different languages understand the meaning of such gestures and postures of sensuous forms. One of the functions of art is to discover, organize, and create the structural forms universally owned by everybody and to imbue the sensuous forms with significance.

The presence, development, and transformation of the perceptual formal stratification of artworks are just the interfusion of a person's physiological, historical, and social functions that occur in sensation through sense organs. These constitute one aspect of the world of art as it cultivates human nature and remolds a person's mind and heart. One reason photography can never take the place of representative painting is that the lines, colors, and compositions drawn by a human hand are not the same as those of natural things. In painting, there are shapes and shadings that derive from a person's technique, which, in some senses, are far superior to natural forms. The colors in the paintings of Qi Baishi and Henri Matisse[5] are not the classical ones that "follow the categories [of the object] in applying colors,"[6] nor are they natural colors; rather, they are emancipated colors, the free expression of a person. These colors are deeply significant. They manifest human uniqueness and the ability of a human to empower a painting, its composition, lines, colors, proportions, and empty spaces with his or her special aesthetic experience.

STRATIFICATION OF FORM IN ARTWORKS CORRESPONDS TO THE HUMANIZATION OF A PERSON'S SENSATION

In summary, the formal stratification of artworks extends itself, based on primitive sedimentation, in two directions. In one direction, the subjective efforts of a creator's and beholder's body and mind approaches, tallies with, and forms isomorphic structures according to the rhythm of nature. This is the naturalization of the human manifested not only in physical activities such as Chinese *qigong*, *taiji*, and *practice for longevity*[7] but also in the formal stratification of artworks, including *qi* (vital force) and *bone-strength*. These do not express natural physiology, but result from human self-cultivation over long periods. In theory, from Mencius's[8] cultivating *qi* to *guqi* (literally means

4. German-born American art theorist and perceptual psychologist (1904–2007).
5. French painter and sculptor (1869–1954). Qi Baishi (1864–1957), Chinese painter famous for his watercolors.
6. Li quotes from Xie He's (c. 500) *Six Canons*. See Jianping Gao, *The Expressive Act in Chinese Art: From Calligraphy to Painting* (Stockholm: Almqvist & Wiksell International, 1996), 127 [translators' note].
7. Different kinds of Chinese exercises for body-mind self-cultivation; each has its distinct style and rationale, but all are predicated on the nurturing of the human *qi* (life force or vital energy).
8. Chinese Confucian philosopher (Mengzi, ca. 371–ca. 289 B.C.E.).

bone-breath, but actually means something near noble vitality), in later times it takes great effort to get the formal stratification of artworks to tally with the rhythm of the universe and thereby to form an isomorphic structure.[9] In Chinese literary works and arts, the emphasis is to embody the Way, exemplified by sayings such as "skill promoting to the Way,"[1] "uncanny workmanship," and "as if created by nature, though made by man." Only through long periods of highly arduous self-cultivation can a person participate in the work of creation with nature. A vast amount of literary data about Chinese artworks testifies both to the difficulty and to the pleasure of achieving this goal.

The other direction in which the formal stratification extends itself refers to the ever-changing objects, events, and relationships that reflect the trends of different times and societies. These features refer to the formal variations, which are only more or less related to the primitive sedimentation. Earlier, I mentioned Worringer's[2] idea that abstract modern art relates to modern life and social psychology. René Wellek compares the relationship between various styles and social psychology.[3] Heinrich Wolfflin[4] shows the different styles of plastic art created in the Renaissance and those created in the Baroque period. The Renaissance is static, distinct, formal, and rational; the Baroque is dynamic, unclear, picturesque, and sensuous. The former appeared in a time of happiness and prosperity, and the latter in a time of depression and solitude.[5] The fact that different historical periods exhibit different styles and forms is the consequence of differing psychological demands, which in turn are affected by the social political life of the time.

How can we account for the transformations in art forms? In traditional Chinese literature, why did the five-character-a-line poetry turn into seven-character-a-line poetry, and the latter into *ci*, the uneven-numbered-character poetry? What is the difference among the artistic atmospheres produced by *shi*, *ci*, and *qu*?[6] Why is it that in Chinese landscape painting the employment of dense blue and green colors turned into that of ink-wash? In addition to detailed drawings of real objects by fine brushwork, why is there the technique of splash-ink? These seem to be changes in the external forms, but in reality, they are deeply imbedded in human psychology and society. For instance, *shi* and *ci* demand implicitness, but *qu* puts stress on explicitness and liveliness. *Qu* took the place of *ci* because, under the oppression of the

9. Zehou Li and Liu Gangji's *The History of Chinese Aesthetics* (vol. 2) provides a detailed discussion of *qi* (vital force) and *gu* (bone). Jianping Gao's *The Expressive Act in Chinese Art* gives an explanation of *gu* and Xie He's *gufa yongbi* after commenting on Susan Bush, Michael Sullivan, William Acker, Wen C. Fong, Zehou Li, and Liu Gangji's relevant views. See *The Expressive Act in Chinese Art*, 176–79 [translators' note].

1. A term from Zhuangzi, "The Secret of Caring for Life," in which the Cook answers to the King's praise by saying "What I care about is the Way, which goes beyond skill." See Burton Watson, trans., *The Complete Works of Chuang Tzu* (New York: Columbia University Press, 1968), 50 [translators' note]. Zhuangzi (or Chuang Tzu, 4th c. B.C.E.), influential Daoist philosopher.

2. Wilhelm Worringer (1881–1965), German art historian.

3. See René Wellek and Austin Warren, *Theory of Literature* (New York: Harcourt Brace Jovanovich, 1977) [translators' note]. Wellek (1903–1995), Czech-born American literary theorist and historian.

4. Swiss art critic (1864–1945).

5. Heinrich Wolfflin, *Principles of Art History: The Problem of the Development of Style in Later Art*, trans. M. D. Hottinger (New York: Dover Publications, 1950) [translators' note]. Baroque art, which developed in Europe in the 17th century, was more dramatic and emotional than that of the Renaissance (14th–17th centuries), which usually displayed a more restrained classicism.

6. *Qu* is a form of poetry that gained popularity during the Yuan Dynasty (1271–1368), a dynasty ruled by the Mongolians. *Qu* can have two forms, one is in the form of short poetry presented independently and the other is a part of a much larger opera [translators' note].

Yuan Dynasty (Mongolians), intellectuals held a very low social position. In addition, owing to the weakening of Confucian teachings of gentleness and mildness,[7] the intellectuals expressed their complaints and indignation through the form of *qu* without hesitancy or reserve. This artistic atmosphere produced the smoothness and clearness of *qu*. In short, the social-political culture appeals to sensation through the formal stratification of art and constitutes the social psychology of a specific time. Conversely, the social psychology of the time, congealed and expressed in the formal stratification of sensation, passes from generation to generation and exerts unceasing and decisive influences on human psychology and sensation. This constitutes the tradition of formal stratification of artworks.

Gombrich's[8] study of the history of fine arts demonstrates that the formal sensation of art relates to its historical and social context and later generations continue the inheritance of the former. Because of the many different social arrangements, religions, ethics, politics, and commerce, societies in different times and places produce different patterns of rhythm, meter, proportion, and balance in the sensuous stratification of art forms. Nevertheless, within these variations lies something inheritable, continual, and conventional. As a result, the history of artistic style is the history of the sensuous psychology of individual cultures as well as that of human beings.

This history retains the primitive sedimentation, which is the basis of the extension toward nature, to form an isomorphic structure in accordance with the universal laws of nature, as well as with social life and ideology. These aspects—primitive sedimentation, nature, and society—intermingle and interact in intricate patterns and, in doing so, form a succession of magnificent aesthetic products. The joint efforts of the three forces constitute the root of art, which is the objective existence of the materialized substance of the human mind and emotion. Herein lies the philosophical and aesthetic mystery of the history of artistic style.

1989, 2006

7. Confucianism was the traditional moral and religious system of China, based on the sayings attributed to the sage known as Confucius (Kongfuzi, 551–479 B.C.E.) and the commentaries on them.

8. Ernst Hans Josef Gombrich (1909–2001), Austrian-born British art historian; his *The Story of Art* (1950) is a very popular introduction to the visual arts.

TONI MORRISON
b. 1931

Toni Morrison is among the most prominent figures of American letters. She is often singled out for her prolific storytelling, which documents the black experience in literature, particularly the black female experience. The philosopher and public intellectual Cornel West has called Morrison "the great storyteller, the great literary artist, of black folk. She's our Tolstoy, our Joyce, our Walter Scott." As an essayist, novelist, lecturer, and educator, Morrison braids together American and African American life, history, and memory. Her work explores gender, sex, sexuality, race, slavery, spirituality, music, and American literary, intellectual, and cultural history. On the one hand, Morrison picks apart the tangles and knots of American history, especially with respect to how black life is shaped and represented artistically, economically, politically, and socially. She addresses pivotal turns in that history, from slavery to the black power movement to U.S. Supreme Court confirmation hearings, while at the same time exposing the ugliness of systemic oppression and the beauty of resilience. On the other hand, Morrison specifically focuses on the black female experience, which is often trapped in the racist-sexist underpinnings of American culture and history and relegated to the periphery of American life. By moving black women to the narrative center, she reintroduces them as integral to the fabric of American life and history. Her novels and criticism give voice to the unspeakable experiences of black human beings and contest discourses that enforce and legitimate racism and oppression.

Morrison was born Chloe Ardelia Wofford in Lorain, Ohio, the second of four children. Her father, George Wofford, was a shipyard welder born in Georgia, and her mother, Ramah (*née* Willis) Wofford, was born in Alabama. By the time she was twelve years old, Morrison had converted to Catholicism; her baptismal name, St. Anthony, is the source of the name Toni. Lorain was a steel town that attracted many immigrants, and Morrison attended integrated schools. In her first grade class, she was the only black student and the only child who could read effortlessly. As she matured, Morrison continued her voracious reading of a great range of authors, from Jane Austen to Ernest Hemingway, Gustave Flaubert to Leo Tolstoy. Her appreciation for African American folk culture, particularly music, was nurtured by her mother, who sang and loved all music, classical music and spirituals alike. After graduating from Lorain High School, in 1949 Morrison enrolled in Howard University in Washington, D.C., the premier historically black university in the United States. The man considered the dean of the Harlem Renaissance, the philosopher Alain Locke, was one of her professors. Morrison was also actively involved with the Howard Repertory Theater, and she took part in a writing workshop where she began to explore the story of a little black girl who wanted blue eyes—a story that twenty years later would become her first novel, *The Bluest Eye* (1970). In 1953, Morrison received her bachelor's degree, with a major in English and a minor in the classics, and began graduate studies at Cornell University. In 1955 she earned her master's in English, writing a thesis that examined how the works of William Faulkner and VIRGINIA WOOLF address despair and suicide.

From 1955 to 1957, Morrison taught at Texas Southern University and then at Howard University from 1957 to 1964. Among her students at Howard were Houston A. Baker Jr., who would become a prominent literary scholar, and Stokely Carmichael, already active in the Student Nonviolent Coordinating Committee and the future honorary prime minister of the Black Panther Party. While on Howard's faculty, Morrison also began writing again. She joined a group of black writers in the Washington, D.C., area that included Claude Brown, who would publish *Manchild in the Promised Land* (1965). During this time she met and married Harold Morrison, a Jamaican architect, with whom she had two sons, Harold Ford Morrison and Kevin Slade Morrison; the couple divorced in 1964. Morrison left Howard University, returned briefly to Lorain, and then moved to Syracuse, New York, where she began editing textbooks for a subsidiary of Random House. In 1967 she was transferred to Random House's headquarters in New York City as a senior editor, a position she would hold for nearly twenty years. There she worked on books by African American authors such as Henry Dumas, Toni Cade Bambara, Angela Davis, Muhammad Ali, and Gayle Jones. She also oversaw the creation of *The Black Book* (1974), a narrative compilation—drawn largely from the collection of Middleton A. Harris—of photographs, slave auction posters, newspaper clippings, and other materials relating to the African American experience in the United States. At the same time, Morrison held a series of academic appointments at the State University of New

York at Purchase, Yale University, and Bard College. She left Random House in 1983, and a year later was named the Albert Schweitzer Professor of the Humanities at the State University of New York at Albany. In 1989 Morrison moved on to Princeton University as the Robert F. Goheen Professor of the Council of the Humanities, becoming professor emerita in 2006. Her papers are in the permanent collections of the Princeton University Library.

Early in her years at Random House, Morrison returned to the story of *The Bluest Eye*, a novel set in an Ohio town just before the outbreak of World War II. Morrison wrote the novel in part as a meditation on a slogan of the black power movement of the 1960s and 1970s, "Black is beautiful," questioning why it was necessary to publicly articulate the idea of black beauty, particularly in opposition to Western beauty ideals of whiteness. She wanted to counter the narrative in American literature that relegated black people—especially little black girls—to the periphery. In her novel, black girls were central characters. Unfortunately, *The Bluest Eye* was published to mixed reviews and it found few readers.

Soon Morrison began working on her second novel, *Sula* (1973), which placed black women in a small town in Ohio at the center of the story. Though *Sula* was nominated for a National Book Award, Morrison was not catapulted to the national stage until the publication of *Song of Solomon* (1977), which featured spectral hauntings, the mythology of flying Africans, and a male narrator. The book became a best seller and won the National Book Critics Circle Award in 1978. It was followed by another best seller—*Tar Baby* (1981), a novel set in a fictional Caribbean village that addressed gender, race, class, and transnationalism—which brought growing national acclaim and popularity.

Morrison's position in American letters was cemented with *Beloved* (1987), which would win both the American Book Award and the Pulitzer Prize for Fiction in 1988, be adapted as a film in 1998, and be named by the *New York Times* in 2006 as the best American novel published in the previous twenty-five years. *Beloved* is inspired in part by the true story of the fugitive slave Margaret Garner; the novel's protagonist, Sethe, is an escaped slave who murders her own daughter, Beloved, rather than consign the child to a life of slavery and sexual abuse. The book's themes include guilt, memory, and the political, sexual, and social implications of slavery and slaveholding.

Morrison has also acted as an important literary, cultural, and social critic. In 1988, she delivered "Unspeakable Things Unspoken: The Afro-American Presence in American Literature," our selection, as the Tanner Lecture on Human Values at the University of Michigan. In this address, later published in the *Michigan Quarterly Review*, Morrison takes up the canon wars raging in the United States: she focuses on the exclusion of black writers from the American literary canon despite the centrality of black people to America's national identity, particularly as their shadowy presence is articulated in the literary imagination of those white writers whose works are considered part of the canon of great American books. Morrison tackles questions of identity, literary quality, and nationhood. She wonders about the definition of "race." Who and what constitutes America and Americanness? What is American literature, and who are its great writers? She challenges literary "standards" that are exclusionary, based solely on a white male norm, as well as those that attribute value on the basis of race rather than mastery of form and feeling. At the same time, Morrison sees ignoring race as a liberal gesture that poses another set of problems. It is precisely the black presence, she suggests, that has enlivened and shaped American literature and the presence of Afro-American literature that raises the stakes and standards for the study of American literature. Literature should be universal—but cannot be if it has room only for white, predominantly male writers. In a nation built on the backs of blacks, the excising of the dark presence as writers and subjects leads to a greatly impoverished national literature.

Morrison turns specifically to Herman Melville's *Moby-Dick* (1851), a novel that she views as haunted and informed by the key issues of its time—namely, slavery, blackness, and whiteness. In Morrison's reading, the contest between Ahab and the white whale is raced. Melville rejects the superiority of whiteness, particularly its deployment in fear to justify human bondage and trafficking. This ideology of whiteness is the unspeakable thing that has long remained unspoken in *Moby-Dick*. With "Unspeakable Things Unspoken," Morrison jumped into the thick of the creative fray around multiculturalism, third world literature, and the canon.

In 1992 Morrison expanded on the themes taken up in "Unspeakable Things Unspoken" in *Playing in the Dark: Whiteness and the Literary Imagination*, a text that drew in part on her William E. Massey Sr. Lectures in the History of American Civilization, delivered in 1990 at Harvard University. Also in 1992, she edited a collection on the raced and gendered implications of the confirmation hearings of Clarence Thomas, an African American judge nominated to the Supreme Court who faced allegations of sexual harassment from Anita Hill, an African American law professor: *Race-ing Justice, En-Gendering Power: Essays on Anita Hill, Clarence Thomas, and the Construction of Social Reality*. Again delving into issues of race, gender, justice, and cultural politics, Morrison co-edited *Birth of a Nation'hood: Gaze, Script, and Spectacle in the O.J. Simpson Case* (1997) with her Princeton colleague Claudia Brodsky Lacour, a professor of comparative literature. In 2017, she published *The Origin of Others*, another series of lectures given at Harvard University, where she addresses, among other ideas, slavery and subsequent European contact/conquest of Africa as originary moments of othering for African Americans.

In recent decades, Morrison has received awards and accolades from around the world, beginning in 1993 with the Nobel Prize in Literature—the first African American and the eighth woman to win that honor. Other awards include an honorary doctorate from Oxford University (2005); France's highest academic honor, the Légion d'Honneur (2010); and the U.S. Presidential Medal of Freedom (2012). Of late, Morrison continues to write and publish novels and opinion editorials, which revisit and refine some of her earlier themes and engage with the political climate of the moment and race.

"Unspeakable Things Unspoken: The Afro-American Presence in American Literature" Keywords: The Canon/Tradition, Identity, Institutional Studies, Literary History, Nationhood, The Novel, Race and Ethnicity Studies

From Unspeakable Things Unspoken: The Afro-American Presence in American Literature

I

I planned to call this paper "Canon Fodder," because the terms put me in mind of a kind of trained muscular response that appears to be on display in some areas of the recent canon debate. But I changed my mind (so many have used the phrase) and hope to make clear the appropriateness of the title I settled on.

My purpose here is to observe the panoply of this most recent and most anxious series of questions concerning what should or does constitute a literary canon in order to suggest ways of addressing the Afro-American presence in American Literature that require neither slaughter nor reification—views that may spring the whole literature of an entire nation from the solitude into which it has been locked. There is something called American literature that, according to conventional wisdom, is certainly not Chicano literature, or Afro-American literature, or Asian-American, or Native American, or . . . It is somehow separate from them and they from it, and in spite of the efforts of recent literary histories, restructured curricula and anthologies, this separate confinement, be it breached or endorsed, is the subject of a large part of these debates. Although the terms used, like the vocabulary of earlier canon debates, refer to literary and/or humanistic value, aesthetic criteria, value-free or socially anchored readings, the contemporary battle plain is most often understood to be the claims of others against the whitemale origins and definitions of those values; whether those definitions reflect an eternal, universal and transcending paradigm or whether they constitute a disguise for a temporal, political and culturally specific program.

Part of the history of this particular debate is located in the successful assault that the feminist scholarship of men and women (black and white) made and continues to make on traditional literary discourse. The male part of the whitemale equation is already deeply engaged, and no one believes the body of literature and its criticism will ever again be what it was in 1965: the protected preserve of the thoughts and works and analytical strategies of whitemen.

It is, however, the "white" part of the question that this paper focuses on, and it is to my great relief that such terms as "white" and "race" can enter serious discussion of literature. Although still a swift and swiftly obeyed call to arms, their use is no longer forbidden.[1] It may appear churlish to doubt the sincerity, or question the proclaimed well-intentioned self-lessness of a 900-year-old academy struggling through decades of chaos to "maintain standards." Yet of what use is it to go on about "quality" being the only criterion for greatness knowing that the definition of quality is itself the subject of much rage and is seldom universally agreed upon by everyone at all times? Is it to appropriate the term for reasons of state; to be in the position to distribute greatness or withhold it? Or to actively pursue the ways and places in which quality surfaces and stuns us into silence or into language worthy enough to describe it? What is possible is to try to recognize, identify and applaud the fight for and triumph of quality when it is revealed to us and to let go the notion that only the dominant culture or gender can make those judgments, identify that quality or produce it.

Those who claim the superiority of Western culture are entitled to that claim only when Western civilization is measured thoroughly against other civilizations and not found wanting, and when Western civilization owns up to its own sources in the cultures that preceded it.

A large part of the satisfaction I have always received from reading Greek tragedy, for example, is in its similarity to Afro-American communal structures (the function of song and chorus, the heroic struggle between the claims of community and individual hubris) and African religion and philosophy. In other words, that is part of the reason it has quality for me—I feel intellectually at home there. But that could hardly be so for those unfamiliar with my "home," and hardly a requisite for the pleasure they take. The point is, the form (Greek tragedy) makes available these varieties of provocative love because *it* is masterly—not because the civilization that is its referent was flawless or superior to all others.

1. Henry Louis Gates, ed., *"Race," Writing, and Difference* (Chicago: University of Chicago Press, 1986) [Morrison's note].

One has the feeling that nights are becoming sleepless in some quarters, and it seems to me obvious that the recoil of traditional "humanists" and some post-modern theorists to this particular aspect of the debate, the "race" aspect, is as severe as it is because the claims for attention come from that segment of scholarly and artistic labor in which the mention of "race" is either inevitable or elaborately, painstakingly masked; and if all of the ramifications that the term demands are taken seriously, the bases of Western civilization will require re-thinking. Thus, in spite of its implicit and explicit acknowledgement, "race" is still a virtually unspeakable thing, as can be seen in the apologies, notes of "special use" and circumscribed definitions that accompany it[2]—not least of which is my own deference in surrounding it with quotation marks. Suddenly (for our purposes, suddenly) "race" does not exist. For three hundred years black Americans insisted that "race" was no usefully distinguishing factor in human relationships. During those same three centuries every academic discipline, including theology, history, and natural science, insisted "race" was *the* determining factor in human development. When blacks discovered they had shaped or become a culturally formed race, and that it had specific and revered difference, suddenly they were told there is no such thing as "race," biological or cultural, that matters and that genuinely intellectual exchange cannot accommodate it.[3] In trying to come to some terms about "race" and writing, I am tempted to throw my hands up. It always seemed to me that the people who invented the hierarchy of "race" when it was convenient for them ought not to be the ones to explain it away, now that it does not suit their purposes for it to exist. But there *is* culture and both gender and "race" inform and are informed by it. Afro-American culture exists and though it is clear (and becoming clearer) how it has responded to Western culture, the instances where and means by which it has shaped Western culture are poorly recognized or understood.

I want to address ways in which the presence of Afro-American literature and the awareness of its culture both resuscitate the study of literature in the United States and raise that study's standards. In pursuit of that goal, it will suit my purposes to contextualize the route canon debates have taken in Western literary criticism.

I do not believe this current anxiety can be attributed solely to the routine, even cyclical arguments within literary communities reflecting unpredictable yet inevitable shifts in taste, relevance or perception. Shifts in which an enthusiasm for and official endorsement of William Dean Howells,[4] for example, withered; or in which the legalization of Mark Twain[5] in critical court rose and fell like the fathoming of a sounding line (for which he may or may not have named himself); or even the slow, delayed but steady swell of attention and devotion on which Emily Dickinson[6] soared to what is now, surely, a permanent crest of respect. No. Those were discoveries,

2. Among many examples, Ivan Van Sertima, *They Came Before Columbus: The African Presence in Ancient America* (New York: Random House, 1976), pp. xvi–xvii [Morrison's note]. Van Sertima (1935–2009), Guyanese-born linguist, literary critic, and anthropologist.

3. TZVETAN TODOROV, "'Race,' Writing, and Culture," trans. Loulou Mack, in Gates, *"Race,"* pp. 370–80 [Morrison's note].

4. American realist novelist (1837–1920).

5. Pen name of the American writer and humorist Samuel Langhorne Clemens (1835–1910); the boatman's phrase "mark twain" signifies water 2 fathoms (12 feet) deep.

6. American poet (1830–1886); only 10 of her almost 1,800 poems were published during her lifetime.

reappraisals of individual artists. Serious but not destabilizing. Such accommodations were simple because the questions they posed were simple: Are there one hundred sterling examples of high literary art in American literature and no more? One hundred and six? If one or two fall into disrepute, is there space, then, for one or two others in the vestibule, waiting like girls for bells chimed by future husbands who alone can promise them security, legitimacy—and in whose hands alone rests the gift of critical longevity? Interesting questions, but, as I say, not endangering.

Nor is this detectable academic sleeplessness the consequence of a much more radical shift, such as the mid-nineteenth century one heralding the authenticity of American literature itself. Or an even earlier upheaval—receding now into the distant past—in which theology and thereby Latin, was displaced for the equally rigorous study of the classics and Greek to be followed by what was considered a strangely arrogant and upstart proposal: that English literature was a suitable course of study for an aristocratic education, and not simply morally instructive fodder designed for the working classes. (The Chaucer Society was founded in 1848, four hundred years after Chaucer[7] died.) No. This exchange seems unusual somehow, keener. It has a more strenuously argued (and felt) defense and a more vigorously insistent attack. And both defenses and attacks have spilled out of the academy into the popular press. Why? Resistance to displacement within or expansion of a canon is not, after all, surprising or unwarranted. That's what canonization is for. (And the question of whether there should be a canon or not seems disingenuous to me—there always is one whether there should be or not—for it is in the interests of the professional critical community to have one.) Certainly a sharp alertness as to *why* a work is or is not worthy of study is the legitimate occupation of the critic, the pedagogue and the artist. What is astonishing in the contemporary debate is not the resistance to displacement of works or to the expansion of genre within it, but the virulent passion that accompanies this resistance and, more importantly, the quality of its defense weaponry. The guns are very big; the trigger-fingers quick. But I am convinced the mechanism of the defenders of the flame is faulty. Not only may the hands of the gun-slinging cowboy-scholars be blown off, not only may the target be missed, but the subject of the conflagration (the sacred texts) is sacrificed, disfigured in the battle. This canon fodder may kill the canon. And I, at least, do not intend to live without Aeschylus or William Shakespeare, or James or Twain or Hawthorne, or Melville,[8] etc., etc., etc. There must be some way to enhance canon readings without enshrining them.

When Milan Kundera,[9] in *The Art of the Novel*, identified the historical territory of the novel by saying "The novel is Europe's creation" and that "The only context for grasping a novel's worth is the history of the European novel," the *New Yorker* reviewer stiffened. Kundera's "personal 'idea of the

7. Geoffrey Chaucer (ca. 1343–1400), English poet.

8. Herman Melville (1819–1891), American novelist. Aeschylus (525–456 B.C.E.), Greek playwright; Shakespeare (1564–1616), English poet and playwright; HENRY JAMES (1843–1916), American-born novelist; Nathaniel Hawthorne (1804–1864), American novelist.

9. Czech-born writer (b. 1929), who in 1994 began publishing in French, the original language of *The Art of the Novel* (1986; trans. 1988).

novel,'" he wrote, "is so profoundly Eurocentric that it's likely to seem exotic, even perverse, to American readers. . . . *The Art of the Novel* gives off the occasional (but pungent) whiff of cultural arrogance, and we may feel that Kundera's discourse . . . reveals an aspect of his character that we'd rather not have known about. . . . In order to become the artist he now is, the Czech novelist had to discover himself a second time, as a European. But what if that second, grander possibility hadn't been there to be discovered? What if Broch, Kafka, Musil[1]—all that reading—had never been a part of his education, or had entered it only as exotic, alien presence? Kundera's polemical fervor in *The Art of the Novel* annoys us, as American readers, because we feel defensive, excluded from the transcendent 'idea of the novel' that for him seems simply to have been there for the taking. (If only he had cited, in his redeeming version of the novel's history, a few more heroes from the New World's culture.) Our novelists don't discover cultural values within themselves; they invent them."[2]

Kundera's views, obliterating American writers (with the exception of William Faulkner[3]) from his own canon, are relegated to a "smugness" that Terrence Rafferty disassociates from Kundera's imaginative work and applies to the "sublime confidence" of his critical prose. The confidence of an exile who has the sentimental education of, and the choice to become, a European.[4]

I was refreshed by Rafferty's comments. With the substitution of certain phrases, his observations and the justifiable umbrage he takes can be appropriated entirely by Afro-American writers regarding their own exclusion from the "transcendent 'idea of the novel.'"

For the present turbulence seems not to be about the flexibility of a canon, its range among and between Western countries, but about its miscegenation. The word is informative here and I do mean its use. A powerful ingredient in this debate concerns the incursion of third-world or so-called minority literature into a Eurocentric stronghold. When the topic of third world culture is raised, unlike the topic of Scandinavian culture, for example, a possible threat to and implicit criticism of the reigning equilibrium is seen to be raised as well. From the seventeenth century to the twentieth, the arguments resisting that incursion have marched in predictable sequence: (1) there is no Afro-American (or third world) art. (2) it exists but is inferior. (3) it exists and is superior when it measures up to the "universal" criteria of Western art. (4) it is not so much "art" as ore—rich ore—that requires a Western or Eurocentric smith to refine it from its "natural" state into an aesthetically complex form.

A few comments on a larger, older, but no less telling academic struggle—an extremely successful one—may be helpful here. It is telling because it sheds light on certain aspects of this current debate and may locate its sources. I made reference above to the radical upheaval in canon-building that took place at the inauguration of classical studies and Greek. This canonical re-

1. Three Austrian writers: Hermann Broch (1886–1951); Franz Kafka (1883–1924), who lived much of his life in Prague; and Robert Musil (1880–1942).
2. Terrence Rafferty, "Articles of Faith," *New Yorker*, May 16, 1988, pp. 110–18 [Morrison's note]. Rafferty (b. 1955), American film critic.
3. American writer (1897–1962).
4. Rafferty, "Articles of Faith," p. 110 [Morrison's note].

routing from scholasticism to humanism, was not merely radical, it must have been (may I say it?) savage. And it took some seventy years to accomplish. Seventy years to eliminate Egypt as the cradle of civilization *and* its model and replace it with Greece. The triumph of that process was that Greece lost its own origins and became itself original. A number of scholars in various disciplines (history, anthropology, ethnobotany, etc.) have put forward their research into cross-cultural and inter-cultural transmissions with varying degrees of success in the reception of their work. I am reminded of the curious publishing history of Ivan van Sertima's work, *They Came Before Columbus*, which researches the African presence in Ancient America. I am reminded of Edward Said's *Orientalism*,[5] and especially the work of Martin Bernal,[6] a linguist, trained in Chinese history, who has defined himself as an interloper in the field of classical civilization but who has offered, in *Black Athena*, a stunning investigation of the field. According to Bernal, there are two "models" of Greek history: one views Greece as Aryan[7] or European (the Aryan Model); the other sees it as Levantine—absorbed by Egyptian and Semitic culture (the Ancient Model). "If I am right," writes Professor Bernal, "in urging the overthrow of the Aryan Model and its replacement by the Revised Ancient one, it will be necessary not only to rethink the fundamental bases of 'Western Civilization' but also to recognize the penetration of racism and 'continental chauvinism' into all our historiography, or philosophy of writing history. The Ancient Model had no major 'internal' deficiencies or weaknesses in explanatory power. It was overthrown for external reasons. For eighteenth and nineteenth century Romantics and racists it was simply intolerable for Greece, which was seen not merely as the epitome of Europe but also as its pure childhood, to have been the result of the mixture of native Europeans and *colonizing* Africans and Semites. Therefore the Ancient Model had to be overthrown and replaced by something more acceptable."[8]

It is difficult not to be persuaded by the weight of documentation Martin Bernal brings to his task and his rather dazzling analytical insights. What struck me in his analysis were the *process* of the fabrication of Ancient Greece and the *motives* for the fabrication. The latter (motive) involved the concept of purity, of progress. The former (process) required mis-reading, pre-determined selectivity of authentic sources, and—silence. From the Christian theological appropriation of Israel (the Levant), to the early nineteenth-century work of the prodigious Karl Müller,[9] work that effectively dismissed the Greeks' own record of their influences and origins as their "Egyptomania," their tendency to be "wonderstruck" by Egyptian culture, a tendency "manifested in the 'delusion' that Egyptians and other non-European 'barbarians' had possessed superior cultures, from which the Greeks had borrowed massively,"[1] on through the Romantic response to

5. Published in 1978. For SAID (1935–2003), a Palestinian-born American literary critic and political activist, see below.
6. British professor of Chinese political history (1937–2013); his *Black Athena* (3 vols., 1987–2006) has been highly controversial among classical scholars.
7. That is, Indo-Iranian.
8. Martin Bernal, *Black Athena: The Afroasiatic Roots of Classical Civilization*, vol. 1, *The Fabrication of Ancient Greece, 1785–1985* (New Brunswick, N.J.: Rutgers University Press, 1987), p. 2 [Morrison's note].
9. German classical scholar (1797–1840), best known for his cultural history of ancient Greek civilizations.
1. Bernal, *Black Athena*, p. 310 [Morrison's note].

the Enlightenment,[2] and the decline into disfavor of the Phoenicians, "the essential force behind the rejection of the tradition of massive Phoenician influence on early Greece was the rise of racial—as opposed to religious—anti-semitism.[3] This was because the Phoenicians were correctly perceived to have been culturally very close to the Jews."[4]

I have quoted at perhaps too great a length from Bernal's text because *motive*, so seldom an element brought to bear on the history of history, is located, delineated and confronted in Bernal's research, and has helped my own thinking about the process and motives of scholarly attention to and an appraisal of Afro-American presence in the literature of the United States.

Canon building is Empire building. Canon defense is national defense, Canon debate, whatever the terrain, nature and range (of criticism, of history, of the history of knowledge, of the definition of language, the universality of aesthetic principles, the sociology of art, the humanistic imagination), is the clash of cultures. And *all* of the interests are vested.

In such a melee as this one—a provocative, healthy, explosive melee—extraordinarily profound work is being done. Some of the controversy, however, has degenerated into *ad hominem* and unwarranted speculation on the personal habits of artists, specious and silly arguments about politics (the destabilizing forces are dismissed as merely political; the status quo sees itself as not—as though the term "*a*political" were only its prefix and not the most obviously political stance imaginable since one of the functions of political ideology is to pass itself off as immutable, natural and "innocent"), and covert expressions of critical inquiry designed to neutralize and disguise the political interests of the discourse. Yet much of the research and analysis has rendered speakable what was formerly unspoken and has made humanistic studies, once again, the place where one has to go to find out what's going on. Cultures, whether silenced or monologistic, whether repressed or repressing, seek meaning in the language and images available to them.

Silences are being broken, lost things have been found and at least two generations of scholars are disentangling received knowledge from the apparatus of control, most notably those who are engaged in investigations of French and British Colonialist Literature, American slave narratives, and the delineation of the Afro-American literary tradition.

Now that Afro-American artistic presence has been "discovered" actually to exist, now that serious scholarship has moved from silencing the witnesses and erasing their meaningful place in and contribution to American culture, it is no longer acceptable merely to imagine us and imagine for us. We have always been imagining ourselves. We are not Isak Dinesen's[5] "aspects of nature," nor Conrad's[6] unspeaking. We are the subjects of our own narrative, witnesses to and participants in our own experience, and, in no way coinci-

2. The emphasis on the emotional, subjective, and irrational that characterized Romanticism (a cultural and intellectual movement of late 18th- to mid-19th-century Europe) was in part a reaction against the rationalism and physical materialism of the Enlightenment (an intellectual movement of the 18th century).
3. Semitic peoples (speakers of one of a group of related languages) include Arabs, Hebrews, and Phoenicians, the sea traders and colonizers who lived in the region corresponding roughly to modern Lebanon.
4. Bernal, *Black Athena*, p. 337 [Morrison's note].
5. Pen name of the Danish writer Karen Blixen (1885–1962); her memoir, *Out of Africa* (1937), focuses on her years in Kenya.
6. Joseph Conrad (1857–1924), Polish-born English novelist; his best-known work, *Heart of Darkness* (1902), is largely set in the Congo Free State.

dentally, in the experience of those with whom we have come in contact. We are not, in fact, "other." We are choices. And to read imaginative literature by and about us is to choose to examine centers of the self and to have the opportunity to compare these centers with the "raceless" one with which we are, all of us, most familiar.

II

* * *

* * * [T]here is a great, ornamental, prescribed absence in early American literature and, I submit, it is instructive. It only seems that the canon of American literature is "naturally" or "inevitably" "white." In fact it is studiously so. In fact these absences of vital presences in Young American literature[7] may be the insistent fruit of the scholarship rather than the text. Perhaps some of these writers, although under current house arrest, have much more to say than has been realized. Perhaps some were not so much transcending politics, or escaping blackness, as they were transforming it into intelligible, accessible, yet artistic modes of discourse. To ignore this possibility by never questioning the strategies of transformation is to disenfranchise the writer, diminish the text and render the bulk of the literature aesthetically and historically incoherent—an exorbitant price for cultural (whitemale) purity, and, I believe, a spendthrift one. The re-examination of founding literature of the United States for the unspeakable unspoken may reveal those texts to have deeper and other meanings, deeper and other power, deeper and other significances.

One such writer, in particular, it has been almost impossible to keep under lock and key is Herman Melville.

Among several astute scholars, Michael Rogin[8] has done one of the most exhaustive studies of how deeply Melville's social thought is woven into his writing. He calls our attention to the connection Melville made between American slavery and American freedom, how heightened the one rendered the other. And he has provided evidence of the impact on the work of Melville's family, milieu, and, most importantly, the raging, all-encompassing conflict of the time: slavery. He has reminded us that it was Melville's father-in-law[9] who had, as judge, decided the case that made the Fugitive Slave Law law, and that "other evidence in *Moby Dick* also suggests the impact of Shaw's ruling on the climax of Melville's tale. Melville conceived the final confrontation between Ahab[1] and the white whale some time in the first half of 1851. He may well have written his last chapters only after returning from a trip to New York in June. [Judge Shaw's decision was handed down in April, 1851]. When New York anti-slavery leaders William Seward and John van Buren[2]

7. Works of writers associated with Young America (a mid-19th-century political and social movement), including Melville and Hawthorne.
8. American political scientist (1937–2001).
9. Lemuel Shaw (1781–1861), chief justice of the Supreme Judicial Court of Massachusetts (1830–60). In 1851, he denied an appeal to release Thomas Sims (ca. 1834–?), a slave who had fled to Boston from Georgia and had been seized in accordance with the Fugitive Slave Act of 1850, which required that any runaway slave be returned from all states and federal territories.
1. In *Moby-Dick* (1851), the captain of a whaling ship, the *Pequod*, who is obsessed with finding the whale who cost him his leg.
2. American lawyer and politician (1810–1866). Seward (1801–1872), American lawyer and politician, later secretary of state (1861–69) under President Abraham Lincoln.

wrote public letters protesting the *Sims* ruling, the New York *Herald*[3] responded. Its attack on "The Anti-Slavery Agitators" began: "Did you ever see a whale? Did you ever see a mighty whale struggling?"[4]

Rogin also traces the chronology of the whale from its "birth in a state of nature" to its final end as commodity.[5] Central to his argument is that Melville in *Moby Dick* was being allegorically and insistently political in his choice of the whale. But within his chronology, one singular whale transcends all others, goes beyond nature, adventure, politics and commodity to an abstraction. What is this abstraction? This "wicked idea"? Interpretation has been varied. It has been viewed as an allegory of the state in which Ahab is Calhoun, or Daniel Webster;[6] an allegory of capitalism and corruption, God and man, the individual and fate, and most commonly, the single allegorical meaning of the white whale is understood to be brute, indifferent Nature, and Ahab the madman who challenges that Nature.

But let us consider, again, the principal actor, Ahab, created by an author who calls himself Typee, signed himself Tawney, identified himself as Ishmael,[7] and who had written several books before *Moby Dick* criticizing missionary forays into various paradises.

Ahab loses sight of the commercial value of his ship's voyage, its point, and pursues an idea in order to destroy it. His intention, revenge, "an audacious, immitigable and supernatural revenge," develops stature—maturity—when we realize that he is not a man mourning his lost leg or a scar on his face. However intense and dislocating his fever and recovery had been after his encounter with the white whale, however satisfactorily "male" this vengeance is read, the vanity of it is almost adolescent. But if the whale is more than blind, indifferent Nature unsubduable by masculine aggression, if it is as much its adjective as it is its noun, we can consider the possibility that Melville's "truth" was his recognition of the moment in America when whiteness became ideology. And if the white whale is the ideology of race, what Ahab has lost to it is personal dismemberment and family and society and his own place as a human in the world. The trauma of racism is, for the racist and the victim, the severe fragmentation of the self, and has always seemed to me a cause (not a symptom) of psychosis—strangely of no interest to psychiatry. Ahab, then, is navigating between an idea of civilization that he renounces and an idea of savagery he must annihilate, because the two cannot co-exist. The former is based on the latter. What is terrible in its complexity is that the idea of savagery is not the missionary one; it is white racial ideology that is savage and if, indeed, a white, nineteenth-century, American male took on not abolition, not the amelioration of racist institutions or their laws, but the very concept of whiteness as an inhuman idea,

3. A proslavery newspaper (published 1835–1924).
4. Michael Paul Rogin, *Subversive Genealogy: The Politics and Art of Herman Melville* (Berkeley: University of California Press, 1985), pp. 107, 142 [Morrison's note].
5. Ibid., p. 112 [Morrison's note].
6. American orator and politician (1782–1852); as a U.S. senator from Massachusetts (1827–41, 1845–50), he defended federal power against those who argued that states could nullify a law they viewed as unconstitutional. The most prominent nullificationist was John C. Calhoun (1782–1850), as vice president (1825–32) and as proslavery senator from South Carolina (1833–50). Both supported the Compromise of 1850, which included the Fugitive Slave Act.
7. The narrator of *Moby-Dick*. Typee was both the title of Melville's first novel (1846) and the name of the Polynesian people he describes in it; Tawney is an old and respected black sailor in his novel *White-Jacket* (1850).

he would be very alone, very desperate, and very doomed. Madness would be the only appropriate description of such audacity, and "he heaves me," the most succinct and appropriate description of that obsession.

I would not like to be understood to argue that Melville was engaged in some simple and simple-minded black/white didacticism, or that he was satanizing white people. Nothing like that. What I am suggesting is that he was overwhelmed by the philosophical and metaphysical inconsistencies of an extraordinary and unprecedented idea that had its fullest manifestation in his own time in his own country, and that that idea was the successful assertion of whiteness as ideology.

On the *Pequod* the multiracial, mainly foreign, proletariat is at work to produce a commodity, but it is diverted and converted from that labor to Ahab's more significant intellectual quest. We leave whale as commerce and confront whale as metaphor. With that interpretation in place, two of the most famous chapters of the book become luminous in a completely new way. One is Chapter 9, The Sermon. In Father Mapple's thrilling rendition of Jonah's trials,[8] emphasis is given to the purpose of Jonah's salvation. He is saved from the fish's belly for one single purpose, "To preach the Truth to the face of Falsehood! That was it!" Only then the reward "Delight"—which strongly calls to mind Ahab's lonely necessity. "Delight is to him . . . who against the proud gods and commodores of this earth, ever stand forth his own inexorable self. . . . Delight is to him whose strong arms yet support him, when the ship of this base treacherous world has gone down beneath him. Delight is to him who gives no quarter in the truth and kills, burns, and destroys all *sin* though he pluck it out from under the robes of Senators and Judges. Delight—top-gallant delight is to him who acknowledges no law or lord, but the Lord his God, and is only a *patriot to heaven*" [italics mine]. No one, I think, has denied that the sermon is designed to be prophetic, but it seems unremarked what the nature of the sin is—the sin that must be destroyed, regardless. Nature? A sin? The terms do not apply. Capitalism? Perhaps. Capitalism fed greed, lent itself inexorably to corruption, but probably was not in and of itself sinful to Melville. Sin suggests a moral outrage within the bounds of man to repair. The concept of racial superiority would fit seamlessly. It is difficult to read those words ("destruction of sin," "patriot to heaven") and not hear in them the description of a different Ahab. Not an adolescent male in adult clothing, a maniacal egocentric, or the "exotic plant" that V. L. Parrington[9] thought Melville was. Not even a morally fine liberal voice adjusting, balancing, compromising with racial institutions. But another Ahab: the only white male American heroic enough to try to slay the monster that was devouring the world as he knew it.

Another chapter that seems freshly lit by this reading is Chapter 42, The Whiteness of the Whale. Melville points to the do-or-die significance of his effort to say something unsayable in this chapter. "I almost despair," he writes, "of putting it in a comprehensive form. It was the whiteness of the whale that above all things appalled me. But how can I hope to explain myself here; and yet in some dim, random way, explain myself I must, *else all these chapters might be naught*" [italics mine]. The language of this chapter

8. That is, the Hebrew prophet's swallowing by a "great fish" (see Jonah 1.17–2.10).

9. Vernon L. Parrington (1871–1929), American literary historian.

ranges between benevolent, beautiful images of whiteness and whiteness as sinister and shocking. After dissecting the ineffable, he concludes: "Therefore . . . symbolize whatever grand or gracious he will by whiteness, no man can deny that in its profoundest *idealized significance* it calls up a peculiar apparition to the soul." I stress "idealized significance" to emphasize and make clear (if such clarity needs stating) that Melville is not exploring white *people*, but whiteness idealized. Then, after informing the reader of his "hope to light upon some chance clue to conduct us to the hidden course we seek," he tries to nail it. To provide the key to the "hidden course." His struggle to do so is gigantic. He cannot. Nor can we. But in nonfigurative language, he identifies the imaginative tools needed to solve the problem: "subtlety appeals to subtlety, and without imagination no man can follow another into these halls." And his final observation reverberates with personal trauma. "This visible [colored] world seems formed in love, the invisible [white] spheres were formed in fright." The necessity for whiteness as privileged "natural" state, the invention of it, was indeed formed in fright.

"Slavery," writes Rogin, "confirmed Melville's isolation, decisively established in *Moby Dick*, from the dominant consciousness of his time."[1] I differ on this point and submit that Melville's hostility and repugnance for slavery would have found company. There were many white Americans of his acquaintance who felt repelled by slavery, wrote journalism about it, spoke about it, legislated on it and were active in abolishing it. His attitude to slavery alone would not have condemned him to the almost autistic separation visited upon him. And if he felt convinced that blacks were worthy of being treated like whites, or that capitalism was dangerous—he had company or could have found it. But to question the very notion of white progress, the very idea of racial superiority, of whiteness as privileged place in the evolutionary ladder of humankind, and to meditate on the fraudulent, self-destroying philosophy of that superiority, to "pluck it out from under the robes of Senators and Judges," to drag the "judge himself to the bar,"[2]—that was dangerous, solitary, radical work. Especially then. Especially now. To be "only a patriot to heaven" is no mean aspiration in Young America for a writer—or the captain of a whaling ship.

A complex, heaving, disorderly, profound text is *Moby Dick*, and among its several meanings it seems to me this "unspeakable" one has remained the "hidden course," the "truth in the Face of Falsehood." To this day no novelist has so wrestled with its subject. To this day literary analyses of canonical texts have shied away from that perspective: the informing and determining Afro-American presence in traditional American literature. The chapters I have made reference to are only a fraction of the instances where the text surrenders such insights, and points a helpful finger toward the ways in which the ghost drives the machine.

Melville is not the only author whose works double their fascination and their power when scoured for this presence and the writerly strategies taken to address or deny it. Edgar Allan Poe[3] will sustain such a reading. So will Nathaniel Hawthorne and Mark Twain; and in the twentieth century, Willa

1. Rogin, *Subversive Genealogy*, p. 150.
2. See *Moby-Dick*, chap. 132.
3. American writer and poet (1809–1849); see above.

Cather, Ernest Hemingway, F. Scott Fitzgerald,[4] and William Faulkner, to name a few. Canonical American literature is begging for such attention. It seems to me a more than fruitful project to produce some cogent analysis showing instances where early American literature identifies itself, risks itself, to assert its antithesis to blackness. How its linguistic gestures prove the intimate relationship to what is being nulled by implying a full descriptive apparatus (identity) to a presence-that-is-assumed-not-to-exist. Afro-American critical inquiry can do this work.

I mentioned earlier that finding or imposing Western influences in/on Afro-American literature had value provided the valued process does not become self-anointing. There is an adjacent project to be undertaken * * *: the examination of contemporary literature (both the sacred and the profane) for the impact Afro-American presence has had on the structure of the work, the linguistic practice, and fictional enterprise in which it is engaged. * * * [T]his critical process must also eschew the pernicious goal of equating the fact of that presence with the achievement of the work. A work does not get better because it is responsive to another culture; nor does it become automatically flawed because of that responsiveness. The point is to clarify, not to enlist. And it does not "go without saying" that a work written by an Afro-American is automatically subsumed by an enforcing Afro-American presence. There is a clear flight from blackness in a great deal of Afro-American literature. In others there is the duel with blackness, and in some cases, as they say, "You'd never know."

1988 1989

4. All canonical American authors: Cather (1873–1947), Hemingway (1899–1961), and Fitzgerald (1896–1940).

RICHARD OHMANN
b. 1931

Few contemporary debates in the humanities have incited as much controversy as those over the literary canon. Deemed "the best that is known and thought" by MATTHEW ARNOLD and his intellectual progeny, the traditional literary canon has been critiqued, attacked, defended, and revised in recent years. The problem, say many literary theorists and critics, is that the canon has been shaped not by eternal or universal standards, but instead by unacknowledged gender, racial, ethnic, and class biases, traditionally favoring, in a memorable phrase, "dead white European males." These critics—feminist, African American, postcolonial, and other—have argued for "opening" the canon to include previously suppressed voices, especially women and people of color. Joining the fray, U.S. conservative political figures such as William Bennett and Lynne Cheney, along with academic allies such as Allan Bloom and HAROLD BLOOM, have blamed efforts to revise the canon for a loss of traditionally revered Western cultural values and a fracturing of a unified culture. In "The Shaping of a Canon: U.S. Fiction, 1960–1975" (1983), Richard Ohmann, a leading contemporary critic of the institution of literature, takes a step back and investigates the preliminary material, historical, and institutional processes that form the literary canon.

Born in Cleveland, Ohmann received his B.A. from Oberlin College in 1952 and his Ph.D. in English literature from Harvard University in 1960. He was a professor and an administrator at Wesleyan University in Connecticut from 1961 until his retirement in 1998. His initial scholarly work focused on literary style and traditional literary figures, like George Bernard Shaw (1856–1950), but through the 1960s he explored new theoretical approaches imported from linguistics; he was one of the first American scholars to introduce speech act theory (developed in the 1950s by the English philosopher of language J. L. AUSTIN) to literary criticism. In the late 1960s his work again shifted, as he began to examine social and political issues involved in the study of literature. He was deeply influenced by the social unrest and leftist politics of the time, and his later work, most notably his landmark book *English in America: A Radical View of the Profession* (1976), arises out of that era's "ruthless critique of all things existing."

English in America is a pioneering study of the social functions of literary study. While we normally justify the teaching of English as developing an appreciation of language and good writing through the study of great works of literature, Ohmann points out less publicized functions of English studies: "We train young people, and those who train young people, in the skills required by a society most of whose work is done on paper and through talk, not by physical labor. We also discipline the young to do assignments, on time, to follow instructions, to turn out uniform products, to observe the etiquette of verbal communication." In other words, university training in English is concerned not just with literary works but with inculcating the values and skills of white-collar work. Ohmann goes on to describe the class bias of English, arguing that despite the ideology of equal opportunity, "we eliminate the less adapted, the ill-trained, the city youth with bad verbal manners, blacks with the wrong dialect . . . and the rebellious of all shapes and sizes." In short, he produces a damning radical critique of the institution of English, which functions as an "instrument" to "maintain social and economic inequalities." Ohmann concludes *English in America* with a critique of the modern American university overall, detailing its connections to business and the military; he argues that universities are not "ivory towers" operating to produce "pure" knowledge, but the instruments of industrial and military research.

"The Shaping of a Canon: U.S. Fiction, 1960–1975" turns from English departments and the university to investigate institutions involved in the material production and distribution of literature, such as publishing houses, advertising firms, and book reviewing outlets, which are usually considered peripheral to discussions of the value and attributes of literary works. Judgments about literature are typically assumed to be a matter for literary critics, who read, criticize, and evaluate it on its autonomous artistic merits. Countering received opinion, Ohmann demonstrates how influential these institutions in fact are in determining merit and the canon.

As a test case, Ohmann examines a group of contemporary U.S. novels published in the 1960s and early 1970s, inspecting normally overlooked aspects of their distribution and consumption, including agenting, editing, marketing, advertising, and reviewing. He argues that this complex set of institutional channels determines which books receive attention, preselecting which texts are ordained as "precanonical," or potential entrants into the canon. The primary criterion of value for these institutions is the capitalist one of marketability rather than abstract aesthetic merit. In particular, Ohmann demonstrates the large role of advertising in determining value and shaping the canon. As he concludes from the evidence compiled, "if a novel did not become a best-seller within three or four weeks of publication, it was unlikely to reach a large readership later on." While not denying that such works might have aesthetic value, Ohmann shows that aesthetic judgments are inflected by capitalist criteria.

Significantly, Ohmann examines the class character of those who work in the institutions of literature. He notes that they are members of the "professional-managerial" class—those who do intellectual rather than blue-collar work—and that their class position informs their judgments of value. They thus attribute value to books that speak to their lives and ideologies, and he speculates that they favor "illness stories," or works that depict the alienation of white-collar life. Continuing his argument that aesthetic judgments are not simply a matter of abstract, artistic value, Ohmann points out that they are shaped by the class divisions of modern capitalism: those in positions of relative power have more influence in determining which books are considered to have literary merit.

Determining the value of artworks is a perennial problem in aesthetic theory, and contemporary debates over the canon pivot on conflicting theories of value. Those who defend the canon typically see its value as universal and timeless, whereas those who attack it generally see it as politically motivated and historically constructed. The eighteenth-century German philosopher IMMANUEL KANT, a founder of aesthetic theory, posited that aesthetic judgments are necessarily universal and disinterested, distinguishing them from the exercise of individual taste. Ohmann dispels just this sense of universality and disinterest through his analysis of the judgments rendered on contemporary U.S. fiction, which testify to specific class interests and are influenced by elements of the capitalist mode of production.

In his analysis of the social construction of aesthetic judgment, Ohmann has affinities with contemporary theorists such as PIERRE BOURDIEU and Barbara Herrnstein Smith. In *Distinction* (1979; see above), Bourdieu conducts a sociological study of contemporary French culture, showing how taste is determined by class. Drawing on the aesthetic theory of the eighteenth-century Scottish philosopher DAVID HUME and of Bourdieu, Smith argues in *Contingencies of Value* (1988) that judgments of value and taste are not universal and timeless, but historically contingent. Ohmann's "Shaping of a Canon" offers a concrete counterpart to Smith's more explicitly theoretical considerations of aesthetic value, providing a case study replete with a "thick description" of historical events illustrating the processes of aesthetic judgment.

Given its focus on class and the social and economic determinants of literary culture, Ohmann's work has been characterized as Marxist and therefore criticized for overstressing material factors and for advocating the radicalization of the profession. Ohmann explains in an interview, however, that he had read few of the Marxist classics at the time he wrote *English in America*; his work arose instead from the collective, radical "Movement" of the 1960s and from his participation in leftist groups such as the Radical Caucus of the Modern Language Association (the central professional organization of academic literary scholars in North America). Ohmann's innovative work in developing a cultural studies approach to literary practices makes him somewhat idiosyncratic in an era when most American critics have been more absorbed in debates over poststructuralist theory. "The Shaping of a Canon" remains a groundbreaking case study of the actual institutions of literature and what has come to be called "print culture."

"The Shaping of a Canon: U.S. Fiction, 1960–1975" Keywords: Aesthetics, The Canon/Tradition, Cultural Studies, Ideology, Institutional Studies, Marxism, The Novel, Print Culture

From The Shaping of a Canon: U.S. Fiction, 1960–1975

Categorical names such as The English Novel, The Modern American Novel, and American Literature often turn up in catalogues as titles of college courses, and we know from them pretty much what to expect. They also have standing in critical discourse, along with allied terms unlikely to serve as course titles: *good writing, great literature, serious fiction, literature* itself. The awareness has grown in recent years that such concepts pose problems, even though we use them with easy enough comprehension when we talk or write to others who share our cultural matrix.

Lately, critics like Raymond Williams[1] have been reminding us that the categories change over time (just as *literature* used to mean all printed books but has come to mean only certain poems, plays, novels, etc.) and that at any given moment categories embody complex social relations and a continuing historical process. That process deeply invests all terms with value: since not everyone's values are the same, the negotiating of such concepts is, among other things, a struggle for dominance—whether between adults and the young, professors and their students, one class and another, or men and women. One doesn't usually notice the power or the conflict, except when some previously weak or silent group seeks a share of the power: for example, when, in the 1960s, American blacks and their supporters insisted that black literature be included in school and college curricula, or when they openly challenged the candidacy of William Styron's *Confessions of Nat Turner*[2] for inclusion in some eventual canon.[3] But the gradual firming up of concepts like, say, postwar American fiction is always a contest for cultural hegemony,[4] even if in our society it is often muted—carried on behind the scenes or in the seemingly neutral marketplace.

Not only do the concepts change, in both intension and extension, but the process of their formation also changes. The English, who had power to do so, admitted *Great Expectations* to the canon by means very different from those used to admit the *Canterbury Tales*[5] by earlier generations of taste-makers. Again, the process may differ from genre to genre even in a particular time and place. For instance, profit and the book market are relatively unimportant in deciding what will be considered modern American poetry, by contrast with their function in defining modern American fiction. As a result, in order to work toward a serviceable theory of canon formation, it is necessary to look at a variety of these processes and at how they impinge on one another.

Here, I attempt to sketch out one of them, the process by which novels written by Americans from about 1960 to 1975 have been sifted and assessed, so that a modest number of them retain the kind of attention and respect that eventually makes them eligible for canonical status.[6] I am going to argue that

1. Welsh literary and cultural critic (1921–1988; see above), whose *Marxism and Literature* (1977) discusses the historical change that Ohmann refers to.
2. This 1967 novel by Styron (1925–2006) depicts a slave rebellion before the American Civil War. It won a Pulitzer Prize but generated controversy because some questioned whether Styron, a southern-born white author, could authentically represent African Americans.
3. See John Henrik Clarke, ed., *William Styron's Nat Turner: Ten Black Writers Respond* (Boston, 1968) [Ohmann's note]. Some of the author's notes have been edited, and some omitted.
4. The manufactured consent that legitimates a dominant group and unifies a society; a Marxist concept articulated by the Italian theorist ANTONIO GRAMSCI (1891–1937).
5. Middle English poem (ca. 1386–1400) by Geoffrey Chaucer; one of the great works of the Middle Ages. *Great Expectations* (1861), English novel by Charles Dickens.
6. I make no large claims for my boundaries. They mark off, crudely, the time when publishing had become part of big business but before subsidiary rights had completely overshadowed hardbound novel publishing. My boundaries also mark the time when people born to one side or the other of 1930 attained cultural dominance and could most strongly advance their reading of the postwar experience. These years roughly enclose the rise and decline of the 1960s movements as well as economic boom and the U.S. intervention in Southeast Asia. Anyhow, things have changed since 1975, both in the great world and in fiction publishing; accordingly I use the past tense when describing the process of canon-formation, even though many of my generalizations still hold true [Ohmann's note].

the emergence of these novels has been a process saturated with class values and interests, a process inseparable from the broader struggle for position and power in our society, from the institutions that mediate that struggle, as well as from legitimation of and challenges to the social order. I will then try to be more specific about the representation of those values and interests in the fiction itself.

Reading and the Book Market

People read books silently, and often in isolation, but reading is nonetheless a social act. As one study concludes:

> Book reading in adult life is sustained . . . by interpersonal situations which minimize the individual's isolation from others. To persist over the years, the act of book reading must be incorporated . . . into a social context. Reading a book becomes meaningful when, after completion, it is shared with others. . . . Social integration . . . sustains a persistent engagement with books. Social isolation, in contrast, is likely to lead to the abandonment of books.[7]

Simone Beserman found, in her study of best-sellers around 1970, that frequent reading of books correlated highly with social interaction—in particular, with the desire to rise in society. Upwardly mobile second- and third-generation Americans were heavy readers of best-sellers.[8]

As you would expect, given the way reading is embedded in and reinforced by social relations, networks of friends and family also contributed in determining which books would be widely read. In her survey, Beserman found that 58 percent of those who read a particular best-seller did so upon recommendation of a friend or relative. Who were these people, so crucial to a book's success? Beserman found that they were of better-than-average education (most had finished college), relatively well-to-do, many of them professionals, in middle life, upwardly mobile, living near New York or oriented, especially through the *New York Times*,[9] to New York cultural life.

These people were responsive to novels where they discovered the values in which they believed or where they found needed moral guidance when shaken in their own beliefs. Saul Bellow's remark, "What Americans want to learn from their writers is how to live,"[1] finds support in Philip H. Ennis's study, *Adult Book Reading in the United States*. Ennis determined that three of the main interests people carried into their reading were a "search for personal meaning, for some kind of map to the moral landscape"; a need to "reinforce or to celebrate beliefs already held, or, when shaken by events, to

7. Jan Hajda, "An American Paradox: People and Books in a Metropolis" (Ph.D. diss., University of Chicago, 1963), p. 218, as cited in Elizabeth Warner McElroy, "Subject Variety in Adult Book Reading" (M.A. thesis, University of Chicago, 1967) [Ohmann's note].

8. See Simone Beserman, "Le Best-seller aux États-Unis de 1961 à 1970: Étude littéraire et sociologique" (Ph.D. diss., University of Paris, 1975), pp. 280–95. Surprisingly, neither this audience nor the ways it integrated novel reading into its social existence seem all that different from their counterparts in early 18th-century England, as described, for example, in chap. 2 of Ian Watt, *The Rise of the Novel: Studies in Defoe, Richardson, and Fielding* (Berkeley, 1957) [Ohmann's note].

9. Arguably the most respected newspaper in the United States.

1. Saul Bellow, in Jason Epstein's interview, "Saul Bellow of Chicago," *New York Times Book Review*, May 9, 1971, p. 16 [Ohmann's note]. Bellow (1915–2005), Canadian-born American novelist; he won the Nobel Prize in Literature in 1976.

provide support in some personal crisis"; and a wish to keep up "with the book talk of friends and neighbors."[2]

The values and beliefs of a small group of people played a disproportionate role in deciding what novels would be widely read in the United States. (Toward the end of this essay, I will turn to those values in some detail.) To underscore their influence, consider two other facts about the book market. First, if a novel did not become a best-seller within three or four weeks of publication, it was unlikely to reach a large readership later on. In the 1960s, only a very few books that were slow starters eventually became best-sellers (in paperback, not hardback). I know of three: *Catch-22, Call It Sleep*, and *I Never Promised You a Rose Garden*, to which we may add the early novels of Vonnegut, which were not published in hard covers, and—if we count its 1970s revival in connection with the film—*One Flew over the Cuckoo's Nest.*[3] To look at the process the other way around, once a new book did make the *New York Times* best-seller list, many other people bought it (and store managers around the country stocked it) *because* it was a best-seller. The process was cumulative. So the early buyers of hardcover books exercised a crucial role in selecting the books that the rest of the country's readers would buy.

Second, best-sellerdom was much more important than suggested by the figures for hardbound sales through bookstores. *Love Story,*[4] for instance, the leading best-seller (in all forms) of the decade sold 450,000 hardback copies in bookstores but more than 700,000 through book clubs, 2.5 million through the *Reader's Digest*, 6.5 million in the *Ladies' Home Journal,*[5] and more than 9,000,000 in paperback—not to mention library circulation or the millions of people who saw the film. Books were adopted by clubs, paperback publishers, film producers, and so forth, in large part because they were best-sellers or because those investing in subsidiary rights thought them likely to become best-sellers. As Victor Navasky rather wryly said:

> Publishers got out of the business of *selling* hardcover books ten or fifteen years ago. The idea now is to publish hardcover books so that they can be reviewed or promoted on television in order to sell paperback rights, movie rights, book club rights, serialization rights, international satellite rights, Barbie doll rights, etc.[6]

The phenomenon of the hardbound best-seller had only modest economic and cultural significance in itself but great significance in triggering reproduction and consumption of the story in other forms.

2. Philip H. Ennis, *Adult Book Reading in the United States*, National Opinion Research Center (University of Chicago, 1965), p. 25. Other main needs were (1) "escape," which also implies a relationship between reading a book and the rest of one's social life (what one is escaping *from*), and (2) information, which I suspect is a need less often fulfilled by novels now than in the time of Defoe and Richardson [Ohmann's note]. Daniel Defoe (1660–1731) and Samuel Richardson (1689–1761) were among the earliest English novelists.

3. A 1962 novel by Ken Kesey (1935–2001), made into an Academy Award–winning film (1975, dir. Milos Forman). *Catch-22* (1961), by Joseph Heller (1923–1999). *Call It Sleep* (1934; reissued 1960), by Henry Roth (1906–1995), Ukrainian-born American novelist. *I Never Promised You a Rose Garden* (1964), by Joanne Greenberg (b. 1932). Kurt Vonnegut (1922–2007), American novelist whose early works include *The Sirens of Titan* (1959), *Mother Night* (1962), and *Cat's Cradle* (1963).

4. A 1970 novel by Erich Segal (1937–2010), published by Harper and Row and made into a movie (dir. Arthur Hiller) that same year.

5. Popular mass-market magazines.

6. Victor Navasky, "Studies in Animal Behavior," *New York Times Book Review*, February 20, 1973, p. 2 [Ohmann's note]. Navasky (b. 1932), American cultural critic and longtime editor of the liberal-left magazine the *Nation*.

A small group of relatively homogeneous readers, then, had a great deal of influence at this preliminary stage. But of course these people did not make *their* decisions freely among the thousands of novels completed each year. They chose among the smaller number actually published. This fact points to an important role in canon formation for literary agents and for editors at the major houses, who belong to the same social stratum as the buyers of hardbound books, and who—as profitability in publishing came to hinge more and more on the achievement of best-sellerdom for a few books—increasingly earned their keep by spotting (and pushing) novels that looked like best-sellers. Here we have a nearly closed circle of marketing and consumption, the simultaneous exploitation and creation of taste, familiar to anyone who has examined marketplace culture under monopoly capitalism.

But, it is clear, influential readers chose not among all novels published but among the few that came to their attention in an urgent or attractive way. How did that happen? As a gesture toward the kind of answer that question requires, I will consider the extraordinary role of the *New York Times*. The *New York Times Book Review* had about a million and a half readers, several times the audience of any other literary periodical. Among them were most bookstore managers, deciding what to stock, and librarians, deciding what to buy, not to mention the well-to-do, well-educated east-coasters who led in establishing hardback best-sellers. The single most important boost a novel could get was a prominent review in the Sunday *New York Times*—better a favorable one than an unfavorable one, but better an unfavorable one than none at all.

Ads complemented the reviews, or perhaps the word is *inundated*: two-thirds of the space in the *Times Book Review* went to ads. According to Richard Kostelanetz, most publishers spent more than half their advertising budgets for space in that journal.[7] They often placed ads in such a way as to reinforce a good *Times* review or offset a bad one with favorable quotations from reviews in other periodicals. And of course reviews and ads were further reinforced by the *Times* best-seller list itself, for the reason already mentioned. Apparently, the publishers' faith in the *Times* was not misplaced. Beserman asked early readers of *Love Story* where they had heard of the book. Most read it on recommendation of another person; Beserman then spoke to *that* person, and so on back to the beginning of the chain of verbal endorsements. At the original source, in more than half the instances, she found the *Times*.[8] (This in spite of the quite unusual impact, for that time, of Segal's appearance on the "Today" show[9] the day of publication—Barbara Walters said the book made her cry all night; Harper was immediately swamped with orders—and of the novel's appearance in the *Ladies' Home Journal* just before book publication.)

7. See Richard Kostelanetz, *The End of Intelligent Writing: Literary Politics in America* (New York, 1974), p. 207. Kostelanetz's estimate was confirmed by some of Beserman's interviews. Allan Green, who handled advertising for a number of publishers, including Viking, told her in 1971 that on the average, 50 to 60 percent of the budget went to the *New York Times Book Review* and another 10 to 20 percent to the daily *New York Times*. M. Stuart Harris, head of publicity at Harper, said he ordinarily channeled 90 percent into the *Times* at the outset, though once a book's success was assured, he distributed advertising more broadly (see Beserman, p. 120) [Ohmann's note].

8. See Beserman, p. 168 [Ohmann's note].

9. The *Today Show*, a popular television show on NBC, debuted in 1952; Walters (b. 1929), television reporter and celebrity, was one of its hosts from 1964 to 1976.

The influence of the *Times Book Review* led publicity departments to direct much of their prepublication effort toward persuading the *Book Review*'s editors that a particular novel was important. It is hard to estimate the power of this suasion, but one thing can be measured: the correlation between advertising in the *Book Review* and being reviewed there. A 1968 study concluded, perhaps unsurprisingly, that the largest advertisers got disproportionately large amounts of review space. Among the large advertisers were, for instance:

	Pages of ads	Pages of reviews
Random House	74	58
Harper	29	22
Little, Brown	29	21

And the smaller ones:

Dutton	16	4
Lippincott	16	4
Harvard	9	"negligible"

During the same year Random House (including Knopf and Pantheon) had nearly three times as many books mentioned in the feature "New and Recommended" as Doubleday or Harper, both of which published as many books as the Random House group.[1]

To summarize: a small group of book buyers formed a screen through which novels passed on their way to commercial success; a handful of agents and editors picked the novels that would compete for the notice of those buyers; and a tight network of advertisers and reviewers, organized around the *New York Times Book Review*, selected from these a few to be recognized as compelling, important, "talked-about."

The Next Stage

So far I have been speaking of a process that led to a mass readership for a few books each year. But most of these were never regarded as serious literature and did not live long in popularity or memory. Books like *Love Story, The Godfather, Jonathan Livingston Seagull*, and the novels of Susann, Robbins, Wouk, Wallace, and Uris[2] would run a predictable course. They had large hardback sales for a few months, tapering off to a trickle in a year or so. Meanwhile, they were reprinted in paper covers and enjoyed two or three years of popularity (often stoked by a film version). After that they disappeared or remained in print to be bought in smaller numbers by, for instance, newly won fans of Wallace who wanted to go back and read his earlier books. There was a similar pattern for mysteries, science fiction, and other specialized genres.

But a few novels survived and continued (in paper covers) to attract buyers and readers for a longer time, and they still do. Why? To answer that the

1. See Kostelanetz, p. 209 [Ohmann's note].
2. Jacqueline Susann (1918–1974), Harold Robbins (1916–1997), Herman Wouk (b. 1915), Irving Wallace (1916–1990) and Leon Uris (1924–2003) were well-known, best-selling authors of the period. *The Godfather* (1969) by Mario Puzo and *Jonathan Livingston Seagull* (1970) by Richard Bach were best-selling American novels.

best novels survive is to beg the question. Excellence is a constantly changing, socially chosen value. Who attributed it to only some novels, and how? I hope now to hint at the way such a judgment took shape.

First, one more word about the *New York Times Book Review.* I have argued that it led in developing a broad audience for fiction. It also began, I believe, the process of distinguishing between ephemeral popular novels and those to be taken seriously over a longer period of time. There was a marked difference in impact between, say, Martin Levin's favorable but mildly condescending (and brief) review of *Love Story* and the kind of front-page review by an Alfred Kazin or an Irving Howe[3] that asked readers to regard a new novel as literature, and that so often helped give the stamp of highbrow approval to books by Bellow, Malamud, Updike, Roth, Doctorow,[4] and so forth. Cultural leaders read the *Times Book Review* too: not only professors but (according to Julie Hoover and Charles Kadushin) 75 percent of our elite intellectuals.[5] By reaching these circles, a major *Times* review could help put a novel on the cultural agenda and ensure that other journals would have to take it seriously.

Among those others, a few carried special weight in forming cultural judgments. In a survey of leading intellectuals, just eight journals—the *New York Review of Books,* the *New Republic*, the *New York Times Book Review*, the *New Yorker, Commentary, Saturday Review, Partisan Review,* and *Harpers*—received almost half the participants' "votes" in response to various questions about influence and importance.[6] In effect, these periodicals were both a communication network among the influentials (where they reviewed one another's books) and an avenue of access to a wider cultural leadership. The elite, writing in these journals, largely determined which books would be seriously debated and which ones permanently valued, as well as what ideas were kept alive, circulated, discussed. Kadushin and his colleagues concluded, from their studies of our intellectual elite and influential journals, that the "top intellectual journals constitute the American equivalent of an Oxbridge establishment, and have served as one of the main gatekeepers for new talent and new ideas."[7]

A novel had to win at least the divided approval of these arbiters in order to remain in the universe of cultural discourse, once past the notoriety of best-sellerdom. The career of *Love Story* is a good example of failure to do so. After some initial favorable reviews (and enormous publicity on television and other media), the intellectuals began cutting it down to size. In the elite journals, it was either panned or ignored. Styron and the rest of the National Book Award[8] fiction panel threatened to quit if it were not removed

3. Kazin (1915–1998) and Howe (1920–1993) were both highly regarded American literary critics affiliated with the New York Intellectuals. Levin (1919–2008), American writer and prolific book critic.

4. All respected "serious" American novelists: Bernard Malamud (1914–1986), John Updike (1932–2009), Philip Roth (b. 1933) and E. L. Doctorow (1931–2015).

5. See Julie Hoover and Charles Kadushin, "Influential Intellectual Journals: A Very Private Club," *Change*, March 1972, p. 41 [Ohmann's note].

6. See Charles Kadushin, Julie Hoover, and Monique Tichy, "How and Where to Find the Intellectual Elite in the United States," *Public Opinion Quarterly*, spring 1971, pp. 1–18. For the method used to identify an intellectual elite, see Kadushin, "Who Are the Elite Intellectuals?" *Public Interest*, fall 1972, pp. 109–25 [Ohmann's note].

7. Kadushin, Hoover, and Tichy, p. 17 [Ohmann's note]. "Oxbridge establishment": English intellectual elite (assumed to be graduates of Oxford or Cambridge University).

8. A prestigious annual book prize, awarded in different genres.

from the list of candidates. And who will read it tomorrow, except on an excursion into the archives of mass culture?

In talking about the *New York Times Book Review*, I suggested a close alliance between reviewing and profit, literary and monetary values. The example of the *New York Review of Books* shows that a similar alliance can exist on the higher ramparts of literary culture. This journal, far and away the most influential among intellectuals (in answer to Kadushin's questions, it was mentioned almost twice as often as the *New Republic*, its nearest competitor), was founded by Jason Epstein, a vice president of Random House, and coedited by his wife, Barbara Epstein.[9] It may be more than coincidental that in 1968 almost one-fourth of the books granted full reviews in the *New York Review* were published by Random House (again, including Knopf and Pantheon)—more than the combined total of books from Viking, Grove, Holt, Harper, Houghton Mifflin, Oxford, Doubleday, Macmillan, and Harvard so honored; or that in the same year one-fourth of the *reviewers* had books in print with Random House and that a third of those were reviewing other Random House books, mainly favorably; or that over a five-year period more than half the regular reviewers (ten or more appearances) were Random House authors.[1] This is not to deny the intellectual strength of the *New York Review*—only to suggest that it sometimes deployed that strength in ways consistent with the financial interest of Random House. One need not subscribe to conspiracy theories in order to see, almost everywhere one looks in the milieu of publishing and reviewing, linkages of fellowship and common interest. Together these networks make up a cultural establishment, inseparable from the market, both influencing and influenced by it.

If a novel was certified in the court of the prestigious journals, it was likely to draw the attention of academic critics in more specialized and academic journals like *Contemporary Literature* and by this route make its way into college curricula, where the very context—course title, academic setting, methodology—gave it de facto recognition as literature. This final step was all but necessary: the college classroom and its counterpart, the academic journal, have become in our society the final arbiters of literary merit and even of survival. It is hard to think of a novel more than twenty-five years old, aside from specialist fiction and *Gone with the Wind*,[2] that still commands a large readership outside of school and college.

I am suggesting that novels moved toward a canonical position only if they attained both large sales (usually, but not always, concentrated enough to place them among the best-sellers for a while) and the right kind of critical attention. On the one side, this hypothesis conflicts with the one most vigorously advanced by Leslie A. Fiedler—that intellectuals are, in the long run, outvoted by the sorts of readers who keep liking *Gone with the Wind*.[3] On the other side, it collides with the hopes or expectations of critics such as Kostelanetz and Jerome Klinkowitz, who promote an avant-garde fiction called postmodernist, postcontemporary, antinovel, or whatever.[4]

9. Jason Epstein (b. 1928) and Barbara Epstein (1928–2006), influential American literary figures.
1. See Kostelanetz, pp. 107–8 [Ohmann's note].
2. One of the most popular American novels of all time, published in 1936 by Margaret Mitchell.
3. See, for instance, Leslie A. Fiedler, *The Inadvertent Epic: From "Uncle Tom's Cabin" to "Roots"* (New York, 1979). Fiedler's *What Was Literature? Class Culture and Mass Society* (New York, 1982) argues again for the primacy of people over professors [Ohmann's note].
4. As Jerome Klinkowitz states in his preface: "For even the well and intelligently read, 'contemporary

Clearly, I need an independent measure of precanonical status, or my argument closes into a circle. Unfortunately, I don't have a very good one, in part, because it is still too early to settle the issue. But let me offer two scraps of pertinent information. First, the editors of *Wilson Quarterly* polled forty-four professors of American literature (in 1977 or 1978, apparently), asking them to rank in order the ten "most important" novels published in the United States after World War II.[5] The editors printed a list of the twenty-one novels rated highest in this survey; eleven of them were published in or after 1960. In rank order, they are *Catch-22, Gravity's Rainbow, Herzog, An American Dream, The Sotweed Factor, Second Skin, Portnoy's Complaint, The Armies of the Night, V, Rabbit Run,*[6] and *One Flew over the Cuckoo's Nest*. All easily meet the criterion of attention from intellectuals. (Again, it doesn't matter that Norman Podhoretz[7] *hates* Updike's novels, so long as he takes them seriously enough to argue with his peers about them.) As for broad readership, all of the novels except *Second Skin* and perhaps *The Sotweed Factor* have sold over half a million copies—and one may be sure that many of those sales occurred through adoption in college courses.[8]

My second cast of the net is much broader. *Contemporary Literary Criticism* abstracts commentary on recent world literature, mainly by American professors and intellectuals. Its coverage includes critical books, respected academic journals, taste-forming magazines, quarterlies, and little magazines. It claims to excerpt from criticism of "work by well-known creative writers," "writers of considerable public interest," who are alive or who died after January 1, 1960. So it constitutes a sampling of the interests of those who set literary standards, and it monitors the intermediate stage in canon formation. During the ten years and twenty-two volumes of its publication, up through 1982, it has run four or more entries (maximum, nine; and the average entry includes excerpts from four or five critical sources) for forty-eight American novelists of the period in question:[9]

American fiction' suggests Ken Kesey, Joseph Heller, John Barth, and Thomas Pynchon at best—and at worst Updike, Roth, Bellow, and Malamud." He contends that such a list misses "the direction which fiction will take, and is taking, as the future unfolds before us" (*Literary Disruptions: The Making of a Post-Contemporary American Fiction*, 2d ed. [Urbana, Ill., 1980], p. ix) [Ohmann's note].

5. Twenty-six of the forty-four responded. The survey accompanies an article by Melvin J. Friedman, "To 'Make It New': The American Novel since 1945," *Wilson Quarterly*, winter 1978, pp. 136–37. I don't know how the professors were selected or who they were, but almost every novel on this list was written by a white male with an elite educational background [Ohmann's note].

6. With their authors, in order: *Gravity's Rainbow* (1973), by Thomas Pynchon (b. 1937); *Herzog* (1964), by Bellow; *An American Dream* (1965), by Norman Mailer (1923–2007); *The Sotweed Factor* (1960), by John Barth (b. 1930); *Second Skin* (1964), by John Hawkes (1925–1998); *Portnoy's Complaint* (1969), by Philip Roth; *The Armies of the Night* (1968), by Mailer; *V* (1963), by Pynchon; and *Rabbit, Run* (1960), by Updike.

7. American essayist and editor (b. 1930).

8. John Hawkes is the outstanding example of a novelist whose work has consistently impressed critics and professors, without ever appealing to a wider audience. Should any of us be around to witness the outcome, it will be interesting to see if any of his books has a place in the canon 40 or 50 years from now [Ohmann's note].

9. I omit novelists still alive in 1960, but whose possibly canonical work belongs to an earlier time—Steinbeck, Dos Passos, Hemingway, etc. I *include* those of an older generation (Porter, McCarthy) who did not publish a precanonical novel until the 1960s. I exclude novelists of foreign origin (Asimov, Kosinski, Nabokov) and writers mainly known for their poetry, plays, or criticism, unless (as with Dickey and Plath) they also produced a precanonical novel during this period [Ohmann's note].

Auchincloss	Elkin	Piercy
Baldwin	Gaddis	Plath
Barth	Gardner	Porter
Barthelme	Gass	Pynchon
Bellow	Hawkes	Rechy
Berger	Heller	Reed
Bradbury	Higgins	Roth
Brautigan	Jong	Salinger
Burroughs	Kesey	Selby
Capote	R. MacDonald	Sorrentino
Cheever	Mailer	Styron
Condon	Malamud	Theroux
de Vries	McCarthy	Updike
Dickey	McMurtry	Vidal
Didion	Oates	Vonnegut
Doctorow	Percy	Walker[1]

Most of these meet my two criteria. All but a few (Bradbury, Condon, MacDonald, perhaps Auchincloss and Higgins) have received ample consideration by influential critics. Yet most novelists promoted by postcontemporary advocates such as Klinkowitz (Sloan, Coover, Wurlitzer, Katz, Federman, Sukenick,[2] etc.) are missing, while the list includes only a few writers who have had elite approval but small readerships (Elkin, Hawkes, Sorrentino, maybe two or three others). In fact, at least thirty-one of these novelists published one book or more between 1960 and 1975 that was a best-seller in hard or paper covers.[3] On the other hand, the list excludes the overwhelming majority of the writers who regularly produced large best-sellers: Puzo, Susann, Wouk, West, Robbins, Wallace, Michener, Krantz, Forsyth, Crichton,[4] and so on and on. I conclude that both the *Contemporary Literary Criticism* selection and the *Wilson Quarterly* survey give modest support to my thesis. Canon formation during this period took place in the interaction between large audiences and gatekeeper intellectuals.

1. Novelists whose dates have not already been given: Louis Auchincloss (1917–2010), James Baldwin (1924–1987), Donald Barthelme (1931–1989), Thomas Berger (1924–2014), Ray Bradbury (1920–2012), Richard Brautigan (1935–1984), William Burroughs (1914–1997), Truman Capote (1924–1984), John Cheever (1912–1982), Richard Condon (1915–1996), Peter De Vries (1910–1993), James Dickey (1923–1997), Joan Didion (b. 1934), Stanley Elkin (1930–1995), William Gaddis (1922–1998), John Gardner (1933–1982), William Gass (b. 1924), George Higgins (1939–1999), Erica Jong (b. 1942), Ross Macdonald (1915–1983), Mary McCarthy (1912–1989), Larry McMurtry (b. 1936), Joyce Carol Oates (b. 1938), Walker Percy (1916–1990), Marge Piercy (b. 1936), Sylvia Plath (1932–1963), Katherine Anne Porter (1890–1980), John Rechy (b. 1931), Ishmael Reed (b. 1938), J. D. Salinger (1919–2010), Hubert Selby Jr. (1928–2004), Gilbert Sorrentino (1929–2006), Paul Theroux (b. 1941), Gore Vidal (1925–2012), and Margaret Walker (1915–1998).

2. American critics and novelists: James Park Sloan (b. 1945), Robert Coover (b. 1932), Rudolph Wurlitzer (b. 1937), Steve Katz (b. 1935), Raymond Federman (1928–2009), and Ronald Sukenick (1932–2004).

3. I got this count by surveying the hardback and paperback best-seller lists in the *New York Times* from 1969 through 1975 and by checking the annual summaries in Alice Payne Hackett and James Henry Burke, *Eighty Years of Best Sellers, 1895–1975* (New York, 1977) for the rest of the 1960s [Ohmann's note].

4. American authors: Paul West (1930–2015), born in England; James Michener (1907–1997); Judith Krantz (b. 1928); Frederick Forsyth (b. 1938), born in England; and Michael Crichton (1942–2008).

Class and the Canon

To return to the main theme, then: I have drawn a sketch of the course a novel had to run in order to lodge itself in our culture as precanonical—as "literature," at least for the moment. It was selected, in turn, by an agent, an editor, a publicity department, a review editor (especially the one at the Sunday *New York Times Book Review*), the New York metropolitan book buyers whose patronage was necessary to commercial success, critics writing for gatekeeper intellectual journals, academic critics, and college teachers. Obviously, the sequence was not rigid, and some steps might on occasion be omitted entirely (as I have indicated with respect to *Catch-22* and *One Flew over the Cuckoo's Nest*). But one would expect the pattern to have become more regular through this period, as publishing was increasingly drawn into the sphere of monopoly capital (with RCA acquiring Random House; ITT, Howard Sams; Time, Inc., Little, Brown; CBS, Holt, Rinehart & Winston; Xerox, Ginn; and so on throughout almost the whole industry). For monopoly capital changed this industry much as it has changed the automobile and the toothpaste industries: by placing much greater emphasis on planned marketing and predictability of profits.[5]

This shift brought publishing into the same arena as many other cultural processes. In fact, the absorption of culture began almost as soon as monopoly capitalism itself, with the emergence of the advertising industry (crucial to planned marketing) in the 1880s and 1890s, and simultaneously with mass-circulation magazines as the main vehicle of national brand advertising.[6] With some variations, cinema, radio, music, sports, newspapers, television, and many lesser forms have followed this path, with books among the last to do so. The change has transformed our culture and the ways we participate in it. It demands rethinking, not only of bourgeois ideas about culture but of central Marxian oppositions like base and superstructure, production and reproduction.[7] Culture cannot, without straining, be understood as a reflex of basic economic activity, when culture is itself a core industry and a major source of capital accumulation. Nor can we bracket culture as reproduction, when it is inseparable from the making and selling of commodities. We have at present a relatively new and rapidly changing cultural process that calls for new and flexible ways of thinking about culture.

My account may, however, have made it sound as if in one respect nothing has changed. Under monopoly capital, even more than when Marx and Engels[8] wrote *The German Ideology*, the "class which has the means of

5. See the analysis in Paul A. Baran and Paul M. Sweezy, *Monopoly Capital: An Essay on the American Economic and Social Order* (New York, 1966). In publishing, the ascendancy of media packaging over simple book publishing has continued apace in recent years. See Thomas Whiteside, *The Blockbuster Complex: Conglomerates, Show Business, and Book Publishing* (Middletown, Conn., 1981). The practices Whiteside describes, along with the growth of national bookstore chains, have further altered the dynamic of publishing, thereby providing another reason for terminating this study somewhere around 1975 [Ohmann's note]. According to Marxist analysis, capitalism inevitably leads to greater monopolistic control and less competition.

6. See Ohmann's later study *Selling Culture: Magazines, Markets, and Class at the Turn of the Century* (New York: Verso, 1996).

7. See, for instance, Raymond Williams, "Base and Superstructure in Marxist Cultural Theory" [Ohmann's note; see above]. The base is the economic structure of society, which provides the foundation for the superstructure of forms of social consciousness (legal, political, artistic, etc.).

8. KARL MARX (1818–1883) and FRIEDRICH ENGELS (1820–1895), German social, economic, and political theorists; they wrote *The German Ideology* (see above) in 1845–46.

material production at its disposal, has control at the same time over the means of mental production." But does it still follow that, "thereby, generally speaking, the ideas of those who lack the means of mental production are subject to" the ruling class?[9] The theory can explain contemporary reality only with an expanded and enriched understanding of "control" and "subject to." For although our ruling class owns the media and controls them formally, it does not exercise direct control over their content—does not now use them in the instrumental and ideological way that Marx and Engels identified 140 years ago. Mobil[1] "idea ads" are the exception, not the rule.

To return to the instance at hand: neither the major stockholders of ITT and Xerox and RCA nor their boards of directors played a significant role in deciding which novels of the 1960s and early 1970s would gain acceptance as literature, and they certainly established no house rules—printing only those books that would advance their outlook on the world. (If they had done so, how could they have allowed, e.g., the Pantheon division of Random House virtually to enlist in the New Left?) They exercised control over publishing in the usual abstract way: they sought a good return on investment and cared little whether it came from a novel by Bellow or by Krantz, or for that matter from novels or computer chips. And very few of the historical actors who did make critical decisions about fiction were members of the haute bourgeoisie.[2] Was class then irrelevant to the early shaping of a canon of fiction? Alternatively, did the working class make its own culture in this sphere?

My argument points toward a conclusion different from both of these, one that still turns upon class but not just upon the two great traditional classes. Intuitively, one can see that literary agents, editors, publicity people, reviewers, buyers of hardbound novels, taste-making intellectuals, critics, professors, most of the students who took literary courses, and, in fact, the writers of the novels themselves, all had social affinities. They went to the same colleges, married one another, lived in the same neighborhoods, talked about the same movies, had to work for their livings (but worked with their minds more than with their hands), and earned pretty good incomes. I hold that they belonged to a common class, one that itself emerged and grew up only with monopoly capitalism. Following Barbara and John Ehrenreich, I call it the professional-managerial class.[3] I characterize it by the affinities just mentioned; by its conflicted relation to the ruling class (intellectuals managed that class's affairs and many of its institutions, and they derived benefits from this position, but they also strove for autonomy and for a somewhat different vision of the future); by its equally mixed relation to the working class (it dominated, supervised, taught, and planned for them, but even in doing so it also served and augmented capital); and by its own marginal position with respect to capital (its members didn't have the wealth to sit back and clip

9. *The Marx-Engels Reader*, ed. Robert C. Tucker (New York, 1972), p. 136 [Ohmann's note].
1. The oil company Mobil Corporation (now Exxon Mobil Corporation).
2. The upper middle class (French).
3. See Barbara and John Ehrenreich, "The Professional-Managerial Class," in Pat Walker, ed., *Between Labor and Capital* (Boston, 1979). Methodologically, I join the Ehrenreichs in holding that the point is not to "define" classes in some ahistorical way and that a notion of class is validated or invalidated by its power in theory, empirical explanation, and political practice. Hence I do not mean to be appropriating a preexisting definition of class in this essay and "applying" it to a particular situation and problem. Rather, I intend my argument and my evidence to help *develop* a more adequate picture of the way class has worked and works in the social process [Ohmann's note]. Barbara Ehrenreich (b. 1941), American social critic and journalist. John Ehrenreich (b. 1943), American psychologist.

coupons, but they had ready access to credit and most could choose—at least at an early stage in their careers—between working for themselves and selling their labor power to others).

People in the professional-managerial class shared one relation to the bourgeoisie and another to the working class: they had many common social experiences and acted out similar styles of life. I hold that they also had—with of course many complexities and much variation—a common understanding of the world and their place in it. In the remainder of this essay, I will look at some of the values, beliefs, and interests that constituted that class perspective, by considering the novels given cultural currency by those class members who produced, marketed, read, interpreted, and taught fiction. My claim is that the needs and values of the professional-managerial class permeate the general form of these novels, as well as their categories of understanding and their means of representation.

For my examples I will draw upon such works as *Franny and Zooey, One Flew over the Cuckoo's Nest, The Bell Jar, Herzog, Portnoy's Complaint*, and Updike's *Rabbit* series.[4] But what I say of these books is true of many other novels from the postwar period that have as yet a chance of becoming canonical. To glance ahead for a moment: these novels told stories of people trying to live a decent life in contemporary social settings, people represented as analogous to "us," rather than as "cases" to be examined and understood from a clinical distance, as in an older realistic convention. They are unhappy people, who move toward happiness, at least a bit, by the ends of their stories.

A premise of this fiction—nothing new to American literature but particularly salient in this period—is that individual consciousness, not the social or historical field, is the locus of significant happening. In passing, note that on the level of style this premise authorizes variety, the pursuit of a unique and personal voice. But on the levels of conceptualization and story, the premise of individual autonomy has an opposite effect: it gives these fictions a common problem and drives their material into narratives that, seen from the middle distance, look very similar. I suggest that much precanonical fiction of this period expresses, in Williams's term, a particular structure of feeling,[5] that that structure of feeling was a common one for the class in question, and that novelists explored its contours before it was articulated in books of social commentary like Philip Slater's *The Pursuit of Loneliness* (1970) and Charles Reich's *The Greening of America* (1970), or in films like *The Graduate*,[6] and certainly, before that structure of feeling informed a broad social movement or entered conversational cliché, in phrases like "a sick society," "the establishment," and "the system." (More avant-garde writers, outside the circuit of best-sellers, had given it earlier expression: the Beats, Mailer in *Advertisements for Myself*, Barth in *The End of the Road*,[7] etc.)

4. The sequels to *Rabbit, Run* are *Rabbit Redux* (1971), *Rabbit Is Rich* (1981), and (after the publication of Ohmann's essay) *Rabbit at Rest* (1990). Novels not already mentioned: *Franny and Zooey* (1961), by J. D. Salinger; *The Bell Jar* (1963), by Sylvia Plath.

5. Williams has used this concept since writing *Culture and Society, 1780–1950* (New York, 1958). Its most exact theoretical formulation is in his *Marxism and Literature* (New York, 1977) [Ohmann's note].

6. An Academy Award–winning film (1967, dir. Mike Nichols), whose somewhat aimless title character is unsure of his career and life plans after college graduation.

7. A novel published in 1958. The Beats: members of a literary and social movement of the 1950s who stressed unconventionality and rebelled against "square" middle-class life. *Advertisements for Myself* (1959), a collection of Mailer's fiction, nonfiction, poems, and plays.

This structure of feeling gathered and strengthened during the postwar period. It became rather intense by the early 1960s. After 1965 it exploded into the wider cultural and political arena, when black rebellions, the student movement, the antiwar movement, and later the women's movement made it clear, right there in the headlines and on television, that not everyone considered ours an age of only "happy problems."[8]

In retrospect it is easy to understand some of the forces that generated this consciousness. To chart the connection, I will take a broad and speculative look at the historical experience of the class that endowed fiction with value and suggest how that experience shaped that class's concerns and needs, before I turn at greater length to the fiction that its members wrote, published, read, and preserved.

Like everyone in the society, people in the professional-managerial class lived through a time when the United States was enjoying the spoils of World War II. It altogether dominated the "free world" for two decades, militarily, politically, and economically. Its power sufficed to give it dominance among its allies and to prevent defections from the capitalist sphere, though the "loss" of China and Cuba[9] gave cause for worried vigilance. Its products and its capital flowed freely through most parts of the world (its very money was the currency of capitalism after the Bretton Woods and Dumbarton Oaks agreements[1]). U.S. values also flowed freely, borne by advertising, television shows, and the *Reader's Digest* more than by propaganda. The confidence one would expect to find in the metropolis of such an empire strengthened the feeling of righteousness that came from having defeated one set of enemies in war and having held at bay another set in peace. Both the war and the cold war fostered a chauvinistic and morally polarized conception of the world. *They* were totalitarian monsters; *we* were an open society of free citizens pursuing a way of life superior to any other, past or present.

Furthermore, that way of life generated a material prosperity that was historically unprecedented and that increased from one year to the next. The pent-up buying power of the war period (never before or since has the broad working class had so much money in the bank) eased the conversion from war production to production for consumers by providing capitalists with an enormous and secure domestic market, and they responded with rapid investment and a flow of old and new products. Affluence, like victory in war, made people confident that they and their society were doing things right.

On top of that, social conflict became muted. Inequality remained as pronounced as it had been before, but no more so, and the working class participated in the steady growth of total product.[2] Though workers could not see any narrowing of the divide between themselves and higher classes, the

8. For a sampling of this consciousness, see Herbert Gold's "The Age of Happy Problems" (1956; rpt. in a book of the same title, New York, 1962) [Ohmann's note].

9. That is, the institution in those countries of communist forms of government in 1949 and 1959, respectively.

1. Proposals drawn up in 1944 (at what was then a private estate in Washington, D.C.) that provided the basic plan for the United Nations, chartered the following year. Bretton Woods: at the United Nations Monetary and Financial Conference at Bretton Woods, N.H., in 1944, the International Monetary Fund and the International Bank for Reconstruction and Development (the World Bank) were created; headquartered in Washington, D.C., they are intended to expand international trade by stabilizing exchange rates and promoting investment, respectively. All calculations at the UN, IMF, and World Bank are based in dollars.

2. For instance, the poorest 40 percent of families in the country received 16.8 percent of the income in 1947 and 16.9 percent in 1960, while the

postwar generation experienced an absolute gain, both from year to year and by comparison with the 1930s; many *perceived* this gain as a softening of class lines. The sense of economic well-being that results from such an experience of history promoted allegiance to the social order, as did the tightening bonds between unions and management, amounting to a truce in class conflict within the assumptions of the welfare state. Cold war propaganda helped make it possible—especially for those who managed the new arrangements and lived in suburbs—to see our society as a harmonious collaboration.

Developments in business additionally gave support to this image of harmony. There was a rapid growth and sophistication of advertising, which not only sold products but continued to shape people into masses, for the purpose of selling those products and advancing a whole way of life whose cornerstones were the suburban home, the family, and the automobile. Leisure and social life became more private, drained of class feeling and even of the feeling of interdependence.

Politics seemed nearly irrelevant to such a life. Moreover, the boundaries of respectable political debate steadily closed in through the 1950s. On one side, socialism was pushed off the agenda by union leaders almost as vigorously as by Truman, McCarthy, the blacklisters, the FBI.[3] On the other side, businessmen gradually abandoned the tough old capitalist principles of laissez-faire and espoused a more benign program of cooperation with labor and government. The spectrum of discussable ideas reached only from corporate liberalism to welfare-state liberalism; no wonder some thought they were witnessing the end of ideology.[4]

Consider the experience of the class that creates the canon of fiction in such an environment. Not only were its numbers and its prosperity growing rapidly along with its institutions but every public voice seemed to be saying to intellectuals, professionals, technical elites, and managers: "History is over, though progress continues. There is no more poverty. Everyone is middle class. The state is a friendly power, capable of smoothing out the abrasions of the economic system, solving its problems one by one through legislation that itself is the product of your ideas and values. You have brought a neutral and a humane rationality to the supervision of public life (exemplified beautifully by that parade of Harvard intellectuals to Washington in 1961[5]). Politics is for experts, not ideologues. You are, therefore, the favored

percentage going to the richest 5 percent went from 17.2 percent to 16.8 percent. The top 1 percent owned 23.3 percent of the nation's *wealth* in 1945 and 27.4 percent in 1962. These figures come from tables complied by Frank Ackerman and Andrew Zimbalist, "Capitalism and Inequality in the United States," in Richard C. Edwards, Michael Reich, and Thomas E. Weisskopf, eds., *The Capitalist System: A Radical Analysis of American Society*, 2d ed. (Englewood Cliffs, N.J., 1978), pp. 298, 301 [Ohmann's note].

3. Representative figures of the cold war: Harry S. Truman (1884–1972), as U.S. president (1945–53), strongly opposed the spread of communist forms of government in the world; Joseph McCarthy (1908–1957), U.S. senator from Wisconsin (1947–57), made largely unsubstantiated charges of Communist infiltration in American government and industry in the early 1950s; "the blacklisters" refused to hire those in the entertainment industry accused of having some connection to communism, following public congressional hearings by the House Committee on Un-American Activities that began in 1947; the Federal Bureau of Investigation secretly and sometimes illegally gathered information about American citizens who were alleged to be subversives.

4. See Daniel Bell, *The End of Ideology* (Glencoe, Ill.: Free Press, 1960).

5. During the presidency of John F. Kennedy (1917–1963; president, 1961–63), many intellectuals from Harvard University and elsewhere were appointed to positions in government.

people, the peacemakers, the technicians of an intelligent society, justly rewarded with quick promotions, respect, and adequate incomes. So carry forward this valued social mission, which in no way conflicts with individual achievement. Enjoy your prestige and comforts. Fulfill yourselves on the terrain of private life."

But because the economic underpinnings of this consciousness were of course *not* unchanging and free of conflict, because material interdependence was an ever more pervasive fact,[6] whether perceived or not, because society cannot be wished away, because freedom on such terms is an illusion—for all these reasons, the individual pursuit of happiness continued to be a problem. Yet myth, ideology, and experience assured the professional-managerial class that no real barriers would prevent personal satisfaction, so it was easy to nourish the suspicion that any perceived lack was one's own fault. If unhappy, one must be personally maladjusted, perhaps even neurotic. I am suggesting that for the people who wrote, read, promoted, and preserved fiction, social contradictions were easily displaced into images of personal illness.[7]

* * *

What I hope to have accomplished * * * is to have given concrete enough form to the following powerful yet vague ideas about culture and value, so that they may be criticized and perhaps developed. (1) A canon—a shared understanding of what literature is worth preserving—takes shape through a troubled historical process. (2) It emerges through specific institutions and practices, not in some historically invariant way. (3) These institutions are likely to have a rather well-defined class base. (4) Although the ruling ideas and myths may indeed be, in every age, the ideas and myths of the ruling class, the ruling class in advanced capitalist societies does not advance its ideas directly through its control of the means of mental production. Rather, a subordinate but influential class shapes culture in ways that express its own interests and experience and that sometimes turn on ruling-class values rather critically—yet in a nonrevolutionary period end up confirming root elements of the dominant ideology, such as the premise of individualism. I hope, in short, to have given a usable and attackable account of the hegemonic process and to have added content to the claim that aesthetic value arises from class conflict.

1983

6. That is, people relied on others, through the intermediary of the market, for more and more goods and services. In an ordinary day's "consuming," each of us depends on the past and present labor of hundreds of millions of workers worldwide. But of course this is easy to forget, since that loaf of bread magically appears on the store shelf and the only labor we *see* is that of the checker and the bagger [Ohmann's note].

7. In the closing section of the essay, omitted here, Ohmann documents specific examples of what he calls "illness stories," such as *The Bell Jar, Franny and Zooey,* and *One Flew over the Cuckoo's Nest,* arguing that their depictions of mental illness represent the social fragmentation wrought by modern U.S. capitalism.

STUART HALL
1932–2014

Stuart Hall, the single most prominent and influential theorist of British cultural studies, embodied the theoretical and political trajectory of late twentieth-century leftist intellectuals. Deeply involved in the New Left's revisionist engagement with Marxism during the 1950s and 1960s, Hall subsequently moved through an encounter with structuralist and poststructuralist thought in the 1970s and 1980s that led to his highly productive reworking of ANTONIO GRAMSCI's theories of hegemony, civil society, and the role of intellectuals. In the 1990s Hall took up issues connected with racial and cultural identities, "the politics of difference," and the African diaspora. Disappointed with the record of the Labour Party after its 1997 return to power following the Thatcher years, Hall became increasingly discouraged about the prospects of leftist politics in Britain and turned his attention after 1998 to contemporary art, especially to video and other emerging urban art forms.

Born in Jamaica to a relatively privileged family, Hall came to Britain as a Rhodes Scholar in 1951 and never left. As he explained it, a combination of vexed family relations and his own intense involvement in the formation of the British New Left made him miss the moment when he might have returned to the Caribbean. His racial and national difference as a black colonial subject in Britain rendered him, in his words, "a familiar stranger," who occupied a "diasporic" position of knowing two "places intimately" (Jamaica and England) while being "not wholly of either place."

Hall's work within New Left circles, including his position as a founding editor of the influential *New Left Review*, kept him from completing his graduate work at Oxford University. The British New Left strove to create a non-Stalinist, noncommunist socialism that could influence Labour Party policies and move intellectual and political paradigms from a sole focus on economic factors to a more complex understanding of the multiple determinants of people's allegiances, attitudes, and beliefs. Interested in popular culture (as were those who laid the groundwork for British cultural studies, E. P. Thompson, RAYMOND WILLIAMS, and Richard Hoggart), Hall worked with the Education Department of the British Film Institute in the early sixties, which in 1961 led to his appointment at the University of London as the first "lecturer in film and mass media studies" in Britain. He moved to the University of Birmingham in 1964 to join Hoggart's newly formed Centre for Contemporary Cultural Studies, remaining there until 1979 and serving as the center's director during much of that time. He spent the years from 1979 until his retirement in 1998 at the Open University.

The Birmingham years have become legendary, with his work done at the Open University only slightly less so. Many figures later important in cultural studies (for instance, DICK HEBDIGE, Hazel Carby, Angela McRobbie, PAUL GILROY, and Larry Grossberg) were students or co-workers of Hall's at some point. Collaborative work was the norm at both places; this founding work in cultural studies characteristically came to the world in the form of edited volumes in which eight to twelve authors address a topic, arguing with each other but also moving toward an overarching delineation of the factors that need to be considered if the topic is to be adequately analyzed.

Hall, like PAUL DE MAN, was a charismatic teacher, and his immense influence is only partially captured in his written work. An essayist, he produced no single distillation of his views, and his pieces are scattered in journals and edited volumes that are often hard to find. But the essay form is suited to his intellectual temperament, which is self-consciously nondogmatic, restless, and open to new ideas and changing social conditions.

To some extent, Hall's intellectual stance bedevils cultural studies, especially as it becomes institutionalized in American universities. The dialogic, multivoiced inception of cultural studies makes it a moving target, engaged in a series of debates with various formalized intellectual paradigms (notably Marxism, anthropological and sociological functionalism, and aestheticist literary criticism), all the while avoiding definitive statements of its own position. Hall advocated a "cultural studies . . . that is always self-reflectively deconstructing itself. . . . Let me put it this way: you have to be sure about a position to teach a class, but you have to be open-minded enough to know that you are going to change your mind by the time you teach it next week." Over the years, Hall's work was influenced by Western Marxism, poststructuralism (especially MICHEL FOUCAULT), critical race theory, and feminism, as he made clear in our selection. Such openness has been characterized by some critics of cultural studies as its willingness and ability to absorb anything, a kind of academic imperialism that lacks intellectual or disciplinary boundaries or values.

Hall's wariness about a codification of cultural studies comes through in our selection, "Cultural Studies and Its Theoretical Legacies" (1992), although certain traits typical of British cultural studies can be identified. The primary feature is a commitment to the political relevance of intellectual work. British cultural studies is an outgrowth of leftist politics, born of the theoretical need for alternatives to a vulgar Marxism that is rooted in class politics and economic determinism. As an offshoot of Marxism, this cultural studies is aligned with Gramsci against the more pessimistic visions of the Frankfurt School (see MAX HORKHEIMER and THEODOR W. ADORNO) and LOUIS ALTHUSSER. Adapting Gramsci's crucial notion of hegemony, Hall emphasized the ways in which the power of ruling elites is constituted and reconstituted within a complex cultural scene that affords various possibilities for action. Rather than stressing the ways that power, through ideology, imposes a mode of life on passive social subjects, he used the concept of hegemony to provide a more dynamic vision of ongoing struggles among all members of society, with only temporary and always fragile victories by any particular group. Hall's interest in connecting intellectuals "organically" to these political struggles also follows Gramsci's lead. But such Gramscian elements in Hall are elaborated through an engagement with Foucault, as he detailed power's dispersion through a whole social order, the processes of subject formation, and the power/knowledge produced by intellectual discourses.

The crucial move in Hall's revisionist leftist theory is his insistence on the role that cultural discourses play in shaping political realities and political possibilities. "My own view," Hall wrote, "is that events, relations, structures do have conditions of existence and real effects, outside the sphere of the discursive; but that only within the discursive, and subject to its specific conditions, limits and modalities, do they have or can they be constructed within meaning." In other words, the "culture" in cultural studies names the various signifying and representational processes through which things acquire meaning. For example, hunger is a biological reality. But what we eat and when and how we eat it, and whether we drink carrot juice or a Coke if we are thirsty, are all products of the cultural elaboration of the necessity of eating. And Hall insisted that "regimes of representation in a culture do play a constitutive, and not merely a reflexive, after-the-event, role." Thus, an American will often refuse to eat horse flesh even if extremely hungry, while the French eat it regularly. Our biological needs are altered by our culture's assignment of values. "This gives questions of culture and ideology, and the scenarios of representation—subjectivity, identity, politics—a formative, not merely an expressive, place in the constitution of social and political life." In this ability of signifying processes to change social and political life, cultural studies has located political hope.

What has confused—and sometimes infuriated—many academics about cultural studies is its refusal to declare a prevailing methodology and a designated object of study, two features required of traditional academic disciplines. Cultural studies strives to analyze the hegemonic practices by which social groups are bound (institutionally, intellectually, emotionally, and economically) to dominant social forms. And it examines how forces of resistance creatively intervene in those practices. Since hegemony works through and on every social site and practice, cultural studies has deemed anything a potential object of study and has adapted any disciplinary methodology that might prove useful, ranging from surveys, case studies, and personal observation to textual explication, institutional analysis, and political critique. Partly in response to intellectual elitism, partly by happenstance, and partly as a form of leftist populism, much cultural studies work has focused on popular, as contrasted to high, culture. But any activity through which people negotiate their relationship to society and to the disparate forces and institutions in their lives is fair game for its attention.

The absence of a prevailing methodology does not mean that cultural studies lacks a theory. Hall's scattered essays have addressed a wide array of theoretical issues and, when taken together, delineate a comprehensive overview of the driving questions and angles of approach followed by many cultural studies practitioners. Processes of identity formation are central, as are the concepts of "conjuncture" and "articulation." Hall, like most Marxists, was a "conflict theorist": one who views the social field as a dynamic site of numerous contending forces. Within that field, he refused to recognize any stable identities—either group (like class) or personal (like ethnicity). Identity for him is always in the process of being constituted by prevailing social norms, institutions, and subject positions, as well as by particular struggles against those would-be determinants. Identity, in other words, is a battleground, where the meaning of social life is being forged and contested. Here as elsewhere, Hall relied on the concept of "conjuncture," the idea that everything exists simultaneously amid specific historical forces in process and amid specific determinant structures. The elements within any conjuncture and the relations of force among them are differently "articulated" at different times and places. Each conjuncture has its own configuration. Social groups, including intellectuals, will work to make their "articulation" of a given constellation of elements prevail.

For Hall, no dominant order could ever provide a seamless, synthetic, permanent vision. All hegemonies must be continually produced by very specific acts of public articulation. Cultural studies is interested in mapping the particular constellation of identities and hegemonic articulations at various social sites; it often focuses on dynamic tensions between mainstream norms and marginalized groups, studying how cultural materials are creatively resignified to fit the nonstandard purposes of such resistant groups. Typical counterhegemonic materials might include a punk 'zine, women's shop-floor gossip, romance novels, and rap poetry. A typical cultural studies research project might examine the circuits of production, distribution, and consumption through which such "discourses" pass.

Critics of Hall's work are divided between traditional leftists who object that he overemphasized a cultural politics of resistance at the expense of a socioeconomic politics focused on systematic inequalities and poststructuralist opponents who see the concept of hegemony as aspiring to a totalized vision that misses the irreducible heterogeneity of the social field. Nevertheless, Hall's—and cultural studies'—importance for contemporary literary studies may rest most crucially on his insistence in "Cultural Studies and Its Theoretical Legacies" that "textuality is never enough." That is to say, Hall insisted on linking literary theory's understanding of meaning production and textual interpretation with social theory's delineation of conflicting forces within the social field. If a literary critic believes that any interpretation of a literary text must consider both the social forces that contribute to the text's production *and* the hegemonic work that the text does, then he or she has taken up the concerns and questions that characterize cultural studies.

"Cultural Studies and Its Theoretical Legacies" Keywords: Cultural Studies, Hegemony, Identity, Institutional Studies, Marxism, Representation, Semiotics

Cultural Studies and Its Theoretical Legacies

This Conference[1] provides us with an opportunity for a moment of self-reflection on cultural studies as a practice, on its institutional positioning, and what Lidia Curti[2] so effectively reminds us is both the marginality and the centrality of its practitioners as critical intellectuals. Inevitably, this involves reflecting on, and intervening in, the project of cultural studies itself.

My title, "Cultural Studies and Its Theoretical Legacies," suggests a look back to the past, to consult and think about the Now and the Future of cultural studies by way of a retrospective glance. It does seem necessary to do some genealogical and archaeological work on the archive. Now the question of the archives is extremely difficult for me because, where cultural studies is concerned, I sometimes feel like a *tableau vivant*,[3] a spirit of the past resurrected, laying claim to the authority of an origin. After all, didn't cultural studies emerge somewhere at that moment when I first met Raymond Williams, or in the glance I exchanged with Richard Hoggart?[4] In that moment, cultural studies was born; it emerged full grown from the head![5] I do want to talk about the past, but definitely not in that way. I don't want to talk about British cultural studies (which is in any case a pretty awkward signifier for me) in a patriarchal way, as the keeper of the conscience of cultural studies, hoping to police you back into line with what it really was if only you knew. That is to say, I want to absolve myself of the many burdens of representation which people carry around—I carry around at least three: I'm expected to speak for the entire black race on all questions theoretical, critical, etc., and sometimes for British politics, as well as for cultural studies. This is what is known as the black person's burden,[6] and I would like to absolve myself of it at this moment.

That means, paradoxically, speaking autobiographically. Autobiography is usually thought of as seizing the authority of authenticity. But in order not to be authoritative, I've got to speak autobiographically. I'm going to tell you about my own take on certain theoretical legacies and moments in cultural studies, not because it is the truth or the only way of telling the history. I myself have told it many other ways before; and I intend to tell it in a different way later. But just at this moment, for this conjuncture, I want to take a position in relation to the "grand narrative"[7] of cultural studies for the purposes of opening up some reflections on cultural studies as a practice, on our institutional position, and on its project. I want to do that by referring to some theoretical legacies or theoretical moments, but in a very particular way. This is not a commentary on the success or effectiveness of different theoretical positions in cultural studies (that is for some other occasion). It is an attempt to say something about what certain theoretical moments in cul-

1. "Cultural Studies Now and in the Future," held in April 1990 at the University of Illinois at Urbana-Champaign.
2. Italian academic working in cultural studies (b. 1947).
3. Living picture (French).
4. Hoggart (1918–2014) and WILLIAMS (1921–1988), both British academics and early practitioners of cultural studies.
5. That is, like Athena (goddess of wisdom) born from the head of Zeus (king of the gods), in Greek mythology.
6. An allusion to "The White Man's Burden" (1899), a poem by Rudyard Kipling that paints imperialism as the duty of the "advanced" peoples.
7. JEAN-FRANÇOIS LYOTARD (1924–1998) defined postmodernism as a skepticism toward any "grand narrative" that offers an all-encompassing vision of history's trajectory.

tural studies have been like for me, and from that position, to take some bearings about the general question of the politics of theory.

Cultural studies is a discursive formation, in Foucault's[8] sense. It has no simple origins, though some of us were present at some point when it first named itself in that way. Much of the work out of which it grew, in my own experience, was already present in the work of other people. Raymond Williams has made the same point, charting the roots of cultural studies in the early adult education movement in his essay on "The Future of Cultural Studies" (1989). "The relation between a project and a formation is always decisive," he says, because they are "different ways of materializing . . . then of describing a common disposition of energy and direction." Cultural studies has multiple discourses; it has a number of different histories. It is a whole set of formations; it has its own different conjunctures and moments in the past. It included many different kinds of work. I want to insist on that! It always was a set of unstable formations. It was "centered" only in quotation marks, in a particular kind of way which I want to define in a moment. It had many trajectories; many people had and have different trajectories through it; it was constructed by a number of different methodologies and theoretical positions, all of them in contention. Theoretical work in the Centre for Contemporary Cultural Studies[9] was more appropriately called theoretical noise. It was accompanied by a great deal of bad feeling, argument, unstable anxieties, and angry silences.

Now, does it follow that cultural studies is not a policed disciplinary area? That it is whatever people do, if they choose to call or locate themselves within the project and practice of cultural studies? I am not happy with that formulation either. Although cultural studies as a project is open-ended, it can't be simply pluralist in that way. Yes, it refuses to be a master discourse or a meta-discourse of any kind. Yes, it is a project that is always open to that which it doesn't yet know, to that which it can't yet name. But it does have some will to connect; it does have some stake in the choices it makes. It does matter whether cultural studies is this or that. It can't be just any old thing which chooses to march under a particular banner. It is a serious enterprise, or project, and that is inscribed in what is sometimes called the "political" aspect of cultural studies. Not that there's one politics already inscribed in it. But there is something *at stake* in cultural studies, in a way that I think, and hope, is not exactly true of many other very important intellectual and critical practices. Here one registers the tension between a refusal to close the field, to police it and, at the same time, a determination to stake out some positions within it and argue for them. That is the tension—the dialogic approach to theory—that I want to try to speak to in a number of different ways in the course of this paper. I don't believe knowledge is closed, but I do believe that politics is impossible without what I have called "the arbitrary closure"; without what Homi Bhabha[1] called social agency as an arbitrary closure. That is to say, I don't understand a practice which aims to make a difference in the world, which doesn't have some points of difference or distinction

8. MICHEL FOUCAULT (1926–1984), French philosopher and historian of ideas.

9. Founded at the University of Birmingham by Richard Hoggart in 1964; Hall served as the center's director from 1968 to 1979.

1. Indian postcolonial theorist and critic (b. 1949); BHABHA makes this point in "The Postcolonial and the Postmodern: A Question of Agency," in *The Location of Culture* (1994).

which it has to stake out, which really matter. It is a question of positionalities. Now, it is true that those positionalities are never final, they're never absolute. They can't be translated intact from one conjuncture to another; they cannot be depended on to remain in the same place. I want to go back to that moment of "staking out a wager" in cultural studies, to those moments in which the positions began to matter.

This is a way of opening the question of the "worldliness" of cultural studies, to borrow a term from Edward Said.[2] I am not dwelling on the secular connotations of the metaphor of worldliness here, but on the worldliness of cultural studies. I'm dwelling on the "dirtiness" of it: the dirtiness of the semiotic game, if I can put it that way. I'm trying to return the project of cultural studies from the clean air of meaning and textuality and theory to the something nasty down below. This involves the difficult exercise of examining some of the key theoretical turns or moments in cultural studies.

The first trace that I want to deconstruct has to do with a view of British cultural studies which often distinguishes it by the fact that, at a certain moment, it became a Marxist critical practice. What exactly does that assignation of cultural studies as a Marxist critical theory mean? How can we think cultural studies at that moment? What moment is it we are speaking of? What does that mean for the theoretical legacies, traces, and aftereffects which Marxism continues to have in cultural studies? There are a number of ways of telling that history, and let me remind you that I'm not proposing this as the only story. But I do want to set it up in what I think may be a slightly surprising way to you.

I entered cultural studies from the New Left, and the New Left always regarded Marxism as a problem, as trouble, as danger, not as a solution. Why? It had nothing to do with theoretical questions as such or in isolation. It had to do with the fact that my own (and its own) political formation occurred in a moment historically very much like the one we are in now—which I am astonished that so few people have addressed—the moment of the disintegration of a certain kind of Marxism. In fact, the first British New Left emerged in 1956 at the moment of the disintegration of an entire historical/political project.[3] In that sense I came into Marxism backwards: against the Soviet tanks in Budapest, as it were. What I mean by that is certainly not that I wasn't profoundly, and that cultural studies then wasn't from the beginning, profoundly influenced by the questions that Marxism as a theoretical project put on the agenda: the power, the global reach and history-making capacities of capital; the question of class; the complex relationships between power, which is an easier term to establish in the discourses of culture than exploitation, and exploitation; the question of a general theory which could, in a critical way, connect together in a critical reflection different domains of life, politics and theory, theory and practice, economic, political, ideological questions, and so on; the notion of critical knowledge itself and the production of critical knowledge as a practice. These important, central questions are what one meant by working within shouting distance of Marxism, working on

2. Palestinian-born American literary and cultural critic and social activist (1935–2003); for SAID's discussion of "worldliness," see chapter 1 of *The World, the Text, and the Critic* (1983).

3. That is, when Soviet troops suppressed a short-lived anti-Communist and anti-Soviet rebellion in Hungary in October 1956.

Marxism, working against Marxism, working with it, working to try to develop Marxism.

There never was a prior moment when cultural studies and Marxism represented a perfect theoretical fit. From the beginning (to use this way of speaking for a moment) there was always-already the question of the great inadequacies, theoretically and politically, the resounding silences, the great evasions of Marxism—the things that Marx did not talk about or seem to understand which were our privileged object of study: culture, ideology, language, the symbolic.[4] These were always-already, instead, the things which had imprisoned Marxism as a mode of thought, as an activity of critical practice—its orthodoxy, its doctrinal character, its determinism, its reductionism, its immutable law of history, its status as a metanarrative. That is to say, the encounter between British cultural studies and Marxism has first to be understood as the engagement with a problem—not a theory, not even a problematic. It begins, and develops through the critique of a certain reductionism and economism, which I think is not extrinsic but intrinsic to Marxism; a contestation with the model of base and superstructure, through which sophisticated and vulgar Marxism alike had tried to think the relationships between society, economy, and culture. It was located and sited in a necessary and prolonged and as yet unending contestation with the question of false consciousness. In my own case, it required a not-yet-completed contestation with the profound Eurocentrism of Marxist theory. I want to make this very precise. It is not just a matter of where Marx happened to be born, and of what he talked about, but of the model at the center of the most developed parts of Marxist theory, which suggested that capitalism evolved organically from within its own transformations. Whereas I came from a society where the profound integument of capitalist society, economy, and culture had been imposed by conquest and colonization. This is a theoretical, not a vulgar critique. I don't blame Marx because of where he was born; I'm questioning the theory for the model around which it is articulated: its Eurocentrism.

I want to suggest a different metaphor for theoretical work: the metaphor of struggle, of wrestling with the angels. The only theory worth having is that which you have to fight off, not that which you speak with profound fluency. I mean to say something later about the astonishing theoretical fluency of cultural studies now. But my own experience of theory—and Marxism is certainly a case in point—is of wrestling with the angels—a metaphor you can take as literally as you like. I remember wrestling with Althusser.[5] I remember looking at the idea of "theoretical practice" in *Reading Capital* and thinking, "I've gone as far in this book as it is proper to go." I felt, I will not give an inch to this profound misreading, this super-structuralist mistranslation, of classical Marxism, unless he beats me down, unless he defeats me in the spirit. He'll have to march over me to convince me. I warred with him, to the death. A long, rambling piece I wrote (Hall, 1974)[6] on Marx's 1857 Introduction to *The Grundrisse*, in which I tried to stake out the difference between

4. On the writings of the German economic and political philosopher KARL MARX (1818–1883) pertaining to culture, see above.

5. LOUIS ALTHUSSER (1918–1990), French philosopher. *Reading Capital* was published in 1965.

6. Stuart Hall, "Marx's Notes on Method: A 'Reading' of the 1857 Introduction," *Working Papers in Cultural Studies* 6 (1974) [Hall's note].

structuralism in Marx's epistemology and Althusser's, was only the tip of the iceberg of this long engagement. And that is not simply a personal question. In the Centre for Contemporary Cultural Studies, for five or six years, long after the anti-theoreticism or resistance to theory of cultural studies had been overcome, and we decided, in a very un-British way, we had to take the plunge into theory, we walked right around the entire circumference of European thought, in order not to be, in any simple capitulation to the *zeitgeist*, Marxists. We read German idealism, we read Weber upside down, we read Hegelian idealism,[7] we read idealistic art criticism. (I've written about this in the article called "The Hinterland of Science: Sociology of Knowledge" [1980] as well as in "Cultural Studies and the Centre: Some Problems and Problematics" [1980].)[8]

So the notion that Marxism and cultural studies slipped into place, recognized an immediate affinity, joined hands in some teleological or Hegelian moment of synthesis, and there was the founding moment of cultural studies, is entirely mistaken. It couldn't have been more different from that. And when, eventually, in the seventies, British cultural studies did advance—in many different ways, it must be said—within the problematic of Marxism, you should hear the term problematic in a genuine way, not just in a formalist-theoretical way: as a problem; as much about struggling against the constraints and limits of that model as about the necessary questions it required us to address. And when, in the end, in my own work, I tried to learn from and work with the theoretical gains of Gramsci,[9] it was only because certain strategies of evasion had forced Gramsci's work, in a number of different ways, to respond to what I can only call (here's another metaphor for theoretical work) the conundrums of theory, the things which Marxist theory couldn't answer, the things about the modern world which Gramsci discovered remained unresolved within the theoretical framework of grand theory—Marxism—in which he continued to work. At a certain point, the questions I still wanted to address in short were inaccessible to me except via a detour through Gramsci. Not because Gramsci resolved them but because he at least addressed many of them. I don't want to go through what it is I personally think cultural studies in the British context, in a certain period, learned from Gramsci: immense amounts about the nature of culture itself, about the discipline of the conjunctural, about the importance of historical specificity, about the enormously productive metaphor of hegemony, about the way in which one can think questions of class relations only by using the displaced notion of ensemble and blocs. These are the particular gains of the "detour" via Gramsci, but I'm not trying to talk about that. I want to say, in this context, about Gramsci, that while Gramsci belonged and belongs to the problematic of Marxism, his importance for this moment of British cultural studies is precisely the degree to which he radically *displaced* some of the inheritances of Marxism in cultural studies. The radical character of Gramsci's "displacement" of Marxism has not yet been understood and probably won't ever be

7. In some respects, Marx's materialism was a reaction against the idealist philosophy of GEORG WILHELM FRIEDRICH HEGEL (1770–1831). Max Weber (1864–1920), German social theorist and a founder of sociology as an academic discipline.

8. "The Hinterland of Science" is in *On Ideology* (1980). "Cultural Studies and the Centre" is in *Culture, Media, Language*, edited by S. Hall et al. (1980) [Hall's note].

9. ANTONIO GRAMSCI (1891–1937), Italian Marxist theorist and cultural critic.

reckoned with, now we are entering the era of post-Marxism. Such is the nature of the movement of history and of intellectual fashion. But Gramsci also did something else for cultural studies, and I want to say a little bit about that because it refers to what I call the need to reflect on our institutional position, and our intellectual practice.

I tried on many occasions, and other people in British cultural studies and at the Centre especially have tried, to describe what it is we thought we were doing with the kind of intellectual work we set in place in the Centre. I have to confess that, though I've read many, more elaborated and sophisticated, accounts, Gramsci's account still seems to me to come closest to expressing what it is I think we were trying to do. Admittedly, there's a problem about his phrase "the production of organic intellectuals."[1] But there is no doubt in my mind that we were trying to find an institutional practice in cultural studies that might produce an organic intellectual. We didn't know previously what that would mean, in the context of Britain in the 1970s, and we weren't sure we would recognize him or her if we managed to produce it. The problem about the concept of an organic intellectual is that it appears to align intellectuals with an emerging historic movement and we couldn't tell then, and can hardly tell now, where that emerging historical movement was to be found. We were organic intellectuals without any organic point of reference; organic intellectuals with a nostalgia or will or hope (to use Gramsci's phrase from another context) that at some point we would be prepared in intellectual work for that kind of relationship, if such a conjuncture ever appeared. More truthfully, we were prepared to imagine or model or simulate such a relationship in its absence: "pessimism of the intellect, optimism of the will."[2]

But I think it is very important that Gramsci's thinking around these questions certainly captures part of what we were about. Because a second aspect of Gramsci's definition of intellectual work, which I think has always been lodged somewhere close to the notion of cultural studies as a project, has been his requirement that the "organic intellectual" must work on two fronts at one and the same time. On the one hand, we had to be at the very forefront of intellectual theoretical work because, as Gramsci says, it is the job of the organic intellectual to know more than the traditional intellectuals do: really know, not just pretend to know, not just to have the facility of knowledge, but to know deeply and profoundly. So often knowledge for Marxism is pure recognition—the production again of what we have always known! If you are in the game of hegemony you have to be smarter than "them." Hence, there are no theoretical limits from which cultural studies can turn back. But the second aspect is just as crucial: that the organic intellectual cannot absolve himself or herself from the responsibility of transmitting those ideas, that knowledge, through the intellectual function, to those who do not belong, professionally, in the intellectual class. And unless those two fronts are operating at the same time, or at least unless those two ambitions are part of the project of cultural studies, you can get enormous theoretical advance without any engagement at the level of the political project.

1. That is, the thinking element that guides their particular class; Gramsci sets organic intellectuals against "traditional intellectuals" (e.g., scientists and academics).

2. Quoted from Gramsci's *Prison Notebooks* (1948–51).

I'm extremely anxious that you should not decode what I'm saying as an anti-theoretical discourse. It is not anti-theory, but it does have something to do with the conditions and problems of developing intellectual and theoretical work as a political practice. It is an extremely difficult road, not resolving the tensions between those two requirements, but living with them. Gramsci never asked us to resolve them, but he gave us a practical example of how to live with them. We never produced organic intellectuals (would that we had) at the Centre. We never connected with that rising historic movement; it was a metaphoric exercise. Nevertheless, metaphors are serious things. They affect one's practice. I'm trying to redescribe cultural studies as theoretical work which must go on and on living with that tension.

I want to look at two other theoretical moments in cultural studies which interrupted the already-interrupted history of its formation. Some of these developments came as it were from outer space: they were not at all generated from the inside, they were not part of an inner-unfolding general theory of culture. Again and again, the so-called unfolding of cultural studies was interrupted by a break, by real ruptures, by exterior forces; the interruption, as it were, of new ideas, which decentered what looked like the accumulating practice of the work. There's another metaphor for theoretical work: theoretical work as interruption.

There were at least two interruptions in the work of the Centre for Contemporary Cultural Studies: The first around feminism, and the second around questions of race. This is not an attempt to sum up the theoretical and political advances and consequences for British cultural studies of the feminist intervention; that is for another time, another place. But I don't want, either, to invoke that moment in an open-ended and casual way. For cultural studies (in addition to many other theoretical projects), the intervention of feminism was specific and decisive. It was ruptural. It reorganized the field in quite concrete ways. First, the opening of the question of the personal as political, and its consequences for changing the object of study in cultural studies, was completely revolutionary in a theoretical and practical way. Second, the radical expansion of the notion of power, which had hitherto been very much developed within the framework of the notion of the public, the public domain, with the effect that we could not use the term power—so key to the earlier problematic of hegemony—in the same way. Third, the centrality of questions of gender and sexuality to the understanding of power itself. Fourth, the opening of many of the questions that we thought we had abolished around the dangerous area of the subjective and the subject, which lodged those questions at the center of cultural studies as a theoretical practice. Fifth, the "re-opening" of the closed frontier between social theory and the theory of the unconscious—psychoanalysis. It's hard to describe the import of the opening of that new continent in cultural studies, marked out by the relationship—or rather, what Jacqueline Rose[3] has called the as yet "unsettled relations"—between feminism, psychoanalysis, and cultural studies, or indeed how it was accomplished.

We know it was, but it's not known generally how and where feminism first broke in. I use the metaphor deliberately. As the thief in the night, it broke in; interrupted, made an unseemly noise, seized the time, crapped on

3. British feminist literary critic (b. 1949).

the table of cultural studies. The title of the volume in which this dawn-raid was first accomplished—*Women Take Issue*[4]—is instructive: for they "took issue" in both senses—took over that year's book and initiated a quarrel. But I want to tell you something else about it. Because of the growing importance of feminist work and the early beginnings of the feminist movement outside in the very early 1970s, many of us in the Centre—mainly, of course, men—thought it was time there was good feminist work in cultural studies. And we indeed tried to buy it in, to import it, to attract good feminist scholars. As you might expect, many of the women in cultural studies weren't terribly interested in this benign project. We were opening the door to feminist studies, being good, transformed men. And yet, when it broke in through the window, every single unsuspected resistance rose to the surface—fully installed patriarchal power, which believed it had disavowed itself. There are no leaders here, we used to say; we are all graduate students and members of staff together, learning how to practice cultural studies. You can decide whatever you want to decide, etc. And yet, when it came to the question of the reading list . . . Now that's where I really discovered about the gendered nature of power. Long, long after I was able to pronounce the words, I encountered the reality of Foucault's profound insight into the individual reciprocity of knowledge and power. Talking about giving up power is a radically different experience from being silenced. That is another way of thinking, and another metaphor for theory: the way feminism broke, and broke into, cultural studies.

Then there is the question of race in cultural studies. I've talked about the important "extrinsic" sources of the formation of cultural studies—for example, in what I called the moment of the New Left, and its original quarrel with Marxism—out of which cultural studies grew. And yet, of course, that was a profoundly English or British moment. Actually getting cultural studies to put on its own agenda the critical questions of race, the politics of race, the resistance to racism, the critical questions of cultural politics, was itself a profound theoretical struggle, a struggle of which *Policing the Crisis*,[5] was, curiously, the first and very late example. It represented a decisive turn in my own theoretical and intellectual work, as well as in that of the Centre. Again, it was only accomplished as the result of a long, and sometimes bitter—certainly bitterly contested—internal struggle against a resounding but unconscious silence. A struggle which continued in what has since come to be known, but only in the rewritten history, as one of the great seminal books of the Centre for Cultural Studies, *The Empire Strikes Back*.[6] In actuality, Paul Gilroy[7] and the group of people who produced the book found it extremely difficult to create the necessary theoretical and political space in the Centre in which to work on the project.

I want to hold to the notion, implicit in both these examples, that movements provoke theoretical moments. And historical conjunctures insist on theories: they are real moments in the evolution of theory. But here I have to stop and retrace my steps. Because I think you could hear, once again, in

4. *Women Take Issue: Aspects of Women's Subordination*, edited by the Women's Studies Group, Centre for Contemporary Cultural Studies (1978).

5. *Policing the Crisis: Mugging, the State, and Law and Order*, edited by Stuart Hall et al. (1978).

6. *The Empire Strikes Back: Race and Racism in 70s Britain*, edited by the Centre for Contemporary Cultural Studies (1982), an important early text in postcolonial theory and criticism.

7. British-Caribbean cultural theorist and critic (b. 1956; see below).

what I'm saying a kind of invocation of a simple-minded anti-theoretical populism, which does not respect and acknowledge the crucial importance, at each point in the moves I'm trying to renarrativize, of what I would call the necessary delay or detour through theory. I want to talk about that "necessary detour" for a moment. What decentered and dislocated the settled path of the Centre for Contemporary Cultural Studies certainly, and British cultural studies to some extent in general, is what is sometimes called "the linguistic turn": the discovery of discursivity, of textuality. There are casualties in the Centre around those names as well. They were wrestled with, in exactly the same way I've tried to describe earlier. But the gains which were made through an engagement with them are crucially important in understanding how theory came to be advanced in that work. And yet, in my view, such theoretical "gains" can never be a self-sufficient moment.

Again, there is no space here to do more than begin to list the theoretical advances which were made by the encounters with structuralist, semiotic, and poststructuralist work: the crucial importance of language and of the linguistic metaphor to *any* study of culture; the expansion of the notion of text and textuality, both as a source of meaning, and as that which escapes and postpones meaning; the recognition of the heterogeneity, of the multiplicity of meanings, of the struggle to close arbitrarily the infinite semiosis beyond meaning; the acknowledgment of textuality and cultural power, of representation itself, as a site of power and regulation; of the symbolic as a source of identity. These are enormous theoretical advances, though of course, it had always attended to questions of language (Raymond Williams's work, long before the semiotic revolution, is central there). Nevertheless, the refiguring of theory, made as a result of having to think questions of culture through the metaphors of language and textuality, represents a point beyond which cultural studies must now always necessarily locate itself. The metaphor of the discursive, of textuality, instantiates a necessary delay, a displacement, which I think is *always* implied in the concept of culture. If you work on culture, or if you've tried to work on some other really important things and you find yourself driven back to culture, if culture happens to be what seizes hold of your soul, you have to recognize that you will always be working in an area of displacement. There's always something decentered about the medium of culture, about language, textuality, and signification, which always escapes and evades the attempt to link it, directly and immediately, with other structures. And yet, at the same time, the shadow, the imprint, the trace, of those other formations, of the intertextuality of texts in their institutional positions, of texts as sources of power, of textuality as a site of representation and resistance, all of those questions can never be erased from cultural studies.

The question is what happens when a field, which I've been trying to describe in a very punctuated, dispersed, and interrupted way, as constantly changing directions, and which is defined as a political project, tries to develop itself as some kind of coherent theoretical intervention? Or, to put the same question in reverse, what happens when an academic and theoretical enterprise tries to engage in pedagogies which enlist the active engagement of individuals and groups, tries to make a difference in the institutional world in which it is located? These are extremely difficult issues to resolve, because what is asked of us is to say "yes" and "no" at one and the same time.

It asks us to assume that culture will always work through its textualities—and at the same time that textuality is never enough. But never enough of what? Never enough for what? That is an extremely difficult question to answer because, philosophically, it has always been impossible in the theoretical field of cultural studies—whether it is conceived either in terms of texts and contexts, of intertextuality, or of the historical formations in which cultural practices are lodged—to get anything like an adequate theoretical account of culture's relations and its effects. Nevertheless I want to insist that until and unless cultural studies learns to live with this tension, a tension that all textual practices must assume—a tension which Said describes as the study of the text in its affiliations with "institutions, offices, agencies, classes, academies, corporations, groups, ideologically defined parties and professions, nations, races, and genders"[8]—it will have renounced its "worldly" vocation. That is to say, unless and until one respects the necessary displacement of culture, and yet is always irritated by its failure to reconcile itself with other questions that matter, with other questions that cannot and can never be fully covered by critical textuality in its elaborations, cultural studies as a project, an intervention, remains incomplete. If you lose hold of the tension, you can do extremely fine intellectual work, but you will have lost intellectual practice as a politics. I offer this to you, not because that's what cultural studies ought to be, or because that's what the Centre managed to do well, but simply because I think that, overall, is what defines cultural studies as a project. Both in the British and the American context, cultural studies has drawn the attention itself, not just because of its sometimes dazzling internal theoretical development, but because it holds theoretical and political questions in an ever irresolvable but permanent tension. It constantly allows the one to irritate, bother, and disturb the other, without insisting on some final theoretical closure.

I've been talking very much in terms of a previous history. But I have been reminded of this tension very forcefully in the discussions on AIDS. AIDS is one of the questions which urgently brings before us our marginality as critical intellectuals in making real effects in the world. And yet it has often been represented for us in contradictory ways. Against the urgency of people dying in the streets, what in God's name is the point of cultural studies? What is the point of the study of representations, if there is no response to the question of what you say to someone who wants to know if they should take a drug and if that means they'll die two days later or a few months earlier? At that point, I think anybody who is into cultural studies seriously as an intellectual practice, must feel, on their pulse, its ephemerality, its insubstantiality, how little it registers, how little we've been able to change anything or get anybody to do anything. If you don't feel that as one tension in the work that you are doing, theory has let you off the hook. On the other hand, in the end, I don't agree with the way in which this dilemma is often posed for us, for it is indeed a more complex and displaced question than just people dying out there. The question of AIDS is an extremely important terrain of struggle and contestation. In addition to the people we know who are dying, or have died, or will, there are the many people dying who are never spoken of. How could we say that the question of AIDS is not also a

8. Said, *The World, the Text, and the Critic*, chap. 1.

question of who gets represented and who does not? AIDS is the site at which the advance of sexual politics is being rolled back. It's a site at which not only people will die, but desire and pleasure will also die if certain metaphors do not survive, or survive in the wrong way. Unless we operate in this tension, we don't know what cultural studies can do, can't, can never do; but also, what it has to do, what it alone has a privileged capacity to do. It has to analyze certain things about the constitutive and political nature of representation itself, about its complexities, about the effects of language, about textuality as a site of life and death. Those are the things cultural studies can address.

I've used that example, not because it's a perfect example, but because it's a specific example, because it has a concrete meaning, because it challenges us in its complexity, and in so doing has things to teach us about the future of serious theoretical work. It preserves the essential nature of intellectual work and critical reflection, the irreducibility of the insights which theory can bring to political practice, insights which cannot be arrived at in any other way. And at the same time, it rivets us to the necessary modesty of theory, the necessary modesty of cultural studies as an intellectual project.

I want to end in two ways. First I want to address the problem of the institutionalization of these two constructions: British cultural studies and American cultural studies. And then, drawing on the metaphors about theoretical work which I tried to launch (not I hope by claiming authority or authenticity but in what inevitably has to be a polemical, positional, political way), to say something about how the field of cultural studies has to be defined.

I don't know what to say about American cultural studies. I am completely dumfounded by it. I think of the struggles to get cultural studies into the institution in the British context, to squeeze three or four jobs for anybody under some heavy disguise, compared with the rapid institutionalization which is going on in the U.S. The comparison is not only valid for cultural studies. If you think of the important work which has been done in feminist history or theory in Britain and ask how many of those women have ever had full-time academic jobs in their lives or are likely to, you get a sense of what marginality is really about. So the enormous explosion of cultural studies in the U.S., its rapid professionalization and institutionalization, is not a moment which any of us who tried to set up a marginalized Centre in a university like Birmingham could, in any simple way, regret. And yet I have to say, in the strongest sense, that it reminds me of the ways in which, in Britain, we are always aware of institutionalization as a moment of profound danger. Now, I've been saying that dangers are not places you run away from but places that you go towards. So I simply want you to know that my own feeling is that the explosion of cultural studies along with other forms of critical theory in the academy represents a moment of extraordinarily profound danger. Why? Well, it would be excessively vulgar to talk about such things as how many jobs there are, how much money there is around, and how much pressure that puts on people to do what they think of as critical political work and intellectual work of a critical kind while also looking over their shoulders at the promotions stakes and the publication stakes, and so on. Let me instead return to the point that I made before: my astonishment at what I called the theoretical fluency of cultural studies in the United States.

Now, the question of theoretical fluency is a difficult and provoking metaphor, and I want only to say one word about it. Some time ago, looking at what one can only call the deconstructive deluge (as opposed to deconstructive turn) which had overtaken American literary studies, in its formalist mode, I tried to distinguish the extremely important theoretical and intellectual work which it had made possible in cultural studies from a mere repetition, a sort of mimicry or deconstructive ventriloquism which sometimes passes as a serious intellectual exercise.[9] My fear at that moment was that if cultural studies gained an equivalent institutionalization in the American context, it would, in rather the same way, formalize out of existence the critical questions of power, history, and politics. Paradoxically, what I mean by theoretical fluency is exactly the reverse. There is no moment now, in American cultural studies, where we are *not* able, extensively and without end, to theorize power—politics, race, class, and gender, subjugation, domination, exclusion, marginality, Otherness, etc. There is hardly anything in cultural studies which isn't so theorized. And yet, there is the nagging doubt that this overwhelming textualization of cultural studies' own discourses somehow constitutes power and politics as exclusively matters of language and textuality itself. Now, this is not to say that I don't think that questions of power and the political have to be and are always lodged within representations, that they are always discursive questions. Nevertheless, there are ways of constituting power as an easy floating signifier which just leaves the crude exercise and connections of power and culture altogether emptied of any signification. That is what I take to be the moment of danger in the institutionalization of cultural studies in this highly rarified and enormously elaborated and well-funded professional world of American academic life. It has nothing whatever to do with cultural studies making itself more like British cultural studies, which is, I think, an entirely false and empty cause to try to propound. I have specifically tried not to speak of the past in an attempt to police the present and the future. But I do want to extract, finally, from the narrative I have constructed of the past some guidelines for my own work and perhaps for some of yours.

I come back to the deadly seriousness of intellectual work. It is a deadly serious matter. I come back to the critical distinction between intellectual work and academic work: they overlap, they abut with one another, they feed off one another, the one provides you with the means to do the other. But they are not the same thing. I come back to the difficulty of instituting a genuine cultural and critical practice, which is intended to produce some kind of organic intellectual political work, which does not try to inscribe itself in the overarching metanarrative of achieved knowledges, within the institutions. I come back to theory and politics, the politics of theory. Not theory as the will to truth, but theory as a set of contested, localized, conjunctural knowledges, which have to be debated in a dialogical way. But also as a practice which always thinks about its intervention in a world in which it would make some difference, in which it would have some effect. Finally, a practice which understands the need for intellectual modesty. I do think

9. See Stuart Hall, "In Defence of Theory," in *People's History and Socialist Theory*, edited by Ralph Samuels (1981).

there is all the difference in the world between understanding the politics of intellectual work and substituting intellectual work for politics.

1990 1992

SUSAN SONTAG
1933–2004

Susan Sontag intended the title of her classic essay "Against Interpretation," first published in 1964 in *Evergreen Review* and reprinted in *Against Interpretation and Other Essays* (1966), to be highly provocative, and she certainly succeeded. Both then and now, many readers have assumed from the title that Sontag is saying something strange, peculiar, perverse. Why should we be opposed to interpretation? Surely interpretation is both desirable and inevitable. But, as the essay makes clear, Sontag is advancing a complex argument, one that describes a specific sense for the term *interpretation* and that lays out a pointed and particular set of claims for why we should be against it.

Sontag had an immediate polemical purpose: she wanted her readers to become more attentive and responsive to the literature, art, and especially film of the 1950s and early 1960s. But at the same time, she located her argument within the long history, classic to contemporary, of literary theory and criticism. Sontag begins with PLATO and ARISTOTLE; she glances at medieval and Renaissance theories of interpretation; she refers to MARX, NIETZSCHE, and FREUD; she invokes T. S. ELIOT and other major modernist writers and critics; and she praises WALTER BENJAMIN, NORTHROP FRYE, ERICH AUERBACH, and ROLAND BARTHES.

"The function of criticism should be to help us experience art more fully," Sontag maintains, "to show *how it is what it is*, even *that it is what it is*, rather than to show *what it means*." But she also insists, in the preface to *Against Interpretation and other Essays*: "What I have been writing is not criticism at all, strictly speaking, but case studies for an aesthetic, a theory of my own sensibility." Concise, forceful, and zealous in its commitments, bold in its claims, and as relevant for our era as it was for the 1960s, "Against Interpretation" organizes and sharpens an understanding of the history and meaning of interpretation and the function of criticism.

Susan Sontag was born Susan Rosenblatt in New York City in 1933, the daughter of first-generation Jewish Americans. Her father, Jack Rosenblatt, was a businessman whose fur-trading work was based in China, and he and his wife Mildred lived there. Mildred returned to the United States to give birth to her daughter, but she then returned to China, and Susan was raised for the first five years of her life in New York and New Jersey by relatives and a nanny. In 1936, Mildred came to the United States a second time to give birth to a second daughter, Judith, and she moved back permanently in late 1938 after Jack's death in China. She and her daughters lived first in Florida, next in New York City, and then settled in Tucson, Arizona—which Sontag later termed the years of her "desert childhood." After Mildred's marriage in 1946 to Nathan Sontag, an army captain, she and her daughters relocated to Sherman Oaks, a suburb of Los Angeles.

In an interview in 1995, Sontag said: "I remember reading real books—biographies, travel books—when I was about six. And then free fall into Poe and Shakespeare and Dickens and the Brontës and Victor Hugo and Schopenhauer and Pater, and so on. I got through my childhood in a delirium of literary exaltations." As a "literature-intoxicated" student at North Hollywood High School, one who in her journal listed more than 100 authors (Faulkner, Dostoyevsky, DANTE, etc.) as "must reads," she became even more fervently attached to American, English, and especially European literature and culture. In an autobiographical piece, "Pilgrimage" (1987), she recalled a visit that she and a friend made in 1947 to the German Nobel Prize–winning novelist and essayist Thomas Mann, who was living in California. Barely a teenager, Sontag already was an intellectual whose "sense of literary vocation," she later explained, "had been shaped by reading literary magazines—*Kenyon Review, Sewanee Review, Hudson Review, Partisan Review*"—and by her voracious reading of challenging works of literature and philosophy.

After graduating from high school at age fifteen, Sontag began undergraduate study in 1949 at the University of California at Berkeley; but after one semester she transferred to the University of Chicago, eager to be part of its humanities-centered Great Books curriculum. One of her teachers was the political philosopher LEO STRAUSS, another was the philosopher and literary scholar Richard McKeon, and still another was the brilliantly idiosyncratic writer, literary theorist, and critic Kenneth Burke. In 1950, Sontag audited a course on Sigmund Freud taught by the sociologist Philip Rieff. He invited her to lunch, and ten days later they married. Sontag completed her undergraduate degree in 1951, and she and Rieff lived briefly in Wisconsin and then moved to the Boston area when he was offered a position at Brandeis University. She gave birth to a son, David, in 1952, and she did graduate work in philosophy at Harvard, receiving her master's degree in 1957.

Sontag left her husband and son behind after winning a fellowship to study at Oxford University, where she intended to work toward a doctorate in philosophy. In December 1957, she traveled to Paris. She decided to live there—she had become involved in a passionate relationship with the writer Harriet Sohmers—and pursued further academic study at the Sorbonne. She immersed herself in French literature and culture, and she responded with much enthusiasm to French and Italian movies. Returning to the United States in late 1958, Sontag ended her marriage and settled with her son in New York City. By the early 1960s, she was well known in intellectual circles for her essays in the *New York Review of Books, Partisan Review,* and *Commentary* on literature, film, and theater and for her first foray into fiction, an experimental novel titled *The Benefactor* (1963), which, as the critic Liam Kennedy has noted, is less a work of fiction than "an extended treatise on subjectivity."

Two of her groundbreaking early essays, "Notes on 'Camp'" (1964) and "Against Interpretation," established her reputation as a major cultural critic who was bringing to the attention of American readers an array of avant-garde European authors and filmmakers. She was a public intellectual and literary celebrity, recognized for her insight and intelligence as well as for her striking appearance: her photo was featured on the covers of *Vanity Fair* and the *New York Times Magazine*. Sontag published widely, saying about her intentions at this time: "I thought of my essays as cultural work. They were written out of a sense of what needed to be written."

Sontag's pioneering, influential essay on the aesthetic of camp has been described as an exploration and affirmation of the "gay sensibility." "Camp," for her, implies a deliberately exaggerated, overstated, and theatrical style, typically for humorous effect—ironic, clever, self-mocking, subversive of conventional norms of gender roles and sexual identities. As Sontag observes in one of the essay's "notes,"

> Camp is a vision of the world in terms of style—but a particular kind of style. It is the love of the exaggerated, the "off," of things-being-what-they-are-not. The best example is in Art Nouveau, the most typical and fully developed

> Camp style. Art Nouveau objects, typically, convert one thing into something else: the lighting fixtures in the form of flowering plants, the living room which is really a grotto. A remarkable example: the Paris Métro entrances designed by Hector Guimard in the late 1890s in the shape of cast-iron orchid stalks.

Camp, she explains, "sees everything in quotation marks. It's not a lamp, but a 'lamp'; not a woman, but a 'woman.' To perceive Camp in objects and persons is to understand Being-as-Playing-a-Role. It is the farthest extension, in sensibility, of the metaphor of life as theater." In its heightened emphasis on style and form, "Notes on 'Camp'" is a companion piece to "Against Interpretation," our selection below.

Sontag wrote a second novel, *Death Kit* (1967), but she attracted greater acclaim and controversy for her political and critical essays, some of which were collected in *Styles of Radical Will* (1969). She was strongly opposed to the Vietnam War, wrote sympathetically about North Vietnam and Cuba, and denounced much about the United States and Europe. In "What's Happening in America" (1967), Sontag declared:

> [T]he quality of American life is an insult to the possibilities of human growth; and the pollution of American space, with gadgetry and cars and TV and box architecture, brutalizes the senses, making gray neurotics of most of us, and perverse spiritual athletes and strident self-transcenders of the best of us. . . . The truth is that Mozart, Pascal, Boolean algebra, Shakespeare, parliamentary government, baroque churches, Newton, the emancipation of women, Kant, Marx, and Balanchine ballets don't redeem what this particular civilization has wrought upon the world. The white race *is* the cancer of human history; it is the white race and it alone—its ideologies and inventions—which eradicates autonomous civilizations wherever it spreads, which has upset the ecological balance of the planet, which now threatens the very existence of life itself.

Other important essays of this period are "The Double Standard of Aging" (1972) and "The Third World of Women" (1973). In an essay collection, *Under the Sign of Saturn* (1980), Sontag considers a range of figures, including the American anarchist philosopher and writer Paul Goodman; the French actor, director, and writer Antonin Artaud; the French critic Roland Barthes; and the German film director and Nazi propagandist Leni Riefenstahl.

Sontag wrote screenplays for and directed a number of films, the most enduring of which is *Promised Lands* (1973), a documentary about Israel and Palestine in the aftermath of the Yom Kippur War of October 1973. This is her only work in any medium that explicitly treats Jewish themes and issues. During a five-year span from the early to mid-1970s, Sontag also crafted essays on the theory and practice of photography; in 1977 these were collected in *On Photography*, a book that won that year's National Book Critics Circle Award for Criticism. Her observations are trenchant: "In America, the photographer is not simply the person who records the past but the one who invents it." She notes that "photographs alter and enlarge our notions of what is worth looking at and what we have a right to observe," elsewhere declaring that "the camera makes everyone a tourist in other people's reality, and eventually in one's own." The images in a photograph can "always . . . be made compatible, even when the realities they depict are not."

This project was all the more challenging for Sontag because at the time she was suffering from, and was being treated for, stage IV breast cancer. In 1975 she was told that she had only a 10 percent chance of surviving for two more years. This grievous affliction and the painful regimen of its treatment prompted Sontag to write *Illness as Metaphor* (1978), which famously begins: "Illness is the night-side of life, a more onerous citizenship. Everyone who is born holds dual citizenship, in the kingdom of the well and the kingdom of the sick." Sontag's cancer responded to treatment but returned in later years, and she continued her commentaries on illness in *AIDS and Its Metaphors* (1989), the short story "The Way We Live Now" (1986), and a play, *Alice in Bed*, about Alice James, the invalid sister of the American philosopher William James and the novelist HENRY JAMES. This play premiered (in translation) in Bonn, Germany, in 1991 and was published in 1993, the same year that, politically active as ever, Sontag directed Samuel Beckett's *Waiting for Godot* (1952) in Sarajevo, during the Bosnian war.

In 1990, Sontag received a MacArthur Foundation Fellowship, popularly called a "genius grant," and from the 1990s to her death in 2004 she was widely honored in the United States and Europe as a public intellectual. Sontag referred to "feminism" as "an empty word," but she also defined herself as a "feminist," noting that "because women are, culturally speaking, a minority, with my minority consciousness I always rejoice in the achievement of women." She spoke in support of the British Indian author Salman Rushdie (who had been sentenced to death by the Iranian leader Ayatollah Khomeini for his "blasphemous" novel *Satanic Verses*); she called for American intervention in the Bosnian war; and she took a strong position on the terrorist attacks of September 11, 2001—insisting that it was wrong to refer to the suicide bombers as "cowards," a statement that angered many Americans in the immediate aftermath of the horrific assaults.

Sontag remained productive even as she battled illness, publishing two successful novels: *The Volcano Lover: A Romance* (1992) and *In America* (2000). In *Regarding the Pain of Others* (2003), she returned to photography and to the question of how to respond "when the subject is looking at other people's pain." She gathered nonfiction pieces from the 1980s and 1990s in *Where the Stress Falls: Essays* (2001), and, after her death, Sontag's publisher collected in *At the Same Time: Essays and Speeches* (2007) more than forty pieces, from her last two decades, on notable figures and topics in film, dance, photography, painting, opera, and theater. Sontag died on December 28, 2004. "With her dies the era," noted an obituary, "of the glamorous public intellectual—and perhaps even the idea of New York as the center of modern literary intelligence."

Sontag produced an impressive body of work; many admire her criticism and novels, and some see her as an inspiration and role model. She has been rebuked, however, for failing to deal more directly with class, gender, race, and ethnicity, and some have claimed that she became more conservative, culturally and politically, in her later years. Sontag's book on AIDS was praised by many members of the gay and lesbian community—Sontag herself was bisexual and the longtime lover of the renowned photographer Annie Leibovitz—but it was harshly attacked by others for its neglect of the urgent social and political contexts and implications of the AIDS crisis. One reviewer noted that while "Sontag alludes to issues of sexuality and discrimination against homosexuals," she "ignores the tremendous response of the homosexual community to the AIDS epidemic through educational programs, health maintenance initiatives, governmental lobbying, and volunteer support services." D. A. Miller, in "Sontag's Urbanity" (*October* 49 [1989]), took aim at her "mandarin aloofness" and concluded that her positions "continue to ratify the prejudice, oppression, and violence that gay people and people with AIDS daily encounter." Sontag was described more than once as a proponent, in her later writings, of an "elegiac modernism," and one critic even identified her as an "eminent Victorian"—"our greatest living Victorian writer."

In "Against Interpretation," writing as a literary theorist and cultural commentator, Sontag argues that critics have focused on content at the expense of form. She believes that the emphasis on interpretation—that is, the extraction of some "content" from a work—disserves literature and art and prevents us from responding to its (at its best) thrilling immediacy. Sontag suggests that we should question whether "there really is such a thing as the content of a work of art." It is this essential question that our ongoing commitment to interpretation fails to acknowledge and engage. In her view, "The modern style of interpretation excavates, and as it excavates, destroys; it digs 'behind' the text, to find a sub-text which is the true one." She judges Marxist and Freudian "doctrines" to be damaging: critics who adhere to those systems of thought impose them on the text, revising and transvaluing it through them, making it into something other than what it is. Such modes of interpretation, she argues, reduce art to thought and privilege utilitarian science over myth and aesthetics. Instead, audiences in our advanced capitalist societies—characterized by overproduction and excess—must employ great care and discrimination. As her essay proceeds, Sontag becomes yet more extreme, claiming that "the very distinction between form and content . . . is, ultimately, an illusion." The work of art thus is its form, is the impact of its form on us, as both modern and contemporary cinema and abstract art vividly demonstrate and as we could see if we could break free from the addiction to interpretation that "poisons our sensibilities."

Sontag lists examples of the type of criticism that she esteems, in which the critic "dissolves considerations of content into those of form"—referring to essays by Frye, Barthes, Auerbach, and others. She neither gives examples of the critical writing that she rejects nor mentions the formalist theory and practice of Anglo-American New Criticism, which resemble her own. At the time Sontag was writing, New Criticism (as employed by CLEANTH BROOKS and W. K. WIMSATT, among others) was the critical approach and procedure that dominated literary journals and had become central to literature departments of colleges and universities.

Perhaps Sontag viewed the New Criticism as simply (and narrowly) academic, linked to pedagogy, and too tied to a limited canon of English and American authors to encompass contemporary and avant-garde European writers and critics and filmmakers. But her failure to assess its formalist emphasis or consider its relationship to her own position creates a glaring absence. Sontag also may underestimate the difficulty of divorcing form from content, which has a way of reappearing in critical discourse, no matter how deliberately the critic seeks to fix his or her attention on form, style, and technique. At one point in the essay, Sontag protests that the misguided emphasis on "interpretation" has led critics to mistakenly describe the main theme of Samuel Beckett's dramas as "modern man's alienation from meaning or from God," but it is not evident that her description of them as "delicate dramas of the withdrawn consciousness" is any less of an interpretation—a statement of content, not of form.

Nevertheless, "Against Interpretation" is and remains a provocation to thought, to our efforts to understand what it means to read, respond to, and interpret a literary text or cultural artifact. "Interpretation is the revenge of the intellect upon art"; "In place of a hermeneutics we need an erotics of art"—such declarations bear witness to the aphoristic brilliance of Sontag's prose and to her skill as a provocateur. She told an interviewer that she aimed in her writing to exemplify an "intelligence" that is "critical, dialectical, skeptical, desimplifying." She also remarked that she defined herself as "a writer"—that is, "someone who pays attention to the world." In this essay and in her work at its most lively and invigorating, Sontag shows the value of paying close attention to the old and the new in culture from top to bottom, and of experiencing the intellectual power and emotional pleasure of both the great tradition and the avant-garde.

"Against Interpretation" Keywords: Aesthetics, Defense of Criticism, Formalism, Hermeneutics, Modernity, Popular Culture

Against Interpretation

Content is a glimpse of something, an encounter like a flash. It's very tiny—very tiny, content.

—Willem de Kooning,[1] in an interview

It is only shallow people who do not judge by appearances. The mystery of the world is the visible, not the invisible.

—Oscar Wilde,[2] in a letter

The earliest *experience* of art must have been that it was incantatory, magical; art was an instrument of ritual. (Cf. the paintings in the caves at Lascaux, Altamira, Niaux, La Pasiega,[3] etc.) The earliest *theory* of art, that of the Greek philosophers, proposed that art was mimesis, imitation of reality.

It is at this point that the peculiar question of the *value* of art arose. For the mimetic theory, by its very terms, challenges art to justify itself.

Plato,[4] who proposed the theory, seems to have done so in order to rule that the value of art is dubious. Since he considered ordinary material things as themselves mimetic objects, imitations of transcendent forms or structures, even the best painting of a bed would be only an "imitation of an imitation." For Plato, art is neither particularly useful (the painting of a bed is no good to sleep on), nor, in the strict sense, true. And Aristotle's[5] arguments in defense of art do not really challenge Plato's view that all art is an elaborate *trompe l'oeil*,[6] and therefore a lie. But he does dispute Plato's idea that art is useless. Lie or no, art has a certain value according to Aristotle because it is a form of therapy. Art is useful, after all, Aristotle counters, medicinally useful in that it arouses and purges dangerous emotions.[7]

In Plato and Aristotle, the mimetic theory of art goes hand in hand with the assumption that art is always figurative. But advocates of the mimetic theory need not close their eyes to decorative and abstract art. The fallacy that art is necessarily a "realism" can be modified or scrapped without ever moving outside the problems delimited by the mimetic theory.

The fact is, all Western consciousness of and reflection upon art have remained within the confines staked out by the Greek theory of art as mimesis or representation. It is through this theory that art as such—above and beyond given works of art—becomes problematic, in need of defense. And it is the defense of art which gives birth to the odd vision by which something we have learned to call "form" is separated off from something we have learned to call "content," and to the well-intentioned move which makes content essential and form accessory.

1. Dutch-born American abstract expressionist painter (1904–1997); this 1960 interview by David Sylvester for the BBC radio was published in *Location* 1 (spring 1963).
2. Irish playwright, critic, and poet (1854–1900; see above). The quotation is actually from his novel *The Picture of Dorian Gray* (1890), chap. 2, which has "true mystery" rather than "mystery."
3. All sites—in southwestern France, northern Spain, southern France, and northern Spain, respectively—famous for their prehistoric cave paintings.
4. Greek philosopher (ca. 427–ca. 347 B.C.E.), who viewed all knowledge and objects as dependent on perfect and immutable transcendent Forms; for his theory of mimesis and art, presented in *Ion* and *Republic* 10, see above.
5. Greek philosopher (384–322 B.C.E.); see his *Poetics* and excerpts from *On Rhetoric*, above.
6. Visual illusion, especially through photographically realistic detail (literally, "deceives the eye"; French).
7. For Aristotle's idea of catharsis, see *Poetics* 6, 1449b.

Even in modern times, when most artists and critics have discarded the theory of art as representation of an outer reality in favor of the theory of art as subjective expression, the main feature of the mimetic theory persists. Whether we conceive of the work of art on the model of a picture (art as a picture of reality) or on the model of a statement (art as the statement of the artist), content still comes first. The content may have changed. It may now be less figurative, less lucidly realistic. But it is still assumed that a work of art *is* its content. Or, as it's usually put today, that a work of art by definition *says* something. ("What X is saying is . . . ," "What X is trying to say is . . . ," "What X said is . . ." etc., etc.)

2

None of us can ever retrieve that innocence before all theory when art knew no need to justify itself, when one did not ask of a work of art what it *said* because one knew (or thought one knew) what it *did*. From now to the end of consciousness, we are stuck with the task of defending art. We can only quarrel with one or another means of defense. Indeed, we have an obligation to overthrow any means of defending and justifying art which becomes particularly obtuse or onerous or insensitive to contemporary needs and practice.

This is the case, today, with the very idea of content itself. Whatever it may have been in the past, the idea of content is today mainly a hindrance, a nuisance, a subtle or not so subtle philistinism.[8]

Though the actual developments in many arts may seem to be leading us away from the idea that a work of art is primarily its content, the idea still exerts an extraordinary hegemony. I want to suggest that this is because the idea is now perpetuated in the guise of a certain way of encountering works of art thoroughly ingrained among most people who take any of the arts seriously. What the overemphasis on the idea of content entails is the perennial, never consummated project of *interpretation*. And, conversely, it is the habit of approaching works of art in order to *interpret* them that sustains the fancy that there really is such a thing as the content of a work of art.

3

Of course, I don't mean interpretation in the broadest sense, the sense in which Nietzsche[9] (rightly) says, "There are no facts, only interpretations." By interpretation, I mean here a conscious act of the mind which illustrates a certain code, certain "rules" of interpretation.

Directed to art, interpretation means plucking a set of elements (the X, the Y, the Z, and so forth) from the whole work. The task of interpretation is virtually one of translation. The interpreter says, Look, don't you see that X is really—or, really means—A? That Y is really B? That Z is really C?

What situation could prompt this curious project for transforming a text? History gives us the materials for an answer. Interpretation first appears

8. That is, disdain for culture and the arts, a term borrowed from MATTHEW ARNOLD's label for the materialist middle classes in "The Function of Criticism at the Present Time" (1864; see above).
9. German philosopher (1844–1900; see above); this statement appears in his notebooks of 1887, published after his death in *The Will to Power* (1901). In *The Portable Nietzsche* (1954), Walter Kaufman translates it as "It is precisely facts that do not exist, only *interpretations*."

in the culture of late classical antiquity, when the power and credibility of myth had been broken by the "realistic" view of the world introduced by scientific enlightenment. Once the question that haunts post-mythic consciousness—that of the *seemliness* of religious symbols—had been asked, the ancient texts were, in their pristine form, no longer acceptable. Then interpretation was summoned, to reconcile the ancient texts to "modern" demands. Thus, the Stoics,[1] to accord with their view that the gods had to be moral, allegorized away the rude features of Zeus and his boisterous clan in Homer's[2] epics. What Homer really designated by the adultery of Zeus with Leto,[3] they explained, was the union between power and wisdom. In the same vein, Philo of Alexandria[4] interpreted the literal historical narratives of the Hebrew Bible as spiritual paradigms. The story of the exodus from Egypt, the wandering in the desert for forty years, and the entry into the promised land, said Philo, was really an allegory of the individual soul's emancipation, tribulations, and final deliverance. Interpretation thus presupposes a discrepancy between the clear meaning of the text and the demands of (later) readers. It seeks to resolve that discrepancy. The situation is that for some reason a text has become unacceptable; yet it cannot be discarded. Interpretation is a radical strategy for conserving an old text, which is thought too precious to repudiate, by revamping it. The interpreter, without actually erasing or rewriting the text, is altering it. But he can't admit to doing this. He claims to be only making it intelligible, by disclosing its true meaning. However far the interpreters alter the text (another notorious example is the Rabbinic and Christian "spiritual" interpretations of the clearly erotic Song of Songs[5]), they must claim to be reading off a sense that is already there.

Interpretation in our own time, however, is even more complex. For the contemporary zeal for the project of interpretation is often prompted not by piety toward the troublesome text (which may conceal an aggression), but by an open aggressiveness, an overt contempt for appearances. The old style of interpretation was insistent, but respectful; it erected another meaning on top of the literal one. The modern style of interpretation excavates, and as it excavates, destroys; it digs "behind" the text, to find a sub-text which is the true one. The most celebrated and influential modern doctrines, those of Marx and Freud,[6] actually amount to elaborate systems of hermeneutics,[7] aggressive and impious theories of interpretation. All observable phenomena are bracketed, in Freud's phrase, as *manifest content*. This manifest content must be probed and pushed aside to find the true meaning—the *latent content*—beneath. For Marx, social events like revolutions and wars; for Freud, the events of individual lives (like neurotic symptoms and slips of

1. Followers of the Greek philosopher Zeno (335–263 B.C.E.).
2. According to tradition, the author of the *Iliad* and the *Odyssey* (8th c. B.C.E.); in those Greek epics, the Olympian gods, whose ruler was Zeus, play an active role.
3. In Greek mythology, a Titan and the mother (by Zeus, whose wife was his sister Hera) of Apollo and Artemis.
4. Hellenistic Jewish philosopher (ca. 20 B.C.E.–ca. 50 C.E.), who attempted to reconcile biblical teaching and Greek philosophy; his works include *Questions and Answers on Exodus*, the second book of the Bible (which tells the story of the Israelites' liberation from slavery in Egypt and the years of wandering in the desert before they entered the Promised Land). Alexandria is in Egypt, then a Roman province.
5. A book of the Hebrew Bible that is a collection of poems of love and courtship (also known as the Song of Solomon, king of Israel, to whom it is traditionally ascribed).
6. SIGMUND FREUD (1856–1939), Austrian neurologist and founder of psychoanalysis; for his concepts of manifest content and latent content, see chapter 6 of *The Interpretation of Dreams* (1900; above). KARL MARX (1818–1883), German economic and political theorist and revolutionary.
7. Theories of interpretation.

the tongue) as well as texts (like a dream or a work of art)—all are treated as occasions for interpretation. According to Marx and Freud, these events only *seem* to be intelligible. Actually, they have no meaning without interpretation. To understand *is* to interpret. And to interpret is to restate the phenomenon, in effect to find an equivalent for it.

Thus, interpretation is not (as most people assume) an absolute value, a gesture of mind situated in some timeless realm of capabilities. Interpretation must itself be evaluated, within a historical view of human consciousness. In some cultural contexts, interpretation is a liberating act. It is a means of revising, of transvaluing, of escaping the dead past. In other cultural contexts, it is reactionary, impertinent, cowardly, stifling.

4

Today is such a time, when the project of interpretation is largely reactionary, stifling. Like the fumes of the automobile and of heavy industry which befoul the urban atmosphere, the effusion of interpretations of art today poisons our sensibilities. In a culture whose already classical dilemma is the hypertrophy of the intellect at the expense of energy and sensual capability, interpretation is the revenge of the intellect upon art.

Even more. It is the revenge of the intellect upon the world. To interpret is to impoverish, to deplete the world—in order to set up a shadow world of "meanings." It is to turn *the* world into *this* world. ("This world"! As if there were any other.)

The world, our world, is depleted, impoverished enough. Away with all duplicates of it, until we again experience more immediately what we have.

5

In most modern instances, interpretation amounts to the philistine refusal to leave the work of art alone. Real art has the capacity to make us nervous. By reducing the work of art to its content and then interpreting *that,* one tames the work of art. Interpretation makes art manageable, comformable.

This philistinism of interpretation is more rife in literature than in any other art. For decades now, literary critics have understood it to be their task to translate the elements of the poem or play or novel or story into something else. Sometimes a writer will be so uneasy before the naked power of his art that he will install within the work itself—albeit with a little shyness, a touch of the good taste of irony—the clear and explicit interpretation of it. Thomas Mann[8] is an example of such an overcooperative author. In the case of more stubborn authors, the critic is only too happy to perform the job.

The work of Kafka,[9] for example, has been subjected to a mass ravishment by no less than three armies of interpreters. Those who read Kafka as a social allegory see case studies of the frustrations and insanity of modern bureaucracy and its ultimate issuance in the totalitarian state. Those who read Kafka as a psychoanalytic allegory see desperate revelations of Kafka's fear of his father, his castration anxieties, his sense of his own impotence,

8. Eminent German novelist and essayist (1875–1955).

9. Franz Kafka (1883–1924), Austrian writer who was born and lived most of his life in Prague; his works often blend the fantastic and realistic. His novels *The Trial* (1925) and *The Castle* (1926) both portray nightmarish bureaucracies.

his thralldom to his dreams. Those who read Kafka as a religious allegory explain that K. in *The Castle* is trying to gain access to heaven, that Joseph K. in *The Trial* is being judged by the inexorable and mysterious justice of God. . . . Another *oeuvre* that has attracted interpreters like leeches is that of Samuel Beckett.[1] Beckett's delicate dramas of the withdrawn consciousness—pared down to essentials, cut off, often represented as physically immobilized—are read as a statement about modern man's alienation from meaning or from God, or as an allegory of psychopathology.

Proust, Joyce, Faulkner, Rilke, Lawrence, Gide[2] . . . one could go on citing author after author; the list is endless of those around whom thick encrustations of interpretation have taken hold. But it should be noted that interpretation is not simply the compliment that mediocrity pays to genius. It is, indeed, *the* modern way of understanding something, and is applied to works of every quality. Thus, in the notes that Elia Kazan[3] published on his production of *A Streetcar Named Desire*, it becomes clear that, in order to direct the play, Kazan had to discover that Stanley Kowalski represented the sensual and vengeful barbarism that was engulfing our culture, while Blanche Du Bois was Western civilization, poetry, delicate apparel, dim lighting, refined feelings and all, though a little the worse for wear to be sure. Tennessee Williams' forceful psychological melodrama now became intelligible: it was *about* something, about the decline of Western civilization. Apparently, were it to go on being a play about a handsome brute named Stanley Kowalski and a faded mangy belle named Blanche Du Bois, it would not be manageable.

6

It doesn't matter whether artists intend, or don't intend, for their works to be interpreted. Perhaps Tennessee Williams thinks *Streetcar* is about what Kazan thinks it to be about. It may be that Cocteau[4] in *The Blood of a Poet* and in *Orpheus* wanted the elaborate readings which have been given these films, in terms of Freudian symbolism and social critique. But the merit of these works certainly lies elsewhere than in their "meanings." Indeed, it is precisely to the extent that Williams' plays and Cocteau's films do suggest these portentous meanings that they are defective, false, contrived, lacking in conviction.

From interviews, it appears that Resnais and Robbe-Grillet[5] consciously designed *Last Year at Marienbad* to accommodate a multiplicity of equally plausible interpretations. But the temptation to interpret *Marienbad*

1. Irish playwright, novelist, and poet (1906–1989); his best-known work is the play *Waiting for Godot* (1952).
2. All major modernist writers: Marcel Proust (1871–1922), French novelist; James Joyce (1882–1941), Irish writer; William Faulkner (1897–1962), American writer; Rainer Maria Rilke (1875–1926), Austrian poet; D. H. Lawrence (1885–1930), English novelist, poet, and essayist; and André Gide (1869–1951), French novelist, essayist, and critic.
3. Turkish-born American director of film and stage (1909–2003). Among his acclaimed productions was *A Streetcar Named Desire*, by the American playwright Tennessee Williams (1911–1983), which he directed first on stage (1947) and then on screen (1951). *Streetcar*'s main characters are Stanley Kowalski and his sister-in-law, Blanche DuBois.
4. Jean Cocteau (1889–1963), French writer, artist, and director. His films include *The Blood of a Poet* (1930) and *Orpheus* (1950).
5. Alain Robbe-Grillet (1922–2008), French writer and director. Alain Resnais (1922–2014), French film director whose works include *Last Year at Marienbad* (1961), for which Robbe-Grillet wrote the screenplay.

should be resisted. What matters in *Marienbad* is the pure, untranslatable, sensuous immediacy of some of its images, and its rigorous if narrow solutions to certain problems of cinematic form.

Again, Ingmar Bergman[6] may have meant the tank rumbling down the empty night street in *The Silence* as a phallic symbol. But if he did, it was a foolish thought. ("Never trust the teller, trust the tale," said Lawrence.[7]) Taken as a brute object, as an immediate sensory equivalent for the mysterious abrupt armored happenings going on inside the hotel, that sequence with the tank is the most striking moment in the film. Those who reach for a Freudian interpretation of the tank are only expressing their lack of response to what is there on the screen.

It is always the case that interpretation of this type indicates a dissatisfaction (conscious or unconscious) with the work, a wish to replace it by something else.

Interpretation, based on the highly dubious theory that a work of art is composed of items of content, violates art. It makes art into an article for use, for arrangement into a mental scheme of categories.

7

Interpretation does not, of course, always prevail. In fact, a great deal of today's art may be understood as motivated by a flight from interpretation. To avoid interpretation, art may become parody. Or it may become abstract. Or it may become ("merely") decorative. Or it may become non-art.

The flight from interpretation seems particularly a feature of modern painting. Abstract painting[8] is the attempt to have, in the ordinary sense, no content; since there is no content, there can be no interpretation. Pop Art[9] works by the opposite means to the same result; using a content so blatant, so "what it is," it, too, ends by being uninterpretable.

A great deal of modern poetry as well, starting from the great experiments of French poetry (including the movement that is misleadingly called Symbolism[1]) to put silence into poems and to reinstate the *magic* of the word, has escaped from the rough grip of interpretation. The most recent revolution in contemporary taste in poetry—the revolution that has deposed Eliot and elevated Pound[2]—represents a turning away from content in

6. Swedish film director and writer (1918–2007); among his many films are *The Silence* (1963) and *Winter Light* (1963, *Nattsvardsgästerna*; also known as *The Communicants*), mentioned below.

7. From Lawrence's *Studies in Classic American Literature* (1923), chap. 1: "Never trust the artist. Trust the tale. The proper function of a critic is to save the tale from the artist who created it."

8. Sontag is referring specifically to abstract expressionism, a variety of nonobjective, nonfigurative art that began in New York in the 1940s and became dominant in the 1950s; prominent painters in the movement included de Kooning and Jackson Pollock.

9. A British and American movement, largely of the mid-1950s and 1960s, in which objects and images from contemporary popular culture and the mass media are the subjects of and are incorporated into artworks. Pop artists, including Andy Warhol and Roy Lichtenstein, reacted against both traditional fine art and abstract expressionism.

1. A literary movement led by French poets and critics in the last third of the 19th century, including Arthur Rimbaud and Stéphane Mallarmé; it emphasized the evocation of subjective emotion, via symbol and metaphor, rather than objective description.

2. Ezra Pound (1885–1972), American poet and critic, a major promoter and shaper of modernist writing, including that of the American-born British poet, critic, and playwright T. S. ELIOT (1888–1965). Sontag is referring here to poets in the post–World War II decades, including Charles Olson, Robert Duncan, Robert Creeley, Allen Ginsberg, Denise Levertov, and Gary Snyder, who defined their theory and practice in relation to the experimental modernist poetry and prose of Pound, rather than to that of T. S. Eliot and the New Critics who endorsed his views and values.

poetry in the old sense, an impatience with what made modern poetry prey to the zeal of interpreters.

I am speaking mainly of the situation in America, of course. Interpretation runs rampant here in those arts with a feeble and negligible avant-garde: fiction and the drama. Most American novelists and playwrights are really either journalists or gentlemen sociologists and psychologists. They are writing the literary equivalent of program music. And so rudimentary, uninspired, and stagnant has been the sense of what might be done with *form* in fiction and drama that even when the content isn't simply information, news, it is still peculiarly visible, handier, more exposed. To the extent that novels and plays (in America), unlike poetry and painting and music, don't reflect any interesting concern with changes in their form, these arts remain prone to assault by interpretation.

But programmatic avant-gardism—which has meant, mostly, experiments with form at the expense of content—is not the only defense against the infestation of art by interpretations. At least, I hope not. For this would be to commit art to being perpetually on the run. (It also perpetuates the very distinction between form and content which is, ultimately, an illusion.) Ideally, it is possible to elude the interpreters in another way, by making works of art whose surface is so unified and clean, whose momentum is so rapid, whose address is so direct that the work can be . . . just what it is. Is this possible now? It does happen in films, I believe. This is why cinema is the most alive, the most exciting, the most important of all art forms right now. Perhaps the way one tells how alive a particular art form is, is by the latitude it gives for making mistakes in it, and still being good. For example, a few of the films of Bergman—though crammed with lame messages about the modern spirit, thereby inviting interpretations—still triumph over the pretentious intentions of their director. In *Winter Light* and *The Silence*, the beauty and visual sophistication of the images subvert before our eyes the callow pseudo-intellectuality of the story and some of the dialogue. (The most remarkable instance of this sort of discrepancy is the work of D. W. Griffith.[3]) In good films, there is always a directness that entirely frees us from the itch to interpret. Many old Hollywood films, like those of Cukor, Walsh, Hawks,[4] and countless other directors, have this liberating anti-symbolic quality, no less than the best work of the new European directors, like Truffaut's *Shoot the Piano Player* and *Jules and Jim*, Godard's *Breathless* and *Vivre Sa Vie*, Antonioni's *L'Avventura*, and Olmi's *The Fiancés*.[5]

The fact that films have not been overrun by interpreters is in part due simply to the newness of cinema as an art. It also owes to the happy accident that films for such a long time were just movies; in other words, that they were understood to be part of mass, as opposed to high, culture, and were left alone by most people with minds. Then, too, there is always some-

3. American film director (1875–1948); his best-known film, *The Birth of a Nation* (1915), is recognized for its brilliant technical and dramatic innovations and notorious for its overt racism.

4. All American directors of the golden age of the Hollywood studios: George Cukor (1899–1983), Raoul Walsh (1887–1980), and Howard Hawks (1896–1977).

5. All adherents of the view that emerged in the mid-1950s that directors are *auteurs* (i.e., authors of the film), and all responsible for more films than are listed here: François Truffaut (1932–1984), French—*Shoot the Piano Player* (1960) and *Jules and Jim* (1962); Jean-Luc Godard (b. 1930), French—*Breathless* (1960) and *Vivre Sa Vie* (1962, *My Life to Live*); Michelangelo Antonioni (1912–2007), Italian—*L'Avventura* (1960, *The Adventure*); and Ermanno Olmi (b. 1931), Italian—*The Fiancés* (1963, *I fidanzati*).

thing other than content in the cinema to grab hold of, for those who want to analyze. For the cinema, unlike the novel, possesses a vocabulary of forms—the explicit, complex, and discussable technology of camera movements, cutting, and composition of the frame that goes into the making of a film.

8

What kind of criticism, of commentary on the arts, is desirable today? For I am not saying that works of art are ineffable, that they cannot be described or paraphrased. They can be. The question is how. What would criticism look like that would serve the work of art, not usurp its place?

What is needed, first, is more attention to form in art. If excessive stress on *content* provokes the arrogance of interpretation, more extended and more thorough descriptions of *form* would silence. What is needed is a vocabulary—a descriptive, rather than prescriptive, vocabulary—for forms.[6] The best criticism, and it is uncommon, is of this sort that dissolves considerations of content into those of form. On film, drama, and painting respectively, I can think of Erwin Panofsky's essay "Style and Medium in the Motion Pictures,"[7] Northrop Frye's essay "A Conspectus of Dramatic Genres,"[8] and Pierre Francastel's essay "The Destruction of a Plastic Space."[9] Roland Barthes' book *On Racine* and his two essays on Robbe-Grillet[1] are examples of formal analysis applied to the work of a single author. (The best essays in Erich Auerbach's *Mimesis*, like "The Scar of Odysseus,"[2] are also of this type.) An example of formal analysis applied simultaneously to genre and author is Walter Benjamin's essay, "The Story Teller: Reflections on the Works of Nicolai Leskov."[3]

Equally valuable would be acts of criticism which would supply a really accurate, sharp, loving description of the appearance of a work of art. This seems even harder to do than formal analysis. Some of Manny Farber's[4] film criticism, Dorothy Van Ghent's essay "The Dickens World: A View from Todgers'."[5] Randall Jarrell's essay on Walt Whitman[6] are among the rare

6. One of the difficulties is that our idea of form is spatial (the Greek metaphors for form are all derived from notions of space). This is why we have a more ready vocabulary of forms for the spatial than for the temporal arts. The exception among the temporal arts, of course, is the drama; perhaps this is because the drama is a narrative (i.e., temporal) form that extends itself visually and pictorially, upon a stage. . . . What we don't have yet is a poetics of the novel, any clear notion of the forms of narration. Perhaps film criticism will be the occasion of a breakthrough here, since films are primarily a visual form, yet they are also a subdivision of literature [Sontag's note].

7. Originally published as "On Movies" (1936), expanded successively under this title (1936, 1947), and reprinted in *Three Essays on Style* (1995), by the German-born American art historian Panofsky (1892–1968).

8. First published in 1951 and later incorporated into *Anatomy of Criticism* (1957), by the Canadian literary critic and theorist FRYE (1912–1991).

9. Essay excerpted from a longer original by the French art historian Francastel (1900–1970) and published in *Art History: An Anthology of Modern Criticism* (ed. Wylie Sypher, 1963).

1. See "There Is No Robbe-Grillet School" and "The Last Word on Robbe-Grillet?" in *Critical Essays* (1964; trans. 1972), by the French literary theorist and critic BARTHES (1915–1980). His *On Racine* (1963; trans. 1964) examines the classical French playwright Jean Racine (1639–1699).

2. For this essay—chapter 1 of *Mimesis: The Representation of Reality in Western Literature* (1946), by the German literary critic AUERBACH (1892–1957)—see above.

3. A 1936 essay included in the collection *Illuminations* (1968), by the German literary and cultural critic BENJAMIN (1892–1940). Nikolai Leskov (1831–1895), Russian novelist and short story writer.

4. American film and art critic and painter (1917–2008).

5. Published (with the subtitle "A View from Todgers's") in *Sewanee Review* 58 (1950); Todgers's is a boardinghouse in *Martin Chuzzlewit* (1843–44), by the English novelist Charles Dickens (1812–1870). Van Ghent (1907–1967), literary scholar.

6. American poet (1819–1892); the essay is "Some Lines from Whitman," in *Poetry and the Age* (1953), by the American poet and critic Jarrell (1914–1965).

examples of what I mean. These are essays which reveal the sensuous surface of art without mucking about in it.

9

Transparence is the highest, most liberating value in art—and in criticism—today. Transparence means experiencing the luminousness of the thing in itself, of things being what they are. This is the greatness of, for example, the films of Bresson and Ozu and Renoir's *The Rules of the Game*.[7]

Once upon a time (say, for Dante[8]), it must have been a revolutionary and creative move to design works of art so that they might be experienced on several levels. Now it is not. It reinforces the principle of redundancy that is the principal affliction of modern life.

Once upon a time (a time when high art was scarce), it must have been a revolutionary and creative move to interpret works of art. Now it is not. What we decidedly do not need now is further to assimilate Art into Thought, or (worse yet) Art into Culture.

Interpretation takes the sensory experience of the work of art for granted, and proceeds from there. This cannot be taken for granted, now. Think of the sheer multiplication of works of art available to every one of us, superadded to the conflicting tastes and odors and sights of the urban environment that bombard our senses. Ours is a culture based on excess, on overproduction; the result is a steady loss of sharpness in our sensory experience. All the conditions of modern life—its material plenitude, its sheer crowdedness—conjoin to dull our sensory faculties. And it is in the light of the condition of our senses, our capacities (rather than those of another age), that the task of the critic must be assessed.

What is important now is to recover our senses. We must learn to *see* more, to *hear* more, to *feel* more.

Our task is not to find the maximum amount of content in a work of art, much less to squeeze more content out of the work than is already there. Our task is to cut back content so that we can see the thing at all.

The aim of all commentary on art now should be to make works of art—and, by analogy, our own experience—more, rather than less, real to us. The function of criticism should be to show *how it is what it is*, even *that it is what it is*, rather than to show *what it means*.

10

In place of a hermeneutics we need an erotics of art.

1964

7. A 1939 film that was the masterpiece of the French director Jean Renoir (1894–1979). Robert Bresson (1901–1999), French film director. Ozu Yasujirō (1903–1963), Japanese film director.

8. DANTE ALIGHIERI (1265–1321), Italian writer of prose and poetry; his masterwork is an allegorical epic poem, *The Divine Comedy* (1307–21).

FREDRIC JAMESON
b. 1934

Although it flourished during the 1930s, Marxist aesthetics and literary criticism all but vanished from critical discourse in the United States after World War II. The cold war consensus stigmatized everything associated with communism, and the dominant methods of the New Criticism practiced by CLEANTH BROOKS and others focused on internal features of works rather than external connections with society, politics, and history. Even when radical cultural criticism reemerged in the social tumult of the 1960s, its main roots were not in Marxism but in new social movements such as feminism, black power, and environmentalism. Against this current, Fredric Jameson almost single-handedly revived Marxist literary studies within the American academy, principally with *Marxism and Form* (1971), which recovered major figures in the Western Marxist tradition, and with his landmark *The Political Unconscious: Narrative as a Socially Symbolic Act* (1981), which outlined his methods for a Marxist literary criticism. An ambitious synthesis of contemporary structuralist theory and Marxism, *The Political Unconscious*, from which we take our first selection, argues that political and economic history form the subtexts and allegorical meanings of literary works. Jameson broadened his focus to examine contemporary culture, and "Postmodernism and Consumer Society" (1988), our second selection, encapsulates his widely influential views on postmodernism, in particular on the relation of art to present-day capitalist production.

Born in Cleveland, Ohio, Jameson was educated at Haverford College, receiving his B.A. in 1954, and at Yale University, where he earned a doctorate in French and comparative literature in 1959. He also spent a formative year in Germany on a Fulbright Fellowship at the Universities of Munich and Berlin (1956–57). After teaching at Harvard University from 1959 to 1967, Jameson moved to the newly created University of California at San Diego, where he encountered Herbert Marcuse, guru for many student radicals and a surviving figure from the Frankfurt School (of which THEODOR W. ADORNO was a central member). Thereafter Jameson held positions at Yale University (1976–83) and the University of California at Santa Cruz (1983–85), settling at Duke University in 1986 as Distinguished Professor of Comparative Literature and director of the Center for Critical Theory.

By the mid-1970s, Jameson and TERRY EAGLETON were being hailed as the most significant Marxist literary critics and theorists in the Anglophone world, but it was not until the publication of *The Political Unconscious* that the originality of Jameson's project became clear. Opening with the famous exhortation "Always historicize!" he sets out the methodological approach he calls "metacommentary," which provides a theoretically sophisticated answer to the perennial question of the relation of aesthetics to social history. In contrast to those practicing more conventional forms of historical criticism, Jameson not only situates cultural texts in relation to their immediate context but also approaches them from the vantage point of hermeneutics, exploring the interpretive strategies that shape how we understand individual works. Unlike other modern theories of interpretation, Jameson's stresses that its object is an analysis of ideology and that Marxism encompasses all other interpretive strategies, showing that their explanations of a text's meaning are only partial.

Jameson holds that a critic wishing to decipher the meaning of a text must proceed through a series of distinct phases, embodied in the text and uncovered through systematic decoding. He draws on a wide array of twentieth-century theoretical sources to do this, from NORTHROP FRYE's four levels of interpretation (which ultimately derive from the medieval interpretive schema of THOMAS AQUINAS), to JACQUES LACAN's theory of the unconscious, to LOUIS ALTHUSSER's account of ideology. Jameson sees Marxist criticism not as exclusionary or separatist but as comprehensive, assimilating a compendium of sources and thereby achieving greater "semantic richness." The critic should examine in turn the political history to which a text refers, social history (conceived in traditional Marxist terms as the history of class struggles), and the history of modes of production. These approaches do not displace but are embedded in each other, building to higher levels of generality and deeper layers of historical causation.

To interpret a text within the horizon of political history, Jameson focuses on "the individual work . . . grasped essentially as a *symbolic act*." For instance, one can read Shakespeare's *Macbeth* (ca. 1606) as a presentation of the burning political issue of its historical moment, royal succession. Shakespeare's contemporaries would have recognized this both as the play's obvious theme (Macbeth as the murderous usurper; Malcolm as the legitimate but feckless heir) and as a matter of immediate political concern—the play was performed at court not long after James VI of Scotland had assumed the English throne as James I, a Stuart supplanting the Tudor dynasty. Details of plot, character, and thought are in this reading understood as allegorical signs referring to historical figures and to Renaissance doctrines about royal power and its legitimacy.

For the second phase of interpretation, the object of investigation is "the *ideologeme*, that is, the smallest intelligible unit of the essentially antagonistic collective discourses of social classes." To take another example from Shakespeare, in a number of the history plays, such as the two parts of *Henry IV* (ca. 1597, 1599), as well as in several of the tragedies, such as *Hamlet* (ca. 1600) and *King Lear* (ca. 1605), the dramatic struggle between the major characters stages the ideological conflict between older, medieval ideals of kingship and the modernizing tendencies of an emergent absolutist power that advances the interests of the bourgeoisie against the prerogatives of powerful feudal landlords. This sociological interpretation does not cancel out the first; one can still recognize the political allegory in *Henry IV*, which justifies Tudor rule by showing the superiority of the modernizing Tudors (embodied in Prince Hal) over both the rebellious English barons and the effeminate French monarchy.

The outermost circle of interpretation, "the ideology of form," links the literary work with the mode of production (characterized, according to KARL MARX, as tribal hordes, Neolithic kinship societies, Oriental despotism, ancient slaveholding societies, feudalism, capitalism, and finally communism). Thus Hamlet's "problems" (famously elaborated by T. S. ELIOT) do not indicate Shakespeare's dramatic failure (as Eliot argued) but rather signify a historical tension between the feudal ideals embodied in Hamlet's father, ideals to which Hamlet owes one sort of allegiance, and the modern habits imbibed by the prince through his university education at Wittenberg. These latter include Hamlet's tendency toward obsessive individualistic reflection, which prevents his carrying out the revenge that his father decreed against the usurping Claudius. This conflict is visible in the play's dramatic form, which overlays a modern psychological drama onto its older source material governed by the conventions of revenge tragedy (a popular form in Shakespeare's day). The play stands, thematically and formally, on the cusp of a major historical transformation—the transition from feudalism to capitalism. Hamlet's fatal actions at the end do not resolve the play's ideological and formal contradictions because no resolution was imaginable in 1600; the triumph of capitalism over feudalism in Britain would not be achieved until near the end of the seventeenth century, with remnants of feudal ideologies persisting long after.

The imaginative limits imposed on an author or a text by its historical moment reveal the operation of history itself, which "sets inexorable limits to individual as well as collective praxis." And though its causes might not be immediately apparent, we can apprehend history in its effects, which are "inaccessible to us except in textual form." Here Jameson espouses a distinctly poststructuralist view, that—as articulated by PAUL DE MAN—"the bases for historical knowledge are not empirical facts but written texts, even if these texts masquerade in the guise of wars or revolutions"; however, he departs from de Man in stressing the text's ideological over its linguistic import.

In "Postmodernism and Consumer Society," which anticipates his magisterial study *Postmodernism, or, The Cultural Logic of Late Capitalism* (1991), Jameson expands his consideration of the ideology of form, moving beyond the literary canon to contemporary culture—including film, experimental poetry, popular fiction, art, and architecture. He identifies two causal conditions for postmodernism across the arts: first, its products "emerge as specific reactions against the established forms of high modernism"; and second, it results from the "erosion of the older distinction between high culture and so-called mass or popular culture." These essentially aesthetic determinations, however, are not postmodernism's ultimate cause. In classically Marxist fashion, Jameson looks to the underlying economic formation: postmodernism "expresses the inner truth of that newly emergent social order of late capitalism," sometimes also called consumer, postindustrial, or multinational capitalism, which arose in the aftermath of World War II and reached both its fulfillment and a moment of crisis during the 1960s and 1970s. For Jameson, "postmodernism" names a historical period, not just a new style or aesthetic. As modernism was a result of the imperial stage of capitalism, so postmodernism is the distinctive "ideology of form" of the contemporary period of consumer capitalism.

Postmodern works exhibit a range of distinctive formal features, such as pastiche and simulation. Focusing on what he calls "the nostalgia mode," Jameson describes the peculiar dehistoricized depthlessness of certain postmodern works, such as the popular film *American Graffiti* (1973) and novels like E. L. Doctorow's *Ragtime* (1975). In a postmodern world, we "seem condemned to seek the historical past through our own pop images and stereotypes about the past, which itself remains forever out of reach." Jameson goes on to analyze one of the exemplary monuments of postmodern architecture, John Portman's Bonaventure Hotel (1977) in downtown Los Angeles. Showing how space is configured in disorienting new ways by Portman's structure, Jameson argues that postmodern architecture embodies an objectively new kind of bewildering hyperspace, which we lack the necessary perceptual and cognitive tools to understand. He concludes by returning to the contrast between high modernist and postmodern works, reemphasizing modernism's oppositional stance toward the dominant culture of the bourgeoisie. About postmodernism, Jameson is more tentative; he suggests that it may be more than the reflection of consumer society, but he ultimately declines to answer the question he has posed about its critical potential.

Recognized as the leading contemporary Marxist critic in the United States as well as a major practitioner of poststructuralist theory, Jameson has drawn both a large following and a great deal of criticism. Some have charged that his writing is overly difficult, obscure, and inaccessible. Theoretically attuned critics have variously questioned his "totalizing" allegorical method of interpretation, his eclectic borrowing from diverse theories, his reductive scheme of historical periods leading to postmodernism, his disregard of feminism and gender dynamics, and his lack of concrete attention to ongoing political struggles. From the Marxist Left, Terry Eagleton questions the connection between theory and politics, pointedly asking of one of Jameson's readings in *The Political Unconscious*: "How is a Marxist-structuralist analysis of a minor novel of Balzac to help shake the foundations of capitalism?" Although Eagleton allows, quoting Althusser, that it contributes to the "class struggle at the level of theory," he concludes that the relation is unclear. Jameson himself answers in an interview that his intention is to make Marxism a central concern in intellectual circles, as well as to redefine it in light of contemporary thought. Though his work may not immediately translate to concrete political practices and policies, Jameson has been a tireless analyst of "the ideology of form" in literary and cultural works, and he is arguably the most influential proponent of Marxism in contemporary criticism.

***The Political Unconscious: Narrative as a Socially Symbolic Act* Keywords:** Ideology, Interpretation Theory, Marxism, Narrative Theory, Poststructuralism, Realism
"Postmodernism and Consumer Society" Keywords: Cultural Studies, Modernity, Popular Culture, Postmodernity, Representation

From The Political Unconscious: Narrative as a Socially Symbolic Act

Preface

Always historicize! This slogan—the one absolute and we may even say "transhistorical" imperative of all dialectical thought[1]—will unsurprisingly turn out to be the moral of *The Political Unconscious* as well. But, as the traditional dialectic teaches us, the historicizing operation can follow two distinct paths, which only ultimately meet in the same place: the path of the object and the path of the subject, the historical origins of the things themselves and that more intangible historicity of the concepts and categories by which we attempt to understand those things. In the area of culture, which is the central field of the present book, we are thus confronted with a choice between study of the nature of the "objective" structures of a given cultural text (the historicity of its forms and of its content, the historical moment of emergence of its linguistic possibilities, the situation-specific function of its aesthetic) and something rather different which would instead foreground the interpretive categories or codes through which we read and receive the text in question. For better or for worse, it is this second path we have chosen to follow here: *The Political Unconscious* accordingly turns on the dynamics of the act of interpretation and presupposes, as its organizational fiction, that we never really confront a text immediately, in all its freshness as a thing-in-itself. Rather, texts come before us as the always-already-read; we apprehend them through sedimented layers of previous interpretations, or—if the text is brand-new—through the sedimented reading habits and categories developed by those inherited interpretive traditions. This presupposition then dictates the use of a method (which I have elsewhere termed the "metacommentary"[2]) according to which our object of study is less the text itself than the interpretations through which we attempt to confront and to appropriate it. Interpretation is here construed as an essentially allegorical act, which consists in rewriting a given text in terms of a particular interpretive master code. The identification of the latter will then lead to an evaluation of such codes or, in other words, of the "methods" or approaches current in American literary and cultural study today. Their juxtaposition with a dialectical or totalizing, properly Marxist ideal of understanding will

1. In Marxist theory, thought that links ideas and cultural forms to their economic foundations.
2. See "Metacommentary" (1971), included in Jameson's *Ideologies of Theory: Essays, 1971–1986*, vol. 1, *Situations of Theory* (Minneapolis: University of Minnesota Press, 1988).

be used to demonstrate the structural limitations of the other interpretive codes, and in particular to show the "local" ways in which they construct their objects of study and the "strategies of containment" whereby they are able to project the illusion that their readings are somehow complete and self-sufficient.

The retrospective illusion of the metacommentary thus has the advantage of allowing us to measure the yield and density of a properly Marxist interpretive act against those of other interpretive methods—the ethical, the psychoanalytic, the myth-critical, the semiotic, the structural, and the theological—against which it must compete in the "pluralism" of the intellectual marketplace today. I will here argue the priority of a Marxian interpretive framework in terms of semantic richness. Marxism cannot today be defended as a mere substitute for such other methods, which would then triumphalistically be consigned to the ashcan of history; the authority of such methods springs from their faithful consonance with this or that local law of a fragmented social life, this or that subsystem of a complex and mushrooming cultural superstructure.[3] In the spirit of a more authentic dialectical tradition, Marxism is here conceived as that "untranscendable horizon" that subsumes such apparently antagonistic or incommensurable critical operations, assigning them an undoubted sectoral validity within itself, and thus at once canceling and preserving them.

Because of the peculiar focus of this retrospective organization, however, it may be worth warning the reader what *The Political Unconscious* is not. The reader should not, in the first place, expect anything like that exploratory projection of what a vital and emergent political culture should be and do which Raymond Williams[4] has rightly proposed as the most urgent task of a Marxist cultural criticism. There are, of course, good and objective historical reasons why contemporary Marxism has been slow in rising to this challenge: the sorry history of Zhdanovite prescription[5] in the arts is one, the fascination with modernisms and "revolutions" in form and language is another, as well as the coming of a whole new political and economic "world system," to which the older Marxist cultural paradigms only imperfectly apply. A provisional conclusion to the present work will spell out some of the challenges Marxist interpretation must anticipate in conceiving those new forms of collective thinking and collective culture which lie beyond the boundaries of our own world. The reader will there find an empty chair reserved for some as yet unrealized, collective, and decentered cultural production of the future, beyond realism and modernism alike.

If this book, then, fails to propose a political or revolutionary aesthetic, it is equally little concerned to raise once again the traditional issues of philosophical aesthetics: the nature and function of art, the specificity of poetic language and of the aesthetic experience, the theory of the beautiful, and so forth. Yet the very absence of such issues may serve as an implicit commentary on them; I have tried to maintain an essentially historicist perspective,

3. According to the German social and political philosopher KARL MARX (1818–1883), all social, political, and cultural forms are part of a society's superstructure, which interacts with but ultimately depends on its economic base.

4. British literary and cultural critic (1921–1988; see above).

5. The censorship by Andrey Zhdanov (1896–1948), a Bolshevik leader during the Russian Revolution who later, as a member of the Soviet Politburo, tightened the guidelines for cultural activities.

in which our readings of the past are vitally dependent on our experience of the present, and in particular on the structural peculiarities of what is sometimes called the *société de consommation* (or the "disaccumulative" moment of late monopoly or consumer or multinational capitalism), what Guy Debord[6] calls the society of the image or of the spectacle. The point is that in such a society, saturated with messages and with "aesthetic" experiences of all kinds, the issues of an older philosophical aesthetics themselves need to be radically historicized, and can be expected to be transformed beyond recognition in the process.

Nor, although literary history is here everywhere implied, should *The Political Unconscious* be taken as paradigmatic work in this discursive form or genre, which is today in crisis. Traditional literary history was a subset of representational narrative, a kind of narrative "realism" become as problematic as its principal exemplars in the history of the novel. The second chapter of the present book, which is concerned with genre criticism, will raise the theoretical problem of the status and possibility of such literary-historical narratives, which in *Marxism and Form* I termed "diachronic[7] constructs"; the subsequent readings of Balzac, Gissing, and Conrad[8] project a diachronic framework—the construction of the bourgeois subject in emergent capitalism and its schizophrenic disintegration in our own time—which is, however, here never fully worked out. Of literary history today we may observe that its task is at one with that proposed by Louis Althusser[9] for historiography in general: not to elaborate some achieved and lifelike simulacrum of its supposed object, but rather to "produce" the latter's "concept." This is indeed what the greatest modern or modernizing literary histories—such as Erich Auerbach's *Mimesis*[1]—have sought to do in their critical practice, if not in their theory.

Is it at least possible, then, that the present work might be taken as an outline or projection of a new kind of critical method? Indeed it would seem to me perfectly appropriate to recast many of its findings in the form of a methodological handbook, but such a manual would have as its object *ideological analysis*, which remains, I believe, the appropriate designation for the critical "method" specific to Marxism. For reasons indicated above, this book is not that manual, which would necessarily settle its accounts with rival "methods" in a far more polemic spirit. Yet the unavoidably Hegelian[2] tone of the retrospective framework of *The Political Unconscious* should not be taken to imply that such polemic interventions are not of the highest priority for Marxist cultural criticism. On the contrary, the latter must necessarily also be what Althusser has demanded of the practice of Marxist philosophy proper, namely "class struggle within theory."

6. French critic (1931–1994), author of *The Society of the Spectacle* (1967), in which he coins these phrases. *Société de consommation*: consumer society (French).

7. Dealing with change over time (a term common in structuralist linguistics, and often paired with the *synchronic*, which focuses on phenomena at one moment of time). *Marxism and Form* was published in 1971.

8. Joseph Conrad (1857–1924), Polish-born English novelist. Honoré de Balzac (1799–1850), French novelist. George Gissing (1857–1903), English novelist.

9. French Marxist philosopher (1918–1990; see above).

1. *Mimesis: The Representation of Reality in Western Literature* (1946; see above), by the German literary critic AUERBACH (1892–1957).

2. Characteristic of GEORG WILHELM FRIEDRICH HEGEL (1770–1831), German idealist philosopher.

For the non-Marxist reader, however, who may well feel that this book is quite polemic enough, I will add what should be unnecessary and underline my debt to the great pioneers of narrative analysis. My theoretical dialogue with them in these pages is not merely to be taken as yet another specimen of the negative critique of "false consciousness"[3] (although it is that too, and, indeed, in the Conclusion I will deal explicitly with the problem of the proper uses of such critical gestures as demystification and ideological unmasking). It should meanwhile be obvious that no work in the area of narrative analysis can afford to ignore the fundamental contributions of Northrop Frye, the codification by A. J. Greimas of the whole Formalist and semiotic traditions, the heritage of a certain Christian hermeneutics, and above all, the indispensable explorations by Freud of the logic of dreams, and by Claude Lévi-Strauss[4] of the logic of "primitive" storytelling and *pensée sauvage*, not to speak of the flawed yet monumental achievements in this area of the greatest Marxist philosopher of modern times, Georg Lukács.[5] These divergent and unequal bodies of work are here interrogated and evaluated from the perspective of the specific critical and interpretive task of the present volume, namely to restructure the problematics of ideology, of the unconscious and of desire, of representation, of history, and of cultural production, around the all-informing process of *narrative*, which I take to be (here using the shorthand of philosophical idealism) the central function or *instance* of the human mind. This perspective may be reformulated in terms of the traditional dialectical code as the study of *Darstellung*:[6] that untranslatable designation in which the current problems of *representation* productively intersect with the quite different ones of *presentation*, or of the essentially narrative and rhetorical movement of language and writing through time.

Last but not least, the reader may well be puzzled as to why a book ostensibly concerned with the interpretive act should devote so little attention to issues of interpretive validity, and to the criteria by which a given interpretation may be faulted or accredited. I happen to feel that no interpretation can be effectively disqualified on its own terms by a simple enumeration of inaccuracies or omissions, or by a list of unanswered questions. Interpretation is not an isolated act, but takes place within a Homeric battlefield, on which a host of interpretive options are either openly or implicitly in conflict. If the positivistic conception of philological accuracy be the only alternative, then I would much prefer to endorse the current provocative celebration of strong misreadings over weak ones.[7] As the Chinese proverb has it, you use one ax handle to hew another: in our context, only another, stronger interpretation can overthrow and practically refute an interpretation already in place.

I would therefore be content to have the theoretical sections of this book judged and tested against its interpretive practice. But this very antithesis

3. A Marxist term referring to an individual's tendency to view reality in ways congruent with the interests of the dominant orthodoxy rather than in ways that reflect his or her own class interest.

4. French structuralist anthropologist (1908–2009; see above), whose works include *La Penseé sauvage* (1962, *The Savage Mind*). FRYE (1912–1991), Canadian literary critic associated with archetypal criticism. Greimas (1917–1992), Lithuanian-born French semiotician. SIGMUND FREUD (1856–1939), Austrian founder of psychoanalysis and author of *The Interpretation of Dreams* (1900).

5. GYÖRGY LUKÁCS (1885–1971), Hungarian literary critic and philosopher.

6. Representation (German).

7. A reference to the theory of literary influence presented by the American critic HAROLD BLOOM in such works as *The Anxiety of Influence* (1973; see above) and *A Map of Misreading* (1975).

marks out the double standard and the formal dilemma of all cultural study today, from which *The Political Unconscious* is scarcely exempt: an uneasy struggle for priority between models and history, between theoretical speculation and textual analysis, in which the former seeks to transform the latter into so many mere examples, adduced to support its abstract propositions, while the latter continues insistently to imply that the theory itself was just so much methodological scaffolding, which can readily be dismantled once the serious business of practical criticism is under way. These two tendencies—theory and literary history—have so often in Western academic thought been felt to be rigorously incompatible that it is worth reminding the reader, in conclusion, of the existence of a third position which transcends both. That position is, of course, Marxism, which, in the form of the dialectic, affirms a primacy of theory which is at one and the same time a recognition of the primacy of History itself.

From *Chapter 1. On Interpretation: Literature as a Socially Symbolic Act*

* * *

III

At this point it might seem appropriate to juxtapose a Marxist method of literary and cultural interpretation with those just outlined, and to document its claims to greater adequacy and validity. For better or for worse, however, as I warned in the Preface, this obvious next step is not the strategy projected by the present book, which rather seeks to argue the perspectives of Marxism as necessary preconditions for adequate literary comprehension. Marxist critical insights will therefore here be defended as something like an ultimate *semantic* precondition for the intelligibility of literary and cultural texts. Even this argument, however, needs a certain specification: in particular we will suggest that such semantic enrichment and enlargement of the inert givens and materials of a particular text must take place within three concentric frameworks, which mark a widening out of the sense of the social ground of a text through the notions, first, of political history, in the narrow sense of punctual event and a chroniclelike sequence of happenings in time; then of society, in the now already less diachronic and time-bound sense of a constitutive tension and struggle between social classes; and, ultimately, of history now conceived in its vastest sense of the sequence of modes of production[8] and the succession and destiny of the various human social formations, from prehistoric life to whatever far future history has in store for us.

These distinct semantic horizons are, to be sure, also distinct moments of the process of interpretation, and may in that sense be understood as dialectical equivalents of what Frye has called the successive "phases" in our reinterpretation—our rereading and rewriting—of the literary text. What we must also note, however, is that each phase or horizon governs a distinct

8. In the Marxist schema, human history progresses through tribal hordes, Neolithic kinship societies, Oriental despotism, ancient slaveholding societies, feudalism, capitalism, and finally to communism.

reconstruction of its object, and construes the very structure of what can now only in a general sense be called "the text" in a different way.

Thus, within the narrower limits of our first, narrowly political or historical, horizon, "the text," the object of study, is still more or less construed as coinciding with the individual literary work or utterance. The difference between the perspective enforced and enabled by this horizon, however, and that of ordinary *explication de texte*, or individual exegesis, is that here the individual work is grasped essentially as a *symbolic act*.

When we pass into the second phase, and find that the semantic horizon within which we grasp a cultural object has widened to include the social order, we will find that the very object of our analysis has itself been thereby dialectically transformed, and that it is no longer construed as an individual "text" or work in the narrow sense, but has been reconstituted in the form of the great collective and class discourses of which a text is little more than an individual *parole* or utterance.[9] Within this new horizon, then, our object of study will prove to be the *ideologeme*, that is, the smallest intelligible unit of the essentially antagonistic collective discourses of social classes.

When finally, even the passions and values of a particular social formation find themselves placed in a new and seemingly relativized perspective by the ultimate horizon of human history as a whole, and by their respective positions in the whole complex sequence of the modes of production, both the individual text and its ideologemes know a final transformation, and must be read in terms of what I will call the *ideology of form*, that is, the symbolic messages transmitted to us by the coexistence of various sign systems which are themselves traces or anticipations of modes of production.

The general movement through these three progressively wider horizons will largely coincide with the shifts in focus of the final chapters in this book, and will be felt, although not narrowly and programmatically underscored, in the methodological transformations determined by the historical transformations of their textual objects, from Balzac to Gissing to Conrad.

We must now briefly characterize each of these semantic or interpretive horizons. We have suggested that it is only in the first narrowly political horizon—in which history is reduced to a series of punctual events and crises in time, to the diachronic agitation of the year-to-year, the chronicle-like annals of the rise and fall of political regimes and social fashions, and the passionate immediacy of struggles between historical individuals—that the "text" or object of study will tend to coincide with the individual literary work or cultural artifact. Yet to specify this individual text as a symbolic act is already fundamentally to transform the categories with which traditional *explication de texte* (whether narrative or poetic) operated and largely still operates.

The model for such an interpretive operation remains the readings of myth and aesthetic structure of Claude Lévi-Strauss as they are codified in his fundamental essay "The Structural Study of Myth."[1] These suggestive, often

9. Structural linguistics follows the distinction first made by the Swiss linguist FERDINAND DE SAUSSURE (1857–1913), often retaining his French terms, between the speech of an individual language user (*parole*) and language as an abstract system (*langue*).

1. Claude Lévi-Strauss, *Structural Anthropology*, trans. C. Jacobson and B. G. Schoepf (New York: Basic, 1963), pp. 206–31 [Jameson's note]. Some of the author's notes have been edited, and some omitted.

sheerly occasional, readings and speculative glosses immediately impose a basic analytical or interpretive principle: the individual narrative, or the individual formal structure, is to be grasped as the imaginary resolution of a real contradiction. Thus, to take only the most dramatic of Lévi-Strauss's analyses—the "interpretation" of the unique facial decorations of the Caduveo Indians[2]—the starting point will be an immanent description of the formal and structural peculiarities of this body art; yet it must be a description already pre-prepared and oriented toward transcending the purely formalistic, a movement which is achieved not by abandoning the formal level for something extrinsic to it—such as some inertly social "content"—but rather immanently, by construing purely formal patterns as a symbolic enactment of the social within the formal and the aesthetic. Such symbolic functions are, however, rarely found by an aimless enumeration of random formal and stylistic features; our discovery of a text's symbolic efficacity must be oriented by a formal description which seeks to grasp it as a determinate structure of still properly formal *contradictions*. Thus, Lévi-Strauss orients his still purely visual analysis of Caduveo facial decorations toward this climactic account of their contradictory dynamic: "the use of a design which is symmetrical but yet lies across an oblique axis . . . a complicated situation based upon two contradictory forms of duality, and resulting in a compromise brought about by a secondary opposition between the ideal axis of the object itself [the human face] and the ideal axis of the figure which it represents."[3] Already on the purely formal level, then, this visual text has been grasped as a contradiction by way of the curiously provisional and asymmetrical resolution it proposes for that contradiction.

Lévi-Strauss's "interpretation" of this formal phenomenon may now, perhaps overhastily, be specified. Caduveo are a hierarchical society, organized in three endogamous groups[4] or castes. In their social development, as in that of their neighbors, this nascent hierarchy is already the place of the emergence, if not of political power in the strict sense, then at least of relations of domination: the inferior status of women, the subordination of youth to elders, and the development of a hereditary aristocracy. Yet whereas this latent power structure is, among the neighboring Guana and Bororo,[5] masked by a division into moieties which cuts across the three castes, and whose exogamous exchange[6] appears to function in a nonhierarchical, essentially egalitarian way, it is openly present in Caduveo life, as surface inequality and conflict. The social institutions of the Guana and Bororo, on the other hand, provide a realm of appearance, in which real hierarchy and inequality are dissimulated by the reciprocity of the moieties, and in which, therefore, "asymmetry of class is balanced . . . by symmetry of 'moieties.'"

As for the Caduveo,

> they were never lucky enough to resolve their contradictions, or to disguise them with the help of institutions artfully devised for that purpose. On the social level, the remedy was lacking . . . but it was never completely

2. A South American indigenous people residing in Argentina, Paraguay, and Brazil.
3. Claude Lévi-Strauss, *Tristes Tropiques*, trans. John Russell (New York: Atheneum, 1971), p. 176 [Jameson's note].
4. Groups whose members intermarry.
5. Other indigenous peoples of the upper Paraguay River.
6. Marriages outside the group.

> out of their grasp. It was within them, never objectively formulated, but present as a source of confusion and disquiet. Yet since they were unable to conceptualize or to live this solution directly, they began to dream it, to project it into the imaginary. . . . We must therefore interpret the graphic art of Caduveo women, and explain its mysterious charm as well as its apparently gratuitous complication, as the fantasy production of a society seeking passionately to give symbolic expression to the institutions it might have had in reality, had not interest and superstition stood in the way.[7]

In this fashion, then, the visual text of Caduveo facial art constitutes a symbolic act, whereby real social contradictions, insurmountable in their own terms, find a purely formal resolution in the aesthetic realm.

This interpretive model thus allows us a first specification of the relationship between ideology and cultural texts or artifacts: a specification still conditioned by the limits of the first, narrowly historical or political horizon in which it is made. We may suggest that from this perspective, ideology is not something which informs or invests symbolic production; rather the aesthetic act is itself ideological, and the production of aesthetic or narrative form is to be seen as an ideological act in its own right, with the function of inventing imaginary or formal "solutions" to unresolvable social contradictions.

Lévi-Strauss's work also suggests a more general defense of the proposition of a political unconscious than we have hitherto been able to present, insofar as it offers the spectacle of so-called primitive peoples perplexed enough by the dynamics and contradictions of their still relatively simple forms of tribal organization to project decorative or mythic resolutions of issues that they are unable to articulate conceptually. But if this is the case for pre-capitalist and even pre-political societies, then how much more must it be true for the citizen of the modern *Gesellschaft*,[8] faced with the great constitutional options of the revolutionary period, and with the corrosive and tradition-annihilating effects of the spread of a money and market economy, with the changing cast of collective characters which oppose the bourgeoisie, now to an embattled aristocracy, now to an urban proletariat, with the great fantasms of the various nationalisms, now themselves virtual "subjects of history" of a rather different kind, with the social homogenization and psychic constriction of the rise of the industrial city and its "masses," the sudden appearance of the great transnational forces of communism and fascism, followed by the advent of the superstates and the onset of that great ideological rivalry between capitalism and communism, which, no less passionate and obsessive than that which, at the dawn of modern times, seethed through the wars of religion, marks the final tension of our now global village? It does not, indeed, seem particularly farfetched to suggest that these texts of history, with their fantasmatic collective "actants,"[9] their narrative organization, and their immense charge of anxiety and libidinal investment, are lived by the contemporary subject as a genuine politico-historical *pensée sauvage* which necessarily informs all of our cultural artifacts, from the literary institutions

7. Lévi-Strauss, *Tristes Tropiques*, pp. 179–80 [Jameson's note].
8. Society of impersonal associations (German); often contrasted with *Gemeinschaft* (a community of organic social relationships).
9. Fundamental factors, such as subject and object, that generate narrative plot (a technical term introduced by Greimas).

of high modernism all the way to the products of mass culture. Under these circumstances, Lévi-Strauss's work suggests that the proposition whereby all cultural artifacts are to be read as symbolic resolutions of real political and social contradictions deserves serious exploration and systematic experimental verification. It will become clear in later chapters of this book that the most readily accessible formal articulation of the operations of a political *pensée sauvage* of this kind will be found in what we will call the structure of a properly political *allegory*, as it develops from networks of topical allusion in Spenser or Milton or Swift[1] to the symbolic narratives of class representatives or "types" in novels like those of Balzac. With political allegory, then, a sometimes repressed ur-narrative[2] or master fantasy about the interaction of collective subjects, we have moved to the very borders of our second horizon, in which what we formerly regarded as individual texts are grasped as "utterances" in an essentially collective or class discourse.

We cannot cross those borders, however, without some final account of the critical operations involved in our first interpretive phase. We have implied that in order to be consequent, the will to read literary or cultural texts as symbolic acts must necessarily grasp them as resolutions of determinate contradictions; and it is clear that the notion of contradiction is central to any Marxist cultural analysis, just as it will remain central in our two subsequent horizons, although it will there take rather different forms. The methodological requirement to articulate a text's fundamental contradiction may then be seen as a test of the completeness of the analysis: this is why, for example, the conventional sociology of literature or culture, which modestly limits itself to the identification of class motifs or values in a given text, and feels that its work is done when it shows how a given artifact "reflects" its social background, is utterly unacceptable. Meanwhile, Kenneth Burke's[3] play of emphases, in which a symbolic act is on the one hand affirmed as a genuine *act*, albeit on the symbolic level, while on the other it is registered as an act which is "merely" symbolic, its resolutions imaginary ones that leave the real untouched, suitably dramatizes the ambiguous status of art and culture.

Still, we need to say a little more about the status of this external reality, of which it will otherwise be thought that it is little more than the traditional notion of "context" familiar in older social or historical criticism. The type of interpretation here proposed is more satisfactorily grasped as the rewriting of the literary text in such a way that the latter may itself be seen as the rewriting or restructuration of a prior historical or ideological *subtext*, it being always understood that that "subtext" is not immediately present as such, not some common-sense external reality, nor even the conventional narratives of history manuals, but rather must itself always be (re)constructed after the fact. The literary or aesthetic act therefore always entertains some active relationship with the Real;[4] yet in order to do so, it cannot simply allow "reality" to persevere inertly in its own being, outside the text and at distance. It

1. All canonical English authors whose works sometimes include topical political references: Edmund Spenser (1552–1599), John Milton (1608–1674), and Jonathan Swift (1667–1745).
2. Prototypical or originary story.
3. American literary critic and rhetorician (1897–1993).
4. A technical term from the theory of the French psychoanalyst JACQUES LACAN (1901–1981); the Real can be studied only in its effects on the Symbolic (and the Imaginary).

must rather draw the Real into its own texture, and the ultimate paradoxes and false problems of linguistics, and most notably of semantics, are to be traced back to this process, whereby language manages to carry the Real within itself as its own intrinsic or immanent subtext. Insofar, in other words, as symbolic action—what Burke will map as "dream," "prayer," or "chart"[5]—is a way of doing something to the world, to that degree what we are calling "world" must inhere within it, as the content it has to take up into itself in order to submit it to the transformations of form. The symbolic act therefore begins by generating and producing its own context in the same moment of emergence in which it steps back from it, taking its measure with a view toward its own projects of transformation. The whole paradox of what we have here called the subtext may be summed up in this, that the literary work or cultural object, as though for the first time, brings into being that very situation to which it is also, at one and the same time, a reaction. It articulates its own situation and textualizes it, thereby encouraging and perpetuating the illusion that the situation itself did not exist before it, that there is nothing but a text, that there never was any extra- or con-textual reality before the text itself generated it in the form of a mirage. One does not have to argue the reality of history: necessity, like Dr. Johnson's stone,[6] does that for us. That history—Althusser's "absent cause," Lacan's "Real"—is *not* a text, for it is fundamentally non-narrative and nonrepresentational; what can be added, however, is the proviso that history is inaccessible to us except in textual form, or in other words, that it can be approached only by way of prior (re)textualization. Thus, to insist on either of the two inseparable yet incommensurable dimensions of the symbolic act without the other: to overemphasize the active way in which the text reorganizes its subtext (in order, presumably, to reach the triumphant conclusion that the "referent" does not exist); or on the other hand to stress the imaginary status of the symbolic act so completely as to reify its social ground, now no longer understood as a subtext but merely as some inert given that the text passively or fantasmatically "reflects"—to overstress either of these functions of the symbolic act at the expense of the other is surely to produce sheer ideology, whether it be, as in the first alternative, the ideology of structuralism, or, in the second, that of vulgar materialism.

Still, this view of the place of the "referent" will be neither complete nor methodologically usable unless we specify a supplementary distinction between several types of subtext to be (re)constructed. We have implied, indeed, that the social contradiction addressed and "resolved" by the formal prestidigitation of narrative must, however reconstructed, remain an absent cause, which cannot be directly or immediately conceptualized by the text. It seems useful, therefore, to distinguish, from this ultimate subtext which is the place of social *contradiction*, a secondary one, which is more properly the place of ideology, and which takes the form of the *aporia* or the *antinomy*:[7]

5. Kenneth Burke, *The Philosophy of Literary Form* (Berkeley: University of California Press, 1973), pp. 5–6 [Jameson's note].

6. That is, the stone famously kicked by the English critic, essayist, and lexicographer SAMUEL JOHNSON (1709–1784) to refute the theory of the nonexistence of matter espoused by George Berkeley.

7. A contradiction between two statements of apparently equal validity. "Aporia": difficulty, logical impasse (a term often used in deconstructive criticism to indicate the point in a text where inherent contradictions render interpretation undecidable).

what can in the former be resolved only through the intervention of praxis here comes before the purely contemplative mind as logical scandal or double bind, the unthinkable and the conceptually paradoxical, that which cannot be unknotted by the operation of pure thought, and which must therefore generate a whole more properly narrative apparatus—the text itself—to square its circles and to dispel, through narrative movement, its intolerable closure. Such a distinction, positing a system of antinomies as the symptomatic expression and conceptual reflex of something quite different, namely a social contradiction, will now allow us to reformulate that coordination between a semiotic and a dialectical method, which was evoked in the preceding section. The operational validity of semiotic analysis, and in particular of the Greimassian semiotic rectangle,[8] derives, as was suggested there, not from its adequacy to nature or being, nor even from its capacity to map all forms of thinking or language, but rather from its vocation specifically to model ideological closure and to articulate the workings of binary oppositions, here the privileged form of what we have called the antinomy. A dialectical reevaluation of the findings of semiotics intervenes, however, at the moment in which this entire system of ideological closure is taken as the symptomatic projection of something quite different, namely of social contradiction.

We may now leave this first textual or interpretive model behind, and pass over into the second horizon, that of the social. The latter becomes visible, and individual phenomena are revealed as social facts and institutions, only at the moment in which the organizing categories of analysis become those of social class. I have in another place described the dynamics of ideology in its constituted form as a function of social class:[9] suffice it only to recall here that for Marxism classes must always be apprehended relationally, and that the ultimate (or ideal) form of class relationship and class struggle is always dichotomous. The constitutive form of class relationships is always that between a dominant and a laboring class: and it is only in terms of this axis that class fractions (for example, the petty bourgeoisie) or ec-centric or dependent classes (such as the peasantry) are positioned. To define class in this way is sharply to differentiate the Marxian model of classes from the conventional sociological analysis of society into strata, subgroups, professional elites and the like, each of which can presumably be studied in isolation from one another in such a way that the analysis of their "values" or their "cultural space" folds back into separate and independent *Weltanschauungen*,[1] each of which inertly reflects its particular "stratum." For Marxism, however, the very content of a class ideology is relational, in the sense that its "values" are always actively in situation with respect to the opposing class, and defined against the latter: normally, a ruling class ideology will explore various strategies of the *legitimation* of its own power position, while an oppositional culture or ideology will, often in covert

8. Dialectical sets of oppositions through which, Greimas theorizes, narratives generate meaning and which he diagrams in a rectangle. Throughout *The Political Unconscious*, Jameson frequently uses Greimassian rectangles in analyzing novels.

9. See my *Marxism and Form: Twentieth-Century Dialectical Theories of Literature* (Princeton: Princeton University Press, 1971), pp. 376–82. The most authoritative contemporary Marxist statement of this view of social class is to be found in E. P. Thompson, *The Making of the English Working Classes* (New York: Vintage, 1966), pp. 9–11 [Jameson's note].

1. Worldviews (German).

and disguised strategies, seek to contest and to undermine the dominant "value system."

This is the sense in which we will say, following Mikhail Bakhtin, that within this horizon class discourse—the categories in terms of which individual texts and cultural phenomena are now rewritten—is essentially *dialogical* in its structure.[2] As Bakhtin's (and Voloshinov's) own work in this field is relatively specialized, focusing primarily on the heterogeneous and explosive pluralism of moments of carnival or festival (moments, for example, such as the immense resurfacing of the whole spectrum of the religious or political sects in the English 1640s or the Soviet 1920s) it will be necessary to add the qualification that the normal form of the dialogical is essentially an *antagonistic* one, and that the dialogue of class struggle is one in which two opposing discourses fight it out within the general unity of a shared code. Thus, for instance, the shared master code of religion becomes in the 1640s in England the place in which the dominant formulations of a hegemonic theology are reappropriated and polemically modified.[3]

Within this new horizon, then, the basic formal requirement of dialectical analysis is maintained, and its elements are still restructured in terms of *contradiction* (this is essentially, as we have said, what distinguishes the rationality of a Marxist class analysis from static analysis of the sociological type). Where the contradiction of the earlier horizon was univocal, however, and limited to the situation of the individual text, to the place of a purely individual symbolic resolution, contradiction here appears in the form of the dialogical as the irreconcilable demands and positions of antagonistic classes. Here again, then, the requirement to prolong interpretation to the point at which this ultimate contradiction begins to appear offers a criterion for the completeness or insufficiency of the analysis.

Yet to rewrite the individual text, the individual cultural artifact, in terms of the antagonistic dialogue of class voices is to perform a rather different operation from the one we have ascribed to our first horizon. Now the individual text will be refocused as a *parole*, or individual utterance, of that vaster system, or *langue*, of class discourse. The individual text retains its formal structure as a symbolic act: yet the value and character of such symbolic action are now significantly modified and enlarged. On this rewriting, the individual utterance or text is grasped as a symbolic move in an essentially polemic and strategic ideological confrontation between the classes, and to describe it in these terms (or to reveal it in this form) demands a whole set of different instruments.

For one thing, the illusion or appearance of isolation or autonomy which a printed text projects must now be systematically undermined. Indeed, since by definition the cultural monuments and masterworks that have survived tend necessarily to perpetuate only a single voice in this class dialogue, the

2. Mikhail Bakhtin, *Problems of Dostoevsky's Poetics*, trans. R. W. Rotsel (Ann Arbor: Ardis, 1973), pp. 153–69. See also Bakhtin's important book on linguistics, written under the name of V. N. Voloshinov, *Marxism and the Philosophy of Language*, trans. L. Matejka and I. R. Titunik (New York: Seminar Press, 1973), pp. 83–98 [Jameson's note]. On the Russian theorist BAKHTIN (1895–1975) and the "dialogical" nature of the novel and discourse, see above. Some believe that to circumvent the suppression of his writings, he published some of his books under the name of a colleague, Valentin N. Vološinov (1895–1936).

3. See Christopher Hill, *The World Turned Upside Down* (London: Temple Smith, 1972) [Jameson's note].

voice of a hegemonic class, they cannot be properly assigned their relational place in a dialogical system without the restoration or artificial reconstruction of the voice to which they were initially opposed, a voice for the most part stifled and reduced to silence, marginalized, its own utterances scattered to the winds, or reappropriated in their turn by the hegemonic culture.

This is the framework in which the reconstruction of so-called popular cultures must properly take place—most notably, from the fragments of essentially peasant cultures: folk songs, fairy tales, popular festivals, occult or oppositional systems of belief such as magic and witchcraft. Such reconstruction is of a piece with the reaffirmation of the existence of marginalized or oppositional cultures in our own time, and the reaudition of the oppositional voices of black or ethnic cultures, women's and gay literature, "naive" or marginalized folk art, and the like. But once again, the affirmation of such nonhegemonic cultural voices remains ineffective if it is limited to the merely "sociological" perspective of the pluralistic rediscovery of other isolated social groups: only an ultimate rewriting of these utterances in terms of their essentially polemic and subversive strategies restores them to their proper place in the dialogical system of the social classes. Thus, for instance, Bloch's[4] reading of the fairy tale, with its magical wish-fulfillments and its Utopian fantasies of plenty and the *pays de Cocagne*, restores the dialogical and antagonistic content of this "form" by exhibiting it as a systematic deconstruction and undermining of the hegemonic aristocratic form of the epic, with its somber ideology of heroism and baleful destiny; thus also the work of Eugene Genovese on black religion restores the vitality of these utterances by reading them, not as the replication of imposed beliefs, but rather as a process whereby the hegemonic Christianity of the slave-owners is appropriated, secretly emptied of its content and subverted to the transmission of quite different oppositional and coded messages.[5]

Moreover, the stress on the dialogical then allows us to reread or rewrite the hegemonic forms themselves; they also can be grasped as a process of the reappropriation and neutralization, the cooptation and class transformation, the cultural universalization, of forms which originally expressed the situation of "popular," subordinate, or dominated groups. So the slave religion of Christianity is transformed into the hegemonic ideological apparatus of the medieval system; while folk music and peasant dance find themselves transmuted into the forms of aristocratic or court festivity and into the cultural visions of the pastoral; and popular narrative from time immemorial—romance, adventure story, melodrama, and the like—is ceaselessly drawn on to restore vitality to an enfeebled and asphyxiating "high culture." Just so, in our own time, the vernacular and its still vital sources of production (as in black language) are reappropriated by the exhausted and media-standardized speech of a hegemonic middle class. In the aesthetic realm, indeed, the process of cultural "universalization" (which implies the repression of the oppositional voice, and the illusion that there is only one genuine "culture") is the specific form taken by what can

4. Ernst Bloch (1885–1977), German philosopher, a Marxist whose "philosophy of hope" sees history ending in utopia, which he calls the *pays de Cocagne* ("land of plenty"; French).

5. Eugene Genovese, *Roll, Jordan, Roll: The World the Slaves Made* (New York: Vintage, 1976), pp. 161–284 [Jameson's note]. Genovese (1930–2012), American historian.

be called the process of legitimation in the realm of ideology and conceptual systems.

Still, this operation of rewriting and of the restoration of an essentially dialogical or class horizon will not be complete until we specify the "units" of this larger system. The linguistic metaphor (rewriting texts in terms of the opposition of a *parole* to a *langue*) cannot, in other words, be particularly fruitful until we are able to convey something of the dynamics proper to a class *langue* itself, which is evidently, in Saussure's sense, something like an ideal construct that is never wholly visible and never fully present in any one of its individual utterances. This larger class discourse can be said to be organized around minimal "units" which we will call *ideologemes*. The advantage of this formulation lies in its capacity to mediate between conceptions of ideology as abstract opinion, class value, and the like, and the narrative materials with which we will be working here. The ideologeme is an amphibious formation, whose essential structural characteristic may be described as its possibility to manifest itself either as a pseudoidea—a conceptual or belief system, an abstract value, an opinion or prejudice—or as a protonarrative, a kind of ultimate class fantasy about the "collective characters" which are the classes in opposition. This duality means that the basic requirement for the full description of the ideologeme is already given in advance: as a construct it must be susceptible to both a conceptual description and a narrative manifestation all at once. The ideologeme can of course be elaborated in either of these directions, taking on the finished appearance of a philosophical system on the one hand, or that of a cultural text on the other; but the ideological analysis of these finished cultural products requires us to demonstrate each one as a complex work of transformation on that ultimate raw material which is the ideologeme in question. The analyst's work is thus first that of the identification of the ideologeme, and, in many cases, of its initial naming in instances where for whatever reason it had not yet been registered as such. The immense preparatory task of identifying and inventorying such ideologemes has scarcely even begun, and to it the present book will make but the most modest contribution: most notably in its isolation of that fundamental nineteenth-century ideologeme which is the "theory" of *ressentiment*,[6] and in its "unmasking" of ethics and the ethical binary opposition of good and evil as one of the fundamental forms of ideological thought in Western culture. However, our stress here and throughout on the fundamentally narrative character of such ideologemes (even where they seem to be articulated only as abstract conceptual beliefs or values) will offer the advantage of restoring the complexity of the transactions between opinion and protonarrative or libidinal fantasy. Thus we will observe, in the case of Balzac, the generation of an overt and constituted ideological and political "value system" out of the operation of an essentially narrative and fantasy dynamic; the chapter on Gissing, on the other hand, will show how an already constituted "narrative paradigm" emits an ideological message in its own right without the mediation of authorial intervention.

This focus or horizon, that of class struggle and its antagonistic discourses, is, as we have already suggested, not the ultimate form a Marxist analysis of

6. Resentment (French); this theory was developed by the German philosopher FRIEDRICH NIETZSCHE (1844–1900).

culture can take. The example just alluded to—that of the seventeenth-century English revolution, in which the various classes and class fractions found themselves obliged to articulate their ideological struggles through the shared medium of a religious master code—can serve to dramatize the shift whereby these objects of study are reconstituted into a structurally distinct "text" specific to this final enlargement of the analytical frame. For the possibility of a displacement in emphasis is already given in this example: we have suggested that within the apparent unity of the theological code, the fundamental difference of antagonistic class positions can be made to emerge. In that case, the inverse move is also possible, and such concrete semantic differences can on the contrary be focused in such a way that what emerges is rather the all-embracing unity of a single code which they must share and which thus characterizes the larger unity of the social system. This new object—code, sign system, or system of the production of signs and codes—thus becomes an index of an entity of study which greatly transcends those earlier ones of the narrowly political (the symbolic act), and the social (class discourse and the ideologeme), and which we have proposed to term the historical in the larger sense of this word. Here the organizing unity will be what the Marxian tradition designates as a *mode of production*.

I have already observed that the "problematic" of modes of production is the most vital new area of Marxist theory in all the disciplines today; not paradoxically, it is also one of the most traditional, and we must therefore, in a brief preliminary way, sketch in the "sequence" of modes of production as classical Marxism, from Marx and Engels to Stalin,[7] tended to enumerate them.[8] These modes, or "stages" of human society, have traditionally included the following: primitive communism or tribal society (the horde), the *gens* or hierarchical kinship societies (neolithic society), the Asiatic mode of production (so-called Oriental despotism), the *polis* or an oligarchical slaveholding society (the ancient mode of production), feudalism, capitalism, and communism (with a good deal of debate as to whether the "transitional" stage between these last—sometimes called "socialism"—is a genuine mode of production in its own right or not). What is more significant in the present context is that even this schematic or mechanical conception of historical "stages" (what the Althusserians have systematically criticized under the term "historicism") includes the notion of a cultural dominant or form of ideological coding specific to each mode of production. Following the same order these have generally been conceived as magic and mythic narrative, kinship, religion or the sacred, "politics" according to the narrower category of citizenship in the ancient city state, relations of personal domination, commodity reification, and (presumably) original and as yet nowhere fully developed forms of collective or communal association.

7. Jameson suggests that "classical Marxism," or a Marxism relying on definite descriptions of classes, class struggle, and so on, was at its height between the time of Marx and his collaborator FRIEDRICH ENGELS (1820–1895) and that of Joseph Stalin (1879–1953), 2d leader of the U.S.S.R. (1924–53).

8. The "classical" texts on modes of production, besides Lewis Henry Morgan's *Ancient Society* (1877), are Karl Marx, *Pre-Capitalist Economic Formations*, a section of the *Grundrisse* (1857–58), and Friedrich Engels, *The Family, Private Property, and the State* (1884). An important recent contribution to the mode of production debate is Étienne Balibar's "The Basic Concepts of Historical Materialism," in Louis Althusser and Balibar, *Reading Capital*, trans. Ben Brewster (London: New Left Books, 1970), pp. 199–308 [Jameson's note]. Balibar (b. 1942), French political philosopher.

Before we can determine the cultural "text" or object of study specific to the horizon of modes of production, however, we must make two preliminary remarks about the methodological problems it raises. The first will bear on whether the concept of "mode of production" is a synchronic one, while the second will address the temptation to use the various modes of production for a classifying or typologizing operation, in which cultural texts are simply dropped into so many separate compartments.

Indeed, a number of theorists have been disturbed by the apparent convergence between the properly Marxian notion of an all-embracing and all-structuring mode of production (which assigns everything within itself—culture, ideological production, class articulation, technology—a specific and unique place), and non-Marxist visions of a "total system" in which the various elements or levels of social life are programmed in some increasingly constricting way. Weber's dramatic notion of the "iron cage" of an increasingly bureaucratic society,[9] Foucault's image of the gridwork of an ever more pervasive "political technology of the body,"[1] but also more traditional "synchronic" accounts of the cultural programming of a given historical "moment," such as those that have variously been proposed from Vico and Hegel to Spengler and Deleuze[2]—all such monolithic models of the cultural unity of a given historical period have tended to confirm the suspicions of a dialectical tradition about the dangers of an emergent "synchronic" thought, in which change and development are relegated to the marginalized category of the merely "diachronic," the contingent or the rigorously nonmeaningful (and this, even where, as with Althusser, such models of cultural unity are attacked as forms of a more properly Hegelian and idealistic "expressive causality"). This theoretical foreboding about the limits of synchronic thought can perhaps be most immediately grasped in the political area, where the model of the "total system" would seem slowly and inexorably to eliminate any possibility of the *negative* as such, and to reintegrate the place of an oppositional or even merely "critical" practice and resistance back into the system as the latter's mere inversion. In particular, everything about class struggle that was anticipatory in the older dialectical framework, and seen as an emergent space for radically new social relations, would seem, in the synchronic model, to reduce itself to practices that in fact tend to reinforce the very system that foresaw and dictated their specific limits. This is the sense

9. "The Puritan wanted to work in a calling; we are forced to do so. For when asceticism was carried out of monastic cells into everyday life, and began to dominate worldly morality, it did its part in building the tremendous cosmos of the modern economic order. This order is now bound to the technical and economic conditions of machine production which today determine the lives of all the individuals who are born into this mechanism, not only those directly concerned with economic acquisition, with irresistible force. Perhaps it will so determine them until the last ton of fossilized coal is burnt. In [one] view the care for external goods should only lie on the shoulders of the saint 'like a light cloak, which can be thrown aside at any moment.' But fate decreed that the cloak should become an iron cage." Max Weber, *The Protestant Ethic and the Spirit of Capitalism*, trans. T. Parsons (New York: Scribners, 1958), p. 181 [Jameson's note]. Weber (1864–1920), German sociologist who helped found the discipline.

1. Michel Foucault, *Discipline and Punish: The Birth of the Prison*, trans. Alan Sheridan (New York: Vintage, 1979), pp. 26ff. [Jameson's note]. FOUCAULT (1926–1984), French philosopher and historian of ideas.

2. All philosophers who made large claims about historical change: the Italian GIAMBATTISTA VICO (1668–1744) viewed historical change as a cycle; Hegel proposed a dialectical model of thesis, antithesis, and synthesis; the German Oswald Spengler (1880–1936) saw a pattern of decline; and the French GILLES DELEUZE (1925–1995) argued for a Nietzschean repetition modified for differences.

in which Jean Baudrillard[3] has suggested that the "total-system" view of contemporary society reduces the options of resistance to anarchist gestures, to the sole remaining ultimate protests of the wildcat strike, terrorism, and death. Meanwhile, in the framework of the analysis of culture also, the latter's integration into a synchronic model would seem to empty cultural production of all its antisystemic capacities, and to "unmask" even the works of an overtly oppositional or political stance as instruments ultimately programmed by the system itself.

It is, however, precisely the notion of a series of enlarging theoretical horizons proposed here that can assign these disturbing synchronic frameworks their appropriate analytical places and dictate their proper use. This notion projects a long view of history which is inconsistent with concrete political action and class struggle only if the specificity of the horizons is not respected; thus, even if the concept of a mode of production is to be considered a synchronic one (and we will see in a moment that things are somewhat more complicated than this), at the level of historical abstraction at which such a concept is properly to be used, the lesson of the "vision" of a total system is for the short run one of the structural limits imposed on praxis rather than the latter's impossibility.

The theoretical problem with the synchronic systems enumerated above lies elsewhere, and less in their analytical framework than in what in a Marxist perspective might be called their infrastructural regrounding. Historically, such systems have tended to fall into two general groups, which one might term respectively the hard and soft visions of the total system. The first group projects a fantasy future of a "totalitarian" type in which the mechanisms of domination—whether these are understood as part of the more general process of bureaucratization, or on the other hand derive more immediately from the deployment of physical and ideological force—are grasped as irrevocable and increasingly pervasive tendencies whose mission is to colonize the last remnants and survivals of human freedom—to occupy and organize, in other words, what still persists of Nature objectively and subjectively (very schematically, the Third World and the Unconscious).

This group of theories can perhaps hastily be associated with the central names of Weber and Foucault; the second group may then be associated with names such as those of Jean Baudrillard and the American theorists of a "post-industrial society."[4] For this second group, the characteristics of the total system of contemporary world society are less those of political domination than those of cultural programming and penetration: not the iron cage, but rather the *société de consommation* with its consumption of images and simulacra, its free-floating signifiers and its effacement of the older structures of social class and traditional ideological hegemony. For both groups, world capitalism is in evolution toward a system which is not socialist in any classical sense, on the one hand the nightmare of total control and on the other the polymorphous or schizophrenic intensities of some ultimate

3. French sociologist (1929–2007; see above), who argues that in postmodern society we deal only with simulations of reality (simulacra), not representations.

4. The most influential statement of the American version of this "end of ideology"/consumer society position is, of course, that of Daniel Bell: see his *Coming of Post-Industrial Society* (New York: Basic, 1973) and *The Cultural Contradictions of Capitalism* (New York: Basic, 1976) [Jameson's note]. Bell (1919–2011), American sociologist.

counterculture (which may be no less disturbing for some than the overtly threatening characteristics of the first vision). What one must add is that neither kind of analysis respects the Marxian injunction of the "ultimately determining instance" of economic organization and tendencies: for both, indeed, economics (or political economy) of that type is in the new total system of the contemporary world at an end, and the economic finds itself in both reassigned to a secondary and nondeterminant position beneath the new dominant of political power or of cultural production respectively.

There exist, however, within Marxism itself precise equivalents to these two non-Marxian visions of the contemporary total system: rewritings, if one likes, of both in specifically Marxian and "economic" terms. These are the analyses of late capitalism in terms of *capitalogic*[5] and of *disaccumulation*,[6] respectively; and while this book is clearly not the place to discuss such theories at any length, it must be observed here that both, seeing the originality of the contemporary situation in terms of systemic tendencies *within* capitalism, reassert the theoretical priority of the organizing concept of the mode of production which we have been concerned to argue.

We must therefore now turn to the second related problem about this third and ultimate horizon, and deal briefly with the objection that cultural analysis pursued within it will tend toward a purely typological or classificatory operation, in which we are called upon to "decide" such issues as whether Milton is to be read within a "precapitalist" or a nascent capitalist context, and so forth. I have insisted elsewhere on the sterility of such classificatory procedures, which may always, it seems to me, be taken as symptoms and indices of the repression of a more genuinely dialectical or historical practice of cultural analysis. This diagnosis may now be expanded to cover all three horizons at issue here, where the practice of homology, that of a merely "sociological" search for some social or class equivalent, and that, finally, of the use of some typology of social and cultural systems, respectively, may stand as examples of the misuse of these three frameworks. Furthermore, just as in our discussion of the first two we have stressed the centrality of the category of contradiction for any Marxist analysis (seen, within the first horizon, as that which the cultural and ideological artifact tries to "resolve," and in the second as the nature of the social and class conflict within which a given work is one act or gesture), so too here we can effectively validate the horizon of the mode of production by showing the form contradiction takes on this level, and the relationship of the cultural object to it.

Before we do so, we must take note of more recent objections to the very concept of the mode of production. The traditional schema of the various modes of production as so many historical "stages" has generally been felt to be unsatisfactory, not least because it encourages the kind of typologizing criticized above, in political quite as much as in cultural analysis. (The form taken in political analysis is evidently the procedure which consists in "decid-

5. See, for a review and critique of the basic literature, Stanley Aronowitz, "Marx, Braverman, and the Logic of Capital," *Insurgent Sociologist* 8, nos. 2/3 (fall 1978): 126–46 [Jameson's note].

6. The basic texts on "disaccumulation theory" are Martin J. Sklar, "On the Proletarian Revolution and the End of Political-Economic Society," *Radical America* 3, no. 3 (May–June 1969): 1–41; Jim O'Connor, "Productive and Unproductive Labor," *Politics and Society* 5 (1975): 297–336; Fred Block and Larry Hirschhorn, "New Productive Forces and the Contradictions of Contemporary Capitalism," *Theory and Society* 7 (1979): 363–95; and Stanley Aronowitz, "The End of Political Economy," *Social Text*, no. 2 (1980): 3–52 [Jameson's note].

ing" whether a given conjuncture[7] is to be assigned to a moment within feudalism—the result being a demand for bourgeois and parliamentary rights—or within capitalism—with the accompanying "reformist" strategy—or, on the contrary, a genuine "revolutionary" moment—in which case the appropriate revolutionary strategy is then deduced.)

On the other hand, it has become increasingly clear to a number of contemporary theorists that such classification of "empirical" materials within this or that abstract category is impermissible in large part because of the level of abstraction of the concept of a mode of production: no historical society has ever "embodied" a mode of production in any pure state (nor is *Capital*[8] the description of a historical society, but rather the construction of the abstract concept of capitalism). This has led certain contemporary theorists, most notably Nicos Poulantzas,[9] to insist on the distinction between a "mode of production" as a purely theoretical construction and a "social formation" that would involve the description of some historical society at a certain moment of its development. This distinction seems inadequate and even misleading, to the degree that it encourages the very empirical thinking which it was concerned to denounce, in other words, subsuming a particular or an empirical "fact" under this or that corresponding "abstraction." Yet one feature of Poulantzas' discussion of the "social formation" may be retained: his suggestion that every social formation or historically existing society has in fact consisted in the overlay and structural coexistence of *several* modes of production all at once, including vestiges and survivals of older modes of production, now relegated to structurally dependent positions within the new, as well as anticipatory tendencies which are potentially inconsistent with the existing system but have not yet generated an autonomous space of their own.

But if this suggestion is valid, then the problems of the "synchronic" system and of the typological temptation are both solved at one stroke. What is synchronic is the "concept" of the mode of production; the moment of the historical coexistence of several modes of production is not synchronic in this sense, but open to history in a dialectical way. The temptation to classify texts according to the appropriate mode of production is thereby removed, since the texts emerge in a space in which we may expect them to be crisscrossed and intersected by a variety of impulses from contradictory modes of cultural production all at once.

Yet we have still not characterized the specific object of study which is constructed by this new and final horizon. It cannot, as we have shown, consist in the concept of an individual mode of production (any more than, in our second horizon, the specific object of study could consist in a particular social class in isolation from the others). We will therefore suggest that this new and ultimate object may be designated, drawing on recent historical experience, as *cultural revolution*, that moment in which the coexistence of various modes of production becomes visibly antagonistic, their contradictions moving to the very center of political, social, and historical

7. Moment in social development at which various antagonistic and sometimes contradictory forces and trends combine.
8. See Marx, *Capital*, vol. 1 (1867).
9. Nicos Poulantzas, *Political Power and Social Classes*, trans. T. O'Hagan (London: New Left Books, 1973), pp. 13–16 [Jameson's note]. Poulantzas (1936–1979), Greek political theorist.

life. The incomplete Chinese experiment with a "proletarian" cultural revolution[1] may be invoked in support of the proposition that previous history has known a whole range of equivalents for similar processes to which the term may legitimately be extended. So the Western Enlightenment may be grasped as part of a properly bourgeois cultural revolution, in which the values and the discourses, the habits and the daily space, of the *ancien régime*[2] were systematically dismantled so that in their place could be set the new conceptualities, habits and life forms, and value systems of a capitalist market society. This process clearly involved a vaster historical rhythm than such punctual historical events as the French Revolution or the Industrial Revolution, and includes in its *longue durée*[3] such phenomena as those described by Weber in *The Protestant Ethic and the Spirit of Capitalism*—a work that can now in its turn be read as a contribution to the study of the bourgeois cultural revolution, just as the corpus of work on romanticism is now repositioned as the study of a significant and ambiguous moment in the resistance to this particular "great transformation," alongside the more specifically "popular" (precapitalist as well as working-class) forms of cultural resistance.

But if this is the case, then we must go further and suggest that all previous modes of production have been accompanied by cultural revolutions specific to them of which the neolithic "cultural revolution," say, the triumph of patriarchy over the older matriarchal or tribal forms, or the victory of Hellenic "justice" and the new legality of the *polis* over the vendetta system are only the most dramatic manifestations. The concept of cultural revolution, then—or more precisely, the reconstruction of the materials of cultural and literary history in the form of this new "text" or object of study which is cultural revolution—may be expected to project a whole new framework for the humanities, in which the study of culture in the widest sense could be placed on a materialist basis.

This description is, however, misleading to the degree to which it suggests that "cultural revolution" is a phenomenon limited to so-called "transitional" periods, during which social formations dominated by one mode of production undergo a radical restructuration in the course of which a different "dominant" emerges. The problem of such "transitions" is a traditional crux of the Marxian problematic of modes of production, nor can it be said that any of the solutions proposed, from Marx's own fragmentary discussions to the recent model of Etienne Balibar, are altogether satisfactory, since in all of them the inconsistency between a "synchronic" description of a given system and a "diachronic" account of the passage from one system to another seems to return with undiminished intensity. But our own discussion began with the idea that a given social formation consisted in the coexistence of various synchronic systems or modes of production, each with its own dynamic or time scheme—a kind of metasynchronicity, if one likes—while we have now shifted to a description of cultural revolution which has been

1. That is, the 1966–76 Cultural Revolution, an attempt to stamp out "bourgeois values" that caused great social and economic disruption in China.

2. That is, the aristocracy.

3. Long duration (French), a phrase used by the French historian Fernand Braudel (1902–1985), whose work emphasized large-scale, long-term changes.

couched in the more diachronic language of systemic transformation. I will therefore suggest that these two apparently inconsistent accounts are simply the twin perspectives which our thinking (and our presentation or *Darstellung* of that thinking) can take on this same vast historical object. Just as overt revolution is no punctual event either, but brings to the surface the innumerable daily struggles and forms of class polarization which are at work in the whole course of social life that precedes it, and which are therefore latent and implicit in "prerevolutionary" social experience, made visible as the latter's deep structure only in such "moments of truth"—so also the overtly "transitional" moments of cultural revolution are themselves but the passage to the surface of a permanent process in human societies, of a permanent struggle between the various coexisting modes of production. The triumphant moment in which a new systemic dominant gains ascendency is therefore only the diachronic manifestation of a constant struggle for the perpetuation and reproduction of its dominance, a struggle which must continue throughout its life course, accompanied at all moments by the systemic or structural antagonism of those older and newer modes of production that resist assimilation or seek deliverance from it. The task of cultural and social analysis thus construed within this final horizon will then clearly be the rewriting of its materials in such a way that this perpetual cultural revolution can be apprehended and read as the deeper and more permanent constitutive structure in which the empirical textual objects know intelligibility.

Cultural revolution thus conceived may be said to be beyond the opposition between synchrony and diachrony, and to correspond roughly to what Ernst Bloch has called the *Ungleichzeitigkeit* (or "nonsynchronous development") of cultural and social life.[4] Such a view imposes a new use of concepts of periodization, and in particular of that older schema of the "linear" stages which is here preserved and canceled all at once. We will deal more fully with the specific problems of periodization in the next chapter: suffice it to say at this point that such categories are produced within an initial diachronic or narrative framework, but become usable only when that initial framework has been annulled, allowing us now to coordinate or articulate categories of diachronic origin (the various distinct modes of production) in what is now a synchronic or metasynchronic way.

We have, however, not yet specified the nature of the textual object which is constructed by this third horizon of cultural revolution, and which would

4. Ernst Bloch, "Nonsynchronism and Dialectics," *New German Critique*, no. 11 (spring 1977): 22–38. The "nonsynchronous" use of the concept of the mode of production outlined above is in my opinion the only way to fulfill Marx's well-known program for dialectical knowledge "of rising from the abstract to the concrete" (1857 Introduction, *Grundrisse*, ed. Eric Hobsbawm [New York: International, 1965], p. 101). Marx there distinguished three stages of knowledge: (1) the notation of the particular (this would correspond to something like empirical history, the collection of data and descriptive materials on the variety of human societies); (2) the conquest of abstraction, the coming into being of a properly "bourgeois" science or of what Hegel called the categories of the Understanding; (3) the transcendence of abstraction by the dialectic, the "rise to the concrete," the setting in motion of hitherto static and typologizing categories by their reinsertion in a concrete historical situation (in the present context, this is achieved by moving from a classificatory use of the categories of modes of production to a perception of their dynamic and contradictory coexistence in a given cultural moment). Althusser's own epistemology, incidentally, is a gloss on this same fundamental passage of the 1857 Introduction, but one which succeeds only too well in eliminating its dialectical spirit (*For Marx*, trans. Ben Brewster [London: Verso, 1990], pp. 183ff.) [Jameson's note].

be the equivalent within this dialectically new framework of the objects of our first two horizons—the symbolic act, and the ideologeme or dialogical organization of class discourse. I will suggest that within this final horizon the individual text or cultural artifact (with its appearance of autonomy which was dissolved in specific and original ways within the first two horizons as well) is here restructured as a field of force in which the dynamics of sign systems of several distinct modes of production can be registered and apprehended. These dynamics—the newly constituted "text" of our third horizon—make up what can be termed *the ideology of form,* that is, the determinate contradiction of the specific messages emitted by the varied sign systems which coexist in a given artistic process as well as in its general social formation.

What must now be stressed is that at this level "form" is apprehended as content. The study of the ideology of form is no doubt grounded on a technical and formalistic analysis in the narrower sense, even though, unlike much traditional formal analysis, it seeks to reveal the active presence within the text of a number of discontinuous and heterogeneous formal processes. But at the level of analysis in question here, a dialectical reversal has taken place in which it has become possible to grasp such formal processes as sedimented content in their own right, as carrying ideological messages of their own, distinct from the ostensible or manifest content of the works; it has become possible, in other words, to display such formal operations from the standpoint of what Louis Hjelmslev[5] will call the "content of form" rather than the latter's "expression," which is generally the object of the various more narrowly formalizing approaches. The simplest and most accessible demonstration of this reversal may be found in the area of literary genre. Our next chapter, indeed, will model the process whereby generic specification and description can, in a given historical text, be transformed into the detection of a host of distinct generic messages—some of them objectified survivals from older modes of cultural production, some anticipatory, but all together projecting a formal conjuncture through which the "conjuncture" of coexisting modes of production at a given historical moment can be detected and allegorically articulated.

Meanwhile, that what we have called the ideology of form is something other than a retreat from social and historical questions into the more narrowly formal may be suggested by the relevance of this final perspective to more overtly political and theoretical concerns; we may take the much debated relation of Marxism to feminism as a particularly revealing illustration. The notion of overlapping modes of production outlined above has indeed the advantage of allowing us to short-circuit the false problem of the priority of the economic over the sexual, or of sexual oppression over that of social class. In our present perspective, it becomes clear that sexism and the patriarchal are to be grasped as the sedimentation and the virulent survival of forms of alienation specific to the oldest mode of production of human history, with its division of labor between men and women, and its division of power between youth and elder. The analysis of the ideology of form, properly completed, should reveal the formal persistence of such archaic structures of

5. Danish linguist (1899–1965).

alienation—and the sign systems specific to them—beneath the overlay of all the more recent and historically original types of alienation—such as political domination and commodity reification—which have become the dominants of that most complex of all cultural revolutions, late capitalism, in which all the earlier modes of production in one way or another structurally coexist. The affirmation of radical feminism, therefore, that to annul the patriarchal is the most *radical* political act—insofar as it includes and subsumes more partial demands, such as the liberation from the commodity form—is thus perfectly consistent with an expanded Marxian framework, for which the transformation of our own dominant mode of production must be accompanied and completed by an equally radical restructuration of all the more archaic modes of production with which it structurally coexists.

With this final horizon, then, we emerge into a space in which History itself becomes the ultimate ground as well as the untranscendable limit of our understanding in general and our textual interpretations in particular. This is, of course, also the moment in which the whole problem of interpretive priorities returns with a vengeance, and in which the practitioners of alternate or rival interpretive codes—far from having been persuaded that History is an interpretive code that includes and transcends all the others—will again assert "History" as simply one more code among others, with no particularly privileged status. This is most succinctly achieved when the critics of Marxist interpretation, borrowing its own traditional terminology, suggest that the Marxian interpretive operation involves a thematization and a reification of "History" which is not markedly different from the process whereby the other interpretive codes produce their own forms of thematic closure and offer themselves as absolute methods.

It should by now be clear that nothing is to be gained by opposing one reified theme—History—by another—Language—in a polemic debate as to ultimate priority of one over the other. The influential forms this debate has taken in recent years—as in Jürgen Habermas' attempt to subsume the "Marxist" model of production beneath a more all-embracing model of "communication" or intersubjectivity,[6] or in Umberto Eco's assertion of the priority of the Symbolic in general over the technological and productive systems which it must organize as *signs* before they can be used as *tools*[7]—are based on the misconception that the Marxian category of a "mode of production" is a form of technological or "productionist" determinism.

It would seem therefore more useful to ask ourselves, in conclusion, how History as a ground and as an absent cause can be conceived in such a way as to resist such thematization or reification, such transformation back into one optional code among others. We may suggest such a possibility obliquely by attention to what the Aristotelians would call the generic satisfaction specific to the form of the great monuments of historiography,[8] or what the semioticians might call the "history-effect" of such narrative texts. Whatever the raw material on which historiographic form works (and we will here only touch

6. See Jürgen Habermas, *Knowledge and Human Interests*, trans. J. Shapiro (Boston: Beacon, 1971), esp. Part I [Jameson's note]. HABERMAS (b. 1929), German philosopher.

7. Umberto Eco, *A Theory of Semiotics* (Bloomington: Indiana University Press, 1976), pp. 21–26 [Jameson's note]. Eco (1932–2016), Italian semiotician and novelist.

8. That is, emphasizing, as does ARISTOTLE in his *Poetics* (ca. 330 B.C.E.; see above), the importance of form.

on that most widespread type of material which is the sheer chronology of fact as it is produced by the rote-drill of the history manual), the "emotion" of great historiographic form can then always be seen as the radical restructuration of that inert material, in this instance the powerful reorganization of otherwise inert chronological and "linear" data in the form of Necessity: why what happened (at first received as "empirical" fact) had to happen the way it did. From this perspective, then, causality is only one of the possible tropes by which this formal restructuration can be achieved, although it has obviously been a privileged and historically significant one. Meanwhile, should it be objected that Marxism is rather a "comic" or "romance" paradigm, one which sees history in the salvational perspective of some ultimate liberation, we must observe that the most powerful realizations of a Marxist historiography—from Marx's own narratives of the 1848 revolution[9] through the rich and varied canonical studies of the dynamics of the Revolution of 1789 all the way to Charles Bettelheim's[1] study of the Soviet revolutionary experience—remain visions of historical Necessity in the sense evoked above. But Necessity is here represented in the form of the inexorable logic involved in the determinate failure of all the revolutions that have taken place in human history: the ultimate Marxian presupposition—that socialist revolution can only be a total and worldwide process (and that this in turn presupposes the completion of the capitalist "revolution" and of the process of commodification on a global scale)—is the perspective in which the failure or the blockage, the contradictory reversal or functional inversion, of this or that local revolutionary process is grasped as "inevitable," and as the operation of objective limits.

History is therefore the experience of Necessity, and it is this alone which can forestall its thematization or reification as a mere object of representation or as one master code among many others. Necessity is not in that sense a type of content, but rather the inexorable *form* of events; it is therefore a narrative category in the enlarged sense of some properly narrative political unconscious which has been argued here, a retextualization of History which does not propose the latter as some new representation or "vision," some new content, but as the formal effects of what Althusser, following Spinoza,[2] calls an "absent cause." Conceived in this sense, History is what hurts, it is what refuses desire and sets inexorable limits to individual as well as collective praxis, which its "ruses" turn into grisly and ironic reversals of their overt intention. But this History can be apprehended only through its effects, and never directly as some reified force. This is indeed the ultimate sense in which History as ground and untranscendable horizon needs no particular theoretical justification: we may be sure that its alienating necessities will not forget us, however much we might prefer to ignore them.

1981

9. The uprising in France that overthrew the constitutional monarchy of Louis-Philippe; Marx wrote about it in a series of articles in 1849–50 published together as *Class Struggles in France* (1895).

1. French economist and social scientist (1913–2006), who wrote *Class Struggles in the USSR* (3 vols., 1974–83).

2. BARUCH SPINOZA (1632–1677), Dutch rationalist philosopher.

Postmodernism and Consumer Society[1]

The concept of postmodernism is not widely accepted or even understood today. Some of the resistance to it may come from the unfamiliarity of the works it covers, which can be found in all the arts: the poetry of John Ashbery,[2] for instance, but also the much simpler talk poetry that came out of the reaction against complex, ironic, academic modernist poetry in the 1960s; the reaction against modern architecture and in particular against the monumental buildings of the International Style, the pop buildings and decorated sheds celebrated by Robert Venturi in his manifesto, *Learning from Las Vegas;*[3] Andy Warhol and Pop art, but also the more recent Photorealism;[4] in music, the moment of John Cage but also the later synthesis of classical and 'popular' styles found in composers like Philip Glass and Terry Riley, and also punk and new-wave rock with such groups as the Clash, Talking Heads and the Gang of Four;[5] in film, everything that comes out of Godard[6]—contemporary vanguard film and video—but also a whole new style of commercial or fiction films, which has its equivalent in contemporary novels as well, where the works of William Burroughs, Thomas Pynchon and Ishmael Reed[7] on the one hand, and the French new novel[8] on the other, are also to be numbered among the varieties of what can be called postmodernism.

This list would seem to make two things clear at once: first, most of the postmodernisms mentioned above emerge as specific reactions against the established forms of high modernism, against this or that dominant high modernism which conquered the university, the museum, the art gallery network, and the foundations. Those formerly subversive and embattled styles—Abstract Expressionism;[9] the great modernist poetry of Pound, Eliot or Wallace Stevens; the International Style (Le Corbusier, Frank Lloyd Wright, Mies); Stravinsky; Joyce, Proust and Mann[1]—felt to be scandalous or shocking by our grandparents are, for the generation which arrives at the gate in the 1960s, felt to be the establishment and the enemy—dead, stifling, canonical,

1. The present text combines elements of two previously published essays: "Postmodernism and Consumer Society," in *The Anti-Aesthetic* (Port Townsend, Wash.: Bay Press, 1983), and "Postmodernism: The Cultural Logic of Late Capitalism," in *New Left Review*, no. 146 (1984) [Jameson's note].

2. American poet (1927–2017) whose work is often obscure and demanding.

3. Published in 1972, by the American eclectic postmodern architect Venturi (b. 1925), Denise Scott Brown, and Steven Izenour. International Style: an architectural style, developed in Europe and the United States during the 1920s and 1930s and dominant by midcentury, characterized by rectilinear forms without ornamentation and by construction in glass and steel.

4. An art movement that flourished in the 1970s; it was an outgrowth of pop art, which came to prominence in the 1960s and also focused on everyday subjects from consumer and popular culture, such as the Campbell's Soup cans depicted by Warhol (1928–1987), its best-known American proponent.

5. Jameson names avant-garde musicians: the American composers Cage (1912–1992), Glass (b. 1937), and Riley (b. 1935); and the British punk band the Clash, the American art rock band Talking Heads, and the British Marxist band Gang of Four, all of whom released debut albums in the late 1970s.

6. Jean-Luc Godard (b. 1930), French film director.

7. All American authors of avant-garde fiction: Burroughs (1914–1997), Pynchon (b. 1937), and Reed (b. 1938).

8. A French literary movement that began in the 1950s and sought to frustrate conventional expectations of plot, character, and dialogue.

9. School of abstract painting that emerged in the United States, during the 1940s, characterized by attention to surface qualities, huge canvases, and the attempt to express pure emotion.

1. All prominent representatives of high modernism: in poetry, Ezra Pound (1885–1972), T. S. ELIOT (1888–1965), and Stevens (1879–1955), all Americans; in architecture, the French Le Corbusier (Charles Édouard Jeanneret, 1887–1965), the American Wright (1867–1959), and the German Ludwig Mies van der Rohe (1886–1969); in music, the Russian composer Igor Stravinsky (1882–1971); and in the novel, the Irish James Joyce (1882–1941), the French Marcel Proust (1871–1922), and the German Thomas Mann (1875–1955).

the reified monuments one has to destroy to do anything new. This means that there will be as many different forms of postmodernism as there were high modernisms in place, since the former are at least initially specific and local reactions *against* those models. That obviously does not make the job of describing postmodernism as a coherent thing any easier, since the unity of this new impulse—if it has one—is given not in itself but in the very modernism it seeks to displace.

The second feature of this list of postmodernisms is the effacement in it of some key boundaries or separations, most notably the erosion of the older distinction between high culture and so-called mass or popular culture. This is perhaps the most distressing development of all from an academic standpoint, which has traditionally had a vested interest in preserving a realm of high or elite culture against the surrounding environment of philistinism,[2] of schlock and kitsch, of TV series and *Reader's Digest* culture, and in transmitting difficult and complex skills of reading, listening and seeing to its initiates. But many of the newer postmodernisms have been fascinated precisely by that whole landscape of advertising and motels, of the Las Vegas strip, of the late show and Grade-B Hollywood film, of so-called paraliterature with its airport paperback categories of the gothic and the romance, the popular biography, the murder mystery and the science fiction or fantasy novel. They no longer 'quote' such 'texts' as a Joyce might have done, or a Mahler;[3] they incorporate them, to the point where the line between high art and commercial forms seems increasingly difficult to draw.

A rather different indication of this effacement of the older categories of genre and discourse can be found in what is sometimes called contemporary theory. A generation ago there was still a technical discourse of professional philosophy—the great systems of Sartre or the phenomenologists, the work of Wittgenstein[4] or analytical or common language philosophy—alongside which one could still distinguish that quite different discourse of the other academic disciplines—of political science, for example, or sociology or literary criticism. Today, increasingly, we have a kind of writing simply called 'theory' which is all or none of those things at once. This new kind of discourse, generally associated with France and so-called French theory, is becoming widespread and marks the end of philosophy as such. Is the work of Michel Foucault,[5] for example, to be called philosophy, history, social theory or political science? It's undecidable, as they say nowadays; and I will suggest that such 'theoretical discourse' is also to be numbered among the manifestations of postmodernism.

Now I must say a word about the proper use of this concept: it is not just another word for the description of a particular style. It is also, at least in my use, a periodizing concept whose function is to correlate the emergence of new formal features in culture with the emergence of a new type of social life and a new economic order—what is often euphemistically called modernization, postindustrial or consumer society, the society of the media or the spectacle, or multinational capitalism. This new moment of capitalism can be

2. Middle-class materialism (a term coined by MATTHEW ARNOLD in "The Function of Criticism at the Present Time," 1864; see above).
3. Gustav Mahler (1860–1911), Austrian composer.
4. Ludwig Wittgenstein (1889–1951), Austrian-born English philosopher whose early work was analytic and whose later work explored the nature of language. Jean-Paul Sartre (1905–1980), French existentialist philosopher, novelist, and dramatist. "Phenomenologists": philosophers who focus introspectively on the contents of consciousness.
5. French philosopher and historian of ideas (1926–1984; see above).

dated from the postwar boom in the United States in the late 1940s and early 1950s or, in France, from the establishment of the Fifth Republic in 1958.[6] The 1960s are in many ways the key transitional period, a period in which the new international order (neocolonialism, the Green Revolution,[7] computerization and electronic information) is at one and the same time set in place and is swept and shaken by its own internal contradictions and by external resistance. I want here to sketch a few of the ways in which the new postmodernism expresses the inner truth of that newly emergent social order of late capitalism, but will have to limit the description to only two of its significant features, which I will call pastiche and schizophrenia; they will give us a chance to sense the specificity of the postmodernist experience of space and time respectively.

Pastiche Eclipses Parody

One of the most significant features or practices in postmodernism today is pastiche. I must first explain this term, which people generally tend to confuse with or assimilate to that related verbal phenomenon called parody. Both pastiche and parody involve the imitation or, better still, the mimicry of other styles and particularly of the mannerisms and stylistic twitches of other styles. It is obvious that modern literature in general offers a very rich field for parody, since the great modern writers have all been defined by the invention or production of rather unique styles: think of the Faulknerian long sentence or of D. H. Lawrence's characteristic nature imagery; think of Wallace Stevens's peculiar way of using abstractions; think also of the mannerisms of the philosophers, of Heidegger for example, or Sartre; think of the musical styles of Mahler or Prokofiev.[8] All of these styles, however different from each other, are comparable in this: each is quite unmistakable; once one is learned, it is not likely to be confused with something else.

Now parody capitalizes on the uniqueness of these styles and seizes on their idiosyncrasies and eccentricities to produce an imitation which mocks the original. I won't say that the satiric impulse is conscious in all forms of parody. In any case, a good or great parodist has to have some secret sympathy for the original, just as a great mimic has to have the capacity to put himself/herself in the place of the person imitated. Still, the general effect of parody is—whether in sympathy or with malice—to cast ridicule on the private nature of these stylistic mannerisms and their excessiveness and eccentricity with respect to the way people normally speak or write. So there remains somewhere behind all parody the feeling that there is a linguistic norm in contrast to which the styles of the great modernists can be mocked.

But what would happen if one no longer believed in the existence of normal language, of ordinary speech, of the linguistic norm (the kind of clarity

6. The government established under a new constitution, written in response to the crisis brought on by France's colonial war in Algeria; Charles de Gaulle (1890–1970) became its first president in 1959.

7. The enormous increase in third world agricultural production (especially in India and Pakistan) in the 1960s made possible by new high-yield varieties of wheat and rice, the use of chemical fertilizers and pesticides, irrigation, and mechanization.

8. All innovators of modernism: the American novelist William Faulkner (1897–1962), the English novelist and poet Lawrence (1885–1930), the German philosopher MARTIN HEIDEGGER (1889–1976), and the Russian composer Sergei Prokofiev (1891–1953).

and communicative power celebrated by Orwell in his famous essay,[9] say)? One could think of it in this way; perhaps the immense fragmentation and privatization of modern literature—its explosion into a host of distinct private styles and mannerisms—foreshadows deeper and more general tendencies in social life as a whole. Supposing that modern art and modernism—far from being a kind of specialized aesthetic curiosity—actually anticipated social developments along these lines; supposing that in the decades since the emergence of the great modern styles society has itself begun to fragment in this way, each group coming to speak a curious private language of its own, each profession developing its private code or idiolect, and finally each individual coming to be a kind of linguistic island, separated from everyone else? But then in that case, the very possibility of any linguistic norm in terms of which one could ridicule private languages and idiosyncratic styles would vanish, and we would have nothing but stylistic diversity and heterogeneity.

That is the moment at which pastiche appears and parody has become impossible. Pastiche is, like parody, the imitation of a peculiar or unique style, the wearing of a stylistic mask, speech in a dead language: but it is a neutral practice of such mimicry, without parody's ulterior motive, without the satirical impulse, without laughter, without that still latent feeling that there exists something *normal* compared to which what is being imitated is rather comic. Pastiche is blank parody, parody that has lost its sense of humor: pastiche is to parody what that curious thing, the modern practice of a kind of blank irony, is to what Wayne Booth[1] calls the stable and comic ironies of, say, the eighteenth century.

The Death of the Subject

But now we need to introduce a new piece into this puzzle, which may help to explain why classical modernism is a thing of the past and why postmodernism should have taken its place. This new component is what is generally called the 'death of the subject'[2] or, to say it in more conventional language, the end of individualism as such. The great modernisms were, as we have said, predicated on the invention of a personal, private style, as unmistakable as your fingerprint, as incomparable as your own body. But this means that the modernist aesthetic is in some way organically linked to the conception of a unique self and private identity, a unique personality and individuality, which can be expected to generate its own unique vision of the world and to forge its own unique, unmistakable style.

Yet today, from any number of distinct perspectives, the social theorists, the psychoanalysts, even the linguists, not to speak of those of us who work in the area of culture and cultural and formal change, are all exploring the notion that that kind of individualism and personal identity is a thing of the past; that the old individual or individualist subject is 'dead'; and that one might even describe the concept of the unique individual and the theoretical basis of individualism as ideological. There are in fact two positions on all this, one of which is more radical than the other. The first one is content to

9. "Politics and the English Language" (1946), by the English novelist and essayist George Orwell (pen name of Eric Arthur Blair, 1903–1950).

1. American literary critic (1921–2005), author of *The Rhetoric of Irony* (1974).

2. Compare ROLAND BARTHES, "The Death of the Author" (1968; see above).

say: yes, once upon a time, in the classic age of competitive capitalism, in the heyday of the nuclear family and the emergence of the bourgeoisie as the hegemonic social class, there was such a thing as individualism, as individual subjects. But today, in the age of corporate capitalism, of the so-called organization man,[3] of bureaucracies in business as well as in the state, of demographic explosion—today, that older bourgeois individual subject no longer exists.

Then there is a second position, the more radical of the two, what one might call the poststructuralist position. It adds: not only is the bourgeois individual subject a thing of the past, it is also a myth; it *never* really existed in the first place; there have never been autonomous subjects of that type. Rather, this construct is merely a philosophical and cultural mystification which sought to persuade people that they 'had' individual subjects and possessed this unique personal identity.

For our purposes, it is not particularly important to decide which of these positions is correct (or rather, which is more interesting and productive). What we have to retain from all this is rather an aesthetic dilemma: because if the experience and the ideology of the unique self, an experience and ideology which informed the stylistic practice of classical modernism, is over and done with, then it is no longer clear what the artists and writers of the present period are supposed to be doing. What is clear is merely that the older models—Picasso,[4] Proust, T. S. Eliot—do not work any more (or are positively harmful), since nobody has that kind of unique private world and style to express any longer. And this is perhaps not merely a 'psychological' matter: we also have to take into account the immense weight of seventy or eighty years of classical modernism itself. There is another sense in which the writers and artists of the present day will no longer be able to invent new styles and worlds—they've already been invented; only a limited number of combinations are possible; the unique ones have been thought of already. So the weight of the whole modernist aesthetic tradition—now dead—also 'weighs like a nightmare on the brains of the living', as Marx said in another context.[5]

Hence, once again, pastiche: in a world in which stylistic innovation is no longer possible, all that is left is to imitate dead styles, to speak through the masks and with the voices of the styles in the imaginary museum. But this means that contemporary or postmodernist art is going to be about art itself in a new kind of way; even more, it means that one of its essential messages will involve the necessary failure of art and the aesthetic, the failure of the new, the imprisonment in the past.

The Nostalgia Mode

As this may seem very abstract, I want to give a few examples, one of which is so omnipresent that we rarely link it with the kinds of developments in high art discussed here. This particular practice of pastiche is not high-cultural but very much within mass culture, and it is generally known as the 'nostalgia film' (what the French neatly call *la mode rétro*—retrospective styling). We must conceive of this category in the broadest way: narrowly, no doubt, it con-

3. See William Whyte, *The Organization Man* (1956).
4. Pablo Picasso (1881–1973), Spanish painter and a pioneer of modernist art, especially cubism.
5. See *The Eighteenth Brumaire of Louis Bonaparte* (1852) by the German social and political philosopher KARL MARX (1818–1883).

sists merely of films about the past and about specific generational moments of that past. Thus, one of the inaugural films in this new 'genre' (if that's what it is) was Lucas's *American Graffiti*, which in 1973 set out to recapture all the atmosphere and stylistic peculiarities of the 1950s United States, the United States of the Eisenhower era. Polanski's great film *Chinatown* does something similar for the 1930s, as does Bertolucci's *The Conformist* for the Italian and European context of the same period, the fascist era in Italy;[6] and so forth. We could go on listing these films for some time: why call them pastiche? Are they not rather work in the more traditional genre known as the historical film—work which can more simply be theorized by extrapolating that other well-known form which is the historical novel?

I have my reasons for thinking that we need new categories for such films. But let me first add some anomalies: supposing I suggested that *Star Wars*[7] is also a nostalgia film. What could that mean? I presume we can agree that this is not a historical film about our own intergalactic past. Let me put it somewhat differently: one of the most important cultural experiences of the generations that grew up from the 1930s to the 1950s was the Saturday afternoon serial of the Buck Rogers[8] type—alien villains, true American heroes, heroines in distress, the death ray or the doomsday box, and the cliffhanger at the end whose miraculous resolution was to be witnessed next Saturday afternoon. *Star Wars* reinvents this experience in the form of a pastiche: that is, there is no longer any point to a parody of such serials since they are long extinct. *Star Wars*, far from being a pointless satire of such now dead forms, satisfies a deep (might I even say repressed?) longing to experience them again: it is a complex object in which on some first level children and adolescents can take the adventures straight, while the adult public is able to gratify a deeper and more properly nostalgic desire to return to that older period and to live its strange old aesthetic artifacts through once again. This film is thus *metonymically*[9] a historical or nostalgia film: unlike *American Graffiti*, it does not reinvent a picture of the past in its lived totality; rather, by reinventing the feel and shape of characteristic art objects of an older period (the serials), it seeks to reawaken a sense of the past associated with those objects. *Raiders of the Lost Ark*,[1] meanwhile, occupies an intermediary position here: on some level it is *about* the 1930s and 1940s, but in reality it too conveys that period metonymically through its own characteristic adventure stories (which are no longer ours).

Now let me discuss another interesting anomaly which may take us further towards understanding nostalgia film in particular and pastiche generally. This one involves a recent film called *Body Heat*,[2] which, as has abundantly been pointed out by the critics, is a kind of distant remake of *The Postman Always Rings Twice* or *Double Indemnity*. (The allusive and elusive plagiarism of older plots is, of course, also a feature of pastiche.) Now *Body Heat* is technically not a nostalgia film, since it takes place in a contemporary setting, in a little Florida village near Miami. On the other hand, this technical contem-

6. All films of the 1970s, set in the relatively recent past: *American Graffiti* (1973), directed by George Lucas (b. 1944), an American; *Chinatown* (1974), directed by Roman Polanski (b. 1933), raised in Poland; and *The Conformist* (1970), written and directed by Bernardo Bertolucci (b. 1940), an Italian.

7. A 1977 film, written and directed by Lucas.

8. Hero of a comic strip created in 1929 featuring science fiction adventures, later popularized in movie serials.

9. Through association, not through resemblance.

1. A 1981 film, directed by Steven Spielberg; the story is by Lucas.

2. This 1981 film, starring William Hurt (b. 1950), follows the same seduction-murder plot line as the films noir named, *The Postman Always Rings Twice* (1946) and *Double Indemnity* (1944).

poraneity is most ambiguous indeed: the credits—always our first cue—are lettered and scripted in a 1930s Art-Deco style which cannot but trigger nostalgic reactions (first to *Chinatown*, no doubt, and then beyond it to some more historical referent). Then the very style of the hero himself is ambiguous: William Hurt is a new star but has nothing of the distinctive style of the preceding generation of male superstars like Steve McQueen or even Jack Nicholson, or rather, his persona here is a kind of mix of their characteristics with an older role of the type generally associated with Clark Gable.[3] So here too there is a faintly archaic feel to all this. The spectator begins to wonder why this story, which could have been situated anywhere, is set in a small Florida town, in spite of its contemporary reference. One begins to realize after a while that the small town setting has a crucial strategic function: it allows the film to do without most of the signals and references which we might associate with the contemporary world, with consumer society—the appliances and artifacts, the high rises, the object world of late capitalism. Technically, then, its objects (its cars, for instance) are 1980s products, but everything in the film conspires to blur that immediate contemporary reference and to make it possible to receive this too as nostalgia work—as a narrative set in some indefinable nostalgic past, an eternal 1930s, say, beyond history. It seems to me exceedingly symptomatic to find the very style of nostalgia films invading and colonizing even those movies today which have contemporary settings: as though, for some reason, we were unable today to focus our own present, as though we have become incapable of achieving aesthetic representations of our own current experience. But if that is so, then it is a terrible indictment of consumer capitalism itself—or, at the very least, an alarming and pathological symptom of a society that has become incapable of dealing with time and history.

So now we come back to the question of why nostalgia film or pastiche is to be considered different from the older historical novel or film. (I should also include in this discussion the major literary example of all this, to my mind: the novels of E. L. Doctorow[4]—*Ragtime*, with its turn-of-the-century atmosphere, and *Loon Lake*, for the most part about our 1930s. But these are, in my opinion, historical novels in appearance only. Doctorow is a serious artist and one of the few genuinely left or radical novelists at work today. It is no disservice to him, however, to suggest that his narratives do not represent our historical past so much as they represent our ideas or cultural stereotypes about that past.) Cultural production has been driven back inside the mind, within the monadic subject: it can no longer look directly out of its eyes at the real world for the referent but must, as in Plato's cave,[5] trace its mental images of the world on its confining walls. If there is any realism left here, it is a 'realism' which springs from the shock of grasping that confinement and of realizing that, for whatever peculiar reasons, we seem condemned to seek the historical past through our own pop images and stereotypes about that past, which itself remains forever out of reach.

3. Gable (1901–1960), like McQueen (1930–1980) and Nicholson (b. 1937), an American leading man.
4. American novelist (1931–2015), who published *Ragtime* in 1975 and *Loon Lake* in 1980.
5. That is, the allegory of the cave that opens book 7 of *Republic* (see above), by the Greek philosopher PLATO (ca. 427–ca. 347 B.C.E.); it describes the majority of humanity as trapped in a cave, seeing only the shadows cast by the representations of real objects (the "real" being the Forms or Ideas of things, located outside the cave). This view is echoed in the argument of the French theorist JEAN BAUDRILLARD (1929–2007) that in postmodernity we deal only with simulations of things (their simulacra), not with the things themselves or even with their representations.

Postmodernism and the City

Now, before I try to offer a somewhat more positive conclusion, I want to sketch the analysis of a full-blown postmodern building—a work which is in many ways uncharacteristic of that postmodern architecture whose principal names are Robert Venturi, Charles Moore, Michael Graves, and more recently Frank Gehry,[6] but which to my mind offers some very striking lessons about the originality of postmodernist space. Let me amplify the figure which has run through the preceding remarks, and make it even more explicit: I am proposing the notion that we are here in the presence of something like a mutation in built space itself. My implication is that we ourselves, the human subjects who happen into this new space, have not kept pace with that evolution; there has been a mutation in the object, unaccompanied as yet by any equivalent mutation in the subject; we do not yet possess the perceptual equipment to match this new hyperspace, as I will call it, in part because our perceptual habits were formed in that older kind of space I have called the space of high modernism. The newer architecture therefore—like many of the other cultural products I have evoked in the preceding remarks—stands as something like an imperative to grow new organs to expand our sensorium and our body to some new, as yet unimaginable, perhaps ultimately impossible, dimensions.

THE BONAVENTURE HOTEL

The building whose features I will very rapidily enumerate in the next few moments is the Bonaventure Hotel, built in the new Los Angeles downtown by the architect and developer John Portman,[7] whose other works include the various Hyatt Regencies, the Peachtree Center in Atlanta, and the Renaissance Center in Detroit. I have mentioned the populist aspect of the rhetorical defence of postmodernism against the elite (and utopian) austerities of the great architectural modernisms: it is generally affirmed, in other words, that these newer building are popular works on the one hand; and that they respect the vernacular of the American city fabric on the other, that is to say, that they no longer attempt, as did the masterworks and monuments of high modernism, to insert a different, a distinct, an elevated, a new utopian language into the tawdry and commercial sign-system of the surrounding city, but rather, on the contrary, seek to speak that very language, using its lexicon and syntax as that has been emblematically 'learned from Las Vegas'.

On the first of these counts, Portman's Bonaventure fully confirms the claim: it is a popular building, visited with enthusiasm by locals and tourists alike (although Portman's other buildings are even more successful in this respect). The populist insertion into the city fabric is, however, another matter, and it is with this that we will begin. There are three entrances to the Bonaventure, one from Figueroa, and the other two by way of elevated gardens on the other side of the hotel, which is built into the remaining slope of the former Beacon Hill. None of these is anything like the old hotel marquee, or the monumental *porte-cochère*[8] with which the sumptuous buildings of yesteryear were wont to stage your passage from city street to the older inte-

6. All prominent American architects: Moore (1925–1993), Graves (1934–2015), and the Canadian-born Gehry (b. 1929).

7. Influential American architect (b. 1924).

8. Coach doorway (French); now, a porch roof extending from an entrance over a driveway.

rior. The entryways of the Bonaventure are as it were lateral and rather back-door affairs: the gardens in the back admit you to the sixth floor of the towers, and even there you must walk down one flight to find the elevator by which you gain access to the lobby. Meanwhile, what one is still tempted to think of as the front entry, on Figueroa, admits you, baggage and all, onto the second-story balcony, from which you must take an escalator down to the main registration desk. More about these elevators and escalators in a moment. What I first want to suggest about these curiously unmarked ways-in is that they seem to have been imposed by some new category of closure governing the inner space of the hotel itself (and this over and above the material constraints under which Portman had to work). I believe that, with a certain number of other characteristic postmodern buildings, such as the Beaubourg in Paris, or the Eaton Centre in Toronto, the Bonaventure aspires to being a total space, a complete world, a kind of miniature city (and I would want to add that to this new total space corresponds a new collective practice, a new mode in which individuals move and congregate, something like the practice of a new and historically original kind of hyper-crowd). In this sense, then, ideally the mini-city of Portman's Bonaventure ought not to have entrances at all, since the entryway is always the seam that links the building to the rest of the city that surrounds it: for it does not wish to be a part of the city, but rather its equivalent and its replacement or substitute. That is, however, obviously not possible or practical, whence the deliberate downplaying and reduction of the entrance function to its bare minimum. But this disjunction from the surrounding city is very different from that of the great monuments of the International Style: there, the act of disjunction was violent, visible, and had a very real symbolic significance—as in Le Corbusier's great *pilotis*[9] whose gesture radically separates the new utopian space of the modern from the degraded and fallen city fabric which it thereby explicitly repudiates (although the gamble of the modern was that this new utopian space, in the virulence of its Novum,[1] would fan out and transform that eventually by the power of its new spatial language). The Bonaventure, however, is content to 'let the fallen city fabric continue to be in its being' (to parody Heidegger[2]); no further effects, no larger protopolitical utopian transformation, is either expected or desired.

This diagnosis is to my mind confirmed by the great reflective glass skin of the Bonaventure, whose function I will now interpret rather differently that I did a moment ago when I saw the phenomenon of reflexion generally as developing a thematics of reproductive technology (the two readings are however not incompatible). Now one would want rather to stress the way in which the glass skin repels the city outside; a repulsion for which we have analogies in those reflector sunglasses which make it impossible for your interlocutor to see your own eyes and thereby achieve a certain aggressivity towards and power over the Other. In a similar way, the glass skin achieves a peculiar and placeless dissociation of the Bonaventure from its neighborhood: it is not even an exterior, inasmuch as when you seek to look at the hotel's outer walls you cannot see the hotel itself, but only the distorted images of everything that surrounds it.

9. Pilings (French), pillars that support a building and make bearing walls unnecessary; Le Corbusier used them to leave the ground floor open.

1. New thing, novelty (Latin).

2. Jameson echoes language often used by Heidegger in *Being and Time* (1927).

Now I want to say a few words about escalators and elevators: given their very real pleasures in Portman, particularly these last, which the artist has termed 'gigantic kinetic sculptures' and which certainly account for much of the spectacle and the excitement of the hotel interior, particularly in the Hyatts, where like great Japanese lanterns or gondolas they ceaselessly rise and fall—given such a deliberate marking and foregrounding in their own right, I believe one has to see such 'people movers' (Portman's own term, adapted from Disney[3]) as something a little more than mere functions and engineering components. We know in any case that recent architectural theory has begun to borrow from narrative analysis in other fields, and to attempt to see our physical trajectories through such buildings as virtual narratives or stories, as dynamic paths and narrative paradigms which we as visitors are asked to fulfill and to complete with our own bodies and movements. In the Bonaventure, however, we find a dialectical heightening of this process: it seems to me that the escalators and elevators here henceforth replace movement but also and above all designate themselves as new reflexive signs and emblems of movement proper (something which will become evident when we come to the whole question of what remains of older forms of movement in this building, most notably walking itself). Here the narrative stroll has been underscored, symbolized, reified and replaced by a transportation machine which becomes the allegorical signifier of that older promenade we are no longer allowed to conduct on our own: and this is a dialectical intensification of the autoreferentiality of all modern culture, which tends to turn upon itself and designate its own cultural production as its content.

I am more at a loss when it comes to conveying the thing itself, the experience of space you undergo when you step off such allegorical devices into the lobby or atrium, with its great central column, surrounded by a miniature lake, the whole positioned between the four symmetrical residential towers with their elevators, and surrounded by rising balconies capped by a kind of greenhouse roof at the sixth level. I am tempted to say that such space makes it impossible for us to use the language of volume or volumes any longer, since these last are impossible to seize. Hanging streamers indeed suffuse this empty space in such a way as to distract systematically and deliberately from whatever form it might be supposed to have; while a constant busyness gives the feeling that emptiness is here absolutely packed, that it is an element within which you yourself are immersed, without any of that distance that formerly enabled the perception of perspective or volume. You are in this hyperspace up to your eyes and your body; and if it seemed to you before that that suppression of depth I spoke of in postmodern painting or literature would necessarily be difficult to achieve in architecture itself, perhaps you may now be willing to see this bewildering immersion as the formal equivalent in the new medium.

Yet escalator and elevator are also in this context dialectical opposites; and we may suggest that the glorious movement of the elevator gondolas is also a dialectical compensation for this filled space of the atrium—it gives us the chance at a radically different, but complementary, spatial experience, that of rapidly shooting up through the ceiling and outside, along one of the four symmetrical towers, with the referent, Los Angeles itself, spread out breathtakingly and even alarmingly before us. But even this vertical movement is

3. Walt Disney (1901–1966), American animator and filmmaker who planned the amusement parks Disneyland and Walt Disney World; they included escalators and monorails, which Disney called "people movers."

contained: the elevator lifts you to one of those revolving cocktail lounges, in which you, seated, are again passively rotated about and offered a contemplative spectacle of the city itself, now transformed into its own images by the glass windows through which you view it.

Let me quickly conclude all this by returning to the central space of the lobby itself (with the passing observation that the hotel rooms are visibly marginalized: the corridors in the residential sections are low-ceilinged and dark, most depressingly functional indeed: while one understands that the rooms are in the worst of taste). The descent is dramatic enough, plummeting back down through the roof to splash down in the lake; what happens when you get there is something else, which I can only try to characterize as milling confusion, something like the vengeance this space takes on those who still seek to walk through it. Given the absolute symmetry of the four towers, it is quite impossible to get your bearings in this lobby; recently, colour coding and directional signals have been added in a pitiful and revealing, rather desperate attempt to restore the coordinates of an older space. I will take as the most dramatic practical result of this spatial mutation the notorious dilemma of the shopkeepers on the various balconies: it has been obvious, since the very opening of the hotel in 1977, that nobody could ever find any of these stores, and even if you located the appropriate boutique, you would be most unlikely to be as fortunate a second time; as a consequence, the commercial tenants are in despair and all the merchandise is marked down to bargain prices. When you recall that Portman is a businessman as well as an architect, and a millionaire developer, an artist who is at one and the same time a capitalist in his own right, you cannot but feel that here too something of a 'return of the repressed' is involved.

So I come finally to my principal point here, that this latest mutation in space—postmodern hyperspace—has finally succeeded in transcending the capacities of the individual human body to locate itself, to organize its immediate surroundings perceptually, and cognitively to map its position in a mappable external world. And I have already suggested that this alarming disjunction point between the body and its built environment—which is to the initial bewilderment of the older modernism as the velocities of spacecraft are to those of the automobile—can itself stand as the symbol and analog of that even sharper dilemma which is the incapacity of our minds, at least at present, to map the great global multinational and decentered communicational network in which we find ourselves caught as individual subjects.

THE NEW MACHINE

But as I am anxious that Portman's space not be perceived as something either exceptional or seemingly marginalized and leisure-specialized on the order of Disneyland, I would like in passing to juxtapose this complacent and entertaining (although bewildering) leisure-time space with its analog in a very different area, namely the space of postmodern warfare, in particular as Michael Herr evokes it in his great book on the experience of Vietnam, called *Dispatches*.[4] The extraordinary linguistic innovations of this work may still be considered postmodern, in the eclectic way in which its language impersonally fuses a whole range of contemporary collective idiolects, most notably rock language and black language: but the fusion is dictated by problems of

4. A memoir published in 1977; Herr (1940–2016) was an American journalist.

content. This first terrible postmodernist war cannot be told in any of the traditional paradigms of the war novel or movie—indeed that breakdown of all previous narrative paradigms is, along with the breakdown of any shared language through which a veteran might convey such experience, among the principal subjects of the book and may be said to open up the place of a whole new reflexivity. Benjamin's account of Baudelaire,[5] and of the emergence of modernism from a new experience of city technology which transcends all the older habits of bodily perception, is both singularly relevant here, and singularly antiquated, in the light of this new and virtually unimaginable quantum leap in technological alienation:

> He was a moving-target-survivor subscriber, a true child of the war, because except for the rare times when you were pinned or stranded the system was geared to keep you mobile, if that was what you thought you wanted. As a technique for staying alive it seemed to make as much sense as anything, given naturally that you were there to begin with and wanted to see it close; it started out sound and straight but it formed a cone as it progressed, because the more you moved the more you saw, the more you saw the more besides death and mutilation you risked, and the more you risked of that the more you would have to let go of one day as a 'survivor'. Some of us moved around the war like crazy people until we couldn't see which way the run was taking us anymore, only the war all over its surface with occasional, unexpected penetration. As long as we could have choppers like taxis it took real exhaustion or depression near shock or a dozen pipes of opium to keep us even apparently quiet, we'd still be running around inside our skins like something was after us, ha, ha, La Vida Loca.[6] In the months after I got back the hundreds of helicopters I'd flown in begin to draw together until they'd formed a collective meta-chopper, and in my mind it was the sexiest thing going; saver-destroyer, provider-waster, right hand-left hand, nimble, fluent, canny and human; hot steel, grease, jungle-saturated canvas webbing, sweat cooling and warming up again, cassette rock and roll in one ear and door-gun fire in the other, fuel, heat, vitality and death, death itself, hardly an intruder.[7]

In this new machine, which does not, like the older modernist machinery of the locomotive or the airplane, represent motion, but which can only be represented *in motion*, something of the mystery of the new postmodernist space is concentrated.

The Aesthetic of Consumer Society

Now I must try very rapidly in conclusion to characterize the relationship of cultural production of this kind to social life in this country today. This will also be the moment to address the principal objection to concepts of postmodernism of the type I have sketched here: namely that all the features we have enumerated are not new at all but abundantly characterized modern-

5. Charles Baudelaire (1821–1867), French poet; the German critic WALTER BENJAMIN (1892–1940) discusses him and 19th-century Paris in his unfinished *Arcades Project* (1983; trans. 1999), part of which was published earlier as *Charles Baudelaire: A Lyric Poet in the Era of High Capitalism* (1969; trans. 1973).

6. The Crazy Life (Spanish).

7. Michael Herr, *Dispatches* (New York: Knopf, 1977), pp. 8–9 [Jameson's note].

ism proper or what I call high modernism. Was not Thomas Mann, after all, interested in the idea of pastiche, and are not certain chapters of *Ulysses* its most obvious realization? Can Flaubert, Mallarmé and Gertrude Stein[8] not be included in an account of postmodernist temporality? What is so new about all of this? Do we really need the concept of *post*modernism?

One kind of answer to this question would raise the whole issue of periodization and of how a historian (literary or other) posits a radical break between two henceforth distinct periods. I must limit myself to the suggestion that radical breaks between periods do not generally involve complete changes of content but rather the restructuring of a certain number of elements already given: features that in an earlier period or system were subordinate now become dominant, and features that had been dominant again become secondary. In this sense, everything we have described here can be found in earlier periods and most notably within modernism proper: my point is that until the present day those things have been secondary or minor features of modernist art, marginal rather than central, and that we have something new when they become the central features of cultural production.

But I can argue this more concretely by turning to the relationship between cultural production and social life generally. The older or classical modernism was an oppositional art; it emerged within the business society of the gilded age[9] as scandalous and offensive to the middle-class public—ugly, dissonant, bohemian, sexually shocking. It was something to make fun of (when the police were not called in to seize the books or close the exhibitions): an offense to good taste and to common sense, or, as Freud and Marcuse[1] would have put it, a provocative challenge to the reigning reality- and performance-principles of early twentieth-century middle-class society. Modernism in general did not go well with over-stuffed Victorian furniture, with Victorian moral taboos, or with the conventions of polite society. This is to say that whatever the explicit political content of the great high modernisms, the latter were always in some mostly implicit ways dangerous and explosive, subversive within the established order.

If then we suddenly return to the present day, we can measure the immensity of the cultural changes that have taken place. Not only are Joyce and Picasso no longer weird and repulsive, they have become classics and now look rather realistic to us. Meanwhile, there is very little in either the form or the content of contemporary art that contemporary society finds intolerable and scandalous. The most offensive forms of this art—punk rock, say, or what is called sexually explicit material—are all taken in stride by society, and they are commercially successful, unlike the productions of the older high modernism. But this means that even if contemporary art has all the same formal features as the older modernism, it has still shifted its position fundamentally within our culture. For one thing, commodity production and in particular our clothing, furniture, buildings and other artifacts are now intimately tied in with styling changes which derive from artistic experimentation; our advertising, for example, is fed by postmodernism in all the arts and inconceivable without it. For another, the classics of high modernism are now part of the

8. American modernist (1874–1946), who was innovative in poetry and prose. *Ulysses* (1922), Joyce's landmark modernist novel. Gustave Flaubert (1821–1880), French novelist. Stéphane Mallarmé (1842–1898), French poet.

9. Era in late 19th-century America of rapid industrial expansion, burgeoning wealth for some, and gaudy materialism (the name is taken from an 1873 novel by Mark Twain and Charles Dudley Warner).

1. Herbert Marcuse (1898–1979), German-born American philosopher and social critic. SIGMUND FREUD (1856–1939), Austrian founder of psychoanalysis.

so-called canon and are taught in schools and universities—which at once empties them of any of their older subversive power. Indeed, one way of marking the break between the periods and of dating the emergence of postmodernism is precisely to be found there: in the moment (the early 1960s, one would think) in which the position of high modernism and its dominant aesthetics become established in the academy and are henceforth felt to be academic by a whole new generation of poets, painters and musicians.

But one can also come at the break from the other side, and describe it in terms of periods of recent social life. As I have suggested, non-Marxists and Marxists alike have come around to the general feeling that at some point following World War II a new kind of society began to emerge (variously described as postindustrial society, multinational capitalism, consumer society, media society and so forth). New types of consumption; planned obsolescence; an ever more rapid rhythm of fashion and styling changes; the penetration of advertising, television and the media generally to a hitherto unparalleled degree throughout society; the replacement of the old tension between city and country, center and province, by the suburb and by universal standardization; the growth of the great networks of superhighways and the arrival of automobile culture—these are some of the features which would seem to mark a radical break with that older prewar society in which high modernism was still an underground force.

I believe that the emergence of postmodernism is closely related to the emergence of this new moment of late, consumer or multinational capitalism. I believe also that its formal features in many ways express the deeper logic of that particular social system. I will only be able, however, to show this for one major theme: namely the disappearance of a sense of history, the way in which our entire contemporary social system has little by little begun to lose its capacity to retain its own past, has begun to live in a perpetual present and in a perpetual change that obliterates traditions of the kind which all earlier social formations have had in one way or another to preserve. Think only of the media exhaustion of news: of how Nixon and, even more so, Kennedy[2] are figures from a now distant past. One is tempted to say that the very function of the news media is to relegate such recent historical experiences as rapidly as possible into the past. The informational function of the media would thus be to help us forget, to serve as the very agents and mechanisms for our historical amnesia.

But in that case the two features of postmodernism on which I have dwelt here—the transformation of reality into images, the fragmentation of time into a series of perpetual presents—are both extraordinarily consonant with this process. My own conclusion here must take the form of a question about the critical value of the newer art. There is some agreement that the older modernism functioned against its society in ways which are variously described as critical, negative, contestatory, subversive, oppositional and the like. Can anything of the sort be affirmed about postmodernism and its social moment? We have seen that there is a way in which postmodernism replicates or reproduces—reinforces—the logic of consumer capitalism; the more significant question is whether there is also a way in which it resists that logic. But that is a question we must leave open.

1988

2. John F. Kennedy (1917–1963), 35th U.S. president (1961–63). Richard Nixon (1913–1994), 37th U.S. president (1969–74), who lost to Kennedy in the 1960 election.

DAVID HARVEY
b. 1935

David Harvey is a leading theorist of contemporary capitalism, updating the Marxist tradition to explain postmodernism and neoliberalism. A geographer by training, he describes how capitalism operates over the expanse of the globe and remakes our spaces, often exploiting labor as well as resources. In our selections from his best-selling *A Brief History of Neoliberalism* (2005), he succinctly defines the policies and practices of neoliberalism, tracing its rise from the 1970s onward and critiquing its tendency toward "accumulation by dispossession," as it draws wealth from poorly paid "disposable workers."

Born in Kent, England, in 1935, Harvey attended Cambridge University (B.A., 1957; Ph.D., 1961). After teaching at the University of Bristol (1961–69), he went to the United States to teach at Johns Hopkins University (1969–87); there he established a seminar studying KARL MARX's *Capital* every year. In 1987 he became the Halford Mackinder Professor of Geography at Oxford, but he returned to Johns Hopkins in 1993. In 2001 he moved to the Graduate Center of the City University of New York as Distinguished Professor of Anthropology.

While Marx declared in *The Communist Manifesto* (1848; see above) that "The history of all hitherto existing society is the history of class struggles," he also distinguished several modes of production, which progressed from ancient hunting and gathering to feudalism and to modern capitalism. Famously, Marx predicted that the next mode of production will be socialism or communism. In more recent years, theorists have distinguished different phases of capitalism itself. In *Late Capitalism* (1972), the radical theorist Ernest Mandel argued that capitalism encompasses three stages: entrepreneurial capitalism in the eighteenth and nineteenth centuries, imperialism in the late nineteenth through the twentieth century, and postindustrial or consumer capitalism after World War II. In "Postmodernism and Consumer Society" (1988; see above), FREDRIC JAMESON applied Mandel's scheme to culture, finding that the first stage corresponded to the European realist novel, the second to modernism, and the third to postmodernism.

In his landmark book *The Condition of Postmodernity: An Enquiry into the Origins of Cultural Change* (1989), Harvey developed his own interpretation of postmodernism, diagnosing the bewildering changes in the economy since the 1970s as "post-Fordism," which exhibits a new form of "flexible accumulation." The previous moment, "Fordism," takes its name from the American pioneering automobile manufacturer Henry Ford, who in the early twentieth century paid his workers a relatively high wage so that they could buy the products they were producing. This general policy is often credited with creating a prosperous American middle class, whose members were paid reasonably well and whose spending in turn could spur the consumer economy. But after a recession and an oil crisis during the 1970s, labor lost power, wages stagnated or fell, and capitalist owners adopted more flexible practices, moving production at will from nationally based businesses to "multinational" ones. As a geographer, Harvey has focused on the movements of capital and labor around the world; rather than relying on a factory fixed in one place manufacturing large stocks, the post-Fordist model emphasizes "just-in-time" production, utilizing the cheapest locations and undermining any concerted power wielded by labor. A car sold in the United States, for instance, might be assembled in Mexico from parts fabricated in China, Korea, and Ohio out of raw materials shipped from various countries in South America and Africa. Rather than accumulating wealth in one stable location—say Detroit, during the heyday of American automobile manufacturing, or Manchester, during the heyday of British industrialism—the model has shifted to flexible accumulation.

Through the 1990s, Harvey turned to look at "neoliberalism," a label he came to prefer to "postmodernism," which has a range of meanings in art and culture as well as political economy. As he explains in our selections, neoliberalism arose from policies put in place in the 1970s in response to the crisis of Western capitalism; these included the paring back of social programs, deregulation rather than governmental oversight, an emphasis on the free market and trade, and the privatization of formerly public services. However reduced, neoliberal government plays a key role in instituting policies that support capitalism, usually favoring finance and constricting unions, and in providing police and military protection to private property. The philosophy of neoliberalism sprang from conservative thinkers such as FRIEDRICH HAYEK and LEO STRAUSS, who reacted against the liberal social welfare programs of the postwar era and stressed individual rights and the benefits of market competition.

In our selections, Harvey begins with the observation that the changes of the late 1970s and early 1980s show a surprising global range, linking not just countries such as the United States and Britain but also their erstwhile opponents China and Russia. After defining this trend, he points out its decisive effects on workers, who have largely lost control of their labor power as companies are likely to move production on short notice and unions have become more restricted. Moreover, workers have experienced declining wages and worsening conditions, as they face perpetual insecurity. Indeed, Harvey asserts that low-wage workers have become "disposable" and that capitalism fosters "accumulation by dispossession"—that is, capitalists profit at the expense of workers in various places around the globe. For instance, as Harvey elaborated in an interview, after the bankruptcy of an American airline, all the flight attendants and service workers lost their pensions, but the senior managers of the company made millions of dollars, as did the bankers who negotiated the deal. Among the other distinctive results of neoliberalism that Harvey points out are new vulnerabilities for women, especially in less developed countries, and the spread of religious fundamentalisms.

Harvey's views have had a great deal of influence in literary and cultural studies, providing a useful description of the political and economic structure of contemporary society. In particular, his idea of disposable workers has resonated with critics of mental labor, such as ANDREW ROSS and MARC BOUSQUET, whose analysis of the current system of academic teaching labor exposes its reliance on casual or term jobs rather than permanent ones. Harvey has also influenced academics working in geography, sociology, and anthropology, but not in mainstream economics, where some dismiss his views as outmoded, fixed on the archaic concepts of Marxism. Moreover, some conservatives argue that despite their problems, human societies today have better conditions than ever before thanks to modernization.

Within cultural studies and allied fields, a few scholars have expressed reservations that Harvey evokes a totalizing view—the kind of grand narrative whose demise has been announced by postmodernist theorists such as JEAN-FRANÇOIS LYOTARD. However, Harvey combines detailed historical analysis with an abstract understanding of capitalism and its processes. As he told his interviewer, "I try to mobilize the power of abstraction and do it in a way that allows me then to connect to the ground" and to the conditions that people experience.

A Brief History of Neoliberalism **Keywords:** Globalization, Hegemony, Marxism, Postmodernity, Religion

From A Brief History of Neoliberalism

Introduction

Future historians may well look upon the years 1978–80 as a revolutionary turning-point in the world's social and economic history. In 1978, Deng Xiaoping[1] took the first momentous steps towards the liberalization of a communist-ruled economy in a country that accounted for a fifth of the world's population. The path that Deng defined was to transform China in two decades from a closed backwater to an open centre of capitalist dynamism with sustained growth rates unparalleled in human history. On the other side of the Pacific, and in quite different circumstances, a relatively obscure (but now renowned) figure named Paul Volcker[2] took command at the US Federal Reserve in July 1979, and within a few months dramatically changed monetary policy. The Fed thereafter took the lead in the fight against inflation no matter what its consequences (particularly as concerned unemployment). Across the Atlantic, Margaret Thatcher had already been elected Prime Minister of Britain in May 1979, with a mandate to curb trade union power and put an end to the miserable inflationary stagnation that had enveloped the country for the preceding decade. Then, in 1980, Ronald Reagan was elected President of the United States and, armed with geniality and personal charisma, set the US on course to revitalize its economy by supporting Volcker's moves at the Fed and adding his own particular blend of policies to curb the power of labour, deregulate industry, agriculture, and resource extraction, and liberate the powers of finance both internally and on the world stage. From these several epicentres, revolutionary impulses seemingly spread and reverberated to remake the world around us in a totally different image.

Transformations of this scope and depth do not occur by accident. So it is pertinent to enquire by what means and paths the new economic configuration—often subsumed under the term 'globalization'—was plucked from the entrails of the old. Volcker, Reagan, Thatcher, and Deng Xiaoping all took minority arguments that had long been in circulation and made them majoritarian (though in no case without a protracted struggle). Reagan brought to life the minority tradition that stretched back within the Republican Party to Barry Goldwater[3] in the early 1960s. Deng saw the rising tide of wealth and influence in Japan, Taiwan, Hong Kong, Singapore, and South Korea and sought to mobilize market socialism instead of central planning to protect and advance the interests of the Chinese state. Volcker and Thatcher both plucked from the shadows of relative obscurity a particular doctrine that went under the name of 'neoliberalism' and transformed it into the central guiding principle of economic thought and man-

1. Chinese Communist leader (1904–1997); though he never held the highest posts in China's government, by 1980 he held the most power (remaining influential even after his official retirement in 1992).

2. American economist (b. 1927); he was chairman of the board of governors of the U.S. Federal Reserve System until 1987.

3. Arizona politician (1909–1998), often viewed as the father of modern U.S. conservativism; he was a U.S. senator (1953–64, 1969–87) and unsuccessful Republican presidential candidate (1964).

agement. And it is with this doctrine—its origins, rise, and implications—that I am here primarily concerned.[4]

Neoliberalism is in the first instance a theory of political economic practices that proposes that human well-being can best be advanced by liberating individual entrepreneurial freedoms and skills within an institutional framework characterized by strong private property rights, free markets, and free trade. The role of the state is to create and preserve an institutional framework appropriate to such practices. The state has to guarantee, for example, the quality and integrity of money. It must also set up those military, defence, police, and legal structures and functions required to secure private property rights and to guarantee, by force if need be, the proper functioning of markets. Furthermore, if markets do not exist (in areas such as land, water, education, health care, social security, or environmental pollution) then they must be created, by state action if necessary. But beyond these tasks the state should not venture. State interventions in markets (once created) must be kept to a bare minimum because, according to the theory, the state cannot possibly possess enough information to second-guess market signals (prices) and because powerful interest groups will inevitably distort and bias state interventions (particularly in democracies) for their own benefit.

There has everywhere been an emphatic turn towards neoliberalism in political-economic practices and thinking since the 1970s. Deregulation, privatization, and withdrawal of the state from many areas of social provision have been all too common. Almost all states, from those newly minted after the collapse of the Soviet Union[5] to old-style social democracies and welfare states such as New Zealand and Sweden, have embraced, sometimes voluntarily and in other instances in response to coercive pressures, some version of neoliberal theory and adjusted at least some policies and practices accordingly. Post-apartheid South Africa quickly embraced neoliberalism, and even contemporary China, as we shall see, appears to be headed in this direction. Furthermore, the advocates of the neoliberal way now occupy positions of considerable influence in education (the universities and many 'think tanks'), in the media, in corporate boardrooms and financial institutions, in key state institutions (treasury departments, the central banks), and also in those international institutions such as the International Monetary Fund (IMF), the World Bank, and the World Trade Organization (WTO) that regulate global finance and trade. Neoliberalism has, in short, become hegemonic as a mode of discourse. It has pervasive effects on ways of thought to the point where it has become incorporated into the common-sense way many of us interpret, live in, and understand the world.

4. S. George, "A Short History of Neoliberalism: Twenty Years of Elite Economics and Emerging Opportunities for Structural Change," in W. Bello, N. Bullard, and K. Malhotra (eds.), *Global Finance: New Thinking on Regulating Capital Markets* (London: Zed Books, 2000), 27–35; G. Duménil and D. Lévy, *Capital Resurgent: Roots of the Neoliberal Revolution*, trans. D. Jeffers (Cambridge, Mass.: Harvard University Press, 2004); J. Peck, "Geography and Public Policy: Constructions of Neoliberalism," *Progress in Human Geography*, 28/3 (2004), 392–405; J. Peck and A. Tickell, "Neoliberalizing Space," *Antipode*, 34/3 (2002), 380–404; P. Treanor, "Neoliberalism: Origins, Theory, Definition," http://web.inter.nl.net/users/Paul.Treanor/neoliberalism.html [Harvey's note].

5. In December 1991, the Union of Soviet Socialist Republics—which had formed in 1922 after the Russian Revolution of 1917—dissolved into three independent nations and twelve republics in the Commonwealth of Independent States.

The process of neoliberalization has, however, entailed much 'creative destruction',[6] not only of prior institutional frameworks and powers (even challenging traditional forms of state sovereignty) but also of divisions of labour, social relations, welfare provisions, technological mixes, ways of life and thought, reproductive activities, attachments to the land and habits of the heart. In so far as neoliberalism values market exchange as 'an ethic in itself, capable of acting as a guide to all human action, and substituting for all previously held ethical beliefs', it emphasizes the significance of contractual relations in the marketplace.[7] It holds that the social good will be maximized by maximizing the reach and frequency of market transactions, and it seeks to bring all human action into the domain of the market. This requires technologies of information creation and capacities to accumulate, store, transfer, analyse, and use massive databases to guide decisions in the global marketplace. Hence neoliberalism's intense interest in and pursuit of information technologies (leading some to proclaim the emergence of a new kind of 'information society'). These technologies have compressed the rising density of market transactions in both space and time. They have produced a particularly intensive burst of what I have elsewhere called 'time-space compression'. The greater the geographical range (hence the emphasis on 'globalization') and the shorter the term of market contracts the better. This latter preference parallels Lyotard's famous description of the postmodern condition as one where 'the temporary contract' supplants 'permanent institutions in the professional, emotional, sexual, cultural, family and international domains, as well as in political affairs'. The cultural consequences of the dominance of such a market ethic are legion, as I earlier showed in *The Condition of Postmodernity*.[8]

While many general accounts of global transformations and their effects are now available, what is generally missing—and this is the gap this book aims to fill—is the political-economic story of where neoliberalization came from and how it proliferated so comprehensively on the world stage. Critical engagement with that story suggests, furthermore, a framework for identifying and constructing alternative political and economic arrangements.

From *Chapter 6. Neoliberalism on Trial*

* * *

Neoliberalization seeks to strip away the protective coverings that embedded liberalism allowed and occasionally nurtured. The general attack against labour has been two-pronged. The powers of trade unions and other working-class institutions are curbed or dismantled within a particular state (by violence if necessary). Flexible labour markets are established. State withdrawal from social welfare provision and technologically induced shifts in job structures that render large segments of the labour force redundant complete the

6. A phrase coined by the Moravian-born American economist and sociologist Joseph Schumpeter in *Capitalism, Socialism, and Democracy* (1942): it describes the incessant process of "industrial mutation" as old economic structures are destroyed and new ones created.
7. Treanor, "Neoliberalism" [Harvey's note].
8. Harvey, *The Condition of Postmodernity* (Oxford: Basil Blackwell, 1989); J.-F. Lyotard, *The Postmodern Condition* (Manchester: Manchester University Press, 1984), 66 [Harvey's note]. For the French philosopher JEAN-FRANÇOIS LYOTARD (1924–1998), see above.

domination of capital over labour in the marketplace. The individualized and relatively powerless worker then confronts a labour market in which only short-term contracts are offered on a customized basis. Security of tenure becomes a thing of the past (Thatcher abolished it in universities, for example). A 'personal responsibility system'[9] (how apt Deng's language was!) is substituted for social protections (pensions, health care, protections against injury) that were formerly an obligation of employers and the state. Individuals buy products in the markets that sell social protections instead. Individual security is therefore a matter of individual choice tied to the affordability of financial products embedded in risky financial markets.

The second prong of attack entails transformations in the spatial and temporal co-ordinates of the labour market. While too much can be made of the 'race to the bottom' to find the cheapest and most docile labour supplies, the geographical mobility of capital permits it to dominate a global labour force whose own geographical mobility is constrained. Captive labour forces abound because immigration is restricted. These barriers can be evaded only by illegal immigration (which creates an easily exploitable labour force) or through short-term contracts that permit, for example, Mexican labourers to work in Californian agribusiness only to be shamelessly shipped back to Mexico when they get sick and even die from the pesticides to which they are exposed.

Under neoliberalization, the figure of 'the disposable worker' emerges as prototypical upon the world stage.[1] Accounts of the appalling conditions of labour and the despotic conditions under which labourers work in the sweatshops of the world abound. In China, the conditions under which migrant young women from rural areas work are nothing short of appalling: 'unbearably long hours, substandard food, cramped dorms, sadistic managers who beat and sexually abuse them, and pay that arrives months late, or sometimes not at all'.[2] In Indonesia, two young women recounted their experiences working for a Singapore-based Levi-Strauss subcontractor as follows:

> We are regularly insulted, as a matter of course. When the boss gets angry he calls the women dogs, pigs, sluts, all of which we have to endure patiently without reacting. We work officially from seven in the morning until three (salary less than $2 a day), but there is often compulsory overtime, sometimes—especially if there is an urgent order to be delivered—until nine. However tired we are, we are not allowed to go home. We may get an extra 200 rupiah (10 US cents) . . . We go on foot to the factory from where we live. Inside it is very hot. The building has a metal roof, and there is not much space for all the workers. It is very cramped. There are over 200 people working there, mostly women, but there is only one toilet for the whole factory . . . when we come home from work, we have no energy left to do anything but eat and sleep . . . [3]

9. A phrase associated with reforms (1979–82) that liberalized rural markets in China, which previously had been controlled entirely by state quotas and prices.

1. K. Bales, *Disposable People: New Slavery in the Global Economy* (Berkeley: University of California Press, 2000); M. Wright, "The Dialectics of Still Life: Murder, Women, and Maquiladoras," *Public Culture*, 11 (1999), 453–74 [Harvey's note].

2. A. Ross, *Low Pay High Profile: The Global Push for Fair Labor* (New York: New Press, 2004), 124 [Harvey's note]. For the American cultural and social critic ANDREW ROSS (b. 1956), see below.

3. J. Seabrook, *In the Cities of the South: Scenes from a Developing World* (London: Verso, 1996), 103 [Harvey's note].

Similar tales come from the Mexican maquila factories,[4] the Taiwanese- and Korean-operated manufacturing plants in Honduras, South Africa, Malaysia, and Thailand. The health hazards, the exposure to a wide range of toxic substances, and death on the job pass by unregulated and unremarked. In Shanghai, the Taiwanese businessman who ran a textile warehouse 'in which 61 workers, locked in the building, died in a fire' received a 'lenient' two-year suspended sentence because he had 'showed repentance' and 'cooperated in the aftermath of the fire'.[5]

Women, for the most part, and sometimes children, bear the brunt of this sort of degrading, debilitating, and dangerous toil.[6] The social consequences of neoliberalization are in fact extreme. Accumulation by dispossession typically undermines whatever powers women may have had within household production/marketing systems and within traditional social structures and relocates everything in male-dominated commodity and credit markets. The paths of women's liberation from traditional patriarchal controls in developing countries lie either through degrading factory labour or through trading on sexuality, which varies from respectable work as hostesses and waitresses to the sex trade (one of the most lucrative of all contemporary industries in which a good deal of slavery is involved). The loss of social protections in advanced capitalist countries has had particularly negative effects on lower-class women, and in many of the ex-communist countries of the Soviet bloc the loss of women's rights through neoliberalization has been nothing short of catastrophic.

So how, then, do disposable workers—women in particular—survive both socially and affectively in a world of flexible labour markets and short-term contracts, chronic job insecurities, lost social protections, and often debilitating labour, amongst the wreckage of collective institutions that once gave them a modicum of dignity and support? For some the increased flexibility in labour markets is a boon, and even when it does not lead to material gains the simple right to change jobs relatively easily and free of the traditional social constraints of patriarchy and family has intangible benefits. For those who successfully negotiate the labour market there are seemingly abundant rewards in the world of a capitalist consumer culture. Unfortunately, that culture, however spectacular, glamorous, and beguiling, perpetually plays with desires without ever conferring satisfactions beyond the limited identity of the shopping mall and the anxieties of status by way of good looks (in the case of women) or of material possessions. 'I shop therefore I am'[7] and possessive individualism together construct a world of pseudo-satisfactions that is superficially exciting but hollow at its core.

But for those who have lost their jobs or who have never managed to move out of the extensive informal economies that now provide a parlous refuge for most of the world's disposable workers, the story is entirely different. With

4. Factories (also called *maquiladoras*) that import components, assemble them using low-wage labor, and then export the finished product (sometimes back to the country that provided the components).

5. J. Sommer, "A Dragon Let Loose on the Land: And Shanghai Is at the Epicenter of China's Economic Boom," *Japan Times*, 26 Oct. 1994, 3 [Harvey's note].

6. C. K. Lee, *Gender and the South China Miracle* (Berkeley: University of California Press, 1998); C. Cartier, *Globalizing South China* (Oxford: Basil Blackwell, 2001), particularly ch. 6 [Harvey's note].

7. A play on "I think, therefore I am," the dictum presented by René Descartes in *Discourse on Method* (1637) as the foundational principle of knowledge.

some 2 billion people condemned to live on less than $2 a day, the taunting world of capitalist consumer culture, the huge bonuses earned in financial services, and the self-congratulatory polemics as to the emancipatory potential of neoliberalization, privatization, and personal responsibility must seem like a cruel joke. From impoverished rural China to the affluent US, the loss of health-care protections and the increasing imposition of all manner of user fees adds considerably to the financial burdens of the poor.[8]

Neoliberalization has transformed the positionality of labour, of women, and of indigenous groups in the social order by emphasizing that labour is a commodity like any other. Stripped of the protective cover of lively democratic institutions and threatened with all manner of social dislocations, a disposable workforce inevitably turns to other institutional forms through which to construct social solidarities and express a collective will. Everything from gangs and criminal cartels, narco-trafficking networks, mini-mafias and favela[9] bosses, through community, grassroots and non-governmental organizations, to secular cults and religious sects proliferate. These are the alternative social forms that fill the void left behind as state powers, political parties, and other institutional forms are actively dismantled or simply wither away as centres of collective endeavour and of social bonding. The marked turn to religion is in this regard of interest. Accounts of the sudden appearance and proliferation of religious sects in the derelict rural regions of China, to say nothing of the emergence of Fulan Gong, are illustrative of this trend.[1] The rapid progress of evangelical proselytizing in the chaotic informal economies that have burgeoned under neoliberalization in Latin America, and the revived and in some instances newly constructed religious tribalism and fundamentalism that structure politics in much of Africa and the Middle East, testify to the need to construct meaningful mechanisms of social solidarity. The progress of fundamentalist evangelical Christianity in the US has some connection with proliferating job insecurities, the loss of other forms of social solidarity, and the hollowness of capitalist consumer culture. In Thomas Frank's account, the religious right took off in Kansas only at the end of the 1980s, after a decade or more of neoliberal restructuring and deindustrialization.[2] Such connections may seem far-fetched. But if Polanyi[3] is right and the treatment of labour as a commodity leads to social dislocation, then moves to rebuild different social networks to defend against such a threat become increasingly likely.

* * *

2005

8. The global impacts are discussed in detail in V. Navarro, *The Political Economy of Social Inequalities: Consequences for Health and the Quality of Life* (Amityville, NY: Baywood, 2002); V. Navarro and C. Muntaner, *Political and Economic Determinants of Population Health and Well-Being* (Amityville, NY: Baywood, 2004) [Harvey's note].

9. A Brazilian shantytown; favelas are discussed by Bales in *Disposable People*.

1. J. Kahn, "Violence Taints Religion's Solace for China's Poor," *New York Times*, 25 Nov. 2004, A1 and A24. [Harvey's note]. Fulan Gong: a Chinese spiritual movement, founded in 1992 by Li Hongzhi as a self-cultivation practice (combining aspects of Buddhism and Daoism); it has been banned by the Chinese government.

2. Frank, *What's the Matter with Kansas: How Conservatives Won the Heart of America* (New York: Metropolitan Books, 2004) [Harvey's note]. Frank (b. 1965), American journalist and historian.

3. Karl Polanyi (1886–1964), Hungarian economist and social theorist; in his best-known work, *The Great Transformation* (1944), he argued that the market economy is by its nature socially divisive.

EDWARD W. SAID
1935–2003

One of the most prominent public intellectuals of recent decades, Edward W. Said was an influential literary critic and theorist as well as a significant political figure, especially as an advocate of the rights of Palestinians. Arguing for a socially engaged criticism against both linguistically oriented theories like deconstruction and ideologically dogmatic positions, he promoted a "worldly," "secular criticism." Beginning with his landmark *Orientalism* (1978), which is often regarded as having established the field of postcolonial studies, his work focused on imperialism and the interplay between the dominant West (the "Occident") and the Middle and Far East (the "Orient"). In the introduction to *Orientialism*, our first selection, Said discusses how European and U.S. literary and cultural representations, academic disciplines, and public perceptions foster biases against non-Western peoples, casting them as oriental Others. In our second selection, excerpted from *Culture and Imperialism* (1993), his major work of literary interpretation, Said examines how a classic literary portrait of British country life, Jane Austen's 1814 novel *Mansfield Park*, surprisingly reveals the ways that empire permeates the colonizers' homeland.

Of Palestinian heritage but educated in British and American colonial schools in Cairo and later in U.S. universities, Said experienced firsthand the complicated relations between the East and Western imperialism. He was born in Jerusalem, Palestine, which had been controlled by Great Britain since 1922 (with a mandate from the League of Nations to help establish a Jewish national home); but in 1947, in the aftermath of World War II, the United Nations divided Palestine into Arab and Jewish territories and placed the city of Jerusalem under its control. The resulting political tension and fighting within Palestine led Said's family to emigrate to Cairo at the end of 1947. When the British mandate expired in 1948, Jewish authorities declared the establishment of the State of Israel, on which all the neighboring Arab countries immediately declared war; hundreds of thousands of Arabs fled what had been Palestine. Though the creation of Israel is celebrated in the West as the restoration of a Jewish homeland, Palestinians call it the *nakbah*, or "disaster"; Said comments, "Israel was established; Palestine was destroyed."

Said's father, Wadie Said, was a prosperous businessman who sold office equipment in Cairo and elsewhere, and Said himself, in the midst of political turmoil, received an elite education. He attended St. George's, an Anglican preparatory school; the American School in Cairo, whose student body was composed primarily of children of U.S. diplomats; and Victoria College, a secondary school where his classmates included the future King Hussein of Jordan. After Said was expelled from school for disciplinary reasons in 1951, his father sent him to Mount Hermon, a preparatory school in Massachusetts, to complete high school and to gain U.S. citizenship. (His father had emigrated to the United States in the 1910s and served in the army in World War I, becoming a naturalized U.S. citizen.) Said became a naturalized citizen in 1953 and attended Princeton University, receiving his B.A. degree in 1957. After a year in Cairo helping with his father's business, he returned to the United States to do doctoral work in English and comparative literature at Harvard University, earning an M.A. in 1960 and a Ph.D. in 1964.

Said's academic career was remarkably successful; after joining the faculty at Columbia University in 1963 he quickly ascended the ladder of academic rank, eventually being appointed to several prestigious chairs. He also held distinguished visiting professorships and fellowships at Harvard, Yale, Princeton, Stanford, and elsewhere, and his books garnered a long list of honors, among them a National Book Critics Circle Award nomination for *Orientalism*. At the same time, Said gained political prominence, translating the first address of Yasir Arafat, longtime leader of the Palestinians, to the General Assembly of the United Nations in 1974; serving as a member of the Palestine National Council from 1977 to 1991 (helping to draft its declaration of Palestinian statehood in 1988); and advocating Palestinian national rights in international news media. While often criticizing Israel's and the United States' refusal to recognize a Palestinian state, he also criticized the leadership and policies of the Palestinian Liberation Organization. He died in 2003 after a long battle with cancer.

In some sense, Said fulfilled the definition of an "organic intellectual"—to use the phrase of the Italian Marxist philosopher ANTONIO GRAMSCI, one of Said's intellectual heroes—developing his criticism of Western representations of Arab culture and his advocacy for the rights of Palestinians out of his personal roots. As he remarked in an interview, however, he always experienced his identity as complicated—as a U.S. citizen as well as a Palestinian, as an "Oriental" as well as a Western scholar educated in the British tradition, and as a renowned academic figure as well as an often dissenting political spokesperson. He felt, as he titled his memoir, "out of place"; this sense of homelessness defined for him the proper stance of the intellectual, who should remain independent of fixed theoretical, disciplinary, professional, and national loyalties, yet always be attentive to social injustice and what he calls the "brute reality" of history.

Said first gained wide attention with the publication of *Beginnings: Intention and Method* (1975), a pioneering comparison of MICHEL FOUCAULT's method of historical "archaeology" and JACQUES DERRIDA's deconstructive critique of language, ultimately favoring Foucault's focus on social forces. A dense meditation on literary "beginnings" and influences, it also conducted an erudite examination of figures from the Western humanistic tradition—GIAMBATTISTA VICO, ERICH AUERBACH, and others. Though already well known in literary circles, Said attained broader prominence across the academic disciplines and among the general public with the publication of his next book, *Orientalism*. Appearing as conflicts in the Middle East were escalating, it provided a timely—and controversial—critical overview of the history of Western understandings of Arab culture. In particular, it voiced a strong dissent against largely pro-Israeli U.S. policies that operated at the expense of Arab peoples.

With *Orientalism*, Said turned to examine more directly the political dimensions of literature and culture. Many critics see this turn as a decisive shift in Said's focus from academic literary theory to actual politics, but in fact his writings display a number of consistent concerns: a grounding in the literary canon; an appreciation of philology and the long humanistic tradition of criticism; research across disciplines, especially history; an overarching concern, influenced by Foucault, with the complex interrelation of culture and the operation of political power; a belief in the value of individual achievements in literature, criticism, and politics; and an assertion of the independent role of the intellectual as someone who eschews orthodoxies both theoretical and political. For Said, literary, philological, and critical texts are always "in the world" and have social resonances.

In our first selection, Said propounds a broad definition of Orientalism, encompassing both Western academic scholarship in disciplines whose field of study is the "Orient"—such as anthropology, philology, history, and area studies—and the general Western image of the "Orient" depicted in novels, political accounts, and contemporary media. He shows how Western writers, archaeologists, linguists, historians, and politicians from the eighteenth century to the present day have "discovered" and in a sense invented the Orient. According to Said, Orientalism reveals more about the West and its fantasies than it does about the actual people, culture, and history of the East; not simply a myth, it is "more particularly valuable as a sign of European-Atlantic power over the Orient than it is as a veridic discourse about the Orient." In effect, the various literary, cultural, and historical discourses of Orientalism participate in the conquest and continuing subjugation of the East. Furthermore, Said's analysis is a sharp warning to scholars and intellectuals, showing how scholarship is sometimes informed by racism and how intellectuals have been complicit in the administration of imperial power.

This examination of Orientalism is particularly indebted to the work of Foucault, as Said adopts Foucault's method of archival research, his focus on cultural and historical knowledges as constituting a system of "discourse," and his tracing of the complex interrelation of power and knowledge. But for Said, the disciplinary institutions of knowledge are not simply embedded in the overarching Foucauldian category of "power": they directly serve the historical interests of European imperialism. Said also diverges from Foucault's generalized, impersonal sense of "discourse," instead retaining a humanistic belief in "the determining imprint of individual writers" and intellectuals. Another poststructuralist influence is Derrida's critique of concepts such as *center* and *margin* and *self* and *Other*. For Said, the "margin" of the East helps define the colonial center of the West, and the Oriental "Other" is a projection of the Western view that constructs it. These and related terms have played a crucial role in the development of postcolonial studies. Said criticizes Derrida's linguistic focus, however, and extends poststructuralist theory to examine its implications for real-world politics—especially in the British rule of India, the European partitioning of the Middle East, and the U.S. intervention in Vietnam.

A less often recognized influence on Said's work is that of RAYMOND WILLIAMS, the British literary and cultural critic. Said praised the work of Williams, particularly his disregard for such traditional academic boundaries as the distinction between literature and history, and followed Williams in his concern with the societal effects of literature and culture. Although Said's *Culture and Imperialism* is often taken as a riposte to MATTHEW ARNOLD's *Culture and Anarchy* (1869) in showing how culture not only improves society but operates in the service of imperialism, its direct forebear is Williams's *Culture and Society* (1958), as well as Williams's *The Country and the City* (1973). In our second selection, "Jane Austen and Empire," Said follows Williams in considering literary works as representing their social world rather than as autonomous objects, but gently corrects Williams's lack of attention to imperialism as he focuses on it.

Culture and Imperialism ranges over a great many literary and artistic works, such as Verdi's opera *Aïda* (1871) and Joseph Conrad's *Heart of Darkness* (1902), that explicitly portray territories under European control. Said's point is that the great works in the European tradition are enmeshed in empire; *Heart of Darkness*, for instance, depicts imperial outposts in Africa. Said uses a more unexpected example when he turns to Jane Austen's novel *Mansfield Park*. Her novels typically depict country life, especially of the middle and upper classes in England around 1800, and their plots center on courtship and marriage. Austen's occasional comments on society tend to be limited to moral advice—for instance, on the proper behavior of the gentry toward their inferiors. Williams, in *The Country and the City*, sees Austen's novels as portraits of British society on the brink of change. Austen is beloved because she presented the passing values of rural English life rather than those of the new order, based in urban centers and industry, that was emerging.

Said demonstrates that though Mansfield Park seems to be an isolated, domestic enclave, it depends on imperialism, which stretches across the Atlantic to the Caribbean. In the midst of the action, the head of the family, Lord Bertram, has to travel twice to Antigua to manage affairs on his plantation. His leaving is usually taken as a plot device: freedom from his watchful eye leads to his children's social entanglements (set aright by the end, when Bertram returns). But Said argues that his leaving foregrounds the colonial situation essential to maintaining Mansfield Park. Much narrative theory, especially of modern literature, focuses on time and time-oriented themes like memory. Said instead calls us to pay attention to location and geography, so that we can see how a house in the countryside of England rested on the global interconnections of empire.

Some critics have claimed that such a reading judges classic works of literature too harshly and anachronistically, foisting contemporary standards on past eras. Said is careful to head off this charge. He notes that representations such as Austen's did not cause imperialism; rather, they record the role of imperialism in their society. Said also unequivocally calls *Mansfield Park* a great work, and he acknowledges the value of the humanistic tradition. In this, he is surprisingly allied with Arnold and his celebration of "the best that is known and thought." However, Said does not mince words about the wrongs that imperialism sponsored, such as the slavery on which plantations like Lord Bertram's relied. This is a more measured position than that of many other postcolonial writers or critics. CHINUA ACHEBE, for example, points out the racism of *Heart of Darkness* and then concludes that we should no longer teach or read the work. In Said's view, we should continue to subject it to interpretation, understanding both its humanistic value and its participation in injustice and oppression.

Said's work has exerted considerable influence, especially in the development of postcolonial studies. *Orientalism* was immediately recognized as a critical classic, with an impact not only on literary studies but also on anthropology, history, international studies, and the discipline known as Orientalism. *Culture and Imperialism* was also hailed as a major work, capping Said's career and showing the reach of imperialism through its erudite readings of a broad selection of literary and other cultural works. Said himself was praised as an exemplary intellectual, having crossed the boundary between the academic world and the public sphere and speaking out on contemporary politics. His advocacy on behalf of a Palestinian state provoked attacks, sometimes vehement. Within the field of literary studies, various scholars criticized different aspects of his work: his residual humanism and belief in individual will, his liberal rather than radical views, his eschewal of professionalism for amateurism, his inattention to feminism, and his primary focus on the high Western literary tradition. However, most critics acknowledge his pivotal role in contemporary theory and his success in forging a path that crossed disciplinary boundaries and in combining political commitment and intellectual work. As demonstrated in *Orientalism*, he persistently underscored the relation of literary study to the world, especially the relation of culture to the "brute reality" of imperialism.

***Orientalism* Keywords:** Cultural Studies, Institutional Studies, Philology, Postcolonial Theory, Poststructuralism, Race and Ethnicity Studies, Representation
***Culture and Imperialism* Keywords:** The Canon/Tradition, Globalization, Literary History, The Novel, Postcolonial Criticism, Representation

From Orientalism

Introduction

I

On a visit to Beirut during the terrible civil war of 1975–1976 a French journalist wrote regretfully of the gutted downtown area that "it had once seemed to belong to . . . the Orient of Chateaubriand and Nerval."[1] He was right

1. Thierry Desjardins, *Le Martyre du Liban* (Paris: Plon, 1976), p. 14 [Said's note]. François-René, vicomte de Chateaubriand (1768–1848), French writer and statesman. Gérard de Nerval (1808–1855), French poet and journalist; he wrote an account of a journey to the Middle East, *Le Voyage en Orient* (1851).

about the place, of course, especially so far as a European was concerned. The Orient was almost a European invention, and had been since antiquity a place of romance, exotic beings, haunting memories and landscapes, remarkable experiences. Now it was disappearing; in a sense it had happened, its time was over. Perhaps it seemed irrelevant that Orientals themselves had something at stake in the process, that even in the time of Chateaubriand and Nerval Orientals had lived there, and that now it was they who were suffering; the main thing for the European visitor was a European representation of the Orient and its contemporary fate, both of which had a privileged communal significance for the journalist and his French readers.

Americans will not feel quite the same about the Orient, which for them is much more likely to be associated very differently with the Far East (China and Japan, mainly). Unlike the Americans, the French and the British—less so the Germans, Russians, Spanish, Portuguese, Italians, and Swiss—have had a long tradition of what I shall be calling *Orientalism*, a way of coming to terms with the Orient that is based on the Orient's special place in European Western experience. The Orient is not only adjacent to Europe; it is also the place of Europe's greatest and richest and oldest colonies, the source of its civilizations and languages, its cultural contestant, and one of its deepest and most recurring images of the Other. In addition, the Orient has helped to define Europe (or the West) as its contrasting image, idea, personality, experience. Yet none of this Orient is merely imaginative. The Orient is an integral part of European *material* civilization and culture. Orientalism expresses and represents that part culturally and even ideologically as a mode of discourse with supporting institutions, vocabulary, scholarship, imagery, doctrines, even colonial bureaucracies and colonial styles. In contrast, the American understanding of the Orient will seem considerably less dense, although our recent Japanese, Korean, and Indochinese adventures[2] ought now to be creating a more sober, more realistic "Oriental" awareness. Moreover, the vastly expanded American political and economic role in the Near East (the Middle East) makes great claims on our understanding of that Orient.

It will be clear to the reader (and will become clearer still throughout the many pages that follow) that by Orientalism I mean several things, all of them, in my opinion, interdependent. The most readily accepted designation for Orientalism is an academic one, and indeed the label still serves in a number of academic institutions. Anyone who teaches, writes about, or researches the Orient—and this applies whether the person is an anthropologist, sociologist, historian, or philologist—either in its specific or its general aspects, is an Orientalist, and what he or she does is Orientalism. Compared with *Oriental studies* or *area studies*, it is true that the term *Orientalism* is less preferred by specialists today, both because it is too vague and general and because it connotes the high-handed executive attitude of nineteenth-century and early-twentieth-century European colonialism. Nevertheless books are written and congresses held with "the Orient" as their main focus, with the Orientalist in his new or old guise as their main authority. The point is that even if it does not survive as it once did, Orientalism lives on

2. That is, the Pacific Theater of World War II (1941–45), the Korean War (1950–53), and the Vietnam War (1964–75), respectively.

academically through its doctrines and theses about the Orient and the Oriental.

Related to this academic tradition, whose fortunes, transmigrations, specializations, and transmissions are in part the subject of this study, is a more general meaning for Orientalism. Orientalism is a style of thought based upon an ontological and epistemological distinction[3] made between "the Orient" and (most of the time) "the Occident." Thus a very large mass of writers, among whom are poets, novelists, philosophers, political theorists, economists, and imperial administrators, have accepted the basic distinction between East and West as the starting point for elaborate theories, epics, novels, social descriptions, and political accounts concerning the Orient, its people, customs, "mind," destiny, and so on. *This* Orientalism can accommodate Aeschylus, say, and Victor Hugo, Dante and Karl Marx.[4] A little later in this introduction I shall deal with the methodological problems one encounters in so broadly construed a "field" as this.

The interchange between the academic and the more or less imaginative meanings of Orientalism is a constant one, and since the late eighteenth century there has been a considerable, quite disciplined—perhaps even regulated—traffic between the two. Here I come to the third meaning of Orientalism, which is something more historically and materially defined than either of the other two. Taking the late eighteenth century as a very roughly defined starting point Orientalism can be discussed and analyzed as the corporate institution for dealing with the Orient—dealing with it by making statements about it, authorizing views of it, describing it, by teaching it, settling it, ruling over it: in short, Orientalism as a Western style for dominating, restructuring, and having authority over the Orient. I have found it useful here to employ Michel Foucault's notion of a discourse, as described by him in *The Archaeology of Knowledge* and in *Discipline and Punish*,[5] to identify Orientalism. My contention is that without examining Orientalism as a discourse one cannot possibly understand the enormously systematic discipline by which European culture was able to manage—and even produce—the Orient politically, sociologically, militarily, ideologically, scientifically, and imaginatively during the post-Enlightenment period. Moreover, so authoritative a position did Orientalism have that I believe no one writing, thinking, or acting on the Orient could do so without taking account of the limitations on thought and action imposed by Orientalism. In brief, because of Orientalism the Orient was not (and is not) a free subject of thought or action. This is not to say that Orientalism unilaterally determines what can be said about the Orient, but that it is the whole network of interests inevitably brought to bear on (and therefore always involved in) any occasion when that peculiar entity "the Orient" is in question. How this happens is what this book tries to demonstrate. It also tries to show that European culture gained in strength and identity by setting itself off against the Orient as a sort of surrogate and even underground self.

3. That is, a difference in their essential being and how they are known.

4. Said names writers not generally viewed as treating the "Oriental": Aeschylus (525–456 B.C.E.), Greek tragedian; Hugo (1802–1885), French Romantic poet, novelist, and dramatist; DANTE ALIGHIERI (1265–1321), Italian poet; and MARX (1818–1883), German economic, social, and political philosopher.

5. Books published in 1969 and 1975, respectively, by FOUCAULT (1926–1984), French philosopher and historian, who explores the connections between knowledge, discourse, and power.

Historically and culturally there is a quantitative as well as a qualitative difference between the Franco-British involvement in the Orient and—until the period of American ascendancy after World War II—the involvement of every other European and Atlantic power. To speak of Orientalism therefore is to speak mainly, although not exclusively, of a British and French cultural enterprise, a project whose dimensions take in such disparate realms as the imagination itself, the whole of India and the Levant,[6] the Biblical texts and the Biblical lands, the spice trade, colonial armies and a long tradition of colonial administrators, a formidable scholarly corpus, innumerable Oriental "experts" and "hands," an Oriental professorate, a complex array of "Oriental" ideas (Oriental despotism, Oriental splendor, cruelty, sensuality), many Eastern sects, philosophies, and wisdoms domesticated for local European use—the list can be extended more or less indefinitely. My point is that Orientalism derives from a particular closeness experienced between Britain and France and the Orient, which until the early nineteenth century had really meant only India and the Bible lands. From the beginning of the nineteenth century until the end of World War II France and Britain dominated the Orient and Orientalism; since World War II America has dominated the Orient, and approaches it as France and Britain once did. Out of that closeness, whose dynamic is enormously productive even if it always demonstrates the comparatively greater strength of the Occident (British, French, or American), comes the large body of texts I call Orientalist.

It should be said at once that even with the generous number of books and authors that I examine, there is a much larger number that I simply have had to leave out. My argument, however, depends neither upon an exhaustive catalogue of texts dealing with the Orient nor upon a clearly delimited set of texts, authors, and ideas that together make up the Orientalist canon. I have depended instead upon a different methodological alternative—whose backbone in a sense is the set of historical generalizations I have so far been making in this Introduction—and it is these I want now to discuss in more analytical detail.

II

I have begun with the assumption that the Orient is not an inert fact of nature. It is not merely *there*, just as the Occident itself is not just *there* either. We must take seriously Vico's[7] great observation that men make their own history; that what they can know is what they have made, and extend it to geography: as both geographical and cultural entities—to say nothing of historical entities—such locales, regions, geographical sectors as "Orient" and "Occident" are man-made. Therefore as much as the West itself, the Orient is an idea that has a history and a tradition of thought, imagery, and vocabulary that have given it reality and presence in and for the West. The two geographical entities thus support and to an extent reflect each other.

6. The countries bordering the eastern coast of the Mediterranean Sea from Turkey to Egypt, including present-day Syria, Lebanon, and Israel.

7. Giambattista Vico (1668–1744), Italian philosopher and historian.

Having said that, one must go on to state a number of reasonable qualifications. In the first place, it would be wrong to conclude that the Orient was *essentially* an idea, or a creation with no corresponding reality. When Disraeli said in his novel *Tancred*[8] that the East was a career, he meant that to be interested in the East was something bright young Westerners would find to be an all-consuming passion; he should not be interpreted as saying that the East was *only* a career for Westerners. There were—and are—cultures and nations whose location is in the East, and their lives, histories, and customs have a brute reality obviously greater than anything that could be said about them in the West. About that fact this study of Orientalism has very little to contribute, except to acknowledge it tacitly. But the phenomenon of Orientalism as I study it here deals principally, not with a correspondence between Orientalism and Orient, but with the internal consistency of Orientalism and its ideas about the Orient (the East as career) despite or beyond any correspondence, or lack thereof, with a "real" Orient. My point is that Disraeli's statement about the East refers mainly to that created consistency, that regular constellation of ideas as the pre-eminent thing about the Orient, and not to its mere being, as Wallace Stevens's[9] phrase has it.

A second qualification is that ideas, cultures, and histories cannot seriously be understood or studied without their force, or more precisely their configurations of power, also being studied. To believe that the Orient was created—or, as I call it, "Orientalized"—and to believe that such things happen simply as a necessity of the imagination, is to be disingenuous. The relationship between Occident and Orient is a relationship of power, of domination, of varying degrees of a complex hegemony, and is quite accurately indicated in the title of K. M. Panikkar's classic *Asia and Western Dominance*.[1] The Orient was Orientalized not only because it was discovered to be "Oriental" in all those ways considered commonplace by an average nineteenth-century European, but also because it *could be*—that is, submitted to being—*made* Oriental. There is very little consent to be found, for example, in the fact that Flaubert's[2] encounter with an Egyptian courtesan produced a widely influential model of the Oriental woman; she never spoke of herself, she never represented her emotions, presence, or history. *He* spoke for and represented her. He was foreign, comparatively wealthy, male, and these were historical facts of domination that allowed him not only to possess Kuchuk Hanem physically but to speak for her and tell his readers in what way she was "typically Oriental." My argument is that Flaubert's situation of strength in relation to Kuchuk Hanem was not an isolated instance. It fairly stands for the pattern of relative strength between East and West, and the discourse about the Orient that it enabled.

This brings us to a third qualification. One ought never to assume that the structure of Orientalism is nothing more than a structure of lies or of myths which, were the truth about them to be told, would simply blow away.

8. An 1847 novel whose hero leaves 19th-century England for the East, by Benjamin Disraeli (1804–1881), English politician and novelist.
9. American poet (1879–1955); one of his poems is titled "Of Mere Being."
1. K. M. Panikkar, *Asia and Western Dominance* (London: Allen and Unwin, 1959) [Said's note]. Panikkar (1895–1963), Indian diplomat and historian.
2. Gustave Flaubert (1821–1880), French novelist; his travels in Egypt and the Orient are recounted in his letters, and his novel *Salammbô* (1862) is set in ancient Carthage (in modern-day Tunisia).

I myself believe that Orientalism is more particularly valuable as a sign of European-Atlantic power over the Orient than it is as a veridic discourse about the Orient (which is what, in its academic or scholarly form, it claims to be). Nevertheless, what we must respect and try to grasp is the sheer knitted-together strength of Orientalist discourse, its very close ties to the enabling socio-economic and political institutions, and its redoubtable durability. After all, any system of ideas that can remain unchanged as teachable wisdom (in academies, books, congresses, universities, foreign-service institutes) from the period of Ernest Renan[3] in the late 1840s until the present in the United States must be something more formidable than a mere collection of lies. Orientalism, therefore, is not an airy European fantasy about the Orient, but a created body of theory and practice in which, for many generations, there has been a considerable material investment. Continued investment made Orientalism, as a system of knowledge about the Orient, an accepted grid for filtering through the Orient into Western consciousness, just as that same investment multiplied—indeed, made truly productive—the statements proliferating out from Orientalism into the general culture.

Gramsci[4] has made the useful analytic distinction between civil and political society in which the former is made up of voluntary (or at least rational and noncoercive) affiliations like schools, families, and unions, the latter of state institutions (the army, the police, the central bureaucracy) whose role in the polity is direct domination. Culture, of course, is to be found operating within civil society, where the influence of ideas, of institutions, and of other persons works not through domination but by what Gramsci calls consent. In any society not totalitarian, then, certain cultural forms predominate over others, just as certain ideas are more influential than others; the form of this cultural leadership is what Gramsci has identified as *hegemony*, an indispensable concept for any understanding of cultural life in the industrial West. It is hegemony, or rather the result of cultural hegemony at work, that gives Orientalism the durability and the strength I have been speaking about so far. Orientalism is never far from what Denys Hay has called the idea of Europe,[5] a collective notion identifying "us" Europeans as against all "those" non-Europeans, and indeed it can be argued that the major component in European culture is precisely what made that culture hegemonic both in and outside Europe: the idea of European identity as a superior one in comparison with all the non-European peoples and cultures. There is in addition the hegemony of European ideas about the Orient, themselves reiterating European superiority over Oriental backwardness, usually overriding the possibility that a more independent, or more skeptical, thinker might have had different views on the matter.

In a quite constant way, Orientalism depends for its strategy on this flexible *positional* superiority, which puts the Westerner in a whole series of possible relationships with the Orient without ever losing him the relative upper hand. And why should it have been otherwise, especially during the period of

3. French historian (1823–1892), who wrote on the Oriental origins of Christianity.
4. Antonio Gramsci (1891–1937), Italian Marxist whose concept of cultural hegemony has been highly influential.
5. Denys Hay, *Europe: The Emergence of an Idea*, 2d ed. (Edinburgh: Edinburgh University Press, 1968) [Said's note].

extraordinary European ascendancy from the late Renaissance to the present? The scientist, the scholar, the missionary, the trader, or the soldier was in, or thought about, the Orient because he *could be there*, or could think about it, with very little resistance on the Orient's part. Under the general heading of knowledge of the Orient, and within the umbrella of Western hegemony over the Orient during the period from the end of the eighteenth century, there emerged a complex Orient suitable for study in the academy, for display in the museum, for reconstruction in the colonial office, for theoretical illustration in anthropological, biological, linguistic, racial, and historical theses about mankind and the universe, for instances of economic and sociological theories of development, revolution, cultural personality, national or religious character. Additionally, the imaginative examination of things Oriental was based more or less exclusively upon a sovereign Western consciousness out of whose unchallenged centrality an Oriental world emerged, first according to general ideas about who or what was an Oriental, then according to a detailed logic governed not simply by empirical reality but by a battery of desires, repressions, investments, and projections. If we can point to great Orientalist works of genuine scholarship like Silvestre de Sacy's *Chrestomathie arabe* or Edward William Lane's *Account of the Manners and Customs of the Modern Egyptians*, we need also to note that Renan's and Gobineau's[6] racial ideas came out of the same impulse, as did a great many Victorian pornographic novels (see the analysis by Steven Marcus of "The Lustful Turk"[7]).

And yet, one must repeatedly ask oneself whether what matters in Orientalism is the general group of ideas overriding the mass of material—about which who could deny that they were shot through with doctrines of European superiority, various kinds of racism, imperialism, and the like, dogmatic views of "the Oriental" as a kind of ideal and unchanging abstraction?—or the much more varied work produced by almost uncountable individual writers, whom one would take up as individual instances of authors dealing with the Orient. In a sense the two alternatives, general and particular, are really two perspectives on the same material: in both instances one would have to deal with pioneers in the field like William Jones,[8] with great artists like Nerval or Flaubert. And why would it not be possible to employ both perspectives together, or one after the other? Isn't there an obvious danger of distortion (of precisely the kind that academic Orientalism has always been prone to) if either too general or too specific a level of description is maintained systematically?

My two fears are distortion and inaccuracy, or rather the kind of inaccuracy produced by too dogmatic a generality and too positivistic a localized focus. In trying to deal with these problems I have tried to deal with three main aspects of my own contemporary reality that seem to me to point the way out of the methodological or perspectival difficulties I have been discussing,

6. Joseph Arthur, comte de Gobineau (1816–1882), French diplomat and author of *Essay on the Inequality of the Human Races* (1853–55). The French Orientalist Antoine-Isaac Silvestre de Sacy (1758–1838) published his *Arab Chrestomathy* in 1806; Lane (1801–1876), an English scholar of Arabic, published his *Account* in 1836.

7. Steven Marcus, *The Other Victorians: A Study of Sexuality and Pornography in Mid-Nineteenth-Century England* (New York: Bantam, 1967), pp. 200–219 [Said's note].

8. English philologist and judge (1746–1794); he was the first to observe the close resemblance of Sanskrit to Greek and Latin.

difficulties that might force one, in the first instance, into writing a coarse polemic on so unacceptably general a level of description as not to be worth the effort, or in the second instance, into writing so detailed and atomistic a series of analyses as to lose all track of the general lines of force informing the field, giving it its special cogency. How then to recognize individuality and to reconcile it with its intelligent, and by no means passive or merely dictatorial, general and hegemonic context?

III

I mentioned three aspects of my contemporary reality: I must explain and briefly discuss them now, so that it can be seen how I was led to a particular course of research and writing.

1. *The distinction between pure and political knowledge.* It is very easy to argue that knowledge about Shakespeare or Wordsworth[9] is not political whereas knowledge about contemporary China or the Soviet Union is. My own formal and professional designation is that of "humanist," a title which indicates the humanities as my field and therefore the unlikely eventuality that there might be anything political about what I do in that field. Of course, all these labels and terms are quite unnuanced as I use them here, but the general truth of what I am pointing to is, I think, widely held. One reason for saying that a humanist who writes about Wordsworth, or an editor whose specialty is Keats,[1] is not involved in anything political is that what he does seems to have no direct political effect upon reality in the everyday sense. A scholar whose field is Soviet economics works in a highly charged area where there is much government interest, and what he might produce in the way of studies or proposals will be taken up by policymakers, government officials, institutional economists, intelligence experts. The distinction between "humanists" and persons whose work has policy implications, or political significance, can be broadened further by saying that the former's ideological color is a matter of incidental importance to politics (although possibly of great moment to his colleagues in the field, who may object to his Stalinism[2] or fascism or too easy liberalism), whereas the ideology of the latter is woven directly into his material—indeed, economics, politics, and sociology in the modern academy are ideological sciences—and therefore taken for granted as being "political."

Nevertheless the determining impingement on most knowledge produced in the contemporary West (and here I speak mainly about the United States) is that it be nonpolitical, that is, scholarly, academic, impartial, above partisan or small-minded doctrinal belief. One can have no quarrel with such an ambition in theory, perhaps, but in practice the reality is much more problematic. No one has ever devised a method for detaching the scholar from the circumstances of life, from the fact of his involvement (conscious or unconscious) with a class, a set of beliefs, a social position, or from the mere activity of being a member of a society. These continue to bear on what he does

9. WILLIAM WORDSWORTH (1770–1850), English Romantic poet.
1. John Keats (1795–1821), English Romantic poet.
2. That is, hard-line authoritarianism similar to that of the oppressive Soviet regime (1924–53) of Joseph Stalin (1879–1953).

professionally, even though naturally enough his research and its fruits do attempt to reach a level of relative freedom from the inhibitions and the restrictions of brute, everyday reality. For there is such a thing as knowledge that is less, rather than more, partial than the individual (with his entangling and distracting life circumstances) who produces it. Yet this knowledge is not therefore automatically nonpolitical.

Whether discussions of literature or of classical philology are fraught with—or have unmediated—political significance is a very large question that I have tried to treat in some detail elsewhere.[3] What I am interested in doing now is suggesting how the general liberal consensus that "true" knowledge is fundamentally nonpolitical (and conversely, that overtly political knowledge is not "true" knowledge) obscures the highly if obscurely organized political circumstances obtaining when knowledge is produced. No one is helped in understanding this today when the adjective "political" is used as a label to discredit any work for daring to violate the protocol of pretended suprapolitical objectivity. We may say, first, that civil society recognizes a gradation of political importance in the various fields of knowledge. To some extent the political importance given a field comes from the possibility of its direct translation into economic terms; but to a greater extent political importance comes from the closeness of a field to ascertainable sources of power in political society. Thus an economic study of long-term Soviet energy potential and its effect on military capability is likely to be commissioned by the Defense Department, and thereafter to acquire a kind of political status impossible for a study of Tolstoi's[4] early fiction financed in part by a foundation. Yet both works belong in what civil society acknowledges to be a similar field, Russian studies, even though one work may be done by a very conservative economist, the other by a radical literary historian. My point here is that "Russia" as a general subject matter has political priority over nicer distinctions such as "economics" and "literary history," because political society in Gramsci's sense reaches into such realms of civil society as the academy and saturates them with significance of direct concern to it.

I do not want to press all this any further on general theoretical grounds: it seems to me that the value and credibility of my case can be demonstrated by being much more specific, in the way, for example, Noam Chomsky has studied the instrumental connection between the Vietnam War and the notion of objective scholarship as it was applied to cover state-sponsored military research.[5] Now because Britain, France, and recently the United States are imperial powers, their political societies impart to their civil societies a sense of urgency, a direct political infusion as it were, where and whenever matters pertaining to their imperial interests abroad are concerned. I doubt that it is controversial, for example, to say that an Englishman in India or Egypt in the later nineteenth century took an interest in those countries that was never far from their status in his mind as British colonies. To say this may seem quite different from saying that all academic

3. See my *The World, the Text, and the Critic* (Cambridge, Mass.: Harvard University Press, 1983) [Said's note].
4. Leo Tolstoy (1828–1910), Russian novelist.
5. Principally in his *American Power and the New Mandarins: Historical and Political Essays* (New York: Pantheon, 1969) and *For Reasons of State* (New York: Pantheon, 1973) [Said's note]. Chomsky (b. 1928), American linguist and radical social critic.

knowledge about India and Egypt is somehow tinged and impressed with, violated by, the gross political fact—and yet *that is what I am saying* in this study of Orientalism. For if it is true that no production of knowledge in the human sciences can ever ignore or disclaim its author's involvement as a human subject in his own circumstances, then it must also be true that for a European or American studying the Orient there can be no disclaiming the main circumstances of *his* actuality: that he comes up against the Orient as a European or American first, as an individual second. And to be a European or an American in such a situation is by no means an inert fact. It meant and means being aware, however dimly, that one belongs to a power with definite interests in the Orient, and more important, that one belongs to a part of the earth with a definite history of involvement in the Orient almost since the time of Homer.[6]

Put in this way, these political actualities are still too undefined and general to be really interesting. Anyone would agree to them without necessarily agreeing also that they mattered very much, for instance, to Flaubert as he wrote *Salammbô*, or to H. A. R. Gibb as he wrote *Modern Trends in Islam*.[7] The trouble is that there is too great a distance between the big dominating fact, as I have described it, and the details of everyday life that govern the minute discipline of a novel or a scholarly text as each is being written. Yet if we eliminate from the start any notion that "big" facts like imperial domination can be applied mechanically and deterministically to such complex matters as culture and ideas, then we will begin to approach an interesting kind of study. My idea is that European and then American interest in the Orient was political according to some of the obvious historical accounts of it that I have given here, but that it was the culture that created that interest, that acted dynamically along with brute political, economic, and military rationales to make the Orient the varied and complicated place that it obviously was in the field I call Orientalism.

Therefore, Orientalism is not a mere political subject matter or field that is reflected passively by culture, scholarship, or institutions; nor is it a large and diffuse collection of texts about the Orient; nor is it representative and expressive of some nefarious "Western" imperialist plot to hold down the "Oriental" world. It is rather a *distribution* of geopolitical awareness into aesthetic, scholarly, economic, sociological, historical, and philological texts; it is an *elaboration* not only of a basic geographical distinction (the world is made up of two unequal halves, Orient and Occident) but also of a whole series of "interests" which, by such means as scholarly discovery, philological reconstruction, psychological analysis, landscape and sociological description, it not only creates but also maintains; it *is*, rather than expresses, a certain *will* or *intention* to understand, in some cases to control, manipulate, even to incorporate, what is a manifestly different (or alternative and novel) world; it is, above all, a discourse that is by no means in direct, corresponding relationship with political power in the raw, but rather is produced and exists in an uneven exchange with various kinds of power, shaped to a degree by the exchange with power political (as with a colonial or imperial establishment), power intellectual (as with reigning sciences like comparative linguistics or

6. Ca. 8th century B.C.E.
7. Published in 1947; Gibb (1895–1971) was an English scholar of Arabic language and history.

anatomy, or any of the modern policy sciences), power cultural (as with orthodoxies and canons of taste, texts, values), power moral (as with ideas about what "we" do and what "they" cannot do or understand as "we" do). Indeed, my real argument is that Orientalism is—and does not simply represent—a considerable dimension of modern political-intellectual culture, and as such has less to do with the Orient than it does with "our" world.

Because Orientalism is a cultural and a political fact, then, it does not exist in some archival vacuum; quite the contrary, I think it can be shown that what is thought, said, or even done about the Orient follows (perhaps occurs within) certain distinct and intellectually knowable lines. Here too a considerable degree of nuance and elaboration can be seen working as between the broad superstructural pressures and the details of composition, the facts of textuality. Most humanistic scholars are, I think, perfectly happy with the notion that texts exist in contexts, that there is such a thing as intertextuality, that the pressures of conventions, predecessors, and rhetorical styles limit what Walter Benjamin once called the "overtaxing of the productive person in the name of . . . the principle of 'creativity,'" in which the poet is believed on his own, and out of his pure mind, to have brought forth his work.[8] Yet there is a reluctance to allow that political, institutional, and ideological constraints act in the same manner on the individual author. A humanist will believe it to be an interesting fact to any interpreter of Balzac that he was influenced in the *Comédie humaine*[9] by the conflict between Geoffroy Saint-Hilaire and Cuvier,[1] but the same sort of pressure on Balzac of deeply reactionary monarchism is felt in some vague way to demean his literary "genius" and therefore to be less worth serious study. Similarly—as Harry Bracken[2] has been tirelessly showing—philosophers will conduct their discussions of Locke, Hume, and empiricism[3] without ever taking into account that there is an explicit connection in these classic writers between their "philosophic" doctrines and racial theory, justifications of slavery, or arguments for colonial exploitation.[4] These are common enough ways by which contemporary scholarship keeps itself pure.

Perhaps it is true that most attempts to rub culture's nose in the mud of politics have been crudely iconoclastic; perhaps also the social interpretation of literature in my own field has simply not kept up with the enormous technical advances in detailed textual analysis. But there is no getting away from the fact that literary studies in general, and American Marxist theorists in particular, have avoided the effort of seriously bridging the gap between the superstructural and the base levels in textual, historical scholarship; on another occasion I have gone so far as to say that the literary-cultural establishment as a whole has declared the serious study of imperialism and culture

8. Walter Benjamin, *Charles Baudelaire: A Lyric Poet in the Era of High Capitalism*, trans. Harry Zohn (London: New Left Books, 1973), p. 71 [Said's note]. BENJAMIN (1892–1940), German literary and cultural critic.
9. *The Human Comedy*, the title given to the totality of his short stories and novels by the French novelist Honoré de Balzac (1799–1850); most portray contemporary French society and many are linked by recurring characters.
1. A debate on comparative anatomy in 1830 between the prominent French zoologists Étienne Geoffroy Saint-Hilaire (1772–1844) and Georges Cuvier (1769–1832).
2. American philosopher (1926–2011).
3. The view, held by the British philosophers John Locke (1632–1704) and DAVID HUME (1711–1776), that all knowledge derives from sensory experience.
4. Harry Bracken, "Essence, Accident, and Race," *Hermathena* 116 (winter 1973): 81–96 [Said's note].

off limits.[5] For Orientalism brings one up directly against that question—that is, to realizing that political imperialism governs an entire field of study, imagination, and scholarly institutions—in such a way as to make its avoidance an intellectual and historical impossibility. Yet there will always remain the perennial escape mechanism of saying that a literary scholar and a philosopher, for example, are trained in literature and philosophy respectively, not in politics or ideological analysis. In other words, the specialist argument can work quite effectively to block the larger and, in my opinion, the more intellectually serious perspective.

Here it seems to me there is a simple two-part answer to be given, at least so far as the study of imperialism and culture (or Orientalism) is concerned. In the first place, nearly every nineteenth-century writer (and the same is true enough of writers in earlier periods) was extraordinarily well aware of the fact of empire: this is a subject not very well studied, but it will not take a modern Victorian specialist long to admit that liberal cultural heroes like John Stuart Mill, Arnold, Carlyle, Newman, Macaulay, Ruskin, George Eliot, and even Dickens[6] had definite views on race and imperialism, which are quite easily to be found at work in their writing. So even a specialist must deal with the knowledge that Mill, for example, made it clear in *On Liberty* and *Representative Government* that his views there could not be applied to India (he was an India Office functionary for a good deal of his life, after all) because the Indians were civilizationally, if not racially, inferior. The same kind of paradox is to be found in Marx, as I try to show in this book. In the second place, to believe that politics in the form of imperialism bears upon the production of literature, scholarship, social theory, and history writing is by no means equivalent to saying that culture is therefore a demeaned or denigrated thing. Quite the contrary: my whole point is to say that we can better understand the persistence and the durability of saturating hegemonic systems like culture when we realize that their internal constraints upon writers and thinkers were *productive*, not unilaterally inhibiting. It is this idea that Gramsci, certainly, and Foucault and Raymond Williams in their very different ways have been trying to illustrate. Even one or two pages by Williams on "the uses of the Empire" in *The Long Revolution* tell us more about nineteenth-century cultural richness than many volumes of hermetic textual analyses.[7]

Therefore I study Orientalism as a dynamic exchange between individual authors and the large political concerns shaped by the three great empires—British, French, American—in whose intellectual and imaginative territory the writing was produced. What interests me most as a scholar is not the gross political verity but the detail, as indeed what interests us in someone

5. In an interview published in *Diacritics* 6, no. 3 (fall 1976): 38 [Said's note]. The terms *superstructure* and *base* allude to the Marxist view that all aspects of a society—literature, arts, politics, and so on—depend on its economic form of production.

6. All major Victorian writers and thinkers: Mill (1806–1873), philosopher and social reformer, who published *On Liberty* in 1859 and *Considerations on Representative Government* in 1861; MATTHEW ARNOLD (1822–1888), poet and critic; Thomas Carlyle (1795–1881), historian and essayist; John Henry Newman (1801–1890), prelate and theologian; Thomas Babington Macaulay (1800–1859), historian and statesman; John Ruskin (1819–1900), art critic; Eliot (pen name of Marian Evans, 1819–1880), novelist; and Charles Dickens (1812–1870), novelist.

7. Raymond Williams, *The Long Revolution* (London: Chatto and Windus, 1961), pp. 66–67 [Said's note]. WILLIAMS (1921–1988), British Marxist literary critic.

like Lane or Flaubert or Renan is not the (to him) indisputable truth that Occidentals are superior to Orientals, but the profoundly worked over and modulated evidence of his detailed work within the very wide space opened up by that truth. One need only remember that Lane's *Manners and Customs of the Modern Egyptians* is a classic of historical and anthropological observation because of its style, its enormously intelligent and brilliant details, not because of its simple reflection of racial superiority, to understand what I am saying here.

The kind of political questions raised by Orientalism, then, are as follows: What other sorts of intellectual, aesthetic, scholarly, and cultural energies went into the making of an imperialist tradition like the Orientalist one? How did philology, lexicography, history, biology, political and economic theory, novel-writing, and lyric poetry come to the service of Orientalism's broadly imperialist view of the world? What changes, modulations, refinements, even revolutions take place within Orientalism? What is the meaning of originality, of continuity, of individuality, in this context? How does Orientalism transmit or reproduce itself from one epoch to another? In fine, how can we treat the cultural, historical phenomenon of Orientalism as a kind of *willed human work*—not of mere unconditioned ratiocination—in all its historical complexity, detail, and worth without at the same time losing sight of the alliance between cultural work, political tendencies, the state, and the specific realities of domination? Governed by such concerns a humanistic study can responsibly address itself to politics *and* culture. But this is not to say that such a study establishes a hard-and-fast rule about the relationship between knowledge and politics. My argument is that each humanistic investigation must formulate the nature of that connection in the specific context of the study, the subject matter, and its historical circumstances.

2. *The methodological question.* In a previous book I gave a good deal of thought and analysis to the methodological importance for work in the human sciences of finding and formulating a first step, a point of departure, a beginning principle.[8] A major lesson I learned and tried to present was that there is no such thing as a merely given, or simply available, starting point: beginnings have to be made for each project in such a way as to *enable* what follows from them. Nowhere in my experience has the difficulty of this lesson been more consciously lived (with what success—or failure—I cannot really say) than in this study of Orientalism. The idea of beginning, indeed the act of beginning, necessarily involves an act of delimitation by which something is cut out of a great mass of material, separated from the mass, and made to stand for, as well as be, a starting point, a beginning; for the student of texts one such notion of inaugural delimitation is Louis Althusser's idea of the *problematic*, a specific determinate unity of a text, or group of texts, which is something given rise to by analysis.[9] Yet in the case of Orientalism (as opposed to the case of Marx's texts, which is what Althusser studies) there is not simply the problem of finding a point of departure, or problematic, but also the question of designating which texts, authors, and periods are the ones best suited for study.

8. In my *Beginnings: Intention and Method* (New York: Basic, 1975) [Said's note].
9. Louis Althusser, *For Marx*, trans. Ben Brewster (New York: Pantheon Books, 1969), pp. 65–67 [Said's note]. ALTHUSSER (1918–1990), French Marxist philosopher.

It has seemed to me foolish to attempt an encyclopedic narrative history of Orientalism, first of all because if my guiding principle was to be "the European idea of the Orient" there would be virtually no limit to the material I would have had to deal with; second, because the narrative model itself did not suit my descriptive and political interests; third, because in such books as Raymond Schwab's *La Renaissance orientale*, Johann Fück's *Die Arabischen Studien in Europa bis in den Anfang des 20. Jahrhunderts*, and more recently, Dorothee Metlitzki's *The Matter of Araby in Medieval England*[1] there already exist encyclopedic works on certain aspects of the European-Oriental encounter such as make the critic's job, in the general political and intellectual context I sketched above, a different one.

There still remained the problem of cutting down a very fat archive to manageable dimensions, and more important, outlining something in the nature of an intellectual order within that group of texts without at the same time following a mindlessly chronological order. My starting point therefore has been the British, French, and American experience of the Orient taken as a unit, what made that experience possible by way of historical and intellectual background, what the quality and character of the experience has been. For reasons I shall discuss presently I limited that already limited (but still inordinately large) set of questions to the Anglo-French-American experience of the Arabs and Islam, which for almost a thousand years together stood for the Orient. Immediately upon doing that, a large part of the Orient seemed to have been eliminated—India, Japan, China, and other sections of the Far East—not because these regions were not important (they obviously have been) but because one could discuss Europe's experience of the Near Orient, or of Islam, apart from its experience of the Far Orient. Yet at certain moments of that general European history of interest in the East, particular parts of the Orient like Egypt, Syria, and Arabia cannot be discussed without also studying Europe's involvement in the more distant parts, of which Persia and India are the most important; a notable case in point is the connection between Egypt and India so far as eighteenth- and nineteenth-century Britain was concerned. Similarly the French role in deciphering the Zend-Avesta, the pre-eminence of Paris as a center of Sanskrit studies during the first decade of the nineteenth century, the fact that Napoleon's[2] interest in the Orient was contingent upon his sense of the British role in India: all these Far Eastern interests directly influenced French interest in the Near East, Islam, and the Arabs.

Britain and France dominated the Eastern Mediterranean from about the end of the seventeenth century on. Yet my discussion of that domination and systematic interest does not do justice to (*a*) the important contributions to Orientalism of Germany, Italy, Russia, Spain, and Portugal and (*b*) the fact that one of the important impulses toward the study of the Orient in the

1. Raymond Schwab, *La Renaissance orientale* [*The Oriental Renaissance*, French] (Paris: Payot, 1950); Johann W. Fück, *Die Arabischen Studien in Europa bis in den Anfang des 20. Jahrhunderts* [*Arabic Studies in Europe from Its Origins through the Twentieth Century*, German] (Leipzig: Otto Harrassowitz, 1955); Dorothee Metlitzki, *The Matter of Araby in Medieval England* (New Haven: Yale University Press, 1977) [Said's note].

2. Napoléon Bonaparte (1769–1821), general and emperor of France (1804–15), who campaigned in Egypt (1798–99) in an attempt to damage Britain's trade with India. The Zend-Avesta: the Avesta, a book of sacred writings from eastern Iran (begun ca. 600 B.C.E., fixed in form ca. 4th–6th c. C.E.) that collects the teachings of the religious leader and prophet Zoroaster.

eighteenth century was the revolution in Biblical studies stimulated by such variously interesting pioneers as Bishop Lowth, Eichhorn, Herder, and Michaelis.[3] In the first place, I had to focus rigorously upon the British-French and later the American material because it seemed inescapably true not only that Britain and France were the pioneer nations in the Orient and in Oriental studies, but that these vanguard positions were held by virtue of the two greatest colonial networks in pre-twentieth-century history; the American Oriental position since World War II has fit—I think, quite self-consciously—in the places excavated by the two earlier European powers. Then too, I believe that the sheer quality, consistency, and mass of British, French, and American writing on the Orient lifts it above the doubtless crucial work done in Germany, Italy, Russia, and elsewhere. But I think it is also true that the major steps in Oriental scholarship were first taken in either Britain and France, then elaborated upon by Germans. Silvestre de Sacy, for example, was not only the first modern and institutional European Orientalist, who worked on Islam, Arabic literature, the Druze religion, and Sassanid Persia; he was also the teacher of Champollion and of Franz Bopp,[4] the founder of German comparative linguistics. A similar claim of priority and subsequent pre-eminence can be made for William Jones and Edward William Lane.

In the second place—and here the failings of my study of Orientalism are amply made up for—there has been some important recent work on the background in Biblical scholarship to the rise of what I have called modern Orientalism. The best and the most illuminatingly relevant is E. S. Shaffer's impressive *"Kubla Khan" and The Fall of Jerusalem,*[5] an indispensable study of the origins of Romanticism, and of the intellectual activity underpinning a great deal of what goes on in Coleridge, Browning,[6] and George Eliot. To some degree Shaffer's work refines upon the outlines provided in Schwab, by articulating the material of relevance to be found in the German Biblical scholars and using that material to read, in an intelligent and always interesting way, the work of three major British writers. Yet what is missing in the book is some sense of the political as well as ideological edge given the Oriental material by the British and French writers I am principally concerned with; in addition, unlike Shaffer I attempt to elucidate subsequent developments in academic as well as literary Orientalism that bear on the connection between British and French Orientalism on the one hand and the rise of an explicitly colonial-minded imperialism on the other. Then too, I wish to show how all these earlier matters are reproduced more or less in American Orientalism after the Second World War.

3. Johann David Michaelis (1717–1791), German theologian. Robert Lowth (1710–1787), English grammarian and biblical translator. Johann Gottfried Eichhorn (1752–1827), German biblical scholar and professor of Oriental languages. Johann Gottfried Herder (1744–1803), German critic and philologist.

4. German philologist and Sanskrit scholar (1791–1867). Druze: a Muslim sect (founded in the early 11th c.) whose members live mainly in the mountains of Lebanon and southern Syria. Sassanid Persia: an empire (224–651) founded by Ardashir I, who made Zoroastrianism the official religion. Jean-François Champollion (1790–1823), French founder of Egyptology, who deciphered the hieroglyphs on the Rosetta Stone.

5. E. S. Shaffer, *"Kubla Khan" and the Fall of Jerusalem: The Mythological School in Biblical Criticism and Secular Literature, 1770–1880* (Cambridge: Cambridge University Press, 1975) [Said's note].

6. Robert Browning (1812–1889), English poet. SAMUEL TAYLOR COLERIDGE (1772–1834), English Romantic poet and critic; his works include "Kubla Khan" (written 1797; published 1816), while *The Fall of Jerusalem* is an epic that he never wrote.

Nevertheless there is a possibly misleading aspect to my study, where, aside from an occasional reference, I do not exhaustively discuss the German developments after the inaugural period dominated by Sacy. Any work that seeks to provide an understanding of academic Orientalism and pays little attention to scholars like Steinthal, Müller, Becker, Goldziher, Brockelmann, Nöldeke[7]—to mention only a handful—needs to be reproached, and I freely reproach myself. I particularly regret not taking more account of the great scientific prestige that accrued to German scholarship by the middle of the nineteenth century, whose neglect was made into a denunciation of insular British scholars by George Eliot. I have in mind Eliot's unforgettable portrait of Mr. Casaubon in *Middlemarch*. One reason Casaubon cannot finish his Key to All Mythologies is, according to his young cousin Will Ladislaw, that he is unacquainted with German scholarship. For not only has Casaubon chosen a subject "as changing as chemistry: new discoveries are constantly making new points of view": he is undertaking a job similar to a refutation of Paracelsus because "he is not an Orientalist, you know."[8]

Eliot was not wrong in implying that by about 1830, which is when *Middlemarch* is set, German scholarship had fully attained its European preeminence. Yet at no time in German scholarship during the first two-thirds of the nineteenth century could a close partnership have developed between Orientalists and a protracted, sustained *national* interest in the Orient. There was nothing in Germany to correspond to the Anglo-French presence in India, the Levant, North Africa. Moreover, the German Orient was almost exclusively a scholarly, or at least a classical, Orient: it was made the subject of lyrics, fantasies, and even novels, but it was never actual, the way Egypt and Syria were actual for Chateaubriand, Lane, Lamartine, Burton,[9] Disraeli, or Nerval. There is some significance in the fact that the two most renowned German works on the Orient, Goethe's *Westöstlicher Diwan* and Friedrich Schlegel's *Über die Sprache und Weisheit der Indier*,[1] were based respectively on a Rhine journey and on hours spent in Paris libraries. What German Oriental scholarship did was to refine and elaborate techniques whose application was to texts, myths, ideas, and languages almost literally gathered from the Orient by imperial Britain and France.

Yet what German Orientalism had in common with Anglo-French and later American Orientalism was a kind of intellectual *authority* over the Orient within Western culture. This authority must in large part be the subject of any description of Orientalism, and it is so in this study. Even the name *Orientalism* suggests a serious, perhaps ponderous style of expertise; when I

7. Except for the Hungarian Goldziher (who also wrote in German), all those named are German: Heymann Steinthal (1823–1899), philologist; Friedrich Max Müller (1823–1900), philologist and scholar of Hinduism and Buddhism; Carl Heinrich Becker (1876–1933), politician and scholar of Islamic civilization; Ignác Goldziher (1850–1921), scholar of Islamic civilization; Carl Brockelmann (1868–1956), scholar of Semitic languages and Arabic literature; and Theodor Nöldeke (1836–1930), scholar of Semitic languages and Arabic history.

8. George Eliot, *Middlemarch: A Study of Provincial Life* [1871–72] (Boston: Houghton Mifflin, 1956), p. 164 [Said's note]. Paracelsus: pseudonym of Theophrastus Bombastus von Hohenheim (1493–1541), German physician and chemist who was obsessed with alchemy.

9. Sir Richard Francis Burton (1821–1890), English explorer and linguist who made a pilgrimage to Mecca in disguise and translated *Arabian Nights* (1885–88). Alphonse de Lamartine (1790–1869), French Romantic poet, historian, and statesman.

1. *On the Language and Wisdom of India* (1808) by the German Romantic critic Friedrich von Schlegel (1772–1829). *West-Eastern Divan* (1819), a volume of lyric poems by the German poet and dramatist Johann Wolfgang von Goethe (1749–1832).

apply it to modern American social scientists (since they do not call themselves Orientalists, my use of the word is anomalous), it is to draw attention to the way Middle East experts can still draw on the vestiges of Orientalism's intellectual position in nineteenth-century Europe.

There is nothing mysterious or natural about authority. It is formed, irradiated, disseminated; it is instrumental, it is persuasive; it has status, it establishes canons of taste and value; it is virtually indistinguishable from certain ideas it dignifies as true, and from traditions, perceptions, and judgments it forms, transmits, reproduces. Above all, authority can, indeed must, be analyzed. All these attributes of authority apply to Orientalism, and much of what I do in this study is to describe both the historical authority in and the personal authorities of Orientalism.

My principal methodological devices for studying authority here are what can be called *strategic location*, which is a way of describing the author's position in a text with regard to the Oriental material he writes about, and *strategic formation*, which is a way of analyzing the relationship between texts and the way in which groups of texts, types of texts, even textual genres, acquire mass, density, and referential power among themselves and thereafter in the culture at large. I use the notion of strategy simply to identify the problem every writer on the Orient has faced: how to get hold of it, how to approach it, how not to be defeated or overwhelmed by its sublimity, its scope, its awful dimensions. Everyone who writes about the Orient must locate himself vis-à-vis the Orient; translated into his text, this location includes the kind of narrative voice he adopts, the type of structure he builds, the kinds of images, themes, motifs that circulate in his text—all of which add up to deliberate ways of addressing the reader, containing the Orient, and finally, representing it or speaking in its behalf. None of this takes place in the abstract, however. Every writer on the Orient (and this is true even of Homer[2]) assumes some Oriental precedent, some previous knowledge of the Orient, to which he refers and on which he relies. Additionally, each work on the Orient *affiliates* itself with other works, with audiences, with institutions, with the Orient itself. The ensemble of relationships between works, audiences, and some particular aspects of the Orient therefore constitutes an analyzable formation—for example, that of philological studies, of anthologies of extracts from Oriental literature, of travel books, of Oriental fantasies—whose presence in time, in discourse, in institutions (schools, libraries, foreign services) gives it strength and authority.

It is clear, I hope, that my concern with authority does not entail analysis of what lies hidden in the Orientalist text, but analysis rather of the text's surface, its exteriority to what it describes. I do not think that this idea can be overemphasized. Orientalism is premised upon exteriority, that is, on the fact that the Orientalist, poet or scholar, makes the Orient speak, describes the Orient, renders its mysteries plain for and to the West. He is never concerned with the Orient except as the first cause of what he says. What he says and writes, by virtue of the fact that it is said or written, is meant to indicate that the Orientalist is outside the Orient, both as an existential and as a moral fact. The principal product of this exteriority is of course

2. Homer's *Iliad* takes place at Troy, in northwestern Asia Minor (present-day Turkey).

representation: as early as Aeschylus's play *The Persians*[3] the Orient is transformed from a very far distant and often threatening Otherness into figures that are relatively familiar (in Aeschylus's case, grieving Asiatic women). The dramatic immediacy of representation in *The Persians* obscures the fact that the audience is watching a highly artificial enactment of what a non-Oriental has made into a symbol for the whole Orient. My analysis of the Orientalist text therefore places emphasis on the evidence, which is by no means invisible, for such representations *as representations*, not as "natural" depictions of the Orient. This evidence is found just as prominently in the so-called truthful text (histories, philological analyses, political treatises) as in the avowedly artistic (i.e., openly imaginative) text. The things to look at are style, figures of speech, setting, narrative devices, historical and social circumstances, *not* the correctness of the representation nor its fidelity to some great original. The exteriority of the representation is always governed by some version of the truism that if the Orient could represent itself, it would; since it cannot, the representation does the job, for the West, and *faute de mieux*,[4] for the poor Orient. "Sie können sich nicht vertreten, sie müssen vertreten werden,"[5] as Marx wrote in *The Eighteenth Brumaire of Louis Bonaparte*.

Another reason for insisting upon exteriority is that I believe it needs to be made clear about cultural discourse and exchange within a culture that what is commonly circulated by it is not "truth" but representations. It hardly needs to be demonstrated again that language itself is a highly organized and encoded system, which employs many devices to express, indicate, exchange messages and information, represent, and so forth. In any instance of at least written language, there is no such thing as a delivered presence, but a *represence*, or a representation. The value, efficacy, strength, apparent veracity of a written statement about the Orient therefore relies very little, and cannot instrumentally depend, on the Orient as such. On the contrary, the written statement is a presence to the reader by virtue of its having excluded, displaced, made supererogatory any such *real thing* as "the Orient." Thus all of Orientalism stands forth and away from the Orient: that Orientalism makes sense at all depends more on the West than on the Orient, and this sense is directly indebted to various Western techniques of representation that make the Orient visible, clear, "there" in discourse about it. And these representations rely upon institutions, traditions, conventions, agreed-upon codes of understanding for their effects, not upon a distant and amorphous Orient.

The difference between representations of the Orient before the last third of the eighteenth century and those after it (that is, those belonging to what I call modern Orientalism) is that the range of representation expanded enormously in the later period. It is true that after William Jones and Anquetil-Duperron,[6] and after Napoleon's Egyptian expedition, Europe came to know the Orient more scientifically, to live in it with greater authority and disci-

3. A tragedy originally staged in 472 B.C.E. that portrays the return of Xerxes, king of Persia, to his capital after his defeat by the Greeks in the second Persian War (482–478).
4. For want of anything better (French).
5. "They cannot represent themselves; they must be represented" (German). *Eighteenth Brumaire* was published in 1852. This quotation is also the epigraph of the entire book.
6. Abraham-Hyacinthe Anquetil-Duperron (1731–1805), French scholar of Oriental languages who translated the Avesta into French in 1771.

pline than ever before. But what mattered to Europe was the expanded scope and the much greater refinement given its techniques for receiving the Orient. When around the turn of the eighteenth century the Orient definitively revealed the age of its languages—thus outdating Hebrew's divine pedigree—it was a group of Europeans who made the discovery, passed it on to other scholars, and preserved the discovery in the new science of Indo-European philology. A new powerful science for viewing the linguistic Orient was born, and with it, as Foucault has shown in *The Order of Things*,[7] a whole web of related scientific interests. Similarly William Beckford, Byron,[8] Goethe, and Hugo restructured the Orient by their art and made its colors, lights, and people visible through their images, rhythms, and motifs. At most, the "real" Orient provoked a writer to his vision; it very rarely guided it.

Orientalism responded more to the culture that produced it than to its putative object, which was also produced by the West. Thus the history of Orientalism has both an internal consistency and a highly articulated set of relationships to the dominant culture surrounding it. My analyses consequently try to show the field's shape and internal organization, its pioneers, patriarchal authorities, canonical texts, doxological[9] ideas, exemplary figures, its followers, elaborators, and new authorities; I try also to explain how Orientalism borrowed and was frequently informed by "strong" ideas, doctrines, and trends ruling the culture. Thus there was (and is) a linguistic Orient, a Freudian Orient, a Spenglerian Orient, a Darwinian Orient,[1] a racist Orient—and so on. Yet never has there been such a thing as a pure, or unconditional, Orient; similarly, never has there been a nonmaterial form of Orientalism, much less something so innocent as an "idea" of the Orient. In this underlying conviction and in its ensuing methodological consequences do I differ from scholars who study the history of ideas. For the emphases and the executive form, above all the material effectiveness, of statements made by Orientalist discourse are possible in ways that any hermetic history of ideas tends completely to scant. Without those emphases and that material effectiveness Orientalism would be just another idea, whereas it is and was much more than that. Therefore I set out to examine not only scholarly works but also works of literature, political tracts, journalistic texts, travel books, religious and philological studies. In other words, my hybrid perspective is broadly historical and "anthropological," given that I believe all texts to be worldly and circumstantial in (of course) ways that vary from genre to genre, and from historical period to historical period.

Yet unlike Michel Foucault, to whose work I am greatly indebted, I do believe in the determining imprint of individual writers upon the otherwise anonymous collective body of texts constituting a discursive formation like

7. Published in 1966 (titled *Les Mots et les choses*, or *The Words and the Things*).
8. George Gordon, Lord Byron (1788–1824), English Romantic poet whose works include such "Eastern tales" as *The Giaour* (1814). Beckford (1760–1844), English travel writer and art collector who also wrote the Gothic novel *Vathek, an Arabian Tale* (1786).
9. Expressing praise to God in established ways.
1. That is, an Orient as perceived through the lenses of the psychological theory of SIGMUND FREUD (1856–1939), Austrian founder of psychoanalysis; the historical theory of Oswald Spengler (1880–1936), German historian who argued in *The Decline of the West* (1918–22) that cultures grow and decay in a natural cycle (the Eastern having given way to the Western, which he believed was itself in its last stage); and the evolutionary theory of Charles Darwin (1809–1882), English naturalist.

Orientalism. The unity of the large ensemble of texts I analyze is due in part to the fact that they frequently refer to each other: Orientalism is after all a system for citing works and authors. Edward William Lane's *Manners and Customs of the Modern Egyptians* was read and cited by such diverse figures as Nerval, Flaubert, and Richard Burton. He was an authority whose use was an imperative for anyone writing or thinking about the Orient, not just about Egypt: when Nerval borrows passages verbatim from *Modern Egyptians* it is to use Lane's authority to assist him in describing village scenes in Syria, not Egypt. Lane's authority and the opportunities provided for citing him discriminately as well as indiscriminately were there because Orientalism could give his text the kind of distributive currency that he acquired. There is no way, however, of understanding Lane's currency without also understanding the peculiar features of *his* text; this is equally true of Renan, Sacy, Lamartine, Schlegel, and a group of other influential writers. Foucault believes that in general the individual text or author counts for very little; empirically, in the case of Orientalism (and perhaps nowhere else) I find this not to be so. Accordingly my analyses employ close textual readings whose goal is to reveal the dialectic between individual text or writer and the complex collective formation to which his work is a contribution.

Yet even though it includes an ample selection of writers, this book is still far from a complete history or general account of Orientalism. Of this failing I am very conscious. The fabric of as thick a discourse as Orientalism has survived and functioned in Western society because of its richness: all I have done is to describe parts of that fabric at certain moments, and merely to suggest the existence of a larger whole, detailed, interesting, dotted with fascinating figures, texts, and events. I have consoled myself with believing that this book is one installment of several, and hope there are scholars and critics who might want to write others. There is still a general essay to be written on imperialism and culture; other studies would go more deeply into the connection between Orientalism and pedagogy, or into Italian, Dutch, German, and Swiss Orientalism, or into the dynamic between scholarship and imaginative writing, or into the relationship between administrative ideas and intellectual discipline. Perhaps the most important task of all would be to undertake studies in contemporary alternatives to Orientalism, to ask how one can study other cultures and peoples from a libertarian, or a nonrepressive and nonmanipulative, perspective. But then one would have to rethink the whole complex problem of knowledge and power. These are all tasks left embarrassingly incomplete in this study.

The last, perhaps self-flattering, observation on method that I want to make here is that I have written this study with several audiences in mind. For students of literature and criticism, Orientalism offers a marvelous instance of the interrelations between society, history, and textuality; moreover, the cultural role played by the Orient in the West connects Orientalism with ideology, politics, and the logic of power, matters of relevance, I think, to the literary community. For contemporary students of the Orient, from university scholars to policymakers, I have written with two ends in mind: one, to present their intellectual genealogy to them in a way that has not been done; two, to criticize—with the hope of stirring discussion—the often unquestioned assumptions on which their work for the most part depends. For the general reader, this study deals with matters that always compel attention, all of them connected not only with Western conceptions and treatments of the Other but also with the singularly important role played by Western culture in what Vico called the world of nations. Lastly, for readers in the so-called Third World,[2] this study proposes itself as a step towards an understanding not so much of Western politics and of the non-Western world in those politics as of the *strength* of Western cultural discourse, a strength too often mistaken as merely decorative or "superstructural." My hope is to illustrate the formidable structure of cultural domination and, specifically for formerly colonized peoples, the dangers and temptations of employing this structure upon themselves or upon others.

The three long chapters and twelve shorter units into which this book is divided are intended to facilitate exposition as much as possible. Chapter One, "The Scope of Orientalism," draws a large circle around all the dimensions of the subject, both in terms of historical time and experiences and in terms of philosophical and political themes. Chapter Two, "Orientalist Structures and Restructures," attempts to trace the development of modern Orientalism by a broadly chronological description, and also by the description of a set of devices common to the work of important poets, artists, and scholars. Chapter Three, "Orientalism Now," begins where its predecessor left off, at around 1870. This is the period of great colonial expansion into the Orient, and it culminates in World War II. The very last section of Chapter Three characterizes the shift from British and French to American hegemony; I attempt there finally to sketch the present intellectual and social realities of Orientalism in the United States.

3. *The personal dimension.* In the *Prison Notebooks* Gramsci says: "The starting-point of critical elaboration is the consciousness of what one really is, and is 'knowing thyself' as a product of the historical process to date, which has deposited in you an infinity of traces, without leaving an inventory." The only available English translation inexplicably leaves Gramsci's comment at that, whereas in fact Gramsci's Italian text concludes by adding, "therefore it is imperative at the outset to compile such an inventory."[3]

Much of the personal investment in this study derives from my awareness of being an "Oriental" as a child growing up in two British colonies. All of my education, in those colonies (Palestine and Egypt) and in the United States, has been Western, and yet that deep early awareness has persisted. In many ways my study of Orientalism has been an attempt to inventory the traces upon me, the Oriental subject, of the culture whose domination has been so powerful a factor in the life of all Orientals. This is why for me the Islamic Orient has had to be the center of attention. Whether what I have achieved is the inventory prescribed by Gramsci is not for me to judge, although I have felt it important to be conscious of trying to produce one. Along the way, as severely and as rationally as I have been able, I have tried to maintain a critical consciousness, as well as employing those instruments of historical, humanistic, and cultural research of which my education has made me the

2. The "underdeveloped" countries, many of them former colonies, now dominated by highly industrialized "first world" (largely Western) nations in a global economy.

3. Antonio Gramsci, *The Prison Notebooks: Selections*, trans. and ed. Quintin Hoare and Geoffrey Nowell Smith (New York: International Publishers, 1971), p. 324 [Said's note].

fortunate beneficiary. In none of that, however, have I ever lost hold of the cultural reality of, the personal involvement in having been constituted as, "an Oriental."

The historical circumstances making such a study possible are fairly complex, and I can only list them schematically here. Anyone resident in the West since the 1950s, particularly in the United States, will have lived through an era of extraordinary turbulence in the relations of East and West. No one will have failed to note how "East" has always signified danger and threat during this period, even as it has meant the traditional Orient as well as Russia. In the universities a growing establishment of area-studies programs and institutes has made the scholarly study of the Orient a branch of national policy. Public affairs in this country include a healthy interest in the Orient, as much for its strategic and economic importance as for its traditional exoticism. If the world has become immediately accessible to a Western citizen living in the electronic age, the Orient too has drawn nearer to him, and is now less a myth perhaps than a place crisscrossed by Western, especially American, interests.

One aspect of the electronic, postmodern world is that there has been a reinforcement of the stereotypes by which the Orient is viewed. Television, the films, and all the media's resources have forced information into more and more standardized molds. So far as the Orient is concerned, standardization and cultural stereotyping have intensified the hold of the nineteenth-century academic and imaginative demonology of "the mysterious Orient." This is nowhere more true than in the ways by which the Near East is grasped. Three things have contributed to making even the simplest perception of the Arabs and Islam into a highly politicized, almost raucous matter: one, the history of popular anti-Arab and anti-Islamic prejudice in the West, which is immediately reflected in the history of Orientalism; two, the struggle between the Arabs and Israeli Zionism,[4] and its effects upon American Jews as well as upon both the liberal culture and the population at large; three, the almost total absence of any cultural position making it possible either to identify with or dispassionately to discuss the Arabs or Islam. Furthermore, it hardly needs saying that because the Middle East is now so identified with Great Power politics, oil economics, and the simple-minded dichotomy of freedom-loving, democratic Israel and evil, totalitarian, and terroristic Arabs, the chances of anything like a clear view of what one talks about in talking about the Near East are depressingly small.

My own experiences of these matters are in part what made me write this book. The life of an Arab Palestinian in the West, particularly in America, is disheartening. There exists here an almost unanimous consensus that politically he does not exist, and when it is allowed that he does, it is either as a nuisance or as an Oriental. The web of racism, cultural stereotypes, political imperialism, dehumanizing ideology holding in the Arab or the Muslim is very strong indeed, and it is this web which every Palestinian has come to feel as his uniquely punishing destiny. It has made matters worse for him to remark that no person academically involved with the Near East—no Orientalist, that is—has ever in the United States culturally and

4. A political movement, originating in central and eastern Europe in the late 19th century, to reestablish and maintain a Jewish national state in Palestine.

politically identified himself wholeheartedly with the Arabs; certainly there have been identifications on some level, but they have never taken an "acceptable" form as has liberal American identification with Zionism, and all too frequently they have been radically flawed by their association either with discredited political and economic interests (oil-company and State Department Arabists, for example) or with religion.

The nexus of knowledge and power creating "the Oriental" and in a sense obliterating him as a human being is therefore not for me an exclusively academic matter. Yet it is an *intellectual* matter of some very obvious importance. I have been able to put to use my humanistic and political concerns for the analysis and description of a very worldly matter, the rise, development, and consolidation of Orientalism. Too often literature and culture are presumed to be politically, even historically innocent; it has regularly seemed otherwise to me, and certainly my study of Orientalism has convinced me (and I hope will convince my literary colleagues) that society and literary culture can only be understood and studied together. In addition, and by an almost inescapable logic, I have found myself writing the history of a strange, secret sharer of Western anti-Semitism. That anti-Semitism and, as I have discussed it in its Islamic branch, Orientalism resemble each other very closely is a historical, cultural, and political truth that needs only to be mentioned to an Arab Palestinian for its irony to be perfectly understood. But what I should like also to have contributed here is a better understanding of the way cultural domination has operated. If this stimulates a new kind of dealing with the Orient, indeed if it eliminates the "Orient" and "Occident" altogether, then we shall have advanced a little in the process of what Raymond Williams has called the "unlearning" of "the inherent dominative mode."[5]

1978

From Culture and Imperialism

From *Chapter Two. Consolidated Vision*

II. JANE AUSTEN AND EMPIRE

We are on solid ground with V. G. Kiernan when he says that "empires must have a mould of ideas or conditioned reflexes to flow into, and youthful nations dream of a great place in the world as young men dream of fame and fortunes."[1] It is, as I have been saying throughout, too simple and reductive to argue that everything in European or American culture therefore prepares for or consolidates the grand idea of empire. It is also, however, historically inaccurate to ignore those tendencies—whether in narrative, political theory, or pictorial technique—that enabled, encouraged, and otherwise assured the West's readiness to assume and enjoy the experience of empire. If there was cultural resistance to the notion of an imperial mission, there was not much support for that resistance in the main departments of cultural thought.

5. Raymond Williams, *Culture and Society, 1780–1950* (London: Chatto and Windus, 1958), p. 376 [Said's note].

1. V. G. Kiernan, *Marxism and Imperialism* (New York: St. Martin's Press, 1974), p. 100 [Said's note]. Kiernan (1913–2009), British historian.

Liberal though he was, John Stuart Mill—as a telling case in point—could still say, "The sacred duties which civilized nations owe to the independence and nationality of each other, are not binding towards those to whom nationality and independence are certain evil, or at best a questionable good."[2] Ideas like this were not original with Mill; they were already current in the English subjugation of Ireland during the sixteenth century and, as Nicholas Canny[3] has persuasively demonstrated, were equally useful in the ideology of English colonization in the Americas. Almost all colonial schemes begin with an assumption of native backwardness and general inadequacy to be independent, "equal," and fit.

Why that should be so, why sacred obligation on one front should not be binding on another, why rights accepted in one may be denied in another, are questions best understood in the terms of a culture well-grounded in moral, economic, and even metaphysical norms designed to approve a satisfying local, that is European, order and to permit the abrogation of the right to a similar order abroad. Such a statement may appear preposterous or extreme. In fact, it formulates the connection between Europe's well-being and cultural identity on the one hand and, on the other, the subjugation of imperial realms overseas rather too fastidiously and circumspectly. Part of our difficulty today in accepting any connection at all is that we tend to reduce this complicated matter to an apparently simple causal one, which in turn produces a rhetoric of blame and defensiveness. I am *not* saying that the major factor in early European culture was that it *caused* late-nineteenth-century imperialism, and I am not implying that all the problems of the formerly colonial world should be blamed on Europe. I am saying, however, that European culture often, if not always, characterized itself in such a way as simultaneously to validate its own preferences while also advocating those preferences in conjunction with distant imperial rule. Mill certainly did: he always recommended that India *not* be given independence. When for various reasons imperial rule concerned Europe more intensely after 1880, this schizophrenic habit became useful.

The first thing to be done now is more or less to jettison simple causality in thinking through the relationship between Europe and the non-European world, and lessening the hold on our thought of the equally simple temporal sequence. We must not admit any notion, for instance, that proposes to show that Wordsworth, Austen, or Coleridge,[4] because they wrote *before* 1857, actually caused the establishment of formal British governmental rule over India *after* 1857. We should try to discern instead a counterpoint between overt patterns in British writing about Britain and representations of the world beyond the British Isles. The inherent mode for this counterpoint is not temporal but spatial. How do writers in the period before the great age of explicit, programmatic colonial expansion—the "scramble for Africa,"[5] say—

2. John Stuart Mill, *Disquisitions and Discussions*, Vol. 3 (London: Longmans, Green, Reader & Dyer, 1875), pp. 167–68. For an earlier version of this see the discussion by Nicholas Canny, "The Ideology of English Colonization: From Ireland to America," *William and Mary Quarterly* 30 (1973), 575–98 [Said's note]. Mill (1806–1873), British philosopher; the quotation comes from "A Few Words on Non-Intervention," an essay that originally appeared in 1859.

3. Irish historian (b. 1944).

4. Samuel Taylor Coleridge (1772–1834) and William Wordsworth (1770–1850), major English poets of the Romantic period. Jane Austen (1775–1817), major English novelist whose works include *Pride and Prejudice* (1813) and *Mansfield Park* (1814), discussed below.

5. The competing attempts by more than a half-dozen European powers to lay claim to African territory at the end of the 19th century.

situate and see themselves and their work in the larger world? We shall find them using striking but careful strategies, many of them derived from expected sources—positive ideas of home, of a nation and its language, of proper order, good behavior, moral values.

But positive ideas of this sort do more than validate "our" world. They also tend to devalue other worlds and, perhaps more significantly from a retrospective point of view, they do not prevent or inhibit or give resistance to horrendously unattractive imperialist practices. No, cultural forms like the novel or the opera do not cause people to go out and imperialize—Carlyle did not drive Rhodes[6] directly, and he certainly cannot be "blamed" for the problems in today's southern Africa—but it is genuinely troubling to see how little Britain's great humanistic ideas, institutions, and monuments, which we still celebrate as having the power ahistorically to command our approval, how little they stand in the way of the accelerating imperial process. We are entitled to ask how this body of humanistic ideas co-existed so comfortably with imperialism, and why—until the resistance to imperialism *in the imperial domain*, among Africans, Asians, Latin Americans, developed—there was little significant opposition or deterrence to empire at home. Perhaps the custom of distinguishing "our" home and order from "theirs" grew into a harsh political rule for accumulating more of "them" to rule, study, and subordinate. In the great, humane ideas and values promulgated by mainstream European culture, we have precisely that "mould of ideas or conditioned reflexes" of which Kiernan speaks, into which the whole business of empire later flowed.

The extent to which these ideas are actually invested in geographical distinctions between real places is the subject of Raymond Williams's richest book, *The Country and the City*.[7] His argument concerning the interplay between rural and urban places in England admits of the most extraordinary transformations—from the pastoral populism of Langland, through Ben Jonson's country-house poems and the novels of Dickens's[8] London, right up to visions of the metropolis in twentieth-century literature. Mainly, of course, the book is about how English culture has dealt with land, its possession, imagination, and organization. And while he does address the export of England to the colonies, Williams does so, as I suggested earlier, in a less focussed way and less expansively than the practice actually warrants. Near the end of *The Country and the City* he volunteers that "from at least the mid-nineteenth century, and with important instances earlier, there was this larger context [the relationship between England and the colonies, whose effects on the English imagination "have gone deeper than can easily be traced"] within which every idea and every image was consciously and unconsciously affected."[9] He goes on quickly to cite "the idea of emigration to the colonies" as one such image prevailing in various novels by Dickens, the

6. Cecil Rhodes (1853–1902), British imperialist who was prime minister of the Cape Town colony in South Africa in the early 1890s and profited from the diamond mines there. Thomas Carlyle (1795–1881), Scottish historian and essayist; in "An Occasional Discourse on the Nigger Question" (1849), he asserted that blacks should be disciplined and governed by whites.

7. Published in 1973 by WILLIAMS (1921–1988), influential British critic and cultural theorist.

8. Charles Dickens (1812–1870), most popular English novelist of the 19th century. William Langland (ca. 1330–1387), probable author of one of the earliest English poems, *Piers Plowman*. Jonson (1572–1637), English poet and playwright.

9. *The Country and the City* (New York: Oxford University Press, 1973), p. 281 [Said's note and brackets].

Brontës, Gaskell,[1] and rightly shows that "new rural societies," all of them colonial, enter the imaginative metropolitan economy of English literature via Kipling, early Orwell, Maugham.[2] After 1880 there comes a "dramatic extension of landscape and social relations": this corresponds more or less exactly with the great age of empire.

It is dangerous to disagree with Williams, yet I would venture to say that if one began to look for something like an imperial map of the world in English literature, it would turn up with amazing insistence and frequency well before the mid-nineteenth century. And turn up not only with the inert regularity suggesting something taken for granted, but—more interestingly—threaded through, forming a vital part of the texture of linguistic and cultural practice. There were established English offshore interests in Ireland, America, the Caribbean, and Asia from the sixteenth century on, and even a quick inventory reveals poets, philosophers, historians, dramatists, statesmen, novelists, travel writers, chroniclers, soldiers, and fabulists who prized, cared for, and traced these interests with continuing concern. (Much of this is well discussed by Peter Hulme in *Colonial Encounters.*)[3] Similar points may be made for France, Spain, and Portugal, not only as overseas powers in their own right, but as competitors with the British. How can we examine these interests at work in modern England before the age of empire, i.e., during the period between 1800 and 1870?

We would do well to follow Williams's lead, and look first at that period of crisis following upon England's wide-scale land enclosure at the end of the eighteenth century. The old organic rural communities were dissolved and new ones forged under the impulse of parliamentary activity, industrialization, and demographic dislocation, but there also occurred a new process of relocating England (and in France, France) within a much larger circle of the world map. During the first half of the eighteenth century, Anglo-French competition in North America and India was intense, in the second half there were numerous violent encounters between England and France in the Americas, the Caribbean, and the Levant, and of course in Europe itself. The major pre-Romantic literature in France and England contains a constant stream of references to the overseas dominions: one thinks not only of various Encyclopedists, the Abbé Raynal, de Brosses, and Volney, but also of Edmund Burke, Beckford, Gibbon, Johnson, and William Jones.[4]

In 1902 J. A. Hobson described imperialism as the expansion of nationality, implying that the process was understandable mainly by considering *expansion* as the more important of the two terms, since "nationality" was a

1. Elizabeth Gaskell (1810–1865), English writer. "The Brontës": Williams discusses the English novels *Shirley* (1849) and *Wuthering Heights* (1847) by the sisters Charlotte (1816–1855) and Emily Brontë (1818–1848).

2. William Somerset Maugham (1874–1965), English novelist. Rudyard Kipling (1865–1936), English novelist and poet known for writings set in India. George Orwell (pen name of Eric Blair, 1903–1950), English novelist and essayist who was an imperial police officer in Burma.

3. Peter Hulme, *Colonial Encounters: Europe and the Native Caribbean, 1492–1797* (London: Methuen, 1986). See also his anthology with Neil L. Whitehead, *Wild Majesty: Encounters with Caribs from Columbus to the Present Day* (Oxford: Clarendon Press, 1992) [Said's note]. Hulme (b. 1948), British cultural critic.

4. English philologist and judge in India (1746–1794). Encyclopedists: 18th-century French intellectuals who attempted to compile a comprehensive encyclopedia. Abbé Raynal (1713–1796), French historian and philosopher. Charles de Brosses (1709–1777), French scholar. Constantin-François Chassebœuf, comte de Volney (1757–1820), French historian and politician. BURKE (1729–1797), British writer and statesman. William Thomas Beckford (1760–1844), English novelist and dilettante. Edward Gibbon (1737–1794), English historian. SAMUEL JOHNSON (1709–1784), English essayist, poet, and lexicographer; his single novel, *Rasselas* (1759), is set in the Orient.

fully formed, fixed quantity,[5] whereas a century before it was still in the process of *being formed*, at home and abroad as well. In *Physics and Politics* (1887) Walter Bagehot[6] speaks with extraordinary relevance of "nation-making." Between France and Britain in the late eighteenth century there were two contests: the battle for strategic gains abroad—in India, the Nile delta, the Western Hemisphere—and the battle for a triumphant nationality. Both battles contrast "Englishness" with "the French," and no matter how intimate and closeted the supposed English or French "essence" appears to be, it was almost always thought of as being (as opposed to already) made, and being fought out with the other great competitor. Thackeray's Becky Sharp,[7] for example, is as much an upstart as she is because of her half-French heritage. Earlier in the century, the upright abolitionist posture of Wilberforce and his allies developed partly out of a desire to make life harder for French hegemony in the Antilles.[8]

These considerations suddenly provide a fascinatingly expanded dimension to *Mansfield Park* (1814), the most explicit in its ideological and moral affirmations of Austen's novels. Williams once again is in general dead right: Austen's novels express an "attainable quality of life," in money and property acquired, moral discriminations made, the right choices put in place, the correct "improvements" implemented, the finely nuanced language affirmed and classified. Yet, Williams continues,

> What [Cobbett] names, riding past on the road, are classes. Jane Austen, from inside the houses, can never see that, for all the intricacy of her social description. All her discrimination is, understandably, internal and exclusive. She is concerned with the conduct of people who, in the complications of improvement, are repeatedly trying to make themselves into a class. But where only one class is seen, no classes are seen.[9]

As a general description of how Austen manages to elevate certain "moral discriminations" into "an independent value," this is excellent. Where *Mansfield Park* is concerned, however, a good deal more needs to be said, giving greater explicitness and width to Williams's survey. Perhaps then Austen, and indeed, pre-imperialist novels generally, will appear to be more implicated in the rationale for imperialist expansion than at first sight they have been.

After Lukács and Proust,[1] we have become so accustomed to thinking of the novel's plot and structure as constituted mainly by temporality that we have overlooked the function of space, geography, and location. For it is not

5. J. A. Hobson, *Imperialism: A Study* (1902; rpt. Ann Arbor: University of Michigan Press, 1972), p. 6 [Said's note]. Hobson (1858–1940), English economist.
6. English economist and critic (1826–1877).
7. The social-climbing antiheroine of *Vanity Fair* (1848), the best-known work by the English novelist William Makepeace Thackeray (1811–1863).
8. This is most memorably discussed in C. L. R. James's *The Black Jacobins: Toussaint L'Ouverture and the San Domingo Revolution* (1938; rpt. New York: Vintage, 1963), especially Chapter 2, "The Owners." See also Robin Blackburn, *The Overthrow of Colonial Slavery 1776–1848* (London: Verso, 1988), pp. 149–53 [Said's note]. James (1901–1989), Trinidadian critic. Blackburn (b. 1940), British historian. William Wilberforce (1759–1833), English politician and abolitionist.
9. Williams, *Country and the City*, p. 117 [Said's note]. William Cobbett (1763–1835), English radical journalist and reformer; his *Rural Rides* (1830) focuses on rural workers.
1. Marcel Proust (1871–1922), French novelist whose great work was the multivolume *À la recherche du temps perdu* (1913–27, *In Search of Lost Time;* first translated into English with the title *Remembrance of Things Past*). GYÖRGY LUKÁCS (1885–1971), Marxist critic and theorist; one of his best-known works is *The Historical Novel* (1955; see above).

only the very young Stephen Dedalus,[2] but every other young protagonist before him as well, who sees himself in a widening spiral at home, in Ireland, in the world. Like many other novels, *Mansfield Park* is very precisely about a series of both small and large dislocations and relocations in space that occur before, at the end of the novel, Fanny Price, the niece, becomes the spiritual mistress of Mansfield Park.[3] And that place itself is located by Austen at the center of an arc of interests and concerns spanning the hemisphere, two major seas, and four continents.

As in Austen's other novels, the central group that finally emerges with marriage and property "ordained" is not based exclusively upon blood. Her novel enacts the disaffiliation (in the literal sense) of some members of a family, and the affiliation between others and one or two chosen and tested outsiders: in other words, blood relationships are not enough to assure continuity, hierarchy, authority, both domestic and international. Thus Fanny Price—the poor niece, the orphaned child from the outlying city of Portsmouth, the neglected, demure, and upright wallflower—gradually acquires a status commensurate with, even superior to, that of most of her more fortunate relatives. In this pattern of affiliation and in her assumption of authority, Fanny Price is relatively passive. She resists the misdemeanors and the importunings of others, and very occasionally she ventures actions on her own: all in all, though, one has the impression that Austen has designs for her that Fanny herself can scarcely comprehend, just as throughout the novel Fanny is thought of by everyone as "comfort" and "acquisition" despite herself. Like Kipling's Kim O'Hara,[4] Fanny is both device and instrument in a larger pattern, as well as a fully fledged novelistic character.

Fanny, like Kim, requires direction, requires the patronage and outside authority that her own impoverished experience cannot provide. Her conscious connections are to some people and to some places, but the novel reveals other connections of which she has faint glimmerings that nevertheless demand her presence and service. She comes into a situation that opens with an intricate set of moves which, taken together, demand sorting out, adjustment, and rearrangement. Sir Thomas Bertram has been captivated by one Ward sister, the others have not done well, and "an absolute breach" opens up; their "circles were so distinct," the distances between them so great that they have been out of touch for eleven years;[5] fallen on hard times, the Prices seek out the Bertrams. Gradually, and even though she is not the eldest, Fanny becomes the focus of attention as she is sent to Mansfield Park, there to begin her new life. Similarly, the Bertrams have given up London (the result of Lady Bertram's "little ill health and a great deal of indolence") and come to reside entirely in the country.

2. The protagonist of *Portrait of the Artist as a Young Man* (1914–15) and *Ulysses* (1922), by James Joyce.

3. The estate of the wealthy Sir Thomas Bertram, in a county about 70 miles northwest of London. Fanny Price, his niece, is the novel's heroine; at age 10, she comes to live at Mansfield Park with her 4 older cousins: Tom, Edmund, Maria, and Julia.

4. The protagonist of Kipling's *Kim* (1901), a novel about the orphaned son of an Irish soldier in India.

5. Jane Austen, *Mansfield Park*, ed. Tony Tanner (1814; rpt. Harmondsworth: Penguin, 1966), p. 42. The best account of the novel is in Tony Tanner's *Jane Austen* (Cambridge, Mass.: Harvard University Press, 1986) [Said's note]. There were three Ward sisters; one married Sir Thomas Bertram, the second his friend the Rev. Mr. Norris (who became minister in a nearby church), and the third an officer in the marines, Mr. Price.

What sustains this life materially is the Bertram estate in Antigua, which is not doing well. Austen takes pains to show us two apparently disparate but actually convergent processes: the growth of Fanny's importance to the Bertrams' economy, including Antigua, and Fanny's own steadfastness in the face of numerous challenges, threats, and surprises. In both, Austen's imagination works with a steel-like rigor through a mode that we might call geographical and spatial clarification. Fanny's ignorance when she arrives at Mansfield as a frightened ten-year-old is signified by her inability to "put the map of Europe together,"[6] and for much of the first half of the novel the action is concerned with a whole range of issues whose common denominator, misused or misunderstood, is space: not only is Sir Thomas in Antigua to make things better there and at home, but at Mansfield Park, Fanny, Edmund, and her aunt Norris negotiate where she is to live, read, and work, where fires are to be lit; the friends and cousins concern themselves with the improvement of estates, and the importance of chapels (i.e., religious authority) to domesticity is envisioned and debated. When, as a device for stirring things up, the Crawfords[7] suggest a play (the tinge of France that hangs a little suspiciously over their background is significant), Fanny's discomfiture is polarizingly acute. She cannot participate, cannot easily accept that rooms for living are turned into theatrical space, although, with all its confusion of roles and purposes, the play, Kotzebue's *Lovers' Vows*,[8] is prepared for anyway.

We are to surmise, I think, that while Sir Thomas is away tending his colonial garden, a number of inevitable mismeasurements (explicitly associated with feminine "lawlessness") will occur. These are apparent not only in innocent strolls by the three pairs of young friends through a park, in which people lose and catch sight of one another unexpectedly, but most clearly in the various flirtations and engagements between the young men and women left without true parental authority, Lady Bertram being indifferent, Mrs. Norris unsuitable. There is sparring, innuendo, perilous taking on of roles: all of this of course crystallizes in preparations for the play, in which something dangerously close to libertinage is about to be (but never is) enacted. Fanny, whose earlier sense of alienation, distance, and fear derives from her first uprooting, now becomes a sort of surrogate conscience about what is right and how far is too much. Yet she has no power to implement her uneasy awareness, and until Sir Thomas suddenly returns from "abroad," the rudderless drift continues.

When he does appear, preparations for the play are immediately stopped, and in a passage remarkable for its executive dispatch, Austen narrates the re-establishment of Sir Thomas's local rule:

> It was a busy morning with him. Conversation with any of them occupied but a small part of it. He had to reinstate himself in all the wonted concerns of his Mansfield life, to see his steward and his bailiff—to examine and compute—and, in the intervals of business, to walk into his

6. Ibid., p. 54 [Said's note].
7. Henry and Mary Crawford, well-off siblings who, as young adults, come to live in Mansfield.
8. A very successful English adaptation (1798) by Elizabeth Inchbald of *Das Kind der Liebe* (1780, *The Child of Love*) by the German playwright August von Kotzebue (1761–1819); the play's subject matter (extramarital sex, illegitimacy) made it particularly unsuitable.

> stables and his gardens, and nearest plantations; but active and methodical, he had not only done all this before he resumed his seat as master of the house at dinner, he had also set the carpenter to work in pulling down what had been so lately put up in the billiard room, and given the scene painter his dismissal, long enough to justify the pleasing belief of his being then at least as far off as Northampton. The scene painter was gone, having spoilt only the floor of one room, ruined all the coachman's sponges, and made five of the under-servants idle and dissatisfied; and Sir Thomas was in hopes that another day or two would suffice to wipe away every outward memento of what had been, even to the destruction of every unbound copy of 'Lovers' Vows' in the house, for he was burning all that met his eye.[9]

The force of this paragraph is unmistakable. Not only is this a Crusoe[1] setting things in order: it is also an early Protestant eliminating all traces of frivolous behavior. There is nothing in *Mansfield Park* that would contradict us, however, were we to assume that Sir Thomas does exactly the same things—on a larger scale—in his Antigua "plantations." Whatever was wrong there—and the internal evidence garnered by Warren Roberts suggests that economic depression, slavery, and competition with France were at issue[2]—Sir Thomas was able to fix, thereby maintaining his control over his colonial domain. More clearly than anywhere else in her fiction, Austen here synchronizes domestic with international authority, making it plain that the values associated with such higher things as ordination, law, and propriety must be grounded firmly in actual rule over and possession of territory. She sees clearly that to hold and rule Mansfield Park is to hold and rule an imperial estate in close, not to say inevitable association with it. What assures the domestic tranquility and attractive harmony of one is the productivity and regulated discipline of the other.

Before both can be fully secured, however, Fanny must become more actively involved in the unfolding action. From frightened and often victimized poor relation she is gradually transformed into a directly participating member of the Bertram household at Mansfield Park. For this, I believe, Austen designed the second part of the book, which contains not only the failure of the Edmund–Mary Crawford romance as well as the disgraceful profligacy of Lydia[3] and Henry Crawford, but Fanny Price's rediscovery and rejection of her Portsmouth home, the injury and incapacitation of Tom Bertram (the eldest son), and the launching of William Price's[4] naval career. This entire ensemble of relationships and events is finally capped with Edmund's marriage to Fanny, whose place in Lady Bertram's household is taken by Susan Price, her sister. It is no exaggeration to interpret the concluding sections of *Mansfield Park* as the coronation of an arguably unnatural (or at very least, illogical) principle at the heart of a desired English order. The audacity

9. Austen, *Mansfield* Park, p. 206 [Said's note].

1. That is, Robinson Crusoe, the title character in Daniel Defoe's 1719 novel about an English castaway who spends 28 years on a deserted island, where he creates a version of British rule.

2. Warren Roberts, *Jane Austen and the French Revolution* (London: Macmillan, 1979), pp. 97–98. See also Avrom Fleishman, *A Reading of Mansfield Park: An Essay in Critical Synthesis* (Minneapolis: University of Minnesota Press, 1967), pp. 36–39 and *passim* [Said's note].

3. Said's error for Maria (Bertram), who, soon after her wedding, leaves her husband for Henry Crawford.

4. Fanny's estimable older brother.

of Austen's vision is disguised a little by her voice, which despite its occasional archness is understated and notably modest. But we should not misconstrue the limited references to the outside world, her lightly stressed allusions to work, process, and class, her apparent ability to abstract (in Raymond Williams's phrase) "an everyday uncompromising morality which is in the end separable from its social basis."[5] In fact Austen is far less diffident, far more severe.

The clues are to be found in Fanny, or rather in how rigorously we are able to consider her. True, her visit to her original Portsmouth home, where her immediate family still resides, upsets the aesthetic and emotional balance she has become accustomed to at Mansfield Park, and true she has begun to take its wonderful luxuries for granted, even as being essential. These are fairly routine and natural consequences of getting used to a new place. But Austen is talking about two other matters we must not mistake. One is Fanny's newly enlarged sense of what it means to be *at home*; when she takes stock of things after she gets to Portsmouth, this is not merely a matter of expanded space.

> Fanny was almost stunned. The smallness of the house, and thinness of the walls, brought every thing so close to her, that, added to the fatigue of her journey, and all her recent agitation, she hardly knew how to bear it. *Within* the room all was tranquil enough, for Susan having disappeared with the others, there were soon only her father and herself remaining; and he taking out a newspaper—the accustomary loan of a neighbour, applied himself to studying it, without seeming to recollect her existence. The solitary candle was held between himself and the paper, without any reference to her possible convenience; but she had nothing to do, and was glad to have the light screened from her aching head, as she sat in bewildered, broken, sorrowful contemplation.
>
> She was at home. But alas! it was not such a home, she had not such a welcome, as—she checked herself; she was unreasonable. . . . A day or two might shew the difference. *She* only was to blame. Yet she thought it would not have been so at Mansfield. No, in her uncle's house there would have been a consideration of times and seasons, a regulation of subject, a propriety, an attention towards every body which there was not here.[6]

In too small a space, you cannot see clearly, you cannot think clearly, you cannot have regulation or attention of the proper sort. The fineness of Austen's detail ("the solitary candle was held between himself and the paper, without any reference to her possible convenience") renders very precisely the dangers of unsociability, of lonely insularity, of diminished awareness that are rectified in larger and better administered spaces.

That such spaces are not available to Fanny by direct inheritance, legal title, by propinquity, contiguity, or adjacence (Mansfield Park and Portsmouth are separated by many hours' journey) is precisely Austen's point. To earn the right to Mansfield Park you must first leave home as a kind of indentured servant or, to put the case in extreme terms, as a kind of transported commodity—this, clearly, is the fate of Fanny and her brother William—but

5. Williams, *The Country and the City*, p. 116.

6. Austen, *Mansfield Park*, pp. 375–76 [Said's note].

then you have the promise of future wealth. I think Austen sees what Fanny does as a domestic or small-scale movement in space that corresponds to the larger, more openly colonial movements of Sir Thomas, her mentor, the man whose estate she inherits. The two movements depend on each other.

The second more complex matter about which Austen speaks, albeit indirectly, raises an interesting theoretical issue. Austen's awareness of empire is obviously very different, alluded to very much more casually, than Conrad's[7] or Kipling's. In her time the British were extremely active in the Caribbean and in South America, notably Brazil and Argentina. Austen seems only vaguely aware of the details of these activities, although the sense that extensive West Indian plantations were important was fairly widespread in metropolitan England. Antigua and Sir Thomas's trip there have a definitive function in *Mansfield Park*, which, I have been saying, is both incidental, referred to only in passing, and absolutely crucial to the action. How are we to assess Austen's few references to Antigua, and what are we to make of them interpretatively?

My contention is that by that very odd combination of casualness and stress, Austen reveals herself to be *assuming* (just as Fanny assumes, in both senses of the word) the importance of an empire to the situation at home. Let me go further. Since Austen refers to and uses Antigua as she does in *Mansfield Park*, there needs to be a commensurate effort on the part of her readers to understand concretely the historical valences in the reference; to put it differently, we should try to understand *what* she referred to, why she gave it the importance she did, and why indeed she made the choice, for she might have done something different to establish Sir Thomas's wealth. Let us now calibrate the signifying power of the references to Antigua in *Mansfield Park*; how do they occupy the place they do, what are they doing there?

According to Austen we are to conclude that no matter how isolated and insulated the English place (e.g., Mansfield Park), it requires overseas sustenance. Sir Thomas's property in the Caribbean would have had to be a sugar plantation maintained by slave labor (not abolished until the 1830s): these are not dead historical facts but, as Austen certainly knew, evident historical realities. Before the Anglo-French competition the major distinguishing characteristic of Western empires (Roman, Spanish, and Portuguese) was that the earlier empires were bent on loot, as Conrad puts it,[8] on the transport of treasure from the colonies to Europe, with very little attention to development, organization, or system within the colonies themselves; Britain and, to a lesser degree, France both wanted to make their empires long-term, profitable, ongoing concerns, and they competed in this enterprise, nowhere more so than in the colonies of the Caribbean, where the transport of slaves, the functioning of large sugar plantations, and the development of sugar markets, which raised the issues of protectionism, monopolies, and price—all these were more or less constantly, competitively at issue.

Far from being nothing much "out there," British colonial possessions in the Antilles and Leeward Islands were during Jane Austen's time a crucial

7. Joseph Conrad (1857–1924), Polish-born English novelist, who worked as a sailor when young and whose novels are almost all set in remote colonies of European powers.

8. In "Geography and Some Explorers" (1924), Conrad calls the carving up of Africa by Europeans the "vilest scramble for loot that ever disfigured the history of human conscience and geographical exploration."

setting for Anglo-French colonial competition. Revolutionary ideas from France were being exported there, and there was a steady decline in British profits: the French sugar plantations were producing more sugar at less cost. However, slave rebellions in and out of Haiti[9] were incapacitating France and spurring British interests to intervene more directly and to gain greater local power. Still, compared with its earlier prominence for the home market, British Caribbean sugar production in the nineteenth century had to compete with alternative sugar-cane supplies in Brazil and Mauritius, the emergence of a European beet-sugar industry, and the gradual dominance of free-trade ideology and practice.

In *Mansfield Park*—both in its formal characteristics and in its contents—a number of these currents converge. The most important is the avowedly complete subordination of colony to metropolis. Sir Thomas, absent from Mansfield Park, is never seen as *present* in Antigua, which elicits at most a half dozen references in the novel. There is a passage, a part of which I quoted earlier, from John Stuart Mill's *Principles of Political Economy* that catches the spirit of Austen's use of Antigua. I quote it here in full:

> These [outlying possessions of ours] are hardly to be looked upon as countries, carrying on an exchange of commodities with other countries, but more properly as outlying agricultural or manufacturing estates belonging to a larger community. Our West Indian colonies, for example, cannot be regarded as countries with a productive capital of their own . . . [but are rather] the place where England finds it convenient to carry on the production of sugar, coffee and a few other tropical commodities. All the capital employed is English capital; almost all the industry is carried on for English uses; there is little production of anything except for staple commodities, and these are sent to England, not to be exchanged for things exported to the colony and consumed by its inhabitants, but to be sold in England for the benefit of the proprietors there. The trade with the West Indies is hardly to be considered an external trade, but more resembles the traffic between town and country.[1]

To some extent Antigua is like London or Portsmouth, a less desirable setting than a country estate like Mansfield Park, but producing goods to be consumed by everyone (by the early nineteenth century every Britisher used sugar), although owned and maintained by a small group of aristocrats and gentry. The Bertrams and the other characters in *Mansfield Park* are a subgroup within the minority, and for them the island is wealth, which Austen regards as being converted to propriety, order, and, at the end of the novel, comfort, an added good. But why "added"? Because, Austen tells us pointedly in the final chapters, she wants to "restore every body, not greatly in fault themselves, to tolerable comfort, and to have done with all the rest."[2]

This can be interpreted to mean first that the novel has done enough in the way of destabilizing the lives of "every body" and must now set them at rest: actually Austen says this explicitly, in a bit of meta-fictional impatience, the

9. Haiti won its independence from France in 1804, after a bloody revolt by mulattoes and freed blacks.

1. John Stuart Mill, *Principles of Political Economy*, Vol. 3, ed. J. M. Robson (Toronto: University of Toronto Press, 1965), p. 693. The passage is quoted in Sidney W. Mintz, *Sweetness and Power: The Place of Sugar in Modern History* (New York: Viking, 1985), p. 42 [Said's note].

2. Austen, *Mansfield Park*, p. 446 [Said's note].

novelist commenting on her own work as having gone on long enough and now needing to be brought to a close. Second, it can mean that "every body" may now be finally permitted to realize what it means to be properly at home, and at rest, without the need to wander about or to come and go. (This does not include young William, who, we assume, will continue to roam the seas in the British navy on whatever commercial and political missions may still be required. Such matters draw from Austen only a last brief gesture, a passing remark about William's "continuing good conduct and rising fame.") As for those finally resident in Mansfield Park itself, more in the way of domesticated advantages is given to these now fully acclimatized souls, and to none more than to Sir Thomas. He understands for the first time what has been missing in his education of his children, and he understands it in the terms paradoxically provided for him by unnamed outside forces, so to speak, the wealth of Antigua and the imported example of Fanny Price. Note here how the curious alternation of outside and inside follows the pattern identified by Mill of the outside *becoming* the inside by use and, to use Austen's word, "disposition":

> Here [in his deficiency of training, of allowing Mrs. Norris too great a role, of letting his children dissemble and repress feeling] had been grievous mismanagement; but, bad as it was, he gradually grew to feel that it had not been the most direful mistake in his plan of education. Some thing must have been wanting *within*, or time would have worn away much of its ill effect. He feared that principle, active principle, had been wanting, that they had never been properly taught to govern their inclinations and tempers, by that sense of duty which can alone suffice. They had been instructed theoretically in their religion, but never required to bring it into daily practice. To be distinguished for elegance and accomplishments—the authorized object of their youth—could have had no useful influence that way, no moral effect on the mind. He had meant them to be good, but his cares had been directed to the understanding and manners, not the disposition; and of the necessity of self-denial and humility, he feared they had never heard from any lips that could profit them.[3]

What was wanting *within* was in fact supplied by the wealth derived from a West Indian plantation and a poor provincial relative, both brought in to Mansfield Park and set to work. Yet on their own, neither the one nor the other could have sufficed; they require each other and then, more important, they need executive disposition, which in turn helps to reform the rest of the Bertram circle. All this Austen leaves to her reader to supply in the way of literal explication.

And that is what reading her entails. But all these things having to do with the outside brought in seem unmistakably *there* in the suggestiveness of her allusive and abstract language. A principle "wanting *within*" is, I believe, intended to evoke for us memories of Sir Thomas's absences in Antigua, or the sentimental and near-whimsical vagary on the part of the three variously deficient Ward sisters by which a niece is displaced from one household to another. But that the Bertrams did become better if not altogether good, that

3. Ibid., p. 448 [Said's note].

some sense of duty was imparted to them, that they learned to govern their inclinations and tempers and brought religion into daily practice, that they "directed disposition": all of this did occur because outside (or rather outlying) factors were lodged properly inward, became native to Mansfield Park, with Fanny the niece its final spiritual mistress, and Edmund the second son its spiritual master.[4]

An additional benefit is that Mrs. Norris is dislodged; this is described as "the great supplementary comfort of Sir Thomas's life."[5] Once the principles have been interiorized, the comforts follow: Fanny is settled for the time being at Thornton Lacey "with every attention to her comfort"; her home later becomes "the home of affection and comfort"; Susan is brought in "first as a comfort to Fanny, then as an auxiliary, and at last as her substitute"[6] when the new import takes Fanny's place by Lady Bertram's side. The pattern established at the outset of the novel clearly continues, only now it has what Austen intended to give it all along, an internalized and retrospectively guaranteed rationale. This is the rationale that Raymond Williams describes as "an everyday, uncompromising morality which is in the end separable from its social basis and which, in other hands, can be turned against it."

I have tried to show that the morality in fact is not separable from its social basis: right up to the last sentence, Austen affirms and repeats the geographical process of expansion involving trade, production, and consumption that predates, underlies, and guarantees the morality. And expansion, as Gallagher reminds us, whether "through colonial rule was liked or disliked, [its] desirability through one mode or another was generally accepted. So in the event there were few domestic constraints upon expansion."[7] Most critics have tended to forget or overlook that process, which has seemed less important to critics than Austen herself seemed to think. But interpreting Jane Austen depends on *who* does the interpreting, *when* it is done, and no less important, from *where* it is done. If with feminists, with great cultural critics sensitive to history and class like Williams, with cultural and stylistic interpreters, we have been sensitized to the issues their interests raise, we should now proceed to regard the geographical division of the world—after all significant to *Mansfield Park*—as not neutral (any more than class and gender are neutral) but as politically charged, beseeching the attention and elucidation its considerable proportions require. The question is thus not only how to understand and with what to connect Austen's morality and its social basis, but also *what* to read of it.

Take once again the casual references to Antigua, the ease with which Sir Thomas's needs in England are met by a Caribbean sojourn, the uninflected, unreflective citations of Antigua (or the Mediterranean, or India, which is where Lady Bertram, in a fit of distracted impatience, requires that William should go "'that I may have a shawl. I think I will have two shawls.'"[8] They stand for a significance "out there" that frames the genuinely important action *here*, but not for a great significance. Yet these signs of "abroad"

4. Fanny and Edmund marry, and at the novel's end they are living in the parsonage in Mansfield (not at Mansfield Park itself).
5. Austen, *Mansfield Park*, p. 450 [Said's note].
6. Ibid., p. 456 [Said's note]. Thornton Lacey: the house attached to Edmund's first post as a clergyman.
7. John Gallagher, *The Decline, Revival and Fall of the British Empire* (Cambridge: Cambridge University Press, 1982), p. 76 [Said's note]. Gallagher (1919–1980) British historian.
8. Austen, *Mansfield Park*, p. 308 [Said's note].

include, even as they repress, a rich and complex history, which has since achieved a status that the Bertrams, the Prices, and Austen herself would not, could not recognize. To call this "the Third World"[9] begins to deal with the realities but by no means exhausts the political or cultural history.

We must first take stock of *Mansfield Park*'s prefigurations of a later English history as registered in fiction. The Bertrams' usable colony in *Mansfield Park* can be read as pointing forward to Charles Gould's San Tomé mine in *Nostromo*, or to the Wilcoxes' Imperial and West African Rubber Company in Forster's *Howards End*, or to any of these distant but convenient treasure spots in *Great Expectations*, Jean Rhys's *Wide Sargasso Sea*, *Heart of Darkness*[1]—resources to be visited, talked about, described, or appreciated for domestic reasons, for local metropolitan benefit. If we think ahead to these other novels, Sir Thomas's Antigua readily acquires a slightly greater density than the discrete, reticent appearances it makes in the pages of *Mansfield Park*. And already our reading of the novel begins to open up at those points where ironically Austen was most economical and her critics most (dare one say it?) negligent. Her "Antigua" is therefore not just a slight but a definite way of marking the outer limits of what Williams calls domestic improvements, or a quick allusion to the mercantile venturesomeness of acquiring overseas dominions as a source for local fortunes, or one reference among many attesting to a historical sensibility suffused not just with manners and courtesies but with contests of ideas, struggles with Napoleonic France,[2] awareness of seismic economic and social change during a revolutionary period in world history.

Second, we must see "Antigua" held in a precise place in Austen's moral geography, and in her prose, by historical changes that her novel rides like a vessel on a mighty sea. The Bertrams could not have been possible without the slave trade, sugar, and the colonial planter class; as a social type Sir Thomas would have been familiar to eighteenth- and early-nineteenth-century readers who knew the powerful influence of the class through politics, plays (like Cumberland's *The West Indian*[3]), and many other public activities (large houses, famous parties and social rituals, well-known commercial enterprises, celebrated marriages). As the old system of protected monopoly gradually disappeared and as a new class of settler-planters displaced the old absentee system, the West Indian interest lost dominance: cotton manufacture, an even more open system of trade, and abolition of the slave trade reduced the power and prestige of people like the Bertrams, whose frequency of sojourn in the Caribbean then decreased.

9. The "underdeveloped" countries, many of them former colonies, now dominated by highly industrialized "first world" (largely Western) nations in a global economy.

1. Conrad's *Heart of Darkness* (1902) is set in the Belgian Congo, from which trading companies extract ivory; his *Nostromo* (1904), set in South America, features a mineral mine controlled by a character named Charles Gould. *Howards End* (1910), by the English novelist E. M. Forster (1879–1970), depicts three families; the richest of them, the Wilcoxes, own the Imperial and West African Rubber Company. The secret benefactor of the protagonist of Dickens's *Great Expectations* (1860–61) is an escaped convict who has made his fortune in Australia. *Wide Sargasso Sea* (1966), by Rhys (1890–1979), a novelist born in Dominica, is a prequel to Charlotte Brontë's *Jane Eyre* (1847); it focuses on a white Creole from Jamaica, the mad first wife of Edward Rochester.

2. That is, France under the rule of Napoléon Bonaparte (1769–1821), who was proclaimed emperor of the French (1804–15); Britain waged war against him from 1803 until his final defeat in 1815.

3. A comedic 1771 play by the English dramatist Richard Cumberland (1732–1811).

Thus Sir Thomas's infrequent trips to Antigua as an absentee plantation owner reflect the diminishment in his class's power, a reduction directly expressed in the title of Lowell Ragatz's[4] classic *The Fall of the Planter Class in the British Caribbean, 1763–1833* (1928). But is what is hidden or allusive in Austen made sufficiently explicit more than one hundred years later in Ragatz? Does the aesthetic silence or discretion of a great novel in 1814 receive adequate explication in a major work of historical research a full century later? Can we assume that the process of interpretation is fulfilled, or will it continue as new material comes to light?

For all his learning Ragatz still finds it in himself to speak of "the Negro race" as having the following characteristics: "he stole, he lied, he was simple, suspicious, inefficient, irresponsible, lazy, superstitious, and loose in his sexual relations."[5] Such "history" as this therefore happily gave way to the revisionary work of Caribbean historians like Eric Williams[6] and C.L.R. James, and more recently Robin Blackburn, in *The Overthrow of Colonial Slavery, 1776–1848*; in these works slavery and empire are shown to have fostered the rise and consolidation of capitalism well beyond the old plantation monopolies, as well as to have been a powerful ideological system whose original connection to specific economic interests may have gone, but whose effects continued for decades.

> The political and moral ideas of the age are to be examined in the very closest relation to the economic development. . . .
> An outworn interest, whose bankruptcy smells to heaven in historical perspective, can exercise an obstructionist and disruptive effect which can only be explained by the powerful services it had previously rendered and the entrenchment previously gained. . . .
> The ideas built on these interests continue long after the interests have been destroyed and work their old mischief, which is all the more mischievous because the interests to which they corresponded no longer exist.[7]

Thus Eric Williams in *Capitalism and Slavery* (1961). The question of interpretation, indeed of writing itself, is tied to the question of interests, which we have seen are at work in aesthetic as well as historical writing, then and now. We must not say that since *Mansfield Park* is a novel, its affiliations with a sordid history are irrelevant or transcended, not only because it is irresponsible to do so, but because we know too much to say so in good faith. Having read *Mansfield Park* as part of the structure of an expanding imperialist venture, one cannot simply restore it to the canon of "great literary masterpieces"—to which it most certainly belongs—and leave it at that. Rather, I think, the novel steadily, if unobtrusively, opens up a broad expanse of domestic imperialist culture without which Britain's subsequent acquisition of territory would not have been possible.

4. American economic historian and pioneer of African studies (1897–1978).
5. Lowell Joseph Ragatz, *The Fall of the Planter Class in the British Caribbean, 1763–1833: A Study in Social and Economic History* (1928; rpt. New York: Octagon, 1963), p. 27 [Said's note].
6. Caribbean historian and first prime minister of independent Trinidad (1911–1981).
7. Eric Williams, *Capitalism and Slavery* (New York: Russell & Russell, 1961), p. 211. See also his *From Columbus to Castro: The History of the Caribbean, 1492–1969* (London: Deutsch, 1970), pp. 177–254 [Said's note].

I have spent time on *Mansfield Park* to illustrate a type of analysis infrequently encountered in mainstream interpretations, or for that matter in readings rigorously based in one or another of the advanced theoretical schools. Yet only in the global perspective implied by Jane Austen and her characters can the novel's quite astonishing general position be made clear. I think of such a reading as completing or complementing others, not discounting or displacing them. And it bears stressing that because *Mansfield Park* connects the actualities of British power overseas to the domestic imbroglio within the Bertram estate, there is no way of doing such readings as mine, no way of understanding the "structure of attitude and reference" except by working through the novel. Without reading it in full, we would fail to understand the strength of that structure and the way it was activated and maintained in literature. But in reading it carefully, we can sense how ideas about dependent races and territories were held both by foreign-office executives, colonial bureaucrats, and military strategists and by intelligent novel-readers educating themselves in the fine points of moral evaluation, literary balance, and stylistic finish.

There is a paradox here in reading Jane Austen which I have been impressed by but can in no way resolve. All the evidence says that even the most routine aspects of holding slaves on a West Indian sugar plantation were cruel stuff. And everything we know about Austen and her values is at odds with the cruelty of slavery. Fanny Price reminds her cousin that after asking Sir Thomas about the slave trade, "There was such a dead silence"[8] as to suggest that one world could not be connected with the other since there simply is no common language for both. That is true. But what stimulates the extraordinary discrepancy into life is the rise, decline, and fall of the British empire itself and, in its aftermath, the emergence of a postcolonial consciousness. In order more accurately to read works like *Mansfield Park*, we have to see them in the main as resisting or avoiding that other setting, which their formal inclusiveness, historical honesty, and prophetic suggestiveness cannot completely hide. In time there would no longer be a dead silence when slavery was spoken of, and the subject became central to a new understanding of what Europe was.

It would be silly to expect Jane Austen to treat slavery with anything like the passion of an abolitionist or a newly liberated slave. Yet what I have called the rhetoric of blame, so often now employed by subaltern,[9] minority, or disadvantaged voices, attacks her, and others like her, retrospectively, for being white, privileged, insensitive, complicit. Yes, Austen belonged to a slave-owning society, but do we therefore jettison her novels as so many trivial exercises in aesthetic frumpery? Not at all, I would argue, if we take seriously our intellectual and interpretative vocation to make connections, to deal with as much of the evidence as possible, fully and actually, to read what is there or not there, above all, to see complementarity and interdependence instead of isolated, venerated, or formalized experience that excludes and forbids the hybridizing intrusions of human history.

8. Austen, *Mansfield Park*, p. 213 [Said's note].
9. A term from the Italian Marxist critic and theorist ANTONIO GRAMSCI (1891–1937), referring to those subordinated by the hegemonic power structure (and, since the 1980s, especially to colonized peoples).

Mansfield Park is a rich work in that its aesthetic intellectual complexity requires that longer and slower analysis that is also required by its geographical problematic, a novel based in an England relying for the maintenance of its style on a Caribbean island. When Sir Thomas goes to and comes from Antigua, where he has property, that is not at all the same thing as coming to and going from Mansfield Park, where his presence, arrivals, and departures have very considerable consequences. But precisely because Austen is so summary in one context, so provocatively rich in the other, precisely because of that imbalance we are able to move in on the novel, reveal and accentuate the interdependence scarcely mentioned on its brilliant pages. A lesser work wears its historical affiliation more plainly; its worldliness is simple and direct, the way a jingoistic ditty during the Mahdist uprising or the 1857 Indian Rebellion[1] connects directly to the situation and constituency that coined it. *Mansfield Park* encodes experiences and does not simply repeat them. From our later perspective we can interpret Sir Thomas's power to come and go in Antigua as stemming from the muted national experience of individual identity, behavior, and "ordination," enacted with such irony and taste at Mansfield Park. The task is to lose neither a true historical sense of the first, nor a full enjoyment or appreciation of the second, all the while seeing both together.

1993

1. Two well-known colonial rebellions: a revolt in Sudan (1882–98) against Anglo-Egyptian rule, initially led by the Muslim religious leader Muhammad Ahmad (the Mahdi), and a widespread uprising (1857–58) by Indian soldiers against the British rule of the East India Company.

MONIQUE WITTIG
1935–2003

When the French writer and radical lesbian theorist Monique Wittig concluded "The Straight Mind," her 1978 presentation at the Modern Language Association convention in New York, with the statement that "lesbians are not women," she was greeted with stunned silence. Not all feminists, or all lesbians, were ready to abandon a division between the sexes that has seemed so natural and inevitable. Most feminists, as Wittig notes in "One Is Not Born a Woman" (1981), "still believe that the basis of women's oppression is biological as well as historical." But for a lesbian like Wittig to refuse to be heterosexual means that she refuses to become a "man" or a "woman"—categories that she regards as political, not as natural givens. For this reason, she has been a central figure in the debate between those feminists who see "woman" as a transhistorical and eternal essence (see, for instance, HÉLÈNE CIXOUS) and those who believe that the idea of "woman" is a social construct (see, for instance, JUDITH BUTLER). Although Wittig is better known for her fiction than her theoretical writing, her fiction frequently blurs the distinction between literature and theory. Feminists have read her second novel, *Les Guérillères* (1969), which describes a postholocaust world where Amazon fighters attempt to create a new society, as an important and inspiring source of theory about language and women's writing.

Wittig was born in Alsace, France, and studied Oriental languages, literatures, history, and philosophy at the Sorbonne in Paris. She won the Prix Medici for her first novel, *L'Opoponax* (1964). Her political views were shaped by the left-wing French intellectual milieu of Paris in the 1950s and 1960s; her participation in the May 1968 student-worker uprisings partly inspired *Les Guérillères.* Active in the French women's movement from its inception, Wittig was a co-founder of the Movement de libération des femmes (MLF, the Women's Liberation Movement), the founder of the Féministes Révolutionaires in 1970, and an active member of Gouines rouges (Red Dykes) in 1971. In 1976 she relocated to the United States, though she continued to explore her materialist theories of lesbianism as a member of the Parisian Marxist-feminist editorial collective Questions Féministes from 1977 until 1980. She received a Ph.D. in literary languages from the Sorbonne in 1986, and she taught at the University of California at Berkeley, the University of Southern California, Vassar College, Duke University, New York University, and the University of Arizona. Wittig served from 1980 to 1991 on the advisory board of *Feminist Issues,* where she published many of her influential essays, including "The Straight Mind" (1980), "The Mark of Gender" (1985), and our selection, "One Is Not Born a Woman." In 1999 she published a collection of stories under the title *Paris-la-politique et autres histoires* (*Paris-Politics and Other Stories*). In 2000, with her partner and collaborator Sande Zieg, she released a film of her English novella "The Girl," her last work before her death in 2003 of a heart attack.

With a nod toward the best-known work of France's most famous feminist, SIMONE DE BEAUVOIR, "One Is Not Born a Woman" rejects biological explanations for inequalities and differences between the sexes. The "immediate given," "the sensible given," even those physical features that appear to constitute the standard categories of sex or race are not, in fact, the result of direct physical perception, as we might intuit; rather they are "mythic constructions," which "reinterpret physical features . . . through the network of relationships in which they are perceived." For this reason, Wittig is critical of feminist speculations about prehistorical matriarchies in which women were the creators of civilization. This approach, she argues, only further imprisons women within the category of sex. From a lesbian vantage point, matriarchy and patriarchy are equally oppressive because equally heterosexist.

All "naturalizing" explanations for the differences between men and women, according to Wittig, presume that the foundation of sex difference is heterosexuality, which she redefines as a tacit, unquestioned, and forced social contract. Because lesbians are not dependent on men, they cannot be "real" women; but because they lack economic, ideological, and political privilege, they cannot be men. Like ADRIENNE RICH, Wittig argues that the very existence of lesbians—a class of individuals who are "not-woman, not-man"—refutes the naturalized division between the sexes that supports institutionalized heterosexuality, thereby exposing the artificiality of the ruling sex/gender system. For this reason, "One Is Not Born a Woman" became a foundational text both for gay and lesbian studies and for queer theory in the 1990s.

The Marxist analysis of class offers, for Wittig, at least a starting point for a nonessentialist feminism in which socioeconomic relations, rather than biological necessity, provide the common ground for political struggle. The Marxist model, however, is not without problems of its own, and Wittig identifies two. First, MARX's analysis of the proletariat (industrial workers) as a class itself depends on an already naturalized sexual division of labor that obscures the class conflict between men and women (constituted not as natural categories but on the basis of their different relations to the economic foundations of society). The subordination of women cannot simply be subsumed under the class conflict between the bourgeoisie and the proletariat; it must rather be understood as an independent, if related, historical development. Second, Marxism has failed to develop a model of subjectivity that might enable women and other oppressed groups to constitute themselves as individual historical subjects. While Marxism allows for class consciousness, it has usefully rejected as idealist the "transcendental subject" of Western philosophy. Wittig sets feminism the difficult task of defining the individual subject of feminist struggle in materialist terms, though she is less clear about how to coordinate the various—sometimes conflicting—class identifications that women have (different races, social classes, nationalities). Just as Marxism occludes the different investments of men and women in economic class, feminism runs the risk of obscuring the different ways in which women of different races and classes experience gender. Yet despite its problems, Wittig's challenging essay remains a central document in the essentialism debate within feminism that has continued since the 1980s.

"One Is Not Born a Woman" Keywords: The Body, Feminist Theory, Gender, Identity, Ideology, Marxism, Queer Theory, Sexuality, Subjectivity

One Is Not Born a Woman

A materialist feminist[1] approach to women's oppression destroys the idea that women are a "natural group": "a racial group of a special kind, a group perceived *as natural*, a group of men considered as materially specific in their bodies."[2] What the analysis accomplishes on the level of ideas, practice makes actual at the level of facts: by its very existence, lesbian society destroys the artificial (social) fact constituting women as a "natural group." A lesbian society[3] pragmatically reveals that the division from men of which women have been the object is a political one and shows that we have been ideologically rebuilt into a "natural group." In the case of women, ideology goes far since our bodies as well as our minds are the product of this manipulation. We have been compelled in our bodies and in our minds to correspond, feature by feature, with the *idea* of nature that has been established for us. Distorted to such an extent that our deformed body is what they call "natural," what is supposed to exist as such before oppression. Distorted to such an extent that in the end oppression seems to be a consequence of this "nature" within ourselves (a nature which is only an *idea*). What a materialist analysis does by reasoning, a lesbian society accomplishes practically: not only is there no natural group "women" (we lesbians are living proof of it), but as individuals as well we question "woman," which for us, as for Simone de Beauvoir, is only a myth. She said: "One is not born, but becomes a woman. No biological, psychological, or economic fate determines the figure that the human female presents in society: it is civilization as a whole that produces this creature, intermediate between male and eunuch, which is described as feminine."[4]

However, most of the feminists and lesbian-feminists in America and elsewhere still believe that the basis of women's oppression *is biological as well as*

1. Christine Delphy, "Pour un féminisme matérialiste," *L'Arc* 61 (1975). Translated as "For a Materialist Feminism," *Feminist Issues* 1, no. 2 (winter 1981) [except as indicated, all notes are Wittig's].
2. Colette Guillaumin, "Race et Nature: Système des marques, idée de groupe naturel et rapports sociaux," *Pluriel*, no. 11 (1977). Translated as "Race and Nature: The System of Marks, the Idea of a Natural Group and Social Relationships," *Feminist Issues* 8, no. 2 (fall 1988).
3. I use the word *society* with an extended anthropological meaning; strictly speaking, it does not refer to societies, in that lesbian societies do not exist completely autonomously from heterosexual social systems.
4. Simone de Beauvoir, *The Second Sex* [trans. H. M. Parshley] (New York: Bantam, 1952), p. 249. [BEAUVOIR (1908–1986), French novelist, philosopher, and feminist—editor's note.]

historical. Some of them even claim to find their sources in Simone de Beauvoir.[5] The belief in mother right and in a "prehistory" when women created civilization (because of a biological predisposition) while the coarse and brutal men hunted (because of a biological predisposition) is symmetrical with the biologizing interpretation of history produced up to now by the class of men. It is still the same method of finding in women and men a biological explanation of their division, outside of social facts. For me this could never constitute a lesbian approach to women's oppression, since it assumes that the basis of society or the beginning of society lies in heterosexuality. Matriarchy is no less heterosexual than patriarchy: it is only the sex of the oppressor that changes. Furthermore, not only is this conception still imprisoned in the categories of sex (woman and man), but it holds onto the idea that the capacity to give birth (biology) is what defines a woman. Although practical facts and ways of living contradict this theory in lesbian society, there are lesbians who affirm that "women and men are different species or races (the words are used interchangeably): men are biologically inferior to women; male violence is a biological inevitability . . ."[6] By doing this, by admitting that there is a "natural" division between women and men, we naturalize history, we assume that "men" and "women" have always existed and will always exist. Not only do we naturalize history, but also consequently we naturalize the social phenomena which express our oppression, making change impossible. For example, instead of seeing giving birth as a forced production, we see it as a "natural," "biological" process, forgetting that in our societies births are planned (demography), forgetting that we ourselves are programmed to produce children, while this is the only social activity "short of war"[7] that presents such a great danger of death. Thus, as long as we will be "unable to abandon by will or impulse a lifelong and centuries-old commitment to childbearing as *the* female creative act,"[8] gaining control of the production of children will mean much more than the mere control of the material means of this production: women will have to abstract themselves from the definition "woman" which is imposed upon them.

A materialist feminist approach shows that what we take for the cause or origin of oppression is in fact only the *mark*[9] imposed by the oppressor: the "myth of woman,"[1] plus its material effects and manifestations in the appropriated consciousness and bodies of women. Thus, this mark does not predate oppression: Colette Guillaumin[2] has shown that before the socioeconomic reality of black slavery, the concept of race did not exist, at least not in its modern meaning, since it was applied to the lineage of families. However, now, race, exactly like sex, is taken as an "immediate given," a "sensible given," "physical features," belonging to a natural order. But what we believe to be a physical and direct perception is only a sophisticated and mythic construction, an "imaginary formation,"[3] which reinterprets physical features (in themselves as neutral as any others but marked by the social system) through

5. Redstockings, *Feminist Revolution* (New York: Random House, 1978), p. 18.
6. Andrea Dworkin, "Biological Superiority: The World's Most Dangerous and Deadly Idea," *Heresies* 6 (1989): 46.
7. Ti-Grace Atkinson, *Amazon Odyssey* (New York: Links Books, 1974), p. 15.
8. Dworkin, op. cit.
9. Guillaumin, op. cit.
1. Beauvoir, op. cit.
2. French sociologist and feminist theorist (1934–2017), author of *Racism, Sexism, Power, and Ideology* (1995) [editor's note].
3. Guillaumin, "Race and Nature."

the network of relationships in which they are perceived. (They are seen as *black*, therefore they *are* black; they are seen as *women*, therefore, they *are* women. But before being *seen* that way, they first had to be *made* that way.) Lesbians should always remember and acknowledge how "unnatural," compelling, totally oppressive, and destructive being "woman" was for us in the old days before the women's liberation movement. It was a political constraint, and those who resisted it were accused of not being "real" women. But then we were proud of it, since in the accusation there was already something like a shadow of victory: the avowal by the oppressor that "woman" is not something that goes without saying, since to be one, one has to be a "real" one. We were at the same time accused of wanting to be men. Today this double accusation has been taken up again with enthusiasm in the context of the women's liberation movement by some feminists and also, alas, by some lesbians whose political goal seems somehow to be becoming more and more "feminine." To refuse to be a woman, however, does not mean that one has to become a man. Besides, if we take as an example the perfect "butch," the classic example which provokes the most horror, whom Proust[4] would have called a woman/man, how is her alienation different from that of someone who wants to become a woman? Tweedledum and Tweedledee.[5] At least for a woman, wanting to become a man proves that she has escaped her initial programming. But even if she would like to, with all her strength, she cannot become a man. For becoming a man would demand from a woman not only a man's external appearance but his consciousness as well, that is, the consciousness of one who disposes by right of at least two "natural" slaves during his life span. This is impossible, and one feature of lesbian oppression consists precisely of making women out of reach for us, since women belong to men. Thus a lesbian *has* to be something else, a not-woman, a not-man, a product of society, not a product of nature, for there is no nature in society.

The refusal to become (or to remain) heterosexual always meant to refuse to become a man or a woman, consciously or not. For a lesbian this goes further than the refusal of the *role* "woman." It is the refusal of the economic, ideological, and political power of a man. This, we lesbians, and nonlesbians as well, knew before the beginning of the lesbian and feminist movement. However, as Andrea Dworkin emphasizes, many lesbians recently "have increasingly tried to transform the very ideology that has enslaved us into a dynamic, religious, psychologically compelling celebration of female biological potential."[6] Thus, some avenues of the feminist and lesbian movement lead us back to the myth of woman which was created by men especially for us, and with it we sink back into a natural group. Having stood up to fight for a sexless society,[7] we now find ourselves entrapped in the familiar deadlock of "woman is wonderful." Simone de Beauvoir underlined particularly the false consciousness[8] which consists of selecting among the

4. Marcel Proust (1871–1922), French novelist [editor's note].
5. Proverbial names for indistinguishable entities, personified as two brothers in Lewis Carroll's *Through the Looking-Glass* (1872) [editor's note].
6. Dworkin, op. cit. [Dworkin (1946–2005), American feminist writer known for opposition to pornography and for the claim that there is no such thing as consensual (heterosexual) sex—editor's note.]
7. Atkinson, p. 6: "If feminism has any logic at all, it must be working for a sexless society."
8. Marxist term referring to the tendency to view reality in ways congruent with the interests of the dominant orthodoxy rather than in ways that reflect an individual's class interest [editor's note].

features of the myth (that women are different from men) those which look good and using them as a definition for women. What the concept "woman is wonderful" accomplishes is that it retains for defining women the best features (best according to whom?) which oppression has granted us, and it does not radically question the categories "man" and "woman," which are political categories and not natural givens. It puts us in a position of fighting within the class "women" not as the other classes do, for the disappearance of our class, but for the defense of "woman" and its reenforcement. It leads us to develop with complacency "new" theories about our specificity: thus, we call our passivity "nonviolence," when the main and emergent point for us is to fight our passivity (our fear, rather, a justified one). The ambiguity of the term "feminist" sums up the whole situation. What does "feminist" mean? Feminist is formed with the word "femme," "woman," and means: someone who fights for women. For many of us it means someone who fights for women as a class and for the disappearance of this class. For many others it means someone who fights for woman and her defense—for the myth, then, and its reenforcement. But why was the word "feminist" chosen if it retains the least ambiguity? We chose to call ourselves "feminists" ten years ago, not in order to support or reenforce the myth of woman, nor to identify ourselves with the oppressor's definition of us, but rather to affirm that our movement had a history and to emphasize the political link with the old feminist movement.

It is, then, this movement that we can put in question for the meaning that it gave to feminism. It so happens that feminism in the last century could never resolve its contradictions on the subject of nature/culture, woman/society. Women started to fight for themselves as a group and rightly considered that they shared common features as a result of oppression. But for them these features were natural and biological rather than social. They went so far as to adopt the Darwinist theory of evolution. They did not believe like Darwin, however, "that women were less evolved than men, but they did believe that male and female natures had diverged in the course of evolutionary development and that society at large reflected this polarization."[9] "The failure of early feminism was that it only attacked the Darwinist charge of female inferiority, while accepting the foundations of this charge—namely, the view of woman as 'unique.'"[1] And finally it was women scholars—and not feminists—who scientifically destroyed this theory. But the early feminists had failed to regard history as a dynamic process which develops from conflicts of interests. Furthermore, they still believed as men do that the cause (origin) of their oppression lay within themselves. And therefore after some astonishing victories the feminists of this first front found themselves at an impasse out of a lack of reasons to fight. They upheld the illogical principle of "equality in difference," an idea now being born again. They fell back into the trap which threatens us once again: the myth of woman.

Thus it is our historical task, and only ours, to define what we call oppression in materialist terms, to make it evident that women are a class, which is to say that the category "woman" as well as the category "man" are political

9. Rosalind Rosenberg, "In Search of Woman's Nature," *Feminist Studies* 3, nos. 1/2 (1975): 144. [Charles Darwin (1809–1882), English naturalist—editor's note.]

1. Ibid., p. 146.

and economic categories not eternal ones. Our fight aims to suppress men as a class, not through a genocidal, but a political struggle. Once the class "men" disappears, "women" as a class will disappear as well, for there are no slaves without masters. Our first task, it seems, is to always thoroughly dissociate "women" (the class within which we fight) and "woman," the myth. For "woman" does not exist for us: it is only an imaginary formation, while "women" is the product of a social relationship. We felt this strongly when everywhere we refused to be called a "*woman's* liberation movement." Furthermore, we have to destroy the myth inside and outside ourselves. "Woman" is not each one of us, but the political and ideological formation which negates "women" (the product of a relation of exploitation). "Woman" is there to confuse us, to hide the reality "women." In order to be aware of being a class and to become a class we first have to kill the myth of "woman" including its most seductive aspects (I think about Virginia Woolf[2] when she said the first task of a woman writer is to kill "the angel in the house"). But to become a class we do not have to suppress our individual selves, and since no individual can be reduced to her/his oppression we are also confronted with the historical necessity of constituting ourselves as the individual subjects of our history as well. I believe this is the reason why all these attempts at "new" definitions of woman are blossoming now. What is at stake (and of course not only for women) is an individual definition as well as a class definition. For once one has acknowledged oppression, one needs to know and experience the fact that one can constitute oneself as a subject (as opposed to an object of oppression), that one can become *someone* in spite of oppression, that one has one's own identity. There is no possible fight for someone deprived of an identity, no internal motivation for fighting, since, although I can fight only with others, first I fight for myself.

The question of the individual subject is historically a difficult one for everybody. Marxism, the last avatar of materialism, the science which has politically formed us, does not want to hear anything about a "subject." Marxism has rejected the transcendental subject, the subject as constitutive of knowledge, the "pure" consciousness. All that thinks per se, before all experience, has ended up in the garbage can of history, because it claimed to exist outside matter, prior to matter, and needed God, spirit, or soul to exist in such a way. This is what is called "idealism." As for individuals, they are only the product of social relations, therefore their consciousness can only be "alienated." (Marx,[3] in *The German Ideology*, says precisely that individuals of the dominating class are also alienated, although they are the direct producers of the ideas that alienate the classes oppressed by them. But since they draw visible advantages from their own alienation they can bear it without too much suffering.) There exists such a thing as class consciousness, but a consciousness which does not refer to a particular subject, except as participating in general conditions of exploitation at the same time as the other subjects of their class, all sharing the same consciousness. As for the practical class problems—outside of the class problems as traditionally defined—

2. English writer (1882–1941). The reference is to WOOLF's "Professions for Women" (lecture, 1931; published 1942); the "Angel" is the Victorian ideal of self-sacrificing womanhood [editor's note].

3. KARL MARX (1818–1883), German economic, social, and political philosopher; *The German Ideology* was written in 1845–46 and published in 1932 [editor's note].

that one could encounter (for example, sexual problems), they were considered "bourgeois" problems that would disappear with the final victory of the class struggle. "Individualistic," "subjectivist," "petit bourgeois," these were the labels given to any person who had shown problems which could not be reduced to the "class struggle" itself.

Thus Marxism has denied the members of oppressed classes the attribute of being a subject. In doing this, Marxism, because of the ideological and political power this "revolutionary science" immediately exercised upon the workers' movement and all other political groups, has prevented all categories of oppressed peoples from constituting themselves historically as subjects (subjects of their struggle, for example). This means that the "masses" did not fight for themselves but for *the* party or its organizations. And when an economic transformation took place (end of private property, constitution of the socialist state), no revolutionary change took place within the new society, because the people themselves did not change.

For women, Marxism had two results. It prevented them from being aware that they are a class and therefore from constituting themselves as a class for a very long time, by leaving the relation "women/men" outside of the social order, by turning it into a natural relation, doubtless for Marxists the only one, along with the relation of mothers to children, to be seen this way, and by hiding the class conflict between men and women behind a natural division of labor (*The German Ideology*). This concerns the theoretical (ideological) level. On the practical level, Lenin,[4] *the* party, all the communist parties up to now, including all the most radical political groups, have always reacted to any attempt on the part of women to reflect and form groups based on their own class problem with an accusation of divisiveness. By uniting, we women are dividing the strength of the people. This means that for the Marxists women *belong* either to the bourgeois class or to the proletariat class, in other words, to the men of these classes. In addition, Marxist theory does not allow women any more than other classes of oppressed people to constitute themselves as historical subjects, because Marxism does not take into account the fact that a class also consists of individuals one by one. Class consciousness is not enough. We must try to understand philosophically (politically) these concepts of "subject" and "class consciousness" and how they work in relation to our history. When we discover that women are the objects of oppression and appropriation, at the very moment that we become able to perceive this, we become subjects in the sense of cognitive subjects, through an operation of abstraction. Consciousness of oppression is not only a reaction to (fight against) oppression. It is also the whole conceptual reevaluation of the social world, its whole reorganization with new concepts, from the point of view of oppression. It is what I would call the science of oppression created by the oppressed. This operation of understanding reality has to be undertaken by every one of us: call it a subjective, cognitive practice. The movement back and forth between the levels of reality (the conceptual reality and the material reality of oppression, which are both social realities) is accomplished through language.

4. V. I. Lenin (1870–1924), Marxist revolutionary leader and theorist of the Bolshevik revolution and first head of the new Soviet government [editor's note].

It is we who historically must undertake the task of defining the individual subject in materialist terms. This certainly seems to be an impossibility since materialism and subjectivity have always been mutually exclusive. Nevertheless, and rather than despairing of ever understanding, we must recognize the *need* to reach subjectivity in the abandonment by many of us to the myth "woman" (the myth of woman being only a snare that holds us up). This real necessity for everyone to exist as an individual, as well as a member of a class, is perhaps the first condition for the accomplishment of a revolution, without which there can be no real fight or transformation. But the opposite is also true; without class and class consciousness there are no real subjects, only alienated individuals. For women to answer the question of the individual subject in materialist terms is first to show, as the lesbians and feminists did, that supposedly "subjective," "individual," "private" problems are in fact social problems, class problems; that sexuality is not for women an individual and subjective expression, but a social institution of violence. But once we have shown that all so-called personal problems are in fact class problems, we will still be left with the question of the subject of each singular woman—not the myth, but each one of us. At this point, let us say that a new personal and subjective definition for all humankind can only be found beyond the categories of sex (woman and man) and that the advent of individual subjects demands first destroying the categories of sex, ending the use of them, and rejecting all sciences which still use these categories as their fundamentals (practically all social sciences).

To destroy "woman" does not mean that we aim, short of physical destruction, to destroy lesbianism simultaneously with the categories of sex, because lesbianism provides for the moment the only social form in which we can live freely. Lesbian is the only concept I know of which is beyond the categories of sex (woman and man), because the designated subject (lesbian) is *not* a woman, either economically, or politically, or ideologically. For what makes a woman is a specific social relation to a man, a relation that we have previously called servitude,[5] a relation which implies personal and physical obligation as well as economic obligation ("forced residence,"[6] domestic corvée, conjugal duties, unlimited production of children, etc.), a relation which lesbians escape by refusing to become or to stay heterosexual. We are escapees from our class in the same way as the American runaway slaves were when escaping slavery and becoming free. For us this is an absolute necessity; our survival demands that we contribute all our strength to the destruction of the class of women within which men appropriate women. This can be accomplished only by the destruction of heterosexuality as a social system which is based on the oppression of women by men and which produces the doctrine of the difference between the sexes to justify this oppression.

1981

5. In an article published in *L'Idiot International* (mai 1970), whose original title was "Pour un mouvement de libération des femmes" (For a Woman's Liberation Movement).
6. Christiane Rochefort, *Les stances à Sophie* (Paris: Grasset, 1963).

BENEDICT ANDERSON
1936–2015

Benedict Anderson's *Imagined Communities* (1983) provides a highly influential account of the origins and causes of nationalism. Anderson defines "the nation" as "an imagined political community—and imagined as both inherently limited and sovereign." The book's title has passed into the theoretical lexicon to designate any group of people who, without knowing each other personally or encountering each other physically, still consider themselves members of the same community. Anderson asks, How is this act of imagination possible? And why, from around 1760 onward, did nationalism become the most potent form in the West of shared membership?

Anderson was born in China to an Irish father and English mother, but grew up mainly in California and Ireland. Following his undergraduate studies at Cambridge University in England, in 1958 he came to Cornell University in upstate New York to pursue Ph.D. research on Indonesia. While working on his doctoral dissertation on post–World War II Indonesian politics, Anderson ran afoul of the country's military leader by challenging Suharto's version of the alleged leftist coup attempt in 1965 that led to his rise to power and the deaths of hundreds of thousands of civilians. Anderson was banned from Indonesia and did not return until after Suharto's resignation from the presidency in 1998. After completing his Ph.D. in 1967, Anderson joined the faculty at Cornell, where he remained until his retirement in 2002. His extensive written work fits mainly under the rubric of Southeast Asian studies. *Imagined Communities* is his most notable foray into more general theoretical speculations and transnational historical accounts. His brother Perry Anderson is a noted Marxist intellectual and longtime editor of the *New Left Review*.

Anderson's work on nationalism came in the wake of EDWARD W. SAID's *Orientalism* (1978), and it reflects an engagement with two historical movements: the pre-twentieth-century establishment by Western powers of colonies around the globe and the late twentieth-century end of most colonialism. FRANTZ FANON, in the 1950s, had already identified nationalist feeling as a potent weapon against the colonizer. Anderson begins with the question of how nationalist sentiment is generated in a geographical territory like a colony that has never been a nation. To answer it, he turns from the colonial situation to the origins of nationalism in Europe itself. Not uniquely, but very influentially, Anderson insists that nationalism appeared first in Europe before manifesting itself elsewhere in the world. Equally crucial is his insistence that nationalism is a *modern* phenomenon, which took shape (after various earlier stirrings) in the eighteenth century. He identifies several key elements of nationalism, including the political institution of the centralized nation-state and its citizens' genuinely felt attachment to that nation. Even when critical of their current government or of a particular set of political leaders, citizens of modern nations are emotionally committed to the preservation and success of their nation. Their act of identification makes their membership in that political entity central to how they understand their own individual identities.

In modern times patriotism has proved a remarkably potent emotion, one that often unleashes demons of intolerance and violence. "The nation," Anderson writes, "is always conceived as a deep, horizontal comradeship. Ultimately it is this fraternity that makes it possible, over the past two centuries, for so many millions of people, not so much to kill, as willingly to die for such limited imaginings." Anderson's wide-ranging historical account of the required conditions for the birth of nationalism places affect near the center. For a nation to exist, a sizable group of people must be able to experience themselves *as* "a people," bound together by special ties and distinct from other peoples. As becomes immediately evident to anyone who tries to identify what "a people" shares, there are some obvious candidates for the unifying principle but no sure winner. In some nations, strong patriotic feelings coexist with ethnic, linguistic, religious, and cultural diversity. No one essential characteristic can be identified that, if missing, makes nationhood impossible. Rather, under different historical, cultural, and geographic circumstances, the shared feeling essential to nationhood can be constructed differently. Likewise, nations can manage to survive while also experiencing considerable racial, regional, religious, ethnic, and class animosities. What does seem crucial is some sense of a common destiny, of the conviction that "we" citizens, for better and for worse, are in the same boat together.

Anderson's great insight is that however it is constructed, fellow feeling must be *imagined*. To use language that Anderson does not, we can say that a nation is always a virtual community. It is never embodied or instantiated in a real time or a real place. It thus stands in contrast to what RAYMOND WILLIAMS called "knowable communities," the small groupings where every member knows each other member through face-to-face interactions. In the nation each citizen's relation to his or her fellow citizens and to the nation as a whole (as an idea) is experienced through an image of simultaneity (I am voting today as millions of my compatriots are) and of shared knowledge and feelings (I vote on the basis of information and a love of country that my compatriots also possess). The nation is an abstraction that is made real only through the actual practices of citizens who imagine those practices as meaningful precisely because of their relation to that abstraction. It is no accident that the broad, often nebulous, concept of culture as a shared way of life dates from the mid-eighteenth century as well. What "culture" struggles to name is individuals' new sense of participating in something larger than themselves when they act, even though it is difficult to specify what that "something larger" actually is.

In our selection, chapter 3 of *Imagined Communities*, Anderson sets out to explain what makes this act of imagination possible. What needs and what historical innovations call this emotional identification into existence? Part of Anderson's answer involves the decline of Catholicism as a single religion prevailing throughout most of Europe. Its loss of control makes possible the rise of more localized political power, leads to the replacement of Latin by various vernaculars as the official languages of church and state, and, most importantly, creates a need for a unifying basis for communal identity. During the Renaissance, Latin becomes increasingly rarefied and the province of humanists. Religious unanimity is gone forever from Europe after the Protestant Reformation, and the modern notion of religious tolerance begins to slowly emerge. To maintain the civil peace, a political version of shared identity is needed that can establish communal bonds among fellow citizens who disagree deeply on religious matters. Religion is still important, but modern political communities are organized around shared identifications with secular states.

In Anderson's view, the mechanism for creating this allegiance to the nation is print capitalism. Europe was a loosely organized congeries of local communities under both the Roman Empire and the Roman Catholic Church; each community was connected hierarchically to Rome, with few ties to one another. Only when aided by print media, Anderson argues, can strangers imagine themselves as partaking simultaneously in the same set of unfolding events. The repetitions and cycles of religious ritual yield to the narrative, linear time of national history. Through the almost instantaneous representation of historical events in newspapers and books, each citizen has the sense of being a participant in the nation's unfolding destiny. This feeling of connection is "limited"—that is, given specific borders—both geographically and linguistically. Print is connected to the establishment of national languages, as the vernacular replaces Latin in almost all contexts and as widely circulated texts stabilize language use and aid in the emergence of a national, standard version of the dominant language. Capitalism is also crucial: the technology of printing did not have the same effects in China as in Europe. Books and newspapers transform society only when they are widely circulated and are connected to money-making enterprises that have a stake in expanding their market by increasing literacy. Nationalism—at least prior to radio and television—depends on a literate citizenry that experiences its membership in the nation through the printed word.

By focusing on the central role of media—whether print journalism, novels, or the nonprint forms of our own time—Anderson emphasizes that a nation groups together people who tell a certain story about themselves. Citizens are at once the producers, subjects, and consumers of this story. Their membership consists in their experience of themselves as both the proper agents and the appropriate audience for these tales. These national stories may be (and in fact usually are) shot through with conflicts and disagreements; members of a nation need not agree with each other, just as they need not share a religion or an ethnicity. But they must each experience themselves as fully entitled participants in the ongoing and unfolding history of the nation—and recognize even their antagonists as similarly fully entitled participants. Civil war, the undoing of the nation, results when any subgroup within the nation (whether religious, regional, ethnic, racial, or tribal) tries to exclude other subgroups as citizens or to separate itself by secession from political unity with other groups. Increasingly since 1800, the nation has become the only internationally recognized form of political organization—and when former colonies gain independence they invariably seek to re-create themselves as nation-states. Yet contemporary separatist movements, ranging from the Scots and Catalans in Europe to the Kurds in the Middle East and indigenous peoples in North and South America, suggest that the nation is not necessarily a very stable or successful political form.

Successful or not as a political form, the nation figures prominently in literature as an emotional fact, whether as a national consciousness some writers want to engender or as an emotional roadblock to alternative visions dear to others. The decision to celebrate or denigrate nationalist feeling does not consistently correspond to the writer's political positions, left or right. Current interest in "cosmopolitanism" does register a sense that nationalism's sometimes murderous passions are inappropriate in a world where mobility across national borders continues to grow. Yet the very persistence of strong national feelings makes claims that we now occupy a "transnational" or "postnational" globalized world seem premature. Perhaps our time is witnessing the final gasp of the nation as it developed between 1500 and 1800 in Europe and then solidified across the globe from 1800 onward. But Benedict Anderson's work will remain indispensable to any understanding of the nation as the crucial political form of modernity, a form closely linked to literacy and print media.

***Imagined Communities* Keywords:** Modernity, Nationhood, Postcolonial Theory, Print Culture, Race and Ethnicity Studies, Vernacular Language

From Imagined Communities

Chapter 3. The Origins of National Consciousness

If the development of print-as-commodity is the key to the generation of wholly new ideas of simultaneity, still, we are simply at the point where communities of the type 'horizontal-secular, transverse-time' become possible.[1]

1. In the previous chapter, Anderson distinguishes secular societies, where lines of authority must be developed from a starting point in which the members are basically equal (horizontal), from those with a vertical hierarchy grounded in a distinction between the sacred and the nonsacred. He also contrasts societies that develop a sense of simultaneity as well as continuity extending beyond a single lifetime from societies that lack such time frames.

Why, within that type, did the nation become so popular? The factors involved are obviously complex and various. But a strong case can be made for the primacy of capitalism.

As already noted, at least 20,000,000 books had already been printed by 1500,[2] signalling the onset of Benjamin's 'age of mechanical reproduction.'[3] If manuscript knowledge was scarce and arcane lore, print knowledge lived by reproducibility and dissemination.[4] If, as Febvre and Martin believe, possibly as many as 200,000,000 volumes had been manufactured by 1600, it is no wonder that Francis Bacon believed that print had changed 'the appearance and state of the world.'[5]

One of the earlier forms of capitalist enterprise, book-publishing felt all of capitalism's restless search for markets. The early printers established branches all over Europe: 'in this way a veritable "international" of publishing houses, which ignored national [sic] frontiers, was created.'[6] And since the years 1500–1550 were a period of exceptional European prosperity, publishing shared in the general boom. 'More than at any other time' it was 'a great industry under the control of wealthy capitalists.'[7] Naturally, 'booksellers were primarily concerned to make a profit and to sell their products, and consequently they sought out first and foremost those works which were of interest to the largest possible number of their contemporaries.'[8]

The initial market was literate Europe, a wide but thin stratum of Latin-readers. Saturation of this market took about a hundred and fifty years. The determinative fact about Latin—aside from its sacrality—was that it was a language of bilinguals. Relatively few were born to speak it and even fewer, one imagines, dreamed in it. In the sixteenth century the proportion of bilinguals within the total population of Europe was quite small; very likely no larger than the proportion in the world's population today, and—proletarian internationalism notwithstanding—in the centuries to come. Then and now the bulk of mankind is monoglot. The logic of capitalism thus meant that once the elite Latin market was saturated, the potentially huge markets represented by the monoglot masses would beckon. To be sure, the Counter-Reformation[9] encouraged a temporary resurgence of Latin-publishing, but by the mid-seventeenth century the movement was in decay, and fervently Catholic libraries replete. Meantime, a Europe-wide shortage of money made printers think more and more of peddling cheap editions in the vernaculars.[1]

2. The population of that Europe where print was then known was about 100,000,000. Lucien Febvre and Henri-Jean Martin, *The Coming of the Book: The Impact of Printing, 1450–1800* (1976), pp. 248–49 [Anderson's note].

3. An allusion to "The Work of Art in the Age of Its Technological Reproducibility" (1936–39; see above), by the German cultural critic WALTER BENJAMIN (1892–1940); as translated in its first publication in English, the essay's title ended "Age of Mechanical Reproduction."

4. Emblematic is Marco Polo's *Travels*, which remained largely unknown till its first printing in 1559 [Anderson's note]. Polo (1254–1324), Venetian traveler; his account of his journey to China, usually known as *The Travels of Marco Polo*, was first published in 1299.

5. Quoted in Elizabeth L. Eisenstein, "Some Conjectures about the Impact of Printing on Western Society and Thought," *Journal of Modern History* 40.1 (March 1968): 56 [Anderson's note]. Bacon (1561–1626), English philospher and scientist; the quotation is from his *Novum Organum* (1620), book I, aphorism 129.

6. Febvre and Martin, *The Coming of the Book*, p. 122 [Anderson's note].

7. Ibid., p. 187 [Anderson's note].

8. "Hence the introduction of printing was in this respect a stage on the road to our present society of mass consumption and standardization." Ibid., pp. 259–60 [Anderson's note].

9. The 16th-century reform movement within the Catholic Church, undertaken in response to the Protestant Reformation—the movement in western Europe critical of the church that led to religious schism and the establishment of Protestant churches.

1. Febvre and Martin, p. 195 [Anderson's note]. "Vernaculars": native languages or dialects in everyday use.

The revolutionary vernacularizing thrust of capitalism was given further impetus by three extraneous factors, two of which contributed directly to the rise of national consciousness. The first, and ultimately the least important, was a change in the character of Latin itself. Thanks to the labours of the Humanists[2] in reviving the broad literature of pre-Christian antiquity and spreading it through the print-market, a new appreciation of the sophisticated stylistic achievements of the ancients was apparent among the trans-European intelligentsia. The Latin they now aspired to write became more and more Ciceronian,[3] and, by the same token, increasingly removed from ecclesiastical and everyday life. In this way it acquired an esoteric quality quite different from that of Church Latin in mediaeval times. For the older Latin was not arcane because of its subject matter or style, but simply because it was written at all, i.e. because of its status as *text*. Now it became arcane because of what was written, because of the language-in-itself.

Second was the impact of the Reformation, which, at the same time, owed much of its success to print-capitalism. Before the age of print, Rome easily won every war against heresy in Western Europe because it always had better internal lines of communication than its challengers. But when in 1517 Martin Luther[4] nailed his theses to the chapel-door in Wittenberg, they were printed up in German translation, and 'within 15 days [had been] seen in every part of the country.'[5] In the two decades 1520–1540 three times as many books were published in German as in the period 1500–1520, an astonishing transformation to which Luther was absolutely central. His works represented no less than one third of *all* German-language books sold between 1518 and 1525. Between 1522 and 1546, a total of 430 editions (whole or partial) of his Biblical translations appeared. 'We have here for the first time a truly mass readership and a popular literature within everybody's reach.'[6] In effect, Luther became the first best-selling author *so known*. Or, to put it another way, the first writer who could 'sell' his *new* books on the basis of his name.[7]

Where Luther led, others quickly followed, opening the colossal religious propaganda war that raged across Europe for the next century. In this titanic 'battle for men's minds', Protestantism was always fundamentally on the offensive, precisely because it knew how to make use of the expanding vernacular print-market being created by capitalism, while the Counter-Reformation defended the citadel of Latin. The emblem for this is the Vatican's *Index Librorum Prohibitorum*[8]—to which there was no Protestant counterpart—a novel catalogue made necessary by the sheer volume of printed subversion. Nothing gives a better sense of this siege mentality than François I's[9] panicked

2. The European scholars who, beginning in the late 14th century, emphasized classical Latin and Greek literature, which had been newly rediscovered.
3. That is, with many subordinate clauses, like the complex style of the great Roman orator and statesman Cicero (106–43 B.C.E.).
4. Religious reformer (1483–1546), whose break with the Catholic Church in 1517 set the Protestant Reformation in motion; he also translated the New Testament into German, and collaborated on a translation of the Old Testament.
5. Febvre and Martin, pp. 289–90 [Anderson's note].
6. Ibid., pp. 291–95 [Anderson's note].
7. From this point it was only a step to the situation in 17th-century France where Corneille, Molière, and La Fontaine could sell their manuscript tragedies and comedies directly to publishers, who bought them as excellent investments in view of their authors' market reputations. Ibid., p. 161 [Anderson's note]. PIERRE CORNEILLE (1606–1684), French tragic playwright. Molière (pen name of Jean-Baptiste Poquelin, 1622–1673), French comic playwright and actor. Jean de La Fontaine (1621–1695), French poet best remembered today for his *Fables*.
8. Index of Forbidden Books (Latin).
9. Catholic king of France (1494–1547; reigned 1515–47).

1535 ban on the printing of *any* books in his realm—on pain of death by hanging! The reason for both the ban and its unenforceability was that by then his realm's eastern borders were ringed with Protestant states and cities producing a massive stream of smugglable print. To take Calvin's[1] Geneva alone: between 1533 and 1540 only 42 editions were published there, but the numbers swelled to 527 between 1550 and 1564, by which latter date no less than 40 separate printing-presses were working overtime.[2]

The coalition between Protestantism and print-capitalism, exploiting cheap popular editions, quickly created large new reading publics—not least among merchants and women, who typically knew little or no Latin—and simultaneously mobilized them for politico-religious purposes. Inevitably, it was not merely the Church that was shaken to its core. The same earthquake produced Europe's first important non-dynastic, non-city states in the Dutch Republic and the Commonwealth of the Puritans.[3] (François I's panic was as much political as religious.)

Third was the slow, geographically uneven, spread of particular vernaculars as instruments of administrative centralization by certain well-positioned would-be absolutist monarchs. Here it is useful to remember that the universality of Latin in mediaeval Western Europe never corresponded to a universal political system. The contrast with Imperial China, where the reach of the mandarinal bureaucracy and of painted characters largely coincided,[4] is instructive. In effect, the political fragmentation of Western Europe after the collapse of the Western Empire[5] meant that no sovereign could monopolize Latin and make it his-and-only-his language-of-state, and thus Latin's religious authority never had a true political analogue.

The birth of administrative vernaculars predated both print and the religious upheaval of the sixteenth century, and must therefore be regarded (at least initially) as an independent factor in the erosion of the sacred imagined community. At the same time, nothing suggests that any deep-seated ideological, let alone proto-national, impulses underlay this vernacularization where it occurred. The case of 'England'—on the northwestern periphery of Latin Europe—is here especially enlightening. Prior to the Norman Conquest,[6] the language of the court, literary and administrative, was Anglo-Saxon. For the next century and a half virtually all royal documents were composed in Latin. Between about 1200 and 1350 this state-Latin was superseded by Norman French. In the meantime, a slow fusion between this language of a foreign ruling class and the Anglo-Saxon of the subject population produced Early English. The fusion made it possible for the new language to take its turn, after 1362, as the language of the courts—and for the opening of Parliament. Wycliffe's vernacular *manuscript* Bible followed

1. John Calvin (1509–1564), French Protestant theologian. Followers of Calvin dominated the government of Geneva during the 1540s and 1550s.

2. Febvre and Martin, pp. 310–15 [Anderson's note].

3. The republic established in 1649 in England following the Civil War and the execution of Charles I; it lasted until the monarchy was restored in 1660. Dutch Republic: the precursor state (1581–1795) of the Netherlands, formed from 7 provinces that declared their independence from Catholic Spain.

4. Beginning in the 7th century, the officials in imperial China (mandarins) were selected by civil examinations that focused on literary and philosophical texts and on knowledge of classical Chinese.

5. The western part of the Roman Empire, whose capital was Rome; the last emperor fell in 476 C.E.

6. The military conquest of England in 1066 by the French (the Normans, or Norsemen, who had earlier conquered Normandy, the northwest region of France).

in 1382.[7] It is essential to bear in mind that this sequence was a series of 'state,' not 'national,' languages; and that the state concerned covered at various times not only today's England and Wales, but also portions of Ireland, Scotland *and France*. Obviously, huge elements of the subject populations knew little or nothing of Latin, Norman French, or Early English.[8] Not till almost a century *after* Early English's political enthronement was London's power swept out of 'France'.

On the Seine,[9] a similar movement took place, if at a slower pace. As Bloch wryly puts it, 'French, that is to say a language which, since it was regarded as merely a corrupt form of Latin, took several centuries to raise itself to literary dignity',[1] only became the official language of the courts of justice in 1539, when François I issued the Edict of Villers-Cotterêts.[2] In other dynastic realms Latin survived much longer—under the Habsburgs[3] well into the nineteenth century. In still others, 'foreign' vernaculars took over: in the eighteenth century the languages of the Romanov court were French and German.[4]

In every instance, the 'choice' of language appears as a gradual, unselfconscious, pragmatic, not to say haphazard development. As such, it was utterly different from the selfconscious language policies pursued by nineteenth-century dynasts confronted with the rise of hostile popular linguistic-nationalisms. One clear sign of the difference is that the old administrative languages were *just that*: languages used by and for officialdoms for their own inner convenience. There was no idea of systematically imposing the language on the dynasts' various subject populations.[5] Nonetheless, the elevation of these vernaculars to the status of languages-of-power, where, in one sense, they were competitors with Latin (French in Paris, [Early] English in London), made its own contribution to the decline of the imagined community of Christendom.

At bottom, it is likely that the esotericization of Latin, the Reformation, and the haphazard development of administrative vernaculars are significant, in the present context, primarily in a negative sense—in their contributions to the dethronement of Latin. It is quite possible to conceive of the emergence of the new imagined national communities without any one, perhaps all, of them being present. What, in a positive sense, made the new communities imaginable was a half-fortuitous, but explosive, interaction between a system of production and productive relations (capitalism), a technology of communications (print), and the fatality of human linguistic diversity.[6]

7. The first translation of the Latin Vulgate Bible into English, promoted (and in part carried out) by the English theologian and reformer John Wycliffe (ca. 1328–1384).

8. Hugh Seton-Watson, *Nations and States: An Inquiry into the Origins of Nations and the Politics of Nationalism* (1977), pp. 28–29; Marc Bloch, *Feudal Society*, trans. I. A. Manyon (1961), vol. I, p. 75 [Anderson's note]. The Welsh, Irish, and Scots had their own languages.

9. River that runs through Paris.

1. Bloch, *Feudal Society*, I, p. 98 [Anderson's note].

2. A law that mandated the use of French, instead of Latin or local dialects, in all official governmental and ecclesiastical documents.

3. The ruling dynasty of Austria from 1282 to 1918.

4. Seton-Watson, *Nations and States*, p. 48 [Anderson's note]. The Romanovs were the ruling dynasty of Russia from 1613 to 1917.

5. An agreeable confirmation of this point is provided by François I, who, as we have seen, banned all printing of books in 1535 and made French the language of his courts four years later! [Anderson's note].

6. It was not the first "accident" of its kind. Febvre and Martin note that while a visible bourgeoisie already existed in Europe by the late 13th century, paper did not come into general use until the end of the 14th. Only paper's smooth plane surface made the mass reproduction of texts and pictures possible—and this did not occur for still another 75 years. But paper was not a European invention. It floated in from another history—China's—through the Islamic world. *The Coming of the Book*, pp. 22, 30, and 45 [Anderson's note].

The element of fatality is essential. For whatever superhuman feats capitalism was capable of, it found in death and languages two tenacious adversaries.[7] Particular languages can die or be wiped out, but there was and is no possibility of humankind's general linguistic unification. Yet this mutual incomprehensibility was historically of only slight importance until capitalism and print created monoglot mass reading publics.

While it is essential to keep in mind an idea of fatality, in the sense of a *general* condition of irremediable linguistic diversity, it would be a mistake to equate this fatality with that common element in nationalist ideologies which stresses the primordial fatality of *particular* languages and their association with *particular* territorial units. The essential thing is the *interplay* between fatality, technology, and capitalism. In pre-print Europe, and, of course, elsewhere in the world, the diversity of spoken languages, those languages that for their speakers were (and are) the warp and woof of their lives, was immense; so immense, indeed, that had print-capitalism sought to exploit each potential oral vernacular market, it would have remained a capitalism of petty proportions. But these varied idiolects were capable of being assembled, within definite limits, into print-languages far fewer in number. The very arbitrariness of any system of signs for sounds facilitated the assembling process.[8] (At the same time, the more ideographic the signs, the vaster the potential assembling zone. One can detect a sort of descending hierarchy here from algebra through Chinese and English, to the regular syllabaries of French or Indonesian.)[9] Nothing served to 'assemble' related vernaculars more than capitalism, which, within the limits imposed by grammars and syntaxes, created mechanically reproduced print-languages capable of dissemination through the market.[1]

These print-languages laid the bases for national consciousnesses in three distinct ways. First and foremost, they created unified fields of exchange and communication below Latin and above the spoken vernaculars. Speakers of the huge variety of Frenches, Englishes, or Spanishes, who might find it difficult or even impossible to understand one another in conversation, became capable of comprehending one another via print and paper. In the process, they gradually became aware of the hundreds of thousands, even millions, of people in their particular language-field, and at the same time that *only those* hundreds of thousands, or millions, so belonged. These fellow-readers, to whom they were connected through print, formed, in their secular, particular, visible invisibility, the embryo of the nationally imagined community.

7. We still have no great multinationals in the world of publishing [Anderson's note]. Perhaps true when Anderson wrote his book in 1983, but certainly not true in recent years.

8. For a useful discussion of this point, see S. H. Steinberg, *Five Hundred Years of Printing* (1966), chapter 5. That the sign *ough* is pronounced differently in the words although, bough, lough, rough, cough, and hiccough, shows both the idiolectic variety out of which the now-standard spelling of English emerged, and the ideographic quality of the final product [Anderson's note].

9. That is, from the purely symbolic representations of algebra to the ideograms of Chinese writing, which represent syllables but not particular sounds, to English spellings that correspond somewhat unpredictably to sounds to the highly regular pronunciation of words spelled in such languages as French and Indonesian. Chinese has a potentially vast "assembling zone," because those whose spoken dialects are mutually incomprehensible can nervertheless read the same text.

1. I say "nothing served . . . more than capitalism" advisedly. Both Steinberg and Eisenstein come close to theomorphizing "print" *qua* print as the genius of modern history. Febvre and Martin never forget that behind print stands printers and publishing firms. It is worth remembering in this context that although printing was invented first in China, possibly 500 years before its appearance in Europe, it had no major, let alone revolutionary impact—precisely because of the absence of capitalism there [Anderson's note].

Second, print-capitalism gave a new fixity to language, which in the long run helped to build that image of antiquity so central to the subjective idea of the nation. As Febvre and Martin remind us, the printed book kept a permanent form, capable of virtually infinite reproduction, temporally and spatially. It was no longer subject to the individualizing and 'unconsciously modernizing' habits of monastic scribes. Thus, while twelfth-century French differed markedly from that written by Villon[2] in the fifteenth, the rate of change slowed decisively in the sixteenth. 'By the 17th century languages in Europe had generally assumed their modern forms.'[3] To put it another way, for three centuries now these stabilized print-languages have been gathering a darkening varnish; the words of our seventeenth-century forebears are accessible to us in a way that to Villon his twelfth-century ancestors were not.

Third, print-capitalism created languages-of-power of a kind different from the older administrative vernaculars. Certain dialects inevitably were 'closer' to each print-language and dominated their final forms. Their disadvantaged cousins, still assimilable to the emerging print-language, lost caste, above all because they were unsuccessful (or only relatively successful) in insisting on their own print-form. 'Northwestern German' became Platt Deutsch, a largely spoken, thus sub-standard, German, because it was assimilable to print-German in a way that Bohemian spoken-Czech was not. High German, the King's English, and, later, Central Thai,[4] were correspondingly elevated to a new politico-cultural eminence. (Hence the struggles in late-twentieth-century Europe by certain 'sub-' nationalities to change their subordinate status by breaking firmly into print—and radio.)

It remains only to emphasize that in their origins, the fixing of print-languages and the differentiation of status between them were largely unself-conscious processes resulting from the explosive interaction between capitalism, technology and human linguistic diversity. But as with so much else in the history of nationalism, once 'there,' they could become formal models to be imitated, and, where expedient, consciously exploited in a Machiavellian spirit.[5] Today, the Thai government actively discourages attempts by foreign missionaries to provide its hill-tribe minorities with their own transcription-systems and to develop publications in their own languages: the same government is largely indifferent to what these minorities *speak*. The fate of the Turkic-speaking peoples in the zones incorporated into today's Turkey, Iran, Iraq, and the USSR is especially exemplary. A family of spoken languages, once everywhere assemblable, thus comprehensible, within an Arabic orthography, has lost that unity as a result of conscious manipulations. To heighten Turkish–Turkey's national consciousness at the expense of any wider Islamic identification, Atatürk imposed compulsory romanization.[6] The Soviet authorities followed suit, first with an anti-Islamic,

2. François Villon (1431–ca. 1473), French poet.
3. Febvre and Martin, *The Coming of the Book*, p. 319 [Anderson's note].
4. All dialects that became the official forms of their respective languages. Platt Deutsch: Low German, spoken in northern Germany.
5. Marked by the amoral cunning and opportunism associated with observations made by the Italian political philosopher Niccolò Machiavelli (1469–1527).
6. Hans Kohn, *The Age of Nationalism* (1962), p. 108. It is probably only fair to add that Kemal also hoped thereby to align Turkish nationalism with the modern, romanized civilization of Western Europe [Anderson's note]. Romanization: use of the Latin alphabet to represent words (Turkish had been written in Arabic script). Kemal Atatürk (1881–1938), Turkish army officer who founded the Republic of Turkey as a secular nation-state after World War I and served as the nation's first prime minister.

anti-Persian compulsory romanization, then, in Stalin's 1930s, with a Russifying compulsory Cyrillicization.[7]

We can summarize the conclusions to be drawn from the argument thus far by saying that the convergence of capitalism and print technology on the fatal diversity of human language created the possibility of a new form of imagined community, which in its basic morphology set the stage for the modern nation. The potential stretch of these communities was inherently limited, and, at the same time, bore none but the most fortuitous relationship to existing political boundaries (which were, on the whole, the highwater marks of dynastic expansionisms).

Yet it is obvious that while today almost all modern self-conceived nations—and also nation-states—have 'national print-languages', many of them have these languages in common, and in others only a tiny fraction of the population 'uses' the national language in conversation or on paper. The nation-states of Spanish America or those of the 'Anglo-Saxon family' are conspicuous examples of the first outcome; many ex-colonial states, particularly in Africa, of the second. In other words, the concrete formation of contemporary nation-states is by no means isomorphic with the determinate reach of particular print-languages. To account for the discontinuity-in-connectedness between print-languages, national consciousness, and nation-states, it is necessary to turn to the large cluster of new political entities that sprang up in the Western hemisphere between 1776 and 1838, all of which selfconsciously defined themselves as nations, and, with the interesting exception of Brazil,[8] as (non-dynastic) republics. For not only were they historically the first such states to emerge on the world stage, and therefore inevitably provided the first real models of what such states should 'look like,' but their numbers and contemporary births offer fruitful ground for comparative enquiry.

1983, 2006

7. Seton-Watson, *Nations and States*, p. 317 [Anderson's note]. Joseph Stalin (1879–1953), Russian revolutionary and leader of the Soviet Union (1924–53); he solidified his rule over the country in the 1930s. Cyrillicization: the use of the Cyrillic (Russian) alphabet to represent words.

8. When Brazil gained its independence from Portugal in 1822, it was ruled by an emperor; a republic was not established until 1889.

SANDRA M. GILBERT
b. 1936

SUSAN GUBAR
b. 1944

Sandra M. Gilbert and Susan Gubar's *Madwoman in the Attic* (1979) is a landmark of 1970s American feminism. The book encapsulates both the strengths and limitations of that first decade of "second-wave feminism." (First-wave feminism produced the Declaration of Women's Rights of 1848 and culminated in the ultimately successful campaign for female suffrage during the early twentieth century.) An outgrowth of the civil rights and student protest movements of the 1960s, second-wave feminism has proved to be among the most durable of the sixties' legacies. In its initial phase, contemporary feminists were pulled between its separatist and assimilationist tendencies. They debated whether women were better off disavowing the given order altogether, choosing instead to form their own communities, or striving for equal treatment within patriarchal institutions while working to reform them. *The Madwoman in the Attic* reflects the pressures from both sides. All parties to the dispute, however, assumed that every woman shares a set of similar experiences and that patriarchy—the male-dominated social order—is everywhere essentially the same. These assumptions became problematic later on, and they have been challenged by feminists such as ADRIENNE RICH, BELL HOOKS, GLORIA ANZALDÚA, and JUDITH BUTLER.

Born in New York City, Sandra M. Gilbert attended Cornell University, where she was active in undergraduate literary circles. She received her M.A. from New York University and her Ph.D. in English literature from Columbia University. The author of nine books of poetry along with her literary criticism, Gilbert has taught at California State University at Hayward, Indiana University, Princeton University, Stanford University, and the University of California at Davis. She and Susan Gubar (who was also born in New York City, and received her Ph.D. from the University of Iowa in 1972) met in 1973; both were young professors at Indiana University, where Gubar taught until her retirement in 2009. *The Madwoman in the Attic* grew out of the course in women's literature that the two team-taught. Gilbert and Gubar continued to collaborate for decades, while also writing single-authored books. They were jointly named *Ms.* magazine's "Woman of the Year" in 1986 for their work as editors of *The Norton Anthology of Literature by Women*. In 2012, they were awarded the Ivan Sandrof Lifetime Achievement Award of the National Book Critics Circle.

Building on the earlier 1970s feminist books by Ellen Moers and Elaine Showalter, *The Madwoman in the Attic* develops the notion that women writers can be understood as a group—and understood as "participat[ing] in a quite different literary subculture from that inhabited by male writers." Such separation is ambiguous: "exhilarating" at its best, "profoundly debilitating" at its worst. Gilbert and Gubar argue that the influential oedipal model developed by HAROLD BLOOM to describe the relation of post-Enlightenment male writers to each other does not fit the entirely different situation of women in a male-dominated literary tradition. The female "anxiety of authorship" described by Gilbert and Gubar was an "isolation that felt like illness, [an] alienation that felt like madness" as women writers of the eighteenth and nineteenth centuries wielded their pens in defiance of the social injunction that writing was not women's work. Each woman writer had to steal (at great risk and great cost to herself) a right to write that society extended only to men—and she looked to earlier women writers to see how such a theft could be pulled off. These "eighteenth- and nineteenth-century foremothers" enable the work of "contemporary women [who] . . . attempt the pen with energy and authority." "We now began to see," Gilbert and Gubar write, that "women of letters from Anne Bradstreet to Anne Brontë and on through Gertrude Stein to Sylvia Plath *had* engaged in a complex, sometimes conspiratorial, sometimes convivial conversation that crossed national as well as temporal boundaries. And that conversation had been far more energetic, indeed far more rebellious, than we had realized."

For the aggression and competitiveness found in Bloom's account of the relation between male authors, Gilbert and Gubar thus substitute "the secret sisterhood" of role models who show that women can write. (Their own collaboration breaks with the model of the isolated, individual scholar.) The connection remains "secret" because the early women writers they discuss still "fear . . . the antagonism of male readers" and "dread" assuming "the patriarchal authority of art." But the tradition of women writers does provide resources for each new woman author.

Gilbert and Gubar famously make evident the high costs women writers pay for success. The madwoman in the attic (a reference to Bertha, Rochester's hidden first wife, in Charlotte Brontë's *Jane Eyre*) stands for everything the woman writer must try to repress—though never with complete success—in order to write books acceptable by male standards. In detailing the various illnesses that women suffer, Gilbert and Gubar open up questions of bodily experience and mainstream medicine that are also pursued by Elaine Showalter, MICHEL FOUCAULT, and SUSAN BORDO. Employing a psychological approach to literature, they focus on the psychic cost of repression and on bodily symptoms that are interpreted as responses to societal oppression. For Gilbert and Gubar, women need to speak and write, but they must do so in a world that strives to keep them silent. The woman who speaks out is branded "an active monster"; the woman who remains silent risks madness.

As feminism moved into the 1980s, Gilbert and Gubar's approach was sometimes derided as "Anglo-American" or "liberal" feminism, defined as the effort to achieve equal status for women within existing social institutions. Their treatment of "woman" as a unitary category was also challenged. In placing Anne Sexton, an American poet of the 1960s, alongside Charlotte Brontë, a Victorian novelist, they looked historically naive, while their omission of nonwhite women writers seemed to point to an additional blind spot. Differences of race, class, sexual orientation, ethnicity, and historical period not only meant that not all women had the same fundamental experiences but also suggested that women writers could not be judged and valued according to one universal standard. The intensified exploration of difference challenged the notion of "sisterhood," the heady 1970s assumption that all woman shared certain basic similarities and would gain political unity through their common experience of being oppressed.

But we should not consign *The Madwoman in the Attic* to a now-surpassed moment of feminism, as is sometimes done. Gilbert and Gubar attend to the strategies women have adopted to survive in a male-dominated society, thus focusing on the world that most women inhabit. The recovery of women's histories and the celebration of women's successes within that male world have proven useful. Traditions are constructed, not discovered, and Gilbert and Gubar offer one remarkable example of how feminist critics can create a usable past, can uncover the achievements and resistances unrecorded by official histories. By being alert both to what women writers have so gloriously done *and* to the high costs paid for those successes, Gilbert and Gubar offer a nuanced view of what it means to dwell in relatively powerless positions within a world one did not make.

***The Madwoman in the Attic: The Woman Writer and the Nineteenth-Century Literary Imagination* Keywords:** Authorship, The Body, The Canon/Tradition, Feminist Criticism, Feminist Theory, Literary History, Sexuality, Women's Literature

From The Madwoman in the Attic: The Woman Writer and the Nineteenth-Century Literary Imagination

From *Chapter 2. Infection in the Sentence: The Woman Writer and the Anxiety of Authorship*

> The man who does not know sick women does not know women.
>
> —S. Weir Mitchell

> I try to describe this long limitation, hoping that with such power as is now mine, and such use of language as is within that power, this will convince any one who cares about it that this "living" of mine had been done under a heavy handicap. . . .
>
> —Charlotte Perkins Gilman

> A Word dropped careless on a Page
> May stimulate an eye
> When folded in perpetual seam

The Wrinkled Maker lie
Infection in the sentence breeds
We may inhale Despair
At distances of Centuries
From the Malaria—

—Emily Dickinson

I stand in the ring
in the dead city
and tie on the red shoes
. . . .
They are not mine,
they are my mother's,
her mother's before,
handed down like an heirloom
but hidden like shameful letters.

—Anne Sexton[1]

What does it mean to be a woman writer in a culture whose fundamental definitions of literary authority are, as we have seen, both overtly and covertly patriarchal? If the vexed and vexing polarities of angel and monster, sweet dumb Snow White and fierce mad Queen, are major images literary tradition offers women, how does such imagery influence the ways in which women attempt the pen? If the Queen's looking glass speaks with the King's voice,[2] how do its perpetual kingly admonitions affect the Queen's own voice? Since his is the chief voice she hears, does the Queen try to sound like the King, imitating his tone, his inflections, his phrasing, his point of view? Or does she "talk back" to him in her own vocabulary, her own timbre, insisting on her own viewpoint? We believe these are basic questions feminist literary criticism—both theoretical and practical—must answer, and consequently they are questions to which we shall turn again and again, not only in this chapter but in all our readings of nineteenth-century literature by women.

That writers assimilate and then consciously or unconsciously affirm or deny the achievements of their predecessors is, of course, a central fact of literary history, a fact whose aesthetic and metaphysical implications have been discussed in detail by theorists as diverse as T. S. Eliot, M. H. Abrams, Erich Auerbach, and Frank Kermode.[3] More recently, some literary theorists have begun to explore what we might call the psychology of literary history—the tensions and anxieties, hostilities and inadequacies writers feel

1. Epigraphs: *Doctor on Patient* (Philadelphia: Lippincott, 1888), quoted in Ilza Veith, *Hysteria: The History of a Disease* (Chicago: University of Chicago Press, 1965), pp. 219–20; *The Living of Charlotte Perkins Gilman* (1935; reprint, New York: Harper and Row, 1975), p. 104; J. 1261 in *The Poems of Emily Dickinson*, ed. Thomas Johnson, 3 vols. (Cambridge, Mass.: Belknap Press of Harvard University Press, 1955); "The Red Shoes," in *The Book of Folly* (Boston: Houghton Mifflin, 1972), pp. 28–29 [Gilbert and Gubar's note; except as indicated, all subsequent notes are theirs]. Mitchell (1829–1914), American physician and author, specializing in nervous diseases. Gilman (1860–1935), American feminist author and lecturer who underwent and strongly criticized Mitchell's "rest cure." Dickinson (1830–1886), American poet. Sexton (1928–1974), American feminist poet.

2. Gilbert and Gubar make this argument in chapter 1 of *Madwoman in the Attic*, "The Queen's Looking Glass" [editor's note].

3. In "Tradition and the Individual Talent" [1919], Eliot of course considers these matters; in *Mimesis* [1946] Auerbach traces the ways in which the realist includes what has been previously excluded from art; and in *The Sense of an Ending* [1967] Frank Kermode shows how poets and novelists lay bare the literariness of their predecessors' forms in order to explore the dissonance between fiction and reality. [Eliot (1888–1965), American-born English poet and critic; for "Tradition and the Individual Talent," see above. Abrams (1912–2015), American literary critic. Auerbach (1892–1957), German literary critic. Kermode (1919–2010), English literary critic—editor's note.]

when they confront not only the achievements of their predecessors but the traditions of genre, style, and metaphor that they inherit from such "forefathers." Increasingly, these critics study the ways in which, as J. Hillis Miller has put it, a literary text "is inhabited . . . by a long chain of parasitical presences, echoes, allusions, guests, ghosts of previous texts."[4]

As Miller himself also notes, the first and foremost student of such literary psychohistory has been Harold Bloom.[5] Applying Freudian structures to literary genealogies, Bloom has postulated that the dynamics of literary history arise from the artist's "anxiety of influence," his fear that he is not his own creator and that the works of his predecessors, existing before and beyond him, assume essential priority over his own writings. In fact, as we pointed out in our discussion of the metaphor of literary paternity, Bloom's paradigm of the sequential historical relationship between literary artists is the relationship of father and son, specifically that relationship as it was defined by Freud. Thus Bloom explains that a "strong poet" must engage in heroic warfare with his "precursor," for, involved as he is in a literary Oedipal struggle, a man can only become a poet by somehow invalidating his poetic father.

Bloom's model of literary history is intensely (even exclusively) male, and necessarily patriarchal. For this reason it has seemed, and no doubt will continue to seem, offensively sexist to some feminist critics. Not only, after all, does Bloom describe literary history as the crucial warfare of fathers and sons, he sees Milton's fiercely masculine fallen Satan as *the* type of the poet in our culture, and he metaphorically defines the poetic process as a sexual encounter between a male poet and his female muse. Where, then, does the female poet fit in? Does she want to annihilate a "forefather" or a "foremother"? What if she can find no models, no precursors? Does she have a muse, and what is its sex? Such questions are inevitable in any female consideration of Bloomian poetics.[6] And yet, from a feminist perspective, their inevitability may be just the point; it may, that is, call our attention not to what is wrong about Bloom's conceptualization of the dynamics of Western literary history, but to what is right (or at least suggestive) about his theory.

For Western literary history *is* overwhelmingly male—or, more accurately, patriarchal—and Bloom analyzes and explains this fact, while other theorists have ignored it, precisely, one supposes, because they assumed literature had to be male. Like Freud, whose psychoanalytic postulates permeate Bloom's literary psychoanalyses of the "anxiety of influence," Bloom has defined processes of interaction that his predecessors did not bother to consider because, among other reasons, they were themselves so caught up in such processes. Like Freud, too, Bloom has insisted on bringing to consciousness assumptions readers and writers do not ordinarily examine. In doing so, he has clarified the implications of the psychosexual and sociosexual contexts

4. J. Hillis Miller, "The Limits of Pluralism, III: The Critic as Host," *Critical Inquiry* 3, no. 3 (spring 1977): 446. [Miller (b. 1928), American literary critic—editor's note.]

5. American literary critic (b. 1930; see above), author of *The Anxiety of Influence* (1972). On SIGMUND FREUD (1856–1939), the Austrian founder of psychoanalysis, see above [editor's note].

6. For a discussion of the woman writer and her place in Bloomian literary history, see Joanne Feit Diehl, "'Come Slowly—Eden': An Exploration of Women Poets and Their Muse," *Signs* 3, no. 3 (spring 1978): 572–87. See also the responses to Diehl in *Signs* 4, no. 1 (autumn 1978): 188–96. [For John Milton's Satan, see *Paradise Lost* (1667)—editor's note.]

by which every literary text is surrounded, and thus the meanings of the "guests" and "ghosts" which inhabit texts themselves. Speaking of Freud, the feminist theorist Juliet Mitchell has remarked that "psychoanalysis is not a recommendation *for* a patriarchal society, but an analysis of one."[7] The same sort of statement could be made about Bloom's model of literary history, which is not a recommendation for but an analysis of the patriarchal poetics (and attendant anxieties) which underlie our culture's chief literary movements.

For our purposes here, however, Bloom's historical construct is useful not only because it helps identify and define the patriarchal psychosexual context in which so much Western literature was authored, but also because it can help us distinguish the anxieties and achievements of female writers from those of male writers. If we return to the question we asked earlier—where does a woman writer "fit in" to the overwhelmingly and essentially male literary history Bloom describes?—we find we have to answer that a woman writer does *not* "fit in." At first glance, indeed, she seems to be anomalous, indefinable, alienated, a freakish outsider. Just as in Freud's theories of male and female psychosexual development there is no symmetry between a boy's growth and a girl's (with, say, the male "Oedipus complex" balanced by a female "Electra complex")[8] so Bloom's male-oriented theory of the "anxiety of influence" cannot be simply reversed or inverted in order to account for the situation of the woman writer.

Certainly if we acquiesce in the patriarchal Bloomian model, we can be sure that the female poet does not experience the "anxiety of influence" in the same way that her male counterpart would, for the simple reason that she must confront precursors who are almost exclusively male, and therefore significantly different from her. Not only do these precursors incarnate patriarchal authority (as our discussion of the metaphor of literary paternity argued), they attempt to enclose her in definitions of her person and her potential which, by reducing her to extreme stereotypes (angel, monster) drastically conflict with her own sense of her self—that is, of her subjectivity, her autonomy, her creativity. On the one hand, therefore, the woman writer's male precursors symbolize authority; on the other hand, despite their authority, they fail to define the ways in which she experiences her own identity as a writer. More, the masculine authority with which they construct their literary personae, as well as the fierce power struggles in which they engage in their efforts of self-creation, seem to the woman writer directly to contradict the terms of her own gender definition. Thus the "anxiety of influence" that a male poet experiences is felt by a female poet as an even more primary "anxiety of authorship"—a radical fear that she cannot create, that because she can never become a "precursor" the act of writing will isolate or destroy her.

This anxiety is, of course, exacerbated by her fear that not only can she not fight a male precursor on "his" terms and win, she cannot "beget" art upon the (female) body of the muse. As Juliet Mitchell notes, in a concise summary

7. Juliet Mitchell, *Psychoanalysis and Feminism* (New York: Vintage, 1975), p. xiii.

8. In Greek mythology, Electra wishes to avenge the death of her father, Agamemnon, whom her mother, Clytemnestra, has helped to murder on his return from leading the Greek armies in the Trojan War. Some psychologists have argued that a girl has an Electra complex that parallels the boy's Oedipus complex, meaning that she feels aggressive toward her mother and desires her father [editor's note].

of the implications Freud's theory of psychosexual development has for women, both a boy and a girl, "as they learn to speak and live within society, want to take the father's [in Bloom's terminology the precursor's] place, and *only the boy will one day be allowed to do so.* Furthermore both sexes are born into the desire of the mother, and as, through cultural heritage, what the mother desires is the phallus-turned-baby, *both* children desire to be the phallus for the mother. Again, *only the boy can fully recognize himself in his mother's desire.* Thus *both* sexes repudiate the implications of femininity," but the girl learns (in relation to her father) "that her subjugation to the law of the father entails her becoming the representative of 'nature' and 'sexuality,' a chaos of spontaneous, intuitive creativity."[9]

Unlike her male counterpart, then, the female artist must first struggle against the effects of a socialization which makes conflict with the will of her (male) precursors seem inexpressibly absurd, futile, or even—as in the case of the Queen in "Little Snow White"—self-annihilating. And just as the male artist's struggle against his precursor takes the form of what Bloom calls revisionary swerves, flights, misreadings, so the female writer's battle for self-creation involves her in a revisionary process. Her battle, however, is not against her (male) precursor's reading of the world but against his reading of *her.* In order to define herself as an author she must redefine the terms of her socialization. Her revisionary struggle, therefore, often becomes a struggle for what Adrienne Rich has called "Re-vision—the act of looking back, of seeing with fresh eyes, of entering an old text from a new critical direction . . . an act of survival."[1] Frequently, moreover, she can begin such a struggle only by actively seeking a *female* precursor who, far from representing a threatening force to be denied or killed, proves by example that a revolt against patriarchal literary authority is possible.

For this reason, as well as for the sound psychoanalytic reasons Mitchell and others give, it would be foolish to lock the woman artist into an Electra pattern matching the Oedipal structure Bloom proposes for male writers. The woman writer—and we shall see women doing this over and over again—searches for a female model not because she wants dutifully to comply with male definitions of her "femininity" but because she must legitimize her own rebellious endeavors. At the same time, like most women in patriarchal society, the woman writer does experience her gender as a painful obstacle, or even a debilitating inadequacy; like most patriarchally conditioned women, in other words, she is victimized by what Mitchell calls "the inferiorized and 'alternative' (second sex) psychology of women under patriarchy."[2] Thus the loneliness of the female artist, her feelings of alienation from male predecessors coupled with her need for sisterly precursors and successors, her urgent sense of her need for a female audience together with her fear of the antagonism of male readers, her culturally conditioned timidity about self-dramatization, her dread of the patriarchal authority of art, her anxiety about the impropriety of female invention—all these phenomena of "inferiorization" mark the woman writer's struggle for artistic self-definition and differentiate her efforts at self-creation from those of her male counterpart.

9. Mitchell, *Psychoanalysis and Feminism*, pp. 404–5.

1. Adrienne Rich, "When We Dead Awaken: Writing as Re-Vision," in *Adrienne Rich's Poetry*, ed. Barbara Charlesworth Gelpi and Albert Gelpi (New York: Norton, 1975), p. 90. [Rich (1929–2012), feminist poet and essayist—editor's note.]

2. Mitchell, *Psychoanalysis and Feminism*, p. 402.

As we shall see, such sociosexual differentiation means that, as Elaine Showalter has suggested, women writers participate in a quite different literary subculture from that inhabited by male writers, a subculture which has its own distinctive literary traditions, even—though it defines itself *in relation to* the "main," male-dominated, literary culture—a distinctive history.[3] At best, the separateness of this female subculture has been exhilarating for women. In recent years, for instance, while male writers seem increasingly to have felt exhausted by the need for revisionism which Bloom's theory of the "anxiety of influence" accurately describes, women writers have seen themselves as pioneers in a creativity so intense that their male counterparts have probably not experienced its analog since the Renaissance, or at least since the Romantic era. The son of many fathers, today's male writer feels hopelessly belated; the daughter of too few mothers, today's female writer feels that she is helping to create a viable tradition which is at last definitively emerging.

There is a darker side of this female literary subculture, however, especially when women's struggles for literary self-creation are seen in the psychosexual context described by Bloom's Freudian theories of patrilineal literary inheritance. As we noted above, for an "anxiety of influence" the woman writer substitutes what we have called an "anxiety of authorship," an anxiety built from complex and often only barely conscious fears of that authority which seems to the female artist to be by definition inappropriate to her sex. Because it is based on the woman's socially determined sense of her own biology, this anxiety of authorship is quite distinct from the anxiety about creativity that could be traced in such male writers as Hawthorne or Dostoevsky. Indeed, to the extent that it forms one of the unique bonds that link women in what we might call the secret sisterhood of their literary subculture, such anxiety in itself constitutes a crucial mark of that subculture.

In comparison to the "male" tradition of strong, father-son combat, however, this female anxiety of authorship is profoundly debilitating. Handed down not from one woman to another but from the stern literary "fathers" of patriarchy to all their "inferiorized" female descendants, it is in many ways the germ of a dis-ease or, at any rate, a disaffection, a disturbance, a distrust, that spreads like a stain throughout the style and structure of much literature by women, especially—as we shall see in this study—throughout literature by women before the twentieth century. For if contemporary women do now attempt the pen with energy and authority, they are able to do so only because their eighteenth- and nineteenth-century foremothers struggled in isolation that felt like illness, alienation that felt like madness, obscurity that felt like paralysis to overcome the anxiety of authorship that was endemic to their literary subculture. Thus, while the recent feminist emphasis on positive role models has undoubtedly helped many women, it should not keep us from realizing the terrible odds against which a creative female subculture was established. Far from reinforcing socially oppressive sexual stereotyping, only a full consideration of such problems can reveal the extraordinary strength of women's literary accomplishments in the eighteenth and nineteenth centuries.

3. See Elaine Showalter, *A Literature of Their Own* (Princeton: Princeton University Press, 1977). [Showalter (b. 1941), American feminist literary critic—editor's note.]

Emily Dickinson's acute observations about "infection in the sentence," quoted in our epigraphs, resonate in a number of different ways, then, for women writers, given the literary woman's special concept of her place in literary psychohistory. To begin with, the words seem to indicate Dickinson's keen consciousness that, in the purest Bloomian or Millerian sense, pernicious "guests" and "ghosts" inhabit all literary texts. For any reader, but especially for a reader who is also a writer, every text can become a "sentence" or weapon in a kind of metaphorical germ warfare. Beyond this, however, the fact that "infection in the sentence *breeds*" suggests Dickinson's recognition that literary texts are coercive, imprisoning, fever-inducing; that, since literature usurps a reader's interiority, it is an invasion of privacy. Moreover, given Dickinson's own gender definition, the sexual ambiguity of her poem's "Wrinkled Maker" is significant. For while, on the one hand, "we" (meaning especially women writers) "may inhale Despair" from all those patriarchal texts which seek to deny female autonomy and authority, on the other hand "we" (meaning especially women writers) "may inhale Despair" from all those "foremothers" who have both overtly and covertly conveyed their traditional authorship anxiety to their bewildered female descendants. Finally, such traditional, metaphorically matrilineal anxiety ensures that even the maker of a text, when she is a woman, may feel imprisoned within texts—folded and "wrinkled" by their pages and thus trapped in their "perpetual seam[s]" which perpetually tell her how she *seems*.

Although contemporary women writers are relatively free of the infection of this "Despair" Dickinson defines (at least in comparison to their nineteenth-century precursors), an anecdote recently related by the American poet and essayist Annie Gottlieb summarizes our point about the ways in which, for all women, "Infection in the sentence breeds":

> When I began to enjoy my powers as a writer, I dreamt that my mother had me sterilized! (Even in dreams we still blame our mothers for the punitive choices our culture forces on us.) I went after the mother-figure in my dream, brandishing a large knife; on its blade was writing. I cried, "Do you know what you are doing? You are destroying my femaleness, my *female power*, which is important to me *because of you*!"[4]

Seeking motherly precursors, says Gottlieb, as if echoing Dickinson, the woman writer may find only infection, debilitation. Yet still she must seek, not seek to subvert, her "*female power*, which is important" to her because of her lost literary matrilineage. In this connection, Dickinson's own words about mothers are revealing, for she alternately claimed that "I never had a mother," that "I always ran Home to Awe as a child. . . . He was an awful Mother but I liked him better than none," and that "a mother [was] a miracle."[5] Yet, as we shall see, her own anxiety of authorship was a "Despair" inhaled not only from the infections suffered by her own ailing physical mother, and her many tormented literary mothers, but from the literary fathers who spoke to her—even "lied" to her—sometimes near at hand, sometimes "at distances of Centuries," from the censorious looking glasses of literary texts.

4. Annie Gottlieb, "Feminists Look at Motherhood," *Mother Jones*, November 1976, p. 53.

5. *The Letters of Emily Dickinson*, ed. Thomas Johnson, 3 vols. (Cambridge, Mass.: Belknap Press of Harvard University Press, 1958), 2:475, 518.

It is debilitating to be *any* woman in a society where women are warned that if they do not behave like angels they must be monsters. Recently, in fact, social scientists and social historians like Jessie Bernard, Phyllis Chesler, Naomi Weisstein, and Pauline Bart have begun to study the ways in which patriarchal socialization literally makes women sick, both physically and mentally.[6] Hysteria, the disease with which Freud so famously began his investigations into the dynamic connections between *psyche* and *soma*,[7] is by definition a "female disease," not so much because it takes its name from the Greek word for womb, *hyster* (the organ which was in the nineteenth century supposed to "cause" this emotional disturbance), but because hysteria did occur mainly among women in turn-of-the-century Vienna, and because throughout the nineteenth century this mental illness, like many other nervous disorders, was thought to be caused by the female reproductive system, as if to elaborate upon Aristotle's notion that femaleness was in and of itself a deformity.[8] And, indeed, such diseases of maladjustment to the physical and social environment as anorexia and agoraphobia did and do strike a disproportionate number of women. Sufferers from anorexia—loss of appetite, self-starvation—are primarily adolescent girls. Sufferers from agoraphobia—fear of open or "public" places—are usually female, most frequently middle-aged housewives, as are sufferers from crippling rheumatoid arthritis.[9]

Such diseases are caused by patriarchal socialization in several ways. Most obviously, of course, any young girl, but especially a lively or imaginative one, is likely to experience her education in docility, submissiveness, self-lessness as in some sense sickening. To be trained in renunciation is almost necessarily to be trained to ill health, since the human animal's first and strongest urge is to his/her *own* survival, pleasure, assertion. In addition, each of the "subjects" in which a young girl is educated may be sickening in a specific way. Learning to become a beautiful object, the girl learns anxiety about—perhaps even loathing of—her own flesh. Peering obsessively into the real as well as metaphoric looking glasses that surround her, she desires literally to "reduce" her own body. In the nineteenth century, as we noted earlier, this desire to be beautiful and "frail" led to tight-lacing and vinegar-drinking. In

6. See Jessie Bernard, "The Paradox of the Happy Marriage," Pauline B. Bart, "Depression in Middle-Aged Women," and Naomi Weisstein, "Psychology Constructs the Female," all in Vivian Gornick and Barbara K. Moran, eds., *Woman in Sexist Society* (New York: Basic Books, 1971). See also Phyllis Chesler, *Women and Madness* (New York: Doubleday, 1972), and—for a summary of all these matters—Barbara Ehrenreich and Deirdre English, *Complaints and Disorders: The Sexual Politics of Sickness* (Old Westbury, N.Y.: Feminist Press, 1973).

7. Body (Greek) [editor's note].

8. In *Hints on Insanity* (1861) John Millar wrote that "Mental derangement frequently occurs in young females from Amenorrhoea, especially in those who have any strong hereditary predisposition to insanity," adding that "an occasional warm hipbath or leeches to the pubis will . . . be followed by complete mental recovery." In 1873, Henry Mauldsey wrote in *Body and Mind* that "the monthly activity of the ovaries . . . has a notable effect upon the mind and body; wherefore it may become an important cause of mental and physical derangement." See especially the medical opinions of John Millar, Henry Maudsley, and Andrew Wynter in *Madness and Morals: Ideas on Insanity in the Nineteenth Century*, ed. Vieda Skultans (London: Routledge and Kegan Paul, 1975), pp. 230–35. [See the Greek philosopher ARISTOTLE (384–322 B.C.E.), *On the Generation of Animals*—editor's note.]

9. See Marlene Boskind-Lodahl, "Cinderella's Stepsisters: A Feminist Perspective on Anorexia Nervosa and Bulimia," *Signs* 2, no. 2 (winter 1976): 342–56; Walter Blum, "The Thirteenth Guest" (on agoraphobia), in *California Living, The San Francisco Sunday Examiner and Chronicle*, 17 April 1977, pp. 8–12; Joan Arehart-Treichel, "Can Your Personality Kill You?" (on female rheumatoid arthritis, among other diseases), *New York* 10, no. 48 (28 November 1977): 45: "According to studies conducted in recent years, four out of five rheumatoid victims are women, and for good reason: The disease appears to arise in those unhappy with the traditional female-sex role."

our own era it has spawned innumerable diets and "controlled" fasts, as well as the extraordinary phenomenon of teenage anorexia.[1] Similarly, it seems inevitable that women reared for, and conditioned to, lives of privacy, reticence, domesticity, might develop pathological fears of public places and unconfined spaces. Like the comb, stay-laces, and apple which the Queen in "Little Snow White" uses as weapons against her hated stepdaughter, such afflictions as anorexia and agoraphobia simply carry patriarchal definitions of "femininity" to absurd extremes, and thus function as essential or at least inescapable parodies of social prescriptions.

In the nineteenth century, however, the complex of social prescriptions these diseases parody did not merely urge women to act in ways which would cause them to become ill; nineteenth-century culture seems to have actually admonished women to *be* ill. In other words, the "female diseases" from which Victorian women suffered were not always byproducts of their training in femininity; they were the goals of such training. As Barbara Ehrenreich and Deirdre English have shown, throughout much of the nineteenth century "Upper- and upper-middle-class women were [defined as] 'sick' [frail, ill]; working-class women were [defined as] 'sickening' [infectious, diseased]." Speaking of the "lady," they go on to point out that "Society agreed that she was frail and sickly," and consequently a "cult of female invalidism" developed in England and America. For the products of such a cult, it was, as Dr. Mary Putnam Jacobi wrote in 1895, "considered natural and almost laudable to break down under all conceivable varieties of strain—a winter dissipation, a houseful of servants, a quarrel with a female friend, not to speak of more legitimate reasons. . . . Constantly considering their nerves, urged to consider them by well-intentioned but short-sighted advisors, [women] pretty soon become nothing but a bundle of nerves."[2]

Given this socially conditioned epidemic of female illness, it is not surprising to find that the angel in the house of literature frequently suffered not just from fear and trembling but from literal and figurative sickness unto death.[3] Although her hyperactive stepmother dances herself into the grave, after all, beautiful Snow White has just barely recovered from a catatonic trance in her glass coffin. And if we return to Goethe's Makarie, the "good" woman of *Wilhelm Meister's Travels* whom Hans Eichner has described as incarnating her author's ideal of "contemplative purity," we find that this "model of selflessness and of purity of heart . . . this embodiment of *das Ewig-Weibliche*, suffers from migraine headaches."[4] Implying ruthless self-suppression, does the "eternal feminine" necessarily imply illness?

1. More recent discussions of the etiology and treatment of anorexia are offered in Hilde Bruch, M.D., *The Golden Cage: The Enigma of Anorexia Nervosa* (Cambridge, Mass.: Harvard University Press, 1978), and in Salvador Minuchin, Bernice L. Rosman, and Lester Baker, *Psychosomatic Families: Anorexia Nervosa in Context* (Cambridge, Mass.: Harvard University Press, 1978). [Gilbert and Gubar discuss "tight-lacing and vinegar-drinking" in chapter 1—editor's note.]
2. Quoted in Ehrenreich and English, *Complaints and Disorders*, p. 19.
3. *Fear and Trembling* (1843) and *The Sickness unto Death* (1849) are works on religious faith and despair by the Danish philosopher Søren Kierkegaard; "the angel in the house" is the heroine of the long poem of that title (1854–63), celebrating domesticity, by Coventry Patmore and is the fictional figure whom Virginia Woolf, in her talk "Professions for Women" (1931; published 1942), declared that she had to kill in order to be free to write [editor's note].
4. Eichner, "The Eternal Female," in *Faust*, ed. Cyrus Hamlin, Norton Critical Edition (New York: W. W. Norton, 1976), p. 620. [Johann Wolfgang von Goethe (1749–1832), German poet, novelist, and playwright, author of *Faust* (1808, 1832) and *Wilhelm Meister's Travels* (1829). *Das Ewig-Weibliche*: the eternal feminine (German)—editor's note.]

If so, we may have found yet another meaning for Dickinson's assertion that "Infection in the sentence breeds." The despair we "inhale" even "at distances of centuries" may be the despair of a life like Makarie's, a life that "*has no story*."

At the same time, however, the despair of the monster-woman is also real, undeniable, and infectious. The Queen's mad tarantella is plainly unhealthy and metaphorically the result of too much storytelling. As the Romantic poets feared, too much imagination may be dangerous to anyone, male or female, but for women in particular patriarchal culture has always assumed mental exercises would have dire consequences. In 1645 John Winthrop, the governor of the Massachusetts Bay Colony, noted in his journal that Anne Hopkins "has fallen into a sad infirmity, the loss of her understanding and reason, which had been growing upon her divers years, by occasion of her giving herself wholly to reading and writing, and had written many books," adding that "if she had attended her household affairs, and such things as belong to women . . . she had kept her wits."[5] And as Wendy Martin has noted

> in the nineteenth century this fear of the intellectual woman became so intense that the phenomenon . . . was recorded in medical annals. A thinking woman was considered such a breach of nature that a Harvard doctor reported during his autopsy on a Radcliffe graduate he discovered that her uterus had shrivelled to the size of a pea.[6]

If, then, as Anne Sexton suggests (in a poem parts of which we have also used here as an epigraph), the red shoes passed furtively down from woman to woman are the shoes of art, the Queen's dancing shoes, it is as sickening to be a Queen who wears them as it is to be an angelic Makarie who repudiates them. Several passages in Sexton's verse express what we have defined as "anxiety of authorship" in the form of a feverish dread of the suicidal tarantella of female creativity:

> And those girls,
> who wore red shoes,
> each boarded a train that would not stop.
> . . . .
> They tore off their ears like safety pins.
> Their arms fell off them and became hats.
> Their heads rolled off and sang down the street.
> And their feet—oh God, their feet in the market place—
> . . . the feet went on.
> The feet could not stop.
> . . . .
> They could not listen.
> They could not stop.
> What they did was the death dance.
> What they did would do them in.

Certainly infection breeds in these sentences, and despair: female art, Sexton suggests, has a "hidden" but crucial tradition of uncontrollable madness.

5. John Winthrop, *The History of New England from 1630 to 1649*, ed. James Savage (Boston, 1826), 2:216.
6. Wendy Martin, "Anne Bradstreet's Poetry: A Study of Subversive Piety," in *Shakespeare's Sisters*, ed. Sandra M. Gilbert and Susan Gubar (Bloomington: Indiana University Press, 1979), pp. 19–31.

Perhaps it was her semi-conscious perception of this tradition that gave Sexton herself "a secret fear" of being "a reincarnation" of Edna Millay,[7] whose reputation seemed based on romance. In a letter to DeWitt Snodgrass she confessed that she had "a fear of writing as a woman writes," adding, "I wish I were a man—I would rather write the way a man writes."[8] After all, dancing the death dance, "all those girls / who wore the red shoes" dismantle their own bodies, like anorexics renouncing the guilty weight of their female flesh. But if their arms, ears, and heads fall off, perhaps their wombs, too, will "shrivel" to "the size of a pea"?

In this connection, a passage from Margaret Atwood's[9] *Lady Oracle* acts almost as a gloss on the conflict between creativity and "femininity" which Sexton's violent imagery embodies (or dis-embodies). Significantly, the protagonist of Atwood's novel is a writer of the sort of fiction that has recently been called "female gothic," and even more significantly she too projects her anxieties of authorship into the fairy-tale metaphor of the red shoes. Stepping in glass, she sees blood on her feet, and suddenly feels that she has discovered

> The real red shoes, the feet punished for dancing. You could dance, or you could have the love of a good man. But you were afraid to dance, because you had this unnatural fear that if you danced they'd cut your feet off so you wouldn't be able to dance. . . . Finally you overcame your fear and danced, and they cut your feet off. The good man went away too, because you wanted to dance.[1]

Whether she is a passive angel or an active monster, in other words, the woman writer feels herself to be literally or figuratively crippled by the debilitating alternatives her culture offers her, and the crippling effects of her conditioning sometimes seem to "breed" like sentences of death in the bloody shoes she inherits from her literary foremothers.

Surrounded as she is by images of disease, traditions of disease, and invitations both to disease and to dis-ease, it is no wonder that the woman writer has held many mirrors up to the discomforts of her own nature. As we shall see, the notion that "Infection in the sentence breeds" has been so central a truth for literary women that the great artistic achievements of nineteenth-century novelists and poets from Austen and Shelley to Dickinson and Barrett Browning[2] are often both literally and figuratively concerned with disease, as if to emphasize the effort with which health and wholeness were won from the infectious "vapors" of despair and fragmentation. Rejecting the poisoned apples her culture offers her, the woman writer often becomes in some sense anorexic, resolutely closing her mouth on silence (since—in the words of Jane Austen's Henry Tilney—"a woman's only power is the power of refusal"[3]), even while she complains of starvation.

7. Edna St. Vincent Millay (1892–1950), American poet [editor's note].
8. "The Uncensored Poet: Letters of Anne Sexton," *Ms.* 6, no. 5 (November 1977): 53.
9. Canadian novelist and poet (b. 1939) [editor's note].
1. Margaret Atwood, *Lady Oracle* (New York: Simon and Schuster, 1976), p. 335.
2. Elizabeth Barrett Browning (1806–1861), English poet. Jane Austen (1775–1817), English novelist. Mary Shelley (1797–1851), English novelist [editor's note].
3. See *Northanger Abbey* [1818], chapter 10: "You will allow, that in both [matrimony and dancing], man has the advantage of choice, woman only the power of refusal."

Thus both Charlotte and Emily Brontë[4] depict the travails of starved or starving anorexic heroines, while Emily Dickinson declares in one breath that she "had been hungry, all the Years," and in another opts for "Sumptuous Destitution." Similarly, Christina Rossetti[5] represents her own anxiety of authorship in the split between one heroine who longs to "suck and suck" on goblin fruit and another who locks her lips fiercely together in a gesture of silent and passionate renunciation. In addition, many of these literary women become in one way or another agoraphobic. Trained to reticence, they fear the vertiginous openness of the literary marketplace and rationalize with Emily Dickinson that "Publication—is the Auction / Of the Mind of Man" or, worse, punningly confess that "Creation seemed a mighty Crack— / To make me visible."[6]

As we shall also see, other diseases and dis-eases accompany the two classic symptoms of anorexia and agoraphobia. Claustrophobia, for instance, agoraphobia's parallel and complementary opposite, is a disturbance we shall encounter again and again in women's writing throughout the nineteenth century. Eye "troubles," moreover, seem to abound in the lives and works of literary women, with Dickinson matter-of-factly noting that her eye got "put out," George Eliot[7] describing patriarchal Rome as "a disease of the retina," Jane Eyre and Aurora Leigh[8] marrying blind men, Charlotte Brontë deliberately writing with her eyes closed, and Mary Elizabeth Coleridge writing about "Blindness" that came because "Absolute and bright, / The Sun's rays smote me till they masked the Sun."[9] Finally, aphasia and amnesia—two illnesses which symbolically represent (and parody) the sort of intellectual incapacity patriarchal culture has traditionally required of women—appear and reappear in women's writings in frankly stated or disguised forms. "Foolish" women characters in Jane Austen's novels (Miss Bates in *Emma*, for instance) express Malapropish confusion about language, while Mary Shelley's monster[1] has to learn language from scratch and Emily Dickinson herself childishly questions the meanings of the most basic English words: "Will there really be a 'Morning'? / Is there such a thing as 'Day'?"[2] At the same time, many women writers manage to imply that the reason for such ignorance of language—as well as the reason for their deep sense of alienation and inescapable feeling of anomie—is that they have *forgotten* something. Deprived of the power that even their pens don't seem to confer, these women resemble Doris Lessing's[3] heroines, who have to fight their internalization of patriarchal strictures for even a faint trace memory of what they might have become.

4. English poet and novelist (1818–1848). Charlotte Brontë (1816–1855), English novelist [editor's note].
5. English poet (1830–1894) [editor's note].
6. See Dickinson, *Poems*, J. 579 ("I had been hungry, all the Years"), J. 709 ("Publication—is the Auction"), and J. 891 ("To my quick ear the Leaves—conferred"); see also Christina Rossetti, "Goblin Market" [1862].
7. English novelist (pen name of Marian Evans, 1819–1880) [editor's note].
8. Heroine of Elizabeth Barrett Browning's "novel in verse" *Aurora Leigh* (1856). Jane Eyre: heroine of Charlotte Brontë's novel *Jane Eyre* (1847) [editor's note].
9. See Dickinson, *Poems*, J. 327 ("Before I got my eye put out), George Eliot, *Middlemarch* [1871–72], book 2, chapter 20, and M. E. Coleridge, "Doubt," in *Poems by Mary E. Coleridge* (London: Elkin Mathews, 1908), p. 40. [Coleridge (1861–1907), English poet and novelist—editor's note.]
1. That is, the monster created in Shelley's novel *Frankenstein* (1818). Malapropish: like Mrs. Malaprop, a character in Richard Sheridan's comic play *The Rivals* (1775), who humorously and unintentionally misuses language [editor's note].
2. See Dickinson, *Poems*, J. 101.
3. Rhodesian and later English novelist (1919–2013) [editor's note].

"Where are the songs I used to know, / Where are the notes I used to sing?" writes Christina Rossetti in "The Key-Note," a poem whose title indicates its significance for her. "I have forgotten everything / I used to know so long ago."[4] As if to make the same point, Charlotte Brontë's Lucy Snowe[5] conveniently "forgets" her own history and even, so it seems, the Christian name of one of the central characters in her story, while Brontë's orphaned Jane Eyre seems to have lost (or symbolically "forgotten") her family heritage. Similarly, too, Emily Brontë's Heathcliff[6] "forgets" or is made to forget who and what he was; Mary Shelley's monster is "born" without either a memory or a family history; and Elizabeth Barrett Browning's Aurora Leigh is early separated from—and thus induced to "forget"—her "mother land" of Italy. As this last example suggests, however, what all these characters and their authors really fear they have forgotten is precisely that aspect of their lives which has been kept from them by patriarchal poetics: their matrilineal heritage of literary strength, their "female power" which, as Annie Gottlieb wrote, is important to them *because of* (not in spite of) their mothers. In order, then, not only to understand the ways in which "Infection in the sentence breeds" for women but also to learn how women have won through disease to artistic health we must begin by redefining Bloom's seminal definitions of the revisionary "anxiety of influence." In doing so, we will have to trace the difficult paths by which nineteenth-century women overcame their "anxiety of authorship," repudiated debilitating patriarchal prescriptions, and recovered or remembered the lost foremothers who could help them find their distinctive female power.

* * *

1979

4. *The Poetical Works of Christina Rossetti*, 2 vols. (Boston: Little, Brown, 1909), 2:11.
5. The heroine of Charlotte Brontë's novel *Villette* (1853) [editor's note].
6. The dark hero of Emily Brontë's novel *Wuthering Heights* (1847) [editor's note].

E. ANN KAPLAN
b. 1936

In the 2009 film *Brothers*, the main character, played by Tobey Maguire, is a Marine captain who returns home to the United States after being captured and tortured by the Taliban in Afghanistan. In the climactic scene, he destroys a new kitchen, holds a gun to his wife and his brother, and threatens suicide. We immediately understand that he suffers from post-traumatic stress disorder (PTSD), a syndrome formally recognized by the American Psychiatric Association only in 1980. Now most often associated with combat, PTSD can also be spurred by other severe events, such as accidents or physical and sexual abuse. While doctors diagnosed some soldiers in World War I with "shell shock," and early psychologists identified "hysteria" in some patients, researchers and scholars from various fields began to explore the effects of trauma more deeply in the aftermath of World War II and the Holocaust. Their work prepared for the emergence in the 1990s of trauma theory, a new field that draws particularly on psychology and psychoanalysis in forming interdisciplinary links between humanists, social scientists, and scientists. In *Trauma Culture: The Politics of Terror and Loss in Media and Literature* (2005), E. Ann Kaplan takes for her point of departure the origins of trauma studies in the writings of SIGMUND FREUD, the founder of psychoanalysis. In our selection, she develops via Freud both an account of trauma and a critique of trauma theory.

Best known for her books in film and cultural studies, Kaplan earned a B.A. in English literature from the University of Birmingham in England (1958), a postgraduate diploma in English from the University of London (1959), and a Ph.D. in comparative literature from Rutgers University (1970). She taught first in England, including as a lecturer in film at London's British Film Institute, before moving to the United States in 1980; she has held positions at Monmouth College, Rutgers University, and the State University of New York at Stony Brook, where since 2005 she has been Distinguished Professor of English and Cultural Analysis and Theory and was also the founding director of the Humanities Institute at Stony Brook (1987–2014). From 2003 to 2005, Kaplan served as president of the Society for Cinema and Media Studies, and she received its Distinguished Career Award in 2009. Much of Kaplan's early work focuses on cinema and feminism; her scope later broadened to popular culture (publishing the first academic study of MTV) and especially trauma in various forms.

Trauma, the Greek word meaning "wound," was at first strictly a specialists' term for an external injury or the condition caused by such an injury, cited by *The Oxford English Dictionary* (*OED*) in a medical dictionary of 1693; the adjective "traumatic" appeared in 1656. It is not included in SAMUEL JOHNSON's great dictionary, published in 1755, but in the nineteenth century its application expanded not just to an internal brain injury, which may result in behavioral change, but also to a psychic injury—cited by the *OED* in this sense ("traumatic psychosis") first in an 1889 translation of the French neurologist Jean-Martin Charcot, with whom Freud briefly studied. The word soon came to refer especially to a psychic injury caused by an "emotional shock the memory of which is repressed and remains unhealed." Trauma is thus a wound either external or internal, as well as the deep distress and disturbance that accompany it. When that disturbance lingers, it can become what we now call PTSD. "The idea," according to the historian Ruth Leys, "is that, owing to the emotions of terror and surprise caused by certain events, the mind is split or dissociated: it is unable to register the wound to the psyche because the ordinary mechanisms of awareness and cognition are destroyed. . . . The experience of the trauma, fixed or frozen in time, refuses to be represented *as* past, but is perpetually re-experienced in a painful, dissociated, traumatic present." As a result, individuals can suffer nightmares, flashbacks, changes in physical and emotional reactions, periods of extreme depression, suicidal impulses, and worse.

The serious theorizing of trauma is a modern phenomenon. But it is tempting simply to say at the outset that the experience of trauma is as old as the human race, with traces everywhere in world literature: for instance, in the combat and aftermath of Homer's *Iliad* and the masterpieces of Greek tragedy. And what could be more traumatic than the experiences of Hamlet and King Lear? In our time, examples abound, both in memoirs—such as the Holocaust testimonies of Eli Wiesel and Primo Levi and the horrifying account of sexual assault recounted by Alice Sebold in *Lucky* (1999)—and in fiction, from Kurt Vonnegut's *Slaughterhouse-Five* (1969), about the firebombing of Dresden in World War II, to TONI MORRISON's *Beloved* (1987), on the ramifications of slavery and the murder of a two-year-old child by her mother.

The range of materials is so extensive and deep, and offers so many perspectives, that the historian Andreas Killen sees trauma as "becoming institutionalized. . . . The aftermath of trauma is being researched in laboratories and analyzed by historians, literary critics and experts in media, law and psychiatry." It is at once profoundly personal, registering its impact on individuals, and also collective, as the brutal history of the twentieth and twenty-first centuries attests—world wars, genocides, atomic bombs, famines, migrations, and natural disasters. Not surprisingly, trauma is collective even when it is personal, because it is so implicated in and woven into familial, social, and political contexts and dependent for its understanding on the interpretive categories brought to it.

Among the theorists and critics who have been active in developing the contemporary field of trauma studies are Cathy Caruth, Shoshana Felman, and Dominick LaCapra. But the inevitable point of departure is much earlier, with Sigmund Freud, as Kaplan indicates in our selection from her *Trauma Culture*, an interdisciplinary study in which she analyzes the artistic, literary, and cinematic forms through which individuals and collectives undergo, represent, and describe the experience of trauma.

Opening her book with a discussion of the terrorist attacks of September 11, 2001, and reflecting on research about the Holocaust, Kaplan proceeds to consider a number of case studies: Freud's *Moses and Monotheism* (1939), Marguerite Duras's *La Douleur* (1985; trans. as *The War: A Memoir*, 1986), Sarah Kofman's *Rue Ordener, Rue Labat* (1994; trans. 1996), Alfred Hitchcock's postwar melodrama *Spellbound* (1945), and Tracey Moffatt's short film *Night Cries: A Rural Tragedy* (1989). Her use of the tools and techniques of literary criticism, media studies, feminist psychoanalysis, and neuroscience in examining them helps to suggest the wide-ranging, interdisciplinary nature of research in this field. Kaplan also devotes attention to media images of Iraq and Rwanda and to films that show the "diverse traumas" experienced by indigenous peoples in the United States and Australia. Yet her primary concern, she explains, is not "the huge catastrophes" that have been extensively and eloquently reported and studied but rather "traumas of loss, abandonment, rejection, betrayal" in specific films and texts.

Kaplan emphasizes the complexity of the term "trauma." In her view, it should be attached not only to victims and survivors but also to those who "suffer terror." Trauma is crucially related to the position of the affected individuals, to social and political contexts, and to institutions (above all, the media) that represent and circulate catastrophe and disaster nationally and internationally. Kaplan speaks of trauma as being "registered" consciously and unconsciously, and she stresses the difficulty—so affected are our lives by all forms of media, social and other—of separating and making distinctions between trauma and vicarious trauma, primary and secondary trauma.

Invoking her own response to 9/11, Kaplan asks whether this event was for her a new trauma or was rather a trigger that recalled her frightening childhood memories of growing up in London during the Blitz. Kaplan also experienced 9/11 directly, as did all Americans—"everyone was in shock": the trauma, in all of its dimensions and reverberations, was at once personal and communal, local and national. It was depicted in stories, commentaries, symbols, and images on TV and radio, in newspapers and magazines, and on the Internet. It was unprecedented, but then again it was not, because for countless people it reverberated with the memories of prior traumas that they had experienced and that remained painfully immediate to them.

The selection below is excerpted from Kaplan's first chapter, "'Why Trauma Now?': Freud and Trauma Studies," where she gives a critical overview of Freud's work on trauma as it emerged gradually from his explorations of sexuality, unconscious motivation, and neurosis. Kaplan reminds us that Freud and his followers were students first of hysteria and that their work on trauma developed from it—or, rather, that the concept of trauma was already implicit in it. Freud and others saw that the symptoms of trauma may arise belatedly, well after the event; and in their studies of women, they connected traumatic memory, repression, fantasy, and hysteria to sexuality and sexual abuse. One of the limitations of their work done in the 1890s and early 1900s, Kaplan observes, is its lack of attention to social constructions of gender, which in cases of sexual trauma lead to different neuroses. We can see a shift in Freud's thinking during World War I and later, when he and others began to study the trauma suffered by soldiers.

Kaplan raises other criticisms of trauma theory. She conceives each case of trauma to be individual—that is, rooted in the singular experience, sensitivity, and unconscious of each afflicted person. Thus one size does not fit all, and in her view diagnoses and treatments have to be individualized. Like Freud, Kaplan is skeptical of the early general application of electric shock therapy and brain surgery and more sympathetic to highly personalized talk cures. Still, Freud comes in for direct critique, for being "wary of mentioning the codes of his social, medical, and political milieu." Kaplan's point is that historical context shapes the experience of trauma, which is why she emphasizes the impacts of the Victorian-era middle-class patriarchal family, the industrial revolution, large-scale mechanized war, and the different social positions of men and women. For all his pioneering insights into trauma, Freud is not immune to this broad criticism—nor is subsequent trauma theory.

To extend her discussion, Kaplan cites the Regeneration Trilogy by the English writer Pat Barker—*Regeneration* (1991), *The Eye in the Door* (1993), and *The Ghost Road* (1995)—an exemplary series of novels that focus on the aftermath of trauma through exploring the history of World War I. Kaplan closes by reflecting on the theory of trauma that Freud articulates in a late work, *Moses and Monotheism*, published in the year of his death. That year also marked the beginning of World War II, whose events remain present in cultural memory and have been extended and reinforced by the traumatic events of subsequent decades.

As much or more than any other field of theory and criticism, trauma studies arises from and is always connected to real-world experiences—the victimization and pain of human beings who have endured and witnessed events which discourse cannot fully express and to which it can never do complete justice. We are more than a century beyond Freud's investigations of trauma, yet in a sense we are still confronting the fundamental questions that he articulated and engaged: what is trauma, how is it experienced, and how do those who suffer from trauma, and who treat the traumatized, speak and write about it? As these questions imply, at the center of trauma studies are issues of and debates about authority and power, the persons who claim to possess the knowledge (and the right) to speak and write about trauma and those living with it, and the institutions where this study, interpretation, and treatment occur.

Trauma Culture: The Politics of Terror and Loss in Media and Literature
Keywords: Affect, The Body, Cultural Studies, Feminist Criticism, Gender, Media, Modernity, Psychoanalysis, Subjectivity

From Trauma Culture: The Politics of Terror and Loss in Media and Literature

From *Chapter 1. "Why Trauma Now?": Freud and Trauma Studies*

FREUD AND TRAUMA

It all begins with Freud, of course. And the more I read of contemporary trauma theories, the more I believe that Freud had already said a great deal.[1]

1. I am not alone in thinking that Freud indeed had anticipated much that is being "discovered" by neuroscientists today. See Fred Guteril's essay, "What Freud Got Right," *Newsweek*, November 11, 2002: 50–52. The subheading reads: "His theories, long discredited, are finding support from neurologists using modern brain imaging," and an insert reads: "Unconscious drives, similar to libido and aggression, have now been located in the most primitive parts of the brain" (50). There is even a

At least, along with Freud's contemporaries and the pioneering clinicians who preceded him, nineteenth- and early twentieth-century thinkers had discovered the basic phenomena and structures of trauma. It took the more sophisticated scientific technologies of the late twentieth century to prove what these pioneers could only theorize about brain circuitry and mechanisms, sometimes, though, at the cost of Freud's insistence on unconscious fantasy as also involved in traumatic effects.

The phenomena of trauma, particularly hysteria, that interested clinicians did not arise in a vacuum. The phenomena were closely linked to modernity, especially to the industrial revolution and its dangerous new machines (the railway, the factory), as well as to the linked growth of the bourgeois family. This family became the site for female hysteria (caused partly by that family's patriarchal and puritanical codes), while industrialization (that required the bourgeois class and was, circularly, produced by that class) provided the social conditions for the train and machine accidents, and for large-scale wars. These in turn prompted attention to the traumatic symptoms such accidents and wars produced in men.[2]

What's interesting is that unlike psychologists and others writing today, Freud and his peers did not set out to write a *theory* of trauma. The concept of trauma emerges in their work on hysteria as if already assumed. It is used to explain processes in hysteria, rather than as a concept that has itself to be theorized. French clinicians, mainly J. M. Charcot and his student Pierre Janet,[3] pioneered research on hysteria and hypnosis. Charcot's research in neuropathology at his Salpètrière clinic (significantly, most of the patients were women, although Charcot argued that men also suffered from hysteria) produced students such as Janet whose case studies were central to ideas of hysteria at the time. Charcot and Janet inspired Freud and Breuer,[4] who visited the Salpètrière in 1890 (see Freud's 1893 moving obituary to Charcot who died soon after), although Breuer, a noted Viennese physician, had already begun research on hysteria in his treatment of Fräulein Anna O. Following the practices developed by Charcot and Janet, Freud and Breuer used hypnosis in their work with their hysterical patients, although shortly thereafter Freud began to experiment with his "talking cure," and in many ways was already moving beyond Charcot.

The influence of French theories and experiments is cited in an essay, "On the Psychical Mechanism of Hysterical Phenomena," written in collabora-

journal, *Neuropsychoanalysis*, and in Guteril's essay Antonio Damasio is quoted as saying that "Freud's insights on the nature of consciousness are consonant with the most advanced contemporary neuroscience views" [Kaplan's note]. Damasio (b. 1944), renowned neuroscientist and director of the Brain and Creativity Institute at the University of Southern California. For SIGMUND FREUD (1856–1939), the Austrian founder of psychoanalysis, see above.

2. Freud developed his theories of trauma from studying female hysteria and then the impact of train accidents and wars. Late in life, he also hypothesized that a violent historical act can remain in cultural consciousness and continue to have a traumatic impact. For more discussion of the history and development of the concept of trauma by Freud, see Cathy Caruth, *Unclaimed Experience: Trauma, Narrative, and History* (Baltimore: Johns Hopkins University Press, 1986). See also essays in Cathy Caruth, ed., *Trauma and Experience: Explorations in Trauma and Memory* (Ithaca, NY: Cornell University Press, 1985) [Kaplan's note].

3. French psychologist, philosopher, and psychotherapist (1859–1947), who focused on dissociation and traumatic memory. Jean-Martin Charcot (1825–1893), French neurologist and professor of anatomical pathology, whose work included research at the Salpêtrière Hospital in Paris.

4. Josef Breuer (1842–1925), Austrian physician; while working with a patient known as Anna O. in the 1880s, he developed the talking cure and helped establish the basis of Freudian psychoanalysis.

tion with Breuer and published in their joint volume, *Studies in Hysteria*.[5] Here the clinicians distinguish between ordinary hysteria and traumatic neuroses, and introduce the concept of "traumatic hysteria." Already the doctors understand that whether a person experiencing a distressing affect "of fright, shame or psychical pain" will be traumatized depends on the particular sensitivity of the person—something even now not sufficiently recognized. In addition, they hint at the belatedness of the onset of symptoms, attributing this to the fact that traumatic memories are not available to the patient in the way his commonplace ones are, but act "as a kind of foreign body" in the psyche, "an affective agent in the present even long after it first penetrated" (6). The famous statement that "hysterics suffer mainly from reminiscences" appears in this essay.

In this work, Freud and Breuer specifically note that the symptoms of hysteria are the result of trauma. The physical phenomena they cite, including what happens to memory in trauma, anticipate by many years the now so familiar litany of effects labeled in American Psychiatric Association's *Diagnostic and Statistical Manual of Mental Disorders: III-R*[6] as Post-Traumatic Stress Disorder (or PTSD). In the same essay in *Studies in Hysteria*, the clinicians note the way in which other ideas including fantasies get attached to the traumatic event. "A memory," they say, "of such a trauma . . . enter[s] the great complex of associations, it comes alongside other experiences, which may contradict it, and is subjected to rectification by other ideas" (9). They note that after an accident, memory of the danger and repetition of the fright "becomes associated with the memory of what happened afterwards—rescue and the consciousness of present safety."

Freud and Breuer implicitly gender trauma in accordance with the way the bourgeois family in Europe was organized in their day: Males largely have traumatic effects from accidents, women from watching by the bedside of sick parents or children, or (at first only implied) from extreme sexual repression. The three early case studies published in *Studies in Hysteria*—those of Anna O. (Breuer), Emily von N. (Freud), and Miss Lucy (Freud)—set the stage for Freud's later case studies while still revealing the legacy of Charcot (especially in Breuer's text) in focusing on detailed descriptions of the women's physical symptoms and treatments with massage, hydrotherapy, and electrotherapy, and in insisting on dissociation as a major symptom. Freud does indicate traumatic sexual origins for the hysteria in his cases, but it was not until the Dora[7] case history that Freud provided a detailed investigation into female hysteria and its traumatic symptoms as occasioned by sexual incidents in an environment of rigid sexual repression such as characterized Freud's nineteenth-century Austria.[8] In the case of Dora, Freud concludes that the hysteria was due to shame triggered by her arousal in response to

5. This volume, published only in German in 1895, was later translated by James Strachey and published in volume 2 of the Standard Edition in 1955. A separate English volume, *Studies in Hysteria*, of the SE section, was published in 1957 [Kaplan's note].

6. Published in 1987 (the current edition is the 5th, 2013).

7. The pseudonym given by Freud to Ida Bauer (1882–1945), a patient whom he treated for hysteria for nearly three months in 1900. He published her "case history" as *An Analysis of a Case of Hysteria* (1905).

8. As the editors of the Standard Edition point out, Freud mentioned in a letter to Fliess at the time that he had omitted reference to the father's abuse of the women in his and Breuer's *Studies in Hysteria* [Kaplan's note]. Wilhelm Fliess (1858–1928), one of Freud's colleagues and an important figure in the history of psychoanalysis.

inappropriate advances of a friend of her father, and further stimulation by attraction to, including sexual discussion with, this man's wife. In Dora's case, hysterical phenomena result from both "seduction" and fantasies.

In their essay introducing *Studies in Hysteria*, Freud and Breuer only mention sexuality as a precipitating cause for traumatic hysteria, asserting that "the determining causes which lead to the *acquisition* of neuroses, their aetiology . . . is to be looked for in *sexual* factors" (257). But a few years later in several papers written in 1894 and 1896 Freud baldly states that sexual abuse lies behind female hysteria. In his paper on "Heredity and the Aetiology of the Neuroses," Freud is fully aware that his audience would find this provocative.[9] He argues that hysteria comes from "memory relating to a sexual life," stating further that "the subject has retained an unconscious memory of *a precocious experience of sexual relations with actual excitement of the genitals, resulting from sexual abuse committed by another person; and the period of life* at which this fatal event takes place is *earliest youth*—the years up to the age of eight to ten, before the child has reached sexual maturity" (154, italics in original).

While these early essays deal mainly with trauma's processes and symptoms rather than their causes, and often imply female patients and situations, they sometimes include examples of male trauma but not hysteria. In "Heredity and the Aetiology of the Neuroses," Freud suggests why women resort to hysteria while men manifest obsessional neuroses by distinguishing the kinds of infantile sexual abuse boys and girls receive (women receive it "passively," males "actively"). Yet he does not realize the implicit acceptance of prevailing concepts of gender in this statement. That is, Freud does not go on to ask how cultural, political, and social roles laid down for men and women produce different neuroses in the case of sexual trauma. Indeed, Freud and others of his time rarely ask if trauma impacts differently on males and females. When the war neuroses force attention to male hysteria, as we'll see, clinicians do not ask if hysteria in men and women is the same. Yet, how the contrasting positions for men and women within national imaginaries result in different traumatic syndromes is important. These are questions I return to throughout this volume.

Trauma, then, was at first closely linked to the sexual experiences of young women within a close-knit bourgeois family and circle of friends such as was common at the turn of the nineteenth century. However, Freud soon questioned the degree to which the trauma depended on actual sexual abuse (not necessarily out of fear of offending his male friends and colleagues whose children he was treating, as is often assumed),[1] and theorized that fantasies of forbidden sexual desires could produce the same symptoms.[2]

9. After stating his notion that all major neuroses "have as their common source the subject's sexual life," he comments: "I am quite sure that this theory will call up a storm of contradictions from contemporary physicians" (Freud, "Heredity," 151) [Kaplan's note].

1. In his essay on "Heredity and the Aetiology of the Neuroses," Freud mentions siblings, other children, and nannies as the figures involved in genital activity with small children. However, this does not prove, as Richard McNally suggests, that Freud was not protecting his colleagues in his later abandoning of the seduction theory, for in a letter to Fliess discussing his patients at the same time, as the editors of the Standard Edition point out, Freud noted that "in every case it was the father who had to be held responsible (for perverse acts with children") (SE 1: 160). Freud later admitted to suppressing the father's abuse in cases in *Studies in Hysteria* (see SE 1: 164) [Kaplan's note]. McNally (b. 1954), American clinical psychologist who studies anxiety disorders.

2. As most readers will know, a huge bibliography surrounds this move by Freud—a bibliography

Freud moved on to develop other aspects of his psychoanalytic theories, and when he returned to trauma, it was now in relation to the symptoms of soldiers in World War I. At this point, interest in trauma focused on men involved in public catastrophes, such as defending the nation at war. A great deal of research and debate in Europe followed the increasing number of soldiers reporting paralysis and other hysterical symptoms preventing them from fighting. Doctors in England, France, and Germany studied these symptoms of soldiers unable to continue in battle (they were often termed "malingerers"). Articles published in the *Lancet*, a British medical journal, between 1895 and 1915 amply reveal the different hypotheses advanced about the soldiers' symptoms, and show how debates drew upon research carried out earlier in regard to industrial accidents and factory workers also described as malingerers.[3]

British doctors faced with traumatized soldiers, apparently applied theories of female hysteria caused by sexual trauma to battle trauma.[4] It is unclear whether they arrived independently at their conclusions about war trauma as hysteria or simply did not mention Freud's views on hysteria because it would require discussion of female sexuality. Elaine Showalter quotes W. H. Rivers[5] in 1917, also in the *Lancet*, noting the "correspondence between Freudian theory and his [Rivers's] clinical practice, and especially the ideas of the unconscious." Rivers concluded that "the advent of the war presented psychiatry with an extraordinary demonstration of the validity of Freudian theory in general" (Showalter, *The Female Malady* 188–189).[6]

---

that reentered public consciousness when issues relating to child abuse surfaced in the United States around highly visible cases in the late 1980s. Trauma theory and PTSD were central to these debates, since the cases relied on traumatic phenomena as evidence of abuse. Many case studies take up other kinds of family traumas, but readers can find a thorough survey of Freud's theories and writings, as well as discussion of the recent so-called "false memory syndrome" in Richard J. McNally's *Remembering Trauma* (Cambridge: Harvard University Press, 2003) [Kaplan's note].

3. War trauma greatly stimulated medical doctors and those interested in psychoanalysis in World War I. While concepts of trauma were first investigated in regard to industrial agents and accidents, it was the research opportunity afforded by traumatized soldiers that impelled work on trauma forward. Indeed, the work done in regard to World War I set the stage for concern about traumatic reactions in World War II, and then most recently and in its most elaborated form, in relation to the Vietnam War, as noted earlier.

See articles dealing with war trauma in the *Lancet*, such as Dr. David Forsyth's essay reviewing ongoing debates, i.e., "Functional Nerve Disease and the Shock of Battle: The So-Called Traumatic Neuroses Arising in Connexion with the War," (*Lancet* 2 [December 25, 1915]: 1399) [Kaplan's note].

4. Since *Studies in Hysteria* was published in 1909 in English, the doctors writing in the *Lancet* were no doubt drawing on Freud and Breuer's ideas (significantly, the English edition, translated by A. A. Brill, omitted the case histories of Anna O., Emmy Von N., and Katharina, as well as Breuer's theoretical chapter). But they were also drawing on much earlier research on railway and industrial accidents, such as 1864 research by J. Eric Erichsen, "On the Concussion of the Spine," mentioned in an article by Thomas R. Glynn, "The Traumatic Neuroses," in the *Lancet* 2 (November 5, 1910): 1332. Glynn awards to two American physicians the insight that since the symptoms of railway spine were cerebral more than spinal disturbances, the term "railway brain" would be more appropriate [Kaplan's note].

5. English anthropologist and psychologist (1864–1922); he treated World War I officers suffering from shell shock. Showalter (b. 1941), American feminist literary critic.

6. In a series of novels, Pat Barker (1991, 1995, 1996) has written convincing fictional accounts of Rivers's psychotherapy with soldiers suffering what was then called "shell shock" in the military hospital in Craiglockhart, Scotland. Doctors were supposed to get these men ready to return to the battlefront, and the soldiers knew this, but Barker shows the very difficult position doctors found themselves in, since their empathy for the men went deep, and they did not necessarily believe in the war. No man wanted to be accused of "malingering." Freud found himself having to judge just such a case, as I go on to show [Kaplan's note]. The three novels by the English writer Pat Barker (b. 1943) are *Regeneration* (1991), *The Ghost Road* (1995), and *The Eye in the Door* (1996). The full title of Showalter's book is *The Female Malady: Women, Madness and English Culture, 1830–1980* (London: Virago, 1987).

It is significant that Freud's development of his ideas about trauma was only belatedly prompted by what happened to soldiers in World War I. His first writings on World War I, namely "Thoughts for the Times on War and Death" and "Why War?" deal with man's binary instincts for love and hate.[7] It is not surprising that both essays reflect the broader cultural and social thinking that Freud developed in his 1920 *Civilization and Its Discontents*, rather than relating to his clinical and more technical research. The essays were written for a broad audience, after all, and one of them was directly addressed to Albert Einstein. Freud often implicitly (if not explicitly) relates his patients' symptoms to the larger cultural (implicitly ideological) thinking that these general essays reveal. Such insights appear in short parentheses (such as reference to the social repression of sexuality). But Freud was wary of mentioning the codes of his social, medical, and political milieu, not wanting to hamper acceptance of his theories by challenging social mores of the day.

Toward the end of World War I Freud and his colleagues published papers that Sandor Ferenczi, Karl Abraham, and Ernst Simmel[8] had presented on war neuroses at the proceedings of the Fifth International Psycho-Analytical Congress, held in Budapest on September 28 and 29, 1918, with an introduction by Freud. The congress was concerned about the treatment of soldiers and, not knowing the war was about to end, wanted to set up special psychoanalytically oriented clinics for traumatized men.

In his short introduction to the volume, Freud observes what essays in the *Lancet* had already observed, namely that war conditions had "an important influence on the spread of psycho-analysis." Freud goes on to note that "medical men who had hitherto held back from any approach to psychoanalytic theories were brought into closer contact with them when, in the course of their duties as army doctors, they were obliged to deal with war neuroses" (Freud, Standard Edition 17: 207). Indeed, Freud takes the opportunity to communicate his irritation with doctors (he may well have some of those in the *Lancet* in mind) who are only ready to use psychoanalysis when it is a matter of the war neuroses, which do not (at least obviously) involve sexuality. In his words, war neuroses do not appear to involve "the conflict between the ego and the sexual instincts which it repudiates" that Freud has been arguing is the basis of "the ordinary neuroses of peace-time" (208).

In the rest of the essay, Freud is at pains to find a link between the traumatic neuroses of war and of peacetime (also termed transference neuroses), which he does by arguing that in both cases there is a conflict in the ego. In the case of war, it is between the soldier's "old peaceful ego and his new warlike one, and it becomes acute as soon as the peace-ego realizes what danger it runs of losing its life owing to the rashness of its newly formed, parasitic double" (209). But Freud does not want to relinquish the possibility that even war trauma has something to do with sexuality, while at the same time fully understanding that he does not have evidence yet of "the relations which

7. "Thoughts for the Times on War and Death" (1915) was written six months after the war began. "Why War?" was part of a 1933 exchange of letters between Freud and Albert Einstein (1879–1955), the German-born theoretical physicist who also was a strong advocate for peace and social justice.

8. All psychoanalysts: Ferenczi (1873–1933), a Hungarian who worked closely with Freud; Abraham (1877–1925), a German; and Simmel (1882–1947), a German who was also a neurologist.

undoubtedly exist between fright, anxiety and narcissistic libido" (210).[9] He tantalizingly ends his essay by asserting that, in the case of both the war and peacetime neuroses, "what is feared is nevertheless an internal enemy" (210). He asserts that it is possible that repression underlies all reaction to trauma, whether sexual or external.

Freud's statements here are "tantalizing" in that he begs the question of whether there is any difference between ordinary neurosis and trauma—a difference that involves the difference between neurotic repression and traumatic dissociation that has plagued recent trauma theorists. But these same comments by Freud are important in linking so-called peacetime neuroses and war neuroses, and in challenging his theory of female hysteria as about repressed fantasies, not *memories*. If hysteria is the result of *fantasies*, then it cannot be the same phenomenon as war trauma, which has a clear external cause. War trauma seemed to be of an entirely different order than female hysteria—closer to the delayed impact of train accidents Freud was later to theorize, and not involving fantasies as such. Yet Freud's early theory that hysterical women suffered from memories of sexual abuse (not fantasies as he later claimed) did match the traumatic phenomenon of soldiers, namely that they too suffered from memories of an overwhelming event that they had been unable to cognitively register at the time it happened.[1]

Freud cannot in the short space of such an introduction go further into the complexities of his thought about links between the peacetime and war neuroses, neatly gendered as they are in Freud's account. There is no evidence that Freud had ever treated any patients suffering from war neuroses (as had Simmel and the others contributing full papers to the volume), but he was nevertheless called upon to be an "Expert Witness" about such neuroses at the investigation of his renowned colleague, Professor Wagner-Jauregg (at the time of the investigation director of the clinic at the Allgemeine Krankenhaus in Vienna).[2] This investigation came about as a result of allegations in a newspaper, *Der Freie Soldat*,[3] about military abuses as World War I came to an end. A commission, presided over by Professor Lofler,[4] was set up to investigate neglect of military duty during the war. Several articles accused the medical profession of "knowingly supporting the army's harsh and inhumane treatment of soldiers during the war" (Eissler 14). Extracts from a diary by Walter Kauders,[5] who was treated by Wagner-Jauregg, had been published, and an investigation began.

Freud's 1915 essay "Thoughts for the Times on War and Death," perhaps, taken together with the introduction discussed above and his status as the

9. Pat Barker's novels are interesting in light of this. More than one of Barker's major characters describe sexual arousal in moving out to a dangerous confrontation with German troops in trenches across from the British ones. Some characters are gay, others bisexual. While Rivers appears to leave such sexual themes unexplored in his therapy sessions, the "data" is there for readers to see [Kaplan's note].

1. Pat Barker's novels, again, dramatize clearly the ways in which traumatic battle events haunt the soldiers in dreams and hallucinations. While sometimes the men can recall the dreams and precipitating events, they prefer not to. Others suffer from total amnesia as a symptom. Partial dissociation, then, is observed in Barker's presenting of Rivers's cases in her fiction [Kaplan's note].

2. For full details of this investigation, see Kurt R. Eissler, *Freud as an Expert Witness: The Discussion of War Neuroses Between Freud and Wagner-Jauregg* (Madison, WI: International University Press, 1986) [Kaplan's note]. Julius Wagner-Jauregg (1857–1940), Austrian physician.

3. *The Free Soldier*, an Austrian Social Democratic weekly.

4. Alexander Löffler (1866–1929), an Austrian criminologist.

5. An Austrian officer who suffered a head injury early in the war and charged that he was subsequently severely mistreated by Wagner-Jauregg and his assistants at a psychological clinic.

"inventor" of psychoanalysis, evidently was seen to qualify him to be an "Expert Witness" in this case. But Freud was in a delicate position in testifying since he could not say anything that would harm the career of this renowned medical man, and yet he also could not agree with the nonpsychoanalytic treatment (usually electrical charges and isolation) that Wagner-Jauregg (like most of his colleagues) used for traumatized soldiers. Freud's "Memorandum on the Electrical Treatment of War Neurotics," submitted to Professor Lofler, allows us to see Freud treading elegantly around similar issues to those that had preoccupied the doctors writing in the *Lancet*. The debate was over whether the soldier's symptoms resulted from organic injuries to the nervous system or were caused by psychic changes such as we understand happens in trauma. Freud comes down clearly on the latter side, noting that "what is known as the psychoanalytic school of psychiatry, which was brought into being by me, had taught for the last twenty-five years that the neuroses of peace could be traced back to disturbances of emotional life. . . . It was therefore easy to infer that the immediate cause of all war neuroses was an unconscious inclination in the soldier to withdraw from the demands, dangerous or outrageous to his feelings, made upon him by active service" (Freud in Eissler 24–25). Freud insists, against claims by Wagner-Jauregg, that only a very small proportion of soldiers with traumatic symptoms were "malingerers." He is careful to note that the physician had a conflict, namely between his duty as a medical man and his military duty to get the soldiers back on the front line, in giving electrical treatment for a "fast fix," as we might say. "Medicine," says Freud, "was serving purposes foreign to its essence" (27). Deaths resulted from the treatment, although Freud will not say that Wagner-Jauregg's clinic used dangerous levels of electrical current. He concludes by referring to Ernst Simmel's success with psychotherapeutic methods ("introduced by me," Freud has to add) in treating war neuroses.

Significantly, Freud found himself returning to the issue of war neuroses in the year following his appearance as an Expert Witness in the Wagner-Jauregg investigation as he was writing *Beyond the Pleasure Principle*.[6] In attempting to understand how the mental apparatus produces pleasure and unpleasure, he began to distinguish between unpleasure from the pressure of internal unsatisfied instincts and unpleasure from an external perception recognized by the mental apparatus as a danger (*Beyond* 28). This leads him to mention the "mechanical concussions, railway disasters and other accidents involving risk to life," that have been given the name of "traumatic neurosis" (28). But his thought immediately turns to the war, as he notes, "The terrible war that has just ended gave rise to a great number of illnesses of this kind," and he footnotes the introduction noted above. Freud continues to reflect on similarities between the traumatic neurosis of war and that of hysteria, as if he continues to be puzzled by these similarities. Referring back to his earliest work with Breuer on female hysteria, Freud notes that war neurotics too "suffer mainly from reminiscences" (29).

6. A 1920 work in which Freud describes the struggle in human beings between eros (sexual love; Greek) and thanatos (death; Greek). It is a revision of his earlier theories.

But at this point he makes a sharp break to discuss child's play and the famous *fort-da* game[7] of his grandson. However, he returns later in the volume to the issue of internal versus external assault on the ego that had led him to the war neuroses in the first place. He is still trying to understand the different kinds of unpleasure involved in the different contexts, only now he theorizes that trauma results from a breach in a protective shield that the mental apparatus sets up to ward against overviolent stimuli. It seems throughout this discussion (52–61) that he has in mind the situation of war for the external assault on the mental apparatus and hysteria for the internal "assault" being theorized. This assumption seems to be valid since Freud refers explicitly again to the war neuroses and to his idea in the 1919 introduction that war neuroses result from a conflict in the ego, as much as from fear or, as he now notes is a more correct term "fright" (62).[8]

But Freud's most significant, and most complete discussion of trauma occurs, not incidentally, at the end of his life, in *Moses and Monotheism*,[9] when Freud was forced to leave his homeland and take up exile in England. At the end of *Moses*, Freud repeats his well-known theories about the etiology of the neuroses, only now in a way never quite articulated before he specifically includes the issue of trauma. He likens the latency of the man who walks away from the train accident apparently unharmed, only later to develop psychical and motor symptoms, to the "forgetting" of monotheism in the Jewish religion, only to have it return later as something insistent. But more importantly, he links common infant traumata to the latency phenomenon. He summarizes: "These three points—early happenings, within the first five years of life, the forgetting, and the characteristic of sexuality and aggressiveness—belong close together. The traumata are either bodily experiences or perceptions, especially those heard or seen." But not everyone responds in the same way to similar experiences, so Freud conceives of a sliding scale and slow series of developments that result in trauma symptoms.[1] It is not too much to infer from what Freud says here that the difference in how soldiers react to similar war traumas may depend on how far the war situation triggered prior psychic conflicts. In war, such internal conflicts, together with intense fear for his life or that of close ones, threatened the soldier's

7. Literally, "there-gone game" (German). In chapter 2 of *Beyond the Pleasure Principle*, Freud describes his 18-month-old grandson throwing a wooden reel out of his cot while exclaiming "o-o-o-o" (interpreted as "fort"), then pulling it back by a string with a joyful "da." This game illustrates the impetus behind repetition compulsions.

8. One of the problems with *Beyond the Pleasure Principle* is that Freud is trying to do too many things. The entire discussion involves Freud's working out of differences among anxiety, fear, and fright (something he will take up later on) and he is also continuing an earlier discussion of the compulsion to repeat. Most significantly, *Beyond* is also where Freud begins to theorize the death drive. However, his introduction of the traumatic war neuroses, when these neuroses are not the main discussion, highlights how bothered Freud was about the challenge to his prior theories that the existence of war neuroses had produced [Kaplan's note].

9. Published in 1939.

1. Juliet Mitchell makes a similar point, perhaps expanding on Freud's insight. Focusing on trauma from the perspective of the person who experiences it, she says: "This means both that the same event will not always be traumatic for different people, and that the experience of different events, if they are experienced as trauma, will be the same whatever the event and whoever the sufferer." Mitchell also seems to agree with Freud's later ideas about trauma when she says that trauma represents a breach in consciousness: "A trauma, whether physical or psychical, must create a breach in a protective covering of such severity that it cannot be coped with by the usual mechanisms by which we deal with pain or loss. . . . In trauma, we are untimely ripped" (121). See her "Trauma, Recognition, and the Place of Language," in *Diacritics* 28, no. 4 (winter 1998): 121–133 [Kaplan's note]. In Shakespeare's play *Macbeth* (1606), Macduff is "from his mother's womb/untimely ripped" (5.8.15–16).

identity and hence the dizzy panic or paralysis that followed, and that is described by many treating such neuroses.

Central to this Freudian theory of trauma is a motivated unconscious. In this case, the traumatic event may trigger early traumatic happenings, already perhaps mingled with fantasy, and shape how the current event is experienced. There may, for instance, in the case of battle trauma, be unconscious guilt at surviving an attack; or events in battle may unconsciously recall childhood violence where the victim wished for a sibling's death, etc. The events may in this case fall into the arena of repression and be recoverable in therapy.[2]

Thus, Freud's ideas about trauma gradually grew in complexity and preciseness from the early *Studies in Hysteria* to *Moses and Monotheism*, the latter work bringing together finally the long nurturing of his early concepts into a theory that anticipates much that clinicians working on combat fatigue and PTSD are now researching. We see Freud, especially in *Beyond the Pleasure Principle*, struggling to develop models of the brain that neuroscientists have only recently been able to produce through new technologies and lab experiments unavailable in Freud's day. Indeed, I have discussed Freud's ideas at such length because they seem to me to still be valuable for the work in this book. The specific complexities of brain circuitry, discussed below in the context of vicarious trauma, Freud could not know, since it has taken intricate modern neuroscience research to determine such circuitry. But he anticipated such circuits without the knowledge new technologies have made possible.

* * *

2005

2. Fictional psychotherapy interviews in Pat Barker's novels between a character modeled on William H. Rivers, the British World War I analyst who treated traumatized soldiers including the poet Siegfried Sassoon, demonstrate precisely this intermixture of fantasy with the traumatic battle happening. Her characters suffer PTSD, and again Barker is able to represent the flashbacks and intrusive memories brilliantly. See, for example, *The Eye in the Door* (Penguin, 1993): 67–76, for an example of such an interview. Following pages provide for examples of PTSD, as does also the earlier novel, *Regeneration* (Viking, 1991), where much of the action takes place in Craiglockhart, the military hospital to which soldiers suffering from war neurosis were sent to be treated by Rivers [Kaplan's note].

HÉLÈNE CIXOUS
b. 1937

"I have nothing to write except what I don't know," says Hélène Cixous in her essay "Coming to Writing" (1977). And in her autobiographical *Rootprints* (1994), she declares: "No sooner do I write . . . it is not true. And yet, I write hanging on to Truth." Like Socrates, Cixous claims to know only that she does not know. Unlike Socrates, she *writes* what she does not know. Transgressing the laws of genre, Cixous's writing defies categorization, but it nevertheless reinvigorates and reexamines many of the conventions of critical essays, novels, plays, and memoirs. In both form and content, Cixous has attempted to put in practice the freedom from any *givenness* that such radical ignorance ("uncovery") entails.

Cixous (pronounced "seek-soo") is known in the English-speaking world primarily as a mid-1970s feminist theorist, a leading practitioner of what is called *écriture féminine*—feminine writing. The word *féminine* has been subject to energetic debates among feminists, nonfeminists, and antifeminists ever since Cixous first published her celebrated manifesto, "The Laugh of the Medusa," in 1975 in a special issue of *L'Arc* magazine devoted to SIMONE DE BEAUVOIR and the women's movement (Cixous's text was translated in a 1976 issue of *Signs: Journal of Women in Culture and Society*, and has been reprinted many times since). Those debates, central to feminist criticism, will be summarized below. But with all the interrogation of the word *féminine*, one sometimes forgets that in France in the late 1960s, it was the word *écriture* (writing) that was the common denominator for a wide range of explosive new practices and publications.

Écriture may be the best name for what distinguishes contemporary "French theory" from "German idealism" or "Anglo-American pragmatism." It describes everything about writing that can neither be subsumed into an idea nor made to correspond exactly to empirical reality. In the late 1960s, a number of important thinkers in France—JACQUES DERRIDA, JULIA KRISTEVA, and ROLAND BARTHES among them—began to investigate what would happen to Western thought if the fact that it exists mainly in *writing* were taken seriously. Philippe Sollers, editor of the journal *Tel Quel*, proclaimed that a new "science of *écriture*," concentrating on the "textuality" of all discourses and inflected by Marxism, promised revolutionary change. The year was 1968, a time of social and political revolt on all levels of French society.

Hélène Cixous, a young English professor, was at the very heart of the intellectual and institutional ferment. Born in Oran, Algeria, to a multicultural, diasporic Jewish family that spoke German and French, she was surrounded by Spanish and Arabic, experienced anti-Semitism during the Vichy regime of the early 1940s, and saw French colonialism firsthand from a position neither French nor Arab. When her father died in 1948, her mother (appropriately named Eve) studied to become a midwife, and was often accompanied by her daughter as she performed her tasks. Hélène, married at eighteen to Guy Berger, with whom she had two children and whom she divorced in 1964, moved to Paris during the Algerian War of Independence, in which her husband was conscripted on the French side while her brother fought for the Algerian side. Pursuing her studies in English, a language not spoken in her family, she became *agrégée* (received the advanced teaching degree) in 1959 and started to teach at the University of Bordeaux, while beginning work on a doctoral dissertation on James Joyce.

Joyce's late style is perhaps the closest thing in the English tradition to *écriture*. As Cixous was writing her dissertation (published in 1969; trans. 1976, *The Exile of James Joyce*), she often discussed Joyce with Derrida, whom she had met in 1962, and with JACQUES LACAN, who was looking for a tutor on Joyce. She went on to teach at the Sorbonne, and then obtained a chair in English literature at the University of Nanterre near Paris, all before having completed her doctorate.

When protests and strikes erupted both within and outside the university in May 1968, Cixous was charged by the minister of education to head a committee to create an experimental branch of the University of Paris (so-called Paris VIII) in the outlying Bois de Vincennes. Many of the country's most innovative writers and thinkers in literature and philosophy came to teach there, including TZVETAN TODOROV, MICHEL FOUCAULT, and GILLES DELEUZE. The first department of psychoanalysis in France was also established there (a department in which the psychoanalytic feminist Luce Irigaray taught until 1974, when she was expelled by the Lacanians for her book *Speculum of the Other Woman*). With Gérard Genette and Todorov, Cixous created the influential journal *Poétique*. At the University of Paris

VIII, first at Vincennes and then at St. Denis, she went on to create and run the only doctoral program in France in *Études Féminines* (Women's Studies), a program that was abolished in the late 1970s by the Barre government and reestablished in the 1980s by the Socialists. But in 1968, she was in the process of completing her *doctorat d'état* in English. She became the youngest "doctor" in France.

So what was this *écriture* that was so much a part of the 1968 moment, and how did it lead to *écriture féminine*?

Ever since Socrates (who did not write) was described in the works of PLATO (who did), writing had been considered a secondary notation of a primary activity, speech. The theory of *écriture*—developed especially in Derrida's *Of Grammatology* (1967) and *Writing and Difference* (1967), where it has come to be known as deconstruction—did not simply reverse the hierarchy between speech and writing; it redefined the terms of that hierarchy. Whereas "speech" had been made to stand for immediacy, presence, truth, Logos (i.e., the "Word"), God, and Oneness (and "writing" had stood for deferral, difference, absence, lack, lawlessness, multiplicity, and heterogeneity), Derrida argued that speech itself had never actually manifested Truth directly; instead, like writing, it was structured through the difference, first named by FERDINAND DE SAUSSURE (1857–1913), between the signifier (the word) and the signified (the meaning). In any act of language, there was a lag, a discrepancy, between a sign and what it meant. To the extent that there was meaning at all, the two things could not be the same. Thus, to the extent that philosophy existed in language (spoken *or* written), it was structured like "writing." No actual language could achieve the simultaneity of signifier and signified, an idealization that was a consequence of the way in which Platonism and Christianity characterized the divine.

Western philosophy after Plato was centered around the impossible but irresistible search for a fundamental Truth or Logos. Derrida calls this search "logocentrism." Brought to clearest conceptualization in the philosophical work of G. W. F. HEGEL in the early nineteenth century, logocentric structures were organized through a series of binary oppositions (mind/matter, light/darkness, presence/absence, nature/culture, good/evil, etc.), the first term of each being desirable and the other shunned. KARL MARX had already claimed to turn Hegel on his head by reversing the relations between materiality and spirituality. But language was neither exactly material nor exactly spiritual. Theorists of *écriture* thus had to find new ways of making readable everything that had been repressed, obscured, or unacknowledged in Western thought.

In the course of that project, many male writers made use of figures of femininity to bring out what had been marginalized from traditional philosophical discourse. These *figures*—veils, shadows, enigmas, figurative language itself—represented resistance to the One, the Light, the Truth, and, implicitly, the idealization of the Male itself. In a way, therefore, we could say that *all écriture* was already *écriture féminine*—it was just being theorized mainly by men.

In part, Cixous aimed at rendering literal the figures of femininity in the theory of *écriture* and exploring the consequences of that literalization. She did not simply privilege the "female" half of an existing binary opposition between "male" and "female"; like other theorists of *écriture*, she questioned the very adequacy of either/or logics to name the complexity of cultural realities. But while Derrida did so by demystifying the "metaphysics of presence" involved in the notion of "voice," Cixous did so by describing the physical (as opposed to metaphysical) sensations of a woman who is speaking for the first time in public. Structuralism had analyzed the fundamental importance of binary oppositions; it now seemed urgent for poststructuralists to analyze all the things that those oppositions had obscured—and not only to analyze them but also to perform them, to transform them.

The real scandal of Cixous's work lay in her insistence on its two incompatible logics. On the one hand, she claimed that *écriture féminine* was characterized by the explicitly female body parts that had been repressed by traditional discourse and were being ex-pressed by the woman writer: "There is always within her at least a little of that good mother's milk. She writes in white ink." Yet on the other hand, she claimed that both men and women could write *écriture féminine*. How can both claims be true at the same time?

The binary logic that structures the opposition between "male" and "female" is set up as a relation not between "A" and "B" but between "A" and "not-A." SIGMUND FREUD's geometrical concept of castration, refined but not substantially changed by Lacan, defines "woman" not in terms of what she *has* but in terms of what she *lacks*—that is, a penis. "Is the fact that Logocentrism subjects thought—all concepts, codes, and values—to a binary system, related to 'the' couple, man/woman?" Cixous asks in "Sorties," published the same year as "The Laugh of the Medusa." Yes, she answers, and the consequences for the structure of *all* thought, not just thought having to do with sexual difference, are far-reaching. One half of the opposition is essentially destroyed for the other half to make "sense." If this is so, then *both* sides of an opposition are defined in terms of *one* of its elements. Thus anyone simply trying to unrepress the obscured term—here, the feminine—is likely to reproduce the very structures he or she is resisting. This is why Cixous declares, "I am not a feminist." Feminism, for her, participates in the same logic of opposition as traditional logocentrism or its companion, phallocentrism (the description of sexual difference as a difference between *having* and *lacking* the phallus).

Nonetheless, she acknowledges, the female body *has* been repressed. Indeed, *any* transgressive, desiring body—and perhaps *the body itself*—has been repressed. But maybe there is no "body itself," only bodies that have had power and bodies that haven't. Granted, power and authority and law have presupposed the male body—but on the condition that no actual body be represented at all. Thus, both men and women would have everything left to say about the body, and that "everything" would no longer fall neatly into any given category. By writing *as if* the female body could be asserted, Cixous's *écriture féminine* frees it from invisibility and, at the same time, does *not* make it into a new model for the universal human being. The new opposition is not between male and female, but between a logic of the One and a logic of heterogeneity and multiplicity.

The incompatibility between *écriture féminine* as assertion of the female body and *écriture féminine* as capable of being written by men creates an impossible logic that *is* *écriture féminine*. Such a writing practice is bound to seem outrageous almost all the time. Responding mainly to "The Laugh of the Medusa," many Anglo-American feminists have accused Cixous of promoting "essentialism"—that is, of equating female writing with an idealized and unhistoricized "femininity." And by making such claims as "women are multiple," "women are open to the other," "women write in white ink," she does seem to be affirming some sort of "essence" of woman. It could be argued that these claims are mythic, performative, and critical rather than descriptive. In her puns (*voler* as "steal" and "fly," *dépenser* as "spend" and "unthink," and *blanc* as both "white" and "blank"), she works on and in language, not in the empirical world. "Essentialism" or "anatomical destiny" is in one sense exactly what Cixous is arguing against.

"The Laugh of the Medusa" Keywords: The Body, Feminist Theory, Gender, Identity, Language, Psychoanalysis, Representation, Sexuality, Subjectivity

The Laugh of the Medusa[1]

I shall speak about women's writing: about *what it will do.* Woman must write her self: must write about women and bring women to writing, from which they have been driven away as violently as from their bodies—for the same reasons, by the same law, with the same fatal goal. Woman must put herself into the text—as into the world and into history—by her own movement.

The future must no longer be determined by the past. I do not deny that the effects of the past are still with us. But I refuse to strengthen them by repeating them, to confer upon them an irremovability the equivalent of destiny, to confuse the biological and the cultural. Anticipation is imperative.

Since these reflections are taking shape in an area just on the point of being discovered, they necessarily bear the mark of our time—a time during which the new breaks away from the old, and, more precisely, the (feminine) new from the old (*la nouvelle de l'ancien*).[2] Thus, as there are no grounds for establishing a discourse, but rather an arid millennial ground to break, what I say has at least two sides and two aims: to break up, to destroy; and to foresee the unforeseeable, to project.

I write this as a woman, toward women. When I say "woman," I'm speaking of woman in her inevitable struggle against conventional man; and of a universal woman subject who must bring women to their senses and to their meaning in history. But first it must be said that in spite of the enormity of the repression that has kept them in the "dark"—that dark which people have been trying to make them accept as their attribute—there is, at this time, no general woman, no one typical woman. What they have *in common* I will say. But what strikes me is the infinite richness of their individual constitutions: you can't talk about a female sexuality, uniform, homogeneous, classifiable into codes—any more than you can talk about one unconscious resembling another. Women's imaginary is inexhaustible, like music, painting, writing: their stream of phantasms is incredible.

I have been amazed more than once by a description a woman gave me of a world all her own which she had been secretly haunting since early childhood. A world of searching, the elaboration of a knowledge, on the basis of a systematic experimentation with the bodily functions, a passionate and precise interrogation of her erotogeneity. This practice, extraordinarily rich and inventive, in particular as concerns masturbation, is prolonged or accompanied by a production of forms, a veritable aesthetic activity, each stage of rapture inscribing a resonant vision, a composition, something beautiful. Beauty will no longer be forbidden.

I wished that that woman would write and proclaim this unique empire so that other women, other unacknowledged sovereigns, might exclaim: I, too, overflow; my desires have invented new desires, my body knows unheard-of songs. Time and again I, too, have felt so full of luminous torrents that I could burst—burst with forms much more beautiful than those

1. Translated by Keith Cohen and Paula Cohen, who occasionally include the original French in parentheses.

2. In French *la nouvelle* (the new, the news) is grammatically feminine, while *l'ancien* (the old, the former) is masculine.

beauty of woman is underrated

which are put up in frames and sold for a stinking fortune. And I, too, said nothing, showed nothing; I didn't open my mouth, I didn't repaint my half of the world. I was ashamed. I was afraid, and I swallowed my shame and my fear. I said to myself: You are mad! What's the meaning of these waves, these floods, these outbursts? Where is the ebullient, infinite woman who, immersed as she was in her naiveté, kept in the dark about herself, led into self-disdain by the great arm of parental-conjugal phallocentrism,[3] hasn't been ashamed of her strength? Who, surprised and horrified by the fantastic tumult of her drives (for she was made to believe that a well-adjusted normal woman has a . . . divine composure), hasn't accused herself of being a monster? Who, feeling a funny desire stirring inside her (to sing, to write, to dare to speak, in short, to bring out something new), hasn't thought she was sick? Well, her shameful sickness is that she resists death, that she makes trouble.

And why don't you write? Write! Writing is for you, you are for you; your body is yours, take it. I know why you haven't written. (And why I didn't write before the age of twenty-seven.) Because writing is at once too high, too great for you, it's reserved for the great—that is, for "great men"; and it's "silly." Besides, you've written a little, but in secret. And it wasn't good, because it was in secret, and because you punished yourself for writing, because you didn't go all the way; or because you wrote, irresistibly, as when we would masturbate in secret, not to go further, but to attenuate the tension a bit, just enough to take the edge off. And then as soon as we come, we go and make ourselves feel guilty—so as to be forgiven; or to forget, to bury it until the next time.

Write, let no one hold you back, let nothing stop you: not man; not the imbecilic capitalist machinery, in which publishing houses are the crafty, obsequious relayers of imperatives handed down by an economy that works against us and off our backs; and not *yourself*. Smug-faced readers, managing editors, and big bosses don't like the true texts of women—female-sexed texts. That kind scares them.

I write woman: woman must write woman. And man, man. So only an oblique consideration will be found here of man; it's up to him to say where his masculinity and femininity are at: this will concern us once men have opened their eyes and seen themselves clearly.[4]

Now women return from afar, from always: from "without," from the heath where witches are kept alive; from below, from beyond "culture"; from their

3. The psychoanalytic system in which sexual difference is defined as the difference between having and lacking the phallus; the term has come to refer to the patriarchal cultural system as a whole insofar as that system privileges the phallus as the symbol and source of power. It is closely related to *logocentrism*, a term coined by the French philosopher JACQUES DERRIDA (1930–2004); the two are sometimes combined as *phallogocentrism*.

4. Men still have everything to say about their sexuality, and everything to write. For what they have said so far, for the most part, stems from the opposition activity/passivity, from the power relation between a fantasized obligatory virility meant to invade, to colonize, and the consequential phantasm of woman as a "dark continent" to penetrate and to "pacify." (We know what "pacify" means in terms of scotomizing the other and misrecognizing the self.) Conquering her, they've made haste to depart from her borders, to get out of sight, out of body. The way man has of getting out of himself and into her whom he takes not for the other but for his own, deprives him, he knows, of his own bodily territory. One can understand how man, confusing himself with his penis and rushing in for the attack, might feel resentment and fear of being "taken" by the woman, of being lost in her, absorbed, or alone [Cixous's note]. "Dark continent": a metaphor used by SIGMUND FREUD in his essay "The Question of Lay Analysis" (1926) to describe woman as unexplored and mysterious. "Scotomizing": forming a mental blind spot about (a psychoanalytic term).

childhood which men have been trying desperately to make them forget, condemning it to "eternal rest." The little girls and their "ill-mannered" bodies immured, well-preserved, intact unto themselves, in the mirror. Frigidified. But are they ever seething underneath! What an effort it takes—there's no end to it—for the sex cops to bar their threatening return. Such a display of forces on both sides that the struggle has for centuries been immobilized in the trembling equilibrium of a deadlock.

Here they are, returning, arriving over and again, because the unconscious is impregnable. They have wandered around in circles, confined to the narrow room in which they've been given a deadly brainwashing. You can incarcerate them, slow them down, get away with the old Apartheid[5] routine, but for a time only. As soon as they begin to speak, at the same time as they're taught their name, they can be taught that their territory is black: because you are Africa, you are black. Your continent is dark. Dark is dangerous. You can't see anything in the dark, you're afraid. Don't move, you might fall. Most of all, don't go into the forest. And so we have internalized this horror of the dark.

Men have committed the greatest crime against women. Insidiously, violently, they have led them to hate women, to be their own enemies, to mobilize their immense strength against themselves, to be the executants of their virile needs. They have made for women an antinarcissism! A narcissism which loves itself only to be loved for what women haven't got! They have constructed the infamous logic of antilove.

We the precocious, we the repressed of culture, our lovely mouths gagged with pollen, our wind knocked out of us, we the labyrinths, the ladders, the trampled spaces, the bevies—we are black and we are beautiful.[6]

We're stormy, and that which is ours breaks loose from us without our fearing any debilitation. Our glances, our smiles, are spent; laughs exude from all our mouths; our blood flows and we extend ourselves without ever reaching an end; we never hold back our thoughts, our signs, our writing; and we're not afraid of lacking.[7]

What happiness for us who are omitted, brushed aside at the scene of inheritances; we inspire ourselves and we expire without running out of breath, we are everywhere!

From now on, who, if we say so, can say no to us? We've come back from always.

It is time to liberate the New Woman from the Old by coming to know her—by loving her for getting by, for getting beyond the Old without delay, by going out ahead of what the New Woman will be, as an arrow quits the bow with a movement that gathers and separates the vibrations musically, in order to be more than her self.

I say that we must, for, with a few rare exceptions, there has not yet been any writing that inscribes femininity; exceptions so rare, in fact, that, after

5. Apartness (Afrikaans), the former official policy of racial segregation and discrimination in South Africa (1948–93).

6. A reference to the Song of Solomon (1.5) and, perhaps, to a slogan of the U.S. black power movement of the 1960s.

7. A reference to the reinterpretation of Freud's theory of sexual difference by the French psychoanalyst JACQUES LACAN (1901–1981). For Freud, men have a penis, and women don't. For Lacan, men and women are both structured through a fundamental "lack," but that lack is first perceived on the body of the mother.

plowing through literature across languages, cultures, and ages,[8] one can only be startled at this vain scouting mission. It is well known that the number of women writers (while having increased very slightly from the nineteenth century on) has always been ridiculously small. This is a useless and deceptive fact unless from their species of female writers we do not first deduct the immense majority whose workmanship is in no way different from male writing, and which either obscures women or reproduces the classic representations of women (as sensitive—intuitive—dreamy, etc.).[9]

Let me insert here a parenthetical remark. I mean it when I speak of male writing. I maintain unequivocally that there is such a thing as *marked* writing; that, until now, far more extensively and repressively than is ever suspected or admitted, writing has been run by a libidinal and cultural—hence political, typically masculine—economy;[1] that this is a locus where the repression of women has been perpetuated, over and over, more or less consciously, and in a manner that's frightening since it's often hidden or adorned with the mystifying charms of fiction; that this locus has grossly exaggerated all the signs of sexual opposition (and not sexual difference), where woman has never *her* turn to speak—this being all the more serious and unpardonable in that writing is precisely *the very possibility of change*, the space that can serve as a springboard for subversive thought, the precursory movement of a transformation of social and cultural structures.

Nearly the entire history of writing is confounded with the history of reason, of which it is at once the effect, the support, and one of the privileged alibis. It has been one with the phallocentric tradition. It is indeed that same self-admiring, self-stimulating, self-congratulatory phallocentrism.

With some exceptions, for there have been failures—and if it weren't for them, I wouldn't be writing (I-woman, escapee)—in that enormous machine that has been operating and turning out its "truth" for centuries. There have been poets who would go to any lengths to slip something by at odds with tradition—men capable of loving love and hence capable of loving others and of wanting them, of imagining the woman who would hold out against oppression and constitute herself as a superb, equal, hence "impossible" subject, untenable in a real social framework. Such a woman the poet could desire only by breaking the codes that negate her. Her appearance would necessarily bring on, if not revolution—for the bastion was supposed to be immutable—at least harrowing explosions. At times it is in the fissure caused by an earthquake, through that radical mutation of things brought on by a material up-heaval when every structure is for a moment thrown off

8. I am speaking here only of the place "reserved" for women by the Western world [Cixous's note].

9. Which works, then, might be called feminine? I'll just point out some examples: one would have to give them full readings to bring out what is pervasively feminine in their significance. Which I shall do elsewhere. In France (have you noted our infinite poverty in this field?—the Anglo-Saxon countries have shown resources of distinctly greater consequence), leafing through what's come out of the 20th century—and it's not much—the only inscriptions of femininity that I have seen were by Colette, Marguerite Duras, . . . and Jean Genet [Cixous's note]. Genet (1910–1986), male French novelist and playwright. Sidonie Gabrielle Colette (1873–1954), French novelist. Duras (pseudonym of Marguerite Donnadieu, 1914–1996), French novelist, screenwriter, playwright, and film director.

1. The "libidinal economy" is the system of exchanges having to do with sexual desire (libido), which Freud characterized as inherently masculine to the extent that it was active, not passive; in this view, only one desire can function at a time.

balance and an ephemeral wildness sweeps order away, that the poet slips something by, for a brief span, of woman. Thus did Kleist[2] expend himself in his yearning for the existence of sister-lovers, maternal daughters, mother-sisters, who never hung their heads in shame. Once the palace of magistrates is restored, it's time to pay: immediate bloody death to the uncontrollable elements.

But only the poets—not the novelists, allies of representationalism. Because poetry involves gaining strength through the unconscious and because the unconscious, that other limitless country, is the place where the repressed manage to survive: women, or as Hoffmann[3] would say, fairies.

She must write her self, because this is the invention of a *new insurgent* writing which, when the moment of her liberation has come, will allow her to carry out the indispensable ruptures and transformations in her history, first at two levels that cannot be separated.

(*a*) Individually. By writing her self, woman will return to the body which has been more than confiscated from her, which has been turned into the uncanny stranger on display—the ailing or dead figure, which so often turns out to be the nasty companion, the cause and location of inhibitions. Censor the body and you censor breath and speech at the same time.

Write your self. Your body must be heard. Only then will the immense resources of the unconscious spring forth. Our naphtha[4] will spread, throughout the world, without dollars—black or gold—nonassessed values that will change the rules of the old game.

To write. An act which will not only "realize" the decensored relation of woman to her sexuality, to her womanly being, giving her access to her native strength; it will give her back her goods, her pleasures, her organs, her immense bodily territories which have been kept under seal; it will tear her away from the superegoized structure[5] in which she has always occupied the place reserved for the guilty (guilty of everything, guilty at every turn: for having desires, for not having any; for being frigid, for being "too hot"; for not being both at once; for being too motherly and not enough; for having children and for not having any; for nursing and for not nursing . . .)—tear her away by means of this research, this job of analysis and illumination, this emancipation of the marvelous text of her self that she must urgently learn to speak. A woman without a body, dumb, blind, can't possibly be a good fighter. She is reduced to being the servant of the militant male, his shadow. We must kill the false woman who is preventing the live one from breathing. Inscribe the breath of the whole woman.

(*b*) An act that will also be marked by woman's *seizing* the occasion to *speak*, hence her shattering entry into history, which has always been based *on her suppression*. To write and thus to forge for herself the antilogos weapon. To become *at will* the taker and initiator, for her own right, in every symbolic system, in every political process.

2. Heinrich von Kleist (1777–1811); German dramatist and poet.

3. E. T. A. Hoffmann (1776–1822), German writer known especially for his fantastic tales (Freud discusses "The Sandman" in his influential 1919 essay "The 'Uncanny'"; see above).

4. A volatile petroleum product; the term was used by alchemists to refer to liquids with low boiling points.

5. The superego, according to Freud, is the part of the psyche that develops through the incorporation of the moral standards of the child's parents and community.

It is time for women to start scoring their feats in written and oral language.

Every woman has known the torment of getting up to speak. Her heart racing, at times entirely lost for words, ground and language slipping away—that's how daring a feat, how great a transgression it is for a woman to speak—even just open her mouth—in public. A double distress, for even if she transgresses, her words fall almost always upon the deaf male ear, which hears in language only that which speaks in the masculine.

It is by writing, from and toward women, and by taking up the challenge of speech which has been governed by the phallus, that women will confirm women in a place other than that which is reserved in and by the symbolic,[6] that is, in a place other than silence. Women should break out of the snare of silence. They shouldn't be conned into accepting a domain which is the margin or the harem.

Listen to a woman speak at a public gathering (if she hasn't painfully lost her wind). She doesn't "speak," she throws her trembling body forward; she lets go of herself, she flies; all of her passes into her voice, and it's with her body that she vitally supports the "logic" of her speech. Her flesh speaks true. She lays herself bare. In fact, she physically materializes what she's thinking; she signifies it with her body. In a certain way she *inscribes* what she's saying, because she doesn't deny her drives the intractable and impassioned part they have in speaking. Her speech, even when "theoretical" or political, is never simple or linear or "objectified," generalized: she draws her story into history.

There is not that scission, that division made by the common man between the logic of oral speech and the logic of the text, bound as he is by his antiquated relation—servile, calculating—to mastery. From which proceeds the niggardly lip service which engages only the tiniest part of the body, plus the mask.

In women's speech, as in their writing, that element which never stops resonating, which, once we've been permeated by it, profoundly and imperceptibly touched by it, retains the power of moving us—that element is the song: first music from the first voice of love which is alive in every woman. Why this privileged relationship with the voice? Because no woman stockpiles as many defenses for countering the drives as does a man. You don't build walls around yourself, you don't forego pleasure as "wisely" as he. Even if phallic mystification has generally contaminated good relationships, a woman is never far from "mother" (I mean outside her role functions: the "mother" as nonname and as source of goods). There is always within her at least a little of that good mother's milk. She writes in white ink.

Woman for women.—There always remains in woman that force which produces/is produced by the other—in particular, the other woman. *In* her, matrix, cradler; herself giver as her mother and child; she is her own sister-daughter. You might object, "What about she who is the hysterical offspring of a bad mother?" Everything will be changed once woman gives woman to the other woman. There is hidden and always ready in woman the source; the

6. A reference to Lacan's theory of the psyche. "The Symbolic" is the dimension of language, law, and the father; in contrast, "the Imaginary" is modeled on the mother-child dyad, or on the relation between an infant and its mirror image.

locus for the other. The mother, too, is a metaphor. It is necessary and sufficient that the best of herself be given to woman by another woman for her to be able to love herself and return in love the body that was "born" to her. Touch me, caress me, you the living no-name, give me my self as myself. The relation to the "mother," in terms of intense pleasure and violence, is curtailed no more than the relation to childhood (the child that she was, that she is, that she makes, remakes, undoes, there at the point where, the same, she others herself). Text: my body—shot through with streams of song; I don't mean the overbearing, clutchy "mother" but, rather, what touches you, the equivoice that affects you, fills your breast with an urge to come to language and launches your force; the rhythm that laughs you; the intimate recipient who makes all metaphors possible and desirable; body (body? bodies?), no more describable than god, the soul, or the Other; that part of you that leaves a space between yourself and urges you to inscribe in language your woman's style. In women there is always more or less of the mother who makes everything all right, who nourishes, and who stands up against separation; a force that will not be cut off but will knock the wind out of the codes. We will rethink womankind beginning with every form and every period of her body. The Americans remind us, "We are all Lesbians";[7] that is, don't denigrate woman, don't make of her what men have made of you.

Because the "economy" of her drives is prodigious, she cannot fail, in seizing the occasion to speak, to transform directly and indirectly *all* systems of exchange based on masculine thrift. Her libido will produce far more radical effects of political and social change than some might like to think.

Because she arrives, vibrant, over and again, we are at the beginning of a new history, or rather of a process of becoming in which several histories intersect with one another. As subject for history, woman always occurs simultaneously in several places. Woman un-thinks[8] the unifying, regulating history that homogenizes and channels forces, herding contradictions into a single battlefield. In woman, personal history blends together with the history of all women, as well as national and world history. As a militant, she is an integral part of all liberations. She must be farsighted, not limited to a blow-by-blow interaction. She foresees that her liberation will do more than modify power relations or toss the ball over to the other camp; she will bring about a mutation in human relations, in thought, in all praxis: hers is not simply a class struggle, which she carries forward into a much vaster movement. Not that in order to be a woman-in-struggle(s) you have to leave the class struggle or repudiate it; but you have to split it open, spread it out, push it forward, fill it with the fundamental struggle so as to prevent the class struggle, or any other struggle for the liberation of a class or people, from operating as a form of repression, pretext for postponing the inevitable, the staggering alteration in power relations and in the production of individualities. This alteration is already upon us—in the United States, for example, where millions of night crawlers are in the process of undermining the family and disintegrating the whole of American sociality.

7. Compare the American feminist slogan attributed to Ti-Grace Atkinson (b. 1938), "Feminism is the theory, lesbianism is the practice"; see also the opening of the Radicalesbians' manifesto, "The Woman-Identified Woman" (1970): "A lesbian is the rage of all women condensed to the point of explosion."

8. "*Dé-pense*," a neologism formed on the verb *penser* [to think], hence "unthinks," but also "spends" (from *dépenser*) [translators' note].

The new history is coming; it's not a dream, though it does extend beyond men's imagination, and for good reason. It's going to deprive them of their conceptual orthopedics,[9] beginning with the destruction of their enticement machine.

It is impossible to *define* a feminine practice of writing, and this is an impossibility that will remain, for this practice can never be theorized, enclosed, coded—which doesn't mean that it doesn't exist. But it will always surpass the discourse that regulates the phallocentric system; it does and will take place in areas other than those subordinated to philosophico-theoretical domination. It will be conceived of only by subjects who are breakers of automatisms, by peripheral figures that no authority can ever subjugate.

Hence the necessity to affirm the flourishes of this writing, to give form to its movement, its near and distant byways. Bear in mind to begin with (1) that sexual opposition, which has always worked for man's profit to the point of reducing writing, too, to his laws, is only a historico-cultural limit. There is, there will be more and more rapidly pervasive now, a fiction that produces irreducible effects of femininity. (2) That it is through ignorance that most readers, critics, and writers of both sexes hesitate to admit or deny outright the possibility or the pertinence of a distinction between feminine and masculine writing. It will usually be said, thus disposing of sexual difference: either that all writing, to the extent that it materializes, is feminine; or, inversely—but it comes to the same thing—that the act of writing is equivalent to masculine masturbation (and so the woman who writes cuts herself out a paper penis); or that writing is bisexual, hence neuter, which again does away with differentiation. To admit that writing is precisely working (in) the in-between, inspecting the process of the same and of the other without which nothing can live, undoing the work of death—to admit this is first to want the two, as well as both, the ensemble of the one and the other, not fixed in sequences of struggle and expulsion or some other form of death but infinitely dynamized by an incessant process of exchange from one subject to another. A process of different subjects knowing one another and beginning one another anew only from the living boundaries of the other: a multiple and inexhaustible course with millions of encounters and transformations of the same into the other and into the in-between, from which woman takes her forms (and man, in his turn; but that's his other history).

In saying "bisexual, hence neuter," I am referring to the classic conception of bisexuality, which, squashed under the emblem of castration fear[1] and along with the fantasy of a "total" being (though composed of two halves), would do away with the difference experienced as an operation incurring loss, as the mark of dreaded sectility.

To this self-effacing, merger-type bisexuality, which would conjure away castration (the writer who puts up his sign: "bisexual written here, come and see," when the odds are good that it's neither one nor the other), I oppose the *other bisexuality* on which every subject not enclosed in the false

9. An allusion to Lacan's term *orthopedic*, which refers to any training process that "corrects" the infant's imagination.

1. The fear that Freud attributes to every male child imagining the punishment for desiring his mother; more generally, the fear of losing something, of not being "whole," that leads men to cling to masculinity for fear of becoming "castrated" like women.

theater of phallocentric representationalism has founded his/her erotic universe. Bisexuality; that is, each one's location in self (*répérage en soi*) of the presence—variously manifest and insistent according to each person, male or female—of both sexes, nonexclusion either of the difference or of one sex, and, from this "self-permission," multiplication of the effects of the inscription of desire, over all parts of my body and the other body.

Now it happens that at present, for historico-cultural reasons, it is women who are opening up to and benefiting from this vatic bisexuality which doesn't annul differences but stirs them up, pursues them, increases their number. In a certain way, "woman is bisexual";[2] man—it's a secret to no one—being poised to keep glorious phallic monosexuality in view. By virtue of affirming the primacy of the phallus and of bringing it into play, phallocratic ideology has claimed more than one victim. As a woman, I've been clouded over by the great shadow of the scepter and been told: idolize it, that which you cannot brandish. But at the same time, man has been handed that grotesque and scarcely enviable destiny (just imagine) of being reduced to a single idol with clay balls. And consumed, as Freud and his followers note, by a fear of being a woman! For, if psychoanalysis was constituted from woman, to repress femininity (and not so successful a repression at that—men have made it clear), its account of masculine sexuality is now hardly refutable; as with all the "human" sciences, it reproduces the masculine view, of which it is one of the effects.

Here we encounter the inevitable man-with-rock, standing erect in his old Freudian realm, in the way that, to take the figure back to the point where linguistics is conceptualizing it "anew," Lacan preserves it in the sanctuary of the phallos (ø)[3] "sheltered" from *castration's lack*! Their "symbolic" exists, it holds power—we, the sowers of disorder, know it only too well. But we are in no way obliged to deposit our lives in their banks of lack, to consider the constitution of the subject in terms of a drama manglingly restaged, to reinstate again and again the religion of the father. Because we don't want that. We don't fawn around the supreme hole. We have no womanly reason to pledge allegiance to the negative. The feminine (as the poets suspected) affirms: ". . . And yes," says Molly, carrying *Ulysses* off beyond any book and toward the new writing; "I said yes, I will Yes."[4]

The Dark Continent is neither dark nor unexplorable.[5]—It is still unexplored only because we've been made to believe that it was too dark to be explorable. And because they want to make us believe that what interests us is the white continent, with its monuments to Lack. And we believed. They riveted us between two horrifying myths: between the Medusa[6] and the

2. Freud claimed that because the mother was the first object of desire for both sexes, women (who had to change their object of desire) were more inherently bisexual than men.
3. The symbol (the Greek letter phi) representing the phallic function, in Lacanian terminology.
4. The final words of James Joyce's *Ulysses* (1922), spoken by Molly Bloom.
5. Qualities suggested by Freud, who also saw female sexuality (the "dark continent") as a "riddle" (see "Femininity," 1932).
6. In Greek mythology, the most famous of the monstrous Gorgon sisters; her head was covered with snakes, and anyone who looked at her was turned to stone (Perseus looked at her reflection in his shield to decapitate her). Freud, in his short essay "Medusa's Head" (1922), associates Medusa with castration (= decapitation) and analyzes the ambiguity of the image: the snakes on her head are a denial of the castration she represents, while the notion of being turned to stone represents both castration and arousal. Cixous may also be referring to Lacan as Perseus, capable of looking at things only in a mirror (see above his famous essay "The Mirror Stage," 1949).

abyss. That would be enough to set half the world laughing, except that it's still going on. For the phallologocentric sublation[7] is with us, and it's militant, regenerating the old patterns, anchored in the dogma of castration. They haven't changed a thing: they've theorized their desire for reality! Let the priests tremble, we're going to show them our sexts![8]

Too bad for them if they fall apart upon discovering that women aren't men, or that the mother doesn't have one. But isn't this fear convenient for them? Wouldn't the worst be, isn't the worst, in truth, that women aren't castrated, that they have only to stop listening to the Sirens[9] (for the Sirens were men) for history to change its meaning? You only have to look at the Medusa straight on to see her. And she's not deadly. She's beautiful and she's laughing.[1]

Men say that there are two unrepresentable things: death and the feminine sex. That's because they need femininity to be associated with death; it's the jitters that gives them a hard-on! for themselves! They need to be afraid of us. Look at the trembling Perseuses moving backward toward us, clad in apotropes.[2] What lovely backs! Not another minute to lose. Let's get out of here.

Let's hurry: the continent is not impenetrably dark. I've been there often. I was overjoyed one day to run into Jean Genet. It was in *Pompes funèbres.*[3] He had come there led by his Jean. There are some men (all too few) who aren't afraid of femininity.

Almost everything is yet to be written by women about femininity: about their sexuality, that is, its infinite and mobile complexity, about their eroticization, sudden turn-ons of a certain minuscule-immense area of their bodies; not about destiny, but about the adventure of such and such a drive, about trips, crossings, trudges, abrupt and gradual awakenings, discoveries of a zone at one time timorous and soon to be forthright. A woman's body, with its thousand and one thresholds of ardor—once, by smashing yokes and censors, she lets it articulate the profusion of meanings that run through it in every direction—will make the old single-grooved mother tongue reverberate with more than one language.

We've been turned away from our bodies, shamefully taught to ignore them, to strike them with that stupid sexual modesty; we've been made victims of the old fool's game: each one will love the other sex. I'll give you your body and you'll give me mine. But who are the men who give women the body that women blindly yield to them? Why so few texts? Because so few women have as yet won back their body. Women must write through their bodies, they must invent the impregnable language that will wreck partitions, classes, and rhetorics, regulations and codes, they must submerge, cut through, get beyond the ultimate reserve-discourse, including the one that laughs at the very idea of pronouncing the word "silence," the

7. The standard English translation of *Aufhebung*, a term used by the German philosopher GEORG WILHELM FRIEDRICH HEGEL (1770–1831) to refer to the dialectical progression from a contradiction to a higher synthesis. Here, "woman" has been sublated into the general category "man," and "man," at first *opposed* to "woman," has risen up to become the generic name for all of humankind.

8. "Showing our sexts" represents a new articulation of sex and text (as does *écriture féminine*), as women who no longer repress their sexuality can talk about everything.

9. In Greek mythology, nymphs with a woman's head and a bird's body who lived on an island surrounded by rocks; the Sirens' enchanting song lured sailors to their death.

1. In redescribing Medusa as beautiful rather than horrible, Cixous is revising the notion of femininity itself.

2. Charms with the power to turn away evil.

3. Jean Genet, *Pompes funèbres* [*Funeral Rites*] (Paris, 1948), p. 185 [Cixous's note].

one that, aiming for the impossible, stops short before the word "impossible" and writes it as "the end."

Such is the strength of women that, sweeping away syntax, breaking that famous thread (just a tiny little thread, they say) which acts for men as a surrogate umbilical cord, assuring them—otherwise they couldn't come—that the old lady is always right behind them,[4] watching them make phallus, women will go right up to the impossible.

When the "repressed" of their culture and their society returns, it's an explosive, *utterly* destructive, staggering return, with a force never yet unleashed and equal to the most forbidding of suppressions. For when the Phallic period comes to an end, women will have been either annihilated or borne up to the highest and most violent incandescence. Muffled throughout their history, they have lived in dreams, in bodies (though muted), in silences, in aphonic[5] revolts.

And with such force in their fragility; a fragility, a vulnerability, equal to their incomparable intensity. Fortunately, they haven't sublimated; they've saved their skin, their energy. They haven't worked at liquidating the impasse of lives without futures. They have furiously inhabited these sumptuous bodies: admirable hysterics who made Freud succumb to many voluptuous moments impossible to confess, bombarding his Mosaic statue[6] with their carnal and passionate body words, haunting him with their inaudible and thundering denunciations, dazzling, more than naked underneath the seven veils of modesty. Those who, with a single word of the body, have inscribed the vertiginous immensity of a history which is sprung like an arrow from the whole history of men and from biblico-capitalist society, are the women, the supplicants of yesterday, who come as forebears of the new women, after whom no intersubjective relation will ever be the same. You, Dora, you the indomitable, the poetic body, you are the true "mistress" of the Signifier.[7] Before long your efficacity will be seen at work when your speech is no longer suppressed, its point turned in against your breast, but written out over against the other.

In body.—More so than men who are coaxed toward social success, toward sublimation, women are body. More body, hence more writing. For a long time it has been in body that women have responded to persecution, to the familial-conjugal enterprise of domestication, to the repeated attempts at castrating them. Those who have turned their tongues 10,000 times seven times before not speaking are either dead from it or more familiar with their tongues and their mouths than anyone else. Now, I-woman am going to blow

4. An allusion to two Greek myths: the story of Theseus, led out of the Minotaur's labyrinth by Ariadne's thread, and the story of the poet Orpheus, who won the release of his dead wife from the underworld on the condition (which he does not keep) that he not turn around and look at her as they ascended.

5. Speechless; an allusion to Freud's patient Dora, one of whose symptoms was aphonia (loss of voice); she is often considered an exemplary case of the misunderstood hysterical woman (Dora left Freud before the end of the analysis).

6. Michelangelo's statue of Moses (ca. 1515), which fascinated Freud, who here stands as the patriarchal Lawgiver himself.

7. The capitalization of the term, coined by the Swiss linguist FERDINAND DE SAUSSURE (1857–1913) to explain the functioning of signs (divided into *signifier*, the form a sign takes, and *signified*, the concept it represents), indicates that Cixous is here referring specifically to Lacan's designation of the phallus as privileged Signifier within the field of sexuality.

up the Law: an explosion henceforth possible and ineluctable; let it be done, right now, *in* language.

Let us not be trapped by an analysis still encumbered with the old automatisms. It's not to be feared that language conceals an invincible adversary, because it's the language of men and their grammar. We mustn't leave them a single place that's any more theirs alone than we are.

If woman has always functioned "within" the discourse of man, a signifier that has always referred back to the opposite signifier which annihilates its specific energy and diminishes or stifles its very different sounds, it is time for her to dislocate this "within," to explode it, turn it around, and seize it; to make it hers, containing it, taking it in her own mouth, biting that tongue with her very own teeth to invent for herself a language to get inside of. And you'll see with what ease she will spring forth from that "within"—the "within" where once she so drowsily crouched—to overflow at the lips she will cover the foam.

Nor is the point to appropriate their instruments, their concepts, their places, or to begrudge them their position of mastery. Just because there's a risk of identification doesn't mean that we'll succumb. Let's leave it to the worriers, to masculine anxiety and its obsession with how to dominate the way things work—knowing "how it works" in order to "make it work." For us the point is not to take possession in order to internalize or manipulate, but rather to dash through and to "fly."[8]

Flying is woman's gesture—flying in language and making it fly. We have all learned the art of flying and its numerous techniques; for centuries we've been able to possess anything only by flying; we've lived in flight, stealing away, finding, when desired, narrow passageways, hidden crossovers. It's no accident that *voler* has a double meaning, that it plays on each of them and thus throws off the agents of sense. It's no accident: women take after birds and robbers just as robbers take after women and birds. They (*illes*)[9] go by, fly the coop, take pleasure in jumbling the order of space, in disorienting it, in changing around the furniture, dislocating things and values, breaking them all up, emptying structures, and turning propriety upside down.

What woman hasn't flown/stolen? Who hasn't felt, dreamt, performed the gesture that jams sociality? Who hasn't crumbled, held up to ridicule, the bar of separation?[1] Who hasn't inscribed with her body the differential, punctured the system of couples and opposition? Who, by some act of transgression, hasn't overthrown successiveness, connection, the wall of circumfusion?

A feminine text cannot fail to be more than subversive. It is volcanic; as it is written it brings about an upheaval of the old property crust, carrier of masculine investments; there's no other way. There's no room for her if she's not a he. If she's a her-she, it's in order to smash everything, to shatter the framework of institutions, to blow up the law, to break up the "truth" with laughter.

8. Also, "to steal." Both meanings of the verb *voler* are played on, as the text itself explains in the following paragraph [translators' note].

9. *Illes* is a fusion of the masculine pronoun *ils*, which refers back to birds and robbers, with the feminine pronoun *elles*, which refers to women [translators' note].

1. An allusion to Lacan's revision of Saussure in "The Agency of the Letter in the Unconscious" (1957; see above): the "bar" between signifier and signified is identical with the structuring function of civilization.

For once she blazes *her* trail in the symbolic, she cannot fail to make of it the chaosmos[2] of the "personal"—in her pronouns, her nouns, and her clique of referents. And for good reason. There will have been the long history of gynocide.[3] This is known by the colonized peoples of yesterday, the workers, the nations, the species off whose backs the history of men has made its gold; those who have known the ignominy of persecution derive from it an obstinate future desire for grandeur; those who are locked up know better than their jailers the taste of free air. Thanks to their history, women today know (how to do and want) what men will be able to conceive of only much later. I say woman overturns the "personal," for if, by means of laws, lies, blackmail, and marriage, her right to herself has been extorted at the same time as her name, she has been able, through the very movement of mortal alienation, to see more closely the inanity of "propriety," the reductive stinginess of the masculine-conjugal subjective economy, which she doubly resists. On the one hand she has constituted herself necessarily as that "person" capable of losing a part of herself without losing her integrity. But secretly, silently, deep down inside, she grows and multiplies, for, on the other hand, she knows far more about living and about the relation between the economy of the drives and the management of the ego than any man. Unlike man, who holds so dearly to his title and his titles, his pouches of value, his cap, crown, and everything connected with his head, woman couldn't care less about the fear of decapitation (or castration), adventuring, without the masculine temerity, into anonymity, which she can merge with without annihilating herself: because she's a giver.

I shall have a great deal to say about the whole deceptive problematic of the gift.[4] Woman is obviously not that woman Nietzsche dreamed of who gives only in order to.[5] Who could ever think of the gift as a gift-that-takes? Who else but man, precisely the one who would like to take everything?

If there is a "propriety of woman," it is paradoxically her capacity to depropriate unselfishly: body without end, without appendage, without principal "parts." If she is a whole, it's a whole composed of parts that are wholes, not simple partial objects but a moving, limitlessly changing ensemble, a cosmos tirelessly traversed by Eros, an immense astral space not organized around any one sun that's any more of a star than the others.

This doesn't mean that she's an undifferentiated magma, but that she doesn't lord it over her body or her desire. Though masculine sexuality gravitates around the penis, engendering that centralized body (in political anatomy) under the dictatorship of its parts, woman does not bring about the same regionalization which serves the couple head/genitals and which is inscribed only within boundaries. Her libido is cosmic, just as her unconscious is worldwide. Her writing can only keep going, without ever inscribing

2. A coinage from James Joyce's *Finnegans Wake* (1939) blending *chaos* and *cosmos*.
3. The killing of women.
4. As explored by the French anthropologist Marcel Mauss in *Essay on the Gift* (1924). A key concept in Cixous's critique of ownership, property, and exchange, the gift functions as excess, as spending, and as abundance—which all become, for Cixous, women's attributes.
5. Reread Derrida's text, "Le Style de la femme," in *Nietzsche aujourd'hui* (Paris: Union Générale d'Editions, Coll. 10/18, [1973]), where the philosopher can be seen operating an *Aufhebung* of all philosophy in its systematic reducing of woman to the place of seduction: she appears as the one who is taken for; the bait in person, all veils unfurled, the one who doesn't give but who gives only in order to (take) [Cixous's note]. Translated in Jacques Derrida, *Spurs: Nietzsche's Styles* (1978). FRIEDRICH NIETZSCHE (1844–1900), German philosopher.

or discerning contours, daring to make these vertiginous crossings of the other(s) ephemeral and passionate sojourns in him, her, them, whom she inhabits long enough to look at from the point closest to their unconscious from the moment they awaken, to love them at the point closest to their drives; and then further, impregnated through and through with these brief, identificatory embraces, she goes and passes into infinity. She alone dares and wishes to know from within, where she, the outcast, has never ceased to hear the resonance of fore-language. She lets the other language speak—the language of 1,000 tongues which knows neither enclosure nor death. To life she refuses nothing. Her language does not contain, it carries; it does not hold back, it makes possible. When id[6] is ambiguously uttered—the wonder of being several—she doesn't defend herself against these unknown women whom she's surprised at becoming, but derives pleasure from this gift of alterability. I am spacious, singing flesh, on which is grafted no one knows which I, more or less human, but alive because of transformation.

Write! and your self-seeking text will know itself better than flesh and blood, rising, insurrectionary dough kneading itself, with sonorous, perfumed ingredients, a lively combination of flying colors, leaves, and rivers plunging into the sea we feed. "Ah, there's her sea," he will say as he holds out to me a basin full of water from the little phallic mother[7] from whom he's inseparable. But look, our seas are what we make of them, full of fish or not, opaque or transparent, red or black, high or smooth, narrow or bankless; and we are ourselves sea, sand, coral, seaweed, beaches, tides, swimmers, children, waves. . . . More or less wavily sea, earth, sky—what matter would rebuff us? We know how to speak them all.

Heterogeneous, yes. For her joyous benefit she is erogenous; she is the erotogeneity of the heterogeneous: airborne swimmer, in flight, she does not cling to herself; she is dispersible, prodigious, stunning, desirous and capable of others, of the other woman that she will be, of the other woman she isn't, of him of you.

Woman be unafraid of any other place, of any same, or any other. My eyes, my tongue, my ears, my nose, my skin, my mouth, my body-for-(the)-other—not that I long for it in order to fill up a hole, to provide against some defect of mine, or because, as fate would have it, I'm spurred on by feminine "jealousy"; not because I've been dragged into the whole chain of substitutions that brings that which is substituted back to its ultimate object. That sort of thing you would expect to come straight out of "Tom Thumb," out of the *Penisneid*[8] whispered to us by old grandmother ogresses, servants to their father-sons. If they believe, in order to muster up some self-importance, if they really need to believe that we're dying of desire, that we are this hole fringed with desire for their penis—that's their immemorial business. Undeniably (we verify it at our own expense—but also to our amusement), it's their

6. The first of three components of the infant's psyche (the others being the ego and superego), as theorized by Freud; it is governed by the most primitive unconscious urges for gratification, ruled by no laws of logic, and unconstrained by external reality.

7. The child's fantasy of what the mother must have been like before she was castrated, theorized by both Freud and Lacan.

8. Penis envy (German); Freud's name for the lifelong wish to have a penis, which he attributed to women. "Tom Thumb": the old nursery tale featuring the diminutive hero of the same name.

business to let us know they're getting a hard-on, so that we'll assure them (we the maternal mistresses of their little pocket signifier) that they still can, that it's still there—that men structure themselves only by being fitted with a feather.[9] In the child it's not the penis that the woman desires, it's not that famous bit of skin around which every man gravitates. Pregnancy cannot be traced back, except within the historical limits of the ancients, to some form of fate, to those mechanical substitutions brought about by the unconscious of some eternal "jealous woman"; not to penis envies; and not to narcissism or to some sort of homosexuality linked to the ever-present mother! Begetting a child doesn't mean that the woman or the man must fall ineluctably into patterns or must recharge the circuit of reproduction. If there's a risk there's not an inevitable trap: may women be spared the pressure, under the guise of consciousness-raising, of a supplement of interdictions. Either you want a kid or you don't—*that's your business.*[1] Let nobody threaten you; in satisfying your desire, let not the fear of becoming the accomplice to a sociality succeed the old-time fear of being "taken." And man, are you still going to bank on everyone's blindness and passivity, afraid lest the child make a father and, consequently, that in having a kid the woman land herself more than one bad deal by engendering all at once child—mother—father—family? No; it's up to you to break the old circuits. It will be up to man and woman to render obsolete the former relationship and all its consequences, to consider the launching of a brand-new subject, alive, with defamilialization. Let us demater-paternalize rather than deny woman, in an effort to avoid the co-optation of procreation, a thrilling era of the body. Let us defetishize. Let's get away from the dialectic which has it that the only good father is a dead one, or that the child is the death of his parents. The child is the other, but the other without violence, bypassing loss, struggle. We're fed up with the reuniting of bonds forever to be severed, with the litany of castration that's handed down and genealogized. We won't advance backward anymore; we're not going to repress something so simple as the desire for life. Oral drive, anal drive, vocal drive—all these drives are our strengths, and among them is the gestation drive—just like the desire to write: a desire to live self from within, a desire for the swollen belly, for language, for blood. We are not going to refuse, if it should happen to strike our fancy, the unsurpassed pleasures of pregnancy which have actually been always exaggerated or conjured away—or cursed—in the classic texts. For if there's one thing that's been repressed here's just the place to find it: in the taboo of the pregnant woman. This says a lot about the power she seems invested with at the time, because it has always been suspected, that, when pregnant, the woman not only doubles her market value, but—what's more important—takes on intrinsic value as a woman in her own eyes and, undeniably, acquires body and sex.

There are thousands of ways of living one's pregnancy; to have or not to have with that still invisible other a relationship of another intensity. And if you don't have that particular yearning, it doesn't mean that you're in any way lacking. Each body distributes in its own special way, without model or

9. In the French *s'empenner*, "to sprout feathers": a reference to PLATO's description of the soul's return to its original perfection by regrowing its lost wings; see *Phaedrus* (ca. 370 B.C.E.), 246a–252a.

1. Abortion was legalized in France in 1974, a year before this essay was published.

norm, the nonfinite and changing totality of its desires. Decide for yourself on your position in the arena of contradictions, where pleasure and reality embrace. Bring the other to life. Women know how to live detachment; giving birth is neither losing nor increasing. It's adding to life an other. Am I dreaming? Am I mis-recognizing? You, the defenders of "theory," the sacrosanct yes-men of Concept, enthroners of the phallus (but not of the penis):

Once more you'll say that all this smacks of "idealism," or what's worse, you'll splutter that I'm a "mystic."

And what about the libido? Haven't I read the "Signification of the Phallus"?[2] And what about separation, what about that bit of self for which, to be born, you undergo an ablation—an ablation, so they say, to be forever commemorated by your desire?

Besides, isn't it evident that the penis gets around in my texts, that I give it a place and appeal? Of course I do. I want all. I want all of me with all of him. Why should I deprive myself of a part of us? I want all of us. Woman of course has a desire for a "loving desire" and not a jealous one. But not because she is gelded; not because she's deprived and needs to be filled out, like some wounded person who wants to console herself or seek vengeance: I don't want a penis to decorate my body with. But I do desire the other for the other,[3] whole and entire, male or female; because living means wanting everything that is, everything that lives, and wanting it alive. Castration? Let others toy with it. What's a desire originating from a lack? A pretty meager desire.

The woman who still allows herself to be threatened by the big dick, who's still impressed by the commotion of the phallic stance, who still leads a loyal master to the beat of the drum: that's the woman of yesterday. They still exist, easy and numerous victims of the oldest of farces: either they're cast in the original silent version in which, as titanesses lying under the mountains they make with their quivering, they never see erected that theoretic monument to the golden phallus looming, in the old manner, over their bodies. Or, coming today out of their *infans*[4] period and into the second, "enlightened" version of their virtuous debasement, they see themselves suddenly assaulted by the builders of the analytic empire and, as soon as they've begun to formulate the new desire, naked, nameless, so happy at making an appearance, they're taken in their bath by the new old men, and then, whoops! Luring them with flashy signifiers, the demon of interpretation—oblique, decked out in modernity—sells them the same old handcuffs, baubles, and chains. Which castration do you prefer? Whose degrading do you like better, the father's or the mother's? Oh, what pwetty eyes, you pwetty little girl. Here, buy my glasses and you'll see the Truth-Me-Myself[5] tell you everything you should know. Put them on your nose and take a fetishist's look (you are me, the other analyst—that's what I'm telling you) at your body and the body of the other. You see? No? Wait, you'll have everything explained to you, and you'll know at last which sort of neurosis you're related to. Hold still, we're going to do your portrait, so that you can begin looking like it right away.

2. A 1958 essay by Jacques Lacan (see above).
3. The non-me, the non-self. In *The Second Sex* (1949), SIMONE DE BEAUVOIR was the first to analyze how society positions woman as man's other.
4. Incapable of speech (Latin). Lacan uses the word to describe the child at the mirror stage.
5. A reference to Lacan, who had written in his essay "The Freudian Thing" (1955), "Moi, la vérité, je parle" (I, the Truth, speak). "My glasses" alludes to the sinister eyeglass salesman in Hoffmann's "Sandman" (1816) whom Freud analyzes in "The 'Uncanny.'"

Yes, the naives to the first and second degree are still legion. If the New Women, arriving now, dare to create outside the theoretical, they're called in by the cops of the signifier, fingerprinted, remonstrated, and brought into the line of order that they are supposed to know; assigned by force of trickery to a precise place in the chain that's always formed for the benefit of a privileged signifier. We are pieced back to the string which leads back, if not to the Name-of-the-Father, then, for a new twist, to the place of the phallic-mother.[6]

Beware, my friend, of the signifier that would take you back to the authority of a signified! Beware of diagnoses that would reduce your generative powers. "Common" nouns are also proper nouns that disparage your singularity by classifying it into species. Break out of the circles; don't remain within the psychoanalytic closure. Take a look around, then cut through!

And if we are legion, it's because the war of liberation has only made as yet a tiny breakthrough. But women are thronging to it. I've seen them, those who will be neither dupe nor domestic, those who will not fear the risk of being a woman; will not fear any risk, any desire, any space still unexplored in themselves, among themselves and others or anywhere else. They do not fetishize, they do not deny, they do not hate. They observe, they approach, they try to see the other woman, the child, the lover—not to strengthen their own narcissism or verify the solidity or weakness of the master, but to make love better, to invent.

Other love.—In the beginning are our differences. The new love dares for the other, wants the other, makes dizzying, precipitous flights between knowledge and invention. The woman arriving over and over again does not stand still; she's everywhere, she exchanges, she is the desire-that-gives. (Not enclosed in the paradox of the gift that takes nor under the illusion of unitary fusion. We're past that.) She comes in, comes-in-between herself me and you, between the other me where one is always infinitely more than one and more than me, without the fear of ever reaching a limit; she thrills in our becoming. And we'll keep on becoming! She cuts through defensive loves, motherages, and devourations: beyond selfish narcissism, in the moving, open, transitional space, she runs her risks. Beyond the struggle-to-the-death that's been removed to the bed, beyond the love-battle that claims to represent exchange, she scorns at an Eros dynamic that would be fed by hatred. Hatred: a heritage, again, a remainder, a duping subservience to the phallus. To love, to watch-think-seek the other in the other, to despecularize, to unhoard. Does this seem difficult? It's not impossible, and this is what nourishes life—a love that has no commerce with the apprehensive desire that provides against the lack and stultifies the strange; a love that rejoices in the exchange that multiplies. Wherever history still unfolds as the history of death, she does not tread. Opposition, hierarchizing exchange, the struggle for mastery which can end only in at least one death (one master—one slave, or two nonmasters ≠ two dead)[7]—all that comes from a period in time governed by phallocentric values. The fact that this period extends into the present doesn't

6. In his seminars of the 1970s, Lacan had attempted to demonstrate the relations among the Imaginary, the Symbolic, and the Real by means of knots made of string. Name-of-the-Father: the Lacanian term for the function of the father in the Symbolic.

7. In the Master-Slave dialectic described by Hegel in *Phenomenology of Spirit* (1807; see above), the master is the one who is willing to fight to the death for freedom; the slave chooses life.

prevent woman from starting the history of life somewhere else. Elsewhere, she gives. She doesn't "know" what she's giving, she doesn't measure it; she gives, though, neither a counterfeit impression nor something she hasn't got. She gives more, with no assurance that she'll get back even some unexpected profit from what she puts out. She gives that there may be life, thought, transformation. This is an "economy" that can no longer be put in economic terms. Wherever she loves, all the old concepts of management are left behind. At the end of a more or less conscious computation, she finds not her sum but her differences. I am for you what you want me to be at the moment you look at me in a way you've never seen me before: at every instant. When I write, it's everything that we don't know we can be that is written out of me, without exclusions, without stipulation, and everything we will be calls us to the unflagging, intoxicating, unappeasable search for love. In one another we will never be lacking.

1975, 1976

GERALD GRAFF
b. 1937

In "Taking Cover in Coverage" (1986), Gerald Graff turns a theoretical eye on the institutional structures within English departments. Why divide literature into separate fields? How do subspecialties affect the way professors work and students learn? Worried, as he declares in *Literature against Itself: Literary Ideas in Modern Society* (1979), that academic approaches to literature have undermined "the power of language to connect us with the world," Graff recommends a novel and subsequently influential method for bringing coherence to what he sees as an increasingly disjointed curriculum, a method he calls "teaching the conflicts."

Born in Chicago, Graff received his B.A. from the University of Chicago in 1959. He did graduate work at Stanford University, where he studied with the New Critic Yvor Winters and the New York Intellectual Irving Howe, receiving his Ph.D. in 1963. He taught at the University of New Mexico from 1963 to 1966, then returned to Illinois to teach at Northwestern University (1966–91) and at the University of Chicago (1991–98). In 1999 he took a deanship at the University of Illinois at Chicago to develop undergraduate curricula and coordinate teacher education programs, retiring in 2016. Among other honors, he served as president of the Modern Language Association in 2008.

In his writing, Graff is an iconoclast. While he has been a prominent participant in debates on contemporary theory, he does not readily fit into any definable camp. He is also an unapologetic polemicist, persistently arguing against literary criticism's disconnection from society. In his early work, he attacked the New Critical axiom that "a poem, as a poem, does not say anything about the world." In his provocative *Literature against Itself*, Graff turned his sights on a range of contemporary theories and claimed that their excessive focus on language fostered the ineffectuality of literary intellectuals. Overall, Graff shows a consistent concern with the social dimensions of intellectual work, without advocating a particular approach and avoiding orthodoxy.

"Taking Cover in Coverage" looks at the ways in which the university institutionally and historically has shaped intellectual work. Graff begins with a defense of theory. His argument is tacitly directed at antitheorists, ranging from traditionalists who believe, in the phrase of the New Critic René Wellek, that contemporary theory is "destroying literary studies" to neopragmatists such as STANLEY FISH, who claims that theory has no consequences. Despite Graff's earlier rough handling of theory, he here sees it as enriching our thought and thus advocates putting it at the center of the curriculum. Although Graff had been an opponent of deconstruction, his defense of theory parallels that in PAUL DE MAN's "Resistance to Theory" (1982), which similarly responds to antitheorists and argues for the importance of theory. However, Graff takes to task much contemporary theory for failing to reflect on its own institutional location, willing to "apply theory within the existing structure but . . . fail[ing] to make a theoretical examination of the structure itself."

Moving to his main topic, Graff gives thumbnail sketches of the history of U.S. English departments (born in the late nineteenth and early twentieth centuries) and the "field coverage" model on which they rely. Specialized fields both engender disconnections and insularities that thwart intellectual community and encourage efficiency, innovation, and autonomy—the benefits that led to the model's success. While institutional structures in English departments have given faculty a relative degree of freedom to pursue new topics (including contemporary theory), they have also essentially quarantined individual scholars in their particular fields; as a result, there is no common ground for discussion, conflicts are suppressed, the curriculum is incoherent, and students lose out. Graff's recommendation to faculty, which has since become something of a slogan, is to "teach the conflicts" and make such divisions the organizing basis of curriculum.

Graff fleshed out his argument about English departments and field coverage in an important book, *Professing Literature: An Institutional History* (1987; 20th anniv. ed., 2007), which traces the discipline's history from the nineteenth century to the 1980s. He sees contemporary conflicts over theory as part of a historical process often alternating between traditionalism and new approaches. In the 1990s Graff focused increasingly on pedagogy. He has responded to public debates over the canon, theory, and "political correctness" by extolling their potential as a resource for teaching. Continuing his argument from "Taking Cover in Coverage," particularly in his popular *Beyond the Culture Wars: How Teaching the Conflicts Can Revitalize Higher Education* (1992), Graff advocates foregrounding critical controversies in the classroom rather than hiding them from students. Citing his own experience as a student, he admits that class discussions of literature bored him until he discovered that literature was something to argue over.

Graff's consistent attention to teaching is unusual among contemporary theorists. It culminated in his coauthoring a textbook, *"They Say/I Say": The Moves That Matter in Academic Writing* (3d ed., 2016), for basic writing classes. His prose style also sets his work apart. Graff argues for theory in plain, colloquial language (such as "literature departments should stop kidding themselves," in our selection) rarely seen in contemporary theory. His book *Clueless in Academe: How Schooling Obscures the Life of the Mind* (2003) emphasizes not conflict but making criticism more comprehensible.

Although Graff's conflictual model has been widely accepted as a productive teaching method and as a useful account of theoretical change, several critics have noted its limitations. Some criticize Graff's nostalgia for a vibrant literary culture outside the university, even as he supplies prescriptions that apply only to the academy. Others note the reductiveness of seeing all change in terms of a repeated conflict between tradition and new movements. Some feminists call for cooperation rather than confrontation and see Graff's embrace of conflict as reflecting a masculinist bias—perhaps making the discipline akin to a contact sport. From a postcolonial perspective, critics like NGUGI WĂ THIONG'O argue that "English" departments propagate imperialism, and therefore call for their abolition. Graff mentions that the division of departments by language is arbitrary, but he does not continue this analysis to critique the nationalistic origins and purposes of English departments. Nevertheless, Graff's history of English departments is a pathbreaking investigation showing how our institutions shape literary thought and proposing how they might be changed.

"Taking Cover in Coverage" Keywords: The Canon/Tradition, Defense of Criticism, Institutional Studies, Rhetoric

Taking Cover in Coverage

In addressing the topic "The Value of Theory in English Studies,"[1] I want to say at the outset that the antagonism usually presumed to exist between literary theory and humanistic tradition has been exaggerated. It is perfectly possible to defend the infusion of theory into the curriculum on traditional grounds, namely, that students need theoretical frameworks in order to conceptualize, and talk about, literature. Until recently, in fact, it was traditionalists like Irving Babbitt and Norman Foerster[2] who called for more "theory," in opposition to the disconnected empiricism of positivist literary history and formalist explication, where the faith seemed to be that "the facts, once in, would of themselves mean something."[3] Most scholars "have left virtually uninspected the theory upon which their practice rests" or have proceeded "as if that theory were an absolute good for all time."[4] While a great deal of current theory does radically attack the premises and values of traditional literary humanism, that attack revives the kinds of questions about literature and its cultural functions that used to concern traditional humanistic critics.

The real enemy of tradition has been the established form of literary study, which has neglected traditional theoretical questions about the ends and social functions of literature and criticism. There is something strange about the belief that we are being traditional when we isolate literary works from their contexts and explicate them in a vacuum or with a modicum of background information. Matthew Arnold[5] would have recognized little traditional or humanistic in these established forms of pedagogy. Obviously I am not saying that recent literary theory is nothing more than the application of Arnoldian culture by other means. What I am saying is that recent theory has reawakened some of the large questions that Arnold raised, while rejecting the Arnoldian answers as no longer sufficient.

In fact, it was the breakdown of agreement on the Arnoldian answers that inspired the current popularity of theory and ensures, I think, that this interest will not be a passing fad. By one definition that seems to me valid, "literary theory" is simply the kind of discourse that is generated when pre-

1. The essay was originally presented at a 1986 seminar run by the Association of Departments of English on this topic.
2. Literary critics and Harvard University professors who espoused the humanistic value of studying literature: Foerster (1887–1972) was a protégé of Babbitt's (1865–1933).
3. Norman Foerster, "The Study of Letters," in *Literary Scholarship: Its Aims and Methods*, by Norman Foerster et al. (Chapel Hill: University of North Carolina Press, 1941), 11–12 [Graff's note].
4. Norman Foerster et al., introduction, in ibid., v [Graff's note].
5. Leading Victorian poet and critic (1822–1888; see above).

suppositions that were once tacitly shared about literature, criticism, and culture become open to question. Theory is what breaks out when agreement about such terms as *text, reading, history, interpretation, tradition*, and *literature* can no longer be taken for granted, so that their meanings have to be formulated and debated. Admittedly, the term *theory* is used here in a very broad sense, denoting an examination of legitimating presuppositions, beliefs, and ideologies. By this definition, even antitheorists like Arnold and F. R. Leavis[6] qualify as theorists, having theorized about the premises of literature and culture and the place of literature and culture in modern societies. And in this sense all teachers of literature operate on theories, whether they choose to examine these theories or not.

Clearly, we need to reserve another sense of *theory* to denote the technical, abstruse, and systematic speculation typical of recent Continental thought. But here is another misconception—that theory is necessarily obscure, technical and abstruse, and therefore too advanced or esoteric for the average college or high school student of literature. This belief fails to recognize that all teaching involves popularization and that even the most difficult current theories are not intrinsically more resistant to popularization than the New Criticism, which had its own abstruse conceptual origins in Kant, Coleridge, and Croce.[7]

It is the average-to-poor student who suffers most from the established curriculum's poverty of theory, for such a student lacks command of the conceptual contexts that make it possible to integrate perceptions and generalize from them. All the close concentration in the world on the particularities of literary texts will not help a student make sense of these particularities without the categories that give them meaning.

Current antitheorists have things exactly backward when they oppose theory to tradition and to close literary analysis and demand that we minister to the ills of literary studies by desisting from theoretical chatter and getting back to teaching literature itself. It was the isolation of "literature itself" in a conceptual vacuum that stranded students without a context for talking about literature and that still forces many of them to resort to *Cliffs Notes* and other such cribs. It is easy to disdain these cribs, but marketing pressures have actually forced their producers to think through the problems facing the average literature student more realistically than have many department curricular planners. *Cliffs Notes* supply students with the generalized things to say about literary works that the literature program takes for granted they will somehow get on their own.

The irony of the current cry of "back to literature itself" is that it was the exclusive concentration on literature itself that helped create a situation in which the *Cliffs Notes* on given works of literature are more readily available in campus bookstores than are the works themselves. Perhaps I am naive to suggest that a more theoretically contextualized curriculum would cause such

6. Influential English literary critic (1895–1978; see above), who extolled "the great tradition."

7. Three important and sometimes abstruse writers on aesthetics: IMMANUEL KANT (1724–1804), a German philosopher; SAMUEL TAYLOR COLERIDGE (1772–1834), a British Romantic poet and theorist; and Benedetto Croce (1866–1952), an Italian philosopher and literary critic. The New Criticism: an approach (championed by CLEANTH BROOKS, WILLIAM K. WIMSATT JR., and others) that emphasizes close reading of the text considered as an autonomous whole; it has greatly influenced teaching from the mid-20th century onward.

cribs to wither away. I can certainly imagine a *Cliffs Notes* on deconstruction, supplementing the ones on Keats and Dickens.[8] But for the moment I think we should view this eventuality as a possibility to be recognized and avoided rather than as an inevitability.

These opening reflections will probably persuade only those who agree with them. My purpose here, however, is not to make a case for theory in the literature program but to point up some difficulties that arise once we have decided that such a goal is desirable. In addressing the pedagogical uses of recent literary theory, we tend to treat the issue as if it were primarily a matter of figuring out how to integrate this theory into individual classrooms. We form conference "workshops," which concentrate on technical questions like how to use reader-response criticism to teach *Hamlet*, or poststructuralist theory to teach the romantic lyric, or feminist critiques of the established canon to restructure the nineteenth-century-novel course. Such reforms can be useful and necessary, but if we do not go beyond them we will limit theory to its instrumental uses, making it into a means of sprucing up ritualized procedures of explication. We will apply theory within the existing structure but will fail to make a theoretical examination of the structure itself.

I want to suggest that one of the first things we need to do with literary theory is to train it on the literature department itself, particularly on the way that the department and other departments and the university are organized. Insofar as a literature department represents a certain organization of literature, it is itself a kind of theory, though it has been largely an incoherent theory, and this incoherence in fact has reinforced the impression that the department has no theory.

In deciding to call ourselves departments of English, French, and German—rather than of literature, cultural studies, or something else—and in subdividing these national units into periods and genres, we have already made significant theoretical choices. But we do not see these choices as choices, much less as theoretical ones, because the categories that mark them—English, eighteenth century, poetry, novel—operate as administrative conveniences and eventually as facts of nature that we can take for granted. We need to recognize that the way we organize and departmentalize literature is not only a crucial theoretical choice but one that largely determines our professional activity and the way students and the laity see it or fail to see it.

To make this statement is not to agree with those who think that the departmentalization of literature itself was a kind of original sin and who look back nostalgically to the days before the creative imagination was bureaucratized. Anyone seriously committed to the idea of democratic mass education has to acknowledge the obvious necessity for some form of bureaucratic departmental organization and the specialized division of labor that that entails. But the form that organization takes is neither self-evident nor inevitable, and it will have a lot to do with considerations of theory.

I use the term *field coverage* as a convenient description of the model of organization that has governed literature departments since the dawn of the modern university, in the last two decades of the nineteenth century. According to the field-coverage model, a department considers itself adequately

8. Charles Dickens (1812–1870), Victorian novelist. John Keats (1795–1821), English Romantic poet.

staffed when it has acquired the personnel to "cover" an adequate number of designated fields of literature, and it assumes that the core of the curriculum will consist of the student's coverage of some portion of those fields. The field-coverage model arose as an adaptation to the modern university's ideal of research specialization, for dividing the territory of literature into fields supervised by specialists imitated the organizational form that had made the sciences efficient in producing advanced research. But the field-coverage principle had a humanistic justification as well, the argument that a student who covered the fields represented by the average department would get a reasonably balanced exposure to the literary-humanistic tradition.

It was the operational advantages, however, that made the field-coverage model irresistible, especially in a newly expanding university where short-term expediency rarely afforded leisure for discussion of first principles and where first principles in any case were becoming increasingly open to dispute. One of the most conspicuous operational advantages was the way field coverage made the department virtually self-regulating. By assigning instructors the roles predetermined by their literary fields, the model created a system in which the job of instruction could proceed as if on automatic pilot, with no need for instructors to confer with their peers or superiors. Assuming that individual instructors had been competently trained—and by about 1900 or so the American system of graduate study had matured sufficiently to see to that—they could be left on their own to carry out their teaching and research jobs without elaborate supervision and management.

A second advantage of the field-coverage model was that it made the department immensely flexible to innovation. By making individuals functionally independent of one another in carrying out their tasks, the model enabled the department to assimilate new subjects, ideas, and methodologies without risking the conflicts that would otherwise have had to be debated and worked through. It thus allowed the modern university to overcome the chronic stagnation that had beset the old nineteenth-century college, where new ideas that challenged the established Christian orthodoxy were usually excluded or suppressed. The coverage model solved the problem of how to make the university open to innovation and diverse viewpoints without incurring paralyzing conflicts.

Unfortunately, these advantages came at a severe cost that we have been paying ever since. The same arrangements that allowed instructors to do their jobs efficiently and independently also relieved them of the need to discuss and reflect on the values and implications of their practices. This form of organization left literature departments without any need to discuss matters of fundamental direction either with their own members or with members of other departments, and it is a rule of bureaucratic organizations that whatever these organizations are not structurally required to do they will tend not to do. Moral exhortation unaccompanied by structural change will be largely wasted. The department was open to innovation as the college had not been before, but under circumstances that were almost as effective in muffling the confrontations provoked by innovation as the old system of repressive control had been. Previously there had been little open debate over first principles because dissenters had been excluded. Now dissenters were invited in, but the departmental structure kept them too isolated from their colleagues for open debate to take place.

Vigorous controversy did arise, but usually only behind the scenes of education, in specialized journals, department meetings, or private gossip—all places where students derived little benefit from it, usually knew nothing of its existence, and certainly did not participate in it. Instructors were freer than they had been from administrative tyranny, but at the sacrifice of certain possibilities of intellectual community.

To put it another way, the field-coverage model solved the problem of theory. Departmental organization took the place of theory, for the presence of an ordered array of fields, fully staffed, made it unnecessary for anyone to have a theory about what the department should do to permit the work of teaching and research to go on. The theoretical choices had already been taken care of in the grid of periods, genres, and other catalog rubrics, which embodied a clear and seemingly uncontroversial conceptualization of what the department was about. With literature courses ranged in periods and genres, instructors did not need to ask what "period" or "genre" meant or what justified the established demarcations. The connections and contrasts between periods and genres, so important for understanding these categories, fell between the cracks, as did other large issues in the university, such as the relation between the sciences and the humanities, which was the responsibility of neither the sciences nor the humanities.

Latent conflicts of method and ideology that had divided the faculty from the outset and the cultural conflicts that these often exemplified did not have to be confronted and taught. Fundamental disagreements over the study of literature were embodied, for example, in the conflict between the research "scholar," who adhered to a positivistic methodology, and the generalist man or woman of letters, who scorned this methodology, and, later, in the conflict between both these types and the hyperanalytical New Critic. But while the department enacted these conflicts, it did not explicitly foreground and engage them. As long as scholars, generalists, and critics covered their turfs within self-enclosed classrooms, the average student did not need to be aware of the clashes of principle, much less use them as a larger context for literary study.

This explanation accounts for the otherwise inexplicable persistence of the fiction of shared humanistic values and purposes during a period when conflicts in method and ideology were becoming progressively more frequent and antagonistic. Since the official premise that humanistic values governed the department did not have to be theorized or subjected to periodical review and discussion, there was no particular reason to acknowledge that the premise was wearing increasingly thin. Not only did the structure provide no necessary occasion for questioning the content of that humanism which, according to the catalog, theoretically held the diverse and conflicting viewpoints of departments together, but the illusion could be maintained that nobody even had a theory.

And of course it was true that the department did not have *a* theory, for it harbored many theories without any clear way to integrate them. Here we arrive at the central problem: How does a department institutionalize theory when there is no agreement on what the theory is to be? The question becomes unanswerable, however, only if it is assumed that a department must achieve theoretical *consensus* before it can achieve theoretical coherence.

The perennial assumption seems to have been that professional and cultural conflicts have to be *resolved* before they can be presented to the students: students, apparently, must be exposed only to the results of the conflicts dividing their teachers, not to the process of conflict itself, which presumably would confuse or demoralize them. Surely one reason why we tend, as I noted earlier, to reduce pedagogical questions to questions about workshop techniques for individual courses is that we doubt the possibility of agreement on larger collective goals. Our doubts are well founded in experience, but why need we assume that we have to agree in order to integrate our activities? Must we have consensus to have coherence?

The unfortunate thing is not that our conflicts of method and ideology have often proved unresolvable but that we have been able to exploit so little of the potential educational value of our unresolved conflicts. Part of the reason stems from the literary mind's temperamental resistance to airing differences; the old-fashioned version of this attitude held that open debate is unseemly, while the more up-to-date version holds that there are no privileged metalanguages, or no fact-of-the-matter outside interpretations, or no "decidable" answers to questions, so that there is nothing to argue about anyway. But even if these sources of resistance to debate were to disappear, there would remain a problem of structure. Our structure prevents exemplary differences of method, ideology, and value from emerging into view even when we want them to.

The literature curriculum mirrors and reproduces the evasion of conflict characteristic of the departmental structure. Hypothetically, the curriculum expresses a unified humanistic tradition, yet anyone who looks at it can see that in every era down to the present it has never expressed a unity of humanistic values but always a set of political trade-offs and compromises among competing professional factions. We need not enter into the now disputed question of whether the curriculum can or should be determined by any more lofty principle than political trade-offs, for again this is precisely the type of theoretical and cultural question that does not have to be resolved in order to play an effective part in education. If the curriculum is going to continue to express political trade-offs, as it seems likely to do unless one faction in the current disciplinary conflict can wholly liquidate its opposition, then why not bring students in on whatever may be instructive in the conflict of political principles involved?

Instead of confronting such conflicts and building them into the curriculum, however, the department (and the university at large) has always responded to pressures by adding new subjects and keeping them safely sealed off from one another. This practice can be justified educationally only on the increasingly hollow pretense that exposure to an aggregate of teachers, periods, genres, methods, and points of view figures to come together in the student's mind as a coherent humanistic experience. The tacit faith is that students will make sense of the aggregate even if their instructors cannot. The surprising thing is that some students manage to do just that, but most do not. Recognition of this failure stimulates further curricular innovation, which in turn, however, is assimilated to the cycle of accretion and marginalization. So we beat on, boats against the current,[9] etc., etc.

9. The last sentence of *The Great Gatsby* (1925), by F. Scott Fitzgerald (it ends, "borne back ceaselessly into the past").

Over the hundred-year span of our institutional history we have had a succession of methodological models, each with a corresponding pedagogy, from linguistic philology to positivist literary history to New Critical explication, all of which now remain as geological strata overlaid by the new theories and methodologies. Each of these revisions has marked a paradigm shift in which the conception of what counts as "literature," "scholarship," and "criticism" altered radically. Yet, as I attempt to show in a forthcoming institutional history of academic literary studies in the United States,[1] the one constant through all this change has been the field-coverage model. The contents have been radically reshuffled, but the envelope has remained the same, and with it the method of assimilating innovation. Arguably the changes represent considerable progress in critical sophistication and cultural range, but if I am correct the benefits for the average student have been less than they might have been.

Nor is it just the students who have paid a price under the field-coverage system, it is the faculty as well. The principles of selection for amassing a literature faculty have systematically screened out intellectual commonality and programmed professional loneliness. A self-destructive principle is built into the mighty effort departments make to achieve a balanced spread of interests. If the interests of candidate X overlap those of faculty member Y, their shared ground is an argument for not hiring X—"We already have Y who does that." The calculus of needs determining appointment priorities thus tends to preselect exactly those instructors who have the least basis for talking to one another. In compensation the department gets a salutary diversity, but the potential benefits of diversity are not really exploited. Nor is the problem merely abstract: the recent proliferation of humanities conferences and symposia suggests that these gatherings have become substitutes for the kind of general discussion that does not take place at home.

The moral is that if the introduction of theory is to make a real difference at the average student's level, we must find some way to modify the field-coverage model, if not to scrap it entirely. Otherwise, theory will be institutionalized as yet another field, equivalent to literary periods and genres—which is to say, it will become one more option that can safely be ignored. We will lose theory's potential for drawing the disconnected parts of the literature curriculum into relation and providing students with the needed contexts. So, I would argue, the real threat that theory faces today comes not from its outright opponents, some of whom are at least willing to argue with it, but from those who are perfectly willing to grant theory an honored place in the scheme of departmental coverage so that they can then forget about it.

This pattern seems to be establishing itself now, as departments clamor to hire theorists to get the new field covered, after which they sit back and assume that the relation of theory to the interests of the rest of the department will take care of itself. In practice, this policy passes the buck to the students, leaving them to figure out how theory courses correlate with the others. And of course as long as theory is conceived as a special field, the rest of the department can go on thinking that its work has no connection with theory.

1. *Professing Literature: An Institutional History* (Chicago: University of Chicago Press, 1987).

Offering students doses of theory in individual courses without helping them make the requisite connections and relations between courses will tend to produce a confused response, which antitheorists will quickly take as proof that theory is inherently over the head of the average student. For the average student to profit from theory, especially from recent theory, the courses that incorporate it must be not only linked with other courses, both theoretical and untheoretical, but also positioned to operate as a central means of correlation and contextualization.

In other words, literature departments should stop kidding themselves. They should stop pretending that, as long as individual courses are reasonably well conceived and well taught, the aggregate can be counted on to take care of itself. If they are serious about incorporating theory, they should not let it remain an option but should make it central to all their activities, not by putting theory specialists in charge but by recognizing that all their members are theorists.

To put it another way, introducing more theory will only compound our problems unless we rethink the assumption that the essential unit of all teaching has to be the single, self-sufficient course that the students correlate with other courses on their own. We can fail just as badly teaching a new canon in a theoretical way as we have failed in teaching an old canon in a nontheoretical way. Unless literature teachers change their means of connecting institutionally with one another, I am afraid that even the most radical theories and canon revisions will not significantly affect the way most students take in what is put before them.

To close, then, I offer a few schematic suggestions:

1. In relation to other courses in the department, theory courses should be central, not peripheral; their function should be to contextualize and pull together the students' work in other courses (outside as well as inside the literature department). Wherever possible, therefore, they should be required courses rather than electives.
2. In taking stock of its strengths, a department should evaluate not just how well it is covering standard fields and approaches but also what potential conflicts of ideological and methodological perspectives it harbors; it should then ask itself what curricular arrangements might exploit these conflicts. There need be no single way of doing this—but one idea (suggested by Brook Thomas[2]) is to couple courses to bring out conceptual relations and contrasts—between, say, views of literature in earlier and modern literary periods or between competing and complementary methodologies of interpretation.
3. A department harboring a conflict between theorists and antitheorists should look for ways to build this conflict into its courses, so that students can situate themselves in relation to the controversy and eventually participate in it. The department should also look for ways such disputes can be used to complicate and challenge period and genre distinctions without necessarily eliminating them.
4. A department should consider the unit of teaching to be the issue or context, not the isolated text; texts to be taught should be chosen not

2. American New Historicist critic (b. 1947).

only for their intrinsic value but for their usefulness in illustrating exemplary problems and issues.
5. As a means of accomplishing goal 4 on a structural scale, the university should subsume literary studies under cultural studies and cultural history, conceived not as a privileged approach but as a framework that encourages ideological dialectic while retaining enough chronological structure to keep focus and continuity from being lost.

The point is that theory is not only a field to be covered, though it is that at one level. It is something that all teachers of literature and all readers practice and that all have a stake in. The worst thing we could do would be to institutionalize theory in a compartmentalized way that would keep theorists and antitheorists from having to hear what they are saying about each other—and would keep students from observing and joining in the battle.

1986

STANLEY E. FISH
b. 1938

Stanley Fish has been the agent provocateur of contemporary American literary theory. The leading critic of John Milton of his generation, the self-proclaimed inventor of reader-response theory, the progenitor of antifoundationalism and neopragmatism in literary studies, a pioneer of critical legal studies, and a spirited defender of the humanities amid public attacks over political correctness, Fish is perhaps best known for the brio of his intellectual style, which he practices with the energy of a sport. Debunking standard notions of interpretation, Fish's essay "How to Recognize a Poem When You See One" (1980) argues for his seminal concept, "interpretive communities," which radically revises interpretive theory by locating meaning not in texts but in readers, and not in individual response but in the protocols of communities.

Fish was born in Providence, Rhode Island, where his father was a plumbing contractor. He attended the University of Pennsylvania, receiving his B.A. in 1959, and went on to do graduate work at Yale University, then the bastion of the American New Critics (such as CLEANTH BROOKS and WILLIAM K. WIMSATT JR.), quickly completing an M.A. and Ph.D., in 1960 and 1962. He taught at the University of California at Berkeley from 1962 to 1974 and published two books before he was thirty, most notably a touchstone of Milton criticism, *Surprised by Sin: The Reader in "Paradise Lost"* (1967; 2d ed., 1999). While at Berkeley, he also wrote *Self-Consuming Artifacts: The Experience of Seventeenth-Century Literature* (1972), which was nominated for a National Book Award. From 1974 to 1985 he was Kenan Professor of English at Johns Hopkins University, publishing another pioneering reader-response work, *Is There a Text in This Class? The Authority of Interpretive Communities* (1980), which includes our selection. Concerned with interpretation and its consequences, at Johns Hopkins he also began to teach in the law school, pursuing an interest in legal theory that became more central to his work through the next two decades.

In 1985 Fish moved to Duke University as Arts and Sciences Distinguished Professor of English and Law and as chair of the English department. As chair, he was instrumental in building the most famous—if sometimes controversial—department of its time. In 1998 he took a position as dean of Arts and Sciences at the University of Illinois at Chicago, where he was again an institutional catalyst, helping to build its programs and reputation. In part because he was both an administrator and a prominent critic, through this latter part of his career Fish became a public spokesperson for the humanities, writing opinion pieces in the *New York Times* and elsewhere, and occasionally appearing on television. Meanwhile he also published several notable books on theory, professionalism, law, and politics. In 2005 he moved to Florida International University as Davidson-Kahn Distinguished University Professor of Humanities and Professor of Law, retiring in 2013.

A formative factor of Fish's work was his response to the New Criticism. Like other theorists who were trained under its auspices, he rebelled against its belief in the autonomy of the text and its sole focus on literary form and language. HAROLD BLOOM, for instance, asserted the centrality of the author and the author's "anxiety of influence" in the face of the New Critical prohibition of the "intentional fallacy"; STEPHEN GREENBLATT, who like Fish and Bloom received his graduate training at Yale University, asserted the significance of historical context against the New Critical view of texts as self-sufficient "verbal icons." Countering Wimsatt and MONROE BEARDSLEY's declaration in "The Affective Fallacy" (1949) that the audience of a literary work is irrelevant, Fish declared that declaration to be a fallacy itself. An abiding concern throughout Fish's work is the rhetorical force of texts and their effects on readers.

In *Surprised by Sin*, Fish focuses on the experience of the reader as he or she encounters Milton's *Paradise Lost*. He upends conventional interpretations of Milton, arguing that the poem's meaning is located not in our final assessment but in the process of struggling through Milton's difficult grammar and rhetoric, which didactically makes readers repeat the Fall. Though he continued to write about literature (and Milton remained a constant point of reference), through the late 1970s and 1980s Fish engaged in broader theoretical speculations on interpretation and rhetoric, exemplified by *Is There a Text in This Class?* In it, he introduces his concept of interpretive communities to explain how readers come to their views—not in idiosyncratic ways, but through social and institutional conventions. He reverses the customary model of interpretation, arguing that we do not discern the inherent features of a literary work but instead construct it through the strategies of our interpretive community.

In "How to Recognize a Poem When You See One," he offers one illustration of this process: he provides students with a list of names, and following his direction they interpret it as a religious poem. A perennial question of literary theory has been what makes a work literary, which is usually thought to be some aspect of literary language or form, distinct from ordinary language, that the critic then explicates. Fish turns this thinking on its head: in his view, literariness stems not from an inherent quality but from the premises that readers bring to a text. Fish's list of names is seemingly unliterary, but it resembles a "found poem"—that is, a poem that comes from language in everyday life, like William Carlos Williams's "This Is Just to Say" (1934), which begins: "I have eaten / the plums / that were in / the icebox." If we see the lines as a poem rather than a personal note, we understand them differently, and Williams's poem is in fact acknowledged as a modern American classic. Literariness arises because of our interpretive conventions, not because it is an innate quality. One can see how this approach might extend to contemporary genres like science fiction: formerly disparaged as a trash genre, it now includes some works that are considered literary.

Claiming the contrary of a standard view, and laying out its argument clearly and step-by-step, "How to Recognize a Poem" epitomizes Fish's style. While some poststructuralist theory can be obscure, Fish uses plain, straightforward terms as he argues almost like a lawyer. He also anticipates a standard attack on reader response, that it relies too much on the subjective and thereby opens the door to allowing anything and everything. Instead, Fish grounds his version of response in interpretive communities, which are social, not individual; institutional, not psychological. Fish does not fully work out how the institution operates—for instance, how many communities exist at any one time, how they form, and how institutions adjudicate among themselves—but he does provide a powerful challenge to formalist theory. Fish also heads off charges of radical relativism: while communities may be variously constituted, they are not arbitrary, and in fact they enact constraints as well as fostering productivity. Interpretation enables a multitude of plays in the sport, but a known number of teams participate in the league of interpretation.

In his later work Fish takes on the perennial problem of the relation of theory to practice. He persistently attacks the assumption that we generate our interpretations from the principles or theories we hold. Instead, in a trademark reversal, he argues that theory stems from our practices, occurs only after the fact, and has no consequences. Extending this notion to law, Fish makes a characteristically provocative claim that judges do not derive their decisions from legal principles, such as the doctrine of free speech, but accrue legal precedents to justify their practical judgments. This view is called antifoundationalism: the denial that practice derives from a predetermined foundation of theory or principle.

Probably because of his contrarian style as well as the nature of his claims, Stanley Fish has prompted both admiration and ire. Traditionalists have denounced him as a relativist who believes in nothing. Leftist critics have attacked him for espousing a circular position that makes principled political action impossible. Defenders of theory have countered that Fish's argument itself has consequences in delegitimating the study of theory in the academy. Critics of his concept of interpretive communities note that it does not explain one's entrance into or departure from a particular community; there are social and political factors that influence what community one might enter. Within the reader-response camp itself, WOLFGANG ISER poses the question: "It is quite true that membership of the community helps to prevent arbitrary ideation, but if there is no subjectivist element in reading, how on earth does Professor Fish account for different interpretations of one and the same text?" Rather than troubling Fish, such rebuttals spur his further argument. His work has indelibly marked contemporary literary theory, especially the concept of interpretation.

Is There a Text in This Class? The Authority of Interpretive Communities
Keywords: Hermeneutics, Institutional Studies, Interpretation Theory, Poetry

From Is There a Text in This Class? The Authority of Interpretive Communities

Chapter 14. How to Recognize a Poem When You See One

Last time[1] I sketched out an argument by which meanings are the property neither of fixed and stable texts nor of free and independent readers but of

1. This was the second of four talks that Fish delivered in April 1979 as part of the John Crowe Ransom Memorial Lectures series at Kenyon College; ironically, RANSOM was a leader of the New Critics, who advocated formalism, whereas Fish argues that meaning resides not in form but in the interpretive conventions that we bring to texts.

interpretive communities that are responsible both for the shape of a reader's activities and for the texts those activities produce. In this lecture I propose to extend that argument so as to account not only for the meanings a poem might be said to have but for the fact of its being recognized as a poem in the first place. And once again I would like to begin with an anecdote.

In the summer of 1971 I was teaching two courses under the joint auspices of the Linguistic Institute of America and the English Department of the State University of New York at Buffalo. I taught these courses in the morning and in the same room. At 9:30 I would meet a group of students who were interested in the relationship between linguistics and literary criticism. Our nominal subject was stylistics[2] but our concerns were finally theoretical and extended to the presuppositions and assumptions which underlie both linguistic and literary practice. At 11:00 these students were replaced by another group whose concerns were exclusively literary and were in fact confined to English religious poetry of the seventeenth century. These students had been learning how to identify Christian symbols and how to recognize typological patterns[3] and how to move from the observation of these symbols and patterns to the specification of a poetic intention that was usually didactic or homiletic. On the day I am thinking about, the only connection between the two classes was an assignment given to the first which was still on the blackboard at the beginning of the second. It read:

Jacobs–Rosenbaum
Levin
Thorne
Hayes
Ohman (?)

I am sure that many of you will already have recognized the names on this list, but for the sake of the record, allow me to identify them. Roderick Jacobs and Peter Rosenbaum are two linguists who have coauthored a number of textbooks and co-edited a number of anthologies. Samuel Levin is a linguist who was one of the first to apply the operations of transformational grammar to literary texts. J. P. Thorne is a linguist at Edinburgh who, like Levin, was attempting to extend the rules of transformational grammar to the notorious irregularities of poetic language. Curtis Hayes is a linguist who was then using transformational grammar in order to establish an objective basis for his intuitive impression that the language of Gibbon's *Rise and Fall of the Roman Empire* is more complex than the language of Hemingway's novels.[4] And Richard Ohmann[5] is the literary critic who, more than any other, was responsible for introducing the vocabulary of transformational

2. A form of literary criticism that draws on developments in linguistics. In the 1960s, it looked especially to Noam Chomsky's recent theory of transformational grammar (language rests on a deep structure, from which sentences in specific languages are generated by processes or transformations).

3. That is, the prefiguration of New Testament persons, objects, or events in the Old Testament, or Hebrew Bible.

4. The American writer Ernest Hemingway (1899–1961) is known for his spare and direct sentences, whereas the British historian Edward Gibbon (1737–1794) has a brilliant but elaborate style. *The History of the Decline and Fall of the Roman Empire* (6 vols., 1776–88) is Gibbon's masterpiece.

5. American critic (b. 1931; see above), whose early work focused on linguistics; he later shifted to institutional studies.

grammar to the literary community. Ohmann's name was spelled as you see it here because I could not remember whether it contained one or two n's. In other words, the question mark in parenthesis signified nothing more than a faulty memory and a desire on my part to appear scrupulous. The fact that the names appeared in a list that was arranged vertically, and that Levin, Thorne, and Hayes formed a column that was more or less centered in relation to the paired names of Jacobs and Rosenbaum, was similarly accidental and was evidence only of a certain compulsiveness if, indeed, it was evidence of anything at all.

In the time between the two classes I made only one change. I drew a frame around the assignment and wrote on the top of that frame "p. 43." When the members of the second class filed in I told them that what they saw on the blackboard was a religious poem of the kind they had been studying and I asked them to interpret it. Immediately they began to perform in a manner that, for reasons which will become clear, was more or less predictable. The first student to speak pointed out that the poem was probably a hieroglyph, although he was not sure whether it was in the shape of a cross or an altar. This question was set aside as the other students, following his lead, began to concentrate on individual words, interrupting each other with suggestions that came so quickly that they seemed spontaneous. The first line of the poem (the very order of events assumed the already constituted status of the object) received the most attention: Jacobs was explicated as a reference to Jacob's ladder,[6] traditionally allegorized as a figure for the Christian ascent to heaven. In this poem, however, or so my students told me, the means of ascent is not a ladder but a tree, a rose tree or rosenbaum.[7] This was seen to be an obvious reference to the Virgin Mary who was often characterized as a rose without thorns, itself an emblem of the immaculate conception.[8] At this point the poem appeared to the students to be operating in the familiar manner of an iconographic riddle. It at once posed the question, "How is it that a man can climb to heaven by means of a rose tree?" and directed the reader to the inevitable answer: by the fruit of that tree, the fruit of Mary's womb, Jesus. Once this interpretation was established it received support from, and conferred significance on, the word "thorne," which could only be an allusion to the crown of thorns, a symbol of the trial suffered by Jesus and of the price he paid to save us all. It was only a short step (really no step at all) from this insight to the recognition of Levin as a double reference, first to the tribe of Levi,[9] of whose priestly function Christ was the fulfillment, and second to the unleavened bread carried by the children of Israel on their exodus from Egypt, the place of sin, and in response to the call of Moses,[1] perhaps the most familiar of the old testament types of Christ. The final word of the poem was given at least three complementary readings: it could be "omen," especially since so much of the poem is concerned with foreshadowing and prophecy; it could be Oh Man, since it is man's story as it intersects with the divine plan that is the poem's subject; and it could, of course, be simply

6. The ladder to heaven of which Jacob dreams in the Hebrew Bible (Genesis 28.12–15).
7. In German, "rose tree."
8. The Christian doctrine that Mary, mother of Jesus, was uniquely born free from the stain of original sin.
9. One of the 12 biblical tribes of ancient Israel, descended from Jacob's son Levi; traditionally, the Levites performed religious functions (members of the priesthood were descendants of Moses's brother Aaron, himself a descendant of Levi).
1. Hebrew prophet who led the exodus; his "call" is his address by God from the burning bush (see Exodus 3.1–4.17).

"amen," the proper conclusion to a poem celebrating the love and mercy shown by a God who gave his only begotten son so that we may live.

In addition to specifying significances for the words of the poem and relating those significances to one another, the students began to discern larger structural patterns. It was noted that of the six names in the poem three—Jacobs, Rosenbaum, and Levin—are Hebrew, two—Thorne and Hayes—are Christian, and one—Ohman—is ambiguous, the ambiguity being marked in the poem itself (as the phrase goes) by the question mark in parenthesis. This division was seen as a reflection of the basic distinction between the old dispensation and the new, the law of sin and the law of love. That distinction, however, is blurred and finally dissolved by the typological perspective which invests the old testament events and heroes with new testament meanings. The structure of the poem, my students concluded, is therefore a double one, establishing and undermining its basic pattern (Hebrew vs. Christian) at the same time. In this context there is finally no pressure to resolve the ambiguity of Ohman since the two possible readings—the name is Hebrew, the name is Christian—are both authorized by the reconciling presence in the poem of Jesus Christ. Finally, I must report that one student took to counting letters and found, to no one's surprise, that the most prominent letters in the poem were S, O, N.

Some of you will have noticed that I have not yet said anything about Hayes. This is because of all the words in the poem it proved the most recalcitrant to interpretation, a fact not without consequence, but one which I will set aside for the moment since I am less interested in the details of the exercise than in the ability of my students to perform it. What is the source of that ability? How is it that they were able to do what they did? What is it that they did? These questions are important because they bear directly on a question often asked in literary theory, What are the distinguishing features of literary language? Or, to put the matter more colloquially, How do you recognize a poem when you see one? The commonsense answer, to which many literary critics and linguists are committed, is that the act of recognition is triggered by the observable presence of distinguishing features. That is, you know a poem when you see one because its language displays the characteristics that you know to be proper to poems. This, however, is a model that quite obviously does not fit the present example. My students did not proceed from the noting of distinguishing features to the recognition that they were confronted by a poem; rather, it was the act of recognition that came first—they knew in advance that they were dealing with a poem—and the distinguishing features then followed.

In other words, acts of recognition, rather than being triggered by formal characteristics, are their source. It is not that the presence of poetic qualities compels a certain kind of attention but that the paying of a certain kind of attention results in the emergence of poetic qualities. As soon as my students were aware that it was poetry they were seeing, they began to look with poetry-seeing eyes, that is, with eyes that saw everything in relation to the properties they knew poems to possess. They knew, for example (because they were told by their teachers), that poems are (or are supposed to be) more densely and intricately organized than ordinary communications; and that knowledge translated itself into a willingness—one might even says a determination—to see connections between one word and another and between every word and the poem's central insight. Moreover, the assumption that there *is* a central insight is itself poetry-specific, and presided over its own realization. Having assumed that the collection of words before them was unified by an informing purpose (because unifying purposes are what poems have), my students proceeded to find one and to formulate it. It was in the light of that purpose (now assumed) that significances for the individual words began to suggest themselves, significances which then fleshed out the assumption that had generated them in the first place. Thus the meanings of the words and the interpretation in which those words were seen to be embedded emerged together, as a consequence of the operations my students began to perform once they were told that this was a poem.

It was almost as if they were following a recipe—if it's a poem do this, if it's a poem, see it that way—and indeed definitions of poetry *are* recipes, for by directing readers as to what to look for in a poem, they instruct them in ways of looking that will produce what they expect to see. If your definition of poetry tells you that the language of poetry is complex, you will scrutinize the language of something identified as a poem in such a way as to bring out the complexity you know to be "there." You will, for example, be on the lookout for latent ambiguities; you will attend to the presence of alliterative and consonantal patterns (there will always be some), and you will try to make something of them (you will always succeed); you will search for meanings that subvert, or exist in a tension with the meanings that first present themselves; and if these operations fail to produce the anticipated complexity, you will even propose a significance for the words that are *not* there, because, as everyone knows, everything about a poem, including its omissions, is significant. Nor, as you do these things, will you have any sense of performing in a willful manner, for you will only be doing what you learned to do in the course of becoming a skilled reader of poetry. Skilled reading is usually thought to be a matter of discerning what is there, but if the example of my students can be generalized, it is a matter of knowing how to *produce* what can thereafter be said to be there. Interpretation is not the art of construing but the art of constructing. Interpreters do not decode poems; they make them.

To many, this will be a distressing conclusion, and there are a number of arguments that could be mounted in order to forestall it. One might point out that the circumstances of my students' performance were special. After all, they had been concerned exclusively with religious poetry for some weeks, and therefore would be uniquely vulnerable to the deception I had practiced on them and uniquely equipped to impose religious themes and patterns on words innocent of either. I must report, however, that I have duplicated this experiment any number of times at nine or ten universities in three countries, and the results were always the same, even when the participants know from the beginning that what they are looking at was originally an assignment. Of course this very fact could itself be turned into an objection: doesn't the reproducibility of the exercise prove that there is something about these words that leads everyone to perform in the same way? Isn't it just a happy accident that names like Thorne and Jacobs have counterparts or near counterparts in biblical names and symbols? And wouldn't my students have been unable to do what they did if the assignment I gave to the first class had been made up of different names? The answer to all of these questions is no.

Given a firm belief that they were confronted by a religious poem, my students would have been able to turn any list of names into the kind of poem we have before us now, because they would have read the names within the assumption that they were informed with Christian significances. (This is nothing more than a literary analogue to Augustine's rule of faith.[2]) You can test this assertion by replacing Jacobs-Rosenbaum, Levin, Thorne, Hayes, and Ohman with names drawn from the faculty of Kenyon College—Temple, Jordan, Seymour, Daniels, Star, Church.[3] I will not exhaust my time or your patience by performing a full-dress analysis, which would involve, of course, the relation between those who saw the River Jordan and those who saw *more* by seeing the Star of Bethlehem,[4] thus fulfilling the prophecy by which the temple of Jerusalem was replaced by the inner temple or church built up in the heart of every Christian. Suffice it to say that it could easily be done (you can take the poem home and do it yourself) and that the shape of its doing would be constrained not by the names but by the interpretive assumptions that gave them a significance even before they were seen. This would be true even if there were no names on the list, if the paper or blackboard were blank; the blankness would present no problem to the interpreter, who would immediately see in it the void out of which God created the earth, or the abyss into which unregenerate sinners fall, or, in the best of all possible poems, both.

Even so, one might reply, all you've done is demonstrate how an interpretation, if it is prosecuted with sufficient vigor, can impose itself on material which has its own proper shape. Basically, at the ground level, in the first place, when all is said and done, "Jacobs-Rosenbaum Levin Thorne Hayes Ohman(?)" is an assignment; it is only a trick that allows you to transform it into a poem, and when the effects of the trick have worn off, it will return to its natural form and be seen as an assignment once again. This is a powerful argument because it seems at once to give interpretation its due (as an act of the will) and to maintain the independence of that on which interpretation works. It allows us, in short, to preserve our commonsense intuition that interpretation must be interpretation of *something.* Unfortunately, the argument will not hold because the assignment we all see is no less the product of interpretation than the poem into which it was turned. That is, it requires just as much work, and work of the same kind, to see this as an assignment as it does to see it as a poem. If this seems counterintuitive, it is only because the work required to see it as an assignment is work we have already done, in the course of acquiring the huge amount of background knowledge that enables you and me to function in the academic world. In order to know what an assigment is, that is, in order to know what to do with something identified as an assignment, you must first know what a class is (know that it isn't an economic grouping) and know that classes meet at specified times for so many weeks, and that one's performance in a class is largely a matter of performing between classes.

2. The early Christian theologian and philosopher AUGUSTINE (354–430 C.E.) defined faith as belief in "things not seen."
3. Faculty members of Kenyon College at the time of Fish's lecture.
4. The star whose appearance signified the birth of Jesus and later led the Magi to him (Matthew 2.2, 7–9). The Jordan was the river that the Israelites crossed to enter the land promised to them by God (Deuteronomy 34.1–4; Joshua 1.13–17). This is presented as another example of typological interpretation.

Think for a moment of how you would explain this last to someone who did not already know it. "Well," you might say, "a class is a group situation in which a number of people are instructed by an informed person in a particular subject." (Of course the notion of "subject" will itself require explication.) "An assignment is something you do when you're not in class." "Oh, I see," your interlocutor might respond, "an assignment is something you do to take your mind off what you've been doing in class." "No, an assignment is a part of a class." "But how can that be if you only do it when the class is not meeting?" Now it would be possible, finally, to answer that question, but only by enlarging the horizons of your explanation to include the very concept of a university, what it is one might be doing there, why one might be doing it instead of doing a thousand other things, and so on. For most of us these matters do not require explanation, and indeed, it is hard for us to imagine someone for whom they do; but that is because our tacit knowledge of what it means to move around in academic life was acquired so gradually and so long ago that it doesn't seem like knowledge at all (and therefore something someone else might *not* know) but a part of the world. You might think that when you're on campus (a phrase that itself requires volumes) that you are simply walking around on the two legs God gave you; but your walking is informed by an internalized awareness of institutional goals and practices, of norms of behavior, of lists of do's and don't's, of invisible lines and the dangers of crossing them; and, as a result, you see everything as *already* organized in relation to those same goals and practices. It would never occur to you, for example, to wonder if the people pouring out of that building are fleeing from a fire; you *know* that they are exiting from a class (what could be more obvious?) and you know that because your perception of their action occurs within a knowledge of what people in a university could possibly be doing and the reasons they could have for doing it (going to the next class, going back to the dorm, meeting someone in the student union). It is within that same knowledge that an assignment becomes intelligible so that it appears to you immediately as an obligation, as a set of directions, as something with parts, some of which may be more significant than others. That is, it is a proper question to ask of an assignment whether some of its parts might be omitted or slighted, whereas readers of poetry know that no part of a poem can be slighted (the rule is "everything counts") and they do not rest until every part has been given a significance.

In a way this amounts to no more than saying what everyone already knows: poems and assignments are different, but my point is that the differences are a result of the different interpretive operations we perform and not of something inherent in one or the other. An assignment no more compels its own recognition than does a poem; rather, as in the case of a poem, the shape of an assignment emerges when someone looks at something identified as one with assignment-seeing eyes, that is, with eyes which are capable of seeing the words as already embedded within the institutional structure that makes it possible for assignments to have a sense. The ability to see, and therefore to make, an assignment is no less a learned ability than the ability to see, and therefore to make, a poem. Both are constructed artifacts, the products and not the producers of interpretation, and while the differences between them are real, they are interpretive and do not have their source in some bedrock level of objectivity.

Of course one might want to argue that there is a bedrock level at which these names constitute neither an assignment or a poem but are merely a list. But that argument too falls because a list is no more a natural object—one that wears its meaning on its face and can be recognized by anyone—than an assignment or a poem. In order to see a list, one must already be equipped with the concepts of seriality, hierarchy, subordination, and so on, and while these are by no mean esoteric concepts and seem available to almost everyone, they are nonetheless learned, and if there were someone who had not learned them, he or she would not be able to see a list. The next recourse is to descend still lower (in the direction of atoms) and to claim objectivity for letters, paper, graphite, black marks on white spaces, and so on; but these entities too have palpability and shape only because of the assumption of some or other system of intelligibility, and they are therefore just as available to a deconstructive dissolution as are poems, assignments, and lists.

The conclusion, therefore, is that all objects are made and not found, and that they are made by the interpretive strategies we set in motion. This does not, however, commit me to subjectivity because the means by which they are made are social and conventional. That is, the "you" who does the interpretative work that puts poems and assignments and lists into the world is a communal you and not an isolated individual. No one of us wakes up in the morning and (in French fashion) reinvents poetry[5] or thinks up a new educational system or decides to reject seriality in favor of some other, wholly original, form of organization. We do not do these things because we could not do them, because the mental operations we can perform are limited by the institutions in which we are *already* embedded. These institutions precede us, and it is only by inhabiting them, or being inhabited by them, that we have access to the public and conventional senses they make. Thus while it is true to say that we create poetry (and assignments and lists), we create it through interpretive strategies that are finally not our own but have their source in a publicly available system of intelligibility. Insofar as the system (in this case a literary system) constrains us, it also fashions us, furnishing us with categories of understanding, with which we in turn fashion the entities to which we can then point. In short, to the list of made or constructed objects we must add ourselves, for we no less than the poems and assignments we see are the products of social and cultural patterns of thought.

To put the matter in this way is to see that the opposition between objectivity and subjectivity is a false one because neither exists in the pure form that would give the opposition its point. This is precisely illustrated by my anecdote in which we do *not* have free-standing readers in a relationship of perceptual adequacy or inadequacy to an equally free-standing text. Rather, we have readers whose consciousnesses are constituted by a set of conventional notions which when put into operation constitute in turn a conventional, and conventionally seen, object. My students could do what they did, and do it in unison, because as members of a literary community they knew what a poem was (their knowledge was public), and that knowledge led them to look in such a way as to populate the landscape with what they knew to be poems.

5. Probably an allusion to Arthur Rimbaud (1854–1891), who was the first important French poet to write in free verse.

Of course poems are not the only objects that are constituted in unison by shared ways of seeing. Every object or event that becomes available within an institutional setting can be so characterized. I am thinking, for example, of something that happened in my classroom just the other day. While I was in the course of vigorously making a point, one of my students, William Newlin by name, was just as vigorously waving his hand. When I asked the other members of the class what it was that Mr. Newlin was doing, they all answered that he was seeking permission to speak. I then asked them how they knew that. The immediate reply was that it was obvious; what else could he be thought to be doing? The meaning of his gesture, in other words, was right there on its surface, available for reading by anyone who had the eyes to see. That meaning, however, would not have been available to someone without any knowledge of what was involved in being a student. Such a person might have thought that Mr. Newlin was pointing to the fluorescent lights hanging from the ceiling, or calling our attention to some object that was about to fall ("the sky is falling," "the sky is falling"[6]). And if the someone in question were a child of elementary or middle-school age, Mr. Newlin might well have been seen as seeking permission not to speak but to go to the bathroom, an interpretation or reading that would never occur to a student at Johns Hopkins or any other institution of "higher learning" (and how would we explain to the uninitiated the meaning of *that* phrase).

The point is the one I have made so many times before: it is neither the case that the significance of Mr. Newlin's gesture is imprinted on its surface where it need only be read off, or that the construction put on the gesture by everyone in the room was individual and idiosyncratic. Rather, the source of our interpretive unanimity was a structure of interests and understood goals, a structure whose categories so filled our individual consciousnesses that they were rendered as one, immediately investing phenomena with the significance they *must* have, given the already-in-place assumptions about what someone could possibly be intending (by word or gesture) in a classroom. By seeing Mr. Newlin's raised hand with a single shaping eye, we were demonstrating what Harvey Sacks has characterized as "the fine power of a culture. It does not, so to speak, merely fill brains in roughly the same way, it fills them so that they are alike in fine detail."[7] The occasion of Sacks's observation was the ability of his hearers to understand a sequence of two sentences—"The baby cried. The mommy picked it up."—exactly as he did (assuming, for example that "the 'mommy' who picks up the 'baby' is the mommy of that baby"), despite the fact that alternative ways of understanding were demonstrably possible. That is, the mommy of the second sentence could well have been the mommy of some other baby, and it need not even have been a baby that this "floating" mommy was picking up. One is tempted to say that in the absence of a specific context we are authorized to take the words literally, which is what Sacks's hearers do; but as Sacks observes, it is within the assumption of a context—one so deeply assumed that we are unaware of it—that the words acquire what seems to be their literal meaning. There is noth-

6. A phrase from the folktale "Henny Penny" (better known in the United States as "Chicken Little"), whose title character warns that the world is ending, panicking because some natural object fell on it.

7. "On the Analysability of Stories by Children," in *Ethnomethodology*, ed. Roy Turner (Baltimore: Penguin, 1974), p. 218 [Fish's note]. Sacks (1935–1975), American sociologist.

ing *in the words* that tells Sacks and his hearers how to relate the mommy and the baby of this story, just as there is nothing *in the form* of Mr. Newlin's gesture that tells his fellow students how to determine its significance. In both cases the determination (of relation and significance) is the work of categories of organization—the family, being a student—that are from the very first giving shape and value to what is heard and seen.

Indeed, these categories are the very shape of seeing itself, in that we are not to imagine a perceptual ground more basic than the one they afford. That is, we are not to imagine a moment when my students "simply see" a physical configuration of atoms and *then* assign that configuration a significance, according to the situation they happen to be in. To be in the situation (this or any other) is to "see" with the eyes of its interests, its goals, its understood practices, values, and norms, and so to be conferring significance *by* seeing, not after it. The categories of my students' vision are the categories by which they understand themselves to be functioning as students (what Sacks might term "doing studenting"), and objects will appear to them in forms related to that way of functioning rather than in some objective or preinterpretive form. (This is true even when an object is seen as not related, since nonrelation is not a pure but a differential category—the specification of something by enumerating what it is not; in short, nonrelation is merely one form of relation, and its perception is always situation-specific.)

Of course, if someone who was not functioning as a student was to walk into my classroom, he might very well see Mr. Newlin's raised hand (and "raised hand" is already an interpretation-laden description) in some other way, as evidence of a disease, as the salute of a political follower, as a muscle-improving exercise, as an attempt to kill flies; but he would always see it in *some* way, and never as purely physical data waiting for his interpretation. And, moreover, the way of seeing, whatever it was, would never be individual or idiosyncratic, since its source would always be the institutional structure of which the "see-er" was an extending agent. This is what Sacks means when he says that a culture fills brains "so that they are alike in fine detail"; it fills them so that no one's interpretive acts are exclusively his own but fall to him by virtue of his position in some socially organized environment and are therefore always shared and public. It follows, then, that the fear of solipsism, of the imposition by the unconstrained self of its own prejudices, is unfounded because the self does not exist apart from the communal or conventional categories of thought that enable its operations (of thinking, seeing, reading). Once one realizes that the conceptions that fill consciousness, including any conception of its own status, are culturally derived, the very notion of an unconstrained self, of a consciousness wholly and dangerously free, becomes incomprehensible.

But without the notion of the unconstrained self, the arguments of Hirsch, Abrams,[8] and the other proponents of objective interpretation are deprived of their urgency. They are afraid that in the absence of the controls

8. M. H. Abrams (1912–2015), American literary critic and founding editor of *The Norton Anthology of English Literature*; in a preface to his lectures, Fish reports that he was responding to Abrams's essay "How to Do Things with Texts" (1978; published 1979). E. D. Hirsch (b. 1928), American educational and literary theorist who elaborated on objective standards in *Validity in Interpretation* (1967); he later became more widely known for his arguments promoting the canon and "cultural literacy."

afforded by a normative system of meanings, the self will simply substitute its own meanings for the meanings (usually identified with the intentions of the author) that texts bring with them, the meanings that texts "*have*"; however, if the self is conceived of not as an independent entity but as a social construct whose operations are delimited by the systems of intelligibility that inform it, then the meanings it confers on texts are not its own but have their source in the interpretive community (or communities) of which it is a function. Moreover, these meanings will be neither subjective nor objective, at least in the terms assumed by those who argue within the traditional framework: they will not be objective because they will always have been the product of a point of view rather than having been simply "read off"; and they will not be subjective because that point of view will always be social or institutional. Or by the same reasoning one could say that they are *both* subjective and objective: they are subjective because they inhere in a particular point of view and are therefore not universal; and they are objective because the point of view that delivers them is public and conventional rather than individual or unique.

To put the matter in either way is to see how unhelpful the terms "subjective" and "objective" finally are. Rather than facilitating inquiry, they close it down, by deciding in advance what shape inquiry can possibly take. Specifically, they assume, without being aware that it is an assumption and therefore open to challenge, the very distinction I have been putting into question, the distinction between interpreters and the objects they interpret. That distinction in turn assumes that interpreters and their objects are two different kinds of *a*contextual entities, and within these twin assumptions the issue can only be one of control: will texts be allowed to constrain their own interpretation or will irresponsible interpreters be allowed to obscure and overwhelm texts. In the spectacle that ensues, the spectacle of Anglo-American critical controversy, texts and selves fight it out in the persons of their respective champions, Abrams, Hirsch, Reichert, Graff on the one hand, Holland, Bleich, Slatoff, and (in some characterizations of him) Barthes[9] on the other. But if selves are constituted by the ways of thinking and seeing that inhere in social organizations, and if these constituted selves in turn constitute texts according to these same ways, then there can be no adversary relationship between text and self because they are the necessarily related products of the same cognitive possibilities. A text cannot be overwhelmed by an irresponsible reader and one need not worry about protecting the purity of a text from a reader's idiosyncracies. It is only the distinction between subject and object that gives rise to these urgencies, and once the distinction is blurred they simply fall away. One can respond with a cheerful yes to the question "Do readers make meanings?" and commit oneself to very little because it would be equally true to say that meanings, in the form of culturally derived interpretive categories, make readers.

9. Those in the latter group focused on the reader and subjectivity in some of their writings: Norman Holland (1927–2017), psychoanalytic and reader-response theorist; David Bleich (b. 1940), American literary critic whose works include *Subjective Criticism* (1978); Walter Slatoff (1922–1991), American reader-response critic; and ROLAND BARTHES (1915–1980), French literary critic. In different ways, Abrams, Hirsch, the American cultural critic GERALD GRAFF (b. 1937), and John Reichert (1935–2004), an American literary critic who argued against Fish's view of interpretive communities in "But That Was in Another Ball Park: A Reply to Stanley Fish" (1979), were invested in defending objective standards in criticism.

Indeed, many things look rather different once the subject–object dichotomy is eliminated as the assumed framework within which critical discussion occurs. Problems disappear, not because they have been solved but because they are shown never to have been problems in the first place. Abrams, for example, wonders how, in the absence of a normative system of stable meanings, two people could ever agree on the interpretation of a work or even of a sentence; but the difficulty is only a difficulty if the two (or more) people are thought of as isolated individuals whose agreement must be compelled by something external to them. (There is something of the police state in Abrams's vision, complete with posted rules and boundaries, watchdogs to enforce them, procedures for identifying their violators as criminals.) But if the understandings of the people in question are informed by the same notions of what counts as a fact, of what is central, peripheral, and worthy of being noticed—in short, by the same interpretive principles—then agreement between them will be assured, and its source will not be a text that enforces its own perception but a way of perceiving that results in the emergence to those who share it (or those whom it shares) of the same text. That text might be a poem, as it was in the case of those who first "saw" "Jacobs-Rosenbaum Levin Hayes Thorne Ohman(?)," or a hand, as it is every day in a thousand classrooms; but whatever it is, the shape and meaning it appears immediately to have will be the "ongoing accomplishment"[1] of those who agree to produce it.

1980

1. A phrase used by the ethnomethodologists to characterize the interpretive activities that create and maintain the features of everyday life. See, for example, Don H. Zimmerman, "Fact as Practical Accomplishment," in *Ethnomethodology*, pp. 128–143 [Fish's note].

NGUGI WĂ THIONG'O b. 1938 · TABAN LO LIYONG b. 1939 · HENRY OWUOR-ANYUMBA 1933–1992

English departments are a relatively recent historical development, arising only in the late nineteenth and early twentieth century. Before that, academic literary study in the West centered on the Greek and Latin classics and focused on elements of rhetoric and philology. During the Victorian era in England, as TERRY EAGLETON points out in the first chapter of *Literary Theory* (1983; see below), English arose as a discipline to foster an appreciation for culture in the less educated classes, who were not trained in Greek and Latin. But as Eagleton also argues, English was enmeshed with nationalism and designed to instill national pride—hence the subject was "English" rather than simply "literature"—particularly in the face of European conflicts (such as World War I) and competition for colonies. Moreover, the teaching of English language and literature was a prominent part of the administration of the British Empire in its many colonies around the globe—in India, Africa, and elsewhere. "On the Abolition of the English Department" (1968), our selection here, stages a revolt against this vestige of British colonial rule: it depicts English not as a neutral or natural subject but as an instrument of imperialism, and promotes the study of indigenous national literatures and languages. Originally a university memorandum, it today is seen as an important inaugural statement of postcolonial literary criticism.

Its lead author, Ngugi wă Thiong'o (James Ngugi), is an internationally renowned novelist, dramatist, and critic. Born in Kenya, which was under British rule from 1895 until 1963, Ngugi witnessed the effects of colonialism firsthand. He attended an independent mission school where the teachers were native Kenyans; but in 1954, in response to the Mau Mau uprising against colonial rule, the British government took control of it and made instruction in English mandatory. In the political turmoil leading to independence, one of his stepbrothers was killed and his mother tortured, and an older brother joined the Mau Mau rebellion. In 1959 Ngugi entered Makerere University in Uganda, receiving his B.A. in 1964; there he also began his writing career, publishing the acclaimed novel *Weep Not, Child* (1964) about the Mau Mau war and East African culture. After attending Leeds University on a British council scholarship (1964–67), he returned to Africa to take a position at Nairobi University, but soon resigned in protest over governmental interference in the university. He rejoined the faculty in 1971, becoming in 1973 head of the Department of Literature, newly formed in response to his and his colleagues' criticism of English. He also renounced his anglicized name, James Ngugi, which he held to be a sign of colonialism; taking his name in his native Kikuyu language, he thereafter wrote first in Kikuyu and then translated his own work into English. In 1977 he was arrested by Kenyan police after the production of one of his plays that was critical of the government. Protests from international literary groups led to his release after he had been imprisoned for a year without being charged. Ngugi eventually left the country, taking professorships at Yale University, New York University, and, since 2004, the University of California at Irvine, where he is now Distinguished Professor of Comparative Literature.

Born in northern Uganda, which was under British rule from 1896 until 1962, Taban lo Liyong received his B.A. from the Ugandan National Teachers College in 1962. He traveled to the United States to study political science, but changed paths in 1965 to attend the prestigious writers' workshop at the University of Iowa; in 1968 he became its first African graduate. He was an important early critic of the paucity of African literature, attributing it to British colonial rule: "I blame the British. The education they came to offer was aimed at recruiting candidates for a Christian Heaven" and at "produc[ing] clerks, teachers, servants." In 1968 he returned to Africa on a fellowship offered by the Institute for African Studies at Nairobi University, where he also lectured in the English department and joined forces with Ngugi and Owuor-Anyumba. Since 1978 he has held positions at the University of Juba in the Sudan.

Born in Kenya, Henry Owuor-Anyumba received a degree in education from the University of East Africa and his B.A. from Cambridge University in 1966. Thereafter he taught at Nairobi University until his death in 1992. Less widely known than his coauthors, he was a folklorist, especially of African music.

After World War II, almost all of the many colonies of the European powers gained their national independence, sometimes through negotiation and sometimes through revolt and war. But political independence did not necessarily entail economic or cultural autonomy, and the effects of colonialism lingered in language, education, and religion, as well as in economic and political structures. The residual effects of imperialism are variously called "postcolonial," "neo-colonial" (the term that Ngugi most frequently uses), or simply "colonial" (the term favored by the celebrated Nigerian novelist CHINUA ACHEBE). Inaugurated as a critique of the results of decolonization, postcolonial studies addresses the perennial theoretical issue of the relation of culture and society, particularly the role that culture—notably language, literature, and education—plays in furthering imperialism. In "Literature and Society" (1973), Ngugi views culture as a central vehicle for continued colonial control, or "cultural imperialism," "which during classical colonialism supplemented direct military and political occupation [but now] becomes the major agency of control under neo-colonialism."

"On the Abolition of the English Department" deals with how literary education and academic institutions have helped implement cultural imperialism in Africa. As Ngugi elaborates in "Literature and Society," "the content of our literature syllabus, its presentation, the machinery for determining the choice of texts and their interpretation were all an integral part of imperialism and domination in the colonial phase, and they are today an integral part of the imperialism and domination in the neo-colonial phase." To remedy this, "On the Abolition of the English Department" offers a straightforward set of proposals for African universities: first, dismantle departments centered on English language and literature; second, create departments centered on the study of indigenous African languages and literature, as well as relevant foreign ones; third, study neglected topics such as the African oral tradition; and, fourth, study modern African literature, which includes Caribbean and African American literature. Ngugi, Liyong, and Owuor-Anyumba are careful not to discredit English or European literature, but argue for the benefits of opening literary study to wider currents. Within the debate over the literary canon, they take an expansionist position, recommending that the canon encompass more texts from different cultures rather than be artificially limited, and that we study representative rather than "classic" texts.

A contentious issue among writers and critics during the early days of decolonization was whether to write in native languages or in the dominant colonial language, usually English or French. European authors similarly had to grapple with the status of vernacular languages in the early Renaissance, when Latin was the dominant language of learning (for example, see JOACHIM DU BELLAY, above). In his other work, Ngugi argues for the primary use of native traditions and languages; in contrast, his coauthor Liyong contends that African writers must write in a European language to capture a wide readership—with the qualification that "we will not have to stick to Queen's English[;] . . . we have to tame the shrew and naturalize her," a point also made by Achebe.

Since the 1980s postcolonial and cultural critics have questioned the nationalistic character of such struggles for independence, arguing that nationalism participates in the logic of imperialism and that it rests on a fictive construct, an "imagined community," without an essential core. Set amid debates over decolonization and Afrocentrism, "On the Abolition of the English Department" provides a glimpse into the political effects of literature and the seemingly neutral institutions of education. Ngugi challenges us to consider such questions more closely, declaring, "Every writer is a writer in politics. The only question is what and whose politics."

"On the Abolition of the English Department" Keywords: The Canon/Tradition, Institutional Studies, Nationhood, Postcolonial Theory, Vernacular Language

On the Abolition of the English Department[1]

1. This is a comment on the paper presented by the Acting Head of the English Department at the University of Nairobi[2] to the 42nd meeting of the Arts Faculty Board on the 20th September, 1968.
2. (*a*) That paper was mainly concerned with possible developments within the Arts Faculty and their relationship with the English Department, particularly:

(i) The place of modern languages, especially French;
(ii) The place and role of the Department of English;
(iii) The emergence of a Department of Linguistics and Languages;
(iv) The place of African languages, especially Swahili.

(*b*) In connection with the above, the paper specifically suggested that a department of Linguistics and Languages, to be closely related to English, be established.
(*c*) A remote possibility of a Department of African literature, or alternatively, that of African literature and culture, was envisaged.
3. The paper raised important problems. It should have been the subject of a more involved debate and discussion, preceding the appointment of a committee with specific tasks, because it raises questions of value, direction and orientation.
4. For instance, the suggestions, as the paper itself admits, question the role and status of an English Department in an African situation and environment. To quote from his paper:

> The English Department has had a long history at this College and has built up a strong syllabus which by its study of the *historic continuity of a single culture throughout the period of emergence of the modern west*, makes it an important companion to History and to Philosophy and Religious Studies. However, *it is bound to become less 'British', more open to other writing in English (American, Caribbean, African, Commonwealth) and also to continental writing, for comparative purposes.*

5. Underlying the suggestions is a basic assumption that the English tradition and the emergence of the modern west is the central root of our consciousness and cultural heritage. Africa becomes an extension of the west, an attitude which, until a radical reassessment, used to dictate the teaching and organization of History in our University.[3] Hence, in fact, the assumed centrality of the English Department, into which other cultures can be admitted from time to time, as fit subjects for study, or from which other satellite departments can

1. This debate resulted in the establishment of two departments: Languages and Literature. In both, African languages and literature were to form the core. In the case of the Literature Department, Caribbean and black American literature were to be emphasized. It thus represents a radical departure in the teaching of literature in Africa [Ngugi, Liyong, and Owuor-Anyumba's note].
2. A focal point of the political tension that continued to beset Kenya after independence was gained in 1964.
3. Then the University of East Africa with three constituent colleges at Makerere, Dar es Salaam, and Nairobi. Since then the three have become autonomous universities [Ngugi, Liyong, and Owuor-Anyumba's note]. Makerere is in Uganda; Dar es Salaam is the capital of Tanzania.

spring as time and money allow. A small example is the current, rather apologetic attempt to smuggle African writing into an English syllabus in our three colleges.

6. Here then, is our main question: If there is need for a 'study of the historic continuity of a single culture', why can't this be African? Why can't African literature be at the centre so that we can view other cultures in relationship to it?

This is not mere rhetoric: already African writing, with the sister connections in the Caribbean and the Afro-American literatures, has played an important role in the African renaissance, and will become even more and more important with time and pressure of events. Just because for reasons of political expediency we have kept English as our official language, there is no need to substitute a study of English culture for our own. We reject the primacy of English literature and culture.

7. The aim, in short, should be to orientate ourselves towards placing Kenya, East Africa, and then Africa in the centre. All other things are to be considered in their relevance to our situation, and their contribution towards understanding ourselves.

8. We therefore suggest:

A. That the English Department be abolished;
B. That a Department of African Literature and Languages be set up in its place.

The primary duty of any literature department is to illuminate the spirit animating a people, to show how it meets new challenges, and to investigate possible areas of development and involvement.

In suggesting this name, we are not rejecting other cultural streams, especially the western stream. We are only clearly mapping out the directions and perspectives the study of culture and literature will inevitably take in an African university.

9. We know that European literatures constitute one source of influence on modern African literatures in English, French, and Portuguese; Swahili,[4] Arabic, and Asian literatures constitute another, an important source, especially here in East Africa; and the African tradition, a tradition as active and alive as ever, constitutes the third and the most significant. This is the stuff on which we grew up, and it is the base from which we make our cultural take-off into the world.

10. Languages and linguistics should be studied in the department because in literature we see the principles of languages and linguistics in action. Conversely, through knowledge of languages and linguistics we can get more from literature. For linguistics not to become eccentric, it should be studied in the Department of African Literature and Languages.

In addition to Swahili, French, and English, whenever feasible other languages such as Arabic, Hindustani, Kikuyu, Luo, Akamba,[5] etc., should be introduced into the syllabus as optional subjects.

4. One of the official languages of Kenya and Tanzania.

5. Some of the diverse languages of the different ethnic groups in and around Kenya.

11. On the literature side, the Department ought to offer roughly:

(a) The oral tradition, which is our primary root;
(b) Swahili literature (with Arabic and Asian literatures): this is another root, especially in East Africa;
(c) A selected course in European literature: yet another root;
(d) Modern African literature.

For the purposes of the Department, a knowledge of Swahili, English, and French should be compulsory. The largest body of writing by Africans is now written in the French language. Africans writing in the French language have also produced most of the best poems and novels. In fact it makes no sense to talk of modern African literature without French.

12. *The Oral Tradition*

The Oral tradition is rich and many-sided. In fact 'Africa is littered with Oral Literature'. But the art did not end yesterday; it is a living tradition. Even now there are songs being sung in political rallies, in churches, in night clubs by guitarists, by accordion players, by dancers, etc. Another point to be observed is the interlinked nature of art forms in traditional practice. Verbal forms are not always distinct from dance, music, etc. For example, in music there is close correspondence between verbal and melodic tones; in 'metrical lyrics' it has been observed that poetic text is inseparable from tune; and the 'folk tale' often bears an 'operatic' form, with sung refrain as an integral part. The distinction between prose and poetry is absent or very fluid.

Though tale, dance, song, myth, etc. can be performed for individual aesthetic enjoyment, they have other social purposes as well. Dance, for example, has been studied 'as symbolic expression of social reality reflecting and influencing the social, cultural and personality systems of which it is a part'. The oral tradition also comments on society because of its intimate relationship and involvement.

The study of the oral tradition at the University should therefore lead to a multi-disciplinary outlook: literature, music, linguistics, Sociology, Anthropology, History, Psychology, Religion, Philosophy. Secondly, its study can lead to fresh approaches by making it possible for the student to be familiar with art forms different in kind and historical development from Western literary forms. Spontaneity and liberty of communication inherent in oral transmission—openness to sounds, sights, rhythms, tones, in life and in the environment—are examples of traditional elements from which the student can draw. More specifically, his familiarity with oral literature could suggest new structures and techniques; and could foster attitudes of mind characterized by the willingness to experiment with new forms, so transcending 'fixed literary patterns' and what that implies—the preconceived ranking of art forms.

The study of the Oral Tradition would therefore supplement (not replace) courses in Modern African Literature. By discovering and proclaiming loyalty to indigenous values, the new literature would on the one hand be set in the stream of history to which it belongs and so be better appreciated; and on the other be better able to embrace and assimilate other thoughts without losing its roots.

13. *Swahili Literature*

There is a large amount of oral and written classical Swahili Literature of high calibre. There is also a growing body of modern Swahili literature: both written and oral.

14. *European Literature*

Europe has influenced Africa, especially through English and French cultures. In our part of Africa there has been an over-concentration on the English side of European life. Even the French side, which is dominant in other countries of Africa, has not received the importance it deserves. We therefore urge for freedom of choice so that a more representative course can be drawn up. We see no reason why English literature should have priority over and above other European literatures where we are concerned. The Russian novel of the nineteenth century should and must be taught. Selections from American, German, and other European literatures should also be introduced. In other words English writings will be taught in their European context and only for their relevance to the East African perspective.

15. *Modern African Literature*

The case for the study of Modern African Literature is self-evident. Its possible scope would embrace:

(a) The African novel written in French and English;
(b) African poetry written in French and English, with relevant translations of works written by Africans in Portuguese and Spanish;
(c) The Caribbean novel and poetry: the Caribbean involvement with Africa can never be over-emphasized. A lot of writers from the West Indies have often had Africa in mind. Their works have had a big impact on the African renaissance—in politics and literature. The poetry of Negritude[6] indeed cannot be understood without studying its Caribbean roots. We must also study Afro-American literature.

16. *Drama*

Since drama is an integral part of literature, as well as being its extension, various dramatic works should be studied as parts of the literature of the people under study. Courses in play-writing, play-acting, directing, lighting, costuming, etc. should be instituted.

17. *Relationship with other Departments*

From things already said in this paper, it is obvious that African Oral and Modern literatures cannot be fully understood without some understanding of social and political ideas in African history. For this, we propose that either with the help of other departments, or within the department, or both, courses on mutually relevant aspects of African thought be offered. For instance, an introductory course on African art—sculpture, painting—could be offered in co-operation with the Department of Design and Architecture.

18. The 3.1.1[7] should be abolished. We think an undergraduate should be exposed to as many general ideas as possible. Any specialization

6. A literary movement of the 1930s through 1950s that began in Paris among black French-speaking African and Caribbean writers; protesting French colonist rule and assimilationist policies, they declared the value of black African identity, culture, and traditions.

7. This is a course for those who want to specialize in literature: 1st year—three subjects; 2d and 3d years—literature only [Ngugi, Liyong, and Owuor-Anyumba's note].

should come in a graduate school where more specialized courses can be offered.

19. In other words we envisage an active Graduate School will develop, which should be organized with such departments as the Institute for Development studies.

20. *Conclusion*

One of the things which has been hindering a radical outlook in our study of literature in Africa is the question of literary excellence; that only works of undisputed literary excellence should be offered. (In this case it meant virtually the study of disputable 'peaks' of English literature.) The question of literary excellence implies a value judgment as to what is literary and what is excellence, and from whose point of view. For any group it is better to study representative works which mirror their society rather than to study a few isolated 'classics', either of their own or of a foreign culture.

To sum up, we have been trying all along to place values where they belong. We have argued the case for the abolition of the present Department of English in the College, and the establishment of a Department of African Literature and Languages. This is not a change of names only. We want to establish the centrality of Africa in the department. This, we have argued, is justifiable on various grounds, the most important one being that education is a means of knowledge about ourselves. Therefore, after we have examined ourselves, we radiate outwards and discover peoples and worlds around us. With Africa at the centre of things, not existing as an appendix or a satellite of other countries and literatures, things must be seen from the African perspective. The dominant object in that perspective is African literature, the major branch of African culture. Its roots go back to past African literatures, European literatures, and Asian literatures. These can only be studied meaningfully in a Department of African Literature and Languages in an African University.

We ask that this paper be accepted in principle; we suggest that a representative committee be appointed to work out the details and harmonize the various suggestions into an administratively workable whole.

1968

TZVETAN TODOROV

1939–2017

A central figure in French structuralism, Tzvetan Todorov is best known for advocating the scientific study of narrative, modeled on linguistics, for which he coined the now-standard term *narratology.* He was responsible for renewing attention to the narrative theory put forth in the early twentieth century by the Russian formalists, such as Boris Eichenbaum and Viktor Shklovsky, and for an effort, with his mentor ROLAND BARTHES, to establish a universal "grammar" of narrative. In "Structural Analysis of Narrative" (1969), Todorov presents a condensed manifesto for the narratological approach.

Born in Bulgaria, Todorov emigrated to France in 1963 to study literature and language at the University of Paris, where he did his doctoral dissertation under the direction of Barthes. From 1968 until his death he held an appointment at the Centre National de la Recherche Scientifique (National Center for Scientific Research) in Paris. His writing was prolific and varied. From the late 1960s through the 1970s, he focused on questions of literary structure; he later turned to questions of interpretation and social history.

The 1960s witnessed a flourishing of structuralism in fields as diverse as anthropology, psychology, philosophy, and literature. Influenced by FERDINAND DE SAUSSURE (1857–1913) as well as by contemporary linguists, structuralists applied the scientific model of linguistics to other aspects of human culture, seeking to chart their underlying structures and rules. For instance, fashion or courtship rituals might be seen as operating according to their own distinctive codes. The Saussurean model treats words and other minimal linguistic elements not as freestanding units but as components of a larger, abstract system; the overall system of language rather than individual speech utterances thus becomes the primary object of analysis. The anthropologist CLAUDE LÉVI-STRAUSS became famous for applying structuralist methods to the analysis of the myths and rituals of the primitive societies he observed, and his "Structural Analysis of Myth" (1958) provided an influential early example for work in literary studies. Defining literary study as one of the "human sciences" instead of a humanistic pursuit, structuralist critics aimed to describe and categorize the systematic operation of literature, whose general codes were exhibited and instantiated in individual literary works.

Encapsulating the tenets of Todorov's books *Grammaire du Décaméron* (1969, *Grammar of the Decameron*) and *Poetics of Prose* (1971; trans. 1977), "Structural Analysis of Narrative" seeks to develop a "poetics," that is, a theoretical study of literary techniques and categories. Todorov is quick to distinguish his version of structural analysis from the New Criticism, the predominant Anglo-American critical approach of the mid-twentieth century. While both focus on internal literary features of works rather than on external concerns such as historical context, he notes that the New Criticism deals only with the individual work itself. The structuralist method proposes instead to understand the overall system in which the work is a part. In his analyses of BOCCACCIO's *Decameron* (1351–53), for example, Todorov's interest is not in any individual tale, but in the general and abstract plot structures that govern all the tales. For Todorov, the New Critical method results only in paraphrase and thus does not create new knowledge; the structuralist method, in contrast, charts the systematic laws and patterns that generate literary works. It therefore yields a scientific knowledge of literature, as physics yields a scientific knowledge of the laws of nature, or as linguistics yields a scientific knowledge of the laws of language.

Following ARISTOTLE's view of plot as the prime category of tragedy, Todorov (and narratology in general) takes plot as the central abstract structure of narrative, analyzing the hundred tales in the *Decameron* on the basis of the similarity of their plots. They lead him to the insight that plot moves from an equilibrium to a disequilibrium—hence the action of the narrative—and concludes in a new equilibrium, which displays either "avoided punishment" or "conversion." As he states, "All of the stories of the *Decameron* can be entered into this very broad schema." In privileging and schematizing plot, Todorov also shows the influence of the Russian formalists, particularly the folklorist Vladimir Propp, whose *Morphology of the Folktale* (1928) charts basic plot motifs or patterns common to folktales. Todorov designates the specific elements of each plot, on the model of the sentence, as subject, predicate, and adjective. In an effort to adopt the technical precision of linguistics, he discerns the "grammar" rather than semantic meaning of narrative.

With the critiques of structuralism and the development of poststructuralism by thinkers such as JACQUES DERRIDA through the 1970s, structuralism waned as a vanguard theoretical approach. However, the structuralist theory of narrative has been less discredited than displaced, supplanted by more socially engaged approaches—among them, Marxism, feminism, the New Historicism, and cultural studies. Todorov's own work broadened to consider larger cultural and interpretive issues, as did that of Barthes, who in the 1970s became a leading proponent of poststructuralist literary criticism, extolling the richness of textual interpretation. Yet as Todorov notes in "Structural Analysis of Narrative," poetics does not deny "the relation between literature and . . . social life"; therefore it does not contradict "external" approaches, but serves a different purpose. Narratology remains an active though technical subfield in literary studies, and Todorov's work is still regarded as foundational.

"Structural Analysis of Narrative" Keywords: Narrative Theory, The Novel, Structuralism

Structural Analysis of Narrative[1]

The theme I propose to deal with is so vast that the few pages which follow will inevitably take the form of a resumé. My title, moreover, contains the word "structural," a word more misleading than enlightening today. To avoid misunderstandings as much as possible, I shall proceed in the following fashion. First, I shall give an abstract description of what I conceive to be the structural approach to literature. This approach will then be illustrated by a concrete problem, that of narrative, and more specifically, that of plot. The examples will all be taken from the *Decameron* of Boccaccio.[2] Finally, I shall attempt to make several general conclusions about the nature of narrative and the principles of its analysis.

First of all, one can contrast two possible attitudes toward literature: a theoretical attitude and a descriptive attitude. The nature of structural analysis will be essentially theoretical and non-descriptive; in other words, the aim of such a study will never be the description of a concrete work. The work will be considered as the manifestation of an abstract structure, merely one of its possible realizations; an understanding of that structure will be the real goal of structural analysis. Thus, the term "structure" has, in this case, a logical rather than spatial significance.

Another opposition will enable us to focus more sharply on the critical position which concerns us. If we contrast the internal approach to a literary work with the external one, structural analysis would represent an internal approach. This opposition is well known to literary critics, and Wellek and Warren have used it as the basis for their *Theory of Literature*.[3] It is necessary, however, to recall it here, because, in labeling all structural analysis "theoretical," I clearly come close to what is generally termed an "external" approach (in imprecise usage, "theoretical" and "external," on the one hand,

1. Translated by Arnold Weinstein.
2. GIOVANNI BOCCACCIO (1313–1375), Italian writer; the *Decameron* (1351–53), his major achievement, is a collection of 100 tales.
3. First published in 1949 and for decades a standard introduction to literary criticism; the coauthors, Austrian-born René Wellek (1903–1995) and Austin Warren (1899–1986), were two American literary critics.

and "descriptive" and "internal," on the other, are synonyms). For example, when Marxists or psychoanalysts deal with a work of literature, they are not interested in a knowledge of the work itself, but in the understanding of an abstract structure, social or psychic, which manifests itself through that work. This attitude is therefore both theoretical and external. On the other hand, a New Critic[4] (imaginary) whose approach is obviously internal, will have no goal other than an understanding of the work itself; the result of his efforts will be a paraphrase of the work, which is supposed to reveal the meaning better than the work itself.

Structural analysis differs from both of these attitudes. Here we can be satisfied neither by a pure description of the work nor by its interpretation in terms that are psychological or sociological or, indeed, philosophical. In other words, structural analysis coincides (in its basic tenets) with theory, with poetics of literature. Its object is the literary discourse rather than works of literature, literature that is virtual rather than real. Such analysis seeks no longer to articulate a paraphrase, a rational resumé of the concrete work, but to propose a theory of the structure and operation of the literary discourse, to present a spectrum of literary possibilities, in such a manner that the existing works of literature appear as particular instances that have been realized.

It must immediately be added that, in practice, structural analysis will also refer to real works: the best stepping-stone toward theory is that of precise, empirical knowledge. But such analysis will discover in each work what it has in common with others (study of genres, of periods, for example), or even with all other works (theory of literature); it would be unable to state the individual specificity of each work. In practice, it is always a question of going continually back and forth, from abstract literary properties to individual works and vice versa. Poetics and description are in fact two complementary activities.

On the other hand, to affirm the internal nature of this approach does not mean a denial of the relation between literature and other homogeneous series, such as philosophy or social life. It is rather a question of establishing a hierarchy: literature must be understood in its specificity, as literature, before we seek to determine its relation with anything else.

It is easily seen that such a conception of literary analysis owes much to the modern notion of science. It can be said that structural analysis of literature is a kind of propaedeutic[5] for a future science of literature. This term "science," used with regard to literature, usually raises a multitude of protests. It will therefore perhaps be fitting to try to answer some of those protests right now.

Let us first of all reread that page from Henry James's[6] famous essay on "The Art of Fiction," which already contains several criticisms: "Nothing, for instance, is more possible than that he [the novelist] be of a turn of mind for which this odd, literal opposition of description and dialogue, incident and description, has little meaning and light. People often talk of these

4. An adherent of the dominant Anglo-American academic approach to literary study in the mid-20th century, which focuses on the text itself and stresses close reading. Prominent New Critics include CLEANTH BROOKS (1906–1994) and WILLIAM K. WIMSATT JR. (1907–1975); Warren and Wellek were loosely associated with the movement.

5. Analysis preliminary to some other study.

6. American novelist and critic (1843–1916); for his programmatic "Art of Fiction" (1884), see above.

things as if they had a kind of internecine distinctness, instead of melting into each other at every breath, and being intimately associated parts of one general effort of expression. I cannot imagine composition existing in a series of blocks, nor conceive, in any novel worth discussing at all, of a passage of description that is not in its intention narrative, a passage of dialogue that is not in its intention descriptive, a touch of truth of any sort that does not partake of the nature of incident, or an incident that derives its interest from any other source than the general and only source of the success of a work of art—that of being illustrative. A novel is a living thing, all one and continuous, like any other organism, and in proportion as it lives will it be found, I think, that in each of the parts there is something of each of the other parts. The critic who over the close texture of a finished work shall pretend to trace a geography of items will mark some frontiers as artificial, I fear, as any that have been known to history."

In this excerpt, the critic who uses such terms as "description," "narration," "dialogue," is accused by Henry James of committing two sins. First, there will never be found, in a real text, a pure dialogue, a pure description, and so on. Secondly, the very use of these terms is unnecessary, even harmful, since the novel is "a living thing, all one and continuous."

The first objection loses all its weight as soon as we put ourselves in the perspective of structural analysis; although it does aim at an understanding of concepts like "description" or "action," there is no need to find them in a pure state. It seems rather natural that abstract concepts cannot be analyzed directly, at the level of empirical reality. In physics, for example, we speak of a property such as temperature although we are unable to isolate it by itself and are forced to observe it in bodies possessing many other qualities also, like resistance and volume. Temperature is a theoretical concept, and it does not need to exist in a pure state; such is also true for description.

The second objection is still more curious. Let us consider the already dubious comparison between a work and a living thing. We all know that any part of our body will contain blood, nerves, muscles—all at the same time; we nonetheless do not require the biologist to abandon these misleading abstractions, designated by the words: blood, nerves, muscles. The fact that we find them together does not prevent us from distinguishing them. If the first argument of James had a positive aspect (it indicated that our objective should be composed of abstract categories and not concrete works), the second represents an absolute refusal to recognize the existence of abstract categories, of whatever is not visible.

There is another very popular argument against the introduction of scientific principles in literary analysis. We are told in this instance that science must be objective, whereas the interpretation of literature is always subjective. In my opinion this crude opposition is untenable. The critic's work can have varying degrees of subjectivity; everything depends on the perspective he has chosen. This degree will be much lower if he tries to ascertain the properties of the work rather than seeking its significance for a given period or milieu. The degree of subjectivity will vary, moreover, when he is examining different strata of the same work. There will be very few discussions concerning the metrical or phonic scheme of a poem; slightly more concerning the nature of its images; still more with regard to the more complex semantic patterns.

On the other hand there is no social science (or science whatsoever) which is totally free of subjectivity. The very choice of one group of theoretical concepts instead of another presupposes a subjective decision; but if we do not make this choice, we achieve nothing at all. The economist, the anthropologist, and the linguist must be subjective also; the only difference is that they are aware of it and they try to limit this subjectivity, to make allowance for it within the theory. One can hardly attempt to repudiate the subjectivity of the social sciences at a time when even the natural sciences are affected by it.

It is now time to stop these theoretical speculations and to give an example of the structural approach to literature. This example will serve as illustration rather than proof: the theories which I have just exposed will not be necessarily contested if there are some imperfections in the concrete analysis based on them.

The abstract literary concept I would like to discuss is that of plot. Of course, that does not mean that literature, for me, is reduced to plot alone. I do think, however, that plot is a notion that critics undervalue and, hence, often disregard. The ordinary reader, however, reads a book above all as the narration of a plot; but this naive reader is uninterested in theoretical problems. My aim is to suggest a certain number of useful categories for examining and describing plots. These categories can thus implement the meager vocabulary at our command with regard to the analysis of narrative; it consists of such terms as action, character, recognition.

The literary examples that I shall use are taken from the *Decameron* of Boccaccio. I do not intend, however, to give an analysis of the *Decameron*: these stories will be used only to display an abstract literary structure, that is, plot. I shall begin by stating the plots of several of the tales.

A monk introduces a young girl into his cell and makes love to her. The abbot detects this misbehavior and plans to punish him severely. But the monk learns of the abbot's discovery and lays a trap for him by leaving his cell. The abbot goes in and succumbs to the charms of the girl, while the monk tries his turn at watching. At the end when the abbot intends to punish him, the monk points out that he has just committed the same sin. Result: the monk is not punished (I,4).[7]

Isabetta, a young nun, is with her lover in her cell. Upon discovering this, the other nuns become jealous and go to wake up the abbess and have Isabetta punished. But the abbess was in bed with an abbot; because she has to come out quickly, she puts the under-shorts of the abbot on her head instead of her coif. Isabetta is led into the church; as the abbess begins to lecture her, Isabetta notices the garment on her head. She brings this evidence to everyone's attention and thus escapes punishment (IX,2).

Peronnella receives her lover while her husband, a poor mason, is absent. But one day he comes home early. Peronnella hides the lover in a cask; when the husband comes in, she tells him that somebody wanted to buy the cask and that this somebody is now in the process of examining it. The husband believes her and is delighted with the sale. The lover pays and leaves with the cask (VII,2).

7. There are 10 characters in the *Decameron*, and each in turn tells one story a day for 10 days; "I,4" refers to the 4th story on the 1st day.

A married woman meets her lover every night in the family's country house, where she is usually alone. But one night the husband returns from town; the lover has not come yet; he arrives a little later and knocks at the door. The wife asserts that this is a ghost who comes to annoy her every night and must be exorcised. The husband pronounces the formula which the wife has improvised; the lover figures out the situation and leaves, pleased with the ingenuity of his mistress (VII,1).

It is easy to recognize that these four plots (and there are many others like them in the *Decameron*) have something in common. In order to express that, I shall use a schematic formulation which retains only the common elements of these plots. The sign → will indicate a relation of entailment between two actions.

$$\text{X violates a law} \rightarrow \text{Y must punish X} \rightarrow \text{X tries to avoid being punished} \rightarrow$$
$$\rightarrow \left\{ \begin{array}{l} \text{Y violates a law} \\ \text{Y believes that X is not violating the law} \end{array} \right. \rightarrow \text{Y does not punish X}$$

This schematic representation requires several explanations.

1. We first notice that the minimal schema of the plot can be shown naturally by a clause. Between the categories of language and those of narrative there is a profound analogy which must be explored.

2. Analysis of this narrative clause leads us to discover the existence of two entities which correspond to the "parts of speech." (a) The agents, designated here by X and Y, correspond to proper nouns. They serve as subject or object of the clause; moreover, they permit identification of their reference without its being described. (b) The predicate, which is always a verb here: violate, punish, avoid. The verbs have a semantic characteristic in common: they denote an action which modifies the preceding situation. (c) An analysis of other stories would have shown us a third part of narrative speech, which corresponds to quality and does not alter the situation in which it appears: the adjective. Thus in I,8: at the beginning of the action Ermino is stingy, whereas Guillaume is generous. Guillaume finds a way to ridicule Ermino's stinginess, and since then Ermino is "the most generous and pleasant of gentlemen." The qualities of the two characters are examples of adjectives.

3. Actions (violate, punish) can have a positive or a negative form; thus, we shall also need the category of status, negation being one possible status.

4. The category of modality[8] is also relevant here. When we say "X must punish Y," we denote thereby an action which has not yet taken place (in the imaginary universe of the story) but which is nonetheless present in a virtual state. André Jolles[9] suggested that entire genres could be characterized by their mood; legends would be the genre of the imperative, to the extent that they offer us an example to follow; the fairy tale is, as is often said, the genre of the optative, of the fulfilled wish.

5. When we write "Y believes that X is not violating the law," we have an example of a verb ("believe") which differs from the others. It is not a ques-

8. That is, the determination of whether a sentence expresses a fact, a command, a wish, and so on, as set by the form (the mood) of the verb and its auxiliaries.

9. Dutch literary and art historian (1874–1946); the reference is to his *Einfache Formen* (1930, *Simple Forms*).

tion of a different action here but of a different perception of the same action. We could therefore speak of a kind of "point of view" which refers not only to the relation between reader and narrator, but also to the characters.

6. There are also relations between the clauses; in our example this is always a causal relation; but a more extensive study would distinguish at least between entailment and presupposition (for example, the relation introducing modal punishment). Analysis of other stories shows that there are also purely temporal relations (succession) and purely spatial ones (parallelism).

7. An organized succession of clauses forms a new syntagmatic pattern,[1] sequence. Sequence is perceived by the reader as a finished story; it is the minimal narrative in a completed form. This impression of completion is caused by a modified repetition of the initial clause; the first and the last clause will be identical but they will either have a different mood or status, for instance, or they will be seen from different points of view. In our example it is punishment which is repeated: first changed in modality, then denied. In a sequence of temporal relations, repetition can be total.

8. We might also ask: is there a way back? How does one get from the abstract, schematic representation to the individual tale? Here, there are three answers:

(a) The same kind of organization can be studied at a more concrete level: each clause of our sequence could be rewritten as an entire sequence itself. We would not thereby change the nature of the analysis, but rather the level of generality.

(b) It is also possible to study the concrete actions that incorporate our abstract pattern. For instance, we may point out the different laws that become violated in the stories of the *Decameron* or the different punishments that are meted out. That would be a thematic study.

(c) Finally, we can examine the verbal medium which composes our abstract patterns. The same action can be expressed by means of dialogue or description, figurative or literal discourse; moreover, each action can be seen from a different point of view. Here we are dealing with a rhetorical study.

These three directions correspond to the three major categories of narrative analysis: study of narrative syntax, study of theme, study of rhetoric.

At this point we may ask: what is the purpose of all this? Has this analysis taught us anything about the stories in question? But that would be a bad question. Our goal is not a knowledge of the *Decameron* (although such analysis will also serve that purpose), but rather an understanding of literature or, in this specific instance, of plot. The categories of plot mentioned here will permit a more extensive and precise description of other plots. The object of our study must be narrative mood, or point of view, or sequence, and not this or that story in and for itself.

From such categories we can move forward and inquire about the possibility of a typology of plots. For the moment it is difficult to offer a valid hypothesis; therefore I must be content to summarize the results of my research on the *Decameron*.

1. The relationship between linguistic items that combine to form a meaningful whole (e.g., the words in a given sentence); in contrast, paradigmatic relationships obtain between items that can be substituted for one another in a given context (e.g., two adverbs).

The minimal complete plot can be seen as the shift from one equilibrium to another. This term "equilibrium," which I am borrowing from genetic psychology, means the existence of a stable but not static relation between the members of a society; it is a social law, a rule of the game, a particular system of exchange. The two moments of equilibrium, similar and different, are separated by a period of imbalance, which is composed of a process of degeneration and a process of improvement.

All of the stories of the *Decameron* can be entered into this very broad schema. From that point, however, we can make a distinction between two kinds of stories. The first can be labeled "avoided punishment"; the four stories I mentioned at the beginning are examples of it. Here we follow a complete cycle: we begin with a state of equilibrium which is broken by a violation of the law. Punishment would have restored the initial balance; the fact that punishment is avoided establishes a new equilibrium.

The other type of story is illustrated by the tale about Ermino (I,8), which we may label "conversion." This story begins in the middle of a complete cycle, with a state of imbalance created by a flaw in one of the characters. The story is basically the description of an improvement process—until the flaw is no longer there.

The categories which help us to describe these types tell us much about the universe of a book. With Boccaccio, the two equilibriums symbolize (for the most part) culture and nature,[2] the social and the individual; the story usually consists in illustrating the superiority of the second term over the first.

We could also seek even greater generalizations. It is possible to contrast a specific plot typology with a game typology and to see them as two variants of a common structure. So little has been done in this direction that we do not even know what kinds of questions to ask.

I would like to return now to the beginning argument and to look at the initial question again: what is the object of structural analysis of literature (or, if you wish, of poetics)? At first glance, it is literature or, as Jakobson[3] would have said, literariness. But let us look more closely. In our discussion of literary phenomena, we have had to introduce a certain number of notions and to create an image of literature; this image constitutes the constant preoccupation of all research on poetics. "Science is concerned not with things but with the system of signs it can substitute for things," wrote Ortega y Gasset.[4] The virtualities which make up the object of poetics (as of all other sciences), these abstract qualities of literature exist only in the discourse of poetics itself. From this perspective, literature becomes only a mediator, a language, which poetics uses for dealing with itself.

We must not, however, conclude that literature is secondary for poetics or that it is not, in a certain sense, the object of poetics. Science is characterized precisely by this ambiguity concerning its object, an ambiguity that need not be resolved, but rather used as the basis for analysis. Poetics, like literature, consists of an uninterrupted movement back and forth between the two poles: the first is auto-reference, preoccupation with itself; the second is what we usually call its object.

2. The opposition between nature and culture is foundational in structuralism, notably in the work of the French anthropologist CLAUDE LÉVI-STRAUSS (1908–2009).

3. ROMAN JAKOBSON (1896–1982), Russian-born American linguist and literary theorist.

4. José Ortega y Gasset (1883–1955), Spanish philosopher and critic.

There is a practical conclusion to be drawn from these speculations. In poetics as elsewhere, discussions of methodology are not a minor area of the larger field, a kind of accidental by-product: they are rather its very center, its principal goal. As Freud[5] said, "The important thing in a scientific work is not the nature of the facts with which it is concerned, but the rigor, the exactness of the method which is prior to the establishment of these facts, and the research of a synthesis as large as possible."

1969

5. SIGMUND FREUD (1856–1939), Austrian founder of psychoanalysis.

KARATANI KŌJIN
b. 1941

Karatani Kōjin is widely regarded as the most influential critic and philosopher of contemporary Japan. His major theme is alterity—understood as a necessarily elusive realm of otherness that can be glimpsed only rarely through ruptures in a world tightly enclosed within the formal systems of signs, Western metaphysics, and capitalism. This pursuit has led to Karatani's engagements with a wide range of disciplines: literature, art and art history, architecture, city planning, linguistics, cultural anthropology, psychoanalysis, mathematics, philosophy, and political economy. From his literary criticism to his rereadings of IMMANUEL KANT and KARL MARX, Karatani's work has been guided by the conviction that true insight derives solely from confrontation with that which is external to the thinking self, to the degree that it is not subsumed by that self. The key is to "see things neither from one's own viewpoint, nor from the viewpoint of others, but to face the reality that is exposed through the difference between the two."

Karatani Yoshio (Karatani is his family name) was born in 1941 in Amagasaki City, midway between the major urban centers of Kobe and Osaka. In 1960, during his freshman year at Tokyo University, he joined a student group called the Communist League, popularly known as the Bund. One of many such groups in Japan in an era of widespread student activism, the Bund disavowed Japanese Communist Party orthodoxy. It was actively supported by the New Left poet and literary critic Yoshimoto Takaaki (1924–2012), whom Karatani has cited as one of the inspirations for his decision to pursue a career as a critic. The year 1960 is pivotal in postwar Japanese history, marked by large-scale but unsuccessful demonstrations against the renewal of the U.S.-Japan Security Treaty of 1951. Karatani's experience of these events and their aftermath forms the basis for his later insights into the relationships between political defeat, the formation of interiority, and the institutionalization of discourse.

Eventually withdrawing from the arena of student political activism, Karatani completed a B.A. in economics in 1964; he continued his studies at Tokyo University, earning an M.A. in English literature in 1967. His career as a public intellectual was launched in 1969, when he was awarded the prestigious Gunzō Literary Prize for an essay on the status of consciousness and nature in the work of Natsume Sōseki (1867–1916), a key figure in modern Japanese literature. Along with Kant, Marx, FRIEDRICH NIETZSCHE, and SIGMUND FREUD, Sōseki would become one of Karatani's major reference points; he took the name "Kōjin" from the title of a Sōseki novel (translated into English as *The Wayfarer*). Karatani taught at Hōsei University in Tokyo from 1970 to 1997, and at Kinki University in Osaka from 1997 until his retirement in 2006. From 1975 to 1977, he was invited to Yale University as a visiting professor of modern Japanese literature, where he met JACQUES DERRIDA, PAUL DE MAN, and FREDRIC JAMESON. Between 1990 and 2004 Karatani also taught regularly at Columbia University as a visiting professor of comparative literature.

It was during his two-year residence at Yale that Karatani initially conceived of *Origins of Modern Japanese Literature* (1980; trans. 1993), the work from which we draw our selection. One of the most widely read and frequently cited texts in Japanese literary studies today, *Origins* was published in translation by Duke University Press in the Post-Contemporary Interventions Series, whose editors include STANLEY FISH and Jameson. Karatani has likened his "existence as a stranger in the United States" to that of Sōseki, who lived in London from 1900 to 1903. This sojourn initiated both a wide-ranging critical inquiry into the meaning of "literature" and a literary practice that, in Karatani's view, resisted the dominant modern epistemological paradigm in which the exterior space of "landscape" and the interior space of "the self" had come to be taken as self-evident realities. Karatani launched his own revisionist account of the origins of modern Japanese literature while reconsidering Sōseki's theoretical work, which had long been dismissed as a "failure" abandoned for the actual writing of literature itself. By resuscitating Sōseki's work as an early twentieth-century Japanese theorist, Karatani implicitly overturned two widespread assumptions: that "theory" is exclusive to "the West" and that "literature" has always existed everywhere in much the same form.

Japan's encounter with the modern West in the late nineteenth century occasioned a profound reorganization of knowledge that affected all fields of intellectual inquiry and cultural practice. It was during this time that the modern Western categories of "literature," "self-expression," and "external object" became firmly established, effacing earlier concepts and practices of writing that were very different. In Europe these categories emerged gradually over two centuries, and thus came to seem completely natural and inevitable. By contrast, Japan's rapid transition threw into doubt the assumed universality of "literature," "self," and "object" in both European and Japanese contexts. It also opened to question the Eurocentric notion of linear historical development that typifies narrative accounts of "modernity."

Origins of Modern Japanese Literature employs the genealogical method of Nietzsche and MICHEL FOUCAULT to expose the historicity of these concepts. In an ironic reversal of the rhetoric of Western expansion—according to which, for instance, Christopher Columbus is said to have "discovered" the Americas—*Origins* presents a series of traumatic discoveries that incorporated the Japanese people into modernity: its chapter titles include "The Discovery of Landscape," "The Discovery of Interiority," and "The Discovery of the Child," implying that these concepts were new to Japan.

In our selection Karatani Kōjin depicts correspondences between a wide array of phenomena occurring during the Meiji era (1868–1912). He establishes links between contact with the West, a changing political system in Japan, the emergence of the isolated individual endowed with an inner life, the rise of psychology, the appearance of landscape painting (an external tableau seen from an individual viewpoint), and new concepts of literature. The subject-object dichotomy of modern (post-1650) Western philosophy sets a self-expressive subject against an inert and measurable external world. This division brought about a new mode of perception—what T. S. ELIOT once called a "dissociation of sensibility"—which displaced the holistic, ordered world of the Middle Ages and Renaissance. Analogous shifts occurred during the late Meiji period, when Japanese seasonal paintings (*shiki-e* and *tsukinami*) became landscapes; written classical language (*gabun*) lost ground to vernacular spoken language (*genbun itchi*); and literature narrowed. In the last case, a broad, varied corpus of texts and styles written in classical Chinese with many Japanese permutations (*kanbungaku*) changed to a smaller, national canon of works in Japanese (*kokubungaku*). What counts as "literature" prior to and after the Meiji era is quite different—but before Karatani, most critics had overlooked this transformation.

While drawing numerous, often unexpected parallels with and contrasts between European and Japanese cultural formations, Karatani does more than simply hold up a Japanese mirror to Western modernity. In "The Discovery of Landscape," our selection, the term *landscape* refers to the notion of "objective description" that has played a central role in modern definitions of literature. The use of a term primarily associated with (Western) painting enables Karatani to identify an overarching structure of modern perception, premised on the split between an interiorized "self" and an exteriorized "outside" from which that self has already been alienated. Once they accepted this split, the general public could see "landscape" as nothing more or less than that which exists outside of themselves. Surprisingly, this modern Western view is contrasted with medieval European and pre-twentieth-century Japanese perceptions of place, which valued the general, often transcendental meanings attached to a location rather than any putatively empirical impressions of it. Karatani thus uses *landscape* deconstructively to signify both a representational practice (the "realistic representation" of "nature") and the transformation of perception that made the practice possible. This transformation, once established, represses its own "origins" or historicity and comes to seem natural.

One of Karatani's signal contributions to the discourse on non-Western modernity is his focus on the ideological role of "literature"—its simultaneous production of the expressing self and of the external objects that the self describes. In the process, he attempts to expose the modern nation-state of Japan itself as a construct, in whose production this aesthetic apparatus played a role. His account connects the origins of landscape in Japan to the emergence of the inner self in the 1890s, not long after the complete suppression of the People's Rights movement by the Japanese state. Both citing and historicizing Freud's theory that consciousness derives from an experience of trauma that redirects the libido inward, Karatani suggests that this political defeat helped create the necessary conditions for a new structure of perception, within which both landscape and the inner self of literature suddenly appeared as a priori givens.

Though modern Japan has been shaped since the late nineteenth century by the threat of Western domination, it was also the first Asian country to join the exclusive club of modern nation-states. This development led to a reversal in its relations with China (regarded by Japan for more than a millennium as the center of civilization); it also led to Japan's aggressive participation in the originally Western project of colonizing Asia, which finally culminated in its disastrous defeat in World War II. During the 1930s and 1940s, Japanese expansion in Asia, China included, was ideologically justified as the liberation of Asia from Western domination, a discursive strategy made possible by Japanese attacks on (Western) modernity. Karatani's steadfast refusal to offer a non-Western alternative to modernity stems from his keen awareness of the ease with which the critique of (Western) modernity—as necessary as it is—can be appropriated by reactionary politics.

Because of its insights into the nature and formation of modern literature in a non-Western context, *Origins* has enjoyed a broad international readership; it has been translated into Korean, Chinese, German, and Turkish in addition to English. The work presents a critical challenge to the story of a gradual, if always somehow incomplete, development of "Western-style" realism and the literary self in Japan—a historiographical approach previously standard on both sides of the Pacific. Indeed, contrary to the author's intentions, this text now serves as the new "standard history" in Japanese literary studies, shaping the work of today's younger critics.

Karatani explicitly defines himself as a critic and not a theorist—a distinction that locates his writings in the context of, and as a critical response to, the present moment, rather than in a purely hypothetical or timeless objective vantage point from which the present and past might be considered. In this regard, Karatani's inquiry into the relationship between landscape, self, literature, and politics in 1890s Japan constitutes his critical response to the discursive space of 1970s Japan, an era that repeats the same "pattern of retreat to interiority and literature after political setback." After he wrote *Origins*, Karatani's own trajectory would move in the opposite direction, away from interiority and literature and toward exteriority and political action. His *Transcritique: On Kant and Marx* (2001; trans. 2003) laid the philosophical groundwork for the ethico-economic New Association Movement (NAM), which he founded in 2000. Boldly proclaiming that "Communism without economic basis is empty, while communism without moral basis is blind," *Transcritique* garnered much attention, particularly in radical philosophy circles, for its alternative vision of Kant and Marx, and for the possibility it raises of superseding capitalism, nation, and state. Although NAM was dissolved in 2003, Karatani has continued his engagement with political activism, most notably in the antinuclear movement that emerged in response to the nuclear disaster that followed Japan's massive earthquake and tsunami of March 11, 2011. A more recent work available in English, *The Structure of World History: From Modes of Production to Modes of Exchange* (2010; trans. with revisions, 2014), builds on core aspects of *Transcritique* by proposing that "rethinking the history of social formations from the perspective of modes of exchange" rather than that of Marx's modes of production is crucial to any attempt to "move beyond the present-day Capital-Nation-State system."

Some scholars have taken issue with Karatani's characterization of Japanese modernity as a fundamental break from the past, citing continuities over Japan's long cultural history. Behind this general objection are two complicated questions. First, does a sharp focus on the rise of modern epistemological constellations in a late-developing nation-state underplay or efface the co-presence of other modes of perception and practice, in effect reproducing the same universalism and homogenization that it seeks to undermine? And second, can the notion of cultural continuity itself be separated from the ideology of modern, linear historiography, with its political interest in locating the origins of modern nations in the distant past?

Because Karatani conceives of history as a series of ruptures that immediately repress their own origins, and because, like Foucault, he characterizes modernity as a system that has "no outside," his work has also been subject to a general epistemological criticism. If a structure of perception is thoroughly ensconced within the epistemological constellation that produced it, then how can anyone within that constellation gain critical insight into it or break from it? Whereas Foucault denies that the individual subject can be a locus of such insight, Karatani privileges the writer Sōseki as the rare example of someone who, caught between historical paradigms, became "aware that the structure of his perceptions had been fundamentally altered." He thus treats Sōseki as an exception to the general rule that epistemological reversals, such as the one that produced the modern concept of "literature," hide themselves as soon as they are established. EDWARD W. SAID also allows such creative individuals to be rare exceptions. In an implicit critique of the Foucauldian approach, Karatani defends this apparent inconsistency by asserting that "it was not my aim to write about the construction of modern Japanese literature from a position of historical transcendence."

Origins of Modern Japanese Literature **Keywords:** Globalization, Literary History, Modernity, Nationhood, New Historicism, Realism, Subjectivity, Vernacular Language

From Origins of Modern Japanese Literature[1]

From *Chapter 1. The Discovery of Landscape*

2

The strongly personal tone of Sōseki's[2] preface to the *Theory of Literature* suggests that the role of theoretician was something he embraced reluctantly and as if perforce. He explains how he came to entertain the question "What is the nature of literature?"

> As a child I enjoyed studying the Chinese classics.[3] Although the time I spent in this kind of study was not long, it was from the Chinese classics that I learned, however vaguely and obscurely, what literature was. In my heart, I hoped that it would be the same way when I read English literature, and that I would not necessarily begrudge giving my whole life, if that were necessary, to its study. I had years ahead of me. I cannot say that I lacked the time to study English literature. But what I resent is that despite my study I never mastered it. When I graduated I was plagued by the fear that somehow I had been cheated by English literature.[4]

There was a basis for Sōseki's fear that he had been "cheated" by English literature. Only those who have come to accept "literature" as natural cannot detect this "cheating." Nor should we invoke vague generalizations about the identity crisis of one who confronts an alien culture. To do this would be to assume there was something self-evident about "literature" and to lose sight of its ideological nature. Sōseki had some inkling of the ideological nature of literature because of his familiarity with *kanbungaku*.[5] Of course, *kanbungaku* as Sōseki knew it was not simply the "literature of China," nor was he attempting to compare it with Western literature. Sōseki was in no position to pursue idle comparisons between *kanbungaku* and Western literature. In point of fact, Sōseki himself could not even grasp *kanbungaku* as a tangible existence, for by his own time it had already become something uncertain and irretrievable, something which could only be imagined on the other shore, as it were, of "literature."

Sōseki uses the term *kanbungaku* in a manner very similar to the way in which the word *sansuiga* (literally, "mountain-water pictures" or "landscape paintings") was used in Meiji Japan[6] to denote paintings of natural scenes done in traditional styles. It was only after the Japanese had been introduced

1. Translated by Brett de Bary, who occasionally retains the Japanese words or adds information in parentheses.
2. Natsume Sōseki (1867–1916), one of the most important novelists of his time; *Theory of Literature* (1906) is based on his lectures on English literature at Tokyo University.
3. Foundational works of history, philosophy, ethics, and poetry, which constituted the core syllabus of elite education in Japan for more than a millennium.
4. Natsume Sōseki, *Bungakuron*, in *Natsume Sōseki zenshū*, vol. 16, pp. 8–9 [translator's note].
5. Both the techniques used to make classical Chinese works accessible to Japanese readers and writing in Japanese that imitates those works. Hence the term neither corresponds to the 19th-century European concept of "literature" nor supports a sharp distinction between "Chinese" and "Japanese" texts.
6. The years of the reign of Mutsuhito (as emperor, he took the reign name Meiji), 1868–1912, which ended Japan's feudalism and began its rise as a modern nation-state.

to Western landscape painting that the word *sansuiga* became widely used. As Usami Keiji[7] wrote in an essay on a recent exhibit of such paintings:

> The word *sansuiga* was not actually used in the period when the works exhibited here were painted. At that time they were referred to as *shiki-e* or *tsukinami* (seasonal paintings). Ernest Fenollosa,[8] who played a leading role in Japan's modernization during the Meiji period, coined the term *sansuiga* and established it as a descriptive category for paintings. The very concept of traditional "landscape paintings" arose out of the disjuncture between Japanese culture and modern Western consciousness.[9]

The same may be said of *kanbungaku*. Although Sōseki uses the term to differentiate certain practices from those of modern literature, it is itself rooted in the consciousness that produced the category "literature" and has no existence apart from it. Literature makes the objectification of *kanbungaku* possible. In this sense to compare *kanbungaku* and English literature is to ignore the historicity of literature itself—of "literature" as a kind of "landscape." It is to fail to take into account the fact that, through the emergence of "literature" and "landscape," the very structure of our perceptions has been transformed.

I would like to propose that the notion of "landscape" developed in Japan sometime during the third decade of the Meiji period.[1] Of course, there were landscapes long before they were "discovered." But "landscapes" as such did not exist prior to the 1890s, and it is only when we think about it in this way that the layers of meaning entailed in the notion of a "discovery of landscape" become apparent.

It was precisely this period of transition that Sōseki lived through. Yet to invoke the concept of a "transitional period" is merely to fall back on a construct of linear history. It was only after Sōseki had already decided to study English literature that he became aware that the structure of his perceptions had been fundamentally altered. Nor was there a kind of static triangular relationship established in Sōseki's mind between himself, English literature, and *kanbungaku*. As with his character Daisuke in the novel *Sore Kara*,[2] it would dawn on Sōseki unpredictably at certain moments that he had already made a decision. Similarly, we cannot describe the Japanese discovery of "landscape" as a process that unfolded in a linear pattern from past to present. "Time" has been refracted and turned upside down.

A person who sees landscape as natural will not perceive this reversal. But it is here that we can find the origin of Sōseki's doubt. Sōseki's fear that he had been cheated by English literature expresses the anxiety of a man who suddenly finds himself in the midst of a "landscape."

It is interesting that Sōseki referred to his native literature as *kanbungaku* rather than *Nihon no bungaku* (Japanese literature). The protests of eigh-

7. Prominent Japanese oil painter (1940–2012), author of several works of art theory and criticism.
8. American poet and art scholar (1853–1908), who served as curator for the Imperial Museum of Japan from 1888 to 1890. He profoundly affected how the concept of "fine art" developed and was institutionalized in Japan.
9. Usami Keiji, "Sansuiga ni zetsubō o miru" (The despair of Japanese landscape painting), *Gendai shisō*, May 1977 [Karatani's note].
1. That is, 1888–1897.
2. Published in 1909 (translated into English as *And Then*, 1978).

teenth century nativist[3] scholars notwithstanding, *kanbungaku* has surely been the orthodox literature of Japan. As Yoshimoto Takaaki[4] has pointed out, even the existence of the first imperial poetry anthology, the *Manyōshū*, in the mid-eighth century can be traced to the impact on Japan of Chinese characters and literature in Chinese.[5] We all recognize that it was in Chinese literature that we were introduced to "flowers, birds, wind, and moon" (*kachō fūgetsu*),[6] yet even those things which nativist scholars posited as purely indigenous were intimately related to the structure of perception we refer to as *kanbungaku*. It was only after this structure of perception crystallized that Japanese in the classical period began to compose *jokei*[7] (敘景 compositions about places)—their equivalent of discovering "landscape." Our search for the origins of writing will never take us beyond writing, beyond écriture.[8]

My discussion is complicated by the fact that the discovery of "landscape" in the third decade of the Meiji period is similar to the premodern discovery of Chinese literature, so that we now confront successive layers of inversions.[9] Just as nativist scholars, when they posited the existence of a literature that existed before Chinese literature, could only do so from *within* the epistemological constellation we now call *kanbungaku*, Meiji Japanese who searched for a landscape that predated "landscape" faced the contradiction of being able to envision it only in relation to "landscape." The very question "What is a Japanese landscape painting?" is by definition predicated on an inversion.

The following remarks by Usami Keiji express a profound awareness of this difficulty:

> We must investigate the nature of "time" and place in *sansuiga* in order to understand its spatial dimension. For the depiction of place in this Japanese landscape painting cannot be reduced to the notion of "position" as defined by European principles of perspective. Position, as established by these principles, is the totality of what can be apprehended by a single person with a fixed point of vision. The relationships between all the things that can be apprehended from this point of view at one instant in time are determined objectively on a grid of coordinates. These are the laws of perspective which have conditioned the modern visual sensibility.

3. The term nativism, or *kokugaku* (often translated as National Learning), refers to the broad-ranging 18th-century discourse which sought to define a distinct Japanese identity while contesting the influence of Chinese culture on Japan [translator's note].
4. Japanese poet and literary critic (1924–2012).
5. The anthology of Japanese poetry (*Collection of a Myriad Ages* or *Myriad Leaves*) was originally written entirely in Chinese characters or ideograms, chosen sometimes for their correspondence to the poem's ideas and sometimes to represent its sounds.
6. A classical Chinese term, used when a speaker of English might say "the beauty of nature."
7. Description of place (Modern Japanese). Karatani gives the term a double meaning by making it also refer to the convention in classical (7th- to 19th-c.) Japanese poetry of alluding to famous places (*meisho*), which in his view displayed greater concern with the figures of writing than with the representation of actual places.
8. An allusion to the inversion of the conventional hierarchy of speech and writing by the French philosopher JACQUES DERRIDA (1930–2004), who showed that *écriture* (any and all forms of inscription) precedes speech.
9. Karatani uses the term *inversion* to signify the reversal of an epistemological or semiotic constellation that, once established, represses its own historicity and assumes an appearance of naturalness or inevitability.

> By contrast to this, *place* in the landscape paintings we now call *sansuiga* is not concerned with the relationship between the individual and "things," but presents a transcendental metaphysical "model." This mode of existence of place, and its transcendental nature, is something *sansuiga* has in common with medieval European painting. In the former, the transcendental place is an ideal realm to which the enlightened sages awakened; in the latter, it is the realm of Scripture and the divine.[1]

In *sansuiga* the painter is not looking at an object but envisioning the transcendental. Similarly, poets like Bashō and Sanetomo[2] were not looking at "landscapes." As Yanagita Kunio[3] has said, there is not a single line of description in Bashō's *Oku no hosomichi* (Narrow road to the deep north, 1694).[4] Even what looks like description is not. If we can follow the subtle yet crucial distinction Yanagita has drawn here, we will be able to see both the process of the Japanese discovery of "landscape" and the literary "history" that paralleled that transformation of perception.

In literature, for example, it was only when Japanese naturalism[5] (and the rejection of Bakin[6]) had become a mainstream trend that Saikaku[7] was discovered to be a "realist." But it is doubtful that Saikaku's writing conformed to our contemporary definition of realism. Saikaku did not "see things as they are" any more than did Shakespeare, whose dramas were based on classical models and written within the framework of the morality play. Similarly, the Meiji poet Shiki praised Buson's[8] haiku for being almost like paintings. But Buson's haiku were in no way related to the sensibility of Shiki and his "sketches"; they were closer in spirit to his own *sansuiga*. This is not to deny that Buson was different from Bashō. But what differentiated them was not what we perceive it to be today. Shiki himself acknowledged this. He described, for example, the "painterly" quality of the poetry produced by Buson's bold incorporation of Chinese compounds into his poetry.[9] The following poem, Shiki held, is enlivened by an intense dynamism because the characters (大河) are not given their Japanese reading (*ōkawa*) but the Sini-

1. Usami Keiji, ibid. [Karatani's note].
2. Minamoto no Sanetomo (1192–1219), third shogun of the Kamakura shogunate (1185–1333) and renowned poet. Matsuo Bashō (1644–1694), Japanese poet, critic, and essayist, best known for his major role in the development of the Japanese genre of poetry called haiku (a 3-unit form, with the syllabic pattern 5-7-5).
3. Bureaucrat and scholar (1875–1962), a major figure in Japanese ethnology and folklore studies.
4. This text is the travel diary recording the poet Matsuo Bashō's journey to the remote northern provinces of the island of Honshu in 1689. The text includes, along with its narrative sections, many famous haiku about sites associated with Japanese literature and history and, allusively, with Chinese poetic and historical texts [translator's note].
5. Naturalism was introduced to Japan from Europe in the early 20th century, when Japanese proponents of the movement dominated both literary criticism and production. Japanese naturalism has been seen as culminating in the dominance of the prose narrative over previously privileged poetic literary forms, of the modern vernacular style over classical written styles, and of conventions of realism [translator's note].
6. Takizawa Bakin (1767–1848), author of fiction that remained highly popular into the early Meiji period; his rejection was signaled by attacks on his work in Tsubouchi Shōyō's *Essence of the Novel* (1885–86), which introduced Western realism to Japan.
7. Ihara Saikaku (1642–1693), influential and prolific writer best known for his *ukiyo zōshi* (literally, "tales of the floating world"), entertaining prose that focused on the lives of merchants and samurai, especially their activities in the pleasure quarters. In the late 19th century, his fiction was championed by Japanese naturalists for its "realistic" depiction of the "nature" of sexuality.
8. Yosa Buson (1716–1783), Japanese painter and master of haiku poetry rich in visual detail. Masaoki Shiki (1867–1902), Japanese poet and author of influential treatises that advocated a realistic, descriptive style of poetry; he attacked the work of Bashō, argued in favor of *shasei* (copying life, sketching), and helped modernize both haiku and tanka (a 5-unit form, in the syllabic pattern 5-7-5-7-7).
9. For centuries, classical Japanese poetic conventions had strictly limited the poetic lexicon to "Japanese" words.

cized reading "taiga."[1] But what this example really reveals is that Buson was fascinated, not so much by landscape, as by the written word.

Early summer rains!
Facing the swollen river
Two houses

Samidare ya	さみだれや
Taiga o mae ni	大河を前に
Ie niken	家二軒

The concept of Japanese literature (*kokubungaku*)[2] took firm root during the third decade of the Meiji period. Needless to say, this was both made possible by and interpreted in terms of the newly institutionalized literature. It is not my aim in this essay to discuss the concept of "the history of Japanese literature." But I do want to point out that this very concept of a history of Japanese literature, which seems so self-evident to us today, took shape in the midst of our discovery of landscape. Perhaps it was only Sōseki who regarded this development with suspicion. Yet it is precisely because our discovery of landscape was the type of phenomenon I have described that I cannot refer to it in terms of the chronological sequence of a so-called "history of Japanese literature." "Meiji literary history" certainly appears to progress according to a temporal sequence. But it is only by distorting this temporal sequence that we can perceive the inversion we have repressed from our memories: our discovery of landscape.

* * *

6

Once a landscape has been established, its origins are repressed from memory. It takes on the appearance of an "object" which has been there, outside us, from the start. An "object," however, can only be constituted within a landscape. The same may be said of the "subject" or self. The philosophical standpoint which distinguishes between subject and object came into existence within what I refer to as "landscape." Rather than existing prior to landscape, subject and object emerge from within it.[3]

It has been said that Edo painting[4] had no concept of landscape, since it lacked techniques for creating depth and perspective. Yet this is also true of medieval European painting (despite the fact that, as I have already suggested, the differences between these two types of painting are more salient.) In both cases developments in painting were paralleled by developments in philosophy. Cartesian philosophy, for example, can be seen as a product of principles of perspective. For the subject of Descartes's "cogito ergo sum"[5] is

1. Many Chinese characters can be given either a Japanese or a Chinese-style (Sinicized) pronunciation; the latter emphasizes the written derivation of the word.
2. Writings in the Japanese language without connections to Chinese (thus a national literature, and distinct from *kanbungaku*).
3. Karatani's assertion rests on his discussion of European landscape painting earlier in the chapter, where the new view of landscape as pure object was described as marking an alienation from the external world—which was also the very precondition for the emergence of the "inner self."
4. That is, painting during the rule of the Tokugawa shogunate, 1603–1867.
5. I think, therefore I am (Latin), the foundational statement of the French philosopher René Descartes (1596–1650)—that is, the occurrence of thought guarantees the existence of the thinker.

confined, ineluctably, within the schema established by the conventions of perspective. It was in precisely the same period that the "object" of thought came to be conceived of as a homogeneous, scientifically measurable entity—that is, as an extension of the principles of perspective. All of these developments paralleled the emergence of "background" as a dehumanized "landscape" in the Mona Lisa.[6]

In her work, *Philosophy in a New Key,* Suzanne Langer[7] described the cul-de-sac of modern European philosophy, which is still preoccupied with the philosophical issues posed by "landscape."

> After several centuries of sterile tradition, logic-chopping, and partisanship in philosophy, the wealth of nameless, heretical, often inconsistent notions born of the Renaissance crystallized into general and ultimate problems. A new outlook on life challenged the human mind to make sense out of its bewildering world; and the Cartesian age of "natural and mental" philosophy succeeded to the realm.
>
> This new epoch had a mighty and revolutionary generative idea: the dichotomy of all reality into *inner experience and outer world,* subject and object, private reality and public truth. The very language of what is now traditional epistemology betrays this basic notion; when we speak of "the given," of "sense data," "the phenomenon," or "other selves," we take for granted the immediacy of an internal experience and the continuity of the external world. Our fundamental questions are framed in these terms: What is actually given to the mind? What guarantees the truth of sense-data? What lies behind the observable order of phenomena? What is the relation of the mind to the brain? How can we know other selves?—All these are familiar problems of today. Their answers have been elaborated into whole systems of thought: empiricism, idealism, realism, phenomenology, *Existenz Philosophie,* and logical positivism. The most complete and characteristic of all these doctrines are the earliest ones: empiricism and idealism. They are the full, unguarded, vigorous formulations of the new generative notion, Experience: their proponents were the enthusiasts inspired by the Cartesian method, and their doctrines are the obvious implications derived by that principle, from such a starting point. Each school in its turn took the intellectual world by storm. Not only universities, but all the literary circles, felt the liberation from time-worn, oppressive concepts, from baffling limits of inquiry, and hailed the new world-picture with a hope of truer orientation in life, art, and action.
>
> After a while, the confusion and shadows inherent in the new vision became apparent, and subsequent doctrines sought in various ways to escape between the horns of the dilemma created by the subject-object dichotomy, which Professor Whitehead[8] has called the "bifurcation of nature." Since then our theories have become more and more refined, circumspect, and clever; no one can be quite frankly an idealist, or go the whole way with empiricism; the early forms of realism are now known as

6. The painting (ca. 1504) by Leonardo da Vinci; earlier in the chapter, Karatani quotes the Dutch psychiatrist Jan Hendrik Van den Berg, who sees the work as breaking sharply with the old view of landscape (*The Changing Nature of Man: Introduction to Historical Psychology, Metabletica,* 1956).

7. American philosopher and aesthetician (1895–1985); *Philosophy in a New Key* (1941) is her best-known work.

8. Alfred North Whitehead (1861–1947), English mathematician and philosopher; the quotation is from *The Concept of Nature* (1920).

> the "naive" varieties, and have been superseded by "critical" or "new" realisms. Many philosophers vehemently deny any systematic Weltanschauung, and repudiate metaphysics in principle.[9]

But will contemporary philosophers, who are trying to break out of a Cartesian weltanschauung even as they operate within it, really succeed in making their escape? Modern artists, when they studied primitive art, or thinkers like Claude Lévi-Strauss,[1] in his work on the "savage mind," faced the same dilemma. Sophisticated technology and Rousseauian romanticism[2] are paradoxically intertwined in Lévi-Strauss's thought. But both these elements had their origins in the modern "landscape." It is the historicity of that landscape that must be exposed.

In Western Europe it was Marx, Nietzsche, and Freud[3] who, albeit from differing perspectives, first exposed the problematic nature of the European conception of landscape. Nietzsche, for example, claimed that European epistemology itself was "an illusion based on the principles of linear perspective." As a product of interiorization, according to Nietzsche, the very notion of linear perspective was "an illusion of itself." The "self," the "inner," "consciousness," and "cogito" in Cartesian philosophy were all based on an inversion of subjectivity.

In order to expose the historicity of European culture Sōseki did not need to look back to ancient Greece, as Nietzsche did. Rather, he maintained within himself a certain attitude toward life that had existed prior to "landscape" and "modern Japanese literature." Sōseki was able to do this because he lived through the discovery of "landscape." We Japanese witnessed with our own eyes and within a limited period of time the occurrence in condensed form of a process which, because it had extended over many centuries, had been repressed from memory in the West.

Various institutions of the modern nation-state were consolidated, in preliminary form, during the third decade of the Meiji period, starting with the promulgation of the Meiji constitution.[4] As Nakamura Mitsuo[5] has written, "if we see the second decade of the Meiji period as one of turbulence, the third was one of unification and stability." In the eyes of those born after the Meiji Restoration,[6] this order appeared to be something that had already solidified. What had been malleable possibilities just after the Restoration now appeared shut off to them. In his *Meiji Literature,* Nakamura Mitsuo describes the People's Rights movement[7] of the 1880s as follows:

> For the movement was a logical extension of that great reform which was the Meiji Restoration, and it had been entrusted with the great hope that this social revolution had awakened in the people. It was

9. Suzanne Langer, *Philosophy in a New Key* (New York: New American Library, 1951), pp. 11–12 [translator's note].
1. French anthropologist (1908–2009; see above); *The Savage Mind* was published in 1962.
2. The philosophy of the Swiss-born French political philosopher Jean-Jacques Rousseau (1712–1778), which idealized the concept of the "noble savage."
3. All figures with enormous influence on modern Western thought: KARL MARX (1818–1883), German economic, social, and political philosopher; FRIEDRICH NIETZSCHE (1844–1900), German philosopher; and SIGMUND FREUD (1856–1939), Austrian founder of psychoanalysis.
4. Japan's first constitution (1889), intended to define Japan as a modern nation on the model of Prussia's constitutional monarchy (it remained in force until 1947).
5. Literary critic and playwright (1911–1988).
6. The revolution (1867–68) that restored the emperor to power and ended the rule of the Tokugawa shogunate.
7. A political movement launched in 1874 that agitated for civil rights, reduced taxes, and an elected legislature.

> through the People's Rights movement that the spirit of the Restoration which until that time had been the sole possession of the warrior class[8] gradually came to infiltrate the popular consciousness. The setback of the movement, therefore, meant the destruction of that vital component of all revolutions, the idealism which is contained within them and which can be transformed into something else at any point in the revolutionary process. The straitened circumstances of the warrior class became a grave social problem in the early years of Meiji. For the few who found themselves in an advantageous situation there were many who had fallen into despair, yet this very fact meant that control of political and cultural life remained the uncontested prerogative of that class. But by 1885 or so, the dissolution of the warrior class became a pronounced trend, the children of commoners began to swell the ranks of students, and Meiji society began to show its true face as a mercantile state created by the offspring of the warrior class.
>
> Vis-à-vis this emerging militarist state dominated by pragmatism and the pursuit of worldly success, the phantoms of freedom and people's rights became the last ideals for which young men who were heirs of the Restoration could risk their lives. The loss of these ideals created a spiritual vacuum which could not be banished and which found expression in a form which was completely different from the political novel.[9]

This insight may also be applied to Sōseki. While contemporary writers like Masaoka Shiki, Futabatei Shimei, Kitamura Tōkoku, and Kunikida Doppo[1] were agonizing over questions of artistic practice, Sōseki stood at the head of the Meiji government's corps of students of the West constantly pursued by a desire to flee from their ranks. What he wrote while he was in their midst had to be "theoretical," for it represented certain conclusions he had reached with reference to the English literature which he had already decided to study. Later, as a novelist, Sōseki appeared obsessed with the phenomenon of the "belated" nature of choice, a problem which he had confronted during this period. In this sense, *kanbungaku* probably symbolized for Sōseki not so much a corpus of texts as a certain atmosphere that existed prior to the establishment of various modern systems. This was during the same period when the political novel was at the height of its popularity. Sōseki's sense that he had been "cheated" by English literature may have corresponded to his observation that the institutions which were set up in the third decade of Meiji were nothing but a sham.

But such interpretive notions as "political disillusionment" or "the influence of Christianity" cannot be interjected into our consideration of the Japanese discovery of "landscape." These ideas suggest a psychological motivation for the process, but the concept of human psychology itself appeared at precisely this time. To treat the psychological as an autonomous sphere, as the science

8. The gentry (samurai), who had ruled Japan during the shogunate (1185–1867).

9. Nakamura Mitsuo, "Meiji bungakushi" (History of Meiji literature), in *Nakamura Mitsuo zenshū* (Tokyo: Chikuma Shobō, 1973), pp. 169–70 [translator's note]. Political novels, extremely popular throughout the 1880s, disseminated the ideas of the People's Rights movement.

1. Influential modern figures: Futabatei (1864–1909), literary critic, translator of Russian fiction, and novelist who pioneered the style known as *genbun itchi* (discussed below); Kitamura (1868–1894), free-verse poet and major theorist of Meiji romanticism; and Kunikida (1871–1908), a writer of poetry and short fiction who was a forerunner of naturalism in Japan.

of psychology does, is a historical, not a timeless, phenomenon. The most significant development in the third decade of the Meiji period was rather the consolidation of modern systems and the emergence of "landscape," not so much as a phenomenon contesting such systems, but as itself a system.

Academic historians of modern literature write of the "modern self'" as if it were something that existed purely within the mind. But certain conditions are necessary for the production of this "self." Freud, like Nietzsche, viewed consciousness not as something which existed from the start, but as a derivative of "introjection."[2] According to Freud, it is at a stage when there is no distinction between inner and outer, when the outer is purely a projection of the inner, that the experience of trauma results in a redirection of the libido inward. With this, for the first time, outer and inner are separated. As Freud wrote in *Totem and Taboo,* "It is only after abstract language and thought come into existence that the perceptual residue of language links up with subjective material in such a way that we first become aware of subjective phenomena."

To speak in Freudian terms, the libido[3] which was once directed toward the People's Rights movement and the writing of political novels lost its object and was redirected inward, at which point "landscape" and "the inner life" appeared. Let me repeat, however, that Freud himself was not aware of the historicity of psychology and of the fact that, like "landscape," it was the product of a specific historical order. The Meiji novelist Mori Ōgai,[4] for example, created characters that appear "a-psychological" in his historical fiction. Toward the end of his life, Ōgai tried as much as possible to return to an awareness that predated modern conceptions of psychology and landscape. We may legitimately use a psychological approach in dealing with writers who emerged after the third decade of the Meiji period, but we must keep in mind that such an approach will not expose the conditions which produced the science of psychology itself.

However, what I find most significant in Freud's thought is the notion of the simultaneous emergence in the human being of the capacity for "abstract thought and language" and of "interiority" (accompanied by an awareness of the external as external). What does "abstract thought and language" correspond to in the Japanese context? Perhaps to the conception of writing which evolved in the Meiji period, known as *genbun itchi*.[5] For *genbun itchi* was a manifestation in the linguistic realm of the establishment, around 1890, of the various institutions of the modern state. It goes without saying that the meaning of this concept was hardly that of bringing "writing" (*bun*) into conformity with "speech" (*gen*), or speech into conformity with writing, as is usually maintained. *Genbun itchi* represented the invention of a new conception of writing as equivalent with speech.[6]

2. The unconscious process by which the outside world is taken into the self and represented in its internal structure; Freud defines this psychoanalytic term in *Totem and Taboo* (1912–13).
3. Instinctual psychic energy that drives all behavior.
4. Writer of criticism, plays, and poetry as well as fiction (1862–1922).
5. Literally, the unification (*itchi*) of speech (*gen*) and writing (*bun*); a neologism widely used by language reform activists, who saw vernacular writing as critical to the spread of literacy and modern education.
6. In chapter 2, "The Discovery of Interiority," Karatani argues that *genbun itchi* is premised on an inversion in the conception of language. Whereas *kanbungaku* placed supreme value in the written word, *genbun itchi* assumed that written language is derivative of, and therefore secondary to, spoken language.

Of course, insofar as *genbun itchi* was an effort towards modernization similar to the Meiji constitution, it could not be a purely "inner" speech. Writers considered to be introverts in the third decade of the Meiji period—Ōgai and Tōkoku, for example—preferred to write in the classical style,[7] and the *genbun itchi* movement quickly lost momentum. Interest did not revive until the end of the decade, which was already the era of Kunikida Doppo and Takahama Kyoshi.[8]

Of course, Futabatei Shimei's novel *Ukigumo* (Drifting clouds),[9] which appeared between 1886 and 1889, may be cited as an exception to this trend. Notions of landscape and the inner self which Futabatei could elaborate when he was writing in Russian,[1] however, seemed to slip through his fingers when he tried to write about them in Japanese, when somehow the language of Shikitei Samba and other *kokkeibon*[2] writers took possession of him. The agony of Futabatei was to have discovered "landscape" without being able to locate it in the Japanese language. By Doppo's time this dilemma had disappeared. What influenced Doppo was not the style of *Ukigumo* but the translation of Turgenev's *Rendez-vous*.[3]

For Doppo the "inner" was the word (the voice), and expression was the projection outward of that voice. In Doppo's work the concept of "expression" came into being for the first time in Japanese literature. Before this time, no one spoke of literature in terms of expression. It was the identification of writing with speech which made such a concept possible. But it was only because Doppo, unlike Futabatei, was oblivious to the fact that *genbun itchi* was a modern system that he was spared the dilemma of Futabatei. That the "inner self" was historical, that it was a system, had by that time been forgotten. Needless to say, we live today on the same soil that Doppo did. In order to know what holds us there, we must uncover its source; we must investigate further this historical period when language was simultaneously exposed and hidden.

1980

7. A style that adhered to ancient models of writing and thus bore little resemblance to spoken Japanese.
8. Novelist and poet (1874–1959), best known for his haiku.
9. One of the first attempts (1887–89) to write fiction in the *genbun itchi* style.
1. An allusion to Futabatei's claim that when he reached an impasse in composing *Ukigumo*, he would write in Russian and then translate the draft into Japanese.
2. Comic or funny book, a genre of fiction popular during the Edo period. Shikitei (1776–1822), writer of popular fiction, including *kokkeibon*.
3. "Svidanie" (1850, "Tryst"), a short story by the Russian novelist and dramatist Ivan Turgenev (1818–1883); Futabatei's 1887 version was the first Japanese literary translation to employ the *genbun itchi* style.

JULIA KRISTEVA
b. 1941

Linguist, literary critic, cultural theorist, and psychoanalyst, Julia Kristeva has been one of the central figures of French intellectual life in the late twentieth and early twenty-first century. Kristeva's main contribution to contemporary theory resides in her elucidation of the processes by which preverbal experience—bodily drives and affects—enters into language and activates creative, transformative, and at times revolutionary modes of cultural production. Like other structuralist and poststructuralist theorists—most notably JACQUES LACAN, ROLAND BARTHES, and JACQUES DERRIDA—Kristeva has a long-standing interest in the relationship of subjectivity to language, in how the speaking subject is both constituted through and threatened by the logic of signification. But Kristeva diverges from other contemporary theorists in her insistence on the corporeal origins of subjectivity and of artistic practice. In contrast to the Saussurean linguistic models of Lacanian psychoanalysis, for instance, Kristeva has emphasized the importance of prelinguistic, instinctual, and sensory components of both subjectivity and signification. Indeed, while Kristeva's thinking has undergone major transformations over the past four decades, progressively moving away from abstract linguistics and toward more classically psychoanalytic concerns, her writings nevertheless exhibit a remarkable degree of continuity insofar as they have consistently sought to articulate—without completely departing from language—the force of the body and its drives.

Born in Bulgaria in 1941, Kristeva arrived in France on a doctoral research fellowship in December 1965. Since her francophone parents were not members of Bulgaria's ruling Communist Party, she had been excluded from the foreign-language schools available to the children of the "red bourgeoisie." Nevertheless, she acquired a French as well as a Bulgarian education from an early age by attending two schools—Bulgarian in the morning and French in the afternoon. In Paris she became a student of Roland Barthes and quickly established herself as a major participant in the lively avant-garde milieu of the late 1960s. By the spring of 1967, Kristeva's articles were being published in such leading journals as *Critique*, *Langages*, and *Tel Quel*, and in 1970 she was appointed to the editorial board of *Tel Quel*, the intellectual venue for the young generation of structuralist and poststructuralist theorists. *Tel Quel* was edited by the charismatic writer and theorist Philippe Sollers, whom she later married and with whom she had a son. In 1974 she was appointed professor of linguistics at the University of Paris VII, where she is now professor emerita and, co-directs the interdisciplinary Centre Roland Barthes, which she created in 2000. In 2004 she was awarded Norway's prestigious Holberg International Memorial Prize for outstanding scholarly work, and in 2008 she was named an Officer of the Legion of Honor.

Besides Barthes, Lucien Goldmann (an influential sociological critic), and CLAUDE LÉVI-STRAUSS, who were her teachers, Kristeva acknowledges intellectual debts to other twentieth-century figures: MIKHAIL BAKHTIN, Émile Benveniste (an important linguist), Jacques Lacan, Melanie Klein (a theorist of pre-oedipal development), and, of course, SIGMUND FREUD. With TZVETAN TODOROV, Kristeva brought the work of Bakhtin into prominence in the French context. In 1970 she published an introduction to the French translation of Bakhtin's work on Dostoyevsky, and she combined his concept of "dialogism" (the idea that a text contains language from more than one "world") with FERDINAND DE SAUSSURE's notebooks on anagrams in poetry (which had recently been discovered and were being published by Jean Starobinski in *Tel Quel*) into a general theory of "intertextuality."

The intertextual sense of the multiplicity of origins and meanings in language informs the theory of the sign set forth in Kristeva's first book, *Σημειωτική*

(Sémeiótiké): Recherches pour une Sémanalyse (1969, *Research toward a Sem-analysis*, where the prefix *sem-* is from the Greek word for "sign"). This was followed in 1974 by *Revolution in Poetic Language*, Kristeva's doctoral dissertation, in which she developed a theory of poetic language based on the writings of Stéphane Mallarmé (1842–1898) and Isidore Ducasse (better known as the comte de Lautréamont, 1846–1870). We print several sections from this book as our selection, below. The "revolution" in poetic language Kristeva analyzed in the work of these late nineteenth-century French poets quickly became a revolution brought about by Kristeva herself in the *analysis* of poetic language as such.

Kristeva finds two forces competing for expression in the language of poetry: the symbolic and the semiotic. The *symbolic* is that aspect of language that allows it to *refer*. It is systematic, propositional, rule-bound, tied to the social order, dependent on a functional separation between the subject and the object, and capable of existing independently of its referent. The linguistics of Saussure focused on this dimension, treating language as a theoretical fiction studied in the absence of any particular speaker. The *semiotic* dimension of language—which cannot be known except in the moments where it breaks through the symbolic—is that aspect that bears the trace of the language user's own body and of the mother's protolinguistic presence—the babbling of the infant who tries out the vocal repertoire before he or she learns to speak, for instance, or the mother's voice prior to the baby's acquisition of language: poetic language in this sense has been called "babble, doodle, and riddle." The "music" of poetry (and indeed prosody itself), Kristeva contends, arises out of this dimension. It is important to avoid two possible misunderstandings of Kristeva's use of these terms. Her "symbolic" is similar to Lacan's, insofar as it is not symbolic *of* anything—not a collection of meaning-filled symbols as, say, Carl Jung might conceive it—but is a *structure*. And "the semiotic" is not the same as *semiotics*, which is the study of the functioning of signs.

In *Revolution in Poetic Language*, Kristeva thus maintains that all signification entails the dialectical interaction of the symbolic and the semiotic. The semiotic represents the discharge of pre-oedipal instinctual energies and drives within language; it is associated with what Kristeva, following PLATO, designates as the *chora* (literally, "space"; Greek)—receptacle, space, womb. This semiotic *chora*, which "precedes and underlies figuration," is, in turn, connected to the maternal body, to the feminine in general, and to what remains mysterious, unintelligible, and unsignifiable. Kristeva's thesis is that the eruption of the semiotic within the symbolic is what provides the creative and innovative impulse of modern poetic language. Ordinary language use depends on a *thetic* or positing structure (Kristeva borrows the term from the German phenomenologist Edmund Husserl, 1859–1938): that is, it is positional and propositional. Artistic practice, capable of transgressing the thetic boundary between the symbolic and the semiotic, fractures and disrupts established modes of signification so as to retrieve the surmounted semiotic energies and thus create an opening for new, polyvalent cultural meanings. This thetic rupture, then, is profoundly subversive, not only implying an upheaval of art forms (such as that effected by Mallarmé and Lautréamont, according to Kristeva, on traditional literary discourse) but also calling for a reconfiguration of the notion of subjectivity. Distinguishing between the *genotext* (the energies that bring a text about) and the *phenotext* (the linguistic structure that results), Kristeva tries to capture the trace of what in a subject brings a text into being, not just what the text signifies. The genotext corresponds roughly to Freud's primary (unconscious) processes—a dream's "latent content." But while a dream's "manifest content" obeys only the rule of representability, a text is shaped by all the linguistic and social structures of the symbolic order.

The "revolution" of Kristeva's title therefore both refers to a transformation in poetic practice and heralds the emergence of what Kristeva, throughout her writings, refers to as the *sujet-en-procès*. *Procès*, in French, means both "process" and "trial."

Hence, this expression can be translated "subject in process" or "subject on trial." The phrase itself expresses what Kristeva sees as the double bind of subjecthood: it combines the incompatible forces of constant change and constant judgment. The subject both *cannot* and *must* present itself in stasis. The semiotic dimension frees the subject from stasis and, according to Kristeva, "gives us a vision of the human venture as a venture of innovation, of creation, of opening, of renewal" (*Interviews*, 1996).

But the breakthroughs of the semiotic have their dark as well as their playful side. The theories of psychoanalysis have enabled Kristeva—who completed her training as a psychoanalyst in 1979—to analyze in more detail the consequences of those breakthroughs for life and writing. Her many book-length studies—treating horror, anti-Semitism, melancholy, and abjection—attend to the destructive as well as the creative consequences of breaking through the symbolic, which is the repository of civilization in both its repressive and its protective guises. Indeed, for Kristeva psychoanalysis is the *practice* of the difficulty in tearing apart the two "sides." The *abject*, for instance, is for her as important to the constitution of the "subject" as its "object." The abject is what the subject's consciousness has to expel or disregard in order to create the proper separation between subject and object. The mother splits into two parts: she is the prototype of subsequent objects that the subject will desire or hate, but she is also the despised ground of infantile dependency and bodily need. Another way of putting this is that the abject is still unconsciously desired and thereby transformed into something undesirable, filthy, and disgusting, like the bodily processes for which it stands. Both matter and mother are *abjects* for the fantasy of self-creation.

Kristeva's publications after 1979 thus take an explicitly psychoanalytic approach to what she calls "the maladies of the soul." *Powers of Horror: An Essay on Abjection* (1980; trans. 1982), *Tales of Love* (1983; trans. 1987), *Black Sun: Depression and Melancholia* (1987; trans. 1989), and *New Maladies of the Soul* (1993; trans. 1995) often feature case studies from her clinical practice. At the same time, Kristeva began enlarging and loosening her compact, difficult, and rather abstract style to attempt new kinds of writing. In a special 1977 issue of *Tel Quel* titled *Recherches féminines* (*Research by and about Women*), she published a celebrated essay about motherhood ("Héréthique de l'amour" or "Love's Herethics[1]"; later translated as "Stabat Mater") written in two columns juxtaposed irregularly on the page. She went on to write several novels, the first of which, *The Samurai* (1990), is a thinly disguised account of the *Tel Quel* milieu. Its Japanese title is a wink at the Chinese title used by SIMONE DE BEAUVOIR (an important precursor for Kristeva) for a similar roman à clef, *The Mandarins* (1954).

Kristeva has published more explicitly political writings as well, from her early *About Chinese Women* (1974)—based on a trip to China taken by several members of *Tel Quel* during its period of interest in Maoism—to the later *Strangers to Ourselves* (1989) and *Nations without Nationalism* (1990). In *Strangers to Ourselves*, Kristeva rediscovers Freud's notion of the "uncanny" in the context of the encounter between the self and the "foreigner": by recognizing that the foreignness lies *within* the self, it might be possible, she suggests, to avoid the violence entailed by its projection outward onto others.

The famous essay "Women's Time" (1979; trans. 1981), a synthesis of Kristeva's analysis of language, the social contract, and feminism, has been much reprinted. It addresses the question of female subjectivity by interrogating the position that women are said to occupy in the social structure. If, according to Lévi-Strauss, women are circulated on the marriage market between men of different groups like the words of a system of communication, what happens when women are seen not as the *objects* but as the *subjects* of communication? If women have had to bear the sacrificial weight of the social contract in patriarchy, does that mean that lifting the weight of patriarchy would provide free, unfettered enjoyment and fulfillment for women? It is

1. Herethics: an ethics tied to the feminine, which would represent a heretical or transgressive ethics.

Kristeva's contention that a liberating change in the social order, however necessary and desirable, would nevertheless not give access to the fulfillment whose attainment appears to be blocked by specific structures of subjectivity. The fantasy of wholeness is a function of those obstacles, not something beyond them. Kristeva's ideal could be said to be postfeminist in the sense that it implies the demolition of "Woman" as an identifiable social category. To the extent that feminism depends on the difference between men and women conceived as an *opposition*, she has resisted being called a "feminist." This has estranged her from some feminists committed to an oppositional notion of political action. When asked what constitutes her distinctiveness, however, she responds by calling herself "a female intellectual," committed to exploring the oxymoronic exclusiveness inherent in the traditional understanding of those categories but refusing to conceive of either one as an "identity."

The attempt to bridge the gap between French and Anglo-American feminisms has contributed to the introduction and dissemination of Kristeva's work to the English-speaking world—see, notably, Toril Moi's *Sexual/Textual Politics: Feminist Literary Theory* (1985)—but Kristeva herself tends to view institutionalized forms of feminism (like all institutionalized groups) as totalizing, at times even as totalitarian, forms of cultural discourse. In "Women's Time" she wonders whether feminism is not in the process of becoming a sort of religion; and she remains highly critical of any feminist politics based on universalist or essentialist notions of femininity. Although Kristeva, in Anglo-American writings, frequently gets grouped together with HÉLÈNE CIXOUS and Luce Irigaray as a representative of "French feminism," the three writers are really very different, united only by the extent to which each is influenced by the 1968 upheaval in French society. Yet Kristeva's rich and provocative writings—particularly her reflections on love, abjection, melancholy, maternity, and the preverbal semiotic—are directly relevant to feminist theorists and continue to generate a sizable body of criticism.

Drawing together linguistics, psychoanalysis, political science, and feminism, Julia Kristeva's work has repeatedly revealed aspects of textuality that literary theory is in danger of glossing over. In insisting that the speaking subject's investment in language is neither transcendental nor entirely conscious, she has enlarged, enriched, and complicated our sense of what goes on in a literary text.

***Revolution in Poetic Language* Keywords:** Affect, The Body, Feminist Theory, Identity, Language, Literary History, Poetry, Psychoanalysis, Semiotics, Subjectivity

From Revolution in Poetic Language[1]

From *Part I. The Semiotic and the Symbolic*

FROM 2. THE SEMIOTIC *CHORA* ORDERING THE DRIVES

We understand the term "semiotic"[2] in its Greek sense: σημεῖον=distinctive mark, trace, index, precursory sign, proof, engraved or written sign, imprint, trace, figuration. This etymological reminder would be a mere archaeological embellishment (and an unconvincing one at that, since the term ultimately encompasses such disparate meanings), were it not for the fact that the preponderant etymological use of the word, the one that implies a *distinctiveness,* allows us to connect it to a precise modality in the signifying

1. Translated by Margaret Waller, who occasionally inserts the original French in brackets.
2. In Kristeva's usage, pre-oedipal—that is, before the infant's discovery of sexual difference—preverbal drives and affects.

process. This modality is the one Freudian psychoanalysis points to in postulating not only the *facilitation* and the structuring *disposition* of drives, but also the so-called *primary processes*[3] which displace and condense both energies and their inscription. Discrete quantities of energy move through the body of the subject who is not yet constituted as such and, in the course of his development, they are arranged according to the various constraints imposed on this body—always already involved in a semiotic process—by family and social structures. In this way the drives, which are "energy" charges as well as "psychical" marks, articulate what we call a *chora*: a nonexpressive totality formed by the drives and their stases in a motility that is as full of movement as it is regulated.

We borrow the term *chora*[4] from Plato's *Timaeus*[5] to denote an essentially mobile and extremely provisional articulation constituted by movements and their ephemeral stases. We differentiate this uncertain and indeterminate *articulation* from a *disposition* that already depends on representation, lends itself to phenomenological, spatial intuition,[6] and gives rise to a geometry. Although our theoretical description of the *chora* is itself part of the discourse of representation that offers it as evidence, the *chora*, as rupture and articulations (rhythm), precedes evidence, verisimilitude, spatiality, and temporality. Our discourse—all discourse—moves with and against the *chora* in the sense that it simultaneously depends upon and refuses it. Although the *chora* can be designated and regulated, it can never be definitively posited: as a result, one can situate the *chora* and, if necessary, lend it a topology, but one can never give it axiomatic form.[7]

The *chora* is not yet a position that represents something for someone (i.e., it is not a sign); nor is it a *position* that represents someone for another position (i.e., it is not yet a signifier either[8]); it is, however, generated in order to attain to this signifying position. Neither model nor copy, the *chora* precedes

3. The most primitive of unconscious mechanisms, according to SIGMUND FREUD (1856–1939), Austrian founder of psychoanalysis. "Facilitation" (French *frayage,* from Freud's German *Bahnung*) and "disposition" are the processes that shape habits of desire.

4. The term "*chora*" has recently been criticized for its ontological essence by Jacques Derrida, *Positions,* trans. and annot. Alan Bass (Chicago: University of Chicago Press, 1981), pp. 75, 106 n. 39 [Kristeva's note]. Some of the author's notes have been omitted. DERRIDA (1930–2004), French philosopher.

5. One of the later dialogues by the Greek philosopher PLATO (ca. 427–ca. 347 B.C.E.).

6. Phenomenology is a philosophical method restricted to analyzing the intellectual processes of which we are introspectively aware (while ignoring external objects, the question of whose existence is "bracketed").

7. Plato emphasizes that the receptacle (ὑποδοχεῖον), which is also called space (χώρα) vis-à-vis reason, is necessary—but not divine since it is unstable, uncertain, ever changing and becoming; it is even unnameable, improbable, bastard: "Space, which is everlasting, not admitting destruction; providing a situation for all things that come into being, but itself apprehended without the senses by a sort of bastard reasoning, and hardly an object of belief. This, indeed, is that which we look upon as in a dream and say that anything that is must needs be in some place and occupy some room . . ." (*Timaeus,* trans. Francis M. Cornford, 52a–b). Is the receptacle a "thing" or a mode of language? Plato's hesitation between the two gives the receptacle an even more uncertain status. It is one of the elements that antedate not only the *universe* but also *names* and even *syllables*: "We speak . . . positing them as original principles, elements (as it were, letters) of the universe; whereas one who has ever so little intelligence should not rank them in this analogy even so low as syllables" (48b). "It is hard to say, with respect to any one of these, which we ought to call really water rather than fire, or indeed which we should call by any given name rather than by all the names together or by each severally, so as to use language in a sound and trustworthy way. . . . Since, then, in this way no one of these things ever makes its appearance as the *same* thing, which of them can we steadfastly affirm to be *this*—whatever it may be—and not something else, without blushing for ourselves? It cannot be done" (49b–d) [Kristeva's note].

8. A reference to the statement by the French psychoanalyst JACQUES LACAN (1901–1981) that "a signifier represents a subject for another signifier"; see Seminar XI (1964), *The Four Fundamental Concepts of Psychoanalysis* (1973; trans. 1977).

and underlies figuration and thus specularization, and is analogous only to vocal or kinetic rhythm. We must restore this motility's gestural and vocal play (to mention only the aspect relevant to language) on the level of the socialized body in order to remove motility from ontology and amorphousness[9] where Plato confines it in an apparent attempt to conceal it from Democritean rhythm.[1] The theory of the subject proposed by the theory of the unconscious will allow us to read in this rhythmic space, which has no thesis and no position, the process by which signifiance[2] is constituted. Plato himself leads us to such a process when he calls this receptacle or *chora* nourishing and maternal,[3] not yet unified in an ordered whole because deity is absent from it. Though deprived of unity, identity, or deity, the *chora* is nevertheless subject to a regulating process [*réglementation*], which is different from that of symbolic law but nevertheless effectuates discontinuities by temporarily articulating them and then starting over, again and again.

The *chora* is a modality of signifiance in which the linguistic sign is not yet articulated as the absence of an object and as the distinction between real and symbolic. We emphasize the regulated aspect of the *chora*: its vocal and gestural organization is subject to what we shall call an objective *ordering* [*ordonnancement*], which is dictated by natural or socio-historical constraints such as the biological difference between the sexes or family structure. We may therefore posit that social organization, always already

9. There is a fundamental ambiguity: on the one hand, the receptacle is mobile and even contradictory, without unity, separable and divisible: presyllable, pre-word. Yet, on the other hand, because this separability and divisibility antecede numbers and forms, the space or receptacle is called *amorphous*; thus its suggested rhythmicity will in a certain sense be erased, for how can one think an articulation of what is not yet singular but is nevertheless necessary? All we may say of it, then, to make it intelligible, is that it is amorphous but that it "is of such and such a quality," not even an index or something in particular ("this" or "that"). Once named, it immediately becomes a container that takes the place of infinitely repeatable separability. This amounts to saying that this repeated separability is "ontologized" the moment a *name* or a *word* replaces it, making it intelligible: "Are we talking idly whenever we say that there is such a thing as an intelligible Form of anything? Is this nothing more than a word?" (*Timaeus* 51c). Is the Platonic *chora* the "nominability" of rhythm (of repeated separation)?

Why then borrow an ontologized term in order to designate an articulation that antecedes positing? First, the Platonic term makes explicit an insurmountable problem for discourse: once it has been named, that functioning, even if it is presymbolic, is brought back into a symbolic position. All discourse can do is differentiate, by means of a "bastard reasoning," the receptacle from the motility, which, by contrast, is not being posited as being "a *certain* something" ["une *telle*"]. Second, this motility is the precondition for symbolicity, heterogeneous to it, yet indispensable. Therefore what needs to be done is to try and differentiate, always through a "bastard reasoning," the specific arrangements of this motility, without seeing them as recipients of accidental singularities, or a *Being* always posited in itself, or a projection of the *One*. Moreover, Plato invites us to differentiate in this fashion when he describes this, while gathering it into the receiving membrane: "But because it was filled with powers that were neither alike nor evenly balanced, there was no equipoise in any region of it; but it was everywhere swayed unevenly and shaken by these things, and its motion shook them in turn. And they, being thus moved, were perpetually being separated and carried in different directions; just as when things are shaken and winnowed by means of winnowing baskets and other instruments for cleaning corn [i.e., wheat] . . . it separated the most unlike kinds farthest apart from one another, and thrust the most alike closest together; whereby the different kinds came to have different regions, even before the ordered whole consisting of them came to be . . . but were altogether in such a condition as we should expect for anything when deity is absent from it" (52d–53b). Indefinite "conjunctions" and "disjunctions" (functioning, devoid of Meaning), the *chora* is governed by a necessity that is not God's law [Kristeva's note].

1. That is, the eternal motion of atoms in haphazard collision postulated by the Greek philosopher Democritus (ca. 460–ca. 370 B.C.E.), a concept here presented as a precursor of the semiotic.

2. Kristeva's coinage: the fact or process of signification, encompassing both the symbolic and the semiotic.

3. The Platonic space or receptacle is a mother and wet nurse: "Indeed we may fittingly compare the Recipient to a mother, the model to a father, and the nature that arises between them to their offspring" (*Timaeus* 50d); "Now the wet nurse of Becoming was made watery and fiery, received the characters of earth and air, and was qualified by all the other affections that go with these . . ." (52d; translation modified) [Kristeva's note].

symbolic, imprints its constraint in a mediated form which organizes the *chora* not according to a *law* (a term we reserve for the symbolic) but through an *ordering*.[4] What is this mediation?

According to a number of psycholinguists, "concrete operations" precede the acquisition of language, and organize preverbal semiotic space according to logical categories, which are thereby shown to precede or transcend language. From their research we shall retain not the principle of an operational state[5] but that of a preverbal functional state that governs the connections between the body (in the process of constituting itself as a body proper), objects, and the protagonists of family structure.[6] But we shall distinguish this functioning from symbolic operations that depend on language as a sign system—whether the language [*langue*][7] is vocalized or gestural (as with deaf-mutes). The kinetic functional stage of the *semiotic* precedes the establishment of the sign; it is not, therefore, cognitive in the sense of being assumed by a knowing, already constituted subject. The genesis of the *functions* organizing the semiotic process can be accurately elucidated only within a theory of the subject that does not reduce the subject to one of understanding, but instead opens up within the subject this other scene of pre-symbolic functions. The Kleinian theory[8] expanding upon Freud's positions on the drives will momentarily serve as a guide.

Drives involve pre-Oedipal semiotic functions and energy discharges that connect and orient the body to the mother. We must emphasize that "drives" are always already ambiguous, simultaneously assimilating and destructive; this dualism, which has been represented as a tetrad[9] or as a double helix, as in the configuration of the DNA and RNA molecule,[1] makes the semiotized body a place of permanent scission. The oral and anal drives,[2] both of which are oriented and structured around the mother's body,[3] dominate

4. "Law," which derives etymologically from *lex* (Latin), necessarily implies the act of judgment whose role in safeguarding society was first developed by the Roman law courts. "Ordering," on the other hand, is closer to the series "rule," "norm" (from the Greek γνώμων, meaning "discerning" [adj.], "carpenter's square" [noun]), etc., which implies a numerical or geometrical necessity. On normativity in linguistics, see Alain Rey, "Usages, judgments et prescriptions linguistiques" [Linguistic Usage, Judgment, and Prescription], *Langue Française* (December 1972), 16:5. But the temporary ordering of the *chora* is not yet even a *rule*: the arsenal of geometry is posterior to the *chora*'s motility; it fixes the *chora* in place and reduces it [Kristeva's note].

5. Operations are, rather, an act of the subject of understanding [Kristeva's note]. Hans G. Furth, in *Piaget and Knowledge: Theoretical Foundations* (Englewood Cliffs, N.J.: Prentice-Hall, 1969), offers the following definition of "concrete operations": "Characteristic of the first stage of operational intelligence. A concrete operation implies underlying general systems or 'groupings' such as classification, seriation, number. Its applicability is limited to objects considered as real (concrete)" (p. 260) [translator's note].

6. Piaget stresses that the roots of sensorimotor operations precede language and that the acquisition of thought is due to the symbolic function, which, for him, is a notion separate from that of language per se. See Jean Piaget, "Language and Symbolic Operations," in *Piaget and Knowledge*, pp. 121–30 [Kristeva's note].

7. That is, language as an abstract system, as distinguished from the speech or hand signs of any particular language user (*parole*)—a distinction first drawn by the Swiss linguist FERDINAND DE SAUSSURE (1857–1913).

8. The theory of mother-child relations held by Melanie Klein (1882–1960), Austrian-born English psychoanalyst.

9. Such a position has been formulated by Lipot Szondi, *Experimental Diagnostic of Drives*, trans. Gertrude Aull (New York: Grune and Stratton, 1952) [Kristeva's note]. "Tetrad": group of four.

1. See James D. Watson, *The Double Helix: A Personal Account of the Discovery of the Structure of DNA* (London: Weidenfeld and Nicolson, 1968) [Kristeva's note].

2. The first and second phases of Freud's discussion of infantile sexuality; the "oral" is associated with sucking, the "anal" with the start of toilet training.

3. Throughout her writings, Melanie Klein emphasizes the "pre-Oedipal" phase, i.e., a period of the subject's development that precedes the "discovery" of castration and the positing of the superego, which itself is subject to (paternal) Law. The processes she describes for this phase correspond, *but on a genetic level*, to what we call the semiotic as opposed to the symbolic, which underlies and conditions the semiotic. Significantly, these pre-Oedipal processes are organized through

this sensorimotor organization. The mother's body is therefore what mediates the symbolic law organizing social relations and becomes the ordering principle of the semiotic *chora*,[4] which is on the path of destruction, aggressivity, and death. For although drives have been described as disunited or contradictory structures, simultaneously "positive" and "negative," this doubling is said to generate a dominant "destructive wave" that is drive's most characteristic trait: Freud notes that the most instinctual drive is the death drive.[5] In this way, the term "drive" denotes waves of attack against stases, which are themselves constituted by the repetition of these charges; together, charges and stases lead to no identity (not even that of the "body proper") that could be seen as a result of their functioning. This is to say that the semiotic *chora* is no more than the place where the subject is both generated and negated, the place where his unity succumbs before the process of charges and stases that produce him. We shall call this process of charges and stases a *negativity* to distinguish it from negation, which is the act of a judging subject (see below, part II).

Checked by the constraints of biological and social structures, the drive charge thus undergoes stases. Drive facilitation, temporarily arrested, marks *discontinuities* in what may be called the various material supports [*matériaux*] susceptible to semiotization: voice, gesture, colors. Phonic (later phonemic), kinetic, or chromatic units and differences are the marks of these stases in the drives. Connections or *functions* are thereby established between these discrete marks which are based on drives and articulated according to their resemblance or opposition, either by slippage or by condensation. Here we find the principles of metonymy and metaphor[6] indissociable from the drive economy underlying them.

Although we recognize the vital role played by the processes of displacement and condensation in the organization of the semiotic, we must also

projection onto the mother's body, for girls as well as for boys: "at this stage of development children of both sexes believe that it is the body of their mother which contains all that is desirable, especially their father's penis." *The Psycho-analysis of Children*, trans. Alix Strachey (London: Hogarth Press, 1932), p. 269. Our own view of this stage is as follows: Without "believing" or "desiring" any "object" whatsoever, the subject is in the process of constituting himself vis-à-vis a non-object. He is in the process of separating from this non-object so as to make that non-object "one" and posit himself as "other": the mother's body is the not-yet-one that the believing and desiring subject will imagine as a "receptacle" [Kristeva's note].

4. As for what situates the mother in symbolic space, we find the phallus again (see Jacques Lacan, "La Relation d'objet et les structures freudiennes" [Object Relations and Freudian Structures], *Bulletin de Psychologie*, April 1957, pp. 426–30), represented by the mother's father, i.e., the subject's maternal grandfather (see Marie-Claire Boons, "Le Meurtre du Père chez Freud" [Killing the Father in Freud], *L'Inconscient*, January–March 1968, 5: 101–29) [Kristeva's note].

5. Though disputed and inconsistent, the Freudian theory of drives is of interest here because of the predominance Freud gives to the death drive in both "living matter" and the "human being." The death drive is transversal to identity and tends to disperse "narcissisms" whose constitution ensures the link between structures and, by extension, life. But at the same time and conversely, narcissism and pleasure are only temporary positions from which the death drive blazes new paths [*se fraye de nouveaux passages*]. Narcissism and pleasure are therefore inveiglings and realizations of the death drive. The semiotic *chora*, converting drive discharges into stases, can be thought of both as a delaying of the death drive and as a possible realization of this drive, which tends to return to a homeostatic state. This hypothesis is consistent with the following remark: "at the beginning of mental life," writes Freud, "the struggle for pleasure was far more intense than later but not so unrestricted: it had to submit to frequent interruptions." *Beyond the Pleasure Principle*, in *The Standard Edition of the Complete Psycho-Analytic Works of Sigmund Freud*, ed. James Strachey (London: Hogarth Press, 1953), 18:63 [Kristeva's note].

6. Two figures (dependent on resemblance and association, respectively), most influentially discussed by the Russian-born American linguist ROMAN JAKOBSON in "Two Aspects of Language and Two Types of Aphasic Disturbances" (1956; see above); Lacan (in "The Agency of the Letter in the Unconscious," 1957; see above) and others connected them to Freud's dream-work processes of condensation and displacement, as described in *The Interpretation of Dreams* (1900; see above).

add to these processes the relations (eventually representable as topological spaces) that connect the zones of the fragmented body to each other and also to "external" "objects" and "subjects," which are not yet constituted as such. This type of relation makes it possible to specify the *semiotic* as a psychosomatic modality of the signifying process; in other words, not a symbolic modality but one articulating (in the largest sense of the word) a continuum: the connections between the (glottal and anal) sphincters in (rhythmic and intonational) vocal modulations, or those between the sphincters and family protagonists, for example.

All these various processes and relations, anterior to sign and syntax, have just been identified from a genetic perspective as previous and necessary to the acquisition of language, but not identical to language. Theory can "situate" such processes and relations diachronically within the process of the constitution of the subject precisely because *they function synchronically within the signifying process of the subject himself,* i.e., the subject of *cogitatio.*[7] Only in *dream* logic, however, have they attracted attention, and only in certain signifying practices, such as the *text,* do they dominate the signifying process.

It may be hypothesized that certain semiotic articulations are transmitted through the biological code or physiological "memory" and thus form the inborn bases of the symbolic function. Indeed, one branch of generative linguistics asserts the principle of innate language universals. As it will become apparent in what follows, however, the *symbolic*—and therefore syntax and all linguistic categories—is a social effect of the relation to the other, established through the objective constraints of biological (including sexual) differences and concrete, historical family structures. Genetic programmings are necessarily semiotic: they include the primary processes such as displacement and condensation, absorption and repulsion, rejection and stasis, all of which function as innate preconditions, "memorizable" by the species, for language acquisition.

Mallarmé[8] calls attention to the semiotic rhythm within language when he speaks of "The Mystery in Literature" ["Le Mystère dans les lettres"]. Indifferent to language, enigmatic and feminine, this space underlying the written is rhythmic, unfettered, irreducible to its intelligible verbal translation; it is musical, anterior to judgment, but restrained by a single guarantee: syntax. As evidence, we could cite "The Mystery in Literature" in its entirety.[9] For now, however, we shall quote only those passages that ally the functioning of that "air or song beneath the text" with woman:

> And the instrument of Darkness, whom they have designated, will not set down a word from then on except to deny that she must have been the enigma; lest she settle matters with a wisk of her skirts; 'I don't get it!'
>
> ....
>
> —They [the critics] play their parts disinterestedly or for a minor gain: leaving our Lady and Patroness exposed to show her dehiscence or lacuna, with respect to certain dreams, as though this were the standard to which everything is reduced.[1]

7. Thinking (Latin).
8. Stéphane Mallarmé (1842–1898), French poet.
9. Mallarmé, *Oeuvres complètes* [*Complete Works*] (Paris: Gallimard, 1945), pp. 382–87 [Kristeva's note].
1. Ibid., p. 383 [Kristeva's note].

To these passages we add others that point to the "mysterious" functioning of literature as a rhythm made intelligible by syntax: "Following the instinct for rhythms that has chosen him, the poet does not deny seeing a lack of proportion between the means let loose and the result." "I know that there are those who would restrict Mystery to Music's domain; when writing aspires to it."[2]

> What pivot is there, I mean within these contrasts, for intelligibility? a guarantee is needed—
>
> Syntax—
>
> . . . an extraordinary appropriation of structure, limpid, to the primitive lightning bolts of logic. A stammering, what the sentence seems, here repressed [. . .]
>
> ....
>
> The debate—whether necessary average clarity deviates in a detail—remains one for grammarians.[3]

Our positing of the semiotic is obviously inseparable from a theory of the subject that takes into account the Freudian positing of the unconscious. We view the subject in language as decentering the transcendental ego,[4] cutting through it, and opening it up to a dialectic in which its syntactic and categorical understanding is merely the liminary moment of the process, which is itself always acted upon by the relation to the other dominated by the death drive and its productive reiteration of the "signifier." We will be attempting to formulate the distinction between *semiotic* and *symbolic* within this perspective, which was introduced by Lacanian analysis, but also within the constraints of a practice—the *text*—which is only of secondary interest to psychoanalysis.

* * *

FROM 5. THE THETIC: RUPTURE AND/OR BOUNDARY

We shall distinguish the semiotic (drives and their articulations) from the realm of signification, which is always that of a proposition or judgment, in other words, a realm of *positions*. This positionality, which Husserlian phenomenology orchestrates through the concepts of *doxa, position,* and *thesis,* is structured as a break in the signifying process, establishing the *identification* of the subject and its object as preconditions of propositionality. We shall call this break, which produces the positing of signification, a *thetic*[5] phase. All enunciation, whether of a word or of a sentence, is thetic. It requires an identification; in other words, the subject must separate from and through his image, from and through his objects. This image and objects must first be posited in a space that becomes symbolic because it connects the two separated positions, recording them or redistributing them in an open combinatorial system.

The child's first so-called holophrastic enunciations include gesture, the object, and vocal emission. Because they are perhaps not yet sentences

2. Ibid., pp. 383, 385 [Kristeva's note].
3. Ibid., pp. 385–86 [Kristeva's note].
4. The autonomous, abstract subject implicit in perception and cognition, as defined by the German philosopher Edmund Husserl (1859–1938), a founder of phenomenology.
5. Propositional (from *thesis*), also a term from Husserl.

(NP-VP),[6] generative grammar is not readily equipped to account for them. Nevertheless, they are already thetic in the sense that they separate an object from the subject, and attribute to it a semiotic fragment, which thereby becomes a signifier. That this attribution is either metaphoric or metonymic ("woof-woof" says the dog, and all animals become "woof-woof") is logically secondary to the fact that it constitutes an *attribution,* which is to say, a positing of identity or difference, and that it represents the nucleus of judgment or proposition.

We shall say that the thetic phase of the signifying process is the "deepest structure" of the possibility of enunciation, in other words, of signification and the proposition. Husserl theologizes this deep logic of signification by making it a productive *origin* of the "free spontaneity" of the Ego:

> Its *free spontaneity and activity* consists in positing, positing on the strength of this or that, positing as an antecedent or a consequent, and so forth; it does not live within the theses as a passive indweller; the theses radiate from it as from a primary source of generation [*Erzeugungen*]. Every thesis begins with a *point of insertion* [*Einsatzpunkt*] with a point at which *the positing has its origin* [*Ursprungssetzung*]; so it is with the first thesis and with each further one in the synthetic nexus. This 'inserting' even belongs to the thesis as such, as a remarkable modus of original actuality. It somewhat resembles the *fiat,*[7] the point of insertion of will and action.[8]

In this sense, *there exists only one signification,* that of the thetic phase, which contains the object as well as the proposition, and the complicity between them. There is no sign that is not thetic and every sign is already the germ of a "sentence," attributing a signifier to an object through a "copula"[9] that will function as a signified. Stoic semiology, which was the first to formulate the matrix of the sign, had already established *this complicity between sign and sentence,* making them proofs of each other.

Modern philosophy recognizes that the right to represent the founding *thesis* of signification (sign and/or proposition) devolves upon the transcendental ego. But only since Freud have we been able to raise the question not of the origin of this thesis but rather of the process of its production. To brand the thetic as the foundation of metaphysics is to risk serving as an antechamber for metaphysics—unless, that is, we specify the way the thetic is produced. In our view, the Freudian theory of the unconscious and its Lacanian development show, precisely, that thetic signification is a stage attained under certain precise conditions during the signifying process, and that it constitutes the subject without being reduced to this process precisely because it is the threshold of language. Such a standpoint constitutes neither a reduction of the subject to the transcendental ego, nor a denial [*dénégation*] of the thetic phase that establishes signification.

6. Noun-phrase, verb-phrase; nomenclature from the generative and transformational grammar of the American linguist Noam Chomsky (b. 1928).
7. Literally "let there be" (Latin); this is the form of God's creative pronouncements in Genesis, in the Vulgate Bible.
8. Edmund Husserl, *Ideas: General Introduction to Pure Phenomenology*, trans. W. R. Boyce Gibson (London: Allen and Unwin, 1969), p. 342 [Kristeva's note].
9. Linking verb (which joins the subject and predicate).

* * *

12. GENOTEXT AND PHENOTEXT

In light of the distinction we have made between the semiotic *chora* and the symbolic, we may now examine the way texts function. What we shall call a *genotext* will include semiotic processes but also the advent of the symbolic. The former includes drives, their disposition, and their division of the body, plus the ecological and social system surrounding the body, such as objects and pre-Oedipal relations with parents. The latter encompasses the emergence of object and subject, and the constitution of nuclei of meaning involving categories: semantic and categorial fields. Designating the genotext in a text requires pointing out the transfers of drive energy that can be detected in phonematic devices (such as the accumulation and repetition of phonemes[1] or rhyme) and melodic devices (such as intonation or rhythm), in the way semantic and categorial fields are set out in syntactic and logical features, or in the economy of mimesis (fantasy, the deferment of denotation, narrative, etc.). The genotext is thus the only transfer of drive energies that organizes a space in which the subject is not *yet* a split unity that will become blurred, giving rise to the symbolic. Instead, the space it organizes is one in which the subject will be *generated* as such by a process of facilitations[2] and marks within the constraints of the biological and social structure.

In other words, even though it can be seen in language, the genotext is not linguistic (in the sense understood by structural or generative linguistics). It is, rather, a *process*, which tends to articulate structures that are ephemeral (unstable, threatened by drive charges, "quanta" rather than "marks") and nonsignifying (devices that do not have a double articulation).[3] It forms these structures out of: (a) instinctual dyads, (b) the corporeal and ecological continuum, (c) the social organism and family structures, which convey the constraints imposed by the mode of production, and (d) matrices of enunciation, which give rise to discursive "genres" (according to literary history), "psychic structures" (according to psychiatry and psychoanalysis), or various arrangements of "the participants in the speech event" (in Jakobson's notion of the linguistics of discourse).[4] We may posit that the matrices of enunciation are the result of the repetition of drive charges (a) within biological, ecological, and socio-familial constraints (b and c), and the stabilization of their facilitation into stases whose surrounding structure accommodates and leaves its mark on symbolization.

The genotext can thus be seen as language's underlying foundation. We shall use the term *phenotext* to denote language that serves to communicate, which linguistics describes in terms of "competence" and "performance."[5] The phenotext is constantly split up and divided, and is irreducible

1. Units of sound. The translator previously noted: "'Device' is Kristeva's own choice for the translation of *dispositif*: something devised or constructed for a particular purpose."
2. The translation of Freud's German *Bahnungen*. According to Freud, it was easier to repeat an experience than to have a new one; repetition thus lays down or "facilitates" a pattern for future experiences.
3. To signify something else, language must both link the sign to the thing (referent) and articulate the two parts of the sign (signifier and signifier).
4. See "Shifters, Verbal Categories, and the Russian Verb," in Roman Jakobson, *Selected Writings*, 2 vols. (The Hague: Mouton, 1971), 2:130–47 [Kristeva's note].
5. Chomsky's terms, corresponding roughly to Saussure's *langue* and *parole*: "competence" is knowledge of language as a system; "performance" involves linguistic acts by particular speakers.

to the semiotic process that works through the genotext. The phenotext is a structure (which can be generated, in generative grammar's sense); it obeys rules of communication and presupposes a subject of enunciation and an addressee. The genotext, on the other hand, is a process; it moves through zones that have relative and transitory borders and constitutes a *path* that is not restricted to the two poles of univocal information between two full-fledged subjects. If these two terms—genotext and phenotext—could be translated into a metalanguage that would convey the difference between them, one might say that the genotext is a matter of topology, whereas the phenotext is one of algebra.[6] This distinction may be illustrated by a particular signifying system: written and spoken Chinese, particularly classical Chinese. Writing represents-articulates the signifying process into specific networks or spaces; *speech* (which may correspond to that writing) restores the diacritical elements necessary for an exchange of meaning between two subjects (temporality, aspect, specification of the protagonists, morpho-semantic identifiers, and so forth).[7]

The signifying process therefore includes both the genotext and the phenotext; indeed it could not do otherwise. For it is in language that all signifying operations are realized (even when linguistic material is not used), and it is on the basis of language that a theoretical approach may attempt to perceive that operation.

In our view, the process we have just described accounts for the way all signifying practices are generated.[8] But every signifying practice does not encompass the infinite totality of that process. Multiple constraints—which are ultimately sociopolitical—stop the signifying process at one or another of the theses that it traverses; they knot it and lock it into a given surface or structure; they discard *practice* under fixed, fragmentary, symbolic *matrices*, the tracings of various social constraints that obliterate the infinity of the process: the phenotext is what conveys these obliterations. Among the capitalist mode of production's numerous signifying practices only certain literary texts of the avant-garde (Mallarmé, Joyce[9]) manage to cover the infinity of the process, that is, reach the semiotic *chora*, which modifies linguistic structures. It must be emphasized, however, that this total exploration of the signifying process generally leaves in abeyance the theses that are characteristic of the social organism, its structures, and their political transformation: the text has a tendency to dispense with political and social signifieds.

It has only been in very recent years or in revolutionary periods that signifying practice has inscribed within the phenotext the plural, heteroge-

6. That is, the genotext is the shape taken by existing space, while the phenotext translates the relations discovered into a formal language.

7. See Joseph Needham, *Science and Civilisation in China*, 4 vols. (Cambridge: Cambridge University Press, 1960), vol. 1 [Kristeva's note].

8. From a similar perspective, Edgar Morin writes: "We can think of magic, mythologies, and ideologies both as mixed systems, making affectivity rational and rationality affective, and as outcomes of combining: (a) fundamental drives, (b) the chancy play of fantasy, and (c) logico-constructive systems. (To our mind, the theory of myth must be based on triunic syncretism rather than unilateral logic.)" He adds, in a note, that "myth does not have a single logic but a synthesis of three kinds of logic." "Le Paradigme perdu: La Nature humaine" [Paradigm Lost: Human Nature], paper presented at the "Invariants biologiques et universaux culturels" [Biological Invariants and Cultural Universals] Colloquium, Royaumont, September 6–9, 1972 [Kristeva's note].

9. James Joyce (1882–1941), Irish writer known for his innovations in the form and language of the novel.

neous, and contradictory process of signification encompassing the flow of drives, material discontinuity, political struggle, and the pulverization of language.[1]

Lacan has delineated four types of discourse in our society: that of the hysteric, the academic, the master, and the analyst.[2] Within the perspective just set forth, we shall posit a different classification, which, in certain respects, intersects these four Lacanian categories, and in others, adds to them. We shall distinguish between the following signifying practices: narrative, metalanguage, contemplation, and text-practice.

Let us state from the outset that this distinction is only provisional and schematic, and that although it corresponds to actual practices, it interests us primarily as a didactic implement [*outil*]—one that will allow us to specify some of the modalities of signifying dispositions. The latter interest us to the extent that they give rise to different practices and are, as a consequence, more or less coded in modes of production. Of course narrative and contemplation could also be seen as devices stemming from (hysterical and obsessional) transference neurosis; and metalanguage and the text as practices allied with psychotic (paranoid and schizoid) economies.[3]

1974

1. An allusion to *Le Poème pulvérisé* (1947, *The Pulverized Poem*), a volume of prose poems by the French poet René Char.
2. Lacan presented this typology of discourse at his 1969 and 1970 seminars [Kristeva's note].
3. Suggesting parallels between creativity and madness, Kristeva connects narrative with hysteria, contemplation with obsession, metalanguage with paranoia, and textuality with schizophrenia.

LAURA MULVEY
b. 1941

The writer and filmmaker Laura Mulvey is widely regarded as one of the most challenging and incisive contemporary feminist cultural theorists. Belonging to the 1970s generation of British film theorists and independent filmmakers, she came to prominence with "Visual Pleasure and Narrative Cinema," a foundational text in feminist film criticism. This essay, published in 1975 in the vanguard British film journal *Screen* and frequently anthologized since, was groundbreaking as one of the earliest pieces of feminist criticism to go beyond cataloguing images of women in films. Extending the psychoanalytic insights of both SIGMUND FREUD and JACQUES LACAN, Mulvey describes how sexual difference and inequality are inscribed not only in the content or subject matter of a film but in its formal visual apparatus—its characteristic ways of looking—as well.

Born in Oxford, England, Mulvey received a B.A. in history from Oxford University in 1963. In 1972, with Claire Johnston and Linda Myles, she organized the women's events at the Edinburgh Film Festival. She has taught classes at Bulmershe College in Reading, England; the London Institute; the University of East Anglia; Cornell University; the University of California at Davis; and the British Film Institute. Since 1999 she has been a professor of film and media studies at Birkbeck, University of London. She has co-directed several avant-garde films with her husband, Peter Wollen, including *Penthesileia: Queen of the Amazons* (1974),

Riddles of the Sphinx (1977), *Amy!* (1980), *Crystal Gazing* (1982), and *The Bad Sister* (1983), all of which attempt to undermine conventional cinematic methods of filming women. With Mark Lewis, she co-directed *Disgraced Monuments* (1991). In addition, her essays on a wide variety of subjects have been published in *Visual and Other Pleasures* (1989) and *Fetishism and Curiosity* (1996).

In 1975 Mulvey's essay on visual pleasure and narrative cinema was revolutionary. It was written at a time when feminist literary criticism was beginning to establish itself as a field of study in many English departments and when women's studies programs were just getting off the ground. Few of the works now considered canonical in feminist literary criticism had been written. Anglo-American feminists, documenting images of women in literature, focused mainly on the content rather than the form of the texts they examined. Furthermore, many were hostile toward psychoanalysis, though a few were already exploring the potential connections between Freud and feminism. In France the theorists who would come to be known in the United States as the French feminists—JULIA KRISTEVA, HÉLÈNE CIXOUS, and Luce Irigaray—were using psychoanalytic theory as a means of exploring sexual difference and inequality, but their work would not begin to have a significant impact on American feminism until the 1980s.

"Visual Pleasure and Narrative Cinema" describes the manner in which the traditional visual apparatus of mainstream Hollywood "narrative" film looks at women as passive objects subordinated to the male gaze. Using a dense but illuminating psychoanalytic framework, Mulvey explores how the male unconscious shapes the erotic pleasures involved in looking. While she concedes that psychoanalysis might not offer a way out of the inequalities between the sexes or the oppression of women, she argues that it does provide a useful political tool for illustrating the mechanisms of pleasure on which the cinematic objectification of women depends.

According to Mulvey, the visual techniques of cinema afford viewers two contradictory pleasures. First, through the process Freud terms *scopophilia* (pleasure in looking), we enjoy making others the object of a controlling gaze. Second, through a process of identification that parallels Lacan's famous mirror stage (theorized in "The Mirror Stage," 1949; see above), we derive pleasure from identifying with an ideal image on the screen. Both have their origins in infantile processes by which we learned to separate ourselves from others. As described to this point, the two processes seem to structure the visual pleasure of men and women in the same way. However, Mulvey argues that because the male viewer cannot bear the burden of sexual objectification, he (the viewer is specifically male) deflects the tension by splitting his gaze between spectacle and narrative. A woman on-screen typically functions as the primary erotic object for both screen characters and audience members, becoming the object of the dominant, male gaze; as such, she exists outside the narrative illusions of time and space the film creates. At the same time, spectators identify with the male protagonist, who acts within the parameters of time and space—the diegesis—created by the film's story line.

The visual apparatus of mainstream film is further complicated because the process of gazing on the female object of desire is both pleasurable and threatening. While film creates an illusionistic world that allows for the free play of desire, in actuality the viewer is never free from the circumstances that gave rise to those desires within the symbolic social order, especially from the castration complex. The female object of the gaze, because she lacks a penis, is associated with the primordial fear of castration; although that threat initiates the male subject's integration into the symbolic social order, it also creates considerable anxiety. For this reason, the controlling male ego must attempt to escape the threat of castration evoked by the very gaze that gives it pleasure. Mulvey maintains that the male unconscious has two means of disarming the threat. The first is a form of voyeurism—investigating the female, demystifying her, and either denouncing, punishing, or saving her. The second is male disavowal, achieved by the substitution of a fetish object that becomes reassuring rather than dangerous. She examines these processes in the films of the directors Josef von Sternberg (1894–1969) and Alfred Hitchcock (1899–1980).

Before the pleasures of mainstream film can be challenged, Mulvey argues, viewers must be able to break down the cinematic codes that create the controlling male gaze and the illusionistic world that satisfies the desires it invokes. The cinema depends on three looks: that of the camera, that of the audience, and that of the film's characters. It achieves its illusion of truth and reality (mimesis) by denying or downplaying the first two (the material process of recording and the critical reading of the viewer) and by emphasizing the last. Only by disrupting the seamlessness of this whole visual illusion can women's subordination to the male gaze be defied.

The visual dynamics described in "Visual Pleasure and Narrative Cinema" have been widely applied not only to film but to other media as well, including photography, advertising, painting, and television, making this essay a landmark text for visual culture and media studies generally. But Mulvey's description of the male gaze has not been without its critics—feminists included—who have pointed out limitations. For many, the spatial logic of the male gaze limits the ways in which vision (and visual pleasure) can be understood. Because the masculine gaze is always posited as the site of mastery and control, while the feminine is marked by submission to the gaze, little room is left within mainstream narrative cinema for resistances or alternative practices. Nor does avant-garde cinema, where Mulvey locates the alternative to the male gaze, offer much evidence of being any more responsive to feminist critique than Hollywood filmmaking. Others argue that her paradigm locks the activity of looking into a traditional oedipal heterosexuality. Moreover, theories drawing on a visual apparatus based on a gendered split between female object and male voyeur cannot describe the visual pleasure of female viewers, or account for the male gaze at another male. Mulvey herself has recognized the validity of such objections, attempting to address many of them in a later essay, "Afterthoughts on 'Visual Pleasure and Narrative Cinema' Inspired by King Vidor's *Duel in the Sun*" (1981). Despite such criticism, Mulvey's 1975 essay continues to inspire important work in feminist film studies.

"Visual Pleasure and Narrative Cinema" Keywords: The Body, Cultural Studies, Feminist Theory, Media, Narrative Theory, Popular Culture, Psychoanalysis, Representation, Sexuality

Visual Pleasure and Narrative Cinema[1]

I. Introduction

(a) a political use of psychoanalysis

This paper intends to use psychoanalysis to discover where and how the fascination of film is reinforced by pre-existing patterns of fascination already at work within the individual subject and the social formations that have moulded him. It takes as its starting-point the way film reflects, reveals and even plays on the straight, socially established interpretation of sexual difference which controls images, erotic ways of looking and spectacle. It is helpful to understand what the cinema has been, how its magic has worked in the past, while attempting a theory and a practice which will challenge this cinema of the past. Psychoanalytic theory is thus appropriated here as a political weapon, demonstrating the way the unconscious of patriarchal society has structured film form.

1. All notes are written by the editor.

The paradox of phallocentrism[2] in all its manifestations is that it depends on the image of the castrated woman to give order and meaning to its world. An idea of woman stands as linchpin to the system: it is her lack that produces the phallus as a symbolic presence, it is her desire to make good the lack that the phallus signifies. Recent writing in *Screen*[3] about psychoanalysis and the cinema has not sufficiently brought out the importance of the representation of the female form in a symbolic order[4] in which, in the last resort, it speaks castration and nothing else. To summarise briefly: the function of woman in forming the patriarchal unconscious is twofold: she firstly symbolises the castration threat by her real lack of a penis and secondly thereby raises her child into the symbolic. Once this has been achieved, her meaning in the process is at an end. It does not last into the world of law and language except as a memory, which oscillates between memory of maternal plenitude and memory of lack. Both are posited on nature (or on anatomy in Freud's famous phrase[5]). Woman's desire is subjugated to her image as bearer of the bleeding wound; she can exist only in relation to castration and cannot transcend it. She turns her child into the signifier of her own desire to possess a penis (the condition, she imagines, of entry into the symbolic). Either she must gracefully give way to the word, the name of the father and the law, or else struggle to keep her child down with her in the half-light of the imaginary. Woman then stands in patriarchal culture as a signifier[6] for the male other, bound by a symbolic order in which man can live out his fantasies and obsessions through linguistic command by imposing them on the silent image of woman still tied to her place as bearer, not maker, of meaning.

There is an obvious interest in this analysis for feminists, a beauty in its exact rendering of the frustration experienced under the phallocentric order. It gets us nearer to the roots of our oppression, it brings closer an articulation of the problem, it faces us with the ultimate challenge: how to fight the unconscious structured like a language (formed critically at the moment of arrival of language) while still caught within the language of the patriarchy? There is no way in which we can produce an alternative out of the blue, but we can begin to make a break by examining patriarchy with the tools it provides, of which psychoanalysis is not the only but an important one. We are still separated by a great gap from important issues for the female unconscious which are scarcely relevant to phallocentric theory: the sexing of the female infant and her relationship to the symbolic, the sexually mature woman as non-mother, maternity outside the signification of the phallus, the vagina.

2. The psychoanalytic system in which sexual difference is defined as the difference between having and lacking the phallus; the term has come to refer to the patriarchal cultural system as a whole insofar as that system privileges the phallus as the symbol and source of power. Because of that privilege, women suffer "penis envy" and men suffer the "castration complex" (the fear of every male child that his desire for his mother will be punished by castration by his father; more generally, the fear of becoming "castrated" like women that leads men to cling to masculinity); both terms are originally from the theories of SIGMUND FREUD (1856–1939).

3. Vanguard British film journal, founded in 1969 by the British Society for Education in Film and Television.

4. In the theories of the psyche put forward by the French psychoanalyst JACQUES LACAN (1901–1981), the Symbolic is the dimension of language, law, and the father; in contrast, the Imaginary is modeled on the preverbal mother-child dyad, or on the relation between an infant and its mirror image.

5. That is, "anatomy is destiny" ("The Dissolution of the Oedipus Complex," 1924).

6. Term used by structuralist and poststructuralist theorists that was coined by the Swiss linguist FERDINAND DE SAUSSURE (1857–1913) to explain the functioning of signs, which he divided into a *signifier* (the form a sign takes) and a *signified* (the concept it represents).

But, at this point, psychoanalytic theory as it now stands can at least advance our understanding of the *status quo*, of the patriarchal order in which we are caught.

(B) DESTRUCTION OF PLEASURE AS A RADICAL WEAPON

As an advanced representation system, the cinema poses questions about the ways the unconscious (formed by the dominant order) structures ways of seeing and pleasure in looking. Cinema has changed over the last few decades. It is no longer the monolithic system based on large capital investment exemplified at its best by Hollywood in the 1930s, 1940s and 1950s. Technological advances (16mm and so on) have changed the economic conditions of cinematic production, which can now be artisanal as well as capitalist. Thus it has been possible for an alternative cinema to develop. However self-conscious and ironic Hollywood managed to be, it always restricted itself to a formal *mise en scène*[7] reflecting the dominant ideological concept of the cinema. The alternative cinema provides a space for the birth of a cinema which is radical in both a political and an aesthetic sense and challenges the basic assumptions of the mainstream film. This is not to reject the latter moralistically, but to highlight the ways in which its formal preoccupations reflect the psychical obsessions of the society which produced it and, further, to stress that the alternative cinema must start specifically by reacting against these obsessions and assumptions. A politically and aesthetically avant-garde cinema is now possible, but it can still only exist as a counterpoint.

The magic of the Hollywood style at its best (and of all the cinema which fell within its sphere of influence) arose, not exclusively, but in one important aspect, from its skilled and satisfying manipulation of visual pleasure. Unchallenged, mainstream film coded the erotic into the language of the dominant patriarchal order. In the highly developed Hollywood cinema it was only through these codes that the alienated subject, torn in his imaginary memory by a sense of loss, by the terror of potential lack in fantasy, came near to finding a glimpse of satisfaction: through its formal beauty and its play on his own formative obsessions. This article will discuss the interweaving of that erotic pleasure in film, its meaning and, in particular, the central place of the image of woman. It is said that analysing pleasure, or beauty, destroys it. That is the intention of this article. The satisfaction and reinforcement of the ego[8] that represent the high point of film history hitherto must be attacked. Not in favour of a reconstructed new pleasure, which cannot exist in the abstract, nor of intellectualised unpleasure, but to make way for a total negation of the ease and plenitude of the narrative fiction film. The alternative is the thrill that comes from leaving the past behind without simply rejecting it, transcending outworn or oppressive forms, and daring to break with normal pleasurable expectations in order to conceive a new language of desire.

7. In film, everything within the frame of a shot, including actors, settings, costumes, action, and lighting.

8. The part of the psyche, as described by Freud, that is conscious, controls behavior, and is in touch with external reality.

II. Pleasure in Looking / Fascination with the Human Form

A The cinema offers a number of possible pleasures. One is scopophilia (pleasure in looking). There are circumstances in which looking itself is a source of pleasure, just as, in the reverse formation, there is pleasure in being looked at. Originally, in his *Three Essays on Sexuality*, Freud isolated scopophilia as one of the component instincts of sexuality which exist as drives quite independently of the erotogenic zones. At this point he associated scopophilia with taking other people as objects, subjecting them to a controlling and curious gaze. His particular examples centre on the voyeuristic activities of children, their desire to see and make sure of the private and forbidden (curiosity about other people's genital and bodily functions, about the presence or absence of the penis and, retrospectively, about the primal scene[9]). In this analysis scopophilia is essentially active. (Later, in 'Instincts and Their Vicissitudes', Freud developed his theory of scopophilia further, attaching it initially to pre-genital auto-eroticism, after which, by analogy, the pleasure of the look is transferred to others. There is a close working here of the relationship between the active instinct and its further development in a narcissistic form.) Although the instinct is modified by other factors, in particular the constitution of the ego, it continues to exist as the erotic basis for pleasure in looking at another person as object. At the extreme, it can become fixated into a perversion, producing obsessive voyeurs and Peeping Toms whose only sexual satisfaction can come from watching, in an active controlling sense, an objectified other.

At first glance, the cinema would seem to be remote from the undercover world of the surreptitious observation of an unknowing and unwilling victim. What is seen on the screen is so manifestly shown. But the mass of mainstream film, and the conventions within which it has consciously evolved, portray a hermetically sealed world which unwinds magically, indifferent to the presence of the audience, producing for them a sense of separation and playing on their voyeuristic fantasy. Moreover the extreme contrast between the darkness in the auditorium (which also isolates the spectators from one another) and the brilliance of the shifting patterns of light and shade on the screen helps to promote the illusion of voyeuristic separation. Although the film is really being shown, is there to be seen, conditions of screening and narrative conventions give the spectator an illusion of looking in on a private world. Among other things, the position of the spectators in the cinema is blatantly one of repression of their exhibitionism and projection of the repressed desire onto the performer.

B The cinema satisfies a primordial wish for pleasurable looking, but it also goes further, developing scopophilia in its narcissistic aspect. The conventions of mainstream film focus attention on the human form. Scale, space, stories are all anthropomorphic. Here, curiosity and the wish to look intermingle with a fascination with likeness and recognition: the human face, the human body, the relationship between the human form and its surroundings, the visible presence of the person in the world. Jacques Lacan has described

9. The scene of the child's parents engaged in sexual intercourse. Freud published *Three Essays on the Theory of Sexuality* in 1905 and "Instincts and Their Vicissitudes" in 1915.

how the moment when a child recognises its own image in the mirror is crucial for the constitution of the ego.[1] Several aspects of this analysis are relevant here. The mirror phase occurs at a time when children's physical ambitions outstrip their motor capacity, with the result that their recognition of themselves is joyous in that they imagine their mirror image to be more complete, more perfect than they experience in their own body. Recognition is thus overlaid with misrecognition: the image recognised is conceived as the reflected body of the self, but its misrecognition as superior projects this body outside itself as an ideal ego, the alienated subject which, re-introjected[2] as an ego ideal, prepares the way for identification with others in the future. This mirror moment predates language for the child.

Important for this article is the fact that it is an image that constitutes the matrix of the imaginary, of recognition/misrecognition and identification, and hence of the first articulation of the I, of subjectivity. This is a moment when an older fascination with looking (at the mother's face, for an obvious example) collides with the initial inklings of self-awareness. Hence it is the birth of the long love affair/despair between image and self-image which has found such intensity of expression in film and such joyous recognition in the cinema audience. Quite apart from the extraneous similarities between screen and mirror (the framing of the human form in its surroundings, for instance), the cinema has structures of fascination strong enough to allow temporary loss of ego while simultaneously reinforcing it. The sense of forgetting the world as the ego has come to perceive it (I forgot who I am and where I was) is nostalgically reminiscent of that pre-subjective moment of image recognition. While at the same time, the cinema has distinguished itself in the production of ego ideals, through the star system for instance. Stars provide a focus or centre both to screen space and screen story where they act out a complex process of likeness and difference (the glamorous impersonates the ordinary).

C Sections A and B have set out two contradictory aspects of the pleasurable structures of looking in the conventional cinematic situation. The first, scopophilic, arises from pleasure in using another person as an object of sexual stimulation through sight. The second, developed through narcissism and the constitution of the ego, comes from identification with the image seen. Thus, in film terms, one implies a separation of the erotic identity of the subject from the object on the screen (active scopophilia), the other demands identification of the ego with the object on the screen through the spectator's fascination with and recognition of his like. The first is a function of the sexual instincts, the second of ego libido.[3] This dichotomy was crucial for Freud. Although he saw the two as interacting and overlaying each other, the tension between instinctual drives and self-preservation polarises in terms of pleasure. But both are formative structures, mechanisms without intrinsic meaning. In themselves they have no signification, unless attached to an idealisation. Both pursue aims in indifference to perceptual reality, and moti-

1. Lacan, in "The Mirror Stage" (1949; see above), describes the development of selfhood in children between 6 and 18 months old.

2. A psychoanalytic term; *introjection* is the unconscious process by which the outside world is taken into the self and represented in its internal structure.

3. Narcissistic libido, a pleasure derived from idealizing the self.

vate eroticised phantasmagoria that affect the subject's perception of the world to make a mockery of empirical objectivity.

During its history, the cinema seems to have evolved a particular illusion of reality in which this contradiction between libido and ego has found a beautifully complementary fantasy world. In *reality* the fantasy world of the screen is subject to the law which produces it. Sexual instincts and identification processes have a meaning within the symbolic order which articulates desire. Desire, born with language, allows the possibility of transcending the instinctual and the imaginary, but its point of reference continually returns to the traumatic moment of its birth: the castration complex. Hence the look, pleasurable in form, can be threatening in content, and it is woman as representation/image that crystallises this paradox.

III. Woman as Image, Man as Bearer of the Look

A In a world ordered by sexual imbalance, pleasure in looking has been split between active/male and passive/female. The determining male gaze projects its fantasy onto the female figure, which is styled accordingly. In their traditional exhibitionist role women are simultaneously looked at and displayed, with their appearance coded for strong visual and erotic impact so that they can be said to connote *to-be-looked-at-ness*. Woman displayed as sexual object is the *leitmotif* of erotic spectacle: from pin-ups to striptease, from Ziegfeld to Busby Berkeley,[4] she holds the look, and plays to and signifies male desire. Mainstream film neatly combines spectacle and narrative. (Note, however, how in the musical song-and-dance numbers interrupt the flow of the diegesis.[5]) The presence of woman is an indispensable element of spectacle in normal narrative film, yet her visual presence tends to work against the development of a story-line, to freeze the flow of action in moments of erotic contemplation. This alien presence then has to be integrated into cohesion with the narrative. As Budd Boetticher[6] has put it:

> What counts is what the heroine provokes, or rather what she represents. She is the one, or rather the love or fear she inspires in the hero, or else the concern he feels for her, who makes him act the way he does. In herself the woman has not the slightest importance.

(A recent tendency in narrative film has been to dispense with this problem altogether; hence the development of what Molly Haskell[7] has called the 'buddy movie', in which the active homosexual eroticism of the central male figures can carry the story without distraction.) Traditionally, the woman displayed has functioned on two levels: as erotic object for the characters within the screen story, and as erotic object for the spectator within the auditorium, with a shifting tension between the looks on either side of the screen. For instance, the device of the show-girl allows the two looks to be unified technically without any apparent break in the diegesis. A woman performs

4. American choreographer and film director (1895–1976), famous for his musical productions. Florenz Ziegfeld Jr. (1867–1932), American theatrical producer, best known for extravagant revues featuring showgirls.
5. The ongoing story or narrative.
6. American film director (1916–2001), best known for his westerns.
7. American film critic (b. 1939); she discusses "buddy movies" in *From Reverence to Rape: The Treatment of Women in the Movies* (1974).

within the narrative; the gaze of the spectator and that of the male characters in the film are neatly combined without breaking narrative verisimilitude. For a moment the sexual impact of the performing woman takes the film into a no man's land outside its own time and space. Thus Marilyn Monroe's first appearance in *The River of No Return* and Lauren Bacall's songs in *To Have and Have Not*.[8] Similarly, conventional close-ups of legs (Dietrich, for instance) or a face (Garbo)[9] integrate into the narrative a different mode of eroticism. One part of a fragmented body destroys the Renaissance space, the illusion of depth demanded by the narrative; it gives flatness, the quality of a cut-out or icon, rather than verisimilitude, to the screen.

B An active/passive heterosexual division of labour has similarly controlled narrative structure. According to the principles of the ruling ideology and the psychical structures that back it up, the male figure cannot bear the burden of sexual objectification. Man is reluctant to gaze at his exhibitionist like. Hence the split between spectacle and narrative supports the man's role as the active one of advancing the story, making things happen. The man controls the film fantasy and also emerges as the representative of power in a further sense: as the bearer of the look of the spectator, transferring it behind the screen to neutralise the extra-diegetic[1] tendencies represented by woman as spectacle. This is made possible through the processes set in motion by structuring the film around a main controlling figure with whom the spectator can identify. As the spectator identifies with the main male protagonist, he projects his look onto that of his like, his screen surrogate, so that the power of the male protagonist as he controls events coincides with the active power of the erotic look, both giving a satisfying sense of omnipotence. A male movie star's glamorous characteristics are thus not those of the erotic object of the gaze, but those of the more perfect, more complete, more powerful ideal ego conceived in the original moment of recognition in front of the mirror. The character in the story can make things happen and control events better than the subject/spectator, just as the image in the mirror was more in control of motor co-ordination.

In contrast to woman as icon, the active male figure (the ego ideal of the identification process) demands a three-dimensional space corresponding to that of the mirror recognition, in which the alienated subject internalised his own representation of his imaginary existence. He is a figure in a landscape. Here the function of film is to reproduce as accurately as possible the so-called natural conditions of human perception. Camera technology (as exemplified by deep focus in particular) and camera movements (determined by the action of the protagonist), combined with invisible editing (demanded by realism), all tend to blur the limits of screen space. The male protagonist is free to command the stage, a stage of spatial illusion in which he articulates the look and creates the action. (There are films with a woman as main protagonist, of course. To analyse this phenomenon seri-

8. The 1944 American film (dir. Howard Hawks) that was the film debut of the actress Bacall (1924–2014). *River of No Return* (dir. Otto Preminger, 1954), American film that stars the actress Monroe (1926–1962) as a beautiful saloon singer.

9. Greta Garbo (1905–1990), Swedish-born American film actress. Marlene Dietrich (1901–1992), German-born American actress.

1. Outside the story or the frame of the camera.

ously here would take me too far afield. Pam Cook and Claire Johnston's study of *The Revolt of Mamie Stover*[2] in Phil Hardy (ed.), *Raoul Walsh* (Edinburgh, 1974), shows in a striking case how the strength of this female protagonist is more apparent than real.)

C1 Sections III A and B have set out a tension between a mode of representation of woman in film and conventions surrounding the diegesis. Each is associated with a look: that of the spectator in direct scopophilic contact with the female form displayed for his enjoyment (connoting male fantasy) and that of the spectator fascinated with the image of his like set in an illusion of natural space, and through him gaining control and possession of the woman within the diegesis. (This tension and the shift from one pole to the other can structure a single text. Thus both in *Only Angels Have Wings*[3] and in *To Have and Have Not*, the film opens with the woman as object of the combined gaze of spectator and all the male protagonists in the film. She is isolated, glamorous, on display, sexualised. But as the narrative progresses she falls in love with the main male protagonist and becomes his property, losing her outward glamorous characteristics, her generalised sexuality, her show-girl connotations; her eroticism is subjected to the male star alone. By means of identification with him, through participation in his power, the spectator can indirectly possess her too.)

But in psychoanalytic terms, the female figure poses a deeper problem. She also connotes something that the look continually circles around but disavows: her lack of a penis, implying a threat of castration and hence unpleasure. Ultimately, the meaning of woman is sexual difference, the visually ascertainable absence of the penis, the material evidence on which is based the castration complex essential for the organisation of entrance to the symbolic order and the law of the father. Thus the woman as icon, displayed for the gaze and enjoyment of men, the active controllers of the look, always threatens to evoke the anxiety it originally signified. The male unconscious has two avenues of escape from this castration anxiety: preoccupation with the re-enactment of the original trauma (investigating the woman, demystifying her mystery), counterbalanced by the devaluation, punishment or saving of the guilty object (an avenue typified by the concerns of the *film noir*[4]); or else complete disavowal of castration by the substitution of a fetish object or turning the represented figure itself into a fetish so that it becomes reassuring rather than dangerous (hence overvaluation, the cult of the female star).

This second avenue, fetishistic scopophilia, builds up the physical beauty of the object, transforming it into something satisfying in itself. The first avenue, voyeurism, on the contrary, has associations with sadism: pleasure lies in ascertaining guilt (immediately associated with castration), asserting control and subjugating the guilty person through punishment or forgiveness. This sadistic side fits in well with narrative. Sadism demands a story, depends on making something happen, forcing a change in another person, a battle of will and strength, victory/defeat, all occurring in a linear time with a

2. A 1956 American film (dir. Raoul Walsh), starring Jane Russell in the title role.
3. A 1939 American film (dir. Howard Hawks); the female "object" is Jean Arthur.
4. Literally, "black film" (French), a post-WWII genre characterized by dark settings, by shady or disturbed characters who are alienated and isolated, and by a view of society from its underside.

beginning and an end. Fetishistic scopophilia, on the other hand, can exist outside linear time as the erotic instinct is focused on the look alone. These contradictions and ambiguities can be illustrated more simply by using works by Hitchcock and Sternberg,[5] both of whom take the look almost as the content or subject matter of many of their films. Hitchcock is the more complex, as he uses both mechanisms. Sternberg's work, on the other hand, provides many pure examples of fetishistic scopophilia.

C2 Sternberg once said he would welcome his films being projected upside-down so that story and character involvement would not interfere with the spectator's undiluted appreciation of the screen image. This statement is revealing but ingenuous: ingenuous in that his films do demand that the figure of the woman (Dietrich, in the cycle of films with her, as the ultimate example) should be identifiable; but revealing in that it emphasises the fact that for him the pictorial space enclosed by the frame is paramount, rather than narrative or identification processes. While Hitchcock goes into the investigative side of voyeurism, Sternberg produces the ultimate fetish, taking it to the point where the powerful look of the male protagonist (characteristic of traditional narrative film) is broken in favour of the image in direct erotic rapport with the spectator. The beauty of the woman as object and the screen space coalesce; she is no longer the bearer of guilt but a perfect product, whose body, stylised and fragmented by close-ups, is the content of the film and the direct recipient of the spectator's look.

Sternberg plays down the illusion of screen depth; his screen tends to be one-dimensional, as light and shade, lace, steam, foliage, net, streamers and so on reduce the visual field. There is little or no mediation of the look through the eyes of the main male protagonist. On the contrary, shadowy presences like La Bessière in *Morocco*[6] act as surrogates for the director, detached as they are from audience identification. Despite Sternberg's insistence that his stories are irrelevant, it is significant that they are concerned with situation, not suspense, and cyclical rather than linear time, while plot complications revolve around misunderstanding rather than conflict. The most important absence is that of the controlling male gaze within the screen scene. The high point of emotional drama in the most typical Dietrich films, her supreme moments of erotic meaning, take place in the absence of the man she loves in the fiction. There are other witnesses, other spectators watching her on the screen, their gaze is one with, not standing in for, that of the audience. At the end of *Morocco*, Tom Brown has already disappeared into the desert when Amy Jolly kicks off her gold sandals and walks after him. At the end of *Dishonoured*,[7] Kranau is indifferent to the fate of Magda. In both cases, the erotic impact, sanctified by death, is displayed as a spectacle for the audience. The male hero misunderstands and, above all, does not see.

In Hitchcock, by contrast, the male hero does see precisely what the audience sees. However, although fascination with an image through scopophilic

5. Josef von Sternberg (1894–1969), Austrian-born American film director; he brought the actress Marlene Dietrich to the United States and featured her in a number of films in the early 1930s. Alfred Hitchcock (1899–1980), English film director known as a master of suspense; many of his most important films were made in Hollywood.

6. A 1930 American film directed by Sternberg; La Bessière is played by Adolphe Menjou, Tom Brown by Gary Cooper, and Amy Jolly by Dietrich.

7. A 1931 American film directed by Sternberg; Kranau is played by Victor McLaglen and Marie (not "Magda"), a spy, by Dietrich.

eroticism can be the subject of the film, it is the role of the hero to portray the contradictions and tensions experienced by the spectator. In *Vertigo* in particular, but also in *Marnie* and *Rear Window*,[8] the look is central to the plot, oscillating between voyeurism and fetishistic fascination. Hitchcock has never concealed his interest in voyeurism, cinematic and non-cinematic. His heroes are exemplary of the symbolic order and the law—a policeman (*Vertigo*), a dominant male possessing money and power (*Marnie*)—but their erotic drives lead them into compromised situations. The power to subject another person to the will sadistically or to the gaze voyeuristically is turned onto the woman as the object of both. Power is backed by a certainty of legal right and the established guilt of the woman (evoking castration, psychoanalytically speaking). True perversion is barely concealed under a shallow mask of ideological correctness—the man is on the right side of the law, the woman on the wrong. Hitchcock's skillful use of identification processes and liberal use of subjective camera from the point of view of the male protagonist draw the spectators deeply into his position, making them share his uneasy gaze. The spectator is absorbed into a voyeuristic situation within the screen scene and diegesis, which parodies his own in the cinema.

In an analysis of *Rear Window*, Douchet[9] takes the film as a metaphor for the cinema. Jeffries is the audience, the events in the apartment block opposite correspond to the screen. As he watches, an erotic dimension is added to his look, a central image to the drama. His girlfriend Lisa had been of little sexual interest to him, more or less a drag, so long as she remained on the spectator side. When she crosses the barrier between his room and the block opposite, their relationship is reborn erotically. He does not merely watch her through his lens, as a distant meaningful image, he also sees her as a guilty intruder exposed by a dangerous man threatening her with punishment, and thus finally giving him the opportunity to save her. Lisa's exhibitionism has already been established by her obsessive interest in dress and style, in being a passive image of visual perfection; Jeffries's voyeurism and activity have also been established through his work as a photo-journalist, a maker of stories and captor of images. However, his enforced inactivity, binding him to his seat as a spectator, puts him squarely in the fantasy position of the cinema audience.

In *Vertigo*, subjective camera predominates. Apart from one flashback from Judy's point of view, the narrative is woven around what Scottie sees or fails to see.[1] The audience follows the growth of his erotic obsession and subsequent despair precisely from his point of view. Scottie's voyeurism is blatant: he falls in love with a woman he follows and spies on without speaking to. Its sadistic side is equally blatant: he has chosen (and freely chosen, for he had been a successful lawyer) to be a policeman, with all the attendant possibilities of pursuit and investigation. As a result, he follows, watches and falls in love with a perfect image of female beauty and mystery.

8. Three American films directed by Hitchcock: *Vertigo* (1958), *Marnie* (1964), and *Rear Window* (1954).

9. Jean Douchet (b. 1929), French film director and critic, author of *Alfred Hitchcock* (1967). Jeffries, temporarily immobilized by a broken leg, is played by James Stewart; Lisa is played by Grace Kelly.

1. Scottie (James Stewart) is hired to watch Madeleine (Kim Novak), a wealthy man's wife; he becomes obsessed with her, and after her suicide, he finds another woman who resembles her (Judy, also played by Novak).

Once he actually confronts her, his erotic drive is to break her down and force her *to tell* by persistent cross-questioning.

In the second part of the film, he re-enacts his obsessive involvement with the image he loved to watch secretly. He reconstructs Judy as Madeleine, forces her to conform in every detail to the actual physical appearance of his fetish. Her exhibitionism, her masochism, make her an ideal passive counterpart to Scottie's active sadistic voyeurism. She knows her part is to perform, and only by playing it through and then replaying it can she keep Scottie's erotic interest. But in the repetition he does break her down and succeeds in exposing her guilt. His curiosity wins through; she is punished.

Thus, in *Vertigo*, erotic involvement with the look boomerangs: the spectator's own fascination is revealed as illicit voyeurism as the narrative content enacts the processes and pleasures that he is himself exercising and enjoying. The Hitchcock hero here is firmly placed within the symbolic order, in narrative terms. He has all the attributes of the patriarchal superego.[2] Hence the spectator, lulled into a false sense of security by the apparent legality of his surrogate, sees through his look and finds himself exposed as complicit, caught in the moral ambiguity of looking. Far from being simply an aside on the perversion of the police, *Vertigo* focuses on the implications of the active/looking, passive/looked-at split in terms of sexual difference and the power of the male symbolic encapsulated in the hero. Marnie, too, performs for Mark Rutland's gaze and masquerades as the perfect to-be-looked-at image.[3] He, too, is on the side of the law until, drawn in by obsession with her guilt, her secret, he longs to see her in the act of committing a crime, make her confess and thus save her. So he, too, becomes complicit as he acts out the implications of his power. He controls money and words; he can have his cake and eat it.

IV. Summary

The psychoanalytic background that has been discussed in this article is relevant to the pleasure and unpleasure offered by traditional narrative film. The scopophilic instinct (pleasure in looking at another person as an erotic object) and, in contradistinction, ego libido (forming identification processes) act as formations, mechanisms, which mould this cinema's formal attributes. The actual image of woman as (passive) raw material for the (active) gaze of man takes the argument a step further into the content and structure of representation, adding a further layer of ideological significance demanded by the patriarchal order in its favourite cinematic form—illusionistic[4] narrative film. The argument must return again to the psychoanalytic background: women in representation can signify castration, and activate voyeuristic or fetishistic mechanisms to circumvent this threat. Although none of these interacting layers is intrinsic to film, it is only in the film form that they can reach a perfect and beautiful contradiction, thanks to the possibility in the cinema of shifting the emphasis of the look. The place of the look defines cinema, the possibility of varying it and exposing it. This is what makes cin-

2. The part of the psyche, as described by Freud, that develops through the incorporation of the moral standards of the parents and community.
3. In *Marnie*, the title character (Tippi Hedren) is a habitual thief and liar who steals from her employers and then changes her identity; Rutland (Sean Connery) hires her despite recognizing her.
4. Relying on illusion to convey realism.

ema quite different in its voyeuristic potential from, say, strip-tease, theatre, shows and so on. Going far beyond highlighting a woman's to-be-looked-at-ness, cinema builds the way she is to be looked at into the spectacle itself. Playing on the tension between film as controlling the dimension of time (editing, narrative) and film as controlling the dimension of space (changes in distance, editing), cinematic codes create a gaze, a world and an object, thereby producing an illusion cut to the measure of desire. It is these cinematic codes and their relationship to formative external structures that must be broken down before mainstream film and the pleasure it provides can be challenged.

To begin with (as an ending), the voyeuristic-scopophilic look that is a crucial part of traditional filmic pleasure can itself be broken down. There are three different looks associated with cinema: that of the camera as it records the pro-filmic event, that of the audience as it watches the final product, and that of the characters at each other within the screen illusion. The conventions of narrative film deny the first two and subordinate them to the third, the conscious aim being always to eliminate intrusive camera presence and prevent a distancing awareness in the audience. Without these two absences (the material existence of the recording process, the critical reading of the spectator), fictional drama cannot achieve reality, obviousness and truth. Nevertheless, as this article has argued, the structure of looking in narrative fiction film contains a contradiction in its own premises: the female image as a castration threat constantly endangers the unity of the diegesis and bursts through the world of illusion as an intrusive, static, one-dimensional fetish. Thus the two looks materially present in time and space are obsessively subordinated to the neurotic needs of the male ego. The camera becomes the mechanism for producing an illusion of Renaissance space, flowing movements compatible with the human eye, an ideology of representation that revolves around the perception of the subject; the camera's look is disavowed in order to create a convincing world in which the spectator's surrogate can perform with verisimilitude. Simultaneously, the look of the audience is denied an intrinsic force: as soon as fetishistic representation of the female image threatens to break the spell of illusion, and the erotic image on the screen appears directly (without mediation) to the spectator, the fact of fetishisation, concealing as it does castration fear, freezes the look, fixates the spectator and prevents him from achieving any distance from the image in front of him.

This complex interaction of looks is specific to film. The first blow against the monolithic accumulation of traditional film conventions (already undertaken by radical film-makers) is to free the look of the camera into its materiality[5] in time and space and the look of the audience into dialectics[6] and passionate detachment. There is no doubt that this destroys the satisfaction, pleasure and privilege of the 'invisible guest', and highlights the way film has depended on voyeuristic active/passive mechanisms. Women, whose image has continually been stolen and used for this end, cannot view the decline of the traditional film form with anything much more than sentimental regret.

1975

5. Actual mechanisms.

6. Analysis of interaction.

GIORGIO AGAMBEN
b. 1942

Written before the events of 9/11 and the subsequent "war on terror," the Italian philosopher Giorgio Agamben's *Homo Sacer* (1995) captures for many the form that state sovereignty and political power have assumed in the current era. Drawing on MICHEL FOUCAULT's concept of "biopower," WALTER BENJAMIN's critique of violence, and the German political theorist Carl Schmitt's work on "the state of exception," Agamben considers how power differentiates between those whose lives should be protected and those who should be stripped of all rights, including a right to live. His pursuit of these questions illuminates the complex political and legal dynamics of modernity and the nation-state. His work contributes to the heightened focus on the term *life* in contemporary theory and to the suspicion of "human rights" discourse among the critics of the war on terror.

Agamben studied law and philosophy at the University of Rome, writing his Ph.D. thesis on the political philosophy of the French mystic and activist Simone Weil. In 1966, 1968, and 1969, he attended small seminars conducted by MARTIN HEIDEGGER in France. He collaborated during the 1960s and '70s on several projects with the Italian filmmaker Pier Paolo Pasolini and the Italian author Italo Calvino. Agamben has taught at several universities in Italy, including the Universities of Macerata and Verona, and at the Collège Internationale de Paris and the European Graduate School in Switzerland. Prior to 9/11 he held visiting positions at the University of California at Berkeley and Northwestern University, among other U.S. institutions. After Congress passed the Homeland Security Act of 2004, which required certain foreign visitors to undergo biometric scanning to receive a visa, Agamben refused to return to America. The writing of *Homo Sacer* in 1995 inaugurated a series on which Agamben worked for twenty years; he published the ninth and final volume of the *Homo Sacer* project, *The Use of Bodies*, in 2014.

In "What Is a Camp?," our first selection, Agamben asserts that the concentration camp is the "*nomos* of the political space in which we live." *Nomos* literally means "law" (Greek) or, more broadly, the prevailing customs and norms of a society. To explain what it means to live, Agamben turns to ARISTOTLE's *Politics*, which he sees as differentiating between two understandings of *life*: *zoē*, which is the physical life of the body and which Agamben calls "bare life" or "naked life," and *bios*, which is the life shaped by an individual as a meaningful product of her interactions with others. Agamben accepts Foucault's contention that in modern societies, the state undertakes to protect and even nurture life. Modern sovereignty rests on this "biopower"—the deployment of power in the name of "life." But Agamben insists, in a theoretical move akin to the logic of deconstruction, that this attention to the life of citizens is enabled, even constituted, by the exclusion of those deemed unworthy of life. The law is always accompanied by a "state of exception," in which its rights and protections are suspended for some people. The favored ones, citizens, benefit from a *bios* guaranteed by law; but the excluded, who are stripped of or denied citizenship, are reduced to "bare life" and removed to a space apart from the legal, political realm, a space called "the camp." Designated as threats to the citizens' ability to live a full life, the inhabitants of the camp are held by a power that can, because it is outside of the law even as it is legally established by that law, do anything to them. Furthermore, the camp is extraterritorial, often located outside the proper jurisdictional territory of the state that establishes it—and thus, in Agamben's reading, quite literally the "outside" that constitutes the "inside." The United States' relegation of suspected terrorists to the Guantánamo Bay prison in Cuba beginning in 2002 provided a dramatic manifestation of the scenario that Agamben outlines.

Our second selection, from *Homo Sacer*, shows how Agamben deploys the Foucauldian notion of biopower. Unlike Foucault, Agamben is mostly interested in the power deployed by the state, and not in nonstate power diffused through any number of social actors and institutions. But like Foucault, he understands power as productive. Biopower uses its focus on life to create a new kind of political subject, one that depends on the state to protect the life of citizens against threats such as epidemics, famine, environmental hazards, and infant mortality. This new kind of power gives the state unprecedented access to the body. It is now a matter of state interest that someone be well fed and free of disease. This "politicization of life" can be based on the notion that "life" is "sacred" and therefore should be protected and preserved, but it also leads to the distinction between "bare life," which is merely bodily and derided as "animalistic," and *bios*, a fully human life. Sovereignty, traditionally the power of the king to order the death of his subjects, has now become the power to provide a fully human life to those subjects. This transformation makes the distinction between subjects (citizens) and nonsubjects momentous. The noncitizen is not entitled to the state-provided means for *bios*, but instead exists only in the realm of bare life. The multiple refugees and displaced persons created by contemporary wars exist in this minimalist condition.

Agamben takes the ancient Roman legal category of the *homo sacer* as the emblem of this fundamental contradiction at the heart of our current situation. An accursed man or outlaw, the *homo sacer* may be killed by anyone who encounters him. But, displaying the fundamental ambivalence of core religious terms, the *homo sacer* is also sacred, since his extralegal status places him outside of worldly power. The state may not sacrifice him, just as he (as a noncitizen) cannot sacrifice himself (as a soldier or otherwise) for his country. As a nonperson, he does not exist for the state, which is why others can kill him with impunity. Agamben contends that biopower cannot exist without this category of the nonperson, the one who has only *zoē* and whose life is not protected.

In the modern era, the *homo sacer* is the inhabitant of the camps. That is why, as HANNAH ARENDT was the first to highlight, the Nazis had to strip German Jews of citizenship before sending them to the camps. Citizens have "rights" that limit what the state can do to them. Agamben links the rise of biopower to the reliance since the American and French Revolutions on the discourse of rights to legitimate political regimes. While rights might be viewed as liberating, in Agamben's view they firmly locate the subject of those rights within the legal system and, hence, make that subject answerable to its demands. That there is barely any life outside of rights is true, but the subjection to rights creates the nation-state's sovereignty. And the notion of rights, Agamben contends, is contradictory from its very origins. Rights are meant, in part, to protect subjects against state tyranny. But the enforcer of rights is the state itself. Furthermore, the state is obliged to protect only the rights of citizens, of its own subjects. So by submitting to the state as its subject, the citizen is supposed to get protection against the state. This doesn't make sense—and, for that reason, the rights enjoyed by virtue of being a citizen are always supplemented by other rights (perhaps more fundamental ones) assumed to be enjoyed by virtue of being human. "Human rights" are contrasted to "political rights," but the idea of human rights (even when the lack the concept is meant to fill is clear) has proved terribly ineffective in protecting those persons that states deem outside the law.

At times, Agamben seems to accept, as do Benjamin and JACQUES DERRIDA, that there is an originary violence at the heart of the law, that the valuing of "life" by biopower must always be shadowed or even constituted by the category of "bare life" and the extralegal *homo sacer*. But as the *Homo Sacer* series has unfolded, Agamben has struggled to imagine ways of being that are nonviolent and offer an alternative to the *nomos* of the state of exception, with its camps. His insistence that democracy and totalitarianism are only inches apart can seem hyperbolic, just as his refusal to acknowledge the successes of rights discourse and humanitarianism in alleviating tyranny and suffering can seem obtuse. But there is no denying that power, concentrated mostly in the hands of nation-states, has persistently over the past one hundred years refused to countenance more than bare life for millions who cannot gain citizenship in the world's more prosperous countries.

Means Without End: Notes on Politics **Keywords:** The Body, Institutional Studies, Modernity, Nationhood, Subjectivity
Homo Sacer: Sovereign Power and Bare Life **Keywords:** The Body, Institutional Studies, Modernity, Nationhood, Subjectivity

From Means Without End: Notes on Politics[1]

What Is a Camp?

What happened in the camps exceeds the juridical concept of crime to such an extent that the specific political-juridical structure within which those events took place has often been left simply unexamined. The camp is the place in which the most absolute *conditio inhumana*[2] ever to appear on Earth was realized: this is ultimately all that counts for the victims as well as for posterity. Here I will deliberately set out in the opposite direction. Rather than deducing the definition of camp from the events that took place there, I will ask instead: *What is a camp? What is its political-juridical structure? How could such events have taken place there?* This will lead us to look at the camp not as a historical fact and an anomaly that—though admittedly still with us—belongs nonetheless to the past, but rather in some sense as the hidden matrix and *nomos*[3] of the political space in which we still live.

Historians debate whether the first appearance of camps ought to be identified with the *campos de concentraciones*[4] that were created in 1896 by the Spaniards in Cuba in order to repress the insurrection of that colony's population, or rather with the *concentration camps* into which the English herded the Boers[5] at the beginning of the twentieth century. What matters here is that in both cases one is dealing with the extension to an entire civilian population of a state of exception[6] linked to a colonial war. The camps, in other words, were not born out of ordinary law, and even less were they the product—as one might have believed—of a transformation and a development of prison law; rather, they were born out of the state of exception and martial law. This is even more evident in the case of the Nazi *Lager*,[7] whose origin and juridical regime is well documented. It is well known that the juridical foundation of internment was not ordinary law but rather the *Schutzhaft* (literally, protective custody), which was a juridical institution of Prussian derivation that Nazi jurists sometimes considered a measure of preventive policing inasmuch as it enabled the "taking into custody" of indi-

1. Translated by Vincenzo Binetti and Cesare Casarino.
2. Inhuman condition (Latin). Agamben is referring to the Nazi concentration camps, first established in 1933 and turned into mass extermination camps during World War II.
3. Law (Greek); more generally, the prevailing customs or norms of a society.
4. Concentration camps (Spanish).
5. South Africans of Dutch, German, and Huguenot descent, defeated by the British in a war (1899–1902) for political dominance of South Africa.
6. For Agamben a key term of governance theory, designating the suspension of legal protection and of rights for certain persons.
7. Concentration camp (literally, "storeroom" or "warehouse"; German).

viduals regardless of any relevant criminal behavior and exclusively in order to avoid threats to the security of the state. The origin of the *Schutzhaft*, however, resides in the Prussian law on the state of siege that was passed on June 4, 1851, and that was extended to the whole of Germany (with the exception of Bavaria) in 1871, as well as in the earlier Prussian law on the "protection of personal freedom" (*Schutz der persönlichen Freiheit*) that was passed on February 12, 1850. Both these laws were applied widely during World War I.

One cannot overestimate the importance of this constitutive nexus between state of exception and concentration camp for a correct understanding of the nature of the camp. Ironically, the "protection" of freedom that is in question in the *Schutzhaft* is a protection against the suspension of the law that characterizes the state of emergency. What is new here is that this institution is dissolved by the state of exception on which it was founded and is allowed to continue to be in force under normal circumstances. *The camp is the space that opens up when the state of exception starts to become the rule.* In it, the state of exception, which was essentially a temporal suspension of the state of law, acquires a permanent spatial arrangement that, as such, remains constantly outside the normal state of law. When Himmler[8] decided, in March 1933, on the occasion of the celebrations of Hitler's election to the chancellorship of the Reich, to create a "concentration camp for political prisoners" at Dachau, this camp was immediately entrusted to the SS and, thanks to the *Schutzhaft*, was placed outside the jurisdiction of criminal law as well as prison law, with which it neither then nor later ever had anything to do. Dachau, as well as the other camps that were soon added to it (Sachsenhausen, Buchenwald, Lichtenberg),[9] remained virtually always operative: the number of inmates varied and during certain periods (in particular, between 1935 and 1937, before the deportation of the Jews began) it decreased to 7,500 people; the camp as such, however, had become a permanent reality in Germany.

One ought to reflect on the paradoxical status of the camp as space of exception: the camp is a piece of territory that is placed outside the normal juridical order; for all that, however, it is not simply an external space. According to the etymological meaning of the term *exception* (*ex-capere*[1]), what is being excluded in the camp is *captured outside*, that is, it is included by virtue of its very exclusion. Thus, what is being captured under the rule of law is first of all the very state of exception. In other words, if sovereign power is founded on the ability to decide on the state of exception, the camp is the structure in which the state of exception is permanently realized. Hannah Arendt[2] observed once that what comes to light in the camps is the principle that supports totalitarian domination and that common sense stubbornly refuses to admit to, namely, the principle according to which anything is possible.

8. Heinrich Himmler (1900–1945), head of the Schutzstaffel (protection squad; German), or SS, the elite paramilitary organization founded as Hitler's personal bodyguard (1925). Eventually members of the SS became responsible for populating and administering the concentration camps, the first of which was Dachau, about 12 miles north of Munich.

9. All concentration camps in Germany itself, established in 1936, 1937, and 1933, respectively.

1. The Latin verb from which "exception" is derived, broken into its components (which literally mean "to seize out of").

2. German-born American political theorist (1906–1975; see above); she makes this observation in *The Origins of Totalitarianism* (1951).

It is only because the camps constitute a space of exception—a space in which the law is completely suspended—that everything is truly possible in them. If one does not understand this particular political-juridical structure of the camps, whose vocation is precisely to realize permanently the exception, the incredible events that took place in them remain entirely unintelligible. The people who entered the camp moved about in a zone of indistinction between the outside and the inside, the exception and the rule, the licit and the illicit, in which every juridical protection had disappeared; moreover, if they were Jews, they had already been deprived of citizenship rights by the Nuremberg Laws[3] and were later completely denationalized at the moment of the "final solution."[4] *Inasmuch as its inhabitants have been stripped of every political status and reduced completely to naked life,*[5] *the camp is also the most absolute biopolitical space that has ever been realized—a space in which power confronts nothing other than pure biological life without any mediation.* The camp is the paradigm itself of political space at the point in which politics becomes biopolitics and the *homo sacer*[6] becomes indistinguishable from the citizen. The correct question regarding the horrors committed in the camps, therefore, is not the question that asks hypocritically how it could have been possible to commit such atrocious horrors against other human beings; it would be more honest, and above all more useful, to investigate carefully how—that is, thanks to what juridical procedures and political devices—human beings could have been so completely deprived of their rights and prerogatives to the point that committing any act toward them would no longer appear as a crime (at this point, in fact, truly anything had become possible).

If this is the case, if the essence of the camp consists in the materialization of the state of exception and in the consequent creation of a space for naked life as such, we will then have to admit to be facing a camp virtually every time that such a structure is created, regardless of the nature of the crimes committed in it and regardless of the denomination and specific topography it might have. The soccer stadium in Bari in which the Italian police temporarily herded Albanian illegal immigrants in 1991 before sending them back to their country, the cycle-racing track in which the Vichy authorities rounded up the Jews before handing them over to the Germans,[7] the refugee camp near the Spanish border where Antonio Machado[8] died in 1939, as well as the *zones d'attente*[9] in French international airports in which foreigners requesting refugee status are detained will all have to be considered camps. In all these cases, an apparently anodyne place (such as the Hotel Arcade near the Paris airport) delimits instead a space in which, for all intents and purposes, the normal rule of law is suspended and in which

3. Laws passed in a 1935 convention in Nürnberg that deprived Jews of German citizenship and banned sexual relations between Jews and those of "German or kindred blood."
4. That is, to the "Jewish question": the solution, adopted in 1942, was to send all Jews within German-controlled territories to labor and extermination camps.
5. Also "bare life," a key term for Agamben: the minimal existence of a human being, apart from any attributes, accomplishments, or rights that attend recognized membership in a political or social community.
6. Sacred/accursed man (Latin): in ancient Roman law, a man who is banned and therefore can be killed with impunity because he is placed outside the law, but who could not be offered as a sacrifice in religious rites.
7. Thousands of Jews were rounded up in Paris by French police on July 16–17, 1942, and most were held in a bicycle racing track and stadium before being shipped to Auschwitz.
8. Spanish poet and playwright (1875–1939); he was fleeing after the Republican defeat in the Spanish Civil War.
9. Waiting zones (French).

the fact that atrocities may or may not be committed does not depend on the law but rather on the civility and ethical sense of the police that act temporarily as sovereign. This is the case, for example, during the four days foreigners may be kept in the *zone d'attente* before the intervention of French judicial authorities. In this sense, even certain outskirts of the great postindustrial cities as well as the gated communities of the United States are beginning today to look like camps, in which naked life and political life, at least in determinate moments, enter a zone of absolute indeterminacy.

From this perspective, the birth of the camp in our time appears to be an event that marks in a decisive way the political space itself of modernity. This birth takes place when the political system of the modern nation-state—founded on the functional nexus between a determinate localization (territory) and a determinate order (the state), which was mediated by automatic regulations for the inscription of life (birth or nation)—enters a period of permanent crisis and the state decides to undertake the management of the biological life of the nation directly as its own task. In other words, if the structure of the nation-state is defined by three elements—*territory, order,* and *birth*—the rupture of the old *nomos* does not take place in the two aspects that, according to Carl Schmitt,[1] used to constitute it (that is, localization, *Ortung*, and order, *Ordnung*),[2] but rather at the site in which naked life is inscribed in them (that is, there where inscription turns *birth* into *nation*). There is something that no longer functions in the traditional mechanisms that used to regulate this inscription, and the camp is the new hidden regulator of the inscription of life in the order—or, rather, it is the sign of the system's inability to function without transforming itself into a lethal machine. It is important to note that the camps appeared at the same time that the new laws on citizenship and on the denationalization of citizens were issued (not only the Nuremberg Laws on citizenship in the Reich but also the laws on the denationalization of citizens that were issued by almost all the European states, including France, between 1915 and 1933).[3] The state of exception, which used to be essentially a temporary suspension of the order, becomes now a new and stable spatial arrangement inhabited by that naked life that increasingly cannot be inscribed into the order. *The increasingly widening gap between birth (naked life) and nation-state is the new fact of the politics of our time and what we are calling "camp" is this disparity.* To an order without localization (that is, the state of exception during which the law is suspended) corresponds now a localization without order (that is, the camp as permanent space of exception). The political system no longer orders forms of life and juridical norms in a determinate space; rather, it contains within itself a *dislocating localization* that exceeds it and in which virtually every form of life and every norm can be captured. The camp intended as a dislocating localization is the hidden matrix of the politics in which we still live, and we must learn to recognize it in all of its metamor-

1. German jurist and political theorist (1888–1985); he is Agamben's source for the concept of "state of exception."
2. Schmitt's terms to designate the key feature of the nation-state: namely, its imposition of order over a specific territory or locality.
3. The French citizenship law of 1933 revoked citizenship by birth, requiring children born in France of non-French parents to request French citizenship upon reaching adulthood at the age of 18. Citizenship requirements were similarly tightened in Great Britain, Italy, and Austria.

phoses. The camp is the fourth and inseparable element that has been added to and has broken up the old trinity of nation (birth), state, and territory.

It is from this perspective that we need to see the reappearance of camps in a form that is, in a certain sense, even more extreme in the territories of the former Yugoslavia.[4] What is happening there is not at all, as some interested observers rushed to declare, a redefinition of the old political system according to new ethnic and territorial arrangements, that is, a simple repetition of the processes that culminated in the constitution of the European nation-states. Rather, we note there an irreparable rupture of the old *nomos* as well as a dislocation of populations and human lives according to entirely new lines of flight. That is why the camps of ethnic rape are so crucially important. If the Nazis never thought of carrying out the "final solution" by impregnating Jewish women, that is because the principle of birth, which ensured the inscription of life in the order of the nation-state, was in some way still functioning, even though it was profoundly transformed. This principle is now adrift: it has entered a process of dislocation in which its functioning is becoming patently impossible and in which we can expect not only new camps but also always new and more delirious normative definitions of the inscription of life in the city. The camp, which is now firmly settled inside it, is the new biopolitical *nomos* of the planet.

1994

From Homo Sacer: Sovereign Power and Bare Life[1]

From *Part Three: The Camp as Biopolitical Paradigm of the Modern*

§1 THE POLITICIZATION OF LIFE

1.1. In the last years of his life, while he was working on the history of sexuality and unmasking the deployments of power at work within it, Michel Foucault[2] began to direct his inquiries with increasing insistence toward the study of what he defined as *biopolitics,* that is, the growing inclusion of man's natural life in the mechanisms and calculations of power. At the end of the first volume of *The History of Sexuality,*[3] Foucault, as we have seen, summarizes the process by which life, at the beginning of the modern age, comes to be what is at stake in politics: "For millennia, man remained what he was for Aristotle: a living animal with the additional capacity for political existence; modern man is an animal whose politics calls his existence as a living being into question."[4] Until the very end, however, Foucault continued to investigate the "processes of subjectivization" that, in the passage from the ancient to the modern world, bring the individual to objectify his own self, constituting himself as a subject and, at the same time, binding him-

4. As part of the ethnic cleansing undertaken by Serbs to drive out or kill Bosnian Muslims and Croats after Yugoslavia broke apart in 1991, mass executions and systematic rapes occurred in concentration camps.

1. Translated by Daniel Heller-Roazen, who occasionally retains Agamben's Italian in square brackets.

2. French historian and philosopher (1926–1984; see above).

3. A 3-volume work (1979–84).

4. *History of Sexuality,* vol. 1, *An Introduction,* trans. Robert Hurley (New York: Vintage, 1980), p. 143. For the Greek philosopher ARISTOTLE (384–322 B.C.E.), see above.

self to a power of external control. Despite what one might have legitimately expected, Foucault never brought his insights to bear on what could well have appeared to be the exemplary place of modern biopolitics: the politics of the great totalitarian states of the twentieth century. The inquiry that began with a reconstruction of the *grand enfermement*[5] in hospitals and prisons did not end with an analysis of the concentration camp.

If, on the other hand, the pertinent studies that Hannah Arendt[6] dedicated to the structure of totalitarian states in the postwar period have a limit, it is precisely the absence of any biopolitical perspective. Arendt very clearly discerns the link between totalitarian rule and the particular condition of life that is the camp: "The supreme goal of all totalitarian states," she writes, in a plan for research on the concentration camps, which, unfortunately, was not carried through, "is not only the freely admitted, long-ranging ambition to global rule, but also the never admitted and immediately realized attempt at total domination. The concentration camps are the laboratories in the experiment of total domination, for human nature being what it is, this goal can be achieved only under the extreme circumstances of human made hell" (*Essays*, p. 240). Yet what escapes Arendt is that the process is in a certain sense the inverse of what she takes it to be, and that precisely the radical transformation of politics into the realm of bare life[7] (that is, into a camp) legitimated and necessitated total domination. Only because politics in our age had been entirely transformed into biopolitics was it possible for politics to be constituted as totalitarian politics to a degree hitherto unknown.

The fact that the two thinkers who may well have reflected most deeply on the political problem of our age were unable to link together their own insights is certainly an index of the difficulty of this problem. The concept of "bare life" or "sacred life" is the focal lens through which we shall try to make their points of view converge. In the notion of bare life the interlacing of politics and life has become so tight that it cannot easily be analyzed. Until we become aware of the political nature of bare life and its modern avatars (biological life, sexuality, etc.), we will not succeed in clarifying the opacity at their center. Conversely, once modern politics enters into an intimate symbiosis with bare life, it loses the intelligibility that still seems to us to characterize the juridico-political foundation of classical politics.

1.2. Karl Löwith[8] was the first to define the fundamental character of totalitarian states as a "politicization of life" and, at the same time, to note the curious contiguity between democracy and totalitarianism:

> Since the emancipation of the third estate,[9] the formation of bourgeois democracy and its transformation into mass industrial democracy, the neutralization of politically relevant differences and postponement of a decision about them has developed to the point of turning into its opposite: a total politicization [*totale Politisierung*] of everything, even

5. Grand (or mass) confinement (French).
6. German-born American political theorist (1906–1975; see above). Agamben quotes from her *Essays in Understanding, 1930–1954: Formation, Exile, and Totalitarianism*, ed. Jerome Kohn (New York: Schocken, 2005).
7. Also "naked life," a key term for Agamben: the minimal existence of a human being, apart from any attributes, accomplishments, or rights that attend recognized membership in a political or social community.
8. German philosopher and intellectual historian (1897–1973).
9. That is, the commons.

> of seemingly neutral domains of life. Thus in Marxist Russia there emerged a worker-state that was "more intensively state-oriented than any absolute monarchy"; in fascist Italy, a corporate state normatively regulating not only national work, but also "after-work" [*Dopolavoro*] and all spiritual life; and, in National Socialist Germany, a wholly integrated state, which, by means of racial laws and so forth, politicizes even the life that had until then been private. (*Der okkasionelle Dezionismus*, p. 33)[1]

The contiguity between mass democracy and totalitarian states, nevertheless, does not have the form of a sudden transformation (as Löwith, here following in Schmitt's[2] footsteps, seems to maintain); before impetuously coming to light in our century, the river of biopolitics that gave *homo sacer*[3] his life runs its course in a hidden but continuous fashion. It is almost as if, starting from a certain point, every decisive political event were double-sided: the spaces, the liberties, and the rights won by individuals in their conflicts with central powers always simultaneously prepared a tacit but increasing inscription of individuals' lives within the state order, thus offering a new and more dreadful foundation for the very sovereign power from which they wanted to liberate themselves. "The 'right' to life," writes Foucault, explaining the importance assumed by sex as a political issue, "to one's body, to health, to happiness, to the satisfaction of needs and, beyond all the oppressions or 'alienation,' the 'right' to rediscover what one is and all that one can be, this 'right'—which the classical juridical system was utterly incapable of comprehending—was the political response to all these new procedures of power" (*La volonté*, p. 191).[4] The fact is that one and the same affirmation of bare life leads, in bourgeois democracy, to a primacy of the private over the public and of individual liberties over collective obligations and yet becomes, in totalitarian states, the decisive political criterion and the exemplary realm of sovereign decisions. And only because biological life and its needs had become the *politically* decisive fact is it possible to understand the otherwise incomprehensible rapidity with which twentieth-century parliamentary democracies were able to turn into totalitarian states and with which this century's totalitarian states were able to be converted, almost without interruption, into parliamentary democracies. In both cases, these transformations were produced in a context in which for quite some time politics had already turned into biopolitics, and in which the only real question to be decided was which form of organization would be best suited to the task of assuring the care, control, and use of bare life. Once their fundamental referent becomes bare life, traditional political distinctions (such as those between Right and Left, liberalism and totalitarianism, private and public) lose their clarity and intelligibility and enter into a zone of indistinction. The ex-communist ruling classes' unexpected fall into the most extreme

1. Löwith, *Der okkasionelle Dezionismus von Carl Schmitt* [*The Opportunistic Decisionism of Carl Schmitt*], in his *Sämtliche Schriften*, ed. Klaus Stichweh and Marc B. de Launey, vol. 8 (Stuttgart: Metzler, 1984).
2. Carl Schmitt (1888–1985), German jurist and political theorist who openly supported Nazism.
3. Sacred/accursed man (Latin); in ancient Roman law, a man who is banned and therefore can be killed with impunity because he is placed outside the law, but who could not be offered as a sacrifice in religious rites.
4. Foucault, *La volonté de savoir* [*The Will to Knowledge*] (Paris: Gallimard, 1976); this is vol. 1 of *History of Sexuality*.

racism (as in the Serbian program of "ethnic cleansing")[5] and the rebirth of new forms of fascism in Europe also have their roots here.

Along with the emergence of biopolitics, we can observe a displacement and gradual expansion beyond the limits of the decision on bare life, in the state of exception, in which sovereignty consisted. If there is a line in every modern state marking the point at which the decision on life becomes a decision on death, and biopolitics can turn into thanatopolitics,[6] this line no longer appears today as a stable border dividing two clearly distinct zones. This line is now in motion and gradually moving into areas other than that of political life, areas in which the sovereign is entering into an ever more intimate symbiosis not only with the jurist but also with the doctor, the scientist, the expert, and the priest. In the pages that follow, we shall try to show that certain events that are fundamental for the political history of modernity (such as the declaration of rights), as well as others that seem instead to represent an incomprehensible intrusion of biologico-scientific principles into the political order (such as National Socialist eugenics and its elimination of "life that is unworthy of being lived," or the contemporary debate on the normative determination of death criteria), acquire their true sense only if they are brought back to the common biopolitical (or thanatopolitical) context to which they belong. From this perspective, the camp—as the pure, absolute, and impassable biopolitical space (insofar as it is founded solely on the state of exception[7])—will appear as the hidden paradigm of the political space of modernity, whose metamorphoses and disguises we will have to learn to recognize.

1.3. The first recording of bare life as the new political subject is already implicit in the document that is generally placed at the foundation of modern democracy: the 1679 writ of *habeas corpus*.[8] Whatever the origin of this formula, used as early as the eighteenth century to assure the physical presence of a person before a court of justice, it is significant that at its center is neither the old subject of feudal relations and liberties nor the future *citoyen*, but rather a pure and simple *corpus*.[9] When John the Landless conceded Magna Carta to his subjects in 1215,[1] he turned his attention to the "archbishops, bishops, abbots, counts, barons, viscounts, provosts, officials and bailiffs," to the "cities, towns, villages," and, more generally, to the "free men of our kingdom," so that they might enjoy "their ancient liberties and free customs" as well as the ones he now specifically recognized. Article 29, whose task was to guarantee the physical freedom of the subjects, reads: "No free man [*homo liber*] may be arrested, imprisoned, dispossessed of his goods, or placed outside the law [*utlagetur*] or molested in any way; we will not place our hands on him nor will have others place their hands on him [*nec super*

5. The Serbian attempt during the Bosnian War (1992–95) to drive out or kill all Muslims and Croats in Bosnia.
6. A politics of death (in Greek, *thanatos*), the reverse of a politics of life (*bios*).
7. The suspension of the law under what are deemed extraordinary circumstances, thereby allowing the state to deprive people of all rights.
8. You should have the body (Latin), the first words of a writ directing the production in court of a person being detained. Although it was in use in England in the Middle Ages, many procedures were formalized in the Habeas Corpus Act of 1679.
9. Body (Latin), as contrasted to a citizen (*citoyen*, French).
1. The "Great Charter," issued to his barons by England's King John (1167–1216), is often seen as the first legal statement of rights granted to citizens by a sovereign.

eum ibimis, nec super eum mittemus], except after a legal judgment by his peers according to the law of the realm." Analogously, an ancient writ that preceded the *habeas corpus* and was understood to assure the presence of the accused in a trial bears the title *de homine replegiando* (or *repigliando*).[2]

Consider instead the formula of the writ that the act of 1679 generalizes and makes into law: *Praecipimus tibi quod Corpus X, in custodia vestra detentum, ut dicitur, una cum causa captionis et detentionis, quodcumque nomine idem X censeatur in eadem, habeas coram nobis, apud Westminster, ad subjiciendum*, "We command that you have before us to show, at Westminster, that body X, by whatsoever name he may be called therein, which is held in your custody, as it is said, as well as the cause of the arrest and the detention." Nothing allows one to measure the difference between ancient and medieval freedom and the freedom at the basis of modern democracy better than this formula. It is not the free man and his statutes and prerogatives, nor even simply *homo*, but rather *corpus* that is the new subject of politics. And democracy is born precisely as the assertion and presentation of this "body": *habeas corpus ad subjiciendum*, "you will have to have a body to show."

The fact that, of the all the various jurisdictional regulations concerned with the protection of individual freedom, it was *habeas corpus* that assumed the form of law and thus became inseparable from the history of Western democracy is surely due to mere circumstance. It is just as certain, however, that nascent European democracy thereby placed at the center of its battle against absolutism not *bios*, the qualified life of the citizen, but *zoē*—the bare, anonymous life that is as such taken into the sovereign ban ("the body of being taken . . . ," as one still reads in one modern formulation of the writ, "by whatsoever name he may be called therein").[3]

What comes to light in order to be exposed *apud Westminster* is, once again, the body of *homo sacer*, which is to say, bare life. This is modern democracy's strength and, at the same time, its inner contradiction: modern democracy does not abolish sacred life but rather shatters it and disseminates it into every individual body, making it into what is at stake in political conflict. And the root of modern democracy's secret biopolitical calling lies here: he who will appear later as the bearer of rights and, according to a curious oxymoron, as the new sovereign subject (*subiectus superaneus*, in other words, what is below and, at the same time, most elevated) can only be constituted as such through the repetition of the sovereign exception and the isolation of *corpus*, bare life, in himself. If it is true that law needs a body in order to be in force, and if one can speak, in this sense, of "law's desire to have a body," democracy responds to this desire by compelling law to assume the care of this body. This ambiguous (or polar) character of democracy appears even more clearly in the *habeas corpus* if one considers the fact that the same legal procedure that was originally intended to assure the presence of the accused at the trial and, therefore, to keep the accused from avoiding judgment, turns—in its new and definitive form—into grounds for the sheriff to detain and exhibit the body of the accused. *Corpus is a two-*

2. For replevying a man: i.e., for releasing a prisoner upon bail.
3. Both *zoē* and *bios* mean "life" in Greek, but Agamben finds in Aristotle's *Politics* a distinction between the terms. *Zoē* (Agamben's "bare life" or "naked life") is physical life, our animal existence; *bios* is our social or political life, the personhood we create (our biography) through our interaction with others.

faced being, the bearer both of subjection to sovereign power and of individual liberties.

This new centrality of the "body" in the sphere of politico-juridical terminology thus coincides with the more general process by which *corpus* is given such a privileged position in the philosophy and science of the Baroque age, from Descartes to Newton, from Leibniz to Spinoza.[4] And yet in political reflection *corpus* always maintains a close tie to bare life, even when it becomes the central metaphor of the political community, as in *Leviathan* or *The Social Contract*.[5] Hobbes's use of the term is particularly instructive in this regard. If it is true that in *De homine*[6] he distinguishes man's natural body from his political body (*homo enim non modo corpus naturale est, sed etiam civitatis, id est, ut ita loquar, corporis politici pars,* "Man is not only a natural body, but also a body of the city, that is, of the so-called political part" [*De homine,* p. 1]), in the *De cive*[7] it is precisely the body's capacity to be killed that founds both the natural equality of men and the necessity of the "Commonwealth":

> If we look at adult men and consider the fragility of the unity of the human body (whose ruin marks the end of every strength, vigor, and force) and the ease with which the weakest man can kill the strongest man, there is no reason for someone to trust in his strength and think himself superior to others by nature. Those who can do the same things to each other are equals. And those who can do the supreme thing—that is, kill—are by nature equal among themselves. (*De cive,* p. 93)

The great metaphor of the Leviathan, whose body is formed out of all the bodies of individuals, must be read in this light. The absolute capacity of the subjects' bodies to be killed forms the new political body of the West.

FROM §2 BIOPOLITICS AND THE RIGHTS OF MAN

2.1. Hannah Arendt entitled the fifth chapter of her book on imperialism,[8] which is dedicated to the problem of refugees, "The Decline of the Nation-State and the End of the Rights of Man." Linking together the fates of the rights of man and of the nation-state, her striking formulation seems to imply the idea of an intimate and necessary connection between the two, though the author herself leaves the question open. The paradox from which Arendt departs is that the very figure who should have embodied the rights of man par excellence—the refugee—signals instead the concept's radical crisis. "The conception of human rights," she states, "based upon the assumed existence of a human being as such, broke down at the very moment when those who professed to believe in it were for the first time confronted with

4. BARUCH SPINOZA (1632–1677), Jewish-born Dutch philosopher. René Descartes (1596–1650), French philosopher. Isaac Newton (1642–1727), English scientist and mathematician. Gottfried Leibniz (1646–1716), German philosopher and mathematician.

5. A classic of political philosophy (1762) by the Swiss-born French philosopher Jean-Jacques Rousseau (1717–1778). *Leviathan* (1651), a work by the English political philosopher Thomas Hobbes (1588–1679); it was the first to suggest that government originates in a social contract of all its members.

6. *Concerning Man* (1658). Agamben quotes the Latin text from Thomas Hobbes, *Opera philosophica quae latine scripsit omnia in unum corpus*, ed. William Molesworth, vol. 2 (London: J. Bohn, 1983).

7. *Concerning the Citizen* (1642); Agamben quotes from *De cive: The Latin Version*, ed. Howard Warrender (Oxford: Clarendon Press, 1983).

8. "Imperialism" is the title of part 2 of Arendt's *Origins of Totalitarianism* (1951; reprint, New York: Harcourt Brace Jovanovich, 1979).

people who had indeed lost all other qualities and specific relationships—except that they were still human" (*Origins*, p. 299). In the system of the nation-state, the so-called sacred and inalienable rights of man show themselves to lack every protection and reality at the moment in which they can no longer take the form of rights belonging to citizens of a state. If one considers the matter, this is in fact implicit in the ambiguity of the very title of the French Declaration of the Rights of Man and Citizen, of 1789. In the phrase *La déclaration des droits de l'homme et du citoyen*, it is not clear whether the two terms *homme* and *citoyen* name two autonomous beings or instead form a unitary system in which the first is always already included in the second. And if the latter is the case, the kind of relation that exists between *homme* and *citoyen* still remains unclear. From this perspective, Burke's *boutade*[9] according to which he preferred his "Rights of an Englishman" to the inalienable rights of man acquires an unsuspected profundity.

Arendt does no more than offer a few, essential hints concerning the link between the rights of man and the nation-state, and her suggestion has therefore not been followed up. In the period after the Second World War, both the instrumental emphasis on the rights of man and the rapid growth of declarations and agreements on the part of international organizations have ultimately made any authentic understanding of the historical significance of the phenomenon almost impossible. Yet it is time to stop regarding declarations of rights as proclamations of eternal, metajuridical[1] values binding the legislator (in fact, without much success) to respect eternal ethical principles, and to begin to consider them according to their real historical function in the modern nation-state. Declarations of rights represent the originary figure of the inscription of natural life in the juridico-political order of the nation-state. The same bare life that in the *ancien regíme*[2] was politically neutral and belonged to God as creaturely life and in the classical world was (at least apparently) clearly distinguished as *zoē* from political life (*bios*) now fully enters into the structure of the state and even becomes the earthly foundation of the state's legitimacy and sovereignty.

A simple examination of the text of the Declaration of 1789 shows that it is precisely bare natural life—which is to say, the pure fact of birth—that appears here as the source and bearer of rights. "Men," the first article declares, "are born and remain free and equal in rights" (from this perspective, the strictest formulation of all is to be found in La Fayette's[3] project elaborated in July 1789: "Every man is born with inalienable and indefeasible rights"). At the same time, however, the very natural life that, inaugurating the biopolitics of modernity, is placed at the foundation of the order vanishes into the figure of the citizen, in whom rights are "preserved" (according to the second article: "The goal of every political association is the preservation of the natural and indefeasible rights of man"). And the Declaration can attribute sovereignty to the "nation" (according to the third article: "The

9. Outburst, sally (French). The English philosopher and statesman EDMUND BURKE (1729–1797) assailed the French Revolution and, specifically, its declaration of rights in *Reflections on the Revolution in France* (1790).

1. Outside or beyond the realm of law established by governmental authority.

2. Old regime (French); specifically, France before the revolution of 1789.

3. The marquis de Lafayette (1757–1834), who after fighting against the British in the American Revolution became a member of France's revolutionary National Assembly, to which in July 1789 he presented his draft of a declaration of rights (written with the aid of Thomas Jefferson).

principle of all sovereignty resides essentially in the nation") precisely because it has already inscribed this element of birth in the very heart of the political community. The nation—the term derives etymologically from *nascere* (to be born)—thus closes the open circle of man's birth.

2.2. Declarations of rights must therefore be viewed as the place in which the passage from divinely authorized royal sovereignty to national sovereignty is accomplished. This passage assures the *exceptio*[4] of life in the new state order that will succeed the collapse of the *ancien régime*. The fact that in this process the "subject" is, as has been noted, transformed into a "citizen" means that birth—which is to say, bare natural life as such—here for the first time becomes (thanks to a transformation whose biopolitical consequences we are only beginning to discern today) the immediate bearer of sovereignty. The principle of nativity and the principle of sovereignty, which were separated in the *ancien régime* (where birth marked only the emergence of a *sujet*, a subject), are now irrevocably united in the body of the "sovereign subject" so that the foundation of the new nation-state may be constituted. It is not possible to understand the "national" and biopolitical development and vocation of the modern state in the nineteenth and twentieth centuries if one forgets that what lies at its basis is not man as a free and conscious political subject but, above all, man's bare life, the simple birth that as such is, in the passage from subject to citizen, invested with the principle of sovereignty. The fiction implicit here is that *birth* immediately becomes *nation* such that there can be no interval of separation [*scarto*] between the two terms. Rights are attributed to man (or originate in him) solely to the extent that man is the immediately vanishing ground (who must never come to light as such) of the citizen.

Only if we understand this essential historical function of the doctrine of rights can we grasp the development and metamorphosis of declarations of rights in our century. When the hidden difference [*scarto*] between birth and nation entered into a lasting crisis following the devastation of Europe's geopolitical order after the First World War, what appeared was Nazism and fascism, that is, two properly biopolitical movements that made of natural life the exemplary place of the sovereign decision. We are used to condensing the essence of National Socialist ideology into the syntagm "blood and soil" (*Blut und Boden*). When Alfred Rosenberg[5] wanted to express his party's vision of the world, it is precisely to this hendiadys[6] that he turned. "The National Socialist vision of the world," he writes, "springs from the conviction that soil and blood constitute what is essential about Germanness, and that it is therefore in reference to these two givens that a cultural and state politics must be directed" (*Blut und Ehre*, p. 242). Yet it has too often been forgotten that this formula, which is so highly determined politically, has, in truth, an innocuous juridical origin. The formula is nothing other than the concise expression of the two criteria that, already in Roman law, served to identify citizenship (that is, the primary inscription of life in the state

4. Exception (Latin).
5. German Nazi ideologist (1893–1946), hanged as a war criminal after the war. Agamben quotes from his *Blut und Ehre, Ein Kampf für deutsche Wiedergeburt: Reden und Aufsätze 1919–1933* [*Blood and Honor, A War for German Rebirth: Speeches and Articles, 1919–1933*] (Munich: F. Eher, 1936).
6. A figure of speech in which a single idea is expressed by two terms joined together by "and," rather than one term modified by the other.

order): *ius soli* (birth in a certain territory) and *ius sanguinis* (birth from citizen parents).[7] In the *ancien régime*, these two traditional juridical criteria had no essential meaning, since they expressed only a relation of subjugation. Yet with the French Revolution they acquire a new and decisive importance. Citizenship now does not simply identify a generic subjugation to royal authority or a determinate system of laws, nor does it simply embody (as Chalier[8] maintained when he suggested to the convention on September 23, 1792, that the title of citizen be substituted for the traditional title *monsieur* or *sieur*[9] in every public act) the new egalitarian principle; citizenship names the new status of life as origin and ground of sovereignty and, therefore, literally identifies—to cite Jean-Denis Lanjuinais's[1] words to the convention—*les members du souverain*, "the members of the sovereign." Hence the centrality (and the ambiguity) of the notion of "citizenship" in modern political thought, which compels Rousseau to say, "No author in France . . . has understood the true meaning of the term 'citizen.'"[2] Hence too, however, the rapid growth in the course of the French Revolution of regulatory provisions specifying which *man* was a *citizen* and which one not, and articulating and gradually restricting the area of the *ius soli* and the *ius sanguinis.* Until this time, the questions "What is French? What is German?" had constituted not a political problem but only one theme among others discussed in philosophical anthropologies. Caught in a constant work of redefinition, these questions now begin to become essentially political, to the point that, with National Socialism, the answer to the question "Who and what is German?" (and also, therefore, "Who and what is not German?") coincides immediately with the highest political task. Fascism and Nazism are, above all, redefinitions of the relations between man and citizen, and become fully intelligible only when situated—no matter how paradoxical it may seem—in the biopolitical context inaugurated by national sovereignty and declarations of rights.

Only this tie between the rights of man and the new biopolitical determination of sovereignty makes it possible to understand the striking fact, which has often been noted by historians of the French Revolution, that at the very moment in which native rights were declared to be inalienable and indefeasible, the rights of man in general were divided into active rights and passive rights. In his *Préliminairé de la constitution*, Sieyès[3] already clearly stated:

> Natural and civil rights are those rights *for* whose preservation society is formed, and political rights are those rights *by* which society is formed. For the sake of clarity, it would be best to call the first ones passive rights, and the second ones active rights. . . . All inhabitants of a country must enjoy the rights of passive citizens . . . all are not active citizens. Women, at least in the present state, children, foreigners, and also those who would not at all contribute to the public establishment must have no active influence on public matters. (*Écrits politiques*, pp. 189–206)

7. Literally, the Latin phrases mean "right of the soil" and "right of blood."
8. Joseph Chalier (1747–1793), French revolutionary.
9. Literally, "my lord" or "lord" (French); in common usage, titles of address roughly equivalent to the English "Mister" and "Sir."
1. French politician and jurist (1753–1827).
2. Rousseau, *Social Contract* 1.6 (Rousseau credits one contemporary author, Jean d'Alembert, with understanding the term).
3. Emmanuel Joseph Sieyès (1748–1836), or Abbé Sieyès: French Roman Catholic cleric and political theorist. Agamben quotes his "Preliminary to the Constitution" (1789) from *Écrits politiques* (Paris: Éditions des Archives contemporains, 1985).

And after defining the *membres du souverain*, the passage of Lanjuinais cited above continues with these words: "Thus children, the insane, minors, women, those condemned to a punishment either restricting personal freedom or bringing disgrace [*punition afflictive ou inflammante*] . . . will not be citizens" (quoted in Sewell, "Le citoyen,"[4] p. 105).

Instead of viewing these distinctions as a simple restriction of the democratic and egalitarian principle, in flagrant contradiction to the spirit and letter of the declarations, we ought first to grasp their coherent biopolitical meaning. One of the essential characteristics of modern biopolitics (which will continue to increase in our century) is its constant need to redefine the threshold in life that distinguishes and separates what is inside from what is outside. Once it crosses over the walls of the *oikos*[5] and penetrates more and more deeply into the city, the foundation of sovereignty—nonpolitical life—is immediately transformed into a line that must be constantly redrawn. Once *zoē* is politicized by declarations of rights, the distinctions and thresholds that make it possible to isolate a sacred life must be newly defined. And when natural life is wholly included in the *polis*—and this much has, by now, already happened—these thresholds pass, as we will see, beyond the dark boundaries separating life from death in order to identify a new living dead man, a new sacred man.

2.3. If refugees (whose number has continued to grow in our century, to the point of including a significant part of humanity today) represent such a disquieting element in the order of the modern nation-state, this is above all because by breaking the continuity between man and citizen, *nativity* and *nationality*, they put the originary fiction of modern sovereignty in crisis. Bringing to light the difference between birth and nation, the refugee causes the secret presupposition of the political domain—bare life—to appear for an instant within that domain. In this sense, the refugee is truly "the man of rights," as Arendt suggests, the first and only real appearance of rights outside the fiction of the citizen that always covers them over. Yet this is precisely what makes the figure of the refugee so hard to define politically.

Since the First World War, the birth-nation link has no longer been capable of performing its legitimating function inside the nation-state, and the two terms have begun to show themselves to be irreparably loosened from each other. From this perspective, the immense increase of refugees and stateless persons in Europe (in a short span of time 1,500,000 White Russians, 700,000 Armenians, 500,000 Bulgarians, 1,000,000 Greeks, and hundreds of thousands of Germans, Hungarians, and Rumanians were displaced from their countries) is one of the two most significant phenomena. The other is the contemporaneous institution by many European states of juridical measures allowing for the mass denaturalization and denationalization of large portions of their own populations. The first introduction of such rules into the juridical order took place in France in 1915 with respect to naturalized citizens of "enemy" origin; in 1922, Belgium followed the

4. W. H. Sewell, "Le citoyen/La citoyenne: Activity, Passivity, and the Revolutionary Concept of Citizenship," in *The French Revolution and the Creation of Modern Political Culture*, ed. Lucas Colin (Oxford: Pergamon, 1988).

5. Household (Greek), a term used by Aristotle in his *Politics* to designate the nonpolitical domestic sphere.

French example and revoked the naturalization of citizens who had committed "antinational" acts during the war; in 1926, the fascist regime issued an analogous law with respect to citizens who had shown themselves to be "unworthy of Italian citizenship"; in 1933, it was Austria's turn; and so it continued until the Nuremberg laws[6] on "citizenship in the Reich" and the "protection of German blood and honor" brought this process to the most extreme point of its development, introducing the principle according to which citizenship was something of which one had to prove oneself worthy and which could therefore always be called into question. And one of the few rules to which the Nazis constantly adhered during the course of the "Final Solution"[7] was that Jews could be sent to the extermination camps only after they had been fully denationalized (stripped even of the residual citizenship left to them after the Nuremberg laws).

These two phenomena—which are, after all, absolutely correlative—show that the birth-nation link, on which the declaration of 1789 had founded national sovereignty, had already lost its mechanical force and power of self-regulation by the time of the First World War. On the one hand, the nation-states become greatly concerned with natural life, discriminating within it between a so-to-speak authentic life and a life lacking every political value. (Nazi racism and eugenics are only comprehensible if they are brought back to this context.) On the other hand, the very rights of man that once made sense as the presupposition of the rights of the citizen are now progressively separated from and used outside the context of citizenship, for the sake of the supposed representation and protection of a bare life that is more and more driven to the margins of the nation-states, ultimately to be recodified into a new national identity. The contradictory character of these processes is certainly one of the reasons for the failure of the attempts of the various committees and organizations by which states, the League of Nations, and, later, the United Nations confronted the problem of refugees and the protection of human rights, from the Bureau Nansen[8] (1922) to the contemporary High Commission for Refugees (1951), whose actions, according to statute, are to have not a political but rather a "solely humanitarian and social" mission. What is essential is that, every time refugees represent not individual cases but—as happens more and more often today—a mass phenomenon, both these organizations and individual states prove themselves, despite their solemn invocations of the "sacred and inalienable" rights of man, absolutely incapable of resolving the problem and even of confronting it adequately.

2.4. The separation between humanitarianism and politics that we are experiencing today is the extreme phase of the separation of the rights of man from the rights of the citizen. In the final analysis, however, humanitarian organizations—which today are more and more supported by international commissions—can only grasp human life in the figure of bare or sacred life,

6. Laws passed in a 1935 convention in Nürnberg that deprived Jews of German citizenship and banned sexual relations between Jews and those of "German or kindred blood."

7. That is, to the "Jewish question": the solution, adopted in 1942, was to send all Jews within German-controlled territories to labor and extermination camps.

8. The office, led by the Norwegian explorer and humanitarian Fridtjof Nansen, that issued travel documents to refugees following World War I.

and therefore, despite themselves, maintain a secret solidarity with the very powers they ought to fight. It takes only a glance at the recent publicity campaigns to gather funds for refugees from Rwanda[9] to realize that here human life is exclusively considered (and there are certainly good reasons for this) as sacred life—which is to say, as life that can be killed but not sacrificed—and that only as such is it made into the object of aid and protection. The "imploring eyes" of the Rwandan child, whose photograph is shown to obtain money but who "is now becoming more and more difficult to find alive," may well be the most telling contemporary cipher of the bare life that humanitarian organizations, in perfect symmetry with state power, need. A humanitarianism separated from politics cannot fail to reproduce the isolation of sacred life at the basis of sovereignty, and the camp—which is to say, the pure space of exception—is the biopolitical paradigm that it cannot master.

The concept of the refugee (and the figure of life that this concept represents) must be resolutely separated from the concept of the rights of man, and we must seriously consider Arendt's claim that the fates of human rights and the nation-state are bound together such that the decline and crisis of the one necessarily implies the end of the other. The refugee must be considered for what he is: nothing less than a limit concept that radically calls into question the fundamental categories of the nation-state, from the birth-nation to the man-citizen link, and that thereby makes it possible to clear the way for a long-overdue renewal of categories in the service of a politics in which bare life is no longer separated and excepted, either in the state order or in the figure of human rights.

* * *

1995

9. Following the genocidal violence in the African nation of Rwanda in 1994, during which as many as 2 million Rwandans fled the country.

GLORIA ANZALDÚA
1942–2004

The Mexican American writer and activist Gloria Anzaldúa self-consciously embodied the longings, critical consciousness, and contradictions of so-called identity politics. She both spoke from her perspective as a lesbian Mexican American *and* contradicted any simple categorization of individuals through their ethnic origins or sexual orientation. We are all mixtures, she insisted, and she called for a new *mestiza* (mixed or hybrid) consciousness to replace "the policy of racial purity that white America practices." Her work simultaneously celebrates and explores the difficulties of multicultural identity.

Anzaldúa came from a seventh-generation Mexican American family that settled in the Rio Grande Valley in southern Texas. After her father died when she was fifteen, she worked as a farm laborer for a time to help support her family. The only member of her family with any education beyond high school, she received her B.A. from Pan-American University in 1969 and an M.A. in English and education from the University of Texas at Austin in 1972. After teaching at a high school for migrant workers in Indiana, Anzaldúa returned to Texas to pursue a Ph.D. in comparative literature, but quit when she met resistance to her desire to focus on Chicano (Mexican American) studies. She subsequently did additional graduate work at the University of California at Santa Cruz while teaching at both San Francisco State University and Santa Cruz. Along with occasional visiting positions at universities, in her later years she devoted herself primarily to writing and social activism. She received a National Endowment for the Arts Fiction Award as well as the 1991 Lesbian Rights Award. When she died from complications from diabetes in 2004, she was a few weeks away from receiving her Ph.D. from UC Santa Cruz.

Anzaldúa's work is important—and has been widely read and taught—not only because she effectively articulates the radical understandings and aspirations of the ethnic, feminist, and gay liberation movements born in the late 1960s and early 1970s, but also because she faced the ambivalences and contradictions of these movements. For literary studies, the most obvious result of such liberation efforts (often referred to as "the new social movements") has been the overt politicization of teaching and criticism. To the bafflement of many and the outrage of some, reading lists and teaching methods in literature classes have been opened to political scrutiny. A formerly vague and innocuous idea—culture—is now a battleground. At stake is "identity"—especially the relative status accorded different identities within a multiethnic society. The new social movements demand not just equal rights and economic opportunity but also respect and recognition. They aim at affirming racial, sexual, and class identities in all their difference from prevailing norms. Anzaldúa's writings speak to this call for affirmation and acknowledgement.

The political energies of the new social movements interacted with developments in literary studies in three especially salient ways. First, the new interest in different identities within American culture arose at the same time that French poststructuralism arrived in literature departments. Although distinct from the "multiculturalist" emphasis on inter- and intracultural differences, the poststructuralist concept of "difference" (especially in the work of JACQUES DERRIDA) provided a favorable theoretical environment for exploring the heterogeneity of identity. In particular, the poststructuralist questioning of boundaries and of the integrity of defined entities encouraged the interest in mixed, hybrid identities found in ethnic theory like Anzaldúa's.

The second conjunction of the new social movements with developments in literary studies centered on the term *voice*. Mid-twentieth-century New Criticism tried to sever the content expressed in literary works from the intention and voice of the author through an insistence on the "intentional fallacy" (see WILLIAM K. WIMSATT JR. and MONROE C. BEARDSLEY), which states that the narrator in a novel or the speaker in a lyric poem is always a mask, a "persona," never the author. With the increasing interest of the 1960s in the personal (culminating in feminism's declaration that "the personal is political") and the growing desire to recover lost and oppressed "voices" in American history, the new social movements stressed the voices of testimony and experience at the exact time when literary critics were striving to reconnect literary expressions to their authors. "Recovery work," which resurrected neglected or forgotten works by nonwhite, nonmale, and nonheterosexual authors, was combined with a new valuing of narratives of personal experience in both historical and contemporary texts. Anzaldúa's text, in our selection taken from her book *Borderlands/La Frontera* (1987), mixes cultural analysis with history, private memories, poems, and politics, demonstrating the stylistic possibilities opened up by the new interest in personal voice. Furthermore, her preoccupation with the difficulties faced by writers who use the "master's tongue" (in her case, English) resonates with similar concerns in postcolonial theory. Anzaldúa wants to combat the suppression of Spanish in America by creating a space for Spanish voices within American literature and culture, but she also recognizes that she must use English to reach the widest possible audience. So her literary voice mixes languages as well as genres. At her request, we have not translated the Spanish phrases and sentences in our selection.

Third, and finally, the dual focus of the new social movements on "identity" and "culture" coincides with the general shift in literary studies after 1965 from text to context, a movement partly reflected in the broad (and often loosely used) term *cultural studies*. The literary work is studied as a product and symptom of its culture or of its author's identity and not as a self-enclosed unit of purely aesthetic elements. In addition, the writing and reading (interpreting) of literary texts are understood as dynamic processes through which identities and cultures are produced, reproduced, maintained, and transformed. Cultural representations are the very stuff of which identities are made, and literature is one crucial arena in which that making is done. As Anzaldúa put it, "culture" is a "story to explain the world and our participation in it, a . . . value system with images and symbols to connect us to each other and to the planets." She saw her cultural work as the production of a "new" culture, a new story with new images.

Cultural representations, such as the stereotypes that undergird contempt for others who are different, can hurt. They are powerful in every sense of that word, coming to us invested with authority and upheld by the social institutions that promulgate them. Those representations, those images, occupy us; they are ours, they are us. That's what it means to be immersed in a culture. For that reason, Anzaldúa insists that the primary political work is "inner." "The struggle," she writes, "has always been inner, and is played out in outer terrains. Awareness of our situation must come before inner changes, which in turn come before changes in society. Nothing happens in the 'real' world unless it first happens in our heads." This focus on changing images and representations is sometimes called "cultural politics," which means emphasizing the transformation of values and beliefs more than changes in elected officials, laws, or working conditions.

It is not surprising that Anzaldúa and other literary people would put their energy and faith into cultural politics. Words and images are their stock-in-trade, what most influences them, and where they have some chance of wielding influence. But cultural politics in the late twentieth-century United States was also a direct response to the civil rights movement, which succeeded in changing the laws and institutional structures of a legally racist society. People discovered, however, that abolishing the legality of racism was hardly the same thing as creating a nonracist society. Cultural politics is often criticized as vague, as nonconcrete, as ignoring bread-and-butter issues. But a cultural politics like Anzaldúa's is developed to foreground and contest the nebulous quality of racism and sexism in her America, prejudices that often do not manifest themselves in overt ways yet have persistent concrete effects in the continued poverty of and the differential opportunities in housing, education, and employment available to nonwhites and women.

Anzaldúa's work, then, is largely concerned with conveying what it feels like for a nonwhite, nonheterosexual woman to live in post–civil rights movement North America. She explores the ambiguities and ambivalences lived by a "hyphenated" Mexican American. The United States both is obsessed with this presence of nonwhites in its midst and tries to act as if they do not exist. On one level, she simply calls for recognition, for the acknowledgment by the culture at large, and Anglos in particular, that she and her people—part Native American, part European, part American—exist. They have been here a long time and are going to be here even longer; meanwhile, "the dominant white culture is killing us slowly with its ignorance." Anzaldúa calls our attention to the 34 million Mexican Americans in the United States.

But on another level, Anzaldúa is arguing that our whole understanding of identity has to be revised. The old notion that we can know who we are by tracing our roots, by referring back to some stable point of origin, has to be abandoned. There is no pure, single source. All identities are hybrids, formed over time through the interaction of multiple cultures and constantly being transformed by new encounters in the "borderlands" between one culture and another. Anzaldúa's work here parallels contemporary postcolonial criticism, particularly that of HOMI K. BHABHA. The nostalgic demand for unitary, isolated cultures can only do harm in a world in which each of us is always already a mixture and we constantly come into contact with, and must live among, others who are mixed in different ways.

Identity politics is often criticized for its contradictions, especially for joining a celebration of difference with simplistic notions of group solidarity. Anzaldúa's work addresses the complex emotional core of identity politics: the deep desire felt throughout the contemporary world for an identity that can be asserted, recognized, affirmed, and respected in the public sphere. In addition, she describes the very forces of cultural mixing and powerful blindnesses that make an unambiguous, clear identity so attractive, especially to those who are least visible within the current order. In trying to negotiate these contrary pressures and achieve a coherent identity in the face of the myriad cultural influences that shape us, Anzaldúa necessarily becomes a writer of ambiguity and ambivalence. "It makes us crazy constantly," she writes, "but if the center holds, we've made some kind of evolutionary step forward."

***Borderlands*/La Frontera: *The New Mestiza* Keywords:** Cultural Studies, Feminist Theory, Identity, Queer Theory, Race and Ethnicity Studies, Vernacular Language

From Borderlands/*La Frontera*: The New Mestiza

Chapter 7. La conciencia de la mestiza/*Towards a New Consciousness*

Por la mujer de mi raza
hablará el espíritu.

José Vasconcelos, Mexican philosopher, envisaged *una raza mestiza, una mezcla de razas afines, una raza de color—la primera raza síntesis del globo.* He called it a cosmic race, *la raza cósmica*, a fifth race embracing the four major races of the world.[1] Opposite to the theory of the pure Aryan, and to the policy of racial purity that white America practices, his theory is one of inclusivity. At the confluence of two or more genetic streams, with chromosomes constantly "crossing over," this mixture of races, rather than resulting in an inferior being, provides hybrid progeny, a mutable, more malleable species with a rich gene pool. From this racial, ideological, cultural and biological cross-pollinization, an "alien" consciousness is presently in the making—a new *mestiza* consciousness, *una conciencia de mujer.* It is a consciousness of the Borderlands.

1. This is my own "take off" on José Vasconcelos' idea. José Vasconcelos, *La Raza Cósmica: Misión de la Raza Ibero-Americana* (Mexico City: Aguilar S.A. de Ediciones, 1961) [Anzaldúa's note]. At Anzaldúa's request, we have not translated the Spanish passages in her text.

UNA LUCHA DE FRONTERAS/A STRUGGLE OF BORDERS

Because I, a *mestiza*,
continually walk out of one culture
and into another,
because I am in all cultures at the same time,
alma entre dos mundos, tres, cuatro,
me zumba la cabeza con lo contradictorio.
Estoy norteada por todas las voces que me hablan
simultáneamente.

The ambivalence from the clash of voices results in mental and emotional states of perplexity. Internal strife results in insecurity and indecisiveness. The *mestiza*'s dual or multiple personality is plagued by psychic restlessness.

In a constant state of mental nepantilism, an Aztec[2] word meaning torn between ways, *la mestiza* is a product of the transfer of the cultural and spiritual values of one group to another. Being tricultural, monolingual, bilingual, or multilingual, speaking a patois, and in a state of perpetual transition, the *mestiza* faces the dilemma of the mixed breed: which collectivity does the daughter of a darkskinned mother listen to?

El choque de un alma atrapado entre el mundo del espíritu y el mundo de la técnica a veces la deja entullada. Cradled in one culture, sandwiched between two cultures, straddling all three cultures and their value systems, *la mestiza* undergoes a struggle of flesh, a struggle of borders, an inner war. Like all people, we perceive the version of reality that our culture communicates. Like others having or living in more than one culture, we get multiple, often opposing messages. The coming together of two self-consistent but habitually incomparable frames of reference[3] causes *un choque*, a cultural collision.

Within us and within *la cultura chicana*,[4] commonly held beliefs of the white culture attack commonly held beliefs of the Mexican culture, and both attack commonly held beliefs of the indigenous culture. Subconsciously, we see an attack on ourselves and our beliefs as a threat and we attempt to block with a counterstance.

But it is not enough to stand on the opposite river bank, shouting questions, challenging patriarchal, white conventions. A counterstance locks one into a duel of oppressor and oppressed; locked in mortal combat, like the cop and the criminal, both are reduced to a common denominator of violence. The counterstance refutes the dominant culture's views and beliefs, and, for this, it is proudly defiant. All reaction is limited by, and dependent on, what it is reacting against. Because the counterstance stems from a problem with authority—outer as well as inner—it's a step towards liberation from cultural domination. But it is not a way of life. At some point, on our way to a new consciousness, we will have to leave the opposite bank, the split between the two mortal combatants somehow healed so that we are on both shores at once and, at once, see through serpent and eagle eyes. Or perhaps we will decide to disengage from the dominant culture, write it off altogether as a lost cause, and cross the border into a wholly new and separate territory. Or

2. One of the major native groups in Mexico before the arrival of Europeans.

3. Arthur Koestler termed this "bisociation." Albert Rothenberg, *The Creative Process in Art, Science, and Other Fields* (Chicago: University of Chicago Press, 1979), 12 [Anzaldúa's note]. Koestler (1905–1983), Hungarian-born English novelist, journalist, and critic.

4. Chicanos are portrayed by Anzaldúa as existing between Anglo (white European) U.S. culture and the indigenous Native American culture of both Mexico and the United States.

we might go another route. The possibilities are numerous once we decide to act and not react.

A TOLERANCE FOR AMBIGUITY

These numerous possibilities leave *la mestiza* floundering in uncharted seas. In perceiving conflicting information and points of view, she is subjected to a swamping of her psychological borders. She has discovered that she can't hold concepts or ideas in rigid boundaries. The borders and walls that are supposed to keep the undesirable ideas out are entrenched habits and patterns of behavior; these habits and patterns are the enemy within. Rigidity means death. Only by remaining flexible is she able to stretch the psyche horizontally and vertically. *La mestiza* constantly has to shift out of habitual formations; from convergent thinking, analytical reasoning that tends to use rationality to move toward a single goal (a Western mode), to divergent thinking,[5] characterized by movement away from set patterns and goals and toward a more whole perspective, one that includes rather than excludes.

The new *mestiza* copes by developing a tolerance for contradictions, a tolerance for ambiguity. She learns to be an Indian in Mexican culture, to be Mexican from an Anglo point of view. She learns to juggle cultures. She has a plural personality, she operates in a pluralistic mode—nothing is thrust out, the good the bad and the ugly, nothing rejected, nothing abandoned. Not only does she sustain contradictions, she turns the ambivalence into something else.

She can be jarred out of ambivalence by an intense, and often painful, emotional event which inverts or resolves the ambivalence. I'm not sure exactly how. The work takes place underground—subconsciously. It is work that the soul performs. That focal point or fulcrum, that juncture where the *mestiza* stands, is where phenomena tend to collide. It is where the possibility of uniting all that is separate occurs. This assembly is not one where severed or separated pieces merely come together. Nor is it a balancing of opposing powers. In attempting to work out a synthesis, the self has added a third element which is greater than the sum of its severed parts. That third element is a new consciousness—a *mestiza* consciousness—and though it is a source of intense pain, its energy comes from continual creative motion that keeps breaking down the unitary aspect of each new paradigm.

En unas pocas centurias, the future will belong to the *mestiza*. Because the future depends on the breaking down of paradigms, it depends on the straddling of two or more cultures. By creating a new mythos—that is, a change in the way we perceive reality, the way we see ourselves, and the ways we behave—*la mestiza* creates a new consciousness.

The work of *mestiza* consciousness is to break down the subject-object duality that keeps her a prisoner and to show in the flesh and through the images in her work how duality is transcended. The answer to the problem between the white race and the colored, between males and females, lies in healing the split that originates in the very foundation of our lives, our culture, our languages, our thoughts. A massive uprooting of dualistic thinking in the individual and collective consciousness is the beginning of a long

5. In part, I derive my definitions for "convergent" and "divergent" thinking from Rothenberg, 12–13 [Anzaldúa's note].

struggle, but one that could, in our best hopes, bring us to the end of rape, of violence, of war.

LA ENCRUCIJADA/THE CROSSROADS

A chicken is being sacrificed
at a crossroads, a simple mound of earth
a mud shrine for *Eshu*,
Yoruba[6] god of indeterminacy,
who blesses her choice of path.
She begins her journey.

Su cuerpo es una bocacalle. La mestiza has gone from being the sacrificial goat to becoming the officiating priestess at the crossroads.

As a *mestiza* I have no country, my homeland cast me out; yet all countries are mine because I am every woman's sister or potential lover. (As a lesbian I have no race, my own people disclaim me; but I am all races because there is the queer of me in all races.) I am cultureless because, as a feminist, I challenge the collective cultural/religious male-derived beliefs of Indo-Hispanics and Anglos; yet I am cultured because I am participating in the creation of yet another culture, a new story to explain the world and our participation in it, a new value system with images and symbols that connect us to each other and to the planet. *Soy un amasamiento*, I am an act of kneading, of uniting and joining that not only has produced both a creature of darkness and a creature of light, but also a creature that questions the definitions of light and dark and gives them new meanings.

We are the people who leap in the dark, we are the people on the knees of the gods. In our very flesh, (r)evolution works out the clash of cultures. It makes us crazy constantly, but if the center holds, we've made some kind of evolutionary step forward. *Nuestra alma el trabajo*, the opus, the great alchemical work; spiritual *mestizaje*, a "morphogenesis,"[7] an inevitable unfolding. We have become the quickening serpent movement.

Indigenous like corn, like corn, the *mestiza* is a product of crossbreeding, designed for preservation under a variety of conditions. Like an ear of corn—a female seed-bearing organ—the *mestiza* is tenacious, tightly wrapped in the husks of her culture. Like kernels she clings to the cob; with thick stalks and strong brace roots, she holds tight to the earth—she will survive the crossroads.

Lavando y remojando el maíz en agua de cal, despojando el pellejo. Moliendo, mixteando, amasando, haciendo tortillas de masa.[8] She steeps the corn

6. One of the three largest ethnic groups in Nigeria; many Caribbean and Latin American blacks are descended from the Yoruba and have retained elements of their ancestral culture.

7. To borrow chemist Ilya Prigogine's theory of "dissipative structures." Prigogine [1917–2003] discovered that substances interact not in predictable ways as it was taught in science, but in different and fluctuating ways to produce new and more complex structures, a kind of birth he called "morphogenesis," which created unpredictable innovation. Harold Gilliam, "Searching for a New World View," *This World*, January 1981, 23 [Anzaldúa's note].

8. *Tortillas de masa*: corn tortillas are of two types, the smooth uniform ones made in a tortilla press and usually bought at a tortilla factory or supermarket, and *gorditas*, made by mixing *masa* with lard or shortening or butter (my mother sometimes puts in bits of bacon or *chicarrones*) [Anzaldúa's note].

in lime, it swells, softens. With stone roller on *metate* she grinds the corn, then grinds again. She kneads and moulds the dough, pats the round balls into *tortillas*.

> We are the porous rock in the stone *metate*
> squatting on the ground
> We are the rolling pin, *el maíz y agua,*
> *la masa harina. Somos el amasijo.*
> *Somos lo molido en el metate.*
> We are the *comal* sizzling hot,
> the hot *tortilla*, the hungry mouth.
> We are the coarse rock.
> We are the grinding motion,
> the mixed potion, *somos el molcajete.*
> We are the pestle, the *comino, ajo, pimienta,*
> We are the *chile colorado,*
> the green shoot that cracks the rock.
> We will abide.

EL CAMINO DE LA MESTIZA/THE MESTIZA WAY

> Caught between the sudden contraction, the breath sucked in and the endless space, the brown woman stands still, looks at the sky. She decides to go down, digging her way along the roots of trees. Sifting through the bones, she shakes them to see if there is any marrow in them. Then, touching the dirt to her forehead, to her tongue, she takes a few bones, leaves the rest in their burial place.
>
> She goes through her backpack, keeps her journal and address book, throws away the muni-bart metromaps.[9] The coins are heavy and they go next, then the greenbacks flutter through the air. She keeps her knife, can opener and eyebrow pencil. She puts bones, pieces of bark, *hierbas*, eagle feather, snakeskin, tape recorder, the rattle and drum in her pack and she sets out to become the complete *tolteca*.[1]

Her first step is to take inventory. *Despojando, desgranando, quitando paja.* Just what did she inherit from her ancestors? This weight on her back—which is the baggage from the Indian mother, which the baggage from the Spanish father, which the baggage from the Anglo?

Pero es difícil differentiating between *lo heredado, lo adquirido, lo impuesto.* She puts history through a sieve, winnows out the lies, looks at the forces that we as a race, as women, have been a part of. *Luego bota lo que no vale, los desmientos, los desencuentos, el embrutecimiento. Aguarda el juicio, hondo y enraízado, de la gente antigua.* This step is a conscious rupture with all oppressive traditions of all cultures and religions. She communicates that rupture, documents the struggle. She reinterprets history and, using new symbols, she shapes new myths. She adopts new perspectives toward the darkskinned, women and queers. She strengthens her tolerance (and intolerance) for ambiguity. She is willing to share, to make herself vulnerable to foreign ways of

9. Maps of San Francisco's bus and subway routes.
1. Gina Valdés, *Puentes y Fronteras: Coplas Chicanas* (Los Angeles Castle Lithograph, 1982), 2 [Anzaldúa's note].

seeing and thinking. She surrenders all notions of safety, of the familiar. Deconstruct, construct. She becomes a *nahual*, able to transform herself into a tree, a coyote, into another person. She learns to transform the small "I" into the total Self. *Se hace moldeadora de su alma. Según la concepción que tiene de sí misma, así será.*

QUE NO SE NOS OLVIDE LOS HOMBRES

> *Tú no sirves pa' nada—*
> you're good for nothing.
> *Eres pura vieja.*

"You're nothing but a woman" means you are defective. Its opposite is to be *un macho*. The modern meaning of the word "machismo," as well as the concept, is actually an Anglo invention. For men like my father, being "macho" meant being strong enough to protect and support my mother and us, yet being able to show love. Today's macho has doubts about his ability to feed and protect his family. His "machismo" is an adaptation to oppression and poverty and low self-esteem. It is the result of hierarchical male dominance. The Anglo, feeling inadequate and inferior and powerless, displaces or transfers these feelings to the Chicano by shaming him. In the Gringo world, the Chicano suffers from excessive humility and self-effacement, shame of self and self-depreciation. Around Latinos he suffers from a sense of language inadequacy and its accompanying discomfort; with Native Americans he suffers from a racial amnesia which ignores our common blood, and from guilt because the Spanish part of him took their land and oppressed them. He has an excessive compensatory hubris when around Mexicans from the other side. It overlays a deep sense of racial shame.

The loss of a sense of dignity and respect in the macho breeds a false machismo which leads him to put down women and even to brutalize them. Coexisting with his sexist behavior is a love for the mother which takes precedence over that of all others. Devoted son, macho pig. To wash down the shame of his acts, of his very being, and to handle the brute in the mirror, he takes to the bottle, the snort, the needle, and the fist.

Though we "understand" the root causes of male hatred and fear, and the subsequent wounding of women, we do not excuse, we do not condone, and we will no longer put up with it. From the men of our race, we demand the admission/acknowledgment/disclosure/testimony that they wound us, violate us, are afraid of us and of our power. We need them to say they will begin to eliminate their hurtful put-down ways. But more than the words, we demand acts. We say to them: We will develop equal power with you and those who have shamed us.

It is imperative that *mestizas* support each other in changing the sexist elements in the Mexican-Indian culture. As long as woman is put down, the Indian and the Black in all of us is put down. The struggle of the *mestiza* is above all a feminist one. As long as *los hombres* think they have to *chingar mujeres* and each other to be men, as long as men are taught that they are superior and therefore culturally favored over *la mujer*, as long as to be a *vieja* is a thing of derision, there can be no real healing of our psyches. We're halfway there—we have such love of the Mother, the good mother. The first step is to unlearn the *puta/virgen* dichotomy and to see *Coatlapopeuh-Coatlicue* in the Mother, *Guadalupe*.[2]

Tenderness, a sign of vulnerability, is so feared that it is showered on women with verbal abuse and blows. Men, even more than women, are fettered to gender roles. Women at least have had the guts to break out of bondage. Only gay men have had the courage to expose themselves to the woman inside them and to challenge the current masculinity. I've encountered a few scattered and isolated gentle straight men, the beginnings of a new breed, but they are confused, and entangled with sexist behaviors that they have not been able to eradicate. We need a new masculinity and the new man needs a movement.

Lumping the males who deviate from the general norm with man, the oppressor, is a gross injustice. *Asombra pensar que nos hemos quedado en ese pozo oscuro donde el mundo encierra a las lesbianas. Asombra pensar que hemos, como femenistas y lesbianas, cerrado nuestros corazónes a los hombres, a nuestros hermanos los jotos, desheredados y marginales como nosotros.* Being the supreme crossers of cultures, homosexuals have strong bonds with the queer white, Black, Asian, Native American, Latino, and with the queer in Italy, Australia and the rest of the planet. We come from all colors, all classes, all races, all time periods. Our role is to link people with each other—the Blacks with Jews with Indians with Asians with whites with extraterrestrials. It is to transfer ideas and information from one culture to another. Colored homosexuals have more knowledge of other cultures; have always been at the forefront (although sometimes in the closet) of all liberation struggles in this country; have suffered more injustices and have survived them despite all odds. Chicanos need to acknowledge the political and artistic contributions of their queer. People, listen to what your *jotería* is saying.

The *mestizo* and the queer exist at this time and point on the evolutionary continuum for a purpose. We are a blending that proves that all blood is intricately woven together, and that we are spawned out of similar souls.

SOMOS UNA GENTE

Hay tantísimas fronteras
que dividen a la gente,
pero por cada frontera
existe también un puente.
—Gina Valdés[3]

Divided Loyalties. Many women and men of color do not want to have any dealings with white people. It takes too much time and energy to explain to the downwardly mobile, white middle-class women that it's okay for us to want to own "possessions," never having had any nice furniture on our dirt floors or "luxuries" like washing machines. Many feel that whites should help their own people rid themselves of race hatred and fear first. I, for one, choose to use some of my energy to serve as mediator. I think we

2. Our Lady of Guadalupe, the Virgin Mary (who is said to have appeared to a Native American in that Mexican city in 1531). *Coatlapopeuh-Coatlicue*: Aztec earth goddess who is the mother of the gods.

3. Valdés, *Puentes y Fronteras*, 2 [Anzaldúa's note].

need to allow whites to be our allies. Through our literature, art, *corridos*, and folktales we must share our history with them so when they set up committees to help Big Mountain Navajos or the Chicano farmworkers or *los Nicaragüenses*[4] they won't turn people away because of their racial fears and ignorances. They will come to see that they are not helping us but following our lead.

Individually, but also as a racial entity, we need to voice our needs. We need to say to white society: We need you to accept the fact that Chicanos are different, to acknowledge your rejection and negation of us. We need you to own the fact that you looked upon us as less than human, that you stole our lands, our personhood, our self-respect. We need you to make public restitution: to say that, to compensate for your own sense of defectiveness, you strive for power over us, you erase our history and our experience because it makes you feel guilty—you'd rather forget your brutish acts. To say you've split yourself from minority groups, that you disown us, that your dual consciousness splits off parts of yourself, transferring the "negative" parts onto us. (Where there is persecution of minorities, there is shadow projection. Where there is violence and war, there is repression of shadow.) To say that you are afraid of us, that to put distance between us, you wear the mask of contempt. Admit that Mexico is your double, that she exists in the shadow of this country, that we are irrevocably tied to her. Gringo, accept the doppelganger in your psyche. By taking back your collective shadow the intracultural split will heal. And finally, tell us what you need from us.

BY YOUR TRUE FACES WE WILL KNOW YOU

I am visible—see this Indian face—yet I am invisible. I both blind them with my beak nose and am their blind spot. But I exist, we exist. They'd like to think I have melted in the pot. But I haven't, we haven't.

The dominant white culture is killing us slowly with its ignorance. By taking away our self-determination, it has made us weak and empty. As a people we have resisted and we have taken expedient positions, but we have never been allowed to develop unencumbered—we have never been allowed to be fully ourselves. The whites in power want us people of color to barricade ourselves behind our separate tribal walls so they can pick us off one at a time with their hidden weapons; so they can whitewash and distort history. Ignorance splits people, creates prejudices. A misinformed people is a subjugated people.

Before the Chicano and the undocumented worker and the Mexican from the other side can come together, before the Chicano can have unity with Native Americans and other groups, we need to know the history of their struggle and they need to know ours. Our mothers, our sisters and brothers, the guys who hang out on street corners, the children in the playgrounds, each of us must know our Indian lineage, our afro-*mestisaje*, our history of resistance.

To the immigrant *mexicano* and the recent arrivals we must teach our history. The 80 million *mexicanos* and the Latinos from Central and South

4. In the 1980s the U.S. government funded paramilitary forces engaged in a guerrilla war against the Sandinista government of Nicaragua.

America must know of our struggles. Each one of us must know basic facts about Nicaragua, Chile and the rest of Latin America.[5] The Latinoist movement (Chicanos, Puerto Ricans, Cubans and other Spanish-speaking people working together to combat racial discrimination in the market place) is good but it is not enough. Other than a common culture we will have nothing to hold us together. We need to meet on a broader communal ground.

The struggle is inner: Chicano, *indio*, American Indian, *mojado, mexicano*, immigrant Latino, Anglo in power, working class Anglo, Black, Asian—our psyches resemble the bordertowns and are populated by the same people. The struggle has always been inner, and is played out in the outer terrains. Awareness of our situation must come before inner changes, which in turn come before changes in society. Nothing happens in the "real" world unless it first happens in the images in our heads.

EL DÍA DE LA CHICANA

I will not be shamed again
Nor will I shame myself.

I am possessed by a vision that we Chicanas and Chicanos have taken back or uncovered our true faces, our dignity and self-respect. It's a validation vision.

Seeing the Chicana anew in light of her history. I seek an exoneration, a seeing through the fictions of white supremacy, a seeing of ourselves in our true guises and not as the false racial personality that has been given to us and that we have given to ourselves. I seek our woman's face, our true features, the positive and the negative seen clearly, free of the tainted biases of male dominance. I seek new images of identity, new beliefs about ourselves, our humanity and worth no longer in question.

> *Estamos viviendo en la noche de la Raza, un tiempo cuando el trabajo se hace a lo quieto, en el oscuro. El día cuando aceptamos tal y como somos y para en donde vamos y porque—ese día será de la Raza. Yo tengo el conpromiso de expresar mi visión, mi sensibilidad, mi percepión de la revalidación de la gente mexicana, su mérito estimación, honra, aprecio, y validez.*

On December 2nd when my sun goes into my first house, I celebrate *el día de la Chicana y el Chicano*. On that day I clean my altars, light my *Coatlalopeuh* candle, burn sage and copal, take *el baño para espantar basura*, sweep my house. On that day I bare my soul, make myself vulnerable to friends and family by expressing my feelings. On that day I affirm who we are.

On that day I look inside our conflicts and our basic introverted racial temperament. I identify our needs, voice them. I acknowledge that the self and the race have been wounded. I recognize the need to take care of our personhood, of our racial self. On that day I gather the splintered and disowned parts of *la gente mexicana* and hold them in my arms. *Todas las partes de nosotros valen.*

5. This history includes U.S. government interventions in Latin and Central American countries from 1950 to 1990, undermining governments thought to be too leftist and supporting right-wing governments.

On that day I say, "Yes, all you people wound us when you reject us. Rejection strips us of self-worth; our vulnerability exposes us to shame. It is our innate identity you find wanting. We are ashamed that we need your good opinion, that we need your acceptance. We can no longer camouflage our needs, can no longer let defenses and fences sprout around us. We can no longer withdraw. To rage and look upon you with contempt is to rage and be contemptuous of ourselves. We can no longer blame you, nor disown the white parts, the male parts, the pathological parts, the queer parts, the vulnerable parts. Here we are weaponless with open arms, with only our magic. Let's try it our way, the *mestiza* way, the Chicana way, the woman way.

On that day, I search for our essential dignity as a people, a people with a sense of purpose—to belong and contribute to something greater than our *pueblo*. On that day I seek to recover and reshape my spiritual identity. *¡Anímate! Raza, a celebrar el día de la Chicana.*

EL RETORNO

All movements are accomplished in six stages,
and the seventh brings return.

—I Ching[6]

Tanto tiempo sin verte casa mía,
mi cuna, mi hondo nido de la huerta.

—"Soledad"[7]

I stand at the river, watch the curving, twisting serpent, a serpent nailed to the fence where the mouth of the Rio Grande empties into the Gulf.

I have come back. *Tanto dolor me costó el alejamiento.* I shade my eyes and look up. The bone beak of a hawk slowly circling over me, checking me out as potential carrion. In its wake a little bird flickering its wings, swimming sporadically like a fish. In the distance the expressway and the slough of traffic like an irritated sow. The sudden pull in my gut, *la tierra, los aguaceros.* My land, *el viento soplando la arena, el lagartijo debajo de un nopalito. Me acuerdo como era antes. Una región desértica de vasta llanuras, costeras de baja altura, de escasa lluvia, de chaparrales formados por mesquites y huizaches.* If I look real hard I can almost see the Spanish fathers who were called "the cavalry of Christ" enter this valley riding their burros, see the clash of cultures commence.

Tierra natal. This is home, the small towns in the Valley, *los pueblitos* with chicken pens and goats picketed to mesquite shrubs. *En las colonias on the other side of the tracks, junk cars line the front yards of hot pink and lavender-trimmed houses—Chicano architecture we call it, self-consciously. I have missed the TV shows where hosts speak in half and half, and where awards are given in the category of Tex-Mex music. I have missed the Mexican cemeteries blooming with artificial flowers, the fields of aloe vera and red pepper, rows of sugar cane, of corn hanging on the stalks, the cloud of polvareda* in the dirt roads behind a speeding pickup truck, *el sabor de tamales de*

6. Richard Wilhelm, *The I Ching or Book of Changes*, trans. Cary F. Baynes (Princeton: Princeton University Press, 1950), 98 [Anzaldúa's note].

7. "Soledad" is sung by the group Haciendo Punto and Otto Son [Anzaldúa's note].

rez y venado. I have missed *la yegua colorada* gnawing the wooden gate of her stall, the smell of horse flesh from Carito's corrals. *He hecho menos las noches calientes sin aire, noches de linternas y lechuzas* making holes in the night.

I still feel the old despair when I look at the unpainted, dilapidated, scrap lumber houses consisting mostly of corrugated aluminum. Some of the poorest people in the U.S. live in the Lower Rio Grande Valley, an arid and semi-arid land of irrigated farming, intense sunlight and heat, citrus groves next to chaparral and cactus. I walk through the elementary school I attended so long ago, that remained segregated until recently. I remember how the white teachers used to punish us for being Mexican.

How I love this tragic valley of South Texas, as Ricardo Sánchez[8] calls it; this borderland between the Nueces and the Rio Grande. This land has survived possession and ill-use by five countries: Spain, Mexico, the Republic of Texas, the U.S., the Confederacy, and the U.S. again. It has survived Anglo-Mexican blood feuds, lynchings, burnings, rapes, pillage.

Today I see the Valley still struggling to survive. Whether it does or not, it will never be as I remember it. The borderlands depression that was set off by the 1982 peso devaluation in Mexico resulted in the closure of hundreds of Valley businesses. Many people lost their homes, cars, land. Prior to 1982, U.S. store owners thrived on retail sales to Mexicans who came across the border for groceries and clothes and appliances. While goods on the U.S. side have become 10, 100, 1000 times more expensive for Mexican buyers, goods on the Mexican side have become 10, 100, 1000 times cheaper for Americans. Because the Valley is heavily dependent on agriculture and Mexican retail trade, it has the highest unemployment rates along the entire border region; it is the Valley that has been hardest hit.[9]

"It's been a bad year for corn," my brother, Nune, says. As he talks, I remember my father scanning the sky for a rain that would end the drought, looking up into the sky, day after day, while the corn withered on its stalk. My father has been dead for 29 years, having worked himself to death. The life span of a Mexican farm laborer is 56—he lived to be 38. It shocks me that I am older than he. I, too, search the sky for rain. Like the ancients, I worship the rain god and the maize goddess, but unlike my father I have recovered their names. Now for rain (irrigation) one offers not a sacrifice of blood, but of money.

"Farming is in a bad way," my brother says. "Two to three thousand small and big farmers went bankrupt in this country last year. Six years ago the price of corn was $8.00 per hundred pounds," he goes on. "This year it is $3.90 per hundred pounds." And, I think to myself, after taking inflation into account, not planting anything puts you ahead.

8. American poet and critic (1941–1995).

9. Out of the 22 border counties in the four border states, Hidalgo County (named for Father Hidalgo who was shot in 1810 after instigating Mexico's revolt against Spain under the banner of *la Virgen de Guadalupe*) is the most poverty-stricken county in the nation as well as the largest home base (along with Imperial in California) for migrant farm-workers. It was here that I was born and raised. I am amazed that both it and I have survived [Anzaldúa's note].

I walk out to the back yard, stare at *los rosales de mamá*. She wants me to help her prune the rose bushes, dig out the carpet grass that is choking them. *Mamagrande Ramona también tenía rosales*. Here every Mexican grows flowers. If they don't have a piece of dirt, they use car tires, jars, cans, shoe boxes. Roses are the Mexican's favorite flower. I think, how symbolic—thorns and all.

Yes, the Chicano and Chicana have always taken care of growing things and the land. Again I see the four of us kids getting off the school bus, changing into our work clothes, walking into the field with Papí and Mamí, all six of us bending to the ground. Below our feet, under the earth lie the watermelon seeds. We cover them with paper plates, putting *terremotes* on top of the plates to keep them from being blown away by the wind. The paper plates keep the freeze away. Next day or the next, we remove the plates, bare the tiny green shoots to the elements. They survive and grow, give fruit hundreds of times the size of the seed. We water them and hoe them. We harvest them. The vines dry, rot, are plowed under. Growth, death, decay, birth. The soil prepared again and again, impregnated, worked on. A constant changing of forms, *renacimientos de la tierra madre*.

This land was Mexican once
was Indian always
and is.
And will be again.

1987

GAYATRI CHAKRAVORTY SPIVAK
b. 1942

Gayatri Chakravorty Spivak is an unsettling voice in literary theory and, especially, postcolonial studies. She has described herself as a "practical deconstructionist feminist Marxist" and as a "gadfly." She uses deconstruction to examine "how truth is constructed" and to deploy the assertions of one intellectual and political position (such as Marxism) to "interrupt" or "bring into crisis" another (feminism, for example). In her work, she combines passionate denunciations of the harm done to women, non-Europeans, and the poor by the privileged West with a persistent questioning of the grounds on which radical critique takes its stand.

Her continual interrogation of assumptions can make Spivak difficult to read. But her restless critiques connect directly to her ethical aspiration for a "politics of the open end," in which deconstruction acts as a "safeguard" against the repression or exclusion of "alterities"—that is, people, events, or ideas that are radically "other" to the dominant worldview. Deconstruction, according to Spivak, "is constantly and persistently looking into how truths are produced. That's why deconstruction doesn't say logocentrism is a pathology, or metaphysical enclosures are something you can escape. Deconstruction, if one wants a formula, is among other things, a persistent critique of what one cannot not want." She writes against the "epistemic violence" done by discourses of knowledge that carve up the world and condemn to oblivion the pieces that do not easily fit. Characteristically, she does not claim to avoid such violence herself; rather, she self-consciously explores structures of violence without assuming a final, settled position.

Spivak was born in Calcutta, India, and received her B.A. from the University of Calcutta. She came to the United States and completed her M.A. and Ph.D. in English literature at Cornell University, where PAUL DE MAN was one of her mentors. She has taught at various American universities, including the University of Iowa, the University of Texas, Emory University, the University of Pittsburgh, and Columbia University. Her earliest important work was her introduction to and translation of JACQUES DERRIDA'S *Of Grammatology* (1977), the first of his major books to be rendered in full into English. Spivak played a key role in introducing French "theory" into North American and British literature departments between 1975 and 1982. Almost from the start, she emphasized how deconstruction's interest in the "violence" of traditional hierarchical binary oppositions (between male and female, the West and the rest, etc.) afforded a passage from literary theory to radical politics. Spivak joined feminism's interest in silenced women to a Marxist global concern with the political, economic, and cultural oppression of nonwhite people. The result was a series of highly influential essays that helped set the agenda for feminism and for postcolonial theory in the 1980s and 1990s. In 1997 Spivak founded the Pares Chandra and Sivani Chakravorty Memorial Literacy Project, a charitable foundation that trains teachers and runs schools in rural India.

"Can the Subaltern Speak?" may be Spivak's best-known essay; it is certainly her most controversial. First given as a lecture in 1983 and published in different versions in 1985 and 1988, Spivak offers a greatly expanded revision (more than one hundred pages) in her *Critique of Postcolonial Reason* (1999). Our selection offers three sections from this revised version, beginning with the sentence in which Spivak poses a central concern: "the possibility that the intellectual is complicit in the persistent constitution of the Other as the Self's shadow." Her essay insists "on marking [critics'] positionality as investigating subjects." Postcolonial critics, like many feminists, want to give silenced others a voice. But Spivak worries that even the most benevolent effort merely repeats the very silencing it aims to combat. The outsider creates the framework within which the "native" speaks and, thus, for Spivak constitutes that native in ways that undermine any claim to authentic contact. After all, colonialists often thought of themselves as well-intentioned. Spivak points to the British outlawing of *sati*, the Hindu practice of burning a widow on her husband's funeral pyre. While this intervention saved some lives and may have given women a modicum of free choice, it also served to secure British power in India and to underscore the asserted difference between British "civilization" and Indian "barbarism." Hindu culture was driven underground, written out of law, denied any legitimacy. Can today's intellectuals avoid a similar condescension when they represent the oppressed?

Spivak articulates her reasons for her worries in the first part of our selection, applying MICHEL FOUCAULT'S understanding of "epistemic violence" to the "remotely orchestrated, far-flung, and heterogeneous project to constitute the colonial subject as Other." Foucault views intellectual power as functioning discursively to produce the very subject over which it then exercises mastery. Of course, no discourse succeeds in obliterating all alternative discourses. Intellectuals have frequently tried to create counterdiscourses that contest the dominant discourses, with the hope of connecting with the oppressed's own acts of resistance. Spivak sees postcolonial studies as a new instance of this attempt to liberate the other and to enable that other to experience and articulate those parts of itself that fall outside what the dominant discourse has constituted as its subjecthood. She asks whether such work can succeed. Can—with or without the intervention of well-intentioned intellectuals—the "subaltern" speak? Her blunt answer is no.

A subaltern, according to the dictionary, is a person holding a subordinate position, originally a junior officer in the British army. But Spivak draws on the term's nuances. It has particularly rich connotations for the Indian subcontinent because the Anglo-Indian writer Rudyard Kipling (1865–1936) so often viewed imperialism from the ambivalent position of the subaltern functionary in the complex colonial hierarchy, caught between detested superiors and feared "natives." The Italian Marxist theorist ANTONIO GRAMSCI later applied the term to the unorganized masses that must be politicized for the workers' revolution to succeed. In the 1980s the Subaltern Studies Group (a collective of radical historians in India with whom Spivak maintains ties) appropriated the term, focusing their attention on the disenfranchised peoples of India. The "subaltern" always stands in an ambiguous relation to power—subordinate to it but never fully consenting to its rule, never adopting the dominant point of view or vocabulary as expressive of its own identity. "One must nevertheless insist that the colonized subaltern *subject* is irretrievably heterogeneous," declares Spivak. Can this difference be articulated? And if so, by whom?

Because subalterns exist, to some extent, outside power, theorists and advocates of political transformation have consistently looked to them as a potential source of change. Marxists speak of and for the proletariat, feminists of and for oppressed women, and anticolonialists of and for third world peoples. In part, Spivak is reacting against the persistent tendency of radical political movements to romanticize the other, especially against the notion that third world peoples must lead the fight against multinational global capitalism. To assign them that role is to repeat colonialism's basic violence, which views non-Europeans as important only insofar as they follow Western scripts. Furthermore, when most of the power resides in the West, why should the least powerful of those caught up in globalization be responsible for halting its advance? Finally, Spivak points out that the suggestion that all third world peoples stand in the same relation to global capitalism and should respond to it in the same way is "essentialist."

Essentialism names the belief that certain people or entities share some essential, unchanging "nature" that secures their membership in a category. In the 1980s, essentialism was the target of much feminist criticism because activists recognized that generalizations about "woman" inevitably exclude some women. One response was "difference feminism," which stressed alliances among women across their differences and hoped to replace a solidarity based on shared essential qualities and experiences. Spivak's landmark contribution to this debate was the concept of "strategic essentialism." In some instances, she argued, it was important *strategically* to make essentialist claims, even while one retained an awareness that those claims were, at best, crude political generalizations. For example, feminists must publicize "the feminization of poverty"—the ways in which employment practices and wages, divorce law and settlements, and social policies ensure that in many societies women make up the majority of poor adults. Of course, many women are not poor, and poverty has causes other than an individual's sex, but to battle effectively against the poverty of some women requires the strategic essentialism of highlighting the gendered nature of economic inequality.

Leftist intellectuals who romanticize the oppressed, Spivak argues, essentialize the subaltern and thus replicate the colonialist discourses they purport to critique. To replace this leftist fantasy of an untouched or essential purity lodged in a particular group, Spivak reminds us (citing Ranajit Guha, a founding member of the Subaltern Studies Group) that a person's or group's identity is relational, a function of its place in a system of differences. There is no true or pure other; instead, the other always already exists in relation to the discourse that would name it as other.

But does the differential position of otherness afford it some resources it can use to articulate its singularity, its nonidentity with power? Spivak seems doubtful; her historical and political analysis describes Western capitalism and colonialism as triumphant. The whole world is now organized economically, politically, and culturally along the lines of Western discourses. Although those discourses are not perfectly aligned, their multiplicity generally reinforces rather than undercuts the marginalization of nonwhite peoples and the dual marginalization of nonwhite women. Given this bleak picture, Spivak turns (in the second part of our selection) to SIGMUND FREUD in an effort to develop an appropriate model of intellectual work.

Freud furthers the analysis of colonialism by helping us see how the very identity of whiteness itself is created in part through the self-proclaimed benevolence of colonial action. More important, he implicitly cautions us against scapegoating or, conversely, creating saviors. Spivak's "sentence"—"White men are saving brown women from brown men"—serves to justify colonial interventions if white men are taken as saviors and brown men are scapegoated as oppressors of brown women. A postcolonialist discourse could just as easily scapegoat white men, with the inevitable consequence of presenting either brown men or brown women as the saviors. Spivak thinks that Freud (as both a positive and a negative example, since he himself didn't always avoid scapegoating) can aid us to keep the "sentence" open, to explore the dynamics of the unfolding human relationships without foreclosing narratives by assigning determinate roles. She remains leery of any attempt to fix and celebrate the subaltern's distinctive voice by claims that the subaltern occupies the position of victim, abjected other, scapegoat, savior, and so on. The critic must remain attentive to the fluidity of possible relations and actions. Spivak's discussion of Freud is offered not "as a solution" but "in acknowledgment of these dangers" of interpreting and representing the other.

Neither Freud nor Spivak is silent. They each make various determinate claims and, Spivak says, reveal their "political interests" in those claims. As intellectuals, both are at home (although their belonging is qualified by Freud's being Jewish and Spivak's being a nonwhite woman) within the dominant discourse. The subaltern is not similarly privileged, and does not speak in a vocabulary that will get a hearing in institutional locations of power. The subaltern enters official and intellectual discourse only rarely and usually through the mediating commentary of someone more at home in those discourses. If the problematic is understood this way, it is hard to see how the subaltern can be capable of speaking.

In the third part of our selection, Spivak offers yet a further twist. She tells the story of Bhubaneswari Bhaduri's suicide not as an example of the Indian woman's inability to speak within Western discourse, but to show that Indian discourse has been so battered by the storms of (colonial) history that it, too, offers no resources for successful communication. Bhubaneswari's suicide is misunderstood by everyone, including her own family—and no one in India seems interested in Spivak's return to and reinterpretation of the event. "Unnerved by this failure of communication," Spivak wrote her "passionate lament: the subaltern cannot speak!" Fifteen years later, Spivak comments: "It was an inadvisable remark."

What scraps of comfort has Spivak unearthed in the meantime to challenge her first, despairing conclusion? She has reminded herself that "speaking" always occurs within the nexus of actions that include listening, responding, interpreting, and qualifying. One's words can be taken up in any number of possible ways. The ongoing effects of an utterance, not its singular expression or any one response, produces its character as a speech act. Much of the point of revisionist history, of returning to scenes of domination and oppression, is to reactivate attempts at speaking that other forces tried to obliterate and keep from having effects. In revisiting Bhubaneswari's suicide, Spivak makes it speak in new ways. To deny that this retelling is a form of speaking would be to hold on to a criterion of "authenticity" that runs counter to Spivak's whole argument about identity. The historian who tries to recover the past should sketch "the itinerary of the trace" that the silenced subaltern has left, should mark the sites where the subaltern was effaced, and should delineate the discourses that did the effacing.

Spivak remains wary of all representations, even while accepting that the opening of "a line of communication" is "to be desired" and "allows us to take pride in our work without making missionary claims." On theoretical and ethical grounds, she insists that any system, any discourse, inevitably excludes something, and she will "reserve" the word *subaltern* to point toward "the sheer heterogeneity of decolonized space." She very much wants the "traces" of those exclusions to haunt us. In every utterance she urges us to hear the faint whisper of what could not be said. And she asks us to be ready to change our current discourse for a new one that would get closer to what the old one leaves unspoken—although the new discourse will have its own silences. This attunement to the unheard is what Spivak, following the philosopher Bimal Krishna Matilal, calls "moral love."

A persistent complaint against Spivak, aside from her difficult style, is that she leaves us no place to stand. Her political pronouncements are unambiguous, but she steadfastly refuses to advocate solutions beyond an openness to the other that can appear vague, undiscriminating, and indeed theatrical. To continually dismantle one's own assumptions seems itself an act of privilege, a deconstructionist's luxury that few can afford, especially those who have to make decisions here and now (a point somewhat conceded by Spivak in her concept of "strategic essentialism"). As an antidote to complacency, however, Spivak's work is exemplary. She never lets anyone, including herself, smugly assume that he or she is on the side of the angels. Her restless probing is unsettling, but invigorating. Like the stranger whose name is "trouble," she shakes things up and gets them moving. No topic is ever quite the same or quite so easy after Spivak has come through town.

***A Critique of Postcolonial Reason* Keywords:** Deconstruction, Feminist Theory, Globalization, Marxism, Postcolonial Theory, Poststructuralism, Psychoanalysis, Representation

From A Critique of Postcolonial Reason

From *Chapter* 3. *History*

[CAN THE SUBALTERN SPEAK?]

* * *

In the face of the possibility that the intellectual is complicit in the persistent constitution of the Other as the Self's shadow, a possibility of political practice for the intellectual would be to put the economic "under erasure," to see the economic factor as irreducible as it reinscribes the social text, even as it is erased, however imperfectly, when it claims to be the final determinant or the transcendental signified.[1]

1. This argument is developed further in Spivak, "Scattered Speculations on the Question of Value," in *In Other Worlds: Essays in Cultural Politics* (New York: Methuen, 1987), pp. 154–75. Once again, the *Anti-Oedipus* did not ignore the economic text, although the treatment was perhaps too allegorical. In this respect, the move from schizo- to rhyzo-analysis in *A Thousand Plateaus* was not, perhaps, salutary [Spivak's note]. Some of the author's notes have been edited, and some omitted. Spivak here argues against regarding the economic as all-powerful *or* as negligible; instead, the economic factor has a discernible impact on society and its discourses (the "social text"). In *A Thousand Plateaus* (1980), the French philosopher GILLES DELEUZE (1925–1995) and the French psychoanalyst FÉLIX GUATTARI (1930–1992) argue for a model of knowledge patterned not on plants with roots (as is traditional) but on fungal rhizomes, which lack centralized control or structure; their earlier *Anti-Oedipus: Capitalism and Schizophrenia* (1972) critiques both orthodox Marxism and institutional Freudianism. Earlier in her book, Spivak faults them for ignoring sociohistorical specificities, an omission that leads them to posit an essentialized psychological "subject of desire" in place of a historically constituted subject.

Until very recently, the clearest available example of such epistemic violence[2] was the remotely orchestrated, far-flung, and heterogeneous project to constitute the colonial subject as Other. This project is also the asymmetrical obliteration of the trace of that Other in its precarious Subjectivity. It is well known that Foucault locates one case of epistemic violence, a complete overhaul of the episteme, in the redefinition of madness at the end of the European eighteenth century.[3] But what if that particular redefinition was only a part of the narrative of history in Europe as well as in the colonies? What if the two projects of epistemic overhaul worked as dislocated and unacknowledged parts of a vast two-handed engine? Perhaps it is no more than to ask that the subtext of the palimpsestic narrative of imperialism be recognized as "subjugated knowledge," "a whole set of knowledges that have been disqualified as inadequate to their task or insufficiently elaborated: naive knowledges, located low down on the hierarchy, beneath the required level of cognition or scientificity."[4]

This is not to describe "the way things really were" or to privilege the narrative of history as imperialism as the best version of history. It is, rather, to continue the account of how *one* explanation and narrative of reality was established as the normative one. A comparable account in the case(s) of Central and Eastern Europe is soon to be launched. To elaborate on this, let us consider for the moment and briefly the underpinnings of the British codification of Hindu Law.

Once again, I am not a South Asianist. I turn to Indian material because I have some accident-of-birth facility there.

Here, then, is a schematic summary of the epistemic violence of the codification of Hindu Law. If it clarifies the notion of epistemic violence, my final discussion of widow-sacrifice[5] may gain added significance.

At the end of the eighteenth century, Hindu Law, insofar as it can be described as a unitary system, operated in terms of four texts that "staged" a four-part episteme defined by the subject's use of memory: *sruti* (the heard), *smriti* (the remembered), *sāstra* (the calculus), and *vyavahāra* (the performance). The origins of what had been heard and what was remembered were not necessarily continuous or identical. Every invocation of *sruti* technically recited (or reopened) the event of originary "hearing" or revelation. The second two texts—the learned and the performed—were seen as dialectically continuous. Legal theorists and practitioners were not in any given case certain if this structure described the body of law or four ways of settling a dispute. The legitimation, through a binary vision, of the polymorphous structure of legal performance, "internally" noncoherent and open at both ends, is the narrative of codification I offer as an example of epistemic violence.[6]

2. That is, the forcible replacement of one structure of beliefs with another; the term is borrowed from the writings of the French philosopher and historian of ideas MICHEL FOUCAULT (1926–1984), who meant by *episteme* (literally, "knowledge"; Greek) the underlying structure of knowledge and beliefs during a historical period.

3. See Foucault, *Madness and Civilization: A History of Insanity in the Age of Reason*, trans. Richard Howard (New York: Pantheon, 1965), pp. 251, 262, 269 [Spivak's note]

4. Foucault, *Power/Knowledge: Selected Interviews and Other Writings, 1972–1977*, ed. Colin Gordon (New York: Pantheon, 1980), p. 82 [Spivak's note].

5. Suttee (from the Hindu *satī*, literally "devoted woman"), the Hindu custom of a widow's being cremated on the funeral pyre of her husband.

6. That is, the British Empire's imposition of "binary vision" in place of the existing set of beliefs, the "polymorphous" Hindu Law.

Consider the often-quoted programmatic lines from Macaulay's infamous "Minute on Indian Education" (1835):

> We must at present do our best to form a class who may be interpreters between us and the millions whom we govern; a class of persons, Indian in blood and colour, but English in taste, in opinions, in morals, and in intellect. To that class we may leave it to refine the vernacular dialects of the country, to enrich those dialects with terms of science borrowed from the Western nomenclature, and to render them by degrees fit vehicles for conveying knowledge to the great mass of the population.[7]

The education of colonial subjects complements their production in law. One effect of establishing a version of the British system was the development of an uneasy separation between disciplinary formation in Sanskrit studies and the native, now alternative, tradition of Sanskirt "high culture." In the first section, I have suggested that within the former, the cultural explanations generated by authoritative scholars matched the epistemic violence of the legal project.[8]

Those authorities would be *the very best* of the sources for the nonspecialist French intellectual's entry into the civilization of the Other.[9] I am, however, not referring to intellectuals and scholars of colonial production, like Shastri,[1] when I say that the Other as Subject is inaccessible to Foucault and Deleuze. I am thinking of the general nonspecialist, nonacademic population across the class spectrum, for whom the episteme operates its silent programming function. Without considering the map of exploitation,[2] on what grid of "oppression" would they place this motley crew?

Let us now move to consider the margins (one can just as well say the silent, silenced center) of the circuit marked out by this epistemic violence, men and women among the illiterate peasantry, Aboriginals, and the lowest strata of the urban subproletariat. According to Foucault and Deleuze (in the First World,[3] under the standardization and regimentation of socialized capital, though they do not seem to recognize this) and mutatis mutandis the metropolitan[4] "third world feminist" only interested in resistance within capital logic, the oppressed, if given the chance (the problem of representation cannot be bypassed here), and on the way to solidarity through alliance politics (a Marxist thematic is at work here) *can speak and know their conditions*. We must now confront the following question: On the other side of

7. Thomas Babington Macaulay, "Minute on Indian Education," in *Selected Writings*, ed. John Clive and Thomas Pinney (Chicago: University of Chicago Press, 1972), p. 249 [Spivak's note]. Macaulay (1800–1859), English historian and statesman.

8. In suggesting that the organization and production of knowledge within academic disciplines acts with and reinforces more overtly political and legal accumulations of power, Spivak follows Foucault.

9. I have discussed this issue in greater detail with reference to Julia Kristeva's *About Chinese Women*, trans. Anita Barrows (New York: Urizen, 1977), in "French Feminism in an International Frame," in *In Other Worlds*, pp. 136–41 [Spivak's note]. KRISTEVA (b. 1941), Bulgarian-born French philosopher and psychoanalyst.

1. Mahamahopadhyaya Shastri (active 1920s), described by Spivak earlier in the chapter as a "learned Indianist, [and] brilliant representative of the indigenous elite within colonial production."

2. That is, the map of the colonized non-Western world, a map absent from Western thought.

3. The highly industrialized (largely Western) nations in a global economy, which dominate the "underdeveloped" countries of the "third world," many of which are former colonies.

4. Of or pertaining to the "mother country," as distinguished from its colony.

the international division of labor from socialized capital, inside *and* outside the circuit of the epistemic violence of imperialist law and education supplementing an earlier economic text, *can the subaltern speak?*

We have already considered the possibility that, given the exigencies of the inauguration of colonial records, the instrumental woman (the Rani of Sirmur) is not fully written.[5]

Antonio Gramsci's[6] work on the "subaltern classes" extends the class-position/class-consciousness argument isolated in *The Eighteenth Brumaire.*[7] Perhaps because Gramsci criticizes the vanguardistic position of the Leninist intellectual,[8] he is concerned with the intellectual's rôle in the subaltern's cultural and political movement into the hegemony. This movement must be made to determine the production of history as narrative (of truth).[9] In texts such as *The Southern Question,* Gramsci considers the movement of historical-political economy in Italy within what can be seen as an allegory of reading taken from or prefiguring an international division of labor.[1] Yet an account of the phased development of the subaltern is thrown out of joint when his cultural macrology[2] is operated, however remotely, by the epistemic interference with legal and disciplinary definitions accompanying the imperialist project. When I move, at the end of this essay, to the question of woman as subaltern, I will suggest that the possibility of collectivity itself is persistently foreclosed through the manipulation of female agency.[3]

The first part of my proposition—that the phased development of the subaltern is complicated by the imperialist project—is confronted by the "Subaltern Studies" group.[4] They *must* ask, Can the subaltern speak? Here we are within Foucault's own discipline of history and with people who acknowledge his influence. Their project is to rethink Indian colonial historiography from the perspective of the discontinuous chain of peasant insurgencies during the colonial occupation. This is indeed the problem of "the permission to narrate" discussed by Said.[5] As Ranajit Guha, the founding editor of the collective, argues,

5. In an earlier chapter, Spivak discusses at length how the British in 1815 prevented the widow-suicide of the widow of the deposed leader of the province of Sirmur, arguing that their intervention was based on a misunderstanding of Hindu practice, served the British's administrative needs in Sirmur, was conducted with an almost parodic British reverence for "legality," and completely obscured the Rani's motives and wishes.

6. Italian Marxist (1891–1937; see above), best known for his notions of "cultural hegemony" (the manufactured consent that legitimates a dominant group and unifies a society) and the "organic intellectual" (someone, regardless of profession, who directs the ideas and aspirations of the particular social class to which he or she "organically" belongs). In his *Prison Notebooks* (published 1948–51), he applies the word *subaltern* to the proletariat.

7. *The Eighteenth Brumaire of Louis Napoleon* (1852), an analysis by the German social, economic, and political theorist KARL MARX (1818–1883) of the dictatorship (later emperorship) declared by President Louis Bonaparte of France in 1851. Spivak argues earlier in her text that Marx explores the "gap" between "class-position" (a group's location in the economic relations of production) and "class-consciousness" (a group's ability to represent to itself the interests that stem from its class position).

8. That is, the position of the Russian revolutionary V. I. Lenin (1870–1924), contrary to Marx's own theory, that the proletarian revolution must be led by a vanguard (i.e., the Bolsheviks).

9. That is, a way of seeing the world shared by those individuals won over to the hegemonic view.

1. Antonio Gramsci, *The Southern Question*, trans. Pasquale Verdicchio (West Lafayette, Ind.: Bordighera, 1995) [Spivak's note].

2. Prolonged discourse.

3. That is, by colonial and postcolonial economic and political arrangements that place women and men at odds with one another.

4. A group of radical historians in India—in particular, the editorial collective of the annual publication *Subaltern Studies* (founded in 1982)—who have worked to recover the struggles of the poor independent of elite nationalism and to reconstruct peasant consciousness.

5. Edward W. Said, "Permission to Narrate," *London Review of Books*, February 16, 1984 [Spivak's note]. SAID (1935–2003), Palestinian-born American theorist of postcolonialism and political activist.

> The historiography of Indian nationalism has for a long time been dominated by elitism—colonialist elitism and bourgeois-nationalist elitism . . . shar[ing] the prejudice that the making of the Indian nation and the development of the consciousness—nationalism—which confirmed this process were exclusively or predominantly elite achievements. In the colonialist and neo-colonialist historiographies these achievements are credited to British colonial rulers, administrators, policies, institutions, and culture; in the nationalist and neo-nationalist writings—to Indian elite personalities, institutions, activities and ideas.[6]

Certain members of the Indian elite are of course native informants for first-world intellectuals interested in the voice of the Other. But one must nevertheless insist that the colonized subaltern *subject* is irretrievably heterogeneous.

Against the indigenous elite we may set what Guha calls "the *politics* of the people," both outside ("this was an *autonomous* domain, for it neither originated from elite politics nor did its existence depend on the latter") and inside ("it continued to operate vigorously in spite of [colonialism], adjusting itself to the conditions prevailing under the Raj[7] and in many respects developing entirely new strains in both form and content") the circuit of colonial production. I cannot entirely endorse this insistence of determinate vigor and full autonomy, for practical historiographic exigencies will not allow such endorsements to privilege subaltern consciousness. Against the possible charge that his approach is essentialist, Guha constructs a definition of the people (the place of that essence) that can be only an identity-in-differential. He proposes a dynamic stratification grid describing colonial social production at large. Even the third group on the list, the buffer group, as it were, between the people and the great macro-structural dominant groups, is itself defined as a place of in-betweenness. The classification falls into: "dominant foreign groups," and "dominant indigenous groups at the all-India and at the regional and local levels" representing the elite; and "[t]he social groups and elements included in [the terms "people" and "subaltern classes"] represent[ing] *the demographic difference between the total Indian population and all those whom we have described as the "elite."*[8]

"The task of research" projected here is "to investigate, identify and measure the *specific* nature and degree of the *deviation* of [the] elements [constituting item 3] from the ideal and situate it historically." "Investigate, identify, and measure the specific": a program could hardly be more essentialist and taxonomic. Yet a curious methodological imperative is at work. I have argued that, in the Foucault-Deleuze conversation, a post-representationalist vocabulary[9] hides an essentialist agenda. In subaltern studies, because of the violence of imperialist epistemic, social, and disciplinary inscription, a project understood in essentialist terms[1] must traffic in a radical textual practice of differences. The object of the group's investigation, in this case not even of the people as such but of the floating buffer zone of the regional elite—is a *deviation* from an *ideal*—the people or subaltern—which is itself defined as a difference from the elite. It is toward this structure that the research is

6. Ranajit Guha, *Subaltern Studies* 1 (1982): 1 [Spivak's note].
7. British colonial rule in India.
8. Guha, pp. 4, 8 [Spivak's note].
9. That is, a vocabulary that champions difference and the undecidable.
1. In terms of a search for the "true" or "essential" voice of Indian resistance to the British.

oriented, a predicament rather different from the self-diagnosed transparency of the first-world radical intellectual. What taxonomy can fix such a space? Whether or not they themselves perceive it—in fact Guha sees his definition of "the people" within the master-slave dialectic[2]—their text articulates the difficult task of rewriting its own conditions of impossibility as the conditions of its possibility. "At the regional and local levels [the dominant indigenous groups] . . . if belonging to social strata hierarchically inferior to those of the dominant all-Indian groups *acted in the interests of the latter and not in conformity to interests corresponding truly to their own social being.*"[3] When these writers speak, in their essentializing language, of a gap between interest and action in the intermediate group, their conclusions are closer to Marx than to the self-conscious naivete of Deleuze's pronouncement on the issue. Guha, like Marx, speaks of interest in terms of the social rather than the libidinal being. The Name-of-the-Father imagery in *The Eighteenth Brumaire* can help to emphasize that, on the level of class or group action, "true correspondence to own being" is as artificial or social as the patronymic.[4]

It is to this intermediate group that the second woman in this chapter belongs.[5] The pattern of domination is here determined mainly by gender rather than class. The subordinated gender following the dominant within the challenge of nationalism while remaining caught within gender oppression is not an unknown story.

For the (gender-unspecified) "true" subaltern group, whose identity is its difference, there is no unrepresentable subaltern subject that can know and speak itself; the intellectual's solution is not to abstain from representation. The problem is that the subject's itinerary[6] has not been left traced so as to offer an object of seduction to the representing intellectual. In the slightly dated language of the Indian group, the question becomes, How can we touch the consciousness of the people, even as we investigate their politics? With what voice-consciousness can the subaltern speak?

My question about how to earn the "secret encounter" with the contemporary hill women of Sirmur[7] is a practical version of this. The woman of whom I will speak in this section was not a "true" subaltern, but a metropolitan middle-class girl. Further, the effort she made to write or speak her body was in the accents of accountable reason, the instrument of self-conscious responsibility. Still her Speech Act[8] was refused. She was made to unspeak herself posthumously, by other women. In an earlier version of this chapter, I had summarized this historical indifference and its results as: the subaltern cannot speak.

The critique by Ajit K. Chaudhury, a West Bengali Marxist, of Guha's search for the subaltern consciousness can be taken as representative of a

2. As set forth by the German philosopher GEORG WILHELM FRIEDRICH HEGEL in *Phenomenology of Spirit* (1807; see above): he tells of two self-consciousnesses that confront each other and fight for mutual recognition. One wins the battle and the other loses, but each gets recognition and thereby identifies him- or herself through the eyes of the other.

3. Guha, 1 [Spivak's note].

4. That is, the Name-of-the-Father, a term used by the French psychoanalyst JACQUES LACAN (1901–1981) to refer to the father in the Symbolic realm (not a biological entity), which marks the child's entrance into language-based experience.

5. Bhunaneswari Bhaduri, discussed later in this selection.

6. That is, the history of its constitution as a subject—and hence the erasure of its heterogeneity—by epistemically violent discourses.

7. That is, the contemporary equivalents of the Rani of Sirmur.

8. An allusion to the speech act theory of the English philosopher J. L. AUSTIN (1911–1960), who considered all the actions typically performed in speaking (here the reverse is suggested: an action serves as an utterance).

moment of the production process that includes the subaltern.[9] Chaudhury's perception that the Marxist view of the transformation of consciousness involves the knowledge of social relations seems, in principle, astute. Yet the heritage of the positivist ideology[1] that has appropriated orthodox Marxism obliges him to add this rider: "This is not to belittle the importance of understanding peasants' consciousness or workers' consciousness *in its pure form*. This enriches our knowledge of the peasant and the worker and, possibly, throws light on how a particular mode takes on different forms in different regions, *which is considered a problem of second order importance in classical Marxism*."[2]

This variety of "internationalist Marxism," which believes in a pure, retrievable form of consciousness only to dismiss it, thus closing off what in Marx remain moments of productive bafflement, can at once be the occasion for Foucault's and Deleuze's rejection of Marxism *and* the source of the critical motivation of the subaltern studies groups. All three are united in the assumption that there *is* a pure form of consciousness. On the French scene, there is a shuffling of signifiers: "the unconscious" or "the subject-in-oppression" clandestinely fills the space of "the pure form of consciousness." In orthodox "internationalist" intellectual Marxism, whether in the First World or the Third, the pure form of consciousness remains, paradoxically, a material effect, and therefore a second-order problem. This often earns it the reputation of racism and sexism. In the subaltern studies group it needs development according to the unacknowledged terms of its own articulation.

Within the effaced itinerary of the subaltern subject, the track of sexual difference is doubly effaced.[3] The question is not of female participation in insurgency, or the ground rules of the sexual division of labor, for both of which there is "evidence." It is, rather, that, both as object of colonialist historiography and as subject of insurgency, the ideological construction of gender keeps the male dominant. If, in the contest of colonial production, the subaltern has no history and cannot speak, the subaltern as female is even more deeply in shadow.

In the first part of this chapter we meditate upon an elusive female figure called into the service of colonialism. In the last part we will look at a comparable figure in anti-colonialist nationalism. The regulative psychobiography of widow self-immolation will be pertinent in both cases. In the interest of the invaginated spaces[4] of this book, let us remind ourselves of the gradual emergence of the new subaltern in the New World Order.[5]

* * *

9. Since then, in the disciplinary fallout after the serious electoral and terrorist augmentation of Hindu nationalism in India, more alarming charges have been leveled at the group. See Aijaz Ahmad, *In Theory: Classes, Nations, Literature* (London: Verso, 1992), pp. 68, 194, 207–11; and Sumit Sarkar, "The Fascism of the Sangh Parivar," *Economic and Political Weekly*, January 30, 1993, pp. 163–67 [Spivak's note].

1. The sociopolitical program that takes knowledge and meaning to derive solely from what can be empirically observed.

2. Ajit K. Chaudhury, "New Wave Social Science," *Frontier* 16.24 (January 28, 1984), p. 10. Emphasis mine [Spivak's note].

3. I do not believe that the recent trend of romanticizing anything written by the Aboriginal or outcaste intellectual has lifted the effacement [Spivak's note].

4. An allusion to the *écriture féminine* (feminine writing) championed by the French feminist HÉLÈNE CIXOUS (b. 1937) and a description of Spivak's method, which folds together various arguments rather than laying them out in a linear progression.

5. A phrase used by George H. W. Bush (b. 1924; 41st U.S. president, 1989–93) to describe what was needed to replace East-West cold war rivalries after the collapse of communism in Eastern Europe.

I am generally sympathetic with the call to make U.S. feminism more "theoretical." It seems, however, that the problem of the muted subject of the subaltern woman, though not solved by an "essentialist" search for lost origins, cannot be served by the call for more theory in Anglo-America either.

That call is often given in the name of a critique of "positivism," which is seen here as identical with "essentialism." Yet Hegel, the modern inaugurator of "the work of the negative," was not a stranger to the notion of essences. For Marx, the curious persistence of essentialism within the dialectic was a profound and productive problem. Thus, the stringent binary opposition between positivism/essentialism (read, U.S.) and "theory" (read, French or Franco-German via Anglo-American) may be spurious. Apart from repressing the ambiguous complicity between essentialism and critiques of positivism (acknowledged by Derrida in "Of Grammatology as a Positive Science"[6]), it also errs by implying that positivism is not a theory. This move allows the emergence of a proper name, a positive essence, Theory. And once again, the position of the investigator remains unquestioned. If and when this territorial debate turns toward the Third World, no change in the question of method is to be discerned. This debate cannot take into account that, in the case of the woman as subaltern, rather few ingredients for the constitution of the itinerary of the trace of a sexed subject (rather than an anthropological object) can be gathered to locate the possibility of dissemination.[7]

Yet I remain generally sympathetic to aligning feminism with the critique of positivism and the defetishization of the concrete. I am also far from averse to learning from the work of Western theorists, though I have learned to insist on marking their positionality as investigating subjects. Given these conditions, and as a literary critic, I tactically confronted the immense problem of the consciousness of the woman as subaltern. I reinvented the problem in a sentence and transformed it into the object of a simple semiosis.[8] What can such a transformation mean?

This gesture of transformation marks the fact that knowledge of the other subject is theoretically impossible. Empirical work in the discipline constantly performs this transformation tacitly. It is a transformation from a first-second person performance to the constatation in the third person.[9] It is, in other words, at once a gesture of control and an acknowledgement of limits. Freud provides a homology[1] for such positional hazards.

Sarah Kofman has suggested that the deep ambiguity of Freud's use of women as a scapegoat may be read as a reaction-formation to an initial and continuing desire to give the hysteric a voice, to transform her into the *subject* of hysteria.[2] The masculine-imperialist ideological formation that shaped

6. A section of *Of Grammatology* (1967; trans. 1977 by Spivak), by the French deconstructive philosopher JACQUES DERRIDA (1930–2004).

7. An allusion to Derrida, one of whose important works is titled *Dissemination* (1972).

8. Process of meaning making, of producing signs. The "sentence," given below, is "White men are saving brown women from brown men."

9. In speech act theory, an utterance that describes a condition, fact, or state of affairs; in contrast, a performative utterance does something (e.g., saying, "I promise to . . ." makes a promise). By writing in the 3d person, Western scholars hide the performative nature of their work, which creates a particular way of seeing the "facts."

1. An example of similarity in structure due to similar development; like the scholars, the psychoanalyst SIGMUND FREUD (1856–1939) turned the performatives of his own 1st-person claims and his patients' appropriated 2d-person accounts into 3d-personal "empirical" statements of scientific "fact."

2. Sarah Kofman, *The Enigma of Woman: Woman in Freud's Writings*, trans. Catherine Porter (Ithaca, N.Y.: Cornell University Press, 1985) [Spivak's note].

that desire into "the daughter's seduction"[3] is part of the same formation that constructs the monolithic "third-world woman." No contemporary metropolitan investigator is not influenced by that formation. Part of our "unlearning" project is to articulate our participation in that formation—by *measuring* silences, if necessary—into the *object* of investigation. Thus, when confronted with the questions, Can the subaltern speak? and Can the subaltern (as woman) speak? our efforts to give the subaltern a voice in history will be doubly open to the dangers run by Freud's discourse. It is in acknowledgment of these dangers rather than as solution to a problem that I put together the sentence "White men are saving brown women from brown men," a sentence that runs like a red thread through today's "gender and development." My impulse is not unlike the one to be encountered in Freud's investigation of the sentence "A child is being beaten."[4]

The use of Freud here does not imply an isomorphic analogy between subject-formation and the behavior of social collectives, a frequent practice, often accompanied by a reference to Reich,[5] in the conversation between Deleuze and Foucault. I am, in other words, not suggesting that "White men are saving brown women from brown men" is a sentence indicating a *collective* fantasy symptomatic of a *collective* itinerary of sadomasochistic repression in a *collective* imperialist enterprise. There is a satisfying symmetry in such an allegory, but I would rather invite the reader to consider it a problem in "wild psychoanalysis" than a clinching solution.[6] Just as Freud's insistence on making the woman the scapegoat in "A child is being beaten" and elsewhere discloses his political interests, however imperfectly, so my insistence on imperialist subject-production as the occasion for this sentence discloses a politics that I cannot step around.

* * *

A young woman of sixteen or seventeen, Bhubaneswari Bhaduri, hanged herself in her father's modest apartment in North Calcutta in 1926. The suicide was a puzzle since, as Bhubaneswari was menstruating at the time, it was clearly not a case of illicit pregnancy. Nearly a decade later, it was discovered, in a letter she had left for her elder sister, that she was a member of one of the many groups involved in the armed struggle for Indian independence. She had been entrusted with a political assassination. Unable to confront the task and yet aware of the practical need for trust, she killed herself.

Bhubaneswari had known that her death would be diagnosed as the outcome of illegitimate passion. She had therefore waited for the onset of menstruation.

3. A reference both to Freud's work on female hysteria (viewed as a symptom of frustrated sexual desire for a male authority figure) and to *The Daughter's Seduction* (1982), a book by Jane Gallop that describes feminist appropriations of Freud.

4. Freud, "'A Child Is Being Beaten': A Contribution to the Study of the Origin of Sexual Perversion," in *The Standard Edition of the Complete Psychological Works of Sigmund Freud*, ed. James Strachey, 24 vols. (London: Hogarth, 1953–74), 17:175–204. For a list of ways in which Western criticism constructs "third world women," see Chandra Talpade Mohanty, "Under Western Eyes: Feminist Scholarship and Colonial Discourses," in *Third World Women and the Politics of Feminism*, ed. Mohanty et al. (Bloomington: Indiana University Press, 1991), pp. 51–80 [Spivak's note].

5. Wilhelm Reich (1897–1957), Austrian psychoanalyst whose *Mass Psychology of Fascism* (1933) exemplifies a radical attempt to psychoanalyze a whole society.

6. Freud, "'Wild' Psycho-Analysis," in *Standard Edition*, 11:221–27. A good deal of psychoanalytic social critique would fit this description [Spivak's note]. Freud warns against "wild" psychoanalysis that jumps to conclusions without the slow accumulation of information and the relationship between patient and therapist necessary for psychoanalytic treatment.

While waiting, Bhubaneswari, the *brahmacārini*[7] who was no doubt looking forward to good wifehood, perhaps rewrote the social text of *sati*-suicide in an interventionist way. (One tentative explanation of her inexplicable act had been a possible melancholia brought on by her father's death and her brother-in-law's repeated taunts that she was too old to be not-yet-a-wife.) She generalized the sanctioned motive for female suicide by taking immense trouble to displace (not merely deny), in the physiological inscription of her body, its imprisonment within legitimate passion by a single male. In the immediate context, her act became absurd, a case of delirium rather than sanity. The displacing gesture—waiting for menstruation—is at first a reversal of the interdict against a menstruating widow's right to immolate herself; the unclean widow must wait, publicly, until the cleansing bath of the fourth day, when she is no longer menstruating, in order to claim her dubious privilege.

In this reading, Bhubaneswari Bhaduri's suicide is an unemphatic, ad hoc, subaltern rewriting of the social text of *sati*-suicide as much as the hegemonic account of the blazing, fighting, familial Durga.[8] The emergent dissenting possibilities of that hegemonic account of the fighting mother are well documented and popularly well remembered through the discourse of the male leaders and participants in the Independence movement. The subaltern as female cannot be heard or read.

I know of Bhubaneswari's life and death through family connections. Before investigating them more thoroughly, I asked a Bengali woman, a philosopher and Sanskritist whose early intellectual production is almost identical to mine, to start the process. Two responses: (a) Why, when her two sisters, Saileswari and Raseswari, led such full and wonderful lives, are you interested in the hapless Bhubaneswari? (b) I asked her nieces. It appears that it was a case of illicit love.

I was so unnerved by this failure of communication that, in the first version of this text, I wrote, in the accents of passionate lament: the subaltern cannot speak! It was an inadvisable remark.

In the intervening years between the publication of the second part of this chapter in essay form and this revision, I have profited greatly from the many published responses to it. I will refer to two of them here: "Can the Subaltern Vote?" and "Silencing Sycorax."[9]

As I have been insisting, Bhubaneswari Bhaduri was not a "true" subaltern. She was a woman of the middle class, with access, however clandestine, to the bourgeois movement for Independence. Indeed the Rani of Sirmur, with her claim to elevated birth, was not a subaltern at all. Part of what I seem to have argued in this chapter is that woman's interception of the claim to subalternity can be staked out across strict lines of definition by virtue of their muting by heterogeneous circumstances. Gulari[1] cannot speak to us because indigenous

7. Female member of the Brahmin (upper) caste (Hindi).
8. In Hindu mythology and religion, one of the many forms of Devi (the divine mother goddess). She is a warrior, often represented with 8 or 10 arms; each hand holds the special weapon of the other gods.
9. Leerom Medovoi et al., "Can the Subaltern Vote?" *Socialist Review* 20.3 (July–September 1990): 133–49; and Abena Busia, "Silencing Sycorax: On African Colonial Discourse and the Unvoiced Female," *Cultural Critique*, no. 14 (winter 1989–90): 81–104 [Spivak's note]. Spivak's original essay was "Can the Subaltern Speak?" in *Marxism and the Interpretation of Culture*, ed. Cary Nelson and Lawrence Grossberg (Urbana: University of Illinois Press, 1988), pp. 271–313.
1. The family name of the Rani of Sirmur.

patriarchal "history" would only keep a record of her funeral and colonial history only needed her as an incidental instrument. Bhubaneswari attempted to "speak" by turning her body into a text of woman/writing. The immediate passion of my declaration "the subaltern cannot speak," came from the despair that, in her own family, among women, in no more than fifty years, her attempt had failed. I am not laying the blame for the muting on the *colonial* authorities here, as Busia seems to think: "Gayatri Spivak's 'Can the Subaltern Speak?'—section 4 of which is a compelling explication of this role of disappearing in the case of Indian women in British legal history."[2]

I am pointing, rather, at her silencing by her own more emancipated granddaughters: a new mainstream. To this can be added two newer groups: one, the liberal multiculturalist metropolitan academy, Susan Barton's[3] great-granddaughters; as follows:

As I have been saying all along, I think it is important to acknowledge our complicity in the muting, in order precisely to be more effective in the long run. Our work cannot succeed if we always have a scapegoat. The postcolonial migrant investigator is touched by the colonial social formations. Busia strikes a positive note for further work when she points out that, after all, I am able to read Bhubaneswari's case, and therefore she *has* spoken in some way. Busia is right, of course. All speaking, even seemingly the most immediate, entails a distanced decipherment by another, which is, at best, an interception. That is what speaking is.

I acknowledge this theoretical point, and also acknowledge the practical importance, for oneself and others, of being upbeat about future work. Yet the moot decipherment by another in an academic institution (willy-nilly a knowledge-production factory) many years later must not be too quickly identified with the "speaking" of the subaltern. It is not a mere tautology to say that the colonial or postcolonial subaltern is defined as the being on the other side of difference, or an epistemic fracture, even from other groupings among the colonized. What is at stake when we insist that the subaltern speaks?

In "Can the Subaltern Vote?" the three authors apply the question of stakes to "political speaking." This seems to me to be a fruitful way of extending my reading of subaltern speech into a collective arena. Access to "citizenship" (civil society) by becoming a voter (in the nation) is indeed the symbolic circuit of the mobilizing of subalternity into hegemony. This terrain, ever negotiating between national liberation and globalization, allows for examining the casting of the vote itself as a performative convention given as constative "speech" of the subaltern subject. It is part of my current concerns to see how this set is manipulated to legitimize globalization; but it is beyond the scope of this book. Here let us remain confined to the field of academic prose, and advance three points:

1. Simply by being postcolonial or the member of an ethnic minority, we are not "subaltern." That word is reserved for the sheer heterogeneity of decolonized space.

2. Busia, "Silencing Sycorax," p. 102 [Spivak's note].
3. The daughter whose mother refuses to acknowledge her as her own in Daniel Defoe's novel *Roxana: The Fortunate Mistress* (1724). The South African writer J. M. Coetzee (b. 1940) uses Susan Barton as the narrator for much (but not all) of his retelling of Defoe's Robinson Crusoe story (1719) in his novel *Foe* (1987), a retelling that Spivak discusses at length in chapter 2 of *A Critique of Postcolonial Reason*.

2. When a line of communication is established between a member of subaltern groups and the circuits of citizenship or institutionality, the subaltern has been inserted into the long road to hegemony. Unless we want to be romantic purists or primitivists about "preserving subalternity"—a contradiction in terms—this is absolutely to be desired. (It goes without saying that museumized or curricularized access to ethnic origin—another battle that must be fought—is not identical with preserving subalternity.) Remembering this allows us to take pride in our work without making missionary claims.
3. This trace-structure (effacement in disclosure) surfaces as the tragic emotions of the political activist, springing not out of superficial utopianism, but out of the depths of what Bimal Krishna Matilal has called "moral love." Mahasweta Devi,[4] herself an indefatigable activist, documents this emotion with exquisite care in "Pterodactyl, Puran Sahay, and Pirtha."

And finally, the third group: Bhubaneswari's elder sister's eldest daughter's eldest daughter's eldest daughter is a new U.S. immigrant and was recently promoted to an executive position in a U.S.-based transnational. She will be helpful in the emerging South Asian market precisely because she is a well-placed Southern diasporic.

> For Europe, the time when the new capitalism *definitely* superseded the old can be established with fair precision: it was the beginning of the twentieth century . . . [With t]he boom at the end of the nineteenth century and the crisis of 1900–03 . . . [c]artels become one of the foundations of the whole of economic life. Capitalism has been transformed into imperialism.[5]

Today's program of global financialization carries on that relay. Bhubaneswari had fought for national liberation. Her great-grandniece works for the New Empire. This too is a historical silencing of the subaltern. When the news of this young woman's promotion was broadcast in the family amidst general jubilation I could not help remarking to the eldest surviving female member: "Bhubaneswari"—her nickname had been Talu—"hanged herself in vain," but not too loudly. Is it any wonder that this young woman is a staunch multiculturalist, believes in natural childbirth, and wears only cotton?

1983 — 1985, 1999

4. Indian author (1926–2016), who wrote in Bengali; some of her work—including "Pterodactyl," in *Imaginary Maps* (1995)—has been translated into English by Spivak. Matilal (1935–1991), Indian philosopher who taught at Oxford University for many years.

5. V. I. Lenin, *Imperialism: The Highest Stage of Capitalism: A Popular Outline* (London: Junius; Chicago: Pluto, 1996), pp. 15, 17 [Spivak's note].

TERRY EAGLETON
b. 1943

Since the 1970s, Terry Eagleton has been perhaps the most prominent and prolific commentator on criticism and theory in English. From an unabashed Marxist perspective, he has taken to task the quietism of other kinds of criticism, and unlike most academically trained critics, he has written with puckish humor and in a variety of genres. For instance, in our first selection, "The Rise of English," from his landmark *Literary Theory: An Introduction* (1983; 3d ed., 2008), he mocks the assumption that culture is edifying, noting instead the use of English literary studies as a form of social control: "If the masses are not thrown a few novels, they may react by throwing up a few barricades." He has in mind the canonical view of MATTHEW ARNOLD (see above), who argued that high culture is ennobling; answering the perennial question of the role of literature in society differently, Eagleton holds that it, like formal religion, helps reproduce the dominant social order. In our second selection, from his book *Culture and the Death of God* (2014), Eagleton turns to condemn postmodern theory in general, finding that it gives up both the ethical core of religion and the critical perspective of modernism.

A student of the Marxist literary and cultural critic RAYMOND WILLIAMS, Eagleton has introduced contemporary theory and its concepts to a wide Anglophone audience, as well as worked as a literary journalist, novelist, and playwright. Born in a working-class community in Salford, England, he attended Cambridge University on a scholarship, receiving his B.A. in 1964 and his Ph.D. in 1968. He taught at Cambridge for a year, held various appointments at Oxford University until 2001, and since has been a distinguished professor at the University of Manchester, Lancaster University, and the University of Notre Dame. During the politically vibrant late 1960s, Eagleton was active in the Catholic Left—among other things, he helped found a journal, *Slant*—and he published three books before he was thirty. It was not until the mid-1970s, however, that he established himself as a leading expositor of Marxism within the emerging field of contemporary literary theory, most notably with *Criticism and Ideology: A Study in Marxist Literary Theory* (1976). It extends LOUIS ALTHUSSER's theory of ideology to literature, revising the conventional Marxist view, espoused by Leon Trotsky, that texts directly reflect social reality; Eagleton argues instead that texts actively produce ideology.

Eagleton subsequently turned away from the pursuit of an overarching theoretical model, or what the American sociologist C. Wright Mills (1916–1962) termed "Grand Theory." As he remarked in a 1990 interview, "I think that back in the seventies we used to suffer from a certain fetishism of method; we used to think that we have to get a certain kind of systematic method right, and this would be *the* way of proceeding. I think some of my early work, certainly *Criticism and Ideology*, would fall within that general approach." Rather than dispensing with Marxism, however, he distinguishes between theoretical methods and political goals: "[A] Marxist has to define certain urgent political goals and allow, as it were, those to determine questions of method rather than the other way around." In eschewing large-scale theoretical models, Eagleton resembles the twentieth-century neopragmatists such as STANLEY FISH, who insists that method cannot be determined in advance but derives from practice. But whereas they argue that literary studies are politically ineffectual, Eagleton advocates a political focus.

Another element of Eagleton's turn from Grand Theory is his style, which is lively, witty, clear, and frequently opinionated, combining theory and literary journalism. Eagleton unabashedly states his opinions—often in audacious one-liners, such as "deconstruction is the death drive at the level of theory"—and injects humor into his writing; for instance, he calls Fish "the Donald Trump of American academia."

In his *Function of Criticism: From the "Spectator" to Post-Structuralism* (1984), Eagleton declares that contemporary criticism has lost its social purpose and become marginalized through the technocratic fetishizing of Grand Theory. Drawing on JÜRGEN HABERMAS's concept of the public sphere, he notes that modern criticism arose in the eighteenth century in opposition to the absolutist state, and he calls for the renewed oppositional role of criticism in the public sphere. To that end, Eagleton became known as the foremost popularizer of contemporary literary theory in the 1980s. His *Literary Theory* has been an academic bestseller and probably the most influential introduction to contemporary theory for students and curious readers. It conducts a knowledgeable but fast-paced, readable, and pithy survey of reader-response and reception theory, structuralism, deconstruction, and psychoanalysis. Rather than presenting a dispassionate history, *Literary Theory* bluntly states Eagleton's preferences and value judgments. Finding fault with most contemporary theories for their lack of attention to politics, he praises Marxist and feminist criticism for their concern with the political effects of literature.

Accessible and polemical, "The Rise of English" illustrates Eagleton's trademark style. It combines broad historical overview and ideological analysis. Eagleton sees English, which became an academic subject only in the late nineteenth century, as an outgrowth of nationalism as well as a replacement for religion as a crucial ideological apparatus. While lacking nuance, Eagleton's analysis succinctly answers a major theoretical question, proposing that literature has social significance not simply as an innocent, pleasurable entertainment but as a primary means of reinforcing the dominant social order.

In our selection from *Culture and the Death of God*, Eagleton tallies up a balance sheet on postmodern theory, and he finds it lacking. As in "The Rise of English," he employs a large historical frame, placing postmodernism in a lineage reaching back to modernism and earlier. In his view, a chief problem with postmodernism—as he suggests here and explains in other books, especially *The Idea of Culture* (2000)—is that its relativism forces it to vacate a critical stance, resulting in an immersion in identity politics rather than class politics. While he acknowledges that the previous mode of modernism was elitist, he finds that its emphasis on *Kulturkritik*, or "culture critique," gave it a stronger position in opposition to capitalism. His assessment differs from that of other figures, notably FREDRIC JAMESON, who sees the critical potential of postmodernism more dialectically at the conclusion of "Postmodernism and Consumer Society" (see above). Eagleton's mode is more polemical than dialectical.

Another element of *Culture and the Death of God* is a focus on religion. As Eagleton remarks in *Reason, Faith, and Revolution: Reflections on the God Debate* (2009), we should not simply dismiss religion as irrational—arguing that it fails according to standards of scientific proof—but should judge it as a different mode of meaning than science. While in our selection he does not assert a faith, he holds that the idea of God presents a more promising view of human potential that postmodernism evacuates. As he remarks in an interview with Matthew Beaumont in *The Task of the Critic: Terry Eagleton in Dialogue* (2009), "I stopped calling myself a Roman Catholic, even though I continue to value aspects of that cultural context and tradition."

In part because of his popularizations of theory, and in part because of the often sweeping, polemical nature of his arguments, Eagleton has occasionally been dismissed by specialist commentators on theory. His influence among theorists is much less pronounced than that of Jameson, the most prominent U.S. Marxist critic. However, Eagleton has made theory accessible to students and nonspecialists, persistently reminding readers of its social role in the public sphere. He has provided a model for younger literary critics who self-consciously choose to write in a more journalistic mode, turning from the dense language and specialist focus of Grand Theory to address a larger public in discussing cultural issues. The tension in criticism between specialization and accessibility, which itself became a central theoretical issue in the 1990s, mirrors a perennial debate in literary studies—whether literature demonstrates special qualities available only to connoisseurs who have expert knowledge of the tradition, as articulated by the modernist T. S. ELIOT, or it can reach the common reader, in what the Romantic poet WILLIAM WORDSWORTH calls "the real language of men."

***Literary Theory: An Introduction* Keywords:** Ideology, Institutional Studies, Literary History, Marxism, Nationhood, Religion
***Culture and the Death of God* Keywords:** Literary History, Modernity, Popular Culture, Postmodernity, Religion, Subjectivity

From Literary Theory: An Introduction

From *Chapter 1. The Rise of English*

* * *

To speak of 'literature and ideology' as two separate phenomena which can be interrelated is, as I hope to have shown, in one sense quite unnecessary. Literature, in the meaning of the word we have inherited, *is* an ideology.[1] It has the most intimate relations to questions of social power. But if the reader is still unconvinced, the narrative of what happened to literature in the later nineteenth century might prove a little more persuasive.

If one were asked to provide a single explanation for the growth of English studies in the later nineteenth century, one could do worse than reply: 'the failure of religion'. By the mid-Victorian period, this traditionally reliable, immensely powerful ideological form was in deep trouble. It was no longer winning the hearts and minds of the masses, and under the twin impacts of scientific discovery and social change its previous unquestioned dominance was in danger of evaporating. This was particularly worrying for the Victorian ruling class, because religion is for all kinds of reasons an extremely effective form of ideological control. Like all successful ideologies, it works much less by explicit concepts or formulated doctrines than by image, symbol, habit, ritual and mythology. It is affective and experiential, entwining itself with the deepest unconscious roots of the human subject; and any social ideology which is unable to engage with such deep-seated a-rational fears and needs, as T. S. Eliot[2] knew, is unlikely to survive very long. Religion, moreover, is capable of operating at every social level: if there is a doctrinal inflection of it for the intellectual elite, there is also a pietistic brand of it for the masses. It provides an excellent social 'cement', encompassing pious peasant, enlightened middle-class liberal and theological intellectual in a single organization. Its ideological power lies in its capacity to 'materialize' beliefs as practices: religion is the sharing of the chalice and the blessing of the harvest, not just abstract argument about

1. That is, a system of specific class beliefs, images, values, and practices that functions to reproduce the dominant social order.

2. American-born English poet, critic, and dramatist (1888–1965; see above).

consubstantiation or hyperdulia.[3] Its ultimate truths, like those mediated by the literary symbol, are conveniently closed to rational demonstration, and thus absolute in their claims. Finally religion, at least in its Victorian forms, is a *pacifying* influence, fostering meekness, self-sacrifice and the contemplative inner life. It is no wonder that the Victorian ruling class looked on the threatened dissolution of this ideological discourse with something less than equanimity.

Fortunately, however, another remarkably similar discourse lay to hand: English literature. George Gordon,[4] early professor of english literature at Oxford, commented in his inaugural lecture that 'England is sick, and . . . English literature must save it. The Churches (as I understand) having failed, and social remedies being slow, English literature has now a triple function: still, I suppose, to delight and instruct us, but also, and above all, to save our souls and heal the State.'[5] Gordon's words were spoken in our own century, but they find a resonance everywhere in Victorian England. It is a striking thought that had it not been for this dramatic crisis in mid-nineteenth-century ideology, we might not today have such a plentiful supply of Jane Austen casebooks and bluffer's guides to Pound.[6] As religion progressively ceases to provide the social 'cement', affective values and basic mythologies by which a socially turbulent class-society can be welded together, 'English' is constructed as a subject to carry this ideological burden from the Victorian period onwards. The key figure here is Matthew Arnold,[7] always preternaturally sensitive to the needs of his social class, and engagingly candid about being so. The urgent social need, as Arnold recognizes, is to 'Hellenize' or cultivate the philistine middle class, who have proved unable to underpin their political and economic power with a suitably rich and subtle ideology. This can be done by transfusing into them something of the traditional style of the aristocracy, who as Arnold shrewdly perceives are ceasing to be the dominant class in England, but who have something of the ideological wherewithal to lend a hand to their middle-class masters. State-established schools, by linking the middle class to 'the best culture of their nation', will confer on them 'a greatness and a noble spirit, which the tone of these classes is not of itself at present adequate to impart'.[8]

The true beauty of this manoeuvre, however, lies in the effect it will have in controlling and incorporating the working class:

> It is of itself a serious calamity for a nation that its tone of feeling and grandeur of spirit should be lowered or dulled. But the calamity appears

3. The particular veneration of the Virgin Mary by Roman Catholics. "Consubstantiation": the Lutheran doctrine that the body and blood of Christ coexist with the elements of bread and wine during Holy Communion (a point of argument with the Roman Catholic belief in transubstantiation, the literal transformation of the consecrated bread and wine into the body and blood of Christ).
4. Oxford professor and critic (1881–1942).
5. Quoted by Chris Baldick, *The Social Mission of English Criticism, 1848–1932* (Oxford, 1983), p. 105 [Eagleton's note]. "To delight and instruct" are the traditional functions of literature; see HORACE, *Ars Poetica* (ca. 10 B.C.E.), lines 343–44, above.
6. Ezra Pound (1885–1972), American poet, editor, and critic, notable for his difficulty and abstruse range of literary references. Austen (1775–1817), English novelist.
7. English critic, poet, and school inspector (1822–1888; see above), who greatly influenced modern views of literature. In *Culture and Anarchy* (1869; see above) he divided England into Barbarians (the aristocracy), Philistines (the materialist middle classes), and the Populace; he also opposed "Hellenism" to "Hebraism," favoring the former (and classical Greek culture generally).
8. "The Popular Education of France," in *Democratic Education*, ed. R. H. Super (Ann Arbor, 1962), p. 22 [Eagleton's note].

> far more serious still when we consider that the middle classes, remaining as they are now, with their narrow, harsh, unintelligent, and unattractive spirit and culture, will almost certainly fail to mould or assimilate the masses below them, whose sympathies are at the present moment actually wider and more liberal than theirs. They arrive, these masses, eager to enter into possession of the world, to gain a more vivid sense of their own life and activity. In this their irrepressible development, their natural educators and initiators are those immediately above them, the middle classes. If these classes cannot win their sympathy or give them their direction, society is in danger of falling into anarchy.[9]

Arnold is refreshingly unhypocritical: there is no feeble pretence that the education of the working class is to be conducted chiefly for their own benefit, or that his concern with their spiritual condition is, in one of his own most cherished terms, in the least 'disinterested'. In the even more disarmingly candid words of a twentieth-century proponent of this view: 'Deny to working-class children any common share in the immaterial, and presently they will grow into the men who demand with menaces a communism of the material'.[1] If the masses are not thrown a few novels, they may react by throwing up a few barricades.

Literature was in several ways a suitable candidate for this ideological enterprise. As a liberal, 'humanizing' pursuit, it could provide a potent antidote to political bigotry and ideological extremism. Since literature, as we know, deals in universal human values rather than in such historical trivia as civil wars, the oppression of women or the dispossession of the English peasantry, it could serve to place in cosmic perspective the petty demands of working people for decent living conditions or greater control over their own lives, and might even with luck come to render them oblivious of such issues in their high-minded contemplation of eternal truths and beauties. English, as a Victorian handbook for English teachers put it, helps to 'promote sympathy and fellow feeling among all classes'; another Victorian writer speaks of literature as opening a 'serene and luminous region of truth where all may meet and expatiate in common', above 'the smoke and stir, the din and turmoil of man's lower life of care and business and debate'.[2] Literature would rehearse the masses in the habits of pluralistic thought and feeling, persuading them to acknowledge that more than one viewpoint than theirs existed—namely, that of their masters. It would communicate to them the moral riches of bourgeois civilization, impress upon them a reverence for middle-class achievements, and, since reading is an essentially solitary, contemplative activity, curb in them any disruptive tendency to collective political action. It would give them a pride in their national language and literature: if scanty education and extensive hours of labour prevented them personally from producing a literary masterpiece, they could take pleasure in the thought that others of their own kind—English people—had done so. The people, according to a study of English literature written in 1891, 'need political culture, instruction, that is to say, in what pertains to their relation to the State, to

9. Ibid., p. 26 [Eagleton's note].

1. George Sampson, *English for the English* (1921), quoted by Baldick, *The Social Mission of English Criticism*, p. 103 [Eagleton's note].

2. H. G. Robinson, "On the Use of English Classical Literature in the Work of Education," *Macmillan's Magazine* 11 (1860), quoted by Baldick, *The Social Mission of English Criticism*, p. 66 [Eagleton's note].

their duties as citizens; and they need also to be impressed sentimentally by having the presentation in legend and history of heroic and patriotic examples brought vividly and attractively before them'.[3] All of this, moreover, could be achieved without the cost and labour of teaching them the Classics: English literature was written in their own language, and so was conveniently available to them.

Like religion, literature works primarily by emotion and experience, and so was admirably well-fitted to carry through the ideological task which religion left off. Indeed by our own time literature had become effectively identical with the opposite of analytical thought and conceptual enquiry: whereas scientists, philosophers and political theorists are saddled with these drably discursive pursuits, students of literature occupy the more prized territory of feeling and experience. Whose experience, and what kinds of feeling, is a different question. Literature from Arnold onwards is the enemy of 'ideological dogma', an attitude which might have come as a surprise to Dante, Milton and Pope;[4] the truth or falsity of beliefs such as that blacks are inferior to whites is less important than what it feels like to experience them. Arnold himself had beliefs, of course, though like everybody else he regarded his own beliefs as reasoned positions rather than ideological dogmas. Even so, it was not the business of literature to communicate such beliefs directly—to argue openly, for example, that private property is the bulwark of liberty. Instead, literature should convey *timeless* truths, thus distracting the masses from their immediate commitments, nurturing in them a spirit of tolerance and generosity, and so ensuring the survival of private property. Just as Arnold attempted in *Literature and Dogma* and *God and the Bible*[5] to dissolve away the embarrassingly doctrinal bits of Christianity into poetically suggestive sonorities, so the pill of middle-class ideology was to be sweetened by the sugar of literature.

There was another sense in which the 'experiential' nature of literature was ideologically convenient. For 'experience' is not only the homeland of ideology, the place where it takes root most effectively; it is also in its literary form a kind of vicarious self-fulfillment. If you do not have the money and leisure to visit the Far East, except perhaps as a soldier in the pay of British imperialism, then you can always 'experience' it at second hand by reading Conrad or Kipling.[6] Indeed according to some literary theories this is even more real than strolling round Bangkok. The actually impoverished experience of the mass of people, an impoverishment bred by their social conditions, can be supplemented by literature: instead of working to change such conditions (which Arnold, to his credit, did more thoroughly than almost any of those who sought to inherit his mantle), you can vicariously fulfil someone's desire for a fuller life by handing them *Pride and Prejudice*.[7]

It is significant, then, that 'English' as an academic subject was first institutionalized not in the Universities, but in the Mechanics' Institutes, working

3. J. C. Collins, *The Study of English Literature* (1891), quoted by Baldick, *The Social Mission of English Criticism*, pp. 64–65 [Eagleton's note].

4. All three major poets—the Italian DANTE ALIGHIERI (1265–1321), the English John Milton (1608–1674), and ALEXANDER POPE (1688–1744)—held strong political views.

5. Published in 1873 and 1875, respectively.

6. Both these English writers—the Polish-born novelist Joseph Conrad (1857–1924) and the short story writer, poet, and novelist Rudyard Kipling (1865–1936)—often set their works in places under colonial rule (though not usually the Far East).

7. Jane Austen's best-known novel (published 1813).

men's colleges and extension lecturing circuits.[8] English was literally the poor man's Classics—a way of providing a cheapish 'liberal' education for those beyond the charmed circles of public school and Oxbridge.[9] From the outset, in the work of 'English' pioneers like F. D. Maurice and Charles Kingsley,[1] the emphasis was on solidarity between the social classes, the cultivation of 'larger sympathies', the instillation of national pride and the transmission of 'moral' values. This last concern—still the distinctive hallmark of literary studies in England, and a frequent source of bemusement to intellectuals from other cultures—was an essential part of the ideological project; indeed the rise of 'English' is more or less concomitant with an historic shift in the very meaning of the term 'moral', of which Arnold, Henry James and F. R. Leavis[2] are the major critical exponents. Morality is no longer to be grasped as a formulated code or explicit ethical system: it is rather a sensitive preoccupation with the whole quality of life itself, with the oblique, nuanced particulars of human experience. Somewhat rephrased, this can be taken as meaning that the old religious ideologies have lost their force, and that a more subtle communication of moral values, one which works by 'dramatic enactment' rather than rebarbative abstraction, is thus in order. Since such values are nowhere more vividly dramatized than in literature, brought home to 'felt experience' with all the unquestionable reality of a blow on the head, literature becomes more than just a handmaiden of moral ideology: it *is* moral ideology for the modern age, as the work of F. R. Leavis was most graphically to evince.

The working class was not the only oppressed layer of Victorian society at whom 'English' was specifically beamed. English literature, reflected a Royal Commission witness in 1877, might be considered a suitable subject for 'women . . . and the second- and third-rate men who [. . .] become schoolmasters.'[3] The 'softening' and 'humanizing' effects of English, terms recurrently used by its early proponents, are within the existing ideological stereotypes of gender clearly feminine. The rise of English in England ran parallel to the gradual, grudging admission of women to the institutions of higher education; and since English was an untaxing sort of affair, concerned with the finer feelings rather than with the more virile topics of *bona fide* academic 'disciplines', it seemed a convenient sort of non-subject to palm off on the ladies, who were in any case excluded from science and the professions. Sir Arthur Quiller Couch,[4] first professor of english at Cambridge University, would open with the word 'Gentlemen' lectures addressed to a hall filled largely with women. Though modern male lecturers may have changed their manners, the ideological conditions which make English a popular University subject for women to read have not.

If English had its feminine aspect, however, it also acquired a masculine one as the century drew on. The era of the academic establishment of English

8. See Lionel Gossman, "Literature and Education," *New Literary History* 13.2 (1982): 341–71. See also D. J. Palmer, *The Rise of English Studies* (London, 1965) [Eagleton's note].

9. Oxford and Cambridge Universities; both date to the 12th century. "Public school": in Great Britain, endowed boarding schools, whose curriculum traditionally has been largely classical.

1. English clergyman, social reformer, and novelist (1819–1875). Maurice (1805–1872), English theologian, clergyman, and writer.

2. English literary critic (1895–1978; see above) and editor of the influential journal *Scrutiny*. JAMES (1843–1916), American novelist and critic.

3. Quoted by Gossman, "Literature and Education," pp. 341–42 [Eagleton's note].

4. English critic (1863–1944).

is also the era of high imperialism in England. As British capitalism became threatened and progressively outstripped by its younger German and American rivals, the squalid, undignified scramble of too much capital chasing too few overseas territories, which was to culminate in 1914 in the first imperialist world war, created the urgent need for a sense of national mission and identity. What was at stake in English studies was less English *literature* than *English* literature: our great 'national poets' Shakespeare and Milton, the sense of an 'organic' national tradition and identity to which new recruits could be admitted by the study of humane letters. The reports of educational bodies and official enquiries into the teaching of English, in this period and in the early twentieth century, are strewn with nostalgic back-references to the 'organic' community of Elizabethan England[5] in which nobles and groundlings found a common meeting-place in the Shakespearian theatre, and which might still be reinvented today. It is no accident that the author of one of the most influential Government reports in this area, *The Teaching of English in England* (1921), was none other than Sir Henry Newbolt,[6] minor jingoist poet and perpetrator of the immortal line 'Play up! play up! and play the game!' Chris Baldick has pointed to the importance of the admission of English literature to the Civil Service examinations in the Victorian period: armed with this conveniently packaged version of their own cultural treasures, the servants of British imperialism could sally forth overseas secure in a sense of their national identity, and able to display that cultural superiority to their envying colonial peoples.[7]

It took rather longer for English, a subject fit for women, workers and those wishing to impress the natives, to penetrate the bastions of ruling-class power in Oxford and Cambridge. English was an upstart, amateurish affair as academic subjects went, hardly able to compete on equal terms with the rigours of Greats or philology;[8] since every English gentleman read his own literature in his spare time anyway, what was the point of submitting it to systematic study? Fierce rearguard actions were fought by both ancient Universities against this distressingly dilettante subject: the definition of an academic subject was what could be examined,[9] and since English was no more than idle gossip about literary taste it was difficult to know how to make it unpleasant enough to qualify as a proper academic pursuit. This, it might be said, is one of the few problems associated with the study of English which have since been effectively resolved. The frivolous contempt for his subject displayed by the first really 'literary' Oxford professor, Sir Walter Raleigh, has to be read to be believed.[1] Raleigh held his post in the years leading up to the First World War; and his relief at the outbreak of the war, an event which allowed him to abandon the feminine vagaries of literature and put his pen to something more manly—war propaganda—is palpable in his writing. The only way in which English seemed likely to justify its existence in the ancient Universities was by systematically mistaking itself

5. That is, England during the reign (1558–1603) of Queen Elizabeth I (1533–1603), the period during which Shakespeare wrote many of his plays.

6. English poet, historian, and novelist (1862–1938); Eagleton quotes "Vitaï Lampada" from *The Island Race* (1898).

7. See Baldick, *The Social Mission of English Criticism*, pp. 70–72 [Eagleton's note].

8. The study of cultures through historical analyses of their languages. "Greats": studies of Greek and Latin literature, history, and philosophy.

9. Tested.

1. See Baldick, *The Social Mission of English Criticism*, pp. 76–79 [Eagleton's note]. Raleigh (1861–1922), English scholar, essayist, and critic.

for the Classics; but the classicists were hardly keen to have this pathetic parody of themselves around.

If the first imperialist world war more or less put paid to Sir Walter Raleigh, providing him with an heroic identity more comfortingly in line with that of his Elizabethan namesake,[2] it also signalled the final victory of English studies at Oxford and Cambridge. One of the most strenuous antagonists of English—philology—was closely bound up with Germanic influence; and since England happened to be passing through a major war with Germany, it was possible to smear classical philology as a form of ponderous Teutonic nonsense with which no self-respecting Englishman should be caught associating.[3] England's victory over Germany meant a renewal of national pride, an upsurge of patriotism which could only aid English's cause; but at the same time the deep trauma of the war, its almost intolerable questioning of every previously held cultural assumption, gave rise to a 'spiritual hungering', as one contemporary commentator described it, for which poetry seemed to provide an answer. It is a chastening thought that we owe the University study of English, in part at least, to a meaningless massacre. The Great War, with its carnage of ruling-class rhetoric, put paid to some of the more strident forms of chauvinism on which English had previously thrived: there could be few more Walter Raleighs after Wilfred Owen.[4] English Literature rode to power on the back of wartime nationalism; but it also represented a search for spiritual solutions on the part of an English ruling class whose sense of identity had been profoundly shaken, whose psyche was ineradicably scarred by the horrors it had endured. Literature would be at once solace and reaffirmation, a familiar ground on which Englishmen could regroup both to explore, and to find some alternative to, the nightmare of history.

* * *

1983

From Culture and the Death of God

From *Chapter 6. Modernism and After*

As the power of religion begins to fail, its various functions are redistributed like a precious legacy to those aspiring to become its heirs. Scientific rationalism takes over its doctrinal certainties, while radical politics inherits its mission to transform the face of the earth. Culture in the aesthetic sense safeguards something of its spiritual depth. Indeed, most aesthetic ideas (creation, inspiration, unity, autonomy, symbol, epiphany and so on) are really displaced fragments of theology. Signs which accomplish what they signify are known as poetry to aesthetics and as sacraments to theology. Meanwhile, culture in the wider sense of the word retains something of

2. The soldier, courtier, and poet Sir Walter Ralegh (1552–1618). "Put paid to": dealt effectually with; put an end to.
3. See Francis Mulhern, *The Moment of "Scrutiny"* (London, 1979), pp. 20–22 [Eagleton's note].
4. English poet (1893–1918), who wrote about his experiences as a soldier in World War I; he died in combat.

religion's communitarian ethos. Science, philosophy, culture and politics, needless to say, survive the decline of religion as enterprises in their own right. Yet they are also called on to shoulder some of its offices, alongside their own proper business.

Like religion, high culture plays a double role, offering a critique of modern civilisation but also a refuge from its degeneracy. * * *

It is remarkable how resilient the faith that art might prove our salvation turns out to be. It is Nietzsche's[1] theme from start to finish. It is a hope which is able to survive the collapse of the high Victorian consensus and the carnage of the First World War. Versions of it are to be found in both Bloomsbury and *Scrutiny*,[2] sworn enemies in so much else. Art is a fortress against an encroaching barbarism. 'Poetry,' writes I. A. Richards with stunning credulity, 'is capable of saving us; it is a perfectly possible means of overcoming chaos.'[3] F. R. Leavis speaks of confronting a crassly materialistic society with the 'religious depth of thought and feeling' to be found in great literature.[4] 'After one has abandoned a belief in God,' remarks Wallace Stevens, 'poetry is that essence which takes its place as life's redemption.'[5] 'Poetry / Exceeding music must take the place / Of empty heaven and its hymns', he writes in 'The Man with the Blue Guitar.' It is a note one can hear sounded as early as Mallarmé,[6] for whom the proper role of art is to succeed religion. Having done service for theology in its time, the aesthetic now makes a bid to supplant it. High modernism is numinous through and through, as the work of art provides one of the last outposts of enchantment in a spiritually degenerate world. Postmodernism, with its notorious absence of affect, is post-numinous. It is also in a sense post-aesthetic, since the aestheticisation of everyday life extends to the point where it undermines the very idea of a special phenomenon known as art. Stretched far enough, the category of the aesthetic cancels itself out.

The imagination as a means of grace is one of modernism's abiding motifs, from the redemptive power of memory in Proust's great novel to the priestly vocation of the Joycean artist.[7] Henry James[8] finds in art a form of saintly self-immolation. Epiphanies of transcendence haunt the fiction of Woolf and the poetry of Rilke.[9] An anthropology based on death, sacrifice and rebirth underlies the most renowned of English modernist poems. Its author will argue later in his *Notes Towards the Definition of Culture*[1] that the culture

1. FRIEDRICH NIETZSCHE (1844–1900), German philosopher who notoriously declared that "God is dead" and debunked metaphysical conceptions of existence; he stressed the value of art and artistry.
2. The most influential English critical journal of its time (active 1932–53), principally edited by F. R. LEAVIS (1895–1978), a major British critic who found fundamental moral value in literature; critics associated with it were somewhat mockingly called "Scrutineers." "Bloomsbury" is shorthand for the Bloomsbury group, a circle of writers, artists, and critics highly skeptical of traditional values (notably the novelist and critic VIRGINIA WOOLF, 1882–1941), several of whom lived near London's Bloomsbury Square, who met from about 1910 to the early 1930s.
3. I. A. Richards, *Science and Poetry* (London, 1926), pp. 82–83 [Eagleton's note]. Richards (1893–1979), English literary critic and theorist.
4. F. R. Leavis, *Two Cultures? The Significance of C. P. Snow* (London, 1962), p. 23 [Eagleton's note].
5. Wallace Stevens, *Opus Posthumous* (New York, 1977), p. 158 [Eagleton's note]. Stevens (1879–1955), American modernist poet.
6. Stéphane Mallarmé (1842–1898), French symbolist poet and critic.
7. In *A Portrait of the Artist as a Young Man* (1916), the Irish novelist James Joyce (1882–1941) sanctifies the role of the writer. The great novel by the French novelist Marcel Proust (1871–1922) is *In Search of Lost Time* (7 vols., 1913–27).
8. Major American writer (1843–1916); see above.
9. Rainer Maria Rilke (1875–1926), Austrian modernist poet.
1. Work of criticism (1948) by T. S. ELIOT (1888–1965), American-born British poet and critic, who converted to the Church of England in 1927. His most renowned poem is *The Waste Land* (1922).

of a people must be founded on religion if it is to thrive. Not many modernist artists, however, happened to be devout Anglo-Catholics, and their preferred strategy was accordingly for culture to replace religion rather than to rest upon it. The shadow of the death of God still falls over the work of one of the most resolutely secular of twentieth-century critics, Frank Kermode, for whose *Sense of an Ending*[2] myths, both religious and political, must give way to self-conscious fictions.

God is not exactly dead, but he has turned his hinderparts to humanity, who can now sense his unbearable presence only in his ominous absence. * * *

With the advent of modernism, the two main senses of culture, aesthetic and anthropological, are increasingly riven apart. They can converge only in such imaginary worlds as Lawrence's Mexico, Yeats's Anglo-Irish estate, the organic society of the Scrutineers, Eliot's stratified Christian society, the aesthetic South of the American New Critics or Heidegger's vision of a philosophical inquiry conducted among the peasantry.[3] (Adorno[4] retorted that one would like to know the peasants' opinion of that.) The contest between culture as art and culture as form of life is one between minority and popular culture, which from now on confront one another as mortal rivals. Modernism is among other things a defensive reaction to the culture industry, with which it was twinned at birth. The dream of the radical Enlightenment—of a culture which would be both learned and popular, resourceful enough to challenge the reigning powers but sufficiently lucid to rally the common people to its standard—would now seem definitively over. So would the radical-Romantic hope of uniting art, culture and politics in a common project. It was a time for distinctions rather than syntheses.

* * *

* * * From the 1980s onward, culture in the sense of art became increasingly populist, streetwise and vernacular, while culture as a form of life was aestheticised from end to end. For the Hellenists and Romantics,[5] the latter meant the kind of common life that was creatively fulfilling; for postmodernism, rather less euphorically, it meant a politics and economy dependent on the image. The long-dreamt-of marriage of art and everyday life, which for the revolutionary avant-garde was consummated in political murals or agitprop theatre, could be found instead in fashion and design, the media and public relations, advertising agencies and recording studios. Culture opened its arms to the everyday life that *Kulturkritik*[6] had regarded as its nemesis.

2. A book (1967) by Kermode (1919–2010), a British literary critic, that describes the modernist feeling of exhaustion.

3. The German philosopher MARTIN HEIDEGGER (1889–1976) presents peasants as closer than others to the relation between earth and world in a major essay, "The Origin of the Work of Art" (1937). The English writer D. H. Lawrence (1885–1930) paints an idealized picture in his travel essays in *Mornings in Mexico* (1927). The ruined castle purchased by the Irish poet W. B. Yeats (1865–1939) was an important symbol in some of his best poems. Eliot espoused hierarchical Anglican views, notably in "The Idea of a Christian Society" (1939). A number of the New Critics, such as JOHN CROWE RANSOM and CLEANTH BROOKS, found special value in the agrarian South of the United States.

4. THEODORE ADORNO (1903–1969), German philosopher and member of the Frankfurt School, which stressed Marxist criticism of mass society.

5. During the late 18th and early 19th centuries, Romantic poets such as WILLIAM WORDSWORTH foregrounded the value of ordinary life and the "language of the common man." Hellenists embraced classical Greece as providing ideals of beauty and democracy.

6. Cultural criticism (German): specifically, a form of it produced in the early 20th century and variously espoused by Adorno, Eliot, and Leavis that, influenced by modernism, excoriated the dangers of mass society and popular taste.

What it gained in democratic terms, however, it abandoned in critical ones. *Kulturkritik*, with its high-minded contempt for everyday habits, was an elitist vein of conservatism; postmodernism, with its fusion of art and commerce, is a populist one. If *Kulturkritik* is too caustic in its view of the commonplace, postmodernism is too complicit. Both look askance at the way of life of the majority—*Kulturkritik* because of what it sees as its dreary mediocrity, postmodernism because it falsely assumes that consensuses and majorities are inherently benighted, and thus has an ideological preference for margins and minorities. *Kulturkritik* is disdainful of such humdrum questions as state, class, economy and political organisation; postmodernism, entranced by the liminal, aberrant and transgressive, can muster scarcely more enthusiasm for them.

* * * Modernism involves a readiness to encounter dark, Dionysian forces,[7] even the possibility of total dissolution, in its zealous pursuit of the truth. Postmodernism sees no such necessity. It is too young to recall a time when there was (so it is alleged) truth, unity, totality, objectivity, universals, absolute values, stable identities and rock-solid foundations, and thus finds nothing disquieting in their apparent absence. It differs in this sense from its modernist precursors, who are close enough to the original catastrophe to be still reeling from the shock waves. For postmodernism, by contrast, there is no fragmentation, since unity was an illusion all along; no false consciousness, because no unequivocal truth; no shaking of the foundations, since there were none to be dislodged. It is not as though truth, identity and foundations are tormentingly elusive, simply that they never were. They have not vanished for ever, leaving only a spectre behind them. There is no phantom limb syndrome here. Their absence is no more palpable than the absence of a hairdryer in the hands of the Mona Lisa.[8] One would no more mourn the lack of these things than one would lament the fact that a pig cannot recite *Paradise Lost*.[9] As Richard Rorty[1] might put it, there is no point in scratching where it doesn't itch.

Whereas modernism experiences the death of God as a trauma, an affront, a source of anguish as well as a cause for celebration, postmodernism does not experience it at all. There is no God-shaped hole at the centre of its universe, as there is at the centre of Kafka, Beckett or even Philip Larkin.[2] Indeed, there is no gap of any kind in its universe. This is one of several reasons why postmodernism is post-tragic. Tragedy involves the possibility of irretrievable loss, whereas for postmodernism there is nothing momentous missing. It is just that we have failed to register this fact in our compulsively idealising hunt for higher, nobler, deeper things. In any case, tragedy is thought to require a certain depth of subjectivity, which is one reason why

7. That is, the frenzied, ecstatic chaotic creative forces associated with Dionysus, the Greek god of wine and vegetation, which Nietzsche sets against Apollonian order and individuation in *The Birth of Tragedy* (1872; see above).

8. Iconic painting of a woman (ca. 1510), seated with folded hands, by Leonardo da Vinci.

9. Epic poem (1667, 1674) by John Milton, generally viewed as one of the greatest poems in the English language.

1. American philosopher (1931–2007) who argued against metaphysical or epistemological foundationalism, favoring instead a form of pragmatism.

2. English poet (1922–1985), known for anti-Romantic, colloquial, and often dark verse. Samuel Beckett (1906–1989), Irish-born writer who published in both English and French; in his best-known work, the play *Waiting for Godot* (1952), two characters vainly await the arrival of "Godot." Franz Kafka (1883–1924), Austrian writer who lived most of his life in Prague and wrote in German; his fictions are often strange and sometimes nightmarish parables of anxiety and alienation.

it might appear to be lacking in Beckett. The postmodern subject is hard-pressed to find enough depth and continuity in itself to be a suitable candidate for tragic self-dispossession. You cannot give away a self you never had. If there is no longer a God, it is partly because there is no longer any secret interior place where he might install himself. Depth and interiority belong to a clapped-out metaphysics, and to eradicate them is to abolish God by rooting out the underground places where he has been concealing himself. For psychoanalysis, by contrast, the human subject is diffused and unstable yet furnished with inner depths. Indeed, the two facts are closely allied. It thus ranks among the latter-day inheritors of the tragic sense, as postmodernism does not.

* * *

If postmodern culture is depthless, anti-tragic, non-linear, anti-numinous, non-foundational and anti-universalist, suspicious of absolutes and averse to interiority, one might claim that it is genuinely post-religious, as modernism most certainly is not. Most religious thought, for example, posits a universal humanity, since a God who concerned himself with only a particular section of the species, say Bosnians or people over five foot eight inches tall, would appear lacking in the impartial benevolence appropriate to a Supreme Being. There must also be some common ground between ourselves and Abraham[3] for the Hebrew Scriptures to make sense. Postmodernism, however, is notoriously nervous of universals, despite its claim that grand narratives have everywhere disappeared from the earth, or that there are no stable identities to be found, wherever one looks. As a current of thought, it inherits most of those aspects of Nietzsche's philosophy that make for atheism; but since in its streetwise style it rejects the notion of the *Übermensch*,[4] it refuses to smuggle in a new form of divinity to replace the old. Sceptical of the whole concept of a universal humanity, it repudiates Man as well as God, and in doing so refuses the quasi-religious consolations of humanism. In this sense, Nietzsche's warning that the Almighty will only rest quiet in his grave when Man lies alongside him is finally taken seriously.

* * *

Since Man is no longer to be seen primarily as agent or creator, he is no longer in danger of being mistaken for the Supreme Being. He has finally attained maturity, but only at the cost of relinquishing his identity. He is not to be seen as self-determining, which is what freedom means for the likes of Kant and Hegel.[5] The self is no longer coherent enough to be so. This is certainly one way in which postmodernism is post-theological, since it is God above all who is One, and who is the ground of his own being. It follows that if you want to be shot of[6] him, you need to refashion the concept of subjectivity itself, which is just what postmodernism seeks to do. It is easier to accomplish this if the capitalist system happens to be in transit from the subject as producer to the subject as consumer. Consumers are passive, dif-

3. The first of the three biblical patriarchs.
4. Overman (German), a concept from Nietzsche's *Thus Spoke Zarathustra* (1883–85) that signifies a goal toward which superior humans should strive.
5. Two major German idealist philosophers, IMMANUEL KANT (1724–1804) and GEORG WILHELM FRIEDRICH HEGEL (1770–1831).
6. Rid of.

fuse, provisional subjects, which is not quite how the Almighty is traditionally portrayed. As long as men and women are seen as producers, labourers, manufacturers or self-fashioners, God can never quite expire. Behind every act of production lurks an image of Creation, and one act of production in particular—art—rivals that of the Almighty himself. Not even he, however, can survive the advent of Man the Eternal Consumer.

Perhaps, then, the latter decades of the twentieth century will be seen as the time when the deity was finally put to death. With the advent of postmodern culture, a nostalgia for the numinous is finally banished. It is not so much that there is no redemption as that there is nothing to be redeemed. Religion, to be sure, lives on, since there is more to late modern civilisation than postmodernism. Even so, after a long succession of botched projects, flawed strategies and theoretical cul-de-sacs, it would not be too much to claim that with the emergence of postmodernism, human history arrives for the first time at an authentic atheism. It is true that postmodern thought pays an enormous price for this coming of age, if coming of age it is. In writing off religion, it also dismisses a good many other momentous questions as so much metaphysical illusion. If it abjures religion, it does so, as we have seen, at the cost of renouncing depth, of which it is notably nervous. It thereby abandons a good deal else of value.

It is true that postmodernism retains the odd trace of transcendence, not least in its somewhat fetishistic cult of otherness. Yet though there is otherness in plenty, there is no Big Other, no grand totality or transcendental signifier. Besides, though other cultures may be incommensurate with one's own, there is no other to culture itself. Culture goes all the way down, as God himself was once thought to do. It is a shamefaced form of foundationalism. Culture is what you cannot peer behind or dig beneath, since the peering and digging would themselves be cultural procedures. It thus operates as a kind of absolute, as culture in a loftier sense of the term did for Arnold.[7] Yet this is culture as transcendental rather than transcendent—as the condition of possibility of all phenomena, rather than as some sacred domain beyond their orbit.

There are also traces of the transcendent in the bogus spirituality of some postmodern cultures. It is the kind of soft-centred, cut-price religiosity one would expect from a thoroughly materialist society. A muddled sense of mystery is the only form of faith to which such hard-headed societies can aspire, rather as broad humour is the only comedy with which the humourless feel at ease. So it is that those who cannot conceive of an end to Wall Street are perfectly capable of believing in Kabbalah.[8] It comes as no surprise that Scientology, packaged Sufism,[9] off-the-peg occultism and ready-to-serve transcendental meditation should figure as fashionable pastimes among the super-rich, or that Hollywood should turn its eyes to Hinduism. The hard-boiled who believe in nothing turn out to be the kind of fantasists who will believe in anything. It is the worldly and well-heeled who think of

7. Matthew Arnold (1822–1888), English poet and critic who stressed—especially in *Culture and Anarchy* (1867; see above)—that culture, composed of "the best that has been known and thought," serves an important social purpose of preventing anarchy.

8. An esoteric school of Jewish mysticism (literally, "Tradition"; Hebrew).

9. Mystical Islamic beliefs and practice. Scientology: a body of religious beliefs promulgated by a church founded in 1954 by the American science fiction author L. Ron Hubbard.

religion as cosmic harmony and esoteric cult, rather as the idea of the artist as a shock-haired bohemian, so James Joyce once pointed out, is the respectable burgher's view of him. Feeding the hungry is too close to filling in one's tax return for those in search of an escape from the mundane. The point of spirituality is to cater for needs that one's stylist or stockbroker cannot fulfil. Yet all this reach-me-down otherworldliness is really a form of atheism. It is a way of feeling uplifted without the gross inconvenience of God.

* * *

2014

STEPHEN J. GREENBLATT
b. 1943

In 1980 literary discussion in the United States was dominated by debates over theory, especially over the status of language, as scholars questioned its referential value and its power to construct or undo meaning. A group of younger critics, several of them at the University of California at Berkeley, were instead turning their attention to the concrete particularities of history. But rather than simply amassing facts, as did traditional literary historians, they used more creative methods, most notably drawing on anecdotes, to illuminate the context of literature. A leading member of that group was Stephen J. Greenblatt, who coined the term "the new historicism" to describe the kind of literary history that he and his colleagues were writing, and who has become the leading critic of Shakespeare of his generation. In our selection, from his essay "Resonance and Wonder" (1990), he explains his sense of literary history, which accounts for the aesthetic wonder that texts arouse as well as their historical resonance.

Born in the Boston area, Greenblatt is the son of a lawyer and grandson of Lithuanian immigrants, as he recounts in some of his essays. He received his B.A. in 1964 from Yale University, where his undergraduate thesis on modern British novelists won a Yale College award and was published in 1965, and where he earned his Ph.D. in 1969. In between undergraduate and graduate work, he spent two years at Cambridge University in England, attending lectures with RAYMOND WILLIAMS and developing his interest in Renaissance literature. He taught at the University of California at Berkeley from 1969 to 1997; he then moved to Harvard University, where he holds a University Professorship of the Humanities. Among his many honors, he served as president of the Modern Language Association in 2002. Building from his studies of Renaissance literature, he has become a prominent public figure in the humanities, serving as general editor of *The Norton Shakespeare* (1997; 3d ed., 2015) and writing the popular biographical study *Will in the World* (2004), which was a finalist for a Pulitzer Prize; taking over the editorship of the major college textbook in English, *The Norton Anthology of English Literature*, in 1999; and lecturing around the globe.

The dominant mode of criticism in the United States when Greenblatt was in college was the New Criticism, and in fact several influential New Critics were at Yale, notably CLEANTH BROOKS and WILLIAM K. WIMSATT JR. They were formalists, holding that literary criticism should attend only to the "verbal icon" and its internal features, and ruling out attention to the work's author, audience, or context. Three Yale Ph.D. students eventually gained fame by turning those formalist prohibitions on their head. In the face of the "intentional fallacy," HAROLD BLOOM focused on the author and his psychic struggle with his predecessors to establish himself in the great tradition. In the face of the "affective fallacy," STANLEY FISH posited that meaning was not in the poem but in the reader. And in the face of bans against considering external matter, Greenblatt focused on both the biographical and historical circumstances surrounding literary works. While not avoiding aesthetic analysis, he showed how history enhanced the interpretation of, for instance, a Shakespeare play. In a famous chapter in *Shakespearean Negotiations* (1988), he tells the story of a trial of a transvestite in France during the Renaissance as a way to explain some of the dilemmas of marriage and gender in Shakespeare's *Twelfth Night* (1601).

Though he named the New Historicism, Greenblatt has been less invested in elaborating a theoretical program than in practical criticism. Still, he has assimilated a variety of theoretical positions along the way. He remarks that studying at Cambridge, especially with Raymond Williams, opened his eyes to the social aspects of literature. But he did not become a Marxist, as Williams was, and he also drew from MICHEL FOUCAULT and from cultural anthropology. Like Foucault's *Discipline and Punish* (1975; see above), which starts its examination of the way that modern society exerts control through subtle discipline rather than overt force with a striking story of an execution, Greenblatt's analyses often begin with an anecdote, unusual detail, or incidental object, like Cardinal Wolsey's cap in "Resonance and Wonder." From Foucault he and many of the New Historicists developed the idea that modern society operates through "subversion and containment"—that is, while it seems that some practices subvert discipline, such resistance is regularly incorporated back into the system. For instance, we might protest an unjust action of our government, but our act of protesting affirms that we have a free society, and therefore reinforces society's overall control rather than disturbing it. From anthropologists, Greenblatt takes ideas of the circulation and exchange of cultural practices, which he uses in showing how a play might represent the dynamics of gender. Greenblatt also is a fellow traveler of poststructuralists, holding that history is textual, constructed, and self-contradictory rather than offering a record of events as they actually happened, as he notes in our selection. We "know" the reign of Henry VIII only through Shakespeare's plays and other texts, and through artifacts like Wolsey's hat.

In "Resonance and Wonder," Greenblatt defines the New Historicism as "an interest . . . in the embeddedness of cultural objects in the contingencies of history." While usually less interested in elaborating a theory than in bringing past texts to life, in this essay Greenblatt programmatically reflects on his position. His stress on history departs from the New Criticism as well as from more recent modes of criticism, like deconstruction, that concentrate on the linguistic attributes of literature. The main target of "Resonance and Wonder," though, is traditional historicism, and he rebuts three standard views. By stressing contingency, Greenblatt distances himself from more deterministic views, such as Marxism, which hold that history follows a teleological path rooted in class struggle. He also counters the idea of scholarly objectivity, the notion that one merely reports facts; rather, New Historicists see their work as interested and aim to intervene in cultural debates—for instance, to dispel rigid, normative ideas of gender. His third attack is on the veneration of history as stable and coherent fact. As he remarks, New Historicists are "as concerned with the margins as with the center," examining the contradictions and conflicts as well as the resolutions.

Though Greenblatt is known for revivifying the study of history, one key that undergirds "Resonance and Wonder" and his work overall is his interest in the literary. While his stress on "resonance" reminds us that literary works are not icons but historical objects spun from a web of cultural practices, his stress on "wonder" forestalls the reduction of a work to its historical context. Rather, it reaffirms the uniqueness of the literary object, through its aesthetic power "to stop the viewer in his tracks." In this regard, Greenblatt represents a revival of literary criticism and aesthetic appreciation over theory; often overlooked is the influence on his work of ERICH AUERBACH, who studied literary masterpieces across Western culture in his classic *Mimesis* (1953; see above). Auerbach opens each chapter with a brief quotation from a literary work, from which he builds his arguments about the shift in cultural representation over two thousand years. As Greenblatt discusses in *Practicing New Historicism* (2000), anecdotes play a similar role for him. They sometimes seem random, but from them Greenblatt builds a sense of an era. Greenblatt's anecdotes try to effect what he has called "the touch of the real," re-creating the social and cultural negotiations of a historical moment.

Although Greenblatt has largely avoided theoretical battles, his work has been criticized on various grounds. Traditionalists appreciate his high valuation of literature, but feel he brings extraneous material into the field. More radical critics, often from the Marxist side, have attacked him for not taking a strong political stand and for having a vague sense of historical causality; he often juxtaposes objects or events that lack a verifiable historical connection—for example, a trial in France and an English play. Ironically, it is probably because he takes a nonpolemical stance, and maintains the importance of literature, that Greenblatt has become a leading representative of literary studies and the world's leading commentator on Shakespeare.

"Resonance and Wonder" Keywords: Aesthetics, The Canon/Tradition, Drama, Formalism, Literary History, Marxism, New Historicism, Poststructuralism

From Resonance and Wonder

In a small glass case in the library of Christ Church, Oxford, there is a round, red priest's hat; a note card identifies it as having belonged to Cardinal Wolsey.[1] It is altogether appropriate that this hat should have wound up at Christ Church, for the college owed its existence to Wolsey, who had decided at the height of his power to found in his own honor a magnificent new Oxford college. But the hat was not a direct bequest; historical forces, as we sometimes say—in this case taking the ominous form of Henry VIII—intervened, and Christ Church, like Hampton Court Palace,[2] was cut off from its original benefactor. Instead, the note informs us, the hat was acquired for Christ Church in the eighteenth century, purchased, we are told, from a company of players. If this miniature history of an artifact is too vague to be of much consequence—I do not know the name of the company of players, or the circumstances in which they acquired their curious stage property, or whether it was ever used, for example, by an actor playing Wolsey in Shakespeare's *Henry VIII*,[3] or when it was placed under glass, or even whether it was anything but a clever fraud—it nonetheless evokes a vision of cultural production that I find compelling. The peregrinations of Wolsey's

1. Thomas Wolsey (ca. 1475–1530), English prelate and statesman who was both a Roman Catholic cardinal (1515–30) and Lord Chancellor (1515–29) under Henry VIII, king of England (1491–1547; reigned 1509–47). Wolsey was charged with treason after failing to obtain the divorce from Catherine of Aragon sought by Henry VIII, but he died before his trial. Wolsey founded Cardinal College in 1525; it was refounded as Christ Church in 1546.
2. A huge palace complex, in outer London, built by Wolsey, then taken over and expanded by Henry VIII.
3. A history play (1613), written in collaboration with John Fletcher.

hat suggest that cultural artifacts do not stay still, that they exist in time, and that they are bound up with personal and institutional conflicts, negotiations, and appropriations.

The term culture has, in the case of the hat, a convenient material referent—a bit of red cloth stitched together—but that referent is only a tiny element in a complex symbolic construction that originally marked the transformation of Wolsey from a butcher's son to a prince of the church. Wolsey's gentleman usher, George Cavendish,[4] has left a remarkably circumstantial contemporary account of that construction, an account that enables us even to glimpse the hat or as Cavendish terms it, the "pillion," in its place, on the Cardinal's head.

> And after Mass he would return in his privy chamber again and, being advertised of the furniture of his chamber without[5] with noblemen and gentlemen . . . , would issue out into them apparelled all in red in the habit of a Cardinal; which was either of fine scarlet or else of crimson satin, taffeta, damask, or caffa [a rich silk cloth], the best that he could get for money; and upon his head a round pillion with a neck of black velvet, set to the same in the inner side. . . . There was also borne before him first the Great Seal of England, and then his Cardinal's hat by a nobleman or some worthy gentleman right solemnly, bareheaded. And as soon as he was entered into his chamber of presence[6] where was attending his coming to await upon him to Westminster Hall, as well noblemen and other worthy gentlemen as noblemen and gentlemen of his own family; thus passing forth with two great crosses of silver borne before him, with also two great pillars of silver, and his sergeant at arms with a great mace of silver gilt. Then his gentlemen ushers cried and said, 'On my lords and masters, make way for my lord's grace!'"[7]

The extraordinary theatricality of this manifestation of clerical power did not escape the notice of the Protestant reformers who called the Catholic church "the Pope's playhouse." When the Reformation in England[8] dismantled the histrionic apparatus of Catholicism, they sold some of its gorgeous properties to the professional players—not only a mark of thrift but a polemical gesture, signifying that the sanctified vestments were in reality mere trumpery whose proper place was a disreputable world of illusion-mongering. In exchange for this polemical service, the theatrical joint-stock companies received more than an attractive, cut-rate wardrobe; they acquired the tarnished but still potent charisma that clung to the old vestments, charisma

4. English poet (1494–ca. 1561); a member of Wolsey's household until the cardinal's death and author of *The Life and Death of Cardinal Wolsey* (written ca. 1554–58, and widely circulated in manuscript; printed 1641).

5. That is, being told that the chamber outside his private room was occupied.

6. That is, the ceremonial room where others waited for (attended) him.

7. George Cavendish, *The Life and Death of Cardinal Wolsey*, in *Two Early Tudor Lives*, ed. Richard S. Sylvester and Davis P. Harding (New Haven and London: Yale University Press, 1962), pp. 24–25. We get another glimpse of the symbolism of hats later in the text, when Wolsey is beginning his precipitous fall from power: "And talking with Master Norris upon his knees in the mire, he would have pulled off his under cap of velvet, but he could not undo the knot under his chin. Wherefore with violence he rent the laces and pulled it from his head and so kneeled bareheaded" (p. 106) [Greenblatt's note]. The Great Seal of England, now the Great Seal of the Realm, is used by the presiding monarch to authorize official documents. Westminster Hall served many governmental purposes and now is where the houses of Parliament meet.

8. The break with the Catholic Church by Henry VIII, who issued the Act of Supremacy (1534) that rejected papal control and created the national Church of England.

that in paradoxical fashion the players at once emptied out and heightened. By the time Wolsey's hat reached the library at Christ Church, its charisma must have been largely exhausted, but the college could confer upon it the prestige of an historical curiosity, as a trophy of the distant founder. And in its glass case it still radiates a tiny quantum of cultural energy.

Tiny indeed—I may already have seemed to make much more of this trivial relic than it deserves. But I am fascinated by transmigrations of the kind I have just sketched here—from theatricalized rituals to the stage to the university library or museum—because they seem to reveal something critically important about the *textual* relics with which my profession is obsessed. They enable us to glimpse the social process through which objects, gestures, rituals, and phrases are fashioned and moved from one zone of display to another. The display cases with which I am most involved—books—characteristically conceal this process, so that we have a misleading impression of fixity and little sense of the historical transactions through which the great texts we study have been fashioned. Let me give a literary example, an appropriately tiny textual equivalent of Wolsey's hat. At the close of Shakespeare's *Midsummer Night's Dream*,[9] the Fairy King Oberon declares that he and his attendants are going to bless the beds of the three couples who have just been married. This ritual of blessing will ensure the happiness of the newlyweds and ward off moles, harelips, and other prodigious marks that would disfigure their offspring. "With this field-dew consecrate," the Fairy King concludes,

> Every fairy take his gait,
> And each several chamber bless,
> Through this palace, with sweet peace,
> And the owner of it blest
> Ever shall in safety rest.
>
> (5.1.415–20)

Oberon himself, we are told, will conduct the blessing upon the "best bride-bed," that of the ruler Theseus and his Amazon queen Hippolyta.

The ceremony—manifestly the sanctification of ownership and caste, as well as marriage—is a witty allusion to the traditional Catholic blessing of the bride-bed with holy water, a ceremony vehemently attacked as pagan superstition and banned by English Protestants. But the conventional critical term "allusion" seems inadequate, for the term usually implies a bloodless, bodiless thing, while even the tiny, incidental detail of the field dew bears a more active charge. Here, as with Wolsey's hat, I want to ask what is at stake in the shift from one zone of social practice to another, from the old religion to public theater, from priests to fairies, from holy water to field dew, or rather to theatrical fairies and theatrical field dew on the London stage. When the Catholic ritual is made into theatrical representation, the transposition at once naturalizes, denaturalizes, mocks, and celebrates. It naturalizes the ritual by transforming the specially sanctified water into ordinary

9. A comedy (ca. 1595) that focuses on the love intrigues of two young couples, framed by the mature relationships of two other couples—the king and queen of the Fairies, Oberon and Titania, as well as Theseus, duke of Athens, and his wife Hippolyta. In Greek mythology, Theseus was king of Athens and had a son with an Amazon whose name is given variously as Antiope, Melanippe, or Hippolyte (who was not the queen).

dew; it denaturalizes the ritual by removing it from human agents and attributing it to the fairies; it mocks Catholic practice by associating it with notorious superstition and then by enacting it on the stage where it is revealed as a histrionic illusion; and it celebrates such practice by reinvesting it with the charismatic magic of the theater.

Several years ago, intending to signal a turn away from the formal, decontextualized analysis that dominates new criticism, I used the term "new historicism"[1] to describe an interest in the kinds of issues I have been raising—in the embeddedness of cultural objects in the contingencies of history—and the term has achieved a certain currency. But like most labels, this one is misleading. The new historicism, like the Holy Roman Empire,[2] constantly belies its own name. *The American Heritage Dictionary* gives three meanings for the term "historicism":

1. The belief that processes are at work in history that man can do little to alter.
2. The theory that the historian must avoid all value judgments in his study of past periods or former cultures.
3. Veneration of the past or of tradition.

Most of the writing labeled new historicist, and certainly my own work, has set itself resolutely against each of these positions.

1. *The belief that processes are at work in history that man can do little to alter.* This formulation rests upon a simultaneous abstraction and evacuation of human agency. The men and women who find themselves making concrete choices in given circumstances at particular times are transformed into something called "man." And this colorless, nameless collective being cannot significantly intervene in the "processes . . . at work in history," processes that are thus mysteriously alienated from all of those who enact them.

New historicism, by contrast, eschews the use of the term "man"; interest lies not in the abstract universal but in particular, contingent cases, the selves fashioned and acting according to the generative rules and conflicts of a given culture. And these selves, conditioned by the expectations of their class, gender, religion, race and national identity, are constantly effecting changes in the course of history. Indeed if there is any inevitability in the new historicism's vision of history it is this insistence on agency, for even inaction or extreme marginality is understood to possess meaning and therefore to imply intention. Every form of behavior, in this view, is a strategy: taking up arms or taking flight is a significant social action, but so is staying put, minding one's business, turning one's face to the wall. Agency is virtually inescapable.

1. A term coined in Greenblatt's introduction to *The Power of Forms in the English Renaissance* (1982). New Criticism: an approach (championed by CLEANTH BROOKS, WILLIAM K. WIMSATT JR., and others) that emphasizes close reading of the text considered as an autonomous whole; it has greatly influenced teaching from the mid-20th century onward.

2. A Germanic union of German territories in western and central Europe, founded by Charlemagne in 800 C.E. and dissolved in 1806 by the last Holy Roman Emperor, Francis II; in 1756 it was famously described by the French writer and philosopher Voltaire as neither holy nor Roman nor an empire.

Inescapable but not simple: new historicism, as I understand it, does not posit historical processes as unalterable and inexorable, but it does tend to discover limits or constraints upon individual intervention. Actions that appear to be single are disclosed as multiple; the apparently isolated power of the individual genius turns out to be bound up with collective, social energy; a gesture of dissent may be an element in a larger legitimation process, while an attempt to stabilize the order of things may turn out to subvert it. And political valences may change, sometimes abruptly: there are no guarantees, no absolute, formal assurances that what seems progressive in one set of contingent circumstances will not come to seem reactionary in another.

The new historicism's insistence on the pervasiveness of agency has apparently led some of its critics to find in it a Nietzschean celebration of the ruthless will to power,[3] while its ironic and skeptical reappraisal of the cult of heroic individualism has led others to find in it a pessimistic doctrine of human helplessness. Hence, for example, from a Marxist perspective one critic characterizes the new historicism as a "liberal disillusionment" that finds that "any apparent site of resistance ultimately serves the interests of power" (33), while from a liberal humanist perspective, another critic proclaims that "anyone who, like me, is reluctant to accept the will to power as the defining human essence will probably have trouble with the critical procedures of the new historicists and with their interpretive conclusions."[4] But the very idea of a "defining human essence" is precisely what new historicists find vacuous and untenable, as I do the counter-claim that love rather than power makes the world go round. The Marxist critique is more plausible, but it rests upon an assertion that new historicism argues that "*any* apparent site of resistance" is ultimately coopted. Some are, some aren't.

I argued in an essay published some years ago that the sites of resistance in Shakespeare's second tetralogy[5] are coopted in the plays' ironic, complex, but finally celebratory affirmation of charismatic kingship. That is, the formal structure and rhetorical strategy of the plays make it difficult for audiences to withhold their consent from the triumph of Prince Hal. Shakespeare shows that the triumph rests upon a claustrophobic narrowing of pleasure, a hypocritical manipulation of appearances, and a systematic betrayal of friendship, and yet these manifestations of bad faith only contrive to heighten the spectators' knowing pleasure and the ratification of applause. The subversive perceptions do not disappear, but insofar as they remain within the structure of the play, they are contained and indeed serve to heighten a power they would appear to question.

3. A central concept in the work of the German philosopher FRIEDRICH NIETZSCHE (1844–1900); the phrase, which supplies the title of his posthumously collected notes, *The Will to Power* (1900), appears in his earlier writings as well.

4. Walter Cohen, "Political Criticism of Shakespeare," in *Shakespeare Reproduced: The Text in History and Ideology*, ed. Jean E. Howard and Marion F. O'Connor (New York and London: Methuen, 1987), p. 33; Edward Pechter, "The New Historicism and Its Discontents," in *PMLA* 102 (1987), p. 301 [Greenblatt's note]. A perspective inspired by the writings of KARL MARX (1818–1883) would not only analyze the dynamic of power but would also emphasize the importance of class struggle and revolution.

5. Shakespeare's tetralogies are 8 plays covering the reigns of English kings from Richard II to Richard III (1377–1485). The second in time of completion (though portraying earlier events) consists of *Richard II* (1595), the 2 parts of *Henry IV* (1597, 1598), and *Henry V* (1599). Prince Hal, the young hero of the *Henry IV* plays, triumphs as he ascends to the throne as Henry V, and then brutally rejects the friendship of his former companion, Falstaff. Greenblatt's essay is "Invisible Bullets: Renaissance Authority and Its Subversion" (1981).

I did not propose that all manifestation of resistance in all literature (or even in all plays by Shakespeare) were coopted—one can readily think of plays where the forces of ideological containment break down. And yet characterizations of this essay in particular, and new historicism in general, repeatedly refer to a supposed argument that any resistance is impossible.[6] A particularizing argument about the subject position projected by a set of plays is at once simplified and turned into a universal principle from which contingency and hence history itself is erased.

Moreover, even my argument about Shakespeare's second tetralogy is misunderstood if it is thought to foreclose the possibility of dissent or change or the radical alteration of the processes of history. The point is that certain aesthetic and political structures work to contain the subversive perceptions they generate, not that those perceptions simply wither away. On the contrary, they may be pried loose from the order with which they were bound up and may serve to fashion a new and radically different set of structures. How else could change ever come about? No one is forced—except perhaps in school—to take aesthetic or political wholes as sacrosanct. The order of things is never simply a given: it takes labor to produce, sustain, reproduce, and transmit the way things are, and this labor may be withheld or transformed. Structures may be broken in pieces, the pieces altered, inverted, rearranged. Everything can be different than it is; everything could have been different than it was. But it will not do to imagine that this alteration is easy, automatic, without cost or obligation. My objection was to the notion that the rich ironies in the history plays were themselves inherently liberating, that to savor the tetralogy's skeptical cunning was to participate in an act of political resistance. In general I find dubious the assertion that certain rhetorical features in much-loved literary works constitute authentic acts of political liberation; the fact that this assertion is now heard from the left, where in my college days it was more often heard from the right, does not make it in most instances any less fatuous and presumptuous. I wished to show, at least in the case of Shakespeare's histories and in several analogous discourses, how a set of representational and political practices in the late sixteenth century could produce and even batten upon what appeared to be their own subversion.

To show this is not to give up on the possibility of altering historical processes—if this is historicism I want no part of it—but rather to eschew an aestheticized and idealized politics of the imagination.

2. *The theory that the historian must avoid all value judgments in his study of past periods or former cultures.* Once again, if this is an essential tenet of historicism, then the new historicism belies its name. My own critical practice and that of many others associated with new historicism was decisively shaped by the American 1960s and early 70s, and especially by the opposi-

6. "The new historicists and cultural materialists," one typical summary puts it, "represent, and by representing, reproduce in their new history of ideas, a world which is hierarchical, authoritarian, hegemonic, unsubvertable. . . . In this world picture, Stephen Greenblatt has poignantly asserted, there can be no subversion—and certainly not for *us*!" [C. T. Neely, "Constructing the Subject: Feminist Practice and the New Renaissance Discourses," *English Literary Renaissance* 18 (1988), p. 10.] Poignantly or otherwise, I asserted no such thing; I argued that the spectator of the history plays was continually tantalized by a resistance simultaneously powerful and deferred [Greenblatt's note].

tion to the Viet Nam War.[7] Writing that was not engaged, that withheld judgments, that failed to connect the present with the past seemed worthless. Such connection could be made either by analogy or causality; that is, a particular set of historical circumstances could be represented in such a way as to bring out homologies with aspects of the present or, alternatively, those circumstances could be analyzed as the generative forces that led to the modern condition. In either mode, value judgments were implicated, because a neutral or indifferent relation to the present seemed impossible. Or rather it seemed overwhelmingly clear that neutrality was itself a political position, a decision to support the official policies in both the state and the academy.

To study the culture of sixteenth-century England did not present itself as an escape from the turmoil of the present; it seemed rather an intervention, a mode of relation. The fascination for me of the Renaissance was that it seemed to be powerfully linked to the present both analogically and causally. This doubled link at once called forth and qualified my value judgments: called them forth because my response to the past was inextricably bound up with my response to the present; qualified them because the analysis of the past revealed the complex, unsettling historical genealogy of the very judgments I was making. To study Renaissance culture then was simultaneously to feel more rooted and more estranged in my own values.[8]

Other critics associated with the new historicism have written directly and forcefully about their own subject position and have made more explicit than I the nature of this engagement.[9] If I have not done so to the same extent, it is not because I believe that my values are somehow suspended in my study of the past but because I believe they are pervasive: in the textual and visual traces I choose to analyze, in the stories I choose to tell, in the cultural conjunctions I attempt to make, in my syntax, adjectives, pronouns. "The new historicism," someone has written in a lively critique, "needs at every point to be more overtly self-conscious of its methods and its theoretical assumptions, since what one discovers about the historical place and function of literary texts is in large measure a function of the angle from which one looks and the assumptions that enable the investigation."[1] I am certainly not opposed to methodological self-consciousness, but I am less inclined to see overtness—an explicit articulation of one's values and methods—as inherently necessary or virtuous. Nor, though I believe that my values are everywhere engaged in my work, do I think that there need be a perfect integration of those values and the objects I am studying. On the contrary, some of the most interesting and powerful ideas in cultural criticism occur precisely at

7. As U.S. involvement in the war between North and South Vietnam escalated throughout the 1960s, opposition to the war also grew, especially among draft-age university students. The last American forces left in 1973, and South Vietnam fell to the communist North in 1975.

8. See my *Renaissance Self-Fashioning: From More to Shakespeare* (Chicago: University of Chicago Press, 1980), pp. 174–75: "We are situated at the close of the cultural movement initiated in the Renaissance; the place in which our social and psychological world seems to be cracking apart are those structural joints visible when it was first constructed" [Greenblatt's note].

9. Louis Adrian Montrose, "Renaissance Literary Studies and the Subject of History," in *English Literary Renaissance* 16 (1986), pp. 5–12; Don Wayne, "Power, Politics, and the Shakespearean Text: Recent Criticism in England and the United States," in *Shakespeare Reproduced: The Text in History and Ideology*, ed. Howard and O'Connor, pp. 47–67; Catherine Gallagher, "Marxism and the New Historicism," in *The New Historicism*, ed. Harold Veeser (New York and London: Routledge, 1989) [Greenblatt's note].

1. Jean E. Howard, "The New Historicism in Renaissance Studies," in *Renaissance Historicism: Selections from "English Literary Renaissance,"* ed. Arthur F. Kinney and Dan S. Collins (Amherst: University of Massachusetts Press, 1987), pp. 32–33 [Greenblatt's note].

moments of disjunction, disintegration, unevenness. A criticism that never encounters obstacles, that celebrates predictable heroines and rounds up the usual suspects, that finds confirmation of its values everywhere it turns, is quite simply boring.[2]

3. *Veneration of the past or of tradition.* The third definition of historicism obviously sits in a strange relation to the second, but they are not simply alternatives. The apparent eschewing of value judgments was often accompanied by a still more apparent admiration, however cloaked as objective description, of the past. One of the more irritating qualities of my own literary training had been its relentlessly celebratory character: literary criticism was and largely remains a kind of secular theodicy. Every decision made by a great artist could be shown to be a brilliant one; works that had seemed flawed and uneven to an earlier generation of critics bent on displaying discriminations in taste were now revealed to be organic masterpieces. A standard critical assignment in my student years was to show how a text that seemed to break in parts was really a complex whole: thousands of pages were dutifully churned out to prove that the bizarre subplot of *The Changeling* was cunningly integrated into the tragic mainplot or that every tedious bit of clowning in *Doctor Faustus*[3] was richly significant. Behind these exercises was the assumption that great works of art were triumphs of resolution, that they were, in Bakhtin's term, monological[4]—the mature expression of a single artistic intention. When this formalism was combined, as it often was, with both ego psychology and historicism, it posited aesthetic integration as the reflection of the artist's psychic integration and posited that psychic integration as the triumphant expression of a healthy, integrated community. Accounts of Shakespeare's relation to Elizabethan culture were particularly prone to this air of veneration, since the Romantic cult of poetic genius could be conjoined with the still older political cult that had been created around the figure of the Virgin Queen.[5]

Here again new historicist critics have swerved in a different direction. They have been more interested in unresolved conflict and contradiction than in integration; they are as concerned with the margins as with the center; and they have turned from a celebration of achieved aesthetic order to an exploration of the ideological and material bases for the production of this order. Traditional formalism and historicism, twin legacies of early nineteenth-century Germany, shared a vision of high culture as a harmoniz-

2. If there is then no suspension of value judgments in the new historicism, there is at the same time a complication of those judgments, what I have called a sense of estrangement. This estrangement is bound up with the abandonment of a belief in historical inevitability, for, with this abandonment, the values of the present could no longer seem the necessary outcome of an irreversible teleological progression, whether of enlightenment or decline. An older historicism that proclaimed self-consciously that it had avoided all value judgments in its account of the past—that it had given us historical reality *wie es eigentlich gewesen* ["as it really was"; German]—did not thereby avoid all value judgments; it simply provided a misleading account of what it had actually done. In this sense the new historicism, for all its acknowledgment of engagement and partiality, may be slightly less likely than the older historicism to impose its values belligerently on the past, for those values seem historically contingent [Greenblatt's note].

3. *The Tragical History of Doctor Faustus* (1604), an English drama by Christopher Marlowe. *The Changeling* (1622), an English tragedy by Thomas Middleton and William Rowley with a comic romantic subplot.

4. See especially "Discourse in the Novel" (1934–35; above), by the Russian theorist MIKHAIL BAKHTIN (1895–1975).

5. That is, Elizabeth I (1533–1603; reigned 1558–1603), who never married and who gave her name to England's Elizabethan era.

ing domain of reconciliation based upon an aesthetic labor that transcends specific economic or political determinants. What is missing is psychic, social, and material resistance, a stubborn, unassimilable otherness, a sense of distance and difference. New historicism has attempted to restore this distance; hence its characteristic concerns have seemed to some critics off-center or strange. "New historicists," writes a Marxist observer, "are likely to seize upon something out of the way, obscure, even bizarre: dreams, popular or aristocratic festivals, denunciations of witchcraft, sexual treatises, diaries and autobiographies, descriptions of clothing, reports on disease, birth and death records, accounts of insanity."[6] What is fascinating to me is that concerns like these should have come to seem bizarre, especially to a critic who is committed to the historical understanding of culture. That they have done so indicates how narrow the boundaries of historical understanding had become, how much these boundaries needed to be broken.

For none of the cultural practices on this list (and one could extend it considerably) is or should be "out of the way" in a study of Renaissance literature or art; on the contrary, each is directly in the way of coming to terms with the period's methods of regulating the body, its conscious and unconscious psychic strategies, its ways of defining and dealing with marginals and deviants, its mechanisms for the display of power and the expression of discontent, its treatment of women. If such concerns have been rendered "obscure," it is because of a disabling idea of causality that confines the legitimate field of historical agency within absurdly restrictive boundaries. The world is parcelled out between a predictable group of stereotypical causes and a large, dimly lit mass of raw materials that the artist chooses to fashion.

The new historicist critics are interested in such cultural expressions as witchcraft accusations, medical manuals, or clothing not as raw materials but as "cooked"[7]—complex symbolic and material articulations of the imaginative and ideological structures of the society that produced them. Consequently, there is a tendency in at least some new historicist writings (certainly in my own) for the focus to be partially displaced from the work of art that is their formal occasion onto the related practices that had been adduced ostensibly in order to illuminate that work. It is difficult to keep those practices in the background if the very concept of historical background has been called into question.

I have tried to deal with the problem of focus by developing a notion of cultural negotiation and exchange, that is, by examining the points at which one cultural practice intersects with another, borrowing its forms and intensities or attempting to ward off unwelcome appropriations or moving texts and artifacts from one place to another. But it would be misleading to imagine that there is a complete homogenization of interest; my own concern remains centrally with imaginative literature, and not only because other cultural structures resonate powerfully within it. If I do not approach works of art in a spirit of veneration, I do approach them in a spirit that is best described as wonder. Wonder has not been alien to literary criticism, but it has been associated (if only implicitly) with formalism rather than histori-

6. Cohen, in *Shakespeare Reproduced*, pp. 33–34 [Greenblatt's note].

7. This distinction between the natural world and the world of human culture was famously drawn by the French anthropologist CLAUDE LÉVI-STRAUSS in *The Raw and the Cooked* (1964).

cism. I wish to extend this wonder beyond the formal boundaries of works of art, just as I wish to intensify resonance within those boundaries.

It will be easier to grasp the concepts of resonance and wonder if we think of the way in which our culture presents to itself not the textual traces of its past but the surviving visual traces, for the latter are put on display in galleries and museums specially designed for the purpose. By resonance I mean the power of the object displayed to reach out beyond its formal boundaries to a larger world, to evoke in the viewer the complex, dynamic cultural forces from which it has emerged and for which as metaphor or more simply as metonymy it may be taken by a viewer to stand. By wonder I mean the power of the object displayed to stop the viewer in his tracks, to convey an arresting sense of uniqueness, to evoke an exalted attention.

The new historicism obviously has distinct affinities with resonance; that is, its concern with literary texts has been to recover as far as possible the historical circumstances of their original production and consumption and to analyze the relationship between these circumstances and our own. New historicist critics have tried to understand the intersecting circumstances not as a stable, prefabricated background against which the literary texts can be placed, but as a dense network of evolving and often contradictory social forces. The idea is not to find outside the work of art some rock onto which literary interpretation can be securely chained but rather to situate the work in relation to other representational practices operative in the culture at a given moment in both its history and our own. In Louis Montrose's[8] convenient formulation, the goal has been to grasp simultaneously the historicity of texts and the textuality of history.

Insofar as this approach, developed for literary interpretation, is at all applicable to visual traces, it would call for an attempt to reduce the isolation of individual "masterpieces," to illuminate the conditions of their making, to disclose the history of their appropriation and the circumstances in which they come to be displayed, to restore the tangibility, the openness, the permeability of boundaries that enabled the objects to come into being in the first place. An actual restoration of tangibility is obviously in most cases impossible, and the frames that enclose pictures are only the ultimate formal confirmation of the closing of the borders that marks the finishing of a work of art. But we need not take that finishing so entirely for granted; museums can and on occasion do make it easier imaginatively to recreate the work in its moment of openness.

That openness is linked to a quality of artifacts that museums obviously dread, their precariousness. But though it is perfectly reasonable for museums to protect their objects—I would not wish it any other way—precariousness is a rich source of resonance. Thomas Greene, who has written a sensitive book on what he calls the "vulnerable text," suggests that the symbolic wounding to which literature is prone may confer upon it power and fecundity. "The vulnerability of poetry," Greene argues, "stems from four basic conditions of language: its historicity, its dialogic function, its referential function, and its

8. Prominent New Historicist critic (b. 1941); his "formulation" appears in "The Elizabethan Subject and the Spenserian Text" (1986).

dependence on figuration."[9] Three of these conditions are different for the visual arts, in ways that would seem to reduce vulnerability: painting and sculpture may be detached more readily than language from both referentiality and figuration, and the pressures of contextual dialogue are diminished by the absence of an inherent *logos*,[1] a constitutive word. But the fourth condition—historicity—is in the case of material artifacts vastly increased, indeed virtually literalized. Museums function, partly by design and partly in spite of themselves, as monuments to the fragility of cultures, to the fall of sustaining institutions and noble houses, the collapse of rituals, the evacuation of myths, the destructive effects of warfare, neglect, and corrosive doubt.

I am fascinated by the signs of alteration, tampering, even destructiveness which many museums try simply to efface: first and most obviously, the act of displacement that is essential for the collection of virtually all older artifacts and most modern ones—pulled out of chapels, peeled off church walls, removed from decaying houses, seized as spoils of war, stolen, "purchased" more or less fairly by the economically ascendent from the economically naïve, the poor, the hard-pressed heirs of fallen dynasties and impoverished religious orders. Then too there are the marks on the artifacts themselves: the attempt to scratch out or deface the image of the devil in numerous late-medieval and Renaissance paintings, the concealing of the genitals in sculptured and painted figures, the iconoclastic[2] smashing of human or divine representations, the evidence of cutting or reshaping to fit a new frame or purpose, the cracks or scorch marks or broken-off noses that indifferently record the grand disasters of history and the random accidents of trivial incompetence. Even these accidents—the marks of a literal fragility—can have their resonance: the climax of an absurdly hagiographical Proust exhibition several years ago was a display case holding a small, patched, modest vase with a notice, "This vase broken by Marcel Proust."[3]

As this comical example suggests, wounded artifacts may be compelling not only as witnesses to the violence of history but as signs of use, marks of the human touch, and hence links with the openness to touch that was the condition of their creation. The most familiar way to recreate the openness of aesthetic artifacts without simply renewing their vulnerability is through a skillful deployment of explanatory texts in the catalogue, on the walls of the exhibit, or on cassettes. The texts so deployed introduce and in effect stand in for the context that has been effaced in the process of moving the object into the museum. But insofar as that context is partially, often primarily, visual as well as verbal, textual contextualism has its limits. Hence the mute eloquence of the display of the palette, brushes, and other implements that an artist of a given period would have employed or of objects that are represented in the exhibited paintings or of materials and images that in some way parallel or intersect with the formal works of art.

Among the most resonant moments are those in which the supposedly contextual objects take on a life of their own, make a claim that rivals that

9. Thomas Greene, *The Vulnerable Text: Essays on Renaissance Literature* (New York: Columbia University Press, 1986), p. 100 [Greenblatt's note]. Greene (1926–2003), American scholar of English and comparative literature.

1. Word, speech; reason (Greek).
2. Literally, "destroying religious images."
3. Marcel Proust (1871–1922), major French novelist.

of the object that is formally privileged. A table, a chair, a map, often seemingly placed only to provide a decorative setting for a grand work, become oddly expressive, significant not as "background" but as compelling representational practices in themselves. These practices may in turn impinge upon the grand work, so that we begin to glimpse a kind of circulation: the cultural practice and social energy implicit in map-making drawn into the aesthetic orbit of a painting which has itself enabled us to register some of the representational significance of the map. Or again the threadbare fabric on the old chair or the gouges in the wood of a cabinet juxtapose the privileged painting or sculpture with marks not only of time but of use, the imprint of the human body on the artifact, and call attention to the deliberate removal of certain exalted aesthetic objects from the threat of that imprint.

For the effect of resonance does not necessarily depend upon a collapse of the distinction between art and non-art; it can be achieved by awakening in the viewer a sense of the cultural and historically contingent construction of art objects, the negotiations, exchanges, swerves, exclusions by which certain representational practices come to be set apart from other representational practices that they partially resemble. A resonant exhibition often pulls the viewer away from the celebration of isolated objects and toward a series of implied, only half-visible relationships and questions. How have the objects come to be displayed? What is at stake in categorizing them as of "museum-quality"? How were they originally used? What cultural and material conditions made possible their production? What were the feelings of those who originally held these objects, cherished them, collected them, possessed them? What is the meaning of my relationship to these same objects now that they are displayed here, in this museum, on this day?

* * *

1990

DONNA HARAWAY
b. 1944

In the introduction to her book *Simians, Cyborgs, and Women: The Reinvention of Nature* (1991), Donna Haraway describes her transformation from a "proper, U.S. socialist feminist, white, female, hominid biologist" into a "multiply marked cyborg feminist" whose writings range freely from cyborgs and monsters to apes and dogs, productive assemblages that in her later work she comes to call "companion species." Haraway's challenging and innovative theoretical work is part of the cultural studies of science and technology, a thriving subdiscipline interested in the history, sociology, and politics of technoscience. Her best-known text, "A Manifesto for Cyborgs" (1985), has been hailed as the central text of cyberfeminism—an often iconoclastic wave of feminist theory and practice that is seeking to reclaim technoscience. As she attempts to understand the place of technology within a postmodern, socialist feminism, Haraway argues that far from being antithetical to the human organism, technology is a material and symbolic apparatus that is already deeply involved in what it means to be human. The old political strategies—Marxist, liberal, and conservative—have become obsolete in the face of a global technoscience that is outpacing the ethical and political mechanisms we have devised for containing it. Her landmark essay is a call for "reconstructing socialist-feminist politics . . . through theory and practice addressed to the social relations of science and technology." In this manifesto, she introduces the mysterious boundary creature and new myth: the cyborg, a "hybrid of machine and organism" that, for Haraway, becomes a metaphor for the "disassembled and reassembled, post-modern collective and personal self" of contemporary cultural theory suited to the West's late capitalist social order.

Haraway's educational history illuminates the broad range of her scholarship. With the aid of a Boettcher Foundation scholarship, she earned a degree in zoology and philosophy in 1966 from Colorado College, where she also fulfilled the requirements for an English major. She studied philosophies of evolution in Paris for a year on a Fulbright scholarship before beginning graduate studies in biology at Yale University; in 1972 she earned a Ph.D. for an interdisciplinary dissertation on the functions of metaphor in shaping twentieth-century research in developmental biology. She has taught at the University of Hawaii and Johns Hopkins University and, from 1980 until her retirement in 2011, in the History of Conciousness Program at the University of California at Santa Cruz. She is also a professor of feminist theory and technoscience in the Media and Communications Program of the European Graduate School in Switzerland.

Although best known for the frequently anthologized "A Manifesto for Cyborgs," Haraway has published on an impressive array of topics, including primatology, science fiction, animal studies, dogs, technoscience, ecofeminism, globalization, and immunity. As befits someone who received a special dispensation to write a dissertation on metaphors in science, what provides coherence to her eclectic body of work is a fascination with the power of tropes—figures of speech, metaphors—to shape and organize the complex interrelationships between the material world and semiosis, the study of signs and meaning. Haraway's writing draws on a series of tropes—the cyborg, the monster, the ape, the dog—to embody the border skirmishes and disarticulated identities that trouble late capitalism. She sees her work as both in alliance and in tension with that of other thinkers of the "posthuman," including N. KATHERINE HAYLES, ROSI BRAIDOTTI, BRUNO LATOUR, and Cary Wolfe. She is particularly interested in bridging the rift between the so-called two cultures—the arts and the sciences—and in bringing science studies to feminism and feminism to science studies. Haraway is at home in the genre of the manifesto, a speculative form of writing that attempts to imagine the world differently, a form that produces risky readings designed to unsettle commonplace ways of thinking about the world.

"A Manifesto for Cyborgs," our first selection, attempts to appropriate the resources of contemporary technoscience as a means of constructing "an ironic political myth faithful to feminism, socialism, and materialism." The icon of this new feminist mythology is the cyborg, the hybrid creation of modern science—part human, part machine. Like the feminist theorist GLORIA ANZALDÚA, Haraway is interested in exploring those boundaries, borders, and borderlands where our jumbled personal and collective identities are constructed and contested. By adopting the cyborg as a political myth, feminism, she believes, might be able to initiate effective political action without recourse to essentialism or identity politics; she argues "for *pleasure* in the confusion of boundaries and for *responsibility* in their construction." While Anzaldúa investigates boundary confusion in geographical space and racial identity, Haraway explores and affirms the breakdowns in three crucial boundaries that have resulted from post–World War II technoscience: those between human and animal, organism and machine, and the physical and non-physical.

Because they are situated on the boundary between organism and machine, Haraway argues, cyborgs do not participate in the various traditional mythologies that have defined the West. Most pernicious among these are the myths of essential identity and original unity—the myth of the garden of Eden, a belief in a pure, coherent social identity that separates the truly human from animals and machines, as well as from other races and ethnic groups. Haraway joins postmodern feminists such as JUDITH BUTLER and EVE KOSOFSKY SEDGWICK in the critique of essentialism, arguing that totalizing formulations of pure identity often associated with Marxism, the feminism of Catharine MacKinnon, and other movements are based on exclusion and marginalization. Because the cyborg is postgender, post-Western, post-Marxist, and post-oedipal, it serves as a viable image for a new partial and heterogeneous subjectivity that reconceptualizes identity politics. Cyborgs, being "wary of holism, but needy for connection," offer a new kind of community and politics based not on unity but on affinity, not on the party but on the coalition, not on the totalized conception of the category "woman" (central to many feminisms) but on partial explanations based on a careful understanding of difference. Yet Haraway warns that "difference" is not inherently liberating: "some differences are playful; some are poles of world historical systems of domination."

Haraway's post-Marxist call for new political strategies follows from her perception of new forms of political domination. The old forms of domination endemic to an industrial society—to white patriarchal capitalism—are rapidly being rendered obsolete by new technologies. The emerging new networks of power, which she calls the "informatics of domination," are adapted to technoscientific economies based on information systems. Haraway's focus on the metaphor of the cyborg does not, as a few of her critics have unfairly charged, ignore the real material oppression of women worldwide—their poverty and exploitation; it is not a flight away from the "real world" into a poststructuralist utopia, even though her poststructuralist language is very difficult and highly theoretical. Her exploration of the informatics of domination rests on an analysis of the social and material relations of science and technology. These real and frequently oppressive relations, promoted by laissez-faire late capitalism, include the "homework economy" (that is, the restructuring and feminization of the workplace), encroaching privatization and the loss of public life, growing insecurity even among the well-to-do, cultural impoverishment, and the "failure of subsistence networks for the most vulnerable."

While best known for the trope of the cyborg, Haraway has always evinced a keen interest in the ways in which the divide between human and animal has been used to determine what it means to be human. Most recently, she has engaged with the emerging field of animal studies, a subject that also occupied JACQUES DERRIDA in his later work (see above). In our excerpt from *The Companion Species Manifesto: Dogs, People, and Significant Otherness* (2003), Haraway argues that dogs and humans have become inextricably interwoven into a single "companion species," a symbiotic relation "in which none of the partners pre-exist the relating." She sees her work on dogs as a "branch of feminist theory." Haraway believes that by taking dog-human relationships seriously as an object of study, we might develop "an ethics and politics committed to the flourishing of significant otherness." The trope of companion species links this essay to her earlier essay on the cyborg, enabling her to trouble the boundaries between "the human and nonhuman, the organic and technological, carbon and silicon, freedom and structure, history and myth, the rich and the poor, the state and the subject, diversity and depletion, modernity and postmodernity, and nature and culture." *The Companion Species Manifesto* marks a significant intervention in the traditional divide between nature and culture. Haraway coins the term *natureculture* to underscore the inextricable entanglements of nature and culture, of the material and semiotic, and of body and mind.

Haraway has been criticized for the exuberance with which she embraces the "monstrous" mixed identity of the cyborg, but her enthusiasm is qualified by sobering discussions of the various impacts of modern and postmodern technoscience on our lives. Where critics sometimes found "Manifesto for Cyborgs" abstruse, they find *The Companion Species Manifesto* cobbled together and inconsistent. Some animal studies scholars have accused her of ignoring animal rights issues, while feminists have complained that she leaves the relationship between dogs and feminism ambiguous. However, Haraway draws on the notion of partial connections, articulated by the anthropologist Marilyn Strathern, insisting that if the parts of her manifestos don't add up to a whole, neither does natureculture. If the relationship to feminism remains latent, it also tantalizes, demanding a response. None of us sees the world as a whole; all we can do is track out networks of connections in a project that is ultimately collaborative.

Haraway's cyborg myth, which recognizes that monsters always mark the limits of community, attempts to integrate women and machines into a new "science" fiction. Her "dog stories" relate tales of biopower and biosociality. Writing and language are crucial to both technoscience and feminist politics. Yet she advocates not the "dream of a common language" embraced by ADRIENNE RICH or the purified *écriture féminine* (feminine writing) described by HÉLÈNE CIXOUS, but a "powerful infidel heteroglossia," derived from the writings of MIKHAIL BAKHTIN, that enables us to theorize the complications of language, the frustrations of communicating experience, and the necessity of negotiating rather than policing boundaries that are becoming increasingly unstable.

"A Manifesto for Cyborgs: Science, Technology, and Socialist Feminism in the 1980s" Keywords: The Body, Cultural Studies, Feminist Theory, Globalization, Marxism, Popular Culture, Postmodernity
***The Companion Species Manifesto: Dogs, People, and Significant Otherness* Keywords:** The Body, Cultural Studies, Feminist Theory, Identity, Ideology, Language, Narrative Theory, Rhetoric

From A Manifesto for Cyborgs: Science, Technology, and Socialist Feminism in the 1980s

An Ironic Dream of a Common Language for Women in the Integrated Circuit[1]

This essay is an effort to build an ironic political myth faithful to feminism, socialism, and materialism. Perhaps more faithful as blasphemy is faithful, than as reverent worship and identification. Blasphemy has always seemed to require taking things very seriously. I know no better stance to adopt from within the secular-religious, evangelical traditions of United States politics, including the politics of socialist-feminism. Blasphemy protects one from the moral majority within, while still insisting on the need for community. Blasphemy is not apostasy. Irony is about contradictions that do not resolve into larger wholes, even dialectically, about the tension of holding incompatible things together because both or all are necessary and true. Irony is about

1. A reference to the feminism of ADRIENNE RICH (1929–2012), author of "Compulsory Heterosexuality and Lesbian Existence" (1980; see above) and of a 1978 collection of poetry titled *The Dream of a Common Language*.

humor and serious play. It is also a rhetorical strategy and a political method, one I would like to see more honored within socialist feminism. At the center of my ironic faith, my blasphemy, is the image of the cyborg.

A cyborg is a cybernetic organism, a hybrid of machine and organism, a creature of social reality as well as a creature of fiction. Social reality is lived social relations, our most important political construction, a world-changing fiction. The international women's movements have constructed "women's experience," as well as uncovered or discovered this crucial collective object. This experience is a fiction and fact of the most crucial, political kind. Liberation rests on the construction of the consciousness, the imaginative apprehension, of oppression, and so of possibility. The cyborg is a matter of fiction and lived experience that changes what counts as women's experience in the late twentieth century. This is a struggle over life and death, but the boundary between science fiction and social reality is an optical illusion.

Contemporary science fiction is full of cyborgs—creatures simultaneously animal and machine, who populate worlds ambiguously natural and crafted. Modern medicine is also full of cyborgs, of couplings between organism and machine, each conceived as coded devices, in an intimacy and with a power that was not generated in the history of sexuality. Cyborg "sex" restores some of the lovely replicative baroque of ferns and invertebrates (such nice organic prophylactics against heterosexism). Cyborg replication is uncoupled from organic reproduction. Modern production seems like a dream of cyborg colonization of work, a dream that makes the nightmare of Taylorism[2] seem idyllic. And modern war is a cyborg orgy, coded by C^3I, command-control-communication-intelligence, an $84 billion item in 1984's U.S. defense budget. I am making an argument for the cyborg as a fiction mapping our social and bodily reality and as an imaginative resource suggesting some very fruitful couplings. Foucault's biopolitics[3] is a flaccid premonition of cyborg politics, a very open field.

By the late twentieth century, our time, a mythic time, we are all chimeras, theorized and fabricated hybrids of machine and organism; in short, we are cyborgs. The cyborg is our ontology;[4] it gives us our politics. The cyborg is a condensed image of both imagination and material reality, the two joined centers structuring any possibility of historical transformation. In the traditions of "Western" science and politics—the tradition of racist, male-dominant capitalism; the tradition of progress; the tradition of the appropriation of nature as resource for the productions of culture; the tradition of reproduction of the self from the reflections of the other—the relation between organism and machine has been a border war. The stakes in the border war have been the territories of production, reproduction, and imagination. This essay is an argument for *pleasure* in the confusion of boundaries and for *responsibility* in their construction. It is also an effort to

2. A system of industrial management, devised by the American inventor and engineer Frederick Taylor (1856–1916), that seeks to maximize workers' efficiency in order to optimize production.

3. A term used in *The History of Sexuality* (1976) by the French philosopher and cultural historian MICHEL FOUCAULT (1926–1984) to describe the social mechanisms of power that regulate the body, extending the methods of power and knowledge over life itself.

4. The branch of philosophy concerned with the nature of being. *Chimera*: in Greek mythology, a female monster with a lion's head, a goat's body, and a serpent's tail; more generally, any monster made of incongruous parts.

contribute to socialist-feminist culture and theory in a post-modernist, non-naturalist mode and in the utopian tradition of imagining a world without gender, which is perhaps a world without genesis, but maybe also a world without end. The cyborg incarnation is outside salvation history.

The cyborg is a creature in a post-gender world; it has no truck with bisexuality, pre-Oedipal symbiosis,[5] unalienated labor,[6] or other seductions to organic wholeness through a final appropriation of all the powers of the parts into a higher unity. In a sense, the cyborg has no origin story in the Western sense; a "final" irony since the cyborg is also the awful apocalyptic *telos* of the "West's" escalating dominations of abstract individuation, an ultimate self untied at last from all dependency, a man in space. An origin story in the "Western," humanist sense depends on the myth of original unity, fullness, bliss and terror, represented by the phallic mother from whom all humans must separate, the task of individual development and of history, the twin potent myths inscribed most powerfully for us in psychoanalysis and Marxism. Hilary Klein has argued[7] that both Marxism and psychoanalysis, in their concepts of labor and of individuation and gender formation, depend on the plot of original unity out of which difference must be produced and enlisted in a drama of escalating domination of woman/nature. The cyborg skips the step of original unity, of identification with nature in the Western sense. This is its illegitimate promise that might lead to subversion of its teleology as star wars.[8]

The cyborg is resolutely committed to partiality, irony, intimacy, and perversity. It is oppositional, utopian, and completely without innocence. No longer structured by the polarity of public and private, the cyborg defines a technological polis based partly on a revolution of social relations in the *oikos*,[9] the household. Nature and culture are reworked; the one can no longer be the resource for appropriation or incorporation by the other. The relationships for forming wholes from parts, including those of polarity and hierarchical domination, are at issue in the cyborg world. Unlike the hopes of Frankenstein's monster,[1] the cyborg does not expect its father to save it through a restoration of the garden; i.e., through the fabrication of a heterosexual mate, through its completion in a finished whole, a city and cosmos. The cyborg does not dream of community on the model of the organic family, this time without the Oedipal project.[2] The cyborg would not recognize the Garden of Eden; it is not made of mud and cannot dream of returning to dust.[3] Perhaps that is why I want to see if cyborgs can subvert the apocalypse of returning to nuclear dust in the manic compulsion to name the Enemy. Cyborgs are not reverent; they do not re-member the cosmos.

5. In psychoanalytic theory, a period of maternal dependence, narcissistic identification, and polymorphous erotic drives that occurs during earliest infancy, preceding the oedipal phase when conflict with the father and the social order emerge. This period of intense attachment to the maternal has been of great interest to contemporary feminist psychoanalytic theorists (e.g., JULIA KRISTEVA and HÉLÈNE CIXOUS).

6. In Marxist theory, labor that does not occur within the exploitative relationships of slavery, feudalism, colonialism, or capitalism.

7. See Klein's "Marxism, Psychoanalysis, and Mother Nature," *Feminist Studies* 15 (1989).

8. The Strategic Defense Initiative, proposed by President Ronald Reagan in 1983, to create a shield against incoming missiles.

9. House (Greek), part of the root of the English word *economy*.

1. That is, the creature constructed in Mary Shelley's novel *Frankenstein* (1818), who begs his creator for a mate.

2. Psychoanalysis describes the task of early childhood—the formation of a distinct ego or identity—as separation from the mother, accomplished through the oedipal stage in which the paternal figure intervenes between the mother-child dyad.

3. The book of Genesis describes the creation of man (in Hebrew, *adam*) from dust (2.7).

They are wary of holism, but needy for connection—they seem to have a natural feel for united front politics, but without the vanguard party.[4] The main trouble with cyborgs, of course, is that they are the illegitimate offspring of militarism and patriarchal capitalism, not to mention state socialism. But illegitimate offspring are often exceedingly unfaithful to their origins. Their fathers, after all, are inessential.

I will return to the science fiction of cyborgs at the end of this essay, but now I want to signal three crucial boundary breakdowns that make the following political fictional (political scientific) analysis possible. By the late twentieth century in United States scientific culture, the boundary between human and animal is thoroughly breached. The last beachheads of uniqueness have been polluted if not turned into amusement parks—language, tool use, social behavior, mental events, nothing really convincingly settles the separation of human and animal. And many people no longer feel the need of such a separation; indeed, many branches of feminist culture affirm the pleasure of connection of human and other living creatures. Movements for animal rights are not irrational denials of human uniqueness; they are clear-sighted recognition of connection across the discredited breach of nature and culture. Biology and evolutionary theory over the last two centuries have simultaneously produced modern organisms as objects of knowledge and reduced the line between humans and animals to a faint trace re-etched in ideological struggle or professional disputes between life and social sciences. Within this framework, teaching modern Christian creationism should be fought as a form of child abuse.

Biological-determinist ideology is only one position opened up in scientific culture for arguing the meanings of human animality. There is much room for radical political people to contest for the meanings of the breached boundary.[5] The cyborg appears in myth precisely where the boundary between human and animal is transgressed. Far from signaling a walling off of people from other living beings, cyborgs signal disturbingly and pleasurably tight coupling. Bestiality has a new status in this cycle of marriage exchange.

The second leaky distinction is between animal-human (organism) and machine. Pre-cybernetic machines could be haunted; there was always the specter of the ghost in the machine.[6] This dualism structured the dialogue

4. Haraway alludes to Soviet history. "Vanguard party": party intended to lead and control the revolution of the workers (e.g., the Bolshevik Party, established during the Russian Revolution). "United front politics": coalitions (e.g., the united fronts set up by the Comintern during the 1930s).

5. Useful references to left and/or feminist radical science movements and theory and to biological/ biotechnological issues include: Ruth Bleier, *Science and Gender: A Critique of Biology and Its Themes on Women* (New York: Pergamon, 1984); Elizabeth Fee, "Critiques of Modern Science: The Relationship of Feminist and Other Radical Epistemologies," and Evelyn Hammonds, "Women of Color, Feminism, and Science," papers for Symposium on Feminist Perspectives on Science, University of Wisconsin, 11–13 April 1985 (proceedings to be published by Pergamon) [Ruth Bleier, ed., *Feminist Approaches to Science* (New York: Pergamon, 1986)]; Stephen J. Gould, *Mismeasure of Man* (New York: Norton, 1981); Ruth Hubbard, Mary Sue Henifin and Barbara Fried, eds., *Biological Woman, the Convenient Myth* (Cambridge, Mass.: Schenkman, 1982); Evelyn Fox Keller, *Reflections on Gender and Science* (New Haven: Yale University Press, 1985); R. C. Lewontin, Steve Rose, and Leon Kamin, *Not in Our Genes* (New York: Pantheon, 1984); *Radical Science Journal*, 26 Freegrove Road, London N7 9RQ; *Science for the People*, 897 Main St., Cambridge, MA 02139 [Haraway's note]. Haraway's original references are, where appropriate, updated in square brackets.

6. The phrase used by the English analytic philosopher Gilbert Ryle (1900–1976) to criticize the mind-body dualism of the French philosopher René Descartes (1596–1650), who separated the publicly observable (material, physical) from the private mind (spiritual).

between materialism and idealism that was settled by a dialectical progeny, called spirit or history, according to taste. But basically machines were not self-moving, self-designing, autonomous. They could not achieve man's dream, only mock it. They were not man, an author to himself, but only a caricature of that masculinist reproductive dream. To think they were otherwise was paranoid. Now we are not so sure. Late-twentieth-century machines have made thoroughly ambiguous the difference between natural and artificial, mind and body, self-developing and externally-designed, and many other distinctions that used to apply to organisms and machines. Our machines are disturbingly lively, and we ourselves frighteningly inert.

Technological determinism is only one ideological space opened up by the reconceptions of machine and organism as coded texts through which we engage in the play of writing and reading the world.[7] "Textualization" of everything in post-structuralist, post-modernist theory has been damned by Marxists and socialist feminists for its utopian disregard for lived relations of domination that ground the "play" of arbitrary reading.[8] It is certainly true that post-modernist strategies, like my cyborg myth, subvert myriad organic wholes (e.g., the poem, the primitive culture, the biological organism). In short, the certainty of what counts as nature—a source of insight and a promise of innocence—is undermined, probably fatally. The transcendent

7. Starting points for left and/or feminist approaches to technology and politics include: Ruth Schwartz Cowan, *More Work for Mother: The Ironies of Household Technology from the Open Hearth to the Microwave* (New York: Basic Books, 1983); Joan Rothschild, *Machina ex Dea: Feminist Perspectives on Technology* (New York: Pergamon, 1983); Sharon Traweek, [*Beamtimes and Lifetimes: The World of High Energy Physics* (Cambridge, Mass.: Harvard University Press, 1988)]; R. M. Young and Les Levidov, eds., *Science, Technology, and the Labour Process*, vols. 1–3 (London: CSE Books); Joseph Weizenbaum, *Computer Power and Human Reason* (San Francisco: Freeman, 1976); Langdon Winner, *Autonomous Technology: Technics out of Control as a Theme in Political Thought* (Cambridge, Mass.: MIT Press, 1977); Langdon Winner, [*The Whale and the Reactor* (Chicago: University of Chicago Press, 1986)]; Jan Zimmerman, ed., *The Technological Woman: Interfacing with Tomorrow* (New York: Praeger, 1983); *Global Electronics Newsletter*, 867 West Dana St., #204, Mountain View, CA 94041; *Processed World*, 55 Sutter St., San Francisco, CA 94104; *ISIS*, Women's International Information and Communication Service, P.O. Box 50 (Cornavin), 1211 Geneva 2, Switzerland, and Via Santa Maria dell'Anima 30, 00186 Rome, Italy. Fundamental approaches to modern social studies of science that do not continue the liberal mystification that it all started with Thomas Kuhn, include: Karin Knorr-Cetina, *The Manufacture of Knowledge* (Oxford: Pergamon, 1981); K. D. Knorr-Cetina and Michael Mulkay, eds., *Science Observed: Perspectives on the Social Study of Science* (Beverly Hills, Calif.: Sage, 1983); BRUNO LATOUR and Steve Woolgar, *Laboratory Life: The Social Construction of Scientific Facts* (Beverly Hills, Calif.: Sage, 1979); Robert M. Young, "Interpreting the Production of Science," *New Scientist*, vol. 29 (March 1979), pp. 1026–28. More is claimed than is known about room for contesting productions of science in the mythic/material space of "the laboratory": the 1984 Directory of the Network for the Ethnographic Study of Science, Technology, and Organizations lists a wide range of people and projects crucial to better radical analysis; available from NBSSTO, P.O. Box 11442, Stanford, CA 94305 [Haraway's note]. Kuhn (1922–1996), American historian of science; his book that some view as starting modern social studies of science is *The Structure of Scientific Revolutions* (1962).

8. Fredric Jameson, "Postmodernism, or, The Cultural Logic of Late Capitalism," *New Left Review*, July/August 1984, pp. 53–94. See Marjorie Perloff, "'Dirty' Language and Scramble Systems," *Sulfur* 11 (1984), pp. 178–83; Kathleen Fraser, *Something (Even Human Voices) in the Foreground, a Lake* (Berkeley, Calif.: Kelsey St. Press, 1984). A provocative, comprehensive argument about the policies and theories of "post-modernism" is made by Fredric Jameson, who argues that post-modernism is not an option, a style among others, but a cultural dominant requiring radical reinvention of left politics from within; there is no longer any place from without that gives meaning to the comforting fiction of critical distance. Jameson also makes clear why one cannot be for or against post-modernism, an essentially moralist move. My position is that feminists (and others) need continuous cultural reinvention, post-modernist critique, and historical materialism; only a cyborg would have a chance. The old dominations of white capitalist patriarchy seem nostalgically innocent now: they normalized heterogeneity, e.g., into man and woman, white and black. "Advanced capitalism" and post-modernism release heterogeneity without a norm, and we are flattened, without subjectivity, which requires depth, even unfriendly and drowning depths. It is time to write *The Death of the Clinic*. The clinic's methods required bodies and works; we have texts and surfaces. Our dominations don't work by medicalization and normalization anymore; they work by networking,

authorization of interpretation is lost, and with it the ontology grounding "Western" epistemology.[9] But the alternative is not cynicism or faithlessness, i.e., some version of abstract existence, like the accounts of technological determinism destroying "man" by the "machine" or "meaningful political action" by the "text." Who cyborgs will be is a radical question; the answers are a matter of survival. Both chimpanzees and artifacts have politics, so why shouldn't we?[1]

The third distinction is a subset of the second: the boundary between physical and non-physical is very imprecise for us. Pop physics books on the consequences of quantum theory and the indeterminacy principle are a kind of popular scientific equivalent to the Harlequin[2] romances as a marker of radical change in American white heterosexuality: they get it wrong, but they are on the right subject. Modern machines are quintessentially microelectronic devices: they are everywhere and they are invisible. Modern machinery is an irreverent upstart god, mocking the Father's ubiquity and spirituality. The silicon chip is a surface for writing; it is etched in molecular scales disturbed only by atomic noise, the ultimate interference for nuclear scores. Writing, power, and technology are old partners in Western stories of the origin of civilization, but miniaturization has changed our experience of mechanism. Miniaturization has turned out to be about power; small is not so much beautiful as pre-eminently dangerous, as in cruise missiles. Contrast the TV sets of the 1950s or the news cameras of the 1970s with the TV wrist bands or hand-sized video cameras now advertised. Our best machines are made of sunshine; they are all light and clean because they are nothing but signals, electromagnetic waves, a section of a spectrum. And these machines are eminently portable, mobile—a matter of immense human pain in Detroit and Singapore. People are nowhere near so fluid, being both material and opaque. Cyborgs are ether, quintessence.[3]

The ubiquity and invisibility of cyborgs is precisely why these sunshine-belt machines are so deadly. They are as hard to see politically as materially. They are about consciousness—or its simulation.[4] They are floating signi-

communications redesign, stress management. Normalization gives way to automation, utter redundancy. Michel Foucault's *Birth of the Clinic* [1963], *History of Sexuality*, and *Discipline and Punish* [1975] name a form of power at its moment of implosion. The discourse of biopolitics gives way to technobabble, the language of the spliced substantive; no noun is left whole by the multinationals. These are their names, listed from one issue of *Science*: Tech-Knowledge, Genentech, Allergen, Hybritech, Compupro, Genencor, Syntex, Allelix, Agrigenetics Corp., Syntro, Codon, Repligen, Micro-Angelo from Scion Corp., Percom Data, Inter Systems, Cyborg Corp., Statcom Corp., Intertec. If we are imprisoned by language, then escape from that prison house requires language poets, a kind of cultural restriction enzyme to cut the code; cyborg heteroglossia is one form of radical culture politics [Haraway's note]. On the American Marxist literary critic JAMESON (b. 1934), whose works include *The Prison-House of Language* (1972), see above. "Heteroglossia": an allusion to the highly influential theories of MIKHAIL M. BAKHTIN (1895–1975).

9. The branch of philosophy concerned with ways of knowing.

1. Frans de Waal, *Chimpanzee Politics: Power and Sex among the Apes* (New York: Harper & Row, 1982); Langdon Winner, "Do Artifacts Have Politics?" *Daedalus*, winter 1980 [Haraway's note].

2. Canada-based publisher that by the 1960s was exclusively publishing mass-market romance novels; over time, its offerings have become more varied and more sexually explicit. "The indeterminacy principle": that is, the theory formulated in 1927 by the German physicist Werner Heisenberg that one cannot specify both the position and momentum of a subatomic particle.

3. In classical and medieval philosophy, the 5th and highest element, which makes up the heavenly bodies (all terrestrial things were believed to be compounds of the other 4 elements).

4. Jean Baudrillard, *Simulations*, trans. P. Foss, P. Patton, P. Beitchman (New York: Semiotext(e), 1983). Jameson ("Postmodernism," p. 66) points out that Plato's definition of the simulacrum is the copy for which there is no original, i.e., the world of advanced capitalism; of pure exchange [Haraway's note]. On the French social critic and theorist BAUDRILLARD (1929–2007) and the Greek philosopher PLATO (ca. 427–ca. 327 B.C.E.), see above.

fiers moving in pickup trucks across Europe, blocked more effectively by the witch-weavings of the displaced and so unnatural Greenham women,[5] who read the cyborg webs of power very well, than by the militant labor of older masculinist politics, whose natural constituency needs defense jobs. Ultimately the "hardest" science is about the realm of greatest boundary confusion, the realm of pure number, pure spirit, C[3]I, cryptography, and the preservation of potent secrets. The new machines are so clean and light. Their engineers are sun-worshipers mediating a new scientific revolution associated with the night dream of post-industrial society. The diseases evoked by these clean machines are "no more" than the miniscule coding changes of an antigen in the immune system, "no more" than the experience of stress. The nimble little fingers of "Oriental" women, the old fascination of little Anglo-Saxon Victorian girls with doll houses, women's enforced attention to the small take on quite new dimensions in this world. There might be a cyborg Alice[6] taking account of these new dimensions. Ironically, it might be the unnatural cyborg women making chips in Asia and spiral dancing in Santa Rita[7] whose constructed unities will guide effective oppositional strategies.

So my cyborg myth is about transgressed boundaries, potent fusions, and dangerous possibilities which progressive people might explore as one part of needed political work. One of my premises is that most American socialists and feminists see deepened dualisms of mind and body, animal and machine, idealism and materialism in the social practices, symbolic formulations, and physical artifacts associated with "high technology" and scientific culture. From *One-Dimensional Man* to *The Death of Nature*,[8] the analytic resources developed by progressives have insisted on the necessary domination of technics and recalled us to an imagined organic body to integrate our resistance. Another of my premises is that the need for unity of people trying to resist worldwide intensification of domination has never been more acute. But a slightly perverse shift of perspective might better enable us to contest for meanings, as well as for other forms of power and pleasure in technologically-mediated societies.

From one perspective, a cyborg world is about the final imposition of a grid of control on the planet, about the final abstraction embodied in a Star War apocalypse waged in the name of defense, about the final appropriation of women's bodies in a masculinist orgy of war.[9] From another perspective, a cyborg world might be about lived social and bodily realities in which people are not afraid of their joint kinship with animals and machines, not afraid of permanently partial identities and contradictory standpoints. The political struggle is to see from both perspectives at once because each reveals both

5. British women's group that protested the placement of nuclear cruise missiles at the U.S. Air Force base at Greenham Common for nearly two decades, beginning in 1982.
6. A reference to the heroine of Lewis Carroll's *Alice's Adventure in Wonderland* (1865), who became both very small and very large.
7. Jail in Alameda County, California, which in 1982 held more than 1,300 antinuclear protestors who were arrested during a nonviolent demonstration at Lawrence Livermore National Laboratory in Livermore, California.
8. Herbert Marcuse, *One-Dimensional Man* (Boston: Beacon, 1964); Carolyn Merchant, *The Death of Nature* (San Francisco: Harper & Row, 1980) [Haraway's note].
9. Zoe Sofia, "Exterminating Fetuses," *Diacritics*, vol. 14, no. 2 (summer 1984), pp. 47–59, and "Jupiter Space" (Pomona, Calif.: American Studies Association, 1984) [Haraway's note].

dominations and possibilities unimaginable from the other vantage point. Single vision produces worse illusions than double vision or many-headed monsters. Cyborg unities are monstrous and illegitimate; in our present political circumstances, we could hardly hope for more potent myths for resistance and recoupling. I like to imagine LAG, the Livermore Action Group,[1] as a kind of cyborg society, dedicated to realistically converting the laboratories that most fiercely embody and spew out the tools of technological apocalypse, and committed to building a political form that actually manages to hold together witches, engineers, elders, perverts, Christians, mothers, and Leninists[2] long enough to disarm the state. Fission Impossible is the name of the affinity group in my town. (Affinity: related not by blood but by choice, the appeal of one chemical nuclear group for another, avidity.)

Fractured Identities

It has become difficult to name one's feminism by a single adjective—or even to insist in every circumstance upon the noun. Consciousness of exclusion through naming is acute. Identities seem contradictory, partial, and strategic. With the hard-won recognition of their social and historical constitution, gender, race, and class cannot provide the basis for belief in "essential" unity. There is nothing about being "female" that naturally binds women. There is not even such a state as "being" female, itself a highly complex category constructed in contested sexual scientific discourses and other social practices. Gender, race, or class consciousness is an achievement forced on us by the terrible historical experience of the contradictory social realities of patriarchy, colonialism, and capitalism. And who counts as "us" in my own rhetoric? Which identities are available to ground such a potent political myth called "us," and what could motivate enlistment in this collectivity? Painful fragmentation among feminists (not to mention among women) along every possible fault line has made the concept of *woman* elusive, an excuse for the matrix of women's dominations of each other. For me—and for many who share a similar historical location in white, professional middle class, female, radical, North American, mid-adult bodies—the sources of a crisis in political identity are legion. The recent history for much of the U.S. left and U.S. feminism has been a response to this kind of crisis by endless splitting and searches for a new essential unity. But there has also been a growing recognition of another response through coalition—affinity, not identity.[3]

* * *

It is important to note that the effort to construct revolutionary standpoints, epistemologies as achievements of people committed to changing the

1. A group organized to protest the development of nuclear weapons technology at Livermore Laboratory.
2. Adherents of the militant offshoot of communism associated with Vladimir Lenin (1870–1924), founder of the Russian Bolshevik Party.
3. Powerful developments of coalition politics emerge from "third world" speakers, speaking from nowhere, the displaced center of the universe, earth: "We live on the third planet from the sun"—*Sun Poem* by Jamaican writer Edward Kamau Braithwaite, review by Nathaniel Mackey, *Sulfur* 11 (1984), pp. 200–205. *Home Girls*, ed. Barbara Smith (New York: Kitchen Table, Women of Color Press, 1983), ironically subverts naturalized identities precisely while constructing a place from which to speak called home. See esp. Bernice Reagan, "Coalition Politics, Turning the Century," pp. 356–68 [Haraway's note].

world, has been part of the process showing the limits of identification. The acid tools of post-modernist theory and the constructive tools of ontological discourse about revolutionary subjects might be seen as ironic allies in dissolving Western selves in the interests of survival. We are excruciatingly conscious of what it means to have a historically constituted body. But with the loss of innocence in our origin, there is no expulsion from the Garden either. Our politics lose the indulgence of guilt with the naïveté of innocence. But what would another political myth for socialist feminism look like? What kind of politics could embrace partial, contradictory, permanently unclosed constructions of personal and collective selves and still be faithful, effective—and, ironically, socialist feminist?

I do not know of any other time in history when there was greater need for political unity to confront effectively the dominations of "race," "gender," "sexuality," and "class." I also do not know of any other time when the kind of unity we might help build could have been possible. None of "us" have any longer the symbolic or material capability of dictating the shape of reality to any of "them." Or at least "we" cannot claim innocence from practicing such dominations. White women, including socialist feminists, discovered (i.e., were forced kicking and screaming to notice) the non-innocence of the category "woman." That consciousness changes the geography of all previous categories; it denatures them as heat denatures a fragile protein. Cyborg feminists have to argue that "we" do not want any more natural matrix of unity and that no construction is whole. Innocence, and the corollary insistence on victimhood as the only ground for insight, has done enough damage. But the constructed revolutionary subject must give late-twentieth-century people pause as well. In the fraying of identities and in the reflexive strategies for constructing them, the possibility opens up for weaving something other than a shroud for the day after the apocalypse that so prophetically ends salvation history.

Both Marxist/socialist feminisms and radical feminisms have simultaneously naturalized and denatured the category "woman" and consciousness of the social lives of "women." Perhaps a schematic caricature can highlight both kinds of moves. Marxian socialism is rooted in an analysis of wage labor which reveals class structure. The consequence of the wage relationship is systematic alienation, as the worker is dissociated from his (sic) product. Abstraction and illusion rule in knowledge, domination rules in practice. Labor is the pre-eminently privileged category enabling the Marxist to overcome illusion and find that point of view which is necessary for changing the world. Labor is the humanizing activity that makes man; labor is an ontological category permitting the knowledge of a subject, and so the knowledge of subjugation and alienation.

In faithful filiation, socialist feminism advanced by allying itself with the basic analytic strategies of Marxism. The main achievement of both Marxist feminists and socialist feminists was to expand the category of labor to accommodate what (some) women did, even when the wage relation was subordinated to a more comprehensive view of labor under capitalist patriarchy. In particular, women's labor in the household and women's activity as mothers generally, i.e., reproduction in the socialist feminist sense, entered theory on the authority of analogy to the Marxian concept of labor. The unity of women here rests on an epistemology based on the ontological structure of "labor." Marxist/socialist feminism does not "naturalize" unity; it is a possible achievement based on a possible standpoint rooted in social relations. The essentializing move is in the ontological structure of labor or of its analogue, women's activity.[4] The inheritance of Marxian humanism, with its pre-eminently Western self, is the difficulty for me. The contribution from these formulations has been the emphasis on the daily responsibility of real women to build unities, rather than to naturalize them.

* * *

The Informatics of Domination

In this attempt at an epistemological and political position, I would like to sketch a picture of possible unity, a picture indebted to socialist and feminist principles of design. The frame for my sketch is set by the extent and importance of rearrangements in worldwide social relations tied to science and technology. I argue for a politics rooted in claims about fundamental changes in the nature of class, race, and gender in an emerging system of world order analogous in its novelty and scope to that created by industrial capitalism; we are living through a movement from an organic, industrial society to a polymorphous, information system—from all work to all play, a deadly game. Simultaneously material and ideological, the dichotomies may be expressed in the following chart of transitions from the comfortable old hierarchical dominations to the scary new networks I have called the informatics of domination:

Representation	Simulation
Bourgeois novel, realism	Science fiction, post-modernism
Organism	Biotic component
Depth, integrity	Surface, boundary
Heat	Noise
Biology as clinical practice	Biology as inscription
Physiology	Communications engineering
Small group	Subsystem
Perfection	Optimization

4. The feminist standpoint argument is being developed by: Jane Flax, "Political Philosophy and the Patriarchal Unconsciousness," in Sandra Harding and Merrill Hintikka, eds., *Discovering Reality* (Dordrecht: Reidel, 1983); Sandra Harding, "The Contradictions and Ambivalence of a Feminist Science," ms.; Harding and Hintikka, *Discovering Reality*; Nancy Hartsock, *Money, Sex, and Power* (New York: Longman, 1983) and "The Feminist Standpoint: Developing the Ground for a Specifically Feminist Historical Materialism," in Harding and Hintikka, *Discovering Reality*; Mary O'Brien, *The Politics of Reproduction* (New York: Routledge & Kegan Paul, 1981); Hilary Rose, "Hand, Brain, and Heart: A Feminist Epistemology for the Natural Sciences," *Signs*, vol. 9, no. 1 (1983), pp. 73–90; Dorothy Smith, "Women's Perspective as a Radical Critique of Sociology," *Sociological Inquiry* 44 (1974), and "A Sociology of Women," in J. Sherman and E. T. Beck, eds., *The Prism of Sex* (Madison: University of Wisconsin Press, 1979). The central role of object-relations versions of psychoanalysis and related strong universalizing moves in discussing reproduction, caring work, and mothering in many approaches to epistemology underline their authors' resistance to what I am calling post-modernism. For me, both the universalizing moves and the versions of psychoanalysis make analysis of "women's place in the integrated circuit" difficult and lead to systematic difficulties in accounting or even seeing major aspects of the construction of gender and gender social life [Haraway's note]. Haraway's main target in object-relations theory is Nancy Chodorow's influential book *The Reproduction of Mothering* (1978).

Eugenics	Population control
Decadence, *Magic Mountain*	Obsolescence, *Future Shock*[5]
Hygiene	Stress Management
Microbiology, tuberculosis	Immunology, AIDS
Organic division of labor	Ergonomics/cybernetics of labor
Functional specialization	Modular construction
Reproduction	Replication
Organic sex role specialization	Optimal genetic strategies
Biological determinism	Evolutionary inertia, constraints
Community ecology	Ecosystem
Racial chain of being	Neo-imperialism, United Nations humanism
Scientific management in home/factory	Global factory/Electronic cottage
Family/Market/Factory	Women in the Integrated Circuit
Family wage	Comparable worth[6]
Public/Private	Cyborg citizenship
Nature/Culture	Fields of difference
Cooperation	Communications enhancement
Freud	Lacan[7]
Sex	Genetic engineering
Labor	Robotics
Mind	Artificial Intelligence
World War II	Star Wars
White Capitalist Patriarchy	Informatics of Domination

This list suggests several interesting things.[8] First, the objects on the right-hand side cannot be coded as "natural," a realization that subverts naturalistic coding for the left-hand side as well. We cannot go back ideologically or materially. It's not just that "god" is dead; so is the "goddess." In relation to objects like biotic components, one must think not in terms of essential properties, but in terms of strategies of design, boundary constraints, rates of flows, systems logics, costs of lowering constraints. Sexual reproduction is one kind of reproductive strategy among many, with costs and benefits as a function of the system environment. Ideologies of sexual reproduction can no longer reasonably call on the notions of sex and sex role as organic aspects in natural objects like organisms and families. Such reasoning will be unmasked as irrational, and ironically corporate executives reading *Playboy* and anti-

5. A 1970 book of social history and production by Alvin Toffler. *The Magic Mountain* (1924), a novel by Thomas Mann set in a tuberculosis sanatorium.

6. The concept that male and female workers holding different jobs that are comparable in difficulty and responsibility should receive equal pay. "Family wage": a wage high enough that a single (usually male) breadwinner can support a family.

7. JACQUES LACAN (1901–1981), French psychoanalyst who argued that the unconscious is structured like a language and claimed to be the intellectual heir of SIGMUND FREUD (1856–1939), the Austrian founder of psychoanalysis.

8. My previous efforts to understand biology as a cybernetic command-control discourse and organisms as "natural-technical objects of knowledge" are: "The High Cost of Information in Post–World War II Evolutionary Biology," *Philosophical Forum*, vol. 13, nos. 2–3 (1979), pp. 206–37; "Signs of Dominance: From a Physiology to a Cybernetics of Primate Society," *Studies in History of Biology* 6 (1983), pp. 129–219; "Class, Race, Sex, Scientific Objects of Knowledge: A Socialist-Feminist Perspective on the Social Construction of Productive Knowledge and Some Political Consequences," in Violet Haas and Carolyn Perucci, eds., *Women in Scientific and Engineering Professions* (Ann Arbor: University of Michigan Press, 1984), pp. 212–29 [Haraway's note].

porn radical feminists will make strange bedfellows in jointly unmasking the irrationalism.

* * *

One should expect control strategies to concentrate on boundary conditions and interfaces, on rates of flow across boundaries—and not on the integrity of natural objects. "Integrity" or "sincerity" of the Western self gives way to decision procedures and expert systems. For example, control strategies applied to women's capacities to give birth to new human beings will be developed in the languages of population control and maximization of goal achievement for individual decision-makers. Control strategies will be formulated in terms of rates, costs of constraints, degrees of freedom. Human beings, like any other component or subsystem, must be localized in a system architecture whose basic modes of operation are probabilistic, statistical. No objects, spaces, or bodies are sacred in themselves; any component can be interfaced with any other if the proper standard, the proper code, can be constructed for processing signals in a common language. Exchange in this world transcends the universal translation effected by capitalist markets that Marx analyzed so well.[9] The privileged pathology affecting all kinds of components in this universe is stress—communications breakdown.[1] The cyborg is not subject to Foucault's biopolitics; the cyborg simulates politics, a much more potent field of operations.

This kind of analysis of scientific and cultural objects of knowledge which have appeared historically since World War II prepares us to notice some important inadequacies in feminist analysis which has proceeded as if the organic, hierarchical dualisms ordering discourse in "the West" since Aristotle[2] still ruled. They have been cannibalized, or as Zoe Sofia (Sofoulis) might put it, they have been "techno-digested." The dichotomies between mind and body, animal and human, organism and machine, public and private, nature and culture, men and women, primitive and civilized are all in question ideologically. The actual situation of women is their integration/exploitation into a world system of production/reproduction and communication called the informatics of domination. The home, workplace, market, public arena, the body itself—all can be dispersed and interfaced in nearly infinite, polymorphous ways, with large consequences for women and others—consequences that themselves are very different for different people and which make potent oppositional international movements difficult to imagine and essential for survival. One important route for reconstructing socialist-feminist politics is through theory and practice addressed to the social relations of science and technology, including crucially the systems of myth and meanings structuring our imaginations. The cyborg is a kind of disassembled and reassembled, post-modern collective and personal self. This is the self feminists must code.

9. That is, the translation of individual labor power into commodities. On the German political theorist, economist, and revolutionary KARL MARX (1818–1883), see above.

1. E. Rusten Hogness, "Why Stress? A Look at the Making of Stress, 1936–56," available from the author, 4437 Mill Creek Rd., Healdsburg, CA 95448 [Haraway's note].

2. Greek philosopher (384–322 B.C.E.; see above) whose scientific system dominated Western thought until the Renaissance.

Communications technologies and biotechnologies are the crucial tools recrafting our bodies. These tools embody and enforce new social relations for women worldwide. Technologies and scientific discourses can be partially understood as formalizations, i.e., as frozen moments, of the fluid social interactions constituting them, but they should also be viewed as instruments for enforcing meanings. The boundary is permeable between tool and myth, instrument and concept, historical systems of social relations and historical anatomies of possible bodies, including objects of knowledge. Indeed, myth and tool mutually constitute each other.

Furthermore, communications sciences and modern biologies are constructed by a common move—*the translation of the world into a problem of coding,* a search for a common language in which all resistance to instrumental control disappears and all heterogeneity can be submitted to disassembly, reassembly, investment, and exchange.

In communications sciences, the translation of the world into a problem in coding can be illustrated by looking at cybernetic (feedback controlled) systems theories applied to telephone technology, computer design, weapons deployment, or data base construction and maintenance. In each case, solution to the key questions rests on a theory of language and control; the key operation is determining the rates, directions, and probabilities of flow of a quantity called information. The world is subdivided by boundaries differentially permeable to information. Information is just that kind of quantifiable element (unit, basis of unity) which allows universal translation, and so unhindered instrumental power (called effective communication). The biggest threat to such power is interruption of communication. Any system breakdown is a function of stress. The fundamentals of this technology can be condensed into the metaphor C^3I, command-control-communication-intelligence, the military's symbol for its operations theory.

In modern biologies, the translation of the world into a problem in coding can be illustrated by molecular genetics, ecology, socio-biological evolutionary theory, and immunobiology. The organism has been translated into problems of genetic coding and read-out. Biotechnology, a writing technology, informs research broadly.[3] In a sense, organisms have ceased to exist as objects of knowledge, giving way to biotic components, i.e., special kinds of information processing devices. The analogous moves in ecology could be examined by probing the history and utility of the concept of the ecosystem. Immunobiology and associated medical practices are rich exemplars of the privilege of coding and recognition systems as objects of knowledge, as constructions of bodily reality for us. Biology is here a kind of cryptography. Research is necessarily a kind of intelligence activity. Ironies abound. A stressed system goes awry; its communication processes break down; it fails to recognize the difference between self and other. Human babies with baboon hearts[4] evoke national ethical perplexity—for animal-rights activists at least as much as for guardians of human purity. Gay men, Haitian

3. A left entry to the biotechnology debate: *GeneWatch, a Bulletin of the Committee for Responsible Genetics*, 5 Doane St. 4th floor, Boston, MA 02109; Susan Wright, ["Recombinant DNA Technology and Its Social Transformation, 1972–82," *Osiris*, 2d ser., vol. 2 (1996), pp. 303–60] and "Recombinant DNA: The Status of Hazards and Controls," *Environment*, July/August 1982; Edward Yoxen, *The Gene Business* (New York: Harper & Row, 1983) [Haraway's note].

4. A transplant performed in 1984; the infant died 21 days later.

immigrants, and intravenous drug users[5] are the "privileged" victims of an awful immune-system disease that marks (inscribes on the body) confusion of boundaries and moral pollution.

But these excursions into communications sciences and biology have been at a rarefied level; there is a mundane, largely economic reality to support my claim that these sciences and technologies indicate fundamental transformations in the structure of the world for us. Communications technologies depend on electronics. Modern states, multinational corporations, military power, welfare-state apparatuses, satellite systems, political processes, fabrication of our imaginations, labor-control systems, medical constructions of our bodies, commercial pornography, the international division of labor, and religious evangelism depend intimately upon electronics. Microelectronics is the technical basis of simulacra, i.e., of copies without originals.

Microelectronics mediates the translations of *labor* into robotics and word processing; *sex* into genetic engineering and reproductive technologies; and *mind* into artificial intelligence and decision procedures. The new biotechnologies concern more than human reproduction. Biology as a powerful engineering science for redesigning materials and processes has revolutionary implications for industry, perhaps most obvious today in areas of fermentation, agriculture, and energy. Communications sciences and biology are constructions of natural-technical objects of knowledge in which the difference between machine and organism is thoroughly blurred; mind, body, and tool are on very intimate terms. The "multinational" material organization of the production and reproduction of daily life and the symbolic organization of the production and reproduction of culture and imagination seem equally implicated. The boundary-maintaining images of base and super-structure,[6] public and private, or material and ideal never seemed more feeble.

I have used Rachel Grossman's image of women in the integrated circuit to name the situation of women in a world so intimately restructured through the social relations of science and technology.[7] I use the odd circumlocution, "the social relations of science and technology," to indicate that we are not dealing with a technological determinism, but with a historical system depending upon structured relations among people. But the phrase should also indicate that science and technology provide fresh sources of power, that we need fresh sources of analysis and political action.[8] Some of the rearrange-

5. These three groups were the focus of medical attention when AIDS was first identified in the 1980s.

6. "Base" and "superstructure" are Marxist terms: a society's base is its economic mode of production, which conditions its superstructure—its social, political, juridical, and intellectual life generally.

7. Starting references for "women in the integrated circuit": Pamela D'Onofrio-Flores and Sheila M. Pfafflin, eds., *Scientific-Technological Change and the Role of Women in Development* (Boulder, Colo.: Westview Press, 1982); Maria Patricia Fernandez-Kelly, *For We Are Sold, I and My People* (Albany, N.Y.: SUNY Press, 1983); Annette Fuentes and Barbara Ehrenreich, *Women in the Global Factory* (Boston: South End Press, 1983), with an especially useful list of resources and organizations; Rachael Grossman, "Women's Place in the Integrated Circuit," *Radical America*, vol. 14, no. 1 (1980), pp. 29–50; June Nash and M. P. Fernandez-Kelly, eds., *Women and Men and the International Division of Labor* (Albany, N.Y.: SUNY Press, 1983); Aihwa Ong, "Japanese Factories, Malay Workers: Industrialization and the Cultural Construction of Gender in West Malaysia," in [Jane Atkinson and Shelly Errington, eds., *Power and Difference: Gender in Island Southeast Asia* (Stanford: Stanford University Press, 1990)]; Science Policy Research Unity, *Microelectronics and Women's Employment in Britain* (University of Sussex, 1982) [Haraway's note].

8. The best example is Bruno Latour, *Les Microbes: Guerre et Paix, suivi de Irréductions* [*Microbes: War and Peace, Followed by Irreductions*] (Paris: Métailié, 1984) [Haraway's note].

ments of race, sex, and class rooted in high-tech-facilitated social relations can make socialist feminism more relevant to effective progressive politics.

The Homework Economy

The "New Industrial Revolution" is producing a new worldwide working class. The extreme mobility of capital and the emerging international division of labor are intertwined with the emergence of new collectivities, and the weakening of familiar groupings. These developments are neither gender- nor race-neutral. White men in advanced industrial societies have become newly vulnerable to permanent job loss, and women are not disappearing from the job rolls at the same rates as men. It is not simply that women in third-world countries are the preferred labor force for the science-based multinationals in the export-processing sectors, particularly in electronics. The picture is more systematic and involves reproduction, sexuality, culture, consumption, and production. In the prototypical Silicon Valley, many women's lives have been structured around employment in electronics-dependent jobs, and their intimate realities include serial heterosexual monogamy, negotiating childcare, distance from extended kin or most other forms of traditional community, a high likelihood of loneliness and extreme economic vulnerability as they age. The ethnic and racial diversity of women in Silicon Valley structures a microcosm of conflicting differences in culture, family, religion, education, language.

Richard Gordon has called this new situation the homework economy.[9] Although he includes the phenomenon of literal homework emerging in connection with electronics assembly, Gordon intends "homework economy" to name a restructuring of work that broadly has the characteristics formerly ascribed to female jobs, jobs literally done only by women. Work is being redefined as both literally female and feminized, whether performed by men or women. To be feminized means to be made extremely vulnerable; able to be disassembled, reassembled, exploited as a reserve labor force; seen less as workers than as servers; subjected to time arrangements on and off the paid job that make a mockery of a limited work day; leading an existence that always borders on being obscene, out of place, and reducible to sex. Deskilling is an old strategy newly applicable to formerly privileged workers. However, the homework economy does not refer only to large-scale deskilling, nor does it deny that new areas of high skill are emerging, even for women and men previously excluded from skilled employment. Rather, the concept indicates that factory, home, and market are integrated on a new scale and that the places of women are crucial—and need to be analyzed

9. For the homework economy and some supporting arguments: Richard Gordon, "The Computerization of Daily Life, the Sexual Division of Labor, and the Homework Economy," in R. Gordon, ed., *Microelectronics in Transition* (Norwood, N.J.: Ablex, 1985); Patricia Hill Collins, "Third World Women in America," and Sara G. Burr, "Woman and Work," in Barbara K. Haber, ed., *The Women's Annual*, 1981 (Boston: G. K. Hall, 1982); Judith Gregory and Karen Nussbaum, "Race against Time: Automation of the Office," *Office: Technology and People* 1 (1982), pp. 197–236; Frances Fox Piven and Richard Cloward, *The New Class War: Reagan's Attack on the Welfare State and Its Consequences* (New York: Pantheon, 1982); Microelectronics Group, *Microelectronics: Capitalist Technology and the Working Class* (London: CSE, 1980); Karin Stallard, Barbara Ehrenreich, and Holly Sklar, *Poverty in the American Dream* (Boston: South End Press, 1983), including a useful organization and resource list [Haraway's note].

for differences among women and for meanings for relations between men and women in various situations.

The homework economy as a world capitalist organizational structure is made possible by (not caused by) the new technologies. The success of the attack on relatively privileged, mostly white, men's unionized jobs is tied to the power of the new communications technologies to integrate and control labor despite extensive dispersion and decentralization. The consequences of the new technologies are felt by women both in the loss of the family (male) wage (if they ever had access to this white privilege) and in the character of their own jobs, which are becoming capital-intensive, e.g., office work and nursing.

The new economic and technological arrangements are also related to the collapsing welfare state and the ensuing intensification of demands on women to sustain daily life for themselves as well as for men, children, and old people. The feminization of poverty—generated by dismantling the welfare state, by the homework economy where stable jobs become the exception, and sustained by the expectation that women's wage will not be matched by a male income for the support of children—has become an urgent focus. The causes of various women-headed households are a function of race, class, or sexuality; but their increasing generality is a ground for coalitions of women on many issues. That women regularly sustain daily life partly as a function of their enforced status as mothers is hardly new; the kind of integration with the overall capitalist and progressively war-based economy is new. The particular pressure, for example, on U.S. black women, who have achieved an escape from (barely) paid domestic service and who now hold clerical and similar jobs in large numbers, has large implications for continued enforced black poverty *with* employment. Teenage women in industrializing areas of the third world increasingly find themselves the sole or major source of a cash wage for their families, while access to land is ever more problematic. These developments must have major consequences in the psychodynamics and politics of gender and race.

Within the framework of three major stages of capitalism (commercial/early industrial, monopoly, multinational)—tied to nationalism, imperialism, and multinationalism, and related to Jameson's three dominant aesthetic periods of realism, modernism, and post-modernism—I would argue that specific forms of families dialectically relate to forms of capital and to its political and cultural concomitants. Although lived problematically and unequally, ideal forms of these families might be schematized as (1) the patriarchal nuclear family, structured by the dichotomy between public and private and accompanied by the white bourgeois ideology of separate spheres[1] and nineteenth-century Anglo-American bourgeois feminism; (2) the modern family mediated (or enforced) by the welfare state and institutions like the family wage, with a flowering of a-feminist heterosexual ideologies, including their radical versions represented in Greenwich Village[2] around World War I; and (3) the "family" of the homework economy with its oxymoronic structure of women-headed households and its explosion of feminisms and the paradoxical intensification and erosion of gender itself.

1. That is, the division of life into the public sphere of work and the private sphere of the home, where authority was said to be held by men and by women, respectively.

2. A neighborhood in New York City (in Lower Manhattan), which for much of the 20th century was associated with unconventional artists and radicals.

This is the context in which the projections for worldwide structural unemployment stemming from the new technologies are part of the picture of the homework economy. As robotics and related technologies put men out of work in "developed" countries and exacerbate failure to generate male jobs in third-world "development," and as the automated office becomes the rule even in labor-surplus countries, the feminization of work intensifies. Black women in the United States have long known what it looks like to face the structural underemployment ("feminization") of black men, as well as their own highly vulnerable position in the wage economy. It is no longer a secret that sexuality, reproduction, family, and community life are interwoven with this economic structure in myriad ways which have also differentiated the situations of white and black women. Many more women and men will contend with similar situations, which will make cross-gender and race alliances on issues of basic life support (with or without jobs) necessary, not just nice.

The new technologies also have a profound effect on hunger and on food production for subsistence worldwide. Rae Lessor Blumberg estimates that women produce about fifty per cent of the world's subsistence food.[3] Women are excluded generally from benefiting from the increased high-tech commodification of food and energy crops, their days are made more arduous because their responsibilities to provide food do not diminish, and their reproductive situations are made more complex. Green Revolution technologies interact with other high-tech industrial production to alter gender divisions of labor and differential gender migration patterns.

The new technologies seem deeply involved in the forms of "privatization" that Ros Petchesky has analyzed, in which militarization, right-wing family ideologies and policies, and intensified definitions of corporate property as private synergistically interact.[4] The new communications technologies are fundamental to the eradication of "public life" for everyone. This facilitates

3. Rae Lessor Blumberg, "A General Theory of Sex and Its Application to the Position of Women in Today's World Economy," paper delivered to Sociology Board, UCSC, February 1983 ["A General Theory of Gender Stratification," *Sociological Theory* 2 (1984): 23–101]. Also Blumberg, *Stratification: Socioeconomic and Sexual Inequality* (Boston: Brown, 1981). See also Sally Hacker, "Doing It the Hard Way: Ethnographic Studies in the Agribusiness and Engineering Classroom," California American Studies Association, Pomona, 1984 [in her *"Doing It the Hard Way": Investigations of Gender and Technology* (Boston: Unwin Hyman, 1990)]; S. Hacker and Lisa Bovit, "Agriculture to Agribusiness: Technical Imperatives and Changing Roles," *Proceedings of the Society for the History of Technology*, Milwaukee, 1981; Lawrence Busch and William Lacy, *Science, Agriculture, and the Politics of Research* (Boulder, Colo.: Westview Press, 1983); Denis Wilfred, "Capital and Agriculture, a Review of Marxian Problematics," *Studies in Political Economy*, no. 7 (1982), pp. 127–54; Carolyn Sachs, *The Invisible Farmers: Women in Agricultural Production* (Totowa, N.J.: Rowman & Allanheld, 1983). Thanks to Elizabeth Bird, "Green Revolution Imperialism," I & II, ms., UCSC, 1984. The conjunction of the Green Revolution's social relations with biotechnologies like plant genetic engineering makes the pressures on land in the third world increasingly intense. AID's [Agency for International Development] estimates (*New York Times*, 14 October 1984) used at the 1984 World Food Day are that in Africa, women produce about 90 per cent of rural food supplies, about 60–80 per cent in Asia, and provide 40 per cent of agricultural labor in the Near East and Latin America. Blumberg charges that world organizations' agricultural politics, as well as those of multinationals and national governments in the third world, generally ignore fundamental issues in the sexual division of labor. The present tragedy of famine in Africa might owe as much to male supremacy as to capitalism, colonialism, and rain patterns. More accurately, capitalism and racism are usually structurally male dominant [Haraway's note]. The Green Revolution: the Western campaign of the 1960s that introduced high-yield varieties of specific staple crops and promoted pesticides to increase food production in developing countries.

4. Cynthia Enloe, "Women Textile Workers in the Militarization of Southeast Asia," in Nash and Fernandez-Kelly, *Women and Men*; Rosalind Petchesky, "Abortion, Anti-Feminism, and the Rise of the New Right," *Feminist Studies*, vol. 7, no. 2 (1981) [Haraway's note].

the mushrooming of a permanent high-tech military establishment at the cultural and economic expense of most people, but especially of women. Technologies like video games and highly miniaturized television seem crucial to production of modern forms of "private life." The culture of video games is heavily oriented to individual competition and extraterrestrial warfare. High-tech, gendered imaginations are produced here, imaginations that can contemplate destruction of the planet and a sci-fi escape from its consequences. More than our imaginations is militarized; and the other realities of electronic and nuclear warfare are inescapable.

The new technologies affect the social relations of both sexuality and of reproduction, and not always in the same ways. The close ties of sexuality and instrumentality, of views of the body as a kind of private satisfaction- and utility-maximizing machine, are described nicely in sociobiological origin stories that stress a genetic calculus and explain the inevitable dialectic of domination of male and female gender roles.[5] These sociobiological stories depend on a high-tech view of the body as a biotic component or cybernetic communications system. Among the many transformations of reproductive situations is the medical one, where women's bodies have boundaries newly permeable to both "visualization" and "intervention." Of course, who controls the interpretation of bodily boundaries in medical hermeneutics is a major feminist issue. The speculum[6] served as an icon of women's claiming their bodies in the 1970s; that hand-craft tool is inadequate to express our needed body politics in the negotiation of reality in the practices of cyborg reproduction. Self-help is not enough. The technologies of visualization recall the important cultural practice of hunting with the camera and the deeply predatory nature of a photographic consciousness.[7] Sex, sexuality, and reproduction are central actors in high-tech myth systems structuring our imaginations of personal and social possibility.

* * *

Women in the Integrated Circuit

Let me summarize the picture of women's historical locations in advanced industrial societies, as these positions have been restructured partly through the social relations of science and technology. If it was ever possible ideologically to characterize women's lives by the distinction of public and private domains—suggested by images of the division of working-class life into

5. For a feminist version of this logic, see Sarah Blaffer Hrdy, *The Woman That Never Evolved* (Cambridge, Mass.: Harvard University Press, 1981). For an analysis of scientific women's storytelling practices, especially in relation to sociobiology, in evolutionary debates around child abuse and infanticide, see Donna Haraway, "The Contest for Primate Nature: Daughters of Man the Hunter in the Field, 1960–80," in Mark Kann, ed., *The Future of American Democracy* (Philadelphia: Temple University Press, 1983), pp. 175–208 [Haraway's note].

6. A medical instrument used in vaginal examinations; feminist books such as *Our Bodies, Ourselves* (3 eds. in the 1970s) advocated self-examination.

7. For the moment of transition of hunting with guns to hunting with cameras in the construction of popular meanings of nature for an American urban immigrant public, see Donna Haraway, "Teddy Bear Patriarchy," *Social Text*, [no. 11 (Winter 1984–85), pp. 20–64]; Roderick Nash, "The Exporting and Importing of Nature: Nature-Appreciation as a Commodity, 1850–1980," *Perspectives in American History*, vol. 3 (1979), pp. 517–60; Susan Sontag, *On Photography* (New York: Dell, 1977); and Douglas Preston, "Shooting in Paradise," *Natural History*, vol. 93, no. 12 (December 1984), pp. 14–19 [Haraway's note].

factory and home, of bourgeois life into market and home, and of gender existence into personal and political realms—it is now a totally misleading ideology, even to show how both terms of these dichotomies construct each other in practice and in theory. I prefer a network ideological image, suggesting the profusion of spaces and identities and the permeability of boundaries in the personal body and in the body politic. "Networking" is both a feminist practice and a multinational corporate strategy—weaving is for oppositional cyborgs.

The only way to characterize the informatics of domination is as a massive intensification of insecurity and cultural impoverishment, with common failure of subsistence networks for the most vulnerable. Since much of this picture interweaves with the social relations of science and technology, the urgency of a socialist-feminist politics addressed to science and technology is plain. There is much now being done, and the grounds for political work are rich. For example, the efforts to develop forms of collective struggle for women in paid work, like SEIU's District 925,[8] should be a high priority for all of us. These efforts are profoundly tied to technical restructuring of labor processes and reformations of working classes. These efforts also are providing understanding of a more comprehensive kind of labor organization, involving community, sexuality, and family issues never privileged in the largely white male industrial unions.

The structural rearrangements related to the social relations of science and technology evoke strong ambivalence. But it is not necessary to be ultimately depressed by the implications of late-twentieth-century women's relation to all aspects of work, culture, production of knowledge, sexuality, and reproduction. For excellent reasons, most Marxisms see domination best and have trouble understanding what can only look like false consciousness[9] and people's complicity in their own domination in late capitalism. It is crucial to remember that what is lost, perhaps especially from women's points of view, is often virulent forms of oppression, nostalgically naturalized in the face of current violation. Ambivalence toward the disrupted unities mediated by high-tech culture requires not sorting consciousness into categories of "clear-sighted critique grounding a solid political epistemology" versus "manipulated false consciousness," but subtle understanding of emerging pleasures, experiences, and powers with serious potential for changing the rules of the game.

There are grounds for hope in the emerging bases for new kinds of unity across race, gender, and class, as these elementary units of socialist-feminist analysis themselves suffer protean transformations. Intensifications of hardship experienced worldwide in connection with the social relations of science and technology are severe. But what people are experiencing is not transparently clear, and we lack sufficiently subtle connections for collectively building effective theories of experience. Present efforts—Marxist, psychoanalytic, feminist, anthropological—to clarify even "our" experience are rudimentary.

8. The division of the Service Employees International Union formed in 1981 that represents librarians, college and university support staff, employees of local government, and other office workers.

9. A Marxist term referring to an individual's tendency to view reality in ways congruent with the interests of the dominant orthodoxy rather than in ways that reflect his or her own class interest.

I am conscious of the odd perspective provided by my historical position—a Ph.D. in biology for an Irish Catholic girl was made possible by Sputnik's[1] impact on U.S. national science-education policy. I have a body and mind as much constructed by the post–World War II arms race and cold war as by the women's movements. There are more grounds for hope by focusing on the contradictory effects of politics designed to produce loyal American technocrats, which as well produced large numbers of dissidents, rather than by focusing on the present defeats.

The permanent partiality of feminist points of view has consequences for our expectations of forms of political organization and participation. We do not need a totality in order to work well. The feminist dream of a common language, like all dreams for a perfectly true language, of perfectly faithful naming of experience, is a totalizing and imperialist one. In that sense, dialectics[2] too is a dream language, longing to resolve contradiction. Perhaps, ironically, we can learn from our fusions with animals and machines how not to be Man, the embodiment of Western logos.[3] From the point of view of pleasure in these potent and taboo fusions, made inevitable by the social relations of science and technology, there might indeed be a feminist science.

Cyborgs: A Myth of Political Identity

* * *

To recapitulate, certain dualisms have been persistent in Western traditions; they have all been systemic to the logics and practices of domination of women, people of color, nature, workers, animals—in short, domination of all constituted as *others,* whose task is to mirror the self. Chief among these troubling dualisms are self/other, mind/body, culture/nature, male/female, civilized/primitive, reality/appearance, whole/part, agent/resource, maker/made, active/passive, right/wrong, truth/illusion, total/partial, God/man. The self is the One who is not dominated, who knows that by the service of the other; the other is the one who holds the future, who knows that by the experience of domination, which gives the lie to the autonomy of the self. To be One is to be autonomous, to be powerful, to be God; but to be One is to be an illusion, and so to be involved in a dialectic of apocalypse with the other. Yet to be other is to be multiple, without clear boundary, frayed, insubstantial. One is too few, but two are too many.

High-tech culture challenges these dualisms in intriguing ways. It is not clear who makes and who is made in the relation between human and machine. It is not clear what is mind and what body in machines that resolve into coding practices. Insofar as we know ourselves in both formal discourse (e.g., biology) and in daily practice (e.g., the homework economy in the integrated circuit), we find ourselves to be cyborgs, hybrids, mosaics, chimeras.

1. The first artificial satellite, launched by the Soviet Union on October 4, 1957; its launch spurred the United States to invest in science and science education and to begin the space race.
2. Marxist dialectics relates society's cultural sphere (its politics, arts, philosophy, and religion) directly to its socioeconomic foundations, depicting society—including its apparent contradictions—as a coherent total system.
3. Haraway alludes to the French philosopher JACQUES DERRIDA (1930–2004), who deconstructs Western logos (literally, "word, discourse, reason," from the Greek) and its partial conception of "Man."

Biological organisms have become biotic systems, communications devices like others. There is no fundamental, ontological separation in our formal knowledge of machine and organism, of technical and organic.

One consequence is that our sense of connection to our tools is heightened. The trance state experienced by many computer users has become a staple of science-fiction film and cultural jokes. Perhaps paraplegics and other severely handicapped people can (and sometimes do) have the most intense experiences of complex hybridization with other communication devices. Anne McCaffrey's *The Ship Who Sang*[4] explored the consciousness of a cyborg, hybrid of girl's brain and complex machinery, formed after the birth of a severely handicapped child. Gender, sexuality, embodiment, skill: all were reconstituted in the story. Why should our bodies end at the skin, or include at best other beings encapsulated by skin? From the seventeenth century till now, machines could be animated—given ghostly souls to make them speak or move or to account for their orderly development and mental capacities. Or organisms could be mechanized—reduced to body understood as resource of mind. These machine/organism relationships are obsolete, unnecessary. For us, in imagination and in other practice, machines can be prosthetic devices, intimate components, friendly selves. We don't need organic holism to give impermeable wholeness, the total woman and her feminist variants (mutants?).

* * *

Monsters have always defined the limits of community in Western imaginations. The Centaurs and Amazons[5] of ancient Greece established the limits of the centered polis of the Greek male human by their disruption of marriage and boundary pollutions of the warrior with animality and woman. Unseparated twins and hermaphrodites were the confused human material in early modern France who grounded discourse on the natural and supernatural, medical and legal, portents and diseases—all crucial to establishing modern identity.[6] The evolutionary and behavioral sciences of monkeys and apes have marked the multiple boundaries of late-twentieth-century industrial identities. Cyborg monsters in feminist science fiction define quite different political possibilities and limits from those proposed by the mundane fiction of Man and Woman.

There are several consequences to taking seriously the imagery of cyborgs as other than our enemies. Our bodies, ourselves; bodies are maps of power and identity. Cyborgs are no exceptions. A cyborg body is not innocent; it was not born in a garden; it does not seek unitary identity and so generate antagonistic dualisms without end (or until the world ends); it takes irony for granted. One is too few, and two is only one possibility. Intense pleasure in skill, machine skill, ceases to be a sin, but an aspect of embodiment. The machine is not an *it* to be animated, worshiped and dominated. The machine

4. A 1969 novel by McCaffrey (1926–2011).

5. In Greek mythology, female warriors. Centaurs: creatures with the body of a horse and the torso and upper body of a man.

6. Page DuBois, *Centaurs and Amazons* (Ann Arbor: University of Michigan Press, 1982); Lorraine Daston and Katharine Park, "Hermaphrodites in Renaissance France," [*Critical Matrix* 1, no. 5 (1985), pp. 1–19]; Katharine Park and Lorraine Daston, "Unnatural Conceptions: The Study of Monsters in 16th and 17th Century France and England," *Past and Present*, no. 92 (August 1981), pp. 20–54 [Haraway's note].

is us, our processes, an aspect of our embodiment. We can be responsible for machines; *they* do not dominate or threaten us. We are responsible for boundaries; we are they. Up till now (once upon a time), female embodiment seemed to be given, organic, necessary; and female embodiment seemed to mean skill in mothering and its metaphoric extensions. Only by being out of place could we take intense pleasure in machines, and then with excuses that this was organic activity after all, appropriate to females. Cyborgs might consider more seriously the partial, fluid, sometimes aspect of sex and sexual embodiment. Gender might not be global identity after all.

The ideologically charged question of what counts as daily activity, as experience, can be approached by exploiting the cyborg image. Feminists have recently claimed that women are given to dailiness, that women more than men somehow sustain daily life, and so have a privileged epistemological position potentially. There is a compelling aspect to this claim, one that makes visible unvalued female activity and names it as the ground of life. But *the* ground of life? What about all the ignorance of women, all the exclusions and failures of knowledge and skill? What about men's access to daily competence, to knowing how to build things, to take them apart, to play? What about other embodiments? Cyborg gender is a local possibility taking a global vengeance. Race, gender, and capital require a cyborg theory of wholes and parts. There is no drive in cyborgs to produce total theory, but there is an intimate experience of boundaries, their construction and deconstruction. There is a myth system waiting to become a political language to ground one way of looking at science and technology and challenging the informatics of domination.

One last image: organisms and organismic, holistic politics depend on metaphors of rebirth and invariably call on the resources of reproductive sex. I would suggest that cyborgs have more to do with regeneration and are suspicious of the reproductive matrix and of most birthing. For salamanders, regeneration after injury, such as the loss of a limb, involves regrowth of structure and restoration of function with the constant possibility of twinning or other odd topographical productions at the site of former injury. The regrown limb can be monstrous, duplicated, potent. We have all been injured, profoundly. We require regeneration, not rebirth, and the possibilities for our reconstitution include the utopian dream of the hope for a monstrous world without gender.

Cyborg imagery can help express two crucial arguments in this essay: (1) the production of universal, totalizing theory is a major mistake that misses most of reality, probably always, but certainly now; (2) taking responsibility for the social relations of science and technology means refusing an antiscience metaphysics, a demonology of technology, and so means embracing the skillful task of reconstructing the boundaries of daily life, in partial connection with others, in communication with all of our parts. It is not just that science and technology are possible means of great human satisfaction, as well as a matrix of complex dominations. Cyborg imagery can suggest a way out of the maze of dualisms in which we have explained our bodies and our tools to ourselves. This is a dream not of a common language, but of a powerful infidel heteroglossia. It is an imagination of a feminist speaking in tongues to strike fear into the circuits of the super-savers of the new right. It means both building and destroying machines, identities, categories, relationships, spaces, stories. Though both are bound in the spiral dance, I would rather be a cyborg than a goddess.

1985

From The Companion Species Manifesto: Dogs, People, and Significant Otherness

Companions

In "The Cyborg Manifesto,"[1] I tried to write a surrogacy agreement, a trope,[2] a figure for living within and honoring the skills and practices of contemporary technoculture without losing touch with the permanent war apparatus of a non-optional, post-nuclear world and its transcendent, very material lies. Cyborgs can be figures for living within contradictions, attentive to the naturecultures[3] of mundane practices, opposed to the dire myths of self-birthing, embracing mortality as the condition for life, and alert to the emergent historical hybridities actually populating the world at all its contingent scales.

However, cyborg refigurations hardly exhaust the tropic work required for ontological[4] choreography in technoscience. I have come to see cyborgs as junior siblings in the much bigger, queer family of companion species, in which reproductive biotechnopolitics are generally a surprise, sometimes even a nice surprise. I know that a US middle-aged white woman with a dog playing the sport of agility is no match for the automated warriors, terrorists, and their transgenic kin in the annals of philosophical inquiry or the ethnography[5] of naturecultures. Besides, (1) self-figuration is not my task; (2) transgenics are not the enemy; and (3) contrary to lots of dangerous and unethical projection in the Western world that makes domestic canines into furry children, dogs are not about oneself. Indeed, that is the beauty of dogs. They are not a projection, nor the realization of an intention, nor the telos of anything. They are dogs; i.e., a species in obligatory, constitutive, historical, protean relationship with human beings. The relationship is not especially nice; it is full of waste, cruelty, indifference, ignorance, and loss, as well as of joy, invention, labor, intelligence, and play. I want to learn how to narrate this co-history and how to inherit the consequences of co-evolution in natureculture.

There cannot be just one companion species; there have to be at least two to make one. It is in the syntax; it is in the flesh. Dogs are about the inescapable, contradictory story of relationships—co-constitutive relationships in which none of the partners pre-exist the relating, and the relating is never done once and for all. Historical specificity and contingent mutability rule

1. "A Manifesto for Cyborgs: Science, Technology, and Socialist Feminism in the 1980s," *Socialist Review* 15.2 (1985): 65–107 (excerpted above).
2. A figure of speech. "Surrogacy agreement": a legal contract of the kind that governs surrogate motherhood.
3. Haraway's coinage that emphasizes the inextricable entanglements of nature and culture, of the material and semiotic, and of body and mind. "Cyborgs": cybernetic organisms, both mechanical and organic.
4. Concerned with the nature of being.
5. Descriptive study of a culture or people (a form of anthropology). "Transgenic kin": those whose genomes have been altered by the addition of a gene from an unrelated species.

all the way down, into nature and culture, into naturecultures. There is no foundation; there are only elephants supporting elephants all the way down.[6]

Companion animals comprise only one kind of companion species, and neither category is very old in American English. In United States English, the term "companion animal" emerges in medical and psycho-sociological work in veterinary schools and related sites from the middle 1970s. This research told us that, except for those few non-dog loving New Yorkers who obsess about unscooped dog shit in the streets, having a dog lowers one's blood pressure and ups one's chances of surviving childhood, surgery, and divorce.

Certainly, references in European languages to animals serving as companions, rather than as working or sporting dogs, predate this US biomedical, techno-scientific literature by centuries. Further, in China, Mexico, and elsewhere in the ancient and contemporary world, the documentary, archaeological, and oral evidence for dogs as pets, in addition to a myriad of other jobs, is strong. In the early Americas dogs assisted in hauling, hunting, and herding for various peoples. For others, dogs were food or a source of fleece. Dog people like to forget that dogs were also lethal guided weapons and instruments of terror in the European conquest of the Americas, as well as in Alexander the Great's[7] paradigm-setting imperial travels. With combat history in Viet Nam as an officer in the US marines,[8] Akita breeder and dog writer John Cargill reminds us that before cyborg warfare, trained dogs were among the best intelligent weapons systems. And tracking hounds terrorized slaves and prisoners, as well as rescued lost children and earthquake victims.

Listing these functions does not begin to get at the heterogeneous history of dogs in symbol and story all over the world, nor does the list of jobs tell us how dogs were treated or how they regarded their human associates. In *A History of Dogs in the Early Americas* (Yale, 1997), Marion Schwartz writes that some American Indian hunting dogs went through similar rituals of preparation as did their humans, including among the Achuar[9] of South America the ingestion of an hallucinogen. In *In the Company of Animals* (Cambridge, 1986), James Serpell relates that for the nineteenth-century Comanche[1] of the Great Plains, horses were of great practical value. But horses were treated in a utilitarian way, while dogs, kept as pets, merited fond stories and warriors mourned their deaths. Some dogs were and are vermin; some were and are buried like people. Contemporary Navajo[2] herding dogs relate to their landscape, their sheep, their people, coyotes, and dog or human strangers in historically specific ways. In cities, villages, and rural areas all over the world, many dogs live parallel lives among people, more or less tolerated, sometimes used and sometimes abused. No one term can do justice to this history.

6. This phrase combines a view about Hindu cosmology—that the world is supported on the backs of elephants who stand on a turtle—with the more common expression of infinite regress, "Turtles all the way down."

7. The greatest general of antiquity (356–323 B.C.E.); king of Macedonia, his conquests extended as far as Egypt and India.

8. U.S. combat troops were overtly engaged in the conflict between North and South Vietnam from 1964 to 1975.

9. Indigenous Amazonian community dwelling on the border between Ecuador and Peru.

1. Indigenous tribe of North America, who in the 18th and 19th centuries were equestrian nomads ranging over the southern Great Plains.

2. An indigenous tribe of the southwestern United States.

However, the term "companion animal" enters US technoculture through the post–Civil War land-grant academic institutions housing the vet schools. That is, "companion animal" has the pedigree of the mating between technoscientific expertise and late industrial pet-keeping practices, with their democratic masses in love with their domestic partners, or at least with the non-human ones. Companion animals can be horses, dogs, cats, or a range of other beings willing to make the leap to the biosociality of service dogs, family members, or team members in cross-species sports. Generally speaking, one does not eat one's companion animals (nor get eaten by them); and one has a hard time shaking colonialist, ethnocentric, ahistorical attitudes toward those who do (eat or get eaten).

From *Species*

"Companion species" is a bigger and more heterogeneous category than companion animal, and not just because one must include such organic beings as rice, bees, tulips, and intestinal flora, all of whom make life for humans what it is—and vice versa. I want to write the keyword entry for "companion species" to insist on four tones simultaneously resonating in the linguistic, historical voice box that enables uttering this term. First, as a dutiful daughter of Darwin,[3] I insist on the tones of the history of evolutionary biology, with its categories of populations, rates of gene flow, variation, selection, and biological species. The debates in the last 150 years about whether the category "species" denotes a real biological entity or merely figures a convenient taxonomic box sound the over- and undertones. Species is about biological kind, and scientific expertise is necessary to that kind of reality. Post-cyborg, what counts as biological kind troubles previous categories of organism. The machinic and the textual are internal to the organic and vice versa in irreversible ways.

Second, schooled by Thomas Aquinas and other Aristotelians,[4] I remain alert to species as generic philosophical kind and category. Species is about defining difference, rooted in polyvocal fugues of doctrines of cause.

Third, my soul indelibly marked by a Catholic formation, I hear in species the doctrine of the Real Presence[5] under both species, bread and wine, the transubstantiated signs of the flesh. Species is about the corporeal join of the material and the semiotic in ways unacceptable to the secular Protestant sensibilities of the American academy and to most versions of the human science of semiotics.

Fourth, converted by Marx and Freud[6] and a sucker for dubious etymologies, I hear in species filthy lucre, specie, gold, shit, filth, wealth. In *Love's Body*, Norman O. Brown[7] taught me about the join of Marx and Freud in shit and gold, in primitive scat and civilized metal, in specie. I met this join

3. Charles Darwin (1809–1882), English naturalist and theorist of evolution.
4. Followers of the Greek philosopher ARISTOTLE (384–322 B.C.E.), whose writings on science dominated European thought until the Renaissance. AQUINAS (1225–1274 C.E.), medieval Scholastic philosopher and Dominican theologian.
5. The belief, in some Christian religions, that the flesh-and-blood Jesus Christ is in reality and not merely symbolically present in Eucharistic bread and wine. In the Catholic Church, this is called the doctrine of transubstantiation.
6. SIGMUND FREUD (1856–1939), Austrian founder of psychoanalysis. KARL MARX (1818–1883), German economic and political theorist and revolutionary.
7. American philosopher (1913–2002) whose work wedded psychoanalysis and Marxism. *Love's Body* (1966) explores the role of eroticism in human history.

again in modern US dog culture, with its exuberant commodity culture; its vibrant practices of love and desire; its structures that tie together the state, civil society, and the liberal individual; its mongrel technologies of purebred subject- and object-making. As I glove my hand in the plastic film—courtesy of the research empires of industrial chemistry—that protects my morning *New York Times* to pick up the microcosmic ecosystems, called scat, produced anew each day by my dogs, I find pooper scoopers quite a joke, one that lands me back in the histories of the incarnation, political economy, technoscience, and biology.

In sum, "companion species" is about a four-part composition, in which co-constitution, finitude, impurity, historicity, and complexity are what is.

The Companion Species Manifesto is, thus, about the implosion of nature and culture in the relentlessly historically specific, joint lives of dogs and people, who are bonded in significant otherness. Many are interpellated into that story, and the tale is instructive also for those who try to keep a hygienic distance. I want to convince my readers that inhabitants of technoculture become who we are in the symbiogenetic tissues of naturecultures, in story and in fact.

I take "interpellation" from the French post-structuralist and Marxist philosopher Louis Althusser's[8] theory for how subjects are constituted from concrete individuals by being "hailed" through ideology into their subject positions in the modern state. Today, through our ideologically loaded narratives of their lives, animals "hail" us to account for the regimes in which they and we must live. We "hail" them into our constructs of nature and culture, with major consequences of life and death, health and illness, longevity and extinction. We also live with each other in the flesh in ways not exhausted by our ideologies. Stories are much bigger than ideologies. In that is our hope.

In this long philosophical introduction, I am violating a major rule of "Notes of a Sports Writer's Daughter," my doggish scribblings in honor of my sports writer father, which pepper this manifesto. The "Notes" require there to be no deviation from the animal stories themselves. Lessons have to be inextricably part of the story; it's a rule of truth as a genre for those of us—practicing and lapsed Catholics and their fellow travelers—who believe that the sign and the flesh are one.

Reporting the facts, telling a true story, I write "Notes of a Sports Writer's Daughter." A sports writer's job is, or at least was, to report the game story. I know this because as a child I sat in the press box in the AAA baseball club's Denver Bears'[9] Stadium late at night watching my father write and file his game stories. A sports writer, perhaps more than other news people, has a curious job—to tell what happened by spinning a story that is just the facts. The more vivid the prose, the better; indeed, if crafted faithfully, the more potent the tropes, the truer the story. My father did not want to have a sports column, a more prestigious activity in the newspaper business. He wanted to write the game stories, to stay close to the action, to tell it like it is, not to look for the scandals and the angles for the meta-story, the column. My father's faith was in the game, where fact and story cohabit.

8. French philosopher (1918–1990); see above.

9. A team that played in Denver, Colorado, in what was called Bears Stadium from 1948 until 1968; it was the highest-level minor league affiliate of a number of different major league teams.

I grew up in the bosom of two major institutions that counter the modernist belief in the no-fault divorce, based on irrevocable differences, of story and fact. Both of these institutions—the Church and the Press—are famously corrupt, famously scorned (if constantly used) by Science, and nonetheless indispensable in cultivating a people's insatiable hunger for truth. Sign and flesh; story and fact. In my natal house, the generative partners could not separate. They were, in down-and-dirty dog talk, tied. No wonder culture and nature imploded for me as an adult. And nowhere did that implosion have more force than in living the relationship and speaking the verb that passes as a noun: companion species. Is this what John meant when he said, "The Word was made flesh"?[1] In the bottom of the ninth inning, the Bears down by two runs, with three on, two out, and two strikes, with the time deadline for filing the story five minutes away?

I also grew up in the house of Science and learned at around the time my breast buds erupted about how many underground passages there are connecting the Estates[2] and how many couplings keep sign and flesh, story and fact, together in the palaces of positive knowledge, falsifiable hypothesis, and synthesizing theory. Because my science was biology, I learned early that accounting for evolution, development, cellular function, genome complexity, the molding of form across time, behavioral ecology, systems communication, cognition—in short, accounting for anything worthy of the name of biology—was not so different from getting a game story filed or living with the conundrums of the incarnation.[3] To do biology with any kind of fidelity, the practitioner *must* tell a story, *must* get the facts, and *must* have the heart to stay hungry for the truth and to abandon a favorite story, a favorite fact, shown to be somehow off the mark. The practitioner must also have the heart to stay with a story through thick and thin, to inherit its discordant resonances, to live its contradictions, when that story gets at a truth about life that matters. Isn't that kind of fidelity what has made the science of evolutionary biology flourish and feed my people's corporeal hunger for knowledge over the last hundred and fifty years?

Etymologically, facts refer to performance, action, deeds done—feats, in short. A fact is a past participle,[4] a thing done, over, fixed, shown, performed, accomplished. Facts have made the deadline for getting into the next edition of the paper. Fiction, etymologically, is very close, but differs by part-of-speech and tense. Like facts, fiction refers to action, but fiction is about the act of fashioning, forming, inventing, as well as feigning or feinting. Drawn from a present participle,[5] fiction is in process and still at stake, not finished, still prone to falling afoul of facts, but also liable to showing something we do not yet know to be true, but will know. Living with animals, inhabiting their/our stories, trying to tell the truth about relationship, cohabiting an active history: that is the work of companion species, for whom "the relation" is the smallest possible unit of analysis.

1. John 1.14, a gospel traditionally attributed to the apostle St. John (1st c. century C.E.). "The Word": identified with Jesus Christ.
2. The orders (*états*) of the realm in France before the Revolution of 1789: the clergy, the nobility, and commoners. (In the 19th century, British writers began referring to the press as the "fourth estate.")
3. The Christian doctrine according to which God "became flesh" in Mary's womb as Jesus Christ, at once fully human and divine.
4. "Fact" is derived from *factum*, the past participle of the Latin verb meaning "to do" (*facere*).
5. "Fiction" is derived from *fictio*, the noun meaning "fashioning, forming," itself derived from the verb "to fashion" (*fingere*).

So, I file dog stories for a living these days. All stories traffic in tropes, i.e., figures of speech necessary to say anything at all. Trope (Greek: *tropós*) means swerving or tripping. All language swerves and trips; there is never direct meaning; only the dogmatic think that trope-free communication is our province. My favorite trope for dog tales is "metaplasm." Metaplasm means a change in a word, for example by adding, omitting, inverting, or transposing its letters, syllables, or sounds. The term is from the Greek *metaplasmos*, meaning remodeling or remolding. Metaplasm is a generic term for almost any kind of alteration in a word, intentional or unintentional. I use metaplasm to mean the remodeling of dog and human flesh, remolding the codes of life, in the history of companion-species relating.

Compare and contrast "protoplasm," "cytoplasm," "neoplasm," and "germplasm."[6] There is a biological taste to "metaplasm"—just what I like in words about words. Flesh and signifier, bodies and words, stories and worlds: these are joined in naturecultures. Metaplasm can signify a mistake, a stumbling, a troping that makes a fleshly difference. For example, a substitution in a string of bases in a nucleic acid[7] can be a metaplasm, changing the meaning of a gene and altering the course of a life. Or, a remolded practice among dog breeders, such as doing more outcrosses and fewer close line breedings,[8] could result from changed meanings of a word like "population" or "diversity." Inverting meanings; transposing the body of communication; remolding, remodeling; swervings that tell the truth: I tell stories about stories, all the way down. Woof.

Implicitly, this manifesto is about more than the relation of dogs and people. Dogs and people figure a universe. Clearly, cyborgs—with their historical congealings of the machinic and the organic in the codes of information, where boundaries are less about skin than about statistically defined densities of signal and noise—fit within the taxon[9] of companion species. That is to say, cyborgs raise all the questions of histories, politics, and ethics that dogs require. Care, flourishing, differences in power, scales of time—these matter for cyborgs. For example, what kind of temporal scale-making could shape labor systems, investment strategies, and consumption patterns in which the generation time of information machines became compatible with the generation times of human, animal, and plant communities and ecosystems? What is the right kind of pooper-scooper for a computer or a personal digital assistant? At the least, we know it is not an electronics dump in Mexico or India, where human scavengers get paid less than nothing for processing the ecologically toxic waste of the well informed.

* * *

So, in *The Companion Species Manifesto*, I want to tell stories about relating in significant otherness, through which the partners come to be who we are in flesh and sign. The following shaggy dog stories about evolution, love, training, and kinds or breeds help me think about living well together with

6. Living genetic material preserved for the purposes of breeding or research. "Protoplasm": a general term for cytoplasm, the liquid that fills all cells and is surrounded by the cell membrane. "Neoplasm": a new or abnormal growth of tissue in the body, generally associated with cancer.

7. A complex organic acid composed of nucleotide chains (e.g., DNA); these acids are the main information-carrying molecules in the cell.

8. The matings of related dogs. "Outcrosses": the matings of unrelated dogs.

9. That is, the classification.

the host of species with whom human beings emerge on this planet at every scale of time, body, and space. The accounts I offer are idiosyncratic and indicative rather than systematic, tendentious more than judicious, and rooted in contingent foundations rather than clear and distinct premises. Dogs are my story here, but they are only one player in the large world of companion species. Parts don't add up to wholes in this manifesto—or in life in naturecultures. Instead, I am looking for Marilyn Strathern's "partial connections,"[1] which are about the counter-intuitive geometries and incongruent translations necessary to getting on together, where the god-tricks of self certainty and deathless communion are not an option.

2003

1. The title of a 1991 book by the British anthropologist Strathern (b. 1941); it argues that our accounts of the relations between entities, people, and cultures are always partial, never whole.

N. KATHERINE HAYLES
b. 1943

Repeating a memorable phrase from William Gibson's *Neuromancer* (1984), the founding novel of cyberpunk fiction, N. Katherine Hayles describes the posthuman body as "data made flesh." She argues that the post–World War II era marks an epistemic shift in the history of science and technology. This new cultural condition of virtuality is characterized by the increasing permeation of material reality by information codes and patterns. In the wake of cybernetic theories that erase the boundaries between human existence and computer simulation, subjectivity comes to be recast in terms of information paradigms. For Hayles, the contemporary technoscientific mutation of subjectivity initiates a dismantling of the liberal humanist individual and the birth of a new age of the posthuman. But unlike other posthumanists, who entertain dehumanizing fantasies of scientific power and of immortality, Hayles stresses the importance of concrete material embodiment. This emphasis ensures that the subject retains both agency and singularity. Literary texts play a central role for Hayles: as cultural documents, revealing and often prophetic, they cast light on today's ongoing transformations at the intersection of technology, the body, and culture. But literary reading in our time has undergone mutations.

Hayles holds degrees in science and literature. She received a B.S. in chemistry from the Rochester Institute of Technology in 1966, an M.S. in chemistry from the California Institute of Technology in 1969, an M.A. in English from Michigan State University in 1970, and a Ph.D. in English from the University of Rochester in 1977. After teaching at Dartmouth College, the University of Missouri at Rolla, the University of Iowa, the California Institute of Technology, and the University of California at Los Angeles, where she was a professor of English and design/media arts from 1992 to 2008, she joined Duke University's Program in Literature. Hayles's numerous honors and awards include two National Endowment for the Humanities Fellowships, a Guggenheim Fellowship, a Fellowship at the National Humanities Center, and a Medal of Honor from the University of Helsinki. Her influential book *How We Became Posthuman: Virtual Bodies in Cybernetics, Literature, and Informatics* (1999) received the René Wellek Prize for the Best Book in Literary

Theory from the American Comparative Literature Association and the Eaton Award for the Best Book in Science Fiction Criticism and Theory from the University of California at Riverside. Hayles is past president of the Society for Literature, Science, and the Arts. She was elected in 2015 to the American Academy of Arts and Sciences.

Like DONNA HARAWAY's pioneering writings on cyborg theory, Hayles's work treats the miscegenation of human and machine as an occasion for reconsidering traditional humanist accounts of subjectivity and reading. While Haraway adopts the cyborg (human+machine) as an "ironic political myth" in the service of socialist feminism, Hayles uses it to examine the philosophical assumptions underlying cybernetic research and textual analysis. In *How We Became Posthuman*, for example, she sees the cyborg as a cultural icon of postmodern society that is closely linked to developments in science—specifically, how "information lost its body." She posits three historical phases of human and machine relations in cybernetics: homeostasis or autonomy of the human body, from 1945 to 1960; reflexivity or integration of machine and body, from 1960 to 1980; and virtuality or symbiosis, from 1980 to the present. The progression is toward increasingly disembodied states of human existence. But Hayles warns against dematerialized definitions of information and corporeality, which she condemns as ill-advised philosophical extensions of the Cartesian separation of mind and body. Characteristically, she seeks balance, reconciliation, and synthesis.

Hayles's posthuman theory resonates with the critique of the unified, universal human subject—a legacy of the Enlightenment—that has been mounted in contemporary times by poststructuralist, feminist, postcolonial, and other postmodern thinkers, notably ROSI BRAIDOTTI. It amplifies the conception of subjectivity as fragmented and heterogeneous, embedded at once in embodied existence, in materialized sets of cultural codes, in social institutions, and in technoscientific devices. In emphasizing posthuman *embodiment*, Hayles sees her project as a "rememory" of the sometimes overlooked engineering as well as broader cultural factors conducive to the condition of virtuality. The multiple interchanges between science and literature help illuminate these historical contingencies of virtuality. To counter abstract models of cybernetics, Hayles draws on narrative fiction such as Bernard Wolfe's *Limbo* (1952) and Philip K. Dick's major novels of the 1960s. These texts offer, in her view, "embodied forms of discourse" that broach a range of social, political, and psychological issues by connecting scientific concepts to particular real-life situations.

Like other leading theorists of the posthuman body, Hayles works in the context of postindustrial society. This is a world in which water is fluoridated; the air inside and outside buildings is tainted by innumerable chemicals (human-made and natural); and food is subjected to genetic modifications as well as other enhancements such as chemical fertilizers and antibiotics. Beginning at an early age, individuals receive multiple immunizations. Prostheses—from dental fillings and contact lenses to stents and hip replacements to transplanted body parts—modify human flesh. Under such conditions the sharply etched classical binary distinctions—man/machine, nature/culture, purity/contamination, private/public—implode and intermix. Where some theorists of the posthuman body see utopia over the horizon, others glimpse dystopia. Hayles characteristically takes a middle road, expressing both exaltation and concern, wonder and anxiety.

In our selection, "How We Read: Close, Hyper, Machine," Hayles argues that digital media create new challenges but also new possibilities when it comes to established reading practices and paradigms that have long defined and shaped literary studies in the United States. Gently casting present-day zealots of print-based close and surface reading as remnants of a bygone era while also cautioning against unbridled faith in digital forms of literacy, such as hyperreading and machine reading, Hayles maintains that all reading practices can and should complement each other, especially if we are to do justice to the tangible cultural and neurological effects of living with and alongside new media. The reality is that students who are expected to develop deep attention by performing close readings of canonical print texts in the classroom may find doing so difficult and even meaningless, for they are in fact already quite skilled in the hyperattention they need in order to skim through the Web in search of keywords and to read fragments of digital texts in truncated contexts. As these new forms of reading have increasingly become mainstream, evidence suggests that digital literacy leads to significant changes in brain architecture in ways that make traditional close reading perhaps more arduous than ever before.

Where others might see an unbridgeable gulf between different modes of reading, however, Hayles discerns new prospects for transforming the discipline of literary studies. In this respect, her work resonates with FRANCO MORETTI's computational criticism, which seeks to find new ways for processing massive amounts of data through distant reading aided by computers. But unlike Moretti, who seems to abandon close reading altogether, Hayles adopts a more balanced approach, one that recognizes distinct advantages and disadvantages of print, digital, and machine literacies, believing the interaction among them to be mutually beneficial and to lead to increased effectiveness in analyzing texts.

As her essay unfolds, Hayles carefully defines close reading, hyperreading, and machine reading in the context of the mounting information overload and distraction of twenty-first-century life. Her aim is to reconfigure reading to encompass all its modes and techniques. As a result, she does not fret, as do some of the respected literacy theorists she cites, over ubiquitous skimming, rapid scrolling, and endless hyperlinks. Yet as broad as her definition of reading turns out to be, Hayles quickly dispatches the "surface reading" famously advocated by STEPHEN BEST and SHARON MARCUS, which she reduces in passing to pleasurable and appreciative reading. Similarly, her plan for reading gives short shrift to ideology critique, also known as symptomatic reading, or cultural critique. In the end, no space is allotted for critical reading, its definition, its dynamics, or its value. But despite these shortcomings, Hayles addresses head-on the growing crisis in present-day traditional literary reading prompted by the rise of both hyper and machine reading while taking into account tweets, blogs, email, and Facebook as well as the powerful computer programs that aggregate keywords, phrase frequencies, and all manner of patterns relevant to literature.

"How We Read: Close, Hyper, Machine" Keywords: The Body, Interpretation Theory, Media, Postmodernity, Print Culture, Reception Theory

How We Read: Close, Hyper, Machine

The evidence is mounting: people in general, and young people in particular, are doing more screen reading of digital materials than ever before. Meanwhile, the reading of print books and of literary genres (novels, plays, and poems) has been declining over the last twenty years. Worse, reading skills (as measured by the ability to identify themes, draw inferences, etc.) have been declining in junior high, high school, college, and even graduate schools for the same period. Two flagship reports from the National Endowment for the Arts,[1] *Reading at Risk*, reporting the results of their own surveys, and *To Read or Not to Read*, drawing together other large-scale surveys,

1. An independent federal agency established by Congress in 1965 that offers funding and support for projects exhibiting artistic excellence.

show that over a wide range of data-gathering instruments the results are consistent: people read less print, and they read print less well [see Works Cited]. This leads the NEA chairman, Dana Gioia,[2] to suggest that the *correlation* between decreased literary reading and poorer reading ability is indeed a *causal* connection. The NEA argues (and I of course agree) that literary reading is a good in itself, insofar as it opens the portals of a rich literary heritage (see Griswold, McDonnell, and Wright for the continued high cultural value placed on reading). When decreased print reading, already a cultural concern, is linked with reading problems, it carries a double whammy.

Fortunately, the news is not all bad. A newer NEA report, *Reading on the Rise*, shows for the first time in more than two decades an uptick in novel reading (but not plays or poems), including among the digitally native young adult cohort (ages 18–24). The uptick may be a result of the Big Read initiative by the NEA and similar programs by other organizations; whatever the reason, it shows that print can still be an alluring medium. At the same time, reading scores among fourth and eighth graders remain flat, despite the No Child Left Behind initiative.[3] Notwithstanding the complexities of the national picture, it seems clear that a critical nexus occurs in the juncture of digital reading (exponentially increasing among all but the oldest cohort) and print reading (downward trending with a slight uptick recently). The crucial questions are these: how to convert the increased digital reading into increased reading ability and how to make effective bridges between digital reading and the literacy traditionally associated with print.

Mark Bauerlein (a consultant on the *Reading at Risk* report), in the offensively titled *The Dumbest Generation: How the Digital Age Stupefies Young Americans and Jeopardizes Our Future*, makes no apology for linking the decline of reading skills directly to a decrease in print reading, issuing a stinging indictment to teachers, professors, and other mentors who think digital reading might encourage skills of its own. Not only is there no transfer between digital reading and print reading skills in his view, but digital reading does not even lead to strong *digital* reading skills (93–111). I found *The Dumbest Generation* intriguing and infuriating in equal measure. The book is valuable for its synthesis of a great deal of empirical evidence, going well beyond the 2009 NEA report in this regard; it is infuriating in its tendentious refusal to admit any salutary effects from digital reading. As Bauerlein moves from the solid longitudinal data on the decline in print reading to the digital realm, the evidence becomes scantier and the anecdotes more frequent, with examples obviously weighted toward showing the inanity of online chats, blogs, and *Facebook*[4] entries. It would, of course, be equally possible to harvest examples showing the depth, profundity, and brilliance of online discourse, so Bauerlein's argument here fails to persuade. The two earlier NEA reports (*Reading at Risk; To Read*) suffer from their own problems; their data do not clearly distinguish between print and digital reading, and they fail to measure how much digital reading is going on or its effects on reading abilities (Kirschenbaum). Nevertheless, despite these lim-

2. American poet and critic (b. 1950); former chairman of the NEA (2003–09).

3. Legislation passed by Congress in 2001 that increased the federal government's role in holding public elementary and secondary schools accountable for student outcomes.

4. The world's largest online and social networking service, launched in 2004.

itations and distortions, few readers are likely to come away unconvinced that there is something like a national crisis in reading and that it is especially acute with teen and young adult readers.

At this point, scholars in literary studies should be jumping on their desks and waving their hands in the air, saying "Hey! Look at us! We know how to read *really* well, and we know how to teach students to read. There's a national crisis in reading? We can help." Yet there is little evidence that the profession of literary studies has made a significant difference in the national picture, including on the college level, where reading abilities continue to decline even into graduate school. This is strange. The inability to address the crisis successfully no doubt has multiple causes, but one in particular strikes me as vitally important. While literary studies continues to teach close reading to students, it does less well in exploiting the trend toward the digital. Students read incessantly in digital media and write in it as well, but only infrequently are they encouraged to do so in literature classes or in environments that encourage the transfer of print reading abilities to digital and vice versa. The two tracks, print and digital, run side by side, but messages from either track do not leap across to the other side.

Close Reading and Disciplinary Identity

To explore why this should be so and open possibilities for synergistic interactions,[5] I begin by revisiting that sacred icon of literary studies, close reading. When literary studies expanded its purview in the 1970s and 1980s, it turned to reading many different kinds of "texts," from Donald Duck[6] to fashion clothing, television programs to prison architecture (see Scholes). This expansion into diverse textual realms meant that literature was no longer the de facto center of the field. Faced with the loss of this traditional center, literary scholars found a replacement in close reading, the one thing virtually all literary scholars know how to do well and agree is important. Close reading then assumed a preeminent role as the essence of the disciplinary identity.

Jane Gallop undoubtedly speaks for many when she writes, "I would argue that the most valuable thing English ever had to offer was the very thing that made us a discipline, that transformed us from cultured gentlemen into a profession [i.e., close reading]. . . . Close reading—learned through practice with literary texts, learned in literature classes—is a widely applicable skill, of real value to students as well as to scholars in other disciplines" (15). Barbara Johnson, in her well-known essay "Teaching Deconstructively," goes further: "This [close reading] is the only teaching that can properly be called literary; anything else is history of ideas, biography, psychology, ethics, or bad philosophy" (140). For Gallop, Johnson, and many others, close reading not only assures the professionalism of the profession but also makes literary studies an important asset to the culture. As such, close reading justifies the discipline's continued existence in the academy, including the monies spent to support literature faculty and departments. More broadly, close reading in this view constitutes the major part of the cultural capital that literary studies relies on to prove its worth to society.

5. That is, interactions of discrete agencies, agents, or conditions such that the total effect is greater than the sum of the individual effects.

6. Cartoon character created in 1934 by Walt Disney, a cartoonist and founder of an entertainment conglomerate.

Literary scholars generally think they know what is meant by *close reading*, but, looked at more closely, it proves not so easy to define or exemplify. Jonathan Culler, quoting Peter Middleton, observes that "close reading is our contemporary term for a heterogeneous and largely unorganized set of practices and assumptions" (20). John Guillory is more specific when he historicizes close reading, arguing that "close reading is a modern academic practice with an inaugural moment, a period of development, and now perhaps a period of decline" ("Close Reading" 8). He locates its prologue in the work of I. A. Richards,[7] noting that Richards contrasted close reading with the media explosion of his day, television. If that McLuhanesque view[8] of media is prologue, then digital technologies, Guillory suggests, may be launching the epilogue. Citing my work on hyperattention (more on that shortly), Guillory sets up a dichotomy between the close reading recognizable to most literary scholars—detailed and precise attention to rhetoric, style, language choice, and so forth through a word-by-word examination of a text's linguistic techniques—to the digital world of fast reading and sporadic sampling. In this he anticipates the close versus digital reading flagrantly on display in Bauerlein's book.

Amid the heterogeneity of close reading techniques, perhaps the dominant one in recent years has been what Stephen Best and Sharon Marcus call "symptomatic reading." In a special issue of *Representations*, Best and Marcus launch a frontal assault on symptomatic reading as it was inaugurated by Fredric Jameson's immensely influential *The Political Unconscious*.[9] For Jameson, with his motto "Always historicize," the text is an alibi for ideological formations that are subtextual. The heroic task of the critic is to wrench a text's ideology into the light, "massy and dripping," as Jameson puts it (245; qtd. in Crane 92), so that it can be unveiled and resisted (see Crane for a close analysis of Jameson's metaphors). The trace of symptomatic reading may be detected in Johnson: listing textual features that merit special attention for close reading, she includes such constructions as "ambiguous words," "undecidable syntax," and "incompatibilities between what a text says and what it does" (141–42). Most if not all these foci are exactly the places where scholars doing symptomatic reading would look for evidence of a text's subsurface ideology.

After more than two decades of symptomatic reading, however, many literary scholars are not finding it a productive practice, perhaps because (like many deconstructive readings[1]) its results have begun to seem formulaic, leading to predictable conclusions rather than compelling insights. In a paraphrase of Gilles Deleuze and Félix Guattari's famous remark, "We are tired of trees,"[2] the *Representations* special issue declared, We are tired of symp-

7. Influential English literary critic and rhetorician (1892–1979) who is often labeled the father of New Criticism, a formalist movement in literary theory that dominated American literary criticism in the mid-20th century.
8. Characteristic of Marshall McLuhan (1911–1980), influential Canadian communications theorist who famously declared that the medium is the message.
9. For this essay by BEST (b. 1967) and MARCUS (b. 1966), see below; for the Marxist critic JAMESON (b. 1934), see above.

1. Philosophical and literary textual analyses of a type developed mainly from the work of the French philosopher JACQUES DERRIDA (1930–2004), involving the inversion and reinscription of a traditional philosophical opposition.
2. A reference to *A Thousand Plateaus: Capitalism and Schizophrenia* (1980; see above), by the French philosopher GILLES DELEUZE (1925–1995) and the French psychoanalyst FÉLIX GUATTARI (1930–1992), who replace the metaphor of the "tree" (a vertical command structure) with the horizontal "rhizome."

tomatic reading. The issue's contributors are not the only ones who feel this way. In panel after panel at the conference sponsored by the National Humanities Center[3] in spring 2010, entitled "The State and Stakes of Literary Studies," presenters expressed similar views and urged a variety of other reading modes, including "surface reading," in which the text is examined not for hidden clues but its overt messages; reading aimed at appreciation and articulation of the text's aesthetic value; and a variety of other reading strategies focusing on affect, pleasure, and cultural value.

Digital and Print Literacies

If one chapter of close reading is drawing to an end, what new possibilities are arising? Given the increase in digital reading, obvious sites for new kinds of reading techniques, pedagogical strategies, and initiatives are the interactions between digital and print literacies. Literary studies has been slow to address these possibilities, however, because it continues to view close reading of print texts as the field's essence. As long as this belief holds sway, digital reading will at best be seen as peripheral to our concerns, pushed to the margins as not "really" reading or at least not compelling or interesting reading. Young people, who vote with their feet in college, are marching in another direction—the digital direction. No doubt those who already read well will take classes based on close reading and benefit from them, but what about others whose print-reading skills are not as highly developed? To reach them, we must start close to where they are, rather than where we imagine or hope they might be. As David Laurence observes, "good teachers deliberately focus on what the reader can do, make sure that both teacher and student recognize and acknowledge it, and use it as a platform of success from which to build" (4).

This principle was codified by the Belarusian psychologist L. S. Vygotsky in the 1930s as the "zone of proximal development." In *Mind in Society: The Development of Higher Psychological Processes*, he defined this zone as "[t]he distance between the actual developmental level as determined by independent problem solving and the level of potential development as determined through problem solving under adult guidance, or in collaboration with more capable peers" (86). The concept implies that if the distance is too great between what one wants someone else to learn and where instruction begins, the teaching will not be effective. Imagine, for example, trying to explain *Hamlet*[4] to a three-year-old (an endless string of "Why?" would no doubt result, the all-purpose response of young children to the mysterious workings of the adult world). More recent work on "scaffolding" (Robertson, Fluck, and Webb) and Ron Tinsley and Kimberly Lebak on the "zone of reflective capacity" extends the idea and amplifies it with specific learning strategies. These authors agree that for learning to occur, the distance between instruction and available skills must be capable of being bridged, either through direct instruction or, as Vygotsky notes, through working with "more capable" peers. Bauerlein instances many responses from young people as they encounter difficult print texts to the effect the works are "boring" or

3. A private, nonprofit U.S. organization dedicated to advanced study in the humanities (established in 1978).

4. English tragedy (ca. 1600) by William Shakespeare, one of the best-known and most exhaustively interpreted works in world literature.

not worth the trouble. How can we convey to such students the deep engagement we feel with challenging literary texts? I argue that we cannot do this effectively if our teaching does not take place in the zone of proximal development, that is, if we are focused exclusively on print close reading. Before opinion solidifies behind new versions of close reading, I want to argue for a disciplinary shift to a broader sense of reading strategies and their interrelation.

In 1999, James Sosnoski presciently introduced the concept of hyperreading, which he defined as "reader-directed, screen-based, computer-assisted reading" (167). Examples include search queries (as in a *Google*[5] search), filtering by keywords, skimming, hyperlinking, "pecking" (pulling out a few items from a longer text), and fragmenting (163–72). Updating his model, we may add juxtaposing, as when several open windows allow one to read across several texts, and scanning, as when one reads rapidly through a blog to identify items of interest. There is considerable evidence that hyperreading differs significantly from typical print reading, and moreover that hyperreading stimulates different brain functions than print reading.

For example, Jakob Nielsen's consulting team, which advises companies and others on effective Web design, does usability research by asking test subjects to deliver running verbal commentaries as they encounter Web pages. Their reactions are recorded by a (human) tester; at the same time, eye-tracking equipment records their eye movements. The research shows that Web pages are typically read in an F pattern (Nielsen, "F-Shaped"). A person reads the first two or three lines across the page, but as the eye travels down the screen, the scanned length gets smaller, and, by the time the bottom of the page is reached, the eye is traveling in a vertical line aligned with the left margin. (Therefore the worst location for important information on a Web page is on the bottom right corner.) In Bauerlein's view, this research confirms that digital reading is sloppy in the extreme; Bauerlein would no doubt appreciate Woody Allen's[6] quip, "I took a speed reading course and was able to read *War and Peace*[7] in twenty minutes. It involves Russia" (qtd. in Dehaene 18). Nevertheless, other research not cited by Bauerlein indicates that this and similar strategies work well to identify pages of interest and to distinguish them from pages with little or no relevance to the topic at hand (Sillence, Briggs, Harris, and Fishwick).

As a strategic response to an information-intensive environment, hyperreading is not without precedent. John Guillory, in "How Scholars Read," notes that "[t]he fact of quantity is an intractable empirical given that must be managed by a determined method if analysis or interpretation is to be undertaken" (13). He is not talking here about digital reading but about archival research that requires a scholar to move through a great deal of material quickly to find the relevant texts or passages. He identifies two techniques in particular, scanning (looking for a particular keyword, image, or other textual feature) and skimming (trying to get the gist quickly). He also mentions the book wheel, a physical device invented in the Renaissance to cope with the information explosion when the number of books increased

5. The software, created by Google, Inc., that is the most commonly used Web search engine.
6. American writer, actor, and director (b. 1935).
7. Leo Tolstoy's great (and very long) Russian novel (1865–69).

exponentially with the advent of print. Resembling a five-foot-high Ferris wheel,[8] the book wheel held several books on different shelves and could be spun around to make different texts accessible, in a predigital print version of hyperreading.

In contemporary digital environments, the information explosion of the Web has again made an exponentially great number of texts available, dwarfing the previous amount of print materials by several orders of magnitude. In digital environments, hyperreading has become a necessity. It enables a reader quickly to construct landscapes of associated research fields and subfields; it shows ranges of possibilities; it identifies texts and passages most relevant to a given query; and it easily juxtaposes many different texts and passages. *Google* searches and keyword filters are now as much part of the scholar's tool kit as hyperreading itself. Yet hyperreading may not sit easily alongside close reading. Recent studies indicate that hyperreading not only requires different reading strategies than close reading but also may be involved with changes in brain architecture that makes close reading more difficult to achieve.

Much of this evidence is summarized by Nicholas Carr in *The Shallows: What the Internet Is Doing to Our Brains.* More judicious than Bauerlein, he readily admits that Web reading has enormously increased the scope of information available, from global politics to scholarly debates. He worries, however, that hyperreading leads to changes in brain function that make sustained concentration more difficult, leaving us in a constant state of distraction in which no problem can be explored for very long before our need for continuous stimulation kicks in and we check e-mail, scan blogs, message someone, or check our RSS feeds.[9] The situation is reminiscent of Kurt Vonnegut's satirical short story "Harrison Bergeron,"[1] in which the pursuit of equality has led to a society that imposes handicaps on anyone with exceptional talents. The handsome, intelligent eponymous protagonist must among other handicaps wear eyeglasses that give him headaches; other brainiacs have radio transmitters implanted in their ears, which emit shrieking sounds two or three times every minute, interrupting their thoughts and preventing sustained concentration. The final satirical punch comes in framing the story from the perspective of Bergeron's parents, Hazel and George, who see their son on TV when he proclaims his anti-handicap manifesto (with fatal results for him), but, hampered by their own handicaps, they cannot concentrate enough to remember it.

The story's publication in 1961 should give us a clue that a media-induced state of distraction is not a new phenomenon. Walter Benjamin[2] in "The Work of Art in the Age of Mechanical Reproduction" (1968), wrote about the ability of mass entertainment forms such as cinema to make distracted viewing into a habit (as opposed to the contemplative viewing of a single work of art). Even though distraction, as Jonathan Crary (2001) has shown, has been a social concern since the late 1800s, there are some new features of

8. A rotating upright wheel carrying seats that remain horizontal as it moves; this amusement park ride, invented by George Ferris, debuted at Chicago's World Columbian Exhibition (1893).

9. Rich Site Summary feeds, which provide subscribers with updated information from sites of their choosing.

1. A dystopian science fiction story (1961) by the American author Vonnegut (1922–2007).

2. German literary and cultural critic (1892–1940); for his influential 1936 essay, under a slightly different title, see above.

Web reading that make it a powerful practice for rewiring the brain (see Greenfield for a summary). Among these are hyperlinks that draw attention away from the linear flow of an article, very short forms such as tweets that encourage distracted forms of reading, small habitual actions such as clicking and navigating that increase the cognitive load, and, most pervasively, the enormous amount of material to be read, leading to the desire to skim everything because there is way too much material to pay close attention to anything for very long.

Reading on the Web

What evidence indicates that these Web-specific effects are making distraction a contemporary cultural condition? Several studies have shown that, contrary to the claims of early hypertext enthusiasts such as George Landow,[3] hyperlinks tend to degrade comprehension rather than enhance it. The following studies, cited by Carr in *The Shallows*, demonstrate the trend. Erping Zhu, coordinator of instructional development at the Center for Research on Learning and Teaching at the University of Michigan, had test subjects read the same online passage but varied the number of links. As the number of links increased, comprehension declined, as measured by writing a summary and completing a multiple-choice test. Similar results were found by two Canadian scholars, David S. Miall and Teresa Dobson, who asked seventy people to read Elizabeth Bowen's short story "The Demon Lover."[4] One group read it in a linear version, and a second group with links. The first group outperformed the second on comprehension and grasp of the story's plot; it also reported liking the story more than the second group. We may object that a print story would of course be best understood in a print-like linear mode; other evidence, however, indicates that a similar pattern obtains for digital-born material. D. S. Niederhauser, R. E. Reynolds, D. J. Salmen, and P. Skolmoski had test subjects read two online articles, one arguing that "knowledge is objective," and the other that "knowledge is relative." Each article had links allowing readers to click between them. The researchers found that those who used the links, far from gaining a richer sense of the merits and limitations of the two positions, understood them less well than readers who chose to read the two in linear fashion. Comparable evidence was found in a review of thirty-eight experiments on hypertext reading by Diana DeStefano and Jo-Anne LeFevre, psychologists with the Centre for Applied Cognitive Research at Canada's Carleton University. Carr summarizes their results, explaining that in general the evidence did not support the claim that hypertext led to "an enriched experience of the text" (qtd. in Carr 129). One of their conclusions was that "increased demands of decision-making and visual processing in hypertext impaired reading performance," especially in relation to "traditional print presentation" (qtd. in Carr 129).

Why should hypertext and Web reading in general lead to poorer comprehension? The answer, Carr believes, lies in the relation of working memory (i.e., the contents of consciousness) to long-term memory. Material is held

3. A scholar of Victorian literature and art history (b. 1940), who helped pioneer hypermedia studies; his book *Hypertext* (1992) was the first to combine literary theory and computer technology.

4. Published in 1941 by the Anglo-Irish novelist and short story writer Bowen (1899–1973).

in working memory for only a few minutes, and the capacity of working memory is severely limited. For a simple example, I think of the cell-phone directory function that allows me to get phone numbers, which are given orally (there is an option to have a text message sent of the number, but for this the company charges an additional fee, and being of a frugal disposition, I don't go for that option). I find that if I repeat the numbers out loud several times so they occupy working memory to the exclusion of other things, I can retain them long enough to punch the number. For retention of more complex matters, the contents of working memory must be transferred to long-term memory, preferably with repetitions to facilitate the integration of the new material with existing knowledge schemas. The small distractions involved with hypertext and Web reading—clicking on links, navigating a page, scrolling down or up, and so on—increase the cognitive load on working memory and thereby reduce the amount of new material it can hold. With linear reading, by contrast, the cognitive load is at a minimum, precisely because eye movements are more routine and fewer decisions need to be made about how to read the material and in what order. Hence the transfer to long-term memory happens more efficiently, especially when readers reread passages and pause to reflect on them as they go along.

Supplementing this research are other studies showing that small habitual actions, repeated over and over, are extraordinarily effective in creating new neural pathways. Carr recounts the story told by Norman Doidge in *The Brain That Changes Itself*[5] of an accident victim, Michael Bernstein, who had a stroke that damaged his brain's right side, rendering his left hand and leg crippled (30–31). He entered an experimental therapy program that had him performing routine tasks with his left arm and leg over and over, such as washing a window and tracing alphabet letters. "The repeated actions," Carr reports, "were a means of coaxing his neurons and synapses to form new circuits that would take over the functions once carried out by the circuits in the damaged area in his brain" (30). Eventually, Bernstein was able to regain most of the functionality of his unresponsive limbs. We may remember in *The Karate Kid* film (1984) when Daniel LaRusso (Ralph Macchio) is made to do the same repetitive tasks over and over again by his kung fu teacher, Mr. Miagi (Pat Morita). In contemporary neurological terms, Mr. Miagi is retraining the young man's neural circuits so he can master the essentials of kung fu movements.

These results are consistent with a large body of research on the impact of (print) reading on brain function. In a study cited by the French neurophysiologist Stanislas Dehaene, a world-renowned expert in this area, researchers sought out siblings from poor Portuguese families that had followed the traditional custom of having an elder sister stay home and watch the infant children while her younger sister went to school. Raised in the same family, the sisters could be assumed to have grown up in very similar environments, thus serving as a way to control other variables. Using as test subjects six pairs of illiterate-literate sisters, researchers found that literacy had strengthened the ability to understand the phonemic structure of language. Functional magnetic resonance (fMRI) scans showed pronounced

5. Best-selling book on neuroplasticity (2007) by the Canadian-born psychiatrist and psychoanalyst Doidge.

differences in the anterior insula, adjacent to Broca's area (a part of the brain associated with language use). "The literate brain," Dehaene summarizes, "obviously engages many more left hemispheric resources than the illiterate brain, even when we only *listen* to speech. . . . The macroscopic finding implies a massive increase in the exchange of information across the two hemispheres" (209).

Equally intriguing is Dehaene's "neural recycling" hypothesis, which suggests that reading repurposes existing brain circuits that evolved independently of reading (because literacy is a mere eye blink in our evolutionary history, it did not play a role in shaping the genetics of our Pleistocene[6] brains but rather affects us epigenetically[7] through environmental factors). Crucial in this regard is an area he calls the brains' "letterbox," located in the left occipito-temporal region at the back of the brain. This area, fMRI data show, is responsible for letter and phonemic recognition, transmitting its results to other distant areas through fiber bundles. He further argues that brain architecture imposes significant constraints on the physical shapes that will be easily legible to us. He draws on research demonstrating that 115 of the world's diverse writing systems (alphabetical and ideographic[8]) use visual symbols consisting mostly of three strokes (plus or minus one). Moreover, the geometry of these strokes mirrors in their distribution the geometry of shapes in the natural environment. The idea, then, is that our writing systems evolved in the context of our ability to recognize natural shapes and that scribal experimentation used this correspondence to craft writing systems that would most effectively repurpose existing neural circuitry. Dehaene thus envisions "a massive selection process: over time, scribes developed increasingly efficient notations that fitted the organization of our brains. In brief, our cortex did not specifically evolve for writing. Rather, writing evolved to fit the cortex" (171).

Current evidence suggests that we are now in a new phase of the dance between epigenetic changes in brain function and the evolution of new reading and writing modalities on the Web. Think, for example, of the F pattern of Web reading that the Nielsen research revealed. Canny Web designers use this information to craft Web pages, and reading such pages further intensifies this mode of reading. How quickly neural circuits may be repurposed by digital reading is suggested by Gary Small's experiments at the University of California, Los Angeles, on the effects of Web reading on brain functionality. Small and his colleagues were looking for digitally naive subjects; they recruited three volunteers in their fifties and sixties who had never performed *Google* searches (Small and Vorgan 15–17). This group was first tested with fMRI brain scans, wearing goggles onto which were projected Web pages. Their scans differed significantly from another group of comparable age and background who were Web savvy. Then the naive group was asked to search the Internet for an hour a day for five days. When retested, their brain scans showed measurable differences in some brain areas, which the exper-

6. That is, earliest human: during this geological epoch, which lasted from about 2.6 million to about 11,700 years ago, the first members of the genus *Homo* appeared and developed into our own species, *Homo sapiens*.

7. That is, through heritable changes in gene function that do not involve changes in the underlying DNA sequence.

8. That is, relying on a picture or symbol to represent a thing or an idea instead of spelling a particular word or phrase.

imenters attributed to new neural pathways catalyzed by Web searching. Citing this study among others, Carr concludes that "[k]nowing what we know today, if you were to set out to invent a medium that would rewire our mental circuits as quickly and thoroughly as possible, you would probably end up designing something that looks and works a lot like the Internet" (116).

How valid is this conclusion? Although Carr's book is replete with many different kinds of studies, we should be cautious about taking his conclusions at face value. For example, in the fMRI study done by Small and his colleagues, many factors might skew the results. I don't know if you have had a brain scan, but I have. As Small mentions, brain scans require that you be shoved into a tube just big enough to accommodate your supine body but not big enough for you to turn over. When the scan begins, supercooled powerful electromagnets generate a strong magnetic field, which, combined with a radio frequency emitter, allows minute changes in blood oxygen levels in the brain to be detected and measured. When the radio frequency emitter begins pulsing, it sounds as though a jackhammer is ripping up pavement next to your ear. These are hardly typical conditions for Web reading. In addition, there is considerable evidence that fMRI scans, valuable as they are, are also subject to a number of interpretive errors and erroneous conclusions (Sanders). Neural activity is not measured directly by fMRI scans (as a microelectrode might, for example). Rather, the most widely used kind of fMRI, BOLD (blood-oxygen-level dependent), measures tiny changes in oxygenated blood as a correlate for brain activity. BOLD research assumes that hardworking neurons require increased flows of oxygen-rich blood and that protons in hemoglobin molecules carrying oxygen respond differently to magnetic fields than protons in oxygen-depleted blood. These differences are tabulated and then statistically transformed into colored images, with different colors showing high levels of oxygen-rich compared with oxygen-depleted blood.

The chain of assumptions that led Small, for example, to conclude that brain function changed as a result of *Google* searches can go wrong in several different ways (see Sanders for a summary of these criticisms). First, researchers assume that the *correlation* between activity in a given brain area is *caused* by a particular stimulus; however, most areas of the brain respond similarly to several different kinds of stimuli, so another stimulus could be activating the change rather than the targeted one. Second, fMRI data sets typically have a lot of noise, and if the experiment is not repeated, the observed phenomenon may be a chimera rather than a genuine result (in Small's case, the experiment was repeated later with eighteen additional volunteers). Because the data sets are large and unwieldy, researchers may resort to using sophisticated statistical software packages they do not entirely understand. Finally, they may be using a circular methodology in which the hypothesis affects how the data is seen (an effect called nonindependence). When one group of researchers went back through fMRI research that had been published in the premier journals *Nature, Science, Nature Neuroscience, Neuron,* and the *Journal of Neuroscience*, it found interpretive errors resulting from nonindependence in forty-two percent of the papers (Sanders).

Relying on summaries of research in books such as Carr's creates additional hazards. I mentioned earlier a review of hypertext experiments (DeStefano and LeFevre) cited by Carr, which he uses to buttress his claim that hypertext reading is not as good as linear reading. Consulting the review itself reveals that Carr has tilted the evidence to support his view. The authors state, for example, that "[t]here may be cases in which enrichment or complexity of the hypertext experience is more desirable than maximizing comprehension and ease of navigation," remarking that this may be especially true for students who already read well. They argue not for abandoning hypertext but rather for "good hypertext design" that takes cognitive load into account "to ensure hypermedia provide *at least as good* a learning environment as more traditional text" (1636; emphasis added). Having read through most of Carr's primary sources, I can testify that he is generally conscientious in reporting research results; nevertheless, the example illustrates the unsurprising fact that reading someone else's synthesis does not give as detailed or precise a picture as reading the primary sources themselves.

The Importance of Anecdotal Evidence

Faced with these complexities, what is a humanist to do? Obviously, few scholars in the humanities have the time—or the expertise—to backtrack through cited studies and evaluate them for correctness and replicability. In my view, these studies may be suggestive indicators but should be subject to the same kind of careful scrutiny we train our students to use with Web research (reliability of sources, consensus among many different researchers, etc.). Perhaps our most valuable yardstick for evaluating these results, however, is our own experience. We know how we react to intensive Web reading, and we know through repeated interactions with our students how they are likely to read, write, and think as they grapple with print and Web materials. As teachers (and parents), we make daily observations that either confirm or disconfirm what we read in the scientific literature. The scientific research is valuable and should not be ignored, but our experiences are also valuable and can tell us a great deal about the advantages and disadvantages of hyperreading compared with close reading, as well as the long-term effects of engaging in either or both of these reading strategies.

Anecdotal evidence hooked me on this topic five years ago, when I was a Phi Beta Scholar[9] for a year and in that capacity visited many different types of colleges and universities. Everywhere I went, I heard teachers reporting similar stories: "I can't get my students to read long novels anymore, so I've taken to assigning short stories"; "My students won't read long books, so now I assign chapters and excerpts." I hypothesized then that a shift in cognitive modes is taking place, from the deep attention characteristic of humanistic inquiry to the hyperattention characteristic of someone scanning Web pages (Hayles, "Hyper and Deep Attention"). I further argued that the shift in cognitive modes is more pronounced the younger the age cohort. Drawing from anecdotal evidence as well as such surveys as the Kaiser Foundation's[1] *Gen M* report (Roberts, Foehr, and Rideout), I suggested that the shift toward hyperattention is now noticeable with college students. Since then, the trend has become even more

9. A participant in a program overseen by Phi Beta Kappa, the U.S. academic honor society for college and university students, in which distinguished scholars lecture at institutions with Phi Beta Kappa chapters.

1. An American nonprofit organization focused on national health issues as well as the U.S. role in global health policy.

apparent, and the flood of surveys, books, and articles on the topic of distraction is now so pervasive as to be, well, distracting.

For me, the topic is much more than the latest research fad, because it hits me where I live: the college classroom. As a literary scholar, I deeply believe in the importance of writing and reading, so any large-scale change in how young people read and write is bound to capture my attention. In my work on hyperattention (published just when the topic was beginning to appear on the national radar), I argued that deep and hyperattention each have distinctive advantages. Deep attention is essential for coping with complex phenomena such as mathematical theorems, challenging literary works, and complex musical compositions; hyperattention is useful for its flexibility in switching between different information streams, its quick grasp of the gist of material, and its ability to move rapidly among and between different kinds of texts.[2] As contemporary environments become more information intensive, it is no surprise that hyperattention (and its associated reading strategy, hyperreading) is growing and that deep attention (and its correlated reading strategy, close reading) is diminishing, particularly among young adults and teens. The problem, as I see it, lies not in hyperattention/hyperreading as such, but rather in the challenges the situation presents for parents and educators to ensure that deep attention and close reading continue to be vibrant components of our reading cultures and interact synergistically with the kind of Web and hyperreading in which our young people are increasingly immersed.

Yet hyper- and close reading are not the whole story. I earlier referred to Sosnoski's definition of hyperreading as "computer-assisted." More precisely, it is computer-assisted human reading. The formulation alerts us to a third component of contemporary reading practices: human-assisted computer reading, that is, computer algorithms used to analyze patterns in large textual corpora where size makes human reading of the entirety impossible. Machine reading ranges from algorithms for word-frequency counts to more sophisticated programs that find and compare phrases, identify topic clusters, and are capable of learning. Given the scope, pervasiveness, and sophistication of contemporary programs used to parse texts, it seems to me quite reasonable to say that machines can read. One could, of course, restrict "read" to human beings, arguing that reading implies comprehension and that machines calculate but do not comprehend. However, some human readers (beginners, for example) may also read with minimum or no comprehension. Moreover, the line between (human) interpretation and (machine) pattern recognition is a porous boundary, with each interacting with the other. Hypotheses about meaning help shape the design of computer algorithms, and the results of algorithmic analyses refine, extend, and occasionally challenge intuitions about meaning that formed the starting point for algorithmic design. Putting human reading in a leakproof container and isolating machine reading in another makes it difficult to see these interactions

2. Researchers in the field of attention studies identify three major types of attention: controlled attention, capable of being focused through conscious effort; stimulus-driven attention, a mode of attentiveness involuntarily attracted by environmental events, such as a loud noise; and arousal, a general level of alertness (see Klingberg 21 for a summary). In these terms, deep attention is a subset of controlled attention, and hyperattention bridges controlled and stimulus-driven attention [Hayles's note].

and understand their complex synergies. Given these considerations, saying computers cannot read is from my point of view merely species chauvinism.

In a field like literary studies, misunderstandings of the efficacy and importance of machine reading are commonplace. Even such a perceptive critic as Culler falls back on caricature when, in writing about close reading, he suggests, "It may be especially important to reflect on the varieties of close reading and even to propose explicit models, in an age where electronic resources make it possible to do literary research without reading at all: find all the instances of the words *beg* and *beggar* in novels by two different authors and write up your conclusions" (24). In other words, close reading is the garlic that will ward off the vampire of machine reading. The anxiety here is palpable, nowhere more so than in his final phrase ("write up your conclusions"), which implies that drawing conclusions from machine analysis is a mechanical exercise devoid of creativity, insight, or literary value. Even Guillory, a brilliant theorist and close reader, while acknowledging that machine reading is a useful "prosthesis for the cognitive skill of scanning," concludes that "the gap in cognitive level between the keyword search and interpretation is for the present immeasurable" ("How" 13). There are two misapprehensions here: that keyword searches exhaust the repertoire of machine reading and that the gap between analysis and interpretation yawns so wide as to form an unbridgeable chasm rather than a dynamic interaction.

Given these misconceptions, explicit recapitulation of the value of machine reading is useful. Although it may be used with a single text and reveal interesting patterns, its more customary use is in analyzing large corpora too vast to be read by a single person. Preeminent in this regard is the work of Franco Moretti,[3] who uses the term "distant reading," an obvious counterpoise to close reading (*Graphs*). Careful reading of his work reveals that this construction lumps together human and machine reading; both count as "distant" if the scale is large. I think it is useful to distinguish between human and machine reading because the two situations (one done by a human assisted by machines, the other done by computer algorithms assisted by humans) have different functionalities, limitations, and possibilities. Hyperreading may not be useful for large corpora, and machine algorithms have limited interpretive capabilities.

If we look carefully at Moretti's methodology, we see how firmly it refutes the misunderstandings referred to above. His algorithmic analysis is usually employed to pose questions. Why are the lifetimes of many different genres limited to about thirty years (*Graphs*)? Why do British novels in the mid–eighteenth century use many words in a title and then, within a few decades, change so that titles are no more than three or four words long ("Style")? How to explain changes in narrative conventions such as free indirect discourse[4] when the novel moves from Britain to British colonies (*Graphs*)? I find Moretti's work intriguing for the patterns he uncovers, but I am flat out delighted by the ingenious explanations he devises to account for them. So far beyond the mechanical exercises Culler imagines are these explanations that

3. Italian literary theorist and historian (b. 1950); his *Graphs, Maps, Trees* is excerpted below.

4. A mode of third-person narration in which characters' thoughts and feelings are reported in their own voice.

I would not hesitate to call many of them brilliant. When the explanations fail to persuade (as Moretti candidly confesses is sometimes the case even for him), the patterns nevertheless stand revealed as entry points for interpretations advanced by other scholars who find them interesting.

I now turn to explore the interrelations between the components of an expanded repertoire of reading strategies that includes close, hyper, and machine reading. The overlaps between them are as revealing as the differences. Close and hyperreading operate synergistically when hyperreading is used to identify passages or to home in on a few texts of interest, whereupon close reading takes over. As Guillory observed, skimming and scanning here alternate with in-depth reading and interpretation ("How"). Hyperreading overlaps with machine reading in identifying patterns. This might be done in the context of a *Google* keyword search, for example when one notices that most of the work on a given topic has been done by X, or it might be done when machine analysis confirms a pattern already detected by hyper (or close) reading. Indeed, skimming, scanning, and pattern identification are likely to occur with all three reading strategies; their prevalence in one or another is a matter of scale and emphasis rather than clear-cut boundary.

Since patterns have now entered the discussion, we may wonder what a pattern is. This is not a trivial question, largely because of the various ways in which patterns become manifest. Patterns in large data sets may be so subtle that only sophisticated statistical analysis can reveal them; complex patterns may nevertheless be apprehended quickly and easily when columns of numbers are translated into visual forms, as with fMRI scans. Verbal patterns may be discerned through the close reading of a single textual passage or grasped through hyperreading of an entire text or many texts. An anecdote may be useful in clarifying the nature of pattern. I once took a pottery class, and the instructor asked each participant to make several objects that would constitute a series. The series might, for example, consist of vases with the same shapes but different sizes, or it might be vases of the same size in which the shapes underwent a consistent set of deformations. The example shows that differences are as important as similarities, for they keep a pattern from being merely a series of identical items. I therefore propose the following definition: a pattern consists of regularities that appear through a series of related differences and similarities.

Related to the idea of pattern is the question of meaning. Since entire books have been written on the subject, I will not attempt to define meaning but merely observe that wherever and however it occurs, meaning is sensitively dependent on context. The same sentence, uttered in two different contexts, may mean something entirely different in one compared with the other. Close reading typically occurs in a mono-local context (that is, with a single text). Here the context is quite rich, including the entire text and other texts connected with it through networks of allusions, citations, and iterative quotations. Hyperreading, by contrast, typically occurs in a multilocal context. Because many textual fragments are juxtaposed, context is truncated, often consisting of a single phrase or sentence, as in a *Google* search. In machine reading, the context may be limited to a few words or eliminated altogether, as in a word-frequency list. Relatively context-poor, machine reading is enriched by context-rich close reading when close reading provides guidance for the construction of algorithms; Margaret Cohen points to this synergy when she observes that for computer programs to be designed, "the patterns still need to be observed [by close reading]" (59). On the other hand, machine reading may reveal patterns overlooked in close reading, a point Willard McCarty makes in relation to his work on personification in Ovid's *Metamorphoses*[5] (53–72). The more the emphasis falls on pattern (as in machine reading), the more likely it is that context must be supplied from outside (by a human interpreter) to connect pattern with meaning; the more the emphasis falls on meaning (as in close reading), the more pattern assumes a subordinate role. In general, the different distributions between pattern, meaning, and context provide a way to think about interrelations between close, hyper, and machine reading.

The larger point is that close, hyper, and machine reading each have distinctive advantages and limitations: nevertheless, they also overlap and can be made to interact synergistically with one another. Maryanne Wolfe reaches a similar conclusion when, at the end of *Proust and the Squid*, she writes,

> We must teach our children to be bitextual or multitextual, able to read and analyze texts flexibly in different ways, with more deliberate instruction at every stage of development on the inferential, demanding aspects of any text. Teaching children to uncover the invisible world that resides in written words needs to be both explicit and part of a dialogue between learner and teacher, if we are to promote the processes that lead to fully formed expert reading in our citizenry. (226)

I agree wholeheartedly with the goal: the question is how, precisely, to accomplish it?

Synergies between Close, Hyper-, and Machine Reading

Starting from a traditional humanistic basis in literature, Alan Liu in the English department at the University of California, Santa Barbara, has been teaching undergraduate and graduate courses that he calls Literature+, which adopt as a pedagogical method the interdisciplinarity facilitated by digital media. He asks students "to choose a literary work and treat it according to one or more of the research paradigms prevalent in other fields of study," including visualization, storyboarding, simulation, and game design. Starting with close reading, he encourages students to compare it with methodologies in other fields, including the sciences and engineering. He also has constructed a "tool kit" on his Web site that includes links to software packages enabling students with little or no programming experience to create different modes of representation of literary texts, including tools for text analysis, visualization, mapping, and social-network diagramming. The approach is threefold: it offers students traditional literary training; it expands their sense of how they can use digital media to analyze literary texts; and it encourages them to connect literary methodologies with those of other fields they

5. The *Metamorphoses* (ca. 10 C.E.) by the Roman poet Ovid (43 B.C.E.–17 C.E.), an epic-length collection of stories from classical myth and legend.

may be entering. It offers close reading not as an unquestioned good but as one methodology among several, with distinctive capabilities and limitations. Moreover, because decisions about how to encode and analyze texts using software programs require precise thinking about priorities, goals, and methodologies, it clarifies the assumptions that undergird close reading by translating them into algorithmic analysis.

An example of how the "Literature+" approach works in practice is the project entitled "*Romeo and Juliet:* A *Facebook* Tragedy" (Skura, Nierle, and Gin). Three students working collaboratively adapted Shakespeare's play to the *Facebook* model, creating maps of social networks using the Friend Wheel[6] (naturally, the Montagues are all "friends" to each other, and so are the Capulets[7]), filling out profiles for the characters (Romeo is interpreted as a depressive personality who has an obsessive attachment to his love object and who has corresponding preferences for music, films, and other cultural artifacts that express this sensibility), and having a fight break out on the message-board forum using a Group called The Streets of Verona. The Wall feature[8] was used to incorporate dialogue in which characters speak directly to one another, and the Photos section allowed one character to comment on the attributes of another. The masque at which Romeo and Juliet meet became an Event,[9] to which Capulet invited friends in his Friend Wheel. From a pedagogical point of view, the students were encouraged to use software with which they were familiar in unfamiliar ways, thus increasing their awareness of its implications. The exercise also required them to make interpretive judgments about which features of the play were most essential (since not everything could be included) and to be precise about interactions between relationships, events, and characters. Linking traditional literary reading skills with digital encoding and analysis, the "Literature+" approach strengthens the ability to understand complex literature at the same time it encourages students to think reflectively on digital capabilities. Here digital and print literacies mutually reinforce and extend each other.

Lev Manovich's "Cultural Analytics" is a series of projects that starts from the premise that algorithmic analyses of large data sets (up to several terabytes in size), originally developed for work in the sciences and social sciences, should be applied to cultural objects, including the analysis of real-time data flows. In many academic institutions, high-end computational facilities have programs that invite faculty members and graduate students in the arts and humanities to use them. For example, at the University of California, San Diego, where Manovich teaches, the Supercomputer Center sponsored a summer workshop in 2006, Cyberinfrastructure for the Humanities, Arts, and Social Sciences. At Duke University, where

6. An application in Facebook that shows in a color diagram the links between all the friends of a particular user.
7. The play's two feuding families, who make peace only after Romeo (a Montague) and Juliet (a Capulet) meet, fall in love, and die.
8. That is, the original profile space where Facebook users' content was displayed until December 2011, when it was replaced by Timeline, the new virtual space in which all the content of Facebook users is organized and shown.
9. Facebook application that enables members to let their friends know about upcoming events in their community and to organize social gatherings.

I teach, the Renaissance Computing Institute (RENCI) offers accounts to faculty members and students in the arts and humanities that allow them to use computationally intense analysis. In my experience, researchers at these kinds of facilities are delighted when humanists come to them with projects. Because their mission is to encourage widespread use across and among campuses and to foster collaborations among academic, government, corporate, and community stakeholders, they see humanistic inquiry and artistic creation as missing parts of the picture that enrich the mix. This opens the door to analysis of large cultural data sets such as visual images, media content, and geospatial mapping combined with various historical and cultural overlays.

An example is Manovich's analysis of *Time* magazine covers from 1923–89. As Manovich observes, ideal sites for cultural analytics are large data sets that are well structured and include metadata about date, publication venue, and so forth. The visualization tools that he uses allow the *Time* covers to be analyzed according to subject (for example, portraits versus other types of covers), color gradients, black-and-white gradients, amount of white space, and in other ways. One feature is particularly useful for building bridges between close reading and machine analysis: the visualization tool allows the user both to see large-scale patterns and to zoom in to see a particular cover in detail, thus enabling analyses across multiple scale levels. Other examples include Manovich's analysis of one million manga pages using the Mondrian software,[1] sorted according to gray-scale values; another project analyzes scene lengths and gray scale values in classic black-and-white films. While large-scale data analyses are not new, their applications in the humanities and arts are still in their infancy, making cultural analytics a frontier of knowledge construction.

Of course, not everyone has access to computation-intensive facilities, including most parents and teachers at smaller colleges and universities. A small-scale example that anyone could implement will be helpful. In teaching an honors writing class, I juxtaposed Mary Shelley's *Frankenstein* with Shelley Jackson's *Patchwork Girl*,[2] an electronic hypertext fiction written in proprietary *Storyspace* software.[3] Since these were honors students, many of them had already read *Frankenstein* and were, moreover, practiced in close reading and literary analysis. When it came to digital reading, however, they were accustomed to the scanning and fast skimming typical of hyperreading; they therefore expected that it might take them, oh, half an hour to go through Jackson's text. They were shocked when I told them a reasonable time to spend with Jackson's text was about the time it would take them to read *Frankenstein*, say, ten hours or so. I divided them into teams and assigned a section of Jackson's text to each team, telling them that I wanted them to discover *all* the lexias (i.e., blocks of digital text) in their section

1. General-purpose statistical data visualization software for interactive data visualization. "Manga": comics originating in a style developed in Japan in the late 19th century (literally, "whimsical, impromptu"; Japanese).
2. A 1995 work by the American author Jackson (b. 1963) that uses as its jumping-off point Shelley's (1797–1851) 1818 tale of the young doctor, Victor Frankenstein, who reanimates a pieced-together human body.
3. Computer program written in the 1980s by Jay David Bolter and Michael Joyce for creating, editing, and reading hypertext fiction.

and warning them that the *Storyspace* software allows certain lexias to be hidden until others are read. Finally, I asked them to diagram interrelations between lexias, drawing on all three views that the *Storyspace* software enables.

As a consequence, the students were not only required to read closely but also to analyze the narrative strategies Jackson uses to construct her text. Jackson focuses some of her textual sections on a narrator modeled on the female creature depicted in *Frankenstein*, when Victor, at the male creature's request, begins to assemble a female body as a companion to his first creation (Hayles, "Invention"). As Victor works, he begins to think about the two creatures mating and creating a race of such creatures. Stricken with sexual nausea, he tears up the female body while the male creature watches, howling, from the window; throws the pieces into a basket; and rows out onto a lake, where he dumps them. In her text Jackson reassembles and reanimates the female creature, playing with the idea of fragmentation as an inescapable condition not only for her narrator but for all human beings. The idea is reinforced by the visual form of the narrative, which (in the *Storyspace* map view) is visualized as a series of titled text blocks connected by webs of lines. Juxtaposing this text with *Frankenstein* encouraged discussions about narrative framing, transitions, strategies, and characterization. By the end the students, who already admired *Frankenstein* and were enthralled by Mary Shelley's narrative, were able to see that electronic literature might be comparably complex and would also repay close attention to its strategies, structure, form, rhetoric, and themes. Here already-existing print literacies were enlisted to promote and extend digital literacy.

These examples merely scratch the surface of what can be done to create productive interactions between close, hyper, and machine reading. Close and hyperreading are already part of a literary scholar's tool kit (although hyperreading may not be recognized or valued as such). Many good programs are now available for machine reading, such as *Wordle*, which creates word clouds[4] to display word-frequency analysis, the advanced version of the *Hermetic Word Frequency Counter*, which has the ability to count words in multiple files and to count phrases as well as words, and other text-analysis tools available through the TAPoR text-analysis portal[5] (http://digitalresearchtools.pbworks.com/Text+Analysis+Tools). Most of these programs are not difficult to use and provide the basis for wide-ranging experimentation by students and teachers alike. As Manovich says about cultural analytics and Moretti proclaims about distant reading, machine analysis opens the door to new kinds of discoveries that were not possible before and that can surprise and intrigue scholars accustomed to the delights of close reading.

What transformed disciplinary coherence might literary studies embrace? Here is a suggestion: literary studies teaches literacies across a range of

4. Visual representations of text data that give greater prominence to words that appear more frequently in the source text (also called "tag clouds" or "weighted lists").

5. Web portal based and developed at McMaster University where researchers can experiment with text analysis tools.

media forms, including print and digital, and focuses on interpretation and analysis of patterns, meaning, and context through close, hyper-, and machine reading practices. Reading has always been constituted through complex and diverse practices. Now it is time to rethink what reading is and how it works in the rich mixtures of words and images, sounds and animations, graphics and letters that constitute the environments of twenty-first-century literacies.

WORKS CITED

Bauerlein, Mark. *The Dumbest Generation: How the Digital Age Stupefies Young Americans and Jeopardizes Our Future.* New York: Penguin, 2009. Print.

Benjamin, Walter. "The Work of Art in the Age of Mechanical Reproduction." *Illuminations.* Ed. Hannah Arendt. Trans. Harry Zohn. New York: Schocken, 1968. 217–51. Print.

Best, Stephen, and Sharon Marcus. "Surface Reading: An Introduction." *The Way We Read Now.* Ed. Best and Marcus. Spec. issue of *Representations* 108 (2009): 1–21. Print.

Carr, Nicholas. *The Shallows: What the Internet Is Doing to Our Brains.* New York: Norton, 2010. Print.

Cohen, Margaret. "Narratology in the Archive of Literature." Spec. issue of *Representations* 108 (2009): 51–75. Print.

Crane, Mary Thomas. "Surface, Depth, and the Spatial Imaginary: A Cognitive Reading of *The Political Unconscious.*" Spec. issue of *Representations* 108 (2009): 76–97. Print.

Crary, Jonathan. *Suspensions of Perception: Attention, Spectacle, and Modern Culture.* Cambridge: MIT P, 2001. Print.

Culler, Jonathan. "The Closeness of Close Reading." *ADE Bulletin* 149 (2010): 20–25. Print.

Dehaene, Stanislas. *Reading in the Brain: The Science and Evolution of a Human Invention.* New York: Viking, 2009. Print.

DeStefano, Diana, and Jo-Anne LeFevre. "Cognitive Load in Hypertext Reading: A Review." *Computers in Human Behavior* 23.3 (2007): 1616–41. Print.

Gallop, Jane. "Close Reading in 2009." *ADE Bulletin* 149 (2010): 15–19. Print.

Greenfield, Patricia M. "Technology and Informal Education: What Is Taught, What Is Learned." *Science* 323.5910 (2009): 69–71. Print.

Griswold, Wendy, Terry McDonnell, and Nathan Wright. "Reading and the Reading Class in the Twenty-First Century." *Annual Review of Sociology* 31 (2005): 127–42. Print.

Guillory, John. "Close Reading: Prologue and Epilogue." *ADE Bulletin* 149 (2010): 8–14. Print.

———. "How Scholars Read." *ADE Bulletin* 146 (2008): 8–17. Print.

Hayles, N. Katherine. "Hyper and Deep Attention: The Generational Divide in Cognitive Modes." *Profession* (2007): 187–99. Print.

———. "The Invention of Copyright and the Birth of Monsters: Flickering Connectivities in Shelley Jackson's *Patchwork Girl.*" *Journal of Postmodern Culture* 10.2 (2001): n. pag. Web. 1 Sept. 2010.

Jameson, Fredric. *The Political Unconscious: Narrative as a Socially Symbolic Act.* Ithaca: Cornell UP, 1981. Print.

Johnson, Barbara. "Teaching Deconstructively." *Writing and Reading Differently: Deconstruction and the Teaching of Composition and Literature.* Ed. G. Douglas Atkins and Michael L. Johnson. Lawrence: UP of Kansas, 1985. 140–48. Print.

Kirschenbaum, Matthew G. "Reading at Risk: A Response." *Learning Technologies*. U of Maryland, 21 July 2004. Web. 1 Sept. 2010.

Klingberg, Torkel. *The Overflowing Brain: Information Overload and the Limits of Working Memory*. Oxford: Oxford UP, 2009. Print.

Laurence, David. "Learning to Read." *ADE Bulletin* 145 (2008): 3–7. Print.

Liu, Alan. "Re-doing Literary Interpretation: A Pedagogy." *Currents in Electronic Literacy*. Digital Writing and Research Lab, U of Texas at Austin, 2008. Web. 1 Sept. 2010.

Manovich, Lev. "Cultural Analytics: Analysis and Visualization of Large Cultural Data Sets." *Manovich.net*. Manovich, 30 Sept. 2007. Web. 1 Sept. 2010.

McCarty, Willard. *Humanities Computing*. London: Palgrave, 2005. Print.

Miall, David S., and Teresa Dobson. "Reading Hypertext and the Experience of Literature." *Journal of Digital Information* 2.1 (2001): n. pag. Web. 1 Sept. 2010.

Moretti, Franco. *Graphs, Maps, Trees: Abstract Models for Literary History*. New York: Verso, 2007. Print.

———. "Style, Inc. Reflections on Seven Thousand Titles (British Novels, 1740–1850)." *Critical Inquiry* 36 (2009): 134–58. Print.

National Endowment for the Arts. *Reading at Risk: A Survey of Literary Reading in America*. NEA, June 2004. Web. 1 Sept. 2010.

———. *Reading on the Rise: A New Chapter in American Literacy*. NEA, Jan. 2009. Web. 1 Sept. 2010.

———. *To Read or Not to Read: A Question of National Consequence*. NEA, Nov. 2007. Web. 27 Aug. 2010.

Niederhauser, D. S., R. E. Reynolds, D. J. Salmen, and P. Skolmoski. "The Influence of Cognitive Load on Learning from Hypertext." *Journal of Educational Computing Research* 23.3 (2000): 237–55. Print.

Nielsen, Jakob. "F-Shaped Pattern for Reading Web Content." *Alertbox* (2006): n. pag. Web. 1 Sept. 2010.

———. "How Little Do Users Read?" *Alertbox* (2008): n. pag. Web. 1 Sept. 2010.

Roberts, D. F., U. G. Foehr, and V. Rideout. *Generation M: Media in the Lives of 8–18 Year Olds: A Kaiser Family Foundation Study*. Kaiser Family Foundation, Mar. 2005. Web. 1 Sept. 2010.

Robertson, Margaret, Andrew Fluck, and Ivan Webb. *Children, On-line Learning and Authentic Teaching Skills in Primary Education. University of Tasmania*. U of Tasmania, n.d. Web. 13 Dec. 2010.

Sanders, Laura. "Trawling the Brain." *Science News* 176.13 (2009): Web. 23 Feb. 2011.

Scholes, Robert. *The Rise and Fall of English: Reconstructing English as a Discipline*. New Haven: Yale UP, 1999. Print.

Sillence, E., P. Briggs, P. R. Harris, and L. Fishwick. "How Do Patients Evaluate and Make Use of Online Health Information?" *Social Science and Medicine* 64 (2007): 1853–62. Print.

Skura, Helen, Katia Nierle, and Gregory Gin. "*Romeo and Juliet*: A *Facebook* Tragedy." *Literature and Cross-Disciplinary Models of Literary Interpretation*. PBWorks, 2008. Web. 1 Sept. 2010.

Small, Gary, and Gigi Vorgan. *iBrain: Surviving the Technological Alteration of the Modern Mind*. New York: Harper, 2008. Print.

Sosnoski, James. "Hyper-readers and Their Reading Engines." *Passions, Pedagogies, and Twenty-First Century Technologies*. Ed. Gail E. Hawisher and Cynthia L. Selfe. Logan: Utah State UP; Urbana: Natl. Council of Teachers of English, 1999. 161–77. Print.

Tinsley, Ron, and Kimberly Lebak. "Expanding the Zone of Reflective Capacity: Taking Separate Journeys Together." *Networks* 11.2 (2009): 1–11. Web. 1 Sept. 2010.

Vonnegut, Kurt. "Harrison Bergeron." *Welcome to the Monkey House.* 1961. New York: Dell, 1998. 7–14. Print.
Vygotsky, L. S. *Mind in Society: The Development of Higher Psychological Processes.* Ed. Michael Cole, Vera John-Steiner, Sylvia Scribner, and Ellen Souberman. 14th ed. Cambridge: Harvard UP, 1978. Print.
Wolf, Maryanne. *Proust and the Squid: The Story and Science of the Reading Brain.* New York: Harper, 2007. Print.
Zhu, Erping. "Hypermedia Interface Design: The Effects of Number of Links and Granularity of Nodes." *Journal of Educational Multimedia and Hypermedia* 8.3 (1999): 331–58. Print.

2010

SUSAN BORDO
b. 1947

Among the founders of "body studies," Susan Bordo stands out for her work's close attention to the ways that cultural images and expectations shape how both sexes understand a female body as "desirable." Although strongly influenced by MICHEL FOUCAULT, Bordo is wary of theory and the academy. She advocates a politically active feminism that highlights the concrete impact of social forces on women's bodies and considers possible forms of resistance. Writing in a steely, lucid prose that reaches out to nonacademic audiences, she works against both cultural self-congratulation ("you've come a long way, baby") and the abstractions of French feminism. She insists on the practical consequences for women's daily lives of feminism's analyses of contemporary culture. Bordo's work introduces a crucial gendered element into contemporary literary and cultural theory's interest in the processes involved in the formation of social subjects.

Bordo was educated at Carleton College and the State University of New York at Stony Brook, from which she received her Ph.D. in 1982. She has taught at Le Moyne College and the University of Kentucky. Her *Unbearable Weight* (1993) was a New York Times Notable Book of the Year. Trained as a philosopher, she now describes her work as "gender studies," which is "part of cultural studies." "But neither gender studies nor cultural studies," she writes, "can be of much significance unless they reach outside the academic world." She calls the "slow unlearning" of the "language" and "arrogance" of the academy her "second and ongoing education."

Bordo's early work explored the exclusionary use of terms such as "rationality" and "objectivity" in the philosophical tradition. Like others studying what came to be called "feminist epistemology," she argued that knowledge is not something achieved by a pure mind that "distances" itself from the object it studies. Rather, knowledge is "embodied," produced from a "standpoint" by a body that is located as a material entity among other material entities. It was a short step from standpoint theory to body studies.

Not all bodies are alike. Different bodies are assigned to different locations, are represented differently in prevailing cultural codes, and are accorded different authority as producers of knowledge. One crucial way to differentiate bodies is, of course, gender. Bordo turns her attention to the ways in which the body is a "text of culture." Prevailing and enforced cultural notions of gender differences are inscribed on the body, as it shapes itself to fit conventions of proper appearance, deportment, and physical activity.

Psychoanalytic feminists tend to discuss the shaping of the girl's body and of her relation to it in generalized terms that posit a triangular familial relation (mother–father–daughter) and an overarching patriarchal Law (the law of the father, compulsory heterosexuality, or the incest taboo). Bordo eschews this focus on the family, contending instead that a variety of social forces converge in the shaping of bodies—and that this constellation of forces shifts over time and from one society to another. The decline in hysteria and the recent rise in anorexia and bulimia point to changes in the cultural nexus within which bodies are produced. Like others who adopt a "social constructivist" position, Bordo argues that the body does not have a fixed and enduring nature; bodies are plastic and change in response to the social demands placed on them.

Bordo follows other contemporary feminists (such as SANDRA M. GILBERT and SUSAN GUBAR) in noting that women over the past two hundred years are more prone than men to suffer from a number of illnesses that occupy an ill-defined terrain between the physical and the psychological. In our selection from her book *Unbearable Weight*, Bordo focuses on three such illnesses: hysteria (extreme emotional excitability), anorexia (inability or refusal to eat), and agoraphobia (inability to enter public places). She strives to demonstrate that these "pathologies of resistance" mark the ways individual women *both* insert their bodies into "the network of practices, institutions, and technologies" within which bodies are produced *and* struggle against those very networks.

Her analysis of anorexia provides an example of this doubleness. Contemporary women in the United States, Bordo argues, are pulled in multiple directions as competing demands are made on them. The anorectic's refusal to eat is tied directly to the peculiar "double bind" in which today's young woman is placed. She is expected to emulate the impossibly thin body that is presented as the ideal in countless media images, while she is also urged—in a kind of demonic parody of feminism—to take control of her own life, to be strong, to become a superwoman. The conflicting message is that only one ideal is acceptable, but you are supposed to be your own woman. Anorexia for Bordo is not solely, as in some popular accounts, the result of an obsession with thinness; it is also, crucially, a comprehensible response to powerlessness. The young woman dramatically enacts her powerlessness by playing the female role to its extreme, making its destructive underpinnings obvious. Paradoxically, this strategy also secures for her a modicum of power as she gains control over her appetite and directly resists (albeit in a self-destructive way) the family, friends, and therapists who urge her to eat.

Bordo is careful to say that cultural images are not everything. "Anorexia," she writes, "clearly contains a dimension of physical addiction to the biochemical effects of starvation." But like Foucault, she focuses on the discourses through which society produces, understands, defines, and interprets the female body. Social codings of beauty, of motherhood, of sexual modesty or its opposite place the individual woman in relation to the prevailing images and conventions. Even if that relation is one of negation and resistance, the power of the categories is still felt as the individual struggles against them. Every body is marked by its relation to the "constitutive mechanisms" of a "power" that "shapes." Femininity, for Bordo, is ideology (a culture's dominant notions of the feminine) inscribed on the body.

In presenting anorexia as a parodic demonstration of the destructive energy stored in our cultural categories, Bordo appears close to JUDITH BUTLER's influential discussion of how homosexual cross-dressing "troubles" gender categories. But Bordo has been sharply critical of Butler because she believes that Butler vastly underestimates the suffering the parodic body endures and vastly overestimates the cultural or political effectiveness of parody. Anorexia, as analyzed by Bordo, may be an eloquent bodily articulation of the unreasonable demands our society places on women, but that articulation through parody can hardly be celebrated or encouraged when its practical effects "utterly defeat rebellion and subvert protest." Anorexia is self-destructive and does nothing in itself to alter the cultural order that calls it forth. Action, Bordo insists, must come on other fronts, especially those of feminist critique and feminist political activism. In this respect, Bordo self-consciously looks back to the feminism of the late 1960s and early 1970s as a model.

The fundamental dispute between Bordo and Butler, or more widely between Anglo-American and French-oriented feminisms, rests on the question of how political and cultural transformation should be attempted. Bordo honors "female praxis": individual and collective action with clear, conscious goals that are pursued through a series of purposive strategies. Similarly, she aims for subjects who are reasonably at home in their bodies, who can experience their bodies as aligned with their purposes and aspirations in life. The anorectic demonstrates how difficult American culture makes it for women to achieve such selfhood and such a relation to their bodies, but the example of the anorectic does not lead Bordo to think the basic goal unattainable. French feminists and those influenced by them believe that such desires for self-unity are themselves symptoms of the repressive patriarchal cultural order of intelligibilty that must be transformed. All ideals of coherence, of unity, of conscious control must be problematized if we are not to repeat endlessly the enforcement of differences that characterizes existing male cultural domination. The two sides share the conviction that cultural codings are powerful and that feminism begins with an analysis of how those codings exercise power, especially over the ongoing social construction of bodies. Their disagreements over the site of the most effective cultural and political interventions continue to resonate throughout feminist theory.

***Unbearable Weight: Feminism, Western Culture, and the Body* Keywords:** The Body, Cultural Studies, Feminist Theory, Gender, Identity, Ideology, Popular Culture

From Unbearable Weight: Feminism, Western Culture, and the Body

Chapter 5. The Body and the Reproduction of Femininity

RECONSTRUCTING FEMINIST DISCOURSE ON THE BODY

The body—what we eat, how we dress, the daily rituals through which we attend to the body—is a medium of culture. The body, as anthropologist Mary Douglas has argued, is a powerful symbolic form, a surface on which the central rules, hierarchies, and even metaphysical commitments of a culture are inscribed and thus reinforced through the concrete language of the body.[1] The body may also operate as a metaphor for culture. From quarters as diverse as Plato and Hobbes to French feminist Luce Irigaray,[2] an imagination of body morphology has provided a blueprint for diagnosis and/or vision of social and political life.

The body is not only a *text* of culture. It is also, as anthropologist Pierre Bourdieu and philosopher Michel Foucault[3] (among others) have argued, a *practical*, direct locus of social control. Banally, through table manners and

1. Mary Douglas, *Natural Symbols* (New York: Pantheon, 1982) and *Purity and Danger* (London: Routledge and Kegan Paul, 1966) [except as indicated, all notes are Bordo's].
2. French feminist theorist (b. 1930). PLATO (ca. 427–ca. 347 B.C.E.), Greek philosopher. Thomas Hobbes (1588–1679), English political philosopher [editor's note].
3. French philosopher and historian of ideas (1926–1984; see above). BOURDIEU (1930–2002), French social theorist [editor's note].

toilet habits, through seemingly trivial routines, rules, and practices, culture is "*made* body," as Bourdieu puts it—converted into automatic, habitual activity. As such it is put "beyond the grasp of consciousness . . . [untouchable] by voluntary, deliberate transformations."[4] Our conscious politics, social commitments, strivings for change may be undermined and betrayed by the life of our bodies—not the craving, instinctual body imagined by Plato, Augustine, and Freud,[5] but what Foucault calls the "docile body," regulated by the norms of cultural life.[6]

Throughout his later "genealogical" works (*Discipline and Punish, The History of Sexuality*), Foucault constantly reminds us of the primacy of practice over belief. Not chiefly through ideology, but through the organization and regulation of the time, space, and movements of our daily lives, our bodies are trained, shaped, and impressed with the stamp of prevailing historical forms of selfhood, desire, masculinity, femininity. Such an emphasis casts a dark and disquieting shadow across the contemporary scene. For women, as study after study shows, are spending more time on the management and discipline of our bodies than we have in a long, long time. In a decade marked by a reopening of the public arena to women, the intensification of such regimens appears diversionary and subverting. Through the pursuit of an ever-changing, homogenizing, elusive ideal of femininity—a pursuit without a terminus, requiring that women constantly attend to minute and often whimsical changes in fashion—female bodies become docile bodies—bodies whose forces and energies are habituated to external regulation, subjection, transformation, "improvement." Through the exacting and normalizing disciplines of diet, makeup, and dress—central organizing principles of time and space in the day of many women—we are rendered less socially oriented and more centripetally focused on self-modification. Through these disciplines, we continue to memorize on our bodies the feel and conviction of lack, of insufficiency, of never being good enough. At the farthest extremes, the practices of femininity may lead us to utter demoralization, debilitation, and death.

Viewed historically, the discipline and normalization of the female body—perhaps the only gender oppression that exercises itself, although to different degrees and in different forms, across age, race, class, and sexual orientation—has to be acknowledged as an amazingly durable and flexible strategy of social control. In our own era, it is difficult to avoid the recognition that the contemporary preoccupation with appearance, which still affects women far more powerfully than men, even in our narcissistic and visually oriented culture, may function as a backlash phenomenon, reasserting existing gender configurations against any attempts to shift or transform power relations.[7]

4. Pierre Bourdieu, *Outline of a Theory of Practice* (Cambridge: Cambridge University Press, 1977), p. 94 (emphasis in original).

5. SIGMUND FREUD (1856–1939), Austrian founder of psychoanalysis. AUGUSTINE (354–430), Christian theologian. The three thinkers all evidenced a disgust with the body, especially the female body [editor's note].

6. On docility, see Michel Foucault, *Discipline and Punish* (New York: Vintage, 1979), pp. 135–69. For a Foucauldian analysis of feminine practice, see Sandra Bartky, "Foucault, Femininity, and the Modernization of Patriarchal Power," in her *Femininity and Domination* (New York: Routledge, 1990); see also Susan Brownmiller, *Femininity* (New York: Ballantine, 1984).

7. During the late 1970s and 1980s, male concern over appearance undeniably increased. Study after study confirms, however, that there is still a large gender gap in this area. Research conducted at the University of Pennsylvania in 1985 found men to be generally satisfied with their appearance, often, in fact, "distorting their perceptions [of themselves] in a positive, self-aggrandizing way" ("Dislike of Own Bodies Found Common among Women," *New York Times*, March 19, 1985, p. C1). Women, however, were found to exhibit extreme negative assessments and distor-

Surely we are in the throes of this backlash today. In newspapers and magazines we daily encounter stories that promote traditional gender relations and prey on anxieties about change: stories about latch-key children, abuse in day-care centers, the "new woman's" troubles with men, her lack of marriageability, and so on. A dominant visual theme in teenage magazines involves women hiding in the shadows of men, seeking solace in their arms, willingly contracting the space they occupy. The last, of course, also describes our contemporary aesthetic ideal for women, an ideal whose obsessive pursuit has become the central torment of many women's lives. In such an era we desperately need an effective political discourse about the female body, a discourse adequate to an analysis of the insidious, and often paradoxical, pathways of modern social control.

Developing such a discourse requires reconstructing the feminist paradigm of the late 1960s and early 1970s, with its political categories of oppressors and oppressed, villains and victims. Here I believe that a feminist appropriation of some of Foucault's later concepts can prove useful. Following Foucault, we must first abandon the idea of power as something possessed by one group and leveled against another; we must instead think of the network of practices, institutions, and technologies that sustain positions of dominance and subordination in a particular domain.

Second, we need an analytics adequate to describe a power whose central mechanisms are not repressive, but *constitutive*: "a power bent on generating forces, making them grow, and ordering them, rather than one dedicated to impeding them, making them submit, or destroying them." Particularly in the realm of femininity, where so much depends on the seemingly willing acceptance of various norms and practices, we need an analysis of power "from below," as Foucault puts it; for example, of the mechanisms that shape and proliferate—rather than repress—desire, generate and focus our energies, construct our conceptions of normalcy and deviance.[8]

And, third, we need a discourse that will enable us to account for the subversion of potential rebellion, a discourse that, while insisting on the necessity of objective analysis of power relations, social hierarchy, political backlash, and so forth, will nonetheless allow us to confront the mechanisms by which the subject at times becomes enmeshed in collusion with forces that sustain her own oppression.

This essay will not attempt to produce a general theory along these lines. Rather, my focus will be the analysis of one particular arena where the interplay of these dynamics is striking and perhaps exemplary. It is a limited and unusual arena, that of a group of gender-related and historically localized

---

tions of body perception. Other studies have suggested that women are judged more harshly than men when they deviate from dominant social standards of attractiveness. Thomas Cash et al., in "The Great American Shape-Up," *Psychology Today*, April 1986, p. 34, report that although the situation for men has changed, the situation for women has more than proportionally worsened. Citing results from 30,000 responses to a 1985 survey of perceptions of body image and comparing similar responses to a 1972 questionnaire, they report that the 1985 respondents were considerably more dissatisfied with their bodies than the 1972 respondents, and they note a marked intensification of concern among men. Among the 1985 group, the group most dissatisfied of all with their appearance, however, were teenage women. Women today constitute by far the largest number of consumers of diet products, attenders of spas and diet centers, and subjects of intestinal by-pass and other fat-reduction operations.

8. Michel Foucault, *The History of Sexuality*, vol. 1, *An Introduction* (New York: Vintage, 1980), pp. 136, 94.

disorders: hysteria, agoraphobia, and anorexia nervosa.[9] I recognize that these disorders have also historically been class- and race-biased, largely (although not exclusively) occurring among white middle- and upper-middle-class women. Nonetheless, anorexia, hysteria, and agoraphobia may provide a paradigm of one way in which potential resistance is not merely undercut but *utilized* in the maintenance and reproduction of existing power relations.[1]

The central mechanism I will describe involves a transformation (or, if you wish, duality) of meaning, through which conditions that are objectively (and, on one level, experientially) constraining, enslaving, and even murderous, come to be experienced as liberating, transforming, and life-giving. I offer this analysis, although limited to a specific domain, as an example of how various contemporary critical discourses may be joined to yield an understanding of the subtle and often unwitting role played by our bodies in the symbolization and reproduction of gender.

THE BODY AS A TEXT OF FEMININITY

The continuum between female disorder and "normal" feminine practice is sharply revealed through a close reading of those disorders to which women have been particularly vulnerable. These, of course, have varied historically: neurasthenia[2] and hysteria in the second half of the nineteenth century; agoraphobia and, most dramatically, anorexia nervosa and bulimia in the second half of the twentieth century. This is not to say that anorectics did not exist in the nineteenth century—many cases were described, usually in the context of diagnoses of hysteria[3]—or that women no longer suffer from classical hysterical symptoms in the twentieth century. But the taking up of eating disorders on a mass scale is as unique to the culture of the 1980s as the epidemic of hysteria was to the Victorian era.[4]

The symptomatology of these disorders reveals itself as textuality. Loss of mobility, loss of voice, inability to leave the home, feeding others while

9. On the gendered and historical nature of these disorders: the number of female to male hysterics has been estimated at anywhere from 2:1 to 4:1, and as many as 80 percent of all agoraphobics are female (Annette Brodsky and Rachel Hare-Mustin, *Women and Psychotherapy* [New York: Guilford Press, 1980], pp. 116, 122). Although more cases of male eating disorders have been reported in the late eighties and early nineties, it is estimated that close to 90 percent of all anorectics are female (Paul Garfinkel and David Garner, *Anorexia Nervosa: A Multidimensional Perspective* [New York: Brunner/Mazel, 1982], pp. 112–13). For a sophisticated account of female psychopathology, with particular attention to nineteenth-century disorders but, unfortunately, little mention of agoraphobia or eating disorders, see Elaine Showalter, *The Female Malady: Women, Madness and English Culture, 1830–1980* (New York: Pantheon, 1985). For a discussion of social and gender issues in agoraphobia, see Robert Seidenberg and Karen DeCrow, *Women Who Marry Houses: Panic and Protest in Agoraphobia* (New York: McGraw-Hill, 1983). On the history of anorexia nervosa, see Joan Jacobs Brumberg, *Fasting Girls: The Emergence of Anorexia Nervosa as a Modern Disease* (Cambridge: Harvard University Press, 1988). ["Hysteria": a psychoneurosis marked by emotional excitability. The word derives from the Greek word for womb; it was thought that such ailments were peculiar to women and caused by disturbances of the uterus–editor's note.]

1. In constructing such a paradigm I do not pretend to do justice to any of these disorders in its individual complexity. My aim is to chart some points of intersection, to describe some similar patterns, as they emerge through a particular reading of the phenomenon—a political reading, if you will.

2. An emotional and psychic disorder characterized by easy fatigability and often by lack of motivation, as well as feelings of inadequacy [editor's note].

3. Showalter, *The Female Malady*, pp. 128–29.

4. On the epidemic of hysteria and neurasthenia, see Showalter, *The Female Malady*; Carroll Smith-Rosenberg, "The Hysterical Woman: Sex Roles and Role Conflict in Nineteenth-Century America," in her *Disorderly Conduct: Visions of Gender in Victorian America* (Oxford: Oxford University Press, 1985).

starving oneself, taking up space, and whittling down the space one's body takes up—all have symbolic meaning, all have *political* meaning under the varying rules governing the historical construction of gender. Working within this framework, we see that whether we look at hysteria, agoraphobia, or anorexia, we find the body of the sufferer deeply inscribed with an ideological construction of femininity emblematic of the period in question. The construction, of course, is always homogenizing and normalizing, erasing racial, class, and other differences and insisting that all women aspire to a coercive, standardized ideal. Strikingly, in these disorders the construction of femininity is written in disturbingly concrete, hyperbolic terms: exaggerated, extremely literal, at times virtually caricatured presentations of the ruling feminine mystique. The bodies of disordered women in this way offer themselves as an aggressively graphic text for the interpreter—a text that insists, actually demands, that it be read as a cultural statement, a statement about gender.

Both nineteenth-century male physicians and twentieth-century feminist critics have seen, in the symptoms of neurasthenia and hysteria (syndromes that became increasingly less differentiated as the century wore on), an exaggeration of stereotypically feminine traits. The nineteenth-century "lady" was idealized in terms of delicacy and dreaminess, sexual passivity, and a charmingly labile and capricious emotionality.[5] Such notions were formalized and scientized in the work of male theorists from Acton and Krafft-Ebing[6] to Freud, who described "normal," mature femininity in such terms.[7] In this context, the dissociations, the drifting and fogging of perception, the nervous tremors and faints, the anesthesias,[8] and the extreme mutability of symptomatology associated with nineteenth-century female disorders can be seen to be concretizations of the feminine mystique of the period, produced according to rules that governed the prevailing construction of femininity. Doctors described what came to be known as the hysterical personality as "impressionable, suggestible, and narcissistic; highly labile, their moods changing suddenly, dramatically, and seemingly for inconsequential reasons . . . egocentric in the extreme . . . essentially asexual and not uncommonly frigid"[9]—all characteristics normative of femininity in this era. As Elaine Showalter points out, the term *hysterical* itself became almost interchangeable with the term *feminine* in the literature of the period.[1]

5. Martha Vicinus, "Introduction: The Perfect Victorian Lady," in Martha Vicinus, ed., *Suffer and Be Still: Women in the Victorian Age* (Bloomington: Indiana University Press, 1972), pp. x–xi.
6. Richard von Krafft-Ebing (1840–1902), German physician who wrote about sexual behavior, especially sexual "pathologies." William Acton (1813–1875), English doctor and civil servant who wrote physician's manuals on sexuality that codify Victorian stereotypes [editor's note].
7. See Carol Nadelson and Malkah Notman, *The Female Patient* (New York: Plenum, 1982), p. 5; E. M. Sigsworth and T. J. Wyke, "A Study of Victorian Prostitution and Venereal Disease," in Vicinus, *Suffer and Be Still*, p. 82. For more general discussions, see Peter Gay, *The Bourgeois Experience: Victoria to Freud*, vol. 1, *Education of the Senses* (New York: Oxford University Press, 1984), esp. pp. 109–68; Showalter, *The Female Malady*, esp. pp. 121–44. The delicate lady, an ideal that had very strong class connotations (as does slenderness today), is not the only conception of femininity to be found in Victorian cultures. But it was arguably the single most powerful ideological representation of femininity in that era, affecting women of all classes, including those without the material means to realize the ideal fully. See Helena Mitchie, *The Flesh Made Word* (New York: Oxford University Press, 1987), for discussions of the control of female appetite and Victorian constructions of femininity.
8. Losses of feeling in various parts of the body [editor's note].
9. Smith-Rosenberg, *Disorderly Conduct*, p. 203.
1. Showalter, *The Female Malady*, p. 129.

The hysteric's embodiment of the feminine mystique of her era, however, seems subtle and ineffable compared to the ingenious literalism of agoraphobia and anorexia. In the context of our culture this literalism makes sense. With the advent of movies and television, the rules for femininity have come to be culturally transmitted more and more through standardized visual images. As a result, femininity itself has come to be largely a matter of constructing, in the manner described by Erving Goffman, the appropriate surface presentation of the self.[2] We are no longer given verbal descriptions or exemplars of what a lady is or of what femininity consists. Rather, we learn the rules directly through bodily discourse: through images that tell us what clothes, body shape, facial expression, movements, and behavior are required.

In agoraphobia and, even more dramatically, in anorexia, the disorder presents itself as a virtual, though tragic, parody of twentieth-century constructions of femininity. The 1950s and early 1960s, when agoraphobia first began to escalate among women, was a period of reassertion of domesticity and dependency as the feminine ideal. *Career woman* became a dirty word, much more so than it had been during the war, when the economy depended on women's willingness to do "men's work." The reigning ideology of femininity, so well described by Betty Friedan and perfectly captured in the movies and television shows of the era, was childlike, nonassertive, helpless without a man, "content in a world of bedroom and kitchen, sex, babies and home."[3] The housebound agoraphobic lives this construction of femininity literally. "You want me in this home? You'll have me in this home—with a vengeance!" The point, upon which many therapists have commented, does not need belaboring. Agoraphobia, as I. G. Fodor has put it, seems "the logical—albeit extreme—extension of the cultural sex-role stereotype for women" in this era.[4]

The emaciated body of the anorectic, of course, immediately presents itself as a caricature of the contemporary ideal of hyperslenderness for women, an ideal that, despite the game resistance of racial and ethnic difference, has become the norm for women today. But slenderness is only the tip of the iceberg, for slenderness itself requires interpretation. "C'est le sens qui fait vendre," said Barthes, speaking of clothing styles—it is meaning that makes the sale.[5] So, too, it is meaning that makes the body admirable. To the degree that anorexia may be said to be "about" slenderness, it is about slenderness, as a citadel of contemporary and historical meaning, not as an empty fashion ideal. As such, the interpretation of slenderness yields multiple readings, some related to gender, some not. For the purposes of this essay I will offer an abbreviated, gender-focused reading. But I must stress that this reading illuminates only partially, and that many other currents not discussed

2. Erving Goffman, *The Presentation of Self in Everyday Life* (Garden City, N.Y.: Anchor Doubleday, 1959).

3. Betty Friedan, *The Feminine Mystique* (New York: Dell, 1962), p. 36. The theme song of one such show ran, in part, "I married Joan . . . What a girl . . . what a whirl . . . what a life! I married Joan . . . What a mind . . . love is blind . . . what a wife!" [From *I Married Joan*, an NBC sitcom (1952–55)—editor's note.]

4. See I. G. Fodor, "The Phobic Syndrome in Women," in V. Franks and V. Burtle, eds., *Women in Therapy* (New York: Brunner/Mazel, 1974), p. 119; see also Kathleen Brehony, "Women and Agoraphobia," in Violet Franks and Esther Rothblum, eds., *The Stereotyping of Women* (New York: Springer, 1983).

5. In Jonathan Culler, *Roland Barthes* (New York: Oxford University Press, 1983), p. 74. [BARTHES (1915–1980), French literary critic—editor's note.]

here—economic, psychosocial, and historical, as well as ethnic and class dimensions—figure prominently.[6]

We begin with the painfully literal inscription, on the anorectic's body, of the rules governing the construction of contemporary femininity. That construction is a double bind[7] that legislates contradictory ideals and directives. On the one hand, our culture still widely advertises domestic conceptions of femininity, the ideological moorings for a rigorously dualistic sexual division of labor that casts woman as chief emotional and physical nurturer. The rules for this construction of femininity (and I speak here in a language both symbolic and literal) require that women learn to feed others, not the self, and to construe any desires for self-nurturance and self-feeding as greedy and excessive.[8] Thus, women must develop a totally other-oriented emotional economy. In this economy, the control of female appetite for food is merely the most concrete expression of the general rule governing the construction of femininity: that female hunger—for public power, for independence, for sexual gratification—be contained, and the public space that women be allowed to take up be circumscribed, limited. * * *[9] [S]lenderness, set off against the resurgent muscularity and bulk of the current male body-ideal, carries connotations of fragility and lack of power in the face of a decisive male occupation of social space. On the body of the anorexic woman such rules are grimly and deeply etched.

On the other hand, even as young women today continue to be taught traditionally "feminine" virtues, to the degree that the professional arena is open to them they must also learn to embody the "masculine" language and values of that arena—self-control, determination, cool, emotional discipline, mastery, and so on. Female bodies now speak symbolically of this necessity in their slender spare shape and the currently fashionable men's-wear look. * * * Our bodies, too, as we trudge to the gym every day and fiercely resist both our hungers and our desire to soothe ourselves, are becoming more and more practiced at the "male" virtues of control and self-mastery. * * * The anorectic pursues these virtues with single-minded, unswerving dedication. "Energy, discipline, my own power will keep me going," says ex-anorectic Aimee Liu, recreating her anorexic days. "I need nothing and no one else. . . . I will be master of my own body, if nothing else, I vow."[1]

The ideal of slenderness, then, and the diet and exercise regimens that have become inseparable from it offer the illusion of meeting, through the body, the contradictory demands of the contemporary ideology of femininity. Popular images reflect this dual demand. In a single issue of *Complete Woman* magazine, two articles appear, one on "Feminine Intuition," the other

6. For other interpretive perspectives on the slenderness ideal, see "Reading the Slender Body" in *Unbearable Weight* (1993); Kim Chernin, *The Obsession: Reflections on the Tyranny of Slenderness* (New York: Harper and Row, 1981); Susie Orbach, *Hunger Strike: The Anorectic's Struggle as a Metaphor for Our Age* (New York: W. W. Norton, 1985).

7. A psychological predicament in which a person receives from a single source conflicting messages that allow no appropriate response. First coined in 1956 by the Scottish psychologist R. D. Laing in his study of schizophrenic children, the term is now used more broadly [editor's note].

8. See my "Hunger as Ideology" in *Unbearable Weight* for a discussion of how this construction of femininity is reproduced in contemporary commercials and advertisements concerning food, eating, and cooking.

9. In this selection, all ellipses replace references to figures not reproduced here [editor's note].

1. Aimee Liu, *Solitaire* (New York: Harper and Row, 1979), p. 123.

asking, "Are You the New Macho Woman?" In *Vision Quest*,[2] the young male hero falls in love with the heroine, as he says, because "she has all the best things I like in girls and all the best things I like in guys," that is, she's tough and cool, but warm and alluring. In the enormously popular *Aliens*, the heroine's personality has been deliberately constructed, with near–comic book explicitness, to embody traditional nurturant femininity alongside breathtaking macho prowess and control; Sigourney Weaver, the actress who portrays her, has called the character "Rambolina."[3]

In the pursuit of slenderness and the denial of appetite the traditional construction of femininity intersects with the new requirement for women to embody the "masculine" values of the public arena. The anorectic, as I have argued, embodies this intersection, this double bind, in a particularly painful and graphic way.[4] I mean *double bind* quite literally here. "Masculinity" and "femininity," at least since the nineteenth century and arguably before, have been constructed through a process of mutual exclusion. One cannot simply add the historically feminine virtues to the historically masculine ones to yield a New Woman, a New Man, a new ethics, or a new culture. Even on the screen or on television, embodied in created characters like the *Aliens* heroine, the result is a parody. Unfortunately, in this image-bedazzled culture, we find it increasingly difficult to discriminate between parodies and possibilities for the self. Explored as a possibility for the self, the "androgynous" ideal ultimately exposes its internal contradiction and becomes a war that tears the subject in two—a war explicitly thematized, by many anorectics, as a battle between male and female sides of the self.[5]

PROTEST AND RETREAT IN THE SAME GESTURE

In hysteria, agoraphobia, and anorexia, then, the woman's body may be viewed as a surface on which conventional constructions of femininity are exposed starkly to view, through their inscription in extreme or hyperliteral form. They are written, of course, in languages of horrible suffering. It is as though these bodies are speaking to us of the pathology and violence that lurks just around the corner, waiting at the horizon of "normal" femininity. It is no wonder that a steady motif in the feminist literature on female disorder is that of pathology as embodied *protest*—unconscious, inchoate, and counterproductive protest without an effective language, voice, or politics, but protest nonetheless.

2. A 1985 film directed by Harold Becker [editor's note].

3. That is, a feminine version of the excessively masculine hero (played by Sylvester Stallone) of the popular Rambo movies: *First Blood* (1982), *Rambo: First Blood Part II* (1985), and *Rambo III* (1988). *Aliens* (1986), a film directed by James Cameron [editor's note].

4. Striking, in connection with this, is Catherine Steiner-Adair's 1984 study of high-school women, which reveals a dramatic association between problems with food and body image and emulation of the cool, professionally "together" and gorgeous superwoman. On the basis of a series of interviews, the high schoolers were classified into two groups: one expressed skepticism over the superwoman ideal, the other thoroughly aspired to it. Later administrations of diagnostic tests revealed that 94 percent of the pro-superwoman group fell into the eating-disordered range of the scale. Of the other group, 100 percent fell into the noneating-disordered range. Media images notwithstanding, young women today appear to sense, either consciously or through their bodies, the impossibility of simultaneously meeting the demands of two spheres whose values have been historically defined in utter opposition to each other.

5. See my "Anorexia Nervosa" in *Unbearable Weight*.

American and French feminists[6] alike have heard the hysteric speaking a language of protest, even or perhaps especially when she was mute. Dianne Hunter interprets Anna O.'s[7] aphasia, which manifested itself in an inability to speak her native German, as a rebellion against the linguistic and cultural rules of the father and a return to the "mother-tongue": the semiotic babble of infancy, the language of the body. For Hunter, and for a number of other feminists working with Lacanian categories, the return to the semiotic level is both regressive and, as Hunter puts it, an "expressive" communication "addressed to patriarchal thought," "a self-repudiating form of feminine discourse in which the body signifies what social conditions make it impossible to state linguistically."[8] "The hysterics are accusing; they are pointing," writes Catherine Clément in *The Newly Born Woman*; they make a "mockery of culture."[9] In the same volume, Hélène Cixous speaks of "those wonderful hysterics, who subjected Freud to so many voluptuous moments too shameful to mention, bombarding his mosaic statute/law of Moses with their carnal, passionate body-words, haunting him with their inaudible thundering denunciations." For Cixous, Dora, who so frustrated Freud, is "the core example of the protesting force in women."[1]

The literature of protest includes functional as well as symbolic approaches. Robert Seidenberg and Karen DeCrow, for example, describe agoraphobia as a "strike" against "the renunciations usually demanded of women" and the expectations of housewifely functions such as shopping, driving the children to school, accompanying their husband to social events.[2] Carroll Smith-Rosenberg presents a similar analysis of hysteria, arguing that by preventing the woman from functioning in the wifely role of caretaker of others, of "ministering angel" to husband and children, hysteria "became one way in which conventional women could express—in most cases unconsciously—dissatisfaction with one or several aspects of their lives."[3] A number of feminist writers, among whom Susie Orbach is the most articulate and forceful, have interpreted anorexia as a species of unconscious feminist protest. The anorectic is engaged in a "hunger strike," as Orbach calls it, stressing that this is a political discourse, in which the action of food refusal and dramatic transformation of body size "expresses with [the] body what [the anorectic] is unable to tell us with words"—her indictment of a culture that disdains and suppresses female hunger, makes women ashamed of their appetites and

6. That is, feminists whose approach is primarily sociological ("American") and feminists whose orientation is more psychoanalytic ("French") [editor's note].

7. The pseudonym for the hysteric patient discussed in Freud's first published case history (cowritten with Joseph Breuer, 1895) [editor's note].

8. Dianne Hunter, "Hysteria, Psychoanalysis and Feminism," in Shirley Garner, Claire Kahane, and Madelon Sprengnether, eds., *The (M)Other Tongue* (Ithaca: Cornell University Press, 1986), p. 42. ["Lacanian": derived from the work of the French psychoanalyst JACQUES LACAN (1901–1981). "Semiotic level": a mother-oriented use of language postulated by the French feminist JULIA KRISTEVA (b. 1941)—editor's note.]

9. Catherine Clément and Hélène Cixous, *The Newly Born Woman*, trans. Betsy Wing (Minneapolis: University of Minnesota Press, 1986), p. 42.

1. Clément and Cixous, *The Newly Born Woman*, p. 95. [Dora: the pseudonym of the patient discussed in Freud's *Dora: An Analysis of a Case of Hysteria* (1904). The case has attracted much feminist attention because Freud discounts what seems the fairly obvious sexual abuse of the young Dora by several older men in her circle while imputing various deviant sexual desires to Dora herself. The French feminist CIXOUS (b. 1937) wrote a play about Dora—editor's note.]

2. Seidenberg and DeCrow, *Women Who Marry Houses*, p. 31.

3. Smith-Rosenberg, *Disorderly Conduct*, p. 208.

needs, and demands that women constantly work on the transformation of their body.[4]

The anorectic, of course, is unaware that she is making a political statement. She may, indeed, be hostile to feminism and any other critical perspectives that she views as disputing her own autonomy and control or questioning the cultural ideals around which her life is organized. Through embodied rather than deliberate demonstration she exposes and indicts those ideals, precisely by pursuing them to the point at which their destructive potential is revealed for all to see.

The same gesture that expresses protest, moreover, can also signal retreat; this, indeed, may be part of the symptom's attraction. Kim Chernin, for example, argues that the debilitating anorexic fixation, by halting or mitigating personal development, assuages this generation's guilt and separation anxiety over the prospect of surpassing our mothers, of living less circumscribed, freer lives.[5] Agoraphobia, too, which often develops shortly after marriage, clearly functions in many cases as a way to cement dependency and attachment in the face of unacceptable stirrings of dissatisfaction and restlessness.

Although we may talk meaningfully of protest, then, I want to emphasize the counterproductive, tragically self-defeating (indeed, self-deconstructing) nature of that protest. Functionally, the symptoms of these disorders isolate, weaken, and undermine the sufferers; at the same time they turn the life of the body into an all-absorbing fetish, beside which all other objects of attention pale into unreality. On the symbolic level, too, the protest collapses into its opposite and proclaims the utter capitulation of the subject to the contracted female world. The muteness of hysterics and their return to the level of pure, primary bodily expressivity have been interpreted, as we have seen, as rejecting the symbolic order of the patriarchy and recovering a lost world of semiotic, maternal value. But *at the same time*, of course, muteness is the condition of the silent, uncomplaining woman—an ideal of patriarchal culture. Protesting the stifling of the female voice through one's own voicelessness—that is, employing the language of femininity to protest the conditions of the female world—will always involve ambiguities of this sort.

4. Orbach, *Hunger Strike*, p. 102. When we look into the many autobiographies and case studies of hysterics, anorectics, and agoraphobics, we find that these are indeed the sorts of women one might expect to be frustrated by the constraints of a specified female role. Sigmund Freud and Joseph Breuer, in *Studies on Hysteria* (New York: Avon, 1966), and Freud, in the later *Dora: An Analysis of a Case of Hysteria* (New York: Macmillan, 1963), constantly remark on the ambitiousness, independence, intellectual ability, and creative strivings of their patients. We know, moreover, that many women who later became leading social activists and feminists of the nineteenth century were among those who fell ill with hysteria and neurasthenia. It has become a virtual cliché that the typical anorectic is a perfectionist, driven to excel in all areas of her life. Though less prominently, a similar theme runs throughout the literature on agoraphobia.

One must keep in mind that in drawing on case studies, one is relying on the perceptions of other acculturated individuals. One suspects, for example, that the popular portrait of the anorectic as a relentless overachiever may be colored by the lingering or perhaps resurgent Victorianism of our culture's attitudes toward ambitious women. One does not escape this hermeneutic problem by turning to autobiography. But in autobiography one is at least dealing with social constructions and attitudes that animate the subject's own psychic reality. In this regard the autobiographical literature on anorexia, drawn on in a variety of places in *Unbearable Weight*, is strikingly full of anxiety about the domestic world and other themes that suggest deep rebellion against traditional notions of femininity.

5. Kim Chernin, *The Hungry Self: Women, Eating, and Identity* (New York: Harper and Row, 1985), esp. pp. 41–93.

Perhaps this is why symptoms crystallized from the language of femininity are so perfectly suited to express the dilemmas of middle-class and upper-middle-class women living in periods poised on the edge of gender change, women who have the social and material resources to carry the traditional construction of femininity to symbolic excess but who also confront the anxieties of new possibilities. The late nineteenth century, the post–World War II period, and the late twentieth century are all periods in which gender becomes an issue to be discussed and in which discourse proliferates about "the Woman Question," "the New Woman," "What Women Want," "What Femininity Is."

COLLUSION, RESISTANCE, AND THE BODY

The pathologies of female protest function, paradoxically, as if in collusion with the cultural conditions that produce them, reproducing rather than transforming precisely that which is being protested. In this connection, the fact that hysteria and anorexia have peaked during historical periods of cultural backlash against attempts at reorganization and redefinition of male and female roles is significant. Female pathology reveals itself here as an extremely interesting social formation through which one source of potential for resistance and rebellion is pressed into the service of maintaining the established order.

In our attempt to explain this formation, objective accounts of power relations fail us. For whatever the objective social conditions are that create a pathology, the symptoms themselves must still be produced (however unconsciously or inadvertently) by the subject. That is, the individual must invest the body with meanings of various sorts. Only by examining this productive process on the part of the subject can we, as Mark Poster has put it, "illuminate the mechanisms of domination in the processes through which meaning is produced in everyday life"; that is, only then can we see how the desires and dreams of the subject become implicated in the matrix of power relations.[6]

Here, examining the context in which the anorexic syndrome is produced may be illuminating. Anorexia will erupt, typically, in the course of what begins as a fairly moderate diet regime, undertaken because someone, often the father, has made a casual critical remark. Anorexia *begins in*, emerges out of, what is, in our time, conventional feminine practice. In the course of that practice, for any number of individual reasons, the practice is pushed a little beyond the parameters of moderate dieting. The young woman discovers what it feels like to crave and want and need and yet, through the exercise of her own will, to triumph over that need. In the process, a new realm of meanings is discovered, a range of values and possibilities that Western culture has traditionally coded as "male" and rarely made available to women: an ethic and aesthetic of self-mastery and self-transcendence, expertise, and power over others through the example of superior will and control. The experience is intoxicating, habit-forming.

At school the anorectic discovers that her steadily shrinking body is admired, not so much as an aesthetic or sexual object, but for the strength of will and self-control it projects. At home she discovers, in the inevitable battles her parents fight to get her to eat, that her actions have enormous power

6. Mark Poster, *Foucault, Marxism, and History* (Cambridge: Polity Press, 1984), p. 28.

over the lives of those around her. As her body begins to lose its traditional feminine curves, its breasts and hips and rounded stomach, begins to feel and look more like a spare, lanky male body, she begins to feel untouchable, out of reach of hurt, "invulnerable, clean and hard as the bones etched into my silhouette," as one student described it in her journal. She despises, in particular, all those parts of her body that continue to mark her as female. "If only I could eliminate [my breasts]," says Liu, "cut them off if need be."[7] For her, as for many anorectics, the breasts represent a bovine, unconscious, vulnerable side of the self. Liu's body symbolism is thoroughly continuous with dominant cultural associations. Brett Silverstein's studies on the "Possible Causes of the Thin Standard of Bodily Attractiveness for Women"[8] testify empirically to what is obvious from every comedy routine involving a dramatically shapely woman: namely, our cultural association of curvaceousness with incompetence. The anorectic is also quite aware, of course, of the social and sexual vulnerability involved in having a female body; many, in fact, were sexually abused as children.

Through her anorexia, by contrast, she has unexpectedly discovered an entry into the privileged male world, a way to become what is valued in our culture, a way to become safe, to rise above it all—for her, they are the same thing. She has discovered this, paradoxically, by pursuing conventional feminine behavior—in this case, the discipline of perfecting the body as an object—to excess. At this point of excess, the conventionally feminine deconstructs, we might say, into its opposite and opens onto those values our culture has coded as male. No wonder the anorexia is experienced as liberating and that she will fight family, friends, and therapists in an effort to hold onto it—fight them to the death, if need be. The anorectic's experience of power is, of course, deeply and dangerously illusory. To reshape one's body into a male body is *not* to put on male power and privilege. To *feel* autonomous and free while harnessing body and soul to an obsessive body-practice is to serve, not transform, a social order that limits female possibilities. And, of course, for the female to become male is only for her to locate herself on the other side of a disfiguring opposition. The new "power look" of female body-building, which encourages women to develop the same hulk-like, triangular shape that has been the norm for male body-builders, is no less determined by a hierarchical, dualistic construction of gender than was the conventionally "feminine" norm that tyrannized female body-builders such as Bev Francis for years.[9]

Although the specific cultural practices and meanings are different, similar mechanisms, I suspect, are at work in hysteria and agoraphobia. In these cases too, the language of femininity, when pushed to excess—when shouted and asserted, when disruptive and demanding—deconstructs into its opposite and makes available to the woman an illusory experience of power previously forbidden to her by virtue of her gender. In the case of nineteenth-century femininity, the forbidden experience may have been the bursting of fetters—particularly moral and emotional fetters. John Conolly, the asylum

7. Liu, *Solitaire*, p. 99.
8. Brett Silverstein, "Possible Causes of the Thin Standard of Bodily Attractiveness for Women," *International Journal of Eating Disorders* 5 (1986): 907–16.
9. Because Francis (b. 1955), a muscular Australian powerlifter, was judged insufficiently "feminine," she repeatedly failed to win major professional bodybuilding competitions [editor's note].

reformer, recommended institutionalization for women who "want that restraint over the passions without which the female character is lost."[1] Hysterics often infuriated male doctors by their lack of precisely this quality. S. Weir Mitchell described these patients as "the despair of physicians," whose "despotic selfishness wrecks the constitution of nurses and devoted relatives, and in unconscious or half-conscious self-indulgence destroys the comfort of everyone around them."[2] It must have given the Victorian patient some illicit pleasure to be viewed as capable of such disruption of the staid nineteenth-century household. A similar form of power, I believe, is part of the experience of agoraphobia.

This does not mean that the primary reality of these disorders is not one of pain and entrapment. Anorexia, too, clearly contains a dimension of physical addiction to the biochemical effects of starvation. But whatever the physiology involved, the ways in which the subject understands and thematizes her experience cannot be reduced to a mechanical process. The anorectic's ability to live with minimal food intake allows her to feel powerful and worthy of admiration in a "world," as Susie Orbach describes it, "from which at the most profound level [she] feels excluded" and unvalued.[3] The literature on both anorexia and hysteria is strewn with battles of will between the sufferer and those trying to "cure" her; the latter, as Orbach points out, very rarely understand that the psychic values she is fighting for are often more important to the woman than life itself.

TEXTUALITY, PRAXIS, AND THE BODY

The "solutions" offered by anorexia, hysteria, and agoraphobia, I have suggested, develop out of the practice of femininity itself, the pursuit of which is still presented as the chief route to acceptance and success for women in our culture. Too aggressively pursued, that practice leads to its own undoing, in one sense. For if femininity is, as Susan Brownmiller has said, at its core a "tradition of imposed limitations,"[4] then an unwillingness to limit oneself, even in the pursuit of femininity, breaks the rules. But, of course, in another sense the rules remain fully in place. The sufferer becomes wedded to an obsessive practice, unable to make any effective change in her life. She remains, as Toril Moi has put it, "gagged and chained to [the] feminine role," a reproducer of the docile body of femininity.[5]

This tension between the psychological meaning of a disorder, which may enact fantasies of rebellion and embody a language of protest, and the practical life of the disordered body, which may utterly defeat rebellion and subvert protest, may be obscured by too exclusive a focus on the symbolic dimension and insufficient attention to praxis. As we have seen in the case of some Lacanian feminist readings of hysteria, the result of this can be a one-sided interpretation that romanticizes the hysteric's symbolic subversion of the phallocentric[6] order while confined to her bed. This is not to say

1. Showalter, *The Female Malady*, p. 48.
2. Smith-Rosenberg, *Disorderly Conduct*, p. 207.
3. Orbach, *Hunger Strike*, p. 103.
4. Brownmiller, *Femininity*, p. 14.
5. Toril Moi, "Representations of Patriarchy: Sex and Epistemology in Freud's *Dora*," in Charles Bernheimer and Claire Kahane, eds., *In Dora's Case: Freud—Hysteria—Feminism* (New York: Columbia University Press, 1985), p. 192.
6. Patriarchal; specifically, characterized by the authority of the phallus in the primal family made up of the dominant father and the subordinate mother and child [editor's note].

that confinement in bed has a transparent, univocal meaning—in powerlessness, debilitation, dependency, and so forth. The "practical" body is no brute biological or material entity. It, too, is a culturally mediated form; its activities are subject to interpretation and description. The shift to the practical dimension is not a turn to biology or nature, but to another "register," as Foucault puts it, of the cultural body, the register of the "useful body" rather than the "intelligible body."[7] The distinction can prove useful, I believe, to feminist discourse.

The intelligible body includes our scientific, philosophic, and aesthetic representations of the body—our cultural *conceptions* of the body, norms of beauty, models of health, and so forth. But the same representations may also be seen as forming a set of *practical* rules and regulations through which the living body is "trained, shaped, obeys, responds," becoming, in short, a socially adapted and "useful body."[8] Consider this particularly clear and appropriate example: the nineteenth-century hourglass figure, emphasizing breasts and hips against a wasp waist, was an intelligible *symbolic* form, representing a domestic, sexualized ideal of femininity. The sharp cultural contrast between the female and the male form, made possible by the use of corsets and bustles, reflected, in symbolic terms, the dualistic division of social and economic life into clearly defined male and female spheres. At the same time, to achieve the specified look, a particular feminine *praxis* was required—straitlacing, minimal eating, reduced mobility—rendering the female body unfit to perform activities outside its designated sphere. This, in Foucauldian terms, would be the "useful body" corresponding to the aesthetic norm.

The intelligible body and the useful body are two arenas of the same discourse; they often mirror and support each other, as in the above illustration. Another example can be found in the seventeenth-century philosophic conception of the body as a machine, mirroring an increasingly more automated productive machinery of labor. But the two bodies may also contradict and mock each other. A range of contemporary representations and images, as noted earlier, have coded the transcendence of female appetite and its public display in the slenderness ideal in terms of power, will, mastery, the possibilities of success in the professional arena. These associations are carried visually by the slender superwomen of prime-time television and popular movies and promoted explicitly in advertisements and articles appearing routinely in women's fashion magazines, diet books, and weight-training publications. Yet the thousands of slender girls and women who strive to embody these images and who in that service suffer from eating disorders, exercise compulsions, and continual self-scrutiny and self-castigation are anything *but* the "masters" of their lives.

Exposure and productive cultural analysis of such contradictory and mystifying relations between image and practice are possible only if the analysis includes attention to and interpretation of the "useful" or, as I prefer to call it, the practical body. Such attention, although often in inchoate and theoretically unsophisticated form, was central to the beginnings of the contemporary feminist movement. In the late 1960s and early 1970s the objectification

7. Foucault, *Discipline and Punish*, p. 136.

8. Foucault, *Discipline and Punish*, p. 136.

of the female body was a serious political issue. All the cultural paraphernalia of femininity, of learning to please visually and sexually through the practices of the body—media imagery, beauty pageants, high heels, girdles, makeup, simulated orgasm—were seen as crucial in maintaining gender domination.

Disquietingly, for the feminists of the present decade, such focus on the politics of feminine praxis, although still maintained in the work of individual feminists, is no longer a centerpiece of feminist cultural critique.[9] On the popular front, we find *Ms.* magazine[1] presenting issues on fitness and "style," the rhetoric reconstructed for the 1980s to pitch "self-expression" and "power." Although feminist theory surely has the tools, it has not provided a critical discourse to dismantle and demystify this rhetoric. The work of French feminists has provided a powerful framework for understanding the inscription of phallocentric, dualistic culture on gendered bodies, but it has offered very little in the way of concrete analyses of the female body as a locus of practical cultural control. Among feminist theorists in this country, the study of cultural representations of the female body has flourished, and it has often been brilliantly illuminating and instrumental to a feminist rereading of culture.[2] But the study of cultural representations alone, divorced from consideration of their relation to the practical lives of bodies, can obscure and mislead.

Here, Helena Mitchie's significantly titled *The Flesh Made Word* offers a striking example. Examining nineteenth-century representations of women, appetite, and eating, Mitchie draws fascinating and astute metaphorical connections between female eating and female sexuality. Female hunger, she argues, and I agree, "figures unspeakable desires for sexuality and power."[3] The Victorian novel's "representational taboo" against depicting women eating (an activity, apparently, that only "happens offstage," as Mitchie puts it) thus functions as a "code" for the suppression of female sexuality, as does the general cultural requirement, exhibited in etiquette and sex manuals of the day, that the well-bred woman eat little and delicately. The same coding is drawn on, Mitchie argues, in contemporary feminist "inversions" of Victorian values, inversions that celebrate female sexuality and power through images exulting in female eating and female hunger, depicting it explicitly, lushly, and joyfully.

Despite the fact that Mitchie's analysis centers on issues concerning women's hunger, food, and eating practices, she makes no mention of the grave eating disorders that surfaced in the late nineteenth century and that are ravaging the lives of young women today. The practical arena of women dieting, fasting, straitlacing, and so forth is, to a certain extent, implicit in her

9. A focus on the politics of sexualization and objectification remains central to the antipornography movement (e.g., in the work of Andrea Dworkin, Catharine MacKinnon). Feminists exploring the politics of appearance include Sandra Bartky, Susan Brownmiller, Wendy Chapkis, Kim Chernin, and Susie Orbach. And a developing feminist interest in the work of Michel Foucault has begun to produce a poststructuralist feminism oriented toward practice; see, for example, Irene Diamond and Lee Quinby, *Feminism and Foucault: Reflections on Resistance* (Boston: Northeastern University Press, 1988).

1. At first a mass-market magazine (founded 1972) that also took a fairly consistent feminist approach, *Ms.* became more and more like a traditional "woman's magazine" before folding in 1989. It was revived in an advertising-free form closer to its original in 1990 [editor's note].

2. See, for example, Susan Suleiman, ed., *The Female Body in Western Culture* (Cambridge: Harvard University Press, 1986).

3. Mitchie, *The Flesh Made Word*, p. 13.

examination of Victorian gender ideology. But when Mitchie turns, at the end of her study, to consider contemporary feminist literature celebrating female eating and female hunger, the absence of even a passing glance at how women are *actually* managing their hungers today leaves her analysis adrift, lacking any concrete social moorings. Mitchie's sole focus is on the inevitable failure of feminist literature to escape "phallic representational codes."[4] But the feminist celebration of the female body did not merely deconstruct on the written page or canvas. Largely located in the feminist counterculture of the 1970s, it has been culturally displaced by a very different contemporary reality. Its celebration of female flesh now presents itself in jarring dissonance with the fact that women, feminists included, are starving themselves to death in our culture.

This is not to deny the benefits of diet, exercise, and other forms of body management. Rather, I view our bodies as a site of struggle, where we must *work* to keep our daily practices in the service of resistance to gender domination, not in the service of docility and gender normalization. This work requires, I believe, a determinedly skeptical attitude toward the routes of seeming liberation and pleasure offered by our culture. It also demands an awareness of the often contradictory relations between image and practice, between rhetoric and reality. Popular representations, as we have seen, may forcefully employ the rhetoric and symbolism of empowerment, personal freedom, "having it all." Yet female bodies, pursuing these ideals, may find themselves as distracted, depressed, and physically ill as female bodies in the nineteenth century were made when pursuing a feminine ideal of dependency, domesticity, and delicacy. The recognition and analysis of such contradictions, and of all the other collusions, subversions, and enticements through which culture enjoins the aid of our bodies in the reproduction of gender, require that we restore a concern for female praxis to its formerly central place in feminist politics.

1989, 1993

4. Mitchie, *The Flesh Made Word*, p. 149.

BRUNO LATOUR
b. 1947

Bruno Latour has been one of the most innovative thinkers in science studies, an interdisciplinary field that situates the sciences within their social, historical, political, and philosophic contexts as it examines how scientific knowledge is created, circulated, and put into practice. While the ostensible subject of most of Latour's writing is technoscience, the consequences of his ideas go beyond disciplinary boundaries. His work draws on and illuminates several important concepts in cultural theory, especially in its reassessment of the relationships between nature and culture, fact and fable, existence and language, and "realism" (the belief in a mind-independent reality) and social constructivism (the idea that reality and knowledge are constructed through human activity). Initially associated with social constructivism, Latour, in recent years, has softened and complicated his position. In "Why Has Critique Run Out of Steam? From Matters of Fact to Matters of Concern" (2004), he laments the appropriation of contemporary critique by conspiracy theorists, global capitalists, and right-wing extremists to such ends as debunking global warming. Both the demystifying iconoclasm and the social constructivism of the modern critique disseminated by university intellectuals, whether stemming from Marxism, psychoanalysis, feminism, deconstruction, postcolonial theory, cultural studies, or some combination of those approaches, have lately lost their critical function and are now used to jeopardize our lives. But despite his suspicion of popularizations of critique, Latour still describes his interdisciplinary project as an attempt "to account for the various ways in which truth is built." Our world, he writes in *We Have Never Been Modern* (1991; trans. 1993), is "simultaneously real, like nature, narrated, like discourse, and collective, like society."

Born in Beaune in Burgundy into a wine-growing family, Latour initially studied philosophy and theology in Dijon. After passing the agrégation, which certified him to teach philosophy, he received a doctorate in philosophy from the University of Tours in 1975. While stationed in Africa for military service, he developed an interest in anthropology, learning through practice by undertaking fieldwork in Côte d'Ivoire. In the mid-1970s he completed an ethnographic study of French methods of industrial education used in the country's largest city and then-capital, Abidjian. In the late 1970s he turned his anthropological lens onto laboratory scientists, attempting the first detailed study of the daily activities of scientists in their natural habitat. It resulted in the 1979 publication of the book that first brought him to prominence: *Laboratory Life: The Social Construction of Scientific Facts*, written with Steve Woolgar. From 1982 until 2006 Latour was a professor at the École Nationale Supérieure des Mines (National Advanced School of Mines) in Paris. In 2006 he moved to the Institute d'Études Politiques de Paris (Institute for Political Studies of Paris, familiarly known as Sciences Po). Since 2013, he has been part-time Centennial Professor at the London School of Economics, as well as Andrew D. White Professor-at-Large at Cornell University. In addition, he has curated two international exhibits in Karlsruhe, Germany, at the Zentrum für Kunst und Medientechnologie (Center for Art and Media Technology): *Iconoclash* (2002) and, with Peter Weibel, *Making Things Public* (2005). Among his numerous awards are the Legion of Honor (2012) and the Holberg Memorial Prize (2013).

Based on two years of ethnographic study at the Salk Institute in California, *Laboratory Life* analyzes scientists at work. This innovative study combined the participant-observer methods of anthropology with paradigms borrowed from the emerging fields of social constructivism and the sociology of scientific knowledge to examine not the ways in which scientists describe what they do—the scientific method—but what scientists working in their laboratories actually do. In the 1980s his focus shifted to history and theory building, and he produced two other groundbreaking studies of science in action. In 1984 he published a volume about France's most famous scientist, Louis Pasteur, and the discovery of microbes titled *Les Microbes: Guerre et paix* (*Microbes: War and Peace*), which challenged the lone genius model of scientific discovery; it was translated into English as *The Pasteurization of France* (1988). In 1987 he published perhaps his most direct statement about how science really works—*Science in Action: How to Follow Scientists and Engineers through Society*; it examines the rhetoric of scientific literature and collaborative networking between human and nonhuman actors. This book is the earliest elaboration of what he later would call Actor Network Theory (ANT). His next major work, *We Have Never Been Modern* (1991; trans. 1993), does not so much abandon science studies as seek to supplement and expand it by uncovering the ways in which modernity was constructed during the Enlightenment on a spurious break between politics and science, culture and nature. Here Latour's readings of the seventeenth-century figures Thomas Hobbes and Robert Boyle, the latter both a political theorist and a chemist, explore the complex interrelations between the two realms. More recently, Latour has begun to question his own social constructivism, complicating it in order to fashion a new realism. In *Pandora's Hope: Essays on the Reality of Science Studies* (1999), Latour revisits the relationship between nature, culture, and artifacts to articulate a view of reality that avoids the oversimplifications both of traditional realism and of constructivism. In *Reassembling the Social: An Introduction to Actor-Network-Theory* (2005), Latour provides a systematic, ordered, and detailed introduction to his material-semiotic approach, ANT. He covers its methodological rules, key concepts, and relationships with other theoretical positions. The work analyzes ANT's consequences—theoretical, methodological, and political—for social theory in general.

Latour's influences are eclectic and wide-ranging. The nineteenth-century French sociologist Gabriel Tarde, who was overshadowed by his younger rival, Émile Durkheim, appeared to Latour to lay the groundwork for Actor Network Theory, especially by arguing that the nature/culture divide is irrelevant to the study of human interaction. In the sciences Latour draws from the English mathematician and philosopher Alfred North Whitehead (1861–1947), founder of process philosophy; from Alan Turing (1912–1954), the English cryptologist and pioneer of computer theory; and from a number of twentieth-century thinkers, including the French philosophers of science Gaston Bachelard and Michel Serres, and the Lithuanian semiotician and linguist A. J. Greimas. While he is sometimes critical of literary theory, Latour's work in science studies bears some resemblance to STANLEY FISH's notion of interpretive communities and MICHEL FOUCAULT's idea of discursive formations. Latour himself has influenced a generation of scholars in the cultural studies of science, including Steve Woolgar and members of the so-called Edinburgh School of the sociology of science studies, as well as DONNA HARAWAY and N. KATHERINE HAYLES.

Our selection, "Why Has Critique Run Out of Steam?," is a good example of Latour's mature attempts to rethink his commitment to the social constructionist viewpoint in the sciences. Social constructivism is a sociological theory of knowledge; it argues that things in the world—from microbes to bodies to gender roles—that appear to have an independent biological existence are the product of ongoing social and historical processes of interaction and thus possess neither fixed meanings nor the status of isolated objects. Latour opposes this perspective to philosophical realism, which posits a reality (or nature) independent of social, psychological, and historical apprehensions and argues for the objective existence of what philosophers call "natural kinds." These two positions set the terms of the so-called science wars—the debate in recent decades between those scholars in the social studies of science who draw on discourse and cultural theory to understand how science works and those who want to hold on to a traditional positivist ideal of science. Though social constructivism has always been controversial in the sciences, it is closely associated in literary theory with poststructuralism, feminism, cultural studies, queer theory, and the New Historicism. In recent years, theorists have relied on social constructivism to deconstruct fixed truths and master narratives based on naturalized facts (about gender, race, law, canons, history, and so on). This process is what Latour calls "critique," whose proponents—especially Stanley Fish and JEAN BAUDRILLARD—are the main unnamed targets of his essay.

Latour also takes to task conservative writers who use simplified versions of social constructivism to dismiss scientific work in areas such as global warming and evolution as merely unproven theories. Having dedicated his career to exploring the lack of scientific certainty inherent in the constitution of scientific facts, he is dismayed by the strategic use of the claim that one cannot know anything in science with certainty to artificially maintain controversies. Latour does not want simply to overlook or dismiss these abuses of critique by individuals who will "use any weapon at hand, naturalized facts when it suits them and social construction when it suits them." Rather, he insists that we should "bring the sword of criticism to criticism itself." Like Donna Haraway, he advocates a more sophisticated understanding of realism that recognizes the historical contingency of knowledge claims and the semiotic technologies for making meaning of the world, but at the same time allows us to make the claim that some versions of reality work better than others, and that some controversies can at least provisionally be considered closed.

In "Why Has Critique Run out of Steam?" Latour attempts to articulate a sophisticated and useful concept of realism by distinguishing between matters of fact and matters of concern. The Enlightenment, he argues, accepted a too uncritical view that reduced reality to matters of fact. Because they are abstractions of reality, generalizable and universal, facts, for Latour, are partial, polemical, and interested renderings of reality: they are reality reduced to a bare minimum. A fact is an utterance that renders invisible a "gathering," a network of human and nonhuman actors, as well as the many controversies, struggles, conflicts, debates, alliances, negotiations, and trials of strength that went into the network's making. So it merely appears that the fact "speaks for itself" and is self-evident. ANT shows otherwise. The task of science studies—and theories of knowledge—should be to unpack the process by which matters of fact emerge out of matters of concern. Here Latour provocatively subverts common sense and understanding. To elucidate the difference between matters of fact and matters of concern, he explores the etymology of the word *thing*, which in all European languages denotes both an object in the world and a "gathering": it refers not just to an object, act, deed, or event but also to an affair, a lawsuit, a case, the subject of debate in an assembly, and the legislative assembly itself (for instance, Iceland's *Althing*, the world's oldest parliament). The word etymologically reconnects the realm of nature (of science and already-constituted objects) to the world of culture (politics, association, and debate).

Broadening his frame, Latour argues that modernity enabled us to forget temporarily the complexity of the Thing. Modernity was constituted by the Enlightenment break between mind and body, subject and object, nature and culture, the spheres of science and politics. It separated a world of social phenomena shaped by human actors (politics) from a natural world that science was supposed to uncover, a world of generalizable facts. At one level, our theories of knowledge struggle to keep these two realms distinct. At another, Latour declares, we have never really been modern, because we are constantly creating monstrous hybrids of nature/culture that trouble all neat epistemological distinctions. "Things" or "gatherings"—like global warming or AIDS drugs—are, of necessity, "simultaneously real, social, and narrative." Either we can continue to hurl rocks at one another to convince ourselves that clear and simple reality exists, or we can more sensibly try to unravel the complex social and technoscientific networks—the gatherings of science, economy, politics, law, religion, technology, and narrative—that make up such controversies as global warming and evolution, or even "things" like moon rocks.

Yet the project of articulating (in both senses of the word) these technoscientific gatherings, these matters of concern, seems often to detract from rather than add to reality. Latour blames this problem, in part, on the excesses of critique, issuing a scathing indictment of what he sees as inconsistencies in the social constructionist debate. Such debates have come to rely on two contradictory critical gestures whose contradictions go unnoticed because the moves are never performed at the same time. In one critical gesture, objects are dismissed as mere fetishes onto which individuals project their own desires. In a second, individuals are shown to be at the mercy of objective forces—genes, drives, race, class, gender—over which they have no control. Thus the rather vague targets of Latour's criticism (he rarely names specific approaches or critics) end up being at one and the same time both constructivist and realist. Latour is not the first theorist to notice the ways in which arguments in the social sciences veer between voluntarism and determinism, between agency and structure, between representations of powerful subjects acting on weak objects and weak subjects being acted on by powerful social forces.

However, the failure to develop more complex conceptions of reality that join matters of fact with matters of concern cannot be blamed solely on the shortcomings of the social sciences. Scientific ways of understanding reality are grounded in a long philosophic tradition, stemming from René Descartes's *Meditations* (1641–42), that sets up the disembodied mind as observer, detached from the very world at which it gazes. This tradition favors the general over the specific, the universal over the particular, the static object over change. It attempts to understand reality at its broadest, most general, most comprehensive level. Such an attitude relegates process to mere accident, history to a mere record. For an alternative tradition Latour looks to Alfred North Whitehead and his process philosophy, in which a plausible account of reality requires not only matters of fact but also matters of concern. Here, critics no longer simply debunk; instead, they gather and assemble. The work of science studies, and by extension of literary theory as well, is to study associations—gatherings of actors, both human and nonhuman, along with their interchanges, conflicts, alliances, negotiations, and trials of strength.

Although Latour has been influential in the emerging fields of science studies and of literature and science, his work has been controversial among scientists, whose response is often an almost visceral rejection. Latour has repeatedly denied that he dismisses reality as mere fiction, asserting that he seeks only a more complex and comprehensive description of reality than that offered by the dominant philosophical tradition. Yet his most vehement critics deplore what they perceive as his refusal to ground science in the investigation of an independent reality, without which, they argue, science becomes meaningless. Latour's casual and, at times, even flippant style contributes at least in part to the extreme reactions to his arguments. Furthermore, despite the sophistication of his ideas and the complexity of the technoscientific networks he tracks, his prose abounds in militaristic metaphors that characterize both science and criticism as arenas of conflict and even open warfare in which only the strongest survive. In spite of the polarized responses he evokes, Latour remains a significant presence in cultural theory for his ingenious attempts to bridge the two-cultures model that divides the humanities from the sciences.

"Why Has Critique Run Out of Steam? From Matters of Fact to Matters of Concern" Keywords: Cultural Studies, Defense of Criticism, Ethics, Institutional Studies, Modernity, Popular Culture, Realism, Representation

Why Has Critique Run Out of Steam?
From Matters of Fact to Matters of Concern

Wars. So many wars. Wars outside and wars inside. Cultural wars, science wars, and wars against terrorism. Wars against poverty and wars against the poor. Wars against ignorance and wars out of ignorance. My question is simple: Should we be at war, too, we, the scholars, the intellectuals? Is it really our duty to add fresh ruins to fields of ruins? Is it really the task of the humanities to add deconstruction to destruction? More iconoclasm to iconoclasm? What has become of the critical spirit? Has it run out of steam?[1]

Quite simply, my worry is that it might not be aiming at the right target. To remain in the metaphorical atmosphere of the time, military experts constantly revise their strategic doctrines, their contingency plans, the size, direction, and technology of their projectiles, their smart bombs, their missiles; I wonder why we, we alone, would be saved from those sorts of revisions. It does not seem to me that we have been as quick, in academia, to prepare ourselves for new threats, new dangers, new tasks, new targets. Are we not like those mechanical toys that endlessly make the same gesture when everything else has changed around them? Would it not be rather terrible if we were still training young kids—yes, young recruits, young cadets—for wars that are no longer possible, fighting enemies long gone, conquering territories that no longer exist, leaving them ill-equipped in the face of threats we had not anticipated, for which we are so thoroughly unprepared? Generals have always been accused of being on the ready one war late—especially French generals,[2] especially these days. Would it be so surprising, after all, if intellectuals were also one war late, one critique late—especially French intellectuals, especially now? It has been a long time, after all, since intellectuals were in the vanguard. Indeed, it has been a long time since the very notion of the avant-garde—the proletariat, the artistic—passed away, pushed aside by other forces, moved to the rear guard, or maybe lumped with the baggage train.[3] We are still able to go through the motions of a critical avant-garde, but is not the spirit gone?

In these most depressing of times, these are some of the issues I want to press, not to depress the reader but to press ahead, to redirect our meager capacities as fast as possible. To prove my point, I have, not exactly facts, but rather tiny cues, nagging doubts, disturbing telltale signs. What has become of critique, I wonder, when an editorial in the *New York Times* contains the following quote?

> Most scientists believe that [global] warming is caused largely by man-made pollutants that require strict regulation. Mr. Luntz [a Republican strategist] seems to acknowledge as much when he says that "the scientific debate is closing against us." His advice, however, is to emphasize that the evidence is not complete.
>
> "Should the public come to believe that the scientific issues are settled," he writes, "their views about global warming will change accordingly.

1. For Graham Harman. This text was written for the Stanford presidential lecture held at the humanities center, 7 Apr. 2003. I warmly thank Harvard history of science doctoral students for many ideas exchanged on those topics during this semester [Latour's note]. Harman (b. 1968), American philosopher of metaphysics.

2. France is often used to exemplify the tendency of generals to "fight the last war"; after World War I, France constructed the Maginot Line, border fortifications that provided little defense against the blitzkrieg—a new form of warfare employed by the Germans in World War II.

3. On what happened to the avant-garde and critique generally, see *Iconoclash: Beyond the Image Wars in Science, Religion, and Art*, ed. Bruno Latour and Peter Weibel (Cambridge, Mass., 2002). This article is very much an exploration of what could happen beyond the image wars [Latour's note]. "Image wars": the simultaneous desire in religion, science, and art to produce and destroy images.

> Therefore, you need to continue to make the *lack of scientific certainty* a primary issue."[4]

Fancy that? An artificially maintained scientific controversy to favor a "brownlash," as Paul and Anne Ehrlich would say.[5]

Do you see why I am worried? I myself have spent some time in the past trying to show "'*the lack of scientific certainty*'" inherent in the construction of facts. I too made it a "'primary issue.'" But I did not exactly aim at fooling the public by obscuring the certainty of a closed argument—or did I? After all, I have been accused of just that sin. Still, I'd like to believe that, on the contrary, I intended to *emancipate* the public from prematurely naturalized objectified facts. Was I foolishly mistaken? Have things changed so fast?

In which case the danger would no longer be coming from an excessive confidence in ideological arguments posturing as matters of fact—as we have learned to combat so efficiently in the past—but from an excessive *distrust* of good matters of fact disguised as bad ideological biases! While we spent years trying to detect the real prejudices hidden behind the appearance of objective statements, do we now have to reveal the real objective and incontrovertible facts hidden behind the *illusion* of prejudices? And yet entire Ph.D. programs are still running to make sure that good American kids are learning the hard way that facts are made up, that there is no such thing as natural, unmediated, unbiased access to truth, that we are always prisoners of language, that we always speak from a particular standpoint, and so on, while dangerous extremists are using the very same argument of social construction to destroy hard-won evidence that could save our lives. Was I wrong to participate in the invention of this field known as science studies?[6] Is it enough to say that we did not really mean what we said? Why does it burn my tongue to say that global warming is a fact whether you like it or not? Why can't I simply say that the argument is closed for good?

Should I reassure myself by simply saying that bad guys can use any weapon at hand, naturalized facts when it suits them and social construction when it suits them? Should we apologize for having been wrong all along? Or should we rather bring the sword of criticism to criticism itself and do a bit of soul-searching here: what were we really after when we were so intent on showing the social construction of scientific facts? Nothing guarantees,

4. "Environmental Word Games," *New York Times*, 15 Mar. 2003, p. A16. Luntz seems to have been very successful; I read later in an editorial in the *Wall Street Journal*:

> There is a better way [than passing a law that restricts business], which is to keep fighting on the merits. There is no scientific consensus that greenhouse gases cause the world's modest global warming trend, much less whether that warming will do more harm than good, or whether we can even do anything about it.
>
> Once Republicans concede that greenhouse gases must be controlled, it will only be a matter of time before they end up endorsing more economically damaging regulation. They could always stand on principle and attempt to educate the public instead. ["A Republican Kyoto," *Wall Street Journal*, 8 Apr. 2003, p. A14.]

And the same publication complains about the "pathological relation" of the "Arab street" with truth! [Latour's note; bracketed material his].

5. Paul R. and Anne H. Ehrlich, *Betrayal of Science and Reason: How Anti-Environmental Rhetoric Threatens Our Future* (Washington D.C., 1997), p. 1 [Latour's note]. Paul (b. 1932) and Anne Ehrlich (b. 1933) are American population researchers; they define "brownlash" as literature that attempts to minimize the seriousness of environmental problems.

6. An interdisciplinary field that situates the sciences within a broad social, historical, cultural, and political context.

after all, that we should be right all the time. There is no sure ground even for criticism.[7] Isn't this what criticism intended to say: that there is no sure ground anywhere? But what does it mean when this lack of sure ground is taken away from us by the worst possible fellows as an argument against the things we cherish?

Artificially maintained controversies are not the only worrying sign. What has critique become when a French general, no, a marshal of critique, namely, Jean Baudrillard, claims in a published book that the Twin Towers destroyed themselves under their own weight, so to speak, undermined by the utter nihilism inherent in capitalism itself—as if the terrorist planes were pulled to suicide by the powerful attraction of this black hole of nothingness?[8] What has become of critique when a book that claims that no plane ever crashed into the Pentagon can be a bestseller? I am ashamed to say that the author was French, too.[9] Remember the good old days when revisionism arrived very late, after the facts had been thoroughly established, decades after bodies of evidence had accumulated? Now we have the benefit of what can be called *instant revisionism*. The smoke of the event has not yet finished settling before dozens of conspiracy theories begin revising the official account, adding even more ruins to the ruins, adding even more smoke to the smoke. What has become of critique when my neighbor in the little Bourbonnais[1] village where I live looks down on me as someone hopelessly naïve because I believe that the United States had been attacked by terrorists? Remember the good old days when university professors could look down on unsophisticated folks because those hillbillies naïvely believed in church, motherhood, and apple pie? Things have changed a lot, at least in my village. I am now the one who naïvely believes in some facts because I am educated, while the other guys are too *un*sophisticated to be gullible: "Where have you been? Don't you know that the Mossad and the CIA did it?"[2] What has become of critique when someone as eminent as Stanley Fish, the "enemy of promises" as Lindsay Waters calls him, believes he defends science studies, my field, by comparing the laws of physics to the rules of baseball?[3] What has become of critique when there is a whole industry denying that the Apollo program landed on the moon? What has become of critique when DARPA uses for its Total Information Awareness project the Baconian slogan *Scientia est potentia*?[4] Didn't I read that somewhere in

7. The metaphor of shifting sand was used by neomodernists in their critique of science studies; see *A House Built on Sand: Exposing Postmodernist Myths about Science*, ed. Noretta Koertge (Oxford, 1998). The problem is that the authors of this book looked backward, attempting to reenter the solid rock castle of modernism, and not forward to what I call, for lack of a better term, nonmodernism [Latour's note].

8. See Jean Baudrillard, *"The Spirit of Terrorism" and "Requiem for the Twin Towers"* (New York, 2002) [Latour's note]. BAUDRILLARD (1929–2007), French sociologist and philosopher; a marshal outranks a general. Twin Towers: One and Two World Trade Center in New York City, destroyed in the terrorist attacks of September 11, 2001.

9. See Thierry Meyssan, *9/11: The Big Lie* (London, 2002). Conspiracy theories have always existed; what is new in instant revisionism is how much scientific proof they claim to imitate [Latour's note].

1. Historical region of central France.

2. That is, the intelligence services of, respectively, Israel and the United States were responsible for 9/11.

3. See Lindsay Waters, *Enemy of Promises* (forthcoming [Chicago, 2004]); see also Nick Paumgarten, "Dept. of Super Slo-Mo: No Flag on the Play," *The New Yorker*, 20 Jan. 2003, p. 32 [Latour's note]. FISH (b. 1938), American literary theorist; his comparison appeared in the *New York Times*, May 21, 1996.

4. Knowledge is power (Latin), a paraphrase of an aphorism by the English statesman and philosopher Francis Bacon (1561–1626), "Knowledge itself is power" (*Religious Meditations*, 1597). The phrase was used in the seal of the Information

Michel Foucault? Has knowledge-slash-power been co-opted of late by the National Security Agency? Has *Discipline and Punish* become the bedtime reading of Mr. Ridge[5]?

Let me be mean for a second. What's the real difference between conspiracists and a popularized, that is a teachable version of social critique inspired by a too quick reading of, let's say, a sociologist as eminent as Pierre Bourdieu[6] (to be polite I will stick with the French field commanders)? In both cases, you have to learn to become suspicious of everything people say because of course we all know that they live in the thralls of a complete *illusio*[7] of their real motives. Then, after disbelief has struck and an explanation is requested for what is really going on, in both cases again it is the same appeal to powerful agents hidden in the dark acting always consistently, continuously, relentlessly. Of course, we in the academy like to use more elevated causes—society, discourse, knowledge-slash-power, fields of forces, empires, capitalism—while conspiracists like to portray a miserable bunch of greedy people with dark intents, but I find something troublingly similar in the structure of the explanation, in the first movement of disbelief and, then, in the wheeling of causal explanations coming out of the deep dark below. What if explanations resorting automatically to power, society, discourse had outlived their usefulness and deteriorated to the point of now feeding the most gullible sort of critique?[8] Maybe I am taking conspiracy theories too seriously, but it worries me to detect, in those mad mixtures of knee-jerk disbelief, punctilious demands for proofs, and free use of powerful explanation from the social neverland many of the weapons of social critique. Of course conspiracy theories are an absurd deformation of our own arguments, but, like weapons smuggled through a fuzzy border to the wrong party, these are our weapons nonetheless. In spite of all the deformations, it is easy to recognize, still burnt in the steel, our trademark: *Made in Criticalland*.

Do you see why I am worried? Threats might have changed so much that we might still be directing all our arsenal east or west while the enemy has now moved to a very different place. After all, masses of atomic missiles are transformed into a huge pile of junk once the question becomes how to defend against militants armed with box cutters or dirty bombs.[9] Why

Awareness Office (2002–03), which lost its funding after only a year of existence when its "Total Information Awareness Program" raised fears of domestic surveillance; it operated within the Defense Advanced Projects Agency (DARPA), which was founded in 1958 to develop advanced technology for the U.S. Department of Defense. (Latour reproduced IAO's seal as figure 1, not included here.) "Apollo program": program (1961–72) undertaken by the U.S. National Aeronautics and Space Administration with the goal—achieved in 1969—of conducting crewed missions to the moon.

5. Thomas J. Ridge (b. 1945), first secretary (2003–05) of the Department of Homeland Security, which was formed in response to the attacks of 9/11. FOUCAULT (1926–1984), French philosopher and historian of ideas; his works include *Discipline and Punish: The Birth of the Prison* (1975) and *Power/Knowledge* (1980).

6. French sociologist (1930–2002; see above).

7. Illusion (Latin).

8. Their serious as well as their popularized versions have the defect of using society as an already existing cause instead of as a possible consequence. This was the critique that Gabriel Tarde always made against Durkheim. It is probably the whole notion of social and society that is responsible for the weakening of critique. I have tried to show that in Latour, "Gabriel Tarde and the End of the Social," in *The Social in Question: New Bearings in History and the Social Sciences*, ed. Patrick Joyce (London, 2002), pp. 117–32 [Latour's note]. Tarde (1843–1904), French sociologist and social psychologist, whom Latour sees as a potential precursor of his Actor Network Theory. Émile Durkheim (1858–1917), French sociologist often viewed as a founder of sociology.

9. Bombs that use conventional explosives to disperse radioactive material. "Box cutters": the weapons used by the 9/11 terrorists to hijack 4 airplanes.

would it not be the same with our critical arsenal, with the neutron bombs of deconstruction, with the missiles of discourse analysis? Or maybe it is that critique has been miniaturized like computers have. I have always fancied that what took great effort, occupied huge rooms, cost a lot of sweat and money, for people like Nietzsche and Benjamin,[1] can be had for nothing, much like the supercomputers of the 1950s, which used to fill large halls and expend a vast amount of electricity and heat, but now are accessible for a dime and no bigger than a fingernail. As the recent advertisement of a Hollywood film[2] proclaimed, "Everything is suspect . . . Everyone is for sale . . . And nothing is what it seems."

What's happening to me, you may wonder? Is this a case of midlife crisis? No, alas, I passed middle age quite a long time ago. Is this a patrician spite for the popularization of critique? As if critique should be reserved for the elite and remain difficult and strenuous, like mountain climbing or yachting, and is no longer worth the trouble if everyone can do it for a nickel? What would be so bad with critique for the people? We have been complaining so much about the gullible masses, swallowing naturalized facts, it would be really unfair to now discredit the same masses for their, what should I call it, gullible criticism? Or could this be a case of radicalism gone mad, as when a revolution swallows its progeny? Or, rather, have we behaved like mad scientists who have let the virus of critique out of the confines of their laboratories and cannot do anything now to limit its deleterious effects; it mutates now, gnawing everything up, even the vessels in which it is contained? Or is it another case of the famed power of capitalism for recycling everything aimed at its destruction? As Luc Boltanski and Eve Chiapello say, the new spirit of capitalism has put to good use the artistic critique that was supposed to destroy it.[3] If the dense and moralist cigar-smoking reactionary bourgeois can transform him- or herself into a free-floating agnostic bohemian, moving opinions, capital, and networks from one end of the planet to the other without attachment, why would he or she not be able to absorb the most sophisticated tools of deconstruction, social construction, discourse analysis, postmodernism, postology[4]?

In spite of my tone, I am not trying to reverse course, to become reactionary, to regret what I have done, to swear that I will never be a constructivist any more. I simply want to do what every good military officer, at regular periods, would do: retest the linkages between the new threats he or she has to face and the equipment and training he or she should have in order to meet them—and, if necessary, to revise from scratch the whole paraphernalia. This does not mean for us any more than it does for the officer that we were wrong, but simply that history changes quickly and that there is no greater intellectual crime than to address with the equipment of an older period the challenges of the present one. Whatever the case, our critical equipment deserves as much critical scrutiny as the Pentagon budget.

1. WALTER BENJAMIN (1892–1940), German literary and cultural theorist. FRIEDRICH NIETZSCHE (1844–1900), German philosopher.
2. *L.A. Confidential* (1997; dir. Curtis Hanson), a film about murder and police corruption in the early 1950s.
3. See Luc Boltanski and Eve Chiapello, *Le Nouvel Esprit du capitalisme* [*The New Spirit of Capitalism*] (Paris, 1999) [Latour's note]. Boltanski (b. 1940), French professor of social sciences. Chiapello (b. 1965), French professor of management and sociology.
4. Latour's comic coinage.

My argument is that a certain form of critical spirit has sent us down the wrong path, encouraging us to fight the wrong enemies and, worst of all, to be considered as friends by the wrong sort of allies because of a little mistake in the definition of its main target. The question was never to get *away* from facts but *closer* to them, not fighting empiricism but, on the contrary, renewing empiricism.

What I am going to argue is that the critical mind, if it is to renew itself and be relevant again, is to be found in the cultivation of a *stubbornly realist attitude*—to speak like William James[5]—but a realism dealing with what I will call *matters of concern*, not *matters of fact*. The mistake we made, the mistake I made, was to believe that there was no efficient way to criticize matters of fact except by moving *away* from them and directing one's attention *toward* the conditions that made them possible. But this meant accepting much too uncritically what matters of fact were. This was remaining too faithful to the unfortunate solution inherited from the philosophy of Immanuel Kant.[6] Critique has not been critical enough in spite of all its sore-scratching. Reality is not defined by matters of fact. Matters of fact are not all that is given in experience. Matters of fact are only very partial and, I would argue, very polemical, very political renderings of matters of concern and only a subset of what could also be called *states of affairs*. It is this second empiricism, this return to the realist attitude, that I'd like to offer as the next task for the critically minded.

To indicate the direction of the argument, I want to show that while the Enlightenment profited largely from the disposition of a very powerful descriptive tool, that of matters of fact, which were excellent for *debunking* quite a lot of beliefs, powers, and illusions, it found itself totally disarmed once matters of fact, in turn, were eaten up by the same debunking impetus. After that, the lights of the Enlightenment were slowly turned off, and some sort of darkness appears to have fallen on campuses. My question is thus: Can we devise another powerful descriptive tool that deals this time with matters of concern and whose import then will no longer be to debunk but to protect and to care, as Donna Haraway[7] would put it? Is it really possible to transform the critical urge in the ethos of someone who *adds* reality to matters of fact and not *subtract* reality? To put it another way, what's the difference between deconstruction and constructivism?

"So far," you could object, "the prospect doesn't look very good, and you, Monsieur Latour, seem the person the least able to deliver on this promise because you spent your life debunking what the other more polite critics had at least respected until then, namely matters of fact and science itself. You can dust your hands with flour as much as you wish, the black fur of the critical wolf will always betray you; your deconstructing teeth have been sharpened on too many of our innocent labs—I mean lambs!—for us to believe you." Well, see, that's just the problem: I have written about a dozen books to inspire respect for, some people have said to uncritically glorify, the objects of science and technology, of art, religion, and, more recently, law, showing every time in great detail the complete

5. American psychologist and philosopher of pragmatism (1842–1910).

6. German philosopher (1724–1804; see above); his "solution" to skepticism about the nature of reality was to set forth the conditions that must be in place within the perceiving subject if the external world is to be apprehended (see *The Critique of Pure Reason*, 1781).

7. American biologist and feminist theorist of science and technology (b. 1944; see above).

implausibility of their being socially explained, and yet the only noise readers hear is the snapping of the wolf's teeth. Is it really impossible to solve the question, to write not matter-of-factually but, how should I say it, in a matter-of-concern way?[8]

Martin Heidegger,[9] as every philosopher knows, has meditated many times on the ancient etymology of the word *thing*. We are now all aware that in all the European languages, including Russian, there is a strong connection between the words for thing and a quasi-judiciary assembly. Icelanders boast of having the oldest Parliament, which they call *Althing*, and you can still visit in many Scandinavian countries assembly places that are designated by the word *Ding* or *Thing*. Now, is this not extraordinary that the banal term we use for designating what is out there, unquestionably, a thing, what lies out of any dispute, out of language, is also the oldest word we all have used to designate the oldest of the sites in which our ancestors did their dealing and tried to settle their disputes?[1] A thing is, in one sense, an object out there and, in another sense, an *issue* very much *in* there, at any rate, a *gathering*. To use the term I introduced earlier now more precisely, the same word *thing* designates matters of fact and matters of concern.

Needless to say, although he develops this etymology at length, this is not the path that Heidegger has taken. On the contrary, all his writing aims to make as sharp a distinction as possible between, on the one hand, objects, *Gegenstand*,[2] and, on the other, the celebrated *Thing*. The handmade jug can be a thing, while the industrially made can of Coke remains an object. While the latter is abandoned to the empty mastery of science and technology, only the former, cradled in the respectful idiom of art, craftsmanship, and poetry, could deploy and gather its rich set of connections.[3] This bifurcation is marked many times but in a decisive way in his book on Kant:

> Up to this hour such questions have been open. Their questionability is concealed by the results and the progress of scientific work. One of these burning questions concerns the justification and limits of mathematical formalism in contrast to the demand for an immediate return to intuitively given nature.[4]

What has happened to those who, like Heidegger, have tried to find their ways in immediacy, in intuition, in nature would be too sad to retell—and is well known anyway. What is certain is that those pathmarks off the beaten track led indeed nowhere. And, yet, Heidegger, when he takes the jug seriously, offers a powerful vocabulary to talk also about the object he despises so much. What would happen, I wonder, if we tried to talk about the object

8. This is the achievement of the great novelist Richard Powers, whose stories are a careful and, in my view, masterful enquiry into this new "realism." Especially relevant for this paper is Richard Powers, *Plowing the Dark* (New York, 2000) [Latour's note]. Powers (b. 1957), American novelist whose work explores the effects of science and technology.

9. German philosopher (1889–1976; see above).

1. See the erudite study by the remarkable French scholar of Roman law, Yan Thomas, "Res, chose, et patrimoine (note sur le rapport sujet-object en droit romain)" ["Matter, Thing, and Inheritance (Note on the Subject-Object Ratio in Roman Law)"], *Archives de philosophie de droit* [*Archives of the Philosophy of Law*] 25 (1980): 413–26 [Latour's note].

2. Object (German): that is, something manufactured rather than handcrafted.

3. See Graham Harman, *Tool-Being: Heidegger and the Metaphysics of Objects* (Chicago, 2002) [Latour's note].

4. Martin Heidegger, *What Is a Thing?* trans. W. B. Barton, Jr., and Vera Deutsch (Chicago, 1967), p. 95 [Latour's note].

of science and technology, the *Gegenstand*, as if it had the rich and complicated qualities of the celebrated *Thing?*

The problem with philosophers is that because their jobs are so hard they drink a lot of coffee and thus use in their arguments an inordinate quantity of pots, mugs, and jugs—to which, sometimes, they might add the occasional rock. But, as Ludwik Fleck remarked long ago, their objects are never complicated enough; more precisely, they are never simultaneously *made* through a complex history and new, real, and *interesting* participants in the universe.[5] Philosophy never deals with the sort of beings we in science studies have dealt with. And that's why the debates between realism and relativism never go anywhere. As Ian Hacking has recently shown, the engagement of a rock in philosophical talk is utterly different if you take a banal rock to make your point[6] (usually to lapidate a passing relativist!) or if you take, for instance, dolomite, as he has done so beautifully.[7] The first can be turned into a matter of fact but not the second. Dolomite is so beautifully complex and entangled that it resists being treated as a matter of fact. It too can be described as a gathering; it too can be seen as engaging the fourfold.[8] Why not try to portray it with the same enthusiasm, engagement, and complexity as the Heideggerian jug? Heidegger's mistake is not to have treated the jug too well, but to have traced a dichotomy between *Gegenstand* and *Thing* that was justified by nothing except the crassest of prejudices.

Several years ago another philosopher, much closer to the history of science, namely Michel Serres,[9] also French, but this time as foreign to critique as one can get, meditated on what it would mean to take objects of science in a serious anthropological and ontological fashion. It is interesting to note that every time a philosopher gets closer to an object of science that is at once historical and interesting, his or her philosophy changes, and the specifications for a realist attitude become, at once, more stringent and completely different from the so-called realist philosophy of science concerned with routine or boring objects. I was reading his passage on the *Challenger* disaster in his book *Statues* when another shuttle, *Columbia,* in early 2003 offered me a tragic instantiation of yet another metamorphosis of an object into a thing.[1]

What else would you call this sudden transformation of a completely mastered, perfectly understood, quite forgotten by the media, taken-for-granted, matter-of-factual projectile into a sudden shower of debris falling on the United States, which thousands of people tried to salvage in the mud and

5. Although Fleck is the founder of science studies, the impact of his work is still very much in the future because he has been so deeply misunderstood by Thomas Kuhn; see Thomas Kuhn, foreword to Ludwik Fleck, *Genesis and Development of a Scientific Fact* (1935; Chicago, 1979), pp. vii–xi [Latour's note]. Fleck (1896–1961), Polish physician and biologist. Kuhn (1922–1996), American historian and philosopher of science; his best-known work is *The Structure of Scientific Revolutions* (1962; 2d ed., 1970).

6. An approach taken perhaps most famously by SAMUEL JOHNSON (1709–1784), who, according to his biographer James Boswell, responded to the idealist philosophy of George Berkeley by kicking a rock mightily and exclaiming, "I refute it *thus*."

7. See Ian Hacking, *The Social Construction of What?* (Cambridge, Mass., 1999), in particular the last chapter [Latour's note]. Hacking (b. 1936), Canadian philosopher of science. "Lapidate": throw stones at.

8. Latour quotes Heidegger on "the fourfold" below.

9. French philosopher of both science and the humanities (b. 1930).

1. See Michel Serres, *Statues: Le Second Livre des fondations* [*Statues: The Second Book of Foundations*] (Paris, 1987). On the reasons why Serres was never critical, see Serres with Latour, *Conversations on Science, Culture, and Time*, trans. Roxanne Lapidus (Ann Arbor, Mich., 1995) [Latour's note]. The *Challenger* disaster: the explosion of the U.S. space shuttle *Challenger* on January 28, 1986, shortly after liftoff. The *Columbia* broke apart over the southern United States during reentry on February 1, 2003. In both cases, all crew members were killed.

rain and collect in a huge hall to serve as so many clues in a judicial scientific investigation? Here, suddenly, in a stroke, an object had become a thing, a matter of fact was considered as a matter of great concern. If a thing is a gathering, as Heidegger says, how striking to see how it can suddenly *disband*. If the "thinging of the thing" is a gathering that always connects the "united four, earth and sky, divinities and mortals, in the simple onefold of their self-unified fourfold,"[2] how could there be a better example of this making and unmaking than this catastrophe unfolding all its thousands of folds? How could we see it as a normal accident of technology when, in his eulogy for the unfortunate victims, your president said: "The crew of the shuttle Columbia did not return safely to Earth; yet we can pray that all are safely home"?[3] As if no shuttle ever moved simply in space, but also always in heaven.

This was on C-Span 1, but on C-Span 2,[4] at the very same time, early February 2003, another extraordinary parallel event was occurring. This time a Thing—with a capital T—was assembled to try to coalesce, to gather in one decision, one object, one projection of force: a military strike against Iraq.[5] Again, it was hard to tell whether this gathering was a tribunal, a parliament, a command-and-control war room, a rich man's club, a scientific congress, or a TV stage. But certainly it was an assembly where matters of great concern were debated and proven—except there was much puzzlement about which type of proofs should be given and how accurate they were. The difference between C-Span 1 and C-Span 2, as I watched them with bewilderment, was that while in the case of *Columbia* we had a perfectly mastered object that suddenly was transformed into a shower of burning debris that was used as so much evidence in an investigation, there, at the United Nations, we had an investigation that tried to coalesce, in one unifying, unanimous, solid, mastered object, masses of people, opinions, and might. In one case the object was metamorphosed into a thing; in the second, the thing was attempting to turn into an object. We could witness, in one case, the head, in another, the tail of the trajectory through which matters of fact emerge out of matters of concern. In both cases we were offered a unique window into the number of *things* that have to participate in the gathering of an *object*. Heidegger was not a very good anthropologist of science and technology; he had only four folds, while the smallest shuttle, the shortest war, has millions. How many gods, passions, controls, institutions, techniques, diplomacies, wits have to be folded to connect "earth and sky, divinities and mortals"—oh yes, especially mortals. (Frightening omen, to launch such a complicated war, just when such a beautifully mastered object as the shuttle disintegrated into thousands of pieces of debris raining down from the sky—but the omen was not heeded; gods nowadays are invoked for convenience only.)

2. Heidegger, "The Thing," *Poetry, Language, Thought*, trans. Albert Hofstadter (New York, 1971), p. 178 [Latour's note].

3. "Bush Talking More about Religion: Faith to Solve the Nation's Problems," CNN website, 18 Feb 2003, www.cnn.com/2003/ALLPOLITICS/02/18/bush.faith/ [Latour's note]. The quotation is from a speech by George W. Bush (b. 1946; 43d U.S. president, 2001–09), given hours after the *Columbia* disaster.

4. Two channels of the nonprofit U.S. cable company that provides public access to governmental proceedings.

5. That is, the second channel was broadcasting the debate at the United Nations on authorizing the use of force against Iraq; though the resolution failed, the United States and a number of allies sent ground troops into Iraq on March 20, 2003.

My point is thus very simple: things have become Things again, objects have reentered the arena, the Thing, in which they have to be gathered first in order to exist later as what *stands apart*. The parenthesis that we can call the modern parenthesis during which we had, on the one hand, a world of objects, *Gegenstand*, out there, unconcerned by any sort of parliament, forum, agora,[6] congress, court and, on the other, a whole set of forums, meeting places, town halls where people debated, has come to a close. What the etymology of the word *thing—chose, causa, res, aitia*[7]—had conserved for us mysteriously as a sort of fabulous and mythical past has now become, for all to see, our most ordinary present. Things are gathered again. Was it not extraordinarily moving to see, for instance, in the lower Manhattan reconstruction project, the long crowds, the angry messages, the passionate emails, the huge agoras, the long editorials that connected so many people to so many variations of the project to replace the Twin Towers? As the architect Daniel Libeskind[8] said a few days before the decision, building will never be the same.

I could open the newspaper and unfold the number of former objects that have become things again, from the global warming case I mentioned earlier to the hormonal treatment of menopause, to the work of Tim Lenoir, the primate studies of Linda Fedigan and Shirley Strum, or the hyenas of my friend Steven Glickman.[9]

Nor are those gatherings limited to the present period as if only recently objects had become so obviously things. Every day historians of science help us realize to what extent we have never been modern because they keep revising every single element of past matters of fact from Mario Biagioli's Galileo, Steven Shapin's Boyle, and Simon Schaffer's Newton, to the incredibly intricate linkages between Einstein and Poincaré that Peter Galison has narrated in his latest masterpiece.[1] Many others of course could be cited, but the crucial point for me now is that what allowed historians, philosophers, humanists, and critics to trace *the* difference between modern and premodern, namely, the sudden and somewhat miraculous appearance of matters of fact, is now thrown into doubt with the merging of matters of fact into highly complex, historically situated, richly diverse matters

6. Marketplace; in Greek city-states, the place of open assembly.
7. All words that mean "thing" (*chose*, French; *res*, Latin) or "cause" (*causa*, Latin; *aitia*, Greek).
8. Polish-born American architect (b. 1946), who in 2003 won the competition to provide the master plan for rebuilding the World Trade Center site after the attacks of 9/11.
9. Serres proposed the word *quasi-object* to cover this intermediary phase between things and objects—a philosophical question much more interesting than the tired old one of the relation between *words* and *worlds*. On the new way animals appear to scientists and the debate it triggers, see *Primate Encounters: Models of Science, Gender, and Society*, ed. Shirley Strum and Linda Fedigan (Chicago, 2000), and Vinciane Despret, *Quand le loup habitera avec l'agneau* [*When the Wolf Lies Down with the Lamb*] (Paris, 2002) [Latour's note]. Lenoir (b. 1948), professor of the history and philosophy of science and technology. Fedigan (b. 1949), professor of primatology. Strum (b. 1947), a primatologist and professor of anthropology, who has collaborated with Latour. Stephen Glickman (b. 1933), professor of biology and director of the Berkeley Spotted Hyena Project.
1. See Peter Galison, *Einstein's Clocks, Poincaré's Maps: Empires of Time* (New York, 2003) [Latour's note]. In addition to the one study named—of the German-born American physicist Albert Einstein (1879–1955) and the French physicist Henri Poincaré (1854–1912), by the American historian of science Galison (b. 1955)—Latour alludes to studies of three other great scientists, Galileo Galilei (1564–1642; Italian), Robert Boyle (1627–1692; British), and Sir Isaac Newton (1642–1727; English): Biagioli's *Galileo, Courtier: The Practice of Science in the Culture of Absolutism* (1993), Shapin and Schaffer's *Leviathan and the Air-Pump: Hobbes, Boyle, and the Experimental Life* (1985), and Schaffer's "Glass Works: Newton's Prisms and the Uses of Experiment" (1989).

of concern. You can do one sort of thing with mugs, jugs, rocks, swans, cats, mats but not with Einstein's Patent Bureau electric coordination of clocks in Bern.[2] Things that gather cannot be thrown at you like objects.

And, yet, I know full well that this is not enough because, no matter what we do, when we try to reconnect scientific objects with their aura, their crown, their web of associations, when we accompany them back to their gathering, we always appear to *weaken* them, not to *strengthen* their claim to reality. I know, I know, we are acting with the best intentions in the world, we want to *add* reality to scientific objects, but, inevitably, through a sort of tragic bias, we seem always to be subtracting some bit from it. Like a clumsy waiter setting plates on a slanted table, every nice dish slides down and crashes on the ground. Why can we never discover the same stubbornness, the same solid realism by bringing out the obviously webby, "thingy" qualities of matters of concern? Why can't we ever counteract the claim of realists that only a fare of matters of fact can satisfy their appetite and that matters of concern are much like nouvelle cuisine—nice to look at but not fit for voracious appetites?

One reason is of course the position objects have been given in most social sciences, a position that is so ridiculously useless that if it is employed, even in a small way, for dealing with science, technology, religion, law, or literature it will make absolutely impossible any serious consideration of objectivity—I mean of "thinginess." Why is this so? Let me try to portray the critical landscape in its ordinary and routine state.[3]

We can summarize, I estimate, 90 percent of the contemporary critical scene by the following series of diagrams that fixate the object at only two positions, what I have called the *fact* position and the *fairy* position—*fact* and *fairy* are etymologically related but I won't develop this point here.[4] The fairy position is very well known and is used over and over again by many social scientists who associate criticism with antifetishism. The role of the critic is then to show that what the naïve believers are doing with objects is simply a projection of their wishes onto a material entity that does nothing at all by itself. Here they have diverted to their petty use the prophetic fulmination against idols "they have mouths and speak not, they have ears and hear not,"[5] but they use this prophecy to decry the very objects of belief—gods, fashion, poetry, sport, desire, you name it—to which naïve believers cling with so much intensity.[6] And then the courageous critic, who alone remains aware and attentive, who never sleeps, turns those false objects into fetishes[7] that are supposed to be nothing but mere empty white screens

2. While working as a patent examiner in Bern (1902–08), Einstein evaluated new inventions to synchronize clocks, and the idea of synchronizing clocks was key to his revolutionary 1905 paper on special relativity.

3. I summarize here some of the results of my already long anthropological inquiry into the iconoclastic gesture, from Latour, *We Have Never Been Modern*, trans. Catherine Porter (Cambridge, Mass., 1993) to *Pandora's Hope: Essays on the Reality of Science Studies* (Cambridge, Mass., 1999) and of course *Iconoclash* [Latour's note].

4. The English word *fact* derives from *facere*, a Latin verb meaning "to do"; *fairy* is usually traced back to *fari*, a Latin verb meaning "to say."

5. Psalm 115.5 ("and" is usually translated "but," in both clauses).

6. See William Pietz, "The Problem of the Fetish, I," *Res* 9 (Spring 1985): 5–17, "The Problem of the Fetish, II: The Origin of the Fetish," *Res* 13 (Spring 1987): 23–45, and "The Problem of the Fetish, IIIa: Bosman's Guinea and the Enlightenment Theory of Fetishism," *Res* 16 (Autumn 1988): 105–23 [Latour's note].

7. Inanimate objects invested with magical, religious, or sexual qualities.

Critical Gesture: Move One
...that merely projects onto an indifferent matter your own power.
You believe in the power of an idol...
...but in fact it is only the power of your own ingenuity...
...to make you do things...

Figure 1

on which is projected the power of society, domination, whatever. The naïve believer has received a first salvo (figure 1).

But, wait, a second salvo is in the offing, and this time it comes from the fact pole. This time it is the poor bloke, again taken aback, whose behavior is now "explained" by the powerful effects of indisputable matters of fact: "You, ordinary fetishists, believe you are free but, in reality, you are acted on by forces you are not conscious of. Look at them, look, you blind idiot" (and here you insert whichever pet facts the social scientists fancy to work with, taking them from economic infrastructure, fields of discourse, social domination, race, class, and gender, maybe throwing in some neurobiology, evolutionary psychology,[8] whatever, provided they act as indisputable facts whose origin, fabrication, mode of development are left unexamined) (figure 2).

Do you see now why it feels so good to be a critical mind? Why critique, this most ambiguous *pharmakon*,[9] has become such a potent euphoric drug? You are always right! When naïve believers are clinging forcefully to their objects, claiming that they are made to do things because of their gods, their poetry, their cherished objects, you can turn all of those attachments into so many fetishes and humiliate all the believers by showing that it is nothing but their own projection, that you, yes you alone, can see. But as soon as naïve believers are thus inflated by some belief in their own importance, in their own projective capacity, you strike them by a second uppercut and humiliate them again, this time by showing that, whatever they think, their behavior is entirely determined by the action of powerful causalities coming from objective reality they don't see, but that you, yes you, the never sleeping critic, alone can see. Isn't this fabulous? Isn't it really worth going to graduate school to study critique? "Enter here, you poor folks. After arduous years of

8. A field of study that attempts to investigate psychological traits, such as memory, perception, or language, in terms of evolutionary processes.

9. Drug, whether healing or harmful (Greek); an allusion to JACQUES DERRIDA's "Plato's Pharmacy," from *Dissemination* (1972; see above).

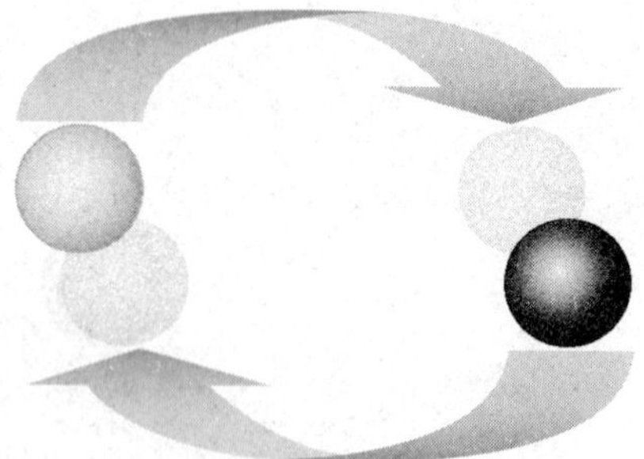
Critical Gesture: Move Two
...to make you do things out of an indifferent matter...
You believe in the free power of your own will...
...but in fact you are unwillingly activated to do things...
...by the necessary power of genes, interests, drives, etc.

Figure 2

reading turgid prose, you will be always right, you will never be taken in any more; no one, no matter how powerful, will be able to accuse you of naïveté, that supreme sin, any longer? Better equipped than Zeus[1] himself you rule alone, striking from above with the salvo of antifetishism in one hand and the solid causality of objectivity in the other." The only loser is the naïve believer, the great unwashed, always caught off balance (figure 3).

Is it so surprising, after all, that with such positions given to the object, the humanities have lost the hearts of their fellow citizens, that they had to retreat year after year, entrenching themselves always further in the narrow barracks left to them by more and more stingy deans? The Zeus of Critique rules absolutely, to be sure, but over a desert.

One thing is clear, not one of us readers would like to see *our* own most cherished objects treated in this way. We would recoil in horror at the mere suggestion of having them socially explained, whether we deal in poetry or robots, stem cells, black holes, or impressionism, whether we are patriots, revolutionaries, or lawyers, whether we pray to God or put our hope in neuroscience. This is why, in my opinion, those of us who tried to portray sciences as matters of concern so often failed to convince; readers have confused the treatment we give of the former matters of fact with the terrible fate of objects processed through the hands of sociology, cultural studies, and so on. And I can't blame our readers. What social scientists do to our favorite objects is so horrific that certainly we don't want them to come any nearer. "Please," we exclaim, "don't touch them at all! Don't try to explain them!" Or we might suggest more politely: "Why don't you go further down the corridor to this other department? *They* have bad facts to account for; why don't you explain away those ones instead of ours?" And this is the reason why, when we want respect, solidity, obstinacy, robustness, we all prefer to stick to the language of matters of fact no matter its well-known defects.

1. In Greek mythology, the king of the gods, whose weapon is the thunderbolt.

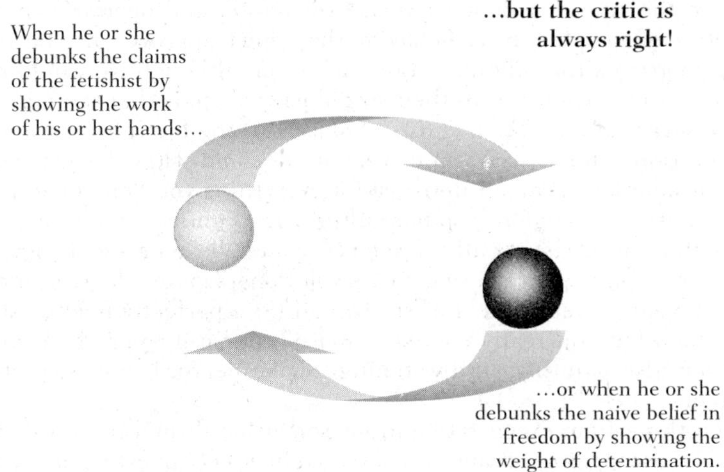

...but the critic is
always right!
When he or she
debunks the claims
of the fetishist by
showing the work
of his or her hands...
...or when he or she
debunks the naive belief in
freedom by showing the
weight of determination.

Figure 3

The Critical Trick: Two Objects–Two Subjects

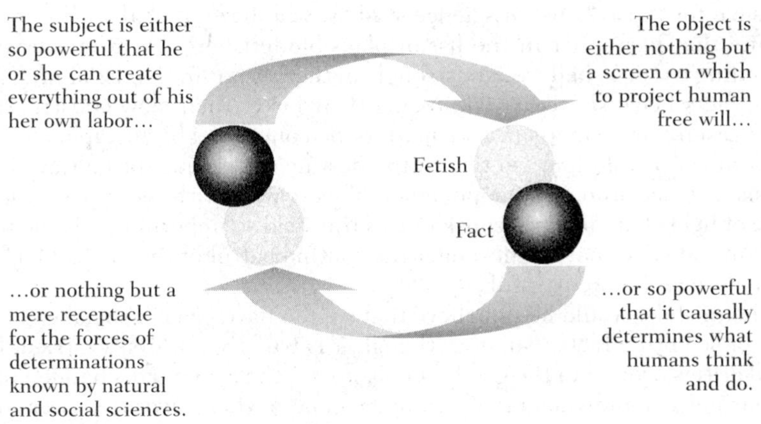

The subject is either

or she can create

her own labor...

a screen on which
to project human

mere receptacle
for the forces of

known by natural

that it causally

humans think

Figure 4

And yet this is not the only way because the cruel treatment objects undergo in the hands of what I'd like to call *critical barbarity* is rather easy to undo. If the critical barbarian appears so powerful, it is because the two mechanisms I have just sketched are never put together in one single diagram (figure 4). Antifetishists debunk objects they don't believe in by showing the productive and projective forces of people; then, without ever making the connection, they use objects they do believe in to resort to the causalist or mechanist explanation and debunk conscious capacities of people whose behavior they don't approve of. The whole rather poor trick that allows critique to go on, although we would never confine our own valuables to their sordid pawnshop, is that there is never any *crossover between the two lists of objects* in the fact position and the fairy position. This is why you can be at once and without even sensing any contradiction (1) an antifetishist for everything you don't believe in—for the most part religion, popular culture, art, politics, and so on; (2) an unrepentant positivist for all the sciences you believe in—sociology, economics, conspiracy theory, genetics, evolutionary psychology, semiotics, just pick your preferred field of study; and (3) a perfectly healthy sturdy realist for what you really cherish—and of course it might be criticism itself, but also painting, bird-watching, Shakespeare, baboons, proteins, and so on.

If you think I am exaggerating in my somewhat dismal portrayal of the critical landscape, it is because we have had in effect almost no occasion so far to detect the total mismatch of the three contradictory repertoires—antifetishism, positivism, realism—because we carefully manage to apply them on *different* topics. We explain the objects we don't approve of by treating them as fetishes; we account for behaviors we don't like by discipline whose makeup we don't examine; and we concentrate our passionate interest on only those things that are for us worthwhile matters of concern. But of course such a cavalier attitude with such contradictory repertoires is not possible for those of us, in science studies, who have to deal with states of affairs that fit neither in the list of plausible fetishes—because everyone, including us, does believe very strongly in them—nor in the list of undisputable facts because we are witnessing their birth, their slow construction, their fascinating emergence as matters of concern. The metaphor of the Copernican revolution,[2] so tied to the destiny of critique, has always been for us, science students, simply moot. This is why, with more than a good dose of field chauvinism, I consider this tiny field so important; it is the little rock in the shoe that might render the routine patrol of the critical barbarians more and more painful.

The mistake would be to believe that we too have given a social explanation of scientific facts. No, even though it is true that at first we tried, like good critics trained in the good schools, to use the armaments handed to us by our betters and elders to crack open—one of their favorite expressions, meaning to destroy—religion, power, discourse, hegemony. But, fortunately (yes, fortunately!), one after the other, we witnessed that the black boxes[3] of science remained closed and that it was rather the tools that lay in the dust of our workshop, disjointed and broken. Put simply, critique was useless against objects of some solidity. You can try the projective game on UFOs or exotic divinities, but don't try it on neurotransmitters, on gravitation, on

2. That is, a paradigm shift in how the world is viewed, similar to the change from the cosmology of the Greek astronomer Ptolemy (active 127–148 C.E.), according to which all heavenly bodies revolved around Earth, to that of the Polish astronomer Nicolaus Copernicus (1473–1543), who argued that the sun is the center of our solar system.

3. In cybernetics, complex systems or devices represented only in terms of input and output, without concern for their internal processes.

Monte Carlo calculations.[4] But critique is also useless when it begins to use the results of one science uncritically, be it sociology itself, or economics, or postimperialism, to account for the behavior of people. You can try to play this miserable game of explaining aggression by invoking the genetic makeup of violent people, but try to do that while dragging in, at the same time, the many controversies in genetics, including evolutionary theories in which geneticists find themselves so thoroughly embroiled.[5]

On both accounts, matters of concern never occupy the two positions left for them by critical barbarity. Objects are much too strong to be treated as fetishes and much too weak to be treated as indisputable causal explanations of some unconscious action. And this is not true of scientific states of affairs only; this is our great discovery, what made science studies commit such a felicitous mistake, such a *felix culpa*.[6] Once you realize that scientific objects cannot be socially explained, then you realize too that the so-called weak objects, those that appear to be candidates for the accusation of antifetishism, were never mere projections on an empty screen either.[7] They too act, they too do things, they too *make you do* things. It is not only the objects of science that resist, but all the others as well, those that were supposed to have been ground to dust by the powerful teeth of automated reflex-action deconstructors. To accuse something of being a fetish is the ultimate gratuitous, disrespectful, insane, and barbarous gesture.[8]

Is it not time for some progress? To the fact position, to the fairy position, why not add a third position, a *fair* position? Is it really asking too much from our collective intellectual life to devise, at least once a century, some *new* critical tools? Should we not be thoroughly humiliated to see that military personnel are more alert, more vigilant, more innovative than we, the pride of academia, the crème de la crème, who go on ceaselessly transforming the whole rest of the world into naïve believers, into fetishists, into hapless victims of domination, while at the same time turning them into the mere superficial consequences of powerful hidden causalities coming from infrastructures whose makeup is never interrogated? All the while being intimately certain that the things really close to our hearts would in no way fit any of those roles. Are you not all tired of those "explanations"? I am, I have always been, when I know, for instance, that the God to whom I pray, the works of art I cherish, the colon cancer I have been fighting, the piece of law I am studying, the desire I feel, indeed, the very book I am writing could in no way be accounted for by fetish or fact, nor by any combination of those two absurd positions.

To retrieve a realist attitude, it is not enough to dismantle critical weapons so uncritically built up by our predecessors as we would obsolete but still

4. A class of computational algorithms whose results are calculated by repeated random sampling; they are used in fields ranging from finance to medicine.

5. For a striking example, see Jean-Jacques Kupiec and Pierre Sonigo, *Ni Dieu ni gène: Pour une autre théorie de l'hérédité* [*Neither God nor Gene: Toward Another Theory of Heredity*] (Paris, 2000); see also Evelyn Fox-Keller, *The Century of the Gene* (Cambridge, Mass., 2000) [Latour's note].

6. Happy or lucky fault (Latin).

7. I have attempted to use this argument recently on two most difficult types of entities, Christian divinities (Latour, *Jubiler ou les tourments de la parole religieuse* [*To Exalt or the Torments of Religious Words*] [Paris, 2002]), and law (Latour, *La Fabrique du droit: Une Ethnographie du Conseil d'État* [*The Fabric of Law: An Ethnography of the Council of State*] [Paris, 2002]) [Latour's note].

8. The exhibition in Karlsruhe, Germany, *Iconoclash*, was a sort of belated ritual in order to atone for so much wanton destruction [Latour's note].

dangerous atomic silos. If we had to dismantle social theory only, it would be a rather simple affair; like the Soviet empire, those big totalities have feet of clay. But the difficulty lies in the fact that they are built on top of a much older philosophy, so that whenever we try to replace matters of fact by matters of concern, we seem to lose something along the way. It is like trying to fill the mythical Danaid's barrel[9]—no matter what we put in it, the level of realism never increases. As long as we have not sealed the leaks, the realist attitude will always be split; matters of fact take the best part, and matters of concern are limited to a rich but essentially void or irrelevant *history*. More will always seem less. Although I wish to keep this paper short, I need to take a few more pages to deal with ways to overcome this bifurcation.

Alfred North Whitehead famously said, "The recourse to metaphysics is like throwing a match into a powder magazine. It blows up the whole arena."[1] I cannot avoid getting into it because I have talked so much about weapon systems, explosions, iconoclasm, and arenas. Of all the modern philosophers who tried to overcome matters of fact, Whitehead is the only one who, instead of taking the path of critique and directing his attention *away* from facts to what makes them possible as Kant did; or adding something to their bare bones as Husserl[2] did; or avoiding the fate of their domination, their *Gestell*,[3] as much as possible as Heidegger did; tried to get *closer* to them or, more exactly, to see through them the reality that requested a new respectful realist attitude. No one is less a critic than Whitehead, in all the meanings of the word, and it's amusing to notice that the only pique he ever directed against someone else was against the other W., the one considered, wrongly in my view, as the greatest philosopher of the twentieth century, not W. as in Bush but W. as in Wittgenstein.[4]

What set Whitehead completely apart and straight on our path is that he considered matters of fact to be a very poor rendering of what is given in experience and something that muddles entirely the question, What is there? with the question, How do we know it? as Isabelle Stengers has shown recently in a major book about Whitehead's philosophy.[5] Those who now mock his philosophy don't understand that they have resigned themselves to what he called the "bifurcation of nature." They have entirely forgotten what it would require if we were to take this incredible sentence seriously: "For natural philosophy everything perceived is in nature. We may not pick up and choose. For us the red glow of the sunset should be as much part of nature as are the molecules and electric waves by which men of science would explain the phenomenon" (*CN*, pp. 28–29).

9. That is, an impossible task. In Greek mythology, all but 1 of the 50 Danaids (daughters of Danaus) killed their husbands on their wedding night; according to the later poets, their eternal punishment in the underworld is to carry water to a leaky jar that they can never fill.

1. Alfred North Whitehead, *The Concept of Nature* (Cambridge, 1920), p. 29; hereafter abbreviated *CN* [Latour's note]. Whitehead (1861–1947), English mathematician and philosopher.

2. Edmund Husserl (1859–1938), German philosopher and founder of phenomenology.

3. A technical term (roughly, "enframing"; German) used by Heidegger to describe the essence of technology as a peculiarly dehumanizing and dangerous orientation to the world.

4. Ludwig Wittgenstein (1889–1951), Austrian-born British philosopher who was highly influential in both philosophy of mind and philosophy of language.

5. See Isabelle Stengers, *Penser avec Whitehead: Une Libre et sauvage creation de concepts* [*Thinking with Whitehead: A Free and Wild Creation of Concepts*] (Paris, 2002), a book which has the great advantage of taking seriously Whitehead's science as well as his theory of God [Latour's note]. Stengers (b. 1949), Belgian philosopher of science.

All subsequent philosophies have done exactly the opposite: they have picked and chosen, and, worse, they have remained content with that limited choice. The solution to this bifurcation is not, as phenomenologists[6] would have it, adding to the boring electric waves the rich lived world of the glowing sun. This would simply make the bifurcation greater. The solution or, rather, the adventure, according to Whitehead, is to dig much further into the realist attitude and to realize that matters of fact are totally implausible, unrealistic, unjustified definitions of what it is to deal with things:

> Thus matter represents the refusal to think away spatial and temporal characteristics and to arrive at the bare concept of an individual entity. It is this refusal which has caused the muddle *of importing the mere procedure of thought into the fact of nature.* The entity, bared of all characteristics except those of space and time, has acquired a physical status as the ultimate texture of nature; so that the course of nature is conceived as being merely the fortunes of matter in its adventure through space. [*CN*, p. 20]

It is not the case that there would exist solid matters of fact and that the next step would be for us to decide whether they will be used to explain something. It is not the case either that the other solution is to attack, criticize, expose, historicize those matters of fact, to show that they are made up, interpreted, flexible. It is not the case that we should rather flee out of them into the mind or add to them symbolic or cultural dimensions; the question is that matters of fact are a poor *proxy* of experience and of experimentation and, I would add, a confusing bundle of polemics, of epistemology, of modernist politics that can in no way claim to represent what is requested by a realist attitude.[7]

Whitehead is not an author known for keeping the reader wide awake, but I want to indicate at least the *direction* of the new critical attitude with which I wish to replace the tired routines of most social theories.

The solution lies, it seems to me, in this promising word *gathering* that Heidegger had introduced to account for the "thingness of the thing." Now, I know very well that Heidegger and Whitehead would have nothing to say to one another, and, yet, the word the latter used in *Process and Reality*[8] to describe "actual occasions," his word for my matters of concern, is the word *societies.* It is also, by the way, the word used by Gabriel Tarde, the real founder of French sociology, to describe all sorts of entities. It is close enough to the word *association* that I have used all along to describe the objects of science and technology. Andrew Pickering would use the words "mangle of practice."[9] Whatever the words, what is presented here is an entirely

6. Philosophers who practice phenomenology, a philosophical method restricted to analyzing the intellectual processes of which we are introspectively aware.

7. That matters of fact represent now a rather rare and complicated historical rendering of experience has been made powerfully clear by many writers; see, for telling segments of this history, Christian Licoppe, *La Formation de la pratique scientifique: Le Discourse de l'expérience en France et en Angleterre (1630–1820)* [*The Formation of Scientific Practice: The Discourse of Experiment in France and England*] (Paris, 1996); Mary Poovey, *A History of the Modern Fact: Problems of Knowledge in the Sciences of Wealth and Society* (Chicago, 1999); Lorraine Daston and Katherine Park, *Wonders and the Order of Nature, 1150–1750* (New York, 1998); and *Picturing Science, Producing Art,* ed. Catherine A. Jones, Galison, and Amy Slaton (New York, 1998) [Latour's note].

8. A work published in 1929, in which Whitehead argues for the primacy of process in constituting objects (reality).

9. See Andrew Pickering, *The Mangle of Practice: Time, Agency, and Science* (Chicago, 1995) [Latour's note]. Pickering (b. ca. 1950), British sociologist and historian of science.

different attitude than the critical one, not a flight into the conditions of possibility of a given matter of fact, not the addition of something more human that the inhumane matters of fact would have missed, but, rather, a multifarious inquiry launched with the tools of anthropology, philosophy, metaphysics, history, sociology to detect *how many participants* are gathered in a *thing* to make it exist and to maintain its existence. Objects are simply a gathering that has failed—a fact that has not been assembled according to due process.[1] The stubbornness of matters of fact in the usual scenography of the rock-kicking objector—"It is there whether you like it or not"—is much like the stubbornness of political demonstrators: "the U.S., love it or leave it," that is, a very poor substitute for any sort of vibrant, articulate, sturdy, decent, long-term existence.[2] A gathering, that is, a thing, an issue, inside a Thing, an arena, can be very sturdy, too, on the condition that the number of its participants, its ingredients, nonhumans as well as humans, not be limited in advance.[3] It is entirely wrong to divide the collective, as I call it, into the sturdy matters of fact, on the one hand, and the dispensable crowds, on the other. Archimedes[4] spoke for a whole tradition when he exclaimed: "Give me one fixed point and I will move the Earth," but am I not speaking for another, much less prestigious but maybe as respectable tradition, if I exclaim in turn "Give me one matter of concern and I will show you the whole earth and heavens that have to be gathered to hold it firmly in place"? For me it makes no sense to reserve the realist vocabulary for the first one only. The critic is not the one who debunks, but the one who assembles. The critic is not the one who lifts the rugs from under the feet of the naïve believers, but the one who offers the participants arenas in which to gather. The critic is not the one who alternates haphazardly between antifetishism and positivism like the drunk iconoclast drawn by Goya,[5] but the one for whom, if something is constructed, then it means it is fragile and thus in great need of care and caution. I am aware that to get at the heart of this argument one would have to renew also what it means to be a constructivist, but I have said enough to indicate the direction of critique, not *away* but *toward* the gathering, the Thing.[6] Not westward, but, so to speak, eastward.[7]

The practical problem we face, if we try to go that new route, is to associate the word *criticism* with a whole set of new positive metaphors, gestures, attitudes, knee-jerk reactions, habits of thoughts. To begin with this new habit forming, I'd like to extract another definition of critique from the most unlikely source, namely, Alan Turing's original paper on thinking

1. See Latour, *Politics of Nature: How to Bridge the Sciences into Democracy*, trans. Porter (Cambridge, Mass., 2004) [Latour's note].
2. See the marvelously funny rendering of the realist gesture in Malcolm Ashmore, Derek Edwards, and Jonathan Potter, "The Bottom Line: The Rhetoric of Reality Demonstrations," *Configurations* 2 (Winter 1994): 1–14 [Latour's note].
3. This is the challenge of a new exhibition I am curating with Peter Weibel in Karlsruhe and that is supposed to take place in 2004 under the provisional title "Making Things Public." This exhibition will explore what *Iconoclash* had simply pointed at, namely, beyond the image wars [Latour's note]. See Latour and Weibel, eds., *Making Things Public: Atmospheres of Democracy* (2005).
4. Greek mathematician and inventor (ca. 287–212 B.C.E.); the quotation is from Simplicius's commentary (6th c. C.E.) on ARISTOTLE's *Physics*.
5. Francisco Goya (1746–1828), Spanish painter.
6. This paper is a companion of another one: Latour, "The Promises of Constructivism," in *Chasing Technoscience: Matrix for Materiality*, ed. Don Ihde and Evan Selinger (Bloomington, Ind., 2003), pp. 27–46 [Latour's note].
7. This is why, although I share all the worries of Thomas de Zengotita, "Common Ground: Finding Our Way Back to the Enlightenment," *Harper's* 306 (Jan. 2003): 33–45, I think he is entirely mistaken in the *direction* of the move he proposes back to the future; to go back to the "natural" attitude is a sign of nostalgia [Latour's note].

machines.[8] I have a good reason for that: here is the typical paper about formalism, here is the origin of one of the icons—to use a cliché of antifetishism—of the contemporary age, namely, the computer, and yet, if you read this paper, it is so baroque, so kitsch, it assembles such an astounding number of metaphors, beings, hypotheses, allusions, that there is no chance that it would be accepted nowadays by any journal. Even *Social Text* would reject it out of hand as another hoax![9] "Not again," they would certainly say, "once bitten, twice shy." Who would take a paper seriously that states somewhere after having spoken of Muslim women, punishment of boys, extrasensory perception: "In attempting to construct such machines we should not be irreverently usurping [God's] power of creating souls, any more than we are in the procreation of children: rather we are, in either case, instruments of His will providing mansions for the souls that He creates" ("CM," p. 443).

Lots of gods, always in machines.[1] Remember how Bush eulogized the crew of the *Columbia* for reaching home in heaven, if not home on earth? Here Turing too cannot avoid mentioning God's creative power when talking of this most mastered machine, the computer that he has invented. That's precisely his point. The computer is in for many surprises; you get out of it much more than you put into it. In the most dramatic way, Turing's paper demonstrates, once again, that all objects are born things, all matters of fact require, in order to exist, a bewildering variety of matters of concern.[2] The surprising result is that we don't master what we, ourselves, have fabricated, the object of this definition of critique.[3]

> Let us return for a moment to Lady Lovelace's[4] objection, which stated that the machine can only do what we tell it to do. One could say that a man can "inject" an idea into the machine, and that it will respond to a certain extent and then drop into quiescence, like a piano string

8. See A. M. Turing, "Computing Machinery and Intelligence," *Mind* 59 (Oct. 1950): 433–60; hereafter abbreviated "CM." See also what Powers in *Galatea 2.2* (New York, 1995) did with this paper; this is critique in the most generous sense of the word. For the context of this paper, see Andrew Hodges, *Alan Turning: The Enigma* (New York, 1983) [Latour's note]. Turing (1912–1954), English mathematician, cryptographer, and pioneer of computer theory.

9. In 1996 the physicist Alan Sokal submitted to the cultural studies journal *Social Text* an article that parodied postmodern science critique; after it was published, he announced the hoax, designed to prove that such analyses were nonsense.

1. The phrase evokes both the *deus ex machina* of classical drama—a god who unexpectedly appears and makes possible a resolution—and "the ghost in the machine," the dismissive phrase applied in *The Concept of Mind* (1949) by the English philosopher Gilbert Ryle to the mind-body dualism proposed by René Descartes (1596–1650).

2. A nonformalist definition of formalism has been proposed by Brian Rotman, *Ad Infinitum: The Ghost in Turing's Machine: Taking God out of Mathematics and Putting the Body Back in* (Stanford, Calif., 1993) [Latour's note].

3. Since Turing can be taken as the first and best programmer, those who believe in defining machines by inputs and outputs should meditate his confession:

> Machines take me by surprise with great frequency. This is largely because I do not do sufficient calculation to decide what to expect them to do, or rather because, although I do a calculation, I do it in a hurried, slipshod fashion, taking risks. Perhaps I say to myself, "I suppose the voltage here ought to be the same as there: anyway let's assume it is." Naturally I am often wrong, and the result is a surprise for me for by the time the experiment is done these assumptions have been forgotten. These admissions lay me open to lectures on the subject of my vicious ways, but do not throw any doubt on my credibility when I testify to the surprises I experience. ("CM," pp. 450–51)

On this nonformalist definition of computers, see Brian Cantwell Smith, *On the Origin of Objects* (Cambridge, Mass., 1997) [Latour's note].

4. Augusta Ada King, countess of Lovelace (1815–1852), an English mathematician and pioneer of early computers, who commented that Charles Babbage's "Analytical Engine has no pretension whatever to originate anything."

> struck by a hammer. Another simile would be an atomic pile of less than critical size: an injected idea is to correspond to a neutron entering the pile from without. Each such neutron will cause a certain disturbance which eventually dies away. If, however, the size of the pile is sufficiently increased, the disturbance caused by such an incoming neutron will very likely go on and on increasing until the whole pile is destroyed. Is there a corresponding phenomenon for minds, and is there one for machines? There does seem to be one for the human mind. The majority of them seem to be "sub-critical," *i.e.* to correspond in this analogy to piles of sub-critical size. An idea presented to such a mind will on average give rise to less than one idea in reply. A smallish proportion are supercritical. An idea presented to such a mind may give rise to a whole "theory" consisting of secondary, tertiary and more remote ideas. Animals' minds seem to be very definitely subcritical. Adhering to this analogy we ask, "Can a machine be made to be super-critical?" ["CM," p. 454]

We all know subcritical minds, that's for sure! What would critique do if it could be associated with *more*, not with *less*, with *multiplication*, not *subtraction*. Critical theory died away long ago; can we become critical again, in the sense here offered by Turing? That is, generating more ideas than we have received, inheriting from a prestigious critical tradition but not letting it die away, or "dropping into quiescence" like a piano no longer struck. This would require that all entities, including computers, cease to be objects defined simply by their inputs and outputs and become again things, mediating, assembling, gathering many more folds than the "united four." If this were possible then we could let the critics come ever closer to the matters of concern we cherish, and then at last we could tell them: "Yes, please, touch them, explain them, deploy them." Then we would have gone for good beyond iconoclasm.

2003, 2004

MARTHA C. NUSSBAUM
b. 1947

Martha C. Nussbaum takes philosophy out of the academic realm and applies it to public issues of our day. While many contemporary philosophers focus on relatively technical issues of language or cognition, Nussbaum explores the therapeutic good that philosophy brings society. In pursuit of this wider aim, she draws on several other fields, such as law, public policy, international development, and, perhaps most surprisingly, literature. In our selections from *Cultivating Humanity: A Classical Defense of Reform in Liberal Education* (1997), Nussbaum argues that American higher education should produce "citizens of the world," and that literature plays a key role in achieving that goal because of its special efficacy in helping us to understand others.

Born in 1947, Nussbaum grew up in the suburbs of Philadelphia, where her father was an attorney. After attending Wellesley College, she completed her B.A.

at New York University in 1969. She did graduate work in classics at Harvard University, earning her M.A. in 1971; she was the first woman to receive a prestigious junior fellowship at Harvard's Society of Fellows, and completed her Ph.D. in 1975. Nussbaum then taught classics and philosophy at Harvard from 1975 to 1983; in 1984 she joined the faculty of Brown University and held a prestigious University Professorship from 1988 to 1995. In addition, she was research adviser to the World Institute for Development Economics Research (WIDER) in Helsinki, a division of the United Nations University, from 1987 to 1993. She moved to the University of Chicago in 1995, where she is the Ernst Freund Distinguished Service Professor of Law and Ethics.

Many contemporary critics have espoused poststructuralist theory, but Nussbaum represents a different tradition of thought, grounding her work in moral philosophy. Touchstones for her are the ancient Stoic philosophers, such as the Roman emperor Marcus Aurelius (121–180 C.E.), who reflected on how to live deliberately and honorably. One of Nussbaum's concerns has been the emotions, particularly their relation to ethics and politics; rather than dismissing them as irrational or irrelevant to judgment, as many thinkers have, she shows their role in evaluation and ethical judgment. For instance, justified anger at inequality, or compassion for those in poverty, works to spur needed social change. Another concern has been the philosophical import of literature, as she has paid particular attention to its capacity to represent emotion and to portray good and bad moral choices.

Much of Nussbaum's work deals with ethics, emotion, and literature, but through the 1990s her work expanded to consider politics more explicitly. Her participation in WIDER and travels to India, where she witnessed the inequalities experienced by many of the women of the world, affected her powerfully; as she remarks in her 2000 book *Women and Human Development*, these influences "transformed my work, making me aware of urgent problems and convincing me that philosophy had a contribution to make toward their solution." In collaboration with the Nobel Prize–winning economist Amartya Sen, she has promoted "the capabilities approach," which redefines social good as assessed not by measuring wealth or a country's per capita gross national product, as many economists and policy makers do, but by determining what capabilities people can exercise and how likely they are to flourish. This new metric entails attention to literacy, health care, and freedom of religion, which she sees as minimal requirements for a decent society.

In foregrounding traditional humanist concerns—in her emphasis on universal human capabilities, as well as in her defense of the tradition of literature and liberal learning—Nussbaum departs from much poststructuralist theory, which espouses antihumanism and stresses the ways in which abstract structures, such as language or ideology, determine human life. Nussbaum also asserts normative standards, believing, for instance, that all people should have health care and "liberty of conscience" (freedom of religion), at a time when much theory rejects normative standards and universal ideals to embrace difference.

A central element in creating a better society for Nussbaum, as it was for PLATO in his *Republic*, is the education of citizens; in our selections from *Cultivating Humanity*, Nussbaum contends that an important purpose of higher education is not just job training but to train citizens of the world who are sensitive to social justice. She believes that one way to achieve such sensitivity is through exposure to literature, especially drama and fiction. Literature makes us better citizens because it helps train us to understand others. Rather than being simply a private pursuit, as is often thought, "narrative imagination is an essential preparation for moral interaction." It makes us more "capable of compassion," which "involves the recognition that another person, in some ways similar to [ourselves], has suffered some significant pain or misfortune." Thus one might vote for universal health care not only out of self-interest but also out of empathy for those who have the misfortune of suffering ill health and lacking insurance.

In the background of Nussbaum's argument are the "culture wars" and debates over the literary canon in the United States during the late 1980s and the 1990s, when conservatives charged that higher education had become politicized and, led by liberals, had abandoned the classics. Nussbaum counters by not only attacking their assumptions about the goal of education but also by grounding her argument that education *should* be political and cosmopolitan in the very tradition that they esteem—the literature and philosophy of the ancient Greeks and Romans. Nussbaum also criticizes the identity politics favored by liberals, asserting that the goals of education are universal. She further diverges from contemporary theorists in refusing to join the widespread critique, inspired by MICHEL FOUCAULT and others, of the Enlightenment and its stress on reason; instead, she strongly defends rational argument and its key role in a deliberative democracy.

One other way that Nussbaum differs from many contemporary theorists is in the accessibility of her writing. She employs philosophical concepts without jargon, determined to convey to a general readership how theory contributes to making a good society. One of her most impassioned critiques, published in the *New Republic* in 1999, was of JUDITH BUTLER, whose writing she finds esoteric and whose arguments for subversion without a vision of normative justice she finds irresponsible, contributing to counterproductive social goals. Nussbaum, in turn, has been criticized from both the right and the left. From the right, she has been attacked for espousing multiculturalism under cover of the classics. From the left, she has been criticized for holding a traditional and unoriginal view of education, as well as for defending normative values. Because Nussbaum advocates cosmopolitanism, the postcolonial theorist GAYATRI CHAKRAVORTY SPIVAK has charged her with carrying out an imperialist, "civilizing mission" directed at other cultures. The pragmatist philosopher Richard Rorty, who joined Nussbaum in calling for the public use of philosophy, nevertheless has criticized her argumentative stance, remarking that "her tone sometimes suggests that to differ from her is to imperil the social bond." Through all of these debates, Nussbaum has been tireless in defending moral values and capabilities, and in insisting on the public role of philosophy and criticism.

Cultivating Humanity: A Classical Defense of Reform in Liberal Education
Keywords: The Canon/Tradition, Classical Theory, Ethics, Institutional Studies, The Novel

From Cultivating Humanity: A Classical Defense of Reform in Liberal Education

From *Introduction. The Old Education and the Think-Academy*

* * *

Our campuses are producing citizens, and this means that we must ask what a good citizen of the present day should be and should know. The present-day world is inescapably multicultural and multinational. Many of our most pressing problems require for their intelligent, cooperative solution a dialogue that brings together people from many different national and cultural and religious backgrounds. Even those issues that seem closest to home—issues, for example, about the structure of the family, the regulation of sexuality, the future of children—need to be approached with a broad historical and cross-cultural understanding. A graduate of a U.S. university or college ought to be the sort of citizen who can become an intelligent participant in debates involving these differences, whether professionally or simply as a voter, a juror, a friend.

When we ask about the relationship of a liberal education to citizenship, we are asking a question with a long history in the Western philosophical tradition. We are drawing on Socrates' concept of "the examined life," on Aristotle's notions of reflective citizenship, and above all on Greek and Roman Stoic notions[1] of an education that is "liberal" in that it liberates the mind from the bondage of habit and custom, producing people who can function with sensitivity and alertness as citizens of the whole world. This is what Seneca[2] means by the cultivation of humanity. The idea of the well-educated person as a "citizen of the world" has had a formative influence on Western thought about education: on David Hume and Adam Smith in the Scottish/English tradition, on Immanuel Kant in the continental Enlightenment tradition, on Thomas Paine[3] and other Founding Fathers in the American tradition. Understanding the classical roots of these ideas helps us to recover powerful arguments that have exercised a formative influence on our own democracy.

Our democracy, indeed, has based its institutions of higher learning on these ideals to a degree unparalleled in the world. In most nations students enter a university to pursue a single subject, and that is all they study. The idea of "liberal education"—a higher education that is a cultivation of the whole human being for the functions of citizenship and life generally—has been taken up most fully in the United States. This noble ideal, however, has not yet been fully realized in our colleges and universities. Some, while using the words "liberal education," subordinate the cultivation of the whole person to technical and vocational education. Even where education is ostensibly "liberal," it may not contain all that a citizen really needs to know. We should ask, then, how well our nation is really fulfilling a goal that it has chosen to make its own. What does the "cultivation of humanity" require?

The classical ideal of the "world citizen" can be understood in two ways, and "cultivation of humanity" along with it. The sterner, more exigent version is the ideal of a citizen whose *primary* loyalty is to human beings the world over, and whose national, local, and varied group loyalties are considered distinctly secondary. Its more relaxed version allows a variety of different views about what our priorities should be but says that, however we order our varied loyalties, we should still be sure that we recognize the worth of human life wherever it occurs and see ourselves as bound by common human abilities and problems to people who lie at a great distance from us. These two different versions have existed at least since ancient Rome, when statesman and philosopher Cicero[4] softened the stern demands of Greek Stoicism for a Roman audience. Although I do sympathize with the sterner thesis, it is the more relaxed and inclusive thesis that will concern me here. What, then, does this inclusive conception ask us to learn?

1. Ideas associated with followers of the Greek philosopher Zeno (335–263 B.C.E.); later, in a passage not included here, Nussbaum observes that the Stoics were interested in "sympathetic perception" and "asked the world citizen to gain an empathic understanding of people who are different." Socrates (469–399 B.C.E.), Greek philosopher known for relentless questioning, as depicted in the dialogues of his pupil PLATO (ca. 427–ca. 347 B.C.E.). ARISTOTLE (384–322 B.C.E.), Greek philosopher who considers citizenship especially in his *Nicomachean Ethics* and *Politics* (both ca. 330 B.C.E.).

2. Roman Stoic philosopher and dramatist (4 B.C.E.–65 C.E.).

3. British-born American political theorist and polemicist for American independence (1737–1809). HUME (1711–1776), Scottish philosopher and historian. Smith (1723–1790), Scottish moral philosopher and founding figure in economics. KANT (1724–1804), German idealist philosopher.

4. The great Roman orator (106–43 B.C.E.).

Three capacities, above all, are essential to the cultivation of humanity in today's world. First is the capacity for critical examination of oneself and one's traditions—for living what, following Socrates, we may call "the examined life." This means a life that accepts no belief as authoritative simply because it has been handed down by tradition or become familiar through habit, a life that questions all beliefs and accepts only those that survive reason's demand for consistency and for justification. Training this capacity requires developing the capacity to reason logically, to test what one reads or says for consistency of reasoning, correctness of fact, and accuracy of judgment. Testing of this sort frequently produces challenges to tradition, as Socrates knew well when he defended himself against the charge of "corrupting the young."[5] But he defended his activity on the grounds that democracy needs citizens who can think for themselves rather than simply deferring to authority, who can reason together about their choices rather than just trading claims and counterclaims. Like a gadfly on the back of a noble but sluggish horse, he said, he was waking democracy up so that it could conduct its business in a more reflective and reasonable way. Our democracy, like ancient Athens, is prone to hasty and sloppy reasoning, and to the substitution of invective for real deliberation. We need Socratic teaching to fulfill the promise of democratic citizenship.

Citizens who cultivate their humanity need, further, an ability to see themselves not simply as citizens of some local region or group but also, and above all, as human beings bound to all other human beings by ties of recognition and concern. The world around us is inescapably international. Issues from business to agriculture, from human rights to the relief of famine, call our imaginations to venture beyond narrow group loyalties and to consider the reality of distant lives. We very easily think of ourselves in group terms—as Americans first and foremost, as human beings second—or, even more narrowly, as Italian-Americans, or heterosexuals, or African-Americans first, Americans second, and human beings third if at all. We neglect needs and capacities that link us to fellow citizens who live at a distance or who look different from ourselves. This means that we are unaware of many prospects of communication and fellowship with them, and also of responsibilities we may have to them. We also sometimes err by neglect of differences, assuming that lives in distant places must be like ours and lacking curiosity about what they are really like. Cultivating our humanity in a complex, interlocking world involves understanding the ways in which common needs and aims are differently realized in different circumstances. This requires a great deal of knowledge that American college students rarely got in previous eras, knowledge of non-Western cultures, of minorities within their own, of differences of gender and sexuality.

But citizens cannot think well on the basis of factual knowledge alone. The third ability of the citizen, closely related to the first two, can be called the narrative imagination. This means the ability to think what it might be like to be in the shoes of a person different from oneself, to be an intelligent reader of that person's story, and to understand the emotions and wishes and desires that someone so placed might have. The narrative imagination is not uncritical, for we always bring ourselves and our own judgments to

5. Tried by an Athenian jury, Socrates was condemned to death. During his trial, recounted in Plato's *Apology* (ca. 395 B.C.E.), he declared that "the unexamined life is not worth living" (38a); for his description of himself as a gadfly, see 30e.

the encounter with another; and when we identify with a character in a novel, or with a distant person whose life story we imagine, we inevitably will not merely identify; we will also judge that story in the light of our own goals and aspirations. But the first step of understanding the world from the point of view of the other is essential to any responsible act of judgment, since we do not know what we are judging until we see the meaning of an action as the person intends it, the meaning of a speech as it expresses something of importance in the context of that person's history and social world. The third ability our students should attain is the ability to decipher such meanings through the use of the imagination.

Intelligent citizenship needs more than these three abilities. Scientific understanding is also of the first importance. My excuse for not dwelling on this aspect of a liberal education is that others are far better placed to describe it than I. The same is true of economics, which I shall approach only in its relationship to philosophy and political theory. I focus on the parts of a liberal education that have by now become associated with "the humanities" and to some extent "the social sciences": above all, then, on philosophy, political science, religious studies, history, anthropology, sociology, literature, art, music, and studies of language and culture. Nor do I describe everything in these areas that a good citizen should know. I focus on areas of current urgency and controversy. (Even within the areas of controversy I am selective, allowing the example of African-American studies to stand for more complex debates about ethnic studies generally. Issues of poverty and social class, which I have treated elsewhere, are treated selectively, within chapters organized along other lines.)

It was through ancient Greek and Roman arguments that I came upon these ideas in my own history. The Greek and Roman versions of these ideas are immensely valuable to us as we pursue these debates today, and I shall focus on that contribution. But ideas of this sort have many sources in many traditions. Closely related notions can be found in India, in Africa, in Latin America, and in China. One of the errors that a diverse education can dispel is the false belief that one's own tradition is the only one that is capable of self-criticism or universal aspiration.

* * *

From *Chapter 3. The Narrative Imagination*

> [There] are many forms of thought and expression within the range of human communications from which the voter derives the knowledge, intelligence, sensitivity to human values: the capacity for sane and objective judgement which, so far as possible, a ballot should express. [The] people do need novels and dramas and paintings and poems, "because they will be called upon to vote."
>
> —Alexander Meiklejohn,[6]
> "The First Amendment Is an Absolute"

The world citizen needs knowledge of history and social fact. We have begun to see how those requirements can be met by curricula of different

6. British-born American philosopher (1872–1964), who as a university president became an influential advocate of a liberal education. The article quoted was published in 1961.

types. But people who know many facts about lives other than their own are still not fully equipped for citizenship. As Heraclitus[7] said 2,500 years ago, "Learning about many things does not produce understanding." Marcus Aurelius[8] insisted that to become world citizens we must not simply amass knowledge; we must also cultivate in ourselves a capacity for sympathetic imagination that will enable us to comprehend the motives and choices of people different from ourselves, seeing them not as forbiddingly alien and other, but as sharing many problems and possibilities with us. Differences of religion, gender, race, class, and national origin make the task of understanding harder, since these differences shape not only the practical choices people face but also their "insides," their desires, thoughts, and ways of looking at the world.

Here the arts play a vital role, cultivating powers of imagination that are essential to citizenship. As Alexander Meiklejohn, the distinguished constitutional scholar and theorist of "deliberative democracy," put it fifty years ago, arguing against an opponent who had denied the political relevance of art, the people of the United States need the arts precisely because they will be called upon to vote. That is not the only reason why the arts are important, but it is one significant reason. The arts cultivate capacities of judgment and sensitivity that can and should be expressed in the choices a citizen makes. To some extent this is true of all the arts. Music, dance, painting and sculpture, architecture—all have a role in shaping our understanding of the people around us. But in a curriculum for world citizenship, literature, with its ability to represent the specific circumstances and problems of people of many different sorts, makes an especially rich contribution. As Aristotle said in chapter 9 of *The Poetics*, literature shows us "not something that has happened, but the kind of thing that might happen."[9] This knowledge of possibilities is an especially valuable resource in the political life.

To begin to understand how literature can develop a citizen's imagination, let us consider two literary works widely separated in place and time. In both cases, the literary work refers to its own distinctive capacity to promote adequate civic perception.

Sophocles'[1] *Philoctetes*, produced in 409 B.C., during a crisis in the Athenian democracy, concerns the proper treatment of a citizen who has become an outcast, crippled by a disfiguring illness. On his way to Troy to fight with the Greeks in the Trojan War, Philoctetes stepped by mistake into a sacred shrine. His foot, bitten by the serpent who guards the shrine, began to ooze with an ulcerous sore, and his cries of pain disrupted the army's religious festivals. So the commanders abandoned him on the deserted island of Lemnos, with no companions and no resources but his bow and arrows. Ten years later, learning that they cannot win the war without his magical bow, they return, determined to ensnare him by a series of lies into participating in the war. The commander Odysseus shows no interest in Philoctetes

7. Greek philosopher (active ca. 500 B.C.E.), best known for his insistence that the only permanent reality is change; Nussbaum quotes his fragment 40.

8. Roman emperor and philosopher (121–180 C.E.; emperor, 161–180); his *Meditations* is an influential expression of Stoic philosophy, emphasizing the ideal of the wise and virtuous man in a society in which all share in a common nature.

9. For Aristotle's *Poetics*, see above.

1. Greek tragedian (ca. 496–406 B.C.E.).

as a person; he speaks of him only as a tool of public ends. The chorus of common soldiers has a different response (lines 169–176):

> For my part, I have compassion for him. Think how
> with no human company or care,
> no sight of a friendly face,
> wretched, always alone,
> he wastes away with that savage disease,
> with no way of meeting his daily needs.
> How, how in the world, does the poor man survive?

Unlike their leader, the men of the chorus vividly and sympathetically imagine the life of a man whom they have never seen, picturing his loneliness, his pain, his struggle for survival. In the process they stand in for, and allude to, the imaginative work of the audience, who are invited by the play as a whole to imagine the sort of needy, homeless life to which prosperous people rarely direct their attention. The drama as a whole, then, cultivates the type of sympathetic vision of which its characters speak. In the play, this kind of vivid imagining prompts a political decision against using Philoctetes as a means, and the audience is led to believe this to be a politically and morally valuable result. In this way, by showing the public benefits of the very sort of sympathy it is currently awakening in its spectators, the drama commends its own resources as valuable for the formation of decent citizenship and informed public choice. Although the good of the whole should not be neglected, that good will not be well served if human beings are seen simply as instruments of one another's purposes.

Ralph Ellison's[2] *Invisible Man* (1952) develops this tradition of reflection about our failures of perception and recognition. Its hero describes himself as "invisible" because throughout the novel he is seen by those he encounters as a vehicle for various race-inflected stereotypes: the poor, humiliated black boy who snatches like an animal at the coins that lie on an electrified mat; the good student trusted to chauffeur a wealthy patron; the listening ear to whom this same patron unburdens his guilt and anxiety; the rabble-rousing activist who energizes an urban revolutionary movement; the violent rapist who gratifies the sexual imagination of a woman brought up on racially charged sexual images—always he is cast in a drama of someone else's making, "never more loved and appreciated" than when he plays his assigned role. The "others," meanwhile, are all "lost in a dream world"—in which they see only what their own minds have created, never the reality of the person who stands before them. "You go along for years knowing something is wrong, then suddenly you discover that you're as transparent as air." Invisibility is "a matter of the construction of their *inner* eyes, those eyes with which they look through their physical eyes upon reality."[3]

Ellison's grotesque, surreal world is very unlike the classical world of Sophocles' play. Its concerns, however, are closely linked: social stratification and injustice, manipulation and use, and above all invisibility and the condition of being transparent to and for one's fellow citizens. Like Sophocles'

2. African American novelist (1914–1994); *Invisible Man*, the only novel he published in his lifetime, is widely recognized as a modern classic.

3. Ralph Ellison, *Invisible Man* (New York: Random House, 1992), pp. 563, 566, 3 [Nussbaum's note].

drama, it explores and savagely excoriates these refusals to see. Like that drama, it invites its readers to know and see more than the unseeing characters. "Being invisible and without substance, a disembodied voice, as it were, what else could I do? What else but try to tell you what was really happening when your eyes were looking through?"[4] In this way, it works upon the inner eyes of the very readers whose moral failures it castigates, although it refuses the easy notion that mutual visibility can be achieved in one heartfelt leap of brotherhood.

Ellison explicitly linked the novelist's art to the possibility of democracy. By representing both visibility and its evasions, both equality and its refusal, a novel, he wrote in an introduction, "could be fashioned as a raft of hope, perception and entertainment that might help keep us afloat as we tried to negotiate the snags and whirlpools that mark our nation's vacillating course toward and away from the democratic idea." This is not, he continued, the only goal for fiction; but it is one proper and urgent goal. For a democracy requires not only institutions and procedures; it also requires a particular quality of vision, in order "to defeat this national tendency to deny the common humanity shared by my character and those who might happen to read of his experience."[5] The novel's mordantly satirical treatment of stereotypes, its fantastic use of image and symbol (in, for example, the bizarre dreamlike sequence in the white-paint factory), and its poignant moments of disappointed hope, all contribute to this end.

As Ellison says, forming the civic imagination is not the only role for literature, but it is one salient role. Narrative art has the power to make us see the lives of the different with more than a casual tourist's interest—with involvement and sympathetic understanding, with anger at our society's refusals of visibility. We come to see how circumstances shape the lives of those who share with us some general goals and projects; and we see that circumstances shape not only people's possibilities for action, but also their aspirations and desires, hopes and fears. All of this seems highly pertinent to decisions we must make as citizens. Understanding, for example, how a history of racial stereotyping can affect self-esteem, achievement, and love enables us to make more informed judgments on issues relating to affirmative action and education.

Higher education should develop students' awareness of literature in many different ways. But literature does play a vital role in educating citizens of the world. It makes sense, then, to ask how it can perform this function as well as possible—what sorts of literary works, and what sort of teaching of those works, our academic institutions should promote in order to foster an informed and compassionate vision of the different. When we ask this question, we find that the goals of world citizenship are best promoted by a literary education that both adds new works to the well-known "canon" of Western literature and considers standard texts in a deliberative and critical spirit.

It is frequently claimed that it is inappropriate to approach literature with a "political agenda." Yet it is hard to justify such a claim without embracing an extreme kind of aesthetic formalism that is sterile and unap-

4. Ibid., p. 572 [Nussbaum's note].

5. Ibid., pp. xxiv–xxv, xxvi [Nussbaum's note].

pealing. The Western aesthetic tradition has had throughout its history an intense concern with character and community. The defense of that tradition in the contemporary "culture wars" should enlist our support.

FANCY AND WONDER

When a child and a parent begin to tell stories together, the child is acquiring essential moral capacities. Even a simple nursery rhyme such as "Twinkle, twinkle little star, how I wonder what you are" leads children to feel wonder—a sense of mystery that mingles curiosity with awe. Children wonder about the little star. In so doing they learn to imagine that a mere shape in the heavens has an inner world, in some ways mysterious, in some ways like their own. They learn to attribute life, emotion, and thought to a form whose insides are hidden. As time goes on, they do this in an increasingly sophisticated way, learning to hear and tell stories about animals and humans. These stories interact with their own attempts to explain the world and their own actions in it. A child deprived of stories is deprived, as well, of certain ways of viewing other people. For the insides of people, like the insides of stars, are not open to view. They must be wondered about. And the conclusion that this set of limbs in front of me has emotions and feelings and thoughts of the sort I attribute to myself will not be reached without the training of the imagination that storytelling promotes.

Narrative play does teach children to view a personlike shape as a house for hope and fear and love and anger, all of which they have known themselves. But the wonder involved in storytelling also makes evident the limits of each person's access to every other. "How I wonder what you are," goes the rhyme. In that simple expression is an acknowledgment of the lack of completeness in one's own grasp of the fear, the love, the sympathy, the anger, of the little star, or of any other creature or person. In fact the child adept at storytelling soon learns that people in stories are frequently easier to know than people in real life, who, as Proust puts it in *The Past Recaptured*,[6] frequently offer "a dead weight that our sensitivity cannot remove," a closed exterior that cannot be penetrated even by a sensitive imagination. The child, wondering about its parents, soon learns about these obstacles, just as it also learns that its parents need not know everything that goes on in its own mind. The habits of wonder promoted by storytelling thus define the other person as spacious and deep, with qualitative differences from oneself and hidden places worthy of respect.

In these various ways, narrative imagination is an essential preparation for moral interaction. Habits of empathy and conjecture conduce to a certain type of citizenship and a certain form of community: one that cultivates a sympathetic responsiveness to another's needs, and understands the way circumstances shape those needs, while respecting separateness and privacy. This is so because of the way in which literary imagining both inspires intense concern with the fate of characters and defines those characters as containing a rich inner life, not all of which is open to view; in the process, the reader learns to have respect for the hidden contents of that

6. The 7th and final volume (1927) of one of the great narratives of the 20th century—*In Search of Lost Time* (1913–27), by the French novelist Marcel Proust (1871–1922).

inner world, seeing its importance in defining a creature as fully human. It is this respect for the inner life of consciousness that literary theorist Lionel Trilling describes when he calls the imagination of the novel-reader a "liberal imagination"[7]—meaning by this that the novel-reader is led to attribute importance to the material conditions of happiness while respecting human freedom.

As children grow older, the moral and social aspects of these literary scenarios become increasingly complex and full of distinctions, so that they gradually learn how to ascribe to others, and recognize in themselves, not only hope and fear, happiness and distress—attitudes that are ubiquitous, and comprehensible without extensive experience—but also more complex traits such as courage, self-restraint, dignity, perseverance, and fairness. These notions might be defined for the child in an abstract way; but to grasp their full meaning in one's own self-development and in social interactions with others requires learning their dynamics in narrative settings.

As children grasp such complex facts in imagination, they become capable of compassion. Compassion involves the recognition that another person, in some ways similar to oneself, has suffered some significant pain or misfortune in a way for which that person is not, or not fully, to blame. As many moral traditions emphasize—the analysis of compassion is remarkably constant in both Western and non-Western philosophy—it requires estimating the significance of the misfortune as accurately as one can—usually in agreement with the sufferer, but sometimes in ways that depart from that person's own judgment. Adam Smith points out that people who lose their mental faculties are the objects of our compassion even though they themselves are not aware of this loss: what is significant is the magnitude of the loss, as the onlooker estimates its role in the life of the loser.[8] This requires, in turn, a highly complex set of moral abilities, including the ability to imagine what it is like to be in that person's place (what we usually call *empathy*), and also the ability to stand back and ask whether the person's own judgment has taken the full measure of what has happened.

Compassion requires one thing more: a sense of one's own vulnerability to misfortune. To respond with compassion, I must be willing to entertain the thought that this suffering person might be me. And this I will be unlikely to do if I am convinced that I am above the ordinary lot and no ill can befall me. There are exceptions to this, in some religious traditions' portrayals of the compassion of God; but philosophers such as Aristotle and Rousseau[9] have plausibly claimed that imperfect human beings need the belief that their own possibilities are similar to those of the suffering person, if they are to respond with compassion to another's plight. This recognition, as they see it, helps explain why compassion so frequently leads to generous support for the needs of others: one thinks, "That might have been me, and that is how I should want to be treated."

7. See Lionel Trilling, *The Liberal Imagination* (New York: Scribner's, 1953) [Nussbaum's note]. Trilling (1905–1975), influential American literary critic during the mid-20th century and leading member of the New York Intellectuals, a group of writers and literary critics.

8. See Smith, *The Theory of Moral Sentiments* (1759), 1.1.1.

9. Jean-Jacques Rousseau (1712–1778), Swiss-born French political philosopher; his writings include *Emile* (1762), a novel that sets forth his theory of education.

Compassion, so understood, promotes an accurate awareness of our common vulnerability. It is true that human beings are needy, incomplete creatures who are in many ways dependent on circumstances beyond their control for the possibility of well-being. As Rousseau argues in *Emile*, people do not fully grasp that fact until they can imagine suffering vividly to themselves, and feel pain at the imagining. In a compassionate response to the suffering of another, one comprehends that being prosperous or powerful does not remove one from the ranks of needy humanity. Such reminders, the tradition argues, are likely to lead to a more beneficent treatment of the weak. Philoctetes, in Sophocles' play, asks for aid by reminding the soldiers that they themselves might suffer what he has suffered. They accept because they are able to imagine his predicament.

It seems, then, to be beneficial for members of a society to see themselves as bound to one another by similar weaknesses and needs, as well as by similar capacities for achievement. As Aristotle argues in chapter 9 of *The Poetics*, literature is "more philosophical than history"—by which he means more conducive to general human understanding—precisely because it acquaints us with "the kind of thing that might happen," general forms of possibility and their impact on human lives.

Compassion requires demarcations: which creatures am I to count as my fellow creatures, sharing possibilities with me? One may be a person of refined feeling and still treat many people in one's world as invisible, their prospects as unrelated to one's own. Rousseau argues that a good education, which acquaints one with all the usual vicissitudes of fortune, will make it difficult to refuse acknowledgment to the poor or the sick, or slaves, or members of lower classes. It is easy to see that any one of those might really have been me, given a change of circumstances. Boundaries of nationality can similarly be transcended in thought, for example by the recognition that one of the frequent hazards of wartime is to lose one's nation. Boundaries of race, of gender, and of sexual orientation prove, historically, more recalcitrant: for there might appear to be little real-life possibility of a man's becoming a woman, a white person's becoming black, or even (*pace* earlier psychiatry) a straight person's becoming gay or lesbian. In these cases, then, it is all the more urgent to cultivate the basis for compassion through the fictional exercise of imagination—for if one cannot in fact change one's race, one can imagine what it is like to inhabit a race different from one's own, and by becoming close to a person of different race or sexual orientation, one can imagine what it would be like for someone one loves to have such a life.

Rousseau thought that people differed only in circumstances: underneath, their desires, aims, and emotions were the same. But in fact one of the things imagining reveals to us is that we are not all brothers under the skin, that circumstances of oppression form desire and emotion and aspiration. Some characters feel like us, and some repel easy identification. But such failures to identify can also be sources of understanding. Both by identification and by its absence, we learn what life has done to people. A society that wants to foster the just treatment of all its members has strong reasons to foster an exercise of the compassionate imagination that crosses social boundaries, or tries to. And this means caring about literature.

* * *

WORLD CITIZENSHIP, RELATIVISM, AND IDENTITY POLITICS

* * *

The really grave cause for concern in the current teaching of literature, however, is not the presence of defective arguments, which can easily be criticized. It is, instead, the prevalence of an approach to literature that questions the very possibility of a sympathy that takes one outside one's group, and of common human needs and interests as a basis for that sympathy. The goal of producing world citizens is profoundly opposed to the spirit of identity politics, which holds that one's primary affiliation is with one's local group, whether religious or ethnic or based on sexuality or gender. Much teaching of literature in the current academy is inspired by the spirit of identity politics. Under the label "multiculturalism"—which can refer to the appropriate recognition of human diversity and cultural complexity—a new antihumanist view has sometimes emerged, one that celebrates difference in an uncritical way and denies the very possibility of common interests and understandings, even of dialogue and debate, that take one outside one's own group. In the world-citizen version of multiculturalism, the ethical argument for adding a work such as *Invisible Man* to the curriculum will be Ellison's own argument: that our nation has a history of racial obtuseness and that this work helps all citizens to perceive racial issues with greater clarity. In the identity-politics version of multiculturalism, by contrast, the argument in favor of *Invisible Man* will be that it affirms the experience of African-American students. This view denies the possibility of the task Ellison set himself: "of revealing the human universals hidden within the plight of one who was both black and American."[1]

These different defenses of literature are connected with different conceptions of democracy. The world-citizen view insists on the need for all citizens to understand differences with which they need to live; it sees citizens as striving to deliberate and to understand across these divisions. It is connected with a conception of democratic debate as deliberation about the common good. The identity-politics view, by contrast, depicts the citizen body as a marketplace of identity-based interest groups jockeying for power, and views difference as something to be affirmed rather than understood. Indeed, it seems a bit hard to blame literature professionals for the current prevalence of identity politics in the academy, when these scholars simply reflect a cultural view that has other, more powerful sources. Dominant economic views of rationality within the political culture have long powerfully promoted the idea that democracy is merely a marketplace of competing interest groups, without any common goals and ends that can be rationally deliberated. Economics has a far more pervasive and formative influence on our lives than does French literary theory, and it is striking that conservative critics who attack the Modern Language Association[2] are slow to criticize the far more powerful sources of such anticosmopolitan ideas when they are presented by market economists. It was no postmod-

1. Ellison, *Invisible Man*, p. xxvi.
2. The primary North American professional organization for academics in English and foreign languages and literatures; at its annual convention, scholarly papers (whose titles on occasion elicit outrage from conservatives) are presented in hundreds of panels.

ernist, but Milton Friedman, who said that about matters of value, "men can ultimately only fight."[3] This statement is false and pernicious. World citizens should vigorously criticize these ideas wherever they occur, insisting that they lead to an impoverished view of democracy.

An especially damaging consequence of identity politics in the literary academy is the belief, which one encounters in both students and scholars, that only a member of a particular oppressed group can write well or, perhaps, even read well about that group's experience. Only female writers understand the experience of women; only African-American writers understand black experience. This claim has a superficial air of plausibility, since it is hard to deny that members of oppressed groups frequently do know things about their lives that other people do not know. Neither individuals or groups are perfect in self-knowledge, and a perceptive outsider may sometimes see what a person immersed in an experience fails to see. But in general, if we want to understand the situation of a group, we do well to begin with the best that has been written by members of that group. We must, however, insist that when we do so it may be possible for us to expand our own understanding—the strongest reason for including such works in the curriculum. We could learn nothing from such works if it were impossible to cross group boundaries in imagination.

Literary interpretation is indeed superficial if it preaches the simplistic message that we are all alike under the skin. Experience and culture shape many aspects of what is "under the skin," as we can easily see if we reflect and read. It is for this reason that literature is so urgently important for the citizen, as an expansion of sympathies that real life cannot cultivate sufficiently. It is the political promise of literature that it can transport us, while remaining ourselves, into the life of another, revealing similarities but also profound differences between the life and thought of that other and myself and making them comprehensible, or at least more nearly comprehensible. Any stance toward criticism that denies that possibility seems to deny the very possibility of literary experience as a human social good. We should energetically oppose these views wherever they are found, insisting on the world-citizen, rather than the identity-politics, form of multiculturalism as the basis for our curricular efforts.

Literature makes many contributions to human life, and the undergraduate curriculum should certainly reflect this plurality. But the great contribution literature has to make to the life of the citizen is its ability to wrest from our frequently obtuse and blunted imaginations an acknowledgment of those who are other than ourselves, both in concrete circumstances and even in thought and emotion. As Ellison put it, a work of fiction may contribute "to defeat this national tendency to deny the common humanity shared by my character and those who might happen to read of his experience."[4] This contribution makes it a key element in higher education.

3. Milton Friedman, "The Methodology of Positive Economics," reprinted in Daniel M. Hausman, ed., *The Philosophy of Economics* (Cambridge: Cambridge University Press, 1984), p. 212 [Nussbaum's note]. Friedman (1912–2006), American economist whose advocacy of free markets was highly influential.

4. Ellison, *Invisible Man*, p. xxvi [Nussbaum's note].

We are now trying to build an academy that will overcome defects of vision and receptivity that marred the humanities departments of earlier eras, an academy in which no group will be invisible in Ellison's sense. That is in its way a radical political agenda; it is always radical, in any society, to insist on the equal worth of all human beings, and people find all sorts of ways to avoid the claim of that ideal, much though they may pay it lip service. The current agenda is radical in the way that Stoic world citizenship was radical in a Rome built on hierarchy and rank, in the way that the Christian idea of love of one's neighbor was and is radical, in a world anxious to deny our common membership in the kingdom of ends or the kingdom of heaven. We should defend that radical agenda as the only one worthy of our conception of democracy and worthy of guiding its future.

1997

HOMI K. BHABHA
b. 1949

A prominent figure in postcolonial studies, Homi K. Bhabha has infused thinking about nationality, ethnicity, and politics with poststructuralist theories of identity and indeterminacy. Drawing on a wide range of theorists, particularly the deconstructive philosopher JACQUES DERRIDA, Bhabha's essay "The Commitment to Theory" (1989) revises conventional notions of nationality and the colonial subject, showing how both are shifting, hybrid cultural constructions. It also provides a powerful argument for the importance of theory, for the indelible link between theory and politics, and for the use of poststructuralist theory in the tacitly anti-imperialist cause of postcolonial studies.

Bhabha was born two years after India gained national independence from British colonial rule, and his life exemplifies some of the hybrid subject positions of the postcolonial world. He was raised in the Parsi community of Bombay, India, where his father was an important constitutional lawyer. After receiving a B.A. from Bombay University, he traveled to England to earn his M.A., M.Phil., and D.Phil. from Oxford University. Beginning in 1978, he taught at Sussex University for sixteen years; he also held visiting appointments in the United States. In 1994 he took a professorship at the University of Chicago, and in 2001 he moved to Harvard University, where he is Anne F. Rothenberg Professor of the Humanities and director of the Humanities Center. He is also Distinguished Visiting Professor in the Humanities at University College, London.

Postcolonial criticism arose in the wake of the turbulent struggles for national independence of many African, Asian, and Latin American countries that were under the rule of European colonial empires through the middle of the twentieth century. Many early anticolonialist critics—among them, C. D. NARASIMHAIAH in India—promoted autonomous, nationalistic literary traditions to counteract the cultural as well as material domination of imperialism. Later, postcolonial theorists turned to analyze the ideological bases of colonial domination. Perhaps the two most influential figures in this development of contemporary postcolonial theory were EDWARD W. SAID and GAYATRI CHAKRAVORTY SPIVAK. In *Orientalism* (1978; see above), a foundational text of postcolonial studies, Said diagnosed the paths of cultural domination that projected non-Western people as the "Other." In "Can the Subaltern Speak?" (1988; see above), Spivak argued that postcolonial subjects have no voice under the dominant regime of colonial discourse.

Extending the work of Said and Spivak, Bhabha starts with a deconstructive critique of the dichotomies of the West and the Orient, the center and the periphery, the empire and the colonized, the oppressor and the oppressed, and the self and the other. He adapts Derrida's analysis of how binary oppositions structure Western thought, arguing that such dichotomies are too reductive because they imply that any national culture is unitary, homogeneous, and defined by "fixity" or an essential core. Instead, Bhabha proposes that nationalities, ethnicities, and identities are dialogic, indeterminate, and characterized by "hybridity"—one of his key terms. In "The Commitment to Theory," he defines hybridity as what "is new, *neither the one nor the other*," which emerges from a "Third Space." To reinforce this fluid sense of nationality and identity, Bhabha employs a vocabulary of process-oriented terms, including *dialogic, translation, negotiation, in-between, cross-reference*, and *ambivalence*.

Although "the wit and wisdom of Jacques Derrida" (as he calls it in another essay) is fundamental to his work, Bhabha draws on a wide array of twentieth-century theorists throughout "The Commitment to Theory." Building on the influential concept of nations set forth by BENEDICT ANDERSON in *Imagined Communities* (1983), Bhabha stresses how nationality is narratively produced, rather than arising from an intrinsic essence. From MIKHAIL M. BAKHTIN, he takes the concept of dialogue to stress that colonialism is not a one-way street but entails an interaction between colonizer and colonized. Regarding identity, he draws on FRANTZ FANON's psychoanalytic model of colonialism and JACQUES LACAN's concepts of "mimicry" and the split subject, arguing that there is always an "excess" in the cultural imitation that the colonial subject is forced to produce. This mimicry in turn both revises colonial discourse and creates a new, hybrid identity for the colonial subject.

The goal of Bhabha's theorizing of hybridity is not simply to modify the terms of debate in postcolonial studies but to make a political intervention. In general, Bhabha contends that theory is not separate from or opposed to political activism, but works hand in hand with it. Employing a deconstructive reversal of the opposition between textuality and the world, Bhabha claims that political events—he uses the example of a famous British strike—are in fact textual and discursive, often generated and spurred by "oppositional *cultural* practices." More specifically, the concept of hybridity militates against "restrictive notions of cultural identity" that result in political separatism, as seen in nationalistic movements or in identity politics. For Bhabha, hybridity fosters the larger goal of "socialist community" while acknowledging cultural differences. Such socialist community arises from the solidarity of different groups and movements working in coalition to create a new, progressive hegemony, as STUART HALL similarly urges.

Although preoccupied with postcolonialism, "The Commitment to Theory" also addresses another field of critical debate. In his unabashed advocacy of poststructuralist theory, Bhabha tacitly responds to many critics of the 1980s and 1990s. Their attacks came both from within the academy and from outside, in claims that theory was too obscure, detracted from literature, and represented a solipsistic academic pursuit. Like PAUL DE MAN's "Resistance to Theory" (1982), which asserts theory's philosophical inevitability, "The Commitment to Theory" offers a staunch defense; but unlike de Man, Bhabha argues for theory's political relevance.

While rooted in contemporary debates, "The Commitment to Theory" also takes part in the larger tradition of defenses of literary practices, which starts with ARISTOTLE's defense of poetry in the *Poetics* (see above) and extends to nineteenth- and twentieth-century defenses of criticism, such as OSCAR WILDE's claims for the artistic value of criticism, "The Critic as Artist" (1890; see above), and JOHN CROWE RANSOM's argument for the value of professional criticism, "Criticism, Inc." (1938; see above). Such works shield literature and criticism against accusations that they lack utility, social relevance, and moral good. Bhabha updates the tradition by declaring the political efficacy of literary theory.

This debate continues to the present day, and Bhabha has frequently been criticized for his embrace of theory at the expense of practice, his dense jargon, and his copiously allusive writing style. His sharpest critics have come from the left, taking to task his view of politics as textual. In particular, the Marxist critic Aijaz Ahmad has criticized him for detaching politics from specific locations and political situations. Ahmad also upbraids him for ignoring class and caste, charging that Bhabha's concept of hybridity applies more aptly to privileged postcolonial intellectuals who have gained success in the Western world, like Bhabha himself, than to those in colonial situations. Other commentators, more concerned with theoretical consistency, have noted that the notion of a hybrid identity is too broad and amorphous, applying ultimately to all identities. But within the context of debates in postcolonial studies, the concept of hybridity has decisively altered thinking about nations and identities.

"The Commitment to Theory" Keywords: Deconstruction, Defense of Criticism, Hegemony, Nationhood, Postcolonial Theory, Poststructuralism, Race and Ethnicity Studies

The Commitment to Theory

I

There is a damaging and self-defeating assumption that theory is necessarily the elite language of the socially and culturally privileged. It is said that the place of the academic critic is inevitably within the Eurocentric archives of an imperialist or neo-colonial West. The Olympian realms of what is mistakenly labelled 'pure theory' are assumed to be eternally insulated from the historical exigencies and tragedies of the wretched of the earth.[1] Must we always polarize in order to polemicize? Are we trapped in a politics of struggle where the representation of social antagonisms and historical contradictions can take no other form than a binarism of theory vs politics? Can the aim of freedom of knowledge be the simple inversion of the relation of oppressor and oppressed, centre and periphery, negative image and positive image? Is our only way out of such dualism the espousal of an implacable oppositionality or the invention of an originary counter-myth of radical purity? Must the project of our liberationist aesthetics be forever part of a totalizing Utopian vision of Being and History that seeks to transcend the contradictions and ambivalences that constitute the very structure of human subjectivity and its systems of cultural representation?

Between what is represented as the 'larceny' and distortion of European 'metatheorizing' and the radical, engaged, activist experience of Third World creativity,[2] one can see the mirror image (albeit reversed in content and intention) of that ahistorical nineteenth-century polarity of Orient and

1. An allusion to *The Wretched of the Earth* (1961; see above), by the Martinique-born French psychoanalyst and postcolonial theorist FRANTZ FANON (1925–1961).

2. See C. Taylor, "Eurocentrics vs. New Thought at Edinburgh," *Framework* 34 (1987), for an illustration of this style of argument. See particularly footnote 1 (p. 148) for an exposition of his use of "larceny" ("the judicious distortion of African truths to fit western prejudices") [Bhabha's note]. Third World: "underdeveloped" nations, many of which were formerly colonies of "First World" nations (countries of the industrialized West).

Occident which, in the name of progress, unleashed the exclusionary imperialist ideologies of self and other. This time round, the term 'critical theory', often untheorized and unargued, is definitely the Other, an otherness that is insistently identified with the vagaries of the depoliticized Eurocentric critic. Is the cause of radical art or critique best served, for instance, by a fulminating professor of film who announces, at a flashpoint in the argument, 'We are not artists, we are political activists?' By obscuring the power of his own practice in the rhetoric of militancy, he fails to draw attention to the specific value of a politics of cultural production; because it makes the surfaces of cinematic signification the grounds of political intervention, it gives depth to the language of social criticism and extends the domain of 'politics' in a direction that will not be entirely dominated by the forces of economic or social control. Forms of popular rebellion and mobilization are often most subversive and transgressive when they are created through oppositional *cultural* practices.

Before I am accused of bourgeois voluntarism, liberal pragmatism, academicist pluralism and all the other '-isms' that are freely bandied about by those who take the most severe exception to 'Eurocentric' theoretic*ism* (Derrideanism, Lacanianism,[3] poststructuralism . . .), I would like to clarify the goals of my opening questions. I am convinced that, in the language of political economy, it is legitimate to represent the relations of exploitation and domination in the discursive division between the First and Third World, the North and the South. Despite the claims to a spurious rhetoric of 'internationalism' on the part of the established multinationals and the networks of the new communications technology industries, such circulations of signs and commodities as there are, are caught in the vicious circuits of surplus value that link First World capital to Third World labour markets through the chains of the international division of labour, and national comprador[4] classes. Gayatri Spivak is right to conclude that it is 'in the interest of capital to preserve the comprador theatre in a state of relatively primitive labour legislation and environmental regulation'.[5]

I am equally convinced that, in the language of international diplomacy, there is a sharp growth in a new Anglo-American nationalism which increasingly articulates its economic and military power in political acts that express a neo-imperialist disregard for the independence and autonomy of peoples and places in the Third World. Think of America's 'backyard' policy towards the Caribbean and Latin America, the patriotic gore and patrician lore of Britain's Falklands Campaign or, more recently, the triumphalism of the American and British forces during the Gulf War.[6] I am further convinced that such economic and political domination has a profound hegemonic influ-

3. The influential poststructuralist lines of thinking inspired by, respectively, the French deconstructive philosopher JACQUES DERRIDA (1930–2004) and the French psychoanalyst JACQUES LACAN (1901–1981).

4. Native intermediary employed by a European business to supervise native employees.

5. G. C. Spivak, *In Other Worlds* (London: Methuen, 1987), pp. 166–67 [Bhabha's note]. SPIVAK (b. 1942), U.S.-based Indian postcolonial theorist.

6. The international conflict (1990–91) triggered by Iraq's August 1990 invasion of oil-rich Kuwait; a U.S.-led coalition decisively defeated the Iraqi forces. The Falklands Campaign: a brief, undeclared war in 1982 between Great Britain and Argentina over control of the Falkland Islands (off the coast of Argentina), occupied and administered by the British since 1833; the ignominious defeat of the Argentine forces led to a landslide victory for Prime Minister Margaret Thatcher's Conservative Party in that year's parliamentary elections in Britain (and to the fall of the military government in Argentina the following year).

ence on the information orders of the Western world, its popular media and its specialized institutions and academics. So much is not in doubt.

What does demand further discussion is whether the 'new' languages of theoretical critique (semiotic, poststructuralist, deconstructionist and the rest) simply reflect those geopolitical divisions and their spheres of influence. Are the interests of 'Western' theory necessarily collusive with the hegemonic role of the West as a power bloc? Is the language of theory merely another power ploy of the culturally privileged Western elite to produce a discourse of the Other that reinforces its own power–knowledge equation?

A large film festival in the West—even an alternative or counter-cultural event such as Edinburgh's 'Third Cinema' Conference[7]—never fails to reveal the disproportionate influence of the West as cultural forum, in all three senses of that word: as place of public exhibition and discussion, as place of judgement, and as market-place. An Indian film about the plight of Bombay's pavement-dwellers wins the Newcastle Festival[8] which then opens up distribution facilities in India. The first searing exposé of the Bhopal disaster is made for Channel Four.[9] A major debate on the politics and theory of Third Cinema first appears in *Screen*, published by the British Film Institute. An archival article on the important history of neo-traditionalism and the 'popular' in Indian cinema sees the light of day in *Framework*.[1] Among the major contributors to the development of the Third Cinema as precept and practice are a number of Third World film-makers and critics who are exiles or *émigrés* in the West and live problematically, often dangerously, on the 'left' margins of a Eurocentric, bourgeois liberal culture. I don't think I need to add individual names or places, or detail the historical reasons why the West carries and exploits what Bourdieu[2] would call its symbolic capital. The condition is all too familiar, and it is not my purpose here to make those important distinctions between different national situations and the disparate political causes and collective histories of cultural exile. I want to take my stand on the shifting margins of cultural displacement—that confounds any profound or 'authentic' sense of a 'national' culture or an 'organic' intellectual[3]—and ask what the function of a committed theoretical perspective might be, once the cultural and historical hybridity of the postcolonial world is taken as the paradigmatic place of departure.

Committed to what? At this stage in the argument, I do not want to identify any specific 'object' of political allegiance—the Third World, the working

7. A showcase for films by Latin American, African, Middle Eastern, and Asian filmmakers at the Edinburgh International Film Festival; Bhabha is referring to the 40th festival (August 11–13, 1986).

8. Arts festival in northeastern England.

9. A British commercially supported network, created in 1982 and intended to increase the representation of minorities on television; it is known for high-quality dramas and documentaries. "Bhopal disaster": the leakage of tons of poisonous gas in December 1984 from a pesticide plant in central India owned by Union Carbide, a U.S. multinational, which was one of the worst industrial disasters in history; thousands died and tens (perhaps hundreds) of thousands were injured.

1. See T. H. Gabriel, "Teaching Third World Cinema," and Julianne Burton, "The Politics of Aesthetic Distance—Sao Bernando," both in *Screen* 24.2 (1983), and A. Rajadhyaksha, "Neo-traditionalism: Film as Popular Art in India," *Framework*, nos. 32/33 (1986) [Bhabha's note].

2. Pierre Bourdieu (1930–2002), French sociologist; one of his key terms is "symbolic capital," the tools used by individuals and institutions within a given environment to gain dominance and thus to reproduce themselves over time.

3. Someone (regardless of profession) who directs the ideas and aspirations of the particular social class to which he or she "organically" belongs, as described by the Italian Marxist theorist Antonio Gramsci (1891–1937). "National culture": a term associated with Fanon.

class, the feminist struggle. Although such an objectification of political activity is crucial and must significantly inform political debate, it is not the only option for those critics or intellectuals who are committed to progressive political change in the direction of a socialist society. It is a sign of political maturity to accept that there are many forms of political writing whose different effects are obscured when they are divided between the 'theoretical' and the 'activist'. It is not as if the leaflet involved in the organization of a strike is short on theory, while a speculative article on the theory of ideology ought to have more practical examples or applications. They are both forms of discourse and to that extent they produce rather than reflect their objects of reference. The difference between them lies in their operational qualities. The leaflet has a specific expository and organizational purpose, temporally bound to the event; the theory of ideology makes its contribution to those embedded political ideas and principles that inform the right to strike. The latter does not justify the former; nor does it necessarily precede it. It exists side by side with it—the one as an enabling part of the other—like the recto and verso of a sheet of paper, to use a common semiotic analogy in the uncommon context of politics.

My concern here is with the process of 'intervening ideologically', as Stuart Hall describes the role of 'imagining' or representation in the practice of politics in his response to the British election of 1987.[4] For Hall, the notion of hegemony implies a politics of *identification* of the imaginary.[5] This occupies a discursive space which is not exclusively delimited by the history of either the right or the left. It exists somehow in-between these political polarities, and also between the familiar divisions of theory and political practice. This approach, as I read it, introduces us to an exciting, neglected moment, or movement, in the 'recognition' of the relation of politics to theory; and confounds the traditional division between them. Such a movement is initiated if we see that relation as determined by the rule of repeatable materiality, which Foucault describes as the process by which statements from one institution can be transcribed in the discourse of another.[6] Despite the schemata of use and application that constitute a field of stabilization for the statement, any change in the statement's conditions of use and reinvestment, any alteration in its field of experience or verification, or indeed any difference in the problems to be solved, can lead to the emergence of a new statement: the difference of the same.

In what hybrid forms, then, may a politics of the theoretical statement emerge? What tensions and ambivalences mark this engimatic place from which theory speaks? Speaking in the name of some counter-authority or horizon of 'the true' (in Foucault's sense of the strategic effects of any apparatus or *dispositif*[7]), the theoretical enterprise has to represent the adversarial authority (of power and/or knowledge) which, in a doubly inscribed move, it simultaneously seeks to subvert and replace. In this complicated

4. S. Hall, "Blue Election, Election Blues," *Marxism Today*, July 1987, pp. 30–35 [Bhabha's note]. HALL (1932–2014), a leading figure in British cultural studies.
5. The notion of hegemony—the manufactured consent that legitimates a dominant group and unifies a society—derives from Gramsci.
6. M. Foucault, *The Archaeology of Knowledge*, [trans. A. M. Sheridan] (London: Tavistock, 1972), pp. 102–5 [Bhabha's note]. MICHEL FOUCAULT (1926–1984), French philosopher and historian of ideas.
7. Apparatus, device (French).

formulation I have tried to indicate something of the boundary and location of the event of theoretical critique which does not *contain* the truth (in polar opposition to totalitarianism, 'bourgeois liberalism' or whatever is supposed to repress it). The 'true' is always marked and informed by the ambivalence of the process of emergence itself, the productivity of meanings that construct counter-knowledges *in medias res,* in the very act of agonism,[8] within the terms of a negotiation (rather than a negation) of oppositional and antagonistic elements. Political positions are not simply identifiable as progressive or reactionary, bourgeois or radical, prior to the act of *critique engagée,*[9] or outside the terms and conditions of their discursive address. It is in this sense that the historical moment of political action must be thought of as part of the history of the form of its writing. This is not to state the obvious, that there is no knowledge—political or otherwise—outside representation. It is to suggest that the dynamics of writing and textuality require us to rethink the logics of causality and determinacy through which we recognize the 'political' as a form of calculation and strategic action dedicated to social transformation.

'What is to be done?'[1] must acknowledge the force of writing, its metaphoricity and its rhetorical discourse, as a productive matrix which defines the 'social' and makes it available as an objective of and for, action. Textuality is not simply a second-order ideological expression or a verbal symptom of a pre-given political subject. That the political subject—as indeed the subject of politics—is a discursive event is nowhere more clearly seen than in a text which has been a formative influence on Western democratic and socialist discourse—Mill's essay 'On Liberty'.[2] His crucial chapter, 'On The Liberty of Thought and Discussion', is an attempt to define political judgement as the problem of finding a form of *public rhetoric* able to represent different and opposing political 'contents' not as a priori preconstituted principles but as a dialogical discursive exchange; a negotiation of terms in the on-going present of the enunciation of the political statement. What is unexpected is the suggestion that a crisis of identification is initiated in the textual performance that displays a certain 'difference' *within* the signification of any single political system, prior to establishing the substantial differences *between* political beliefs. A knowledge can only become political through an agonistic process: dissensus, alterity and otherness are the discursive conditions for the circulation and recognition of a politicized subject and a public 'truth':

> [If] opponents of all important truths do not exist, it is indispensable to imagine them . . . [He] must feel the whole force of the difficulty which the true view of the subject has to encounter and dispose of; *else he will never really possess himself of the portion of truth which meets and removes that difficulty*. . . . Their conclusion may be true, but it might be false for anything they know: they have never thrown themselves into the *mental position* of those who think differently from them . . . and consequently

8. Combat, contest. *In medias res*: in the middle of things (Latin); usually, in the midst of a narrative.
9. Engaged criticism (French), a term associated with the French philosopher, playwright, and political activist Jean-Paul Sartre (1905–1980).
1. The title of a famous 1902 pamphlet by the Russian Marxist revolutionary V. I. Lenin.
2. Published in 1859 by the English philosopher and social reformer John Stuart Mill (1806–1873).

> they do not, in any proper sense of the word, *know the doctrine which they themselves profess.*[3] (My emphases)

It is true that Mill's 'rationality' permits, or requires, such forms of contention and contradiction in order to enhance his vision of the inherently progressive and evolutionary bent of *human* judgement. (This makes it possible for contradictions to be resolved and also generates a sense of the 'whole truth' which reflects the natural, organic bent of the human mind.) It is also true that Mill always reserves, in society as in his argument, the unreal neutral space of the Third Person as the representative of the 'people', who witnesses the debate from an 'epistemological distance' and draws a reasonable conclusion. Even so, in his attempt to describe the political as a form of debate and dialogue—as the process of public rhetoric—that is crucially mediated through this ambivalent and antagonistic faculty of a political 'imagination', Mill exceeds the usual mimetic sense of the battle of ideas. He suggests something much more dialogical: the realization of the political idea at the ambivalent point of textual address, its emergence through a form of political projection.

Rereading Mill through the stategies of 'writing' that I have suggested, reveals that one cannot passively follow the line of argument running through the logic of the opposing ideology. The textual process of political antagonism initiates a contradictory process of reading between the lines; the agent of the discourse becomes, in the same time of utterance, the inverted, projected object of the argument, turned against itself. It is, Mill insists, only by effectively assuming the mental position of the antagonist and working through the displacing and decentring force of that discursive difficulty that the politicized 'portion of truth' is produced. This is a different dynamic from the ethic of tolerance in liberal ideology which has to imagine opposition in order to contain it and demonstrate its enlightened relativism or humanism. Reading Mill, against the grain, suggests that politics can only become representative, a truly public discourse, through a splitting in the signification of the subject of representation; through an ambivalence at the point of the enunciation of a politics.

I have chosen to demonstrate the importance of the space of writing, and the problematic of address, at the very heart of the liberal tradition because it is here that the myth of the 'transparency' of the human agent and the reasonableness of political action is most forcefully asserted. Despite the more radical political alternatives of the right and the left, the popular, commonsense view of the place of the individual in relation to the social is still substantially thought and lived in ethical terms moulded by liberal beliefs. What the attention to rhetoric and writing reveals is the discursive ambivalence that makes 'the political' possible. From such a perspective, the problematic of political judgement cannot be represented as an epistemological problem of appearance and reality or theory and practice or word and thing. Nor can it be represented as a dialectical problem or a symptomatic contradiction constitutive of the materiality of the 'real'. On the contrary, we are made excruciatingly aware of the ambivalent juxtaposition, the dangerous interstitial relation of the factual and the projective, and, beyond that, of the crucial

3. J. S. Mill, "On Liberty," in *Utilitarianism, Liberty, Representative Government* (London: Dent and Sons, 1972), pp. 93–94 [Bhabha's note].

function of the textual and the rhetorical. It is those vicissitudes of the movement of the signifier,[4] in the fixing of the factual and the closure of the real, that ensure the efficacy of stategic thinking in the discourses of *Realpolitik*. It is this to-and-fro, this *fort/da*[5] of the symbolic process of political negotiation, that constitutes a politics of address. Its importance goes beyond the unsettling of the essentialism or logocentricism of a received political tradition, in the name of an abstract free play of the signifier.[6]

A critical discourse does not yield a *new* political object, or aim, or knowledge, which is simply a mimetic reflection of an a priori political principle or theoretical commitment. We should not demand of it a pure teleology of analysis whereby the prior principle is simply augmented, its rationality smoothly developed, its identity as socialist or materialist (as opposed to neo-imperialist or humanist) consistently confirmed in each oppositional stage of the argument. Such identikit[7] political idealism may be the gesture of great individual fervour, but it lacks the deeper, if dangerous, sense of what is entailed by the *passage* of history in theoretical discourse. The language of critique is effective not because it keeps forever separate the terms of the master and the slave,[8] the mercantilist and the Marxist, but to the extent to which it overcomes the given grounds of opposition and opens up a space of translation: a place of hybridity, figuratively speaking, where the construction of a political object that is new, *neither the one nor the other*, properly alienates our political expectations, and changes, as it must, the very forms of our recognition of the moment of politics. The challenge lies in conceiving of the time of political action and understanding as opening up a space that can accept and regulate the differential structure of the moment of intervention without rushing to produce a unity of the social antagonism or contradiction. This is a sign that history is *happening*—within the pages of theory, within the systems and structures we construct to figure the passage of the historical.

When I talk of *negotiation* rather than *negation*, it is to convey a temporality that makes it possible to conceive of the articulation of antagonistic or contradictory elements: a dialectic without the emergence of a teleological or transcendent History,[9] and beyond the prescriptive form of symptomatic reading where the nervous tics on the surface of ideology reveal the 'real materialist contradiction' that History embodies. In such a discursive temporality, the event of theory becomes the *negotiation* of contradictory and antagonistic instances that open up hybrid sites and objectives of struggle, and

4. The symbol or sound that conveys meaning (what is conveyed is the signified), as described in the analysis of signs by the Swiss linguist Ferdinand de Saussure (1857–1913).

5. Gone/here (German). In *Beyond the Pleasure Principle* (1920), Sigmund Freud describes how his 18-month-old nephew would throw a spool tied to a piece of yarn, saying "Fort," and then pull it back in, saying "Da"; for Freud this game was a way for the child to work out his anxiety about his mother's absence. In "The Mirror Stage" (1949; see above), Lacan argues that the game is about the child's entry into the Symbolic (the structure of language itself).

6. "The free play of the signifier," like "logocentrism" (the privileging of speech, the assumption that knowledge is organized around some central Truth), is a concept developed by Jacques Derrida in *Of Grammatology* (1967).

7. Likeness of a person's face constructed from descriptions (used by the police to help identify a suspect).

8. An allusion to the Master-Slave dialectic developed by the German philosopher Georg Friedrich Wilhelm Hegel in *Phenomenology of Spirit* (1807; see above), which describes two self-consciousnesses that confront each other and fight for mutual recognition; each identifies him- or herself through the eyes of the other as ruler and ruled.

9. That is, a process of change through contest of opposites that—unlike in the systems of Hegel or the German political and economic theorist Karl Marx (1818–1883), in which the dialectic plays a key role—does not necessarily lead to a predetermined end.

destroy those negative polarities between knowledge and its objects, and between theory and practical-political reason.[1] If I have argued against a primordial and previsionary division of right or left, progressive or reactionary, it has been only to stress the fully historical and discursive *différance*[2] between them. I would not like my notion of negotiation to be confused with some syndicalist sense of reformism because that is not the political level that is being explored here. By negotiation I attempt to draw attention to the structure of *iteration*[3] which informs political movements that attempt to articulate antagonistic and oppositional elements without the redemptive rationality of sublation or transcendence.[4]

The temporality of negotiation or translation, as I have sketched it, has two main advantages. First, it acknowledges the historical connectedness between the subject and object of critique so that there can be no simplistic, essentialist opposition between ideological miscognition and revolutionary truth. The progressive reading is crucially determined by the adversarial or agonistic situation itself; it is effective because it uses the subversive, messy mask of camouflage and does not come like a pure avenging angel speaking the truth of a radical historicity and pure oppositionality. If one is aware of this heterogeneous emergence (not origin) of radical critique, then—and this is my second point—the function of theory within the political process becomes double-edged. It makes us aware that our political referents and priorities—the people, the community, class struggle, anti-racism, gender difference, the assertion of an anti-imperialist, black or third perspective—are not there in some primordial, naturalistic sense. Nor do they reflect a unitary or homogeneous political object. They make sense as they come to be constructed in the discourse of feminism or Marxism or the Third Cinema[5] or whatever, whose objects of priority—class or sexuality or 'the new ethnicity'—are always in historical and philosophical tension, or cross-reference with other objectives.

Indeed, the whole history of socialist thought which seeks to 'make it new and better' seems to be a different process of articulating priorities whose political objects can be recalcitrant and contradictory. Within contemporary Marxism, for example, witness the continual tension between the English, humanist, labourist faction and the 'theoreticist', structuralist, new left tendencies. Within feminism, there is again a marked difference of emphasis between the psychoanalytic/semiotic tradition and the Marxist articulation of gender and class through a theory of cultural and ideological interpellation.[6] I have presented these differences in broad brush-strokes, often using the language of polemic to suggest that each position is always a process of

1. For a significant elaboration of a similar argument, see E. Laclau and C. Mouffe, *Hegemony and Socialist Strategy*, [trans. W. Moore and P. Cammack] (London: Verso, 1985), chap. 3 [Bhabha's note]. Ernesto Laclau (1935–2014), Argentine political theorist, and his wife Chantal Mouffe (b. 1943), Belgian political theorist, are known for their elaboration of "post-Marxism."

2. Derrida's term, drawing on the two senses of the French verb *différer*, that combines spatial difference and temporal deferral.

3. Repetition; Derrida applies the term to the repetitious structure of signification.

4. For a philosophical underpinning of some of the concepts I am proposing here see R. Gasché, *The Tain of the Mirror* (Cambridge, Mass.: Harvard University Press, 1986) [Bhabha's note]. "Sublation": in Hegel, the negation but partial incorporation of an element in the dialectic process.

5. A movement calling for political, anticolonial filmmaking in the third world, independent of commercial models; it began in Latin America in the late 1960s.

6. The term used by the French Marxist philosopher LOUIS ALTHUSSER (1918–1990) to refer to how ideology "hails" or creates individuals as subjects, in "Ideology and Ideological State Apparatuses" (1970; see above).

translation and transference of meaning. Each objective is constructed on the trace of that perspective that it puts under erasure; each political object is determined in relation to the other, and displaced in that critical act. Too often these theoretical issues are peremptorily transposed into organizational terms and represented as sectarianism. I am suggesting that such contradictions and conflicts, which often thwart political intentions and make the question of commitment complex and difficult, are rooted in the process of translation and displacement in which the object of politics is inscribed. The effect is not stasis or a sapping of the will. It is, on the contrary, the spur of the negotiation of socialist democratic politics and policies which demand that questions of organization are theorized and socialist theory is 'organized', *because there is no given community or body of the people whose inherent, radical historicity emits the right signs.*

This emphasis on the representation of the political, on the construction of discourse, is the radical contribution of the translation of theory. Its conceptual vigilance never allows a simple identity between the political objective and its means of representation. This emphasis on the necessity of heterogeneity and the double inscription of the political objective is not merely the repetition of a general truth about discourse introduced into the political field. Denying an essentialist logic and a mimetic referent to political representation is a strong, principled argument against political separatism of any colour, and cuts through the moralism that usually accompanies such claims. There is literally, and figuratively, no space for the unitary or organic political objective which would offend against the sense of a socialist *community* of interest and articulation.

In Britain, in the 1980s, no political struggle was fought more powerfully, and sustained more poignantly, on the values and traditions of a socialist community than the miners' strike of 1984–5.[7] The battalions of monetarist figures and forecasts on the profitability of the pits were starkly ranged against the most illustrious standards of the British labour movement, the most cohesive cultural communities of the working class. The choice was clearly between the dawning world of the new Thatcherite city gent and a long history of the working man, or so it seemed to the traditional left and the new right. In these class terms the mining women involved in the strike were applauded for the heroic supporting role they played, for their endurance and initiative. But the revolutionary impulse, it seemed, belonged securely to the working-class male. Then, to commemorate the first anniversary of the strike, Beatrix Campbell,[8] in the *Guardian*, interviewed a group of women who had been involved in the strike. It was clear that their experience of the historical struggle, their understanding of the historic choice to be made, was startlingly different and more complex. Their testimonies would not be contained simply or singly within the priorities of the politics of class or the histories of industrial struggle. Many of the women began to question their

7. A yearlong struggle, sometimes violent, between the United Kingdom's Conservative government and the National Union of Mineworkers, which went on strike after the government announced that it would close uneconomic coal pits; the union defeat capped Margaret Thatcher's efforts, begun when she became prime minister in 1979, to impose legal restrictions on British unions.

8. English journalist, feminist, and socialist (b. 1947); the *Guardian* is a major daily newspaper in England.

roles within the family and the community—the two central institutions which articulated the meanings and mores of the *tradition* of the labouring classes around which ideological battle was enjoined. Some challenged the symbols and authorities of the culture they fought to defend. Others disrupted the homes they had struggled to sustain. For most of them there was no return, no going back to the 'good old days'. It would be simplistic to suggest either that this considerable social change was a spin-off from the class struggle or that it was a repudiation of the politics of class from a socialist-feminist perspective. There is no simple political or social truth to be learned, for there is no unitary representation of a political agency, no fixed hierarchy of political values and effects.

My illustration attempts to display the importance of the hybrid moment of political change. Here the transformational value of change lies in the rearticulation, or translation, of elements that are *neither the One* (unitary working class) *nor the Other* (the politics of gender) *but something else besides*, which contests the terms and territories of both. There is a negotiation between gender and class, where each formation encounters the displaced, differentiated boundaries of its group representation and enunciative sites in which the limits and limitations of social power are encountered in an agonistic relation. When it is suggested that the British Labour Party should seek to produce a socialist alliance among progressive forces that are widely dispersed and distributed across a range of class, culture and occupational forces—without a unifying sense of the class for itself—the kind of hybridity that I have attempted to identify is being acknowledged as a historical necessity. We need a little less pietistic articulation of political principle (around class and nation); a little more of the principle of political *negotiation*.

This seems to be the theoretical issue at the heart of Stuart Hall's arguments for the construction of a counter-hegemonic power bloc through which a socialist party might construct its majority, its constituency; and the Labour Party might (in)conceivably improve its image. The unemployed, semi-skilled and unskilled, part-time workers, male and female, the low paid, black people, underclasses: these signs of the fragmentation of class and cultural consensus represent both the historical experience of contemporary social divisions, and a structure of heterogeneity upon which to construct a theoretical and political alternative. For Hall, the imperative is to construct a new social bloc of different constituencies, through the production of a form of symbolic identification that would result in a collective will. The Labour Party, with its desire to reinstate its traditionalist image—white, male, working class, trade union based—is not hegemonic enough, Hall writes. He is right; what remains unanswered is whether the rationalism and intentionality that propel the collective will are compatible with the language of symbolic image and fragmentary identification that represents, for Hall and for 'hegemony'/ 'counter-hegemony', the fundamental political issue. Can there ever be hegemony enough, except in the sense that a two-thirds majority will elect us a socialist government?

It is by intervening in Hall's argument that the necessities of negotiation are revealed. The interest of Hall's position lies in his acknowledgement, remarkable for the British left, that, though influential, 'material interests on their own have no necessary class belongingness.'[9] This has two significant effects. It enables Hall to see the agents of political change as discontinuous, divided subjects caught in conflicting interests and identities. Equally, at the historical level of a Thatcherite population, he asserts that divisive rather than solidary forms of identification are the rule, resulting in undecidabilities and aporia[1] of political judgement. What does a working woman put first? Which of her identities is the one that determines her political choices? The answers to such questions are defined, according to Hall, in the ideological definition of materialist interests; a process of symbolic identification achieved through a political technology of imaging that hegemonically produces a social bloc of the right or the left. Not only is the social bloc heterogeneous, but, as I see it, the work of hegemony is itself the process of iteration and differentiation. It depends on the production of alternative or antagonistic images that are always produced side by side and in competition with each other. It is this side-by-side nature, this partial presence, or metonymy of antagonism, and its effective significations, that give meaning (quite literally) to a politics of struggle *as the struggle of identifications* and the war of positions. It is therefore problematic to think of it as sublated into an image of the collective will.

Hegemony requires iteration and alterity to be effective, to be productive of politicized populations: the (non-homogeneous) symbolic–social bloc needs to represent itself in a solidary collective will—a modern image of the future—if those populations are to produce a progressive government. Both may be necessary but they do not easily follow from each other, for in each case the mode of representation and its temporality are different. The contribution of negotiation is to display the 'in-between' of this crucial argument; it is *not* self-contradictory but significantly performs, in the process of its discussion, the problems of judgement and identification that inform the political space of its enunciation.

For the moment, the act of negotiation will only be interrogatory. Can such split subjects and differentiated social movements, which display ambivalent and divided forms of identification, be represented in a collective will that distinctively echoes Gramsci's enlightenment inheritance and its rationalism?[2] How does the language of the will accommodate the vicissitudes of its representation, its construction through a symbolic majority where the have-nots identify themselves from the position of the haves? How do we construct a politics based on such a displacement of affect or strategic elaboration (Foucault), where political positioning is ambivalently grounded in an acting-out of political fantasies that require repeated passages across the differential boundaries between one symbolic bloc *and an other*, and the positions available to each? If such is the case, then how do we fix the counter-image of socialist hegemony to reflect the divided will, the fragmented population? If the policy of hegemony is, quite literally, *unsignifiable* without the metonymic representation of its agonistic and ambivalent structure of articulation, then how does the collective will stabilize and unify its address as an agency of *representation*, as representative of a people? How do we avoid the mixing

9. Hall, "Blue Election," p. 33 [Bhabha's note].

1. Difficulty, logical impasse (a term often used in deconstructive criticism to indicate the point in a text where inherent contradictions render interpretation undecidable).

2. I owe this point to Martin Thom [Bhabha's note].

or overlap of images, the split screen, the failure to synchronize sound and image? Perhaps we need to change the ocular language of the image in order to talk of the social and political identifications or representations of a people. It is worth noting that Laclau and Mouffe have turned to the language of textuality and discourse, to *différance* and enunciative modalities, in attempting to understand the structure of hegemony.[3] Paul Gilroy also refers to Bakhtin's theory of narrative when he describes the performance of black expressive cultures as an attempt to transform the relationship between performer and crowd 'in *dialogic* rituals so that spectators acquire the active role of participants in collective processes which are sometimes cathartic and which may symbolize or even create a community' (my emphasis).[4]

Such negotiations between politics and theory make it impossible to think of the place of the theoretical as a metanarrative claiming a more total form of generality. Nor is it possible to claim a certain familiar epistemological distance between the *time and place* of the intellectual and the activitist, as Fanon suggests when he observes that 'while politicians situate their action in actual present-day events, men of culture take their stand in the field of history'.[5] It is precisely that popular binarism between theory and politics, whose foundational basis is a view of knowledge as totalizing generality and everyday life as experience, subjectivity or false consciousness,[6] that I have tried to erase. It is a distinction that even Sartre subscribes to when he describes the committed intellectual as the theoretician of practical knowledge whose defining criterion is rationality and whose first project is to combat the irrationality of ideology.[7] From the perspective of negotiation and translation, *contra* Fanon and Sartre, there can be no final discursive *closure* of theory. It does not foreclose on the political, even though battles for power-knowledge[8] may be won or lost to great effect. The corollary is that there is no first or final act of revolutionary social (or socialist) transformation.

I hope it is clear that this erasure of the traditional boundary between theory/politics, and my resistance to the en-*closure* of the theoretical, whether it is read negatively as elitism or positively as radical supra-rationality, do not turn on the good or bad faith of the activist agent or the intellectual *agent provocateur.* I am primarily concerned with the conceptual structuring of the terms—the theoretical/the political—that inform a range of debates around the place and time of the committed intellectual. I have therefore argued for a certain relation to knowledge which I think is crucial in structuring our sense of what the *object* of theory may be in the act of determining our specific political *objectives*.

3. Laclau and Mouffe, *Hegemony and Socialist Strategy*, chap. 3 [Bhabha's note].
4. P. Gilroy, *There Ain't No Black in the Union Jack* (London: Hutchinson, 1987), p. 214 [Bhabha's note]. GILROY (b. 1956), British cultural critic. MIKHAIL M. BAKHTIN (1895–1975), Russian literary theorist and philosopher of language, associated with the "dialogic."
5. F. Fanon, *The Wretched of the Earth* (Harmondsworth: Penguin, 1967), p. 168 [Bhabha's note].
6. A Marxist term referring to an individual's tendency to view reality in ways congruent with the interests of the dominant orthodoxy rather than in ways that reflect his or her own class interest.
7. J.-P. Sartre, *Politics and Literature* [trans. J. A. Underwood, J. Calder] (London: Calder and Boyars, 1973), pp. 16–17 [Bhabha's note].
8. An allusion to the work of Foucault, which investigates the interrelation of political power and disciplines of knowledge.

II

What is at stake in the naming of critical theory as 'Western'? It is, obviously, a designation of institutional power and ideological Eurocentricity. Critical theory often engages with texts within the familiar traditions and conditions of colonial anthropology either to universalize their meaning within its own cultural and academic discourse, or to sharpen its internal critique of the Western logocentric sign, the idealist subject, or indeed the illusions and delusions of civil society. This is a familiar manoeuvre of theoretical knowledge, where, having opened up the chasm of cultural difference, a mediator or metaphor of otherness must be found to contain the effects of difference. In order to be institutionally effective as a discipline, the knowledge of cultural difference must be made to foreclose on the Other; difference and otherness thus become the fantasy of a certain cultural space or, indeed, the certainty of a form of theoretical knowledge that deconstructs the epistemological 'edge' of the West.

More significantly, the site of cultural difference can become the mere phantom of a dire disciplinary struggle in which it has no space or power. Montesquieu's Turkish Despot, Barthes's Japan, Kristeva's China, Derrida's Nambikwara Indians, Lyotard's Cashinahua pagans[9] are part of this strategy of containment where the Other text is forever the exegetical horizon of difference, never the active agent of articulation. The Other is cited, quoted, framed, illuminated, encased in the shot/reverse-shot strategy of a serial enlightenment. Narrative and the *cultural* politics of difference become the closed circle of interpretation. The Other loses its power to signify, to negate, to initiate its historic desire, to establish its own institutional and oppositional discourse. However impeccably the content of an 'other' culture may be known, however anti-ethnocentrically it is represented, it is its *location* as the closure of grand theories, the demand that, in analytic terms, it be always the good object of knowledge, the docile body of difference, that reproduces a relation of domination and is the most serious indictment of the institutional powers of critical theory.

There is, however, a distinction to be made between the institutional history of critical theory and its conceptual potential for change and innovation. Althusser's critique of the temporal structure of the Hegelian-Marxist expressive totality, despite its functionalist limitations, opens up the possibilities of thinking the relations of production in a time of differential histories. Lacan's location of the signifier of desire, on the cusp of language and the law, allows the elaboration of a form of social representation that is alive to the ambivalent structure of subjectivity and sociality. Foucault's archaeology of the emergence of modern, Western man as a problem of finitude, inextricable from its afterbirth, its Other, enables the linear, progressivist claims of the social

9. Bhabha gives examples of cultural others used by French cultural critics and philosophers to further their own arguments: Charles-Louis de Secondat, baron de la Brède et de Montesquieu (1689–1755), employs the "Turkish Despot" in his *Persian Letters* (1721), which satirizes French society; his observations on Japan, presented in *Empire of Signs* (1970), convinced ROLAND BARTHES (1915–1980) that some signs have no signified; JULIA KRISTEVA (b. 1941) treats China in *About Chinese Women* (1974); in *Of Grammatology*, Derrida finds in CLAUDE LÉVI-STRAUSS's anthropological descriptions of Brazil's Nambikwara in *Tristes Tropiques* (1955; see above) evidence of internal resistance to coercive naming practices; and JEAN-FRANÇOIS LYOTARD (1925–1998) discusses the storytelling of the tribal Cashinahua of Peru in *The Postmodern Condition* (1979).

sciences—the major imperializing discourses—to be confronted by their own historicist limitations. These arguments and modes of analysis can be dismissed as internal squabbles around Hegelian causality, psychic representation or sociological theory. Alternatively, they can be subjected to a translation, a transformation of value as part of the questioning of the project of modernity in the great, revolutionary tradition of C. L. R. James—*contra* Trotsky[1] or Fanon, *contra* phenomenology and existentialist psychoanalysis. In 1952, it was Fanon who suggested that an oppositional, differential reading of Lacan's Other might be more relevant for the colonial condition than the Marxisant[2] reading of the master-slave dialectic.

It may be possible to produce such a translation or transformation if we understand the tension within critical theory between its institutional containment and its revisionary force. The continual reference to the horizon of other cultures which I have mentioned earlier is ambivalent. It is a site of citation, but it is also a sign that such critical theory cannot forever sustain its position in the academy as the adversarial cutting edge of Western idealism. What is required is to demonstrate another territory of translation, another testimony of analytical argument, a different engagement in the politics of and around cultural domination. What this other site for theory might be will become clearer if we first see that many poststructuralist ideas are themselves opposed to Enlightenment humanism and aesthetics. They constitute no less than a deconstruction of the moment of the modern, its legal values, its literary tastes, its philosophical and political categorical imperatives. Secondly, and more importantly, we must rehistoricize the moment of 'the emergence of the sign', or 'the question of the subject', or the 'discursive construction of social reality' to quote a few popular topics of contemporary theory. This can only happen if we relocate the referential and institutional demands of such theoretical work in the field of cultural difference—*not cultural diversity*.

Such a reorientation may be found in the historical texts of the colonial moment in the late eighteenth and early nineteenth centuries. For at the same time as the question of cultural difference emerged in the colonial text, discourses of civility were defining the doubling moment of the emergence of Western modernity. Thus the political and theoretical genealogy of modernity lies not only in the origins of the *idea* of civility, but in this history of the colonial moment. It is to be found in the resistance of the colonized populations to the Word of God and Man—Christianity and the English language. The transmutations and translations of indigenous traditions in their opposition to colonial authority demonstrate how the desire of the signifier, the indeterminacy of intertextuality, can be deeply engaged in the postcolonial struggle against dominant relations of power and knowledge. In the following words of the missionary master we hear, quite distinctly, the oppositional voices of a culture of resistance; but we also hear the uncertain and threatening process of cultural transformation. I quote from A. Duff's[3] influential *India and India Missions* (1839):

1. Leon Trotsky (1879–1940), Russian Marxist revolutionary and theorist. James (1901–1989), Trinidadian political activist and critic of colonialism.
2. Marxism-influenced. Bhabha is referring to Fanon's *Black Skin, White Masks* (1952; see above).
3. Alexander Duff (1806–1878), Scottish missionary to India from the Free Church of Scotland.

> Come to some doctrine which you believe to be peculiar to Revelation; tell the people that they must be regenerated or born again, else they can never 'see God'. Before you are aware, they may go away saying, 'Oh, there is nothing new or strange here; our own Shastras[4] tell us the same thing; we know and believe that we must be born again; it is our fate to be so.' But what do they understand by the expression? It is that they are to be born again and again, in some other form, agreeably to their own system of transmigration or reiterated births. To avoid the appearance of countenancing so absurd and pernicious a doctrine, you vary your language, and tell them that there must be a second birth—that they must be twice-born. Now it so happens that this, and all similar phraseology, is preoccupied. The sons of a Brahman have to undergo various purificatory and initiatory ceremonial rites, before they attain to full Brahmanhood. The last of these is the investiture with the sacred thread; which is followed by the communication of the Gayatri, or most sacred verse in the Vedas. This ceremonial constitutes, 'religiously and metaphorically, their second birth'; henceforward their distinctive and peculiar appellation is that of the twice-born, or regenerated men. *Hence it is your improved language might only convey the impression that all must become perfect Brahmans, ere they can 'see God'.*[5] (My emphasis)

The grounds of evangelical certitude are opposed not by the simple assertion of an antagonistic cultural tradition. The process of translation is the opening up of another contentious political and cultural site at the heart of colonial representation. Here the word of divine authority is deeply flawed by the assertion of the indigenous sign, and in the very practice of domination the language of the master becomes hybrid—neither the one thing nor the other. The incalculable colonized subject—half acquiescent, half oppositional, always untrustworthy—produces an unresolvable problem of cultural difference for the very address of colonial cultural authority. The 'subtile system of Hinduism', as the missionaries in the early nineteenth century called it, generated tremendous policy implications for the institutions of Christian conversion. The written authority of the Bible was challenged and together with it a postenlightenment notion of the 'evidence of Christianity' and its historical priority, which was central to evangelical colonialism. The Word could no longer be trusted to carry the truth when written or spoken in the colonial world by the European missionary. Native catechists therefore had to be found, who brought with them their own cultural and political ambivalences and contradictions, often under great pressure from their families and communities.

This revision of the history of critical theory rests, I have said, on the notion of cultural difference, not cultural diversity. Cultural diversity is an epistemological object—culture as an object of empirical knowledge—whereas cultural difference is the process of the *enunciation* of culture as 'knowledge*able*', authoritative, adequate to the construction of systems of cultural identifica-

4. Sutras, or precepts summarizing Vedic teachings; the Vedas are the sacred literature of Hinduism.

5. Rev. A. Duff, *India and India Missions: Including Sketches of the Gigantic System of Hinduism* (Edinburgh: John Johnstone; London: John Hunter, 1839), p. 560 [Bhabha's note].

tion. If cultural diversity is a category of comparative ethics, aesthetics or ethnology, cultural difference is a process of signification through which statements *of* culture or *on* culture differentiate, discriminate and authorize the production of fields of force, reference, applicability and capacity. Cultural diversity is the recognition of pre-given cultural contents and customs; held in a time-frame of relativism it gives rise to liberal notions of multiculturalism, cultural exchange or the culture of humanity. Cultural diversity is also the representation of a radical rhetoric of the separation of totalized cultures that live unsullied by the intertextuality of their historical locations, safe in the Utopianism of a mythic memory of a unique collective identity. Cultural diversity may even emerge as a system of the articulation and exchange of cultural signs in certain early structuralist accounts of anthropology.

Through the concept of cultural difference I want to draw attention to the common ground and lost territory of contemporary critical debates. For they all recognize that the problem of cultural interaction emerges only at the significatory boundaries of cultures, where meanings and values are (mis)read or signs are misappropriated. Culture only emerges as a problem, or a problematic, at the point at which there is a loss of meaning in the contestation and articulation of everyday life, between classes, genders, races, nations. Yet the reality of the limit or limit-text of culture is rarely theorized outside of well-intentioned moralist polemics against prejudice and stereotype, or the blanket assertion of individual or institutional racism—that describe the effect rather than the structure of the problem. The need to think the limit of culture as a problem of the enunciation of cultural difference is disavowed.

The concept of cultural difference focuses on the problem of the ambivalence of cultural authority: the attempt to dominate in the *name* of a cultural supremacy which is itself produced only in the moment of differentiation. And it is the very authority of culture as a knowledge of referential truth which is at issue in the concept and moment of *enunciation*. The enunciative process introduces a split in the performative present of cultural identification; a split between the traditional culturalist demand for a model, a tradition, a community, a stable system of reference, and the necessary negation of the certitude in the articulation of new cultural demands, meanings, strategies in the political present, as a practice of domination, or resistance. The struggle is often between the historicist teleological or mythical time and narrative of traditionalism—of the right or the left—and the shifting, strategically displaced time of the articulation of a historical politics of negotiation which I suggested above. The time of liberation is, as Fanon powerfully evokes, a time of cultural uncertainty, and, most crucially, of significatory or representational undecidability:

> But [native intellectuals] forget that the forms of thought and what [they] feed . . . on, together with modern techniques of information, language and dress, have dialectically reorganized the people's intelligences and *the constant principles (of national art)* which acted as safeguards during the colonial period are now undergoing extremely radical changes. . . . [We] must join the people in that fluctuating movement which they are *just* giving a shape to . . . which will be the signal for

> everything to be called into question . . . it is to the zone of *occult instability* where the people dwell that we must come.[6] (My emphases)

The enunciation of cultural difference problematizes the binary division of past and present, tradition and modernity, at the level of cultural representation and its authoritative address. It is the problem of how, in signifying the present, something comes to be repeated, relocated and translated in the name of tradition, in the guise of a pastness that is not necessarily a faithful sign of historical memory but a strategy of representing authority in terms of the artifice of the archaic. That iteration negates our sense of the origins of the struggle. It undermines our sense of the homogenizing effects of cultural symbols and icons, by questioning our sense of the authority of cultural synthesis in general.

This demands that we rethink our perspective on the identity of culture. Here Fanon's passage—somewhat reinterpreted—may be helpful. What is implied by his juxtaposition of the constant national principles with his view of culture-as-political-struggle, which he so enigmatically and beautifully describes as 'the zone of occult instability where the people dwell'? These ideas not only help to explain the nature of colonial struggle; they also suggest a possible critique of the positive aesthetic and political values we ascribe to the unity or totality of cultures, especially those that have known long and tyrannical histories of domination and misrecognition. Cultures are never unitary in themselves, nor simply dualistic in the relation of Self to Other. This is not because of some humanistic nostrum that beyond individual cultures we all belong to the human culture of mankind; nor is it because of an ethical relativism which suggests that in our cultural capacity to speak of and judge others we necessarily 'place ourselves in their position', in a kind of relativism of distance of which Bernard Williams has written at length.[7]

The reason a cultural text or system of meaning cannot be sufficient unto itself is that the act of cultural enunciation—the *place of utterance*—is crossed by the *différance* of writing. This has less to do with what anthropologists might describe as varying attitudes to symbolic systems within different cultures than with the structure of symbolic representation itself—not the content of the symbol or its social function, but the structure of symbolization. It is this difference in the process of language that is crucial to the production of meaning and ensures, at the same time, that meaning is never simply mimetic and transparent.

The linguistic difference that informs any cultural performance is dramatized in the common semiotic account of the disjuncture between the subject of a proposition (*énoncé*) and the subject of enunciation, which is not represented in the statement but which is the acknowledgement of its discursive embeddedness and address, its cultural positionality, its reference to a present time and a specific space. The pact of interpretation is never simply an act of communication between the I and the You designated in the statement. The production of meaning requires that these two places be mobilized in the passage through a Third Space, which represents both the general condi-

6. Fanon, *The Wretched of the Earth*, pp. 182–83 [Bhabha's note].

7. B. Williams, *Ethics and the Limits of Philosophy* (London: Fontana, 1985), chap. 9 [Bhabha's note]. Williams (1929–2003), English moral philosopher.

tions of language and the specific implication of the utterance in a performative and institutional strategy of which it cannot 'in itself' be conscious. What this unconscious relation introduces is an ambivalence in the act of interpretation. The pronominal I of the proposition cannot be made to address—in its own words—the subject of enunciation, for this is not personable, but remains a spatial relation within the schemata and strategies of discourse. The meaning of the utterance is quite literally neither the one nor the other. This ambivalence is emphasized when we realize that there is no way that the content of the proposition will reveal the structure of its positionality; no way that context can be mimetically read off from the content.

The implication of this enunciative split for cultural analysis that I especially want to emphasize is its temporal dimension. The splitting of the subject of enunciation destroys the logics of synchronicity and evolution which traditionally authorize the subject of cultural knowledge. It is often taken for granted in materialist and idealist problematics that the value of culture as an object of study, and the value of any analytic activity that is considered cultural, lie in a capacity to produce a cross-referential, generalizable unity that signifies a progression or evolution of ideas-in-time, as well as a critical self-reflection on their premisses or determinants. It would not be relevant to pursue the detail of this argument here except to demonstrate—via Marshall Sahlins's *Culture and Practical Reason*—the validity of my general characterization of the Western expectation of culture as a disciplinary practice of writing. I quote Sahlins at the point at which he attempts to define the difference of Western bourgeois culture:

> We have to do not so much with functional dominance as with structural—with different structures of symbolic *integration*. And to this gross difference in design correspond differences in symbolic performance: between an *open, expanding* code, responsive by *continuous* permutation to events it has itself staged, and an apparently *static* one that seems to know not events, but only its own preconceptions. The gross distinction between 'hot' societies and 'cold', development and underdevelopment, societies with and without history—and so between large societies and small, expanding and self-contained, colonizing and colonized.[8] (My emphases)

The intervention of the Third Space of enunciation, which makes the structure of meaning and reference an ambivalent process, destroys this mirror of representation in which cultural knowledge is customarily revealed as an integrated, open, expanding code. Such an intervention quite properly challenges our sense of the historical identity of culture as a homogenizing, unifying force, authenticated by the originary Past, kept alive in the national tradition of the People. In other words, the disruptive temporality of enunciation displaces the narrative of the Western nation which Benedict Anderson so perceptively describes as being written in homogeneous, serial time.[9]

8. M. Sahlins, *Culture and Practical Reason* (Chicago: University of Chicago Press, 1976), p. 211 [Bhabha's note]. Sahlins (b. 1930), American anthropologist.

9. B. Anderson, *Imagined Communities* (London: Verso, 1983), chap. 1 [Bhabha's note]. ANDERSON (1936–2015), American-based British historian; for *Imagined Communities*, see above.

It is only when we understand that all cultural statements and systems are constructed in this contradictory and ambivalent space of enunciation, that we begin to understand why hierarchical claims to the inherent originality or 'purity' of cultures are untenable, even before we resort to empirical historical instances that demonstrate their hybridity. Fanon's vision of revolutionary cultural and political change as a 'fluctuating movement' of occult instability could not be articulated as cultural *practice* without an acknowledgement of this indeterminate space of the subject(s) of enunciation. It is that Third Space, though unrepresentable in itself, which constitutes the discursive conditions of enunciation that ensure that the meaning and symbols of culture have no primordial unity or fixity; that even the same signs can be appropriated, translated, rehistoricized and read anew.

Fanon's moving metaphor—when reinterpreted for a theory of cultural signification—enables us to see not only the necessity of theory, but also the restrictive notions of cultural identity with which we burden our visions of political change. For Fanon, the liberatory people who initiate the productive instability of revolutionary cultural change are themselves the bearers of a hybrid identity. They are caught in the discontinuous time of translation and negotiation, in the sense in which I have been attempting to recast these words. In the moment of liberatory struggle, the Algerian people destroy the continuities and constancies of the nationalist tradition which provided a safeguard against colonial cultural imposition. They are now free to negotiate and translate their cultural identities in a discontinuous intertextual temporality of cultural difference. The native intellectual who identifies the people with the true national culture will be disappointed. The people are now the very principle of 'dialectical reorganization' and they construct their culture from the national text translated into modern Western forms of information technology, language, dress. The changed political and historical site of enunciation transforms the meanings of the colonial inheritance into the liberatory signs of a free people of the future.

> I have been stressing a certain void or misgiving attending every assimilation of contraries—I have been stressing this in order to expose what seems to me a fantastic mythological congruence of elements. . . . And if indeed therefore any real sense is to be made of material change it can only occur with an acceptance of a concurrent void and with a willingness to descend into that void wherein, as it were, one may begin to come into confrontation with a spectre of invocation whose freedom to participate in an alien territory and wilderness has become a necessity for one's reason or salvation.[1]

This meditation by the great Guyanese writer Wilson Harris on the void of misgiving in the textuality of colonial history reveals the cultural and historical dimension of that Third Space of enunciations which I have made the precondition for the articulation of cultural difference. He sees it as accompanying the 'assimilation of contraries' and creating that occult instability which presages powerful cultural changes. It is significant that the productive capacities of this Third Space have a colonial or postcolonial provenance. For

1. W. Harris, *Tradition, the Writer, and Society* (London: New Beacon, 1973), pp. 60–63 [Bhabha's note].

a willingness to descend into that alien territory—where I have led you—may reveal that the theoretical recognition of the split-space of enunciation may open the way to conceptualizing an *inter*national culture, based not on the exoticism of multiculturalism or the *diversity* of cultures, but on the inscription and articulation of culture's *hybridity*. To that end we should remember that it is the 'inter'—the cutting edge of translation and negotiation, the *in-between* space—that carries the burden of the meaning of culture. It makes it possible to begin envisaging national, anti-nationalist histories of the 'people'. And by exploring this Third Space, we may elude the politics of polarity and emerge as the others of our selves.

1989

LENNARD J. DAVIS
b. 1949

The 1980s and early 1990s saw the rise of identity studies, as critics emphasized the diverse ways that race, class, gender, ethnicity, sexuality, and location shape our identities. Yet Lennard J. Davis pointed to a significant gap in this critical turn; as he charges in his book *Enforcing Normalcy: Disability, Deafness, and the Body* (1995), disability was largely ignored, if not "relegated to a sideshow, a freak show at that, far away from the academic midway of progressive ideas and concerns." With *Enforcing Normalcy* and his anthology, *The Disabilities Studies Reader* (1997; 5th ed., 2016), Davis pioneered the field of disability studies in criticism and theory. In those works and several books since, he has focused on the "biopolitics" involved in our understanding of our bodies, in particular how a coercive ideology of "normalcy" specifies a "normal body" and stigmatizes any divergence from that norm, even though bodies have many variations. In our selection from *Enforcing Normalcy*, "Visualizing the Disabled Body: The Classical Nude and the Fragmented Torso," Davis melds literary analysis and contemporary theory, especially from psychoanalysis, to show the many (and often unnoticed) images of disability appearing in art, fiction, and film and to expose the negative effects of "normalcy," enforced through the almost unattainable projection of a "normal ideal."

Davis experienced the politics of disability while growing up with deaf, working-class Jewish parents in the Bronx, as he saw how his family was isolated and demeaned simply because of the cultural view of deafness. He attended Columbia University, receiving a B.A. in 1970 and a Ph.D. in 1976, writing his doctoral dissertation under the supervision of EDWARD W. SAID. He also attended courses in the early 1970s at the École Pratique des Hautes Études in Paris, where he studied with ROLAND BARTHES. Davis has taught at Columbia, at the State University of New York at Binghamton, and since 2000 at the University of Illinois at Chicago, where he helped found one of the first programs in disability studies. He published his first two books on the history of the novel, but his research interests shifted in the early 1990s when he became a member of Children of Deaf Adults (CODA). Thereafter he has concentrated on deafness and disability, co-founding the Modern Language Association's Committee on Disability Issues in the Profession and writing on disability in academic venues as well as more mainstream ones such as the *Nation* and the *New York Times*.

Like other versions of identity studies, disability studies focuses on the way that identity relates to the body and on the social constructions of marginality and normality. It draws on a wide array of contemporary theoretical sources, including psychoanalysis, cultural studies, feminism, and especially body studies. Beginning with the work of MICHEL FOUCAULT, who examined the disciplining and medicalization of the body as a form of social control, the body has emerged as a central theoretical category, often replacing the concern with subjectivity that was prominent in the 1970s and 1980s. In particular, feminist theorists such as SUSAN BORDO have exposed the frequently negative body images enforced on women. In a different vein, DONNA HARAWAY's "Manifesto for Cyborgs" (1985; see above) has also influenced disability studies by promoting a postmodern view of the body as a technologically constructed "cyborg."

Demonstrating how the body is a social construction rather than a universal constant, Davis—and disability studies—starts with a critique of "normalcy," which functions to stigmatize as abnormal those with different or limited abilities. In *Enforcing Normalcy*, he traces the history of the idea of the normal, initiated in the eighteenth century with eugenics and statistics, which mandated that people fit within the limits of a "normal curve." Before that time, Davis argues, the "ideal" was the primary model in Western culture, which assumed that all bodies were less than ideal, and there was therefore less stigma attached to disability. Some disability theorists trace the emphasis on the normal body to industrial capitalism, which required a standardized body for factory work and labeled other bodies as abnormal, relegating them to marginal status. In our own era we have seen the rise of the "normal ideal," especially in Hollywood movies, which depict ideal bodies as normal and less-than-ideal bodies as abnormal.

Our selection from "Visualizing the Disabled Body" analyzes the frequent depiction of disability and normalcy in art, literature, and film. Beginning with a striking comparison between a famous classical Greek statue, the Venus de Milo, and a contemporary woman with disabilities, Davis questions aesthetic and social preconceptions that lead us to think an armless statue beautiful and a living woman without arms ugly, deformed, and de-eroticized. After deconstructing this dichotomy, he investigates the images of disability prevalent in a range of works of art and literature, including Mary Shelley's novel *Frankenstein* (1818), the photography of Diane Arbus (1923–1971) and others, and films such as *Frankenstein* (1931) and *Born on the Fourth of July* (1989). Davis finds that the "visual arts have done a magnificent job of centralizing normalcy and of marginalizing different bodies."

Turning to psychoanalysis, Davis draws on JACQUES LACAN's notion of the primordial "fragmented body" to understand the persistence of images of disabled bodies. The abnormal body suggests that one's coherent identity is actually a fantasy construction concealing the fundamentally fragmentary nature of identity. In particular, Davis considers *Frankenstein* in terms of the fragmented, grotesque body, finding the scientist's creation representative of a person with disabilities. The creature is horrible because he is a composite made from disparate body parts, thereby literalizing the notion we hold from early infancy of the primordial fragmented body.

Disability theorists like Davis aim not only at making a theoretical intervention but at changing community views of disability and removing its social stigma. Just as feminism, queer studies, and African American studies arose out of political mobilizations, so disability studies is connected with a movement that seeks greater rights for people with disabilities. As Davis argued in his introduction to the first *Disability Studies Reader*, "people with disabilities have been an oppressed and repressed group. People with disabilities have been isolated, incarcerated, . . . institutionalized, and controlled to a degree probably unequal to that experienced by any other minority group. As fifteen percent of the population, people with disabilities make up the largest physical minority within the United States." Construed as one among many minority groups, disabled people can demand equal treatment as a matter of human rights whose denial is a form of unjust discrimination.

A problematic issue for disability theorists is that of definition. The central critique launched by disability studies aims to break down the dichotomy of abled/disabled and normal/abnormal, offering instead a wide conceptual continuum encompassing persons of varying abilities. At the same time, however, disability is cast as a specific identity defined narrowly enough that most people (e.g., the nearsighted) are not considered disabled. This narrower definition invokes "the disabled" as a category designed to convey minority status and legal rights. The tension between wide and narrow definitions of disability mirrors a tension in other identity-based studies—whether focusing on race, ethnicity, gender, or sexuality—between deconstructing conventional categories that marginalize individuals and asserting a separate status to remedy losses of rights. Perhaps it reflects less a contradiction than a two-pronged strategy, aiming ideologically to dispel prejudice and pragmatically to assert the rights of those injured by prejudice. In concentrating on these tasks, Davis's work and disability studies compellingly reconfigure concepts of identity, the body, and normalcy.

Enforcing Normalcy: Disability, Deafness, and the Body **Keywords:** The Body, Cultural Studies, Identity, The Novel, Popular Culture, Psychoanalysis, Representation

From Enforcing Normalcy: Disability, Deafness, and the Body

From *Chapter 6. Visualizing the Disabled Body: The Classical Nude and the Fragmented Torso*

> A human being who is first of all an invalid is *all* body, therein lies his inhumanity and his debasement. In most cases he is little better than a carcass—.
>
> —Thomas Mann, *The Magic Mountain*[1]

> . . . the female is as it were a deformed male.
>
> —Aristotle, *Generation of Animals*[2]

> When I begin to wish I were crippled—even though I am perfectly healthy—or rather that I would have been better off crippled, that is the first step towards *butoh*.
>
> —Tatsumi Hijikata,[3] co-founder of the Japanese performance art/dance form *butoh*

She has no arms or hands, although the stump of her upper right arm extends just to her breast. Her left foot has been severed, and her face is badly scarred, with her nose torn at the tip, and her lower lip gouged out. Fortunately, her facial mutilations have been treated and are barely visible, except for minor scarring visible only up close. The big toe of her right foot

1. The 1924 masterpiece by the German novelist Mann (1875–1955); the novel is set in a tuberculosis sanatorium.
2. One of the zoological works of the Greek philosopher (384–322 B.C.E.; see above), who set the course of Western science for centuries.
3. Japanese dancer, teacher, and choreographer (1928–1986); his style featured dancers with distorted, emaciated bodies, shaved heads, and white-plastered faces.

has been cut off, and her torso is covered with scars, including a particularly large one between her shoulder blades, one that covers her shoulder, and one covering the tip of her breast where her left nipple was torn out.

Yet she is considered one of the most beautiful female figures in the world. When the romantic poet Heinrich Heine saw her he called her 'Notre-Dame de la Beauté.'[4]

He was referring to the Venus de Milo.[5]

Consider too Pam Herbert, a quadriplegic with muscular dystrophy, writing her memoir by pressing her tongue on a computer keyboard, who describes herself at twenty-eight years old:

> I weigh about 130 pounds; I'm about four feet tall. It's pretty hard to get an accurate measurement on me because both of my knees are permanently bent and my spine is curved, so 4' is an estimate. I wear size two tennis shoes and strong glasses; my hair is dishwater blonde and shoulder length.[6]

In this memoir, she describes her wedding night:

> We got to the room and Mark laid me down on the bed because I was so tired from sitting all day. Anyway, I hadn't gone to the bathroom all day so Mark had to catheterize me. I had been having trouble going to the bathroom for many years, so it was nothing new to Mark, he had done it lots of times before.
>
> It was time for the biggest moment of my life, making love. Of course, I was a little nervous and scared. Mark was very gentle with me. He started undressing me and kissing me. We tried making love in the normal fashion with Mark on top and me on the bottom. Well, that position didn't work at all, so then we tried laying on our sides coming in from behind. That was a little better. Anyway, we went to sleep that night a little discouraged because we didn't have a very good lovemaking session. You would have thought that it would be great, but sometimes things don't always go the way we want them to. We didn't get the hang of making love for about two months. It hurt for a long time.[7]

I take the liberty of bringing these two women's bodies together. Both have disabilities. The statue is considered the ideal of Western beauty and eroticism, although it is armless and disfigured. The living woman might be considered by many 'normal' people to be physically repulsive, and certainly without erotic allure. The question I wish to ask is why does the impairment of the Venus de Milo in no way prevent 'normal' people from considering her beauty, while Pam Herbert's disability becomes the focal point for horror and pity?

In asking this question, I am really raising a complex issue. On a social level, the question has to do with how people with disabilities are seen and

4. Our Lady of Beauty (French). Heine (1797–1856), German Romantic poet and journalist.
5. Famous classical statue of Aphrodite (called Venus by the Romans), Greek goddess of love (2d c. B.C.E. copy of a 4th c. original), found on the island of Melos in 1820; it is now displayed in the Louvre, the national art museum of France.
6. In S. E. Browne, D. Connors, and N. Stern, eds., *With the Power of Each Breath: A Disabled Women's Anthology* (Pittsburgh: Cleis Press, 1985), p. 147 [Davis's note]. Some of the author's notes have been edited, and some omitted.
7. Ibid., p. 155 [Davis's note].

why, by and large, they are de-eroticized. If, as I mentioned earlier, disability is a cultural phenomenon rooted in the senses, one needs to inquire how a disability occupies a field of vision, of touch, of hearing; and how that disruption or distress in the sensory field translates into psycho-dynamic representations. This is more a question about the nature of the subject than about the qualities of the object, more about the observer than the observed. The 'problem' of the disabled has been put at the feet of people with disabilities for too long.

Normalcy, rather than being a degree zero of existence, is more accurately a location of bio-power, as Foucault[8] would use the term. The 'normal' person (clinging to that title) has a network of traditional ableist assumptions and social supports that empowers the gaze[9] and interaction. The person with disabilities, until fairly recently, had only his or her own individual force or will. Classically, the encounter has been, and remains, an uneven one. Anne Finger describes it in strikingly visual terms by relating an imagined meeting between Rosa Luxemburg and Antonio Gramsci,[1] each of whom was a person with disabilities, although Rosa is given the temporary power of the abled gaze:

> We can measure Rosa's startled reaction as she glimpses him the misshapen dwarf limping towards her in a second-hand black suit so worn that the cuffs are frayed and the fabric is turning green with age, her eye immediately drawn to this disruption in the visual field; the unconscious flinch; the realization that she is staring at him, and the too-rapid turning away of the head. And then, the moment after, the consciousness that the quick aversion of the gaze was as much of an insult as the stare, so she turns her head back but tries to make her focus general, not a sharp gape. Comrade Rosa, would you have felt a slight flicker of embarrassment? shame? revulsion? dread? of a feeling that can have no name?[2]

In this encounter what is suppressed, at least in this moment, is the fact that Rosa Luxemburg herself is physically impaired (she walked with a limp for her whole life). The emphasis then shifts from the cultural norm to the deviation; Luxemburg, now the gazing subject, places herself in the empowered position of the norm, even if that position is not warranted.

Disability, in this and other encounters, is a disruption in the visual, auditory, or perceptual field as it relates to the power of the gaze. As such, the disruption, the rebellion of the visual, must be regulated, rationalized, contained. Why the modern binary—normal/abnormal—must be maintained is a complex question. But we can begin by accounting for the desire to split bodies into two immutable categories: whole and incomplete, abled and disabled, normal and abnormal, functional and dysfunctional.

8. MICHEL FOUCAULT (1926–1984), French philosopher and historian of ideas; the study of bio-power (as a political technology for manipulating the body) is a major theme in his work.

9. A term associated with the psychoanalytic theory of JACQUES LACAN (1901–1981) and, more specifically, with Lacan-influenced film studies (e.g., LAURA MULVEY's 1975 "Visual Pleasure and Narrative Cinema"; see above).

1. Italian Marxist philosopher (1891–1937; see above). Luxemburg (1871–1919), Polish-born German Marxist revolutionary.

2. Anne Finger, "Comrade Luxemburg and Comrade Gramsci Pass Each Other at a Congress of the Second International in Switzerland on the 10th of March, 1912," unpublished manuscript, 1994 [Davis's note]. Finger (b. 1951), American activist in the disabilities movement and writer of fiction and nonfiction.

In the most general sense, cultures perform an act of splitting (*Spaltung*,[3] to use Freud's term). These violent cleavages of consciousness are as primitive as our thought processes can be. The young infant splits the good parent from the bad parent—although the parent is the same entity. When the child is satisfied by the parent, the parent is the good parent; when the child is not satisfied, the parent is bad. As a child grows out of the earliest phases of infancy, she learns to combine those split images into a single parent who is sometimes good and sometimes not. The residue of *Spaltung* remains in our inner life, personal and collective, to produce monsters and evil stepmothers as well as noble princes and fairy godmothers.

In this same primitive vein, culture tends to split bodies into good and bad parts. Some cultural norms are considered good and others bad. Everyone is familiar with the 'bad' body: too short or tall, too fat or thin, not masculine or feminine enough, not enough or too much hair on the head or other parts of the body, penis or breasts too small or (excepting the penis) too big. Furthermore, each individual assigns good and bad labels to body parts—good: hair, face, lips, eyes, hands; bad: sexual organs, excretory organs, underarms.

The psychological explanation may provide a reason why it is imperative for society at large to engage in *Spaltung*. The divisions whole/incomplete, able/disabled neatly cover up the frightening writing on the wall that reminds the hallucinated whole being that its wholeness is in fact a hallucination, a developmental fiction. *Spaltung* creates the absolute categories of abled and disabled, with concomitant defenses against the repressed fragmented body.

But a psychological explanation alone is finally insufficient. Historical specificity makes us understand that disability is a social process with an origin. So, why certain disabilities are labeled negatively while others have a less negative connotation is a question tied to complex social forces (some of which I have tried to lay out in earlier chapters). It is fair to say, in general, that disabilities would be most dysfunctional in postindustrial countries, where the ability to perambulate or manipulate is so concretely tied to productivity, which in itself is tied to production. The body of the average worker, as we have seen, becomes the new measure of man and woman. Michael Oliver, citing Ryan and Thomas (1980), notes:

> With the rise of the factory . . . [during industrialization] many more disabled people were excluded from the production process for 'The speed of factory work, the enforced discipline, the time-keeping and production norms—all these were a highly unfavourable change from the slower, more self-determined and flexible methods of work into which many handicapped people had been integrated.'[4]

3. Crack; splitting, division (German). The term is used by SIGMUND FREUD (1856–1939) in discussing psychosis and fetishism, especially in "Splitting of the Ego in the Process of Defense" (1940) and "Fetishism" (1927; see above); more important for the point made here, Lacan makes the concept fundamental to subjectivity itself.

4. J. Ryan and F. Thomas, *The Politics of Mental Handicap* (Harmondsworth: Penguin, 1980), ctd. in Michael Oliver, *The Politics of Disablement: A Sociological Approach* (New York: St. Martin's, 1990), p. 27 [Davis's note].

Both industrial production and the concomitant standardization of the human body have had a profound impact on how we split up bodies.

We tend to group impairments into the categories either of 'disabling' (bad) or just 'limiting' (good). For example, wearing a hearing aid is seen as much more disabling than wearing glasses, although both serve to amplify a deficient sense. But loss of hearing is associated with aging in a way that nearsightedness is not. Breast removal is seen as an impairment of femininity and sexuality, whereas the removal of a foreskin is not seen as a diminution of masculinity. The coding of body parts and the importance attached to their selective function or dysfunction is part of a much larger system of signs and meanings in society, and is constructed as such.

'Splitting' may help us to understand one way in which disability is seen as part of a system in which value is attributed to body parts. The disabling of the body part or function is then part of a removal of value. The gradations of value are socially determined, but what is striking is the way that rather than being incremental or graduated, the assignment of the term 'disabled,' and the consequent devaluation are total. That is, the concept of disabled seems to be an absolute rather than a gradient one. One is either disabled or not. Value is tied to the ability to earn money. If one's body is productive, it is not disabled. People with disabilities continue to earn less than 'normal' people and, even after the passage of the Americans with Disabilities Act, 69 percent of Americans with disabilities were unemployed.[5] Women and men with disabilites are seen as less attractive, less able to marry and be involved in domestic production.

The ideology of the assigning of value to the body goes back to preindustrial times. Myths of beauty and ugliness have laid the foundations for normalcy. In particular, the Venus myth is one that is dialectically linked to another. This embodiment of beauty and desire is tied to the story of the embodiment of ugliness and repulsion. So the appropriate mythological character to compare the armless Venus with is Medusa.[6] Medusa was once a beautiful sea goddess who, because she had sexual intercourse with Poseidon at one of Athene's temples, was turned by Athene into a winged monster with glaring eyes, huge teeth, protruding tongue, brazen claws, and writhing snakes for hair. Her hideous appearance has the power to turn people into stone, and Athene eventually completes her revenge by having Perseus kill Medusa. He finds Medusa by stealing the one eye and one tooth shared by the Graiae until they agree to help him. Perseus then kills Medusa by decapitating her while looking into his brightly polished shield, which neutralizes the power of her appearance; he then puts her head into a magic

5. *New York Times*, October 27, 1994, A22 [Davis's note]. The Americans with Disabilities Act was passed in 1990.

6. The pairing of beauty with ugliness is further carried out in Venus's marriage to Vulcan, who is himself both ugly and disabled by his lameness. Lameness tends also to be associated in an ableist way with impotence—as it is, for example, in W. Somerset Maugham's *Of Human Bondage* [1915; Davis's note]. Davis gives one version of the myth. In most accounts, Medusa is one of three monstrous sisters, the Gorgons, the sight of whom turns the gazer to stone. The hero Perseus (the son of Zeus, king of the gods, and the mortal Danaë) is able to kill her, helped by the gods and by the coerced Graiae, the Gorgons' sisters. Poseidon is the Greek god of the sea; Athene (Athena), the Greek goddess of war, the arts and crafts, and wisdom. Vulcan is an Italian fire-god, identified with the Greek Hephaestus, god of fire and especially the forge.

wallet that shields onlookers from its effects. When Athene receives the booty, she uses Medusa's head and skin to fashion her own shield.

In the Venus tradition, Medusa is a poignant double. She is the necessary counter in the dialectic of beauty and ugliness, desire and repulsion, wholeness and fragmentation. Medusa is the disabled woman to Venus's perfect body. The story is a kind of allegory of a 'normal' person's intersection with the disabled body. This intersection is marked by the power of the visual. The 'normal' person sees the disabled person and is turned to stone, in some sense, by the visual interaction. In this moment, the normal person suddenly feels self-conscious, rigid, unable to look but equally drawn to look. The visual field becomes problematic, dangerous, treacherous. The disability becomes a power derived from its otherness, its monstrosity, in the eyes of the 'normal' person. The disability must be decapitated and then contained in a variety of magic wallets. Rationality, for which Athene stands, is one of the devices for containing, controlling, and reforming the disabled body so that it no longer has the power to terrorize. And the issue of mutilation comes up as well because the disabled body is always the reminder of the whole body about to come apart at the seams. It provides a vision of, a caution about, the body as a construct held together willfully, always threatening to become its individual parts—cells, organs, limbs, perceptions—like the fragmented, shared eye and tooth that Perseus ransoms back to the Graiae.

In order to understand better how normalcy is bred into ways of viewing the body, it might be productive to think about the body as it appears in art, photography, and the other visual media. There has been a powerful tradition in Western art of representing the body in a way that serves to solidify, rather early on in history, a preferred mode of envisioning the body. This tradition, identified by Kenneth Clark, has been most clearly articulated in the 'nude'. The nude, as Clark makes clear, is not a literal depiction of the human body but rather a set of conventions about the body: 'the nude is not the subject of art, but a form of art.' Or, as he says, the nude is 'the body re-formed.'[7] If that is the case, then the nude is really part of the development of a set of idealized conventions about the way the body is supposed to look.

While some nudes may be male, when people talk about 'the nude' they most often mean the female nude. Lynda Nead, in a feminist correction of Clark, points out that 'more than any other subject, the female nude connotes "Art."'[8] And in that tradition, the Venus becomes the vortex for thinking about the female body. The Venus is, rather than a subject, a masculine way of fashioning the female body, or of remaking it into a conceptual whole.

I emphasize the word 'whole,' because the irony of the Venus tradition is that virtually no Venuses have been preserved intact from antiquity. Indeed, one of the reasons for the popularity of the Venus de Milo was

7. Kenneth Clark, *The Nude: A Study in Ideal Form* (New York: Pantheon, 1964), pp. 5, 3 [Davis's note]. Clark (1903–1983), English art historian.

8. Lynda Nead, *The Female Nude: Art, Obscenity, and Sexuality* (London: Routledge, 1992), p. i [Davis's note].

that from the time it was discovered in 1820 until 1893 when Furtwängler's[9] scholarship revealed otherwise, the statue was, according to Clark, 'believed to be an original of the fifth century and the only free-standing figure of a woman that had come down from the great period with the advantage of a head.'[1]

The mutilation of the statues is made more ironic by the fact that their headless and armless state is usually overlooked by art historians—barely referred to at all by Clark, for example, in the entirety of his book. The art historian does not *see* the absence and so fills the absence with a presence. This compensation leads us to understand that in the discourse of the nude, one is dealing not simply with art history but with the reception of disability, the way that the 'normal' observer compensates or defends against the presence of difference. This is a 'way of seeing' not often discussed in art criticism. Of course, one can consider that art historians are really just making the best of a bad situation, but it is possible to make a number of further observations.

First of all, the headlessness and armlessness of Venuses link them, structurally, with the Medusa tradition. Many of these Venuses have in effect been decapitated. There seems to be a reciprocal relationship between the decapitations of Medusa in myth and of Venus in reality. It seems that the Venus is really only made possible in coordination with the Medusa—that Aphrodite can romp because Medusa can kill. So it is a fitting dialectic that Medusa's beheading is contained within every broken Venus. The speechlessness of the art historian about the mutilation of his objects of beauty and desire is the effect of his metaphoric transformation to stone. This lapsus[2] in speech is really an avoidance, a wish to avoid the castrating, terrifying vision of Medusa—the disabled, the monster, who is also the disabler. In a larger sense, as Nead suggests, all visions of the female nude, particularly in the Venus tradition, are attempts by male artists and critics to gird themselves against the irrationality and chaos of the body—particularly the female body:

> It begins to speak of a deep-seated fear and disgust of the female body and of femininity within patriarchal culture and of a construction of masculinity around the related fear of the contamination and dissolution of the male ego.[3]

In thinking about disability, one can extend this argument and say that the fear of the unwhole body, of the altered body, is kept at bay by depictions of whole, systematized bodies—the nudes of Western art. The unwhole body is the unholy body. Or as Kaja Silverman points out[4] about images of the body in film, society creates a 'protective shield' that insulates it against the possibility of mutilation, fragmentation, castration.

9. Adolf Furtwängler (1853–1907), German classical archaeologist; see his *Meisterwerke der Griechischen Plastik* (1893, *Masterworks of Greek Sculpture*).
1. Clark, *The Nude*, p. 89 [Davis's note].
2. Falling, slip (Latin); slips of the tongue are discussed by Freud in *The Psychopathology of Everyday Life* (1901).
3. Nead, *The Female Nude*, pp. 17–18 [Davis's note].
4. Kaja Silverman, "Historical Trauma and Male Subjectivity," in *Psychoanalysis and Cinema*, ed. E. Ann Kaplan (New York: Routledge, 1990), p. 14 [Davis's note].

Indeed, the systematization of the body by artist and critic suggests a linearity, a regularity, a completeness that belie the fragmentary, explosive way the body is constitutively experienced. Clark exemplifies this systematic approach in discussing the Esquiline Venus of the fifth century, the first embodiment of these conventions.

> But she is solidly desirable, compact, proportionate; and, in fact, her proportions have been calculated on a simple mathematical scale. The unit of measurement is her head. She is seven heads tall; there is the length of one head between her breasts, one from breast to navel, and one from the navel to the division of the legs . . . fundamentally this is the architecture of the body that will control the observations of classically minded artists till the end of the nineteenth century.[5]

The amnesia of art historians to the subject of mutilation and decapitation (the Esquiline Venus has no head) is not accidental. The most we get from Clark in his entire book is one wistful mention of a Greco-Roman depiction of the three graces as 'a relief in the Louvre, headless, alas.'[6] The 'alas' speaks volumes. This amnesia, this looking away from incompleteness, an averting of the attention, a sigh, is the tip of a defensive mechanism that allows the art historian still to see the statue as an object of desire. So the critic's aim is to restore the damage, bring back the limbs, through an act of imagination.[7] This phenomenon is not unlike the experience of 'phantom limb,' the paradoxical effect that amputees experience of sensing their missing limb. In the case of the art historian, the statue is seen as complete with phantom limbs and head. The art historian does not see the lack, the presence of an impairment, but rather mentally reforms the outline of the Venus so that the historian can return the damaged woman in stone to a pristine origin of wholeness. His is an act of reformation of the visual field, a sanitizing of the disruption in perception.

This is the same act of imagination, or one might say control, that bans from the nude the representation of normal biological processes. For example, there are no pregnant Venuses, there are no paintings of Venuses who are menstruating, micturating, defecating—lactating and lacrimating[8] being the only recognized activities of idealized women. There are no old Venuses (with the exception of a Diana by Rembrandt[9]). One might think of a pregnant Venus as a temporarily disabled woman, and as such banned from the reconstruction of the body we call 'the nude.' Clark distinguishes between prehistoric fertility goddesses, like the Willendorf Venus,[1] images

5. Clark, *The Nude*, p. 75 [Davis's note].

6. Ibid., p. 91 [Davis's note]. The Graces: daughters of Zeus who personified beauty and grace, they were the constant attendants of Aphrodite/Venus.

7. This phenomenon corresponds to the filmgoer's experience of watching stories of disability. As Martin Norden points out, when disability is depicted in film, there is a strong tendency to erase or fix the "problem" by the end of the film (*Cinema of Isolation: A History of Physical Disability in the Movies* [New Brunswick, N.J.: Rutgers University Press, 1994], pp. 59ff.). For instance, no one recalls that Luke Skywalker in *Star Wars* [*The Empire Strikes Back*, 1980] lost his lower arm in a battle with his father, Darth Vader. At the end of the film, a techno-intensive prosthesis is fitted on his stump, and for the sequels he acts as if his hand had grown back. No short-circuits or balky fingers are ever a problem in the sequels [Davis's note].

8. Weeping.

9. Rembrandt van Rijn (1606–1669), Dutch painter. Diana: a Roman goddess identified with the Greek Artemis, goddess of the hunt.

1. A 4" limestone statue of a woman (ca. 25,000 B.C.E.), found near the Austrian town of Willendorf in 1908; its head is covered with a braided pattern, and it is obese, with huge breasts.

of fertility and pregnancy, and the differently ideal Grecian versions which are never pregnant. As Nead notes, 'Clark alludes to this image of the female body [the Willendorf Venus] as undisciplined, out of control; it is excluded from the proper concerns of art in favour of the smooth, uninterrupted line of the Cycladic [Greek] figure.'[2] As artists and art historians shun the fluids and changes in shape that are incompatible with the process of forming the 'regular' body, the evidentiary record of mutilated Venuses must be repressed by a similar process.

A cautionary word must be said on the decapitated and armless Venuses. While it is true that male statues equally are truncated, the incompleteness of the female statues suggests another obvious point that has been repressed for so long—violence. Did all these statues lose their arms and heads by sheer accident, were the structurally fragile head and limbs more likely to deteriorate than the torso, were there random acts of vandalism, or was a particular kind of symbolic brutality committed on these stone women? Did vandals, warriors, and adolescent males amuse themselves by committing focused acts of violence, of sexual bravado and mockery on these embodiments of desire? An armless woman is a symbol of sexual allure without the ability to resist, a headless nude captures a certain kind of male fantasy of submission without the complication of the individuality and the authority granted by a face, even an idealized one. We do not know and will probably never know what happened to these statues, although the destruction of the Parthenon[3] figures has been documented as done by occupying soldiers. The point is that the violence against the body, the acts of hacking, mutilation and so on, have to be put in the context we have been discussing. An act of violence against a female statue is constitutively different from that against a male statue—and these are acts that can be placed in a range of terrorist acts against women during war. Such acts create disabled people, and so, in a sense, these Venuses are the disabled women of art. To forget that is again to commit acts of omission of a rather damning nature.

Of course, a statue is not a person. But as representations of women, the Venus statues carry a powerful cultural signification. The reaction to such statues, both by critics and other viewers, tells much about the way in which we consider the body both as a whole and as incomplete. One point to note is that the art historian, like Clark, tends to perform a complex double act. On the one hand, the critic sees the incomplete statue as whole, imagines the phantom limbs in order to defend against incompleteness, castration, the chaotic or 'grotesque body,' as Peter Stallybrass and Allon White have, using Bakhtinian terminology, called it.[4] On the other hand (if indeed our standard is *two* hands), the critic and the artist are constantly faced with the fragmentary nature of the body, analyzing parts, facing the gaze of the missing part that must be argued into existence.

2. Nead, *The Female Nude*, p. 19 [Davis's note].

3. The chief temple to Athena, built (447–432 B.C.E.) on Athens' Acropolis; the Acropolis was seized by the Turks in 1458, and during a Venetian bombardment in 1687 the explosion of a powder magazine in the temple destroyed the center of the building. Many sculptures decorated the structure.

4. See Peter Stallybrass and Allon White, *The Politics and Poetics of Transgression* (Chicago: University of Chicago Press, 1987) [Davis's note]. The Russian theorist MIKHAIL BAKHTIN (1895–1975) discusses the "carnivalesque" and the "grotesque body" in *Rabelais and His World* (1965).

The model for the fragmentary nature of the nude is best illustrated by the famous story of Zeuxis, as told by Pliny.[5] When Zeuxis painted his version of Aphrodite, he constructed her from the parts of five beautiful young women of his town of Kroton. His vision of the wholeness of Aphrodite was really an assemblage of unrelated parts. Likewise, the critic in regarding the whole nude must always be speaking of parts: 'their torsos have grown so long that the distance from the breasts to the division of the legs is three units instead of two, the pelvis is wide, the thighs are absurdly short.'[6] The whole can only be known by the sum of its parts—even when those parts are missing. John Barrell has detailed the reactions of eighteenth-century men to the Venus de' Medici, and noted how they tended to examine every detail of the statue.[7] Edward Wright, for example, tells observers to 'strictly examine every part' and a typical account read thus:

> One might very well insist on the beauty of the breasts. . . . They are small, distinct, and delicate to the highest degree; with an idea of softness. . . . And yet with all that softness, they have a firmness too. . . . From her breasts, her shape begins to diminish gradually down to her waist; . . . Her legs are neat and slender; the small of them is finely rounded; and her feet are little, white, and pretty.[8]

Another carped:

> The head is something too little for the Body, especially for the Hips and Thighs; the Fingers excessively long and taper, and no match for the Knuckles, except for the little Finger of the Right-Hand.[9]

These analyses perform a juggling act between the fragmentation of the body and its reunification into an hallucinated erotic whole.[1] In imagining the broken statues, the critic must mentally replace the arms and the head, then criticize any other restoration, as does Clark in attacking the reconstruction of the Venus of Arles: 'the sculptor Girardon[2] . . . not only added the arms and changed the angle of the head, but smoothed down the whole body, since the King was offended by the sight of ribs and muscles.'[3] The point here is that the attempt of the critic to keep the body in some systematic whole is really based on a repression of the fragmentary nature of the body.

One might also want to recall that for the Greeks these statues, while certainly works of art, were also to be venerated, since they were representations of deities. For the Greeks, Aphrodite was not a myth; she was a goddess whose domain was desire. It somehow seems appropriate that the ritualistic or reverential attitude toward these statues, pointed out by

5. Pliny the Elder (23/4–79 C.E.), Roman historian and scientific encyclopedist; he gave this account of the Greek painter Zeuxis (active in Athens ca. 400 B.C.E.) in his *Natural History* 35.36.
6. Clark, *The Nude*, p. 91 [Davis's note].
7. John Barrell, "'The Dangerous Goddess': Masculinity, Prestige, and the Aesthetic in Early Eighteenth-Century Britain," *Cultural Critique* 12 (1989): 101–31 [Davis's note]. Venus de' Medici: a Roman copy (1st c. B.C.E.) of a Greek original (4th c. B.C.E.), discovered in Rome in the 16th century (now in the Uffizi Gallery, Florence).
8. Ctd. in ibid., p. 127 [Davis's note].
9. Ibid. [Davis's note].
1. The Medici Venus had been reconstructed, so the 18th-century men did not have to face the incompleteness of their erotic ideal [Davis's note].
2. François Girardon (1628–1715), French sculptor. Venus of Arles: a Roman copy (1st c. B.C.E.) of a Greek original (ca. 359–340 B.C.E.) by Praxiteles (now in the Louvre).
3. Clark, *The Nude*, p. 87 [Davis's note].

Walter Benjamin,[4] indeed their very appearance in stone (which Page Dubois sees as a cultic representation of the bones of the female spirits[5]), has been reproduced in the attitude of that most secular of worshippers, the art critic. For the Venus has a double function: she is both a physical and a spiritual incarnation of desire. In that double sense, the critic must emphasize her spiritual existence by going beyond her physical incarnation in fallible stone, and her mutilations, to the essential body, the body of Desire, the body of the Other.

We can put this paradox in Lacanian terms. For Lacan, the most primitive, the earliest experience of the body is actually of the fragmented body (*corps morcelé*).[6] The infant experiences his or her body as separate parts or pieces, as 'turbulent movements.' For the infant, rather than a whole, the body is an assemblage of arms, legs, surfaces. These representations/images of fragmented body parts Lacan calls *imagos* because they are 'constituted for the "instincts" themselves.'

> Among these *imagos* are some that represent the elective vectors of aggressive intentions, which they provide with an efficacity that might be called magical. These are the images of castration, mutilation, dismemberment, dislocation, evisceration, devouring, bursting open of the body, in short, the *imagos* that I have grouped together under the apparently structural term of *imagos of the fragmented body*.[7]

The process that builds a self involves the enforced unifying of these fragments through the hallucination of a whole body, 'a Gestalt, that is to say, in an exteriority,' as Lacan has pointed out. The process 'extends from a fragmented body-image to a form of its totality . . . and, lastly, to the assumption of the armour of an alienating identity.'[8] When the child points to an image in the mirror—at that stage Lacan calls 'the mirror phase'—the child recognizes (actually misrecognizes) that unified image as his or her self. That identification is really the donning of an identity, an 'armor' against the chaotic or fragmentary body.

In this sense, the disabled body is a direct *imago* of the repressed fragmented body. The disabled body causes a kind of hallucination of the mirror phase gone wrong. The subject looks at the disabled body and has a moment of cognitive dissonance, or should we say a moment of cognitive resonance with the earlier state of fragmentation. Rather than seeing the whole body in the mirror, the subject sees the repressed fragmented body; rather than seeing the object of desire, as controlled by the Other, the subject sees the true self of the fragmented body. For Lacan, because the child first saw its body as a 'collection of discrete part-objects, adults can never perceive their bodies in a complete fashion in later life.'[9] This

4. "The Work of Art in the Age of Mechanical Reproduction" (1936), in *Illuminations*, ed. Hannah Arendt, trans. Harry Zohn (New York: Schocken, 1969), pp. 223–24 [Davis's note]. BENJAMIN (1892–1940), German theorist and aesthetician; for this essay, see above.

5. Page duBois, *Sowing the Body: Psychoanalysis and Ancient Representations of Women* (Chicago: University of Chicago Press, 1988) [Davis's note].

6. The term *corps morcelé* is a bit more vivid than "fragmented body," the now-standard translation of the term into English. *Morceler* is defined as "to divide up into pieces." It more actively carries the concept of chopping, cutting, or hacking. Thus the *corps morcelé* might more accurately be called "the cut-up body." However, I will retain the standard usage, for the sake of uniformity [Davis's note].

7. Lacan, "The Mirror Stage" [see above], in *Écrits: A Selection*, trans. Alan Sheridan (New York: Norton, 1977), pp. 2, 11 [Davis's note].

8. Ibid., pp. 2, 4 [Davis's note].

9. Ellie Ragland-Sullivan, *Jacques Lacan and the Philosophy of Psychoanalysis* (Urbana: University of Illinois Press, 1987), p. 21 [Davis's note].

repressed truth of self-perception revolves around a prohibited central, specular moment—of seeing the disabled body—in which the 'normal' person views the Medusa image, in which the Venus-nude cannot be sustained as a viable armor. In Lacanian terms, the *moi*[1] is threatened with a breaking-up, literally, of its structure, is threatened with a reminder of its incompleteness. In a specular, face-to-face moment, the ego is involved in what J. B. Pontalis calls 'death work,' which involves the 'fundamental process of unbinding [of the ego], of fragmentation, of breaking up, of separation, of bursting.'[2] Thus the specular moment between the armored, unified self and its repressed double—the fragmented body—is characterized by a kind of death-work, repetition compulsion in which the unified self continuously sees itself undone—castrated, mutilated, perforated, made partial. In this context, it is worth noting that the Venus tradition involves castration at its very origin. Aphrodite is said to have been born from the foam of Uranus's genitals which Cronus threw into the sea after castrating his father.[3] The dynamic is clear. Male mutilation is mitigated by the creation of the desirable female body. The disabled body is corrected by the wholeness of the constructed body of the nude. But, as has been noted, the emphasis on wholeness never entirely erases the foundation of the Venus tradition in the idea of mutilation, fragmented bodies, decapitation, amputation.

If we follow these terms, the disabled Venus serves as an unwanted reminder that the 'real' body, the 'normal body,' the observer's body, is in fact always already a 'fragmented body.' The linking together of all the disparate bodily sensations and locations is an act of will, a hallucination that always threatens to fall apart. The mutilated Venus and the disabled person, particularly the disabled person who is missing limbs or body parts, will become in fantasy visual echoes of the primal fragmented body—a signifier of castration and lack of wholeness. Missing senses, blindness, deafness, aphasia, in that sense, will point to missing bodily parts or functions. The art historian in essence dons or retains the armor of identity, needs the armor as does Perseus who must see Medusa through the polished shield. The art historian's defense is that mirror-like shield that conjures wholeness through a misrecognition linking the parts into a whole.

What this analysis tells us is that the 'disabled body' belongs to no one, just as the normal body, or even the 'phallus' belongs to no one. Even a person who is missing a limb, or is physically 'different,' still has to put on, assume, the disabled body and identify with it.[4] The disabled body, far from being the body of some small group of 'victims,' is an entity from the earli-

1. Me (French), a Lacanian term for the self.

2. Ctd. in Ragland-Sullivan, *Jacques Lacan*, p. 70 [Davis's note]. Pontalis (1924–2013), French psychoanalyst.

3. Robert Graves, *The Greek Myths* (New York: Penguin, 1957), p. 49 [Davis's note]. Uranus (literally, "Sky"; Greek), the first ruler of the world, was born from Gaia (Earth); Cronus was the youngest of their children (and was himself overthrown by Zeus).

4. Irving Kenneth Zola pointed out that people with disabilities are mostly born into "normal" families. Thus they are socialized into ableist culture and have to adopt their disabled identity. "We think of ourselves in the shadows of the external world. The very vocabulary we use to describe ourselves is borrowed from the society. We are *de*-formed, *dis*-eased, *dis*-abled, *dis*-ordered, *ab*-normal, and most of all an *in*-valid" ("Communication Barriers between 'the Able-Bodied' and 'the Handicapped,'" in *Psychological and Social Impact of Physical Disability*, ed. Robert P. Marinelli and Arthur E. Dell Orto [New York: Springer, 1984], p. 144) [Davis's note].

est of childhood instincts, a body that is common to all humans, as Lacan would have it. The 'normal' body is actually the body we develop later. It is in effect a Gestalt—and therefore in the realm of what Lacan calls the Imaginary. The realm of the 'Real' in Lacanian terms is where the fragmented body is found because it is the body that precedes the ruse of identity and wholeness. Artists often paint this vision, and it often appears in dreams 'in the form of disjointed limbs, or of those organs represented in exoscopy . . . the very same that the visionary Hieronymus Bosch has fixed for all time.'[5]

In understanding this point, we can perhaps see how the issue of disability transcends the rather narrow category to which it has been confined. Just as, I claim, we readers are all deaf, participating in a deafened moment, likewise, we all—first and foremost—have fragmented bodies. It is in tracing our tactical and self-constructing (deluding) journeys away from that originary self that we come to conceive and construct that phantom goddess of wholeness, normalcy, and unity—the nude.

One might even add that the element of repulsion and fear associated with fragmentation and disability may in fact come from the very act of repressing the primal fragmentariness of the body. As Freud wrote, 'the uncanny is in reality nothing new or foreign, but something familiar and old-established in the mind that has been estranged only [in] the process of repression.'[6] The feelings of repulsion associated with the uncanny, *das Unheimlich,* the unfamiliar, are not unlike the emotions of the 'normal' when they are visualizing the disabled. The key to the idea of the uncanny is in its relation to the normal. *Heimlich* is a word associated with the home, with familiarity—and with the comfortable predictability of the home. The disabled body is seen as *unheimlich* because it is the familiar gone wrong. Disability is seen as something that does not belong at home, not to be associated with the home. Freud notes that the terror or repulsion of the uncanny is ambivalent, is found precisely in its relation to and yet deviance from the familiar. That the uncanny can be related to disability is made clear when Freud cites specifically 'dismembered limbs, a severed head, a hand cut off at the wrist' as *unheimlich*.[7] What is uncanny about dismemberment seems to be the familiarity of the body part that is then made *unheimlich* by its severing. As Freud wrote, 'the *unheimlich* is what was once *heimisch,* homelike, familiar; the prefix "un" is the token of repression.'[8]

But in this equation I think Freud is actually missing the earlier repression of the inherently fragmentary nature of the original body *imago.* The homeyness of the body, its familiarity as whole, complete, contained, is based on a dynamic act of repression. Freud is assuming that the whole body is an *a priori* given, as he had done with the concept of the ego. But as Lacan has shown more than adequately, the ego is a multifaceted structure

5. Lacan, "The Mirror Stage," p. 4 [Davis's note]. "Exoscopy": a view from the outside. Bosch (ca. 1460–1516), Dutch painter whose best-known works feature grotesque figures that sometimes combine human, animal, vegetable, and inanimate parts.

6. Freud, "The Uncanny" [see above], in *Studies in Parapsychology* (New York: Collier, 1963), p. 47 [Davis's note].

7. Ibid., p. 49 [Davis's note].

8. Ibid., p. 51 [Davis's note].

to be understood in its philosophical complexity. Likewise the ground of the body, its materiality given by Freud, needs a re-analysis. The route of disability studies allows for this revisioning. In this process, the *heimisch* body becomes the *unheimlich* body, and the fragment, the disabled parts, can be seen as the originary, familiar body made unfamiliar by repression. Dominant culture has an investment in seeing the disabled, therefore, as uncanny, as something found outside the home, unfamiliar, while in fact where is the disabled body found if not at home?

I have been concentrating on the physical body, but it is worth considering for a moment the issue of madness. While mental illness is by definition not related to the intactness of the body, nevertheless, it shows up as a disruption in the visual field. We 'see' that someone is insane by her physical behavior, communication, and so on. Yet the fear is that the mind is fragmenting, breaking up, falling apart, losing itself—all terms we associate with becoming mad. With the considerable information we have about the biological roots of mental illness, we begin to see the disease again as a breaking up of 'normal' body chemistry: amino acid production gone awry, depleted levels of certain polypeptide chains or hormones. Language production can become fragmentary, broken, in schizophrenic speech production. David Rothman[9] points out that in eighteenth- and nineteenth-century America, insanity was seen as being caused by the fragmented nature of 'modern' life—particularly the pressures brought to bear on people by a society in which economic boundaries were disappearing. This fragmenting of society produced a fragmentation of the individual person. So the asylums that sprung up during this period recommended a cure that involved a removal from the urban, alienated, fragmented environment to rural hospitals in which order and precision could be restored. 'A precise schedule and regular work became the two characteristics of the best private and public institutions. . . . The structure of the mental hospital would counteract the debilitating influences of the community.' As Rothman notes, 'Precision, certainty, regularity, order' were the words that were seen as embodying the essence of cure.[1] The mind would be restored to 'wholeness' by restoring the body through manual labor. However, needless to add, one had to have a whole body to have a whole mind. The general metaphor here continues to be a notion of wholeness; order, clean boundaries, as opposed to fragmentations, disordered bodies, messy boundaries.

If people with disabilities are considered anything, they are or have been considered creatures of disorder—monsters, monstrous. Leslie Fiedler has taken some pains to show this in his book *Freaks.*[2] If we look at Mary Shelley's *Frankenstein,*[3] we find some of the themes we have been discussing emerge in novelistic form. First, we might want to note that we have no name for

9. American social and medical historian (b. 1937).

1. David J. Rothman, *The Discovery of the Asylum: Social Order and Disorder in the Early Republic* (Boston: Little Brown, 1971), pp. 144, 145 [Davis's note].

2. *Freaks: Myths and Images of the Secret Self* (New York: Simon and Schuster, 1978); Fiedler (1917–2003) was an American literary and cultural critic.

3. The 1818 tale of horror by Mary Shelley (1791–1851), English novelist and wife of PERCY BYSSHE SHELLEY.

the creation of Dr. Frankenstein other than 'monster.' (This linguistic lapsus is usually made up for in popular culture by referring to the creature itself as 'Frankenstein,' a terminology that confuses the creator with the created.) In reading the novel, or speaking about it, we can only call the creature 'the monster.' This linguistic limitation is worth noting because it encourages the reader to consider the creature a monster rather than a person with disabilities.

We do not often think of the monster in Mary Shelley's work as disabled, but what else is he? The characteristic of his disability is a difference in appearance. He is more than anything a disruption in the visual field. There is nothing else different about him—he can see, hear, talk, think, ambulate, and so on. It is worth noting that in popular culture, largely through the early film versions of the novel, the monster is inarticulate, somewhat mentally slow, and walks with a kind of physical impairment.[4] In addition, the film versions add Ygor, the hunchbacked criminal who echoes the monster's disability in his own. Even in the recent film version by Kenneth Branagh, the creature walks with a limp and speaks with an impediment.[5] One cannot dismiss this filtering of the creature through the lens of multiple disability. In order for the audience to fear and loathe the creature, he must be made to transcend the pathos of a single disability. Of course, it would be unseemly for a village to chase and torment a paraplegic or a person with acromegaly. Disabled people are to be pitied and ostracized; monsters are to be destroyed; audiences must not confuse the two.

In the novel, it is clear that Dr. Frankenstein cannot abide his creation for only one reason—its hideous appearance. Indeed, the creature's only positive human contact is with the blind old man De Lacey, who cannot see the unsightly features. When De Lacey's family catches a glimpse of the creature, the women faint or run, and the men beat and pursue him. His body is a zone of repulsion; the reaction he evokes is fear and loathing. The question one wants to ask is why does a physical difference produce such a profound response?

The answer, I believe, is twofold. First, what is really hideous about the creature is not so much his physiognomy as what that appearance suggests. The *corps morcelé* makes its appearance immediately in the construction of the monster. Ironically, Dr. Frankenstein adapts Zeuxis's notion of taking ideal parts from individuals to create the ideal whole body. As he says, 'I collected bones from charnel houses. . . . The dissecting room and the slaughter house furnished many of my materials.'[6] From these fragments, seen as loathsome and disgusting, Frankenstein assembles what he wishes to create—a perfect human. It is instructive in this regard to distinguish

4. According to Norden, Robert Florey, a writer who contributed to the original *Frankenstein* script, came up with the idea of having Dr. Frankenstein's assistant Fritz break into medical school to steal a brain. He finds the "normal" brain the doctor wanted but then drops it and takes one marked "abnormal" instead [Davis's note]. The French-born writer and director Florey (1900–1979) worked on the best-known (through not earliest) film version, directed by James Whale (1931).

5. *Mary Shelley's Frankenstein* (1994), which also starred the Irish director Branagh (b. 1960) as Victor Frankenstein.

6. Mary Shelley, *Frankenstein, or The Modern Prometheus* (Oxford: Oxford University Press, 1990), pp. 54–55 [Davis's note]. Prometheus, the Titan punished for giving mortals fire stolen from the gods, is sometimes also credited with creating the human race from mud.

the Boris Karloff incarnation of the creature[7]—with the bolt through his neck—or Branagh's grotesquely sewn creature, from the image that Mary Shelley would have us imagine. Dr. Frankenstein tells us:

> His limbs were in proportion, and I had selected his features as beautiful. Beautiful!—Great God! His yellow skin scarcely covered the work of muscles and arteries beneath; his hair was of a lustrous black and flowing; his teeth of a pearly whiteness; but these luxuriances only formed a more horrid contrast with his watery eyes, that seemed almost of the same colour as the dun white sockets in which they were set, his shrivelled complexion and straight black lips.[8]

What then constitutes the horror? If we add up the details, what we see is a well-proportioned man with long black hair, pearly white teeth, whose skin is somewhat deformed—resulting in jaundice and perhaps a tightness or thinness of the skin, a lack of circulation perhaps causing shriveling, watery eyes and darkened lips. This hardly seems to constitute horror rather than, say, pathos.[9]

What is found to be truly horrifying about Frankenstein's creature is its composite quality, which is too evocative of the fragmented body. Frankenstein's reaction to this living *corps morcelé* is repulsion: 'the beauty of the dream vanished, and breathless horror and disgust filled my heart.'[1] Frankenstein attempted to create a unified nude, an object of beauty and harmony—a Venus, in effect. He ended up with a Medusa whose existence reveals the inhering and enduring nature of the archaic fragmented body, endlessly repressed but endlessly reappearing.

Why does the appearance of the monster produce so powerful an affect? Routinely, one might view a deformed person, even a multiply deformed one, without desiring to kill that person. Here we see a man whose skin is strange or unnatural being transposed into the category 'monster.' The element of skin reminds us that the monster as a disturbance in the visual field is linked to the tactile field. The disruption in the skin's surface immediately translates into a threat of touching, of being touched. The idea of touch always initiates a dialectic of attraction and repulsion, of fear, hatred, or erotic attraction. Indeed, from a psychoanalytic viewpoint there is not much difference between these choices. So, inevitably, the disabled body becomes a site of the erotic, as instantly it is perceived in either the Venus or the Medusa scenarios.[2] In Shelley's novel, after the creation, Dr. Frankenstein

7. In *Frankenstein* (1931), *Bride of Frankenstein* (1935), and *Son of Frankenstein* (1939); the English actor Karloff (born William Henry Pratt, 1887–1969) is best remembered for his roles in these and other horror films.

8. Shelley, *Frankenstein*, p. 57 [Davis's note].

9. Indeed, one could argue that this function of horror films is to remove the element of pity in the visual transaction between "normal" viewer and disabled object. In the place of pity, pure repulsion is made allowable by turning the object with a disability into a criminal, a horror, a monstrosity. While everyone may enjoy a good horror movie now and then, there is a case to be made that horror films involving physically disabled characters are in fact the equivalent of racist films. The counterbalanced compassionate films showing people with disabilities triumphing over their disability is just the other moment of the same dialectic [Davis's note].

1. Shelley, *Frankenstein*, p. 57 [Davis's note].

2. Women with disabilities are often the target of sexual or physical abuse; children with disabilities or Deaf children are often the victims of child abuse. This impulse to touch is unfortunately seen quite dramatically in these situations [Davis's note].

has rather a peculiar response—he goes to sleep and has a dream about his fiancée:

> I thought I saw Elizabeth, in the bloom of health, walking in the streets of Ingolstadt. Delighted and surprised, I embraced her, but as I imprinted the first kiss on her lips, they became livid with the hue of death; her features appeared to change, and I thought that I held the corpse of my dead mother in my arms; a shroud enveloped her form, and I saw the grave-worms crawling in the folds of the flannel.[3]

The rather incredible set of associations made by Dr. Frankenstein would take pages to explore thoroughly, but what we might want to note here is that the immediate flight from the Medusa image of the monster's fragmented body leads immediately to the Venus body of Elizabeth, seen as frankly erotic. However, upon the first sexual contact the Venus myth immediately deconstructs, and Elizabeth's body initially changes to a corpse, then to the decomposing corpse of Frankenstein's dead mother. The visual leads to the tactile, which then contaminates the normal body. And all these moments lead back to the decomposing, fragmenting body. Later in the novel, when the creature demands a spouse, Frankenstein again creates the fragmented, now female, body. But at the last minute 'trembling with passion, [I] tore to pieces the thing on which I was engaged.'[4] Frankenstein's explicit reason for failing to give the monster a mate is fear that a race of deformed creatures would populate the earth and threaten the human race.[5] Thus the risk of the erotic touch, of the frankly erotic agenda for the creature, is seen as a contaminating danger to 'normal' people. So, the fragmented body is hacked up, exploded, into the fragments that make it up.

* * *

In no area is this set of cultural values related to the visual more compelling than in film. Film is a medium whose main goal, one might say, is the construction and reconstruction of the body. The abnormal body plays a major role in the defining of the normal body, and so one might assume that film would be concerned with the issue of disability. Martin F. Norden has recently published the most complete account to date of disability in the film industry, *The Cinema of Isolation: A History of Physical Disability in the Movies* (1994). The remarkable thing about this book is the staggering number of films that have been made about the issue of disability. When I first began to consider the issue of how the disabled body is depicted in film, I came up with my own list of twenty or so films, and I thought that I would mention the occasional way in which the disabled were included in a film industry that mainly focused on the normal body. In other words, I thought

3. Shelley, *Frankenstein*, p. 58 [Davis's note].
4. Ibid., p. 168 [Davis's note].
5. Later in the century Alexander Graham Bell would raise the same specter in regard to a deaf race taking over should deaf people be allowed to marry each other [Davis's note]. Bell (1847–1922), Scottish-born American inventor best known for producing the first telephone; Davis is referring to his *Memoirs upon the Formation of a Deaf Variety of the Human Race* (1884). Bell's wife was deaf and his mother was nearly deaf, and he was keenly interested in the education of the deaf and in eugenics.

I was dealing with a parallel situation to, say, the depiction in cinema of African-Americans—a marginalized group who rarely appeared in Hollywood films until recently and, if they did, played mainly minor characters or supernumerary roles.

But the facts about the depiction of disability are quite the opposite of what I had thought. The film industry has been obsessed with the depiction of the disabled body from the earliest silent films. The blind, the deaf, the physically disabled were singled out from the very beginning of cinema. * * *

Norden's book lists about six hundred disability-related films in its index, a far cry from my twenty or so. And if one stops and thinks about the subject, one realizes that films concerning people with disabilities are almost always playing at any given time. For example, at the moment I write this sentence on 5 January 1995, I can go see movies about the deaf Beethoven in *Immortal Beloved,* the linguistically deprived girl in Jodie Foster's *Nell,* the emotionally impaired monarch in *The Madness of King George,* and of course the lovable, mentally challenged *Forrest Gump.* In recent years films like *My Left Foot, Lorenzo's Oil, Rainman, Children of a Lesser God, Elephant Man, Mask, Awakenings, Stanley and Iris,* to name only a few better-known films, have become major hits. In addition to films centrally about disabled people, there are hundreds of films in which characters, mainly evil, are depicted as using wheelchairs, missing limbs or eyes, walking with a limp, stuttering, and so on.

The point that Norden's book made clear to me is that the cinematic experience, far from including disabilities in an ancillary way, is powerfully arranged around the management and deployment of disabled and 'normal' bodies. Disabled stories, stories of people's bodies or minds going wrong, make compelling tales. But more than that, as with any obsession, there has to be an underlying reason why films are drawn obsessively to the topic of disability. In order to understand why film makers routinely incorporate disabled bodies into films, it might be relevant to ask what else routinely appears in films. The answer is more than obvious: sex and violence. While it is fashionable for liberals to decry the violent content of films, and conservatives to decry the sexual, it might be more accurate for them to think of films as vehicles for the delivery of images of the body in extreme circumstances. The inherent voyeuristic nature of film makes it a commodity that works by visualizing for viewers the body in attitudes that it is otherwise difficult to see. Few people in quotidian life see couples making love on a regular basis, but that is a routine experience to filmgoers. Likewise, most middle-class citizens rarely see dead, mutilated, bleeding bodies, but the average viewer has no shortage of such images.

So films, one could say, are a streamlined delivery system that produces dramatically these bodily images in exchange for a sum of money (as the Coca-Cola industry can be said to be a system for delivering caffeine and sugar, or as cigarettes are really time-release delivery systems for nicotine administration). As novels were seen to be mechanisms for the cultural production of normativity, so films have to be seen in the same regard, with the addition that the phantasm of the body is particularly subject to these normativizing activities.

Films enforce the normal body, but through a rather strange process. The normal body, invented in the nineteenth century as a departure from the ideal body, has shifted over to a new concept: the normal ideal. This normal ideal body is the one we see on the screen. It is the commodified body of the eroticized male or female star. This body is not actually the norm, but it is the fantasized, hypostatized body of commodified desire. In order to generate this body and proliferate its images, films have constantly to police and to regulate the variety of bodily differences. These bodies are the modern equivalents of the nude Venuses, and to keep them viable, to think on and obsess about them, the Medusa body has constantly to be shown, reshown, placed, categorized, itemized, and anatomized. In short, we cannot have Sharon Stone without Linda Hunt; we cannot have Tom Cruise without Ron Kovic;[6] we cannot have the fantasy of the erotic *femme fatale's* body without having the sickened, disabled, deformed person's story testifying to the universal power of the human spirit to overcome adversity. As Norden points out, when films about disabled people are made, more often than not the disabled characters get cured by the end of the film.[7] The tension between the whole and the fragmented body, between the erotic, complete body and the uncanny, incomplete body, must be constantly deployed and resolved through films.

* * *

Throughout this chapter, I have tried to show that the concept of disability is a crucial part of the very way we conceive of and live in our bodies. In art, photography, film, and other media in which the body is represented, the 'normal' body always exists in a dialectical play with the disabled body. Indeed, our representations of the body are really investigations of and defenses against the notion that the body is anything but a seamless whole, a complete, unfragmented entity. In addition to the terms of race, class, gender, sexual preference and so on—all of which are factors in the social construction of the body—the concept of disability adds a background of somatic concerns. But disability is more than a background. It is in some sense the basis on which the 'normal' body is constructed: disability defines the negative space the body must not occupy, it is the Manichean binary[8] in contention with normality. But this dialectic is one that is enforced by a set of social conditions and is not natural in any sense. Only when disability is made visible as a compulsory term in a hegemonic process, only when the binary is exposed and the continuum acknowledged, only when the body is seen apart from its existence as an object of production or consumption—only then will normalcy cease being a term of enforcement in a somatic judicial system.

1995

6. The paraplegic veteran (b. 1946) of the Vietnam War whose autobiography, *Born on the Fourth of July* (1984), was made into a film (dir. Oliver Stone, 1989) starring Cruise (b. 1962), one of the biggest box-office draws of his generation. Sharon Stone (b. 1958), 5'9", is known for sexy leading roles, while the 4'9" Hunt (b. 1945) is a highly regarded "character" actor.

7. Norden, *The Cinema of Isolation*, p. 59 [Davis's note].

8. The converse in a dualistic worldview; Manichaeism sees the world as divided between good and evil, light and darkness, spirit and matter.

GAYLE RUBIN
b. 1949

Political activist, sex dissident, cultural anthropologist, ethnographer of gay communities, feminist, and queer theorist, Gayle Rubin is a groundbreaking figure in the fields of feminism, lesbian and gay studies, and queer theory. Her work accounts for the mechanisms by which gender and compulsory heterosexuality are produced, as well as the inequalities that these systems create, while it challenges the gap between scholarship and activism. More than many scholars working in theory today, Rubin is able to bring theoretical analysis to bear on complex empirical data drawn from the methods of ethnography, drawing theory and data into productive association. As committed to political action as to scholarship, she produced her two landmark essays, "The Traffic in Women: Notes on the 'Political Economy' of Sex" (1975) and "Thinking Sex: Notes for a Radical Theory of the Politics of Sexuality" (1984), while still a graduate student; each alone is enough to secure her position in the canon of feminist theory.

Born in 1949, Rubin grew up in South Carolina and enrolled at the University of Michigan in 1966, becoming involved in local New Left, feminist, and gay politics. "The Traffic in Women" began as a term paper written in a class with the American anthropologist Marshall Sahlins, where Rubin first read the structuralist theories of CLAUDE LÉVI-STRAUSS and JACQUES LACAN that underpin that essay. In 1969 Rubin became the University of Michigan's first women's studies major, a program she designed herself. She began graduate studies at the University of Michigan and, in 1978, moved to San Francisco to undertake a study of gay male leather culture. There, with the writer and transsexual activist Pat Califia and sixteen others, she founded Samois (a name they borrowed from the estate of Anne-Marie, a lesbian dominatrix in Pauline Réage's 1954 novel, *The Story of O*), the first political organization devoted to lesbian sadomasochism. The group disbanded in 1983, and in 1984 Rubin founded a new lesbian S/M organization, the Outcasts, which split up in 1997. During the 1990s, Rubin taught women's studies at the University of California at Santa Cruz. In 1994 she completed her Ph.D. in anthropology at the University of Michigan, with a dissertation on gay leather culture in San Francisco. She is currently an associate professor of anthropology and women's studies at the University of Michigan.

Early on, Rubin was a "pro-sex" activist, becoming prominent in the so-called sex wars of the 1980s—the acrimonious debate that split and continues to divide the feminist movement over the issues surrounding sexuality, especially pornography, sadomasochism, butch/femme roles, and sex work. On the other side of this debate were antipornography groups such as Women Against Pornography and Women Against Violence in Pornography and Media—led by Andrea Dworkin, ADRIENNE RICH, and Catharine MacKinnon—which targeted sex activists, including Rubin and Califia. The disagreement came to a head in 1982 at the ninth conference in "The Scholar and the Feminist" series, held at Barnard College in New York City: its organizing theme was "sexuality." Antipornography groups picketed the conference, handing out leaflets attacking some of the speakers as sexual deviants, while those inside heard papers and attended workshops on an array of controversial topics. Rubin presented an early version of "Thinking Sex," titled "Concepts for a Radical Politics of Sex."

Rubin's two best-known essays, both frequently reprinted in anthologies and readers, have achieved prominence because they effectively articulate major theoretical and historical shifts within the feminist and gay liberation movements. "The Traffic in Women," published in the collection *Toward an Anthropology of Women* (1975), marks the beginning of a shift away from the activism of movement feminism and toward the academic feminism that would come to dominate feminist work in the 1980s as women's studies programs were institutionalized in American universities. In it Rubin famously coins the term "sex/gender system" to describe "the set of arrangements by which a society transforms biological sexuality into products of human activity, and in which these transformed sexual needs are satisfied." The essay, drawing on theoretical models derived from structuralism (Lévi-Strauss) and psychoanalysis (SIGMUND FREUD and Lacan), also articulates a shift from a feminism rooted in the Marxism of the 1960s New Left toward the poststructuralism that would soon dominate academic feminism. "Thinking Sex," published in 1984 in the Scholar and the Feminist conference proceedings, *Pleasure and Danger: Exploring Female Sexuality*, reflects the emerging interest in cultural politics in the 1980s and 1990s, as well as the movement from gay and lesbian studies to queer theory, which focused less on gay identity than on the heterogeneity of sexual practices and identities. Heavily influenced by MICHEL FOUCAULT's *History of Sexuality* (1976; trans. 1978), "Thinking Sex" rejects not only the anti-sex politics of Catharine MacKinnon and Andrea Dworkin but also the lesbian feminism represented by Adrienne Rich's notion of a "lesbian continuum." Whereas Rich's formulation tends to minimize sex and treat all forms of same-sex bonding alike, "Thinking Sex" aims to restore sex to lesbian theory and politics. In this regard Rubin aligns herself with feminists and lesbians who have promoted a progressive sexual politics, including BELL HOOKS, Cherríe Moraga, Joan Nestle, and Esther Newton. The essay anticipates key features of queer theory's agenda that were later articulated by JUDITH BUTLER, EVE KOSOFSKY SEDGWICK, and LAUREN BERLANT and MICHAEL WARNER.

Our selection, "Thinking Sex: Notes for a Radical Theory of the Politics of Sexuality," was written in response not only to the damaging views of antipornography feminists but also to the political ascendency of the New Right, which was mobilizing in opposition to homosexuality, feminism, abortion, contraception, premarital sex, and the perceived corruption of the young. Antipornography feminists had entered into an uneasy alliance with moral conservatives, such as the commission appointed to investigate pornography in 1985 by President Ronald Reagan and headed by then Attorney General Edwin Meese. In her essay, Rubin attempts to think through the repressive consequences of conservatives' anti-sex position and, at the same time, to articulate "an accurate, humane, and genuinely liberatory body of thought about sexuality."

In times of great social stress, sexuality often takes on a symbolic value beyond its own significance. So Rubin begins with a detailed historical account of several periods in history (the late nineteenth century, the 1950s, and the 1970s and 1980s) when sexuality became a vehicle on which were displaced other anxieties and fears, especially about poverty, disease, warfare, and global annihilation. Long after the details of such struggles are forgotten, they continue to leave their mark in the form of laws, social practices, and ideologies that affect how individuals experience sexuality. Central to Rubin's thesis is the claim that sexuality is not simply a biological function, a private preference, or a psychological state of health or illness; it is also a realm of politics, inequality, and oppression.

Having begun by examining the historical evidence for sexual repression in modern Western societies, Rubin then describes the conceptual tools required for a radical theory of sexuality—one that could identify, explain, and denounce "erotic injustice and sexual oppression." The first task of such a theory is to challenge the conceptual stranglehold of sexual essentialism. Though it is tempting to see sexuality as a purely natural force that has been subjected to artificial social and institutional repression, such a position is neither tenable after Foucault nor particularly helpful in challenging sexual oppression. Drawing on the work of Foucault, of feminist historians such as Judith Walkowitz, and of gay historians such as Alan

Bérubé, Jeffrey Weeks, and John D'Emilio, Rubin argues for a constructivist view of sex: it allows a place for biology and the body, but at the same time recognizes that our experiences of both are always mediated by historically specific cultural conventions, values, and practices. From this perspective, it is possible to question sexual ideologies that constrain our understanding of sexuality within such narrow and rigidly defined categories as male and female, heterosexual and homosexual.

Rubin identifies five ideologies, beyond sexual essentialism, that need to be challenged: sex negativity, the belief that sex is a dangerous and destructive force that must be controlled; the fallacy of misplaced scale, in which small differences in value or behavior are inflated into "cosmic threats"; the hierarchical ordering of sex acts, which distinguishes between those that are labeled good, natural, or normal and those that are considered bad, unnatural, or abnormal; the domino theory of sexual peril, which casts any infraction of the normative as catastrophic for the entire system; and the absence of any concept of benign sexual variation. These are the key components of a nuanced, hegemonic system of status and caste that characterizes and disciplines sexual behaviors. At every level, the dominant system is enforced by social institutions, including the family, law, and religion; by psychoanalysis, psychiatry, and psychology; by popular opinion and the media; and, sadly, by antiporn feminists. In defending nonhegemonic sexual practices and communities, Rubin seeks autonomy to counteract the society-wide pathologization, persecution, stigmatization, demonization, and scapegoating of sexual minorities.

Rubin concludes with a discussion of the three positions that came to dominate the sex wars in U.S. feminism during the 1980s: anti-sex authoritarianism, pro-sex libertarianism, and the so-called moderate position, the belief that the truth lies somewhere between the two extremes. Rubin challenges this middle position with particular force, arguing that it rests on the false assumption that the poles of the debate are equally extreme, thereby mystifying the institutional power of sex negativity and marginalizing radical thought. She pushes her readers to test the limits of their tolerance for sexualities usually labeled perverse, including not only homosexuality and the consumption of pornography but also sadomasochism, pedophilia, and incest.

The failure of feminists to develop a radical theory of sexuality leads Rubin to her most far-reaching and perhaps most misunderstood position in the essay. She argues, as does Sedgwick later in *Epistemology of the Closet* (1990), that theorizing about sexuality needs to be disentangled from theorizing about gender, that feminism cannot be the sole or privileged site of theories about sex. This position revises her analysis of the sex/gender system proposed in "Traffic in Women" without entirely repudiating it. Sexuality cannot be reduced either to biological sex or to socially constructed gender. While gender, anatomical sex, and sexuality are undoubtedly intertwined and while feminism will continue to theorize about sexuality in relation to both gender and biological sex, the binary gender system on which feminist theory relies cannot encompass the kind of sexual diversity Rubin believes to be required by a radical theory of sexuality. Sexuality cuts across systems of oppression, and is thus too complex and diverse to be contained within feminism.

Critics of Rubin's theory of sexuality interrogate her utopian tendencies from two directions. Queer theorists question whether any theory of sexuality, however radical, is elastic enough to embrace all sexual minorities, and feminists point to problems with Rubin's separation of feminist theory and theories of sexuality. Antipornography feminists, moreover, argue that she either ignores or downplays the issue of consent in sex. They accuse her of promoting a libertarian approach to sex and thereby abandoning the historical analysis that characterizes her writing about sexual repression. They also charge her with ahistoricism in drawing on biology to discuss sexual diversity. Such an analysis, they believe, ignores the social, political, cultural, and economic forms of coercion that women continue to face and that frequently—as in rape and battery—make the question of consent meaningless. Yet in spite of, or perhaps because of, these utopian tendencies, Rubin remains one of the most original voices in both feminist and queer theory.

"Thinking Sex: Notes for a Radical Theory of the Politics of Sexuality" Keywords: The Body, Feminist Theory, Gender, Hegemony, Identity, Institutional Studies, Popular Culture, Queer Theory, Religion, Sexuality

From Thinking Sex: Notes for a Radical Theory of the Politics of Sexuality

I. The Sex Wars

> Asked his advice, Dr. J. Guerin affirmed that, after all other treatments had failed, he had succeeded in curing young girls affected by the vice of onanism by burning the clitoris with a hot iron. . . . I apply the hot point three times to each of the large labia and another on the clitoris. . . . After the first operation, from forty to fifty times a day, the number of voluptuous spasms was reduced to three or four. . . . We believe, then, that in cases similar to those submitted to your consideration, one should not hesitate to resort to the hot iron, and at an early hour, in order to combat clitoral and vaginal onanism in little girls.
>
> —Demetrius Zambaco[1]

The time has come to think about sex. To some, sexuality may seem to be an unimportant topic, a frivolous diversion from the more critical problems of poverty, war, disease, racism, famine, or nuclear annihilation. But it is precisely at times such as these, when we live with the possibility of unthinkable destruction, that people are likely to become dangerously crazy about sexuality. Contemporary conflicts over sexual values and erotic conduct have much in common with the religious disputes of earlier centuries. They acquire immense symbolic weight. Disputes over sexual behavior often become the vehicles for displacing social anxieties, and discharging their attendant emotional intensity. Consequently, sexuality should be treated with special respect in times of great social stress.

The realm of sexuality also has its own internal politics, inequities, and modes of oppression. As with other aspects of human behavior, the concrete institutional forms of sexuality at any given time and place are products of human activity. They are imbued with conflicts of interest and political maneuvering, both deliberate and incidental. In that sense, sex is always political. But there are also historical periods in which sexuality is more sharply contested and more overtly politicized. In such periods, the domain of erotic life is, in effect, renegotiated.

1. Demetrius Zambaco, "Onanism and Nervous Disorders in Two Little Girls," in François Peraldi (ed.), *Polysexuality, Semiotext(e)*, vol. 4, no. 1, 1981, pp. 31, 38 [Rubin's note]. Zambaco (1832–1913), physician born in Constantinople; he advocated radical treatment of masturbation in girls. Jules Guérin (1801–1886), French physician who coined the term "social medicine" and promoted aggressive treatment of masturbation.

In England and the United States, the late nineteenth century was one such era. During that time, powerful social movements focused on "vices" of all sorts. There were educational and political campaigns to encourage chastity, to eliminate prostitution, and to discourage masturbation, especially among the young. Morality crusaders attacked obscene literature, nude paintings, music halls, abortion, birth control information, and public dancing.[2] The consolidation of Victorian morality, and its apparatus of social, medical, and legal enforcement, was the outcome of a long period of struggle whose results have been bitterly contested ever since.

The consequences of these great nineteenth-century moral paroxysms are still with us. They have left a deep imprint on attitudes about sex, medical practice, child-rearing, parental anxieties, police conduct, and sex law.

The idea that masturbation is an unhealthy practice is part of that heritage. During the nineteenth century, it was commonly thought that "premature" interest in sex, sexual excitement, and, above all, sexual release, would impair the health and maturation of a child. Theorists differed on the actual consequences of sexual precocity. Some thought it led to insanity, while others merely predicted stunted growth. To protect the young from premature arousal, parents tied children down at night so they would not touch themselves; doctors excised the clitorises of onanistic little girls.[3] Although the more gruesome techniques have been abandoned, the attitudes that produced them persist. The notion that sex *per se* is harmful to the young has been chiseled into extensive social and legal structures designed to insulate minors from sexual knowledge and experience.

Much of the sex law currently on the books also dates from the nineteenth-century morality crusades. The first federal anti-obscenity law in the United States was passed in 1873. The Comstock Act—named for Anthony Comstock, an ancestral anti-porn activist and the founder of the New York Society for the Suppression of Vice—made it a federal crime to make, advertise, sell, possess, send through the mails, or import books or pictures deemed obscene. The law also banned contraceptive or abortifacient drugs and devices and information about them.[4] In the wake of the federal statute, most states passed their own anti-obscenity laws.

The Supreme Court began to whittle down both federal and state Comstock laws during the 1950s. By 1975, the prohibition of materials used for, and information about, contraception and abortion had been ruled unconstitutional. However, although the obscenity provisions have been modified, their fundamental constitutionality has been upheld. Thus it

2. Linda Gordon and Ellen Dubois, "Seeking Ecstasy on the Battlefield: Danger and Pleasure in Nineteenth-Century Feminist Sexual Thought," *Feminist Studies*, vol. 9, no. 1, Spring 1983; Steven Marcus, *The Other Victorians*, New York, New American Library, 1974; Mary Ryan, "The Power of Women's Networks: A Case Study of Female Moral Reform in America," *Feminist Studies*, vol. 5, no. 1, 1979; Judith R. Walkowitz, *Prostitution and Victorian Society*, Cambridge, Cambridge University Press, 1980; Judith R. Walkowitz, "Male Vice and Feminist Virtue: Feminism and the Politics of Prostitution in Nineteenth-Century Britain," *History Workshop Journal*, no. 13, Spring 1982; Jeffrey Weeks, *Sex, Politics and Society: The Regulation of Sexuality Since 1800*, New York, Longman, 1981 [Rubin's note].

3. G. J. Barker-Benfield, *The Horrors of the Half-Known Life*, New York, Harper Colophon, 1976; Marcus, op. cit.; Weeks, op. cit., especially pages 48–52; Zambaco, op. cit. [Rubin's note].

4. Sarah Senefeld Beserra, Sterling G. Franklin, and Norma Clevenger (eds.), *Sex Code of California*, Sacramento, Planned Parenthood Affiliates of California, 1977, p. 113 [Rubin's note]. Comstock (1844–1915), U.S. reformer and crusader against vice who influenced first the N.Y. state legislature and then Congress to pass laws against sending "obscene materials" through the mail.

remains a crime to make, sell, mail, or import material which has no purpose other than sexual arousal.[5]

Although sodomy statutes date from older strata of the law, when elements of canon law were adopted into civil codes, most of the laws used to arrest homosexuals and prostitutes come out of the Victorian campaigns against "white slavery." These campaigns produced myriad prohibitions against solicitation, lewd behavior, loitering for immoral purposes, age offenses, and brothels and bawdy houses.

In her discussion of the British "white slave" scare, historian Judith Walkowitz observes that: "Recent research delineates the vast discrepancy between lurid journalistic accounts and the reality of prostitution. Evidence of widespread entrapment of British girls in London and abroad is slim."[6] However, public furor over this ostensible problem

> forced the passage of the Criminal Law Amendment Act of 1885, a particularly nasty and pernicious piece of omnibus legislation. The 1885 Act raised the age of consent for girls from 13 to 16, but it also gave police far greater summary jurisdiction over poor working-class women and children . . . it contained a clause making indecent acts between consenting male adults a crime, thus forming the basis of legal prosecution of male homosexuals in Britain until 1967 . . . the clauses of the new bill were mainly enforced against working-class women, and regulated adult rather than youthful sexual behaviour.[7]

In the United States, the Mann Act, also known as the White Slave Traffic Act, was passed in 1910. Subsequently, every state in the union passed anti-prostitution legislation.[8]

In the 1950s, in the United States, major shifts in the organization of sexuality took place. Instead of focusing on prostitution or masturbation, the anxieties of the 1950s condensed most specifically around the image of the "homosexual menace" and the dubious specter of the "sex offender." Just before and after World War II, the "sex offender" became an object of public fear and scrutiny. Many states and cities, including Massachusetts, New Hampshire, New Jersey, New York State, New York City and Michigan, launched investigations to gather information about this menace to public safety.[9] The term "sex offender" sometimes applied to rapists, sometimes to "child molesters," and eventually functioned as a code for homosexuals. In its bureaucratic, medical, and popular versions, the sex offender discourse

5. Ibid., pp. 113–17 [Rubin's note].
6. Walkowitz, "Male Vice and Feminist Virtue," op. cit., p. 83. Walkowitz's entire discussion of the *Maiden Tribute of Modern Babylon* and its aftermath are illuminating [Rubin's note]. *Maiden Tribute of Modern Babylon*, a series of newspaper articles by W. T. Stead on child prostitution, appeared in England's *Pall Mall Gazette* in July 1885; their veracity was later called into question. Walkowitz (b. 1945), American historian specializing in modern European, British, and women's history.
7. Walkowitz, "Male Vice and Feminist Virtue," op. cit., p. 85 [Rubin's note].
8. Beserra et al., op. cit., pp. 106–7 [Rubin's note].
9. Commonwealth of Massachusetts, *Preliminary Report of the Special Commission Investigating the Prevalence of Sex Crimes*, 1947; State of New Hampshire, *Report of the Interim Commission of the State of New Hampshire to Study the Cause and Prevention of Serious Sex Crimes*, 1949; City of New York, *Report of the Mayor's Committee for the Study of Sex Offenses*, 1939; State of New York, *Report to the Governor on a Study of 102 Sex Offenders at Sing Sing Prison*, 1950; Samuel Hartwell, *A Citizen's Handbook of Sexual Abnormalities and the Mental Hygiene Approach to Theory Prevention*, State of Michigan, 1950; State of Michigan, *Report of the Governor's Study Commission on the Deviated Criminal Sex Offender*, 1951. This is merely a sampler [Rubin's note].

tended to blur distinctions between violent sexual assault and illegal but consensual acts such as sodomy. The criminal justice system incorporated these concepts when an epidemic of sexual psychopath laws swept through state legislatures.[1] These laws gave the psychological professions increased police powers over homosexuals and other sexual "deviants."

From the late 1940s until the early 1960s, erotic communities whose activities did not fit the postwar American dream drew intense persecution. Homosexuals were, along with communists, the objects of federal witch hunts and purges. Congressional investigations, executive orders, and sensational exposés in the media aimed to root out homosexuals employed by the government. Thousands lost their jobs, and restrictions on federal employment of homosexuals persist to this day.[2] The FBI began systematic surveillance and harassment of homosexuals which lasted at least into the 1970s.[3]

Many states and large cities conducted their own investigations, and the federal witch-hunts were reflected in a variety of local crackdowns. In Boise, Idaho, in 1955, a schoolteacher sat down to breakfast with his morning paper and read that the vice-president of the Idaho First National Bank had been arrested on felony sodomy charges; the local prosecutor said that he intended to eliminate all homosexuality from the community. The teacher never finished his breakfast. "He jumped up from his seat, pulled out his suitcases, packed as fast as he could, got into his car, and drove straight to San Francisco. . . . The cold eggs, coffee, and toast remained on his table for two days before someone from his school came by to see what had happened."[4]

In San Francisco, police and media waged war on homosexuals throughout the 1950s. Police raided bars, patrolled cruising areas, conducted street sweeps, and trumpeted their intention of driving the queers out of San Francisco.[5] Crackdowns against gay individuals, bars, and social areas occurred throughout the country. Although anti-homosexual crusades are the best-documented examples of erotic repression in the 1950s, future research should reveal similar patterns of increased harassment against pornographic materials, prostitutes, and erotic deviants of all sorts. Research is needed to determine the full scope of both police persecution and regulatory reform.[6]

1. Estelle B. Freedman, "'Uncontrolled Desire': The Threat of the Sexual Psychopath in America, 1935–1960," paper presented at the Annual Meeting of the American Historical Association, San Francisco, December 1983 [Rubin's note].

2. Allan Bérubé, "Behind the Spectre of San Francisco," *Body Politic*, April, 1981; Allan Bérubé, "Marching to a Different Drummer," *Advocate*, October 15, 1981; John D'Emilio, *Sexual Politics, Sexual Communities: The Making of the Homosexual Minority in the United States, 1940–1970*, Chicago, University of Chicago Press, 1983; Jonathan Katz, *Gay American History*, New York, Thomas Y. Crowell, 1976 [Rubin's note].

3. D'Emilio, op. cit, pp. 46–47; Alan Bérubé, personal communication [Rubin's note].

4. John Gerassi, *The Boys of Boise*, New York, Collier, 1968, p. 14. I am indebted to Allan Bérubé for calling my attention to this incident [Rubin's note].

5. Allan Bérubé, personal communication; D'Emilio, op. cit.; John D'Emilio, "Gay Politics, Gay Community; San Francisco's Experience," *Socialist Review*, no. 55, January–February, 1981 [Rubin's note].

6. The following examples suggest avenues for additional research. A local crackdown at the University of Michigan is documented in Daniel Tsang, "Gay Ann Arbor Purges," *Midwest Gay Academic Journal*, vol. 1, no. 1, 1977; and Daniel Tsang, "Ann Arbor Gay Purges," part 2, *Midwest Gay Academic Journal*, vol. 1, no. 2, 1977. At the University of Michigan, the number of faculty dismissed for alleged homosexuality appears to rival the number fired for alleged communist tendencies. It would be interesting to have figures comparing the number of professors who lost their positions during this period due to sexual and political offenses. On regulatory reform, many states passed laws during this period prohibiting the sale of alcoholic beverages to "known sex perverts" or providing that bars which catered to "sex perverts" be closed. Such a law was passed in California in 1955, and declared unconstitutional by the state supreme court in 1959 (Allan

The current period bears some uncomfortable similarities to the 1880s and the 1950s. The 1977 campaign to repeal the Dade County, Florida, gay rights ordinance[7] inaugurated a new wave of violence, state persecution, and legal initiatives directed against minority sexual populations and the commercial sex industry. For the last six years, the United States and Canada have undergone an extensive sexual repression in the political, not the psychological, sense. In the spring of 1977, a few weeks before the Dade County vote, the news media were suddenly full of reports of raids on gay cruising areas, arrests for prostitution, and investigations into the manufacture and distribution of pornographic materials. Since then, police activity against the gay community has increased exponentially. The gay press has documented hundreds of arrests, from the libraries of Boston to the streets of Houston and the beaches of San Francisco. Even the large, organized, and relatively powerful urban gay communities have been unable to stop these depredations. Gay bars and bath houses have been busted with alarming frequency, and police have gotten bolder. In one especially dramatic incident, police in Toronto raided all four of the city's gay baths. They broke into cubicles with crowbars and hauled almost 300 men out into the winter streets, clad in their bath towels. Even "liberated" San Francisco has not been immune. There have been proceedings against several bars, countless arrests in the parks, and, in the fall of 1981, police arrested over 400 people in a series of sweeps of Polk Street, one of the thoroughfares of local gay nightlife. Queerbashing has become a significant recreational activity for young urban males. They come into gay neighborhoods armed with baseball bats and looking for trouble, knowing that the adults in their lives either secretly approve or will look the other way.

The police crackdown has not been limited to homosexuals. Since 1977, enforcement of existing laws against prostitution and obscenity has been stepped up. Moreover, states and municipalities have been passing new and tighter regulations on commercial sex. Restrictive ordinances have been passed, zoning laws altered, licensing and safety codes amended, sentences increased, and evidentiary requirements relaxed. This subtle legal codification of more stringent controls over adult sexual behavior has gone largely unnoticed outside of the gay press.

For over a century, no tactic for stirring up erotic hysteria has been as reliable as the appeal to protect children. The current wave of erotic terror has reached deepest into those areas bordered in some way, if only symbolically,

---

Bérubé, personal communication). It would be of great interest to know exactly which states passed such statutes, the dates of their enactment, the discussion that preceded them, and how many are still on the books. On the persecution of other erotic populations, evidence indicates that John Willie and Irving Klaw, the two premier producers and distributors of bondage erotica in the United States from the late 1940s through the early 1960s, encountered frequent police harassment and that Klaw, at least, was affected by a congressional investigation conducted by the Kefauver Committee. I am indebted to personal communication from J. B. Rund for information on the careers of Willie and Klaw. Published sources are scarce, but see John Willie, *The Adventures of Sweet Gwendoline*, New York, Belier Press, 1974; J. B. Rund, "Preface," *Bizarre Comix*, vol. 8, New York, Belier Press, 1977; J. B. Rund, "Preface," *Bizarre Fotos*, vol. 1, New York, Belier Press, 1978; and J. B. Rund, "Preface," *Bizarre Katalogs*, vol. 1, New York, Belier Press, 1979. It would be useful to have more systematic information on legal shifts and police activity affecting non-gay erotic dissidence [Rubin's note]. Kefauver Committee: the U.S. Senate Special Committee to Investigate Crime in Interstate Commerce, chaired by Senator Estes Kefauver (D-Tenn.), which held nationally televised hearings to investigate organized crime (1950–51).

7. This successful nationally publicized campaign was led by Anita Bryant, a singer who performed in commercials for Florida orange juice.

by the sexuality of the young. The motto of the Dade County repeal campaign was "Save Our Children" from alleged homosexual recruitment. In February 1977, shortly before the Dade County vote, a sudden concern with "child pornography" swept the national media. In May, the *Chicago Tribune* ran a lurid four-day series with three-inch headlines, which claimed to expose a national vice ring organized to lure young boys into prostitution and pornography.[8] Newspapers across the country ran similar stories, most of them worthy of the *National Enquirer*.[9] By the end of May, a congressional investigation was underway. Within weeks, the federal government had enacted a sweeping bill against "child pornography" and many of the states followed with bills of their own. These laws have reestablished restrictions on sexual materials that had been relaxed by some of the important Supreme Court decisions. For instance, the Court ruled that neither nudity nor sexual activity *per se* were obscene. But the child pornography laws define as obscene any depiction of minors who are nude or engaged in sexual activity. This means that photographs of naked children in anthropology textbooks and many of the ethnographic movies shown in college classes are technically illegal in several states. In fact, the instructors are liable to an additional felony charge for showing such images to each student under the age of 18. Although the Supreme Court has also ruled that it is a constitutional right to possess obscene material for private use, the child pornography laws prohibit even the private possession of any sexual material involving minors.

The laws produced by the child porn panic are ill-conceived and misdirected. They represent far-reaching alterations in the regulation of sexual behavior and abrogate important sexual civil liberties. But hardly anyone noticed as they swept through Congress and state legislatures. With the exception of the North American Man/Boy Love Association and the American Civil Liberties Union, no one raised a peep of protest.[1]

A new and even tougher federal child pornography bill has just reached House-Senate conference. It removes any requirement that prosecutors must prove that alleged child pornography was distributed for commercial sale. Once this bill becomes law, a person merely possessing a nude snapshot of a 17-year-old lover or friend may go to jail for fifteen years, and be fined $100,000. This bill passed the House 400 to 1.[2]

The experiences of art photographer Jacqueline Livingston exemplify the climate created by the child porn panic. An assistant professor of photography at Cornell University, Livingston was fired in 1978 after exhibiting pictures of

8. "Chicago Is Center of National Child Porno Ring: The Child Predators," "Child Sex: Square in New Town Tells It All," "U.S. Orders Hearings on Child Pornography: Rodino Calls Sex Racket an 'Outrage,'" "Hunt Six Men, Twenty Boys in Crackdown," *Chicago Tribune*, May 16, 1977; "Dentist Seized in Child Sex Raid: Cary to Open Probe," "How Ruses Lure Victims to Child Pornographers," *Chicago Tribune*, May 17, 1977; "Child Pornographers Thrive on Legal Confusion," "U.S. Raids Hit Porn Sellers," *Chicago Tribune*, May 18, 1977 [Rubin's note].

9. American supermarket tabloid (founded 1926).

1. For more information on the "kiddie porn panic" see Pat Califia, "The Great Kiddy Porn Scare of '77 and Its Aftermath," *Advocate*, October 16, 1980; Pat Califia, "A Thorny Issue Splits a Movement," *Advocate*, October 30, 1980; Mitzel, *The Boston Sex Scandal*, Boston, Glad Day Books, 1980; Gayle Rubin, "Sexual Politics, the New Right, and the Sexual Fringe," in Daniel Tseng (ed.), *The Age Taboo*, Boston, Alyson Publications, 1981; on the issue of cross-generational relationships, see also Roger Moody, *Indecent Assault*, London, Word Is Out Press, 1980; Tom O'Carroll, *Paedophilia: The Radical Case*, London: Peter Owen, 1980; Tseng, *The Age Taboo*, op. cit.; and Paul Wilson, *The Man They Called a Monster*, New South Wales, Cassell Australia, 1981 [Rubin's note].

2. "House Passes Tough Bill on Child Porn," *San Francisco Chronicle*, November 15, 1983, p. 14 [Rubin's note]. The bill became law in 1984.

male nudes which included photographs of her seven-year-old son masturbating. *Ms. Magazine*, *Chrysalis*, and *Art News* all refused to run ads for Livingston's posters of male nudes. At one point, Kodak confiscated some of her film, and for several months, Livingston lived with the threat of prosecution under the child pornography laws. The Tompkins County Department of Social Services investigated her fitness as a parent. Livingston's posters have been collected by the Museum of Modern Art, the Metropolitan, and other major museums. But she has paid a high cost in harassment and anxiety for her efforts to capture on film the uncensored male body at different ages.[3]

It is easy to see someone like Livingston as a victim of the child porn wars. It is harder for most people to sympathize with actual boy-lovers. Like communists and homosexuals in the 1950s, boy-lovers are so stigmatized that it is difficult to find defenders for their civil liberties, let alone for their erotic orientation. Consequently, the police have feasted on them. Local police, the FBI, and watchdog postal inspectors have joined to build a huge apparatus whose sole aim is to wipe out the community of men who love underaged youth. In twenty years or so, when some of the smoke has cleared, it will be much easier to show that these men have been the victims of a savage and undeserved witch-hunt. A lot of people will be embarrassed by their collaboration with this persecution, but it will be too late to do much good for those men who have spent their lives in prison.

While the misery of the boy-lovers affects very few, the other long-term legacy of the Dade County repeal affects almost everyone. The success of the anti-gay campaign ignited long-simmering passions of the American right, and sparked an extensive movement to compress the boundaries of acceptable sexual behavior.

Right-wing ideology linking non-familial sex with communism and political weakness is nothing new. During the McCarthy period, Alfred Kinsey and his Institute for Sex Research were attacked for weakening the moral fiber of Americans and rendering them more vulnerable to communist influence. After congressional investigations and bad publicity, Kinsey's Rockefeller grant was terminated in 1954.[4]

Around 1969, the extreme right discovered the Sex Information and Education Council of the United States (SIECUS). In books and pamphlets, such as *The Sex Education Racket: Pornography in the Schools* and *SIECUS: Corrupter of Youth*, the right attacked SIECUS and sex education as communist plots to destroy the family and sap the national will.[5] Another pamphlet, *Pavlov's Children (They May Be Yours)*, claims that the United

3. George Stambolian, "Creating the New Man: A Conversation with Jacqueline Livingston," *Christopher Street*, May 1980; "Jacqueline Livingston," *Clothed with the Sun*, vol. 3, no. 1, May 1983 [Rubin's note].

4. Paul H. Gebhard, "The Institute," in Martin S. Weinberg (ed.), *Sex Research: Studies from the Kinsey Institute*, New York, Oxford University Press, 1976 [Rubin's note]. Kinsey (1894–1965), American biologist and sex researcher; in 1941 he secured funding from the Rockefeller Foundation, and in 1947 he founded the Institute for Sex Research of Indiana University (now the Kinsey Institute for Research in Sex, Gender, and Reproduction); its first two publications, *Sexual Behavior in the Human Male* (1948) and *Sexual Behavior in the Human Female* (1953), were best sellers. Joseph McCarthy (1908–1957), as Republican U.S. senator from Wisconsin (1947–57), gained national attention with his sensational and unsubstantiated claims that the State Department and other parts of the government had been infiltrated by Communists; he helped create an atmosphere of suspicion and fear in which all nonconformity became suspect.

5. Phoebe Courtney, *The Sex Education Racket: Pornography in the Schools (An Exposé)*, New Orleans, Free Men Speak, 1969; Dr. Gordon V. Drake, *SIECUS: Corrupter of Youth*, Tulsa, Oklahoma, Christian Crusade Publications, 1969 [Rubin's note].

Nations Educational, Scientific and Cultural Organization (UNESCO) is in cahoots with SIECUS to undermine religious taboos, to promote the acceptance of abnormal sexual relations, to downgrade absolute moral standards, and to "destroy racial cohesion," by exposing white people (especially white women) to the alleged "lower" sexual standards of black people.[6]

New Right and neo-conservative ideology has updated these themes, and leans heavily on linking "immoral" sexual behavior to putative declines in American power. In 1977, Norman Podhoretz wrote an essay blaming homosexuals for the alleged inability of the United States to stand up to the Russians.[7] He thus neatly linked "the anti-gay fight in the domestic arena and the anti-communist battles in foreign policy."[8]

Right-wing opposition to sex education, homosexuality, pornography, abortion, and pre-marital sex moved from the extreme fringes to the political center stage after 1977, when right-wing strategists and fundamentalist religious crusaders discovered that these issues had mass appeal. Sexual reaction played a significant role in the right's electoral success in 1980.[9] Organizations like the Moral Majority and Citizens for Decency[1] have acquired mass followings, immense financial resources, and unanticipated clout. The Equal Rights Amendment has been defeated, legislation has been passed that mandates new restrictions on abortion, and funding for programs like Planned Parenthood[2] and sex education has been slashed. Laws and regulations making it more difficult for teenage girls to obtain contraceptives or abortions have been promulgated. Sexual backlash was exploited in successful attacks on the Women's Studies Program at California State University at Long Beach.

The most ambitious right-wing legislative initiative has been the Family Protection Act (FPA), introduced in Congress in 1979. The Family Protection Act is a broad assault on feminism, homosexuals, non-traditional families, and teenage sexual privacy.[3] The Family Protection Act has not and probably will not pass, but conservative members of Congress continue to pursue its agenda in a more piecemeal fashion. Perhaps the most glaring

6. *Pavlov's Children (They May Be Yours)*, Impact Publishers, Los Angeles California, 1969 [Rubin's note].

7. Norman Podhoretz, "The Culture of Appeasement," *Harper's*, October 1977 [Rubin's note]. Podhoretz (b. 1930), prominent American neoconservative and longtime editor of *Commentary* magazine (1960–95).

8. Alan Wolfe and Jerry Sanders, "Resurgent Cold War Ideology: The Case of the Committee on the Present Danger," in Richard Fagen (ed.), *Capitalism and the State in U.S.-Latin American Relations*, Stanford, Stanford University Press, 1979 [Rubin's note].

9. Jimmy Breslin, "The Moral Majority in Your Motel Room," *San Francisco Chronicle*, January 22, 1981; Linda Gordon and Allen Hunter, "Sex, Family, and the New Right," *Radical America*, Winter 1977–78; Sasha Gregory-Lewis, "The Neo-Right Political Apparatus," *Advocate*, February 8, 1977; Sasha Gregory-Lewis, "Right Wing Finds New Organizing Tactic," *Advocate*, June 23, 1977; Sasha Gregory-Lewis, "Unravelling the Anti-Gay Network," *Advocate*, September 7, 1977; Andrew Kopkind, "America's New Right," *New Times*, September 30, 1977; Rosalind Pollack-Petchesky, "Anti-abortion, Anti-feminism, and the Rise of the New Right," *Feminist Studies*, vol. 7, no. 2, summer 1981 [Rubin's note].

1. Citizens for Decency through Law, a U.S. anti-pornography organization (founded in 1956; after 1993, it ceased to function on a national scale). Moral Majority: an organization (1979–89) founded by Jerry Falwell and other evangelicals to mobilize social conservatives politically (revived in 2004 as the Moral Majority Coalition).

2. Organization founded in 1923 (as the American Birth Control League) to provide comprehensive reproductive health care and education services. Equal Rights Amendment: though Congress passed a constitutional amendment in 1972 guaranteeing that equality of rights under the law not be abridged or denied on account of sex, the measure did not take effect, because it failed to gain the required ratification by three-quarters of the states by the 1982 deadline.

3. Rhonda Brown, "Blueprint for a Moral America," *Nation*, May 23, 1981 [Rubin's note].

sign of the times is the Adolescent Family Life Program. Also known as the Teen Chastity Program, it gets some 15 million federal dollars to encourage teenagers to refrain from sexual intercourse, and to discourage them from using contraceptives if they do have sex, and from having abortions if they get pregnant. In the last few years, there have been countless local confrontations over gay rights, sex education, abortion rights, adult bookstores, and public school curricula. It is unlikely that the anti-sex backlash is over, or that it has even peaked. Unless something changes dramatically, it is likely that the next few years will bring more of the same.

Periods such as the 1880s in England, and the 1950s in the United States, recodify the relations of sexuality. The struggles that were fought leave a residue in the form of laws, social practices, and ideologies which then affect the way in which sexuality is experienced long after the immediate conflicts have faded. All the signs indicate that the present era is another of those watersheds in the politics of sex. The settlements that emerge from the 1980s will have an impact far into the future. It is therefore imperative to understand what is going on and what is at stake in order to make informed decisions about what policies to support and oppose.

It is difficult to make such decisions in the absence of a coherent and intelligent body of radical thought about sex. Unfortunately, progressive political analysis of sexuality is relatively underdeveloped. Much of what is available from the feminist movement has simply added to the mystification that shrouds the subject. There is an urgent need to develop radical perspectives on sexuality.

Paradoxically, an explosion of exciting scholarship and political writing about sex has been generated in these bleak years. In the 1950s, the early gay rights movement began and prospered while the bars were being raided and anti-gay laws were being passed. In the last six years, new erotic communities, political alliances, and analyses have been developed in the midst of the repression. In this essay, I will propose elements of a descriptive and conceptual framework for thinking about sex and its politics. I hope to contribute to the pressing task of creating an accurate, humane, and genuinely liberatory body of thought about sexuality.

From *II. Sexual Thoughts*

> "You see, Tim," Phillip said suddenly, "your argument isn't reasonable. Suppose I granted your first point that homosexuality is justifiable in certain instances and under certain controls. Then there is the catch: where does justification end and degeneracy begin? Society must condemn to protect. Permit even the intellectual homosexual a place of respect and the first bar is down. Then comes the next and the next until the sadist, the flagellist, the criminally insane demand their places, and society ceases to exist. So I ask again: where is the line drawn? Where does degeneracy begin if not at the beginning of individual freedom in such matters?"
>
> —Fragment from a discussion between two gay men trying to decide if they may love each other, from a novel published in 1950[4]

4. James Barr, *Quatrefoil*, New York, Greenberg, 1950, p. 310 [Rubin's note].

A radical theory of sex must identify, describe, explain, and denounce erotic injustice and sexual oppression. Such a theory needs refined conceptual tools which can grasp the subject and hold it in view. It must build rich descriptions of sexuality as it exists in society and history. It requires a convincing critical language that can convey the barbarity of sexual persecution.

Several persistent features of thought about sex inhibit the development of such a theory. These assumptions are so pervasive in Western culture that they are rarely questioned. Thus, they tend to reappear in different political contexts, acquiring new rhetorical expressions but reproducing fundamental axioms.

One such axiom is sexual essentialism—the idea that sex is a natural force that exists prior to social life and shapes institutions. Sexual essentialism is embedded in the folk wisdoms of Western societies, which consider sex to be eternally unchanging, asocial, and transhistorical. Dominated for over a century by medicine, psychiatry, and psychology, the academic study of sex has reproduced essentialism. These fields classify sex as a property of individuals. It may reside in their hormones or their psyches. It may be construed as physiological or psychological. But within these ethnoscientific categories, sexuality has no history and no significant social determinants.

During the last five years, a sophisticated historical and theoretical scholarship has challenged sexual essentialism both explicitly and implicitly. Gay history, particularly the work of Jeffrey Weeks, has led this assault by showing that homosexuality as we know it is a relatively modern institutional complex.[5] Many historians have come to see the contemporary institutional forms of heterosexuality as an even more recent development.[6] An important contributor to the new scholarship is Judith Walkowitz, whose research has demonstrated the extent to which prostitution was transformed around the turn of the century. She provides meticulous descriptions of how the interplay of social forces such as ideology, fear, political agitation, legal reform, and medical practice can change the structure of sexual behavior and alter its consequences.[7]

Michel Foucault's *The History of Sexuality* has been the most influential and emblematic text of the new scholarship on sex. Foucault criticizes the traditional understanding of sexuality as a natural libido yearning to break free of social constraint. He argues that desires are not preexisting biological entities, but rather, that they are constituted in the course of historically specific social practices. He emphasizes the generative aspects of the social organization of sex rather than its repressive elements by pointing out that new sexualities are constantly produced. And he points to a major discontinuity between kinship based systems of sexuality and more modern forms.[8]

5. This insight was first articulated by Mary McIntosh, "The Homosexual Role," *Social Problems*, vol. 16, no. 2, Fall 1968; the idea has been developed in Jeffrey Weeks, *Coming Out: Homosexual Politics in Britain from the Nineteenth Century to the Present*, New York, Quartet, 1977, and in Weeks, *Sex, Politics, and Society*, op. cit.; see also D'Emilio, *Sexual Politics, Sexual Communities*, op. cit.; and Gayle Rubin, "Introduction" to Renée Vivien, *A Woman Appeared to Me*, Weatherby Lake, Mo., Naiad Press, 1979 [Rubin's note]. Weeks (b. 1945), British sociologist.

6. Bert Hansen, "The Historical Construction of Homosexuality," *Radical History Review*, no. 20, Spring/Summer, 1979 [Rubin's note].

7. Walkowitz, *Prostitution and Victorian Society*, op. cit.; and Walkowitz, "Male Vice and Female Virtue," op. cit. [Rubin's note].

8. Michel Foucault, *The History of Sexuality*, New York, Pantheon, 1978 [Rubin's note]. FOUCAULT (1926–1984), French philosopher and historian of ideas. For *The History of Sexuality* (1976), see above.

The new scholarship on sexual behavior has given sex a history and created a constructivist alternative to sexual essentialism. Underlying this body of work is an assumption that sexuality is constituted in society and history, not biologically ordained.[9] This does not mean the biological capacities are not prerequisites for human sexuality. It does mean that human sexuality is not comprehensible in purely biological terms. Human organisms with human brains are necessary for human cultures, but no examination of the body or its parts can explain the nature and variety of human social systems. The belly's hunger gives no clues as to the complexities of cuisine. The body, the brain, the genitalia, and the capacity for language are all necessary for human sexuality. But they do not determine its content, its experiences, or its institutional forms. Moreover, we never encounter the body unmediated by the meanings that cultures give to it. To paraphrase Lévi-Strauss, my position on the relationship between biology and sexuality is a "Kantianism without a transcendental libido."[1]

It is impossible to think with any clarity about the politics of race or gender as long as these are thought of as biological entities rather than as social constructs. Similarly, sexuality is impervious to political analysis as long as it is primarily conceived as a biological phenomenon or an aspect of individual psychology. Sexuality is as much a human product as are diets, methods of transportation, systems of etiquette, forms of labor, types of entertainment, processes of production, and modes of oppression. Once sex is understood in terms of social analysis and historical understanding, a more realistic politics of sex becomes possible. One may then think of sexual politics in terms of such phenomena as populations, neighborhoods, settlement patterns, migration, urban conflict, epidemiology, and police technology. These are more fruitful categories of thought than the more traditional ones of sin, disease, neurosis, pathology, decadence, pollution, or the decline and fall of empires.

By detailing the relationships between stigmatized erotic populations and the social forces which regulate them, work such as that of Allan Bérubé, John D'Emilio,[2] Jeffrey Weeks, and Judith Walkowitz contains implicit categories of political analysis and criticism. Nevertheless, the constructivist perspective has displayed some political weaknesses. This has been most evident in misconstructions of Foucault's position.

Because of his emphasis on the ways that sexuality is produced, Foucault has been vulnerable to interpretations that deny or minimize the reality of sexual repression in the more political sense. Foucault makes it abundantly clear that he is not denying the existence of sexual repression so much as inscribing it within a large dynamic.[3] Sexuality in Western societies has been structured within an extremely punitive social framework, and has been subjected to very real formal and informal controls. It is necessary to recognize repressive phenomena without resorting to the essentialist assumptions

9. A very useful discussion of these issues can be found in Robert Padgug, "Sexual Matters: On Conceptualizing Sexuality in History," *Radical History Review*, no. 20, Spring/Summer 1979 [Rubin's note].

1. Claude Lévi-Strauss, "A Confrontation," *New Left Review*, no. 62, July–August, 1970. In this conversation, Lévi-Strauss calls his position "a Kantianism without a transcendental subject" [Rubin's note]. LÉVI-STRAUSS (1908–2009), French anthropologist. The German philosopher IMMANUEL KANT sets forth his concept of the transcendental subject of thought—about which nothing of an empirical nature can be known—in *The Critique of Pure Reason* (1781).

2. American historian (b. 1948). Bérubé (1946–2007), American historian.

3. Foucault, op. cit., 11 [Rubin's note].

of the language of libido. It is important to hold repressive sexual practices in focus, even while situating them within a different totality and a more refined terminology.[4]

Most radical thought about sex has been embedded within a model of the instincts and their restraints. Concepts of sexual oppression have been lodged within that more biological understanding of sexuality. It is often easier to fall back on the notion of a natural libido subjected to inhumane repression than to reformulate concepts of sexual injustice within a more constructivist framework. But it is essential that we do so. We need a radical critique of sexual arrangements that has the conceptual elegance of Foucault and the evocative passion of Reich.[5]

The new scholarship on sex has brought a welcome insistence that sexual terms be restricted to their proper historical and social contexts, and a cautionary scepticism towards sweeping generalizations. But it is important to be able to indicate groupings of erotic behavior and general trends within erotic discourse. In addition to sexual essentialism, there are at least five other ideological formations whose grip on sexual thought is so strong that to fail to discuss them is to remain enmeshed within them. These are sex negativity, the fallacy of misplaced scale, the hierarchical valuation of sex acts, the domino theory of sexual peril, and the lack of a concept of benign sexual variation.

Of these five, the most important is sex negativity. Western cultures generally consider sex to be a dangerous, destructive, negative force.[6] Most Christian tradition, following Paul,[7] holds that sex is inherently sinful. It may be redeemed if performed within marriage for procreative purposes and if the pleasurable aspects are not enjoyed too much. In turn, this idea rests on the assumption that the genitalia are an intrinsically inferior part of the body, much lower and less holy than the mind, the "soul," the "heart," or even the upper part of the digestive system (the status of the excretory organs is close to that of the genitalia).[8] Such notions have by now acquired a life of their own and no longer depend solely on religion for their perseverance.

This culture always treats sex with suspicion. It construes and judges almost any sexual practice in terms of its worst possible expression. Sex is presumed guilty until proven innocent. Virtually all erotic behavior is considered bad unless a specific reason to exempt it has been established. The most acceptable excuses are marriage, reproduction, and love. Sometimes scientific curiosity, aesthetic experience, or a long-term intimate relationship may serve. But the exercise of erotic capacity, intelligence, curiosity, or creativity all require pretexts that are unnecessary for other pleasures, such as the enjoyment of food, fiction, or astronomy.

4. See the discussion in Weeks, *Sex, Politics and Society*, op. cit., p. 9 [Rubin's note].

5. Wilhelm Reich (1897–1957), Austrian psychoanalyst who setted in the United States in 1939; author of *The Function of the Orgasm* (1927) and *The Sexual Revolution* (1936), he argued that the release of "orgone energy" through sexual activity is necessary for individual and societal health.

6. See Weeks, *Sex, Politics and Society*, op. cit., p. 22 [Rubin's note]

7. St. Paul (d. ca. 67 C.E.), born a Roman Jew; he wrote, "It is good for a man not to touch a woman," but for those who cannot be abstinent "it is better to marry than to burn" (1 Corinthians 7.1, 9).

8. See, for example, "Pope Praises Couples for Self-Control," *San Francisco Chronicle*, October 13, 1980, p. 5; "Pope Says Sexual Arousal Isn't a Sin If It's Ethical," *San Francisco Chronicle*, November 6, 1980, p. 33; "Pope Condemns 'Carnal Lust' As Abuse of Human Freedom," *San Francisco Chronicle*, January 15, 1981, p. 2; "Pope Again Hits Abortion, Birth Control," *San Francisco Chronicle*, January 16, 1981, p. 13; and "Sexuality, not Sex in Heaven," *San Francisco Chronicle*, December 3, 1981, p. 50 [Rubin's note].

What I call the fallacy of misplaced scale is a corollary of sex negativity. Susan Sontag once commented that since Christianity focused "on sexual behavior as the root of virtue, everything pertaining to sex has been a 'special case' in our culture."[9] Sex law has incorporated the religious attitude that heretical sex is an especially heinous sin that deserves the harshest punishments. Throughout much of European and American history, a single act of consensual anal penetration was grounds for execution. In some states, sodomy still carries twenty-year prison sentences.[1] Outside the law, sex is also a marked category. Small differences in value or behavior are often experienced as cosmic threats. Although people can be intolerant, silly, or pushy about what constitutes proper diet, differences in menu rarely provoke the kinds of rage, anxiety, and sheer terror that routinely accompany differences in erotic taste. Sexual acts are burdened with an excess of significance.

Modern Western societies appraise sex acts according to a hierarchical system of sexual value. Marital, reproductive heterosexuals are alone at the top of the erotic pyramid. Clamoring below are unmarried monogamous heterosexuals in couples, followed by most other heterosexuals. Solitary sex floats ambiguously. The powerful nineteenth-century stigma on masturbation lingers in less potent, modified forms, such as the idea that masturbation is an inferior substitute for partnered encounters. Stable, long-term lesbian and gay male couples are verging on respectability, but bar dykes and promiscuous gay men are hovering just above the groups at the very bottom of the pyramid. The most despised sexual castes currently include transsexuals, transvestites, fetishists, sadomasochists, sex workers such as prostitutes and porn models, and the lowliest of all, those whose eroticism transgresses generational boundaries.

Individuals whose behavior stands high in this hierarchy are rewarded with certified mental health, respectability, legality, social and physical mobility, institutional support, and material benefits. As sexual behaviors or occupations fall lower on the scale, the individuals who practice them are subjected to a presumption of mental illness, disreputability, criminality, restricted social and physical mobility, loss of institutional support, and economic sanctions.

Extreme and punitive stigma maintains some sexual behaviors as low status and is an effective sanction against those who engage in them. The intensity of this stigma is rooted in Western religious traditions. But most of its contemporary content derives from medical and psychiatric opprobrium.

The old religious taboos were primarily based on kinship forms of social organization. They were meant to deter inappropriate unions and to provide proper kin. Sex laws derived from Biblical pronouncements were aimed at preventing the acquisition of the wrong kinds of affinal partners: consanguineous kin (incest), the same gender (homosexuality), or the wrong species (bestiality). When medicine and psychiatry acquired extensive powers over sexuality, they were less concerned with unsuitable mates than with unfit forms of desire. If taboos against incest best characterized kinship systems of sexual organization, then the shift to an emphasis on taboos against

9. Susan Sontag, *Styles of Radical Will*, New York, Farrar, Straus, & Giroux, 1969, p. 46 [Rubin's note]. SONTAG (1933–2004), American novelist, filmmaker, and literary and cultural critic.

1. In 2003 the Supreme Court struck down anti-sodomy laws, reversing a 1986 ruling that had affirmed their constitutionality.

masturbation was more apposite to the newer systems organized around qualities of erotic experience.[2]

Medicine and psychiatry multiplied the categories of sexual misconduct. The section on psychosexual disorders in the *Diagnostic and Statistical Manual of Mental Disorders (DSM)* of the American Psychiatric Association (APA) is a fairly reliable map of the current moral hierarchy of sexual activities. The APA list is much more elaborate than the traditional condemnations of whoring, sodomy, and adultery. The most recent edition, *DSM-III*, removed homosexuality from the roster of mental disorders after a long political struggle. But fetishism, sadism, masochism, transsexuality, transvestism, exhibitionism, voyeurism, and pedophilia are quite firmly entrenched as psychological malfunctions.[3] Books are still being written about the genesis, etiology, treatment, and cure of these assorted "pathologies."

Psychiatric condemnation of sexual behaviors invokes concepts of mental and emotional inferiority rather than categories of sexual sin. Low status sex practices are vilified as mental diseases or symptoms of defective personality integration. In addition, psychological terms conflate difficulties of psychodynamic functioning with modes of erotic conduct. They equate sexual masochism with self-destructive personality patterns, sexual sadism with emotional aggression, and homoeroticism with immaturity. These terminological muddles have become powerful stereotypes that are indiscriminately applied to individuals on the basis of their sexual orientations.

Popular culture is permeated with ideas that erotic variety is dangerous, unhealthy, depraved, and a menace to everything from small children to national security. Popular sexual ideology is a noxious stew made up of ideas of sexual sin, concepts of psychological inferiority, anti-communism, mob hysteria, accusations of witchcraft, and xenophobia. The mass media nourish these attitudes with relentless propaganda. I would call this system of erotic stigma the last socially respectable form of prejudice if the old forms did not show such obstinate vitality, and new ones did not continually become apparent.

All these hierarchies of sexual value—religious, psychiatric, and popular—function in much the same ways as do ideological systems of racism, ethnocentrism, and religious chauvinism. They rationalize the well-being of the sexually privileged and the adversity of the sexual rabble.

Figure 1 diagrams a general version of the sexual value system. According to this system, sexuality that is "good," "normal" and "natural" should ideally be heterosexual, marital, monogamous, reproductive, and non-commercial. It should be coupled, relational, within the same generation, and occur at home. It should not involve pornography, fetish objects, sex toys of any sort, or roles other than male and female. Any sex that violates these rules is "bad," "abnormal," or "unnatural." Bad sex may be homosexual, unmarried, promiscuous, non-procreative, or commercial. It may be masturbatory or take place at orgies, may be casual, may cross generational lines, and may take place in "public," or at least in the bushes or the baths. It may involve the use of pornography, fetish objects, sex toys, or unusual roles (see Figure 1).

2. See Foucault, op. cit., pp. 106–7 [Rubin's note].
3. American Psychiatric Association, *Diagnostic and Statistical Manual of Mental and Physical Disorders*, 3rd edn, Washington, D.C., American Psychiatric Association [Rubin's note].

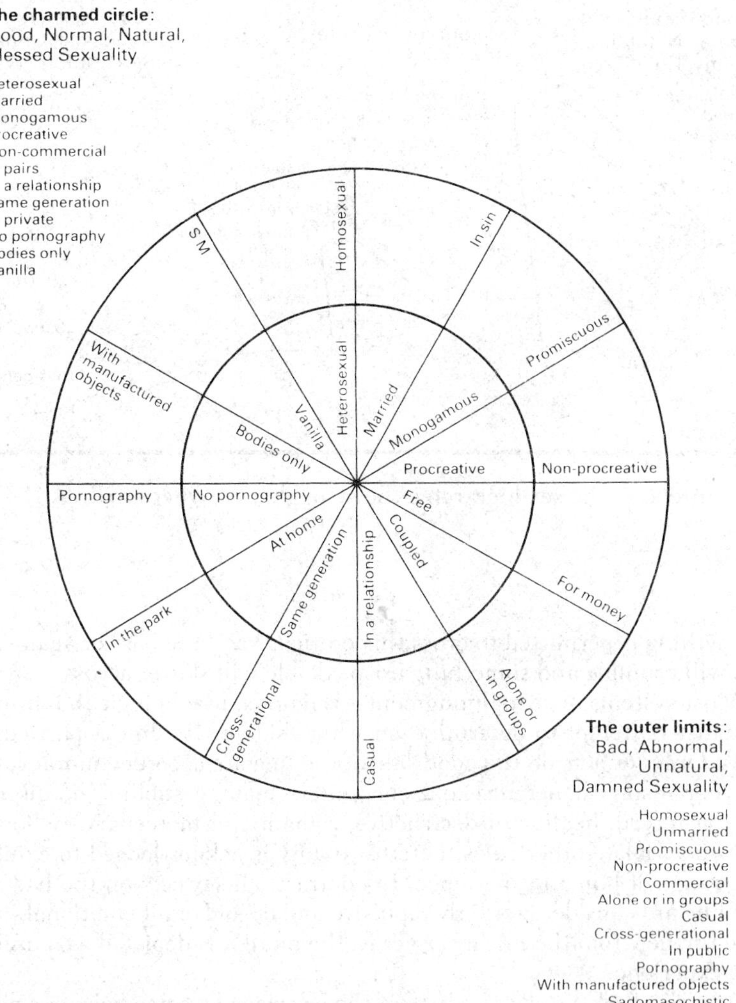

Figure 1. The sex hierarchy: the charmed circle vs the outer limits

Figure 2 diagrams another aspect of the sexual hierarchy: the need to draw and maintain an imaginary line between good and bad sex. Most of the discourses on sex, be they religious, psychiatric, popular, or political, delimit a very small portion of human sexual capacity as sanctifiable, safe, healthy, mature, legal, or politically correct. The "line" distinguishes these from all other erotic behaviors, which are understood to be the work of the devil, dangerous, psychopathological, infantile, or politically reprehensible. Arguments are then conducted over "where to draw the line," and to determine what other activities, if any, may be permitted to cross over into acceptability.

All these models assume a domino theory of sexual peril. The line appears to stand between sexual order and chaos. It expresses the fear that

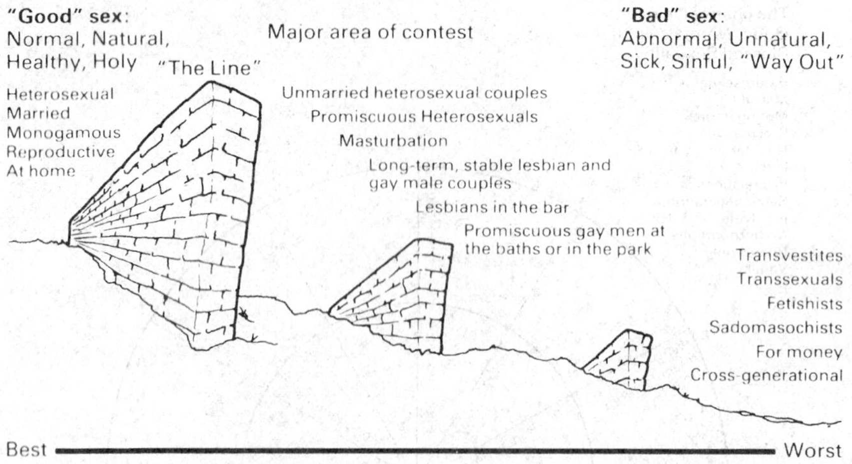

Figure 2. The sex hierarchy: the struggle over where to draw the line

if anything is permitted to cross this erotic DMZ,[4] the barrier against scary sex will crumble and something unspeakable will skitter across.

Most systems of sexual judgment—religious, psychological, feminist, or socialist—attempt to determine on which side of the line a particular act falls. Only sex acts on the good side of the line are accorded moral complexity. For instance, heterosexual encounters may be sublime or disgusting, free or forced, healing or destructive, romantic or mercenary. As long as it does not violate other rules, heterosexuality is acknowledged to exhibit the full range of human experience. In contrast, all sex acts on the bad side of the line are considered utterly repulsive and devoid of all emotional nuance. The further from the line a sex act is, the more it is depicted as a uniformly bad experience.

As a result of the sex conflicts of the last decade, some behavior near the border is inching across it. Unmarried couples living together, masturbation, and some forms of homosexuality are moving in the direction of respectability (see Figure 2). Most homosexuality is still on the bad side of the line. But if it is coupled and monogamous, the society is beginning to recognize that it includes the full range of human interaction. Promiscuous homosexuality, sadomasochism, fetishism, transsexuality, and cross-generational encounters are still viewed as unmodulated horrors incapable of involving affection, love, free choice, kindness, or transcendence.

This kind of sexual morality has more in common with ideologies of racism than with true ethics. It grants virtue to the dominant groups, and relegates vice to the underprivileged. A democratic morality should judge sexual acts by the way partners treat one another, the level of mutual consideration, the presence or absence of coercion, and the quantity and quality of the pleasures they provide. Whether sex acts are gay or straight,

4. Demilitarized zone, the boundary between two military powers.

coupled or in groups, naked or in underwear, commercial or free, with or without video, should not be ethical concerns.

It is difficult to develop a pluralistic sexual ethics without a concept of benign sexual variation. Variation is a fundamental property of all life, from the simplest biological organisms to the most complex human social formations. Yet sexuality is supposed to conform to a single standard. One of the most tenacious ideas about sex is that there is one best way to do it, and that everyone should do it that way.

Most people find it difficult to grasp that whatever they like to do sexually will be thoroughly repulsive to someone else, and that whatever repels them sexually will be the most treasured delight of someone, somewhere. One need not like or perform a particular sex act in order to recognize that someone else will, and that this difference does not indicate a lack of good taste, mental health, or intelligence in either party. Most people mistake their sexual preferences for a universal system that will or should work for everyone.

This notion of a single ideal sexuality characterizes most systems of thought about sex. For religion, the ideal is procreative marriage. For psychology, it is mature heterosexuality. Although its content varies, the format of a single sexual standard is continually reconstituted within other rhetorical frameworks, including feminism and socialism. It is just as objectionable to insist that everyone should be lesbian, non-monogamous, or kinky, as to believe that everyone should be heterosexual, married, or vanilla—though the latter set of opinions are backed by considerably more coercive power than the former.

Progressives who would be ashamed to display cultural chauvinism in other areas routinely exhibit it towards sexual differences. We have learned to cherish different cultures as unique expressions of human inventiveness rather than as the inferior or disgusting habits of savages. We need a similarly anthropological understanding of different sexual cultures.

Empirical sex research is the one field that does incorporate a positive concept of sexual variation. Alfred Kinsey approached the study of sex with the same uninhibited curiosity he had previously applied to examining a species of wasp. His scientific detachment gave his work a refreshing neutrality that enraged moralists and caused immense controversy.[5] Among Kinsey's successors, John Gagnon and William Simon have pioneered the application of sociological understandings to erotic variety.[6] Even some of the older sexology is useful. Although his work is imbued with unappetizing eugenic beliefs, Havelock Ellis was an acute and sympathetic observer. His monumental *Studies in the Psychology of Sex* is resplendent with detail.[7]

Much political writing on sexuality reveals complete ignorance of both classical sexology and modern sex research. Perhaps this is because so few colleges and universities bother to teach human sexuality, and because so

5. Alfred Kinsey, Wardell Pomeroy, and Clyde Martin, *Sexual Behavior in the Human Male*, Philadelphia, W. B. Saunders, 1948; Alfred Kinsey, Wardell Pomeroy, Clyde Martin, and Paul Gebhard, *Sexual Behavior in the Human Female*, Philadelphia, W. B. Saunders, 1953 [Rubin's note].

6. John Gagnon and William Simon, *Sexual Deviance*, New York, Harper & Row, 1967; John Gagnon and William Simon, *The Sexual Scene*, Chicago, Transaction Books, Aldine, 1970; John Gagnon, *Human Sexualities*, Glenview, Illinois, Scott, Foresman, 1977 [Rubin's note]. Gagnon (1931–2016) and Simon (1930–2000), American sociologists.

7. Havelock Ellis, *Studies in the Psychology of Sex* (two volumes), New York, Random House, 1936 [Rubin's note]. Ellis (1859–1939), British physician and pioneer of sexology.

much stigma adheres even to scholarly investigation of sex. Neither sexology nor sex research has been immune to the prevailing sexual value system. Both contain assumptions and information which should not be accepted uncritically. But sexology and sex research provide abundant detail, a welcome posture of calm, and a well developed ability to treat sexual variety as something that exists rather than as something to be exterminated. These fields can provide an empirical grounding for a radical theory of sexuality more useful than the combination of psychoanalysis and feminist first principles to which so many texts resort.

* * *

From *VI. The Limits of Feminism*

> We know that in an overwhelmingly large number of cases, sex crime is associated with pornography. We know that sex criminals read it, are clearly influenced by it. I believe that, if we can eliminate the distribution of such items among impressionable children, we shall greatly reduce our frightening sex-crime rate.
>
> —J. Edgar Hoover[8]

In the absence of a more articulated radical theory of sex, most progressives have turned to feminism for guidance. But the relationship between feminism and sex is complex. Because sexuality is a nexus of the relationships between genders, much of the oppression of women is borne by, mediated through, and constituted within, sexuality. Feminism has always been vitally interested in sex. But there have been two strains of feminist thought on the subject. One tendency has criticized the restrictions on women's sexual behavior and denounced the high costs imposed on women for being sexually active. This tradition of feminist sexual thought has called for a sexual liberation that would work for women as well as for men. The second tendency has considered sexual liberalization to be inherently a mere extension of male privilege. This tradition resonates with conservative, anti-sexual discourse. With the advent of the anti-pornography movement, it achieved temporary hegemony over feminist analysis.

The anti-pornography movement and its texts have been the most extensive expression of this discourse.[9] In addition, proponents of this viewpoint have condemned virtually every variant of sexual expression as anti-feminist. Within this framework, monogamous lesbianism that occurs within long-term, intimate relationships, and which does not involve playing with polarized roles, has replaced married, procreative heterosexuality at the top of the value hierarchy. Heterosexuality has been demoted to somewhere in the middle. Apart from this change, everything else looks more or less familiar. The lower depths are occupied by the usual groups and behaviors: prostitu-

8. Cited in H. Montgomery Hyde, *A History of Pornography*, New York, Dell, 1965, p. 31 [Rubin's note]. Hoover (1895–1972), made director in 1924 of the Bureau of Investigation, renamed the Federal Bureau of Investigation in 1935, a position he held until his death. (Rumors that he was a homosexual have circulated for decades.)

9. See, for example, Laura Lederer (ed.), *Take Back the Night*, New York, William Morrow, 1980; Andrea Dworkin, *Pornography*, New York, Perigee, 1981. The *Newspage* of San Francisco's Women Against Violence in Pornography and Media and the *Newsreport* of New York Women Against Pornography are excellent sources [Rubin's note].

tion, transsexuality, sadomasochism, and cross-generational activities.[1] Most gay male conduct, all casual sex, promiscuity, and lesbian behavior that does involve roles or kink or non-monogamy are also censured.[2] Even sexual fantasy during masturbation is denounced as a phallocentric hold-over.[3]

This discourse on sexuality is less a sexology than a demonology. It presents most sexual behavior in the worst possible light. Its descriptions of erotic conduct always use the worst available example as if it were representative. It presents the most disgusting pornography, the most exploited forms of prostitution, and the least palatable or most shocking manifestations of sexual variation. This rhetorical tactic consistently misrepresents human sexuality in all its forms. The picture of human sexuality that emerges from this literature is unremittingly ugly.

In addition, this anti-porn rhetoric is a massive exercise in scapegoating. It criticizes non-routine acts of love rather than routine acts of oppression, exploitation, or violence. This demon sexology directs legitimate anger at women's lack of personal safety against innocent individuals, practices, and communities. Anti-porn propaganda often implies that sexism originates within the commercial sex industry and subsequently infects the rest of society. This is sociologically nonsensical. The sex industry is hardly a feminist utopia. It reflects the sexism that exists in the society as a whole. We need to analyze and oppose the manifestations of gender inequality specific to the sex industry. But this is not the same as attempting to wipe out commercial sex.

Similarly, erotic minorities such as sadomasochists and transsexuals are as likely to exhibit sexist attitudes or behavior as any other politically random social grouping. But to claim that they are inherently anti-feminist is sheer fantasy. A good deal of current feminist literature attributes the oppression of women to graphic representations of sex, prostitution, sex education, sadomasochism, male homosexuality, and transsexualism. Whatever happened to the family, religion, education, child-rearing practices, the media, the state, psychiatry, job discrimination, and unequal pay?

Finally, this so-called feminist discourse recreates a very conservative sexual morality. For over a century, battles have been waged over just how much shame, distress, and punishment should be incurred by sexual activity.

1. Kathleen Barry, *Female Sexual Slavery*, Englewood Cliffs, New Jersey, Prentice-Hall, 1979; Janice Raymond, *The Transsexual Empire*, Boston, Beacon, 1979; Kathleen Barry, "Sadomasochism: The New Backlash to Feminism," *Trivia*, no. 1, fall 1982; Robin Ruth Linden, Darlene R. Pagano, Diana E. H. Russell, and Susan Leigh Starr (eds.), *Against Sadomasochism*, East Palo Alto, CA, Frog in the Wall, 1982; and Florence Rush, *The Best Kept Secret*, New York, McGraw-Hill, 1980 [Rubin's note].

2. Sally Gearhart, "An Open Letter to the Voters in District 5 and San Francisco's Gay Community," 1979; ADRIENNE RICH, *On Lies, Secrets, and Silence*, New York, W. W. Norton, 1979, p. 225 ("On the other hand, there is homosexual patriarchal culture, a culture created by homosexual men, reflecting such male stereotypes as dominance and submission as modes of relationship, and the separation of sex from emotional involvement—a culture tainted by profound hatred for women. The male 'gay' culture has offered lesbians the imitation role–stereotypes of 'butch' and 'femme,' 'active' and 'passive,' cruising, sadomasochism, and the violent, self-destructive world of 'gay' bars"); Judith Pasternak, "The Strangest Bedfellows: Lesbian Feminism and the Sexual Revolution," *WomanNews*, October, 1983; Adrienne Rich, "Compulsory Heterosexuality and Lesbian Existence," in Ann Snitow, Christine Stansell, and Sharon Thompson (eds.), *Powers of Desire: The Politics of Sexuality*, New York, Monthly Review Press, 1983 [Rubin's note]. For Rich's essay "Compulsory Heterosexuality" (1980), see above.

3. Julia Penelope, "And Now For the Really Hard Questions," *Sinister Wisdom*, no. 15, Fall 1980, p. 103 [Rubin's note].

The conservative tradition has promoted opposition to pornography, prostitution, homosexuality, all erotic variation, sex education, sex research, abortion, and contraception. The opposing, pro-sex tradition has included individuals like Havelock Ellis, Magnus Hirshfeld, Alfred Kinsey, and Victoria Woodhull,[4] as well as the sex education movement, organizations of militant prostitutes and homosexuals, the reproductive rights movement, and organizations such as the Sexual Reform League of the 1960s. This motley collection of sex reformers, sex educators, and sexual militants has mixed records on both sexual and feminist issues. But surely they are closer to the spirit of modern feminism than are moral crusaders, the social purity movement, and anti-vice organizations. Nevertheless, the current feminist sexual demonology generally elevates the anti-vice crusaders to positions of ancestral honor, while condemning the more liberatory tradition as anti-feminist. In an essay that exemplifies some of these trends, Sheila Jeffreys blames Havelock Ellis, Edward Carpenter, Alexandra Kollantai, "believers in the joy of sex of every possible political persuasion," and the 1929 congress of the World League for Sex Reform for making "a great contribution to the defeat of militant feminism."[5]

The anti-pornography movement and its avatars have claimed to speak for all feminism. Fortunately, they do not. Sexual liberation has been and continues to be a feminist goal. The women's movement may have produced some of the most retrogressive sexual thinking this side of the Vatican. But it has also produced an exciting, innovative, and articulate defense of sexual pleasure and erotic justice. This "pro-sex" feminism has been spearheaded by lesbians whose sexuality does not conform to movement standards of purity (primarily lesbian sadomasochists and butch/femme dykes), by unapologetic heterosexuals, and by women who adhere to classic radical feminism rather than to the revisionist celebrations of femininity which have become so common.[6] Although the anti-porn forces have

4. American reformer, agitator for women's suffrage, and advocate of free love (1838–1927). Hirschfeld (1868–1935), German physician, sexologist, and founder of the first homosexual rights organization, the Scientific Humanitarian Committee (1897), and the World League for Sexual Reform (1921).

5. Sheila Jeffreys, "The Spinster and Her Enemies: Sexuality and the Last Wave of Feminism," *Scarlet Woman*, no. 13, part 2, July, 1981, p. 26; a further elaboration of this tendency can be found in Judith Pasternak, op. cit. [Rubin's note]. Jeffreys (b. 1948), British professor of political science and feminist activist. Carpenter (1844–1929), English socialist reformer who wrote extensively and positively about homosexuality. Kollantai (1872–1952), Russian revolutionary, novelist, and advocate for free love and women's rights.

6. Pat Califia, "Feminism vs. Sex: A New Conservative Wave," *Advocate*, February 21, 1980; Pat Califia, "Among Us, Against Us—The New Puritans," *Advocate*, April 17, 1980; Califia, "The Great Kiddy Porn Scare of '77 and Its Aftermath," op. cit.; Califia, "A Thorny Issue Splits a Movement," op. cit.; Pat Califia, *Sapphistry*, Tallahassee, Florida, Naiad, 1980; Pat Califia, "What Is Gay Liberation," *Advocate*, June 25, 1981; Pat Califia, "Feminism and Sadomasochism," *Co-Evolution Quarterly*, no. 33, Spring 1981; Pat Califia, "Response to Dorchen Leidholdt," *New Women's Times*, October 1982; Pat Califia, "Public Sex," *Advocate*, September 30, 1982; Pat Califia, "Doing It Together: Gay Men, Lesbians, and Sex," *Advocate*, July 7, 1983; Pat Califia, "Gender-Bending," *Advocate*, September 15, 1983; Pat Califia, "The Sex Industry," *Advocate*, October 13, 1983; Deirdre English, Amber Hollibaugh, and Gayle Rubin, "Talking Sex," *Socialist Review*, July–August, 1981; "Sex Issue," *Heresies*, no. 12, 1981; Amber Hollibaugh, "The Erotophobic Voice of Women: Building a Movement for the Nineteenth Century," *New York Native*, September 26–October 9, 1983; Maxine Holz, "Porn: Turn On or Put Down, Some Thoughts on Sexuality," *Processed World*, no. 7, Spring 1983; Barbara O'Dair, "Sex, Love, and Desire: Feminists Struggle Over the Portrayal of Sex," *Alternative Media*, Spring, 1983; Lisa Orlando, "Bad Girls and 'Good' Politics," *Village Voice*, Literary Supplement, December 1982; Joanna Russ, "Being Against Pornography," *Thirteenth Moon*, vol. VI, nos. 1 and 2, 1982; Samois, *What Color Is Your Handkerchief*, Berkeley, Samois, 1979; Samois, *Coming to Power*, Boston, Alyson, 1982; Deborah Sundahl, "Stripping for a Living," *Advocate*, October 13, 1983; Nancy Wechsler, "Interview with Pat Califia and Gayle

attempted to weed anyone who disagrees with them out of the movement, the fact remains that feminist thought about sex is profoundly polarized.[7]

Whenever there is polarization, there is an unhappy tendency to think the truth lies somewhere in between. Ellen Willis has commented sarcastically that "the feminist bias is that women are equal to men and the male chauvinist bias is that women are inferior. The unbiased view is that the truth lies somewhere in between."[8] The most recent development in the feminist sex wars is the emergence of a "middle" that seeks to evade the dangers of anti-porn fascism, on the one hand, and a supposed "anything goes" libertarianism, on the other.[9] Although it is hard to criticize a position that is not yet fully formed, I want to draw attention to some incipient problems.

The emergent middle is based on a false characterization of the poles of the debate, construing both sides as equally extremist. According to B. Ruby Rich, "the desire for a language of sexuality has led feminists into locations (pornography, sadomasochism) too narrow or overdetermined for a fruitful discussion. Debate has collapsed into a rumble."[1] True, the fights between Women Against Pornography (WAP)[2] and lesbian sadomasochists have resembled gang warfare. But the responsibility for this lies primarily with the anti-porn movement, and its refusal to engage in principled discussion. S/M lesbians have been forced into a struggle to maintain their membership in the movement, and to defend themselves against slander. No major spokeswoman for lesbian S/M has argued for any kind of S/M supremacy, or advocated that everyone should be a sadomasochist. In addition to self-defense, S/M lesbians have called for appreciation for erotic diversity and more open discussion of sexuality.[3] Trying to find a middle course between WAP and Samois[4] is a bit like saying that the truth about homosexuality lies somewhere between the positions of the Moral Majority and those of the gay movement.

In political life, it is all too easy to marginalize radicals, and to attempt to buy acceptance for a moderate position by portraying others as extremists. Liberals have done this for years to communists. Sexual radicals have opened up the sex debates. It is shameful to deny their contribution, misrepresent their positions, and further their stigmatization.

Rubin," part I, *Gay Community News*, Book Review, July 18, 1981, and part II, *Gay Community News*, August 15, 1981; Ellen Willis, *Beginning to See the Light*, New York, Knopf, 1981; for an excellent overview of the history of the ideological shifts in feminism which have affected the sex debates, see Alice Echols, "Cultural Feminism: Feminist Capitalism and the Anti-Pornography Movement," *Social Text*, no. 7, Spring and Summer 1983 [Rubin's note].

7. Lisa Orlando, "Lust at Last! Spandex Invades the Academy," *Gay Community News*, May 15, 1982; Ellen Willis, "Who Is a Feminist? An Open Letter to Robin Morgan," *Village Voice*, Literary Supplement, December 1982 [Rubin's note].

8. Ellen Willis, *Beginning to See the Light*, op. cit., p. 146. I am indebted to Jeanne Bergman for calling my attention to this quote [Rubin's note]. Willis (1941–2006), radical feminist, cultural critic, and co-founder in 1969 of the radical feminist group Redstockings.

9. See, for example, Jessica Benjamin, "Master and Slave: The Fantasy of Erotic Domination," in Snitow et al., op. cit., p. 297; and B. Ruby Rich, review of *Powers of Desire*, *In These Times*, November 16–22, 1983 [Rubin's note].

1. B. Ruby Rich, op. cit., p. 76 [Rubin's note]. Rich (b. 1948), American cultural theorist and film critic.

2. Radical feminist activist group, founded in 1978; it gained attention in the 1980s by leading organized tours of sex shops and pornographic theaters.

3. Samois, *What Color Is Your Handkerchief*, op. cit.; Samois, *Coming to Power*, op. cit.; Pat Califia, "Feminism and Sadomasochism," op. cit.; Pat Califia, *Sapphistry*, op. cit. [Rubin's note].

4. Organization of lesbian-feminist sadomasochists (1978–83), co-founded in San Francisco by Rubin.

In contrast to cultural feminists,[5] who simply want to purge sexual dissidents, the sexual moderates are willing to defend the rights of erotic nonconformists to political participation. Yet this defense of political rights is linked to an implicit system of ideological condescension. The argument has two major parts. The first is an accusation that sexual dissidents have not paid close enough attention to the meaning, sources, or historical construction of their sexuality. This emphasis on meaning appears to function in much the same way that the question of etiology has functioned in discussions of homosexuality. That is, homosexuality, sadomasochism, prostitution, or boy-love are taken to be mysterious and problematic in some way that more respectable sexualities are not. The search for a cause is a search for something that could change so that these "problematic" eroticisms would simply not occur. Sexual militants have replied to such exercises that although the question of etiology or cause is of intellectual interest, it is not high on the political agenda and that, moreover, the privileging of such questions is itself a regressive political choice.

The second part of the "moderate" position focuses on questions of consent. Sexual radicals of all varieties have demanded the legal and social legitimation of consenting sexual behavior. Feminists have criticized them for ostensibly finessing questions about "the limits of consent" and "structural constraints" on consent.[6] Although there are deep problems with the political discourse of consent, and although there are certainly structural constraints on sexual choice, this criticism has been consistently misapplied in the sex debates. It does not take into account the very specific semantic content that consent has in sex law and sex practice.

As I mentioned earlier, a great deal of sex law does not distinguish between consensual and coercive behavior. Only rape law contains such a distinction. Rape law is based on the assumption, correct in my view, that heterosexual activity may be freely chosen or forcibly coerced. One has the legal right to engage in heterosexual behavior as long as it does not fall under the purview of other statutes and as long as it is agreeable to both parties.

This is not the case for most other sexual acts. Sodomy laws, as I mentioned above, are based on the assumption that the forbidden acts are an "abominable and detestable crime against nature." Criminality is intrinsic to the acts themselves, no matter what the desires of the participants. "Unlike rape, sodomy or an unnatural or perverted sexual act may be committed between two persons both of whom consent, and regardless of which is the aggressor, both may be prosecuted."[7] Before the consenting adults statute was passed in California in 1976, lesbian lovers could have been prosecuted for committing oral copulation. If both participants were capable of consent, both were equally guilty.[8]

5. Those who valorize women's essential differences from men.

6. Lisa Orlando, "Power Plays: Coming to Terms with Lesbian S/M," *Village Voice*, July 26, 1983; Elizabeth Wilson, "The Context of *Between Pleasure and Danger*: the Barnard Conference on Sexuality," *Feminist Review*, no. 13, Spring 1983, especially pp. 35–41 [Rubin's note].

7. *Taylor v. State*, 214 Md. 156, 165, 133 A. 2d 414, 418 [1957]. This quote is from a dissenting opinion, but it is a statement of prevailing law [Rubin's note].

8. Sarah Senefeld Beserra, Nancy M. Jewel, Melody West Matthews, and Elizabeth R. Gatov (eds.), Sacramento, *Sex Code of California*, Public Education and Research Committee of California, 1973, pp. 163–5 [Rubin's note].

Adult incest statutes operate in a similar fashion. Contrary to popular mythology, the incest statutes have little to do with protecting children from rape by close relatives. The incest statutes themselves prohibit marriage or sexual intercourse between adults who are closely related. Prosecutions are rare, but two were reported recently. In 1979, a 19-year-old Marine met his 42-year-old mother, from whom he had been separated at birth. The two fell in love and got married. They were charged and found guilty of incest, which under Virginia law carries a maximum ten-year sentence. During their trial, the Marine testified, "I love her very much. I feel that two people who love each other should be able to live together."[9] In another case, a brother and sister who had been raised separately met and decided to get married. They were arrested and pleaded guilty to felony incest in return for probation. A condition of probation was that they not live together as husband and wife. Had they not accepted, they would have faced twenty years in prison.[1]

In a famous S/M case, a man was convicted of aggravated assault for a whipping administered in an S/M scene. There was no complaining victim. The session had been filmed and he was prosecuted on the basis of the film. The man appealed his conviction by arguing that he had been involved in a consensual sexual encounter and had assaulted no one. In rejecting his appeal, the court ruled that one may not consent to an assault or battery "except in a situation involving ordinary physical contact or blows incident to sports such as football, boxing, or wrestling."[2] The court went on to note that the "consent of a person without legal capacity to give consent, such as a child or insane person, is ineffective," and that "It is a matter of common knowledge that a normal person in full possession of his mental faculties does not freely consent to the use, upon himself, of force likely to produce great bodily injury."[3] Therefore, anyone who would consent to a whipping would be presumed *non compos mentis*[4] and legally incapable of consenting. S/M sex generally involves a much lower level of force than the average football game, and results in far fewer injuries than most sports. But the court ruled that football players are sane, whereas masochists are not.

Sodomy laws, adult incest laws, and legal interpretations such as the one above clearly interfere with consensual behavior and impose criminal penalties on it. Within the law, consent is a privilege enjoyed only by those who engage in the highest-status sexual behavior. Those who enjoy low-status sexual behavior do not have the legal right to engage in it. In addition, economic sanctions, family pressures, erotic stigma, social discrimination, negative ideology, and the paucity of information about erotic behavior, all serve to make it difficult for people to make unconventional sexual choices. There certainly are structural constraints that impede free sexual choice, but they hardly operate to coerce anyone into being a pervert. On the contrary, they operate to coerce everyone toward normality.

The "brainwash theory" explains erotic diversity by assuming that some sexual acts are so disgusting that no one would willingly perform them. Therefore, the reasoning goes, anyone who does so must have been forced or

9. "Marine and Mom Guilty of Incest," *San Francisco Chronicle*, November 16, 1979, p. 16 [Rubin's note].
1. Clark Norton, "Sex in America," *Inquiry*, October 5, 1981, p. 18 [Rubin's note].
2. *People v. Samuels*, 250 Cal. App. 2d 501, 513, 58 Cal. Rptr. 439, 447 (1967) [Rubin's note].
3. *People v. Samuels*, 250 Cal. App. 2d at 513–514, 58 Cal. Rptr. at 447 [Rubin's note].
4. Not of sound mind (Latin).

fooled. Even constructivist sexual theory has been pressed into the service of explaining away why otherwise rational individuals might engage in variant sexual behavior. Another position that is not yet fully formed uses the ideas of Foucault and Weeks to imply that the "perversions" are an especially unsavory or problematic aspect of the construction of modern sexuality.[5] This is yet another version of the notion that sexual dissidents are victims of the subtle machinations of the social system. Weeks and Foucault would not accept such an interpretation, since they consider all sexuality to be constructed, the conventional no less than the deviant.

Psychology is the last resort of those who refuse to acknowledge that sexual dissidents are as conscious and free as any other group of sexual actors. If deviants are not responding to the manipulations of the social system, then perhaps the source of their incomprehensible choices can be found in a bad childhood, unsuccessful socialization, or inadequate identity formation. In her essay on erotic domination, Jessica Benjamin draws upon psychoanalysis and philosophy to explain why what she calls "sadomasochism" is alienated, distorted, unsatisfactory, numb, purposeless, and an attempt to "relieve an original effort at differentiation that failed."[6] This essay substitutes a psychophilosophical inferiority for the more usual means of devaluing dissident eroticism. One reviewer has already construed Benjamin's argument as showing that sadomasochism is merely an "obsessive replay of the infant power struggle."[7]

The position which defends the political rights of perverts but which seeks to understand their "alienated" sexuality is certainly preferable to the WAP-style bloodbaths. But for the most part, the sexual moderates have not confronted their discomfort with erotic choices that differ from their own. Erotic chauvinism cannot be redeemed by tarting it up in Marxist drag, sophisticated constructivist theory, or retro-psychobabble.

Whichever feminist position on sexuality—right, left, or center—eventually attains dominance, the existence of such a rich discussion is evidence that the feminist movement will always be a source of interesting thought about sex. Nevertheless, I want to challenge the assumption that feminism is or should be the privileged site of a theory of sexuality. Feminism is the theory of gender oppression. To automatically assume that this makes it the theory of sexual oppression is to fail to distinguish between gender, on the one hand, and erotic desire, on the other.

In the English language, the word "sex" has two very different meanings. It means gender and gender identity, as in "the female sex" or "the male sex." But sex also refers to sexual activity, lust, intercourse, and arousal, as in "to have sex." This semantic merging reflects a cultural assumption that sexuality is reducible to sexual intercourse and that it is a function of the relations between women and men. The cultural fusion of gender with sexuality has given rise to the idea that a theory of sexuality may be derived directly out of a theory of gender.

In an earlier essay, "The Traffic in Women," I used the concept of a sex/gender system, defined as a "set of arrangements by which a society trans-

5. Mariana Valverde, "Feminism Meets Fist-Fucking: Getting Lost in Lesbian S & M," *Body Politic*, February 1980; Wilson, op. cit., p. 38 [Rubin's note].

6. Benjamin, op. cit., p. 292, but see also pp. 286, 291–7 [Rubin's note]. Benjamin (b. 1946), American feminist and psychoanalyst.

7. Barbara Ehrenreich, "What Is This Thing Called Sex," *Nation*, September 24, 1983, p. 247 [Rubin's note].

forms biological sexuality into products of human activity."[8] I went on to argue that "Sex as we know it—gender identity, sexual desire and fantasy, concepts of childhood—is itself a social product."[9] In that essay, I did not distinguish between lust and gender, treating both as modalities of the same underlying social process.

"The Traffic in Women" was inspired by the literature on kin-based systems of social organization. It appeared to me at the time that gender and desire were systemically intertwined in such social formations. This may or may not be an accurate assessment of the relationship between sex and gender in tribal organizations. But it is surely not an adequate formulation for sexuality in Western industrial societies. As Foucault has pointed out, a system of sexuality has emerged out of earlier kinship forms and has acquired significant autonomy.

> Particularly from the eighteenth century onward, Western societies created and deployed a new apparatus which was superimposed on the previous one, and which, without completely supplanting the latter, helped to reduce its importance. I am speaking of the deployment of *sexuality*. . . . For the first [kinship], what is pertinent is the link between partners and definite statutes; the second [sexuality] is concerned with the sensations of the body, the quality of pleasures, and the nature of impressions.[1]

The development of this sexual system has taken place in the context of gender relations. Part of the modern ideology of sex is that lust is the province of men, purity that of women. Women have been to some extent excluded from the modern sexual system. It is no accident that pornography and the perversions have been considered part of the male domain. In the sex industry, women have been excluded from most production and consumption, and allowed to participate primarily as workers. In order to participate in the "perversions," women have had to overcome serious limitations on their social mobility, their economic resources, and their sexual freedoms. Gender affects the operation of the sexual system, and the sexual system has had gender-specific manifestations. But although sex and gender are related, they are not the same thing, and they form the basis of two distinct arenas of social practice.

In contrast to my perspective in "The Traffic in Women," I am now arguing that it is essential to separate gender and sexuality analytically to more accurately reflect their separate social existence. This goes against the grain of much contemporary feminist thought, which treats sexuality as a derivation of gender. For instance, lesbian feminist ideology has mostly analyzed the oppression of lesbians in terms of the oppression of women. However, lesbians are also oppressed as queers and perverts, by the operation of sexual, not gender, stratification. Although it pains many lesbians to think about it, the fact is that lesbians have shared many of the sociological features and suffered from many of the same social penalties as have gay men, sadomasochists, transvestites, and prostitutes.

Catharine MacKinnon has made the most explicit theoretical attempt to subsume sexuality under feminist thought. According to MacKinnon, "Sexuality

8. Gayle Rubin, "The Traffic in Women," in Rayna R. Reiter (ed.), *Toward an Anthropology of Women*, New York, Monthly Review Press, 1975, p. 159 [Rubin's note].

9. Rubin, "The Traffic in Women," op. cit., p. 166 [Rubin's note].

1. Foucault, op. cit., p. 106 [Rubin's note].

is to feminism what work is to marxism . . . the molding, direction, and expression of sexuality organizes society into two sexes, women and men."[2] This analytic strategy in turn rests on a decision to "use sex and gender relatively interchangeably."[3] It is this definitional fusion that I want to challenge.

There is an instructive analogy in the history of the differentiation of contemporary feminist thought from Marxism. Marxism is probably the most supple and powerful conceptual system extant for analyzing social inequality. But attempts to make Marxism the sole explanatory system for all social inequalities have been dismal exercises. Marxism is most successful in the areas of social life for which it was originally developed—class relations under capitalism.

In the early days of the contemporary women's movement, a theoretical conflict took place over the applicability of Marxism to gender stratification. Since Marxist theory is relatively powerful, it does in fact detect important and interesting aspects of gender oppression. It works best for those issues of gender most closely related to issues of class and the organization of labor. The issues more specific to the social structure of gender were not amenable to Marxist analysis.

The relationship between feminism and a radical theory of sexual oppression is similar. Feminist conceptual tools were developed to detect and analyze gender-based hierarchies. To the extent that these overlap with erotic stratifications, feminist theory has some explanatory power. But as issues become less those of gender and more those of sexuality, feminist analysis becomes irrelevant and often misleading. Feminist thought simply lacks angles of vision which can encompass the social organization of sexuality. The criteria of relevance in feminist thought do not allow it to see or assess critical power relations in the area of sexuality.

In the long run, feminism's critique of gender hierarchy must be incorporated into a radical theory of sex, and the critique of sexual oppression should enrich feminism. But an autonomous theory and politics specific to sexuality must be developed.

It is a mistake to substitute feminism for Marxism as the last word in social theory. Feminism is no more capable than Marxism of being the ultimate and complete account of all social inequality. Nor is feminism the residual theory which can take care of everything to which Marx did not attend. These critical tools were fashioned to handle very specific areas of social activity. Other areas of social life, their forms of power, and their characteristic modes of oppression, need their own conceptual implements. In this essay, I have argued for theoretical as well as sexual pluralism.

* * *

1984

2. Catharine MacKinnon, "Feminism, Marxism, Method and the State: An Agenda for Theory," *Signs*, vol. 7, no. 3, Spring 1982, pp. 515–16 [Rubin's note].

3. Catharine MacKinnon, "Feminism, Marxism, Method, and the State: Toward Feminist Jurisprudence," *Signs*, vol. 8, no. 4, Summer 1983, p. 635 [Rubin's note].

SLAVOJ ŽIŽEK
b. 1949

By turns maddening, hilarious, politically incorrect, obscure, insightful, tedious, and provocative, the Slovenian philosopher, sociologist, and cultural critic Slavoj Žižek has been likened in the popular press to an academic rock star. The author of more than fifty books since 1989 when his first book, *The Sublime Object of Ideology*, brought him to the attention of critics in the West, he has appeared on talk shows, in the popular press, and in YouTube videos; been the subject of an art installation (*Slavoj Žižek Does Not Exist*); and starred in two movies (*Žižek!* and *The Pervert's Guide to Cinema*). Applying the difficult psychoanalytic theories of JACQUES LACAN through a dizzying array of pop cultural references, Žižek's works realize the convergence of high and low culture that FREDRIC JAMESON describes as a chief characteristic of the postmodern. Predictably iconoclastic, Žižek's intellectual thought has, throughout his career, been marked by a resistance to the dogmas of official culture, whether Marxist, capitalist, Christian, poststructuralist, or psychoanalytic.

Born in Ljubljana, the capital of Slovenia and once part of Yugoslavia, Žižek attended Bežigrad High School and in 1967 enrolled at the University of Ljubljana. There he studied sociology and philosophy, earning a bachelor of arts in 1971 and a master of arts in philosophy in 1975. His master's thesis analyzed the growing influence on European intellectual life of the French structuralists and poststructuralists, including Lacan, JACQUES DERRIDA, JULIA KRISTEVA, CLAUDE LÉVI-STRAUSS, and GILLES DELEUZE. Unable to find work in Communist Yugoslavia because of his connections to dissident intellectuals, Žižek spent two years in Karlovac, discharging his national service in the Yugoslav army. In 1977 he secured a post at the Central Committee of the League of Slovene Communists. During these years Žižek fell in with a group of Slovenian scholars interested in Lacanian psychoanalysis; with them he created the Society for Theoretical Psychoanalysis, the so-called Ljubljana school, whose best-known members include Mladen Dolar, Alenka Zupančič, and Žižek's second wife, Renata Salecl. The group published a journal called *Problemi* and a book series called Analecta. In 1979 his friends secured him a better position as researcher at the University of Ljubljana's Institute for Sociology, where he was able to pursue his research interests free from the obligations of teaching and bureaucracy. In 1981 he received a doctor of arts in philosophy from the University of Ljubljana. He then moved to Paris, where he studied psychoanalysis and was analyzed by Lacan's son-in-law, Jacques-Alain Miller. Žižek completed his second doctorate (in psychoanalysis) at the Université Paris-VIII in 1985, after which he returned to Slovenia.

Against the tumultuous backdrop of the dissolution of the former Soviet empire, the establishment of a new Slovenian state, and the emergence of violent nationalist conflicts in the former Yugoslavia, Žižek emerged as a powerful independent voice. In 1990 the first democratic elections were held in Slovenia, and Žižek stood for the presidency as a Liberal Democrat, coming in fifth. He became ambassador of science for the Republic of Slovenia in 1991. Since then, Žižek has held posts at the Institute for Social Sciences at the University of Ljubljana and is currently international director of the Birkbeck Institute for the Humanities, Birkbeck, University of London. He has held visiting positions in the United States at SUNY Buffalo, the University of Minnesota, Tulane University, the Cardozo Law School, Columbia University, Princeton University, the New School for Social Research, the University of Michigan, and Georgetown University.

The role of both European popular culture and Continental theory in Slovenia as forms of resistance to the Communist government influenced Žižek's thinking, accounting for the peculiar blend of politics, pop culture, and high theory that characterizes his writing. Like other cultural critics, Žižek has written on a broad array of topics, ranging from philosophy and psychoanalysis to theology, film, opera, religion, politics, and literature. Because of the volume of his output, the shape of Žižek's career is difficult to characterize. His books, all written in English, seem less to evince a chronological development than to circle restlessly around a few key topics. *The Sublime Object of Ideology*, which launched Žižek's career in 1989, and several subsequent volumes have continued a critique of ideology: they include *Tarrying with the Negative* (1993); *The Plague of Fantasies* (1997), which explores the place of fantasy in ideological critique; *The Ticklish Subject: The Absent Centre of Political Ontology* (1999), which attempts to rehabilitate the Cartesian subject; and *The Parallax View* (2006). Beginning with his 1991 *Looking Awry: An Introduction to Jacques Lacan through Popular Culture*, from which our selection is drawn, much of Žižek's work has focused on using popular culture to elucidate concepts from Lacanian psychoanalysis. While this thread is a constant in Žižek's writing, it is especially central to *Enjoy Your Symptom! Jacques Lacan in Hollywood and Out* (1992; rev. ed., 2001); *The Fright of Real Tears: Krzysztof Kieślowski between Theory and Post-Theory* (2001), which uses the films of the Polish director to defend psychoanalytic film theory against the critique of cognitive film scholars; *Opera's Second Death*, with Mladen Dolar (2001); and *How to Read Lacan* (2007). Žižek turned his hand to religion in *The Fragile Absolute, or Why Is the Christian Legacy Worth Fighting For?* (2000) and *The Puppet and the Dwarf: The Perverse Core of Christianity* (2003). He explored the aftermath of the attacks of September 11, 2001, in *Welcome to the Desert of the Real* (2002) and the second Gulf war in *Iraq: The Borrowed Kettle* (2004). He explores the post-9/11 world in *Violence: Six Sideways Reflections* (2008), *First as Tragedy, Then as Farce* (2009), *The Year of Dreaming Dangerously* (2012), and *Trouble in Paradise: From the End of History to the End of Capitalism* (2014). Religion and politics come together in *Living in the End Times* (2010). In *Event: Philosophy in Transit* (2014) and *Absolute Recoil: Towards a New Foundation of Dialectical Materialism* (2014), Žižek investigates the nature of challenging problems in contemporary philosophy. *Incontinence of the Void: Economico-Philosophical Spandrels* (2017) works at the intersections of philosophy, psychoanalysis, and the critique of political economy, providing new contexts for old Žižekian themes. Other volumes examine the work of such philosophers as the apostle St. Paul, F. W. J. Schelling, GEORG WILHELM FRIEDRICH HEGEL, and Gilles Deleuze. Increasingly Žižek's writing has been in collaboration and debate with contemporary philosophers, including JUDITH BUTLER and GIORGIO AGAMBEN.

The most important influences on Žižek's work have been Hegel in philosophy, KARL MARX in politics, and Lacan in psychoanalysis. From Hegel he takes and extends the concept of the dialectic, the process in which the confrontation between a thesis and its opposite (antithesis) produces a synthesis by means of "overcoming" (*aufgehoben*). Viewed through the lens of psychoanalysis, however, the dialectic produces not synthesis but the realization that contradiction is the necessary condition of identity. The truth is found in the clash of oppositions, in contradiction. Žižek articulates his revision of the Hegelian dialectic most fully in *The Parallax View*, and this attitude toward contradiction accounts for the strong contrarian thread that runs through most of his writing. A self-described Marxist, Žižek owes much of his political thinking to Marxist analytics, in particular its criticism of capitalism, its belief in the possibility of an alternative to global capitalism, and its critique of ideology. Although *ideology* is sometimes perceived as false consciousness, as an error in understanding that can be corrected, for Žižek it forms the horizon and limit of thought. Moreover, he provides a model to explain how the ideologies that, according to Marxists, structure social formations find their way into the psyches of the individuals subject to those ideologies. For this he turns to the psychoanalytic thought of Jacques Lacan as a means of salvaging the "Cartesian subject."

Žižek understands the "cogito," or subject articulated by René Descartes (1596–1650), not as the usual substantial, transparent, and fully self-conscious "I," or as an effect of the structure of discourses, but as the empty space left when the rest of the world has been expelled from itself. "Cogito ergo sum," wrote Descartes (I think, therefore I am). Žižek's subject or cogito is Cartesian in a way that would have surprised Descartes, who focused on human consciousness and rationality. Žižek, in contrast, delves into the complex psychodynamics of the unconscious and irrationality—the libido (desire), fantasy, and human perversity.

In his early writing, one of Žižek's favorite pop culture examples for the psychodynamics of the subject are the films of the British director Alfred Hitchcock, best known for such psychological thrillers as *Psycho* (1960) and *The Birds* (1963). Because Hitchcock's films draw heavily on psychoanalytic themes, exploring unconscious processes, fantasies, and perversions, they have been favorite texts for psychoanalytic film theorists. Much as *Rear Window* (1954) and *Vertigo* (1958) provided LAURA MULVEY texts through which to work out the cinematic mechanisms that constitute the male gaze, these films offer Žižek a means of elucidating some basic Lacanian concepts. Our selection, "The Hitchcockian Blot," which appeared in a series of chapters on Hitchcock in *Looking Awry*, offers a compelling Lacanian reading of Hitchcock's oeuvre.

To understand Žižek's argument, we must map out Lacan's three psychic orders—the Imaginary, the Symbolic, and the Real—which situate subjectivity in dialogue with the external and internal worlds. The Imaginary is the internalized image of an ideal self, or imago, organized around the idea of wholeness rather than fragmentation. Lacan argues that in early childhood, the subject passes through the "mirror stage": it must externalize itself (view itself in a mirror) if it is to be coherent. Such externalization opens up a gap between the fiction of totality provided by the image and the actual fragmentation that signals the impossibility of ever attaining that ideal image. The Symbolic constitutes most of what we usually call "reality," or the social order, including the realm of language, symbol, and law. This is the sphere of the signifier, as defined by FERDINAND DE SAUSSURE. Though its elements—signifier and signified—have no simple positive existence, because they are determined by their mutual differences in a structure of relations, they exert a binding social force on the subject.

While many Lacanian theorists have concentrated on articulating the relationships between the Imaginary and Symbolic orders, Žižek investigates the importance of the Real and its interactions with the Symbolic in the formation of the subject. The Real is somewhat harder to grasp than the other two Lacanian terms. Perhaps it is most helpful to think of it as that which resists incorporation into the Symbolic. In one sense, it is the world before it is carved up by language; thus it is inaccessible to us after our entrance into the Symbolic social world. In our selection, Žižek argues that the Symbolic introduces a cut into the Real, thereby rendering the Real meaningless and senseless; it simply persists as a void in the Symbolic around which the Symbolic structures itself. It is momentarily discernible only when the subject is "looking awry"; it can only be glimpsed in the uncanny eerie effects of an anamorphosis (distorted perspective), in the detail that, "when viewed straightforwardly, remains a meaningless stain, but which, as soon as we look at the picture from a precisely determined lateral perspective, all of a sudden acquires well-known contours." What Žižek will call the anamorphic blot is that which "sticks out" from a representation and so renders it strange. Hitchcock's films offer an array of such moments in which the ordinary is rendered uncanny by the director's manipulation of the image.

Waggishly noting that what "sticks out" is precisely the phallocentric, Žižek locates the Lacanian Real not in details of the plot, not in the film's narrative, but in its formal apparatus. At stake in the characteristic Hollywood mechanisms for suturing time and space in film—that is, montage—are psychic processes. Žižek begins by mapping Freud's oral, anal, and phallic stages onto the film technique of montage, techniques of editing by which filmmakers create continuity by suturing (joining) shots together. The phallic stage complicates Mulvey's "male" gaze (though Žižek does not explicitly refer to her essay) by reversing its direction. Žižek's focus is not, like Mulvey's, the woman on the screen as the object of a controlling male gaze. For him, the thing that "sticks out" is the gaze of the other, the point at which the inert image looks back at the spectator, producing "total ambiguity," "denaturing" the image and rendering it uncanny. Žižek demonstrates the gaze of the other in Hitchcock's *Rear Window*; in that film, the window through which the protagonist spies on his neighbors is a "fantasy window," which is rendered strange the moment he meets the gaze of the murderer across the yard. Hitchcock's most characteristic technique for revealing the blot is the tracking shot, which eerily subjectivizes the camera's usually objective gaze, zeroing in on the gaze of the other. Žižek isolates three types of tracking shot in Hitchcock's films.

For Žižek the anamorphic blot "announces an agency that perturbs and hinders the rule of the Name-of-the-Father," namely the maternal superego. The essay tracks a shift in the development of Hitchcock's filmmaking from the "Oedipal journey," which represents the obstacles placed in the way of the heteronormative couple, as in his 1930s films (for example *The Thirty-Nine Step*), to the "pathological narcissism" represented in later films dominated by the maternal superego (*Psycho, The Birds*). In these later films, the protagonist is blocked from developing a "normal" heterosexual relation by the possessive mother's arbitrary demands: the paternal—the law—is ineffectual and the vacuum is filled by an "irrational" maternal.

Finally, Žižek turns to sociology and the modern American family. He tracks the transformation of capitalist society and hegemony from the autonomous individual of the Protestant ethic to the other-oriented organization man of the era just after World War II to the pathological narcissist of later decades. He argues that the domestic dramas and love triangles of Hitchcock's films reflect this social transformation and the disorders that it prompts in family and sexual relations, especially affecting the role of the maternal function.

Žižek's critics argue that his style is uneven and sometimes obscure, that his arguments tend to get lost in the dizzying array of disparate texts he discusses, that his politics remains fixed in traditional categories (especially those of Marxist class analysis), that his work is based on willful misreadings of Lacan and Hegel, and that Lacan ends up too easily as the last word on every contemporary problem, from capitalism to racism. Feminists criticize Žižek's account of the maternal superego as both phallocratic and heterosexist. It seems to draw on a philosophical tradition that sees the masculine (paternal) as rational and the feminine (maternal) as irrational. Yet even though he interprets Hitchcock's films almost entirely through these phallocentric categories, Žižek does offer feminist theory an intriguing and important reading of the key fantasy structures of misogyny and heterosexual love.

Looking Awry: An Introduction to Jacques Lacan through Popular Culture
Keywords: Cultural Studies, Hegemony, Identity, Marxism, Media, Popular Culture, Psychoanalysis, Sexuality, Subjectivity

From Looking Awry: An Introduction to Jacques Lacan through Popular Culture

Chapter 5. The Hitchcockian Blot

THE PHALLIC ANAMORPHOSIS[1]

Oral, Anal, Phallic

In *Foreign Correspondent*,[2] there is a short scene that exemplifies what might be called the elementary cell, the basic matrix of the Hitchcockian procedure. In pursuit of the kidnappers of a diplomat, the hero finds himself in an idyllic Dutch countryside with fields of tulips and windmills. All of a sudden he notices that one of the mills rotates against the direction of the wind. Here we have the effect of what Lacan calls the *point de capiton* (the quilting point)[3] in its purest: a perfectly "natural" and "familiar" situation is denatured, becomes "uncanny," loaded with horror and threatening possibilities, as soon as we add to it a small supplementary feature, a detail that "does not belong," that sticks out, is "out of place," does not make any sense within the frame of the idyllic scene. This "pure" signifier without signified[4] stirs the germination of a supplementary, metaphorical meaning for all other elements: the same situations, the same events that, till then, have been perceived as perfectly ordinary acquire an air of strangeness. Suddenly we enter the realm of double meaning, everything seems to contain some hidden meaning that is to be interpreted by the Hitchcockian hero, "the man who knows too much." The horror is thus internalized, it reposes on the *gaze* of him who "knows too much."[5]

Hitchcock is often reproached for his "phallocentrism";[6] although meant as a criticism, this designation is quite adequate—on condition that we locate

1. *Anamorphosis* is the process of making distorted images that are legible only when viewed from a particular perspective or with a particular restorative device (e.g., a cylindrical mirror); also, the image produced by such a process.
2. A 1940 film directed by the British filmmaker Alfred Hitchcock (1899–1980). All films mentioned in this essay are Hitchcock's, unless otherwise specified.
3. Literally, the point of attachment of an upholstery button. The French psychoanalyst JACQUES LACAN (1901–1981) uses the term to indicate the point at which the signifier and signified are "knotted together" in discourse to stabilize the sliding of the signifier.
4. The sign was divided into *signified* (the meaning conveyed) and *signifier* (the symbol or sound that conveys that meaning) by the Swiss linguist FERDINAND DE SAUSSURE (1857–1913).
5. From this perspective, the denouement of *Dial M for Murder* [1954] is extremely interesting insofar as it *reverses* the usual situation of Hitchcock's films: "the man who knew too much" is not the hero foreboding some terrifying secret behind the idyllic surface, but *the murderer himself*. That is to say, the inspector traps the murderous husband of Grace Kelly through a certain surplus knowledge—the murderer is caught knowing something that it would not be possible for him to know if he were innocent (the hiding place of the other key to his apartment). The irony of the denouement is that what provokes the downfall of the murderer is precisely his quick and clever reasoning. If he had been just a little bit more slow-witted, i.e., if, after the key in his jacket had failed to open the door to his apartment, he had been unable to deduce quickly what must have happened, he would have been forever safe from the hand of justice. In the way he sets the trap for the murderer, the inspector acts like a real Lacanian analyst: the crucial ingredient of his success is not his ability to "penetrate the other," to understand him, to adapt to his reasoning, but rather his capacity to take into account the structuring role of a certain object that circulates among the subjects and entangles them in a network that they cannot dominate—the key in *Dial M for Murder* (and in *Notorious* [1946], the letter in Edgar Allan Poe's "The Purloined Letter," etc. [Žižek's note]. Kelly (1929–1982), American actor who appeared in several Hitchcock films. POE (1809–1849), American writer of poetry, tales, and criticism; the authorized version of his story "The Purloined Letter" was published in 1845. "The man who knew too much" is the title of a film made and remade by Hitchcock (1934, 1956).
6. The psychoanalytic system in which sexual difference is defined as the difference between having and lacking the phallus; the term has come to refer to patriarchal cultural as a whole insofar

the phallic dimension precisely in this supplementary feature that "sticks out." To explain, let us articulate three successive ways of presenting an event onscreen, three ways that correspond to the succession of "oral," "anal," and "phallic" stages in the subject's libidinal economy.[7]

The "oral" stage is, so to speak, the zero degree of filmmaking: we simply shoot an event and as spectators we "devour it with our eyes"; the montage[8] has no function in organizing narrative tensions. Its prototype is the silent, slapstick film. The effect of "naturalness," of direct "rendering of reality," is, of course, false: even at this stage, a certain "choice" is at work, part of reality is enframed and extracted from the space-time continuum. What we see is the result of a certain "manipulation," the succession of shots partakes of a *metonymical*[9] movement. We see only parts, fragments of a never-shown whole, which is why we are already caught in a dialectic of seen and unseen, of the field (enframed by the camera) and its outside, giving rise to the desire to see what is not shown. For all that, we remain captive of the illusion that we witness a homogeneous continuity of action registered by the "neutral" camera.

In the "anal" stage montage enters. It cuts up, fragments, multiplies the action; the illusion of homogeneous continuity is forever lost. Montage can combine elements of a wholly heterogeneous nature and thus create new *metaphorical* meaning having nothing whatsoever to do with the "literal" value of its component parts (compare Eisenstein's concept of "intellectual montage"[1]). The exemplary display of what montage can achieve at the level of traditional narration is, of course, the case of "parallel montage": we show in alternation two interconnected courses of action, transforming the linear deployment of events into the horizontal coexistence of two lines of action, thus creating an additional tension between the two. Let us take, for example, a scene depicting the isolated home of a rich family encircled by a gang of robbers preparing to attack it; the scene gains enormously in effectiveness if we contrast the idyllic everyday life within the house with the threatening preparations of the criminals outside: if we show in alternation the happy family at dinner, the boisterousness of the children, father's benevolent reprimands, etc., and the "sadistic" smile of a robber, another checking his knife or gun, a third already grasping the house's balustrade . . .

In what would the passage to the "phallic" stage consist? In other words, how would *Hitchcock* shoot the same scene? The first thing to remark is that the content of this scene does not lend itself to Hitchcockian suspense insofar as it rests upon a simple counterpoint of idyllic interior and threatening exterior. We should therefore transpose this "flat," horizontal doubling of the action onto a *vertical* level: the menacing horror should not be placed *outside, next to* the idyllic interior, but well *within* it, more precisely: *under* it, as its "repressed" underside. Let us imagine, for example, the same happy

as that system privileges the phallus as the symbol and source of power. It is closely related to *logocentrism*, a term coined by the French philosopher JACQUES DERRIDA (1930–2004), and the two are sometimes combined as *phallogocentrism*.

7. According to SIGMUND FREUD (1856–1939), the Austrian founder of psychoanalysis, the developmental stages through which childhood sexuality passes are the oral, anal, phallic, and (if the oedipal complex is successfully resolved) genital (i.e., mature sexuality).

8. The assembling of distinct images or sounds into a sequence (a film-editing technique).

9. That is, displaying a connection through association rather than through resemblance (metaphorical).

1. A form of montage that relies on metaphor, not metonymy, in juxtaposing images. The Russian director Sergei Eisenstein (1898–1948) was an early innovator in cinematic technique.

family dinner shown from the point of view of a rich uncle, their invited guest. In the midst of dinner, the guest (and together with him ourselves, the public) suddenly "sees too much," observes what he was not supposed to notice, some incongruous detail arousing in him the suspicion that the hosts plan to poison him in order to inherit his fortune. Such a "surplus knowledge" has so to speak an abyssal effect[2] on the perspective of the host (and ours with it): the action is in a way *redoubled in itself,* endlessly reflected in itself as in a double mirror play. The most common, everyday events are suddenly loaded with terrifying undertones, "everything becomes suspicious": the kind mistress of the house asking if we feel well after dinner wants perhaps to learn if the poison has already taken effect; the children who run around in innocent joy are perhaps excited because the parents have hinted that they would soon be able to afford a luxurious voyage . . . things appear in a totally different light, although they stay the same.

Such a "vertical" doubling entails a radical change in the libidinal economy: the "true" action is repressed, internalized, subjectivized, i.e., presented in the form of the subject's desires, hallucinations, suspicions, obsessions, feelings of guilt. What we actually see becomes nothing but a deceptive surface beneath which swarms an undergrowth of perverse and obscene implications, the domain of what is *prohibited*. The more we find ourselves in total ambiguity, not knowing where "reality" ends and "hallucination" (i.e., desire) begins, the more menacing this domain appears. Incomparably more threatening than the savage cries of the enemy is his calm and cold gaze, or—to transpose the same inversion into the field of sexuality—incomparably more exciting than the openly provocative brunette is the cold blonde who, as Hitchcock reminds us, knows how to do many things once we find ourselves alone with her in the back seat of a taxi. What is crucial here is this inversion by means of which silence begins to function as the most horrifying menace, where the appearance of a cold indifference promises the most passionate pleasures—in short, where the prohibition against passing over into action opens up the space of a hallucinatory desire that, once set off, cannot be satisfied by any "reality" whatsoever.

But what has this inversion to do with the "phallic" stage? "Phallic" is precisely the detail that "does not fit," that "sticks out" from the idyllic surface scene and denatures it, renders it uncanny. It is the point of *anamorphosis* in a picture: the element that, when viewed straightforwardly, remains a meaningless stain, but which, as soon as we look at the picture from a precisely determined lateral perspective, all of a sudden acquires well-known contours. Lacan's constant point of reference is Holbein's *Ambassadors*[3]: at the bottom of the picture, under the figures of the two ambassadors, a viewer catches sight of an amorphous, extended, "erected" spot. It is only when, on the very threshold of the room in which the picture is exposed, the visitor casts a final lateral glance at it that this spot acquires the contours of a skull, disclosing thus the true meaning of the picture—the nullity of all terrestrial goods, objects of art and knowledge that fill out the rest of the picture. This is the way Lacan defines the phallic signifier, as a "signifier without signified" which, as such,

2. Žižek refers to Derrida's *mise en abyme*.
3. Cf., for example, Lacan, *The Four Fundamental Concepts of Psycho-Analysis* (London: Hogarth Press, 1977), p. 92 [Žižek's note]. *The Ambassadors* (1533), a painting by the German artist Hans Holbein the Younger (1497–1543).

renders possible the effects of the signified: the "phallic" element of a picture is a meaningless stain that "denatures" it, rendering all its constituents "suspicious," and thus opens up the abyss of the search for a meaning—nothing is what it seems to be, everything is to be interpreted, everything is supposed to possess some supplementary meaning. The ground of the established, familiar signification opens up; we find ourselves in a realm of total ambiguity, but this very lack propels us to produce ever new "hidden meanings": it is a driving force of endless compulsion. The oscillation between lack and surplus meaning constitutes the proper dimension of subjectivity. In other words, it is by means of the "phallic" spot that the observed picture is subjectivized: this paradoxical point undermines our position as "neutral," "objective" observer, pinning us to the observed object itself. This is the point at which the observer is already included, inscribed in the observed scene—in a way, it is the point from which the picture itself looks back at us.[4]

The Blot as the Gaze of the Other

The finale of *Rear Window*[5] demonstrates perfectly how the fascinating object that drives the interpretive movement is ultimately the gaze itself: this interpretive movement is suspended when Jeff's (James Stewart's) gaze, inspecting what goes on in the mysterious apartment across the yard, meets the gaze of the other (the murderer). At this point, Jeff loses his position as neutral, distant observer and is caught up in the affair, i.e., he becomes part of what he observed. More precisely, he is forced to confront the question of his own desire: what does he really want from this affair? This *Che vuoi?*[6] is literally pronounced during the final confrontation between him and the perplexed murderer who asks him again and again: "Who are you? What do you want from me?" The whole final scene, in which the murderer approaches as Jeff attempts desperately to stop him by the dazzle of flashbulbs, is shot in a remarkable, totally "unrealistic" way. Where we would expect rapid movement, an intense, swift clash, we get hindered, slowed-down, protracted movement, as if the "normal" rhythm of events had undergone a kind of anamorphotic deformation. This renders perfectly the immobilizing, crippling

4. We must be attentive to the diversity of the ways this motif of the "uncanny" detail is at work in Hitchcock's films. Note just five of its variations:

- *Rope* [1948]: here, we have the spot *first* (the traumatic act of murder) and *then* the idyllic everyday situation (the party) constructed to conceal it.
- *The Man Who Knew Too Much* [1956]: in a short scene in which the hero (James Stewart) makes his way to the taxidermist Ambrose Chappell, the street the hero traverses is depicted as charged with a sinister atmosphere; but in fact things are precisely what they seem to be (the street is just an ordinary suburban London street, etc.), so that the only "stain" in the picture is *the hero himself,* his suspicious gaze that sees threats everywhere.
- *The Trouble with Harry* [1955]: a "stain" (a body) smears the idyllic Vermont countryside, but instead of provoking traumatic reactions, people who stumble upon it merely treat it as a minor inconvenience and pursue their daily affairs.
- *Shadow of a Doubt* [1943]: the "stain" here is uncle Charlie, the film's central character, a pathological murderer who rejoins his sister's family in a small American town. In the eyes of the townsfolk, he is a friendly, rich benefactor; it is only his niece Charlie who "knows too much" and sees him as he is—why? The answer is found in the identity of their names: the two of them constitute two parts of the same personality (like Marion and Norman in *Psycho* [1960], where the identity is indicated by the fact that the two names reflect each other in an inverted form).
- And finally *The Birds* [1963], where—in what is surely Hitchcock's final irony—the "unnatural" element that disturbs everyday life is the birds, i.e., *nature itself* [Žižek's note].

The American actor Stewart (1908–1997) appears in several Hitchcock films.

5. Released in 1954.

6. What do you want? (Italian). In Lacanian terms, desire belongs never to the subject but only to the other. But as others in turn do not know what they want, this question triggers an infinite regress.

effect the fantasy object has upon the subject: from the interpretive movement induced by the ambiguous register of symptoms, we have passed over to the register of fantasy, the inert presence of which suspends the movement of interpretation.

Where does this power of fascination come from? Why does the neighbor who killed his wife function for the hero as the object of his desire? There is only one answer possible: *the neighbor realizes Jeff's desire*. The hero's desire is to elude the sexual relation at any price, i.e., to get rid of the unfortunate Grace Kelly. What happens on *this side* of the window, in the hero's apartment—the amorous misadventures of Stewart and Kelly—is by no means a simple subplot, an amusing diversion with no bearing on the central motif on the film, but on the contrary, its very center of gravity. Jeff's (and our) fascination with what goes on in the other apartment functions to make Jeff (and us) overlook the crucial importance of what goes on on this side of the window, in the very place from which he looks. *Rear Window* is ultimately the story of a subject who eludes a sexual relation by transforming his effective impotence into power by means of the gaze, by means of secret observation: he "regresses" to an infantile curiosity in order to shirk his responsibility toward the beautiful woman who offers herself to him (the film is at this point very unequivocal—note the scene where Grace Kelly changes into a transparent nightgown). What we encounter here is, again, one of Hitchcock's fundamental "complexes," the interconnection of the gaze and the couple power/impotence. In this respect, *Rear Window* reads like an ironic reversal of Bentham's "Panopticon" as exploited by Foucault.[7] For Bentham, the horrifying efficacity of the Panopticon is due to the fact that the subjects (prisoners, patients, schoolboys, factory workers) can never know for sure if they are actually observed from the all-seeing central control tower—this very uncertainty intensifies the feeling of menace, of the impossibility of escape from the gaze of the Other. In *Rear Window,* the inhabitants of the apartments across the yard are actually observed all the time by Stewart's watchful eye, but far from being terrorized, they simply ignore it and go on with their daily business. On the contrary, it is Stewart himself, the center of the Panopticon, its all-pervasive eye, who is terrorized, constantly looking out the window, anxious not to miss some crucial detail. Why?

The rear window is essentially a fantasy window (the phantasmatic value of the window in painting has already been pointed out by Lacan):[8] incapable of motivating himself to action, Jeff puts off indefinitely the (sexual) act, and what he sees through the window are precisely *fantasy figurations of what could happen to him and Grace Kelly*. They could become happy newlyweds; he could abandon Grace Kelly, who would then become an eccentric artist or lead a desperate, secluded life like Miss Lonely Hearts; they could spend their time together like the ordinary couple with a small dog, yielding to an everyday routine that barely conceals their underlying despair; or, finally, he could *kill* her. In short, the meaning of what the hero perceives

7. French philosopher and historian of ideas (1926–1984; see above). The English philosopher and reformer Jeremy Bentham (1748–1832) designed an ideal circular prison, which he called the Panopticon (all seeing), in which prisoners could be kept under constant surveillance by a single guard in a central tower; for Foucault, in *Discipline and Punish* (1975), it is a metaphor for the disciplinary mechanisms of modern society.

8. In Lacan's unpublished 1965–66 seminars, *The Object of Psychoanalysis*.

beyond the window depends on his actual situation this side of the window: he has just to "look through the window" to see on display a multitude of imaginary solutions to his actual impasse.

Careful attention to the film's soundtrack, especially if we approach *Rear Window* in retrospect, on the basis of Hitchcock's subsequent films, also reveals unmistakably the agency that hinders the hero's "normal" sexual relation: the *maternal superego* embodied in a *voix acousmatique,* a free-floating voice that is not assigned to any bearer. Michel Chion[9] has already drawn attention to a peculiarity of the film's soundtrack, more precisely, its background sounds: we hear a diversity of voices to which we are always able to assign bearers, i.e., emitters. All *except one,* the voice of an unidentified soprano practicing scales and generally emerging just in time to prevent the fulfillment of sexual union between Stewart and Kelly. This mysterious voice does not originate from a person living on the other side of the courtyard, visible through the window, so the camera never shows the singer: the voice remains *acousmatique* and uncannily close to us, as if its origins were within us.[1] It is on account of this feature that *Rear Window* announces *The Man Who Knew Too Much, Psycho,* and *The Birds*: this voice transmutes first into the awkwardly pathetic song by means of which Doris Day reaches her kidnapped son (the famous *Que será será*[2]), then into the voice of the dead mother taking possession of Norman Bates, until it finally dissolves into the chaotic croaking of the birds.

The Tracking Shot[3]

The standard Hitchcockian *formal* procedure for isolating the stain, this remainder of the real that "sticks out," is, of course, his famous tracking shot. Its logic can be grasped only if we take into account the whole range of variations to which this procedure is submitted. Let us begin with a scene from *The Birds* in which the hero's mother, peering into a room that has been ravaged by the birds, sees a pajama-clad body with its eyes torn out. The camera first shows us the entire body; we then expect it to track forward slowly into the fascinating detail, the bloody sockets of the missing eyes. But Hitchcock instead gives us an *inversion* of the process we expect: instead of slowing down, he drastically *speeds up*; with two abrupt cuts, each bringing us closer to the subject, he quickly shows us the corpse's head. The subversive effect of these quickly advancing shots is created by the way in which they frustrate us even as they indulge our desire to view the terrifying object more closely: we approach it too quickly, skipping over the "time for understanding," the pause needed to "digest," to integrate the brute perception of the object.

Unlike the usual tracking shot that endows the object-blot with a particular weight by slowing down the "normal" speed and by *deferring* the approach, here the object is "missed" precisely insofar as we approach it

9. French composer of experimental music (b. 1947); in his book *Audio-Vision: Sound on Screen* (1990), he applies the term "acousmatic" (*acousmatique*) to sounds that one hears without seeing their source.

1. Cf. Michel Chion, "Le quatrième côté" ["The Fourth Side"] in *Cahiers du cinema* 356 (1984), pp. 6–7 [Žižek's note].

2. Whatever will be will be (Spanish), the title of a song composed by Jay Livingston (1915–2001) and the lyricist Ray Evans (1915–2007); in the film, it is sung by the American actor and singer Day (b. 1922).

3. Shot filmed from a camera mounted on a dolly and pushed on rails.

precipitously, too quickly. Thus, if the usual tracking shot is obsessional, forcing us to fix on a detail that is made to function as a blot because of the slow motion of the tracking, the precipitous approach to the object reveals its own hysterical basis: we "miss" the object because of the speed, because this object is already empty in itself, hollow—it cannot be evoked other than "too slowly" or "too swiftly," because in its "proper time" it is nothing. So delay and precipitousness are two modes of capturing the object-cause of desire, object small *a*,[4] the "nothingness" of pure seeming. We thereby touch upon the *objectal* dimension of the Hitchcockian "blot" or "stain": the signifying dimension of the blot, its effect of doubling meaning, of conferring on every element of the image a supplementary meaning that makes the interpretative movement work. None of this should blind us to its other aspect, however, that of an inert, opaque object that must drop out or sink for any symbolic reality to emerge. In other words, the Hitchcockian tracking shot that produces the blot in an idyllic picture is achieved as though to illustrate the Lacanian thesis: "The field of reality rests upon the extraction of the object *a*, which nevertheless frames it."[5] Or, to quote Jacques-Alain Miller's precise commentary:

> We understand that the covert setting aside of the object as real conditions the stabilization of reality, as "a bit of reality." But if the object *a* is absent, how can it still frame reality?
>
> 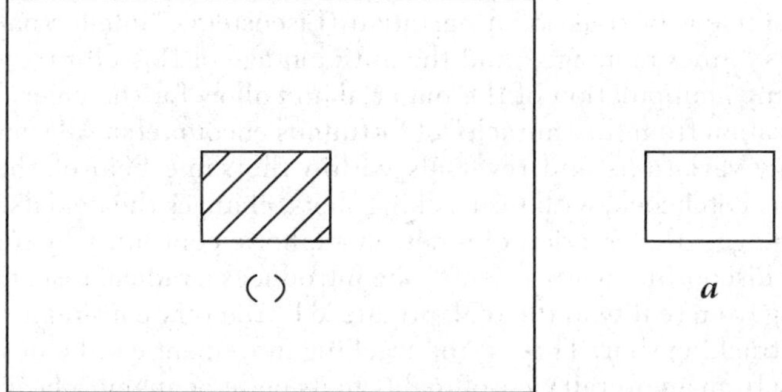
>
>
> It is precisely *because* the object *a* is removed from the field of reality that it frames it. If I withdraw from the surface of this picture the piece I represent by a shaded square, I get what we might call a frame: a frame for a hole, but also a frame of the rest of the surface. Such a frame could be created by any window. So object *a* is such a surface fragment, and it is its subtraction from reality that frames it. The subject, as barred subject—as want-of-being—is this hole. As being, it is nothing but the subtracted bit. Whence the equivalency of the subject and object *a*.[6]

4. Lacan's *objet petit a* (the *a* abbreviates *autre*, French for "other") is the unattainable or lost object of desire that the subject never had, the loss brought into being by symbolization itself.
5. Jacques Lacan, *Ecrits* (Paris: Seuil, 1966), p. 554 [Žižek's note].
6. Jacques-Alain Miller, "Montré à Premontré," in *Analytica* 37 (1984), pp. 28–29 [Žižek's note]. Miller (b. 1944), French psychoanalyst, Lacan's son-in-law, and editor of his seminars. "Barred subject": the subject split by language and the unconscious.

We can read Miller's schema as the schema of the Hitchcockian tracking shot: from an overall view of reality, we advance toward the blot that provides it with its frame (the hatched square). The advance of the Hitchcockian tracking shot is reminiscent of the structure of a Moebius strip:[7] by moving away from the side of reality, we find ourselves suddenly alongside the real whose extraction constitutes reality. Here the process inverts the dialectic of montage: there it was a matter of producing, through the discontinuity of the cuts, the continuity of a new signification, of a new diegetic reality,[8] linking the disconnected fragments, whereas here the continual advance itself produces an effect of banking, of radical discontinuity, by showing us the heterogeneous element that must remain an inert, nonsensical "blot" if the rest of the picture is to acquire the consistency of a symbolic reality.

Whence we could return to the succession of "anal" and "phallic" stages in the organization of filmic material: if montage is the "anal" process *par excellence*, the Hitchcockian tracking shot represents the point at which the "anal" economy becomes "phallic." Montage entails the production of a supplementary, metaphorical signification that emerges from the juxtaposition of connected fragments, and, as Lacan emphasized in *The Four Fundamental Concepts of Psycho-Analysis*, metaphor is, in its libidinal economy, an eminently anal process: we give something (shit) to fill out the nothing, that is, to make up for what we do not have.[9] In addition to montage within the framework of traditional narration (as typified by "parallel montage") we have a whole series of "excessive" strategies that are designed to subvert the linear movement of traditional narration (Eisenstein's "intellectual montage," Welles's "inner montage," and the antimontage of Rossellini,[1] who tried to forgo any manipulation of the material and allow for the emergence of the signification from the "miracle" of fortuitous encounters). All such processes are only variations and reversals within the same field of the montage, whereas Hitchcock, with his tracking shots, changes the field itself: in place of montage—the creation of a new metaphoric continuity by the combination of discontinuous fragments—he introduces a radical discontinuity, the shifting from reality to the real, produced by the very continuous movement of the tracking shot. That is, the tracking movement can be described as a moving from an overall view of reality to its point of anamorphosis. To return to Holbein's *Ambassadors*, the Hitchcockian tracking shot would advance from the total area of the picture toward the erected, "phallic" element in the background that must fall away, remain simply a demented stain—the skull, the inert fantasy-object as the "impossible" equivalent of the subject itself ($\$\diamond a$),[2] and it is no accident that we find this same object in several instances in Hitchcock's own work (*Under Capricorn*,[3] *Psycho*). In Hitchcock this real object, the blot, the terminal point of the tracking shot, can assume two principal forms: either the gaze of the other insofar as our posi-

7. A continuous one-sided surface formed by affixing the ends of a rectangular strip after giving one of the ends a half twist (discovered independently in 1858 by two German mathematicians, one of whom was August Ferdinand Möbius).
8. That is, reality as presented in the total world of the film.
9. "The anal level is the locus of metaphor—one object for another, give the faeces in place of the phallus" (Lacan, *The Four Fundamental Concepts of Psycho-Analysis*, p. 104) [Žižek's note].
1. Roberto Rossellini (1906–1977), Italian filmmaker and a leader of the neorealist movement in cinema. Orson Welles (1915–1985), American actor, writer, and innovative director; "inner montage" maintains spatial and temporal continuity.
2. Lacan's formula for the fantasy, read as the relationship between the barred subject and the object of desire (*objet petit a*).
3. Released in 1949.

tion as spectator is already inscribed within the film—i.e., the point from which the picture itself gazes at us (the eye sockets in the skull, not to mention the most celebrated of Hitchcock's tracking shots, the shot into the drummer's blinking eyes in *Young and Innocent*[4])—or the Hitchcockian object *par excellence,* the nonspecularizable object of exchange, the "piece of the real" that circulates from one subject to another, embodying and guaranteeing the structural network of symbolic exchanges between them (the most famous example: the long tracking shot in *Notorious,* from the overall view of the entrance hall down to the key in Ingrid Bergman's hand).

We can categorize Hitchcock's tracking shots, however, without reference to the nature of their terminal object, that is, based on variations in the formal process itself. In addition to the zero degree of tracking (which moves from the overall view of reality to its real point of anamorphosis), we have at least three other variants in Hitchcock:

- The precipitous, "hystericized" tracking shot: see the example from *The Birds* analyzed above, in which the camera draws into the blot too quickly, through jump cuts.
- The reverse tracking shot, which begins at the uncanny detail and pulls back to the overall view of reality: witness the long shot in *Shadow of a Doubt* that starts with the hand of Teresa Wright holding the ring given her by her murdering uncle, and pulls back and up to the overall view of the library reading room in which she appears as nothing but a small dot in the center of the frame; or the famous reverse tracking shot in *Frenzy.*[5]
- Lastly, the paradox of the "immobile tracking shot," in which the camera does not move: the shift from reality to the real is accomplished by the intrusion into the frame of a heterogeneous object. For an example, we can return to *The Birds,* in which such a shift is achieved during one long, fixed shot. A fire caused by a cigarette butt dropped into some gasoline breaks out in the small town threatened by the birds. After a series of short and "dynamic" close-ups and medium shots that draw us immediately into the action, the camera pulls back and up and we are given an overall shot of the entire town taken from high above. In the first instant we read this overall shot as an "objective," "epic" panorama shot, separating us from the immediate drama going on down below and enabling us to disengage ourselves from the action. This distancing at first produces a certain "pacifying" effect; it allows us to view the action from what might be called a "metalinguistic" distance. Then, suddenly, a bird enters the frame from the right, as if coming from behind the camera and thus from behind our own backs, and then three birds, and finally an entire flock. The same shot takes on a totally different aspect, it undergoes a radical *subjectivization*: the camera's elevated eye ceases to be that of a netural, "objective" onlooker gazing down upon a panoramic landscape and suddenly becomes the subjective and threatening gaze of the birds as they zero in on their prey.[6]

4. Released in 1937.
5. Released in 1972.
6. This scene, creating as it does a phantasmatic effect, also illustrates the thesis that the subject is not necessarily inscribed in the phantasmatic scene as observer, but can also be one of the objects observed. The birds' subjective view of the town creates a menacing effect, even though our view—the camera's view—is that of the birds and not that of their prey, because we are inscribed in the scene as inhabitants of the town, i.e., we identify with the menaced inhabitants [Žižek's note].

THE MATERNAL SUPEREGO

Why Do the Birds Attack?

What we must bear in mind is the libidinal content of this Hitchcockian stain: although its logic is phallic, it announces an agency that perturbs and hinders the rule of the Name-of-the-Father—in other words, the stain materializes the *maternal superego*.[7] To prove it, let us return to the last of the above-mentioned cases: that of *The Birds*. Why do they attack? Robin Wood suggests three possible readings of this inexplicable, "irrational" act by which the idyllic, daily life of a small northern California town is derailed: "cosmological," "ecological," "familial."[8]

According to the first, "cosmological" reading, the attack of the birds can be viewed as embodying Hitchcock's vision of the universe, of the (human) cosmos as system—peaceful on the surface, ordinary in its course—that can be upset at any time, that can be thrown into chaos by the intervention of pure chance. Its order is always deceiving; at any moment some ineffable terror can emerge, some traumatic real erupt to disturb the symbolic circuit. Such a reading can be supported by references to many other Hitchcock films, including the most somber of them, *The Wrong Man*,[9] in which the mistaken identification of the hero as a thief, which happens purely by chance, turns his daily life into a hell of humiliation and costs his wife her sanity—the entering into play of the theological dimension in Hitchcock's work, the vision of a cruel, arbitrary, and impenetrable God who can bring down catastrophe at any moment.

For the second, "ecological" reading, the film's title could have been *Birds of the World, Unite!*: in this reading, the birds function as a condensation of exploited nature that finally rises up against man's heedless exploitation. In support of this interpretation, we can cite the fact that Hitchcock selected his attacking birds almost exclusively from species known for their gentle, nonaggressive nature: sparrows, seagulls, a few crows.

The third reading sees the key to the film in the intersubjective relations between the main characters (Melanie, Mitch, and his mother), which are far from being merely an insignificant sideline to the "true" plot, the attack of the birds: the attacking birds only "embody" a fundamental discord, a disturbance, a derailment in those relations. The pertinence of this interpretation emerges if we consider *The Birds* within the context of Hitchcock's earlier (and later) films; in other words, to play on one of Lacan's homophonies, if we are to take the films seriously, we can only do so if we take them serially.[1]

In writing of Poe's "The Purloined Letter," Lacan makes reference to a game of logic: we take a random series of 0s and 1s—100101100, for example—and as soon as the series is articulated into linked triads (100,001,010, etc.), rules of succession will emerge (a triad with 0 at the end

7. The part of the psyche, as described by Freud, that develops by incorporating the moral standards of the parents and community. Since the symbolic in which Hitchcock's characters exist is patriarchal, the superego is paternal and rational. When the paternal function is absent, the maternal superego is given free rein; Žižek characterizes the maternal superego as irrational and arbitrary, blocking normal heterosexual relationships.

8. Robin Wood, *Hitchcock's Films* (New York: A. S. Barnes and Co., 1977), p. 116 [Žižek's note].

9. Released in 1956.

1. Lacan, *Le seminaire, livre XX: Encore* (Paris: Seuil, 1975), p. 23 [Žižek's note].

cannot be followed by a triad that has 1 as its middle term, and so on).[2] The same is true of Hitchcock's films: if we consider them as a whole we have an accidental, random series, but as soon as we separate them into linked triads (and exclude those films that are not part of the "Hitchcockian universe," the "exceptions," the results of various compromises), each triad can then be seen to be linked by some theme, some common structuring principle. For example take the following five films: *The Wrong Man, Vertigo, North by Northwest,*[3] *Psycho,* and *The Birds*: no single theme can be found to link all the films in such a series, yet such themes can be found if we consider them in groups of three. The first triad concerns "false identity": in *The Wrong Man,* the hero is wrongly identified as the burglar; in *Vertigo* the hero is mistaken about the identity of the false Madeleine; in *North by Northwest* Soviet spies mistakenly identify the film's hero as the mysterious CIA agent "George Kaplan." As for the great trilogy *Vertigo, North by Northwest,* and *Psycho,* it is very tempting to regard these three key Hitchcock films as the articulation of three different versions of filling the gap in the Other. Their formal problem is the same: the relationship between a lack and a factor (a person) that tries to compensate for it. In *Vertigo,* the hero attempts to compensate for the absence of the woman he loves, an apparent suicide, on a level that is literally *imaginary*: he tries, by means of dress, hairstyle, and so forth, to recreate the image of the lost woman. In *North by Northwest,* we are on the *symbolic* level: we are dealing with an empty name, the name of a nonexistent person ("Kaplan"), a signifier without a bearer, which becomes attached to the hero out of sheer chance. In *Psycho,* finally, we reach the level of the *real*: Norman Bates, who dresses in his mother's clothes, speaks with her voice, etc., wants neither to resuscitate her image nor act in her name; he wants to take her place in the real—evidence of a psychotic state.

If the middle triad, therefore, is that of the "empty place," the final one is in its turn united around the motif of the *maternal superego*: the heroes of these three films are fatherless, they have a mother who is "strong," who is "possessive," who disturbs the "normal" sexual relationship. At the very beginning of *North by Northwest* the film's hero, Roger Thornhill (Cary Grant), is shown with his scornful, mocking mother, and it is not difficult to guess why he has been four times divorced; in *Psycho,* Norman Bates (Anthony Perkins) is directly controlled by the voice of his dead mother, which instructs him to kill any woman to whom he is sexually attracted; in the case of the mother of Mitch Brenner (Rod Taylor),[4] hero of *The Birds,* mocking disdain is replaced by a zealous concern for her son's fate, a concern that is perhaps even more effective in blocking any lasting relationship he might have with a woman.

There is another trait common to these three films: from one film to the next, the figure of a threat in the shape of birds assumes greater prominence. In *North by Northwest* we have what is perhaps the most famous Hitchcockian scene, the attack by the plane—a steel bird—that pursues the hero across a flat, sun-baked landscape; in *Psycho,* Norman's room is filled with stuffed mounted birds, and even the body of his mummified mother reminds us of

2. Lacan, *Ecrits*, pp. 54–59 [Žižek's note].
3. Released in 1959; *Vertigo*, in 1958.
4. Australian-born television and film actor (1930–2015). Grant (1904–1986), English actor who appears in several Hitchcock films. Perkins (1932–1992), American actor best known for his portrayal of Norman Bates.

a stuffed bird; in *The Birds,* after the (metaphorical) steel bird and the (metonymic) stuffed birds, we finally have actual live birds attacking the town.

The decisive thing is to perceive the link between the two traits: the terrifying figure of the birds is actually the embodiment in the real of a discord, an unresolved tension in intersubjective relations. In the film, the birds are like the plague in Oedipus's Thebes:[5] they are the incarnation of a fundamental disorder in family relationships—the father is absent, the paternal function (the function of pacifying law, the Name-of-the-Father) is suspended and that vacuum is filled by the "irrational" maternal superego, arbitrary, wicked, blocking "normal" sexual relationship (only possible under the sign of the paternal metaphor). The dead end *The Birds* is really about is, of course, that of the modern American family: the deficient paternal ego-ideal makes the law "regress" toward a ferocious maternal superego, affecting sexual enjoyment—the decisive trait of the libidinal structure of "pathological narcissism": "Their unconscious impressions of the mother are so overblown and so heavily influenced by aggressive impulses, and the quality of her care is so little attuned to the child's needs, that in the child's fantasies the mother appears as a devouring bird."[6]

From the Oedipal Journey to the "Pathological Narcissist"

How should we locate this figuration of the maternal superego in the totality of Hitchcock's work? The three main stages of Hitchcock's career can be conceived precisely as three variations on the theme of the impossibility of the sexual relationship. Let us begin with the first Hitchcockian classic, *The Thirty-Nine Steps:*[7] all the animated action of the film should not deceive us for a minute—its function is ultimately just to put the love couple to the test and thus render possible their final reunion. It is on account of this feature that *The Thirty-Nine Steps* starts the series of Hitchcock's English films of the second half of the 1930s, all of which, with the exception of the last (*Jamaica Inn*),[8] relate the same story of the *initiation of an amorous couple.* They are all stories of a couple tied (sometimes literally: note the role of handcuffs in *The Thirty-Nine Steps*) by accident and then maturing through a series of ordeals. All these films are thus actually variations on the fundamental motif of the bourgeois ideology of marriage, gaining its first and perhaps noblest expression in Mozart's *Magic Flute.*[9] The parallel could be here expanded to details: the mysterious woman who charges the hero with his mission (the stranger killed in Hannay's apartment in *The Thirty-Nine Steps*; the nice old lady who vanishes in the film of the same title), is she not a kind of reincarnation of the "Queen of the Night"? The black Monostatos, is he not reincarnated in the murderous drummer with blackened face in *Young and Innocent*? In *The Lady Vanishes,*[1] the hero attracts the attention of his future love by playing what?—a flute, of course!

5. In Greek mythology, Thebes was struck by plague because the murderer of Thebes' previous king was in the city; Oedipus, as king, swore to drive the killer out, not knowing that he himself was the murderer and that he had killed his own father.

6. Christopher Lasch, *The Culture of Narcissism* (London: Abacus, 1980), p. 176 [Žižek's note].

7. Released in 1935.

8. Released in 1939.

9. One of the most famous operas (1791) of Wolfgang Amadeus Mozart (1756–1791); its characters include the Queen of the Night and Monostatos.

1. Released in 1938.

The innocence lost on this voyage of initiation is best presented in the remarkable figure of Mr. Memory, whose number in the music hall opens and closes the film. He is a man who "remembers everything," a personification of pure automatism and, at the same time, the absolute ethic of the signifier (in the film's final scene, he answers Hannay's question "What are 'the thirty-nine steps'?", although he knows the answer could cost him his life—he is simply obliged to honor his public engagement, to answer any question whatsoever). There is something of the fairy tale in this figure of a Good Dwarf who must die in order that the liaison of the amorous couple finally be established. Mr. Memory embodies a pure, asexual gapless knowledge, a signifying chain that works absolutely automatically, without any traumatic stumbling block hindering its course. What we must be careful about is the precise moment of his death: he dies after answering the question "What are 'the thirty-nine steps'?", i.e., after revealing the McGuffin,[2] the secret propelling the story. By disclosing it to the public in the music hall (which stands here for the big Other of common opinion), he delivers Hannay from the awkward position of "persecuted persecutor." The two circles (that of the police chasing Hannay and that of Hannay himself in pursuit of the real culprit) rejoin, Hannay is exonerated in the eyes of the big Other, and the real culprits are unmasked. At this point, the story could end since it was sustained solely by this intermediary state, by Hannay's ambiguous position vis-a-vis the big Other: guilty in the eyes of the big Other, he is at the same time on the track of the real culprits.

It is this position of the "persecuted persecutor" that already displays the motif of the "transference of guilt": Hannay is falsely accused, the guilt is transferred onto him—but whose guilt is it? The guilt of the *obscene, "anal" father* personified by the mysterious leader of the spy network. At the film's end, we witness *two* consecutive deaths: first the leader of the spy ring kills Mr. Memory, then the police, this instrument of the big Other, shoot down the leader, who falls from his theater box onto the podium (this is an exemplary place of denouement in Hitchcock's films: *Murder, Stage Fright, I Confess*[3]). Mr. Memory and the leader of the spy ring represent the two sides of the same pre-Oedipal conjunction: the Good Dwarf with his gapless undivided knowledge, and the mean "anal father," the master who pulls the strings of this knowledge-automaton, a father who exhibits in an obscene way his shortened little finger—an ironic allusion to his castration. (We encounter a homologous split in Robert Rossen's *The Hustler,* in the relationship between the professional billiard player, an incarnation of the pure ethic of the game [Jackie Gleason], and his corrupt boss [George C. Scott].[4]) The story begins with an act of "interpellation"[5] that subjectivizes the hero, i.e., it constitutes him as desiring by evoking the McGuffin, the object-cause of his desire (the message of the "Queen of the Night," the mysterious stranger who is slaughtered in Hannay's apartment). The Oedipal voyage in

2. Hitchcock's term for a particular plot device: a desired object or goal that catches (and distracts) the viewer's attention but is ultimately of no real importance.

3. Released in 1930, 1950, and 1953, respectively.

4. American stage and film actor (1927–1999). Rossen (1908–1966), American screenwriter, director, and producer; *The Hustler* (1961) is his best-known film. Gleason (1916–1987), American comedian, actor, and composer.

5. The term used by the French Marxist philosopher LOUIS ALTHUSSER (1918–1990) to refer to ideology's ability to "hail" or summon individuals as subjects.

pursuit of the father, which constitutes the bulk of the film, ends with the "anal" father's death. By means of his death, he can assume his place as metaphor, as the Name-of-the-Father, thus rendering possible the amorous couple's final reunion, their "normal" sexual relation which, according to Lacan, can take place only under the sign of the paternal metaphor.

In addition to Hannay and Pamela in *The Thirty-Nine Steps,* couples tied by chance and reunited through ordeal are Ashenden and Elsa in *The Secret Agent,* Robert and Erica in *Young and Innocent,* Gilbert and Iris in *The Lady Vanishes*—with the notable exception of *Sabotage,*[6] where the triangle of Sylvia, her criminal husband Verloc, and the detective Ted foreshadows the conjuncture characteristic of Hitchcock's next stage (the Selznick period[7]). Here, the story is, as a rule, narrated from the point of view of a woman divided between two men, the elderly figure of a villain (her father or her aged husband, embodying one of the typical Hitchcockian figures, that of a villain who is aware of the evil in himself and who strives after his own destruction) and the younger, somewhat insipid "good guy" whom she chooses at the end.[8] In addition to Sylvia, Verloc, and Ted in *Sabotage,* the main cases of such triangles are Carol Fisher, divided between loyalty to her pro-Nazi father and love for the young American journalist, in *Foreign Correspondent*; Charlie, divided between her murderous uncle of the same name and the detective Jack, in *Shadow of a Doubt*; and, of course, Alicia, divided between her aged husband Sebastian and Devlin, in *Notorious.* (The notable exception here is *Under Capricorn,* where the heroine resists the charm of a young seducer and returns to her aged, criminal husband after confessing that the crime her husband was convicted for was her own.) The third stage again shifts the accent to the male hero to whom the maternal superego blocks access, thus prohibiting a "normal" sexual relation (from Bruno in *Strangers on a Train* to the "necktie murderer" in *Frenzy*).

Where should we look for the wider frame of reference enabling us to confer a kind of theoretical consistency on this succession of the three forms of (the impossibility of) sexual relationship? Here, we are tempted to venture a somewhat quick "sociological" answer by invoking the three successive forms of the libidinal structure of the subject exhibited in capitalist society during the past century: the "autonomous" individual of the Protestant ethic, the heteronomous "organization man,"[9] and the type gaining predominance today, the "pathological narcissist." The crucial thing to emphasize here is that the so-called "decline of the Protestant ethic" and the appearance of the "organization man," i.e., the replacement of the ethic of individual responsibility by the ethic of the heteronomous individual, oriented toward others, leaves intact the underlying frame of the ego-ideal. It is merely its contents that change: the ego-ideal becomes "externalized" as the expecta-

6. Released in 1936.
7. That is, Hitchcock's first years in Hollywood (1940–47), after he signed a long-term contract with the American producer and studio executive David O. Selznick (1902–1965).
8. Here it is crucial to grasp the logic of the connection between the woman's perspective and the figure of the resigned, impotent Master. Lacan's answer to Freud's famous question "*Was will das Weib?* What does the (hysterical) woman want?" is: *a Master, but one whom she could dominate.* The perfect figuration of this hysterical fantasy is Charlotte Brontë's *Jane Eyre* where, at the end of the novel, the heroine is happily married to the blinded, helpless fatherlike figure (*Rebecca* [1940 film], of course, belongs to the same tradition) [Žižek's note]. *Jane Eyre* (1847), first novel published by the English writer Brontë (1816–1855).
9. As described in William H. Whyte's best-selling book on corporate life, *The Organization Man* (1956). The classic study of the "Protestant ethic" is Max Weber's *The Protestant Ethic and the Spirit of Capitalism* (1905).

tions of the social group to which the individual belongs. The source of moral satisfaction is no longer the feeling that we resisted the pressure of our milieu and remained true to ourselves (i.e., to our paternal ego-ideal), but rather the feeling of loyalty to the group. The subject looks at himself through the eyes of the group, he strives to merit its love and esteem.

The third stage, the arrival of the "pathological narcissist," breaks precisely with this underlying frame of the ego-ideal common to the first two forms. Instead of the integration of a symbolic *law,* we have a multitude of *rules* to follow—rules of accommodation telling us "how to succeed." The narcissistic subject knows only the "rules of the (social) game" enabling him to manipulate others; social relations constitute for him a playing field in which he assumes "roles," not proper symbolic mandates; he stays clear of any kind of binding commitment that would imply a proper symbolic identification. He is a radical *conformist* who paradoxically experiences himself as an *outlaw.* All this is, of course, already a commonplace of social psychology; what usually goes unnoticed, however, is that this disintegration of the ego-ideal entails the installation of a "maternal" superego that does not prohibit enjoyment but, on the contrary, imposes it and punishes "social failure" in a far more cruel and severe way, through an unbearable and self-destructive anxiety. All the babble about the "decline of paternal authority" merely conceals the resurgence of this incomparably more oppressive agency. Today's "permissive" society is certainly not less "repressive" than the epoch of the "organization man," that obsessive servant of the bureaucratic institution; the sole difference lies in the fact that in a "society that demands submission to the rules of social intercourse but refuses to ground those rules in a code of moral conduct,"[1] i.e., in the ego-ideal, the social demand assumes the form of a harsh, punitive superego.

We could also approach "pathological narcissism" on the basis of Saul Kripke's criticism of the theory of descriptions, i.e., from his premise that the meaning of a name (proper or of a natural kind) can never be reduced to a set of descriptive features that characterize the object denoted by it. The name always functions as a "rigid designator," referring to the same object even if all properties contained in its meaning prove false.[2] Needless to say, the Kripkian notion of the "rigid designator" overlaps perfectly with the Lacanian notion of the "master signifier," i.e., of a signifier that does not denote some positive property of the object but establishes, by means of its own act of enunciation, a new intersubjective relation between speaker and hearer. If, for example, I tell somebody "You are my master!", I confer upon him a certain symbolic "mandate" that is not contained in the set of his positive properties but results from the very performative force of my utterance, and I create thereby a new symbolic reality, that of a master-disciple relationship between the two of us, within which each of us assumes a certain commitment. The paradox of the "pathological narcissist" is, however, that *for him, language does indeed function according to the theory of descriptions*: the meaning of words is reduced to the positive features of the denoted object, above all those that concern his narcissistic interests. Let us exemplify this apropos of the eternally tedious feminine question: "Why do you love me?" In love proper, this question is, of

1. Lasch, *The Culture of Narcissism*, p. 12 [Žižek's note].
2. Cf. Saul Kripke, *Naming and Necessity* (Cambridge, Mass.: Harvard University Press, 1972) [Žižek's note]. Kripke (b. 1940), American philosopher and logician.

course, unanswerable (which is why women ask it in the first place), i.e., the only appropriate answer is "Because there is something in you more than yourself, some indefinite X that attracts me, but that cannot be pinned down to any positive quality." In other words, if we answer it with a catalogue of positive properties ("I love you because of the shape of your breasts, because of the way you smile"), this is at best a mocking imitation of love proper. The "pathological narcissist" is, on the other hand, somebody who *is* able to answer such a question by enumerating a definite list of properties: for him, the idea that love is a commitment transcending an attachment to a series of qualities that could gratify his wishes is simply beyond comprehension.[3] And the way to hystericize the "pathological narcissist" is precisely to force upon him some symbolic mandate that cannot be grounded in its properties. Such a confrontation brings about the hysterical question, "Why am I what you are saying that I am?" Think of Roger O. Thornhill in Hitchcock's *North by Northwest*, a pure "pathological narcissist" if ever there was one, who all of a sudden, without any apparent reason, finds himself pinned to the signifier "Kaplan"; the shock of this encounter derails his narcissistic economy and opens up to him the road of gradual access to "normal" sexual relations under the sign of the Name-of-the-Father (which is why *North by Northwest* is a variation of the formula of *The Thirty-Nine Steps*).[4]

We can now see how the three versions of the impossibility of sexual relationship in Hitchcock's films refer to these three types of libidinal economy. The couple's initiating voyage, with its obstacles stirring the desire of reunification, is firmly grounded in the classical ideology of the "autonomous" subject strengthened through ordeal; the resigned paternal figure of Hitchcock's next stage evokes the decline of this "autonomous" subject to whom is opposed the victorious, insipid "heteronomous" hero; and, finally, it is not difficult to recognize in the typical Hitchcockian hero of the 1950s and '60s the features of the "pathological narcissist" dominated by the obscene figure of the maternal superego. Hitchcock is thus staging again and again the vicissitudes of the family in late-capitalist society; the real "secret" of his films is ultimately always the family secret, its tenebrous reverse.

A Mental Experiment: *The Birds* without Birds

Although Hitchcock's birds do give body to the agency of the maternal superego, the essential thing is nevertheless *not* to seize upon the link between the two traits we have noted—the appearance of the ferocious assailant birds, the blockage of "normal" sexual relations by the intervention of the maternal superego—as a sign relationship, as a correlative between a "symbol" and its "signification": the birds do not "signify" the maternal superego, they do not

3. It is against the background of this problem that we could perhaps locate the lesson to be drawn from Stanley Cavell's *Pursuits of Happiness: The Hollywood Comedies of Remarriage* (Cambridge, Mass.: Harvard University Press, 1981), namely a version of the Hegelian theory of repetition in history: the only proper marriage is the second one. First we marry the other *qua* our narcissistic complement; it is only when his/her delusive charm fades that we can engage in marriage as an attachment to the other beyond his/her imaginary properties [Žižek's note]. For the German philosopher GEORG WILHELM FRIEDRICH HEGEL (1770–1831), see above.

4. It is because *North by Northwest* repeats the logic of the Oedipal journey that it offers us a kind of spectral analysis of the function of the father, dividing it into three figures: Roger Thornhill's *imaginary* father (the UN diplomat stabbed in the hall of the General Assembly), his *symbolic* father (the CIA "Professor" who invented the *name* "Kaplan" to which Thornhill is tied), and his *real* father, i.e., the resigned, perverse villain Van Damm [Žižek's note].

"symbolize" blocked sexual relations, the "possessive" mother, and so on; they are, rather, the making present in the real, the objectivization, the incarnation of the fact that, on the symbolizing level, something "has not worked out," in short, the objectivization-positivization of a *failed* symbolization. In the terrifying presence of the attacking birds, a certain lack, a certain failure assumes positive existence. At first glance, this distinction may appear factitious, vague; that is why we shall try to explicate it by means of a fairly elementary test question: how might the film have been constructed if the birds were to function *in fact* as the "symbol" of blocked sexual relations?

The answer is simple: first, we must imagine *The Birds* as a film *without birds*. We would then have a typically American drama about a family in which the son goes from one woman to another because he is unable to free himself from the pressure exerted by a possessive mother, a drama similar to dozens of others that have appeared on American stages and screens, particularly in the 1950s: the tragedy of a son playing with the chaos of his sexual life for what was in those days referred to as the mother's inability to "live her own life," to "expend her vital energy," and the mother's emotional breakdown when some woman finally manages to take away her son, all seasoned with a touch of "psychoanalytic" salt à la Eugene O'Neill or Tennessee Williams and acted, if possible, in a psychologistic, Actors' Studio[5] style—the common ground of the American theater at midcentury.

Next, in such a drama we must imagine the appearance from time to time, particularly at crucial moments of emotional intrigue (the son's first encounter with his future wife, the mother's breakdown, etc.), of birds—in the background, as part of the ambience: the opening scene (the meeting of Mitch and Melanie in the pet shop, the purchase of the lovebirds) could perhaps remain as it is; and, after the emotion-charged scene of conflict between mother and son, when the sorrowing mother withdraws to the seacoast, we might hear the cawing of birds. In such a film, the birds, even though or, rather, *because* they do not play a direct role in the development of the story, would be "symbols," they would "symbolize" the tragic necessity of the mother's renunciation, her helplessness, or whatever—and everyone would know what the birds signified, everyone would clearly recognize that the film was depicting an emotional drama of a son facing up to a possessive mother who is trying to transfer onto him the price of her own failure, and the "symbolic" role of the birds would be indicated by the title, which would remain unchanged: *The Birds*.

Now, what did Hitchcock do? In his film, the birds are not "symbols" at all, they play a direct part in the story as something inexplicable, as something outside the rational chain of events, as a *lawless* impossible real. The diegetic action of the film is so influenced by the birds that their massive presence completely overshadows the domestic drama: the drama—literally—*loses its significance*. The "spontaneous" spectator does not perceive *The Birds* as a domestic family drama in which the role of the birds is "symbolic" of intersubjective relationships and tensions; the accent is put totally on the traumatic

5. A professional actors' workshop, founded in 1947; under its longtime director Lee Strasberg (1948–68) it became identified with method acting, in which actors draw on their own experiences and emotional memories. The great 20th-century American dramatists O'Neill (1888–1953) and Williams (1911–1983) wrote many plays dealing with family conflict and thwarted desires.

attacks by the birds, and, within that framework, the emotional intrigue is mere pretext, part of the undifferentiated tissue of everyday incidents of which the first half of the film is made up, so that, against that background, the weird, inexplicable fury of the birds can be made to stand out even more strongly. Thus the birds, far from functioning as a "symbol" whose "signification" can be detected, on the contrary *block, mask,* by their massive presence, the film's "signification," their function being to make us *forget,* during their vertiginous and dazzling attacks, with what, in the end, we are dealing: the triangle of a mother, her son, and the woman he loves. If the "spontaneous" spectator had been supposed to perceive the film's "signification" easily, then the birds should quite simply have been *left out.*

There is a key detail that supports our reading; at the very end of the film, Mitch's mother "accepts" Melanie as her son's wife, gives her consent, and abandons her superego role (as indicated by the fleeting smile she and Melanie exchange in the car)—and that is why, at that moment, they are all able to leave the property that is being threatened by the birds: the birds are no longer needed, their role is finished. The end of the film—the last shot of the car driving away surrounded by hordes of calm birds—is for that reason wholly coherent and not at all the result of some kind of "compromise"; the fact that Hitchcock himself spread the rumor that he would have preferred another ending (the car arriving at a Golden Gate Bridge totally blackened by the birds perched on it) and was forced to accede to studio pressure, is just another of the many myths fomented by the director, who was at pains to dissimulate what was really at stake in his work.

It is clear, therefore, why *The Birds*—according to François Regnault[6]—is the film that closes the Hitchcockian system: the birds, the ultimate incarnation in Hitchcock of the Bad Object, are the counterpart of the reign of maternal law, and it is precisely this conjunction of the Bad Object of fascination and the maternal law that defines the kernel of the Hitchcockian fantasy.

1991

6. Cf. François Regnault, "Systeme formel d'Hitchcock," in *Cahiers du cinema,* hors-serie 8 [Žižek's note].

HENRY LOUIS GATES JR.

b. 1950

One of the best-known cultural critics in America, Henry Louis Gates Jr. has played a vital role in establishing an African American literary canon. A tireless impresario, he has also helped build institutional structures to study African American literature and has disseminated his views of race and culture through mainstream media, writing for such magazines as *Newsweek* and the *New Yorker* and frequently appearing on television. Our selection, "Talking Black: Critical Signs of the Times" (1988), sets out his credo for present-day African American literary theory, which borrows from but revises mainstream theory with infusions of African American modes of thought and vernacular discourse.

Gates was born and raised in Keyser, West Virginia. After high school, he attended Potomac State Community College but was encouraged by an English instructor to transfer to Yale University, from which he received his B.A. in 1973. While an undergraduate (1970–71), Gates traveled to Africa on a fellowship, visiting fifteen countries and learning about African culture. On his return to the United States he worked as a director of student affairs for the West Virginia gubernatorial campaign of John D. Rockefeller IV, later writing his senior honors thesis on the campaign. He received Mellon and Ford Foundation fellowships that enabled him to undertake graduate study at Cambridge University, where he earned his M.A. in 1974 and Ph.D. in 1979. At Cambridge he worked with the Nigerian writer Wole Soyinka, who exposed him to Yoruba myths and interpretive modes. While in England he also began a journalistic career, working as a London correspondent for *Time* magazine from 1973 to 1975. In 1975 he returned to the United States, attending Yale Law School for a month before changing paths to pursue literary studies. He began teaching at Yale in 1976 as a lecturer in English; by the time he left, in 1985, he had become a full professor and had received several prestigious awards, including a 1981 MacArthur Fellowship. After teaching at Cornell and Duke Universities, in 1991 he moved to Harvard University as W. E. B. Du Bois Professor of the Humanities, director of the W. E. B. Du Bois Institute for African and African American Research, and chair of the Department of African and African American Studies. While chair from 1991 to 2006, he gathered what he called a "dream team" of prominent scholars from several disciplines. In 2006 Harvard appointed him to a prestigious University Professorship.

Gates's work shows the influence of the two poles of his education: the sophisticated reading practices and deconstructive literary theories of the critics affiliated with Yale University in the 1970s, such as PAUL DE MAN, JACQUES DERRIDA, and Geoffrey Hartman, and the indigenous African tradition of literature and interpretation introduced to him by Soyinka. His early critical writing draws on an array of contemporary theory, from sources as diverse as MIKHAIL M. BAKHTIN, NORTHROP FRYE, and Derrida, which he applies to readings of African American literature in an attempt to revalue it and to construct a canon. In his innovative book *The Signifying Monkey: A Theory of African-American Literary Criticism* (1988), he melds the poststructuralist theory of signification rooted in the linguistics of FERDINAND DE SAUSSURE with the African vernacular tradition of "signifyin(g)," which derives from Yoruba oral literature. The latter tradition is evident in present-day practices such as "the dozens" (a game of verbal one-upsmanship) and jazz improvisation. Gates stresses that he uses theory provisionally; his intention is "to develop theories of criticism indigenous to our literatures" by drawing on "black textual tradition."

By blending contemporary Euro-American theory with African tradition, Gates positions himself as an intermediary between dominant Anglo-American and minority African American literary cultures. Against the conservative view that African American literature lacks aesthetic merit and is valuable only as a social report, Gates urges us to gauge it on its own aesthetic terms, within the vernacular black tradition. Using these criteria, he establishes an African American canon. Against radical black separatist arguments for the exclusive study of African American literature, or Afrocentrism, Gates argues instead for "cultural tolerance," and he freely makes use of mainstream literary theory as a means to specific ends. Between traditionalists and radicals, between assimilationists and separatists, and between antitheorists and theorists, Gates negotiates a middle path. His ultimate goal is institutional as well as theoretical. As he puts it in our selection, he aims to forge a place for black writing and criticism in "the broader, larger institution of literature."

"Talking Black" exemplifies Gates's intermediary role, drawing on two competing poles in African American cultural politics—assimilationist and separatist—as well as asserting the status of black writing in mainstream literary culture. Characteristically, Gates calls for simultaneously using critical theory and injecting African American tradition. He foregrounds the example of the early African American intellectual and religious leader Alexander Crummell (1819–1898), who advocated studying classical languages and obtaining a traditional white education. Most African American critics view this position as overly accommodating, and Gates distances himself from it, stressing that his amalgam of contemporary theoretical approaches and black tradition transforms the theory it employs. "Talking Black," which originally appeared in the New York–based weekly the *Village Voice*, also exemplifies Gates's efforts to bridge the gap between the specialized sphere of academic criticism and the public sphere of journalism, efforts that have been remarkably successful.

This middle-of-the-road position has helped win Gates a high degree of public visibility and success, but it has also generated much criticism. Traditionalists believe that the effort to create a separate African American canon degrades the Western canon, whose value, they argue, has been confirmed over time. Some dedicated theorists see Gates's mainstream writings as a watering-down of his scholarship. On the other hand, Afrocentrist critics consider it a means of accommodating white culture, in effect claiming that Gates has become a latter-day Crummell. Other radical critics judge that he focuses too exclusively on literature and culture rather than on the material conditions of African Americans. Gates unapologetically defines his role as that of a literary critic and argues that attention to black literary tradition and heritage carries an implicit politics, fostering greater cultural recognition for African Americans. Ironically, Gates's intermediary position, both intellectual and stylistic, fuels his popular influence as well as the attacks of his most cogent detractors.

"Talking Black: Critical Signs of the Times" Keywords: The Canon/Tradition, Identity, Literary History, Race and Ethnicity Studies, Representation, Vernacular Language

Talking Black: Critical Signs of the Times

> For a language acts in diverse ways, upon the spirit of a people; even as the spirit of a people acts with a creative and spiritualizing force upon a language.
>
> —Alexander Crummell,[1] 1860

> A new vision began gradually to replace the dream of political power—a powerful movement, the rise of another ideal to guide the unguided, another pillar of fire by night after a clouded day. It was the ideal of "book-learning"; the curiosity, born of compulsory ignorance, to know and test the power of the cabalistic letters of the white man, the longing to know. Here at last seemed to have been discovered the mountain path to Canaan; longer than the highway of Emancipation and law, steep and rugged, but straight, leading to heights high enough to overlook life.
>
> —W. E. B. Du Bois,[2] 1903

> The knowledge which would teach the white world was Greek to his own flesh and blood . . . and he could not articulate the message of another people.
>
> —W. E. B. Du Bois, 1903

1. African American Episcopalian minister (1819–1898), who earned a degree from Cambridge University (1853) and cultivated scholarship among young blacks. The quotation is from "The English Language in Liberia," an address delivered in Liberia.

2. African American historian and sociologist (1868–1963; see above), co-founder of the NAACP and the foremost voice of black protest in the early 20th century. Both his epigraphs are from chapter 1 of *The Souls of Black Folk* (1903).

Alexander Crummell, a pioneering nineteenth-century Pan-Africanist,[3] statesman, and missionary who spent the bulk of his creative years as an Anglican minister in Liberia, was also a pioneering intellectual and philosopher of language, founding the American Negro Academy[4] in 1897 and serving as the intellectual godfather of W. E. B. Du Bois. For his first annual address as president of the academy, delivered on December 28, 1897, Crummell selected as his topic "The Attitude of the American Mind Toward the Negro Intellect." Given the occasion of the first annual meeting of the great intellectuals of the race, he could not have chosen a more timely or appropriate subject.

Crummell wished to attack, he said, "the denial of intellectuality in the Negro; the assertion that he was not a human being, that he did not belong to the human race." He argued that the desire "to becloud and stamp out the intellect of the Negro" had led to the enactment of "laws and Statutes, closing the pages of every book printed to the eyes of Negroes; barring the doors of every school-room against them!" This, he concluded, "was the systematized method of the intellect of the South, to stamp out the brains of the Negro!"—a program that created an "almost Egyptian darkness[5] [which] fell upon the mind of the race, throughout the whole land."

Crummell next shared with his audience a conversation between two Boston lawyers which he had overheard when he was "an errand boy in the Anti-slavery office in New York City" in 1833 or 1834:

> While at the Capitol they happened to dine in the company of the great John C. Calhoun,[6] then senator from South Carolina. It was a period of great ferment upon the question of Slavery, States' Rights, and Nullification; and consequently the Negro was the topic of conversation at the table. One of the utterances of Mr. Calhoun was to this effect—"That if he could find a Negro who knew the Greek syntax, he would then believe that the Negro was a human being and should be treated as a man."

"Just think of the crude asininity," Crummell concluded rather generously, "of even a great man!"

The salient sign of the black person's humanity—indeed, the only sign for Calhoun—would be the mastering of the very essence of Western civilization, of the very foundation of the complex fiction upon which white Western culture had been constructed. It is likely that "Greek syntax," for John C. Calhoun, was merely a hyperbolic figure of speech, a trope of virtual impossibility; he felt driven to the hyperbolic mode, perhaps, because of the long racist tradition in Western letters of demanding that black people *prove* their full humanity. We know this tradition all too well, dotted as it is with the names of the great intellectual Western racialists, such as Francis Bacon, David Hume, Immanuel Kant, Thomas Jefferson, and G. W. F. Hegel.[7]

3. A believer in the innate unity of all black Africans and their overseas descendants; more especially, one active in the movement for the unity and independence of African states (as was Du Bois, beginning in 1900 with the Pan-African Congress in London).

4. A learned society for African Americans that promoted civil rights through scholarly work on African American culture and history.

5. An allusion to one of the plagues said to have been brought by God against the Egyptians who were holding the Israelites in slavery (Exodus 10.21–23).

6. Prominent American political leader (1782–1850) and the 7th U.S. vice president (1825–32); he was a strong advocate of states' rights and of slavery.

7. Major thinkers who generally (save the slaveholding Jefferson) are not thought of as "racialist": Bacon (1561–1626), English philosopher, scientist,

Whereas each of these figures demanded that blacks write poetry to prove their humanity, Calhoun—writing in a post–Phillis Wheatley[8] era—took refuge in, yes, Greek syntax.

In typical African-American fashion, a brilliant black intellectual accepted Calhoun's challenge. The anecdote Crummell shared with his fellow black academicians turned out to be his shaping scene of instruction. For Crummell himself jumped on a boat, sailed to England, and matriculated at Queens' College, Cambridge, where he mastered the intricacies of Greek syntax. Calhoun, we suspect, was not impressed.

Crummell never stopped believing that mastering the master's tongue was the sole path to civilization, intellectual freedom, and social equality for the black person. It was Western "culture," he insisted, that the black person "must claim as his rightful heritage, as a man—not stinted training, not a caste education, not," he concluded prophetically, "a Negro curriculum." As he argued so passionately in his speech of 1860, "The English Language in Liberia," the acquisition of the English language, along with Christianity, is the wonderful sign of God's providence encoded in the nightmare of African enslavement in the racist wilderness of the New World. English, for Crummell, was "the speech of Chaucer and Shakespeare, of Milton and Wordsworth, of Bacon and Burke, of Franklin and Webster,"[9] and its potential mastery was "this one item of compensation" that "the Almighty has bestowed upon us" in exchange for "the exile of our fathers from their African homes to America." In the English language are embodied "the noblest theories of liberty" and "the grandest ideas of humanity." If black people master the master's tongue, these great and grand ideas will become African ideas, because "ideas conserve men, and keep alive the vitality of nations."

In dark contrast to the splendors of the English language, Crummell set the African vernacular languages, which, he wrote, have "definite marks of inferiority connected with them all, which place them at the widest distances from civilized languages." Any effort to render the master's discourse in our own black tongue is an egregious error, for we cannot translate sublime utterances "in[to] broken English—a miserable caricature of their noble tongue." We must abandon forever both indigenous African vernacular languages and the neo-African vernacular languages that our people have produced in the New World:

> All low, inferior, and barbarous tongues are, doubtless, but the lees and dregs of noble languages, which have gradually, as the soul of a nation has died out, sunk down to degradation and ruin. We must not suffer this decay on these shores, in this nation. We have been made, providentially, the deposit of a noble trust; and we should be proud to show our appreciation of it. Having come to the heritage of this language we

and statesman; HUME (1711–1776), Scottish philosopher and historian; KANT (1724–1804), German idealist philosopher; Jefferson (1743–1826), drafter of the Declaration of Independence, Founding Father, and 3d president (1801–09) of the United States; HEGEL (1770–1831), German idealist philosopher.

8. The first black American woman poet in the United States (ca. 1753–1784), born probably in Senegal and sold as a slave to a Boston family.

9. Crummell names English and American men famed for their skill with words: the English poet Geoffrey Chaucer (ca. 1343–1400) and the poet/dramatist William Shakespeare (1564–1616); two poets, John Milton (1608–1674) and WILLIAM WORDSWORTH (1770–1850); two philosopher/statesmen, Bacon and EDMUND BURKE (1729–1797); and two American politicians, the popular author, inventor, and ambassador Benjamin Franklin (1706–1790) and the great orator Daniel Webster (1782–1852).

must cherish its spirit, as well as retain its letter. We must cultivate it among ourselves; we must strive to infuse its spirit among our reclaimed and aspiring natives.

I cite the examples of John C. Calhoun and Alexander Crummell as metaphors for the relation between the critic of black writing and the broader, larger institution of literature. Learning the master's tongue, for our generation of critics, has been an act of empowerment, whether that tongue be New Criticism, humanism, structuralism, Marxism, poststructuralism, feminism, new historicism,[1] or any other "ism." Each of these critical discourses arises from a specific set of texts within the Western tradition. At least for the past decade, many of us have busied ourselves with the necessary task of learning about these movements in criticism, drawing upon their modes of reading to explicate the texts in our own tradition.

This is an exciting time for critics of Afro-American literature. More critical essays and books are being produced than ever before, and there have never been more jobs available teaching Afro-American literature in white colleges and universities. In a few years, we shall at last have our very own Norton anthology,[2] a sure sign that the teaching of Afro-American literature is being institutionalized. Our pressing question now becomes this. In what languages shall we choose to speak, and write, our own criticisms? What are we now to do with the enabling masks of empowerment that we have donned as we have practiced one mode of formal criticism or another?

There is a long history of resistance to (white) theory in the (black) tradition. Unlike almost every other, the Afro-American literary tradition was generated as a response to allegations that its authors did not, and *could not* create literature, considered the signal measure of a race's innate "humanity." The African living in Europe or in the New World seems to have felt compelled to create a literature not only to demonstrate that blacks did indeed possess the intellectual ability to create a written art, but also to indict the several social and economic institutions that delimited the "humanity" of all black people in Western cultures.

So insistent did these racist allegations prove to be, at least from the eighteenth to the early twentieth century, that it is fair to describe the subtext of the history of black letters in terms of the urge to refute them. Even as late as 1911, when J. E. Casely-Hayford[3] published *Ethiopia Unbound* (the "first" African novel), he felt it necessary to address this matter in the first two paragraphs of this text. "At the dawn of the twentieth century," the novel opens, "men of light and leading both in Europe and in America had not yet made up their minds as to what place to assign to the spiritual aspirations of the black man." Few literary traditions have begun with such a complex and curious relation to criticism: allegations of an absence led directly to a presence, a literature often inextricably bound in a dialogue with its harshest critics.

Black literature and its criticism, then, have been put to uses that were not primarily aesthetic; rather, they have formed part of a larger discourse on the nature of the black, and of his or her role in the order of things. The

1. Major critical schools of 20th-century U.S. literary studies.
2. *The Norton Anthology of African American Literature* (1997), whose general editors were Gates and Nellie Y. McKay.
3. Ghanaian lawyer, writer, and advocate of African nationalism (1866–1930).

relation among theory, tradition, and integrity within black culture has not been, and perhaps cannot be, a straightforward matter.

Despite the fact that critics of black literature are often attacked for using theory and that some black readers respond to their work by remarking that it's all Greek to them, it is probably true that critics of Afro-American literature are more concerned with the complex relation between literature and theory than ever before. There are many reasons for this, not the least of which is our increasingly central role in "the profession" precisely when our colleagues are engulfed in their own extensive debates about the intellectual merit of so much theorizing. Theory, as a second-order reflection upon a primary gesture, has *always* been viewed with suspicion by scholars who find it presumptuous and even decadent when criticism claims the right to stand on its own: theoretical texts breed equally "decadent" theoretical responses in a creative process that can be very far removed from a poem or a novel.

For the critic of Afro-American literature, this process is even more perilous because most of the contemporary literary theory derives from critics of Western European languages and literatures. Is the use of theory to write about Afro-American literature merely another form of intellectual indenture, a mental servitude as pernicious in its intellectual implications as any other kind of enslavement? The key word implied in this panel discussion[4] is *integrity*. To quote the *Oxford English Dictionary*'s definition of the word, does theorizing about a text or a literary tradition "mar," "violate," "impair," or "corrupt" the "soundness" of an "original perfect state" of a black text or of the black tradition? To argue that it does is to align oneself with the New Critics[5]—who often seem not to have cared particularly for, or about, the writing of Afro-Americans—and with their view that texts are "organic wholes" in the first place. This is a critical error.

The sense of "integrity" as it seems to arise in the Afro-American tradition is more akin to the notion of "ringing true," or to Houston Baker's[6] concept of "sounding." (One of the most frequently used critical judgments in the African-American tradition is "That just don't sound right," or, as Alice Walker puts it in *The Color Purple*,[7] "Look like to me only a fool would want to talk in a way that feel peculiar to your mind.") That is the sense that black nationalists[8] call on here, without understanding how problematic this can be. Doubleness, alienation, equivocality—since the turn of the century at least, these have been recurrent tropes for the black tradition.

To be sure, this matter of criticism and "integrity" has a long and rather tortured history in black letters. It was David Hume, after all, who called Francis Williams,[9] the Jamaican poet of Latin verse, "a parrot who merely speaks a few words plainly." Phillis Wheatley, too, has long suffered from the spurious attacks of black and white critics alike for being the *rara avis*[1] of a

4. The panel "Integrity and the Black Tradition," where this essay was originally presented at the 1987 convention of the Modern Language Association (the primary North American professional organization for scholars in English and foreign languages and literatures).
5. Those literary interpreters (CLEANTH BROOKS, WILLIAM K. WIMSATT JR., etc.) who emphasize close reading of the text as an autonomous ("organic") whole; they dominated Anglo-American criticism in the mid-20th century.
6. A leading African American literary theorist (b. 1943).
7. A 1982 novel by Walker (b. 1944), African American novelist and poet.
8. Those who advocate a separatist black culture and political organization, a stance associated with the black power and Black Arts movements of the 1960s through mid-1970s.
9. Jamaican poet (1700–1770).
1. Rare bird (Latin).

school of so-called mockingbird poets, whose use of European and American literary conventions has been considered a corruption of a "purer" black expression, found in forms such as the blues, signifying, spirituals, and Afro-American dance. Can we, as critics, escape a "mockingbird" relation to theory? And can we escape the racism of so many critical theorists, from Hume and Kant through the Southern Agrarians and the Frankfurt school?[2]

Only recently have some scholars attempted to convince critics of black literature that we can. Perhaps predictably, a number of these attempts share a concern with that which has been most repressed in the received tradition of Afro-American criticism: close readings of the texts themselves. My advocacy of theory's value for such readings is meant as a prelude to the definition of critical principles peculiar to the black literary traditions, related to contemporary theory generally and yet, as Robert Farris Thompson[3] puts it, "indelibly black." I have tried to work through contemporary theories of literature not to "apply" them to black texts, but to transform by translating them into a new rhetorical realm—to re-create, through revision, the critical theory at hand. As our familiarity with the black tradition and with literary theory expands, we shall invent our own black, text-specific theories, as some of us have begun to do. We must learn to read a black text within a black formal cultural matrix, as well as its "white" matrix.

This is necessary because the existence of a black canon is a historically contingent phenomenon; it is not inherent in the nature of "blackness," not vouchsafed by the metaphysics of some racial essence. The black tradition exists only insofar as black artists enact it. Only because black writers have read and responded to other black writers with a sense of recognition and acknowledgment can we speak of a black literary inheritance, with all the burdens and ironies that has entailed. Race is a text (an array of discursive practices), not an essence. It must be *read* with painstaking care and suspicion, not imbibed.

I have tried to employ contemporary theory to defamiliarize[4] the texts of the black tradition: ironically, it is necessary to create distance between reader and texts in order to go beyond reflexive responses and achieve critical insight into and intimacy with their formal workings. I have done this to respect the "integrity" of these texts, by trying to avoid confusing my experience as an Afro-American with the act of language that defines a black text. This is the challenge of the critic of black literature in the 1980s: not to shy away from white power—that is, literary theory—but to translate it into the black idiom, *renaming* principles of criticism where appropriate, but especially *naming* indigenous black principles of criticism and applying them to our own texts. *Any* tool that enables the critic to explain the complex workings of the language of a text is appropriate here. For it is language, the black

2. German social and aesthetic theorists who gathered at Frankfurt's Institute for Social Research (founded in 1923); prominent members include THEODOR ADORNO and MAX HORKHEIMER. Southern Agrarians: also known as the Fugitives, a group of Southern poets and critics (many, including JOHN CROWE RANSOM, were associated with Vanderbilt University in the 1920s) who were politically conservative and viewed works of literature as autonomous verbal structures; their manifesto was *I'll Take My Stand: The South and the Agrarian Tradition by Twelve Southerners* (1930).

3. African American art historian (b. 1932).

4. A term from the Russian formalist Viktor Shklovsky (1893–1984); defamiliarization is the process through which an object of art "makes strange" what is familiar, so our response to it is not routine and it can be appreciated not as imitative but as an independent work.

language of black texts, that expresses the distinctive quality of our literary tradition. Once it may have seemed that the only critical implements black critics needed were the pom-pom and the twirled baton; in fact, there is no deeper form of literary disrespect. We will not protect the "integrity" of our tradition by remaining afraid of, or naive about, literary theory; rather, we will inflict upon it the violation of reflexive, stereotypical readings—or non-reading. We are the keepers of the black literary tradition. No matter what theories we embrace, we have more in common with each other than we do with any other critic of any other literature. We write for each other, and for our own contemporary writers. This relation is a critical trust.

It is also *political* trust. How can the demonstration that our texts sustain ever closer and more sophisticated readings *not* be political at a time when all sorts of so-called canonical critics mediate their racism through calls for "purity" of the "tradition," demands as implicitly racist as anything the Southern Agrarians said? How can the deconstruction of the forms of racism itself not be political? How can the use of literary analysis to explicate the racist social text in which we still find ourselves be anything *but* political? To be political, however, does not mean that I have to write at the level of a Marvel comic book. My task, as I see it, is to help guarantee that black and so-called Third World literature[5] is taught to black and Third World and white students by black and Third World and white professors in heretofore white mainstream departments of literature, and to train students to think, to read, and to write clearly, to expose false uses of language, fraudulent claims, and muddled arguments, propaganda, and vicious lies—from all of which our people have suffered just as surely as we have from an economic order in which we were zeros and a metaphysical order in which we were absences. These are the "values" which should be transmitted through critical theory.

In the December 1986 issue of the *Voice Literary Supplement*, in an essay entitled "Cult-Nats Meet Freaky-Deke," Greg Tate[6] argued cogently and compellingly that "black aestheticians need to develop a coherent criticism to communicate the complexities of our culture. There's no periodical on black cultural phenomena equivalent to *The Village Voice* or *Artforum*, no publication that provides journalism on black visual art, philosophy, politics, economics, media, literature, linguistics, psychology, sexuality, spirituality, and pop culture. Though there are certainly black editors, journalists, and academics capable of producing such a journal, the disintegration of the black cultural nationalist movement and the brain-drain of black intellectuals to white institutions have destroyed the vociferous public dialogue that used to exist between them." While I would argue that *Sage, Callaloo,* and *Black American Literature Forum (BALF)* are indeed fulfilling that function for academic critics, I am afraid that the truth of Tate's claim is irresistible.

But his most important contribution to the future of black criticism is to be found in his most damning allegation. "What's unfortunate," he writes, "is that while black artists have opened up the entire 'text of blackness' for fun and games, not many black critics have produced writing as fecund, eclectic, and freaky-deke as the art, let alone the culture, itself. . . . For

5. Literature from the "underdeveloped" countries, many of them former colonies, now dominated by highly industrialized "first world" (largely Western) nations in a global economy.

6. African American cultural critic and journalist.

those who prefer exegesis with a polemical bent, just imagine how critics as fluent in black and Western culture as the postliberated artists could strike terror into that bastion of white supremacist thinking, the Western art [and literary] world[s]." To which I can only say, echoing Shug in Alice Walker's *The Color Purple*, "Amen. Amen."

Tate's challenge is a serious one because neither ideology nor criticism nor blackness can exist as entities of themselves, outside the forms of their texts. This is the central theme of Ralph Ellison's *Invisible Man* and Ishmael Reed's *Mumbo Jumbo*,[7] for example. But how can we write or read the text of "Black Theory"? What language(s) do black people use to represent their critical or ideological positions? In what forms of language do we speak or write? Can we derive a valid, integral "black" text or criticism or ideology from borrowed or appropriated forms? Can a black woman's text emerge "authentically" as borrowed, or "liberated," or revised, from the patriarchal forms of the slave narratives, on the one hand, or from the white matriarchal forms of the sentimental novel, on the other, as Harriet Jacobs and Harriet Wilson attempted to do in *Incidents in the Life of a Slave Girl* (1861) and *Our Nig* (1859)?[8] Where lies the liberation in revision, the ideological integrity of defining freedom in the modes and forms of difference charted so cogently by so many poststructural critics of black literature?

For it is in these spaces of difference that black literature has dwelled. And while it is crucial to read these patterns of difference closely, we must understand as well that the quest was lost, in a major sense, before it had even begun, simply because the terms of our own self-representation have been provided by the master. It is not enough for us to show that refutation, negation, and revision exist, and to define them as satisfactory gestures of ideological independence. Our next concern must be to address the black political signified, that is, the cultural vision and the critical language that underpin the search through literature and art for a profound reordering and humanizing of everyday existence. We must urge our writers and critics to undertake the fullest and most ironic exploration of the manner and matter, the content and form, the structure and sensibility so familiar and poignant to us in our most sublime form of art, black music, where ideology and art are one, whether we listen to Bessie Smith or to postmodern and poststructural John Coltrane.[9]

Just as we must urge our writers to meet this challenge, we as critics must turn to our own peculiarly black structures of thought and feeling to develop our own languages of criticism. We must do so by drawing on the black vernacular, the language we use to speak to each other when no outsiders are around. Unless we look to the vernacular to ground our theories and modes of reading, we will surely sink in the mire of Nella Larsen's quicksand,[1] remain alienated in the isolation of Harriet Jacob's garret, or masked in the received stereotype of the Black Other helping Huck to return to the raft, singing

7. The best-known novel (1972) by Reed (b. 1938), African American novelist and poet. *Invisible Man* (1952) is the masterpiece of Ellison (1914–1994), African American writer of fiction, essays, and criticism.

8. Accounts of slave life by Jacobs (1813–1877) and Wilson (1808–ca. 1870). Jacobs writes of hiding for nearly 7 years in a small, cramped attic; this is the "garret" to which Gates later refers.

9. American jazz saxophonist and composer (1926–1967). Smith (ca. 1894–1937), American blues singer.

1. *Quicksand* (1928) was the first novel by the African American writer Larsen (1891–1964).

"China Gate" with Nat King Cole under the Da Nang moon, or reflecting our bald heads in the shining flash of Mr. T's[2] signifying gold chains.

We must redefine theory itself from within our own black cultures, refusing to grant the racist premise that theory is something that white people do, so that we are doomed to imitate our white colleagues, like reverse black minstrel critics done up in whiteface. We are all heirs to critical theory, but critics are also heir to the black vernacular critical tradition as well. We must not succumb, as did Alexander Crummell, to the tragic lure of white power, the mistake of accepting the empowering language of white critical theory as "universal" or as our only language, the mistake of confusing the enabling mask of theory with our own black faces. Each of us has, in some literal or figurative manner, boarded a ship and sailed to a metaphorical Cambridge, seeking to master the master's tools. (I myself, being quite literal-minded, booked passage some fourteen years ago on the *QE2*.[3]) Now we must at last don the empowering mask of blackness and talk *that* talk, the language of black difference. While it is true that we must, as Du Bois said so long ago, "know and test the power of the cabalistic letters of the white man," we must also know and test the dark secrets of a black discursive universe that awaits its disclosure through the black arts of interpretation. For the future of theory, in the remainder of this century, is black indeed.

1988

2. Lawrence Tureaud (b. 1952), popular African American television and film actor of the 1980s, generally seen in a Mohawk haircut and copious gold jewelry. Huck: title character of Mark Twain's *Adventures of Huckleberry Finn* (1884), who is helped by the runaway slave Jim back to the raft traveling down the Mississippi River. Cole (1919–1965), innovative African American pianist and leading popular singer of the 1950s and 1960s, who had a small role (and sang the title song) in the 1957 film *China Gate* (dir. Samuel Fuller), which was set in the last days of the French war in Vietnam; Da Nang, in central Vietnam, later became a major American military base.

3. *Queen Elizabeth* 2, a Cunard liner put into service in 1969; until it was replaced by the *Queen Mary II* in 2008, it provided the only regularly scheduled luxury passenger service across the Atlantic. Gates pursued his graduate studies at Cambridge University.

FRANCO MORETTI
b. 1950

A whole lifetime dedicated to reading would be insufficient to explore all the novels that have been published. In attempting a systematic study of such an immense body of works, Franco Moretti argues that close reading is useless for reasons not only of time but of methodology. The extraordinary size of the corpus, declares Moretti, requires a new, quantitative model of literary history: a "distant reading," which strategically subjects the genre to a process of scientific observation and analysis focused on the total phenomenon rather than on individual cases. He sees the rise and fall of novelistic genres not as a series of unrelated events but as a system of temporary structures organized into thirty-year cyclical patterns of dominant forms. Combining structuralist analysis with the Annales historiography of Fernand Braudel (1902–1985), Moretti invokes morphology to help explain the transitory historical dominance of hitherto neglected novelistic subgenres. Drawing on models taken from the natural and the social sciences—most notably geography, demography, and quantitative history—he seeks to elucidate the dynamic interplay between social history and literary form. Moretti aims to construct a rational theory of the history of the novel, which can supplant the dominance of individual works with diverse systems of genres.

Born in Italy, Franco Moretti received his Ph.D. in modern literature from the University of Rome in 1972. After teaching at various Italian universities, he joined the faculty of Columbia University as a professor of comparative literature from 1990 to 1999; in 2000 he accepted the Danily C. and Laura Louise Bell Professorship at Stanford University. That same year, he founded the Stanford Center for the Study of the Novel, an interdisciplinary institute dedicated to promoting discussions on the novel that cut across history and cultures. Founded by Moretti, the Stanford Literary Lab offers a space for collaborative research projects that apply computational criticism to the study of literature. His notion of computational criticism is based on the crucial role of computers in processing massive amounts of data for a quantitative literary analysis.

Moretti gave the Gauss Seminar in Criticism at Princeton University in 1991, the Beckman Lectures at the University of California at Berkeley in 2002, and the Carpenter Lectures at the University of Chicago in 2008. In 2006 he was named to the American Academy of Arts and Sciences. He has also been a fellow at the Wissenschaftskolleg zu Berlin and a scientific adviser to the French Ministry of Research.

Moretti first came to prominence with the publication of *The Way of the World: The Bildungsroman in European Culture* (1987), an influential study that memorably mixes social history and narrative theory. Influenced in part by GYÖRGY LUKÁCS's Marxist theory of the novel, Moretti argues that the coming of age novel is a symptomatic form of modernity—a product of the shifting socioeconomic conditions which mark the period between the French Revolution of 1789 and the numerous national uprisings that convulsed Europe in 1848. From Johann Wolfgang von Goethe's *Wilhelm Meister* (1795–96) to Gustave Flaubert's *Sentimental Education* (1869) and George Eliot's *Daniel Deronda* (1876), the classic bildungsroman registers the reigning contradictions in the rise of the modern bourgeoisie. For Moretti, the bildungsroman is the aesthetic form of modernity par excellence because it reflects a new balance between socialization and individuality and also between mobility and interiority. The genre suggests a picture of bourgeois culture that is multivocal and precarious rather than monologic and static. The relative social freedom of middle-class man rests on a principle of normality that itself requires internalization: each individual must perceive the norm as his own. For Moretti, the bildungsroman confirms a major claim that his subsequent writings develop: "the most profoundly social aspect of literature is its form."

Moretti focuses on roughly the same period in *Atlas of the European Novel, 1800–1900* (1997), which contains one hundred maps depicting the spatial distribution of nineteenth-century novels. The data he collects throw light on a range of issues that traditional literary histories have not engaged. For example, used as analytic tools, maps of London reveal the city's secret cultural geography; they also uncover relationships between fictional settings and national identities. In *Graphs, Maps, Trees: Abstract Models for a Literary History* (2005), three interconnected essays, Moretti seeks to transform the study of literature by setting forth a scientific model of literary history. "Graphs," the first chapter and our selection, traces literature through time ("Maps" does the same through space, and "Trees" combines the two in an evolutionary theory concentrating on the morphology of literary genres). In it Moretti argues that literary history is segmented into successive cycles as genres replace each other at intervals of about thirty years. Identifying forty-four British novelistic subgenres over the period between 1740 and 1900, Moretti shows that they emerged largely clustered "in six major bursts of creativity: the late 1760s, early 1790s, late 1820s, 1850, early 1870s, and mid–late 1880s." Patterns of disappearance are similarly regular. Although there are social and political explanations for the historical dominance of a few types of novels, they cannot account for the simultaneous rise and fall of most others.

According to Moretti, the cyclical rhythm of dominant genres is conditioned by the sequence of generations. Drawing on the work of Karl Mannheim (1893–1947), one of the founders of sociology, Moretti assigns intellectual and aesthetic functions to a generational bond that operates across modern history. Entire systems of genres suddenly vanish from the literary field not primarily through obsolescence—they no longer accurately represent contemporary reality—but because their readers disappear. These formal oscillations reveal, in Moretti's view, a "hidden pendulum of literary history" that also swings between high and low genres, as well as between male and female authors.

The cornerstone of Moretti's literary theory is its methodology, as he shifts focus from individual novels to groups of subgenres. Here he follows the Russian formalists, especially Viktor Shklovsky (1893–1984). Such a broad expansion of the textual corpus renders the list of acknowledged Great Books a tiny speck in a much larger pattern of generic cycles. For Moretti, morphology is not an artistic end in itself but a means of illuminating a neglected "middle layer" of literary studies concerned neither with singular historical events nor with very large periods (the Middle Ages, Renaissance, Enlightenment, etc.). It enables the scientific charting of literature through graphs. A productive marriage of mid-twentieth-century Annales historiography and structuralism, Moretti's theory incorporates socioeconomic and demographic factors into a quantitative formal analysis that recasts seemingly unrelated individual phenomena as elements of a collective system of recurrent structures. He rejects the traditional division of literature into distinct periods, proposing instead a cyclical model of literary history. He thereby mirrors the shift made by Annales historians, who turned their attention from narrow analyses of isolated events to comprehensive accounts of historical structures of long duration (the so-called *longue durée*).

The wide-ranging effects of this theoretical reconfiguration are exemplified in *The Novel* (2 vols., 2006), a selection in English of essays originally published in Italian in *Il Romanzo* (2001–03), five volumes edited by Moretti and containing more than one hundred essays by dozens of literary scholars. This landmark publication of formal, statistical, thematic, and historical analyses offers the first truly global assessment of the novel. It shows the novel, Moretti argues, to be a complex "planetary form" that reaches across time from the ancient Greeks to the present day and spans national borders. "Countless are the novels of the world," Moretti claims in the preface to this pioneering work, which offers a rational reconception of literary history, as cultural geography and aesthetic form are fused.

Sometimes called a literary heretic, Moretti has been charged with positivism and criticized for relying on tenuous connections between literary history and the sciences. Other major criticisms can also be leveled against him. His staunch advocacy of structuralist models and quantitative analysis eliminates the autonomy and singularity of individual literary texts. The broad geographic and historical expansion of novelistic genres to include immense numbers of peripheral works discounts the specificity of historical context, eliminating not just close reading but also cultural critique. His omissions are also significant: he overlooks the psychological, moral, and aesthetic functions of literature. Nevertheless, Moretti's theory of novelistic cycles presents an innovative and bold alternative to traditional literary history.

Graphs, Maps, Trees: Abstract Models for a Literary History **Keywords:** Globalization, Literary History, Modernity, The Novel, Print Culture, Structuralism

From Graphs, Maps, Trees: Abstract Models for a Literary History

Chapter 1. Graphs

Before the advent of the Annales, Krzysztof Pomian once wrote,

> the gaze of the historian [was directed] towards extraordinary events . . . historians resembled collectors: both gathered only rare and curious objects, disregarding whatever looked banal, everyday, normal . . . History was an idiographic discipline, having as its object that which does not repeat itself.[1]

History *was* . . . Pomian speaks in the past tense here, as is probably accurate in the case of social history, but certainly not for its literary counterpart, where the collector of rare and curious works, that do not repeat themselves, exceptional—and which close reading makes even more exceptional, by emphasizing the uniqueness of exactly *this* word and *this* sentence here—is still by far the dominant figure. But what would happen if literary historians, too, decided to 'shift their gaze' (Pomian again) 'from the extraordinary to the everyday, from exceptional events to the large mass of facts'? What literature would we find, in 'the large mass of facts'?

All questions that occurred to me some years ago, when the study of national bibliographies made me realize what a minimal fraction of the literary field we all work on: a canon of two hundred novels, for instance, sounds very large for nineteenth-century Britain (and *is* much larger than the current one), but is still less than one per cent of the novels that were actually published: twenty thousand, thirty, more, no one really knows—and close reading won't help here, a novel a day every day of the year would take a century or so . . . And it's not even a matter of time, but of method: a field this large cannot be understood by stitching together separate bits of knowledge about individual cases, because it *isn't* a sum of individual cases: it's a collective system, that should be grasped as such, as a whole—and the graphs that follow are one way to begin doing this. Or as Fernand Braudel[2] put it in the lecture on history he gave to his companions in the German prison camp near Lübeck:

> An incredible number of dice, always rolling, dominate and determine each individual existence: uncertainty, then, in the realm of individual history; but in that of collective history . . . simplicity and consistency. History is indeed 'a poor little conjectural science' when it selects individuals as its objects . . . but much more rational in its procedures and results, when it examines groups and repetitions.[3]

A more rational literary history. That is the idea.

1. Krzysztof Pomian, 'L'histoire des structures', in Jacques Le Goff, Roger Chartier, Jacques Revel, eds., *La nouvelle histoire*, Paris 1978, pp. 115–16 [Moretti's note]. Pomian (b. 1934), Polish philosopher, historian, and essayist. The *Annales*: the interdisciplinary journal founded in 1929 by the French historians Marc Bloch and Lucien Febvre, who advocated the study not of exceptional political or military events but of historical structures over the long term (*la longue durée*) in a comprehensive approach that incorporated economy, geography, and the sociology of everyday life. Their influential approach to historiography became known as the Annales School.

2. French historian (1902–1985), leading second-generation member of the Annales School. During World War II, he spent 5 years as a prisoner of war in Germany.

3. Fernand Braudel, 'L'histoire, mesure du monde', in *Les écrits de Fernand Braudel*, vol. II, Paris 1997 [Moretti's note].

I

The quantitative approach to literature can take several different forms—from computational stylistics to thematic databases, book history, and more. For reasons of space, I will here limit myself to book history, building on work originally done by McBurney, Beasley, Raven, Garside and Block for Britain;[4] Angus, Mylne and Frautschi for France;[5] Zwicker for Japan; Petersen for Denmark; Ragone for Italy;[6] Martí-Lopez and Santana for Spain;[7] Joshi for India; and Griswold for Nigeria.[8] And I mention these names right away because quantitative work is truly *cooperation*: not only in the pragmatic sense that it takes forever to gather the data, but because such data are ideally independent from any individual researcher, and can thus be shared by others, and combined in more than one way. Figure 1,[9] which charts the take-off of the novel in Britain, Japan, Italy, Spain and Nigeria, is a case in point. See how similar those shapes are: five countries, three continents, over two centuries apart, and it's really the same pattern, the same old metaphor of the 'rise' of the novel come alive: in twenty years or so (in Britain, 1720–40; Japan, 1745–65; Italy, 1820–40; Spain, 1845 to early 1860s; Nigeria, 1965–80), the graph leaps from five–ten new titles per year, which means one new novel every month or two, to one new novel *per week*. And at this point, the horizon of novel-reading changes. As long as only a handful of new titles are published each year, I mean, novels remain unreliable products, that disappear for long stretches of time, and cannot really command the loyalty of the reading public; they are commodities, yes—but commodities still waiting for a fully developed market. A new novel per week, by contrast, is already the great capitalist oxymoron of the *regular novelty*: the unexpected that is produced with such efficiency and punctuality that readers become unable to do without it. The novel 'becomes a necessity of life', to paraphrase the title of a book[1] by William Gilmore-Lehne, and the jeremiads that immediately multiply around it—novels make readers lazy, stupid, dissolute, insane, insubordinate: exactly like films two centuries later—are the clearest sign of its symbolic triumph.

II

The rise of the novel, then; or, better, *one* rise in a history which had begun many centuries earlier, and will go through several other accelerations, as emerges quite clearly from the data on the publication of new novels in Brit-

4. In listing these names, Moretti is referring to specific works (grouped in the notes for ease of reading): William Harlin McBurney, *Check List of English Prose Fiction, 1700–1739* (1960); Jerry C. Beasley, *The Novels of the 1740s* (1982); Peter Garside, James Raven, and Rainer Schöwerling, eds., *The English Novel, 1770–1829*, 2 vols. (2000); and Andrew Block, *The English Novel, 1740–1850* (1961).

5. Angus Martin, Vivienne Mylne, and Richard L. Frautschi, eds., *Bibliographie du genre romanesque français 1751–1800* (1977).

6. Jonathan Zwicker, "The Long Nineteenth Century of the Japanese Novel," in Franco Moretti, ed., *The Novel* (2006), vol. 1; Erland Munch-Petersen, *Die Übersetzungsliteratur als Unterhaltung des romantischen Lesers* (1991); and Giovanni Ragone, "Italy 1815–1870," in Moretti, ed., *The Novel*, vol. 1.

7. Elisa Martí-Lopez and Mario Santana, "Spain 1843–1900," in Moretti, *The Novel*, vol. 1.

8. Priya Joshi, "India 1850–1900," in Moretti, *The Novel*, vol. 1, and Wendy Griswold, "Nigeria 1950–2000," in ibid.

9. Note to figure 1: BARTHES (1915–1980), French literary theorist, critic, and semiotician; the article cited was published in *Annales* in 1960.

1. *Reading Becomes a Necessity of Life: Material and Cultural Life in Rural New England, 1780–1835* (1989). Gilmore-Lehne (1945–1999), American historian.

To enrich our literary chronicles with a few new historical ingredients . . . would be pointless: it's the presuppositions which must change, and the object transform itself. To abolish the individual from literature! It's a laceration, clearly, even a paradox. But a literary history is possible only at this price.

Roland Barthes, 'History or Literature?'

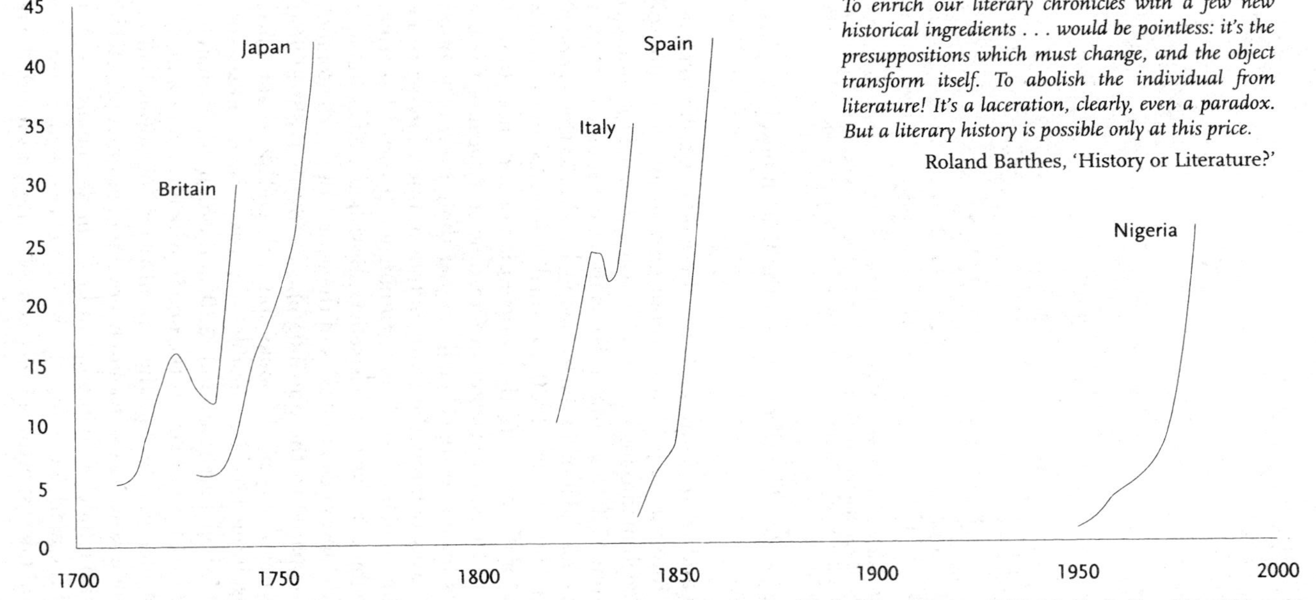

New novels per year, by 5-year average. Sources: For Britain: W. H. McBurney, *A Check List of English Prose Fiction, 1700–39*, Cambridge, MA 1960, and J. C. Beasley, *The Novels of the 1740s*, Athens, GA 1982; both partly revised by James Raven, *British Fiction 1750–70: A Chronological Check-List of Prose Fiction Printed in Britain and Ireland*, London 1987. For Japan: Jonathan Zwicker, 'Il lungo Ottocento del romanzo gíapponese', in *Il romanzo*, vol. III, *Storia e geografis*, Torino 2002. For Italy: Giovanni Ragone, 'Italia 1815–70', in *Il romanzo*, vol. III. For Spain: Elisa Marti-Lopez and Mario Santana, 'Spagna 1843–1900', *Il romanzo*, vol. III. For Nigeria: Wendy Griswold, 'Nigeria 1950–2000', *Il romanzo*, vol. III.

Figure 1. The rise of the novel, 18th to 20th century

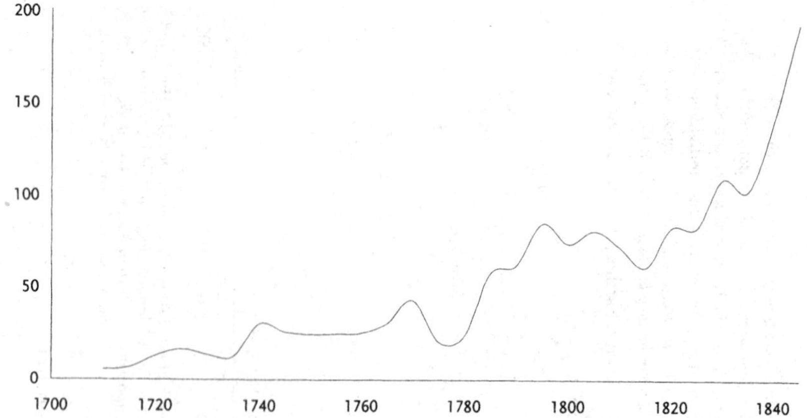

New novels per year, by 5-year average. Sources: McBurney, *Check List of English Prose Fiction, 1700–39;* Beasley, *The Novels of the 1740s;* Raven, *British Fiction 1759–70;* Peter Garside, James Raven and Rainer Schöwerling, eds., *The English Novel 1770–1829,* 2 vols., Oxford 2000; Andrew Block, *The English Novel, 1740–1850,* London 1961.

Figure 2. The three rises of the British novel

ain between 1710 and 1850 (figure 2). Here, three phases seem to stand out, each subdivided into a first period of rapid growth and a second one of stabilization, and each modifying in a specific way the social role of the novel. The first phase, from 1720 to around 1770, is the one discussed above: a leap in 1720–40, and a consolidation in the following decades. In the second phase, which runs from 1770 to around 1820, the further increase in the number of new titles induces for its part a drastic reorientation of audiences towards the present. Up to then, I mean, the 'extensive' reading so typical of the novel—reading many texts once and superficially, rather than a few texts often and intensely—would easily outgrow the yearly output of titles, forcing readers to turn to the past for (much of) their entertainment: all sorts of reprints and abridgements of eighteenth-century bestsellers, British as well as foreign, plus the old, and even the few ancient classics of the genre. But as the total of new novels doubles, compared to the previous phase—80 in 1788; 91 in 1796; 111 in 1808—the popularity of old books suddenly collapses, and novelistic audiences turn resolutely (and irreversibly) towards the current season.[2]

The third phase, which begins around 1820, and which unfortunately I can only follow for the first thirty years, is the one in which the *internal composition* of the market changes. So far, the typical reader of novels had been a 'generalist'—someone 'who reads absolutely anything, at random', as Thibaudet was to write with a touch of contempt in *Le liseur de romans.*[3] Now, however, the growth of the market creates all sorts of niches for 'specialist' readers and genres (nautical tales, sporting novels, school stories, *mystères*): the books

2. 'In Italy,' writes Giovanni Ragone, 'in the first twenty years of the nineteenth century virtually all the bestsellers of the previous century disappear'; 'Italia 1815–1870', in *Il romanzo*, vol. III, pp. 343–54. A similar shift seems to occur in France, where, however, the caesura of the revolution [of 1789] offers a very strong alternative explanation. The 'pastness of the past' is of course the key message of the two genres—gothic, and then historical novels—most responsible for the turn towards the present [Moretti's note].

3. Albert Thibaudet, *Il lettore di romanzi* [*The Reader of Novels*] [1925], Napoli 2000, p. 49 [Moretti's note]. Thibaudet (1874–1936), French essayist and literary critic.

aimed at urban workers in the second quarter of the nineteenth century, or at boys, and then girls, in the following generation, are simply the most visible instances of this larger process, which culminates at the turn of the century in the super-niches of detective fiction and then science fiction.

Abstract models for literary history . . . and we certainly have abstraction here: *Pamela, The Monk, The Wild Irish Girl, Persuasion, Oliver Twist*[4]—where are they? five tiny dots in the graph of figure 2, indistinguishable from all others. But graphs are not really *models*; they are not simplified, intuitive versions of a theoretical structure in the way maps and (especially) evolutionary trees will be in the next two chapters.

Quantitative research provides a type of data which is ideally independent of interpretations, I said earlier, and that is of course also its limit: it provides *data*, not interpretation. That figure 2 shows a first 'rise' (when the novel becomes a necessity of life), and then a second (the shift from the past to the present), and then a third (the multiplication of market niches), seems to me a good account of the data, but is certainly far from inevitable. Quantitative data can tell us when Britain produced one new novel per month, or week, or day, or hour for that matter, but where the significant turning points lie along the continuum—and why—is something that must be decided on a different basis.

III

A—multiple—rise of the novel. But with an interesting twist, which is particularly visible in the Japanese case of figure 3:[5] after the rise from one novel per month in the mid-1740s to one per week twenty years later (and even more in the following years: between 1750 and 1820, in fact, many more novels are published in Japan than in Britain; a fact which deserves a good explanation!)—several equally rapid downturns occur in 1780–90, the 1810s to the 1830s, and in 1860–70. The fall of the novel. And the reason behind the downturns seems to be always the same: politics—a direct, virulent censorship during the Kansei and Tempo periods, and an indirect influence in the years leading up to the Meiji Restoration,[6] when there was no specific repression of the book trade, and the crisis was thus probably due to a more general dissonance between the rhythm of political crises and the writing of novels. It's the same in Denmark during the Napoleonic wars[7] (figure 4), or in France and Italy (better, Milan) in comparable situations (figure 5):[8] after 1789, the publication of French novels drops about 80 per cent; after the first Risorgimento war,[9] the Milanese downturn is around 90 per cent, with only 3 novels published in the course of 1849, against 43 in 1842.

4. All novels (a mix of genres) written in English: *Pamela* (1740), by Samuel Richardson; *The Monk* (1796), by Matthew Gregory Lewis; *The Wild Irish Girl* (1806), by Sydney Owenson (Lady Morgan); *Persuasion* (1817), by Jane Austen; and *Oliver Twist* (1838), by Charles Dickens.
5. Note to figure 3: Sadanobu (1759–1829), Japanese feudal ruler who became the shogun's chief minister.
6. The restoration of the emperorship after the long period of rule by shoguns (1192–1868); the reign of the Meiji emperor (1868–1912) was a period of revolutionary political, economic, and social changes, as Japan opened to the West and modernized. Both the Kansei (1789–1801) and Tempo periods were eras of reactionary restrictions.
7. Series of wars (1803–15) waged by and against the French military and political leader Napoléon Bonaparte (1769–1821; emperor, 1804–15), who sought to conquer all of Europe and England.
8. Note to figure 5: in 1917 revolutions were occurring in Russia and in Mexico.
9. The Risorgimento (Resurgence, Italian) was the 19th-century nationalist movement in Italy that led to the country's unification. In 1848–49, brief revolutions against Austrian rule broke out from Sicily to Venice, and in their support the independent kingdom of Sardinia unsuccessfully sent its army against Austrian forces.

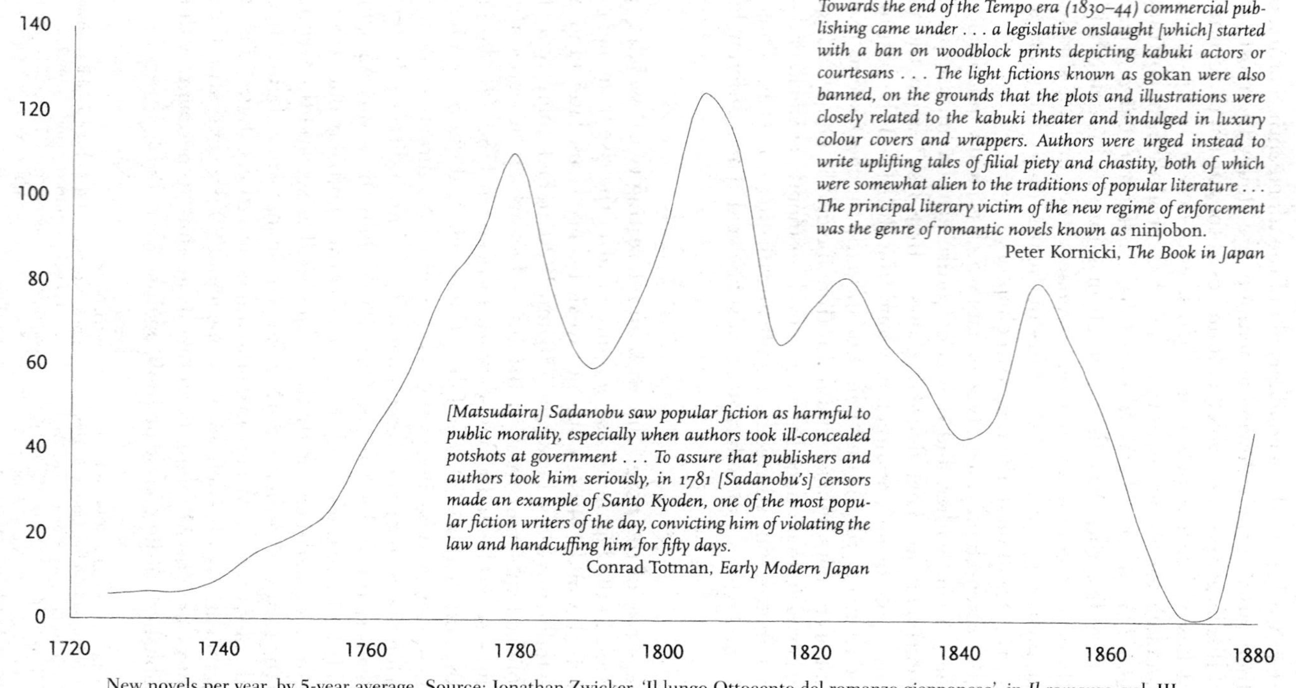

140
120
100
80
60
40
20
0
1720
1740
1760
1780
1800
1820
1840
1860
1880
Towards the end of the Tempo era (1830–44) commercial publishing came under . . . a legislative onslaught [which] started with a ban on woodblock prints depicting kabuki actors or courtesans . . . The light fictions known as gokan *were also banned, on the grounds that the plots and illustrations were closely related to the kabuki theater and indulged in luxury colour covers and wrappers. Authors were urged instead to write uplifting tales of filial piety and chastity, both of which were somewhat alien to the traditions of popular literature . . . The principal literary victim of the new regime of enforcement was the genre of romantic novels known as* ninjobon.
Peter Kornicki, *The Book in Japan*
[Matsudaira] Sadanobu saw popular fiction as harmful to public morality, especially when authors took ill-concealed potshots at government . . . To assure that publishers and authors took him seriously, in 1781 [Sadanobu's] censors made an example of Santo Kyoden, one of the most popular fiction writers of the day, convicting him of violating the law and handcuffing him for fifty days.
Conrad Totman, *Early Modern Japan*

New novels per year, by 5-year average. Source: Jonathan Zwicker, 'Il lungo Ottocento del romanzo giapponese', in *Il romanzo*, vol. III. See also Totman, *Early Modern Japan*, Berkeley 1993; Kornicki, *The Book in Japan*, Leiden 1998.

Figure 3. The fall of the novel: Japan

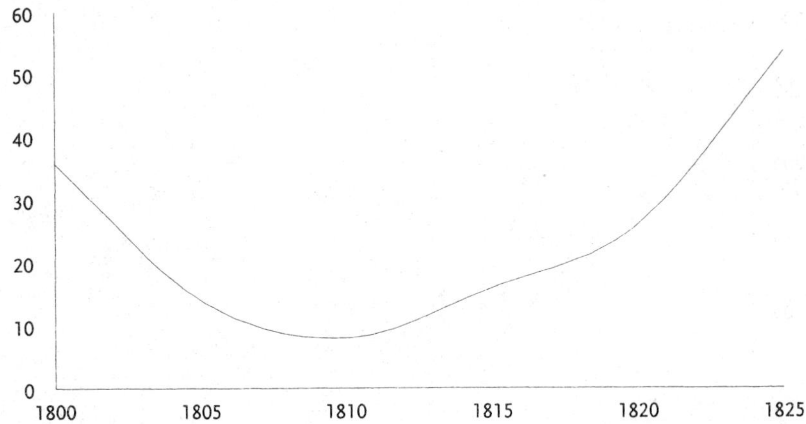

New novels per year, by 5-year average. Source: Erland Munch-Petersen, *Die Übersetzungsliteratur als Unterhaltung des romantischen Lesers,* Wiesbaden 1991.

Figure 4. The fall of the novel: Denmark

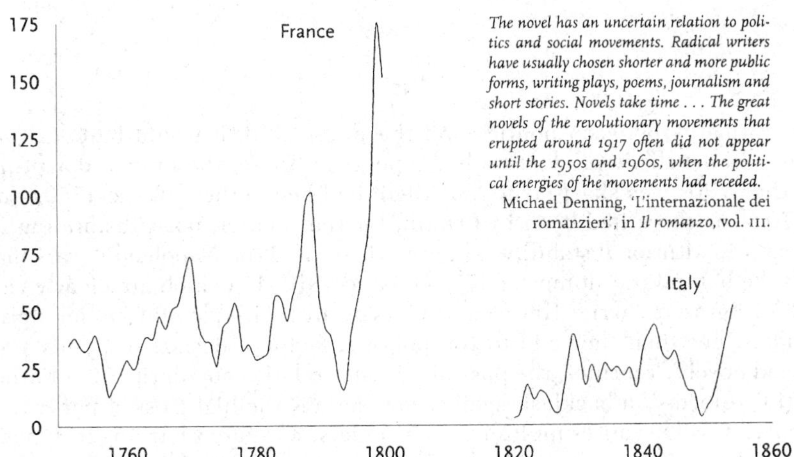

The novel has an uncertain relation to politics and social movements. Radical writers have usually chosen shorter and more public forms, writing plays, poems, journalism and short stories. Novels take time . . . The great novels of the revolutionary movements that erupted around 1917 often did not appear until the 1950s and 1960s, when the political energies of the movements had receded.
Michael Denning, 'L'internazionale dei romanzieri', in *Il romanzo,* vol. III.

New novels per year. Sources: For France: Angus Martin, Vivienne G. Mylne and Richard Frautschi, eds., *Bibliographic du genre romanesque français 1751–1800,* Paris 1977. For Milan: Giovanni Ragone, 'Italia 1815–70', in *Il romanzo,* vol. III, and *Catalogo dei libri italiani dell'Ottocento,* Milano 1991.

Figure 5. The fall of the novel: France, Italy

The only exception I know to this pattern is the import of British books into India charted by Priya Joshi (figure 6), which rises sharply after the 1857 rebellion;[1] but as Joshi points out, the logic of a colonial relationship is reversed, and the peak is a sign of Britain suddenly accelerating the pace of symbolic hegemony; then, once the crisis is over, the flow returns to its pre-1857 levels.

1. The widespread uprising (1857–58) by Indian soldiers against the British rule of the East India Company.

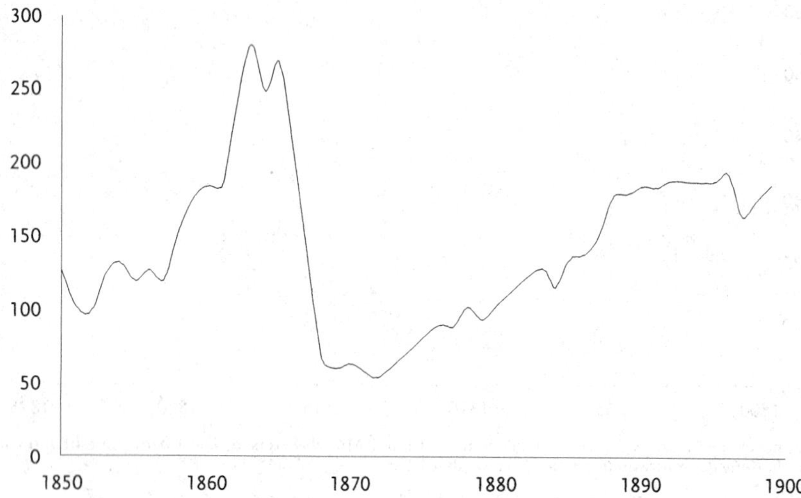

Thousands of pounds sterling. Source: Priya Joshi, *In Another Country: Colonialism, Culture, and the English Novel in India,* New York 2002.

Figure 6. Book imports into India

IV

An antipathy between politics and the novel. Still, it would be odd if *all* crises in novelistic production had a political origin: the French downturn of the 1790s was sharp, true, but there had been others in the 1750s and 1770s—as there had been in Britain, for that matter, notwithstanding its greater institutional stability. The American[2] and the Napoleonic wars may well be behind the slumps of 1775–83 and 1810–17 (which are clearly visible in figure 2), write Raven and Garside in their splendid bibliographic studies; but then they add to the political factor 'a decade of poorly produced novels', 'reprints', the possible 'greater relative popularity . . . of other fictional forms', 'a backlash against low fiction', the high cost of paper . . .[3] And as possible causes multiply, one wonders: what are we trying to explain here—two *unrelated individual events*, or two moments *in a recurring pattern of ups and downs*? Because if the downturns are individual events, then looking for individual causes (Napoleon, reprints, the cost of paper, whatever) makes perfect sense; but if they are parts of a pattern, then what we must explain is *the pattern as a whole,* not just one of its phases.

The whole pattern; or, as some historians would say, the whole cycle: 'An increasingly clear idea has emerged . . . of the multiplicity of time', writes Braudel in the essay on *longue durée*:

> Traditional history, with its concern for the short time span, for the individual and the event, has long accustomed us to the headlong, dramatic, breathless rush of its narrative . . . The new economic and social history

2. That is, the American Revolution (1775–83).
3. James Raven, 'Historical Introduction: The Novel Comes of Age', and Peter Garside, 'The English Novel in the Romantic Era: Consolidation and Dispersal', in Garside, Raven, and Schöwerling, eds., *The English Novel 1770–1829;* vol. I, p. 27, and vol. II, p. 44 [Moretti's note].

> puts cyclical movement in the forefront of its research . . . large sections of the past, ten, twenty, fifty years at a stretch . . . Far beyond this . . . we find a history capable of traversing even greater distances . . . to be measured in centuries . . . the long, even the very long time span, the *longue durée*.[4]

Event, cycle, *longue durée*: three time frames which have fared very unevenly in literary studies. Most critics are perfectly at ease with the first one, the circumscribed domain of the event and of the individual case; most theorists are at home at the opposite end of the temporal spectrum, in the very long span of nearly unchanging structures. But the middle level has remained somewhat unexplored by literary historians; and it's not even that we don't work within that time frame, it's that we haven't yet fully understood its specificity: the fact, I mean, that cycles constitute *temporary structures within the historical flow*. That is, after all, the hidden logic behind Braudel's tripartition: the short span is all flow and no structure, the *longue durée* all structure and no flow, and cycles are the—unstable—border country between them. Structures, because they introduce repetition in history, and hence regularity, order, pattern; and temporary, because they're short (ten, twenty, fifty years, this depends on the theory).

Now, 'temporary structures' is also a good definition for—genres: morphological arrangements that *last* in time, but always only for *some* time. Janus-like[5] creatures, with one face turned to history and the other to form, genres are thus the true protagonists of this middle layer of literary history—this more 'rational' layer where flow and form meet. It's the regularity of figures 7 and 8, with their three waves of epistolary novels from 1760 to 1790, and then gothic novels from 1790 to 1815, and then historical novels from 1815 to the 1840s. Each wave produces more or less the same number of novels per year, and lasts the same 25–30 years, and each also rises only after the previous wave has begun to ebb away (see how the up- and down-ward trends intersect around 1790 and 1815). 'The new form makes its appearance to replace an old form that has outlived its artistic usefulness', writes Shklovsky,[6] and the decline of a ruling genre seems indeed here to be the necessary precondition for its successor's take-off. Which may explain those odd 'latency periods' in the early history of genres: *Pamela* is published in 1740, and *The Castle of Otranto*[7] in 1764, but very few epistolary or gothic novels are written until 1760 and 1790 respectively. Why the lag? Almost certainly, because as long as a hegemonic form has not lost its 'artistic usefulness', there is not much that a rival form can do: there can always be an exceptional text, yes, but the exception *will not change the system*. It's only when Ptolemaic astronomy begins to generate one 'monstrosity' after another, writes Kuhn in *The Structure of Scientific Revolutions*,[8] that 'the time comes to give a competitor

4. Fernand Braudel, 'History and the Social Sciences: The *longue durée*', in *On History*, Chicago 1980, p. 27. The first extended treatment of economic cycles was of course Nikolai Kondratiev's *The Long Wave Cycle*, written between 1922 and 1928 [Moretti's note]. *Longue durée*: long period (French), a key concept of the Annales School.
5. That is, with 2 faces looking in opposite directions, like many statues of Janus, the Roman god of entrances and gates and of beginnings.
6. "The Connection of Devices of Plot Formation with General Devices of Style" (1919), by Viktor Shklovsky (1893–1984), Russian formalist literary critic.
7. An English novel (1764) by Horace Walpole, the first Gothic romance. *Pamela* is the first epistolary novel.
8. The landmark publication (1962; 3d ed., 1996) by the American historian and philosopher of science Thomas S. Kuhn (1922–1996); his idea of a "paradigm shift" (e.g., from the Ptolemaic, or geocentric, to the Copernican, or heliocentric, view of the solar system), when the definition of "normal science" changes, has influenced many later thinkers.

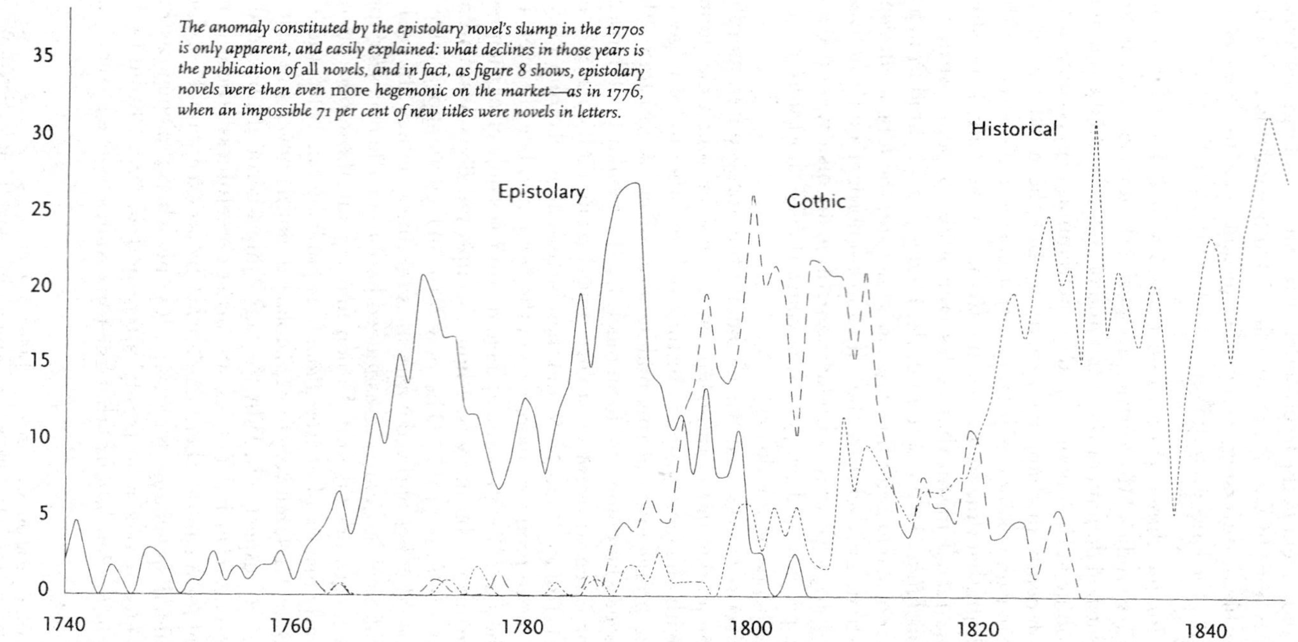
The anomaly constituted by the epistolary novel's slump in the 1770s is only apparent, and easily explained: what declines in those years is the publication of all novels, and in fact, as figure 8 shows, epistolary novels were then even more hegemonic on the market—as in 1776, when an impossible 71 per cent of new titles were novels in letters.
35
30
25
20
15
10
5
0
1740
1760
1780
1800
1820
1840
Epistolary
Gothic
Historical

New novels per year. Sources: For the epistolary novel: James Raven, 'Gran Bretagna 1750–1830', in *Il romanzo*, vol. III, pp. 311–12. For the gothic novel: Maurice Lévy, *Le roman 'gothique' anglais*, Paris 1995. For the historical novel, I have taken as the basis the checklist provided by Rainer Schöwerling ('Sir Walter Scott and the Tradition of the Historical Novel before 1814', in Uwe Böker, Manfred Markus, Rainer Schöwerling, eds., *The Living Middle Ages*, Stuttgart 1989), and subtracted those texts that also appear in Lévy's bibliography of the gothic; for the later period, I have also used Block, *The English Novel, 1740–1850*.

Figure 7. British hegemonic forms, 1760–1850

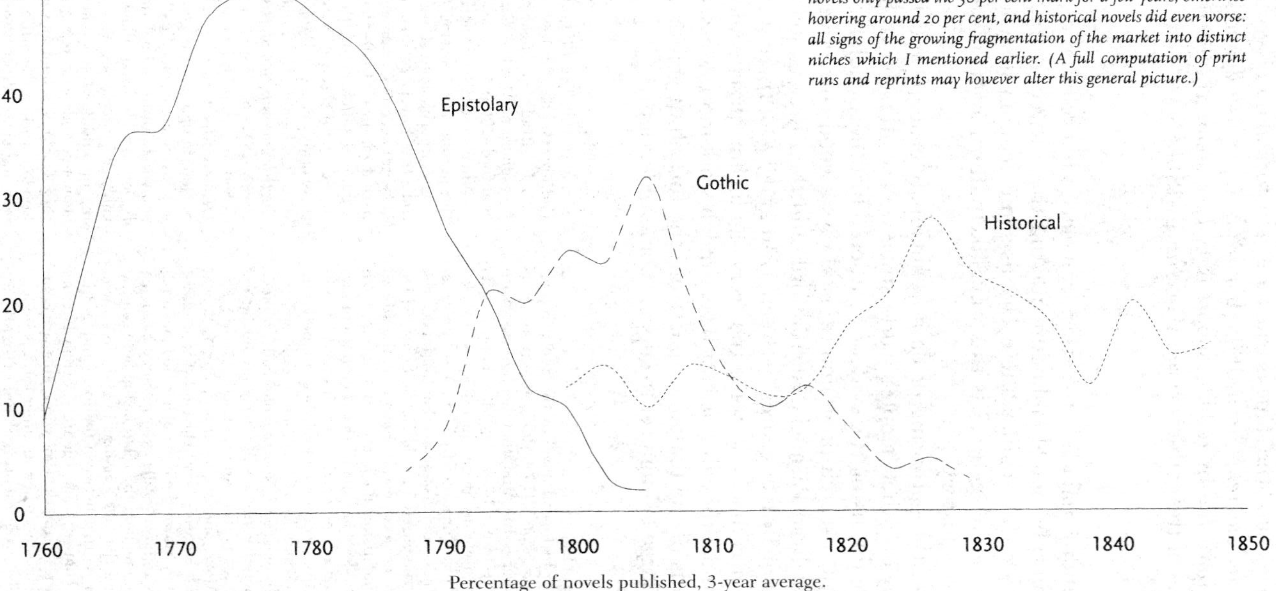

All works of art, and not only parodies, are created either as a parallel or an antithesis to some model. The new form makes its appearance not in order to express a new content, but rather to replace an old form that has already outlived its artistic usefulness.
Viktor Shklovsky, *A Theory of Prose*
As more and more novels are published every year, the hegemony of a single genre tends to become less and less absolute: whereas epistolary novels amounted to 30 per cent or more of the market for twenty-five years (and over 50 per cent in the late 1770s), gothic novels only passed the 30 per cent mark for a few years, otherwise hovering around 20 per cent, and historical novels did even worse: all signs of the growing fragmentation of the market into distinct niches which I mentioned earlier. (A full computation of print runs and reprints may however alter this general picture.)
50
40
30
20
10
0
Epistolary
Gothic
Historical
1760
1770
1780
1790
1800
1810
1820
1830
1840
1850
Percentage of novels published, 3-year average.

Figure 8. Market quotas of British hegemonic forms, 1760–1850

a chance'—and the same is true here: a historical novel written in 1800, such as *Castle Rackrent*[9] (or in 1805, like *Waverley*'s[1] abandoned first draft) simply didn't have the incredible opportunity to reshape the literary field that the collapse of the gothic offered *Waverley* in 1814.[2]

V

From individual cases to series; from series to cycles, and then to genres as their morphological embodiment. And these three genres seem indeed to follow a rather regular 'life-cycle', as some economists would call it. These genres—or *all* genres? Is this wave-like pattern a sort of hidden pendulum of literary history?

Here, the gathering of data is obviously crucial, and I decided to rely entirely on other people's work: since we are all eager to find what we are looking for, using the evidence gathered by other scholars, with completely different research programmes, is always a good corrective to one's desires. So, first Brad Pasanek,[3] at Stanford, and then I, consulted over a hundred studies of British genres between 1740 and 1900; there were some dubious cases, of course, and some (not very significant) disagreements in periodization,[4] and although this is still very much work-in-progress, especially at the two ends of the temporal spectrum, the forty-four genres of figure 9[5] provide a large enough set to support some reflections.

9. By Maria Edgeworth.

1. An 1814 historical novel by the Scottish poet Sir Walter Scott (1771–1832) that was enormously successful (and that he followed with many more in a similar vein); it was not, as its first chapter claims, begun in 1805.

2. A few more words on why a form loses its 'artistic usefulness' and disappears. For Shklovsky, the reason is the purely inner dialectic of art, which begins in creative estrangement, and ends in stale automatism: 'Each art form travels down the inevitable road from birth to death; from seeing and sensory perception, when every detail in the object is savoured and relished, to mere recognition, when form becomes a dull epigone which our senses register mechanically, a piece of merchandise not visible even to the buyer.' (The passage is from an article collected in *The Knight's Move*, and is quoted by Victor Erlich in *Russian Formalism*, New Haven 1955, p. 252.) This journey 'down the inevitable road from birth to death' can however also be explained by focusing, not so much on the relationship between the 'young' and the 'old' versions of the same form, but rather on that between the form and its historical context: a genre exhausts its potentialities—and the time comes to give a competitor a chance—when its inner form is no longer capable of representing the most significant aspects of contemporary reality. At which point, either the genre loses its form under the impact of reality, thereby disintegrating, or it turns its back to reality in the name of form, becoming a 'dull epigone' indeed. (I develop this point in the appendix to the new edition of *The Way of the World*, '"A useless longing for myself": The crisis of the European *Bildungsroman*, 1898–1914', London 2000.) But we will soon see another, more draconian explanation for the disappearance of forms [Moretti's note]. Moretti, *The Way of the World: The Bildungsroman in European Culture* (1st ed., 1987).

3. See Brad Pasanek, "Eighteenth-Century Metaphors of Mind: A Dictionary" (Ph.D. diss., Stanford, 2006).

4. When specialists disagreed, I always opted for the periodization arising out of the more convincing morphological argument: in the case of industrial novels, for instance, I followed Gallagher rather than Cazamian, although the latter's periodization of 1830–50 would have fitted my argument much better than Gallagher's 1832–67. For details, see 'A Note on the Taxonomy of the Forms', p. 2275 [Moretti's note]. See Catherine Gallagher, *The Industrial Reformation of English Fiction: Social Discourse and Narrative Form, 1832–67* (1985); Louis Cazamian, *The Social Novel in England, 1830–50: Dickens, Disraeli, Mrs. Gaskell, Kingsley* (1903).

5. Note to figure 9: the genres named by Moretti are associated specifically with the periods shown. Kailyard school: movement in Scottish fiction that idealized village life (a "kail-yard" is a cabbage garden). New Woman novel: novel focusing on middle-class women seeking social and economic independence at the turn of the century. Cockney school: novelists who wrote about London working-class life. Chartist novel: novel focusing on the British working-class movement (1838–48) that took its name from a petition, the People's Charter, calling for such reforms as universal male suffrage. Conversion novel: that is, a novel of religious conversion (usually from Anglicanism to Roman Catholicism). Newgate novel: novel that features criminals as main characters (Newgate was a famous London prison). Silver-fork novel: novel focusing on the elegance of aristocratic high society. Anti-Jacobin and Jacobin novels: novels against and in favor of the extreme supporters of the French Revolution.

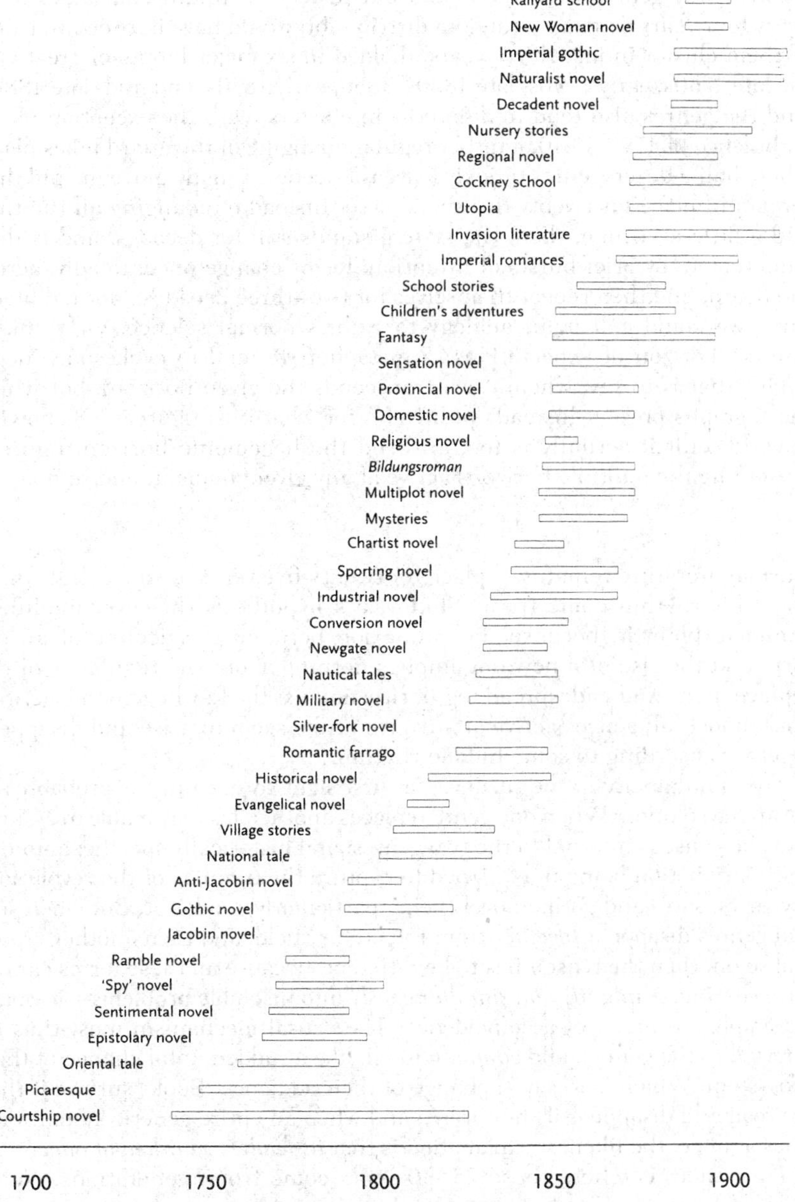

For sources, see 'A Note on the Taxonomy of the Forms' on page 2275.

Figure 9. British novelistic genres, 1740–1900

Forty-four genres over 160 years; but instead of finding one new genre every four years or so, as a random distribution would have it, over two thirds of them cluster in just thirty years, divided in six major bursts of creativity: the late 1760s, early 1790s, late 1820s, 1850, early 1870s, and mid–late 1880s. And the genres also tend to *disappear* in clusters: with the exception of the turbulence of 1790–1810, a rather regular changing of the guard takes place, where half a dozen genres quickly leave the scene, as many move in, and then remain in place for twenty-five years or so. Instead of changing all the time and a little at a time, then, the system stands still for decades, and is then 'punctuated' by brief bursts of invention: forms change once, rapidly, across the board, and then repeat themselves for two–three decades: 'normal literature', we could call it, in analogy to Kuhn's normal science. Or think of Jauss's[6] 'horizon of expectations': a metaphor we tend to evoke only 'negatively' (that is to say, when a text transcends the given horizon), but which these graphs present instead, 'positively', for what it is: figures 7–8 showing how difficult it actually is to transcend the hegemonic horizon, figure 9 presenting the multiple horizons active at any given moment, and so on.

VI

Normal literature remains in place for twenty-five years or so . . . But where does this rhythm come from? Shklovsky's hypothesis (however modified) cannot explain it, because the connexion between the decline of an old form and the rise of a new one implies nothing about the regularity of the replacement. And widespread regularity: not just the few hegemonic genres, but (almost) all genres active at any given time seem to arise and disappear together according to some hidden rhythm.

The simultaneity of the turnover, at first sight so uncanny, is probably the key to the solution. When one genre replaces another, it's reasonable to assume that the cause is internal to the two genres, and historically specific: amorous epistolary fiction being ill-equipped to capture the traumas of the revolutionary years, say—and gothic novels being particularly good at it. But when several genres disappear *together* from the literary field, and then another group, and so on, then the reason has to be different, because all these forms cannot have run *independently and simultaneously* into insoluble problems—it would be simply too much of a coincidence. The causal mechanism must thus be *external* to the genres, and *common* to all: like a sudden, total change of their ecosystem. Which is to say: a change of their audience. Books survive if they are read and disappear if they aren't: and when an entire generic system vanishes at once, the likeliest explanation is that *its readers vanished at once*.

This, then, is where those 25–30 years come from: generations. Not a concept I am very fond of, actually, but the only one that seems to make sense of figure 9. And indeed, in Mannheim's[7] great essay of 1927, the best evidence for his thesis comes precisely from the aesthetic sphere: 'a rhythm in the sequence of generations', he writes, following Mentré's *Les générations sociales*,[8] published a few years earlier,

> is far more apparent in the realm of the *séries libres*—free human groupings such as salons and literary circles—than in the realm of the

6. Hans Robert Jauss (1921–1997), German literary theorist.
7. Karl Mannheim (1893–1947), Hungarian-born German sociologist.
8. *Social Generations* (1920), a thesis by the French historian François Mentré (1877–1950).

> institutions, which for the most part lay down a lasting pattern of behaviour, either by prescriptions or by the organization of collective undertakings, thus preventing the new generation from showing its originality . . . The aesthetic sphere is perhaps the most appropriate to reflect overall changes of mental climate.[9]

Overall changes of the mental climate: the five, six shifts in the British novelistic field between 1740 and 1900. But since people are born every day, not every twenty-five years, on what basis can the biological continuum be segmented into discrete units? Mannheim again:

> Whether a new *generation style* emerges every year, every thirty, every hundred years, or whether it emerges rhythmically at all, depends entirely on the trigger action of the social and cultural process . . . We shall therefore speak of a *generation as an actuality* only where a concrete bond is created between members of a generation by their being exposed to the social and intellectual symptoms of a process of dynamic destabilization.[1]

A bond due to a process of dynamic destabilization; and one who was eighteen in 1968[2] understands. But again, this cannot possibly explain the *regularity* of generational replacement, unless one assumes—absurdly—that the 'destabilizations' themselves occur punctually every twenty-five or thirty years. And so, I close on a note of perplexity: *faute de mieux*,[3] some kind of generational mechanism seems the best way to account for the regularity of the novelistic cycle—but 'generation' is itself a very questionable concept. Clearly, we must do better.[4]

VII

Normal literature remains in place for a generation or so . . . It's the central group of figure 10,[5] which rearranges the forty-four genres according to their duration, and where about two thirds of them last indeed between 23 and 35 years.[6] The one large exception is formed by those genres—nine years, ten, twelve—on the left end of the spectrum: why so short-lived? Almost certainly,

9. Karl Mannheim, 'The Problem of Generations', in *Essays on the Sociology of Knowledge*, London 1952, p. 279 [Moretti's note].

1. *Essays on the Sociology of Knowledge*, pp. 303, 310 [Moretti's note].

2. From Mexico City to Belgrade, 1968 was marked by numerous student uprisings—especially in France, where demonstrations in Paris grew into a massive revolt, joined by a general strike of millions of workers.

3. For lack of something better (French).

4. A possible solution: at some point, a particularly significant 'destabilization' gives rise to a clearly defined generation, which occupies centre stage for 20–30 years, attracting within its orbit, and shaping after its mould, slightly younger or older individuals. Once biological age pushes this generation to the periphery of the cultural system, there is suddenly room for a new generation, which comes into being simply *because it can*, destabilization or not; and so on, and on. A regular series would thus emerge even without a 'trigger action' *for each new generation*: once the generational clock has been set in motion, it will run its course—for some time at least. (This is in fact Mentré's approach to the problem, especially in the long chapter in which he sketches an unbroken series of generations throughout French literature from 1515 to 1915) [Moretti's note].

5. Note to figure 10: see Katherine Sobba Green, *The Courtship Novel, 1740–1820* (1991). *Cecilia* (1782) was the second novel by the English novelist and diarist Fanny Burney (1752–1840); her extremely popular first publication, *Evelina* (1778), was an epistolary novel.

6. A first look at French literature from the 17th to the 19th century suggests that most of its narrative genres have a similar 30-year span: pastoral and heroic novels, the *nouvelle historique* [short historical novel], *romans galants* [courtly novels] and *contes philosophiques* [philosophical tales], sentimental novels, the *Bildungsroman*, the *roman gai* [coarse comic fiction], the two main phases ('heroic' and 'sentimental') of the *roman-feuilleton* [serialized fiction] . . . On the other hand, Sandra Guardini Vasconcelos and other Brazilian literary historians have pointed out that when a country *imports* most of its novels, the regular turnover of the Anglo-French generations

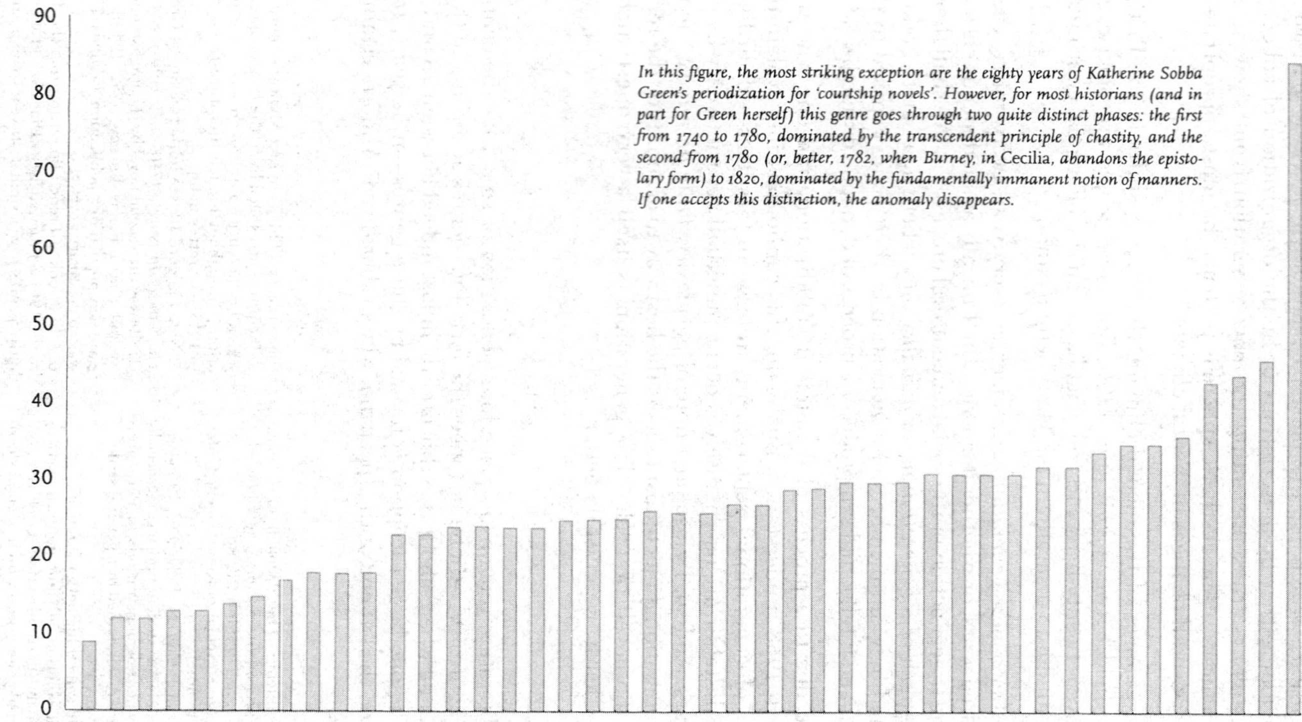

90
80
70
60
50
40
30
20
10
0
In this figure, the most striking exception are the eighty years of Katherine Sobba Green's periodization for 'courtship novels'. However, for most historians (and in part for Green herself) this genre goes through two quite distinct phases: the first from 1740 to 1780, dominated by the transcendent principle of chastity, and the second from 1780 (or, better, 1782, when Burney, in Cecilia, *abandons the epistolary form) to 1820, dominated by the fundamentally immanent notion of manners. If one accepts this distinction, the anomaly disappears.*

For sources, see 'A Note on the Taxonomy of the Forms' on page 2275.

Figure 10. British novelistic genres, 1740–1915 (duration in years)

because of politics again: Jacobin, anti-Jacobin, evangelical novels around the turn of the century, Chartist and religious narratives in the 1840s, New Woman novels in the 1890s . . . And as often happens with politics and the novel, the outcome is a string of explicit ideological declarations: Jacobin novels trying to reform their villains by 'discussion and reasoning', as Gary Kelly puts it; Right Reason, adds Marilyn Butler in *Jane Austen and the War of Ideas*:[7] a 'puzzling' choice, she goes on, the great 'missed opportunity' of the Jacobin novel as a form. Missed opportunity, yes, but puzzling, perhaps not: if a novel wants to engage the political sphere directly, a series of unambiguous statements, however narratively dull, is a perfectly rational choice. And then, ideological exchanges are an easy way to capture Braudel's 'dramatic rush of the event': to turn a book into *A tale of the times, A tale of the day, The philosophy of the day,* to quote some typical 1790s subtitles. But the conjunction of course works both ways: if what most attracts readers is the drama of the day, then, once the day is over, so is the novel . . .

VIII

Why did most British genres last 25–30 years, then, but some of them only ten? Because these 'political' forms subordinated narrative logic to the tempo of the short span, I have conjectured, and thus they also disappeared with the short span; and I hope the answer sounds plausible. But the real point, here, is less the specific answer, than the total *heterogeneity of problem and solution*: to make sense of quantitative data, I had to abandon the quantitative universe, and turn to morphology: evoke form, in order to explain figures. Here, the figures of the literary market. But when I studied the international impact of American films, I encountered exactly the same problematic: in the sample decade (1986–95), comedies amounted to 20% of the top box office hits within the United States, whereas elsewhere, as figure 11 shows, they were a lot less successful (especially in Asia and in the Mediterranean).[8] The figures were crystal clear. But if one then wondered *why* this was so—why, in other words, comedies were so much harder to export than, say, action films—percentages offered no help, and the explanation had to be sought once again in the realm of form: as contemporary comedies make large use of jokes, which are often lost in translation, American comedies are quite simply a lot less funny in Japanese or Egyptian or Spanish than in English. (Not for nothing, the great international age of comic films—Chaplin, Keaton, Lloyd, Laurel and Hardy[9]—coincided with silent cinema.)[1]

is replaced by a much more accelerated and possibly uneven tempo. If they are right—and I think they are—then the Western European case would once more be the exception rather than the rule of world literature [Moretti's note].

7. Published in 1975. Gary Kelly, *The English Jacobin Novel, 1780–1805* (1976).

8. Franco Moretti, 'Planet Hollywood', *New Left Review* 9, May–June 2001, pp. 90–101 [Moretti's note]. Moretti has published extensively in *New Left Review*, a U.K. leftist political journal also known as *NLR*.

9. American comedy team, the British-born Stan Laurel (Arthur Stanley Jefferson, 1890–1965) and Oliver Hardy (1892–1957). Charlie Chaplin (1889–1977), English director and film star. Joseph Frank "Buster" Keaton (1895–1966), American writer, director, and star of silent film. Harold Clayton Lloyd (1893–1971), American film actor and producer, best known for silent comedies.

1. See here how a quantitative history of literature is also a profoundly formalist one—especially at the beginning and at the end of the research process. At the end, because it must account for the data; and at the beginning, because a formal concept is usually what makes quantification possible in the first place: since a series must be composed of homogeneous objects, a morphological category is needed— 'novel', 'anti-Jacobin novel', 'comedy', etc.—to establish such homogeneity [Moretti's note].

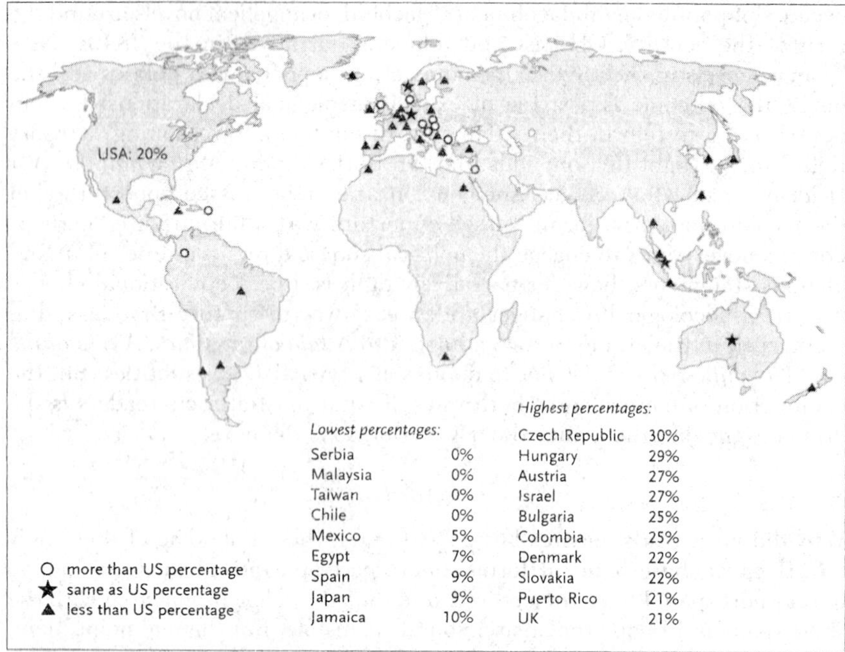

Figure 11. US comedies as a percentage of top five box office hits, 1986–95

Quantification poses the problem, then, and form offers the solution. But let me add: if you are lucky. Because the asymmetry of a quantitative *explanandum* and a qualitative *explanans*[2] leaves you often with a perfectly clear problem—and no idea of a solution. In 'Planet Hollywood', for instance, it turned out that absolutely *all* Italian box office hits of the sample decade were comedies; why that was so, however, was completely unclear. I felt I had to say something, so I presented an 'explanation', and NLR indulgently printed it; but it was silly of me, because the most interesting aspect of those data was that *I had found a problem for which I had absolutely no solution.* And problems without a solution are exactly what we need in a field like ours, where we are used to asking only those questions for which we already have an answer. 'I have noticed,' says Brecht's Herr Keuner,[3] 'that we put many people off our teaching because we have an answer to everything. Could we not, in the interest of propaganda, draw up a list of the questions that appear to us completely unsolved?'

IX

Two brief theoretical conclusions. The first is again on the cycle as the hidden thread of literary history. 'For the elevation of the novel to occur', writes William Warner in *Licensing Entertainment*, 'the novel of amorous intrigue must . . . disappear'; it is 'the Great Gender Shift' of the mid-eighteenth

2. Explaining element (Latin). *Explanandum*: that which must be explained (Latin).
3. A character in *Stories of Mr. Keuner* (1965), a collection of short stories, aphorisms, and parables that the German Marxist playwright and theater director Bertolt Brecht (1898–1956) began publishing in 1930.

century, adds April Alliston: the disappearance of earlier fiction by women writers, with the related increase in the number of male novelists. And it's all true, except for the article: *the* shift? The third quarter of the nineteenth century, write Tuchman and Fortin in *Edging Women Out,* was 'the period of invasion' of the novelistic field by male authors, who eventually 'edge out' their female competitors.[4]

But, clearly, a mid-Victorian 'invasion' presupposes a reversal of the gender shift of the 1740s. And, in fact, this is what the historical record shows: if between 1750 and 1780, as a result of the initial shift, men publish indeed twice as many novels as women, in the late 1780s a second shift reverses the gender ratio, as one can see in Garside's breakdown for a slightly later period (figure 12),[5] in which women novelists (among them Burney, Radcliffe, Edgeworth,[6] Austen) remain the majority until a third shift occurs, around 1820, towards male writers (Scott; then Bulwer, Dickens, Thackeray[7]), to be followed by a fourth shift back to women in mid-century (the Brontës, Gaskell, Braddon, Eliot[8]), and then by a fifth one—the 'edging out'—in the 1870s. Similar data are beginning to emerge for France, Spain, the US, and it's fascinating to see how researchers are convinced that they are all describing something unique (*the* gender shift, *the* elevation of the novel, *the* gentrification, *the* invention of high and low, *the* feminization, *the* sentimental education, *the* invasion . . .), whereas in all likelihood they are all observing the same comet that keeps crossing and recrossing the sky: the same *literary cycle*, where gender and genre are probably in synchrony with each other—a generation of military novels, nautical tales, and historical novels *à la* Scott attracting male writers, one of domestic, provincial and sensation novels attracting women writers, and so on.

Now, let me be clear, saying that these studies describe the return of the same literary cycle is not an objection: quite the opposite, my thesis *depends* on their findings, and it even corroborates them somehow, by finding the common mechanism which is at work in all those instances. But it's also true that if one reframes individual instances as moments of a cycle, then the nature of the questions changes: 'Events don't interest Lucien Febvre for what in them is unique', writes Pomian, but 'as units in a series, which reveal the conjunctural variations in . . . a conflict that remains constant throughout the period.'[9]

Variations in a conflict that remains constant: this is what emerges at the level of the cycle—and if the conflict remains constant, then the point is not who prevails in this or that skirmish, but exactly the opposite: no victory is ever definitive, neither men nor women writers 'occupy' the British

4. William B. Warner, *Licensing Entertainment: The Elevation of Novel Reading in Britain, 1685–1750*, Berkeley 1998, p. 44; April Alliston, 'Love in Excess', in *Il romanzo,* vol. I, *La cultura del romanzo*, Torino 2001, p. 650; Gaye Tuchman and Nina Fortin, *Edging Women Out*, New Haven 1989, pp. 7–8 [Moretti's note].
5. Note to figure 12: Austen (1775–1817) published 6 novels between 1813 and 1817.
6. Maria Edgeworth (1767–1849), best known today for novels of Irish life. Ann Radcliffe (1764–1823), pioneer of the Gothic novel.
7. All popular novelists: Edward Bulwer-Lytton (1803–1873), politician and author of historical and romantic novels; Charles Dickens (1812–1870), most popular English novelist of the 19th century; and William Makepeace Thackeray (1811–1863), best known for his satirical writings.
8. Prominent names in 19th-century British fiction: the three Brontë sisters, Charlotte (1816–1855), Emily (1818–1848), and Anne (1820–1849); Elizabeth Gaskell (1810–1865); Mary Elizabeth Braddon (1837–1915); and George Eliot (pen name of Marian Evans, 1819–1880).
9. Pomian, 'L'histoire des structures', p. 117 [Moretti's note].

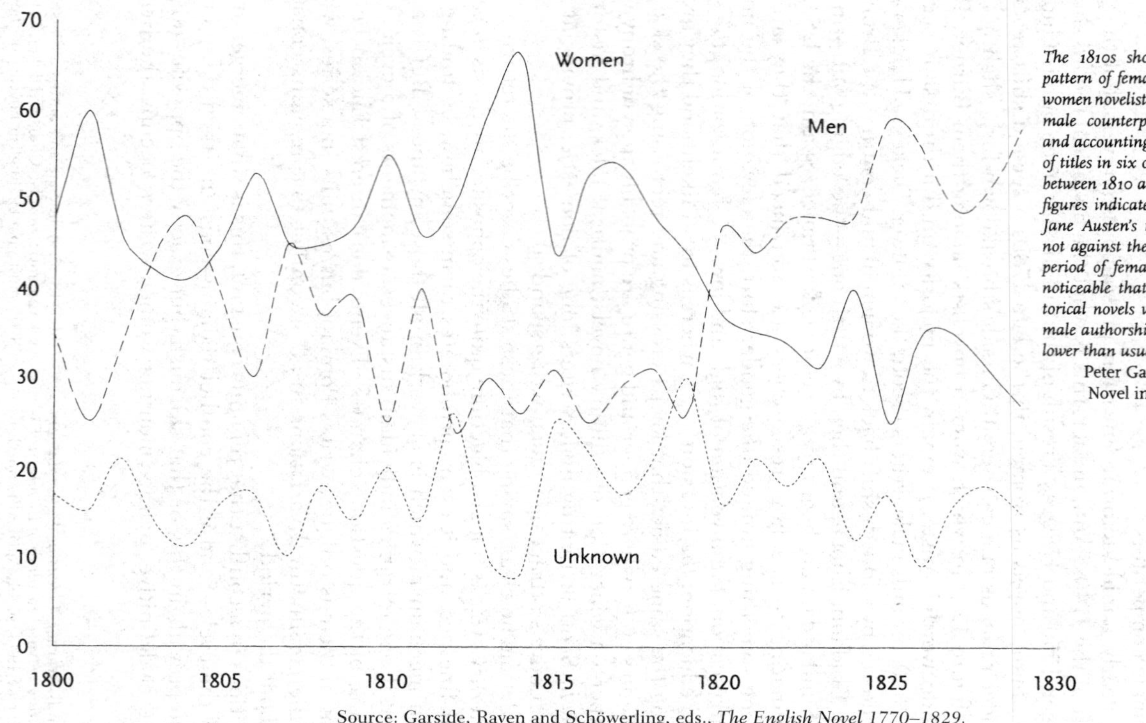

The 1810s show an even clearer pattern of female dominance, with women novelists out-producing their male counterparts in every year, and accounting for over 50 per cent of titles in six out of the eight years between 1810 and 1817 . . . As these figures indicate, the publication of Jane Austen's novels was achieved not against the grain but during a period of female ascendancy. It is noticeable that Scott's earliest historical novels were launched when male authorship of fiction was at a lower than usual ebb.

Peter Garside, 'The English Novel in the Romantic Era'

Source: Garside, Raven and Schöwerling, eds., *The English Novel 1770–1829.*

Figure 12. Authorship of new novels, Britain 1800–1829: gender breakdown (percentage)

novel once and for all, and the form keeps oscillating back and forth between the two groups. And if this sounds like nothing is happening, no, what is happening *is the oscillation*, which allows the novel to use a double pool of talents and of forms, thereby boosting its productivity, and giving it an edge over its many competitors. But this process can only be glimpsed *at the level of the cycle*: individual episodes tend, if anything, to conceal it, and only the abstract pattern reveals the true nature of the historical process.[1]

x

Do cycles and genres explain everything, in the history of the novel? Of course not. But they bring to light its hidden tempo, and suggest some questions on what we could call its internal shape. For most literary historians, I mean, there is a categorical difference between 'the novel' and the various 'novelistic (sub)genres': the novel is, so to speak, the substance of the form, and deserves a full general theory; subgenres are more like accidents, and their study, however interesting, remains local in character, without real theoretical consequences. The forty-four genres of figure 9, however, suggest a different historical picture, where the novel does not develop as a single entity—where is 'the' novel, there?—but by periodically generating a whole set of genres, and then another, and another . . . Both synchronically and diachronically, in other words, the novel is *the system of its genres*: the whole diagram, not one privileged part of it. Some genres are morphologically more significant, of course, or more popular, or both—and we must account for this: but not by pretending that they are the only ones that exist. And instead, all great theories of the novel have precisely reduced the novel to one basic form only (realism, the dialogic, romance, meta-novels . . .); and if the reduction has given them their elegance and power, it has also erased nine tenths of literary history. Too much.

I began this chapter by saying that quantitative data are useful because they are independent of interpretation; then, that they are challenging because they often demand an interpretation that transcends the quantitative realm; now, most radically, we see them *falsify* existing theoretical explanations, and ask for a theory, not so much of 'the' novel, but of *a whole family of novelistic forms.* A theory—of diversity. What this may mean, will be the topic of my third chapter.

A NOTE ON THE TAXONOMY OF THE FORMS

The genres of figures 9 and 10 are listed below in the following way: current definition (in capitals); dates of beginning and end; and critical study from which I have drawn the chosen (and not always explicit) periodization. Since both figures are meant as a first panorama of a very large territory,

1. A comparable oscillation is probably at work between High and Low forms, whose simultaneous existence is a well-known, if often ignored, fact of novelistic history: from the Hellenistic beginnings (divided between 'subliterary' and 'idealized' genres) through the Middle Ages, the 17th century (the *Bibliothèque Bleue*, and aristocratic novels), 18th (Warner's pair of 'entertainment' and 'elevation'), 19th (*feuilletons*, railway novels—and 'serious realism'), and 20th century (pulp fiction—modernist experiments). Here, too, the strength of the novel is not to be found in *one* of the two positions, but in its rhythmical oscillation between them: the novel is not hegemonic because it makes it into High Culture (it does, yes, but it's so desperately professorial to be awed by this fact), but for the opposite reason: it is never *only* in High Culture, and it can keep playing on two tables, preserving its double nature, where vulgar and refined are almost inextricable [Moretti's note].

soon to be improved by further work, a few words of caution are in order. First, except for the (rare) cases in which quantitative data or full bibliographies are available, the initial date refers to the genre's first recognizable example rather than to its genuine take-off, which occurs usually several years later; as our knowledge improves, therefore, it is likely that the chronological span of novelistic genres will turn out to be significantly shorter than the one given here. On the other hand, a few genres experience brief but intense revivals decades after their original peak, like the oriental tale in 1819–25, or the gothic after 1885, or the historical novel (more than once). How to account for these Draculaesque[2] reawakenings is a fascinating topic, which however will have to wait for another occasion. Finally, the chart shows neither detective fiction nor science fiction; although both genres achieve their modern form around 1890 (Doyle and Wells[3]), and undergo a major change in the 1920s, in step with the overall pattern, their peculiar long duration seems to require a different approach.

courtship novel, 1740–1820: Katherine Sobba Green, *The Courtship Novel 1740–1820,* Kentucky 1991. picaresque, 1748–90: F. W. Chandler, *The Literature of Roguery,* London 1907. oriental tale, 1759–87: Ernest Baker, *The History of the English Novel,* London 1924, vol. v. epistolary novel, 1766–95: James Raven, 'Historical Introduction', in Garside, Raven and Schöwerling, eds., *The English Novel 1770–1829,* vol. i. sentimental novel, 1768–90: John Mullan, 'Sentimental Novels', in John Richetti, ed., *The Cambridge Companion to the Eighteenth-Century Novel,* Cambridge 1996. 'spy' novel, 1770–1800: Christopher Flint, 'Speaking Objects: The Circulation of Stories in Eighteenth-Century Prose Fiction', *PMLA* 113 (2), March 1998, pp. 212–26. ramble novel, 1773–90: Simon Dickie, *The Mid-Century 'Ramble' Novels,* PhD dissertation, Stanford 2000. jacobin novel, 1789–1805: Gary Kelly, *The English Jacobin Novel* 1780–1805, Oxford 1976. gothic novel, 1790–1820: Peter Garside, 'The English Novel in the Romantic Era', in Garside, Raven and Schöwerling, eds., *The English Novel* 1770–1829, vol. ii. anti-jacobin novel, 1791–1805: M. O. Grenby, *The Anti-Jacobin Novel,* Cambridge 2001. national tale, 1800–31: Katie Trumpener, 'National Tale', in Paul Schellinger, ed., *The Encyclopedia of the Novel,* Chicago 1998, vol. ii. village stories, 1804–32: Gary Kelly, *English Fiction of the Romantic Period,* 1789–1830, London 1989. evangelical novel, 1808–19: Peter Garside, 'The English Novel in the Romantic Era'. historical novel, 1814–48: Nicholas Rance, *The Historical Novel and Popular Politics in Nineteenth-Century England,* New York 1975. romantic farrago, 1822–47: Gary Kelly, *English Fiction of the Romantic Period.* silver-fork novel, 1825–42: Alison Adburgham, *Silver Fork Society,* London 1983. military novel, 1826–50: Peter Garside, 'The English Novel in the Romantic Era'. nautical tales, 1828–50: Michael Wheeler, *English Fiction of the Victorian Period: 1830–90,* London 1985. newgate novel, 1830–47: Keith Hollingsworth, *The Newgate Novel, 1830–47,* Detroit 1963. conversion novel, 1830–53: Sarah Gracombe, *Anxieties of Influence: Jewishness and English Culture in the Victorian Novel,* PhD dissertation, Columbia University 2003.

2. Like the title character of Bram Stoker's *Dracula* (1897); a vampire who comes back from the dead.

3. H. G. Wells (1866–1946), English social thinker, historian, and pioneer of science fiction. Sir Arthur Conan Doyle (1859–1930), Scottish author best known as the creator of Sherlock Holmes.

INDUSTRIAL NOVEL, 1832–67: Catherine Gallagher, *The Industrial Reformation of English Fiction,* Chicago 1985. SPORTING NOVEL, 1838–67: John Sutherland, *The Stanford Companion to Victorian Literature,* Stanford 1989. CHARTIST NOVEL, 1839–52: Gustav Klaus, *The Literature of Labour,* New York 1985. MYSTERIES, 1846–70: Richard Maxwell, *The Mysteries of Paris and London,* Charlottesville, VA 1992. MULTIPLOT NOVEL, 1846–72: Crisi Benford, *The Multiplot Novel and Victorian Culture,* PhD dissertation, Stanford 2003. *BILDUNGSROMAN,* 1847–72: Michael Minden, 'Bildungsroman', in Schellinger, ed., *The Encyclopedia of the Novel,* vol. II. RELIGIOUS NOVEL, 1848–56: Wheeler, *English Fiction of the Victorian Period.* DOMESTIC NOVEL, 1849–72: Sutherland, *Stanford Companion to Victorian Literature.* PROVINCIAL NOVEL, 1850–73: Ian Duncan, 'The Provincial or Regional Novel', in Patrick Brantlinger and William Thesing, eds., *A Companion to the Victorian Novel,* Oxford 2003. SENSATION NOVEL, 1850–76: Nicholas Rance, *Wilkie Collins and Other Sensation Novelists,* London 1991. FANTASY, 1850–95: C. N. Manlove, *Modern Fantasy: Five Studies,* Cambridge 1975. CHILDREN'S ADVENTURES, 1851–83: Sutherland, *Stanford Companion to Victorian Literature.* SCHOOL STORIES, 1857–81: Isabel Quigly, *The Heirs of Tom Brown,* London 1982. IMPERIAL ROMANCES, 1868–1902: Joseph Bristow, *Empire Boys,* London 1991. INVASION LITERATURE, 1871–14: I. F. Clarke, *The Tale of the Next Great War,* 1871–1914, Liverpool 1995. UTOPIA, 1872–1901: Wheeler, *English Fiction of the Victorian Period.* COCKNEY SCHOOL, 1872–97: Sutherland, *Stanford Companion to Victorian Literature.* REGIONAL NOVEL, 1873–96: Duncan, 'The Provincial or Regional Novel'. NURSERY STORIES, 1876–1906: Gillian Avery, *Nineteenth Century Children,* London 1965. DECADENT NOVEL, 1884–1906: A. A. Mandal, 'Decadent Novel', in Schellinger, ed., *The Encyclopedia of the Novel,* vol. I. NATURALIST NOVEL, 1885–1915: William Frierson, *L'influence du naturalisme français sur les romanciers anglais de 1885 à 1990,* Paris 1925. IMPERIAL GOTHIC, 1885–1916: Patrick Brantlinger, *Rule of Darkness,* Ithaca 1988. NEW WOMAN NOVEL, 1888–99: Ann L. Ardis, *New Women, New Novels,* New Brunswick 1990. KAILYARD SCHOOL, 1888–1900: Sutherland, *Stanford Companion to Victorian Literature.*

2003, 2005

EVE KOSOFSKY SEDGWICK
1950–2009

In the 1992 preface to the second edition of *Between Men: English Literature and Male Homosocial Desire* (1985), Eve Sedgwick writes about the emergence in the late 1980s and early 1990s of queer theory, a new paradigm of literary theory that owes its productivity to the "gorgeous generativity, the speculative generosity and daring, the permeability, and the activism that have long been lodged in the multiple histories of queer *reading.*" In the aftermath of the famous Stonewall riots, when gay men and lesbians fought back against a police raid on a gay bar in New York City in the summer of 1969, and often under the umbrella of feminist and then gender studies, an increasingly vocal gay and lesbian liberation movements took shape. In the 1970s, the work of literary theorists such as ADRIENNE RICH, Bonnie Zimmerman, Barbara Smith, GLORIA ANZALDÚA, Louie Crew, and Rictor Norton had begun to define gay and lesbian studies in the academy based on the identity politics that had well served both feminists and civil rights activists. The 1980s, however, saw a reappraisal of political strategies and the emergence of a "highly productive queer community whose explicit basis [was] the criss-crossing of the lines of identification and desire among genders, races and sexual definitions." By the early 1990s, it was possible to talk about queer theory as a vital new area of literary theory, built on the pioneering work of theorists such as MICHEL FOUCAULT, GAYLE RUBIN, JUDITH BUTLER, MONIQUE WITTIG, and Sedgwick herself; its aim was to expose incoherencies in the supposedly stable definitions of male and female sexuality, to include not only gay and lesbian but also transgender subjects, and to explore topics such as cross-dressing, gender ambiguity, transsexuality, and deviance.

Born in Dayton, Ohio, Sedgwick received her B.A. from Cornell University and went on to earn an M.Phil. and in 1975 a Ph.D. from Yale University. She taught at a number of colleges and universities and held major fellowships from the Mellon Foundation (1976–78), the Bunting Institute at Radcliffe College (1983–84), the Guggenheim Foundation (1987–88), and the National Humanities Center (1991–92). From 1998 until her death in 2009, she was a Distinguished Professor of English at the Graduate Center at the City University of New York.

In *Between Men* Sedgwick explores the phenomenon of *homosociality*, a term she applied to the social bonds formed between persons of the same sex. While these bonds can be distinguished from homosexuality—sexual desire between persons of the same sex—they exist on a continuum with it. The structures of male and female homosocial bonds are, Sedgwick argues, quite distinct. The continuum between male homosocial and homosexual desire is disrupted by the often intense homophobia (fear of homosexuality) that marks rituals of male bonding in our culture. But the opposition between homosocial and homosexual is much less pronounced, much less dichotomous, observes Sedgwick, for women than it is for men (see, for instance, Adrienne Rich's famous notion of a "lesbian continuum" in "Compulsory Heterosexuality and Lesbian Existence," above). *Between Men* examines how male homosociality gets constructed and reflected in European literary texts from 1600 to 1850. In particular, Sedgwick is interested in the ways in which homosocial desire is constituted in Western literature between men whose bonding is forged through their rivalry over a woman who mediates their relationship and deflects any taint of homoeroticism. A popular example of this phenomenon might be the triangle formed between Arthur, Guinevere, and Lancelot in Arthurian literature.

In *Epistemology of the Closet* (1990), Sedgwick points out that the versions of modern lesbian and gay history recounted by gay liberation movements following Stonewall were all based on a metaphor of "the closet," which created what she calls the regime of the "open secret" that has dominated lesbian and gay life for more than a century. She suggests that this regime, with its contradictory and constraining rules about privacy and disclosure, public and private, awareness and ignorance, has shaped the way in which many questions of value and epistemology (knowledge) have been conceived and addressed not only in gay subculture but in modern Western society as a whole. In her book's introduction, which she titles "Axiomatic," Sedgwick explores this problem through seven "axioms." The second axiom, included in our selection below, argues that while sexuality and gender may be implicated in one another, they constitute conceptually distinct realms (on the relationship between sex and gender, see also Gayle Rubin). To treat sexuality as a part of gender perpetuates heterosexist assumptions about sexuality, foreclosing other as yet unarticulated ways of understanding. For Sedgwick, it follows that while lesbian, gay, and antihomophobic scholarship have much to learn from feminism, one cannot assume that the interests of the various actors coincide. Any alliances among movements to end oppression are strategic and political, not natural.

Sedgwick's criticism exhibits the strong influence of feminist, Foucauldian, and deconstructive (see JACQUES DERRIDA) modes of analysis and, like many poststructuralist critics, she writes in a philosophical prose that is often challenging. Yet while some critics have voiced the familiar complaint about the impenetrability of poststructuralist prose, others have been more concerned with the political stakes involved in her argument. Some fear that queer theory seeks to dissolve familiar identity categories such as gay and lesbian, creating an apolitical movement that ignores the real material conditions of gay life. Others suspect that queer theory will once more render women and lesbians invisible under the guise of a gender-neutral politics. These vexing political issues aside, Sedgwick's groundbreaking theoretical work raises important questions about the limits of identity politics, as it reshapes our understanding of the relationships between literature and sexuality.

Between Men: English Literature and Male Homosocial Desire **Keywords:** Feminist Theory, Gender, The Novel, Psychoanalysis, Queer Theory, Sexuality
Epistemology of the Closet **Keywords:** Feminist Theory, Gender, Psychoanalysis, Queer Theory, Sexuality

From Between Men: English Literature and Male Homosocial Desire

From *Introduction*

1. HOMOSOCIAL DESIRE

The subject of this book is a relatively short, recent, and accessible passage of English culture, chiefly as embodied in the mid-eighteenth- to mid-nineteenth-century novel. The attraction of the period to theorists of many disciplines is obvious: condensed, self-reflective, and widely influential change in economic, ideological, and gender arrangements. I will be arguing that concomitant changes in the structure of the continuum of male "homosocial desire" were tightly, often causally bound up with the other more visible changes; that the emerging pattern of male friendship, mentorship, entitlement, rivalry, and hetero- and homosexuality was in an intimate and shifting relation to class; and that no element of that pattern can be understood outside of its relation to women and the gender system as a whole.

"Male homosocial desire": the phrase in the title of this study is intended to mark both discriminations and paradoxes. "Homosocial desire," to begin with, is a kind of oxymoron. "Homosocial" is a word occasionally used in history and the social sciences, where it describes social bonds between persons of the same sex; it is a neologism, obviously formed by analogy with "homosexual," and just as obviously meant to be distinguished from "homosexual." In fact, it is applied to such activities as "male bonding," which may, as in our society, be characterized by intense homophobia, fear and hatred of homosexuality.[1] To draw the "homosocial" back into the orbit of "desire," of the

1. The notion of "homophobia" is itself fraught with difficulties. To begin with, the word is etymologically nonsensical. A more serious problem is that the linking of fear and hatred in the "-phobia" suffix, and in the word's usage, does tend to prejudge the question of the cause of homosexual oppression: it is attributed to fear, as opposed to (for example) a desire for power, privilege, or material goods. An alternative term that is more suggestive of collective, structurally inscribed, perhaps materially based oppression is "heterosexism." This study will, however, continue to use "homophobia," for three reasons. First, it will be an important concern here to question, rather

potentially erotic, then, is to hypothesize the potential unbrokenness of a continuum between homosocial and homosexual—a continuum whose visibility, for men, in our society, is radically disrupted. It will become clear, in the course of my argument, that my hypothesis of the unbrokenness of this continuum is not a *genetic* one—I do not mean to discuss genital homosexual desire as "at the root of" other forms of male homosociality—but rather a strategy for making generalizations about, and marking historical differences in, the *structure* of men's relations with other men. "Male homosocial desire" is the name this book will give to the entire continuum.

I have chosen the word "desire" rather than "love" to mark the erotic emphasis because, in literary critical and related discourse, "love" is more easily used to name a particular emotion, and "desire" to name a structure; in this study, a series of arguments about the structural permutations of social impulses fuels the critical dialectic. For the most part, I will be using "desire" in a way analogous to the psychoanalytic use of "libido"[2]—not for a particular affective state or emotion, but for the affective or social force, the glue, even when its manifestation is hostility or hatred or something less emotively charged, that shapes an important relationship. How far this force is properly sexual (what, historically, it means for something to be "sexual") will be an active question.

The title is specific about *male* homosocial desire partly in order to acknowledge from the beginning (and stress the seriousness of) a limitation of my subject; but there is a more positive and substantial reason, as well. It is one of the main projects of this study to explore the ways in which the shapes of sexuality, and what *counts* as sexuality, both depend on and affect historical power relationships.[3] A corollary is that in a society where men and women differ in their access to power, there will be important gender differences, as well, in the structure and constitution of sexuality.

For instance, the diacritical[4] opposition between the "homosocial" and the "homosexual" seems to be much less thorough and dichotomous for women, in our society, than for men. At this particular historical moment, an intelligible continuum of aims, emotions, and valuations links lesbianism with the other forms of women's attention to women: the bond of mother and daughter, for instance, the bond of sister and sister, women's friendship, "networking," and the active struggles of feminism.[5] The continuum is crisscrossed with deep discontinuities—with much homophobia, with conflicts of race and class—but its intelligibility seems now a matter of simple common sense.

---

than to reinforce, the presumptively symmetrical opposition between homo- and heterosexuality, which seems to be implicit in the term "heterosexism." Second, the etiology of individual people's attitudes toward male homosexuality will not be a focus of discussion. And third, the ideological and thematic treatments of male homosexuality to be discussed from the late eighteenth century onward do combine fear and hatred in a way that is appropriately called phobic. For a good summary of social science research on the concept of homophobia, see Stephen M. Morin and Ellen M. Garfinkle, "Male Homophobia," in *Gayspeak: Gay Male and Lesbian Communication*, ed. James W. Chesebro (New York: Pilgrim Press, 1981), pp. 117–29 [except as indicated, all notes are Sedgwick's].

2. Psychic drive or energy associated with the sexual instinct but also inherent in other mental desires and drives [editor's note].

3. For a good survey of the background to this assertion, see Jeffrey Weeks, *Sex, Politics, and Society: The Regulation of Sexuality Since 1800* (London: Longman, 1981), pp. 1–18.

4. Distinctive; serving as a distinguishing feature [editor's note].

5. Adrienne Rich describes these bonds as forming a "lesbian continuum," in her essay "Compulsory Heterosexuality and Lesbian Existence," *Signs* 5 (1980): 631–60. [Rich (1929–2012), American feminist poet and essayist; for this essay, see above—editor's note.]

However agonistic the politics, however conflicted the feelings, it seems at this moment to make an obvious kind of sense to say that women in our society who love women, women who teach, study, nurture, suckle, write about, march for, vote for, give jobs to, or otherwise promote the interests of other women, are pursuing congruent and closely related activities. Thus the adjective "homosocial" as applied to women's bonds (by, for example, historian Carroll Smith-Rosenberg)[6] need not be pointedly dichotomized as against "homosexual"; it can intelligibly denominate the entire continuum.

The apparent simplicity—the unity—of the continuum between "women loving women" and "women promoting the interests of women," extending over the erotic, social, familial, economic, and political realms, would not be so striking if it were not in strong contrast to the arrangement among males. When Ronald Reagan and Jesse Helms[7] get down to serious logrolling on "family policy," they are men promoting men's interests. (In fact, they embody Heidi Hartmann's definition of patriarchy: "relations between men, which have a material base, and which, though hierarchical, establish or create interdependence and solidarity among men that enable them to dominate women.")[8] Is their bond in any way congruent with the bond of a loving gay male couple? Reagan and Helms would say no—disgustedly. Most gay couples would say no—disgustedly. But why not? Doesn't the continuum between "men-loving-men" and "men-promoting-the-interests-of-men" have the same intuitive force that it has for women?

Quite the contrary: much of the most useful recent writing about patriarchal structures suggests that "obligatory heterosexuality" is built into male-dominated kinship systems, or that homophobia is a *necessary* consequence of such patriarchal institutions as heterosexual marriage.[9] Clearly, however convenient it might be to group together all the bonds that link males to males, and by which males enhance the status of males—usefully symmetrical as it would be, that grouping meets with a prohibitive structural obstacle. From the vantage point of our own society, at any rate, it has apparently been impossible to imagine a form of patriarchy that was not homophobic. Gayle Rubin writes, for instance, "The suppression of the homosexual component of human sexuality, and by corollary, the oppression of homosexuals, is . . . a product of the same system whose rules and relations oppress women."[1]

The historical manifestations of this patriarchal oppression of homosexuals have been savage and nearly endless. Louis Crompton makes a detailed case for describing the history as genocidal.[2] Our own society is brutally

6. "The Female World of Love and Ritual," in *A Heritage of Her Own: Toward a New Social History of American Women*, ed. Nancy F. Cott and Elizabeth H. Pleck (New York: Simon and Schuster, 1979), pp. 311–42; usage appears on, e.g., pp. 316, 317.

7. Senator (1921–2008) from North Carolina (1973–2002). Reagan (1911–2004), 40th president of the United States (1981–89). Both conservative Republicans were well known for their vocal support of "family values" during the 1980s [editor's note].

8. "The Unhappy Marriage of Marxism and Feminism: Toward a More Progressive Union," in *Women and Revolution: A Discussion of the Unhappy Marriage of Marxism and Feminism*, ed. Lydia Sargent (Boston: South End Press, 1981), pp. 1–41; the quotation is from p. 14.

9. See, for example, Gayle Rubin, "The Traffic in Women: Notes toward a 'Political Economy' of Sex," in *Toward an Anthropology of Women*, ed. Rayna Reiter (New York: Monthly Review Press, 1975), pp. 182–83. [Rubin (b. 1949), American anthropologist and queer theorist—editor's note.]

1. Rubin, "Traffic," p. 180.

2. Louis Crompton, "Gay Genocide: From Leviticus to Hitler," in *The Gay Academic*, ed. Louie Crew (Palm Springs, Calif.: ETC Publications, 1978), pp. 67–91; but see chapter 5 [of *Between Men*] for a discussion of the limitations of "genocide" as an understanding of the fate of homosexual men.

homophobic; and the homophobia directed against both males and females is not arbitrary or gratuitous, but tightly knit into the texture of family, gender, age, class, and race relations. Our society could not cease to be homophobic and have its economic and political structures remain unchanged.

Nevertheless, it has yet to be demonstrated that, because most patriarchies structurally include homophobia, therefore patriarchy structurally *requires* homophobia. K. J. Dover's recent study, *Greek Homosexuality*, seems to give a strong counterexample in classical Greece. Male homosexuality, according to Dover's evidence, was a widespread, licit, and very influential part of the culture. Highly structured along lines of class, and within the citizen class along lines of age, the pursuit of the adolescent boy by the older man was described by stereotypes that we associate with romantic heterosexual love (conquest, surrender, the "cruel fair," the absence of desire in the love object), with the passive part going to the boy. At the same time, however, because the boy was destined in turn to grow into manhood, the assignment of roles was not permanent.[3] Thus the love relationship, while temporarily oppressive to the object, had a strongly educational function; Dover quotes Pausanias in Plato's *Symposium* as saying "that it would be right for him [the boy] to perform any service for one who improves him in mind and character."[4] Along with its erotic component, then, this was a bond of mentorship; the boys were apprentices in the ways and virtues of Athenian citizenship, whose privileges they inherited. These privileges included the power to command the labor of slaves of both sexes, and of women of any class including their own. "Women and slaves belonged and lived together," Hannah Arendt writes. The system of sharp class and gender subordination was a necessary part of what the male culture valued most in itself: "Contempt for laboring originally [arose] out of a passionate striving for freedom from necessity and a no less passionate impatience with every effort that left no trace, no monument, no great work worthy to remembrance";[5] so the contemptible labor was left to women and slaves.

The example of the Greeks demonstrates, I think, that while heterosexuality is necessary for the maintenance of any patriarchy, homophobia, against males at any rate, is not. In fact, for the Greeks, the continuum between "men loving men" and "men promoting the interests of men" appears to have been quite seamless. It is as if, in our terms, there were no perceived discontinuity between the male bonds at the Continental Baths and the male bonds at the Bohemian Grove[6] or in the board room or Senate cloakroom.

It is clear, then, that there is an asymmetry in our present society between, on the one hand, the relatively continuous relation of female homosocial and

3. On this, see Jean Baker Miller, *Toward a New Psychology of Women* (Boston: Beacon Press, 1976), chap. 1.

4. K. J. Dover, *Greek Homosexuality* (New York: Random House–Vintage, 1980), p. 91. [Dover's quotation is from PLATO, *Symposium* 184d—editor's note.]

5. Hannah Arendt, *The Human Condition* (Chicago: University of Chicago Press, 1958), p. 83; quoted in Adrienne Rich, *On Lies, Secrets, and Silence: Selected Prose, 1966–1978* (New York: Norton, 1979), p. 206. [ARENDT (1906–1975), German-born American political theorist—editor's note.]

6. On the Bohemian Grove, an all-male summer camp for American ruling-class men, see G. William Domhoff, *The Bohemian Grove and Other Retreats: A Study in Ruling-Class Cohesiveness* (New York: Harper and Row, 1974); and a more vivid, although homophobic, account, John van der Zee, *The Greatest Men's Party on Earth: Inside the Bohemian Grove* (New York: Harcourt Brace Jovanovich, 1974). [The Continental Baths: a gay bathhouse/club, very popular in the 1970s, located on Manhattan's Upper West Side—editor's note.]

homosexual bonds, and, on the other hand, the radically discontinuous relation of male homosocial and homosexual bonds. The example of the Greeks (and of other, tribal cultures, such as the New Guinea "Sambia" studied by G. H. Herdt[7]) shows, in addition, that the structure of homosocial continuums is culturally contingent, not an innate feature of either "maleness" or "femaleness." Indeed, closely tied though it obviously is to questions of male vs. female power, the explanation will require a more exact mode of historical categorization than "patriarchy," as well, since patriarchal power structures (in Hartmann's sense) characterize both Athenian and American societies. Nevertheless, we may take as an explicit axiom that the historically differential shapes of male and female homosociality—much as they themselves may vary over time—will always be articulations and mechanisms of the enduring inequality of power between women and men.

Why should the different shapes of the homosocial continuum be an interesting question? Why should it be a *literary* question? Its importance for the practical politics of the gay movement as a minority rights movement is already obvious from the recent history of strategic and philosophical differences between lesbians and gay men. In addition, it is theoretically interesting partly as a way of approaching a larger question of "sexual politics": What does it mean—what difference does it make—when a social or political relationship is sexualized? If the relation of homosocial to homosexual bonds is so shifty, then what theoretical framework do we have for drawing any links between sexual and power relationships?

* * *

1985

From Epistemology of the Closet

From *Introduction: Axiomatic*

* * *

AXIOM 2: THE STUDY OF SEXUALITY IS NOT COEXTENSIVE WITH THE STUDY OF GENDER; CORRESPONDINGLY, ANTIHOMOPHOBIC INQUIRY IS NOT COEXTENSIVE WITH FEMINIST INQUIRY. BUT WE CAN'T KNOW IN ADVANCE HOW THEY WILL BE DIFFERENT.

Sex, gender, sexuality: three terms whose usage relations and analytical relations are almost irremediably slippery. The charting of a space between something called "sex" and something called "gender" has been one of the most influential and successful undertakings of feminist thought. For the purposes of that undertaking, "sex" has had the meaning of a certain group of irreducible, biological differentiations between members of the species Homo sapiens who have XX and those who have XY chromosomes. These include (or are ordinarily thought to include) more or less marked dimorphisms of genital formation, hair growth (in populations that have body hair),

7. American anthropologist (b. 1949), author of *Guardians of the Flute: Idioms of Masculinity* (1981) [editor's note].

fat distribution, hormonal function, and reproductive capacity. "Sex" in this sense—what I'll demarcate as "chromosomal sex"—is seen as the relatively minimal raw material on which is then based the social construction of *gender*. Gender, then, is the far more elaborated, more fully and rigidly dichotomized social production and reproduction of male and female identities and behaviors—of male and female *persons*—in a cultural system for which "male/female" functions as a primary and perhaps model binarism affecting the structure and meaning of many, many other binarisms whose apparent connection to chromosomal sex will often be exiguous or nonexistent. Compared to chromosomal sex, which is seen (by these definitions) as tending to be immutable, immanent in the individual, and biologically based, the meaning of gender is seen as culturally mutable and variable, highly relational (in the sense that each of the binarized genders is defined primarily by its relation to the other), and inextricable from a history of power differentials between genders. This feminist charting of what Gayle Rubin refers to as a "sex/gender system,"[1] the system by which chromosomal sex is turned into, and processed as, cultural gender, has tended to minimize the attribution of people's various behaviors and identities to chromosomal sex and to maximize their attribution to socialized gender constructs. The purpose of that strategy has been to gain analytic and critical leverage on the female-disadvantaging social arrangements that prevail at a given time in a given society, by throwing into question their legitimative ideological grounding in biologically based narratives of the "natural."

"Sex" is, however, a term that extends indefinitely beyond chromosomal sex. That its history of usage often overlaps with what might, now, more properly be called "gender" is only one problem. ("I can only love someone of my own sex." Shouldn't "sex" be "gender" in such a sentence? "M. saw that the person who approached was of the opposite sex." Genders—insofar as there are two and they are defined in contradistinction to one another—may be said to be opposite; but in what sense is XX the opposite of XY?) Beyond chromosomes, however, the association of "sex," precisely through the physical body, with reproduction and with genital activity and sensation keeps offering new challenges to the conceptual clarity or even possibility of sex/gender differentiation. There is a powerful argument to be made that a primary (or *the* primary) issue in gender differentiation and gender struggle is the question of who is to have control of women's (biologically) distinctive reproductive capability. Indeed, the intimacy of the association between several of the most signal forms of gender oppression and "the facts" of women's bodies and women's reproductive activity has led some radical feminists to question, more or less explicitly, the usefulness of insisting on a sex/gender distinction. For these reasons, even usages involving the "sex/gender system" within feminist theory are able to use "sex/gender" only to delineate a problematical *space* rather than a crisp distinction. My own loose usage in this book will be to denominate that problematized space of the sex/gender system, the whole package of physical and cultural distinctions between women and men, more simply under the rubric "gender." I do this in order to reduce the likelihood of confusion between

1. Gayle Rubin, "The Traffic in Women: Notes toward a 'Political Economy' of Sex," in *Toward an Anthropology of Women*, ed. Rayna Reiter (New York: Monthly Review Press, 1975), pp. 157–210 [except as indicated, all notes are Sedgwick's]. [RUBIN (b. 1949), American anthropologist and queer theorist—editor's note.]

Biological Essential Individually immanent		Cultural Constructed Relational
	Constructivist Feminist Analysis	
chromosomal sex	——————	gender gender inequality
	Radical Feminist Analysis	
chromosomal sex reproductive relations sexual inequality	——————	reproductive relations sexual inequality
	Foucault-influenced Analysis	
chromosomal sex	——— reproduction ———	sexuality

Figure 1. Some Mappings of Sex, Gender, and Sexuality

"sex" in the sense of "the space of differences between male and female" (what I'll be grouping under "gender") and "sex" in the sense of sexuality.

For meanwhile the whole realm of what modern culture refers to as "sexuality" and *also* calls "sex"—the array of acts, expectations, narratives, pleasures, identity-formations, and knowledges, in both women and men, that tends to cluster most densely around certain genital sensations but is not adequately defined by them—that realm is virtually impossible to situate on a map delimited by the feminist-defined sex/gender distinction. To the degree that it has a center or starting point in certain physical sites, acts, and rhythms associated (however contingently) with procreation or the potential for it, "sexuality" in this sense may seem to be of a piece with "chromosomal sex": biologically necessary to species survival, tending toward the individually immanent, the socially immutable, the given. But to the extent that, as Freud argued and Foucault[2] assumed, the distinctively sexual nature of human sexuality has to do precisely with its excess over or potential difference from the bare choreographies of procreation, "sexuality" might be the very opposite of what we originally referred to as (chromosomal-based) sex: it could occupy, instead, even more than "gender" the polar position of the relational, the social/symbolic, the constructed, the variable, the representational (see Figure 1). To note that, according to these different findings, *something* legitimately called sex or sexuality is all over the experiential and conceptual map is to record a problem less resolvable than a necessary choice of analytic paradigms or a determinate slippage of semantic meaning; it is rather, I would say, true to quite a range of contemporary worldviews and intuitions to find that sex/sexuality *does* tend to represent the full spectrum of positions between the most intimate and the most social, the most predetermined and the most aleatory, the most physically rooted and the most symbolically infused, the most innate and the most learned, the most autonomous and the most relational traits of being.

2. MICHEL FOUCAULT (1926–1984), French philosopher and historian of ideas. SIGMUND FREUD (1856–1939), Austrian founder of psychoanalysis [editor's note].

If all this is true of the definitional nexus between sex and sexuality, how much less simple, even, must be that between sexuality and gender. It will be an assumption of this study that there is always at least the potential for an analytic distance between gender and sexuality, even if particular manifestations or features of particular sexualities are among the things that plunge women and men most ineluctably into the discursive, institutional, and bodily enmeshments of gender definition, gender relation, and gender inequality. This, too, has been posed by Gayle Rubin:

> I want to challenge the assumption that feminism is or should be the privileged site of a theory of sexuality. Feminism is the theory of gender oppression. . . . Gender affects the operation of the sexual system, and the sexual system has had gender-specific manifestations. But although sex and gender are related, they are not the same thing.[3]

This book will hypothesize, with Rubin, that the question of gender and the question of sexuality, inextricable from one another though they are in that each can be expressed only in the terms of the other, are nonetheless not the same question, that in twentieth-century Western culture gender and sexuality represent two analytic axes that may productively be imagined as being as distinct from one another as, say, gender and class, or class and race. Distinct, that is to say, no more than minimally, but nonetheless usefully.

Under this hypothesis, then, just as one has learned to assume that every issue of racial meaning must be embodied through the specificity of a particular class position—and every issue of class, for instance, through the specificity of a particular gender position—so every issue of gender would necessarily be embodied through the specifity of a particular sexuality, and vice versa; but nonetheless there could be use in keeping the analytic axes distinct.

An objection to this analogy might be that gender is *definitionally* built into determinations of sexuality, in a way that neither of them is definitionally intertwined with, for instance, determinations of class or race. It is certainly true that without a concept of gender there could be, quite simply, no concept of homo- or heterosexuality. But many other dimensions of sexual choice (auto- or alloerotic,[4] within or between generations, species, etc.) have no such distinctive, explicit definitional connection with gender; indeed, some dimensions of sexuality might be tied, not to gender, but *instead* to differences or similarities of race or class. The definitional narrowing-down in this century of sexuality as a whole to a binarized calculus of *homo-* or *hetero-*sexuality is a weighty fact but an entirely historical one. To use that fait accompli as a reason for analytically conflating sexuality per se with gender would obscure the degree to which the fact itself requires explanation. It would also, I think, risk obscuring yet again the extreme intimacy with which all these available analytic axes do after all mutually constitute one another: to assume the distinctiveness of the *intimacy* between sexuality and gender might well risk assuming too much about the definitional *separability* of either of them from determinations of, say, class or race.

3. Gayle Rubin, "Thinking Sex: Notes for a Radical Theory of the Politics of Sexuality," in *Pleasure and Danger: Exploring Female Sexuality*, ed. Carole S. Vance (Boston: Routledge & Kegan Paul, 1984), pp. 307–8. [For this essay, see above—editor's note.]

4. Based in eroticism focused on the other. "Autoerotic": based in eroticism focused on the self [editor's note].

It may be, as well, that a damaging bias toward heterosocial[5] or heterosexist assumptions inheres unavoidably in the very concept of gender. This bias would be built into any gender-based analytic perspective to the extent that gender definition and gender identity are necessarily relational between genders—to the extent, that is, that in any gender system, female identity or definition is constructed by analogy, supplementarity, or contrast to male, or vice versa. Although many gender-based forms of analysis do involve accounts, sometimes fairly rich ones, of intragender behaviors and relations, the ultimate definitional appeal in many gender-based analysis must necessarily be to the diacritical[6] frontier between different genders. This gives heterosocial and heterosexual relations a conceptual privilege of incalculable consequence. Undeniably, residues, markers, tracks, signs referring to that diacritical frontier between genders are everywhere, as well, internal to and determinative of the experience of each gender and its intragender relations; gender-based analysis can never be dispensed with in even the most purely intragender context. Nevertheless it seems predictable that the analytic bite of a purely gender-based account will grow less incisive and direct as the distance of its subject from a social interface between different genders increases. It is unrealistic to expect a close, textured analysis of same-sex relations through an optic calibrated in the first place to the coarser stigmata of gender difference.[7] The development of an alternative analytic axis—call it sexuality—might well be, therefore, a particularly urgent project for gay/lesbian and antihomophobic inquiry.

It would be a natural corollary to Axiom 2 to hypothesize, then, that gay/lesbian and antihomophobic inquiry still has a lot to learn from asking questions that feminist inquiry has learned to ask—but only so long as we don't demand to receive the same answers in both interlocutions. In a comparison of feminist and gay theory as they currently stand, the newness and consequent relative underdevelopment of gay theory are seen most clearly in two manifestations. First, we are by now very used to asking as feminists what we aren't yet used to asking as antihomophobic readers: how a variety of forms of oppression intertwine systemically with each other; and especially how the person who is disabled through one set of oppressions may *by the same positioning* be enabled through others. For instance, the understated demeanor of educated women in our society tends to mark both their deference to educated men and their expectation of deference from women and men of lower class. Again, a woman's use of a married name makes graphic at the same time her subordination as a woman and her privilege as a presumptive heterosexual. Or, again, the distinctive vulnerability to rape of women of all races has become in this country a powerful tool for the racist enforcement by which white people, including women, are privileged at the expense of Black people of both genders. That one is *either* oppressed *or* an oppressor, or that if one happens to be both, the two are not likely to

5. A term used to described social bonds between persons of different genders, by analogy with *homosocial*, the notion Sedgwick explores in *Between Men* (1985; see above) [editor's note].

6. Distinctive; serving as a distinguishing feature [editor's note].

7. For valuable related discussions, see Katie King, "The Situation of Lesbianism as Feminism's Magical Sign: Contests for Meaning and the US Women's Movement, 1968–1972," *Communication* 9 (1986): 65–91, special issue, "Feminist Critiques of Popular Culture," ed. Paula A. Treichler and Ellen Wartella; and Teresa de Lauretis, "Sexual Indifference and Lesbian Representation," *Theatre Journal* 40 (May 1988): 155–77.

have much to do with each other, still seems to be a common assumption, however, in at any rate male gay writing and activism,[8] as it hasn't for a long time been in careful feminist work.

Indeed, it was the long, painful realization, *not* that all oppressions are congruent, but that they are *differently* structured and so must intersect in complex embodiments that was the first great heuristic[9] breakthrough of socialist-feminist thought and of the thought of women of color.[1] This realization has as its corollary that the comparison of different axes of oppression is a crucial task, not for any purpose of ranking oppressions, but to the contrary because each oppression is likely to be in a uniquely indicative relation to certain distinctive nodes of cultural organization. The *special* centrality of homophobic oppression in the twentieth century, I will be arguing, has resulted from its inextricability from the question of knowledge and the processes of knowing in modern Western culture at large.

The second and perhaps even greater heuristic leap of feminism has been the recognition that categories of gender and, hence, oppressions of gender can have a structuring force for nodes of thought, for axes of cultural discrimination, whose thematic subject isn't explicitly gendered at all. Through a series of developments structured by the deconstructive understandings and procedures sketched above, we have now learned as feminist readers that dichotomies in a given text of culture as opposed to nature, public as opposed to private, mind as opposed to body, activity as opposed to passivity, etc. etc., are, under particular pressures of culture and history, likely places to look for implicit allegories of the relations of men to women; more, that to fail to analyze such nominally ungendered constructs in gender terms can itself be a gravely tendentious move in the gender politics of reading. This has given us ways to ask the question of gender about texts even where the culturally "marked" gender (female) is not present as either author or thematic.

8. Gay male–centered work that uses more complex models to investigate the intersection of different oppressions includes Gay Left Collective, eds., *Homosexuality: Power and Politics* (London: Allison & Busby, 1980); Paul Hoch, *White Hero Black Beast: Racism, Sexism, and the Mask of Masculinity* (London: Pluto, 1979); Guy Hocquenghem, *Homosexual Desire*, trans. Daniella Dangoor (London: Allison & Busby, 1978); Mario Mieli, *Homosexuality and Liberation: Elements of a Gay Critique*, trans. David Fernbach (London: Gay Men's Press, 1980); D. A. Miller, *The Novel and the Police* (Berkeley: University of California Press, 1988); Michael Moon, "'The Gentle Boy from the Dangerous Classes': Pederasty, Domesticity, and Capitalism in Horatio Alger," *Representations*, no. 19 (summer 1987): 87–110; Michael Moon, *Disseminating Whitman* (Cambridge: Harvard University Press, 1990); and Jeffrey Weeks, *Sexuality and Its Discontents: Meanings, Myths, and Modern Sexualities* (London: Longman, 1980).

9. Explanatory, serving as an aid to problem solving [editor's note].

1. The influential socialist-feminist investigations have included Michèle Barrett, *Women's Oppression Today: Problems in Marxist Feminist Analysis* (London: Verso, 1980); Zillah Eisenstein, ed., *Capitalist Patriarchy and the Case for Socialist Feminism* (New York: Monthly Review Press, 1979); and Juliet Mitchell, *Women's Estate* (New York: Vintage, 1973). On the intersections of racial with gender and sexual oppressions, see, for example, Elly Bulkin, Barbara Smith, and Minnie Bruce Pratt, *Yours in Struggle: Three Feminist Perspectives on Anti-Semitism and Racism* (New York: Long Haul Press, 1984); BELL HOOKS [Gloria Watkins], *Feminist Theory: From Margin to Center* (Boston: South End Press, 1984); Katie King, "Audre Lorde's Lacquered Layerings: The Lesbian Bar as a Site of Literary Production," *Cultural Studies* 2, no. 3 (1988): 321–42; Audre Lorde, *Sister Outsider: Essays and Speeches* (Trumansburg, N.Y.: Crossing Press, 1984); Cherríe Moraga, *Loving in the War Years: Lo que nunca paso por sus labios* (Boston: South End Press, 1938); Cherrié Moraga and GLORIA ANZALDÚA, eds., *This Bridge Called My Back: Writings by Radical Women of Color* (Watertown: Persephone, 1981; rpt. ed., New York: Kitchen Table, Women of Color Press, 1983); and Barbara Smith, ed., *Home Girls: A Black Feminist Anthology* (New York: Kitchen Table, Women of Color Press, 1983). Good overviews of several of these intersections as they relate to women and in particular to lesbians, can be found in Ann Snitow, Christine Stansell, and Sharon Thompson, eds., *The Powers of Desire: The Politics of Sexuality* (New York: Monthly Review/New Feminist Library, 1983); Vance, *Pleasure and Danger*; and de Lauretis, "Sexual Indifference."

The dichotomy heterosexual/homosexual, as it has emerged through the last century of Western discourse, would seem to lend itself peculiarly neatly to a set of analytic moves learned from this deconstructive moment in feminist theory. In fact, the dichotomy heterosexual/homosexual fits the deconstructive template much more neatly than male/female itself does, and hence, importantly differently. The most dramatic difference between gender and sexual orientation—that virtually all people are publicly and unalterably assigned to one or the other gender, and from birth—seems if anything to mean that it is, rather, sexual orientation, with its far greater potential for rearrangement, ambiguity, and representational doubleness, that would offer the apter deconstructive object. An essentialism of sexual object-choice is far less easy to maintain, far more visibly incoherent, more visibly stressed and challenged at every point in the culture than any essentialism of gender. This is not an argument for any epistemological or ontological privileging of an axis of sexuality over an axis of gender; but it is a powerful argument for their potential distinctness one from the other.

Even given the imperative of constructing an account of sexuality irreducible to gender, however, it should already be clear that there are certain distortions necessarily built into the relation of gay/lesbian and antihomophobic theory to a larger project of conceiving a theory of sexuality as a whole. The two can after all scarcely be coextensive. And this is true not because "gay/lesbian and antihomophobic theory" would fail to cover heterosexual as well as same-sex object-choice (any more than "feminist theory" would fail to cover men as well as women), but rather because, as we have noted, sexuality extends along so many dimensions that aren't well described in terms of the gender of object-choice at all. Some of these dimensions are habitually condensed under the rubrics of object-choice, so that certain discriminations of (for instance) *act* or of (for another instance) *erotic localization* come into play, however implicitly and however incoherently, when categories of object-choice are mobilized. One used, for instance, to hear a lot about a high developmental stage called "heterosexual genitality," as though cross-gender object-choice automatically erased desires attaching to mouth, anus, breasts, feet, etc.; a certain anal-erotic salience of male homosexuality is if anything increasingly strong under the glare of heterosexist AIDS-phobia; and several different historical influences have led to the de-genitalization and bodily diffusion of many popular, and indeed many lesbian, understandings of lesbian sexuality. Other dimensions of sexuality, however, distinguish object-choice quite differently (e.g., human/animal, adult/child, singular/plural, autoerotic/alloerotic) or are not even about object choice (e.g., orgasmic/nonorgasmic, noncommercial/commercial, using bodies only/using manufactured objects, in private/in public, spontaneous/scripted).[2] Some of these other dimensions of sexuality have had high diacritical importance in different historical contexts (e.g., human/animal, autoerotic/alloerotic). Others, like adult/child object choice, visibly do have such importance today, but without being very fully subsumed under the hetero/homosexual binarism. Still others, including a host of them I haven't mentioned or couldn't think of, subsist in this culture as nondiacritical differences, differences that seem to make little difference beyond themselves—except that the hyperintensive structuring of sexuality in our culture sets several of them, for instance, at

2. This list owes something to Rubin, "Thinking Sex," esp. pp. 281–82.

the exact border between legal and illegal. What I mean at any rate to emphasize is that the implicit condensation of "sexual theory" into "gay/lesbian and antihomophobic theory," which corresponds roughly to our by now unquestioned reading of the phrase "sexual orientation" to mean "gender of object-choice," is at the very least damagingly skewed by the specificity of its historical placement.

* * *

1990

HAMID DABASHI
b. 1951

Hamid Dabashi is a literary historian and cultural critic who both criticizes and reconfigures contemporary postcolonial theory. He does so by focusing on the changing geographical and historical fortunes of Persian literature over a tumultuous fourteen-century span during which empires and forms of imperialism rose and fell while borders expanded and contracted. From its earliest days, Persian literature was—and remains—transnational, multiethnic, cosmopolitan, and resistant. Viewed historically, the human subject position of the Persian-language writer is characterized not by ethnic or national sovereignty but by fluidity, which leads to a distinctive and supple literary humanism. The comparatively recent arrivals in central Asia of modern European imperialism, Orientalism, and nationalism at present distort the contours of Persian culture. Dabashi argues, "Because it emerged and thrived in multiple and multinational empires, Persian literary humanism does not exclusively belong to any single, contemporary, postcolonial nation-state. Afghanistan, India, Iran, Pakistan, Tajikistan, and any number of other central Asian states have identical claim on its long and meandering history—and rightly so."

Dabashi was born in Ahvaz, a city in southwest Iran in the oil-rich province of Khuzestan. After graduating from college in Tehran, he moved to the United States to complete his graduate studies, and in 1984 he received a dual doctoral degree in sociology of culture and Islamic studies from the University of Pennsylvania. His dissertation, which he completed under the guidance of the Freudian cultural critic Philip Rieff, examined Max Weber's theory of charismatic authority. Today Dabashi is the Hagop Kevorkian Professor of Iranian Studies and Comparative Literature at Columbia University, and his interests and expertise span areas as diverse as Islamism, politics, cinema, the performing arts, and literature. As a social activist, he has supported progressive and reform movements in the Middle East and has written extensive commentaries on them.

Dabashi has published two dozen books on a variety of subjects, including religion, history, cinema, and social criticism. Our selection comes from his book *The World of Persian Literary Humanism* (2012), in which he recasts the classical Persian tradition known as *adab*, a word that combines literature and etiquette, as Persian literary humanism. According to Dabashi, this humanism was "a normative and moral *space* consistently cultivated within an imperial imaginary rather than a mere ethnic uprising replicating Arab tribalism." By explicitly avoiding the usual Persian/Arabic dualism, this formulation enables us to observe a literature facing numerous challenges over time, independent of any cultural confinements such as Arab domination. Dabashi traces the epochs of Persian literature as it transforms over time from tribal ethnos (*nezhad*) to logos (*sokhan*) in the earliest period, when the Persian language was a shared tongue through most of the Islamic world, to a later period, after the Mongol invasion, when a universalizing ethos (*hanjar*) supported linguistic autonomy and self-reference. The huge resulting body of work that also included other forms of arts eventually resulted in "chaos" (*ashub*) when artists encountered Europe in the modern period and when the crumbling royal courts and religious institutions no longer sponsored creativity—which, once emancipated, flourished in the new public sphere.

The World of Persian Literary Humanism begins by asking about the meaning of "being human." It then contends that the question has been approached mostly from a Western perspective. To pose it from a non-European point of view, Dabashi examines the 1,400-year Persian literary tradition, conceptualized as the subversive subconscious of Islamic civilization. When the Islamic conquests began in the seventh century, the Arab invaders disparaged Persian culture for effeminate frailty and sexual wrongdoing, among other things. Consequently, Persian literary humanism has long spoken from a hidden and defiant viewpoint, encapsulating a subversive protean subjectivity and creativity. The subversive humanistic views expressed by the poets Sa'di (ca. 1213–1292) and Ferdowsi (ca. 935–ca. 1020), for example, stand in contrast to the transcendental Islamic scholasticism of the medieval period. Dabashi criticizes Eurocentric and Orientalist scholars for ignoring these aspects of history, an oversight he sees as shared by today's departments of comparative literature and English. In discussing matters related to Persian literary humanism, he therefore engages throughout the book with European and American cultural critics such as THEODOR ADORNO, FREDRIC JAMESON, and EDWARD W. SAID.

Dabashi is critical of reigning concepts not only of world literature and third world literature but also of nationalism and globalization. Imposed on Persian literature, these modern Eurocentric formulations distort its long distinctive history. In addition, he is critical of the racialization of multiracial Persian literature currently associated with the Islamic Republic of Iran (established in 1979). Along the way Dabashi finds fault for similar reasons with previous histories of Persian literature, singling out E. G. Browne's *A Literary History of Persia*, vol. 1 (1902), and Zabihullah Safa's five-volume *Tarikh-e Adabiyat dar Iran* (1959–89, *History of Literature in Iran*).

Dabashi himself is open to criticism on various counts, including a failure to take into account the earliest Persian writers. The literature produced in the Persian Empire (whose boundaries stretched beyond those of contemporary Iran in all directions) is often conveniently divided by scholars into three periods: ancient or pre-Islamic (before 651 C.E.), medieval or classical (tenth century to the end of the nineteenth century), and contemporary or modern. Dabashi avoids the error of ignoring the vast body of works produced by Persian speakers after their conquest by Arab Muslims (in 651) that were written in Arabic, the language of the victor. Yet he does not examine works produced before the medieval period in earlier forms of the Persian language, Old Persian and Pahlavi (Middle Persian). That body of pre-Islamic work had an affinity with Zoroastrianism and other Iranian ancient religions. The roots of the "resistance" or the subconscious component subverting "Arab imperialism" that Dabashi sees in medieval Persian humanism can also be sought in pre-Islamic culture and civilization, which to this day continue to inform some important social formulations, including Dabashi's own dichotomy of humanism and scholasticism. A scrutiny in *The World of Persian Literary Humanism* of ancient texts, added to its examination of Iranians' works in Arabic, would have strengthened its findings.

Nevertheless, Dabashi's formulation helps us see Persian literary criticism in a new light. When Abd al-Qaher Jorjani (d. 1078) attempted to write a theory of literary criticism in *Mysteries of Eloquence*, Persian poetry had begun to flourish in areas where the local Persians had managed to establish rule independent of the central Islamic caliphate. Classical poetry, often associated at the time with the court (in Dabashi's formulation, the pre-chaotic ethos stage), sees itself as autonomous and self-aware, a vibrant arena for debates regarding concrete forms of literary criticism. A number of poets, including Farrukhi Sistani (d. 1037), Unsuri Balkhi (d. 1039), and Ferdowsi, commented on and at times criticized the works of their rivals and predecessors, participating in criticism and theory within the genre of poetry itself. Many of these classical literary men viewed criticism as the act of distinguishing between the desirable and undesirable, the good and the bad, structure and disorder, poetry and prose—distinctions all in some way informed by ancient but still vital pre-Islamic Zoroastrian dichotomies.

Such debates continue into modern and contemporary times. Contemporary Persian literature, including its schools of literary criticism, has often engaged, both in support and in opposition, with the dominant ideology of its time. Here, what Dabashi calls "Persian literary humanism" has itself become part of an ideological school, displaying a sort of modern scholasticism. In the decades prior to the 1979 Iranian Revolution, for example, literary criticism—like the production of literature itself—was highly influenced by Marxist literary theory. Since the end of the nineteenth century, nationalism, Islam, and feminism have also significantly affected the critical approaches to Persian literary humanism. Such movements contributed heavily to the formation of leftist discourse and to the social turmoil that led to popular uprisings in the late 1970s and ended the rule of the shah, Mohammad Reza (which was immediately replaced by conservative clerical rule). As Dabashi and others have noted, the Persian word for literature, *adabiyat*, comes from the word *adab*, meaning "culture," "proper behavior," "politeness," and "pleasant demeanor": Persian literature remains intricately tied to Persian ethics, politics, and history.

The World of Persian Literary Humanism **Keywords:** Globalization, Literary History, Modernity, Nationhood, Postcolonial Theory, Vernacular Language

From The World of Persian Literary Humanism

From *Conclusion: Literary Humanism as an Alternative Theory to Modernity*

* * *

A COSMOPOLITAN WORLDLINESS

How do people become "human"—and what does that exactly mean? I have thought this question through a literary humanism that expands over 1,400 years, extends over vast global empires that culminate in the Mongol conquest of the vastest imperial territory in human history, and finally divides into three magnificent Muslim empires of the Mughals, the Safavids, and the Ottomans,[1] before it faces the catalytic effects of the mighty European imperialism. My central thesis in this book is predicated on a systematic

1. The Mughals (1526–1759), of Turkic-Mongol origin, ruled most of northern India; the Safavids (1501–1736) ruled Iran, establishing Shiite Islam as the state religion; and the Ottoman Empire (1299–1922), also of Turkic-Mongol origins, was created in Asia Minor (modern Turkey) but at its height, under the rule of Suleiman the Magnificent (1494–1566), controlled land on several continents. Under Genghis Khan (1162–1227) and his sons and grandsons, the Mongols, a people of central Asia, stretched west to Europe and east to China; their empire reached its greatest extent in 1368.

articulation of a theory of subjection (how do people become human?) embedded in the heart of Persian literary humanism—a theory that proposes a *metamorphic sublation*[2] of a succession of defining tropes that lead it from one phase to another, from its initial *ethnos/nezhad* when it was formed in opposition to Arab imperialism of the seventh century, to its definitive *logos/sokhan* when an expansive number of transnational empires took over the region, to its transformative *ethos/hanjar* when the fragile knowing subject at the heart of Persian poetic imagination became self-evident, and ultimately to its defiant *chaos/ashub* when it exited its habitual habitat at royal courts under the duress of its fateful encounter with European imperialism and perforce crafted for itself a *public space* it called *vatan* (homeland, nation). The self-transformative disposition of this fragile subject has been at the heart of Persian literary humanism and its cosmopolitan worldliness. My principal objection to the present state of literary studies is that the current location of this panoramic development under the self-designated "Western" hegemony has hitherto preempted the theoretical assessment of its metamorphic history. I have sought to expose and overcome this blind spot.

I propose this *metamorphic transformation* of the central tropes of Persian literary humanism to be a far more thematically accurate register of normative subjection and moral agency than a generic, Eurocentric, or even anticolonial mode of subject formation, which is the most recent globalized context in which Persian literary humanism has found itself, performing in the shadow of European imperialism. This imperialism should not be privileged over all the preceding forms of imperialism—from the Achamanids and the Sassanids[3] in the pre-Islamic period to the Arabs in the seventh century to the Mongols in the thirteenth century or the Mughals or the Ottomans in the sixteenth century. I have sought to give historical depth and geographical range to our understanding of literary humanism as the modus operandi of subjection. When the transnational empires of the Ghaznavids and Seljuqids took over from the early Iranian dynasties of the Saffarids and the Samanids,[4] they forced the early transformation of *ethnos* into *logos* because *sokhan*[5] was now the paramount factor of Persian literary humanism and not the presumed ethnicity of the poet or the literati. When the global empire of the Mongols took over, the *logos* of Persian literary humanism was at the center of its self-universalizing literary cosmopolitanism and pushed the *logos* toward the formation of an *ethos* as the matrix of the multiple measures of being human. From the Timurid period[6] forward, the eventual formation of a *paralingual semiosis*[7] at the juncture of Persian poetry and painting extended the potential transmutation of *ethos* into *chaos* in the context of the four adjacent empires of the Mughals, the Safavids, the Otto-

2. Explained by Dabashi as a transformative negation of dominant historical realities and associated tropes, which affected *ethnos* (Persian ethnic identity), *logos* (Persian language), *ethos* (Persian mind-set/character), and "chaos" (the rise of modern Persian nationalism and the public sphere).
3. The last pre-Islamic Persian empire (224–651). The Achamanids, or Achaemenians (559–330 B.C.E.), were an ancient Persian dynasty.
4. The Saffarids (861–900) ruled a large area in what is now eastern Iran, and the Samanids (819–999) were based in eastern Iran and Uzbekistan. The Ghaznavids (977–1186), of Turkic origin, ruled northeastern Iran, Afghanistan, and northern India, while the empire of the Seljuqids or Seljuqs (1016–1157) included Mesopotamia, Syria, Palestine, and most of Iran.
5. Proper and beautiful speech: *sokhan* became the dominant discourse (*logos*) of the people (*ethnos*).
6. That is, 1370–1507; the Timurid dynasty encompassed modern-day Iran, Iraq, and most of Syria and Afghanistan and was heavily influenced by Persian culture.
7. That is, the full geographical, linguistic, and cultural richness of its historical discourse including pitch, rhythm, and body language.

mans, and the Russians, where the tropic transfusion was exacerbated in the context of encounter with a fifth, aterritorial, constellation of empires, approaching from Europe. This latest encounter finally forced Persian literary humanism out of its habitat inside the royal court, while disallowing it entrance into the new imperial formation, which was decidedly against any privileging of the Persian language and literature—as best evident in the Macaulay Act (English Education Act) of 1835.[8] This fortuitous development finally resolved the historical paradox of Persian literary humanism and forced it to craft and cultivate a tertiary space—between its own courts that it had abandoned and the European courts that did not welcome it—which became the public space it now termed *nation* and *nationalism*, in which Persian literary humanism effectively set up its own edifice, finally in its new home, where it belonged.

This whole process has resulted in a manner of literary subjection as a self-conscious worlding of the world that European Orientalism and American literary criticism alike have silenced by their respective narrative urges to flatten out the world against the presumed centrality of the allegory of "the West" that they habitually take for real by way of allegorizing the rest of the world. The literary nationalism of the postcolonial world has unknowingly corroborated this episteme[9] by competing in producing ethnic nationalist historiographies of their own. Contrary to the very grain of this train of thinking about literary history and theory, the locus classicus[1] of the first three phases of Persian literary humanism—from *ethnos* to *logos* to *ethos*—has been the royal courts of vast empires, while the location of the very last phase, *chaos*, is the public space that Persian literary imagination has termed *vatan* (homeland, nation) and *vatanparasti* (nationalism) and carved in between the courts it exited and the courts into which it had no entry. Both European Orientalism and American literary criticism have misread this notion of *vatan* (homeland, nation)—one by *ethnicizing* Persian literary humanism in its entirety and the other by colonizing it as "Third World literature," or even worse "world literature," and thus declaring "all Third World texts . . . are national allegories."[2] This collusion of false readings is an expression of nothing more innocent/sinister than simply being embedded in one imperial imaginary—the one that calls itself "the West"—that has imperially overcome and glossed over the historical fact and continued resonance of other worldly empires—and is now casting its extended shadow over the long history that has preceded it.

The final phase of Persian literary humanism in its encounter with European imperialism was in fact a liberating and emancipatory moment in its long and adventurous history. Persian literary humanism was formed and coagulated in an initial encounter with Arab imperialism in *ethnic* terms (Persian vs. Arab). It went through multiple transformative phases and was finally delivered to a renewed cosmopolitan worldliness in its encounter

8. An act of the (British) Council of India that required English, rather than native tongues (Sanskrit and Persian), to be the language of instruction in British-funded schools.

9. The underlying structure of knowledge and beliefs during a historical period (an important term in the writings of the French philosopher and historian of ideas MICHEL FOUCAULT); literally, "knowledge" (Greek).

1. Usually "classic example," but here *locus* has its more literal Latin meaning of "place."

2. FREDRIC JAMESON, "Third World Literature in an Age of Multinational Capitalism," *Social Text* 15 (Autumn 1986): 69 [Dabashi's note]. Third World: the "under developed" countries, many of them former colonies, now dominated by highly industrialized "First World" (largely Western) nations in a global economy.

with European imperialism—though this time around it was not confined within the royal courts but acted from the assured centrality of a public space it had in fact envisioned, imagined, articulated, and inhabited. The success of the Constitutional Revolution of 1906–1911 was interrupted by a corrupt monarchy (the Pahlavis) and an even more tyrannical theocracy (the Islamic Republic)[3]—a historical development that was nevertheless necessary to get rid of two overriding illusions that the monarchy and the theocracy had any claim over that public space, which was not theirs. The royal courts and the juridical scholasticism had been identically overcome and run over by that public space. Successive revolutionary uprisings in Iran from the mid-nineteenth century forward effectively claimed that public space for the democratic aspirations that had initiated it in the first place and filled it with poets, musicians, dramatists, filmmakers, journalists, scholars, each in his or her own way articulating the specifics of that public sphere.

The cosmopolitan worldliness embedded in Persian literary humanism enters a renewed pact with its history in this final phase. By *chaos/ashub* in this phase I mean a morphological transmutation of the *ethos/hanjar* of Persian literary humanism into multiple registers, thematically and formally alternating and unstable in its multiple formations, positing a dissipative mood of creativity that dismantles any regime of *knowledge/power* production and its presumed subject.[4] *Chaos* is a condition of dissolute creativity whereby the positivist epistemes of *systematicity, longevity, endurance,* or even *coherence* finally yield to the open-ended expanse of a dissipative alterity. Poetry, fiction, drama, journalism, photography, music, and film keep producing, exhausting, and overcoming one another's capacities. Creative turbulence and formal disequilibria become the markers of a *mood* in the literary act that breaks any appearance of symmetry or systematicity and becomes negatively stochastic, formally disruptive—as perhaps best evident in Nima's poetic revolution, Hedayat's subversive fiction, or Kiarostami's[5] fusion of fact and fantasy in his cinema. The creative mood remains constant in its synergy but keeps changing from prose to poetry, from complicated to simplified verse, from metric prosody to Nimaic revolt, from poetry to painting, from fiction to film, from painting to photography, from scholarship to journalism, etc. The more unstable these systems become, the more tyrannical and solid do appear the ruling regimes—which are farthest removed from the destablizing fact of these alternating subsystems. In its varied and evasive forms, literary humanism keeps dodging power and metamorphosizing itself, from one genre to another, so that no *ruling regime* ever would be able to lay any claim to it. The transmutation of *ethos* into *chaos* is the last and most creatively dissipative disposition of Persian liter-

3. The Pahlavi dynasty began in 1925 with Reza Shah (1878–1944), who had led a military coup; his son Mohammad Reza was driven out of the country by the 1978–79 uprising that ended in the founding of the Islamic Republic of Iran, led by a Shiite cleric.

4. This notion of *chaos*, which I detect as the last mode of subjection in Persian literary humanism, is very much akin to what [Barbara] Riebling theorizes in her "Remodeling Truth, Power, and Society: Implications of Chaos Theory, Nonequilibrium Dynamics, and Systems Science for the Study of Politics and Literature," in *After Poststructuralism: Interdisciplinarity and Literary Theory*, ed. Nancy Easterlin and Riebling (Evanston, Ill.: Northwestern University Press, 1993), pp. 177–201 [Dabashi's note].

5. Abbas Kiarostami (1940–2016), a prominent Iranian filmmaker. Nima Yushij (1895–1960), father of modern Persian poetry. Sadeq Hedayat (1903–1951), Persian novelist.

ary humanism—a creative effervescence corresponding to the globality of the public space that it has crafted and that it commands.

* * *

AN ALTERNATIVE THEORY TO MODERNITY

As both a philosophical predicament and a social phenomenon, "modernity" was and remains a principally European problem—while grappling with it in either hermeneutic or postmodern directions provides comparative clues as to how the question of the subject is to be understood or overcome on the colonial domains of that globally presumptuous "modernity." To the degree that it became a global issue, whether by the colonized imagination of those who wanted "to modernize," or else the modernity of the means of colonial conquest and domination,[6] it has cast a European imperial map on the mind, body, soul, and history of the people thus dominated, "modernized," and ruled. Even in the moments of their defiance, colonized people under the normative and imaginative spell of "the modern West" have reversely corroborated the European condition of "modernity" as their problem too.

What I have offered in this book on Persian literary humanism (*Adab*)[7] is not in opposition to the European project of modernity—which remains a perfectly valid and thriving issue in its immediate European context (however falsely globalized). What I have outlined in some historical and textual detail is an alternative vision of subjection, whereby humans become human, in the very last stages of which, when the literary manner of subjection moved from the centrality of *ethnos,* to *logos,* to *ethos,* to *chaos* it was in fact eventually located and articulated within the European imperial context—carrying (obviously) the stamp of its previous imperial framings into newer encounters. In doing so, I have altogether discarded the "tradition *versus* modernity" binary—itself a manufactured opposition superimposed on Persian literary humanism to further universalize the European project of modernity. The far more accurate, grounded, and nuanced morphological succession of *ethnos, logos, ethos,* and *chaos* within successive imperial contexts includes, but does not privilege, the encounter of this humanism with European empires. It does not deny the historic significance of European imperialism—but it does not privilege it with deciding the entire history of the human race. What I have offered here, as a result, is not a theory of alternative modernity—but an alternative theory *to* modernity, the vision of an inner dynamic to the logic and rhetoric, poetic and aesthetic of Persian literary humanism, of its manner of subjection, of how was it that it made humans all too human.

Though I have narrated my story within the vast imperial context of Persian literary humanism, it would still be an exercise in futility and entirely self-delusional to purpose any idea of "humanism" a decade into the twenty-first century and not to confront the traumatizing matter of European philosophical antihumanism or pretend that it did not exist, or otherwise

6. The best example of how "modernizing" was "colonizing" for the non-European world is in Timothy Mitchell's classical study, *Colonizing Egypt* (Berkeley: University of California Press, 1991) [Dabashi's note].

7. Literature, excellent literature; also, good manners (Persian).

introduce and treat the masterpieces of a rich literary tradition like relics of bygone ages gathered in a museum. My intention has been to produce an account of Persian literary humanism that will speak directly to the challenging traumas of our time and not turn a magnificent literary heritage into an object of Orientalist curiosity, fetishized items of a nationalized literary history, or else the exclusive and privileged scholarly preoccupation of academically secluded "Persianists." I have offered a theory of Persian literary humanism as the modus operandi of a sustained historical mode of subjection as an alternative theory of European modernity, and I have defended the case of a literary humanism based on the particular, contingent, and unstable mode of subjection integral to this humanism. At the receiving end of European imperialism and perforce its philosophical predicaments, the normative hegemony of European humanism and antihumanism requires a sustained argument from within the context of historical experiences silenced precisely by that hegemony.

In making my case, I have also suggested that the literary act creates its own autonomous and even sovereign truth claims, so that through a Bakhtinian act of *heteroglossia*[8] it becomes self-propelling, a kind of detranscendentalized alterity, its signs meaning nothing outside their signature in the text they signal, whereby everything that is said is said through an always already decentered and mislaid knowing subject that denies itself evident agency precisely at the moment that it authors itself. The mortal fragility of *Adami* (human) that keeps historicism at bay but incorporates history into the literary is such that the literary become self-revelatory, positing an evident historicality to the literary act. The autonomous fragility of *Adami* at the heart of Persian literary humanism joins the parabolic prose and poetry that Saʿdi[9] had made proverbial to stage the indeterminacy of the knowing subject and the effective dissolution of the narrator to present it as not just autonomous of the scholastic but in fact defiant of its own sovereignty over the fate of successive empires it served and subverted at one and the same time.

The problem of antihumanism is internal to the European philosophical crisis, globalized by virtue of the power of philosophical narratives that have subsumed the non-European philosophical domains to their self-assured dominance. Positing literary humanism by way of overcoming the problem of the subject points to the evident fact that the self-revelatory disposition of Persian *Adab* has no false self-systematizing subject to authorize or deauthorize it. Edward Said could not resolve the problem of humanism because he remained very much limited within Aristotelian (Western) mimesis[1] and never worked seriously through any other literary tradition than English—Arabic or otherwise. So theoretically he opted for a *quantitative* resolution of the problem of the subject by asking that more "world literature" be added to the repository of English and comparative literature project. This does not resolve the issue—it in fact exacerbates it if it ends up assimilating other wordly literatures into what the English and comparative literature programs call "world literature." English and comparative literature in fact

8. In the theory of the Russian literary theorist MIKHAIL M. BAKHTIN (1895–1975), the complex stratification of a language into different social dialects, class dialects, generational dialects, professional jargons, and so on.

9. Persian poet (ca. 1213–1292), a major figure in classical Persian literature.

1. See the *Poetics* of ARISTOTLE (384–322 B.C.E.), above. SAID (1935–2003), Palestinian-born American literary and cultural critic and social activist.

digests and absorbs anything that comes its way—whether through Franco Moretti's "distant reading,"[2] Gayatri Spivak's "close reading,"[3] David Damrosch's "world literature,"[4] or Edward Said's "critical humanism"[5]—all housed and launched in and from the English and comparative literature departments. The sovereign subject (falsely self-conscious) continues to gobble up all you feed it into something the (European) knowing subject can grasp and thus devour. The whole idea of "world literature" is an English and comparative literature department menu of exotic appetizers to wet the dulled appetites of their professors (there is only so much Dickens and Austen[6] that one can have)—and scarce has anything to do with worldly literatures they thus carve up and serve to one another. Said's idea of including more "world literature" in the arsenal of "Western humanism" not only does not cure that gluttonous appetite for exotic food—it positively fattens the self-totalizing subject to disfigured proportions.

Working the problem through Persian literature (or the writing idiomaticity[7] and reading protocols of any other non-European literature) reveals a variety of ways in which the sovereign subject is never formed to falsely organize any knowledge to begin with, for it to be in need of an antihumanism to dismantle it, for the "human" at the heart of (Persian) literary humanism is no knowing subject you can corner and name. The self-signifying literary act is always cognizant of its idiomaticity and as such has no false systematizing subject at its center to decenter, for its shifting, lyrical "heart" cannot hold, for its mimetic acts are always already momentary and indivisible into subject and object, and ipso facto self-destruct, for that "self" is always already somewhere else.

LITERATURE AND TRANSNATIONAL EMPIRES

To come to terms with the cosmopolitan worldliness of Persian literary humanism and the enduring significance of the manner in which it has posited the very fragile notion of *human*, it is imperative not to reduce it to a "national literature" and at this stage in fact to reverse the combined distortions of the Orientalist and nationalist readings of it back to its imperial history, and thus come to terms with its transnational, and even more accurately non-national, origins and disposition. The idea will be unsettling to ethnic nationalists of all sorts—Iranians, Afghans, Tajiks, Indians, Turks, Arabs,[8] and so on—but the transnational and imperial context of this literary humanism is written into the very textual and contextual facts of its history, the very global disposition of its idiomaticities.

Because it emerged and thrived in multiple and multinational empires, Persian literary humanism does not exclusively belong to any single, contemporary, postcolonial nation-state. Afghanistan, India, Iran, Pakistan,

2. For FRANCO MORETTI's notion of "distant reading," see his "Conjectures on World Literature," *New Left Review* 1 (January–February 2000) [Dabashi's note].
3. For a rebuttal to Moretti's position on "distant reading" and articulation of her notion of "close reading," see GAYATRI CHAKRAVORTY SPIVAK, *Death of a Discipline* (New York: Columbia University Press, 2005) [Dabashi's note].
4. See David Damrosch, *What Is World Literature?* (Princeton, N.J.: Princeton University Press, 2003) [Dabashi's note].
5. See Edward W. Said, *Humanism and Democratic Criticism* (New York: Columbia University Press, 2004) [Dabashi's note].
6. Two English novelists who are staples of the canon, Charles Dickens (1812–1870) and Jane Austen (1775–1817).
7. Idiomatic quality.
8. All peoples who were at different times part of Persian imperial formations.

Tajikistan, and any number of other central Asian states have identical claim on its long and meandering history—and rightly so. Ferdowsi, Nezami, Rumi, Sa'di, Hafez,[9] and so on—these are the master practitioners of Persian poetry performed within multiple imperial contexts, having emerged on a continuum that has thrived on the primacy of *logos* and not *ethnos*—so that by "Persian" we mean, and we can only mean, a *language* and not any false pretense to a *race* or *ethnicity*, which in this case is entirely meaningless. There are no people, no nation, no race, and no ethnicity called "Persian." Any such assumption is entirely fictitious. There is only a language called *Farsi,* or *Dari,* or *Tajik* in Iran, Afghanistan, or Tajikistan, respectively—for all of which there is only one word in English: Persian.

It is thus fundamentally flawed to call Ferdowsi's *Shahnameh,*[1] for example, an "Iranian national epic." It is not. It is as much Afghanistan or Tajikistan's "national epic" as it is Iran's—if we are to commit the fallacy of attributing a product of an *imperial* age to a postcolonial nation-state. Ferdowsi's *Shahnameh* is not a *national* epic of Iran or any other postcolonial nation-state. It is an *imperial* epic, like all other epics, as indeed all epics are products of imperial imaginations—empires that by nature are transnational—in this case Iranians, Turks, Mongols, Indians, and so on. The contemporary Iran, Afghanistan, Tajikistan, Pakistan, India, and so on, have been integral to multiple empires over the last 1,400 years and beyond. It is that historic fact that must inform our reading of their literary products, and not the postcolonial nation-states that are, without a single exception, the product of the encounter of the last of those empires with European imperialism. Ferdowsi's *Shahnameh* belongs to Persian literary humanism so far as "Persian" is the linguistic designation of a *literary* tradition and not the *racial* register of any postcolonial nation and its anxiety of longevity and authenticity. Today when we say "English literature" it will have to include anything from Shakespeare to Hemingway, to Salman Rushdie, to Nadine Gordimer, to V. S. Naipaul[2]—meaning various literary expressions in English and within the real or imaginative contours of the British Empire, and thus "English" here means a language and not a race, an ethnicity, or a breed. The same is true for French or Spanish literature. Spanish literature includes anything from Cervantes to Juan Goytisolo, to Gabriel García Márquez, to Mario Vargas Llosa.[3] It is a literary allusion predicated on a language that was made imperially global, and certainly not on a race. The same is true for "Persian literature"—it can only mean the language, for there are no people called "Persians." Today, there are Iranians, Indians, Pakistanis, Afghans, Tajiks, and so on, as the nationals of various postcolonial nation-states—and they all have identical claims on various stages of Persian literature. Understood in its own terms, Ferdowsi's *Shahnameh* was and remains an imperial epic, produced in the context of

9. Classical Persian poets: Ferdowsi (ca. 935–ca. 1020), Nezami or Nizami (ca. 1141–1209), Rumi (1207–1273), and Hafez or Hafiz (1325/26–1390).

1. *The Book of Kings* (977–1010), a long epic poem that presents a history of the kings of Persia and is the most beloved of classical Persian works, celebrated not just in Iran but throughout the region influenced by Persian culture.

2. All writers in the English language, though only William Shakespeare (1564–1616) was born in England: Ernest Hemingway (1899–1961) is American; Rushdie (b. 1947), born in India; Nadine Gordimer (1923–2014), South African; and Naipaul (b. 1932), born in Trinidad.

3. Peruvian writer (b. 1936). Miguel de Cervantes (1547–1616), Spanish novelist. Goytisolo (1931–2017), Spanish writer who lived in self-imposed exile in France and Morocco. García Márquez (1927–2014), Colombian novelist.

two successive and transnational empires, about another forgone imperial age—half-legendary and half-historical. This is not to rob Iranians, Afghans, and so on, of their "national epic"—it is to give it back to them with a far more global imaginary in which they should read their epic.

Ferdowsi's *Shahnameh* was and has remained an imperial epic, transnational, multinational, cross-national, and thus nonnational, for the simple reason that the current postcolonial national boundaries have been drawn over and against multiple imperial mappings from the Samanids to the Safavids down to the Qajars.[4] *Shahnameh* is the product and the manifestation of an imperial imagination. The problem becomes particularly jarring when contemporary Iranian scholars, staunch and fanatical nationalists against the very grain of historical facts, call *Shahnameh* "their" national epic, and then if the Turks or the Afghans call Rumi "their" poet or the Azerbaijanis call Nezami "their" poet, the nationalists get very angry. Ferdowsi's birth and death place of Tus is much closer to Herat and Samarqand than it is to Tehran or Shiraz or Ahvaz.[5] By what authority or reason can an Isfahani or a Tabrizi or an Ahvazi[6] have a claim to the *Shahnameh* that a resident of Herat or Samarqand or Dushanbe[7] does not? If the fact that Ferdowsi's birthplace is within the current borders of Iran were to be the measure, then Iranians will instantly lose Rumi who was born in Balkh in Afghanistan and died in Konya in Turkey. And if they were to cite the fact that Rumi wrote much of his poetry in Persian, they would then instantly lose Avicenna and al-Ghazali and al-Tabari[8] who wrote most of their significant work in Arabic—and thus Iraqis, Egyptians, Kuwaitis, Bahrainis, and Qataris have more right to them than would the people of Hamadhan, Tabarestan,[9] or Tus.

All of these false problems arise when we juxtapose the colonially calibrated postcolonial map of the world—a gift of European colonialism that keeps giving—on the historical mapping of the world in which these poets and by extension Persian literary humanism wrote and was produced. The historical experience of Persian literary humanism is predicated on the fact that it began as the ethnic assumption of Iranians in juxtaposition to a racialized Arab sense of superiority in the late Umayyad and early Abbasid[1] dynasties. But as soon as the Saffarids and Samanid dynasties yielded power to the Turkic empires of the Ghaznavids and the Seljuqids, that *ethnos* as the trope of Persian literary humanism had moved to become a *logos* and "Persian" meant language, not race or ethnicity, for it was, in discourse and disposition, the imperial language and culture of vastly transnational—if we were to use the term *national* ahistorically here—empires. But even that *logos* did not stand still, and because of developments internal to Persian literary humanism and external to its varied imperial contexts, it transmuted

4. A Turkmen dynasty (1785–1925) that ruled over Persia, but defeats in 19th-century wars with Russia reduced its territory to Iran's present-day limits.

5. Tehran, Shiraz, and Ahvaz are in present-day Iran, as is Tus, while Herat is in Afghanistan and Samarqand is in Uzbekistan.

6. A resident of Ahvaz. Isfahan is a city in west-central Iran; Tabriz is a city in extreme northwestern Iran.

7. Capital of Tajikistan.

8. All major Muslim intellectual figures born in Iran. Avicenna (the Latin name of Ibn Sina, 980–1037) was a philosopher, scientist, and physician; al-Ghazali (1058–1111), a theologian and mystic; and al-Tabari (ca. 839–923), the author of a foundational commentary on the Qur'an.

9. Region of northern Iran. Hamadhan: region of western Iran.

1. The second Muslim dynasty (750–1258), which traced its lineage back to an uncle of the Prophet Muhammad; it overthrew the first, the Umayyad (661–750), which was descended from a clan of the Quraysh tribe and established itself after a fierce struggle following the death of Muhammad.

to *ethos* during the Timurid period—a development that was exacerbated during the Mughal, Safavid, Ottoman, and Russian[2] empires. But even that *ethos,* put into full practice in the crucible of its encounter with European imperialism, initially in India but later in the rest of the Persianate world, eventually transmuted into *chaos/ashub* as the productive trope of Persian literary humanism in the age of its active interface with colonial domination in the age of European imperialism. Precisely at the moment of its highest self-transcendence, European Orientalism recast it in *ethnic* terms and, in the work of E. G. Browne[3] in particular, drew it toward *ethnos.* In this flawed and misbegotten (even catastrophic) development, European Orientalists like Browne were still infinitely superior to American postmodernist (even Marxist) literary theorists like Fredric Jameson—for if the ethnicizing of Persian literary humanism by the Orientalists was predicated on deep knowledge but poor theory, the postmodernists misapplied European theories that were, and have remained, constitutionally blind to alternative imperial maps of the world before their empire took over and shaped their critical imagination.

The problem with nationalist literary history is not just historical. It is also categorical. It creates much confusion and anarchy for the literary historian who insists on forcefully nationalizing a transnational history. Here is the late Zabihollah Safa, the preeminent Iranian literary historian, trying to explain what he is doing in tracing that history in India:

> A point that needs to be explained is that in this chapter more than in others the domain of my discussions will cross the boundaries of Iran and extend to all those lands/sarzamins that Persian poetry and Adab has reached. I will go after Persian speaking/Farsi-guy poets, writers, and their patrons and those who have served Persian Adab anywhere in Asia Minor/Rum, India, and Transoxiana,[4] that is necessary. I will discuss the life and work of any master Persian-speaker that I find in these lands, whether Iranian, Indian, or from Asia Minor/Rum. Every patron of Persian poets and prose stylists in these discussions is like a brother to me, who has arisen from my Kuy-o-Barzan/ neighborhood and has lived with me—be he a Turk, a Tajik, someone from Asia Minor, or an Indian. I very much hope that this task, which is diluted by no political intentions, will not become an excuse for [scurrilous] interpretations of the sort we have known and recognize—and that no dust of gloom is caused by the steps taken by my thoughts.[5]

This anxiety is caused when the literary historian crosses the current borders of Iran and moves to India to complete his historical narrative. But that anxiety becomes entirely misplaced when we remember that Persian literature produced in the Mughal court or in south Asia had a perfectly natural habitat within an empire adjacent to the Safavid and Ottoman empires, long

2. The empire lasted from 1721 to 1917.
3. British scholar of the Middle East and Orientalist professor of Eastern languages (1862–1926); he traveled much in Persia and wrote numerous books, most notably *A Literary History of Persia* (4 vols., 1902–24).
4. Literally, the region beyond the Oxus River (the Amu Darya, in central and west Asia); it corresponds roughly to modern Uzbekistan and parts of Turkmenistan, Tajikistan, and Kazakhstan. It was part of the Achaemenid Persian empire.
5. See Zabihollah Safa, *Tarikh-e Adabiyat dar Iran* (*History of Literature in Iran*) (Tehran: Tehran University [and other] Press, 1959–89), 5: 1:420 [Dabashi's note].

before the European empires eventually took them over and redrew the map of the world, within which Zabihollah Safa found himself when writing his history. Literary historians must be able freely to navigate from the Timurids to the Mughals back to the Qajars and so on without the slightest sense of anxiety if they cross over the political boundaries of the map that European empires have imposed on them and their world. Without that crossing over something constitutional, something definitive to Persian literary cosmopolitanism will be lost to the historian.

Another effect of this forced nationalization of literature is the racialization of literary taste, as is evident in the expression *Sabk-e Hendi,*[6] propagated at the height of Reza Shah's ultra-nativist nationalism by the Iranian literary critic Mohammad Taqi Bahar,[7] who in a poem said:

> Their thoughts were weak and their imagination weird;
> Poetry was filled with themes but non-attractive—
> Devoid of elegance.
> Every poet was carrying the burden of meaning;
> Much painfully—
> For which reason Sabk-e Hendi was so garish.[8]

Upon this racialized characterization and dismissal of a literary taste in the Mughal court, yet another literary historian, Yahya Aryanpour, further adds his own gloss and in fact endorses it by saying that at this point "poetry [had] left the royal court and degenerated in the hands of the masses (*beh dast-e ammeh oftad*)."[9]

The same racialization of literary taste is also evident in the thinking of Orientalist scholar Jan Marek about Persian literature in India: "It might indeed be difficult to point out a comparable example in the history of the world literature of a language being adopted, and to find another country having mastered a foreign language to such a degree as was the case with Persian in India. The Indians have contributed very really to the rise of Persian literature, and to them we owe many of its most brilliant pages."[1] Persian was not "adopted" in the Mughal court, nor was it a "foreign language" to its domain. Indians have as much contributed to Persian, Hindi, or English literature as to Bengali, Guajarati, or Marathi—and they are all "their own languages." Here is the perfect example of how Orientalist ethnic nationalization of Persian literature completely distorts the imperial (transnational) context of Persian language and alienates people from their own language and literature.

Against the grain of these false categories, and placing Persian literary humanism in its proper context of successive empires, I have suggested in the unfolding of Persian literary humanism as a historic event the successive formation of four nodal tropes—*ethnos, logos, ethos,* and *chaos.* If I were to give a comparative example of this idea it would be Hayden White's *Metahistory,* in which he suggests the historical unfolding of four major tropes

6. Persian language poets in India.
7. Noteworthy professor, poet, journalist, historian, and politician (1884–1951), whose works exhibit Iranian nationalistic fervor. For Reza Shah Pahlavi, see p. 2295, n. 3.
8. See Yahya Aryanpour, *Az Saba ta Nima* (*From Saba to Nima*) (Tehran: Zavvar, 1972–95), 1:9 [Dabashi's note].
9. Ibid., 1:8 [Dabashi's note].
1. See Jan Rypka, ed., *History of Iranian Literature* (Dordrecht, Holland: D. Reidel, 1968), 732–33 [Dabashi's note].

(from *metaphor* to *metonymy*, to *synecdoche*, and finally *irony*).[2] White offers these tropes by way of alerting historians to the use of linguistic devices in the writing of history. I offer these four morphological tropes by way of an historical unfolding of the modus operandi of literary production, moving from one imperial setting to another, and thus repositing the un/knowing subject at the heart of the literary act. This succession of the tropics of subjection in Persian literary imagination is to me a far more accurate and rooted grounding of historical agency than the European project of modernity. If we follow this train of thought and course of development internal to the logic and rhetoric of Persian literary humanism in multiple imperial contexts over a period of 1,400 years, the question is no longer the possibility of an alternative modernity, but the fact that this course of development is an entirely indifferent, autonomous matrix of subjection to the European philosophical problem of modernity and its contingent crisis of the subject. The imperial and discursive force of European modernity and particularly its gestation as "colonial modernity" have forced themselves on our reading of the non-European worlding in those imported and super/imposed terms. The question here is not to disregard, bypass, or ignore the historical fact of European imperialism, but not to privilege it over all the other previous imperial settings in which Persian literary humanism has been acted out. The Seljuqid, Mongol, Timurid, Mughal, and Safavid empires each had their own distinct impact on Persian literary humanism. Against the grain and texture of this history, the "nationalization" of Persian literature has been instrumental in deworlding it—unplugging it from its historical habitat and casting it into a postcolonial context that assigns it a "Third World" status and glosses over its historic worldliness. My insistence in this book on restoring its historicity and denationalizing its imperial context is to retrieve its cosmopolitan worldliness and its multiple manner of subjection that includes *ethnos* but is not limited to it.

FAREWELL TO OUR ORIENTALISTS

The enduring impact of Orientalism, ethnic nationalism, and area studies on the study of Persian (and all other non-European) literary humanism has been quite dire. Up until now, the study of Persian literature, both classical and modern, has suffered from a depth of theoretical poverty that it has inherited from Orientalism and extended into nativist nationalism—an aversion to theory that mirrors a tired and belabored face-off between the two overlapping narratives of Orientalism and ethnic nationalism. This poverty of insight is a closed-circuit system that has now degenerated into an Islamic Republic giving lip service to "the glorious Iranian culture" by way of covering up its atrocious abuses of a world religion. Exceedingly competent textual criticism has of course created reliable and heavily glossed texts—from Ferdowsi's *Shahnameh* to Mehdi Akhavan Sales's[3] poetry—but the reading

2. See HAYDEN WHITE, *Metahistory: The Historical Imagination in Nineteenth-Century Europe* (Baltimore: Johns Hopkins University Press, 1975) [Dabashi's note]. The four figures of speech are not usually viewed as forming a historical progression. *Metaphor* implies comparison between two unlike entities; in *metonymy*, one word is used to mean another to which it is connected by any way other than similarity; *synecdoche*, a form of metonymy, is a naming of a part of something for its whole, or vice versa; and in *irony*, the real meaning is hidden or contradicted by the literal meaning of the words.

3. A pioneer in Persian free verse (1929–1990).

of those texts very much suffers from an analytical positivism that has very little beyond a nativist-nationalist, analytical regurgitation of old-fashioned Orientalism. Outside Iran the scene is not any better with a bizarre combination of watered-down Orientalism and literary comparatist cross-breeding in the impoverished field of "Iranian Studies." The answer to all of this is not an "application" of high theory to "Third World literature"—an even more paralyzing cliché. What is needed is theorization of the history of this literature from within itself, predicated on a detailed textual hermeneutics[4] that is informed by larger theoretical concerns in an organic (not mechanical) way—and always in conversation with other literary settings but not beholden to them.

As Orientalism alienated and othered Persian literature to its own authorship and readership, Iranian literary nativism allegorized it for a nationalist politics, both concealing the worldliness of Persian literary humanism—which in the twentieth century ran away from strictly literary terms and manifested itself in cinema, art, music, drama, and so on. The driving forces of Persian literary humanism became runaway metaphors—decentering it into multiple subject formation. While Orientalist and ethnic nationalist narratives assimilated Persian literary humanism into the colonial and postcolonial world, in parallel terms, English and comparative literature de-worlded it altogether by considering it part of "the Third World Literature." What I have sought to do in this book is to retrieve its historic worldliness, a worldly cosmopolitanism that extends from India through Iran to the Mediterranean basin. That world is now lost to the overextended narratives of Orientalism and ethnic nationalism competing, complementing, and even cross-metaphorizing each other.

The European Orientalist writing on Persian literary history, best exemplified by E. G. Browne and continued to this day with full force and through multivolume projects, has categorically glossed over the inner dynamics of its emotive universes and assimilated downward toward the colonial context of its reception. Browne and other European Orientalists cast Persian literary humanism in ethnic nationalist terms precisely at a moment when for more than 1,000 years after the successful transmutation of its *ethnos* into *logos* and then to *ethos*, it had finally reached a momentous point of self-transmutation into *chaos*—bringing the paralingual semiosis it had achieved during the Timurid and Safavid eras to full literary production within the European imperial context and the creative formation of a public space. Entirely blinded to this tropic development, E. G. Browne and other Orientalists, deeply learned as they were, wasted their vast knowledge of Persian literature on a theoretically flat-footed narration of Persian literary humanism in an *ethnos* tone from beginning to end.

Recasting the masterpieces and thereby the history of Persian literature into a decidedly different narrative than the one canonized by Orientalists and exacerbated by the nativist nationalists, I have offered literary humanism as a key concept in comparative literary studies. I use and locate the concept of "literary humanism" somewhere between its articulation by the detailed textual hermeneutics of George Makdisi[5] and its later compara-

4. Theory of interpretation.
5. Prominent American scholar of Islamic studies (1920–2002).

tive theorization by Edward Said and then extend it into a specifically Persian literary context. Persian literature has historically been cast into the shadow of Arabic literary humanism, which in turn prevented George Makdisi from seeing and realizing that humanism was a reality sui generis and should not be framed in the shadow of "Western" literary humanism or Islamic scholasticism. The domain of Persian (or Arabic, Turkish, Urdu) literary humanism was the vast arena of worldly literatures (in the plurality of worlds they have occupied) and most certainly not as "world literature," a historical fact that Edward Said never seriously studied during his lifelong preoccupation with humanism, with a mode of knowledge production that did not implicate an all-knowing, imperial, subject position. My objective has been to posit literary humanism as a reality sui generis, autonomous of any alterity to "Western humanism," and adjacent to Islamic scholasticism (my conversation with George Makdisi), and to predicate it on an autonormative constellation of subject positions that posits humanism without implicating an all-knowing subject in the making of a cosmopolitan worldliness (my conversation with Edward Said). Thus, in conversation with two monumental figures in the study of literary humanism, I have sought to make my case.

2012

DICK HEBDIGE
b. 1951

In his sharp yet sympathetic examinations of youth subcultures, Dick Hebdige displays the theoretical and political commitments of cultural studies. His work—along with that of STUART HALL—exemplifies cultural studies in its contemporary British incarnation. Hebdige combines semiotic analysis with questions of political resistance and effectiveness in his famous study of marginalized subcultures like punk. The result is a cultural studies approach resembling but distinct both from sociological investigations of deviance and from mainstream literary criticism of printed texts.

Born into a London working-class family, Hebdige received an M.A. from the celebrated University of Birmingham Centre for Contemporary Cultural Studies during its 1970s heyday. He taught at Goldsmith's College of the University of London from 1984 to 1992 before moving to the United States to become dean of Critical Studies at the California Institute of the Arts; he subsequently taught in the Film and Media Studies Department at the University of California at Santa Barbara.

Our selection from *Subculture: The Meaning of Style* (1979) illustrates cultural studies' effort to engage analytically and politically with popular culture. How can the cultural critic, either from the outside or as a participant-observer, honor the expressive products of a subculture while also realistically assessing the relation of those expressed values, beliefs, and feelings to mainstream culture? The last thing that Hebdige wants is to repeat the condescending conclusion often found in radical Marxist analyses, which reflexively fault various marginalized groups for diverting their attention from the "real" site of political struggle to invest their energy in sideshows and trivialities. The rebellious attitudes of punk and other youth subcultures—expressed through music, dance, dress, and slang—should be taken seriously in their own right and not viewed as allegories or displaced symptoms of class struggle. Instead, repeating a strategy akin to that adopted by the Dada movement after World War I, Hebdige characterizes much subcultural expression as "noise." Post–World War II British youth subcultures deliberately and provocatively eschew meaning, and even try to destroy it. All attempts at explanation—whether by Marxists focused on class struggle, or by sociologists with their talk of juvenile delinquency, or by psychologists preoccupied with dysfunctional families—that seek to clarify a subculture's behavior and expressive forms represent efforts to co-opt, incorporate, or tame what aspires to stand as radically disruptive, as irreducibly alien. An almost inevitable dialectic is set in motion. The more the experts (speaking in the newspapers or from positions in academia or the government) try to explain the outsiders, the more outrageous the outsiders are pushed to become in their desire to transcend all explanation.

Besides mobilizing the connections between punk and the historical avant-gardes of Dada and surrealism, Hebdige also appropriates the concept of "moral panic" from the sociologist Stan Cohen to explain anxious and hysterical societal responses to radical disruptions of normal meanings. The heightened rhetorics of denunciation that characterize moral panics serve to consolidate approved models of behavior and justify the punitive actions taken against deviants. Not surprisingly, queer theorists such as EVE KOSOFSKY SEDGWICK have also considered the dynamics of moral panics. Hebdige shows that initial attempts to mark the deviant Other as beyond the pale are almost always accompanied by follow-up efforts to domesticate those same deviants. He points to newspaper articles about punks and their mothers that situate the deviant within the family structure and consumer society.

Hebdige's sympathy with the anarchistic urge to disrupt established signification, to produce "noise," stands in tension with the general semiotic basis of his own analysis. The main claim of semiotics is that every object, practice, and relation within human societies is enmeshed in a systemic web of codes and conventions that constitute the specific item's meaning and value. Like Stuart Hall, Hebdige understands "culture" to designate the semiotic processes and practices through which people, actions, and things acquire significance. Against MATTHEW ARNOLD's view of culture as the best that has been said and known, cultural studies considers culture to include the whole way of life of a people or a subset of that people. In RAYMOND WILLIAMS's phrase, "culture is ordinary." In this understanding of culture, that a woman has blond hair is a fact; but the meaning of being "a blonde" is culturally produced and varies in different cultures or in different subcultures. Thus, to be "a blonde" could be an advantage in Hollywood and a disadvantage at Harvard. Different societies vary not just in what they do but in how they understand and value what they do. Influenced by semiotics, cultural studies attends both to the significance attached to various objects and activities in a particular society *and* to the linguistic and symbolic processes through which significance is produced. It sets code breaking and deviance against preexisting cultural conventions and norms.

Two further consequences of cultural studies' semiotic approach should be noted. Literary texts, like other artworks, are neither more nor less important than any other cultural artifact or practice. Keeping the emphasis on how cultural meanings are produced, circulated, and consumed, the investigator will focus on art or literature insofar as such works connect with broader social factors, not because they possess some intrinsic interest or special aesthetic value. The subsumption of literature into the broader cultural field explains the widespread perception that cultural studies poses a threat to literary criticism.

In addition, the turn to semiotics connects British cultural studies to structuralism and poststructuralism, especially in elevating social codes to a position of importance over individual speakers. The production of significance is not simply a subjective or individual process; it is communal. Meanings are assigned within language, not by selves but within systems, and things come to us already laden with meanings. Even when semioticians view this process as dynamic, with meanings being constantly created and reconfigured, the conflicts that generate change are not between selves but between larger social forces. Hebdige reads punk as a social symptom, not as an isolated outbreak or as the production of a few geniuses or rebels.

Many of the British cultural studies writers, however, retain a leftist populism that wants to celebrate the creative and resistant political agency of ordinary men and women. As a result, Hebdige, like Hall, is less ready than are some French theorists to jettison all faith in small-scale action and choice. This reluctance explains his focus on "subcultural style," which can be defined as the creative and often oppositional variations that come into existence as marginal groups reshape the meanings made available by preexisting dominant codes. In the terms of FERDINAND DE SAUSSURE's influential linguistic theory, style is *parole*, the utterances of actual speakers: they use the words and grammatical structures of the already-existing *langue* (language system), but they still have considerable latitude in how they combine its elements at any particular moment.

Yet the semiotic and structuralist framework makes it impossible to step outside of signifying practices altogether. It is therefore unclear how the anarchist (or Dadaist or punk musician) could avoid signifying and actually produce pure noise. The radical's gestures still acquire meaning through their relationship (a hostile one in this case) to prevailing modes of meaning. Thus, it is not surprising that Hebdige, in our selection, turns quickly from the notion of "noise" to the mechanics of "incorporation." The discussion thereby shifts from a battle between meaning and nonmeaning to a struggle over how the punk musician's antics will be understood. What meanings will punk acquire in the cultural processes of meaning making, and whose understanding of punk will come to dominate? At this point in his argument, Hebdige appears quite pessimistic. The strategies by which the mainstream and dominant culture can incorporate and thus tame the challenging subcultures appear destined to win.

The reasons for this pessimism are complex—and probably better understood as marking the site of a troubled theoretical and political nexus than as supporting any kind of definitive judgment. In many ways, Hebdige is tackling the same questions that take center stage in JUDITH BUTLER's feminist work. What room is available for selves to maneuver within the signifying systems that constitute them and the conditions within which they live and act? "Commodities," Hebdige writes, "can be symbolically 'repossessed' in everyday life, and endowed with implicitly oppositional meanings." The famous punk safety pin stuck through an eyebrow would be an example. A focus on the creative "resignification" of received commodities, practices, institutions, and values recurs throughout the work of cultural studies scholars, and opposition and resistance preoccupy their research. Against any and all images of passive consumers or silent majorities, they note that contemporary populations regularly work within constrained circumstances to turn what society offers them into something that, to at least some extent, serves their own needs and purposes. Hebdige is considering the extent to which resignification simultaneously occurs within the prevailing systems of signification, using the materials available within those systems, *and* is capable of transforming received materials and even prevailing systems by expressing things "differently." Thus, for example, while he worries that punk is always already working in the dominant commodity form of consumer capitalism, he also wants to avoid claiming that punk therefore cannot be transformative in any way.

We might say that the underlying problem in Hebdige's own work is how to provide a convincing portrait of social transformation once the notion of revolution is tacitly abandoned. Changes will be incremental (it seems), will always involve some steps sideways for every step forward, and will be difficult to assess at any particular social site. So the process of conflict "invariably ends with the simultaneous diffusion and defusion of the subcultural style." That result is simultaneously progressive (more people are now party to this radical critique) and regressive (the critique itself is less radical than it was at first). For cultural studies, media and market play a big role in disseminating and blunting the forces of social opposition.

Hebdige's—and cultural studies'—residual Marxism is apparent when he turns to the concept of "ideology" at the end of our selection. He accepts the French post-structuralists' critique of the orthodox Marxist definition of ideology as the inevitable dominance in a given society of the ideas, beliefs, and values of the ruling class. From ROLAND BARTHES, Hebdige takes the idea that ideology "naturalizes." In other words, ideology obscures the class orientation of dominant beliefs, habits, practices, and social structures by presenting all of these things as inevitable, as just the way (the only possible way) things are, as "natural." But he uses Barthes's theory of ideology to make a traditional Marxist observation, pointing out that the dominant ideology rewrites the punk subculture to obscure its origins in and protest against a set of "real historical contradictions" manifest in "unemployment . . . and narrow options." In the ideological rewriting carried out by the media and through the official discourses of experts and government bureaucrats, a collective protest against those economic contradictions is turned into the expressive talents displayed by individual musicians who have no connection to the neighborhoods, social class, and subcultures from which they emerge. The success of the few who become "stars" serves as proof of an "open society" that rewards hard work and merit. Ideology renders thinking of achievement in individualistic terms "natural," and thereby obscures the social conditions that largely determine the chances for "success."

Hebdige's use of the concept of ideology indicates that he is no simple celebrant of youth culture. Symbolic repossessions are not, in themselves, effective acts of political resistance. Though "implicitly" oppositional, they are not direct challenges to the powers that be. In particular, the challenges offered by contemporary youth subcultures, notably punks, are "expressed obliquely, in style"—particularly in visual styles suited to a society in which television, advertising, and film foster spectacle. Because these gestures are oblique, an analyst like Hebdige is needed to interpret and translate them into political statements. At minimum, he implies that the disenchanted young can become effective political agents only if they attain some self-understanding of the larger social field, if they are not blinded by ideological obfuscations.

Hebdige here touches by implication on one of the most conflicted topics in cultural studies. Some practitioners of cultural studies worry that presenting the activities of subcultures as either inchoate or misplaced resistance, which require an intellectual to transform them into something truly political, is elitist. Conversely, to simply celebrate a marginal group's creativity and spectacular acts of resistance leaves everything as it is, within a contemporary scene that hardly appears to be transformed by various acts of "symbolic repossession." Yet we should also wonder just how and when we would be able to detect social transformation. What yardstick would differentiate "real" or "substantial" from "superficial" changes? There are no easy answers to these questions. In part, the relation of the aesthetic to the political is at issue. A concern with style is, after all, a traditional aesthetic concern. To what extent can style—or any kind of artistic expression today—be an articulation of a socially critical position or, more dramatically, a potentially transformative political act?

Subculture: The Meaning of Style **Keywords:** Cultural Studies, Ideology, Institutional Studies, Marxism, Media, Popular Culture, Semiotics

From Subculture: The Meaning of Style

Chapter 6

SUBCULTURE: THE UNNATURAL BREAK

I felt unclean for about 48 hours.
—G.L.C. councillor after seeing a concert by the Sex Pistols[1]
(reported *New Musical Express*, 18 July 1977)

[Language is] of all social institutions, the least amenable to initiative. It blends with the life of society, and the latter, inert by nature, is a prime conservative force.
—Saussure,[2] *Course in General Linguistics* (1974)

Subcultures represent 'noise' (as opposed to sound): interference in the orderly sequence which leads from real events and phenomena to their representation in the media. We should therefore not underestimate the signifying power of the spectacular subculture not only as a metaphor for potential anarchy 'out there' but as an actual mechanism of semantic disorder: a kind of temporary blockage in the system of representation. As John Mepham has written:

> Distinctions and identities may be so deeply embedded in our discourse and thought about the world whether this be because of their role in our practical lives, or because they are cognitively powerful and are an important aspect of the way in which we appear to make sense of our experience, that the theoretical challenge to them can be quite startling.[3]

Any elision, truncation or convergence of prevailing linguistic and ideological categories can have profoundly disorienting effects. These deviations briefly expose the arbitrary nature of the codes which underlie and shape all forms of discourse. As Stuart Hall has written (here in the context of explicitly political deviance):

> New . . . developments which are both dramatic and 'meaningless' within the consensually validated norms, pose a challenge to the normative world. They render problematic not only how the . . . world is defined, but how it ought to be. They 'breach our expectancies'. . . .[4]

Notions concerning the sanctity of language are intimately bound up with ideas of social order. The limits of acceptable linguistic expression are prescribed by a number of apparently universal taboos. These taboos guarantee the continuing 'transparency' (the taken-for-grantedness) of meaning.

Predictably then, violations of the authorized codes through which the social world is organized and experienced have considerable power to provoke and disturb. They are generally condemned, in Mary Douglas' words, as 'contrary to holiness' and Lévi-Strauss has noted how, in certain primitive myths,

1. Rock band (1975–78), fronted by Sid Vicious and Johnny Rotten, that epitomized punk music: aggressive, antiestablishment, and nihilistic. G.L.C.: the Greater London Council, which governed the city of London.
2. FERDINAND DE SAUSSURE (1857–1913), Swiss linguist; for his *Course in General Linguistics*, originally published in 1915, see above.
3. John Mepham, "The Theory of Ideology in Capital," *Working Papers in Cultural Studies* 6 (1974), University of Birmingham [Hebdige's note].
4. Stuart Hall, "Deviancy, Politics and Media," in P. Rock and M. McIntosh (eds.), *Deviance and Social Control* (Tavistock, 1974) [Hebdige's note]. HALL (1932–2014), Jamaican-born British cultural critic.

the mispronunciation of words and the misuse of language are classified along with incest as horrendous aberrations capable of 'unleashing storm and tempest'.[5] Similarly, spectacular subcultures express forbidden contents (consciousness of class, consciousness of difference) in forbidden forms (transgressions of sartorial and behavioural codes, law breaking, etc.). They are profane articulations, and they are often and significantly defined as 'unnatural'. The terms used in the tabloid press to describe those youngsters who, in their conduct or clothing, proclaim subcultural membership ('freaks', 'animals . . . who find courage, like rats, in hunting in packs'[6]) would seem to suggest that the most primitive anxieties concerning the sacred distinction between nature and culture can be summoned up by the emergence of such a group. No doubt, the breaking of rules is confused with the 'absence of rules' which, according to Lévi-Strauss, 'seems to provide the surest criteria for distinguishing a natural from a cultural process'.[7] Certainly, the official reaction to the punk subculture, particularly to the Sex Pistols' use of 'foul language' on television[8] and record,[9] and to the vomiting and spitting incidents at Heathrow Airport[1] would seem to indicate that these basic taboos are no less deeply sedimented in contemporary British society.

TWO FORMS OF INCORPORATION

> Has not this society, glutted with aestheticism, already integrated former romanticisms, surrealism, existentialism and even Marxism to a point? It has, indeed, through trade, in the form of commodities. That which yesterday was reviled today becomes cultural consumer-goods, consumption thus engulfs what was intended to give meaning and direction.[2]

5. Mary Douglas, *Purity and Danger* (Penguin, 1967), and Claude Lévi-Strauss, *The Elementary Structures of Kinship* ([1949; trans.] Eyre and Spottiswoode, 1969) [Hebdige's note]. Douglas (1921–2007), British cultural anthropologist. Lévi-Strauss (1908–2009), French structuralist anthropologist.
6. This was part of a speech made by Dr. George Simpson, a Margate magistrate, after the mod–rocker clashes of Whitsun, 1964. For sociologists of deviance, this speech has become *the* classic example of rhetorical overkill and deserves quoting in full: "These long-haired, mentally unstable, petty little hoodlums, these sawdust Caesars who can only find courage like rats, in hunting in packs" (quoted in P. Cohen, "Sub-cultural Conflict and Working Class Community," *Working Papers in Cultural Studies* 2 [1972], University of Birmingham) [Hebdige's note]. "Mod–rocker clashes": fights between 2 subcultures, the clean-cut and motor scooter–riding "mods" and the leather-clad, motorcycle-riding "rockers," that broke out in Margate and other beach resorts in southern England in May 1964 over a holiday weekend (in observance of Whitsunday, or Pentacost, the 7th Sunday after Easter).
7. Lévi-Strauss, *The Elementary Structures of Kinship* [Hebdige's note].
8. On 1 December 1976 the Sex Pistols appeared on the Thames twilight programme *Today*. During the course of the interview with Bill Grundy they used the words 'sod,' 'bastard' and 'fuck.' The papers carried stories of jammed switchboards, shocked parents etc. and there were some unusual refinements. The *Daily Mirror* (2 December) contained a story about a lorry driver who had been so incensed by the Sex Pistols' performance that he had kicked in the screen of his colour television: "I can swear as well as anyone, but I don't want this sort of muck coming into my home at teatime" [Hebdige's note]. Thames: formerly an independent television network (1968–92), based in London.
9. The police brought an unsuccessful action for obscenity against the Sex Pistols after their first LP *Never Mind the Bollocks* was released in 1977 [Hebdige's note]. "Bollocks": vulgar British slang equivalent to the American "balls" (i.e., testicles).
1. On 4 January 1977 the Sex Pistols caused an incident at Heathrow Airport by spitting and vomiting in front of airline staff. The *Evening News* quoted a check-in desk girl as saying: "The group are the most revolting people I have ever seen in my life. They were disgusting, sick and obscene." Two days after this incident was reported in the newspapers, EMI terminated the group's contract [Hebdige's note]. EMI: British music company, one of the largest record companies and the largest music publisher in the world.
2. Henri Lefebvre, *Everyday Life in the Modern World* ([1968; trans.] Allen Lane, 1971) [Hebdige's note]. Lefebvre (1901–1991), French sociologist.

We have seen how subcultures 'breach our expectancies', how they represent symbolic challenges to a symbolic order. But can subcultures always be effectively incorporated and if so, how? The emergence of a spectacular subculture is invariably accompanied by a wave of hysteria in the press. This hysteria is typically ambivalent: it fluctuates between dread and fascination, outrage and amusement. Shock and horror headlines dominate the front page (e.g. 'Rotten Razored', *Daily Mirror*, 28 June 1977) while, inside, the editorials positively bristle with 'serious' commentary[3] and the centrespreads or supplements contain delirious accounts of the latest fads and rituals (see, for example, *Observer* colour supplements 30 January, 10 July 1977, 12 February 1978). Style in particular provokes a double response: it is alternately celebrated (in the fashion page) and ridiculed or reviled (in those articles which define subcultures as social problems).

In most cases, it is the subculture's stylistic innovations which first attract the media's attention. Subsequently deviant or 'anti-social' acts—vandalism, swearing, fighting, 'animal behaviour'—are 'discovered' by the police, the judiciary, the press; and these acts are used to 'explain' the subculture's original transgression of sartorial codes. In fact, either deviant behaviour or the identification of a distinctive uniform (or more typically a combination of the two) can provide the catalyst for a moral panic. In the case of the punks, the media's sighting of punk style virtually coincided with the discovery or invention of punk deviance. The *Daily Mirror* ran its first series of alarmist centrespreads on the subculture, concentrating on the bizarre clothing and jewellery during the week (29 Nov–3 Dec 1977) in which the Sex Pistols exploded into the public eye on the Thames *Today* programme. On the other hand, the mods, perhaps because of the muted character of their style, were not identified as a group until the Bank Holiday[4] clashes of 1964, although the subculture was, by then, fully developed, at least in London. Whichever item opens the amplifying sequence, it invariably ends with the simultaneous diffusion and defusion of the subcultural style.

As the subculture begins to strike its own eminently marketable pose, as its vocabulary (both visual and verbal) becomes more and more familiar, so the referential context to which it can be most conveniently assigned is made increasingly apparent. Eventually, the mods, the punks, the glitter rockers can be incorporated, brought back into line, located on the preferred 'map of problematic social reality' at the point where boys in lipstick are 'just kids dressing up', where girls in rubber dresses are 'daughters just like yours'.[5] The media, as Stuart Hall has argued, not only record resistance,

3. The 1 August 1977 edition of the *Daily Mirror* contained just such an example of dubious editorial concern. Giving 'serious' consideration to the problem of ted-punk violence along the King's Road, the writer makes the obvious comparison with the seaside disturbances of the previous decade: "[The clashes] must not be allowed to grow into the pitched battles like the mods and rockers confrontations at several seaside towns a few years back." Moral panics can be recycled; even the same events can be recalled in the same prophetic terms to mobilize the same sense of outrage [Hebdige's note]. The teds, or teddy boys, were British youth who embraced American black rhythm and blues and wore smart clothing, including Edwardian-style jackets. The British punks, associated with punk rock, aggressively staged themselves as alienated outcasts, wearing rough clothes and favoring body piercings, dyed hair, and tattoos. The King's Road: a major street in West London that in the 1970s became a center of the punk movement.

4. In England, one of a number of legal holidays on which banks are closed (in this case, the Monday after Whitsunday).

5. Clifford Geertz, "Ideology as Cultural System," in D. E. Apter (ed.), *Ideology and Discontent* (Free Press, 1964); see pp. 98–99, 158–59 n. 8 [Hebdige's note].

they 'situate it within the dominant framework of meanings' and those young people who choose to inhabit a spectacular youth culture are simultaneously *returned*, as they are represented on TV and in the newspapers, to the place where common sense would have them fit (as 'animals' certainly, but also 'in the family', 'out of work', 'up to date', etc.).[6] It is through this continual process of recuperation that the fractured order is repaired and the subculture incorporated as a diverting spectacle within the dominant mythology from which it in part emanates: as 'folk devil', as Other, as Enemy. The process of recuperation takes two characteristic forms:

(1) The conversion of subcultural signs (dress, music, etc.) into mass-produced objects (i.e. the commodity form);
(2) The 'labelling' and re-definition of deviant behaviour by dominant groups—the police, the media, the judiciary (i.e. the ideological form).

The Commodity Form

The first has been comprehensively handled by both journalists and academics. The relationship between the spectacular subculture and the various industries which service and exploit it is notoriously ambiguous. After all, such a subculture is concerned first and foremost with consumption. It operates exclusively in the leisure sphere ('I wouldn't wear my punk outfit for work—there's a time and a place for everything'). It communicates through commodities even if the meanings attached to those commodities are purposefully distorted or overthrown. It is therefore difficult in this case to maintain any absolute distinction between commercial exploitation on the one hand and creativity/originality on the other, even though these categories are emphatically opposed in the value systems of most subcultures. Indeed, the creation and diffusion of new styles is inextricably bound up with the process of production, publicity and packaging which must inevitably lead to the defusion of the subculture's subversive power—both mod and punk innovations fed back directly into high fashion and mainstream fashion. Each new subculture establishes new trends, generates new looks and sounds which feed back into the appropriate industries. As John Clarke has observed:

> The diffusion of youth styles from the subcultures to the fashion market is not simply a 'cultural process', but a real network or infrastructure of new kinds of commercial and economic institutions. The small-scale record shops, recording companies, the boutiques and one- or two-woman manufacturing companies—these versions of artisan capitalism, rather than more generalised and unspecific phenomena, situate the dialectic of commercial 'manipulation'.[7]

However, it would be mistaken to insist on the absolute autonomy of 'cultural' and commercial processes. As Lefebvre puts it: 'Trade is . . . both a

6. Stuart Hall, "Culture, the Media and the 'Ideological Effect,'" in J. Curran et al. (eds.), *Mass Communication and Society* (Arnold, 1977) [Hebdige's note].

7. John Clarke, "Style," in Stuart Hall et al. (eds.), *Resistance through Rituals* (Hutchinson, 1976) [Hebdige's note].

social and an intellectual phenomenon',[8] and commodities arrive at the market-place already laden with significance. They are, in Marx's words, 'social hieroglyphs'[9] and their meanings are inflected by conventional usage.

Thus, as soon as the original innovations which signify 'subculture' are translated into commodities and made generally available, they become 'frozen'. Once removed from their private contexts by the small entrepreneurs and big fashion interests who produce them on a mass scale, they become codified, made comprehensible, rendered at once public property and profitable merchandise. In this way, the two forms of incorporation (the semantic/ideological and the 'real'/commercial) can be said to converge on the commodity form. Youth cultural styles may begin by issuing symbolic challenges, but they must inevitably end by establishing new sets of conventions; by creating new commodities, new industries or rejuvenating old ones (think of the boost punk must have given haberdashery!). This occurs irrespective of the subculture's political orientation: the macrobiotic restaurants, craft shops and 'antique markets' of the hippie era were easily converted into punk boutiques and record shops. It also happens irrespective of the startling content of the style: punk clothing and insignia could be bought mail-order by the summer of 1977, and in September of that year *Cosmopolitan* ran a review of Zandra Rhodes'[1] latest collection of couture follies which consisted entirely of variations on the punk theme. Models smouldered beneath mountains of safety pins and plastic (the pins were jewelled, the 'plastic' wet-look satin) and the accompanying article ended with an aphorism—'To shock is chic'—which presaged the subculture's imminent demise.

The Ideological Form

The second form of incorporation—the ideological—has been most adequately treated by those sociologists who operate a transactional model of deviant behaviour. For example, Stan Cohen has described in detail how one particular moral panic (surrounding the mod–rocker conflict of the mid-60s) was launched and sustained.[2] Although this type of analysis can often provide

8. Lefebvre, *Everyday Life in the Modern World* [Hebdige's note].

9. "The characters that stamp products as commodities, and whose establishment is a necessary preliminary to the circulation of commodities, have already acquired the stability of natural, self-understood forms of social life before man seeks to decipher, not their historical character, for in his eyes they are immutable, but their meaning." KARL MARX and FRIEDRICH ENGELS, *The German Ideology* ([written 1845–46; trans.] Lawrence and Wishart, 1970) [Hebdige's note].

1. British fashion designer (b. 1940), who came to prominence in the 1970s.

2. The definitive study of a moral panic is Stan Cohen's *Folk Devils and Moral Panics* (MacGibbon and Kee, 1972). The mods and rockers were just two of the "folk devils"—"the gallery of types that society erects to show its members which roles should be avoided"—which periodically become the centre of a "moral panic." "Societies appear to be subject, every now and then, to periods of moral panic. A condition, episode, person or group of persons emerges to become defined as a threat to societal values and interests; its nature is presented in a stylized and stereotypical fashion by the mass media; the moral barricades are manned by editors, bishops, politicians and other right-thinking people, socially accredited experts pronounce their diagnoses and solutions; ways of coping are evolved or (more often) resorted to; the condition then disappears, submerges or deteriorates and becomes more visible" (Cohen). Official reaction to the punk subculture betrayed all the classic symptoms of a moral panic. Concerts were cancelled; clergymen, politicians and pundits unanimously denounced the degeneracy of youth. Among the choicer reactions, Marcus Lipton, the late MP for Lambeth North, declared: "If pop music is going to be used to destroy our established institutions, then it ought to be destroyed first." Bernard Brook-Partridge, MP for Havering Romford, stormed, "I think the Sex Pistols are absolutely bloody revolting. I think their whole attitude is calculated to incite people to misbehavior. . . . It is a deliberate incitement to anti-social behavior and conduct" (quoted in *New Musical Express*, 15 July 1977) [Hebdige's note]. Cohen (1942–2013), South African–born British sociologist. MP: member of Parliament.

an extremely sophisticated explanation of why spectacular subcultures consistently provoke such hysterical outbursts, it tends to overlook the subtler mechanisms through which potentially threatening phenomena are handled and contained. As the use of the term 'folk devil' suggests, rather too much weight tends to be given to the sensational excesses of the tabloid press at the expense of the ambiguous reactions which are, after all, more typical. As we have seen, the way in which subcultures are represented in the media makes them both more *and less* exotic than they actually are. They are seen to contain both dangerous aliens and boisterous kids, wild animals and wayward pets. Roland Barthes furnishes a key to this paradox in his description of 'identification'—one of the seven rhetorical figures which, according to Barthes, distinguish the meta-language of bourgeois mythology. He characterizes the petit-bourgeois as a person '. . . unable to imagine the Other . . . the Other is a scandal which threatens his existence'.[3]

Two basic strategies have been evolved for dealing with this threat. First, the Other can be trivialized, naturalized, domesticated. Here, the difference is simply denied ('Otherness is reduced to sameness'). Alternatively, the Other can be transformed into meaningless exotica, a 'pure object, a spectacle, a clown'.[4] In this case, the difference is consigned to a place beyond analysis. Spectacular subcultures are continually being defined in precisely these terms. Soccer hooligans, for example, are typically placed beyond 'the bounds of common decency' and are classified as 'animals'. ('These people aren't human beings', football club manager quoted on the *News at Ten*, Sunday, 12 March 1977.)[5] On the other hand, the punks tended to be resituated by the press in the family, perhaps because members of the subculture deliberately obscured their origins, refused the family and willingly played the part of folk devil, presenting themselves as pure objects, as villainous clowns. Certainly, like every other youth culture, punk was perceived as a threat to the family. Occasionally this threat was represented in literal terms. For example, the *Daily Mirror* (1 August 1977) carried a photograph of a child lying in the road after a punk–ted confrontation under the headline 'VICTIM OF THE PUNK ROCK PUNCH-UP: THE BOY WHO FELL FOUL OF THE MOB'. In this case, punk's threat to the family was made 'real' (that could be my child!) through the ideological framing of photographic evidence which is popularly regarded as unproblematic.

None the less, on other occasions, the opposite line was taken. For whatever reason, the inevitable glut of articles gleefully denouncing the latest punk outrage was counterbalanced by an equal number of items devoted to the small details of punk family life. For instance, the 15 October 1977 issue of *Woman's Own* carried an article entitled 'Punks and Mothers' which stressed the classless, fancy dress aspects of punk.[6] Photographs depicting

3. Roland Barthes, *Mythologies* ([1957; trans.] Paladin, 1972) [Hebdige's note]. BARTHES (1915–1980), French literary and cultural critic and semiologist.

4. Ibid. [Hebdige's note].

5. See Stuart Hall's treatment of the press coverage of football hooligans in Roger Ingham, ed., *Football Hooliganism* (Inter-action Imprint, 1978) [Hebdige's note].

6. See also "Punks Have Mothers Too: They Tell Us a Few Home Truths" in *Woman* (15 April 1978) and "Punks and Mothers" in *Woman's Own* (15 October 1977). These articles draw editorial comment (a sign of recognition of the staff of the need to reassure the challenged expectations of the reader?). The following anecdote appeared beneath a photograph of two dancing teddy boys: "The other day I overheard two elderly ladies, cringing as a gang of alarming looking punks passed them, say in tones of horror, 'Just imagine what their children will be like.' I'm sure a lot of people must have said exactly the same thing

punks with smiling mothers, reclining next to the family pool, playing with the family dog, were placed above a text which dwelt on the ordinariness of individual punks: 'It's not as rocky horror as it appears' . . . 'punk can be a family affair' . . . 'punks as it happens are non-political', and, most insidiously, albeit accurately, 'Johnny Rotten is as big a household name as Hughie Green'.[7] Throughout the summer of 1977, the *People* and the *News of the World*[8] ran items on punk babies, punk brothers, and punk–ted weddings. All these articles served to minimize the Otherness so stridently proclaimed in punk style, and defined the subculture in precisely those terms which it sought most vehemently to resist and deny.

Once again, we should avoid making any absolute distinction between the ideological and commercial 'manipulations' of subculture. The symbolic restoration of daughters to the family, of deviants to the fold, was undertaken at a time when the widespread 'capitulation' of punk musicians to market forces was being used throughout the media to illustrate the fact that punks were 'only human after all'. The music papers were filled with the familiar success stories describing the route from rags to rags and riches—of punk musicians flying to America, of bank clerks become magazine editors or record producers, of harrassed seamstresses turned overnight into successful business women. Of course, these success stories had ambiguous implications. As with every other 'youth revolution' (e.g. the beat boom,[9] the mod explosion and the Swinging Sixties) the relative success of a few individuals created an impression of energy, expansion and limitless upward mobility. This ultimately reinforced the image of the open society which the very presence of the punk subculture—with its rhetorical emphasis on unemployment, high-rise living and narrow options—had originally contradicted. As Barthes has written: 'myth can always, as a last resort, signify the resistance which is brought to bear against it'[1] and it does so typically by imposing its own ideological terms, by substituting in this case 'the fairy tale of the artist's creativity'[2] for an art form 'within the compass of every consciousness',[3] a 'music' to be judged, dismissed or marketed for 'noise'—a logically consistent, self-constituted chaos. It does so finally by replacing a subculture engendered by history, a product of real historical contradictions, with a handful of brilliant

about the Teddy Boys, like the ones pictured . . . and Mods and Rockers. That made me wonder what had happened to them when the phase passed. I reckon they put away their drape suits or scooters and settled down to respectable, quiet lives, bringing up kids and desperately hoping they won't get involved in any of these terrible Punk goings-on" [Hebdige's note].

7. British television game and talent show host (1920–1997).

8. Two British weekly tabloids.

9. British pop music of the early 1960s (which gave rise to the "British invasion" of the United States, most notably by the Beatles).

1. Barthes, *Mythologies* [Hebdige's note].

2. "The fairy-tale of the artist's creativity is western culture's last superstition. One of Surrealism's revolutionary acts was to attack this myth . . ." (Max Ernst, "What Is Surrealism," in *Surrealists on Art* (Spectrum, 1970), edited by L. Lippard) [Hebdige's note].

3. "Surrealism is within the compass of every consciousness" (surrealist tract quoted in Lippard). See also Paul Eluard, *Food for Vision* (Editions Galliard, 1933): "We have passed the period of individual exercises." The solemn and extremely reverential exhibition of Surrealism mounted at London's Hayward Gallery in 1978 ironically sought to establish the reputation of individual surrealists as artists and was designed to win public recognition of their "genius." For a comparison of punk and surrealism, see below the sections entitled "Style as Bricolage" and "Revolting Style" [in chapter 7 of *Subculture*]. It is fitting that punk should be absorbed into high fashion at the same time as the first major exhibition of Dada and surrealism in Britain was being launched [Hebdige's note]. Surrealism: an experimental literary and artistic movement founded in France in 1924; inspired in part by SIGMUND FREUD, surrealists sought to express subconscious thought and feeling. Dadaism, a precursor to surrealism, is an artistic movement that protested the insanity of World War I by demolishing the tenets of art, philosophy, and logic.

nonconformists, satanic geniuses who, to use the words of Sir John Read, Chairman of EMI 'become in the fullness of time, wholly acceptable and can contribute greatly to the development of modern music'.[4]

1979

4. On 7 December, one month before EMI terminated its contract with the Sex Pistols, Sir John Read, the record company's Chairman, made the following statement at the annual general meeting:

> Throughout its history as a recording company, EMI has always sought to behave within contemporary limits of decency and good taste—taking into account not only the traditional rigid conventions of one section of society, but also the increasingly liberal attitudes of other (perhaps larger) sections . . . at any given time . . . What is decent or in good taste compared to the attitudes of, say, 20 or even 10 years ago?
>
> It is against this present-day social background that EMI has to make value judgments about the content of records . . . Sex Pistols is a pop group devoted to a new form of music known as "punk rock." It was contracted for recording purposes by EMI . . . in October, 1976 . . . In this context, it must be remembered that the recording industry has signed many pop groups, initially controversial, who have in the fullness of time become wholly acceptable and contributed greatly to the development of modern music . . . EMI should not set itself up as a public censor, but it does seek to encourage restraint. (quoted in F. Vermorel, *The Sex Pistols*, 1978)

Despite the eventual loss of face (and some £40,000 paid out to the Pistols when the contract was terminated) EMI and the other record companies tended to shrug off the apparent contradictions involved in signing up groups who openly admitted to a lack of professionalism, musicianship, and commitment to the profit motive. During the Clash's famous performance of "White Riot" at the Rainbow in 1977 when seats were ripped out and thrown at the stage, the last two rows of the theatre (left, of course, intact) were occupied almost exclusively by record executives and talent scouts: CBS paid for the damage without complaint. There could be no clearer demonstration of the fact that symbolic assaults leave real institutions intact. Nonetheless, the record companies did not have everything their own way. The Sex Pistols received five-figure sums in compensation from both A&M and EMI and when their LP (recorded at last by Virgin) finally did reach the shops, it contained a scathing attack on EMI delivered in Rotten's venomous nasal whine:

> You thought that we were faking
> That we were all just money-making
> You don't believe that we're for real
> Or you would lose your cheap appeal.
> Who?
> EMI—EMI
>
> Blind acceptance is a sign
> Of stupid fools who stand in line
> Like EMI—EMI ("EMI," Virgin, 1977)
> [Hebdige's note].

The Clash: punk rock group (1976–86), known for its leftist political ideology.

BELL HOOKS

b. Gloria Jean Watkins, 1952

bell hooks first emerged in the 1980s as a trenchant critical voice among African American intellectuals. Her wide-ranging essays about U.S. culture offer critiques on issues ranging from the academy to the environmental crisis, from the media to masculinity, from racism to sexism, while exploring the unique problems and perspectives of black women and the underprivileged. Within feminism, much of her writing has been devoted to articulating the intersections of race, class, and gender oppression. In *Feminist Theory: From Margin to Center* (1984) she writes, "Feminism is the struggle to end sexist oppression. Its aim is not to benefit solely any specific group of women, any particular race or class of women. It does not privilege women over men. It has the power to transform in a meaningful way all our lives."

Born into a rural black working-class family in Hopkinsville, Kentucky, Gloria Jean Watkins suffered a turbulent childhood but found inspiration in books and solace in imagination. When, as an adult, she took the name "bell hooks," it was to honor her outspoken great-grandmother and the legacy of her past. hooks received a B.A. from Stanford University in 1973, an M.A. from the University of Wisconsin in 1976, and a Ph.D. from the University of California at Santa Cruz in 1983. She taught African American studies and English at Yale University in the 1980s, English and women's studies at Oberlin College from 1988 until 1993, and English at the City University of New York Graduate Center from 1993 until 2004. Since 2004, she has been a distinguished professor in residence at Berea College in Kentucky.

hooks gained prominence as a social critic with the publication of her first book, *Ain't I a Woman: Black Women and Feminism* (1981), begun when she was only nineteen and published while she was still a graduate student. An extremely prolific writer, she has published several dozen books since then on topics as varied as feminist theory, racism, film, black masculinity, spirituality, teaching, and cultural studies. With the publication of *Bone Black: Memories of Girlhood* (1996) and *Wounds of Passion: A Writing Life* (1997), she turned to the genre of autobiography to explore more fully her interest in capturing "the authority of experience" that she examines in our selection, "Postmodern Blackness." Like Cornel West, with whom she collaborated on *Breaking Bread: Insurgent Black Intellectual Life* (1991), hooks has sought a niche as a public intellectual on the left, attempting to reach a wider audience outside of academia for her cultural criticism while remaining connected to her underclass black community. As an essayist, she follows in the rich tradition of twentieth-century black intellectuals such as W. E. B. DU BOIS, C. L. R. James, and ZORA NEALE HURSTON, although doubtless hooks would also include in any list of intellectual forebears earlier black women such as Anna Cooper (the nineteenth-century author of *A Voice from the South by a Black Woman of the South*) and Sojourner Truth.

In "Postmodern Blackness," which appears in her *Yearning: Race, Gender, and Cultural Politics* (1990), hooks asks why African Americans should have any interest in "postmodern theory." She applies this label to the philosophic critique of modernity that celebrates difference and otherness, that advocates radical liberation and political equality, that finds fault with rigid concepts of identity, and that criticizes so-called master narratives (for example, those about the inevitable progress of human reason, the eventual triumph of the proletariat, or the ending of the world on Judgment Day). For hooks and other cultural critics, postmodernity also evokes late twentieth-century postindustrial society with its job restructuring, ubiquitous media and popular culture, and new social movements and protest groups. Like the African American feminist critic Barbara Christian, hooks believes that the abstract philosophical discourse of postmodernism—as defined by French theorists such as JACQUES DERRIDA, JEAN-FRANÇOIS LYOTARD, and JEAN BAUDRILLARD—is dominated by white male intellectuals. These academic elites speak to one another, oblivious to the concerns of black people. Despite its invocation of "difference," she argues, postmodernism is exclusionary: while using the concepts of difference and marginality to legitimate itself in the face of accusations of irrelevance, it seems unwilling to engage the experiences or writings of the truly marginalized—black women, for example. In its celebration of indeterminacy and free play in language and in its focus on deconstructing identity, postmodernism fails to offer useful analyses of the power relations that shape discourse. Without "adequate concrete knowledge" of and contact with oppressed and marginalized groups, white theorists risk impeding rather than supporting "radical liberation struggle."

Because she discerns in those silenced by the "master narratives" of Western culture a "yearning"—what she describes as a "longing for critical voice"—hooks, unlike Christian and some other minority intellectuals, is not willing to abandon postmodernism to the intellectual elites. She identifies the intersection of "identity politics" and the postmodern critique of human essence as a particularly significant site of struggle for African Americans, who, she argues, need to resist outmoded notions of essential blackness in much the same way as feminist critics have contested the idea of the essentially female (see JUDITH BUTLER, MONIQUE WITTIG, and JULIA KRISTEVA). hooks is critical of the concept of essential blackness whether imposed from without as racist stereotype or from within as prescription for an "authentic black identity," an identity that refuses to recognize the multiplicities of black experiences that ground "diverse cultural productions." At the same time, hooks argues, the postmodern critique of essence ought not to be used to dismiss black and feminist identity politics. hooks worries about the potential within postmodernist discourse to deny a critical voice to those who have been "subjected to" colonization or domination. She is suspicious that the postmodern call to dismantle identity comes at a historical moment when subjugated peoples are beginning to assert their own identity and to act collectively in its name. hooks's solution is to embrace the postmodern critique of essentialism while emphasizing the traditional humanistic "authority of experience."

The dangers hooks exposes in the discourse of postmodernism are real, though it is worth noting that hooks here treats "postmodernism" not as a historical period but as a single set of monologic discourses that mean the same thing to everyone. Postmodern theory is a wide-ranging and diverse set of practices, texts, and discourses no more easily reducible to one set of essential meanings than is "blackness." Both terms in hooks's title must be seen as equally under interrogation, and much work remains to be done to understand the relations between them. Greater precision about the complex meanings within postmodern discourse of such terms as *identity, subjectivity*, and *experience* might break the impasse she describes between a desire to reclaim a common black history, culture, and experience and the need to avoid imposing restrictive and damaging stereotypes on diverse experiences. hooks is in agreement with the best "oppositional practices" of postmodernism, however, when she suggests that it is in the gaps, ruptures, and contradictions of Western master narratives that the struggles for liberation and for coalition politics will discover effective forms of resistance and new forms of community.

"Postmodern Blackness" Keywords: Cultural Studies, Feminist Theory, Identity, Postmodernity, Race and Ethnicity Studies, Subjectivity

Postmodern Blackness

Postmodernist discourses are often exclusionary even as they call attention to, appropriate even, the experience of "difference" and "Otherness" to provide oppositional political meaning, legitimacy, and immediacy when they are accused of lacking concrete relevance. Very few African-American intellectuals have talked or written about postmodernism. At a dinner party I talked about trying to grapple with the significance of postmodernism for contemporary black experience. It was one of those social gatherings where only one other black person was present. The setting quickly became a field of contestation. I was told by the other black person that I was wasting my time, that "this stuff does not relate in any way to what's happening with black people." Speaking in the presence of a group of white onlookers, staring at us as though this encounter were staged for their benefit, we engaged in a passionate discussion about black experience. Apparently, no one sympathized with my insistence that racism is perpetuated when blackness is associated solely with concrete gut level experience conceived as either opposing or having no connection to abstract thinking and the production of critical theory. The idea that there is no meaningful connection between black experience and critical thinking about aesthetics or culture must be continually interrogated.

My defense of postmodernism and its relevance to black folks sounded good, but I worried that I lacked conviction, largely because I approach the subject cautiously and with suspicion.

Disturbed not so much by the "sense" of postmodernism but by the conventional language used when it is written or talked about and by those who speak it, I find myself on the outside of the discourse looking in. As a discursive practice it is dominated primarily by the voices of white male intellectuals and/or academic elites who speak to and about one another with coded familiarity. Reading and studying their writing to understand postmodernism in its multiple manifestations, I appreciate it but feel little inclination to ally myself with the academic hierarchy and exclusivity pervasive in the movement today.

Critical of most writing on postmodernism, I perhaps am more conscious of the way in which the focus on "Otherness and difference" that is often alluded to in these works seems to have little concrete impact as an analysis or standpoint that might change the nature and direction of postmodernist theory. Since much of this theory has been constructed in reaction to and against high modernism, there is seldom any mention of black experience or writings by black people in this work, specifically black women (though in more recent work one may see a reference to Cornel West, the black male scholar who has most engaged postmodernist discourse). Even if an aspect of black culture is the subject of postmodern critical writing, the works cited will usually be those of black men. A work that comes immediately to mind is Andrew Ross's chapter "Hip, and the Long Front of Color" in *No Respect: Intellectuals and Popular Culture*;[1] while it is an interesting reading, it constructs black culture as though black women have had no role in black cultural production. At the end of Meaghan Morris' discussion of postmodernism in her collection of essays *The Pirate's Fiancée: Feminism, Reading, Postmodernism*, she provides a bibliography of works by women, identifying them as important contributions to a discourse on postmodernism that offer new insight as well as challenging male theoretical hegemony.[2] Even though many of the works do not directly address postmodernism, they address similar concerns. There are no references to works by black women.

The failure to recognize a critical black presence in the culture and in most scholarship and writing on postmodernism compels a black reader, particularly a black female reader, to interrogate her interest in a subject where those who discuss and write about it seem not to know black women exist or even to consider the possibility that we might be somewhere writing or saying something that should be listened to, or producing art that should be seen, heard, approached with intellectual seriousness. This is especially the case with works that go on and on about the way in which postmodernist discourse has opened up a theoretical terrain where "difference and Otherness" can be considered legitimate issues in the academy. Confronting both the absence of recognition of black female presence that much

1. ANDREW ROSS, *No Respect: Intellectuals and Popular Culture* (New York: Routledge, 1989).
2. Meaghan Morris, *The Pirate's Fiancée: Feminism, Reading, Postmodernism* (London: Verso, 1988).

postmodernist theory re-inscribes and the resistance on the part of most black folks to hearing about real connection between postmodernism and black experience, I enter a discourse, a practice, where there may be no ready audience for my words, no clear listener, uncertain then, that my voice can or will be heard.

During the sixties, the black power movement was influenced by perspectives that could easily be labeled modernist. Certainly many of the ways black folks addressed issues of identity conformed to a modernist universalizing agenda. There was little critique of patriarchy as a master narrative among black militants. Despite the fact that black power ideology reflected a modernist sensibility, these elements were soon rendered irrelevant as militant protest was stifled by a powerful, repressive postmodern state. The period directly after the black power movement was a time when major news magazines carried articles with cocky headlines like "Whatever Happened to Black America?" This response was an ironic reply to the aggressive, unmet demand by decentered, marginalized black subjects who had at least momentarily successfully demanded a hearing, who had made it possible for black liberation to be on the national political agenda. In the wake of the black power movement, after so many rebels were slaughtered and lost, many of these voices were silenced by a repressive state; others became inarticulate. It has become necessary to find new avenues to transmit the messages of black liberation struggle, new ways to talk about racism and other politics of domination. Radical postmodernist practice, most powerfully conceptualized as a "politics of difference," should incorporate the voices of displaced, marginalized, exploited, and oppressed black people. It is sadly ironic that the contemporary discourse which talks the most about heterogeneity, the decentered subject, declaring breakthroughs that allow recognition of Otherness, still directs its critical voice primarily to a specialized audience that shares a common language rooted in the very master narratives it claims to challenge. If radical postmodernist thinking is to have a transformative impact, then a critical break with the notion of "authority" as "mastery over" must not simply be a rhetorical device. It must be reflected in habits of being, including styles of writing as well as chosen subject matter. Third world nationals, elites, and white critics who passively absorb white supremacist thinking, and therefore never notice or look at black people on the streets or at their jobs, who render us invisible with their gaze in all areas of daily life, are not likely to produce liberatory theory that will challenge racist domination, or promote a breakdown in traditional ways of seeing and thinking about reality, ways of constructing aesthetic theory and practice. From a different standpoint, Robert Storr makes a similar critique in the global issue of *Art in America* when he asserts:

> To be sure, much postmodernist critical inquiry has centered precisely on the issues of "difference" and "Otherness." On the purely theoretical plane the exploration of these concepts has produced some important results, but in the absence of any sustained research into what artists of color and others outside the mainstream might be up to, such discussions become rootless instead of radical. Endless second guessing about the latent imperialism of intruding upon other cultures only compounded matters, preventing or excusing these theorists from

> investigating what black, Hispanic, Asian and Native American artists were actually doing.[3]

Without adequate concrete knowledge of and contact with the non-white "Other," white theorists may move in discursive theoretical directions that are threatening and potentially disruptive of that critical practice which would support radical liberation struggle.

The postmodern critique of "identity," though relevant for renewed black liberation struggle, is often posed in ways that are problematic. Given a pervasive politic of white supremacy which seeks to prevent the formation of radical black subjectivity, we cannot cavalierly dismiss a concern with identity politics. Any critic exploring the radical potential of postmodernism as it relates to racial difference and racial domination would need to consider the implications of a critique of identity for oppressed groups. Many of us are struggling to find new strategies of resistance. We must engage decolonization as a critical practice if we are to have meaningful chances of survival even as we must simultaneously cope with the loss of political grounding which made radical activism more possible. I am thinking here about the postmodernist critique of essentialism as it pertains to the construction of "identity" as one example.

Postmodern theory that is not seeking to simply appropriate the experience of "Otherness" to enhance the discourse or to be radically chic should not separate the "politics of difference" from the politics of racism. To take racism seriously one must consider the plight of underclass people of color, a vast majority of whom are black. For African-Americans our collective condition prior to the advent of postmodernism and perhaps more tragically expressed under current postmodern conditions has been and is characterized by continued displacement, profound alienation, and despair. Writing about blacks and postmodernism, Cornel West describes our collective plight:

> There is increasing class division and differentiation, creating on the one hand a significant black middle-class, highly anxiety-ridden, insecure, willing to be co-opted and incorporated into the powers that be, concerned with racism to the degree that it poses contraints on upward social mobility; and, on the other, a vast and growing black underclass, an underclass that embodies a kind of walking nihilism of pervasive drug addiction, pervasive alcoholism, pervasive homicide, and an exponential rise in suicide. Now because of the deindustrialization, we also have a devastated black industrial working class. We are talking here about tremendous hopelessness.[4]

This hopelessness creates longing for insight and strategies for change that can renew spirits and reconstruct grounds for collective black liberation struggle. The overall impact of postmodernism is that many other groups now share with black folks a sense of deep alienation, despair, uncertainty, loss of a sense of grounding even if it is not informed by shared circumstance. Radical postmodernism calls attention to those shared sensibilities which cross the bound-

3. Robert Storr, "The Global Issue: A Symposium," *Art in America* 77 (1989): 88.
4. Cornel West, "Interview with Cornel West," by Anders Stephanson (1989), reprinted as "The Public Intellectual" in *The Cornel West Reader* (New York: Basic Civitas Books, 1999), p. 284.

aries of class, gender, race, etc., that could be fertile ground for the construction of empathy—ties that would promote recognition of common commitments, and serve as a base for solidarity and coalition.

Yearning is the word that best describes a common psychological state shared by many of us, cutting across boundaries of race, class, gender, and sexual practice. Specifically, in relation to the post-modernist deconstruction of "master" narratives, the yearning that wells in the hearts and minds of those whom such narratives have silenced is the longing for critical voice. It is no accident that "rap" has usurped the primary position of rhythm and blues music among young black folks as the most desired sound or that it began as a form of "testimony" for the underclass. It has enabled underclass black youth to develop a critical voice, as a group of young black men told me, a "common literacy." Rap projects a critical voice, explaining, demanding, urging. Working with this insight in his essay "Putting the Pop Back into Postmodernism," Lawrence Grossberg comments:

> The postmodern sensibility appropriates practices as boasts that announce their own—and consequently our own—existence, like a rap song boasting of the imaginary (or real—it makes no difference) accomplishments of the rapper. They offer forms of empowerment not only in the face of nihilism but precisely through the forms of nihilism itself: an empowering nihilism, a moment of positivity through the production and structuring of affective relations.[5]

Considering that it is as subject one comes to voice, then the postmodernist focus on the critique of identity appears at first glance to threaten and close down the possibility that this discourse and practice will allow those who have suffered the crippling effects of colonization and domination to gain or regain a hearing. Even if this sense of threat and the fear it evokes are based on a misunderstanding of the postmodernist political project, they nevertheless shape responses. It never surprises me when black folks respond to the critique of essentialism, especially when it denies the validity of identity politics by saying, "Yeah, it's easy to give up identity, when you got one." Should we not be suspicious of postmodern critiques of the "subject" when they surface at a historical moment when many subjugated people feel themselves coming to voice for the first time? Though an apt and oftentimes appropriate comeback, it does not really intervene in the discourse in a way that alters and transforms.

Criticisms of directions in postmodern thinking should not obscure insights it may offer that open up our understanding of African-American experience. The critique of essentialism encouraged by postmodernist thought is useful for African-Americans concerned with reformulating outmoded notions of identity. We have too long had imposed upon us from both the outside and the inside a narrow, constricting notion of blackness. Postmodern critiques of essentialism which challenge notions of universality and static over-determined identity within mass culture and mass consciousness can open up new possibilities for the construction of self and the assertion of agency.

5. Lawrence Grossberg, "Putting the Pop Back into Postmodernism," in *Universal Abandon: The Politics of Postmodernism*, ed. Andrew Ross (Minneapolis: University of Minnesota Press, 1988), p. 181.

Employing a critique of essentialism allows African-Americans to acknowledge the way in which class mobility has altered collective black experience so that racism does not necessarily have the same impact on our lives. Such a critique allows us to affirm multiple black identities, varied black experience. It also challenges colonial imperialist paradigms of black identity which represent blackness one-dimensionally in ways that reinforce and sustain white supremacy. This discourse created the idea of the "primitive" and promoted the notion of an "authentic" experience, seeing as "natural" those expressions of black life which conformed to a pre-existing pattern or stereotype. Abandoning essentialist notions would be a serious challenge to racism. Contemporary African-American resistance struggle must be rooted in a process of decolonization that continually opposes re-inscribing notions of "authentic" black identity. This critique should not be made synonymous with a dismissal of the struggle of oppressed and exploited peoples to make ourselves subjects. Nor should it deny that in certain circumstances this experience affords us a privileged critical location from which to speak. This is not a re-inscription of modernist master narratives of authority which privilege some voices by denying voice to others. Part of our struggle for radical black subjectivity is the quest to find ways to construct self and identity that are oppositional and liberatory. The unwillingness to critique essentialism on the part of many African-Americans is rooted in the fear that it will cause folks to lose sight of the specific history and experience of African-Americans and the unique sensibilities and culture that arise from that experience. An adequate response to this concern is to critique essentialism while emphasizing the significance of "the authority of experience."[6] There is a radical difference between a repudiation of the idea that there is a black "essence" and recognition of the way black identity has been specifically constituted in the experience of exile and struggle.

When black folks critique essentialism, we are empowered to recognize multiple experiences of black identity that are the lived conditions which make diverse cultural productions possible. When this diversity is ignored, it is easy to see black folks as falling into two categories: nationalist or assimilationist, black-identified or white-identified. Coming to terms with the impact of postmodernism for black experience, particularly as it changes our sense of identity, means that we must and can rearticulate the basis for collective bonding. Given the various crises facing African-Americans (economic, spiritual, escalating racial violence, etc.), we are compelled by circumstance to reassess our relationship to popular culture and resistance struggle. Many of us are as reluctant to face this task as many non-black postmodern thinkers who focus theoretically on the issue of "difference" are to confront the issue of race and racism.

Music is the cultural product created by African-Americans that has most attracted postmodern theorists. It is rarely acknowledged that there is far greater censorship and restriction of other forms of cultural production by black folks—literary, critical writing, etc. Attempts on the part of editors and publishing houses to control and manipulate the representation of black culture, as well as the desire to promote the creation of products that will attract

6. The title of a 1977 collection of essays of feminist criticism, edited by Arlyn Diamond and Lee R. Edwards.

the widest audience, limit in a crippling and stifling way the kind of work many black folks feel we can do and still receive recognition. Using myself as an example, that creative writing I do which I consider to be most reflective of a postmodern oppositional sensibility, work that is abstract, fragmented, non-linear narrative, is constantly rejected by editors and publishers. It does not conform to the type of writing they think black women should be doing or the type of writing they believe will sell. Certainly I do not think I am the only black person engaged in forms of cultural production, especially experimental ones, who is constrained by the lack of an audience for certain kinds of work. It is important for postmodern thinkers and theorists to constitute themselves as an audience for such work. To do this they must assert power and privilege within the space of critical writing to open up the field so that it will be more inclusive. To change the exclusionary practice of postmodern critical discourse is to enact a postmodernism of resistance. Part of this intervention entails black intellectual participation in the discourse.

In his essay "Postmodernism and Black America," Cornel West suggests that black intellectuals "are marginal—usually languishing at the interface of Black and white cultures or thoroughly ensconced in Euro-American settings." He cannot see this group as potential producers of radical postmodernist thought. While I generally agree with this assessment, black intellectuals must proceed with the understanding that we are not condemned to the margins. The way we work and what we do can determine whether or not what we produce will be meaningful to a wider audience, one that includes all classes of black people. West suggests that black intellectuals lack "any organic link with most of Black life" and that this "diminishes their value to Black resistance." This statement bears traces of essentialism. Perhaps we need to focus more on those black intellectuals, however rare our presence, who do not feel this lack and whose work is primarily directed towards the enhancement of black critical consciousness and the strengthening of our collective capacity to engage in meaningful resistance struggle. Theoretical ideas and critical thinking need not be transmitted solely in written work or solely in the academy. While I work in a predominantly white institution, I remain intimately and passionately engaged with black community. It's not like I'm going to talk about writing and thinking about postmodernism with other academics and/or intellectuals and not discuss these ideas with underclass non-academic black folks who are family, friends, and comrades. Since I have not broken the ties that bind me to underclass poor black community, I have seen that knowledge, especially that which enhances daily life and strengthens our capacity to survive, can be shared. It means that critics, writers, and academics have to give the same critical attention to nurturing and cultivating our ties to black community that we give to writing articles, teaching, and lecturing. Here again I am really talking about cultivating habits of being that reinforce awareness that knowledge can be disseminated and shared on a number of fronts. The extent to which knowledge is made available, accessible, etc. depends on the nature of one's political commitments.

Postmodern culture with its decentered subject can be the space where ties are severed or it can provide the occasion for new and varied forms of bonding. To some extent, ruptures, surfaces, contextuality, and a host of other happenings create gaps that make space for oppositional practices which no longer require intellectuals to be confined by narrow separate spheres with no meaningful connection to the world of the everyday. Much postmodern engagement with culture emerges from the yearning to do intellectual work that connects with habits of being, forms of artistic expression, and aesthetics that inform the daily life of writers and scholars as well as a mass population. On the terrain of culture, one can participate in critical dialogue with the uneducated poor, the black underclass who are thinking about aesthetics. One can talk about what we are seeing, thinking, or listening to; a space is there for critical exchange. It's exciting to think, write, talk about, and create art that reflects passionate engagement with popular culture, because this may very well be "the" central future location of resistance struggle, a meeting place where new and radical happenings can occur.

1990

ROSI BRAIDOTTI
b. 1954

Rosi Braidotti opens *The Posthuman* (2013) by declaring, "Not all of us can say, with any degree of certainty, that we have always been human, or that we are only that." Her words define the central premise of the posthuman turn in literary and cultural theory. The word *posthuman* emerged in the mid-1990s in philosophy, cultural criticism, and literary theory, becoming an umbrella term for a variety of movements and schools of thought responding to technological and scientific developments, as well as to philosophic critiques of the traditional humanist subject, that call for a redefinition of what it means to be human. Its roots, as Braidotti declares, are in post-1968 antihumanism and arguably even further back in cybernetics, systems theory, and the environmental movement, which together began a process of decentering the human from its privileged position as chief arbiter of meaning and as the classical "measure of all things." Braidotti sees this reappraisal of both humanism and the human not simply as another in a long line of theoretical "posts" but as a "qualitative shift in our thinking about . . . the basic unit of common reference for our species, our polity and our relationship to the other inhabitants of the planet." Acknowledging that a number of terms have marked the limits of the human, including "the non-human, the inhuman, the anti-human, [and] the inhumane," she follows other posthumanist theorists (such as Cary Wolfe) in distinguishing posthumanism from "transhumanism"—a belief in human enhancement through technoscience that dreams of transcending embodiment. By contrast, the starting point for the posthuman is "the vital, self-organizing and yet non-naturalistic structure of living matter itself." Moving away from beliefs that the human marks a privileged position in the world, posthumanism seeks to demonstrate humans' continuity with both the biological and the technological domains.

Born in Italy in 1954, and raised in Australia, Braidotti received a first-class honors degree in 1977 from the Australian National University in Canberra. She did graduate work at the Sorbonne in Paris, receiving a Ph.D. in philosophy in 1981. In 1988 she was appointed the first professor in women's studies at the University of Utrecht in the Netherlands. Between 1995 and 2005, she was the director of the Netherlands Research School of Women's Studies (now Gender Studies). Braidotti has been a pioneer in linking women's studies programs and feminist projects throughout Europe through the Thematic Network for Women's Studies. She has held several distinguished visiting positions, including Fellow in the School of Social Science at Princeton's Institute for Advanced Study (1994), Jean Monnet Professor at the European University Institute in Florence (2002–03), Leverhulme Trust Visiting Professor at London's Birkbeck College (2005–06), and Matteo Ricci Visiting Professorship, Faculty of the Humanities, University of Macerata (Italy, 2016). She is currently Distinguished University Professor at Utrecht University, where she is founding director of the Centre for the Humanities. Braidotti has received many honors, including a Royal Knighthood from Queen Beatrix of the Netherlands in 2005, the University Medal from the University of Lodz in Poland in 2006, and honorary degrees from Helsinki University in 2007 and Linköping University, Sweden, in 2013. In 2009, she was elected an Honorary Fellow of the Australian Academy of the Humanities.

Braidotti has published in Italian, French, and English. Her written work—which demonstrates an interdisciplinary engagement with political theory, feminist theory, ethnic studies, animal studies, and technoscience—falls within the tradition of Continental (i.e., European) philosophy and draws on a variety of theoretical approaches: phenomenology, structuralism, poststructuralism, French feminism, psychoanalysis, and Marxism. Braidotti defines her own philosophical project as an attempt to think positively about difference (including gender, race, and ethnicity), freeing it from the dualism that marks it as the negative of sameness. Her first book, *Patterns of Dissonance: A Study of Women in Contemporary Philosophy* (1991), explores the ways in which male philosophers such as JACQUES DERRIDA and MICHEL FOUCAULT use the concept of the feminine to critique classical philosophic thought, as well as the efforts of contemporary feminist philosophers like Luce Irigaray to articulate the significance of women for philosophy.

Over the next decade, Braidotti would develop the theoretical concept for which she is best known, the nomadic subject, through a trilogy of books that explore alternative views of subjectivity and difference. Extending the concept of the nomad developed by GILLES DELEUZE and FÉLIX GUATTARI in *A Thousand Plateaus* (1980; see above), Braidotti's second book, *Nomadic Subjects: Embodiment and Sexual Difference in Contemporary Feminist Theory* (1994; 2d ed., 2011), argues for a female and feminist subjectivity that opposes the falsely universalizing subject of modern liberal individualism, with its dualistic oppositions—between self and other, male and female, citizen and alien—that create an "illusion of unity, mastery, and self-transparence" through violence and exclusion. The postmodern nomadic subject is a performative subject, always in flux, always in the process of becoming, aware of both the creative and the destructive possibilities of power relations. Braidotti's interest in nomadism is unsurprising, given her own biography as a "polyglot nomadic intellectual" who speaks and writes several languages and calls no one country her home. With *Metamorphoses: Towards a Materialist Theory of Becoming* (2002), Braidotti extends her work on sexual difference to include other differences: the racial and ethnic differences that increasingly inflect European politics, and also, like DONNA HARAWAY, the boundaries between the human and animal, the human and monstrous, the human and machine. *Transpositions: On Nomadic Ethics* (2006) investigates the ethical consequences that follow from the nomadic subject.

In *The Posthuman*, Braidotti resituates her feminist critique of the subject within current work on the posthuman, without abandoning her commitments to a politically engaged feminist philosophy. In the opening chapter, she outlines the intellectual and historical genealogies of posthumanism, locating it first in the critique of reason and universalism developed in the 1960s and '70s by feminist thinkers, who questioned the norm of "man" as the epitome of the human and developed theoretical models for situated knowledge rooted in analyses of power, and then in the antihumanism articulated by the generation of philosophers who came of age as intellectuals in the wake of failed 1968 student and worker uprisings in France. Unlike earlier philosophers of inequality such as Jean-Paul Sartre, SIMONE DE BEAUVOIR, and the anticolonialist FRANTZ FANON, who sought to conserve the humanist discourse of reason as they criticized sexism or colonialism, the so-called poststructuralist generation—which includes Foucault, Derrida, Deleuze and Guattari, JACQUES LACAN, and LOUIS ALTHUSSER, as well as the French feminists Irigaray, HÉLÈNE CIXOUS, and JULIA KRISTEVA—rejected notions of the human inherited from humanism and the Enlightenment, particularly the autonomy and unity of the human subject. A third intellectual influence on posthumanism comes from postcolonial thinkers such as EDWARD W. SAID, GAYATRI CHAKRAVORTY SPIVAK, and HOMI K. BHABHA, who have challenged the Eurocentric bias of Enlightenment humanism.

Our selection focuses primarily on the critique of humanism. Braidotti channels this critique through Vitruvian Man, Leonardo da Vinci's famous sketch showing the proportions of the human (that is, male) body—an iconic image of human perfectibility. Vitruvian Man provides an emblem for a set of discourses and representations that create a very particular view of what it means to be human: that is, to exercise rationality in the service of a "teleologically ordained" progress. European Renaissance humanism and the Enlightenment installed the autonomous, self-regulating, unified subject as the measure of all things. This eventually becomes the secular subject of the liberal individualism that accompanied the emergence of constitutional democracies in the age of revolutions and that pitched its claims toward a universal "citizen," specifically embodied as male and European. By the nineteenth century, she argues, reason, individualism, and progress had become synonymous with Europe, setting it apart from the rest of the world, while difference from what is a white European male norm resulted in exclusion, inferiority, and "otherness." While Braidotti recognizes that humanism has promoted important values such as emancipation, human dignity, and social justice, which have fueled the projects of those "othered" by humanism (women as well as racial and nonhuman others), she maintains that these virtues cannot be entirely disentangled from the epistemic violence it has legitimated. The abstract conception of "rational man," so central to Western humanism, becomes, in the end, a "systematized standard of recognition," a regulatory regime that often consigns sexualized, racialized, and naturalized "others" to what the Italian philosopher GIORGIO AGAMBEN calls "bare life"; they become disposable bodies. The posthuman critique of humanism posits that the universal ideal of reason is neither universal nor natural law, but instead "a historical construct and as such contingent as to values and locations." "Individualism is not an intrinsic part of 'human nature,' but rather a historically and culturally specific discursive formation" that is becoming increasingly difficult to sustain. To highlight her argument, Braidotti intersperses throughout the book a series of images that playfully upend the icon of Vitruvian Man, calling attention to humanism's exclusions: Vitruvian woman, Vitruvian rat, Vitruvian dog, Vitruvian robot.

Posthumanism is a response both to the exclusions created in the name of humanism and to challenges to the human posed by technoscientific advances that undercut age-old distinctions between human and nonhuman. Braidotti maps out three responses to these challenges, three strands of posthumanism, remarking that all share the view that science and technology have profoundly altered "the very fibre and structure of the living." At the same time, however, she is critical of the initial two strands. The first is best represented by the moral philosophy of MARTHA NUSSBAUM, who, rejecting the antihumanist critique, argues that the cure for the ills created by technology and globalization is a revitalized humanism. Nussbaum embraces the universal values, rationality, and individualism that are the hallmark of classic liberalism. The second strand, "analytic posthumanism," emerges from the interdisciplinary fields of science and technology studies. As the interface between human subjects and technological artifacts becomes increasingly porous, as complex webs of interdependence between human and nonhuman entities emerge, the basic building blocks of humanism—secularism, universalism, the unitary subject, and rationality—become increasingly untenable. Analytic posthumanism looks not nostalgically back to humanist values, as Nussbaum does, but forward to speculation about "the morality of things." Ethicists have begun to imagine nonhuman forms of moral consciousness: for instance, robots that could make life-and-death decisions. Braidotti criticizes both strands of posthumanism for, among other things, failing to offer an adequate account of the subject of posthumanism.

Braidotti calls the third strand (her own version) "critical posthumanism." Because it is sensitive to issues of power and privilege, giving voice to the "others" silenced by Eurocentrism, masculinism, and anthropocentrism, critical posthumanism is in conversation with postcolonial and race theorists, including Said, Bhabha, and PAUL GILROY, as well as feminists and environmental theorists such as Maria Mies and Vandana Shiva. It engages with the work of other posthumanist theorists, such as Wolfe, Haraway, and N. KATHERINE HAYLES. Braidotti's most significant contribution to posthumanism is her call to replace the unitary subject of humanism with the "nomadic subject," a "more complex and relational subject framed by embodiment, sexuality, affectivity, empathy and desire." This subject would be fully embodied but also relationally embedded in networks or, following BRUNO LATOUR, in assemblages of human and nonhuman actors. It would be both internally differentiated and able to work across difference. It would be accountable, but part of a community. From these new subjectivities, critical posthumanism must develop a new affirmative ethics and politics capable of imagining a sustainable future. To do so, she argues, requires the displacement of the human/nonhuman distinction that props up the unity of the subject. To effect this displacement and to debunk the age-old philosophic argument for human exceptionalism (the belief that human life is set apart from other forms of life), she rehabilitates Agamben's *zoe* (bare life) as the vital and self-organizing power of life (including nonhuman life).

Braidotti is one of the pioneers of the "new materialism"—a theory that, critical of the "linguistic turn" in poststructuralism because it privileges language and culture over matter and nature, gives special attention to matter, which its proponents believe has been neglected by a long philosophical tradition of dualism that devalues the material. But some find troublesome the new materialists' mischaracterization of the linguistic turn. Like many of the new materialists (Latour, JANE BENNETT, IAN BOGOST), Braidotti attributes to poststructuralism a categorical distinction—privileging culture over nature and language over matter—that its adherents actually sought to deconstruct. Other critics find her antihumanism troubling: while she admits ambivalence about humanism, noting that it is "complicitous with genocides and crimes on the one hand, supportive of enormous hopes and aspirations to freedom on the other," she dismisses the possibility that humanism could be rehabilitated to serve liberatory ends. For both groups, Braidotti appears to risk throwing out the methodological tools that the humanities might best bring to bear on technoscience, global capitalism, and neoliberalism. Can the humanities exist without humans and humanism? In dismissing the "linguistic frame of reference," do those of us in the humanities sacrifice the ability to contribute to these debates by unpacking the work done by representation, symbolic meaning, and discourse in sustaining and contesting systems of oppression?

Such criticisms notwithstanding, Braidotti's posthumanism brings a crucial feminist lens to bear on contemporary debates about the human and about the shifts in subjectivity and ethics posed by technoscience and globalization.

***The Posthuman* Keywords:** The Body, Cultural Studies, Deconstruction, Feminist Theory, Postcolonial Theory, Postmodernity, Poststructuralism, Religion, Subjectivity

From The Posthuman

From *Introduction*

Not all of us can say, with any degree of certainty, that we have always been human, or that we are only that. Some of us are not even considered fully human now, let alone at previous moments of Western social, political and scientific history. Not if by 'human' we mean that creature familiar to us from the Enlightenment and its legacy: 'The Cartesian subject of the cogito, the Kantian "community of reasonable beings", or, in more sociological terms, the subject as citizen, rights-holder, property-owner, and so on'.[1] And yet the term enjoys widespread consensus and it maintains the re-assuring familiarity of common sense. We assert our attachment to the species as if it were a matter of fact, a given. So much so that we construct a fundamental notion of Rights around the Human. But is it so?

While conservative, religious social forces today often labour to re-inscribe the human within a paradigm of natural law, the concept of the human has exploded under the double pressure of contemporary scientific advances and global economic concerns. After the postmodern, the post-colonial, the post-industrial, the post-communist and even the much contested post-feminist conditions, we seem to have entered the post-human predicament. Far from being the nth variation in a sequence of prefixes that may appear both endless and somehow arbitrary, the posthuman condition introduces a qualitative shift in our thinking about what exactly is the basic unit of common reference for our species, our polity and our relationship to the other inhabitants of this planet. This issue raises serious questions as to the very structures of our shared identity—as humans—amidst the complexity of contemporary science, politics and international relations. Discourses and representations of the non-human, the inhuman, the anti-human, the inhumane and the posthuman proliferate and overlap in our globalized, technologically mediated societies.

The debates in mainstream culture range from hard-nosed business discussions of robotics, prosthetic technologies, neuroscience and bio-genetic capital to fuzzier new age visions of trans-humanism and techno-transcendence.[2] Human enhancement is at the core of these debates. In academic culture, on the other hand, the posthuman is alternatively celebrated as the next frontier in critical and cultural theory or shunned as the latest in a series of annoying 'post' fads. The posthuman provokes elation but also anxiety[3] about the possibility of a serious de-centring of 'Man', the former measure of all things. There is widespread concern about the loss of relevance and mastery suffered by the dominant vision of the human subject and by the field of scholarship centred on it, namely the Humanities.

1. Cary Wolfe, "Posthumanities," 2010; available at: http:www.carywolfe.com/post_about.html (accessed 2 January 2012) [except as indicated, all notes are Braidotti's]. ["Cogito": I think (Latin), the starting point of the metaphysics of the French philosopher and mathematician René Descartes (1596–1650)—the occurrence of thought guarantees the existence of the thinker. "Community of reasonable beings": the German philosopher IMMANUEL KANT (1724–1804) limited direct ethical obligations to reasonable beings, implicitly excluding the nonhuman—editor's note.]

2. A belief that, in some future, human and machine will be indistinguishable, as humanity is utterly transformed by technology [editor's note].

3. JÜRGEN HABERMAS, *The Future of Human Nature* (Cambridge: Polity Press, 2003).

In my view, the common denominator for the posthuman condition is an assumption about the vital, self-organizing and yet non-naturalistic structure of living matter itself. This nature–culture continuum is the shared starting point for my take on posthuman theory. Whether this post-naturalistic assumption subsequently results in playful experimentations with the boundaries of perfectibility of the body, in moral panic about the disruption of centuries-old beliefs about human 'nature' or in exploitative and profit-minded pursuit of genetic and neural capital, remains however to be seen. In this book I will try to examine these approaches and engage critically with them, while arguing my case for posthuman subjectivity.

What does this nature–culture continuum amount to? It marks a scientific paradigm that takes its distance from the social constructivist approach, which has enjoyed widespread consensus. This approach posits a categorical distinction between the given (nature) and the constructed (culture). The distinction allows for a sharper focus in social analysis and it provides robust foundations to study and critique the social mechanisms that support the construction of key identities, institutions and practices. In progressive politics, social constructivist methods sustain the efforts to de-naturalize social differences and thus show their man-made and historically contingent structure. Just think of the world-changing effect of Simone de Beauvoir's statement that 'one is not born, one becomes a woman'.[4] This insight into the socially bound and therefore historically variable nature of social inequalities paves the road to their resolution by human intervention through social policy and activism.

My point is that this approach, which rests on the binary opposition between the given and the constructed, is currently being replaced by a non-dualistic understanding of nature–culture interaction. In my view the latter is associated to and supported by a monistic philosophy,[5] which rejects dualism, especially the opposition nature–culture and stresses instead the self-organizing (or auto-poietic) force of living matter. The boundaries between the categories of the natural and the cultural have been displaced and to a large extent blurred by the effects of scientific and technological advances. This book starts from the assumption that social theory needs to take stock of the transformation of concepts, methods and political practices brought about by this change of paradigm. Conversely, the question of what kind of political analysis and which progressive politics is supported by the approach based on the nature–culture continuum is central to the agenda of the posthuman predicament.

* * *

* * * I want to approach posthuman theory as both a genealogical[6] and a navigational tool. I find it useful as a term to explore ways of engaging affirmatively with the present, accounting for some of its features in a manner that is empirically grounded without being reductive and remains critical while avoiding negativity. I want to map out some of the ways in which the

4. The remark that opens vol. 2 of *The Second Sex* (1949), by the French existential philosopher and feminist BEAUVOIR (1908–1986) [editor's note].
5. The view that reality can be reduced to one substance [editor's note].
6. A key term in the work of the French philosopher MICHEL FOUCAULT (1926–1984): this method of historical and critical analysis is designed to demonstrate that a given institution or system of thought resulted from contingencies of history (rather than being inevitable) [editor's note].

posthuman is circulating as a dominant term in our globally linked and technologically mediated societies. More specifically, posthuman theory is a generative tool to help us re-think the basic unit of reference for the human in the bio-genetic age known as 'anthropocene', the historical moment when the Human has become a geological force capable of affecting all life on this planet. By extension, it can also help us re-think the basic tenets of our interaction with both human and non-human agents on a planetary scale.

* * *

From *Chapter 1. Post-Humanism: Life beyond the Self*

At the start of it all there is He: the classical ideal of 'Man', formulated first by Protagoras as 'the measure of all things', later renewed in the Italian Renaissance as a universal model and represented in Leonardo da Vinci's Vitruvian Man.[7] An ideal of bodily perfection which, in keeping with the classical dictum *mens sana in corpore sano*,[8] doubles up as a set of mental, discursive and spiritual values. Together they uphold a specific view of what is 'human' about humanity. Moreover, they assert with unshakable certainty the almost boundless capacity of humans to pursue their individual and collective perfectibility. That iconic image is the emblem of Humanism as a doctrine that combines the biological, discursive and moral expansion of human capabilities into an idea of teleologically ordained, rational progress. Faith in the unique, self-regulating and intrinsically moral powers of human reason forms an integral part of this high-humanistic creed, which was essentially predicated on eighteenth- and nineteenth-century renditions of classical Antiquity and Italian Renaissance ideals.

This model sets standards not only for individuals, but also for their cultures. Humanism historically developed into a civilizational model, which shaped a certain idea of Europe as coinciding with the universalizing powers of self-reflexive reason. The mutation of the Humanistic ideal into a hegemonic cultural model was canonized by Hegel's[9] philosophy of history. This self-aggrandizing vision assumes that Europe is not just a geo-political location, but rather a universal attribute of the human mind that can lend its quality to any suitable object. This is the view espoused by Edmund Husserl in his celebrated essay 'The crisis of European sciences',[1] which is a passionate defence of the universal powers of reason against the intellectual and moral decline symbolized by the rising threat of European fascism in the 1930s. In Husserl's view, Europe announces itself as the site of origin of critical reason and self-reflexivity, both qualities resting on the Humanistic norm. Equal only to itself, Europe as universal consciousness transcends its specificity, or, rather, posits the power of transcendence as its distinctive

7. A famous sketch (1492) by the Italian artist Leonardo da Vinci (1452–1519), showing the proportions of the male body. Protagoras (5th c. B.C.E.), Greek philosopher whose work survives only in fragments; his statement that man is the measure of all things is discussed by PLATO in *Theaetetus* 152a–d [editor's note].

8. A sound mind in a sound body (Latin) [editor's note].

9. GEORG FRIEDRICH WILHELM HEGEL (1770–1831), German philosopher; see especially his *Lectures on the Philosophy of World History* (1837) [editor's note].

1. Edmund Husserl, *The Crisis of European Sciences and Transcendental Phenomenology* (Evanston, Ill.: Northwestern University Press, 1970). [Husserl (1859–1938), German philosopher and principal founder of phenomenology—editor's note.]

characteristic and humanistic universalism as its particularity. This makes Eurocentrism into more than just a contingent matter of attitude: it is a structural element of our cultural practice, which is also embedded in both theory and institutional and pedagogical practices. As a civilizational ideal, Humanism fuelled 'the imperial destinies of nineteenth-century Germany, France and, supremely, Great Britain'.[2]

This Eurocentric paradigm implies the dialectics of self and other, and the binary logic of identity and otherness as respectively the motor for and the cultural logic of universal Humanism. Central to this universalistic posture and its binary logic is the notion of 'difference' as pejoration. Subjectivity is equated with consciousness, universal rationality, and self-regulating ethical behaviour, whereas Otherness is defined as its negative and specular counterpart. In so far as difference spells inferiority, it acquires both essentialist and lethal connotations for people who get branded as 'others'. These are the sexualized, racialized, and naturalized others, who are reduced to the less than human status of disposable bodies. We are all humans, but some of us are just more mortal than others. Because their history in Europe and elsewhere has been one of lethal exclusions and fatal disqualifications, these 'others' raise issues of power and exclusion. We need more ethical accountability in dealing with the legacy of Humanism. Tony Davies puts it lucidly: 'All Humanisms, until now, have been imperial. They speak of the human in the accents and the interests of a class, a sex, a race, a genome. Their embrace suffocates those whom it does not ignore. [. . .] It is almost impossible to think of a crime that has not been committed in the name of humanity'.[3] * * *

Humanism's restricted notion of what counts as the human is one of the keys to understand how we got to a post-human turn at all. The itinerary is far from simple or predictable. Edward Said, for instance, complicates the picture by introducing a post-colonial angle: 'Humanism as protective or even defensive nationalism is [. . .] a mixed blessing for its [. . .] ideological ferocity and triumphalism, although it is sometimes inevitable. In a colonial setting for example, a revival of the suppressed languages and cultures, the attempts at national assertion through cultural tradition and glorious ancestors [. . .] are explainable and understandable'.[4] This qualification is crucial in pointing out the importance of where one is actually speaking from. Differences of location between centres and margins matter greatly, especially in relation to the legacy of something as complex and multi-faceted as Humanism. Complicitous with genocides and crimes on the one hand, supportive of enormous hopes and aspirations to freedom on the other, Humanism somehow defeats linear criticism. This protean quality is partly responsible for its longevity.

ANTI-HUMANISM

Let me put my cards on the table at this early stage of the argument: I am none too fond of Humanism or of the idea of the human which it implicitly upholds. Anti-humanism is so much part of my intellectual and personal

2. Tony Davies, *Humanism* (London: Routledge, 1997), 23.
3. Davis, *Humanism*, 141.
4. Edward W. Said, *Humanism and Democratic Criticism* (New York: Columbia University Press, 2004), 37. [SAID (1935–2003), Palestinian-born American literary and cultural critic and social activist—editor's note.]

genealogy, as well as family background, that for me the crisis of Humanism is almost a banality. Why?

Politics and philosophy are the main reasons for the glee with which I have always greeted the notion of the historical decline of Humanism, with its Eurocentric core and imperial tendencies. Of course, the historical context has a lot to do with it. I came of age intellectually and politically in the turbulent years after the Second World War, when the Humanist ideal came to be questioned quite radically. Throughout the 1960s and 1970s an activist brand of anti-Humanism was developed by the new social movements and the youth cultures of the day: feminism, de-colonization and anti-racism, anti-nuclear and pacifist movements. Chronologically linked to the social and cultural politics of the generation known as the baby-boomers, these social movements produced radical political, social theories and new epistemologies. They challenged the platitudes of Cold War rhetoric, with its emphasis on Western democracy, liberal individualism and the freedom they allegedly ensured for all.

* * *

Up until the 1960s, philosophical reason had escaped relatively unscathed from the question of its responsibilities in perpetuating historical models of domination and exclusion. Both Sartre[5] and de Beauvoir, influenced by Marxist theories of alienation and ideology, did connect the triumph of reason with the might of dominant powers, thus disclosing the complicity between philosophical ratio[6] and real-life social practices of injustice. They continued, however, to defend a universalist idea of reason and to rely on a dialectical model for the resolution of these contradictions. This methodological approach, while being critical of hegemonic models of violent appropriation and consumption of the 'others', also defined the task of philosophy as a privileged and culturally hegemonic tool of political analysis. With Sartre and de Beauvoir, the image of the philosopher-king[7] is built into the general picture, albeit in a critical mode. As a critic of ideology and the conscience of the oppressed, the philosopher is a thinking human being who continues to pursue grand theoretical systems and overarching truths. Sartre and de Beauvoir consider humanistic universalism as the distinctive trait of Western culture, i.e. its specific form of particularism. They use the conceptual tools provided by Humanism to precipitate a confrontation of philosophy with its own historical responsibilities and conceptual power-brokering.

This humanistic universalism, coupled with the social constructivist emphasis on the man-made and historically variable nature of social inequalities, lays the grounds for a robust political ontology. For instance, de Beauvoir's emancipatory feminism builds on the Humanist principle that 'Woman is the measure of all things female'[8] and that to account for herself, the feminist philosopher needs to take into account the situation of all women. This creates on the theoretical level a productive synthesis of self and others. Politically, the Vitruvian female forged a bond of solidarity between one and

5. Jean-Paul Sartre (1905–1980), French existential philosopher, and Beauvoir's lifelong associate and lover [editor's note].
6. Reason [editor's note].
7. The ideal presented in Plato's *Republic* (ca. 375 B.C.E.) [editor's note].
8. Braidotti here inserts an illustration of "Vitruvian Woman," an answer to Vitruvian Man (neither figure is included in this excerpt) [editor's note].

the many, which in the hands of the second feminist wave in the 1960s[9] was to grow into the principle of political sisterhood. This posits a common grounding among women, taking being-women-in-the-world as the starting point for all critical reflection and jointly articulated political praxis.

Humanist feminism introduced a new brand of materialism, of the embodied and embedded kind.[1] The cornerstone of this theoretical innovation is a specific brand of situated epistemology,[2] which evolved from the practice of 'the politics of locations'[3] and infused standpoint feminist theory and the subsequent debates with postmodernist feminism throughout the 1990s.[4] The theoretical premise of humanist feminism is a materialist notion of embodiment that spells the premises of new and more accurate analyses of power. These are based on the radical critique of masculinist universalism, but are still dependent on a form of activist and equality-minded Humanism.

Feminist theory and practice worked faster and more efficiently than most social movements of the 1970s. It developed original tools and methods of analysis that allowed for more incisive accounts of how power works. Feminists also explicitly targeted the masculinism and the sexist habits of the allegedly 'revolutionary' Left and denounced them as contradictory with their ideology, as well as intrinsically offensive.

Within the mainstream Left, however, a new generation of post-war thinkers had other priorities. They rebelled against the high moral status of post-war European Communist parties in Western Europe, as well as in the Soviet empire. This had resulted in an authoritarian hold over the interpretation of Marxist texts and their key philosophical concepts. The new forms of philosophical radicalism developed in France and throughout Europe in the late 1960s expressed a vocal critique of the dogmatic structure of Communist thought and practice. They included a critique of the political alliance between philosophers like Sartre and de Beauvoir and the Communist Left,[5] which lasted at least until the Hungarian insurrection of 1956.[6] In response to the dogma and the violence of Communism, the generation of 1968[7] appealed directly to the subversive potential of the texts of Marx, so as to recover their anti-institutional roots. Their radicalism was expressed in terms of a critique of the humanistic implications and the political conservatism of the institutions that embodied Marxist dogma.

Anti-humanism emerged as the rallying cry of this generation of radical thinkers who later were to become world-famous as the 'post-structuralist generation'. In fact, they were post-communists *avant la letter*.[8] They stepped

9. A movement that sought equal rights and opportunities for women in every sphere (economic, personal, and political). First-wave feminism, in the 18th and early 19th century, focused on women's legal rights, particularly suffrage [editor's note].

1. Rosi Braidotti, *Patterns of Dissonance* (Cambridge: Polity Press, 1991).

2. DONNA HARAWAY, "Situated Knowledges: The Science Question in Feminism as a Site of Discourse on the Privilege of Partial Perspective," *Feminist Studies* 14.3 (1988): 575–99.

3. ADRIENNE RICH, *Blood, Bread and Poetry* (London: Virago Press, 1987).

4. Sandra Harding, *Whose Science? Whose Knowledge?* (Ithaca, N.Y.: Cornell University Press, 1991).

5. Although Sartre and de Beauvoir were not members of the French Communist Party [editor's note].

6. A national revolt against the Soviet-dominated Communist government, which began as a peaceful demonstration on October 23, 1956; it ended on November 10, 1956, after Soviet soldiers and tanks intervened [editor's note].

7. A year of worldwide protests, particularly in France (student protests leading to a general strike), Germany (student protests), Italy (student protests), and the United States (antiwar and civil rights protests by students and others, especially following the assassination of Martin Luther King Jr.) [editor's note].

8. Before the letter (French); that is, before the term existed [editor's note].

out of the dialectical oppositional thinking and developed a third way to deal with changing understandings of human subjectivity. By the time Michel Foucault published his ground-breaking critique of Humanism in *The Order of Things* (1970),[9] the question of what, if anything, was the idea of 'the human' was circulating in the radical discourses of the time and had set the anti-humanist agenda for an array of political groups. The 'death of Man', announced by Foucault formalizes an epistemological and moral crisis that goes beyond binary oppositions and cuts across the different poles of the political spectrum. What is targeted is the implicit Humanism of Marxism, more specifically the humanistic arrogance of continuing to place Man at the centre of world history. Even Marxism, under the cover of a master theory of historical materialism, continued to define the subject of European thought as unitary and hegemonic and to assign him (the gender is no coincidence) a royal place as the motor of human history. Anti-humanism consists in de-linking the human agent from this universalistic posture, calling him to task, so to speak, on the concrete actions he is enacting. Different and sharper power relations emerge, once this formerly dominant subject is freed from his delusions of grandeur and is no longer allegedly in charge of historical progress.

The radical thinkers of the post-1968 generation rejected Humanism both in its classical and its socialist versions. The Vitruvian ideal of Man as the standard of both perfection and perfectibility was literally pulled down from his pedestal and deconstructed. This humanistic ideal constituted, in fact, the core of a liberal individualistic view of the subject, which defined perfectibility in terms of autonomy and self-determination. These are precisely the qualifications the post-structuralists objected to.

It turned out that this Man, far from being the canon of perfect proportions, spelling out a universalistic ideal that by now had reached the status of a natural law, was in fact a historical construct and as such contingent as to values and locations. Individualism is not an intrinsic part of 'human nature', as liberal thinkers are prone to believe, but rather a historically and culturally specific discursive formation, one which, moreover, is becoming increasingly problematic. The deconstructive brand of social constructivism introduced by post-structuralist thinkers like Jacques Derrida[1] also contributed to a radical revision of the Humanist tenets. An entire philosophical generation called for insubordination from received Humanist ideas of 'human nature'.

Feminists like Luce Irigaray[2] pointed out that the allegedly abstract ideal of Man as a symbol of classical Humanity is very much a male of the species: it is a he. Moreover, he is white, European, handsome and able-bodied; of his sexuality nothing much can be guessed, though plenty of speculation surrounds that of its painter, Leonardo da Vinci. What this ideal model may

9. Michel Foucault, *The Order of Things: An Archaeology of the Human Sciences* (New York: Pantheon Books, 1970).
1. Jacques Derrida, *Writing and Difference* [trans. Alan Bass] ([1978; repr.,] New York: Routledge, 2001). [DERRIDA (1930–2004), French deconstructionist philosopher and critic—editor's note.]
2. Luce Irigaray, *Speculum of the Other Woman* [trans. Gillian C. Gill] (Ithaca, N.Y.: Cornell University Press, 1985); *This Sex Which Is Not One* [trans. Catherine Porter with Carolyn Burke] (Ithaca, N.Y.: Cornell University Press, 1985). [Irigaray (b. 1930), Belgian-born French linguist, philosopher, and psychoanalyst; Anglo-American feminists frequently group her together with HÉLÈNE CIXOUS and JULIA KRISTEVA as representative of "French feminism"—editor's note.]

have in common with the statistical average of most members of the species and the civilization he is supposed to represent is a very good question indeed. Feminist critiques of patriarchal posturing through abstract masculinity[3] and triumphant whiteness[4] argued that this Humanist universalism is objectionable not only on epistemological, but also on ethical and political grounds.

Anti-colonial thinkers adopted a similar critical stance by questioning the primacy of whiteness in the Vitruvian ideal as the aesthetic canon of beauty. Re-grounding such lofty claims onto the history of colonialism, anti-racist and post-colonial thinkers explicitly questioned the relevance of the Humanistic ideal, in view of the obvious contradictions imposed by its Eurocentric assumptions, but at the same time they did not entirely cast it aside. They held the Europeans accountable for the uses and abuses of this ideal by looking at colonial history and the violent domination of other cultures, but still upheld its basic premises. Frantz Fanon,[5] for instance, wanted to rescue Humanism from its European perpetuators arguing that we have betrayed and misused the humanist ideal. As Sartre put it in his preface to Fanon's *The Wretched of the Earth*: the yellow and black voices still spoke of our Humanism, but only to reproach us with our inhumanity'.[6] Post-colonial thought asserts that if Humanism has a future at all, it has to come from outside the Western world and by-pass the limitations of Eurocentrism. By extension, the claim to universality by scientific rationality is challenged on both epistemological and political grounds,[7] all knowledge claims being expressions of Western culture and of its drive to mastery.

French post-structuralist philosophers pursued the same post-colonial aim through different routes and means.[8] They argued that in the aftermath of colonialism, Auschwitz, Hiroshima and the Gulag[9]—to mention but a few of the horrors of modern history—we Europeans need to develop a critique of Europe's delusion of grandeur in positing ourselves as the moral guardian of the world and as the motor of human evolution. Thus, the philosophical generation of the 1970s, that proclaimed the 'death of Man' was anti-fascist, post-communist, post-colonial and post-humanist, in a variety of different combinations of the terms. They led to the rejection of the classical definition of European identity in terms of Humanism, rationality and

3. Nancy Hartsock, "The Feminist Standpoint: Developing the Ground for a Specifically Feminist Historical Materialism," in Sandra Harding, ed., *Feminism and Methodology* (London: Open University Press, 1987).

4. bell hooks, *Ain't I a Woman* (Boston: South End Press, 1981); Vron Ware, *Beyond the Pale: White Women, Racism and History* (London: Verso, 1992).

5. Martinique-born French psychoanalyst and postcolonial theorist (1925–1961; see above) [editor's note].

6. Jean-Paul Sartre, preface, in Frantz Fanon, *The Wretched of the Earth* (London: Penguin Books, 1963), 7.

7. Gayatri Chakravorty Spivak, *A Critique of Postcolonial Reason: Toward a History of the Vanishing Present* (Cambridge, Mass.: Harvard University Press, 1999); Said, *Humanism and Democratic Criticism*.

8. This line is pursued in philosophy by Deleuze's rejection of the transcendental vision of the subject [*Difference and Repetition* (London: Athlone Press, 1994)]; Irigaray's decentering of phallogocentrism [*Speculum of the Other Woman* and *This Sex Which Is Not One*]; Foucault's critique of Humanism [*Discipline and Punish: The Birth of the Prison*, trans. Alan Sheridan (New York: Pantheon Books, 1977)] and Derrida's deconstruction of Eurocentrism [*The Other Heading: Reflections on Today's Europe*, trans. Pascale-Anne Brault and Michael B. Naas (Bloomington: Indiana University Press, 1992)]. [Gilles Deleuze (1925–1995), French philosopher—editor's note.]

9. The Russian acronym for "Main Administration of Corrective Labor Camps," a system of labor and prison camps for criminals and political prisoners in the Soviet Union (1919–57) that reached its height under the rule of Joseph Stalin (1929–53). Both Auschwitz (in Poland), the largest of the Nazi concentration camps, and Hiroshima, the Japanese city on which the United States dropped the first atomic bomb in 1945, are associated with World War II [editor's note].

the universal. The feminist philosophies of sexual difference,[1] through the spectrum of the critique of dominant masculinity, also stressed the ethnocentric nature of European claims to universalism. They advocated the need to open it up to the 'others within'[2] in such a way as to re-locate diversity and multiple belongings to a central position as a structural component of European subjectivity.

Anti-humanism is consequently an important source for posthuman thought. It is by no means the only one, nor is the connection between anti-humanism and the posthuman logically necessary or historically inevitable. And yet it turned out to be so for my own work, although this story is still unfinished and in some ways, as I will argue in the next section, my relation to Humanism remains unresolved.

THE DEATH OF MAN, THE DECONSTRUCTION OF WOMAN

As indicated in the genealogical itinerary I have just sketched, anti-humanism is one of the historical and theoretical paths that can lead to the posthuman. I owe my anti-humanism to my beloved post-1968 teachers, some of whom were amazing philosophers whose legacy I continue to respect and admire: Foucault, Irigaray and Deleuze especially. The human of Humanism is neither an ideal nor an objective statistical average or middle ground. It rather spells out a systematized standard of recognizability—of Sameness—by which all others can be assessed, regulated and allotted to a designated social location. The human is a normative convention, which does not make it inherently negative, just highly regulatory and hence instrumental to practices of exclusion and discrimination. The human norm stands for normality, normalcy and normativity. It functions by transposing a specific mode of being human into a generalized standard, which acquires transcendent values as *the* human: from male to masculine and onto human as the universalized format of humanity. This standard is posited as categorically and qualitatively distinct from the sexualized, racialized, naturalized others and also in opposition to the technological artefact. The human is a historical construct that became a social convention about 'human nature'.

My anti-humanism leads me to object to the unitary subject of Humanism, including its socialist variables, and to replace it with a more complex and relational subject framed by embodiment, sexuality, affectivity, empathy and desire as core qualities. Equally central to this approach is the insight I learned from Foucault on power as both a restrictive (*potestas*) and productive (*potentia*) force. This means that power formations not only function at the material level but are also expressed in systems of theoretical and cultural representation, political and normative narratives and social modes of identification. These are neither coherent, nor rational and their makeshift nature is instrumental to their hegemonic force. The awareness of the instability and the lack of coherence of the narratives that compose the social structures and relations, far from resulting in a suspension of political and moral action, become the starting point to elaborate new forms of resistance

1. See, for instance, Irigaray [*An Ethics of Sexual Difference*, trans. Carolyn Burke and Gillian C. Gill (Ithaca, N.Y.: Cornell University Press, 1993)], Cixous ["Mon Algeriance," *Les Inrockuptibles*, magazine archive nr. 115 (August 20, 1997), p. 70], and Braidotti (*Patterns of Dissonance*).

2. Julia Kristeva, *Strangers to Ourselves* [trans. Leon S. Roudiez] (New York: Columbia University Press, 1991).

suited to the polycentric and dynamic structure of contemporary power.[3] This engenders a pragmatic form of micro-politics that reflects the complex and nomadic nature of contemporary social systems and of the subjects that inhabit them. If power is complex, scattered and productive, so must be our resistance to it. Once this deconstructive move is activated, both the standard notion of Man and his second sex, Woman, are challenged in terms of their internal complexities.

This clearly affects the task and the methods status of theory. Discourse, as Michel Foucault argues in *Discipline and Punish* (1977), is about the political currency that is attributed to certain meanings, or systems of meaning, in such a way as to invest them with scientific legitimacy; there is nothing neutral or given about it. Thus, a critical, materialist link is established between scientific truth, discursive currency and power relations. This approach of discourse analysis primarily aims at dislodging the belief in the 'natural' foundations of socially coded and enforced 'differences' and of the systems of scientific validity, ethical values and representation which they support.[4]

Feminist anti-Humanism, also known as postmodernist feminism, rejected the unitary identities indexed on that Eurocentric and normative humanist ideal of 'Man'.[5] It went further, however, and argued that it is impossible to speak in one unified voice about women, natives and other marginal subjects. The emphasis falls instead on issues of diversity and differences among them and on the internal fractures of each category. In this respect, anti-humanism rejects the dialectical scheme of thought, where difference or otherness played a constitutive role, marking off the sexualized other (woman), the racialized other (the native) and the naturalized other (animals, the environment or earth). These others were constitutive in that they fulfilled a mirror function that confirmed the Same in His superior position.[6] This political economy of difference resulted in passing off entire categories of human beings as devalued and therefore disposable others: to be 'different from' came to mean to be 'less than'. The dominant norm of the subject was positioned at the pinnacle of a hierarchical scale that rewarded the ideal of zero-degree of difference.[7] This is the former 'Man' of classical Humanism.

* * *

3. Paul Patton, *Deleuze and the Political* (London: Routledge, 2000).
4. Rosalind Coward and John Ellis, *Language and Materialism: Developments in Semiology and the Theory of the Subject* (London: Routledge & Kegan Paul, 1977). This approach has also been adopted by intersectional analysis, which argues for the methodological parallelism of gender, race, class and sexual factors, without flattening out any differences between them but rather investing politically the question of their complex interaction (Kimberlé Crenshaw, "Intersectionality and Identity Politics: Learning from Violence against Women of Color," in Kimberlé Crenshaw, Neil Gotanda, Gary Peller, and Kendall Thomas, eds., *Critical Race Theory* [New York: New Press, 1995]).
5. Rosi Braidotti, *Metamorphoses: Towards a Materialist Theory of Becoming* (Cambridge: Polity Press, 2002).
6. Rosi Braidotti, *Transpositions: On Nomadic Ethics* (Cambridge: Polity Press, 2006).
7. Deleuze calls it "the Majority subject" or the Molar centre of being (Gilles Deleuze and Félix Guattari, *A Thousand Plateaus: Capitalism and Schizophrenia* (Minneapolis: University of Minnesota Press, 1987). Irigaray calls it "the Same," or the hyper-inflated, falsely universal "He" (Irigaray, *This Sex Which Is Not One* and *An Ethics of Sexual Difference*), whereas Hill Collins calls to account the white and Eurocentric bias of this particular subject of humanistic knowledge (Patricia Hill Collins, *Black Feminist Thought: Knowledge, Consciousness and the Politics of Empowerment* [New York: Routledge, 1991]).

Having practically grown up with theories about the death of God (Nietzsche), the end of Man (Foucault) and the decline of ideologies (Fukuyama),[8] it took me a while to realize that, actually, one touches humanism at one's own risk and peril. The anti-humanist position is certainly not free of contradictions. As Badmington wisely reminds us: 'Apocalyptic accounts of the end of "man" [. . .] ignore Humanism's capacity for regeneration and, quite literally, recapitulation'.[9] The Vitruvian Man rises over and over again from his ashes, continues to uphold universal standards and to exercise a fatal attraction.

The thought did occur to me, as I was listening to Diamanda Galas' 'Plague Mass' (1991)[1] for the victims of AIDS: it is one thing to loudly announce an anti-humanist stance, quite another to act accordingly, with a modicum of consistency. Anti-humanism is a position fraught with such contradictions that the more one tries to overcome them, the more slippery it gets. Not only do anti-humanists often end up espousing humanist ideals—freedom being my favourite one—but also, in some ways, the work of critical thought is supported by intrinsic humanist discursive values.[2] Somehow, neither humanism nor anti-humanism is adequate to the task.

The best example of the intrinsic contradictions generated by the anti-humanist stance is emancipation and progressive politics in general, which I consider one of the most valuable aspects of the humanistic tradition and its most enduring legacy. Across the political spectrum, Humanism has supported on the liberal side individualism, autonomy, responsibility and self-determination.[3] On the more radical front, it has promoted solidarity, community-bonding, social justice and principles of equality. Profoundly secular in orientation, Humanism promotes respect for science and culture, against the authority of holy texts and religious dogma. It also contains an adventurous element, a curiosity-driven yearning for discovery and a project-oriented approach that is extremely valuable in its pragmatism. These principles are so deeply entrenched in our habits of thought that it is difficult to leave them behind altogether.

And why should we? Anti-humanism criticizes the implicit assumptions about the human subject that are upheld by the humanist image of Man, but this does not amount to a complete rejection.

For me it is impossible, both intellectually and ethically, to disengage the positive elements of Humanism from their problematic counterparts: individualism breeds egotism and self-centredness; self-determination can turn to arrogance and domination; and science is not free from its own dogmatic tendencies. The difficulties inherent in trying to overcome Humanism as an intellectual tradition, a normative frame and an institutionalized practice,

8. Francis Fukuyama (b. 1952), neoconservative American political scientist and economist who in *The End of History and the Last Man* (1992) predicted that liberal democracies and capitalism marked the end of human development. FRIEDRICH NIETZSCHE (1844–1900), German philosopher and poet who first announced that God is dead in the prologue to *Thus Spoke Zarathustra* (1885) [editor's note].

9. Neil Badmington, "Theorizing Posthumanism," *Cultural Critique*, no. 53 (2003): 11.

1. A live album by the American avant-garde singer and composer Galas (b. 1955), recorded in 1990 at the Cathedral Church of St. John the Divine in New York City; it criticizes the Catholic Church for its indifference to the AIDS epidemic [editor's note].

2. Kate Soper, *Humanism and Anti-Humanism* (LaSalle, Ill.: Open Court Press, 1986).

3. TZVETAN TODOROV, *Imperfect Garden: The Legacy of Humanism* [trans. Carol Cosman] (Princeton, N.J.: Princeton University Press, 2002).

lie at the core of the deconstructive approach to the posthuman. Derrida opened this discussion by pointing out the violence implicit in the assignation of meaning.[4] His followers pressed the case further: 'the assertion that Humanism can be decisively left behind ironically subscribes to a basic humanist assumption with regard to volition and agency, as if the "end" of Humanism might be subjected to human control, as if we bear the capacity to erase the traces of Humanism from either the present or an imagined future'.[5] The emphasis falls therefore on the difficulty of erasing the trace of the epistemic violence by which a non-humanist position might be carved out of the institutions of Humanism. The acknowledgment of epistemic violence goes hand in hand with the recognition of the real-life violence which was and still is practised against non-human animals and the dehumanized social and political 'others' of the humanist norm. In this deconstructive tradition, Cary Wolfe[6] is especially interesting, as he attempts to strike a new position that combines sensitivity to epistemic and word-historical violence with a distinctly trans-humanist faith[7] in the potential of the post-human condition as conducive to human enhancement.

I have great respect for deconstruction, but also some impatience with the limitations of its linguistic frame of reference. I prefer to take a more materialist route to deal with the complexities of the posthuman as a key feature of our historicity. That road, too, is fraught with perils, as we shall see in the next section.

THE POSTSECULAR TURN

As a progressive political creed, Humanism bears a privileged relation to two other interlocked ideas: human emancipation in the pursuit of equality, and secularism through rational governance. These two premises emerge from the concept of Humanism just like the classical goddess Athena is raised from Zeus' head, fully clad and armed for battle.[8] As John Gray argued: 'Humanism is the transformation of the Christian doctrine of salvation into a project of universal human emancipation. The idea of progress is a secular version of the Christian belief in providence. That is why among the ancient pagans it was unknown'.[9] It is not surprising, therefore, that one of the side-effects of the decline of Humanism is the rise of the post-secular condition.[1]

If the death of Man proved to be a bit of a hasty statement, that of God turned out to be positively delusional. The first cracks in the edifice of self-assured secularity appeared at the end of the 1970s. As the revolutionary zeal cooled off and social movements started to dissipate, conform or mutate, former militant agnostics joined a wave of conversions to a variety of conventional monotheistic or imported Eastern religions. This turn of events

4. Derrida, *Writing and Difference*.
5. Christopher Peterson, "The Posthumanism to Come," *Angelaki: Journal of the Theoretical Humanities* 16.2 (2011): 128.
6. Cary Wolfe, *What Is Posthumanism?* (Minneapolis: University of Minnesota Press, 2010).
7. Nick Bostrom, "A History of Transhuman Thought," *Journal of Evolution and Technology* 14.1 (2005): 1–25.
8. This is the account given in Greek mythology: Athena, goddess of wisdom and war, was born full-grown, without a mother, from the head of Zeus, king of the Olympian gods [editor's note].
9. John Gray, *Straw Dogs* (London: Granta Books, 2002), xiii.
1. Rosi Braidotti, "In Spite of the Times: The Postsecular Turn in Feminism," *Theory, Culture & Society* 25.6 (2008): 1–24; Jürgen Habermas, "Notes on a Post-secular Society," *New Perspectives Quarterly* 25.4 (2008): 17–29.

raised serious doubts as to the future of secularity. The doubt crept into the collective and individual mind: how secular are 'we'—feminists, anti-racists, post-colonialists, environmentalists, etc.—really?

The doubt was even sharper for intellectual activists. Science is intrinsically secular, secularity being a key tenet of Humanism, alongside universalism, the unitary subject and the primacy of rationality. Science itself, however, in spite of its secular foundations, is far from immune from its own forms of dogmatism. Freud[2] was one of the first critical thinkers to warn us against the fanatical atheism of the supporters of scientific reason. In *The Future of an Illusion* (1928), Freud compares different forms of rigid dogmatism, classifying rationalist scientism alongside religion as a source of superstitious belief, a position best illustrated today by the extremism with which Richard Dawkins defends his atheist faith.[3] Moreover, the much-celebrated objectivity of science has also been shown to be quite flawed. The uses and abuses of scientific experimentation under Fascism and in the colonial era prove that science is not immunized against nationalist, racist and hegemonic discourses and practices. Any claim to scientific purity, objectivity and autonomy needs therefore to be firmly resisted. Where does that leave Humanism and its anti-humanist critics?

Secularity is one of the pillars of Western Humanism, thus an instinctive form of aversion to religion and to the church is historically an integral aspect of emancipatory politics. The socialist humanist tradition, which was so central to the European Left and the women's movements in Europe since the eighteenth century, is justified in claiming to be secular in the narrow sense of the term: to be agnostic if not atheist and to descend from the Enlightenment critique of religious dogma and clerical authority. Like other emancipatory philosophies and political practices, the feminist struggle for women's rights in Europe has historically built on secular foundations. The lasting influence exercised by existentialist feminism,[4] and Marxist or socialist feminisms[5] on the second feminist wave, may also account for the perpetuation of this position. As the secular and rebellious daughters of the Enlightenment, European feminists were raised in rational argumentation and detached self-irony. The feminist belief-system is accordingly civic, not theistic and viscerally opposed to authoritarianism and orthodoxy. Feminist politics is also and at the same time a double-edged vision[6] that combines rational arguments with political passions and creates alternative social blueprints and value systems.

However proud twentieth-century feminism may be of its secular roots, it is nonetheless the case that it has historically produced various alternative spiritual practices alongside and often in antagonism to the mainstream

2. SIGMUND FREUD (1856–1939), the Austrian founder of psychoanalysis [editor's note].
3. Richard Dawkins, *The Selfish Gene* (Oxford: Oxford University Press, 1976). [Dawkins (b. 1941), British evolutionary biologist who has become an anti-religion and pro-atheism polemicist—editor's note.]
4. Simone de Beauvoir, *The Second Sex* [trans. H. M. Parshley] ([1952; repr.,] New York: Bantam Books, 1973).
5. Central figures in this tradition are: Shulamith Firestone, *The Dialectic of Sex* (New York: Bantam Books, 1970); Sheila Rowbotham, *Women, Resistance and Revolution* (New York: Random House, 1973); Juliet Mitchell, *Psychoanalysis and Feminism* (New York: Pantheon, 1974); Michèle Barrett, *Women's Oppression Today* (London: Verso Books, 1980); Angela Davis, *Women, Race and Class* (New York: Random House, 1981); Rosalind Coward, *Patriarchal Precedents* (London: Routledge, 1983); and Christine Delphy, *Close to Home. A Materialist Analysis of Women's Oppression* (Amherst: University of Massachusetts Press, 1984).
6. Joan Kelly, "The Double-edged Vision of Feminist Theory," *Feminist Studies* 5.1 (1979): 216–27.

political secularist line. Major writers in the radical feminist tradition of the second American wave, notably Audre Lorde, Alice Walker, and Adrienne Rich,[7] acknowledged the importance of the spiritual dimension of women's struggle for equality and symbolic recognition. The work of Mary Daly, Schussler Fiorenza, and Luce Irigaray,[8] to name but a few, highlights a specific feminist tradition of non-male-centred spiritual and religious practices. Feminist theology in the Christian, Muslim, and Judaic traditions[9] produced well-established communities of both critical resistance and affirmation of creative alternatives. The call for new rituals and ceremonies makes the fortune of the witches' movement, currently best exemplified by Starhawk and reclaimed among others by the epistemologist Stengers.[1] Neo-pagan elements have also emerged in technologically mediated cyber-culture, producing various brands of posthuman techno-asceticism.[2]

Black and post-colonial theories have never been loudly secular. In the very religious context of the USA, African-American women's literature is filled with references to Christianity, as bell hooks and Cornel West demonstrate.[3]

* * *

Let me approach the limits of the feminist secular position from another angle. My monistic philosophy of becomings rests on the idea that matter, including the specific slice of matter that is human embodiment, is intelligent and self-organizing. This means that matter is not dialectically opposed to culture, nor to technological mediation, but continuous with them. This produces a different scheme of emancipation and a non-dialectical politics of human liberation. This position has another important corollary, namely that political agency need not be critical in the negative sense of oppositional and thus may not be aimed solely or primarily at the production of counter-subjectivities. Subjectivity is rather a process of auto-poiesis or self-styling, which involves complex and continuous negotiations with dominant norms and values and hence also multiple forms of accountability.[4] This process-oriented political ontology can accommodate a post-secular turn, a position that is also defended within feminism by a variety of thinkers, such as Harding and Mahmood.[5] The double challenge of linking political subjectivity to religious agency and of disengaging both from oppositional consciousness,

7. Audre Lorde, *Sister Outsider* (Trumansburg, N.Y.: Crossing Press, 1984); Alice Walker, *In Search of Our Mothers' Gardens* (London: Women's Press, 1984); Rich, *Blood, Bread and Poetry*.

8. Mary Daly, *Beyond God the Father: Toward a Theory of Women's Liberation* (Boston: Beacon Press, 1973); Elizabeth Schüssler Fiorenza, *In Memory of Her: A Feminist Theological Reconstruction of Christian Origins* (New York: Crossroads, 1983); Irigaray, *An Ethics of Sexual Difference*.

9. Christian: Catherine Keller, "Christianity," in Alison M. Jaggar and Iris M. Young, eds., *A Companion to Feminist Philosophy* (Oxford: Blackwell, 1998); Muslim: Amina Wadud, *Qur'an and Woman: Rereading the Sacred Text from a Woman's Perspective* (Oxford: Oxford University Press, 1999), and Basharat Tayyab, "Islam," in Jaggar and Young, *A Companion to Feminist Philosophy*; and Judaic: Rachel Adler, "Judaism," in Jaggar and Young, *A Companion to Feminist Philosophy*.

1. Starhawk, *The Spiral Dance* (San Francisco: Harper Books, 1999); Isabelle Stengers, *D'une science à l'autre. Des concepts nomades* [*From One Science to Another: The Concept of Nomadism*] (Paris: Seuil, 1987).

2. Judith Halberstam and Ira Livingston, eds., *Posthuman Bodies* (Bloomington: Indiana University Press, 1995); Braidotti, *Metamorphoses*.

3. bell hooks, "Postmodern Blackness," in *Yearning: Race, Gender and Cultural Politics* (Toronto: Between the Lines, 1990); Cornel West, *Prophetic Thought in Postmodern Times* (Monroe, Me.: Common Courage Press, 1994).

4. Braidotti, *Transpositions*, 2006.

5. Sandra Harding, *The Book of Jerry Falwell: Fundamentalist Language and Politics* (Princeton, N.J.: Princeton University Press, 2000); Saba Mahmood, *Politics of Piety: The Islamic Revival and the Feminist Subject* (Princeton, N.J.: Princeton University Press, 2005).

and from critique defined as negativity, is one of the main issues raised by the posthumanist condition.

Things around Humanism, however, are always more complex than one expects them to be. The return of religion in the public sphere and the strident tone reached by the global public debate on the 'clash of civilizations',[6] not to speak of the permanent state of war on terror that ensued from this context, took many anti-humanists by surprise. To speak of a 'return' of religion is inappropriate, as it suggests a regressive movement. What we are experiencing at present is a more complicated situation. The crisis of secularism, defined as the essentialist belief in the axioms of secularity, is a phenomenon that takes place within the social and political horizon of late globalized post-modernity, not in pre-modern times. It is of the here and now. Moreover, it spreads across all religions, amidst both second and third generation descendants of Muslim immigrants; and amidst born-again fundamentalist Christians and by Hindi, Hebrew and others.

This is the paradoxical and violent global context where the posture of Western 'exceptionalism' has taken the form of self-aggrandizing praise of the Enlightenment Humanist legacy. This claim to an exceptional cultural status foregrounds the emancipation of women, gays and lesbians as the defining feature of the West, coupled with extensive geo-political armed interventions against the rest. Humanism has once again become enlisted in a civilizational crusade. Simultaneously over-estimated in its emancipatory historical role and manipulated for xenophobic purposes by populist politicians across Europe, Humanism may need to be rescued from these oversimplifications and violent abuses. I wonder, therefore, whether nowadays one can continue to uphold a simple anti-humanist position. Is a residual form of Humanism inevitable, intellectually, politically and methodologically, after all? If the new belligerent discourses about the alleged superiority of the West are expressed in terms of the legacy of secular Humanism, while the most vehement opposition to them takes the form of post-secular practices of politicized religion, where can an anti-humanist position rest? To be simply secular would be complicitous with neo-colonial Western supremacist positions, while rejecting the Enlightenment legacy would be inherently contradictory for any critical project. The vicious circle is stifling.

It is out of contradictions of this magnitude that the seemingly endless polemic between Humanism and anti-humanism reaches a dead-end. This position is not only unproductive; it also actively prevents an adequate reading of our immediate context. Leaving behind the tensions that surround Humanism and its self-contradictory refutation is now a priority. Another option becomes increasingly desirable and necessary: posthumanism as a move beyond these lethal binaries. Let us turn to it next.

THE POSTHUMAN CHALLENGE

Posthumanism is the historical moment that marks the end of the opposition between Humanism and anti-humanism and traces a different discur-

6. The title (with a question mark) of a controversial essay (*Foreign Affairs* 72.3 [1993]) by the American political scientist Samuel P. Huntington, who argues (partly in response to his student Francis Fukuyama) that in the aftermath of the fall of the Soviet Union, Islam would become the greatest obstacle to the West's hegemony; he extended his argument in a book, *The Clash of Civilizations and the Remaking of World Order* (1996) [editor's note].

sive framework, looking more affirmatively towards new alternatives. The starting point for me is the anti-humanist death of Wo/Man which marks the decline of some of the fundamental premises of the Enlightenment, namely the progress of mankind through a self-regulatory and teleological ordained use of reason and of secular scientific rationality allegedly aimed at the perfectibility of 'Man'. The posthumanist perspective rests on the assumption of the historical decline of Humanism but goes further in exploring alternatives, without sinking into the rhetoric of the crisis of Man. It works instead towards elaborating alternative ways of conceptualizing the human subject. I will emphasize the priority of the issue of posthuman subjectivity throughout this book.

The crisis of Humanism means that the structural others of the modern humanistic subject re-emerge with a vengeance in postmodernity.[7] It is a historical fact that the great emancipatory movements of postmodernity are driven and fuelled by the resurgent 'others': the women's rights movement; the anti-racism and de-colonization movements; the anti-nuclear and pro-environment movements are the voices of the structural Others of modernity. They inevitably mark the crisis of the former humanist 'centre' or dominant subject-position and are not merely anti-humanist, but move beyond it to an altogether novel, posthuman project. These social and political movements are simultaneously the symptom of the crisis of the subject, and for conservatives even its 'cause', and also the expression of positive, proactive alternatives. In the language of my nomadic theory,[8] they express both the crisis of the majority and the patterns of becoming of the minorities. The challenge for critical theory consists in being able to tell the difference between these different flows of mutation.

In other words, the posthumanist position I am defending builds on the anti-humanist legacy, more specifically on the epistemological and political foundations of the post-structuralist generation, and moves further. The alternative views about the human and the new formations of subjectivity that have emerged from the radical epistemologies of Continental philosophy in the last thirty years do not merely oppose Humanism but create other visions of the self. Sexualized, racialized and naturalized differences, far from being the categorical boundary-keepers of the subject of Humanism, have evolved into fully fledged alternative models of the human subject. * * * I want to emphasize this shift away from anti-Humanism towards an affirmative posthuman position and examine critically some of its components.

I see three major strands in contemporary posthuman thought: the first comes from moral philosophy and develops a reactive form of the posthuman; the second, from science and technology studies, enforces an analytic form of the posthuman; and the third, from my own tradition of anti-humanist philosophies of subjectivity, proposes a critical post-humanism. Let us look at each of these in turn.

7. Braidotti, *Metamorphoses*.

8. Rosi Braidotti, *Nomadic Subjects: Embodiment and Sexual Difference in Contemporary Feminist Theory*, 2d ed. (New York: Columbia University Press, 2011), and *Nomadic Theory: The Portable Rosi Braidotti* (New York: Columbia University Press, 2011).

The reactive approach to the posthuman is defended, both conceptually and politically, by contemporary liberal thinkers like Martha Nussbaum.[9] She develops a thorough contemporary defence of Humanism as the guarantee of democracy, freedom and the respect for human dignity, and rejects the very idea of a crisis of European Humanism, let alone the possibility of its historical decline. Nussbaum does acknowledge the challenges presented by contemporary, technology-driven global economies, but responds to them by reasserting classical humanist ideals and progressive liberal politics. She defends the need for universal humanistic values as a remedy for the fragmentation and the relativistic drift of our times, which is the result of globalization itself. Humanistic cosmopolitan universalism is also presented as an antidote against nationalism and ethnocentrism, which plague the contemporary world, and to the prevailing American attitude of ignorance of the rest of the world.

Central to the reactive or negative post-humanism of Nussbaum is the idea that one of the effects of globalization is a sort of re-contextualization induced by the market economy. This produces a new sense of inter-connection which in turn calls for a neo-humanist ethics. For Nussbaum, abstract universalism is the only stance that is capable of providing solid foundations for moral values such as compassion and respect for others, which she firmly attaches to the tradition of American liberal individualism. I am very happy that Nussbaum stresses the importance of subjectivity, but less happy about the fact that she re-attaches it to a universalistic belief in individualism, fixed identities, steady locations and moral ties that bind.

In other words, Nussbaum rejects the insights of the radical anti-humanist philosophies of the last thirty years. Notably, she embraces universalism over and against the feminist and post-colonial insights about the importance of the politics of location and careful grounding in geo-political terms. By embracing dis-embedded universalism, Nussbaum ends up being paradoxically parochial in her vision of what counts as the human.[1] There is no room for experimenting with new models of the self; for Nussbaum the posthuman condition can be solved by restoring a humanist vision of the subject. As we shall see in the next section, whereas Nussbaum fills the ethical vacuum of the globalized world with classical Humanistic norms, critical posthumanists take the experimental path. They attempt to devise renewed claims to community and belonging by singular subjects who have taken critical distance from humanist individualism.

A second significant posthuman development comes from science and technology studies. This contemporary interdisciplinary field raises crucial ethical and conceptual questions about the status of the human, but is generally reluctant to undertake a full study of their implications for a theory of subjectivity. The influence of Bruno Latour's[2] anti-epistemology and anti-subjectivity position accounts partly for this reluctance. Concretely, it results in parallel and non-communicating lines of posthuman enquiry.

9. MARTHA C. NUSSBAUM, *Cultivating Humanity: A Classical Defense of Reform in Liberal Education* (Cambridge, Mass.: Harvard University Press, 1999) and *Not for Profit: Why Democracy Needs the Humanities* (Princeton, N.J.: Princeton University Press, 2010).

1. HOMI K. BHABHA, "Unpacking my library . . . again," in Iain Chambers and Lidia Curti, eds., *The Post-Colonial Question: Common Skies, Divided Horizons* (London: Routledge, 1996).

2. French anthropologist and sociologist of science (b. 1947; see above) [editor's note].

A new segregation of knowledge is produced, along the dividing lines of the 'two cultures',[3] the Humanities and the Sciences. * * *

For now, let me stress that there is a posthuman agreement that contemporary science and biotechnologies affect the very fibre and structure of the living and have altered dramatically our understanding of what counts as the basic frame of reference for the human today. Technological intervention upon all living matter creates a negative unity and mutual dependence among humans and other species. The Human Genome Project,[4] for instance, unifies all the human species on the basis of a thorough grasp of our genetic structure. This point of consensus, however, generates diverging paths of enquiry. The Humanities continue to ask the question of the epistemological and political implications of the posthuman predicament for our understanding of the human subject. They also raise deep anxieties both about the moral status of the human and express the political desire to resist commercially owned and profit-minded abuses of the new genetic know-how.

Contemporary science and technology studies, on the other hand, adopt a different agenda. They have developed an analytic form of posthuman theory. For instance, Franklin, Lury and Stacey, working within a socio-cultural frame of reference, refer to the technologically mediated world of today as 'panhumanity'.[5] This indicates a global sense of inter-connection among all humans, but also between the human and the non-human environment, including the urban, social and political, which creates a web of intricate inter-dependences. This new pan-humanity is paradoxical in two ways: firstly, because a great deal of its inter-connections are negative and based on a shared sense of vulnerability and fear of imminent catastrophes and, secondly, because this new global proximity does not always breed tolerance and peaceful co-existence; on the contrary, forms of xenophobic rejection of otherness and increasing armed violence are key features of our times. * * *

* * *

Another significant case for analytic post-humanism is advocated by Peter-Paul Verbeek.[6] Starting from the recognition of the intimate and productive association between human subjects and technological artefacts, as well as the theoretical impossibility of keeping them apart, Verbeek hints at the need for a post-anthropological turn that links humans to non-humans, but he is also very careful not to trespass certain limits. His analytic form of post-humanism is immediately qualified by a profoundly humanist and thus normative approach to technology itself. Verbeek's main argument is that 'technologies contribute actively to how humans do ethics';[7] a revised and updated form of humanist ethics gets superimposed on post-humanist technologies.

In order to defend the humanist principle at the heart of contemporary technologies, Verbeek emphasizes the moral nature of technological tools

3. "The Two Cultures" (1956) was an article by the English scientist and novelist C. P. Snow, later expanded and published as *The Two Cultures and the Scientific Revolution* (1959) [editor's note].
4. An international scientific project (1990–2003) that successfully determined and published the sequences of the genetic content of human chromosomes [editor's note].
5. Sarah Franklin, Celia Lury, and Jackie Stacey, *Global Nature, Global Culture* (London: Sage, 2000), 26.
6. Peter-Paul Verbeek, *Moralizing Technology: Understanding and Designing the Morality of Things* (Chicago: University of Chicago Press, 2011).
7. Verbeek, *Moralizing Technology*, 5.

as agents that can guide human decision making on normative issues. He also introduces multiple forms of machinic intentionality, all of them indexed on non-human forms of moral consciousness. Only by taking seriously the morality of things, argues Verbeek, can we hope to integrate our technology into the wider social community and bring a posthuman brand of Humanism into the twenty-first century. This results in shifting the location of traditional moral intentionality from autonomous transcendental consciousness to the technological artefacts themselves.

The analytic post-humanism of science and technology studies is one of the most important elements of the contemporary posthuman landscape. In terms of critical theories of the subject, which is the focus of my position, however, this position falls wide of the mark, because it introduces selected segments of humanistic values without addressing the contradictions engendered by such a grafting exercise.

The pride in technological achievements and in the wealth that comes with them must not prevent us from seeing the great contradictions and the forms of social and moral inequality engendered by our advanced technologies. Not addressing them, in the name of either scientific neutrality or of a hastily reconstructed sense of the pan-human bond induced by globalization, simply begs the question.

In my eyes, what is striking about the science and technology studies approach, whether it relies theoretically on moral philosophy or on sociocultural theory, is the high degree of political neutrality it expresses about the posthuman predicament. Both Rose and Franklin et al.,[8] for instance, make it clear that the focus of their research is analytic and aims to achieve a better, more thorough and in some ways intimate ethnographic understanding of how these new technologies actually function. Science and technology studies tend to dismiss the implications of their positions for a revised vision of the subject. Subjectivity is out of the picture and, with it, a sustained political analysis of the posthuman condition. In my view, a focus on subjectivity is necessary because this notion enables us to string together issues that are currently scattered across a number of domains. For instance, issues such as norms and values, forms of community bonding and social belonging as well as questions of political governance both assume and require a notion of the subject. Critical posthuman thought wants to reassemble a discursive community out of the different, fragmented contemporary strands of posthumanism.

* * *

There is another fundamental problem with the residual humanism of the analytically posthuman attempts to moralize technology and sideline experiments with new forms of subjectivity, namely their over-confidence about the moral intentionality of the technology itself. More specifically, they neglect the current state of autonomy reached by the machines. The complexity of our smart technologies lies at the core of the post-anthropocentric turn. * * * Let us consider just one aspect of our technological smartness.

8. Nicholas Rose, *The Politics of Life Itself: Biomedicine, Power and Subjectivity in the Twenty-First Century* (Princeton, N.J.: Princeton University Press, 2007); Franklin, Lury, and Stacey, *Global Nature, Global Culture*.

A recent issue of the weekly magazine *The Economist* (2 June 2012) on 'Morals and the machine' raises some pertinent issues about the degree of autonomy reached by robots and calls for society to develop new rules to manage them. The analysis is significant: in contrast to the modernist idea of the robot as subservient to the human, as exemplified by Isaac Asimov's 'three laws of robotics' formulated in 1942,[9] we are now confronted by a new situation, which makes human intervention rather peripheral if not completely irrelevant. *The Economist* argues:

> As robots become more autonomous, the notion of computer-controlled machines facing ethical decisions is moving out of the realm of science fiction and into the real world.[1]

Most of these new robots are military in purpose * * * but many others are used for perfectly reasonable civilian purposes. All of them share a crucial feature: they have made it technologically feasible to by-pass human decision making at both the operational and the moral levels. According to this report, humans will increasingly operate not 'in the loop' but 'on the loop', monitoring armed and working robots rather than fully controlling them. Only ethical and legal issues remain to be solved to grant responsibility to autonomous machines' decision making, while the cognitive capacities are already in place.

As they become smarter and more widespread, autonomous machines are bound to make life-or-death decisions and thus assume agency. Whether this high degree of autonomy, however, results in moral decision making is at best an open question. Against claims to the in-built moral intentionality of the technology, I would claim that it is normatively neutral. Take some burning issues, such as: should an unmanned flying vehicle, also known as a drone, fire on a house where a target is known to be hiding, which also shelters civilians? Should robots involved in disaster relief tell people the truth about their conditions, thus causing panic and pain? Such questions lead to the field of 'machine ethics', which aims to give machines the ability to make such choices appropriately, in other words, to tell right from wrong. And who is to decide?

According to *The Economist*, a new ethical approach needs to be developed by active experiments. They should focus on three areas especially: firstly, the rule of Laws to determine whether the designer, the programmer, the manufacturer, or the operator is at fault if a machine goes wrong. To allocate responsibility, a detailed logs system is needed so that it can explain the reasoning behind the decision-making process. This has implications for design, with a preference for systems that obey pre-defined rules rather than decision-making systems. Secondly, when ethical systems are embedded in robots, the judgements they make need to be ones that seem right to most

9. These three laws are: (1) A robot may not injure a human being or, through inaction, allow a human being to come to harm. (2) A robot must obey the orders given to it by human beings, except where such orders would conflict with the First Law. (3) A robot must protect its own existence as long as such protection does not conflict with the First or Second Laws. These rules were set up by Isaac Asimov in a short story in 1942 and then re-printed in the world best-seller: *I, Robot*, in 1950. They became foundational notions in cyber-studies. Later, Asimov added a fourth law which precedes all others: (0) A robot may not harm humanity, or, by inaction, allow humanity to come to harm. [Asimov (1920–1992), American biochemist and author, best known for his science fiction—editor's note.]

1. "Morals and the Machine," *The Economist*, June 2, 2012, p. 11.

people. The techniques of experimental philosophy, which studies how people respond to ethical dilemmas, should be able to help. Thirdly, new interdisciplinary collaboration is required between engineers, ethicists, lawyers and policy-makers, all of whom would draw up very different rules if left to their own devices. They all stand to gain by working with each other.

What is posthuman about the situation outlined in *The Economist* is that it does not assume a human, individualized self as the deciding factor of main subject. It rather envisages what I would call a transversal interconnection or an 'assemblage' of human and non-human actors, not unlike Latour's Actor Network Theory.[2] It is significant that a rather cautious and conservative journal like *The Economist*, faced with the challenge of the posthuman powers of the technologies we have developed, does not call for a return to humanist values, but for pragmatic experimentation. This prompts three comments on my part: firstly, that I could not agree more that this is no time for nostalgic longings for the humanist past, but for forward-looking experiments with new forms of subjectivity. Secondly, I want to emphasize the normatively neutral structure of contemporary technologies: they are not endowed with intrinsic humanistic agency. Thirdly, I note that the advocates of advanced capitalism seem to be faster in grasping the creative potential of the posthuman than some of the well-meaning and progressive neo-humanist opponents of this system. * * *

CRITICAL POSTHUMANISM

The third strand of posthuman thought, my own variation, shows no conceptual or normative ambivalence towards posthumanism. I want to move beyond analytic posthumanism and develop affirmative perspectives on the posthuman subject. My inspiration for taking the jump into critical posthumanism comes from my anti-humanist roots, of course. More specifically, the current of thought that has gone further in unfolding the productive potential of the posthuman predicament can be genealogically traced back to the poststructuralists, the anti-universalism of feminism and the anti-colonial phenomenology of Frantz Fanon and of his teacher Aimé Césaire.[3] What they have in common in a sustained commitment to work out the implications of posthumanism for our shared understandings of the human subject and of humanity as a whole.

The work of post-colonial and race theorists displays a situated cosmopolitan posthumanism that is supported as much by the European tradition as by non-Western sources of moral and intellectual inspiration. The examples are manifold and deserve more in-depth analysis than I can grant them here; for now, let me pick out the main gist of it.[4]

2. John Law and John Hassard, eds., *Actor Network Theory and After* (Oxford: Blackwell, 1999). [Actor Network Theory: a theoretical approach to understanding technoscience that follows "actors" (either human or nonhuman) to understand the "networks" or assemblages that they create, which can coalesce into scientific facts. This methodology yields more complex accounts of scientific discovery than those that feature a "hero"—editor's note.]

3. Frantz Fanon, *Black Skin, White Masks* (New York: Grove Press, 1967); Aimé Césaire, *Discours sur le colonialisme* [*Discourse on Colonialism*] (Paris: Presence Africain, 1955). [Césaire (1913–2008), Martinican politician and author, one of the founders of the *négritude* movement in Francophone literature that asserted black and African pride—editor's note.]

4. Significant examples are: Avtar Brah's diasporic ethics in *Cartographies of Diaspora: Contesting Identities* (New York: Routledge, 1996) echoes Vandana Shiva's anti-global neo-Humanism in *Biopiracy: The Plunder of Nature and Knowledge* (Boston: South End Press, 1997).

Edward Said[5] was among the first to alert critical theorists in the West to the need to develop a reasoned scholarly account of Enlightenment-based secular Humanism, which would take into account the colonial experience, its violent abuses and structural injustice, as well as post-colonial existence. Post-colonial theory developed this insight into the notion that ideals of reason, secular tolerance, equality under the Law and democratic rule, need not be, and indeed historically have not been, mutually exclusive with European practices of violent domination, exclusion and systematic and instrumental use of terror. Acknowledging that reason and barbarism are not self-contradictory, nor are Enlightenment and horror, need not result in either cultural relativism, or in moral nihilism, but rather in a radical critique of the notion of Humanism and its link with both democratic criticism and secularism. Edward Said defends the idea that:

> It is possible to be critical of Humanism in the name of Humanism and that, schooled in its abuses by the experience of Eurocentrism and empire, one could fashion a different kind of Humanism that was cosmopolitan and text-and-language bound in ways that absorbed the great lessons of the past [. . .] and still remain attuned to the emergent voices and currents of the present, many of them exilic, extraterritorial, and unhoused.[6]

Fighting for such subaltern secular spaces is a priority for a posthuman quest for what is known in some quarters as a 'global ethic for global politics and economics'.[7]

Paul Gilroy's planetary cosmopolitanism[8] also proposes a productive form of contemporary critical posthumanism. Gilroy holds Europe and the Europeans accountable for our collective failure in implementing the ideals of the humanist Enlightenment. Like the feminists, race theorists are suspicious of deconstructing a subject-position, which historically they never gained the right to. Gilroy considers colonialism and fascism as a betrayal of the European ideal of the Enlightenment, which he is determined to defend, holding Europeans accountable for their ethical and political failings. Racism splits common humanity and disengages whites from any ethical sensibility, reducing them to an infrahuman moral status. It also reduces non-whites to a subhuman ontological status that exposes them to murderous violence. Taking a strong stand against the return of fundamentalist appeals to ethnic differences by a variety of white, black, Serbian, Rwandan, Texan and other nationalists, Gilroy denounces what Deleuze calls 'micro-fascisms'[9] as the epidemics of our globalized times. He locates the site of the ethical transformation in the critique of each nationalistic cate-

African Humanism or Ubuntu is receiving more attention, from Patricia Hill Collins (*Black Feminist Thought*) to Drucilla Cornell in *The Ubuntu Project with Stellenbosch University*, www.fehe.org/index.php?id=281 (2002) (accessed 2 January 2007). In a more nomadic vein, Edouard Glissant's politics of relations in *Poetics of Relation* [trans. Betsy Wing] (Ann Arbor: University of Michigan Press, 1997) inscribed multi-lingual hybridity at the heart of the contemporary posthuman condition. Homi Bhabha's "subaltern secularism" in *The Location of Culture* (London: Routledge, 1994) builds on the huge legacy of Edward Said.

5. Edward Said, *Orientalism* (Harmondsworth: Penguin Books, 1978).

6. Said, *Humanism and Democratic Criticism*, 11.

7. Hans Kung, *A Global Ethic for Global Politics and Economics* (Oxford: Oxford University Press, 1998).

8. Paul Gilroy, *Against Race: Imagining Political Culture beyond the Color Line* (Cambridge, Mass.: Harvard University Press, 2000). [Gilroy (b. 1956), British-born scholar of cultural studies and the Black Atlantic diaspora—editor's note.]

9. Deleuze and Guattari, *A Thousand Plateaus*.

gory, not in the assertion of a new dominant one. He sets diasporic mobility and the transcultural interconnections up against the forces of nationalism. This is a theory of mixture, hybridity and cosmopolitanism that is resolutely non-racial. Against the enduring power of nation states, Gilroy posits instead the affirmative politics of transversal movements, such as anti-slavery, feminism, Médécins sans frontières[1] and the like.

An altogether different and powerful source of inspiration for contemporary re-configurations of critical posthumanism is ecology and environmentalism. They rest on an enlarged sense of inter-connection between self and others, including the non-human or 'earth' others. This practice of relating to others requires and is enhanced by the rejection of self-centred individualism. It produces a new way of combining self-interests with the well-being of an enlarged community, based on environmental inter-connections.

Environmental theory stresses the link between the humanistic emphasis on Man as the measure of all things and the domination and exploitation of nature and condemns the abuses of science and technology. Both of them involve epistemic and physical violence over the structural 'others' and are related to the European Enlightenment ideal of 'reason'. The worldview which equated Mastery with rational scientific control over 'others' also militated against the respect for the diversity of living matters and of human cultures.[2] The environmental alternative is a new holistic approach that combines cosmology with anthropology and post-secular, mostly feminist spirituality, to assert the need for loving respect for diversity in both its human and non-human forms. Significantly, Shiva and Mies stress the importance of life-sustaining spirituality in this struggle for new concrete forms of universality: a reverence for the sacredness of life, of deeply seated respect for all that lives. This attitude is opposed to Western Humanism and to the West's investment in rationality and secularity as the pre-condition for development through science and technology. In a holistic perspective, they call for the 're-enchantment of the world'[3] or for healing the Earth and that which has been so cruelly disconnected. Instead of the emphasis on emancipation from the realm of natural necessity, Shiva pleads for a form of emancipation that occurs within that realm and in harmony with it. From this shift of perspective there follows a critique of the ideal of equality as the emulation of masculine modes of behaviour and also the rejection of the model of development that is built upon this ideal and is compatible with world-wide forms of market domination.

Although ecological posthumanists like Shiva take great care to distance themselves from anything that is even remotely related to 'post'-modernism, post-colonialism, or post-feminism, paradoxically, they share in the epistemic premises of posthuman critiques. For instance, they agree with the post-structuralist generation on the critique of the homogenization of cultures under the effects of globalized advanced capitalism. They propose as an alternative a robust type of environmentalism, based on non-Western neo-humanism. What matters for Mies and Shiva is the reassertion of the need for new universal values in the sense of interconnectedness among humans,

1. Doctors without Borders (French), an independent international nonprofit medical humanitarian organization [editor's note].

2. Maria Mies and Vandana Shiva, *Ecofeminism* (London: Zed Books, 1993).

3. Mies and Shiva, *Ecofeminism*, 18.

on a worldwide scale. Thus, universal needs are amalgamated to universal rights and they cover as much basic and concrete necessities, such as food, shelter, health, safety, as higher cultural needs, like education, identity, dignity, knowledge, affection, joy and care. These constitute the material grounding of the situated claims to new ethical values.

A new ecological posthumanism thus raises issues of power and entitlement in the age of globalization and calls for self-reflexivity on the part of the subjects who occupy the former humanist centre, but also those who dwell in one of the many scattered centres of power of advanced post-modernity.[4]

In my own work, I define the critical posthuman subject within an eco-philosophy of multiple belongings, as a relational subject constituted in and by multiplicity, that is to say a subject that works across differences and is also internally differentiated, but still grounded and accountable. Posthuman subjectivity expresses an embodied and embedded and hence partial form of accountability, based on a strong sense of collectivity, relationality and hence community building.

My position is in favour of complexity and promotes radical posthuman subjectivity, resting on the ethics of becoming. * * * The focus is shifted accordingly from unitary to nomadic subjectivity, thus running against the grain of high humanism and its contemporary variations. This view rejects individualism, but also asserts an equally strong distance from relativism or nihilistic defeatism. It promotes an ethical bond of an altogether different sort from the self-interests of an individual subject, as defined along the canonical lines of classical Humanism. A posthuman ethics for a non-unitary subject proposes an enlarged sense of inter-connection between self and others, including the non-human or 'earth' others, by removing the obstacle of self-centred individualism. As we saw earlier, contemporary bio-genetic capitalism generates a global form of reactive mutual inter-dependence of all living organisms, including non-humans. This sort of unity tends to be of the negative kind, as a shared form of vulnerability, that is to say a global sense of inter-connection between the human and the non-human environment in the face of common threats. The posthuman recomposition of human interaction that I propose is not the same as the reactive bond of vulnerability, but is an affirmative bond that locates the subject in the flow of relations with multiple others.

* * * For me there is a necessary link between critical posthumanism and the move beyond anthropocentrism. I refer to this move as expanding the notion of Life towards the non-human or *zoe*.[5] This results in radical posthumanism as a position that transposes hybridity, nomadism, diasporas and creolization processes into means of re-grounding claims to subjectivity, connections and community among subjects of the human and the non-human kind. * * *

2013

4. Inderpal Grewal and Caren Kaplan, eds., *Scattered Hegemonies: Postmodernity and Transnational Feminist Practices* (Minneapolis: University of Minnesota Press, 1994).

5. Life (Greek). A number of contemporary theorists (most notably GIORGIO AGAMBEN) find a distinction in Aristotle's *Politics* between *zōē* (bare or biological life) and *bios* (life meaningfully shaped in interactions with others) [editor's note].

ROB NIXON
b. 1954

Rob Nixon is a public intellectual whose work in ecological criticism and postcolonial literature has established him as a leading figure in the interdisciplinary field of environmental humanities. By precept and by example, he urges that scholarly and public writing be married to concrete struggles for justice.

Nixon was born in South Africa, where he earned a B.A. from Rhodes University (1978). Rejecting South Africa's then-dominant apartheid regime, Nixon expatriated and earned an M.A. in English from the University of Iowa (1982) followed by an M.Phil. and Ph.D. in English from Columbia University (1984, 1989). While in graduate school, Nixon began publishing journalistic essays in magazines such as the *Nation*, *Border/lines*, and the *Village Voice* in addition to scholarly articles in journals such as *Critical Arts* and *English in Africa*. After receiving his Ph.D., Nixon taught at Columbia University and the University of Wisconsin–Madison. In 2015, he became Currie C. and Thomas A. Barron Family Professor in the Humanities and the Environment at Princeton University. Throughout his career, Nixon has pursued both public and scholarly writing; that breadth has enabled him to make the ideas of ecological and postcolonial theory accessible to wide audiences, as he has frequently published in outlets such as the *New York Times*, the *Atlantic*, and the *London Review of Books*. His books similarly range from academic cultural criticism to creative nonfiction.

Our first selection is from the introduction to Nixon's book *Slow Violence and the Environmentalism of the Poor* (2011). The book highlights forms of environmental violence that are easily ignored because they occur over long periods of time and are spatially dispersed. As an example of such "slow violence," Nixon describes how in the 1980s mothers in the Marshall Islands were still giving birth to "headless, eyeless, limbless human infants who would live just a few hours" because of the long-term effects of radiation contamination from atmospheric nuclear tests conducted there from 1948 to 1958. The decades-long delay between an action (nuclear tests) and its violent effects (malformed infants) could easily function to obscure the public perception of the causal relationship between the two. This problem is made more acute by what Nixon calls "the flickering attention spans" of people living in wealthy twenty-first-century capitalist nations. The combination of spectacle-driven ephemeral corporate media, time-saving domestic technologies, and the habit of expecting instant gratification of consumer desires has made it difficult for such individuals to attend to atrocities that are committed gradually. To people accustomed to the spectacles of war and sudden natural disasters, violence that is inflicted over the course of decades seems unreal. At the same time, industrial technologies have made it possible for humans to affect local and global ecologies more dramatically than ever before, as is demonstrated by numerous instances of slow violence, including toxic drift, deforestation, ocean acidification, and climate change. The consequent risk of widespread suffering due to adverse ecological effects makes attending to slow violence a matter of grave importance.

The urgent task of drawing public and political attention to the problem of slow violence leads Nixon to promote the work of activist writers who tell stories and create images that are capable of shining a spotlight on acts of violence that are not easily reduced to media spectacles. In particular, he highlights the work of environmentalist writers who give "scientific and imaginative testimony" to ecological injustices in a way that captures public attention, stirs emotion, and inspires concrete political action. In Nixon's view, the social importance of such public intellectuals often requires them to cross the traditional boundaries between academic disciplines as well as the boundaries between academic and journalistic writing. Along these lines, Nixon is particularly invested in the "environmental humanities," an interdisciplinary field in which historians and literary critics with a concern for ecological justice are joining scholars in the hard and social sciences to "testify on issues of world urgency." Nixon's work seeks to forge such alliances for the purpose of creative communication that can raise consciousness and stir action regarding ecological issues of great consequence on a global scale.

That scale leads to the major theme suggested in the second half of Nixon's book title: the environmentalism of the poor. Nixon asserts that the people most threatened by slow violence are those who lack resources, especially the impoverished peoples of the global South. In previous generations, environmental activism was dominated by the inhabitants of rich nations for whom environmentalism was often a "planetary abstraction" disconnected from the concrete struggles of the poor; consequently, their activism was viewed with suspicion by poor non-Westerners. However, Nixon argues that the intensification of ecological exploitation due to globalization and neoliberal capitalism has provoked an intensification of resistance from the poor. Many impoverished people and groups who have long depended on local resources that are being exploited by global capitalists are now becoming "resource rebels" who "experience environmental threat not as a planetary abstraction but as a set of inhabited risks." Nixon argues that the future of the biosphere depends in large part on the relations among environmentalists, writer-activists, and the resource rebels of the global poor whose voices desperately need to be heard.

Our second selection from Nixon, "The Anthropocene: The Promise and Pitfalls of an Epochal Idea" (2014), considers a concept in environmental studies that seeks to highlight the massive impact that humans in the modern era are having on the present and future of the planet. The term *Anthropocene*, which was popularized in 2000 by the atmospheric chemist Paul Crutzen and the ecologist Eugene Stoermer, refers to a proposed new geological epoch that began in the late eighteenth century and is defined by massive human impacts on the earth's geophysical and biophysical systems. Though the concept is useful, Nixon points out its potential problems, such as the danger of ignoring the massive inequities between the world's rich and poor in a reductive master narrative about how "humanity" has changed the planet. He also expresses concern about "Anthropocene optimists" who tell a hubristic story about humans emerging as demigods who will increasingly excel at bending the planet to their collective will. Against these tendencies, Nixon advocates learning to tell two different kinds of narratives held in tension. The first describes humanity's increasing impact on a planet that nonetheless remains outside of humanity's control, and the second focuses on the many frictions and diversities characterizing humans' ways of relating to the planet in an age of "the uber-rich and the ultra-poor." Nixon again calls for academics, public intellectuals, and other creative communicators to develop stories and images that can help a growing number of people see, feel, and respond appropriately to the reality of massive ecological changes that humans have slowly brought about over the course of centuries.

Nixon's arguments are open to criticism from several angles. Some have suggested that his concept of slow violence inadvertently obscures the rapid impact of the environmental degradations he describes, and that the term *violence* oversimplifies matters by implying conscious, malevolent intent on the part of persons responsible for these degradations. Furthermore, those who are more critical than Nixon of the notion of the Anthropocene might argue that it betrays "presentist" or anthropocentric biases by exaggerating the role of modern humans in shaping the earth. Despite such criticisms, Nixon's work has won wide praise for its insightful synthesis of ecocriticism with postcolonial theory. Nixon's insistence on viewing slow violence from the perspective of people in postimperial situations illuminates the connections between environmental activists and theorists such as EDWARD W. SAID, whom Nixon cites as a major inspiration. Moreover, the arguments of ecological theorists such as

TIMOTHY MORTON, who emphasizes the profound interconnectedness of all life, can be further developed by Nixon's stress on the spatially and temporally dispersed connections that exist between people in different generations and on different continents. Nixon's exploration of the intersections between environmental and postcolonial theory demonstrates that the two fields have much to offer one another.

Slow Violence and the Environmentalism of the Poor **Keywords:** Cultural Studies, Ethics, Globalization, Media, Postcolonial Criticism, Postcolonial Theory, Representation
"The Anthropocene: The Promise and Pitfalls of an Epochal Idea" Keywords: Ethics, Globalization, Modernity

From Slow Violence and the Environmentalism of the Poor

From *Introduction*

> I think of globalization like a light which shines brighter and brighter on a few people and the rest are in darkness, wiped out. They simply can't be seen. Once you get used to not seeing something, then, slowly, it's no longer possible to see it.
>
> —Arundhati Roy[1]

> I think the economic logic behind dumping a load of toxic waste in the lowest wage country is impeccable and we should face up to that. . . . I've always thought that countries in Africa are vastly under polluted; their air quality is probably vastly inefficiently low compared to Los Angeles. . . . Just between you and me, shouldn't the World Bank be encouraging more migration of the dirty industries to the Least Developed Countries?
>
> —Lawrence Summers, confidential World Bank memo, December 12, 1991

When Lawrence Summers, then president of the World Bank, advocated that the bank develop a scheme to export rich nation garbage, toxic waste, and heavily polluting industries to Africa, he did so in the calm voice of global managerial reasoning.[2] Such a scheme, Summers elaborated, would help correct an inefficient global imbalance in toxicity. Underlying his plan is an overlooked but crucial subsidiary benefit that he outlined: offloading rich-nation toxins onto the world's poorest continent would help ease the growing pressure from rich-nation environmentalists who were campaigning against garbage dumps and industrial effluent that they condemned as health threats and found aesthetically offensive. Summers thus rationalized his poison-redistribution ethic as offering a double gain: it would benefit the United States and Europe economically, while helping appease the rising

1. Indian author and political activist (b. 1961), well-known for her novel *The God of Small Things* (1997) [editor's note; except as indicated, all notes are Nixon's].
2. Philip Arestis, "Furor on Memo at World Bank," *New York Times*, February 7, 1992. For insightful commentary on Summers' proposal, see also Upamanyu Pablo Mukherjee, *Postcolonial Environments: Nature, Culture and the Contemporary Indian Novel in English* (London: Palgrave Macmillan, 2010). [The World Bank is an international financial institution that provides capital loans to developing countries with the stated goal of reducing poverty; it has been criticized for requiring countries to implement major changes to their economic structures—editor's note.]

discontent of rich-nation environmentalists. Summers' arguments assumed a direct link between aesthetically unsightly waste and Africa as an out-of-sight continent, a place remote from green activists' terrain of concern. In Summers' win-win scenario for the global North, the African recipients of his plan were triply discounted: discounted as political agents, discounted as long-term casualties of what I call in this book "slow violence," and discounted as cultures possessing environmental practices and concerns of their own. I begin with Summers' extraordinary proposal because it captures the strategic and representational challenges posed by slow violence as it impacts the environments—and the environmentalism—of the poor.

Three primary concerns animate this book, chief among them my conviction that we urgently need to rethink—politically, imaginatively, and theoretically—what I call "slow violence." By slow violence I mean a violence that occurs gradually and out of sight, a violence of delayed destruction that is dispersed across time and space, an attritional violence that is typically not viewed as violence at all. Violence is customarily conceived as an event or action that is immediate in time, explosive and spectacular in space, and as erupting into instant sensational visibility. We need, I believe, to engage a different kind of violence, a violence that is neither spectacular nor instantaneous, but rather incremental and accretive, its calamitous repercussions playing out across a range of temporal scales. In so doing, we also need to engage the representational, narrative, and strategic challenges posed by the relative invisibility of slow violence. Climate change, the thawing cryosphere, toxic drift, biomagnification,[3] deforestation, the radioactive aftermaths of wars, acidifying oceans, and a host of other slowly unfolding environmental catastrophes present formidable representational obstacles that can hinder our efforts to mobilize and act decisively. The long dyings—the staggered and staggeringly discounted casualties, both human and ecological that result from war's toxic aftermaths or climate change—are underrepresented in strategic planning as well as in human memory.

Had Summers advocated invading Africa with weapons of mass destruction, his proposal would have fallen under conventional definitions of violence and been perceived as a military or even an imperial invasion. Advocating invading countries with mass forms of slow-motion toxicity, however, requires rethinking our accepted assumptions of violence to include slow violence. Such a rethinking requires that we complicate conventional assumptions about violence as a highly visible act that is newsworthy because it is event focused, time bound, and body bound. We need to account for how the temporal dispersion of slow violence affects the way we perceive and respond to a variety of social afflictions—from domestic abuse to post-traumatic stress and, in particular, environmental calamities. A major challenge is representational: how to devise arresting stories, images, and symbols adequate to the pervasive but elusive violence of delayed effects. Crucially, slow violence is often not just attritional but also exponential, operating as a major threat multiplier; it can fuel long-term, proliferating conflicts in situations where the conditions for sustaining life become increasingly but gradually degraded.

3. The process by which a compound becomes more concentrated in the tissues of organisms as it travels up the food chain. "Cryosphere": that part of the earth's surface that is permanently frozen [editor's note].

Politically and emotionally, different kinds of disaster possess unequal heft. Falling bodies, burning towers, exploding heads, avalanches, volcanoes, and tsunamis have a visceral, eye-catching and page-turning power that tales of slow violence, unfolding over years, decades, even centuries, cannot match. Stories of toxic buildup, massing greenhouse gases, and accelerated species loss due to ravaged habitats are all cataclysmic, but they are scientifically convoluted cataclysms in which casualties are postponed, often for generations. In an age when the media venerate the spectacular, when public policy is shaped primarily around perceived immediate need, a central question is strategic and representational: how can we convert into image and narrative the disasters that are slow moving and long in the making, disasters that are anonymous and that star nobody, disasters that are attritional and of indifferent interest to the sensation-driven technologies of our image-world? How can we turn the long emergencies of slow violence into stories dramatic enough to rouse public sentiment and warrant political intervention, these emergencies whose repercussions have given rise to some of the most critical challenges of our time?

This book's second, related focus concerns the environmentalism of the poor, for it is those people lacking resources who are the principal casualties of slow violence. Their unseen poverty is compounded by the invisibility of the slow violence that permeates so many of their lives. Our media bias toward spectacular violence exacerbates the vulnerability of ecosystems treated as disposable by turbo-capitalism while simultaneously exacerbating the vulnerability of those whom Kevin Bales, in another context, has called "disposable people."[4] It is against such conjoined ecological and human disposability that we have witnessed a resurgent environmentalism of the poor, particularly (though not exclusively) across the so-called global South. So a central issue that emerges is strategic: if the neoliberal era[5] has intensified assaults on resources, it has also intensified resistance, whether through isolated site-specific struggles or through activism that has reached across national boundaries in an effort to build translocal alliances.

"The poor" is a compendious category subject to almost infinite local variation as well as to fracture along fault lines of ethnicity, gender, race, class, region, religion, and generation. Confronted with the militarization of both commerce and development, impoverished communities are often assailed by coercion and bribery that test their cohesive resilience. How much control will, say, a poor hardwood forest community have over the mix of subsistence and market strategies it deploys in attempts at adaptive survival? How will that community negotiate competing definitions of its own poverty and long-term wealth when the guns, the bulldozers, and the moneymen arrive? Such communities typically have to patch together threadbare improvised alliances against vastly superior military, corporate, and media forces. As such, impoverished resource rebels can seldom afford to be single-issue activists: their green commitments are seamed through with other economic and cultural causes as they experience environmental threat not

4. Kevin Bales, *Disposable People: New Slavery in the Global Economy* (Berkeley: University of California Press, 2004). [Bales (b. 1952), American activist and scholar whose focus is modern slavery—editor's note.]

5. The late twentieth-century global resurgence of laissez-faire economic liberalism. The term is used mainly by critics of this economic system; its proponents emphasize deregulation, privatization, and free trade [editor's note].

as a planetary abstraction but as a set of inhabited risks, some imminent, others obscurely long term.

The status of environmental activism among the poor in the global South has shifted significantly in recent years. Where green or environmental discourses were once frequently regarded with skepticism as neocolonial, Western impositions inimical to the resource priorities of the poor in the global South, such attitudes have been tempered by the gathering visibility and credibility of environmental justice movements that have pushed back against an antihuman environmentalism that too often sought (under the banner of universalism) to impose green agendas dominated by rich nations and Western NGOs. Among those who inhabit the frontlines of the global resource wars, suspicions that environmentalism is another guise of what Andrew Ross calls "planetary management" have not, of course, been wholly allayed.[6] But those suspicions have eased somewhat as the spectrum of what counts as environmentalism has broadened. Western activists are now more prone to recognize, engage, and learn from resource insurrections among the global poor that might previously have been discounted as not properly environmental.[7] Indeed, I believe that the fate of environmentalism—and more decisively, the character of the biosphere itself—will be shaped significantly in decades to come by the tension between what Ramachandra Guha and Joan Martinez-Alier have called "full-stomach" and "empty-belly" environmentalism.[8]

The challenge of visibility that links slow violence to the environmentalism of the poor connects directly to this book's third circulating concern—the complex, often vexed figure of the environmental writer-activist. In the chapters that follow I address not just literary but more broadly rhetorical and visual challenges posed by slow violence; however, I place particular emphasis on combative writers who have deployed their imaginative agility and worldly ardor to help amplify the media-marginalized causes of the environmentally dispossessed. I have sought to stress those places where writers and social movements, often in complicated tandem, have strategized against attritional disasters that afflict embattled communities. The writers I engage are geographically wide ranging—from various parts of the African continent, from the Middle East, India, the Caribbean, the United States, and Britain—and work across a variety of forms. Figures like Wangari Maathai, Arundhati Roy, Indra Sinha, Ken Saro-Wiwa, Abdulrahman Munif, Njabulo Ndebele, Nadine Gordimer, Jamaica Kincaid, Rachel Carson, and June Jordan[9] are alive to the inhabited impact of corrosive trans-

6. Andrew Ross, *Strange Weather: Culture, Science, and Technology in the Age of Limits* (New York: Verso, 1991), 207–12. [Ross (b. 1956), Scottish-born social critic, academic, and activist—editor's note.]

7. The term "West" is inevitably shorthand. The environmentalism of the poor within North American and Europe, although not the focus of this book, helped goad affluent environmentalists in the global North to diversify their vision of what counts as environmentalism and to recognize—in the present and retrospectively—third-world-generated activism as a vital force and potential ally in the global resource wars. That said, as I indicate in my penultimate chapter on the ecological threats posed by so-called precision warfare, it is often very difficult to articulate as a single narrative of risk the threat slow violence poses to the health of troops conscripted from the rich-nation poor and the threat to the even more impoverished people who inhabit war zones long term, war zones that are overwhelmingly located in the global South. The very difficulty of integrating such conjoined (if unequal) threats is symptomatic of the layered invisibility that defines slow violence. The poor, of course, are hardly restricted to the global South, but they are dramatically, disproportionately concentrated there.

8. Ramachandra Guha and Joan Martinez-Alier, *Varieties of Environmentalism: Essays North and South* (London: Earthscan, 1997), 12.

9. Renowned activists and authors from around the world. Maathai (1940–2011), a Kenyan, founded the Green Belt Movement and advocated for environmental conservation and women's

national forces, including petro-imperialism, the megadam industry, outsourced toxicity, neocolonial tourism, antihuman conservation practices, corporate and environmental deregulation, and the militarization of commerce forces that disproportionately jeopardize the livelihoods, prospects, and memory banks of the global poor. Among the writers I consider, some have testified in relative isolation, some have helped instigate movements for environmental justice, and yet others, in aligning themselves with preexisting movements, have given imaginative definition to the issues at stake while enhancing the public visibility of the cause.

Relations between movements and writers are often fraught and frictional, not least because such movements themselves are susceptible to fracture from both external and internal pressures.[1] That said, the writers I consider are enraged by injustices they wish to see redressed, injustices they believe they can help expose, silences they can help dismantle through testimonial protest, rhetorical inventiveness, and counterhistories in the face of formidable odds. Most are restless, versatile writers ready to pit their energies against what Edward Said called "the normalized quiet of unseen power."[2] This normalized quiet is of particular pertinence to the hushed havoc and injurious invisibility that trail slow violence.

SLOW VIOLENCE

In this book, I have sought to address our inattention to calamities that are slow and long lasting, calamities that patiently dispense their devastation while remaining outside our flickering attention spans—and outside the purview of a spectacle-driven corporate media. The insidious workings of slow violence derive largely from the unequal attention given to spectacular and unspectacular time. In an age that venerates instant spectacle, slow violence is deficient in the recognizable special effects that fill movie theaters and boost ratings on TV. Chemical and radiological violence, for example, is driven inward, somatized into cellular dramas of mutation that—particularly

rights; she was awarded the 2004 Nobel Peace Prize. Sinha (b. 1950), a British author of Indian and English descent, has focused public attention on those harmed by the 1984 chemical leak in Bhopal, India. Saro-Wiwa (1941–1995), a Nigerian novelist and journalist, supported environmentalism and minority ethnic rights. Abdul Rahman Munif (1933–2004), a Saudi, was a political novelist. Ndebele (b. 1948), a South African, is a novelist, cultural critic, and academic; he is currently chancellor of the University of Johannesburg. Gordimer (1923–2014), a South African, was a writer of fiction and anti-apartheid activist; she was awarded the 1991 Nobel Prize in Literature. Kincaid (b. 1949), an Antiguan-born American, often explores themes related to colonialism and postcolonialism in her fiction. Carson (1907–1964), an American, was a marine biologist whose writing on environmental pollution helped spur the global conservation movement. Jordan (1936–2002), an American born of West Indian immigrants, was a poet, journalist, activist, and feminist theorist [editor's note].

1. Arundhati Roy has expressed some unease toward the very notion of the writer-activist. Yet her concerns—that the term makes activist writers sound exceptional, that it risks institutionalizing them as experts, and risks narrowing our perception of both writers and activists—need to be taken with a grain of salt, as an exercise in self-protectiveness and false modesty, given her ineluctably institutionalized role in the media as professional (albeit dissident professional) go-between. The fact is only a tiny minority of writers assume an overtly activist public role and that minority—especially when they shuttle between the novel or poetry on the one hand and engaged nonfiction on the other—are routinely skittish, insisting on their imaginative autonomy from ideological obligation while also declaring their political commitments. Such balancing acts between avowal and disavowal surface in the writings of Albert Camus, Jean-Paul Sartre, James Baldwin, Langston Hughes, Wole Soyinka, Derek Walcott, Gabriel Garcia Marquez, Carolyn Forché, Joseph Brodsky, Paul Muldoon, Mahmoud Darwish, and Nadine Gordimer to name but a few. For Roy's take on writer-activism, see *The Algebra of Infinite Justice* (London: HarperCollins, 2002), 186–87.

2. Edward Said, "The Public Role of Writers and Intellectuals," *The Nation*, September 17, 2001, 10. [SAID (1935–2003), Palestinian-born American literary and cultural critic and social activist—editor's note.]

in the bodies of the poor—remain largely unobserved, undiagnosed, and untreated. From a narrative perspective, such invisible, mutagenic theater is slow paced and open ended, eluding the tidy closure, the containment, imposed by the visual orthodoxies of victory and defeat.

Let me ground this point by referring, in conjunction, to Rachel Carson's *Silent Spring* and Frantz Fanon's *The Wretched of the Earth*.[3] In 1962 *Silent Spring* jolted a broad international public into an awareness of the protracted, cryptic, and indiscriminate casualties inflicted by dichlorodiphenyltrichloroethane (DDT).[4] Yet, just one year earlier, Fanon, in the opening pages of *Wretched of the Earth*, had comfortably invoked DDT as an affirmative metaphor for anticolonial violence: he called for a DDT-filled spray gun to be wielded as a weapon against the "parasites" spread by the colonials' Christian church.[5] Fanon's drama of decolonization is, of course, studded with the overt weaponry whereby subjugation is maintained ("by dint of a great array of bayonets and cannons") or overthrown ("by the searing bullets and bloodstained knives") after "a murderous and decisive struggle between the two protagonists."[6] Yet his temporal vision of violence—and of what Aimé Césaire[7] called "the rendezvous of victory"—was uncomplicated by the concerns that an as-yet inchoate environmental justice movement (catalyzed in part by *Silent Spring*) would raise about lopsided risks that permeate the land long term, blurring the clean lines between defeat and victory, between colonial dispossession and official national self-determination.[8] We can certainly read Fanon, in his concern with land as property and as fount of native dignity, retrospectively with an environmental eye. But our theories of violence today must be informed by a science unavailable to Fanon, a science that addresses environmentally embedded violence that is often difficult to source, oppose, and once set in motion, to reverse.

Attritional catastrophes that overspill clear boundaries in time and space are marked above all by displacements—temporal, geographical, rhetorical, and technological displacements that simplify violence and underestimate, in advance and in retrospect, the human and environmental costs. Such displacements smooth the way for amnesia, as places are rendered irretrievable to those who once inhabited them, places that ordinarily pass unmourned in the corporate media. Places like the Marshall Islands, subjected between 1948 and 1958 to sixty-seven American atmospheric nuclear "tests," the largest of them equal in force to 1,000 Hiroshima-sized bombs. In 1956 the Atomic Energy Commission declared the Marshall Islands "by far the most

3. Published in 1963 (see above); FANON (1925–1961), born in Martinique, was a psychiatrist, political theorist, and advocate for Algerian independence [editor's note].

4. A pesticide that came into widespread use in the mid-20th century; because of its toxicity to wildlife, its agricultural use was banned in the United States in 1972 and worldwide in 2004 [editor's note].

5. Frantz Fanon, *The Wretched of the Earth*, trans. Constance Farrington (1963; repr., New York: Grove, 1968), 42.

6. Ibid., 36–37.

7. Martinican politician and author (1913–2008), one of the founders of the *négritude* movement in Francophone literature that asserted black and African pride; he was also an early mentor of Fanon. The quotation, which refers to the revolutionary struggle for liberation—"There is a place for all at the rendezvous of victory"—is from his book-length poem *Cahier d'un retour au pays natal* (1939, *Notebook of a Return to My Native Land*) [editor's note].

8. If historically Fanon was in no position to write about the slow violence of inequitably distributed environmental threats, he was, of course, alive to the psychological seepage of colonial values that could sustain neocolonialism. Furthermore, in "Colonial War and Mental Disorders" he is attuned to the slow violence that results from colonial "pacification," the psychological effects far outlasting specific acts of discernible violence. See *The Wretched of the Earth*, 249–316.

contaminated place in the world," a condition that would compromise independence in the long term, despite the islands' formal ascent in 1979 into the ranks of self-governing nations.[9] The island republic was still in part governed by an irradiated past: well into the 1980s its history of nuclear colonialism, long forgotten by the colonizers, was still delivering into the world "jellyfish babies"—headless, eyeless, limbless human infants who would live for just a few hours.[1]

If as Said notes, struggles over geography are never reducible to armed struggle but have a profound symbolic and narrative component as well, and if, as Michael Watts insists, we must attend to the "violent geographies of fast capitalism," we need to supplement both these injunctions with a deeper understanding of the slow violence of delayed effects that structures so many of our most consequential forgettings.[2] Violence, above all environmental violence, needs to be seen—and deeply considered—as a contest not only over space, or bodies, or labor, or resources, but also over time. We need to bear in mind Faulkner's dictum that "the past is never dead. It's not even past."[3] His words resonate with particular force across landscapes permeated by slow violence, landscapes of temporal overspill that elude rhetorical cleanup operations with their sanitary beginnings and endings.

Kwame Anthony Appiah famously asked, "Is the 'Post-' in 'Postcolonial' the 'Post-' in 'Postmodern'?"[4] As environmentalists we might ask similarly searching questions of the "post" in postindustrial, post–Cold War, and postconflict.[5] For if the past of slow violence is never past, so too the post is never fully post: industrial particulates and effluents live on in the environmental elements we inhabit and in our very bodies, which epidemiologically and ecologically are never our simple contemporaries.[6] Something similar applies to so-called postconflict societies whose leaders may annually commemorate, as marked on the calendar, the official cessation of hostilities, while ongoing intergenerational slow violence (inflicted by, say, unexploded landmines or carcinogens from an arms dump) may continue hostilities by other means.

Ours is an age of onrushing turbo-capitalism, wherein the present feels more abbreviated than it used to—at least for the world's privileged classes who live surrounded by technological time-savers that often compound the

9. Quoted in Stephanie Cooke, *In Mortal Hands: A Cautionary History of the Nuclear Age* (New York: Bloomsbury, 2009), 168.

1. Zohl dé Ishtar, *Daughters of the Pacific* (Melbourne: Spinifex Press, 1994), 24. In the nuclear exceptionalism upheld by mainstream Japanese memory, amnesia persists about Micronesian and Polynesian casualties of what were, in terms of the environmental and epidemiological *longue durée*, effectively American and French nuclear attacks. [*Longue durée*: long duration (French), a phrase used by the French historian Fernand Braudel (1902–1985), whose work emphasized large-scale, long-term changes—editor's note.]

2. Edward W. Said, *Culture and Imperialism* (London: Chatto and Windus, 1992), 17; Michael J. Watts, *Struggles over Geography: Violence, Freedom, and Development at the Millennium* (Hettner Lectures no. 3, University of Heidelberg, Department of Geography, 2000), 8.

3. Faulkner's oft-misquoted remark appears in *Requiem for a Nun* (1951; repr., New York: Routledge, 1987), 17. [William Faulkner (1897–1962), American writer of fiction, much of it imbued with the aftershocks of the Civil War—editor's note.]

4. The title of an article in *Critical Inquiry* 17 (1991). Appiah (b. 1954), born in London to Ghanaian and English parents, is an American philosopher, novelist, and cultural theorist [editor's note].

5. Anne McClintock, Aamir Mufti, and Ella Shohat, eds., *Dangerous Liaisons* (Minneapolis: University of Minnesota Press, 1997), 420–44.

6. For an astute examination of the impact of particulate residues on the timelines of environmental thinking—as well as on Victorian literary genres—see Jesse Oak Taylor's dissertation, "A Sky of Our Manufacture: Literature, Modernity, and the London Fog from Dickens to Conrad" (Ph.D. diss., University of Wisconsin–Madison, 2009).

sensation of not having enough time. Consequently, one of the most pressing challenges of our age is how to adjust our rapidly eroding attention spans to the slow erosions of environmental justice. If, under neoliberalism, the gulf between enclaved rich and outcast poor has become ever more pronounced, ours is also an era of enclaved time wherein for many speed has become a self-justifying, propulsive ethic that renders "uneventful" violence (to those who live remote from its attritional lethality) a weak claimant on our time. The attosecond pace of our age, with its restless technologies of infinite promise and infinite disappointment, prompts us to keep flicking and clicking distractedly in an insatiable—and often insensate—quest for quicker sensation.

The oxymoronic notion of slow violence poses a number of challenges: scientific, legal, political, and representational. In the long arc between the emergence of slow violence and its delayed effects, both the causes and the memory of catastrophe readily fade from view as the casualties incurred typically pass untallied and unremembered. Such discounting in turn makes it far more difficult to secure effective legal measures for prevention, restitution, and redress. Casualties from slow violence are, moreover, out of sync not only with our narrative and media expectations but also with the swift seasons of electoral change. Politicians routinely adopt a "last in, first out" stance toward environmental issues, admitting them when times are flush, dumping them as soon as times get tight. Because preventative or remedial environmental legislation typically targets slow violence, it cannot deliver dependable electoral cycle results, even though those results may ultimately be life saving. Relative to bankable pocketbook actions—there'll be a tax rebate check in the mail next August—environmental payouts seem to lurk on a distant horizon. Many politicians—and indeed many voters—routinely treat environmental action as critical yet not urgent. And so generation after generation of two- or four-year cycle politicians add to the pileup of deferrable actions deferred. With rare exceptions, in the domain of slow violence "yes, but not now, not yet" becomes the modus operandi.

How can leaders be goaded to avert catastrophe when the political rewards of their actions will not accrue to them but will be reaped on someone else's watch decades, even centuries, from now? How can environmental activists and storytellers work to counter the potent political, corporate, and even scientific forces invested in immediate self-interest, procrastination, and dissembling? We see such dissembling at work, for instance, in the afterword to Michael Crichton's 2004 environmental conspiracy novel, *State of Fear*, wherein he argued that we needed twenty more years of data gathering on climate change before any policy decisions could be ventured.[7] Although the National Academy of Sciences had assured former president George W. Bush that humans were indeed causing the earth to warm, Bush shopped around for views that accorded with his own skepticism and found them in a private meeting with Crichton, whom he described as "an expert scientist."

To address the challenges of slow violence is to confront the dilemma Rachel Carson faced almost half a century ago as she sought to dramatize

7. Michael Crichton, *State of Fear* (New York: Avon, 2004), 626. [Crichton (1942–2008), American physician and author of popular novels (especially science fiction thrillers)—editor's note.]

what she eloquently called "death by indirection."[8] Carson's subjects were biomagnification and toxic drift, forms of oblique, slow-acting violence that, like climate change, pose formidable imaginative difficulties for writers and activists alike. In struggling to give shape to amorphous menace, both Carson and reviewers of *Silent Spring* resorted to a narrative vocabulary: one reviewer portrayed the book as exposing "the new, unplotted and mysterious dangers we insist upon creating all around us,"[9] while Carson herself wrote of "a shadow that is no less ominous because it is formless and obscure."[1] To confront slow violence requires, then, that we plot and give figurative shape to formless threats whose fatal repercussions are dispersed across space and time. The representational challenges are acute, requiring creative ways of drawing public attention to catastrophic acts that are low in instant spectacle but high in long-term effects. To intervene representationally entails devising iconic symbols that embody amorphous calamities as well as narrative forms that infuse those symbols with dramatic urgency.

SLOW VIOLENCE AND STRUCTURAL VIOLENCE

Seven years after Rachel Carson turned our attention to the lethal mechanisms of "death by indirection," Johan Galtung, the influential Norwegian mathematician and sociologist, coined the term "indirect or structural violence."[2] Galtung's theory of structural violence is pertinent here because some of his concerns overlap with the concerns that animate this book, while others help throw into relief the rather different features I have sought to highlight by introducing the term "slow violence." Structural violence, for Galtung, stands in opposition to the more familiar personal violence that dominates our conceptions of what counts as violence per se.[3] Galtung was concerned, as I am, with widening the field of what constitutes violence. He sought to foreground the vast structures that can give rise to acts of personal violence and constitute forms of violence in and of themselves. Such structural violence may range from the unequal morbidity that results from a commodified health care system, to racism itself. What I share with Galtung's line of thought is a concern with social justice, hidden agency, and certain forms of violence that are imperceptible.

In these terms, for example, we can recognize that the structural violence embodied by a neoliberal order of austerity measures, structural adjustment, rampant deregulation, corporate megamergers, and a widening gulf between rich and poor is a form of covert violence in its own right that is often a catalyst for more recognizably overt violence. For an expressly environmental example of structural violence, one might cite Wangari Maathai's insistence that the systemic burdens of national debt to the IMF and World Bank borne by many so-called developing nations constitute a major impediment to environmental sustainability.[4] So, too, feminist earth

8. Rachel Carson, *Silent Spring* (1963; repr., Boston: Houghton Mifflin, 1992), 32.
9. Eric Sevareid, "An Explosive Book," *Washington D.C. Star*, October 9, 1962, 3.
1. Carson, *Silent Spring*, 238.
2. Johan Galtung, "Violence, Peace, and Peace Research," *Journal of Peace Research* 6 (1969): 167–91.
3. This is not the place for a full assessment of Galtung's prodigious writings about peace and violence. At a later point in his thinking, for instance, Galtung complicated his theory of structural violence by introducing the notion of cultural violence.
4. Wangari Maathai, *The Challenge for Africa* (New York: Pantheon, 2009), 83ff.

scientist Jill Schneiderman, one of our finest thinkers about environmental time, has written about the way in which environmental degradation may "masquerade as inevitable."[5]

For all the continuing pertinence of the theory of structural violence and for all the modifications the theory has undergone, the notion bears the impress of its genesis during the high era of structuralist thinking that tended toward a static determinism. We see this, for example, in Galtung's insistence that "structural violence is silent, it does not show—it is essentially static, it is the tranquil waters."[6] In contrast to the static connotations of structural violence, I have sought, through the notion of slow violence, to foreground questions of time, movement, and change, however gradual. The explicitly temporal emphasis of slow violence allows us to keep front and center the representational challenges and imaginative dilemmas posed not just by imperceptible violence but by imperceptible change whereby violence is decoupled from its original causes by the workings of time. Time becomes an actor in complicated ways, not least because the temporal templates of our spectacle-driven, 24/7 media life have shifted massively since Galtung first advanced his theory of structural violence some forty years ago. To talk about slow violence, then, is to engage directly with our contemporary politics of speed.

Simply put, structural violence is a theory that entails rethinking different notions of causation and agency with respect to violent effects. Slow violence, by contrast, might well include forms of structural violence, but has a wider descriptive range in calling attention, not simply to questions of agency, but to broader, more complex descriptive categories of violence enacted slowly over time. The shift in the relationship between human agency and time is most dramatically evident in our enhanced understanding of the accelerated changes occurring at two scalar extremes—in the life-sustaining circuits of planetary biophysics and in the wired brain's neural circuitry. The idea of structural violence predated both sophisticated contemporary ice-core sampling methods and the emergence of cyber technology. My concept of slow violence thus seeks to respond both to recent, radical changes in our geological perception and our changing technological experiences of time.

Let me address the geological aspect first. In 2000, Paul Crutzen, the Nobel Prize–winning atmospheric chemist, introduced the term "the Anthropocene Age" (which he dated to James Watt's[7] invention of the steam engine). Through the notion of "the Anthropocene Age," Crutzen sought to theorize an unprecedented epochal effect: the massive impact by the human species, from the industrial era onward, on our planet's life systems, an impact that, as his term suggests, is geomorphic, equal in force and in long-term implications to a major geological event.[8] Crutzen's attempt to capture

5. Jill S. Schneiderman, "Buddhist Living in the Anthropocene" (unpublished essay, 2010), 7. I am especially grateful to Schneiderman for a rich set of exchanges—including a comparison between Galtung's ideas and my own—in response to a talk I gave at Vassar College in 2008.

6. Galtung, "Violence, Peace, and Peace Research," 173.

7. Scottish inventor (1736–1819); his improvements on earlier versions of the steam engine helped make possible the Industrial Revolution [editor's note].

8. In an indicative convergence of the tectonic shifts in geological thinking about speed and media technologies of speed, one notes that Crutzen first advanced his idea of the Anthropocene Age on his blog rather than going through the slower medium of a peer-reviewed academic journal.

the epochal scale of human activity's impact on the planet was followed by Will Steffen's elaboration, in conjunction with Crutzen and John McNeill,[9] of what they dubbed the Great Acceleration, a second stage of the Anthropocene Age that they dated to the mid-twentieth century. Writing in 2007, Steffen et al. noted how "nearly three-quarters of the anthropogenically driven rise in CO_2 concentration has occurred since 1950 (from about 310 to 380 ppm), and about half of the total rise (48 ppm) has occurred in just the last 30 years."[1] The Australian environmental historian Libby Robin has put the case succinctly: "We have recently entered a new geological epoch, the Anthropocene. There is now considerable evidence that humanity has altered the biophysical systems of Earth, not just the carbon cycle . . . but also the nitrogen cycle and ultimately the atmosphere and climate of the whole globe."[2] What, then, are the consequences for our experience of time of this newfound recognition that we have inadvertently, through our unprecedented biophysical species power, inaugurated an Anthropocene Age and are now engaged in (and subject to) the hurtling changes of the Great Acceleration?

Over the past two decades, this high-speed planetary modification has been accompanied (at least for those increasing billions who have access to the Internet) by rapid modifications to the human cortex. It is difficult, but necessary, to consider simultaneously a geologically-paced plasticity, however relatively rapid, and the plasticity of brain circuits reprogrammed by a digital world that threatens to "info-whelm" us into a state of perpetual distraction. If an awareness of the Great Acceleration is (to put it mildly) unevenly distributed, the experience of accelerated connectivity (and the paradoxical disconnects that can accompany it) is increasingly widespread. In an age of degraded attention spans it becomes doubly difficult yet increasingly urgent that we focus on the toll exacted, over time, by the slow violence of ecological degradation. We live, writes Cory Doctorow, in an era when the electronic screen has become an "ecosystem of interruption technologies."[3] Or as former Microsoft executive Linda Stone puts it, we now live in an age of "continuous partial attention."[4] Fast is faster than it used to be, and story units have become concomitantly shorter. In this cultural milieu of digitally speeded up time, and foreshortened narrative, the intergenerational aftermath becomes a harder sell. So to render slow violence visible entails, among other things, redefining speed: we see such efforts in talk of accelerated species loss, rapid climate change, and in attempts to recast "glacial"—once a dead metaphor for "slow"—as a rousing, iconic image of unacceptably fast loss.

Efforts to make forms of slow violence more urgently visible suffered a setback in the United States in the aftermath of 9/11, which reinforced a spectacular, immediately sensational, and instantly hyper-visible image of what constitutes a violent threat. The fiery spectacle of the collapsing towers was burned into the national psyche as *the* definitive image of violence,

9. American environmental historian (b. 1954). Steffen (b. 1947), an American chemist who has spent much of his career in Australia.
1. Will Steffen, Paul J. Crutzen, and John R. McNeill, "The Anthropocene: Are Humans Now Overwhelming the Great Forces of Nature?" *Ambio* 36 (2007): 618.
2. Libby Robin, "The Eco-humanities as Literature: A New Genre?" *Australian Literary Studies* 23 (2008): 290.
3. Cory Doctorow, "Writing in the Age of Distraction," *Locus Magazine*, January 7, 2009, http://www.locusmag.com/Features/2009/01/cory-doctorow-writing-in-age-of.html. [Doctorow (b. 1971), Canadian-born British journalist and science fiction author—editor's note.]
4. Quoted in Thomas Friedman, "The Age of Interruption," *New York Times*, July 5, 2006, A27.

setting back by years attempts to rally public sentiment against climate change, a threat that is incremental, exponential, and far less sensationally visible. Condoleezza Rice's[5] strategic fantasy of a mushroom cloud looming over America if the United States failed to invade Iraq gave further visual definition to cataclysmic violence as something explosive and instantaneous, a recognizably cinematic, immediately sensational, pyrotechnic event.

The representational bias against slow violence has, furthermore, a critically dangerous impact on what counts as a casualty in the first place. Casualties of slow violence—human and environmental—are the casualties most likely not to be seen, not to be counted. Casualties of slow violence become light-weight, disposable casualties, with dire consequences for the ways wars are remembered, which in turn has dire consequences for the projected casualties from future wars. We can observe this bias at work in the way wars, whose lethal repercussions spread across space and time, are tidily bookended in the historical record. Thus, for instance, a 2003 *New York Times* editorial on Vietnam declared that "during our dozen years there, the U.S. killed and helped kill at least 15 million people."[6] But that simple phrase "during our dozen years there" shrinks the toll, foreshortening the ongoing slow-motion slaughter: hundreds of thousands survived the official war years, only to slowly lose their lives later to Agent Orange.[7] In a 2002 study, the environmental scientist Arnold Schecter recorded dioxin levels in the bloodstreams of Bien Hoa residents at 135 times the levels of Hanoi's inhabitants, who lived far north of the spraying.[8] The afflicted include thousands of children born decades after the war's end. More than thirty years after the last spray run, Agent Orange continues to wreak havoc as, through biomagnification, dioxins build up in the fatty tissues of pivotal foods such as duck and fish and pass from the natural world into the cooking pot and from there to ensuing human generations. An Institute of Medicine committee has by now linked seventeen medical conditions to Agent Orange; indeed, as recently as 2009 it uncovered fresh evidence that exposure to the chemical increases the likelihood of developing Parkinson's disease and ischemic heart disease.[9] Under such circumstances, wherein long-term risks continue to emerge, to bookend a war's casualties with the phrase "during our dozen years there" is misleading: that small, seemingly innocent phrase is a powerful reminder of how our rhetorical conventions for bracketing violence routinely ignore ongoing, belated casualties.

SLOW VIOLENCE AND STRATEGIES OF REPRESENTATION: WRITER-ACTIVISM

How do we bring home—and bring emotionally to life—threats that take time to wreak their havoc, threats that never materialize in one spectacu-

5. American political scientist and diplomat (b. 1954); she made her remark about a possible mushroom cloud in 2002, while serving as national security advisor (2001–05) during the presidency of George W. Bush. She later (2005–09) served as his secretary of state [editor's note].
6. "Vietnam in Retrospect," *New York Times*, March 23, 2003, A25.
7. A defoliant, millions of gallons of which were sprayed in Vietnam by U.S. forces between 1962 and 1971. It has been linked to cancers, high rates of miscarriage, and birth defects [editor's note].
8. Arnold Schecter et al., "Agent Orange and the Vietnamese: The Persistence of Elevated Dioxin Levels in Human Tissues," *American Journal of Public Health* 85 (1995): 516–22.
9. Janie Lorber, "Defoliant May Be Tied to New List of Illnesses," *New York Times*, July 25, 2009, A8.

lar, explosive, cinematic scene? *Apprehension* is a critical word here, a crossover term that draws together the domains of perception, emotion, and action. To engage slow violence is to confront layered predicaments of apprehension: to apprehend—to arrest, or at least mitigate—often imperceptible threats requires rendering them apprehensible to the senses through the work of scientific and imaginative testimony. An influential lineage of environmental thought gives primacy to immediate sensory apprehension, to sight above all, as foundational for any environmental ethics of place. George Perkins Marsh, the mid-nineteenth-century environmental pioneer, argued in *Man and Nature* that "the power most important to cultivate, and, at the same time, hardest to acquire, is that of seeing what is before him."[1] Aldo Leopold similarly insisted that "we can be ethical only toward what we can see."[2] But what happens when we are unsighted, when what extends before us—in the space and time that we most deeply inhabit—remains invisible? How, indeed, are we to act ethically toward human and biotic communities that lie beyond our sensory ken? What then, in the fullest sense of the phrase, is the place of seeing in the world that we now inhabit? What, moreover, is the place of the other senses? How do we both make slow violence visible yet also challenge the privileging of the visible?

Such questions have profound consequences for the apprehension of slow violence, whether on a cellular or a transnational scale. Planetary consciousness (a notion that has undergone a host of theoretical formulations) becomes pertinent here, perhaps most usefully in the sense in which Mary Louise Pratt[3] elaborates it, linking questions of power and perspective, keeping front and center the often latent, often invisible violence in the view. Who gets to see, and from where? When and how does such empowered seeing become normative? And what perspectives—not least those of the poor or women or the colonized—do hegemonic sight conventions of visuality obscure? Pratt's formulation of planetary consciousness remains invaluable because it allows us to connect forms of apprehension to forms of imperial violence.[4]

Against this backdrop, I want to introduce the third central concern of this book. Alongside slow violence and the environmentalism of the poor, the chapters that follow are critically concerned with the political, imaginative, and strategic role of environmental writer-activists. Writer-activists can help us apprehend threats imaginatively that remain imperceptible to the senses, either because they are geographically remote, too vast or too minute in scale, or are played out across a time span that exceeds the instance of observation or even the physiological life of the human observer. In a world permeated by insidious, yet unseen or imperceptible violence, imaginative writing can help make the unapparent appear, making it accessible and tangible by humanizing drawn-out threats inaccessible to the immediate

1. George Perkins Marsh, *Man and Nature*, ed. David Lowenthal (1864; repr., Seattle: University of Washington Press, 2003), 15.

2. Leopold's address at the June 1934 dedication of the University of Wisconsin Arboretum, quoted in Scott Russell Sanders, "Speaking for the Land: Aldo Leopold as a Writer" [2009], author's personal website, www.scottrussellsanders.com/SRS%20entries/SRS_on_Leopold.htm. Leopold was inconsistent on this point, sometimes emphasizing an ethics of immediacy grounded in local knowledge and sometimes emphasizing an intergenerational ethics less rooted in the moment or in a visible locale. [Leopold (1887–1948), American environmentalist and founder of the Wilderness Society—editor's note.]

3. Prominent scholar of Spanish and Portuguese literature (b. 1948) [editor's note].

4. Mary Louise Pratt, *Imperial Eyes: Travel Writing and Transculturation* (New York: Routledge, 1992), 15–37.

senses. Writing can challenge perceptual habits that downplay the damage slow violence inflicts and bring into imaginative focus apprehensions that elude sensory corroboration. The narrative imaginings of writer-activists may thus offer us a different kind of witnessing: of sights unseen.

To allay states of apprehension—trepidations, forebodings, shadows cast by the invisible—entails facing the challenge, at once imaginative and scientific, of giving the unapparent a materiality upon which we can act. Yet poor communities, often disproportionately exposed to the force fields of slow violence—be they military residues or imported e-waste or the rising tides of climate change—are the communities least likely to attract sustained scientific inquiry into causes, effects, and potential redress. Such poor communities are abandoned to sporadic science at best and usually no science at all; they are also disproportionately subjected to involuntary pharmaceutical experiments. Indeed, when such communities raise concerns, they often become targets of well-funded antiscience by forces that have a legal or commercial interest in manufacturing and disseminating doubt.[5] Such embattled communities, beset by officially unacknowledged hazards, must find ways to broadcast their inhabited fears, their lived sense of a corroded environment, within the broader global struggles over apprehension. It is here that writers, filmmakers, and digital activists may play a mediating role in helping counter the layered invisibility that results from insidious threats, from temporal protractedness, and from the fact that the afflicted are people whose quality of life—and often whose very existence—is of indifferent interest to the corporate media.

To address violence discounted by dominant structures of apprehension is necessarily to engage the culturally variable issue of *who counts as a witness*. Contests over what counts as violence are intimately entangled with conflicts over who bears the social authority of witness, which entails much more than simply seeing or not seeing. The entangled politics of spectacle and witnessing have implications that stretch well beyond environmental slow violence. In domestic abuse, for instance, violence may be life threatening but slow, bloodless, and brutal in ways that are not always immediately fatal: a broken nose constitutes a different order of evidence from food or access to medical treatment or human company withheld over an extended period. A locked door can be a weapon. Doors for women are often long-term, nonlethal weapons that leave no telltale bloody trail; doors don't bear witness to a single, decisive blow. In many cultures, moreover, rape isn't defined as rape if it is inflicted by a husband. And in some societies, a rape isn't rape unless three adult men are present to witness it. As the journalistic chestnut has it, "if it bleeds, it leads." And as a corollary, if it's bloodless, slow-motion violence, the story is more likely to be buried, particularly if it's relayed by people whose witnessing authority is culturally discounted.

* * *

2011

5. See especially David Michaels, *Doubt Is Their Product: How Industry's Assault on Science Threatens Your Health* (New York: Oxford University Press, 2008); Naomi Oreskes and Erik M. Conway, *Merchants of Doubt: How a Handful of Scientists Obscured the Truth on Issues from Tobacco Smoke to Global Warming* (New York: Bloomsbury, 2010); and James Hoggan, *Climate Cover-Up: The Crusade to Deny Global Warming* (Vancouver: Greystone Books, 2009).

The Anthropocene: The Promise and Pitfalls of an Epochal Idea

What would it mean to imagine *Homo sapiens*[1] as not merely a historical but a geological actor, a force of such magnitude that our impacts are being written into the fossil record? What would it mean to acknowledge that, for the first time in Earth's history, a sentient species, our own, has shaken Earth's life systems with a profundity that paleontologist Anthony Barnosky has likened to an asteroid strike?[2] How might that perceptual shift disturb widespread assumptions about human history, ethics, power, and responsibility?

Such consequential questions follow from the turn to the Anthropocene, a hypothesis advanced by Nobel Prize-winning atmospheric chemist Paul Crutzen and ecologist Eugene Stoermer in 2000.[3] They argued that the Holocene[4] was history: the Earth had entered a new, unprecedented geological epoch, triggered by human actions.

Crutzen and Stoermer dated this rupture to the late eighteenth century beginnings of the industrial revolution. So according to the dominant Anthropocene script, over the past two-and-a-quarter centuries we have been laying down in stone a durable archive of human impacts to Earth's geophysical and biophysical systems. Those long-term impacts have become particularly acute since 1950 during the so-called Great Acceleration.

We have decisively altered the carbon cycle, the nitrogen cycle and the rate of extinction. We have created unprecedented atomic isotopes and fossilized plastics. We have erected megacities that will leave an enduring footprint long after they have ceased to function as cities. We have changed the pH of the oceans and have shunted so many life forms around the globe—inadvertently and intentionally—that we are creating novel ecosystems everywhere. Of vertebrate terrestrial life, humans and our domesticated animals now constitute over 90% by weight, with less than 10% comprised by wild creatures.

When Crutzen and Stoermer advanced their hypothesis, they couldn't possibly have imagined what an immense, omnivorous idea it would become. It took a while, but by the millennium's second decade those enthralled and appalled by the Anthropocene were being sucked, in their interdisciplinary masses, into its cavernous maw. Enthusiasts and skeptics poured in from paleobotany and postcolonial studies, from nanotechnology and bioethics, from Egyptology, evolutionary robotics, feminist psychology, geophysics, agronomy, post-humanism[5] and druidic studies. The classicists arrived alongside the futurists, where they mingled with students of everything from plastiglomerates[6] to romantic prosody, from ruins to rewilding.

1. The scientific name of the species to which all modern humans belong (literally, "wise person"; Latin).
2. Quoted in "Science & Environment: Leaving Our Mark: What Will Be Left of Our Cities?" BBC News, November 1, 2012, www.bbc.com/news/science-environment-20154030 [Nixon's note].
3. Paul J. Crutzen and Eugene F. Stoermer, "The 'Anthropocene,'" *Global Change Newsletter*, no. 41 (May 2000): 17–18 [Nixon's note].
4. The postglacial geological epoch of the past 10 to 12 thousand years.
5. A branch of cultural theory that is critical of both the philosophical presuppositions and the legacy of humanism.
6. Artificial "stones," formed of melted plastic, beach sediment, basaltic lava fragments, and organic debris; the term was coined in Patricia L. Corcoran, Charles J. Moore, and Kelly Jazva, "An Anthropogenic Marker Horizon in the Future Rock Record," *GSA Today* 24.6 (2014), which proposed that the material could mark the beginning of human pollution in the geological record.

This has arguably been the most generative feature of the Anthropocene turn: the myriad exchanges it has stimulated across the earth and life sciences, the social sciences, the humanities and the arts, bringing into conversation scholars who have been lured out of their specialist bubbles to engage energetically with unfamiliar interlocutors. The humanities and arts have become vital to this conversational mix, which is as it should be. For the Anthropocene hypothesis shakes the very idea of what it means to be human. If, collectively, we're a hurtling hunk of rock that feels, what does that mean for the stories we tell about our species and our place in life on Earth? What does it mean for the ethics of human actions? What are the imaginative and emotional pressures of opening up the human to geological time scales? We're simply not accustomed—maybe even equipped—to conceive of human consequences across such a vastly expanded temporal stage. How can we begin to internalize our role as Anthropocene actors, to inhabit that role feelingly?

To such imaginative questions we must add political ones. The Anthropocene—often for good reason—has proven hugely controversial. Let's focus on a few crucial disagreements. First, what is lost and gained by adopting the Anthropocene's grand species perspective on the human? Does this epic vantage point risk suppressing—historically and in the present—unequal human impacts, unequal human agency, and unequal human vulnerabilities? Does lumping together under the sign of the human the average twenty-first century Liberian and the average American as agents of planetary change risk concealing more than it reveals?

So a crucial challenge facing us is this: how do we tell two large stories that can often seem in tension with each other, a convergent story and a divergent one? First, a collective story about humanity's impacts that will be legible in the earth's geophysical systems for millennia to come. Second, a much more fractured narrative. For the species-centered Anthropocene meme has arisen in the twenty-first century, a period in which most human societies have experienced a deepening schism between the uber-rich and the ultra-poor. In terms of the history of ideas, what does it mean that the Anthropocene as a grand explanatory species story has taken hold during a plutocratic age? And from an imaginative perspective, how can we counter the centripetal force of the dominant Anthropocene species story with centrifugal stories that acknowledge immense inequalities in planet-altering powers? (Not to speak of inequalities in access to resources and exposures to risk in a time of deepening disparities.) We may all be in the Anthropocene but we're not all in it in the same way.

A second controversy separates those who might be called command-and-control Anthropocene optimists and those who are skeptical of such a mindset. In the former camp stands geographer Erle Ellis, who believes "we must not see the Anthropocene as a crisis, but as the beginning of a new geological epoch ripe with human-directed opportunity."[7] Ranked alongside him are science journalists Mark Lynas (author of *The God Species*) and Ronald Bailey, who insists that "over time, we will only get better at being

7. Erle Ellis, "The Planet of No Return: Human Resilience on an Artificial Earth," *The Breakthrough*, no. 2 (2011), at https://thebreakthrough.org/journal [Nixon's note].

the guardian gods of the earth."[8] As their mantra, these Anthropocene optimists cite Stewart Brand's exhortation: "we are as gods and must get good at it."[9]

But for others, talk of *Homo sapiens* as god species, as Earth's surrogate divinity, is positively chilling. Hasn't a hubristic mindset of earth mastery, of dominion over nature, gotten us into this mess as unwitting geological actors? Earth mastery, moreover, conjures up disturbing associations with the race, gender and class hierarchies of the selective enlightenment. For the climatologist Mike Hulme, there is a direct line between such megalomaniacal thinking and the reckless adventurism of a small, powerful set of geo-engineers and their billionaire backers who harbor ambitions to "reset the global thermostat." To which I'd add this: we should not equate human planetary impact with human planetary control, as either a possibility or an ideal. Moreover, humility before the incalculable complexities of a rapidly changing Earth is not the same as quietism.

Science writer Elizabeth Kolbert has tweeted: "two words that probably should not be used in sequence: 'good' & 'anthropocene.'" Environmental philosopher Kathleen Dean Moore goes further, suggesting that the Anthropocene would have been better named the Unforgiveable-crimescene.[1]

Concern over hubristic responses to the Anthropocene leads us to a third controversy. Does the very notion of an Age of Humans risk encouraging species narcissism? It's one thing to recognize that *Homo sapiens* has accrued massive bio- and geomorphic powers. But it's another thing altogether to fixate on human agency to a degree that downplays the imperfectly understood, infinitely elaborate webs of non-human agency, from the microbiome to the movement of tectonic plates, that continue to shape Earth's life systems. To be sure, humans—especially the wealthiest of us—possess planet-altering powers, but we do not exercise those powers in isolation from other forces.

"Geologically, the Anthropocene is a remarkable episode in the history of the planet," says paleontologist Jan Zalasiewicz.[2] But what began as a data-driven scientific debate over how to measure and project the human fingerprint in the fossil record has spread to almost every imaginable scholarly field. The power of the Anthropocene—by turns illuminating, exasperating, alarming—is not reducible to metrics. As environmental historian Libby Robert observes, "the question is how people can take responsibility for and respond to their changed world. And the answer is not simply scientific and technological, but also social, cultural, political and ecological."

To that end, we are witnessing the Anthropocene's transition from a robustly disputed interdisciplinary idea to one that is permeating the public sphere. We see this in special Anthropocene issues of *The Economist, Nature,*

8. Ronald Bailey, "Better to Be Potent Than Not," *New York Times*, May 23, 2011 [Nixon's note].
9. Note: Stewart Brand originally said, "We are as gods and might as well get good at it" (1968), which he changed to: "We are as gods and must get good at it" (2009). Quoted by Diane Ackerman, *The Age of Humans* [*The Human Age: The World Shaped by Us* (New York: W. W. Norton, 2014)], p. 152 [Nixon's note]. Brand (b. 1938), American author and pioneering environmentalist; in *Whole Earth Discipline: An Ecopragmatist Manifesto* (2009) he argues that technology can be green.
1. Kathleen Dean Moore, "Anthropocene Is the Wrong Word," *Earth Island Journal* 27.4 (2013), at www.earthisland.org/journal/ [Nixon's note].
2. Quoted in "The Dawn of a New Epoch?" Press release, University of Leicester, March 26, 2010, www.le.ac.uk/ebulletin-archive/ebulletin/news/press-releases/2010-2019/2010/03/nparticle.2010-03-26.html [Nixon's note].

and *The Smithsonian*. We see it in the way bloggers, filmmakers, public intellectuals, and curators are trying to reimagine, through the prism of the Anthropocene, what geographer Doreen Massey calls "the ancient manoeverings of life and rock."

To give the Anthropocene a public resonance involves choosing objects, images, and stories that will make visceral those tumultuous geologic processes that now happen on human time scales. With this in mind, the Anthropocene Cabinet of Curiosities Slam[3] has assembled a lively array of object-driven stories. The work on display here seeks to give immense biomorphic and geomorphic changes a granular intimacy. Collectively, these Anthropocene stories have the power to disturb and to surprise, hopefully goading us toward new ways of thinking and feeling about the planet we have inherited and the planet we will bequeath.

2014

3. http://nelson.wisc.edu/che/anthroslam/ [Nixon's note]. "The Anthropocene Slam: A Cabinet of Curiosities" was a creative event for scholars and artists hosted by the Nelson Institute Center for Culture, History and Environment at the University of Wisconsin–Madison on November 8–10, 2014.

JUDITH BUTLER
b. 1956

Judith Butler's *Gender Trouble: Feminism and the Subversion of Identity* (1990), arguably the most influential theoretical text of the 1990s, is a founding document of queer theory and a key statement of "performative" accounts of cultural meaning. Butler's work distills forty years of French theory—from the pioneer feminist SIMONE DE BEAUVOIR to JULIA KRISTEVA, and from JACQUES LACAN and LOUIS ALTHUSSER to JACQUES DERRIDA and MICHEL FOUCAULT—to explore how gendered identity is socially produced through repetitions of ordinary daily activities. Her goal is to uncover the assumptions that "restrict the meaning of gender to received notions of masculinity and femininity." In opening up "the field of possibility for gender," Butler aims for a feminism that avoids "exclusionary gender norms" and fixed identities in favor of a more fluid and dynamic understanding of desires and selves.

Trained in philosophy, Judith Butler received her undergraduate and graduate degrees at Yale University. She has taught in interdisciplinary programs her whole career, first at Johns Hopkins University and then at the University of California at Berkeley. While continuing her affiliation with Berkeley, she has also taught frequently at Columbia University. *Gender Trouble* made Butler something between a celebrity and a cult figure, especially in gay and lesbian subcultures, and she has responded by jealously guarding her personal life from public scrutiny. Her longtime partner, Wendy Brown, is a prominent political theorist, and she and Butler have collaborated on a number of projects. Butler's work since 9/11 has often been directly political; she has written extensively on the U.S. wars in Afghanistan and Iraq, and on the troubled relations between the state of Israel and the Palestinian people.

In *Gender Trouble*, Butler insists that nothing is natural, including sexual identity and sexual desire. Feminists have sometimes distinguished between "sex" as the anatomical difference between male and female bodies and "gender" as the meanings and conventions attached to those bodily differences in various cultures. Butler argues that even anatomical differences can be experienced only through the categories and expectations set out by the culture's signifying order. Moreover, anatomical differences are mapped to expectations about sexual desire, specifically to society's "compulsory heterosexuality" (a term Butler borrows from ADRIENNE RICH), which posits that there are two sexes and that desire runs from one sex to the other. Modern Western culture's understanding of sexuality is ill-equipped, therefore, to recognize bodies that confound the strict binary division between male and female, or desires that cross, combine, or otherwise fail to conform to a fairly narrow understanding of sex as genital intercourse between two people, one "naturally" female, the other "naturally" male.

Following Foucault's work in *The History of Sexuality* (1976; see above), Butler stresses that modern culture sees sexuality as a fundamental constituent of identity. Our sex and our sexual desires and activities are understood as profound indices of who we are. And, like Foucault, Butler hopes to disrupt that linkage. The norms of both acceptable sexual desires and of identity construction and maintenance are oppressive, forcing the polymorphous perversity described by SIGMUND FREUD into the straitjacket of the prevailing heterosexual categories. The established and conventional connections between anatomy and desire, and between sexual activities and ascriptions of identity, are not inevitable; they have been different in other cultures and in other historical eras, and they are open to revision or, to use one of Butler's favorite words, "resignification." The meanings and categories by which we understand and live our daily existence can be altered.

Such alteration does not come easily, however. "Those naturalized and reified notions of gender that support masculine hegemony and heterosexist power" are written into our very psyches as well as into the dominant institutions of political and social life. Butler follows the accounts of subject formation found in Foucault and Lacan. For Foucault, discourse (the articulated categories of thought) orders knowledge along lines that produce subjects open to power's control. Such power, he stresses, works at the level of daily routine. For Lacan, individuals achieve an identity, a recognized place in the social order, by passing into the Law (the culture's signifying order)—at the cost of creating the unconscious and establishing a permanent split, an alienation of self from desire, within the subject.

To Foucault's account of power's "micro-physics" and Lacan's description of subject formation, Butler adds Derrida's understanding of "performative speech acts." She believes "the performative" offers her a model of action within theories that often seem to allow subjects no room for resistance to power. Derrida develops his notion of the performative in an essay on J. L. AUSTIN, the twentieth-century Oxford philosopher who invented the term, and in a later debate with the American philosopher John Searle. Austin comes from an Anglo-American tradition (dating back to John Locke) that sees the meaning of language as grounded in the way that words refer to already existing objects. I speak of a certain blue chair, and my words are meaningful and true insofar as they conform to the facts of the matter. But Austin realized that some utterances are creative: they make something come into existence, rather than referring to something that already exists. Anyone who makes a promise, or a judge who sentences someone to prison, creates a fact (the promise, the sentence) through the act of speaking. Such speech acts are performatives.

Surprisingly, as Austin pursues this notion he finds it increasingly difficult to distinguish performatives from referential speech acts. Derrida picks up on this difficulty and adds the concepts of "citation" and "repetition" to the analysis. Every speech act, Derrida argues, succeeds in meaning anything at all only by virtue of its "citing" previous uses of the term it now employs. In other words, language works because the speakers of that language have a prior knowledge of its terms and its prevailing usages (both syntactic and semantic). Every new speech act is a repetition, using old words and structures in this new instance. There are thus fairly strict limits on novelty. An utterance that departs too far from received understandings will be incomprehensible. But exact repetition does not occur very often either. After all, we are using the old words in new contexts. Each separate use of a word tweaks it in this or that direction in relation to a variety of pressures: the context, the audience, conscious or unconscious purposes. Thus, each speech act has a performative dimension; while repeating or referring to preexisting meanings in its "citation" of a previously used word, it also alters, if always within limits, the meaning of that word. Languages are reproduced, are kept alive and functioning, through innumerable acts of use; but those acts also constantly change the language. Most changes are inadvertent by-products of use, but some may be conscious, such as contemporary efforts to abandon "man" as the generic word referring to all human beings.

Butler proposes that we understand "sex" and "gender" as citational repetitions. Various cultural discourses converge in a prevailing (although never fully homogeneous or monolithic) understanding of what "boy" and "girl," "man" and "woman" signify. Individual actions then "cite" these meanings, playing off them in various ways. Power functions pervasively through these meanings. The little boy learns that his crying is not masculine; he must grow into his masculinity by imitating the behavior designated as "male" to the point that such behavior becomes "second nature." The little girl learns that some ways of acting make her a tomboy, and she is encouraged to dress the part of "femininity." In Butler's view, we feel our way into these roles, slowly establishing (under the watchful eyes of powerful social forces) the way we will occupy them. Given our prevailing categories, we experience this process as discovering our identity. Butler believes identity is a trap, a hardening into rigid, binarized categories of much more fluid and heterogeneous possibilities. She calls for actions that will "resignify" our received meanings—actions that will lead to a "proliferation" of the "constitutive categories" into which all selves are now constrained to fit.

The costs of identity's straitjacket, Butler believes, are high—both for those who fit the categories comfortably and those who don't. "Deviants" (such as homosexuals, bisexuals, hermaphrodites, or other less recognizable nonidentities) are inevitable, according to Butler, although her reasons for this claim are not completely clear. For her, discursive power is never fully effective. It cannot create all individuals in its preferred image, in part because any social field is traversed by various discourses, none of which ever achieves full domination. In any case, compulsory heterosexuality cannot erase all nonheterosexual desires or acts. But the price paid by those labeled deviant for such desires and acts—in internalized guilt and external sanctions—is exorbitant. On the side of "normality," heterosexual identity can be achieved only through the forceful exclusion or "disavowal" of all nonheterosexual desires, in keeping with commonplace obsessional notions of identity as consistent in all places and at all times. Socially, this disavowal is expressed through homophobia and other discourses of "abjection" (Kristeva's famous term) that single out deviants as worthy targets of aggression and punishment.

Butler calls for a loosening of the categories, a relaxation of our fixation on identity. Power uses identity to latch on to us, and normative identity calls for a homogeneity too difficult to live. Butler believes that feminism has been hurt by its attempt to find an identity that would designate something common to everyone in the movement. She calls instead for a coalitional politics that avoids the fights over purity (of identity, of doctrine, of commitment) that often tear apart movements dependent on complete agreement among members over long periods of time. Thus, while Butler's work grows out of feminism, she is against any "identity politics" that sees political groupings and beliefs as grounded in a shared identity, whether ethnic, racial, sexual, national, or economic. All forms of identity politics, she believes, are prone to aggressions used to enforce rigid consistencies.

How do we begin to loosen the hold of identity, especially at a time when the passions attached to identity and its preservation are fervent and pervasive? An initial step, Butler says, is to make evident identity's construction; it is not inevitable (even if social power hardly leaves us much freedom to choose our ways of being in the world). Identity is not something planted in us to be discovered, but something that is performatively produced by acts that "effectively constitute the identity they are said to express or reveal." At the end of *Gender Trouble*, Butler advocates parody in general and drag performances in particular because such "subversive" performances "destabilize the naturalized categories of identity and desire." It is here that queer theory makes its appearance. Such theory is interested in any and all acts, images, and ideas that "trouble," violate, cross, mix, or otherwise confound established boundaries between male and female, normal and abnormal, self and other. In a limited sense, the goal is to create more space for and recognition of the various actions performed daily in a social landscape blinded and hostile to variety. But the broader goal is a general troubling, an attempted unfixing, of the links between acts, categories, representations, desires, and identities.

The main objections to Butler's position echo the objections often made to poststructuralist work. Key questions focus on agency, power, and ethics, while her difficult style and specialized terminology seem to guarantee a small audience for work that aims to have political consequences. To what extent does Butler believe that conscious, purposive action is possible if she posits an all-encompassing discursive power that shapes us at such a deep, unconscious level? How are we to understand "compulsory heterosexuality," "masculine hegemony," "phallogocentrism" (Derrida's term for the masculine power at the origin of the Law), and other terms by which she designates power? Have there been societies in which these forms of power have not been dominant? Is the formation of subjectivity entirely a matter of the self's relation to power, or do intersubjective relationships have any important role to play? What enables the critical enterprise itself, the ability to describe the processes of subject formation? Within ongoing debates over the details, however, a new interest in violations of received categories and the performative reproduction and transformation of culture attests to Butler's impact on literary studies.

***Gender Trouble* Keywords:** The Body, Deconstruction, Feminist Theory, Gender, Hegemony, Identity, Poststructuralism, Queer Theory, Sexuality

From Gender Trouble

From *Preface*

Contemporary feminist debates over the meanings of gender lead time and again to a certain sense of trouble, as if the indeterminacy of gender might eventually culminate in the failure of feminism. Perhaps trouble need not carry such a negative valence. To make trouble was, within the reigning discourse of my childhood, something one should never do precisely because that would get one *in* trouble. The rebellion and its reprimand seemed to be caught up in the same terms, a phenomenon that gave rise to my first critical insight into the subtle ruse of power: the prevailing law threatened one with trouble, even put one in trouble, all to keep one out of trouble. Hence, I concluded that trouble is inevitable and the task, how best to make it, what best way to be in it. As time went by, further ambiguities arrived on the critical scene. I noted that trouble sometimes euphemized some fundamentally mysterious problem usually related to the alleged mystery of all things feminine.

I read Beauvoir[1] who explained that to be a woman within the terms of a masculinist culture is to be a source of mystery and unknowability for men, and this seemed confirmed somehow when I read Sartre[2] for whom all desire, problematically presumed as heterosexual and masculine, was defined as *trouble*. For that masculine subject of desire, trouble became a scandal with the sudden intrusion, the unanticipated agency, of a female "object" who inexplicably returns the glance, reverses the gaze, and contests the place and authority of the masculine position. The radical dependency of the masculine subject on the female "Other" suddenly exposes his autonomy as illusory. That particular dialectical reversal of power, however, couldn't quite hold my attention—although others surely did. Power seemed to be more than an exchange between subjects or a relation of constant inversion between a subject and an Other; indeed, power appeared to operate in the production of that very binary frame for thinking about gender. I asked, what configuration of power constructs the subject and the Other, that binary relation between "men" and "women," and the internal stability of those terms? What restriction is here at work? Are those terms untroubling only to the extent that they conform to a heterosexual matrix for conceptualizing gender and desire? What happens to the subject and to the stability of gender categories when the epistemic regime of presumptive heterosexuality is unmasked as that which produces and reifies these ostensible categories of ontology?

But how can an epistemic/ontological regime be brought into question? What best way to trouble the gender categories that support gender hierarchy and compulsory heterosexuality? Consider the fate of "female trouble," that historical configuration of a nameless female indisposition, which thinly veiled the notion that being female is a natural indisposition. Serious as the medicalization of women's bodies is, the term is also laughable, and laughter in the face of serious categories is indispensable for feminism. Without a doubt, feminism continues to require its own forms of serious play. *Female Trouble* is also the title of the John Waters film that features Divine, the hero/heroine of *Hairspray*[3] as well, whose impersonation of women implicitly suggests that gender is a kind of persistent impersonation that passes as the real. Her/his performance destabilizes the very distinctions between the natural and the artificial, depth and surface, inner and outer through which discourse about genders almost always operates. Is drag the imitation of gender, or does it dramatize the signifying gestures through which gender itself is established? Does being female constitute a "natural fact" or a cultural performance, or is "naturalness" constituted through discursively constrained performative acts that produce the body through and within the categories of sex? Divine notwithstanding, gender practices within gay and lesbian cultures often thematize "the natural" in parodic contexts that bring into relief the performative construction of an original and true sex. What other foundational categories of identity—the binary of sex, gender, and the body—can be shown as productions that create the effect of the natural, the original, and the inevitable?

1. SIMONE DE BEAUVOIR (1908–1986), French existentialist philosopher and feminist writer.
2. Jean-Paul Sartre (1905–1980), French existentialist philosopher.
3. *Hairspray* (1988) and *Female Trouble* (1974), films by the independent producer/director/screenwriter John Waters (b. 1946). Divine (born Harris Glenn Milstead, 1945–1988), a 300-pound cross-dresser who starred in many of Waters's films.

To expose the foundational categories of sex, gender, and desire as effects of a specific formation of power requires a form of critical inquiry that Foucault, reformulating Nietzsche,[4] designates as "genealogy." A genealogical critique refuses to search for the origins of gender, the inner truth of female desire, a genuine or authentic sexual identity that repression has kept from view; rather, genealogy investigates the political stakes in designating as an *origin* and *cause* those identity categories that are in fact the *effects* of institutions, practices, discourses with multiple and diffuse points of origin. The task of this inquiry is to center on—and decenter—such defining institutions: phallogocentrism and compulsory heterosexuality.[5]

Precisely because "female" no longer appears to be a stable notion, its meaning is as troubled and unfixed as "women," and because both terms gain their troubled significations only as relational terms, this inquiry takes as its focus gender and the relational analysis it suggests. Further, it is no longer clear that feminist theory ought to try to settle the questions of primary identity in order to get on with the task of politics. Instead, we ought to ask, what political possibilities are the consequence of a radical critique of the categories of identity. What new shape of politics emerges when identity as a common ground no longer constrains the discourse on feminist politics? And to what extent does the effort to locate a common identity as the foundation for a feminist politics preclude a radical inquiry into the political construction and regulation of identity itself?

* * *

From *Chapter 3. Subversive Bodily Acts*

* * *

BODILY INSCRIPTIONS, PERFORMATIVE SUBVERSIONS

> Garbo "got in drag" whenever she took some heavy glamour part, whenever she melted in or out of a man's arms, whenever she simply let that heavenly-flexed neck . . . bear the weight of her thrown-back head. . . . How resplendent seems the art of acting! It is all *impersonation*, whether the sex underneath is true or not.
>
> —Parker Tyler, "The Garbo Image,"
> quoted in Esther Newton, *Mother Camp*[6]

Categories of true sex, discrete gender, and specific sexuality have constituted the stable point of reference for a great deal of feminist theory and politics. These constructs of identity serve as the points of epistemic departure from which theory emerges and politics itself is shaped. In the case of

4. FRIEDRICH NIETZSCHE (1844–1900), German philosopher. MICHEL FOUCAULT (1926–1984), French philosopher and historian of ideas.

5. A term coined by the American feminist poet ADRIENNE RICH (1929–2012) to indicate society's injunction against all homosexual desires and acts. "Phallogocentrism": a term coined by the French philosopher JACQUES DERRIDA (1930–2004) for the patriarchal dominance of sexuality and the legal system.

6. *Mother Camp: Female Impersonators in America* (Chicago: University of Chicago Press, 1972). Greta Garbo (1905–1990), Swedish-born American film star.

feminism, politics is ostensibly shaped to express the interests, the perspectives, of "women." But is there a political shape to "women," as it were, that precedes and prefigures the political elaboration of their interests and epistemic point of view? How is that identity shaped, and is it a political shaping that takes the very morphology and boundary of the sexed body as the ground, surface, or site of cultural inscription? What circumscribes that site as "the female body"? Is "the body" or "the sexed body" the firm foundation on which gender and systems of compulsory sexuality operate? Or is "the body" itself shaped by political forces with strategic interests in keeping that body bounded and constituted by the markers of sex?

The sex/gender distinction and the category of sex itself appear to presuppose a generalization of "the body" that preexists the acquisition of its sexed significance. This "body" often appears to be a passive medium that is signified by an inscription from a cultural source figured as "external" to that body. Any theory of the culturally constructed body, however, ought to question "the body" as a construct of suspect generality when it is figured as passive and prior to discourse. There are Christian and Cartesian precedents[7] to such views which, prior to the emergence of vitalistic biologies in the nineteenth century, understand "the body" as so much inert matter, signifying nothing or, more specifically, signifying a profane void, the fallen state: deception, sin, the premonitional metaphorics of hell and the eternal feminine. There are many occasions in both Sartre's and Beauvoir's work where "the body" is figured as a mute facticity, anticipating some meaning that can be attributed only by a transcendent consciousness, understood in Cartesian terms as radically immaterial. But what establishes this dualism for us? What separates off "the body" as indifferent to signification, and signification itself as the act of a radically disembodied consciousness or, rather, the act that radically disembodies that consciousness? To what extent is that Cartesian dualism presupposed in phenomenology[8] adapted to the structuralist frame in which mind/body is redescribed as culture/nature? With respect to gender discourse, to what extent do these problematic dualisms still operate within the very descriptions that are supposed to lead us out of that binarism and its implicit hierarchy? How are the contours of the body clearly marked as the taken-for-granted ground or surface upon which gender significations are inscribed, a mere facticity devoid of value, prior to significance?

Wittig[9] suggests that a culturally specific epistemic *a priori* establishes the naturalness of "sex." But by what enigmatic means has "the body" been accepted as a *prima facie* given that admits of no genealogy? Even within Foucault's essay on the very theme of genealogy, the body is figured as a surface and the scene of a cultural inscription: "the body is the inscribed surface of events."[1] The task of genealogy, he claims, is "to expose a body totally imprinted by history." His sentence continues, however, by referring

7. In the dualistic system of the French philosopher René Descartes (1596–1650), spirit and matter are mutually exclusive.

8. A philosophical method restricted to analyzing the intellectual processes of which we are introspectively aware (while ignoring external objects, the question of whose existence is "bracketed").

9. Monique Wittig (1935–2003), French feminist theorist and novelist.

1. Michel Foucault, "Nietzsche, Genealogy, History," in *Language, Counter-Memory, Practice*, ed. Donald F. Bouchard, trans. Donald F. Bouchard and Sherry Simon (Ithaca: Cornell University Press, 1977), p. 148 [Butler's note]. Some of the author's notes are edited, and some omitted.

to the goal of "history"—here clearly understood on the model of Freud's "civilization"—as the "destruction of the body" (148). Forces and impulses with multiple directionalities are precisely that which history both destroys and preserves through the *entstehung* (historical event) of inscription. As "a volume in perpetual disintegration" (148), the body is always under siege, suffering destruction by the very terms of history. And history is the creation of values and meanings by a signifying practice that requires the subjection of the body. This corporeal destruction is necessary to produce the speaking subject and its significations. This is a body, described through the language of surface and force, weakened through a "single drama" of domination, inscription, and creation (150). This is not the *modus vivendi* of one kind of history rather than another, but is, for Foucault, "history" (148) in its essential and repressive gesture.

Although Foucault writes, "Nothing in man [*sic*]—not even his body—is sufficiently stable to serve as the basis for self-recognition or for understanding other men [*sic*]" (153), he nevertheless points to the constancy of cultural inscription as a "single drama" that acts on the body. If the creation of values, that historical mode of signification, requires the destruction of the body, much as the instrument of torture in Kafka's *In the Penal Colony*[2] destroys the body on which it writes, then there must be a body prior to that inscription, stable and self-identical, subject to that sacrificial destruction. In a sense, for Foucault, as for Nietzsche, cultural values emerge as the result of an inscription on the body, understood as a medium, indeed, a blank page; in order for this inscription to signify, however, that medium must itself be destroyed—that is, fully transvaluated into a sublimated domain of values. Within the metaphorics of this notion of cultural values is the figure of history as a relentless writing instrument, and the body as the medium which must be destroyed and transfigured in order for "culture" to emerge.

By maintaining a body prior to its cultural inscription, Foucault appears to assume a materiality prior to signification and form. Because this distinction operates as essential to the task of genealogy as he defines it, the distinction itself is precluded as an object of genealogical investigation. Occasionally in his analysis of Herculine,[3] Foucault subscribes to a prediscursive multiplicity of bodily forces that break through the surface of the body to disrupt the regulating practices of cultural coherence imposed upon that body by a power regime, understood as a vicissitude of "history." If the presumption of some kind of precategorial source of disruption is refused, is it still possible to give a genealogical account of the demarcation of the body as such as a signifying practice? This demarcation is not initiated by a reified history or by a subject. This marking is the result of a diffuse and active structuring of the social field. This signifying practice effects a social space for and of the body within certain regulatory grids of intelligibility.

Mary Douglas' *Purity and Danger* suggests that the very contours of "the body" are established through markings that seek to establish specific codes of cultural coherence. Any discourse that establishes the boundaries of the body serves the purpose of instating and naturalizing certain taboos regard-

2. A 1919 story by Franz Kafka (1883–1924), Austrian writer who was born and lived most of his life in Prague.

3. Herculine Barbin, a 19th-century French hermaphrodite whose memoirs were published in 1978 with an introduction by Foucault (discussed by Butler earlier in this chapter).

ing the appropriate limits, postures, and modes of exchange that define what it is that constitutes bodies:

> ideas about separating, purifying, demarcating and punishing transgressions have as their main function to impose system on an inherently untidy experience. It is only by exaggerating the difference between within and without, above and below, male and female, with and against, that a semblance of order is created.[4]

Although Douglas clearly subscribes to a structuralist distinction between an inherently unruly nature and an order imposed by cultural means, the "untidiness" to which she refers can be redescribed as a region of *cultural* unruliness and disorder. Assuming the inevitably binary structure of the nature/culture distinction, Douglas cannot point toward an alternative configuration of culture in which such distinctions become malleable or proliferate beyond the binary frame. Her analysis, however, provides a possible point of departure for understanding the relationship by which social taboos institute and maintain the boundaries of the body as such. Her analysis suggests that what constitutes the limit of the body is never merely material, but that the surface, the skin, is systemically signified by taboos and anticipated transgressions; indeed, the boundaries of the body become, within her analysis, the limits of the social *per se*. A poststructuralist appropriation of her view might well understand the boundaries of the body as the limits of the socially *hegemonic*. In a variety of cultures, she maintains, there are

> pollution powers which inhere in the structure of ideas itself and which punish a symbolic breaking of that which should be joined or joining of that which should be separate. It follows from this that pollution is a type of danger which is not likely to occur except where the lines of structure, cosmic or social, are clearly defined.
>
> A polluting person is always in the wrong. He [*sic*] has developed some wrong condition or simply crossed over some line which should not have been crossed and this displacement unleashes danger for someone.[5]

In a sense, Simon Watney has identified the contemporary construction of "the polluting person" as the person with AIDS in his *Policing Desire: AIDS, Pornography, and the Media*.[6] Not only is the illness figured as the "gay disease," but throughout the media's hysterical and homophobic response to the illness there is a tactical construction of a continuity between the polluted status of the homosexual by virtue of the boundary-trespass that *is* homosexuality and the disease as a specific modality of homosexual pollution. That the disease is transmitted through the exchange of bodily fluids suggests within the sensationalist graphics of homophobic signifying systems the dangers that permeable bodily boundaries present to the social order as such. Douglas remarks that "the body is a model that can stand for any bounded system. Its boundaries can represent any boundaries which are threatened or precarious."[7] And she asks a question which one might have

4. Mary Douglas, *Purity and Danger* (London: Routledge and Kegan Paul, 1969) p. 4 [Butler's note]. Douglas (1921–2007), British anthropologist.
5. Ibid., p. 113 [Butler's note].
6. Simon Watney, *Policing Desire: AIDS, Pornography, and the Media* (Minneapolis: University of Minnesota Press, 1988) [Butler's note].
7. Douglas, *Purity and Danger,* p. 115 [Butler's note].

expected to read in Foucault: "Why should bodily margins be thought to be specifically invested with power and danger?"[8]

Douglas suggests that all social systems are vulnerable at their margins, and that all margins are accordingly considered dangerous. If the body is synecdochal for the social system *per se* or a site in which open systems converge, then any kind of unregulated permeability constitutes a site of pollution and endangerment. Since anal and oral sex among men clearly establishes certain kinds of bodily permeabilities unsanctioned by the hegemonic order, male homosexuality would, within such a hegemonic point of view, constitute a site of danger and pollution, prior to and regardless of the cultural presence of AIDS. Similarly, the "polluted" status of lesbians, regardless of their low-risk status with respect to AIDS, brings into relief the dangers of their bodily exchanges. Significantly, being "outside" the hegemonic order does not signify being "in" a state of filthy and untidy nature. Paradoxically, homosexuality is almost always conceived within the homophobic signifying economy as *both* uncivilized and unnatural.

The construction of stable bodily contours relies upon fixed sites of corporeal permeability and impermeability. Those sexual practices in both homosexual and heterosexual contexts that open surfaces and orifices to erotic signification or close down others effectively reinscribe the boundaries of the body along new cultural lines. Anal sex among men is an example, as is the radical re-membering of the body in Wittig's *The Lesbian Body*.[9] Douglas alludes to "a kind of sex pollution which expresses a desire to keep the body (physical and social) intact,"[1] suggesting that the naturalized notion of "the" body is itself a consequence of taboos that render that body discrete by virtue of its stable boundaries. Further, the rites of passage that govern various bodily orifices presuppose a heterosexual construction of gendered exchange, positions, and erotic possibilities. The deregulation of such exchanges accordingly disrupts the very boundaries that determine what it is to be a body at all. Indeed, the critical inquiry that traces the regulatory practices within which bodily contours are constructed constitutes precisely the genealogy of "the body" in its discreteness that might further radicalize Foucault's theory.[2]

Significantly, Kristeva's discussion of abjection in *The Powers of Horror* begins to suggest the uses of this structuralist notion of a boundary-constituting taboo for the purposes of constructing a discrete subject through exclusion.[3] The "abject" designates that which has been expelled from the body, discharged as excrement, literally rendered "Other." This appears as an expulsion of alien elements, but the alien is effectively established through

8. Ibid., p. 121 [Butler's note].
9. Published in 1973.
1. Douglas, *Purity and Danger*, p. 140 [Butler's note].
2. Foucault's essay "A Preface to Transgression" (in *Language, Counter-Memory, Practice*) does provide an interesting juxtaposition with Douglas's notion of body boundaries constituted by incest taboos. Originally written in honor of Georges Bataille, this essay explores in part the metaphorical "dirt" of transgressive pleasures and the association of the forbidden orifice with the dirt-covered tomb. See pp. 46–48 [Butler's note]. Bataille (1897–1962), French novelist and philosopher.
3. Kristeva discusses Mary Douglas's work in a short section of *The Powers of Horror: An Essay on Abjection*, trans. Leon Roudiez (New York: Columbia University Press, 1982), originally published as *Pouvoirs de l'horreur* (1980). Assimilating Douglas's insights to her own reformulation of Lacan, Kristeva writes, "Defilement is what is jettisoned from the *symbolic system*. It is what escapes that social rationality, that logical order on which a social aggregate is based, which then becomes differentiated from a temporary agglomeration of individuals and, in short, constitutes a *classification system* or a *structure*" (p. 65) [Butler's note]. JULIA KRISTEVA (b. 1941), French feminist literary critic and psychoanalyst.

this expulsion. The construction of the "not-me" as the abject establishes the boundaries of the body which are also the first contours of the subject. Kristeva writes:

> *nausea* makes me balk at that milk cream, separates me from the mother and father who proffer it. "I" want none of that element, sign of their desire; "I" do not want to listen, "I" do not assimilate it, "I" expel it. But since the food is not an "other" for "me," who am only in their desire, I expel *myself*, I spit *myself* out, I abject *myself* within the same motion through which "I" claim to establish myself.[4]

The boundary of the body as well as the distinction between internal and external is established through the ejection and transvaluation of something originally part of identity into a defiling otherness. As Iris Young has suggested in her use of Kristeva to understand sexism, homophobia, and racism, the repudiation of bodies for their sex, sexuality, and/or color is an "expulsion" followed by a "repulsion" that founds and consolidates culturally hegemonic identities along sex/race/sexuality axes of differentiation.[5] Young's appropriation of Kristeva shows how the operation of repulsion can consolidate "identities" founded on the instituting of the "Other" or a set of Others through exclusion and domination. What constitutes through division the "inner" and "outer" worlds of the subject is a border and boundary tenuously maintained for the purposes of social regulation and control. The boundary between the inner and outer is confounded by those excremental passages in which the inner effectively becomes outer, and this excreting function becomes, as it were, the model by which other forms of identity-differentiation are accomplished. In effect, this is the mode by which Others become shit. For inner and outer worlds to remain utterly distinct, the entire surface of the body would have to achieve an impossible impermeability. This sealing of its surfaces would constitute the seamless boundary of the subject; but this enclosure would invariably be exploded by precisely that excremental filth that it fears.

Regardless of the compelling metaphors of the spatial distinctions of inner and outer, they remain linguistic terms that facilitate and articulate a set of fantasies, feared and desired. "Inner" and "outer" make sense only with reference to a mediating boundary that strives for stability. And this stability, this coherence, is determined in large part by cultural orders that sanction the subject and compel its differentiation from the abject. Hence, "inner" and "outer" constitute a binary distinction that stabilizes and consolidates the coherent subject. When that subject is challenged, the meaning and necessity of the terms are subject to displacement. If the "inner world" no longer designates a topos,[6] then the internal fixity of the self and, indeed, the internal locale of gender identity, become similarly suspect. The critical question is not *how* did that identity become *internalized*? as if internalization were a process or a mechanism that might be descriptively reconstructed. Rather,

4. Ibid., p. 3 [Butler's note].
5. Iris Marion Young, "Abjection and Oppression: Unconscious Dynamics of Racism, Sexism, and Homophobia," paper presented at the Society of Phenomenology and Existential Philosophy Meetings, Northwestern University, 1988. The paper is included as part of a larger chapter [chapter 5] in *Justice and the Politics of Difference* (1990) [Butler's note]. Young (1949–2006), American feminist political philosopher.
6. Place (Greek).

the question is: From what strategic position in public discourse and for what reasons has the trope of interiority and the disjunctive binary of inner/outer taken hold? In what language is "inner space" figured? What kind of figuration is it, and through what figure of the body is it signified? How does a body figure on its surface the very invisibility of its hidden depth?

From Interiority to Gender Performatives

In *Discipline and Punish* Foucault challenges the language of internalization as it operates in the service of the disciplinary regime of the subjection and subjectivation of criminals. Although Foucault objected to what he understood to be the psychoanalytic belief in the "inner" truth of sex in *The History of Sexuality*, he turns to a criticism of the doctrine of internalization for separate purposes in the context of his history of criminology. In a sense, *Discipline and Punish* can be read as Foucault's effort to rewrite Nietzsche's doctrine of internalization in *On the Genealogy of Morals* on the model of *inscription*. In the context of prisoners, Foucault writes, the strategy has been not to enforce a repression of their desires, but to compel their bodies to signify the prohibitive law as their very essence, style, and necessity. That law is not literally internalized, but incorporated, with the consequence that bodies are produced which signify that law on and through the body; there the law is manifest as the essence of their selves, the meaning of their soul, their conscience, the law of their desire. In effect, the law is at once fully manifest and fully latent, for it never appears as external to the bodies it subjects and subjectivates. Foucault writes:

> It would be wrong to say that the soul is an illusion, or an ideological effect. On the contrary, it exists, it has a reality, it is produced permanently *around, on, within*, the body by the functioning of a power that is exercised on those that are punished [my emphasis].[7]

The figure of the interior soul understood as "within" the body is signified through its inscription *on* the body, even though its primary mode of signification is through its very absence, its potent invisibility. The effect of a structuring inner space is produced through the signification of a body as a vital and sacred enclosure. The soul is precisely what the body lacks; hence, the body presents itself as a signifying lack. That lack which *is* the body signifies the soul as that which cannot show. In this sense, then, the soul is a surface signification that contests and displaces the inner/outer distinction itself, a figure of interior psychic space inscribed *on* the body as a social signification that perpetually renounces itself as such. In Foucault's terms, the soul is not imprisoned by or within the body, as some Christian imagery would suggest, but "the soul is the prison of the body."[8]

The redescription of intrapsychic processes in terms of the surface politics of the body implies a corollary redescription of gender as the disciplinary production of the figures of fantasy through the play of presence and absence on the body's surface, the construction of the gendered body through a series of exclusions and denials, signifying absences. But what

7. Michel Foucault, *Discipline and Punish: The Birth of the Prison*, trans. Alan Sheridan (New York: Vintage, 1979), p. 29 [Butler's note]. *The History of Sexuality* was published in 1976, *On the Genealogy of Morals* in 1887.

8. Ibid., p. 30 [Butler's note].

determines the manifest and latent text of the body politic? What is the prohibitive law that generates the corporeal stylization of gender, the fantasied and fantastic figuration of the body? We have already considered the incest taboo and the prior taboo against homosexuality as the generative moments of gender identity,[9] the prohibitions that produce identity along the culturally intelligible grids of an idealized and compulsory heterosexuality. That disciplinary production of gender effects a false stabilization of gender in the interests of the heterosexual construction and regulation of sexuality within the reproductive domain. The construction of coherence conceals the gender discontinuities that run rampant within heterosexual, bisexual, and gay and lesbian contexts in which gender does not necessarily follow from sex, and desire, or sexuality generally, does not seem to follow from gender—indeed, where none of these dimensions of significant corporeality express or reflect one another. When the disorganization and disaggregation of the field of bodies disrupt the regulatory fiction of heterosexual coherence, it seems that the expressive model loses its descriptive force. That regulatory ideal is then exposed as a norm and a fiction that disguises itself as a developmental law regulating the sexual field that it purports to describe.

According to the understanding of identification as an enacted fantasy or incorporation, however, it is clear that coherence is desired, wished for, idealized, and that this idealization is an effect of a corporeal signification. In other words, acts, gestures, and desire produce the effect of an internal core or substance, but produce this *on the surface* of the body, through the play of signifying absences that suggest, but never reveal, the organizing principle of identity as a cause. Such acts, gestures, enactments, generally construed, are *performative* in the sense that the essence or identity that they otherwise purport to express are *fabrications* manufactured and sustained through corporeal signs and other discursive means. That the gendered body is performative suggests that it has no ontological status apart from the various acts which constitute its reality. This also suggests that if that reality is fabricated as an interior essence, that very interiority is an effect and function of a decidedly public and social discourse, the public regulation of fantasy through the surface politics of the body, the gender border control that differentiates inner from outer, and so institutes the "integrity" of the subject. In other words, acts and gestures, articulated and enacted desires create the illusion of an interior and organizing gender core, an illusion discursively maintained for the purposes of the regulation of sexuality within the obligatory frame of reproductive heterosexuality. If the "cause" of desire, gesture, and act can be localized within the "self" of the actor, then the political regulations and disciplinary practices which produce that ostensibly coherent gender are effectively displaced from view. The displacement of a political and discursive origin of gender identity onto a psychological "core" precludes an analysis of the political constitution of the gendered subject and its fabricated notions about the ineffable interiority of its sex or of its true identity.

If the inner truth of gender is a fabrication and if a true gender is a fantasy instituted and inscribed on the surface of bodies, then it seems that genders can be neither true nor false, but are only produced as the truth effects of a discourse of primary and stable identity. In *Mother Camp: Female Impersonators in America*, anthropologist Esther Newton suggests that the structure

9. In chapter 2 of *Gender Trouble*.

of impersonation reveals one of the key fabricating mechanisms through which the social construction of gender takes place. I would suggest as well that drag fully subverts the distinction between inner and outer psychic space and effectively mocks both the expressive model of gender and the notion of a true gender identity. Newton writes:

> At its most complex, [drag] is a double inversion that says, "appearance is an illusion." Drag says [Newton's curious personification] "my 'outside' appearance is feminine, but my essence 'inside' [the body] is masculine." At the same time it symbolizes the opposite inversion; "my appearance 'outside' [my body, my gender] is masculine but my essence 'inside' [myself] is feminine."[1]

Both claims to truth contradict one another and so displace the entire enactment of gender significations from the discourse of truth and falsity.

The notion of an original or primary gender identity is often parodied within the cultural practices of drag, cross-dressing, and the sexual stylization of butch/femme identities. Within feminist theory, such parodic identities have been understood to be either degrading to women, in the case of drag and cross-dressing, or an uncritical appropriation of sex-role stereotyping from within the practice of heterosexuality, especially in the case of butch/femme lesbian identities. But the relation between the "imitation" and the "original" is, I think, more complicated than that critique generally allows. Moreover, it gives us a clue to the way in which the relationship between primary identification—that is, the original meanings accorded to gender—and subsequent gender experience might be reframed. The performance of drag plays upon the distinction between the anatomy of the performer and the gender that is being performed. But we are actually in the presence of three contingent dimensions of significant corporeality: anatomical sex, gender identity, and gender performance. If the anatomy of the performer is already distinct from the gender of the performer, and both of those are distinct from the gender of the performance, then the performance suggests a dissonance not only between sex and performance, but sex and gender, and gender and performance. As much as drag creates a unified picture of "woman" (what its critics often oppose), it also reveals the distinctness of those aspects of gendered experience which are falsely naturalized as a unity through the regulatory fiction of heterosexual coherence. *In imitating gender, drag implicitly reveals the imitative structure of gender itself—as well as its contingency.* Indeed, part of the pleasure, the giddiness of the performance is in the recognition of a radical contingency in the relation between sex and gender in the face of cultural configurations of causal unities that are regularly assumed to be natural and necessary. In the place of the law of heterosexual coherence, we see sex and gender denaturalized by means of a performance which avows their distinctness and dramatizes the cultural mechanism of their fabricated unity.

The notion of gender parody defended here does not assume that there is an original which such parodic identities imitate. Indeed, the parody is *of* the very notion of an original; just as the psychoanalytic notion of gender identification is constituted by a fantasy of a fantasy, the transfiguration of an Other who is always already a "figure" in that double sense, so gender

1. Newton, *Mother Camp*, p. 103 [Butler's note].

parody reveals that the original identity after which gender fashions itself is an imitation without an origin. To be more precise, it is a production which, in effect—that is, in its effect—postures as an imitation. This perpetual displacement constitutes a fluidity of identities that suggests an openness to resignification and recontextualization; parodic proliferation deprives hegemonic culture and its critics of the claim to naturalized or essentialist gender identities. Although the gender meanings taken up in these parodic styles are clearly part of hegemonic, misogynist culture, they are nevertheless denaturalized and mobilized through their parodic recontextualization. As imitations which effectively displace the meaning of the original, they imitate the myth of originality itself. In the place of an original identification which serves as a determining cause, gender identity might be reconceived as a personal/cultural history of received meanings subject to a set of imitative practices which refer laterally to other imitations and which, jointly, construct the illusion of a primary and interior gendered self or parody the mechanism of that construction.

According to Fredric Jameson's "Postmodernism and Consumer Society," the imitation that mocks the notion of an original is characteristic of pastiche rather than parody:

> Pastiche is, like parody, the imitation of a peculiar or unique style, the wearing of a stylistic mask, speech in a dead language: but it is a neutral practice of mimicry, without parody's ulterior motive, without the satirical impulse, without laughter, without that still latent feeling that there exists something *normal* compared to which what is being imitated is rather comic. Pastiche is blank parody, parody that has lost its humor.[2]

The loss of the sense of "the normal," however, can be its own occasion for laughter, especially when "the normal," "the original" is revealed to be a copy, and an inevitably failed one, an ideal that no one *can* embody. In this sense, laughter emerges in the realization that all along the original was derived.

Parody by itself is not subversive, and there must be a way to understand what makes certain kinds of parodic repetitions effectively disruptive, truly troubling, and which repetitions become domesticated and recirculated as instruments of cultural hegemony.[3] A typology of actions would clearly not suffice, for parodic displacement, indeed, parodic laughter, depends on a context and reception in which subversive confusions can be fostered. What performance where will invert the inner/outer distinction and compel a radical rethinking of the psychological presuppositions of gender identity and sexuality? What performance where will compel a reconsideration of the *place* and stability of the masculine and the feminine? And what kind of gender performance will enact and reveal the performativity of gender itself in a way that destabilizes the naturalized categories of identity and desire.

If the body is not a "being," but a variable boundary, a surface whose permeability is politically regulated, a signifying practice within a cultural field of

2. Fredric Jameson, "Postmodernism and Consumer Society," in *The Anti-Aesthetic: Essays on Postmodern Culture,* ed. Hal Foster (Port Townshend, Wash.: Bay Press, 1983), p. 114 [Butler's note]. JAMESON (b. 1934), American Marxist literary critic.

3. The manufactured consent that legitimates a dominant group and unifies a society, as theorized by the Italian Marxist ANTONIO GRAMSCI (1891–1937).

gender hierarchy and compulsory heterosexuality, then what language is left for understanding this corporeal enactment, gender, that constitutes its "interior" signification on its surface? Sartre would perhaps have called this act "a style of being," Foucault, "a stylistics of existence." And in my earlier reading of Beauvoir,[4] I suggest that gendered bodies are so many "styles of the flesh." These styles are never fully self-styled, for styles have a history, and those histories condition and limit the possibilities. Consider gender, for instance, as *a corporeal style*, an "act," as it were, which is both intentional and performative, where "*performative*" suggests a dramatic and contingent construction of meaning.

Wittig understands gender as the workings of "sex," where "sex" is an obligatory injunction for the body to become a cultural sign, to materialize itself in obedience to a historically delimited possibility, and to do this, not once or twice, but as a sustained and repeated corporeal project. The notion of a "project," however, suggests the originating force of a radical will, and because gender is a project which has cultural survival as its end, the term *strategy* better suggests the situation of duress under which gender performance always and variously occurs. Hence, as a strategy of survival within compulsory systems, gender is a performance with clearly punitive consequences. Discrete genders are part of what "humanizes" individuals within contemporary culture; indeed, we regularly punish those who fail to do their gender right. Because there is neither an "essence" that gender expresses or externalizes nor an objective ideal to which gender aspires, and because gender is not a fact, the various acts of gender create the idea of gender, and without those acts, there would be no gender at all. Gender is, thus, a construction that regularly conceals its genesis; the tacit collective agreement to perform, produce, and sustain discrete and polar genders as cultural fictions is obscured by the credibility of those productions—and the punishments that attend not agreeing to believe in them; the construction "compels" our belief in its necessity and naturalness. The historical possibilities materialized through various corporeal styles are nothing other than those punitively regulated cultural fictions alternately embodied and deflected under duress.

Consider that a sedimentation of gender norms produces the peculiar phenomenon of a "natural sex" or a "real woman" or any number of prevalent and compelling social fictions, and that this is a sedimentation that over time has produced a set of corporeal styles which, in reified form, appear as the natural configuration of bodies into sexes existing in a binary relation to one another. If these styles are enacted, and if they produce the coherent gendered subjects who pose as their originators, what kind of performance might reveal this ostensible "cause" to be an "effect"?

In what senses, then, is gender an act? As in other ritual social dramas, the action of gender requires a performance that is *repeated*. This repetition is at once a reenactment and reexperiencing of a set of meanings already socially established; and it is the mundane and ritualized form of their legitimation.[5] Although there are individual bodies that enact these significations by becoming stylized into gendered modes, this "action" is a public action. There are temporal and collective dimensions to these actions, and

4. In chapter 1 of *Gender Trouble*.
5. See Victor Turner, *Dramas, Fields, and Metaphors* (Ithaca: Cornell University Press, 1974). See also Clifford Geertz, "Blurred Genres: The Refiguration of Thought," in *Local Knowledge: Further Essays in Interpretive Anthropology* (New York: Basic Books, 1983) [Butler's note].

their public character is not inconsequential; indeed, the performance is effected with the strategic aim of maintaining gender within its binary frame—an aim that cannot be attributed to a subject, but, rather, must be understood to found and consolidate the subject.

Gender ought not to be construed as a stable identity or locus of agency from which various acts follow; rather, gender is an identity tenuously constituted in time, instituted in an exterior space through a *stylized repetition of acts*. The effect of gender is produced through the stylization of the body and, hence, must be understood as the mundane way in which bodily gestures, movements, and styles of various kinds constitute the illusion of an abiding gendered self. This formulation moves the conception of gender off the ground of a substantial model of identity to one that requires a conception of gender as a constituted *social temporality*. Significantly, if gender is instituted through acts which are internally discontinuous, then the *appearance of substance* is precisely that, a constructed identity, a performative accomplishment which the mundane social audience, including the actors themselves, come to believe and to perform in the mode of belief. Gender is also a norm that can never be fully internalized; "the internal" is a surface signification, and gender norms are finally phantasmatic, impossible to embody. If the ground of gender identity is the stylized repetition of acts through time and not a seemingly seamless identity, then the spatial metaphor of a "ground" will be displaced and revealed as a stylized configuration, indeed, a gendered corporealization of time. The abiding gendered self will then be shown to be structured by repeated acts that seek to approximate the ideal of a substantial ground of identity, but which, in their occasional *dis*continuity, reveal the temporal and contingent groundlessness of this "ground." The possibilities of gender transformation are to be found precisely in the arbitrary relation between such acts, in the possibility of a failure to repeat, a de-formity, or a parodic repetition that exposes the phantasmatic effect of abiding identity as a politically tenuous construction.

If gender attributes, however, are not expressive but performative, then these attributes effectively constitute the identity they are said to express or reveal. The distinction between expression and performativeness is crucial. If gender attributes and acts, the various ways in which a body shows or produces its cultural signification, are performative, then there is no preexisting identity by which an act or attribute might be measured; there would be no true or false, real or distorted acts of gender, and the postulation of a true gender identity would be revealed as a regulatory fiction. That gender reality is created through sustained social performances means that the very notions of an essential sex and a true or abiding masculinity or femininity are also constituted as part of the strategy that conceals gender's performative character and the performative possibilities for proliferating gender configurations outside the restricting frames of masculinist domination and compulsory heterosexuality.

Genders can be neither true nor false, neither real nor apparent, neither original nor derived. As credible bearers of those attributes, however, genders can also be rendered thoroughly and radically *incredible*.

1990

PAUL GILROY
b. 1956

Paul Gilroy's provocative work on race, transnationalism, and culture has strongly influenced contemporary cultural studies and postcolonial theory. A sociologist by training, Gilroy is a leading scholar of cultural studies whose multidisciplinary approach blends historicism, Marxism, and critical race studies; he uses literature, art, and music as lenses for examining black Atlantic diasporic culture in the Western hemisphere. While he did not coin the term "Black Atlantic," he has brought the concept into common usage. In defining the Black Atlantic, Gilroy posits that "there is a culture that is not specifically African, American, Caribbean, or British, but all of these at once; a black Atlantic culture whose themes and techniques transcend ethnicity and nationality to produce something new and, until now, unremarked." For Gilroy, nationalism and ethnocentrism in the academy and in popular culture are dangerous constructs for which the Black Atlantic is a corrective. Together with such scholars as W. E. B. DU BOIS, STUART HALL, C. L. R. James, and HENRY LOUIS GATES JR., Gilroy draws attention to the transnational character of modern black culture. Ultimately, he advocates that we banish race and nation as organizing structures for identity and culture.

Paul Gilroy was born in London; his father is British and his mother is the award-winning Guyanese author Beryl Gilroy. Gilroy earned a B.A. from Sussex University in 1978 and a Ph.D. from the pioneering Centre for Contemporary Cultural Studies (CCCS) at Birmingham University in 1986. Following his graduation, he held positions at South Bank University and Essex University. In 1991 he began teaching at Goldsmiths College and became a professor of sociology and cultural studies in 1995. Gilroy then taught at Yale University as the Charlotte Marion Saden Professor of Sociology and African American Studies, serving as the chair of the Department of African American Studies. Between 2005 and 2012 he served on the faculty at the London School of Economics, where he was the inaugural Anthony Giddens Professor in Social Theory. Since 2012 he has been at King's College London's Department of English. His career has been varied and interdisciplinary. He has worked for the Greater London Council and been a guest curator for the Tate Gallery and for the House of World Cultures in Berlin. Gilroy is a prolific speaker, delivering talks on both sides of the Atlantic, and he has also been a music DJ.

According to Gilroy, while working within postmodernism, we must not wholly reject the concept of modernity in and of itself. To begin with, we should recognize slavery and diaspora as previously unacknowledged cornerstones of modernity. Because modernity is necessarily tied to inhumanity and violence, the modern concepts of freedom and reason are paradoxically but inescapably juxtaposed to coercion and terror. The connections are particularly clear, he asserts, when we acknowledge that fascism was a major political occurrence within the past century—and the one with the furthest-reaching effects. Gilroy claims that fascism is alive and well in our current cultural experiences: it emerges when cultural groups and individuals make "spectacles" of their differences, including national and racial differences. For good and ill, modern legacies live on in our postmodern world.

Following World War II, waves of people of color came to England from British colonies in Africa, Asia, and the Caribbean. These Britons, often referred to collectively as "black Britons," created their own syncretic culture and affected the mainstream. Among them was the Jamaican-born Stuart Hall, a leading figure of the British New Left during the 1950s, major figure at the CCCS in Birmingham from 1964 to 1979, and mentor to Paul Gilroy. Not surprisingly, Gilroy positions himself in our selection and elsewhere as a second-generation cultural studies scholar and black Briton as well as an outsider. He is critical not only of the European Enlightenment (Marxism included) and its racist aesthetics and canon, but also of contemporary British cultural studies and its continuation of modern ethnonationalism. As a self-conscious postnational countercultural agent, Gilroy deplores ethnic and nationalist absolutisms and champions transnational hybridities, particularly their forgotten histories, many of which are in need of scholarly recovery. The full history of the black diaspora and its impact on culture, notes Gilroy, remains to be written. With this conclusion Gilroy follows a long line of black intellectuals—Du Bois, LANGSTON HUGHES, and the Martinican journalist Paulette Nardal among them.

In his best-known book, the highly influential *The Black Atlantic: Modernity and Double Consciousness* (1993), Gilroy builds on the concept of the Black Atlantic, first developed by Robert Farris Thompson, an American historian of African Atlantic art and music. Gilroy argues that this transatlantic culture transcends ethnicity and national heritage, and that its participation in the Master-Slave dialectic described by G. F. W. HEGEL makes it part of modernity. Ultimately, he questions the uses of historical periodization as well as racial purity. In our selection, from the first chapter, Gilroy sets the terms of his analysis by taking up the hybrid identity or "double consciousness"—a term borrowed from Du Bois's *The Souls of Black Folk* (1903)—involved in "striving to be both European and black." Though there are continuities between these two categories, he notes that they are frequently viewed as mutually exclusive and thus the attempt to combine them is read as politically defiant. He attempts to bridge the divide between Europeanness and blackness by examining the transmutations, contemporary and historical, that occur within hybrid identities. Gilroy begins by criticizing first English and then African American cultural studies, as well as leftist politics and its Enlightenment legacies, for their emphasis on nationalism and national purity, which are antithetical to the long-standing transcultural makeup of the Black Atlantic. Throughout the selection, he employs the metaphor of ships in motion, which travel across the spaces between Europe, the Americas, Africa, and the Caribbean; circulate ideas and artifacts in ways that link those regions together; and break down divisions that position race and nationality as separate, potentially oppositional categories.

Gilroy's book has received extensive commentary, and it has been criticized on a number of grounds. Some point out that it focuses solely on the modern age and ignores the number and complexity of hybrid black identities and cultures both across the Black Atlantic and around the globe. For example, it fails to address interactions of black and Islamic or Indian or indigenous societies. Because he ignores Africa, observe his critics, Gilroy invariably treats black communities as oppressed minorities. Moreover, his emphasis on the transnational leads him to slight the local. His criticisms of African American cultural studies as nationalist, ethnocentric, and hegemonic have drawn particular fire, as has his appropriation of Du Bois's idea of "double consciousness," which overlooks other key features of identity—most obviously gender and sexuality. Nevertheless, *Black Atlantic* is a distinctive contribution to the field of transatlantic studies, which succeeds in helping to make black studies more global.

The Black Atlantic: Modernity and Double Consciousness **Keywords:** Cultural Studies, Globalization, Identity, Marxism, Modernity, Nationhood, New Historicism, Postcolonial Theory, Race and Ethnicity Studies

From The Black Atlantic: Modernity and Double Consciousness

From *Chapter 1. The Black Atlantic as a Counterculture of Modernity*

We who are homeless,—Among Europeans today there is no lack of those who are entitled to call themselves homeless in a distinctive and honourable sense . . . We children of the future, how could we be at home in this today? We feel disfavour for all ideals that might lead one to feel at home even in this fragile, broken time of transition; as for "realities," we do not believe that they will last. The ice that still supports people today has become very thin; the wind that brings the thaw is blowing; we ourselves who are homeless constitute a force that breaks open ice and other all too thin "realities."

—Nietzsche[1]

On the notion of modernity. It is a vexed question. Is not every era "modern" in relation to the preceding one? It seems that at least one of the components of "our" modernity is the spread of the awareness we have of it. The awareness of our awareness (the double, the second degree) is our source of strength and our torment.

—Edouard Glissant[2]

Striving to be both European and black requires some specific forms of double consciousness.[3] By saying this I do not mean to suggest that taking on either or both of these unfinished identities necessarily exhausts the subjective resources of any particular individual. However, where racist, nationalist, or ethnically absolutist discourses orchestrate political relationships so that these identities appear to be mutually exclusive, occupying the space between them or trying to demonstrate their continuity has been viewed as a provocative and even oppositional act of political insubordination.

The contemporary black English, like the Anglo-Africans of earlier generations and perhaps, like all blacks in the West, stand between (at least) two great cultural assemblages, both of which have mutated through the course of the modern world that formed them and assumed new configurations. At present, they remain locked symbiotically in an antagonistic relationship marked out by the symbolism of colours which adds to the conspicuous cultural power of their central Manichean[4] dynamic—black and white. These colours support a special rhetoric that has grown to be associated with a language of nationality and national belonging as well as the languages of "race" and ethnic identity.

Though largely ignored by recent debates over modernity and its discontents, these ideas about nationality, ethnicity, authenticity, and cultural integrity are characteristically modern phenomena that have profound implications for cultural criticism and cultural history. They crystallised

1. FRIEDRICH NIETZSCHE (1844–1900), German philosopher; quoted from *The Gay Science*, translated by Walter Kaufman (New York: Vintage, 1974), Book V, sec. 377.
2. Martinican poet, novelist, and theorist (1928–2011); translated from the novel *Malemort* (Paris: Seuil, 1981).
3. A term borrowed from W. E. B. DU BOIS, who wrote in *The Souls of Black Folk* (1903) of the "twoness" that results ("an American, a Negro") when one constantly looks at oneself through others' eyes.
4. That is, dualistic.

with the revolutionary transformations of the West at the end of the eighteenth and the beginning of the nineteenth centuries and involved novel typologies and modes of identification. Any shift towards a postmodern condition should not, however, mean that the conspicuous power of these modern subjectivities and the movements they articulated has been left behind. Their power has, if anything, grown, and their ubiquity as a means to make political sense of the world is currently unparalleled by the languages of class and socialism by which they once appeared to have been surpassed. My concern here is less with explaining their longevity and enduring appeal than with exploring some of the special political problems that arise from the fatal junction of the concept of nationality with the concept of culture and the affinities and affiliations which link the blacks of the West to one of their adoptive, parental cultures: the intellectual heritage of the West since the Enlightenment. I have become fascinated with how successive generations of black intellectuals have understood this connection and how they have projected it in their writing and speaking in pursuit of freedom, citizenship, and social and political autonomy.

If this appears to be little more than a roundabout way of saying that the reflexive cultures and consciousness of the European settlers and those of the Africans they enslaved, the "Indians" they slaughtered, and the Asians they indentured were not, even in situations of the most extreme brutality, sealed off hermetically from each other, then so be it. This seems as though it ought to be an obvious and self-evident observation, but its stark character has been systematically obscured by commentators from all sides of political opinion. Regardless of their affiliation to the right, left, or centre, groups have fallen back on the idea of cultural nationalism, on the overintegrated conceptions of culture which present immutable, ethnic differences as an absolute break in the histories and experiences of "black" and "white" people. Against this choice stands another, more difficult option: the theorisation of creolisation, métissage, mestizaje,[5] and hybridity. From the viewpoint of ethnic absolutism, this would be a litany of pollution and impurity. These terms are rather unsatisfactory ways of naming the processes of cultural mutation and restless (dis)continuity that exceed racial discourse and avoid capture by its agents.

This book addresses one small area in the grand consequence of this historical conjunction—the stereophonic, bilingual, or bifocal cultural forms originated by, but no longer the exclusive property of, blacks dispersed within the structures of feeling, producing, communicating, and remembering that I have heuristically called the black Atlantic world. This chapter is therefore rooted in and routed through the special stress that grows with the effort involved in trying to face (at least) two ways at once.

My concerns at this stage are primarily conceptual: I have tried to address the continuing lure of ethnic absolutisms in cultural criticism produced both by blacks and by whites. In particular, this chapter seeks to explore the special relationships between "race," culture, nationality, and ethnicity which have a bearing on the histories and political cultures of Britain's black citizens. I have argued elsewhere that the cultures of this group have been produced in a syncretic pattern in which the styles and forms of the Caribbean,

5. Mixture (Spanish); specifically, the fusion of European, African, African American, and indigenous peoples in Central and South America. "Métissage": cross-breeding, racial mixing (French).

the United States, and Africa have been reworked and reinscribed in the novel context of modern Britain's own untidy ensemble of regional and class-oriented conflicts.[6] Rather than make the invigorating flux of those mongrel cultural forms my focal concern here, I want instead to look at broader questions of ethnic identity that have contributed to the scholarship and the political strategies that Britain's black settlers have generated and to the underlying sense of England as a cohesive cultural community against which their self-conception has so often been defined. Here the ideas of nation, nationality, national belonging, and nationalism are paramount. They are extensively supported by a clutch of rhetorical strategies that can be named "cultural insiderism."[7] The essential trademark of cultural insiderism which also supplies the key to its popularity is an absolute sense of ethnic difference. This is maximised so that it distinguishes people from one another and at the same time acquires an incontestable priority over all other dimensions of their social and historical experience, cultures, and identities. Characteristically, these claims are associated with the idea of national belonging or the aspiration to nationality and other more local but equivalent forms of cultural kinship. The range and complexity of these ideas in English cultural life defies simple summary or exposition. However, the forms of cultural insiderism they sanction typically construct the nation as an ethnically homogeneous object and invoke ethnicity a second time in the hermeneutic procedures deployed to make sense of its distinctive cultural content.

The intellectual seam in which English cultural studies has positioned itself—through innovative work in the fields of social history and literary criticism—can be indicted here. The statist modalities of Marxist analysis[8] that view modes of material production and political domination as exclusively *national* entities are only one source of this problem. Another factor, more evasive but nonetheless potent for its intangible ubiquity, is a quiet cultural nationalism which pervades the work of some radical thinkers. This crypto-nationalism means that they are often disinclined to consider the cross catalytic or transverse dynamics of racial politics as a significant element in the formation and reproduction of English national identities. These formations are treated as if they spring, fully formed, from their own special viscera.[9]

My search for resources with which to comprehend the doubleness and cultural intermixture that distinguish the experience of black Britons in contemporary Europe required me to seek inspiration from other sources and, in effect, to make an intellectual journey across the Atlantic. In black America's histories of cultural and political debate and organisation I found another, second perspective with which to orient my own position. Here too the lure of ethnic particularism and nationalism has provided an ever-present danger. But that narrowness of vision which is content with the merely national has also been challenged from within that black community by thinkers who were prepared to renounce the easy claims of African-American exceptionalism in

6. See Gilroy's *There Ain't No Black in the Union Jack: The Cultural Politics of Race and Nation* (1991), and *Small Acts: Thoughts on the Politics of Black Cultures* (1993).

7. Werner Sollors, *Beyond Ethnicity* (New York and Oxford: Oxford University Press, 1986) [Gilroy's note].

8. That is, analysis derived from the writings of the German political and economic theorist KARL MARX (1818–1883).

9. An allusion to the story in Greek mythology of the birth of Athena, goddess of wisdom, who sprang fully formed from the head of her father, Zeus.

favour of a global, coalitional politics in which anti-imperialism and anti-racism might be seen to interact if not to fuse. The work of some of those thinkers will be examined in subsequent chapters.

This chapter also proposes some new chronotopes[1] that might fit with a theory that was less intimidated by and respectful of the boundaries and integrity of modern nation states than either English or African-American cultural studies have so far been. I have settled on the image of ships in motion across the spaces between Europe, America, Africa, and the Caribbean as a central organising symbol for this enterprise and as my starting point. The image of the ship—a living, micro-cultural, micro-political system in motion—is especially important for historical and theoretical reasons that I hope will become clearer below. Ships immediately focus attention on the middle passage,[2] on the various projects for redemptive return to an African homeland, on the circulation of ideas and activists as well as the movement of key cultural and political artefacts: tracts, books, gramophone records, and choirs.

The rest of this chapter falls into three sections. The first part addresses some conceptual problems common to English and African-American versions of cultural studies which, I argue, share a nationalistic focus that is antithetical to the rhizomorphic,[3] fractal structure of the transcultural, international formation I call the black Atlantic. The second section uses the life and writings of Martin Robison Delany,[4] an early architect of black nationalism whose influence still registers in contemporary political movements, to bring the black Atlantic to life and to extend the general arguments by introducing a number of key themes that will be used to map the responses to modernity's promises and failures produced by later thinkers. The final section explores the specific counterculture of modernity produced by black intellectuals and makes some preliminary points about the internality of blacks to the West. It initiates a polemic which runs through the rest of the book against the ethnic absolutism that currently dominates black political culture.

CULTURAL STUDIES IN BLACK AND WHITE

Any satisfaction to be experienced from the recent spectacular growth of cultural studies as an academic project should not obscure its conspicuous problems with ethnocentrism and nationalism. Understanding these difficulties might commence with a critical evaluation of the ways in which notions of ethnicity have been mobilised, often by default rather than design, as part of the distinctive hermeneutics of cultural studies or with the unthinking assumption that cultures always flow into patterns congruent with the borders of essentially homogeneous nation states. The marketing and inevitable reification of cultural studies as a discrete academic

1. "A unit of analysis for studying texts according to the ratio and nature of the temporal and spatial categories represented . . . The chronotope is an optic for reading texts as x-rays of the forces at work in the culture system from which they spring." M. M. BAKHTIN, *The Dialogic Imagination*, edited and translated by Michael Holquist (Austin: University of Texas Press, 1981), p. 426 [Gilroy's note]. MIKHAIL M. BAKHTIN (1895–1975), Russian literary theorist.

2. The sea passage of newly enslaved Africans across the Atlantic to the Americas.

3. In the form of a fungus, with multiple connections—the antihierarchical perspective (as opposed to the traditional structural model, the rooted tree) championed by GILLES DELEUZE and FÉLIX GUATTARI; see the introduction to *A Thousand Plateaus: Capitalism and Schizophrenia* (1980; see above).

4. African American abolitionist and novelist (1812–1885), an early proponent of African unity and the elimination of colonialism.

subject also has what might be called a secondary ethnic aspect. The project of cultural studies is a more or less attractive candidate for institutionalisation according to the ethnic garb in which it appears. The question of whose cultures are being studied is therefore an important one, as is the issue of where the instruments which will make that study possible are going to come from. In these circumstances it is hard not to wonder how much of the recent international enthusiasm for cultural studies is generated by its profound associations with England and ideas of Englishness. This possibility can be used as a point of entry into consideration of the ethno-historical specificity of the discourse of cultural studies itself.

Looking at cultural studies from an ethnohistorical perspective requires more than just noting its association with English literature, history, and New Left[5] politics. It necessitates constructing an account of the borrowings made by these English initiatives from wider, modern, European traditions of thinking about culture, and at every stage examining the place which these cultural perspectives provide for the images of their racialised[6] others as objects of knowledge, power, and cultural criticism. It is imperative, though very hard, to combine thinking about these issues with consideration of the pressing need to get black cultural expressions, analyses, and histories taken seriously in academic circles rather than assigned via the idea of "race relations" to sociology and thence abandoned to the elephants' graveyard to which intractable policy issues go to await their expiry. These two important conversations pull in different directions and sometimes threaten to cancel each other out, but it is the struggle to have blacks perceived as agents, as people with cognitive capacities and even with an intellectual history—attributes denied by modern racism—that is for me the primary reason for writing this book. It provides a valuable warrant for questioning some of the ways in which ethnicity is appealed to in the English idioms of cultural theory and history, and in the scholarly productions of black America. Understanding the political culture of blacks in Britain demands close attention to both these traditions. This book is situated on their cusp.

Histories of cultural studies seldom acknowledge how the politically radical and openly interventionist aspirations found in the best of its scholarship are already articulated to black cultural history and theory. These links are rarely seen or accorded any significance. In England, the work of figures like C. L. R. James and Stuart Hall[7] offers a wealth of both symbols and concrete evidence for the practical links between these critical political projects. In the United States the work of interventionist scholars like bell hooks and Cornel West as well as that of more orthodox academics like Henry Louis Gates, Jr., Houston A. Baker, Jr., Anthony Appiah, and Hazel Carby,[8] points to similar convergences. The position of these thinkers in the contested "con-

5. Marxists and radicals who in the 1950s reacted against the pro-Soviet "Old Left" and its model of state socialism.

6. The concept of racialisation is developed by FRANTZ FANON in his essay "On National Culture" in *The Wretched of the Earth* (Harmondsworth: Penguin, 1967), pp. 170–71. See also Robert Miles, *Racism* (New York and London: Routledge, 1989), pp. 73–77 [Gilroy's note].

7. Jamaican-born theorist of British cultural studies (1932–2014; see above). James (1901–1989), Trinidadian writer, Marxist, and leading proponent of anticolonialism, who spent many years in Britain and the United States.

8. All black scholars active in the United States: HOOKS (b. 1952), American feminist scholar and cultural studies critic; West (b. 1953), American philosopher and activist; GATES (b. 1950), American literary critic and public intellectual; Baker (b. 1943), American literary and cultural critic; Appiah (b. 1954), Ghanaian-born philosopher and critical race theorist; and Carby (b. 1948), American literary scholar.

tact zones"[9] between cultures and histories is not, however, as exceptional as it might appear at first. We shall see below that successive generations of black intellectuals (especially those whose lives, like James's, crisscrossed the Atlantic Ocean) noted this intercultural positionality and accorded it a special significance before launching their distinct modes of cultural and political critique. They were often urged on in their labour by the brutal absurdity of racial classification that derives from and also celebrates racially exclusive conceptions of national identity from which blacks were excluded as either non-humans or non-citizens. I shall try to show that their marginal endeavours point to some new analytic possibilities with a general significance far beyond the well-policed borders of black particularity. For example, this body of work offers intermediate concepts, lodged between the local and the global, which have a wider applicability in cultural history and politics precisely because they offer an alternative to the nationalist focus which dominates cultural criticism. These intermediate concepts, especially the undertheorised idea of diaspora examined in Chapter 6, are exemplary precisely because they break the dogmatic focus on discrete *national* dynamics which has characterised so much modern Euro-American cultural thought.

Getting beyond these national and nationalistic perspectives has become essential for two additional reasons. The first arises from the urgent obligation to reevaluate the significance of the modern nation state as a political, economic, and cultural unit. Neither political nor economic structures of domination are still simply co-extensive with national borders. This has a special significance in contemporary Europe, where new political and economic relations are being created seemingly day by day, but it is a world-wide phenomenon with significant consequences for the relationship between the politics of information and the practices of capital accumulation. Its effects underpin more recognisably political changes like the growing centrality of transnational ecological movements which, through their insistence on the association of sustainability and justice, do so much to shift the moral and scientific precepts on which the modern separation of politics and ethics was built. The second reason relates to the tragic popularity of ideas about the integrity and purity of cultures. In particular, it concerns the relationship between nationality and ethnicity. This too currently has a special force in Europe, but it is also reflected directly in the post-colonial histories and complex, transcultural, political trajectories of Britain's black settlers.

What might be called the peculiarity of the black English requires attention to the intermixture of a variety of distinct cultural forms. Previously separated political and intellectual traditions converged and, in their coming together, overdetermined the process of black Britain's social and historical formation. This blending is misunderstood if it is conceived in simple ethnic terms, but right and left, racist and anti-racist, black and white tacitly share a view of it as little more than a collision between fully formed and mutually exclusive cultural communities. This has become the dominant view where black history and culture are perceived, like black settlers themselves, as an illegitimate intrusion into a vision of authentic British national life that, prior to their arrival, was as stable and as peaceful as it was ethnically undifferentiated. Considering this history points to issues of power and knowledge that

9. Mary Louise Pratt, *Imperial Eyes* (London and New York: Routledge, 1992) [Gilroy's note].

are beyond the scope of this book. However, though it arises from present rather than past conditions, contemporary British racism bears the imprint of the past in many ways. The especially crude and reductive notions of culture that form the substance of racial politics today are clearly associated with an older discourse of racial and ethnic difference which is everywhere entangled in the history of the idea of culture in the modern West. This history has itself become hotly contested since debates about multiculturalism, cultural pluralism, and the responses to them that are sometimes dismissively called "political correctness" arrived to query the ease and speed with which European particularisms are still being translated into absolute, universal standards for human achievement, norms, and aspirations.

It is significant that prior to the consolidation of scientific racism in the nineteenth century,[1] the term "race" was used very much in the way that the word "culture" is used today. But in the attempts to differentiate the true, the good, and the beautiful which characterise the junction point of capitalism, industrialisation, and political democracy and give substance to the discourse of western modernity, it is important to appreciate that scientists did not monopolise either the image of the black or the emergent concept of biologically based racial difference. As far as the future of cultural studies is concerned, it should be equally important that both were centrally employed in those European attempts to think through beauty, taste, and aesthetic judgement that are the precursors of contemporary cultural criticism.

Tracing the racial signs from which the discourse of cultural value was constructed and their conditions of existence in relation to European aesthetics and philosophy as well as European science can contribute much to an ethnohistorical reading of the aspirations of western modernity as a whole and to the critique of Enlightenment assumptions in particular. It is certainly the case that ideas about "race," ethnicity, and nationality form an important seam of continuity linking English cultural studies with one of its sources of inspiration—the doctrines of modern European aesthetics that are consistently configured by the appeal to national and often racial particularity.[2]

This is not the place to go deeply into the broader dimensions of this intellectual inheritance. Valuable work has already been done by Sander Gilman,[3] Henry Louis Gates, Jr.,[4] and others on the history and role of the image of the black in the discussions which found modern cultural axiology. Gilman points out usefully that the figure of the black appears in different forms in the aesthetics of Hegel, Schopenhauer,[5] and Nietzsche (among others) as a marker for moments of cultural relativism and to support the production of aesthetic judgements of a supposedly universal character to

1. Nancy Stepan, *The Idea of Race in Science: Great Britain, 1800–1960* (Basingstoke, Hampshire, and London: Macmillan, 1982); Michael Banton, *Racial Theories* (Cambridge: Cambridge University Press, 1987) [Gilroy's note].

2. George Mosse, *Nationalism and Sexuality: Middle-Class Morality and Sexual Norms in Modern Europe* (Madison and London: University of Wisconsin Press, 1985); Reinhold Grimm and Jost Hermand, eds., *Blacks and German Culture* (Madison and London: University of Wisconsin Press, 1986) [Gilroy's note].

3. Sander Gilman, *On Blackness without Blacks* (Boston: G. K. Hall, 1982) [Gilroy's note].

4. See Henry Louis Gates, Jr., "The History and Theory of Afro-American Literary Criticism, 1773–1831: The Arts, Aesthetic Theory and the Nature of the African" (doctoral thesis, Clare College, Cambridge University, 1978); David Brion Davis, *The Problem of Slavery in Western Culture* (Ithaca: Cornell University Press, 1975); and Eva Beatrice Dykes, *The Negro in English Romantic Thought; or, A Study of Sympathy for the Oppressed* (Washington, DC: Associated Publishers, 1942) [Gilroy's note].

5. Arthur Schopenhauer (1788–1860), German philosopher. G. W. F. HEGEL (1770–1831), German philosopher.

differentiate, for example, between authentic music and, as Hegel puts it, "the most detestable noise."[6] Gates emphasises a complex genealogy in which ambiguities in Montesquieu's discussion of slavery prompt responses in Hume[7] that can be related, in turn, to philosophical debates over the nature of beauty and sublimity found in the work of Burke and Kant.[8] Critical evaluation of these representations of blackness might also be connected to the controversies over the place of racism and anti-Semitism in the work of Enlightenment figures like Kant and Voltaire.[9] These issues deserve an extended treatment that cannot be provided here. What is essential for the purposes of this opening chapter is that debates of this sort should not be brought to an end simply by denouncing those who raise awkward or embarrassing issues as totalitarian forces working to legitimate their own political line. Nor should important enquiries into the contiguity of racialised reason and unreasonable racism be dismissed as trivial matters. These issues go to the heart of contemporary debates about what constitutes the canon of western civilisation and how this precious legacy should be taught.

In these embattled circumstances, it is regrettable that questions of "race" and representation have been so regularly banished from orthodox histories of western aesthetic judgement, taste, and cultural value.[1] There is a plea here that further enquiries should be made into precisely how discussions of "race," beauty, ethnicity, and culture have contributed to the critical thinking that eventually gave rise to cultural studies. The use of the concept of fetishism in Marxism and psychoanalytic studies is one obvious means to open up this problem.[2] The emphatically national character ascribed to the concept of modes of production[3] (cultural and otherwise) is another fundamental question which demonstrates the ethnohistorical specificity of dominant approaches to cultural politics, social movements, and oppositional consciousnesses.

6. G. W. F. Hegel, *Aesthetics: Lectures on Fine Art*, trans. T. M. Knox (New York: Oxford University Press, 1998), vol. 1, ch. 6, sec. iii, p. 43.

7. David Hume (1711–1776), Scottish philosopher and historian; in the second edition of "Of National Characters" (1753), he suggests that "negroes" are naturally "inferior" to whites, though he does not accept the argument of the French political thinker Charles-Louis de Secondat, baron de La Brède et de Montesquieu (1689–1755), in *The Spirit of the Laws* (1748)—a work that advocates against slavery—that a region's climate affects the nature of its inhabitants.

8. Immanuel Kant (1724–1804), German philosopher; his major work of aesthetics is *Critique of Judgment* (1790; see above). Edmund Burke (1729–1797), British statesman and author of *A Philosophical Enquiry into the Origin of Our Ideas of the Sublime and Beautiful* (1757; see above).

9. Leon Poliakov, *The Aryan Myth* (London: Sussex University Press, 1974), ch. 8, and "Racism from the Enlightenment to the Age of Imperialism," in Robert Ross, ed., *Racism and Colonialism: Essays on Ideology and Social Structure* (The Hague: Martinus Nijhoff, 1982); Richard Popkin, "The Philosophical Basis of Eighteenth Century Racism," in *Studies in Eighteenth Century Culture*, vol. 3: *Racism in the Eighteenth Century* (Cleveland and London: Case Western Reserve University Press, 1973); Harry Bracken, "Philosophy and Racism," *Philosophia* 8, nos. 2–3, November 1978. In some respects this pioneering work foreshadows the debates about Heidegger's fascism [Gilroy's note]. Voltaire (pen name of François-Marie Arouet, 1694–1778), French Enlightenment philosopher; see his *Essay on the Manners and Spirit of Nations* (1756).

1. Hugh Honour's contribution to the DeMenil Foundation Project, *The Representation of the Black in Western Art* (London and Cambridge, Mass.: Harvard University Press, 1989), is a welcome exception to this amnesia [Gilroy's note].

2. W. Pietz, "The Problem of the Fetish, I," *Res* 9 (Spring 1985) [Gilroy's note]. Marx connected fetishism with commodities viewed as independent beings: "This I call the Fetishism which attaches itself to the products of labour, so soon as they are produced as commodities" (chap. 1, sec. 4 of *Capital*, vol. 1, 1867; see above). In psychoanalytic theory, as Sigmund Freud explains in "Fetishism" (1927; see above), the fetish is an object, perceived as a substitute for the "missing" penis of the mother, that becomes the focus of sexual interest.

3. According to Marx, a society's economic mode of production (feudalism, capitalism, etc.) determines its social, political, and intellectual life, and all modes are associated with distinctive epochs.

These general issues appear in a specific form in the distinctive English idioms of cultural reflection. Here too, the moral and political problem of slavery loomed large not least because it was once recognised as *internal* to the structure of western civilisation and appeared as a central political and philosophical concept in the emergent discourse of modern English cultural uniqueness.[4] Notions of the primitive and the civilised which had been integral to pre-modern understanding of "ethnic" differences became fundamental cognitive and aesthetic markers in the processes which generated a constellation of subject positions in which Englishness, Christianity, and other ethnic and racialised attributes would finally give way to the dislocating dazzle of "whiteness."[5] A small but telling insight into this can be found in Edmund Burke's discussion of the sublime, which has achieved a certain currency lately. He makes elaborate use of the association of darkness with blackness, linking them to the skin of a real, live black woman. Seeing her produces a sublime feeling of terror in a boy whose sight has been restored to him by a surgical operation.

> Perhaps it may appear on enquiry, that blackness and darkness are in some degree painful by their natural operation, independent of any associations whatever. I must observe that the ideas of blackness and darkness are much the same; and they differ only in this, that blackness is a more confined idea.
>
> Mr Cheselden has given us a very curious story of a boy who had been born blind, and continued so until he was thirteen or fourteen years old; he was then couched for a cataract, by which operation he received his sight . . . Cheselden tells us that the first time the boy saw a black object, it gave him great uneasiness; and that some time after, upon accidentally seeing a negro woman, he was struck with great horror at the sight.[6]

Burke, who opposed slavery and argued for its gradual abolition, stands at the doorway of the tradition of enquiry mapped by Raymond Williams[7] which is also the infrastructure on which much of English cultural studies came to be founded. This origin is part of the explanation of how some of the contemporary manifestations of this tradition lapse into what can only be called a morbid celebration of England and Englishness. These modes of subjectivity and identification acquire a renewed political charge in the post-imperial history that saw black settlers from Britain's colonies take up their citizenship rights as subjects in the United Kingdom. The entry of blacks into national life was itself a powerful factor contributing to the circumstances in which the formation of both cultural studies and New Left politics became possible. It indexes the profound transformations of British social and cultural life in the 1950s and stands, again usually unacknowledged, at the heart of laments for a more human scale of social living that seemed no longer practicable after the 1939–45 war.

4. Robin Blackburn, *The Overthrow of Colonial Slavery, 1776–1848* (London and New York: Verso, 1988) [Gilroy's note].
5. Winthrop D. Jordan, *White over Black* (New York: W. W. Norton, 1977) [Gilroy's note].
6. Edmund Burke, *A Philosophical Enquiry into the Origin of Our Ideas of the Sublime and Beautiful*, edited by James T. Boulton (Oxford: Basil Blackwell, 1987) [Gilroy's note].
7. British Marxist literary critic and activist (1921–1988; see above), a founding figure of British cultural studies.

The convoluted history of black settlement need not be recapitulated here. One recent fragment from it, the struggle over Salman Rushdie's book *The Satanic Verses,*[8] is sufficient to demonstrate that racialised conflict over the meaning of English culture is still very much alive and to show that these antagonisms have become enmeshed in a second series of struggles in which Enlightenment assumptions about culture, cultural value, and aesthetics go on being tested by those who do not accept them as universal moral standards. These conflicts are, in a sense, the outcome of a distinct historical period in which a new, ethnically absolute and culturalist racism was produced. It would explain the burning of books on English streets as manifestations of irreducible cultural differences that signposted the path to domestic racial catastrophe. This new racism was generated in part by the move towards a political discourse which aligned "race" closely with the idea of national belonging and which stressed complex cultural difference rather than simple biological hierarchy. These strange conflicts emerged in circumstances where blackness and Englishness appeared suddenly to be mutually exclusive attributes and where the conspicuous antagonism between them proceeded on the terrain of culture, not that of politics. Whatever view of Rushdie one holds, his fate offers another small, but significant, omen of the extent to which the almost metaphysical values of England and Englishness are currently being contested through their connection to "race" and ethnicity. His experiences are also a reminder of the difficulties involved in attempts to construct a more pluralistic, post-colonial sense of British culture and national identity. In this context, locating and answering the nationalism if not the racism and ethnocentrism of English cultural studies has itself become a directly political issue.

Returning to the imperial figures who supplied Raymond Williams with the raw material for his own brilliant critical reconstruction of English intellectual life is instructive. Apart from Burke, Thomas Carlyle, John Ruskin, Charles Kingsley,[9] and the rest of Williams's cast of worthy characters can become valuable not simply in attempts to purge cultural studies of its doggedly ethnocentric focus but in the more ambitious and more useful task of actively reshaping contemporary England by reinterpreting the cultural core of its supposedly authentic national life. In the work of reinterpretation and reconstruction, reinscription and relocation required to transform England and Englishness, discussion of the cleavage in the Victorian intelligentsia around the response to Governor Eyre's handling of the Morant Bay Rebellion in Jamaica in 1865 is likely to be prominent.[1] Like the English responses to the 1857 uprising in India examined by Jenny Sharpe,[2] it may well turn

8. A 1988 novel by the Indian-born British novelist Rushdie (b. 1947); its allegedly blasphemous references to the Prophet Muhammad led to violent protests, book burnings, and a religious decree (fatwa) calling for Muslims to kill Rushdie and others involved in publishing the book. Rushdie spent more than 5 years in hiding.

9. Three major British social critics: Carlyle (1795–1881), Scottish essayist and historian; Ruskin (1819–1900), English art critic; and Kingsley (1819–1875), English clergyman and novelist, a founder of Christian Socialism.

1. Catherine Hall, *White, Male, and Middle-Class* (Cambridge: Polity Press, 1992) [Gilroy's note]. After unrest spread following a violent confrontation in Morant Bay, the capital of an eastern parish of Jamaica, between militia and blacks (freed by the British Emancipation Act of 1834), Edward John Eyre (1815–1901) responded by declaring martial law; hundreds died as the rebellion was forcefully put down, and his main political opponent was hanged despite the lack of evidence of any complicity.

2. Jenny Sharpe, "The Unspeakable Limits of Rape: Colonial Violence and Counter-Insurgency," *Genders*, no. 10 (Spring 1999): 25–46, and "Figures of Colonial Resistance," *Modern Fiction Studies* 35:1 (Spring 1989) [Gilroy's note]. The widespread uprising by Indian soldiers (1857–58) against the British rule of the East India Company led to the direct governance of India by the British government.

out to be a much more formative moment than has so far been appreciated. Morant Bay is doubly significant because it represents an instance of metropolitan,[3] internal conflict that emanates directly from an external colonial experience. These crises in imperial power demonstrate their continuity. It is part of my argument that this inside/outside relationship should be recognised as a more powerful, more complex, and more contested element in the historical, social, and cultural memory of our glorious nation than has previously been supposed.

I am suggesting that even the laudable, radical varieties of English cultural sensibility examined by Williams and celebrated by Edward Thompson[4] and others were not produced spontaneously from their own internal and intrinsic dynamics. The fact that some of the most potent conceptions of Englishness have been constructed by alien outsiders like Carlyle, Swift, Scott, or Eliot[5] should augment the note of caution sounded here. The most heroic, subaltern[6] English nationalisms and countercultural patriotisms are perhaps better understood as having been generated in a complex pattern of antagonistic relationships with the supra-national and imperial world for which the ideas of "race," nationality, and national culture provide the primary (though not the only) indices. This approach would obviously bring William Blake's[7] work into a rather different focus from that supplied by orthodox cultural history, and, as Peter Linebaugh has suggested, this overdue reassessment can be readily complemented by charting the long-neglected involvement of black slaves and their descendants in the radical history of our country in general and its working-class movements in particular.[8] Olaudah Equiano,[9] whose involvement in the beginnings of organised working-class politics is now being widely recognised; the anarchist, Jacobin, ultra-radical, and Methodist heretic Robert Wedderburn;[1] William Davidson, son of Jamaica's attorney general, hanged for his role in the Cato Street conspiracy to blow up the British cabinet in 1819;[2] and the Chartist William Cuffay[3] are only the most urgent, obvious candidates for rehabilitation. Their lives offer invaluable means of seeing how thinking with and through the discourses and the imagery of "race" appears in the core rather than at the fringes of English political life. Davidson's speech from the scaffold before being subject to the last public decapitation in England is, for example, one moving appropriation of the rights of dissident freeborn Englishmen that is not widely read today.

3. Of or pertaining to the "mother country," as distinguished from its colony.
4. E. P. Thompson (1924–1993), English historian and influential member of the British New Left.
5. T. S. ELIOT (1888–1965), American-born poet and critic who lived most of his life in London. Carlyle was Scottish, as was the poet and novelist Sir Walter Scott (1771–1832); the cleric and satirist Jonathan Swift (1667–1745) was born in Ireland.
6. A term from the Italian Marxist critic and theorist ANTONIO GRAMSCI (1891–1937), referring to those subordinated by the hegemonic power structure (and, since the 1980s, especially to colonized peoples).
7. English poet, artist, and radical (1757–1827).
8. Peter Linebaugh, "All the Atlantic Mountains Shook," *Labour/Le Travailleur* 10 (Autumn 1982): 87–121 [Gilroy's note].
9. African (ca. 1745–1797), also known as Gustavus Vassa; enslaved as a child, he bought his freedom, wrote his autobiography, and became an abolitionist.
1. British abolitionist (1762–ca. 1835).
2. Peter Fryer, *Staying Power* (London: Pluto Press, 1980), p. 219 [Gilroy's note]. Davidson (1781–1820), also the son of an unnamed black woman. Cato Street: location of the building in London where the conspirators were captured.
3. Trade unionist (1788–1870), a founder of the Metropolitan Tailors' Charter Association (1839); his grandfather was an African slave. Chartism was a British working-class movement (1838–48) that took its name from a petition, the People's Charter, calling for such reforms as universal male suffrage.

Of this infamous trio, Wedderburn is perhaps the best known, thanks to the efforts of Peter Linebaugh and Iain McCalman.[4] The child of a slave dealer, James Wedderburn, and a slave woman, Robert was brought up by a Kingston conjure woman who acted as an agent for smugglers. He migrated to London at the age of seventeen in 1778. There, having published a number of disreputable ultra-radical tracts as part of his subversive political labours, he presented himself as a living embodiment of the horrors of slavery in a debating chapel in Hopkins Street near the Haymarket, where he preached a version of chiliastic anarchism based on the teachings of Thomas Spence[5] and infused with deliberate blasphemy. In one of the debates held in his "ruinous hayloft with 200 persons of the lowest description," Wedderburn defended the inherent rights of the Caribbean slave to slay his master, promising to write home and "tell them to murder their masters as soon as they please." After this occasion he was tried and acquitted on a charge of blasphemy after persuading the jury that he had not been uttering sedition but merely practising the "true and infallible genius of prophetic skill."[6]

It is particularly significant for the direction of my overall argument that both Wedderburn and his sometime associate Davidson had been sailors, moving to and fro between nations, crossing borders in modern machines that were themselves micro-systems of linguistic and political hybridity. Their relationship to the sea may turn out to be especially important for both the early politics and poetics of the black Atlantic world that I wish to counterpose against the narrow nationalism of so much English historiography. Wedderburn served in the Royal Navy and as a privateer, while Davidson, who ran away to sea instead of studying law, was pressed into naval service on two subsequent occasions. Davidson inhabited the same ultra-radical subculture as Wedderburn and was an active participant in the Marylebone Reading Society, a radical body formed in 1819 after the Peterloo massacre.[7] He is known to have acted as the custodian of their black flag, which significantly bore a skull and crossbones with the legend "Let us die like men and not be sold as slaves," at an open air meeting in Smithfield later that year.[8] The precise details of how radical ideologies articulated the culture of the London poor before the institution of the factory system to the insubordinate maritime culture of pirates and other pre-industrial workers of the world will have to await the innovative labours of Peter Linebaugh and Marcus Rediker.[9] However, it has been estimated that at the end of the eighteenth century a quarter of the British navy was composed of Africans for whom the experience of slavery was a powerful orientation to the ideologies of liberty and justice. Looking for similar patterns on the other side of the Atlantic network

4. *The Horrors of Slavery and Other Writings by Robert Wedderburn*, ed. Iain McCalman (Edinburgh: Edinburgh University Press, 1992) [Gilroy's note].

5. Bookseller and radical (1750–1814), advocate of the common ownership of land.

6. Iain McCalman, "Anti-Slavery and Ultra Radicalism in Early Nineteenth-Century England: The Case of Robert Wedderburn," *Slavery and Abolition* 7 (1986) [Gilroy's note].

7. The cavalry charge against 60,000 men, women, and children assembled in St. Peter's Field, Manchester, on August 16, 1819, to petition for parliamentary reform and the repeal of grain tariffs; 11 were killed and hundreds injured. The name plays on Waterloo, a great victory by the British and their allies in Belgium that marked the final defeat of Napoléon Bonaparte in 1815.

8. Fryer, *Staying Power*, p. 219; Public Records Office, London: PRO Ho 44/5/202, PRO Ho 42/199 [Gilroy's note]. Smithfield: site of a livestock market in central London, a large open space often used for public gatherings.

9. Their article "The Many Headed Hydra," *Journal of Historical Sociology* 3, no. 3 (September 1990): 225–53, gives a foretaste of these arguments [Gilroy's note].

we can locate Crispus Attucks[1] at the head of his "motley rabble of saucy boys, negroes, mulattoes, Irish teagues and outlandish jack tars"[2] and can track Denmark Vesey[3] sailing the Caribbean and picking up inspirational stories of the Haitian revolution (one of his co-conspirators testified that he had said they would "not spare one white skin alive for this was the plan they pursued in San Domingo").[4] There is also the shining example of Frederick Douglass,[5] whose autobiographies reveal that he learnt of freedom in the North from Irish sailors while working as a ship's caulker in Baltimore. He had less to say about the embarrassing fact that the vessels he readied for the ocean—Baltimore Clippers—were slavers, the fastest ships in the world and the only craft capable of outrunning the British blockade. Douglass, who played a neglected role in English anti-slavery activity, escaped from bondage disguised as a sailor and put this success down to his ability to "talk sailor like an old salt."[6] These are only a few of the nineteenth-century examples. The involvement of Marcus Garvey, George Padmore, Claude McKay, and Langston Hughes[7] with ships and sailors lends additional support to Linebaugh's prescient suggestion that "the ship remained perhaps the most important conduit of Pan-African communication before the appearance of the long-playing record."[8]

Ships and other maritime scenes have a special place in the work of J. M. W. Turner,[9] an artist whose pictures represent, in the view of many contemporary critics, the pinnacle of achievement in the English school in painting. Any visitor to London will testify to the importance of the Clore Gallery[1] as a national institution and of the place of Turner's art as an enduring expression of the very essence of English civilisation. Turner was secured on the summit of critical appreciation by John Ruskin, who, as we have seen, occupies a special place in Williams's constellation of great Englishmen. Turner's celebrated

1. Perhaps the son of an African and a Native American (ca. 1723–1770), thought to be the first man killed by British soldiers on March 5, 1770, in what became known as the Boston Massacre. Some believe he had served as a sailor.
2. John Adams quoted by Linebaugh in "Atlantic Mountains," p. 112 [Gilroy's note]. Adams (1735–1826; 2d U.S. president, 1797–1801), a Boston lawyer who was a central figure in the American Revolution, successfully defended the British soldiers against murder charges.
3. Leader of a foiled slave rebellion in Charleston, South Carolina (ca. 1767–1822), born in Africa and enslaved.
4. Alfred N. Hunt, *Haiti's Influence on Antebellum America* (Baton Rouge and London: Louisiana State University Press, 1988), p. 119 [Gilroy's note]. After a series of slave and mulatto rebellions, Haiti won its independence from France in 1804; Santo Domingo was invaded and its slaves freed in 1801.
5. African American abolitionist (ca. 1818–1895), who escaped from slavery in 1835 and became a prominent publisher and orator; he published *Narrative of the Life of Frederick Douglass* in 1845.
6. Douglass's own account of this is best set out in Frederick Douglass, *Life and Times of Frederick Douglass* (New York: Macmillan, 1962), p. 199. See also Philip M. Hamer, "Great Britain, the United States and the Negro Seamen's Acts" and "British Consuls and the Negro Seamen's Acts, 1850–1860," *Journal of Southern History* 1 (1935): 3–28, 138–68. Introduced after Denmark Vesey's rebellion, these interesting pieces of legislation required free black sailors to be jailed while their ships were in dock as a way of minimizing the political contagion their presence in the ports was bound to transmit [Gilroy's note].
7. All blacks who were prominent figures in the United States in the 20th century: Garvey (1887–1940), Jamaican black nationalist who founded an organization to encourage racial pride, the Universal Negro Improvement Organization, and promoted a back-to-Africa movement and Pan-Africanism (the union of all black peoples), a combination that became known as "Garveyism"; Padmore (professional name of Malcolm Ivan Meredith Nurse, 1902–1959), Trinidadian political activist and Pan-Africanist; McKay (1889–1948), Jamaican-born poet and novelist who played a major role in the Harlem Renaissance, a vibrant African American movement in the literary, visual, and performing arts centered in New York City in the 1920s and early 1930s; and HUGHES (1902–1967), American poet, playwright, and author of fiction who was the most famous writer associated with the Harlem Renaissance.
8. Linebaugh, "Atlantic Mountains," p. 119 [Gilroy's note].
9. Joseph Mallord William Turner (1775–1851), foremost English landscape painter of his time.
1. The 1987 annex to the Tate Gallery, in London, which was built to house the Turner collection.

picture of a slave ship[2] throwing overboard its dead and dying as a storm comes on was exhibited at the Royal Academy to coincide with the world anti-slavery convention held in London in 1840. The picture, owned by Ruskin for some twenty-eight years, was rather more than an answer to the absentee Caribbean landlords who had commissioned its creator to record the tainted splendour of their country houses, which, as Patrick Wright has eloquently demonstrated, became an important signifier of the contemporary, ruralist distillate of national life.[3] It offered a powerful protest against the direction and moral tone of English politics. This was made explicit in an epigraph Turner took from his own poetry and which has itself retained a political inflection: "Hope, hope, fallacious hope where is thy market now?"[4] Three years after his extensive involvement in the campaign to defend Governor Eyre,[5] Ruskin put the slave ship painting up for sale at Christie's. It is said that he had begun to find it too painful to live with. No buyer was found at that time, and he sold the picture to an American three years later. The painting has remained in the United States ever since. Its exile in Boston is yet another pointer towards the shape of the Atlantic as a system of cultural exchanges. It is more important, though, to draw attention to Ruskin's inability to discuss the picture except in terms of what it revealed about the aesthetics of painting water. He relegated the information that the vessel was a slave ship to a footnote in the first volume of *Modern Painters*.[6]

In spite of lapses like this, the New Left heirs to the aesthetic and cultural tradition in which Turner and Ruskin stand compounded and reproduced its nationalism and its ethnocentrism by denying imaginary, invented Englishness any external referents whatsoever. England ceaselessly gives birth to itself, seemingly from Britannia's[7] head. The political affiliations and cultural preferences of this New Left group amplified these problems. They are most visible and most intense in the radical historiography that supplied a counterpart to Williams's subtle literary reflections. For all their enthusiasm for the work of C. L. R. James, the influential British Communist Party's historians' group[8] is culpable here. Their predilections for the image of the freeborn Englishman and the dream of socialism in one country that framed their work are both to be found wanting when it comes to nationalism. This uncomfortable pairing can be traced through the work of Edward Thompson and Eric Hobsbawm,[9] visionary writers who contributed so much to the strong foundations of English cultural studies and who share a non-reductive Marxian approach to economic, social, and cultural history in which the nation—understood as a stable receptacle for counter-

2. Paul Gilroy, "Art of Darkness, Black Art, and the Problem of Belonging to England," *Third Text* 10 (1990). A very different interpretation of Turner's painting is given in Albert Boime's *The Art of Exclusion: Representing Blacks in the Nineteenth Century* (London: Thames and Hudson, 1990) [Gilroy's note]. The painting is *Slavers Throwing Overboard the Dead and Dying—Typhoon Coming On* (1840), also called *Slave Ship*.

3. Patrick Wright, *On Living in an Old Country* (London: Verso, 1985) [Gilroy's note].

4. Quoted from Turner's unpublished poem "Fallacies of Hope." Verses from the poem accompanied many of his later works.

5. Bernard Semmel, *Jamaican Blood and the Victorian Conscience* (Westport: Greenwood Press, 1976). See also Gillian Workman, "Thomas Carlyle and the Governor Eyre Controversy," *Victorian Studies* 18, no. 1 (1974): 77–102 [Gilroy's note].

6. Vol. 1, sec. 5, ch. 3, sec. 39 [1843]. W. E. B. Du Bois reprinted this commentary while he was editor of *The Crisis*; see vol. 15 (1918): 239 [Gilroy's note].

7. The personification of Britain.

8. Eric Hobsbawm, "The Historians' Group of the Communist Party," in M. Cornforth, ed., *Essays in Honour of A. L. Morton* (Atlantic Highlands: Humanities Press, 1979) [Gilroy's note].

9. A British Marxist historian of revolution and the working classes (1917–2012).

hegemonic class struggle—is the primary focus. These problems within English cultural studies form at its junction point with practical politics and instantiate wider difficulties with nationalism and with the discursive slippage or connotative resonance between "race," ethnicity, and nation.

Similar problems appear in rather different form in African-American letters where an equally volkish[1] popular cultural nationalism is featured in the work of several generations of radical scholars and an equal number of not so radical ones. We will see below that absolutist conceptions of cultural difference allied to a culturalist understanding of "race" and ethnicity can be found in this location too.

In opposition to both of these nationalist or ethnically absolute approaches, I want to develop the suggestion that cultural historians could take the Atlantic as one single, complex unit of analysis in their discussions of the modern world and use it to produce an explicitly transnational and intercultural perspective.[2] Apart from the confrontation with English historiography and literary history this entails a challenge to the ways in which black American cultural and political histories have so far been conceived. I want to suggest that much of the precious intellectual legacy claimed by African-American intellectuals as the substance of their particularity is in fact only partly their absolute ethnic property. No less than in the case of the English New Left, the idea of the black Atlantic can be used to show that there are other claims to it which can be based on the structure of the African diaspora into the western hemisphere. A concern with the Atlantic as a cultural and political system has been forced on black historiography and intellectual history by the economic and historical matrix in which plantation slavery—"capitalism with its clothes off"[3]—was one special moment. The fractal patterns of cultural and political exchange and transformation that we try and specify through manifestly inadequate theoretical terms like creolisation and syncretism indicate how both ethnicities and political cultures have been made anew in ways that are significant not simply for the peoples of the Caribbean but for Europe, for Africa, especially Liberia and Sierra Leone,[4] and of course, for black America.

It bears repetition that Britain's black settler communities have forged a compound culture from disparate sources. Elements of political sensibility and cultural expression transmitted from black America over a long period of time have been reaccentuated in Britain. They are central, though no longer dominant, within the increasingly novel configurations that characterise another newer black vernacular culture. This is not content to be either dependent upon or simply imitative of the African diaspora cultures of America and the Caribbean. The rise and rise of Jazzie B and Soul II Soul[5] at the turn of the last decade constituted one valuable sign of this new assertive mood. North London's Funki Dreds, whose name itself projects a newly hybridised identity, have projected the distinct culture and rhythm of life of

1. That is, rooted in the idea of a *Volk*, or people (German), a term that has racial connotations and is associated with ethnic nationalism.

2. Linebaugh, "Atlantic Mountains." This is also the strategy pursued by Marcus Rediker in his brilliant book *Between the Devil and the Deep Blue Sea* (Cambridge: Cambridge University Press, 1987) [Gilroy's note].

3. H. Orlando Patterson, "Slavery in Human History," *New Left Review*, no. 117 (Nov.–Dec. 1979): 51.

4. In the 19th century, thousands of freed blacks from the United States settled in both Liberia and Sierra Leone.

5. British music group—also known as the Funki Dreds, from their clothing and hairstyle—named in 1982 by one of its founding members, the black Briton Jazzie B (Trevor Beresford Romeo, b. 1963); one of its hit singles was "Keep on Movin'" (1989).

black Britain outwards into the world. Their song "Keep On Moving" was notable for having been produced in England by the children of Caribbean settlers and then re-mixed in a (Jamaican) dub format in the United States by Teddy Riley, an African-American. It included segments or samples of music taken from American and Jamaican records by the JBs and Mikey Dread respectively. This formal unity of diverse cultural elements was more than just a powerful symbol. It encapsulated the playful diasporic intimacy that has been a marked feature of transnational black Atlantic creativity. The record and its extraordinary popularity enacted the ties of affiliation and affect which articulated the discontinuous histories of black settlers in the new world. The fundamental injunction to "Keep On Moving" also expressed the restlessness of spirit which makes that diaspora culture vital. The contemporary black arts movement in film, visual arts, and theatre as well as music, which provided the background to the musical release, have created a new topography of loyalty and identity in which the structures and presuppositions of the nation state have been left behind because they are seen to be outmoded. It is important to remember that these recent black Atlantic phenomena may not be as novel as their digital encoding via the transnational force of north London's Soul II Soul suggests. Columbus's[6] pilot, Pedro Nino, was also an African. The history of the black Atlantic since then, continually crisscrossed by the movements of black people—not only as commodities but engaged in various struggles towards emancipation, autonomy, and citizenship—provides a means to reexamine the problems of nationality, location, identity, and historical memory. They all emerge from it with special clarity if we contrast the national, nationalistic, and ethnically absolute paradigms of cultural criticism to be found in England and America with those hidden expressions, both residual and emergent, that attempt to be global or outer-national in nature. These traditions have supported countercultures of modernity that touched the workers' movement but are not reducible to it. They supplied important foundations on which it could build.

Turner's extraordinary painting of the slave ship remains a useful image not only for its self-conscious moral power and the striking way that it aims directly for the sublime in its invocation of racial terror, commerce, and England's ethico-political degeneration. It should be emphasised that ships were the living means by which the points within that Atlantic world were joined. They were mobile elements that stood for the shifting spaces in between the fixed places that they connected.[7] Accordingly they need to be thought of as cultural and political units rather than abstract embodiments of the triangular trade. They were something more—a means to conduct political dissent and possibly a distinct mode of cultural production. The ship provides a chance to explore the articulations between the discontinuous histories of England's ports, its interfaces with the wider world.[8] Ships also

6. The Genoese explorer Christopher Columbus (1451–1506).

7. "A space exists when one takes into consideration vectors of direction, velocities, and time variables. Thus space is composed of intersections of mobile elements. It is in a sense articulated by the ensemble of movements deployed within it." Michel de Certeau, *The Practice of Everyday Life* (Berkeley and London: University of California Press, 1984), p. 117 [Gilroy's note].

8. See Michael Cohn and Michael K. Platzer, *Black Men of the Sea* (New York: Dodd, Mead, 1978). I have been heavily reliant on George Francis Dow's anthology *Slave Ships and Slaving*, publication no. 15 of the Marine Research Society (1927; rpt. Cambridge, Md.: Cornell Maritime

refer us back to the middle passage, to the half-remembered micro-politics of the slave trade and its relationship to both industrialisation and modernisation. As it were, getting on board promises a means to reconceptualise the orthodox relationship between modernity and what passes for its prehistory. It provides a different sense of where modernity might itself be thought to begin in the constitutive relationships with outsiders that both found and temper a self-conscious sense of western civilisation.[9] For all these reasons, the ship is the first of the novel chronotopes presupposed by my attempts to rethink modernity via the history of the black Atlantic and the African diaspora into the western hemisphere.

In the venturesome spirit proposed by James Clifford in his influential work on travelling culture,[1] I want to consider the impact that this outernational, transcultural reconceptualisation might have on the political and cultural history of black Americans and that of blacks in Europe. In recent history, this will certainly mean reevaluating Garvey and Garveyism, pan-Africanism, and Black Power as hemispheric if not global phenomena. In periodising modern black politics it will require fresh thinking about the importance of Haiti and its revolution for the development of African-American political thought and movements of resistance. From the European side, it will no doubt be necessary to reconsider Frederick Douglass's relationship to English and Scottish radicalisms and to meditate on the significance of William Wells Brown's five years in Europe as a fugitive slave, on Alexander Crummell's[2] living and studying in Cambridge, and upon Martin Delany's experiences at the London congress of the International Statistical Congress in 1860.[3] It will require comprehension of such difficult and complex questions as W. E. B. Du Bois's childhood interest in Bismarck, his investment in modelling his dress and moustache on that of Kaiser Wilhelm II, his likely thoughts while sitting in Heinrich Von Treitschke's seminars,[4] and the use his tragic heroes make of European culture.

Press, 1968), which includes extracts from valuable 18th- and 19th-century material. On England, I have found the anonymously published study *Liverpool and Slavery* (Liverpool: A. Bowker and Sons, 1884) to be very valuable. Memoirs produced by black sea captains also point to a number of new intercultural and transcultural research problems. Captain Harry Dean's *The Pedro Gorino: Adventures of a Negro Sea Captain in Africa and on the Seven Seas in His Attempts to Found an Ethiopian Empire* (Boston and New York: Houghton Mifflin, 1929) contains interesting material on the practical politics of Pan-Africanism that go unrecorded elsewhere. Captain Hugh Malzac's autobiography, *A Star to Steer By* (New York: International Publishers, 1963), includes valuable observations on the role of ships in the Garvey movement. Some pointers towards what a black Atlantic rereading of the history of Rastafari might involve are to be found in Robert A. Hill's important essay which accentuates the complex post-slavery relations between Jamaica and Africa: "Dread History: Leonard P. Howell and Millenarian Visions in Early Rastafari Religions in Jamaica," *Epoché: Journal of the History of Religions at UCLA* 9 (1981): 30–71 [Gilroy's note]. Among the tenets of Rastafarianism, a cultural and religious movement that began in Jamaica in the 1930s, is the eventual return of blacks to Africa.

9. Stephen Greenblatt, *Marvellous Possessions* (Oxford: Oxford University Press, 1992). See also Pratt, *Imperial Eyes* [Gilroy's note].

1. James T. Clifford, "Travelling Cultures," in *Cultural Studies*, ed. Lawrence Grossberg et al. (New York and London: Routledge, 1992), and "Notes on Theory and Travel," *Inscriptions* 5 (1989) [Gilroy's note].

2. African American abolitionist, minister, educator, and black nationalist (1819–1898). Brown (1814–1884), African American abolitionist, novelist, and playwright.

3. *Manchester Weekly Advertiser*, July 21, 1860; *Punch*, July 28, 1860; *The Morning Star*, July 18, 1860; and F. A. Rollin, *Life and Public Services of Martin R. Delany* (Lee and Shepard: Boston, 1868), p. 102 [Gilroy's note].

4. Peter Winzen, "Treitschke's Influence on the Rise of Imperialist and Anti-British Nationalism in Germany," in P. Kennedy and A. Nicholls, eds., *Nationalist and Racialist Movements in Britain and Germany Before 1914* (Basingstoke: Macmillan, 1981) [Gilroy's note]. Otto von Bismarck (1815–1898), Prussian statesman and advocate of German unification. Kaiser Wilhelm II (1859–1941; reigned 1888–1918), the last emperor of Germany and king of Prussia. Treitschke (1834–1896), German historian who advocated authoritarianism and colonial expansion.

Notable black American travellers, from the poet Phyllis Wheatley[5] onwards, went to Europe and had their perceptions of America and racial domination shifted as a result of their experiences there. This had important consequences for their understanding of racial identities. The radical journalist and political organiser Ida B. Wells is typical, describing her productive times in England as like "being born again in a new condition."[6] Lucy Parsons is a more problematic figure in the political history of black America,[7] but how might her encounters with William Morris, Annie Besant, and Peter Kropotkin[8] impact upon a rewriting of the history of English radicalism? What of Nella Larsen's[9] relationship to Denmark, where George Padmore was held in jail during the early 1930s and which was also the home base of his banned paper the *Negro Worker,* circulated across the world by its supporters in the Colonial Seamen's Association?[1] What of Sarah Parker Remond's work as a medical practitioner in Italy and the life of Edmonia Lewis,[2] the sculptor, who made her home in Rome? What effects did living in Paris have upon Anna Cooper, Jessie Fauset, Gwendolyn Bennett,[3] and Lois Maillou Jones?[4]

It would appear that there are large questions raised about the direction and character of black culture and art if we take the powerful effects of even temporary experiences of exile, relocation, and displacement into account. How, for example, was the course of the black vernacular art of jazz changed by what happened to Quincy Jones in Sweden and Donald Byrd[5] in Paris? This is especially interesting because both men played powerful roles in the remaking of jazz as a popular form in the early 1970s. Byrd describes his sense of Europe's appeal as something that grew out of the view of Canada he developed as a young man growing up in Detroit:

> That's why Europe was so important to me. Living across the river from Canada as a kid, I used to go down and sit and look at Windsor, Ontario. Windsor represented Europe to me. That was the rest of the world that was foreign to me. So I always had a feeling for the foreign, the Euro-

5. African-born slave (ca. 1753–1784), sold in Boston, who gained fame in her teens for her poetry.
6. Ida B. Wells quoted in Vron Ware, *Beyond the Pale: White Women, Racism, and History* (London and New York: Verso, 1992). p. 177 [Gilroy's note]. Wells (1862–1931), African American crusader against lynching.
7. Carolyn Ashbaugh, *Lucy Parsons: American Revolutionary* (Chicago: Charles H. Kerr, 1976). I must thank Tommy Lott for this reference [Gilroy's note]. Parsons (1853–1942), labor activist associated with anarchist, socialist, and communist organizations; her heritage was Mexican, Native American, and almost certainly (though she denied it) African.
8. Russian revolutionary and anarchist (1842–1921). Morris (1834–1896), English poet, artist, and socialist. Besant (1847–1933), British socialist, orator, Theosophist, and advocate of Indian home rule.
9. African American novelist (1891–1964), whose mother was Danish and father was West Indian; she was raised by a Danish stepfather, and lived in Denmark for 3 years, beginning at age 16.
1. Frank Hooker, *Black Revolutionary: George Padmore's Path from Communism to Pan Africanism* (London: Pall Mall Library of African Affairs, 1967) [Gilroy's note].
2. William S. McFeely, *Frederick Douglass* (New York: W. W. Norton, 1991), p. 329 [Gilroy's note]. Remond (1826–1894), African American physician, antislavery lecturer, and advocate of women's rights. Lewis (ca. 1845–1911), African American and Native American sculptor.
3. Michel Fabre, *Black American Writers in France, 1840–1980* (Urbana and Chicago: University of Illinois Press, 1991) [Gilroy's note]. Anna Julia Cooper (1858–1964), author and educator, who received her Ph.D. from the Sorbonne in Paris in 1925. Fauset (ca. 1882–1961), novelist and editor, who earned an M.A. in French and studied at the Sorbonne for 6 months. Bennett (1902–1981), Harlem Renaissance writer and artist, who studied art in Paris.
4. Painter and longtime professor of design and watercolor painting at Howard University (1905–1998), who spent many summers in Paris.
5. Jazz and rhythm-and-blues trumpeter (1932–2013). Jones (b. 1933), jazz trumpeter, composer, and music producer.

> pean thing, because Canada was right there. We used to go to Canada. For black people, you see, Canada was a place that treated you better than America, the North. For my father Detroit was better than the South, to me born in the North, Canada was better. At least that was what I thought. Later on I found out otherwise, but anyway, Canada represented for me something foreign, exotic, that was not the United States.[6]

Richard Wright's life in exile, which has been written off as a betrayal of his authenticity and as a process of seduction by philosophical traditions supposedly outside his narrow ethnic compass,[7] will be explored below as an exemplary instance of how the politics of location and the politics of identity get inscribed in analyses of black culture. Many of the figures listed here will be dealt with in later chapters. They are all potential candidates for inclusion in the latest African-American cultural canon, a canon that is conditional on and possibly required by the academic packaging of black cultural studies.[8] Chapter 4 will discuss what version of the politics and philosophy of W. E. B. Du Bois will be constructed for that canon from the rich transnational textures of his long and nomadic life. Du Bois's travel experiences raise in the sharpest possible form a question common to the lives of almost all these figures who begin as African-Americans or Caribbean people and are then changed into something else which evades those specific labels and with them all fixed notions of nationality and national identity. Whether their experience of exile is enforced or chosen, temporary or permanent, these intellectuals and activists, writers, speakers, poets, and artists repeatedly articulate a desire to escape the restrictive bonds of ethnicity, national identification, and sometimes even "race" itself. Some speak, like Wells and Wright, in terms of the rebirth that Europe offered them. Whether they dissolved their African-American sensibility into an explicitly pan-Africanist discourse or political commitment, their relationship to the land of their birth and their ethnic political constituency was absolutely transformed. The specificity of the modern political and cultural formation I want to call the black Atlantic can be defined, on one level, through this desire to transcend both the structures of the nation state and the constraints of ethnicity and national particularity.

* * *

1993

6. Ursula Broschke Davis, *Paris without Regret* (Iowa City: University of Iowa Press, 1986), p. 102 [Gilroy's note].

7. I challenge this view in Chapter 5 [Gilroy's note]. Wright (1908–1960), novelist and writer of nonfiction; he moved to Paris after World War II.

8. Some of the problems associated with this strategy have been discussed by Cornel West in "Minority Discourse and the Pitfalls of Canon Formation," *Yale Journal of Criticism* 1, no. 1 (Fall 1987): 193–201 [Gilroy's note].

ANDREW ROSS
b. 1956

To many, Andrew Ross personifies cultural studies in the United States. One reason is that he examines popular as well as high culture and does not hesitate to cross disciplinary boundaries, writing on topics ranging from modernist poetry to Madonna, the New York Intellectuals to Disney, and the university to the Weather Channel. In addition, he has attained a great deal of visibility; he has published trade as well as academic books, written articles for magazines such as the *Nation* and *Artforum*, and been the subject of profiles in major media, notably the *New York Times Magazine*. However, his writing does not simply embrace popular culture but investigates the politics inherent in cultural aspects of science, technology, and labor. His essay "The Mental Labor Problem" (2004), from which we take our selection, is an original analysis of the way in which labor has been refashioned in recent years, as knowledge workers adopt the work profile of musicians and other artists—a cultural construal that results in less pay and security than are offered by traditional white-collar jobs. The essay also criticizes the infusion of corporate practices into academe, and calls for unionization to protect academic labor and to ensure humane workplaces.

Born in Scotland, Ross was educated at Aberdeen University (M.A., 1978) and the University of Kent (Ph.D., 1984). He first came to the United States in 1980, teaching at Illinois State University and elsewhere until 1985, when he took an appointment at Princeton University. In 1993 he moved to New York University, where he helped found the Department of Social and Cultural Analysis, which conjoins American, race, gender, sexuality, and ethnicity studies.

Much criticism through the 1970s and 1980s was absorbed in debates over "theory," especially over language, social structures, and psychoanalytic concepts like the subject. Trained in literature during that time, Ross began as a theoretically oriented critic, taking a psychoanalytic approach to modern poetry. In the late 1980s, however, he turned to an examination of technology, ecology, popular culture, and intellectual history, becoming a pacesetter for a rising generation of critics. As he remarks in an essay, "I took the opportunity to liberate myself, professionally, from the teaching of literature, and self-apprenticed in the kinds of social and cultural analysis" familiar in influential British cultural studies figures like STUART HALL. Sometimes cultural studies is seen as simply applying the tools of literary studies to other media and popular culture, but Ross has stressed that he was particularly interested in "researching the traditions of cultural citizenship," as he decided to remain in the United States.

Ross's method also differs from that of influential theorists like PAUL DE MAN, who espoused deconstruction and was perhaps the representative figure of literary theory in the United States during the late 1970s and early 1980s. Rather than focusing on the interpretation of literary and philosophical texts, as de Man does, Ross developed an ethnographic approach, or what he calls "scholarly reporting." In books addressed to nonacademic audiences, such as *No-Collar: The Humane Workplace and Its Hidden Costs* (2003), he has reported on the work conditions of contemporary capitalism in the developed world. His method combines detailed interviews and observations, undertaken at a deeper level than most journalism, with scholarly research (for instance, into labor history) to expose features of employment in our world. To do this, he notes that he had to retrain himself from being a reader of texts to a listener (he remarks that his literary training had made him "not a very good listener"), and from being an "armchair theorist" to an empirically oriented observer.

"The Mental Labor Problem" offers an eye-opening account of the reconfiguration of labor, from blue-collar and white-collar—that is, physical labor and mental labor—to devalued "no-collar" jobs. In the first half of our selection, Ross investigates how jobs requiring mental labor now often adopt the cultural ethos of the bohemian artist, which had typically been seen as antithetical to a proper work attitude. Artists presumably do their work because they love it, rather than for pay, of which most receive notoriously little; Ross designates this "the cultural discount." Many current jobs, notably in high-tech firms, have been imbued with this ethos, but this "freedom" is actually designed to encourage workers to produce more labor for less pay. One might add to the examples that Ross names the unpaid or minimally paid internships held by many university students.

Ross also looks at what economists have called "the cost disease." To increase their profits, businesses expect productivity to rise and costs to decrease over time, relying on such advances as improved technology on a production line. But mental labor seems immune from this kind of speedup. Faster computers do not necessarily translate into faster, better, or more profitable ideas. Thus for those who manage businesses, the answer again is to discount and encourage free mental labor.

At its core, Ross's argument is a defense of fair and just work conditions. In an interview, he remarked that one of his chief influences is Marxist theory, and his analysis subtly shows how contemporary neoliberal capitalism extracts more time from workers. But Ross also notes that another of his influences is anarchism; a key value for him is human liberation. "The Mental Labor Problem" points to the bitter irony that current labor practices not only constrain workers but do so while claiming to liberate them to do what they love. One of Ross's more trenchant charges is that many current jobs return to the conditions of the sweatshop, mobilizing cultural ideas of enjoyable work to extract long hours for low pay.

In the latter half of our selection, Ross shifts from analyzing the projection of the artistic ethos onto white-collar jobs to describing the imposition of corporate labor structures on academic jobs. Rather than being an ivory tower, the contemporary university participates in corporate practices like sweatshop labor to reduce its costs, particularly in its use of poorly paid "adjuncts," the part-time laborers who, according to current statistics, teach more than half the courses in universities in the United States. This practice draws on the ethos of the medieval monk as well as the Romantic artist; since university teachers presumably love and are prepared to make sacrifices for their fields, they will accept low pay. It also draws on the modernist disdain for the marketplace, often adopted by academics who therefore see bread-and-butter issues like wages as irrelevant or unworthy of their attention. To counter the devaluation of teaching, Ross advocates campaigning for fair wages and benefits as well as embracing the traditional tool of labor, unionization.

In this essay and much of his work since the late 1990s, Ross shines light on the often-confusing effects of the postindustrial economy. Times have not been good for most workers. Beginning in the 1970s, many jobs have disappeared through "outsourcing," while others have been "casualized" or made temporary; health and retirement benefits have been pared away; and many protections, notably those afforded by union membership, have been lost. Many remaining jobs have been "deskilled" and therefore command less pay, and workers are increasingly subject to underemployment or overwork. Ross shows how professional jobs, which formerly conferred more benefits, have become subject to the same pressures as blue-collar jobs: "brainwork," particularly in academic or creative jobs, no longer is accorded a special status. Those with creative jobs are encouraged to conceive of themselves as individual contractors, seeking short-term employment in less definable roles than before—hence "no-collar" rather than blue- or white-collar work. Such jobs presumably grant individuals more freedom, but also create more insecurity and more pressure for overwork. In short, Ross demonstrates how recent shifts in the socioeconomic landscape operate not for the social good but to produce more exploitation, inequality, and social insecurity.

Ross's style is a distinctive one. He often makes pithy remarks to put ordinary practices in a new perspective. For instance, to emphasize that the American research university is not an altruistic enclave, he notes that after World War II it served "as a money-launderer for the Department of Defense's permanent war economy," receiving large amounts of funding for military research. To those who view the current conditions of academic labor as a function of "supply and demand," he points out that there is "no shortage of work, only a shortage of decent jobs." He also takes on the conventional wisdom that philanthropists have provided the most support to the arts, arguing that artists themselves have given the largest donation, in the form of their unpaid labor.

Probably because of his high profile as well as his fearlessness in addressing topics outside the discipline of literature, Ross has been subject to public criticism to a degree experienced by few academics; in one instance, he was attacked in the fashion magazine *GQ* as a member of "Hackademia." In particular, Ross's forays into science have proved quite controversial, and he has been accused of being a postmodern relativist who would deny basic scientific principles like gravity. Ross, however, makes arguments not about scientific knowledge but about the cultural position and social use of science. He does not comment on, say, the physics or engineering of fighter planes; rather, he notes that their funding and development rely on social institutions, public policy, and political decisions. As he retorts in a 1996 essay, "Cultural Studies and the Challenge of Science," "If you are a nonprofessional, of course you will never know enough to satisfy your scientist interlocutors. . . . But how much do you need to know about nuclear fission to know that nuclear reactors are an insane idea?" While this claim is debatable, his fundamental point is that the goals and uses of science, rather than the methods of scientific knowledge, deserve public discussion in a democratic society. This stance is similar to that of EDWARD W. SAID, who argues in his book *Representations of the Intellectual* (1994) that a chief impediment to criticism is the cult of expertise, which allows only Orientalists to comment on Middle Eastern politics, or scientists to comment on the social uses of science.

Within the liberal-left camp, Ross has been criticized for his concentration on culture. In a prominent attack, the pragmatist philosopher Richard Rorty charged that Ross's focus on "cultural politics" has deflected attention from "real politics" and concrete political issues like health care. Ross replies that society, and inequality in it, "reproduces itself culturally as well as economically," through such institutions as education and media, and through social rituals and values. Though he left behind "armchair theory," in his focus on the formative effects of culture he joins a distinguished line of thinkers who examine the relation of culture to the underlying material structure of society and to social relations, notably ANTONIO GRAMSCI and RAYMOND WILLIAMS. In "The Mental Labor Problem," Ross shows how culture creates the conditions for jobs. Ross has been one of the strongest voices in contemporary criticism urging that attention be paid to the culture of work and that action be taken to ensure more humane and equitable working conditions in late capitalism.

"The Mental Labor Problem" Keywords: Cultural Studies, Ideology, Institutional Studies, Marxism, Popular Culture

From The Mental Labor Problem

* * *

The great divide between the high arts and popular culture has, of course, been discussed to death (including by this author) as a measure of changes in the aesthetic life and mass social organization of modern times. The corresponding change in the nature of cultural labor has received much less attention. Even within the literature that could be grouped together under the heading of cultural policy, the lion's share is given over to the "funding problem" of the arts, such as changes in the sources and traditions of patronage and institutional money supply. By contrast, there is relatively little focus on the "labor problem" of the arts.[1] Among the exceptions to this rule I have chosen to briefly outline two quite different, but not untypical, approaches to this topic of cultural labor—the cultural discount and the cost disease.

The Cultural Discount

In the first approach, the cultural labor problem figures primarily as the challenge of maintaining a steady supply of workers willing to discount the price of their labor for love of their craft. This might be characterized as the culture vulture's version of "how difficult it is to find good help these days." The most incisive version of this thesis can be found in San Francisco Foundation executive John Kreidler's useful account of the rise and decline of the nonprofit arts foundation. Central to Kreidler's analysis is the principle of the *cultural discount*, by which artists and other arts workers accept nonmonetary rewards—the gratification of producing art—as compensation for their work, thereby discounting the cash price of their labor.[2]

In the nineteenth century, Kreidler points out that it was the model of individual proprietorship that characterized most theaters, orchestras, opera companies, performing arts impresarios, and many museums. The separation between high and low, or elite and popular, as Lawrence Levine and others have shown, was much less distinct in this period.[3] While these for-profit proprietorships had to meet the test of the marketplace to survive, they were still heavily subsidized and sustained by the willingness of cultural workers to accept deeply discounted compensation for their labor. Indeed, it is fair to say that the largest subsidy to the arts has always come from workers themselves. To this day, all such workers, even those employed on market-driven contracts, tend to earn compensation well below that commensurate with their skills and levels of educational attainment. The rough justice of the marketplace does not seem to deter the chronically discounted. Indeed, and largely because of artists' traditions of sacrifice, it often appears to spur them on in ways that would be regarded as self-destructive in any other economic sector.

Kreidler observes that, lately, arts organizations have begun to worry about the depletion of this discount labor supply. Today's youth, he suggests, are less attracted to the ethos of public service or service to the arts that equates to personal sacrifice, an ethos that was more appealing to relatively affluent,

1. Some titles, predominantly relating to the for-profit sector, include: Lois Gray and Ronald Seeber, eds., *Under the Stars: Essays on Labor Relations in Arts and Entertainment* (Ithaca, NY: ILR/Cornell University Press, 1996); Michael Storper, "The Transition to Flexible Specialization in the U.S. Film Industry," *Cambridge Journal of Economics* 13 (1989), 273–305; Toby Miller, *Technologies of Truth: Cultural Citizenship and the Popular Media* (Minneapolis: University of Minnesota Press, 1998) and "Television and Citizenship: A New International Division of Cultural Labor," in Andrew Calabrese and Jean-Claude Burgelman, eds., *Communication, Citizenship, and Social Policy: Rethinking the Limits of the Welfare State* (Lanham, MD: Rowman and Littlefield, 1999), 279–92 [Ross's note].

2. John Kreidler, "Leverage Lost: The Nonprofit Arts in the Post-Ford Era," *In Motion Magazine* (www.inmotionmagazine.com/lost.html) [Ross's note].

3. Lawrence Levine, *Highbrow/Lowbrow: The Emergence of Cultural Hierarchy in America* (Cambridge, MA: Harvard University Press, 1988) [Ross's note]. Levine (1933–2006), American cultural historian.

white baby boomers in the post-Kennedy period[4] at the height of nonprofit funding of the arts. As that funding pipeline has sharply reduced its flow, and as leisure time has declined radically for most people in the U.S. in the last two decades, the arts economy faces an uncertain future. The older proprietary models have mostly been subsumed by the commercial culture industries, and the traditional dependence on volunteer, discounted labor to support the arts can no longer be taken for granted. Subtle improvements in the money supply, he concludes, are not likely to offset the long-term impact of labor attrition.

Since Kreidler assumes that the status and levels of comparative compensation enjoyed by artists have not changed significantly since the entrepreneurial heyday of the nineteenth-century arts proprietor, the root of the current arts crisis must therefore lie in the "selfish gene"[5] pool of the boomer parent. Although he does not identify the problem in quite this candid way, it is not unfair to see his conclusion as akin to parental indictments of Gen X[6] apathy. The labor crisis of the arts can thus be laid at the door of youngsters who will not commit to an ideal higher than their own self-absorbed, material interests. Presumably the moral calling of the arts is not well-served by a generation distinguished by its cultivation of types like the world-class slacker or the IPO-seeking dotcommer.[7] If we flesh out this line of argument, we can almost hear the grouchy tones of the parental scold, chiding the listless offspring with mawkish tales about his own hardships of yore, nobly borne in cold-water apartments and fixtureless lofts. Kreidler's description of the cultural discount is a very useful contribution, but his belief that sacrificial labor is morally sustaining for youth is little short of a recipe for exploitation. Reasoning that appeals to the moral fiber of generational temperament may be consoling, especially to those above the boomer waterline, but it will not provide a cogent assessment of the state of cultural labor. Not when the percentage of employees identified as artists, in national labor statistics, is higher than ever. Not when the principle of the cultural discount, as I will shortly show, is more and more utilized on a semi-industrial scale in sectors of the knowledge industries.

The Cost Disease

A second kind of explanation of the labor crisis, with proven historical impact on arts funding, has been advanced by arts economists. Professionally challenged by evidence of productive activity that does not observe the all-powerful laws of market supply and demand, liberal economists have been drawn to offer a structural explanation for the "income gap" between the arts and other professions. One influential example was offered by William Baumol in a 1966 study of the performing arts co-authored with fellow

4. That is, the period after the presidency of John F. Kennedy (1917–1963; 35th U.S. president, 1961–63). "Baby boomers": Americans born during the marked rise in birthrate after World War II (usually dated 1946–64).

5. An allusion to *The Selfish Gene* (1976), Richard Dawkins's best seller that presented a theory of cultural transmission grounded in sociobiological evolution.

6. Generation X, the generation that followed the baby boomers (born 1964–ca. 1979).

7. The owner of a company that markets its products or services on the Internet (such as those that characterized the "dot-com bubble" of the 1990s) who seeks investment capital through an initial public offering (IPO) of stock.

Princeton economist William Bowen.[8] With the help of their faculty spouses, who did much of the empirical research, Baumol and Bowen set out to reveal how and why the performing arts have failed to keep up with the impressive productivity gains, measured in outputs per man hour, that have been recorded by other sectors of American industry in the course of the century.

For their purposes, they propose to assess the labor cost per unit of the arts as if the arts functioned like any other service-sector industry: "It is helpful to treat the arts, not as an intangible manifestation of the human spirit, but as a productive activity which provides services to the community: one which, in this respect, does not differ from the manufacture of electricity or the supply of transportation or house-cleaning services."[9] Viewed from this angle, Baumol and Bowen find that the performing arts do not behave at all like other sectors of the service economy, primarily because they cannot, by their nature, exploit the productivity gains that come with advances in technology. In terms of its technological conditions of production, a contemporary performance of *Macbeth*[1] is not substantially different from its Elizabethan equivalent. "It will be seen," Baumol and Bowen write, "that the tendency for costs to rise and for prices to lag behind is neither a matter of bad luck nor mismanagement. Rather, it is an inescapable result of the technology of live performance, which will continue to contribute to the widening of the income gaps of the performing organizations."

While the costs of performing will continue to rise without an increase in productivity, Baumol and Bowen conclude, more auspiciously, that productivity in other sectors of economy will provide workers with more leisure time to consume and participate in the arts, and thereby alleviate some of the economic pressure. This cheerful rider, so indicative of the mid-1960s American climate of chipper expectations, would have a much more consequential echo in Bowen's infamous report on a different service profession, twenty-three years later. His 1989 study of graduate education forecast widespread tenure-track job openings in the professoriat by the middle of the 1990s and may have bootlessly lured thousands into doctoral programs with its misconceived assurances of a buoyant future in college teaching.[2]

Baumol and Bowen's 1966 arts forecast foundered almost as quickly as the education one offered by Bowen in 1989. A decline in the leisure time available to the general U.S. workforce set in from the early 1970s and has not been stemmed, not even by the boom economy of the 1990s, which only triggered even higher levels of performance anxiety. Overwork, as opposed to joblessness, became the most chronic feature of the labor landscape. Nonetheless, the impact of the 1966 study helped to fuel the clamor for

8. Former president of Princeton University and of the Mellon Foundation (1933–2016). Baumol (1922–2017), American economist.

9. William Baumol and William Bowen, *Performing Arts—The Economic Dilemma: A Study of Problems Common to Theatre, Opera, Music, and Dance* (New York: Twentieth-Century Fund, 1966), 162 [Ross's note].

1. A 1606 play by William Shakespeare.

2. William Bowen and Julie Ann Sosa, *Prospects for Faculty in the Arts and Sciences: A Study of Factors Affecting Supply and Demand, 1987 to 2012* (Princeton: Princeton University Press, 1989); and the later study, William Bowen and Neil Rudenstine, *In Pursuit of the Ph.D.* (Princeton: Princeton University Press, 1992). It has been argued that Bowen's forecast of abundant jobs would have been realized if universities had not embarked, in the 1990s, on a full-scale program of casualizing its faculty workforce. If colleges were still hiring full-time tenure-track professors, instead of part-timers and adjuncts, today's labor supply would more closely approximate employer demand [Ross's note].

increased state funding for the arts, revived that same year, after a hiatus of almost three decades, with the creation of the National Endowment for the Arts. Baumol's "cost disease" model, as it came to be known (the cost disease condemns the cost per live performance to rise at a rate persistently faster than that of a typically manufactured good), provided empirical support for state intervention in the arts, and subsequently became a staple principle of welfare economics.

But his cost disease does not apply solely to the arts. It is shared, he points out, by other "stagnant sectors" like health and education, whose capacity to provide services is impaired by increasing relative costs.[3] Handicapped from the outset by the cost disease, the arts, in Baumol's opinion, can either join the productive sector—by emulating the culture industries in their adaptation of advanced technologies—or hew more and more to the model of social services, like health or education (or national defense for that matter), which produce a subsidized public good under the heavy hand of bureaucratic supervision.

In some respects, both of these outcomes have come to pass. The institutional divide between the high and low arts has continued to blur, and more and more live performance has come to serve a merely promotional function for cultural product available to remote consumers in some other technologically mediated format. So too, as George Yudice[4] has analyzed, the new profile of the artist as a glorified social service worker has supplanted the autonomous avant-garde innovator as a fundable type, increasingly sponsored through local arts agencies. The all-purpose artist-citizen, whose work can help to preserve rural and inner-city communities at risk and stimulate efforts to revive their economies, is increasingly viewed as a means to create jobs through cultural tourism, to promote urban renewal through the competitive siting of museums and arts centers, to save teenagers from substance abuse, or generally to enhance public education through an infusion of communicative skills.[5]

New Model Workers

* * *

The "mentality" of artists' work is more and more in demand, and is steadily being relocated from its traditional position at the social margins of the productive economy into roles closer to the economic centers of production. Indeed, the traditional profile of the artist as unattached and adaptable to circumstance is surely now coming into its own as the ideal definition of the postindustrial knowledge worker. What is the profile of this new kind of worker who behaves and thinks like an artist? Someone who is comfortable in an ever-changing environment that often demands creative shifts in communication with different kinds of employers, clients, and colleagues; who is attitudinally geared toward work that requires long, and often unsocial, hours; who dedicates their time and energy to distinct projects, rather

3. Ruth Towse, ed., *Baumol's Cost Disease: The Arts and Other Victims* (Northampton, MA: Edward Elgar, 1997) [Ross's note].
4. American cultural critic (b. 1948).
5. George Yudice, "The Privatization of Culture," *Social Text*, no. 59 (Spring 1999), 17–34 [Ross's note].

than to a steady flow of production; who exercises self-management, if not self-employment, in the execution of their work; and who is accustomed to a contingent and casual work environment, without overt supervision or judgment from above.

The best example of these employment patterns could be found in the New Economy companies that emerged in urban downtown centers from the mid-1990s. Borne along by the boom in Internet services, these new media start-ups capitalized on a surplus of creative labor and depressed real estate prices to recruit and nurture a neo-bohemian workforce that satisfied the profile of the "fast company" in a creative ferment, throwing off innovative ideas from a nonconformist mold. In *No-Collar*, my ethnographic study of two of these companies, I observed the efforts, on the part of company managers, to develop templates that could standardize the fitful rhythms of creative labor.[6] This involved the attempt to fashion a business that imitated all of the attributes of artists—their habitats, lifestyles, clothing, work patterns, and custom individuality—and incorporate them into a tempo and a work temperament that could be recognized by clients as a reliable industrial process. The disposition of artists to undertake sacrifical labor was a blessing to a start-up economy that demanded of its workforce a legendary outlay of time and energy on the promise of deferred bounties: most employees in the new media industries invested a massive share of "sweat equity" in the mostly futile hope that their stock options would pay off. More important, even, than this apprenticeship in sacrifice was the flexibility of artists' work patterns to a corporate economy that had placed flexibility at the heart of its restructuring efforts the last two decades.

In the workplaces I observed, employee concentration on the job was variable, often erratic. It was a style of work (which the casual observers could easily misconstrue as goofing off) where stints of inspired self-application alternated with vivid socializing, and with those intervals of undirected play and dreamy indolence that Henry James[7] once called the "unstrenuous brooding sort of attention" that is required to produce art. Employees were not producing anything that Henry James would have cared to acknowledge as art, but they were doing their work in a way that he might have recognized. Company managers were faced with the formidable task of trying to accommodate these spasmodic rhythms. Play and recreation were encouraged in the workplace because they were perceived to add value to the work product. Employees were encouraged to work as and when the spirit took them, on the premise that ideas and creativity were as likely to surface at home or in other locations. In return for ceding freedom of movement to employees along with control over their work schedule, a no-collar company exercised the right to collect returns from areas of their lives that lay far beyond the physical workplace. A traditional industrial model derives value from workers where and when the company can control their labor. In the realm of no-collar work, the goal is to extract value from any waking moment of an employee's day. In this way, the most free of all impulses—the most unmoored of all thoughts—could become snared in the work process.

6. Andrew Ross, *No-Collar: The Humane Workplace and Its Hidden Costs* (New York: Basic Books, 2003) [Ross's note].

7. American novelist and critic (1843–1916; see above).

In these knowledge companies, the ethos of creative autonomy was lavishly supported by the principle of self-management. While this precept released employees from the indignity of constant supervision and other work rituals of subordination, it also required them to shoulder the full brunt of risks and responsibilities that are ordinarily borne by middle managers. Self-directed employees were newly vulnerable, experiencing the kind of raw exposure to the market that would ordinarily have been mediated by organizational higher-ups. The result of this liberalization of the workplace was not unlike the liberalization of the economy. It had been accompanied by a stripping away, or shredding, of layers of protection and social insurance against risk and insecurity. In the absence of safeguards and protections, the ultra-humane workplace could easily turn into a medium of self-exploitation—with bottomless seventy-hour-plus workweeks, and a dissolution of all boundaries between company and personal time.

The Internet industries of the New Economy hosted a fusion of work traditions drawn from the technology industries, on the one hand, and urban bohemia, on the other. They offered an advanced profile of the neoliberal world of work, where the worker, like the traditional artist, is a freelance thinker, operating in a deregulated environment that has banished stifling bureaucracy. In return for the opportunity to pursue personally gratifying work, the liberated individual takes over, from state institutions or company organizations, all responsibility for his or her economic survival and welfare. The creative entrepreneur is no longer alienated; there are no structures to be alienated from.[8]

Artists Cannot Afford to Be Rewarded Well?

Capitalist history is full of vicious little time warps, where archaic or long foresworn practices and conceptions of work are reinvented in a fresh context to suit some new economic arrangement. The "sweating" system of putting out work to competing contractors in the nineteenth-century garment industry was disdained as a preindustrial relic by the apostles of scientific management, yet this form of subcontracting is now a basic principle of almost every sector of the postindustrial economy and has emerged as the number-one weapon in capital's arsenal of labor cost-cutting and union-busting. So too the ethos of the autonomous artist, once so fiercely removed from industry's dark satanic mills[9] and from the soiled hand of commerce, has been recouped and revamped as a convenient, even alluring, esprit de corps for contingent work in today's de-structured knowledge industries. Indeed, the "voluntary poverty" of the déclassé bohemian artist—an ex-bourgeois descendant, more often than not, of the self-exiled Romantic poet—may turn out to be an inadvertent forerunner of the discounted labor of the new industrial landscape.

How does the legacy of these nineteenth-century traditions enter into the analyses of the cultural economists? In their 1966 study, Baumol and Bowen

8. Building on her studies of petty entrepreneurs in the British fashion industry, Angela McRobbie offers an analysis of the creative work as the new entrepreneurial model in "Clubs to Companies: Notes on the Decline of Political Culture in Speeded Up Creative Worlds," *Cultural Studies* 16:4 (2002), 516–31; and "Everyone Is Creative: Artists as Pioneers of the New Economy" (August 30, 2001), www.opendemocracy.net/themes/article-7-652.jsp [Ross's note].

9. That is, the early factories of the industrial revolution; "dark Satanic Mills" is a phrase from William Blake's poem (ca. 1804–10) that later became a hymn titled "Jerusalem."

have little to say about the impact of Romantic artist mythology, except to note that the parlous condition of artist compensation "seems only to elicit apathy from a public whose responses have been dulled by the stereotyped and somewhat romantic notion of the engarreted and starving artist."[1] In considering arguments against government support of the arts, they also refer to the

> antediluvian manifestation that poverty is good for the arts and stimulates creativity. "We want to develop a hungry theater" said one witness at the [1962] House Hearings on economic conditions in the performing arts, who went on to assert that only a hungry man feels compelled to say "what's in him."[2]

Antediluvian this may well be, yet popular wisdom is full of gimcrack rationales for paying people less than they deserve. Many are distorted hand-me-down versions of formerly principled positions about the worth of labor and the dignity of expression. Others are more candid judgments about the expendability of workers. When they circulate as common sense, they do have some real impact on net income levels, but not in a way that the empirical economist can safely measure. These nuggets of ideology are often at their most antediluvian when viewed from the perspective of the rational science of neoclassical economics, which cannot break down their influence on labor markets into hard numbers. Who could compute the impact of popular prejudices about race and gender on the kind of heavily segmented work that women or immigrants are expected to take on, at depressed wage levels? Yet market supply and demand cannot explain alone those features of labor segmentation that consign women and immigrants to specialized locations in the secondary labor market.

It may be worth taking the time, briefly, to review some of the history of what Baumol and Bowen refer to as the "antediluvian manifestation" of the starving artist. Ever since the name of the artist was attached to artworks, patrons have been extracting personal prestige and profit from their own association with the labor of art. In part, to maintain and inflate this prestige, artistic labor was elevated to a rank above and beyond the mere workmanship of craft and trade. It was the royal, papal, and noble patrons of the Renaissance who, for their own gain, invented the concept of the artist-genius in emulation of alchemists who, through their craft, might turn the dross of mere custom into the gold of lavish repute. Traces of this precapitalist prestige survive in those successive phases of patronage characterized by the bourgeois public, the mass market, and the state subsidy (nation-states can claim status on the global landscape on the basis of the great artists they have produced). As for the work of art itself, Marx's distinction between the value of labor and labor power[3]—the value added to a product, in this case, primarily the artist's name—is extremely consequential. The autonomous artist, who emerges in the nineteenth century as a solo entrepreneur working for a largely anonymous public audience, can benefit, in principle, from the surplus value that the name adds to his or her labor. But the name's value

1. Baumol and Bowen, 99 [Ross's note].
2. Ibid., 371 [Ross's note].
3. That is, between the actual value of the laborer's activity (the value of the goods or services produced) and his or her capacity to work, sold as a commodity; the difference between them, according to the German political philosopher and economist KARL MARX (1818–1883), is surplus value (the capitalist's profit).

tends to increase with the formal estrangement of the artistic soul from the bargaining and haggling of the marketplace. Any taint of mercenary involvement with market supply and demand can diminish the worth of that name.

For the most part, then, this surplus value accrues in reality to the publisher, dealer, promoter, producer, or owner-manager. To say the least, it is in their own pecuniary interest to endorse their clients' remove from matters of commerce. The personal agent emerges as the artist's best shot at recouping some of this value. When literary agents first sought to strengthen writers' bargaining power in the literary marketplace of the late nineteenth century, publishers complained that this "philistine" intervention disrupted the sacred bond between writer and publisher.[4] Yet these agents were realizing their clients' labor power in much the same way as fledgling trade unionists. (In bargaining for hours and wages, the unionists were also accused of "intruding" on the benevolent capitalist's relationship with his workers.) Did the result amount to the cheapening or commercialization of culture, as publishers had warned? To some degree, yes, but nowhere nearly as much as the behavior of publishers themselves, already covetous of the popular market, and well-primed to pattern the book trade in the mold of the mass media industries that would dominate the twentieth century.

The noble ethos of the unattached artist was conceived in the struggle to break free from aristocratic patronage and was clearly compromised by the simultaneous birth of a mass commercial audience from the womb of the bourgeois public. Most fatefully, from the perspective of the artist wage, this ethos was soaked in the full torrent of Romantic thought about the separation of art and culture from the commodity production of industrialization. As the industrial division of labor everywhere sought to convert artisans into machine operatives, artists recoiled from being treated like any other trade producer. At the very least, the artist would be an independent skilled worker producing a marginal commodity of taste, but the higher calling of the Romantic imagination demanded something more. The artist was called on to represent, if not wholly embody, those imaginative qualities, skills, and virtues that industrial civilization was systematically destroying. Ironically, then, the artistic sensibility that was so opposed to utility could not afford to be directly rewarded by trade, yet the commodity value of the artwork rose in direct relation to the artist's remoteness from trade. In time, the highest value could be attached to the work of those—Van Gogh[5] is the quintessential example—who were most detached, reclusive, ignored, or pauperized by bourgeois society. To some degree, this value could appreciate in inverse proportion to the depression of their labor value while alive. As the moving legacy of Romantic ideas collided and meshed with the evolving arts economy, a curious, and perhaps unique, condition of labor emerged. *The artist cannot afford to be rewarded well.* High-caliber compensation proves fatal to the peer appraisal of an artist's achievement; pecuniary neglect, by that same token, translates into cultural credit.

4. Linda Marie Fritschner, "Literary Agents and Literary Traditions: The Role of the Philistine," in Judith Huggins Balfe, ed., *Paying the Piper: Causes and Consequences of Art Patronage* (Urbana: University of Illinois Press, 1993), 54–72. Also James Hepburn, *The Author's Empty Purse and the Rise of the Literary Agent* (London: Oxford University Press, 1968) [Ross's note]. "Philistine": that is, characteristic of the materialist middle classes—a term used by MATTHEW ARNOLD in "The Function of Criticism at the Present Time" (1865; see above).

5. Vincent van Gogh (1853–1890), Dutch painter whose works are now among the most valuable in the world, though in his lifetime he sold only one painting and was extremely poor.

With the subsequent development of urban, bohemian quarters in low-income districts, this formula would have a geographical basis in the rent economy of the industrializing city and would endure through several decades of suburban flight and urban renewal until the waves of gentrification finally washed over its center-city habitat. The special condition of artistic labor, however, persists in all sorts of vestigial ways. Aside from its increasing use as a rationale for flexible labor in the new postindustrial workplace, in its traditional form it may well serve a general function in a capitalist society as an alleviator of liberal guilt for living in an exchange economy that puts a market price on everything. This social sanctioning of discounted arts labor is quite distinct from the pro bono work built into the pricing system of other, more highly paid, professions like the law. Alpha professionals, like lawyers, occasionally work for free because they can afford to do so, or because their complicity with structural injustice would otherwise be too conspicuous. This is no less the case for the highest-paid arts workers in the commercial sector, like pop musicians, whose continued regard often depends on high-profile appearances at benefit concerts where their fees are seen to be waived for a higher cause. But artists in general are expected, and are therefore inclined, to put in time gratis for love of their art in contexts that would require overtime pay for most other workers.

To compound matters, there persists an ingrained prejudice on the left against being well-paid occupationally, whether in the arts or in the academy. According to this reasoning, an underpaid intelligentsia can identify more readily with those living in low-wage conditions or abject poverty. Material self-denial and voluntary poverty are the monkish markers of conscience and left-wing integrity in a reward economy. Compassion and commitment may well flow from this posture, but they are hardly dependent on it. Ultimately, there is something quite patronizing about this ascetic credo, redolent, as it is, of middle-class fantasies about the lives and aspirations of working people. Nothing could be further from the raw thrust of ameliorative laborism, typified by Wobbly chieftain Big Bill Haywood's[6] pronouncement (when asked about the fat cigars he smoked) that "nothing's too good for the proletariat."

For a modern version of Haywood's bravura, consider the priority placed on "getting paid in full," which has been a constant strain in hip-hop, and never more so than in the quixotic materialism of today's alpha rapper scene. The champagne-and-Bentley fantasy of the high life may be a crass nouveau riche version of American success, but it cannot be divorced entirely from the claim for reparations for almost a full century in which black artists had been robbed blind of their rights and royalties by the music industry. Golden-age rappers from the late 1980s were perhaps more articulate about the reparations claim than today's gilded celebrities, but the industrial streamlining of rap's genres in the intervening years has only made the choices more limited. Sustainable careers in hip-hop are ever harder to come by. Top-billers tend to be commercial champions for only a short period of time before they fall to fresh contenders (which rapper can honestly envisage a career in the mold of B.B. King,[7] earning a livelihood from performing at a ripe old age?). Rappers who enjoy the limelight temporarily are obliged to be conspicuous consumers; their flaunting of wealth is a kind of potlatch, and

6. William Dudley Haywood (1869–1928), founding member and leader of the Industrial Workers of the World (IWW, or Wobblies), a revolutionary socialist industrial union founded in 1905.

7. Blues musician (1925–2015), whose career spanned 8 decades.

they lose their status if they cannot spend flamboyantly, even if the habit threatens to drive them prematurely into poverty. Even as they fill the swaggering role of cartoon figments of the casino capitalist imagination, they must remind us that the choice between "selling out" and preserving one's artistic purity has never been an equal option for black performers, and was only really adopted as a litmus test of integrity by advocates for a white rock fraternity who elevated it to an unlikely, and mostly impractical criterion of faith for most working musicians, let alone African American ones. Yet the search for music untouched by the taint of lucre goes on, rather like the search for undeveloped beaches. Deprived, since the "discovery" of the Delta bluesmen,[8] of a supply of domestic primitives, well-meaning liberal rockists (Paul Simon, Sting, David Byrne[9]) have patronized Third World[1] musicians hitherto remote from any direct contact with the dollar economy. Ry Cooder's *Buena Vista Social Club*[2] of Cuba's aging, "forgotten" legends is the most recent, and perhaps the best, example of this search for purity of performance unsullied by high exchange rates.

The bohemian option has always been much less meaningful for artists of color. In communities with a history of being starved of any kind of resources, voluntary poverty is not generally regarded as a virtue, and least of all as a heroic, or romantic act of self-invention. Whenever a black bohemia has emerged, as in the case of the bebop jazz enclave, it was almost instantly converted into super-bohemian capital by white emulators like the Beats, hepcats,[3] and street-corner juveniles of the 1950s. By contrast, material success for black artists has been much more closely tied to status for those few who can rise above the competition. The often blunt focus on compensation—it's all about the Benjamins[4]—contrasts with the predominantly cultural prestige that the white indie artist is trained to extract from the thin wages of bohemia. That is why getting paid in full has had to mean as much to the rapper as the stage conventions of "keeping it real." That is why the militant "rebel without a pause"[5] of late 1980s hip-hop, who came the closest to meeting the romantic profile of the rock rebel, was still expected to be up-front in expressing opinions about the terms and conditions of his recording contracts. No surprise, then, that it was Chuck D, the paragon of the rebel without a pause, who was one of the first recording artists, a decade later, to make a preemptive strike against the industry by seizing on MP3 as a way of outfoxing the majors by bypassing traditional distribution routes.[6]

* * *

8. Blues musicians from the Mississippi Delta, who were "discovered" in the 1950s and early 1960s by white American and European bands.
9. All world-famous rock musicians: Simon (b. 1941), American; Sting (Gordon Sumner, b. 1951), British; and Byrne (b. 1952), American.
1. The "underdeveloped" countries, many of them former colonies, now dominated by highly industrialized "first world" (largely Western) nations in a global economy.
2. A 1999 movie (dir. Wim Wender), featuring long-retired musicians brought together to perform by the American guitarist Cooder (b. 1947).
3. Hipsters (especially jazz enthusiasts). The Beats: anarchic American writers of the 1950s.
4. That is, hundred-dollar bills, which bear the portrait of the American statesman and writer Benjamin Franklin (1706–1790).
5. A play on the title of an American movie about a rebellious youth, *Rebel without a Cause* (1955; dir. Nicholas Ray).
6. Partly in response to the disastrous consequences of the 1996 Telecommunications Act, which opened the way for rapid concentration of media interests in a range of industries, the Future of Music Coalition was formed to petition for musicians' rights on a broad front. Composed of "musicians, lawyers, academics, policymakers and music industry executives," the coalition, according to its Web site (www.futureofmusic.org), aims to debate and lobby on "some of the most contentious issues surrounding digital technology,

The Service Ideal

* * *

When the American labor market took its flexible turn in the early 1980s, and union organizing eroded as a fundamental right, blue-collar unions took a direct hit, but white-collar and professional organizing was still on the rise. The new knowledge industries, either comprising the higher-education sector or in corporate parks built around a university research complex, provided a natural union base for salaried employees with less and less control over their own workplace. In the 1990s, the corporatization of higher education set in for real, and casualization began to take a heavy toll on institutions nominally built on tenure, academic freedom, and faculty governance. The tenure-track appointment, hitherto a staple contract in the profession, would soon become a highly privileged exception to the rule. Professional academics, long accustomed to regarding their workplace as a non-worldly realm, beholden to different rules and standards from those observed in more "secular" employment sectors, had a rude awakening. In no time at all, it seemed, higher education had became one of the more advanced examples, among the professions, of the adjunct contract workplace, where a large percentage of its part-time labor force was soon struggling to earn any kind of living wage.

A Volunteer Low-Wage Army?

The rapidity with which the low-wage revolution swept through higher education was clearly hastened along by conditions amenable to discounting mental labor. For one thing, the willingness of adjuncts (whether as graduate students or postdoctoral employees) to accept a discounted wage out of "love for their subject" has helped not only to sustain the cheap labor supply but also to magnify its strength and volume. Like artists and performers, academics are inclined by training to sacrifice earnings for the opportunity to exercise the teaching craft. While other traditional professional industries, like law or medicine, depend to some degree on intern labor, none rely economically on the self-sacrifice of their accredited members to anything like the same degree.

Employers have long relied on the existence of a reserve army of unemployed to keep wages down in any labor market. Institutions of higher education have now entered this business with a vengeance. In addition—and this is the significant element—their managers increasingly draw on a *volunteer low-wage army*. By this I do not mean to suggest that adjunct and part-timer educators actually invite their underpayment and lack of benefits or job security. These conditions are, first and foremost, a direct result of managerial policy. Nor are they inactive in protesting and organizing for their interests. Like the jazz musicians at the New School, they are forming unions and bargaining units (my own institution now boasts the largest adjunct union of any

artists' rights and the current state of the music industry" [Ross's note]. Chuck D (Carlton Ridenhour, b. 1960), African American writer, producer, and leading figure in rap music, a founding member of the politically conscious rap group Public Enemy. MP3, a digital audio encoding format, enabled music files to be easily shared over the Internet, outside the control of the major record labels.

private university).[7] Rather, I choose the phrase to describe the structural eventuality of being trained in the habit of embracing nonmonetary rewards—job gratification is self-actualizing—as compensation. As a result of this training, low compensation for a high workload can become a rationalized feature of the job. In the most perverse extension of this logic, underpayment can even be interpreted as proof of the worth of the academic vocation—as the ultimate gauge of the selfless teacher and/or the disinterested seeker of knowledge.

Vestiges of the amateur ideal of the scholar are a contributing element. Indeed, one of the uncommon privileges traditionally enjoyed by academic scholars was the right to pursue their work in full ignorance of its economic underpinnings. Money matters were considered too vulgar and trivial to be understood, let alone handled, by faculty. Such pecuniary concerns befouled the noble quest for knowledge and truth. No doubt, this customary feature of the profession has made it easy for power to shift inexorably to managers and administrators, whose ready grasp of fiscal affairs renders their decisions unassailable by faculty members. Ultimately, the comfort offered by job security in the form of tenure was a recipe for complacency on the part of those who might have resisted the casualization measures, much earlier and more vigorously. Submission to the selfless, disinterested devotions of the scholar's calling almost inevitably led to the sacrifice of younger "apprentices" on the altar of an anachronistic faith.[8]

In the restructured economy of the American higher education system, the net result of this professional ethos has been rapid deprofessionalization, not the revival of Veblen's virtuous ideal of Idle Curiosity.[9] It has contributed, directly or otherwise, to policies of casualization pursued in the name of belt-tightening and aimed at redistributing academic work out of the realm of regular tenure-track lines. Two generations of scholars now form a semipermanent cadre of independent contractors, with little or no prospect of advancement into regular, full-time employment. For most graduate students, as Marc Bousquet points out, the attainment of a degree is not the beginning, but the end of their teaching career; they are not a product, but a by-product, of graduate education; their degree holding is not a credential to practice, but rather it "represents a disqualification from practice."[1] As for regular faculty, their salaries have stagnated against the average wage, and

7. Since 1993 Ross has taught at New York University, where in 2002 the adjunct faculty unionized. In the beginning of this essay (not included here), Ross discusses the successful unionization of part-time jazz faculty at New York's New School and its significance.

8. For analysis in general of these developments see Cary Nelson, ed., *Will Teach for Food: Academic Labor in Crisis* (Minneapolis: University of Minnesota Press, 1997); Randy Martin, ed., *Chalk Lines: The Politics of Work in the Managed University* (Durham, NC: Duke University Press, 1998); Cary Nelson and Stephen Watt, *Academic Keywords: A Devil's Dictionary for Higher Education* (New York: Routledge, 1999); Stanley Aronowitz, *The Knowledge Factory: Dismantling the Corporate University and Creating True Higher Learning* (Boston: Beacon, 2000); Benjamin Johnson, Patrick Kavanagh, and Kevin Mattson, eds., *Steal This University: The Rise of the Corporate University and the Academic Labor Movement* (New York: Routledge, 2003); Sheila Slaughter and Larry Leslie, *Academic Capitalism: Politics, Policies, and the Entrepreneurial University* (Baltimore: Johns Hopkins University Press, 1997); Gary Rhoades, *Managed Professionals: Unionized Faculty and Restructuring Academic Labor* (Albany: SUNY Press, 1998); all of the issues of *Workplace: A Journal for Academic Labor*, and the special issue of *Social Text* 20:1 (Spring 2002) [Ross's note].

9. In an earlier passage not included here, Ross discusses *The Higher Learning in America: A Memorandum on the Conduct of University by Business Men* (1919), by the American economist and social critic Thorstein Veblen (1857–1929), who argues that ideally universities should pursue "Idle Curiosity."

1. Marc Bousquet, "The Waste Product of Graduate Education: Toward a Dictatorship of the Flexible," *Social Text* 20:1 (Spring 2002), 81–104 [Ross's note]. Bousquet (b. 1963), American critic of higher education; for this essay, see below.

they retain control over a profession that can no longer ensure, or control, its means of reproduction. Increasingly, their job security serves as window dressing for a system designed to ensure a continuous flow of cheap, easily replaceable labor.

What forms of self-rationalization motivate adjuncts to contribute so selflessly to a workplace where they are regarded as untouchables? Comparing their organizing efforts to a process of recovery from codependency, Mickie McGee describes how she and her fellow "teachaholics" and "ad-junk-ties" diagnosed the early symptoms of their "high-functioning addiction" as a way of understanding their need to unionize. They came to realize that their self-sacrificing love of teaching, combined with the intoxicating fantasy of universities as cachet-rich havens from the marketplace, had led them into a spiral of addiction and self-exploitation.

McGee recalls "the damage that adjuncting did to my life":

> Somehow, in spite of my adjuncting habit, I'd managed to become pregnant. My partner and I were thrilled. At that point, my teaching habit was so all-consuming that we'd all but given up hopes of ever starting a family. I was expecting and I was delighted. But still I wouldn't give up my teaching habit. Even in the final months of the pregnancy, when my doctor urged me to remain in bed to control pregnancy hypertension, I couldn't do it. Fearful that I'd lose my classes, or seem "unprofessional," I was in the classroom, dizzy with high blood pressure, the week before my daughter was born, not surprisingly by emergency C-section. This was insanity. This was an addict's insanity.[2]

In some respect, the peripatetic life of the part-timer, offering her skills hither and thither (a large majority are female), on one freeway exit after another, is germane to the eccentric work schedule of the traditional academic, who commonly observes no clear boundaries between being on and off the job, and for whom there is often little distinction between paid work and free labor. For the professionally active full-timer, this habitual schedule means that she can take on a range of tasks and obligations that will easily fill out a sixty-hour workweek.[3] For the part-timer, desperate to savor the prestige of being a college teacher at an institution with brand-name cachet, the identity of being a switched-on, round-the-clock thinker, eager to impart knowledge, and in a position to freely extend her mental labor, feeds directly into the psychology of casualized work and underpayment. The industrial worker, by comparison, is not beset by such occupational hazards.

What we see here is the fabrication of a model "flexible employee" out of the cloth of the profession's nonconcentric habits and beliefs, a worker whose customary training in the service ideals and irregular routines of mental labor can be roundly exploited by cost-cutting managers. In this way, we can see how and why fundamentally characteristic features of the academic work style, like those of artists, whom I earlier depicted, conform to the demands of a contingent labor profile. Most fateful of all, perhaps, is

2. Mickie McGee, "Hooked on Higher Education and Other Tales from Adjunct Faculty Organizing," *Social Text* 20:1 (Spring 2002), 61–80 [Ross's note].

3. A recent study of full-time faculty at sixteen midsized colleges and universities found faculty members worked an average of 53.6 hours per week. "Nota bene," *Academe*, July–August 1999, 11 [Ross's note]. "Nota bene": note well (Latin).

the elective ingredient of this recipe for exploitation. Again, I do not mean to suggest that individuals are drawn toward this predicament, nor indeed that they are directly responsible for their own exploitation. For the most part, the patterns of casualization chosen by academic managers have more or less emulated the policy behavior of corporate managers. (Partly, as a result, graduate students have been able to win legal recognition for their perception that they hold the status of an employee.) Nonetheless, I am proposing that academic labor has been casualized in ways that directly complement the habits and compulsions of the academic work mentality, and this has made it all the easier to accomplish. It is in this respect that we can speak, structurally, of a volunteer army of underemployed, low-wage contract labor. As part of its ceaseless search for ways to induct workers in their own exploitation, capital, it might be said, has found the makings of a *self-justifying*, low-wage workforce, at the very heart of the knowledge industries so crucial to its growth and development.

It is no small irony that artists and academics, who would have been borderline, even oddball, features of an older labor landscape, are now more like exemplary figures, occupying frontline positions on the leading edge of neoliberal penetration.[4] With the relocation overseas of core manufacturing, value-adding sectors have become key to First World economies. Artists and academics are value-adding paragons. In the past, their work traditions and privileges have been marked by an impermeability to the mainstream rhythms of industrial process. Now, their customary work life increasingly lies at the center of industrial attention. Indeed, it may come to serve soon as a core industrial personality of the early twenty-first century.

In this respect, it is hardly surprising that higher education has become a battleground for labor. Too many bullish forces in the corporate sector see higher education as a huge, untapped market for selling goods and services on the basis of the prestigious brand names of universities. At the primary and secondary levels, the spoils of the public school system have long been coveted by "education entrepreneurs," touting the "discipline" of the marketplace over the "inefficiency" of the public realm, and normalizing the rhetoric of corporate management—the public as customer, education as competitive product, learning as efficiency tool. Remember Lamar Alexander's declaration, shortly before becoming George Bush's secretary of education, that Burger King and Federal Express should set up schools to show how the private sector would run things.[5] School-business partnerships opened the door not just to total quality management[6] but to every corporate huckster looking for ways to promote and build brand loyalty in the "K–12 marketplace." Tax-supported school vouchers and union-free charter schools[7] were introduced, respectively, as the fast and the slow track toward privatization.

4. Neoliberalism, a revival of the classical liberal economic thought of the 18th and 19th centuries, became dominant in Britain and the United States in the 1980s; it stresses the virtues of the free market.

5. Alex Molnar, *Giving Kids the Business: The Commercialization of America's Schools* (Boulder, CO: Westview Press, 1996), 3 [Ross's note]. Alexander (b. 1940), elected U.S. senator from Tennessee in 2002, served as education secretary (1991–93) under George H. W. Bush (b. 1924; 41st U.S. president, 1989–93).

6. A management strategy that became a corporate buzz phrase in the 1980s.

7. Tax-supported schools that, once the relevant authority grants them a charter to achieve specified goals, are allowed to operate free of many of the regulations that apply to other public schools. "Vouchers": government-issued certificates that can be used to pay for children's education at the schools of their choice.

If your local high school hasn't yet been bought out by McDonald's, many educators there probably already use teaching aids and packets of materials, "donated" by companies, that are crammed with industry propaganda designed to instill product awareness among young consumers: lessons about the history of the potato chip, sponsored by the Snack Food Association, or literacy programs that reward students who reach monthly reading goals with Pizza Hut slices.[8]

In addition to serving as magnets for corporate sponsorship, the economy of scale and the fiscal autonomy enjoyed by many institutions of higher education allow them to function like corporations in their own right. On the labor front, they have adopted many of the same tactics of union-busting, downsizing, and outsourcing, and they hire the same antiunion law firms. In their respective campaigns against graduate-student organizing, NYU, Yale, and Columbia all retained the notorious legal firm Proskauer, Rose, which openly advertises its antiunion services on the company Web site—("With respect to union relationships, we counsel clients how to avoid, and where appropriate, resist union organization among employees"). In addition, the modern, neo-corporate research university is no longer simply a vehicle, as it was in the Cold War period, for socializing the costs of training, research, and technological development on behalf of capital.[9] Far from serving as a money-launderer for the Department of Defense's permanent war economy, the research university has now become a site of capital accumulation in its own right, where the profitability of research and teaching programs and the marketability of learning products is fast coming to the fore as the primary driving force behind academic policy at many institutions. Corporate sponsorship increasingly buys faculty and entire research programs, while the patenting and selling of online courses promises a bonanza of low-cost yields.

In many cases, cost-cutting employment policies are also instruments for establishing administrative control over curricular content. Recently digitized programs of distance learning, for example, were eagerly championed by administrators and state legislators itching to switch their fixed investment in temperamental bodies and impetuous minds over to the sleek machinery of digital pipes with mega bandwidth. In a milieu where education is viewed as a product to be delivered without risk, it is easy to see how the most compelling corporate vision would be that of the wired, tenureless university, where contract hands prepare or administer online courses pumped out to a remote, disaggregated student body. Faculty attempts to establish control over online instruction are not simply struggles to stave off the automation of jobs, they are also frontline battles in the culture wars over the right to determine and influence curriculum.[1]

While the economic payoffs of digitized instruction appear to be self-evident, these technology-assisted programs have less to do with increased efficiency or cost-effectiveness than with control over the workforce and, potentially, the curriculum. The elimination of the social and cultural services ministered by full-time, flesh-and-blood faculty inevitably results in a

8. Molnar, chapter two [Ross's note].

9. See Richard Lewontin's persuasive survey of the growth of the Cold War university in tandem with the defense needs of the national security state, "The Cold War and the Transformation of the Academy," in Noam Chomsky, Richard Lewontin, et al., *The Cold War and the University* (New York: New Press, 1997), 1–34 [Ross's note].

1. David F. Noble, *Digital Diploma Mills: The Automation of Higher Education* (New York: Monthly Review Press, 2001) [Ross's note].

sharp drop in the quality of education. Any cost-benefit analysis of online instruction should have to assess the challenge of delivering a product of comparable quality. Based on this criterion, no one has ever been able to identify clear gains in productivity or cost-effectiveness from the computerization of work. I am referring here to the phenomenon of the productivity paradox, an IT update of the technology trap first identified by business economists in the fledgling years of automation forty years ago. As economist Robert Solow[2] put it, in a famous throwaway line, "You can see the computer age everywhere except in the productivity statistics." "Downstream benefits" have not exactly flowed from the habit of throwing "upstream" money into IT systems, applications, upgrades, management, and maintenance that do not serve the practical needs of businesses or other employee organizations. Promotional hype, technological obsolescence, communication overload, and widespread downtime outages caused by worker sabotage are only some of the factors that inhibit productivity.[3] The economic failure of many online programs (NYU threw away $25 million on its version) was not simply a casualty of the downturn in the Internet economy. It also stemmed from a miscalculation of the economic benefits to be won over and against the high, and therefore unproductive, cost of widespread faculty resistance to the idea of virtual education.

Second Thoughts

With or without its virtual arm, how efficient will the newly restructured academic sectors prove to be in servicing the labor markets of industrialized knowledge? Higher education is in a pivotal position in this regard. Not only is it now a massive anchorage for discounted labor among its own workforce, it is also a training site, responsible for reproducing the discounted labor force among the next generation of knowledge workers. Are educators contributing involuntarily to the problem when they urge students, in pursuing their career goals, to place principles of selflessness (public interest or collective political agency or creative expression) well above the pursuit of material security? In an economy so heavily under the sway of neoliberal business models, is it fair to say that this service ideal invites, if it does not vindicate, the manipulation of inexpensive labor?

Fifteen years ago, this suggestion would have seemed ludicrous. Labor freely offered in the service of some common benefit or mental ideal has always been the informal economic backbone that supports political, cultural, and educational activities in the nonprofit or public-interest sectors. Selfless labor of this sort is also a source of great pleasure. The world that we value most—the world that is not in thrall to market dictates—would not exist without this kind of donated effort. But what happens when some version of this disinterested labor moves, as I have suggested here, from the social margins to core sectors of capital accumulation? When the opportunity to pursue mentally gratifying work becomes a rationale for discounted

2. American economist (b. 1924), in the *New York Times Book Review*, July 12, 1987. IT: information technology.

3. Henry C. Lucas Jr., *Information Technology and the Productivity Paradox: Assessing the Value of the Investment in IT* (New York: Oxford University Press, 1999); John Thorp, *The Information Paradox: Realizing the Business Benefits of Information Technology* (New York: McGraw-Hill, 1999); Leslie Willcocks and Stephanie Lester, eds., *Beyond the IT Productivity Paradox: Assessment Issues* (New York: John Wiley, 1999); Jessica Keyes, *Solving the Productivity Paradox: TQM for Computer Professionals* (New York: McGraw-Hill, 1994) [Ross's note].

labor at the heart of the key knowledge industries, is it not time to rethink some of our bedrock pedagogical values? Does the new landscape of mental labor demand more than the usual call for modernizing the politics of labor? What is to be done with the anxiety generated by such questions?

First and foremost, we must remember that the problem lies not in how people choose to operate within an economy, but rather in how that economy is structured to limit their choices. As ever, the educational system is playing its role in creating and rationalizing the gulf between those in the de-skilled lower tiers, destined for low-wage service sector jobs, and those in the skilled strata, who are tracked into credentialed fractions of the mental labor economy. Currently, managers of national and global economies tell us that education is the only passport to economic mobility or security in a knowledge society. And yet people with advanced degrees are waiting tables, driving taxicabs, or functioning as Microserf[4] temps, while most service jobs in the secondary labor market (with absolutely no prospect of advancement) require little more than basic literacy accompanied by a modest facility in pleasing customers. In the academy, just as in the neoliberal economy as a whole, there is no shortage of work, only a shortage of decent jobs. The accumulation of real skills means little in a system that underproduces real jobs. In the Fordist era[5] of the two-tier labor system, it was the simple presence of trade union power, and not gaps in skills, that separated the decent high-wage jobs in the primary labor markets from those in the low-wage secondary labor markets.

The education system (both at the high school and collegiate levels) is overdeveloped in relation to the needs of an economy that will only provide so many meaningful jobs that pay a living wage. Accordingly, there exists a cruel disconnect between the managerial promises and the opportunities on the ground. While this disparity generates its share of social discontent, the expectations raised by these promises play a crucial role in regulating labor markets. In the sectors of mental work I have looked at here, the prospect of meaningful work provides a rationale for de-professionalizing while helping to maintain a degraded labor market that disciplines and sets the wage floors of those precariously positioned in the core segments immediately above. In addition, and at a time (quite distinct from the Fordist era) when creative gratification is more and more touted as an obligatory feature of the realm of no-collar work, the collective educational capital that once stimulated and supported consumption and leisure time is more and more invested in gray areas of unwaged work that the new cultural economy is creating. For example, Tiziana Terranova has outlined the role that free labor played in creating the Web site infrastructure of digital capitalism and in contributing directly to its development, as in the Open Source model of software improvement, where corporations now take advantage of amateur users to locate bugs and suggest refinements and upgrades.[6] All in all, the creation of the World Wide Web has been the most massive, uncoordinated effort in the history of unwaged work. Education is not, then, wasted, as it appears at

4. That is, a young, low-paid programmer working for Microsoft (or, by extension, for another computing company), a term coined by Douglas Coupland in his novel *Microserfs* (1995).

5. That is, the 1940s–1960s, when the U.S. economy was characterized by mass consumption and mass production, associated with the development of the assembly line by the automobile manufacturer Henry Ford (1863–1947).

6. Tiziana Terranova, "Free Labor: Producing Culture for the Digital Economy," *Social Text*, no. 63 (Spring 2000), 33–58 [Ross's note]. Terranova (b. 1967), Italian sociologist and media theorist.

first sight. Rather, it is being unsystematically converted into un- or under-compensated labor in ways that remain to be adequately charted (just as the hidden costs of unwaged domestic labor of women have sustained the economy for so much longer).

Insofar as we participate in the knowledge economy as scholars, writers, and artists, there now exists an explicit responsibility to recognize the cost of our traditionally cherished beliefs in aesthetic or educational ideals. These ideals come at a price, and managers of the new economy are taking full advantage of our disregard of that price. When the outcome is discounted labor on an industrial scale, our traditions of studied indifference to the world of trade and waged labor can no longer only be savored as expressions of faith in some purer life of the mind, or as charming eccentricities to be deemed objects of tourist interest in bohemia or the ivory tower. Those days are over.

Historically, we have found it too challenging, and professionally limiting, to see ourselves as workers. Academics have often viewed their daily teaching and service obligations as an obligatory, even menial, chore that permits them to pursue the true life of the mind in their research—their "real" work—on sabbatical or in summer breaks. Artists contracted by federal or local government programs such as the Comprehensive Employment and Training Act (CETA—in the 1970s, the biggest public commitment to arts-employment subsidies since the WPA) routinely have made a distinction between what they do for a living in the realm of public and community arts, and their own after-hours work as expressive individuals.[7] Even in the WPA years, many artists who qualified for poor relief refused federal assistance through the artists programs because they were averse to being classed as laborers (while others saw the program as a conspiracy to shut them up by offering full-time work). Writers of all stripes continue to regard part-time commercial work as a vile meal ticket that expedites their true calling.

There are, of course, sound reasons for abiding by such distinctions. Unpopular forms of intellectual, artistic, and political expression cannot and will not thrive unless they are independent of commercial or bureaucratic dictates. But these conditions of independence can no longer be defended stubbornly and solely as a matter of humanistic principle, or as a freestanding right within a civilized society. When capital-intensive industry is concentrated around vast culture trading sectors (copyright is now the U.S.'s single largest export), when media Goliaths feed off their control of intellectual property, and when the new Vested Interests[8] routinely barter discount wages for creative satisfaction on the job, the expressive traditions of mental labor are no longer "ours" simply to claim, not when informal versions of them are daily being bought off and refined into high-octane fuel for the next generation of knowledge factories.

The new labor landscape is now hosting efforts to organize sectors where professional identity has been based, in part, on a sharp indifference to being organized. Campaigns can and should build on the recognition that both artists and educators draw on an intimate and shared experience of the tradi-

7. See Steven Dubin's study of Chicago's artists-in-residence programs funded by the Comprehensive Employment and Training Act (CETA) in the late 1970s, *Bureaucratizing the Muse: Public Funds and the Cultural Worker* (Chicago: University of Chicago Press, 1987) [Ross's note]. In a section of the essay not included here, Ross discusses the Depression-era programs that, through the Work Progress Administration, directly employed jobless artists and writers.

8. An echo of *The Vested Interests and the State of the Industrial Arts* (1919), by Thorstein Veblen.

tions of sacrificial labor.[9] The outcome will help to modernize labor politics in the age of mental labor (the age of the Yale Corporation, the Microserf, and the consolidated push of Time Warner-Bertelsmann-Disney-CNN-Hachette-Paramount-NewsCorp), and it will depend on recognizing the special conditions that apply to pricing wages for thought. We have always known that aesthetics comes at a price, especially for those who do not benefit from the prestige it confers. Now we must learn to recognize that aesthetics is part of a price system, to use a pet phrase of Thorstein Veblen's. No one has really thought this out properly. If we don't, then others, with less to lose and a world of lucrative copyrights to gain, will do it for us.

2000, 2004

9. NVAG, the National Visual Artists Guild, has set up an organizing committee to liaise with the National Writers Guild, the Graphic Artists Guild, UNITE [Union of Needletrades, Industrial, and Textile Employees], the UAW, and the steel workers union [Ross's note].

JANE BENNETT
b. 1957

An early proponent of the new materialism, Jane Bennett is one of a group of cultural theorists and philosophers who, repudiating the linguistic turn of much twentieth-century philosophy and literary theory, have since 2000 taken up the study of objects or "things" as autonomous and independent of human manipulation. Variously referred to as object-oriented ontology or as speculative realism, the new materialism champions a realist philosophy based on objects untethered from discourse and the anthropocentrism of human projects. "I believe it is wrong to deny vitality to nonhuman bodies, forces, and forms," writes Bennett, "and that a careful course of anthropomorphization can help reveal that vitality, even though it resists full translation and exceeds my comprehensive grasp. I believe that encounters with lively matter can chasten my fantasies of human mastery, highlight the common materiality of all that is, expose a wider distribution of agency, and reshape the self and its interests." A political theorist, Bennett has written extensively on the relations between the environment and politics, striving in her published work to counter the disenchantment of modern life by opening up a space for wonder and enchantment, affects that tend to get lost in the rationality that has been the hallmark of literary criticism since the 1980s.

Bennett received a B.A. from Siena College in 1979 and a Ph.D. in political science from the University of Massachusetts in 1986. From 1988 until 2004 she taught at Goucher College. Since 2004 Bennett has been a professor of political science at Johns Hopkins University, and in 2013 she served as director of the School for Criticism and Theory at Cornell University. She has been a fellow of Keble College Oxford (2011), Birkbeck Institute for the Humanities, University of London (2010), University of Nottingham (2007), Australian National University (2000), and the Humanities Research Center, Australian National University (1997). She was a visiting professor at the University of Exeter in 2003. One of the founders of the journal *Theory and Event*, she is currently the editor of *Political Theory: An International Journal of Political Philosophy*.

Bennett is the author of four books. *Unthinking Faith and Enlightenment: Nature and the State in a Post-Hegelian Era* (1987) engages with contemporary debates over the environment and the state. *Thoreau's Nature: Ethics, Politics, and the Wild* (1994) stages a series of dialogues between Thoreau and contemporary theorists to explore his concept of "the Wild," which she defines as an openness to the foreignness of things. *The Enchantment of Modern Life: Attachments, Crossings, and Ethics* (2001) continues this investigation of wonder, attempting to rehabilitate enchantment for a disenchanted modern world. In *Vibrant Matter: A Political Ecology of Things* (2010), from which our selection is drawn, Bennett shifts her attention from the human experience of the world to things themselves. This focus is characteristic of the "new materialism," a phrase that describes the work of a number of philosophers and theorists writing after the turn of the century, including Graham Harman, BRUNO LATOUR, TIMOTHY MORTON, and IAN BOGOST, who share a desire to bring "things-in-themselves" back into philosophical debate to counter the dominance of poststructuralist theories of language and discourse in the last decades of the twentieth century. These theorists share with posthumanists such as DONNA HARAWAY, N. KATHERINE HAYLES, ROSI BRAIDOTTI, and Elizabeth Grosz a desire to decenter the human, and with ecocritics such as Cary Wolfe and ROB NIXON the desire to create more sustainable accounts of the earth to counter environmental depredation.

To understand what is new about the new materialism, it helps to differentiate it from older forms of materialism. KARL MARX posited a material basis for reality, arguing that human consciousness and culture develop out of that material base (the means of production). The materialism of British cultural studies (as championed by RAYMOND WILLIAMS and STUART HALL, for instance) questioned the Marxist claim that the economic base precedes and determines the cultural superstructure, casting the cultural and material as co-constitutive. The new materialists criticize both forms of materialism as "correlationist," a term coined by the philosopher Quentin Meillassoux to refer to systems of thought in which objects have meaning only in relation to human activity and perception.

While all new materialists put objects at the center of their work, they are a diverse lot. Most would agree with Bennett on the "recalcitrance of things" as well as on their "positive, productive power." Rather than understanding objects as "conglomerates of human designs and practices (discourses)," practitioners "highlight the active role of nonhuman materials in public life." Bennett calls these first principles "thing-power." While these tenets are easy enough to articulate, the philosophical debates they engage about the vexed relationships of language to objects, concepts to things, culture to nature, humans to nonhumans, and animate to inanimate have very long and complicated philosophical histories. Bennett revisits discredited forms of vitalism, from the atomism of the Roman poet Lucretius (ca. 94–55 B.C.E.) to the *conatus* that the philosopher BARUCH SPINOZA describes in the seventeenth century as an "active impulsion" or tendency of things to persist to Henry David Thoreau's nineteenth-century concept of the Wild as the "uncanny presence that met him in the Concord woods and atop Mount Ktaadn." She departs from more Heideggerian object-oriented ontologists like Graham Harman, who argues that objects "withdraw," not only from humans but from each other. In such a view, things-in-themselves can be thought but not known, and causation occurs only indirectly. Bennett argues that this way of thinking about objects threatens to "overstate the . . . fixed stability of materiality." She is less interested in objects in and of themselves than in the assemblages they form with other human and nonhuman actants, a distributed form of agency she takes from Latour, as well as from the work of GILLES DELEUZE and FÉLIX GUATTARI. Things act not alone but in assemblages with other things, both human and nonhuman.

In our selection, "The Force of Things," the first chapter of *Vibrant Matter: A Political Ecology of Things*, Bennett lays out her philosophy of "thing-power." Although her primary interest is in relations rather than objects, this essay begins with things as a way to think the "outside" of human experience, "to raise the volume on the vitality of materiality per se." Thing-power, or "vital materialism," attests to the "strange ability" of ordinary things—a collection of debris glimpsed in a storm drain, a strange and strangely animated toy from a Kafka short story, and a legal "thing," a gunpowder residue sampler—"to act as quasi-agents or forces with trajectories, propensities, or tendencies of their own." Objects have the capacity to "animate, to produce effects dramatic and subtle." We are used to thinking that things get done when agents or actors (usually people) act. Bennett takes the concepts of "actant" from Latour and of "operator" from Deleuze: both terms describe any "thing" that modifies something else through its actions. Neither term implies any necessary intention or teleology; both merely describe action. Bennett uses these terms to introduce a concept of distributive agency that does away with clear distinctions between subject and object, actor and acted upon. Actants can be either human or nonhuman; in any given assemblage, more likely than not they are both. Here Bennett is describing what the new materialists call *flat ontology*: all objects equally exist. Those who embrace flat ontology do not claim that there are no differences between humans and nonhuman objects. The point, which Bennett shares with most new materialists, is instead to move away from a perspective "that places humans at the ontological center or hierarchical apex." While she acknowledges critics who argue that decentering the human could have the deleterious effect of objectifying some humans, she maintains that extending the political sphere beyond the human creates the potential to generate new forms of political action and so encourage a less exploitative stance toward the nonhuman world.

But Bennett's argument is not merely ontological; it is epistemological as well. Like other new materialists, she questions whether humans can ever have direct knowledge of things-in-themselves. Concepts are not objects, and "objects do not go into their concepts without leaving a remainder." THEODOR ADORNO's *Negative Dialectics* (1966) offers Bennett a method for imagining this "nonidentity" (what we cannot know of things-in-themselves). It suggests practices that might "cultivate a more careful attentiveness to the out-side" of human experience. For Bennett, however, Adorno falls short of vital materialism, because for him "objects are always 'entwined' with human subjectivity." Bennett recommends revisiting philosophies such as animism, vitalism, and anthropomorphism. "How," she asks, "would political responses to public problems change were we to take seriously the vitality of (non-human) bodies?" To counter the "mechanism" of most accounts of the natural world, she advocates a "strategic anthropomorphism"—which she defines as the idea that human agency has some echoes in nonhuman nature—as a means to counter the "narcissism" of human domination of the natural world.

While it is possible to see the political stakes of Bennett's argument—once myths about human dominance are exploded, we might have a less exploitative attitude toward the natural world—nothing seems further from literature, with its emphasis on language and artistic (i.e., human) intention. What would a literary criticism based on objects look like? Bennett's analysis of Kafka's "The Cares of a Family Man" (1919) gestures toward a literary criticism based in things. Her reading of the protagonist, an old spool of thread, requires a capacious definition of "object" to respond to the criticism that what the story presents is only a representation of an old spool of thread, a linguistic construct. In a flat ontology, however, objects might be corporeal (e.g., bread, beds, and the moon), incorporeal (e.g., dream visions and unicorns), real (e.g., bubbles, hotels, and dolphins), or imaginary (e.g., vampires, grails, and ghosts). Objects in literary texts, then, would have the same existence as objects in the world. But the most promising approach to an object-oriented literary theory begins by replacing a focus on the *meaning* of the text with attention to the *materiality* of the text. In this view, texts are objects that circulate and interact with other objects, including human objects. As such, they create assemblages that act in the world. Here object-oriented literary theory would intersect with the concepts of thinkers such as Marshall McLuhan and

Friedrich Kittler, whose theoretical work begins with the assumption that the physical medium is the message.

Critics of the new materialism point to a troublesome mischaracterization of the "linguistic turn" in literary theory, a tendency to attribute to poststructuralism a categorical distinction privileging culture over nature and language over matter that its adherents—particularly JACQUES DERRIDA—sought to deconstruct. Furthermore, object-oriented ontologies run the risk of treating language, and indeed representation, as if it were transparent, allowing unmediated access to objects. Such an approach ignores not only the materiality of linguistic signs but also the enmeshment of material objects in signification. Another criticism is that the new materialism replaces critique with enchantment, falling into a kind of anthropomorphism that is simply another way of projecting human meaning onto the physical world. Since objects cannot speak for themselves, object-oriented ontologists will speak for them. Finally, although the decentering of the human may focus more attention on the human exploitation of nonhuman entities, the move to a larger geological scale may obscure the injustices that result from humans oppressing other humans, and perhaps even offer an escape from thinking about those intractable forms of inequality based in gender, race, class, or sexuality. Despite these criticisms, *Vibrant Matter* contributes to several important strands in contemporary theory, including discussions of posthumanism, the reconsideration of social constructivism, and the desire to engage in an ecocriticism that ethically challenges our relation to the nonhuman world.

Vibrant Matter: A Political Ecology of Things **Keywords:** Aesthetics, Ethics, Phenomenology, Realism, Subjectivity

From Vibrant Matter: A Political Ecology of Things

Chapter 1. The Force of Things

In the wake of Michel Foucault's death in 1984, there was an explosion of scholarship on the body and its social construction, on the operations of biopower.[1] These genealogical (in the Nietzschean sense) studies exposed the various micropolitical and macropolitical techniques[2] through which the human body was disciplined, normalized, sped up and slowed down, gendered, sexed, nationalized, globalized, rendered disposable, or otherwise composed. The initial insight was to reveal how cultural practices produce what is experienced as the "natural," but many theorists also insisted on the *material recalcitrance* of such cultural productions.[3] Though gender, for example, was a congealed bodily effect of historical norms and repetitions, its status as artifact does *not* imply an easy susceptibility to

1. Techniques for achieving the subjugations of bodies and the control of populations described by FOUCAULT (1926–1984), French poststructuralist philosopher and historian of ideas [editor's note—except as indicated, all notes are Bennett's].
2. The macropolitical pertains to large-scale political structures and forces; the micropolitical, smaller-scale interventions at the level of individuals and groups. Foucault is indebted to the idea of genealogy as a method of analysis developed by the German philosopher FRIEDRICH NIETZSCHE (1844–1900) [editor's note].
3. There is too much good work in feminist theory, queer studies, and cultural studies to cite here. The three volumes of Michael Feher, Ramona Naddaff, and Nadia Tazi, eds., *Fragments for a History of the Human Body*, 3 vols. (New York: Zone, 1989), offer one map of the terrain. See also Momin Rahman and Anne Witz, "What Really Matters? The Elusive Quality of the Material in Feminist Thought," *Feminist Theory* 4.3 (2003): 243–61; JUDITH BUTLER, *Bodies That Matter: On the Discursive Limits of "Sex"* (New York: Routledge, 1993); Judith Butler, "Merely Cultural," *New Left Review*, no. 227 (1998): 33–44; Wendy Brown, *States of Injury: Power and Freedom in Late Modernity* (Princeton: Princeton University Press, 1995); Kathy E. Ferguson, *Man Question: Visions of Subjectivity in Feminist Theory* (Berkeley: University of California Press, 1993); and Moira Gatens, *Imaginary Bodies: Ethics, Power, and Corporeality* (New York: Routledge, 1996).

human understanding, reform, or control. The point was that cultural forms are themselves powerful, material assemblages with *resistant force*.

In what follows, I, too, will feature the negative power or recalcitrance of things. But I will also seek to highlight a positive, productive power of their own. And, instead of focusing on collectives conceived primarily as conglomerates of *human* designs and practices ("discourse"), I will highlight the active role of *nonhuman* materials in public life. In short, I will try to give voice to a thing-power. As W. J. T. Mitchell notes, "objects are the way things appear to a subject—that is, with a name, an identity, a gestalt or stereotypical template. . . . Things, on the other hand, . . . [signal] the moment when the object becomes the Other, when the sardine can looks back, when the mute idol speaks, when the subject experiences the object as uncanny and feels the need for what Foucault calls 'a metaphysics of the object, or, more exactly, a metaphysics of that never objectifiable depth from which objects rise up toward our superficial knowledge.'"[4]

THING-POWER, OR THE OUT-SIDE

Spinoza ascribes to bodies a peculiar vitality: "Each thing [*res*], as far as it can by its own power, strives [*conatur*] to persevere in its own being."[5] *Conatus* names an "active impulsion" or trending tendency to persist.[6] Although Spinoza distinguishes the human body from other bodies by noting that its "virtue" consists in "nothing other than to live by the guidance of reason,"[7] every nonhuman body shares with every human body a conative nature (and thus a "virtue" appropriate to its material configuration). Conatus names a power present in *every* body: "Any thing whatsoever, whether it be more perfect or less perfect, will always be able to persist in existing with that same force whereby it begins to exist, so that in this respect all things are equal."[8] Even a falling stone, writes Spinoza, "is endeavoring, as far as in it lies, to continue in its motion."[9] As Nancy Levene notes, "Spinoza continually stresses this continuity between human and other beings," for "not only do human beings not form a separate imperium unto themselves; they do not even command the imperium, nature, of which they are a part."[1]

4. W. J. T. Mitchell, *What Do Pictures Want? The Lives and Loves of Images* (Chicago: University of Chicago Press, 2005), 156–57.

5. Baruch Spinoza, *Ethics: Treatise on the Emendation of the Intellect, and Selected Letters*, trans. Samuel Shirley, ed. Seymour Feldman (Indianapolis: Hackett, 1992), pt. 3, proposition 6. [SPINOZA (1632–1677), Jewish-born Dutch philosopher; an important early rationalist, he wrote in Latin—editor's note.]

6. Freya Mathews, *For Love of Matter: A Contemporary Panpsychism* (Albany: State University of New York, 2003), 48.

7. Spinoza, *Ethics*, pt. 4, proposition 37, scholium 1.

8. Ibid., 4, preface.

9. Spinoza links, in this famous letter, his theory of conatus to a critique of the notion of human free will: "Now this stone, since it is conscious only of its endeavor [conatus] and is not at all indifferent, will surely think that it is completely free, and that it continues in motion for no other reason than it so wishes. This, then, is that human freedom which all men boast of possessing, and which consists solely in this, that men are conscious of their desire and unaware of the causes by which they are determined" (Spinoza, *The Letters*, trans. Samuel Shirley [Indianapolis: Hackett, 1995], epistle 58). Hasana Sharp argues that the analogy between humans and stones "is not as hyperbolic as it seems at first glance. For Spinoza, all beings, including stones, . . . include a power of thinking that corresponds exactly to the power of their bodies to be disposed in different ways, to act and be acted upon. . . . Likewise every being, to the extent that it preserves its integrity amidst infinitely many other beings, as a stone surely does, is endowed with . . . a desire to . . . preserve and enhance its life to the extent that its nature allows" (Hasana Sharp, "The Force of Ideas in Spinoza," *Political Theory* 35, no. 6 [2007], 740).

1. Nancy K. Levene, *Spinoza's Revelation: Religion, Democracy, and Reason* (Cambridge: Cambridge University Press, 2004), 3. Yitzhak Melamed goes further to say that "since the doctrine of the *conatus* . . . provide[s] the foundations for Spinoza's moral theory, it seems likely that we could even construct a moral theory for hippopotamuses and rocks" (Yitzhak Melamed, "Spinoza's Anti-Humanism," *The Rationalists*, ed. C. Fraenkel, D. Perinetti, and J. Smith [New York: Kluwer, 2011], 161 n59).

The idea of thing-power bears a family resemblance to Spinoza's conatus, as well as to what Henry David Thoreau called the Wild or that uncanny presence that met him in the Concord woods and atop Mount Ktaadn[2] and also resided in/as that monster called the railroad and that alien called his Genius. Wildness was a not-quite-human force that addled and altered human and other bodies. It named an irreducibly strange dimension of matter, an *out-side*. Thing-power is also kin to what Hent de Vries, in the context of political theology, called "the absolute" or that "intangible and imponderable" recalcitrance.[3] Though the absolute is often equated with God, especially in theologies emphasizing divine omnipotence or radical alterity, de Vries defines it more open-endedly as "that which tends to loosen its ties to existing contexts."[4] This definition makes sense when we look at the etymology of *absolute*: *ab* (off) + *solver* (to loosen). The absolute is that which is *loosened off* and on the loose. When, for example, a Catholic priest performs the act of ab-solution, he is the vehicle of a divine agency that loosens sins from their attachment to a particular soul: sins now stand apart, displaced foreigners living a strange, impersonal life of their own. When de Vries speaks of the absolute, he thus tries to point to what no speaker could possibly see, that is, a some-thing that is not an object of knowledge, that is detached or radically free from representation, and thus no-thing at all. Nothing but the force or effectivity of the detachment, that is.

De Vries's notion of the absolute, like the thing-power I will seek to express, seeks to acknowledge that which refuses to dissolve completely into the milieu of human knowledge. But there is also a difference in emphasis. De Vries conceives this exteriority, this out-side, primarily as an epistemological limit: in the presence of the absolute, we cannot *know*. It is from human thinking that the absolute has detached; the absolute names the limits of *intelligibility*. De Vries's formulations thus give priority to humans as knowing bodies, while tending to overlook things and what *they* can do. The notion of thing-power aims instead to attend to the it as actant; I will try, impossibly, to name the moment of independence (from subjectivity) possessed by things, a moment that must be there, since things do in fact affect other bodies, enhancing or weakening their power. I will shift from the language of epistemology to that of ontology, from a focus on an elusive recalcitrance hovering between immanence and transcendence (the absolute) to an active, earthy, not-quite-human capaciousness (vibrant matter). I will try to give voice to a vitality intrinsic to materiality, in the process absolving matter from its long history of attachment to automatism or mechanism.[5]

The strangely vital things that will rise up to meet us in this chapter—a dead rat, a plastic cap, a spool of thread—are characters in a speculative

2. Katahdin, the highest mountain in Maine. The American poet and essayist Thoreau (1817–1862) climbed it in 1840, recording his ascent in "Ktaadn and the Maine Woods" (1848; revised and expanded in *The Maine Woods*, 1864). Concord woods: where Thoreau lived for two years by the shore of Walden Pond, as he describes in *Walden, or Life in the Woods* (1854) [editor's note].

3. Hent de Vries, introduction to *Political Theologies: Public Religions in a Post-secular World*, ed. Hent de Vries and Lawrence Sullivan, 1–88 (New York: Fordham University Press, 2006), 42. [De Vries (b. 1958), Dutch philosopher—editor's note.]

4. Ibid., 6.

5. De Vries seems to affirm this association when he wonders whether Baruch Spinoza's picture of interacting, conatus-driven *bodies* could possibly account for the creative emergence of the new: "It would seem that excess, gift, the event . . . have no place here" (de Vries, introduction to *Political Theologies*, 22). Why? Because the only plausible locus of creativity is, for de Vries, one that is "quasi-spiritual," hence Spinoza's second attribute of God/Nature, that is, *thought* or ideas. But what if materiality itself harbors creative vitality?

onto-story.[6] The tale hazards an account of materiality, even though it is both too alien and too close to see clearly and even though linguistic means prove inadequate to the task. The story will highlight the extent to which human being and thinghood overlap, the extent to which the us and the it slip-slide into each other. One moral of the story is that we are also nonhuman and that things, too, are vital players in the world. The hope is that the story will enhance receptivity to the impersonal life that surrounds and infuses us, will generate a more subtle awareness of the complicated web of dissonant connections between bodies, and will enable wiser interventions into that ecology.

THING-POWER I: DEBRIS

On a sunny Tuesday morning on 4 June in the grate over the storm drain to the Chesapeake Bay in front of Sam's Bagels on Cold Spring Lane in Baltimore, there was:

one large men's black plastic work glove
one dense mat of oak pollen
one unblemished dead rat
one white plastic bottle cap
one smooth stick of wood

Glove, pollen, rat, cap, stick. As I encountered these items, they shimmied back and forth between debris and thing—between, on the one hand, stuff to ignore, except insofar as it betokened human activity (the workman's efforts, the litterer's toss, the rat-poisoner's success), and, on the other hand, stuff that commanded attention in its own right, as existents in excess of their association with human meanings, habits, or projects. In the second moment, stuff exhibited its thing-power: it issued a call, even if I did not quite understand what it was saying. At the very least, it provoked affects in me: I was repelled by the dead (or was it merely sleeping?) rat and dismayed by the litter, but I also felt something else: a nameless awareness of the impossible singularity of *that* rat, *that* configuration of pollen, *that* otherwise utterly banal, mass-produced plastic water-bottle cap.

I was struck by what Stephen Jay Gould called the "excruciating complexity and intractability" of nonhuman bodies,[7] but, in being *struck*, I realized that the capacity of these bodies was not restricted to a passive "intractability" but also included the ability to make things happen, to produce effects. When the materiality of the glove, the rat, the pollen, the bottle cap, and the stick started to shimmer and spark, it was in part because of the contingent tableau that they formed with each other, with the street, with the weather that morning, with me. For had the sun not glinted on the black glove, I might not have seen the rat; had the rat not been there, I might not have noted the bottle cap, and so on. But they *were* all there just as they were, and so I caught a glimpse of an energetic vitality inside each of these things, things that I generally conceived as inert. In this assemblage, *objects*

6. That is, a story of ontology, the branch of philosophy concerned with the nature of being [editor's note].
7. Stephen J. Gould, *Structure of Evolutionary Theory* (Cambridge: Harvard University Press, 2002), 1338. [Gould (1941–2002), American evolutionary biologist and science writer—editor's note.]

appeared as *things*, that is, as vivid entities not entirely reducible to the contexts in which (human) subjects set them, never entirely exhausted by their semiotics. In my encounter with the gutter on Cold Spring Lane, I glimpsed a culture of things irreducible to the culture of objects.[8] I achieved, for a moment, what Thoreau had made his life's goal: to be able, as Thomas Dumm puts it, "to be surprised by what we see."[9]

This window onto an eccentric out-side was made possible by the fortuity of that particular assemblage, but also by a certain anticipatory readiness on my in-side, by a perceptual style open to the appearance of thing-power. For I came on the glove-pollen-rat-cap-stick with Thoreau in my head, who had encouraged me to practice "the discipline of looking always at what is to be seen"; with Spinoza's claim that all things are "animate, albeit in different degrees"; and with Maurice Merleau-Ponty, whose *Phenomenology of Perception* had disclosed for me "an immanent or incipient significance in the living body [which] extends, . . . to the whole sensible world" and which had shown me how "our gaze, prompted by the experience of our own body, will discover in all other 'objects' the miracle of expression."[1]

As I have already noted, the items on the ground that day were vibratory—at one moment disclosing themselves as dead stuff and at the next as live presence: junk, then claimant; inert matter, then live wire. It hit me then in a visceral way how American materialism, which requires buying ever-increasing numbers of products purchased in ever-shorter cycles, is *anti*materiality.[2] The sheer volume of commodities, and the hyperconsumptive necessity of junking them to make room for new ones, conceals the vitality of matter. In *The Meadowlands*, a late twentieth-century, Thoreauian travelogue of the New Jersey garbage hills outside Manhattan, Robert Sullivan describes the vitality that persists even in trash:

> The . . . garbage hills are alive. . . . there are billions of microscopic organisms thriving underground in dark, oxygen-free communities. . . . After having ingested the tiniest portion of leftover New Jersey or New York, these cells then exhale huge underground plumes of carbon dioxide and of warm moist methane, giant stillborn tropical winds that seep through the ground to feed the Meadlowlands' fires, or creep up into the atmosphere, where they eat away at the . . . ozone. . . . One afternoon I . . . walked along the edge of a garbage hill, a forty-foot drumlin of compacted trash that owed its topography to the waste of

8. On the effectivity of trash, see the fascinating Tim Edensor, "Waste Matter: The Debris of Industrial Ruins and the Disordering of the Material World," *Journal of Material Culture* 10, no. 3 (2005): 311–32; and Gay Hawkins, *The Ethics of Waste: How We Relate to Rubbish* (Sydney: University of New South Wales Press, 2006).

9. See Thomas L. Dumm, *Politics of the Ordinary* (New York: New York University Press, 1999), 7, for a subtle reckoning with the "obscure power of the ordinary." My attempt to speak on behalf of "things" is a companion project to Dumm's attempt to mine the ordinary as a potential site of resistance to conventional and normalizing practices.

1. Thoreau, *The Writings of Henry David Thoreau*, ed. J. Lyndon Shanley (Princeton: Princeton University Press, 1973), 111 (Thoreau trained his gaze on things with the faith that "the perception of surfaces will always have the effect of miracle to a sane sense" [Thoreau, *The Journal of Henry David Thoreau*, vol. 2, ed. Bradford Torrey and Francis H. Allen (New York: Houghton Mifflin, 1949), 313]); Spinoza, *Ethics*, pt. 2, proposition 13, scholium 72; Maurice Merleau-Ponty, *The Phenomenology of Perception*, trans. Colin Smith (New York: Routledge and Kegan Paul, 1981), 197. [Merleau-Ponty (1908–1961), French philosopher of phenomenology, whose work focused primarily on the body as a site of knowledge—editor's note.]

2. For a good analysis of the implications of the trash-and-waste culture for democracy, see John Buell and Tom DeLuca, *Sustainable Democracy: Individuality and the Politics of the Environment* (Thousand Oaks, Calif.: Sage, 1996).

> the city of Newark. . . . There had been rain the night before, so it wasn't long before I found a little leachate seep, a black ooze trickling down the slope of the hill, an espresso of refuse. In a few hours, this stream would find its way down into the . . . groundwater of the Meadowlands; it would mingle with toxic streams. . . . But in this moment, here at its birth, . . . this little seep was pure pollution, a pristine stew of oil and grease, of cyanide and arsenic, of cadmium, chromium, copper, lead, nickel, silver, mercury, and zinc. I touched this fluid—my fingertip was a bluish caramel color—and it was warm and fresh. A few yards away, where the stream collected into a benzene-scented pool, a mallard swam alone.[3]

Sullivan reminds us that a vital materiality can never really be thrown "away," for it continues its activities even as a discarded or unwanted commodity. For Sullivan that day, as for me on that June morning, thing-power rose from a pile of trash. Not Flower Power, or Black Power, or Girl Power,[4] but *Thing-Power*: the curious ability of inanimate things to animate, to act, to produce effects dramatic and subtle.

THING-POWER II: ODRADEK'S NONORGANIC LIFE

A dead rat, some oak pollen, and a stick of wood stopped me in my tracks. But so did the plastic glove and the bottle cap: thing-power arises from bodies inorganic as well as organic. In support of this contention, Manuel De Landa notes how even inorganic matter can "self-organize":

> Inorganic matter-energy has a wider range of alternatives for the generation of structure than just simple phase transitions. . . . In other words, even the humblest forms of matter and energy have the potential for *self-organization* beyond the relatively simple type involved in the creation of crystals. There are, for instance, those coherent waves called solitons which form in many different types of materials, ranging from ocean waters (where they are called tsunamis) to lasers. Then there are . . . stable states (or attractors), which can sustain coherent cyclic activity. . . . Finally, and unlike the previous examples of nonlinear self-organization where true innovation cannot occur, there [are] . . . the different combinations into which entities derived from the previous processes (crystals, coherent pulses, cyclic patterns) may enter. When put together, these forms of spontaneous structural generation suggest that inorganic matter is much more variable and creative than we ever imagined. And this insight into matter's inherent creativity needs to be fully incorporated into our new materialist philosophies.[5]

I will in chapter 4 try to wrestle philosophically with the idea of impersonal or nonorganic life, but here I would like to draw attention to a literary

3. Robert Sullivan, *Meadowlands: Wilderness Adventures on the Edge of a City* (New York: Doubleday, 1998), 96–97.
4. Slogans of different U.S. groups: "Flower Power" was associated with nonviolent protesters against the Vietnam War and with the counterculture in the mid- and late 1960s; "Black Power" emphasized racial pride and self-determination among African Americans in the late 1960s and early 1970s; and "Girl Power," celebrating female empowerment, began in punk culture in the early 1990s and spread to wider popular culture over the next decade [editor's note].
5. Manuel De Landa, *A Thousand Years of Nonlinear History* (New York: Zone, 1997), 16.

dramatization of this idea: to Odradek, the protagonist of Franz Kafka's[6] short story "Cares of a Family Man." Odradek is a spool of thread who/that can run and laugh; this animate wood exercises an impersonal form of vitality. De Landa speaks of a "spontaneous structural generation" that happens, for example, when chemical systems at far-from-equilibrium states inexplicably choose one path of development rather than another. Like these systems, the material configuration that is Odradek straddles the line between inert matter and vital life.

For this reason Kafka's narrator has trouble assigning Odradek to an ontological category. Is Odradek a cultural artifact, a tool of some sort? Perhaps, but if so, its purpose is obscure: "It looks like a flat star-shaped spool of thread, and indeed it does seem to have thread wound upon it; to be sure, these are only old, broken-off bits of thread, knotted and tangled together, of the most varied sorts and colors. . . . One is tempted to believe that the creature once had some sort of intelligible shape and is now only a broken-down remnant. Yet this does not seem to be the case; . . . nowhere is there an unfinished or unbroken surface to suggest anything of the kind: the whole thing looks senseless enough, but in its own way perfectly finished."[7]

Or perhaps Odradek is more a subject than an object—an organic creature, a little person? But if so, his/her/its embodiment seems rather unnatural: from the center of Odradek's star protrudes a small wooden crossbar, and "by means of this latter rod . . . and one of the points of the star . . . , the whole thing can stand upright as if on two legs."[8]

On the one hand, like an active organism, Odradek appears to move deliberately (he is "extraordinarily nimble") and to speak intelligibly: "He lurks by turns in the garret, the stairway, the lobbies, the entrance hall. Often for months on end he is not to be seen; then he has presumably moved into other houses; but he always comes faithfully back to our house again. Many a time when you go out of the door and he happens just to be leaning directly beneath you against the banisters you feel inclined to speak to him. Of course, you put no difficult questions to him, you treat him—he is so diminutive that you cannot help it—rather like a child. 'Well, what's your name?' you ask him. 'Odradek,' he says. 'And where do you live?' 'No fixed abode,' he says and laughs." And yet, on the other hand, like an inanimate object, Odradek produced a so-called laughter that "has no lungs behind it" and "sounds rather like the rustling of fallen leaves. And that is usually the end of the conversation. Even these answers are not always forthcoming; often he stays mute for a long time, as wooden as his appearance."[9]

Wooden yet lively, verbal yet vegetal, alive yet inert, Odradek is ontologically multiple.[1] He/it is a vital materiality and exhibits what Gilles Deleuze has described as the persistent "hint of the animate in plants, and of the vegetable in animals."[2] The late-nineteenth-century Russian scientist Vladimir Ivanovich Vernadsky, who also refused any sharp distinction

6. Austrian writer who lived most of his life in Prague and wrote in German (1883–1924); "Cares of a Family Man" was written between 1914 and 1917 and first published in 1919 [editor's note].

7. Kafka, "Cares of a Family Man," in *Complete Stories*, ed. Nahum N. Glatzer (New York: Schocken, 1971), 428.

8. Ibid.

9. Ibid.

1. That is, multiple in forms of being [editor's note].

2. GILLES DELEUZE, *Bergsonism*, trans. Hugh Tomlinson and Barbara Habberjam (New York: Zone, 1991), 95.

between life and matter, defined organisms as "special, distributed forms of the common mineral, water. . . . Emphasizing the continuity of watery life and rocks, such as that evident in coal or fossil limestone reefs, Vernadsky noted how these apparently inert strata are 'traces of bygone biospheres.'"[3] Odradek exposes this continuity of watery life and rocks; he/it brings to the fore the becoming of things.

THING-POWER III: LEGAL ACTANTS

I may have met a relative of Odradek while serving on a jury, again in Baltimore, for a man on trial for attempted homicide. It was a small glass vial with an adhesive-covered metal lid: the Gunpowder Residue Sampler. This object/witness had been dabbed on the accused's hand hours after the shooting and now offered to the jury its microscopic evidence that the hand had either fired a gun or been within three feet of a gun firing. Expert witnesses showed the sampler to the jury several times, and with each appearance it exercised more force, until it became vital to the verdict. This composite of glass, skin cells, glue, words, laws, metals, and human emotions had become an actant. *Actant,* recall, is Bruno Latour's term for a source of action; an actant can be human or not, or, most likely, a combination of both. Latour defines it as "something that acts or to which activity is granted by others. It implies no special motivation of human individual actors, nor of humans in general."[4] An actant is neither an object nor a subject but an "intervener,"[5] akin to the Deleuzean "quasi-causal operator."[6] An operator is that which, by virtue of its particular location in an assemblage and the fortuity of being in the right place at the right time, makes the difference, makes things happen, becomes the decisive force catalyzing an event.

Actant and *operator* are substitute words for what in a more subject-centered vocabulary are called agents. Agentic capacity is now seen as differentially distributed across a wider range of ontological types. This idea is also expressed in the notion of "deodand," a figure of English law from about 1200 until it was abolished in 1846. In cases of accidental death or injury to a human, the nonhuman actant, for example, the carving knife that fell into human flesh or the carriage that trampled the leg of a pedestrian—became deodand (literally, "that which must be given to God"). In recognition of *its* peculiar efficacy (a power that is less masterful than agency but more active than recalcitrance), the deodand, a materiality "suspended between human and thing,"[7] was surrendered to the crown to be used (or sold) to compensate for the harm done. According to William Pietz, "any culture must establish some procedure of compensation, expiation, or

3. Lynn Margulis and Dorion Sagan, *What Is Life?* (Berkeley: University of California Press, 2000), 50.
4. BRUNO LATOUR, "On Actor-Network Theory: A Few Clarifications," *Soziale Welt* 47, no. 4 (1996): 369–81.
5. Latour, *The Politics of Nature: How to Bring the Sciences into Democracy*, trans. Catherine Porter (Cambridge: Harvard University Press, 2004), 75.
6. Manuel De Landa, *Intensive Science and Virtual Philosophy* (London: Continuum, 2002), 123. [De Landa (b. 1952), Mexican-born philosopher and artist—editor's note.]
7. Daniel Tiffany, "Lyric Substance: On Riddles, Materialism, and Poetic Obscurity," *Critical Inquiry* 28, no. 1 (2001): 74. Tiffany draws an analogy between riddles and materiality per se: both are suspended between subject and object and engage in "transubstantiations" from the organic to the inorganic and from the earthly to the divine. In developing his materialism out of an analysis of literary forms, Tiffany challenges the long-standing norm that regards science as "the sole arbiter in the determination of matter" (75). He wants to pick "the lock that currently bars the literary critic from addressing the problem of material substance" (77).

punishment to settle the debt created by unintended human deaths whose direct cause is not a morally accountable person, but a nonhuman material object. This was the issue thematized in public discourse by . . . the law of deodand."[8]

There are of course differences between the knife that impales and the man impaled, between the technician who dabs the sampler and the sampler, between the array of items in the gutter of Cold Spring Lane and me, the narrator of their vitality. But I agree with John Frow that these differences need "to be flattened, read horizontally as a juxtaposition rather than vertically as a hierarchy of being. It's a feature of our world that we can and do distinguish . . . things from persons. But the sort of world we live in makes it constantly possible for these two sets of kinds to exchange properties."[9] And to note this fact explicitly, which is also to begin to *experience* the relationship between persons and other materialities more horizontally, is to take a step toward a more ecological sensibility.

THING-POWER IV: WALKING, TALKING MINERALS

Odradek, a gunpowder residue sampler, and some junk on the street can be fascinating to people and can thus seem to come alive. But is this evanescence a property of the stuff or of people? Was the thing-power of the debris I encountered but a function of the subjective and intersubjective connotations, memories, and affects that had accumulated around my ideas of these items? Was the real agent of my temporary immobilization on the street that day *humanity*, that is, the cultural meanings of "rat," "plastic," and "wood" in conjunction with my own idiosyncratic biography? It could be. But what if the swarming activity inside my head was *itself* an instance of the vital materiality that also constituted the trash?

I have been trying to raise the volume on the vitality of materiality per se, pursuing this task so far by focusing on nonhuman bodies, by, that is, depicting them as actants rather than as objects. But the case for matter as active needs also to readjust the status of human actants: not by denying humanity's awesome, awful powers, but by presenting these powers as evidence of our own constitution as vital materiality. In other words, human power is itself a kind of thing-power. At one level this claim is uncontroversial: it is easy to acknowledge that humans are composed of various material parts (the minerality of our bones, or the metal of our blood, or the electricity of our neurons). But it is more challenging to conceive of these materials as lively and self-organizing,[1] rather than as passive or mechanical means under the direction of something nonmaterial, that is, an active soul or mind.

Perhaps the claim to a vitality intrinsic to matter itself becomes more plausible if one takes a long view of time. If one adopts the perspective of evolutionary rather than biographical time, for example, a mineral efficacy becomes visible. Here is De Landa's account of the emergence of our bones: "Soft tissue (gels and aerosols, muscle and nerve) reigned supreme until

8. William Pietz, "Death of the Deodand: Accursed Objects and the Money Value of Human Life," "The Abject," ed. Francesco Pellizzi, special issue, *Res*, no. 31 (1997): 97–108.

9. John Frow, "A Pebble, a Camera, a Man Who Turns into a Telegraph Pole," *Critical Inquiry* 28, no. 1 (2001): 283.

1. Creating order in a disorganized system out of the interactions of smaller component parts, as in crystallization or as in animals' swarming (a term from the sciences) [editor's note].

5000 million years ago. At that point, some of the conglomerations of fleshy matter-energy that made up life underwent a sudden *mineralization*, and a new material for constructing living creatures emerged: bone. It is almost as if the mineral world that had served as a substratum for the emergence of biological creatures was reasserting itself."[2] Mineralization names the creative agency by which bone was produced, and bones then "made new forms of movement control possible among animals, freeing them from many constraints and literally setting them into motion to conquer every available niche in the air, in water, and on land."[3] In the long and slow time of evolution, then, mineral material appears as the mover and shaker, the active power, and the human beings, with their much-lauded capacity for self-directed action, appear as *its* product.[4] Vernadsky seconds this view in his description of humankind as a particularly potent mix of minerals: "What struck [Vernadsky] most was that the material of Earth's crust has been packaged into myriad moving beings whose reproduction and growth build and break down matter on a global scale. People, for example, redistribute and concentrate oxygen . . . and other elements of Earth's crust into two-legged, upright forms that have an amazing propensity to wander across, dig into and in countless other ways alter Earth's surface. *We are walking, talking minerals*."[5]

Kafka, De Landa, and Vernadsky suggest that human individuals are themselves composed of vital materials, that our powers are thing-power. These vital materialists do not claim that there are no differences between humans and bones, only that there is no necessity to describe these differences in a way that places humans at the ontological center or hierarchical apex. Humanity can be distinguished, instead, as Jean-François Lyotard suggests, as a *particularly rich and complex* collection of materials: "Humankind is taken for a complex material system; consciousness, for an effect of language; and language for a highly complex material system."[6] Richard Rorty similarly defines humans as very complex animals, rather than as animals "with an extra added ingredient called 'intellect' or 'the rational soul.'"[7]

The fear is that in failing to affirm human uniqueness, such views authorize the treatment of people as mere things; in other words, that a strong distinction between subjects and objects is needed to prevent the instrumentalization of humans. Yes, such critics continue, objects possess a certain power of action (as when bacteria or pharmaceuticals enact hostile or symbiotic projects inside the human body), and yes, some subject-on-subject objectifications are permissible (as when persons consent to use and be used as a means to sexual pleasure), but the *ontological* divide between persons and things must remain lest one have no *moral* grounds for privileging man over germ or for condemning pernicious forms of human-on-human instrumentalization (as when powerful humans exploit illegal, poor, young, or otherwise weaker humans).

2. De Landa, *A Thousand Years of Nonlinear History*, 26; my emphasis.
3. Ibid., 26–27.
4. Although, as I will argue in chapter 2, it is more accurate to say that this efficacy belongs less to minerals alone than to the combined activities of a variety of bodies and forces acting as an agentic assemblage.
5. Margulis and Sagan, *What Is Life?*, 49; my emphasis.
6. Jean-François Lyotard, *Postmodern Fables*, trans. Georges van den Abbeele (Minneapolis: University of Minnesota Press, 1997), 98. [LYOTARD (1924–1998), French postmodernist philosopher—editor's note.]
7. Richard Rorty, *Rorty and Pragmatism: The Philosopher Responds to His Critics*, ed. Herman J. Saatkamp Jr. (Nashville, Tenn.: Vanderbilt University Press, 1995), 199. [Rorty (1931–2007), American pragmatist philosopher—editor's note.]

How can the vital materialist respond to this important concern? First, by acknowledging that the framework of subject versus object has indeed at times worked to prevent or ameliorate human suffering and to promote human happiness or well-being. Second, by noting that its successes come at the price of an instrumentalization of nonhuman nature that can itself be unethical and can itself undermine long-term human interests. Third, by pointing out that the Kantian imperative to treat humanity always as an end-in-itself and never merely as a means[8] does not have a stellar record of success in preventing human suffering or promoting human well-being: it is important to raise the question of its actual, historical efficacy in order to open up space for forms of ethical practice that do not rely upon the image of an intrinsically *hierarchical* order of things. Here the materialist speaks of promoting healthy and enabling instrumentalizations, rather than of treating people as ends-in-themselves, because to face up to the compound nature of the human self is to find it difficult even to make sense of the notion of a single end-in-itself. What instead appears is a swarm of competing ends being pursued simultaneously in each individual, some of which are healthy to the whole, some of which are not. Here the vital materialist, taking a cue from Nietzsche's and Spinoza's ethics, favors physiological over moral descriptors because she fears that moralism can itself become a source of unnecessary human suffering.[9]

We are now in a better position to name that other way to promote human health and happiness: *to raise the status of the materiality of which we are composed.* Each human is a heterogeneous compound of wonderfully vibrant, dangerously vibrant, matter. If matter itself is lively, then not only is the difference between subjects and objects minimized, but the status of the shared materiality of all things is elevated. All bodies become more than mere objects, as the thing-powers of resistance and protean agency are brought into sharper relief. Vital materialism would thus set up a kind of safety net for those humans who are now, in a world where Kantian morality is the standard, routinely made to suffer because they do not conform to a particular (Euro-American, bourgeois, theocentric, or other) model of personhood. The ethical aim becomes to distribute value more generously, to bodies as such. Such a newfound attentiveness to matter and its powers will not solve the problem of human exploitation or oppression, but it can inspire a greater sense of the extent to which all bodies are kin in the sense of inextricably enmeshed in a dense network of relations. And in a knotted world of vibrant matter, to harm one section of the web may very well be to harm oneself. Such an enlightened or expanded notion of self-interest is *good for humans.* As I will argue further in chapter 8, a vital materialism does not reject self-interest as a motivation for ethical behavior, though it does seek to cultivate a broader definition of self and of interest.

8. In his *Groundwork of the Metaphysics of Morals* (1785), the German philosopher IMMANUEL KANT (1724–1804) declared as a fundamental moral principle that humanity, whether in one's own person or in any other, must never be treated simply as a means to an end [editor's note].

9. I will also argue, at the end of chapter 2, that the efficacy of moralism in addressing social problems is overrated. The antimoralism that is one of the implications of a vital materialism is a dangerous game to play, and not one I wish to play out to its logical extreme. I aim not to eliminate the practice of moral judgment but to increase the friction against the moralistic reflex.

THING-POWER V: THING-POWER AND ADORNO'S NONIDENTITY

But perhaps the very idea of thing-power or vibrant matter claims too much: to know more than it is possible to know. Or, to put the criticism in Theodor Adorno's[1] terms, does it exemplify the violent hubris of Western philosophy, a tradition that has consistently failed to mind the gap between concept and reality, object and thing? For Adorno this gap is ineradicable, and the most that can be said with confidence about the thing is that it eludes capture by the concept, that there is always a "nonidentity" between it and any representation. And yet, as I shall argue, even Adorno continues to seek a way to access—however darkly, crudely, or fleetingly—this out-side. One can detect a trace of this longing in the following quotation from *Negative Dialectics*: "What we may call the thing itself is not positively and immediately at hand. He who wants to know it must think more, not less."[2] Adorno clearly rejects the possibility of any direct, sensuous apprehension ("the thing itself is not positively and immediately at hand"), but he does not reject all modes of encounter, for there is one mode, "thinking more, not less," that holds promise. In this section I will explore some of the affinities between Adorno's nonidentity and my thing-power and, more generally, between his "specific materialism" (*ND*, 203) and a vital materialism.

Nonidentity is the name Adorno gives to that which is not subject to knowledge but is instead "heterogeneous" to all concepts. This elusive force is not, however, wholly outside human experience, for Adorno describes nonidentity as a presence that acts upon us: we knowers are haunted, he says, by a painful, nagging feeling that something's being forgotten or left out. This discomfiting sense of the inadequacy of representation remains no matter how refined or analytically precise one's concepts become. "Negative dialectics" is the method Adorno designs to teach us how to *accentuate* this discomforting experience and how to give it a meaning. When practiced correctly, negative dialectics will render the static buzz of nonidentity into a powerful reminder that "objects do not go into their concepts without leaving a remainder" and thus that life will always exceed our knowledge and control. The ethical project par excellence, as Adorno sees it, is to keep remembering this and to learn how to accept it. Only then can we stop raging against a world that refuses to offer us the "reconcilement" that we, according to Adorno, crave (*ND*, 5).[3]

For the vital materialist, however, the starting point of ethics is less the acceptance of the impossibility of "reconcilement" and more the recognition of human participation in a shared, vital materiality. We *are* vital materiality and we are surrounded by it, though we do not always see it that way. The ethical task at hand here is to cultivate the ability to discern nonhuman vitality, to become perceptually open to it. In a parallel manner, Adorno's "specific materialism" also recommends a set of practical techniques for

1. German philosopher and cultural critic (1903–1969); see above [editor's note].
2. Theodor Adorno, *Negative Dialectics*, trans. E. B. Ashton (New York: Continuum, 1973), 189. Further references to this title will be made in the running text as *ND*.
3. Romand Coles offers a sustained interpretation of Adorno as an ethical theorist: negative dialectics is a "morality of thinking" that can foster generosity toward others and toward the nonidentical in oneself. Coles argues that Adorno seeks a way to acknowledge and thereby mitigate the violence done by conceptualization and the suffering imposed by the quest to know and control all things. Romand Coles, *Rethinking Generosity: Critical Theory and the Politics of Caritas* (Ithaca: Cornell University Press, 1997), chap. 2.

training oneself to better detect and accept nonidentity. Negative dialectics is, in other words, the pedagogy inside Adorno's materialism.

This pedagogy includes intellectual as well as aesthetic exercises. The intellectual practice consists in the attempt to make the very process of conceptualization an explicit object of thought. The goal here is to become more cognizant that conceptualization automatically obscures the inadequacy of its concepts. Adorno believes that critical reflection can expose this cloaking mechanism and that the exposure will intensify the felt presence of nonidentity. The treatment is homeopathic:[4] we must develop a *concept* of nonidentity to cure the hubris of conceptualization. The treatment can work because, however distorting, concepts still "refer to nonconceptualities." This is "because concepts on their part are moments of the reality that requires their formation" (*ND*, 12). Concepts can never provide a clear view of things in themselves, but the "discriminating man," who "in the matter and its concept can distinguish even the infinitesimal, that which escapes the concept" (*ND*, 45), can do a better job of gesturing toward them. Note that the discriminating man (adept at negative dialectics) both subjects his conceptualizations to second-order reflection and pays close *aesthetic* attention to the object's "qualitative moments" (*ND*, 43), for these open a window onto nonidentity.

A second technique of the pedagogy is to exercise one's utopian imagination. The negative dialectician should imaginatively re-create what has been obscured by the distortion of conceptualization: "The means employed in negative dialectics for the penetration of its hardened objects is possibility—the possibility of which their reality has cheated the objects and which is nonetheless visible in each one" (*ND*, 52). Nonidentity resides in those denied possibilities, in the invisible field that surrounds and infuses the world of objects.

A third technique is to admit a "playful element" into one's thinking and to be willing to play the fool. The negative dialectician "knows how far he remains from" knowing nonidentity, "and yet he must always talk as if he had it entirely. This brings him to the point of clowning. He must not deny his clownish traits, least of all since they alone can give him hope for what is denied him" (*ND*, 14).

The self-criticism of conceptualization, a sensory attentiveness to the qualitative singularities of the object, the exercise of an unrealistic imagination, and the courage of a clown: by means of such practices one might replace the "rage" against nonidentity with a respect for it, a respect that chastens our will to mastery. That rage is for Adorno the driving force behind interhuman acts of cruelty and violence. Adorno goes even further to suggest that negative dialectics can transmute the anguish of nonidentity into a will to ameliorative political action: the thing thwarts our desire for conceptual and practical mastery and this refusal angers us; but it also offers us an ethical injunction, according to which "suffering ought not to be, . . . things should be different. Woe speaks: 'Go.' Hence the convergence of specific materialism with criticism, with social change in practice" (*ND*, 202–3).[5]

4. That is, like the treatment of illnesses that uses a highly diluted dose of the substance that causes particular symptoms to cure those symptoms [editor's note].

5. Adorno also describes this pain as the "guilt of a life which purely as a fact will strangle other life" (*ND*, 364). Coles calls it the "ongoing discomfort that solicits our critical efforts" (Coles, *Rethinking Generosity*, 89). Adorno does not elaborate or defend his claim that the pain of conceptual failure can provoke or motivate an ethical will to redress the pain of social injustice. But surely some defense is needed, for history has shown that even if the pangs of nonidentity engender in the self the idea that "things should be different," this moral awakening does not

Adorno founds his ethics on an intellectual and aesthetic attentiveness that, though it will always fail to see its object clearly, nevertheless has salutory effects on the bodies straining to see. Adorno willingly plays the fool by questing after what I would call thing-power, but which he calls "the preponderance of the object" (*ND*, 183). Humans encounter a world in which nonhuman materialities have power, a power that the "bourgeois I," with its pretensions to autonomy, denies.[6] It is at this point that Adorno identifies negative dialectics as a materialism: it is only "by passing to the object's preponderance that dialectics is rendered materialistic" (*ND*, 192).

Adorno dares to affirm something like thing-power, but he does not want to play the fool for *too* long. He is quick—too quick from the point of view of the vital materialist—to remind the reader that objects are always "entwined" with human subjectivity and that he has no desire "to place the object on the orphaned royal throne once occupied by the subject. On that throne the object would be nothing but an idol" (*ND*, 181). Adorno is reluctant to say too much about nonhuman vitality, for the more said, the more it recedes from view. Nevertheless, Adorno does try to attend somehow to this reclusive reality, by means of a negative dialectics. Negative dialectics has an affinity with negative theology: negative dialectics honors nonidentity as one would honor an unknowable god; Adorno's "specific materialism" includes the possibility that there is divinity behind or within the reality that withdraws. Adorno rejects any naive picture of transcendence, such as that of a loving God who designed the world ("metaphysics cannot rise again" [*ND*, 404] after Auschwitz[7]), but the desire for transcendence cannot, he believes, be eliminated: "Nothing could be experienced as truly alive if something that transcends life were not promised also. . . . The transcendent is, and it is not" (*ND*, 375).[8] Adorno honors nonidentity as an *absent* absolute, as a messianic promise.[9]

always result in "social change in practice." In other words, there seems to be a second gap, alongside the one between concept and thing, that needs to be addressed: the gap between recognizing the suffering of others and engaging in ameliorative action. Elsewhere I have argued that one source of the energy required is a love of the world or an enchantment with a world of vital materiality; Adorno sees more ethical potential in suffering and a sense of loss. He "disdained the passage to affirmation," contending that the experience of the "fullness of life" is "inseparable from . . . a desire in which violence and subjugation are inherent. . . . There is no fullness without biceps-flexing" (*ND* 385, 378). Nonidentity is dark and brooding, and it makes itself known with the least distortion in the form of an unarticulated feeling of resistance, suffering, or pain. From the perspective of the vital materialist, Adorno teeters on the edge of what Thomas Dumm has described as "the overwhelming sense of loss that could swamp us when we approach [the thing's] unknowable vastness" (Dumm, *Politics of the Ordinary*, 169). On enchantment with the world, see [Bennett's] *The Enchantment of Modern Life: Attachments, Crossings, and Ethics* (2001), see especially p. 10.

6. "Preponderance of the object is a thought of which any pretentious philosophy will be suspicious. . . . [Such] protestations . . . seek to drown out the festering suspicion that heteronomy might be mightier than the autonomy of which Kant . . . taught. . . . Such philosophical subjectivism is the ideological accompaniment of the . . . bourgeois I" (*ND*, 189).

7. The largest Nazi concentration camp of World War II, located in Poland; Adorno famously wrote in "Cultural Criticism and Society" (1951) that "to write poetry after Auschwitz is barbaric" [editor's note].

8. The gap between concept and thing can never be closed, and, according to Albrecht Wellmer, Adorno believes that this lack of conciliation can be withstood only "in the *name* of an absolute, which, although it is veiled in black, is not nothing. Between the being and the non-being of the absolute there remains an infinitely narrow crack through which a glimmer of light falls upon the world, the light of an absolute which is yet to come into being" (Albrecht Wellmer, *Endgames: The Irreconcilable Nature of Modernity*, trans. David Midgley [Cambridge: MIT Press, 1998], 171; my emphasis).

9. Thanks to Lars Tønder for alerting me to the messianic dimension of Adorno's thinking. One can here note Adorno's admiration for Kant, who Adorno read as having found a way to assign transcendence an important role while making it inaccessible in principle: "What finite beings say about transcendence is the semblance of transcendence; but as Kant well knew, it is a necessary semblance. Hence the incomparable

Adorno struggles to describe a force that is *material* in its resistance to human concepts but *spiritual* insofar as it might be a dark promise of an absolute-to-come. A vital materialism is more thoroughly nontheistic in presentation: the out-side has no messianic promise.[1] But a philosophy of nonidentity and a vital materialism nevertheless share an urge to cultivate a more careful attentiveness to the out-side.

THE NAIVE AMBITION OF VITAL MATERIALISM

Adorno reminds us that humans can experience the out-side only indirectly, only through vague, aporetic,[2] or unstable images and impressions. But when he says that even distorting concepts still "refer to nonconceptualities, because concepts on their part are moments of the reality that requires their formation" (*ND*, 12), Adorno also acknowledges that human experience nevertheless includes encounters with an out-side that is active, forceful, and (quasi)independent. This out-side can operate at a distance from our bodies or it can operate as a foreign power internal to them, as when we feel the discomfort of nonidentity, hear the naysaying voice of Socrates's demon, or are moved by what Lucretius described as that "something in our breast" capable of fighting and resisting.[3] There is a strong tendency among modern, secular, well-educated humans to refer such signs back to a human agency conceived as its ultimate source. This impulse toward cultural, linguistic, or historical constructivism, which interprets any expression of thing-power as an effect of culture and the play of human powers, politicizes moralistic and oppressive appeals to "nature." And that is a good thing. But the constructivist response to the world also tends to obscure from view whatever thing-power there may be. There is thus something to be said for moments of methodological naiveté, for the postponement of a genealogical critique of objects.[4] This delay might render manifest a subsistent world of

metaphysical relevance of the rescue of semblance, the object of esthetics" (*ND*, 393). For Adorno, "the idea of truth is supreme among the metaphysical ideas, and this is why . . . one who believes in God cannot believe in God, why the possibility represented by the divine name is maintained, rather, by him who does not believe" (*ND*, 401–2). According to Coles, it does not matter to Adorno whether the transcendent realm actually exists; what matters is the "demand . . . placed on thought" by its promise (Coles, *Rethinking Generosity*, 114).

1. There is, of course, no definitive way to prove either ontological imaginary. Morton Schoolman argues that Adorno's approach, which explicitly leaves open the possibility of a divine power of transcendence, is thus preferable to a materialism that seems to close the question. See Morton Schoolman, *Reason and Horror: Critical Theory, Democracy, and Aesthetic Individuality* (New York: Routledge, 2001).

2. Undecidable [editor's note].

3. Lucretius, "On the Nature of the Universe," in *The Epicurean Philosophers*, trans. C. Bailey, R. D. Dicks, and J. C. A. Gaskin, ed. John Gaskin (London: J. M. Dent, 1995), 128. [Lucretius (ca. 94–55 B.C.E.), Roman poet whose only extant work, *De rerum natura* (*On the Nature of Things*), is an epic on Epicurean philosophy; the Greek philosopher Epicurus (341–270 B.C.E.) held that the gods had nothing to do with human affairs. "Socrates' demon": in the account of his trial for impiety written by his pupil PLATO, the Greek philosopher Socrates (469–399 B.C.E.) explains that since childhood, a kind of voice has come to him, "something godlike and spiritual" (*theion ti kai daimonion*), that holds him back from action but never urges him forward (*Apology* 31c–d)—editor's note.]

4. In response to Foucault's claim that "perhaps one day, this century will be known as Deleuzean," Deleuze described his own work as "naive": "[Foucault] may perhaps have meant that I was the most naive philosopher of our generation. In all of us you find themes like multiplicity, difference, repetition. But I put forward almost raw concepts of these, while others work with more mediations. I've never worried about going beyond metaphysics. . . . I've never renounced a kind of empiricism. . . . Maybe that's what Foucault meant: I wasn't better than the others, but more naive, producing a kind of *art brut*, so to speak, not the most profound but the most innocent" (Gilles Deleuze, *Negotiations*, trans. Martin Joughin [New York: Columbia University Press, 1995]), 88–89). My thanks to Paul Patton for this reference. [*Art brut*: rough or raw art (French): art created outside the academic or official tradition—editor's note.]

nonhuman vitality. To "render manifest" is both to receive and to participate in the shape given to that which is received. What is manifest arrives through humans but not entirely because of them.

Vital materialists will thus try to linger in those moments during which they find themselves fascinated by objects, taking them as clues to the material vitality that they share with them. This sense of a strange and incomplete commonality with the out-side may induce vital materialists to treat nonhumans—animals, plants, earth, even artifacts and commodities—more carefully, more strategically, more ecologically. But how to develop this capacity for naiveté? One tactic might be to revisit and become temporarily infected by discredited philosophies of nature, risking "the taint of superstition, animism, vitalism, anthropomorphism, and other premodern attitudes."[5] I will venture into vitalism in chapters 5 and 6, but let me here make a brief stop at the ancient atomism of Lucretius, the Roman devotee of Epicurus.

Lucretius tells of bodies falling in a void, bodies that are not lifeless stuff but matter on the go, entering and leaving assemblages, swerving into each other: "*At times quite undetermined and at undetermined spots they push a little from their path*: yet only just so much as you could call a change of trend. [For if they did not] . . . swerve, all things would fall downwards through the deep void like drops of rain, nor could collision come to be, nor a blow brought to pass for the primordia: so nature would never have brought anything into existence."[6] Louis Althusser described this as a "materialism of the encounter," according to which political events are born from chance meetings of atoms.[7] A primordial swerve says that the world is not determined, that an element of chanciness resides at the heart of things, but it also affirms that so-called inanimate things have a life, that deep within is an inexplicable vitality or energy, a moment of independence from and resistance to us and other bodies: a kind of thing-power.

The rhetoric of *De Rerum Natura* is realist, speaking in an authoritative voice, claiming to describe a nature that preexists and outlives us: here are the smallest constituent parts of being ("primordia") and here are the principles of association governing them.[8] It is easy to criticize this realism: Lucretius quests for the thing itself, but there is no there there—or, at least, no way for us to grasp or know it, for the thing is always already humanized; its object status arises at the very instant something comes into our awareness. Adorno levels this charge explicitly against Martin Heidegger's phenomenology, which Adorno interprets as a "realism" that "seeks to breach the walls which thought has built around itself, to pierce the interjected layer of

5. Mitchell, *What Do Pictures Want?*, 149. ["Animism": the belief that nonhuman entities—animals, plants, and inanimate object—possess a spirit or soul; "vitalism": the theory that life processes arise from or contain a nonmaterial vital force and cannot be explained entirely as physical and chemical phenomena—editor's note.]

6. Lucretius, "On the Nature of the Universe," 126. There are no supernatural bodies or forces for Lucretius, and if we sometimes seem to have spiritual experiences, that is only because some kinds and collections of bodies exist below the threshold of human sense perception.

7. Louis Althusser, "Underground Current of the Materialism of the Encounter," in *Philosophy of the Encounter: Later Writings, 1978–87*, trans. G. M. Goshgarian, ed. François Matheron (New York: Verso, 2006), 169. "Without swerve and encounter, [primordia] would be nothing but *abstract* elements. . . . So much so that we can say that [prior to] . . . *the swerve and the encounter* . . . they led only a phantom existence" (ibid.). [ALTHUSSER (1918–1990), French philosopher—editor's note.]

8. Lucretian physics is the basis for his rejection of religion, his presentation of death as a reconfiguration of primordia made necessary by the essential motility of matter, and his ethical advice on how to live well while existing in one's current material configuration.

subjective positions that have become a second nature." Heidegger's aim "to philosophize formlessly, so to speak, purely on the ground of things" (*ND*, 78)[9] is for Adorno futile, and it is productive of a violent "rage" against nonidentity.[1]

But Lucretius's poem—like Kafka's stories, Sullivan's travelogue, Vernadsky's speculations, and my account of the gutter of Cold Spring Lane—does offer this potential benefit: it can direct sensory, linguistic, and imaginative attention toward a material vitality. The advantage of such tales, with their ambitious naiveté, is that though they "disavow . . . the tropological work, the psychological work, and the phenomenological work entailed in the human production of materiality," they do so "in the name of *avowing* the force of questions that have been too readily foreclosed by more familiar fetishizations: the fetishization of the subject, the image, the word."[2]

2010

9. For Adorno, Heidegger, "weary of the subjective jail of cognition," became "convinced that what is transcendent to subjectivity is immediate for subjectivity, without being conceptually stained by subjectivity" (*ND*, 78). But it does not seem to me that Heidegger makes a claim to immediacy. See Heidegger, *What Is a Thing?*, trans. W. B. Barton Jr. and Vera Deutsch (South Bend, Ill.: Gateway, 1967). [HEIDEGGER (1889–1976), major 20th-century German philosopher—editor's note.]

1. For Marx, too, naive realism was the philosophy to overcome. He wrote his doctoral dissertation on the "metaphysical materialism" of Democritus, and it was against that naive objectivism that Marx would eventually define his own "historical materialism." Historical materialism would not focus on matter but on human power-laden socioeconomic structures. [KARL MARX (1818–1883), German philosopher, political economist, and revolutionary—editor's note.]

2. This is Bill Brown's account of Arjun Appadurai's *The Social Life of Things*, in "Thing Theory," *Critical Inquiry* 28, no. 1 (2001): 6–7.

LAUREN BERLANT
b. 1957

MICHAEL WARNER
b. 1958

"Heteronormativity is a fundamental motor of social organization," assert Lauren Berlant and Michael Warner, and it produces "unequal and exploitative relations throughout even straight society." With their essay "Sex in Public" (1998), our selection, Berlant and Warner elaborate a new category of analysis—heteronormativity—that works, alongside race, class, and gender, to create the social distinctions that structure American culture. Focusing on the public associations attached to sexuality as well as the possibilities of "counterpublics," the essay has become a manifesto of queer theory.

Berlant and Warner are leading figures in the generation of American critics and theorists that came to prominence in the 1990s. Berlant grew up in the Philadelphia area, but a formative time for her, she notes in an interview, was her teenage participation in the Twin Oaks commune in Virginia. She went on to Oberlin College, receiving her B.A. in 1979, and to Cornell University, earning her Ph.D. in 1985. Since 1984 she has taught at the University of Chicago, where she is the George M. Pullman Professor of English. Michael Warner, as he recounts in a brief memoir, was brought up in a Pentecostal family and attended Oral Roberts University as an undergraduate (B.A., 1980). From there he went to the University of Wisconsin (M.A., 1981) and Johns Hopkins University, from which he received his Ph.D. in 1985. He has taught at Northwestern and Rutgers Universities, and since 2007 at Yale University, where he is Seymour H. Knox Professor of English.

Having undergone graduate training during the heyday of debates over literary theory, notably deconstruction, both Berlant and Warner are versed in its terms and concerns, but they direct it, like many of their generation, toward investigating public culture and contemporary politics as well as literary texts. Warner, extending JÜRGEN HABERMAS's conception of the public sphere, has done pathbreaking work on early American institutions of publishing in the eighteenth century. For her part, Berlant has produced significant work on nineteenth-century literature and sentimentalism, focusing on citizenship and how contemporary American political discourse interweaves the public and private. Both Berlant and Warner examine how presumably intimate things like sex are public issues, and how political issues are privatized and reduced to personal feeling. In "Sex in Public," their conception of queer theory points out the ways in which not only do standard sexual categories deconstruct into contradictions but also those contradictions affect American society, with real and often pernicious consequences for people.

The term *heteronormativity* was first coined by Warner in the early 1990s. As he and Berlant develop it here, heteronormativity prescribes both certain sex acts and "many practices that are not sex," such as what constitutes a family, romance, legal rights of partners, citizenship, property ownership and zoning, and national character. They are responding to the coercive ways in which heterosexual norms isolate and demonize people in U.S. society. Part of the hegemonic order, heteronormativity projects a "monoculture" that dominates all alternative sexual cultures or groups. Sexuality is not just a personal choice or lifestyle, but is as determinative of one's place in American social life as are racial designations. The authors take the lesson of MICHEL FOUCAULT, whose *History of Sexuality* (1976; see above) exposes the discursive regime clustered around sex in the Victorian era, and show its applicability to contemporary American culture.

Berlant and Warner are also responding to trends in gender theory, especially gay and lesbian theory. Through the 1970s and 1980s scholars employed gender as a central concept to designate identity, with the aim of establishing status for minority identities. Queer theory, notably in the work of GAYLE RUBIN, EVE KOSOFSKY SEDGWICK, and JUDITH BUTLER, developed from this project, but it has not simply expanded the pool of identities. Rather, it has deconstructed such identities as gay or straight, showing how they are not unitary or fixed. As Berlant and Warner point out, any such identity "consolidates . . . widely differing practices." Among those who claim a heterosexual identity there is enormous variation; for instance, some have sex often, some rarely; some use the missionary position, some practice sadomasochism; some consider oral sex sodomy, some not. This is why Berlant and Warner choose the word "queer," for a heterosexual couple such as the one they mention in "Sex in Public" might not fit the narrow image of heteronormativity.

"Sex in Public" concludes with a startling depiction of a performance at a leather bar (serving a subculture usually associated with S and M), where one man induces another, at a climactic moment, to vomit. While such a scene might disturb or offend some, Berlant and Warner's point is to illustrate the value of counterpublic spaces, as well as to underscore the range of acts that people practice. Though the essay is largely in the mode of critique, it also suggests the democratic role if not utopian possibilities of counterpublics. The idea of counterpublics stems from amendments to Habermas's seemingly monolithic notion of the public sphere, here replaced with the idea of numerous public spheres, some of which are alternative, minor, or antagonistic to the mainstream. Berlant and Warner emphasize the way in which many cities foster counterpublic spaces for nonnormative culture—for instance, New York's Greenwich Village for gay culture. Their point is not only that these counterpublics must be tolerated but also that they are necessary to break through the constraints of normative strictures.

Berlant and Warner have had a great deal of influence on the way that contemporary critics conceive of the public sphere, citizenship, and sexuality in the United

States. They have spearheaded thinking about what it means "to queer" theory as well as practice. Predictably, though unusually for most in academe, they have been attacked in mainstream media for encouraging homosexuality, and Warner has been labeled a "dangerous professor" by a right-wing pundit. Within academic circles, they have been criticized for targeting normativity. Some, like MARTHA NUSSBAUM, argue that one has to have a tacit sense of the normative to judge whether violence, for instance, is wrong. Berlant and Warner head off this charge in "Sex in Public," declaring that "To be against heteronormativity is not to be against norms." Although they don't explicitly declare the norms they hold, they implicitly value a full sense of democracy, which fosters various counterpublics and which, conversely, such counterpublics make possible. Within queer theory, they take a radical rather than liberal position. For instance, they are unlikely to embrace gay marriage as an ultimate goal, because its apparent conferral of equal rights in fact merely apes heteronormative forms. Rather, they suggest more far-reaching change for all who live under normative strictures. Debates within political theory usually set reform against revolution, but the aim of Berlant and Warner might be better understood as utopian: removing the obstacles to liberated forms of human world making.

"Sex in Public" Keywords: Affect, The Body, Cultural Studies, Hegemony, Identity, Ideology, Queer Theory, Sexuality, Subjectivity

Sex in Public

There Is Nothing More Public Than Privacy

An essay titled "Sex in Public" teases with the obscurity of its object and the twisted aim of its narrative. In this essay, we talk not about the sex people already have clarity about, or identities and acts,[1] or a wildness in need of derepression;[2] rather, we talk about sex as it is mediated by publics. Some of these publics have an obvious relation to sex: pornographic cinema, phone sex, "adult" markets for print, lap dancing. Others are organized around sex but not necessarily sex *acts* in the usual sense: queer zones and other worlds estranged from heterosexual culture, but also more tacit scenes of sexuality like official national culture, which depends on a notion of privacy to cloak its sexualization of national membership.

The aim of this essay is to describe what we want to promote as the radical aspirations of queer culture building: not just a safe zone for queer sex, but the changed possibilities of identity, intelligibility, publics, culture, and sex that appear when the heterosexual couple is no longer the referent or privileged example of sexual culture. Queer social practices like sex and theory

1. On "public sex" in the standard sense, see Pat Califia, *Public Sex: The Culture of Radical Sex* (Pittsburgh, PA: Cleis Press, 1994). On "identities and acts," see Janet Halley, "The Status/Conduct Distinction in the 1993 Revisions to Military Antigay Policy: A Legal Archaeology," *GLQ* 3 (1996), pp. 159–252 [except as indicated, all notes are Berlant and Warner's].

2. The classic political argument for sexual derepression as a condition of freedom is put forth in Herbert Marcuse, *Eros and Civilization: A Philosophical Inquiry into Freud* (Boston: Beacon Press, 1966). In contemporary pro-sex thought inspired by Michel Foucault's *History of Sexuality*, vol. 1, trans. Robert Hurley (New York: Vintage, 1978), the denunciation of "erotic injustice and sexual oppression" is situated less in the freedom of individuals than in analyses of the normative and coercive relations between specific "populations" and the institutions created to manage them (Gayle Rubin, "Thinking Sex," in *Pleasure and Danger: Exploring Female Sexuality* [Boston: Pandora Press, 1984], p. 275). [For *The History of Sexuality* (1976), by the French philosopher and historian of ideas FOUCAULT (1926–1984), and for "Thinking Sex," by the American anthropologist and queer theorist RUBIN (b. 1949), see above—editor's note.]

try to unsettle the garbled but powerful norms supporting that privilege—including the project of normalization that has made heterosexuality hegemonic—as well as those material practices that, though not explicitly sexual, are implicated in the hierarchies of property and propriety that we will describe as heteronormative.[3] We open with two scenes of sex in public.

SCENE ONE

In 1993, *Time* magazine published a special issue about immigration called "The New Face of America."[4] The cover girl of this issue was morphed via computer from head shots representing a range of U.S. immigrant groups: an amalgam of "Middle Eastern," "Italian," "African," "Vietnamese," "Anglo-Saxon," "Chinese," and "Hispanic" faces. The new face of America is supposed to represent what the model citizen will look like when, in the year 2004, there will no longer be a white statistical majority in the United States. Naked, smiling, and just off-white, *Time*'s divine Frankenstein[5] aims to organize hegemonic optimism about citizenship and the national future. *Time*'s theory is that by the twenty-first century interracial reproductive sex will have taken place in the United States on such a mass scale that racial difference itself will be finally replaced by a kind of family feeling based on blood relations. In the twenty-first century, *Time* imagines, hundreds of millions of hybrid faces will erase American racism altogether: the nation will become a happy racial monoculture made up of "one mixed blood."[6]

The publication of this special issue caused a brief flurry of interest but had no important effects; its very banality calls us to understand the technologies that produce its ordinariness. The fantasy banalized by the image is one that reverberates in the law and the most intimate crevices of everyday life. Its explicit aim is to help its public process the threat to "normal" or "core" national culture currently phrased as "the problem of immigration."[7] But this crisis image of immigrants is also a *racial mirage* generated by a white-dominated society, supplying a concrete phobia to organize its public so that a more substantial discussion of exploitation in the United States can

3. By heteronormativity we mean the institutions, structures of understanding, and practical orientations that make heterosexuality seem not only coherent—that is, organized as a sexuality—but also privileged. Its coherence is always provisional, and its privilege can take several (sometimes contradictory) forms: unmarked as the basic idiom of the personal and the social; or marked as a natural state; or projected as an ideal or moral accomplishment. It consists less of norms that could be summarized as a body of doctrine than of a sense of rightness produced in contradictory manifestations—often unconscious, immanent to practice or to institutions. Contexts that have little visible relation to sex practice, such as life narrative and generational identity, can be heteronormative in this sense, while in other contexts forms of sex between men and women might *not* be heteronormative. Heteronormativity is thus a concept distinct from heterosexuality. One of the most conspicuous differences is that it has no parallel, the way heterosexuality organizes homosexuality as its opposite. Because homosexuality can never have the invisible, tacit, society-founding rightness that heterosexuality has, it would not be possible to speak of "homonormativity" in the same sense. See Michael Warner, "Fear of a Queer Planet," *Social Text*, no. 29 (1991), pp. 3–17.

4. *Time*, special issue, 142.21 (Fall 1993). This analysis reworks materials in Lauren Berlant, *The Queen of America Goes to Washington City: Essays on Sex and Citizenship* (Durham, NC: Duke University Press, 1997), pp. 200–208.

5. That is, a construct created out of pieces, like the unnamed monster in Mary Shelley's novel *Frankenstein* (1818) [editor's note].

6. For a treatment of the centrality of "blood" to U.S. nationalist discourse, see Bonnie Honig, *No Place Like Home: Democracy and the Politics of Foreignness* (Princeton, NJ: Princeton University Press, 1998).

7. See, for example, William Bennett, *The De-Valuing of America: The Fight for Our Culture and Our Children* (New York: Simon and Schuster, 1992); Peter Brimelow, *Alien Nation: Common Sense about America's Immigration Disaster* (New York: Random House, 1995); and William A. Henry III, *In Defense of Elitism* (New York: Doubleday, 1994).

be avoided and then remaindered to the part of collective memory sanctified not by nostalgia but by mass aversion. Let's call this the amnesia archive. The motto above the door is: "Memory is the amnesia you like."

But more than exploitation and racism are forgotten in this whirl of projection and suppression. Central to the transfiguration of the immigrant as a nostalgic image to shore up core national culture and allay white fears of minoritization is something that cannot speak its name,[8] though its signature is everywhere: national heterosexuality. National heterosexuality is the mechanism by which a core national culture can be imagined as a sanitized space of sentimental feeling and immaculate behavior, a space of pure citizenship. A familial model of society displaces recognition of structural racism and other systemic inequalities. This is not entirely new: the family form has functioned as a mediator and metaphor of national existence in the United States since the eighteenth century.[9] We are arguing that its contemporary deployment increasingly supports the governmentality of the welfare state by separating the aspirations of national belonging from the critical culture of the public sphere and from political citizenship.[1] Immigration crises have also previously produced feminine icons that function as prostheses for the state—most famously, the Statue of Liberty, which symbolized seamless immigrant assimilation to the metaculture of the United States. In *Time*'s face, it is not symbolic femininity but practical heterosexuality that guarantees the monocultural nation.

The nostalgic family-values covenant of contemporary American politics stipulates a privatization of citizenship and sex in a number of ways. In law and political ideology, for example, the fetus and the child have been spectacularly elevated to the place of sanctified nationality. The state now sponsors stings and laws to purify the Internet on behalf of children. New welfare and tax "reforms" passed under the cooperation between the Contract with America and Clintonian familialism[2] seek to increase the legal and economic privileges of married couples and parents. Vouchers and privatization rezone education as the domain of parents rather than of citizens. Meanwhile, senators such as Ted Kennedy and Jesse Helms[3] support amendments that refuse federal funds to organizations that "promote, disseminate, or produce materials that are obscene or that depict or describe, in a patently

8. An allusion to "the Love that dare not speak its name" (i.e., love between men)—a phrase that ends "Two Loves," a poem by Lord Alfred Douglas that entered into the 1895 libel trial of his lover, Oscar Wilde [editor's note].

9. On the family form in national rhetoric, see Jay Fliegelman, *Prodigals and Pilgrims: The American Revolution against Patriarchal Authority, 1750–1800* (Cambridge, UK: Cambridge University Press, 1982); and Shirley Samuels, *Romances of the Republic: Women, the Family, and Violence in the Literature of the Early American Nation* (New York: Oxford University Press, 1996). On fantasies of genetic assimilation, see Robert S. Tilton, *Pocahontas: The Evolution of an American Narrative* (Cambridge, UK: Cambridge University Press, 1994), pp. 9–33; and Elise Lemire, "Making Miscegenation" (Ph.D. diss., Rutgers University, 1996).

1. The concept of welfare-state governmentality has a growing literature. For a concise statement, see Jürgen Habermas, "The New Obscurity: The Crisis of the Welfare State and the Exhaustion of the Utopian Energies," *The New Conservatism: Cultural Criticism and the Historians' Debate*, trans. Shierry Nicholsen (Cambridge, MA: MIT Press, 1990), pp. 48–70. Michael Warner has discussed the relation between this analysis and queer culture in his "Something Queer about the Nation-State," chapter 6, *Publics and Counterpublics* (New York: Zone Books, 2002). [Habermas (b. 1929), German philosopher—editor's note.]

2. The policies of the administration of Bill Clinton (b. 1946; 42nd U.S. president, 1993–2001), a Democrat. "Contract with America": the principles set forth by the Republicans, led by Speaker of the House Newt Gingrich, in the 1994 midterm campaign [editor's note].

3. That is, both the most liberal, such as the Democrat Edward Kennedy of Massachusetts (1932–2009; U.S. senator, 1962–2009), and the most conservative, such as the Republican Helms of North Carolina (1921–2008; U.S. senator, 1973–2003) [editor's note].

offensive way, sexual or excretory activities or organs, including but not limited to obscene depictions of sadomasochism, homo-eroticism, the sexual exploitation of children, or any individuals engaged in sexual intercourse."[4] These developments, though distinct, are linked in the way they organize a hegemonic national public around sex. But because this sex public officially claims to act only in order to protect the zone of heterosexual privacy, the institutions of economic privilege and social reproduction informing its practices and organizing its ideal world are protected by the spectacular demonization of any represented sex.

SCENE TWO

In October 1995, the New York City Council passed a new zoning law by a forty-one-to-nine vote. The Zoning Text Amendment covers adult book and video stores, eating and drinking establishments, theaters, and other businesses. It allows these businesses only in certain nonresidential zoning areas, most of which turn out to be on the waterfront. Within the new reserved districts, adult businesses are disallowed within five hundred feet of another adult establishment or within five hundred feet of a house of worship, school, or day-care center. They are limited to one per lot and limited in size to ten thousand square feet. Signs are limited in size, placement, and illumination. All other adult businesses are required to close within a year. Of the estimated 177 adult businesses in the city, all but 28 may have to close under this law. Enforcement of the bill is entrusted to building inspectors.

The court challenge to the bill was brought by a coalition that also fought it in the political process: anticensorship groups such as the New York Civil Liberties Union, Feminists for Free Expression, People for the American Way, and the National Coalition Against Censorship, as well as gay and lesbian organizations such as the Lambda Legal Defense and Education Fund, the Empire State Pride Agenda, and the AIDS Prevention Action League. (An appeal was still pending as of July 1997.)[5] These latter groups joined the anticensorship groups for a simple reason: the impact of rezoning on businesses catering to queers, especially to gay men, will be devastating. All five of the adult businesses on Christopher Street[6] will be shut down, along with the principal venues where men meet men for sex. None of these businesses has been a target of local complaints. Gay men have come to take for granted the availability of explicit sexual materials, theaters, and clubs. That is how they have learned to find each other, to map a commonly accessible world, to construct the architecture of queer space in a homophobic environment, and, for the last fifteen years, to cultivate a collective ethos of safer sex. All of that is about to change. Now gay men who want sexual materials, or who want to meet men for sex, will have two choices: they can cathect the privatized virtual public of phone sex and the Internet; or they can travel to small, inaccessible, little-trafficked, badly lit areas, remote from public transportation and from any residences, mostly on the waterfront, where heterosexual porn

4. *Congressional Record*, 1st sess., 1989, vol. 135, no. 134, S12967.

5. The Court of Appeals upheld the zoning law, but it also upheld a legal loophole that allows sex shops to remain open if no more than 40 percent of their floor space is devoted to sexual material or activity [editor's note].

6. A street in the West Village that has long been the focus of gay life in New York City (it is the location of the Stonewall Inn, the site of the 1969 riots often seen as marking the beginning of the modern gay rights movement) [editor's note].

users will also be relocated and where risk of violence will consequently be higher.[7] In either case, the result will be a sense of isolation and diminished expectations for queer life, as well as an attenuated capacity for political community. The nascent lesbian sexual culture, including the Clit Club and the only video-rental club catering to lesbians, will also disappear. The impact of the sexual purification of New York will fall unequally on those who already have the fewest publicly accessible resources.

Normativity and Sexual Culture

Heterosexuality is not a thing. We speak of heterosexual culture rather than heterosexuality because that culture never has more than a provisional unity.[8] It is neither a single Symbolic nor a single ideology nor a unified set of shared beliefs.[9] The conflicts between these strands are seldom more than dimly perceived in practice, where the givenness of male-female sexual relations is part of the ordinary rightness of the world, its fragility masked in shows of solemn rectitude. Such conflicts have also gone unrecognized in theory, partly because of the metacultural work of the very category of heterosexuality, which consolidates as *a sexuality* widely differing practices, norms, and institutions, and partly because the sciences of social knowledge are themselves so deeply anchored in the process of normalization to which Foucault attributes so much of modern sexuality.[1] Thus when we say that the

7. Political geography in this way produces systematic effects of violence. Queers are forced to find each other in untrafficked areas because of the combined pressures of propriety, stigma, the closet, and state regulation such as laws against public lewdness. The same areas are known to gay bashers and other criminals. And they are disregarded by police. The effect is to make both violence and police neglect seem natural hazards, voluntarily courted by queers. As the 1997 documentary film *Licensed to Kill* [dir. Arthur Dong] illustrates, antigay violence has been difficult to combat by legal means; victims are reluctant to come forward in any public and prosecutorial framework, while bashers can appeal to the geographic circumstances to implicate the victims themselves. The legal means has helped to produce the violence it is called upon to remedy.

8. EVE KOSOFSKY SEDGWICK, *The Epistemology of the Closet* (Berkeley: University of California Press, 1992). [For *Epistemology of the Closet*, see above—editor's note.]

9. Gay and lesbian theory, especially in the humanities, frequently emphasizes psychoanalytic or psychoanalytic-style models of subject formation, the differences among which are significant and yet all of which tend to block out the difference between the categories male/female and the process and project of heteronormativity. Three propositional paradigms are relevant here: those that propose that human identity itself is fundamentally organized by gender identifications that are hardwired into infants; those that equate the clarities of gender identity with the domination of a relatively coherent and vertically stable "straight" ideology; and those that focus on a phallocentric Symbolic order that produces gendered subjects who live out the destiny of their positioning in it. The psychoanalytic and philosophical insights and limits of these models (which, we feel, underdescribe the practices, institutions, and incongruities of heteronormativity) require further engagement. For the time being, these works stand in as the most challenging relevant archive: JUDITH BUTLER, *Bodies That Matter: On the Discursive Limits of "Sex"* (New York: Routledge, 1993); Luce Irigaray, *Speculum of the Other Woman* (Ithaca, NY: Cornell University Press, 1985) and *The Sex Which Is Not One* (Ithaca, NY: Cornell University Press, 1985); Teresa de Lauretis, *The Practice of Love* (Bloomington: Indiana University Press, 1994); Kaja Silverman, *Male Subjectivity at the Margin* (New York: Routledge, 1992); MONIQUE WITTIG, *The Straight Mind and Other Essays* (Boston: Beacon Press, 1992). Psychoanalytic work on sexuality does not always latch acts and inclinations to natural or constructed "identity"; see, for example, Leo Bersani, *Homos* (Cambridge, MA: Harvard University Press, 1995) and "Is the Rectum a Grave?" in Douglas Crimp, ed., *AIDS: Cultural Analysis, Cultural Activism* (Cambridge, MA: MIT Press, 1988). [The Symbolic: in the theories of the psyche put forward by the French psychoanalyst JACQUES LACAN (1901–1981), the Symbolic is the dimension of language, law, and the father—editor's note.]

1. The notion of metaculture we borrow from Greg Urban; see his *Toward a Discourse-Centered Approach to Culture* (Austin: University of Texas Press, 1991) and *Noumenal Community: Myth and Reality in an Amerindian Brazilian Society* (Austin: University of Texas Press, 1996). On normalization, see Michel Foucault, *Discipline and Punish*, trans. Alan Sheridan (New York: Vintage, 1979), pp. 184–85; and *The History of Sexuality*, p. 144. Foucault derives his argument here from the revised version of Georges Canguilhem, *The Normal and the Pathological*, trans. Carolyn R. Fawcett (New York: Zone Books, 1991).

contemporary United States is saturated by the project of constructing national heterosexuality, we do not mean that national heterosexuality is anything like a simple monoculture. Hegemonies are nothing if not elastic alliances, involving dispersed and contradictory strategies for self-maintenance and reproduction.

Heterosexual culture achieves much of its metacultural intelligibility through the ideologies and institutions of intimacy. We want to argue here that although the intimate relations of private personhood appear to be the realm of sexuality itself, allowing "sex in public" to appear like matter out of place, intimacy is itself publicly mediated, in several senses. First, its conventional spaces presuppose a structural differentiation of "personal life" from work, politics, and the public sphere.[2] Second, the normativity of heterosexual culture links intimacy only to the institutions of personal life, making them the privileged institutions of social reproduction, the accumulation and transfer of capital, and self-development. Third, by making sex seem irrelevant or merely personal, heteronormative conventions of intimacy block the building of nonnormative or explicit public sexual cultures. Finally, those conventions conjure a mirage: a home base of pre-political humanity from which citizens are thought to come into political discourse and to which they are expected to return in the (always imaginary) future after political conflict. Intimate life is the endlessly cited *elsewhere* of political public discourse, a promised haven that distracts citizens from the unequal conditions of their political and economic lives, consoles them for the damaged humanity of mass society, and shames them for any divergence between their lives and the intimate sphere that is alleged to be simple personhood.

Ideologies and institutions of intimacy are increasingly offered as a vision of the good life for the destabilized and struggling citizenry of the United States, the only (fantasy) zone in which a future might be thought and willed, the only (imaginary) place where good citizens might be produced away from the confusing and unsettling distractions and contradictions of capitalism and politics. Indeed, one of the unforeseen paradoxes of national-capitalist privatization has been that citizens have been led through heterosexual culture to identify both themselves *and their politics* with privacy. In the official public, this involves making sex private; reintensifying *blood* as a psychic base for identification; replacing state mandates for social justice with a privatized ethics of responsibility, charity, atonement, and "values"; and enforcing boundaries between moral persons and economic ones.[3]

A complex cluster of sexual practices gets confused, in heterosexual culture, with the love plot of intimacy and familialism that signifies belonging to society in a deep and normal way. Community is imagined through scenes of

2. Here we are influenced by Eli Zaretsky, *Capitalism, the Family, and Personal Life*, rev. ed. (New York: Harper and Row, 1986), and Stephanie Coontz, *The Social Origins of Private Life: A History of American Families, 1600–1900* (London: Verso, 1988), though heteronormativity is a problem not often made visible in Coontz's work.

3. On privatization and intimacy politics, see Berlant, *Queen of America*, pp. 1–24, and "Feminism and the Institutions of Intimacy," in E. Ann Kaplan and George Levine, eds., *The Politics of Research* (New Brunswick, NJ: Rutgers University Press, 1997); Honig, *No Place Like Home*; Rosalind Pollack Petchesky, "The Body as Property," in Faye D. Ginsburg and Rayna Rapp, eds., *Conceiving the New World Order: The Global Politics of Reproduction* (Berkeley: University of California Press, 1995). On privatization and national capitalism, see David Harvey, *The Condition of Postmodernity* (Oxford: Blackwell, 1989); and Mike Davis, *City of Quartz: Excavating the Future in Los Angeles* (New York: Verso, 1992).

intimacy, coupling, and kinship.[4] And a historical relation to futurity is restricted to generational narrative and reproduction. A whole field of social relations becomes intelligible as heterosexuality, and this privatized sexual culture bestows on its sexual practices a tacit sense of rightness and normalcy. This sense of rightness—embedded in things and not just in sex—is what we call heteronormativity. Heteronormativity is more than ideology, or prejudice, or phobia against gays and lesbians; it is produced in almost every aspect of the forms and arrangements of social life: nationality, the state, and the law; commerce; medicine; education; plus the conventions and affects of narrativity, romance, and other protected spaces of culture. It is hard to see these fields as heteronormative because the sexual culture straight people inhabit is so diffuse, a mix of languages they are just developing with notions of sexuality so ancient that their material conditions feel hardwired into personhood.

But intimacy has not always had the meaning it has for contemporary heteronormative culture. Along with Foucault and other historians, the classicist David Halperin, for example, has shown that in ancient Athens, sex was a transitive act rather than a fundamental dimension of personhood or an expression of intimacy. The verb for having sex appears on a late antique list of things that are not done in regard to or through others: "namely, speaking, singing, dancing, fist-fighting, competing, hanging oneself, dying, being crucified, diving, finding a treasure, having sex, vomiting, moving one's bowels, sleeping, laughing, crying, talking to the gods, and the like."[5] Halperin points out that the inclusion of fucking on this list shows that sex is not here "knit up in a web of mutuality." In contrast, modern heterosexuality is supposed to refer to relations of intimacy and identification with other persons, and sex acts are supposed to be the most intimate communication of them all.[6] The sex act protected in the zone of privacy is the affectional nimbus that

4. This language for community is a problem for gay historiography. In otherwise fine and important studies such as Esther Newton's *Cherry Grove, Fire Island: Sixty Years in America's First Gay and Lesbian Town* (Boston: Beacon Press, 1993), or Elizabeth Lapovsky Kennedy and Madeline D. Davis's *Boots of Leather, Slippers of Gold: The History of a Lesbian Community* (New York: Routledge, 1993), or even George Chauncey's *Gay New York: Gender, Urban Culture, and the Makings of the Gay Male World, 1890–1940* (New York: Basic Books, 1994), community is imagined as whole-person, face-to-face relations—local, experiential, proximate, and saturating. But queer worlds seldom manifest themselves in such forms. Cherry Grove—a seasonal resort depending heavily on weekend visits by New Yorkers—may be typical less of a "gay and lesbian town" than of the way queer sites are specialized spaces in which transits can project alternative worlds. John D'Emilio's *Sexual Politics, Sexual Communities: The Making of a Homosexual Minority in the United States, 1940–1970* (Chicago: University of Chicago Press, 1983) is an especially interesting example of the imaginative power of the idealization of local community for queers. The book charts the separate tracks of political organizing and local scenes such as bar life, showing that when the "movement" and the "subculture" began to converge in San Francisco, the result was a new formation with a new utopian appeal: "A 'community,'" D'Emilio writes, "was in fact forming around a shared sexual orientation" (p. 195). D'Emilio (wisely) keeps quotation marks around "community" in the very sentence declaring it to exist in fact.

5. David M. Halperin, "Sex before Sexuality: Pederasty, Politics, and Power in Classical Athens," in Martin Bauml Duberman, Martha Vicinus, and George Chauncey, eds., *Hidden from History: Reclaiming the Gay and Lesbian Past* (New York: New American Library, 1989), p. 49. The list Halperin cites is from Artemidorus, *Oneirocritica* 1.2 (pp. 8.21–9.4 Pack). [Halperin (b. 1952), American classical scholar—editor's note.]

6. Studies of intimacy that do not assume this "web of mutuality," either as the self-evident nature of intimacy or as a human value, are rare. ROLAND BARTHES's *A Lover's Discourse*, trans. Richard Howard (New York: Farrar, Straus, and Giroux, 1978), and Niklas Luhmann's *Love as Passion*, trans. Jeremy Gaines and Doris Jones (Cambridge, MA: Harvard University Press, 1986), both try, in very different ways, to describe the production of intimacy analytically. More typical is Anthony Giddens's attempt to theorize intimacy as "pure relationship" in *The Transformation of Intimacy: Sexuality, Love, and Eroticism in Modern Societies* (Stanford, CA: Stanford University Press, 1992). There, ironically, it is "the gays who are the pioneers" in separating the "pure relationship" of love from extraneous institutions and contexts such as marriage and reproduction.

heterosexual culture protects and from which it abstracts its model of ethics; but this utopia of social belonging is also supported and extended by acts less commonly recognized as part of sexual culture: paying taxes, being disgusted, philandering, bequeathing, celebrating a holiday, investing for the future, teaching, disposing of a corpse, carrying wallet photos, buying economy size, being nepotistic, running for president, divorcing, or owning anything "His" and "Hers."

The elaboration of this list is a project for further study. Meanwhile, to make it, and to laugh at it, is not immediately to label any practice as oppressive, uncool, or definitive. We are describing a constellation of practices that everywhere disperses heterosexual privilege as a tacit but central organizing index of social membership. Exposing it inevitably produces what we have elsewhere called a wrenching sense of recontextualization as its subjects, even its gay and lesbian subjects, begin to piece together how it is that social and economic discourses, institutions, and practices that don't feel especially sexual or familial collaborate to produce as a social norm and ideal an extremely narrow context for living.[7] Heterosexual culture cannot recognize, validate, sustain, incorporate, or remember much of what people know and experience about the cruelty of normal culture even to the people who identify with it.

But that cruelty does not go unregistered. Intimacy, for example, has a whole public environment of therapeutic genres dedicated to witnessing the constant failure of heterosexual ideologies and institutions. Every day in many countries now, people's failure to sustain or be sustained by institutions of privacy is testified to on talk shows, in scandal journalism, even in the ordinary course of mainstream journalism addressed to middlebrow culture. We can learn a lot from these stories of love plots that have gone astray: about the ways quotidian violence is linked to complex pressures from money, racism, histories of sexual violence, cross-generational tensions. We can learn a lot from listening to the increasing demands on love to deliver the good life it promises. And we can learn a lot from the extremely punitive responses that tend to emerge when people seem not to suffer enough for their transgressions and failures.

Maybe we would learn too much. Recently the proliferation of evidence for heterosexuality's failings has produced a backlash against talk-show therapy. It has even brought William Bennett to the podium; but rather than confessing his transgressions or making a complaint about someone else's, he calls for boycotts and suppression of heterosexual therapy culture altogether. Recognition of heterosexuality's daily failures agitates him as much as queerness. "We've forgotten that civilization depends on keeping some of this stuff under wraps," he said. "This is a tropism toward the toilet."[8]

But does civilization need to cover its ass? Or does heterosexual culture actually secure itself through banalizing intimacy? Does belief that normal life is actually possible *require* amnesia and the ludicrous stereotyping of a bottom-feeding culture apparently inadequate to intimacy? On these shows,

7. See our "What Does Queer Theory Teach Us about X?" *PMLA* 110.3 (May 1995), pp. 343–49.
8. William Bennett, quoted in *New York Times*, Oct. 26, 1995, p. A25. [Bennett (b. 1943), conservative academic who gained national attention as chair of the National Endowment for the Humanities (1981–85) and secretary of education (1985–89) critical of the academic establishment—editor's note.]

no one ever blames the ideology and institutions of heterosexuality. Every day, even the talk-show hosts are newly astonished to find that people who are committed to hetero intimacy are nevertheless unhappy. After all is said and done, the prospects and promises of heterosexual culture still represent the optimism for optimism, a hope to which people apparently have already pledged their consent—at least in public.

Biddy Martin has written that some queer social theorists have produced a reductive and pseudo-radical antinormativity by actively repudiating the institutions of heterosexuality that have come to oversaturate the social imaginary. She shows that the kinds of arguments that crop up in the writings of people like Andrew Sullivan are not just right-wing fantasies. "In some queer work," she writes, "the very fact of attachment has been cast as only punitive and constraining because already socially constructed. . . . Radical anti-normativity throws out a lot of babies with a lot of bathwater. . . . An enormous fear of ordinariness or normalcy results in superficial accounts of the complex imbrication of sexuality with other aspects of social and psychic life, and in far too little attention to the dilemmas of the average people that we also are."[9]

We think our friend Biddy might be referring to us, although in this segment she cites no one in particular. We would like to clarify the argument. To be against heteronormativity is not to be against norms. To be against the processes of normalization is not to be afraid of ordinariness. Nor is it to advocate the "life without limit" she sees as produced by bad Foucauldians. Nor is it to decide that sentimental identifications with family and children are waste or garbage, or make people into waste or garbage. Nor is it to say that any sex called "lovemaking" isn't lovemaking; whatever the ideological or historical burdens of sexuality have been, they have not excluded, and indeed may have entailed, the ability of sex to count as intimacy and care. What we have been arguing here is that the space of sexual culture has become obnoxiously cramped from doing the work of maintaining a normal metaculture. When Martin calls us to recognize ourselves as "average people," to relax from an artificially stimulated "fear of . . . normalcy," the image of average personhood appears to be simply descriptive. But its averageness is also normative, in exactly the sense that Foucault meant by "normalization": not the imposition of an alien will, but a distribution around a statistically imagined norm. This deceptive appeal of the average remains heteronormative, measuring deviance from the mass. It can also be consoling, an expression of a utopian desire for unconflicted personhood. But this desire cannot be satisfied in the current conditions of privacy. People feel that the price they must pay for social membership and a relation to the future is identification with the heterosexual life narrative; that they are individually responsible for the rages, instabilities, ambivalences, and failures they experience in their intimate lives, while the fractures of the contemporary United States shame and sabotage them everywhere. Heterosexuality involves so many practices that are not sex that a world in which this hegemonic cluster would not be dominant is, at this point, unimaginable. We are trying to bring that world into being.

9. Biddy Martin, "Extraordinary Homosexuals and the Fear of Being Ordinary," *Differences* 6.2/3 (Summer–Fall 1994), pp. 122–23. [Martin (b. 1951), American lesbian theorist and university administrator. Sullivan (b. 1963), British-born American gay conservative journalist and editor—editor's note.]

Queer Counterpublics

By queer culture we mean a world-making project, where world, like public, differs from community or group because it necessarily includes more people than can be identified, more spaces than can be mapped beyond a few reference points, modes of feeling that can be learned rather than experienced as birthright. The queer world is a space of entrances, exits, unsystematized lines of acquaintance, projected horizons, typifying examples, alternate routes, blockages, incommensurate geographies.[1] World making, as much in the mode of dirty talk as of print-mediated representation, is dispersed through incommensurate registers, by definition *unrealizable* as community or identity. Every cultural form, be it a novel or an after-hours club or an academic lecture, indexes a virtual social world in ways that range from a repertoire of styles and speech genres to referential metaculture. A novel like *Dancer from the Dance*[2] relies much more heavily on referential metaculture than does an after-hours club that survives on word of mouth and may be a major scene because it is only barely coherent *as* a scene. Yet for all their differences, both allow for the concretization of a queer counterpublic. We are trying to promote this world-making project, and a first step in doing so is to recognize that queer culture constitutes itself in many ways other than through the official publics of opinion culture and the state or through the privatized forms normally associated with sexuality.

Queer and other insurgents have long striven, often dangerously or scandalously, to cultivate what good folks used to call criminal intimacies. We have developed relations and narratives that are only recognized as intimate in queer culture: girlfriends, gal pals, fuckbuddies, tricks. Queer culture has learned not only how to sexualize these and other relations but also how to use them as a context for witnessing intense and personal affect while elaborating a public world of belonging and transformation. Making a queer world has required the development of kinds of intimacy that bear no necessary relation to domestic space, to kinship, to the couple form, to property, or to the nation. These intimacies *do* bear a necessary relation to a counterpublic—an indefinitely accessible world conscious of its subordinate relation. They are typical both of the inventiveness of queer world making and of the queer world's fragility.

Nonstandard intimacies would seem less criminal and less fleeting if, as used to be the case, normal intimacies included everything from consorts to courtiers, friends, amours, associates, and co-conspirators.[3] Along with the

1. In some traditions of social theory, the process of world making as we describe it here is seen as common to all social actors. See, for example, Alfred Schutz's emphasis on the practices of typification and projects of action involved in ordinary knowledge of the social, in *The Phenomenology of the Social World*, trans. George Walsh and Frederick Lehnert (Evanston, IL: Northwestern University Press, 1967). Yet in most contexts, the social world is understood not as constructed by reference to types or projects but as an instantiated whole in a form capable of reproducing itself. The family, the state, a neighborhood, the human species, or institutions such as schools and churches—such images of social being share an appearance of plenitude seldom approached in contexts of queer world making. However much the latter might resemble the process of world construction in ordinary contexts, queer worlds do not have the power to represent a taken-for-granted social existence.

2. A 1978 novel by Andrew Holleran (pseudonym of Eric Garber) [editor's note].

3. See, for example, Alan Bray, "Homosexuality and the Signs of Male Friendship in Elizabethan England," *History Workshop Journal* 29 (Spring 1990), pp. 1–19; Laurie J. Shannon, "Emilia's Argument: Friendship and 'Human Title' in *The Two Noble Kinsmen*," *ELH* 64.3 (Fall 1997); and Roger Chartier, ed., *Passions of the Renaissance*, trans. Arthur Goldhammer, vol. 3 of *A History of Private Life*, ed. Philippe Ariès and Georges Duby (Cambridge, MA: Harvard University Press, 1989).

sex it legitimates, intimacy has been privatized; the discourse contexts that narrate true personhood have been segregated from those that represent citizens, workers, or professionals.

This transformation in the cultural forms of intimacy is related both to the history of the modern public sphere and to the modern discourse of sexuality as a fundamental human capacity. In *The Structural Transformation of the Public Sphere*, Habermas shows that the institutions and forms of domestic intimacy made private people private, members of the public sphere of private society rather than the market or the state. Intimacy grounded abstract, disembodied citizens in a sense of universal humanity. In *The History of Sexuality*, Foucault describes the personalization of sex from the other direction: confessional and expert discourses of civil society continually posit an inner personal essence, equating this true personhood with sex, and surrounding that sex with dramas of secrecy and disclosure. There is an instructive convergence here in two thinkers who otherwise seem to be describing different planets.[4] Habermas overlooks the administrative and normalizing dimensions of privatized sex in sciences of social knowledge because he is interested in the norm of a critical relation between state and civil society. Foucault overlooks the critical culture that might enable transformation of sex and other private relations because he wants to show that modern epistemologies of sexual personhood, far from bringing sexual publics into being, are techniques of isolation; they identify persons as normal or perverse for the purpose of medicalizing or otherwise administering them as individuals. Yet both Habermas and Foucault point to the way a hegemonic public has founded itself by a privatization of sex and the sexualization of private personhood. Both identify the conditions in which sexuality seems a property of subjectivity rather than a publicly or counterpublicly accessible culture.

Like most ideologies, normal intimacy may never have been an accurate description of how people actually live. It was from the beginning mediated not only by a structural separation of economic and domestic space but also by opinion culture, correspondence, novels, and romances; Rousseau's *Confessions*[5] is typical both of the ideology and of its reliance on mediation by print and by new, hybrid forms of life narrative. Habermas notes, "Subjectivity, as the innermost core of the private, was always oriented to an audience," adding that the structure of this intimacy includes a fundamentally contradictory relation to the economy:

> To the autonomy of property owners in the market corresponded a self-presentation of human beings in the family. The latter's intimacy, apparently set free from the constraint of society, was the seal on the truth of a private autonomy exercised in competition. Thus it was a private autonomy denying its economic origins . . . that provided the bourgeois family with its consciousness of itself.[6]

This structural relation is no less normative for being imperfect in practice. Its force is to prevent the recognition, memory, elaboration, or institutionaliza-

4. On the relation between Foucault and Habermas, we take inspiration from Tom McCarthy, *Ideals and Illusions* (Cambridge, MA: MIT Press, 1991), pp. 47–75.

5. Autobiographical work (1782) by the Swiss-born French political philosopher Jean-Jacques Rousseau (1712–1778) [editor's note].

6. Jürgen Habermas, *The Structural Transformation of the Public Sphere: An Inquiry into a Category of Bourgeois Society*, trans. Thomas Burger (Cambridge, MA: MIT Press, 1989), pp. 49 and 46.

tion of all the nonstandard intimacies that people have in everyday life. Affective life slops over onto work and political life; people have key self-constitutive relations with strangers and acquaintances; and they have eroticism, if not sex, outside the couple form. These border intimacies give people tremendous pleasure. But when that pleasure is called sexuality, the spillage of eroticism into everyday social life seems transgressive in a way that provokes normal aversion, a hygienic recoil even as contemporary consumer and media cultures increasingly trope toiletward, splattering the matter of intimate life at the highest levels of national culture.

In gay male culture, the principal scenes of criminal intimacy have been tearooms, streets, sex clubs, and parks—a tropism toward the public toilet.[7] Promiscuity is so heavily stigmatized as nonintimate that it is often called anonymous, whether names are used or not. One of the most commonly forgotten lessons of AIDS is that this promiscuous intimacy turned out to be a lifesaving public resource. Unbidden by experts, gay people invented safer sex; and as Douglas Crimp wrote in 1987:

> We were able to invent safe sex because we have always known that sex is not, in an epidemic or not, limited to penetrative sex. Our promiscuity taught us many things, not only about the pleasures of sex, but about the great multiplicity of those pleasures. It is that psychic preparation, that experimentation, that conscious work on our own sexualities that has allowed many of us to change our sexual behaviors—something that brutal "behavioral therapies" tried unsuccessfully for over a century to force us to do—very quickly and very dramatically. . . . All those who contend that gay male promiscuity is merely sexual *compulsion* resulting from fear of intimacy are now faced with very strong evidence against their prejudices. . . . Gay male promiscuity should be seen instead as a positive model of how sexual pleasures might be pursued by and granted to everyone if those pleasures were not confined within the narrow limits of institutionalized sexuality.[8]

AIDS is a special case, and this model of sexual culture has been typically male. But sexual practice is only one kind of counterintimacy. More important is the critical practical knowledge that allows such relations to count as intimate, to be not empty release or transgression but a common language of self-cultivation, shared knowledge, and the exchange of inwardness.

Queer culture has found it necessary to develop this knowledge in mobile sites of drag, youth culture, music, dance, parades, flaunting, and cruising—sites whose mobility makes them possible but also renders them hard to recognize as world making because they are so fragile and ephemeral. They are paradigmatically trivialized as "lifestyle." But to understand them only as self-expression or as a demand for recognition would be to misrecognize the fundamentally unequal material conditions whereby the institutions of

7. On the centrality of semipublic spaces like tearooms, bathrooms, and bathhouses to gay male life, see Chauncey, *Gay New York*; Lee Edelman, "Tearooms and Sympathy, or, Epistemology of the Water Closet," in Andrew Parker, Mary Russo, Doris Sommer, and Patricia Yaeger, eds., *Nationalisms and Sexualities* (New York: Routledge, 1992), pp. 263–84. The spaces of both gay and lesbian semipublic sexual practices are investigated in David Bell and Gill Valentine, eds., *Mapping Desire: Geographies of Sexualities* (New York: Routledge, 1995).

8. Douglas Crimp, "How to Have Promiscuity in an Epidemic," *October*, no. 43 (Winter 1987), p. 253. [Crimp (b. 1944), American art and cultural critic—editor's note.]

social reproduction are coupled to the forms of hetero culture.[9] Contexts of queer world making depend on parasitic and fugitive elaboration through gossip, dance clubs, softball leagues, and the phone-sex ads that increasingly are the commercial support for print-mediated left culture in general.[1] Queer is difficult to entextualize *as* culture.

This is particularly true of intimate culture. Heteronormative forms of intimacy are supported, as we have argued, not only referentially, in overt discourse such as love plots and sentimentality, but materially, in marriage and family law, in the architecture of the domestic, in the zoning of work and politics. Queer culture, by contrast, has almost no institutional matrix for its counterintimacies. In the absence of marriage and the rituals that organize life around matrimony, improvisation is always necessary for the speech act of pledging, or the narrative practice of dating, or for such apparently noneconomic economies as joint checking. The heteronormativity in such practices may seem weak and indirect. After all, same-sex couples have sometimes been able to invent versions of such practices. But they have done so only by betrothing the couple form and its language of personal significance, leaving untransformed the material and ideological conditions that divide intimacy from history, politics, and publics. The queer project we imagine is not just to destigmatize those average intimacies, not just to give access to the sentimentality of the couple for persons of the same sex, and definitely not to certify as properly private the personal lives of gays and lesbians.[2] Rather, it is to support forms of affective, erotic, and personal living that are public in the sense of accessible, available to memory, and sustained through collective activity.

Because the heteronormative culture of intimacy leaves queer culture especially dependent on ephemeral elaborations in urban space and print culture, queer publics are also peculiarly vulnerable to initiatives such as Mayor Rudolph Giuliani's[3] zoning law. The law aims to restrict any counterpublic sexual culture by regulating its economic conditions; its effects will reach far beyond the adult businesses it explicitly controls. The gay bars on Christopher Street draw customers from people who come there because of its sex trade. The street is cruisier because of the sex shops. The boutiques that sell freedom rings[4] and Don't Panic T-shirts do more business for the

9. The notion of a demand for recognition has been recently advanced by a number of thinkers as a way of understanding multicultural politics. See, for example, Axel Honneth, *The Struggle for Recognition* (Cambridge, UK: Polity Press, 1995); and Charles Taylor, *Multiculturalism* (Princeton, NJ: Princeton University Press, 1994). We are suggesting that although queer politics does contest the terrain of recognition, it cannot be conceived as a politics of recognition *as opposed to* an issue of distributive justice; this is the distinction proposed in Nancy Fraser's "From Redistribution to Recognition? Dilemmas of Justice in a 'Postsocialist' Age," *New Left Review*, no. 212 (July–Aug. 1995), pp. 68–93, reprinted in her *Justice Interruptus: Critical Reflections on the 'Postsocialist' Condition* (New York: Routledge, 1997).

1. See Sedgwick, *Epistemology of the Closet*, and Yvonne Zipter, *Diamonds Are a Dyke's Best Friend: Reflections, Reminiscences, and Reports from the Field on the Lesbian National Pastime* (Ithaca, NY: Firebrand Books, 1988).

2. Such a politics is increasingly recommended within the gay movement. See, for example, Andrew Sullivan, *Same-Sex Marriage, Pro and Con* (New York: Vintage, 1997); Michelangelo Signorile, *Life Outside* (New York: HarperCollins, 1997); Gabriel Rotello, *Sexual Ecology: AIDS and the Destiny of Gay Men* (New York: Dutton, 1997); William N. Eskridge Jr., *The Case for Same-Sex Marriage: From Sexual Liberty to Civilized Commitment* (New York: Free Press, 1996); Robert M. Baird and Stuart E. Rosenbaum, eds., *Same-Sex Marriage: The Moral and Legal Debate* (Amherst, NY: Prometheus Books, 1996); and Mark Strasser, *Legally Wed: Same-Sex Marriage and the Constitution* (Ithaca, NY: Cornell University Press, 1997).

3. Republican mayor of New York (b. 1944; mayor, 1994–2001) known for his tough approach to crime and for "cleaning up" the city [editor's note].

4. Six metal rings in the colors of the rainbow flag representative of gay pride, first sold in 1991 [editor's note].

same reasons. Not all of the thousands who migrate or make pilgrimages to Christopher Street use the porn shops, but all benefit from the fact that some do. After a certain point, a quantitative change is a qualitative change. A critical mass develops. The street becomes queer. It develops a dense, publicly accessible sexual culture. It therefore becomes a base for nonporn businesses, like the Oscar Wilde Bookshop. And it becomes a political base from which to pressure politicians with a gay voting bloc.

No group is more dependent on this kind of pattern in urban space than queers. If we could not concentrate a publicly accessible culture somewhere, we would always be outnumbered and overwhelmed. And because what brings us together is sexual culture, there are very few places in the world that have assembled much of a queer population without a base in sex commerce; and even those that do exist, such as the lesbian culture in Northampton, Massachusetts, are stronger because of their ties to places like the West Village, Dupont Circle, West Hollywood, and the Castro.[5] Respectable gays like to think that they owe nothing to the sexual subculture they think of as sleazy. But their success, their way of living, their political rights, and their very identities would never have been possible but for the existence of the public sexual culture they now despise. Extinguish it, and almost all *out* gay or queer culture will wither on the vine. No one knows this connection better than the right. Conservatives would not so flagrantly contradict their stated belief in a market free from government interference if they did not see this kind of hyperregulation as an important victory.

The point here is not that queer politics needs more free-market ideology but that heteronormative forms, so central to the accumulation and reproduction of capital, also depend on heavy interventions in the regulation of capital. One of the most disturbing fantasies in the zoning scheme, for example, is the idea that an urban locale is a community of shared interest based on residence and property. The ideology of the neighborhood is politically unchallengeable in the current debate, which is dominated by a fantasy that sexual subjects only reside, that the space relevant to sexual politics is the neighborhood. But a district like Christopher Street is not just a neighborhood affair. The local character of the neighborhood depends on the daily presence of thousands of nonresidents. Those who actually live in the West Village should not forget their debt to these mostly queer pilgrims. And we should not make the mistake of confusing the class of citizens with the class of property owners. Many of those who hang out on Christopher Street—typically young, queer, and African-American—couldn't possibly afford to live there. Urban space is always a host space. The right to the city extends to those who use the city.[6] It is not limited to property owners. It is not because of a fluke in the politics of zoning that urban space is so deeply misrecognized; normal sexuality requires such misrecognitions, including their economic and legal enforcement, in order to sustain its illusion of humanity.

5. Predominantly gay areas in New York City; in Washington, D.C.; west of Los Angeles; and in San Francisco, respectively [editor's note].

6. The phrase "the right to the city" is Henri Lefebvre's, from his 1968 *Le Droit à la ville*, trans. Eleonore Kofman and Elizabeth Lebas, in Henri Lefebvre, *Writings on Cities* (Oxford, UK: Blackwell, 1996). See also Manuel Castells, *The City and the Grassroots* (Berkeley: University of California Press, 1983).

Tweaking and Thwacking

Queer social theory is committed to sexuality as an inescapable category of analysis, agitation, and refunctioning: like class relations, which in this moment are mainly visible in the polarized embodiments of identity forms, heteronormativity is a fundamental motor of social organization in the United States, a founding condition of unequal and exploitative relations throughout even straight society. Any social theory that miscomprehends this participates in their reproduction.

The project of thinking about sex in public does not only engage sex when it is disavowed or suppressed. Even if sex practice is not the object domain of queer studies, sex is everywhere present. But where is the tweaking, thwacking, thumping, sliming, and rubbing you might have expected—or dreaded—in an essay on sex? We close with two scenes that might have happened on the same day in our wanderings around the city. One afternoon, we were riding with a young straight couple we know in their station wagon. Gingerly, after much circumlocution, they brought the conversation around to vibrators. These are people whose reproductivity governs their lives, their aspirations, their relations to money and entailment, mediating their relations to everyone and everything else. But the woman in this couple had recently read an article in a women's magazine about sex toys and other forms of nonreproductive eroticism. She and her husband did some mail-order shopping and became increasingly involved in what from most points of view would count as queer sex practices: their bodies have become disorganized and exciting to them. They said to us: you're the only people we can talk to about this; to all of our straight friends, this would make us perverts. In order not to feel like perverts, they had to make *us* into a kind of sex public.

Later, the question of aversion and perversion came up again. This time, we were in a bar that on most nights is a garden-variety leather bar but that on Wednesday nights hosts a sex-performance event called "Pork." Shows typically include spanking, flagellation, shaving, branding, laceration, bondage, humiliation, wrestling—you know, the usual: amateur, everyday practitioners strutting for everyone else's gratification, not unlike an academic conference. This night, word was circulating that the performance was to be erotic vomiting. This sounded like an appetite spoiler, and the thought of leaving early occurred to us but was overcome by a simple curiosity: What would the foreplay be like? Let's stay until it gets messy. Then we can leave.

A boy, twentyish, very skateboard, comes on the low stage at one end of the bar, wearing Lycra shorts and a dog collar. He sits loosely in a restraining chair. His partner, the vomiting top, comes out and tilts the bottom's head up to the ceiling, stretching out his throat. Behind them is an array of foods. The top begins pouring milk down the boy's throat, then food, then more milk. It spills over, down his chest and onto the floor. A dynamic is established between them in which they carefully keep at the threshold of gagging. The bottom struggles to keep taking in more than he really can. The top is careful to give him just enough to stretch his capacities. From time to time, a baby bottle is offered as a respite, but soon the rhythm intensifies. The boy's stomach is beginning to rise and pulse, almost convulsively.

It is at this point that we realize we cannot leave, cannot even look away. No one can. The crowd is transfixed by the scene of intimacy and display, control and abandon, ferocity and abjection. People are moaning softly with admiration, then whistling, stomping, screaming encouragements. They have pressed forward in a compact and intimate group. Finally, as the top inserts two, then three fingers in the bottom's throat, insistently offering his own stomach for the repeated climaxes, we realize that we have never seen such a display of trust and violation. We are breathless. But, good academics that we are, we also have some questions to ask. Word has gone around that the boy is straight. We want to know: What does that mean in this context? How did you discover that this is what you want to do? How did you find a male top to do it with? How did you come to do it in a leather bar? Where else do you do this? How do you feel about your new partners, this audience?

We did not get to ask these questions, but we have others that we can pose now about these scenes where sex appears more sublime than narration itself, neither redemptive nor transgressive, moral nor immoral, hetero nor homo, or sutured to any axis of social legitimation. We have been arguing that sex opens a wedge to the transformation of those social norms that require only its static intelligibility or its *deadness* as a source of meaning.[7] In these cases, though, paths through publicity led to the production of nonheteronormative bodily contexts. They intended nonheteronormative worlds because they refused to pretend that privacy was their ground; because they were forms of sociability that delinked money and family from the scene of the good life; because they made sex the consequence of public mediations and collective self-activity in a way that made for unpredicted pleasures; because, in turn, they attempted to make a context of support for their practices; because their pleasures were not purchased by a redemptive pastoralism of sex or by mandatory amnesia about failure, shame, and aversion.[8]

We are used to thinking about sexuality as a form of intimacy and subjectivity, and we have just demonstrated how limited that representation is. But the heteronormativity of U.S. culture is not something that can easily be rezoned or disavowed by individual acts of will, by a subversiveness imagined only as personal rather than as the basis of public formation, or even by the lyric moments that interrupt the hostile cultural narrative that we have been staging here. Remembering the utopian wish behind normal intimate life, we also want to remember that we aren't married to it.

1998

7. On "deadness" as an affect and aspiration of normative social membership, see "Live Sex Acts," in Berlant, *Queen of America*, pp. 59–60 and 79–81.

8. The argument against the redemptive sex pastoralism of normative sexual ideology is made in Bersani, "Is the Rectum a Grave?"; on redemptive visions more generally, see his *The Culture of Redemption* (Cambridge, MA: Harvard University Press, 1990).

REY CHOW
b. 1957

FREDRIC JAMESON has remarked that "Rey Chow completely restructures the problem of ethnicity; all future discussions and debates will have to come to terms with [her work]." A comparatist and cultural theorist, Rey Chow draws on and reworks a number of theoretical perspectives, including poststructuralism, feminism, and postcolonialism, as she seeks to illuminate topics such as identity politics, film, gender, and ethics. Her theoretical work challenges conventional Western representations of China as "a mark of absolute difference," by insisting on "the very instability upon which the dialectic between 'Chinese' and 'Western' is played." She reads and writes, as the subtitle of her first book, *Woman and Chinese Modernity*, suggests, "between East and West." Significantly, her work elucidates a transition in recent decades from a postcolonial feminism that largely examined women from within national frameworks to a transnational feminism savvy about the points of connection between nations in global circuits of exchange.

Born in Hong Kong to Muslim parents, Rey Chow earned a bachelor's degree from the University of Hong Kong (1979), where she received what she describes as a "classical colonial education" that focused on English language and literature. Her interest in poststructuralism led her to graduate work in the United States, where she received an M.A. (1982) and a Ph.D. (1986) from Stanford University. From 1987 until 1992, she taught comparative literature at the University of Minnesota. In 1992, she became a professor in the Department of Comparative Literature at the University of California at Irvine. From 2000 to 2009 she was the Andrew W. Mellon Professor of the Humanities at Brown University, where she held appointments in the Departments of Comparative Literature, English, and Modern Culture and Media. Since 2010, she has been the Anne Firor Scott Professor and Director of the Program in Literature at Duke University. In addition, she has held visiting positions at Smith College, the University of Queensland in Australia, and Princeton University, where in 2008 she was the Class of 1932 Fellow in English. In 1986–87, she was a postdoctoral fellow at the Pembroke Center for Research and Teaching on Women at Brown University. She was awarded a John Simon Guggenheim Memorial Foundation Fellowship in 1992. In 2002 she was a fellow at the Center for Advanced Study in the Behavioral Sciences, and in 2005 she was a research fellow at the Radcliff Institute. She won a Fulbright Scholarship in 2008.

While Chow's interest in English literature and theory grew out of her Hong Kong education, after her graduate work in English literature and theory she gradually returned to a consideration of Chinese literature and culture. She is the author of nine books and the editor of one that focus on the cultural, linguistic, and political interchanges between China and the West. Her first book, *Woman and Chinese Modernity: The Politics of Reading between West and East* (1991), explored gender and sexuality, popular literature, film, and commodity fetishism, focusing on "feminized space" in the West's representations of China, as well as in China's responses to Western modernity. *Writing Diaspora: Tactics of Intervention in Contemporary Cultural Studies* (1993) is a collection of eight essays in which she examines the West's attitude toward China from a "diasporic consciousness"—that is, from the perspective of those Chinese who live outside of China. With *Primitive Passions: Visuality, Sexuality, Ethnography, and Contemporary Chinese Cinema* (1995), awarded the James Russell Lowell Prize by the Modern Language Association, Chow began to bring her postcolonial lens to cinema and contemporary visual technologies. In her next five books, she explored ethnicity, ethics, media, and disciplinarity in *Ethics after Idealism: Theory–Culture–Ethnicity–Reading* (1998), the edited collection *Modern Chinese Literary and Cultural Studies in the Age of Theory: Reimagining a Field* (2000), *The Protestant Ethnic and the Spirit of Capitalism* (2002), *The Age of the World Target: Self-Referentiality in War, Theory, and Comparative Work* (2006), and *Entanglements, or Transmedial Thinking about Capture* (2012). *Sentimental Fabulations, Contemporary Chinese Films: Attachment in the Age of Global Visibility* (2007), from which our selection is drawn, examines the sentimental in nine contemporary Chinese directors whose accomplishments have brought Chinese film to the attention of world cinema. In *Not Like a Native Speaker: On Languaging as a Postcolonial Experience* (2014), Chow investigates the experiences of intellectuals like herself, including FRANZ FANON, JACQUES DERRIDA, CHINUA ACHEBE, and NGUGI WĂ THIONG'O, for whom racialization has followed from the loss of the native tongue and the experience of learning the colonist's language.

As a postcolonial theorist, Chow offers critiques of Orientalism, racism, and sexism that draw on Marxist, deconstructive, and feminist theories. Well-read in the works of Derrida, GILLES DELEUZE, and MICHEL FOUCAULT, she brings poststructural analyses of discourse, alterity, and supplementarity to bear on questions of identity and ethnicity. But hers is not an uncritical poststructuralism; it is marked by critical engagement with feminist theorists such as LAURA MULVEY, GAYATRI CHAKRAVORTY SPIVAK, and Teresa de Lauretis; postcolonial writers such as Fanon, Spivak, EDWARD W. SAID, and PAUL GILROY; and STUART HALL's cultural studies. Turning a poststructuralist lens on her precursors, she deconstructs the investments of postwar French intellectuals such as Derrida, ROLAND BARTHES, LOUIS ALTHUSSER, and JULIA KRISTEVA in romanticized views of China as a political alternative to the West's capitalist ideology. Most important, whatever her subject matter, Chow brings an intersectional analysis to her writing, in which "race and ethnicity are . . . coterminous with sexuality, just as sexuality is implicated in race and ethnicity. . . . [I]t is their categorical enmeshment—their categorical miscegenation, so to speak—that needs to be foregrounded."

Our selection, from the introduction to *Sentimental Fabulations*, illustrates Chow's theoretical writing on film—in particular, on Chinese film. The book explores the work of a group of Chinese filmmakers from mainland China, Taiwan, and Hong Kong—of whom Ang Lee (b. 1954) and Zhang Yimou (b. 1951) are the best known in the West—whose films brought Chinese filmmaking out of the art house and into the multiplex, where they could find a global audience. The legacy of Mao Zedong's China, especially the Cultural Revolution of 1966–76; the opening of China to the West after President Richard Nixon's 1972 visit; the privatization of state industries—including the film industry—that began in the 1980s and continues apace; and the country's emergence as an economic superpower led up to and made possible the so-called Fifth Generation filmmakers of mainland China, the Taiwanese New Wave, and Hong Kong Second Wave filmmakers, all contributors to the growing international popularity of Chinese film after 1980. Chow's introduction theorizes this new wave of Chinese filmmaking within the context of Western cinema both to avoid the tendency of Western scholars to ghettoize non-Western film industries and to counter Orientalisms that posit some authentic version of Asianness that would underwrite the images on the screen. In our selection, Chow describes the relationship of Chinese films not only to the ongoing and dynamic development of Chinese culture but, more significantly, to the complexities of intercultural exchange in an age of global media, where diasporic populations help support international cinemas and Asianness becomes a "commodified and reproducible value . . . sustained by and contributing to the flows of capital."

Chow begins, "Where is the movie about me?" Rather than attempting to answer her question, she uses the query as a springboard to unpack the complexities of ethnic identity formation, illustrating the vexed role of representation—and of film—in this process. Her question condenses with elegant simplicity a paradigm shift within Western film theory that began in the 1970s with the development of feminist film theory and continued through the 1990s as various groups (defined by nationality, gender, sexual orientation, religion, race, or ethnicity) took up this question and film studies became increasingly concerned with group cultures. The theoretical question Chow poses is how to move beyond classifying group identities to interrogate the role cinema necessarily has in the process of any group's coming into visibility.

An examination of Mulvey's landmark 1975 essay, "Visual Pleasure and Narrative Cinema" (see above), sets the terms of Chow's argument. Mulvey was the first to split the seemingly unified cinematic image, with its transparency and its untroubled referentiality to an objective world, by articulating what remains invisible in it: the apparatus that she called the male gaze. In Hollywood films, the camera and the framing of the mise-en-scène tend to promote particular views of "reality"—for Mulvey, patriarchal views—over others. Rooted in a distrust of images as deceptive because constructed to privilege particular (in this case masculine) fantasies, Mulvey's split between image and gaze opened up film to the study of cultural difference and ideological critique. While feminist film theory has continued to interrogate the patriarchal gaze, other cultural groups formed around race, ethnicity, nationality, and sexuality began to use this gap between gaze and image to critique dominant (Western) modes of representation and value.

Building on Gilles Deleuze's argument in his book on Foucault, however, Chow argues that there is more to the "becoming visible" of subordinated groups than simply replacing bad representations with good and presumably authentic ones. She uses the term "visuality" to describe a key epistemic process: a discursive formation—what Foucault would call an apparatus or grid of intelligibility—that becomes "the condition of possibility for what becomes visible." That is, what we can see is largely dependent on what we can know. Attention to this "discursive politics" in the "fraught" context of a globalized media shifts the focus away from an "anthropomorphic realism" that confuses the image of a subordinated cultural group with the group itself toward a deconstruction of the image and its fantasies. Thus, Chow maintains, Western film theorists fascinated with Chinese cinema must abandon the dream of authentic Chineseness, in order to understand the myriad ways in which Chineseness has become a commodity in a transnational market that includes not only movies but also "economic rivalry, exotic cuisine, herbal medicine, spiritual and physical exercise, sex trade, female child adoption, model minority politics, illegal immigration, and so on."

Today Chinese films are produced and distributed by multinational corporations, employ multinational casts and crews, compete internationally for awards, and attract audiences from around the world, activities all abetted by the transnational movements of people, capital, media, and goods across the globe. Yet the new international Chinese cinema does not simply slot itself into the conventional categories of Western film theory. Rather, Chow argues, it challenges long-held values. She points, for example, to the perceived connection between political progressivism and the avant-garde, which she sees promoted by the German dramatist Bertolt Brecht (1898–1956), but which also is found in the Frankfurt School critics, such as THEODOR ADORNO and MAX HORKHEIMER, as well as in Mulvey's essay. Avant-garde art does not necessarily serve progressive political ends, nor are popular genres always politically regressive.

What unites the disparate filmmakers that make up the new international Chinese cinema, Chow contends, is the persistence of the sentimental, a term most frequently dismissed as "affective excess" in the West; in film it is mostly associated with "women's films" and derogated accordingly. She examines the Western genealogy of the term in the moral philosophy and literature of the eighteenth century, specifically in the philosophy of FRIEDRICH VON SCHILLER. She concludes that far from being merely affective excess, in the Euro-American context the sentimental, whether as elegiac lament for lost ideals or, more recently, as a means of focalizing struggles for social justice, engages the ethics of sociality in literature and art. Sentimentality, in this regard, might be a mechanism of intercultural exchange between West and East. The sentimental, translated into Chinese as *wenqing zhuyi* (warm sentiment-ism), is a recurrent mode in Chinese cinema as well; there, however, it carries with it a sense of moderation (being between hot and cold) that the European term lacks. The sentimental in Chinese films designates "an inclination or a disposition toward making compromises and toward making-do with even—and especially—that which is oppressive and unbearable." As in the West, it tends to circle around domestic themes: home, the family, and kinship ties. As Chow interrogates the sentimental she refuses to label it as either socially progressive or ideologically suspect. Her dialectical treatment highlights regressive and progressive features of sentimentality in Chinese cinema. She links it on the one hand with a collective nostalgia for ancestral traditions and, on the other, with inevitable life-enhancing escapes from and disruptions of such traditions. Chow argues, moreover, that the traditional anachronistic focus on personal modesty and individual restraint in Chinese cinema now serves positive protective functions in a global era of increasing individual visibility, spectacle, and personal aggrandizement.

Critics interested in the study of Chinese cinema have sometimes dismissed Chow's theoretical apparatus, which draws heavily on Continental theories, as unnecessary to her otherwise excellent readings of the films, while others criticize her dense language, which is characteristic of poststructuralism. In addition, some have found her characterization of the sentimental a bit too broad to hold together the variety of films she examines. There can be little doubt, however, that Chow's is a major voice in contemporary film theory. Through her elegant syntheses of media studies, feminism, and poststructuralism, her work stages powerful interventions into ethnicity, postcolonialism, and Chinese cultural studies, illuminating both the opportunities and the inequalities that mark intercultural exchanges in an increasingly transnational world.

Sentimental Fabulations, Contemporary Chinese Films: Attachment in the Age of Global Visibility **Keywords:** Affect, Cultural Studies, Ethics, Feminist Theory, Globalization, Media, Postcolonial Theory, Poststructuralism, Psychoanalysis

From Sentimental Fabulations, Contemporary Chinese Films: Attachment in the Age of Global Visibility

From *Introduction*

Where is the movie about me?

In the academic study of cinema, this is one of the most commonly encountered questions in recent years. Versions of it include some of the following: Where in this discipline am I? How come I am not represented? What does it mean for me and my group to be unseen? What does it mean for me and my group to be seen in this manner—what has been left out? These questions of becoming visible pertain, of course, to the prevalence of the politics of identification, to the relation between representational forms and their articulation of subjective histories and locations. It is one reason the study of cinema, like the study of literature and history, has become increasingly caught up in the study of group cultures: every group (be it defined by nationality, class, gender, ethnicity, sexual orientation, religion, or disability), it seems, produces a local variant of the universal that is cinema, requiring critics to engage with the specificities of particular collectivities even as they talk about the generalities of the filmic apparatus. According to one report, for instance, at the Society of Cinema Studies Annual Conference of 1998, "nearly half the over four hundred papers (read from morning to night in nine rooms) treated the politics of representing ethnicity, gender, and sexuality."[1] Western film studies, as Christine Gledhill and Linda Williams write, is currently faced with its own "impending dissolution . . . in . . . transnational theorization."[2] How did this state of affairs arise? How might we approach it not simply empirically, by way of numerical classifications, but also theoretically, by probing visibility as a problematic, to which film, because of its palpably visual modes of signification, may serve as a privileged point of entry?

Transnational theorization was, in fact, already an acute part of the reflections of non-Western authors on film experiences during the 1900s, 1910s, and 1920s. When contemplating the effects of the filmic spectacle, for instance, Lu Xun and Tanizaki Junichiro,[3] writing self-consciously as Chinese and Japanese nationals, readily raised questions of what it meant to be—and to be visible as—Chinese and Japanese in the modern world. The visual immediacy of Chinese and Japanese figures and faces, conveyed on the screen as they had never been before, was experienced by these authors not only as scientific advancement but simultaneously as a type of racially marked signification—specifically, as representations in which their own cultures appeared inferior and disadvantaged vis-à-vis a newly global, mediatized gaze.[4]

In light of these early reflections—reflections that are, strictly speaking, part of the history of film but which have hitherto been relegated to the margins of the West—the current preoccupation with group identities in film studies is perhaps only a belated reenactment of a longstanding set of issues pertaining to the fraught relationship between film and cultural identity. * * *

HIGHLIGHTS OF A WESTERN DISCIPLINE

* * *

In her groundbreaking essay of 1975, "Visual Pleasure and Narrative Cinema," Laura Mulvey turned the question of the cinematic image (and its implications of time) into a story, one that, she revealed, was far from being

1. Dudley Andrew, "The 'Three Ages' of Cinema Studies and the Age to Come," *PMLA* 115.3 (2000): 348. Andrew offers this information as part of a discussion of the history of cinema studies [except as indicated, all notes are Chow's; some of her notes have been edited and some omitted].

2. Christine Gledhill and Linda Williams, introduction to *Reinventing Film Studies*, ed. Christine Gledhill and Linda Williams (London: Arnold, 2000), 1.

3. Popular Japanese novelist (1886–1965). Lu Xun (pen name of Zhou Shuren, 1881–1936), a major figure in modern Chinese literature [editor's note].

4. See my discussion of Lu Xun's famous reactions to a slide show of an execution of a Chinese man (which he happened to watch during 1904–5 in Japan), reactions that led him to abandon medical studies and become a writer, at the beginning of part 1 of *Primitive Passions: Visuality, Sexuality, Ethnography, and Contemporary Chinese Cinema* (New York: Columbia UP, 1995). Tanizaki, for his part, noted how, in contrast to Western faces, Japanese faces appeared hideous and repulsive on film. For in-depth commentaries on as well as translations of some of Tanizaki's film essays and stories (written during the 1910s and 1920s), see Thomas LaMarre, *Shadows on the Screen: Tanizaki Junichiro on Cinema and "Oriental" Aesthetics* (Ann Arbor: Center for Japanese Studies, University of Michigan, 2005), in particular chaps. 7 and 8. It should be added, however, that Tanizaki's emphases were largely aesthetic—indeed, synesthetic, as LaMarre argues—in orientation, whereas Lu Xun's emphases were motivated by his sense of shock at his countrymen's apathy as bystanders and geared toward the urgency of national reform. For a major historical study of early East Asian cinema that elaborates the sensorial aspects of cinematic modernity, see Zhang Zhen, *An Amorous History of the Silver Screen: Shanghai Cinema, 1896–1937* (Chicago: U of Chicago P, 2005).

sexually neutral or innocent.[5] Rather than treating the cinematic image as a single entity, Mulvey approached it in a deconstructive move, in which what seems visually obvious and unified is taken apart by the reintroduction of narrative. The part of the narrative that determines how specific images are looked at while remaining itself hidden and invisible, Mulvey called the gaze. Most critically, Mulvey gave the temporal differential between image and gaze the name of patriarchy, so that, in the case of classical Hollywood melodrama at least, she charged, masculinist scopophilia underwrote the imperative of gazing, while women were cast, as a result, as passive, fetishized objects,[6] as beautiful images to be looked at. Mulvey was formidably direct about her goal: "It is said that analysing pleasure, or beauty, destroys it. That is the intention of this article."[7] As Maggie Humm puts it, "Mulvey's essay marked a huge conceptual leap in film theory: a jump from the ungendered and formalistic analyses of semiotics to the understanding that film viewing always involves gendered identities."[8] By arguing that cinema is irreducibly structured by (hetero) sexual difference, Mulvey succeeded in doing something that her fellow male critics were uninterested in doing—prying the filmic image open and away from its hitherto spontaneous, reified status and reinserting in it the drama of the ongoing cultural struggle between men and women, the drama of narrative coercions and ideological interpellations.[9]

In its justifiable distrust of the cinematic image as deceptive and usurpatory and in its courageous effort to forge a politics that would prevent the woman spectator from completely collapsing, at her own peril, into the cinematic image of femininity produced by men, was feminist film theory, in spite of itself, an unwitting ally to an intellectual tradition that is, to borrow a term from Martin Jay's study of modern French theory, iconophobic?[1] I tend to think so, but it is necessary to add that this iconophobia was a theoretically and institutionally productive one.[2] (Among other things, it posed a crucial question within the politics of film production: how could

5. Laura Mulvey, "Visual Pleasure and Narrative Cinema," in *Visual and Other Pleasures* (Bloomington: Indiana UP, 1989), 14–26. Mulvey was not alone in her effort to theorize narrativity in relation to film. Among her fellow travelers were Jean-Louis Baudry, Christian Metz, Stephen Heath, and Paul Willemen, who each did substantive work with film narrative during the same period. See Jean-Louis Baudry, "The Apparatus," in *Narrative, Apparatus, Ideology: A Film Theory Reader*, ed. Philip Rosen (New York: Columbia UP, 1986), 299–319; Christian Metz, *Film Language: A Semiotics of the Cinema* (New York: Oxford UP, 1974) and *Language and Cinema*, trans. Donna Jean Umiker-Sebeok (The Hague: Mouton, 1974); Stephen Heath, "Narrative Space," *Screen* 17.3 (1976): 68–112, and *Questions of Cinema* (Bloomington: Indiana UP, 1981); and Paul Willemen, *Looks and Frictions: Essays on Cultural Studies and Film Theory* (Bloomington: Indiana UP, 1994). Mulvey, however, was the one who raised the issue of sexual politics. [MULVEY (b. 1941), feminist film theorist and filmmaker; for the essay cited, see above—editor's note.]

6. Objects invested with magical, religious, or sexual qualities. "Scopophilia": pleasure in looking [editor's note].

7. Mulvey, "Visual Pleasure and Narrative Cinema," 16.

8. Maggie Humm, *Feminism and Film* (Bloomington: Indiana UP, 1997), 17. Humm's book offers a thoughtful account that places Mulvey's essay in its historical context of the United Kingdom in 1960s and 1970s, when the British intellectual left encountered the burgeoning of feminist theory.

9. *Interpellation* is a term used by the French Marxist philosopher LOUIS ALTHUSSER (1918–1990) to describe the process by which ideology "hails" and incorporates the individual [editor's note].

1. Martin Jay, *Downcast Eyes: The Denigration of Vision in Modern French Thought* (Berkeley: U of California P, 1993). ["Iconophobic": affected by fear or hatred of images—editor's note.]

2. Many criticisms of Mulvey's polemic piece, including feminist criticisms of the 1980s, revolve around her point about destroying pleasure and, as a counterargument, attempt to recuperate the positive value of pleasure, especially for women spectators. My argument is quite different in that it is about the intellectually and institutionally productive—that is, reproducible—nature of Mulvey's original negative move (of deconstructing the image) and how this is thought-provokingly bound up with the iconophobia of our (image-studded) culture at large.

one make a differently narrativized kind of film?) It was precisely its momentum of negativity, manifested in the belief that the cinematic image has somehow repressed something existing beyond it, that became the characteristic force with which the study of film has since then spread—first to English departments, in which film is often accepted as a kind of pop culture; then to foreign language and literature departments, in which film becomes yet another method of learning about other cultures; and finally to the currently fashionable discussions, in social science as well as humanities programs across the university, of so-called global media.

Feminist film theory, in other words, inaugurated the institutional dissemination of cinema studies in the Anglo-American world with something akin to what Michel Foucault, in his work on the history of sexuality in the West, called the repressive hypothesis, whereby the conceptualization of what is repressive—together with its investment in lack and castration—is reinforced simultaneously by the incessant generation and proliferation of discourses about what is supposedly repressed.[3] (It was no mere coincidence that the political weapon on which Mulvey relied for attacking phallocentrism was Freudian psychoanalysis.)[4] But what was unique—and remarkable—in this instance was the articulation of the repressive hypothesis to the visual field, an articulation wherein the visually full (presence and plenitude of the) cinematic image has become itself the very evidence/sign of repression and lack.

IMAGE, TIME, IDENTITY: TRAJECTORIES OF BECOMING VISIBLE

Because it was underwritten with the push of the repressive hypothesis, the paradigm shift within the cinematic visual field toward the study of narrativity and ideology led to consequences that have gone considerably beyond (the Western parameters of) film studies. Such a paradigm shift harked back to the heightened sense of group self-consciousness already felt by non-Western writers such as Lu Xun and Tanizaki about film technology in the early twentieth century and logically made way, in academia, for the study of differences dispersed along multiple lines of inquiry. In the decades since Mulvey's essay was first published,[5] film and cultural critics have been extending the implications of her work (often in simplified terms) by devoting themselves to problematizing the naturalness of the cinematic image. Rather than being on the image itself, its magic, or its tendency toward monumentalization, the focus in theorizing and analyzing film has increasingly been on identifying and critiquing the multiple narrative and ideological processes that go into the image's production. Bill Nichols sums up this general trend succinctly: "The visual is no longer a means of verifying the certainty of facts pertaining to an objective, external world and truths about

3. See Michel Foucault, *The History of Sexuality*, vol. 1, trans. Robert Hurley (New York: Pantheon, 1978). [Foucault (1926–1984), French philosopher and historian of ideas; for *The History of Sexuality*, see above—editor's note.]

4. Mulvey, "Visual Pleasure and Narrative Cinema," 14. ["Phallocentrism": the psychoanalytic system in which sexual difference is defined as the difference between having and lacking the phallus; the term has come to refer to the patriarchal cultural system as a whole insofar as that system privileges the phallus as the symbol and source of power, and it is associated with the theories of Sigmund Freud (1856–1939), the Austrian founder of psychoanalysis—editor's note.]

5. To her credit, Mulvey herself has, with historical hindsight, critiqued the binarism of her earlier polemical argument and revised her observations. See the chapter "Changes: Thoughts on Myth, Narrative and Historical Experience" (first published in 1985), in *Visual and Other Pleasures*, 159–76.

this world conveyed linguistically. The visual now constitutes the terrain of subjective experience as the locus of knowledge, and power."[6] Whereas feminist critics, following Mulvey, elaborate and refine women-centered modes of interrogating patriarchy, other critics, equipped with other types of social queries, would complicate the differential between gaze and image in terms of class, race, ethnicity, nationality, and sexual preference in order to expose the repressive effects of dominant modes of visuality and identification. (Think, for instance, of the numerous critiques in postcolonial studies of orientalist representations.) Concurrently, they also theorize the ambiguities inherent in various forms of spectatorship and, by implication, in various forms of seeing and subjectivity.[7]

In these collective endeavors to destroy the pleasure of the beautiful image, what has happened to the problematic of time? At one level, time is infinitely diversified and relativized: as every group of spectators comes forward with its demands, interrogations, and political agendas, one can no longer speak of the image as such but must become willing to subject the image to processes of re-viewing, reimaging, and reassembling. This is perhaps one reason there are so many publications on filmmaking and film reception in different cultures (Brazilian, Chinese, French, German, Hong Kong, Indian, Iranian, Israeli, Italian, Japanese, Korean, and Spanish, just to name some commonly encountered examples). At the same time, in this culturally pluralized way of theorizing the filmic image, one cannot help feeling that a certain predictability has set in and that, despite their local differences, the theoretical moves made by different cultural groups vis-à-vis the cinematic image often share a similar kind of critical prerogative. Borrowing again from Nichols, we may describe this prerogative in this manner: "The rise of distinct cultures to a condition of visibility accompanies a radical shift away from democratic ideals of universalism (equality under the law for all regardless of gender, color, sexual orientation and so on) toward a particularism that insists on equality precisely in relation to differences of gender, color, sexual orientation and the like."[8] "Differences of gender, color, sexual orientation and the like," it follows, all generate research agendas, competition for institutional space and funding, and self-reproductive mechanisms such as publications and the training and placing of students. The questions of identity politics with which I began this discussion are therefore, arguably, some of the *temporal* outcomes of the proliferating and disseminating mechanisms that characterize the repressive hypothesis as it has been mobilized around the cinematic visual field.

In this light, the ambivalent logics exemplified by feminist film theory from the very beginning may be seen as constitutive, perhaps paradigmatic, of the process of a subordinated group's rise to visibility. When feminist film theory alerted us to the cinematically fetishized status of women, its apparent

6. Bill Nichols, "Film Theory and the Revolt against Master Narratives," in *Reinventing Film Studies*, 42.
7. See, for instance, essays in the following collections: *Unthinking Eurocentrism: Multiculturalism and the Media*, ed. Ella Shohat and Robert Stam (New York: Routledge, 1994); *Fugitive Images: From Photography to Video*, ed. Patrice Petro (Bloomington: Indiana UP, 1995); *The Image in Dispute*, ed. Dudley Andrew with Sally Shafto (Austin: U of Texas P, 1997); *The Oxford Guide to Film Studies*, ed. John Hill and Pamela Church Gibson (Oxford: Oxford UP, 1998); *Visual Culture: The Reader*, ed. Jessica Evans and Stuart Hall (London: Sage, 1999); and *Keyframes: Popular Film and Cultural Studies*, ed. Matthew Tinkcom and Amy Villarejo (New York: Routledge, 2001).
8. Nichols, "Film Theory and the Revolt against Master Narratives," 40.

iconophobia shared important affinities with the moral charge that accompanied Western political activisms of the 1960s and early 1970s, with their demands for an end to imperialism and military violence and for the granting of civil rights to disenfranchised populations. At the same time, like the mass protests so self-consciously staged during that era, feminist film theory was delivering another message. This was the message that the politics of gender and sexuality (together with the politics of race, class, and ethnicity) was, in fact, none other than the politics of commodified media spectacles, a politics constituted by the demonstrative forces of public display.[9] Indeed, the determination with which feminist critics sought to subvert the widespread "false" representations of women—by actively competing for the right to transform, possess, and manage the visual field; to fabricate women's images; to broadcast women's stories—suggested that the dynamics of late capitalist simulacra[1] was assuming center stage. The mechanically and then electronically produced images; the instantly transmitted, spectacular "reality" shows: these were henceforth going to be the actual, ubiquitous political battleground.

The attempt to anchor one's identity definitively in what Mulvey called to-be-looked-at-ness (on the screen as well as off) is, in view of this history, a newly fetishistic practice in an exponentially expanding and accelerating virtual field of global visibility. (This is, I believe, one reason that those who traditionally would have concentrated on the study of prose fiction have been migrating steadily toward the study of film and visual cultures.) Moreover, this fetishistic practice and its countless simulacra—in so many varieties of "Look at me! Look at us!"—are no longer confined to the realm of gender politics but also repeated and reproduced widely across the disciplines, in which the morally impassioned rebuke of images always goes hand in hand with the massive production and circulation of more images—be those images about classes, races, nations, or persons of different sexual orientations.

Pursued in close relation to a controversial visual medium, feminist film theory since Mulvey hence reveals (in a handy manner) something crucial about the condition of visibility in general. In the course of feminist critique, the immediately present, visible object—the image of woman in classical Hollywood narrative cinema—is delimited or bracketed in an intervention that, notably, cannot abandon the visible as such but instead moves it into a different frame (women's world). This move makes it possible to include that which has hitherto remained invisible and thereby to reinvent the very terms of the relation between the visible and the invisible. In this process, however, becoming visible is no longer simply a matter of becoming visible in the visual sense (as an image or object) but also a matter of participating in a discursive politics of (re)configuring the relation between center and margins, a politics in which what is visible may be a key but not the exclusive

9. As Nancy Armstrong writes: "The sixties saw an important shift in the theater of political activism from the plane of physical action and conflicts that we persist in designating as real to the plane of discourse, representation, and performance, where conflicts determine how we imagine our relation to the real" ("Who's Afraid of the Cultural Turn?" *differences* 12.1 [Spring 2001]: 42). Her essay offers an interesting discussion of the linkage between the iconophobic legacy of Victorianism and the so-called cultural turn set off by the media-oriented activist events of the 1960s in the United States.

1. Simulations of reality, copies without originals; this term is associated with writings of the French social critic and theorist JEAN BAUDRILLARD (1929–2007) [editor's note].

determinant. *There is, in other words, a visibility of visibility—a visibility that is the condition of possibility for what becomes visible, that may derive a certain intelligibility from the latter but cannot be simply reduced to it.* It is to this other, epistemic sense of visibility—of visibility as the structuration of knowability—that Gilles Deleuze[2] alerts us in his fascinating study of Foucault. As Deleuze writes in different passages, "Visibilities are not to be confused with elements that are visible or more generally perceptible, such as qualities, things, objects, compounds of objects. . . . Visibilities are not forms of objects, nor even forms that would show up under light, but rather forms of luminosity which are created by the light itself and allow a thing or object to exist only as a flash, sparkle or shimmer"; "Visibilities are neither the acts of a seeing subject nor the data of a visual meaning"; "Visibilities are not defined by sight but are complexes of actions and passions, actions and reactions, multisensorial complexes, which emerge into the light of day."[3]

If we follow Deleuze's thinking along these lines, the question of anyone's or any group's rise to the condition of visibility would turn out to be much more complicated than an attainment of quantifiable image time or even of the empirical status of being represented or seen. Instead, such a question would need to involve a consideration of the less immediately or sensorially detectable elements helping to propel, enhance, or obstruct such visibility in the first place and, even where visibility has occurred, a consideration of the often vacillating relations between the visible and the invisible that may well continue at different levels.

Tied as it is to the problematic of becoming visible (understood in these terms), the fetishization of identity as it is currently found in the study of cinematic images thus tends to proceed with a Janus-faced[4] logic. There are those who, mistaking simple visual presence for (the entirety of) visibility, will always insist on investing artificial images with an anthropomorphic realism—the very thing that the iconoclasm of film, as its early theorists observed, fundamentally undid—and moreover to equate such images with the lives and histories of "real" cultural groups. ("National allegory" readings are one good example of this.) This line of thinking has its productive moments, to be sure, but it is ultimately limited in what it can offer. Meanwhile, for those who remember that what is on the screen are not real people but images, a suspension of such insistence on literal, positivistic identifications can mean a turn, more interestingly, to the specific materialities of image, affect, and fantasy, on the one hand, and the fraught complexities of globalized visibility, on the other.

With respect to the recent Western European and North American fascination with East Asian cinema,[5] the first question to ask, then, is this: should we try to direct such fascination back at some authentic, continuous Asianness lying beyond the alluring cinematic images, or would it not be more

2. French philosopher (1925–1995); see above [editor's note].
3. Gilles Deleuze, *Foucault*, trans. Sean Hand, foreword by Paul Bove (Minneapolis: U of Minnesota P, 1988), 52, 58, and 59.
4. That is, looking in opposite directions, like the Roman two-faced god of transitions, time, gates, and doorways [editor's note].
5. See, for instance, Charles Tesson, "L'Asie majeure," *Cahiers du cinema* 553 (January 2001): 5; Dave Kehr, "In Theaters Now: The Asian Alternative," *New York Times*, January 14, 2001, 2:1, 30. Apart from being featured at film festivals around the world, at which they have been receiving major awards, East Asian films, directors, and actors and actresses have also steadily made their way into mainstream cinematic venues in Western Europe and North America.

pertinent to see Asianness itself as a commodified and reproducible value, made tantalizingly visible and accessible not only by the filmic genres of the action or martial arts comedy, the love story, and the historical saga but also by an entire network of contemporary media discourses—economic rivalry, exotic cuisine, herbal medicine, spiritual and physical exercise, sex trade, female child adoption, model minority politics, illegal immigration, and so on—that are at once sustained by and contributing to the flows of capital? Part of my goal in this study is to argue that Chinese cinema since the 1980s—a cinema that is often characterized by multinational corporate production and distribution, multinational cast and crew collaboration, international award competition activity, and multicultural, multiethnic reception, as well as being accompanied by a steady stream of English-language publications, written (not infrequently by those who do not speak or read Chinese or consult Chinese-language sources) for an English-reading market—is an inherent part of a contemporary global problematic of becoming visible. As much as belonging in the history of Chinese culture, the films involved should also, I contend, be seen as belonging in the history of Western cinema studies, in the same manner that modern Asia, Africa, and Latin America, properly speaking, belong in the history of modern European studies.[6]

DEFINING THE SENTIMENTAL IN RELATION TO CONTEMPORARY CHINESE CINEMA

To the extent that one implicit aim of her criticism of classical Hollywood cinema was to eradicate conventional Western images altogether, Mulvey's early work can be seen as a British rejoinder to the political aspirations of the French nouvelle vague filmmakers (such as Jean-Luc Godard) and the theorists associated with the French journal *Tel quel*, who in the 1960s and 1970s mobilized critiques of Western thinking, often by way of looking east, especially to Mao Zedong's China.[7] Just as Mao and his cohort, following a native revolutionary tradition that began with the May Fourth Movement of 1919, sought to radicalize Chinese society by attacking its most basic social unit—the Chinese family[8]—so, too, did Anglo-American feminist film the-

6. For an account of the study of Chinese cinema in the West, see the chapter "The Rise of Chinese Film Studies in the West," in Yingjin Zhang, *Screening China: Interventions, Cinematic Reconfigurations, and the Transnational Imaginary in Contemporary Chinese Cinema* (Ann Arbor: U of Michigan P, 2002), 43–113.

7. Notable examples of films include Godard's *La chinoise* (1967) [*The Chinese*; French], *Le vent d'Est* (*Wind from the East* [French]) (1969), and *Tout va bien* [*All's Well*; French] (1972), while Chris Marker's *Sunday in Peking* (1956) was among the first European documentaries to chronicle China under Mao (even though Marker is not considered a representative of the *nouvelle vague*). Among the more well-known publications by members of *Tel quel* on China, see, for instance, JULIA KRISTEVA, *About Chinese Women*, trans. Anita Barrows (New York: Urizen, 1977); and ROLAND BARTHES, *Alors la Chine?* [*Then China?*, French] (Paris: C. Bourgois, 1975). Among other well-known European endeavors to engage with China during this period and not too long afterward, see JACQUES DERRIDA, *Of Grammatology*, trans. GAYATRI CHAKRAVORTY SPIVAK (Baltimore: Johns Hopkins UP, 1976); the film *Chung Kuo/Cina*, directed by Michelangelo Antonioni (1972); and the film *The Last Emperor*, directed by Bernardo Bertolucci (1987). [*Tel quel*: literally, "as is" or "as such" (French), an avant-garde literary magazine published in Paris (1960–82) that from 1966 to 1970 represented a Maoist version of Marxism. *Nouveau vague*: New Wave (French), a group of French avant-garde filmmakers of the late 1950s and 1960s, including Godard (b. 1930), known for their documentary realism and spare style. Mao (1893–1976), principal Marxist theorist of China's communist revolution and the leader of the People's Republic of China from its founding in 1949 until his death—editor's note.]

8. It should, however, be noted that although the Chinese Communist Party was always eager to emphasize that loyalty to the party and the state must come before the family (in case of contradiction), efforts were often made to ensure that the patriarchal family system and the party could coexist in harmony. In other, words, communism in China did not in actuality supplant or eradicate

ory of the mid-twentieth century leave some of its most pronounced critical marks on melodrama, the film genre that is, arguably, most intimately linked to the middle-class nuclear family and its demands for female self-sacrifice.[9] But the Chinese connection, if it may be so called, did not stop at the attempt to deconstruct the family, East or West. As the consequences of Chinese communism began to be questioned by organic intellectuals in China—and as the disasters spawned by Mao's political idealism (which reached its frenzied heights during the Cultural Revolution of 1966–76)[1] became a subject of reflective critique by those who had spent their formative youthful years living under the mainland Chinese regime—Chinese cinema became, for the first time, globally visible. In the astonishing films made by mainland Fifth Generation directors such as Chen Kaige, Zhang Yimou, Tian Zhuangzhuang, and their classmates, as well as by their contemporaries in Hong Kong and Taiwan such as Tsui Hark, Hou Hsiao-Hsien, Ann Hui, Ang Lee, Edward Yang, Stanley Kwan, Clara Law, Wong Kar-wai, and Tsai Ming-liang, Chinese cinema has since the 1980s become an event with which the entire world has to reckon.[2] Appearing first in international film festivals and art house theaters, then gradually in undergraduate curricula across college campuses in the English-speaking world, and finally in mainstream Hollywood productions, China—in the form of films, directors, actors and actresses, cinematographic techniques, and special effects—has helped to revitalize cinematic discourse in the West and made it necessary, once again, for Western intellectuals to come to terms with aspects of what in so many ways still remains an exotic culture.

---

loyalty to the patriarchal family. [May Fourth Movement: a student-led protest and reform movement that attacked traditional Confucian values and promoted national independence and Western ideas—editor's note.]

9. See, for instance, some of the essays by Mulvey in *Visual and Other Pleasures*; Tania Modleski, *Loving with a Vengeance: Mass-Produced Fantasies for Women* (Hamden, Conn.: Archon, 1982); Ien Ang, *Watching Dallas: Soap Opera and the Melodramatic Imagination*, trans. Della Couling (London: Methuen, 1985); Mary Ann Doane, *The Desire to Desire: The Woman's Film of the 1940s* (Bloomington: Indiana UP, 1987); Thomas Elsaesser, "Tales of Sound and Fury: Observations on the Family Melodrama," in *Movies and Methods*, ed. Bill Nichols (Berkeley: U of California P, 1985), 2:165–89; Geoffrey Nowell Smith, "Minnelli and Melodrama," in *Movies and Methods*, 2:190–94; and Christine Gledhill, "Genre and Gender: The Case of Soap Opera," in *Representation: Cultural Representations and Signifying Practices*, ed. Stuart Hall (London: Sage in association with the Open University, 2003), 337–85. See also some of the essays in the following collections: *Home Is Where the Heart Is: Studies in Melodrama and the Woman's Film*, ed. Christine Gledhill (London: British Film Institute, 1987); *Melodrama: Stage, Picture, Screen*, ed. Jacky Bratton, Jim Cook, and Christine Gledhill (London: British Film Institute, 1994); and *Feminism and Film*, ed. E. Ann Kaplan (Oxford: Oxford UP, 2000). For an informative account that argues melodrama's close affiliations to genres of action and suspense (in contrast to the standard view that sees it as primarily linked to genres of passion and femininity), see Steve Neale, *Genre and Hollywood* (London: Routledge, 2000), 179–204.

1. A campaign launched by Mao to rekindle revolutionary fervor by removing counterrevolutionary elements from the Communist Party and from society in general; the repeated purges resulted in factionalism, violence, and chaos [editor's note].

2. Before the 1980s, a large number of Chinese films had been produced during various time periods—for example, the silent films from the late 1890s to the early 1930s; the nation-building patriotic films of the 1930s and beyond; films produced on the mainland during and after the reign of Mao Zedong; films in Cantonese, Chaozhouhua (Chiu Chow), Xiamenhua (Amoy), and Minnanhua (Taiwanese) as well as in Mandarin, produced in Shanghai, Taiwan, Hong Kong, and southeast Asia in the decades of the 1940s to the early 1980s. * * * Before the 1980s, it was not uncommon for Chinese films to be shown at regional (especially Asian) film festivals, but few participated in international film festivals involving European and American audiences. [The "Fifth Generation" Chinese filmmakers—Chen (b. 1952), Zhang (b. 1951), and Tian (b. 1952)—all graduated from the Beijing Film Academy and, beginning in the mid-1980s, increasingly drew international attention to Chinese cinema. Tsui (b. 1950), Hui (b. 1947), Lee (b. 1954), Kwan (b. 1957), Law (b. 1957), and Wong (b. 1958) represent the Hong Kong Second New Wave, while Hou (b. 1947), Yang (b. 1947), and Tsai (b. 1957) are the best known of the Taiwanese New Wave filmmakers—editor's note.]

What does this becoming-visible of contemporary Chinese cinema signify in light of the small history of the discipline of film studies that I eclectically outlined above, including the critical moment of Anglo-American feminist critique? Many things can be said in response to this question,[3] but I'd like to foreground something that is central to my readings in some of the chapters to follow. Whereas contemporary cultural theory in the West, including feminist film theory, has thrived on an inextricable linkage (itself a legacy from Bertolt Brecht) between political consciousness raising, on the one hand, and an aesthetic-cum-theoretical avant-gardism,[4] on the other, the emergence of Chinese cinema renders this particular linkage a historical—and culturally specific—occurrence rather than a universal or absolute necessity. That is to say, although for left-leaning Western intellectuals since the post–Second World War period, "China" has often stood for a set of political aspirations alternative to the right, when China enters the world picture in the form of a contemporary cinema, it does not necessarily comply with such presumptions. Consciousness raising, contemporary Chinese cinema suggests, does not have to take the route of the avant-garde; conversely, aesthetic and theoretical avant-gardism, so valued in certain academic sectors for purposes of intellectual renewal and regeneration, does not necessarily lead to a progressive or democratic politics. In particular, the persistence of a predominant affective mode,[5] a mode I will describe as the sentimental, indicates that contemporary Chinese cinema, even as its contents fully partake of contemporary film and cultural problematics such as explicit sex, women's lives, gay male relationships, extramarital liaisons, immigrant tragedies and comedies, reproduction, and so forth, simultaneously brings with it fundamental challenges to the cornerstones of Western progressivist theoretical thinking. To engage productively with the global visibility of contemporary Chinese cinema, it is therefore important to work conceptually and speculatively, at a level beyond the (obviously invaluable) documenting and inventorying efforts and the geographical and chronological compartmentalization exercises that currently seem to dominate developments in this fledgling field. To put it bluntly, it is important to aim at goals other than information retrieval and canonization, and other than a monumentalizing of film periods (as tradition) and film directors (as individual talents).

What do I mean, then, by the recurrent sentimental in contemporary Chinese films? It would be helpful to begin with a conventional understanding—namely, of the sentimental as an affective orientation/tendency, one that is often characterized by apparent emotional excess, in the form of exaggerated

3. In the Chinese language, various publications have debated the becoming visible of Chinese cinema in sophisticated terms, though, understandably, these publications tend not to take into consideration the history of film studies in the English-speaking world in which I am locating my inquiry.

4. For an informed reappraisal, based on knowledge of the Chinese language as well as of German and French, of the work of Brecht and the journal *Tel quel* in relation to Chinese art and politics, see Eric Hayot, *Chinese Dreams: Pound, Brecht, Tel Quel* (Ann Arbor: U of Michigan P, 2004), 54–102, 103–75. [Brecht (1898–1956), German poet and playwright, a theorist and practitioner of a provocative and highly political drama that rejected tradition and convention—editor's note.]

5. John Frow, referring to Alastair Fowler's *Kinds of Literature: An Introduction to the Theory of Genres and Modes* (Cambridge: Harvard UP, 1982), has provided a succinct formulation of the term "mode" that I find helpful: "What I would . . . like to suggest is that the term 'mode' be reserved for use in . . . the 'adjectival' sense . . . , in which modes are understood as the extensions of certain genres beyond specific and time-bound formal structures to a broader specification of 'tone'" (*Genre* [London: Routledge, 2006], 65).

grief or dejection or a propensity toward shedding tears.[6] But when examined closely, such emotional excess is only a clue to a much broader range of issues.

In his famous discussion, in 1795–96, of naive and sentimental poetry, the German-speaking philosopher and writer Friedrich Schiller[7] defined the sentimental as a modern creative attitude marked by a particular self-consciousness of loss. To reiterate Schiller's statements in simple terms: while the poet who writes "naively" *is* nature, the poet who writes "sentimentally" *seeks* nature; the latter's "feeling for nature is like the feeling of an invalid for health."[8] The sentimental relation to nature (the condition of simple and sensuous wholeness that, because it is lost, will henceforth become a moral ideal) is, in other words, no longer spontaneous but reflexive—suffused with feelings of longing and characterized by the imaginative infiniteness of thought. What remains instructive in this classic European account is its attempt to understand the sentimental not only as an instance of affect but also as a relation of time: as an affective state triggered by a sense of loss, sentimentalism was, for Schiller, the symptom of the apprehension of an irreversible temporal differentiation or the passing of time. As well, this symptom was mediated by and accessible through aesthetic and cultural form: it was poetry (or "the poetic mood"), which Schiller considered "an independent whole in which all distinctions and all shortcomings vanish,"[9] that seemed generically appropriate for conveying the moral rigor pertaining to the naive and sentimental as contrastive but deeply bonded spiritual states.

Although Schiller's writings are typically classified under the rubric of German romanticism—he wrote about the sentimental belatedly, at a time when the term had already become pejorative in connotations; his formulation of the sentimental (as the awareness of the loss of spontaneous feeling) was also quite distinct from the views advanced in previous decades, as for instance in mid-eighteenth century England—his emphasis on the reflexive character of the sentimental—that is, the character whereby the mind does not receive any impressions without simultaneously observing its own activity and reflection—was illustrative of the general tenets of the well-established debates in eighteenth-century European moral philosophy and literature about the sentiments.[1] Conducted in the vocabulary of sensibility, pity, sympathy, compassion, virtue, refined and delicate feeling, and so forth,[2] some of these debates have also evolved around what in retrospect might be called

6. Sir Leslie Stephen defined the sentimental as "the name of the mood in which we make a luxury of grief" in *English Thought in the Eighteenth Century* (London: Smith, Elder, 1902), 2:436, quoted in Janet Todd, *Sensibility: An Introduction* (London: Methuen, 1986), 7.

7. German poet, dramatist, and historian (1759–1805); see above [editor's note].

8. Friedrich Schiller, *On Naïve and Sentimental Poetry* (1795–96), trans. Julius A. Elias (slightly modified), excerpted in *The Origins of Modern Critical Thought: German Aesthetic and Literary Criticism from Lessing to Hegel*, ed. David Simpson (Cambridge: Cambridge UP, 1988), 148–73; the quoted statements can be found on 155, 156, 158.

9. Ibid., 170.

1. See RAYMOND WILLIAMS, *Keywords: A Vocabulary of Culture and Society*, rev. ed. (London: Fontana, 1983), 280–83, for a brief account of the evolution of the word "sensibility," including its important relation to the word "sentimental" in the 18th and 19th centuries. In the English-speaking world, a classic treatise is Adam Smith, *The Theory of Moral Sentiments* (1759), ed. Knud Haakonssen (Cambridge: Cambridge UP, 2002), in which Smith, extending the work of moral-sense philosophers such as Francis Hutcheson [1694–1746] and DAVID HUME [1711–1776], elaborated the notions of sympathy—an imaginative sharing or agreement of feelings that is not simply benevolence—and of the mental construct of an impartial spectator as bases for his theory of conscience and moral judgment.

2. For an informative study of the controversy of sentimentalism in British writings, see Markman Ellis, *The Politics of Sensibility: Race, Commerce and the Sentimental Novel* (Cambridge: Cambridge UP, 1996).

a dialectical relationship between sentimentality and its darker underside, as discourses about the philanthropic function of benevolence were shown to be regularly underpinned by a fascination with monstrosity, cruelty, violence, and the pleasures of inflicting pain on others. For some scholars, this dialectical relationship constitutes a definition of humanity that is ridden with ambiguity and puts the European Enlightenment's presumed (arrival at) rationality into serious question.[3]

In Anglo-American literary and cinematic studies, this rich historical backdrop of intellectual controversies over the unresolved tensions between compassion and cruelty, between altruism and sadism gave way to a type of articulation about the sentiments that links them explicitly with the dynamics of social power struggles. When studied in relation to modern narrative fiction and film melodrama, in particular, the sentimental, which for many still carries derogative meanings such as effeminacy and sensationalist self-indulgence, often becomes a means to focalize issues about the politics of identity. From the novels of Samuel Richardson and Charlotte Brontë to those of Toni Morrison,[4] to the woman-centered narrative films of Hollywood, and to the media representations of nonwhite peoples, sentimentalism has, beginning with feminist revisionist scholarship of the 1970s and 1980s, increasingly been analyzed in conjunction with the agency of those (most typically, white middle-class women confined to domesticity) who occupy a marginalized social status and read as an alternative form of power attainment based, ironically, on the emotional cathexes produced by experiences of social deprivation, subordination, and exclusion.[5] In such reversal of social hierarchy, what used to be considered trivial and weak is accordingly reread as dazzle and strength: the seeming passivity or minoritization of those who are inmates of their environments are thus reconceptualized as possessing a manipulable potentiality that was previously dismissed or ignored. In this manner, sentimentalism, rather than designating the passing of time or the melancholy sensitivity of a lone lyric consciousness, becomes instead a vindicated instrument in (the reinterpretation of) social entanglements, often providing new clues as to who is actually in control.

Although far from being a unitary or unified concept, the sentimental in modern Euro-American humanistic studies clearly occupies a place that has much to do with *the enduringly fraught ethics of human sociality as mediated by art and fiction*, be that ethics conceived negatively, in the form of an individual consciousness's satirical or elegiac longing for an ideal whose attainment is always deferred, or affirmatively, in the form of (collective) identity empowerment and the fight for social justice.[6] And even where the sentimental reveals

3. For a comparative study that discusses the English, French, and German literary and philosophical contributions to these debates, see James A. Steintrager, *Cruel Delight: Enlightenment Culture and the Inhuman* (Bloomington: Indiana UP, 2004).

4. African American novelist and essayist (b. 1931); see above. Richardson (1689–1761), English novelist credited with writing the earliest sentimental novel, *Pamela* (1740). Brontë (1816–1855), English novelist whose best-known work, *Jane Eyre* (1847), was an enormously influential narrative of a woman triumphing over "social deprivation, subordination, and exclusion" [editor's note].

5. Ben Singer, *Melodrama and Modernity: Early Sensational Cinema and Its Contexts* (New York: Columbia UP, 2001) (see in particular chap. 2, in which the author elaborates five primary features as characteristic of melodrama—pathos, emotionalism, moral polarization, nonclassical narrative form, and graphic sensationalism).

6. As Ellis puts it in regard to the sentimental novel: "Paradoxically, . . . by addressing an audience that was disenfranchised and lacking power in political life, the sentimental novel effectively created a new political role for literature" (*The Politics of Sensibility*, 3).

itself to be much more intimately entwined with sadism and malevolence than the feeble-minded would prefer, its function in gauging the textures and nuances of a society's moral duplicity seems indisputable. The pertinent question to be derived from these cross-cultural considerations is not exactly how to apply them to Chinese film or how such "Western theory" does not fit "Chinese reality" but rather the question of a particular discursive relation: how can the symptoms of prominent affective tendencies, as detectable in certain films, be theorized in relation to the foundations and practices of social interaction? With this question in the foreground, the sentimental, instead of being equated with the occurrence of affective excess per se, can more fruitfully be rethought as a discursive constellation—one that traverses affect, time, identity, and social mores, and whose contours tend to shift and morph under different cultural circumstances and likely with different genres, forms, and media.[7] To this extent, this book could perhaps be seen as participating in a larger trend in recent film studies of a (re)turn to the historical relationship between medium and ontology, a (re)-turn that has been triggered in part by digitization's radical altering and obsoleting of film's materiality and that has led scholars to rethink the medium-specific and oftentimes somatic, as well as imaginary, effects of cinematic signification itself.

In the Chinese language, as can be expected, more than one term has been used for "sentimentalism," but the term *wenqing zhuyi* (溫情主義)—literally, "warm sentiment-ism"—seems to me to shed light on something unique to the Chinese discursive constellation. "Warm sentiment," of course, does conjure up all the touchy-feely, lachrymose effusiveness that is conventionally associated with the sentimental. At the same time, a rather different connotation is being evoked: being warm, to be exact, is being in the middle between the extremes of hot and cold, bespeaking a kind of moderation that is, interestingly, not quite the affective outpour that is the typical definition of sentimentalism. This alternative emphasis on being moderate, which readily translates into affiliate notions of being mild, tender, tolerant, obliging, and forbearing, was the reason *wenqing zhuyi* used to be targeted for criticism as bourgeois ideology by the Chinese communists. *Wenqing* was suspect because it signals an accepting attitude that is the opposite of a clear-cut determination to reject and expel.[8]

With this crucial sense of moderation in the foreground, the sentimental may thus be specified as *an inclination or a disposition toward making compromises and toward making-do with even—and especially—that which is oppressive and unbearable.* Whereas a Freudian or proto-Freudian approach to the emotions often sees them in hydraulic terms (in what Foucault has

7. For comparative interest, see Singer, *Melodrama and Modernity,* in particular chap. 2. Singer defines melodrama as a "cluster concept"—"a term whose meaning varies from case to case in relation to different configurations of a range of basic features or constitutive factors" (44). * * * Although I have found the melodramatic and the sentimental to intersect on some occasions, I do not consider them to be identical phenomena.

8. Although it is conceivable to trace the notion of *qing* (alternately translated as inner experience, emotion, sentiment, or personal nature) in Chinese usage all the way back to the ancients, such a genealogy of ideas is not exactly the point of my discussion, which is to come to grips with the sentimentalism in some contemporary Chinese films as a noticeable affective symptom emerging both from global modernity and from cinematic mediation. My interest, in other words, is not in the elaboration of the nuances of *qing* in the sense of a natural or cultivated form of interiority (or self) but rather in sentimentalism or *wenqing* as a manifestation, in the context of global visibility, of evolving inter- as well as intra-cultural politics.

called the repressive hypothesis), as an overflow of what has been repressed, the sentimental is rather about what keeps and preserves, what holds things together. For this reason, the sentimental is perhaps best described as *a mood of endurance*, a mode whose contours tend to remain fuzzy rather than sharply delineated and whose effects may more easily be apprehended as (a prevailing) *tone*. From this perspective, it is not at all surprising that the film hailed by contemporary Chinese directors and audiences alike as the sentimental masterpiece *sans pareil* is Fei Mu's[9] *Xiaocheng zhichun* (*Springtime in a Small Town*, 1948; remake, 2002, by Tian Zhuangzhuang), a story in which disruptive emotional energies, triggered by the entry of an outsider (the wife's former intimate male friend), come into play only to result, finally, in the restoration of the status quo of a familial situation already in ruins. (Fei Mu's remarkably stylized film, now considered a classic, was denounced as decadent and reactionary at the height of communist orthodoxy in the People's Republic.)

Still, why does so much of the drama of the sentimental have to do with domesticity, the household, and the home?

Borrowing from Harry Harootunian's discussion of the twentieth-century Japanese philosopher Watsuji Tetsuro's[1] writings on *fudo* (climate, culture, and history), I believe the interior of the house may help illuminate things at this juncture. As Harootunian writes (in explication of Watsuji), "The house constitutes the spatial container of the most primordial relationships guiding conduct in the everyday. . . . It calls attention to the space of relationality among the members of the household and to a form that derived from the most archaic experience."[2] As the material structure basic to human existence, the house is lived, we may say, as a boundary differentiating an inside holding the comfortable apart from the uncomfortable, and hence as a home—a refuge from a tyrannical world. Because it functions as a refuge, this inside also tends to take on the import of a timeless, undifferentiated, and infinitely adaptable (interpersonal) time/space whereby conflicts ought to be resolved and opposites ought to be reconciled. The modes of human relationships affectively rooted in this imagined inside—an inside whose depths of feeling tend to become intensified with the perceived aggressive challenges posed by modernity—are what I would argue as sentimental.

The English-language lexicon "accommodation" provides a felicitous encapsulation of the issues involved: as *wenqing* or moderation, the sentimental is ultimately about being accommodating and being accommodated, about the delineation and elaboration of a comfortable/homely interiority, replete with the implications of exclusion that such delineation and elaboration by necessity entail. Accordingly, what is excluded, what is banished to the outside, is believed to be antagonistic, dangerous, and evil. Reformulated in this manner, the affective excess usually attributed to the sentimental should be grasped, more precisely, as a symptom of the emotional demands—alternating between the polarized extremes of forbearance and xenophobia—exacted by the imaginary, and very much lived, relations to

9. Major Chinese filmmaker of the pre-Communist era (1906–1951). *Sans pareil*: without equal (French) [editor's note].

1. Japanese philosopher and intellectual historian (1889–1960); his 1935 book, translated as *A Climate: A Philosophical Study* (or *Climate and Culture*), argued for an essential relationship between the environment and human culture [editor's note].

2. Harry Harootunian, "Time's Envelope," forthcoming in his book-in-progress *Borrowed Time: History in Search of Temporality*, MS page 37.

such interiority and its outside. The gravest problems arise, of course, when the homely—what is inside—too, is revealed to be oppressive and unbearable—indeed, uninhabitable. * * *

THE SENTIMENTAL IN THE AGE OF GLOBAL VISIBILITY

* * *

In a cinema in which even renegade directors are given their places in a hierarchical filial system (as the names "Fifth Generation," "Sixth Generation," and so forth clearly indicate),[3] the oft-encountered affective excesses surrounding domestic and familial stories would seem at first to amount to an obvious case of ideological manipulation. * * * The heart-wrenching situations that many films dramatize include poverty, interpersonal and intergenerational conflicts, separation, exile, illness, death, and loneliness—situations in which quotidian living itself can take on the weight of imprisonment or assault, and the most ordinary scenarios (the memory of a pond filled with lotuses in the autumn sun; an illegal immigrant accidentally shot to death by gangsters in a cold foreign land; the glimpse of a proud but aging father dozing off before breakfast in his son's apartment; a hungry country boy wandering in the streets of the big city, staring at shop windows . . .)[4] can become imbued with melancholy connotations of helplessness, loss, belatedness, or regret. From the perspective of a stringent ideology critique, such focalizations on physical or material deprivation and psychological destitution can easily be read as ways to (re)affirm the necessity and virtue of the interior, the organic connectedness that is the patriarchal family, clan, village, nation, or ethnic group, whose demands often give rise to a profound sense of entrapment yet whose dispersal and disunity are dreaded as a kind of invasive otherness, to be dispelled at all costs. As tragicomic stories of human fragility unfold with moving effects, what seems perpetuated sentimentally is the myth of the continuous growth, expansion, and reproductive power of an indomitable collective will, above and beyond individual difference and dissent. This is why it is possible to argue that *at the heart of Chinese sentimentalism lies the idealization of filiality*: as a predominant mode of subjectivization, filial piety is not simply a matter of respecting one's biological or cultural elders but also an age-old moral apparatus for interpellating individuals into the hierarchy-conscious conduct of identifying with—and submitting to—whatever preexists them—from the ancestral family to the ancestral land, the province, the country, and the ethnic community in a foreign nation—as authoritative and thus beyond challenge.

Although such sentimental situations are readily identifiable in the films, however, my objective is not merely to subject sentimentalism to yet another barrage of criticism by simply exposing its ideology-ridden assumptions. Rather than offering a strictly demythifying approach to the sentimental, I am also invested in articulating the ideological assumptions with the fictive

3. For two fairly recent, informative studies of the Fifth Generation directors and their works that place them in historical perspective, see Ni Zhen, *Memoirs of the Beijing Film Academy: The Genesis of China's Fifth Generation*, trans. Chris Berry (Durham, N.C.: Duke UP, 2002), and Paul Clark, *Reinventing China: A Generation and Its Films* (Hong Kong: Chinese UP, 2005).

4. These four examples are taken respectively from the films *Song of the Exile* [Ann Hui, 1990], *Comrades: Almost a Love Story* [Peter Chan, 1996], *The Wedding Banquet* [Ang Lee, 1993], and *Not One Less* [Zhang Yimou, 1999].

but intense processes of identity negotiation. In other words, much as I am, like many of my fellow academics, suspicious of the maudlin extravagances and containment strategies that are considered a hallmark of the sentimental, my readings of the selected films are really attempts to think through the fantasy structures of accommodation and endurance that develop and multiply around such extravagances and strategies: the economic and moral forms of submission and subjectivization they solicit, the imaginary resolutions they supply to social antagonisms, and, most important, the formal and cognitive ruptures within them that, however tangentially or even unnoticeably, signal possibilities for perversion, subversion, and diversion.

Let me also formulate my interest in the sentimental in closer relation to the preceding parts of this introduction. If contemporary cultures are caught up in what I have been referring to as global visibility—the ongoing, late capitalist phenomenon of mediatized spectacularization in which the endeavor to seek social recognition amounts to an incessant production and consumption of oneself and one's group as images on display, a phenomenon in which subjectivity has become, willy-nilly, object-ivity—how do we come to terms with older—or increasingly estranged—forms of interpellations such as self-restraint, frugality, filial piety, compliance with collective obligations, inconspicuous consumption, modesty about exhibiting and thrusting oneself (including one's body parts and sexual interests) forward as a cause in public, and so forth, wherein the key is not exactly—perhaps exactly not—becoming visible? How might we go about handling the tenacity, in the midst of global visibility—itself a new kind of aggressive, oftentimes oppressive, reality—of residual significatory traces of a different kind of social behavioral order? Such traces, often emergent in the form of a vaguely anachronistic affect whose mere survival points to another modality of attachment and identification—and whose noncontemporaneity stands in mute contrast to the glamour of global visibility—are among the things I would like to see encompassed within the conceptual parameters of this study.[5]

Defined in these terms, the sentimental is thought-provoking not exactly because it allows us to rediscover something old. It is rather that the old, now lingering in the enigmatic form of an intensity (in the form of some emotionally guarded and clung-to inside) that seems neither timely nor fully communicable—especially not across cultures—should nonetheless also be acknowledged as an inherent link to the nexus of becoming visible—in the specific sense of visibility that Deleuze argues. In other words, more than simply a matter of excavating historical layers of meaning embedded in cinematic images, what I would like to get at is the process in which this second, epistemic sense of visibility—that is, a trajectory of objectification, recognition, and knowledge that may be made palpable by visual objects such as filmic images but cannot in the end be reduced to them—materializes

5. In using the terms "residual" and "emergent," I am indebted to Raymond Williams's influential discussion of the categories residual, dominant, and emergent, pertaining to what he has famously called "structures of feeling" in *Marxism and Literature* (Oxford: Oxford UP, 1977). Although both the residual and the emergent contain elements that can be incorporated within the dominant, Williams argues that they also signify experiences and practices that have an alternative or oppositional relation to the dominant culture. Whereas the residual refers to meanings and values that were formed in the past but are still active in the present cultural process, the emergent "is never only a matter of immediate practice; indeed it depends crucially on finding new forms or adaptations of form" (126). In the context of contemporary Chinese films, I see the residual and the emergent as thoroughly entangled categories.

not only in relation to the visible that is the images but also in the very sentimental interstices—the remains of a collective cultural scaffold—that lend the images their support.

* * *

2007

KENNETH W. WARREN
b. 1957

When Kenneth W. Warren proclaimed that "the collective enterprise we call African-American or black literature . . . has already come to an end," he set off a firestorm of criticism. Warren, who had previously been comfortably ensconced in the halls of academe, garnering little attention, landed in the pages of the *Los Angeles Review of Books*' symposium with the publication of *What Was African American Literature?* (2011). After his hair-raising essay summarizing the book's primary thesis was featured in the *Chronicle of Higher Education*, that journal printed a spirited response by the literary historian Gene Andrew Jarrett and a "Live Chat" between Warren and his critics.

The Fairfax M. Cone Distinguished Service Professor of English Language and Literature at the University of Chicago, where he has been a faculty member since 1991, Kenneth Warren has also served as deputy provost for research and minority issues. His research focuses on African American and American literature from the nineteenth century to the mid-twentieth century, in particular tracking these works against cultural, social, and political change. Born in 1957, Warren had a somewhat itinerant childhood because of his father's service in the Air Force. He grew up primarily in Colorado and Albuquerque, New Mexico, where he went to high school. At Harvard College he took his first course on the history of literary theory, graduating in 1980. At Stanford University, where he received his Ph.D. in 1988, he studied with the Americanist Jay Fliegelman. From 1987 to 1991, he taught at Northwestern University.

Warren is not an especially theory-driven literary critic, though he is well informed about theory. As a matter of practice, his work has been concerned with giving context to the literary text. History and the archive have been especially critical to this process, and he has occasionally found himself at odds with those who argue that analysis should be primarily restricted to the literary text itself.

Black and White Strangers: Race and American Literary Realism (1993), Warren's first book, examines late nineteenth-century literary realism by several authors, including HENRY JAMES and William Dean Howells. Here he contends that postbellum racial politics influenced these literary works while simultaneously informing the retrograde segregationist politics and policies of the era. In a second book of literary criticism, *So Black and Blue: Ralph Ellison and the Occasion of Criticism* (2003), Warren explores Ellison's intellectual life and work. According to Warren, in his masterwork, *Invisible Man* (1952), Ellison was so deeply engaged with responding to Jim Crow, the era that began with the first post-Reconstruction laws enforcing racial segregation in 1877, that when Jim Crow gave way to a new era of social change and civil rights legislation he was unable to complete his highly anticipated second novel. Warren continues tracking the interrelated themes of Jim Crow and African American literary output in *What Was African American Literature?*, which developed out of the W. E. B. Du Bois Lectures that he delivered at Harvard University in 2007. In addition to his three books and a number of scholarly articles and book chapters that revolve around historicizing African American and American literature, Warren has co-edited two collections. With the political scientist Adolph Reed Jr., Warren published *Renewing Black Intellectual History: The Ideological and Material Foundations of African American Thought* (2010). It reexamines black intellectual history and traditional understandings of race and racism in the context of how the well-meaning have used them, knowingly and unwittingly, in ways that have worked to maintain elite interests and capitalist inequality. *Jim Crow, Literature, and the Legacy of Sutton E. Griggs* (2013), a volume co-edited with Tess Chakkalakal, a literary critic and professor of English, examines the work of the Baptist preacher and author Sutton Elbert Griggs (1872–1933).

Warren's "Does African-American Literature Exist?" (2011), our selection, puts forth what is for many a controversial thesis: African American literature can no longer be written, because it no longer exists. Drawing from ERICH AUERBACH's *Literary Language and Its Public in Late Latin Antiquity and in the Middle Ages* (1958; trans. 1993), Warren posits that African American literature began with the 1896 *Plessy v. Ferguson* ruling that legalized the doctrine of "separate but equal" in the United States and ended with the emergence during the 1950s and 1960s of juridical civil rights for blacks that opened the door to desegregation and recognition of equal rights. African American literature is a historical response to the exigencies and restrictions of Jim Crow America. With the end of de jure Jim Crow and with the conditions that called the literature into existence no longer present, African American literature no longer *needed* to exist. The contemporary black novelists Colson Whitehead, Paul Beatty, Danzy Senna, and Alice Randall, according to Warren, embody this new phase in African American literary production—whatever it may be named.

Like history, literature is not static but ever-changing, responding to and shaping its time. Warren's attempt to periodize African American literature is not without problems, however. We are left wondering when exactly Jim Crow ended, since it was historically coterminous with efforts to usher in black rights. Historicizing African American literature as a discrete historical phenomenon that emerged during the late nineteenth century necessarily ignores literary production before *Plessy*. And while de jure segregation is illegal, what about de facto segregation and its supporting apparatus, which are still at work, though less overtly? Such new conditions should produce a different call and thus a different set of literary responses, but those responses have unfortunately become entangled with the hangovers of an old problem. Warren rightly resists the notion that race is the almost exclusive mediator of contemporary African American life and literature, as it seems to have been during Jim Crow America. Social class now plays a key role. Though his argument does not lead him to embrace the debatable idea of a postracial literature in a postracial America, it does tend to ignore a treasure trove of pre– and post–Jim Crow literary criticism and literature premised on intersectionality, as well as the textured variety of African American literatures produced during the era of de jure racial segregation.

"Does African-American Literature Exist?" Keywords: The Canon/Tradition, Identity, Literary History, Print Culture, Race and Ethnicity Studies

Does African-American Literature Exist?

I'd like to make a claim that runs counter to much of literary scholarship. Historically speaking, the collective enterprise we call African-American or black literature is of recent vintage—in fact, it's just a little more than a century old. Further, it has already come to an end. And the latter is a fact we should neither regret nor lament.

African-American literature was the literature of a distinct historical period, namely, the era of constitutionally sanctioned segregation known as Jim Crow.[1] Punctuated by state constitutional amendments that disfranchised black Americans throughout much of the South, legitimated by the U.S. Supreme Court in 1896 with the infamous "separate but equal" ruling in *Plessy v. Ferguson*, and stumbling into decline in the 1950s, 60s, and early 70s, Jim Crow and the fight against it gave rise to—and shaped—African-American literary practice as we have come to know it. Like it or not, African-American literature was a Jim Crow phenomenon, which is to say, speaking from the standpoint of a post-Jim Crow world, African-American literature is history. While one can (and students of American literature certainly should) write *about* African-American literature as an object of study, one can no longer *write* African-American literature, any more than one can currently write Elizabethan literature.

That this fact should occasion no lament is because the society that gave us what we know as African-American literature is a society that black Americans did not want then and certainly don't want now. In consolidating Jim Crow through violence, state statutes, and judicial decisions, Southern states foreclosed on many of the avenues of political and social participation that had opened up for Southern blacks during Reconstruction and had managed to survive various forms of opposition during the two decades after the 1877 Hayes-Tilden compromise[2] effectively ended Radical Reconstruction. It was in response to the rising tide of disfranchisement and segregation that calls for black Americans to produce a distinct literature began to proliferate and to shape black literary practice.

In light of recent literary criticism, my assertion may seem wrongheaded. Much scholarship has sought to justify taking a longer view of African-American literature: Some work argues that what defines African-American literary texts is the way black authors, consciously or unconsciously, have reworked rhetorical practices, myths, folklore, and traditions deriving from the African continent. Others have defined African-American literature by its prolonged argument with slavery, seeing even contemporary black literature as indelibly marked by the ways that enslaved blacks coped with the brutalities of the Middle Passage.[3] To be sure, before the Civil War, abolitionists had cited and encouraged black achievement in literature to refute charges of black inferiority. For the most part, however, they wanted to demonstrate that blacks could produce literature, not that they needed to produce a distinct literature.

By the end of the 19th century, though, that had changed. From an array of writers—including Frances E.W. Harper, Anna Julia Cooper, W.E.B.

1. The name is taken from Thomas "Jim Crow" Rice (1808–1860), a white actor who gained international fame for his performances in blackface.
2. The unwritten agreement that settled the disputed results of the presidential election of 1876; the Democratic candidate, Samuel Tilden (1814–1886), who had won the majority of the popular vote, acceded to the findings of an electoral commission that awarded the electoral votes to the Republican, Rutherford B. Hayes (1822–1893), on the condition that federal troops withdraw from the South. This withdrawal effectively ended Reconstruction, the period (1865–77) after the Civil War when the federal government sought to reincorporate the Confederate states into the union while protecting and aiding blacks who were dealing with the legacy of slavery. So-called Radical Republicans were committed to the equal treatment and enfranchisement of former slaves.
3. The voyage of newly enslaved Africans across the Atlantic Ocean to the New World.

Du Bois, and Sutton E. Griggs[4]—came exhortations to blacks to write a literature by and for themselves. Not only had literature been enlisted in the fight against Jim Crow as a way to challenge the enforcement and justification of segregation, but with so many black Americans effectively shut out from the political process, literature, and writers themselves, could play an outsized role in what became a seemingly endless round of trying to figure out just what it was that "the Negro" wanted. The question mattered because defenders of the white South were insisting they had created a society that conformed to the natural order of things, while critics of the region's sociopolitical order were trying to determine how far down the road of equality the nation would need to go to appease its aggrieved black citizens. Both sides solicited black voices for confirmation or denial.

When, in 1944, the University of North Carolina Press brought out an anthology under the title *What the Negro Wants*, featuring essays by 14 black authors and edited by the African-American historian Rayford W. Logan, the press's publisher, a white man named W.T. Couch,[5] felt compelled to include an introduction telling the reader: "This book was written at the request of the Press. The idea back of the request was that the country, and particularly the South, ought to know what the Negro wants, and that statements from leading Negroes might throw some light on this important question." Among the 14 "leading Negroes" were four whose fame rested significantly on their literary productions: Du Bois, George S. Schuyler, Langston Hughes, and Sterling A. Brown.[6]

In sum, what produced African-American literature as we know it was that, in a Jim Crow society, black writers and their works could plausibly be perceived as voices for a largely silenced population.

As a consequence, literary work by black writers came to be discussed in terms of how well it served (or failed to serve) as an instrument in the fight against Jim Crow and in terms of what it showed about the development (or lack thereof) of black literature, the race as a whole, or the nation's progress in accepting African-Americans as full and equal citizens. Of course, not every black writer accepted or embraced those terms; some objected to the demands being placed on them as writers.

Many critics of black literature also cited such expectations as imposing a considerable liability on black literature. Writing in 1942 in the short-lived journal *Negro Quarterly: A Review of Negro Life and Culture*, edited by Angelo Herndon and Ralph Ellison, for example, the upstart young black critic Edward Bland[7] lamented the lack of literary accomplishment among Harlem Renaissance[8] authors in the 1920s: "One of the outstanding features of the Negro novels that appeared during the twenties was their literary incompetence." Attributing that alleged incompetence to the political burden

4. All African American activists of differing sorts: Harper (1825–1911), abolitionist and advocate for women's suffrage; Cooper (1858–1964), educator and voice for black women; DU BOIS (1868–1963), historian and sociologist; and Griggs (1872–1933), Baptist minister.

5. American editor who served as director of the University of North Carolina Press and the University of Chicago Press. Logan (1897–1982), historian, Pan-Africanist, and longtime associate of Du Bois.

6. Poet and literary critic (1901–1989). Schuyler (1895–1977), journalist and cultural critic. HUGHES (1902–1967), poet, playwright, and fiction writer.

7. Composer (1926–2013). Herndon (1913–1997), labor activist until he left the Communist Party in the late 1940s. Ellison (1914–1994), teacher and writer of prose.

8. Vibrant African American movement in the literary, visual, and performing arts centered in New York City in the 1920s and early 1930s.

imposed on black writers by the black middle class, Bland complained that for the black petit-bourgeois reader, "literature was a medium through which the black man could state his case to the world and exhibit those details of Negro life that would redound to the credit and goodwill of the race. Writing became a function of changing the world through what became explicit propaganda; and the primary consideration governing its subject matter and presentation was the welfare of the race."

Bland was far from alone in making that sort of criticism. Many Harlem Renaissance authors had themselves faulted their predecessors in similar terms. And many writers after Bland did so as well. The point here is not to agree or disagree with such withering assessments of black fiction. Rather, it is to recognize that the impulse to offer those assessments reveals how inextricably black literature and the social conditions imposed by Jim Crow were tied together. In every instance, the critique expressed a hope that black literature could shed the very qualities that had previously identified it as black literature. Sometimes the argument was that in doing so, it could finally become what it had striven to be at the outset—truly representative of black people and a true index of the creativity and capacity of the race. Others argued that after Jim Crow, black writers could be freed entirely from the burden of representing a race—writers would at last be free to be themselves.

Despite the differences in the answers they produced, both lines of argument were responses to the same questions. Just what would the status of black literature be when at last the walls of Jim Crow came tumbling down? Would the true contours of black difference finally shine forth? Or would racial difference and the need for a distinct literature prove to have been only a function of a system of imposed inequality?

While one might have expected those issues to have become salient during the late 1940s and early 1950s, as the modern civil-rights movement began to achieve the victories that signaled the coming end of constitutionally sanctioned segregation, the truth is otherwise. From the inception of black literature, at the beginning of the 20th century, Frances Harper, Du Bois, Zora Neale Hurston,[9] and Ellison were only some of the writers to pose the question explicitly. The tour de force response, and the literary work that truly, and paradoxically, sits at the center of African-American literature, is George S. Schuyler's controversial 1931 satiric novel on racial difference, *Black No More: Being an Account of the Strange and Wonderful Workings of Science in the Land of the Free, A.D. 1933–1940.*

Schuyler conjured up a scientist, the ominously named Dr. Junius Crookman, who invents an effective and inexpensive method to make blacks indistinguishable in appearance from whites. Crookman markets his invention as the solution to the race problem, and in the brave new world of Schuyler's novel, blacks decide en masse to take advantage of the opportunity to be black no more, leaving virtually no visually black people remaining in the United States.

Schuyler, a prickly, prideful individual, and an archconservative, pitched his satire as, in part, an indictment of black self-hatred and racial shame. But as it unfolds, *Black No More* becomes something different. For if race were more than skin deep, a new skin color would prove to be an insufficient

9. Folklorist, anthropologist, and writer of fiction (1891–1960); see above.

disguise; some cultural dissembling would be in order for the trick to play out. As it turns out in Schuyler's story, however, if blacks can't be physically identified as different, then they simply aren't all that different. In the main, blacks in the novel become black no more not because they feel their culture is inferior to that of whites. They make the change because they are tired of being shut out of good jobs, good housing, and decent services solely on the basis of skin color.

Tellingly, it is the elites of both races who speak most fervently in the book on behalf of racial differences. Unable to be demagogues on the basis of skin color, white Southern politicians scramble desperately to reconstruct some basis of racial difference, probing into genealogies in hopes of determining once and for all who is black and who is white. But here they meet with disastrous results because they discover that most American whites turn out to be tarred somewhere on their family tree with the brush of black ancestry. Paralleling the distress of white segregationists is the plight of black leaders, whom Schuyler sends up in a series of scathing caricatures of figures like Marcus Garvey, James Weldon Johnson, Madam C.J. Walker,[1] and Du Bois—caricatures that did not prevent Du Bois and Alain Locke,[2] a key force in the Harlem Renaissance, from reviewing the book favorably. Despite the fact that he and his ilk were among the novel's targets, Du Bois, for one, felt strongly that the health of Negro literature depended on freeing black authors to write about the race in whatever manner they pleased, even if the results were unflattering. On that score, *Black No More* delivered marvelously.

But it is the novel's delineation of the class commitment to the race line that helps make apparent why it is proper to see African-American literature as having come to an end. Although *Black No More* is unsparing in its negative depiction of all civil-rights and protest organizations, Schuyler's plot device underscores Jim Crow's role in forging a link between the actions and writings of elite blacks and the nation's black population as a whole. The novel shows that, whether for good or for ill, the activities of the group whom Du Bois deemed the Talented Tenth[3] could serve to represent all black Americans only in a world in which Jim Crow could be enforced. Because segregation rested informally on claims and beliefs about racial difference and inequality, it lent coherence to the notion of a collective race interest. That also meant that the publication of a work of literature or the success of a particular black individual could call attention to the falsity of racist beliefs and, through argument or demonstration, conceivably affect all blacks regardless of their class status.

The present moment is different. As rendered vividly in a work like Michael Thomas's[4] 2007 novel, *Man Gone Down*, which was awarded the 2009 International Impac Dublin Literary Award, racism still stings. Tracing the four-day odyssey in post 9/11[5] New York City of an unnamed black protagonist

1. Entrepreneur and philanthropist (born Sarah Breedlove, 1867–1919). Garvey (1887–1940), Jamaican political leader, publisher, and founder of the pan-African Universal Negro Improvement Association. Johnson (1871–1938), poet, diplomat, and civil rights activist.
2. Influential philosopher and critic (1886–1954).
3. A term popularized by Du Bois (the title of a 1903 essay), referring to the educated class that must be developed to lead African Americans in the 20th century.
4. African American author and teacher (b. 1967). The Impac Dublin award, administered by the city government of Dublin, Ireland, is for fiction written in any language; works are nominated by public libraries.
5. The 2001 terrorist attacks whose targets included the Twin Towers of New York City's World Trade Center.

and former English Ph.D. student with an ancestry as mixed as Du Bois's, it shows how discrimination remains a problem. It is, for example, infuriating for Thomas's protagonist that white patrons at trendy markets react with surprise upon encountering a black male shopping alongside them as if he belonged there. Yet, as Thomas notes, it is also clear that a society that takes in stride the appearance of blacks in upscale markets, neighborhoods, and schools, or a society that recognizes black literary achievement, can also be a society that tolerates a great deal of poverty and inequality. Again, in itself, that observation is nothing new. Langston Hughes, in his 1940 autobiography *The Big Sea,* mercilessly panned his Harlem Renaissance contemporaries for having believed "the race problem had at last been solved through Art plus Gladys Bentley,"[6] and that "the New Negro would lead a new life from then on in green pastures of tolerance created by Countee Cullen, Ethel Waters, Claude McKay, Duke Ellington, Bojangles,[7] and Alain Locke." Hughes then continued, acerbically, if somewhat disingenuously, "I don't know what made any Negroes think that—except that they were mostly intellectuals doing the thinking. The ordinary Negroes hadn't heard of the Harlem Renaissance. And if they had, it hadn't raised their wages any."

Of course it hadn't, and at some level Hughes recognized the injustice of his criticism. The targets of his censure were not as naïve as he made them out to be. But he knew where the knife's edge was keenest. What made work by a select group of blacks African-American literature was the claim and belief that their work had something to do with the welfare of black Americans generally. Sever that connection, and works, however accomplished, would settle into the literary universe according to style, theme, genre, or whatever. Writing in the 1940s, Hughes knew that the connection hadn't been severed yet. American society was still a Jim Crow society, and writing by black Americans was African-American literature.

Under Jim Crow, by helping to draw attention to the wrongs of segregation, the literary artists who gave us African-American literature assisted in establishing a politics based on appealing to a white-power structure, putatively on behalf of the whole race, to proclaim (to quote Du Bois's most well-known text, *The Souls of Black Folk*[8]) that "the problem of the Twentieth Century is the problem of the color line." That politics was limited by being a politics of elite appeal rather than of direct action. In truth, that was because racial discrimination, enforced by violence and by statute, impeded most black Americans in the South from effectively being able to act politically on their own behalf.

At present, however, a literature insisting that the problem of the 21st century remains the problem of the color line paradoxically obscures the economic and political problems facing many black Americans, unless those problems can be attributed to racial discrimination. If the nation's black citizens are suffering largely for the same reasons its white citizens are suffering, then that is a problem about which such politics has nothing to say. In the world we inhabit, discrimination stands out most blatantly as the problem to

6. African American blues singer and pianist (1907–1960).

7. All prominent African American writers and entertainers: Cullen (1903–1946), poet; Waters (1896–1977), blues and jazz singer and actor; McKay (1889–1948), Jamaican-born poet and novelist; Ellington (born Edward Kennedy Ellington, 1899–1974), jazz composer and pianist; and Bill "Bojangles" Robinson (1878–1949), actor and tap dancer.

8. Published in 1903 (see above); the quotation is found in its first paragraph.

be addressed when you've got a lot of life's other problems whittled down to a manageable size—which is why college professors being snubbed by cab drivers and accosted by police officers in their own homes, or wealthy celebrities being dissed by upscale retailers,[9] have become iconic figures in demonstrating that race still matters.

A literature highlighting discrimination is a literature of that class stratum. And make no mistake, the late 20th and early 21st centuries have seen the publication of many very fine novels and poems by writers like Thomas, Colson Whitehead, Paul Beatty, Danzy Senna, Andrea Lee, and Carl Phillips,[1] to name a few. By the criteria we use to determine matters of racial identity, all of these authors may indeed be African-American. The works they've written, however, are not.

2011

9. In 2005, the African American entrepreneur and television personality Oprah Winfrey, one of the richest individuals in America, was denied entrance to a Hermes boutique in Paris shortly after it closed (but while customers were still inside). In an even more notorious incident in 2009, HENRY LOUIS GATES JR., an African American literary critic and Harvard professor, was arrested outside his own house following a confrontation with a police officer who had received a report that a break-in was in progress.

1. Contemporary African American writers: Whitehead (b. 1969), novelist; Beatty (b. 1962), poet and novelist; Senna (b. 1970), novelist; Lee (b. 1953), novelist and memoirist; and Phillips (b. 1959), poet and literary critic.

KELLY OLIVER
b. 1958

An American feminist philosopher, Kelly Oliver engages nineteenth- and twentieth-century Continental and contemporary French philosophy, feminism, and psychoanalysis; in her work she also explores film theory, theories of oppression, and ethical, social, and political philosophy. Building on key Continental figures such as MARTIN HEIDEGGER, Maurice Merleau-Ponty, JACQUES DERRIDA, GIORGIO AGAMBEN, SIGMUND FREUD, JACQUES LACAN, and JULIA KRISTEVA, she investigates connections between language, subjectivity, and responsibility. Her theoretical work has often been informed by, and formed through, engagements with contemporary issues, such as reproductive technologies, affirmative action, stereotypes of absent fathers and earth mothers, U.S. debates around multiculturalism and English-only policies, institutional sexism and racism, war, depression, animal rights, and environmentalism. She is currently the W. Alton Jones Professor of Philosophy at Vanderbilt University, with appointments in African-American Diaspora Studies, Film Studies, and Women's and Gender Studies. Previously, she taught at the State University of New York at Stony Brook and the University of Texas.

Born to working-class parents in Spokane, Washington, Oliver was the first of four children. She spent her childhood in Montana and Idaho, where her paternal grandfather was a logger and her maternal grandfather was a forest ranger. Although her family was not religious, she attended a Jesuit college, Gonzaga University, from which she graduated cum laude in three years with a double major in philosophy and communications.

At age twenty, she began graduate studies in philosophy at Northwestern University, and she earned her Ph.D. in 1987. It was not until late in her graduate career—more specifically, not until the feminist philosopher Nancy Fraser arrived at Northwestern as an assistant professor—that Oliver encountered a woman professor. Her experience in graduate school with all male professors and mostly male peers pushed her toward feminist studies. She had struggled to write her dissertation under the direction of the phenomenologist David Levin, but after making Fraser her director she wrote a feminist dissertation on language, poetry, and music in FRIEDRICH NIETZSCHE.

Oliver's training at Northwestern was focused on Continental philosophers, primarily GEORG WILHELM FRIEDRICH HEGEL and Edmund Husserl. Already finished with course work by the time Fraser arrived, Oliver audited seminars in which she was introduced to French feminists—Luce Irigaray, HÉLÈNE CIXOUS, and Julia Kristeva—whose work was just being translated into English. Her first book, *Reading Kristeva: Unraveling the Double-bind* (1993), is an outgrowth of those seminars. It examines the relationship between language, ethics, subjectivity, and sexual difference in Kristeva's body of work. In particular, Oliver parses Kristeva's distinctions between the semiotic and symbolic dimensions of language, exploring the liberatory potential for political revolution that lies in poetic language. A substantially revised version of her dissertation was published as *Womanizing Nietzsche: Philosophy's Relation to the "Feminine"* (1995). Her next book, *Family Values: Subjects between Nature and Culture* (1997), explores the ways in which primary family relations affect subjectivity, intersubjectivity, and ethical relations.

In 1991, Oliver obtained her first tenure-track job at the University of Texas at Austin, in a department more sympathetic to Anglo-American analytic philosophy—the tradition dominant in the United States since World War II—than to feminism and Continental philosophy. Although she had already written three books and dozens of articles by the time she came up for tenure in 1997, the department approved her by only a narrow margin.

Undeterred, she followed up her work on family relations with *Subjectivity without Subjects: From Abject Fathers to Desiring Mothers* (1998), which debates the complex relationship between images of maternity, paternity, rhetoric, subjectivity, and ethics. During the subsequent decade she continued publishing on a wide range of topics. Her next book was *Noir Anxiety* (2002), co-authored with her husband, Benigo Trigo, a professor of Spanish and Portuguese at Vanderbilt University. In it they interpret what others have called the free-floating anxiety of film noir as a symptom of concrete anxieties over race, sex, maternity, and national origin that threaten the very possibility of identity by undermining its boundaries. *The Colonization of Psychic Space: A Psychoanalytic Social Theory of Oppression* (2004) engages with works by the political theorists and psychiatrists FRANTZ FANON, Kristeva, and others, while *Women as Weapons of War: Iraq, Sex, and the Media* (2007) analyzes the actual and metaphorical involvement of women in war, specifically in the U.S. campaigns in Afghanistan and Iraq. *Animal Lessons: How They Teach Us to Be Human* (2009) represents Oliver's Derridean turn toward animal studies, as she explores the various ways throughout the history of philosophy that humanity has been defined against animality. *Knock Me Up, Knock Me Down: Images of Pregnancy in Hollywood Films* (2012) continues her interest in film and film theory and the latter's intersection with women's and gender studies.

Oliver was one of the founding members of PhiloSophia, a Continental feminist society established in 2006; she is also one of the founders in 2011 of the Kristeva Circle, and she currently serves as one of its directors.

Our selection, "Witnessing and Testimony" (2004), is a crystallization of Oliver's frequently cited *Witnessing: Beyond Recognition* (2001). Derived from Hegel's analysis of the Master-Slave dialectic, recognition models of identity and subjectivity, she argues, promote false oppositions and hostilities, including the split between subjectivity and agency. Oliver observes that the demand for recognition is a symptom of the pathology of oppression that perpetuates subject-object, same-other, and master-slave hierarchies. Moreover, though theories of misrecognition challenge us to be vigilant in exposing illusions of familiarity or sameness, most of them still propose an antagonistic subject-object, master-slave relationship. Even contemporary theories of recognition concerned with difference and the other do not move us beyond subject-centered notions of relationships. Rather than talk about "the other"—a discursive move that perpetuates the subject-other hierarchy—Oliver urges us to diagnose othered subjectivity. She proposes developing a theory of subjectivity that takes othered subjectivity as a starting point. As an alternative to theories of recognition, Oliver posits a theory of witnessing subjectivity. Here she postulates that the notion of witnessing, with its double meaning as either being an eyewitness or bearing witness (testimony) to the unseen, offers a promising approach for describing the onset and sustenance of subjectivity. Subjectivity is born out of and sustained by the process of witnessing—the possibility of addressability and response-ability—which puts ethical obligations at its heart.

At the close of her essay, Oliver reveals that it is twenty-first-century U.S. war making that motivates her, as it is steeped in extreme and irresponsible individualism, isolationism, and arrogance. In this context, her argument to recast identity so that it includes both subject position (social standing) and subjectivity (unconscious social sources of agency) highlights not only the heterogeneous social foundations of the self but also the grounds of human interaction, dialogue, and responsibility. Taking a position against contemporary domination, oppression, and torture, Oliver calls in the end for "hyperbolic ethics" of responsibility to and for the self and others.

For all its subtleties and strengths, Oliver's argument fails to confront the redistribution side of the recognition-redistribution debates of recent decades famously launched by her mentor Nancy Fraser, Axel Honneth, and others. What about economic equality and justice? After projecting "an ethics of responsibility without sovereignty and ownership" in the penultimate paragraph, she falls silent on that note. Nor does she address the vexing ethical roles played today by religion and media. Nevertheless, Kelly Oliver here develops a sophisticated, nuanced, and multifaceted theory of subjectivity suited to our times.

"Witnessing and Testimony" Keywords: Affect, Ethics, Identity, Phenomenology, Poststructuralism, Psychoanalysis, Subjectivity

Witnessing and Testimony

Contemporary debates in social theory around issues of multiculturalism have focused on the demand or struggle for recognition by marginalized or oppressed people, groups, and cultures. The work of Charles Taylor and Axel Honneth, in particular, have crystallized issues of multiculturalism and justice around the notion of recognition.[1] In *Witnessing: Beyond Recognition,* I challenge what has become a fundamental tenet of this trend in debates over multiculturalism, namely, that the social struggles manifest in critical race theory, queer theory, feminist theory, and various social movements are struggles for recognition.[2] Testimonies from the aftermath of the Holocaust and

1. See Axel Honneth, *The Struggle for Recognition*, trans. Joel Anderson (Boston: MIT Press, 1996) and Charles Taylor, "The Politics of Recognition," in *Multiculturalism*, ed. Amy Gutman (Princeton, NJ: Princeton University Press, 1994) [except as indicated, all notes are Oliver's]. [Taylor (b. 1931), Canadian philosopher. Honneth (b. 1949), German philosopher—editor's note.]

2. These insights about the discourse of multiculturalism are indebted to comments by Cynthia Willett.

slavery do not merely articulate a demand to be recognized or to be seen. Rather, they witness to pathos beyond recognition. The victims of oppression, slavery, and torture are not merely seeking visibility and recognition, but they are also seeking witnesses to horrors beyond recognition. The demand for recognition manifest in testimonies from those othered by dominant culture is transformed by the accompanying demands for retribution and compassion.

If, as I suggest, those othered by dominant culture are seeking not only, or even primarily, recognition but also witnessing to something beyond recognition, then our notions of recognition must be reevaluated. Certainly notions of recognition that throw us back into a Hegelian master-slave relationship[3] do not help us to overcome domination. If recognition is conceived as being conferred on others by the dominant group, then it merely repeats the dynamic of hierarchies, privilege, and domination. Even if oppressed people are making demands for recognition, insofar as those who are dominant are empowered to confer it, we are thrown back into the hierarchy of domination. This is to say that if the operations of recognition require a recognizer and a recognizee then we have done no more than replicate the master-slave, subject-other/object hierarchy in this new form.

Additionally, the need to demand recognition from the dominant culture or group is a symptom of the pathology of oppression. Oppression creates the need and demand for recognition. It is not just that the injustices of oppression create the need for justice. More than this, the pathology of oppression creates the need in the oppressed to be recognized by their oppressor, the very people most likely not to recognize them. The internalization of stereotypes of inferiority and superiority leave the oppressed with the sense that they are lacking something that only their superior dominators have or can give them. The very notion of recognition as it is deployed in various contemporary theoretical contexts is, then, a symptom of the pathology of oppression itself. Implied in this diagnosis is the conclusion that struggles for recognition and theories that embrace those struggles may indeed presuppose and thereby perpetuate the very hierarchies, domination, and injustice that they attempt to overcome.

The notion of recognition becomes more problematic in models where what is recognized is always only something familiar to the subject.[4] In this case, the subject and what is known to him and his experience are once again privileged. Any real contact with difference or otherness becomes impossible because recognition requires the assimilation of difference into something familiar. When recognition repeats the master-slave or subject-object hierarchy, then it is also bound to assimilate difference back into sameness. The subject recognizes the other only when he can see something familiar in that other; for example, when he can see that the other is a person too. Only when we begin to think of the recognition of what is beyond recognition can we begin to think of the recognition of difference.

3. In *Phenomenology of Spirit* (1807; see above), by the German philosopher GEORG WILHELM FRIEDRICH HEGEL (1770–1831), the story of two self-consciousnesses that confront each other and fight for mutual recognition: one wins the battle and the other loses, but each gets recognition and thereby identifies him- or herself through the eyes of the other [editor's note].

4. In *Witnessing: Beyond Recognition* (Minneapolis: University of Minnesota Press, 2001) I argue that Charles Taylor and Maria Lugones present such models. [Lugones is an Argentinean feminist philosopher, currently an associate professor of comparative literature and women's studies at Binghamton University, State University of New York—editor's note.]

Some contemporary theorists seem to think that we can begin to move beyond recognition by focusing on misrecognition. But, it makes sense to talk about misrecognition only if recognition is still the ideal.[5] Misrecognition or the misfire of recognition presuppose an idea of successful recognition. While theories of misrecognition have the advantage of challenging us to be vigilant in exposing the illusion of familiarity or sameness, most of them also propose an antagonistic subject-object/other relationship. Influenced by Lacan's account of misrecognition in the mirror stage, theorists like Julia Kristeva and Judith Butler propose that identity and one's sense of oneself as a subject come from abjecting or excluding otherness.[6] Otherness and difference are abjected in order to secure the subject's always precarious boundaries against the threat of fragmentation. In this type of scenario, we fortify ourselves on the level of individual subjective identity as well as group and national identity by drawing artificial but strict boundaries between ourselves and others. Whatever characteristics we prefer not to associate with ourselves—those characteristics we deem unacceptable, dirty, or improper—we project onto the others. Others and otherness become threats to our very sense of ourselves as subjects. While this neo-Hegelian model is very effective in *explaining* the existence of war and oppression, if *normalized* it makes it impossible to imagine peaceful compassionate relations with others across or through differences.

In *Witnessing: Beyond Recognition*, I associate the pathos beyond recognition inherent in struggles for recognition and testimony to atrocity with witnessing in its full and double sense. Rather than extolling the virtues of testimony per se, I am developing a theory of subjectivity modeled on witnessing in its double sense of eye-witness and bearing witness to what cannot be seen. Although I use examples of testimony in order to show how the structure of witnessing operates in all subjectivity, I do not reduce subjectivity to testimony. Rather, I develop a model of subjectivity based on the address-response structure of witnessing in its double sense. Moreover, the purpose of my discussion of the therapeutic or transformative effects of witnessing is not to promote public testimonies or the practice of psychoanalysis but rather to demonstrate on the one hand how oppression and victimization undermine subjectivity by attacking the ability for address and response and on the other hand how the structure of address and response is the lynch-pin of subjectivity.

There is a tension inherent in the notion of witnessing in the sense of eye-witness to historical facts or accuracy on the one hand, witnessing in the sense of bearing witness to a truth about humanity and suffering that transcends those facts. It is important to note that witnessing has both the juridical connotations of seeing with one's own eyes and the religious or now political connotations of testifying to that which cannot be seen, or *bearing witness*. It is this double meaning that makes witnessing such a powerful

5. Some examples of theorists of misrecognition with whom I engage in *Witnessing* are Judith Butler, Julia Kristeva, and Jacques Lacan. [BUTLER (b. 1956), American philosopher and gender theorist. KRISTEVA (b. 1941), Bulgarian-born French psychoanalyst and critic. LACAN (1901–1981), French psychoanalyst—editor's note.]

6. For example, see Julia Kristeva, *Powers of Horror*, trans. Leon Roudiez (New York: Columbia University Press, 1982), and Judith Butler, *The Psychic: Life of Power* (Stanford: Stanford University Press, 1997). ["Mirror stage": according to Lacan, the pivotal stage in character development when an infant recognizes him- or herself in a mirror; see his essay "The Mirror Stage" (1949), above—editor's note.]

alternative to recognition in reconceiving subjectivity and thereby ethical relations. The tension between eyewitness testimony and bearing witness, between historical facts and what we might call psychoanalytic or phenomenological truth, between subject position and subjectivity is the dynamic operator that moves us beyond the melancholic choice between either dead historical facts or traumatic repetition of violence.

Using this double-sided witnessing as a model, I propose that the subject is constituted by virtue of a tension between finite historical contexts that constitute subject position on the one hand and the structure of infinite addressability and response-ability of subjectivity on the other. The tendency on the part of my critics, and perhaps on my own part, to read my notion of subjectivity and identity as reduced to one pole or the other is a symptom of the difficulty in thinking the heterogeneity and otherness inherent in identity and subjectivity. More specifically, the difficulty is how to articulate fluid and mobile relationships within and between subjects and identities in a theoretical language where grammar requires fixing both sameness and difference into discrete units of meaning whose relationships are limited by logical connections 'and', 'or', 'not', etc. . . . The central question is: How can we conceive of the tension between social and historical context with its differential power relations on the one hand and what makes us beings who mean on the other? In *Witnessing* I addressed this question by negotiating between philosophies of liberation—feminism, race theory, holocaust studies—and phenomenologies of subjectivity.[7] Here, I would like to take up this question by focusing on the pivotal distinction between the two senses of witnessing that I develop and the concomitant distinction between subject position and subjectivity. It will be necessary to further delineate the differences between testimony and witnessing and the differences between the phenomenological subject and the psychoanalytic subject. Whereas testimony is usually a spoken or written account of something seen or experienced, here witnessing refers to the structure of subjectivity itself, the very structure that makes testimony possible. Whereas the phenomenological subject can become conscious of its self-consciousness and its motives, desires and fears, which it owns, the psychoanalytic subject is continually an encounter with the otherness of the unconscious, which cannot completely come to consciousness or be owned up to, let alone owned. These differences bear on the history of subject position and the historicity of subjectivity or the distinction between beings and meaning.

Invoking the double meaning of witnessing, in *Witnessing* I develop a theory of the subject that connects the historically localizable subject position of particular subjects with the infinite response-ability that makes subjectivity possible. By bringing together subject position and the structure of subjectivity as witnessing, I attempt to navigate between the extremes of conceiving of the subject either as the foundation for action apart from social circumstance on the one hand, or as the simple effect of social context on the other. The notion of witnessing brings together the historical context with the witnessing structure that makes subjectivity an infinite open

7. *Witnessing: Beyond Recognition* (Minneapolis: University of Minnesota Press, 2001). [Phenomenology is a philosophical method restricted to analyzing the intellectual processes of which we are introspectively aware—editor's note.]

system of response. As we will see, by so doing, it both politicizes the subject à la subject position and insists on a fundamental ethical obligation at the heart of subjectivity itself.

Any theory of subjectivity must also consider subject position. Subjects, subjectivity and agency always exist only in a political and social context that affects them at the foundation of their constitution. One's social position and history profoundly influence one's very sense of oneself as an active agent in the world. Yet, the contradictions and inconsistencies in historical and social circumstances guarantee that we are never completely determined by our subject position. It is possible to develop a sense of agency in spite of, or in resistance to, an oppressive social situation. Subject positions, although mobile, are constituted in our social interactions and our positions within our culture and context. They are determined by history and circumstance. Subject positions are our relations to the finite world of human history—what we might call politics. Subjectivity, on the other hand, is experienced as the sense of agency and response-ability that are constituted in the infinite encounter with otherness, which is fundamentally ethical. And, although subjectivity is logically prior to any possible subject position, in our experience, they are always profoundly interconnected. This is why our experience of our own subjectivity is the result of the productive tension between finite subject position and infinite response-ability of the structure of subjectivity itself.

By *subjectivity* I mean one's sense of oneself as an 'I', as an agent. By *subject position* I mean one's position in society and history as developed through various social relationships. The structure of subjectivity is the structure that makes taking oneself as an agent or a self possible. The structure of subjectivity is what I am calling a witnessing structure that is founded on the possibility of address and response; it is a fundamentally dialogic structure. Subject position, on the other hand, is not the very possibility of one's sense of oneself as an agent or an 'I' per se, but the particular sense of one's kind of agency, so to speak, that comes through one's social position and historical context. While distinct, subject position and subjectivity are also intimately related. For example, if you are a black woman within a racist and sexist culture, then your subject position as oppressed could undermine your subjectivity, your sense of yourself as an agent. If you are a white man within a racist and sexist culture, then your subject position as privileged could shore up your subjectivity and promote your sense of yourself as an agent.

The subject is a dynamic yet stable structure that results from the interaction between two forces, finitude, being and history (which I identify with subject position) at the one pole and infinity, meaning and historicity (which I identify with subjectivity) at the other. As an analogy, consider that architects and engineers have worked with the principle of tension loaded structures that use the tension as support. A classic example is the Brooklyn bridge.[8] We could say that the subject is a tension loaded structure, but its flexibility makes it more like what architects call a *tensile structure*. Architect Frei Otto's description of the difference between the two structures is suggestive: He says, 'the capacity to transmit forces and moments by tension-loaded materials is found in animate and inanimate nature' while tensile

8. The first steel suspension bridge (opened in 1883), linking two boroughs in New York City, Manhattan and Brooklyn [editor's note].

structures 'are found more frequently in animate nature. . . . Flexible tension-resisting skins and sinews are necessary whenever the supporting system is movable'.[9] The stability of tensile structures is the result of opposing forces pulling in two directions, through which a membrane's double curvature receives its structure and resistance. Subjectivity is analogous to the structure and resistance that result from a membrane or skin being stretched in two directions and held together by tension. Like Frei Otto's famous architectural design using the tension of two opposing axis of force to support a fabric (which architects refer to as a membrane or a 'flexible stretched skin'[1]) the subject too is a kind of tensile structure. The two axis of force whose tension supports the subject are subject position and subjectivity.

An example recounted in Dori Laub's *Testimony: Crises of Witnessing in Literature, Psychoanalysis and History* illustrates the productive tension between subject position and subjectivity, between eye-witness and historical accuracy and another level of truth, a truth beyond recognition, the truth of witnessing to what cannot be seen.[2] Laub, a psychoanalyst interviewing survivors as part of the Video Archive for Holocaust Testimonies at Yale, remarks on a tension between historians and psychoanalysts involved in the project. He describes a lively debate that began after the group watched the taped testimony of a woman who was an eyewitness to the Auschwitz uprising in which prisoners set fire to the camp. The woman reported four chimneys going up in flames and exploding, but historians insisted that since there was only one chimney blown up, her testimony was incorrect and should be discredited in its entirety because she proved herself an unreliable witness. One historian suggested that her testimony should be discounted because she 'ascribes importance to an attempt that, historically, made no difference'.[3] The psychoanalysts responded that the woman was not testifying to the number of chimneys blown up but to something more 'radical' and more 'crucial', namely, the seemingly unimaginable occurrence of Jewish resistance at Auschwitz, that is to say, the historical truth of Jewish resistance at Auschwitz. Laub concludes that what the historians could not hear, listening for empirical facts, was the 'very secret of survival and of resistance to extermination'.[4] The Auschwitz survivor saw something unfamiliar, Jewish resistance, which gave her the courage to resist. She saw something that in one sense did not happen—four chimneys blowing up—but in another made all the difference to what happened. Seeing the impossible—what did not happen—gave her the strength to make what seemed impossible possible, surviving the Holocaust.

From his work with Holocaust survivors, and being a survivor himself, Dori Laub concludes that psychic survival depends on an addressable other, what he calls an 'inner witness'. The inner witness is produced and sustained by dialogic (and I would add nonlinguistic forms of communicative) interaction with other people. In order to think, talk, act as an agent, the inner witness must be in place. This is to say that we learn to 'talk to ourselves'—to think—by talking to others. Our experience is meaningful for us only if

9. Frei Otto, "Basic Concepts and Survey of Tensile Structures," in *Tensile Structures*, ed. Frei Otto, volume 2, trans. D. Ben-Yaakov and T. Pelz (Cambridge, MA: MIT Press, 1969), p. 15.

1. Otto, "Basic Concepts and Survey of Tensile Structures," p. 12.

2. See Shoshana Felman and Dori Laub, *Testimony: Crises of Witnessing in Literature, Psychoanalysis, and History* (New York: Routledge, 1992).

3. Felman and Laub, *Testimony*, p. 61.

4. Felman and Laub, *Testimony*, p. 62.

we can imagine that it is meaningful for others. And, our sense of what is meaningful, our sense of meaning itself, comes through our relationships with others. Creating or finding meaning for oneself is possible only through the internalization of meaning for others.[5] Over simplifying somewhat, we can say that address and response are possible because the interpersonal dialogue is interiorized.

On my account, subjectivity is the ability to address oneself to others combined with the ability to respond to others. One can only address oneself to oneself, or respond to oneself, if one has first addressed or been addressed by and responded to others. At its core, subjectivity is relational and formed and sustained by addressability (the ability to address others and be addressed by them) and response-ability (the ability to respond to others and oneself). It is the possibility of address that sustains psychic life and the sense of subjective agency. If the possibility of address is undermined or annihilated, then subjectivity is also undermined or annihilated. To conceive of oneself as a subject is to have the ability to address oneself to another, real or imaginary, actual or potential. This address and response structure develops in infancy from birth and sustains psychic and social life. I call this address-response structure witnessing and argue that oppression, domination, enslavement, and torture work to undermine and destroy the ability to respond and thereby undermine and destroy subjectivity. Part of the psychoanalyst's task in treating survivors is reconstructing the addressability that makes witnessing subjectivity possible.

If one's subject position is the socio-historical position in which one finds oneself, and one's subjectivity is the structure of witnessing as infinite response-ability, then the inner witness is where subject position and subjectivity meet. If the inner witness is on the one hand the ability to address oneself or to be self-reflective that is 'learned' through addressing and being addressed by others, and it is also 'learned' in a particular historical and social situation, then it is going to be both a prerequisite for a sense of agency per se and a governing factor in the particularities of and restrictions on that sense of agency. We internalize our relationships with others, which empowers us with a sense of our own agency but can also leave us with a sense of the limitations of our own agency if we are in marginal or oppressed social positions or power relations.

As Laub's example points up, psychoanalysis attends to the address-ability and response-ability pole of witnessing, while history attends to the pole of the eye-witness. The double meaning of witness can help to theorize the Holocaust survivor's testimony and witnessing to the Jewish uprising at Auschwitz. As an *eyewitness*, she testifies (incorrectly) to the events of that particular day when prisoners blew up a chimney. In addition, however, she *bears witness* to something that in itself cannot be seen, the conditions of possibility of Jewish resistance and survival. As an eyewitness she occupies a particular historical position in a concrete context that constitutes her actuality as well as her possibilities. She was a Jew in the midst of deadly anti-Semitism. She was a prisoner in a concentration camp. She was a woman in the mid-Twentieth Century. Her position as a subject is related to the particularities

5. In my book *The Colonization of Psychic Space* ([Minneapolis: University of Minnesota Press,] 2004), I identify this internalization of meaning as a form of sublimation.

of her historical and social circumstance. In order to evaluate her testimony as an eyewitness, it is crucial to consider her socio-historical subject-position and not just the 'accuracy' of her testimony. Indeed, the 'accuracy' of her testimony has everything to do with her subject position. It is, in fact, her subject position that makes historians particularly interested in her testimony as a Holocaust survivor. Her testimony is unique because she was an eyewitness; she was there. But, it is not just because she was there, but why and how she was there that makes her testimony unique. The testimony of another eye-witness to the same event—a Nazi guard at the camp, or someone outside the camp who noticed flames in the air—would have a very different meaning, even if he also claimed to see four chimneys blowing up. Perhaps within the context of the Holocaust Testimonies at Yale, surrounded by mostly male professors, the fact that this witness was a woman makes a difference to how she speaks and how she is heard. Only by considering her subject-position can we learn something about the 'truth' of history even from the 'inaccuracies' of her testimony. In this regard, the facts of history cannot disclose the significance or meaning of historical context. Moreover, insofar as she is also bearing witness to what cannot be seen—agency and resistance—she testifies to the process of witnessing itself.

Consider the recent controversy over the accuracy of Rigoberta Menchu's[6] testimony to the atrocities of the Guatemalan army's cruelty, which also points to the distinction between historical accuracy and another level of meaning and truth, the truth of suffering that cannot be reduced to historical facts. Although undeniably powerful in their impact, the empirical facts of the Holocaust, or of the atrocities of the civil war in Guatemala, are dead not only to the truth of suffering but also to the response-ability that the process of witnessing presupposes. The process of witnessing, always in tension with eyewitness testimony, complicates the notion of historical truth and moves us beyond any easy dichotomy between history and psychoanalysis. This is not to say that we can or should discount historical accuracy or historical truth, on the contrary. We need both poles of witnessing. But, we need to critically analyze the meaning of history and context. Our inaccuracies and false beliefs also have meaning that can reveal something true about our desires and fears. This truth is not always liberatory, it is not always the truth of suffering, but may be the truth of hatred and discrimination or even what I call in *Witnessing* false witnessing. We need to investigate the conditions of possibility of meaning, whether it is the meaning of historical facts or of subjective testimony, with its inaccuracies and falsehoods.

My insistence on considering subject position and socio-historical context in any discussion of subjectivity is meant as a corrective to both phenomenological and psychoanalytic theories of subjectivity that do not attend to history. While phenomenology and psychoanalytic theory have been instructive in formulating a theory of subjectivity as intersubjectivity, traditionally they have neglected subject position and thereby sacrificed not only social, political and historical relevance but also its truth, not to mention its accuracy. My insistence on subjectivity as response-ability, on the other hand, is meant as

6. Guatemalan indigenous civil rights activist (b. 1959); her widely translated book *I, Rigoberta Menchú* (1983) drew international attention to government abuses of peasants, especially during Guatemala's civil war (1960–96). She was awarded the Nobel Peace Prize in 1992, but in the late 1990s questions were raised about the truthfulness of her autobiography [editor's note].

a corrective to political theories that begin with a subject essentially either isolated from, or opposed to, objects including other people. My engagement with psychoanalysis in particular is meant to move behind the scenes of the subject-object relation to what makes it possible, which I elaborate as the structure of address and response through which subjectivity and objectivity emerge. In a primary sense, the address-response structure must be formed or at least figured before the subject-object distinction is possible. Subjects distinguish themselves from the world and others by virtue of responsive relations with other people. Recognition too depends on responsivity between infants and their environments and care-takers. For example, recent studies in psychology by Nicholas Meltzoff and Keith Moore show that infants are responsive to facial and manual gestures from birth, prior to recognition of objects.[7] Following this work, Shaun Gallagher and Meltzoff conclude that 'recent studies of newborn imitation suggest that an experiential connection between self and others exists right from birth' that 'is already an experience of pre-verbal communication in the language of gesture and action'.[8]

At the most fundamental level, this relationality or responsivity is neither intellectual nor perceptual but operates through unconscious processes of transference. This means that in a strict sense, our primary relations are neither subjective nor intersubjective but prior to, and prerequisites for, either. This brings us to an ontological level on which subjectivity is essentially relational and dependent, always formed through a primordial 'we'. From this primordial we, follows an ethics of response-ability that entails an ethical obligation to our founding possibility, which is responsivity. Reformulating Eva Kittay's analysis of relations of dependency, we could say that a subject who 'refuses to support this bond absolves itself from its most fundamental obligation—its obligation to its founding possibility'.[9] In terms of my analysis, this fundamental obligation is to respond to others in ways that open up rather than close off their response. This Levinasian move gives us an ethics even more radical than Sartre's[1] insistence on our responsibility for our emotions. We are not only responsible for our own feelings and actions but also for others'. As Levinas says 'communication would be impossible if it should have to begin in the ego, a free subject, to whom every other would be only a limitation that invited war, domination, precaution and information. To communicate is indeed to open oneself, but the openness is not complete if it is on the watch for recognition. It is complete not in the opening to the spectacle of or the recognition of the other, but in becoming a responsibility for him'.[2] With Levinas, we are also responsible for the other's response; which entails at least taking responsibility for the effects of our actions and emotions on others as indicated in their responses. This principle couldn't be more relevant today as we try to understand anti-American sentiment throughout the world. Of course this does not mean that others are not or should not be held responsible for their own actions. Rather, this hyperbolic ethics, as we might call it

7. Andrew Meltzoff and Keith Moore, "Imitation of Facial and Manual Gestures by Human Neonates," *Science* 198 (1977): 75–78; see also "Newborn Infants Imitate Adult Facial Gestures," *Child Development* 54 (1983): 702–9.

8. Shaun Gallagher and Andrew Meltzoff, "The Earliest Sense of Self and Others: Merleau-Ponty and Recent Developmental Studies," *Philosophical Psychology* 9 (1996): 211–36, pp. 212, 227.

9. Eva Kittay, "Welfare, Dependency, and a Public Ethic of Care," *Social Justice* 25.1 (Spring 1998): 131.

1. Jean-Paul Sartre (1905–1980), French existential philosopher [editor's note].

2. Emmanuel Levinas, *Otherwise Than Being*, trans. Alphonso Lingis (Boston: Nijhoff, 1991), p. 119. [Lévinas (1906–1995), Lithuanian-born French philosopher.]

following Derrida,[3] puts the burden of responsibility primarily on the subject, who *is* by virtue of her relations to others. And, it is this indebtedness to others and otherness that grounds a hyperbolic ethics of difference.

As I argue elsewhere, however, this Levinasian or Derridian hyperbolic ethics is not radical enough without accounting for the unconscious.[4] We can articulate an ethics and/or a politics of otherness or difference only by accounting for the unconscious. In order to make responsibility radical enough, which is to say ethical enough, we need a notion of the unconscious, which makes us responsible even for motives, desires and fears unknown to us. The fundamental imperative of hyperbolic ethics is that we should never be content with ourselves. It is an imperative to be self-critical especially with our responses to others, most especially because there are those others whom we may not even recognize. We can never stop interrogating our notions of justice, democracy, and freedom, which means that we can never stop asking ourselves why we do what we do, why we value what we value, why we desire what we desire, why we fear what we fear. Yet, without engaging the unconscious our self-interrogation will never be vigilant enough. Only by postulating the existence of the unconscious will we be humble enough to continue to question our own motives, fears, and desires.

Only the notion of the unconscious gives us an ethics of responsibility without sovereignty and ownership. We are responsible for what we cannot and do not control, for our unconscious fears and desires and their affective representations. In addition, we are responsible for the effects of those fears, desires and affects on others. As Levinas says, we are responsible for the other's response. This means, for example, that if the United States is resented and hated throughout the world, we must ask why and take responsibility for the actions that cause that resentment and hatred. This impossible responsibility entails the imperative to question ourselves and constantly engage in self-critical hermeneutics. And, it is this critical interpretation that also gives meaning to our lives and allows for the sublimation of bodily drives and affects.[5]

Responsible ethics and politics requires that we account for the unconscious. Without doing so we risk self-righteously adhering to deadly principles in the name of freedom and justice. We risk taking the defensive posture of isolationism and individualism that protects itself by attacking others, becoming absolutely unforgiving in its attempts to silence others and cut off their ability to respond. Individualism is based on the denial of the fundamental ethical relationality and response-ability that is subjectivity. It adopts a defensive unforgiving unresponsive posture that denies, even fears the singularity that is the unconscious. It maintains control by denying the existence of the unconscious or unconscious motives, desires and fears. Yet, only by acknowledging our unconscious fears, phobias, and desires, can we hope to be self-reflective enough to contemplate an ethical response to others. Perhaps by acknowledging the death drive[6] within ourselves, we can begin to prevent killing and find a third way between murder and suicide.

2004

3. JACQUES DERRIDA (1930–2004), French deconstructionist philosopher; for his "hyperbolic ethics," see "On Forgiveness" (1999), in his *On Cosmopolitanism and Forgiveness* (2001) [editor's note].

4. See my book *The Colonization of Psychic Space*.

5. For an elaboration of this thesis, see my *The Colonization of Psychic Space*.

6. In psychoanalytic theory, the drive toward chaos and self-destruction [editor's note].

MICHAEL HARDT
b. 1960

ANTONIO NEGRI
b. 1933

The closing decades of the twentieth century brought a sea change in international relations and world economies. The cold war ended with the collapse of the Berlin Wall in 1989 and the dissolution of the Soviet Union in 1991. Starting with the decoupling of the American dollar from the gold standard in 1971 and the first oil crisis of the mid-1970s and continuing with the rise of Japan and then China as economic giants, "globalization" dramatically altered economic and political relations between the West and the rest. All these portentous changes were suggestive of irreversible change, and U.S. President George H. W. Bush, in a speech delivered before Congress in September 1990 on the eve of the first Gulf War, famously predicted the coming of a "new world order." Published a decade later, *Empire* (2000), the collaborative best seller by the American theorist Michael Hardt and the Italian political philosopher and radical activist Antonio Negri, names this world order and articulates its structure, dominant features, and driving forces.

Born in Washington, D.C., Hardt began his academic training in engineering. As an undergraduate at Swarthmore College in Pennsylvania, where he earned his B.S. in 1983, Hardt studied alternative energy development, in the belief that empowering third world nations would be "a way of doing politics that would get out of all [the] campus political posing that [he] hated." Continuing to seek out opportunities for political engagement, Hardt worked on political and humanitarian projects for nongovernmental organizations in Central and South America after his graduation. Over the 1980s Hardt studied comparative literature, earning his master's degree in 1986 and his Ph.D. in 1990 from the University of Washington and writing a dissertation on Negri and GILLES DELEUZE. During this time Hardt also translated Negri's *The Savage Anomaly: The Power of Spinoza's Metaphysics and Politics* (1981; trans. 1991). After briefly taking a position at the University of Southern California, Hardt was hired at Duke University in 1993, where he currently teaches literature and Italian.

Like Hardt's, Negri's career has intertwined academic work and political activism. Negri earned his *laurea,* roughly analogous to but somewhat more demanding than a bachelor's degree, at the University of Padua in 1956, the same year that he joined the Italian Communist Party. Also in 1956—at the age of twenty-three—he was appointed to the faculty of jurisprudence at the University of Padua. Two years later Negri earned his *libera docenza,* the Italian equivalent of a Ph.D., in the philosophy of law at the University of Padua. His political activities during the 1960s accompanied his professional advancement. He left the Communist Party in 1963 and helped found the Italian Operaismo (Workerism) movement, was promoted to chair in state doctrine (in Padua's political science department) in 1966, and in 1967 was named director of the University of Padua's Institute of Political Science. His controversial arrest in 1979 ended his tenure as professor at the University of Padua, but it did not stop his academic career or political commitments. From 1983 to 1997 Negri lived in exile in Paris, continuing to teach in the University of Paris system and to publish. It was during this time that Negri met Hardt, who was then working on his translation of Negri's book. Their meeting inaugurated a fruitful partnership that has produced six co-written volumes and a new critical vocabulary for analyzing the dynamics of contemporary global capitalism—a set of economic, legal, political, social, and cultural relations that they term Empire.

Hardt and Negri's concept of Empire arises from the twin contexts of French poststructuralism, especially the theories developed by Deleuze and FÉLIX GUATTARI in *A Thousand Plateaus: Capitalism and Schizophrenia* (1980), and the Italian tradition of radical social and political movements—notably the Potere Operaio

(Workers' Power) and Autonomia Operaio (Workers' Autonomy) movements of the 1960s and 1970s, in which Negri was deeply involved. Negri's relation to these revolutionary movements has shaped his biography, career, and international reputation. In 1978 the armed faction Brigate Rosse (Red Brigades) kidnapped and killed the former Italian prime minister Aldo Moro; on April 7, 1979, Negri and several of his colleagues at the University of Padua's Institute of Political Science were arrested under suspicion of having masterminded the abduction and assassination. Drawing on laws dating from Benito Mussolini's fascist regime that had remained on the books after the 1945 Allied liberation of Italy—the same laws that Mussolini's government used to arrest ANTONIO GRAMSCI in 1926—the state detained Negri for years before finally taking him to trial in 1983. Negri had never been involved with the Red Brigades, and the prosecution's case against him rested on selective quotations from his political pamphlets of the 1970s. The attempt at criminalizing Negri's writings prompted MICHEL FOUCAULT to famously quip: "Isn't he in prison for being an intellectual?"

With his trial finally under way in 1983, Negri gained a reprieve from his confinement when his election as a Radical Party representative in the Chamber of Deputies won him parliamentary immunity from criminal proceedings. However, the chamber voted by a narrow margin (300–293) to revoke Negri's immunity and return him to prison; the day before the vote, Negri fled to France. In 1997 Negri returned to Italy to serve the remainder of his sentence—originally thirty years but reduced on appeal to thirteen—at Rome's Rebibbia Prison; after a year of full imprisonment, two years of work release, and three years of various forms of house arrest, he was granted full parole in 2003.

It was while Negri was an exile in France that he began to collaborate with Hardt, whose dissertation led to the book *Gilles Deleuze: An Apprenticeship in Philosophy* (1993). The influence of Deleuze and Guattari is unmistakable in Hardt and Negri's two key concepts, Empire and multitude, which denote, respectively, the juridical-economic structure of the expanding global capitalist order and the collective oppositional subject poised against global capital. According to Hardt and Negri, globalization involves not only a global expansion of capital, with its saturation of world markets, but also a tendency toward the progressive obsolescence of modern conceptions of nation-state sovereignty. No longer confined to the striated space centered on the metropoles of modern imperialism, Empire functions in smooth space, across ever-more-permeable boundaries, national borders, and cultural divides. Under globalization, Hardt and Negri claim, national sovereignty has been superseded by the supranational sovereignty of Empire, which disperses power horizontally according to the model of a rhizomatic network. In other words, power and authority are to be found not in individual nation-state actors but in contemporary supranational structures such as the World Trade Organization (WTO), the Group of Seven (G7), and the World Bank.

Antagonistic to this supranational sovereignty of Empire is the multitude. Just as the modern capitalism of the nation-state was opposed by the industrial proletariat, so the multitude, according to Hardt and Negri, is the oppositional postmodern subject against Empire. They describe the multitude as a collectivity that both includes and exceeds more limited earlier configurations of oppositional subjectivities such as the proletariat (the industrial working class) and the Communist Party. Rejecting these older configurations' hierarchical chains of command and exclusionary notions of membership, the multitude—in an inverted mirror image of Empire—functions through the networking and coordination of "singularities" that, much like DONNA HARAWAY's coalitions, join in common projects and share affinities but do not subsume those singularities under some unified banner of homogeneous identity. Consider, for example, the famous protests at the 1999 WTO summit in Seattle, which Hardt and Negri discuss at some length in their follow-up book, *Multitude: War and Democracy in the Age of Empire* (2004): the protests were shaped not by a centralized leadership dictating a single agenda to an identifiable, exclusionary group but by the coordinated democratic planning of separate, autonomous interest groups; though each had unique concerns, they shared an opposition to the WTO's unelected, antidemocratic structure. The Seattle protests conjoined such strange bedfellows as labor unionists, environmentalists, anarchists, and church groups, without setting any one of these groups and its goals above others. In the years since the publication of *Empire* and *Multitude*, other oppositional movements, such as Occupy, Black Lives Matter, and the minimum wage activists 15 Now and OUR Walmart, have likewise eschewed the vertically integrated authority of older leftist movements in favor of a horizontal distribution of democratic decision making. Only the coming communism (small "c") of the multitude, Hardt and Negri argue, offers real hope for a global democracy.

Hardt and Negri's first collaboration, *Labor of Dionysus: A Critique of the State-Form* (1994), laid the groundwork for their theorization of Empire and the multitude, but the watershed event for globalization studies was the 2000 publication of *Empire*. The book achieved remarkably high sales for an academic text, appearing briefly on the *Washington Post* best-seller list, and was reviewed extensively in the popular press. (At one point, *Empire* was in such high demand, with so many back orders, that a free digital copy of the text was made available online.) Moreover, *Empire* also widely introduced Negri to a new generation of academics and dramatically enhanced Hardt's visibility and reputation in the American university system.

Empire is not without its critics, however. On the right, most attacks are from conservatives assailing the leftist orientation of university intellectuals; and there are many critiques from the left as well. Academic Marxists such as Malcolm Bull and Giovanni Arrighi object to Hardt and Negri's use of Deleuze and Guattari, arguing that today's late capitalism, far from producing a smooth space that would allow for unimpeded transit across borders, actually imprisons labor in increasingly rigid structures of exploitation, outsourcing, and offshoring. Other leftists criticize Hardt and Negri for being too celebratory of the advent of globalization—just as KARL MARX had earlier viewed nascent capitalism as a step forward for workers from feudalism. Insofar as capitalism produces its own possibilities for resistance and revolution, Hardt and Negri perceive postmodern Empire as a similar improvement over the modern capitalism of the nation-state. Like the factory discipline of industrial capitalism, the global structures of coordination and communication that serve Empire are also the same tools that make possible the global sociality of the multitude. In response, Ellen Meiksins Wood reads *Empire* not as a twenty-first-century *Communist Manifesto*, as the book has been called, but as "a manifesto for global capitalism." Still others, such as Atilio A. Boron, point to the unilateral U.S. invasion and occupation of Iraq, dating from 2003, as evidence that the sovereignty of the traditional nation-state is as hegemonic as ever, despite the claims of *Empire*.

Notwithstanding these and other critiques, Hardt and Negri's influential book remains required reading for students of postmodernity and globalization, particularly for their repositioning and reevaluation of theories of the postmodern. Hardt and Negri follow the lead of Marxists such as Haraway, the geographer DAVID HARVEY, and the cultural critic and theorist FREDRIC JAMESON in viewing contemporary capitalism as a distinctly and thoroughly postmodern phenomenon. What makes globalization postmodern and sets it off from previous capitalist systems of economic organization and exploitation is what Marx called the "real subsumption" of capital, in contradistinction to its "formal subsumption." (Significantly, Negri had first begun his sustained investigation of real subsumption in *Marx beyond Marx: Lessons on the "Grundrisse"* [1979], the outgrowth of a seminar he led at l'École Normale in Paris at the invitation of LOUIS ALTHUSSER.) The formal subsumption of capital, according to Marx, entails capitalism's *extensive* incorporation of processes of production and labor that originated outside its domain, while the real subsumption, which Hardt and Negri identify as a necessary condition for a world market, signifies capital's *intensive* transformation of the relations of production and processes of labor themselves. An example of this dynamic would be the transition from peasant agricultural labor based on traditional farming practices, which is incorporated into market exchange (formal subsumption), to contemporary factory farming, in which the very process of agricultural labor is transformed (real subsumption). For Hardt and Negri, postmodernity and real subsumption occupy one and the same historical period. Occasionally, they call the increasing dominance of communicative and intellectual labor the "postmodernization" of labor.

But Hardt and Negri are ambivalent toward the postmodern. Although they situate globalization squarely within the historical period of postmodernity, they are critical of theories collected under the rubric of postmodernism, with the *-ism* here best understood as signifying a form of ideological or political commitment to putatively liberatory projects founded on such celebrated facets of postmodernist theory as mobility, hybridity, and difference. In "Symptoms of Passage," our selection taken from part 2 of *Empire*, Hardt and Negri argue that postmodernist theory, as identified with the figures of JEAN-FRANÇOIS LYOTARD, JEAN BAUDRILLARD, and JACQUES DERRIDA, loses its efficacy as a form of critique after the advent of real subsumption. Worse still, in its attempts to oppose capital it can actually serve the interests of global capitalism. According to Hardt and Negri, the key problem is postmodernism's conceptualization of difference. Here and elsewhere, postmodernism is characterized by a celebration and affirmation of difference in the face of the homogenizing and totalitarian discourses, the master narratives, of modernity and the Enlightenment. Followers of the French poststructuralist thinkers named above believe that by opening up hegemonic discourses to the play of difference, they undermine the foundations of the exclusionary, oppressive, binaristic thought characteristic of modern European colonialism, racism, and sexism. For Hardt and Negri, however, difference is already the weave and woof of the market logic of Empire, exemplified in today's niche marketing and diversity management that identify and target highly specific demographics—"one [strategy] for gay Latino males between the ages of eighteen and twenty-two, another for Chinese-American teenage girls, and so forth." They similarly criticize postcolonial theory, represented here by HOMI K. BHABHA: postcolonial theory privileges conceptions of identity predicated on difference and hybridity, but these are precisely the concepts that undergird the logic of the global capitalist economy. As Hardt and Negri put it, capitalism joins with postmodernism and elitist postcolonial theory in the battle cry "Long live difference! Down with essentialist binaries!"

Yet for all their criticism of postmodernist and postcolonial theory, Hardt and Negri are not wholly dismissive of them. Rather, they view these theories as "symptoms of passage" from modernity to postmodernity, as signs of the current transition from national to global economies and from nationalist sovereignty to Empire. In the selection Hardt and Negri identify another symptom of postmodern passage: the contemporary global proliferation of religious fundamentalisms. Fundamentalism, which affirms an apparently "premodern" notion of fixed identity and insists on traditional if not archaic forms of social organization, might at first seem a very unlikely corollary to postmodernist and postcolonial theory, with their strident antiessentialism and egalitarian celebration of difference. But contemporary fundamentalisms, according to Hardt and Negri, are tied to the postmodern globalization that they so strongly reject: what seem to be premodern elements "are really directed in reaction to the present social order." Thus postmodernism and fundamentalism are two sides of the same coin, one "appeal[ing] primarily to the winners in the processes of globalization," the other "to the losers." Both cases are symptomatic of the same historical moment. (Significantly, Hardt and Negri widen their definition of fundamentalisms to include not only religious but also nationalist, racist, and economistic fundamentalisms in their later book, *Commonwealth* [2009].)

In making their diagnosis, though, Hardt and Negri's critique relies on oversimplifications of "postmodernism" and "postcolonialism." Paradoxically, their use of

Bhabha's treatment of difference and hybridity elides the difference and hybridity that inhere within the field of postcolonial studies itself. Similarly, the selection's discussion of postmodernism reduces an entire corpus of discourse to three prolific figures whose theories, in turn, are represented by what seem to be slogans, with scant attention to how those thinkers actually complicate Hardt and Negri's representation of postmodernist theory. For instance, Hardt and Negri highlight postmodernism's hostility toward Enlightenment thinking as a signal trait, but they neglect to mention Derrida's interrogations of the Enlightenment and his frequent invocations of an "Enlightenment-to-come." Nevertheless, their insistence on the need for theory to scrutinize itself and its reigning paradigms and methodologies is salutary. Insofar as difference and hybridity, free play and simulation remain the privileged gestures of postmodernist theory, such theory will appear to aid and abet the development of global capitalism and its power of cooptation.

Empire **Keywords:** Globalization, Ideology, Marxism, Modernity, Postcolonial Theory, Postmodernity, Poststructuralism, Religion

From Empire

From *Part 2. Passages of Sovereignty*

FROM SECTION 4. SYMPTOMS OF PASSAGE

> Here then is the man outside our people, outside our humanity. He is continually starving, nothing belongs to him but the instant, the prolonged instant of torture . . . He always has only one thing: his suffering, but there is nothing on the entire face of the earth that could serve as a remedy for him, there is no ground on which to plant his two feet, no support for his two hands to grasp, and thus there is so much less for him than there is for the music-hall trapeze artist who is at least hanging by a thread.
>
> —Franz Kafka[1]

The end of colonialism and the declining powers of the nation are indicative of a general passage from the paradigm of modern sovereignty toward the paradigm of imperial sovereignty.[2] The various postmodernist and postcolonialist theories that have emerged since the 1980s give us a first view of this passage, but the perspective they offer proves to be quite limited. As the prefix "post-" should indicate, postmodernist and postcolonialist theorists never tire of critiquing and seeking liberation from the past forms of rule and their legacies in the present. Postmodernists continually return to the lingering influence of the Enlightenment as the source of domination; postcolonialist theorists combat the remnants of colonialist thinking.

We suspect that postmodernist and postcolonialist theories may end up in a dead end because they fail to recognize adequately the contemporary

1. Jewish Austrian writer (1883–1924), who lived most of his life in Prague and wrote in German, often focusing on the alienation and isolation of the modern individual; the quotation is from *Diaries, 1910–1923* (1951).

2. Throughout *Empire* Hardt and Negri contrast modern and postmodern sovereignty. Whereas modern sovereignty functioned through hierarchical chains of command, centered on localizable national capitals and imperialist metropoles, postmodern sovereignty is articulated in a decentered network structure that disperses power across multiple nodes and operates through the horizontal coordination of interconnected supranational entities and organizations. The adjective *imperial* refers to postmodernity's Empire (to refer to modernity's imperialism, Hardt and Negri use *imperialist*).

object of critique, that is, they mistake today's real enemy. What if the modern form of power these critics (and we ourselves) have taken such pains to describe and contest no longer holds sway in our society? What if these theorists are so intent on combating the remnants of a past form of domination that they fail to recognize the new form that is looming over them in the present? What if the dominating powers that are the intended object of critique have mutated in such a way as to depotentialize any such postmodernist challenge? In short, what if a new paradigm of power, a postmodern sovereignty, has come to replace the modern paradigm and rule through differential hierarchies of the hybrid and fragmentary subjectivities that these theorists celebrate? In this case, modern forms of sovereignty would no longer be at issue, and the postmodernist and postcolonialist strategies that appear to be liberatory would not challenge but in fact coincide with and even unwittingly reinforce the new strategies of rule!

When we begin to consider the ideologies of corporate capital and the world market, it certainly appears that the postmodernist and postcolonialist theorists who advocate a politics of difference, fluidity, and hybridity in order to challenge the binaries and essentialism of modern sovereignty have been outflanked by the strategies of power. Power has evacuated the bastion they are attacking and has circled around to their rear to join them in the assault in the name of difference. These theorists thus find themselves pushing against an open door. We do not mean to suggest that postmodernist and/or postcolonialist theorists are somehow the lackeys of global capital and the world market. Anthony Appiah and Arif Dirlik are ungenerous when they cast these authors in the position of "a comprador intelligentsia" and "the intelligentsia of global capitalism."[3] There is no need to doubt the democratic, egalitarian, and even at times anticapitalist desires that motivate large segments of these fields of work, but it is important to investigate the utility of these theories in the context of the new paradigm of power. This new enemy not only is resistant to the old weapons but actually thrives on them, and thus joins its would-be antagonists in applying them to the fullest. Long live difference! Down with essentialist binaries!

To a certain extent postmodernist and postcolonialist theories are important *effects* that reflect or trace the expansion of the world market and the passage of the form of sovereignty. These theories point toward Empire,[4] but in a vague and confused way, with no awareness of the paradigmatic leap that this passage constitutes. We have to delve deep into this passage, elaborate its terms, and make clear the lineaments that constitute the new Empire. Recognizing the value and limitations of postmodernist and postcolonialist theories is a first step in this project.

Politics of Difference

In order to appreciate fully the critical powers of postmodernist discourses, one must first focus on the modern forms of sovereignty. As we saw in the

3. Arif Dirlik, *The Postcolonial Aura: Third World Criticism in the Age of Global Capitalism* (Boulder: Westview Press, 1997), pp. 52–83; quotation p. 77 [Hardt and Negri's note]. Kwame Anthony Appiah (b. 1954), American theorist, cultural critic, and political philosopher of British and Ghanaian descent. Dirlik (1940–2017), Turkish-born Marxist historian.

4. Hardt and Negri's term for the global network configuration of postmodern sovereignty.

previous sections, the world of modern sovereignty is a Manichaean world, divided by a series of binary oppositions that define Self and Other, white and black, inside and outside, ruler and ruled. Postmodernist thought challenges precisely this binary logic of modernity and in this respect provides important resources for those who are struggling to challenge modern discourses of patriarchy, colonialism, and racism. In the context of postmodernist theories, the hybridity and ambivalences of our cultures and our senses of belonging seem to challenge the binary logic of Self and Other that stands behind modern colonialist, sexist, and racist constructions. Similarly, the postmodernist insistence on difference and specificity defies the totalitarianism of universalizing discourses and structures of power; the affirmation of fragmented social identities appears as a means of contesting the sovereignty of both the modern subject and the modern nation-state, along with all the hierarchies they imply. This postmodernist critical sensibility is extremely important in this regard because it constitutes the proposition (or the symptom) of a break with respect to the entire development of modern sovereignty.

It is difficult to generalize about the numerous discourses that go under the banner of postmodernism, but most of them draw at least indirectly on Jean-François Lyotard's critique of modernist master narratives, Jean Baudrillard's affirmations of cultural simulacra, or Jacques Derrida's critique of Western metaphysics.[5] In the most basic and reductive formulation, postmodernist theories are defined by many of their proponents as sharing one single common denominator, a generalized attack on the Enlightenment.[6] From this perspective the call to action is clear: Enlightenment is the problem and postmodernism is the solution.

We should take care, however, to look more closely at what exactly is intended by "Enlightenment" or "modernity" from this postmodernist perspective.[7] We argued earlier[8] that modernity should be understood not as uniform and homogeneous, but rather as constituted by at least two distinct and conflicting traditions. The first tradition is that initiated by the revolution of Renaissance humanism, from Duns Scotus to Spinoza,[9] with the discovery of the place of immanence and the celebration of singularity and difference. The second tradition, the Thermidor[1] of the Renaissance revolution, seeks to control the utopian forces of the first through the construction and mediation of dualisms, and arrives finally at the concept of modern sovereignty as a provisional solution. When postmodernists propose their opposition to a modernity and an Enlightenment that exalt the universality of reason only to sustain white male European supremacy, it should be clear that they are really attacking the second tradition of our schema (and unfortunately ignoring or eclipsing the first). It would be more accurate, in other words, to pose postmodernist theory as a challenge neither to the Enlightenment nor to modernity in toto

5. LYOTARD (1924–1998), BAUDRILLARD (1929–2007), and DERRIDA (1930–2004) are leading figures in French postmodernist and poststructuralist theory.

6. See, for example, Jane Flax, *Thinking Fragments* (Berkeley: University of California Press, 1990), p. 29 [Hardt and Negri's note].

7. For an explanation of how many postmodernist theorists conflate the varieties of modernist thought under the single rubric of "the Enlightenment," see Kathi Weeks, *Constituting Feminist Subjects* (Ithaca: Cornell University Press, 1998), chap. 2 [Hardt and Negri's note].

8. In section 1 of part 2, "Two Europes, Two Modernities," not included here.

9. BARUCH SPINOZA (1632–1677), Dutch philosopher of Portuguese Jewish descent and an important early rationalist philosopher. John Duns Scotus (ca. 1266–1308), prominent Scottish philosopher and scholastic theologian.

1. That is, a reactionary period after a revolution (literally, the month of the 1794 coup that ended the French Revolution's Reign of Terror with the execution of Maximilien Robespierre).

but specifically to the tradition of modern sovereignty. More precisely still, these various theoretical contestations are brought together most coherently in a challenge to the dialectic[2] as the central logic of modern domination, exclusion, and command—for both its relegating the multiplicity of difference to binary oppositions and its subsequent subsumption of these differences in a unitary order. If modern power itself is dialectical, the logic goes, then the postmodernist project must be nondialectical.

Once we recognize postmodernist discourses as an attack on the dialectical form of modern sovereignty, then we can see more clearly how they contest systems of domination such as racism and sexism by deconstructing the boundaries that maintain the hierarchies between white and black, masculine and feminine, and so forth. This is how postmodernists can conceive their theoretical practice as heir to an entire spectrum of modern and contemporary liberation struggles. The history of challenges to European political-economic hegemony and its colonial rule, the successes of national liberation movements, women's movements, and antiracist struggles, are all interpreted as the heritage of postmodernist politics because they, too, aim at disrupting the order and the dualisms of modern sovereignty. If the modern is the field of power of the white, the male, and the European, then in perfectly symmetrical fashion the postmodern will be the field of liberation of the non-white, the non-male, and the non-European. As bell hooks says, in its best form radical postmodernist practice, a politics of difference, incorporates the values and voices of the displaced, the marginalized, the exploited, and the oppressed.[3] The binaries and dualisms of modern sovereignty are not disrupted only to establish new ones; rather, the very power of binaries is dissolved as "we set differences to play across boundaries."[4]

Postmodernist thinking has been received by a wide range of scholars as a clarion call to a new paradigm of academic and intellectual practice, and as a real opportunity to dislodge the dominant paradigms of scholarship in their own field.[5] One of the most important examples from our perspective is the postmodernist challenge in the field of international relations.[6] Here the

2. The central process in the philosophical system developed by G. W. F. HEGEL (1770–1831), in which history unfolds through contradictions between theses and antitheses (cast as neat binaries), resulting in syntheses (unities and totalities), which in turn give rise to their own antitheses, and so forth, in an orderly way.

3. bell hooks, *Yearning: Race, Gender, and Cultural Politics* (Boston: South End Press, 1990), p. 25 [Hardt and Negri's note]. HOOKS (b. 1952), African American cultural critic and theorist of race, gender, and class.

4. Jane Flax, *Disputed Subjects* (London: Routledge, 1993), p. 91 [Hardt and Negri's note].

5. What is necessary for a postmodernist critique is first to identify what "modernist" means in the field and then to pose a successor paradigm that is in some way consistent with some form of postmodernist thinking. Consider, for example, a field that might at first sight seem an unlikely candidate for such an operation: public administration, that is, the study of bureaucracies. The modernist paradigm of research that dominates the field is defined by a "prescription of neutral public administration ascribed to Wilson (separation of politics from administration), Taylor (scientific management), and Weber (hierarchical command)." Charles Fox and Hugh Miller, *Postmodern Public Administration: Toward Discourse* (Thousand Oaks, Calif.: Sage, 1995), p. 3. Scholars who are convinced that this paradigm is outdated and leads to undemocratic governmental practice can use postmodernist thinking as a weapon to transform the field. In this case, they propose "non-foundational discourse theory" as a postmodernist model that will create more active public interactions and thus democratize bureaucracy (p. 75) [Hardt and Negri's note]. Woodrow Wilson (1856–1924), 28th U.S. president (1913–21). Frederick Winslow Taylor (1856–1915), American engineer and pioneer of scientific time management. Max Weber (1864–1920), German sociologist regarded as a founder of sociology.

6. See James Der Derian and Michael Shapiro, eds., *International/Intertextual Relations: Postmodern Readings of World Politics* (Lexington, Mass.: Lexington Books, 1989); Jim George, *Discourses of Global Politics: A Critical (Re)Introduction to International Relations* (Boulder: Lynne Rienner Publications, 1994); and Michael Shapiro and Hayward Alker, eds., *Territorial Identities and Global Flows* (Minneapolis: University of Minnesota Press, 1996) [Hardt and Negri's note].

"modernist" paradigm of research is more or less identified with the methods of realism and neorealism, and thus centered on the concept of sovereignty, commonly understood as synonymous with the power of nation-states, the legitimate use of state violence, and territorial integrity. From a postmodernist perspective, this "modernist" international relations, because of its acceptance of and focus on these boundaries, tends to support the dominant power and the sovereignty of nation-states. Authors in this field thus make a clear connection between the critique of the binary dualisms of the "Enlightenment" developed in the context of the philosophical and literary postmodernists and the challenge to the fixed boundaries of modern state sovereignty. Postmodernist international relations theorists strive to challenge the sovereignty of states by deconstructing the boundaries of the ruling powers, highlighting irregular and uncontrolled international movements and flows, and thus fracturing stable unities and oppositions. "Discourse" and "interpretation" are presented as powerful weapons against the institutional rigidities of the modernist perspectives. The resulting postmodernist analyses point toward the possibility of a global politics of difference, a politics of deterritorialized flows across a smooth world, free of the rigid striation of state boundaries.[7]

Although many of the various postmodernist theorists are lucid in their refusal of the logics of modern sovereignty, they are in general extremely confused about the nature of our potential liberation from it—perhaps precisely because they cannot recognize clearly the forms of power that have today come to supplant it. When they present their theories as part of a project of political liberation, in other words, postmodernists are still waging battle against the shadows of old enemies: the Enlightenment, or really modern forms of sovereignty and its binary reductions of difference and multiplicity to a single alternative between Same and Other. The affirmation of hybridities and the free play of differences across boundaries, however, is liberatory only in a context where power poses hierarchy exclusively though essential identities, binary divisions, and stable oppositions. The structures and logics of power in the contemporary world are entirely immune to the "liberatory" weapons of the postmodernist politics of difference. In fact, Empire too is bent on doing away with those modern forms of sovereignty and on setting differences to play across boundaries. Despite the best intentions, then, the postmodernist politics of difference not only is ineffective against but can even coincide with and support the functions and practices of imperial rule. The danger is that postmodernist theories focus their attention so resolutely on the old forms of power they are running from, with their heads turned backwards, that they tumble unwittingly into the welcoming arms of the new power. From this perspective the celebratory affirmations of postmodernists can easily appear naive, when not purely mystificatory.

What we find most important in the various postmodernist currents of thought is the historical phenomenon they represent: they are the symptom

7. Hardt and Negri take the notions of striated and smooth space from GILLES DELEUZE and FÉLIX GUATTARI's *A Thousand Plateaus: Capitalism and Schizophrenia* (1980). According to Hardt and Negri, modern sovereignty operated in the striated—that is, rigidly organized, clearly demarcated, and territorially limited—space of the nation-state, whereas the postmodern sovereignty of Empire constructs a smooth space that facilitates "deterritorialized flows" of trade, finance, and capital across national borders and throughout the globe.

of a rupture in the tradition of modern sovereignty. There is, of course, a long tradition of "anti-modern" thought that opposes modern sovereignty, including the great thinkers of the Frankfurt School[8] (along with the entire republican line we have traced back to Renaissance humanism). What is new, however, is that postmodernist theorists point to the *end* of modern sovereignty and demonstrate a new capacity to think outside the framework of modern binaries and modern identities, a thought of plurality and multiplicity. However confusedly or unconsciously, they indicate the passage toward the constitution of Empire.

The Liberation of Hybridities, or Beyond Colonial Binaries

A certain stream of postcolonial studies also proposes a global politics of difference and might be well situated in line with postmodernist theory. Our analysis of modern sovereignty in the preceding sections poses already a strong potential rationale for an accord between postcolonialist and postmodernist theories. Insofar as modern sovereignty was identified with Europe's tendency toward global domination, and more important, insofar as colonial administration and imperialist practices were central components in the constitution of modern sovereignty, postmodernist and postcolonialist theories do indeed share a common enemy. Postmodernism appears in this light to be fundamentally post-Eurocentric.

Postcolonial studies encompasses a wide and varied group of discourses, but we want to focus here on the work of Homi Bhabha[9] because it presents the clearest and best-articulated example of the continuity between postmodernist and postcolonialist discourses. One of the primary and constant objects of Bhabha's attack are *binary divisions*. In fact, the entire postcolonial project as he presents it is defined by its refusal of the binary divisions on which the colonialist worldview is predicated. The world is not divided in two and segmented in opposing camps (center versus periphery, First versus Third World[1]), but rather it is and has always been defined by innumerable partial and mobile differences. Bhabha's refusal to see the world in terms of binary divisions leads him to reject also theories of totality and theories of the identity, homogeneity, and essentialism of social subjects. These various refusals are very closely linked. The binary conception of the world implies the essentialism and homogeneity of the identities on its two halves, and, through the relationship across that central boundary, implies the subsumption of all experience within a coherent social totality. In short, the specter that haunts Bhabha's analysis and that coherently links together these various opponents is the Hegelian dialectic, that is, the dialectic that subsumes within a coherent totality the essential social identities that face each other in opposition. In this sense one could say that postcolonial theory (or at least this version of it) is, along with postmodernist theories, defined above all by its being nondialectical.

8. A group of Western Marxist cultural critics and theorists associated with the Institute for Social Research at the University of Frankfurt whose projects focused on political economy, sociology, and the work of KARL MARX (1818–1883) and FRIEDRICH ENGELS (1820–1895); they include THEODOR W. ADORNO (1903–1969), WALTER BENJAMIN (1892–1940), JÜRGEN HABERMAS (b. 1929), and MAX HORKHEIMER (1895–1973).

9. Indian-born postcolonial theorist (b. 1949; see above).

1. The "underdeveloped" countries, many of them former colonies, now dominated by highly industrialized "first world" (largely Western) nations in a global economy.

Bhabha's critique of the dialectic—that is, his attack on binary divisions, essential identities, and totalization—is both a sociological claim about the real nature of societies and a political project aimed at social change. The former is in fact a condition of possibility of the latter. Social identities and nations were never really coherent imagined communities;[2] the colonized's mimicry of the colonizer's discourse rearticulates the whole notion of identity and alienates it from essence; cultures are always already partial and hybrid formations. This social fact is the basis on which a subversive political project can be conducted to destroy the binary structure of power and identity. In summary form, then, Bhabha's logic of liberation runs like this: Power, or forces of social oppression, function by imposing binary structures and totalizing logics on social subjectivities, repressing their difference. These oppressive structures, however, are never total, and differences are always in some way expressed (through mimicry, ambivalence, hybridization, fractured identities, and so forth). The postcolonial political project, then, is to affirm the multiplicity of differences so as to subvert the power of the ruling binary structures.

The utopia Bhabha points toward after the binary and totalizing structures of power have been fractured and displaced is not an isolated and fragmentary existence but a new form of community, a community of the "unhomely," a new internationalism,[3] a gathering of people in the diaspora. The affirmation of difference and hybridity is itself, according to Bhabha, an affirmation of community: "To live in the unhomely world, to find its ambivalences and ambiguities enacted in the house of fiction, or its sundering and splitting performed in the work of art, is also to affirm a profound desire for social solidarity."[4] The seeds of the alternative community, he believes, arise out of close attention to the locality of culture, its hybridity, and its resistance to the binary structuring of social hierarchies.

We should be careful to recognize the form of the dominating power that serves as the enemy (and really the negative foundation) in this postcolonialist framework. Power is assumed to operate exclusively through a dialectical and binary structure. The only form of domination Bhabha recognizes, in other words, is that of modern sovereignty. This is why, for example, he can say "hierarchical or binary" as if the two terms were interchangeable: from his perspective hierarchy as such is necessarily grounded in binary divisions, so that the mere fact of hybridity has the power to destroy hierarchy *tout court*.[5] Hybridity itself is a realized politics of difference, setting differences to play across boundaries. This is where the postcolonial and the postmodern most powerfully meet: in the united attack on the dialectics of modern sovereignty and the proposition of liberation as a politics of difference.

Like the postmodernist theorists, postcolonial theorists such as Bhabha interest us primarily insofar as they are symptoms of the epochal shift we

2. An allusion to BENEDICT ANDERSON's *Imagined Communities: Reflections on the Origin and Spread of Nationalism* (1983; see above).
3. In his book *Specters of Marx: The State of the Debt, the Work of Mourning, and the New International* (1993; trans. 1994), Derrida provocatively used the term "the new international" to refer to a postcapitalist revolutionary collectivity that, like Hardt and Negri's multitude, preserves a revolutionary spirit of Marxism without subsuming the identities of its constituents under a unifying banner such as "the party," "the vanguard," etc.
4. Homi Bhabha, *The Location of Culture* (London: Routledge, 1994), p. 18 [Hardt and Negri's note].
5. Simply (French).

are undergoing, that is, the passage to Empire. Perhaps the discourses themselves are possible only when the regimes of modern sovereignty are already on the wane. Like postmodernists too, however, postcolonialist theorists in general give a very confused view of this passage because they remain fixated on attacking an old form of power and propose a strategy of liberation that could be effective only on that old terrain. The postcolonialist perspective remains primarily concerned with colonial sovereignty. As Gyan Prakash says, "The postcolonial exists as an aftermath, as an after—after being worked over by colonialism."[6] This may make postcolonialist theory a very productive tool for rereading history, but it is entirely insufficient for theorizing contemporary global power. Edward Said, certainly one of the most brilliant to go under the label of postcolonial theory, manages to condemn the current global power structures only to the extent that they perpetuate cultural and ideological remnants of European colonialist rule.[7] He charges that "the tactics of the great empires [that is, the European imperialisms], which were dismantled after the first world war, are being replicated by the U.S."[8] What is missing here is a recognition of the novelty of the structures and logics of power that order the contemporary world. Empire is not a weak echo of modern imperialisms but a fundamentally new form of rule.

Fundamentalism and/or Postmodernism

Another symptom of the historical passage already in process in the final decades of the twentieth century is the rise of so-called fundamentalisms. Since the collapse of the Soviet Union, the great ideologues of geopolitics and the theoreticians of the end of history[9] have consistently posed fundamentalisms as the primary danger facing global order and stability. Fundamentalism, however, is a poor and confused category that groups together widely disparate phenomena. In general, one might say that fundamentalisms, diverse though they may be, are linked by their being understood both from within and outside as anti-modernist movements, resurgences of primordial identities and values; they are conceived as a kind of historical backflow, a de-modernization. It is more accurate and more useful, however, to understand the various fundamentalisms not as the re-creation of a premodern world, but rather as a powerful refusal of the contemporary historical passage in course. In this sense, then, like postmodernist and postcolonialist theories, fundamentalisms too are a symptom of the passage to Empire.

Often today in the media the term "fundamentalism" reduces the variety of social formations that go by that name and refers exclusively to Islamic fundamentalism, the complexity of which is in turn reduced to a violent and intolerant religious fanaticism that is above all "anti-Western." Islamic fundamentalism itself, of course, takes various forms and has a long history

6. Gyan Prakash, "Postcolonial Criticism and Indian Historiography," *Social Text*, no. 31/32 (1992), 8 [Hardt and Negri's note]. Prakash (b. 1952), Indian-born historian of South Asia, urban, and postcolonial studies.

7. See Edward Said, *Culture and Imperialism* (New York: Vintage, 1993), pp. 282–303 [Hardt and Negri's note]. SAID (1935–2003), Palestinian-born American postcolonial theorist and literary and cultural critic widely known for his critique of Eurocentric Orientalism.

8. Edward Said, "Arabesque," *New Statesman and Society*, 7 (September 1990), 32 [Hardt and Negri's note].

9. See especially Francis Fukuyama's *The End of History and the Last Man* (1992), which argues that the end of the cold war, leaving the United States the world's sole superpower, signified the end of the contradictions that had driven the Hegelian dialectic of history.

extending throughout the modern era. Islamic revivalism and reformism were strong at different times in the eighteenth and nineteenth centuries, and the current forms of Islamic radicalism bear distinct similarities to those previous movements. Islamic fundamentalisms are most coherently united, however, in their being *resolutely opposed to modernity and modernization*. Insofar as political and cultural modernization has been a process of secularization, Islamic fundamentalisms oppose it by posing sacred texts at the center of political constitutions and religious leaders, both priests and jurists, in positions of political power. In terms, too, of gender roles, family structures, and cultural forms, an unchanging, traditional religious norm is commonly meant to stand against the progressively changing secular forms of modernity. Counter to modernism's dynamic and secular society, fundamentalism seems to pose a static and religious one. In this light, then, as an anti-modernism, Islamic fundamentalisms seem to be engaged in an effort to reverse the process of social modernization, separate from the global flows of modernity, and re-create a premodern world. The Iranian revolution of 1979,[1] for example, would from this perspective be seen as an anti-revolution, resurrecting an ancient order.

Christian fundamentalisms in the United States also present themselves as movements against social modernization, re-creating what is imagined to be a past social formation based on sacred texts. These movements should certainly be situated in line with the long U.S. tradition of projects to create in America a new Jerusalem, a Christian community separate from both the corruption of Europe and the savagery of the "uncivilized" world.[2] The most prominent social agenda of the current Christian fundamentalist groups is centered on the (re)creation of the stable and hierarchical nuclear family, which is imagined to have existed in a previous era, and thus they are driven specifically in their crusades against abortion and homosexuality. Christian fundamentalisms in the United States have also continuously been oriented (in different times and different regions more or less overtly) toward a project of white supremacy and racial purity. The new Jerusalem has almost always been imagined as a white and patriarchal Jerusalem.

These common characterizations of fundamentalisms as a return to a premodern or traditional world and its social values, however, obscure more than they illuminate. In fact, fundamentalist visions of a return to the past are generally based on historical illusions. The purity and wholesomeness of the stable, nuclear heterosexual family heralded by Christian fundamentalists, for example, never existed in the United States. The "traditional family" that serves as their ideological foundation is merely a pastiche of values and practices that derives more from television programs than from any real historical experiences within the institution of the family.[3] It is a

1. The religion-based uprising that led to the abdication of Iran's shah, Mohammad Reza Shah Pahlevi, and the establishment of an "Islamic republic"; its first "supreme leader" was the Ayatollah Ruhollah Khomeini, a conservative Shiite cleric.

2. Anders Stephanson gives an excellent account of the conceptions of the United States as a "new Jerusalem" in *Manifest Destiny: American Expansionism and the Empire of Right* (New York: Hill and Wang, 1995) [Hardt and Negri's note].

3. "Like most visions of a 'golden age,' the 'traditional family' . . . evaporates upon close examination. It is an ahistorical amalgam of structures, values, and behaviors that never co-existed in the same time and place." Stephanie Coontz, *The Way We Never Were: American Families and the Nostalgia Trap* (New York: Basic Books, 1992), p. 9 [Hardt and Negri's note]. The idea of postmodern pastiche recalls FREDRIC JAMESON's "Postmodernism and Consumer Society" (1988; see above).

fictional image projected on the past, like Main Street U.S.A. at Disneyland,[4] constructed retrospectively through the lens of contemporary anxieties and fears. The "return to the traditional family" of the Christian fundamentalists is not backward-looking at all, but rather a new invention that is part of a political project against the contemporary social order.

Similarly, the current forms of Islamic fundamentalism should not be understood as a return to past social forms and values, not even from the perspective of the practitioners. According to Fazlur Rahman: "Actually it is even something of a misnomer to call such phenomena in Islam 'fundamentalist' except insofar as they emphasize the basis of Islam as being the two original sources: the Qur'an and the Sunna of the Prophet Muhammed. Otherwise they emphasize ijtihad, original thought."[5] Contemporary Islamic radicalisms are indeed primarily based on "original thought" and the invention of original values and practices, which perhaps echo those of other periods of revivalism or fundamentalism but are really directed in reaction to the present social order. In both cases, then, the fundamentalist "return to tradition" is really a new invention.[6]

The anti-modern thrust that defines fundamentalisms might be better understood, then, not as a *pre*modern but as a *post*modern project. The postmodernity of fundamentalism has to be recognized primarily in its refusal of modernity as a weapon of Euro-American hegemony—and in this regard Islamic fundamentalism is indeed the paradigmatic case. In the context of Islamic traditions, fundamentalism is postmodern insofar as it rejects the tradition of Islamic modernism for which modernity was always overcoded as assimilation or submission to Euro-American hegemony. "If modern meant the pursuit of Western education, technology and industrialization in the first flush of the post-colonial period," Akbar Ahmed writes, "postmodern would mean a reversion to traditional Muslim values and a rejection of modernism."[7] Considered simply in cultural terms, Islamic fundamentalism is a paradoxical kind of postmodernist theory—postmodern only because it chronologically follows and opposes Islamic modernism. It is more properly postmodernist, however, when considered in geopolitical terms. Rahman writes: "The current postmodernist fundamentalism, in an important way, is novel because its basic élan is anti-Western . . . Hence its condemnation of classical modernism as a purely Westernizing force."[8] Certainly, powerful segments of Islam have been in some sense "anti-Western" since the religion's inception. What is novel in the contemporary resurgence of funda-

4. The theme park in Anaheim, California, operated by the Walt Disney Company; its Main Street is discussed by Baudrillard as well.
5. Fazlur Rahman, *Islam and Modernity: Transformation of an Intellectual Tradition* (Chicago: University of Chicago Press, 1984), p. 142 [Hardt and Negri's note]. Rahman (1919–1988), scholar of Islam born in West Pakistan. Sunna: literally, "course, rule" (Arabic); the body of sayings and customs attributed to Muhammad that supplement the Qur'an.
6. "The fundamentalism of the humiliated Islamic world is not a tradition of the past but a postmodern phenomenon: the inevitable ideological reaction to the failure of Western modernization." Robert Kurz, "Die Krise, die aus dem Osten Kam" [The crisis that came from the East], translated into Italian in *L'onore perduto del lavaro*, trans. Anselm Jappe and Maria Teresa Ricci (Rome: Manifestolibri, 1994), p. 16. More generally, on contemporary fallacies around notions of tradition and group identity, see Arjun Appadurai, "Life after Primordialism," in *Modernity at Large* (Minneapolis: University of Minnesota Press, 1996), pp. 139–57 [Hardt and Negri's note]. Arjun Appadurai (b. 1949), Indian-born American anthropologist and globalization theorist.
7. Akbar Ahmed, *Postmodernism and Islam* (New York: Routledge, 1992), p. 32 [Hardt and Negri's note]. Ahmed (b. 1943), Pakistani anthropologist and scholar of contemporary Islam.
8. Rahman, *Islam and Modernity*, p. 136 [Hardt and Negri's note].

mentalism is really the refusal of the powers that are emerging in the new imperial order. From this perspective, then, insofar as the Iranian revolution was a powerful rejection of the world market, we might think of it as the first postmodernist revolution.

This marriage between postmodernism and fundamentalism is certainly an odd coupling considering that postmodernist and fundamentalist discourses stand in most respects in polar opposition: hybridity versus purity, difference versus identity, mobility versus stasis. It seems to us that postmodernists and the current wave of fundamentalists have arisen not only at the same time but also in response to the same situation, only at opposite poles of the global hierarchy, according to a striking geographical distribution. Simplifying a great deal, one could argue that postmodernist discourses appeal primarily to the winners in the processes of globalization and fundamentalist discourses to the losers. In other words, the current global tendencies toward increased mobility, indeterminacy, and hybridity are experienced by some as a kind of liberation but by others as an exacerbation of their suffering. Certainly, bands of popular support for fundamentalist projects—from the Front National in France and Christian fundamentalism in the United States to the Islamic Brothers[9]—have spread most widely among those who have been further subordinated and excluded by the recent transformations of the global economy and who are most threatened by the increased mobility of capital. The losers in the processes of globalization might indeed be the ones who give us the strongest indication of the transformation in progress.

The Ideology of the World Market

Many of the concepts dear to postmodernists and postcolonialists find a perfect correspondence in the current ideology of corporate capital and the world market. The ideology of the world market has always been the anti-foundational and anti-essentialist discourse par excellence. Circulation, mobility, diversity, and mixture are its very conditions of possibility. Trade brings differences together and the more the merrier! Differences (of commodities, populations, cultures, and so forth) seem to multiply infinitely in the world market, which attacks nothing more violently than fixed boundaries: it overwhelms any binary division with its infinite multiplicities.

As the world market today is realized ever more completely, it tends to deconstruct the boundaries of the nation-state. In a previous period, nation-states were the primary actors in the modern imperialist organization of global production and exchange, but to the world market they appear increasingly as mere obstacles. Robert Reich, former U.S. secretary of labor, is in an excellent position to recognize and celebrate the overcoming of national boundaries in the world market. He contends that "as almost every factor of production—money, technology, factories, and equipment—moves effortlessly across borders, the very idea of a [national] economy is becoming meaningless." In the future "there will be no *national* products or technologies, no national corporations, no national industries. There will no

9. The Muslim Brotherhood (founded in Egypt, 1928), a militant international political organization of fundamentalist Sunni Muslims. Front National: the National Front (French), a right-wing nationalist French political party, founded in 1971, with a platform of social conservatism, economic protectionism, and racial purity.

longer be national economies, as least as we have come to understand that concept."[1] With the decline of national boundaries, the world market is liberated from the kind of binary divisions that nation-states had imposed, and in this new free space a myriad of differences appears. These differences of course do not play freely across a smooth global space, but rather are regimented in global networks of power consisting of highly differentiated and mobile structures. Arjun Appadurai captures the new quality of these structures with the analogy of landscapes, or better, seascapes: in the contemporary world he sees finanscapes, technoscapes, ethnoscapes, and so forth.[2] The suffix "-scape" allows us on the one hand to point to the fluidity and irregularity of these various fields and on the other to indicate formal commonalities among such diverse domains as finance, culture, commodities, and demography. The world market establishes a real politics of difference.

The various -scapes of the world market provide capital with potentials on a scale previously unimaginable. It should be no surprise, then, that postmodernist thinking and its central concepts have flourished in the various fields of practice and theory proper to capital, such as marketing, management organization, and the organization of production. Postmodernism is indeed the logic by which global capital operates. Marketing has perhaps the clearest relation to postmodernist theories, and one could even say that the capitalist marketing strategies have long been postmodernist, *avant la lettre*.[3] On the one hand, marketing practices and consumer consumption are prime terrain for developing postmodernist thinking: certain postmodernist theorists, for example, see perpetual shopping and the consumption of commodities and commodified images as the paradigmatic and defining activities of postmodern experience, our collective journeys through hyperreality.[4] On the other hand, postmodernist thinking—with its emphasis on concepts such as difference and multiplicity, its celebration of fetishism and simulacra, its continual fascination with the new and with fashion—is an excellent description of the ideal capitalist schemes of commodity consumption and thus provides an opportunity to perfect marketing strategies. As a marketing theorist says, there are clear "parallels between contemporary market practices and the precepts of postmodernism."[5]

Marketing itself is a practice based on differences, and the more differences that are given, the more marketing strategies can develop. Ever more hybrid and differentiated populations present a proliferating number of "target markets" that can each be addressed by specific marketing strategies—one for gay Latino males between the ages of eighteen and twenty-two, another for

1. Robert Reich, *The Work of Nations* (New York: Random House, 1992), pp. 8 and 3 [Hardt and Negri's note]. Reich (b. 1946), American academic and economist; he served as secretary of labor (1993–97) under President Bill Clinton.

2. See Arjun Appadurai, "Disjuncture and Difference in the Global Cultural Economy," in *Modernity at Large* (Minneapolis: University of Minnesota Press, 1996), pp. 27–47 [Hardt and Negri's note].

3. Before the letter (French); that is, before the term existed.

4. See, for example, Jean Baudrillard, *Selected Writings*, ed. Mark Poster (Oxford: Blackwell, 1988); and Umberto Eco, *Travels in Hyper-reality*, trans. William Weaver (London: Picador, 1986), pp. 3–58 [Hardt and Negri's note]. "Hyperreality": the ability of images and simulacra to displace reality and appear "more real" than reality itself. Eco (1932–2016), Italian literary theorist, novelist, and philosopher.

5. Stephen Brown, *Postmodern Marketing* (London: Routledge, 1995), p. 157. Whereas marketing practice is postmodernist, Brown points out, marketing theory remains stubbornly "modernist" (which here means positivistic). Elizabeth Hirschman and Morris Holbrook also bemoan the resistance of marketing theory and consumer research to postmodernist thinking in *Postmodern Consumer Research: The Study of Consumption as Text* (Newbury Park, Calif.: Sage, 1992) [Hardt and Negri's note].

Chinese-American teenage girls, and so forth. Postmodern marketing recognizes the difference of each commodity and each segment of the population, fashioning its strategies accordingly.[6] Every difference is an opportunity.

Postmodern marketing practices represent the consumption cycle of contemporary capital, its external face, but we are even more interested in the postmodernist tendencies within the cycle of capitalist production. In the productive sphere, postmodernist thinking has perhaps had the largest direct impact in the field of management and organization theory. Authors in this field argue that large and complex modern organizations, with their rigid boundaries and homogeneous units, are not adequate for doing business in the postmodern world. "The postmodern organization," one theorist writes, "has certain distinctive features—notably, an emphasis on small-to-moderate size and complexity and adoption of flexible structures and modes of interinstitutional cooperation to meet turbulent organizational and environmental conditions."[7] Postmodern organizations are thus imagined either as located on the boundaries between different systems and cultures or as internally hybrid. What is essential for postmodern management is that organizations be mobile, flexible, and able to deal with difference. Here postmodernist theories pave the way for the transformation of the internal structures of capitalist organizations.

The "culture" within these organizations has also adopted the precepts of postmodernist thinking. The great transnational corporations that straddle national boundaries and link the global system are themselves internally much more diverse and fluid culturally than the parochial modern corporations of previous years. The contemporary gurus of corporate culture who are employed by management as consultants and strategy planners preach the efficiency and profitability of diversity and multiculturalism within corporations.[8] When one looks closely at U.S. corporate ideology (and, to a lesser but still significant extent, at U.S. corporate practice), it is clear that corporations do not operate simply by excluding the gendered and/or racialized Other. In fact, the old modernist forms of racist and sexist theory are the explicit enemies of this new corporate culture. The corporations seek to include difference within their realm and thus aim to maximize creativity, free play, and diversity in the corporate workplace. People of all different races, sexes, and sexual orientations should potentially be included in the corporation; the daily routine of the workplace should be rejuvenated with unexpected changes and an atmosphere of fun. Break down the old boundaries and let one hundred flowers bloom![9] The task of the boss, subsequently, is to organize these energies and differences in the interests of profit. This project is aptly called "diversity management." In this light, the corporations

6. See George Yúdice, "Civil Society, Consumption, and Governmentality in an Age of Global Restructuring: An Introduction," *Social Text*, no. 45 (Winter 1995), 1–25 [Hardt and Negri's note].
7. William Bergquist, *The Postmodern Organization: Mastering the Art of Irreversible Change* (San Francisco: Jossey-Bass, 1993), p. xiii. See also the essays in David Boje, Robert Gephart Jr., and Tojo Joseph Thatchenkery, eds., *Postmodern Management and Organizational Theory* (Thousand Oaks, Calif.: Sage, 1996) [Hardt and Negri's note].
8. See Avery Gordon, "The Work of Corporate Culture: Diversity Management," *Social Text*, no. 44, vol. 13, no. 3 (Fall/Winter 1995), 3–30 [Hardt and Negri's note].
9. See Chris Newfield, "Corporate Pleasures for a Corporate Planet," *Social Text*, no. 44, vol. 13, no. 3 (Fall/Winter 1995), 31–44 [Hardt and Negri's note]. "Let one hundred flowers bloom": that is, let diverse voices and perspectives be put to use. The slogan was employed by Mao Zedong in a campaign (1956–57) that urged Chinese intellectuals to criticize the state.

appear not only "progressive" but also "postmodernist," as leaders in a very real politics of difference.

The production processes of capital have also taken forms that echo postmodernist projects. We will have ample opportunity to analyze (particularly in Section 3.4[1]) how production has come to be organized in flexible and hybrid networks. This is, in our view, the most important respect in which the contemporary transformations of capital and the world market constitute a real process of postmodernization.

We certainly agree with those contemporary theorists, such as David Harvey and Fredric Jameson, who see postmodernity as a new phase of capitalist accumulation and commodification that accompanies the contemporary realization of the world market.[2] The global politics of difference established by the world market is defined not by free play and equality, but by the imposition of new hierarchies, or really by a constant process of hierarchization. Postmodernist and postcolonialist theories (and fundamentalisms in a very different way) are really sentinels that signal this passage in course, and in this regard are indispensable.

Truth Commissions

It is salutary to remind ourselves that postmodernist and postcolonial discourses are effective only in very specific geographical locations and among a certain class of the population. As a political discourse, postmodernism has a certain currency in Europe, Japan, and Latin America, but its primary site of application is within an elite segment of the U.S. intelligentsia. Similarly, the postcolonial theory that shares certain postmodernist tendencies has been developed primarily among a cosmopolitan set that moves among the metropolises and major universities of Europe and the United States. This specificity does not invalidate the theoretical perspectives, but it should make us pause for a moment to reflect on their political implications and practical effects. Numerous genuinely progressive and liberatory discourses have emerged throughout history among elite groups, and we have no intention here of questioning the vocation of such theorizing *tout court*. More important than the specificity of these theorists are the resonances their concepts stimulate in different geographical and class locations.

Certainly from the standpoint of many around the world, hybridity, mobility, and difference do not immediately appear as liberatory in themselves. Huge populations see mobility as an aspect of their suffering because they are displaced at an increasing speed in dire circumstances. For several decades, as part of the modernization process there have been massive migrations from rural areas to metropolitan centers within each country and across the globe. The international flow of labor has only increased in recent years, not only from south to north, in the form of legal and illegal guest workers or immigrants, but also from south to south, that is, the temporary or semipermanent worker migrations among southern regions, such as that of South Asian workers in the Persian Gulf. Even these massive

1. Titled "Postmodernization, or The Informatization of Production."
2. See Fredric Jameson, *Postmodernism, Or, The Cultural Logic of Late Capitalism* (Durham: Duke University Press, 1991); and David Harvey, *The Condition of Postmodernity* (Oxford: Blackwell, 1989) [Hardt and Negri's note]. HARVEY (b. 1935), British geographer and Marxist theorist.

worker migrations, however, are dwarfed in terms of numbers and misery by those forced from their homes and land by famine and war. Just a cursory glance around the world, from Central America to Central Africa and from the Balkans to Southeast Asia, will reveal the desperate plight of those on whom such mobility has been imposed. For them, mobility across boundaries often amounts to forced migration in poverty and is hardly liberatory. In fact, a stable and defined place in which to live, a certain immobility, can on the contrary appear as the most urgent need.

The postmodernist epistemological challenge to "the Enlightenment"—its attack on master narratives and its critique of truth—also loses its liberatory aura when transposed outside the elite intellectual strata of Europe and North America. Consider, for example, the mandate of the Truth Commission formed at the end of the civil war in El Salvador,[3] or the similar institutions that have been established in the post-dictatorial and post-authoritarian regimes of Latin America and South Africa. In the context of state terror and mystification, clinging to the primacy of the concept of truth can be a powerful and necessary form of resistance. Establishing and making public the truth of the recent past—attributing responsibility to state officials for specific acts and in some cases exacting retribution—appears here as the ineluctable precondition for any democratic future. The master narratives of the Enlightenment do not seem particularly repressive here, and the concept of truth is not fluid or unstable—on the contrary! The truth is that this general ordered the torture and assassination of that union leader, and this colonel led the massacre of that village. Making public such truths is an exemplary Enlightenment project of modernist politics, and the critique of it in these contexts could serve only to aid the mystificatory and repressive powers of the regime under attack.

In our present imperial world, the liberatory potential of the postmodernist and postcolonial discourses that we have described only resonates with the situation of an elite population that enjoys certain rights, a certain level of wealth, and a certain position in the global hierarchy. One should not take this recognition, however, as a complete refutation. It is not really a matter of either/or. Difference, hybridity, and mobility are not liberatory in themselves, but neither are truth, purity, and stasis. The real revolutionary practice refers to the level of *production.* Truth will not make us free, but taking control of the production of truth will. Mobility and hybridity are not liberatory, but taking control of the production of mobility and stasis, purities and mixtures is. The real truth commissions of Empire will be constituent assemblies of the multitude, social factories for the production of truth.

* * *

2000

3. The civil war in El Salvador followed a military coup in 1979; it lasted until peace accords were signed in January 1992. That treaty established the Commission on the Truth for El Salvador, whose U.N.-appointed commissioners investigated civil rights abuses by all participants in the conflict (about 85 percent of the acts of violence were attributed to agents of the state).

JUDITH JACK HALBERSTAM
b. 1961

Judith Jack Halberstam combines queer theory, cultural studies, and popular culture to speak to activist as well as academic audiences. Building on the work of such theorists as LOUIS ALTHUSSER, JUDITH BUTLER, and EVE KOSOFSKY SEDGWICK, Halberstam shows that intellectuals can draw on the experience of everyday life to deconstruct narrow binary systems of gender and sexuality and generate new, more expansive understandings. Her work examines texts ranging from Victorian literature to 1980s lesbian pornography to contemporary novels and Hollywood films. "Masculinity" is a category of behaviors, asserts Halberstam, that can be studied and understood apart from individual men. Furthermore, masculinity can be performed by and linked to bodies other than those of white heterosexual males (the dominant model in Western culture). Women can access masculinity as well, and they can do so without surgically altering their bodies. The category of "female masculinity" is Halberstam's major critical contribution. By separating masculinity from the male body, Halberstam restructures popular and frequently negative portrayals of masculine women, particularly so-called butch women. Such work has implications that reach beyond the academy; by using personal and popular culture narratives of sexuality it can, in Halberstam's words, both "rewrite . . . psychoanalytic theories of desire and scientific theories of sexuality" and dispel "homogenizing notions of gay and lesbian desire."

Halberstam earned a B.A. in English from the University of California at Berkeley in 1985 and a Ph.D. in English literature from the University of Minnesota in 1991. The author of six books to date and numerous articles, Halberstam is currently a professor of English, American studies and ethnicity, comparative literature, and gender studies at the University of Southern California, where she has served as the director of the Center for Feminist Research. In addition to lecturing at universities across the United States and Europe, Halberstam has been a visiting professor at Duke University, Harvard University, Yale University, and the University of Basel in Switzerland. Her book *Female Masculinity* (1998) received the Publisher's Triangle Judy Grahn Award for Lesbian Non-Fiction in 1999, and *In a Queer Time and Place* (2005) was nominated for a Lambda Award in 2006.

Drawing on the critical theories of ANTONIO GRAMSCI and MICHEL FOUCAULT, among others, Halberstam not only dissects hegemonic gender systems and their operations but also "theorizes the alternative" (the counterhegemonic). She uses gender, queer, and cultural theory to address the "silly archive"—animated movies, television shows, and other popular culture texts that might seem far removed from theory and socially significant interpretation. Halberstam's method, which engages both scholarly and popular audiences, addresses a frequent criticism of queer theory: that its reliance on complex deconstructive and psychoanalytic terminology obscures meaning and alienates nonacademic readers. In interviews, Halberstam explains that her drive to connect to a broad audience emerges, in part, from a sense that her work represents a community. This sense links her style and approach to that of African American scholars such as HENRY LOUIS GATES JR. and BELL HOOKS.

Halberstam's work—most notably in *Female Masculinity*, whose introduction appears below—resembles that of Gramsci in stressing counterhegemonic groups. At the same time, it embraces the Foucauldian notion that medical and scientific categories attain cultural "realness" when individuals embody them as elements of their identities. Gender is one such category that is taught and performed in the process of socialization. Whereas Butler acknowledges this reality and evinces suspicion toward the taxonomical boundaries of gender (which she links to dominant heteronormative values), Halberstam surprisingly retains the existing taxonomy but seeks increased complexity within it. Masculinity and femininity, as performative acts and codes that can be associated with numerous kinds of bodies, allow *all* bodies to disrupt gender or to represent queer deviance. We see this especially in Halberstam's discussion of bathroom problems and gender policing for those who do not perform or conform to social expectations of femininity or masculinity. Halberstam's designation "female masculinity" is fluid and complex, identifying a frequently ignored or abjected category of identity. Her "taxonomical impulse" to retain the categories of masculine and feminine leads not to confinement but to the recognition of varied erotic and identity categories, and she focuses especially on cross-identifying females who do not fit into categories of "transgender" or "transsexual": masculine females. She associates them with female sports icons, butch roles, lesbian fatherhood, tomboys, and drag kings. In this regard, Halberstam aligns herself with Eve Sedgwick, whose influential *Epistemology of the Closet* (1990) lists methods of categorizing desire beyond the hetero/homo binary. Rather than completely deconstructing gender, Halberstam makes nameable identities that were previously unacknowledged or disenfranchised.

In arguing for gender variance and gender preference and against mandatory masculine/feminine identity, Halberstam is critical of mainstream dominant masculinity reserved for males. Characteristically coded as white and heroic, it is associated (vis-à-vis femininity) with power, privilege, and legitimacy as well as freedom and mobility. To broaden both the definition and the reach of masculinity, Halberstam advocates a "scavenger methodology" that mixes and matches ethnography, textual studies, and queer historical inquiry with critique of the shortcomings of earlier research and publication on masculinity. Her conclusion: female masculinity exists in multiple forms. At the end of her section on "constructing masculinities," Halberstam pivots in a personal direction and reveals that her "book is an attempt to make my own female masculinity plausible, credible, real."

While Halberstam's work has been widely praised and deployed by queer theorists, it has not been accepted by all critics. Some question the language of Halberstam's gender taxonomies, objecting to her use of the terms "masculine" and "feminine," binaries that are always already hierarchically ranked. A number of critics also point out that not all disruptive gender performances are "queer" in the sense of being counternormative. Others assert that queer theory should work to disavow and deconstruct gender identities rather than freezing them within categories that, though they may seem more fluid, are ultimately just as limiting and rigid as those they are intended to replace.

***Female Masculinity* Keywords:** The Body, Cultural Studies, Feminist Criticism, Gender, Hegemony, Identity, Queer Theory, Race and Ethnicity Studies, Sexuality

From Female Masculinity

From *Chapter 1. An Introduction to Female Masculinity: Masculinity without Men*

What's the use of being a little boy if you are going to grow up to be a man?
—Gertrude Stein,[1] *Everybody's Autobiography* (1937)

THE REAL THING

What is "masculinity"? This has been probably the most common question that I have faced over the past five years while writing on the topic of female masculinity. If masculinity is not the social and cultural and indeed political expression of maleness, then what is it? I do not claim to have any definitive answer to this question, but I do have a few proposals about why masculinity must not and cannot and should not reduce down to the male body and its effects. I also venture to assert that although we seem to have a difficult time defining masculinity, as a society we have little trouble in recognizing it, and indeed we spend massive amounts of time and money ratifying and supporting the versions of masculinity that we enjoy and trust; many of these "heroic masculinities" depend absolutely on the subordination of alternative masculinities. I claim in this book that far from being an imitation of maleness, female masculinity actually affords us a glimpse of how masculinity is constructed as masculinity. In other words, female masculinities are framed as the rejected scraps of dominant masculinity in order that male masculinity may appear to be the real thing. But what we understand as heroic masculinity has been produced by and across both male and female bodies.

This opening chapter does not simply offer a conventional theoretical introduction to the enterprise of conceptualizing masculinity without men; rather, it attempts to compile the myths and fantasies about masculinity that have ensured that masculinity and maleness are profoundly difficult to pry apart. I then offer, by way of a preliminary attempt to re-imagine masculinity, numerous examples of alternative masculinities in fiction, film, and lived experience. These examples are mostly queer and female, and they show clearly how important it is to recognize alternative masculinities when and where they emerge. Throughout this introduction, I detail the many ways in which female masculinity has been blatantly ignored both in the culture at large and within academic studies of masculinity. This widespread indifference to female masculinity, I suggest, has clearly ideological motivations and has sustained the complex social structures that wed masculinity to maleness and to power and domination. I firmly believe that a sustained examination of female masculinity can make crucial interventions within gender studies, cultural studies, queer studies, and mainstream discussions of gender in general.

Masculinity in this society inevitably conjures up notions of power and legitimacy and privilege; it often symbolically refers to the power of the state

1. Avant-garde American writer (1874–1946), an important figure in modernist and lesbian literature.

and to uneven distributions of wealth. Masculinity seems to extend outward into patriarchy and inward into the family; masculinity represents the power of inheritance, the consequences of the traffic in women, and the promise of social privilege. But, obviously, many other lines of identification traverse the terrain of masculinity, dividing its power into complicated differentials of class, race, sexuality, and gender. If what we call "dominant masculinity" appears to be a naturalized relation between maleness and power, then it makes little sense to examine men for the contours of that masculinity's social construction. Masculinity, this book will claim, becomes legible as masculinity where and when it leaves the white male middle-class body. Arguments about excessive masculinity tend to focus on black bodies (male and female), latino/a bodies, or working-class bodies, and insufficient masculinity is all too often figured by Asian bodies or upper-class bodies; these stereotypical constructions of variable masculinity mark the process by which masculinity becomes dominant in the sphere of white middle-class maleness. But all too many studies that currently attempt to account for the power of white masculinity recenter this white male body by concentrating all their analytical efforts on detailing the forms and expressions of white male dominance. Numerous studies of Elvis,[2] white male youth, white male feminism, men and marriage, and domestications of maleness amass information about a subject whom we know intimately and ad nauseam. This study professes a degree of indifference to the whiteness of the male and the masculinity of the white male and the project of naming his power: male masculinity figures in my project as a hermeneutic, and as a counterexample to the kinds of masculinity that seem most informative about gender relations and most generative of social change. This book seeks Elvis only in the female Elvis impersonator Elvis Herselvis; it searches for the political contours of masculine privilege not in men but in the lives of aristocratic European cross-dressing women in the 1920s; it describes the details of masculine difference by comparing not men and women but butch lesbians and female-to-male transsexuals; it examines masculinity's iconicity not in the male matinee idol but in a history of butches in cinema; it finds, ultimately, that the shapes and forms of modern masculinity are best showcased within female masculinity.

How else to begin a book on female masculinity but by deposing one of the most persistent of male heroes: Bond, James Bond.[3] To illustrate my point that modern masculinity is most easily recognized as female masculinity, consider the James Bond action film, in which male masculinity very often appears as only a shadow of a more powerful and convincing alternative masculinity. In *Goldeneye* (1995), for example, Bond battles the usual array of bad guys: Commies, Nazis, mercenaries, and a superaggressive violent femme type. He puts on his usual performance of debonair action adventure hero, and he has his usual supply of gadgetry to aid him—a retractable belt, a bomb disguised as a pen, a laser weapon watch, and so on. But there's something curiously lacking in *Goldeneye*, namely, credible masculine power. Bond's boss, M, is a noticeably butch older woman who calls Bond a dinosaur and chastises him for being a misogynist and a sexist. His secretary,

2. Elvis Presley (1935–1977), American singer and actor, a 1950s teen idol, and an enduring cultural icon.

3. Spy hero featured in 12 novels by the English author Ian Fleming (1908–1964), the first in 1953, and 26 films to date.

Miss Moneypenny, accuses him of sexual harassment, his male buddy betrays him and calls him a dupe, and ultimately women seem not to go for his charms—bad suits and lots of sexual innuendo—which seem as old and as ineffective as his gadgets.

Masculinity, in this rather actionless film, is primarily prosthetic and, in this and countless other action films, has little if anything to do with biological maleness and signifies more often as a technical special effect. In *Goldeneye* it is M who most convincingly performs masculinity, and she does so partly by exposing the sham of Bond's own performance. It is M who convinces us that sexism and misogyny are not necessarily part and parcel of masculinity, even though historically it has become difficult, if not impossible, to untangle masculinity from the oppression of women. The action adventure hero should embody an extreme version of normative masculinity, but instead we find that excessive masculinity turns into a parody or exposure of the norm. Because masculinity tends to manifest as natural gender itself, the action flick, with its emphases on prosthetic extension, actually undermines the heterosexuality of the hero even as it extends his masculinity. So, in *Goldeneye*, for example, Bond's masculinity is linked not only to a profoundly unnatural form of masculine embodiment but also to gay masculinities. In the scene in which Bond goes to pick up his newest set of gadgets, a campy and almost queeny science nerd gives Bond his brand-new accessories and demonstrates each one with great enthusiasm. It is no accident that the science nerd is called Agent Q. We might read Agent Q as a perfect model of the interpenetration of queer and dominant regimes—Q is precisely an agent, a queer subject who exposes the workings of dominant heterosexual masculinity. The gay masculinity of Agent Q and the female masculinity of M provide a remarkable representation of the absolute dependence of dominant masculinities on minority masculinities.

When you take his toys away, Bond has very little propping up his performance of masculinity. Without the slick suit, the half smile, the cigarette lighter that transforms into a laser gun, our James is a hero without the action or the adventure. The masculinity of the white male, what we might call "epic masculinity," depends absolutely, as any Bond flick demonstrates, on a vast subterranean network of secret government groups, well-funded scientists, the army, and an endless supply of both beautiful bad babes and beautiful good babes, and finally it relies heavily on an immediately recognizable "bad guy." The "bad guy" is a standard generic feature of epic masculinity narratives: think only of *Paradise Lost*[4] and its eschatological separation between God and Devil; Satan, if you like, is the original bad guy. Which is not to say that the bad guy's masculinity bars him from the rewards of male privilege—on the contrary, bad guys may also look like winners, but they just tend to die more quickly. Indeed, there is currently a line of clothing called Bad Boy that revels in the particular power of the bad guy and reveals how quickly transgression adds up to nothing more than consumerism in the sphere of the white male. Another line of clothing that indulges in the consumer potential of male rebellion is No Fear gear. This label features advertisements with skydiving, surfing, car-racing men who show their manliness by wearing the No Fear logo and practicing death-defying stunts in their

4. John Milton's great epic English poem (1667, 1674).

leisure time. To test how domesticated this label actually is, we have only to imagine what No Fear might mean for women. It might mean learning how to shoot a gun or working out or taking up a martial art, but it would hardly translate into skydiving. Obviously, then, No Fear is a luxury and can in no way be equated with any form of social rebellion.

There is also a long literary and cinematic history that celebrates the rebellion of the male. If James Stewart, Gregory Peck, and Fred Astaire represent a few faces of good-guy appeal, James Dean, Marlon Brando, and Robert De Niro[5] represent the bad-guy appeal, and really it becomes quite hard to separate one group from the other. Obviously, bad-boy representations in the 1950s captured something of a white working-class rebellion against middle-class society and against particular forms of domestication, but today's rebel without a cause is tomorrow's investment banker, and male rebellion tends toward respectability as the rewards for conformity quickly come to outweigh the rewards for social rebellion. To paraphrase Gertrude Stein, what's the point of being a rebel boy if you are going to grow up to be a man? Obviously, where and when rebellion ceases to be white middle-class male rebellion (individualized and localized within the lone male or even generalized into the boy gang) and becomes class rebellion or race rebellion, a very different threat emerges.

TOMBOYS

What happens when boy rebellion is located not in the testosterone-induced pout of the hooligan but in the sneer of the tomboy? Tomboyism generally describes an extended childhood period of female masculinity. If we are to believe general accounts of childhood behavior, tomboyism is quite common for girls and does not generally give rise to parental fears. Because comparable cross-identification behaviors in boys do often give rise to quite hysterical responses, we tend to believe that female gender deviance is much more tolerated than male gender deviance.[6] I am not sure that tolerance in such matters can be measured or at any rate that responses to childhood gender behaviors necessarily tell us anything concrete about the permitted parameters of adult male and female gender deviance. Tomboyism tends to be associated with a "natural" desire for the greater freedoms and mobilities enjoyed by boys. Very often it is read as a sign of independence and self-motivation, and tomboyism may even be encouraged to the extent that it remains comfortably linked to a stable sense of a girl identity. Tomboyism is punished, however, when it appears to be the sign of extreme male identification (taking a boy's name or refusing girl clothing of any type) and when it threatens to extend beyond childhood and into adolescence.[7] Teenage tomboyism presents a problem and tends to be subject to the most severe efforts to reorient. We could say that tomboyism is tolerated as long as the child

5. All American leading men in film: Stewart (1908–1997), Peck (1916–2003), Astaire (1899–1987), Dean (1931–1955), Brando (1924–2004), and De Niro (b. 1943).

6. For an extension of this discussion of tomboys see my article "Oh Bondage Up Yours: Female Masculinity and the Tomboy," in *Sissies and Tomboys: A CLAGS Reader* (New York: New York University Press, 1999) [Halberstam's note].

7. For more on the punishment of tomboys see Phyllis Burke, *Gender Shock: Exploding the Myths of Male and Female* (New York: Anchor Books, 1996). Burke analyzes some recent case histories of so-called GID or Gender Identity Disorder, in which little girls are carefully conditioned out of male behavior and into exceedingly constrictive forms of femininity [Halberstam's note].

remains prepubescent; as soon as puberty begins, however, the full force of gender conformity descends on the girl. Gender conformity is pressed onto all girls, not just tomboys, and this is where it becomes hard to uphold the notion that male femininity presents a greater threat to social and familial stability than female masculinity. Female adolescence represents the crisis of coming of age as a girl in a male-dominated society. If adolescence for boys represents a rite of passage (much celebrated in Western literature in the form of the bildungsroman), and an ascension to some version (however attenuated) of social power, for girls, adolescence is a lesson in restraint, punishment, and repression. It is in the context of female adolescence that the tomboy instincts of millions of girls are remodeled into compliant forms of femininity.

That any girls do emerge at the end of adolescence as masculine women is quite amazing. The growing visibility and indeed respectability of lesbian communities to some degree facilitate the emergence of masculine young women. But as even a cursory survey of popular cinema confirms, the image of the tomboy can be tolerated only within a narrative of blossoming womanhood; within such a narrative, tomboyism represents a resistance to adulthood itself rather than to adult femininity. In both the novel and film versions of the classic tomboy narrative *The Member of the Wedding*, by Carson McCullers,[8] tomboy Frankie Addams fights a losing battle against womanhood, and the text locates womanhood or femininity as a crisis of representation that confronts the heroine with unacceptable life options. As her brother's wedding approaches, Frankie Addams pronounces herself mired in a realm of unbelonging, outside the symbolic partnership of the wedding but also alienated from belonging in almost every category that might describe her. McCullers writes: "It happened that green and crazy summer when Frankie was twelve years old. This was the summer when for a long time she had not been a member. She belonged to no club and was a member of nothing in the world. Frankie was an unjoined person who hung around in doorways, and she was afraid."[9] McCullers positions Frankie on the verge of adolescence ("when Frankie was twelve years old") and in the midst of an enduring state of being "unjoined": "She belonged to no club and was a member of nothing in the world." While childhood in general may qualify as a period of "unbelonging," for the boyish girl arriving on the doorstep of womanhood, her status as "unjoined" marks her out for all manner of social violence and opprobrium. As she dawdles in the last light of childhood, Frankie Addams has become a tomboy who "hung around in doorways, and she was afraid."

As a genre, the tomboy film, as I show in chapter 6, "Looking Butch," suggests that the categories available to women for racial, gendered, and sexual identification are simply inadequate. In her novel, McCullers shows this inadequacy to be a direct result of the tyranny of language—a structure that fixes people and things in place artificially but securely. Frankie tries to change her identity by changing her name: "Why is it against the law to change your name?" she asks Berenice (107). Berenice answers: "Because things

8. American writer of fiction (1917–1967); the movie version of her *The Member of the Wedding* (1946) was released in 1952.

9. Carson McCullers, *The Member of the Wedding* (1946; reprint, New York: Bantam, 1973), 1 [Halberstam's note].

accumulate around your name," and she stresses that without names, confusion would reign and "the whole world would go crazy." But Berenice also acknowledges that the fixity conferred by names also traps people into many different identities, racial as well as gendered: "We all of us somehow caught. . . . And maybe we wants to widen and bust free. But no matter what we do we still caught" (113). Frankie thinks that naming represents the power of definition, and name changing confers the power to reimagine identity, place, relation, and even gender. "I wonder if it is against the law to change your name," says Frankie, "Or add to it. . . . Well I don't care. . . . F. Jasmine Addams" (15).

Psychoanalysis posits a crucial relationship between language and desire such that language structures desire and expresses therefore both the fullness and the futility of human desire—full because we always desire, futile because we are never satisfied. Frankie in particular understands desire and sexuality to be the most regimented forms of social conformity—we are supposed to desire only certain people and only in certain ways, but her desire does not work that way, and she finds herself torn between longing and belonging. Because she does not desire in conventional ways, Frankie seeks to avoid desire altogether. Her struggle with language, her attempts to remake herself through naming and remake the world with a new order of being, are ultimately heroic, but unsuccessful. McCullers's pessimism has to do with a sense of the overwhelming "order of things," an order that cannot be affected by the individual, and works through things as basic as language, and forces nonmembers into memberships they cannot fulfill.

My book refuses the futility long associated with the tomboy narrative and instead seizes on the opportunity to recognize and ratify differently gendered bodies and subjectivities. Moving from the nineteenth century to the present and examining diaries, court cases, novels, letters, films, performances, events, critical essays, videos, news items, and testimonies, this book argues for the production of new taxonomies, what Eve K. Sedgwick[1] humorously called "nonce taxonomies" in *Epistemology of the Closet*, classifications of desire, physicality, and subjectivity that attempt to intervene in hegemonic processes of naming and defining. Nonce taxonomies are categories that we use daily to make sense of our worlds but that work so well that we actually fail to recognize them. In this book, I attempt to bring some of the nonce taxonomies of female masculinity into view, and I detail the histories of the suppression of these categories. Here, and in the rest of the book, I am using the topic of female masculinity to explore a queer subject position that can successfully challenge hegemonic models of gender conformity. Female masculinity is a particularly fruitful site of investigation because it has been vilified by heterosexist and feminist/womanist programs alike; unlike male femininity, which fulfills a kind of ritual function in male homosocial cultures, female masculinity is generally received by hetero- and homo-normative cultures as a pathological sign of misidentification and maladjustment, as a longing to be and to have a power that is always just out of reach. Within a lesbian context, female masculinity has been situated as the place where patriarchy goes to work on the female psyche and reproduces misogyny

1. American scholar of gender studies and queer theory (1950–2009); *Epistemology of the Closet* (1990) is excerpted above.

within femaleness. There have been to date remarkably few studies or theories about the inevitable effects of a fully articulated female masculinity on a seemingly fortified male masculinity. Sometimes female masculinity coincides with the excesses of male supremacy, and sometimes it codifies a unique form of social rebellion; often female masculinity is the sign of sexual alterity, but occasionally it marks heterosexual variation; sometimes female masculinity marks the place of pathology, and every now and then it represents the healthful alternative to what are considered the histrionics of conventional femininities.

I want to carefully produce a model of female masculinity that remarks on its multiple forms but also calls for new and self-conscious affirmations of different gender taxonomies. Such affirmations begin not by subverting masculine power or taking up a position against masculine power but by turning a blind eye to conventional masculinities and refusing to engage. Frankie Addams, for example, constitutes her rebellion not in opposition to the law but through indifference to the law: she recognizes that it may be against the law to change one's name or add to it, but she also has a simple response to such illegal activity: "Well, I don't care." I am not suggesting in this book that we follow the futile path of what Foucault[2] calls "saying no to power," but I am asserting that power may inhere within different forms of refusal: "Well, I don't care."

QUEER METHODOLOGIES

This book deploys numerous methodologies in order to pursue the multiple forms of gender variance presented within female masculinity. On account of the interdisciplinary nature of my project, I have had to craft a methodology out of available disciplinary methods. Deploying what I would call a "queer methodology," I have used some combination of textual criticism, ethnography, historical survey, archival research, and the production of taxonomies. I call this methodology "queer" because it attempts to remain supple enough to respond to the various locations of information on female masculinity and betrays a certain disloyalty to conventional disciplinary methods. Obviously, I could have produced methodological consistency by confining myself to literary texts, but the queer methodology used here, then, typifies just one of the forms of refusal that I discussed in my last section.

Although some of the most informative work on alternative sexual communities has come in the form of ethnography, and although autobiographies and narrative histories tend to be the material that we turn to for information on sexual identities, there is nonetheless some disagreement among queer scholars about how we should collect and interpret such information on sexual identity. Indeed, some of the most bitter and long-lasting disagreements within queer studies have been about disciplinarity and methodology. Whereas some cultural studies proponents have argued that social science methods of collecting, collating, and presenting sexual data through surveys and other methods of social research tend to rediscover the sexual systems they already know rather than finding out about those they do not, social science proponents argue that cultural studies scholars do not pay enough

2. MICHEL FOUCAULT (1926–1984), French philosopher and historian of ideas.

attention to the material realities of queer life. And while there has been plenty of discussion in the academy about the need for interdisciplinary work, there has been far less support for such work in the university at large. A project such as this one, therefore, risks drawing criticism from historians for not providing a proper history, from literary critics for not focusing on literary texts, and from social scientists for not deploying the traditional tools of social science research. While I take full responsibility for all the errors I may make in my attempts to produce readings and histories and ethnography, I also recognize that this book exemplifies the problem confronted by queer studies itself: How do we forge queer methodologies while as scholars we reside in traditional departments?

At least one method of sex research that I reject in creating a queer methodology is the traditional social science project of surveying people and expecting to squeeze truth from raw data. In a review essay in the *New York Review of Books* about a series of new sex surveys, R. C. Lewontin comments on the difficulty associated with this social science approach to sexuality: "Given the social circumstances of sexual activity, there seems no way to find out what people do 'in the bedroom' except to ask them. But the answers they give cannot be put to the test of incredulity."[3] Lewontin suggests that people tend not to be truthful when it comes to reporting on their own sexual behavior (men exaggerate and women downplay, for example), and there are no ways to make allowances for personal distortion within social science methods. Furthermore, social scientists seem not to be concerned with the high levels of untruth in relation to sexuality but spend all their energy on solving methodological problems. Ultimately, Lewontin claims—and I think he has a point—social science surveys are "demonstrations of what their planners already believed they knew to be true" (25). At a time when the humanities are under severe scrutiny and attack, it is important to point to the reliance of social science methods on strategies such as narrative analysis, interpretation, and speculation. As Lewontin says in his conclusion: "How then can there be a social science? The answer surely is to be less ambitious and stop trying to make sociology into a natural science although it is, indeed, the study of natural objects" (29). This is not to say, however, that traditional social science research methods such as questionnaires are never appropriate. Indeed, there are certain questions that can be answered only by survey methods in the realm of sexuality (i.e., how many lesbians are using dental dams?[4] What age-groups or social classes do these lesbians belong to?), but all too often surveys are used to try to gather far less factual information, and all subtlety tends to be lost.[5]

There is some irony in the apparent impossibility of applying traditional social science methods to the study of sex because as queer sociologists are

3. R. C. Lewontin, "Sex, Lies, and Social Science," New *York Review of Books* 42, no. 7 (20 April 1995): 24 [Halberstam's note]. Richard C. Lewontin (b. 1929), American evolutionary biologist and geneticist.

4. Thin sheets of latex used for protection against sexually transmitted diseases during oral sex.

5. Thanks to Esther Newton for making this point and suggesting when and how survey methods are useful. For an example of the kinds of questions used in sex surveys see John Gagnon et al., *Sex in America* (Boston: Little Brown, 1994). This particular volume is remarkable because the explicit questions it asks about the kinds of sex people were having focus obsessively on the couple, and the study links certain activities definitely to certain identities. So, for example, questions about anal sex are directed only at male/female and male/male couples because anal sex is defined as "when a man's penis is inside his partner's anus or rectum" (260). There are no questions directed specifically at female/female couples and no questions about sex toys or use of dildos or hands in this section [Halberstam's note].

all too quick to point out, many of the theoretical systems that we use to talk about sex, such as social constructionism, come from sociology. In a recent "queer" issue of *Sociological Theory*, a group of sociologists attempted to account for the currently strained relations between sociological theory and queer theory. Steven Epstein pointed out that sociology asserted that sexuality was socially constructed and indeed that "without seeking to minimize the importance of other disciplines, I would suggest that neither queer theory nor lesbian and gay studies in general could be imagined in their present forms without the contributions of sociological theory."[6] Arlene Stein and Ken Plummer continue Epstein's line of inquiry and add a critique of the present state of queer theory:

> Queer theorists . . . appreciate the extent to which the texts of literature and mass culture shape sexuality, but their weakness is that they rarely, if ever, move beyond the text. There is a dangerous tendency for the new queer theorists to ignore "real" queer life as it is materially experienced across the world, while they play with the free-floating signifiers of texts.[7]

In an effort to restore sociology to its proper place within the study of sexuality, Stein and Plummer have reinvested here in a clear and verifiable difference between the real and the textual, and they designate textual analysis as a totally insular activity with no referent, no material consequences, and no intellectual gain. But as Lewontin's review suggested, it is precisely this belief in the real and the material as separate from the represented and the textual that creates the problems of survey analysis. To be fair, Stein and Plummer are clearly not suggesting merely a quantitative approach to the study of sexuality and queer subcultures, but they do, on some level, seem to have re-created some essential divide between the truth of sexual behavior and the fiction of textual analysis.

The answer to the problem of how to study sexuality, I am trying to suggest, must lie to some extent in an interdisciplinary approach that can combine information culled from people with information culled from texts. So, whereas Cindy Patton, for example, in "Tremble Hetero Swine," remarks with dismay on the dominance of "textually based forms of queer theory," we must question whether there is a form of queer theory or sexual theory that is not textually based.[8] Isn't a sexual ethnographer studying texts? And doesn't a social historian collate evidence from texts? Sometimes the texts are oral histories, sometimes they might be interview material, sometimes they might be fiction or autobiography, but given our basic formulation of sex as "private," something that happens when other people are not around, there is no way to objectively observe "in the bedroom." Conversely, readings of texts also require historical contexts and some relation to the lived experience of subjects. The text-based methodologies err on the side of abstraction, and the sociological studies err on the side of overly rationalizing sexual behavior. Finally, although some have criticized literary or cultural studies approaches to identity construction as apolitical or ahistorical, theories that

6. Steven Epstein, "A Queer Encounter: Sociology and the Study of Sexuality," *Sociological Theory* 12, no. 2 (July 1994): 189 [Halberstam's note].

7. Arlene Stein and Ken Plummer, "I Can't Even Think Straight: Queer Theory and the Missing Revolution in Sociology," *Sociological Theory* 12, no. 2 (July 1994): 184 [Halberstam's note].

8. Cindy Patton, "Tremble Hetero Swine," in *Fear of a Queer Planet: Queer Politics and Social Theory*, ed. Michael Warner (Minneapolis: University of Minnesota Press, 1993), 165 [Halberstam's note].

tie the history of sexuality unproblematically to economics or the movement of capital tend to produce exactly the linear narratives of rational progress and modernization that sexuality seems to resist.

A queer methodology, in a way, is a scavenger methodology that uses different methods to collect and produce information on subjects who have been deliberately or accidentally excluded from traditional studies of human behavior. The queer methodology attempts to combine methods that are often cast as being at odds with each other, and it refuses the academic compulsion toward disciplinary coherence. Although this book will be immediately recognizable as a work of cultural studies, it will not shy away from the more empirical methods associated with ethnographic research.

CONSTRUCTING MASCULINITIES

Within cultural studies itself, masculinity has recently become a favorite topic. I want to try here to account for the growing popularity of a body of work on masculinity that evinces absolutely no interest in masculinity without men. I first noticed the unprecedented interest in masculinity in April 1994 when the DIA Center for the Performing Arts convened a group of important intellectuals to hold forth on the topic of masculinities. On the opening night of this event, one commentator wondered, "Why masculinity, why now?" Several others, male critics and scholars, gave eloquent papers about their memories of being young boys and about their relationships with their fathers. The one lesbian on the panel, a poet, read a moving poem about rape. At the end of the evening, only one panelist had commented on the limitations of a discussion of masculinity that interpreted "masculinity" as a synonym for men or maleness.[9] This lonely intervention highlighted the gap between mainstream discussions of masculinity and men and ongoing queer discussions about masculinity, which extend far beyond the male body. Indeed, in answer to the naive question that began the evening, "Why masculinities, why now?" one might state: Because masculinity in the 1990s has finally been recognized as, at least in part, a construction by female- as well as male-born people.[1]

The anthology that the conference produced provides more evidence of the thoroughgoing association that the editors have made between masculinity and maleness. The title page features a small photographic illustration of a store sign advertising clothing as "Fixings for Men." This illustration has been placed just below the title, *Constructing Masculinity*, and forces the reader to understand the construction of masculinity as the outfitting of males within culture. The introduction to the volume attempts to diversify this definition of masculinity by using Judith Butler's[2] and Eve Sedgwick's contributions to suggest that the anthology recognizes the challenges made

9. The conference papers were collected in a volume called *Constructing Masculinity*, ed. Maurice Berger, Brian Wallis, and Simon Watson (New York: Routledge, 1996), and the one intervention on behalf of nonmale masculinities was made by Eve Kosofsky Sedgwick [Halberstam's note]. The conference was held in New York City.

1. I am using the terms "female born" and "male born" to indicate a social practice of assigning one of two genders to babies at birth. My terminology suggests that these assignations may not hold for the lifetime of the individual, and it suggests from the outset that binary gender continues to dominate our cultural and scientific notions of gender but that individuals inevitably fail to find themselves in only one of two options [Halberstam's note].

2. American philosopher and queer theorist (b. 1956); see above.

by gays, lesbians, and queers to the terms of gender normativity. The editors insist that masculinity is multiple and that "far from just being about men, the idea of masculinity engages, inflects, and shapes everyone."[3] The commitment to the representation of masculinity as multiple is certainly borne out in the first essay in the volume, by Eve Sedgwick, in which she proposes that masculinity may have little to do with men, and is somewhat extended by Butler's essay "Melancholy Gender." But Sedgwick also critiques the editors for having proposed a book and a conference on masculinity that remain committed to linking masculinity to maleness. Although the introduction suggests that the editors have heeded Sedgwick's call for gender diversity, the rest of the volume suggests otherwise. There are many fascinating essays in this anthology, but there are no essays specifically on female masculinity. Although gender-queer images by Loren Cameron and Cathy Opie[4] adorn the pages of the book, the text contains no discussions of these images. The book circles around discussions of male icons such as Clint Eastwood and Steven Seagal;[5] it addresses the complex relations between fathers and sons; it examines topics such as how science defines men and masculinity and the law. The volume concludes with an essay by Stanley Aronowitz[6] titled "My Masculinity," an autobiographically inflected consideration of various forms of male power.

None of my analysis here is to say that this is an uninteresting anthology or that the essays are somehow wrong or misguided, but I am trying to point out that the editorial statement at the beginning of the volume is less a prologue to what follows and more of an epilogue that describes what a volume on masculinity *should* do as opposed to what the anthology does do. Even when the need for an analysis of female masculinity has been acknowledged, in other words, it seems remarkably difficult to follow through on. What is it then that, to paraphrase Eve Sedgwick's essay, makes it so difficult *not* to presume an essential relation between masculinity and men?[7]

By beginning with this examination of the *Constructing Masculinity* conference and anthology, I do not want to give the impression that the topic of female masculinities must always be related to some larger topic, some more general set of masculinities that has been, and continues to be, about men. Nor do I want to suggest that gender theory is the true origin of gender knowledges. Rather, this conference and book merely emphasize the lag between community knowledges and practices and academic discourses.[8] I believe it is both helpful and important to contextualize a discussion of female and lesbian masculinities in direct opposition to a more generalized discussion of masculinity within cultural studies that seems intent on insisting that masculinity remain the property of male bodies. The continued refusal in

3. Berger, Wallis, and Watson, introduction to *Constructing Masculinity*, 7 [Halberstam's note].
4. American fine-art photographer and professor (b. 1961). Cameron (b. 1959), American photographer and transsexual activist.
5. American actor and martial artist (b. 1952). Eastwood (b. 1930), American actor and director.
6. American sociologist and scholar of cultural studies (b. 1933).
7. More and more journals are putting together special issues on masculinity, but I have yet to locate a single special issue with a single essay about female masculinity. The latest journal announcement that found its way to me was from *The Velvet Light Trap: A Critical Journal of Film and Television*. They announced an issue on "New Masculinities" that featured essays titled "The 'New Masculinity' in *Tootsie*," "On Fathers and Sons, Sex and Death," "Male Melodrama and the Feeling Man," and so forth. This is not to say that such topics are not interesting, only that the "new masculinities" sound remarkably like the old ones. See *The Velvet Light Trap*, "New Masculinities," no. 38 (fall 1996) [Halberstam's note].
8. Berger, Wallis, and Watson, *Constructing Masculinity* [Halberstam's note].

Western society to admit ambiguously gendered bodies into functional social relations (evidenced, for example, by our continued use of either/or bathrooms, either women or men) is, I will claim, sustained by a conservative and protectionist attitude by men in general toward masculinity. Such an attitude has been bolstered by a more general disbelief in female masculinity. I can only describe such disbelief in terms of a failure in a collective imagination: in other words, female-born people have been making convincing and powerful assaults on the coherence of male masculinity for well over a hundred years; what prevents these assaults from taking hold and accomplishing the diminution of the bonds between masculinity and men? Somehow, despite multiple images of strong women (such as bodybuilder Bev Francis or tennis player Martina Navratilova), of cross-identifying women (Radclyffe Hall or Ethel Smyth), of masculine-coded public figures (Janet Reno), of butch superstars (k. d. lang), of muscular and athletic women (Jackie Joyner-Kersee), of female-born transgendered people (Leslie Feinberg),[9] there is still no general acceptance or even recognition of masculine women and boyish girls. This book addresses itself to this collective failure to imagine and ratify the masculinity produced by, for, and within women.

In case my concerns about the current discussions of masculinity in cultural studies sound too dismissive, I want to look in an extended way at what happens when academic discussions of male masculinity take place to the exclusion of discussions of more wide-ranging masculinities. While it may seem that I am giving an inordinate amount of attention to what is after all just one intervention into current discussions, I am using one book as representative of a whole slew of other studies of masculinity that replicate the intentions and the mistakes of this one. In an anthology called *Boys: Masculinities in Contemporary Culture*, edited by Paul Smith for a Cultural Studies series, Smith suggests that masculinity must always be thought of "in the plural" as masculinities "defined and cut through by differences and contradictions of all sorts."[1] The plurality of masculinities for Smith encompasses a dominant white masculinity that is crisscrossed by its others, gay, bisexual, black, Asian, and Latino masculinities. Although the recognition of a host of masculinities makes sense, Smith chooses to focus on dominant white masculinity to the exclusion of the other masculinities he has listed. Smith, predictably, warns the reader not to fall into the trap of simply critiquing dominant masculinity or simply celebrating minority masculinities, and then he makes the following foundational statement:

> And it may well be the case, as some influential voices often tell us, that masculinity or masculinities are in some real sense not the exclusive "property" of biologically male subjects—it's true that many female subjects lay claim to masculinity as their property. Yet in terms of cul-

9. A range of figures active in the 20th century: Francis (b. 1955), Australian-born American former professional bodybuilder; Navratilova (b. 1956), Czech-born American former tennis player; Hall (1880–1943), English writer who, like the English composer Smyth (1858–1944), wore male-tailored ties and jackets; Reno (1938–2016), the first woman to serve as U.S. attorney general (1993–2001); Lang (b. 1961), Canadian singer and songwriter; Joyner-Kersee (b. 1962), American Olympic medalist in track and field; Feinberg (1949–2014), American activist and writer whose novel *Stone Butch Blues* (1993) is later discussed by Halberstam.

1. Paul Smith, ed., *Boys: Masculinities in Contemporary Culture* (Boulder, Colo.: Westview Press, 1996), 3 [Halberstam's note].

> tural and political *power*, it still makes a difference when masculinity coincides with biological maleness. (4)

What is immediately noticeable to me here is the odd attribution of immense power to those "influential voices" who keep telling us that masculinity is not the property of men. There is no naming of these influential voices, and we are left supposing that "influence" has rendered the "female masculinity theorists" so powerful that names are irrelevant: these voices, one might suppose, are hegemonic. Smith goes on to plead with the reader, asking us to admit that the intersection of maleness and masculinity does "still" make a difference. His appeal here to common sense allows him to sound as if he is trying to reassert some kind of rationality to a debate that is spinning off into totally inconsequential discussions. Smith is really arguing that we must turn to dominant masculinity to begin deconstructing masculinity because it is the equation of maleness plus masculinity that adds up to social legitimacy. As I argued earlier in this chapter, however, precisely because white male masculinity has obscured all other masculinities, we have to turn away from its construction to bring other more mobile forms of masculinity to light. Smith's purpose in his reassertion of the difference that male masculinity makes is to uncover the "cultural and political *power*" of this union in order to direct our attention to the power of patriarchy. The second part of the paragraph makes this all too clear:

> Biological men—male-sexed beings—are after all, in varying degrees, the bearers of privilege and power within the systems against which women still struggle. The privilege and power are, of course, different for different men, endlessly diversified through the markers of class, nation, race, sexual preference and so on. But I'd deny that there are any men who are entirely outside of the ambit, let's say, of power and privilege *in relation to women*. In that sense it has to be useful to our thinking to recall that masculinities are not only a function of dominant notions of masculinity and not constituted solely in resistant notions of "other" masculinities. In fact, masculinities exist inevitably in relation to what feminisms have construed as the system of patriarchy and patriarchal relations.[2]

The most noticeable feature of this paragraph is the remarkable stability of the terms "women" and "men." Smith advances here a slightly old-fashioned feminism that understands women as endlessly victimized within systems of male power. Woman, within such a model, is the name for those subjects within patriarchy who have no access to male power and who are regulated and confined by patriarchal structures. But what would Smith say to Monique Wittig's claim that lesbians are not women because they are not involved in the heterosexual matrix that produces sexual difference as a power relation? What can Smith add to Judith Butler's influential theory of "gender trouble," which suggests that "gender is a copy with no original" and that dominant sexualities and genders are in some sense imbued with a pathetic dependence on their others that puts them perpetually at risk? What would Smith say to Jacob Hale's claim that the genders we use as reference points

2. Paul Smith, introduction to *Boys: Masculinities in Contemporary Culture*, 4–5 [Halberstam's note].

in gender theory fall far behind community productions of alternative genderings?[3] Are butch dykes women? Are male transvestites men? How does gender variance disrupt the flow of powers presumed by patriarchy in relations between men and women? Smith, in other words, cannot take female masculinity into account because he sees it as inconsequential and secondary to much more important questions about male privilege. Again, this sounds more like a plaintive assertion that men *do* still access male power within patriarchy (don't they?), and it conveniently ignores the ways in which gender relations are scrambled where and when gender variance comes into play.

Smith's attempt to shore up male masculinity by dismissing the importance of other masculinities finds further expression in his attempt to take racialized masculinities into consideration. His introductory essay opens with a meditation on the complications of the O.J. Simpson case,[4] and Smith wonders at the way popular discourse on the O.J. case sidesteps issues of masculinity and male domination in favor of race. When he hears a black male caller to a radio talk show link O.J.'s case to an ongoing conspiracy against black men in this country, Smith ponders: "His spluttering about the attempted genocide of black men reminded me, somehow, that another feature of the O.J. case was the way it had started with the prosecution trying to establish the relevance of O.J.'s record as a wife beater" (Smith, *Boys,* 1). Noting that the callers to the talk show did not have much to say about this leads Smith to wonder whether race can constitute a collective identity but masculinity cannot, and finally he suggests that although "it might be difficult to talk about race in this country, it is even more difficult to talk about masculinity" (1). If you are a white man, it is probably extremely difficult to talk about either race or masculinity let alone both at the same time. But, of course, race and masculinity, especially in the case of O.J., are not separable into tidy categories. Indeed, one might say that the caller's "spluttering" about conspiracies against black men constituted a far more credible race analysis in this case than Smith's articulation of the relations between race and masculinity. For Smith, masculinity in the case of O.J. constitutes a flow of domination that comes up against his blackness as a flow of subordination. There is no discussion here of the injustices of the legal system, the role of class and money in the trial, or the complicated history of relations between black men and white women. Smith uses O.J. as shorthand for a model that is supposed to suggest power and disempowerment in the same location.

I am taking so much time and effort to discount Smith's introduction to *Boys* because there is a casualness to his essay that both indicates his lack of any real investment in the project of alternative masculinities and suggests an unwillingness to think through the messy identifications that make up contemporary power relations around gender, race, and class. The book that Smith introduces also proves to have nothing much to offer to new discussions of masculinity, and we quickly find ourselves, from the opening

3. See Monique Wittig, "The Straight Mind," in *The Straight Mind and Other Essays* (Boston: Beacon Press, 1992); Judith Butler, "Imitation and Gender Insubordination," in *Inside/Out: Lesbian Theories, Gay Theories*, ed. Diana Fuss (New York: Routledge, 1991), 13–31; Jacob Hale, "Are Lesbians Women?" *Hypatia* 11, no. 2 (spring 1996): 94–121 [Halberstam's note]. WITTIG (1935–2003), French lesbian feminist writer and activist. Hale (b. ca. 1980), American philosopher who works in transgender studies.

4. The 1995 trial of the American former football player and celebrity Simpson (b. 1947) for the 1994 murder of his ex-wife and a man who was her friend; reactions to his acquittal were sharply and racially divided.

essay on, in the familiar territory of men, boys, and their fathers. The first essay, for example, by Fred Pfeil,[5] "A Buffalo, New York Story," tells a pitiful tale about father-son relations in the 1950s. In one memorable moment from the memoir, he (Fred) and Dad have cozied up on the couch to watch *Bonanza*[6] while Mom and Sis are doing the dishes in the kitchen. Boy asks Dad "why bad guys were always so stupid," and Dad laughs and explains "because they were bad" (10). The story goes on to detail the innocent young boy's first brushes with his male relatives' racism and his own painful struggle with car sickness. Besides taking apart the dynamics of fathers and sons cozying up together to watch *Bonanza*, there most certainly are a multitude of important things to say about men and masculinity in patriarchy, but Smith and some of his contributors choose not to say them. We could be producing ethnographies on the aggressive and indeed protofascist masculinities produced by male sports fans.[7] Much work still remains to be done on the socialization (or lack thereof) of young men in high schools, on (particularly rich white male) domestic abusers, on the new sexism embodied by "sensitive men," on the men who participate in the traffic in mail-order brides and sex tourism (including a study of privileged white gay masculinity). But studies in male masculinity are predictably not so interested in taking apart the patriarchal bonds between white maleness and privilege; they are much more concerned to detail the fragilities of male socialization, the pains of manhood, and the fear of female empowerment.[8]

Because I have criticized Smith for his apparent lack of investment in the project of producing alternative masculinities, let me take a moment to make my own investments clear. Although I make my own masculinity the topic of my last chapter, it seems important to state that this book is an attempt to make my own female masculinity plausible, credible, and real. For a large part of my life, I have been stigmatized by a masculinity that marked me as ambiguous and illegible. Like many other tomboys, I was mistaken for a boy throughout my childhood, and like many other tomboy adolescents, I was forced into some semblance of femininity for my teenage years. When gender-ambiguous children are constantly challenged about their gender identity, the chain of misrecognitions can actually produce a new recognition: in other words, to be constantly mistaken for a boy, for many tomboys, can contribute to the production of a masculine identity. It was not until my midtwenties that I finally found a word for my particular gender configuration: butch. In my final chapter, "Raging Bull (Dyke)," I address the ways in which butches manage to affirm their masculinity despite the multiple sites in which that masculinity is challenged, denied, threatened, and violated.

5. American writer, teacher, and political activist (1949–2005).

6. Popular American television series (1959–73), the first western broadcast in color.

7. Indeed, one such ethnography has been carried out, but significantly it took English soccer hooligans as its topic. See Bill Buford's remarkable *Among the Thugs* (New York: Norton, 1992). A similar work on American male fans would be extremely useful [Halberstam's note].

8. For verification of such topics of concern just check out the men's sections that are popping up in your local bookstores. More specifically see the work of Michael Kimmel and Victor Seidler: Michael Kimmel, *Manhood in America: A Cultural History* (New York: Free Press, 1996); Victor J. Seidler, *Unreasonable Men: Masculinity and Social Theory* (New York: Routledge, 1994) [Halberstam's note].

THE BATHROOM PROBLEM

If three decades of feminist theorizing about gender has thoroughly dislodged the notion that anatomy is destiny, that gender is natural, and that male and female are the only options, why do we still operate in a world that assumes that people who are not male are female, and people who are not female are male (and even that people who are not male are not people!). If gender has been so thoroughly defamiliarized, in other words, why do we not have multiple gender options, multiple gender categories, and real-life nonmale and nonfemale options for embodiment and identification? In a way, gender's very flexibility and seeming fluidity is precisely what allows dimorphic gender to hold sway. Because so few people actually match any given community standards for male or female, in other words, gender can be imprecise and therefore multiply relayed through a solidly binary system. At the same time, because the definitional boundaries of male and female are so elastic, there are very few people in any given public space who are completely unreadable in terms of their gender.

Ambiguous gender, when and where it does appear, is inevitably transformed into deviance, thirdness, or a blurred version of either male or female. As an example, in public bathrooms for women, various bathroom users tend to fail to measure up to expectations of femininity, and those of us who present in some ambiguous way are routinely questioned and challenged about our presence in the "wrong" bathroom. For example, recently, on my way to give a talk in Minneapolis, I was making a connection at Chicago's O'Hare airport. I strode purposefully into the women's bathroom. No sooner had I entered the stall than someone was knocking at the door: "Open up, security here!" I understood immediately what had happened. I had, once again, been mistaken for a man or a boy, and some woman had called security. As soon as I spoke, the two guards at the bathroom stall realized their error, mumbled apologies, and took off. On the way home from the same trip, in the Denver airport, the same sequence of events was repeated. Needless to say, the policing of gender within the bathroom is intensified in the space of the airport, where people are literally moving through space and time in ways that cause them to want to stabilize some boundaries (gender) even as they traverse others (national). However, having one's gender challenged in the women's rest room is a frequent occurrence in the lives of many androgynous or masculine women; indeed, it is so frequent that one wonders whether the category "woman," when used to designate public functions, is completely outmoded.[9]

It is no accident, then, that travel hubs become zones of intense scrutiny and observation. But gender policing within airport bathrooms is merely an intensified version of a larger "bathroom problem." For some gender-

9. The continued viability of the category "woman" has been challenged in a variety of academic locations already: Monique Wittig, most notably, argued that "lesbians are not women" in her essay "The Straight Mind," 121. Wittig claims that because lesbians are refusing primary relations to men, they cannot occupy the position "woman." In another philosophical challenge to the category "woman," transgender philosopher Jacob Hale uses Monique Wittig's radical claim to theorize the possibility of gendered embodiments that exceed male and female (see Hale, "Are Lesbians Women?"). Elsewhere, Cheshire Calhoun suggests that the category "woman" may actually "operate as a lesbian closet" (see Cheshire Calhoun, "The Gender Closet: Lesbian Disappearance under the Sign 'Women,'" *Feminist Studies* 21, no. 1 [spring 1995]: 7–34) [Halberstam's note].

ambiguous women, it is relatively easy to "prove" their right to use the women's bathroom—they can reveal some decisive gender trait (a high voice, breasts), and the challenger will generally back off. For others (possibly low-voiced or hairy or breastless people), it is quite difficult to justify their presence in the women's bathroom, and these people may tend to use the men's bathroom, where scrutiny is far less intense. Obviously, in these bathroom confrontations, the gender-ambiguous person first appears as not-woman ("You are in the wrong bathroom!"), but then the person appears as something actually even more scary, not-man ("No, I am not," spoken in a voice recognized as not-male). Not-man and not-woman, the gender-ambiguous bathroom user is also not androgynous or in-between; this person is gender deviant.

For many gender deviants, the notion of passing is singularly unhelpful. Passing as a narrative assumes that there is a self that masquerades as another kind of self and does so successfully; at various moments, the successful pass may cohere into something akin to identity. At such a moment, the passer has *become*. What of a biological female who presents as butch, passes as male in some circumstances and reads as butch in others, and considers herself not to be a woman but maintains distance from the category "man"? For such a subject, identity might best be described as process with multiple sites for becoming and being. To understand such a process, we would need to do more than map psychic and physical journeys between male and female and within queer and straight space; we would need, in fact, to think in fractal terms and about gender geometries. Furthermore, I argue in chapter 4, in my discussion of the stone butch, when and where we discuss the sexualities at stake in certain gender definitions, very different identifications between sexuality, gender, and the body emerge. The stone butch, for example, in her self-definition as a non-feminine, sexually untouchable female, complicates the idea that lesbians share female sexual practices or women share female sexual desires or even that masculine women share a sense of what animates their particular masculinities.

I want to focus on what I am calling "the bathroom problem" because I believe it illustrates in remarkably clear ways the flourishing existence of gender binarism despite rumors of its demise. Furthermore, many normatively gendered women have no idea that a bathroom problem even exists and claim to be completely ignorant about the trials and tribulations that face the butch woman who needs to use a public bathroom. But queer literature is littered with references to the bathroom problem, and it would not be an exaggeration to call it a standard feature of the butch narrative. For example, Leslie Feinberg provides clear illustrations of the dimensions of the bathroom problem in *Stone Butch Blues*. In this narrative of the life of the he-she factory worker, Jess Goldberg, Jess recounts many occasions in which she has to make crucial decisions about whether she can afford to use the women's bathroom. On a shopping outing with some drag queens, Jess tells Peaches: "I gotta use the bathroom. God, I wish I could wait, but I can't." Jess takes a deep breath and enters the ladies room:

> Two women were freshening their makeup in front of the mirror. One glanced at the other and finished applying her lipstick. "Is that a man or a woman?" She said to her friend as I passed them.

> The other woman turned to me. "This is the woman's bathroom," she informed me.
>
> I nodded. "I know."
>
> I locked the stall door behind me. Their laughter cut me to the bone. "You don't really know if that is a man or not," one woman said to the other. "We should call security to make sure."
>
> I flushed the toilet and fumbled with my zipper in fear. Maybe it was just an idle threat. Maybe they really would call security. I hurried out of the bathroom as soon as I heard both women leave.[1]

For Jess, the bathroom represents a limit to her ability to move around in the public sphere. Her body, with its needs and physical functions, imposes a limit on her attempts to function normally despite her variant gender presentation. The women in the rest room, furthermore, are depicted as spiteful, rather than fearful. They toy with Jess by calling into question her right to use the rest room and threatening to call the police. As Jess puts it: "They never would have made fun of a guy like that." In other words, if the women were truly anxious for their safety, they would not have toyed with the intruder, and they would not have hesitated to call the police. Their casualness about calling security indicates that they know Jess is a woman but want to punish her for her inappropriate self-presentation.

Another chronicle of butch life, *Throw It to the River*, by Nice Rodriguez, a Filipina-Canadian writer, also tells of the bathroom encounter. In a story called "Every Full Moon," Rodriguez tells a romantic tale about a butch bus conductor called Remedios who falls in love with a former nun called Julianita. Remedios is "muscular around the arms and shoulders," and her "toughness allows her to bully anyone who will not pay the fare."[2] She aggressively flirts with Julianita until Julianita agrees to go to a movie with Remedios. To prepare for her date, Remedios dresses herself up, carefully flattening out her chest with Band-Aids over the nipples: "She bought a white shirt in Divisoria just for this date. Now she worries that the cloth may be too thin and transparent, and that Julianita will be turned off when her nipples protrude out like dice" (33). With her "well-ironed jeans," her smooth chest, and even a man's manicure, Remedios heads out for her date. However, once out with Julianita, Remedios, now dressed in her butch best, has to be careful about public spaces. After the movie, Julianita rushes off to the washroom, but Remedios waits outside for her:

> She has a strange fear of ladies rooms. She wishes there was another washroom somewhere between the mens' and the ladies' for queers like her. Most of the time she holds her pee—sometimes as long as half a day—until she finds a washroom where the users are familiar with her. Strangers take to her unkindly, especially elder women who inspect her from head to toe. (40–41)

Another time, Remedios tells of being chased from a ladies' room and beaten by a bouncer. The bathroom problem for Remedios and for Jess severely limits their ability to circulate in public spaces and actually brings them into

1. Leslie Feinberg, *Stone Butch Blues: A Novel* (Ithaca, N.Y.: Firebrand, 1993), 59 [Halberstam's note].

2. Nice Rodriguez, *Throw It to the River* (Toronto, Canada: Women's Press, 1993), 25–26 [Halberstam's note].

contact with physical violence as a result of having violated a cardinal rule of gender: one must be readable at a glance. After Remedios is beaten for having entered a ladies' room, her father tells her to be more careful, and Rodriguez notes: "She realized that being cautious means swaying her hips and parading her boobs when she enters any ladies room" (30).

If we use the paradigm of the bathroom as a limit of gender identification, we can measure the distance between binary gender schema and lived multiple gendered experiences. The accusation "you're in the wrong bathroom" really says two different things. First, it announces that your gender seems at odds with your sex (your apparent masculinity or androgyny is at odds with your supposed femaleness); second, it suggests that single-gender bathrooms are only for those who fit clearly into one category (male) or the other (female). Either we need open-access bathrooms or multigendered bathrooms, or we need wider parameters for gender identification. The bathroom, as we know it, actually represents the crumbling edifice of gender in the twentieth century. The frequency with which gender-deviant "women" are mistaken for men in public bathrooms suggests that a large number of feminine women spend a large amount of time and energy policing masculine women. Something very different happens, of course, in the men's public toilet, where the space is more likely to become a sexual cruising zone than a site for gender repression. Lee Edelman, in an essay about the interpenetration of nationalism and sexuality, argues that "the institutional men's room constitutes a site at which the zones of public and private cross with a distinctive psychic charge."[3] The men's room, in other words, constitutes both an architecture of surveillance and an incitement to desire, a space of homosocial interaction and of homoerotic interaction.

So, whereas men's rest rooms tend to operate as a highly charged sexual space in which sexual interactions are both encouraged and punished, women's rest rooms tend to operate as an arena for the enforcement of gender conformity. Sex-segregated bathrooms continue to be necessary to protect women from male predations but also produce and extend a rather outdated notion of a public-private split between male and female society. The bathroom is a domestic space beyond the home that comes to represent domestic order, or a parody of it, out in the world. The women's bathroom accordingly becomes a sanctuary of enhanced femininity, a "little girl's room" to which one retreats to powder one's nose or fix one's hair. The men's bathroom signifies as the extension of the public nature of masculinity—it is precisely not domestic even though the names given to the sexual function of the bathroom—such as cottage or tearoom—suggest it is a parody of the domestic. The codes that dominate within the women's bathroom are primarily gender codes; in the men's room, they are sexual codes. Public sex versus private gender, openly sexual versus discreetly repressive, bathrooms beyond the home take on the proportions of a gender factory.

Marjorie Garber comments on the liminality of the bathroom in *Vested Interests* in a chapter on the perils and privileges of cross-dressing. She discusses the very different modes of passing and cross-dressing for cross-

3. Lee Edelman, "Tearooms and Sympathy, or The Epistemology of the Water Closet," in *Homographesis: Essays in Gay Literary and Cultural Theory* (New York: Routledge, 1994), 158 [Halberstam's note]. Edelman (b. 1953), American literary critic and queer theorist.

identified genetic males and females, and she observes that the restroom is a "potential waterloo" for both female-to-male (FTM) and male-to-female (MTF) cross-dressers and transsexuals.[4] For the FTM, the men's room represents the most severe test of his ability to pass, and advice frequently circulates within FTM communities about how to go unnoticed in male-only spaces. Garber notes: "The cultural paranoia of being caught in the ultimately wrong place, which may be inseparable from the pleasure of 'passing' in that same place, depends in part on the same cultural binarism, the idea that gender categories are sufficiently uncomplicated to permit self-assortment into one of the two 'rooms' without deconstructive reading" (47). It is worth pointing out here (if only because Garber does not) that the perils for passing FTMS in the men's room are very different from the perils of passing MTFS in the women's room. On the one hand, the FTM in the men's room is likely to be less scrutinized because men are not quite as vigilant about intruders as women for obvious reasons. On the other hand, if caught, the FTM may face some version of gender panic from the man who discovers him, and it is quite reasonable to expect and fear violence in the wake of such a discovery. The MTF, by comparison, will be more scrutinized in the women's room but possibly less open to punishment if caught. Because the FTM ventures into male territory with the potential threat of violence hanging over his head, it is crucial to recognize that the bathroom problem is much more than a glitch in the machinery of gender segregation and is better described in terms of the violent enforcement of our current gender system.

Garber's reading of the perilous use of rest rooms by both FTMS and MTFS develops out of her introductory discussion of what Lacan calls "urinary segregation." Lacan used the term to describe the relations between identities and signifiers, and he ultimately used the simple diagram of the rest room signs "Ladies" and "Gentlemen" to show that within the production of sexual difference, primacy is granted to the signifier over that which it signifies; in more simple terms, naming confers, rather than reflects, meaning.[5] In the same way, the system of urinary segregation creates the very functionality of the categories "men" and "women." Although restroom signs seem to serve and ratify distinctions that already exist, in actual fact these markers produce identifications within these constructed categories. Garber latches on to the notion of "urinary segregation" because it helps her to describe the processes of cultural binarism within the production of gender; for Garber, transvestites and transsexuals challenge this system by resisting the literal translation of the signs "Ladies" and "Gentlemen." Garber uses the figures of the transvestite and the transsexual to show the obvious flaws and gaps in a binary gender system; the transvestite, as interloper, creates a

4. Marjorie Garber, *Vested Interests: Cross-Dressing and Cultural Anxiety* (New York: Routledge, 1992), 47. Obviously Garber's use of the term "waterloo" makes a pun out of the drama of bathroom surveillance. Although the pun is clever and even amusing, it is also troubling to see how often Garber turns to punning in her analyses. The constant use of puns throughout the book has the overall effect of making gender crossing sound like a game or at least trivializes the often life-or-death processes involved in cross-identification. This is not to say gender can never be a "laughing matter" and must always be treated seriously but only to question the use of the pun here as a theoretical method. [Halberstam's note]. Garber (b. 1944), American scholar of Shakespeare and of cultural studies. Her pun plays on the meanings of "waterloo," a disastrous defeat (from the village in Belgium where Napoleon was finally defeated in 1815), and of "loo"—British slang for "toilet."

5. See Jacques Lacan, "The Agency of the Letter in the Unconscious," in *Ecrits: A Selection*, trans. Alan Sheridan (New York: Norton, 1977), 151 [Halberstam's note]. LACAN (1901–1981), French psychoanalyst; for this essay, see above.

third space of possibility within which all binaries become unstable. Unfortunately, as in all attempts to break a binary by producing a third term, Garber's third space tends to stabilize the other two. In "Tearooms and Sympathy," Lee Edelman also turns to Lacan's term "urinary segregation," but Edelman uses Lacan's diagram to mark heterosexual anxiety "about the potential inscriptions of homosexual desire and about the possibility of knowing or recognizing whatever might constitute 'homosexual difference'" (160). Whereas for Garber it is the transvestite who marks the instability of the markers "Ladies" and "Gentlemen," for Edelman it is not the passing transvestite but the passing homosexual.

Both Garber and Edelman, interestingly enough, seem to fix on the men's room as the site of these various destabilizing performances. As I am arguing here, however, focusing exclusively on the drama of the men's room avoids the much more complicated theater of the women's room. Garber writes of urinary segregation: "For transvestites and transsexuals, the 'men's room' problem is really a challenge to the way in which such cultural binarism is read" (14). She goes on to list some cinematic examples of the perils of urinary segregation and discusses scenes from *Tootsie* (1982), *Cabaret* (1972), and the *Female Impersonator Pageant* (1975). Garber's examples are odd illustrations of what she calls "the men's room problem" if only because at least one of her examples (*Tootsie*) demonstrates gender policing in the women's room. Also, Garber makes it sound as if vigorous gender policing happens in the men's room while the women's room is more of a benign zone for gender enforcement. She notes: "In fact, the urinal has appeared in a number of fairly recent films as a marker of the ultimate 'difference'—or studied indifference" (14). Obviously, Garber is drawing a parallel here between the conventions of gender attribution within which the penis marks the "ultimate difference"; however, by not moving beyond this remarkably predictable description of gender differentiation, Garber overlooks the main distinction between gender policing in the men's room and in the women's room. Namely, in the women's room, it is not only the MTF but *all* gender-ambiguous females who are scrutinized, whereas in the men's room, biological men are rarely deemed out of place. Garber's insistence that there is "a third space of possibility" occupied by the transvestite has closed down the possibility that there may be a fourth, fifth, sixth, or one hundredth space beyond the binary. The "women's room problem" (as opposed to the "men's room problem") indicates a multiplicity of gender displays even within the supposedly stable category of "woman."

So what gender are the hundreds of female-born people who are consistently not read as female in the women's room? And because so many women clearly fail the women's room test, why have we not begun to count and name the genders that are clearly emerging at this time? One could answer this question in two ways: On the one hand, we do not name and notice new genders because as a society we are committed to maintaining a binary gender system. On the other hand, we could also say that the failure of "male" and "female" to exhaust the field of gender variation actually ensures the continued dominance of these terms. Precisely because virtually nobody fits the definitions of male and female, the categories gain power and currency from their impossibility. In other words, the very flexibility and elasticity of the terms "man" and "woman" ensures their longevity. To test this proposition, look around any public space and notice how few people present formulaic versions of gender and yet how few are unreadable or totally ambiguous. The "It's Pat" character on a *Saturday Night Live*[6] skit dramatized the ways in which people insist on attributing gender in terms of male or female on even the most undecidable characters. The "It's Pat" character produced laughs by consistently sidestepping gender fixity—Pat's partner had a neutral name, and everything Pat did or said was designed to be read either way. Of course, the enigma that Pat represented could have been solved very easily; Pat's coworkers could simply have asked Pat what gender s/he was or preferred. This project on female masculinity is designed to produce more than two answers to that question and even to argue for a concept of "gender preference" as opposed to compulsory gender binarism. The human potential for incredibly precise classifications has been demonstrated in multiple arenas; why then do we settle for a paucity of classifications when it comes to gender? A system of gender preferences would allow for gender neutrality until such a time when the child or young adult announces his or her or its gender. Even if we could not let go of a binary gender system, there are still ways to make gender optional—people could come out as a gender in the way they come out as a sexuality. The point here is that there are many ways to depathologize gender variance and to account for the multiple genders that we already produce and sustain. Finally, as I suggested in relation to Garber's arguments about transvestism, "thirdness" merely balances the binary system and, furthermore, tends to homogenize many different gender variations under the banner of "other."

It is remarkably easy in this society not to look like a woman. It is relatively difficult, by comparison, not to look like a man: the threats faced by men who do not gender conform are somewhat different than for women. Unless men are consciously trying to look like women, men are less likely than women to fail to pass in the rest room. So one question posed by the bathroom problem asks, what makes femininity so approximate and masculinity so precise? Or to pose the question with a different spin, why is femininity easily impersonated or performed while masculinity seems resilient to imitation? Of course, this formulation does not easily hold and indeed quickly collapses into the exact opposite: why is it, in the case of the masculine woman in the bathroom, for example, that one finds the limits of femininity so quickly, whereas the limits of masculinity in the men's room seem fairly expansive?

We might tackle these questions by thinking about the effects, social and cultural, of reversed gender typing. In other words, what are the implications of male femininity and female masculinity? One might imagine that even a hint of femininity sullies or lowers the social value of maleness while all masculine forms of femaleness should result in an elevation of status.[7] My bathroom example alone proves that this is far from true. Furthermore, if we think of popular examples of approved female masculinity like a buffed Linda Hamilton in *Terminator 2* (1991) or a lean and mean Sigourney Weaver

6. American late night television variety and comedy sketch show; Pat (Julie Sweeney) was featured in episodes between 1990 and 1994.

7. Susan Bordo argues this in "Reading the Male Body," *Michigan Quarterly Review* 32, no. 4 (fall 1993). She writes: "When masculinity gets 'undone' in this culture, the deconstruction nearly always lands us in the territory of the degraded: when femininity gets symbolically undone, the result is an immense elevation of status" (721) [Halberstam's note].

in *Aliens*,[8] it is not hard to see that what renders these performances of female masculinity quite tame is their resolute heterosexuality. Indeed, in *Alien Resurrection* (1997), Sigourney Weaver combines her hard body with some light flirtation with co-star Winona Ryder[9] and her masculinity immediately becomes far more threatening and indeed "alien." In other words, when and where female masculinity conjoins with possibly queer identities, it is far less likely to meet with approval. Because female masculinity seems to be at its most threatening when coupled with lesbian desire, in this book I concentrate on queer female masculinity almost to the exclusion of heterosexual female masculinity. I have no doubt that heterosexual female masculinity menaces gender conformity in its own way, but all too often it represents an acceptable degree of female masculinity as compared to the excessive masculinity of the dyke. It is important when thinking about gender variations such as male femininity and female masculinity not simply to create another binary in which masculinity always signifies power; in alternative models of gender variation, female masculinity is not simply the opposite of female femininity, nor is it a female version of male masculinity.

* * *

1998

8. Released in 1986. Both Hamilton (b. 1956) and Weaver (b. 1949) are American actors.

9. American actor (b. 1971).

DAVID HERMAN
b. 1962

David Herman blends late twentieth-century cognitive psychology and narrative theory, promoting a new field at the outset of the twenty-first century: cognitive narratology. This project is indebted to but self-consciously surpasses the postwar classical narratology of ROLAND BARTHES, TZVETAN TODOROV, and others as well as the first-wave 1950s cognitive theory of Jerome Bruner, Noam Chomsky, and others. Herman describes his work as "postclassical narratology" steeped in the "second cognitive revolution" that commenced in the 1980s.

David Herman earned a B.A. in English and philosophy in 1985 from the University of North Carolina at Greensboro, followed by an M.A. (1988) and a Ph.D. (1992) from the University of Pennsylvania. He has taught at several institutions, including North Carolina State University, Purdue University, and Ohio State University, where he co-founded and served as the inaugural director of the Project Narrative initiative; and more recently at the Institute of Advanced Study at Durham University in the United Kingdom. In addition, he served as founding editor of *Storyworlds: A Journal of Narrative Studies* and Frontiers of Narrative, a book series from the University of Nebraska Press. He was co-winner of the Perkins Prize, awarded by the Society for the Study of Narrative Literature to the book making "the most significant contribution to narrative studies," for his *Story Logic: Problems and Possibilities of Narrative* (2002).

In our selection, "Narrative Theory after the Second Cognitive Revolution," originally published in *Introduction to Cognitive Cultural Studies* (edited by Lisa Zunshine, 2010), Herman employs recent psychological research in order to develop an updated approach to narrative study. Through an analysis of Ernest Hemingway's short story "Hills Like White Elephants" (1927), he explores ways in which recent discursive psychology can add to narrative theory in the broad context of cognitive science-oriented cultural studies. "Focusing on scenes of talk as a point of convergence for narrative theory and discursive psychology," he argues that "Hemingway's and other authors' representations of discourse practices—their staging of 'scenes of talk'—bear importantly on the tradition(s) of research that locate cognitive processes not in the heads of solitary thinkers but rather in sociocommunicative processes unfolding within richly material settings." Not surprisingly, a main objective of "Narrative Theory after the Second Cognitive Revolution" is to develop productive interchanges between strategies used to analyze face-to-face interactions and tools used to study written narrative texts. Among influential forerunners theorizing the discourse of conversation, Herman mentions the Russian psychologist Lev Vygotsy and the Austrian-born British philosopher Ludwig Wittgenstein, and he points to the sociological methods of ethnography and participant observation.

By scrutinizing the storytelling techniques of Hemingway's "Hills Like White Elephants," Herman investigates how narrative literature and discursive psychology can inform one another. His premise is that "cognitive processes can be lodged not just in reports about characters' behaviors, utterances, and experiences but also in modes of narration, types of perspective, and details about the spatial and temporal contexts of narrated situations and events." The Hemingway story centers on discourse between the female character Jig and an unnamed male character who presumably impregnated her. At the heart of this dialogue is the prospect of abortion. The symbolic setting is a train station in hot Spain, "in a valley through which the Ebro River flows." Waiting to take the train to Madrid, the two characters converse and Jig observes that "the hills across the valley look like white elephants." While the story has an uncertain ending, Herman judges the female character to be under stress and the male protagonist to be unsympathetic and cynical. For him it's a matter of subtly conflicting story lines.

To explain what he means by "the second cognitive revolution" of his title, Herman turns to Cartesian dualism as a starting point. The famous argument of René Descartes (1596–1650) about the separation of the mind and the world has long caused problems in the philosophy of mind. This dualism, Herman notes, has shaped much theory that comes after it, for theorists find themselves choosing between an emphasis on the mind and an emphasis on the external world. Regardless of which standpoint they adopt, they maintain the binary opposition, leading to two philosophies. First, introspectionism denotes "*the mind in here*" stance, featured in prominent modern philosophical and psychological discourse and taken by Franz Brentano (1838–1917), among other theorists. Second, behaviorism results from the adoption of "*the world out there*" position. Its advocates, most notably the American psychologists John B. Watson (1878–1958) and B. F. Skinner (1904–1990), argue, in Herman's summary, that "the world out there is the only thing that can be studied and known; the mind in here is epiphenomenal or, at best, an explanatory fiction postulated on the basis of observable, outward behaviors of material bodies."

Herman lays out the difference between the first and the second cognitive revolutions. The first, sometimes referred to simply as cognitivism, shifts "from behaviorism to the study of cognition," construing people's speeches and actions as caused by their "mental processes." It bears witness to a focus both on the mind in here and on the constant interaction between the mind and the surrounding world. The mind is perceived "as an information-processing device." According to the second cognitive revolution, "the mind is *both* in here *and* out there; so is the world." Although the second cognitive revolution still emphasizes cognitive processes, it views them as "immanent in . . . discourse practices"—that is, a hierarchical relationship between mind and discourse is no longer assumed. Its philosophy, then, is that "the mind does not preexist discourse, but is ongoingly accomplished in and through its production and interpretation."

From the second cognitive revolution Herman extrapolates five concepts to broaden narrative theory: positioning, embodiment, distributed mind, emotion discourse (emotionology), and qualia. In Hemingway's "Hills Like White Elephants," *positioning* happens on two levels: how the characters engage and position one another and how the reader engages and positions the narrative. Analyzing these positioning acts, Herman highlights two conflicting story lines developed by the male and female characters. He suggests that entrenched positions, master narratives, and socially recurrent story lines constitute ideology, and he wonders if narrative means exist to disrupt such ideological positioning. *Embodiment*, in the hands of the second cognitive revolution, means "that the mind is always and inalienably embodied; minds should be viewed as the nexus of brain, body, and environment (or world)." Focusing on Hemingway's text, Herman singles out subtle symbolic roles played by space, time, and perceptual flows across the storyworld. Settings matter. *Distributed mind* means that minds are not closed off internal entities: they constantly form and grow on the basis of their interactions with discourses, participants, and environments. Thus, in Hemingway's story Herman tracks the unfolding, often seemingly tangential, movements of judgments, inferences, and memories generated by characters. In discussing *emotion discourse* and *emotionology*, Herman first reviews three main approaches to emotion: naturalist (inherent unvarying emotions across the whole world), constructionist (culturally specific emotions), and a reconciliation of the two. The third approach has led to the useful concept of emotionology, introduced in the 1980s by the social scientists Peter Stearns and Carol Stearns. Herman defines "emotionologies" as culturally specific "systems of emotion terms and concepts deployed by participants in discourse to ascribe emotions to themselves as well as their cohorts." He shows in Hemingway's narrative how particular nonverbal actions and pregnant silences perform emotional functions, judging that the female character is an emotional innovator and the masculine character is a stereotypical selfish male. *Qualia*, as defined in a range of disciplines but especially philosophy, designate the subjective properties of conscious experience. In that regard, Herman argues, Hemingway creates "a story about the active, ongoing construction, through the discursive means available to the participants in this scene of talk, of the felt, experienced meaning of events." As a result and by implication, narrative literature captures moment-by-moment qualia in distinctive and memorable ways.

For all its suggestiveness, David Herman's work surprisingly omits discussion of economics and social class. As much as he applies psychology, he hesitates to psychologize—that is, to diagnose emotional dysfunctions and psychopathologies of characters. Nor does he show any interest in psychoanalysis; for example, he does not consider the role of the unconscious in character formation and storytelling. He explicitly downplays the dedication of literary criticism to questions of artistic craft and to the dynamics of individual reader responses. By taking such an approach, however, he expands the scope of narrative theory beyond long-standing preoccupations with formal technique, such as plot construction and point of view. In addition, he materializes and puts flesh on thinking and discourse, treating them as equally fundamental and portraying them as agnostic. Last but not least, Herman's focus on qualia, however tentative, seeks to bring human singularity into more robust forms of literary discourse analysis and cognitive narratology.

"Narrative Theory after the Second Cognitive Revolution" Keywords: Affect, The Body, Cultural Studies, Language, Narrative Theory

Narrative Theory after the Second Cognitive Revolution

In parallel with the other contributors' adoption of ideas from cognitive science for the purposes of textual and more broadly cultural analysis, the present chapter uses social-psychological research to outline one strategy for developing "postclassical" approaches to the study of narrative. At issue are frameworks for narrative research that build on the work of classical, structuralist narratologists but supplement that work with concepts and methods that were unavailable to story analysts such as Roland Barthes, Gerard Genette, A. J. Greimas, and Tzvetan Todorov during the heyday of the structuralist revolution.[1] One such framework, or cluster of frameworks, has begun to take shape under the rubric of "cognitive narratology," and my chapter seeks to contribute to this emergent area of narrative inquiry by focusing on the nexus between narrative and mind.[2]

The particular strand of social-psychological research on which I draw in order to explore this nexus is sometimes referred to as "discursive psychology." In Derek Edwards and Jonathan Potter's characterization, a basic contrast can be drawn between, on the one hand, "cognitivist approaches to language, where texts, sentences, and descriptions are taken as depictions of an externally given world, or as realizations of underlying cognitive representations of that world,"[3] and, on the other hand, the discursive approach:

> The focus of discursive psychology is the action orientation of talk and writing. . . . We are concerned with the nature of knowledge, cognition and reality: with how events are described and explained, how factual reports are constructed, how cognitive states are attributed. These are defined as discursive topics, things people topicalize or orientate themselves to, or imply, in their discourse. And rather than seeing such discursive constructions as expressions of speakers' underlying cognitive states, they are examined in the context of their occurrence as situated and occasioned constructions whose precise nature makes sense, to participants and analysts alike, in terms of the social actions those descriptions accomplish.[4]

Theorists working in this tradition, including Molly Andrews, Michael Bamberg, Michael Billig, Jerome Bruner, Derek Edwards, Grant Gillett, Rom Harré, Jonathan Potter, Peter Stearns, and Margaret Wetherell, have collectively sought to make a case for what Harré has termed the "second

1. For a fuller account of classical versus postclassical approaches to narrative theory, see David Herman, "Introduction," *Narratologies: New Perspectives on Narrative Analysis* (Columbus: Ohio State University Press, 1999), 1–30. For accounts of the structuralist revolution and of the way it shaped structuralist theories of narrative in particular, see David Herman, "Histories of Narrative Theory (1): A Genealogy of Early Developments," *The Blackwell Companion to Narrative Theory*, ed. James Phelan and Peter J. Rabinowitz (Malden, MA: Blackwell, 2005), 19–35, and François Dosse, *History of Structuralism*, 2 vols., trans. Deborah Glassman (Minneapolis: University of Minneapolis Press, 1997) [except as indicated, all notes are Herman's]. [Herman names important figures in French structuralism: BARTHES (1915–1980); Genette (b. 1930); Greimas (1917–1992), originally Lithuanian; and TODOROV (1939–2017), born in Bulgaria—editor's note.]
2. For a synoptic account of developments in cognitive narratology, see Manfred Jahn, "Cognitive Narratology," *Routledge Encyclopedia of Narrative Theory*, ed. David Herman, Manfred Jahn, and Marie-Laure Ryan (London: Routledge, 2005), 67–71; see also David Herman, *Narrative Theory and the Cognitive Sciences* (Stanford: Publications of the Center for the Study of Language and Information, 2003).
3. Derek Edwards and Jonathan Potter, *Discursive Psychology* (London: Sage, 1992), 3.
4. Edwards and Potter, *Discursive Psychology*, 2.

cognitive revolution."[5] The first cognitive revolution marked a shift away from behaviorism to the study of cognition, postulating that "there are mental processes 'behind' what people say and do, that these processes are to be classified as 'information processing,' and that the best model for the cognitively active human being is the computer when it is running a program."[6] In contrast, although the second cognitive revolution also accepts that there are cognitive processes, it views them as immanent in discourse practices. From this perspective, the mind does not preexist discourse, but is ongoingly accomplished in and through its production and interpretation. Hence the designation "*discursive* psychology."

My chapter uses an illustrative literary narrative—namely, Ernest Hemingway's[7] 1927 story "Hills Like White Elephants"—to test out the productiveness of broadly discursive-psychological research for cognitive cultural studies; one of my goals is to show how ideas geared mainly to the study of intelligent activity in face-to-face interaction can also illuminate analyses of written narrative texts (and vice versa). Sketching a thumbnail history of the developments that have led discursive psychologists to speak of a second cognitive revolution, I outline five key concepts that have emerged from this rethinking of the nature of thinking and use Hemingway's text as a case study to show how those concepts are relevant for narrative inquiry. I also indicate ways in which the study of literary texts like Hemingway's can inform discursive-psychological research—research premised on the idea that minds are always already grounded in discourse. Hemingway's and other authors' representations of discourse practices—their staging of "scenes of talk"—bear importantly on the tradition(s) of research that locate cognitive processes not in the heads of solitary thinkers but rather in sociocommunicative processes unfolding within richly material settings.[8]

"Hills Like White Elephants": Key Aspects

Hemingway's brief story—it has fewer than fifteen hundred words—focuses on a conversation between an unnamed male character and Jig, the woman who has been impregnated by the male character (the reader assumes). The story is set on a hot day at a train station in Spain, in a valley through which the Ebro River flows. As they wait for the train to Madrid, the two characters briefly discuss the appearance of the landscape surrounding them (specifically, Jig mentions that the hills across the valley look like white elephants), then order drinks and engage in a sometimes tense conversational exchange about the possibility of Jig's having an abortion. When the story ends, with the characters expecting the train to arrive momentarily, it remains unclear what course of action they will pursue—although the closing lines perhaps suggest that Jig has acceded to the male character's suggestion that she get the abortion or at least decided that any further discussion

5. See Rom Harré, "Introduction: The Second Cognitive Revolution," *American Behavioral Scientist* 36 (1992): 5–7, and also the website maintained by Andrew Lock at Massey University in New Zealand: www.massey.ac.nz/~alock/virtual/welcome.htm.

6. Harré, "Introduction," 5; cf. Rom Harré and Grant Gillett, *The Discursive Mind* (London: Sage, 1994), 1–17.

7. American novelist and short story writer (1899–1961). Herman later quotes "Hills Like White Elephants" from *The Complete Short Stories of Ernest Hemingway* (New York: Scribner's, 1987), 211–14 [editor's note].

8. See also David Herman, "Dialogue in a Discourse Context: Scenes of Talk in Fictional Narrative," *Narrative Inquiry* 16.1 (2006): 75–84.

of the matter with him would be fruitless. I discuss the story in greater detail below, but some key issues raised by Hemingway's storytelling method can be highlighted at the outset.

Although Hemingway's fiction in general and "Hills Like White Elephants" in particular might be construed as instances of "behaviorist" narrative, presenting only overt, surface behaviors of the characters and omitting narratorial commentary on more or less fugitive internal states (dispositions, thoughts, attitudes, memories, etc.), as the characters' conversation unfolds in the story a rich context of perceptions, inferences, and emotional responses emerges.[9] Here one might cite Hemingway's statement about his own tip-of-the-iceberg method of composition: "I always try to write on the principle of the iceberg. . . . There is seven-eighths of it underwater for every part that shows."[1] In lieu of this surface-and-depth metaphor, however, the story itself suggests the advantages of a more "lateralized," or distributed, model. Memory, perception, emotion—in short, the mind—do not reside beneath the surface of the characters' verbal and nonverbal actions but are rather spread out as a distributional flow in what they do and say (as well as what they do not do and do not say), the material setting that constitutes part of their interaction, the method of narratorial mediation used to present the characters' verbal and nonverbal activities, and readers' own engagement with all of these representational structures. One of the chief tasks for postclassical narrative theory is to develop tools for studying the mind relevance of all these dimensions of stories and storytelling. The question is how cognitive processes can be lodged not just in reports about characters' behaviors, utterances, and experiences but also in modes of narration, types of perspective, and details about the spatial and temporal contexts of narrated situations and events. I argue in what follows that ideas from the field of discursive psychology can contribute at least some of the tools needed to explore the mind relevance of these aspects of narrative structure, though story analysts will also need to draw on other, complementary, frameworks that study the interrelations among language, mind, and world.[2]

My next section provides further context for understanding the disciplinary origins and explanatory aims of discursive psychology itself. In other words, to grasp why theorists in this tradition have sought to define mind as discourse, it is necessary to recall part of the recent history of discourse about minds.

Recent Conceptions of Mind: Some Swings of the Post-Cartesian Pendulum

Research concerned with the nature of the mind spans millennia and ranges across multiple fields of inquiry, including neuroscience; cognitive linguistics; the philosophy of mind; cognitive anthropology; artificial intelligence;

9. On problems with the very notion zero-degree "behaviorist narrative"—that is, a mode of narration utterly devoid of clues about characters' dispositions, inferences, attitudes, and so forth—see Alan Palmer, *Fictional Minds* (Lincoln: University of Nebraska Press, 2004), 205–39.
1. Quoted by Kenneth G. Johnston, *The Tip of the Iceberg: Hemingway and the Short Story* (Greenwood, FL: Penkevill, 1987), 31.
2. See David Herman, "Cognitive Narratology," *Living Handbook of Narratology*, ed. John Pier, Wolf Schmid, Jörg Schönert, and Peter Hühn (Berlin: Walter de Gruyter, 2009), 30–43.

cognitive, social, and evolutionary psychology; and, as the current volume[3] attests, humanistic scholarship that is increasingly drawing on concepts from these other areas of study to examine cultural processes and artifacts. Although I cannot hope to do justice to this immense body of work here, several recent accounts converge in identifying key junctures in the study of mind since the time of Descartes.[4]

- *Cartesian dualism*: Descartes' account of the mind as immaterial and unextended, and his opposition between the mind and the extended matter constituting the physical world, codified a dualistic conception that can be traced back to Plato[5] (e.g., the *Meno*) and that can be abbreviated with a formula: *the mind in here; the world out there*. As Anthony Freeman discusses in his overview of theories of consciousness, this dualistic model leads to a number of paradoxes in the philosophy of mind.[6] Yet Descartes' bifurcated conception of the mental versus the physical nonetheless set the terms for subsequent debates about the nature of mental phenomena. Specifically, his dichotomization of the mind in here and the world out there created two poles, or end points, of a spectrum between which subsequent theories had to position themselves, even when those theories were anti-Cartesian in spirit, as was the case with behaviorism (see below).[7]
- *Introspectionism* (the pendulum swings toward one end of the Cartesian spectrum, *the mind in here*): Cartesian dualism licensed the introspectionism that characterized philosophical as well as psychological discourse in the late nineteenth and early twentieth centuries (Franz Brentano, Edmund Husserl, Wilhelm Wundt, William James).[8] If one assumes that the mind is in here, then introspective analysis constitutes a legitimate source of data about the mind's nature and workings. The legacy of introspectionism carries over into the first cognitive revolution, that is, the heyday of cognitive science after it emerged in the mid-twentieth century as a constellation of disciplines that included

3. *Introduction to Cognitive Cultural Studies*, ed. Lisa Zunshine (Baltimore: Johns Hopkins University Press, 2010), where this essay originally appeared [editor's note].
4. Sources consulted in this context include Philip E. Agre, *Computation and Human Experience* (Cambridge: Cambridge University Press, 1997); William Bechtel and George Graham, eds., *A Companion to Cognitive Science* (Oxford: Blackwell, 1998); Ned Block, Owen Flanagan, and Güven Güzeldere, eds., *The Nature of Consciousness: Philosophical Debates* (Cambridge, MA: MIT Press, 1997); Andy Clark, *Being There: Putting Brain, Body, and World Together Again* (Cambridge, MA: MIT, 1997); Antonio R. Damasio, *Descartes' Error: Emotion, Reason, and the Human Brain* (New York: G. P. Putnam, 1994); Derek Edwards, *Discourse and Cognition* (London: Sage, 1997); Donald Freeman, "'According to My Bond': *King Lear* and Re-Cognition," *Language and Literature* 2 (1993): 1–18; Howard Gardner, *The Mind's New Science: A History of the Cognitive Revolution* (New York: Basic Books, 1985); Rom Harré, "The Discursive Turn in Social Psychology," *The Handbook of Discourse Analysis*, ed. Deborah Schiffrin, Deborah Tannen, and Heidi E. Hamilton (Oxford: Blackwell, 2001), 688–706; and Harré and Gillett, *The Discursive Mind*. [René Descartes (1596–1650), French mathematician and philosopher whose theory of mind led to the classic formulation of the modern mind-body problem—editor's note.]
5. Greek philosopher (ca. 427–ca. 347 B.C.E.); see above [editor's note].
6. Anthony Freeman, *Consciousness: A Guide to Debates* (Santa Barbara: ABC-CLIO, 2003). See, for example, chaps. 5 and 12.
7. For a comic account of Cartesian dualism and its implications for attempts to understand the nature of the mind, see Samuel Beckett, *Murphy*, chap. 6. [Beckett (1906–1989), Irish author of fiction, plays, and criticism; *Murphy* (1938) is a novel—editor's note.]
8. Important figures in early psychology: Brentano (1838–1917), German philosopher and founder of act psychology; Husserl (1859–1938), German philosopher and founder of phenomenology; Wundt (1832–1920), German physiologist and founder of experimental psychology; and James (1842–1910), American philosopher and psychologist [editor's note].

computer science, cognitive psychology, linguistics, neurophysiology, and so forth.[9] As Andy Clark has argued, certain strands of such first-wave cognitive science continued to treat "the mind as a privileged and insulated inner arena" and "body and world as mere bit-players on the cognitive stage."[1]

- *Behaviorism* (the pendulum swings to other end of the Cartesian spectrum, *the world out there*): As a reaction against introspectionism, early twentieth-century behaviorism (John B. Watson, B. F. Skinner)[2] holds that the world out there is the only thing that can be studied and known; the mind in here is epiphenomenal or, at best, an explanatory fiction postulated on the basis of observable, outward behaviors of material bodies. Chomsky's theory of transformational generative grammar, which constitutes one of the key developments in the first cognitive revolution, emerged against the backdrop of what Chomsky viewed as the impoverished conception of language available within a behaviorist framework.[3]
- *The first cognitive revolution* (the pendulum swings back once more to the "mind" end of the spectrum): As a reaction against behaviorism, first-wave cognitive science is sometimes also termed "cognitivism" by its critics.[4] An inherently interdisciplinary enterprise, the first cognitive revolution marks a return to the mind in here, but now the mind is viewed as an information-processing device—the dominant metaphor being, according to Rom Harré and Grant Gillett, the mind as a software program that runs on the "hardware" of the physical brain.[5]
- *The second cognitive revolution* (the mind is *both* in here *and* out there; so is the world): To reiterate, the basic claim made by discursive psychologists is that cognitive processes exist, but that they are immanent in—that they emerge from—discourse practices. From this vantage point, people acquire the status of psychological beings just by participating in discourse, in normatively accountable ways.[6] Further, for theorists working in this tradition, discourse itself can be defined in broadly Wittgensteinian terms as the rule-based manipulation of symbols in multiperson episodes that unfold within material settings.[7]

But what developments helped precipitate the shift from first-wave, cognitivist models of mind to the second-wave, discursively oriented models? Research contributing to this second revolution in thinking about thinking,

9. Howard Gardner, *The Mind's New Science: A History of the Cognitive Revolution* (New York: Basic Books, 1985).
1. Andy Clark, "Embodied, Situated, and Distributed Cognition," *A Companion to Cognitive Science*, 508.
2. Two American psychologists who were influential theorists of behaviorism, Watson (1878–1958) and Skinner (1904–1990) [editor's note].
3. See Noam Chomsky, *Review of Verbal Behavior* by B. F. Skinner, *Language* 35 (1959), 26–58.
4. Cf. Edwards, *Discourse and Cognition*.
5. Harré and Gillett, *The Discursive Mind*, 17–34. See Gardner, *The Mind's New Science*, for a rich account of the historical and intellectual contexts from which first-wave cognitive science emerged as well as for a description of the overall program for research that defined the first cognitive revolution.
6. See Edwards, *Discourse and Cognition* and "Discursive Psychology," *Handbook of Language and Social Interaction*, ed. Kristine L. Fitch and Robert E. Sanders (Mahwah, NJ: Lawrence Erlbaum, 2005), 257–73; and Harré and Gillett, *The Discursive Mind*.
7. See Rom Harré, "The Discursive Turn in Social Psychology," *The Handbook of Discourse Analysis*, 688–706; Ludwig Wittgenstein, *Philosophical Investigations,* 3d ed., ed. G. E. M. Anscombe and Rush Rhees, trans. G. E. M. Anscombe (Oxford: Blackwell, 1953). [Wittgenstein (1889–1951), Austrian-born British philosopher of language—editor's note.]

which began to unfold in the late 1980s, emanated from several sources. One source was Vygotsky's work on the social roots of human intelligence; his hypothesis that, in the development of individuals, intramental thinking derives from shared, or intermental, thinking has led to a broader interest in socially distributed cognition—as I discuss more fully in my next section.[8] Another source was the approach to discourse analysis (sometimes called "Conversation Analysis") that can be traced back to the ethnomethodological or participant-centered theories of the sociologist Harold Garfinkel. According to this work, participants index their understandings of an ongoing interaction precisely by making particular kinds of contributions to the course of the interaction itself and thereby jointly constructing it as the *kind* of interaction that they understand it to be.[9] Knowing and doing, cognition and discourse, are thus inextricably interlinked. A similar emphasis on the discourse grounding of cognitive processes can be found in a third important source in this context, namely, the philosophy of the later Wittgenstein. Emphasizing the embeddedness of humans' meaning-making practices in larger "forms of life," Wittgenstein characterized meaning as use; in this account, utterances have meanings by virtue of how they are used in particular communicative situations. He also argued that pain and other mental phenomena should be thought of as anchored not in a private, inner language but rather in rule-oriented displays within normative contexts specifying how and when such displays can be produced and interpreted as such.

What links these research initiatives, as diverse as they are, is a shared attempt to nudge the post-Cartesian pendulum away from the "mind in here" pole but without allowing it to swing all the way back to the "world out there" pole at which the behaviorists sought to arrest it. In turn, the discursive-psychological research that builds on these and other analytic frameworks has major implications for the study of the mind-discourse nexus in general and of the cognitive dimensions of narrative discourse in particular. In the next section, I use Hemingway's story to outline specific strategies by which narrative scholars might harness this tradition of inquiry to reconfigure narrative theory after the second cognitive revolution—and to develop ideas that may also be productive for discursive-psychological inquiry.

Hemingway and the Discursive Mind

Putting Hemingway's story into dialogue with discursive-psychological research highlights five key concepts that can productively inform (and be informed by) narrative theory. The first four concepts have emerged directly from the second cognitive revolution; the fifth concept, although it might

8. Research on distributed cognition that was inspired by Vygotsky includes Agre, *Computation and Human Experience*; David Herman, "Genette Meets Vygotsky: Narrative Embedding and Distributed Intelligence," *Language and Literature* 15.4 (2006): 375–98; Edwin Hutchins, *Cognition in the Wild* (Cambridge, MA: MIT Press, 1995); Jean Lave and Etienne Wenger, *Situated Learning: Legitimate Peripheral Practice* (Cambridge: Cambridge University Press, 1991); and Barbara Rogoff, *Apprenticeship in Thinking: Cognitive Development in Social Context* (New York: Oxford University Press, 1991). [Lev Vygotsky (1896–1934), Russian psychologist—editor's note.]

9. For foundational work in this tradition, see Paul Drew and John Heritage, ed., *Talk at Work* (Cambridge: Cambridge University Press, 1992); Harold Garfinkel, *Studies in Ethnomethodology* (Englewood Cliffs, NJ: Prentice-Hall, 1967); Harvey Sacks, *Lectures on Conversation*, vols. 1 and 2, ed. Gail Jefferson (Oxford: Blackwell, 1992); and Emanuel A. Schegloff, "Notes on Conversational Practice: Formulating Place," *Studies in Social Interaction*, ed. David Sudnow (New York: Free Press, 1972), 75–119.

seem to be orthogonal or even opposed to discursive-psychological research, nonetheless connects up with it in ways that have not been adequately explored, though narrative analysts have begun to sketch some of the links. The five concepts are: (1) positioning; (2) embodiment; (3) the distributed versus localized nature of mind; (4) emotion discourse and "emotionology"; and (5) qualia, or the idea that conscious experiences have ineliminably subjective properties, a distinctive sense or feeling of what it is like for someone or something to experience them.

POSITIONING THEORY

The first key concept is the notion that we make sense of our own and other minds through *positioning*. In Harré and van Langenhove's account,[1] one can position oneself or be positioned in discourse as powerful or powerless, admirable or blameworthy, and so forth. In turn, a position can be specified by characterizing how a speaker's contributions are taken as bearing on these and other "polarities of character" in the context of an overarching storyline—a narrative of self and other(s) being jointly elaborated (or disputed) by participants via self-positioning and other positioning speech acts. Hence positions are selections made by participants in discourse, who use position-assigning speech acts to build "storylines" in terms of which the assignments make sense. Reciprocally, the storylines provide context in terms of which speech acts can be construed as having a position-assigning force.

In "Hills," positioning is a relevant parameter for analysis on at least two levels: the level of the characters and, given Hemingway's narrative techniques, the level of the reader's engagement with the text.[2] At the first level, the story portrays the unnamed male character and Jig as engaged in both self- and other-positioning acts. At the second level Hemingway's mode of narration—in particular, his use of what F. K. Stanzel[3] would characterize as figural narration (= third-person or heterodiegetic narration in which events are refracted through the vantage point of a particular consciousness or "reflector")—works to position readers.

Consider this early exchange between the characters regarding the appearance of the hills on the other side of the valley:

> "They look like white elephants," she said.
> "I've never seen one," the man drank his beer.
> "No, you wouldn't have."
> "I might have," the man said. "Just because you say I wouldn't have doesn't prove anything." (211)

Here the male character explicitly rejects the storyline in which Jig seeks to position him. However, given the way the story unfolds and the double entendre embedded in its title, the storyline evoked by Jig's comment does acquire legitimacy. This is a person who doesn't have the ability to contextualize, let alone accept, unwanted gifts—or unwanted children.

1. Rom Harré and Luk van Langenhove, eds., *Positioning Theory* (Oxford: Blackwell, 1999).
2. Cf. Michael Bamberg, "Positioning," *Routledge Encyclopedia of Narrative Theory*, 445–46.
3. Franz Karl Stanzel, *A Theory of Narrative*, trans. Charlotte Goedsche (Cambridge: Cambridge University Press, 1984). [Stanzel (b. 1923), Austrian narratologist—editor's note.]

Conversely, the male character fails in his own attempt to position Jig within a storyline, one that she questions and exposes as grounded in the male character's self-interest, not in his concern for their shared life and happiness together. The key passage is the following:

> "I'll go with you and I'll stay with you all the time. They just let the air in and then it's all perfectly natural."
> "Then what will we do afterward?"
> "We'll be fine afterward. Just like we were before."
> "What makes you think so?"
> "That's the only thing that bothers us. It's the only thing that's made us unhappy." (212)

Jig's subsequent remarks, including her ironic comment about the happiness of all women who have abortions, work to invalidate the storyline in which the male character tries to position them—a story in which they were a happy couple for whom everything was going well and would go well again, provided the abortion takes place. In other words, the man tries to other-position Jig as part of an "us" to which Jig does not position herself as belonging. She momentarily adopts the male character's language but then repositions herself and other-positions him within a different kind of storyline, one in which things will not necessarily work out in the way that her interlocutor suggests. Similarly, at the very end of the story, the male character tries to emplot their current interaction as one in which Jig, after going through a brief period of feeling "unwell," recovers her equilibrium. Jig rejects this storyline, which is based on an attempt to position her in terms of the polarity feeling worse/feeling better; but she does not necessarily project a storyline of her own vis-à-vis their recent interaction:

> "Do you feel better?" he asked.
> "I feel fine," she said. "There's nothing wrong with me. I feel fine." (214)

Jig thus rejects the presupposition of the male character's question but does not engage in a self-positioning act that might lend a sense of closure to their recent dispute—or to the narrative itself.

At another level Hemingway's mode of narration positions readers vis-à-vis the (inter)action unfolding within the storyworld. Although there are shifts of perspective over the course of the story, the male character functions as the main internal focalizer or reflector figure, whose vantage point provides a window on the action being recounted. Thus, almost all of the nonverbal actions recounted in the story are performed by Jig, confirming that the dominant reflector or perceiver (the one witnessing Jig's actions) is the male character. The use of the male character as the focalizer tends to align the reader with his vantage point: we literally see things through his eyes. Yet, as already discussed, the text ultimately invalidates both the storyline he proposes and his attempt at other-positioning Jig in terms of that storyline. This creates a kind of dissonance in the positioning logic of the story. And whatever Hemingway's conscious stance toward dominant conceptions of gender in the epoch during which he wrote, the technique of positioning readers simultaneously with and against the male character serves to disrupt sexist master narratives in which men are the repositories of authoritative knowledge and sound judgments while women lack these attributes and are therefore unreliable.[4]

Thus the idea of positioning, although originally developed for the purposes of analyzing everyday communicative interactions, can also throw light on processes of self- and other-identification in literary narratives like Hemingway's. At the same time, concepts and methods originating in literary narratology, such as figural narration and internal focalization, can lead to finer-grained analyses of positioning logic itself. Combining the resources of these research traditions allows us to formulate a number of questions that could not have been posed by classical narrative theory: How do the stories we tell about ourselves and others, as well as written literary narratives, position us, our interlocutors, authors, narrators, characters, and readers in networks of presuppositions and norms? Can a person's mind be described as, in part, a byproduct of how he or she is situated at the intersection of multiple storylines? Conversely, how do storylines emerge over the course of sequences of position assignments? Can ideology in general, and gender ideologies in particular, be redefined as entrenched storylines—master narratives that arise through an iterative process of assigning the same position, repeatedly, to the same kind of agent, until the agent and his or her position appear to be indissolubly linked? And if so, how can we best use the formal tools developed by narratologists to show how literary narratives sometimes work to interrupt or even derail this process—to uncouple positions and types of agents and thereby "unwrite" dominant storylines—no matter what the conscious aims of the texts' authors?

EMBODIMENT

The second key concept emerging from the second cognitive revolution and taken up in discursive-psychological research concerns the mind's embodiment. Second-wave cognitive science resists both the cognitivist hierarchicalization of mind over body and the behaviorist prioritization of body over mind. Instead, it holds that the mind is always and inalienably embodied; minds should be viewed as the nexus of brain, body, and environment (or world).[5] By putting mind on the same footing as the world in which we think, act, and communicate, second-wave cognitive science avoids making underlying cognitive processes wholly explanatory of overt verbal as well as nonverbal behaviors. Those behaviors, rather, help constitute the cognitive processes themselves, with which they are related in a feedback loop.

In the field of cognitive linguistics, scholars such as George Lakoff, Mark Johnson, Ronald Langacker, and Leonard Talmy have explored ways the structure of language is grounded in (and constitutes a ground for) embodied human experience.[6] For example, this mind-body-language nexus mani-

4. For feminist (and other) critiques of Hemingway, see contributions to the volumes assembled by Jackson J. Benson, ed., *New Critical Approaches to the Short Stories of Ernest Hemingway* (Durham: Duke University Press, 1990), and by Linda Wagner-Martin, ed., *Ernest Hemingway: Seven Decades of Criticism* (East Lansing: Michigan State University Press, 1998).

5. See Clark, *Being There*, and his "Embodied, Situated, and Distributed Cognition."

6. For an overview of this work, see William Croft and Alan D. Cruse, *Cognitive Linguistics* (Cambridge: Cambridge University Press, 2004). For a critique of some aspects of cognitive-linguistic research from a discursive-psychological perspective, see Derek Edwards, "Categories Are for Talking: On the Cognitive and Discursive Bases of Categorization," *Theory and Psychology* 1.4 (1991): 515–42, and his *Discourse and Cognition*, 202–62. [See, e.g., George Lakoff, *Women, Fire, and Dangerous Things: What Categories Reveal about the Mind* (1987); Mark Johnson, *The Body*

fests itself in metaphor systems deriving from the experience of navigating the world in, preferably, an upright position. Thus, in English, "up" is generally valorized as positive and "down" as negative (contrast "Today was a real high point for me" with "I'm feeling really low today"). But it is not just that the structures of language can be *correlated with* the physical embodiment of the mind. What is more, as Hemingway's text suggests, stories help *constitute* characters (and character-narrators) as embodied: the process of narration constructs the experiencing self as inalienably linked to a spatially and temporally oriented body-in-the-world. Thus, in "Hills" the use of internal focalization (that is, the filtering of the action through particularized agents of perception in the storyworld) affords an expressive resource by which the text locates the characters' experiences in space and time. The opening sentence of the story—"The hills across the valley of the Ebro were long and white" (211)—encodes a particular perceptual position: the spatial preposition *across* indicates that the viewers, the man and Jig, are located on one side of the valley and are looking out from the train station across at the other side. The text enacts the situated nature of all perception, both in the passage just quoted and also more globally, given that the role of focalizer shifts from the man to Jig and back to the man again over the course of the story. Not only does "Hills" suggest that what can be seen, what is known about the world, alters with the spatial coordinates of the embodied self that is doing the looking; more than this, it suggests that a self is in part constituted by what it sees and by when and where it sees it—with narrative being one of the principal means for tracing this perceptual flux.

Note, too, that the story also carefully situates the characters in time, using the train schedule to mark off increments of their unfolding interaction. In addition, in disputing the male character's attempt to position her as part of a couple that will regain its equanimity and happiness after the operation, Jig indicates her awareness of time's irreversibility and the constraints such linearity imposes on human decisions and relationships.

MIND AS DISTRIBUTED

In synergy with the concepts of positioning and embodiment, the discursive turn in (social-) psychological research suggests that key properties of mind cannot be grasped without an understanding of the mind as distributed. In other words, minds are spread out among participants in discourse, their speech acts, and the objects in their material environment. From this perspective, cognition should be viewed as a supra- or trans-individual activity distributed across groups functioning in specific contexts rather than as a wholly internal process unfolding within the minds of solitary, autonomous, and desituated cognizers. Hence, instead of being abstract, individualistic, and constant across all contexts, thinking in its

---

in the Mind: The Bodily Basis of Meaning, Imagination, and Reason (1987); Lakoff and Johnson, *Metaphors We Live By* (1980) and *Philosophy in the Flesh: The Embodied Mind and Its Challenge to Western Thought* (1999); Ronald W. Langacker, *Foundations of Cognitive Grammar*, vol. 1, *Theoretical Prerequisites* (1978); and Leonard Talmy, *Toward a Cognitive Semantics* (2 vols., 2000)—editor's note.]

most basic form is grounded in particular situations, socially distributed, and domain specific.[7]

Although they help organize intelligent behavior in a different way than do stories told in face-to-face interaction, literary narratives like Hemingway's not only represent but also enable the distribution of mind across participants, places, and times. For one thing, the title of the story signals how cognitive processes are constituted through discourse; they are grounded in the characters' relation with one another and with their surrounding social and material environment.[8] Jig's observation that the hills across the valley look like white elephants prompts the exchange in which she positions the man as never having seen a white elephant. This exchange precedes Jig's and the man's conversation about the abortion, but in light of their subsequent remarks Jig's other-positioning utterance can be interpreted as setting into play a chain of metaphorical equations—the hills are like white elephants; white elephants are metaphoric equivalents for unwanted gifts; the baby with which Jig is pregnant is an unwanted gift; hence, the baby is a white elephant—of the sort that the male character has been careful to avoid in the past. In this way, besides *portraying* the distribution of mind across participants, their speech acts, and their larger environment for acting and interacting, the story *vehiculates*[9] distributed cognition of this sort. The communicative and cognitive processes internal to the storyworld function as models for readers, who are cued to use structures of the narrative text as interpretive affordances, just as Jig and the male character use features of the setting to "triangulate" what is going on and how they understand and feel about their situation.[1]

Similarly, when the narrator reports that the male character looks at his and Jig's suitcases and sees "labels on them from all the hotels where they had spent nights" (214), this reference to a feature of the characters' environment suggests how the suitcases do part of the male character's thinking for him, triggering what Erving Goffman[2] would call a lamination of past and present time frames and at the same time supporting readers' inferences concerning the characters' relationship and the causal sequence leading up to their present situation. The same process of lamination, and the same distribution of mind across time, space, and social interactants, at once structures and emerges from the characters' conversational exchange. Thus, in response to the male character's attempt to minimize the likely emotional impact of the abortion, Jig ironically alludes to the life stories of other women who have had the procedure. Her contribution in turn prompts the male character to reposition both Jig and himself: here the man's use of the discourse marker "Well" signals an effort to manage problems with the recep-

7. See Lev S. Vygotsky, *Mind in Society: The Development of Higher Psychological Processes*, ed. Michael Cole, Vera John-Steiner, Sylvia Scribner, and Ellen Souberman (Cambridge, MA: Harvard University Press, 1978), and the items listed in n. 8, p. 2557. For more discussion of distributed cognition and also of the systems of emotion concepts or "emotionologies" that I examine in the next section, see Alan Palmer's "Storyworlds and Groups," *Introduction to Cognitive Cultural Studies*, 176–92.

8. For more on the role of "setting" in Hemingway's text, see Johnston, *The Tip of the Iceberg*, 125–34. My analysis, however, questions the traditional division of narrative representations into character and setting, because features of Jig's and the man's material environment factor into the sense-making activities represented in the story.

9. Carries, conveys [editor's note].

1. Cf. Herman, "Genette."

2. Canadian sociologist (1922–1982) who worked mainly in the United States. Goffman's research focused on social interactions; here, see especially his *Frame Analysis: An Essay on the Organization of Experience* (1974) [editor's note].

tion of his previous utterance and also a shift in his tactics for storyline construction, though his overall strategy remains the same:[3]

> "You don't have to be afraid. I've known lots of people that have done it."
> "So have I," said the girl. "And afterward they were all so happy."
> "Well," the man said, "if you don't want to you don't have to. I wouldn't have you do it if you didn't want to. But I know it's perfectly simple." (213)

The point is that the characters' construal of their situation is jointly (if oppositionally) accomplished and that it recruits from features of their environment as well as from the experiences of others with whom they have engaged in similarly collaborative cognition.

More generally, discursive-psychological research again suggests the need for narrative theorists to expand the scope of what they consider to be mind-relevant dimensions of stories and storytelling. Study of the judgments, inferences, and memories of characters, narrators, and readers can be folded into a broader investigation of the cognitive properties associated with narrative gestalts, that is, with narratively organized systems for making sense of experience. Expressive resources such as deixis ("I," "this," "here," "now"), shifts in point of view, and the embedding of one story inside another allow narratives to represent the distribution of mind across spaces, times, participants, and objects in the environments in which stories are told, a distribution that they represent in the form of storyworlds. Conversely, the process of storytelling facilitates just this sort of distribution. It involves the coordinated interplay of minds whose distinctive profile emerges from the nature and extent of their participation in such interplay.

Emotion Discourse and Emotionology

In research on emotion, as Stearns points out, there is a basic tension between naturalist and constructionist approaches. Naturalists argue for the existence of innate, biologically grounded emotions that are more or less uniform across cultures and subcultures. By contrast, constructionists argue that emotions are culturally specific—that "context and function determine emotional life and that these vary."[4] As Ralph Adolphs notes,[5] however, the naturalist and constructionist positions can be reconciled if emotions are viewed as (1) shaped by evolutionary processes and implemented in the brain but also (2) situated in a complex network of stimuli, behavior, and other cognitive states. Because of (2), the shared stock of emotional responses are mediated by culturally specific learning processes. In turn, to explore the contribution of cultural contexts to humans' emotional life, analysts can study "[e]motion discourse [as] an integral feature of talk about events, mental states, mind and body, personal dispositions, and social relations."[6]

3. On discourse markers, see Deborah Schiffrin, *Discourse Markers* (Cambridge: Cambridge University Press, 1987), 102–27.
4. Peter Stearns, "Emotion," *Discursive Psychology in Practice*, ed. Rom Harré and Peter Stearns (Thousand Oaks: Sage, 1995), 41.
5. Ralph Adolphs, "Could a Robot Have Emotions? Theoretical Perspectives from Social Cognitive Neuroscience," *Who Needs Emotions: The Brain Meets the Robot*, ed. Michael Arbib and Jean-Marc Fellous (Oxford: Oxford University Press, 2005), 9–28.
6. Edwards, *Discourse and Cognition*, 170.

This approach gave rise to the concept of "emotionology," which was proposed by Peter Stearns and Carol Stearns as a way of referring to the collective emotional standards of a culture as opposed to the experience of emotion itself.[7] The term functions in parallel with recent usages of the term "ontology" to designate a model of the entities, together with their properties and relations, that exist within a particular domain. Possessed by every culture and subculture, emotionologies are systems of emotion terms and concepts deployed by participants in discourse to ascribe emotions to themselves as well as their cohorts. At issue is a framework for conceptualizing emotions, their causes, and how participants in discourse are likely to display them. Further, narratives at once ground themselves in and help build frameworks of this sort, as when ghost stories and romance novels link particular kinds of emotions to recurrent narrative scenarios. Stories' emotionological profile, like their positioning logic, can thus be investigated both at the level of the characters' interactions with one another and at the level of readers' interactions with the text; that is, stories both represent and are interpreted in light of models of emotion. It should be noted further that even narratives that background or suppress emotion terms necessarily orient themselves to an emotionology. Emotionological conclusions can be drawn from the absence of emotion terms and categories in contexts where, in other cultural and communicative settings (and other modes of narration), the terms and categories would generally be deployed.

Gerald Prince cites Hemingway's "The Killers" as a paradigmatic instance of behaviorist narrative "limited to the conveyance of the characters' behavior (words and actions but not thought or feelings), their appearance, and the setting against which they come to the fore."[8] Although "Hills Like White Elephants" might therefore be expected to engage in a similar systematic suppression of the lexicon of emotion, in fact it grounds itself in an emotionology not just lexically but also structurally through the way it sequences the characters' speech acts as well as their silences and nonverbal actions. In other words, Hemingway's story points to the discursive bases of mind by anchoring the characters' emotional responses in what they say and do not say, as well as in the nonverbal actions they perform, at particular junctures over the course of their interaction. Indeed, readers are able to understand the characters' *behaviors* as *actions* in part because of the models of emotion on which they rely to interpret the text. An emotionology specifies that when an event X inducing an emotion Y occurs, an agent is likely to engage in Z sorts of actions, where Z constitutes a fuzzy set of more or less prototypical responses. For example, police detectives were recently led to conclude that a mother had played a role in her own children's death because of her atypically gleeful behavior at their gravesite. Likewise, a discourse

7. See, in addition to Peter Stearns and Carol Stearns, "Emotionology: Clarifying the History of Emotions and Emotional Standards," *American Historical Review* 90 (1985): 13–36; Christina Kotchemidova, "From Good Cheer to 'Drive-By Smiling': A Social History of Cheerfulness," *Journal of Social History* 39.1 (2005): 5–37; Edwards, *Discourse and Cognition*, 170–201; Harré and Gillett, *The Discursive Mind*, 144–61; Penny Lee, "'Feelings of the Mind' in Talk about Thinking in English," *Cognitive Linguistics* 14.2/3 (2003): 221–49; and Stearns, "Emotion." For an account of emotion that derives from the tradition of narrative semiotics, see A. J. Greimas and Jacques Fontamille, *The Semiotics of Passions: From States of Affairs to States of Feeling*, trans. Paul Perron and Frank Collins (Minneapolis: University of Minnesota Press, 1993).

8. Gerald Prince, *A Dictionary of Narratology*, 2d ed. (Lincoln: University of Nebraska Press, 2003), 10; cf. Herman, "Cognitive Narratology." ["The Killers" was published in 1927—editor's note.]

such as Hemingway's acquires coherence, comes across as more than a set of sentences, by virtue of its relationship to a larger emotionological context. The characters' activities can be construed as more than just a series of individual, unrelated doings because of the assumption, licensed by a model of emotions, that those behaviors constitute a coherent *class*. At stake is a class of actions in which one is more or less likely to engage when motivated by anxiety about committing to a relationship or by resentment over another's manipulative attempts to avoid such commitment, as the case may be.

At the lexical level, "Hills Like White Elephants" represents the characters drawing on a quite extensive vocabulary of emotion to make sense of one another's minds *as* minds. Early in the story, the characters engage in a verbal exchange that begins with an utterance by the male character:

> "Well, let's try and have a fine time."
> "All right. I was trying, I said the mountains looked like white elephants. Wasn't that bright?"
> "That was bright." (212)

Here Jig overtly thematizes the emotion terms and categories that appear to be holdovers from their previous interactions, thereby drawing attention to how, in the face of the complex issues now facing her and the male character, the terms have become hackneyed, overgeneral descriptors, incapable of helping them make sense of themselves and of what is going on. As the conversation proceeds, Jig continues to press against the limits of the emotionology on which the male character by contrast seems content to fall back, perhaps for cynical, manipulative reasons—namely, so that he can hold the more problematic, self-incriminating aspects of his position at a distance while still trying to convince Jig that he has her interests (and not just his own) at heart. Whereas the male character takes cover in the emotionological status quo, so to speak. Jig tries to find a language with which to express her concerns. At one point she uses a childlike locution that seems designed to strip the situation down to its most basic form, so that she can work toward a clearer understanding of its emotional ramifications: "But if I do it, then it will be nice again if I say things are like white elephants, and you'll like it?" (213). A moment later, referring to the characters' natural surroundings, Jig resorts to strategic vagueness to imply an amorphous, difficult-to-express sense of frustration or defeat: "'And we could have all this,' she said. 'And we could have everything and every day we make it more impossible'" (213). Toward the end of their conversation, after the male character ignores Jig's request that they stop talking, Jig uses verbal repetition to underscore the emotional urgency of her request: "Would you please please please please please please please stop talking?" (214). As these passages reveal, there is no direct mapping from form to function when it comes to emotionology: depending on context, words that do not designate emotional states can nonetheless perform emotionological functions. Indeed, in contrast with those of the male character, Jig's lexical choices are marked by an attempt to exploit this looseness of fit between form and function, perhaps in an effort to engage in emotionological innovation, to find patterns of usage adequate to the complex dynamics of the characters' current interaction.

Furthermore, and as should already be apparent, emotion discourse goes beyond individual words and includes whole utterances as well as the sequential patterning of multiple utterances. At the most global level, the male character tries unsuccessfully to project a storyline in which the abortion will enable the couple to move from unhappiness to happiness. Jig's noncommittal response to the man's question at the end of the story—"Do you feel better?"—signals her rejection of both that storyline and its emotional premises: "I feel fine. . . . There's nothing wrong with me. I feel fine" (214). At a less global level, subsets of interconnected utterances within the overall conversation, as well as places where speech might be expected to occur but does not, suggest the discursive grounding of emotions. Thus, in the three utterances contained in the following exchange, Jig's speech act (ii) construes the man's speech act (i) as a reflection on his dispositions and attitudes and not just as a report about his past experiences, whereas the man's rejoinder (iii) in turn construes Jig's construal as biased and projects an offended (and defensive) emotional posture:

(i) "I've never seen one [i.e., a white elephant]," the man drank his beer.
(ii) "No, you wouldn't have."
(iii) "I might have," the man said. "Just because you say I wouldn't have doesn't prove anything." (211)

The mind-constructing function of each utterance, in other words, depends on its place in the larger sequence of utterances being co-constructed by the characters in incremental fashion. In turn, readers can understand this series of verbal performances as a conversational sequence by virtue of models of emotion that overlap, more or less extensively, with those used by the characters in the storyworld.

Consider, finally, the passage where the male character first broaches the topic of the abortion:

(i) "It's really an awfully simple operation, Jig," the man said. "It's not really an operation at all."
(ii) The girl looked at the ground the table legs rested on.
(iii) "I know you wouldn't mind it, Jig. It's really not anything. It's just to let the air in."
(iv) The girl did not say anything. (212)

In this case it is the absence of a speech production by Jig in slots (ii) and (iv) and the text's substitution of reports of Jig's act of looking at the ground and of *not* speaking that have implications for emotionology. These empty slots in the characters' discourse suggest not only that Jig is experiencing an emotional disturbance but also that she may be chafing against the limits of the emotion discourse that she and her interlocutor have used hitherto. A task for postclassical narratology is to explore the degree to which gender asymmetry of the kind we see in Hemingway's story—which portrays Jig as an emotionological innovator and the male character as cynically hiding his self-interest behind established emotion categories—structures other narrative discourse as well, in fictional texts as well as everyday interactions. More generally, narrative analysts can investigate the power of stories to (re)shape emotionology itself. Narrative therapy, for example, involves the construction of stories about the self in which the emotional charge habitually carried by particular actions or routines can be defused or redirected, allowing people to prise apart emotion-action linkages that have become inimical to their psychological well-being.[9] Similarly, by staging the way behaviors are dovetailed with emotions and thereby interpreted as actions, stories like Hemingway's may promote greater reflexivity and self-awareness about emotionologies circulating in the broader culture.

THE PROBLEM OF QUALIA

As Janet Levin notes, "[t]he terms *quale* and *qualia* (pl.) are most commonly used to characterize the qualitative, experiential, or felt properties of mental states."[1] Or, as Daniel Dennett puts it, "'qualia' is an unfamiliar term for something that could not be more familiar to each of us: *the ways things seem to us*."[2] In Thomas Nagel's terms, qualia arise from the sense or feeling of *what it is like* to be someone or something having a given experience.[3] In the philosophy of mind, the notion of qualia continues to be debated among scholars who have adopted a range of positions on their status. Physicalists argue for the possibility of reducing qualia to brain states.[4] Antireductionists argue that there is an irreducible explanatory gap between accounts of brain physiology and the phenomenology of conscious experience.[5] For their part, functionalists argue that qualia are "multiply physically realizable"—they could in principle be emulated on a computer system, for example, and are therefore not specific to an individual brain.[6] Although the particulars of these philosophical arguments are beyond the scope of the present chapter, the general, underlying issues they tap into are directly relevant to my discussion. The key question is whether the notion of qualia, defined as subjective or "first person" properties of conscious experience, can be reconciled with the conception of mind as constituted in and through discourse.

Here it should be noted that Monika Fludernik has made *experientiality*, or the impact of narrated situations and events on an experiencing consciousness, a core property of narrative itself.[7] Fludernik's account suggests that unless a text or a discourse registers the pressure of events on an embodied human or at least a humanlike consciousness, then that text or discourse will not be construed by interpreters as a full-fledged narrative but rather (at best) as a report or chronicle. On the one hand, this account makes qualia a necessary condition for narrative, suggesting that stories are irreducibly tied to subjective states of mind. Stories are premised on minds. But on the other hand, the approach also grounds qualia in discourse practices, specifically, in the design and interpretation of narratively organized discourse. Minds are an emergent result of stories. Again we encounter important research questions for narrative theory after the second cognitive revolution:

9. See Linda Mills, "Narrative Therapy," *Routledge Encyclopedia of Narrative Theory*, 375–76.
1. Janet Levin, "Qualia," *MIT Encyclopedia of the Cognitive Sciences*, ed. Robert A. Wilson and Frank C. Keil (Cambridge, MA: MIT Press, 1999), 693.
2. Daniel Dennett, "Quining Qualia," *The Nature of Consciousness*, 619.
3. See Thomas Nagel, "What Is It Like to Be a Bat?," *Philosophical Review* 83.4 (1974): 435–50, for a classic study.
4. Dennett, "Quining Qualia."
5. See Frank Jackson, "Epiphenomenal Qualia," *Philosophical Quarterly* 32 (1982): 127–36, and also Joseph Levine, "Materialism and Qualia: The Explanatory Gap," *Pacific Philosophical Quarterly* 64.4 (1983): 354–61.
6. See Michael Tye, "Qualia," *The Stanford Encyclopedia of Philosophy* (Summer 2003 ed.), ed. Edward N. Zalta, https://plato.stanford.edu/archives/sum2003/entries/qualia/, sec. 4.
7. Monika Fludernik, *Towards a "Natural" Narratology* (London: Routledge, 1996).

Can stories not only encapsulate but also provide access to qualia, pace Nagel? That is, do stories in fact enable us to know "what it is like" to be someone else, and maybe also ourselves? More radically, could we even have a notion of the felt quality of experience without narrative?[8]

In Hemingway's story, qualia enter directly into plot: the conflict at the heart of the narrative concerns what an experience will or would be like for the person who must undergo that experience. In other words, "Hills" portrays an interaction in which one of the participants seeks to manage and minimize the felt experience of events from his interlocutor's vantage point. In the storyline that he seeks to project, the subjectively experienced character of those events is at odds with the character that Jig herself senses they will have; Jig therefore rejects the male character's other-positioning strategies. She is of another mind. Hemingway's text is thus a story about the active, ongoing construction, through the discursive means available to the participants in this scene of talk, of the felt, experienced meaning of events. Rather than preceding their interaction, the experiential profile of events emerges from the participants' use of verbal as well as nonverbal acts, in a richly material setting, to engage in processes of self- and other-positioning in the discursive construction of mind.

Horizons for Cognitive Narratology

Focusing on scenes of talk as a point of convergence for narrative theory and discursive psychology, this chapter has attempted to outline directions for further research—both for cognitive cultural studies in general and for cognitive narratology in particular. But the program for research sketched here constitutes only a beginning. Ideas from discursive psychology will need to be brought to bear on aspects of narrative structure and narrative interpretation besides the ones foregrounded here. In addition, narrative theorists will need to explore the extent to which discursive-psychological concepts can be brought into dialogue with other models for understanding the nexus between narrative and mind. How might discursive psychology contextualize research on the acquisition of narratives by children, for example?[9] By the same token, is it possible to harmonize quantitative methods for narrative study with the mainly qualitative, case-study-based approach of discursive psychology?[1] How can discursive psychology inform the study of narrative across media and be used to illuminate the mind-relevance of storytelling

8. Significantly, many of the arguments about qualia in the philosophy of mind are couched in the form of stories or storylike thought experiments. Thus Jackson's "knowledge argument" centers around Mary, the neuroscientist, who encounters a qualitative difference between what she knows through her study of the physiology of brains experiencing color, on the one hand, and the subjective, phenomenological knowledge of color that she herself acquires when she is finally let out of her windowless, colorless laboratory, on the other hand (Jackson, "Epiphenomenal Qualia"). In a similar vein, David Chalmers in *The Conscious Mind: In Search of a Fundamental Theory* (New York: Oxford University Press, 1996) uses an imagined race of zombies (humanoid beings exactly like us except that they have no conscious experiences) to argue against both strict physicalist and functionalist critiques of the concept of qualia (cf. Robert Kirk, "Zombies," *The Stanford Encyclopedia of Philosophy* [Fall 2003 ed.], ed. Edward N. Zalta, https://plato.stanford.edu/archives/fall2003/entries/zombies/).

9. See Ruth A. Berman and Dan I. Slobin, ed., *Relating Events in Narrative: A Cross-Linguistic Developmental Study* (Mahwah, NJ: Lawrence Erlbaum, 1994).

1. For a discussion of quantitative techniques, see David Herman, "Quantitative Methods in Narratology: A Corpus-Based Study of Motion Events in Stories," *Narratology beyond Literary Criticism*, ed. Jan Christoph Meister (Berlin: Walter de Gruyter, 2005), 125–49.

processes in semiotic systems other than those associated with written and spoken language? Finally, how might we work toward a rapprochement between (1) discourse-oriented approaches to the mind as a situated interactional achievement and (2) the work in cognitive grammar and cognitive semantics that likewise promises to throw light on the mind relevance of narrative structures but that focuses on discourse productions by individual speakers?[2] The scope of these questions suggests both the challenges and the opportunities facing narrative theory after the second cognitive revolution.[3]

2010

2. See Ronald W. Langacker, *Foundations of Cognitive Grammar*, vol. 1, *Theoretical Prerequisites* (Stanford: Stanford University Press, 1987); Leonard Talmy, *Toward a Cognitive Semantics*, vols. 1 and 2 (Cambridge, MA: MIT Press, 2000); and John Taylor, *Cognitive Grammar* (Oxford: Oxford University Press, 2002).

3. A different version of material included in this chapter was incorporated into David Herman, *Basic Elements of Narratives* (Malden, MA: Wiley-Blackwell, 2009).

MARC BOUSQUET
b. 1963

Marc Bousquet turns the tools of criticism and theory toward the university itself, especially toward academic labor. We customarily think that university students have a special position, seeing undergraduate education as offering wide exposure to different fields of knowledge and personal self-exploration, as well as preparation for a career, and postgraduate education as providing an apprenticeship, particularly in the humanities, for becoming a professor. Bousquet debunks those assumptions, arguing that the category of the student has frequently been used since the 1980s as a way to exploit labor. Our selection, from "The Waste Product of Graduate Education: Toward a Dictatorship of the Flexible" (2002), points out that in teaching-intensive fields like English, doctoral training in most cases functions no longer as a path to a professorial job but as a way to provide cheap labor for higher education. In fact, many are disqualified from teaching after receiving the Ph.D., thereby becoming "waste products," in Bousquet's provocative formulation. Since its appearance, "The Waste Product of Graduate Education" has been a lightning rod for graduate student and contingent faculty movements. It has also been a foundational text for contemporary criticism of the corporatizaton of higher education.

Born in Buffalo, New York, Bousquet studied at Yale University (B.A., 1985), where he took courses with HAROLD BLOOM and other members of the Yale School, a prominent group of critics during the 1970s and 1980s, many espousing deconstruction or other radical views of interpretation. After college Bousquet moved to New York City to write, working part-time as an advertising copywriter and ghostwriter, but in 1991 he returned to academe, studying English at the City University of New York (Ph.D., 1997). While working on a dissertation on nineteenth-century American literature and culture, he was also active in the graduate student union movement there and in the Modern Language Association (MLA). After graduate school, he has taught English at the University of Louisville, Santa Clara University, and Emory University; since 2015 at Emory University, he has been an associate professor in the Department of Film and Media Studies.

In the period after World War II, American universities expanded severalfold, admitting unprecedented numbers of new students and hiring new faculty. The system was built on substantial support from state and federal governments, which enabled low tuition and fees for students and good job conditions for professors. However, things started changing in the 1970s, and from the 1980s onward governmental support declined in relative terms, tuition and fees increased sharply, and the number of full-fledged professorial positions shrank. One result was that many Ph.D.s in fields like English could no longer attain a full-fledged professorial position, and soon there were twice as many new Ph.D.s as there were advertised professorships. At first, some hypothesized that the problem was temporary, as an older generation, hired in the 1950s and 1960s during the expansion, formed a kind of labor bubble that would resolve in the 1990s when that cohort retired. However, even after they retired, the problem intensified: by 2010 only one-fourth of teaching positions were held by full-fledged faculty. What had happened was that university teaching positions had been reconfigured—instead of putting a professor in most classrooms, higher education management turned to using contingent or "casual" (adjunct, part-time, or nontenureable) teaching labor, installing a system of what Bousquet calls "perma-temping."

Confronting these changes, a new wave of criticism arose in the 1990s that looked at politics and culture in academe itself. (The movement started somewhat later in the United Kingdom, where more state support was sustained, but it appeared after the turn of the century, gaining strength particularly after an enormous increase of fees in 2010.) It had ties to graduate student union movements active in the late 1980s and 1990s that aimed for better working conditions for graduate students, who do a significant portion of the teaching, particularly at state colleges and universities in the United States, often teaching two courses (of English composition, for instance) each term while pursuing their own studies. Bousquet became involved in the union at City University and also in the Graduate Student Caucus of the MLA, of which he was for a time president and which urged professional organizations such as the MLA to devote more attention to the state of their graduate students. Initially, faculty and those in professional organizations, operating under outdated or overly optimistic expectations, were often ignorant of or in denial about the actual situation: they resisted seeing graduate students as workers, instead saying that teaching was not labor but part of graduate education.

"The Waste Product of Graduate Education" comes out of this context, characterized not only by pinched job prospects but by a lack of critical understanding of these conditions. Most commentators simply invoked the laws of supply and demand—there were fewer jobs, so there must be less demand. But that explanation was misguided, as the number of undergraduate students—the demand for education—increased steadily through the past century. In a sense, Bousquet turns the tools of deconstruction on the figure of the graduate student, showing how the conventional figure of an apprentice was a mystification and asking a basic question: if one is actually not going to get a job, then what is the real position that one holds? He also deconstructs the idea of the "job market." The figure of the market makes academic hiring appear to be a natural process whose workings are inevitable and, over time, self-balancing. However, Bousquet suggests that the idea of the market functions ideologically, masking what is really going on: deliberate labor strategies geared toward the accumulation of capital at the expense of labor, intensified under contemporary neoliberalism, as diagnosed by DAVID HARVEY, which disrupts secure employment to offer "just-in-time" services or products and privatizes public institutions like education. Bousquet's solution is that workers should have control—hence his subtitle, "the dictatorship of the flexible," which plays off the Marxist goal of the dictatorship of the proletariat, updated with the contemporary idea of flexible labor.

Though Bousquet's deconstruction of the logic of academic labor centers on English—which is typically one of the largest departments on campuses because almost all students in U.S. universities are required to take a composition class—it struck a nerve for graduate students in many disciplines. In the sciences, for instance, graduate students often work as research assistants in labs where they are subject to sometimes exploitive or substandard conditions, with a limited hope of gaining a professorial job; and in history or mathematics, graduate students teach many lower-level courses and suffer similarly daunting job prospects. Bousquet's analysis also resonated with those who held contingent positions, as it explained their situation and pointed to one way to respond—to organize into what has come to be called "the new faculty majority."

One other significant element of Bousquet's argument is his moral outrage. When we read theory, we usually encounter a more distant and dispassionate tone. But Bousquet moves between a careful analysis of the system and discernable anger at its effects on those subject to its policies. One might cringe at the crude but unforgettable metaphor of treating graduate students like "a waste product," but Bousquet's outrage stems from his humanist assumption that people should not be treated that way. He not only criticizes the theoretical system of labor but holds responsible those who have instituted it, particularly executive administrators who invented and implement it. As he puts it, "cheap teaching is not a victimless crime." He also mocks the tendency of some permanent faculty to offer sympathy ("I feel your pain"), because the clear solution is not mere compassion but political action.

From an organic focus on graduate labor, Bousquet expanded his critique to consider other elements of the current system, notably management (at the other side of the table from labor) and the plight of undergraduates, in his book *How the University Works: Higher Education and the Low-Wage Nation* (2008), as well as in essays and columns in the *Chronicle of Higher Education*, *Inside Higher Ed*, and his website, howtheuniversityworks.com. Bousquet observes that because most permanent faculty in composition do not teach but have become managers of contingent teachers, tenure ironically offers greater protection to administrators than to most faculty. In the phrase of a chapter title of *How the University Works*, he points out that undergraduate "students are already workers," and he demonstrates that rather than holding a special status, students—particularly those at public colleges and universities—currently work record numbers of hours, a burden that lowers completion rates and impedes academic success. As he did in deconstructing the image of graduate students as apprentices, he shows how companies use the category of "student" to exploit young laborers, so that they don't have to pay higher wages or provide normal job protections and benefits.

The exposure of the real conditions of academe follows in the line of institutional criticism of RICHARD OHMANN, who argued in his groundbreaking *English in America: A Radical View of the Profession* (1976) that English functions not just to cultivate literary values but to inculcate white-collar discipline—one works on paper rather than doing physical labor, one does assignments independently but on time, and one should follow polite etiquette. It also dovetails with ANDREW ROSS's analysis of "mental labor" (see "The Mental Labor Problem," 2004, above), showing how contemporary tech jobs share characteristics with those in the academy, drawing on love of a pursuit in order to exploit or gain discounted labor. Overall, Bousquet's work forms a major plank in the emerging field of what Jeffrey J. Williams has called "Critical University Studies." Like the 1980s movement critical legal studies, which sought to expose the way that presumably neutral institutions actually operate in the service of power, critical university studies aims to expose the practices of higher education that support corporate business rather than educational or socially progressive goals. As Bousquet remarks at the close of "The Waste Product of Graduate Education," the university is not exempt from neoliberal capitalism but in fact enables it and adopts some of its most pernicious practices.

Provocatively framed, Bousquet's theories of academic labor have incited a great deal of debate. Bousquet has been a hero to those in graduate student or contingent positions, but a scourge to those more concerned with administration. Many in the middle acknowledge the difficulties of academic working conditions, but refuse to see graduate students as labor. And some suggest that while Bousquet underscores a significant problem, his solutions are too idealistic and not pragmatically possible. Nonetheless, while his analysis of "the waste product of graduate education" was first met with controversy, his recognition of the problems of academic labor has become generally accepted, spurring reports from professional organizations, expressions of concern from administrators, and organizing efforts among graduate student and contingent faculty.

"The Waste Product of Graduate Education: Toward a Dictatorship of the Flexible" Keywords: Cultural Studies, Ethics, Ideology, Institutional Studies, Marxism

From The Waste Product of Graduate Education: Toward a Dictatorship of the Flexible

* * *

Like many scholars of my cohort, I entered graduate school in 1991 informed by a common sense about academic work significantly influenced by the projections of the 1989 Bowen report, which projected what it emphasized would be "a *substantial* excess demand for faculty in the arts and sciences" by the mid-1990s, with the consequence that early in the new millennium we could expect "roughly four candidates for every five positions."[1] The department administrators who recruited me into the profession were of the thoughtful and concerned variety: they were up on the literature and very glad to inform me that something called the "job market" would radically improve just six years in the future. There had been a cycle of bad times for holders of the Ph.D., they admitted, but prosperity was just around the corner. During the early 1990s, buoyed in part by the election of a Democrat to the White House,[2] liberal newspapers and major disciplinary associations recirculated the Bowen projections with a sense of relief and general optimism: with the certain onset of universal health coverage, could full employment for English faculty be far behind? David Laurence, MLA's staffer for its association of chairs of English departments (ADE), wrote with typical emotion when he enthused, "Friends, the future we've all been waiting for is about to arrive."[3] As late as 1995, disciplinary associations and scholars on the state of the profession such as David Damrosch gave serious credence to the Bowen projections of "increased demand" for the academic employment of holders of the doctoral degree.[4] (In fact, as of this writing, the report

1. William G. Bowen and Julie Ann Sosa, *Prospects for the Faculty in the Arts and Sciences: A Study of Factors Affecting Demand and Supply, 1987 to 2012* (Princeton, N.J.: Princeton University Press, 1989) [Bousquet's note]. Bowen (1933–2016), economist and educator who served as president of Princeton University (1972–88) and of the Mellon Foundation (1988–2006).
2. Bill Clinton (b. 1946; U.S. president, 1993–2001), elected president in 1992, followed 12 years of Republicans holding the office.
3. David Laurence, "From the Editor," *ADE Bulletin* 94 (1989): 1 [Bousquet's note]. The Modern Language Association (MLA) is the chief North American professional organization for scholars of English and other modern languages and literatures; within it, the Associated Departments of English (ADE) advocates for English departments.
4. David Damrosch, *We Scholars: Changing the Culture of the University* (Cambridge, Mass.: Harvard University Press, 1995) [Bousquet's note]. Damrosch (b. 1953), American scholar of comparative literature and Harvard University professor.

of the American Philosophical Association on employment issues, republished on many department Web sites, still gives credence to the Bowen projections.[5]) It wasn't until 1994 that the *Chronicle of Higher Education* finally ran a short item questioning the validity of the report.[6] Over the next couple of years, most disciplinary associations, somewhat reluctantly, gave up citing the Bowen projections of a rosy future.

It is easy enough to measure the difference between the five jobs for every four candidates projected by Bowen and the reality of .25 or .30 jobs per candidate. The reporters of the *Chronicle* and one or two angry reviewers of Bowen's subsequent work have made a point of revisiting the rather startling gap between projection and reality.[7] But the more important and interesting question is analytical: what was wrong with Bowen's assumptions that he strayed so outrageously into fantasy? And what was it about these projections that generated such a warm and uncritical welcome? Essentially, Bowen's "method" was to impose neoliberal market ideology[8] on data that attest, instead, to the unfolding process of casualization. Most egregiously, for instance, when confronted with data that increasing numbers of doctoral degree holders had been taking nonacademic work since the 1970s, Bowen ignores the abundant testimony by graduate students that this dislocation from the academy was involuntary and imposes the ideology of "free choice" on the phenomenon, generating the claim that this ever-upward "trend" shows that even more people will "choose" similarly, with the result that he projects a need to *increase* graduate school admissions (to compensate for the ever-increasing numbers of people who "choose" nonacademic work). This error is only one element in an overall methodological neoliberalism that assumes the academic labor system operates as a "market" that, by unwarranted analogy to other markets in the business cycle, has a "natural" boom-bust pattern. In order to manufacture an empirically existing "job market" out of data that indicate a labor system running on the continual substitution of student and casual labor for faculty, Bowen has to virtually exclude the labor of students, full-time lecturers, and part-time faculty from his model of the labor system. This is like modeling the solar system without the sun: he populates his "universe of faculty" with only twelve thousand part-timers, whereas the National Study of the Post-Secondary Faculty (NSOPF) saw more than a quarter million (and felt its numbers deeply under-counted).[9] Furthermore, Bowen's projections rest on the counterfactual assumption that "institutions always *want* to have more faculty and will add faculty positions *when they can afford to do so*"[1]—when every nook and cranny of the public discourse on the question holds reams of evidence attesting that what institutions "want" is to accumulate capital and conserve

5. Statement to Prospective Graduate Students (American Philosophical Association, n.d.) [Bousquet's note].

6. Denise Magner, "Job Market Blues: Instead of the Anticipated Demand, New Ph.D.'s Are Finding Few Openings," *Chronicle of Higher Education*, 27 April 1994, A17 [Bousquet's note].

7. Ibid.; William Craig Rice, "The Robert McNamara of the American Academy," *The Idler*, 2 August 1999 [Bousquet's note].

8. Neoliberalism, a dominant contemporary political view inspired by the conservative thinkers FRIEDRICH HAYEK and LEO STRAUSS and criticized by the Marxist theorist DAVID HARVEY (see selections above), stresses that the chief purpose of government is to encourage the capitalist market and calls for reducing the government's role in providing welfare and other public benefits to citizens. It also emphasizes freedom of choice over other principles.

9. National Center for Education Statistics, "National Study of Postsecondary Faculty" (1993), nces.ed.gov/surveys/nsopf [Bousquet's note].

1. Bowen and Sosa, *Prospects for the Faculty in the Arts and Sciences*, p. 153 (emphasis theirs) [Bousquet's note].

labor costs by casualizing faculty positions by any means available: early retirement, expanded graduate programs, outsourcing, distance education, deskilling, and the like. Bowen's response to the "bear market"[2] in academic hiring 1970–89 was, in a sense, predetermined: he started out looking for the complementary swing of the pendulum, what he viewed as the inevitable bull market in academic hiring, and he found it.

But Bowen is hardly alone in erroneously imposing market ideology on data about the structure and relations of academic labor. The interpretive engine driving Bowen's projections—the notion that there is a "job market" in academic labor (a notion that has to be held distinct from true "labor market" analyses) is nearly universal throughout the academy.

* * *

Theorizing Blockage

Under the general neoliberal onslaught, the notion of "market" serves as the only available heuristic for thinking at the level of totality: in this airless environment, even the slightest displacement of market logic yields insight into a very different underlying reality. One doesn't have to become wildly unconventional to accomplish this displacement. For instance: it is perfectly conventional for scholars of professional work more generally to employ the heuristic of a labor monopoly rather than a labor "market." (The best application of a labor-market mode of analysis to academic work might include the concept of segmentation: asking, for example, how is it that women comprise a vast majority in the casual sector and a distinct minority in the tenured sector.) Monopoly control of professional labor generally reflects a social bargain made by professional associations that exchange a service mission with the public for substantial control over the conditions of their work, generally including deciding who gets to practice. In a professionalized police culture, for instance, only the graduates of police academies may practice, and the police unions, like professional associations, supervise this instruction and apprenticeship and safeguard the employment conditions of these recruits against the depredations of would-be amateur and volunteer police practitioners. From this perspective, the ideological literalization of the "job-market" analogy may be seen as having obscured the very useful possibility of describing the academic labor system in perfectly scholarly and conventional terms as a failed monopoly of professional labor. That is: postsecondary educators generally fulfill the service mission that constitutes their half of the bargain, and society in return continues to grant them monopoly control over degrees, but the labor monopoly fails because degree holding no longer represents control over who may practice.[3]

2. That is, a declining market—a term from securities trading, as is "bull market" (a market in which prices and values rise).

3. On the failure of professional associations to exert even modest influence upon university employers, see Watt's entry, "The Modern Language Association," in Cary Nelson and Stephen Watt, *Academic Keywords: A Devil's Dictionary for Higher Education* (New York: Routledge, 1999), 169–78, and his "What Is an 'Organization Like the MLA'? From Gentleman's Club to Professional Association," *Workplace*, no. 1 (1998): 27–35. As Lennard Davis observes in his "manifesto" against them, "the obvious thing about professional organizations in general is how well they dovetail with institutional agendas" ("Dancing in the Dark: A Manifesto against Professional Organizations," *Minnesota Review*, nos. 45/46 [1995–96]: 197) [Bousquet's note]. DAVIS (b. 1949), American literary and cultural critic.

Indeed, the inescapable observation must be this: under casualization, *degree holding increasingly represents a disqualification from practice*. The ultimate refutation to job market theory is that, in observing that the holder of the doctoral degree is the "waste product of graduate education," we are only moving toward an acknowledgment of simple fact.

For most graduate employees, the receipt of the Ph.D. signifies the end—and not the beginning—of a long teaching career. Degree holders frequently serve as university teachers for eight or ten years before earning their doctorate. In English departments, a degree holder will have taught many writing classes, perhaps also a literature survey or theme class, even an upper-division seminar related to his or her field of study. Many degree holders have served as adjunct lecturers at other campuses, sometimes teaching M.A. students and advising their theses en route to their own degrees. Some will have taught thirty to forty sections, or the equivalent of five to seven years' full-time teaching work. During this time, they received frequent mentoring and regular evaluation; most will have a large portfolio of enthusiastic observations and warm student commendations. A large fraction will have published essays and book reviews and authored their departmental Web pages. Yet at precisely the juncture that this "preparation" should end and regular employment begin—the acquisition of the Ph.D.—the system embarrasses itself and discloses a horrible truth that every recent degree holder knows and few administrators wish to acknowledge: under the actually existing system of graduate education, the terminal degree is no longer the beginning of one's teaching career but the logical end of that career.

Acknowledging that the receipt of the doctorate names the end of many long teaching careers asks us to confront the reality of casualization. As presently constructed, the system of academic work requires persons who have the terminal M.A. or the M.Phil., or who are ABD[4]—ideally persons who have a well-paid partner or other means of support enabling them to teach for wages below the poverty line for an extended period of time without undue suffering.[5] Without a degree and presupposing another source of income, persons of this description can and do teach virtually forever. The system cannot run without persons who are doing or who have done graduate study, quite frequently persons who can be represented as on some long trajectory toward the terminal doctorate. For our analysis, the inescapable point must be this: all of these nondegreed persons—graduate employees and former graduate employees working on an adjunct basis—are the "products" of the system of graduate education in the same way that persons who hold the Ph.D. are its product. Indeed, these other "products" are what the labor system produces to sustain itself. The system "really needs" a continuous flow of replaceable nondegreed labor. As presently constructed, the academic labor system requires few if any new degree holders—but it gasps and sputters when there is a tiny interruption in the steady stream of new

4. All but dissertation: the stage in the process of attaining a doctorate after course work and qualifying examinations are successfully completed but before a dissertation is written.

5. The most recent surveys on the question of wages for casual academic teachers are those conducted by the Coalition on the Academic Work Force (see American Historical Association, "Summary of Data from Surveys by the Coalition on the Academic Workforce," November 2000). In English composition, fewer than one-third of the responding programs paid more than $2,500 a class. Nearly half (47.6 percent) paid less than $2,000 per class: teaching a full-time load or eight classes nets less than $16,000 annually, usually without benefits [Bousquet's note].

graduate students (hence the appearance of employment contracts in admittance packets).[6]

What needs to be quite clear is that this is not a "system out of control," a machine with a thrown rod or blown gasket. Quite the contrary: it's a smoothly functioning new system with its own easily apprehensible logic, a logic premised entirely on the continual replacement of degree holders with nondegreed labor. The plight of recent degree holders encapsulates this logic. Let us say that Jane Doe has taught sections 101-97 and 101-98 for the past seven years and, for the past four, women's studies 205, a special topics course fulfilling a university-wide diversity requirement. Upon earning the degree (or in many circumstances much earlier), Doe becomes ineligible to teach those sections, unless given a special waiver or postdoctoral invitation. The reason most universities limit the number of years a graduate student is "eligible to teach" is to ensure a smooth flow of new persons into the system. The many "exceptions" to these eligibility rules are the expression of this labor pool's flexibility, enabling the administration to be confident that it can deliver low-cost teaching labor "just in time"[7] to any point on the factory floor.

This system has no trouble bringing persons in through its primary gateways: admission to a graduate program at a research university. Its only problem is disposing of them after it has extracted six to ten years of their labor, to make room for new cheap teachers. This logic of replacement creates many local ironies. Because persons who are declared "ineligible to teach" by a graduate program frequently serve as flexible labor at other campuses, it is often at the junior colleges and other less-prestigious locations that the most experienced and dedicated flexible faculty can be found. That is: whereas the flexible labor at research universities with graduate programs will typically have between zero and five years of experience, the flexible labor at junior colleges will typically have between five and twenty years of experience. These local ironies are important because they make clear that the system's logic is not designed to provide better teaching even at the richest schools: it is designed to accommodate capital accumulation, which transpires with greater efficiency at the richest schools.

To the extent that our understanding of casualization continues to be grafted onto the assumptions of the job market theory of graduate education, we have continued to flounder epistemologically. Thinking about casualization means abandoning the vividly counterfactual job market premise, that doctoral education functions primarily to create a "supply" of teachers with the Ph.D., and asking instead: What does it mean that the primary

6. This can be described as a system of "all but unwaged" work or a kind of volunteerism, like the Peace Corps, increasingly approachable through an ethos of service or creativity, as with the "avocational" and "supplemental" activities that generate a large fraction of Web content. Recently, Tiziana Terranova, "Free Labor: Producing Culture for the Digital Economy," *Social Text*, no. 63 (2000): 33–58, and Andrew Ross, "The Mental Labor Problem," *Social Text*, no. 63 (2000): 1–31, have attempted to chart the strategic exploitation of "free labor" in both digital capitalism and the occupations of mental work more generally. As Ross observes, from the point of view of accumulation, the phenomenon of doctoral degree holders driving taxicabs does not represent a "waste" of education but testifies instead to the ruthless and systematic conversion of it to "un- or undercompensated labor" in ways we have yet to fully chart (27) [Bousquet's note]. Terranova (b. 1967), Italian media theorist; Ross (b. 1956), Scottish-born American cultural critic (for the essay cited, see above).

7. A term that originated in manufacturing practices of the 1960s and 1970s (now common) that save money by reducing the costs associated with overproduction and excessive inventory; such manufacturing relies on on-demand production.

function of the vast web of doctoral education is to provide the university with teachers who *don't* hold the doctorate?

Any real examination of graduate education and casualization leads inescapably to the conclusion that the real "labor market" in the academy is a market in the labor of persons without the terminal degree. And if this is true, the creation of persons holding the doctorate may be more properly named a "by-product" of the graduate employee system: persons who don't hold the degree are inherently more "marketable" than persons who do. That is, this is a system that creates holders of the Ph.D. but doesn't have much use for them. Indeed, the buildup of degree holders in the system represents a potentially toxic blockage. The academic labor system produces degree holders largely in the sense that a car's engine produces heat—a tiny fraction of which is recycled into the car's interior by the cabin heater, but the vast majority of which figures as waste energy that the system urgently requires to be radiated away. The system of academic labor creates degree holders only out of a tiny fraction of the employees it takes in by way of graduate education: leaving aside the use of M.A. students as instructional staff, doctoral programs in the humanities typically award the Ph.D. to between 20 and 40 percent of their entrants. And the system employs only perhaps a third of the degree holders it makes. Like a car's engine idling in the takeout food line, the system's greatest urgency is to dispel most of the degree-holding waste product.

From the perspective of casualization, the possibility of a toxic buildup of degree holders is not, as commonly maintained by job market theorists, the result of "too many" graduate students. On the contrary, it is precisely the nature of perma-temping to arrange that there are always "just enough" graduate students and other nondegreed flex workers to be delivered "just in time" to serve the university's labor needs. It is in the interest and logic of the system to have as many graduate students as it can employ while producing the fewest number of degrees—or, better yet, to produce persons with degrees who don't make a claim for permanent academic employment. This is one of the reasons why graduate school administrations have recently promoted the Marie Antoinette or "let them eat cake" theory of graduate education: "Why, if they cannot find teaching work, let them be screenwriters!"[8] This is a kind of excrement theory for managers, through which the degree holder figures as a horrible stain or blot, an embarrassment that the system is hysterically trying to scrape from its shoes. By institutionalizing the practice of preparing degree holders for "alternate careers," the system's managers are creating a radiator or waste pipe to flush away persons whose teaching services are no longer required—precisely because they now hold the degree.

In suggesting the need for an "excrement theory" to replace market theories of graduate education, I am in a way only insisting upon the urgency of recognizing the already excremental circumstance of the degree holder. Persons who actually hold the terminal degree are the traumatic

8. A reference to proposals for alternative careers ("alt-ac") for those with advanced academic degrees—in particular, the suggestion by then MLA president Elaine Showalter in 1998 that Ph.D.s might pursue work in the film industry. Marie-Antoinette (1755–1793), queen of France executed with Louis XVI after the French Revolution; she is popularly believed to have said "Let them eat cake" after hearing that the people had no bread to eat.

Real[9] puncturing the collective fantasy powering this system. Degree in hand, loans coming due, the working partner expecting a more fair financial contribution, perhaps the question of children growing relevant, the degree holder asks a question to which the system has no answer: if I have been a splendid teacher and scholar while nondegreed for the past ten years, why am I suddenly unsuitable? The answer to this question is the one that makes us writhe with humiliation: only the degree itself renders the previously splendid teacher suddenly an undesirable waste product.

Nearly all of the administrative responses to the degree holder can already be understood as responses to waste: flush it, ship it to the provinces, recycle it through another industry, keep it away from the fresh meat. Until graduate employees have an excrement theory of their own, they will continue to grasp their circumstance incompletely—that is, that they feel "treated like shit"—without grasping the systemic reality that they *are* waste. Insofar as graduate employees feel "treated like" waste, they can maintain the fantasy that they really exist elsewhere, in some place other than the overwhelmingly excremental testimony of their experience. This fantasy becomes an alibi for inaction, because in this construction agency lies elsewhere, with the administrative touch on the flush-chain. The affect of people who feel "treated like" waste is an appeal to some other agent: please stop treating us this way. Which is to say to that outside agent, "please recognize that we are not waste," even when that benevolent recognition is contrary to the testimony of our understanding. (And it is of course only good management to tell the exploited and super-exploited, "Yes, I recognize your dignity. You are special.") Persons who have the grasp of the totality of the system that proceeds from the understanding that they are indeed the waste of that system—persons who know they are not merely "treated like" waste but are in fact the actual shit of the system, being churned inexorably toward the outside, not merely "dispos*able*" labor but labor *that must be disposed of* for the system to work—these are persons who can perform acts of blockage. They are the system's constitutive exterior: without expelling the degree holder, the system could not be what it is. The difference in consciousness between feeling treated like waste and knowing one's excremental condition is the difference between experiencing casualization as "local disorder" (which authority will soon rectify) and having the grasp of one's potential for transforming the systemic realities of an actually existing new order. Where the degree-holding waste product understands its capacity for blockage and refuses to be expelled, the system organizing the inside must rapidly succumb.

There are obviously many ways of writing about the casualization of academic work. The larger picture is of the corporatization of the university and the informationalization of higher education (so that some pale fraud going by the name of education can be delivered in the way information is delivered: "just in time" and "on demand"). I wish to state unequivocally: To these problems generally and to the specific pressure point of graduate student

9. Psychoanalytic term from JACQUES LACAN, who theorized that while the Real situates the Imaginary (modeled on the preverbal mother-child dyad, or on the relation between an infant and its mirror image) and the Symbolic (the dimension of language, law, and the father) in their respective positions, it is by definition impossible to talk about and can be studied only in its effects on the other two dimensions.

experience, the only solution is the continual mobilization of a united and activist movement of faculty, graduate employees, and students consistent with the most inclusive forms of unionization. And the specific philosophies of mobilization appropriate to unionism by members of the academic community will inevitably be those that seek to bring down the barriers between academic work and other kinds of work, to struggle with the exceptionalism associated with "mental" labor generally.[1] The affiliation of many of the UC graduate employee locals with UAW and the social-movement unionism of CUNY[2] Professional Staff Congress's New Caucus instantiate these achieved and continuously achievable realities. Ultimately, the most helpful standpoint from which to initiate action will be one that sees contingent labor as the experience of two generations of young people in North America and globally, one that sees the university as a dynamic node of post-Fordist[3] employment from the sweatshop to the classroom.

In this enlarged context, it is fair to ask: Why bother to talk about the doctoral degree holder at all, when the experience of contingency is general, or at least generational? Isn't it frivolous to speak of an "excrement theory" of graduate education when the democratic promise of higher education is eroding everywhere around us? Don't we just need more clear positive knowledge regarding flex work? In the big picture, just how important are the problems of underemployed holders of doctoral degrees anyway?

Insisting on the need for an excrement theory of graduate education is in a way making an argument for privileging the systemic location of the degree holder. Without a theory of the waste product—the system's constitutive exterior—we have so far utterly failed to see that the effects of academic casualization are immanent throughout the system (not merely "local" to the casualized). For thirty years the bad knowledge of "markets" for degree holders has enabled faculty unions and disciplinary associations alike to accommodate the creation of a two-tier labor system, the most dramatically tiered labor system in North America. With the exception of the City University of New York, no faculty labor union has ever bargained for graduate students and other flex workers under the basic principle of collective bargaining: parity, or equal pay for equal work. Faculty bargaining agents have accepted the collective fantasy regarding the waste of the labor system, that graduate employees are being "trained" for future jobs, not toiling in the only academic job they will ever have. Subtract the largely

1. On academic unionism, professional work, and social movements, see Gary Rhoades, *Managed Professionals: Unionized Faculty and Restructuring Academic Labor* (Albany: State University of New York Press, 1998); Randy Martin, "Stat(e)ing the Obvious," *Workplace*, no. 4 (1999): 10–15, and Martin, ed., *Chalk Lines: The Politics of Work in the Managed University* (Durham, N.C.: Duke University Press, 2000); Vincent Tirelli, "Adjuncts and More Adjuncts: Labor Segmentation and the Transformation of Higher Education," in *Chalk Lines*, 181–201; Stanley Aronowitz, *The Knowledge Factory: Dismantling the Corporate University and Creating True Higher Learning* (Boston: Beacon, 2000); Cary Nelson, *Manifesto of a Tenured Radical* (New York: NYU Press, 1997), and Nelson, ed., *Will Teach for Food: Academic Labor in Crisis* (Minneapolis: University of Minnesota Press, 1997); Nelson and Watt, *Academic Keywords*; Robin D. G. Kelley, "The Proletariat Goes to College," in *Will Teach for Food*, 145–52; Barbara Bowen, "This Old House: Renovating the House of Labor at the City University of New York," *Workplace*, no. 1 (1998): 52–58 [Bousquet's note].

2. City University of New York. UC: University of California. UAW: United Auto Workers (union).

3. After the era of modern industrial production that has been called "Fordism" (notably in the writings of David Harvey). In the 1920s, Henry Ford paid his workers relatively high wages and offered secure full-time jobs so that they could buy expensive consumer products such as the cars they were manufacturing; this "Fordist" strategy is credited with helping to create a middle class. Since the 1970s, companies have moved away from that model toward just-in-time production by casualized labor.

imaginary relationship of most graduate employee labor to a future job, and the systemic effects of that labor are visible as the effects of casualized second-tier labor in any workplace: management domination of the work rules, speedup, moonlighting, grossly depressed wages for everyone.

Without a theory of the specificity of the degree holder's location in the system, the logic of replacement governing this system of disposable labor has been consistently mistaken as a problem only for the relatively small constituency of the graduate student. For instance, the total compatibility of the cheap teaching system with capital accumulation has enabled most schools (or the public funding them) to spend money on other things besides teaching labor—to engage in vast building programs, to create enormous endowments, to launch new programs and services, and so on. From this perspective, one might sentimentally deplore the way that graduate students are exploited by being cycled out of the system after a period of service and debt accumulation but go on to feel that "other constituencies" are surely benefiting from new stadiums, business centers, and prisons. The money saved by cheap teaching surely benefits some people, and if the only people harmed are a few graduate students, or persons whose other sources of income allow them to teach as a kind of philanthropy, what's the big deal?

One of the most useful aspects of the knowledge of graduate employee unionists is the way it addresses the system as a totality, enabling us to see that no one working, learning, or even investing in the education ecology really benefits from the system of cheap teaching.

From "I Feel Your Pain" to "Oh, Shit! Your Problem Is My Problem!"

* * *

In recognizing that their work is—in fact—labor, graduate employees have been able to get beyond the fetish of "the economy," "the market," and "the law" that bedevils second-wave knowledge.[4] Graduate employees understand that all of these forces exist not in a distant field of titans but in the arena of everyday struggle with the employer for control of the workplace. For the graduate employees, it has not been a question—as for the dominant discourse—of forecasting the economy or learning the limits established by the law—but rather of making the law responsive to their understanding. Despite setbacks in state courts and before the National Labor Relations Board (NLRB)[5] in the 1970s and the extraordinary, sustained, and frequently illegal opposition by university employers, graduate employee unionists have throughout the 1990s continually won victories writing their knowledge ("we work") into law. At public universities, the organization of graduate employee unions is subject to state law. In order to win recognition, organizers have had to initiate multiyear legislative campaigns—the ongoing

4. In an omitted passage, Bousquet characterizes academic labor in the United States as moving from a first wave of secure conditions catalyzed by faculty unionization movements in the 1960s and 1970s to a second wave of casualization inspired by neoliberalism in the 1980s and 1990s, and he projects a third wave propelled by graduate employee unions (GEUs).

5. An independent agency of the U.S. government charged with regulating elections for labor unions and investigating unfair labor practices.

litigation of the UAW-affiliated University of California unions is finally bringing to a close seventeen years of foot-dragging by the university employer. In decisions involving unionists at private universities (Yale and NYU) between 1996 and 2001, the National Labor Relations Board essentially reversed itself on previous holdings (1972, 1974, 1976) regarding the workplace status of graduate employees: under these decisions, graduate students working as teachers and various postdoctoral employees have the right to bargain their working conditions, opening the way to organizing drives at more than a dozen private universities. The will and capacity of university employers to defy the law rival the most ruthless union busting of any other commercial enterprise. When in March 2000 the Illinois House of Representatives passed a bill written by the University of Illinois graduate employees, granting them the right to collectively bargain their working conditions, the support of the state Public Employment Relations Board has meant that even this special act of the legislature has not ended the university's continuing refusal to recognize the union.

Implicit in the understanding "we work" and the corollary understanding that the consciousness of work has to be materialized in law, social policy, and workplace practice are a set of important realizations.

1. We are not "overproducing Ph.D.s"; we are underproducing jobs. There is plenty of work in higher education for everyone who wants to do it. The problem is that this enormous quantity of work no longer comes in the bundle of tenure, dignity, scholarship, and a living wage that we call "a job." The concrete aura of the claim that degree holders are "overproduced" conceals the necessary understanding that there is in fact a huge shortage of degree holders. If degree holders were doing the teaching, there'd be far too few of them. Graduate employees understand that "labor markets" are socially structured: with a single stroke (by, say, recovering the tenure lines lost in either New York or California since 1972), all of the "surplus" degree holders could be immediately employed. Even a modest "reconversion" plan designed to re-create jobs out of part-time piecework would swiftly generate a real shortage of degreed persons. The intervening official knowledge, informed by liberal economic determinism (what I call vulgar liberalism), works to conceal the operation of a policy universe (social, legal, institutional) shaping academic working conditions—a policy universe that organized graduate employees understand that they can and must transform.
2. Cheap teaching is not a victimless crime. Graduate employees understand that the system of cheap teaching hurts everyone, not just the persons who teach cheaply. The cheapness of their labor holds down salaries in the ladder ranks: professorial salaries have stagnated 50 percent against per capita gains since 1970 and have stagnated most in the disciplines most reliant upon graduate employee labor. In this period, tenured faculty have stagnated more in real wages than any other group besides persons without a college education. The cheapness and disorganization of flexible labor supports speed up throughout the system: assistant and associate professors teach more, serve more, and publish more in return for lower compensation than any previous

generation of faculty. Senior faculty suffer as well. At my institution,[6] as in many other locations, the phenomenon of salary compression is so bad that newly hired junior faculty frequently earn wages similar to or higher than those of associate professors and within spitting distance of the wages of full professors: nearly everyone in the ladder ranks of departments like mine earns between $40,000 and $60,000—regardless of rank, distinction, or term of service. This means that a sixty-year-old distinguished scholar with a national reputation and three books (and three children in college) earns a salary similar to that of junior faculty in many other disciplines. Because salary compression is really also salary depression, it also means that this distinguished scholar earns about as much as a good accountant with two or three years of experience or a twenty-five-year-old district attorney. At the end of a career covered with distinction, this professor earns about half of what moderately accomplished professionals in law and medicine earn at the beginning of their careers. He or she frequently earns less than a secondary school teacher, civil servant, factory employee, or bartender with the same term of service. In many ways, he or she also has less control over work and fewer rights to due process, despite the fantasies of unfireable tenured faculty. You have to look pretty hard to find other avenues of employment where sixty-year-old persons who've distinguished themselves at their work get paid less than college faculty. And cheap teaching hasn't only reduced salaries: it has diminished the dignity, research support, and academic freedom of the tenured, as well as affecting their morale and their capacity to govern the academy.

The system of graduate education has also radically altered the experience of general education for nearly all undergraduate students. Ask any thirty-seven-year-old graduate employee with ten or more years of service, who is just beginning to peak in pedagogical and scholarly powers, yet soon to be replaced by a twenty-two-year-old M.A. candidate: Is this a system that teaches well? And that graduate employee will answer: Heck, no, it is just a system that teaches cheaply. Accomplishing its marvelous cheapness by allocating an ever-larger section of the curriculum to flexible instructors who typically have between zero and four years of teaching experience, or who have brought their graduate studies to early termination, the system replaces its most experienced and accomplished teachers with persons who are less accomplished and less experienced. In English departments it is now typical for students to take nearly all first-year classes, many lower-division survey courses, and some advanced topics courses from nondegreed persons who are imperfectly attuned to disciplinary knowledge, who may or may not have an active research agenda, who may or may not have a future in the profession. The whole zone of general education—that is, the education that most persons who go to college have in common with each other—has been radically evacuated. The proletarianized teachers who will be the only experience that most students have of a language department generally don't even enjoy

6. The University of Louisville, where Bousquet was an assistant professor.

such necessities as offices, telephones, or photocopying privileges—much less the protections of due process that guarantee academic freedom. It is usual practice for administrations to simply dispense with the services of flexible teachers who exercise academic freedom: those who teach controversial material, of course, but also those who generate student complaints by teaching difficult material. Flexible teachers cannot afford to provide an obstacle to the advancing administrative ideal of an ultimately education-free transfer of cash for course credits. Most citizens wouldn't dream of employing an accountant without an office or a telephone—or go to a lawyer who practiced avocationally—but they regularly send their children for writing and liberal arts instruction by a person working out of the trunk of a car.

To paraphrase Emma Goldman,[7] cheap teaching is a social crime and failure. This is true even if the injuries to all persons who teach are excluded from the equation. Even the persons who seemingly "benefit" from the labor savings—students and the public they serve and also become—are substantially injured. Nor is it just a matter of teaching. The whole complex of research production is diminished by the elimination of tenurable faculty positions. Casualization systematically replaces the scholarly activity of the professoriat with new management tasks and profoundly degrades the undergraduate educational experience—producing such "efficiencies" as a reduced variety of course offerings, reduced access to faculty doing active scholarship in their field, and the regular replacement of experienced professionals with students and avocational labor.

3. Casualization is an issue of racial, gendered, and class justice. Frequently the cheap teachers are persons who can afford to teach with little or no compensation, as idealized in the recent financial services commercial illustrating the corporate employee taking a plush early retirement so he can "afford" to realize his "dream" of being a teacher. What does it mean that increasingly only persons who can "afford to teach" are entering higher education as a profession? Surely one reason the neoliberal second-wave knowledge took such hold of the academy during the 1980s and 1990s is the degree to which academic casualization has increasingly closed the profession to persons who rely on waged work to live—and replaced them with persons for whom teaching figures as a secondary income. If it typically requires family support to become a teacher, how do factors such as class and the racialized wealth gap affect the composition of the professoriat? Today's graduate employee unionists are at least half women, and they understand that casualization is a feminist issue. The recent Coalition of Graduate Employee Unions' "Casual Nation" report (2000) headlines the fact that women take about 40 percent of the doctorates but represent about 58 percent of the full-time temporary instructors and only 25 percent of senior professors. There is a sharp generational break: women who joined the faculty from 1985 to 1992 were much less likely to join the faculty as members of the ladder ranks than women

7. Russian-born American anarchist and writer (1869–1940); in 1917 she published an essay titled "Prisons: A Social Crime and Failure."

who joined the faculty in earlier cohorts. Despite a plentiful "surplus" of women holding the doctorate, junior faculty women are substantially more likely to work in poorer-paying and less-satisfying sectors of higher education than junior faculty men. The NSOPF "New Entrants" analysis shows that fewer than half of the women who began full-time work from 1985 to 1992 held the Ph.D.: women were about as likely to hold the M.A. (44.2 percent) as the Ph.D. (48.4 percent), whereas male "new entrants" overwhelmingly hold the Ph.D (71.0 percent).[8] The only fields in which women have achieved near parity in numbers with male faculty in the upper ranks are the most ill-paid fields, primarily language, literature, and writing instruction. The sectors in which women outnumber men in the academy are uniformly the worst paid, frequently involving lessened autonomy (as in writing instruction, where the largely female staff is generally not rewarded for research, usually excluded from governance and even union representation, and frequently barred even from such basic expressions of academic discretion as choosing course texts, syllabi, requirements, and pedagogy).

4. Late capitalism[9] doesn't just happen to the university; the university makes late capitalism happen. The flexible faculty are just one dimension of an informationalized higher ed—the transformation of the university into an efficient and thoroughly accountable environment through which streaming education can be made available in the way that information is delivered: just in time, on demand, in spasms synchronized to the work rhythm of student labor on the shop floor. The university has not only casualized its own labor force: it operates as a kind of fusion reactor for casualization more generally, directly serving the casual economy by supplying it with flexible student labor (which is to say: by providing flex workers with the identity of "student"), normalizing and generalizing the experience of casual work. The casualization of the higher education teacher has been accompanied by the wholesale reinventing of what it means to be an undergraduate: the identity of "student" has been disarticulated from the concept and possibility of leisure and vigorously rearticulated to contingent labor. In the twenty-first century, "being a student" names a way of work. The graduate employee understands that the gen-x[1] structure of feeling proceeds from the generational register of the economic order: insofar as casualization colonizes the experience and possibilities of "youth," cheerfully extending the term of youth and youthful "enjoyment" into the fourth decade of life—because youth now delimits a term of availability for super-exploitation.

* * *

8. M. J. Finkelstein, R. Seal, and J. H. Schuster, "New Entrants to the Full-Time Faculty of Higher Education Institutions" (Washington, D.C.: National Center for Education Statistics, 1998), 98–252 [Bousquet's note].

9. A Marxist term for capitalism after World War II, characterized by a shift from industrial production to mass consumption, globalized markets, and commodified information, consonant with neoliberalism; see, e.g., Fredric Jameson's *Postmodernism, or the Cultural Logic of Late Capitalism* (1991).

1. Generation X, the American cohort born between, roughly, the mid-1960s and 1980.

Moving from the discourse of "I feel your pain" to the collective recognition that our problems are mutual ultimately means acknowledging the intellectual and political leadership of the graduate employee union movement. Acting at the level of system means acting as graduate employees have acted, writing their knowledge into law and policy at every level of social organization, from the campus and community to state and federal statute, developing linkages to labor on a global scale. This means that everyone else implicated in the system of academic work will benefit from "acting with" the graduate employee (rather than "sounding like" them while "acting with" administration). Against the dominative totality of higher ed marketization—the flexible dictatorship of university administration—the possibility of antagonism at the same level of systemic totality is emergent in the GEU movement. Acting with the GEU movement, we are privileging the perspective of the graduate employee (as incipient degree holder) and doing so in the belief that accomplishing the particular agenda of the graduate employee will address the problems that are general to the system (but feel "specific" to other locations). That is, in re-creating jobs out of the piecework done by the graduate employees and other incipient degree holders, we address with one stroke the problems experienced by everyone else: tenure-stream faculty benefit because eliminating cheap teaching raises the price of experienced teaching and reinstalls the value of research in pedagogy; undergraduates benefit by receiving experienced, secure faculty (who "do knowledge" rather than "provide information") in the first two years, when they are most vulnerable; other movement activists benefit from a more diverse and de-marketized professoriat; the public, taxpayers, and employers receive a more literate, accomplished, thoughtful, and civically oriented citizenry—the embodied and political subjects of education, not the reactive "meatware" of information capitalism. We of the academic system would in a way, then, be submitting to a "dictatorship of the flexible," saying instead of "I feel your pain" something more like this: "Oh heck, now I realize that your problems are intimately related to my own difficulties. Solving your problem *is* solving my problem." This is an accession to the moral and political imperative of the incipient degree holders, acknowledging their marginality as a constitutive exterior, where actions have effects immanent throughout the system as a whole. And to the extent that the system of academic labor is a system interlocking in a plane with other systems, it seems plausible that a dictatorship of the knowledge proletariat could be articulated to the proletarian struggles elaborating themselves elsewhere. (The GEU movement, for instance, might be the basis for an important evolution in the undergraduate movement against sweatshops, which in my view would acquire even greater vitality by becoming conscious of the North American student's own status as flexible labor.) The articulation of the GEU movement to other proletarian movements will necessarily take place on the equal relation of the shared consciousness of work rather than the hierarchical relation of expertise. But the articulation of the GEU movement within "the knowledge class" itself *will* take place in a hierarchical relation—a revived apprenticeship, if you will—except that this apprenticeship runs on the opposite trajectory: we can only have a workers' movement in the academy when the professoriat (and their unions and institutions) are willing to politically and intellectually indenture themselves to the graduate employee.

2002

MARK McGURL
b. 1966

Mark McGurl has defined the contemporary period in American literature as "the Program Era." From the time of the Romantic poets, such as WILLIAM WORDSWORTH, we have tended to think of literature as arising from solitary genius; but since World War II most writers in the United States have attended a creative writing program, and many teach in them. Some see this institutional setting as a constraint, thwarting originality, but McGurl argues that the expansion of the American university system for the most part has fostered good conditions for writers and precipitated a remarkable flourishing of fiction. Blending the systems theory of the German sociologist Niklas Luhmann with literary history, in "The Program Era: Pluralisms of Postwar American Fiction" (2005) McGurl examines how writing programs work through autopoiesis—that is, how they reflexively generate writing, often about writers and writing itself. The system cultivates modernist literary values and techniques in an era of mass media and technology, resulting in what he terms "technomodernism," and it also encourages "high cultural pluralism," valuing the diverse identities of individual writers.

Born in Connecticut, McGurl attended Phillips Exeter Academy and Harvard University (B.A., 1989). He then explored a career in literary journalism and publishing, working for the *New York Times* and *New York Review of Books* and doing freelance writing, including an essay on the ecologically oriented criticism of ANDREW ROSS in *Lingua franca* (1994). However, as he recounts in an interview, he decided that he was best suited to work as a literary scholar, so he entered the graduate program at Johns Hopkins University, where he studied with the New Historicist critic Walter Benn Michaels and the art historian Michael Fried, receiving his Ph.D. in 1998. He has taught at UCLA and, since 2011, Stanford University, where he is Albert Guérard Professor of Literature.

McGurl represents a generation of scholars who are reconsidering American literary history. During the 1980s and early '90s, when he started graduate school, the New Historicism, practiced by STEPHEN GREENBLATT, Michaels, and others, was a leading approach: it drew on MICHEL FOUCAULT's theories of the way that modern institutions, such as schools, hospitals, and the census bureau, perpetuate a culture of discipline and surveillance. New Historicists emphasized how texts, even if expressing progressive views, frequently played out "subversion and containment"—that is, a text might seem to dissent from and thus subvert capitalism, for example, but in actuality it was still a product of capitalism, did not alter the relations of power, and tacitly reinforced capitalism's disciplinary hold. In contrast, McGurl sees institutions more neutrally. Turning to Luhmann rather than Foucault, he explains how writing programs spur writing in a kind of feedback loop, or autopoiesis. Though bounded as a game might be, the system enables creativity. Put a lot of people in a workshop and some will write good stories and novels.

Like many influential critical insights, McGurl's starts with a simple observation that others seem to have missed or misinterpreted: perhaps the most significant development in contemporary American literature has been the rise of creative writing programs. The first such program was founded at the University of Iowa in 1936, and particularly from the 1960s onward, as U.S. universities expanded, these programs multiplied; their numbers climbed to more than 300 by 2000. Their establishment changed the way writers were trained: before World War II, most writers worked in journalism or other jobs, whereas by the latter part of the century, most had significant connections with university creative writing programs. This shift has prompted complaints that contemporary writing has become too routinized and that writers have only a small world to portray, as they have spent most of their time in academe.

McGurl provocatively turns the tables on this bias against creative writing in his essay "The Program Era," whose thesis he further elaborates in his book *The Program Era: Postwar Fiction and the Rise of Creative Writing* (2010), which won the Truman Capote Prize for Literary Criticism. In our selection, he surveys the historical facts of the modern American university system and the rise of creative writing in it. To counter negative views of these programs, he points out their overall excellence and the productivity of their participants. Driven by autopoiesis, the system encourages "portraits of the artist" and other self-representations that center on education. As modernist authors became a key part of the canon in American higher education through the mid- and late twentieth century, modernism became a dominant value of the system; the result, combined with awareness of contemporary mass media and technology, has been what McGurl calls technomodernism, a label that might describe the work of postmodern authors like Thomas Pynchon but also extends to more recent writers such as David Foster Wallace and Karen Tei Yamashita. A second and interrelated line of fiction falls under what McGurl calls "high cultural pluralism." The value of diversity, foregrounded by the postwar "multiversity," was internalized by fiction coming from the program, which stressed individuality not just in ethnicity and race but in region, class, and other factors. The lower-middle-class modernism evident in writers such as Raymond Carver and Joyce Carol Oates reflects the adoption of highbrow modernist modes by students who were outside the traditional elites and were welcomed into the postwar U.S. university education system.

In addition to defending creative writing, "The Program Era" revises the standard definition of the current period—as seen, for instance, in FREDRIC JAMESON's Marxist theory of postmodernism. For Jameson, post-1945 literature and other arts reflect the current mode of capitalism, which he identifies as consumer or postindustrial capitalism. McGurl does not necessarily disagree with this view, but he finds that the more specific institutional history of creative writing offers a better explanation of the tendencies of contemporary fiction. He turns to a sociology of the institution rather than to the macro history of capitalism.

The first decade of the twenty-first century saw the rise of new sociological approaches to literature in place of linguistic or other historical focuses, and McGurl forges a distinctive sociological approach. In his first book, *The Novel Art: Elevation of Fiction after Henry James* (2001), McGurl uses PIERRE BOURDIEU's concept of cultural capital to explain the embrace of elitist techniques in modernist fiction during the first half of the twentieth century—in effect, making the novel "high art." To explain the situation after World War II, he finds systems theory more relevant, as it illuminates how complex natural and institutional systems generate their effects. This version of the sociology of American literature differs from that of RICHARD OHMANN, perhaps the leading U.S. critic of the institution of literature, whose *English in America: A Radical View of the Profession* (1976) examines literary studies in terms not of literature per se but of the ways in which literary instruction supports the status quo and reinforces class differences. Ohmann has likewise looked at the institutions surrounding contemporary fiction in "The Shaping of the Canon: American Fiction, 1960–1975" (1983; see above), focusing particularly on publishing and reviewing and on the work done by agents, editors, advertisers, reviewers, and professors, who all contribute to produce a book. For Ohmann, fiction is heavily influenced by the professional-managerial class position of those who create it, as they elevate fiction that assumes their values, taste, and sensibility. In "The Program Era," McGurl sees fiction almost entirely in terms of its academic location, in a self-enclosed feedback loop.

"The Program Era" has drawn a great deal of response, both positive and negative, and almost immediately was regarded as a major contribution to the discussion.

One rebuttal pointed out that it was too limited in its account and in fact many writers worked independently of academe. Calling the division "MFA vs. NYC," the novelist Chad Harbach observed that there are actually two leagues of fiction writers, those who have M.F.A.s and earn their livelihood teaching, and those who live primarily in New York and earn their livelihood writing. The former favor short stories, the latter novels; the former lean toward complexity, the latter toward readability; the former are more oriented toward an academic audience, the latter toward a larger public; the former see books as a credential, the latter as a living.

Other critics have faulted the narrow focus of the systems framework, which sets to the side other sociological concerns, such as publishing, as well as historical forces like capitalism. In addition, it is not clear how McGurl's thesis applies to poetry, which forms a significant part of writing programs and has a markedly different social and professional position than fiction. Nonetheless, McGurl is acknowledged—notably by Jameson himself—to have proposed a new paradigm for considering contemporary literature, and his thesis has opened a new approach for research on the ways in which writing programs have influenced contemporary literature.

"The Program Era: Pluralisms of Postwar American Fiction" Keywords: Institutional Studies, Literary History, Modernity, The Novel, Postmodernity

From The Program Era: Pluralisms of Postwar American Fiction

It had to be U.

—Richard Powers,[1] *Galatea* 2.2 (1995)

1. Getting with the Program

The American writer's intimacy with the university in our time is not an entirely unprecedented phenomenon. If only as students, occasionally as teachers, writers have been spotted on campus before now. The gradual conjoining of the activities of literary production and teaching over the course of the postwar period is, however, in the sheer scale of the institutional program building upon which it has depended and in the striking reversal of attitudes that it suggests about as close to a genuine literary historical novelty as one could hope to see. Once perceived as the stuffy enemy of modernist innovation in the arts, the last place a self-respecting artist would want, or be welcomed, to ply his or her trade, the university has with the rise and spread of classroom instruction in creative writing—and with it the creative writing professorship and other forms of writer-in-residency—become perhaps the most important patron of artistically ambitious literary practice in the United States, the sine qua non of countless careers. "All this represents a very great change," wrote Alfred Kazin in the mid-1950s, already amazed by the transformation he was witnessing: "When I was in college in the 'thirties, it was still well understood that scholars were one class and writers quite another. They did not belong to the same order of mind, they

1. Celebrated American novelist (b. 1957); *Galatea 2.2* is a novel set in a university where a researcher is trying to develop artificial intelligence capable of passing an M.A. qualifying exam in English literature.

seemed quite antithetical in purpose and temperament, and at the very least, they needed different places to work in."[2]

Of course there were some obvious exceptions to Kazin's rule—most importantly the New Critics,[3] who had previously convened in the environs of Vanderbilt in the 1920s as the Fugitive poets and whose later promotion of the practice of close reading of literary texts in the classroom would harmonize conspicuously well with the obsessive concern for "craft" that began to define writing programs at roughly the same time.[4] The New Critics began as relatively marginal figures in academia, with low status even at places like Vanderbilt, but lived to see their ideas lodged at the core of American literary studies in the postwar period; in this they can be taken as emblematic of American writers more broadly, who, since the founding of the Iowa Writers' Workshop in the late 1930s, have gradually seen the "extramural" consciousness of their modernist predecessors turned inside out—or, rather, outside in. The handful of creative writing programs that existed in the 1940s had, by 1970, increased to forty-four in number. By 1980 there would be more than one hundred, and as of 2000 there were more than three hundred creative writing programs in the United States, all of them staffed by practicing writers, most of whom, by now, are themselves holders of an M.F.A. degree in creative writing.[5] You don't have to be a dogmatic historical materialist to believe that a transformation of the institutional context of literary production as fundamental as this one might matter to a reading of postwar American literature.

Indeed, one might imagine that the rise of the writing program would have already attracted considerable attention from literary scholars, who have after all been on hand to watch it occur at close range. But in fact—perhaps as a result of its occurring at too close range—it is only a small exaggeration to say that the rise of the creative writing program has been ignored in historicist studies of the postwar period. Discussion of the writer's relation to the university has instead largely been confined to the domain of literary journalism and to the question of whether the rise of the writing program has been good or bad for American writers.[6] Whether couched in populist

2. Alfred Kazin, *The Inmost Leaf: A Selection of Essays* (New York, 1956), p. 244 [McGurl's note; some of the author's notes are abridged, and some omitted]. Kazin (1915–1998), American literary critic and member of the group called the New York Intellectuals.

3. Group named and led by the poet and critic JOHN CROWE RANSOM, which included his onetime students CLEANTH BROOKS and Robert Penn Warren (1905–1989); they first gathered in the 1920s as the Fugitive poets at Vanderbilt University, celebrating the agrarian values of the U.S. South against those of the industrial North.

4. One of the original Fugitive-Agrarians, novelist Andrew Lytle, would teach fiction writing at Iowa for a time, where he was a mentor of his fellow southerner Flannery O'Connor [McGurl's note]. O'Connor (1925–1964), major American fiction writer.

5. These figures are reported in David Gershom Myers, *The Elephants Teach: Creative Writing since 1880* (Englewood Cliffs, N.J., 1996), p. 146. Figures from 2000 are gleaned from the Associated Writing Programs, *AWP Official Guide to Writing Programs*, 10th ed. (New York, 2002). As Myers notes, the formation of the AWP in 1967, coming some 80 years after the formation of the Modern Language Association, itself marks an important moment in the history of creative writing programs [McGurl's note].

6. Mainly focused on the six decades leading up to World War II, Myers's *The Elephants Teach* is to my knowledge the best account of the historical emergence of the ideas and institutions of creative writing instruction in the U.S. and has been of help in establishing the background of my project here. Some initial steps toward an analysis of the postwar writer's relation to the university are taken in *The American Writer and the University*, ed. Ben Siegel (Newark, N.J., 1989). A theoretically assertive account of the workshop is available in Donald Morton and Mas'ud Zavarzadeh, "The Cultural Politics of the Fiction Workshop," *Cultural Critique*, no. 11 (Winter 1988–89): 155–73, which argues that the writing program's commitment to realism betrays its efforts to "keep intact the legitimacy of bourgeois values" (p. 159). The weakness in this left-formalist argument is not in the claim that the writing program is a bourgeois enterprise, which

or elitist terms, the suspicion running throughout these discussions is that there may be something inherently wrong with artistic activity being, as critics ominously say, institutionalized in such a way. Published to considerable fanfare in *Harper's* magazine in 1989, Tom Wolfe's "manifesto" for a new social realism, "Stalking the Billion-Footed Beast," is perhaps the most notorious of these critiques, complaining of "writers in the university writing programs" who in "long, phenomenological discussions" have "decided that the act of writing words on a page" is the "real thing and the so-called real world of America" is the fiction.[7] In place of this effete and tedious navel-gazing, Wolfe would have writers return to the robust example of nineteenth-century naturalism, as in Zola,[8] where the practices of novel writing partially converged with those of investigative journalism.

Others such as John W. Aldridge[9] have given thumbs down to the writing program, not only for its removal of writers from the manifold stimulations of the real world, but for the damage it has done to the originality of the individual authorial voice. Demonstrating the continuing appeal of the romantic conception of the artist as an original genius, Aldridge blames "assembly-line" writing programs for producing a standardized aesthetic, a corporate literary style that makes a writer identifiable as, say, an Iowa writer. The claim here is that the collective pursuit of perfectly crafted, "workshopped" prose has the effect of eliminating the salutary unpredictability of the students in question, ironically reproducing the machine-made quality of formulaic genre fiction on another, slightly more elevated or rarefied cultural level. The result, according to Aldridge, is that products of the writing program become, not writers, but "clonal fabrications of writers" who can only be expected to produce "small, sleek, clonal fabrications of literature."[1]

A nervousness surrounding these issues is evident even in the official history of the illustrious program at Iowa, available on its website, whose rhetorical curlicues are a typical response to the simple but difficult questions that have haunted creative writing programs since their inception:

> Though we agree in part with the popular insistence that writing cannot be taught, we exist and proceed on the assumption that talent can be developed, and we see our possibilities and our limitations as a school in that light. If one can "learn" to play the violin or to paint, one can "learn" to write, though no processes of externally induced training can ensure that one will do it well. Accordingly, the fact that the Workshop can claim as alumni nationally and internationally prominent poets, novelists, and short story writers is, we believe, more the result of what they brought here than of what they gained from us. We continue to look for the most promising talent in the country, in our conviction that writing cannot be taught but that writers can be encouraged.[2]

---

it most certainly is, but in the assumption that antirealist fiction (hardly absent from the writing program establishment in any case) would necessarily be a nonbourgeois enterprise [McGurl's note].

7. Wolfe, "Stalking the Billion-Footed Beast: A Literary Manifesto for the New Social Novel," *Harper's Magazine* (Nov. 1989): 49 [McGurl's note]. Wolfe (b. 1931), American writer known for combining the techniques of journalism and fiction.

8. Émile Zola (1840–1902), French writer who pioneered "naturalism," a literary movement that combines realism with scientific determinism, so that characters are portrayed as determined by their social environment.

9. American literary critic (1922–2007).

1. John W. Aldridge, *Talents and Technicians: Literary Chic and the New Assembly-Line Fiction* (New York, 1992), p. 28 [McGurl's note].

2. https://writersworkshop.uiowa.edu/about/about-workshop/philosophy [McGurl's note, with URL updated].

Tilling the symbolic ground between teaching and development, teaching and encouragement, this cannily argued document manages on the one hand to pay respect to the "popular" idea of natural individual genius and to communicate a strong sense of Iowa's considerable historical importance and continuing prestige. The point here, indeed, is to make populism and elitism indistinguishable. The same sort of fusion is evident in the creative writer's distinct claim to prestige in the English departments to which creative writing programs tend to be attached; although typically somewhat undereducated, he or she may actually be known to a nonacademic readership. Combined with the spiritual privilege derived from the writer's intimate commerce with the Muse, this offsets to some degree the intramural dominance of Ph.D. scholars who largely run the place but who are famous, if at all, only to each other.

Writing programs: pro or con? There is nothing wrong with this debate, but surely it's time for the museless pedants to have their say. What is needed now, that is, are studies that take the rise and spread of the creative writing program not as an occasion for praise or lamentation but as an established fact in need of historical interpretation: how, why, and to what end has the writing program reorganized American literary production in the postwar period? How might it be brought to bear on a reading of the literature itself? Focusing on fiction at the expense of the equally interesting (and potentially interilluminating) cases of poetry and the other arts, this essay will take some modest steps toward answering these large questions. It will do so precisely by taking the two charges most frequently heard against program fiction in literary journalism—that it is self-involved, that it is unoriginal—as occasions for a nonpartisan examination of the reflexivity and systematicity of American fiction in the Program Era.[3] Unpacking, in turn, some of the contents of that well-travelled portmanteau *postmodernism*, this production will be described as being governed by the interaction of two aesthetic formations called, respectively, high cultural pluralism and technomodernism. Only in conclusion will we return to the important question of aesthetic value judgments, seeing if the studiously neutral scholarly account I will have begun to sketch here can be made to intersect meaningfully with a debate from which, until now, scholars have mostly absented themselves.

2. *In Studentdom*

It's hard to say when exactly the presence of creative writers on campus came to seem natural—assuming that it ever has. Certainly as late as the mid-1960s, by which time creative writing programs were beginning to multiply exponentially, the sense of strangeness hovering about this juxtaposition of scholars and writers had not yet diminished. This can be gauged from the prefatory "Cover-Letter to the Editors and Publisher" attached to the long, bizarre, comic novel *Giles Goat-Boy* (1966), where John Barth notes that "like most of our authors these days I support myself by preaching what I practice."[4]

* * *

3. McGurl is playing off the title of a major critical book on modernist writers, *The Pound Era* (1971), by Hugh Kenner; that era, according to Kenner, was the modernist period of the early 20th century, at whose center he placed Ezra Pound (1885–1972).

4. John Barth, *Giles Goat-Boy or, The Revised New Syllabus* (Garden City, N.Y., 1966), p. xviii; hereafter abbreviated *GGB* [McGurl's note]. Barth (b. 1930), American novelist.

John Barth began to write *Giles Goat-Boy* at Pennsylvania State University, a land-grant institution where, as he later explained, "in an English department of nearly one hundred members" he taught his "classes not far from an experimental nuclear reactor, a water tunnel for testing the hull forms of missile submarines, laboratories for ice-cream research and mushroom development, a lavishly produced football program . . . , a barn-size computer with elaborate cooling systems . . . and the literal and splendid barns of the animal husbandry departments."[5]

Massively infused with federal funding for the support of cold war weapons technology and other scientific research but still catering to a regional and state economy (and its large football fan base), the secular university has become, for Barth, comically expanded and diversified in its worldly pursuits, nothing like the pious gentleman's college of yore. In this Barth echoes what was no doubt the most influential and widely read account of higher educational institutions in the early sixties, Clark Kerr's *The Uses of the University* (1963), which proposed the neologism "multiversity" as a description of these institutions that are, as Kerr later reiterated, "pluralistic in several senses: in having several purposes, not one; in having several centers of power, not one; in serving several clienteles, not one." The multiversity, in short, "worship[s] no single God" and "constitute[s] no single, unified community."[6]

* * *

* * * Barth's disciplinary allegory works in both directions. If it reimagines the secular research university in terms of a spiritually elevated literary tradition, it also strongly associates the "preaching" and practice of literature in the university with the scientific research being conducted in the same institutional space. Clark Kerr had done the same when he had begun to rationalize the presence of creative writers and other artists on campus by linking them to scientists:

> Another field ready to bloom is that of the creative arts, hitherto the ugly ducklings or Cinderellas of the academic world. America is bursting with creativity in painting, music, literature, the theater with a vigor equaled in few other parts of the world today. . . . In the arts the universities have been more hospitable to the historian and the critic than to the creator; he has found his havens elsewhere. *Yet it is the creativity of science that has given science its prestige in the university.* Perhaps creativity will do the same again for the humanities, though . . . the tests of value are far less precise [than in the sciences].[7]

Updating the traditional term, Barth associates creative writing in the university not with the dusty workshop but with the modern cold war laboratory. Often labeled postmodernist, this sprawling enterprise would, I think, more helpfully be described as technomodernist. This term reasserts the

5. Barth, "Four Forewords: *Giles Goat-Boy*," *Further Fridays: Essays, Lectures, and Other Nonfiction, 1984–1994* (Boston, 1995), p. 269 [McGurl's note].
6. Kerr, *The Uses of the University* (Cambridge, Mass., 1972), p. 136 [McGurl's note]. Kerr (1911–2003), American economist who, as chancellor of the University of California at Berkeley (1952–58) and then president of the entire University of California system (1958–67), oversaw its massive expansion.
7. Kerr, *The Uses of the University*, pp. 112–13 [McGurl's note].

obvious continuity of much postwar American fiction with the modernist project of systematic experimentation with narrative form, even as it registers a growing acknowledgment of the "scandalous" continuity of the literary techne[8] (craft) with technology in the grosser sense—including, most importantly, mass media technology. Seen in the sickly light cast by the latter, modernist narrative becomes visible not as the antithesis of debased genre fiction but as a genre in its own right called literary fiction—which relativization does not, it should be noted, disable the distinction between high and low (one common account of what postmodernism entails) but situates it in a larger cultural industrial system.[9] The potential for such an acknowledgment of kinship between high literary techne and media technology was already latent in an earlier modernist fascination with technology explored by Hugh Kenner in *The Mechanic Muse* (1987) and in the high literary appropriation of low media one sees in John Dos Passos's *U.S.A.* trilogy (1930–36).[1] And while the term is most easily applied to those writers who have gained prominence by featuring techno-mediatic themes—that is, mostly white males like Barth, Thomas Pynchon, Don DeLillo, Robert Coover, Joseph McElroy, Richard Powers, and so on—experimental narratives like Samuel Delany's *Dhalgren* (1975) and Karen Tei Yamashita's[2] *Tropic of Orange* (1997), with their depictions of simultaneously ethnicized and media-saturated landscapes and their ethnically marked authorship, suggest a broader reach. The most literal instantiation of technomodernism, meanwhile, is found in the emergent field of electronic literature (including hypertext fictions like Shelley Jackson's[3] *Patchwork Girl* [1995]), strongly associated with Brown University and with the pedagogy of Coover. Remediating the values and practices of textual modernism (the fragmentation, difficulty, and general "literariness" still so abundant in Coover's own print productions), electronic literature replays the venerable modernism/mass culture dialectic in its status war with a nonliterary commercial variant, the video game.

* * *

3. *Autopoetics*

Giles Goat-Boy is only one of the odder of innumerable examples of a conspicuously flourishing genre in the postwar period, the campus novel. Typically written as satire, this genre usually registers not the metaphysics but, more humbly, the ironies of institutionalization. The proliferation of universities as settings for novels is what we might call a thematic symptom of a larger shift in the institutional arrangements of postwar literary production as such. The question is whether and to what degree all novels aspiring to

8. The Greek word (*technē*) that also means "art, skill."
9. Indeed the high/low distinction floats everywhere in this system, internally differentiating genre-fiction categories (science fiction, detective fiction, spy novels, fantasy novels, romances, and so on) and literary fiction alike along various scales, including those of greater or lesser consumability, originality, and/or self-conscious attention to craft [McGurl's note].
1. The novel sequence by the American novelist Dos Passos (1896–1970)—*The 42nd Parallel* (1930), *1919* (1932), and *The Big Money* (1936)—includes newspaper headlines and other popular forms.
2. Japanese American novelist (b. 1951). The "white males"—Barth, Pynchon (b. 1937), DeLillo (b. 1936), Coover (b. 1932), and McElroy (b. 1930)—are well-known literary novelists; Delany (b. 1942), an African American writer, is best known for his science fiction.
3. American writer (b. 1963).

the honorific status of literature must now be considered campus novels of a sort. Beyond the question of a novel's setting, for instance, how might we see the metafictional reflexivity of so much postwar fiction as being related to its production in and around a programmatically analytical and pedagogical environment? That, certainly, was Wolfe's implication in "Stalking the Billion-Footed Beast." Pursuing this line of inquiry, but setting aside Wolfe's negative evaluation of the phenomenon, we could read the reflexive prose experiments of academic creative writers such as Barth not as radically "deconstructive," as they sometimes are, but as radically conventional, as testaments to the continuing interest of literary forms as objects of a certain kind of professional research.

At least one contemporary strand of theoretical endeavor, systems theory, would insist that we understand reflexivity, not as an invitation to the abyss, but as a necessary component of any system's self-constitution, its "autopoiesis."[4] Self-reference in this view is perfectly routine, not impeding but participating in the making and organizing of things, including literature, whose construction of autonomous fictional realities serves, according to Niklas Luhmann, to make visible "the inevitability of order as such."[5] While reflexivity, as systems theory sees it, is the general condition of reflexive modernity—this is why Mark Seltzer can produce such a powerful diagnosis of what he calls the pathological public sphere from a reading of the lowly true crime genre—a particular aura of intellectual sophistication still attaches to overtly reflexive (that is, reflexively reflexive) projects, inviting critics to take them seriously as participating in the modernist/postmodernist high literary tradition.[6] Holding up a flattering mirror to the critic's own sophistication, these invitations are often accepted, but at the risk of the critic's experiencing his or her tiresome redundancy.

What this means is that, in the modernist tradition, the portrait of the artist is not only an important single book and an important genre but also an indication of the routine operations of literary modernism. For the modernist artist, that is, the reflexive production of the "modernist artist"—the job description itself—is a large part of the job. This reveals itself most obviously on the level of theme. Flouting the strictures against personality proposed by T. S. Eliot in "Tradition and the Individual Talent," works like Joyce's *Portrait of the Artist as a Young Man*, or Thomas Wolfe's *Look Homeward, Angel* (1929), or—looking ahead to a profusion of postwar examples—Maxine Hong Kingston's[7] *The Woman Warrior* (1976) stage the autobiographical drama of heroic self-authorization that accounts, in circular fashion, for its

4. This term was coined by the neurophysiologist Humberto Maturana to describe the self-making activities of the biological organism, which in his account lives in the solipsistic domain of its own structures of sense perception. See, for instance, Humberto R. Maturana and Francisco J. Varela, *The Tree of Knowledge: The Biological Roots of Human Understanding* (Boston, 1992). Systems theory borrows the term to describe the self-referential closure of all systems, biological, social, or otherwise [McGurl's note].

5. Niklas Luhmann, *Art as a Social System*, trans. Eva M. Knodt (Stanford, Calif., 2000), p. 149 [McGurl's note]. Luhmann (1927–1998), German sociologist and social theorist.

6. See Mark Seltzer, "The Crime System," *Critical Inquiry* 30 (Spring 2004): 557–83. Witness how, in Stephen King, a notorious desire to be thought literary coincides with the obsessive reflexivity of his bestselling horror oeuvre, where novelists are tortured in various ways by their popularity [McGurl's note]. Seltzer (b. 1951), American literary critic; King (b. 1947), bestselling American novelist.

7. Chinese American writer (b. 1940). Eliot (1888–1965), American-born British poet and critic; for "Tradition and the Individual Talent" (1919), see above. James Joyce (1882–1941), Irish writer; the A *Portrait of the Artist* (1914–15) was his first novel. Wolfe (1900–1938), American novelist.

own existence. Taking the suggestion of Barth's notionally computer-generated heroism in *Giles Goat-Boy,* we might understand these acts of authorial self-making neither—or not merely—as the feats of individuation they often represent themselves to be, nor as evidence of a postheroic, postmodern dispersal of subjectivity in and across the mediasphere, but as moments in the operation, the autopoiesis, of a larger system geared for the production of self-expressive originality. Taking advantage of a common Greek root in *autopoiesis* (self-making) and *poetics*, and forcing an obvious but helpful pun, we can call the routinely reflexive operations of literature *autopoetics*.

The ways and means of interwar literary modernism were modified in the postwar university, where it was codified in the pedagogy of New Criticism and then disseminated to a range of student populations previously under-represented in the writing profession. Among other effects, the institutionalization of modernism conspicuously strengthened and broadened its social functionality by coupling it with the educational system. Once the product of urban coteries, circulating in the tiny sphere of little magazines, now the texts of the modernist tradition reside helpfully on the syllabus as objects of study; its canon of literary practices, including a demand for self-conscious attention to technique, are pursued across the land in classes in creative writing; and its latter-day practitioners, sometimes called postmodernists, attend faculty meetings. For a small percentage of these practitioners—Kingston, Toni Morrison, Sandra Cisneros, Tim O'Brien,[8] and others—this coupling has created a significant student market for their wares. The rest exhibit the same more or less vexed relation to the publishing market as their modernist forebears, selling relatively modest numbers of books, not intentionally, exactly, but by design. Meanwhile the autopoetic thematization of authorship in the various projects of postwar literary fiction has continued unabated.

Consider the case of Philip Roth,[9] who between 1959 and 2005, even as he has frequently associated himself with colleges and universities (including, briefly, the Iowa Writers' Workshop) as an adjunct faculty member, has published some twenty-five novels and other books. In that period he has developed what it seems fair to call a singular authorial persona, where an unmistakably forceful and mostly invariant writing style—a "foaming confluence," as he puts it in *The Anatomy Lesson* (1983), of "diatribe, alibi, anecdote, confession, expostulation, promotion, pedagogy, philosophy, assault, apologia, denunciation"—is matched with an obsessive attachment to a small constellation of patently autobiographical themes: masculinity, family, Jewishness, and authorship itself.[1] Even beyond the explicitly interrelated Zuckerman novels,[2] the internal coherence and serial continuity of this autopoetic enterprise over so many years and so many novels is astonishing. Roth can seem by turns endlessly inventive in finding new ways to manipulate its few terms and yet abysmally unimaginative, a nasty narcissist lost in a highly polished hall of mirrors. The hall of mirrors effect is most forcefully introduced into the system by the Zuckerman novels, which provide a kind of

8. American novelist (b. 1946). MORRISON (b. 1931), African American novelist and essayist. Cisneros (b. 1954), Latina American novelist.
9. American novelist (b. 1933).
1. Philip Roth, *The Anatomy Lesson* (New York, 1983), p. 233; hereafter abbreviated *AL* [McGurl's note].
2. *The Ghost Writer* (1979), *Zuckerman Unbound* (1981), *The Anatomy Lesson*, the novella *The Prague Orgy* (1985), *The Counterlife* (1993), *American Pastoral* (1997), *I Married a Communist* (1998), *The Human Stain* (2000), and, after the publication of McGurl's article, *Exit Ghost* (2007).

running commentary on the life and career of a Jewish American novelist named Nathan Zuckerman, who, we are given to understand, has written his own versions of Roth's non-Zuckerman books, including most importantly the controversial National Book Award winner, *Goodbye, Columbus* (1959; Zuckerman's *Higher Education*) and the hugely best-selling *Portnoy's Complaint* (1969; renamed *Carnovsky*).

* * *

4. *High Cultural Pluralism*

Another way to get at the impressive typicality of the figure of Philip Roth would be to note how, seen against the forty-year backdrop of the field he has inhabited, he can seem to figure either as a culturally conservative white male writer, staunchly upholding high modernist literary values, or, as was more plainly the case in the 1960s, as a conspicuously "ethnic" writer ("The Jew You Can't Permit into the Parlor") who introduces cultural difference into that system. Braiding these roles together, he could be said to personify the aesthetic ideology of postwar literary fiction that I will call high cultural pluralism, which combines the routine operation of modernist autopoetics with a rhetorical performance of cultural group membership preeminently, though by no means exclusively, marked as ethnic. Paired with and against the complementary aesthetic of technomodernism, high cultural pluralism has governed the production of a very wide swath of postwar American fiction.

Cultural pluralism is of course a term historically associated with figures like Randolph Bourne, Alain Locke, and especially Horace Kallen, the American pragmatist philosopher and Zionist who began in the early twentieth century to transpose the philosophical pluralism of his teacher at Harvard, William James,[3] into the domain of cultural identity. Decades later, but with no mention of race or ethnicity, Kerr would also trace the intellectual origins of his conception of the multiversity back to James's philosophical pluralism. No wonder, then, that cultural pluralism and the multiversity have coupled so nicely. Both are driven by the logic of expansion and differentiation; the continual birth of new scientific subdisciplines is echoed, on the other side of campus, in the emergence of ethnic and women's and cultural studies and, within English departments, in the demarcated study of alternative literary canons.

High cultural pluralism enacts a layering of positively marked differences. In the modernist tradition, it understands its self-consciously "crafted" and intellectually substantial products as importantly distinct from mass culture or genre fiction, although in practice—for example, when Joyce Carol Oates[4] flirts with low genres, or when Roth produces a best seller on the titanic scale of *Portnoy's Complaint*, or when Morrison's *Beloved* (1987) is read by Oprah's book club[5]—this distinction is often blurred or intentionally put at

3. American philosopher and psychologist (1842–1910). Bourne (1886–1918), American critic and essayist. Locke (1886–1954), African American philosopher and critic. Kallen (1882–1974), American philosopher who coined the term "cultural pluralism" to replace the image of the American "melting pot."

4. Prolific American author in a wide range of styles and genres (b. 1938).

5. Influential book club featuring books chosen by the American entrepreneur and television personality Oprah Winfrey (b. 1954); originally a segment on her popular talk show, *The Oprah Winfrey Show* (1996–2010), and since 2012, somewhat more irregularly, promoted on social media platforms.

risk. The high cultural pluralist writer is additionally called upon to testify as a member of a hyphenated culture, synthesizing the particularity of the ethnic—or analogously marked—voice with the elevated idiom of literary modernism. Thus, while one path to literary distinction in the postwar period has been to assert the themes of technomodernism, another, though sometimes overlapping, path has been to forge a career in literary cultural pluralism, from the Jewish American writers who emerged in force in the early postwar period, such as Saul Bellow[6] and Roth; to the Native American renaissance that began with N. Scott Momaday's *House Made of Dawn* (1968) and continues through the novels of Leslie Marmon Silko, Louise Erdrich,[7] and many others; to the appearance of a growing number of celebrated Asian American writers from Kingston to Chang-Rae Lee;[8] to the distinctly theory-inflected field of Chicana/o literature, most prominently represented by Cisneros; to—and all along—the African American experience as it has been represented by writers working in the modernist tradition, from Ralph Ellison to Ishmael Reed[9] to Morrison. All of these writers are widely taught, and all were or remain significantly connected to universities.

Occurring in the broader context of the rise of mass higher education in the U.S., high cultural pluralism is the product of a certain institutional history, the most important feature of which has been the partially overlapping institutionalizations of elitist high modernism and cultural pluralism in university English departments of the postwar period. The result could be described either as a partially democratized modernism, which would emphasize the conditioning effect of a liberal-progressive (at least as compared to other American institutions) institutional context on an elitist aesthetic discourse, or, because universities are still a long way from offering unrestricted social access to the masses, as an elitist pluralism in which the lucky ones, among their other privileges, are taught to savor their own open-mindedness; or, yet again, it can be described simply as an enterprise that makes for unprecedented amounts of good reading. But let's save these judgments for later. For now we can simply observe that, associating the individual writer with a group from which he or she draws a claim to personal literary distinction, high cultural pluralism becomes one model, in the university environment, for the productive mediation of "group-think" and "individual genius."

Describing his own initiation into the modernist tradition at a largely Protestant liberal arts college in the early 1950s, Roth notes how at first it "did not dawn on" him that the "anecdotes and observations" of his boyhood in Newark, with which he entertained his highbrow friends, "might be made into literature. . . . Thomas Wolfe's exploitation of Asheville or Joyce's of Dublin suggested nothing." Instead the "stories I *wrote*, set absolutely nowhere, were mournful little things about sensitive children, sensitive adolescents, and sensitive young men crushed by coarse life. . . . The Jew was nowhere to be seen; there were no Jews in the stories, no Newark, and not a sign of comedy."[1] This would soon change. Like so many other writers of

6. Canadian-born American novelist (1915–2005).
7. Three Native American novelists: Momaday (b. 1934), Silko (b. 1948), and Erdrich (b. 1954).
8. Korean-born American novelist (b. 1965).
9. African American poet, playwright, and satirical novelist (b. 1938). Ellison (1914–1994), African American author of a single novel in his lifetime, the classic *Invisible Man* (1952).
1. Roth, *The Facts: A Novelist's Autobiography* (New York, 1988), pp. 59–60 [McGurl's note].

the postwar period, Roth would learn to join the modernist literary sophistication of his higher educational training with the ethnic experiential specificity of his upbringing, the late modernist version of writing what you know.

While the privileged marker of difference here is a racial or ethnic one, it would be a serious mistake to think that writers with no strong ethnic associations have been shut out of the high cultural pluralist enterprise; they are merely (and ironically) "minoritized" to a small degree. The exquisitely refined lower middle-class ordinariness of "K-mart Realism" seen in the work of Raymond Carver and his many students gets inflected by the "hidden injuries" of social class.[2] In Tim O'Brien's Veteran American fiction, the psychic wounds of war experience, marking their author as different, become foundational to a career. A form of analogy that generally hasn't worked, it should be noted in this context, is identification with the wounds of female experience alone, perhaps because, as detailed by Sandra Gilbert and Susan Gubar, the category of woman writer was precisely the category, associated with sentimental fiction, against which modernist fiction had originally defined itself.[3] What has worked, though, has been the form of alignment by analogy visible in the many writers, from Wallace Stegner to William Kennedy to Cormac McCarthy,[4] who have staged their careers in the continuing tradition of literary regionalism.

Regionalist fiction has always been cultural pluralist in the sense that it is a form of appreciation of diversity within a larger national whole. Here, for instance, Flannery O'Connor, a white Southerner returning from the workshop in Iowa to her home in Milledgeville, Georgia, associates her fiction with a cultural entity understood to be significantly different from American culture as such. Doing so, she achieves the logical equivalent of an ethnic difference within the system. In one of her essays, echoing Roth's assessment of his own earliest collegiate fiction, she notes disapprovingly how she "read some stories at one of the colleges not long ago . . . [and] with the exception of one story, they might all have originated in some synthetic place that could have been anywhere or nowhere."[5] In another essay she establishes the importance of Southern cultural difference for her fiction in strong, if negative, terms, noting how Southern writers

> are all known to be anguished. [And some editorialists] suggest that our anguish is a result of our isolation from the rest of the country. I feel that this would be news to most Southern writers. The anguish that most of us [feel] . . . has been caused not by the fact that the South is alienated from the rest of the country, but by the fact that it is not alienated enough, that every day we are getting more and more like the rest of the country, that we are being forced out not only of our many sins, but of our few virtues.[6]

2. An allusion to the celebrated study *The Hidden Injuries of Class* (1972) by Jonathan Cobb and Richard Sennett. Carver (1938–1988), major American short story writer.

3. See Sandra M. Gilbert and Susan Gubar, *No Man's Land: The Place of the Woman Writer in the Twentieth Century*, 3 vols. (New Haven, Conn., 1988–94) [McGurl's note]. Gilbert (b. 1936) and Gubar (b. 1944), American feminist literary critics.

4. The fiction of Stegner (1909–1993) is often set in the West; of Kennedy (b. 1928), in Albany, New York; and of McCarthy (b. 1933), in the Southwest.

5. O'Connor, "The Regional Writer," *Mystery and Manners: Occasional Prose*, ed. Sally and Robert Fitzgerald (New York, 1969), p. 56 [McGurl's note].

6. O'Connor, "The Fiction Writer and His Country," *Mystery and Manners*, pp. 28–29 [McGurl's note].

Written during the civil rights era, when the South was beginning to be pressed into conformity with federal law,[7] O'Connor's anguished appeal to and for the maintenance of difference would reinstall *southern culture* as one of the terms in the developing cultural pluralist aesthetic program of the 1960s, promoting southern writing as, in effect, a white minority discourse that resists assimilation into the American mainstream.[8]

At the very limits of the high cultural pluralist enterprise, where the space it inhabits begins to curve, one encounters technomodernism, its unmarked dialectical reversal. One sometimes hears of a postwar literary field divided cleanly into postmodernist and ethnic realist traditions. Apart from the descriptive weakness of this notion—as though there could be either a more "postmodernist" or a more "black" writer than Ishmael Reed—this way of conceiving things misses the profound complementarity of high cultural pluralism and technomodernism, each of which contains, in latent form, the other's primary term. If we apply interpretative pressure to overtly pluralist fiction to make visible the machinery involved in its production of difference, with overtly machinic technomodernism we can apply it in the opposite direction. Doing so, we see how even the whitest-seeming technomodernism can function as a discourse of difference, producing a symbolic placeholder for a paradoxically nonethnic ethnicity that might as well be called (with apologies to John Guillory) "technicity."[9] Put baldly, what Roth knows about Jewishness, and Morrison knows about blackness, writers like Powers, DeLillo, and Pynchon know about the second law of thermodynamics, cybernetic causality, communications and media theory, and the like, and it is on that basis that they, too, are put on the syllabus. That technicity, no less than ethnicity, might be imagined to be lodged in the body is suggested by Pynchon's intensely collegiate, occasionally even sophomoric *Gravity's Rainbow* (1973), where it is the distinction of the character Tyrone Slothrop, who imagines inscribing his name on a missile, to become sexually aroused at the sites of future rocket blasts. Registering the dialectical interpenetration of high cultural pluralism and technomodernism in this way, we still need to locate these inheritors of the modernist tradition in relation to the broader institutional structures of the multiversity that has become its primary institutional patron.

* * *

6. *Systematic Excellence*

What is creative writing to the university? Inheritor of the New Critical positioning of aesthetic value as something that might be produced, as well as appreciated, in an academic environment, creative writing is an odd but, to all appearances, healthy duck. Unlike recent literary scholarship, which, in rekindling the eagerly fact-gathering historicism of an earlier era, has swerved

7. "The Regional Writer" was originally published in 1963; "The Fiction Writer and His Country," in 1957.

8. See my fuller discussion of this issue in McGurl, "Faulkner's Ambit: Modernism, Regionalism, and the Location of Cultural Capital," *The Novel Art: Elevations of American Fiction after Henry James* (Princeton, N.J., 2001), pp. 135–57 [McGurl's note].

9. For Guillory, "technicity" is a linguistic phenomenon arising from intellectual specialization. See John Guillory, "The Memo and Modernity," *Critical Inquiry* 31 (Autumn 2004): 130. [McGurl's note]. Guillory (b. 1952), American literary theorist.

at least part of the way back into sync with the scientism of its wider institutional environment, creative writing might seem to have no ties at all to the pursuit of positive knowledge. It is, rather, an exercise in subjectivity. Symptomatically, the very genre that would seem to bind the arts and sciences at the level of theme, science fiction, is only minimally represented in the creative writing program establishment. Privileging ideas and adventures over disciplined elevations of literary form, this genre is often brainy but is only rarely considered literary. Furthermore, commercially successful writers like Stephenson[1] have little financial incentive to seek the patronage (that is, don the shackles) of the university. What role, then, is the creative writer playing there?

One way to answer this question is, first, to ask another question: If the modern university is an assemblage of centrifugal pluralisms—of splintered knowledges, divergent research agendas, and multiplying bureaucratic expressions of cultural and other forms of difference—how does the system hold together? Once it was supposed to be the domain of "culture," the quasi-sacred arts, which offered the secular institution an avenue back to the unity of specialized knowledges in God, but no longer. Nor has a unity founded in national purpose, expressed in the intellectual exploration of a national culture, been the prize possession of the American university, even during the cold war. The typically strong regional and state affiliations of American higher educational institutions—the U.S. does not even have a national university—and their tendency to oppositional liberal intellectualism have meant that its most impressive contributions to the nation-qua-nation have taken the form of technical assistance. (That assistance has of course been massive and very well paid.) In his compellingly bleak and extremist analysis of the situation, *The University in Ruins*, Bill Readings suggests that the new God of the university is "excellence":

> Generally, we hear a lot of talk from University administrators about excellence, because it has become the unifying principle of the contemporary University. C. P. Snow's "Two Cultures" have become "Two Excellences," the humanistic and the scientific. As an integrating principle, excellence has the singular advantage of being entirely meaningless, or to put it more precisely, non-referential. . . . Today, all departments of the University can be urged to strive for excellence, since the general applicability of the notion is in direct relation to its emptiness.[2]

The University Readings describes is one that has begun to behave like a corporation, integrating new management techniques and market valuations into its wholly self-referential, self-reproducing practices. In this scheme, excellence is the "integrating principle that allows 'diversity' (the other watchword of the University prospectus) to be tolerated without threatening the unity of the system." A "unit of value entirely internal" to that system, marking "nothing more than the moment of technology's self-reflection,"

1. Neal Stephenson (b. 1959), American writer best known for his science fiction.
2. Bill Readings, *The University in Ruins* (Cambridge, 1996), pp. 22–23 [McGurl's note]. Readings (1960–1994), British literary critic. The British scientist and novelist Snow (1905–1980) argued in his 1956 essay (expanded in 1959 as *The Two Cultures and the Scientific Revolution*) that the modern university had developed "two cultures," each ignorant and sometimes scornful of the other: that of the sciences and that of the humanities.

it is a sign, above all, of bureaucratic efficiency, the smooth running of the pluralist machine.[3]

Readings is right to see Excellence as the new God of the university and as a marker of institutional self-reflection, but crucially wrong, I think, in seeing it as a measure of bureaucratic efficiency alone. For one thing, as his own documentation shows, the rhetoric of excellence in the university tends to appear in contexts where what is at issue is competition—say, between one funding application and another—or reputation, as in the hierarchically arranged schools in the *U.S. News and World Report* rankings. If this is not yet "referential" to something wholly outside the educational system itself, it is nonetheless profoundly and importantly relational, a measure of relative "distinction" that, among other effects, cashes out in the workplace as the relative value of a degree from a given institution. In the early twentieth century Thorstein Veblen had a lot to say about the orientation of higher education toward business interests that echoes even now in Readings's account of the university in ruins; but Veblen, even more importantly, drew our attention to the excessive symbolic activity (that is, showing off) entailed in the creation and maintenance of such invidious distinctions.[4] Knowing this we should be on guard against assuming that appeals to excellence are, as Readings claims, a matter only of technocratic efficiency.

On the contrary, keying off his observation that the university increasingly functions as an "autonomous system" with little direct involvement in extracurricular agendas, we might say that the "excellence" of the university is an index not of its functional efficiency but of its more or less impressive capacity to waste. *Excellence* in this view is a primarily aesthetic term, the guise in which judgments of beauty-as-superiority reappear in an otherwise efficiency-oriented university environment. Readings is wrong, therefore, to say that the disappearance of a referential appeal to national culture has occasioned the "ruin" of the traditional university in our time, at least in the United States. Indeed, insofar as American culture has become a corporate culture, the rhetoric of excellence could be understood as a deep expression of that national culture and seems for now to be holding educational institutions together quite well.

It is safe to say, then, that creative writing in the university will exist as long as it seems simply too excellent to resist. The ideologues of science can make no effective arguments against this excellence, a form of beauty they worship every bit as fervently and irrationally as do the arts. Still less can academic administrators afford to be insensitive to the beauty of excellence; they often must judge the value of highly specialized research at second hand by measuring the evidence of its relative prestige. Not only this, but an impressive creative writing program can be had for what amounts, as against particle accelerators and the like, to chump change, much of which is returned (as with master's programs in general) in the form of healthy tuition payments. Thus, while academic creative writers have often perceived themselves as outsiders to the institution that houses them, it is not hard to

3. Readings, "For a Heteronomous Cultural Politics: The University, Culture, and the State," *Oxford Literary Review* 15, nos. 1–2 (1993): 168 [McGurl's note].

4. The relevant texts are Thorstein Veblen, *The Higher Learning in America: A Memorandum on the Conduct of University by Business Men* (1918; New York, 1992) and *The Theory of the Leisure Class* (1899; New York, 1994) [McGurl's note]. Veblen (1857–1929), American economist and pioneering sociologist.

enumerate their uses beyond the obvious one of teaching students something about writing. Inwardly, their job as teachers is to stand as inspiring exemplars of the unalienated laborer. In this sense, every artist on campus is half a performance artist; making his name, doing her job, owning the product of his or her labor of "self-expression," the artist or writer-in-residence is in a sense the purest version of the kind of worker, the professional, that so many college students are preparing themselves to be.[5] Alternatively, but relatedly, the artist can be seen as offering a form of educational therapy to some of these students, the "creative types," in advance of their lifelong capture by the usual cubicle. Outwardly the task of the academic creative writer is to produce, in his or her writings, unconscious allegories of institutional quality, aesthetically pure because luxuriously useless. More simply, they contribute a certain form of prestige to the university's overall portfolio of cultural capital, adding their bit to the market value of the degrees it confers. In this role they are somewhat like varsity athletes, but whereas varsity athletics typically symbolizes the excellence of competitive teamwork, creative writing and the other arts testify to the institution's systematic hospitality to the excellence of individual self-expression.

And isn't postwar American fiction, after all, unprecedented in its excellence? If I could, I would ask this concluding question with two voices in counterpoint, and only one of them sarcastic. The conservative modernism of T. S. Eliot and his ilk has ingrained in us the notion that art never improves, and judgments of postwar American literature, including critiques of the writing program, habitually see it in sad decline from the heroic heights of the as-yet-unprogrammed interwar modernist era. But perhaps, in the interest of dislodging some tedious prejudices, and for love of the educational system that has made most of us what we are, or maybe just for the fun of it, it's time to resist this notion.

One way to do so would be to convert historical materialism[6] into a mode of aesthetic judgment, putting literary production in line with other human enterprises, such as technology and sports, where few would deny that systematic investments of capital over time have produced a continual elevation of performance. Granted there is no way, these days, to engage in strenuous aesthetic appreciation as a literary scholar without sounding goofily anachronistic, so call the effort what you will. Call it a strategic triumphalism. Owing to the tremendous expansion of the literary talent pool coincident to the advent of mass higher education; and to the wide distribution, therein, of elevated literary ambitions; and to cultivation in these newly vocal, vainglorious masses of the habits of self-conscious attention to craft through which these ambitions might plausibly be realized; is it not true that owing to the organized efforts of the program, owing to the simple fact of our trying harder than ever before, there has been a system-wide rise in the excellence of American literature in the postwar period?

5. A few of these students, of course, will become professional writers, the creative writing instructors of tomorrow. Modeling unalienated labor, the function of creative writing seems continuous, in some ways, with its proletarianized alter ego, composition, which when taught on the influential Peter Elbow model is also seen as an exercise in autonomy, of "tak[ing] charge of yourself as you write" (Peter Elbow, *Writing with Power: Techniques for Mastering the Writing Process* [New York, 1981], p. 8). It is however possible to see a gulf between the two disciplines, the first emphasizing open-ended self-creation, the second a process of self-disciplining more immediately useful in the workplace [McGurl's note].

6. Mode of analysis developed by Karl Marx in which society is viewed as determined by economic forces.

Granted, we can only measure literary excellence on our own terms, and the task of elevating individual authors high above their numerous accomplished peers has become increasingly difficult. This may have produced, as with the disappearance of the .400 hitter in professional baseball, a kind of optical illusion of encroaching mediocrity; being the dominant figure in Shakespeare's or even Pound's time was, by comparison to today, as easy as cake.[7] But seriously, laying aside our anachronistic prejudices for the One over the Many Ones, moving our minds from the Pound Era into the Program Era, do we not bear daily witness to a surfeit of literary excellence, an embarrassment of riches? Is there not more excellent fiction being produced now than anyone (especially considering the excellence of television) has time to read?

What kind of traitor to the mission of mass higher education would you have to be to think otherwise?

2005

7. See Stephen Jay Gould, *Full House: The Spread of Excellence from Plato to Darwin* (New York, 1996). Granted, literature has nothing as convenient as baseball's numerical batting average to measure "excellence," the very definition of which, in literature, is subject to dispute [McGurl's note]. The last major league baseball player to hit over .400 for the season was Ted Williams (.406) in 1941.

STEPHEN BEST b. 1969 / SHARON MARCUS b. 1966

Most literary critics do a form of "reading." However, much debate centers on what kind of reading they choose to do and how they characterize it. From the 1940s through the 1970s, the New Critics, such as JOHN CROWE RANSOM and CLEANTH BROOKS, advocated "close reading" of the language and form of literary texts over historical or other approaches. From the 1960s through the 1990s, critics shifted to reading from specific theoretical perspectives, conducting Marxist, feminist, psychoanalytic, and other kinds of readings to expose the linguistic, political, or psychological meaning underlying texts. This general practice has been called "symptomatic reading" because it looks at the statements in texts as symptoms of underlying causes—for instance, the unconscious in FREDRIC JAMESON's landmark book *The Political Unconscious* (1981)—making it the critic's task to bring those hidden meanings to light. In "Surface Reading: An Introduction" (2009), from which we take our selection, Stephen Best and Sharon Marcus declare that we have overemphasized symptomatic reading and propose that we should attend to texts' manifest meaning. Their call has galvanized a great deal of controversy, in part because it has been taken to prescribe the end of theory.

Attending graduate school in the late 1980s and early 1990s, Best and Marcus entered literary studies after major theoretical movements such as deconstruction, Marxism, and feminism had won central place in the field. Though trained in theory, they both gravitated toward literary and cultural history, Best focusing on law and African American literature and history, and Marcus on nineteenth-century British and French literature and culture. Early in their careers they also worked for several years as colleagues at the University of California at Berkeley, and their collaboration on "Surface Reading" is an outgrowth of that period. Best attended

Williams College (B.A., 1989) and the University of Pennsylvania (M.A., 1992; Ph.D., 1997), and he has taught at Berkeley since 1997. His book *The Fugitive's Properties: Law and the Poetics of Possession* (2004) elaborates the legal context of slavery, and he is on the editorial board of *Representations*, a major critical journal affiliated with Berkeley that published "Surface Reading."

Marcus was born in 1966 in Queens, New York, and attended Brown University (B.A., 1986) and Johns Hopkins University (Ph.D., 1995). She first taught at Berkeley (1994–2003), moving in 2003 to Columbia University, where in 2008 she became Orlando Harriman Professor of English and Comparative Literature. She is also the co-founder and editor of *Public Books*, an online literary review. Her first book, *Apartment Stories: City and Home in Nineteenth-Century Paris and London* (1999), is a historical study of buildings, architecture, and urban planning in England and France, examining how they appear in the novel and how they revise our notion of domestic space. Her next book, *Between Women: Friendship, Desire, and Marriage in Victorian England* (2007), conducts a similarly erudite historical investigation of the relations that women had in the era—often loving and sometimes sexual but usually not secret or hidden for the critic to detect and uncover. In one chapter, she sets out her idea of "just reading," which presages "surface reading": it emphasizes the manifest rather than allegorical meaning of texts (their meaning when they are "just read"), in contrast with Jameson's insistence on looking to the unconscious.

Symptomatic reading reflects a modern stance that the French philosopher Paul Ricoeur termed "the hermeneutics of suspicion." According to Ricoeur, beginning in the late nineteenth and early twentieth century with NIETZSCHE, MARX, and FREUD, many modern thinkers start with a mistrust of the conventional bases of language, the concept of truth itself, society, and the psyche. The hermeneutics of suspicion runs through much contemporary literary theory. For instance, MICHEL FOUCAULT argues that power and discipline control society without our conscious choice; PAUL DE MAN finds that language deconstructs efforts to discern a stable meaning, requiring the critic to uncover the "mystifications" of meaning; and Jameson sees modern culture as expressing capitalist ideology. While the New Historicists, led by STEPHEN GREENBLATT, showed a renewed interest in history beginning in the 1980s, they adopted poststructuralist ideas of textuality, and one of their common moves was to reveal how texts express "subversion and containment"—that is, even if a text purports to criticize or subvert dominant power, it is contained by power. In other words, they continued the hermeneutics of suspicion, applying it to literary texts that claimed to be radical and finding the opposite.

By the 1990s a number of critics began casting doubt on poststructuralist theory, some turning "against theory," some embracing the more literary modes of personal or autobiographical criticism, and some urging a less obscure and more accessible criticism. Questions were raised even among influential critics associated with theoretical critique. The queer theorist EVE KOSOFSKY SEDGWICK speculated that a good deal of theory veered toward "paranoid reading," assuming a kind of conspiracy underlying texts, and she called for a more recuperative stance of "reparative reading." The sociologist of science BRUNO LATOUR crystallized reservations about the hermeneutics of suspicion in "Why Has Critique Run Out of Steam? From Matters of Fact to Matters of Concern" (2003, 2004; see above), contending that we have put too much stress on a negative critical perspective at the expense of any positive value. He argues that while theory has debunked the idea of objective truth, it does not follow that no way exists to ascertain relative truths—for example, about issues like climate change.

"Surface Reading" calls for a nonparanoid, more constructive sense of interpretation. The title of Marcus's *Between Women*, in which she proposes "just reading," plays on the title of Sedgwick's *Between Men: English Literature and Male Homosocial Desire* (1985), a pioneering work of gay and lesbian theory that uncovered in many texts a latent homosociality among the male characters. Marcus tacitly pays homage to Sedgwick but shifts ground, arguing that the relationships between women were manifest rather than latent or hidden. In fact, part of her feminist argument is that they did not need to be hidden, because women's relationships were generally not valued; the task of interpretation is thus to bring texts' manifest meaning to the fore. As a formulation from our selection puts it, we should look at rather than see through texts.

Beyond their own practices, in "Surface Reading: An Introduction" Best and Marcus survey a number of other critics and find several allies in the turn to this new mode of reading. Indeed, the critics included in the special issue that the essay prefaces variously advocate a renewed poetics or "new formalism," narratology, the history of the book, and other material textual approaches. Another approach in the background is "distant reading," promoted by FRANCO MORETTI: that is, looking at large numbers of texts through quantitative and other means. While Moretti focuses on the evolution of the novel, many who work under the rubric of digital humanities also tend toward surface rather than close or symptomatic reading (for example, N. KATHERINE HAYLES). One aspect of the surface reading movement might be generational, as our selection asserts, but in a subsequent interview Marcus qualified this view, noting that the turn toward the surface does not necessarily track along lines of age. Moretti, for instance, is of an earlier generation but has energetically pioneered new approaches using statistical modeling.

At first glance, "Surface Reading" might seem to be "against theory," and that is how a number of respondents have taken it. Yet it does not renounce theory for the more concrete realm of history; rather, it tempers some of the assertions made about the political effect of criticism. A Marxist reading, or a feminist reading, or a Foucauldian reading typically is framed as an attack on hierarchy, power, and normative society, and theorists often claim to "make an intervention," suggesting that their work produces a political change. In doing so, they are positioning themselves at the end of a long line of thinking about the relation of literature and society, stretching from PERCY BYSSHE SHELLEY, who deemed poets the "unacknowledged legislators" of society, to the New York Intellectuals of the mid-twentieth century, who believed, in LIONEL TRILLING's words, that criticism has an "adversarial" relation to culture. Best and Marcus call for a more measured sense of the actual political effects of criticism, which are often very small, deflating the notion of the critic as an oppositional hero that seemed to hold sway in the heyday of theory during the closing decades of the twentieth century.

Because of its political reservations, "Surface Reading" has drawn rebuttals from critics on the left, who maintain the importance of symptomatic reading and charge that "surface reading" expresses a kind of resignation to the corporatized university. The essay has incited some Victorianists to form the V21 Collective (seeking to revitalize Victorian studies for the twenty-first century), whose manifesto attacks the "accumulation of mere information" through surface approaches and reasserts the need for speculative methods. More sympathetic critics draw on Best and Marcus's diagnosis to argue for the renewed use of description in criticism, in particular as it contributes to a "new sociology" of literature. Others see their diagnosis as a defense of formalist methods and literature against theory. Overall, "Surface Reading" takes stock of the possibilities of criticism in its moment, as well as auguring a shift to "surface" methods.

"Surface Reading: An Introduction" Keywords: Defense of Criticism, Hermeneutics, Interpretation Theory, Marxism, Psychoanalysis

From Surface Reading: An Introduction

Reading "The Way We Read Now"

The title of this special issue[1] raises many questions. To begin with, who are "we"? Although *Representations* is a multidisciplinary journal, this issue's contributors and editors constitute a relatively homogeneous group of scholars who received doctoral degrees in either English or comparative literature after 1983. Our shared training delimits what we mean and don't mean by the term "read." As literary critics, we were trained to equate reading with interpretation: with assigning a meaning to a text or set of texts. As scholars formed in the era of interdisciplinarity, we take for granted that the texts we read and interpret include canonical and non-canonical literary works. We also feel licensed to study objects other than literary ones, using paradigms drawn from anthropology, history, and political theory, which themselves borrowed from literary criticism an emphasis on close reading and interpretation after the linguistic turn of the 1970s.

One factor enabling exchanges between disciplines in the 1970s and 1980s was the acceptance of psychoanalysis and Marxism as metalanguages. It was not just any idea of interpretation that circulated among the disciplines, but a specific type that took meaning to be hidden, repressed, deep, and in need of detection and disclosure by an interpreter. This "way" of interpreting went by the name of "symptomatic reading."[2] We were trained in symptomatic reading, became attached to the power it gave to the act of interpreting, and find it hard to let go of the belief that texts and their readers have an unconscious.

So much for the way we read. What about "now"? In the last decade or so, we have been drawn to modes of reading that attend to the surfaces of texts rather than plumb their depths. Perhaps this is because, at the end of the first decade of the twenty-first century, so much seems to be on the surface. "If everything were transparent, then no ideology would be possible, and no domination either," wrote Fredric Jameson in 1981, explaining why interpretation could never operate on the assumption that "the text means just what it says."[3] The assumption that domination can only do its work when veiled, which may once have sounded almost paranoid, now has a nostalgic, even utopian ring to it. Those of us who cut our intellectual teeth on deconstruction, ideology critique, and the hermeneutics of suspicion[4] have often found those demystifying protocols superfluous in an era when images of torture at Abu Ghraib and elsewhere were immediately circulated on the internet; the real-time coverage of Hurricane Katrina[5] showed in ways that

1. This essay originally introduced *The Way We Read Now*, a special issue of the journal *Representations* (no. 108 [2009]) that contained essays by the literary critics Anne Anlin Cheng, Margaret Cohen, Mary Thomas Crane, Christopher Nealon, and Leah Price, with an afterword by Emily Apter and Elaine Freedgood [editor's note; except as indicated, all notes are Best and Marcus's—some have been edited and some omitted].
2. Any mode of interpretation according to which texts exhibit symptoms stemming from unconscious motivations that the analyst seeks to uncover (an extension of the psychoanalytic terms of SIGMUND FREUD) [editor's note].
3. Fredric Jameson, *The Political Unconscious: Narrative as a Socially Symbolic Act* (Ithaca, 1981), 61. Page references in the text. [JAMESON (b. 1934), American Marxist literary theorist—editor's note.]
4. Phrase coined by the French philosopher Paul Ricoeur (1913–2005) to characterize the stance of suspicion in the major 19th- and early 20th-century theorists FRIEDRICH NIETZSCHE, KARL MARX, and Freud [editor's note].
5. A major storm in August 2005 that devastated the Gulf Coast and caused massive flooding in New Orleans after the levees gave way; more than 1,000 died, and the slow federal response led to widespread criticism of President George W. Bush (b. 1946; president 2001–09). The Bush

required little explication the state's abandonment of its African American citizens; and many people instantly recognized as lies political statements such as "mission accomplished."[6] Eight years of the Bush regime may have hammered home the point that not all situations require the subtle ingenuity associated with symptomatic reading, and they may also have inspired us to imagine that alongside nascent fascism there might be better ways of thinking and being simply there for the taking, in both the past and the present. We find ourselves the heirs of Michel Foucault,[7] skeptical about the very possibility of radical freedom and dubious that literature or its criticism can explain our oppression or provide the keys to our liberation. Where it had become common for literary scholars to equate their work with political activism, the disasters and triumphs of the last decade have shown that literary criticism alone is not sufficient to effect change. This in turn raises the question of why literary criticism matters if it is not political activism by another name, a question to which we return in the last section of this essay.

We have chosen our title for its resonance but are aware of the many readers and ways of reading that our contributors do not discuss at all, some of which our co-editors address in the afterword. "The Way We Read Now" calls to mind the title of Anthony Trollope's 1875 novel *The Way We Live Now*, echoed in recent books by Amanda Anderson (*The Way We Argue Now*) and Elaine Freedgood (in the coda to *The Ideas in Things*, entitled "Victorian Thing Culture and the Way We Read Now").[8] As a rubric, the phrase announces that we plan to perform a self-assessment, to survey the present—the deictic "now" carrying with it a note of urgency. It connotes change, the sense that now we do things a bit differently than they did back then. These essays also incorporate a site-specific "now" and "then," since the majority were first delivered at a 2008 conference jointly sponsored by Columbia University and New York University, which in turn emerged from a 2006 American Comparative Literature Association seminar convened to mark the twenty-fifth anniversary of Fredric Jameson's publication of *The Political Unconscious* (1981), the book that popularized symptomatic reading among U.S. literary critics. The 2008 conference invited speakers to reflect on the current place of symptomatic reading, but in asking our contributors to expand their talks into essays, we set a somewhat different agenda, requesting that they articulate what alternatives to symptomatic reading currently shape their work, and how those alternatives might pose new ways of reading.

administration was similarly held responsible for the torture of Iraqi detainees by U.S. personnel at Iraq's Abu Ghraib prison, which had been taken over by the United States in 2003 after the invasion of Iraq; the abuses were exposed in late 2003, with photographs published in 2004 [editor's note].

6. We note that there remain things that government powers go to extraordinary lengths to keep hidden, to keep as state secrets, "extraordinary rendition" being one of them. A hermeneutics of suspicion in which understanding requires a subtle reading of the situation thus remains readily pertinent to the work of critique. See, for example, Trevor Paglen, *Blank Spots on the Map: The Dark Geography of the Pentagon's Secret World* (New York, 2009). ["Extraordinary rendition": the kidnapping by agents of one country of individuals who are transferred to another country. "Mission accomplished": the statement on a banner behind President Bush as he announced in May 2003, on the deck of an aircraft carrier, that "major combat operations in Iraq have ended"; U.S. involvement continued until 2011, and most casualties occurred after that speech—editor's note.]

7. French philosopher and cultural historian (1926–1984, see above), who suggested that resistance was assimilated by disciplinary structures of power [editor's note].

8. Amanda Anderson, *The Way We Argue Now: A Study in the Cultures of Theory* (Princeton, 2006); Elaine Freedgood, *The Ideas in Things: Fugitive Meaning in the Victorian Novel* (Chicago, 2006). [Trollope (1815–1882), English novelist; *The Way We Live Now* looks critically at economic speculation in England during his time—editor's note.]

These essays represent neither a polemic against nor a postmortem of symptomatic reading. Our contributors trace nascent practices in the text-based disciplines, some of which evolve from symptomatic reading, some of which break from it. The "way" of our title should not be construed as a unitary mode or a pilgrimage to a single point, but as a road branching in multiple directions, like Jorge Luis Borges's garden of forking paths.[9] It would be inaccurate, however, to call this issue "the *ways* we read now," because these articles demonstrate significant overlap among our contributors. To that extent, a different literary allusion is also apt for picturing how these articles are related, that of Swann's way, which initially appears separate from the Guermantes way[1] but turns out to be connected to it at key points.

Symptomatic Reading

All of the contributors to this volume are responding to a particular notion of interpretation that came to be known as symptomatic reading. Broadly speaking, this practice encompasses an interpretive method that argues that the most interesting aspect of a text is what it represses, and that, as Fredric Jameson argued, interpretation should therefore seek "a latent meaning behind a manifest one" (60). The interpreter "rewrite[s] the surface categories of a text in the stronger language of a more fundamental interpretive code" (60) and reveals truths that "remain unrealized in the surface of the text" (48). As the letter of invitation to the 2008 conference put it, symptomatic reading asserts that "what a text means lies in what it does not say, which can then be used to rewrite the text in terms of a master code. By disclosing the absent cause that structures the text's inclusions and exclusions, the critic restores to the surface the deep history that the text represses."[2]

When symptomatic readers focus on elements present in the text, they construe them as symbolic of something latent or concealed; for example, a queer symptomatic reading might interpret the closet, or ghosts, as surface signs of the deep truth of a homosexuality that cannot be overtly depicted. Symptomatic readings also often locate outright absences, gaps, and ellipses in texts, and then ask what those absences mean, what forces create them, and how they signify the questions that motivate the text, but that the text itself cannot articulate.[3] Symptomatic reading thus often conflates three pairs of oppositions: present/absent, manifest/latent, and surface/depth. Strictly speaking, these are not compatible sets of terms. What is absent is simply not there; what is latent is present but invisible, unrecognized either because it is concealed or because it is undeveloped; what is deep is fully present and thus theoretically visible, but is positioned so far down, in, or back relative to a viewer, or is so completely covered by an opaque surface, that it can only be detected by an extreme degree of penetration or insight. The different connotations of manifest and surface are especially significant.

9. "The Garden of Forking Paths" (1941), short story by the Argentine writer Borges (1899–1986) [editor's note].

1. An allusion to the first (*Swann's Way*) and third (*The Guermantes Way*) volumes of Marcel Proust's 7-volume *À la recherche du temps perdu* (1913–27, *In Search of Lost Time*; French) [editor's note].

2. The conference proposal was written by Emily Apter, Elaine Freedgood, and Sharon Marcus [editor's note].

3. As Ellen Rooney has put it, symptomatic reading produces "the absent question . . . that the reading . . . establishes as unthinkable within the text's own problematic"; "Better Read Than Dead: Althusser and the Fetish of Ideology," *Yale French Studies* 88 (1995): 187.

The surface is associated with the superficial and deceptive, with what can be perceived without close examination and, implicitly, would turn out to be false upon closer scrutiny. The manifest has more positive connotations, as what is truthful, obvious, and clearly revealed.

The notion underlying all forms of symptomatic reading, that the most significant truths are not immediately apprehensible and may be veiled or invisible, has a very long history. Umberto Eco traces it back to the Gnostics in the second century CE, who, in contrast to Greek philosophers who defined reason as noncontradiction, posited truth as secret, deep, and mysterious, and language as inadequate to meaning.[4] Eco might also have noted, however, the equally Greek roots of the idea that truth does not lie in evidence directly available to the senses, since this was the point of Plato's parable of the cave, which influenced not only the Gnostics but also Christians such as Paul, and led to their emphasis on allegory.[5] Symptomatic reading thus has links to what Eco calls the hermetic theory of interpretation: the idea that words "hide the untold" and the secret of meaning is its impossibility (39–40). The notion of truth as recessive was not limited, however, to ancient mystics; as Mary Crane explains in her contribution to this volume,[6] the idea that meaning and verity must be deep and inaccessible to view was also promoted by a technique that had close ties to science: the development of perspective in early modern European painting.

The nineteenth-century roots of symptomatic reading lie with Marx's interest in ideology and the commodity and Freud's in the unconscious and dreams.[7] In an important essay entitled "Clues: Roots of an Evidential Paradigm," Carlo Ginzburg noted that Freud was "accustomed to divine secret and concealed things from unconsidered or unnoticed details"; in psychoanalysis, "infinitesimal traces permit the comprehension of a deeper, otherwise unattainable reality."[8] Those traces are clues, symptoms, details on the surface that indicate the form and content of hidden depths to the trained and intuitive interpreter. In *Freud and Philosophy: An Essay on Interpretation* (1970), Paul Ricoeur showed how Freud's model of interpretation was particularly suited to symbolic language, which he defined as any form of language "where another meaning is both given and hidden in an immediate meaning." Ricoeur defined the symbolic function as "to mean something other than what is said," and posited that "to interpret is to understand a double meaning." What he called a "hermeneutics of suspicion" in Freud described a method of understanding double meaning based not on the

4. Umberto Eco, "Interpretation and History," in *Interpretation and Overinterpretation*, ed. Stefan Collini (Cambridge, 1992), 31. [Eco (1932–2016), Italian theorist and novelist. Gnostics: early Christians who believed that salvation requires an esoteric knowledge of spiritual truths—editor's note.]

5. See Plato, *The Republic*, trans. G. M. A. Grube (Indianapolis, 1992), and Daniel Boyarin, *A Radical Jew: Paul and the Politics of Identity* (Berkeley, 1994). [The allegory of the cave in *Republic* 7 (see above), by the Greek philosopher PLATO (ca. 427–ca. 347 B.C.E.), describes the majority of humanity as trapped in a cave, seeing only the shadows cast by the representations of real objects (the "real" being the Forms or Ideas of things, located outside the cave). Paul (d. ca. 64 C.E.), a leader of the first generation of Christians, to whom 13 books of the New Testament are attributed; originally a prosecutor of Christians, he converted after he had a vision (Galatians 1.16; 1 Corinthians 9.1)—editor's note.]

6. "Surface, Depth, and the Cognitive Reading of *The Political Unconscious*" [editor's note].

7. On the interpretive homology between Marx's analysis of the commodity and Freud's analysis of dreams, see SLAVOJ ŽIŽEK, "How Did Marx Invent the Symptom?" *Mapping Ideology*, ed. Žižek (New York, 1995), 296–331.

8. Carlo Ginzburg, "Clues: Roots of an Evidential Paradigm," in *Clues, Myths, and the Historical Method*, trans. John and Anne C. Tedeschi (Baltimore, 1989), 99, 101. [Ginzburg (b. 1939), Italian historian—editor's note.]

religious model of revealed meaning but on the demystification of illusion.[9] This hermeneutics of suspicion became a general property of literary criticism even for those who did not adhere strictly to psychoanalysis.

The other set of critics invested in symptomatic reading were Marxists engaged with the writings of Louis Althusser.[1] In *Reading Capital* (published in French in 1968, in English translation in 1970), Althusser unfolded a method of symptomatic reading that he found in Marx and used to read Marx, one that "divulges the undivulged event in the text it reads, and in the same movement relates it to a different text, present as a necessary absence in the first."[2] For Althusser, symptomatic reading makes "lacunae perceptible" (86); it assumes that texts are shaped by questions they do not themselves pose and contain symptoms that help interpreters articulate those questions, which lie outside texts as their absent causes. Althusser dismissed "the religious phantasm of epiphanic transparency" (35), the theory of reading as one of logos, in which each part immediately expresses the whole and there is no split between manifest and latent meaning. Although Althusser equated religious reading with instantaneous transparency, his theory actually harkens back to the Gnostic concept of truth as too complex to describe, because he defined history as what could not be read in manifest discourse, as "the inaudible and illegible notation of the effects of a structure of structures" (17). This concept of truth as antilogos, as what cannot be immediately understood, also resonates with Jacques Derrida's[3] critique of truth as presence.

In *The Political Unconscious* (1981), Fredric Jameson argued that only weak, descriptive, empirical, ideologically complicit readers attend to the surface of the text. In an affirmative version of symptomatic reading, Jameson insisted that the "strong" critic must rewrite narrative in terms of master codes, disclosing its status as ideology, as an imaginary resolution of real contradictions (13). Like Althusser, Jameson saw the text as shaped by absence, but unlike Althusser, Jameson saw only one absent cause, history itself, and insisted that interpretation should seek a repressed, mystified, latent meaning behind a manifest one (60). For Jameson, interpretation is "unmasking"; meaning is the allegorical difference between surface and depth; and the critic restores to the surface the history that the text represses (20). That restoration entails the "semantic enrichment and enlargement of the *inert* givens and materials of a particular text" (75, emphasis added). Jameson's image of the critic as wresting meaning from a resisting text or inserting it into a lifeless one had enormous influence in the United States, perhaps because it presented professional literary criticism as a strenuous and heroic endeavor, one more akin to activism and labor than to leisure, and therefore fully deserving of remuneration.[4] The influence of Jameson's version of symptomatic reading can be felt in the centrality of two scholarly texts from the 1990s: Eve Kosofsky Sedgwick's *Epistemology of the Closet*

9. Paul Ricoeur, *Freud and Philosophy: An Essay on Interpretation*, trans. Denis Savage (New Haven, 1979), 7, 12, 8, 56.
1. French Marxist philosopher (1918–1990); see above [editor's note].
2. Louis Althusser and Etienne Balibar, *Reading Capital*, trans. Ben Brewster (London, 1997), 28.
3. French deconstructionist philosopher and critic (1930–2004); see above [editor's note].
4. Mary Poovey argues that this account of reading as work originated with John Ruskin, who tended to cast meaning "not as self-evident because simply denoted by the author's words but as *difficult* and *evasive*." See her *Genres of the Credit Economy: Mediating Value in Eighteenth- and Nineteenth-Century Britain* (Chicago, 2007), 312–13. [Ruskin (1819–1900), English critic and artist—editor's note.]

(1991), which crystallized the emergent field of queer theory, and Toni Morrison's[5] *Playing in the Dark: Whiteness and the Literary Imagination* (1992), which set forth an agenda for studying the structuring role of race in American literature. Both showed that one could read a text's silences, gaps, style, tone, and imagery as symptoms of the queerness or race absent only apparently from its pages.

* * *

Surface Reading

Surface looms large in the vocabulary of our contributors,[6] but rarely do they mean the literal surface of texts: paper, binding, typography, the sounds of words read aloud. Nor do they construe surface as symptomatic readers often have—as a layer that conceals, as clothing does skin, or encloses, as a building's facade does its interior. Following the lead of our contributors, we take surface to mean what is evident, perceptible, apprehensible in texts; what is neither hidden nor hiding; what, in the geometrical sense, has length and breadth but no thickness, and therefore covers no depth. A surface is what insists on being looked *at* rather than what we must train ourselves to see *through*.

Many types of reading, some quite old, some fairly new, might come under the rubric of "surface reading."

Surface as materiality. This kind of surface emerges primarily in two forms—in the history of the book and in cognitive reading. Bibliography attends to the literal surfaces of books themselves, making signs inseparable from their material supports. Histories of reading, publication, and circulation study books as things that link their producers, sellers, and users. Cognitive studies of literature attend to the material workings of the brain during the reading process and show how writing prompts readers to imitate what Elaine Scarry calls "the material conditions" that structure perception.[7] Scarry shows that we can best produce mental images of depth and solidity by picturing one surface passing in front of another, because surfaces are easier to imagine than three-dimensional objects (10–12). The verbal arts, Scarry points out, are often associated with immateriality because they are "counterfactual" and ask us to picture what does not exist, but they are also significantly "counterfictional," because they infuse our ordinarily pallid imaginings with vivacity (38). Crucial to this process are objects, such as flowers, that we can easily envision and that thus become "the tissue of the mental images themselves—not the thing pictured, but the [mental] surfaces on which the images will get made" (48).

Surface as the intricate verbal structure of literary language. This understanding of surface produces close readings that do not seek hidden meanings, but focus on unraveling what Samuel Otter, in a recent account of New Formalism, has called the "linguistic density" and "verbal complexity"

5. American novelist and essayist (b. 1931); see above. SEDGWICK (1950–2009), American critic and theorist [editor's note].
6. In the omitted section, Best and Marcus summarize the five essays in the special issue [editor's note].
7. Elaine Scarry, *Dreaming by the Book* (New York, 1999), 9. [Scarry (b. 1946), prominent American literary and cultural critic—editor's note.]

of literary texts.[8] This type of surface reading, as Otter shows, would move slowly, if at all, from text to context, from parsing meaning to interpreting significance.[9] This valorization of surface reading as willed, sustained proximity to the text recalls the aims of New Criticism,[1] which insisted that the key to understanding a text's meaning lay within the text itself, particularly in its formal properties. Formalisms new and old argue against the traditional association of the surface with what is too simple to merit notice. As I. A. Richards pointed out, though such criticism "is very largely . . . an exercise in navigation" it still requires great skill. Since most readers have trouble construing the sensuous form and literal sense of poetry, simply paraphrasing a text or understanding its verbal meaning is a demanding "craft."[2]

Embrace of the surface as an affective and ethical stance. Such an embrace involves accepting texts, deferring to them instead of mastering or using them as objects, and refuses the depth model of truth, which dismisses surfaces as inessential and deceptive. An early and influential statement of this approach was Susan Sontag's "Against Interpretation" (1966), which argued that interpreters do not disclose the text's true meaning but alter it. Instead of saying, "Look, don't you see that X is really—or, really means—A?" Sontag admonished, the critic of a work should "show it is what it is, even that it is what it is, rather than . . . show what it means." Sontag's manifesto against the model of interpretation drawn from Freud and Marx refused the notion that meaning and content define the work of art and proposed that we set aside the theory of mimesis in favor of the experience of art in its "pure, untranslatable, sensuous immediacy," a stance that she also called an "erotics of art."[3] Such an erotics can take the form of attending to the text, or to one's affective responses to it. Other versions of receptiveness and fidelity to the text's surface, as opposed to suspicious and aggressive attacks on its concealed depths, include Eve Kosofsky Sedgwick's "reparative reading" (discussed in the afterword to this issue), Timothy Bewes's "reading with the grain," and Jane Gallop's meditation on the ethics of close reading.[4]

8. Samuel Otter, "An Aesthetics in All Things," *Representations*, no. 104 (Fall 2008): 116–25, 119. [Otter (b. 1956), American scholar of American literature. New Formalism: a movement among poets and critics, arising in the decades before and after the turn of the 21st century, that renews the focus on literary language and form—aspects to which New Historicism (dominant from roughly the 1980s) had paid little attention—editor's note.]

9. The distinction between meaning and significance belongs properly to E. D. Hirsch, for whom the former describes what an author means by a chosen sign sequence, whereas the latter names a relationship between that meaning "and a person, or a conception, or a situation, or indeed anything imaginable." E. D. Hirsch Jr., *Validity in Interpretation* (New Haven, 1967), 8. [Hirsch (b. 1928), American theorist of hermeneutics and education, best known for his advocacy of cultural literacy—editor's note.]

1. The dominant critical practice in North American and British universities from the 1940s through the 1960s, which advocated "close reading" and attention to verbal texture and literary structure; it was named by JOHN CROWE RANSOM [editor's note].

2. I. A. Richards, *Practical Criticism: A Study of Literary Judgment* (1929; reprint, London, 1973), 312, 11. [Richards (1893–1979), English critic and poet who strongly influenced the American New Critics—editor's note.]

3. Susan Sontag, "Against Interpretation," in *Against Interpretation and Other Essays* (New York, 1966), 6, 5, 14. [SONTAG (1933–2004), American critic and novelist; for this essay (1964), see above—editor's note.]

4. Eve Kosofsky Sedgwick, "Paranoid Reading and Reparative Reading, or, You're So Paranoid, You Probably Think This Essay Is about You," in *Touching Feeling: Affect, Pedagogy, Performativity* (Durham, 2003), 123–51; Timothy Bewes, "Reading with the Grain," unpublished manuscript, presented at 2006 ACLA seminar on symptomatic reading and later expanded; Jane Gallop, "The Ethics of Reading: Close Encounters," *Journal of Curriculum Theorizing* 16, no. 3 (2000): 7–18.

To these we would add three other ways of doing surface reading that deeply interest us and that we hope will generate more discussion:

Attention to surface as a practice of critical description. This focus assumes that texts can reveal their own truths because texts mediate themselves; what we think theory brings to texts (form, structure, meaning) is already present in them. Description sees no need to translate the text into a theoretical or historical metalanguage in order to make the text meaningful. The purpose of criticism is thus a relatively modest one: to indicate what the text says about itself. Though we would not endorse Paul de Man's insistence on the "void that separates" poetic intent from reality, we remain intrigued by his observation that poetry is the "foreknowledge" of criticism, and that the interpreter therefore "discloses poetry for what it is" and articulates "what was already there in full light."[5] Similarly, Joel Fineman's *Shakespeare's Perjured Eye* argued that the traditional questions *for* criticism of the sonnets are already questions *in* the sonnets themselves; there is no need for a critical metalanguage to explain the sonnets because, as Aaron Kunin has recently observed, "the poems provide the most accurate description of their own operations."[6] Here, depth is not to be found outside the text or beneath its surface (as its context, horizon, unconscious, or history); rather, depth is continuous with surface and is thus an effect of immanence.

Surface as the location of patterns that exist within and across texts. This notion includes narratology, thematic criticism, genre criticism, and discourse analysis. Symptomatic reading looks for patterns in order to break free of and reach beyond them to a deep truth too abstract to be visible or even locatable in a single text. Jameson thus urges interpreters to sketch the ideological rectangles that structure texts only in order to move toward what lies outside them. Surface readers, by contrast, find value in the rectangles themselves and locate narrative structures and abstract patterns on the surface, as aggregates of what is manifest in multiple texts as cognitively latent but semantically continuous with an individual text's presented meaning. In this type of surface reading, the critic becomes an anatomist breaking down texts or discourses into their components, or a taxonomist arranging and categorizing texts into larger groups. The anatomist and taxonomist rearrange texts into new forms but nonetheless attend to what is present rather than privilege what is absent. Examples of this kind of work include Clifford Siskin's demonstration that large-scale shifts in how literature defines reality coincide with epochal changes in media history, and Marc Angenot's study of "social discourse," in which he looks at everything published in France in a particular year in order to chart "a global typology of the prevailing sayable."[7] Unconvinced that literature differs significantly from other kinds of writing, Angenot places literary surfaces

5. Paul de Man, *Blindness and Insight* (New York, 1971), 34, 31. [DE MAN (1919–1983), Belgian-born literary theorist of deconstruction—editor's note.]

6. Joel Fineman, *Shakespeare's Perjured Eye* (Berkeley, 1986), 324 n.15; Aaron Kunin, "Shakespeare's Preservation Fantasy," *PMLA* 124 (January 2009): 95.

7. Clifford Siskin, "Textual Culture in the History of the Real," *Textual Culture* 2, no. 2 (Autumn 2007): 118–30; Marc Angenot, "Social Discourse Analysis: Outlines of a Research Project," *Yale Journal of Criticism* 17 (2004): 199–215, 200. [Angenot (b. 1941), Belgian-born literary critic and social theorist—editor's note.]

on the same plane as "social discourse," defined as "the total network of meaning."[8] For Angenot, what defines ideology is its dispersal, and to understand it we must chart its extent as a commonplace worldview, not expose its falsity.

Surface as literal meaning. What Sharon Marcus has called "just reading" accounts for what is in the text "without construing presence as absence or affirmation as negation."[9] Her example is female friendship in Victorian novels, which has often been read as a cover story for an otherwise unspeakable desire between women. Because critics assume that novels ending in marriage eliminate lesbian desire, they have also assumed that courtship plots exile female friendship to the narrative margins. In fact, Marcus shows, female friends rarely lose their centrality in novels with marriage plots, but critics have overlooked this out of an insistence on reading female friendship as something other than it is. Taking friendship in novels to signify friendship is thus not mere tautology; it highlights something true and visible on the text's surface that symptomatic reading had ironically rendered invisible. Similarly, Benjamin Kahan argues that, rather than interpret celibacy as repressed homosexuality, we adopt a "depthless hermeneutic" that would take celibacy as "the 'absence' of sex that it is."[1] Ann Stoler, in *Along the Archival Grain*, looks at imperial violence that was never hidden, and attends to the colonial state's interests in family life as a genuine preoccupation, not as "metaphors for something else."[2]

Other examples suggest an emerging interest in literal readings that take texts at face value. In his study of rumor in the archive, Stephen Best reads first-person testimony by Caribbean slaves who believed that the British monarch had freed them, viewing their words neither as evidence irredeemably corrupted by the sovereign power that extracted them, nor as verbatim speech through which we can recover subjects lost to history. Those words are, rather, exactly what they appear to be: "impossible speech" that oscillates between loyalty and insurgency, speech and paraphrase, fact and prophecy, confession and coercion, and in that sense reflects back to us the deeply felt uncertainty of the enslaved. Attention to the rumors on the surface of the archive challenges our conception of the latter as a repository of latent voices and "hidden transcripts," and requires that we reconsider whether the story of slavery can ever be narrated "from below" if our aim is to register what is inaccessible in the voice of the enslaved.[3] Elisa Tamarkin similarly reads the American love of hierarchy, caste, and British traditions as meaning what it said. Unlike cultural historians who have read Anglophilia symptomatically, as a "guilty conscience that will not own [the egalitarian democracy] it has fought to gain," Tamarkin takes Anglophilia

8. Angenot, *Ce que l'on dit des Juifs en 1889. Antisémitisme et discours social* [*What Was Said about the Jews in 1889: Anti-Semitism and Social Discourse*; French] (Saint-Denis, 1989), 177, translation ours.

9. Marcus, *Between Women: Friendship, Desire, and Marriage in Victorian England* (Princeton, 2007), 75.

1. Benjamin Kahan, "'The Viper's Traffic-Knot': Celibacy and Queerness in the 'Late' Marianne Moore," *GLQ* 14, no. 4 (2008): 510, 512.

2. Ann Stoler, *Along the Archival Grain: Epistemic Anxieties and Colonial Common Sense* (Princeton, 2009), 63.

3. Stephen Best, "Rumor in the Archive," unpublished manuscript, presented at "The Way We Read Now: Symptomatic Reading and Its Aftermath," Columbia University and New York University, May 2008.

literally, as a statement of American national character that comprises attachment to deference as well as allegiance to independence.[4]

These understandings of what one can learn from surfaces resonate with a rarely cited statement Foucault made about his relationship to archives: rather than dig for "relations that are secret, hidden, more silent or deeper than . . . consciousness," he described himself as seeking "to define the relations on the very surface of discourse" and "to make visible what is invisible only because it's too much on the surface of things."[5] Just reading sees ghosts as presences, not absences, and lets ghosts be ghosts, instead of saying what they are ghosts *of*.

Freedom in Attentiveness

If criticism is not the excavation of hidden truths, what can it add to our experience of texts? Can surface reading be anything other than a tacit endorsement of the status quo, the academic version of resignation's latest mantra, "It is what it is"? These questions are especially urgent because many of our most powerful critical models see criticism as a practice of freedom by locating autonomy, self-reflexiveness, detachment, and liberatory potential either in the artwork itself or in the valiant labor of the critic. In the former case, a measure of heroism is attributed to the artwork due to its autonomy from ideology; the latter makes the critic a hero who performs interpretive feats of demystification. The surface readers in this volume place noticeably less faith than many other critics in the heroic qualities of art, and they understand their critical activity as something other than wresting truths from the hidden depths of resisting texts. We feel it is important, therefore, to situate this volume in relation to dominant tendencies and to significant emergent moments within recent literary criticism that position themselves in relation to the two poles of critical freedom.

First, the dominant trends. One of the most emphatic recent articulations of the notion that freedom lies in aesthetic objects and aesthetic play can be found in the broad field styled as "New Formalist." As Marjorie Levinson describes in her recent review essay on the movement, a common assumption in much New Formalist work is that we do not need to criticize artworks, because they contain their own "critical (and self-critical) agency." New Formalists characterize the task of the critic as restoring the artwork to its "original, compositional complexity," a position that corresponds by and large to the aims of the old New Criticism and distances itself from what it perceives as attacks on literary form by New Historicism.[6] In this essentially modernist view of art as a locus of critical autonomy, reading becomes what Levinson calls "learned submission," which is not as submissive as it sounds, because in submitting to the artwork, we come to share its freedom, by experiencing "the deep challenge that the artwork poses to ideology, or to the flattening, routinizing, absorptive effects associated with ideological regimes" (560). Immersion in texts frees us from the apathy and instrumentality of

4. Elisa Tamarkin, *Anglophilia: Deference, Devotion, and Antebellum America* (Chicago, 2008), xxiv, xxvi–xxvii.

5. *Foucault Live: Interviews, 1961–84*, ed. Sylvère Lotringer, trans. John Johnston (New York, 1989), 57–58.

6. Marjorie Levinson, "What Is New Formalism?" *PMLA* 122, no. 2 (March 2007): 558–69, 560.

capitalism by allowing us to bathe in the artwork's disinterested purposelessness.

* * *

At our most speculative and exploratory, we want to ask what it might mean to stay close to our objects of study, without citing as our reason for doing so a belief that those objects encapsulate freedom. We pose this question, in part, out of a sense of political realism about the revolutionary capacities of both texts and critics, and doubts about whether we could ever attain the heightened perspicacity that would allow us to see fully beyond ideology. We also detect in current criticism a skepticism about the very project of freedom, or about any kind of transcendent value we might use to justify intellectual work. A variety of critical styles in the second half of the twentieth century were marked by a utopian strain and a striving for redemption. Sontag subscribed to the "cult of art," Jameson expressed the divine aspirations of revolutionary critics, and those pursuing various forms of identity politics (feminism, queer studies, critical race studies) believed in the authority imbedded in particular subject positions. Across these various styles, the project of freedom came to be associated with what Christopher Nealon calls a "comportment"; he points out that for long it seemed to be the mandated task of either the artwork or the critic's theories about it to provide a finite array of stances from among which we had to choose "the one that will count as resistant, or subversive."[7] This appears to be less the case now if we take our contributors as at all representative. All seem to be relatively neutral about their objects of study, which they tend less to evaluate than to describe, and which they situate in landscapes neither utopian nor dystopian. * * *

Surface reading, which strives to describe texts accurately, might easily be dismissed as politically quietist, too willing to accept things as they are. We want to reclaim from this tradition the accent on immersion in texts (without paranoia or suspicion about their merit or value), for we understand that attentiveness to the artwork as itself a kind of freedom. This strikes an ideal expressed most succinctly by Charles Altieri: "an ideal of being able not to worry about performing the self so that one can pursue potentials within the range of ongoing practices that are blocked by worries about identity and authenticity . . . [a freedom to be able] to enjoy what and where one is without having to produce any supplemental claims that promise some 'significance' not immediately evident."[8] To some ears this might sound like a desire to be free from having a political agenda that determines in advance how we interpret texts, and in some respects it is exactly that. We think, however, that a true openness to all the potentials made available by texts is also prerequisite to an attentiveness that does not reduce them to instrumental means to an end and is the best way to say anything accurate and true about them. Criticism that valorizes the freedom of the critic has often assumed that an adversarial relation to the object of criticism is the only

7. Christopher Nealon, "Un-Militant Thinking," unpublished manuscript, delivered at "The Way We Read Now: Symptomatic Reading and Its Aftermath," Columbia University and New York University, May 2008.

8. Charles Altieri, "Cavell's Imperfect Perfectionism," in *Ordinary Language Criticism: Literary Thinking after Cavell after Wittgenstein*, ed. Kenneth Dauber and Walter Jost (Evanston, 2003), 216.

way for the critic to free himself from the text's deceptive, ideological surface and uncover the truth that the text conceals. We want to suggest that, in relinquishing the freedom dream that accompanies the work of demystification, we might be groping toward some equally valuable, if less glamorous, states of mind.

This brings us to two emergent styles of doing literary criticism that resonate with the work in this volume—work that attends as much to the complexities of the critic's position as to those of the artwork, but seeks to occupy a paradoxical space of minimal critical agency.

We have in mind here, first, the recent turn toward computers, databases, and other forms of machine intelligence across a range of fields and practices, from book history to distant reading. Where the heroic critic corrects the text, a nonheroic critic might aim instead to correct for her critical subjectivity, by using machines to bypass it, in the hopes that doing so will produce more accurate knowledge about texts. Where the heroic text commands admiration of its unique features, computers can help us to find features that texts have in common in ways that our brains alone cannot. Computers are weak interpreters but potent describers, anatomizers, taxonomists. New media create new forms of knowledge, and digital modes of reading may be the inspiration for the hope that we could bypass the selectivity and evaluative energy that have been considered the hallmarks of good criticism, in order to attain what has almost become taboo in literary studies: objectivity, validity, truth. This might raise alarm that we are destroying existing rationales for studying the humanities: critical thinking, the uniqueness of art and culture, and the correspondingly distinctive ways that humanist disciplines study them. But to suggest that there might be ways of studying culture that would neither attack nor defend it is not to suggest that we abandon the study of culture altogether. It is to propose that rather than evaluate culture as masterworks of genius or documents of barbarism, we instead define what is unique about the disciplines that study culture as their interest in human artifacts, in contrast to the sciences, which focus on processes beyond our creation and control. To adopt some of the methods of science to the study of culture is not to say that scientists would be the better students of it, for scientists not only have little interest in studying cultural objects but also lack training in how to study them qualitatively. We are not envisioning a world in which computers replace literary critics but are curious about one in which we work with them to expand what we do.

We are thinking, second, of a critic like Anne-Lise François and her interest in a form of reading whose minimal agency would match that of certain textual moments of silence, deferral, acceptance, "complaisance without hope."[9] Taking its distance from the recuperative ethos of earlier styles that seemed capable of reading only "for hidden meanings and lost histories" (32), this type of criticism highlights "the agency of the act of bearing witness to the given" (35). Instead of turning to literature for models of how to overcome constraint, or for a right way to live under capital, or to register the difference between our critical freedom and the limits placed on others, we are interested in how to register the ways that constraints structure existence as much as breaking free of them does. The neutrality of description

9. Anne-Lise François, *Open Secrets: The Literature of Uncounted Experience* (Stanford, 2008), xix.

is thus not neutrality about the constraints themselves, which we may find ourselves moved to deplore, but neutrality about the existences entwined with them, which we would like to be able to recognize without judging. Just as many dismiss surface reading as obvious, but find themselves unable to sustain the slow pace, receptiveness, and fixed attention it requires, many readers might find that to refuse to celebrate or condemn their objects of study is, in practice, both difficult and discomfiting.

The essays that follow remind us that as much as our objects of study may conceal the structures that give rise to them, they also wear them on their sleeves; that the moments that arrest us in texts need not be considered symptoms, whose true cause exists on another plane of reality, but can themselves indicate important and overlooked truths. As Edgar Allan Poe's story "The Purloined Letter"[1] continues to teach us, what lies in plain sight is worthy of attention but often eludes observation—especially by deeply suspicious detectives who look past the surface in order to root out what is underneath it. These essays also gesture toward a future for literary criticism that does not involve the untenable claim that we are always more free than those who produce the texts we study and that our insights and methods therefore have the power to confer freedom. At the same time, we would suggest that to begin to challenge the state of things, or the distortions of ideology, we must strive to produce undistorted, complete descriptions of them. Of course, one of the great questions of the last two centuries has been whether we can ever set aside our responses in order to produce undistorted accounts of things, since our responses are often unconscious and unknowable. Without fully answering that question, we believe that even if we cannot exhaustively explain what causes our responses, we can strive to describe them accurately, and that there is nothing inherently truthful or misleading about them. Sometimes our subjectivity will help us see a text more clearly, and sometimes it will not.

In closing, we want to underscore two points: that to see more clearly does not require that we plumb hidden depths and that producing accurate accounts of surfaces is not antithetical to critique; indeed, it may be, as Bruno Latour has recently suggested, the best way to move past the impasses created by what has become an excessive emphasis on ideological demystification. Referring to the ease with which conservatives question global warming by referring to it as a social construction rather than a scientific truth, he asks, "While we spent years trying to detect the real prejudices hidden behind the appearance of objective statements, do we now have to reveal the real objective and incontrovertible facts hidden behind the *illusion* of prejudices?"[2] Latour reminds us that "the question was never to get *away* from facts but *closer* to them" (231) and notes that the critic "is not the one who debunks, but the one who assembles" (246). We began this essay by asserting the distance we would like to take from the type of symptomatic reading we inherited from psychoanalysis and Marxism, but in concluding we note that the work of assembly and the desire for a more complete

1. Detective story (1844) about a letter that is hidden in plain sight, by the American writer POE (1809–1849); it is the focus of JACQUES LACAN's celebrated "Seminar on 'The Purloined Letter'" (1966) [editor's note].

2. Bruno Latour, "Why Has Critique Run Out of Steam? From Matters of Fact to Matters of Concern," *Critical Inquiry* 30, no. 2 (Winter 2004): 227. [LATOUR (b. 1947), French sociologist of science; for this essay, see above—editor's note.]

view of reality are also aims of both schools of thought, which is one reason they remain central to the critics whose works we have assembled here. We hope these reflections on the way we read now give us a clearer view of the past and open up fertile paths of inquiry in the future.

2009

TIMOTHY MORTON
b. 1968

In his influential book *The Environmental Imagination* (1996), the Harvard University professor Lawrence Buell defines *ecocriticism* as "study of the relation between literature and environment conducted in a spirit of commitment to environmentalist praxis." In his book *The Ecological Thought* (2010), from which our selection is taken, Timothy Morton complains that "Ecocriticism has overlooked the way in which all art—not just explicitly ecological art—hardwires the environment into its *form*." Morton highlights problems with existing ecocritical theories, particularly how representations of ecology in literature reflect a narrow-minded perception of nature. In response, Morton develops a distinctive mode of materialist ecological thinking based on the interconnectedness of all beings, living and nonliving.

Timothy Morton was born in London in 1968. He earned his B.A. and his D.Phil. in English from Oxford University, studying at Magdalen College. His dissertation, "Re-Imagining the Body: Shelley and the Languages of Diet," examined diet, temperance, and consumption in the works of PERCY BYSSHE SHELLEY (1792–1822). Over the years, Morton has worked for several institutions: he was a tutor at Oxford's Magdalen College and Lincoln College. He held the positions of visiting fellow at Princeton University and visiting assistant professor at New York University. He worked as an assistant professor at the University of Colorado at Boulder, where he later became an associate professor. He taught at the University of California at Davis. Since 2012, he has been the Rita Shea Guffey Chair in English at Rice University. While Morton's interests span a wide array of contemporary fields, his writings focus on theories of ecology, food studies, and Romanticism.

In *The Ecological Thought*, Morton wonders: "Is the ecological thought thinking about ecology?" He answers, "Yes and no. It is a thinking that is ecological, a contemplating that is a doing." The book explores the interrelatedness of various forms of life and thinking. Morton uses the awkward phrase "the ecological thought" to refer to the ability to perceive "interconnectedness." Dwelling on the concept of the ecological thought, the book builds on existing approaches to ecocriticism in order to liberate the discipline from problematic conservative and ideological thinking. It argues that ecology not only addresses global warming, wastewater recycling, and wind power but extends to space and time, emotions, and other features of culture. Ecology, Morton maintains, is not a description of nature; it is "coexistence," "interconnectedness," and ongoing mobility and mutability. Ecological thinking therefore prompts wide-ranging questions, explores ideas, and rejects fixed resolutions; it confronts the damage done to thinking by modernity; it "has to do with amazement, open-mindedness, and wonder. It has to do with doubt, confusion, and skepticism."

The Ecological Thought deconstructs nature as an ideology and a commodified object. The book argues that the traditional concept of "Nature" fails to serve ecology well. Morton capitalizes the N in "Nature" in order to defamiliarize our perception that nature is a thing with default "hierarchy, authority, harmony, purity, neutrality, and mystery." Nature, according to Morton, is always interconnected with all other things and persons in the universe, and therefore is constantly changing. He advocates an ecology without reified Nature.

Timothy Morton argues that the ecological thought is available only to modern society, because its apparent "totality" was not accessible to premodern humans. Yet modernity's understanding of ecology, with its narrow account of totality, is problematic: its ideal and pure image of nature, stemming from the Enlightenment era, has prevented the progress of the ecological thought, making the act of thinking of secondary importance to "Nature." Here, Morton agrees with Emmanuel Lévinas's (1906–1995) astute critique of MARTIN HEIDEGGER to the effect that "our concepts of 'faceless generous mother nature' are based on 'sedentary' agricultural societies with their idea of 'possession.'" He observes that through the contemporary spread of mobile consumerism and capitalism, the modern individual is getting well rid of this idea of "pristine" nature. Modern "human beings are past the point at which Nature is a help." In his discussion of the numerous contents and forms of the ecological thought and in his urgent and copious lyrical style, Morton self-consciously enacts Lévinas's maxim that he uses as his book's epigraph: "Infinity overflows the thought that thinks it."

While developing his account of the ecological thought, which globalization is helping to force upon us, Morton reassesses the nature of art. Art manifests to us how to think ecologically. Morton explains: "Ecological art, and the ecological-ness of all art," is not defined by the portrayal of objects in nature; rather, art is ecological by virtue of its phenomenological substance and its location—it is made from and takes place in "the world." Art "*is* something"; for example, poems are written on paper, which comes from trees. Simultaneously, art "*does* something"; it forms the environment—for instance, the way in which a poem looks on paper shapes our perception of that paper. When we read, our body occupies space and adopts a certain stance. "The poem organizes space." In short, the environment is embedded in art; absence of overt references to it does not mean that it is not there. Morton argues that "all texts—all artworks, indeed—have an irreducibly ecological form. Ecology permeates all forms."

As he proceeds, Morton runs into problems that he quickly and self-consciously acknowledges. He admits to a tendency to a leveling vitalism, in which all existence is equally animated with positive life forces. Here ontological hierarchies collapse in the name of radical openness to all modes of being, an outcome characteristic of twenty-first-century object-oriented ontology and new materialism (as in the work of JANE BENNETT and IAN BOGOST). In this context, distinctions of race, class, and gender go unmentioned. Morton admits to a commitment to theory, to its powers and complexities, though he simultaneously tries to push it aside in order to reach a wider audience. His prose style mixes the accessible vocabulary of the public intellectual with the theory jargon of a Continental philosopher. Nevertheless, Morton's critique of the modern ideology of Nature and his materialist phenomenology of "the ecological thought," a new mode of interconnected thinking for our twenty-first-century condition, work to open up new views for contemporary arts and sciences.

***The Ecological Thought* Keywords:** Aesthetics, Affect, Cultural Studies, Ethics, Modernity, Phenomenology

From The Ecological Thought

From *Introduction: Critical Thinking*

The ecological crisis we face is so obvious that it becomes easy—for some, strangely or frighteningly easy—to join the dots and see that everything is interconnected. This is *the ecological thought*. And the more we consider it, the more our world opens up.

We usually think of ecology as having to do with science and social policy. But as the poet Percy Shelley said, regarding developments in science, "We want the creative faculty to imagine that which we know."[1] Ecology seems earthy, pedestrian. It's something to do with global warming, recycling, and solar power; something to do with quotidian relationships between humans and nonhumans. Sometimes we associate ecology with fervent beliefs that are often explicitly religious: the Animal Liberation Front or Earth First! To the extent that we don't yet have a truly ecological world, religion cries aloud in a green voice.[2] But what would an ecological society look like? What would an ecological mind think? What kinds of art would an ecologically minded person enjoy? All these questions have one thing in common: *the ecological thought*.

As the success of the 2008 Pixar masterpiece *Wall•E* demonstrated, the question is on everyone's mind: what is ecological awareness?[3] How do we restart Spaceship Earth with the pieces we have to hand? How do we move forward from the melancholy of a poisoned planet? *Wall•E* begins several hundred years into the future, with the depressing scene of a little garbage-compacting robot piling skyscraper-high towers of human detritus. There's something wrong with "his" software, something that manifests as an obsessive collecting. It looks like he's searching for some key to humanness among the Rubik's Cubes, the video of *Hello Dolly*,[4] the tiny sprout in a flowerpot. *Wall•E* happily shows that the "broken" software, the mental disorder of the little robot, is the viral code that reboots Earth: this time around, we evolve from memes, not genes. Yet isn't his obsessive compulsion, so like a manifestation of grief (from where we sit in the cinema at least, spectators to future ruin), exactly our situation right now? How do we begin? Where do we go from here? Is that the sound of something calling us from within the grief—the sound of the ecological thought?

The ecological thought is a virus that infects all other areas of thinking. (Yet viruses, and virulence, are shunned in environmental ideology.) This book argues that ecology isn't just about global warming, recycling, and solar power—and also not just to do with everyday relationships between humans and nonhumans. It has to do with love, loss, despair, and compassion. It has to do with depression and psychosis. It has to do with capitalism and with what might exist after capitalism. It has to do with amazement,

1. Percy Shelley, "A Defence of Poetry," *Shelley's Poetry and Prose*, ed. Donald H. Reiman and Neil Fraistat (New York: Norton, 2002), 530 [except as indicated, all notes are Morton's]. [SHELLEY (1792–1822), major English poet; for this essay (1821), see above—editor's note.]
2. For example, see the Church of Deep Ecology: churchofdeepecology.org.
3. Andrew Stanton, dir., *Wall•E* (Pixar Animation Studios, 2008).
4. A 1964 musical, by Jerry Herman and Michael Stewart; the film version of the romantic comedy, directed by Gene Kelly, was released in 1969. Rubik's Cubes: three-dimensional puzzle toys invented by Erno Rubik, a Hungarian professor of design; they were popular in the 1980s [editor's note].

open-mindedness, and wonder. It has to do with doubt, confusion, and skepticism. It has to do with concepts of space and time. It has to do with delight, beauty, ugliness, disgust, irony, and pain. It has to do with consciousness and awareness. It has to do with ideology and critique. It has to do with reading and writing. It has to do with race, class, and gender. It has to do with sexuality. It has to do with ideas of self and the weird paradoxes of subjectivity. It has to do with society. It has to do with coexistence.

Like the shadow of an idea not yet fully thought, a shadow from the future (another wonderful phrase of Shelley's), the ecological thought creeps over other ideas until nowhere is left untouched by its dark presence.[5] Darwin trusted the theory of evolutionary impermanence so much that he was prepared to suspend his disbelief in continental permanence, although in his day there was no tectonic plate theory.[6] Such is the force of the ecological thought. As one philosopher put it (see this book's epigraph), "infinity overflows the thought that thinks it."[7]

You could think of *The Ecological Thought* as the prequel to my previous book, *Ecology without Nature*. What must I have been thinking in order to realize that in order to have "ecology," we have to let go of "nature"?[8] You can't make a prequel until you have made the "original" movie. In some strong sense, the ecological thought rigorously comes afterward—it is always to come, somewhere in the future. In its fullest scope, it *will have been thought* at some undefined future point. You find yourself caught in its tractor beam (it's like a mathematical "attractor"). You didn't mean to. You must have been thinking it all along. But you had no idea. The ecological thought sneaks up on you from the future, a picture of what will have had to be there, already, for "ecology without nature" to make sense.

Like archaeologists of the future, we must piece together what will have been thought. Ultimately, the ecological thought surpasses what passes for environmentalism. It thinks otherwise than small-minded, and big-minded, manipulation. It goes beyond thinking "How many other living beings must we kill in order to be around next winter?" It goes beyond "Whatever is, is right."[9] It goes beyond "Let it be, let it be."[1] It goes beyond self, Nature, and species. It goes beyond survival, Being, destiny, and essence. Yet like a virus, like the lowest of the lowest (are they even alive?), like the tiny macromolecules in our cells, in our very DNA, the ecological thought has been there all along.

Why "ecology without nature"? "Nature" fails to serve ecology well. I shall sometimes use a capital *N* to highlight its "unnatural" qualities, namely (but not limited to), hierarchy, authority, harmony, purity, neutrality, and mystery. Ecology can do without a concept of a something, a thing of some kind,

5. Percy Shelley, "A Defence of Poetry," 535.

6. Charles Darwin, *The Origin of Species*, ed. Gillian Beer (Oxford: Oxford University Press, 1990), 248–51. [Darwin (1809–1882), English naturalist and theorist of evolution—editor's note.]

7. Emmanuel Levinas, *Totality and Infinity: An Essay on Exteriority*, trans. Alphonso Lingis (Pittsburgh: Duquesne University Press, 1969), 25. [Lévinas (1906–1995), French philosopher; the quotation here is also the book's epigraph—editor's note.]

8. Timothy Morton, *Ecology without Nature: Rethinking Environmental Aesthetics* (Cambridge, MA: Harvard University Press, 2007), 204–5.

9. Alexander Pope, *Essay on Man* 1.294, in *The Poems of Alexander Pope: A One-Volume Edition of the Twickenham Text, with Selected Annotations*, ed. John Butt (London: Routledge, 1989). [Pope (1688–1744), major English poet—editor's note.]

1. Paul McCartney (and Martin Heidegger), "Let It Be," *Let It Be* (Apple Records, 1970). [MARTIN HEIDEGGER'S (1889–1976) environmental ethics is frequently translated to the imperative "Let it be." The song, the title track of the Beatles' final album, was one of the band's most popular—editor's note.]

"over yonder," called Nature. Yet thinking, including ecological thinking, has set up "Nature" as a reified thing in the distance, under the sidewalk, on the other side where the grass is always greener, preferably in the mountains, in the wild. One of the things that modern society has damaged, along with ecosystems and species and the global climate, is thinking. Like a dam, Nature contained thinking for a while, but in the current historical situation, thinking is about to spill over the edge.

Ecological thinking might be quite different from our assumptions about it. It isn't just to do with the sciences of ecology. Ecological thinking is to do with art, philosophy, literature, music, and culture. Ecological thinking has as much to do with the humanities wing of modern universities as with the sciences, and it also has to do with factories, transportation, architecture, and economics. Ecology includes all the ways we imagine how we live together. Ecology is profoundly about coexistence. Existence is always coexistence. No man is an island.[2] Human beings need each other as much as they need an environment. Human beings *are* each others' environment. Thinking ecologically isn't simply about nonhuman things. Ecology has to do with you and me.

Why call this book *The Ecological Thought*? Why not *An Ecological Thought* or *Some Ecological Thoughts*? Or more modestly, *Notes toward Ecological Thinking*? Or just *Ecological Thought*? Of course there are ecological thoughts. And this book has no monopoly on ecological thinking. But there is a particular kind of thinking that I call *the* ecological thought. It runs like a strand of DNA code through thousands of other kinds of thoughts. Moreover, the *form* of the ecological thought is at least as important as its *content*. It's not simply a matter of *what* you're thinking about. It's also a matter of *how* you think. Once you start to think the ecological thought, you can't unthink it: it's a sphincter—once it's open, there's no closing.

THE SCOPE OF THE DAMAGE

Modern economic structures have drastically affected the environment. Yet they have had an equally damaging effect on thinking itself. I don't mean that before now we thought ecologically and properly. The ecological thought in its full richness and depth was unavailable to nonmodern humans. Even now, on the brink—over the brink, indeed—of climate catastrophe, we're only just capable of glimpsing its magnitude and profundity. The modern age compels us to think big, in the words of the first chapter.[3] Any thinking that avoids this "totality" is part of the problem. So we have to face it. Something about modern life has prevented us from thinking "totality" as big as we could. Now we can't help but think it. Totality looms like a giant skyscraper shadow into the flimsiest thought about, say, today's weather. We may need to think bigger than totality itself, if totality means something closed, something we can be sure of, something that remains the same. It might be harder to imagine four and a half billion years[4] than abstract eternity. It might be harder to imagine evolution than to imagine abstract

2. John Donne, "Meditation 17" [1624], in *Major Works: Including Songs and Sonnets and Sermons*, ed. John Carey (Oxford: Oxford University Press, 2000), 344.

3. Chapter 1 is titled "Thinking Big" [editor's note].

4. The estimated age of Earth [editor's note].

infinity. It's a little humiliating. This "concrete" infinity directly confronts us in the actuality of life on Earth. Facing it is one of the profound tasks to which the ecological thought summons us.

We've gotten it wrong so far—that's the truth of climate disruption and mass extinction. I don't advocate a return to premodern thinking. The ecological thought is modern. The paradox is that the modern era—let's say it began around the late eighteenth century—impeded its own access to the ecological thought, even though the ecological thought will have been one of its lasting legacies. As far as ecology goes, modernity spent the last two and a half centuries tilting at windmills. The ghost of "Nature," a brand new entity dressed up like a relic from a past age, haunted the modernity in which it was born.[5] This ghostly Nature inhibited the growth of the ecological thought. Only now, when contemporary capitalism and consumerism cover the entire Earth and reach deeply into its life forms, is it possible, ironically and at last, to let go of this nonexistent ghost. Exorcise is good for you, and human beings are past the point at which Nature is a help. Our continued survival, and therefore the survival of the planet we're now dominating beyond all doubt, depends on our thinking past Nature.

Modern thinkers had taken it for granted that the ghost of Nature, rattling its chains, would remind them of a time without industry, a time without "technology," as if we had never used flint or wheat. But in looking at the ghost of Nature, modern humans were looking in a mirror. In Nature, they saw the reflected, inverted image of their own age—and the grass is always greener on the other side. Nature was always "over yonder," alien and alienated.[6] Just like a reflection, we can never actually reach it and touch it and belong to it. Nature was an ideal image, a self-contained form suspended afar, shimmering and naked behind glass like an expensive painting. In the idea of pristine wilderness, we can make out the mirror image of private property: Keep off the Grass, Do Not Touch, Not for Sale. Nature was a special kind of private property, without an owner, exhibited in a specially constructed art gallery. The gallery was Nature itself, revealed through visual technology in the eighteenth century as "picturesque"—looking like a picture.[7] The "new and improved" version is art without an object, just an aura: the glow of value.[8] Nature isn't what it claims to be.

While we're on the subject of Nature and "new and improved" upgrades, this book makes a rigorous distinction between *environmentalism* and *ecology*. By the time you finish, you may feel that there are good reasons for advocating not just ecology without nature but also *ecology without environmentalism*.

In *Reflections on the Edge of Askja*, Pall Skulason tells us why we need Nature:

> To live, to be able to exist, the mind must connect itself with some kind of order. It must apprehend reality as an independent whole . . . and

5. Morton, *Ecology without Nature*, 14, 18–19, 83–92.
6. See Steven Vogel, *Against Nature: The Concept of Nature in Critical Theory* (Albany: State University of New York Press, 1996).
7. John Barrell, *The Idea of Landscape and the Sense of Place, 1730–1840: An Approach to the Poetry of John Clare* (Cambridge: Cambridge University Press, 1972); and *The Dark Side of the Landscape: The Rural Poor in English Painting, 1730–1840* (Cambridge: Cambridge University Press, 1980).
8. Morton, *Ecology without Nature*, 20–21, 22, 52–53, 67, 80–81, 105–6, 114–15, 142, 155, 168.

> must bind itself in a stable fashion to certain features of what we call reality. It cannot bind itself to the ordinary world of everyday experience, except by taking it on faith that reality forms an objective whole, a whole which exists independently of the mind. The mind lives, and we live, in a relationship of faith with reality itself. This relationship is likewise one of confidence in a detached reality, a reality which is different and other than the mind. We live and exist in this relationship of confidence, which is always by its nature uncertain and insecure. . . . [This] relationship of confidence . . . is originally, and truly, always a relationship with reality as a natural totality: as Nature.[9]

It isn't hard to detect in this passage the violent, repetitive actions of someone desperate to restart a broken machine. Skulason cranks handles, attaches jumper cables, rolls it down a hill . . . it's not just what he says or even how he says it. It's the attitude with which he says it, the "subject position." From the tone of hope and fear, you can tell that the game is up and that he knows it. He is indulging in magical thinking: "If I just keep saying this in the right way, it'll be okay. Nature will exist." The desperation is legible in the sheer amount of writing. It goes on and on, waiting for something that never comes. It's Nature writing reduced to *Waiting for Godot:*[1] "I must keep going. I can will Nature into existence, write it into the script." Skulason is trying to cheer us up in the middle of the slow motion disaster we're facing. The more he says, the worse it gets.

In the name of ecology, we must scrutinize Nature with all the suspicion a modern person can muster. Let the buyer beware. Nature has turned out to be a plastic knockoff of the real thing. As Emmanuel Levinas puts it in an astonishing passage that is among other things a passionate critique of deep ecology's favorite philosopher, Martin Heidegger, our concepts of "faceless generous mother nature" are based on "sedentary" agricultural societies with their idea of "possession." The myth of the faceless mother provides the very motivation for our exploitation of Earth, seen as "inexhaustible matter for things."[2] Wilderness areas are giant, abstract versions of the products hanging in mall windows. Even when we've tried to preserve an enclave of safety from the ravages of the modern age, we've been getting it all wrong, on a more profound level.

Can we get over our addiction to possession and the myth of the faceless mother? What is the real thing? We can get a sense of it, to be sure, though it will upgrade our ideas of "real" and "thing" to boot. Ecology shows us that all beings are connected. *The ecological thought* is the thinking of interconnectedness. The ecological thought is a thought about ecology, but it's also a thinking that is ecological. Thinking the ecological thought is part of an ecological project. The ecological thought doesn't just occur "in the mind." It's a practice and a process of becoming fully aware of how human beings are connected with other beings—animal, vegetable, or mineral. Ultimately, this includes thinking about democracy. What would a truly democratic

9. Pall Skulason, *Reflections at the Edge of Askja: On Man's Relation to Nature* (Reykjavik: University of Iceland Press, 2006), 11. See SLAVOJ ŽIŽEK, *In Defense of Lost Causes* (London: Verso, 2008), 444. [Skúlason (1945–2015), Icelandic philosopher; Askja is a volcanic crater in the highlands of Iceland—editor's note.]

1. Samuel Beckett's absurdist play, originally written in French (1952), in which the two main characters hope in vain for someone named "Godot" to arrive [editor's note].

2. Levinas, *Totality and Infinity*, 46.

encounter between truly equal beings look like, what would it be—can we even imagine it?

When we start looking, we find the ecological thought everywhere. This isn't surprising, since the ecological thought is interconnectedness in the fullest and deepest sense. Even Descartes' infamous "I think therefore I am" takes place in an environment, and this environment is present in the very text of the cogito. Descartes begins the *Meditations* by describing himself sitting by a fire, holding in his hand the paper on which he is writing.[3] Environmentalist thinking frequently condemns Cartesianism as a prototype of the dreaded dualism that separates mind and body, self and world, subject and object. Descartes is framed as environmental public enemy number one. The ecological thought insists that we're deeply connected even when we say we're not. Thinking itself is an ecological event. The kind of environmentalist ideology that wishes that we had never started to think—ruthlessly immediate, aggressively masculine, ruggedly anti-intellectual, afraid of humor and irony—is dubious at best. In fact, it's part of the problem. The constant assertion that we're "embedded" in a lifeworld is, paradoxically, a symptom of drastic separation.[4]

When we think the ecological thought, we encounter all kinds of beings that are not strictly "natural." This isn't surprising either, since what we call "nature" is a "denatured," unnatural, uncanny sequence of mutations and catastrophic events: just read Darwin. The ecological view to come isn't a picture of some bounded object or "restrictive economy," a closed system.[5] It is a vast, sprawling mesh of interconnection without a definite center or edge. It is radical intimacy, coexistence with other beings, sentient and otherwise—and how can we so clearly tell the difference? The ecological thought fans out into questions concerning cyborgs, artificial intelligence, and the irreducible uncertainty over what counts as a person.[6] Being a person means never being sure that you're one. In an age of ecology without Nature, we would treat many more beings as people while deconstructing our ideas about what counts as people. Think *Blade Runner* or *Frankenstein:*[7] the ethics of the ecological thought is to regard beings as people even when they aren't people. Ancient animisms treat beings as people, without a concept of Nature. Perhaps I'm aiming for an upgraded version of animism. (I'm also aiming for another good excuse to write about my favorite film, *Blade Runner.*)

OPENING MOVES

Thinking the ecological thought is difficult: it involves becoming open, radically open—open forever, without the possibility of closing again. Studying

3. René Descartes, *Meditations and Other Metaphysical Writings*, trans. with an intro. by Desmond M. Clarke (London: Penguin, 2000), 19. ["I think therefore I am" (in Latin, *cogito ergo sum*)—that is, the occurrence of thought guarantees the existence of the thinker—is the foundational statement of the French philosopher Descartes (1596–1650); his *Meditations* were published in 1641—editor's note.]
4. Morton, *Ecology without Nature*, 4–5, 63–64, 80–81, 124–25, 129, 128–35, 164, 168.
5. I borrow "restrictive economy" from Georges Bataille, *The Accursed Share: An Essay on General Economy*, trans. Robert Hurley (New York: Zone Books, 1988), 1:19–26 (25).
6. The "cyborg" represents personhood in an age of digital and ecological interconnectedness: see DONNA HARAWAY, "A Cyborg Manifesto: Science, Technology, and Socialist-Feminism in the Late Twentieth Century," in *Simians, Cyborgs, Women: The Reinvention of Nature* (London: Routledge, 1991), 149–81. [For this essay, see above—editor's note.]
7. Two American films: the artificial "replicants" hunted in *Blade Runner* (1982, dir. Ridley Scott) and the "monster" created in *Frankenstein* (1931, dir. James Whale) insist on their humanity [editor's note].

art provides a platform, because the environment is partly a matter of perception. Art forms have something to tell us about the environment, because they can make us question reality. I would like to stay for as long as possible in an open, questioning mode. This open mode is intrinsic to whatever we inadequately call the environment.[8] Is the ecological thought thinking about ecology? Yes and no. It is a thinking that is ecological, a contemplating that is a doing. Reframing our world, our problems, and ourselves is part of the ecological project. This is what *praxis* means—action that is thoughtful and thought that is active. Aristotle asserted that the highest form of praxis was contemplation.[9] We shouldn't be afraid to withdraw and reflect.

The ecological thought is also difficult because it brings to light aspects of our existence that have remained unconscious for a long time; we don't like to recall them. It isn't *like* thinking about where your toilet waste goes. It *is* thinking about where your toilet waste goes. Anxiety over wastewater treatment provides a good example. In the United States, many people now drink recycled wastewater. Some people simply don't want to know that their water is recycled excrement. It is public policy to tune out this fact. Yet recycled water is less unclean than "naturally" filtered water. We lose not only our undisturbed dreams of civilized cleanliness through this process but also our sense of Nature as pristine and nonartificial. Nature becomes wastewater treatment version 1.0.[1] Freud[2] described the unconscious as a wilderness area. Wilderness areas are the unconscious of modern society, places we can go to keep our dreams undisturbed. The very form of modern consciousness is itself this dream.

In Lakewood, Colorado, residents objected to the construction of a solar array in a park in 2008, because it didn't look "natural."[3] Objections to wind farms are similar—made not because of the risk to birds but because they "spoil the view." A 2008 plan to put a wind farm near a remote Scottish island was, well, scotched, because residents complained that their view would be destroyed. This is truly a case of the aesthetics of Nature impeding ecology and a good argument for why ecology must be without Nature. Why is a wind turbine less beautiful than an oil pipe? Why does it "spoil the view" any more than pipes and roads?

You could see turbines as environmental art. Wind chimes play in the wind; some environmental sculptures sway and rock in the breeze. Wind farms have a slightly frightening size and magnificence. One could easily read them as embodying the aesthetics of the sublime (rather than the beautiful).[4] But it's an ethical sublime that says, "We humans choose not to use carbon"—a choice visible in gigantic turbines. Perhaps it's this very visibility of choice that makes wind farms disturbing: visible choice, rather than secret pipes, running under an apparently undisturbed "landscape" (a word

8. See, for example, Timothy Morton, "John Clare and the Question of Place," in *Romanticism's Debatable Lands*, ed. Claire Lamont and Michael Rossington (London: Palgrave, 2007), 105–17.
9. See Erich Fromm, *To Have or to Be?* (London: Continuum, 2007), 75. [ARISTOTLE (384–322 B.C.E.), Greek philosopher; see especially *Nicomachean Ethics* 10.8, 1178b20–22—editor's note.]
1. See Elizabeth Royte, "A Tall, Cool Drink of . . . Sewage?" *New York Times Magazine*, August 10, 2008, 30–33.
2. SIGMUND FREUD (1856–1939), Austrian founder of psychoanalysis [editor's note].
3. Ryan Parker, "Residents Upset about Park Proposal," *Lakewood Sentinel*, July 31, 2008; "Solar Foes Focus in the Dark," Editorial, August 7, 2008; and August 14, 2008, 1, 4.
4. On the distinction between the sublime and the beautiful, see especially EDMUND BURKE's *A Philosophical Enquiry into the Origin of Our Ideas of the Sublime and Beautiful* (1757, 1759), excerpted above [editor's note].

for a painting, not actual trees and water). As a poster in the office of Mulder in the television series *The X-Files*[5] used to read, "The Truth Is Out There." Ideology isn't just in your head. It's in the shape of a Coke bottle. It's in the way some things appear "natural"—rolling hills and greenery—as if the Industrial Revolution had never occurred. These fake landscapes are the original greenwashing. What the Scots are saying, in objecting to wind farms, isn't "Save the environment!" but "Leave our dreams undisturbed!"

If you're a parent, you will understand our resistance to cleaning things up. Ecology talks about areas of life that we find annoying, boring, and embarrassing. Art can help us, because it's a place in our culture that deals with intensity, shame, abjection, and loss. It also deals with reality and unreality, being and seeming. If ecology is about radical coexistence, then we must challenge our sense of what is real and what is unreal, what counts as existent and what counts as nonexistent. The idea of Nature as a holistic, healthy, real thing avoids this challenge.

We must face some puzzling questions. What is an environment? Is there such a thing as *the environment*? Is it everything "around" us? At what point do we stop, if at all, drawing the line between *environment* and *non-environment*: The atmosphere? Earth's gravitational field? Earth's magnetic field, without which everything would be scorched by solar winds? The sun, without which we wouldn't be alive at all? The Galaxy? Does the environment include or exclude us? Is it natural or artificial, or both? Can we put it in a conceptual box? Might the word *environment* be the wrong word? *Environment*, the upgrade of *Nature*, is fraught with difficulty. This is ironic, since what we often call the environment is being changed, degraded, and eroded (and destroyed) by global forces of industry and capitalism. Just when we need to know what it is, it's disappearing.

Along with the ecological crisis goes an equally powerful and urgent opening up of our view of who we are and where we are. What, therefore, is environmental art? If what we inadequately call the environment entails a radical openness, how does this appear in art forms? Are there environmental ways of reading and doing criticism that account for this radical openness? Various kinds of ecocriticism have emerged to explore the role of ecology in literature. In particular, Romantic literature, from the beginning of the modern age of industry and capitalism, has served as a touchstone for ecocriticism.[6] This brand of criticism, however, restricts the radical openness the ecological thought implies, employing a prepackaged conceptual container labeled "Nature." Ironically, Romantic "Nature" is an artificial construct. And extra-ironically, Romantic-period art itself already thought

5. Originally aired 1993–2002; the FBI agent Fox Mulder believed in paranormal and extraterrestrial activities [editor's note].

6. See, for example, Lawrence Buell, *The Environmental Imagination: Thoreau, Nature Writing, and the Formation of American Culture* (Cambridge, MA: Harvard University Press, 1995); Jonathan Bate, *Romantic Ecology: Wordsworth and the Environmental Tradition* (London: Routledge, 1991); Bate, *The Song of the Earth* (Cambridge, MA: Harvard University Press, 2000); James McKusick, *Green Writing: Romanticism and Ecology* (New York: St. Martin's Press, 2000); and Karl Kroeber, *Ecological Literary Criticism: Romantic Imagining and the Biology of Mind* (New York: Columbia University Press, 1994). See also Greg Garrard, *Ecocriticism* (London: Routledge, 2004); Kevin Hutchings, *Imagining Nature: Blake's Environmental Poetics* (Montreal: McGill-Queen's University Press, 2003); Ralph Pite, "How Green Were the Romantics?" *Studies in Romanticism* 35, no. 3 (Spring 1996): 357–73; Kate Rigby, *Topographies of the Sacred: The Poetics of Place in British Romanticism* (Charlottesville: University of Virginia Press, 2004); Onno Oerlemans, *Romanticism and the Materiality of Nature* (Toronto: University of Toronto Press, 2002).

about the environment in ways that were decisively "out of the box." We will thus find it helpful to explore Romantic literature in *The Ecological Thought*.[7] Nothing much has changed since. There is more concrete, more plastic, more democracy, more intense science and technology, more GDP, more alienation, and more self-consciousness about whether writing poems really can change the world. These are quantitative differences, not qualitative ones.

A truly ecological reading practice would think the environment beyond rigid conceptual categories—it would include as much as possible of the radical openness of the ecological thought. Ecocriticism has overlooked the way in which all art—not just explicitly ecological art—hardwires the environment into its *form*. Ecological art, and the ecological-ness of all art, isn't just *about* something (trees, mountains, animals, pollution, and so forth). Ecological art *is* something, or maybe it *does* something. Art is ecological insofar as it is made from materials and exists in the world. It exists, for instance, as a poem on a page made of paper from trees, which you hold in your hand while sitting in a chair in a certain room of a house that rests on a hill in the suburbs of a polluted city. But there is more to its ecological quality than that. The shape of the stanzas and the length of the lines determine the way you appreciate the blank paper around them. Reading the poem aloud makes you aware of the shape and size of the space around you (some forms, such as yodeling, do this deliberately). The poem organizes space. Seen like this, all texts—all artworks, indeed—have an irreducibly ecological form. Ecology permeates all forms. Nowadays we're used to wondering what a poem says about race or gender, even if the poem makes no explicit mention of race or gender. We will soon be accustomed to wondering what any text says about the environment even if no animals or trees or mountains appear in it.[8]

The ecological thought affects all aspects of life, culture, and society. Aside from art and science, we must build the ecological thought from what we find in philosophy, history, sociology, anthropology, religion, cultural studies, and critical theory. I shall combine empirical evolution theory with "Continental" thinking about being and existence. This seems perverse: "high" philosophy merging shamelessly with "vulgar" materialism. There are pretty good boundaries between science and humanities departments and within the humanities themselves. This won't be to everyone's taste. Daniel Dennett, a Darwinist cognition theorist, pooh-poohs deconstruction.[9] Much Continental thinking assumes that there is no continuity between humans and animals, adopting a haughty "everyone knows that" tone and declaring that thinking otherwise is "asinane" (worse than asinine—and worse because we're behaving like donkeys).[1] This is condescending exclusivity. Some insist

7. See Morton, *Ecology without Nature*, 73–76, 194–95.
8. For an analysis of environmental form, see Timothy Morton, "Of Matter and Meter: Environmental Form in Coleridge's 'Effusion 35' and 'The Eolian Harp,'" *Literature Compass Romanticism* 5 (January 2008).
9. Daniel C. Dennett, *Darwin's Dangerous Idea: Evolution and the Meanings of Life* (New York: Simon & Schuster, 1995), 115, n. 10.
1. The word sometimes used is "continuism," from Jacques Derrida, *The Animal That Therefore I Am*, ed. Marie-Louise Mallet, trans. David Wills (New York: Fordham University Press, 2008), 30. The assumption that Derrida always knows what he is talking about is not Derridean. Derrida is also responsible for "asinane" (18, 31). Derrida finds himself in company with Luc Ferry, "Neither Man nor Stone," in Peter Atterton and Matthew Calarco, eds., *Animal Philosophy: Ethics and Identity* (London: Continuum, 2007), 147–56 (155). For a different view, see Felipe Fernández-Armesto, *So You Think You're Human? A Brief History of Humankind* (Oxford: Oxford University Press, 2004), 37. [DERRIDA (1930–2004), French deconstructionist philosopher and critic; for *The Animal That Therefore I Am*, see above—editor's note.]

proudly that they "refuse to accept the theory of evolution," which to a biologist sounds like refusing to accept that the Earth is round.[2] Even creationists take evolution more seriously than that. It doesn't have to be like this. No less a figure than Derrida maintained that deconstruction was a form of radical empiricism.[3] You want anti-essentialism and antibiologism? Just read Darwin.

Taken at their trivial and ideological worst, the humanities is hamstrung by "factoids," quasi- or pseudofacts that haven't been well thought out, while the sciences are held in the sway of unconscious "opinions." Humanities and sciences hold broken pieces of a jigsaw puzzle, pieces that might not fit together. Like William Blake I'm suspicious of "fitting & fitted."[4] The ecological thought must interrogate both the attitude of science, its detached authoritarian coldness; and the nihilistic, baselessly anthropocentric arguments in the humanities as well as humanist refusals to see the big picture, often justified by self-limiting arguments against "totalization"—talk about shooting yourself in the foot.[5] The ecological thought is about warmth and strangeness, infinity and proximity, tantalizing "thereness" and head-popping, wordless openness.

The ecological thought is intrinsically open, so it doesn't really matter where you begin. There are good reasons for trusting the biases and specialties that I bring to this task. Studying art is important, because art sometimes gives voice to what is unspeakable elsewhere, either temporarily—one day we will find the words—or intrinsically—words are impossible. Since the ecological thought is so new and so open, and therefore so difficult, we should expect art to show us some of the way. The ecological thought supplies good reasons to study culture and philosophy. Ecology is a matter of human experience. Humanities research can ask questions that science should address, questions that scientists may not have asked yet. For its part, science is about being able to admit that you're wrong. This means that if we want to live in a science-based society, we will have to live in the shadow of the possibility of wrongness. A questioning attitude needs to become habitual. Philosophy and critical theory in the humanities can help. Some people, including left humanities scholars who should know better, either think that scientists should be left to get on with their work, or even when they don't, the net effect of their beliefs is that science is untouched.[6] We have a responsibility to examine, participate in, support, and criticize scientific experiments: to that end, this book shall propose some.

For example, are nonhumans capable of aesthetic contemplation? Can they enjoy art? Fascinating research projects, to say the least, are beginning find out whether the beings we call animals are capable of this. If they were, it would be essential to find out whether this contemplation was an advanced

2. Peter Atterton, "Ethical Cynicism," Atterton and Calarco, eds., *Animal Philosophy*, 51–61 (61). GILLES DELEUZE and FÉLIX GUATTARI assert that they are beyond evolution in proposing the codevelopment of all beings in "alliance": "Becoming-Animal," in Atterton and Calarco, eds., *Animal Philosophy*, 87–100 (88). On the contrary, symbiosis, far from being the opposite of evolution, is deeply entrenched in it.

3. Jacques Derrida, *Of Grammatology*, trans. Gayatri Chakravorty Spivak (Baltimore: Johns Hopkins University Press, 1987), 162.

4. William Blake, *The Complete Poetry and Prose of William Blake*, ed. D. V. Erdman (New York: Doubleday, 1988), 667.

5. By "attitude" I mean what Lacanian ideology theory calls "subject position."

6. See, for instance, Slavoj Žižek, "Ecology without Nature," talk given at Panteion University, Athens [October 3, 2007].

cognitive state or a simple one, if not the simplest. Is our capacity to enjoy art one of those things that makes us uniquely human (along with hands, tools, laughter, and dancing, all of which have been discovered in nonhumans)? Or do we share this capacity with nonhuman beings? These questions get to the heart of some of our cultural and political assumptions regarding nonhuman beings.

While it's deeply informed by critical theory, this book won't be talking very explicitly about theory. Why? Not because I want to dumb down the argument. I do this because people who aren't members of the in crowd of specialists familiar with the language of theory (and the kinds of things that are cool to say with it) badly need to read this book. Otherwise the ecological thought separates theory haves from have-nots. Humanities scholars have some very good and important ideas, if only they would let others read them. We simply can't leave environmentalism to the anti-intellectualists. If you're interested, this book does engage with theory in the notes. Or you can read my essays, perhaps starting with "Queer Ecology" in *PMLA*, and also *Ecology without Nature*.[7] I won't be doing a lot of green close reading either. You can find some examples, based on the view this book lays out, by following this note.[8]

* * *

2010

7. Timothy Morton, "Queer Ecology," *PMLA* 125, no. 2 (March 2010): 273–82; "Thinking Ecology: The Mesh and the Strange Stranger," *Collapse* 6 (2010): 265–93; "Ecologocentrism: Unworking Animals," *SubStance* 37, no. 3 (2008): 37–61.

8. Timothy Morton, "Of Matter and Meter," "John Clare and the Question of Place," and "Shelley, Nature and Culture," in *The Cambridge Companion to Shelley*, ed. Timothy Morton (Cambridge: Cambridge University Press, 2006), 185–207; "Wordsworth Digs the Lawn," *European Romantic Review* 15, no. 2 (March 2004): 317–27; "Why Ambient Poetics?" *The Wordsworth Circle* 33, no. 1 (Winter 2002): 52–56.

ALONDRA NELSON
b. 1968

Alondra Nelson is among a group of critical theorists committed to studying and discussing the theoretical and cultural aesthetic called Afrofuturism. It engages the intersections between race and technology, between technoculture and the histories and futures of the African diaspora. Nelson is professor of sociology and gender studies at Columbia University, where she also has served as inaugural dean of social science for the Faculty of Arts and Sciences and director of the Institute for Research on Women, Gender, and Sexuality. An interdisciplinary social scientist, Nelson publishes writings at the intersections of sociology and history, gender and sexuality, race and technology, medicine and inequality, and art and new media. She has appeared on radio and television's popular science-oriented *Star Talk Live*, hosted by the cosmologist and astrophysicist Neil deGrasse Tyson.

Born to middle-class parents in Bethesda, Maryland, Nelson moved as a child with her family to San Diego, California. Nelson's interest in science and technology developed from her parents: her father served as a technician in the U.S. Navy, and her mother, an immigrant from Jamaica, was a cryptologist for the U.S. Army. She studied anthropology at the University of California at San Diego, receiving her B.A. magna cum laude. She earned a Ph.D. in American studies from New York University in 2003. Her first position was at Yale, where she taught in the Departments of African American Studies and Sociology before leaving for Columbia in 2009.

While at New York University, Nelson enrolled in a semester-long course on FRANTZ FANON offered by the art historian Kobena Mercer. Fanon's work on science and technology as critical apparatuses and his political and critical interventions as a medical doctor greatly affected Nelson's dissertation, "Black Power, Biopolitics and the Politics of Knowledge." That dissertation would form the basis of her first scholarly monograph, *Body and Soul: The Black Panther Party and the Fight against Medical Discrimination* (2011), a social and political history of the Black Panther Party from its founding in 1966 to its formal end in 1980 that won four awards: Distinguished Book Contribution to Scholarship from the American Sociological Association, the Association for Humanist Sociology Book Award, the Letitia Woods Brown Memorial Book Award, and the Mirra Komarovsky Book Award. While the Panthers are most often remembered for their revolutionary rhetoric and militant action, Nelson deftly recovers a lesser-known but indispensable aspect of their broader struggle for social justice: the battle for access to health care.

In 1998, Nelson was instrumental in building an Internet online community around Afrofuturism—a term coined by Mark Dery in "Black to the Future" (1993). That essay, which contains interviews with the scholar Tricia Rose, journalist Greg Tate, and science fiction writer Samuel R. Delany, attempts to frame black identity and the black experience in science and technology—in effect, to historicize black technoculture. It resonated with Nelson's work. In 2002, she curated and edited *Afrofuturism*, a special issue of *Social Text*, a leading U.S. journal of cultural studies. In it, several authors address the intersections between African diasporic culture and technology through literature, poetry, science fiction and speculative fiction, music, visual art, and the Internet. The issue demonstrates that racial identity fundamentally influences technocultural practices.

Nelson's "AfroFuturism: Past-Future Visions" (2000), our selection, articulates Afrofuturism's narrative, sonic, and visual components while namechecking its practitioners and innovators. Innovation and improvisation, she argues, are at the heart of black technoculture and of African diasporic peoples' histories and futures. For Nelson, history may inform the future of the African diaspora, but it does not wholly define it. Here Afrofuturists are vital as they envision those alternative tomorrows, sometimes utopic and at other times dystopic.

Along the way, Nelson highlights Afrodiasporic technical innovations in jazz, hip-hop, film, and especially photography. The pioneering work of the Nigerian-born photographer Fatimah Tuggar receives special attention. Tuggar's digital artistry creates works of contrast. Her photography captures what we think we know about Africa, a continent so vast and varied, but here reimagined as a place of decided technological and economic underdevelopment mixed with development. We see rural Nigerian women in domestic spaces and in traditional dress as well as Nigerian women involved in the global production of goods, services, and information via work in data processing and on assembly lines. For Nelson, Tuggar's photography and the women it pictures represent the past, present, and future possibilities of women's soft power, their facility with global digital and technological innovations in private and public spaces on a continent now gripped by Chinese soft power, a distilled form of neocolonialism that promises development and cooperation yet is revealed in Tuggar's work as uneven.

"AfroFuturism: Past-Future Visions" Keywords: Cultural Studies, Identity, Ideology, Media, Popular Culture, Postcolonial Theory, Race and Ethnicity Studies

AfroFuturism: Past-Future Visions

Visions of the future abound, celebrating progress, speed, and the empowering presence of technology in our lives, often accompanied by pronouncements about a brave new world coming into being—a world free from race, class, and gender conflicts. But how utopian are visions of new gizmos and gadgets fueled by commercial imperatives? And to whom do these futures belong?

They say you can't see race in cyberspace, but it is certainly not a coincidence that post-identity sentiments thrive in a climate intolerant to appeals for social and racial justice. Cyber-libertarian ideology holds that assertions of race, class, or gender difference in technologically enabled environments are like broaching politics at a dinner party—the epitome of bad taste. As a result, a false opposition is created, placing women and people of color on one side of the utopian equation, and technoculture on the other.

This split is partly a function of the "digital divide"—a gap that, not surprisingly, falls along race and class lines. Even in the midst of a digital revolution, the social conditions produced by the new information order have much in common with those that shaped the old industrial order. So the digital divide has become a call-to-arms for many African Americans, activists and entrepreneurs alike. But while it speaks to very material concerns that require real solutions, the digital divide is also ideological. This gap has become a self-fulfilling prophecy, reinforcing stereotypes of black technophobia; it confirms that African Americans can't keep pace in a hi-tech world that threatens to outstrip them. Focusing on the digital divide has paralyzed the thinking even of those who seek to bridge it.

Why don't we look at the innovations in technique and communication that can be found throughout black diasporic culture? Technology speaks to identity, but identity also speaks to technology. While identifying the class, race, and gender inequities that structure the so-called digital divide, we can also identify glimpses of creative possibility in the application of African diasporic cultural traditions to technology.

AfroFuturism has emerged as a term of convenience to describe the analysis, criticism, and cultural production that addresses the intersections between race and technology. Neither a mantra nor a movement, AfroFuturism is a critical perspective that opens up inquiry into the many overlaps between technoculture and black diasporic histories. AfroFuturism looks across popular culture—jazz, hip-hop, and techno music; experimental film; graffiti art; new photography—to find models of expression that transform spaces of alienation into novel forms of creative potential. In the process, it reclaims theorizing about the future.

New Icons, New Heroes, New Futures

In response to prevailing views about race, culture, and technology, alternative AfroFuturist narratives insist that who we've been and where we've traveled is always an integral component of who we can become. They provide novel takes on lived experience in a technologized world, perspectives that open up space for new ideas about politics and new visions of black life: new icons, new heroes, new futures.

AfroFuturist communiques are issued in the writing of Ishmael Reed, Octavia Butler, Ralph Ellison, Samuel R. Delany, and Nalo Hopkinson;[1] they are delivered in the music of Sun Ra and the Omniverse Arkestra, George Clinton, 4 Hero, Underground Resistance, Lee "Scratch" Perry, Missy Elliot, and DJ Spooky;[2] they are made manifest in the imagery weaved by video maker Hype Williams, independent director John Akomfrah, and filmmaker Julie Dash;[3] and they are revealed in the visual speculation of artists Rammellzee, Jean-Michel Basquiat, Fatimah Tuggar, and Keith Piper.[4]

These artists are self-styled mavericks whose creations reflect the long and impressive history of African diasporic culture, but also push the envelope of these traditions. They garner text, sound, and image in the service of reimagining black life. They create reflections on the African diasporic past and renderings of our possible futures. These are past-future visions, and in this sense, AfroFuturism is an antidote to unbridled, raceless future-lust.

Envisioning the Future

Cultural production can produce social reflection. Art that attends to themes of science and technology offers particularly sharp models of social reflection, for it is in the realm of art—with its ability to bring heightened perception and a critical distance to bear on lived experience—that we are better able to consider how technology is significant in everyday life. And AfroFuturist narratives in which time collapses into a single plane are not necessarily unconcerned with history.

The work of digital artist Fatimah Tuggar might best be characterized as "cyborg[5] realism": a body of work that is equally true to the traditions of the Nigerian communities that she photographs and to shifting social relations in an increasingly technological world. Tuggar's unlikely cyborgs are most often rural African women engaged in domestic activities.

Tuggar's method tricks the eye. At first glance, her digitally modified and U.V. laminated images seem to depict familiar visions of Africa: Nigerian women in traditional dress and rural villages bereft of modern influence and modern comforts. These images are seductive, drawing the viewer's eye with rich hues and tones. They are also deceptive. Tuggar's images seem to provide confirmation of the "real Africa" we already know, that place where

1. All writers of color: Reed (b. 1938), American playwright, novelist, and poet; Butler (1947–2006), American author of science fiction; Ellison (1914–1994), American novelist; Delany (b. 1942), American author best known for his science fiction; Hopkinson (b. 1960), Jamaican-born author of science fiction and fantasy.
2. Musicians in a range of genres: Sun Ra (born Herman Poole Blount, 1914–1993), American jazz composer and leader of the Arkestra, an ensemble; Clinton (b. 1941), American funk singer, songwriter, and music producer; 4hero: an electronic music group from London formed in 1989; Underground Resistance: a highly political techno music collective from Detroit, Michigan, formed in 1989; Perry (b. 1936), Jamaican music producer; Elliott (b. 1971), American rapper and music producer; and DJ Spooky (Paul D. Miller, b. 1970), American electronic and hip-hop musician.
3. American film director, writer, and producer (b. 1952). Harold "Hype" Williams (b. 1970), American screenwriter and director and producer of films and music videos. Akomfrah (b. 1957), Ghanaian-born British artist and film director.
4. Maltese-born British multimedia artist and curator (b. 1960), a founding member of the BLK Art Group. Rammellzee (1960–2010), American visual, graffiti, and hip-hop artist. Basquiat (1960–1988), American expressionist artist. Tuggar (b. 1967), Nigerian-born visual artist who often creates Web-based interactive works, computer montages, and video collages.
5. On the cyborg, see DONNA HARAWAY'S "A Manifesto for Cyborgs: Science, Technology, and Socialist Feminism in the 1980s" (1985), excerpted above.

technology has never existed, that dark continent that is the opposite of the West.

But, in fact, the surreal settings she composes exist in "no place." For these are images of a virtual Africa—virtual because they are digitally built environments and because, in their juxtaposition of hi-tech artifacts with rural African life, they depict scenarios that are unimaginable, and therefore unreal, to many Western eyes. The result is a body of utopian, and sometimes dystopian, reflections on Africa and modernity.

Tuggar also deals with domestic and information technologies that are coded as feminine. Her collaged images bring into relief the contradictions and the ambiguities of post-modern progress, simultaneously exploring the important role that non-Western women play in the free trade zone assembly lines, or rural data processing outposts, and their desire for modern convenience. Her method allows her to consider, side-by-side, the contradiction between the sometimes tragic history of modernity and colonialism in Nigeria, and the power that digital technologies offer to better connect Africa to the global flow of goods, services, and information.

In this sense, her work responds to what she keenly terms "soft power," the flow of electronics and information that enables neo-colonial power, despite the absence of physical proximity. Tuggar believes that soft power must be battled with soft power. She exercises her own by creating images of African women at ease with technology in the public and private sphere, women who own and desire technological gadgets and the power that they can wield. Her representations are not blanket indictments of technological advance, but rather an opportunity for the viewer to consider the incongruities and contradictions of uneven development. They examine soft power as both a tool of domination and a tool of possibility.

With her digital photomontage, Tuggar provides alternative, critical icons for the digital revolution that look neither like the hyper-aestheticized cyborg women of television, film, or photography nor like the white male "pirates of Silicon Valley."[6] Her unlikely cyborgs, rather than indulging in the glamour of the posthuman, offer images and reflections on the effect of technology upon women's everyday lives. Tuggar's images revisit the past, redefine the probable, and forecast the possible.

Alien Nation

The central focus of AfroFuturist thought is in defining the relationships between race and technology through the many places where they intersect, including fiction and digital art. But there is no consensus among critics about the absolute significance of these associations. Like the cultural productions they write about, the strength of what we might cautiously call AfroFuturist criticism lies in the speculative and fragmented nature of the ideas. Mark Dery[7] coined the word "AfroFuturism" in a 1993 essay, first published in *South Atlantic Quarterly*, called "Black to the Future." Dery argued that "African American voices have other stories to tell about culture, technology, and things to come." He continued, "If there is an AfroFuturism, it must be sought in unlikely places, constellated from far-flung points."

6. The title of a 1999 made-for-television biographical film about the founders of Apple Computer and of Microsoft, Steve Jobs and Bill Gates.

7. American cultural critic (b. 1959).

Surveying black cultural production in film, music, literature, genre fiction, comics, and the arts, Dery assembled these "other stories," models of subjectivity which resonated with African American history due to their uncanny parallels with the geographic dislocations and abuses of chattel slavery. In an oft-quoted passage, Dery wrote, "African Americans, in a very real sense, are the descendants of alien abductees; they inhabit a sci-fi nightmare in which unseen but no less impassable force fields of intolerance frustrate their movements; official histories undo what has been done; and technology is too often brought to bear on black bodies (branding, forced sterilization, the Tuskegee [syphilis] experiment[8] and tasers come readily to mind)."

Was there ever anyone more "alien" than the black men and women abducted from Africa and brought to the New World against their will? Wasn't the history of black Americans a "sci-fi nightmare" in which the tools of the future were continually turned against black people? In posing these questions, Dery brilliantly elucidated recurring themes in black culture that crossed genres and forged paths for further inquiry.

But he leaves the full depth of Afrodiasporic technoculture underexplored. We are presented with an abject people with escapist visions. By virtue of their historically subjugated relationship to technology, blacks are given more of a reactionary than a constitutive relationship to technoculture in Dery's account. The affiliation he established between AfroFuturist artists is limited to their shared racial background rather than to the improvisation and innovation of black diasporic culture. These artists are notable more because they appropriate images of technology than because of the use of technologies in their work. By focusing on themes rather than techniques, Dery underappreciates the history of black technological innovation.

Free at Last—Of History?

Much of that innovation has occurred in music production, so it's not surprising that another strain of AfroFuturist thought has developed in music writing and criticism. In hip-hop, the separation and machination of break beats, achieved with turntables and sampling technology, become the building blocks for new combinations of sound. For cultural critic Tricia Rose, author of *Black Noise: Rap Music and Black Culture in Contemporary America*,[9] these technological innovations express the Afro-diasporic "cultural priorities" of rhythmic layering and rupture. Other experimental and electronic music forms like electro, techno, and drum-and-bass have built on these innovations. These often lyric-less musics marry science fiction themes in song titles and futurist imagery on cover art, with a post-industrial soundtrack of synthetic sounds and noises. Because the lyrics or narrative elements of these musics are pared down or absent, the techniques that make them possible are often brought to the forefront.

8. A notorious example of unethical medical experimentation on human subjects, examining the course of untreated syphilis in black men. This study (1932–72), conducted by the U.S. Public Health Service, involved 600 poor sharecroppers, who were never informed of the real purpose of the study and were told they would receive free health care; those infected with syphilis were not given the option of effective treatment, which became available in the mid-1940s.

9. Published in 1994.

For Kodwo Eshun,[1] author of *More Brilliant than the Sun*, the complexity of these compositions, and the high level of aptitude required of the music makers, deserve nothing less than the name "science." "Breakbeat science" describes the application of scientific technique to the production of music. Eshun even extends the term "science" to musics that existed before the advent of this "sampladelia," like the music of John Coltrane[2] and Sun Ra. In this clever formulation, Eshun duly recognizes the artists' ingenuity of aesthetic and technique. Eshun is also interested in the philosophical possibilities of the "break." Musical innovations always begin as breaks with tradition, as stark discontinuities with how music had been made prior to the point of innovation. For Eshun, such breaks are irrevocable, they mark an unbridgeable distance between the past and the future. What is produced stands alone in the sphere of novelty.

Tradition, Eshun argues, hinders our ability to experience the "new." Eshun wants "to reverse traditional accounts of Black Music. Traditionally, they've been autobiographical or biographical, or they've been heavily social or political. My aim is to suspend all of that absolutely, and then, in the shock of these absences, this huge world is opened up." But, despite Eshun's focus on what is usually called Black Music—a term that he rejects—the effect of this position is to negate the constitutive role of racial histories in shaping representations of the future and uses of technology. Race disappears into technology and the "Afro" in AfroFuturism is deconstructed until its effects are negligible.

If with Dery, AfroFuturism leads down a path to the constraints of history, with Eshun the future holds a new, improved, and dispersed "blackness," free of the weight of the historical past. Eshun's disposable history reacts to theories of black culture that place all Afrodiasporic cultural production in a linear and strictly chronological trajectory, that fail to recognize the borrowed and hybrid melange from which these creative efforts spring.

Beyond Reality

Though Eshun can be taken to task for his dismissal of any semblance of a unified black cultural tradition, he does rightly critique what might be called "black authenticity"—the tendency to believe that there are real and true ways of uniformly representing the collectivity of black diasporic experience. Black creative life has too often been determined by this impulse to "keep it real." In order to be taken seriously, we have fostered and encouraged a long tradition of social realism in our cultural production. And we feared that to stop keeping things real was to lose the ability to recognize and protest the very real inequities in the social world. But we created a cultural environment often hostile to speculation, experimentation, and abstraction.

Yet future vision is a necessary complement to realism, for the reality of oppression without utopianism will surely lead to nihilism. And we should not think of speculative cultural production as only "escapist," but rather as

1. British Ghanaian writer and filmmaker (b. 1967); *More Brilliant Than the Sun* (1998) examines the development of "sampladelia," a form of dance music that uses sampling and other digital technologies.

2. African American virtuoso jazz saxophonist, composer, and bandleader (1926–1967).

holding important insights about people's lived conditions. Uniting the strengths of Eshun and Dery, from a decidedly feminist perspective, Fatimah Tuggar's "cyborg realism" projects the future as a hybrid of times, places, influences, and techniques; novelty and tradition exist simultaneously.

Here imagination becomes crucial. As science fiction writer and theorist Samuel R. Delany suggests: "We need images of tomorrow; and our people [black people] need them more than most. Without an image of tomorrow, one is trapped by blind history, economics, and politics, beyond our control. One is tied up in a web, in a net, with no way to struggle free. Only by having clear and vital images of the many alternatives, good and bad, of where one can go, will we have any control over the way we may actually get there in a reality tomorrow will bring all too quickly."[3]

The future is neither an uncritical embrace of the past nor a singular conception of what lies ahead. It's ours for the imagining.

2002

3. Quoted from a 1978 lecture published as "The Necessity of Tomorrows," in Samuel R. Delany, *Starboard Wine: More Notes on the Language of Science Fiction* (Pleasantville, N.Y.: Dragon Press, 1984), p. 35.

SIANNE NGAI
b. 1971

One of the most remarkable things about literature is its ability to create very real feelings in response to imaginary events. Although there is a long history of speculation on literature's capacity to arouse emotion, from the ancient Greeks (GORGIAS, PLATO, and ARISTOTLE) all the way down to SIGMUND FREUD, much twentieth-century literary theory avoided explicitly theorizing emotion, viewing it as too subjective to be easily available for theoretical scrutiny. The New Critics banished it with the doctrine of the affective fallacy. It was too personal for structuralism's positivism or deconstruction's withering interrogation of the categories of the "subject" and "experience." Critiques of ideology (Marxism, feminism, critical race theory) that drew on a "hermeneutics of suspicion" sought to demystify oppressive social relations. Only psychoanalysis, some early myth criticism, and reader-response theory offered terms for theorizing literature's emotional impact. Around 2000, however, a number of theorists, including EVE KOSOFSKY SEDGWICK, LAUREN BERLANT, and Brian Massumi, returned to the question of literature's affective qualities, its ability to arouse feelings and emotions. Sianne Ngai has been praised as one of the most insightful and inventive theorists of this turn to affect. But rather than taking on the great emotions of the literary canon—rage, love, joy, hatred—her first book, *Ugly Feelings* (2005), focuses instead on the smaller and meaner feelings that seem to pervade late modernity, such as envy, irritation, anxiety, paranoia, and disgust. "If *Ugly Feelings* is a bestiary of affects," Ngai writes, "it is one filled with rats and possums rather than lions, its categories of feeling generally being, well, weaker and nastier."

Ngai was born in California and raised in Hawaii. She earned a B.A. (1993) and an M.F.A. (1995) from Brown University, and she received her Ph.D. from Harvard University (2000). From 2000 until 2007, she was an assistant professor of English at Stanford University; from 2007 until 2011, she was an associate professor of English at UCLA. She has been a professor of English at Stanford University since 2011. Ngai received a 2007–08 Charles A. Ryskamp Fellowship from the American Council of Learned Societies and in 2014–15 was a fellow at the Institute of Advanced Studies in Berlin, Germany. In 2015 she was awarded an honorary D.Phil. in Humanities from the University of Copenhagen. She is the author of two books, both major studies, and several articles. Her published work—including *Ugly Feelings* and *Our Aesthetic Categories: Zany, Cute, Interesting* (2012), which won both the MLA James Russell Lowell Prize and the PCA/ACA Ray and Pat Browne award for Best Reference or Best Primary Source Work—consistently engages with the minor, unappreciated, and overlooked. Ngai is also an accomplished poet and avant-garde fiction writer.

Affect theory follows and builds on the work of trauma theorists such as Cathy Caruth, E. ANN KAPLAN, and KELLY OLIVER by exploring emotional responses to more mundane events. While literary theorists have long attempted to objectify literary emotions through concepts such as John Dewey's "esthetic emotion" or T. S. ELIOT's "art emotion," what characterizes this most recent return to emotion is the distinction drawn between affect and emotion. Ngai notes that the concept of affect, which owes something to the philosophy of BARUCH SPINOZA, took on its contemporary meaning in the field of psychoanalysis as a means of characterizing "feeling described from an observer's (analyst's) perspective," as opposed to emotion, "designating feeling that 'belongs' to the speaker" or patient. That is, it attempts to separate what is objective about emotion from what is subjective, providing a way to put emotion into therapeutic discourse. The concept was further elaborated by GILLES DELEUZE and FÉLIX GUATTARI to emphasize bodily experience independent of a subject. Drawing on the work of the psychologist Silvan Tomkins (1911–1991), affect theorists such as Sedgwick and Massumi argue that while emotion is rooted in an experiencing subject, affect preexists the subject. Affect theory, then, designates feelings as personal, emotions as social, and affects per se as the biological substrate of emotion, which, according to Tomkins, is "hard-wired, pre-programmed, and genetically transmitted." Because affect, in this theory, is prior to and outside of consciousness, it eludes representation in language or signs. Once affect has been given social meaning, it becomes an emotion. This distinction between affect and emotion enables affect theorists to rebut the charge that the study of emotion is subjective and idiosyncratic. By creating a proper object of study, an authentic locus of feeling, they create a more objective approach to emotion—an approach rooted in biological bodies rather than idiosyncratic individuals.

Not all affect theorists accept such a hard-and-fast distinction, however; some, like Ngai, use the two words more or less interchangeably. Ngai acknowledges that the problem of sorting out what is subjective or objective about emotion remains; at the same time, she insists that for her purposes, "the difference between affect and emotion is taken as a modal difference of intensity or degree, rather than a formal difference of quality or kind." Affect, for her, is less "sociolinguistically fixed" than emotion, but not outside of meaning or language. If affect did elude language, how could it become an object of discourse? In our selection, from the introduction to *Ugly Feelings*, Ngai describes emotions/affects as "unusually knotted or condensed 'interpretations of predicaments.'" Within a literary text, affects or emotions provide a focal point for condensing problems that are at once formal, ideological, and sociohistorical. These knots correspond to the somewhat amorphous literary critical concept of "tone," which she defines as a text's "global or organizing affect, its general disposition or orientation toward its audience and the world." What makes tone such a difficult literary concept is that it is almost impossible to determine whether a text's affect is produced by the text (objective) or by its reader (subjective): thus, tone recapitulates the very subject/object problem that the emotion/affect distinction tries to resolve. By untying these knots (for example, by paying attention to tone), Ngai seeks to connect the formal features of literary texts and their ideological and sociocultural contexts—contexts that include entanglements of race and gender. In doing so, she fashions a method of reading emotion that balances formal analysis of texts with contemporary cultural and political issues.

The particular knots she chooses for her study are those typical of what THEODOR ADORNO called "the fully administered world of late modernity," in which individuals may feel a sense of "obstructed agency" that spawns enervation rather than action. Ngai turns to what she calls ugly feelings; these are emotions or affects that are "explicitly amoral and noncathartic, offering no satisfactions of virtue, however oblique, nor any therapeutic or purifying release"—emotions like envy, irritation, and paranoia. She even invents two previously unnamed "knots," which she calls *animatedness* (the representation of the black subject as an excessively emotional and expressive subject) and *stuplimity* ("an amalgamation of shock and boredom"). These ugly feelings are negative in three ways. They are experientially negative in evoking pain or displeasure, they are syntactically negative in repelling rather than attracting, and they are semantically negative in carrying socially stigmatized meanings.

These negative feelings or "sentiments of disenchantment," perhaps because they are repulsive (both unpleasant and repelling), tend to attach themselves not to canonical texts, which probe the strong emotions on which philosophers have tended to focus, but to minor literatures: Herman Melville's "tonally ambiguous" *Confidence-Man* (1857) rather than *Moby-Dick* (1851), Samuel Beckett's "exhausting" poetry rather than the Romantic lyric. The cultural canon, writes Ngai, "seems to prefer higher passions and emotions—as if minor or ugly feelings were not only incapable of producing 'major' works, but somehow disabled the works they do drive from acquiring canonical distinction." The presiding genius of *Ugly Feelings* is Melville's inscrutable Bartleby—the titular character of his "Bartleby, the Scrivener" (1853), a short story about a clerk working on Wall Street. Bartleby's all-encompassing refrain, "I prefer not to," serves as a motto for the sense of blocked agency that gives rise to ugly feelings in modern society.

Ugly feelings focalize the problem of art's own limited agency in the modern world. Following Adorno, Ngai argues that in our highly differentiated society, art is cordoned off from the "empirical," the utilitarian. Art's powerlessness in the political sphere, for Ngai, makes it an ideal space for theorizing political resistance. Extending the thinking of the contemporary Italian Marxist philosopher Paolo Virno, Ngai treats ugly feelings as socially symptomatic of capitalist society—as ideological material. At the same time, she recognizes that ugly feelings are ambiguous enough, being amoral and nonvirtuous, that they might be mobilized for either progressive or regressive ends, by the Right as easily as by the Left. This contradiction tends to make her claims for the efficacy of ugly feelings as a form of political praxis weaker. Some critics have characterized her claims as "doomed to failure," given the pervasive powerlessness so well illustrated by Ngai's book. For these critics, art is not the handmaiden of politics and should not be measured by its ability to initiate political resistance. Yet even her critics recognize that Ngai's sensitivity to the complex paradoxes produced by ugly feelings leads to nuanced readings of both literature and popular culture.

Ugly Feelings Keywords: Aesthetics, Affect, Cultural Studies, Ideology, Marxism, Modernity, Psychoanalysis, Subjectivity

From Ugly Feelings

From *Introduction*

This book presents a series of studies in the aesthetics of negative emotions, examining their politically ambiguous work in a range of cultural artifacts produced in what T. W. Adorno calls the fully "administered world" of late modernity.[1] This is the world already depicted by Herman Melville[2] with startling clarity in "Bartleby, the Scrivener: A Story of Wall Street" (1853)—a fiction in which the interpretive problems posed by an American office worker's *affective* equivocality seem pointedly directed at the *political* equivocality of his unnervingly passive form of dissent. What, if anything, is this inexpressive character feeling? Is Bartleby's unyielding passivity, even in the polemical act of withholding his labor ("I prefer not to"), radical or reactionary? Should we read his inertness as part of a volitional strategy that anticipates styles of nonviolent political activism to come, or merely as a sign of what we now call depression? In Melvillean fashion, the following chapters dwell on affective gaps and illegibilities, dysphoric feelings, and other sites of emotional negativity in literature, film, and theoretical writing, to explore similarly ambivalent situations of suspended agency. They thus draw together two seemingly disparate philosophical definitions—Hannah Arendt's claim that "what makes man a political being is his faculty of action" and Baruch Spinoza's description of emotions as "waverings of the mind" that can either increase or diminish one's power to act—and attend to the aesthetics of the ugly feelings that index these suspensions.[3]

Recalling the corner of the office in which Melville's scrivener is wedged and cordoned off by a screen, we might think of this book's project as Bartlebyan in a more reflexive sense, in that it privileges the circumscribed standpoint of the literary to examine problems whose greatest import arguably lies beyond the sphere of the aesthetic per se. For Bartleby's powerful powerlessness can also be thought of as exemplified by literature or art itself, as a relatively autonomous, more or less cordoned-off domain in an increasingly specialized and differentiated society. As Adorno's analysis of the historical origins of this aesthetic autonomy suggests, the separateness from "empirical society" which art gains as a consequence of the bourgeois revolution ironically coincides with its growing awareness of its inability to significantly change that society—a powerlessness that then becomes the privileged object of the newly autonomous art's "guilty" self-reflection (*AT*, 225). Yet one could argue that bourgeois art's reflexive preoccupation with its *own* "powerlessness and superfluity in the empirical world" is precisely what makes it capable of theorizing social powerlessness in a manner unrivaled by other forms of cultural praxis (104). In this manner, the discussion

1. Theodor W. Adorno, *Aesthetic Theory*, ed. and trans. Robert Hullot-Kentor (Minneapolis: University of Minnesota Press, 1997), 31. Hereafter designated *AT* [except as indicated, all notes are Ngai's]. [ADORNO (1903–1969), German philosopher and cultural critic—editor's note.]
2. American novelist and poet (1819–1891) [editor's note].
3. Hannah Arendt, *On Violence* (New York: Harcourt Brace, 1969), 82. Baruch Spinoza, *Ethics*, as translated and cited in Cheshire Calhoun and Robert C. Solomon, eds., *What Is an Emotion? Classic Readings in Philosophical Psychology* (New York: Oxford University Press, 1984), 85. [ARENDT (1906–1975), German-born American political theorist. SPINOZA (1632–1677), Dutch philosopher and theologian—editor's note.]

of aesthetic autonomy in *Aesthetic Theory* suggests that literature may in fact be the ideal space to investigate ugly feelings that obviously ramify beyond the domain of the aesthetic proper, since the situation of restricted agency from which all of them ensue is one that describes art's own position in a highly differentiated and totally commodified society.

Each of the feelings explored in the following chapters—envy, anxiety, paranoia, irritation, a racialized affect I call "animatedness," and a strange amalgamation of shock and boredom I call "stuplimity"—can thus be thought of as a mediation between the aesthetic and the political in a nontrivial way. As a whole, the book approaches emotions as unusually knotted or condensed "interpretations of predicaments"—that is, signs that not only render visible different registers of problem (formal, ideological, sociohistorical) but conjoin these problems in a distinctive manner.[4] My exclusive focus, however, is on the negative affects that read the predicaments posed by a general state of obstructed agency with respect to other human actors or to the social as such—a dilemma I take as charged with political meaning regardless of whether the obstruction is actual or fantasized, or whether the agency obstructed is individual or collective. These situations of passivity, as uniquely disclosed and interpreted by ignoble feelings like envy (of the disempowered for the powerful) or paranoia (about one's perceived status as a small subject in a "total system"), can also be thought of as allegories for an autonomous or bourgeois art's increasingly resigned and pessimistic understanding of its *own* relationship to political action. At the core of *Ugly Feelings,* then, is a very old predicament—the question of relevance—that has often haunted the discipline of literary and cultural criticism. The evidence here would suggest that the very effort of thinking the aesthetic and political together—a task whose urgency seems to increase in proportion to its difficulty in a increasingly anti-utopian and functionally differentiated society—is a prime occasion for ugly feelings.

Yet I want immediately to emphasize the deeply equivocal status of the ugly feelings featured in this study. For although dysphoric affects often seem to be the psychic fuel on which capitalist society runs, envy, paranoia, and all the emotional idioms I examine are marked by an ambivalence that will enable them to resist, on the one hand, their reduction to mere expressions of class *ressentiment,*[5] and on the other, their counter-valorization as therapeutic "solutions" to the problems they highlight and condense. Admittedly it is part of this book's agenda to recuperate several of these negative affects for their *critical* productivity, but no one warns us better about the danger of romanticizing them than Paolo Virno, for whom the classic "sentiments of disenchantment" that once marked positions of radical alienation from the system of wage labor—anxiety, distraction, and cynicism—are now perversely integrated, from the factory to the office, into contemporary capitalist production itself: "Fears of particular dangers, if only virtual ones, haunt the workday like a mood that cannot be escaped. This fear, however, is transformed into *an operational requirement,* a special tool of the trade. Insecurity about one's

4. Rei Terada, *Feeling in Theory: Emotion after the "Death of the Subject"* (Cambridge, Mass.: Harvard University Press, 2001), 57.

5. Resentment (French), a key concept in the philosophy of FRIEDRICH NIETZSCHE (1844–1900) [editor's note].

place during periodic innovation, fear of losing recently gained privileges, and anxiety over being 'left behind' translate into flexibility, adaptability, and a readiness to reconfigure oneself."[6] Here we see how capitalism's classic affects of disaffection (and thus of potential social conflict and political antagonism) are neatly reabsorbed by the wage system and reconfigured into professional ideals. Nothing could be further from Fredric Jameson's more widely known thesis about the "waning" of negative affect in our contemporary moment.[7] Instead, Virno shows how central and perversely *functional* such affective attitudes and dispositions have become, as the very lubricants of the economic system which they originally came into being to oppose.[8] Yet while irreversibly integrated into the contemporary, post-Fordist organization of labor,[9] these ugly feelings remain, for Virno, "open to radically conflicting developments" ("AD," 26). For example, while there is nothing redeeming about the "eager" disposition of opportunism, its "'truth' . . . what might be called its neutral kernel, resides in the fact that our relation with the world tends to articulate itself primarily through possibilities, opportunities, and chances, instead of according to linear and univocal directions." As Virno points out, "This modality of experience, even if it nourishes opportunism, does not necessarily result in it" (25). For other kinds of behavior, and even kinds diametrically opposed to opportunism, "might also be inscribed within an experience fundamentally structured by these same possibilities and fleeting opportunities. We can discern such radical and transformative behavior, however, only by tracing in the opportunism so widespread today the specific modality of experience to which this behavior might indeed be correlated, even if in a completely different way" (25). Indeed, one could extrapolate from Virno's claims to argue that in the transnational stage of capitalism that defines our contemporary moment, our emotions no longer link up as securely as they once did with the models of social action and transformation theorized by Aristotle, Thomas Hobbes,[1] and others under the signs of relatively unambiguous emotions like anger or fear. In other words, the nature of the sociopolitical itself has changed in a manner that both calls forth and calls upon a new set of feelings—ones less powerful than the classical political passions, though perhaps more suited, in their ambient, Bartlebyan, but still diagnostic nature, for models of subjectivity, collectivity, and agency not entirely foreseen by past theorists of the common-

6. Paolo Virno, "The Ambivalence of Disenchantment," in Paolo Virno and Michael Hardt, eds., *Radical Thought in Italy* (Minneapolis: University of Minnesota Press, 1996), 17, italics added. Hereafter designated "AD." [Virno (b. 1952), Italian Marxist, philosopher, and semiologist—editor's note.]

7. Fredric Jameson, *Postmodernism, or, The Cultural Logic of Late Capitalism* (Durham: Duke University Press, 1991), 15. [JAMESON (b. 1934), American Marxist literary theorist—editor's note.]

8. In fact, according to Virno, nothing currently unites "the software technician, the autoworker, and the illegal laborer" more than a process of socialization that, in teaching "habitual mobility, the ability to keep pace with extremely rapid conversions, adaptability in every enterprise, [and] flexibility in moving from one group of rules to another" ("Ambivalence of Disenchantment,"14), effectively runs on the affects of fear (which prompts mobility in the form of flight), opportunism (which relies on flexibility and adaptability), and cynicism (which arises from a particular intimacy with rules).

9. That is, after the era of modern industrial production that has been called "Fordism" (notably in the writings of DAVID HARVEY). In the 1920s, Henry Ford paid his workers relatively high wages and offered secure full-time jobs so that they could buy expensive consumer products such as the cars they were manufacturing; this "Fordist" strategy is credited with helping to create a middle class. Since the 1970s, companies have moved away from that model toward just-in-time production by casualized labor [editor's note].

1. English political philosopher (1588–1679). ARISTOTLE (384–322 B.C.E.), Greek philosopher [editor's note].

wealth. This is why, for Virno, even an unattractive feeling like opportunism can provide the "kernel" from which to shape "transforative behavior." For all its pettiness, the feeling calls attention to a real social experience and a certain kind of historical truth.

While this book makes a similar if more modest claim for the social significance of its own fundamentally ambivalent "sentiments of disenchantment" (an ambivalence demonstrated by the fact that all are mobilized as easily by the political right as by the left, as the histories of disgust and paranoia illustrate so well), it is useful to recall that with notable exceptions like Hobbes or Niccolò Machiavelli, who made fear central to their theories of modern sovereignty and the state, it is the discourse of philosophical aesthetics, rather than that of political philosophy or economy, in which emotions have traditionally played the most pivotal role—from Longinus to Immanuel Kant[2] on the sublime (perhaps the first "ugly" or explicitly non-beautiful feeling appearing in theories of aesthetic judgment), to the twentieth-century mutation of this affect I describe in my chapter on stuplimity. Or, to trace another exemplary arc, from the seventeenth-century "Affect Theorists" who tried to systematize the correlation of musical forms and genres to specific emotions, to Susanne Langer's[3] analysis of music as a "tonal analogue of emotive life" in *Philosophy in a New Key,* to my own attempt to reanimate the concept of literary "tone" by means of the atonal but no less musical concept of noise. The investigation of how new theories of affect might expand the discourse of aesthetics thus continues a long-standing intellectual project, even as it sets this book apart from cultural histories of specific emotions (as, for instance, *American Nervousness, 1903: An Anecdotal History,* by Tom Lutz; *Anatomy of Disgust,* by William Ian Miller; and *Cato's Tears and the Making of Anglo-American Emotion,* by Julie Ellison), as well as from new philosophies of emotion that inquire into what feeling is (*Parables for the Virtual,* by Brian Massumi; *Feeling in Theory,* by Rei Terada; and *The Vehement Passions,* by Philip Fisher). In a sense, the book's turn to ugly feelings to reanimate aesthetics is simply the flip side of its privileging of the aesthetic domain as the ideal site to examine the politically ambiguous work of negative emotions.

More specifically, this book turns to ugly feelings to expand and transform the category of "aesthetic emotions," or feelings unique to our encounters with artworks—a concept whose oldest and best-known example is Aristotle's discussion of catharsis in *Poetics*.[4] Yet this particular aesthetic emotion, the arousal and eventual purgation of pity and fear made possible by the genre of tragic drama, actually serves as a useful foil for the studies that follow. For in keeping with the spirit of a book in which minor and generally unprestigious feelings are deliberately favored over grander passions like anger and fear (cornerstones of the philosophical discourse of emotions, from Aristotle to the present), as well as over potentially ennobling or mor-

2. German philosopher (1724–1804); for his "Analytic of the Sublime" in *Critique of Judgment* (1790), see above. Machiavelli (1469–1527), Italian statesman and political philosopher who wrote about fear in *The Prince* (1513). LONGINUS (1st c. C.E.), Greek rhetorician to whom the treatise *On Sublimity* is attributed (see above) [editor's note].

3. American philosopher who wrote on linguistic analysis and aesthetics (1895–1985); *Philosophy in a New Key* (1957) is her best-known book [editor's note].

4. Aristotle, *Poetics* 6, 1449b (see above) [editor's note].

ally beatific states like sympathy, melancholia, and shame (the emotions given the most attention in literary criticism's recent turn to ethics), the feelings I examine here are explicitly *a*moral and *non*cathartic, offering no satisfactions of virtue, however oblique, nor any therapeutic or purifying release. In fact, most of these feelings tend to interfere with the outpouring of other emotions. Moods like irritation and anxiety, for instance, are defined by a flatness or ongoingness entirely opposed to the "suddenness" on which Aristotle's aesthetics of fear depends.[5] And unlike rage, which cannot be sustained indefinitely, less dramatic feelings like envy and paranoia have a remarkable capacity for duration. If *Ugly Feelings* is a bestiary of affects, in other words, it is one filled with rats and possums rather than lions, its categories of feeling generally being, well, weaker and nastier.

* * *

The equivocality of the Bartlebyan aesthetic suggests that there is a special relationship between ugly feelings and irony, a rhetorical attitude with a decidedly affective dimension, if not a "feeling" per se. For the morally degraded and seemingly unjustifiable status of these feelings tends to produce an unpleasurable feeling *about* the feeling (a reflexive response taking the form of "I feel ashamed about feeling envious" or "I feel anxious about my enviousness") that significantly parallels the doubleness on which irony, as an evaluative stance hinging on a relationship between the said and the unsaid, fundamentally depends.[6] In their tendency to promote what Susan Feagin calls "meta-responses" (since it is hard to feel envy without feeling that one should *not* be feeling envy, reinforcing the negativity of the original emotion), there is a sense in which ugly feelings can be described as conducive to producing ironic distance in a way that the grander and more prestigious passions, or even the moral emotions associated with sentimental literature, do not.[7] This is why the aesthetic examples in this book tend *not* to be drawn from the more recognizably "emotional" genres—such as melodrama, sentimental fiction, tales of supernatural horror, or lyric poetry—to which literary critics interested in such matters have traditionally turned. While the ironic as well as the noncathartic aspect of ugly feelings drives this book's preference for "constructivist" rather than "expressivist" forms as ideal sites for examining the social and symbolic productivity of emotion in general, it is another key aspect of these negative feelings—that of being noticeably weaker in intensity than what Philip Fisher calls the "vehement passions" underwriting canonically major forms and genres like Homeric epic and Shakespearean tragedy—which informs its preference for texts that even seem oddly impassive: texts that, like "Bartleby," foreground the absence of a strong emotion where we are led to expect one, or turn entirely on the interpretive problems posed by an emotional illegibility. The fact that this book reads the tonally ambiguous *Confidence-Man* rather than the rage-driven epic *Moby-Dick,* Nella Larsen's superficially "irritated" *Quicksand* but not the melodrama of jealousy that is *Passing,* and

5. Philip Fisher, *The Vehement Passions* (Princeton: Princeton University Press, 2001), 137. Hereafter designated *VP*.
6. Linda Hutcheon, *Irony's Edge: The Theory and Politics of Irony* (New York: Routledge, 1994).
7. Susan L. Feagin, "The Pleasures of Tragedy," *American Philosophical Quarterly*, 20 (1983), cited in Susan Feagin and Patrick Maynard, eds., *Aesthetics* (Oxford: Oxford University Press, 1997), 305–13.

Beckett's[8] exhausting poetry of permutations and combinations as opposed to the Romantic lyric, proceeds directly from its emphasis on the ignoble cousins of the philosophically canonical emotions featured in Fisher's study. With the turn to the ambiguous affects of the administered world's many "Sub-Subs"—Melville's appellation for the minor employee, or "mere painstaking burrower and grub-worm," who dutifully assembles the cetological "Extracts" that open *Moby-Dick*[9]—rather than those of more iconic figures such as Ahab, Othello, or Lear,[1] my focus will be on irritation *instead of* anger, envy *rather than* jealousy, and "stuplimity" *as opposed to* the transcendent feeling of the sublime. It is interesting to note here that while the texts chosen for the way they highlight these feelings are drawn from both high and mass culture, all are canonically minor. Something about the cultural canon itself seems to prefer higher passions and emotions—as if minor or ugly feelings were not only incapable of producing "major" works, but somehow disabled the works they do drive from acquiring canonical distinction.

Still, while partly a response to one philosopher's call for a study of feeling with a more idiosyncratic focus than those that "concentrate on analyzing the features of a handful of classic emotions,"[2] the "negativity" of the feelings in this book obtains at several levels that the classic emotions share. Like rage and fear, ugly feelings such as envy can be described as dysphoric or experientially negative, in the sense that they evoke pain or displeasure. They can also be described as "semantically" negative, in the sense that they are saturated with socially stigmatizing meanings and values (such as the "pettiness" one traditionally associates with envy); and as "syntactically" negative, in the sense that they are organized by trajectories of repulsion rather than attraction, by phobic strivings "away from" rather than philic strivings "toward." In the case of these explicitly agonistic emotions, informed by what one psychoanalyst calls the global affect of "against," the negativity at stake is algorithmic or operational, rather than value- or meaning-based, involving processes of aversion, exclusion, and of course negation.[3] It is these multiple levels of negativity that make the ugly feelings in this study so useful for *conjoining* predicaments from multiple registers—showing how sociohistorical and ideological dilemmas, in particular, produce formal or representational ones. The affect I call animatedness, for instance, will allow us to take the disturbingly enduring representation of the African-American as at once an excessively "lively" subject and a pliant body unusually susceptible to external control and link this representation to the rhetorical figure of apostrophe (in which a speaker animates or "gives life" to nonhuman objects by addressing them as subjects capable of response), and, further, to connect these to a symptomatic controversy surrounding the televisual aesthetics of dimensional animation, a technique in which clay or foam

8. Samuel Beckett (1906–1989), Irish author best known for his plays, but also a writer of criticism, novels, and poetry. *The Confidence-Man: His Masquerade* (1857), the final novel published in Melville's lifetime; *Moby-Dick* (1851) is his best-known work. Larsen (1891–1964), black American author of two novels, *Quicksand* (1928) and *Passing* (1929) [editor's note].

9. Herman Melville, *Moby-Dick, or The Whale* (New York: Penguin, 1992), xxxix.

1. The tragic heroes of, respectively, *Moby-Dick*, Shakespeare's *Othello* (1604), and Shakespeare's *King Lear* (1605) [editor's note].

2. Sue Campbell, *Interpreting the Personal: Expression and the Formation of Feelings* (Ithaca: Cornell University Press, 1997), 4.

3. Rene Spitz, *No and Yes: On the Genesis of Human Communication* (New York: International Universities Press, 1957), 50.

puppets are similarly brought to "life" as racialized characters by being physically manipulated and ventriloquized.

* * *

* * * The question of feeling's objective or subjective status has in fact been central to numerous philosophical investigations into the exact role and status of emotion in the aesthetic encounter. These investigations include debates over whether Aristotle uses *katharsin*[4] to refer to something that takes place in the audience or that takes place in the tragic drama (that is, whether it refers to a response undergone by the viewing subject or to an event presented in the object viewed); John Dewey's[5] effort to divorce expression from "the mere issuing forth or discharge of raw material" by describing "esthetic emotion" as "objectified" emotion; T. S. Eliot's[6] closely related attempt to separate "personal emotion" from "art emotion," which he describes as a mixture or cocktail producing "feelings which are not in actual emotions at all"; the counterintuitive effort, on the part of Edmund Burke[7] and other Enlightenment empiricists, to use emotional qualities to "objectify" or standardize judgments of taste (so as to avoid the problem of relativism it inevitably poses); and Gérard Genette's[8] unapologetically subjectivist theory of aesthetic judgment as a mode of illusory projection, in which a quality or value reflecting the negative or positive feeling inspired by an object's appearance, in what amounts to a fundamentally subjective appraisal, is treated "as if" it were one of the object's own intrinsic properties.[9] For Genette, who claims to "out-Kant" Kant by fully acknowledging the relativism Kant's subjectivist theory of aesthetic judgment attempted to sidestep (by asserting the claim for universality in the judgment itself), aesthetic judgment *is* this illusory objectification. It is this process that produces what Genette calls "aesthetic predicates," affective-aesthetic values like "precious," "stilted," "monotonous," or "imperious," created from, or based upon, the feeling of pleasure or displeasure that accompanies our initial perception of the aesthetic object (*AR*, 90). Genette in fact describes these objectifying predicates, which bear a close resemblance to what I. A. Richards called "aesthetic or 'projectile' adjectives," as descriptive terms that "sneak in" evaluations of the object based on *feelings* about the object.[1] There is thus a sense in which the "aesthetic relation," which for Genette is more or less synonymous with "objectification," can be understood as an oblique effort to justify the presence of feeling in every aesthetic encounter.

4. Catharsis (Greek); this form of the noun (as object) appears in Aristotle, *Poetics* 6, 1449b28 [editor's note].
5. American philosopher and educational reformer (1859–1952) [editor's note].
6. Anglo-American poet and critic (1888–1965); the quotation is from "Tradition and the Individual Talent" (1919; see above) [editor's note].
7. British philosopher and statesman (1729–1797); see above [editor's note].
8. French literary theorist (b. 1930) [editor's note].
9. For a useful summary of the *katharsin* debate, as staged between the interpretations offered by Gerard F. Else in *Aristotle's Poetics: The Argument* (Cambridge, 1957) and those put forward by S. H. Butcher in *Aristotle's Theory of Poetry and Fine Art* (London, 1923), see Monroe C. Beardsley, *Aesthetics from Classical Greece to the Present* (Tuscaloosa: University of Alabama Press, 1966), 64–67. John Dewey, *Art as Experience* (New York: Perigee Books, 1980), 64, 78. T. S. Eliot, "Tradition and the Individual Talent," in *The Norton Anthology of Theory and Criticism* (New York: Norton, 2000), 1097. Gérard Genette, *The Aesthetic Relation*, trans. G. M. Goshgarian (Ithaca: Cornell University Press, 1999), 71, hereafter designated *AR*.
1. I. A. Richards, *Practical Criticism: A Study of Literary Judgement* (New York: Harcourt Brace Jovanovich, 1929), 336–40. [Richards (1893–1979), English literary theorist—editor's note.]

The subjective-objective problematic, magnified by the relativism of aesthetic judgment and other classic problems in the discourse of aesthetics (including the contested notion of special "aesthetic feelings"), is central, as we have seen, to the ugly feelings in this book, as well as to the artistic forms and genres they generate. It will be a particular concern in my discussion of "tone" (Chapter 1), the affective-aesthetic concept that will implicitly inform all the analyses of the aesthetics of specific feelings that follow. Yet the subjective/objective problematic so central to the philosophy of aesthetics can also be traced back to the philosophy of *emotion* in general. It has become the über-question of recent theoretical writing on feeling in particular, as evinced in the analysis of emotion after "the death of the subject" (Rei Terada) or attempts to differentiate "emotion" and "affect" on the grounds that the former requires a subject while the latter does not (Lawrence Grossberg, Brian Massumi).[2] These questions reflect the extent to which the subjective dimension of feeling, in particular, in seeming to undercut its validity as an object of *materialist* inquiry, has posed a difficulty for contemporary theorists. The present spotlight on emotion in literary criticism can be understood partly as an attempt to redress its earlier exclusion on such "subjectivist" grounds, including its failure to be grasped by the more positivistic kinds of cultural-historical analysis and the more dryly technical kinds of semiotic analysis that dominated literary studies in the 1970s and 1980s, as well as by poststructuralist theories of literary language prevailing in the 1980s and early 1990s. In the former case, feeling's marginalization stemmed from its perceived incompatibility with "concrete" social experiences; in the latter (as Terada most fully examines), from its perceived incompatibility with poststructuralism's skeptical interrogation of the category of experience itself. Though emotion once posed an embarrassment to these very different critics for very different reasons, most critics today accept that far from being merely private or idiosyncratic phenomena, or reflecting a "romantically raw domain of primitive experiential richness" that materialist analysis will be unable to grasp (Massumi, *PV*, 29), feelings are as fundamentally "social" as the institutions and collective practices that have been the more traditional objects of historicist criticism (as Raymond Williams[3] was perhaps the earliest to argue, in his analyses of "structures of feeling"), and as "material" as the linguistic signs and significations that have been the more traditional objects of literary formalism. Although feeling is not reducible to these institutions, collective practices, or discursive significations, it is nonetheless as socially real and "infrastructural" in its effects "as a factory" (Massumi, *PV*, 45).

The affect/emotion split originated in psychoanalysis for the practical purpose of distinguishing third-person from first-person representations of feeling, with "affect" designating feeling described from an observer's (analyst's) perspective, and "emotion" designating feeling that "belongs" to the

2. See Brian Massumi, "The Autonomy of Affect," in idem, *Parables for the Virtual* (Durham: Duke University Press, 2002), 23–45, hereafter designated *PV*; and Lawrence Grossberg, "Mapping Popular Culture," in *We Gotta Get out of This Place: Popular Conservatism and Postmodern Culture* (New York: Routledge, 1992), 69–87. [Massumi (b. 1956), U.S.-born Canadian social and communications theorist. Terada (b. 1962), scholar of comparative literature. Grossberg (b. 1947), American scholar of media and communications studies and cultural studies—editor's note.]

3. British Marxist cultural theorist (1921–1988); see above [editor's note].

speaker or analysand's "I." Yet Massumi and Grossberg have made claims for a stronger distinction, arguing not just that emotion requires a subject while affect does not, but that the former designates feeling given "function and meaning" while the latter remains "unformed and unstructured" (Massumi, *PV*, 260, note 3).[4] As Grossberg puts it, "Unlike emotions, affective states are neither structured narratively nor organized in response to our interpretations of situations."[5] Similarly, Massumi argues that while emotion is "a subjective content, the sociolinguistic fixing of the quality of an experience which is from that point onward defined as personal," affect is feeling or "intensity" disconnected from "meaningful sequencing, from narration" (*PV*, 28). The difficulty affective "intensity" poses for analysis is thus strikingly analogous to the analytical difficulty which Williams coined his term "structures of feeling" to address—that is, the kind posed by social experiences which "do not have to await definition, classification, or rationalization before they exert palpable pressures and set effective limits on experience and action."[6] In escaping qualification much like Williams' structures of feeling, which as "social experiences in solution" lie "at the very edge of semantic availability" (*ML*, 132), affective intensity clearly creates difficulties for more positivistic kinds of materialist analysis, even as it always remains highly *analyzable* in or as effect (Massumi, *PV*, 260, note 3).

While strong arguments have thus been made—primarily on the basis of a subjective/objective divide, but also in terms of oppositions like narrative/nonnarrative or semiotic/asignifying—for the idea that emotion and affect "follow different logics and pertain to different orders," some aspects of this taxonomic division will be more useful and important to this book than others (Massumi, *PV*, 27). Certainly less narratively structured, in the sense of being less object- or goal-directed, the intentionally weak and therefore often politically ambiguous feelings in this book are in fact much more like affects, in accordance with the definitions above, than emotions—which, for Martha Nussbaum, are "closely connected with action; few facts about them are more obvious."[7] Tied intimately, in contrast, with situations of what Dewey calls "being withheld from doing,"[8] the feelings in this book are obviously not as strategic as the emotions classically associated with political action; with their indeterminate or undifferentiated objects, in particular, they are less than ideally suited for setting and realizing clearly defined goals. Whereas Hobbes and Aristotle have shown how the principle of mutual fear actively binds men into the contracts that support the political commonwealth, and how anger advances the redressing of perceived injustices

4. On the psychoanalytical origins of the emotion/affect taxonomy, see Donna M. Orange, "Affect and Emotional Life," in *Emotional Understanding: Studies in Psychoanalytic Epistemology* (New York: Guilford, 1995), 90.

5. Grossberg, *We Gotta Get out of This Place*, 81.

6. Raymond Williams, "Structures of Feeling," in idem, *Marxism and Literature* (Oxford: Oxford University Press, 1977), 128. Hereafter designated *ML*. It should be clarified that in "Structures of Feeling" Williams is not really talking about emotions or even affects. For while "structures of feeling" do designate "affective elements of consciousness and relationships" or "social content of [a] present and affective kind" (132, 133), Williams defines them more broadly (and at the same time much more precisely) as "structured formation[s] . . . at the very edge of semantic availability" (132). His term thus represents a "cultural hypothesis" derived from efforts to understand "a social experience which is still in process" (132), and thus has "many of the characteristics of a pre-formation, until specific articulations—new semantic figures—are discovered in material practice" (134).

7. MARTHA NUSSBAUM, *Upheavals of Thought: The Intelligence of Emotions* (Cambridge: Cambridge University Press, 2001), 135.

8. Dewey, *Art as Experience*, 16.

through retaliation,[9] it is difficult to imagine how either of these actions might be advanced by an affective state like, say, irritation. While one can be irritated without realizing it, or knowing exactly what one is irritated about, there can be nothing ambiguous about one's rage or terror, or about what one is terrified of or enraged about. Yet the unsuitability of these weakly intentional feelings for forceful or unambiguous action is precisely what amplifies their power to diagnose situations, and situations marked by blocked or thwarted action in particular.

While the distinction between affect and emotion is thus helpful here in a number of ways, I will not be theoretically leaning on it to the extent that others have—as may be apparent from the way in which I use the two terms more or less interchangeably. In the chapters that follow, the difference between affect and emotion is taken as a modal difference of intensity or degree, rather than a formal difference of quality or kind. My assumption is that affects are *less* formed and structured than emotions, but not lacking form or structure altogether; *less* "sociolinguistically fixed," but by no means code-free or meaningless; *less* "organized in response to our interpretations of situations," but by no means entirely devoid of organization or diagnostic powers. As suggested above, ambient affects may in fact be better suited to interpreting ongoing states of affairs. What the switch from formal to modal difference enables is an analysis of the *transitions* from one pole to the other: the passages whereby affects acquire the semantic density and narrative complexity of emotions, and emotions conversely denature into affects. At the end of the day, the difference between emotion and affect is still intended to solve the same basic and fundamentally descriptive problem it was coined in psychoanalytic practice to solve: that of distinguishing first-person from third-person feeling, and, by extension, feeling that is contained by an identity from feeling that is not. Rather than also trying to dissolve this subjective/objective problematic by creating two distinct categories of feeling, this study aims to preserve it for its aesthetic productivity.

* * *

2005

9. On mutual fear and the social contract, see Hobbes, *Leviathan* (1651), 2.17; on anger and retaliation, see Aristotle, *Rhetoric* 2.2, 1378a [editor's note].

IAN BOGOST

b. 1976

A video game designer, cultural theorist, and public intellectual, Ian Bogost has emerged as one of the world's leading experts on the cultural significance of video games. Bogost is a gaming guru who eschews the isolation of "game studies" from other academic disciplines. His work in a variety of genres has consistently made connections between poetry, cinema, and visual art as well as philosophy, literary criticism, and information technology. Perhaps more than any other contemporary theorist, Bogost continues to demonstrate and interrogate the marriage of art and technology that has become a representative feature of postmodern culture.

Bogost's own video game creations began appearing in numerous festivals and curated exhibits around 2005, shortly after he finished doctoral work in comparative literature at the University of California at Los Angeles (2004). He had previously earned a B.A. in philosophy and comparative literature from the University of Southern California (1998), an M.A. in comparative literature from UCLA (2001), and a Diplôme Approfondi de Langue Français from the Centre International d'Etudes Pédagogique in Sèvres, France (1997). His early video game creations—such as *Howard Dean for Iowa* (2003), *Take Back Illinois* (2004), *Horde of Directors* (2004), and *Airport Insecurity* (2005)—garnered critical praise for the complex ways in which they make social and political arguments. For example, *Airport Insecurity* invites players to navigate impatient fellow passengers, incompetent security officers, and humiliating searches in American airports while attempting to carry their personal effects—including contraband items such as scissors and guns—past security checkpoints. Though completing this process is harrowing for even the most innocent of passengers, smuggling dangerous items onto the plane turns out to be surprisingly easy. Based on data regarding airport security gathered by the Transportation Security Administration (TSA) and investigative journalists, the game puts pressure on those who play to reconsider political justifications for the violation of travelers' personal privacy while it exposes just how ineffective the airport security system really is at guaranteeing their safety. Created in the wake of 9/11 and the USA PATRIOT Act of 2001, the game raises broader questions regarding trade-offs between national security and personal rights. As Bogost has repeatedly argued, the procedures that constitute such games invite players to think in fresh ways about the systems in which they live and to imagine alternative social possibilities.

Shortly after Bogost's games began receiving widespread critical attention, he published his first book, *Unit Operations* (2006). It draws on influential contemporary theorists such as Alain Badiou and SLAVOJ ŽIŽEK—in addition to classical philosophy and information technology—to argue that insights from the humanities and technology studies can be combined to develop productive new tools for analyzing a wide array of human artifacts. In the book, Bogost employs his innovative fusion of technical and literary theories to analyze video games such as *Half-Life* (first release, 1998) and *The Legend of Zelda* (first release, 1986) as well as literary works such as Gustave Flaubert's *Madame Bovary* (1857) and James Joyce's *Ulysses* (1922). Though *Unit Operations* yields numerous valuable insights, such as the connections between structuralism and the processes of computation, its most important contribution is perhaps its groundbreaking demonstration that deep interdisciplinary dialogue between literary theory and information technology can bring about new ways to interpret the world, a task that seems particularly urgent given the ubiquitous presence of technologically mediated cultural expressions in the contemporary era.

Bogost's subsequent work has continued to explore new frontiers through both genre-mixing creative projects and interdisciplinary cultural theory. For example, his 2010 release, *A Slow Year,* consists of four "game poems"—each of which invites readers into meditative observations corresponding to the four seasons of the year—accompanied by two essays about the connections between video games and poetry. Meanwhile, Bogost has continued to publish academic books that demonstrate how the analysis of games can produce new insights of broad cultural and philosophical significance. *How to Do Things with Video Games* (2011) draws inspiration from the speech-act theory of J. L. AUSTIN in order to further develop Bogost's theory of games as creative interventions with the potential to dramatically transform human cultures. Venturing into the realm of metaphysics, Bogost's *Alien Phenomenology, or What It's Like to Be a Thing* (2012) proposes an "object-oriented ontology" that draws on his experiences as a video game designer. In addition to producing avant-garde games and heady academic treatises, Bogost is a public intellectual who writes and lectures in a variety of venues, including *The Atlantic*, for which he is a contributing editor. The breadth and reach of this work demonstrate that both video games and the once-esoteric field of game studies have become mainstream phenomena with which contemporary cultural theorists and students need to grapple.

In our selection, "The Rhetoric of Video Games" (2007), Bogost argues that video games can and do make claims about the world. Though such games often employ images and have narrative components, Bogost does not situate his argument within the theoretical domains of visual rhetoric or narratology. Instead, he proposes that we should analyze games through the lens of "procedural rhetoric," which he defines as "the practice of using processes persuasively." He contends that games make assertions by presenting rule-based models and representations of reality—procedures—that players must learn to interpret and evaluate. Rules, which are the basis of all computation, simultaneously create the possibility of play and construct the meaning of the game. The concept of procedural rhetoric opens up fresh possibilities for analyzing games as well as other human artifacts.

Central to Bogost's argument in this essay is his insistence that we need to challenge conventional ideas about the nature and significance of "play." Though the word is often associated with childhood or leisure and used to signify the opposite of "serious work," Bogost argues that a broader and more positive theory of play has the power to illuminate all kinds of cultural activities in new ways. He builds on Katie Salen and Eric Zimmerman's definition of play as "the free space of movement within a rigid structure" in order to draw connections between the rhetoric of video games and other forms of art. For example, Bogost notes that much poetry may be understood as individual poets' exploitation of the unique opportunities for free expression afforded by rule-based genres such as the haiku. As such observations make clear, Bogost's work has important points of contact with structuralism, genre theory, and poetics. In fact, Bogost's argument about the ways that rules create "possibility spaces" for creative play has broad philosophical implications, which he subsequently examined in *Play Anything: The Pleasure of Limits, the Uses of Boredom, and the Secret of Games* (2016). As it turns out, play is a serious matter.

One important application of Bogost's theories of play and procedural rhetoric becomes apparent when, in an expanded definition of literacy, he demonstrates that they can be used for ideological criticism of video games. He draws on both PLATO and KARL MARX in order to articulate his own theory of ideology and then subjects several games to ideological analyses. For instance, the procedures of *America's Army: Operations* (a game developed by the U.S. Army as a recruitment tool; first release, 2002) are designed to communicate that the military conducts itself according to a code of honor that is founded on soldiers' following strict rules of engagement. Unlike many first-person shooter games, in which indiscriminate violence is rewarded, the rules of this game heavily punish such behavior while rewarding those actions that are considered honorable. However, Bogost points out that "honor" in this context signifies unquestioning submission to authority, and the game's politically decontextualized mission assignments discourage players from considering the moral or social implications of the orders themselves. For contrast, Bogost also analyzes the ways in which more subversive games wield procedural rhetoric to expose problematic elements of systems that range from neoliberal capitalism and the fast-food industry in *The McDonald's Videogame* (2006) to the treacherous social terrain of a high school populated by bullies, jocks, and nerds in *Bully* (2006). Such analyses reveal how video games have the potential to reinforce, obscure, expose, or challenge the sociopolitical status quo.

Bogost's argument here is open to criticism and further development. For example, his insistence that games may carry ideological messages with or without the conscious knowledge of their creators shows awareness of the problems associated with authorial intentionality; but this argument also needs to take into account how authorship is complicated by the collaborative nature of game development: many are created by large teams of designers and artists, who may invest the final product with conflicting values and ideas. Moreover, as theorists in the field of game studies continue to debate the ways in which narrative, visual rhetoric, and procedural rhetoric interact in video games, some may not be convinced that the last is always dominant in how games communicate. From a different angle, Bogost's argument that games can be conscious political interventions in the world may invite questions about the principles guiding his own decision to create games commissioned by both Republicans and Democrats for the explicit purpose of helping to elect their respective candidates for public office. Nevertheless, it is clear that Bogost is both a sophisticated artist and an important theorist whose work breaks new ground through the interdisciplinary interaction of literary criticism, philosophy, and information technology.

"The Rhetoric of Video Games" Keywords: Cultural Studies, Ideology, Media, Popular Culture, Representation, Rhetoric

The Rhetoric of Video Games

Animal Crossing is an "animal village simulator" for the Nintendo GameCube and DS video game consoles.[1] As the game begins, the player has just left home to move to the game's small village. There he meets a host of cartoonish animal residents and settles into a new life. The player is penniless upon arrival, and the game quickly thrusts him into the reality of making ends meet. The village's resident real estate tycoon and shopkeeper, Tom Nook, helps the player out, offering him a small shack to live in and a job of planting trees, delivering goods, and creating marketing materials on the town notice board. After completing these chores, Nook releases the player to explore the town on his own. He may then work, trade, and personalize his environment. The game offers a series of innocuous, even mundane activities like bug catching, gardening, and wallpaper designing.

One of the more challenging projects in the game is paying off the mortgage on one's house. *Animal Crossing* allows players to upgrade their homes, but doing so requires paying off a large note the player must take out to start the game in the first place. The player must then pay down renovation mortgages for even larger sums.[2] While the game omits some of the more punitive intricacies of long-term debt, such as compounding interest, improving one's home does require consistent work in the game world. Catching fish, hunting for fossils, finding insects, and doing jobs for other townsfolk all produce income that can be used to pay off mortgage debt or to buy carpets, furniture, and objects to decorate one's house.

When my then five-year-old began playing the game seriously, he quickly recognized the dilemma he faced. On the one hand, he wanted to spend the money he had earned from collecting fruit and bugs on new furniture,

1. Nintendo, *Animal Crossing* (Kyoto, Japan: Nintendo, 2002); and idem, *Animal Crossing: Wild World* (Kyoto, Japan: Nintendo, 2005) [except as indicated, all notes are Bogost's].

2. Just to give the reader a sense of the magnitude of work that faces players of *Animal Crossing*, the final renovation mortgage is over 700,000 "bells" (the currency unit in the game). The most lucrative fish and insects one can catch in the game sell for 10,000 bells, but they are quite rare. More typical items sell for 300–1,000 bells.

carpets, and shirts. On the other hand, he wanted to pay off his house so he could get a bigger one like mine. Once he managed to amass enough savings to pay off his mortgage, Tom Nook offered to expand his house. While it is possible to refrain from upgrading, the unassuming raccoon continues to offer renovations as frequently as the player visits his store. My son began to realize the dilemma facing him: the more material possessions he took on, the more space he needed, and the more debt he had to assume to provide that space. And the additional space just fueled more material acquisitions, continuing the loop. This link between debt and acquisition gives form to a routine that many mortgage holders fail to recognize: buying more living space not only creates more debt, it also drives the impulse to acquire more goods. More goods demand even more space, creating a vicious cycle.

In real life, when we pay our mortgage bill we don't see where that money ends up. But in *Animal Crossing,* the player experiences the way his debt makes bankers wealthy. After a player makes a major payment to his mortgage, Tom Nook closes his shop and upgrades it: the game starts with Nook's Cranny, a wooden shack general store, and ends with Nookington's, a two-story department store. Each upgrade allows Tom Nook to sell more goods. None of the townsfolk ever appear in Tom Nook's shop, although they occasionally refer to it somewhat disdainfully; the animals seem to have little drive to consume. *Animal Crossing*'s nonplayer characters (NPCs) are much less materialistic. The cute animals that occupy the village sternly berate the player if they haven't seen him around for many days, but they seem to have no concern for the quantity or type of material properties that the players possess. Occasionally, animals will express desire for a shirt or furniture item the player carries with him around the village, and they will offer to trade for it. But this type of transaction is both rare and charming; the animals frame their requests in terms of inveterate longing—"I've always wanted a Modern Lamp!"—quite a different refrain from the mallgoer's "one overriding interest, to spend money."[3]

In contrast, the player participates in a full consumer regimen: he pays off debt, buys and sells goods. Tom Nook buys the player's goods, which he converts to wealth. As the player pays off debt and upgrades his home to store more goods, he sees Tom Nook convert that wealth into increased commercial leverage—one's own debt makes the bank rich. Tom Nook then leverages that wealth to draw more capital out of the player, whose resources remain effectively constant. While the player spends more, Nook makes more. By condensing all of the environment's financial transactions into one flow between the player and Tom Nook, the game models the redistribution of wealth in a way even young children like my five-year-old can understand. Tom Nook is a condensation of the corporate bourgeoisie.[4]

Animal Crossing simulates the social dynamics of a small town, complete with the material demands of keeping up with the Joneses. As such, the game serves as a sandbox for experimenting with the ways one can recombine personal wealth. While the player diligently works to pay off that new upstairs

3. John de Graaf, David Wann, and Thomas H. Naylor, *Affluenza: The All-Consuming Epidemic* (San Francisco: Berrett Koehler, 2005).

4. That is, middle-class capitalists who own the means of production and become wealthy by exploiting the labor of the working classes (a term from Marxist theory) [editor's note].

addition, the other animals retain their small shacks perpetually. They never sell old belongings or acquire new ones, seemingly unconcerned that their homes are filled only with fish, or rocks, or fruit furniture. *Animal Crossing*'s animals enjoy walks outdoors. They snooze on their porches at twilight. They stop to watch the player fish. They meander aimlessly and take great care to partake in the community events that transpire on holidays. They are not consumers but naturalists, more Henry David Thoreau than Paris Hilton.[5]

Animal Crossing is a game about everyday life in a small town. It is a game about customizing and caring for an environment. It is a game about making friends and about collecting insects. But *Animal Crossing* is also a game about long-term debt. It is a game about the repetition of mundane work necessary to support contemporary material property ideals. It is a game about the bittersweet consequences of acquiring goods and keeping up with the Joneses. *Animal Crossing* accomplishes this feat not through moralistic regulation, but by creating a model of commerce and debt in which the player can experience and discover such consequences. In its model, the game simplifies the real world in order to draw attention to relevant aspects of that world.

We often think that video games have a unique ethos. Video game players have their own culture and values. Video game players often self-identify as "gamers" and devote a major part of their leisure time to video games. They discuss games online, follow new trends, and adopt new technology early. Video game play could be understood as a "community of practice," a name Jean Lave and Etienne Wenger have given to a common social situation around which people collaborate to develop ideas.[6] In this sense, the people who play video games develop values, strategies, and approaches to the practice of play itself. For example, a large group of *Animal Crossing* players contribute to an online community called Animal Crossing Community (ACC for short) to discuss the game, share things they've made, find strategies, or look up the value of different fish, insects, or furniture.[7] Within this community, as in all communities, cultural values develop, both by design and by evolution. For example, ACC offers players the option of "getting adopted." A veteran "Scout" is assigned to a new member as a "foster buddy" to help the newbie "learn the ropes of ACC . . . They'll also help you with any of your Animal Crossing questions, and may even give you a free item as a welcoming gift!"[8] Venues like ACC show that video game play is a cultural activity where values develop over time.

But the values of a video game community like ACC exist *outside* the game. While the neighborliness of the foster buddy program might suggest a carryover of values from the video game, the ACC is primarily focused on the social practices *of playing* the game, rather than the social practices *represented in* the game. This is an important distinction: video games are

5. American model, TV personality, and socialite (b. 1981), a symbol of conspicuous consumption and inherited wealth. Thoreau (1817–1862), American author, poet, and philosopher, best known for his experiment in basic living that he documented in *Walden; or, Life in the Woods* (1854) [editor's note].

6. Jean Lave and Etienne Wenger, *Situated Learning: Legitimate Peripheral Participation* (Cambridge: Cambridge University Press, 1991).

7. See www.animalcrossingcommunity.com. Accessed June 1, 2006.

8. See www.animalcrossingcommunity.com/gettingstarted.asp. Accessed June 1, 2006.

not just stages that facilitate cultural, social, or political practices; they are also media where cultural values themselves can be represented—for critique, satire, education, or commentary. When understood in this way, we can learn to read games as deliberate expressions of particular perspectives. In other words, video games make claims about the world, which players can understand, evaluate, and deliberate. Game developers can learn to create games that make deliberate expressions about the world. Players can learn to read and critique these models, deliberating the implications of such claims. Teachers can learn to help students address real-world issues by playing and critiquing the video games they play. And educators can also help students imagine and design games based on their own opinions of the world. When games are used in this fashion, they can become part of a whole range of subjects.

Play

One of the reasons we tend not to consider video games as legitimate venues for learning to take place is precisely because they are *games,* playthings. Play is often considered a children's activity, a trifle that occupies or distracts kids and which they eventually grow out of, turning to more serious pursuits. Play and learning have been segregated from one another in contemporary schooling, further cementing their perceived disparity. Children learn while seated in desks, listening attentively to a teacher or reading from a book. This sort of valid learning is interrupted by recess where children are allowed to play. Understood in this way, play is a distraction useful only to let off the necessary steam to allow kids (or adults) to get back to the serious business of learning (or working).

Video games also subscribe to this value model. They are a part of the "entertainment software" industry, and they are generally considered a leisure practice by players and the general public alike. Video game play is considered an unproductive expenditure of time, time that fills the breaks between work. This goes for children playing games at home after school as well as adults playing games after work. Parents might worry about their children playing video games after school instead of doing their homework or playing outside. Video games are perceived to interrupt learning and social life, acting as a leech on normal childhood development. During the 1990s dot-com boom,[9] many offices teeming with young workers took lunch or after-work breaks to play networked games on the office computers, taking respite from the "productive" practices of work. While it is rarely discussed directly, this conflation of work and play at the office serves as an archetype for the ill-founded business acumen of that era. These early internet companies failed because they weren't serious; they were merely "playing" at business.

But this association of video games with leisure is not a necessary condition. It is, rather, a by-product of a misunderstanding of the nature of play. Instead of understanding play as child's activity, or as the means to consume

9. The surge of speculative investment in Internet and e-commerce companies in the late 1990s, causing a financial bubble that was followed by the "dot-com crash" [editor's note].

games, or even as the shifting centers of meaning in poststructuralist thought, I suggest adopting Katie Salen and Eric Zimmerman's useful, abstract definition of the term: "play is the free space of movement within a more rigid structure."[1] Understood in this sense, play refers to the "possibility space" created by constraints of all kinds. Play activities are not rooted in one social practice, but in many social and material practices. For example, Salen and Zimmerman use the example of the play in a mechanism like a steering column, in which the meshing gears create "play" in the wheel before the turning gesture causes the gears to couple.

The possibility space of play includes all of the gestures made possible by a set of rules. As Salen and Zimmerman explain, imposing rules does not suffocate play, but makes it possible in the first place. On a playground, the possibility space refers to the physical properties of the play space, as well as the equipment, time allotted, and number and type of children. Kids are particularly adept at inventing new games based on the constraints of their environment; if one listens closely to children at play, one of the most common things to overhear is the establishment of new rules ("Now you be the monster." "This square is safe!"). When children play, they constantly renegotiate their relationship with a possibility space.

In more traditional media like poetry, the possibility space refers to the expressive opportunities afforded by rules of composition, form, or genre. For example, the poetic form of haiku enforces three lines of five, seven, and five syllables each.[2] The imposition of these restrictions constrains poetic authorship. To write haiku means exploring configurations of language that intersect with these rules of composition.

While possibility spaces like haiku develop over time (in this case, dating from a linked verse style of the fifteenth century), other literary practices have invented new possibility spaces with the specific purpose of creating new forms of expression. The artistic movement known as Oulipo (*Ouvroir de littérature potentielle*),[3] founded in Paris in 1960, adopted precisely this practice. The group's members invented, revived, or adopted forms for literary expression, each of which changes the possibility space of literary expression. One familiar example is the palindrome, a word or phrase that reads the same forward and backward. Georges Perec wrote "Le Grand Palindrome" of roughly 1,500 words,[4] although writers Nick Montfort and William Gillespie topped Perec's record with 2002, a palindromic novel of 2,002 words, authored in the year 2002.[5] Another Oulipian construct is the lipogram, a text in which use of a particular letter is forbidden. The most famous lipogrammatic text is Georges Perec's *La Disparition*, a lipogram in *E* (i.e., the letter *e* appears nowhere in the work).[6] The prisoner's constraint

1. Katie Salen and Eric Zimmerman, *Rules of Play: Game Design Fundamentals* (Cambridge, MA: MIT Press, 2004).
2. In Japanese, the divisions are not precisely commensurate with English syllables, although this is usually the way we adapt haiku for Western languages.
3. Workshop for potential literature (French) [editor's note].
4. Georges Perec, "Le Grand Palindrome," in *La clôture et autres poèmes* [Closure and other poems] (Paris: Hachette/Collection POL, 1980).
5. Montfort and Gillespie's *2002: A Palindrome Story in 2002 Words* (Urbana, IL: Spineless Books, 2002) was written with the assistance of a computer program called Deep Speed [editor's note].
6. Georges Perec, *La disparition* (1969; reprint Paris: Gallimard, 1990); and idem, *A Void*, trans. Gilbert Adair (1994; reprint Boston: Verba Mundi, 2005).

is a lipogram in ascenders and descenders; that is, letters that stick up or down from the line are forbidden (*b, d, f, g, h, j, k, l, p, q, t,* and *y*).

The constrained forms of Oulipo practitioners impose even more stringent restrictions than those of natural grammar and "ordinary" literary convention, but more importantly these artists deliberately *invented* new constraints, rather than adopting the forms provided by a particular historical and cultural moment. By designing the rules of literary composition, Oulipian writers share much in common with children on a playground: first they create a possibility space, then they fill that space with meaning by exploring the free movement within the rigid structure of literary rules. Likewise, readers of work like Perec's must take into account the rules of its composition, which tightly couple to the meaning of the work ("la disparition" means "the disappearance"; the novel follows a group of people who cannot find a hunting companion). Likewise, the rules children adopt in playground play alter the experience and meaning of the play. For example, consider a game of hide-and-seek in which an older player must count for a longer time to allow younger players a better chance to hide more cleverly. This rule is not merely instrumental; it suggests a value of equity in the game and its players.

In a video game, the possibility space refers to the myriad configurations the player might construct to see the ways the processes inscribed in the system work. This is really what we do when we *play* video games: we explore the possibility space its rules afford by manipulating the symbolic systems the game provides. The rules do not merely create the experience of play—they also construct the meaning of the game. That is to say, the gestures, experiences, and interactions a game's rules allow (and disallow) make up the game's significance. Video games represent processes in the material world—war, urban planning, sports, and so forth—and create new possibility spaces for exploring those topics. That representation is composed of the rules themselves. We encounter the meaning of games by exploring their possibility spaces. And we explore their possibility spaces through play.

Procedurality

We rely on the practice of *procedurality* to craft representations through rules, which in turn create possibility spaces that can be explored through play. Procedurality is a somewhat technical term that requires explanation. The term *procedure* itself does not usually give rise to positive reactions. We typically understand procedures as established, entrenched ways of doing things. *Procedure* often invokes notions of officialdom, even bureaucracy. In common parlance, a procedure is a static course of action, perhaps one established long ago and in need of revision. Often, we talk about procedures only when they go wrong: *after several complaints, we decided to review our procedures for creating new accounts*. But in fact, procedures in this sense of the word structure behavior of all types. Procedures (or processes) are sets of constraints that create possibility spaces, which can be explored through play.

In her influential book *Hamlet on the Holodeck,* Janet Murray defines four essential properties of digital artifacts: procedurality, participation, spatiality, and encyclopedic scope.[7] Murray uses the term *procedural* to refer to the computer's "defining ability to execute a series of rules."[8] Procedurality in this sense refers to the core practice of software authorship. Software is composed of algorithms that model the way things behave. To write procedurally, one authors code that enforces rules to generate some kind of representation, rather than authoring the representation itself. Procedural systems generate behaviors based on rule-based models; they are machines capable of producing many outcomes, each conforming to the same overall guidelines. The "brain" or "heart" of a computer is its *processor,* the chip that executes instructions. *Procedurality* gets its name from the function of the processor—procedurality is the principal value of the computer, which creates meaning through the interaction of algorithms. While Murray places procedurality alongside three other properties, these properties are not equivalent. The computer, she writes, "was designed . . . to embody complex, contingent behaviors. To be a computer scientist is to think in terms of algorithms and heuristics, that is, to be constantly identifying the exact or general rules of behavior that describe any process, from running a payroll to flying an airplane."[9] This ability to execute computationally a series of rules fundamentally separates computers from other media.

Among computer-based media, video games tend to emphasize procedurality more than other types of software programs. Chris Crawford has used the term *process intensity* to refer to the "degree to which a program emphasizes processes instead of data."[1] Higher process intensity—or in Crawford's words a higher "crunch per bit ratio"—suggests that a program has greater potential for meaningful expression. That is to say, video games more frequently and more deeply exploit the property of the computer that creates the kind of possibility spaces that we can explore through play. Furthermore, unlike productivity software such as word processors and spreadsheets, video games are usually created with some expressive purpose in mind; they represent models of systems or spaces that players can inhabit, rather than serving as mere tools.

Video games depict real and imagined systems by creating procedural models of those systems, that is, by imposing sets of rules that create particular possibility spaces for play. Often, when we think of video games we think of the themes of fantasy and power, like the space marine of *Doom* who must combat demons to save the world.[2] But these themes represent only part of the expressive capacity of games. Other games go beyond models of fantasy worlds, creating representations of the ordinary world that might give players new perspectives on the world they inhabit. For example, *Animal Crossing* creates a representation of everyday life in which labor and debt are a part. When video games represent things—anything from space demons to long-term debt—they do so through procedurality, by construct-

7. Janet Murray, *Hamlet on the Holodeck* (New York: Free Press, 1997), 71. [Murray (b. 1946), American theorist of digital media and pioneer in integrating computer science and the humanities—editor's note.]

8. Ibid.

9. Ibid., 72.

1. Chris Crawford, "Process Intensity," *The Journal of Computer Game Development* 1, no. 5 (1987). www.erasmatazz.com/library/the-journal-of-computer/jcgd-volume-1/process-intensity.html. [URL updated—editor's note.]

2. iD Software, *Doom* (Mesquite, TX: iD Software, 1993). [*Doom*: a series of first-person shooter games famous for pioneering such features as three-dimensional spatiality and networked multiplayer gameplay—editor's note.]

ing rule-based models of their chosen topics. In *Doom*'s model of the world, emphasis is placed on the trajectory and power of weaponry. In *Animal Crossing*'s model of the world, emphasis is placed on work, trade, and arrangement of the environment.

In the context of digital media and learning, video games offer two overlapping opportunities. In one, players can learn about aspects of the world that particular games model, such as consumption in *Animal Crossing* or urban planning in *Sim City*.[3] This is a kind of subject-centered literacy focused on examples of human practice. In the other, players can learn about procedurality itself, an inscriptive practice that will become more important only as computers continue to expand their role in society.

Rhetoric

Some games' procedural representations serve mostly to create an entertainment experience, a fantastic situation that transports the player to another world. But other games use procedurality to make claims about the cultural, social, or material aspects of human experience. Some do this deliberately, while others do it inadvertently. When we talk about making claims or arguments about things, we enter the domain of *rhetoric,* the field of communication that deals with persuasive speech. I would like to take a brief historical detour through the field of rhetoric in order to connect it to procedurality, learning, and to video games in turn.

Like procedurality, rhetoric is not an esteemed term. Despite its two-and-a-half-millennia-long history, today rhetoric invokes largely negative connotations. We often speak of "empty rhetoric," elaborate and well-crafted speech that is nevertheless devoid of actual meaning. Rhetoric might conjure the impression of *hot* air, as in the case of a fast-talking con who crafts pretentious language to hide barren or deceitful intentions. Academics and politicians are particularly susceptible to this sort of criticism, perhaps because we (and they) tend to use flourish and lexis[4] when coherence runs thin, as in this very sentence. Rhetoric is often equated with a type of smoke screen; it is language used to occlude, confuse, or manipulate the listener.

However, turgidity and extravagance are relatively recent inflections to this term, which originally referred only to persuasive speech, or oratory. The term rhetoric (ῥητωρική) first appears in Plato's *Gorgias*,[5] written some 2,500 years ago, in reference to the art of persuasion. The term itself derives from the rhetor (ῥήτωρ), or orator, and his practice, oratory (ῥήτωρεύω).[6] Rhetoric in ancient Greece meant public speaking for civic purposes.

Because of the importance of public speech in Golden Age Athens, rhetorical training became a promising business opportunity. Technical rhetoric, as this type is sometimes called, is useful for the everyman but perhaps too simplistic for the professional orator. Skilled orators developed numerous other techniques in much the same way as motivational business

3. Maxis, *Sim City* (Alameda, CA: Brøderbund, 1989).

4. That is, elaborate diction or vocabulary [editor's note].

5. Dialogue (ca. 385 B.C.E.) by the Greek philosopher PLATO (ca. 427–ca. 347 B.C.E.); it features GORGIAS OF LEONTINI (ca. 483–376 B.C.E.), a prominent teacher of rhetoric, and argues that rhetoric needs moral guidance from philosophy [editor's note].

6. Plato, *Plato: Complete Works* (New York: Hackett, 1997), 453a. [*Rhētōreuō* literally means "I practice oratory" (Greek)—editor's note.]

speakers do today. These experts charged for their services, and were called *sophists*. The popularity of books and sophistry bred critique. Such approaches motivated the work of Socrates[7] and Plato, who rejected the social and political contingency of the court and the assembly in favor of more lasting philosophical truths.

Responding to Plato, Aristotle attempts a systematic, philosophical approach to the art of persuasive oratory;[8] he argues that rhetorical practice has the final cause of persuasion to correct judgment. For Aristotle, rhetoric is "the faculty of observing in any given case the available means of persuasion."[9] The adept rhetorician does not merely follow a list of instructions for composing an oratory (technical rhetoric), nor does he merely parrot the style or words of an expert (sophistic rhetoric), but rather he musters reason to discover the available means of persuasion in any particular case. This variety of rhetoric implies an understanding of both the reasons to persuade and the tools available to achieve that end.

Classical rhetoric passed into the Middle Ages and modern times with considerable alteration. Civil rhetoric never disappeared entirely, and indeed it remains a common form of rhetoric today. But the concept of rhetoric expanded to account for new modes of inscription—especially literary and artistic modes. Writers and artists have expressive goals, and they deploy techniques to accomplish those goals. Here, persuasion shifts from the simple achievement of desired ends to the effective arrangement of a work so as to create a desirable possibility space for interpretation. In contemporary rhetoric, the goal of persuasion is largely underplayed or even omitted as a defining feature of the field, replaced by the more general notion of elegance, clarity, and creativity in communication. In this sense, rhetoric "provides ways of emphasizing ideas or making them vivid."[1] Success means effective expression, not necessarily effective influence.

Twentieth-century rhetorician Kenneth Burke identifies the need to identify with others as the ancestor of the practice of rhetoric. He extends rhetoric beyond persuasion, instead suggesting "identification" as a key term for the practice.[2] We use symbolic systems like language, says Burke, as a way to achieve this identification. While rhetoric still entails persuasion for Burke, he greatly expands its purview, arguing that it facilitates human action in general. In addition to expanding the conception of rhetoric, Burke expands its domain. In the tradition of oral and written rhetoric, language remains central. But Burke's understanding of humans as creators and consumers of symbolic systems expands rhetoric to include nonverbal domains known and yet to be invented or discovered.

The wide latitude Burke affords to rhetoric won him both champions and critics, but his expansion of the concept is particularly useful for our interest in video game rhetoric.[3] Thanks to the influence of Burke, and amplified by

7. Greek philosopher (469–399 B.C.E.), Plato's teacher and usually the main interlocutor in his dialogues, including *Gorgias* [editor's note].
8. In *On Rhetoric* (excerpted above), the highly influential treatise by the Greek philosopher ARISTOTLE (384–322 B.C.E.) [editor's note].
9. Aristotle, *The Rhetoric and Poetics of Aristotle* (New York: McGraw Hill, 1984), 24, see 1.2, 1355b26.

1. George A. Kennedy, *Classical Rhetoric and Its Christian and Secular Tradition* (Chapel Hill: University of North Carolina Press, 1999), 3.
2. Kenneth Burke, *A Rhetoric of Motives* (Berkeley: University of California Press, 1969), 19.
3. Sonja K. Foss, Karen A. Foss, and Robert Trapp, *Contemporary Perspectives on Rhetoric* (Prospect Heights, IL: Waveland Press, 1985), 214.

the increasingly inescapable presence of nonoral, nonverbal media, increasing interest has mounted around efforts to understand these other, newer modes of inscription that also appear to serve rhetorical ends. In particular, the emergence of photographic and cinematic expression in the nineteenth and twentieth centuries suggested a need to understand how those new, nonverbal media mount arguments. This subfield is called *visual rhetoric*. Visual communication cannot simply adopt the figures and forms of oral and written expression, so a new form of rhetoric must be created to accommodate these media forms.

Visual rhetoric offers a useful lesson in the creation of new forms of rhetoric in the general sense. One would be hard pressed to deny that advertisements, photographs, illustrations, and other optical phenomena have no effect on their viewers. To be sure, visual rhetoric is often at work in video games, a medium that deploys both still and moving images. But visual rhetoric does not account for procedural representation. This is not a flaw in the subfield of visual rhetoric; in procedural media like video games, images are frequently constructed, selected, or sequenced in code, making the stock tools of visual rhetoric inadequate. Image is subordinate to process.

Other efforts to unite computers and rhetoric do not make appeals even to visual rhetoric, instead remaining firmly planted in the traditional frame of verbal and written rhetoric. *Digital rhetoric* often abstracts the computer as a consideration, focusing on the text and image content a machine might host and the communities of practice in which that content is created and used. E-mail, Web sites, message boards, blogs, and wikis[4] are examples of these targets. To be sure, all of these digital forms can function rhetorically, and they are worthy of study. James P. Zappen begins his integrated theory of digital rhetoric on this very note: "Studies of digital rhetoric," he writes, "help to explain how traditional rhetorical strategies of persuasion function and are being reconfigured in digital spaces."[5] But for scholars of digital rhetoric, to "function in digital spaces" often means mistaking subordinate properties of the computer for primary ones. Other digital rhetoricians likewise focus on the use of digital computers to carry out culturally modified versions of existing oral and written discourse; letters become e-mails, conversations become instant message sessions.

Procedural Rhetoric

I suggest the name *procedural rhetoric* for the practice of using processes persuasively, just as verbal rhetoric is the practice of using oratory persuasively and visual rhetoric is the practice of using images persuasively.[6] Procedural rhetoric is a general name for the practice of authoring arguments through processes. Following the classical model, procedural rhetoric entails persuasion—to change opinion or action. Following the contemporary model, procedural rhetoric entails expression—to convey ideas effectively. Procedural rhetoric is a subdomain of procedural authorship; its arguments are made not

4. Websites that allow visitors to make changes or corrections. "Blogs": personal online journals (weblogs) [editor's note].

5. James P. Zappen, "Digital Rhetoric: Toward an Integrated Theory," *Technical Communication Quarterly* 14, no. 3 (2005): 319.

6. A much more detailed version of this argument, with additional examples from the domains of politics, advertising, and education, can be found in my book on the subject, Ian Bogost, *Persuasive Games* (Cambridge, MA: MIT Press, 2007).

through the construction of words or images, but through the authorship of rules of behavior, the construction of dynamic models. In computation, those rules are authored in code, through the practice of programming.

My rationale for suggesting a new rhetorical domain is very similar to the one that motivates visual rhetoricians. Just as photography, motion graphics, moving images, and illustrations have become pervasive in contemporary society, so have computer hardware, software, and video games. Just as visual rhetoricians argue that verbal and written rhetorics inadequately account for the unique properties of the visual expression, so I argue that verbal, written, and visual rhetorics inadequately account for the unique properties of procedural expression. A theory of procedural rhetoric is needed to make commensurate judgments about the software systems we encounter everyday and to allow a more sophisticated procedural authorship with both persuasion and expression as its goal. As a high process intensity medium, video games can benefit significantly from a study of procedural rhetoric.

Procedural rhetoric affords a new and promising way to make claims about *how things work*. As I argued earlier, video games do not simply distract or entertain with empty, meaningless content. Rather, video games can make claims about the world. But when they do so, they do it not with oral speech, nor in writing, nor even with images. Rather, video games make argument with *processes*. Procedural rhetoric is the practice of effective persuasion and expression using processes. Since assembling rules together to describe the function of systems produces procedural representation, assembling particular rules that suggest a particular function of a particular system characterizes procedural rhetoric.

Another way to understand procedural representation is in terms of *models*. When we build models, we normally attempt to describe the function of some material system accurately—for example, in this volume James Paul Gee offers a number of ways one might create a model of a plane, from child's toy to engineer's wind tunnel stress test.[7] Models of all kinds can be thought of as examples of procedural rhetoric; they are devices that attempt to persuade their creators or users that a machine works in a certain way. Video games too can adopt this type of goal; for example, a flight simulator program attempts to model how the mechanical and professional rules of aviation work. But since procedurality is a symbolic medium rather than a material one, procedural rhetorics can also make arguments about conceptual systems, like the model of consumer capitalism in *Animal Crossing*. Gee argues that modeling allows "specific aspects of experience to be interrogated and used for problem solving in ways that lead from concreteness to abstraction."[8] Games like *Animal Crossing* demonstrate that such models include, but extend far beyond physical and formal models to include, arguments about how social, cultural, and political processes work as well.

Artifacts that deploy procedural rhetoric can also make arguments about how things *don't* work just as easily as they can make arguments about how they do. Consider a particularly sophisticated example, *The McDonald's Videogame*.[9] The game is a critique of McDonald's business practices by Italian

7. James Paul Gee, "Learning and Games," in *The Ecology of Games: Connecting Youth, Games, and Learning*, ed. Katie Salen (Cambridge, MA: MIT Press, 2007), 21–40. [Bogost's essay was originally published in this book—editor's note.]
8. Ibid.
9. Released in 2006 [editor's note].

art collective Molleindustria, an example of a genre I call anti-advergames, games created to censure or disparage a company rather than support it. The player controls four separate aspects of the McDonald's production environment, each of which he has to manage simultaneously: the third-world pasture where cattle are raised as cheaply as possible; the slaughterhouse where cattle are fattened for slaughter; the restaurant where burgers are sold; and the corporate offices where lobbying, PR, and marketing are managed. In each sector, the player must make difficult business choices, but more importantly he must make difficult moral choices. In the pasture, the player must create enough cattle grazing land and soy crops to produce the meat required to run the business. But only a limited number of fields are available; to acquire more land, the player must bribe the local governor for rights to convert his people's crops into corporate ones. More extreme tactics are also available: the player can bulldoze rain forest or dismantle indigenous settlements to clear space for grazing. These tactics correspond with the questionable business practices the developers want to critique.

To enforce the corrupt nature of these tactics, public interest groups can censure or sue the player for violations. For example, bulldozing indigenous rainforest settlements yields complaints from antiglobalization groups. Overusing fields reduces their effectiveness as soil or pasture; too much use without crop cycling creates dead earth, which angers environmentalists. However, those groups can be managed through PR and lobbying in the corporate sector. Corrupting a climatologist may dig into profits, but it ensures fewer complaints in the future. Regular corruption of this kind is required to maintain allegiance. Likewise, in the slaughterhouse players can use growth hormones to fatten cows faster, and they can choose whether to kill diseased cows or let them go through the slaughter process. Removing cattle from the production process reduces material product thereby reducing supply and thereby again reducing profit. Growth hormones offend health critics, but they also allow the rapid production necessary to meet demand in the restaurant sector. Feeding cattle animal by-products cheapens the fattening process, but is more likely to cause disease. Allowing diseased meat to be made into burgers may spawn complaints and fines from health officers, but those groups too can be bribed through lobbying. The restaurant sector demands similar trade-offs, including balancing a need to fire incorrigible employees with local politician's complaints about labor practices.

The McDonald's Videogame mounts a procedural rhetoric about the necessity of corruption in the global fast food business, and the overwhelming temptation of greed, which leads to more corruption. In order to succeed in the long-term, the player must use growth hormones, he must coerce banana republics, and he must mount PR and lobbying campaigns. Furthermore, the temptation to destroy indigenous villages, launch bribery campaigns, recycle animal parts, and cover-up health risks is tremendous, although the financial benefit from doing so is only marginal. As Patrick Dugan explains, the game imposes "constraints simulating necessary evils on one hand, and on the other hand . . . business practices that are self-defeating and, really just stupid."[1] Players learn to "read" this argument in the system of

1. Patrick Dugan, "Hot off the Grill: la Molleindustria's Paolo Pedercini on *The McDonald's Video Game*," *Gamasutra*, February 27, 2006. www.gamasutra.com/view/feature/130980/hot_off_the_grill_la_.php. [URL updated—editor's note.]

play and can interpret the relevance of the argument in the context of their own lives.

Ways of Using Procedural Rhetoric: Interrogating Ideology

I have argued for procedural rhetoric as a representational form, and as the specific communication practice at work in games like *Animal Crossing* and *The McDonald's Videogame.* But to use games for learning purposes requires general approaches that might be applied to many games and many subjects. As such, it is worth sketching a few of the different ways video games can be used rhetorically, whether for design, critique, or learning.

One use of procedural rhetoric is to expose and explain the hidden ways of thinking that often drive social, political, or cultural behavior. We often call such logics *ideology,* a term with a long and conflicted intellectual history. In Plato's famous parable of the cave in the *Republic,* humans' understanding of the world is likened to prisoners watching shadows cast on the wall of a cave by objects and agents passing above. The prisoners see only a flawed shadow of the ideal form (*εἶδος*) of the object.[2] For Plato, the disparity between the ideal and material realms can only be reconciled through a recollection of the forms, a claim that assumes that our souls were once connected to these forms and, therefore, are also immortal. The term *ideology* itself can be traced to eighteenth-century French revolutionary Antoine Destutt de Tracy, who conceived of it as a science of the origin of ideas, that is, of how humans access the ideal realm from the material.[3] As Raymond Boudon clarifies, it was Napoleon's response to de Tracy that gave ideology its more familiar meaning.

> When Destutt de Tracy and Volney tried to thwart Napoleon's imperial ambitions, he scornfully called them *ideologues,* meaning people who wanted to substitute abstract considerations for *real* politics, as it was later called. From that time on, ideology signified those abstract (and rather dubious) theories allegedly based on reason or science, which tried to map out the social order and guide political action.[4]

Karl Marx understood the concept this way, and gave it perhaps its most famous characterization, "they aren't aware of it, but they do it [*Sie wissen das nicht, aber sie tun es*]."[5] Ideology thus lost the sense of a weapon against entrenched ideas and gained a decidedly negative connotation, as the very entrenchment of those ideas.

Like all cultural artifacts, no video game is produced in a cultural vacuum. All bear the biases of their creators. Video games can help shed light on these ideological biases. Sometimes these biases are inadvertent and deeply hidden. Other times, the artifacts themselves hope to expose their creators' biases as positive ones, but which of course can then be read in support or opposition.

2. Plato, 515a–16a. [The allegory of the cave appears in *Republic* 7 (see above)—editor's note.]
3. Raymond Boudon, *The Analysis of Ideology* (Chicago: University of Chicago Press, 1989), 25.
4. Ibid. [Constantin-François de Chassebœuf, comte de Volney (1757–1820), French historian and philosopher. Napoléon Bonaparte (1769–1821), French general who named himself emperor of the French (1804–15) and sought to conquer Europe—editor's note.]
5. Karl Marx, *Capital: Vol. 1, A Critique of Political Economy,* trans. Ben Fowkes (New York: Penguin, 1992), 166–67. The translation here has been modified. [MARX (1818–1883), German philosopher, political economist, and revolutionary—editor's note.]

In 2002, the U.S. Army released an unprecedented government-funded first-person shooter (FPS) game. *America's Army: Operations*[6] was conceived and openly publicized as an Army recruiting and communications tool, one crafted "to recreate the US Army for the benefit of young civilians."[7] The game represented a major step for the military-entertainment complex; it was created on the then-current Unreal 2 engine, a costly professional-grade game engine, and released for free on the Army's Web site. Within the first six months, over a million users had registered, of which over 600,000 had completed the game's basic rifle marksmanship and combat training (BCT), a necessary step before gaining access to combat missions.[8]

While *America's Army* shares a genre with other popular multiplayer FPS games, the Army's desire to offer "a realistic look at army personal and career opportunities via sophisticated role-playing" altered or eliminated many of the conventions of movement in both conventional and tactical first-person shooters.[9] But the game's political simulation is more interesting than its mechanical and physical simulation. *America's Army* enforces strict Army Rules of Engagement (ROE), preventing the brouhaha of typical squad-based fighting games. Whereas *Counter-Strike*[1] encourages the player to log as many kills as possible, *America's Army* players collaborate in short missions, such as rescuing a prisoner of war, capturing an enemy building, or assaulting an enemy installation. The ROE guides play with an iron fist. Writing about the game, designers Michael Zyda et al. explain:

> All players abide by rules of warfare. If a player violates the Uniform Code of Military Justice, rules of engagement, or laws of land warfare, reprisal is instant. He will find himself in a cell at Fort Leavenworth, accompanied by a mournful harmonica playing the blues. Continued violation of the rules may cause a player to be eliminated from the game. To rejoin he must create a new ID and restart.[2]

Many players discover this constraint in basic training; turning a weapon on one's drill sergeant immediately lands the player in the brig. The direct mapping of in-game behavior to the very ability to continue playing serves as a convincing procedural rhetoric for the chain of command, the principal structure new recruits must understand immediately. Even the use of foul language is grounds for in-game discipline.

But the game also ties ROE and chain of command directly to the moral imperative of the U.S. Army. As in many similar games, when players successfully complete levels, they earn points that persist on Web-based global statistics boards. At specified point targets, a player character's Honor statistic increases. Since Honor telegraphs commitment and expertise, disincentives to violate the ROE and chain of command become especially strong; losing a character through violation would require considerable effort to rebuild.

6. Modeling, Simulation, and Virtual Environments Institute (MOVES), *America's Army: Operations* (Washington, DC: U.S. Army, 2002).
7. Michael Zyda, John Hiles, Alex Mayberry, Casey Wardynski, Michael V. Capps, Brian Osborn, Russell Shilling, Martin Robaszewski, and Margaret J. Davis, "Entertainment R&D for Defense," *IEEE Computer Graphics and Applications* 23, no. 1 (2003): 28–36.
8. Ibid., 34.
9. Ibid., 28.
1. First-person shooter videogame, originally released by Valve Corporation in 1999 [editor's note].
2. Zyda et al., "Entertainment R&D for Defense," 30.

The correlation of honor with the performance of arbitrary and politically decontextualized missions offers particular insight into the social reality of the U.S. Army. While the use of arbitrary honor points may seem contrived at first, the system bears much in common with the practice of military decoration. Ribbons, medals, and other designations reward successful completion of military objectives. Training, professional development, wounds, completion of missions, and many other events earn soldiers decorations, which when worn on a dress uniform speak to the honor and nobility of the bearer. The average citizen's lack of familiarity with the specific actions that warrant a ribbon or medal ensure that these designations signify the soldier's abstract worth rather than his individual achievements. *America's Army*'s Honor mechanic successfully proceduralizes this value system. As Zyda et al. summarize, "The game insists on the mission orientation of the US Army. Above all, soldiers must be team players, following army values and rules."[3]

This approach is similar to, but different from, the idea of epistemic games advanced by David Williamson Shaffer.[4] Shaffer argues that games can model how professions work, offering an incomplete, yet embodied experience of real-world jobs. As Gee explains in this volume, these types of games "already give us a good indication that even young learners, through video games embedded inside a well-organized curriculum, can be inducted into professional practices as a form of value-laden deep learning that transfers to school-based skills and conceptual understandings."[5] On first blush, *America's Army* would appear to be a superb example of epistemic games: the game models the values and practices of the army, giving the player an embodied experience of the recruit. However, *America's Army* also shows that epistemic games bear a risk: sometimes, we may want to question the values of professional practices rather than assume those values blindly. Procedural rhetoric offers an approach to do so.

Ways of Using Procedural Rhetoric: Making and Unpacking an Argument

Video games that expose ideology may or may not do so intentionally. But video games can also be created to make explicit claims about the way a material or conceptual system works. *The McDonald's Videogame* is an example of such a one, albeit a satire and a political commentary meant to critique the processes employed in the fast food business. Other games strive to explain and support a particular method for accomplishing a political or social goal; these games use procedural rhetoric to make an argument, and players unpack that argument through play.

In the early fall 2004, the Illinois House Republicans commissioned a game I designed to represent their positions on several public policy issues at the center of their 2004 state legislative election. These issues—medical malpractice tort reform, education standards policy, and local economic development—are abstract and dry at best. As such, citizens were even less

3. Ibid.
4. David Williamson Shaffer, "Epistemic Games," *Innovate* 1, no. 6 (2005); and idem, *How Computer Games Help Children Learn* (New York: Palgrave/MacMillan, 2007).
5. Gee, "Learning and Games."

likely to engage with them in the public or private forum, which provided only soapbox sound bites or lengthy, unreadable policy documentation. Moreover these topics, like most public policy issues, are tightly interwoven. Educational quality affects job qualification, which in turn affects economic welfare. *Take Back Illinois* attempts to create a complex, interrelated procedural rhetoric that communicated the candidates' positions on these topics.[6]

Four subgames comprise the game, three for each of the policy issues and one game about citizen participation. These subgames interrelate; play in one affects performance in the others. Each subgame provides a goal for the player to reach. For example, in the medical malpractice reform subgame, the player must raise the public health level to a predefined target. The subgame goal and the player's progress toward it are displayed directly under the game field. A small calendar serves as a timer for the game, starting at January 1, and counts up one day for every few seconds of game time. To win, the player must reach the goal before the calendar reaches the end of the year. Faster success yields a lower, and therefore better, score.

The procedural rhetoric for each policy issue was designed to compress as much detail into the smallest possible rule-set. For example, in the medical malpractice reform subgame, a representation of a city was filled with citizens of varying health—healthy, ill, gravely ill. Unwell citizens were contagious, and healthy citizens nearby them would eventually become ill themselves. If left untreated, gravely ill citizens would die. The city contained several medical offices, and the player could send sick citizens to those offices for treatment. However, Illinois suffered higher medical malpractice insurance rates than its neighboring states. The candidates' positions on tort reform were partially motivated by the potential reduction in insurance rates such changes would encourage. The game provides a "policy panel" that allows the player to change simple public policy settings for the game environment. In this case, the player could alter maximum noneconomic damages awarded in medical malpractice lawsuits as well as investment in medical research to prevent repeat tragedies. In the medical malpractice subgame, maintaining a high threshold on noneconomic damages keeps insurance rates high, which is likely to cause doctors to leave the state. Once this happens, the medical office dims and the player can no longer treat citizens there.

The other policy subgames created similar procedural rhetorics for each of the issues. In the education reform subgame, players simultaneously manage a handful of school districts across the state. Some districts start out with different educational standards in place, while other districts enjoy disproportionate funding and teacher-to-student ratios. To play the game, the player has to "teach" in each district by keying in a Simon-like[7] memory sequence that corresponds with the educational standard in each district. This procedural rhetoric embodies the candidate's policy position: maintaining multiple standards across the state made the educational system on the

6. Persuasive Games, *Take Back Illinois* (Atlanta, GA: Persuasive Games/Illinois House Republicans, 2004). [In 2004, both the Illinois house and senate had Democratic majorities (Republicans had lost the majority in the senate in 2002)—editor's note.]

7. *Simon* is an electronic game, first released by Milton Bradley in 1978, that requires players to memorize sequential patterns [editor's note].

whole difficult to manage. Players would quickly understand this position upon being forced to remember four or five different memory sequences for all the schools. To play more efficiently, the player could reassign standards on a district-by-district basis by changing policy. The player could also reassign funding to needy schools in order to raise their educational output.

In public forums, policy issues are often discussed independently, even though most are bound to one another in significant ways. To communicate the rhetoric of interrelations, *Take Back Illinois* maintained a set of scores for each subgame and used those scores as inputs for settings in other games. For example, higher performance in the educational reform subgame increased the efficiency of job training centers in the economic development game. The parameterized interaction between simulation models serves as a rudimentary procedural rhetoric for the interrelationship of these issues in particular, and other issues by extension.

To play the game successfully, the player is forced to acknowledge the campaign's position on the issues it represents—for example, it is impossible to win the medical malpractice reform subgame without reducing maximum noneconomic damages for malpractice lawsuits (although reducing them beyond reason decreases the likelihood of faults). The game's procedural rhetoric is a compressed version of the campaign's policy position. In playing the game, the player is not "brainwashed" or otherwise fooled into adopting the candidates' policy position. Rather he is afforded an understanding of that position for further inquiry, agreement, or disapproval. However, none of the subgames argue that policy change alone is sufficient to create social change. In each of the games, the player must perform nontrivial actions to accomplish goals like improved health care and education. These actions trace the interconnectedness of political conditions.

Take Back Illinois and *The McDonald's Game* are specialty titles, created for specific purposes in which their persuasion outweighs entertainment. But procedural rhetoric is not limited to the narrow domain of educational or political games; the same properties can be found in commercial titles as well.

Consider *Bully,* from Rockstar Games, the creators of the *Grand Theft Auto* series.[8] In *Bully,* the player takes the role of Jimmy Hopkins, an adolescent just dropped off at Bullworth Academy by his disinterested mother and stepfather, who are on the way to their lavish honeymoon. The school is riddled with bullies and troublemakers, and Jimmy struggles to get by amidst the conflicted social situation of high school politics. The game has been reviled for supposedly glorifying bullying, but the experience it creates is anything but celebratory. Even if the player struggles to steer Jimmy away from trouble, it catches up to him thanks to the petty malevolence of his peers. Students mill in the quad and buildings, either verbally and physically abusing each other or receding from verbal and physical attacks. Staying out of the way of the bullies (bullies in the game conveniently have their own clique, and all wear the same clothes) allows a player to avoid tussles. If a player stands in front of the wrong locker, he or she should expect to get

8. Rockstar Games, *Grand Theft Auto III* (New York: Take Two Interactive, 2001); idem, *Grand Theft Auto: Vice City* (New York: Take Two Interactive, 2003); idem, *Grand Theft Auto: San Andreas* (New York: Take Two Interactive, 2004); and Rockstar Vancouver, *Bully* (New York: Take Two, 2006).

shoved out of the way. *Bully* models the social environment of high school through an expressive system of rules, and makes a procedural argument for the necessity of confrontation. Confronting bullies is not a desirable or noble action in the game, but it is necessary if one wants to restore justice. The game privileges the underdogs—nerds and girls—and the player spends most of his time undermining the bullies and the jocks in order to even the social pecking order.

Bully is part social commentary, part satire. But it also bears the usual features of an entertainment title. While games like *The McDonald's Game* are more didactic, games like *Bully* are more subtly expressive. Neither technique is inherently more or less valid than the other, but each accomplishes a different kind of video-game-based speech, each of which might be more or less appropriate in different circumstances.

Rockstar does not generally discuss or acknowledge the procedural rhetorics they build into games like *Bully*. But other designers make more deliberate efforts to frame the ideas they put forward in their games. Consider the Will Wright/Maxis game *Spore*.[9] In *Spore,* the player starts with a microorganism and grows it into a complex sentient creature, then a civilization, then a military power, and finally a space-traveling superrace. The game is a rich and complex one that clearly addresses a number of topics, most notably the tension between evolution and natural selection (creatures evolve, but the player carefully designs their attributes). But in a discussion of the game at the annual Game Developers Conference, Wright explained that the real topic he hoped to address in the game was astrobiology, the study of life throughout the cosmos.[1] Often when we wonder if there is intelligent alien life in the universe, we assume that life arises naturally and evolves slowly. Thus the chance of finding intelligent life seems remarkably small; to do so would require the greatest of coincidences in a place as large as the (ever expanding) universe. In the theory Wright hopes to advance in his video game, intelligent life does not occur and grow naturally, but is cultured and transported from planet to planet by other, more advanced civilizations. The perspective on astrobiology Wright advocates borrows the concept of seed spread by wind or other environmental factors; these reproductive structures are called *spores*. *Spore* adopts the logic of this particular view on astrobiology, subtly arguing through its game play that the spread of life in the universe is most likely caused by sentient beings transporting other creatures from star to star. While a book might make this argument by explaining the process, in *Spore* the player discovers the argument by playing in the possibility space the game's rules create. This act of discovering a procedural argument through play is endemic to procedural rhetoric.

Learning from Procedural Rhetoric

Video games are models of real and imagined systems. We always *play* when we use video games, but the sort of play that we perform is not always the

9. Maxis, *Spore* (Redwood Shores, CA: Electronic Arts, forthcoming). As of this writing, *Spore* is expected to be released in 2009. [Will Wright (b. 1960), American video game designer and co-founder of the company Maxis, best known for designing *SimCity* and *The Sims*; *Spore* was released in 2008—editor's note.]

1. Will Wright, "What's Next in Content?" Paper presented at the Game Developers Conference, San Jose, CA, 2006.

stuff of leisure. Rather, when we play, we explore the possibility space of a set of rules—we learn to understand and evaluate a game's meaning. Video games make arguments about how social or cultural systems work in the world—or how they could work, or don't work. Video games like *Spore* and *Take Back Illinois* make arguments about abstract, conceptual systems the way mechanical models make them about material ones. When we play video games, we can interpret these arguments and consider their place in our lives.

In this way, playing video games is a kind of literacy. Not the literacy that helps us read books or write term papers, but the kind of literacy that helps us make or critique the systems we live in. By "system," I don't just mean large-scale, impersonal things like political systems. Any social or cultural practice can be understood as a set of processes, and our understanding of each of them can be taught, supported, or challenged through video games. *Animal Crossing* presents a model of consumer capitalism that players might embrace, reinforcing their interest in property in the material world. Or, through their experience of the game, players might question the goals they set for themselves, particularly the often endless feedback loop between the desire for material goods and the work needed to support it. When we learn to play games with an eye toward uncovering their procedural rhetorics, we learn to ask questions about the models such games present.

The kind of technology literacy that procedural rhetoric offers is becoming increasingly necessary for kids and adults alike. As more of our cultural attention moves from linear media like books and film to procedural, random-access media like software and video games, we need to become better critics of the latter kind. This process starts at home where parents can help their kids play games critically, just as they might help their kids understand novels or films by virtue of their own familiarity with those media. Of course, such a future requires parents who are themselves literate in the medium of video games. Parents of all kinds can learn to play video games, but those who grew up with video games themselves are already raising the next generation of children—a six-year-old who played the Atari VCS[2] in 1978 was thirty-five years old in 2007. These parents must play games with their kids just as a previous generation watched westerns or read comic books with them. And before they do so, they must begin playing games critically themselves, perhaps unlearning decades of treating video games as mere distraction.

Educators also have a role to play. When video games are used in schools, we often think that they should be used pedagogically. That is, if video games have any purpose in schools, it is for supplementing or replacing lesson plans for concrete, factual learning, such as principles of chemistry. But once we understand video games as procedural representations that make arguments about systems in the world, they resemble creative artifacts as much as—and perhaps more so—than they do pedagogical tools. Educators should consider adopting video games as artifacts to be discussed alongside traditional media in subjects like literature, language arts, history, and art, teaching game playing as an argumentative and expressive practice alongside reading, writing, and debating.

2. The first hugely successful home video console (released in 1977) [editor's note].

Finally, procedural rhetoric has a role to play in the way we teach programming and video game development. As interest in games as a cultural activity increases, and as the importance of computing itself has increased, some educators have hoped to teach game development as an entry point into computer science.[3] Video games are appealing, kids want to play them, and they also want to make them. By luring kids into computer science through video game development, we can attempt to increase dwindling interest in math, science, and technology.

This is not a bad approach to programming education. But unfortunately, such approaches risk assuming that creating any kind of video game offers the same pedagogical value. Programming education must take care to ensure that it supports sophisticated responses to the medium, rather than reinforcing the idea that play is equivalent to leisure, and that video games are intended to produce fun and distraction rather than critical response. In addition to using video games to teach kids how to write computer programs (procedural literacy), we can use them to teach kids how to write computer arguments (procedural rhetoric). When kids program, just as when they write, they can learn to make their own claims about the world in the form of processes. Such a practice reframes video game development as a rhetorical practice, not just a craft practice or a technical practice. By actively teaching kids to mount arguments in procedural form—even simple ones like models of their everyday life—video games can become a carrot medium for both programming and expression. Work in teaching kids to program games has already begun (examples include MIT's Scratch,[4] the MacArthur-funded University of Wisconsin/Gamelab Game Designer project,[5] the London Knowledge Lab's Making Games Project,[6] Carnegie Mellon University's Alice,[7] among others). Efforts like these can be used as the basis for a combined program in procedural literacy and rhetoric.

Video games are not mere trifles, artifacts created only to distract or to amuse. But they are also not *automatically* rich, sophisticated statements about the world around us. Video games have the power to make arguments to persuade, to express ideas. But they do not do so inevitably. As we evolve our relationship with video games, one of the most important steps we can take is to learn to play them critically, to suss out the meaning they carry, both on and under the surface. To do this requires a fluency in procedurality, the core representational form of computing. But programming or using computers is not the sole answer to such a charge. Rather, we need to play video games in order to understand the possibility spaces their rules create, and then to explore those possibility spaces and accept, challenge, or reject them in our daily lives.

2007

3. For examples, cf. Brenda Cantwell Wilson and Sharon Shrock, "Contributing to Success in an Introductory Computer Science Course: A Study of Twelve Factors," *ACM SIGCSE Bulletin* 33, no. 1 (2001): 184–88; and Randolph M. Jones, "Design and Implementation of Computer Games: A Capstone Course for Undergraduate Computer Science Education," *ACM SIGCSE Bulletin* 32, no. 1 (2000): 260–64.

4. See http://scratch.mit.edu/. Accessed March 1, 2007.

5. As of this writing, the Game Designer project is still in the early stages of development. An overview of the project can be found at http://website.education.wisc.edu/gls/research.gamedesigner.htm. Accessed March 1, 2007. [The game in this project became Gamestar Mechanic: see https://gamestarmechanic.com/teachers/about—editor's note.]

6. See www.lkl.ac.uk/research/pelletier.html. Accessed March 1, 2007.

7. See www.alice.org. Accessed February 1, 2018.

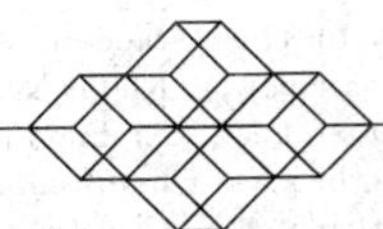

Author Bibliographies

Chinua Achebe

Called "the father of the African novel," Chinua Achebe is best known for his fiction foregrounding the political struggles of Nigeria. His novels include *Things Fall Apart* (1958), *No Longer at Ease* (1960), *Arrow of God* (1964), *A Man of the People* (1966), and *Anthills of the Savannah* (1987). He also published two short story collections, three volumes of poetry, four works of juvenile literature, and several edited collections of African literature. *Morning Yet on Creation Day: Essays* (1975) and *Hopes and Impediments: Selected Essays, 1965–1987* (1988) are overlapping collections of his literary criticism, primarily dealing with the role of the African writer in society. Both include "An Image of Africa." His other criticism includes the slim volumes *A Tribute to James Baldwin* (1989) and *Home and Exile* (2000), and three volumes directly addressing Nigerian politics: *The Trouble with Nigeria* (1983), *The World of the Ogbanje* (1986), and *The University and the Leadership Factor in Nigerian Politics* (1988). He also published a short memoir, *There Was a Country: A Personal History of Biafra* (2012). The interviews collected in *Conversations with Chinua Achebe*, edited by Bernth Lindfors (1997), record Achebe's views on literature and politics.

The large secondary literature on Achebe deals primarily with his career as a novelist. Ezenwa-Ohaeto's *Chinua Achebe: A Biography* (1997) is a detailed account of Achebe's life and travels. Catherine Innes's *Chinua Achebe* (1990) offers the best critical survey of his novels as well as his other writings. Though focused on Achebe's novels, Simon Gikandi's *Reading Chinua Achebe: Language and Ideology in Fiction* (1991) examines them in relation to the critical essays. *The Chinua Achebe Encyclopedia*, edited by M. Keith Booker (2003), is a comprehensive guide to many facets of his life and work. *Achebe and Friends at Umuahia: The Making of a Literary Elite* (2015), by Terri Ochiagha, gives a detailed account of the formation of a cohort of pioneering African writers.

There are many entries in the debate over "An Image of Africa": defenders of Conrad include Caribbean writer Wilson Harris in "The Frontier on Which *Heart of Darkness* Stands," *Research on African Literatures* 12 (1981), and Hunt Hawkins, "The Issue of Racism in *Heart of Darkness,*" *Conradiana* (1982); following Achebe is Frances B. Singh, "The Colonialistic Bias of *Heart of Darkness,*" *Conradiana* 10 (1978); and compromise views are offered by the postcolonial critic Benita Parry in *Conrad and Imperialism* (1983), and Patrick Brantlinger, "*Heart of Darkness*: Anti-Imperialism, Racism, or Impressionism?," *Criticism* 27 (1985). The collections *Conrad in Africa: New Essays on "Heart of Darkness,"* edited by Attie de Lange and Gail Fincham (2002), and *Approaches to Teaching Conrad's "Heart of Darkness" and "The Secret Sharer,"* edited by Hunt Hawkins and Brian W. Shaffer (2002), both offer notable reassessments of the controversy and comment on the ethics of reading *Heart of Darkness* in the twenty-first century. Ezenwa-Ohaeto's *Chinua Achebe* (cited above) contains a useful bibliography of his writing and of selected secondary sources, and the *Achebe Encyclopedia* (cited above) includes a comprehensive bibliography.

Joseph Addison

Donald F. Bond prepared modern editions of *The Spectator* (5 vols., 1965) and *The Tatler* (3 vols., 1987). One-volume editions include *Addison and Steele: Selections from "The Tatler" and "The Spectator,"* edited by R. J. Allen (1957); *Selected Essays from "The Tatler," "The Spectator," and "The Guardian,"* edited by Daniel McDonald (1973); and *Selections from the "Tatler" and the "Spectator" of Steele and Addison*, edited by Angus Ross (1982). For texts and contexts, and a biographical and literary overview, see *The Commerce of Everyday Life: Selections from "The Tatler" and "The Spectator,"* edited by Erin Mackie (1998). For Addison's correspondence, see *Letters*, edited by Walter Graham (1941).

A good biography is Peter Smithers, *The Life of Joseph Addison* (2d ed., 1968). For a cogent brief overview, consult Robert M. Otten, *Joseph Addison* (1982). Helpful critical studies include Lee Andrew Elioseff, *The Cultural Milieu of Addison's Literary Criticism* (1963); Edward A. Bloom and Lillian D. Bloom, *Joseph Addison's Sociable Animal: In the Market Place, on the Hustings, in the Pulpit* (1971); and Michael G. Ketcham, *Transparent Designs: Reading, Performance, and*

Form in the "Spectator" Papers (1985). In *The Constitution of Literature: Literacy, Democracy, and Early English Literary Criticism* (2008), Lee Morrissey discusses theories of reading in the seventeenth and eighteenth centuries, as articulated in *The Spectator* and in the writings of Dryden, Hume, and Johnson. Other resources include *Addison and Steele: The Critical Heritage*, edited by Edward A. Bloom and Lillian D. Bloom (1980), and Charles A. Knight, *Joseph Addison and Richard Steele: A Reference Guide, 1730–1991* (1994).

Adūnīs

Adūnīs is a prolific literary critic, historian, editor, and theorist as well as being one of the Arab world's most renowned poets. Over a half dozen of his more than thirty books of poetry are available in English, including two of his more influential collections: *Mihyar of Damascus: His Songs* (2008) and *A Time between Ashes and Roses* (2004). The latter contains, in addition to the poems, a particularly fine biographical and critical study by the translator, Shawkat M. Toorawa, of Adūnīs as both critic and poet and provides a lengthy bibliography of his more important works. Many of his own critical reflections and manifestos have appeared in the Lebanese literary journal *Shiʿr* (1957–70), which he co-founded, and later *Mawāqif*, which he founded in 1968. To date, two books of his writings in prose have been translated into English: *An Introduction to Arab Poetics* (1985; trans. 1990), which was originally a series of lectures given at the Collège de France in Paris, and *Sufism and Surrealism* (1995; trans. 2005). His major works of criticism and literary history in Arabic include *Muqaddima li-al-shiʿr al-ʿArabī* (1971, *An Introduction to Arabic Poetry*)—not to be confused with the later *An Introduction to Arab Poetics*—and *Al-Thābit wa-al-mutahawwil* (1974, *The Static and the Dynamic*).

Later Adūnīs combined his various interests and functions in an experimental work, *Al-Kitāb ams al-makān al-ān: mak-htūta tunsabu ilā al-Mutanabbī* (1995, *The Book Yesterday the Place Now: A Manuscript Attributed to al-Mutanabbi*), in which he blends the roles of poet and critic in his commentary on a poem by his forebear al-Mutanabbī. This volume continues the critical impulse begun by Adūnīs in *Dīwān al-shiʿr al-ʿArabī* (1964, *Collection of Arabic Poetry*), his selections of the most significant poets and poetry in the Arabic literary heritage.

Adūnīs's *Al-Thābit* (1974) elicited an attentive, often admiring, and sometimes contentious response from many of his contemporaries. The outlines of this immediate response can be profitably traced in articles written by three Arab critics and academics working mostly in English: Issa J. Boullata, Mounah A. Khouri, and Kamal Abu-Deeb. Particularly helpful in situating Adūnīs's work in *Al-Thābit* are Boullata's "Adonis: Revolt in Modern Arabic Poetics," *Edebiyat* 2.1 (1977), and Khouri's "A Critique of Adonis's Perspectives on Arabic Literature and Culture," a chapter in his *Studies in Contemporary Arabic Poetry and Criticism* (1987). Abu-Deeb—himself a central figure in Arabic modernism—has published several fine studies of the broader impact of Adūnīs's theories about Arabic literature on his contemporaries. The most accessible and informative of these is probably "The Collapse of Totalizing Discourse and the Rise of Marginalized/Minority Discourses," in *Tradition, Modernity and Postmodernity in Arabic Literature: Essays in Honor of Professor Issa J. Boullata* (ed. Kamal Abdel-Malek and Wael Hallaq, 2000), which examines in detail Adūnīs's concept of "modernity" and tracks its influence on others.

For broader studies of Adūnīs that link the poetic and critical aspects of his work, consult the rewarding articles of Kamal Abu-Deeb in various journals and Festschrifts, as well as Muhsin J. al-Musawi's fine survey *Arabic Poetry: Trajectories of Modernity and Tradition* (2006), which refers throughout to Adūnīs's critical legacy and poetic example. For other assessments, see Roger Allen, *The Arabic Literary Heritage* (1998) and *An Introduction to Arabic Literature* (2000), especially the sections titled "Poetry" and "The Critical Tradition"; M. M. Badawi, *A Critical Introduction to Modern Arabic Poetry* (1975); Salma Khadra Jayyusi, *Trends and Movements in Modern Arabic Poetry* (2 vols., 1977); Mohammad Mohmoud Khazali, "Modernity: A Study of Adūnīs' Theory and Poetry" (Ph.D. diss., 1983); and Atif Y. Faddul, *The Poetics of T. S. Eliot and Adunis: A Comparative Study* (1992). The role of Adūnīs in the broader intellectual debates concerning decline and renewal in Arabic culture has been admirably traced by Elizabeth Suzanne Kassab in her *Contemporary Arab Thought: Cultural Critique in Comparative Perspective* (2010), which can be supplemented by her valuable and lucid study of the intellectual reaction to the 2011 Arab uprisings, "Critics and Rebels: Older Arab Intellectuals Reflect on the Uprisings," *British Journal of Middle Eastern Studies* 41 (2014).

For further biographical details on Adūnīs—besides those found in Shawkat Toorawa's afterword to *A Time between Ashes and Roses* (cited above)—see the entries in *Modern Arabic Literature* (ed. Roger Allen, 1987) and *Encyclopedia of Arabic Literature* (ed. Julie Scott Meisami and Paul Starkey, 1998).

Giorgio Agamben

Almost all Agamben's work has been translated into English; the major works, in order of English publication (with the date of the original Italian listed first, where applicable), are *Language and Death: The Place of Negativity* (1982; 1991), *The Coming Community* (1990; 1993), *Stanzas: Word and Phantasm in Western Culture* (1977; 1993), *Idea of Prose* (1985; 1995), *The End of the Poem: Studies in Poetics* (1996; 1999), *The Man without*

Content (1970; 1999), *Potentialities: Collected Essays in Philosophy* (2000), *Means without End: Notes on Politics* (1996; 2000), *The Open: Man and Animal* (2002; 2004), *The Time That Remains: A Commentary on the Letter to the Romans* (2000; 2005), *Infancy and History: On the Destruction of Experience* (1978, new ed. 2001; 1993, 2007), *Profanations* (2005; 2007), *What Is an Apparatus? And Other Essays* (2009), *The Signature of All Things: On Method* (2008; 2009), *Nudities* (2009; 2011), *The Church and the Kingdom* (2010; 2012), *Nymphs* (2007; 2013), *The Unspeakable Girl: The Myth and Mystery of Kore* (2010; 2014), *Pilate and Jesus* (2013; 2015), *The Fire and the Tale* (2015; 2017), *The Mystery of Evil: Benedict XVI and the End of Days* (2013, 2017), *What Is Philosophy?* (2016, 2017), and *Karman: A Brief Treatise on Action, Guilt, and Gesture* (2017, 2018). The nine volumes of the *Homo Sacer* series (listed here by their order in the sequence, not by date of publication) are *Homo Sacer: Sovereign Power and Bare Life* (1995; 1998), *State of Exception* (2003; 2005), *Stasis: Civil War as Political Paradigm* (2015; 2015), *The Sacrament of Language: An Archaeology of the Oath* (2008; 2010), *The Kingdom and the Glory: For a Theological Genealogy of Economy and Government* (2007; 2011), *Opus Dei: An Archaeology of Duty* (2012; 2013), *Remnants of Auschwitz: The Witness and the Archive* (1998; 1999), *The Highest Poverty: Monastic Rules and Form-of-Life* (2011; 2013), and *The Use of Bodies* (2014; 2016). The full *Homo Sacer* series has now been collected in one volume, *The Omnibus Homo Sacer* (2017). The best source for biographical information is Juliette Cerf's interview with Agamben found at www.versobooks.com/blogs/1612-thought-is-the-courage-of-hopelessness-an-interview-with-philosopher-giorgio-agamben (accessed September 15, 2017). Agamben explains his refusal to come back to the United States after 9/11 in "No to Biopolitical Tattooing," *Le Monde*, January 10, 2004.

The best single-volume introduction is Leland de la Durantaye's *Giorgio Agamben: A Critical Introduction* (2009). See also de la Durantaye's superb essay "To Be and to Do: The Life's Work of Giorgio Agamben," *Boston Review*, January 26, 2016. Catherine Mill's *The Philosophy of Agamben* (2008); *The Agamben Dictionary*, edited by Alex Murray and Jessica Whyte (2011); and Claire Colebrook and Jason Maxwell's *Agamben* (2016) also provide useful overviews. Jacques Derrida's engagement with Agamben's work can be found in *The Beast and the Sovereign*, vol. 1 (2009). Of the more specialized monographs, of special interest to literary theorists are William Watkin's *The Literary Agamben: Adventures in Logopoiesis* (2010), Thanos Zartaloudis's *Giorgio Agamben: Power, Law and the Uses of Criticism* (2010), and Kevin Attell's *Giorgio Agamben: Beyond the Threshold of Deconstruction* (2015). Three superb collection of essays on Agamben's work are *Politics, Metaphysics, and Death: Essays on Giorgio Agamben's "Homo Sacer,"* edited by Andrew Norris (2005); *Giorgio Agamben: Sovereignty and Life*, edited by Matthew Calarco and Steven DeCaroli (2007); and *Towards the Critique of Violence: Walter Benjamin and Giorgio Agamben*, edited by Brendan Moran and Carlo Salzani (2015). Calarco and DeCaroli's volume has the most complete bibliography of Agamben's work; it can be supplemented with the more recent bibliography in de la Durantaye's book, which also can be consulted for secondary sources.

Louis Althusser

Althusser's major essays are collected in three influential books: *For Marx* (1965; trans. 1969); *Lenin and Philosophy and Other Essays* (1969; trans. 1971), which contains "Ideology and Ideological State Apparatuses"; and *Reading Capital*, a reconsideration of Marx's masterwork written with his student Étienne Balibar (1968; trans. 1970). Subsequent collections in English, gathering his many essays, are *Politics and History: Montesquieu, Rousseau, Hegel, and Marx* (1972), which includes the long essay published as his first book, *Montesquieu: Politics and History* (1959); *Essays in Self-Criticism* (1974; trans. 1976); *Philosophy and the Spontaneous Philosophy of the Scientists, and Other Essays* (1974; trans. 1990); *Essays on Ideology* (1984); *Writings on Psychoanalysis: Freud and Lacan* (1993; trans. 1996); *On the Reproduction of Capitalism: Ideology and Ideological State Apparatuses* (1995; trans. 2014), which presents material (including "Ideology and Ideological State Apparatuses") from two unfinished book manuscripts; *The Spectre of Hegel: Early Writings* (1997); *Machiavelli and Us* (1999); *The Humanist Controversy and Other Writings (1966–67)* (2003); *Philosophy of the Encounter: Later Writings, 1978–1987* (2006); the short selection *On Ideology* (2008), which includes "Ideology and Ideological State Apparatuses"; a series of lectures, *Psychoanalysis and the Human Sciences* (trans. 2016); and *Philosophy for Non-Philosophers* (trans. 2016). *Journal de captivité: Stalag XA 1940–1945* (1992, *Journal of Captivity*) records Althusser's experiences as a prisoner of war. Written during the mid-1980s, the autobiographical texts collected in *The Future Lasts Forever*, edited by Olivier Corpet and Yann Moulier Boutang (1992; trans. 1993), should be approached with caution, since many passages bear witness to Althusser's mental decline. The definitive biography is Yann Moulier Boutang, *Louis Althusser: Une Biographie (Louis Althusser: A Biography)*; only the first volume, *La Formation du mythe (1918–1956)* (1992, *The Formation of the Myth*), has appeared to date.

Warren Montag's *Louis Althusser* (2003) and Luke Ferretter's *Louis Althusser* (2006) provide useful introductions, as well as selective annotated bibliographies. There was a great deal of sometimes contentious discussion of Althusser through the 1970s and early 1980s. The philosopher Jacques

Rancière, a onetime student of Althusser's, criticized him from a Maoist perspective for adhering to theory over practice, in his book *Althusser's Lesson* (1974; trans. 2011), whereas the English historian E. P. Thompson, in "The Poverty of Theory or an Orrery of Errors" (1978), declared Althusserian theory to be Stalinist. In *Althusser: The Detour of Theory* (1987), Gregory Elliott helpfully traces the political background that shaped Althusser's work.

Elliott also edited an excellent collection of critical essays from a range of political and theoretical perspectives, *Althusser: A Critical Reader* (1994); see especially the essay by Francis Mulhern considering Althusser's impact on literary studies. *The Althusserian Legacy*, edited by E. Ann Kaplan and Michael Sprinker (1994), contains a revealing interview with his onetime student Jacques Derrida, conducted by Sprinker. See also *Postmodern Materialism and the Future of Marxist Theory: Essays in the Althusserian Tradition*, edited by Antonio Callari and David F. Ruccio (1996).

Since 2000, there has been a new wave of commentary. William S. Lewis, *Louis Althusser and the Traditions of French Marxism* (2005), places Althusser's work in historical context. In contrast to earlier interpretations, commentators have focused on the influence of Spinoza on Althusser's version of materialism, notably Montag's *Louis Althusser*. Montag's subsequent study, *Althusser and His Contemporaries: Philosophy's Perpetual War* (2013), is a major reevaluation of Althusser in relation to French theory. See also *Encountering Althusser: Politics and Materialism in Contemporary Radical Thought*, edited by Katja Diefenbach et al. (2013). Elliot's *Althusser: A Critical Reader* includes a comprehensive bibliography of all Althusser's publications up to 1993.

Benedict Anderson

Apart from his specialized works on Southeast Asian politics and history, Anderson wrote several books relevant to students of nationalism and postcolonialism: *Imagined Communities: Reflections on the Origin and Spread of Nationalism* (1983; 2d ed., 1991; 3d ed., 2006), *Language and Power: Exploring Political Cultures in Indonesia* (1990), *The Spectre of Comparisons: Nationalism, Southeast Asia, and the World* (1998), *The Age of Globalization: Anarchists and the Anticolonial Imagination* (2005, as *Under Three Flags*; 2d ed., 2013), and a memoir, *A Life beyond Boundaries* (2016). Biographical information, as well as a sense of Anderson's influence, can be found in the obituaries published in the *New York Times* (December 14, 2015), *The New Republic* (December 13, 2015), and the *Guardian* (January 1, 2016).

Two collections of essays specifically address Anderson's work: *Grounds of Comparison: Around the Work of Benedict Anderson*, edited by Pheng Cheah and Jonathan Culler (2003), and *Southeast Asia over Three Generations: Essays Presented to Benedict R. O'G. Anderson*, edited by James T. Siegel and Audrey R. Kahin (2003). Umut Özkırımlı's *Theories of Nationalism: A Critical Introduction* (2d ed., 2010) is a good place to start on the topic and pays particular attention to Anderson's work. Other valuable studies include Craig Calhoun's *Nations Matter: Culture, History, and the Cosmopolitan Dream* (2007), Anthony D. Smith's *Nationalism: Theory, Ideology, History* (2d ed., 2010), Partha Chatterjee's *Empire and Nation: Selected Essays* (2010), Bernard Yack's *Nationalism and the Moral Psychology of Community* (2012), and John Coakley's *Nationalism, Ethnicity and the State: Making and Breaking Nations* (2012). Two very useful reference works on the topic are *Nationality and Nationalism*, edited by Athena S. Leoussi and Steven Grosby, vol. 1, *Theoretical Studies* (2004), and *The SAGE Handbook of Nations and Nationalism*, edited by Gerard Delanty and Krishan Kumar (2006). Özkırımlı's book provides a good working bibliography.

Gloria Anzaldúa

Anzaldúa's books include *Speaking in Tongues: A Letter to Third World Women Writers* (1983), *Borderlands/La Frontera: The New Mestiza* (1987), *Towards a New Consciousness* (1990), and three children's books, *Prietita Has a Friend* (1991), *Friends from the Other Side/Amigos del otro lado* (1993), and *Prietita and the Ghost Woman/Prietita y la Llorona* (1996). She is also the co-editor (with Cherríe Moraga) of *This Bridge Called My Back: Writings by Radical Women of Color* (1981; 3d revised ed., 2002), editor of *Making Face, Making Soul / Haciendo caras: Creative and Critical Perspectives by Women of Color* (1990), and co-editor (with AnaLouise Keating) of *This Bridge We Call Home: Radical Visions for Transformation* (2002), three highly influential collections. *The Gloria Anzaldúa Reader,* edited by AnaLouise Keating (2009) collects writings from across her life, while *Light in the Dark=Luz en lo oscuro: Rewriting Identity, Spirituality, Reality* (2015), also edited by Keating, offers late essays and stories, including some works in progress. The detailed chronology of Anzaldúa's life found in *The Gloria Anzaldúa Reader* is best supplemented with the autobiographical reflections found in *Interviews/Entrevistas,* edited by Keating (2000), a collection of interviews with Anzaldúa.

Anzaldúa's work has generated numerous responses that address issues of ethnicity, sexuality, feminism, hybridity, and identity politics. The best place to start are the retrospective essays found in the section devoted to Anzaldúa in *PMLA* 121 (2006). Collections of essays that offer reflections on her work include *Other Sisterhoods: Literary Theory and U.S. Women of Color,* edited by Sandra Kumamoto Stanley (1998); *Chicana Feminisms: A Critical Reader,* edited by Gabriela F. Arredondo et al. (2003); *Entre Mundos/Among Worlds: New Perspectives on Gloria*

Anzaldúa, edited by AnaLouise Keating (2005); and *Bridging: How Gloria Anzaldúa's Life and Work Transformed Our Own*, edited by AnaLouise Keating and Gloria González-López (2011). Three monographs that devote significant attention to Anzaldúa's work are Arturo J. Aldama's *Disrupting Savagism: Intersecting Chicana/o, Mexican Immigrant. and Native American Struggles for Self-Representation* (2001), Sheila Marie Contreras's *Blood Lines: Myth, Indigenism, and Chicana/o Literature* (2008), and Theresa Delgadillo's *Spiritual Mestizaje: Religion, Gender, Race, and Nation in Contemporary Chicana Narrative* (2011). *The Gloria Anzaldúa Reader* provides a complete bibliography of Anzaldúa's own writings and an extensive bibliography of secondary works. Anzaldúa's manuscripts, letters, and unpublished writings are housed at the Nettie Lee Benson Latin American Collection at the University of Texas at Austin.

Hannah Arendt

The major works published during Arendt's lifetime are *The Origins of Totalitarianism* (1951; 3d ed., 1966), *The Human Condition* (1958), *Rahel Varnhagen: The Life of a Jewess* (1957; rev. ed., 1974), *Between Past and Future: Eight Exercises in Political Thought* (1961; enlarged ed., 1968), *On Revolution* (1963), *Eichmann in Jerusalem: A Report on the Banality of Evil* (1963), *Men in Dark Times* (1968), and *Crises of the Republic: Lying in Politics; Civil Disobedience; On Violence; Thoughts on Politics and Revolution* (1972). *The Life of the Mind: Thinking and Willing*, left unfinished at Arendt's death, was published in 1978. Most of Arendt's essays and occasional pieces have now been collected in books: *The Jew as Pariah: Jewish Identity and Politics in the Modern Age* (1978), *Lectures on Kant's Political Philosophy* (1982), *Essays in Understanding, 1930–1954* (1994), *Responsibility and Judgment* (2003), *The Promise of Politics* (2005), *Reflections on Literature and Culture* (2007), and *The Jewish Writings* (2007), as well as a translation of her 1929 doctoral dissertation, *Love and Saint Augustine* (1996). There are also five volumes of letters: *Hannah Arendt Karl Jaspers Correspondence* (1985; trans. 1992), *Between Friends: The Correspondence of Hannah Arendt and Mary McCarthy, 1949–1975* (1995), *Within Four Walls: The Correspondence between Hannah Arendt and Heinrich Blücher, 1936–1968* (1996; trans. 2000), *Letters, 1925–1975*, by Hannah Arendt and Martin Heidegger (1998; trans. 2004), and *The Correspondence of Hannah Arendt and Gershom Scholem* (2017). Her papers are held at the Library of Congress. Biographical material can be found in *Hannah Arendt: The Last Interview and Other Conversations* (2013). Margarethe von Trotta's excellent film *Hannah Arendt* (2012) provides a good rendition of the controversy surrounding the Eichmann book. Elisabeth Young-Bruehl's full-scale biography, *Hannah Arendt: For Love of the World* (1982; 2d ed., 2004), is superb; nothing more recent compares to it.

The secondary literature is immense. The best place to start is Elisabeth Young-Bruehl's *Why Arendt Matters* (2006). Simon Swift's *Hannah Arendt* (2009) and *Hannah Arendt: Key Concepts*, edited by Patrick Hayden (2014), are good introductory overviews. To get a sense of the critical response, consult the following collections of essays by diverse hands: *The Cambridge Companion to Hannah Arendt*, edited by Dana Villa (2000); *Thinking in Dark Times: Hannah Arendt on Ethics and Politics*, edited by Roger Berkowitz, Jeffrey Katz, and Thomas Keenan (2010); *Politics in Dark Times: Encounters with Hannah Arendt*, edited by Seyla Benhabib (2010); *Action and Appearance: Ethics and the Politics of Writing in Hannah Arendt*, edited by Anna Yeatman (2011); and *Arendt and Adorno: Political and Philosophical Investigations*, edited by Lars Rensmann and Samir Gandesha (2012). Among the monographs of special interest to literary theorists are Seyla Benhabib's *The Reluctant Modernism of Hannah Arendt* (1996), Julia Kristeva's *Hannah Arendt* (1999; trans. 2001), Hanna Fenichel Pitkin's *The Attack of the Blob: Hannah Arendt's Concept of the Social* (2002), Judith Butler's *Notes toward a Performative Theory of Assembly* (2015), and Roberto Esposito's *The Origin of the Political: Hannah Arendt or Simone Weil?* (2017). Of more general note are Steve Buckler's *Hannah Arendt and Political Theory: Challenging the Tradition* (2011) and Richard H. King's *Arendt and America* (2015). Hayden's *Hannah Arendt: Key Concepts* has a fairly comprehensive bibliography of primary and secondary works.

Aristotle

There are a vast number of editions and translations of Aristotle's works, from the medieval period to the present. Our text of the *Poetics* comes from *Aristotle's Poetics*, admirably translated into discursive English by James Hutton (1982), which is based on the standard edition of Rudolf Kassel, *Aristotelis "De Arte Poetica Liber"* (1965). Our selection from *On Rhetoric* is taken from the definitive present-day English version, *On Rhetoric: A Theory of Civic Discourse*, translated and annotated by George A. Kennedy (1991; 2d ed., 2007), which also includes useful commentary. It draws on an amalgam of Greek texts, including *Aristotelis "Ars Rhetorica,"* edited by W. David Ross (1959); *Aristote, "Rhétorique,"* edited by Médéric Dufour and André Wartelle (3 vols., 1960–73); and *Aristotelis "Ars Rhetorica,"* edited by Rudolf Kassel (1976). *The Complete Works of Aristotle*, edited by Jonathan Barnes (2 vols., 1984), contains the best compendium of Aristotle's works in English.

Jonathan Barnes's *Aristotle* (1982) is a brief, accessible overview of Aristotle's life and works. In a crowded field, Abraham Edel's *Aristotle and His Philosophy* (1982) and John M. Rist's *Mind of*

Aristotle (1989) also stand out as good basic introductions. *The Cambridge Companion to Aristotle*, edited by Barnes (1995), contains chapters on important phases of Aristotle's philosophical project, including a survey of his life and work by Barnes. See also *A Companion to Aristotle*, edited by Georgios Anagnostopoulos (2009), a collection of forty essays covering the range of Aristotle's work. Carlo Natali, *Aristotle: His Life and School* (1991; trans. 2013), sorts through conjectures about Aristotle's biography; in addition, it includes a bibliography of ancient sources.

On the *Poetics*, Stephen Halliwell's *Aristotle's "Poetics"* (1986) is the authoritative contemporary interpretation; see also Halliwell's chapter, "Aristotle's Poetics," in *The Cambridge History of Literary Criticism*, vol. 1, *Classical Criticism*, edited by George A. Kennedy (1989). Gerald F. Else, *Aristotle's "Poetics": The Argument* (1957), provides a detailed commentary on the text, and his *Plato and Aristotle on Poetry* (1986) is a useful comparative study. D. W. Lucas's *Aristotle—"Poetics"* (1968) offers significant commentary as well as the Kassel edition of the Greek text. Martha Nussbaum's *Fragility of Goodness: Luck and Ethics in Greek Philosophy* (1986) contains an influential modification of the argument about catharsis. *Aristotle's "Poetics" and English Literature: A Collection of Critical Essays*, edited by Elder Olson (1965), gathers views from the eighteenth century through the 1960s. *Essays on Aristotle's "Poetics,"* edited by Amélie Oksenberg Rorty (1992), is an excellent contemporary collection by philosophers and scholars of Aristotle, clarifying concepts such as mimesis, catharsis, and comedy. Though contemporary narrative theory has developed more sophisticated distinctions than Aristotle's basic ones of plot and character, the *Poetics* still has significant influence among filmmakers; see Ari Hiltunen, *Aristotle in Hollywood: The Anatomy of Successful Storytelling* (2002). *Ancient Literary Criticism*, edited by Andrew Laird (2006), reprints three older essays on the *Poetics*. In *The Lost Second Book of Aristotle's "Poetics"* (2012), Walter Watson attempts to reconstruct Aristotle's view of comedy and the laughable as a counterpart to his view of tragedy and the pitiable. Malcolm Heath, *Ancient Philosophical Poetics* (2013), compares Plato's and Aristotle's poetics and emphasizes Aristotle's grounding in biology. The *Routledge Philosophy Guidebook to Aristotle and the "Poetics"* (2016), by Angela Curran, offers detailed commentary.

For *On Rhetoric*, W. M. A. Grimaldi's *Aristotle, "Rhetoric": A Commentary* (1980) is a useful exposition. *Essays on Aristotle's "Rhetoric"* (1996), edited by Amélie Oksenberg Rorty as a companion to her volume on the *Poetics*, provides an excellent range of contemporary interpretations and reevaluations of the text. Alexander Nehamas's "Pity and Fear in the *Rhetoric* and *Poetics*," in *Aristotle's "Rhetoric": Philosophical Essays* (ed. David J. Furley and Nehamas, 1994), cogently compares Aristotle's treatment of emotion in both texts and, in a provocative argument, claims that catharsis refers to the internal resolution of a tragic plot itself rather than to the response of the audience. Our translator, George A. Kennedy, has written standard histories of rhetoric; see his *Classical Rhetoric and Its Christian and Secular Tradition from Ancient to Modern Times* (2d ed., 1999), which has a useful discussion of Aristotle's development of a "philosophical rhetoric." See also *Rereading Aristotle's "Rhetoric,"* edited by Alan G. Gross and Arthur E. Walzer (2000). Dana LaCourse Munteanu, *Tragic Pathos: Pity and Fear in Greek Philosophy and Tragedy* (2012), represents another effort to reinterpret catharsis, drawing on the *Rhetoric* as well as the *Poetics*.

The "Poetics" of Aristotle and the "Tractatus Coislinianus": A Bibliography from about 900 till 1996, compiled by Omert J. Schrier (1998), testifies to the massive literature relating to the *Poetics*. *Aristotle's "Rhetoric": Five Centuries of Philological Research*, compiled by Keith V. Erickson (1975), covers the many studies of *On Rhetoric*. *The Cambridge Companion to Aristotle* contains an excellent bibliography on all of Aristotle's work, with individual sections on the *Poetics* and *On Rhetoric*. Halliwell's *Aristotle's Poetics* and Kennedy's edition of *On Rhetoric* include selective bibliographies on their respective texts. The Rorty collections on the *Poetics* and *On Rhetoric* also include good selective bibliographies.

Matthew Arnold

The Complete Prose Works of Matthew Arnold, edited by R. H. Super (11 vols., 1960–77), offers a definitive text and excellent notes. P. J. Keating (1970) and Christopher Ricks (1972) have edited collections of Arnold's critical writings. For the poetry and prose, the editions by Lionel Trilling (1949) and A. Dwight Culler (1961) are useful, though thin in their annotations. For the correspondence, *Letters, 1848–1888*, edited by George W. E. Russell (2 vols., 1895), remains important, although this edition and other selections have been superseded by *Letters of Matthew Arnold*, edited by Cecil Y. Lang (6 vols., 1996–2001). Excellent biographies include Park Honan, *Matthew Arnold: A Life* (1981); Nicholas Murray, *A Life of Matthew Arnold* (1995); and Ian Hamilton, *A Gift Imprisoned: The Poetic Life of Matthew Arnold* (1999).

For critical overviews, see Lionel Trilling, *Matthew Arnold* (1939); Douglas Bush, *Matthew Arnold: A Survey of His Poetry and Prose* (1971), a cogent and informative survey of Arnold's life and literary career; and Stefan Collini, *Matthew Arnold: A Critical Portrait* (2008). Also helpful is a collection of essays, *Matthew Arnold*, edited by Kenneth Allott (1976).

Critical studies that focus on Arnold's prose include John Holloway, *The Victorian Sage: Studies in Argument* (1953), insightful on Arnold's style and rhetorical strategies; Raymond Williams, *Culture and Society: 1780–1950* (1958), a landmark history of British cultural criticism that includes a substantial discussion of Arnold; Vincent Buckley, *Poetry and Morality: Studies on the Criticism of Matthew Arnold, T. S. Eliot, and F. R. Leavis* (1959); Leon Gottfried, *Matthew Arnold and the Romantics* (1963); David J. DeLaura, *Hebrew and Hellene in Victorian England: Newman, Arnold, and Pater* (1969), which explicates the affinities and differences between Arnold and his contemporaries and successors; Fred G. Walcott, *The Origins of Culture and Anarchy: Matthew Arnold and Popular Education in England* (1970); Sidney Coulling, *Matthew Arnold and His Critics: A Study of Arnold's Controversies* (1974), which provides historical context; Joseph Carroll, *The Cultural Theory of Matthew Arnold* (1982), an excellent study of Arnold's main themes and ideas; and Ruth apRoberts, *Arnold and God* (1983). For responses to Arnold by his contemporaries, see *Matthew Arnold—Prose Writings: The Critical Heritage*, edited by Carl Dawson and John Pfordresher (1979). Edward W. Said, in *The World, the Text, and the Critic* (1983), and Geoffrey H. Hartman, in *Criticism in the Wilderness: The Study of Literature Today* (1980), are among the important contemporary literary theorists who have assessed Arnold's impact on the academy. Additional commentaries can be found in an edition of *Culture and Anarchy* prepared by Samuel Lipman (1994). In *Ethnicity and Cultural Authority: From Arnold to Du Bois* (2006), Daniel G. Williams studies Arnold in a transatlantic context, showing how he, William Dean Howells, W. B. Yeats, and W. E. B. Du Bois draw on ethnicity and race in their cultural and literary criticism. Also stimulating are Antony H. Harrison, *The Cultural Production of Matthew Arnold* (2009), which situates Arnold as a poet and an elite male literary intellectual in social, political, literary, and gender/sexual identity contexts in the 1840s/1850s and later, and James Walter Caufield, *Overcoming Matthew Arnold: Ethics in Culture and Criticism* (2012), which examines Arnold's literary and cultural criticism and religious essays.

Concentrating on Arnold's poetry but including pertinent commentary on the prose are A. Dwight Culler, *Imaginative Reason: The Poetry of Matthew Arnold* (1961); Alan Roper, *Arnold's Poetic Landscapes* (1969); and David G. Riede, *Matthew Arnold and the Betrayal of Language* (1988).

Thomas Burnett Smart has compiled *The Bibliography of Matthew Arnold* (1892); it should be supplemented by the listing in *The Works of Matthew Arnold*, vol. 15 (1903–04). See also Clinton Machann, *The Essential Matthew Arnold: An Annotated Bibliography of Major Modern Studies* (1993). For more recent work, consult the bibliography in Caufield's *Overcoming Matthew Arnold* (see above).

Erich Auerbach

Auerbach's earliest scholarly work was a German translation of Vico's *New Science* (1926). His first monograph, *Dante: Poet of the Secular World* (1929; trans. 1961), is still considered one of the best introductions to Dante's work. *Mimesis: The Representation of Reality in Western Literature* (1946), the work for which Auerbach is best remembered, was translated into English in 1953; the fiftieth anniversary of the book's translation saw the release of a new edition with a preface by Edward W. Said (2003). Other books include *Introduction to Romance Languages and Literature* (1953; trans. 1961) and *Literary Language and Its Public in Late Latin Antiquity and in the Middle Ages* (1953; trans. 1965). Auerbach's last book, *Scenes from the Drama of European Literature* (1959; trans. 1984), contains the essay "Figura," considered his definitive statement on figural history. *Time, History, and Literature: Selected Essays of Erich Auerbach*, edited by James I. Porter and translated by Jane O. Newman (2014), collects twenty essays by Auerbach, including twelve that have never before been translated into English and one previously unpublished work.

Geoffrey Green's *Literary Criticism and the Structures of History: Erich Auerbach and Leo Spitzer* (1982) is a useful introduction to Auerbach that provides an intellectual biography. Geoffrey Hartman's *A Scholar's Tale: Intellectual Journey of a Displaced Child of Europe* (2007) ends with an extended meditation on his encounters with Auerbach at Yale during the late 1950s. Renewed interest in Auerbach's response to Nazi oppressions, which he experienced firsthand, was sparked by Martin Elsky, Martin Vialon, and Robert Stein's translation in *PMLA* 122 (2007) of a series of letters written by Auerbach during the war years to, among others, his student Martin Hellweg, to Karl Vossler, and to Walter Benjamin.

Edward W. Said discusses Auerbach's legacy in the introductory chapter to his *The World, the Text, and the Critic* (1983), and the central chapters of Paul Bové's *Intellectuals in Power: A Genealogy of Critical Humanism* (1986) are devoted to Auerbach. With the approach of a new century, reevaluations of Auerbach's legacy focused on the place of philology in literary criticism, on his status as a German Jew in exile in Istanbul during the Holocaust, and on his brush there with Orientalism. Aamir R. Mufti explores the importance of Auerbach for Edward W. Said's notion of "secular criticism" in "Auerbach in Istanbul: Edward Said, Secular Criticism, and the Question of Minority Culture," *Critical Inquiry* 25 (1998). In *East-West Mimesis: Auerbach in Turkey* (2010), Kader Konuk challenges the standard narrative of Auerbach's exile in Istanbul, arguing that there was a reciprocal exchange of knowledge and culture between the German émigrés and their host Muslim culture. The essays collected in *Literary*

History and the Challenge of Philology: The Legacy of Erich Auerbach, edited by Seth Lerer (1996), examine Auerbach's work in the context of nineteenth- and twentieth-century philology, the European discipline that studies cultures through historical analyses of their languages. *Poetics Today* devoted a special issue (20.1) to Auerbach, *Erich Auerbach and Literary Representation* (1998). In "Literary History and the Sublime in Erich Auerbach's *Mimesis*," *New Literary History* 38 (2007), Robert Doran places Romance philology within the critical tradition, derived from Longinus, of the sublime. In "Erich Auerbach and the Judaizing of Philology," *Critical Inquiry* 35 (2008), James I. Porter reads in Auerbach's contrast in "Odysseus' Scar" between Jewish and Greek forms of representation a challenge to Germanic philology from the perspective of a secular Jewish intellectual writing during and in the immediate aftermath of the Holocaust. A selective but up-to-date bibliography, including recent trends in Auerbach scholarship, is provided by Porter in *Time, History, and Literature* (see above).

Augustine of Hippo

Augustine's complete works in Latin can be found in his *Opera Omnia* (14 vols., 1830–38). More up-to-date editions of some works appear in the unfinished *Bibliothèque Augustinienne* (1947–). English translations of Augustine's major works are included in Catholic University's *Fathers of the Church* series (1947–). In the past D. W. Robertson Jr.'s 1958 translation of *On Christian Doctrine* was usually favored by scholars. R. P. H. Green's 1997 *On Christian Teaching* has become the preferred version. John Healey's 1940 translation of *The City of God* is widely cited, as is John K. Ryan's 1960 translation of *The Confessions*, Augustine's chronicle of his own life. The Loeb dual-language edition of this work has been reissued (2 vols., 2014–16), newly edited and translated by Carolyn J.-B. Hammond. James J. O'Donnell's *Augustine: A New Biography* (2005) offers not only a readable introduction to the saint's life, based on newly discovered material, but also a sustained meditation on the saint's own self-fashioning.

Eugene Portalie's *Guide to the Thought of St. Augustine* (1960) is an accessible and carefully indexed guide to Augustine's writings. *What Are They Saying about Augustine?* (2014) by Joseph T. Kelly provides an accessible overview of Augustine's life and thought for those new to Augustinian studies. D. W. Robertson's *Preface to Chaucer* (1963), controversial since its publication, is a learned and useful introduction to Augustinian aesthetics. Marcia L. Colish's *Mirror of Language: A Study in the Medieval Theory of Knowledge* (1968) cogently draws out the implications of Augustinian sign theory for later medieval theorists such as Thomas Aquinas and Dante. *De doctrina christiana: A Classic of Western Culture*, edited by Duane W. H. Arnold and Pamela Bright (1995), provides a range of critical views. Extrapolating from Augustinian sign theory, Brian Stock explores Augustine's theory of reading and its implications for later medieval writers in two books, *Augustine the Reader: Meditation, Self-Knowledge, and the Ethics of Interpretation* (1996) and *After Augustine: The Meditative Reader and the Text* (2001). Augustine's influence on the later Middle Ages is examined in *Reading and Wisdom: The De doctrina christiana of Augustine in the Middle Ages*, edited by E. D. English (1995). Brent D. Shaw's *Sacred Violence: African Christians and Sectarian Hatred in the Age of Augustine* (2011) examines the sectarian politics of late fourth- and early fifth-century Christianity in Augustine's native Africa. *A Companion to Augustine*, edited by Mark Vessey (2012), collects essays that view the saint as product of his own culture, as well as a cultural influence in his own right. *The Cambridge Companion to Augustine*, edited by Eleonore Stump and Norman Kretzmann (2001), was revised in 2014 by Stump and David Vincent Meconi, SJ. This second edition contains significant new material, including a section on Augustine's writing about language and faith. Several other books explore Augustinian theories of language, rhetoric, and poetics, including Edward Morgan, *The Incarnation of the Word: The Theology of Language of Augustine of Hippo* (2010); James A. Andrews, *Hermeneutics and the Church: In Dialogue with Augustine* (2012); and Simone Marchesi, *Dante and Augustine: Linguistics, Poetics, Hermeneutics* (2011), which examines the influence of the saint on the poet Dante. Among other works on Augustinian interpretation are Michael Cameron's *Christ Meets Me Everywhere: Augustine's Early Figurative Exegesis* (2012); Susannah Ticciati's *A New Apophaticism: Augustine and the Redemption of Signs* (2013); Mark F. M. Clavier's *Eloquent Wisdom: Rhetoric, Cosmology and Delight in the Theology of Augustine of Hippo* (2014); and a collection of essays edited by Calvin L. Troup, *Augustine for the Philosophers: The Rhetor of Hippo, the "Confessions," and the Continentals* (2014), which looks at the saint's influence on several philosophers, including Martin Heidegger, Hannah Arendt, Albert Camus, Jean-François Lyotard, and Paul Ricoeur. The *Augustinus-Lexicon* (1985–), when completed (vols. 1–3 are currently available), will become the standard reference work, containing encyclopedic articles on Augustine's life, works, and doctrine. The *Fichier Augustinien* (1972) offers a comprehensive bibliography to 1970, with one supplemental volume (1978). See also the substantial bibliography in *The Cambridge Companion to Augustine* (2d ed., 2014).

J. L. Austin

Austin's two posthumously published sets of lectures are *How to Do Things with Words* (1962) and

Sense and Sensibilia (1962). His essays are collected in *Philosophical Papers* (3d ed., 1979). G. J. Warnock's "John Langshaw Austin, A Biographical Sketch," in *Symposium on J. L. Austin* (ed. K. T. Fann, 1969), is the most useful biographical source. The Fann volume, along with John Searle, *Speech Acts* (1969); Isaiah Berlin et al., *Essays on J. L. Austin* (1973); *Speech Act Theory and Pragmatics*, edited by John Searle, Ferenc Kiefer, and Manfred Bierwisch (1980); and *The Philosophy of J. L. Austin*, edited by Martin Gustafsson and Richard Sørli (2011), provide good overviews of Austin's reception within Anglo-American philosophy. G. J. Warnock's *J. L. Austin* (1989) is an excellent, concise introductory text. Mary Louise Pratt's *Toward a Speech Act Theory of Literary Discourse* (1977), Charles Altieri's *Act and Quality* (1981), and Sandy Petrey's *Speech Acts and Literary Theory* (1990) are the most influential uses of Austin to account for the capacities of literary texts. For more general reflections on theoretical issues arising out of Austin's work, see Stanley Fish, *Is There a Text in This Class? The Authority of Interpretive Communities* (1980); Alice Crary, "'The Happy Truth': J. L. Austin's *How to Do Things with Words*," *Inquiry* 45 (2002); Michael J. Golec, "'The Thinking's Man Filter': J. L. Austin's Ordinary Language Philosophy as Cultural Criticism," *Cultural Critique*, no. 72 (2009); and Maximilian de Gaynesford, "How Not to Do Things with Words: J. L. Austin on Poetry," *British Journal of Aesthetics* 51 (2011). Jacques Derrida's essay on Austin and his side in the debate with Searle is collected in *Limited INC* (1988); for Searle's side, one must go to "Reiterating the Difference: A Reply to Derrida," *Glyph* 1 (1977). The most original American disciple of Austin is Stanley Cavell, a philosopher who is also a major literary and film critic. He has revisited the Derrida-Searle debate in his *Philosophical Passages: Wittgenstein, Emerson, Austin, Derrida* (1995). Cavell and Judith Butler contribute commentaries to Shoshana Felman's *The Scandal of the Speaking Body: Don Juan with J. L. Austin, or Seduction in Two Languages* (1980; trans. 2002). The best available bibliography can be found in Gustafsson and Sørli's *Philosophy of J. L. Austin*, but it is incomplete and limited to work in Anglo-American philosophy.

Mikhail M. Bakhtin

The standard Russian-language edition of Bakhtin's works is *Sobranie sochinenii*, edited by S. G. Bocharov et al. (7 vols., 1996–2012). The earliest works survive only in fragments, collected and translated into English by Vadim Liapunov as *Art and Answerability* (1990) and *Toward a Philosophy of the Act* (1993). *Problems of Dostoevsky's Poetics*, first published in 1929, was revised and reissued in Russian in 1963; Caryl Emerson translated it into English in 1984. Bakhtin's dissertation of the 1930s and 1940s, finally published in 1965, was translated by Hélène Iswolsky as *Rabelais and His World* (1968). The important group of lengthy essays Bakhtin wrote between 1934 and 1941—including "Discourse in the Novel"—was not published in Russia until 1973; they were translated by Caryl Emerson and Michael Holquist as *The Dialogic Imagination: Four Essays* (1981). Fragments of Bakhtin's late—and largely unfinished—works were collected in a Russian volume and translated into English as *Speech Genres and Other Late Essays* (1986). Works attributed to Bakhtin by some scholars though their title pages list other authors include V. N. Vološinov, *Freudianism: A Marxist Critique* (1926; trans. 1976); P. N. Medvedev, *The Formal Method in Literary Scholarship* (1928; trans. 1978); and Vološinov, *Marxism and the Philosophy of Language* (1929; trans. 1973). For selections of works by members of the Bakhtin circle, see *The Bakhtin Reader: Selected Writings of Bakhtin, Medvedev, and Voloshinov*, edited by Pam Morris (1994).

The standard biography is Katerina Clark and Michael Holquist, *Mikhail Bakhtin* (1984). Gary Saul Morson edited one of the first English collections of essays, *Bakhtin: Essays and Dialogues on His Work* (1981), still valuable for its critical readings. Tzvetan Todorov, who, with Julia Kristeva, was instrumental in bringing Bakhtin's work to the attention of the West, provides a useful brief introduction to Bakhtinian dialogics in *Mikhail Bakhtin: The Dialogic Principle* (1981; trans. 1984). Two collections of essays—*Bakhtin and Cultural Theory*, edited by Ken Hirschkop and David Shepherd (1989; 2d ed., 2001), and *Rethinking Bakhtin: Extensions and Challenges*, edited by Gary Saul Morson and Caryl Emerson (1989)—offer readings of Bakhtin across a range of theoretical and political positions. For the feminist reception of Bakhtin, see Dale Bauer and Susan McKinstry, *Feminism, Bakhtin, and the Dialogic* (1991). Michael Holquist's *Dialogism: Bakhtin and His World* (1991; 2d ed., 2002) provides a comprehensive overview of Bakhtin's work. Gary Saul Morson and Caryl Emerson's *Mikhail Bakhtin: Creation of a Prosaics* (1990) is the single most thorough and authoritative book-length study of Bakhtin's writing and should be the starting point for more advanced study of his work. With the end of the cold war in 1989, the work of Russian scholars on Bakhtin has become available for the first time, notably in *Face to Face: Bakhtin in Russia and the West*, edited by Carol Adlam (1997), which collects essays from a 1995 Bakhtin conference in Moscow. Sue Vice's *Introducing Bakhtin* (1997) and Alastair Renfrew's *Mikhail Bakhtin* (2015) may be more accessible introductions than Todorov's for students new to Bakhtin's thought. For a retrospective on Bakhtin's works that places him in the context of twentieth-century Russian thought, see Caryl Emerson, *The First One Hundred Years of Mikhail Bakhtin* (1997), as well as *Critical Essays on Bakhtin*, edited by Emerson (1999). Ken Hirschkop's *Mikhail Bakhtin: An Aesthetic for Democracy*

(1999), drawing on the new Russian scholarship, challenges many of the myths about Bakhtin's life and work to explore in a more nuanced fashion his contributions to an ethical and democratic cultural theory. *The Bakhtin Circle: In the Master's Absence*, edited by Craig Brandist, David Shepherd, and Galin Tihanov (2004), offers new translations and studies of texts produced by the Bakhtin Circle, as well as new archival material related to their activity, highlighting the distinctiveness of works by such theorists as Vološinov and Medvedev, who have been closely identified with Bakhtin. *Bakhtin's Theory of the Literary Chronotope: Reflections, Applications, Perspectives*, edited by Nele Bemong et al. (2010), collects theoretical and critical essays on the chronotope. *Dialogues with Bakhtinian Theory: Proceedings of the Thirteenth International Mikhail Bakhtin Conference*, edited by Mykola Polyuha, Clive Robert Thomson, and Anthony J. Wall (2012), features essays by Bakhtin scholars from around the world. *Bakhtin and His Others: (Inter)subjectivity, Chronotope, Dialogism*, edited by Liisa Steinby and Tintti Klapuri (2013), considers Bakhtinian ethics over his sociological poetics in the wake of scholarship on Bakhtin's German sources. As readers of Bakhtin have examined his debts to German philosophers in his earlier works, they have become more interested in Bakhtin as a philosopher of ethics than as a theorist of aesthetics and literature (since most Bakhtinians have considered works like *Discourse in the Novel* to be about literary concerns). Daphna Erdinast-Vulcan's *Between Philosophy and Literature: Bakhtin and the Question of the Subject* (2014) reads Bakhtin alongside philosophers such as Henri Bergson, Maurice Merleau-Ponty, and Emmanuel Lévinas. In *Difference, Dialogue, and Development: A Bakhtinian World* (2016), Lakshmi Bandlamudi, a developmental psychologist, offers a reading of Bakhtin's dialogism from the perspective of development. Julio Peiró Sempere, in *The Influence of Mikhail Bakhtin on the Formation and Development of the Yale School of Deconstruction* (2014), argues that Bakhtin's philosophical and ethical approach to interpretation should be understood as one of the antecedents of deconstructive criticism.

The Annotated Bakhtin Bibliography, edited by Carol Adlam and David Shepherd (2000), is the most up-to-date print bibliography, drawing on the extensive resources of the online Bakhtin Archive, which is maintained by the Bakhtin Center at the University of Sheffield. It can be supplemented by Donald L. Anderson, "Mikhail Bakhtin" (2015), in the online Oxford Bibliographies.

Roland Barthes

Roland Barthes wrote fourteen books: *Writing Degree Zero* (1953; trans. 1967), *Michelet* (1954; trans. 1987), *Mythologies* (1957; trans. 1972, 2012), *On Racine* (1963; trans. 1964), *Elements of Semiology* (1964; trans. 1968), *The Fashion System* (1967; trans. 1983), *S/Z* (1970; trans. 1974), *The Empire of Signs* (1970; trans. 1982), *The Pleasure of the Text* (1973; trans. 1975), *Roland Barthes by Roland Barthes* (1975; trans. 1977), *A Lover's Discourse: Fragments* (1977; trans. 1978), *Leçon* (1978; trans. 1979), *Camera Lucida: Reflections on Photography* (1980; trans. 1981), and *Incidents* (1987; trans. 1992). In addition, there are several volumes of Barthes's essays available in English. Barthes published four collections of essays in French, which have all been translated by Richard Howard (*Critical Essays*, 1972; *New Critical Essays*, 1980; *The Responsibility of Forms*, 1986; and *The Rustle of Language*, 1986). Howard has also translated *What Is Sport?* (2004; trans. 2007), a posthumous book developed from Barthes's text for a short TV documentary (1960), as well as *Mourning* (2009; trans. 2010), a private journal that chronicles Barthes's mourning after the death of his mother. Rosalind E. Krauss and Denis Hollier have translated *The Neutral: Lecture Course at the Collège de France, 1977–1978* (2002; trans. 2005). Columbia University Press has published *Album* (2018), a collection of Barthes's correspondences from adolescence to his last years, as well as two translations of lectures delivered before Barthes's death: *The Preparation of the Novel: Lecture Courses and Seminars at the Collège de France, 1978–1979 and 1979–1980* (2003; trans. 2011) and *How to Live Together: Novelistic Simulations of Some Everyday Spaces* (2002; trans. 2012). *A Barthes Reader*, edited by Susan Sontag (1982), has a good selection but does not include some of the best-known essays. The collection edited by Stephen Heath, *Image, Music, Text* (1977), is perhaps the best short selection available. Andy Stafford and Michael Carter have edited and translated a collection of all of Barthes's writings on fashion, *The Language of Fashion* (2006). A collection of interviews, *The Grain of the Voice: Interviews, 1962–1980*, was translated by Linda Coverdale (1985), and an additional informative interview published in *Tel Quel* has been translated in *The "Tel Quel" Reader* (ed. Patrick ffrench and Roland-François Lack, 1998). Seagull Books has made available a five-volume set of Barthes's interviews and essays: *"A Very Fine Gift": And Other Writings on Theory*, vol. 1 (2015); *"The 'Scandal' of Marxism" and Other Writings on Politics*, vol. 2 (2015); *"Masculine, Feminine, Neuter" and Other Writings on Literature*, vol. 3 (2016); *Signs and Images: Writings on Art, Cinema and Photography*, vol. 4 (2016); and *Simply a Particular Contemporary: Interviews, 1970–79*, vol. 5 (2016). Éditions du Seuil has published Barthes's complete works in French in chronological order, *Oeuvres complètes* (5 vols., 2002); his 1974 impressions of Mao's China as *Carnets du voyage en Chine* (2009, *Travels in China*); and *Album: Inédits, correspondances et varia* (2015, *Album: Unedited Writings, Correspondence, and Miscellaneous Works*), which was published by Columbia University Press (see above).

There are numerous studies of Barthes's life and work. The biography by Louis-Jean Calvet, *Roland Barthes: A Biography* (1990; trans. 1994), is excellent. Andy Stafford's *Roland Barthes, Phenomenon and Myth: An Intellectual Biography* (1998) is thoroughgoing. Two recent biographies introduce previously unpublished materials about Barthes's life and work: Andy Stafford's *Roland Barthes* (2015) and Tiphaine Samoyault's *Barthes: A Biography* (2015; trans. 2017). Philippe Sollers chronicles his friendship with Barthes in the epistolary biography, *The Friendship of Roland Barthes* (2015; trans. 2017). Of the general introductions to Barthes's work as a whole, the following are brief and meaty: the essay on Barthes by John Sturrock in *Structuralism and Since* (ed. John Sturrock, 1979); Jonathan Culler, *Roland Barthes* (1983); Mireille Ribière, *Barthes: A Beginner's Guide* (2002); and Graham Allen, *Roland Barthes* (2003). Longer studies include books—all called *Roland Barthes*—by Philip Thody (1977, rev. 1983; an early conservative reading), Annette Lavers (1982; an early admirer and expositor), Steven Ungar (1983; focusing on Barthes as "professor of desire"), and Mike and Nicholas Gane (3 vols., 2004; an edited collection of many assessments of Barthes's career). Other studies—still called *Roland Barthes*—include those by Michael Moriarty (1991; closely argued and extensive) and Rick Rylance (1994; readable and useful, organized in terms of Barthes's "hot" and "cold" writing). Among the numerous critical studies, *The Barthes Effect: The Essay as Reflective Text* by Réda Bensmaïa (1986; trans. 1987) deserves mention as an interesting study of the essay in Barthes and Montaigne. See also Timothy Sheie's fascinating *Performance Degree Zero: Roland Barthes and Theatre* (2006) and the British journal *Paragraph*'s wide-ranging special issue on Barthes, *Roland Barthes Retroactively*, edited by Jürgen Pieters and Kris Pint (2008). Published in a set together with Barthes's posthumous *Incidents* (see above) is D. A. Miller's *Bringing Out Roland Barthes*, an analysis of the movement of gay desire through Barthes's texts. The annotated bibliography published by Sandford Freedman and Carole Anne Taylor, *Roland Barthes: A Bibliographical Reader's Guide* (1983), is useful but dated. Comprehensive bibliographies are provided by Allen's *Roland Barthes*, Samoyault's and Stafford's bibliographies, and the collection *Album*.

Jean Baudrillard

Baudrillard's books (with French publication date first, followed by the date of the English translation) are *The System of Objects* (1968; 1996), *The Consumer Society* (1970; 1998), *For a Critique of the Political Economy of the Sign* (1972; 1981), *The Mirror of Production* (1973; 1983), *Symbolic Exchange and Death* (1976; 1993), *The Beauborg Effect* (1977; 1982), *Forget Foucault* (1977; 1978), *In the Shadow of the Silent Majorities* (1978; 1983), *Seduction* (1979; 1990), *Simulations* (1981; 1983), *Fatal Strategies* (1983; 1990), *America* (1986; 1988), *The Ecstasy of Communication* (1987; 1988), *Cool Memories, 1980–1985* (1987; 1990), *The Transparency of Evil* (1990; 1993), *Cool Memories II, 1987–1990* (1990; 1996), *The Gulf War Did Not Take Place* (1991; 1995), *The Illusion of the End* (1992; 1994), *The Perfect Crime* (1993; 1996), *Fragments: Cool Memories III, 1990–1995* (1995; 1997), *Impossible Exchange* (1999; 2001), *Passwords* (2000; 2003), *Cool Memories IV: 1995–2000* (2000; 2005), *The Spirit of Terrorism and Other Essays* (2002; 2003), *The Intelligence of Evil, or the Lucidity Pact* (2004; 2005), *Cool Memories V: 2000–2004* (2005; 2006), *Exiles from Dialogue*, with Enrique Valiente Noailles (2005; 2007), and *Why Hasn't Everything Already Disappeared?* (2009). There are also five selections of Baudrillard's work in translation: *The Revenge of the Crystal: Selected Writings on the Modern Object and Its Destiny, 1968–1983*, edited by Paul Foss and Julian Pefanis (1990); *Jean Baudrillard: Selected Writings*, edited by Mark Poster (2d ed., 2001); *The Uncollected Baudrillard*, edited by Gary Genosko (2001); *Mass, Identity, Architecture: Architectural Writings of Jean Baudrillard*, edited by Francesco Proto (new ed., 2006); and *The Jean Baudrillard Reader*, edited by Steve Redhead (2008). Five books collect interviews with Baudrillard: *Baudrillard Live: Selected Interviews*, edited by Mike Gane (1993); *Paroxysm: Interviews with Philippe Petit* (1997; trans. 1998); *Fragments: Conversations with François L'Yvonnet* (2001; trans. 2004); *Jean Baudrillard: From Hyperreality to Disappearance: Uncollected Interviews*, edited by Richard G. Smith and David B. Clarke (2015); and *The Disappearance of Culture*, also edited by Smith and Clarke (2017). The best biographical sources are the entry in *Current Biography Yearbook* (1993) and the introduction to Redhead's *The Jean Baudrillard Reader*.

Four excellent overviews of Baudrillard's career and ideas are the best places to start: Mike Gane's *Jean Baudrillard: In Radical Uncertainty* (2000), Paul Hegarty's *Jean Baudrillard: Live Theory* (2004), William Pawlett's *Jean Baudrillard: Against Banality* (2007), and Richard J. Lane's *Jean Baudrillard* (2d ed., 2009). William Merrin's more specialized *Baudrillard and the Media: A Critical Introduction* (2005) is also recommended. Kim Toffoletti's *Baudrillard Reframed: Interpreting Key Thinkers for the Arts* (2011) considers Baudrillard's influence on contemporary art, while Mihail Evans's *The Singular Politics of Derrida and Baudrillard* (2014) provides a good understanding of Baudrillard's work in relation to French theory after World War II. Among numerous volumes of collected critical essays on Baudrillard's work, *Baudrillard: A Critical Reader*, edited by Douglas Kellner (1994); *Baudrillard Now: Current Perspectives in Baudrillard Studies*, edited by Ryan Bishop (2009); and *Jean Baudrillard: Fatal Theories*, edited by David B. Clarke et al. (2009), are particularly useful. *The Baudrillard Dictionary*, edited by Richard G. Smith (2010), offers succinct accounts of key concepts in Baudrillard's work. It also contains a comprehensive bibliography of all Baudrillard's work, both in French and in English translation, along with a good, although not complete, bibliography of secondary work in English on Baudrillard.

Simone de Beauvoir

First published in France as *Le Deuxième Sexe* (1949), *The Second Sex* (1952) was published in the United States in an incomplete translation by a zoologist, H. M. Parshley. A new translation, marking the sixtieth anniversary of its publication, appeared in 2009, restoring a third of the original work. Besides her six novels, short stories, and play, Beauvoir wrote several books of philosophy and cultural criticism, including *Pyrrhus et Cinéas* (1944); *The Ethics of Ambiguity* (1947; trans. 1948); *L'Existentialisme et la sagesse des nations* (1948, *Existentialism and Popular Wisdom*); *America Day by Day* (1948; trans. 1948); *Must We Burn Sade?* (1951–52; trans. 1953); *The Long March* (1957; trans. 1958); *Brigitte Bardot and the Lolita Syndrome* (1959; trans. 1960); *Djamila Boupacha: The Story of a Young Algerian Girl Which Shocked Liberal French Opinion*, with Gisele Halimi (1962; trans. 1962); and *Old Age* (1970; trans. 1972). Margaret Simon's multivolume Beauvoir Series, produced in consultation with Sylvie Le Bon de Beauvoir, Beauvoir's adopted daughter and literary executor, aims to make available in English translation previously unpublished and little-known works by Beauvoir. Initial volumes include *Philosophical Writings*, edited by Margaret Simons with Marybeth Timmermann and Mary Beth Mader (2004), which includes scholarly translations of twelve essays that span Beauvoir's career, and *Diary of a Philosophy Student*, volume 1, *1926–27*, edited by Barbara Klaw, Sylvie Le Bon de Beauvoir, and Margaret A. Simons, with Marybeth Timmerman (2006), which makes available for the first time Beauvoir's preoccupations with key philosophic issues as early as 1926 and 1927, before she met Sartre. Newer volumes, all edited by Simons and Timmermann, collect Beauvoir's literary writing in *"The Useless Mouths," and Other Literary Writings* (2011), her political essays in *Political Writings* (2012), and her other writing about women in *Feminist Writings* (2015). Beauvoir's extensive autobiographical writing—*Memories of a Dutiful Daughter* (1958; trans. 1959), *The Prime of Life* (1960; trans. 1962), *Force of Circumstances* (1963; trans. 1964), *A Very Easy Death* (1972; trans. 1973), *All Said and Done* (1972; trans. 1974), and *Adieux: A Farewell to Sartre* (1981; trans. 1984)—have supplied most of the information for her biographers. Deirdre Bair's *Simone de Beauvoir: A Biography* (1990) remains the most authoritative biography of the philosopher. 2017 saw the publication of a new biography, *Simone de Beauvoir: Creating a Feminist Existence in the World*, by Sadrine Sanos, that explores Beauvoir's complicated relationship to colonial, transnational, and postcolonial politics and their influences on her philosophy.

For excellent introductions to Beauvoir's writing, see Ursula Tidd, *Simone de Beauvoir* (2004), and Stella Sandford, *How to Read Beauvoir* (2006). *The Cambridge Companion to Simone de Beauvoir*, edited by Claudia Card (2003), will appeal to more advanced students. One of the most astute French writers on Beauvoir is Michèle le Doeuff, who discusses Beauvoir in the context of women's relationship to philosophy in *Hipparchia's Choice: An Essay Concerning Women, Philosophy, etc.* (1989; trans. 1991). The decade leading up to the centennial of Beauvoir's birth (2008) saw a virtual explosion of scholarship on the philosopher. Attempts to extricate Beauvoir's reputation from its dependence on Sartre have proved especially fertile for revisionary scholarship, the most radical rethinking being Edward Fullbrook and Kate Fullbrook's *Sex and Philosophy: Rethinking de Beauvoir and Sartre* (2008). Toril Moi's considerable contributions to Beauvoir scholarship include *Feminist Theory and Simone de Beauvoir* (1990), *Simone de Beauvoir: The Making of an Intellectual Woman* (1994; 2d ed., 2008), and *Sex, Gender, and the Body: The Student Edition of "What Is a Woman?"* (2005), a critical study that explores Beauvoir's contributions to ongoing feminist debates about sex and gender and about the place of the personal in philosophical thought. Fredrika Scarth, *The Other Within: Ethics, Politics, and the Body in Simone de Beauvoir* (2004), examines Beauvoir's reformulation of the Cartesian subject from a feminist ethical perspective. Several collections of essays attest to the vibrancy of Beauvoir scholarship: see *Beauvoir and "The Second Sex": Feminism, Race, and the Origins of Existentialism* (1999) and *The Philosophy of Simone de Beauvoir: Critical Essays* (2006), both edited by Margaret A. Simons; *The Legacy of Simone de Beauvoir*, edited by Emily R. Grosholz (2004); *A Companion to Simone de Beauvoir* (2017), edited by Laura Hengehold and Nancy Bauer; *Proceedings of the 18th Conference of the Simone de Beauvoir Society: Yesterday, Today and Tomorrow* (2017), edited by Andrea Duranti and Matteo Tuvari; *Differences: Rereading Beauvoir and Irigaray* (2017), edited by Emily Parker and Anne van Leeuwen; and *"On ne naît pas femme: on le deviant . . .": The Life of a Sentence* (2017), edited by Bonnie Mann and Martina Ferrari, in which a group of philosophers, translators, literary scholars and historians debate the meaning of Beauvoir's most famous sentence. In *Simone de Beauvoir's Philosophy of Individuation: The Problem of the Second Sex* (2017), Laura Hengehold offers a Deleuzian reading of both *The Second Sex* and Beauvoir's novels. *Politics with Beauvoir: Freedom in the Encounter* (2017), by Lori Jo Marso, and *A New Dawn for the Second*

Sex: Women's Freedom Practices in World Perspective (2017), by Karen Vintges, both examine the role of freedom in Simone de Beauvoir's feminism and political theory. Edward Fullbrook and Margaret Simons's "Simone de Beauvoir," in the online *Oxford Bibliographies* (2015), offers the most up-to-date bibliography.

Aphra Behn

The standard text of Behn's works is the seven-volume edition by Janet M. Todd, *The Works of Aphra Behn* (1992–96). For two valuable biographies of Behn, see Maureen Duffy, *The Passionate Shepherdess: Aphra Behn, 1640–1689* (1977; rpt. 2000), and Janet Todd, *The Secret Life of Aphra Behn* (1999). Frederick M. Link's *Aphra Behn* (1968) offers a useful introduction to Behn's work. Tanya Claire Tenkarian describes Behn's contributions to the development of the novel in *Aphra Behn and the Rise of the English Novel: Gender and Genre* (1993). Two fine anthologies of essays, with contributions by several prominent Behn scholars, are *Rereading Aphra Behn: History, Theory, and Criticism*, edited by Heidi Hutner (1993), and *The Cambridge Companion to Aphra Behn*, edited by Derek Hughes and Janet M. Todd (2004). Todd describes Behn's literary reputation in *The Critical Fortunes of Aphra Behn* (1998), while Jane Spencer explores Behn's legacy in the eighteenth century in *Aphra Behn's Afterlife* (2000). In *Aphra Behn and Her Female Successors*, edited by Margarete Rubik (2011), contributors explore Behn's literary reputation, examining intertextual relations and literary parallels with other women writers. *Aphra Behn Online: An Interactive Journal for Women in the Arts, 1640–1830* (2011–) is an open access scholarly journal sponsored by the Aphra Behn Society. Two recent special issues of the journal *Women's Writing* have been devoted to Behn's work; *Aphra Behn*, edited by Margarete Rubik (19.2 [2012]), and *Aphra Behn, New Questions and Contexts*, edited by Claire Bowditch and Elaine Hobby (22.1 [2015]).

For bibliography, see Mary Ann O'Donnell, *Aphra Behn: An Annotated Bibliography of Primary and Secondary Sources* (2d ed., 2004).

Walter Benjamin

Not until decades after his death did Benjamin's diverse work become readily available in German and later in English. In addition to his two dissertations, *The Concept of Criticism in German Romanticism* (1920) and *The Origin of German Tragic Drama* (1928; trans. 1977), he published many essays and articles and left several unfinished book manuscripts. The first collected edition in German, the two-volume *Schriften* (*Writings*), edited by Theodor Adorno and Gershom Scholem (1955), brought renewed attention to Benjamin's work. The standard scholarly edition of the complete writings in German is *Gesammelte Schriften*, edited by Rolf Tiedemann and Hermann Schweppenhäuser (7 vols., 1972–89). The first selection of essays in English, *Illuminations*, was edited by Hannah Arendt (1968); it includes an early, popular translation of our selection, "The Work of Art in the Age of Its Technological Reproducibility." A string of English collections followed, most notably *Reflections: Essays, Aphorisms, Autobiographical Writings*, edited by Peter Demetz (1978), and *One-Way Street and Other Writings* (1979). In the 1990s, Harvard University Press began publishing a wide array of Benjamin's writings in English, foremost four volumes of *Selected Writings*, under the general editorship of Michael W. Jennings: volume 1, *1913–1926* (1996); volume 2, *1927–1934* (1999); volume 3, *1935–1938* (2002); and volume 4, *1938–1940* (2003). The press also published Benjamin's massive but incomplete *Arcades Project* (1999) and a series of short, spin-off collections, among them *Berlin Childhood around 1900* (1950; trans. 2006), *On Hashish* (2006), *The Writer of Modern Life: Essays on Charles Baudelaire* (2006), *The Work of Art in the Age of Its Technological Reproducibility, and Other Writings on Media* (2008), and *Early Writings (1910–1917)* (2011).

Our selection, "The Work of Art in the Age of Its Technological Reproducibility," comes from the last volume of the *Selected Writings*. There are several versions and translations of the essay, and scholars continue to debate which is the closest to Benjamin's intentions and is the best rendering. Benjamin began the essay in the mid-1930s, completing a first version in 1935. He then prepared a second version that appeared in French translation in 1936; the latter text was the only version published in his lifetime. However, Benjamin continued to revise the essay, as he did with most of his work, up to the spring of 1939. This later, unfinished version, called the third version, is what Adorno included in the 1955 edition of Benjamin's writings, the basis of both the well-known 1968 translation in *Illuminations* and our translation. We chose this version because, though unfinished, it presumably most closely represents Benjamin's final intentions. It includes a larger selection of quotations, reliance on which being one of Benjamin's signature habits—for instance, the opening and very relevant epigraph from the modern French poet Paul Valéry. The Benjamin scholar Esther Leslie notes of the third version "that the Brechtian elements are amplified." The most prominent advocate of the second version is the film scholar Miriam Hansen, who argues that it better conveys Benjamin's intention because it was completed and is more consistent. See Howard Caygill, *Walter Benjamin: The Colour of Experience* (1998), for an extended comparison of the two versions. Caygill believes that Benjamin "refined and improved" his views in the 1939 version, while perhaps playing down the stronger political claims about magic in the earlier version. We use the 2003 translation because it more closely follows Benjamin's German (beginning with the title, which renders *technischen Reproduzierbarkeit* literally as "technological reproducibility" rather than using the more idiomatic English phrase "mechanical reproduction").

Among several collections of letters, the most comprehensive is *The Correspondence of Walter Benjamin, 1910–1940*, edited by Scholem and Adorno (1966; trans. 1994). For Adorno's as well as Benjamin's letters, see Adorno and Benjamin, *The Complete Correspondence, 1928–1940* (1999). *Walter Benjamin's Archive*, edited by Ursula Marx et al. (2007), reprints manuscript pages, notes, pictures, and other curiosities from Benjamin memorabilia.

The standard biography is Momme Brodersen's *Walter Benjamin: A Biography* (1990; trans. 1996), although Howard Eiland and Michael W. Jennings's *Walter Benjamin: A Critical Life* (2014) promises to become the new standard. Gershom Scholem's *Walter Benjamin: The Story of a Friendship* (1975; trans. 1981) offers a firsthand personal account.

The secondary literature on Benjamin in English is extensive. Fredric Jameson provided an influential introduction of Benjamin in *Marxism and Form: Twentieth-Century Dialectical Theories of Literature* (1971). Susan Buck-Morss's *The Origin of Negative Dialectics: Theodor W. Adorno, Walter Benjamin, and the Frankfurt School* (1977) roots Benjamin's work in the context of the Frankfurt School. A spirited attempt to recapture Benjamin for the Left was undertaken by Terry Eagleton in *Walter Benjamin, or Towards a Revolutionary Criticism* (1981). Much of the criticism on Benjamin, such as Richard Wolin, *Walter Benjamin: An Aesthetic of Redemption* (1982; 2d ed., 1994), follows the mystical interpretation inaugurated by Scholem. *On Walter Benjamin: Critical Essays and Recollections*, edited by Gary Smith (1988), contains important texts by Benjamin's contemporaries Adorno, Scholem, and Ernst Bloch and an assessment by the philosopher Jürgen Habermas. In addition, there have been more than twenty special issues of journals on Benjamin; Noah Isenberg's "The Work of Walter Benjamin in the Age of Information," in a special issue of *New German Critique* (no. 83 [2001]), reviews the outpouring of criticism up to that point.

More recently Esther Leslie, *Walter Benjamin: Overpowering Conformism* (2000), provides a good overview; see also Graeme Gilloch, *Walter Benjamin: Critical Constellations* (2002). *The Cambridge Companion to Walter Benjamin*, edited by David S. Ferris (2004), covers the range of Benjamin's work. The compendium *Walter Benjamin: Critical Evaluations in Cultural Theory*, edited by Peter Osborne (3 vols., 2005), reprints key essays on many facets of Benjamin's work. See also David Ferris, *The Cambridge Introduction to Walter Benjamin* (2008). Uwe Steiner's *Walter Benjamin: An Introduction to His Work and Thought* (2004; trans. 2010) offers a good survey. Testifying to the influence Benjamin has on contemporary culture, there are also a few fictionalized accounts—notably Jay Parini's novel *Benjamin's Crossing* (1997).

For works focusing on aesthetics, see Caygill's *Walter Benjamin*, cited above; Lutz Koepnick, *Walter Benjamin and the Aesthetics of Power* (1999); *Benjamin's Ghosts: Interventions in Contemporary Literary and Cultural Theory*, edited by Gerhard Richter (2002); *Mapping Benjamin: The Work of Art in the Digital Age*, edited by Hans Ulrich Gumbrecht and Michael Marrinan (2003); and *Walter Benjamin and Art*, edited by Beatrice Hanssen and Andrew Benjamin (2005). Specifically on our selection, see Miriam Hansen, "Benjamin, Cinema, and Experience," *New German Critique*, no. 40 (winter 1987); Susan Buck-Morss, "Aesthetics and Anaesthetics: Walter Benjamin's Artwork Essay Reconsidered," *October*, no. 62 (fall 1992); and Hansen, "Room-for-Play: Benjamin's Gamble with Cinema," *October*, no. 109 (summer 2004). The first two are collected in Osborne, *Walter Benjamin*; the latter contains Hansen's argument for the second version of the "Work of Art" essay. See also Hansen's *Cinema and Experience: Siegfried Kracauer, Walter Benjamin, and Theodor W. Adorno* (2012) and Jaeho Kang's *Walter Benjamin and the Media: The Spectacle of Modernity* (2014).

The standard bibliography in German is *Walter Benjamin: Eine kommentierte Bibliographie*, compiled by Momme Brodersen et al. (1996), which includes a section on Benjamin's work in English. Gary Smith's *Benjamin* (cited above) includes a bibliography of Benjamin's work and selected secondary material up to 1988. The *Cambridge Companion*, Gilloch's *Walter Benjamin*, and Steiner's *Walter Benjamin* include selected bibliographies of Benjamin's writing and criticism on it.

Jane Bennett

Jane Bennett is the author of four books and dozens of articles. *Unthinking Faith and Enlightenment: Nature and the State in a Post-Hegelian Era* (1987) engages with contemporary debates over the environment and the state; *Thoreau's Nature: Ethics, Politics, and the Wild* (1994) stages a series of dialogues between Thoreau and contemporary theorists to explore his concept of "the Wild," which she defines as an openness to the foreignness of things; *The Enchantment of Modern Life: Attachments, Crossings, and Ethics* (2001) continues this investigation of wonder, attempting to rehabilitate enchantment for a disenchanted modern world; and *Vibrant Matter: A Political Ecology of Things* (2010) offers a manifesto for a politics of the nonhuman. In addition, she has edited, with William Chaloupka, *In the Nature of Things: Language, Politics, and the Environment* (1993) and, with Michael J. Shapiro, *The Politics of Moralizing* (2002). In "Systems and Things: A Response to Graham Harman and Timothy Morton," *New Literary History* 43 (2012), Bennett outlines some of the differences among proponents of the new materialism.

Interviews provide a good entry into Bennett's work; see Gulshan Khan, "Agency, Nature and

Emergent Properties: An Interview with Jane Bennett," *Contemporary Political Theory* 8 (2009), and Janell Watson, "Eco-Sensibilities: An Interview with Jane Bennett," *Minnesota Review*, no. 81 (2013). Steven Shaviro's *The Universe of Things: On Speculative Realism* (2014) is a more advanced theoretical exploration of speculative realism, including its philosophical history. *The Nonhuman Turn*, edited by Richard Grusin (2015), offers an introduction to a range of theoretical and philosophical work decentering the human, including actor-network theory, animal studies, and speculative realism. It includes essays by Bennett, Shaviro, Ian Bogost, and Timothy Morton. On object-oriented literary criticism, see Graham Harman, "The Well-Wrought Broken Hammer: Object-Oriented Literary Criticism," *New Literary History* 43 (2012). For critiques of the new materialism, see Andrew Cole, "The Call of Things: A Critique of Object-Oriented Ontologies," *Minnesota Review*, no. 80 (2013), and Andrew Galloway, "The Poverty of Philosophy: Realism and Post-Fordism," *Critical Inquiry* 39 (2013).

Lauren Berlant and Michael Warner

Lauren Berlant's first three books constitute a trilogy on feeling, national form, and citizenship: *The Anatomy of National Fantasy: Hawthorne, Utopia, and Everyday Life* (1991), which began as her dissertation; *The Queen of America Goes to Washington City: Essays on Sex and Citizenship* (1997); and *The Female Complaint: The Unfinished Business of Sentimentality in American Culture* (2008). She followed them with a major book on affect theory, *Cruel Optimism* (2011), as well as the brief meditation *Desire/Love* (2012) and a dialogue on queer theory with Lee Edelman, *Sex, or the Unbearable* (2014). She has also edited several books, including *Intimacy* (2000), *Our Monica, Ourselves: The Clinton Affair and the National Interest* (co-edited with Lisa Duggan, 2001), and *Compassion: The Culture and Politics of an Emotion* (2004). In addition, she has introduced a volume of photographs by Laura Letinsky, *Venus Inferred* (2000). For an account of her work and life, see the interviews "The Promise of Lauren Berlant," by Imogen Tyler and Elena Loizidou, *Cultural Values* 4 (2000), and "Citizen Berlant," by Andrew Hoberek, in *Critics at Work: Interviews, 1993–2003* (ed. Jeffrey J. Williams, 2004).

Michael Warner began as an early Americanist, and his first book was the influential *The Letters of the Republic: Publication and the Public Sphere in Eighteenth-Century America* (1990). While continuing to write on American literature, he became known as a queer theorist with the edited collection *Fear of a Queer Planet: Queer Politics and Social Theory* (1993), which drew essays from a special issue of the journal *Social Text* (1991) and introduced the concept of "heteronormativity," and with his crossover book, *The Trouble with Normal: Sex, Politics, and the Ethics of Queer Life* (1999). He developed his ideas about the public sphere in *Publics and Counterpublics* (2002); the book includes "Sex in Public," which originally appeared in *Critical Inquiry* 24 (1998). In addition, Warner has edited a number of volumes, including *The Origins of Literary Study in America: A Documentary Anthology*, with Gerald Graff (1989); *The English Literatures of America: 1500–1800*, with Myra Jehlen (1997); *American Sermons: The Pilgrims to Martin Luther King, Jr.* (1999); *The Portable Walt Whitman* (2003); and *Varieties of Secularism in a Secular Age*, with Jonathan VanAntwerpen and Craig Calhoun (2010). He has also written for less academic audiences in magazines such as the *Nation*, the *Village Voice*, and the *Advocate*. For an account of his religious upbringing, see "Tongues Untied: Memoirs of a Pentecostal Boyhood," in *Curioser: On the Queerness of Children* (ed. Steven Bruhm and Natasha Hurley, 2004); see also the interview "Queer World Making," by Annamarie Jagose, *Genders*, no. 31 (2000).

Both Berlant and Warner are regularly referred to in queer theory, discussions of the public sphere, and recent publications in American studies, although there are not yet individual studies of their works. Their analysis of heteronormativity has influenced contemporary thought in education, sociology, and anthropology as well as literary and cultural studies. For instance, see Suzanne Fraser, "Poetic World-Making: *Queer as Folk*, Counterpublic Speech and the 'Reader,'" *Sexualities* 9 (2006). For an early assessment of Berlant's work, see Lora Romero, "Making History," *Novel* 26 (1993); on her work on sentimental narrative, see Kathleen Woodward, "Calculating Compassion," *Indiana Law Journal* 77 (2002); and on her work on trauma, see John Johnston, "*The Intuitionist* and *Pattern Recognition*: A Response to Lauren Berlant," *American Literary History* 20 (2008). *Life Writing as Intimate Publics*, edited by Margaretta Jolly, a special issue of *Biography* (34.1 [2011]), starts from Berlant's ideas of sentimentality, affect, and the public. For a less-sympathetic response, see Tim Dean, "No Sex Please, We're American," *American Literary History* 27 (2015). For responses to Warner's influential work in queer theory, see John Nguyet Erni, "Eternal Excesses: Toward a Queer Mode of Articulation in Social Theory," *American Literary History* 8 (1996); and Jeffrey Escoffier, chapter 8 of *American Homo: Community and Perversity* (1998). For considerations of Warner's analysis of the public sphere, see Jodi Dean, "The Lure of the Public," *Theory and Event* 6.3 (2003), and Sandra M. Gustafson, "American Literature and the Public Sphere," *American Literary History* 20 (2008). There are no bibliographies of Berlant and Warner to date.

Stephen Best and Sharon Marcus

Stephen Best examines law and literature, particularly in relation to slavery, in a number of essays and in *The Fugitive's Properties: Law and the Poetics of Possession* (2004). He also serves on the editorial board of *Representations* and co-edited its special issue *Redress* (no. 92 [2005]), as well as *The Way We Read Now* (no. 108 [2009]), for which he co-wrote our selection, "Surface Reading: An Introduction," with Sharon Marcus. Marcus is a scholar of comparative literature, studying nineteenth-century literature and culture in England and France. Her first book, *Apartment Stories: City and Home in Nineteenth-Century Paris and London* (1999), examines architecture, planning, and the domestic sphere; her next book, *Between Women: Friendship, Desire, and Marriage in Victorian England* (2007), studies the relations that women had in the era. In *Between Women*, she explains the value of "just reading" as opposed to Fredric Jameson's and other theorists' symptomatic approaches. She has also examined the rise of modern celebrity in articles such as "Salomé!! Sarah Bernhardt, Oscar Wilde, and the Drama of Celebrity," *PMLA* 126 (2011). For her thinking about the controversy over "surface reading" as well as her work overall, see Jeffrey J. Williams's "Ways of Reading: An Interview with Sharon Marcus," *Minnesota Review*, no. 89 (2017).

Though "Surface Reading" was an introduction to a special issue, not a featured article, it has drawn a great deal of response. For criticism of the absence of politics in it, see Crystal Bartolovich, "Humanities of Scale: Marxism, Surface Reading—and Milton," *PMLA* 127 (2012), and Ellen Rooney, "Live Free or Describe: The Reading Effect and the Persistence of Form," *differences* 21.3 (2010). Carolyn Lesjak's "Reading Dialectically," *Criticism* 55 (2013), provides a useful survey of the different senses of "reading," finally arguing against reading on the surface. The journal *Eighteenth Century* 54 (2013) featured a cluster of five responses, and in 2015 a group of Victorianists under the name "V21" ("21" indicates their stance in the twenty-first century) issued an online "Manifesto of the V21 Collective" criticizing the "positivist historicism" suggested by surface reading and reasserting the importance of theory.

A more sympathetic line of response has agreed with surface reading's eschewal of "critique" and its nod to emerging methods. N. Katherine Hayles, in "How We Read: Close, Hyper, Machine," *ADE Bulletin* 150 (2010), places surface reading in the context of digital approaches. For Heather Love, in "Close But Not Deep: Literary Ethics and the Descriptive Turn," *NLH* 41 (2010), it accords with her interest in sociological description rather than critique. Rita Felski, in both "Suspicious Minds," *Poetics Today* 32 (2011), and *The Limits of Critique* (2015), finds surface reading to be a salutary sign of moving past the "hermeneutics of suspicion." For a general account, see Jeffrey J. Williams, "The New Modesty in Literary Criticism," *Chronicle of Higher Education*, January 5, 2015.

Homi K. Bhabha

Bhabha's reputation primarily rests on his essays, twelve of which are collected in his book *The Location of Culture* (1994; new ed., 2004), which includes "The Commitment to Theory." He has also edited an influential anthology on the cultural construction of nationality, *Nation and Narration* (1990). Many of his later essays, as yet uncollected, focus on globalization, identity, and what he calls "vernacular cosmopolitanism." In addition, he was among four editors of the collection *Cosmopolitanism* (2002) and co-edited, with W. J. T. Mitchell, *Edward Said: Continuing the Conversation* (2005), to which he contributed an essay, "Adagio." He also writes regularly on art, with contributions to *Artforum* and a number of exhibition catalogs or collections, including *Negotiating Rapture: The Power of Art to Transform Lives* (ed. Richard Francis, 1996), *Intervention Architecture: Building for Change* ([ed. Aga Khan Foundation,] 2007), *Iranian Photography Now* (ed. Rose Issa, 2009), *Anish Kapoor* (2009), *Midnight to the Boom: Painting in India after Independence* (ed. Susan S. Bean, 2013), and *Matthew Barney: River of Fundament* (ed. Okwui Enwezor, 2014).

Bhabha is the subject of a growing body of criticism. Robert Young's "The Ambivalence of Bhabha," in his *White Mythologies: Writing History and the West* (1990), is a useful discussion of Bhabha's overall project. From the left, Aijaz Ahmad's "The Politics of Literary Postcoloniality," *Race and Class* 36.3 (1995), criticizes Bhabha's philosophical conception of politics and his elision of the concrete relations of class and caste. Bart Moore-Gilbert, in *Postcolonial Theory: Contexts, Practices, Politics* (1997), situates Bhabha's work among that of other prominent postcolonial theorists and comments on its "babelian" or many-voiced performance. Anthony Easthope's "Bhabha, Hybridity, and Identity," *Textual Practice* 12.2 (1998), uncovering its Derridean roots, criticizes the amorphous nature of "hybridity." Two books titled *Homi K. Bhabha*, by David Huddart (2006) and Eleanor Byrne (2009), provide useful overviews. Patricia Pisters's "Homi K. Bhabha," in *Film, Theory and Philosophy: The Key Thinkers* (ed. Felicity Coleman, 2009), assesses Bhabha's relevance to film and art criticism; see also Felix Hernández, *Bhabha for Architects* (2010). Shai Ginsburg, "Signs and Wonders: Fetishism and Hybridity in Homi Bhabha's *The Location of Culture*," *New Centennial Review* 9.3 (2009), argues that Bhabha does not escape conventional thinking about colonialism with his neologisms but instead produces a new fetish for theory. Alan Ramón Ward, "Sartre as Silent Partner: Reading Bhabha's Existential Turn," *Cultural Critique* 83 (2013), explores a surprising connection to the French philosopher Jean-Paul Sartre, via Bhabha's use of Fanon and Lacan. See also a special section of *PMLA* 132.1 (2017) reassessing Bhabha's *Location of Culture*. Huddart's volume includes a good selected, annotated bibliography of Bhabha's work and critical responses to it.

Harold Bloom

Bloom began as a critic of Romantic poetry, with *Shelley's Mythmaking* (1959), *The Visionary Company: A Reading of English Romantic Poetry* (1961; rev. ed., 1971), *Blake's Apocalypse: A Study in Poetic Argument* (1963), *Yeats* (1970), *Romanticism and Consciousness: Essays in Criticism* (1970), and *The Ringers in the Tower: Studies in Romantic Tradition* (1971). *The Anxiety of Influence: A Theory of Poetry* (1973; 2d ed., 1997) introduced his theoretical view of the poet's struggle with tradition, which was elaborated in *A Map of Misreading* (1975), *Kabbalah and Criticism* (1975), *Poetry and Repression: Revisionism from Blake to Stevens* (1976), *Figures of Capable Imagination* (1976), and *Agon: Towards a Theory of Revisionism* (1982). Other books are *Wallace Stevens: The Poems of Our Climate* (1977), the novel *The Flight to Lucifer: A Gnostic Fantasy* (1979), *The Breaking of the Vessels* (1982), *Ruin the Sacred Truths: Poetry and Belief from the Bible to the Present* (1989), *The Book of J* (1990), *The American Religion: The Emergence of a Post-Christian Nation* (1992), *The Western Canon: The Books and School of the Ages* (1994), *Omens of Millennium: The Gnosis of Angels, Dreams, and Resurrection* (1996), *Shakespeare: The Invention of the Human* (1998), *How to Read and Why* (2000), *Genius: A Mosaic of One Hundred Exemplary Creative Minds* (2002), *Hamlet: Poem Unlimited* (2003), *Where Shall Wisdom Be Found?* (2004), *The Art of Reading Poetry* (2005), *Jesus and Yahweh: The Names Divine* (2005), *Fallen Angels* (2007), *The Shadow of a Great Rock: A Literary Appreciation of the King James Bible* (2011), *The Anatomy of Influence: Literature as a Way of Life* (2011), and *The Daemon Knows: Literary Greatness and the American Sublime* (2015). Two excellent interviews are the best place to find biographical information and to sample Bloom's characteristic tone and obsessions: with Cassandra Atherton in *Writing on the Edge* 17 (2007), and with Adam Fitzgerald in *Boston Review*, April 27, 2011.

Graham Allen's *Harold Bloom: A Poetics of Conflict* (1994) offers the fullest engagement with Bloom's works on poetic influence. *The Salt Companion to Harold Bloom*, edited by Allen and Roy Sellars (2007), provides a generous sampling of critical responses to Bloom's work and can be paired with *Reading, Writing, and the Influence of Harold Bloom*, edited by Alan Rawes and Jonathon Shears (2010). Two specialized monographs serve those interested in Bloom's place in contemporary theory: Agata Bielik-Robson's *The Saving Lie: Harold Bloom and Deconstruction* (2011) and Alistair Heys's *The Anatomy of Bloom: Harold Bloom and the Study of Influence and Anxiety* (2014). Cynthia Ozick's shrewd evaluation of Bloom's whole career in her review of *The Daemon Knows* (*New York Times*, May 18, 2015) is well worth consulting.

Giovanni Boccaccio

A modern Italian edition of the complete works of Giovanni Boccaccio was published under the editorial direction of Vittore Branca, *Tutte le opere di Giovanni Boccaccio* (10 vols., 1964–98). For the Latin text of *Genealogy of the Gentile Gods*, consult the definitive edition by Vincenzo Romano (1951). Jon Solomon is preparing a new English translation of *Genealogy of the Pagan Gods*; volume 1 (2011) contains books 1–5. An English translation of books 14 and 15 of *Genealogy of the Gentile Gods* is available in Charles G. Osgood, *Boccaccio on Poetry* (1930). Other of Boccaccio's critical works in English include his *Life of Dante*, translated by J. G. Nichols (2002); *Famous Women*, edited and translated by Virginia Brown (2001); and *De casibus: The Fates of Illustrious Men*, translated in an abridged version by Louis Brewer Hall (1965). For an intellectual biography of Boccaccio in English with important primary material translated, see Vittore Branca, *Boccaccio: The Man and His Works* (1976).

Much of the secondary criticism of Boccaccio focuses on the *Decameron*. The introduction to Charles Osgood's *Boccaccio on Poetry* is an indispensable guide to Boccaccio's literary criticism. Erich Auerbach's chapter on Boccaccio in *Mimesis* (1953) offers a fundamental discussion of realism in his writing. Herbert G. Wright traces Boccaccio's considerable influence on English poets in *Boccaccio in England: From Chaucer to Tennyson* (1957). Filippo Andrei's *Boccaccio the Philosopher* (2017) explores the relationship between literary production and epistemology in *Decameron*, documenting his engagement with contemporary thinkers like Dante, Petrarch, and Thomas Aquinas. For a general introduction to Boccaccio and his work, see Judith Powers Serafini-Sauli, *Giovanni Boccaccio* (1982), and *The Cambridge Companion to Boccaccio*, edited by Guyda Armstrong, Rhiannon Daniels, and Stephen J. Milner (2015). Thomas Hyde's essay "Boccaccio and the Genealogies of Myth," *PMLA* 100 (1985), offers a close analysis of the *Genealogy of the Gentile Gods*. Gregory Stone provides an advanced study of Boccaccio's literary criticism in *The Ethics of Nature in the Middle Ages: On Boccaccio's Poetaphysics* (1998), as does Lina Insana in "Redefining *Dulce et utile*: Boccaccio's Organization of Literature on Economic Terms," *Heliotropia* 2.1 (2004). For a study of the *Genealogy of the Gentile Gods*, see Jon Solomon's "Historian and Humanist: Gods, Greeks, and Poetry (*Genealogia deorum gentilium*)," in *Boccaccio: A Critical Guide to the Complete Works* (ed. Victoria Kirkham, Michael Sherberg, and Janet Levarie Smarr, 2013). For a bibliography, consult Joseph P. Consoli, *Giovanni Boccaccio: An Annotated Bibliography* (1992), and "Giovanni Boccaccio Bibliography" by Jason Houston, in the online *Oxford Bibliographies* (2014).

Ian Bogost

In addition to creating video games and authoring scholarly and popular articles, Ian Bogost has written a broad array of academic books. *Unit Operations: An Approach to Videogame Criticism* (2006) is a pioneering work that integrates literary theory with information technology in order to generate new interpretive modes for understanding both video games and older forms of art and literature. *Persuasive Games: The Expressive Power of Videogames* (2007) offers an extended account of the argument—introduced in our selection, "The Rhetoric of Video Games" (2007)—that games employ "procedural rhetoric." Co-authored with Nick Montfort, Bogost's *Racing the Beam: The Atari Video Computer System* (2009) makes a contribution to scholarly understanding of the history of video games by offering a technical and cultural analysis of the pioneering Atari system. A second co-authored book, *Newsgames: Journalism at Play* (2010)—written with Simon Ferrari and Bobby Schweizer—argues that games can provide new possibilities for journalism by creating interactive models that enable people to encounter and interpret the news for themselves in ways that are not possible in traditional media. Bogost's *How to Do Things with Videogames* (2011) seeks to move beyond denouncing games as mindless entertainment or defending them as serious aesthetic objects in order to show how games have already begun to permeate every aspect of culture and how they will continue to do so with culturally transformative effects. *A Slow Year: Game Poems* (2010) contains four poetic video games plus two essays on the relationship between games and poetry, and *Alien Phenomenology, or, What It's Like to Be a Thing* (2012) develops an object-oriented ontology while drawing on Bogost's creative experiences as a game designer for illustrative material. Bogost teamed up with nine other authors to collaborate on the highly innovative (and esoterically titled) *10 PRINT CHR $(205.5+RND(1)); : GOTO 10* (2012), which offers diverse analyses of programming language (especially that of the landmark BASIC program for the Commodore 64) as a kind of cultural text with linguistic, aesthetic, and social implications. In *The Geek's Chihuahua: Living with Apple* (2015), Bogost perceptively explores the dark side of widespread addiction to contemporary technologies such as the iPhone, which he argues have complex effects on human existence, such as burdening consumers with stress and anxiety. Bogost's *How to Talk about Videogames* (2015) is a probing analysis both of how video games (which he describes as inhabiting a space between "art" and "appliance") continue to shape human lives in ever-evolving ways and of the danger that academic "game criticism" runs by cutting itself off from the dynamic phenomena of play it seeks to understand. A related philosophical inquiry, *Play Anything: The Pleasure of Limits, the Uses of Boredom, and the Secret of Games* (2016), draws on his theory of play to suggest how playfulness can help contemporary people live with creativity and joy in the midst of the systems and constraints that define our social existence. Bogost maintains an up-to-date bibliography as well as a gallery of his games and other creative projects on his personal website, bogost.com.

Theorists have offered critical analyses of the concept of procedural rhetoric that Ian Bogost develops in our selection and in his book *Persuasive Games*. For example, Jennifer deWinter, in a review of *Persuasive Games* in *Kairos: A Journal for Rhetoric, Technology, and Pedagogy* 14.1 (2009), praises Bogost's concept of procedural rhetoric but argues that he overemphasizes the purposes and intentions of authors to the exclusion of considering how players actively participate in the process of determining the meaning of games. Consequently, deWinter suggests that many who play the video games that Bogost analyzes may understand the games as carrying messages very different than those suggested in his own sophisticated ideological analyses. Similarly, in "Procedural Rhetoric and Expression," *JAC: A Journal of Composition Theory* 30 (2010), Annette Vee favorably assesses Bogost's theory of procedural rhetoric but implies that his sanguine faith in the ability of players to critically evaluate how games represent the world may be disconnected from the actual experiences and interpretations of many who play games.

Susan Bordo

Bordo is the author of *The Flight to Objectivity: Essays on Cartesianism and Culture* (1987), *Unbearable Weight: Feminism, Western Culture, and the Body* (1993), *Twilight Zones: The Hidden Life of Cultural Images from Plato to O.J.* (1997), *The Male Body: A New Look at Men in Public and in Private* (1999), *The Creation of Anne Boleyn: A New Look at England's Most Notorious Queen* (2013), and *The Destruction of Hillary Clinton* (2017). She is co-editor of two collections—with Alison M. Jaggar, *Gender/Body/Knowledge: Feminist Reconstructions of Being and Knowing* (1989), and with Cristina Alcalde and Ellen Rosenman, *Provocations: A Transnational Reader in the History of Feminist Thought* (2015)—as well as the sole editor of *Feminist Interpretations of René Descartes* (1999). Representative reviews of *Unbearable Weight* can be found in the *New York Times Book Review*, September 26, 1993 (by Maud Ellmann); the *London Review of Books*, March 10, 1994 (by Carol Gilligan); *Hypatia* 10 (1995) (by Susan Hekman); and *Ethics* 105 (1995) (by Rosemarie Tong). Ellen Rooney, "What Can the Matter Be?," *American Literary History* 8 (1996), and Susan Hekman, "Material Bodies," in *Body and Flesh: A Philosophical Reader* (ed. Donn Welton, 1998), offer fuller engagements with Bordo's work. See also the chapter on Bordo in Michael P. Spikes, *Understanding Contemporary American Literary Theory* (rev. ed., 2003). Reviews of Bordo's work after *Unbearable Weight* include the *New York Times*, September 12, 1999 (of *The Male Body*, by Jesse Green), and

April 14, 2013 (all of *The Creation of Anne Boleyn*, by Jennifer Schuessler); the *Daily Beast*, April 25, 2013 (by Lauren Elkin); and the *Telegraph*, January 6, 2014 (by Anna Whitelock). Margo DeMello's excellent *Body Studies: An Introduction* (2014) discusses Bordo's work in the context of this new field.

Pierre Bourdieu

Bourdieu's published works (almost all of which are available in English; the date of the original French is given first) fall into three groups: his work in sociological and anthropological theory; his work on art, intellectuals, and the school system; and his directly political works. In the first group, the major texts are *Outline of a Theory of Practice* (1972; 1977); *The Logic of Practice* (1980; 1990); *Sociology in Question* (1980; 1993); *In Other Words: Essays towards a Reflexive Sociology* (1987; 1990); *An Invitation to Reflexive Sociology*, with Löic Wacquant (1992); *Practical Reason: On the Theory of Action* (1994; 1998); *Pascalian Meditations* (1997; 2000); *The Social Structures of the Economy* (2000; 2005); and *Science of Science and Reflexivity* (2001; 2004). On intellectuals, art, and schooling the major books are *Photography: A Middle-brow Art*, with Luc Boltanski et al. (1965; 1990); *Academic Discourse: Linguistic Misunderstanding and Professorial Power*, with Jean-Claude Passeron and Monique de Saint Martin (1965; 1994); *Reproduction in Education, Society, and Culture*, with Jean-Claude Passeron (1970; 1977); *Distinction: A Social Critique of the Judgement of Taste* (1979; 1984); *Language and Symbolic Power* (1982; 1991); *Homo Academicus* (1984; 1988); *The State Nobility: Elite Schools in the Field of Power* (1989; 1996); *The Rules of Art: Genesis and Structure of the Literary Field* (1992; 1995); *Free Exchange*, with the artist Hans Haacke (1993; 1995); and *On Television* (1996; 1998). His political writings include *The Political Ontology of Martin Heidegger* (1988; 1991); *The Weight of the World: Social Suffering in Contemporary Society*, with Alain Accardo et al. (1993; 1999); *Acts of Resistance: Against the New Myths of Our Time* (1998; 1998); *Masculine Domination* (1998; 2001); *Firing Back: Against the Tyranny of the Market 2* (2001; 2003); and *Political Interventions: Social Science and Political Action* (2002; 2008). An important selection of translated essays has been collected in *The Field of Cultural Production: Essays on Art and Literature*, edited by Randal Johnson (1993). Four posthumous collections gather essays and interviews: *Sketch for a Self-Analysis* (2004; 2007) comes close to an autobiography, while *Picturing Algeria* (2003; 2012), *Algerian Sketches* (2013), and *The Sociologist and the Historian* (2010; 2015) cover a variety of topics and Bourdieu's whole career. Transcripts of some of Bourdieu's lectures have been published in French as *Sur l'état: Cours au Collège de France, 1898–1992* (2012, *On the State: Lectures from the Collège du France*). Another set of lectures has been published in English as *Manet: A Symbolic Revolution* (2017). The most detailed biography is *Pierre Bourdieu: Vers une économie du bonheur* (2008, *Toward an Economy of Happiness*) by Marie-Anne Lescourret. The English reader will find a succinct biography in the very useful reference book *Pierre Bourdieu: Key Concepts*, edited by Michael Grenfell (2012).

Richard Jenkins's *Pierre Bourdieu* (rev. ed., 2002) is an excellent general introduction. John Guillory's influential *Cultural Capital: The Problem of Literary Canon Formation* (1993) addresses the changing shape of literary studies in ways that creatively employ and expand Bourdieu's work. Three noteworthy full-length monographs are John R. W. Speller's *Bourdieu and Literature* (2011), David Gartman's *Culture, Class, and Critical Theory: Between Bourdieu and the Frankfurt School* (2013), and David Swartz's superb *Symbolic Power, Politics, and Intellectuals: The Political Sociology of Pierre Bourdieu* (2013). Several collections of essays provide good overviews of various responses and approaches to Bourdieu's work: *Pierre Bourdieu 2*, edited by Derek Robbins (4 vols., 2005); *The Legacy of Pierre Bourdieu: Critical Essays*, edited by Simon Susen and Bryan S. Turner (2011); *The Routledge Companion to Bourdieu's "Distinction,"* edited by Philippe Coulangeon and Julien Duval (2014); *Bourdieu's Theory of Social Fields: Concepts and Applications*, edited by Mathieu Hilgers and Eric Mangez (2015); and the essays collected in *Beyond Bourdieu and Other Essays*, a special issue of *New Literary History* (46.3 [2015]). A good, although not exhaustive, bibliography of primary and secondary works can be found in Grenfell's *Key Concepts*.

Marc Bousquet

Marc Bousquet's dissertation was on nineteenth-century American literature, and several of his initial scholarly articles dealt with canonical authors such as Henry James, but since the late 1990s he has focused on academic labor. He published several groundbreaking essays on the plight of graduate students, the managerial turn of professors (particularly in service fields like English composition), and the corporatization of higher education, culminating in his book *How the University Works: Higher Education and the Low-Wage Nation* (2008). In conjunction with his focus on labor, he co-founded *Workplace: A Journal for Academic Labor*, whose first issue appeared in February 1998. In addition, he has co-edited, with Katherine Wills, *The Politics of Information: The Electronic Mediation of Social Change* (2003) and, with Tony Scott and Leo Parascondola, *Tenured Bosses and Disposable Teachers: Writing Instruction in the Managed University* (2004). For a discussion of his background and work, see "Higher Exploitation: An Interview with Marc Bousquet," by Jeffrey J. Williams, *Minnesota Review*, nos. 71–72 (2009).

Bousquet's writing has received a great deal of response. His initial arguments about graduate education and labor almost immediately drew rebuttals, notably in a special issue of *Journal of Advanced Composition* (22.4 [2002]), which includes responses from those in the composition community, some questioning his credentials to talk about the field. A more considered, wide-ranging assessment of his work appears in *Information University: Rise of the Education Management Organization*, edited by Teresa Derrickson, a lengthy special issue of *Works and Days* (21.1–2 [2003]) that gathers fourteen essays, as well as reprinting five of his previous essays, among them "The Waste Product of Graduate Education."

Several subsequent evaluations place his work in the tradition of criticism and theory: see Vincent B. Leitch, "Work Theory," *Critical Inquiry* 31 (2005), and Jeffrey J. Williams, "The Post-Welfare State University," *American Literary History* 18 (2006). In addition, Williams's "The Academic Devolution," *Dissent* (fall 2009), examines *How the University Works*, comparing it favorably to accounts of higher education that display more resignation, and Williams's "The Need for Critical University Studies," in *A New Deal for the Humanities: Liberal Arts and the Future of Public Higher Education* (ed. Gordon Hutner and Feisal G. Mohamed, 2016), inducts Bousquet into this new critical movement. See also *Graduate Education in English Studies*, edited by Leonard Cassuto, a special issue of *Pedagogy* (15.1 [2015]) that includes essays responding to Bousquet as well as an essay by him.

Rosi Braidotti

Braidotti has written widely in several languages. Her most important early books in English are *Patterns of Dissonance: A Study of Women in Contemporary Philosophy* (1991), *Nomadic Subjects: Embodiment and Sexual Difference in Contemporary Feminist Theory* (1994; 2d ed., 2011), *Metamorphoses: Towards a Materialist Theory of Becoming* (2002), *Transpositions: On Nomadic Ethics* (2006), and *The Posthuman* (2013). *Nomadic Theory: The Portable Rosi Braidotti* (2011) collects thirteen of her essays. Braidotti co-authored *Women, the Environment and Sustainable Development: Towards a Theoretical Synthesis* (1994) with Ewa Charkiewicz, Sabine Hausler, and Saskia Wieringa, and she has co-edited many collections of essays: *Between Monsters, Goddesses and Cyborgs: Feminist Confrontations with Science, Medicine, and Cyberspace* (1996), with Nina Lykke; *Thinking Differently: A Reader in European Women's Studies* (2002), with Gabriele Griffin; *Deleuze and Law: Forensic Futures* (2009), with Claire Colebrook and Patrick Hanafin; *Revisiting Normativity with Deleuze* (2012), with Patricia Pisters; *After Cosmopolitanism* (2013), with Patrick Hanafin and Bolette Blaagaard; *This Deleuzian Century: Art, Activism, Life* (2014), with Rick Dolphijn; *Transformations of Religion and the Public Sphere: Postsecular Publics* (2014), with Bolette Blaagaard, Tobijn de Graauw, and Eva Midden; and *Conflicting Humanities* (2016), with Paul Gilroy.

Braidotti is perhaps better known in Europe than in the United States. For an introduction to her work, see two interviews: "Nomadic Philosopher: A Conversation with Rosi Braidotti," by Kathleen O'Grady, *Women's Education des femmes* 12.1 (1996); and "Nomadism, the European Union, and Embedding Identities: An Interview with Rosi Braidotti," by Thea Arnold, Mina Karavanta, and Robert P. Marzec, *Crossings: A Counter-Disciplinary Journal*, no. 2 (1998). In the 1990s several articles examined Braidotti's feminism, including Irene Gedalof, "Can Nomads Learn to Count to Four? Rosi Braidotti and the Space for Difference in Feminist Theory," *Women: A Cultural Review* 7 (1996); Inge E. Boer, "The World beyond Our Window: Nomads, Travelling Theories and the Function of Boundaries," *Parallax* 2.2 (1996); and Pelagia Goulimari, "A Minoritarian Feminism? Things to Do with Deleuze and Guattari," *Hypatia: A Journal of Feminist Philosophy* 14.2 (1999). *(Post)Human Lives*, edited by Gillian Whitlock, a special issue of *Biography* (35.1 [2012]), explores work on the posthuman, including Braidotti's, that challenges the very notion of biography—a genre dependent on the ideas of the human that posthumanism challenges. In a substantive review of *The Posthuman* published in the open access journal *Culture Machine* (2013), Stefan Herbrechter situates Braidotti's work within the broad landscape of posthumanism. *The Subject of Rosi Braidotti: Politics and Concepts*, edited by Bolette Blaagaard and Iris van der Tuin (2014), offers a comprehensive evaluation of Braidotti's work in twenty-eight essays; among the contributors are Judith Butler, Catherine Stimpson, and Genevieve Lloyd, as well as several of her collaborators and Braidotti herself. It includes a section on Braidotti's work on the posthuman and also an extensive bibliography.

Cleanth Brooks

Brooks's most noteworthy books are *Modern Poetry and the Tradition* (1939), *The Well Wrought Urn: Studies in the Structure of Poetry* (1947), and the textbook on poetry he co-edited with Robert Penn Warren, *Understanding Poetry* (1938). See also his *William Faulkner: The Yoknapatawpha Country* (1963) and *William Faulkner: Toward Yoknapatawpha and Beyond* (1978). He also coauthored, with William K. Wimsatt Jr., *Literary Criticism: A Short History* (1957); with Warren and R. W. B. Lewis, he co-edited *American Literature: The Makers and the Making* (1973), a two-volume, 3,000-page anthology. Collections of his essays include *The Hidden God: Studies in Hemingway, Faulkner, Yeats, Eliot, and Warren* (1963), *A Shaping Joy: Studies in the Writer's Craft* (1971), *Historical*

Evidence and the Reading of Seventeenth-Century Poetry (1991), and *Community, Religion, and Literature: Essays* (1995). Another important source is *Cleanth Brooks and Robert Penn Warren: A Literary Correspondence*, edited by James A. Grimshaw (1998). See also *Cleanth Brooks and Allen Tate: Collected Letters, 1933–1976*, edited by Alphonse Vinh (1998). For an excellent biography, consult Mark Royden Winchell, *Cleanth Brooks and the Rise of Modern Criticism* (1996).

The Possibilities of Order: Cleanth Brooks and His Work, edited by Lewis P. Simpson (1976), is a valuable collection of critical essays that includes an interview with Brooks conducted by Robert Penn Warren. For cogent discussions of Brooks in the context of Anglo-American New Criticism, see Grant Webster, *The Republic of Letters: A History of Postwar American Literary Opinion* (1979), and James J. Sosnoski, *Token Professionals and Master Critics: A Critique of Orthodoxy in Literary Studies* (1994). See also Thomas W. Cutrer, *Parnassus on the Mississippi: "The Southern Review" and the Baton Rouge Literary Community, 1935–1942* (1984); Mark Jancovich, *The Cultural Politics of the New Criticism* (1993), which considers Brooks in relation to John Crowe Ransom, Robert Penn Warren, and Allen Tate; and John Michael Walsh, *Cleanth Brooks: An Annotated Bibliography* (1990). Another good resource is *Rereading the New Criticism*, edited by Miranda B. Hickman and John D. McIntyre (2012), a collection of essays on the New Critics, their influences (e.g., T. S. Eliot), their relation to some of their contemporaries (e.g., Theodor Adorno), and the theory and practice of "close reading."

Edmund Burke

For complete editions of Burke, see *Writings and Speeches of Edmund Burke*, edited by Paul Langford (9 vols., 1980–2015); *Works* (9 vols., 1839); and *Works* (8 vols., 1868–80). An important source is the *Correspondence* (10 vols., 1958–78). A selection of the letters has been edited by Harvey C. Mansfield (1984). There are two annotated editions of *A Philosophical Enquiry into the Origin of Our Ideas of the Sublime and Beautiful*, the first by James T. Boulton (1958), the second by Adam Phillips (1990). For Burke's biography, consult Alice P. Miller, *Edmund Burke and His World* (1979), and Stanley Ayling, *Edmund Burke: His Life and Opinions* (1988). For a detailed, measured assessment, see F. P. Lock's study *Edmund Burke* (2 vols., 1998–2006). David Bromwich, *The Intellectual Life of Edmund Burke: From the Sublime and Beautiful to American Independence* (2014), the first part of a two-volume intellectual biography, is essential. So too is Richard Bourke's *Empire and Revolution: The Political Life of Edmund Burke* (2015), which depicts Burke as a philosopher-in-action who evaluated the political realities of the day through the lens of Enlightenment thought.

Contemporary literary critics have paid much attention to Burke as a thinker and writer. Good discussions can be found in David Bromwich, *A Choice of Inheritance: Self and Community from Edmund Burke to Robert Frost* (1989); Terry Eagleton, *The Ideology of the Aesthetic* (1990); Frances Ferguson, *Solitude and the Sublime: Romanticism and the Aesthetics of Individuation* (1992), a study of Burke, Kant, and eighteenth- and nineteenth-century aesthetic theory; and Tom Furniss, *Edmund Burke's Aesthetic Ideology: Language, Gender, and Political Economy in Revolution* (1993). Luke Gibbons, in *Edmund Burke and Ireland: Aesthetics, Politics, and the Colonial Sublime* (2003), treats Burke's contribution to aesthetic theory, in the context of the role of sensibility within Enlightenment thought and the politics of the eighteenth century.

For background, see *The Sublime: A Reader in British Eighteenth-Century Aesthetic Theory*, edited by Andrew Ashfield and Peter de Bolla (1996). *The Sublime: From Antiquity to the Present*, edited by Timothy M. Costelloe (2012), includes a challenging essay on Burke by Rodolphe Gasché. Also recommended are Mark Canuel, *Justice, Dissent, and the Sublime* (2012); Cian Duffy, *The Landscapes of the Sublime, 1700–1830: Classic Ground* (2013), a fascinating study of the "natural sublime" encountered by British and European travelers and explorers (the Alps; the Italian volcanoes, Vesuvius and Etna; the Arctic and the Antarctic; the deserts of central and southern Africa; and the universe being revealed by the new astronomy); and Emily Brady, *The Sublime in Modern Philosophy: Aesthetics, Ethics, and Nature* (2014). For a detailed, rigorous survey, consult Robert Doran, *The Theory of the Sublime from Longinus to Kant* (2015); he examines how theories of sublimity are united by a common structure—the paradoxical experience of being at once overwhelmed and exalted—and a common concern: the preservation of a notion of transcendence in the midst of the secularization of modern culture.

Recent studies of Burke are diverse and intellectually rich. Clearly written, balanced, and stimulating is Yuval Levin, *The Great Debate: Edmund Burke, Thomas Paine, and the Birth of Right and Left* (2014). *The Cambridge Companion to Edmund Burke*, edited by David Dwan and Christopher J. Insole (2012), is a valuable resource that contains an excellent essay on Burke's "aesthetic psychology" by Paddy Bullard. Ian Crowe, *Patriotism and Public Spirit: Edmund Burke and the Role of the Critic in Mid-Eighteenth-Century Britain* (2012), is informative on the political and cultural contexts of the 1750s and on early philosophical and literary influences on Burke's thought. Bibliographical resources on Burke include William B. Todd, *A Bibliography of Edmund Burke* (1964); Clara I. Gandy, *Edmund Burke: A Bibliography of Secondary Studies to 1982* (1983); and Leonard W. Cowie, *Edmund Burke, 1729–1797: A Bibliography* (1994).

Judith Butler

Butler's first book, *Subjects of Desire: Hegelian Reflections in Twentieth-Century France* (1987), traces French theories of subject formation as influenced by the nineteenth-century German philosopher G. F. W. Hegel. Her first three books after *Gender Trouble: Feminism and the Subversion of Identity* (1990)—*Bodies That Matter: On the Discursive Limits of "Sex"* (1993), *Excitable Speech: A Politics of the Performative* (1996), and *The Psychic Life of Power* (1997)—address various objections to her work and further develop her performative model of subject formation. Her subsequent works—*Antigone's Claim: Kinship between Life and Death* (2000), *Precarious Life: The Powers of Mourning and Violence* (2004), *Giving an Account of Oneself: A Critique of Ethical Violence* (2005), *Frames of War: When Is Life Grievable?* (2009), *Parting Ways: Jewishness and the Critique of Zionism* (2012), and *Dispossession: The Performative in the Political* (2013)—turn to questions of mourning, violence, and responsibility, often in response to events in the Middle East since 2001. Of the later works, *Undoing Gender* (2004) and *Senses of the Subject* (2015) are more directly tied to the themes explored in *Gender Trouble*, while *Notes Toward a Performative Theory of Assembly* (2015) deploys her interest in the performative to consider contemporary political movements.

Butler has participated in a number of published interchanges with other theorists: *Feminist Contentions: A Philosophical Exchange*, by Seyla Benhabib et al. (1995); *Contingency, Hegemony, and Universality: Contemporary Dialogues on the Left*, by Butler, Ernesto Laclau, and Slavoj Žižek (2000); *Who Sings the Nation-State? Language, Politics, Belonging*, by Butler and Gayatri Chakravorty Spivak (2007); *Is Critique Secular? Blasphemy, Injury, and Free Speech*, by Talal Asad et al. (2009); *The Power of Religion in the Public Sphere*, by Butler et al. (2011); and *What Is a People?*, by Alain Badiou et al. (2013; trans. 2016). She has also co-edited a number of collections of essays, including, with Joan Scott, *Feminists Theorize the Political* (1992); with Elizabeth Weed, *The Question of Gender: Joan W. Scott's Critical Feminism* (2011); and, with Zeynep Gambetti and Leticia Sabsay, *Vulnerability in Resistance* (2016). *The Judith Butler Reader* (2004), edited by Sara Salih with Butler's assistance, provides selections from the first five books, along with other essays and an illuminating interview. For other useful interviews, see Butler, Lynne Segal, and Peter Osborne, "Gender as Performance," *Radical Philosophy* 67 (1994), and Vicki Kirby, *Judith Butler: Live Theory* (2006). For two autobiographical accounts of Butler's intellectual formation, see her new preface to the tenth anniversary edition of *Gender Trouble* (1999) and the chapter "Can the 'Other' of Philosophy Speak?" in *Undoing Gender*.

The best single-volume introduction is Moya Lloyd's *Judith Butler: From Norms to Politics* (2007). Kirby's book and Anita Brady's *Understanding Judith Butler* (2011) are also useful. Annika Thiem's *Unbecoming Subjects: Judith Butler, Moral Philosophy, and Critical Responsibility* (2008), Arthur Kroker's *Body Drift: Butler, Hayles, Haraway* (2012), and Birgit Schippers's *The Political Philosophy of Judith Butler* (2014) offer more focused discussions of her work. Two collections of essays attend to the whole of Butler's career: *Judith Butler's Precarious Politics: Critical Encounters*, edited by Terrell Carver and Samuel A. Chambers (2008), and *Butler and Ethics*, edited by Moya Lloyd (2015), while *Butler Matters: Judith Butler's Impact on Feminist and Queer Studies*, edited by Margaret Sönser Breen and Warren J. Blumenfeld (2016), focuses more on issues raised by *Gender Trouble*.

Rey Chow

Rey Chow is the author of nine books and the editor of one collection of essays. *Woman and Chinese Modernity: The Politics of Reading between West and East* (1991) explores gender and sexuality, popular literature and film. *Writing Diaspora: Tactics of Intervention in Contemporary Cultural Studies* (1993) examines the West's attitude toward China from a "diasporic consciousness"—that is, from the perspective of those Chinese who live outside of China. With *Primitive Passions: Visuality, Sexuality, Ethnography, and Contemporary Chinese Cinema* (1995), Chow brings a postcolonial lens to cinema and contemporary visual technologies. *Ethics after Idealism: Theory–Culture–Ethnicity–Reading* (1998) argues for a critique of the idealism that underwrites identity politics. Chow's edited collection, *Modern Chinese Literary and Cultural Studies in the Age of Theory: Reimagining a Field* (2000), continues to illuminate ethnicity, as does her *The Protestant Ethnic and the Spirit of Capitalism* (2002). In *The Age of the World Target: Self-Referentiality in War, Theory, and Comparative Work* (2006), she reflects on area studies, poststructuralism, and comparative literature, historicizing these influential fields within the U.S. academy. *Sentimental Fabulations, Contemporary Chinese Films: Attachment in the Age of Global Visibility* (2007) examines the sentimental in twelve contemporary Chinese films from the 1990s. *Entanglements, or Transmedial Thinking about Capture* (2012) highlights the crucial importance of the mediatized image in transnational modes of connection. In *Not Like a Native Speaker: On Languaging as a Postcolonial Experience* (2014), Chow investigates the experiences of intellectuals for whom racialization has followed from the experience of learning the colonists' language. A generous selection of Chow's work is available in *The Rey Chow Reader* (2010), edited by Paul Bowman. For an account of Chow's life, see her essay "The Postcolonial Difference: Lessons in Cultural Legitimation," *Postcolonial Studies* 1 (1998).

Paul Bowman's introduction to the *Rey Chow Reader* is the best introduction to Chow's theoretical writing. Bowman has also edited special issues on Chow in two journals: *Rey Chow and Postcolonial Social Semiotics* (*Social Semiotics* 20.4 [2010]), a selection of eight articles by prominent scholars assessing the significance of Chow's work in postcolonialism, feminism, and visual culture, and *Postcoloniality and Interdisciplinarity* (*Postcolonial Studies* 13.3 [2010]), which focuses on Chow's contributions to interdisciplinarity in postcolonial studies. For a book-length critical study, see Bowman's *Reading Rey Chow: Visuality, Postcoloniality, Ethnicity, Sexuality* (2013), which contains a bibliography.

Christine de Pizan

Perhaps the surest sign of the critical neglect of Christine de Pizan is the lack of any editions or translations of her collected works. Maurice Roy edited *Oeuvres poétiques de Christine de Pisan* (1886–89), but it excludes the prose works for which Christine is best known. Charity Canon Willard edited a selection of Christine's works in translation, *The Writings of Christine de Pizan* (1992), which better captures the diversity of her writing. Generally, it is easier to find translations than editions of individual works. Eric Hicks edited the "Quarrel of the *Rose*" as *Le Débat sur le Roman de la Rose* (1977). All of the letters in the debate were finally made available in English in *Debating the "Roman de la rose,"* edited by Christine McWebb and translated by McWebb and Earl Jeffrey Richards (2007); the volume includes both the original texts and their English translations. In 2010, David F. Hult also published a dual-language edition of these letters in *The Debate of the "Romance of the Rose."* The only edition of *The Book of the City of Ladies* in the original Old French is Maureen Curnow's 1975 Ph.D. dissertation, "The *Livre de la Cité des Dames*: A Critical Edition," which Earl Jeffrey Richards translated as *The Book of the City of Ladies* in 1982. A new translation by Rosalind Brown-Grant appeared in 1999. The earliest English translation of *City of Ladies*, Brian Anslay's sixteenth-century *The Boke of the Cyte of Ladyes*, has been edited by Hope Johnston (2015). Much of what we know about Christine's life comes to us from her own autobiographical writing, especially *Christine's Vision*, translated by Glenda K. McLeod (1993). Charity Canon Willard offers the best modern biography in *Christine de Pizan: Her Life and Works* (1984).

Nadia Margolis's *An Introduction to Christine de Pizan* (2011) is the first comprehensive introduction to Christine's works. Critical interest in Christine and her writing increased exponentially in the 1980s and 1990s, largely because of the influence of feminist criticism. Sandra Hindman's *Christine de Pizan's "Epistre d'Othea": Painting and Politics at the Court of Charles VI* (1986) offers a richly detailed description of the social context of Christine's writing. Sheila Delany's controversial essay "Mothers to Think Back Through: Who Are They? The Ambiguous Example of Christine de Pizan," in *Medieval Texts, Contemporary Readers* (ed. Laurie A. Finke and Martin B. Shichtman, 1987), was instrumental in raising questions about feminist appropriations of Christine. Maureen Quilligan's *Allegory of Female Authority: Christine de Pizan's "Cité des Dames"* (1991) offers a sophisticated theoretical analysis of *The City of Ladies*. Two studies shed light on the relationship between Christine's participation in the debate over the *Roman de la Rose* and her defense of women in *The City of Ladies*. In *Christine de Pizan and the Moral Defense of Women: Reading beyond Gender* (1999), Rosalind Brown-Grant considers the evolution of Christine's attack on misogyny and her defense of women throughout her career, while Douglas Kelly, in *Christine de Pizan's Changing Opinion: A Quest for Certainty in the Midst of Chaos* (2007), positions Christine's writing within a medieval philosophical tradition of opinion at a time of great political and intellectual upheaval. The variety of contemporary critical responses to Christine's writing is usefully represented by collections of essays; the best include *Christine de Pizan and the Categories of Difference*, edited by Marilynn Desmond (1998), and *Christine de Pizan: A Casebook*, edited by Barbara K. Altmann and Deborah L. McGrady (2003). Sarah Kay's "Allegory and Melancholy in Luce Irigaray, Julia Kristeva, and Christine de Pizan," which appeared in *Provocation and Negotiation: Essays in Comparative Criticism* (ed. Gesche Ipsen, Timothy Mathews, and Dragana Obradović, 2013), uses *City of Ladies* to elucidate the psychoanalytic work of Irigaray and Kristeva. Finally, Tracy Adams's *Christine de Pizan and the Fight for France* (2014) examines Christine's literary engagement with the French politics of her time. The most up-to-date bibliography is Angus J. Kennedy, *Christine de Pizan: A Bibliographical Guide* (1984; supplements 1994, 2004).

Hélène Cixous

In 1969 Cixous won the prestigious Medici Prize for her first novel, *Dedans* (trans. 1986, *Inside*), and she has published many writings since, first called novels, then called fictions, then often not characterized; among those available in English are *Angst* (1977; trans. 1985), *The Book of Promethea* (1983; trans. 1991), *Manna, for the Mandelstams for the Mandelas* (1988; trans. 1993), *Manhattan: Letters from Prehistory* (2002; trans. 2007), *So Close* (2007; trans. 2009), *Philippines* (2009; trans. 2011), *Hemlock: Old Women in Bloom* (2008; trans. 2011), and *Eve Escapes: Ruins and Life* (2009; trans. 2012). These are part mythic autobiography, part meditation, part philosophy, and part poetry, and the mobility of her style gives pronouns and structures of address a range far beyond any person or character. She has written a number of plays as well, including *Portrait of Dora* (1976; trans. 1979) and two historical dramas, one on Cambodia and one on India, which she wrote in collaboration with Ariane Mnouchkine's celebrated Théâtre du Soleil. Eric Prenowitz's *Selected Plays of Hélène Cixous* (2004) is a collection of four plays, three of which had never before been translated into English. Cixous is the author of more than fifty books, including the bilingual edition of *The Writing Notebooks of Hélène Cixous*, edited and translated by Susan Sellers (2004); it contains a very informative interview with Cixous. Other interviews from three decades are collected in her *White Ink: Interviews on Sex, Text, and Politics*, edited by Susan Sellers (2008).

"The Laugh of the Medusa" forms part of a larger project Cixous was working on in 1975, another part of which ("Sorties") she published in collaboration with the more historicist feminist Catherine Clément as *La Jeune née* (trans. 1986, *The Newly Born Woman*). These are the texts in which Cixous speaks most explicitly about *écriture féminine*, and they are the best-known works by her in English. In addition to *The Exile of James Joyce* (1969; trans. 1976), she has also written a book on the contemporary Brazilian writer Clarice Lispector, translated as *Reading with Clarice Lispector* (1989; trans. 1990). Two volumes of her other literary criticism and theory have been published as *Coming to Writing and Other Essays*, edited by Deborah Jenson (1991), and *Readings: The Poetics of Blanchot, Joyce, Kleist, Kafka, Lispector, and Tsvetayeva*, edited by Verena Andermatt Conley (1991). Her essay in *The Future of Literary Theory* (ed. Ralph Cohen, 1989), titled "From the Scene of the Unconscious to the Scene of History," gives a good overview of Cixous's own poetics. A collection, *The Hélène Cixous Reader*, with a preface by Cixous and a foreword by Derrida, was edited in 1994 by Susan Sellers. It consists of short extracts from a large number of works, mainly "fictional." *The Portable Cixous*, edited by Marta Segarra (2010), brings together a mix of Cixous's theoretical, autobiographical, theatrical, and fictional writings. The fifteen essays in *Volleys of Humanity: Essays 1972–2009*, edited by Eric Prenowitz (2011), which include six previously unpublished and five newly published in English, also provide insight into Cixous's oeuvre. Although there is no full-length biography, Cixous has written a partly autobiographical text, complete with family histories and photographs, with Mireille Calle-Gruber called *Hélène Cixous, Photos de racines* (1994; trans. 1997, *Hélène Cixous, Rootprints: Memory and Life Writing*).

There are many critical studies devoted to the work of Cixous. For a good introduction and bibliography for students, see *Hélène Cixous: Live Theory* (2004), by Ian Blyth with Susan Sellers. Two books by Verena Andermatt Conley, *Hélène Cixous: Writing the Feminine* (1984) and *Hélène Cixous* (1992), also provide excellent introductions. *Hélène Cixous: A Politics of Writing* (1991) by Morag Shiach presents a somewhat critical assessment but discusses aspects of Cixous's work not often mentioned in Anglo-American theory, while Susan Sellers's *Hélène Cixous: Authorship, Autobiography, and Love* (1996) presents a more admiring view. Discussions of Cixous in the context of other "French feminists" (a designation that exists only in English) began with the 1981 anthology called *New French Feminisms*, painstakingly and far-reachingly edited by Elaine Marks and Isabelle de Courtivron. Alice Jardine's *Gynesis: Configurations of Women and Modernity* (1985) analyzes how post-structuralist male theorists in France made use of the figure of woman in their attempts to articulate what had been marginalized from traditional philosophical discourse. Susan Sellers, in her *Language and Sexual Difference: Feminist Writing in France* (1991), sees Cixous as the central theorist of feminine writing. And in a larger study of French thought around 1968, *Logics of Failed Revolt: French Theory after May '68* (1995), Peter Starr sees Cixous as the theorist of a "hysteria" that might be politically enabling. For bibliographies, see the entry on Cixous by Verena Andermatt Conley in *French Women Writers: A Bio-Bibliographic Source Book* (ed. Eva Martin Sartori and Dorothy Wynne Zimmerman, 1991); *French Feminist Theory (III): Luce Irigaray and Hélène Cixous: A Bibliography* (1996), by Joan Nordquist; Blyth and Sellers, *Hélène Cixous*; and Segarra's selected bibliography in *The Portable Cixous*.

Samuel Taylor Coleridge

Primary sources include *The Collected Works of Samuel Taylor Coleridge*, general editor Kathleen Coburn (23 vols., 1969–2002), published by the Bollingen Foundation and Princeton University Press, superbly edited and with comprehensive introductions; *The Collected Letters*, edited by Earl Leslie Griggs (6 vols., 1956–71); and *Selected Letters*, edited by H. J. Jackson (1987). Also illuminating are *The Notebooks*, edited primarily by Kathleen Coburn (5 vols., 1957–2002). Collections of Coleridge's criticism include *Shakespearean Criticism* (2 vols., 1930) and *Miscellaneous Criticism* (1936), both edited by T. M. Raysor. See also *Coleridge on the Seventeenth Century*, edited by Roberta Florence Brinkley (1955), and *Writings on Shakespeare: A Selection of the Essays, Notes, and Lectures*, edited by Terence Hawkes (1959). A compilation of Coleridge's prose, organized by theme, is *Coleridge's Responses: Selected Writings on Literary Criticism, the Bible, and Nature*, edited by John Beer et al. (3 vols., 2008). A good collection of primary and secondary sources is *Coleridge's Poetry and Prose: Authoritative Texts, Criticism*, edited by Nicholas Halmi, Paul Magnuson, and Raimonda Modiano (2003).

Walter Jackson Bate, *Coleridge* (1968), is a fine introduction to the life and works; two volumes by Richard Holmes, *Coleridge: Early Visions, 1772–1804* (1989) and *Coleridge: Darker Reflections, 1804–1834* (1999), constitute the best biography. Rosemary Ashton, *The Life of Samuel Taylor Coleridge: A Critical Biography* (1996), is astute.

Adam Sisman's *The Friendship: Wordsworth and Coleridge* (2006) is an engaging biographical and intellectual overview. Norman Fruman, *Coleridge: The Damaged Archangel* (1971), assembles the evidence of Coleridge's plagiarisms. Additional resources include *The Oxford Handbook of Samuel Taylor Coleridge*, edited by Frederick Burwick (2009), and John Worthen, *The Cambridge Introduction to Samuel Taylor Coleridge* (2010), a concise survey of the life, poetry, and literary criticism.

The best point of departure for studying Coleridge's criticism is the *Biographia Literaria*. See especially the editions by James Engell and Walter Jackson Bate, vol. 7 of the Bollingen *Samuel Taylor Coleridge* (1983), and by John Shawcross (2 vols., 1907). Scholarly studies of *Biographia Literaria* include Kathleen M. Wheeler, *Sources, Processes, and Methods in Coleridge's "Biographia Literaria"* (1980); Catherine Miles Wallace, *The Design of "Biographia Literaria"* (1983); and *Coleridge's "Biographia Literaria": Text and Meaning*, edited by Frederick Burwick (1989), which presents fourteen essays on major themes of the text and on its style, sources, significance for the history of Romanticism, and connections to contemporary literary theory. For critical responses to Coleridge to the year 1900, consult *Coleridge: The Critical Heritage*, edited by J. R. de J. Jackson (2 vols., 1970–91).

There are many fine books on Coleridge's literary theory: J. A. Appleyard, *Coleridge's Philosophy of Literature: The Development of a Concept of Poetry, 1791–1819* (1965); Thomas McFarland, *Coleridge and the Pantheist Tradition* (1969), which includes cogent chapters on Coleridge's plagiarisms and pantheist beliefs; J. R. de J. Jackson, *Method and Imagination in Coleridge's Criticism* (1969); J. Robert Barth, *The Symbolic Imagination: Coleridge and the Romantic Tradition* (1977); and Jerome C. Christensen, *Coleridge's Blessed Machine of Language* (1981). On Coleridge's theories of literary language and poetic diction, see Emerson R. Marks, *Coleridge on the Language of Verse* (1981), a treatment of Coleridge's interest in language "as an artistic medium"; Timothy Corrigan, *Coleridge, Language, and Criticism* (1982); Paul Hamilton, *Coleridge's Poetics* (1983), an insightful study of Coleridge's significant influence on post-Romantic literary criticism; James C. McKusick, *Coleridge's Philosophy of Language* (1986); and A. C. Goodson, *Verbal Imagination: Coleridge and the Language of Modern Criticism* (1988), which relates Coleridge's theory of poetry to the development of modern literary criticism. The following are also recommended: John B. Beer, *Coleridge's Play of Mind* (2010), a stimulating exploration of the relationship between the life and the work, with pertinent chapters on the literary criticism and lectures on Shakespeare; Gregory Leadbetter, *Coleridge and the Daemonic Imagination* (2011), which explores the themes of exaltation and transgression in Coleridge's poetry and philosophy; J. C. C. Mays, *Coleridge's Experimental Poetics* (2013); and David Ward, *Coleridge and the Nature of Imagination: Evolution, Engagement with the World, and Poetry* (2013). On Coleridge and the sublime, a major topic in the Romantic period, see Christopher Stokes, *Coleridge, Language and the Sublime: From Transcendence to Finitude* (2010), and Murray J. Evans, *Sublime Coleridge: The Opus Maximum* (2012).

For bibliographies, see *Samuel Taylor Coleridge: An Annotated Bibliography of Criticism and Scholarship*, edited by Richard and Josephine Haven and Maurianne Adams (2 vols., 1976–83), which covers work to 1939. See also Jefferson D. Caskey and Melinda M. Capper, *Samuel Taylor Coleridge: A Selective Bibliography of Criticism, 1935–1977* (1978). A guide to further reading can be found in *The Cambridge Companion to Coleridge*, edited by Lucy Newlyn (2002), as well as cogent essays on Coleridge's criticism, philosophy, and political and religious thought. Suggestions for further reading are also included in Worthen's *Cambridge Introduction* (see above).

Pierre Corneille

Corneille's third *Discours* is the one most often reprinted, in part because its title, "Of the Three Unities of Time, Place, and Action," is so closely associated with the theory of classical drama. The three *Discours* do not exist in a single English edition. The first, "On the Uses and Elements of Dramatic Poetry," is translated by Beatrice Stewart MacClintock in *European Theories of the Drama* (ed. Barrett H. Clark, 1965). The second, "Discourse on Tragedy and of the Methods of Treating It, according to Probability and Necessity," can be found in *Dramatic Essays of the Neoclassic Age* (ed. Henry Hitch Adams and Baxter Hathaway, 1950). The third, our selection, is found in *The Continental Model* (ed. Scott Elledge and Donald Schier, 1960). The three essays are published together in French, with a helpful introduction and notes in English, in *Pierre Corneille: Writings on the Theatre*, edited by H. T. Barnwell (1965).

Two notable introductory works are P. J. Yarrow, *Corneille* (1963), and Claire L. Carlin, *Pierre Corneille Revisited* (1998); the latter offers a biographical chapter. Mitchell Greenberg's *Corneille, Classicism, and the Ruses of Symmetry* (1986) is an invaluable study of Corneille's tragic universe. David R. Clarke, *Pierre Corneille: Poetics and Political Drama under Louis XIII* (1992), and John Lyons, *The Tragedy of Origins: Pierre Corneille and Historical Perspective* (1996), provide two different interpretations of the nature of "history" in Corneille's plays. Three comparative studies—Benedetto Croce's classic *Ariosto, Shakespeare, and Corneille* (1920), A. Donald Sellstrom's more speculative *Corneille, Tasso, and Modern Poetics* (1986), and Richard E. Goodkin's provocative *Birth Marks: The Tragedy of Primogeniture in Pierre Corneille, Thomas*

Corneille, and Jean Racine (2000)—are of interest. Timothy Hampton's *Fictions of Embassy: Literature and Diplomacy in Early Modern Europe* (2009) explores the fluidity between politics and aesthetics in the author's oeuvre, with particular attention to Corneille as dramatist of geopolitics, while John D. Lyons revisits Corneille's poetics of tragedy, engaging *The Three Discourses* and the concepts of fortune, randomness, and chance in chapter 1 of *The Phantom of Chance: From Fortune to Randomness in Seventeenth-Century French Literature* (2012). The best bibliography of Corneille studies is the Corneille chapter in *A Critical Bibliography of French Literature*, vol. 3A, *The Seventeenth Century* (ed. Marc Fumaroli and Gwyneth Castor, 1983).

Hamid Dabashi

Hamid Dabashi has published two dozen books, four edited volumes, and numerous articles and chapters. *The World Is My Home: A Hamid Dabashi Reader* (2010), edited by Andrew Davison and Himadeep Muppidi, conveniently brings together some of his main ideas. In *Theology of Discontent: The Ideological Foundations of the Islamic Revolution in Iran* (1993), which displays his intimate familiarity with Islam and with poststructural and postmodern concepts, Dabashi argues that the global rise of Islamism is a form of liberation theology. He presses here to see beyond the standard viewpoints of Western scholars, which he often depicts as having only some of the truth at hand. In *Truth and Narrative: The Untimely Thoughts of 'Ayn al-Quḍāt al-Hamadhānī* (1999), Dabashi deconstructs the essentialist conceptions of Islam propounded by Orientalists as well as by Islamists, proposing instead a "polyfocal" conception of Islam in which three narratives, readings, and institutions of authority compete simultaneously. He believes that these three readings of "Islam" encompass the vast majority of Muslims' moral, political, and intellectual history. In *Staging a Revolution: The Art of Persuasion in the Islamic Republic of Iran* (1999), Dabashi and Peter Chelkowski examine the public myths and collective symbols that contributed to the making of Iran's Islamic Revolution of 1978–79, commenting on the effects of its war with Iraq (1980–88) on the evolution of the country's postrevolutionary politics. In his polemical article "For the Last Time: Civilizations," *International Sociology* 16 (2001), Dabashi postulates a dichotomy between "Islam and the West" and casts European modernity as a constructed center in relation to the rest of the world.

At the start of the twenty-first century, Dabashi's interests expanded into Iranian cinema; in *Close Up: Iranian Cinema, Past, Present, Future* (2001), he presents Iranian national cinema as a form of cultural modernity. A few years later he edited *Dreams of a Nation: On Palestinian Cinema* (2006), whose essays and interviews reflect on the challenges of film production and the impact of Palestinian films; his introduction and essay focus on Palestinian cinema as the most important artistic expression of "a much-maligned people." In *Masters and Masterpieces of Iranian Cinema* (2007), Dabashi guides the reader on an exploration of twelve Iranian films, each subjected to combined formal, historical, and textual analyses.

In more recent years, Dabashi has published several major books. *Iran: A People Interrupted* (2007) traces the country's history, cultural trends, and political developments over two hundred years, up to the collapse of the Green Movement of 2009. In it, Dabashi contends that "Iran needs to be understood as the site of an ongoing contest between two contrasting visions of modernity, one colonial, the other anticolonial." Dabashi's *Post-Orientalism: Knowledge and Power in a Time of Terror* (2009) extends Edward W. Said's critical portrait of Orientalism by focusing less on colonial misrepresentation and domination and more on postcolonial agency and resistance. His *Shi'ism: A Religion of Protest* (2011) provides Western readers with an understanding of Islam and its Shiite branch as a religion of protest, offering critical analyses and extended discussions of Shia Islam's doctrine, historical development, visual and performing arts, and three largest areas of concentration (Iran, Iraq, and Lebanon). *The World of Persian Literary Humanism* (2012) surveys the multinational history of Persian literature from the seventh to the twenty-first centuries, taking into unsparing critical account both Arab imperialism and European Orientalism and colonialism, plus much modern literary criticism and cultural theory. *The Arab Spring: The End of Postcolonialism* (2012) explains the movements in a number of countries that together came to be labeled the Arab Spring, which has led to a rethinking of the Middle East from within as well as without. Dabashi argues that the revolutionary uprisings that have consumed several countries in the Middle East were driven by a "delayed defiance," a rebellion against local tyranny and globalized disempowerment. *Corpus Anarchicum: Political Protest, Suicidal Violence, and the Making of the Posthuman Body* (2012) examines suicidal violence in the decade between 2001 and 2011, highlighting the attacks of 9/11, led by Muhammad Atta, and the suicide in 2010 of the Tunisian street vendor Mohamed Bouazizi, which sparked the Arab Spring. Dabashi contends that though suicidal violence is specific neither to Islam nor to the contemporary era, it is today entirely different because it is perpetrated on what he calls the contour of a posthuman body. In *Being a Muslim in the World* (2013), Dabashi addresses the question of what it means to be a Muslim in what he calls the "post-Western world," where Islam and the West no longer constitute a binary opposition and the West no longer holds "the same normative hegemony." He argues that today the task facing Muslims is to gain self-consciousness and not self-alienation.

In *Can Non-Europeans Think?* (2015), a collection of philosophical explorations, Dabashi returns to his earliest concerns, especially the sociology of culture, discussing important thinkers whom he sees as regularly marginalized, patronized, and misrepresented, because they lack the pedigree of European philosophy, and offering a new perspective in "postcolonial theory" by examining how intellectual debate reinforces a "hidden colonial system of knowledge." Dabashi's *Persophilia: Persian Culture on the Global Scene* (2015) argues that Persian culture has been integral to European history since the biblical period and classical antiquity through the Renaissance and the Enlightenment. That is, European artists, poets, and thinkers have looked to Persian culture and history for inspiration and ideas that have helped shape both Western views of Iran and Iranian's views of themselves. In his argument, Dabashi draws on Jürgen Habermas's theory of "the public sphere" to trace the formation of a civil discourse in Iran that led to the creation of a modern nation-state out of an ancient civilization. As always, Dabashi connects his arguments to the history of European colonialism, even though Iran was never formally colonized. The wide-ranging and provocative book refers to such seminal works as Xenophon's *Cyropaedia*, Nietzsche's *Thus Spoke Zarathustra*, Handel's *Xerxes*, and Puccini's *Turandot*, as well as analyzing Gauguin's and Matisse's fascination with Persian art. In *Iran without Borders: Towards a Critique of the Postcolonial Nation* (2016), Dabashi depicts Iran from the eighteenth century onward as a modern cosmopolitan nation, while in *Iran: The Rebirth of a Nation* (2016), he reflects on the contemporary history of Iran, emphasizing the profound difference between the nation and the state.

Dabashi's critics raise a number of points. In a review, "Iran: A People Interrupted," *Comparative Studies of South Asia, Africa and the Middle East* 28 (2008), Kouross Esmaeli notes that Dabashi fails to define some key concepts, including *cosmopolitanism*, resulting in a conflation of "the consciously internationalist nature of the pre-1979 political life of Iran with the cosmopolitanism of his own early-twenty-first-century New York milieu." In her review of Dabashi's *Shi'ism: A Religion of Protest* in *Journal of Shi'a Islamic Studies* 6 (2013), Amina Inloes highlights "the unspoken assumption that Shi'ism is Iranian, and, hence, anything Iranian is relevant to Shi'ism." Some critics note that in *The World of Persian Literary Humanism*, Dabashi does not engage with a number of important prior works on classical Persian literature. In "Alternative Versions of Being Human: 'The World of Persian Literary Humanism,'" *PopMatters* (2013; www.popmatters.com/), Subashini Navaratnam addresses many concerns at once: "But Persian literature was also in service of its own empires, and here Dabashi tends to gloss over the factors of class and elitism that powered much of Persian *adab* (court poets and philosophers and members of the aristocracy were more likely than not to be its central figures) and fumbles when he talks about the 'creative consciousness' that makes up the subject of Persian literary humanism." And, like others, Navaratnam faults Dabashi's tendency to at times "pontificate from within the confines of an insular, self-absorbed language of high theory." Nevertheless, she acknowledges that "*Persian Literary Humanism* not only maps out the production and formation of Persian *adab* from within the spaces and regions from which it grew, but is also in conversation with European and American cultural critics like Theodor Adorno and Fredric Jameson."

Dabashi's books and articles have been translated into more than a dozen other languages, from Catalan to Urdu. A select bibliography is available in *The World Is My Home* (cited above).

Dante Alighieri

Dante's literary criticism can be found in the Italian *Opere minori di Dante Alighieri* (1986). The standard Italian edition of *Il Convivio* was edited by Maria Simonelli (1966). Two recent English translations of *Il Convivio*, by Christopher Ryan (1989) and by Richard H. Lansing (1990), both based on the Simonelli edition, are superior to earlier translations. *The Letters of Dante* (1920), with Latin text, edited and with English translation by Paget Toynbee, is the standard edition of Dante's letters. The best translation of the "Letter to Can Grande" can be found in Robert S. Haller's *Literary Criticism of Dante Alighieri* (1973), which also contains *Eloquence in the Vernacular Tongue* and other critical statements. Barbara Reynolds's *Dante: The Poet, the Political Thinker, the Man* (2006) offers a reassessment of the poet's life and times.

For an introduction, see *Dante: A Very Short Introduction* (2015), by Peter Hainsworth and David Robey. Dante has been the subject of commentaries by important poet-critics, the most prominent among them T. S. Eliot's *Dante* (1928). Major statements about Dante by modern poets have been collected in *The Poet's Dante: Twentieth-Century Responses*, edited by Peter S. Hawkins and Rachel Jacoff (2001). Erich Auerbach, in *Dante: Poet of the Secular World* (1929) and *Mimesis: The Representation of Reality in Western Literature* (1953), argues that Dante's comments on allegorical reading are central to an interpretation of *The Divine Comedy*. For important introductions to Dantean poetics, see Robert Hollander's *Dante: A Life in Works* (2001) and *The Cambridge Companion to Dante*, edited by Rachel Jacoff (2d ed., 2007). Peter Dronke, in *Dante and the Medieval Latin Tradition* (1986), and Henry Ansgar Kelly, in *Tragedy and Comedy from Dante to Pseudo-Dante* (1989), have both questioned the authenticity of the letter to Can Grande, arguing that Auerbach's insistence on a figural reading of *The Divine Comedy* based on that letter is mistaken. J. F. Took's *Dante, Lyric Poet and Philosopher: An Introduction to the Minor Works* (1990) contains an important chapter on *Il Convivio.* In *Dante's Epistle to Cangrande* (1993), Robert Hollander summarizes the debate over the letter to Can Grande, while defending Dante's authorship and its relevance to the allegorical reading of *The Divine Comedy. Dante in Context*, edited by Zygmunt G. Barański and Lino Pertile (2015), collects essays that locate the poet in his historical, cultural, and intellectual context, including literary culture and literary theory and criticism. Essays by the translator and Dante scholar John Freccero on Dante and his influence on later poets have been collected in *Dante's Wake: Reading from Medieval to Modern in the Augustinian Tradition* (2015), edited by Danielle Callegari and Melissa Swain. For a bibliography on Dante, consult "American Dante Bibliography," published annually in *Dante Studies* (1953–).

Lennard J. Davis

Lennard Davis's first two books, *Factual Fictions: The Origins of the Novel* (1983; rpt. 1997) and *Resisting Novels: Ideology and Fiction* (1987), focus on the history of the novel. With M. Bella Mirabella, he also co-edited *Left Politics and the Literary Profession* (1990). He turned to disability studies in his pathbreaking book *Enforcing Normalcy: Disability, Deafness, and the Body* (1995) and his anthology, *The Disability Studies Reader* (1997; 5th ed., 2016), which has defined the field. In addition, Davis edited his parents' correspondence, published as *Shall I Say a Kiss?: Courtship Letters of a Deaf Couple, 1936–1938* (1999), which conveys the experience of two deaf people in England just before World War II. He has expanded his analysis of disability in several books: *Bending Over Backwards: Disability, Dismodernism, and Other Difficult Positions* (2002), *The End of Normal: Identity in a Biocultural Era* (2013), and *Enabling Acts: The Hidden Story of How the American with Disabilities Act Gave the Largest US Minority Its Rights* (2015), a book for a general audience. He also elaborated his view of psychoanalysis in *Obsession: A History* (2008) and co-edited, with Dan Goodley and Bill Hughes, the collection *Disability and Social Theory: New Developments and Directions* (2012).

Alongside his academic work, he has tried his hand at fiction in *The Sonnets: A Novel* (2001) and has published articles in mainstream magazines and newspapers, including the *Nation*, the *New York Times*, *McCall's*, and *Redbook*. The best biographical source about Davis is his autobiography, *My Sense of Silence: Memoirs of a Childhood with Deafness* (2000), as well as his memoir *Go Ask Your Father: One Man's Obsession with Finding His Origins through DNA Testing* (2009).

Davis's investigation of the origin of the novel has received significant attention, notably in Catherine Gallagher's *Nobody's Story: The Vanishing Act of Women Writers in the Marketplace, 1679–1820* (1994). On disability, Rachel Adams's "Enabling Differences: New Work in Disability Studies," *Michigan Quarterly Review* 37 (1998), praises Davis's critique of normalcy but faults his failure to take into account the "differences between deafness and other forms of physical impairment." Brenda Jo Brueggeman draws on Davis's work in *Lend Me Your Ear: Rhetorical Constructions of Deafness* (1999). In "What a Difference a Decade Makes: Reflections on Doing 'Emancipatory' Disability Research," *Disability and Society* 18 (2003), Colin Barnes assesses Davis's political position. David Bolt, in "Social Encounters, Cultural Representation and Critical Avoidance," in *Routledge Handbook of Disability Studies* (ed. Nick Watson, Alan Roulstone, and Carol Thomas, 2012), surveys Davis's formative work in the field; see also Dan Goodley, *Disability Studies: An Interdisciplinary Introduction* (2011). In *The Biopolitics of Disability: Neoliberalism, Ablenationalism, and Peripheral Embodiment* (2015), David T. Mitchell and Sharon L. Snyder draw on Davis's concept of dismodernism but find that it tends to level social difference.

Gilles Deleuze and Félix Guattari

Deleuze and Guattari are best known for their *Anti-Oedipus* (1972; trans. 1983, 2009), *Kafka: Toward a Minor Literature* (1975; trans. 1986), *A Thousand Plateaus* (1980; trans. 1987), and *What Is Philosophy?* (1991; trans. 1994). In addition to the books mentioned above, Gilles Deleuze's writings, most of which are available in English, include *Proust and Signs* (1964; trans. 1972); *Masochism: An Interpretation of Coldness and Cruelty* (1967; trans. 1971); *Kant's Critical Philosophy* (1971; trans. 1984); *Dialogues*, with Claire Parnet (1977; trans. 1987), on the relation between culture and politics; *Foucault* (1986; trans. 1988); *Essays Critical and Clinical* (1993; trans. 1997), with chapters on Alfred Jarry, Herman Melville, and Walt Whitman; *The Abecedaire of Gilles Deleuze* (1997), a set of taped television interviews; *Desert Islands and Other Texts, 1953–1974* (2004); and *Two Regimes of Madness, 1975–1995* (2006). *The Deleuze Reader*, edited and introduced by Constantin V. Boundas, was published in 1993. Félix Guattari's works include, in addition to the titles mentioned in the headnote, *Molecular Revolution: Psychiatry and Politics* (1977; trans. 1984); "A Liberation of Desire," in *Homosexualities and French Literature* (ed. George Stambolian and Elaine Marks, 1979); *Chaosmosis* (1992; trans. 1995); and *The Anti-Oedipus Papers* (2004; trans. 2006). *The Guattari Reader*, edited and introduced by Gary Genosko, was published in 1996. *Gilles Deleuze and Félix Guattari: Intersecting Lives* (2007; trans. 2010), by François Dosse, devotes more than 600 pages to chronicling the intellectual and personal lives of the two, while Frida Beckman's *Gilles Deleuze* (2017) traces Deleuze's life and intellectual journey.

Brian Massumi's *User's Guide to Capitalism and Schizophrenia: Deviations from Deleuze and Guattari* (1992) is a sprightly, provocative reading that both explains a revolutionary Deleuze and Guattari and deviates from them. Eleanor Kaufman and Kevin Jon Heller's *Deleuze and Guattari: New Mappings in Politics, Philosophy, and Culture* (1998) contains a variety of articles, including Bruno Bosteel's detailed account of Guattari's relation to language and Aden Evens et al.'s cogent discussion of difference and creativity. Charles J. Stivale's *The Two-Fold Thought of Deleuze and Guattari* (1998) is also useful. A three-volume collection of criticism titled *Critical Assessments: Deleuze and Guattari*, edited by Gary Genosko (2000), gives a wide range of responses. Ian Buchanan's *Deleuze and Guattari's "Anti-Oedipus": A Reader's Guide* (2008), with its suggestions for further reading and bibliography, is a very useful introduction for students, as is Eugene W. Holland's *Deleuze and Guattari: 'A Thousand Plateaus': A Reader's Guide* (2013).

Criticism on Deleuze includes Michael Hardt, *Gilles Deleuze: An Apprenticeship in Philosophy* (1993), which presents a concrete and existential Deleuze, and *Gilles Deleuze and the Theater of Philosophy*, edited by Constantin V. Boundas and Dorothea Olkowski (1994), which is a good sampler of readings of Deleuze's work; it includes a terse analysis by the French philosopher Alain Badiou, who has since published *Deleuze: The Clamor of Being* (1997; trans. 2000). Other collections of criticism are *Deleuze: A Critical Reader*, edited by Paul Patton (1996), and *Gilles Deleuze: Image and Text*, edited by Eugene W. Holland, Daniel W. Smith, and Charles J. Stivale (2009). A good overview of Deleuze's involvement with film is provided by David Rodowick in *The Time-Machine* (1997). See also Gregory Flaxman's collection *The Brain Is the Screen: Deleuze and the Philosophy of Cinema* (2000) and Richard Rushton's comprehensive study, *Cinema After Deleuze* (2012). Feminists, who initially rejected Deleuze and Guattari for robbing women of being with their insistence on becoming, are now revising earlier views. An entire volume, *Deleuze and Feminism*, edited by Ian Buchanan and Claire Colebrook (2000), includes a fresh look at Deleuze by a dozen feminists. See also Buchanan's collection *Gilles Deleuze: A Philosopher for Our Century?* (2000). The best bibliographies are Timothy S. Murphy's "Bibliography of the Works of Gilles Deleuze" in Patton's *Deleuze*, cited above; *The Guattari Effect*, edited by Eric Alliez and Andrew Goffey (2011); and Gary Genosko's bibliography in *Félix Guattari: An Aberrant Introduction* (2002). Eugene B. Young's *The Deleuze and Guattari Dictionary* (2013) also has an updated bibliography.

Paul de Man

De Man's early reputation derived primarily from his essays, which were collected in books published later in his life or posthumously. His first book, *Blindness and Insight: Essays in the Rhetoric of Contemporary Criticism* (1971; 2d ed., 1983), surveys a range of important critics and argues that criticism is frequently predicated on a blindness to its own rhetoric, which paradoxically also enables its insight; it includes a famous critique of Derrida, "The Rhetoric of Blindness" (1971). His most unified book, *Allegories of Reading: Figural Language in Rousseau, Nietzsche, Rilke, and Proust* (1979), best exemplifies his deconstructive reading methods and has been extremely influential. The remainder of de Man's books, gathering numerous essays, were published after his death; they include *The Rhetoric of Romanticism* (1984); *The Resistance to Theory* (1986); *Critical Writings, 1953–1978*, edited by Lindsay Waters (1989); *Romanticism and Contemporary Criticism: The Gauss Seminars and Other Papers*, edited by E. S. Burt, Kevin Newmark, and Andrzej Warminski (1992); *Aesthetic Ideology*, edited by Andrzej Warminski (1996); and several volumes of miscellaneous writings, such as *The Post-Romantic Predicament*, edited by Martin McQuillan (2012), and *The Paul de Man Notebooks*, edited by McQuillan (2014). His controversial journalism dating from World War II is included in *Wartime Journalism, 1939–1943*, edited by Werner Hamacher, Neil Hertz, and Thomas Keenan (1988).

De Man's work has drawn a large body of commentary. Ortwin de Graef's *Serenity in Crisis: A Preface to Paul de Man, 1939–1960* (1993) and *Titanic Light: Paul de Man's Post-Romanticism, 1960–1969* (1995) review de Man's intellectual career, though the best biographical recounting is Lindsay Waters's lengthy introduction to *Critical Writings*, "Paul de Man: Life and Works." Evelyn Barish, *The Double Life of Paul de Man* (2014), attacks de Man's character while admitting little knowledge of his work. A useful factual chronology of de Man's early life is offered in *Responses: On Paul de Man's Wartime Journalism*, edited by Hamacher, Hertz, and Keenan (1989), their companion volume to *Wartime Journalism*. Robert Moynihan, "Interview with Paul de Man," *Yale Review* 73 (1984), is accessible and illuminating.

Important early critical responses include Frank Lentricchia's critique of de Man's "rhetoric of authority" in *After the New Criticism* (1980); Rodolphe Gasché's "'*Setzung*' and '*Übersetzung*': Notes on Paul de Man," *Diacritics* 11 (1981), which compares de Man's use of deconstruction unfavorably with that of Derrida; and Barbara Johnson's "Gender Theory and the Yale School" (1984), collected in her *World of Difference* (1987), which notes the lack of consideration of gender among Yale critics.

Immediately after de Man's death, there was a spate of publications largely sympathetic to his work. See *The Lesson of Paul de Man*, a special issue of *Yale French Studies*, no. 69 (1985); Jacques Derrida's *Mémoires: For Paul de Man* (1986), a moving meditation on de Man's project that distinguishes his focus on literature and allegory from Derrida's version of deconstruction; and *Reading de Man Reading*, edited by Lindsay Waters and Wlad Godzich (1989). Following the publication of his wartime writings, the criticism on de Man changed markedly. *Responses* (cited above) records the range of debate, from condemnations to defenses.

A new wave of reconsiderations of de Man's work began in the 1990s. In his *Cultural Capital: The Problem of Literary Canon Formation* (1993), John Guillory devotes a chapter to de Man's influence as a teacher. Rodolphe Gasché's *The Wild Card of Reading: On Paul de Man* (1998) focuses, often critically, on de Man's use of philosophy (it also reprints the 1981 essay noted above). Gathering contributions by Derrida, Judith Butler, Johnson, and others, *Material Events: Paul de Man and the Afterlife of Theory*, edited by Tom Cohen, Barbara Cohen, J. Hillis Miller, and Andrzej Warminski (2000), proposes new directions for the study of de Man. Martin McQuillan's *Paul de Man* (2001) is an accessible introduction. *Legacies of Paul de Man*, edited by Marc Redfield (2007), gathers eight essays reassessing de Man. See also *The Political Archive of Paul de Man: Property, Sovereignty, and the Theotropic*, edited by McQuillan (2012), which collects essays by leading critics. Redfield's *Theory at Yale: The Strange Case of Deconstruction in America* (2016) is a major reassessment of the central role of theory in the institution of American literary study, and particularly of de Man's influence in establishing his version of theory. The 1985 special issue of *Yale French Studies* cited above and de Man's posthumous *Resistance to Theory* provide complete bibliographical lists of his work up to 1985; de Graef (see above) lists de Man's publications up to 1983, as well as more recent secondary sources. In addition, McQuillan's *Paul de Man* includes a selective annotated bibliography.

Jacques Derrida

Derrida's analysis of the nontransparency of writing did not slow publication by him or by those inspired (or incensed) by his writing. Derrida's first published book was a translation with a lengthy introduction, *Edmund Husserl's "Origin of Geometry": An Introduction* (1962; trans. 1978). In 1967 Derrida published three books: *La Voix et le phénomène* (trans. 1973, *Speech and Phenomena*), *De la grammatologie* (trans. 1976, *Of Grammatology*; rev. trans. 2016), and *L'Écriture et la différence* (trans. 1978, *Writing and Difference*). In 1972 he published three more books: *La Dissémination* (trans. 1981, *Dissemination*), *Positions* (trans. 1981, *Positions*), and *Marges—de la philosophie* (trans. 1982, *Margins of Philosophy*).

Glas (1974; trans. 1986, *Glas*), a huge book written in two columns broken up in various ways on the page, discusses the works of the German philosopher Hegel and the transgressive French playwright and novelist Jean Genet; one of the translators, John P. Leavey Jr., published an accompanying volume, *Glassary* (1986). *Éperons: Les Styles de Nietzsche* (1976, 1978; trans. 1979, *Spurs: Nietzsche's Styles*), in which Derrida analyzes how certain philosophers have used concepts of sexual difference, has had an impact on feminist criticism. In *La Vérité en peinture* (1978; trans. 1987, *The Truth in Painting*), he discusses Heidegger, Kant, van Gogh, and art criticism. *La Carte postale de Socrate à Freud et au-delà* (1980; trans. 1987, *The Post Card*) continues the discussions of Plato and Socrates, speech and writing, that Derrida began in "Plato's Pharmacy" and includes a groundbreaking reading of Freud's *Beyond the Pleasure Principle*; it also contains "Le facteur de la vérité" ("The Purveyor of Truth"; *facteur* means "mailman" as well as "factor"), Derrida's famous critical reading of Jacques Lacan's seminar on "The Purloined Letter" by Edgar Allan Poe.

Derrida's next publication, *Signéponge/Signsponge* (1983), was a bilingual study of the work of Francis Ponge in which he unpacked the French poet's signature ("anagrammatically") from the poet's works. *Memoires: For Paul de Man*, a collection of lectures that appeared in English in 1986, was revised in 1989 to comment on de Man's wartime journalism.

To simplify the increasingly complex publication history of the later writings only the English titles of Derrida's important works are given hereafter, unless they appeared in French under a different title. In 1988 Gerald Graff edited *Limited, Inc.*, in which appeared an exchange between Derrida and the philosopher John Searle (first collected in the journal *Glyph* in 1977) about the nature of performative language, with additional texts by Derrida. "Declarations of Independence," *New Political Science* 15 (1986), an influential reading of the American Declaration of Independence, first appeared in French in *Otobiographies: L'enseignement de Nietzsche et la politique du nom propre* (1984). Many essays on Heidegger, Roland Barthes, Emmanuel Levinas, and Paul de Man and on such topics as racism, translation, and metaphor were published in *Psyche: Inventions of the Other* (2 vols., 1987–2003; trans., 2007–08). Derrida's thesis defense, "The Time of a Thesis: Punctuations," in *Philosophy in France Today* (ed. Alan Montefiore, 1983), was published among other texts addressing the institutions of philosophy in *Eyes of the University: Right to Philosophy 2* (1990; trans. 2004); the companion volume is *Who's Afraid of Philosophy? Right to Philosophy 1* (1990; trans. 2002). *The Other Heading: Reflections on Today's Europe* (1991; trans. 1992) took up political issues, as did Derrida's long-awaited engagement with the texts of Karl Marx, *Specters of Marx: The State of the Debt, the Work of Mourning, and the New International* (1993; trans. 1994). *Advances* (1995; trans. 2018), a slim volume, offers reflections on temporality, religion, and eco-politics. Derrida responded to 9/11 in *Philosophy in a Time of Terror: Dialogues with Jürgen Habermas and Jacques Derrida*, interviewed by Giovanna Borradori (2003), and investigated democracy in *Rogues: Two Essays on Reason* (2003; trans. 2005).

His meditations on the *gift* and *givenness* can be found in his *Given Time: I, Counterfeit Money* (1991; trans. 1992), which focuses on Baudelaire and Heidegger, and *The Gift of Death* (1992; trans. 1995), one of Derrida's most explicit discussions of religion; on that subject, see also the collection *Acts of Religion*, edited by Gil Anidjar (2002). In 1995 three short works (*Passions, Sauf le nom,* and *Khôra*) were translated under the title *On the Name*. *Archive Fever: A Freudian Impression* (1995; trans. 1996), on Freud's *Moses and Monotheism*, was followed by *The Politics of Friendship* (1994; trans. 1997). And two translations appeared in 1998: *Monolingualism of the Other, or, The Prosthesis of Origin* (1996) and *Resistances of Psychoanalysis* (1996).

Between 2000 and his death in 2004, Derrida continued lecturing and publishing prodigiously. Many seminars and volumes were published and translated, some posthumously. *Of Hospitality* (1997; trans. 2000), a compilation of two seminar lectures given in Paris in January 1996, examines the concept of hospitality as it relates to political and ethical dilemmas. *A Taste for the Secret*, with Maurizio Ferraris (1997; trans. 2001), a set of conversations, provides both an autobiographical and a theoretical overview of Derridean thought. *On Cosmopolitanism and Forgiveness* (1997; trans. 2001) is a lean but penetrating exegesis on forgiveness, healing, truth and reconciliation, and world events; *Without Alibi* (2002) is collection of long pieces, a number of which focus on sovereignty. In *On Touching: Jean-Luc Nancy* (2000; trans. 2005), Derrida engages in a philosophical investigation of touching, grounded in the work of the philosopher Nancy. *The Work of Mourning*, edited by Pascale-Anne Brault and Michael Naas (2001), is a meditation on friendship and the passing of French intellectual luminaries such as Louis Althusser and Roland Barthes, among others. *For What Tomorrow . . . : A Dialogue* (2001; trans. 2004), with his friend the historian Elisabeth Roudinesco, offers accessible and wide-ranging insights into Derrida's intellectual and political evolution. *Paper Machine* (2001; trans. 2005) investigates the archive, writing, and media. *Negotiations: Interventions and Interviews, 1971–2001*, edited by Elizabeth Rottenberg (2002), a disparate collection of many essays and some interviews, provides biographical as well as intellectual insights often on political topics. Derrida published two late volumes on his friend the writer Hélène Cixous: *H.C. for Life, That Is to Say—* (2002; trans. 2006) and *Geneses, Genealogies, Genres, and Genius: The Secrets of the Archive* (2003; trans. 2006). In the literary treatise *Demeure: Fiction and Testimony* (1998), published together in English (2000) with the essay by Maurice Blanchot to which it responds, *The Instant of My Death* (1994), Derrida discusses literature, witnessing, and memory as it relates to truth. With the essays collected in *Sovereignties in Question: The Poetics of Paul Celan* (2005), another foray into literature, Derrida explores the poetics of the twentieth-century poet Paul Celan, a Romanian-French Jew who wrote in German. In *Learning to Live Finally: The Last Interview* (2005; trans. 2007), Derrida reflects on death, dying, and living in an interview with the *Le Monde* journalist Jean Birnbaum. And in *The Animal That Therefore I Am*, edited by Marie-Louise Mallet (2006; trans. 2008), a seminar, Derrida considers the roles played by animals throughout his corpus, delving into animal life and rights.

Derrida's annual seminars are being published in France and rapidly issued in English by the University of Chicago Press. The series started with *The Beast and the Sovereign* (2 vols., 2008–10; trans. 2009–11), followed by *The Death Penalty* (2 vols., 2012–15; trans. 2014–17) and *Heidegger: The Question of Being and History* (2013; trans. 2016); several dozen more volumes are projected.

As the selection above suggests, Derrida participated in many interviews and dialogues, which often clarified his work and his positions. The first interviews were collected in *Positions*, which was followed by *Points—: Interviews, 1974–1994*, edited by Elisabeth Weber (1992; trans. 1995 [with two added articles]), and *Negotiations*. Among the most revealing and informative dialogues, all cited above, are *A Taste for the Secret, For What Tomorrow*, and *Philosophy in a Time of Terror*.

Five readers in English provide useful starting points: *A Derrida Reader: Between the Blinds*, edited by Peggy Kamuf (1991), gives a good overall sample of his writing; *Acts of Literature*, edited by Derek Attridge (1992), and *The Derrida Reader: Writing Performances*, edited by Julian Wolfreys (1998), are more explicitly geared toward literature; and *Jacques Derrida: Basic Writings*, edited by Barry Stocker (2007), addresses topics in philosophy, while John W. P. Phillips's *Derrida Now: Current Perspectives in Derrida Studies* offers a sweeping introductory look into the major themes in his work (2016).

A good source of biographical information is *Jacques Derrida*, coauthored by Geoffrey Bennington and Jacques Derrida (1991; trans. 1993, rev. 1999). Bennington's exposition of Derrida's work, titled "Derridabase," is at the top of each page; Derrida's autobiographical commentary, "Circumfession," is at the bottom. The book also provides photographs, a chronology, and a good bibliography. *Jacques Derrida: A Biography* (2006) by Jason Powell is an introduction more to his philosophy than to his life. Benoît Peeters's *Derrida: A Biography* (2010; trans. 2013) covers Derrida's life and work in great depth, as well as providing an excellent bibliography. Several documentary films take the philosopher as their subject; *Derrida* (2002), directed by Kirby Dick and Amy Ziering Kofman, offers a very personal view.

Christopher Norris's *Derrida* (1987) remains a fine introduction to Derrida's early work. *The*

Cambridge Introduction to Jacques Derrida, edited by Leslie Hill (2007), and Nicholas Royle's *Jacques Derrida* (2003) are also very accessible. Simon Glendinning's *Derrida: A Very Short Introduction* (2011) unpacks and relates the difficulties and significance of Derrida's philosophical contributions. *Working through Derrida*, edited by Gary B. Madison (1993), presents very well the divisions around Derrida in Anglo-American philosophy, from John Searle's critique to explications and extensions of Derrida by the leading philosophers Barry Allen, John D. Caputo, and Drucilla Cornell, with Nancy Fraser and Richard Rorty falling somewhere in between. The four-volume *Jacques Derrida*, edited by Christopher Norris and David Roden (2003), reprints sixty-five pieces of critical reaction spanning three decades, with a focus on philosophers and philosophy. Another collection, *Deconstruction and the Possibility of Justice*, edited by Drucilla Cornell, Michel Rosenfeld, and David Gray Carlson (1992), considers his work's political implications; it begins with an essay by Derrida. Samir Haddad's *Derrida and the Inheritance of Democracy* (2013) also explores Derrida's political writings, with particular attention to the nature of democracy and democratic traditions in conversation with issues of violence and justice, while *Derrida and Our Animal Others: Derrida's Final Seminar, "The Beast and the Sovereign"* (2013) by David Farrell Krell engages Derrida's ideas on animals, humans, and political sovereignty. Allison Weiner and Simon Morgan Wertham have put together an interesting collection of essays on the future of deconstruction, *Encountering Derrida: Legacies and Futures of Deconstruction* (2007).

Exceptional monographs on Derrida include Rodolphe Gasché, *Inventions of Difference: On Jacques Derrida* (1994), which takes seriously Derrida's philosophical critique of reflexivity and specularity and distinguishes between Derrida's deconstruction and American deconstructive literary criticism; Marion Hobson, *Jacques Derrida: Opening Lines* (1998), a difficult but worthwhile reading of the inseparability of Derrida's writing strategies from his arguments; and Christina Howells, *Derrida: Deconstruction from Phenomenology to Ethics* (1999), a readable introduction to Derrida, but with particular attention to the parallel writings of Jean-Paul Sartre. For a substantial sympathetic scholarly account of the late Derrida, see J. Hillis Miller, *For Derrida* (2009).

Two constant critical engagements with deconstruction have come from feminism and Marxism. See, in particular, Diane Elam, *Feminism and Deconstruction: Ms. en Abyme* (1994); *Feminist Interpretations of Jacques Derrida*, edited by Nancy J. Holland (1997); and *Derrida and Feminism: Recasting the Question of Woman*, edited by Ellen K. Feder, Mary C. Rawlinson, and Emily Zakin (1997). More recent turns in feminist engagements with Derrida revolve around pornography, reproductive freedom, and transgender rights. See, for instance, Christopher Morris, "Derrida on Pornography: Putting (It) Up for Sale," *Derrida Today* 6 (2013), and Shannon Hoff, "Translating Principle into Practice: On Derrida and the Terms of Feminism," *Journal of Speculative Philosophy* 29 (2015). The response from Marxism has been divided: in *Marxism and Deconstruction: A Critical Articulation* (1982), Michael Ryan discusses analytical strategies common to Marx and Derrida as inheritors of Hegel; Terry Eagleton, in contrast, attacks deconstruction in his *Literary Theory: An Introduction* (1983; 2d ed., 1996) for not being political. Bill Martin, in *Humanism and Its Aftermath: The Shared Fate of Deconstruction and Politics* (1995), argues that deconstruction *is* political but doesn't go as far as it could. And after Derrida published *Specters of Marx*, Michael Sprinkler organized a symposium around the work, "Ghostly Demarcations," whose proceedings were published under the same title (1999). For critiques of deconstruction from more traditional standpoints, see John Ellis, *Against Deconstruction* (1989); David H. Hirsch, *The Deconstruction of Literature: Criticism after Auschwitz* (1991); and M. C. Dillon, *Semiological Reductionism: A Critique of the Deconstructionist Movement in Postmodern Thought* (1995).

Studies that extend Derrida's writings in various directions include Jasper Neel, *Plato, Derrida, and Writing* (1988), which investigates the relevance of Derrida's reading of Plato to composition theory; *Writing the Politics of Difference*, edited by Hugh J. Silverman (1991); Jonathan Loesberg, *Aestheticism and Deconstruction: Pater, Derrida, and de Man* (1991); Simon Critchley, *The Ethics of Deconstruction: Derrida and Levinas* (1992; 2d ed., 1999); Morag Patrick, *Derrida, Responsibility, and Politics* (1997); Joseph G. Kronick, *Derrida and the Future of Literature* (1999); Christine van Boheemen-Saaf, *Joyce, Derrida, Lacan, and the Trauma of History: Reading, Narrative, and Postcolonialism* (1999); and Peter Pericles Trifonas, *The Ethics of Writing: Derrida, Deconstruction, and Pedagogy* (2000). Both Joanna Hodge, *Derrida on Time* (2007), and David Wood, *Time after Time* (2007), contrast Derrida's use of temporality with that of Heidegger, Lévinas, and others.

William Schultz's *Jacques Derrida: An Annotated Primary and Secondary Bibliography* (1992) is useful up to 1992. *Jacques Derrida (II): A Bibliography*, compiled by Joan Nordquist (1995), goes up to 1995. For more recent bibliographies, see Bennington and Derrida, *Jacques Derrida*; Royle, *Jacques Derrida*; *The Cambridge Introduction to Jacques Derrida*; and Peeter's *Derrida: A Biography*, as well as Glendinning's *Derrida: A Very Short Introduction*.

John Dryden

For many years the standard edition of Dryden was the eighteen-volume collection first published in 1808 and revised in 1882–93. It has been replaced by the University of California Press edition, edited E. N. Hooker, H. T. Swedenberg Jr., et al. (20 vols., 1956–2002). There are two well-annotated collections of Dryden's criticism, the first edited by W. P. Ker (2 vols., 1900), the second by George Watson (2 vols., 1962). Other helpful collections include John Aden, *Critical Opinions of John Dryden* (1963); *Literary Criticism of John Dryden*, edited by Arthur C. Kirsch (1966); H. James Jensen, *A Glossary of John Dryden's Critical Terms* (1969); and *John Dryden: Selected Criticism*, edited by James Kinsley and George Parfitt (1970).

The best biography is James Anderson Winn, *John Dryden and His World* (1987). Also valuable are James Marshall Osborn, *John Dryden: Some Biographical Facts and Problems* (rev. ed., 1965), and Winn, *"When Beauty Fires the Blood": Love and the Arts in the Age of Dryden* (1992). A good survey of the life and works is Paul Hammond, *John Dryden: A Literary Life* (1991).

Important modern studies of Dryden include T. S. Eliot, *Homage to John Dryden* (1924) and *John Dryden: The Poet, the Dramatist, the Critic* (1932); and Louis I. Bredvold, *The Intellectual Milieu of John Dryden* (1934). The best books on the criticism are Edward Pechter, *Dryden's Classical Theory of Literature* (1975), and James Engell, *Forming the Critical Mind: Dryden to Coleridge* (1989). Philip Harth, *Contexts of Dryden's Thought* (1968), is the standard work on Dryden's philosophical and religious views; Harth's *Pen for a Party: Dryden's Tory Propaganda in Its Contexts* (1993) is also valuable. Michael Werth Gelber, *The Just and the Lively: The Literary Criticism of John Dryden* (1999), analyzes the criticism as a full and coherent body of literary theory. The essays included in *The Cambridge Companion to John Dryden*, edited by Steven N. Zwicker (2004), examine Dryden's work as a poet, playwright, and literary critic in its political and cultural contexts. *Dryden, Pope, Johnson, Malone*, edited by Claude Rawson (2010), in the Great Shakespeareans series, includes a cogent essay by Harold Love on Shakespeare's impact on Dryden's contribution to the interpretation and appreciation of Shakespeare's work. Philip Smallwood, in *Critical Occasions: Dryden, Pope, Johnson, and the History of Criticism* (2011), situates Dryden's criticism in relation both to the critics he read (e.g., Thomas Rymer, Nicolas Boileau) and to modern critics, theorists, and historians (e.g., R. G. Collingwood, Hans-George Gadamer, Paul Ricoeur).

For bibliographic works, see Hugh Macdonald, *John Dryden: A Bibliography of Early Editions and Drydeniana* (1939); *John Dryden: The Critical Heritage*, edited by James Kinsley and Helen Kinsley (1971); *An Annotated Bibliography of John Dryden: Texts and Studies, 1949–1973*, edited by John A. Zamonski (1975); *John Dryden: A Survey and Bibliography of Critical Studies, 1895–1974*, edited by David J. Latt and Samuel Holt Monk (1976); and James M. Hall, *John Dryden: A Reference Guide* (1984). For more recent bibliography of primary and secondary sources, consult Zwicker's *Cambridge Companion* (see above).

Joachim du Bellay

Little of du Bellay's work has been translated into English: the *Defense* is available in an English translation by Gladys M. Turquet (1939), as is *Regrets*, translated by C. H. Sisson (1984). Richard Helgerson has put together a bilingual edition of du Bellay's work that includes *Regrets, Antiquities*, and the *Defense* (2006). Our selection is taken from Helgerson's volume. *Joachim du Bellay* (1971) by L. Clark Keating includes a biography as well as a general introduction.

There are relatively few book-length studies of du Bellay in English; however, many books on Renaissance poetics contain chapters on him. Walter Pater's chapter on du Bellay in *The Renaissance: Studies in Art and Poetry* (1877) and Arthur Tilley's *The Literature of the French Renaissance* (2 vols., 1904) represent some of the earliest studies on du Bellay's poetry. Especially useful are the chapters in W. F. Patterson's *Three Centuries of French Poetic Theory: A Critical History of the Chief Arts of Poetry in France (1328–1630)* (1935) and in S. J. Holyoake's concise study, *An Introduction to French Sixteenth Century Poetic Theory* (1972). The chapter on du Bellay in Margaret Ferguson's *Trials of Desire: Renaissance Defenses of Poetry* (1983) examines the political and historical context of the *Defense*, as well as the implications of du Bellay's own "borrowing" from Italian treatises. Hassan Melehy's *The Poetics of Literary Transfer in Early Modern France and England* (2010), a critical comparative study, has a chapter on du Bellay's *Defense*, examining the literary interplay and interrelationship between early modern and medieval writers and their attention to classical poetics. For a theoretical discussion of the Pléiade poets as a whole, see Grahame Castor's *Pléiade Poetics: A Study in Sixteenth-Century Thought and Terminology* (1964). Other good general studies include Dorothy Coleman, *The Chaste Muse: A Study of Joachim Du Bellay's Poetry* (1980), and David Hartley, *Patriotism in the Work of Joachim Du Bellay: A Study of the Relationship between the Poet and France* (1993). Margaret Brady Wells has compiled an extensive unannotated bibliography: *Du Bellay, a Bibliography* (1974). Helgerson's bilingual edition, mentioned above, has a robust bibliography related to the *Defense*.

W. E. B. Du Bois

The Complete Published Works of W. E. B. Du Bois has been edited by Herbert Aptheker (36 vols., 1973–86). It is supplemented by two other works edited by Aptheker: *The Correspondence of W. E. B. Du Bois* (3 vols., 1973–78) and *Against Racism: Unpublished Essays, Papers, Addresses, 1887–1961* (1985). The Du Bois volume in the Library of America series, edited by Nathan Irvin Huggins (1986), includes *The Suppression of the*

African Slave Trade, *The Souls of Black Folk*, and *Dusk of Dawn*, as well as a number of essays. A range of selections is also available in *W. E. B. Du Bois: A Reader*, edited by David Levering Lewis (1995), and *The Oxford W. E. B. Du Bois Reader*, edited by Eric J. Sundquist (1996).

There are several excellent biographies: Manning Marable, *W. E. B. Du Bois, Black Radical Democrat* (1986), a cogently written survey by an author fully familiar with Du Bois's writings and the major issues in African American social and political history; Gerald Horne, *Black and Red: W. E. B. Du Bois and the Afro-American Response to the Cold War, 1944–1963* (1986), a detailed account of the final phase of Du Bois's career; and David L. Lewis, *W. E. B. Du Bois*, a comprehensive two-volume biography: *Biography of a Race, 1868–1919* (1993) and *The Fight for Equality and the American Century, 1919–1963* (2000).

The best study of Du Bois as a writer is Arnold Rampersad's *Art and Imagination of W. E. B. Du Bois* (1976), which explores all of Du Bois's major books. See also the extensive chapter on Du Bois in Eric J. Sundquist, *To Wake the Nations: Race in the Making of American Literature* (1993); Keith Eldon Byerman, *Seizing the Word: History, Art, and Self in the Work of W. E. B. Du Bois* (1994); Shamoon Zamir, *Dark Voices: W. E. B. Du Bois and American Thought, 1888–1903* (1995); Adolph Reed Jr., *W. E. B. Du Bois and American Political Thought: Fabianism and the Color Line* (1997); and Raymond Wolters, *Du Bois and His Rivals* (2002), which examines Du Bois's ideological disputes with Booker T. Washington and Marcus Garvey. Other helpful resources include two collections: *Critical Essays on W. E. B. Du Bois*, edited by William L. Andrews (1985), and *W. E. B. Du Bois on Race and Culture*, edited by Bernard W. Bell, Emily R. Grosholz, and James B. Stewart (1996), which sheds light on Du Bois's attitudes toward race, gender equality, and Pan-Africanism.

For primary sources leading up to *The Souls of Black Folk*, see *The Problem of the Color Line at the Turn of the Twentieth Century: The Essential Early Essays*, edited by Nahum Dimitri Chandler (2015). Also valuable for context and interpretation is Stephanie J. Shaw, *W. E. B. Du Bois and "The Souls of Black Folk"* (2013); she contends that Du Bois appropriates Hegelian idealism in order to include the United States, the nineteenth century, and African Americans in the historical narrative of Hegel's philosophy of history.

Recent studies of Du Bois have situated him in relation to modern and contemporary issues of world history and democracy. See Eric Porter, *The Problem of the Future World: W. E. B. Du Bois and the Race Concept at Midcentury* (2010), which brings forward and reassesses Du Bois's writings of the 1940s and 1950s; Katharine Lawrence Balfour, *Democracy's Reconstruction: Thinking Politically with W. E. B. Du Bois* (2011), a cogent treatment of Du Bois as a political theorist; Terrence L. Johnson, *Tragic Soul-Life: W. E. B. Du Bois and the Moral Crisis Facing American Democracy* (2012), which locates Du Bois in the midst of ongoing debates about race, politics, and religion; Kwame Anthony Appiah, *Lines of Descent: W. E. B. Du Bois and the Emergence of Identity* (2014), a keen consideration of Du Bois's educational experiences at Harvard and at the University of Berlin; and Bill V. Mullen, *Un-American: W. E. B. Du Bois and the Century of World Revolution* (2015), on Du Bois's revolutionary vision and commitment to human liberation.

For other dimensions of Du Bois's career, see *Protest and Propaganda: W. E. B. Du Bois, "The Crisis," and American History*, edited by Amy Helene Kirschke and Phillip Luke Sinitiere (2014), examining how the essays, columns, and visuals in *The Crisis*, a magazine published by the NAACP and edited by Du Bois from 1910 to 1934, changed perceptions and even laws in the United States; see also Aldon D. Morris, *The Scholar Denied: W. E. B. Du Bois and the Birth of Modern Sociology* (2015), a major study of Du Bois's role in the development of scientific sociology and his relationships with Booker T. Washington, Robert Park, and other members of the Chicago school, and with the preeminent social scientist Max Weber. Key bibliographic sources include Herbert Aptheker, *Annotated Bibliography of the Published Writings of W. E. B. Du Bois* (1973), and Paul G. Partington, *W. E. B. Du Bois: A Bibliography of His Published Writings* (1979). For additional bibliography, reference, and context, see *W. E. B. Du Bois: An Encyclopedia*, edited by Gerald Horne and Mary Young (2001), and *The Cambridge Companion to W. E. B. Du Bois*, edited by Shamoon Zamir (2008), which includes excellent essays on *The Souls of Black Folk* and on Du Bois's place in American and European intellectual history.

Terry Eagleton

Eagleton has been prolific, writing more than forty critical books, scores of pieces of literary journalism, several plays, and a novel. In this he follows the model of his teacher Raymond Williams, though he has focused primarily on literary criticism and theory rather than cultural and media studies. Eagleton's early books include *Shakespeare and Society: Critical Studies in Shakespearean Drama* (1967), *Exiles and Emigres: Studies in Modern Literature* (1970), and *The Body as Language: Outline of a "New Left" Theology* (1970). He also edited collections that reflect his involvement in the Catholic Left, including *Directions: Pointers for the Post-Conciliar Church* (1968) and, with Brian Wicker, *From Culture to Revolution: The "Slant" Symposium, 1967* (1968). In the 1970s and early 1980s he published three works of Marxist theory: *Marxism and Literary Criticism* (1976), a superb short survey of major Marxist critics and debates; *Criticism and Ideology:*

A Study in Marxist Literary Theory (1976); and *Walter Benjamin; or, Towards a Revolutionary Criticism* (1981). He also published two works of literary criticism, *Myths of Power: A Marxist Study of the Brontës* (1975; 2d ed., 1988) and *The Rape of Clarissa: Writing, Sexuality, and Class Struggle in Samuel Richardson* (1982), which is notable for its engagement with feminism.

In the mid-1980s Eagleton published the popular overview *Literary Theory: An Introduction* (1983; 3d ed., 2008) and a short history, *The Function of Criticism: From the "Spectator" to Post-Structuralism* (1984), which is perhaps the best place to start reading his work. He also published *William Shakespeare* (1986); a collection of his essays, *Against the Grain: Essays, 1975–1985* (1986); and a fine edited collection assessing the influence of his teacher, *Raymond Williams: A Critical Reader* (1989). In the 1990s, Eagleton published *The Ideology of the Aesthetic* (1990), an engaging survey of aesthetic theory from the eighteenth century to the twentieth, and several guides to Marxist theory, including *Ideology: An Introduction* (1991), the brief *Marx* (1999), and the anthology *Marxist Literary Theory: A Reader*, co-edited with Drew Milne (1996). Of Irish ancestry, he also explored Irish culture in three works, *Heathcliff and the Great Hunger: Studies in Irish Culture* (1995), *Crazy John and the Bishop and Other Essays on Irish Culture* (1998), and *Scholars and Rebels in Nineteenth-Century Ireland* (1999). His creative work includes the novel *Saints and Scholars* (1987); a script, *Wittgenstein: The Terry Eagleton Script, the Derek Jarman Film* (1993); and plays, *Saint Oscar and Other Plays* (1997).

At the century's end, Eagleton complained about much contemporary theory, in *The Illusions of Postmodernism* (1996), *The Idea of Culture* (2000), and *After Theory* (2003), and collected his pithy reviews in *Figures of Dissent: Critical Essays on Fish, Spivak, Žižek and Others* (2003). Through the 2000s he concentrated on traditional literary topics in *Sweet Violence: The Idea of the Tragic* (2003), *The English Novel: An Introduction* (2004), *How to Read a Poem* (2007), *The Event of Literature* (2012), and *How to Read Literature* (2013). He also returned to his early concern with religion, in *Holy Terror* (2005), *The Meaning of Life* (2007), his substantial introduction to *Jesus Christ: The Gospels* (2007), *Reason, Faith, and Revolution: Reflections on the God Debate* (2009), *Trouble with Strangers: A Study of Ethics* (2009), *On Evil* (2010), *Culture and the Death of God* (2014), and *Hope without Optimism* (2015). In addition, he continued to write on Marxism in *Why Marx Was Right* (2011) and on the confused definitions of culture in *Culture* (2016), and he wryly commented on the United States in *Across the Pond: An Englishman's View of America* (2013). *The Gatekeeper: A Memoir* (2001) offers some information on Eagleton's early biography but is otherwise unrevealing; much more informative is the substantial series of interviews with Matthew Beaumont, *The Task of the Critic: Terry Eagleton in Dialogue* (2009).

The Eagleton Reader, edited by Stephen Regan (1998), provides an excellent sampler of Eagleton's work, as well as a complete bibliography of both his writing and commentary on him up to 1996. A special issue of *The Year's Work in Critical and Cultural Theory* 1 (1994) includes nine essays and shorter pieces reflecting on Eagleton's style and career. Two volumes titled *Terry Eagleton*, by David Alderson (2004) and James Smith (2008), provide useful overviews; Smith includes a composite bibliography. See also Ola Sigurdson, *Theology and Marxism in Eagleton and Žižek: A Conspiracy of Hope* (2012), for a study of Eagleton's view of religion, as well as John E. O'Brien, *Critical Practice from Voltaire to Foucault, Eagleton, and Beyond: Contested Perspectives* (2014), which surveys the span of Eagleton's work. Beaumont's *The Task of the Critic* includes a comprehensive bibliography of works by and about Eagleton.

T. S. Eliot

Among Eliot's books of criticism, the key texts are *The Sacred Wood* (1920), *Selected Essays* (3d ed., 1972), and *On Poetry and Poets* (1957). Other important publications include *Homage to John Dryden* (1924), in which appear the brilliant essays "John Dryden," "The Metaphysical Poets," and "Andrew Marvell." A good selection is *Selected Prose of T. S. Eliot*, edited by Frank Kermode (1975). There are hundreds of reviews, introductions to books, essays, and other critical pieces that have not yet been collected in book form. For further insight into Eliot's development as a critic, one should also consult the posthumous book *The Varieties of Metaphysical Poetry*, edited by Ronald Schuchard (1993).

Eliot did not want to be made the subject of a biography, and much source material is either sealed or is unavailable for citation. Despite these limitations, Peter Ackroyd's *T. S. Eliot* (1984) is a valuable, crisply written book. Also useful are Lyndall Gordon, *Eliot's Early Years* (1977) and *Eliot's New Life* (1988); she presents Eliot's life as a spiritual journey and is perceptive on the poetry, but pays little attention to the criticism. Tony Sharpe, *T. S. Eliot: A Literary Life* (1991), is also recommended. Recent scholarship on Eliot includes important primary sources: *The Letters of T. S. Eliot*, edited by Valerie Eliot, Hugh Haughton, and John Haffenden (7 vols. to date, 2011–); *The Complete Prose of T. S. Eliot: The Critical Edition*, general editor Ronald Schuchard (6 vols. to date, 2014–), a tremendous online resource; and *The Poems of T. S. Eliot*, edited by Christopher Ricks and Jim McCue (2 vols., 2015). Robert Crawford's *Young Eliot: From St. Louis to "The Waste Land"* (2015) is the first volume of a new biography, comprehensive and lucidly written. An excellent complement to it is *T. S. Eliot in Context*, edited by Jason Harding (2011), a wide-ranging survey of Eliot's life and times, which includes helpful essays on his literary journalism and on his social, political, and cultural writings. Steven Matthews, *T. S. Eliot and Early Modern Literature* (2013), is helpful on the relationship between Eliot's early poetry and his literary criticism. *The New Cambridge Companion to T. S. Eliot*, edited by Jason Harding (2017), offers separate chapters on Eliot as a literary critic and as a social critic, as well as on the roles of gender and sexuality in his work.

A good place to begin study of Eliot is *T. S. Eliot: Critical Assessments*, edited by Graham Clarke (4 vols., 1990). The fourth volume includes commentaries on Eliot's critical writings. A number of older studies, which include discussion of Eliot's criticism, remain useful: F. O. Matthiessen, *The Achievement of T. S. Eliot: An Essay on the Nature of Poetry* (1935; 3d ed., 1958); Hugh Kenner, *The Invisible Poet: T. S. Eliot* (1959); Northrop Frye, *T. S. Eliot* (1967); and Bernard Bergonzi, *T. S. Eliot* (1972).

On Eliot and the modernist movement in literature, see John D. Margolis, *T. S. Eliot's Intellectual Development, 1922–1939* (1972); Piers Gray, *T. S. Eliot's Intellectual and Poetic Development, 1909–1922* (1982); Sanford Schwartz, *The Matrix of Modernism: Pound, Eliot, and Early Twentieth-Century Thought* (1985); Louis Menand, *Discovering Modernism: T. S. Eliot and His Context* (1987; 2d ed., 2007); *T. S. Eliot: The Modernist in History*, edited by Ronald Bush (1991), which includes a good essay by Michael North on Eliot and György Lukács; Gail McDonald, *Learning to Be Modern: Pound, Eliot, and the American University* (1993); and Jewel Spears Brooker, *Mastery and Escape: T. S. Eliot and the Dialectic of Modernism* (1994). Though somewhat dated in approach, C. K. Stead's *New Poetic: Yeats to Eliot* (rev. ed., 1987) and *Pound, Yeats, Eliot, and the Modernist Movement* (1986) are informative and acute in judgment. Of the many collections of essays on Eliot, the best is the special issue of the *Southern Review* 21.4 (autumn 1985).

The studies of Eliot's criticism are disappointing, but some good work can be found in *The Literary Criticism of T. S. Eliot: New Essays*, edited by David Newton-Molina (1977). In *T. S. Eliot and the Philosophy of Criticism* (1988), Richard Shusterman describes Eliot as a postmodernist and relates his work to that of Theodor Adorno, Richard Rorty, Jacques Derrida, and other philosophers and theorists. The social, cultural, and economic contexts for Eliot's poetry and criticism and the modernist movement are described in Lawrence Rainey, *Institutions of Modernism: Literary Elites and Public Culture* (1998). *T. S. Eliot and the Concept of Tradition*, edited by Giovanni Cianci and Jason Harding (2007), includes a number of essays on "Tradition and the Individual Talent."

Other resources include *The Cambridge Companion to T. S. Eliot*, edited by A. D. Moody (1994); Caroline Behr, *T. S. Eliot: A Chronology of His Life and Works* (1983); and *T. S. Eliot: The Critical Heritage*, edited by Michael Grant (1982). For bibliography, see Donald Gallup, *T. S. Eliot: A Bibliography* (rev. ed., 1969); Mildred Martin, *A Half-Century of Eliot Criticism: An Annotated Bibliography of Books and Articles in English, 1916–1965* (1972); and Beatrice Ricks, *T. S. Eliot: A Bibliography of Secondary Works* (1980). For further reading, consult the bibliography in Harding's *T. S. Eliot in Context* (see above).

Ralph Waldo Emerson

The standard editions are *The Collected Works of Ralph Waldo Emerson*, edited by Robert Spiller et al. (10 vols., 1971–2013); *The Early Lectures*, edited by Stephen Whicher, Robert Spiller, and Wallace E. Williams (3 vols., 1959–72); *Journals and Miscellaneous Notebooks*, edited by William H. Gilman et al. (16 vols., 1960–84); and *Letters*, edited by Ralph L. Rusk (6 vols., 1939). For excellent single-volume collections (which include annotations), consult *Emerson's Literary Criticism*, edited by Eric W. Carlson (1979), and *Ralph Waldo Emerson*, edited by Richard Poirier, in the Oxford Authors series (1990). Also recommended are *The Annotated Emerson*, edited by David Mikics (2012), which includes both prose and poetry, and *Ralph Waldo Emerson: The Major Prose*, edited by Ronald A. Bosco and Joel Myerson (2015), with selections from sermons, lectures, addresses, and essays. For more wide-ranging selections, see the Emerson volumes in the Library of America series, especially *Essays and Lectures* (1983). For selections from the journals, refer to *Emerson in His Journals*, edited by Joel Porte (1982). *Selected Journals*, edited by Lawrence Rosenwald (2 vols., 2010), offers a fuller sampling.

Ralph L. Rusk's *Life of Ralph Waldo Emerson* (1949) remains a basic starting point. Biographies have also been written by Gay Wilson Allen, *Waldo Emerson: A Biography* (1981), and John McAleer, *Ralph Waldo Emerson: Days of Encounter* (1984). Robert D. Richardson, *Emerson: The Mind on Fire* (1995), explores Emerson's career as an American scholar, reader, and writer. Another keen study that combines biography and literary analysis, and that explores Emerson's work as a poet, essayist, literary critic and theorist, religious thinker, and philosopher, is Lawrence Buell, *Emerson* (2003). For an account of Emerson's friends and contemporaries, see Carlos Baker, *Emerson among the Eccentrics: A Group Portrait* (1996). For incisive commentaries on Emerson's style and strategies as a writer, turn to Warner Berthoff, introduction to his edition of *Nature* (1968); Alfred Kazin, *An American Procession* (1984); Richard Poirier, *The Renewal of Literature: Emersonian Reflections* (1984); and Poirier, *Poetry and Pragmatism* (1992).

Many books have been written on Emerson; particularly worthy of attention are Barbara L. Packer, *Emerson's Fall: A New Interpretation of the Major Essays* (1982), an analysis of Emerson's uses of language; Julie Ellison, *Emerson's Romantic Style* (1984); Irving Howe, *The American Newness: Culture and Politics in the Age of Emerson* (1986), a suggestive book that relates Emerson to his contemporaries; David Van Leer, *Emerson's Epistemology: The Argument of the Essays* (1986), a cogent investigation of Emerson's theory of knowledge; Richard A. Grusin, *Transcendentalist Hermeneutics: Institutional Authority and the Higher Criticism of the Bible* (1991), which is helpful on religious contexts; Merton M. Sealts, *Emerson on the Scholar* (1992); George J. Stack, *Nietzsche and Emerson: An Elective Affinity* (1992), an argument for the German philosopher's deep indebtedness to Emerson's ideas; Christina Zwarg, *Feminist Conversations: Fuller, Emerson, and the Play of Reading* (1995); Stanley Cavell, *Philosophical Passages: Wittgenstein, Emerson, Austin, Derrida* (1995), a rewarding meditation on Emerson's significance for twentieth-century philosophy; and Pamela Schirmeister, *Less Legible Meanings: Between Poetry and Philosophy in the Work of Emerson* (1999), which scrutinizes Emerson's conception of the act of reading and his literary and cultural project for American letters. Recent studies include James M. Albrecht, *Reconstructing Individualism: A Pragmatic Tradition from Emerson to Ellison* (2012), on selfhood and social reform in Emerson, William James, John Dewey, and Ralph Ellison; David Greenham, *Emerson's Transatlantic Romanticism* (2012), on Emerson's creative debts to British and European writers, including Samuel Taylor Coleridge and Thomas Carlyle; and Samantha C. Harvey, *Transatlantic Transcendentalism: Coleridge, Emerson, and Nature* (2013), which examines Coleridge's literary, philosophical, and theological influences on Emerson. For a richly detailed, vivid study of the period, see David Reynolds, *Beneath the American Renaissance: The Subversive Imagination in the Age of Emerson and Melville* (1988; rpt. with new foreword, 2011). Also valuable are *Emerson and Thoreau: The Contemporary Reviews*, edited by Joel Myerson (1992), and *Critical Essays on Ralph Waldo Emerson*, edited by Robert E. Burkholder and Joel Myerson (1983).

Joel Myerson has prepared a bibliography of Emerson's writings, *Ralph Waldo Emerson: A Descriptive Bibliography* (1982), and, with Robert E. Burkholder, two bibliographies of secondary sources: *A Secondary Bibliography of Ralph Waldo Emerson* (1985) and *Ralph Waldo Emerson: An Annotated Bibliography of Criticism, 1980–1991* (1994). Albert J. Von Frank, *An Emerson Chronology* (1994), is an indispensable reference. Also helpful are Tiffany K. Wayne, *Critical Companion to Ralph Waldo Emerson: A Literary Reference to His Life and Work* (2010), and *Ralph Waldo Emerson in Context*, edited by Wesley T. Mott (2014), which includes a detailed chronology and a wide range of essays on Emerson's travels, intellectual influences, interests in many fields, and other topics.

Frantz Fanon

Fanon's major works are *Black Skin, White Masks* (1952; trans. 1967), *A Dying Colonialism* (1959; trans. 1965), *The Wretched of the Earth* (1961; trans. 1963), and *Toward the African Revolution* (1964; trans. 1976). For a good, brief introduction to Fanon's life and ideas, see David Caute's *Frantz Fanon* (1970). For more detailed biographies, see Peter Geismar's *Fanon* (1971) and David Macey's *Frantz Fanon: A Life* (2000). Fanon's life is also the subject of the documentary film *Frantz Fanon: Black Skin, White Mask* (1995), directed by Isaac Julien. For studies that combine biographical detail with critical analysis of Fanon's thought, see Richard C. Onwuanibe, *A Critique of Revolutionary Humanism: Frantz Fanon* (1983); Hussein Abadilahi Bulhan, *Frantz Fanon and the Psychology of Oppression* (1985); *Frantz Fanon's "Black Skin, Whites Masks": New Interdisciplinary Essays*, edited by Max Silverman (2005); and Lewis R. Gordon's *What Fanon Said: A Philosophical Introduction to His Life and Thought* (2015).

Other useful critical studies include Irene Gendzier, *Frantz Fanon: A Critical Study* (1973); Renate Zahar, *Frantz Fanon: Colonialism and Alienation* (1969; trans. 1974); Lewis Gordon, *Frantz Fanon and the Crisis of European Man* (1995); and Ato Sekyi-Otu, *Fanon's Dialectic of Experience* (1996). For a feminist engagement with Fanon's work, see "Dark Continents: Epistemologies of Racial and Sexual Difference in Psychoanalysis and the Cinema," a chapter in Mary Ann Doane's *Femmes Fatales: Feminism, Film Theory, Psychoanalysis* (1991) that critiques Fanon's psychoanalytic reading of miscegenation and the repressed desire for interracial sex as rape, and, more sympathetically, T. Denean Sharpley-Whiting's *Frantz Fanon: Conflicts and Feminisms* (1998) and Ashley Bohrer's "Fanon and Feminism: The Discourse of Colonization in Italian Feminism," *Interventions: International Journal of Postcolonial Studies* 17 (2015). Several essay collections of the 1990s marked a resurgence of interest in Fanon's thought: see *Frantz Fanon: Critical Perspectives*, edited by Anthony Alessandrini (1999); *Rethinking Fanon: The Continuing Dialogue*, edited by Nigel Gibson (1999); and *Fanon: A Critical Reader*, edited by Lewis Gordon, T. Denean Sharpley-Whiting, and Renee White (1996). The last of these also includes a particularly extensive bibliography; see also the primary and secondary bibliographies in Nigel Gibson's *Fanon: The Postcolonial Imagination* (2003) and Silverman's *Frantz Fanon's "Black Skin, Whites Masks"* (cited above).

Stanley E. Fish

Grounded in the study of seventeenth-century literature, Fish's early books are *John Skelton's Poetry* (1965), *Surprised by Sin: The Reader in "Paradise*

Lost" (1967; 2d ed., 1999), *Self-Consuming Artifacts: The Experience of Seventeenth-Century Literature* (1972), and *The Living Temple: George Herbert and Catechizing* (1978). *Is There a Text in This Class? The Authority of Interpretive Communities* (1980) expands his early consideration of the reader to more general discussions of interpretation and theory. Thereafter Fish broadened his field of inquiry to encompass law, pragmatism, and professionalism, as well as literature and literary theory, in three collections of essays: *Doing What Comes Naturally: Change, Rhetoric, and the Practice of Theory in Literary and Legal Studies* (1989), *There's No Such Thing as Free Speech . . . and It's a Good Thing, Too* (1994), and *The Trouble with Principle* (1999). Fish's *Professional Correctness: Literary Studies and Political Change* (1995) and subsequent *Save the World on Your Own Time* (2008) chastise contemporary critics, holding that politics are not a part of literary criticism. *How Milton Works* (2001) culminates Fish's thinking on the writer, and *Versions of Antihumanism: Milton and Others* (2012) collects essays from several decades. Fish has increasingly reached out beyond an academic audience in *How to Write a Sentence: And How to Read One* (2011), *The Fugitive in Flight: Faith, Liberalism, and Law in a Classic TV Show* (2011), *Versions of Academic Freedom: From Professionalism to Revolution* (2014), and *Think Again: Contrarian Reflections on Life, Culture, Politics, Religion, Law, and Education* (2015), a collection drawn from his columns in the *New York Times* (1995–2013). *The Stanley Fish Reader*, edited by H. Aram Veeser (1999), offers a diverse selection of his work. Gary A. Olson's *Stanley Fish, America's Enfant Terrible: The Authorized Biography* (2016) is merely a celebrity profile, lacking notes or bibliography. For an account of some aspects of his career, see "Stanley Agonistes: An Interview with Stanley Fish," conducted by Jeffrey J. Williams, in *Critics at Work: Interviews 1993–2003* (ed. Williams, 2004).

The first wave of commentary on Fish deals with reader-response theory. A famous debate between Fish and Wolfgang Iser appeared in *Diacritics* 11 (1981). The best discussion of Fish's concept of interpretive communities is Steven Mailloux's *Interpretive Conventions: The Reader in the Study of American Fiction* (1982). A leftist assessment of Fish is Mary Louise Pratt, "Interpretive Strategies/Strategic Interpretation: On Anglo-American Reader Response Criticism," *Boundary 2* 2.11 (1982/83). Important early critiques also include Gerald Graff's "Interpretation on Tlon: A Response to Stanley Fish," *New Literary History* 17 (1985), and a chapter in Ellen Rooney's *Seductive Reasoning: Pluralism as the Problematic of Contemporary Literary Theory* (1989).

The later commentary on Fish primarily deals with his antifoundationalism. Christopher Norris's *What's Wrong with Postmodernism: Critical Theory and the Ends of Philosophy* (1990) includes a representative critique of the circularity of Fish's argument that theory has "no consequences." In "The Estate Agent," *London Review of Books*, March 2, 2000, the Marxist critic Terry Eagleton calls Fish "a brash, noisy entrepreneur of the intellect" and criticizes the apolitical outcome of Fish's "no consequences" argument. Gary A. Olson's *Justifying Belief: Stanley Fish and the Work of Rhetoric* (2002) is a good account of Fish's nonliterary work, and concludes with two interviews and a chronological bibliography of Fish's writing. See also *Postmodern Sophistry: Stanley Fish and the Critical Enterprise*, edited by Olson and Lynn Worsham (2004), which collects fifteen essays on Fish's work, including reassessments by Graff and Mailloux and Eagleton's "Estate Agent." *Stanley Fish on Philosophy, Politics, and Law: How Fish Works* (2014), by Michael Robertson, studies Fish's influence in legal theory.

Michel Foucault

Foucault's books published during his lifetime include *Madness and Civilization* (1961; trans. 1965); *The Birth of the Clinic* (1963; trans. 1973); *Death and the Labyrinth: The World of Raymond Roussel* (1963; trans. 1986); *The Order of Things* (1966; trans. 1970); *The Archaeology of Knowledge* (1969; trans. 1972); *This Is Not a Pipe* (1973; trans. 1981); *Discipline and Punish: The Birth of the Prison* (1975; trans. 1977); and the three volumes of *The History of Sexuality*: *An Introduction* (1976; trans. 1978), *The Use of Pleasure* (1984; trans. 1985), and *The Care of the Self* (1984; trans. 1986). Essays and interviews are collected in *Language, Counter-Memory, and Practice: Selected Essays and Interviews*, edited by Daniel Bouchard (1977); *Power/Knowledge*, edited by Colin Gordon (1980); *Technologies of the Self: A Seminar with Michel Foucault*, edited by Luther H. Martin, Huck Gutman, and Patrick H. Hutton (1988); *Politics, Philosophy, Culture: Interviews and Other Writings, 1977–1984*, edited by Lawrence Kritzman (1988); *Foucault Live: Interviews, 1966–1984*, edited by Sylvère Lotringer (1989; 2d ed., 1996); *The Foucault Effect: Studies in Governmentality*, edited by Graham Burchell, Colin Gordon, and Peter Miller (1991); *The Politics of Truth*, edited by Sylvère Lotringer (1997); a three-volume collection of essays and interviews, *The Essential Works of Michel Foucault, 1954–1984*, edited by Paul Rabinow (1997–2000); *Introduction to Kant's Anthropology* (2008; trans. 2008); *Speech Begins after Death* (2011; trans. 2013); and *Language, Madness, and Desire: On Literature* (2013; trans. 2015). Foucault's annual course lectures at the Collège de France have been translated and published in English: *Abnormal, 1974–1975* (2003), *"Society Must Be Defended," 1975–1976* (2003), *The Hermeneutics of the Subject, 1981–1982* (2005), *Security, Territory, Population, 1977–1978* (2007), *Psychiatric Power, 1973–1974* (2008), *The Birth of Biopolitics, 1978–1979* (2008), *The Government of Self and Others, 1982–1983* (2011), *The*

Courage of Truth, 1983–1984 (2011), *Lectures on the Will to Know, 1970–1971* (2013), *On the Government of the Living, 1979–1980* (2014), and *On the Punitive Society, 1972–1973* (2015). Foucault also edited three books: *I, Pierre Rivière, Having Slaughtered My Mother, My Sister, and My Brother . . . : A Case of Parricide in the 19th Century* (1973; trans. 1975), *Herculine Barbin: Being the Recently Discovered Memoirs of a Nineteenth-Century French Hermaphrodite* (1978; trans. 1980), and *Disorderly Families: Infamous Letters from the Bastille Archive* (1982; trans. 2017). Didier Eribon's sober and reliable biography *Michel Foucault* (1989, trans. 1991; 2d French ed., 2011) can be supplemented with Stuart Elden's more detailed intellectual biographies *Foucault's Last Decade* (2016) and *Foucault: The Birth of Power* (2017).

The critical commentary on Foucault is extensive. Lisa Downing, *Cambridge Introduction to Foucault* (2008); *Michel Foucault: Key Concepts*, edited by Dianna Taylor (2011); *A Companion to Foucault*, edited by Christopher Falzon, Timothy O'Leary, and Jana Sawicki (2013); *Cambridge Foucault Lexicon*, edited by Leonard Lawler and John Nale (2014); and *The Routledge Guidebook to Foucault's the History of Sexuality*, edited by Chloë Taylor (2017) are all reliable places to start. David M. Halperin's *Saint Foucault: Towards a Gay Hagiography* (1995) examines Foucault's gay activism and the impact of his work on queer theory. Béatrice Han's *Foucault's Critical Project: Between the Transcendental and the Historical* (1998; trans. 2002) addresses Foucault's methodology by tracing his debts to and differences from Kant, Nietzsche, and Heidegger. Jeffrey T. Nealon's *Foucault beyond Foucault: Power and Its Intensifications since 1984* (2008) offers a revisionist reading of Foucault's work on power. Four highly influential works that engage Foucault's Collège de France lectures are Giorgio Agamben's *Homo Sacer: Sovereign Power and Bare Life* (1995; trans. 1998), Roberto Esposito's *Bios: Biopolitics and Philosophy* (2004; trans. 2008), Nikolas Rose's *The Politics of Life Itself: Biomedicine, Power and Subjectivity in the Twenty-First Century* (2007), and Wendy Brown's *Undoing the Demos: Neoliberalism's Stealth Revolution* (2015). A good way to start studying Foucault is to read through the many collections of essays on his work, which include *Foucault Now: Current Perspectives in Foucault Studies*, edited by James D. Faubion (2014); *The Government of Life: Foucault, Biopolitics, and Neoliberalism*, edited by Vanessa Lemm and Miguel Vatter (2014); *Biopower: Foucault and Beyond*, edited by Vernon W. Cisney and Nicolae Morar (2016); and *Foucault and Neoliberalism*, edited by Daniel Zamora and Michael C. Behrent (2016). Taylor's *Key Concepts* volume has a superb bibliography of Foucault's work, while both it and Falzon's *Companion to Foucault* have good bibliographies of secondary work.

Sigmund Freud

The English translation of Freud's collected works, carried out under the direction of James Strachey for Leonard and Virginia Woolf's Hogarth Press, has become in many ways more authoritative than any collected works in German. This *Standard Edition of the Complete Psychological Works of Sigmund Freud* (24 vols., 1953–74) is thus the edition most often cited. A handy collection of Freud's literary and artistic essays was edited by Neil Hertz in 1997 under the title *Writings on Art and Literature*. For more general purposes, see Peter Gay's *Freud Reader* (1989) and Elisabeth Young-Bruehl's *Freud on Women* (1990). Many volumes of Freud's copious correspondence (he never left a letter unanswered) have also been published. A monumental three-volume biography, *The Life and Work of Sigmund Freud*, was published by Ernest Jones, who knew Freud well (1953–57; abridged into one volume, 1961). *Freud: A Life for Our Time* (1988) by Peter Gay is excellent; his invaluable bibliographical essays appended to each chapter delineate all the major debates. In *Freud: Darkness in the Midst of Vision* (2000), the psychoanalyst Louis Breger engages with Freud and his work in unexpected and new ways. For an intriguing study of Freud's final years in London and how he was affected by the rise of totalitarian figures like Hitler, see Mark Edmundson's *The Death of Sigmund Freud: The Legacy of His Last Days* (2004).

Philip Rieff's *Freud: The Mind of the Moralist* (1959) and Peter Gay's *Reading Freud* (1990) are good introductions, the latter more literary. See also Paul Ricoeur's *Freud and Philosophy: An Essay on Interpretation* (1970) and Steven Marcus's *Freud and the Culture of Psychoanalysis: Studies in the Transition from Victorian Humanism to Modernity* (1984). For a collection of essays critical of Freud, see *Unauthorized Freud: Doubters Confront a Legend*, edited by Frederick C. Crews (1998).

On the centrality of Freud to contemporary critical theory, see the works of Jacques Lacan and Jacques Derrida. Related developments can be found in *The Literary Freud: Mechanisms of Defense and the Poetic Will*, edited by Joseph H. Smith (1980); Malcolm Bowie, *Psychoanalysis and the Future of Theory* (1993), speculates about Freud's continuing impact on discussions of art; while *Freud and Forbidden Knowledge*, edited by Peter L. Rudnytsky and Ellen Handler Spitz (1994), investigates the literary and religious sources of Freud's concepts. See also Graham Frankland's *Freud's Literary Culture* (2000).

For a good general approach to early feminist responses to Freud, see Juliet Mitchell's *Psychoanalysis and Feminism* (1974). A related work by Lisa Appignanesi and John Forrester, *Freud's Women* (1992), analyzes both the historical and the theoretical importance of femininity and of the many women who surrounded Freud as analysts and patients. Luce Irigaray, in *Speculum of the Other Woman* (1974; trans. 1985), and Sarah Kofman, in *The Enigma of Woman* (1980; trans. 1985), revisit Freud's writings on femininity from a French poststructuralist perspective. For a good overview of the intersection of Freud, feminism, and literary studies, see *In Dora's Case: Freud—Hysteria—Feminism*, edited by Charles Bernheimer and Claire Kahane (2d ed., 1990). A fascinating compilation by Susan Stanford Friedman, *Analyzing Freud: Letters of H.D., Bryher, and Their Circle* (2002), provides insight into Freud's mind as well as the minds of the modernist woman writer H.D. and her correspondents. In *Scenes of Projection: Recasting the Enlightenment Subject* (2015), Jill H. Casid engages Freudian psychoanalysis and feminist and queer theories to explore modernity, the modern subject, colonialism, and the history of projection.

On Freud's *Interpretation of Dreams*, see Lawrence M. Porter, *The Interpretation of Dreams: Freud's Theories Revisited* (1987); Alexander Welsh, *Freud's Wishful Dream Book* (1994); Harvie Ferguson, *The Lure of Dreams: Sigmund Freud and the Construction of Modernity* (1996); and the collection of interdisciplinary essays edited by Laura Marcus, *Sigmund Freud's "The Interpretation of Dreams": New Interdisciplinary Essays* (1999). Mary Bergstein's *Mirrors of Memory: Freud, Photography, and the History of Art* (2010) is a sweeping study of how Freud's photograph-filled library affected the psychoanalyst's unconscious, his interpretation of dreams, and the field itself.

Two essays on Freud's "Uncanny" deserve special note: Hélène Cixous, "Fiction and Its Phantoms," *New Literary History* 7 (1976), and "Freud and the Sandman" by Neil Hertz, published in his study of the sublime, *The End of the Line: Essays on Psychoanalysis and the Sublime* (1985). Contemporary literary studies have been greatly affected by Freud's notion of the uncanny, from those focusing on the Renaissance (Marjorie Garber, *Shakespeare's Ghost Writers: Literature as Uncanny Causality*, 1984) to the Enlightenment (Terry Castle, *The Female Thermometer: Eighteenth-Century Culture and the Invention of the Uncanny*, 1995) to the posthuman Gothic (Judith Halberstam, *Skin Shows: Gothic Horror and the Technology of Monsters*, 1995). Julia Kristeva, in *Strangers to Ourselves* (1988; trans. 1991), applies the notion to political science, while Anthony Vidler, in *The Architectural Uncanny: Essays in the Modern Unhomely* (1994), explores it in architecture.

E. L. McCallum's *Object Lessons: How to Do Things with Fetishism* (1999) offers a full-scale analysis of Freud's notion. Two books attempt to combine the Freudian and the Marxian versions of fetishism: Slavoj Žižek's *The Sublime Object of Ideology* (1989) and Rachel Bowlby's *Shopping with Freud* (1993). Alistair Rolls's *Paris and the Fetish: Primal Crime Scenes* (2014) uses Freud to explore fetishism in the French crime scenes, the novel, and poetics of Charles Baudelaire.

Much research deals with Freud's Jewishness: Marthe Robert's *From Oedipus to Moses: Freud's Jewish Identity* (1974; trans. 1976) and Susan Handelman's *Slayers of Moses: The Emergence of Rabbinic Interpretation in Modern Literary Theory* (1982) give two early versions of this analysis, later taken in other directions by Sander Gilman in both *Freud, Race, and Gender* (1993) and *The Case of Sigmund Freud: Medicine and Identity at the Fin de Siècle* (1993). Jay Geller's *On Freud's Jewish Body: Mitigating Circumcisions* (2007) and Adam Phillips's *Becoming Freud: The Making of a Psychoanalyst* (2014) continue this trend. Diana Fuss's *Identification Papers* (1995) reads Freud through the lenses of queer and postcolonial theory. Fuss also has written a superior comparative study of Freud's interior life in *The Sense of an Interior: Four Writers and the Rooms That Shaped Them* (2004). Stefan Bird-Pollan's *Hegel, Freud, Fanon: The Dialectic of Emancipation* (2015) brings Freudian theories in conversation with Hegelian and Fanonian dialectics of recognition and liberation.

The Cambridge Companion to Freud, edited by Jerome Neu (1991), is a useful resource. Among the bibliographies available in English, by far the best for the period up to 1988 is the bibliographical survey in Peter Gay's biography. An excellent synthesis of subsequent bibliographic materials and resources is provided by Breger's biography cited above, *Freud*. Breger's follow-up to *Freud*, *A Dream of Undying Fame: How Freud Betrayed His Mentor and Invented Psychoanalysis* (2009), provides an updated bibliography on Freud and the history of psychoanalysis.

Northrop Frye

Frye's major books include *Fearful Symmetry* (1947), *Anatomy of Criticism* (1957), *T. S. Eliot* (1963), *The Return of Eden: Five Essays on Milton's Epics* (1965), and *A Study of English Romanticism* (1968). He also wrote a number of books on Shakespeare, including *Fools of Time: Studies in Shakespearean Tragedy* (1967) and *Northrop Frye on Shakespeare* (1986). Among his collections of essays on diverse topics are *Fables of Identity: Studies in Poetic Mythology* (1963), *The Stubborn Structure: Essays on Criticism and Society* (1970), and *Spiritus Mundi: Essays on Literature, Myth, and Society* (1976). See also *Reading the World: Selected Writings, 1935–1976*, edited by Robert D. Denham (1990). In addition, Frye has been a significant force in turning the attention of literary scholars to the narratives and structural patterns of the Bible; his books on this subject include *The Great Code: The Bible and Literature* (1982) and *Words with Power: Being a Second Study of the Bible and Literature* (1990).

The University of Toronto Press has published the Collected Works of Northrop Frye in thirty volumes (1996–2012), under the general editorship of Alvin A. Lee; volume 30 is an index to the collection. See also *Northrop Frye's Uncollected Prose*, edited by Robert D. Denham (2015). Frye gave many interviews about his life, work, and career; see, for example, the collection *Northrop Frye in Conversation*, edited by David Cayley (1996). Also valuable is John Ayre's *Northrop Frye: A Biography* (1989). For further biographical contexts, see *Remembering Northrop Frye: Recollections by His Students and Others in the 1940s and 1950s*, edited by Robert D. Denham (2010); and Robert D. Denham, *Northrop Frye and Others: Twelve Writers Who Helped Shape His Thinking* (2015), on the impact of Aristotle, Longinus, and other writers, philosophers, and theologians on Frye's work. Another good resource is *The Northrop Frye Quote Book*, compiled by John Robert Colombo (2014).

Good brief overviews include Robert D. Denham, *Northrop Frye and Critical Method* (1974); David Cook, *Northrop Frye: A Vision of the New World* (1986); Ian Balfour, *Northrop Frye* (1988); and Joseph Adamson, *Northrop Frye: A Visionary Life* (1993). The most comprehensive studies are A. C. Hamilton, *Northrop Frye: An Anatomy of His Criticism* (1990), and Jonathan Locke Hart, *Northrop Frye: The Theoretical Imagination* (1994).

There are a number of helpful collections: *Northrop Frye in Modern Criticism*, edited by Murray Krieger (1966), which includes essays by Krieger, Angus Fletcher, William K. Wimsatt Jr., and Geoffrey H. Hartman, comments by Frye, and a checklist of his writings; *Centre and Labyrinth: Essays in Honour of Northrop Frye*, edited by Eleanor Cook et al. (1983); *Northrop Frye and Eighteenth-Century Studies*, edited by Howard D. Weinbrot—a special issue of *Eighteenth-Century Studies* 24 (winter 1990–91); *Visionary Poetics: Essays on Northrop Frye's Criticism*, edited by Robert D. Denham and Thomas Willard (1991); *The Legacy of Northrop Frye*, edited by Alvin A. Lee and Robert D. Denham (1994), which is especially useful in describing Frye's contributions to Canadian culture and his work on Romanticism, modernism, and religion; and Caterina Nella Cotrupi, *Northrop Frye and the Poetics of Process* (2000). Another excellent collection is *Rereading Frye*, edited by David Boyd and Imre Salusinsky (1999). In *The Twentieth-Century Humanist Critics: From Spitzer to Frye* (2007), William Calin examines Frye, Leo Spitzer, Erich Auerbach, C. S. Lewis, and others in the contexts of canon formation, humanism, and modernism. Recent scholarship includes *Northrop Frye's Canadian Literary Criticism and Its Influence*, edited by Branko Gorjup (2009); Michael Sinding, *Body of Vision: Northrop Frye and the Poetics of Mind* (2014), which connects Frye's studies of the imagination to cognitive poetics and cultural mythology; Brian Russell Graham, *The Necessary Unity of Opposites: The Dialectical Thinking of Northrop Frye* (2011), on Frye's dialectical approach to thought and effort to transcend binary constructs in his considerations of literature, politics, and society; and *Educating the Imagination: Northrop Frye Past, Present, and Future*, edited by Alan Bewell, Neil ten Kortenaar, and Germaine Warkentin (2015), which includes essays on Frye's symbolism; utopianism; similarities to and differences from Fredric Jameson, Paul de Man, and Jacques Derrida; and other topics.

See also Robert D. Denham, *Northrop Frye: An Annotated Bibliography of Primary and Secondary Sources* (1987), and the essays and bibliographies in the *Northrop Frye Newsletter*. The Northrop Frye Centre was established in 1988 at the University of Toronto. Also helpful is the bibliography in Bewell, ten Kortenaar, and Warkentin's *Educating the Imagination* (see above).

Henry Louis Gates Jr.

Gates first had an impact on literary studies through his editorial work: he rediscovered the earliest novel by an African American, Harriet E. Wilson's *Our Nig: Or, Sketches from the Life of a Free Black, in a Two Story White House, North* (1983), which had been privately printed in 1859. He also edited three important anthologies of contemporary criticism: *Black Literature and Literary Theory* (1984), *"Race," Writing, and Difference* (1986), and *Reading Black, Reading Feminist: A Critical Anthology* (1990). Gates's first two books of his own, *Figures in Black: Words, Signs, and the "Racial" Self* (1987), a collection of essays, and *The Signifying Monkey: A Theory of African-American Literary Criticism* (1988), which won the 1989 American Book Award, innovatively combine poststructuralist literary theory and indigenous African literary sources. His next book, *Loose Canons: Notes on the Culture Wars* (1992), which includes "Talking Black," collects Gates's essays from the late 1980s through the early 1990s on the canon, race, and criticism. Though focused on scholarly debates, it shows Gates's move from poststructural theory toward broader cultural issues, and from a dense, academic style toward a more lively one, accessible to a wider public.

Through the 1990s Gates shifted to address mainstream, popular audiences. His *Colored People: A Memoir* (1994) is an interesting account of his childhood in a small town in West Virginia. *The Future of the Race* (1996) is a dialogue between Gates and the philosopher Cornel West on the social possibilities for African Americans. Subsequently, Gates published a series of books composed of vignettes of notable African Americans, including *Thirteen Ways of Looking at a Black Man* (1997); *The African-American Century: How Black Americans Have Shaped Our Country*, with Cornel West (2000); and the brief and fascinating *The Trials of Phillis Wheatley: America's First Black Poet and Her Encounters with the Founding Fathers* (2003). In addition, he has looked at the wide legacy of the African diaspora in *Tradition and the Black Atlantic: Critical Theory in the African*

Diaspora (2010), *Black in Latin America* (2011), and *Life upon These Shores: Looking at African American History, 1513–2008* (2011). *The Henry Louis Gates, Jr. Reader*, edited by Abby Wolf (2012), collects primarily shorter essays, several reflecting on his family and career, and also includes five interviews.

A number of his projects since the late 1990s derive from television specials; in 1999 he wrote and narrated the six-part series *Wonders of the African World*, which was published as a book of the same title (1999). Among other projects, he has explored the often surprising genealogies of African Americans, resulting in *Finding Oprah's Roots: Finding Your Own* (2007), *Faces of America: How 12 Extraordinary People Discovered Their Pasts* (2010), and *Finding Your Roots: The Official Companion to the PBS Series* (2014). He also wrote, with Donald Yacovone, *The African Americans: Many Rivers to Cross* (2013), the companion to his six-part PBS documentary.

One of Gates's major goals is to increase the institutional presence of African American writers; thus he and Nellie Y. McKay were general editors of *The Norton Anthology of African American Literature* (1997; 3d ed., 2014). He is the editor of the Schomburg Library of Nineteenth-Century Black Women Writers, the Amistad Critical Studies in African American Literature (with K. Anthony Appiah), and the Black Periodical Literature Project, and he has edited or co-edited more than sixty volumes of African American writing and criticism on African American literature and culture. One of his most important editorial achievements has been producing, with Kwame Anthony Appiah, *Encarta Africana* (2000)—an encyclopedia in electronic format, on the model of the *Encyclopaedia Britannica*, of African American experience. It was published as *Africana* (1999) and subsequently expanded to the five-volume *Africana: The Encyclopedia of the African and African-American Experience* (2d ed., 2005). He also co-edited, with Evelyn Brooks-Higginbotham, the eight-volume *The African American National Biography* (2008), and, with David Bindman, the five-volume *The Image of the Black in Western Art* (2010–14).

Meg Greene's *Henry Louis Gates, Jr.: A Biography* (2012) provides a sketch of his life and career. In addition, Gates has also been the subject of two biographies for young adults.

Joyce A. Joyce's "'Who the Cap Fit': Unconsciousness and Unconscionableness in the Criticism of Houston A. Baker, Jr. and Henry Louis Gates, Jr.," *New Literary History* 18 (1987), charges Gates with elitism; it drew a sharp answer from Gates, distinguishing the different voices he uses in academic and public forums. In "Henry Louis Gates, Jr., and African American Literary Discourse," *New England Quarterly* 62 (1989), Wahneema Lubiano offers a balanced assessment of Gates's theory, which she defines as "precisely a theory of literary history," and argues against the charge that it is apolitical. Kenneth W. Warren's "Delimiting America: The Legacy of Du Bois," *American Literary History* 1 (1989), criticizes Gates's reliance on the image of professionalistic pluralism "to establish some non-political notion of black unity." Sandra Adell, in *Double-Consciousness/Double Bind: Theoretical Issues in Twentieth-Century Black Literature* (1994), relevantly compares Gates and Baker. Adolph L. Reed, in *W. E. B. Du Bois and American Political Thought: Fabianism and the Color Line* (1997), castigates Gates, especially in his later work, as a center-right apologist. Phillip M. Richards, *Black Heart: The Moral Life of Recent African American Letters* (2006), discusses Gates's influence and criticizes his separation of African American culture from the broader humanistic tradition. The prominent critic Houston A. Baker Jr., in *Betrayal: How Black Intellectuals Have Abandoned the Ideals of the Civil Rights Era* (2008), attacks Gates's centrism. Charles J. Ogletree Jr., in *The Presumption of Guilt: The Arrest of Henry Louis Gates, Jr. and Race, Class, and Crime in America* (2010), gives a detailed account of a controversial case when Gates was arrested for disorderly conduct after forcing open a door of his own home in Cambridge, Massachusetts. Greene's biography includes a selective bibliography of Gates's work.

Sandra M. Gilbert and Susan Gubar

Gilbert and Gubar have co-edited *Shakespeare's Sisters: Feminist Essays on Women Poets* (1979), *The Norton Anthology of Literature by Women: The Traditions in English* (1985; 3d ed., 2007), *The Female Imagination and the Modernist Aesthetic* (1986), *Mothersongs: Poems for, by, and about Mothers* (1995), and *Feminist Literary Theory and Criticism: A Reader* (2007). They also coauthored a three-volume sequel to their *Madwoman in the Attic* (1979) on women and modernism titled *No Man's Land: The Place of the Woman Writer in the Twentieth Century*, containing *The War of the Words* (1988), *Sexchanges* (1989), and *Letters from the Front* (1994). Paying more attention than *Madwoman in the Attic* did to the historical and ideological context of literary works and focusing less on masterpieces by great writers, *No Man's Land* reflects the changes in feminism and prevailing critical models during the 1980s. Gilbert and Gubar's satire of contemporary academic critical schools and movements, *Masterpiece Theatre: An Academic Melodrama*, was published in 1995. A second edition of *Madwoman in the Attic* was published in 2000 and features an indispensable introduction that traces the origins and reception of the book.

Sandra M. Gilbert's works are *Acts of Attention: The Poems of D. H. Lawrence* (1973); the nonfiction account of the death of her husband, *Wrongful Death: A Medical Tragedy* (1995), and *Death's Door: Modern Dying and the Way We Grieve*

(2006); *Rereading Women; Thirty Years of Exploring Our Literary Traditions (2011); The Culinary Imagination: From Myth to Modernity* (2014); and nine books of poetry: *In the Fourth World* (1978), *Summer Kitchen* (1983), *Emily's Bread* (1984), *Blood Pressure* (1988), *Ghost Volcano* (1995), *Kissing the Bread* (2000), *The Italian Collection: Poems of Heritage* (2003), *Belongings* (2005), and *Aftermath* (2011). Biographical information can be found in *Contemporary Authors, New Revision Series* 106 (2002).

Susan Gubar has co-edited *For Adult Users Only: The Dilemmas of Violent Pornography* (1989), with Joan Hoff; and *English Inside and Out: The Places of Literary Criticism* (1992), with Jonathan Kamholtz. She is the author of *Racechanges: White Skin, Black Face in American Culture* (1997), *Critical Condition: Feminism at the Turn of the Century* (2000), *Poetry after Auschwitz: Remembering What One Never Knew* (2003), *Rooms of Our Own* (2006), *Judas: A Biography* (2008), *Memoir of a Debulked Women: Enduring Ovarian Cancer* (2012), and *Reading and Writing Cancer: How Words Heal* (2016). Biographical information can be found in *Contemporary Authors, New Revision Series* 70 (1999) and in Robin Wilson's "A Feminist Professor's Closing Chapters," *Chronicle of Higher Education*, April 22, 2012.

Toril Moi's famous critique of *Madwoman in the Attic* in her *Sexual/Textual Politics* (1985) encapsulates the "French feminist" objections to Gilbert and Gubar's work. Elizabeth Rosdeitcher's "Interview with Sandra M. Gilbert and Susan Gubar," *Critical Texts* 6.1 (1989), is a good place to start in studying their work. A range of critical responses can be traced in Laura E. Donaldson, "The Miranda Complex: Colonialism and the Question of Feminist Reading," *Diacritics* 18.3 (1988); Jane Marcus, "The Asylums of Antaeus: Women, War, and Madness," in *The New Historicism* (ed. H. Aram Veeser, 1989); and *Making Feminist History: The Literary Scholarship of Sandra M. Gilbert and Susan Gubar*, edited by William E. Cain (1994). Annette R. Federico's edited collection *Gilbert and Gubar's "The Madwoman in the Attic" after Thirty Years* (2009) provides valuable reflections on that work's legacy and an important introduction by Gilbert. Also useful are Jacqueline Vaught Brogan's interview with Gilbert in *Women's Studies* 38 (2009) and Janet Gezari's "Sandra M. Gilbert and Susan Gubar's *The Madwoman in the Attic*," *Essays in Criticism* 56 (2006).

Paul Gilroy

To date Paul Gilroy has written eight books. *There Ain't No Black in the Union Jack: The Cultural Politics of Race and Nation* (1987; new intro., 2002), his first, examines a twenty-year evolution in postwar British racial politics. Emphasizing the interrelations among discourses of race, class, and nation, he argues that British politicians and scholars on both sides of the political divide fail to take account of insidious racial dynamics. In *Small Acts: Thoughts on the Politics of Black Cultures* (1993), published in the same year as *The Black Atlantic*, discussed above in the headnote, Gilroy combines photos, art reviews, speeches, and interviews with bell hooks, Toni Morrison, and others to highlight differences between black British culture and the diverse black community in the United States. In *Between Camps: Race, Identity and Nationalism at the End of the Colour Line* (2000), he claims that individuals currently live in "camps"—defined in terms of race, nationality, culture, and religion—and looks to the concept of diaspora, which decouples territory and identity, to heal the rifts between them. *Against Race: Imagining Political Culture beyond the Color Line* (2000), a revised version of *Between Camps* for an American audience, continues to argue against race as an organizing principle in collective human experience. In his *After Empire: Melancholia or Convivial Culture?* (2004), published in the United States with the subtitle *Multiculture of Postcolonial Melancholia*, Gilroy examines race hierarchies and their consequences, notably involvements in colonialism and fascism. *Black Britain—A Photographic History* (2007), with a preface by Stuart Hall, uses photography to trace the cultural role of African and Caribbean descendents living in Great Britain. Originally delivered as the W. E. B. Du Bois Lectures at Harvard University, *Darker Than Blue: On the Moral Economies of Black Atlantic Culture* (2010) examines at once the global influence of black American culture, particularly music, and the acquisitive nature of American consumer capitalism, which has done harm to black political cultures as the right to acquire things, lauded in the music, has replaced the demands for black rights and social and restorative justice in the music of the civil rights and black power generation.

While Gilroy's calls for cosmopolitan and utopian conceptions of race, culture, and identity have been widely influential, they have also generated a great deal of controversy among academics and activists. Among articles and book chapters focusing on *The Black Atlantic* are Nadi Edwards's "Roots, and Some Routes Not Taken," *Found Object* 4 (1994), which faults Gilroy for equating "black community" with "oppressed"; Louis Chude-sokei's "The Black Atlantic Paradigm: Paul Gilroy and the Fractured Landscape of 'Race,'" *American Quarterly* 48 (1996), a book review that finds Gilroy's view of Black Atlantic identities too narrow; J. Blaine Hudson's "The African Diaspora and the 'Black Atlantic': An African American Perspective," *Negro History Bulletin* 60 (1997), which maintains that Gilroy's construct is not valid for exploring the historical dimensions of African diaspora before 1800; and Colin Palmer's "Defining and Studying the Modern African Diaspora," *Perspectives: A Newsletter of the American Historical Association* 36.6

(1998), which contends that Gilroy pays insufficient attention to the African continent and to African diasporic movement outside the Atlantic. In *Monsters and Revolutionaries: Colonial Family Romance and Métissage* (1999), Françoise Vergès raises the same criticisms as Chude-sokei and Hudson, adding that an exclusive focus on the Atlantic slave trade hinders the explorations of other areas, such as forced migrations across the Indian Ocean and the interactions of diasporic Africans with the Islamic world. Houston Baker, in *Turning South Again: Re-thinking Modernism/Re-reading Booker T.* (2001), takes issue with Gilroy's neglect of American blackness and also asserts that his discussion of modernity is limiting. Other critiques of Paul Gilroy's approach, such as Cheryl Johnson-Odim's "From Both Sides Now: Gendering the Black Atlantic," in *Women in African Studies: Scholarly Publishing* (ed. Cassandra Rachel Veney and Paul Tiyambe Zeleza, 2001), take up the issue of race and gender. Edited anthologies that critically examine Gilroy's theoretical frameworks and his condemnations of ethnicity and nationality include *Beyond the Black Atlantic: Relocating Modernization and Technology*, edited by Walter Goebel and Saskia Schabio (2006), and *Recharting the Black Atlantic: Modern Cultures, Local Communities, Global Connections*, edited by Annalisa Oboe and Anna Scacchi (2008). Criticism of Gilroy's Anglophone-centered Black Atlantic can be found in *Comparative Perspectives on the Black Atlantic*, edited by Jossianna Arroyo and Elizabeth Marchant, a special issue of *Comparative Literature Studies* (49.2 [2012]); its articles expand Gilroy's concept of the Black Atlantic world and the African diaspora to include Latin America and the Caribbean as well as Luso-Africa and the Cape Verde Islands, while *Retrieving the Human: Reading Paul Gilroy*, edited by Rebecka Rutledge Fisher and Jay Garcia (2014), moves beyond *The Black Atlantic* to examine a range of Gilroy's interrogations of neoliberal politics, identity politics, empire, Frantz Fanon's theories of oppression, among other matters.

As part of the Routledge Critical Thinkers series, Paul Williams's *Paul Gilroy* (2013) engages Gilroy's work in its totality as well as the various influences on his thought. The volume provides a useful annotated bibliography of his work.

Gorgias of Leontini

D. M. MacDowell has published the Greek text of the *Encomium on Helen* with a parallel English translation (1989). Michael Gagarin and Paul Woodruff include all the extant fragments attributed to Gorgias in *Early Greek Political Thought from Homer to the Sophists* (1995). Their translations are based on the Greek text established by Thomas Buchheim in his edition with German translation, *Reden, Fragmente, und Testimonien* (1989). The standard account of the sophists is *The Sophists* by W. K. C. Guthrie; the volume, published separately in 1971, was originally part of volume 3 of his *History of Greek Philosophy* (6 vols., 1962–81). George Kerferd offers a comprehensive interpretation of the whole movement in *The Sophistic Movement* (1981). Susan C. Jarratt's *Rereading the Sophists: Classical Rhetoric Refigured* (1991) reads the sophists with and against contemporary literary theories, including feminism and deconstruction. In *The Birth of Rhetoric: Gorgias, Plato and Their Successors* (1996), Robert Wardy sets Gorgias's radical epistemological relativism against Plato's defense of philosophy in his dialogue *Gorgias*, arguing that sophist and philosopher set the terms of later debates about the relationship between rhetoric and philosophy. Bruce McComiskey's *Gorgias and the New Sophistic Rhetoric* (2002) places Gorgias's antifoundationalism, his refusal to ground philosophy in a preexisting truth or reality, in the context of fifth- and fourth-century B.C.E. Athenian politics, arguing that Plato's advocacy of philosophical truth served the interests of oligarchic government, while Gorgias's antifoundationalism promoted democracy. C. J. Classen's *Sophistik* (1976) includes a thorough and useful bibliography. More recently, in her book on Helen of Troy, *Helen of Troy: Beauty, Myth, Devastation* (2013), Ruby Blondell situates Gorgias's encomium within a Greek tradition of writing about Helen. Her chapter on Gorgias proffers a reading that explores his failure to challenge the gender dynamics of the Greek culture in which he wrote while engaging with serious philosophical debates about human agency, moral responsibility, and the power of persuasive discourse.

Gerald Graff

Stemming from his doctoral dissertation, Graff's first book, *Poetic Statement and Critical Dogma* (1970), attacks the lack of social concern evinced by the New Criticism and other approaches. *Literature against Itself: Literary Ideas in Modern Society* (1979) extends his polemic to contemporary theory. Through the 1980s Graff turned his attention more concertedly to the university, in 1985 co-editing (with Reginald Gibbons) a collection, *Criticism in the University*; publishing *Professing Literature: An Institutional History* (1987; 20th anniv. ed., 2007), regarded as the standard history of the discipline; and compiling (with Michael Warner) a collection, *The Origins of Literary Studies in America: A Documentary History* (1988). *Beyond the Culture Wars: How Teaching the Conflicts Can Revitalize Higher Education* (1992) presents his program for "teaching the conflicts." His program inspired two casebooks co-edited with James Phelan, *Adventures of Huckleberry Finn: A Case Study in Critical Controversy* (1995) and *The Tempest: A Case Study in Critical Controversy* (2000). Through the 1990s, Graff focused more on the accessibility of academic work, publishing

Clueless in Academe: How Schooling Obscures the Life of the Mind (2003) and a slim textbook, *"They Say/I Say": The Moves That Matter in Academic Writing* (2006; 3d ed., 2014), co-written with his spouse, Cathy Birkenstein, which provides easily understood "templates" to help people write.

Graff's views have been widely discussed. A special issue of the journal *Critical Exchange* (23 [1987]) responds to his early work. The collection *Teaching the Conflicts: Gerald Graff, Curricular Reform, and the Culture Wars*, edited by William E. Cain (1994), gathers eleven essays assessing Graff's conflictual method; Cain's introduction provides an excellent survey. In *University in Ruins* (1996), Bill Readings assimilates Graff's conflictual model in recommending that the university be a community of "dissensus," but he argues that Graff's model itself becomes "a unified object of professional discourse." Don Bialostosky, in "Is Gerald Graff Machiavellian?" *Style* 33 (1999), provocatively compares Graff's notion of the productive uses of conflict with Machiavelli's prescriptions for power. See also the symposium "Teaching the Conflicts at Twenty Years," *Pedagogy* 3 (2003), and a roundtable on his book *Clueless in Academe* in *Pedagogy* 5 (2005). Amanda Anderson sympathetically considers Graff's focus on how we argue, but finds that we need a stronger sense of disciplinary commitments in "The Way We Talk About the Way We Teach Now," *Profession* (2009). "Only Connect: An Interview with Gerald Graff," conducted by Jeffrey J. Williams, reviews Graff's career; it is collected in *Critics at Work: Interviews 1993–2003* (ed. Williams, 2004).

Antonio Gramsci

The complete *Prison Notebooks*, edited by Joseph A. Buttigieg (3 vols., 1992–2007), with an indispensable introduction and superb scholarly apparatus, is the scholarly edition. But *Selections from the Prison Notebooks*, edited by Quentin Hoare and Geoffrey Newell Smith (1971), remains the most accessible text for the general reader. *The Gramsci Reader: Selected Writings, 1916–1935*, edited by David Forgacs (2000), is also a good place to start. *Letters from Prison*, edited by Frank Rosengarten (2 vols., 1994), is an informative supplement to the *Prison Notebooks*. Parts of Gramsci's work before the prison years have been translated, including *Selections from Political Writings*, edited by Quintin Hoare (2 vols., 1977–78); *Selections from Cultural Writings*, edited by David Forgacs and Geoffrey Nowell Smith (1991); and *Pre-Prison Writings*, edited by Richard Bellamy (1994). There are two biographies: Arnold Davidson's *Antonio Gramsci: Toward an Intellectual Biography* (1977) focuses on Gramsci's intellectual development, while Giuseppe Fiori's *Antonio Gramsci: Life of a Revolutionary* (1966; trans., rev. ed. 1990) uses new sources to offer the most comprehensive account of Gramsci's life.

Three excellent general introductions are Steve Jones's *Antonio Gramsci* (2006), John Schwarzmantel's *The Routledge Guidebook to Gramsci's "Prison Notebooks"* (2015), and George Hoare and Nathan Sperber's *An Introduction to Antonio Gramsci* (2016). Broader engagements with Gramsci's work can be found in Walter L. Adamson's *Hegemony and Revolution: A Study of Antonio Gramsci's Political and Cultural Theory* (1980), Anne Showstack Sassoon's *Gramsci and Contemporary Politics: Beyond Pessimism of the Intellect* (2000), and Peter D. Thomas's *The Gramscian Moment: Philosophy, Hegemony and Marxism* (2009). The four volumes of essays collected in *Antonio Gramsci: Critical Assessments of Leading Political Philosophers*, edited by James Martin (2002), contain many important and illuminating responses to and expansions on Gramsci's ideas. Perry Anderson's *Considerations on Western Marxism* (1976), a key place to begin looking into Western Marxism, discusses Gramsci at some length. Ernesto Laclau and Chantal Mouffe's *Hegemony and Socialist Strategy* (1985) joins Gramsci with poststructuralist thought to provide a fundamental rethinking of Marxist theory. The selections by Stuart Hall and Dick Hebdige in this anthology record the influence of Gramsci on cultural studies; David Harris's *From Class Struggle to the Politics of Pleasure: The Effects of Gramscianism on Cultural Studies* (1993) and *Stuart Hall: Critical Dialogues in Cultural Studies*, edited by David Morley and Kuan-Hsing Chen (1996), explore this connection further. A good, although incomplete, bibliography can be found in Schwarzmantel's *Routledge Guide* (see above).

Stephen J. Greenblatt

Stephen Greenblatt's first interest was the modern novel, and his undergraduate thesis, *Three Modern Satirists: Waugh, Orwell, and Huxley* (1965), was published in the Yale College Series. During graduate school he turned to Renaissance literature, resulting in his second book, *Sir Walter Ralegh: The Renaissance Man and His Roles* (1973), which derived from his dissertation and discussed what would prove a recurrent theme: how authors fashion their personas. With his next book, *Renaissance Self-Fashioning: From More to Shakespeare* (1980), Greenblatt captured wide attention in literary studies. During the 1980s he was involved in developing the New Historicism, notably through the journal *Representations*, which he founded with colleagues at Berkeley in 1982. Greenblatt also had a hand in editing several collections, including *Allegory and Representation* (1981), with a lead essay by Paul de Man; *The Power of Forms in the English Renaissance* (1982), which introduced the phrase "the new historicism"; and two collections of essays selected from

Representations, *Representing the English Renaissance* (1988) and *New World Encounters* (1993). His own *Shakespearean Negotiations: The Circulation of Social Energy in Renaissance England* (1988) provides models of New Historical reading in five influential and often-reprinted chapters on different Shakespeare plays. *Learning to Curse: Essays in Early Modern Culture* (1990) gathers essays practicing and reflecting on the New Historicism, including "Resonance and Wonder." *Marvelous Possessions: The Wonder of the New World* (1991) develops Greenblatt's concept of wonder in literature focusing on the New World.

Through the 1990s Greenblatt became a prominent public figure representing literary studies. He served as president of the Modern Language Association, co-editing (with Giles Gunn) *Redrawing the Boundaries: The Transformation of English and American Literary Studies* (1992), and became general editor of *The Norton Shakespeare* (1997; 3d ed., 2015) and general editor of *The Norton Anthology of English Literature* (9th ed., 2012). In 2000 Greenblatt wrote, with Catherine Gallagher (a Berkeley colleague on the board of *Representations*), a book defining his mode of criticism, *Practicing New Historicism*. His international standing as today's leading scholar of Shakespeare has been cemented by *Hamlet in Purgatory* (2001); the popular book *Will in the World: How Shakespeare Became Shakespeare* (2004), which was a finalist for the Pulitzer Prize; and *Shakespeare's Freedom* (2010). He also tried his hand at drama, co-writing *Cardenio* (performed 2008), and has since focused on cultural transmission, in the co-written volume *Cultural Mobility: A Manifesto* (2010) and in two trade books, *The Swerve: How the World Became Modern* (2011) and *The Rise and Fall of Adam and Eve* (2017). *The Greenblatt Reader*, edited by Michael Payne (2005), provides a good sampling of his writing. For an account of his background and early career in his own words, see "Critical Self-Fashioning: An Interview with Stephen J. Greenblatt," conducted by Jeffrey J. Williams, *Minnesota Review*, n.s. 71–72 (2009).

There is a large body of commentary on Greenblatt's work. Many responses have followed his model, especially in early modern scholarship, though some (especially Marxist critics) question his political stance. Donald Pease, "Toward a Sociology of Literary Knowledge: Greenblatt, Colonialism, and the New Historicism," in *Consequences of Theory* (ed. Jonathan Arac and Barbara Johnson, 1991), is a careful exposition of Greenblatt that criticizes him for perpetuating a linguistic colonialism, despite his disclaimers. Chapters of Scott Wilson's *Cultural Materialism: Theory and Practice* (1995) and Claire Colebrook's *New Literary Histories: New Historicism and Contemporary Criticism* (1997) provide useful overviews. *Critical Self-Fashioning: Stephen Greenblatt and the New Historicism*, edited by Jürgen Pieters (1999), gathers several essays from European scholars assessing Greenblatt; see also Pieters's own *Moments of Negotiation: The New Historicism of Stephen Greenblatt* (2001), which puts Greenblatt's work in a vast theoretical frame. *The Touch of the Real: Essays in Early Modern Culture*, edited by Philippa Kelly (2002), presents essays in honor of Greenblatt from Australian scholars, though it focuses more broadly on extending historicist work. For an intriguing account of Greenblatt's method, see Ivo Kamps, "New Historicizing the New Historicism; or, Did Stephen Greenblatt Watch the Evening News in Early 1968?" in *Historicizing Theory* (ed. Peter C. Herman, 2004); in the same volume, see also Jonathan Gil Harris, "Stephen Greenblatt's 'X'-Files: The Rhetoric of Containment and Invasive Disease in 'Invisible Bullets' and 'The Sources of Soviet Conduct.'" Mark Robson's *Stephen Greenblatt* (2008) offers a short overview. See also Neema Parvini, *Shakespeare and Contemporary Theory: New Historicism and Cultural Materialism* (2012).

The Greenblatt Reader provides a complete list of Greenblatt's publications up to 2003, and Robson's *Stephen Greenblatt* includes a selected, annotated bibliography of Greenblatt's work and commentary on him.

Jürgen Habermas

Almost all of Habermas's major works have been translated into English (below, the German publication date is followed by the date of the translation). For those coming to Habermas for the first time, the interviews with him collected in *Autonomy and Solidarity*, edited by Peter Dews (1986), offer an accessible overview; in *The Philosophical Discourse of Modernity* (1985; 1987), Habermas articulates his basic position vis-à-vis the attacks on reason by Nietzsche, Adorno, Derrida, and Foucault. His other works include *The Structural Transformation of the Public Sphere: An Inquiry into a Category of Bourgeois Society* (1962; 1989); *On the Logic of the Social Sciences* (1967; 1988); *Knowledge and Human Interests* (1968; 1971); *Legitimation Crisis* (1973; 1975); *Communication and the Evolution of Society* (1976; 1979); *The Theory of Communicative Action* (2 vols., 1981; 1984–87); *Moral Consciousness and Communicative Action* (1983; 1990); *The New Conservatism: Cultural Criticism and the Historians' Debate* (1985, 1987; 1989); *Between Facts and Norms: Contributions to a Discourse Theory of Law and Democracy* (1992; 1996); *The Inclusion of the Other: Studies in Political Theory* (1996; 1998); *The Postnational Constellation: Political Essays* (1998; 2001); *Truth and Justification* (1999; 2003); *The Future of Human Nature* (2001; 2003); *Time of Transitions* (2001; 2006); *The Divided West* (2004; 2006); *Dialectics of Secularization: On Reason and Religion*, with Pope Benedict XVI (2005; 2006); *Europe: The Faltering Project* (2009); *An Awareness of What Is Missing: Faith and Reason in a Post-Secular Age* (2008; 2010); *The Lure of Technocracy* (2015); *Postmetaphysical Thinking II* (2017); and *Philosophical Introductions* (2017). Eight volumes gather English translations of Habermas's essays written at various times: *Philosophical-Political Profiles* (1983), *Postmetaphysical Thinking: Philosophical Essays* (1994), *Justification and Application: Remarks on Discourse Ethics* (1993), *A Berlin Republic: Writings on Germany* (1997), *On the Pragmatics of Communication* (1998), *The Liberating Power of Symbols: Philosophical Essays* (2001), *Religion and Rationality: Essays on Reason, God, and Modernity* (2002), and *Between Naturalism and Religion: Philosophical Essays* (2005; 2008). Two books both collect and contextualize discussions between Habermas and Derrida: *Philosophy in a Time of Terror: Dialogues with Jürgen Habermas and Jacques Derrida*, interviewed by Giovanna Borradori (2003), and *The Derrida-Habermas Reader*, edited by Lasse Thomassen (2006). Biographical information can be found in Egbert Klautk's entry on Habermas in *Encyclopedia of Modern Political Thought* (ed. Gregory Claeys, 2013). Stefan Müller-Doohm's *Habermas: A Biography* (2014; trans. 2016) is the first full-length biography.

There are several superb overviews of Habermas's work, whose different emphases are indicated by their titles: Andrew Edgar's *The Philosophy of Habermas* (2005), Luke Goode's *Jürgen Habermas: Democracy and the Public Sphere* (2005), Pauline Johnson's *Habermas: Rescuing the Public Sphere* (2006), Uwe Steinhoff's *The Philosophy of Jürgen Habermas* (2009, an abridged trans. of a 2006 work), and the most comprehensive of the lot, *The Habermas Handbook*, edited by Hauke Brunkhorst, Regina Kreide, and Cristina Lafont (2018). Of the in-depth studies of Habermas, two of particular interest to literary studies are J. M. Bernstein's *Recovering Ethical Life: Jürgen Habermas and the Future of Critical Theory* (1995) and Pieter Duvenage's *Habermas and Aesthetics: The Limits of Communicative Reason* (2003). Of special value is David Couzens Hoy and Thomas A. McCarthy's *Critical Theory* (1994), which lays out the case for each side in the Habermas/poststructuralist debate. The best place to encounter the debates sparked by Habermas's work is in the large number of collections of responses to it. Noteworthy are *Habermas and Modernity*, edited by Richard J. Bernstein (1985); *Habermas and the Public Sphere*, edited by Craig Calhoun (1992), which contains the highly influential essay "Rethinking the Public Sphere: A Contribution to the Critique of Actually Existing Democracy," by the feminist philosopher Nancy Fraser; *The Cambridge Companion to Habermas*, edited by Stephen K. White (1995); *Feminists Read Habermas: Gendering the Subject of Discourse*, edited by Johanna Meehan (1995); *Habermas and the Unfinished Project of Modernity: Critical Essays on "The Philosophical Discourse of Modernity,"* edited by Maurizio Passerin d'Entrèves and Seyla Benhabib (1997); *Habermas: A Critical Reader*, edited by Peter Dews (1999); and a very comprehensive four-volume collection, *Jürgen Habermas*, edited by David M. Rasmussen and James Swindal (2002). The Bernstein and Calhoun collections have proved particularly influential in shaping the reception of Habermas's work. *Jürgen Habermas: Key Concepts*, edited by Barbara Fultner (2011), provides an excellent overview of Habermas's work along with a complete bibliography of his work and a substantial bibliography of secondary works.

Judith Jack Halberstam

Halberstam's first book, *Skin Shows: Gothic Horror and the Technology of Monsters* (1995), traces the cultural object of the monster from nineteenth-century Gothic novels like Mary Shelley's *Frankenstein* up to contemporary Hollywood movies like *Texas Chainsaw Massacre*. Using this broad range of texts, she argues both that the monster is rewritten over time to reflect "historically and culturally conditioned fears" which emerge from ideas about otherness and difference and that graphic violence empowers readers. Her second book—and her most influential—is *Female Masculinity* (1998), which explores butch/femme lesbian roles, transsexual and "transgender dyke" communities, and contemporary drag king performances, as she articulates her larger project of examining gender construction and pursuing a concept of masculinity without men. *The Drag King Book* (1999), which Halberstam coauthored with Del LaGrace Volcano under the name "Judith 'Jack' Halberstam," investigates drag king communities and performances for a broad audience. Her next book, *In a Queer Time and Place: Transgender Bodies, Subcultural Lives* (2005), considers the transgendered body's representation in the media and in queer art, while *The Queer Art of Failure* (2011) critiques the logic of failure and success in our culture and argues that failing offers creative possibilities, freedom, and other rewards through its resistance, subversion, and unmaking of punishing norms. Halberstam's sixth book, *Gaga Feminism: Sex, Gender and the End of Normal* (2012), analyzes the pop feminist icon Lady Gaga as a way to explore gender identity and sexuality in twenty-first-century feminism.

One important critical response to Halberstam is Pat Califia's "Dildo Envy and Other Phallic Adventures," in *A Dick for a Day: What Would You Do If You Had One?* (ed. Fiona Giles, 1997). Taking issue with Halberstam's classification "butch" (which straddles the line between lesbian and transgendered), Califia claims that it blocks the flow of desire and reflects self-hate rather than self-definition and understanding. Halberstam responds to Califia's criticisms in *Female Masculinity*, in a chapter titled "Lesbian Masculinity:

Even Stone Butches Get the Blues." Chris Beasley's *Gender and Sexuality: Critical Theory, Critical Thinkers* (2005) argues that Halberstam's work on masculinity "stands at an interesting remove from Queer": because her work enables and includes transgender desire and all its physical manifestations, her position is distinct from that of other queer theorists, who set "queer" and "transgender" in opposition to one another. Halberstam addresses some of these issues in "Within the New Moment," an interview by Vicki Crowley in *Discourse* 25 (2004). In *Beauty and Misogyny: Harmful Cultural Practices in the West* (2005), Sheila Jeffreys asserts that Halberstam's notion of female masculinity is both apolitical, in that it fails to grapple with masculinity as "the product of male dominance," and antifeminist, in that liberation for women is identified with performing masculinity and disavowing feminity.

Several interviews helpfully introduce and supplement Halberstam's written work; see Annmarie Jagose's detailed "Masculinity without Men," *Genders*, no. 29 (1999); Mathias Danbolt's "The Eccentric Archive," *Trikster—Nordic Queer Journal*, no. 1 (2008), in which Halberstam discusses the rationale behind her choice of texts; and Jeffrey J. Williams's "The Drag of Masculinity: An Interview with Judith 'Jack' Halberstam," *symplokē* 19 (2011), which offers a wide-ranging back-and-forth conversation about Halberstam's biography, concepts, and writings, plus feminist politics.

Stuart Hall

Stuart Hall's work (scattered in numerous journals and edited volumes) is slowly being collected in book form in a series titled Stuart Hall: Selected Writings, to be published by Duke University Press under the general editorship of Bill Schwarz and Catherine Hall; already in print (with more promised) are *The Hard Road to Renewal* (1988); *Cultural Studies 1983: A Theoretical History*, edited by Jennifer Darryl Slack and Lawrence Grossberg (2016); *Selected Political Writings: The Great Moving Right Show and Other Essays*, edited by Sally Davison, David Featherstone, Michael Rustin, and Bill Schwarz (2017); and *The Popular Arts* (2018). *The Fateful Triangle: Race, Ethnicity, Nation*, edited by Kobena Mercer (2017), is drawn from lectures delivered at Harvard in 1994. *Familiar Stranger: A Life Between Two Islands* (2017) collects his autobiographical reflections. The most influential collaborative texts done by various British cultural studies groups working with Hall (volumes that usually contain essays by Hall) are *The Popular Arts*, edited by Stuart Hall and Paddy Whannel (1964); *Resistance through Rituals: Youth Subcultures in Post-War Britain*, edited by Stuart Hall and Tony Jefferson (1976); *Policing the Crisis: Mugging, the State, and Law and Order*, edited by Stuart Hall et al. (1978); *Culture, Media, Language: Working Papers in Cultural Studies*, edited by Stuart Hall et al. (1980); *New Times: The Changing Face of Politics in the 1990s*, edited by Stuart Hall and Martin Jacques (1990); *Questions of Cultural Identity*, edited by Stuart Hall and Paul du Gay (1996); *Modernity: An Introduction to Modern Societies*, edited by Stuart Hall et al. (1996); and *Representation: Cultural Representations and Signifying Practices*, edited by Stuart Hall (1997). *Different* (2001) is a collection of contemporary photographs by people of color selected by Hall along with explanatory text by him. *Women Take Issue: Aspects of Women's Subordination*, edited by the Women's Studies Group, Centre for Contemporary Cultural Studies (1978), and *The Empire Strikes Back: Race and Racism in 70s Britain*, edited by the Centre for Contemporary Cultural Studies (1982), are important early collections that extend cultural studies into studies of gender, race, and postcolonialism. The best biographical source is Hall's own *Familiar Stranger* (2017), which can be supplemented with Caryl Philip's "Interview with Stuart Hall," *Bomb*, no. 58 (1997). Also of biographical interest is the film *The Stuart Hall Project* (2013, dir. John Akomfrah).

Chris Rojek's *Stuart Hall* (2003) is by far the best overview of Hall's life and work, although Helen Davis's *Understanding Stuart Hall* (2004) is also worth consulting. *Stuart Hall: Critical Dialogues in Cultural Studies*, edited by David Morley and Kuan-Hsing Chen (1996), collects several key essays by Hall along with responses to his work; it can be supplemented by *Without Guarantees: In Honour of Stuart Hall*, edited by Paul Gilroy, Lawrence Grossberg, and Angela McRobbie (2000), a collection of essays that includes responses to Hall's work by Judith Butler and Gayatri Chakravorty Spivak among many others. Fredric Jameson, "On Cultural Studies" (1993), in *The Identity in Question* (ed. John Rajchman, 1995), provides a sophisticated short introduction to cultural studies. Dennis Dworkin's *Cultural Marxism in Postwar Britain: History, the New Left, and the Origins of Cultural Studies* (1997) and Lawrence Grossberg's *Cultural Studies in the Future Tense* (2010) usefully locate Hall's work in the context of cultural studies more generally. Michael Bérubé's *The Left at War* (2009) mobilizes Hall's work as a guide for thinking about the Left's responses to neoconservatism. The essays published after Hall's death in the online journal *Open Democracy* (www.opendemocracy.net/ourkingdom/collections/stuart-hall-cultural-theorist-1932-2014; accessed July 12, 2017) offer a valuable overview of his career and influence; the obituaries by Robin Blackburn (in *New Left Review*, no. 86 [2014]) and Geoff Eley (in *History Workshop Journal*, no. 79 [2015]) along with the collection of responses to his work in *South Atlantic Quarterly*, no. 115 (October 2016), and Hua Hsu's essay, "Stuart Hall and the Rise of Cultural Studies," *New Yorker*, July 17, 2017, offer further reflections on his work and its impact. While waiting for the Duke University Press series to be completed, an assiduous reader can compile a fairly complete list of Hall's scattered writings by consulting the bibliographies in the books of Morley and Chen, Rojek, and Davis, cited above.

Donna Haraway

Haraway's dissertation appeared as *Crystals, Fabrics, and Fields: Metaphors of Organicism in Twentieth-Century Developmental Biology* (1976). Her "Manifesto for Cyborgs" (1985), first published in the journal *Socialist Review*, has been reprinted many times. *Primate Visions: Gender, Race, and Nature in the World of Modern Science* (1989), Haraway's second book, examines the cultural and ideological ramifications of twentieth-century primatology. In addition, she has published two collections of her early essays: *Simians, Cyborgs, and Women: The Reinvention of Nature* (1991) and *Modest_Witness@Second_Millennium. FemaleMan©Meets OncoMouse™* (1997). Haraway's most celebrated essays have been collected in *The Haraway Reader* (2004). Her more recent work includes *The Companion Species Manifesto: Dogs, People, and Significant Otherness* (2003) and *When Species Meet* (2008). *How Like a Leaf* (2000) is a book-length interview of Haraway by a former student, Thyrza Goodeve, that explores the relationships between Haraway's life, her teaching, and her scholarship. *Manifestly Haraway* (2016) bundles "Cyborg Manifesto" with "Companion Species Manifesto," together with a conversation between Haraway and Cary Wolfe that explores the manifesto as a theoretical genre.

During the 1990s most critical engagement with Haraway's writing came in the form of articles. Among the earliest evaluations is Allison Fraiberg's "Of AIDS, Cyborgs, and Other Indiscretions: Resurfacing the Body in the Postmodern" (1991), published in the online journal *Postmodern Culture* (vol. 1), together with a response by David Porush. A 1993 special issue of the journal *Genders*, titled *Cyberpunk: Technologies of Cultural Identity*, examines the ways in which Haraway's analysis of the cyborg figures in several cyberpunk texts. For a more advanced evaluation of Haraway's manifesto, see Chela Sandoval, "Re-Entering Cyberspace: Sciences of Resistance," *Dispositio/n: American Journal of Cultural Histories and Theories* 19 (1994). Rosi Braidotti's "Cyberfeminism with a Difference," *New Formations* 29 (1996), uses Haraway's notion of the "informatics of domination" to investigate the politics of cyberfeminism. Jonathan Crewe examines Haraway's handling of postmodern theory in "Transcoding the World: Haraway's Postmodernism," *Signs* 22 (1997). After 2000, several book-length studies appeared. Useful introductions include Joseph Schneider's *Donna Haraway: Live Theory* (2005), which contains the most complete bibliography, and David Bell's *Cyberculture Theorists: Manuel Castells and Donna Haraway* (2007), which introduces Haraway's foundational ideas about technoscience in relation to such cyberculture theorists as Sherry Turkle and Sean Cubitt. Arthur Kroker's *Body Drift: Butler, Hayes, Haraway* (2012) maps out a posthuman future for the body in the works of these three feminist thinkers. In *Beyond the Cyborg: Adventures with Donna Haraway* (2013), Margret Grebowicz and Helen Merrick resituate "Manifesto for Cyborgs" within a more nuanced reading of the body of Haraway's scholarship, including her recent work on companion species.

Michael Hardt and Antonio Negri

Michael Hardt and Antonio Negri have collaborated on six books: *Labor of Dionysus: A Critique of the State-Form* (1994), which collects four previously published essays by Negri as well as three co-authored essays; *Empire* (2000), their first systematic articulation of their theory of global capitalism; *Multitude: War and Democracy in the Age of Empire* (2004), which elaborates on the multitude, Hardt and Negri's contemporary model of revolutionary subjectivity; *Commonwealth* (2009), an extended analysis of "the common" that provides the conceptual and material basis for their understanding of communism; *Declaration* (2012), which extends earlier analyses of the multitude and the common to examine contemporary forms of resistance such as the Arab Spring and the Occupy Movement (which both began in 2011); and *Assembly* (2017), which proposes the concept of "assembly" as a means for inventing models of social organization necessary for the longevity and efficacy of so-called leaderless movements in an age of resurgent right-wing political regimes and the continued dominance of neoliberal capitalism.

Michael Hardt has also written *Gilles Deleuze: An Apprenticeship in Philosophy* (1993), which examines Deleuze's "philosophical apprenticeship" undertaken in his early works on Henri Bergson, Friedrich Nietzsche, and Baruch Spinoza. In addition to this book on Deleuze and his work with Negri, Hardt is the author of many articles on political theory and on globalization, including most importantly "The Withering of Civil Society," *Social Text*, no. 45 (1995), reprinted in *Deleuze and Guattari: New Mappings in Politics, Philosophy, and Culture* (ed. Eleanor Kaufman and Kevin Jon Heller, 1998); "The Global Society of Control," *Discourse* 20.3 (1998); "Affective Labor," *boundary 2* 26.2 (1999); "Jefferson and Democracy," *American Quarterly* 59 (2007); and "The Power to Be Affected," *International Journal of Politics, Culture, and Society* 28 (2015). Hardt co-edited both *Radical Thought in Italy: A Potential Politics* (with Paolo Virno, 1996)—which includes Negri's essay "Constituent Republic" as well as "Do You Remember Revolution?," coauthored by Negri and ten other figures from the Italian Left—and *The Jameson Reader* (with Kathi Weeks, 2000).

Antonio Negri has produced a large body of written work, much of it translated into English. He is particularly known in the Anglophone world for three things: his role as a leading contemporary commentator on Spinoza; his political and theoretical writings within the Italian Left, especially the Autonomia movement; and his revolutionary theories of contemporary oppositional subjectivities under global capital. On Spinoza, the most important books are *The Savage Anomaly: The Power of Spinoza's Metaphysics and Politics* (1981; trans. 1991) and *Subversive Spinoza: (Un)contemporary Variations*, edited by Timothy S. Murphy (1992; trans. 2004). Negri's writings in the context of the Italian Left of the 1960s to the 1980s include *Revolution Retrieved: Selected Writings on Marx, Keynes, Capitalist Crisis and New Social Subjects, 1967–1983* (1988) and *Books for Burning: War and Democracy in 1970s Italy* (1997; trans. 2005), which consists of five political pamphlets written from 1971 to 1977. Quotations from these pamphlets were used by the prosecutor in Negri's trial following his April 1979 arrest. Negri's *Pipeline: Letters from Prison* (1983; trans. 2014) collects twenty letters written by Negri from October 1981 to April 1982, while he was incarcerated at Rebibbia prison in Rome; in these letters Negri reflects on his own development as a radical theorist and activist and recounts the events leading to his accusation, trial, and imprisonment. For Negri's most important theorizations of resistance and revolution, see especially *Marx beyond Marx: Lessons on the "Grundrisse"* (1979; trans. 1984), which views not *Capital* but the *Grundrisse* of Marx as the fundamental revolutionary text of classical Marxism, identifying Marx's concept of the real subsumption of capital as the key to understanding contemporary capitalism; *The Politics of Subversion: A Manifesto for the Twenty-First Century* (1988; trans. 1989; 2d ed., 2005), a precursor to Negri and Hardt's theoretical work in their collaborative books; *Insurgencies: Constituent Power and the Modern State* (1992; trans. 1999), which analyzes the canceling out of revolutionary constituent power by the constituted power of the state in the English, American, French, and Russian revolutions; *Time for Revolution* (1997; trans. 2003), a phenomenological account of the temporality of antagonism, resistance, and revolt; and *Marx and Foucault* (2017), a collection of essays analyzing the influence and role of Foucault and other poststructuralists in Marxian and leftist theory and praxis from May 1968 to the Obama administration in the United States. Negri has also written a number of books that further elaborate and develop the arguments made with Hardt, including *Reflections on Empire* (2003; trans. 2008) and *The Porcelain Workshop: For a New Grammar of Politics* (2008). In addition, Negri has made forays into both literature and literary criticism: his *Trilogy of Resistance* (2009; trans. 2011) collects three of his plays (*Swarm: Didactics of the Multitude, The Bent Man: Didactics of the Rebel*, and *Cithaeron: Didactics of Exodus*) that symbolically enact the formation of the multitude and the common, while *Flower of the Desert: Giacomo Leopardi's Poetic Ontology* (1987; trans. 2015) mounts a materialist rereading of the nineteenth-century Italian poet.

Although there are no book-length biographies of Negri in English, the film *Antonio Negri: A Revolt That Never Ends*, directed by Alexandra Weltz and Andreas Pichler (2005), follows Negri's career as an activist and theorist from his early involvement in Potere Operaio to his April 2003 release from prison. Biographical information can also be found in the translators' prefaces to *Marx beyond Marx* as well as in two encyclopedia articles on Negri by Timothy S. Murphy: one in the *Edinburgh Dictionary of Continental Philosophy* (ed. John Protevi, 2005) and the other in the *Encyclopedia of Literature and Politics: Censorship, Revolution, and Writing* (ed. M. Keith Booker, 2005). In connection with Negri's arrest, trial, and imprisonment, see Murphy's editor's introduction to *Books for Burning*; Rowan Wilson, "Inside the Radiant City," *The Philosophers' Magazine* (autumn 1999) and several of the essays included in *Autonomia: Post-Political Politics*, edited by Sylvère Lotringer and Christian Marazzi (2d ed., 2007). Interview collections include *Negri on Negri*, with Anne Dufourmantelle (2004; trans. 2004), and *Goodbye Mr. Socialism*, edited by Raf Valvola Scelsi (2006; trans. 2008). There is currently little biographical information available on Hardt, although in an interview with Caleb Smith and Enrico Minardi published in the *Minnesota Review*, nos. 61–62 (2004), he describes his entry into political thought via his work on alternative energy as an engineering student.

The 2000 publication of *Empire* prompted numerous critical responses. A "dossier" on *Empire* that constitutes a special issue of *Rethinking Marxism*, edited by Abdul-Karim Mustapha and Bülent Eken (13.3–4 [2001]); *Debating Empire*, edited by Gopal Balakrishnan (2003); and *Empire's New Clothes: Reading Hardt and Negri*, edited by Paul A. Passavant and Jodi Dean (2004), offer collections of responses to *Empire*, ranging from Saskia Sassen's sympathetic interpretation in *Empire's New Clothes* to Malcolm Bull's hostile rebuttals in all volumes. Atilio A. Boron's *Empire and Imperialism: A Critical Reading of Michael Hardt and Antonio Negri* (2005) mounts an "empirical refutation" of Hardt and Negri's postnationalist account of globalization, citing as counterexamples the actions undertaken during the administration of George W. Bush, including the U.S. military occupation of Iraq.

Timothy S. Murphy's *Antonio Negri: Modernity and the Multitude* (2012) provides a comprehensive overview of Negri's theoretical and political work. Another excellent secondary source on Negri is the two-volume *The Philosophy of Antonio Negri*, edited by Timothy S. Murphy and Abdul-

Karim Mustapha (2005–07), which also contains a very useful, but not exhaustive, bibliography of Negri's work. The bibliography in Negri's *Time for Revolution* is more scant, but still useful. There are no detailed bibliographies of Hardt's work in print.

David Harvey

After his first book, *Explanation in Geography* (1969), which deals with methodological debates among geographers, David Harvey more directly confronted social issues and engaged with Marxism, particularly in relation to the city, in *Social Justice and the City* (1973; rev. ed., 2009), *Limits to Capital* (1982; new ed., 2006), and the paired volumes *The Urbanization of Capital: Studies in the History and Theory of Capitalist Urbanization* (1985) and *Consciousness and the Urban Experience: Studies in the History and Theory of Urbanization* (1985), which were together abridged as *The Urban Experience* (1989). Through the 1990s he addressed postmodernism and cultural difference, while continuing his revision of Marxism, in *The Condition of Postmodernity: An Enquiry into the Origins of Cultural Change* (1989), *Justice, Nature, and the Geography of Difference* (1996), *Spaces of Hope* (2000), *Spaces of Capital: Towards a Critical Geography* (2001), and *Paris: Capital of Modernity* (2003).

Beginning in the 2000s, Harvey turned toward analyzing contemporary imperialism and neoliberalism rather than postmodernism in *The New Imperialism* (2003), *A Brief History of Neoliberalism* (2005), *Spaces of Global Capitalism: Towards a Theory of Uneven Geographical Development* (2006), *Cosmopolitanism and the Geographies of Freedom* (2009), *The Enigma of Capital: And the Crises of Capitalism* (2010), *Rebel Cities: From the Right to the City to the Urban Revolution* (2012), and *The Ways of the World* (2016). He also published a sequence of exegeses of Marx: *A Companion to Marx's "Capital"* (2010), *A Companion to Marx's "Capital," Volume 2* (2013), and *Seventeen Contradictions and the End of Capitalism* (2014). For an overview of his career in his own words, see "Reinventing Geography," an interview conducted by the editors of *New Left Review*, n.s. 4 (2000), and "The Geography of Accumulation: An Interview with David Harvey," conducted by Jeffrey J. Williams, *Minnesota Review*, n.s. 69 (2007).

John L. Paterson's *David Harvey's Geography* (1984) is an early account of Harvey's adoption of Marxist methods. The cultural studies scholar Meaghan Morris analyzes Harvey's assumptions about culture's reflection of material conditions in "The Man in the Mirror: David Harvey's 'Condition' of Postmodernity," *Theory, Culture and Society* 9.1 (1992). Derek Gregory's *Geographical Imaginations* (1994) offers a good synopsis of Harvey's project to that point. In "Spaced Out," *London Review of Books*, April 24, 1997, Terry Eagleton observes Harvey's tendency toward large-scale abstractions. John Paul Jones's *David Harvey: Live Theory* (2004) is a cursory overview. For the best overview of Harvey's work, provided by thirteen contributors, see *David Harvey: A Critical Reader*, edited by Noel Castree and Derek Gregory (2006). Loïc Wacquant offers a pointed criticism of Harvey, noting that his account of neoliberalism focuses on economic factors but misses the huge neoliberal expansion of prisons, in "Crafting the Neoliberal State: Workfare, Prisonfare, and Social Insecurity," *Sociological Forum* 25 (2010). Jamie Peck, *Constructions of Neoliberal Reason* (2010), draws on Harvey in surveying neoliberalism. Castree and Gregory's *David Harvey* includes a complete list of Harvey's publications up to 2006.

Friedrich A. Hayek

Hayek's major works are *Prices and Production* (1931; 2d ed., 1935), *Profits, Interest, and Investment, and Other Essays on the Theory of Industrial Fluctuations* (1939), *The Pure Theory of Capital* (1941), *The Road to Serfdom* (1944), *Individualism and Economic Order* (1948), *John Stuart Mill and Harriet Taylor: Their Correspondence and Subsequent Marriage* (1951), *The Sensory Order: An Inquiry into the Foundations of Theoretical Psychology* (1952), *The Counter-Revolution of Science: Studies on the Abuse of Reason* (1952; 2d ed., 1979), *The Constitution of Liberty* (1960), *Studies in Philosophy, Politics, and Economics* (1967), *The Mirage of Social Justice* (1976), *New Studies in Philosophy, Politics, Economics, and the History of Ideas* (1978), *The Political Order of a Free People* (1979), and *Knowledge, Evolution and Society* (1983). *The Collected Works of F. A. Hayek*, being published by the University of Chicago Press in nineteen volumes (1988–), will contain all the major works as well as occasional essays, reviews, and interviews, and stands as the definitive scholarly edition. Edited transcripts of a series of interviews with Hayek about his life and work are published under the title *Hayek on Hayek: An Autobiographical Dialogue*, edited by Stephen Kresge and Leif Wenar (1994). Bruce Caldwell's *Hayek's Challenge: An Intellectual Biography of F. A. Hayek* (2004) is not only the best biography but also the best overall account of his ideas.

Two excellent shorter introductions are G. R. Steele's *The Economics of Friedrich Hayek* (1993; 2d ed., 2007) and A. J. Tebble's *F. A. Hayek* (2010). Andrew Gamble's *Hayek: The Iron Cage of Liberty* (1996) and John Gray's *Hayek on Liberty* (1984; 3d ed., 1998)—the first critical, the second sympathetic—evaluate Hayek's arguments about the conditions required to secure liberty in any political and economic order. Michel Foucault's discussion of Hayek in *The Birth of Biopolitics: Lectures at the Collège de France, 1978–1979* (2008) has greatly influenced literary theorists' understanding of neoliberalism. *Friedrich A. Hayek: Critical Assessments of Contemporary Economists, Second*

Series, edited by John C. Wood and Robert D. Wood (4 vols., 2004), offers a comprehensive overview of responses to Hayek's work. *The Road from Mont Pèlerin: The Making of the Neoliberal Thought Collective*, edited by Philip Mirowski and Dieter Plehwe (2009), is an indispensable (albeit hostile) history of the development of neoliberal thought and its rise to political influence. *The Cambridge Companion to Hayek*, edited by Edward Feser (2006), provides superb introductory essays on all facets of Hayek's work and influence as well as a good working bibliography.

N. Katherine Hayles

In her first book, *The Cosmic Web: Scientific Field Models and Literary Strategies in the Twentieth Century* (1984), Hayles argues that early twentieth-century "field theory" introduces a dynamic and integrated perspective on reality that constitutes a paradigm shift in science, philosophy, and literature. A sequel and complement to her first book, *Chaos Bound: Orderly Disorder in Contemporary Literature and Science* (1990) shows how contemporary scientific chaos theory offers a cultural matrix that can be shared by science and literature, treating chaos not as simply meaningless disorder but as a productive means of generating higher orders of information and complexity. *How We Became Posthuman: Virtual Bodies in Cybernetics, Literature, and Informatics* (1999) examines the fate of human embodiment in a world increasingly dominated by information technology. Hayles here investigates three related aspects of the information age: the story of how information lost its body, the development of the cultural icon of the cyborg, and the emergence of posthuman identities. In *Writing Machines* (2002), whose page layouts sometimes resemble computer screens and abstract information patterns, Hayles playfully and creatively illustrates her notion of "flickering signifiers." Focusing on the complex ways in which various forms of media interpenetrate, she insists on the materiality of different kinds of literary artifacts such as hyperfiction, the artist's book, and the traditional novel. *My Mother Was a Computer: Digital Subjects and Literary Texts* (2005) offers new ways of understanding the relationships between language and code. It investigates processes of intermediation through which traditional cultural practices interact with digital media. Hayles's *Electronic Literature: New Horizons for the Literary* (2008) provides a systematic survey of the field of electronic literature, isolating major genres and central theoretical issues pertaining to networked and programmable media. It is accompanied by a CD featuring volume 1 of the *Electronic Literature Collection*, coedited by Hayles with Nick Montfort, Scott Rettberg, and Stephanie Strickland; the collection of sixty works is intended for courses on contemporary electronic literature. In *How We Think: Digital Media and Contemporary Technogenesis* (2012), Hayles argues that contemporary technogenesis—the idea that humans and technics are coevolving—is changing the ways we think about academic research, teaching, and publication. Tracing the neurological implications of working in digital media, she investigates the limitations and possibilities of new forms of analysis such as "hyperreading" and reading through machine algorithms. Mindful that the vast amount of digital material she had developed far exceeds the scope of her printed books, Hayles has made this voluminous material available on her website (http://nkhayles.com) and in *How We Think: A Digital Companion* (http://howwethink.nkhayles.com, 2013), which enables readers to put into practice new forms of reading and draw their own conclusions. In her *Unthought: The Power of the Cognitive Nonconscious* (2017), Hayles redefines cognition to include not only processes inaccessible to consciousness but also mechanisms governing other forms of life such as unicellular organisms and plants, in addition to human technical assemblages: for example, urban traffic control systems and the trading algorithms of financial markets. Working at the intersections of neuroscience, cognitive science, cognitive biology, and literature, Hayles traces the dynamics of what she calls a "planetary cognitive ecology," while arguing for a broader and more thorough understanding of the role humans might play in making the environment more sustainable for all forms of life. In addition to her own books, Hayles has edited the essay collection *Chaos and Order: Complex Dynamics in Literature and Science* (1991); guest edited *Technocriticism and Hypernarrative* (1997), a special issue of *Modern Fiction Studies* (43.3); and edited both *Nanoculture: Implications of the New Technoscience* (2004) and *Comparative Textual Media: Transforming the Humanities in the Postprint Era* (2013). She has also published numerous articles in books and journals on literature, computer culture, cyborg theory, and the history of technology.

Notable assessments of Hayles's work have come, for example, from literary critics concentrating on science fiction and on feminist theory. Istvan Csicsery-Ronay Jr.'s "Till We Have Interfaces," *Science Fiction Studies* 26 (1999), offers a pointed review of *How We Became Posthuman*. While praising Hayles as a sharp diagnostician of the social and cultural implications of information technologies, Csicsery-Ronay observes that her theory of the posthuman ends in anxiety and uncertainty, failing to indicate what comes after the demise of the liberal humanist subject. In "How We Think When We Think about Science Fiction," *Science Fiction Studies* 40 (2013), Paweł Prelik notes that Hayles's *How We Think* does not offer a definitive conclusion about the complex effects or the future of technogenesis; he also points out that this very open-endedness may prove to be especially promising for the rethinking of the relationship within science fiction studies between human and machine. In "How We Think about Technology (Without Thinking about Politics)," *the b20 review*, November 4, 2015, R. Joshua Scannell faults Hayles for failing to fully engage with the social and political ramifications of her theory, including the hidden motivations of hyper and machine reading in strengthening the corporate university and the large-scale troubling transformation of labor in postindustrial capitalism.

Dick Hebdige

Hebdige's books are *Subculture: The Meaning of Style* (1979), *Cut 'n' Mix: Culture, Identity, and Caribbean Music* (1987), and *Hiding in the Light: On Images and Things* (1988).

In a series of essays responding to and growing out of Hebdige's work, Angela McRobbie, a leading figure of British cultural studies, has questioned the male focus of the subcultures Hebdige describes and has pondered the political effectiveness of subcultural resistance. See her "Settling Accounts with Subcultures: A Feminist Critique," *Screen Education* 34 (1980); "Postmodernism and Popular Culture," *Journal of Communication Inquiry* 10 (1986); and "New Times in Cultural Studies," *New Formations* 13 (1991). Further reactions to Hebdige's work can be found in Anne Beezer's "Dick Hebdige, *Subculture: The Meaning of Style*," in *Reading into Cultural Studies* (ed. Martin Barker and Anne Beezer, 1992); Vincent B. Leitch, *Cultural Criticism, Literary Theory, Poststructuralism* (1992); and Neil Nehring, *Flowers in the Dustbin: Culture, Anarchy, and Postwar England* (1993). Two excellent overviews of the history and theoretical outlook of cultural studies that discuss Hebdige's work are Simon During's *Cultural Studies: A Critical Introduction* (2005) and Chris Rojek's *Cultural Studies* (2007). Hebdige offers his reflections on *Subculture* and its impact in an interview, "Dick Hebdige: Unplugged and Greased Back," by Timothy Dugdale, *Post Identity* 4.1 (2004), and an article, "Contemporizing 'Subculture': 30 Years to Life," *European Journal of Cultural Studies* 15 (2012). Hebdige also contributed the essay "The Worldliness of Cultural Studies" to the important symposium on cultural studies published in the journal *Cultural Studies* 29 (2015).

Georg Wilhelm Friedrich Hegel

Edited by Eva Moldenhauer and Karl Markus Michel, Hegel's *Werke* (22 vols., 1969–72) is a complete German edition of his writings. Most of his work has been translated into English, though there is no standard scholarly edition of the complete works. Of special relevance to students of literature are *Philosophy of Right*, translated by T. M. Knox (1942); *Hegel's Aesthetics: Lectures on Fine Art*, translated by T. M. Knox (2 vols., 1975); *Lectures on the Philosophy of World History*, edited by H. B. Nisbet (1975); *Phenomenology of Spirit*, translated by A. V. Miller (1977); and *Lectures on the History of Philosophy*, edited by Robert Brown (3 vols., 1990). *The Hegel Reader*, edited by Stephen Houlgate (1998), offers selections covering the breadth of Hegel's interests. The best biography is Terry Pinkard's *Hegel: A Biography* (2000).

The secondary literature on Hegel is immense; thus the following bibliography is extremely selective. Jean Hyppolite's *Genesis and Structure of Hegel's "Phenomenology of Spirit"* (1946; trans. 1974) and Alexandre Kojève's *Introduction to the Reading of Hegel* (1947; trans. 1969) are two French works that shaped the existentialist and poststructuralist understandings of Hegel.

The single best, and most influential, overview remains Charles Taylor's *Hegel* (1975), which also comes in a slimmer, more reader-friendly version titled *Hegel and Modern Society* (1979). *G. W. F. Hegel: Key Concepts*, edited by Michael Baur (2015), and Stephen Houlgate, *Hegel's "Phenomenology of Spirit": A Reader's Guide* (2013), along with *The Cambridge Companion to Hegel and Nineteenth-Century Philosophy*, edited by Frederick C. Beiser (2008), are recommended for those coming to Hegel for the first time. Jacques Derrida's *Glas* (1981; trans. 1986) is the most important of many poststructuralist encounters with Hegel. Judith Butler's *Subjects of Desire: Hegelian Reflections in Twentieth-Century France* (1987), Slavoj Žižek's *Less Than Nothing: Hegel and the Shadow of Dialectical Materialism* (2012), and Andrew Cole's *The Birth of Theory* (2014) all display Hegel's presence in contemporary theory. The theme of "recognition" has been the subject of much debate; major contributions to the discussion include Patchen P. Markell's *Bound by Recognition: The Politics of Identity after Hegel* (2003), Paul Ricoeur's *The Course of Recognition* (2005), and Axel Honneth's *The I in We: Studies in the Theory of Recognition* (2012). Three excellent books that address Hegel's aesthetics are Alan Speight's *Hegel, Literature, and the Problem of Agency* (2001), Theodore D. George's *Tragedies of Spirit: Tracing Finitude in Hegel's "Phenomenology"* (2006), and *Hegel and the Arts*, edited by Stephen Houlgate (2007).

Kurt Steinhauser's massive German/English *Hegel Bibliographie* (1980, 1998) covers almost all the secondary literature from 1802 to the end of the twentieth century. A more manageable and recent bibliography, arranged by topic, can be found in *The Cambridge Companion to Hegel and Nineteenth-Century Philosophy*.

Martin Heidegger

The standard edition of Heidegger's collected works in German is the *Gesamtausgabe* (1976–), which is projected to reach 102 volumes. About a dozen remain unpublished. An introductory collection of texts in English is available in *Basic*

Writings: From "Being and Time" (1927) to "The Task of Thinking" (1964), translated by various hands and edited by David Farrell Krell (rev. and expanded, 2008). English versions of Heidegger's writings bearing directly on his understanding of poetry and language are available in *Existence and Being*, edited by Werner Brock and translated by Douglas Scott (1949); *Poetry, Language, Thought*, edited and translated by Albert Hofstadter (1971); and *On the Way to Language*, translated by Peter D. Hertz and Joan Stambaugh (1971). Philosophical texts translated into English (with the date of German publication given first) include *What Is Philosophy?* (1956; 1956); *An Introduction to Metaphysics*, translated first by Ralph Manheim (1953; 1959), and then (as *Introduction to Metaphysics*) by Gregory Fried and Richard Polt (2000); *Being and Time*, translated first by John Macquarrie and Edward Robinson (1927; 1962), and then by Joan Stambaugh (1996); *What Is a Thing?* (1962; 1967); *Identity and Difference* (1957; 1969); *On Time and Being* (1969; 1972); *The Question Concerning Technology and Other Essays*, translated by William Lovitt (1977); *Nietzsche* (2 vols., 1961; 4 vols., 1979–87); *History of the Concept of Time: Prolegomena* (1979; 1985); *Hegel's Phenomenology of Spirit* (1980; 1988); *Kant and the Problem of Metaphysics* (1929; 1990); *The Concept of Time* (1992; 1992); *Basic Concepts* (1981; 1993); *The Fundamental Concepts of Metaphysics: World, Finitude, Solitude* (1983; 1995); *Pathmarks* (1967; 1998); *Contributions to Philosophy: From Enowning* [a term that translates *Ereignis*, "appropriation"] (1989; 1999); *Towards the Definition of Philosophy* (1987; 2000); *Supplements: From the Earliest Essays to "Being and Time" and Beyond*, edited by John van Buren (2002); *Four Seminars* (1977; 2003); *Mindfulness* (1997; 2006); *Hegel* (2015), which collects an array of Heidegger's interpretations of Hegel's writings; and Heidegger's long-running intellectual diary *Schwarze Hefte*, edited by Peter Tawny (2014, *Black Notebooks*), which has been translated as *Ponderings II–VI: 1931–38* (2016), *Ponderings VII–XI: 1938–39* (2017), and *Ponderings XII–XV: 1939–41* (2017). A translation of Heidegger's interview on his Nazi past, "Only a God Can Save Us Now," can be found in the journal *Philosophy Today* 20 (winter 1976). For biographical sources, see Hugo Ott's *Martin Heidegger: A Political Life* (1993); Rüdiger Safranski's *Martin Heidegger: Between Good and Evil* (1994; trans. 1998); and James K. Lyon's *Paul Celan and Martin Heidegger: An Unresolved Conversation, 1951–1970* (2006), which draws on documentary material to offer the first systematic analysis of the troubled and unfinished relationship between the two.

For general introductions, see George Steiner's *Martin Heidegger* (2d ed., 1991); Michael Inwood's *Heidegger* (1997); *Heidegger Reexamined*, edited by Hubert Dreyfus and Mark Wrathall (4 vols., 2002); *The Cambridge Companion to Heidegger*, edited by Charles B. Guignon (2d ed., 2006); and John Richardson's *Heidegger* (2012). Among the important studies and applications of Heidegger's views on language and poetry are *On Heidegger and Language*, edited by Joseph J. Kockelmans (1972); David A. White, *Heidegger and the Language of Poetry* (1978); *Martin Heidegger and the Question of Literature: Toward a Postmodern Literary Hermeneutics*, edited by William V. Spanos (1979); Paul A. Bové, *Destructive Poetics: Heidegger and Modern American Poetry* (1980); David Halliburton, *Poetic Thinking: An Approach to Heidegger* (1981); Joseph Kockelmans, *Heidegger on Art and Art Works* (1985); Gerald L. Bruns, *Heidegger's Estrangements: Language, Truth, and Poetry in the Later Writings* (1989); Hans-Georg Gadamer, *Heidegger's Ways* (1983; trans. 1994); Marc Froment-Meurice, *That Is to Say: Heidegger's Poetics* (1996; trans. 1998); Philippe Lacoue-Labarthe, *Heidegger and the Politics of Poetry* (2002; trans. 2007); Jennifer Anna Gosetti-Ferencei, *Heidegger, Hölderin, and the Subject of Poetic Language: Toward a New Poetics of Dasein* (2004); Mark A. Wrathall, *Heidegger and Unconcealment: Truth, Language, and History* (2010); and Richard Capobianco, *Heidegger's Way of Being* (2015), which develops a well-informed rebuttal of antirealist interpretations of Heidegger's thought that reduce his concept of "being" to "human meaning-making." On Heidegger and the Nazi question, see Pierre Bourdieu, *The Political Ontology of Martin Heidegger* (1975; trans. 1991); Victor Farias, *Heidegger and Nazism* (1987; trans. 1990); Jacques Derrida, *Of Spirit: Heidegger and the Question* (1987; trans. 1990); Philippe Lacoue-Labarthe, *Heidegger, Art, and Politics: The Fiction of the Political* (1987; trans. 1990); Jean-François Lyotard, *Heidegger and "the Jews"* (1988; trans. 1990); *The Heidegger Controversy: A Critical Reader*, edited by Richard Wolin (1992); Fred Dallmayr, *The Other Heidegger* (1993); Hans D. Sluga, *Heidegger's Crisis: Philosophy and Politics in Nazi Germany* (1993); Julian Young, *Heidegger, Philosophy, Nazism* (1997); Miguel de Beistegui, *Heidegger & the Political: Dystopias* (1998); James Phillips, *Heidegger's Volk: Between National Socialism and Poetry* (2005); Peter Trawny, *Heidegger and the Myth of A Jewish World Conspiracy* (2014; trans. 2015), which draws on Heidegger's *Black Notebooks* to argue that anti-Semitism plays an integral role in Heidegger's philosophy of history; and Jean-Luc Nancy's *The Banality of Heidegger* (2015; trans. 2017), which criticizes Heidegger and broadly argues anti-Semitism is Western self-hatred. For bibliographies, see Hans-Martin Sass, *Martin Heidegger: Bibliography and Glossary* (1982); Joan Nordquist, *Martin Heidegger: A Bibliography* (1990) and *Martin Heidegger (II): A Bibliography* (1996); Miles Groth, *The Voice That Thinks: Heidegger Studies with a Bibliography of English Translations, 1949–1996* (1997); and *The Cambridge Companion to Heidegger*, cited above.

David Herman

David Herman has published numerous articles, chapters, review essays, and reviews, as well as five books and nine edited volumes in the areas of narrative theory, modern and postmodern fiction, and storytelling across media. His books are *Universal Grammar and Narrative Form* (1995); *Story Logic: Problems and Possibilities of Narrative* (2002); *Basic Elements of Narrative* (2009); with James Phelan, Peter J. Rabinowitz, Brian Richardson, and Robyn Warhol, *Narrative Theory: Core Concepts and Debate* (2010); and *Storytelling and the Sciences of Mind* (2013). He has edited or co-edited *Narratologies: New Perspectives on Narrative Analysis* (1999); *Narrative Theory and Cognitive Sciences* (2003); with Manfred Jahn and Marie-Laure Ryan, *Routledge Encyclopedia of Narrative Theory* (2005); *The Cambridge Companion to Narrative* (2007); *Muriel Spark: Twenty-First-Century Perspectives* (2010); with Brian McHale and James Phelan, *Teaching Narrative Theory* (2010); *The Emergence of Mind: Representations of Consciousness in Narrative Discourse in English* (2011); *Creatural Fictions: Human-Animal Relationships in Twentieth- and Twenty-First-Century Literature* (2016); and *Animal Comics: Multispecies Storyworlds in Graphic Narratives* (2017). For particularly informative interviews with Herman, see Shang Biwu's, http://cf.hum/uva.nl/narratology/all_an_interview_with_david_herman.htm (2005), in which Herman discusses his use of postclassical narratology and storyworlds, and Barry Mazur's, http://thalesandfriends.org/2007/07/22/interview-with-david-herman/ (2007), which examines Herman's "panoptic view of the field of narratology" and analyzes the experimental mathematical approach that Herman uses in one of his essays to create an interdisciplinary discourse between mathematics and narrative theory.

While reviewers of Herman's work sometimes complain about his use of technical vocabulary and his preference for theory, most critics praise his interdisciplinary efforts, especially in bringing cognitive theory to literary narratology. See, for example, Jan Baetens, who in his review of Herman's *Storytelling and the Sciences of Mind* in *Leonardo* 47.5 (2014), deems the book an "important attempt to bridge the gap between several subdisciplinary approaches." Along the way Baetens points out some key issues unaddressed by Herman, such as the role in narratives of implied readers and implied authors as well as authorial intentions.

bell hooks

hooks's early critical writing, mainly essay collections, include, on feminist theory, *Ain't I a Woman: Black Women and Feminism* (1981), *Feminist Theory: From Margin to Center* (1984; 2d ed., 2000), *Talking Back: Thinking Feminist, Thinking Black* (1989), and *Sisters of the Yam: Black Women and Self-Recovery* (1993); on race, *Breaking Bread: Insurgent Black Intellectual Life* (with Cornel West, 1991), *Black Looks: Race and Representation* (1992), *Killing Rage: Ending Racism* (1995), and *Writing Beyond Race: Living Theory and Practice* (2012); on teaching, *Teaching to Transgress: Education as the Practice of Freedom* (1994) and *Teaching Critical Thinking: Practical Wisdom* (2010); on film, *Reel to Real: Race, Sex, and Class at the Movies* (1996); and on cultural studies, *Yearning: Race, Gender, and Cultural Politics* (1990), *Outlaw Culture: Resisting Representation* (1994), *Art on My Mind: Visual Politics* (1995), and *Belonging: A Culture of Place* (2009). Her memoirs—*Bone Black: Memories of Girlhood* (1996), *Wounds of Passion: A Writing Life* (1997), and *Remembering Rapture: The Writer at Work* (1999)—are good sources of information on her life. hooks's most recent works include *Feminism Is for Everybody: Passionate Politics* (2000), *Where We Stand: Class Matters* (2000), *All About Love: New Versions* (2001), *Salvation: Black People and Love* (2001), *Communion: The Female Search for Love* (2002), *Teaching Community: A Pedagogy of Hope* (2003), *Rock My Soul: Black People and Self-esteem* (2003), *The Will to Change: Men, Masculinity, and Love* (2004), *We Real Cool: Black Men and Masculinity* (2004), *Homegrown: Engaged Cultural Criticism*, with Amalia Mesa-Bains (2006), and *Uncut Funk: A Contemplative Dialogue* (2017), with Stuart Hall. She has also written three books of poetry, *And There We Wept: Poems* (1978), *When Angels Speak of Love: Poems* (2007), and *Appalachian Elegy: Poetry and Place* (2012), plus five children's books. For a biographical sketch, see the entry by Ondine E. Le Blanc and Margaret L. Moser in *Contemporary Black Biography*, vol. 90 (2011).

A number of critical articles on hooks have appeared. Of most interest to students of literary criticism are Cassie Premo, "When the Difference Becomes Too Great: Images of the Self and Survival in a Postmodern World," *Genre* 28 (1995); Clive Thomson, "Culture, Identity, and Dialogue: bell hooks and Gayatri Chakravorty Spivak," in *Dialogism and Cultural Criticism* (ed. Thomson and Hans Raj Dau, 1995); and Marilyn Edelstein, "Resisting Postmodernism; or, 'A Postmodernism of Resistance': bell hooks and the Theory Debates," in *Other Sisterhoods: Literary Theory and U.S. Women of Color* (ed. Sandra Kumamoto Stanley, 1998). hooks's essays about teaching have also been of interest to critics, including Gary Olson and Elizabeth Hirsh, "Feminist Praxis and the Politics of Literacy: A Conversation with bell hooks," in *Women Writing Culture* (ed. Olson and Hirsch, 1995); Namulundah Florence, *bell hooks' Engaged Pedagogy: A Transgressive Education for Critical Consciousness* (1998); and Linda Strong-Leek, "bell hooks, Carter G. Woodson, and African American Education," *Journal of Black Studies* 38 (2008). Recent books on hooks's cultural criticism include *Critical Perspectives on bell hooks*, edited by Maria del Guadalupe Davidson and

George Yancy (2009), and Catherine R. Squires, *bell hooks: A Critical Introduction to Media and Communication Theory* (2013). Sut Jhally features hooks in his documentary film *bell hooks: Cultural Criticism and Transformation* (1997). Bibliographical information on hooks may be found in Genevieve Fabre's "Selected Bibliography of Essays on Black Women and Black Feminist Criticism," *Revue Française d'Études Americaines* 24 (1986), as well as in the Schomburg Center for Research in Black Studies' *Bibliographic Guide to Black Studies* (2003).

Horace

The complete Latin works of Horace are collected in *Q. Horati Flacci Opera*, edited by D. R. Shackleton Bailey (4th ed., 2001). The standard Latin edition of the *Ars Poetica* with English commentary can be found in *Epistles Book II and Epistle to the Pisones*, edited by Niall Rudd (1989). This text also includes the important "Epistle to Augustus" and the "Epistle to Florus." *The Complete Works of Horace*, edited by Charles E. Passage (1983), offers an English translation of Horace's collected poetry, including the *Ars Poetica*. There are a number of very accessible prose translations of *Ars Poetica*: D. A. Russell's in *Ancient Literary Criticism* (1972); Leon Golden's in O. B. Hardison and Leon Golden's *Horace for Students of Literature: The "Ars Poetica" and Its Tradition* (1995), which also includes a series of documents that demonstrate the influence of Horace's epistle throughout the history of Western literary criticism; and Ross S. Kilpatrick's eminently readable translation in *The Poetry of Criticism: Horace, Epistles II and the Ars Poetica* (1990), which we use here. A Latin *Life of Horace* exists; it is attributed to the Roman historian Suetonius (ca. 69–140 C.E.). For an English biography, see Peter Levi's *Horace: A Life* (1997).

D. A. Russell's essay on the *Ars Poetica* in *Horace* (ed. C. D. N. Costa, 1973) provides a useful and brief introduction to the poem. It is reprinted in *Ancient Literary Criticism* (ed. Andrew Laird, 2006). S. J. Harrison's *Horace* (2014) is also indispensable for the beginning student of Horace. Charles O. Brink's monumental three-volume study, *Horace on Poetry* (1963–82), is the standard text for advanced study of Horace's critical principles; it includes texts and commentaries on the *Ars Poetica*, the "Epistle to Augustus," and the "Epistle to Florus." Ross Kilpatrick, in *The Poetry of Criticism* (see above), examines the relationships between Horace's epistles on poetry, providing an account of the major themes of the *Ars Poetica*. Bernard Frischer, in *Shifting Paradigms: New Approaches to Horace's "Ars Poetica"* (1991), presents a detailed statistical analysis of the epistle's many controversies. Several collections of essays on Horace offer introductions to the life and works of Horace, as well as specific chapters on *Ars Poetica*; these include essays by Andrew Laird in *The Cambridge Companion to Horace*, edited by S. J. Harrison (2007); by Ellen Oliensis in *Horace, Satires and Epistles*, edited by Kirk Freudenburg (2009); by W. R. Johnson and Leon Golden in *A Companion to Horace*, edited by Gregson Davis (2010); and by Tobias Reinhardt in *Brill's Companion to Horace*, edited by Hans-Christian Günther (2013). Ellen Oliensis's *Horace and the Rhetoric of Authority* (1998) includes a chapter on self-fashioning in the *Ars Poetica*, which is reprinted in Freudenburg's collection. In *Horace's Iambic Criticism: Casting Blame (Iambikē Poiēsis)* (2012), Timothy S. Johnson offers a more advanced examination of Horace's use and criticism of iambic meter in his literary practice.

Volume 3 of Brink's *Horace on Poetry* (cited above) contains an extensive bibliography of primary and secondary sources on Horace's literary criticism. *Horace* by S. J. Harrison (cited above) offers a complete survey of the scholarly literature on Horace since 1957.

Max Horkheimer and Theodor W. Adorno

The authoritative German edition of Adorno's collected works is the twenty-one-volume *Gesammelte Schriften*, edited by Rolf Tiedemann with Gretel Adorno, Susan Buck-Morss, and Klaus Schultz (1970–86). English translations of Adorno's writings on music theory, history, and criticism (with their original publication date given first) include *Philosophy of Modern Music* (1949; 1973 and 2006 [two trans.]), *Introduction to the Sociology of Music* (1962; 1976), *In Search of Wagner* (1952; 1981), *Alban Berg: Master of the Smallest Link* (1968; 1991), *Mahler: A Musical Physiognomy* (1960; 1992), *Quasi Una Fantasia: Essays on Modern Music* (1963; 1992), *Composing for the Films* (1994), *Sound Figures* (1959; 1998), *Beethoven: The Philosophy of Music* (1993; 1998), *Towards a Theory of Musical Reproduction: Notes, a Draft and Two Schemata* (2001; 2006), and *Current of Music: Elements of a Radio Theory* (2006; 2009). A substantial number of English translations of Adorno's sociological writings are readily available, including *Prisms* (1955; 1967), *Dialectic of Enlightenment* (1947; 1972 and 2002), *Aspects of Sociology* (1956; 1972), *Minima Moralia: Reflections from a Damaged Life* (1951; 1974), *The Positivist Dispute in German Sociology* (1976), *Culture Industry: Selected Essays on Mass Culture* (1991), *Stars Come Down to Earth and Other Essays on the Irrational* (1994), and *Critical Models: Interventions and Catchwords* (1963–69; 1998). Translations into English of works focusing on philosophy, aesthetics, and literature include *The Jargon of Authenticity* (1964; 1973), *Negative Dialectics* (1966; 1973), *Against Epistemology* (1956; 1982), *Kierkegaard: Construction of the Aesthetic* (1933; 1989), *Notes to Literature* (4 vols., 1958–74; 2 vols., 1991), *Hegel: Three Studies* (1963; 1993), *Aesthetic Theory* (1970; 1984 and 1997), *Problems of Moral Philosophy* (1963; 2000), *Kant's "Critique of Pure Reason"* (1959; 2001), *Metaphysics: Concept and Problems* (1965; 2000), *Can One Live After Auschwitz? A Philosophical*

Reader (1997; 2003), and *Aesthetics: 1958/59* (2017). See also *The Authoritarian Personality* (1950), by Adorno and others. For a selection, see *The Adorno Reader*, edited by Brian O'Connor (2000). English translations of Adorno's letters include Adorno and Alban Berg, *Correspondence, 1925–1935* (2006), and *Letters to His Parents, 1939–1951* (2006). A selection of Adorno's writings on his dreams, spanning the last twenty-five years of his life, appears in *Dream Notes* (2005; 2007). For the best introductory biography, see Martin Jay's *Adorno* (1984). More recent ones include Stefan Müller-Doohm's *Adorno: A Biography* (2003; trans. 2005), the most comprehensive account of Adorno's life and work; Lorenz Jäger's *Adorno: A Political Biography* (2003; trans. 2004), which is the first attempt to evaluate Adorno's philosophical and literary work in its political contexts; and Detlev Claussen's *Theodor W. Adorno: One Last Genius* (2003; trans. 2008), providing the best biographical account of primary texts written by Adorno.

The nineteen-volume *Gesammelte Schriften* of Horkheimer, edited by Alfred Schmidt and Gunzelin Schmid Noerr (1985–96), is the definitive German edition of his work. The major English translations of his writings are *Eclipse of Reason* (1947), *Critical Theory: Selected Essays* (1972), *Critique of Instrumental Reason: Lectures and Essays Since the End of World War II* (1974), *Dawn and Decline: Notes 1926–1931 and 1950–1969* (1974), and *Between Philosophy and Social Science: Selected Early Writings* (1993). For an English translation of Horkheimer's letters, see *A Life in Letters: Selected Correspondence*, edited and translated by Manfred R. Jacobson and Evelyn M. Jacobson (2007). The most comprehensive intellectual biography of Horkheimer is John Abromeit's *Max Horkheimer and the Foundations of the Frankfurt School* (2011), which includes a thorough survey of relevant secondary literary as well as interpretive analyses of Horkheimer's major works that are supplemented by insights from Abromeit's extensive archival research.

For a discussion of Adorno and Horkheimer's early involvement with the Frankfurt School, see Martin Jay's *Dialectical Imagination: A History of the Frankfurt School and the Institute of Social Research, 1923–1950* (1973). Susan Buck-Morss's *Origin of Negative Dialectics: Theodor W. Adorno, Walter Benjamin, and the Frankfurt Institute* (1977) provides a historical account of the beginnings of Critical Theory. For useful studies of Adorno, Horkheimer, Critical Theory, and the work of the Frankfurt School as a whole, see David Held's *Introduction to Critical Theory: Horkheimer to Habermas* (1980); *Foundations of the Frankfurt School of Social Research*, edited by Judith Marcus and Zoltán Tar (1984); and Stuart Jeffries's *Grand Hotel Abyss: The Lives of the Frankfurt School* (2016). Zoltán Tar's critical analysis, *The Frankfurt School: The Critical Theories of Max Horkheimer and Theodor W. Adorno* (1977; rev. ed., 2011), attempts to understand Horkheimer and Adorno's theories in light of their experience as Jewish émigré intellectuals confronting fascism.

Gillian Rose's *Melancholy Science: An Introduction to the Thought of Theodor W. Adorno* (1978) offers a wide-ranging study of Adorno's work. Fredric Jameson's controversial *Late Marxism: Adorno, or, the Persistence of the Dialectic* (1990) demonstrates the relevance of Adorno to postmodern times. Peter Uwe Hohendahl's *Prismatic Thought: Theodor W. Adorno* (1995) provides a general overview, while Deborah Cook's *The Culture Industry Revisited: Theodor W. Adorno on Mass Culture* (1996) gives a comprehensive study of Adorno's writings on the culture industry. More recent studies include *Adorno: A Critical Reader*, edited by Nigel Gibson and Andrew Rubin (2001); Robert W. Witkin, *Adorno on Popular Culture* (2003); *The Cambridge Companion to Adorno*, edited by Thomas Huhn (2004); *Adorno and Literature*, edited by David Cunningham and Nigel Mapp (2006); *Feminist Interpretations of Theodor Adorno*, edited by Renée Heberle (2006); Berthold Hoeckner, *Apparitions: New Perspectives on Adorno and Twentieth-Century Music* (2006); *Adorno and Heidegger: Philosophical Questions*, edited by Iain Macdonald and Krzysztof Ziarek (2008); and Brian O'Connor's highly accessible *Adorno* (2013). For a bibliography of Horkheimer's work, along with a critical overview, see *On Max Horkheimer*, edited by Seyla Benhabib et al. (1993). Bibliographical information on Adorno is available in Müller-Doohm's biography and the *Cambridge Companion*, mentioned above.

Langston Hughes

Hughes published ten books of poetry, eight of fiction, and twenty of nonfiction prose (several coauthored). His social and literary criticism appeared in *A New Song* (1938), *Freedom's Plow* (1943), *Jim Crow's Last Stand* (1943), *Laughing to Keep from Crying* (1952), *Black Misery* (1969), and *Good Morning Revolution: Uncollected Social Protest Writings by Langston Hughes*, edited by Faith Berry (1973). His correspondence with the influential black writer and editor Arna Bontemps has been published in *Arna Bontemps–Langston Hughes Letters, 1925–1967*, edited by Charles H. Nichols (1980). A selection from all his work is available in *The Langston Hughes Reader* (1958), and *The Selected Letters of Langston Hughes*, edited by Arnold Rampersad and David Roessel (2015), covers his whole life, while *Letters from Langston: From the Harlem Renaissance to the Red Scare and Beyond*, edited by Evelyn Louise Crawford and MaryLouise Patterson (2016), documents his political opinions and affiliations. Hughes also edited many works, among them the important literary anthologies *The Poetry of the Negro* (1949), with Arna Bontemps; *The Book of Negro Folklore* (1958), with Arna Bontemps; *New Negro Poets: USA* (1964); and *The Best Short Stories by Negro Writers* (1967).

Hughes wrote two autobiographies, *The Big Sea* (1940) and *I Wonder as I Wander* (1956). Two biographies are Faith Berry's *Langston Hughes: Before and Beyond Harlem* (1983) and Arnold Rampersad's authoritative two-volume *Life of Langston Hughes* (1986–88). Critical studies that attend to Hughes's nonpoetical works include W. Jason Miller's *Langston Hughes and American Lynching Culture* (2011), Vera M. Kutzinski's *The Worlds of Langston Hughes: Modernism and Translation in the Americas* (2012), and David E. Chinitz's *Which Sin to Bear? Authenticity and Compromise in Langston Hughes* (2013). Three collections of essays are useful for giving a sense of Hughes's place in American letters and the range of responses to his work: *Montage of a Dream: The Art and Life of Langston Hughes*, edited by John Edgar Tidwell and Cheryl R. Ragan (2007); *Langston Hughes*, edited by Harold Bloom (new ed., 2008); and *Langston Hughes*, edited by R. Baxter Miller (2013). This last volume is a particularly good place to start, and also has an excellent bibliography covering Hughes's own works and the secondary literature on him.

David Hume

For Hume's writings, see *The Essays, Moral, Political, and Literary*, edited by T. H. Green and T. H. Grose (4 vols., 1874–75), and *The Philosophical Works of David Hume*, edited by T. H. Green and T. H. Grose (4 vols., 1882–86; rpt. 1964). Eugene F. Miller has prepared a good modern edition of Hume's essays (rev. ed., 1987). For a one-volume collection, see *The Essential David Hume*, edited by Robert Paul Wolff (1969). *Essays and Treatises on Philosophical Subjects*, edited by Lorne Falkenstein and Neil McArthur (2013), with detailed notes and contextual materials, is the first edition in over a century to present Hume's *Enquiry Concerning Human Understanding, Dissertation on the Passions, Enquiry Concerning the Principles of Morals*, and *Natural History of Religion* in the format he intended—collected together in a single volume. The correspondence is available in *The Letters of David Hume*, edited by J. Y. T. Greig (2 vols., 1932), and *New Letters of David Hume*, edited by Raymond Klibansky and Ernest C. Mossner (1954). The standard biography is Ernest C. Mossner, *The Life of David Hume* (2d ed., 1980). In *Hume: An Intellectual Biography* (2015), James A. Harris focuses on Hume's intentions as a philosophical analyst of human nature, politics, commerce, English history, and religion; he also examines Hume's intellectual relations with his contemporaries. Don Garrett's *Hume* (2015) is a full account of the life and work, with an excellent chapter on the influence and legacy of Hume's thought today.

Introductions to Hume's work include D. G. C. MacNabb, *David Hume: His Theory of Knowledge and Morality* (2d ed., 1966); Terence Penelhum, *Hume* (1975); Barry Stroud, *Hume* (1977); and A. J. Ayer, *Hume* (1980). For more detailed discussions, see Norman Kemp Smith, *The Philosophy of David Hume: A Critical Study of Its Origins and Central Doctrines* (1966); James Noxon, *Hume's Philosophical Development* (1973); John Passmore, *Hume's Intentions* (3d ed., 1980); Donald W. Livingston, *Hume's Philosophy of Common Life* (1984); and Anthony Flew, *David Hume, Philosopher of Moral Science* (1986). On the empiricist tradition, see Jonathan Francis Bennett, *Locke, Berkeley, Hume: Central Themes* (1971). Recent studies include *David Hume: Historical Thinker, Historical Writer*, edited by Mark G. Spencer (2013), a very good collection on Hume's historical writings and their intersections with his work on philosophy and literature; Dennis C. Rasmussen, *The Pragmatic Enlightenment: Recovering the Liberalism of Hume, Smith, Montesquieu, and Voltaire* (2014), on morality, reason, and eighteenth-century political theory; Thomas W. Merrill, *Hume and the Politics of Enlightenment* (2015); and Jacqueline Anne Taylor, *Reflecting Subjects: Passion, Sympathy, and Society in Hume's Philosophy* (2015), which deals with Hume's social theory, focusing on the passions and imagination in relation to institutions such as government and the economy.

On Hume as a literary critic and theorist, see Teddy Brunius, *David Hume on Criticism* (1952), and Jan Wilbanks, *Hume's Theory of Imagination* (1968). Chapter 2 in Terry Eagleton, *The Ideology of the Aesthetic* (1990), examining Hume, Shaftesbury, and Burke, is provocative. Hume has also received much attention as a literary artist in his own right; see Leo Braudy, *Narrative Form in History and Fiction: Hume, Fielding, and Gibbon* (1970); John J. Richetti, *Philosophical Writing: Locke, Berkeley, Hume* (1983); Jerome Christensen, *Practicing Enlightenment: Hume and the Formation of a Literary Career* (1987); Leopold Damrosch, *Fictions of Reality in the Age of Hume and Johnson* (1989); M. A. Box, *The Suasive Art of David Hume* (1990); Adam Potkay, *The Fate of Eloquence in the Age of Hume* (1994); and Adela Pinch, *Strange Fits of Passion: Epistemologies of Emotion, Hume to Austen* (1996). On Hume's work and the empiricist background of aesthetics in the eighteenth century, Dabney Townsend's *Hume's Aesthetic Theory: Taste and Sentiment* (2001) is illuminating. *The Continuum Companion to Hume*, edited by Alan Bailey and Dan O'Brien (2012), offers wide-ranging coverage and includes an essay by M. W. Rowe on "Of the Standard of Taste."

An excellent resource is *The Cambridge Companion to Hume*, edited by David Norton and Jacqueline Taylor (2d ed., 2008), which includes an essay by Peter Jones on Hume's account of the arts and taste, plus a selected bibliography. See also T. E. Jessop, *A Bibliography of David Hume and of Scottish Philosophy from Frances Hutcheson to Lord Balfour* (1938); Roland Hall,

A Hume Bibliography, from 1930 (1971); the bibliographical essay in *Hume and the Enlightenment*, edited by William B. Todd (1974); and Roland Hall, *Fifty Years of Hume Scholarship: A Bibliographical Guide* (1978).

Zora Neale Hurston

Hurston's novels, stories, folklore, memoirs, and other writings are available from the Library of America in two volumes edited by Cheryl A. Wall, *Novels and Stories* and *Folklore, Memoirs, and Other Writings* (1995). See also *I Love Myself: A Zora Neale Hurston Reader*, edited by Alice Walker (1979).

Robert Hemenway's *Zora Neale Hurston* (1977) is an indispensable biography that has done much to spark interest in Hurston's work. Lillie P. Howard's *Zora Neale Hurston* (1980) is a concise survey of Hurston's life and writings. In addition, *Zora Neale Hurston: A Life in Letters*, edited by Carla Kaplan (2002), includes more than 600 letters that span nearly forty years of Hurston's life. Virginia Lynn Moylan's *Zora Neale Hurston's Final Decade* (2011) recounts the writer's turbulent last years. The best studies of Hurston are Karla F. C. Holloway, *The Character of the Word: The Texts of Zora Neale Hurston* (1987); Lynda Marion Hill, *Social Rituals and the Verbal Art of Zora Neale Hurston* (1996); Susan Edwards Meisenhelder, *Hitting a Straight Lick with a Crooked Stick: Race and Gender in the Work of Zora Neale Hurston* (1999); and Tiffany Ruby Patterson, *Zora Neale Hurston and a History of Southern Life* (2005).

Cheryl A. Wall's *Women of the Harlem Renaissance* (1995) places Hurston within a wider cultural and literary context. On the relation of Hurston's work to contemporary literary theory and African American cultural and literary studies, see Barbara Johnson, *A World of Difference* (1987), and Henry Louis Gates Jr., *The Signifying Monkey: A Theory of Afro-American Literary Criticism* (1988). A helpful collection of essays is *Zora Neale Hurston: Perspectives Past and Present*, edited by Henry Louis Gates Jr. and K. A. Appiah (1993). The documentary *Zora Neale Hurston: Jump at the Sun* (2008), produced and written by Kristy Andersen, is informative and moving. For bibliography, see Adele S. Newson, *Zora Neale Hurston: A Reference Guide* (1987); Rose Parkman Davis, *Zora Neale Hurston: An Annotated Bibliography and Reference Guide* (1997); and Cynthia Davis and Verner D. Mitchell's *Zora Neale Hurston: An Annotated Bibliography of Works and Criticism* (2013).

Wolfgang Iser

Iser's early works, *Die Weltanschauung Henry Fieldings* (1952, *Henry Fielding's Worldview*) and *Walter Pater: The Aesthetic Moment* (1960; trans. 1987), are traditional scholarly studies. He first developed his views of reader response in *Die Appell-struktur der Text* (1970, *The Affective Structure of the Text*), *The Implied Reader: Patterns of Communication in Prose Fiction from Bunyan to Beckett* (1972; trans. 1974), and *The Act of Reading: A Theory of Aesthetic Response* (1976; trans. 1978). Thereafter, Iser published two literary studies, *Laurence Sterne: Tristram Shandy* (1987; trans. 1988) and *Staging Politics: The Lasting Impact of Shakespeare's Histories* (1988; trans. 1993). In *Prospecting: From Reader Response to Literary Anthropology* (1989), *The Fictive and the Imaginary: Charting Literary Anthropology* (1991; trans. 1993), and *The Range of Interpretation* (2000), Iser moved to develop "literary anthropology," examining why (rather than how) people read and exploring how fiction is a necessary human activity. Iser also published an introductory guide, *How to Do Theory* (2006); his brief *Stepping Forward: Essays, Lectures and Interviews* (2008) collects several previously unpublished pieces.

An early, notable response by Stanley Fish, "Why No One Is Afraid of Wolfgang Iser," appeared in *Diacritics* 11 (1981). Steven Mailloux's *Interpretive Conventions: The Reader in the Study of American Fiction* (1982) includes a good discussion of Iser's relation to the New Criticism and a pointed comparison between Iser and Fish. Robert Holub's "Reception Theory: School of Constance," in *The Cambridge History of Literary Criticism*, vol. 8, *From Formalism to Poststructuralism* (ed. Raman Selden, 1995), provides an excellent overview of Iser's work and the Constance School, noting its influence on a second generation of reception theorists. Michael Bérubé's "There Is Nothing Inside the Text, or, Why No One's Heard of Wolfgang Iser," in *Postmodern Sophistry: Stanley Fish and the Critical Enterprise* (ed. Gary A. Olson and Lynn Worsham, 2004), speculates that Fish's takedown turned attention away from Iser. Still, there has been a good deal of criticism reassessing his work since 2000. A special issue of *New Literary History* 31 (2000)—*On the Writings of Wolfgang Iser*, edited by John Paul Riquelme—gathers ten substantial essays on aspects of Iser's work and career; it includes Brook Thomas's "Restaging the Reception of Iser's Early Work, or Sides Not Taken in Discussions of the Aesthetic," which usefully contextualizes Iser's entrance on the American critical scene, and Winfried Fluck's dense but informative "The Search for Distance: Negation and Negativity in Wolfgang Iser's Literary Theory," which comments on Iser's interest in aesthetics as a generational response to the situation in Germany after World War II. Craig Hamilton and Ralf Schneider, "From Iser to Turner and Beyond: Reception Theory Meets Cognitive Criticism," *Style* 36 (2002), includes a substantial review of Iser's work and looks at how contemporary cognitive theory has developed from reception theory. Robert Folkenflik's "Wolfgang Iser's Eighteenth

Century," *Poetics Today* 27 (2006), examines the way that eighteenth-century British novels, one of Iser's specialties, influenced his views. See also Brook Thomas, "The Fictive and the Imaginary: Charting Literary Anthropology, or, What's Literature Have to Do with It?" *American Literary History* 20 (2008), which rebuts Bérubé and surveys recent work on Iser.

On Iser's theory in pedagogy, see Olga M. Hubard, "The Act of Looking: Wolfgang Iser's Literary Theory and Meaning Making in the Visual Arts," *International Journal of Art and Design Education* 27 (2008), and Lisa Schade Eckert, "Bridging the Pedagogical Gap: Intersections between Literary and Reading Theories in Secondary and Postsecondary Literacy Instruction," *Journal of Adolescent and Adult Literacy* 52 (2008). Two articles amend Iser's concept of "the implied reader," showing its relevance to queer theory and cognitive theory: Hanna Kubowitz, "The Default Reader and a Model of Queer Reading and Writing Strategies Or: Obituary for the Implied Reader," *Style* 46 (2012), and Karin Kukkonen, "Presence and Prediction: The Embodied Reader's Cascades of Cognition," *Style* 48 (2014). Ben De Bruyn, *Wolfgang Iser: A Companion* (2012), surveys Iser's work and includes a selected bibliography.

Roman Jakobson

The best single collection of Jakobson's writings on literature is *Language in Literature*, edited by Krystyna Pomorska and Stephen Rudy (1987). A more complete selection is available in *Selected Writings* (7 vols., 1971–84), each volume of which is introduced with a "retrospective" by Jakobson himself. Biographical information is both plentiful and scant. The closest thing to a biography is a volume of conversations between Jakobson and Krystyna Pomorska, his third wife, titled *Dialogues* (1983); it perfectly illustrates Jakobson's "mythic" concept of autobiography: both participants are focused on displaying the charisma of Jakobson's intellectual, not personal, life.

Good introductions to Jakobson's work are Elmar Holenstein's *Roman Jakobson's Approach to Language: Phenomenological Structuralism* (1974; trans. 1976) and Richard Bradford's *Roman Jakobson: Life, Language, Art* (1994). For two excellent and different accounts of Russian formalism in context, see Victor Erlich, *Russian Formalism: History—Doctrine* (1955; 3d ed., 1981) and Fredric Jameson, *The Prison-House of Language: A Critical Account of Structuralism and Russian Formalism* (1972). *Roman Jakobson: Echoes of His Scholarship*, edited by Daniel Armstrong and C. H. Van Schooneveld (1977), gives a good general sense of the many directions those pursuing Jakobson's interests have taken. Svetlana Boym's *Death in Quotation Marks: Cultural Myths of the Modern Poet* (1991) furthers Jakobson's analysis of mythic biography. For a bibliography of works by Jakobson, see Stephen Rudy, *Roman Jakobson: A Complete Bibliography of His Writings, 1912–1982* (1985); for critical writings about Jakobson, see the annotated overview in Bradford's book along with bibliographies in the book by Holenstein and in *Language, Poetry, and Poetics: The Generation of the 1890s—Jakobson, Trubetszkoy, Majakovskij*, edited by Krystyna Pomorska, Elzbieta Chodakowska, Hugh McLean, and Brent Vine (1987).

Henry James

James's literary criticism has been collected by the Library of America in two volumes, titled *Essays, American and English Writers* and *European Writers and the Prefaces* (1984). This is an essential collection for the student of James's work. Selections can be found in *Literary Reviews and Essays on American, English, and French Literature*, edited by Albert Mordell (1957); *Henry James: Selected Literary Criticism*, edited by Morris Shapira (1963); *Theory of Fiction: Henry James*, edited by James E. Miller Jr. (1972), arranged according to topics and categories; *The House of Fiction: Essays on the Novel*, edited by Leon Edel (1973); *The Art of Criticism: Henry James on the Theory and the Practice of Fiction*, edited by William Veeder and Susan M. Griffin (1986), which includes excellent discussion of and detailed notes for each selection; and *The Critical Muse: Selected Literary Criticism of Henry James*, edited by Roger Gard (1988), which is the best selection for an overview of James's achievement in criticism and theory. Also important is *The Art of the Novel: Critical Prefaces by Henry James*, with an introduction by R. P. Blackmur (new ed., 1984), which gathers the prefaces that James wrote for the New York Edition. Additional primary sources include *Henry James: Autobiography*, edited by F. W. Dupee (1956), written in James's late labyrinthine, evocative manner; *The Complete Notebooks of Henry James*, edited by Leon Edel and Lyall H. Powers (1987); and *Letters*, edited by Leon Edel (4 vols., 1974–84). *William and Henry James: Selected Letters*, edited by Ignas K. Skrupskelis and Elizabeth M. Berkeley (1997), is a fascinating collection. A new, complete edition of James's letters, edited by Pierre A. Walker and Greg W. Zacharias, is now in progress (11 vols. to date, 2006–). Another valuable resource is Edgar F. Harden, *A Henry James Chronology* (2005).

The definitive biography is *Henry James*, variously subtitled, in five volumes by Leon Edel (1953–72); it is condensed and updated in the single volume *Henry James: A Life* (1985). Other excellent biographies include Fred Kaplan, *Henry James: The Imagination of Genius: A Biography* (1992), and Kenneth Graham, *Henry James: A Literary Life* (1995). Lyndall Gordon, *A Private Life of Henry James: Two Women and His Art* (1999), probes the impact on James's writing of two important relationships: one with his cousin Minnie Temple, the other with the author Constance Fenimore Woolson. Sheldon M. Novick, in *Henry James: The Young Master* (1996) and *Henry James: The Mature Master* (2007), examines the work and the life, including a speculative, and controversial, account of James's homosexuality. In *House of Wits: An Intimate Portrait of the James Family* (2008), Paul Fisher provides a keen study of the entire James family in the context of nineteenth- and twentieth-century society and culture. See also *A Historical Guide to Henry James*, edited by John Carlos Rowe and Eric Haralson (2012), which includes essays on race and empire, sexuality, gender, and other topics.

The best scholarly writings on James as a critic and theorist are Sarah B. Daugherty, *The Literary Criticism of Henry James* (1981), and Vivien Jones, *James the Critic* (1984). Also helpful are Adeline Tintner, *The Book World of Henry James: Appropriating the Classics* (1987); Jonathan Freedman, *Professions of Taste: Henry James, British Aestheticism, and Commodity Culture* (1990), which makes cogent connections among James, Walter Pater, and Oscar Wilde; Edwin S. Fussell, *The French Side of Henry James* (1990); Tony Tanner, *Henry James and the Art of Nonfiction* (1995), which includes a chapter on the criticism; and Pierre A. Walker, *Reading Henry James in French Cultural Contexts* (1995).

Among the many books on James's fiction, the most pertinent to his critical writings and context are Laurence Bedwell Holland, *The Expense of Vision: Essays on the Craft of Henry James* (1964), a brilliant analysis of the novels that relates them to the criticism, especially to the prefaces; John Carlos Rowe, *The Theoretical Dimensions of Henry James* (1984); Michael Anesko, *"Friction with the Market": Henry James and the Profession of Authorship* (1986), on the pressures that James faced in struggling to meet but not surrender to the demands of the literary marketplace; Sharon Cameron, *Thinking in Henry James* (1989); Ross Posnock, *The Trial of Curiosity: Henry James, William James, and the Challenge of Modernity* (1991), a wide-ranging comparison of the James brothers' attitudes toward the challenges of modernity; Garry Hagberg, *Meaning and Interpretation: Wittgenstein, Henry James, and Literary Knowledge* (1994); and Eric Haralson, *Henry James and Queer Modernity* (2003), rewarding for its analysis of sexual politics and aesthetic theory and practice in James, Willa Cather, Gertrude Stein, and Ernest Hemingway. For comparisons of James and other significant critics, see Rob Davidson, *The Master and the Dean: The Literary Criticism of Henry James and William Dean Howells* (2005), and Michèle Mendelssohn, *Henry James, Oscar Wilde and Aesthetic Culture* (2007). Recent scholarly work includes Kevin Ohi, *Henry James and the Queerness of Style* (2011), which gives subtle consideration to James's later writings in the context of queer theory; Lisi Schoenbach, *Pragmatic Modernism* (2012), a stimulating exploration of pragmatist philosophy and its keywords (habit, institution, etc.), with interpretations of James, Gertrude Stein, Marcel Proust, and other writers; and Michael Anesko, *Monopolizing the Master: Henry James and the Politics of Modern Literary Scholarship* (2012), an excellent examination of James and the literary marketplace and the critical reception of his writings, especially the groundbreaking biographical and critical interpretations by Percy Lubbock, Leon Edel, and others.

See also *A Bibliography of Henry James*, by Leon Edel and Dan H. Laurence, revised with the assistance of James Rambeau (3d ed., 1982). Secondary sources are listed in Linda J. Taylor, *Henry James, 1866–1916: A Reference Guide* (1982); Kristin Pruitt McColgan, *Henry James, 1917–1959: A Reference Guide* (1979); Dorothy McInnis Scura, *Henry James, 1960–1974: A Reference Guide* (1979); and Judith E. Funston, *Henry James: A Reference Guide, 1975–1987* (1991). Consult also the excellent bibliographical essay in Rowe and Haralson's *Historical Guide* (see above).

Fredric Jameson

Largely focused on stylistics rather than Jean-Paul Sartre's Marxist politics, Jameson's first book, *Sartre: The Origins of a Style* (1961), a revision of his doctoral dissertation, offered scant indication of his subsequent work. The two major studies of the early 1970s, *Marxism and Form: Twentieth-Century Dialectical Theories of Literature* (1971) and *The Prison-House of Language: A Critical Account of Structuralism and Russian Formalism* (1972), respectively introduced the work of the Frankfurt School and other European Marxists and the work of the Russian formalists and early French structuralists to the English-speaking world before much of it was available in translation. After writing a short book on the English modernist Wyndham Lewis, *Fables of Aggression: Wyndham Lewis, the Modernist as Fascist* (1979), Jameson captured the attention of Anglophone intellectual circles with *The Political Unconscious: Narrative as a Socially Symbolic Act* (1981), which solidified his position as the leading representative of Marxist theory. It was followed by a two-volume collection of previously published pieces, *The Ideologies of Theory: Essays, 1971–1986* (1988), which includes his succinct "Metacommentary" (1971) and his programmatic reflections on historical method, "Marxism and Historicism" (1980). *Late Marxism: Adorno, or, the Persistence of the Dialectic* (1990) extends his survey of Marxist figures begun in *Marxism and Form*.

In the 1990s Jameson turned increasingly to film and popular culture. *Signatures of the Visible* (1990) collects writings on film, concluding with an important essay theorizing its development from the silent era onward. *Postmodernism, or, The Cultural Logic of Late Capitalism* (1991) has had wide influence in defining the postmodern era and its art. There followed a collection of essays on contemporary cinema, *The Geopolitical Aesthetic: Cinema and Space in the World System* (1992). Jameson also published two books assembled from lectures: *The Seeds of Time* (Wellek Library Lectures, 1994) and *Theory of Culture: Lectures at Rikkyo* (1994). The useful collection *The Cultural Turn: Selected Writings on the Postmodern, 1983–98* (1998), which includes "Postmodernism and Consumer Society," records his developing views on postmodernism. *Brecht and Method* (1998) takes the German dramatist Bertolt Brecht (rather than Adorno) as an exemplary figure for reviving Marxism in the era of late capitalism, and *A Singular Modernity: Essay on the Ontology of the Present* (2002) is a short reconsideration of the idea of the modern. Two hefty collections, *The Modernist Papers* (2007) and *Archaeologies of the Future: The Desire Called Utopia and Other Science Fictions* (2005), gather Jameson's essays from three decades on modern literature and on science fiction.

Since then, Jameson has readdressed major theoretical issues in *Valences of the Dialectic* (2009) and two studies focused on particular works, *The Hegel Variations: On the "Phenomenology of Spirit"* (2010) and *Representing "Capital": A Reading of Volume One* (2011). In addition, *The Antinomies of Realism* (2013) revisits the question of realism and the historical novel, *The Ancients and the Postmoderns: On the Historicity of Forms* (2015) looks at art and the question of the classic and the modern, and *Raymond Chandler: The Detections of Totality* (2016) is a short study of the detective genre. *The Jameson Reader*, edited by Michael Hardt and Kathi Weeks (2000), provides an excellent selection of Jameson's work, and *Jameson on Jameson: Conversations on Cultural Marxism*, edited by Ian Buchanan (2007), gathers interviews from three decades.

Jameson's writings have drawn a substantial though uneven body of criticism. Perhaps the best early accounts are by Terry Eagleton, "The Idealism of American Criticism" (1981) and "Frederic Jameson: The Politics of Style" (1982), both collected in his *Against the Grain: Selected Essays* (1986). Two critical journals devoted special issues to *The Political Unconscious: Diacritics* 12 (1982), which includes essays by the historian Hayden White, Eagleton (cited above), and others, and *New Orleans Review* 11 (1984), which includes a response by Jean-François Lyotard. Mike Davis offers a celebrated challenge to Jameson's account of postmodern architecture in "Urban Renaissance and the Spirit of Postmodernism," *New Left Review*, no. 151 (1985). *Postmodernism/Jameson/Critique*, edited by Douglas Kellner (1989), gathers diverse essays as well as Jameson's response to his critics. A famous riposte, Aijaz Ahmad's "Jameson's Rhetoric of Otherness and the 'National Allegory'" (1987), polemically critiques Jameson's notion of third world literature; it has been reprinted in Ahmad's *In Theory: Classes, Nations, Literatures* (1992). Perry Anderson's *Origins of Postmodernity* (1998) is a short overview by a leading British Marxist; in addition, Sean Homer, *Fredric Jameson: Marxism, Hermeneutics, Postmodernism* (1998); Adam Roberts, *Fredric Jameson* (2000); and Ian Buchanan, *Fredric Jameson: Live Theory* (2006), provide useful introductions. The collections *Fredric Jameson: A Critical Reader*, edited by Sean Homer and Douglas Kellner (2004), and *On Jameson: From Postmodernism to Globalism*, edited by Caren Irr and Ian Buchanan (2006), investigate, respectively, the range of Jameson's work and his more recent attention to globalism. Looking to his earlier work rather than to his analysis of postmodernism, *The Political Unconscious of Architecture: Re-opening Jameson's "Narrative,"* edited by Nadir Lahiji (2011), collects fourteen essays on architecture. Two studies by former students, Robert T. Tally Jr.'s *Fredric Jameson: The Project of Dialectical Criticism* (2014) and Phillip E. Wegner's *Periodizing Jameson: Dialectics, the University, and the Desire for Narrative* (2014), offer good surveys of his work over his career. *An American Utopia: Dual Power and the Universal Army*, edited by Slavoj Žižek (2016), includes the title essay by Jameson and responses by Žižek and eight other critics.

Homer, *Fredric Jameson*, contains a bibliography of primary and selected secondary texts. *The Jameson Reader* and *Jameson on Jameson* include comprehensive bibliographies of Jameson's writings.

Samuel Johnson

The standard edition has been *The Works of Samuel Johnson* (11 vols., 1825; reprinted in 1970 as *Dr. Johnson's Works*). It is being superseded by *The Yale Edition of the Works of Samuel Johnson* (22 vols. to date, 1958–). Other valuable editions of Johnson's works include *The Lives of the English Poets*, edited by George Birkbeck Hill (3 vols., 1905); *Johnson's "Lives of the Poets": A Selection*, edited by J. P. Hardy (1971); and *The Life of Richard Savage*, edited by Clarence Tracy (1971). An important recent work in Johnson studies is Roger Lonsdale's superb four-volume edition of *The Lives of the English Poets* (2006), which presents the primary texts; describes the origins, composition, and textual history of the *Lives*; and assesses Johnson's assumptions and aim as biographer and critic. Also valuable is the excellent set of the *Lives* edited by John H. Middendorf (2010), volumes 21–23 of the Yale edition. *The Letters of Samuel Johnson*, edited by Bruce Redford (5 vols., 1992–94), known as the Hyde Edition, is an indispensable resource. *The Complete English Poems*, edited by J. D. Fleeman (1971), is a well-edited collection. The best one-volume selection of Johnson's poetry and prose is *Samuel Johnson*, edited by Donald J. Greene (1984). A good single volume of the prose is *Selected Writings*, edited by Peter Martin (2009). On Johnson's critical outlook, see *The Critical Opinions of Samuel Johnson*, a topical anthology compiled by Joseph Epes Brown (1926), and *Johnson on the English Language*, edited by Gwin J. Kolb and Robert DeMaria Jr. (2005), volume 18 of the Yale edition.

The points of departure for biography are James Boswell, *The Journal of a Tour to the Hebrides* (1785) and *The Life of Samuel Johnson, LL.D.* (1791). Of the many editions of these works—often published together—the best, with detailed notes, is by George Birkbeck Hill, revised and enlarged by L. F. Powell (6 vols., 1934–50, 1964). A paperback edition, with a cogent introduction and notes, has been prepared by David Womersley (2008). There are a number of excellent modern biographies: James L. Clifford, *Young Sam* [or *Samuel*] *Johnson* (1955), and his *Dictionary Johnson: Samuel Johnson's Middle Years* (1979); Walter Jackson Bate, *Samuel Johnson* (1977), which includes expert commentary on Johnson's writings; Thomas Kaminski, *The Early Career of Samuel Johnson* (1987); John Wain, *Samuel Johnson* (rev. ed., 1988), a vivid portrait of Johnson as a literary professional; Robert DeMaria Jr., *The Life of Samuel Johnson: A Critical Biography* (1993), a first-rate survey of Johnson's literary career; Richard Holmes, *Dr. Johnson and Mr. Savage* (1993); and Lawrence I. Lipking, *Samuel Johnson: The Life of an Author* (1998). Donald Greene, *Samuel Johnson* (rev. ed., 1989), offers a fine briefer treatment. Also useful are Norman Page, *A Dr. Johnson Chronology* (1990), and Pat Rogers, *The Samuel Johnson Encyclopedia* (1996). Recent biographies by Peter Martin, *Samuel Johnson: A Biography* (2008), and by Jeffrey Meyers, *Samuel Johnson: The Struggle* (2008), are enlightening; Martin is especially good on historical context and social background, while Meyers, taking a more literary point of view, deals expertly with Johnson as a writer. David Nokes, *Samuel Johnson: A Life* (2009), is solid on the facts and gives a good account of the *Dictionary*, the edition of Shakespeare, and the *Lives of the Poets*. See also John B. Radner, *Johnson and Boswell: A Biography of Friendship* (2012), and Nicholas Hudson, *A Political Biography of Samuel Johnson* (2013), which surveys Johnson's moral and political views during an era of revolutionary transition in the eighteenth century.

For a range of critical opinion, see Walter Jackson Bate, *The Achievement of Samuel Johnson* (1958); Paul Fussell, *Samuel Johnson and the Life of Writing* (1971), filled with sharp perceptions about Johnson's rhetoric and relation to his readers; and Thomas Reinert, *Regulating Confusion: Samuel Johnson and the Crowd* (1996), which explores Johnson's attitudes toward the crowd, the city, and urban culture. Nicholas Hudson, *Samuel Johnson and the Making of Modern England* (2003), examines the impact of Johnson's literary criticism and other writings on the creation of modern English identity. Early critical reception is collected in *Johnson: The Critical Heritage*, edited by James T. Boulton (1971). Collections of criticism include *Samuel Johnson: New Critical Essays*, edited by Isobel Grundy (1984); *Johnson and His Age*, edited by James Engell (1984); and *Johnson after Two Hundred Years*, edited by Paul J. Korshin (1986).

On Johnson's literary criticism, see Jean H. Hagstrum, *Samuel Johnson's Literary Criticism* (1952), a good overview of Johnson's attitudes toward nature, the sublime, wit, and other key topics; Leopold Damrosch Jr., *The Uses of Johnson's Criticism* (1976); Morris R. Brownell, *Samuel Johnson's Attitude to the Arts* (1989), which astutely examines Johnson's positions on music, art, and architecture; Steven Lynn, *Samuel Johnson after Deconstruction: Rhetoric and "The Rambler"* (1992), with interesting comparisons between Johnson and Harold Bloom, Jacques Derrida, and other contemporary theorists; Charles Hinnant, *"Steel for the Mind": Samuel Johnson and Critical Discourse* (1994), which relates Johnson's work to recent debates in literary theory; and Robert DeMaria Jr., *Samuel Johnson and the Life of Reading* (1997). Examinations of Johnson's critical work on Shakespeare include G. F. Parker, *Johnson's Shakespeare* (1989), which includes cogent analysis of responses to Johnson by Romantic poets and critics, and Edward Tomarken, *Samuel Johnson on Shakespeare: The Discipline of Criticism* (1991). On Johnson as biographer of poets, consult Robert Folkenflik, *Samuel Johnson, Biographer* (1978); Martin Maner, *The Philosophical Biographer: Doubt and Dialectic in Johnson's "Lives of the Poets"* (1988); and Catherine Neal Parke, *Samuel Johnson and Biographical Thinking* (1991). Also recommended are the following collections of essays: *The Interpretation of Samuel Johnson*, edited by Jonathan Clark and Howard Erskine-Hill (2012), noteworthy for Erskine-Hill's essay on the *Lives of the Poets*; *Samuel Johnson: The Arc of the Pendulum*, edited by Freya Johnston and Lynda Mugglestone (2012); *Samuel Johnson in Context*, edited by Jack Lynch (2012), valuable on a wide range of topics, including a fine essay by Philip Smallwood on Johnson's literary criticism; and *Samuel Johnson: New Contexts for a New Century*, edited by Howard D. Weinbrot (2014), illuminating in its coverage of Johnson's writings, life, and relationships.

The standard bibliography is William P. Courtney and David Nichol Smith, *A Bibliography of Samuel Johnson* (1915). It is supplemented by R. W. Chapman and Allen T. Hazen, "Johnsonian Bibliography: A Supplement to Courtney," in *Oxford Bibliographical Society, Proceedings and Papers*, vol. 5, pt. 3 (1938). James L. Clifford and Donald J. Greene, *Samuel Johnson: A Survey and Bibliography of Critical Studies* (1970), contains 4,000 items. See also Donald J. Greene and John A. Vance, *A Bibliography of Johnsonian Studies, 1970–1985* (1987). *The Cambridge Companion to Samuel Johnson*, edited by Greg Clingham (1997), offers a selective guide to further reading. Compiled by J. D. Fleeman, *A Bibliography of the*

Works of Samuel Johnson (2 vols., 2000) treats the published items up to 1984. Johnson's *The Major Works*, edited by Donald J. Greene (rev. ed., 2008), provides a concise list of further reading.

Immanuel Kant

The Cambridge edition of the works of Immanuel Kant (1992–) offers the first complete scholarly edition in English of all of Kant's writing (in the list below, all translations published after 1991 belong to this edition). *Theoretical Philosophy, 1755–1770*, edited by David Walford (1992), contains much of Kant's early work (although not his 1764 book on aesthetics), while *Practical Philosophy*, edited by Mary J. Gregor (1996), collects the major works on morality (including *Groundwork of the Metaphysics of Morals*, 1785; *Critique of Practical Reason*, 1788; and *The Metaphysics of Morals*, 1797, along with the important essays "What Is Enlightenment?," 1784, and "Toward Perpetual Peace," 1795). Kant's major individual works are *Observations on the Feeling of the Beautiful and Sublime* (1764; trans. 1960); *Critique of Pure Reason* (1781; trans. 1998); *Prolegomena to Any Future Metaphysics* (1783; trans. 1997); *Metaphysical Foundations of Natural Science* (1786; trans. 2004); *Critique of Judgment* (1790; trans. 1987 and 2000); *Religion within the Boundaries of Mere Reason* (1793; trans. 1998); *The Conflict of Faculties* (1798; trans. 1992); and *Anthropology from a Pragmatic Point of View* (1798; trans. 2006). Kant's essays, lectures, and letters can be found in *Kant: On History*, edited by Louis White Beck (1963); *Selected Pre-Critical Writings and Correspondence with Beck*, edited by G. B. Kerferd and D. E. Walford (1968); *Kant's Political Writings*, edited by Hans Reiss (1970); *Lectures on Philosophical Theology*, edited by Allen W. Wood and Gertrude M. Clark (1978); *Perpetual Peace and Other Essays on Politics, History, and Morals*, edited by Ted Humphrey (1983); *Lectures on Logic*, edited by J. Michael Young (1992); *Lectures on Ethics*, edited by Peter Heath and J. B. Schneewind (1997); *Lectures on Metaphysics*, edited by Karl Ameriks and Steve Naragon (1997); and *Correspondence*, edited by Arnulf Zweig (1999). Ernst Cassirer's *Kant's Life and Thought* (1921; trans. 1981) remains of interest, but the standard biography is now Manfred Kuehn's *Kant* (2001).

The secondary literature on Kant is immense. Paul Guyer's *Kant* (2d ed., 2014) is a superb one-volume overview of Kant's entire work. Douglas Burnham's *An Introduction to Kant's "Critique of Judgement"* (2000), Christian Helmut Wenzel's *An Introduction to Kant's Aesthetics: Core Concepts and Problems* (2005), and Fiona Hughes's *Kant's "Critique of Aesthetic Judgement": A Reader's Guide* (2010) offer accessible guides to Kant's views on beauty, taste, the sublime, and art. *Kant's "Critique of the Power of Judgment": Critical Essays*, edited by Paul Guyer (2003), gathers a variety of responses to Kant's aesthetics, while *The Cambridge Companion to Kant*, edited by Paul Guyer (1992), offers essays that cover Kant's whole career. See also *The Sublime and Its Teleology: Kant, German Idealism, and Phenomenology*, edited by Donald Loose (2012). Of the many encounters with Kant's work in contemporary theory, the following have been especially influential: Jacques Derrida, *The Truth in Painting* (1978; trans. 1987); Pierre Bourdieu, *Distinction: A Social Critique of the Judgement of Taste* (1979; trans. 1984); Hannah Arendt, *Lectures on Kant's Political Philosophy* (1982); Barbara Herrnstein Smith, *Contingencies of Value* (1988); Terry Eagleton, *The Ideology of the Aesthetic* (1990); Jean-François Lyotard, *Lessons on the Analytic of the Sublime* (1991; trans. 1994); J. M. Bernstein, *The Fate of Art: Aesthetic Alienation from Kant to Derrida and Adorno* (1992); and Rodolphe Gasché, *The Idea of Form: Rethinking Kant's Aesthetics* (2003). Within the Anglo-American philosophical tradition, the best treatments of Kant's aesthetics are Paul Guyer's *Kant and the Claims of Taste* (2d ed., 1997), Henry E. Allison's *Kant's Theory of Taste: A Reading of the "Critique of Aesthetic Judgment"* (2001), Eli Friedlander's *Expressions of Judgment: An Essay on Kant's Aesthetics* (2015), and Hannah Ginsborg's *The Normativity of Nature: Essays on Kant's "Critique of Judgement"* (2015). *Kant's "Critique of the Power of Judgment": Critical Essays* offers an annotated bibliography of commentaries on Kant's aesthetics; Christian Wenzet's "Kant's Aesthetics: Overview and Recent Literature," *Philosophy Compass* 4 (2009), provides another listing of secondary sources, as does Guyer's *Kant* (2014).

E. Ann Kaplan

E. Ann Kaplan began her career with studies of film, notably its relation to feminism, in *Talking about the Cinema* (1966; 2d ed., 1974), co-authored (as Ann Mercer) with Jim Kitses; *Fritz Lang: A Guide to References and Resources* (1981); and *Women and Film: Both Sides of the Camera* (1983). She took a broader view of popular culture in *Rocking around the Clock: Music Television, Postmodernism, and Consumer Culture* (1987), the first academic study of the new form of MTV, and *Motherhood and Representation: The Mother in Popular Culture and Melodrama* (1992; rpt. 2013), while continuing her research on film in *Looking for the Other: Feminism, Film, and the Imperial Gaze* (1997). In a turn linked with her interest in psychoanalysis, she examines trauma in *Trauma Culture: The Politics of Terror and Loss in Media and Literature* (2005), her most important and influential work, where she analyzes the artistic, literary, and cinematic forms through which individuals and collectives undergo, represent, and describe the experience of trauma. Also significant is *Climate Trauma: Foreseeing the Future in Dystopian Film and Fic-*

tion (2016), which explores expressions of "pre-traumatic stress disorder" in depictions of environmental and other crises in such films as *Soylent Green* (1973), *The Road* (2009), and *The Book of Eli* (2010) and in documentaries on climate change.

Kaplan has also edited or co-edited twelve books, including *Women in Film Noir* (1978; rev. and expanded ed., 1998); *Regarding Television: Critical Approaches—An Anthology* (1983); *Postmodernism and Its Discontents: Theories, Practices* (1988); *Psychoanalysis and Cinema* (1990); *Generations: Academic Feminists in Dialogue* (1997), with Devoney Looser; *Feminism and Film* (2000); and *Trauma and Cinema: Cross-Cultural Explorations* (2008), with Ban Wang. Biographical information is available in several interviews with Kaplan. See "Instituting Cultural Studies," in *Critics at Work: Interviews, 1993–2003*, edited by Jeffrey J. Williams (2004), where Kaplan talks about her relations with British cultural studies, and an interview in *Americana: The Journal of American Popular Culture, 1900 to Present* 4.1 (2005) in which Kaplan discusses her family in the context of her book *Motherhood and Representation* and addresses more broadly the roles in her work of feminism, psychoanalysis, and postmodernism.

Trauma studies reaches into many disciplines and fields; for contemporary literary theory and criticism, important points of departure noted in Kaplan's book include Shoshana Felman and Dori Laub, *Testimony: Crises of Witnessing in Literature, Psychoanalysis, and History* (1991); Dominick LaCapra, *Representing the Holocaust: History, Theory, Trauma* (1994); *Trauma: Explorations in Memory*, edited by Cathy Caruth (1995); Caruth, *Unclaimed Experience: Trauma, Narrative, and History* (1996); and Shoshana Felman, *The Juridical Unconscious: Trials and Traumas in the Twentieth Century* (2002). See also Kali Tal, *Worlds of Hurt: Reading the Literatures of Trauma* (1996); Marianne Hirsch, *Family Frames: Photography Narrative and Postmemory* (1997); and Anne Whitehead, *Trauma Fiction* (2004). Also for students of literature, see *Postcolonial Trauma Novels*, edited by Stef Craps and Gert Buelens, a special issue of *Studies in the Novel* (40.1–2 [2008]).

For further discussion, see *Ethics and Trauma in Contemporary British Fiction* (2011) and *Trauma and Romance in Contemporary British Literature* (2013), both edited by Jean-Michel Ganteau and Susana Onega. See also *The Future of Trauma Theory: Contemporary Literary and Cultural Criticism*, edited by Gert Buelens, Sam Durrant, and Robert Eaglestone (2013); Alan Gibbs's *Contemporary American Trauma Narratives* (2014); and Michael Richardson's *Gestures of Testimony: Torture, Trauma, and Affect in Literature* (2016). Another good resource is *Contemporary Approaches in Literary Trauma Theory*, edited by Michelle Balaev (2014); the introductory chapter surveys the field and includes a bibliography.

Karatani Kōjin

Karatani Kōjin has written more than twenty books that cross disciplinary boundaries as a matter of principle; more than half a dozen are available in English. *Origins of Modern Japanese Literature* (1980; trans. 1993) is his most influential work as a literary critic self-consciously operating in New Historicist and deconstructionist modes. *Architecture as Metaphor: Language, Number, Money* (1983; trans. 1995) moves away from literary analysis to take on the problems of form and formalization in a broad array of domains, arguing that "the will to architecture" is the foundation of all manifestations of Western thought. *Transcritique: On Kant and Marx* (2001; trans. 2003), a rereading of Kant via Marx and Marx via Kant, seeks to establish a theoretical basis for collective resistance against global capital, nation, and state. *Nation and Aesthetics: On Kant and Freud* (2004; trans. 2017), a collection of essays, extends Karatani's analysis on nationalism explored in *Transcritique*. *History and Repetition* (2004; trans. 2012) encompasses economic, historical, and literary analysis across the East–West divide; essays on Marx's *The Eighteenth Brumaire of Louis Bonaparte* and on the thorny issue of periodicity in modern Japan lay the foundation for penetrating insights into the works of the Nobel Prize–winning novelist Kenzaburo Oe and the best-selling novelist Haruki Murakami. *The Structure of World History: From Modes of Production to Modes of Exchange* (2010; trans. with revisions, 2014) marks Karatani's shift from densely layered textual analysis of literary and philosophical forebears to a boldly independent assertion that the key to understanding movements in social history, and the best chance we have for future progress, is to replace Marx's analysis of modes of production with analysis of modes of exchange. A follow-up to *The Structure of World History*, Karatani's *Isonomia and the Origins of Philosophy* (2012; trans. 2017) resituates the birth of Western philosophy and democracy in the ancient Greek colonies of Ionia (present-day Turkey) against the standard idealized narrative about Athens. As opposed to Athenian elitist democracy and its philosophical idealism, *Isonomia* embodies an earlier materialist egalitarian social vision.

Many works remain unavailable in English. Karatani's major texts of literary criticism are *Ifu suru ningen* (1972, *Man in Awe*), *Imi to iu yamai* (1975, *The Sickness Called Meaning*), *Han-bungaku ron* (1979, *Against Literature*), *Hihyō to posutomodan* (1985, *Criticism and the Postmodern*), *Kotoba to higeki* (1989, *Language and Tragedy*), *Sakaguchi Ango to Nakagami Kenji* (1996, *Sakaguchi Ango and Nakagami Kenji*), *Zōho Sōseki ron shūsei* (2001, *Writings on Sōseki*, expanded ed.), and *Kindai bungaku no owari* (2005, *The End of Modern Literature*). His main philosophical books include *Marukusu sono kanōsei no chūshin* (1978, *Marx: The Center of His Possibilities*), a pivotal attempt to read Marx's *Capital* on its own terms; *Naisei to sokō*

(1985, *Introspection and Retrospection*); and *Tankyū* (2 vols., 1986–89, *Philosophical Inquiries*), the latter two works being sustained philosophical inquiries into the problems and possibilities of alterity, difference, and the other. The essays collected in *Hyūmoa to shite no yuibutsuron* (1993, *Materialism as Humor*) integrate inquiry into Western philosophical questions with analyses of modern Japanese history, politics, and literature. The essays collected in *Senzen no shikō* (1994, *Thinking before the War*) focus on overtly political issues such as imperialism, nationalism, democratic representation, the Japanese constitution, and the Gulf War. *Sekai kyōwakoku e: Shihon nēshon kokka o koete* (2006, *Toward a World Republic: Beyond the Trinity of Capital, Nation, and State*) marks a late development in Karatani's theory of capital, nation, and state as an interlocking system of mutually reinforcing entities. *Yūdorōn: Yanagida Kunio to Yamabito* (2014, *On Nomadism: Yanagida Kunio and Mountain People*) and *Teikoku no kōzō: chūshin, shūhen, ashūhen* (2014, *The Structure of Empire: Center, Periphery, A-Periphery*) form a trilogy with *The Structure of World History* to elaborate Karatani's later theories of capital, nation, and state and the central importance of modes of exchange.

Karatani has also published numerous articles and interviews in journals and books on issues related to Japan and to Western philosophy. In English, see especially "One Spirit, Two Nineteenth Centuries," in *Postmodernism and Japan* (ed. Masao Miyoshi and H. D. Harootunian, 1989); "The Discursive Space of Modern Japan," in *Japan in the World* (ed. Masao Miyoshi and H. D. Harootunian, 1993), originally a special issue of *boundary 2* (18.3 [1991]); "Non-Cartesian Cogito, or Cogito as Difference," *Discours Social/Social Discourse* 6.1 (1994); "Nationalism and Écriture," *Surfaces* 5 (1995); "The Uses of Aesthetics: After *Orientalism*," in *Edward Said and the Work of the Critic: Speaking Truth to Power* (ed. Paul A. Bové, 2000), originally a special issue of *boundary 2* (25.2 [1998]); "Edo Exegesis and the Present," in *Modern Japanese Aesthetics: A Reader* (ed. Michele Marra, 1999); "Japan as Art Museum: Okakura Tenshin and Ernest Fenellosa," in *A History of Modern Japanese Aesthetics* (ed. Michael F. Marra, 2001); "Sōseki's Diversity: On *Kokoro*" and "Overcoming Modernity," in *Contemporary Japanese Thought* (ed. Richard F. Calichman, 2005); "Rethinking Sōseki's Theory," *Japan Forum* 20 (2008); "The Irrational Will to Reason: The Praxis of Sakaguchi Ango," in *Literary Mischief: Sakaguchi Ango, Culture, and the War* (ed. James Dorsey and Doug Slaymaker, 2010); "How Catastrophe Heralds a New Japan," in *Counterpunch*, March 24, 2011 (www.counterpunch.org/2011/03/24/how-catastrophe-heralds-a-new-japan/); "'Critique Is Impossible without Moves': An Interview of Kojin Karatani by Joel Wainright," *Dialogues in Human Geography* 2 (2012); and "Rethinking City Planning and Utopianism," in *The Political Unconscious of Architecture: Re-opening Jameson's Narrative* (ed. Nadir Lahiji, 2011).

Fredric Jameson's foreword to the English translation of *Origins of Modern Japanese Literature*, "In the Mirror of Alternate Modernities," is an important introduction to the work within the Western critical context (first published in *South Atlantic Quarterly* 92 [1993]); Brett de Bary's "Karatani Kōjin's *Origins of Modern Japanese Literature*," in *Postmodernism and Japan* (ed. Miyoshi and Harootunian, 1989), is an excellent analysis of the critical context, rhetorical strategies, and broader significance of the work. In "Exteriority and Transcritique: Karatani Kōjin and the Impact of the 1990s," *Japanese Studies* 27 (2007), Carl Cassegard provides a very useful account of Karatani's shift from deconstruction to social activism; and in "From Withdrawal to Resistance: The Rhetoric of Exit in Yoshimoto Takaaki and Karatani Kōjin," *Japan Focus*, March 4, 2008, he analyzes the role of 1960s social movements in Japan for Karatani's thought. Hosea Hirata's *Discourses of Seduction: History, Evil, Desire, and Modern Japanese Literature* (2005) contains a provocative comparison of Karatani's work to that of the contemporary Japanese novelist Murakami Haruki. Slavoj Žižek's "The Parallax View," *New Left Review*, ser. 2, no. 25 (2004), remains the most influential reading of *Transcritique: On Kant and Marx*; Giuseppe Tassone's "Antinomies of Transcritique and Virtue Ethics: An Adornian Critique," *Philosophy and Social Criticism* 34 (2008), pits Karatani's *Transcritique* against Adorno's critique of moral philosophy.

Julia Kristeva

Kristeva's writings first became widely available in English through the publication of the 1980 collection *Desire in Language*, edited by Leon S. Roudiez (who was also responsible for inviting Kristeva to be a regular visitor at Columbia University) and translated by Thomas Gora, Alice Jardine, and Roudiez. This collection, which does not correspond to any book in French, contains essays from her *Séméiótiké* (1969) and from her *Polylogue* (1977). Margaret Waller's English translation of *Revolution in Poetic Language* (1984) reproduces the first half of the original 1974 French text. The best-known translation of "Women's Time" is by Alice Jardine and Harry Blake, and was originally published in the journal *Signs* 7 (1981). Another translation, slightly updated by Kristeva, was produced by Ross Mitchell Guberman for the English translation of *New Maladies of the Soul* (1995). All of the work that derives from Kristeva's "psychoanalytic" period is deeply literary as well, grappling with such authors as Louis-Ferdinand Céline (1894–1961), Gérard de Nerval (1808–1855), Plotinus (ca. 204/5–ca. 270), and Charles Baudelaire (1821–1867). *Powers of Horror* (1980; trans. 1982), *Tales of Love* (1983; trans. 1987), and *Black Sun* (1987; trans. 1989) have been influential in literary studies. Among her other writings are *Language:*

The Unknown (1981; trans. 1989) and *Time and Sense: Proust and the Experience of Literature* (1994; trans. 1996). More recently she has turned her psychoanalytic lens on issues of religion and belief; on hatred, love, and forgiveness; and on the severed human head in art as an avenue to understand violence and desire in, respectively, *This Incredible Need to Believe* (2006; trans. 2009), *Hatred as Forgiveness* (2005; trans. 2010), and *The Severed Head: Capital Visions* (1998; trans. 2012). Kristeva has written what can be described as a series of studies of great female intellectuals: *Hannah Arendt* (1999; trans. 2001), on the philosopher; *Melanie Klein* (2000; trans. 2001), on the psychoanalyst; and *Colette* (2002; trans. 2004), on the novelist. The latest is a sizable book, *Thérèse mon amour: Sainte Thérèse d'Avila* (2008; trans. 2014 as *Teresa, My Love: An Imagined Life of the Saint of Avila*). In addition, she has engaged Simone de Beauvoir and feminism in a series of recent essays: "Beauvoir and the Risks of Freedom," *PMLA* 124 (2009); "Liberty, Equality, Fraternity, and . . . Vulnerability," *Women's Studies Quarterly* 38.1/2 (2010); and "Reading *The Second Sex* Sixty Years Later," *PhiloSOPHIA* 1.2 (2011). *Passions of the Times* (2018), a collection of essays by Kristeva, meditates on time and a range of issues or passions of our times—disability, Islam, French culture and diversity, and humanism. Kristeva has also written a number of novels and a series of reflections on the limits of psychoanalysis. Toril Moi's *Kristeva Reader* (1986) and Kelly Oliver's *Portable Kristeva* (1997) present good selections and substantial introductions to Kristeva's writings. Two books contain biographical information: *Julia Kristeva: Interviews*, edited by Ross Mitchell Guberman (1996), and, with a grain of salt, *The Samurai* (1990; trans. 1992).

There exist a number of helpful explications of Kristeva's work. John Lechte and Maria Margaroni, *Julia Kristeva: Live Theory* (2004), provides a nice introduction to Kristeva, as does *The Kristeva Critical Reader*, edited by Lechte and Mary Zournazi (2003). Elizabeth Grosz's *Sexual Subversions: Three French Feminists* (1989) places Kristeva in the context of French philosophy and feminism, while Birgit Schipper's *Julia Kristeva and Feminist Thought* (2011) explores Kristeva's relationship more broadly to feminist thought. Michael Payne's *Reading Theory: An Introduction to Lacan, Derrida, and Kristeva* (1993) has a chapter devoted to *Revolution in Poetic Language*. John Lechte, *Julia Kristeva* (1990); Kelly Oliver, *Reading Kristeva: Unraveling the Double-Bind* (1993); Anna Smith, *Julia Kristeva: Readings of Exile and Estrangement* (1996); and Anne-Marie Smith, *Julia Kristeva: Speaking the Unspeakable* (1998), all provide overviews of Kristeva's main arguments and concepts. The critical literature on Kristeva is represented in numerous collections of essays, the most notable of which include *Abjection, Melancholia, and Love: The Work of Julia Kristeva*, edited by John Fletcher and Andrew Benjamin (1990); *Body / Text in Julia Kristeva: Religion, Women, and Psychoanalysis*, edited by David Crownfield (1992); *Ethics, Politics, and Difference in Julia Kristeva's Writing*, edited by Kelly Oliver (1993); *After the Revolution: On Kristeva*, edited by John Lechte and Mary Zournazi (1998); and *Psychoanalysis, Aesthetics, and Politics in the Work of Julia Kristeva*, edited by Oliver and S. K. Keltner (2009).

French Feminist Criticism: Women, Language, and Literature, by Elissa D. Gelfand and Virginia Thorndike Hules (1985), contains a dated but well-annotated bibliography of the early Kristeva. Joan Nordquist's *Julia Kristeva: A Bibliography* (1995) provides a comprehensive list of Kristeva's books and essays as well as of relevant critical literature published in English. See also the generous and more recent bibliography in the book by Lechte and Margaroni, as well as in the collection edited by Lechte and Zournazi, both cited above. *Head Cases: Julia Kristeva in Philosophy and Art in Depressed Times* (2014), by Elaine P. Miller, also has an up-to-date Kristeva bibliography.

Jacques Lacan

The literature on Lacan illustrates the axiom that the more difficult the text, the more extensive the bibliography. In addition to his thesis, *De la psychose paranoïaque dans ses rapports avec la personnalité* (1932, *On Paranoiac Psychosis in Its Relations with the Personality*; not yet translated), Lacan published *Écrits* (1966), a small selection of which appeared in English as *Ecrits: A Selection*, translated by Alan Sheridan (1977). Bruce Fink offers a judicious translation of *Écrits* in the aptly titled *Écrits: The First Complete Edition in English* (2006), as well as translating *The Triumph of Religion* (2016) and two lectures collectively titled *On the Names-of-the-Father* (2013). A series of lectures given at the Chapel at Sainte-Anne Hospital has been translated by Adrian Price as *Talking to Brick Walls* (2017). The "Seminar on 'The Purloined Letter'" as it appears in the French *Écrits* can be found, translated by Jeffrey Mehlman, in *The Purloined Poe*, edited by John Muller and William Richardson (1988), an excellent casebook containing essays by Jacques Derrida, Barbara Johnson, and many others. Another notable early translation of and commentary on one of Lacan's essays is Anthony Wilden, *The Language of the Self* (1968), which treats Lacan's "Rome discourse," "Fonction et champ de la parole et du langage en psychanalyse" (1953, "The Function of Language in Psychoanalysis"). A selection of Lacan's writings on female sexuality with two substantial introductions was published as *Feminine Sexuality*, edited by Juliet Mitchell and Jacqueline Rose (1982). To date, the annual seminars of Lacan that have been translated into English are book 1, *Freud's Papers on Technique, 1953–54* (1988); book 2, *The Ego in Freud's Theory and in the Technique of Psychoanalysis, 1954–55* (1988); book 3, *The Psychoses* (1993); book 5, *Formations of the Unconscious* (2017); book 7, *The Ethics of Psychoanalysis, 1959–60*

(1992); book 8, *Transference* (2015); book 10, *Anxiety* (2014); book 11, *The Four Fundamental Concepts of Psycho-Analysis* (1977), a series of lectures given in 1964; book 17, *The Other Side of Psychoanalysis* (2007); book 19, *. . . or Worse* (2017); book 20, *On Feminine Sexuality: The Limits of Love and Knowledge* (1998); and book 23, *The Sinthome* (2016). Several others have appeared in French. Lacan's *My Teaching*, translated by David Macey (2008), contains three lectures directed at those who are not psychoanalysts.

For an information-packed, fascinating biography, see the work of Elisabeth Roudinesco; volume 2 of her two-volume history of psychoanalysis in France (*La Bataille de cent ans*, 1982–86), devoted to Lacan, has been translated as *Jacques Lacan & Co.* (1990), and a separate work, *Jacques Lacan*, has also been translated (1993; trans. 1997). For a shorter but equally zesty account of psychoanalysis in France centered on Lacan's life and works, see Sherry Turkle, *Psychoanalytic Politics* (1978; rev. ed., 1992). The pithy biobibliography offered by Lacan's son-in-law, Jacques-Alain Miller, in *On the Names-of-the-Father* (see above) provides some interesting insights into the psychoanalyst's life and work processes. Miller has also published in French *Vie de Lacan* (2011, *Life of Lacan*), which examines previously unexplored aspects of Lacan's life in relation to his working through his psychoanalytic theories.

There are many introductions to Lacan's thought. The most useful for the nonspecialist are Elizabeth Grosz, *Jacques Lacan: A Feminist Introduction* (1990); Malcolm Bowie, *Lacan* (1991), a book that focuses particularly on Lacan's style; *Lacan and the Subject of Language*, edited by Ellie Ragland-Sullivan and Mark Bracher (1991); Madan Sarup, *Jacques Lacan* (1992), an introduction to Lacan in cultural context; Michael Payne, *Reading Theory: An Introduction to Lacan, Derrida, and Kristeva* (1993); and Bruce Fink, The *Lacanian Subject* (1995), *Lacan to the Letter: Reading "Écrits" Closely* (2004), and *Lacan on Love: An Exploration of Lacan's Seminar VIII, Transference* (2016), for a Lacanian understanding of love and the key concept of transference. Students should also consult Sean Homer's *Jacques Lacan* (2005), which engages key Lacanian concepts and suggests useful further readings. For advanced engagements with the process of reading Lacan, see Jane Gallop's *Reading Lacan* (1985) and Shoshana Felman's *Jacques Lacan and the Adventure of Insight* (1987). For a good explanation of the differences between Lacanian and American psychoanalysis, see *The Subject and the Self: Lacan and American Psychoanalysis*, edited by Judith Feher Gurewich and Michel Tort (1996). On Lacan's importance for cultural and historical studies, see Juliet Flower MacCannell's *Figuring Lacan* (1986) and Teresa Brennan's *History after Lacan* (1993).

There are many critical and polemical books about Lacan. Some of the most interesting are Philippe Lacoue-Labarthe and Jean-Luc Nancy, *The Title of the Letter* (1973; trans. 1992), which continues the famous critique Jacques Derrida had begun in his reading of Lacan's seminar on "The Purloined Letter" (see "The Purveyor of Truth" in *The Purloined Poe*); François Roustang, *Dire Mastery* (1976; trans. 1982), which considers the combination of the religionlike nature of psychoanalysis and the tyrannical power of Jacques Lacan; and Mikkel Borch-Jacobsen, *Lacan: The Absolute Master* (1990; trans. 1991), a more restrained but still thoroughgoing critique of the effects of power in Lacan's theory. A theorist whose work is an ongoing reinterpretation of the work of Lacan is Slavoj Žižek; see his 1992 *Everything You've Ever Wanted to Know about Lacan (But Were Afraid to Ask Hitchcock), How to Read Lacan* (2007), and other works. *Culture/Clinic 1: "We're All Mad Here,"* edited by Jacques-Alain Miller and Maire Jaanus (2013), is a collective thematic volume that inaugurates the book series Culture/Clinic: Applied Lacanian Psychoanalysis; the collection explores Lacan's theories and concepts at the intersections of cultural studies and clinical practice.

For a dated but annotated bibliography, see Michael Clark, *Jacques Lacan: An Annotated Bibliography* (1988). Dylan Evans has published *An Introductory Dictionary of Lacanian Psychoanalysis* (1996), which is extremely useful and contains a good bibliography. Also worth consulting are the suggested readings in Homer's *Jacques Lacan;* in addition, *The Cambridge Companion to Lacan*, edited by Jean-Michel Rabaté (2003), has a solid bibliography, as does Bruce Fink's *Against Understanding*, vol. 1, *Commentary and Critique in a Lacanian Key* (2014).

Bruno Latour

Latour has written more than a dozen books in both English and French (for books translated into English, the date of the original French publication is given first), catalogues for two exhibits, and countless articles and reviews. His first anthropological investigation of scientists in action, *Laboratory Life: The Construction of Scientific Facts*, which he co-authored with Steve Woolgar in English, was published in 1979. It was followed by a study of Louis Pasteur and microbes, *The Pasteurization of France* (1984; 1988), and *Science in Action: How to Follow Scientists and Engineers through Society* (1987). *Conversations on Science, Culture, and Time* (1992; 1995), records his discussions with the French philosopher Michel Serres; *Aramis, or the Love of Technology* (1992; 1996) examines a failed transit initiative; and *We Have Never Been Modern* (1993) extends his exploration of the sciences to include political theory. *Politics of Nature: How to Bring the Sciences into Democracy* (1999; 2005) offers a radical rethinking of environmentalism and "political ecology." *Pandora's Hope: Essays on the Reality of Science Studies* (1999) is a collection of essays that articulates Latour's ideas about reality. In response to the attacks of 9/11, he published a small pamphlet, *War of the Worlds: What about Peace?* (2002). That same year, he co-edited, with Peter Weibel, a collection of essays on the so-called image wars, *Iconoclash: Beyond the Image Wars in Science, Religion, and Art* (2002); he also returned to more traditional areas of anthropological study with books on religion and on law, *Rejoicing: Or the Torments of Religious Speech* (2002; 2013) and *The Making of Law: An Ethnography of the Conseil d'État* (2002; 2010). The latter is a three-year study of the French Conseil d'État (a body that provides legal advice to the executive branch of the French government and serves as the final court of appeal for administrative law courts) that also marks his return to the methodology of ethnography. In 2005, Latour's English introduction to his Actor Network Theory appeared with the title *Reassembling the Social: An Introduction to Actor-Network-Theory*. In that same year he co-edited a second collection of essays with Peter Weibel, based on an exhibit they curated: *Making Things Public: Atmospheres of Democracy*, which attempts to redefine politics as not just a profession or a system of institutions, but as a concern for "things" brought to the attention of a public. *The Science of Passionate Interests: An Introduction to Gabriel Tarde's Economic Anthropology* (2008; 2009) was written with Vincent Antonin Lépinay. *On the Modern Cult of the Factish Gods* (2010), *An Inquiry into Modes of Existence: An Anthropology of the Moderns* (2012; 2013), and *Reset Modernity!*, edited by Latour, with Christophe Leclerq (2016), all continue and elaborate on ideas articulated in *We Have Never Been Modern*. *Facing Gaia: Eight Lectures on the New Climatic Regime* (2017), collects Latour's 2013 Gifford lectures delivered at Edinburgh University. For a biography, see *Bruno Latour in Pieces: An Intellectual Biography* (2011; trans. 2015) by Henning Schmidgen.

T. Hugh Crawford's extensive interview with Latour, published in *Configurations* 1.2 (1993), a journal dedicated to the cultural studies of science, explores his life, his intellectual influences, and his shifting focus from empirical research to philosophy to theory in the late 1980s. Ian Hacking, a philosopher of science who has written extensively on realism, offers an insightful reading of *Laboratory Life* in "The Participant Irrealist at Large in the Laboratory," *British Journal of the Philosophy of Science* 39 (1988). For substantive critical analyses that connect Latour's work in technoscience with literary theory, see Ronald Schleifer's "Disciplinarity and Collaboration in the Science and Humanities," *College English* 59 (1997). Criticism of Latour's position has been most forcefully articulated by essays in *The Flight from Science and Reason*, edited by Paul R. Gross, Norman Levitt, and Martin W. Lewis (1997). For a response to their arguments, see Robert Markley, "After the Science Wars: From Old Battles to New Directions in the Cultural Studies of Science," in *After the Disciplines: The Emergence of Cultural Studies* (ed. Michael Peters, 1999). Essays in a collection edited by John Law and John Hassard, *Actor Network Theory and After* (1999), provide elaborations of Latour's theoretical model of the sciences. For a feminist perspective, see Vicki Kirby, "Natural Convers(at)-ions: Or, What If Culture Was Really Nature All Along?," in *Material Feminisms* (ed. Stacy Alaimo and Susan Hekman, 2008). In *Prince of Networks: Bruno Latour and Metaphysics* (2009), Graham Harman provides a philosophical account of Latour's metaphysics, while in *Bruno Latour: Reassembling the Political* (2014), he explores Latour's political philosophy. On Latour's legal thinking, see Kyle McGee, *Bruno Latour: The Normativity of Networks* (2014), and *Latour and the Passage of Law*, edited by McGee (2015). Gerard de Vries's *Bruno Latour* (2016) provides a comprehensive overview of Latour's writing, from the early ethnographies to the more recent philosophical works. Schmidgen's *Bruno Latour in Pieces* (see above) contains a bibliography.

F. R. Leavis

Leavis's published work focuses on English poetry and fiction from 1800 to 1930, along with reflections on university education. He never finished a proposed survey of critical practices. His books are *New Bearings in English Poetry: A Study of the Contemporary Situation* (1932); with Denys Thompson, *Culture and Environment: The Training of Critical Awareness* (1933); *Revaluation: Tradition and Development in English Poetry* (1936); *Education and the University: A Sketch for an "English School"* (1943; 2d ed., 1979); *The Great Tradition: George Eliot, Henry James, Joseph Conrad* (1948); *D. H. Lawrence, Novelist* (1955); *Two Cultures? The Significance of C. P. Snow* (1962); *English Literature in Our Time and the University* (1969); with Q. D. Leavis, *Dickens: The Novelist* (1970); *The Living Principle: English as a Discipline of Thought* (1975); and *Thought, Words and Creativity: Art and Thought in Lawrence* (1976). There are many collections of Leavis's essays: *For Continuity* (1933); the influential *The Common Pursuit* (1952); *Anna Karenina and Other Essays* (1967); with Q. D. Leavis, *Lectures in America* (1969); *Nor Shall My Sword: Discourses on Pluralism, Compassion and Social Hope* (1972); *Letters in Criticism*, edited by John Tasker (1974); *The Critic as Anti-Philosopher: Essays and Papers*, edited by G. Singh (1982); *Valuation in Criticism and Other Essays*, edited by G. Singh (1986); and *F. R. Leavis: Essays and Documents*, edited by Ian MacKillop and Richard Storer (1995). The standard biography is Ian MacKillop's *F. R. Leavis: A Life in Criticism* (1995). The beginning reader will find Ronald Hayman's briefer treatment, *Leavis* (1976), more useful.

Francis Mulhern's *The Moment of 'Scrutiny'* (1979) is far and away the best in-depth study of Leavis's cultural significance. Ted Striphas's essay, "Known-Unknowns: Matthew Arnold, F. R. Leavis, and the Government of Culture," *Cultural Studies* 31 (spring 2017), considers Leavis's influence on cultural studies. Michael Bell's *F. R. Leavis* (1988) and Richard Storer's *F. R. Leavis* (2009) provide good short overviews. Gary Day's *Re-reading Leavis: Culture and Literary Criticism* (1996) is an ambitious attempt to evaluate Leavis in relation to developments in literary theory after 1970. Stefan Collini's *Absent Minds: Intellectuals in Britain* (2006), Guy Ortolano's *The Two Cultures Controversy: Science, Literature and Cultural Politics in Postwar Britain* (2009), Christopher Hilliard's *English as a Vocation: The "Scrutiny" Movement* (2012), and David Ellis's *Memoirs of a Leavisite: The Decline and Fall of Cambridge English* (2013) all attest to the ongoing interest in Leavis's central place in British letters and education in the mid-twentieth century. *F. R. Leavis and Q. D. Leavis: An Annotated Bibliography*, edited by M. B. Kinch, William Baker, and John Kimber (1989), lists and comments on everything written by the Leavises and all that was written about them up to 1988. The bibliography in Hilliard's *English as a Vocation* covers more recent work on Leavis and his legacy.

Gotthold Ephraim Lessing

Lessing's *Laokoon* (1766) has been translated into English many times. The most easily accessible edition was published in 1962 as *Laocoön: An Essay on the Limits of Painting and Poetry*, translated with an introduction and useful notes by Edward Allen McCormick. Many of Lessing's other theoretical works, however, are available only in German. The best selection of Lessing's works, heavily oriented toward theater, is *Nathan the Wise, Minna von Barnhelm, and Other Plays and Writings*, edited by Peter Demetz (1991). For Lessing's drama theory, see *Hamburg Dramaturgy*, edited by Victor Lange (1962). See also *Lessing's Theological Writings*, edited by Henry Chadwick (1956). A more complete English translation was undertaken by E. C. Beasley and Helen Zimmern, under the editorship of Edward Bell, more than a century ago: *Selected Prose Works of G. E. Lessing* (1890). H. B. Nisbet's *Lessing: Philosophical and Theological Writings* (2005) includes some newly translated materials as well as overviews that provide useful context. Also see Nisbet's *Gotthold Ephraim Lessing: His Life, Works, and Thought* (2013). Good general studies devoted to Lessing's life and works are H. B. Garland, *Lessing: The Founder of Modern German Literature* (1962), and Edward M. Batley, *Catalyst of Enlightenment: Gotthold Ephraim Lessing* (1990). Studies situating Lessing in a larger context include a very useful collected volume edited by Alexej Ugrinsky called *Lessing and the Enlightenment* (1986), Robert S. Leventhal's *Disciplines of Interpretation: Lessing, Herder, Schlegel, and Hermeneutics in Germany, 1750–1800* (1994), the anthology edited by Barbara Fischer and Thomas C. Fox titled *A Companion to the Works of Gotthold Ephraim Lessing* (2005), and Avi Lifschitz and Michael Squire's co-edited, *Rethinking Lessing's Laocoon: Antiquity, Enlightenment, and the "Limits" of Painting and Poetry* (2017). Early in the twentieth century, Irving Babbitt's *New Laokoon: An Essay on the Confusion of the Arts* (1910) attempted to restore Lessing's sense of distinction to a world led astray by Romanticism's tendency to cross or blur boundaries. E. H. Gombrich's short *Lessing* (1957) paints a brilliant portrait of a man whose dialectical mind had no real use for visual art.

The publication in 1984 of David Wellbery's *Lessing's "Laocoön": Semiotics and Aesthetics in the Age of Reason* brought Lessing into post-Saussurian discussions of sign theory. Simon Richter's *Laocoön's Body and the Aesthetics of Pain: Winckelmann, Lessing, Herder, Moritz, Goethe* (1992) provides an interesting analysis of the relation between pain and beauty. Carol Jacobs offers a good analysis of the rhetoric of Lessing's polemics in "Fictional Histories: Lessing's *Laocoön*," in her *Telling Time* (1993). Susan Gustafson's *Absent Mothers and Orphaned Fathers: Narcissism and Abjection in Lessing's Aesthetic and Dramatic Production* (1995) combines a discussion of Lessing's plays with a reading of the *Laocoön* that uses Julia Kristeva's theory of maternal erasure, or "abjection," in a daring feminist psychoanalysis. A special issue of *Poetics Today* on Lessing (20.2 [1999]) offers a very interesting collection of essays, particularly striking for the debates about gender as a category of analysis. The volume concludes with a long, energetic, polemical review of the literature on Lessing by Meir Sternberg. For debates about ecphrasis, see Murray Krieger's 1967 essay "*Ekphrasis* and the Still Movement of Poetry; or, *Laokoön* Revisited," later collected in Krieger's *Ekphrasis: The Illusion of the Natural Sign* (1992); W. J. T. Mitchell's 1984 essay "Space and Time: Lessing's *Laocoön* and the Politics of Genre," later collected in his *Iconology: Image, Text, Ideology* (1986); and James Heffernan's *Museum of Words* (1993). There is a bibliography in German on Lessing by Doris Kuhles, *Lessing-Bibliographie 1971–1985* (1988). See also the updated bibliography in *Rethinking Lessing's Laocoön, A Companion to the Works of Gotthold Ephraim Lessing*, and Nisbet's *Gotthold Ephraim Lessing: His Life, His Works, and Thought*.

Claude Lévi-Strauss

In addition to the works discussed in the headnote, Lévi-Strauss's notable publications include *The Savage Mind* (1962; trans. 1966); *Totemism* (1962; trans. 1963); "The Scope of Anthropology" (his 1960 inaugural lecture at the Collège de France;

trans. 1967); *Mythologiques* (4 vols., 1964–71; trans. 1969–81 as *Introduction to the Science of Mythology*, with the individual volumes titled *The Raw and the Cooked, From Honey to Ashes, The Origin of Table Manners*, and *The Naked Man*); *Myth and Meaning* (1978), a short and very accessible introduction to the structural analysis of myth; *Anthropology and Myth* (1984; trans. 1986); and several additional volumes on myth. *Anthropology Confronts the Problems of the Modern World* (2013) is an English translation of a collection of lectures delivered in 1986 in Tokyo on structural anthropology. In honor of Lévi-Strauss's turning 100 in 2008, Gallimard published a 2,000-page collection of his work, *Oeuvres*, while Penguin issued an English edition of *Tristes Tropiques* (2012) with a new introduction. An assembled collection of Lévi-Strauss's essays, *We Are All Cannibals: And Other Essays* (2013; trans. 2016), comparatively explores customs, myths, and rituals. Besides the autobiographical *Tristes Tropiques* (1955), the best sources of biographical information available in English are two books of interviews, the first set with Georges Charbonnier (1961; trans. 1969), the second with Didier Eribon (1988; trans. 1991), each published under the title *Conversations with Claude Lévi-Strauss*. See also Christopher Johnson, *Claude Lévi-Strauss: The Formative Years* (2003).

Good introductions to Lévi-Strauss's work include Edmund Leach's respectfully critical *Claude Lévi-Strauss* (1970), which is particularly useful for situating Lévi-Strauss in relation to the discipline of anthropology; David Pace, *Claude Lévi-Strauss: The Bearer of Ashes* (1983); Roland Champagne, *Claude Lévi-Strauss* (1987); and Marcel Hénaff, *Claude Lévi-Strauss and the Making of Structural Anthropology* (1991; trans. 1998). In 2008 UNESCO devoted a special issue of its flagship journal, *The Courier*, to the man and his work.

Theoretically crucial readings of Lévi-Strauss's structuralism in general and *Tristes Tropiques* in particular have been published by Jacques Derrida in *Of Grammatology* (1967; trans. 1976) and *Writing and Difference* (1967; trans. 1978) and by Clifford Geertz in *The Interpretation of Cultures* (1973) and *Works and Lives: The Anthropologist as Author* (1988). Also noteworthy are several highly influential essays analyzing the sexual politics of Lévi-Strauss's kinship theory: Gayle Rubin, "The Traffic in Women: Notes on the 'Political Economy' of Sex," in *Toward an Anthropology of Women* (ed. Rayna Reiter, 1975); Hélène Cixous and Catherine Clément, *The Newly Born Woman* (1975; trans. 1986); and Luce Irigaray, *This Sex Which Is Not One* (1977; trans. 1985). Cleo McNelly's "Natives, Women, and Claude Lévi-Strauss," *Massachusetts Review* 16 (1975), addresses questions of race and gender in *Tristes Tropiques*, drawing comparisons with Charles Baudelaire and Joseph Conrad; other aspects of Lévi-Strauss's participation in literary trends are explored by James Boon's *From Symbolism to Structuralism: Lévi-Strauss in a Literary Tradition* (1972), and by *Rethinking Claude Lévi-Strauss (1908–2009)*, edited by Robert Doran, a special issue of *Yale French Studies*, no. 123 (2013). The interdisciplinary essays in *The Cambridge Companion to Lévi-Strauss*, edited by Boris Wiseman (2009), examine his body of ideas in relationship to aesthetics, anthropology, language, and literature. In "The Ethnic Ethnographer: Judaism in *Tristes Tropiques*," *Representations*, no. 15 (1995), David Damrosch discusses the specter of Nazi terror and Lévi-Strauss's ambivalent treatment of his own ethnicity in *Tristes Tropiques*. In "Lévi-Strauss: The Writing Lesson Revisited," *Modern Language Review* 92 (1997), Christopher Johnson reexamines Lévi-Strauss's framing of the writing lesson episode and proposes a recontextualized interpretation of it. For bibliographies, see Joan Nordquist's *Claude Lévi-Strauss: A Bibliography* (1987), which covers publications in English, and Marcel Hénaff's book (cited above), which provides a selective but nevertheless extensive bibliography. See also the impressive bibliography in Johnson, *Claude Lévi-Strauss* and the *Cambridge Companion*.

Li Zehou

Li Zehou has written two dozen books in Chinese, and several of his major works have been translated into Japanese, Korean, English, German, and other languages. The first to become available in English was his most popular study of Chinese history and theory of art, *Mei de licheng* (1981; trans. 1988, 2d ed., 1994, *The Path of Beauty*). The English version of *Meixue sijing* (1989, *Four Lectures on Aesthetics*), published in 2006 with the title *Four Essays on Aesthetics: Toward a Global View*, is a joint rendering by Li and Jane Cauvel. It differs significantly from the Chinese text, omitting many sections of the original. A third book translated into English is *Huaxia Meixue* (1989; trans. 2010, *The Chinese Aesthetic Tradition*). Translations of several other books are in process. A dozen of Li Zehou's essays are available in English, including "The Philosophy of Kant and a Theory of Subjectivity," *Analecta Husserliana* 21 (1986); "A Discourse on Zhuangzi and Chan Buddhism," *Social Sciences in China* 1 (1987); "Human Nature and Human Future: A Combination of Marx and Confucius," in *Chinese Thought in a Global Context: A Dialogue between China and Western Philosophical Approaches* (ed. Karl-Heinz Pohl, 1999); and "Subjectivity and 'Subjectality': A Response," *Philosophy East and West* 49.2 (1999), which succinctly summarizes his major philosophical and aesthetic ideas. In addition, a selection of his writings were published as a special issue of *Contemporary Chinese Thought* (32.2 [2000]) titled *Li Zehou*.

Li Zehou's writings fall into three categories: philosophy and aesthetics, studies of Chinese intellectual and art history, and studies of Chinese culture and society. Major works in the first group (titles given in English) are *Critique of Critical Philosophy* (1979), *Collection of Essays on Aesthetics* (1979), *The*

Path of Beauty (1981), *Selected Writings on Philosophy and Aesthetics by Li Zehou* (1985), *The Chinese Aesthetic Tradition* (1989), *Four Lectures on Aesthetics* (1989), *An Outline of My Philosophy* (1990), *The Anthropo-historical Ontology* (2008), *Ethics* (2010), *A Response to Michael Sandel and Other Matters* (2014), and *What Is Morality?* (2015). In the second group are *A Study of the Thought of Kang Youwei and Tan Sitong* (1958); *On the History of Modern Chinese Intellectual Thought* (1979); *On the History of Ancient Chinese Intellectual Thought* (1985); *On the History of Contemporary Chinese Intellectual Thought* (1987); *History of Chinese Aesthetics*, with Liu Gangji (2 vols., 1984–87); and *From Shamanism to Ritual Regulation and Humaneness* (2015). The third group includes *Walk My Own Path* (1986), *Marxism in China* (1993), *New Dreams of the Century* (1998), *Reading Confucian Analects Today* (1998), *Five Essays from 1999* (1999), *Pragmatic Reason and the Culture of Optimism* (2005), *Should Chinese Philosophy Go on Stage?* (2011), *How Can Chinese Philosophy Go on Stage?* (2012), and *Collected Dialogues of Li Zehou* (7 vols., 2014). He has also published many miscellaneous essays in Chinese journals and newspapers.

Because of Li Zehou's prominence in China as a contemporary thinker, his works have been subjected to numerous studies and critiques in Chinese. In English, see the special section devoted to his ideas about philosophy and aesthetics in *Philosophy East and West* 49.2 (1999). A general introduction to Li's ideas and works is offered by Woei Lien Chong, "History as the Realization of Beauty: Li Zehou's Aesthetic Marxism," *Contemporary Chinese Thought* 32.2 (2000), and John Zijiang Ding, "Li Zehou: Chinese Aesthetics from a Post-Marxist and Confucian Perspective," in *Contemporary Chinese Philosophy* (ed. Chung-Ying Cheng and Nicholas Bunnin, 2002). For a critical assessment, see the lengthy article by Gu Xin, "Subjectivity, Modernity, and Chinese Hegelian Marxism: A Study of Li Zehou's Philosophical Ideas from a Comparative Perspective," *Philosophy East and West* 46.2 (1996). While acknowledging Li's contributions to philosophy and aesthetics through his efforts to transform Kant's idealistic doctrine of subjectivity into a materialistic one that denies the duality of matter and mind, Gu argues that Li's system of thought—despite his declared aim—remains within a Hegelian-Lukácsian Marxist framework. Ding's essay contains a useful bibliography of Li Zehou's complete works up to 2002.

Longinus

The original Greek text with valuable critical commentary can be found in *"Longinus" on the Sublime* (1964), edited by the leading Longinus scholar D. A. Russell. English translations include W. R. Roberts's *Longinus on the Sublime* (1899); W. H. Fyfe's Loeb Classical Library edition (vol. 199, 1927); and, most notably, D. A. Russell's version in *Ancient Literary Criticism: The Principal Texts in New Translations* (1972) and in *Classical Literary Criticism* (1989), both edited by Russell and M. Winterbottom. Fyfe's translation has also been revised by Russell in the more recent Loeb edition (1995). Both of Russell's translations offer useful and authoritative introductions and annotations. A more recent version, also with notes, appears in the new edition of *Classical Literary Criticism* (2000), edited by Penelope Murray and T. S. Dorsch.

Works of criticism focusing on the English reception of Longinus include T. R. Henn's *Longinus and English Criticism* (1934) and S. H. Monk's *The Sublime: A Study of Critical Theories in Eighteenth-Century England* (1935). J. W. H. Atkins's *Literary Criticism in Antiquity, A Sketch of Its Development*, volume 2, *Graeco-Roman* (1934), and G. M. A. Grube's *Greek and Roman Critics* (1965) offer comprehensive discussions of the text of *On Sublimity*, covering important social and historical contexts. M. H. Abrams's *The Mirror and the Lamp: Romantic Theory and the Critical Tradition* (1953) and Thomas Weiskel's *The Romantic Sublime: Studies in The Structure and Psychology of Transcendence* (1976) include insightful comments on Longinus's relationship to the emergence of Romanticism, while Jules Brody's *Boileau and Longinus* (1958) concentrates on the poet-critic who with his late seventeenth-century French translation contributed the most to Longinus's great reputation in Europe. *Classical Criticism*, volume 1 of *The Cambridge History of Literary Criticism*, includes an informative short piece on Longinus by D. A. Russell (ed. George A. Kennedy, 1989). Yun Lee Too's *The Idea of Ancient Literary Criticism* (1998) places Longinus's theory of the sublime within the context of ancient criticism from its origins in archaic Greek poetry to the early Christian era. Adnan K. Abdulla's *A Comparative Study of Longinus and Al-Jurjani: The Interrelationships between Medieval Arabic Literary Criticism and Graeco-Roman Poetics* (2004) investigates the similarities and differences in how two major critics with different cultural backgrounds describe at disparate times the origin and the reception of sublime art. *Ancient Literary Criticism*, edited by Andrew Laird (2005), is a useful companion to the Russell and Winterbottom anthology, offering a collection of important scholarship on canonical texts of ancient rhetoric and poetics, including Longinus's *On Sublimity*. Emma Gilby's *Sublime Worlds: Early Modern French Literature* (2006) provides close readings of Longinus's theory of the sublime, tracing his influence on three major French authors: Pierre Corneille, Blaise Pascal, and Nicolas Boileau. Karl Axelsson's *The Sublime: Precursors and British Eighteenth-Century Conceptions* (2007) explores the ways in which Longinus's Greek treatise shaped much of late seventeenth- and eighteenth-century British criticism. For an overview of theories of the sublime, see *The Sublime: A Reader*, edited by Andrew Ashfield and Peter De Bolla (1993), and Philip Shaw's *The Sublime*

(2006). The wide-ranging essays in *The Sublime: From Antiquity to the Present*, edited by Timothy M. Costelloe (2012), demonstrate the array of important cultural and philosophical issues connected with the concept of sublimity. Robert Doran provides a well-informed and carefully nuanced analysis of Longinus and his eighteenth-century reception in *The Theory of the Sublime from Longinus to Kant* (2015). For bibliographic information, see Demetrio St. Marin's *Bibliography of the Essay on the Sublime* (1967) and Thomas Gwinup and Fidelia Dickinson's *Greek and Roman Authors: A Checklist of Criticism* (1982), as well as the bibliographies included in Castelloe's *The Sublime: From Antiquity to the Present* and Doran's *The Theory of the Sublime from Longinus to Kant.*

György Lukács

The standard edition of Lukács's writings is the German *Georg Lukács Werke* (18 vols., 1926–86). A number of scholarly edited texts are also available in Hungarian. A substantial collection of his letters, taped interviews, photos, unpublished works, and miscellaneous materials, plus his 10,000-volume personal library, is housed in the Lukács Archive in Budapest. English translations are *Soul and Form* (1910; trans. 1974), *The Theory of the Novel* (1916; trans. 1971), *History and Class Consciousness* (1923; trans. 1971), *Lenin: A Study on the Unity of His Thought* (1924; trans. 1971), *The Historical Novel* (1937; trans. 1962), *Studies in European Realism: A Sociological Survey of the Writings of Balzac, Stendhal, Zola, Tolstoy, Gorki, and Others* (1945; trans. 1950), *Goethe and His Age* (1947; trans. 1978), *Essays on Thomas Mann* (1947; trans. 1965), *The Young Hegel: Studies in the Relations between Dialectics and Economics* (1948; trans. 1976), *Essays on Realism* (1948; trans. 1981), *German Realists in the Nineteenth Century* (1951; trans. 1993), *The Destruction of Reason* (1954; trans. 1981), *The Meaning of Contemporary Realism* (1958; trans. 1963), *Conversations with Lukács* (1967; trans. 1975), *Tactics and Ethics: Political Writings, 1919–1929* (1968; trans. 1972), *Solzhenitsyn* (1969; trans. 1971), *Writer and Critic and Other Essays* (trans. 1970), *The Ontology of Social Being* (2 vols., 1976; trans. 1978), *Record of a Life: An Autobiographical Sketch* (1981; trans. 1983), *The Process of Democratization* (1985; trans. 1991), and *A Defence of History and Class Consciousness: Tailism and the Dialectic* (1996; trans. 2000). A sampling of essays is available in *The Lukács Reader*, edited by Arpad Kadarkay (1995). Lukács's essays on democracy from the post–World War II period, including those in his influential volume *Literature and Democracy* (1947), are available in *The Culture of People's Democracy: Hungarian Essays on Literature, Art, and Democratic Transition, 1945–1948*, edited and translated by Tyrus Miller (2013). For a detailed biography, see Kadarkay's *Georg Lukács: Life, Thought, and Politics* (1991).

On Lukács's theory of the novel, see Lucien Goldmann, *Towards a Sociology of the Novel* (1964; trans. 1975), and J. M. Bernstein, *The Philosophy of the Novel: Lukács, Marxism, and the Dialectic of Form* (1984). For critical responses to Lukács's involvement in the realism debate, see the essays by Theodor Adorno, Walter Benjamin, Bertolt Brecht, and Ernst Bloch in the often-cited *Aesthetics and Politics*, edited by the *New Left Review* (1977). Also helpful in this regard is Eugene Lunn's *Marxism and Modernism: An Historical Study of Lukács, Brecht, Benjamin, and Adorno* (1982). Fredric Jameson's most developed account of Lukács's work appears in his *Marxism and Form* (1971). Béla Királyfalvi's *Aesthetics of György Lukács* (1975) offers a systematic examination of Lukács's aesthetic theories, while Terry Eagleton's introductory *Marxism and Literary Criticism* (1976) and his *Ideology of the Aesthetic* (1990) present some suggestive critical remarks on Lukács. Andrew Arato and Paul Breines's *The Young Lukács and the Origins of Western Marxism* (1979) and Martin Jay's *Marxism and Totality: The Adventures of a Concept from Lukács to Habermas* (1984) situate Lukács's work within the tradition of Western Marxism. Galin Tihanov's *The Master and the Slave: Lukács, Bakhtin, and the Ideas of Their Time* (2000) offers a comparative study focusing on intellectual background and historical context, while also introducing unknown archival material and overlooked texts by Lukács and Bakhtin. János Kelemen's *The Rationalism of Georg Lukács* (2014) explores the central motif of the defense of reason in Lukács's oeuvre by drawing on a number of his untranslated, lesser-known writings. For a survey of contemporary Marxist critics' assessments of Lukács, see the interviews gathered in *Lukács After Communism*, edited by Eva L. Corredor (1997). Bibliographies of Lukács's writing and criticism of it can be found in Peter Murphy's *Writings by and about Georg Lukács: A Bibliography* (1976), François Lapointe's *Georg Lukács and His Critics (1910–1982)* (1983), and Kadarkay's reader and biography mentioned above.

Jean-François Lyotard

Much, but not all, of Lyotard's work has been translated into English (the date of French publication is given first, where appropriate): *Phenomenology* (1954; 1991); *Discourse, Figure* (1971; 2011); *Libidinal Economy* (1974; 1993); *Duchamps's Trans/Formers* (1977; 1990); *The Pacific Wall* (1975; 1990); *The Postmodern Condition* (1979; 1984); *Just Gaming*, with Jean-Loup Thébaud (1979; 1985); *The Differend* (1983; 1988); *The Postmodern Explained* (1986; 1992); *Enthusiasm: The Kantian Critique of History* (1986; 2009); *The Inhuman: Reflections on Time* (1988; 1991); *Peregrinations: Law, Form, Event* (1988); *Heidegger and "the jews"* (1988; 1990); *Lessons on the Analytic of the Sublime* (1991; 1994); *Postmodern Fables* (1993; 1997); *Signed, Malraux* (1996; 1999); *Soundproof Room: Malraux's Anti-Aesthetics*

(1998; 2001); *The Confession of Augustine* (1998; 2000); *The Hyphen: Between Judaism and Christianity* (1999); and *Why Philosophize* (2012; 2013). There are five collections of work spanning Lyotard's career: *Driftworks*, edited by Roger McKeon (1984); *The Lyotard Reader*, edited by Andrew Benjamin (1989); *Political Writings*, edited by Bill Readings (1993); *Toward the Postmodern*, edited by Robert Harvey and Mark S. Roberts (1993); and *Music/Ideology: Resisting the Aesthetic*, edited by Adam Krims (1998). The untranslated works are *Dérive à partir de Marx et Freud* (1973, *Starting from Marx and Freud*); *Des dispositifs pulsionnels* (1973, *Driving Impulses*); *Instructions païennes* (1977, *Pagan Instructions*); *Récits tremblants* (1977, *Trembling Stories*); *La Guerre des Algériens: Écrits 1956–63* (1988, *The Algerian War: Writings, 1956–63*); and *Misère de la philosophie* (2000, *Poverty of Philosophy*). Stuart Sim's *Jean-François Lyotard* (1996) places Lyotard's work in historical and intellectual context. The most comprehensive biography is Kiff Bamford's *Jean-François Lyotard* (2017).

The best short introduction is Simon Malpas's *Jean François Lyotard* (2003). David Carroll's *Paraesthetics: Foucault, Lyotard, Derrida* (1987) details Lyotard's connections with poststructuralism. Three excellent collections of essays on Lyotard's work are *Judging Lyotard*, edited by Andrew Benjamin (1992); *The Politics of Jean-François Lyotard*, edited by Chris Rojek and Bryan S. Turner (1998); and *Minima Memoria: In the Wake of Jean-François Lyotard*, edited by Claire Novel, Zrinka Stahuljak, and Kent Still (2007). *The Lyotard Dictionary*, edited by Stuart Sim (2011), offers succinct accounts of the major themes in Lyotard's work, while Dylan Sawyer's *Lyotard, Literature and the Trauma of the "differend"* (2014) examines Lyotard's relevance to literary criticism. *The Lyotard Dictionary* has a complete bibliography of Lyotard's work, along with a good, although not fully comprehensive, bibliography of secondary works in English.

Moses Maimonides

The modern Arabic edition of *The Guide of the Perplexed (Dalalat al-Ha'irin)* was compiled in 1929 by S. Munk and translated into English by Shlomo Pines (1963); Joseph Kafih's three-volume edition (1972) offers parallel Arabic and Hebrew versions. Large sections of the *Mishneh Torah* as well as other writings by Maimonides are available in English translation in *The Maimonides Reader*, edited by Isadore Twersky (1972). Ilil Arbel's *Maimonides: A Spiritual Biography* (2001) is an excellent popular introduction to Maimonides' life, while Joel L. Kraemer's *Maimonides: The Life and World of One of Civilization's Greatest Minds* (2008) is a more scholarly biography. Moshe Halbertal's *Maimonides: Life and Thought* (2009; trans. 2014), originally published in Hebrew, is an accessible introduction to both the philosopher's life and his work.

For beginners as well as scholars, Alfred L. Ivry's *Maimonides Guide of the Perplexed: A Philosophical Guide* (2016) provides a new introduction to *Guide of the Perplexed* that includes an explication of each chapter of the Pines translation, as well as paraphrases that clarify key terms and concepts, and analyses of the philosophical issues raised by the text. Leo Strauss's essay "The Literary Character of *The Guide for the Perplexed*," originally included in *Essays on Maimonides: An Octocentennial Volume* (ed. Salo W. Baron, 1941) and later reprinted in *Maimonides: A Collection of Critical Essays* (ed. Joseph A. Buijs, 1988), is an indispensable introduction to Maimonides' method in *The Guide*. Several recent volumes document the significance of the political philosopher Leo Strauss, whose work on Maimonides was instrumental in restoring the medieval philosopher's reputation in the twentieth century. Kenneth Hart Green, in *Leo Strauss on Maimonides: The Complete Writing* (2013), brings together in an annotated collection all Strauss's writing on Maimonides—a total of sixteen essays, three published in English for the first time. Aryeh Tepper's *Progressive Minds, Conservative Politics: Leo Strauss's Later Writings on Maimonides* (2013) identifies in Strauss's later writing a new focus on Maimonides' esoteric teaching on progress as a means to go beyond conflicts not only between reason and revelation but also between progressivism and conservatism in contemporary politics. Joshua Parens, in *Leo Strauss and the Recovery of Medieval Political Philosophy* (2016), focuses on Strauss's engagement with medieval political philosophy to offer a new interpretation of Strauss's understanding of *Guide of the Perplexed*. Susan A. Handelman, in *The Slayers of Moses: The Emergence of Rabbinic Interpretation in Modern Literary Theory* (1982), examines the relationship between early Jewish biblical hermeneutics and contemporary deconstructive literary theory. The collection of essays edited by Geoffrey H. Hartman and Sanford Budick, *Midrash and Literature* (1986), also examines the relationships between Jewish hermeneutics and literary theory. For an advanced introduction, see *The Cambridge Companion to Maimonides*, edited by Kenneth Seeskin (2005). Since the octacentennial of Maimonides' death there has been a virtual explosion of scholarship on the Jewish thinker. Menachem Kellner explores Maimonides' critique of Jewish mysticism in *Maimonides' Confrontation with Mysticism* (2006). Donald McCallum's *Maimonides' Guide for the Perplexed: Silence and Salvation* (2007) provides an overview of Maimonides scholarship. *Maimonides after 800 Years: Essays on Maimonides and His Influence*, edited by Jay M. Harris (2007), contains essays by leading scholars in the field. Recent volumes focus on the importance of hermeneutics and biblical exegesis in *The Guide of the Perplexed*, including *Maimonides as Biblical Interpreter* (2011), by Sara Klein-Braslavy, and *Method and Metaphysics in Maimonides' "Guide for the Perplexed"* (2011), by

Daniel Davies. *The Matter and Form of Maimonides' "Guide"* (2013), by Josef Stern, attempts to provide a unified interpretation of the *Guide* through the philosophies of matter and form. In *Philo's Heirs: Moses Maimonides and Thomas Aquinas* (2017), Luis Cortest examines the influence of Philo of Alexandria, the first century Jewish philosopher on the philosophical works of Maimonides and Thomas Aquinas, and in doing so highlights the relationships between the two medieval philosophers. Volumes on the reception of Maimonides include James Arthur Diamond's *Maimonides and the Shaping of the Jewish Canon* (2014), which describes the philosopher's reception in Jewish intellectual history, and Howard Kriesel's *Judaism as Philosophy: Studies in Maimonides and the Medieval Jewish Philosophers of Provence* (2015), which examines his reception among medieval Jewish philosophers. Micah Goodman's *Maimonides and the Book That Changed Judaism: Secrets of "The Guide for the Perplexed"* (2010; trans. 2015), a best-selling book in Israel, offers an interpretation of the *Guide* that puts it into dialogue with contemporary religious thought, demonstrating the relevance of Maimonides not only to Jewish culture and identity but to Western philosophy as well. James T. Robinson, "Moses Maimonides," in the online *Oxford Bibliographies* (2015), is the most up-to-date bibliography.

Karl Marx and Friedrich Engels

The English translation of the collected works of Marx and Engels fills fifty volumes, *Karl Marx, Frederick Engels: Collected Works* (1975–2005). The best single-volume editions are David McLellan's *Karl Marx: Selected Writings* (1977) and Robert C. Tucker's *Marx-Engels Reader* (2d ed., 1978). For Marx's letters, see *Correspondence*, edited by Saul K. Padover (1979). Helpful introductions to Marx's life and writings include David McLellan, *Karl Marx: His Life and Thought* (1973); Isaiah Berlin, *Karl Marx: His Life and Environment* (4th ed., 1978); Francis Wheen, *Karl Marx* (1999); and Jonathan Sperber, *Karl Marx: A Nineteenth-Century Life* (2013). On Engels, see Steven Marcus, *Engels, Manchester, and the Working Class* (1974), an excellent work of cultural history; W. O. Henderson, *The Life of Friedrich Engels* (1976); Terrell Carver, *Engels* (1981), a good overview; and Carver, *Marx and Engels: The Intellectual Relationship* (1983). An excellent recent biography is Tristram Hunt, *Marx's General: The Revolutionary Life of Friedrich Engels* (2009).

There is a vast secondary literature on Marx and Engels's views on literature and criticism and on the long line of theorists and critics who belong to the Marxist tradition. Essay collections provide a good starting point: see *Radical Perspectives in the Arts*, edited by Lee Baxandall (1972); *Marxism and Art: Writings in Aesthetics and Criticism*, edited by Berel Lang and Forrest Williams (1972); *Marxism and Art: Essays Classic and Contemporary*, edited by Maynard Solomon (1973); *Karl Marx and Frederick Engels on Literature and Art: A Selection of Writings*, edited by Lee Baxandall and Stefan Morawski (1974); and *Marxists on Literature: An Anthology*, edited by David Craig (1975). More up-to-date are *Contemporary Marxist Literary Criticism*, edited by Francis Mulhern (1992), and *Marxist Literary Theory: A Reader*, edited by Terry Eagleton and Drew Milne (1996). See also *Aesthetics and Politics*, edited by Ernst Bloch (1977), and *Marxism and the Interpretation of Culture*, edited by Cary Nelson and Lawrence Grossberg (1988). Also stimulating are the essays included in *Marxist Shakespeares*, edited by Jean E. Howard and Scott Cutler Shershow (2001). Robert Paul Wolff, *Understanding Marx: A Reconstruction and Critique of "Capital"* (1984); *A Dictionary of Marxist Thought*, edited by Tom Bottomore (2d ed., 1991); and Peter Singer, *Marx: A Very Short Introduction* (rev. ed., 2000), are all insightful. On Marx's relevance for the twenty-first century, see Jonathan Wolff, *Why Read Marx Today?* (2002), and Terry Eagleton, *Why Marx Was Right* (2011), which seeks to refute common objections to Marxism (that it leads to political tyranny, that it reduces everything to the economic and historical determinism, etc.). Cogent studies of Marx's social, political, and economic thought include Vincent Barnett, *Marx* (2009); Amy E. Wendling, *Karl Marx on Technology and Alienation* (2009); and David Harvey, *A Companion to Marx's "Capital"* (2010).

On the history of Marx and Engels's interest in and response to literature, Peter Demetz's *Marx, Engels, and the Poets: Origins of Marxist Literary Criticism* (1967) and S. S. Prawer's *Karl Marx and World Literature* (1976) are informative. A concise and popular survey of Marxist literary criticism is Terry Eagleton, *Marxism and Literary Criticism* (1976). Tony Bennett, *Formalism and Marxism* (1979), deals well with Russian formalism and Marxist theory and criticism; and Fredric Jameson, *Marxism and Form: Twentieth-Century Dialectical Theories of Literature* (1971), examines several leading twentieth-century intellectuals influenced by Marx's writings. In *The Ideology of the Aesthetic* (1990) and *Ideology: An Introduction* (1991), Eagleton studies the meanings and implications of two key terms in Marxist criticism, *ideology* and *aesthetics*. *Marxism, Modernity and Postcolonial Studies*, edited by Crystal Bartolovich and Neil Lazarus (2002), also merits attention.

For studies of literature and culture that bear witness to Marx's influence, see Kevin Floyd, *The Reification of Desire: Toward a Queer Marxism* (2009), with provocative discussions of György Lukács, Michel Foucault, Judith Butler, Herbert Marcuse, and other writers and theorists; Orrin N. C. Wang, *Romantic Sobriety: Sensation, Revolution, Commodification, History* (2011), exploring the relationship among Romanticism, deconstruction, and Marxism through the themes of sensation and sobriety in Romantic literature and contemporary literary theory; John F. Lavelle, *Blue Collar, Theoretically: A Post-Marxist Approach to Working Class Literature* (2012), drawing on sociology, cognitive science, anthropology, and psychology, and supported by interpretations of literary texts by Stephen Crane and F. Scott Fitzgerald; and *Marx at the Movies: Revisiting History, Theory and Practice*, edited by Ewa Mazierska and Lars Kristensen (2014), which includes essays on Sergei Eisenstein, Orson Welles, and other American and European filmmakers and their films.

On the relationships between Marxism and recent theories of literature and criticism, consult Michael Ryan, *Marxism and Deconstruction: A Critical Articulation* (1982); John Frow, *Marxism and Literary History* (1986); and Scott Wilson, *Cultural Materialism: Theory and Practice* (1995). Dated but worth consulting are Lee Baxandall, *Marxism and Aesthetics: A Selective Annotated Bibliography* (1968), and Chris Bullock and David Peck, *Guide to Marxist Literary Criticism* (1980). There is a helpful, concise bibliography in Richard Schmitt's *Introduction to Marx and Engels: A Critical Reconstruction* (2d ed., 1997). See also Cecil L. Eubanks, *Karl Marx and Friedrich Engels: An Analytical Bibliography* (2d ed., 1984), and the bibliography included in David McLellan, *Karl Marx: A Biography* (4th ed., 2006).

Giacopo Mazzoni

There is no complete English translation of *On the Defense of the "Comedy" of Dante*. A book-length English rendering of its "Introduction and Summary" can be found in *On the Defense of the "Comedy" of Dante: Introduction and Summary*, translated by Robert L. Montgomery (1983), who also provides detailed scholarly annotations plus a superb preface covering textual, historical, biographical, and critical matters. The standard modern Italian edition is *Introduzione della Difesa della "Commedia" di Dante*, edited by Enrico Musacchio and Gigino Pellegrini (1982). A generous selection of excerpted passages from other parts of *On the Defense of the "Comedy" of Dante* appears in *Literary Criticism: Plato to Dryden* (ed. and trans. Allan H. Gilbert, 1940). A dated biography in Italian exists, Pierantonio Serassi's *La Vita di Jacopo Mazzoni, Patrizio Cesenate* (1790). Illuminating biographical details can be found in Montgomery's preface.

A comprehensive and authoritative critical overview of Mazzoni's work appears in Bernard Weinberg's magisterial *History of Literary Criticism in the Italian Renaissance* (2 vols., 1961). Also useful are Baxter Hathaway's *Age of Criticism: The Late Renaissance in Italy* (1962) and his *Marvels and Commonplaces: Renaissance Literary Criticism* (1968). The former contextualizes Mazzoni's work in relationship to five leading issues of his time, while the latter narrows its context to the debates surrounding imitation. A formalist critique of how Mazzoni evades defining poetry can be found in Robin Louis McAllister's "Meaning, Language, and Conceptualization: Alternatives in Mazzoni and Dante," *Language and Style* 5 (1971). Frederick Purnell's dissertation "Jacopo Mazzoni and His Comparison of Plato and Aristotle" (1971) offers a detailed study of Mazzoni in the context of Renaissance debates about classical philosophy. For a New Critical perspective on Mazzoni that accentuates the novelty of his treatment of the image, see Murray Krieger's "Jacopo Mazzoni, Repository of Diverse Critical Traditions or Source of a New One?" in his *Poetic Presence and Illusion: Essays in Critical History and Theory* (1979). A limited bibliography of criticism can be found in Montgomery's book; for a bibliography of primary texts, see Weinberg's history.

Mark McGurl

McGurl's first book, *The Novel Art: Elevations of American Fiction after Henry James* (2001), examines American fiction from the late nineteenth century through World War II, showing how in that period the novel aspired to be high art. Drawing on Pierre Bourdieu's theory of cultural capital, it points to the ways in which modernist works distinguished themselves from mainstream fiction. His next book, *The Program Era: Postwar Fiction and the Rise of Creative Writing* (2009), starts where his previous account left off, taking up the second half of the century. Rather than examining the small, elite networks of modernism, it looks at the mass institution of creative writing and adopts systems theory to explain its operation. For an account of McGurl's career and thinking in his own words, see Jeffrey J. Williams, "With the Program: An Interview with Mark McGurl," *Contemporary Literature* 57 (2016).

The Program Era was immediately hailed as a major interpretation of contemporary American fiction. It received substantial treatment from influential critics such as Louis Menand, in "Show or Tell," *New Yorker*, June 8, 2009, and Fredric Jameson, in "Dirty Little Secret: The Programme Era," *London Review of Books*, November 22, 2012. It was also attacked by the writer Elif Batuman in "Get a Real Degree: Down with Creative Writing," *London Review of Books*, September 23, 2010; in "MFA vs. NYC," *n+1*, no. 10 (2010), Chad Harbach (identified as "the editors") pointed out that it left out a significant group of writers who responded to the popular rather than academic market. His essay is the anchor of *MFA vs. NYC: The Two Cultures of American Fiction*, edited by Harbach (2014), which also collects Batuman's essay, Jameson's review, and sixteen other pieces. See also Eric Bennett, *Workshops of Empire: Stegner, Engle, and American Creative Writing during the Cold War* (2015), which takes a less positive view than McGurl's, arguing that the workshop flattened fiction and served postwar U.S. politics. In addition, Chris Findeisen, "Injuries of Class: Mass Education and the American Campus Novel," *PMLA* 130 (2015), criticizes McGurl's overly positive view of higher education's ability to level classes.

Franco Moretti

Franco Moretti's first book—a collection of essays translated from Italian, *Signs Taken for Wonders: Essays in the Sociology of Literary Forms* (1983)—offers an analysis of the relations between high and mass culture, ranging across genres from horror and tragedy to detective fiction and classic realism. In his next book, *The Way of the World: The Bildungsroman in European Culture* (1986; trans. 1987, new ed. 2000), he argues that the bildungsroman is the exemplary aesthetic form of modernity, a product of Europe's shifting socioeconomic conditions. In *Modern Epic: The World System from Goethe to García Márquez* (1994; trans. 1996), Moretti proposes a new genre, "modern epic," which includes canonical works that stretch from Goethe's *Faust* (1808–32) to García Márquez's *One Hundred Years of Solitude* (1967). To account for the continuity of this genre, Moretti uses a Darwinian-style evolutionary paradigm. His project to construct a scientific materialist history of literary genres is elaborated in his next two books: *Atlas of the European Novel, 1800–1900* (1997; trans. 1998) and *Graphs, Maps, Trees: Abstract Models for a Literary History* (2005). During this period, Moretti served as chief editor of *Il Romanzo* (5 vols., 2001–03), a collection of more than one hundred essays by leading contemporary critics that provide an international reassessment of the novel. Selections have been translated into English as *The Novel* (2 vols., 2006), which provides a detailed argument for understanding the genre as a "planetary form." Moretti's *The Bourgeois: Between History and Literature* (2013) explores the vicissitudes of bourgeois culture in modern European literature by analyzing both particular keywords (such as "useful," "earnest," "efficiency," and "influence") and specific formal mutations of prose. In the ten essays collected in *Distant Reading* (2013), Moretti reconstructs the intellectual trajectory of his theory of "distant reading" and his data-centric study of literature, summarizing two decades of critical work. In its regular section on "Theories and Methodologies" *PMLA* 132.3 (May 2017), Moretti responds to ten assessments of *Distant Reading*. While reiterating his "fascination with (nonliterary) conceptual models," he highlights the creative potential for literary study of the shifts from proximity to distance; from actual history to simulations of theoretical models; from the concrete reader to conventions and abstract institutions; and from close reading to "quantitative formalism." In addition to his books, Moretti has written numerous articles and is a frequent contributor to the *New Left Review*.

Critical evaluations of Moretti's work come from scholars working in literary history, the novel, and genre theory. In "How the Mule Got Its Tale: Moretti's Darwinian Bricolage," *Diacritics* 29.2 (1999), a review of *Atlas of the European Novel*, Geoffrey Winthrop-Young praises Moretti but also points out methodological limitations, arguing that Moretti's recourse to biological and cultural evolutionary models is arbitrary and tenuous. In "Anglo-Globalism?" *New Left Review*, 2d ser., no. 16 (2002), Jonathan Arac commends Moretti's global reach; he notes, however, that Moretti's theory of the novel as a "planetary form" risks strengthening the cultural hegemony of the English language as a deceptively transparent medium for analyzing diverse national literatures. In "Evolution and Literary History: A Response to Franco Moretti," *New Left Review*, 2d ser., no. 34 (2005), Christopher Prendergast discusses in detail the strengths of Moretti's theory of graphs, maps, and trees, while also indicating potential logical flaws and argumentative ellipses. In particular, Prendergast questions the causal links between form, time, and space that sustain Moretti's morphology of literary genres. In "The Dangers of Distant Reading: Reassessing Moretti's Approach to Literary Genres," *Genre: Forms of Discourse and Culture* 47 (2014), Maurizio Ascari contests the purported scientific objectivity of Moretti's method of inquiry, arguing that distant reading might in fact lead to biased interpretations of a pseudoscientific nature. In "Plotting Devices: Literary Darwinism in the Laboratory," in *Evolutionary Aesthetics*, a special issue of *Philosophy and Literature* (38.1A [2014]), John Hay argues that Moretti's quantitative analysis of the history of literary form might provide the missing link enabling literary Darwinism to realize its full scientific potential as "a more consilient literary criticism."

Toni Morrison

Toni Morrison's books of cultural and literary criticism include *The Black Book* (1974; reprinted 2009), a scrapbook on African American experiences that includes photographs, slave auction posters, newspaper clippings, and related materials, co-edited by Toni Morrison, Middleton A. Harris, and others; *Playing in the Dark: Whiteness and the Literary Imagination* (1992); *What Moves at the Margin: Selected Nonfiction*, edited by Carolyn C. Denard (2008), containing several dozen essays and reviews; and *The Origin of Others* (2017). Two of Morrison's award speeches have been published as pamphlets: *Lecture and Speech of Acceptance, upon the Award of the Nobel Prize for Literature, Delivered in Stockholm on the Seventh of December, Nineteen Hundred and Ninety-three* (1994) and *The Dancing Mind: Speech upon Acceptance of the National Book Foundation Medal for Distinguished Contribution to American Letters on the Sixth of November, Nineteen Hundred and Ninety-six* (1996). She has edited three collections: *Race-ing Justice, En-Gendering Power: Essays on Anita Hill, Clarence Thomas, and the Construction of Social Reality* (1992); with Claudia Brodsky Lacour, *Birth of a Nation'hood: Gaze,*

Script, and Spectacle in the O.J. Simpson Case (1997); and *Burn This Book: PEN Writers Speak Out on the Power of the Word* (2009), a collection addressing literature and censorship.

Morrison has written eleven novels: *The Bluest Eye* (1970), *Sula* (1973), *Song of Solomon* (1977), *Tar Baby* (1981), *Beloved* (1987), *Jazz* (1992), *Paradise* (1997), *Love* (2003), *A Mercy* (2008), *Home* (2012), and *God Help the Child* (2015). Her only short story, "Recitatif," was published in *Confirmation: An Anthology of African American Women* (1983), a collection co-edited by Black Arts movement poet and playwright Amiri Baraka and Amina Baraka, his wife. Morrison has also written two plays: *Dreaming Emmett* (1986), about the teenager (Emmett Till) whose 1955 murder helped catalyze the civil rights movement, and *Desdemona* (2012), which features Shakespeare's Desdemona and her African nursemaid. Morrison has written the libretto for the opera *Margaret Garner* (2005) as well as eleven children's books—all, except *Remember: The Journey to School Integration* (2004), co-written with her late son, Slade Morrison: *The Big Box* (1999); *The Book of Mean People* (2002); a number of adaptations of Aesop's fables under the series title Who's Got Game, *The Ant or the Grasshopper?* (2003), *Poppy or the Snake* (2003), *The Lion or the Mouse* (2003), and *The Mirror or the Glass* (2007); *Peeny Butter Fudge* (2009); *Little Cloud and Lady Wind* (2010); *The Tortoise or the Hare* (2010); and *Please, Louise* (2014).

Morrison's fiction and criticism have engendered numerous scholarly articles, monographs, and collections, and not all responses have been positive. The grounds for objections to her fiction range from liberties taken with the historical record—a charge aimed mostly at her use of Margaret Garner's story in *Beloved*—to her depictions of black male characters to her use of violence as part of her novels' narrative structures. Similarly, her criticism has been faulted for not accounting for gender and sexuality (*Playing in the Dark*), for skewering Clarence Thomas (*Race-ing Justice, En-Gendering Power*), and for erasing the body of Nicole Brown-Simpson (*Birth of a Nation'hood*).

A number of works provide good general introductions to Toni Morrison's life and work: Linda Wagner-Martin's *Toni Morrison: A Literary Life* (2015) is a good starting point. *Toni Morrison: Memory and Meaning*, edited by Adrienne Lanier Seward and Justine Tally (2014), has a foreword by Carolyn C. Denard, founder of the Toni Morrison Society, and essays that take up all manner of themes in Morrison's body of ideas; biographical insights are provided by Dana A. Williams's "To Make a Humanist Black: Toni Wofford's Howard Years." Tessa Roynon's *The Cambridge Introduction to Toni Morrison* (2013) is part biography, part close textual analysis of Morrison's fiction and engagement with her critical reception. Morrison's *What Moves at the Margin: Selected Nonfiction*, edited and with an introduction by Carolyn C. Denard (2008), a compilation of Morrison's commentaries, musings on her family history, and speeches, includes "The Nobel Lecture in Literature" (1994) and "The Dancing Mind" (1996), both of which have been published separately as well (see above). Other solid resources are *The Cambridge Companion to Toni Morrison*, edited by Justine Tally (2007), which is divided into sections that treat Morrison's fiction and nonfiction (particularly insightful is Cheryl A. Wall's essay on Morrison's legacy as an editor who nurtured the careers of African American writers, "Toni Morrison, Editor and Teacher"), and the classic *Critical Essays on Toni Morrison*, edited by Nellie Y. McKay (1988). See also *Toni Morrison: Conversations*, edited by Carolyn C. Denard (2008), which relies on interviews and conversations over a span of years to offer insights into Morrison's life, work, motivations, and literary inspirations; and Elizabeth A. Beaulieu's *The Toni Morrison Encyclopedia*, edited by Elizabeth Ann Beaulieu (2003), which helps identify and define key themes and trends in her oeuvre.

For compelling examinations of Morrison's *Playing in the Dark*, see Nathaniel F. Mills, "Playing in the Dark, on the Left, and Out of Bounds: Nelson Algren, World War II, and the Cross-Racial Imagination of Blackness," *MELUS* 38.4 (2013); Catherine Hall, "*Playing in the Dark* . . . and Racing Englishness," *European Journal of Women's Studies* 18 (2011); Sanyat Sattar, "*Playing in the Dark* and the Quest of Identity: Morrison Painting the True Colours of Americanness," *Shiron*, no. 45 (2010); and Roynon's close reading in *The Cambridge Introduction to Toni Morrison* (see above). Harold Bloom, one of the leading partisans in the culture and canon wars, engages with debates on American literature, the canon, and Morrison's own mastery of the American novel as form in "Two African-American Masters of the American Novel," *Journal of Blacks in Higher Education*, no. 28 (2000).

Over the years, Morrison's edited collection on the Clarence Thomas–Anita Hill controversy, *Race-ing Justice, En-Gendering Power*, has elicited scholarship across a variety of disciplines. Luke Charles Harris's "Lessons Still Unlearned: The Continuing Sounds of Silence," *Du Bois Review* 10 (2013), provides a retrospective overview of the issues relating to black women, silence, justice, power, and intersectionality that its essays sought to engage.

The anthology on the O.J. Simpson saga edited by Morrison and Lacour, *Birth of a Nation'hood*, whose title plays on that of the American filmmaker D. W. Griffith's racially charged silent epic, *The Birth of a Nation* (1915)—itself inspired by Thomas F. Dixon Jr.'s novel *The Clansman* (1905)—led to two noteworthy articles on interracial sex, spectacle, black masculinity, and violence: Riché Richardson's "'The Birth of Nation'hood': Lessons from Thomas Dixon and D. W. Griffith to William

Bradford Huie and *The Klansman*, O.J. Simpson's First Movie," *Mississippi Quarterly* 56 (2002/2003), and Rinaldo Walcott's "Deceived: The Unreadability of the O.J. Simpson Case," *Canadian Review of American Studies/Revue Canadienne d'Etudes Américaines* 28.2 (1998).

"Toni Morrison Remembers" (2015, dir. Jill Nichols), an episode in the BBC series *Imagine* featuring Morrison herself, provides intimate insights into her life and work. For further reading, the bibliographies in Wagner-Martin's *Toni Morrison: A Literary Life* and Roynon's *Cambridge Introduction to Toni Morrison* are quite extensive. In addition to hosting a biennial conference, the Toni Morrison Society publishes an annual bibliography.

Timothy Morton

Timothy Morton is the author of eight books, coauthor of two, editor of four, and co-editor of one. His *Shelley and the Revolution in Taste: The Body and the Natural World* (1994), described by the critic Charles J. Rzepka as a "magical mystery tour of a gargantuan subject largely unexamined in relation to its important role in shaping the modern Western world and English literature," discusses the topics of food and drink in the works of Percy Bysshe Shelley and Mary Wollstonecraft Shelley, offering new perspectives on recent theories of medicine and diet while treating food as a cultural construct. *The Poetics of Spice: Romantic Consumerism and the Exotic* (2000) studies the importance of spice and the spice trade, extending scholarship on the impact of consumerism and capitalism to Romantic writers. Defining spice as a "discourse, not an object, naively transparent to itself," the book makes use of Jacques Derrida's *pharmakon* in its reading of spice as a multifaceted "sign" and in its description of the ideological relationships dominating the spice trade. It also employs Slavoj Žižek's political philosophy. Morton edited *Radical Food: The Culture and Politics of Eating and Drinking, 1780–1830* (3 vols., 2000), *Mary Shelley's "Frankenstein": A Sourcebook* (2002), *Cultures of Taste/Theories of Appetite: Eating Romanticism* (2004), and *The Cambridge Companion to Shelley* (2006). With Nigel Smith, Morton co-edited *Radicalism in British Literary Culture, 1650–1830: From Revolution to Revolution* (2002). Morton's *The Ecological Thought* (2010) represents an extension of his *Ecology without Nature: Rethinking Environmental Aesthetics* (2007); the earlier work explores possible "political and social thinking, making, and doing" for our interaction with the environment. *Hyperobjects: Philosophy and Ecology after the End of the World* (2013) discusses the meaning of hyperobjects, such as global warming, radioactive plutonium, and climate change, and explores an ethicopolitics that acknowledges human weakness, lameness, and hypocrisy. His *Realist Magic: Objects, Ontology, Causality* (2013) offers innovative ways to perceive causality. With Marcus Boon and Eric Cazdyn, Morton wrote *Nothing: Three Inquiries in Buddhism* (2015); his emails with Björk Guðmundsdóttir make up *Björk*, vol. 4, *This Huge Sunlit Abyss from the Future Right There Next to You* (2015). His *Dark Ecology: For a Logic of Future Coexistence* (2016) questions the purity of nature, encouraging readers to quit looking for the "origin point" at which nature has stopped being natural and, instead, inviting them to think ecologically: "we must think each state of affairs as entwined with one another and as consisting of nested loops of other states entwined with one another: humans within ecosystems, thoughts within brains." Here he defines "ecological awareness" as "a loop because human interference has a loop form, because ecological and biological systems are loops." Morton's *Humankind: Solidarity with Nonhuman People* (2017) mounts a radical call for solidarity and kindness between humans and nonhumans and for overcoming the ironclad notion of species in the interest of symbiosis and ecological coexistence. In addition, it aims to liberate current academic discourse on ecology from dominant cultural conservatism and hostility to theory, both of which should include humans and nonhumans alike.

Morton's "Guest Column: Queer Ecology," *PMLA* 125 (2010), imagines a field of study in which ecological and queer theories coexist and lays out some hypotheses regarding the interrelatedness of the two existing fields: "Ecology and queer theory are intimate. It's not that ecological thinking would benefit from an injection of queer theory from the outside. It's that, fully and properly, ecology is queer theory and queer theory is ecology: queer ecology." Morton has done several dozen interviews; for insight into his intellectual biography, see the February 2011 interview on the blog "New APPS: Art, Politics, Philosophy, Science" (www.newappsblog.com/2011/02/new-apps-interview-timothy-morton.html).

Timothy Morton's work has received much attention, both appreciative and critical. Eric Gidal's review of *The Ecological Thought* in *Studies in Romanticism* 50 (2011) acknowledges Morton's view of shared responsibility regarding ecological problems such as global warming but disagrees with the ways in which Morton applies his theory. Morton, not unlike other humanists, Gidal argues, prefers thinking to acting, rendering his work inaccessible to a general audience. In his review of *The Ecological Thought* in *Christianity and Literature* 61 (2012), Jeffrey Bilbro takes issue with the book's lack of "close textual analysis" and its "high-level theory," finding deficiencies in Morton's handling of choice and identity. Gregers Andersen's "Greening the Sphere: Towards an Eco-Ethics for the Local and Artificial," *symplokē* 21 (2013), sets Morton's global "eco-ethics" against Heidegger's "local eco-ethics." He recommends a middle ground between these two positions: "it is in the abyss between the old Heideggerian imperative to save authentic local nature, and the abstract recognition of the strange strangers of an artificial world, suggested by Morton, that ecocriticism should seek its future place for action." Morton maintains a personal blog, "Ecology without Nature" (http://ecologywithoutnature.blogspot.com/), which contains an up-to-date résumé plus lists of interviews and talks.

Laura Mulvey

Although "Visual Pleasure and Narrative Cinema" (1975) is her most frequently anthologized essay, Mulvey has written widely on film theory and criticism and media studies. She has published four books: *Visual and Other Pleasures* (1989; 2d ed., 2009) collects her essays on a wide range of topics; *Citizen Kane* (1992) explores what is perhaps the most celebrated American film; *Fetishism and Curiosity* (1996) examines how the concept of fetishism as it has been developed by Karl Marx and Freud relates to artistic texts; and *Death 24x a Second: Stillness and the Moving Image* (2006) discusses new forms of spectatorship created by new media technologies, such as the DVD. She has also contributed, with Michael Rush and Philippe-Alain Michaud, to a volume on the filmmaker Mark Lewis, *Mark Lewis* (2006). She has co-edited four collections of essays: *Experimental British Television* (2007), with Jamie Sexon; a critical reappraisal of the French filmmaker Jean-Luc Godard, *Godard's Contempt: Essays from the London Consortium* (2012), with Colin MacCabe; *Feminisms: Diversity, Difference and Multiplicity in Contemporary Film Cultures* (2015), with Anna Backman Rogers; and *Other Cinemas: Politics, Culture and Experimental Film in the 1970s* (2017), with Sue Clayton. For biographical information on Mulvey, see her entry in *Movies in American History: An Encyclopedia* (ed. Philip C. DiMare, 2011).

David Sorfa's "Laura Mulvey," in *Film, Theory and Philosophy: The Key Thinkers* (ed. Felicity Colman, 2009), provides an introductory account of Mulvey's work. A great deal of feminist film criticism since 1975 has been written in response to Mulvey's essay. Among the most notable analyses are E. Ann Kaplan, *Women and Film: Both Sides of the Camera* (1983); *Re-vision: Essays in Feminist Film Criticism*, edited by Mary Ann Doane, Patricia Mellencamp, and Linda Williams (1984); Kaplan, *Rocking around the Clock: Music Television, Postmodernism, and Consumer Culture* (1987), which examines MTV and the popular music video, in another extension and critique of Mulvey's argument; and Mary Ann Doane, *The Desire to Desire: The Woman's Film of the 1940s* (1987). An anthology that demonstrates Mulvey's considerable influence on feminist film criticism is *Female Spectators: Looking at Film and Television*, edited by E. Deidre Pribram (1988). Several major psychoanalytic books on film assess Mulvey's contributions, including Kaja Silverman, *The Acoustic Mirror: The Female Voice in Psychoanalysis and Cinema* (1988); *Psychoanalysis and Cinema*, edited by E. Ann Kaplan (1990); and *Femmes Fatales: Feminism, Film Theory, Psychoanalysis*, edited by Mary Ann Doane (1991). *Viewing Positions: Ways of Seeing Films*, edited by Linda Williams (1995), offers a major reassessment of Mulvey's theories of film spectatorship. *Feminist Film Theorists: Laura Mulvey, Kaja Silverman, Teresa de Lauretis, Barbara Creed*, edited by Shohini Chaudhuri (2006), explores connections between Mulvey's work and that of other feminist film theorists. Interviews that illuminate Mulvey's cinematic and critical practices include Jacquelyn Suter and Sandy Flitterman, "Textual Riddles: Women as Enigma or Site of Social Meanings? An Interview with Laura Mulvey," *Discourse* 1 (1979); Juan Suarez and Millicent Manglis, "Cinema, Gender, and the Topography of Enigmas: A Conversation with Laura Mulvey," *Cinefocus* 3 (1995); and Roberta Sassatelli, "Interview with Laura Mulvey: Gender, Gaze and Technology in Film Culture," *Theory, Culture and Society* 28.5 (2011).

C. D. Narasimhaiah

C. D. Narasimhaiah's main interest, beginning with his seminal collection of essays *The Swan and the Eagle* (1969; 3d ed., 1999), was comparing Indian and contemporary Western theories of criticism. Among his other books on literary criticism in India are *The Function of Criticism in India: Essays on Indian Response to Literature* (1987), *The Indian Critical Scene: Controversial Essays* (1990), *English Studies in India: Widening Horizons* (2002), and *An Inquiry into the Indianness of Indian English* (2003), and he edited or co-edited numerous collections, including *A Common Poetic for Indian Literatures* (with C. N. Srinath, 1984), *East-West Poetics at Work* (1991), and *Makers of Indian English Literature* (2000). He published extensively on literature of other Commonwealth nations, including *An Introduction to Australian Literatures* (ed., 1965), *Awakened Conscience: Studies in Commonwealth Literature* (1978), and *Essays in Commonwealth Literature: Heirloom of Multiple Heritage* (1995).

Narasimhaiah wrote and edited books on single authors, including *Better Literary History and Better Literary Criticism: The Work of F. R. Leavis and How It Strikes an Indian* (1963), *Raja Rao* (1973), *Ananda Coomaraswamy: Centenary Essays* (ed., 1982), and *T. S. Eliot and the Indian Literary Scene* (edited with C. N. Srinath, 1990). He also did much work on India's first prime minister, Jawaharlal Nehru: he collected a selection of Nehru's speeches in 1963, abridged Nehru's *The Discovery of India* (1946) in 1975, and wrote a biography, *Jawaharlal Nehru: The Statesman as Writer* (2001).

Narasimhaiah titled his life story *"N" for Nobody: An Autobiography of an English Teacher* (1991). He was honored by several festschrifts, notably *Theory in Practice: Essays in Honour of C. D. Narasimhaiah*, edited by D. A. Shankar, V. K. Natraj, and M. Sathyanarayana Rao (2001), and *Critical Spectrum: Essays in Literary Culture (in Honour of C. D. Narasimhaiah)*, edited by Satish C. Aikant (2004).

Narasimhaiah's work has drawn both approval and condemnation from Indian critics. Feroza Jussawalla's *Family Quarrels: Towards a Criticism of Indian Writing in English* (1985) assesses both his handling of Indian writers and his use of European critics (especially F. R. Leavis and I. A. Richards). In the popular *The Empire Writes Back: Theory and Practice in Post-colonial Literature* (1989; 2d ed., 2002), the Australian critics Bill Ashcroft, Gareth Griffiths, and Helen Tiffen fault the Sanskrit-based aesthetic for trying to recover "the illusory essence of Indianness." Criticism of Narasimhaiah and other postcolonial and postmodern theorists for perpetuating colonialist discourse is widespread, especially on Internet blogs. In his conference paper "Decolonizing the Indian Mind" (2001), available online, Kapil Kapoor very broadly criticizes Anglicized and Americanized Indian critics for internalizing Western critical practices and defends Sanskritist theories. In "Indigenous Education and Brahminical Hegemony in Bengal," in *The Transmission of Knowledge of South Asia: Essays on Education, Religion, History, and Politics* (ed. Nigel Crook, 1996), Poromesh Acharya claims that Sanskritist theories lend support to the ancient Indian caste system.

Much work is being done, both in India and overseas, on the Sanskritist concepts of criticism that Narasimhaiah helped resurrect. At the Dhvanyaloka Centre, which he helped found, scholars engage at the same time with Indian critical theories and Western theories. Ragini Ramachandra's article "Rasa-Dhvani and British Formalism: Some Random Thoughts," *Dialogue* 7.1 (June 2011), and Uma Alladi's collection *The Study of Aesthetics: An Indian Perspective* (2007), which includes Mohan Ramanan's "C. D. Narasimhaiah's Contribution to Literary Criticism and Aesthetics," illustrate the continuing interest in bridging the two different critical traditions. In "From Downing to Dhvanyaloka: Leavis, Nationalism and Sanskrit Poetics," *Literary Criterion* (Diamond Jubilee Year Special Issue, 2012), T. J. Cribb continues the conversation between F. R. Leavis and Sanskritist poetics. Narasimhaiah's work is also the subject of a book coauthored by Bandana and L. R. Sharma, *The Twain Shall Meet—West East: Indian Criticism and C. D. Narasimhaiah* (1998).

Narasimhaiah's ideas have influenced some leading works of postcolonial criticism, such as *Reworlding: The Literature of the Indian Diaspora*, edited by Emmanuel S. Nelson (1992); Priya Joshi's *In Another Country: Colonialism, Culture, and the English Novel in India* (2002); and Srinivas Aravamudan's *Guru English: South Asian Religion in a Cosmopolitan Language* (2006). Another fruitful line of influence brings postcolonial studies to bear on the idea of Commonwealth literature, as in *Postcolonizing the Commonwealth: Studies in Literature and Culture*, edited by Rowland Smith (2000), a project pioneered by Narasimhaiah in his collection *Awakened Conscience*. Significantly, in his recent work the prominent postcolonial critic Ashish Nandy has revived and applied *rasa-dhvani*. Other works that develop these concepts include G. N. Devy's *Indian Literary Criticism: Theory and Interpretation* (2002) and Revathi Krishnaswamy's "Toward World Literary Knowledges: Theory in the Age of Globalization," *Comparative Literature* 62 (2010). For more on Narasimhaiah's work and the concepts of *rasa* and *dhvani*, see John C. Hawley, *Encyclopedia of Postcolonial Studies* (2001), and *The Johns Hopkins Guide to Literary Theory and Criticism*, edited by Michael Groden, Martin Kreiswirth, and Imre Szeman (2d ed., 2005). *A Common Poetic for Indian Literatures* contains a bibliography of Narasimhaiah's work up to 1984.

Alondra Nelson

Alondra Nelson's books are *Body and Soul: The Black Panther Party and the Fight against Medical Discrimination* (2011) and *The Social Life of DNA: Race, Reparations, and Reconciliation after the Genome* (2016), which examines genetic genealogy as a new tool for addressing old and enduring issues around race, including grappling with the unfinished business of slavery, establishing ties with African ancestral homelands, and making legal claims for slavery reparations. Nelson edited *Technicolor: Race, Technology, and Everyday Life* (2001), which looks at the cultural impact of new information and communication technologies and how they have been constant topics of debate while questions of race and ethnicity fail to be raised; *Afrofuturism*, a special issue of *Social Text* (no. 71 [2002]); and, with the sociologist Catherine Lee and the historian Keith Wailoo, *Genetics and the Unsettled Past: The Collision of DNA, Race, and History* (2012), which explores how our genetic markers have come to be regarded as portals to the past. There is to date little secondary literature on Nelson's work.

Jalondra Davis Brown highlights the African American–centric dimensions of Afrofuturism as proposed by Nelson and others in "Imagining Africa," *Science Fiction Studies* 41 (2014). In his review of *Genetics and the Unsettled Past* in *Contemporary Sociology* 44 (2015), B. Ricardo Brown notes that Nelson's contribution to that collection, "Reconciliation Projects: From Kinship to Justice" (which formed the basis of her book *The Social Life of DNA*), suggests that the "genomic era" of heightened knowledge about DNA and genealogy may make possible "recognition and reconciliation in locations of intense social conflict." The most up-to-date bibliography of Nelson's writings can be found on her departmental website.

Sianne Ngai

Ngai is the author of two books. *Ugly Feelings* (2005) examines in art and popular culture the relatively small emotions of irritation, envy, anxiety, paranoia, and disgust, as well as two "feelings" to which Ngai gives the names "animatedness" and "stuplimity." *Our Aesthetic Categories: Zany, Cute, Interesting* (2012) continues her exploration of less exalted art forms, investigating the ways in which the zany, cute, and interesting saturate contemporary commodity culture, including its art. Her articles have appeared in *PMLA*, *Critical Inquiry*, *American Literature*, and other prestigious journals. See, for example, "The Cuteness of the Avant-Garde," *Critical Inquiry* 31 (2005); "Merely Interesting," *Critical Inquiry* 34 (2008); and "Visceral Abstractions," *GLQ: A Journal of Lesbian and Gay Studies* 21.1 (2015). She discusses her work in "Our Aesthetic Categories: An Interview with Sianne Ngai," by Adam Jasper, in *Cabinet*, no. 43 (fall 2011).

For a brief introduction to affect theory, see Marta Figlerowicz's introduction to *Affect Theory Dossier*, a special issue of *Qui Parle* (20.2 [2012]). *The Affect Theory Reader*, edited by Melissa Gregg and Gregory J. Seigworth (2010), collects major statements on affect by contemporary theorists. Ruth Leys critiques the scientism of affect theory in "The Turn to Affect: A Critique," *Critical Inquiry* 37 (2011). In "*Ugly Feelings*, Powerful Sensibilities," *Contemporary Literature* 27 (2006), Charles Altieri calls Ngai's first book "stunning in its depth and range, exemplary in its learning, and almost continually surprising in its inventiveness," although he criticizes as a "doomed strategy" Ngai's focus "on art's powerlessness in the political sphere as her means of locating its possible power." Jennifer Fleissner, reviewing the book for *Modernism/modernity* 13 (2006), expresses irritation at its occasional inaccessibility, while at the same time calling it "one of the most intellectually dazzling and wide-ranging critical studies to appear in years." Ngai's influential work has been used by other scholars to illuminate topics as diverse as the West Indian novelist Jean Rhys in Anne Cunningham's "'Get On or Get Out': Failure and Negative Femininity in Jean Rhys's *Voyage in the Dark*," *Modern Fiction Studies* 59 (2013); Asian cinema in Jonathan Beller's "The Martial Art of 'Cinema': Modes of Virtuosity à la Hong Kong and the Philippines," *Positions: East Asia Cultures Critique* 19 (2011); and festivity in Naomi Milthorpe's "'Heavy Jokes': Festive Unpleasure in the Interwar Novel," *Journal of Modern Literature* 38.3 (2015).

Ngugi wă Thiong'o, Taban Lo Liyong, and Henry Owuor-Anyumba

Ngugi wă Thiong'o has published numerous critical essays on African literature, education, and politics, collected in *Homecoming: Essays on African and Caribbean Literature, Culture and Politics* (1973), which includes "On the Abolition of the English Department"; *Writers in Politics: Essays* (1981; rev. ed., 1997); *Education for a National Culture* (1981); *Barrel of a Pen: Resistance to Repression in Neo-Colonial Kenya* (1983); *Decolonising the Mind: The Politics of Language in African Literature* (1986); *Moving the Centre: The Struggle for Cultural Freedom* (1993); *Penpoints, Gunpoints, and Dreams: Towards a Critical Theory of the Arts and the State of Africa* (1998); *Something Torn and New: An African Renaissance* (2009); and *Globalectics: Theory and the Politics of Knowing* (2012), which reflects on the context of "On the Abolition of the English Department," written after British atrocities. He has also written several memoirs, including *Detained: A Writer's Prison Diary* (1981), *Dreams in a Time of War: A Childhood Memoir* (2010), and *In the House of the Interpreter: A Memoir* (2012). See also *Ngũgĩ wa Thiong'o Speaks: Interviews with the Kenyan Writer*, edited by Reinhard Sander and Bernth Lindfors (2005). Ngugi also has an international reputation as a novelist depicting twentieth-century Kenya; his best-known novels are *Weep Not, Child* (1964), *A Grain of Wheat* (1967), *Petals of Blood* (1977), and *Wizard of the Crow* (2006).

Published primarily in Africa, Taban lo Liyong is a prolific writer of poetry, short stories, and criticism. His most notable books in English are *The Last Word: Cultural Synthesism* (1969), the first book of literary criticism specifically focused on African literature, and *Fixions* (1968), a collection of short stories that contain elements of African oral tradition. Other works include *Eating Chiefs: Lwo Culture from Lolwe to Malkal* (1970), *Thirteen Offensives: Against Our Enemies* (1973), and *Carrying Knowledge up a Palm Tree* (1997), a collection of poems. Henry Owuor-Anyumba's publications in English include a collection, *Kikuyu Folktales*, co-edited with Rose N. Gecau (1970), and the monograph *A Musical Profile of Some Kalenjin Songs* (1973).

Carol Sicherman's "Revolutionizing the Literature Curriculum at the University of East Africa: Literature and the Soul of the Nation," *Research in African Literatures* 29.3 (1998), details the context out of which "On the Abolition of the English Department" arose and its subsequent impact on African literary study. See also Apollo Obonyo Amoko, *Postcolonialism in the Wake of the Nairobi Revolution: Ngugi Wa Thiong'o and the Idea of African Literature* (2010). There is a great deal of scholarship on Ngugi's work, especially his fiction. *Ngugi wă Thiong'o: The Making of a Rebel: A Source Book in Kenyan Literature and Resistance*, edited by Carol Sicherman (1989), is a helpful reference work. Simon Gikandi, *Ngugi wă Thiong'o* (2000), is a useful study, as is Oliver Lovesey, *Ngũgĩ wa Thiong'o* (2000), which provides biographical information as well as a good bibliography. *Ngugi wă Thiong'o: A Bibliography of Primary and Secondary Works, 1957–1987*, compiled by Carol Sicherman (1991), is comprehensive but needs updating. There is to date little criticism and bibliography in English on Liyong or Owuor-Anyumba.

Friedrich Nietzsche

The standard German edition of Nietzsche's work is *Werke: Kritische Gesamtausgabe*, edited by Giorgio Colli and Mazzo Montinari (50+ vols., 1967–present). It is available online at www.nietzschesource.org/ (accessed Nov. 22, 2015). All of Nietzsche's major works and much of his occasional unpublished works and notebooks have been translated, but the history of English editions of his works is vexed. After World War II, Random House published most of his major works in translations by Walter Kaufmann and R. J. Hollingdale, but Kaufmann especially has been criticized for heavy-handed editing. Since the 1990s, both Stanford University Press and Cambridge University Press have been engaged in issuing new translations that are based on the texts in the standard German edition. Here we list the Cambridge University edition where one exists and the Random House version where it still remains the most readily available (the original date of publication is given first, followed by the date of the English translation): *The Birth of Tragedy* (1872; 1999), *On the Advantages and Disadvantages of History for Life* (1877; 1980), *Daybreak: Thoughts on the Prejudices of Morality* (1881; 1997), *The Gay Science* (1882; 2001), *Thus Spoke Zarathustra* (1885; 2006), *Beyond Good and Evil* (1886; 2001), *Genealogy of Morals* (1887; 2007), and *The Case of Wagner* (1888; 1966). Three short late works, all written in 1888, are translated in the Cambridge University Press volume *The Anti-Christ, Ecce Homo, Twilight of the Idols, and Other Writings* (2005). *The Will to Power*, edited by Walter Kaufmann and R. J. Hollingdale (1967), is an important collection of entries from Nietzsche's notebooks, but the work is controversial because it was collated by Nietzsche's sister. The more recent *Writings from the Late Notebooks*, edited by Rüdiger Bittner (2003), explains the controversy in its introduction and attempts to provide a less tendentious selection of work that Nietzsche left unpublished. *Nietzsche on Rhetoric and Language*, edited by Sandor Gilman, Carole Blair, and David J. Parent (1989), collects work of particular interest to literary critics. *The Nietzsche Reader*, edited by Keith Ansell Pearson and Duncan Large (2006), offers generous selections from the whole range of Nietzsche's career. *Selected Letters of Friedrich Nietzsche*, edited by Christopher Middleton (1969), is the most useful collection of letters. *Ecce Homo* (1888) is Nietzsche's half-mad and fascinating autobiography; the most succinct biography is Ronald Hayman's *Nietzsche: A Critical Life* (1980), but Rüdiger Safranski's more comprehensive intellectual biography, *Nietzsche: A Philosophical Biography* (2000; trans. 2002), is essential for a full engagement with Nietzsche's life and thought. Also worth consulting are Thomas H. Brobjer, *Nietzsche's Philosophical Context: An Intellectual Biography* (2008), and Julian Young, *Friedrich Nietzsche: A Philosophical Biography* (2010).

The secondary literature is immense and we can touch here only on works likely to interest those coming to Nietzsche through an engagement with literary theory. Gianni Vattimo's *Nietzsche: An Introduction* (1985; trans. 2001) and Alexander Nehamas's influential *Nietzsche: Life as Literature* (1985) are good places to start. Martin Heidegger's four-volume *Nietzsche* (1961; trans. 1979–86) is a major document of twentieth-century philosophy as well as a powerful, if idiosyncratic, interpretation of Nietzsche. Many poststructuralists have written extensively on Nietzsche. A partial list includes Gilles Deleuze, *Nietzsche and Philosophy* (1962; trans. 1983); Sarah Kofman, *Nietzsche and Metaphor* (1972; trans. 1993); Michel Foucault, *Language, Counter-Memory, Practice* (1977); Jacques Derrida, *Spurs: Nietzsche's Styles* (1978; trans. 1979); and Paul de Man, *Allegories of Reading* (1979). Five works that particularly address Nietzsche's aesthetics are James I. Porter's *The Invention of Dionysus: An Essay on "The Birth of Tragedy"* (2000), Matthew Rampley's *Nietzsche, Aesthetics and Modernity* (2000), Peter Sloterdijk's *Nietzsche Apostle* (2000; trans. 2013), Douglas Burnham and Martin Jesinghausen's *Nietzsche's "The Birth of Tragedy": A Reader's Guide* (2010), Robert R. William's *Tragedy, Recognition, and the Death of God: Studies in Hegel and Nietzsche* (2012), and *Nietzsche on Art and Life*, edited by Daniel Came (2014). Malcolm Bull's *Anti-Nietzsche* (2011) has been widely read and discussed, while Jennifer Ratner-Rosenhagen's *American Nietzsche: A History of an Icon and His Ideas* (2012) is a fascinating history of Nietzsche's reception in the United States. Peter R. Sedgwick, *Nietzsche: The Key Concepts* (2009); *Introductions to Nietzsche*, edited by Robert B. Pippin (2012); *The Oxford Handbook of Nietzsche*, edited by Ken Gemes and John Richardson (2013); and Douglas Burnham, *The Nietzsche Dictionary* (2015), are all useful reference works. *Nietzsche: Godfather of Fascism? On the Uses and Abuses of a Philosophy*, edited by Jacob Golomb and Robert S. Wistrich (2002), offers essays that explore Nietzsche's relation to National Socialism, including an important reassessment by Robert C. Holub of the notion that Nietzsche's sister is to blame for the Nazis' appropriation of Nietzsche's work. William H. Schaberg's *The Nietzsche Canon: A Publication History and Bibliography* (1995) carefully traces the history of all Nietzsche's texts. Useful bibliographies of secondary works can be found in Pearson and Large's *Nietzsche Reader* and Pippin's *Introductions to Nietzsche*.

Rob Nixon

In addition to numerous articles and reviews in academic and popular journals, Rob Nixon has published four books. *London Calling: V. S. Naipaul, Postcolonial Mandarin* (1992) is a scathing reassessment of the works of the Nobel Prize–winning author Naipaul, who has been celebrated for bridging cross-cultural divides between the West and postcolonial nations, but whom Nixon castigates for upholding an imperialistic representation of the "third world" as existing in parasitic dependence on the creative and productive cultures of the West. In *Homelands, Harlem and Hollywood: South African Culture and the World Beyond* (1994), Nixon examines the anticolonialist and anti-apartheid struggles of South Africa while exploring the ways in which South Africa and the United States have mutually influenced one another. *Dreambirds: The Strange History of the Ostrich in Fashion, Food, and Fortune* (2000) is a partially autobiographical work of creative nonfiction in which Nixon raises probing personal, historical, and ethical questions while analyzing the strange obsessions with the ostrich that he encountered in both South Africa and the United States. Nixon's interests in environmental and postcolonial theory intersect in *Slow Violence and the Environmentalism of the Poor* (2011), which analyzes both the slow environmental devastations caused by capitalist and imperialist forces and the movements of ecological justice in the global South that have emerged to resist these forces. An extended interview with Nixon by Robert P. Marzec and Allison Carruth in *Public Culture* 26 (2014) includes discussions of the concept of slow violence as well as of the intersections between environmentalism and postcolonialism.

Several reviews of *Slow Violence and the Environmentalism of the Poor* help demonstrate its significance and offer constructive criticisms. In a favorable review published in the *Times Higher Education Supplement*, September 15, 2011, Jules Pretty praises Nixon's analysis of the intersections between imperialism, war, and environmental degradation, but argues that the concept of slow violence may hide the fast impacts of environmental degradation while reductively implying that such degradations are always caused by the violent intentions of malevolent persons. In *Research in African Literatures* 43.1 (2012), Byron Caminero-Santangelo celebrates Nixon as a member of a vanguard movement that attunes ecocriticism to the realities of imperialism. Caminero-Santangelo also claims that Nixon fills a gap in the work of Edward W. Said by demonstrating the environmental aspects of colonialism. In "The Varieties of Environmental Violence," *Los Angeles Review of Books*, November 22, 2013, Subhankar Banerjee praises Nixon's work for its fresh reframing of important theoretical concepts and its lucid prose while suggesting that his analysis should be extended both to address writer-activists outside of the global South and to situate the works of individual activists within the broader communities from which their activism emerges.

Martha C. Nussbaum

Martha Nussbaum is one of the most prolific scholars of her generation; she has written or edited more than forty books; published more than 300 articles, as well as over fifty reviews in prominent magazines such as the *New Republic* and the *New York Review of Books*; and given scores of public lectures. Her first book, *Aristotle's De Motu Animalium: Text with Translation, Commentary, and Interpretive Essays* (1978), was a revision of her dissertation. It was with her next book, *The Fragility of Goodness: Luck and Ethics in Greek Tragedy and Philosophy* (1986; rev. ed., 2001) that she gained wide attention. It inaugurated a cluster of works that deal with classical philosophy, ethics, emotion, and literature, including *Love's Knowledge: Essays on Philosophy and Literature* (1990), *The Therapy of Desire: Theory and Practice in Hellenistic Ethics* (1994), *Poetic Justice: The Literary Imagination and Public Life* (1995), and *Cultivating Humanity: A Classical Defense of Reform in Liberal Education* (1997), from which we draw our selection. While continuing her focus on ethics, her next wave of books more explicitly address politics and human rights; they include *Sex and Social Justice* (1999), *Women and Human Development: The Capabilities Approach* (2000), *Upheavals of Thought: The Intelligence of Emotions* (2001), *Hiding from Humanity: Disgust, Shame, and the Law* (2004), and *Frontiers of Justice: Disability, Nationality, Species Membership* (2006). She also examined religion and its effect on politics, in *The Clash Within: Democracy, Religious Violence, and India's Future* (2007), *Liberty of Conscience: In Defense of America's Tradition of Religious Equality* (2008), and *The New Religious Intolerance: Overcoming the Politics of Fear in an Anxious Age* (2012). She followed *Cultivating Humanity* with a polemic against the corporate university in *Not for Profit: Why Democracy Needs the Humanities* (2010), and continued her reflections on social justice and emotions in a succession of short books: *From Disgust to Humanity: Sexual Orientation and Constitutional Law* (2010), *Creating Capabilities: The Human Development Approach* (2011), *Political Emotions: Why Love Matters for Justice* (2013), and *Anger and Forgiveness: Resentment, Generosity, Justice* (2016). In addition, she collected essays in *Philosophical Interventions: Reviews 1986–2011* (2012).

Nussbaum has co-edited more than a dozen collections, among them several on ancient philosophy; several deriving from her work with the United Nations University, such as *The Quality of Life* (with Amartya Sen, 1993), and *Women, Culture, and Development: A Study of Human Capabilities* (with Jonathan Glover, 1995); several on topical issues, including *Sexual Orientation and Human Rights in American Religious Discourse* (with Saul Olyan, 1998) and *Animal Rights: Current Debates and New Directions* (with Cass R. Sunstein, 2004); and several on literature, including *Subversion and Sympathy: Gender, Law, and the British Novel* (with Alison LaCroix, 2013). For an account of her work in her own words, see "The Capability of Philosophy: An Interview with Martha C. Nussbaum," conducted by Jeffrey J. Williams, *Minnesota Review*, n.s. 71–72 (2009).

The critical commentary on Nussbaum is sizable, ranging from scholarly disputations on classical philosophy to engagement in public debates on politics and religion; she has appeared in television interviews and been the subject of a *New York Times Magazine* feature article by Robert S. Boynton, "Who Needs Philosophy?" November 21, 1999. A special issue of *New Literary History* 15 (1983), titled *Literature and/as Moral Philosophy*, focused on Nussbaum's reading of Henry James; it includes essays by the philosophers Richard Wollheim and Hilary Putnam. *For Love of Country?* (1996; new ed., 2002), edited by Joshua Cohen, contains sixteen responses to Nussbaum's essay "Patriotism and Cosmopolitanism" by leading philosophers and critics, among them Judith Butler; the issue of *Boston Review* 19 (1994) where it was originally published contained twenty-nine responses. A review attacking the multicultural leanings of *Cultivating Humanity* by the prominent conservative critic David Frum appears in *Public Interest*, spring 1998. A substantial section of Ronald L. Hall's *The Human Embrace: The Love of Philosophy and the Philosophy of Love: Kierkegaard, Cavell, Nussbaum* (2000) considers Nussbaum's focus on emotion. A special issue of *Ethics* 111 (2000) features "Symposium on Martha Nussbaum's Political Philosophy." For studies of her philosophical positions, see Peter Johnson, *Moral Philosophers and the Novel: A Study of Winch, Nussbaum, and Rorty* (2004), and John M. Alexander, *Capabilities and Social Justice: The Political Philosophy of Amartya Sen and Martha Nussbaum* (2008). Geoffrey Galt Harpham's "Criticism as Therapy: The Hunger of Martha Nussbaum," in his *The Character of Criticism* (2006), offers a good synthetic account of Nussbaum's career. An exchange in *California Law Review* 98 (2010) on gay marriage features an essay by Nussbaum and an interesting response by the queer theorist Michael Warner. See also *Honoring the Contributions of Professor Martha Nussbaum to the Scholarship and Practice of Gender and Sexuality Law*, a symposium volume of *Columbia Journal of Gender and Law* 19 (2010). Specifically addressing her theories of education, see Jon Nixon, *Interpretive Pedagogies for Higher Education: Arendt, Berger, Said, Nussbaum and Their Legacies* (2012). See also *Capabilities, Gender, Equality: Towards Fundamental Entitlements*, edited by Flavio Comim and Nussbaum (2014), which includes a number of responses to Nussbaum's positions on social justice.

Richard Ohmann

Richard Ohmann's early work includes *Shaw: The Style and the Man* (1962), the edited collection *The Making of Myth* (1962), two coauthored textbooks on rhetoric and composition, and several influential essays employing speech act theory to analyze the style of literary works. After the late 1960s, he turned to focus on the politics of the profession and the socioinstitutional context of literature, publishing *English in America: A Radical View of the Profession* (1976; reissued in 1996 with a foreword by Gerald Graff and a new introduction by Ohmann) and a series of essays collected in *Politics of Letters* (1987), which includes "The Shaping of a Canon." Expanding his research to more general issues of literary culture, Ohmann's *Selling Culture: Magazines, Markets, and Class at the Turn of the Century* (1996), a prominent work of American cultural studies, examines the correlated rise of popular literary magazines and advertising in the late nineteenth and early twentieth century in the United States. In a related effort, Ohmann edited the collection *Making and Selling Culture* (1996), which includes essays by publishers and filmmakers as well as academics. He gathered his later essays in *Politics of Knowledge: The Commercialization of the University, the Professions, and Print Culture* (2003), a sequel to *Politics of Letters*. From 1966 through 1978, Ohmann also edited the influential journal *College English*, sponsoring innovative issues on feminism, gay studies, and other topics. His collection co-edited with W. B. Coley, *Ideas for English 101: Teaching Writing in College* (1975), derives from *College English*. "English in America Updated: An Interview with Richard Ohmann," conducted by Jeffrey Williams, recounts Ohmann's career and his embrace of radical politics; it is collected in *Critics at Work: Interviews, 1993–2003* (ed. Williams, 2004), as well as in Ohmann's *Politics of Knowledge*.

Notable responses to Ohmann include Gerald Graff's criticism of the radical assumptions of *English in America* in *Literature against Itself: Literary Ideas in Modern Society* (1979). In *Doing What Comes Naturally: Change, Rhetoric, and the Practice of Theory in Literary and Legal Studies* (1989), Stanley Fish finds a self-contradictory antiprofessional strand in Ohmann's critique of the profession. "The Shaping of a Canon" has provided a model for subsequent reception studies of the contemporary American canon and the "book market." In "Courses and Canons: The Post-1945 U.S. Novel," *Critique: Studies in Contemporary Fiction* 31 (1990), Raymond Mazurek expands on Ohmann's account to survey the recent canon taught in university courses, while noting the limitations of the category of "illness stories." A special issue of *Works and Days* 23 (2005) gathers fourteen essays assessing Ohmann's work, testifying to his influence in composition studies, American cultural studies, and the politics of literary studies. James F. English, "Everywhere and Nowhere: The Sociology of Literature after 'the Sociology of Literature,'" *New Literary History* 41.2 (2010), notes Ohmann's central work in developing a sociological approach. Jeffrey J. Williams, "The Rise of the Academic Novel," *American Literary History* 24 (2012), extends Ohmann's focus on fiction that dwells on the anxiety of the professional-managerial class.

Kelly Oliver
During the first two decades of her career, Oliver wrote ten books: *Reading Kristeva: Unraveling the Double-bind* (1993); *Womanizing Nietzsche: Philosophy's Relation to the "Feminine"* (1995); *Family Values: Subjects between Nature and Culture* (1997); *Subjectivity without Subjects: From Abject Fathers to Desiring Mothers* (1998); *Witnessing: Beyond Recognition* (2001); with Benigno Trigo, *Noir Anxiety* (2002); *The Colonization of Psychic Space: A Psychoanalytic Social Theory of Oppression* (2004); *Women as Weapons of War: Iraq, Sex, and the Media* (2007); *Animal Lessons: How They Teach Us to Be Human* (2009); and *Knock Me Up, Knock Me Down: Images of Pregnancy in Hollywood Films* (2012). More recently, *Technologies of Life and Death: From Cloning to Capital Punishment* (2013) analyzes the extremes of birth and death in their mediation by technologies of life and death. *Earth and World: Philosophy after the Apollo Missions* (2015) takes up discussions occurring within Continental philosophy about humanity's complex relationship to the earth and the environment. *Hunting Girls: Sexual Violence from "The Hunger Games" to Campus Rape* (2016) examines sexual violence and rape culture on-screen and offscreen. In *Carceral Humanitarianism: Logics of Refugee Detention* (2017), Oliver argues that humanitarian aid and rights rhetoric is never neutral and often betrays partisan politics. Books edited or co-edited by Oliver are *Ethics, Politics, and Difference in Julia Kristeva's Writing* (1993); *The Portable Kristeva* (1997; updated ed., 2002); with Marilyn Pearsall, *Feminist Interpretations of Nietzsche* (1998); with Christina Hendricks, *Language and Liberation: Feminism, Philosophy, and Language* (1999); with Penelope Deutsche, *Enigmas: The Writing of Sarah Kofman* (1999); *French Feminism Reader* (2000); with Steve Edwin, *Between the Psyche and the Social: Psychoanalytic Social Theory* (2002); with Lisa Walsh, *Contemporary French Feminism* (2004); with Alice A. Jardine and Shannon Lundeen, *Living Attention: On Teresa Brennan* (2007); and, with S. K. Keltner, *Psychoanalysis, Aesthetics, and Politics in the Work of Julia Kristeva* (2009).

A range of secondary scholarship responds to Oliver's work, especially on Nietzsche and feminism, Kristeva, and her theory of witnessing and testimony. Mae Henderson's *Speaking in Tongues and Dancing Diaspora: Black Women Writing and Performing* (2014) favorably extends Oliver's body of ideas on witnessing, recognition, and "response-ability" and "address-ability." Ewa Płonowska Ziarek's *An Ethics of Dissensus: Postmodernity, Feminism and the Politics of Radical Democracy* (2001) critically engages Oliver's theorizing on trauma, feminism, and Kristeva. In her review in *Hypatia* 20.2 (2005), Debra Bergoffen argues that Oliver's *Witnessing* would have been strengthened and challenged by engagements with Simone de Beauvoir and Martin Buber, particularly with regard to her wholesale rejection of subject-object relationships. For a representative list of Oliver's journal publications, see her faculty page at Vanderbilt University's Philosophy Department.

Walter Pater
Primary sources include *The Works of Walter Pater* (10 vols., 1910; rpt. 1967) and *Letters*, edited by Lawrence Evans (1970). See also *Walter Pater: Three Major Texts*, edited by William E. Buckler (1986), which includes *Studies in the History of the Renaissance, Appreciations*, and *Imaginary Portraits*. For a good selection, see *The Selected Writings of Walter Pater*, edited by Harold Bloom (1974). Thomas Wright's biography, *The Life of Walter Pater* (2 vols., 1907), is informative but not always reliable. Overviews of the life and work are provided by Ian Fletcher, *Walter Pater* (rev. ed., 1972), and Gerald Monsman, *Walter Pater* (1977).

For background and annotations for *Studies in the History of the Renaissance*, consult the editions by Adam Phillips (1986) and Donald L. Hill (1980). Context and analysis are offered by Paul Barolsky, *Walter Pater's Renaissance* (1987). Another useful resource is Billie Andrew Inman, *Walter Pater and His Reading, 1874–1877, with a Bibliography of His Library Borrowings, 1878–1894* (1990).

On Pater's criticism, see David J. DeLaura, *Hebrew and Hellene in Victorian England: Newman, Arnold, and Pater* (1969); William E. Buckler, *Walter Pater: The Critic as Artist of Ideas* (1987); and Jonathan Loesberg, *Aestheticism and Deconstruction: Pater, Derrida, and de Man* (1991), which argues for the philosophical and political force of Pater's aestheticist views in *Studies in the History of the Renaissance* and other works. Critical studies include Wolfgang Iser, *Walter Pater: The Aesthetic Moment* (1960; trans. 1987); Robert Keefe, *Walter Pater and the Gods of Disorder* (1988), on Pater's interest in Greek culture and mythology; Carolyn Williams, *Transfigured World: Walter Pater's Aesthetic Historicism* (1989), illuminating on Pater's narrative and rhetorical strategies in his criticism and fiction; Jay Fellows, *Tombs, Despoiled and Haunted: "Under-Textures" and "After-Thoughts" in Walter Pater* (1991); Denis Donoghue, *Walter Pater: Lover of Strange Souls* (1995), a suggestive study of Pater as a writer who sees criticism as "an opportunity for the exercise of self-consciousness"; and William Shuter, *Rereading Walter Pater* (1997), especially cogent on the influence of Heraclitus, Plato, and Hegel on Pater's thought. Kenneth Daley, in *The Rescue of Roman-*

ticism: Walter Pater and John Ruskin (2001), offers a stimulating account of Pater's response to and interpretation of the Romantic movement. Recent studies include *Victorian Aesthetic Conditions: Pater across the Arts*, edited by Elicia Clements and Lesley J. Higgins (2010), which provides interdisciplinary essays on Pater and art, music, theater, and literature; and Kate Hext, *Walter Pater: Individualism and Aesthetic Philosophy* (2013), on Pater's conception of the individual and self-identity and its relation to his aesthetic philosophy.

Walter Pater: An Imaginative Sense of Fact, edited by Philip Dodd (1981), collects papers presented at the First International Pater Conference, held in Oxford in 1980. Another good collection is *Pater in the 1990s*, edited by Laurel Brake and Ian Small (1991). *Comparative Criticism*, vol. 17, edited by E. S. Shaffer (1995), includes excellent essays on Pater by Denis Donoghue, Richard Wollheim, and others. For his contemporaries' responses to Pater's writings, see *Walter Pater: The Critical Heritage*, edited by R. M. Seiler (1980). See also *Walter Pater: An Annotated Bibliography of Writings about Him*, edited by Franklin Court (1979).

Plato

The standard Greek edition of the entire works of Plato, including those of dubious authorship, is *Platonis Opera*, edited by John Burnet (5 vols., 1900–1907). This edition is being updated by a team of scholars led by E. A. Duke (2 vols. to date, 1995–). For a handy one-volume English translation of selected dialogues by various translators, see *The Collected Dialogues of Plato*, edited by Edith Hamilton and Huntington Cairns (1961; rpt. 1989). *Plato: Complete Works*, edited by John M. Cooper (1997), is the most complete one-volume collection, with the best translations available (done by various hands). The best translation of *Republic* is Robin Waterfield's (1993).

A. E. Taylor's *Plato, the Man and His Work* (1926; 7th ed., 1969) contains a complete translation of Diogenes Laërtius's third-century C.E. life of Plato, which has served as the basis for modern reconstructions of the philosopher's life. For a general introduction, see *Plato: A Very Short Introduction* (2003), by Julia Annas. Several books provide good introductions to Plato's aesthetic theory, including Iris Murdoch, *The Fire and the Sun: Why Plato Banished the Artists* (1977), which attempts to defend Plato's view of the arts; and Morriss Henry Partee, *Plato's Poetics: The Authority of Beauty* (1981). Gerald F. Else, *Plato and Aristotle on Poetry* (1986), is a comparative study of the aesthetic theory of Greece's two greatest philosophers. In *Postmodern Platos* (1985), Catherine H. Zuckert examines the centrality of Platonic thought to theorists from Friedrich Nietzsche to Jacques Derrida. Other books dealing with Plato's importance to poststructuralist criticism include Jasper Neel, *Plato, Derrida, and Writing* (1988), and *Plato and Postmodernism*, edited by Steven Shankman (1994). For feminist readings of Plato, see *Feminist Interpretations of Plato*, edited by Nancy Tuala (1994). *The Cambridge Companion to Plato*, edited by Richard Kraut (1992), contains essays on several aspects of Plato's thought, including aesthetics. Andrea Wilson Nightingale's *Genres in Dialogue: Plato and the Construct of Philosophy* (1996) examines Plato's integration of Greek poetry and rhetoric into his dialogues. In *The Play of Character in Plato's Dialogues* (2002), Ruby Blondell explores the literary and philosophical questions raised by Plato's use of the dialogue form. *The Cambridge Companion to Plato's Republic*, edited by G. R. F. Ferrari (2007), offers a more advanced introduction to Plato's central work. Charles Griswold's article "Plato on Rhetoric and Poetry," in *The Stanford Encyclopedia of Philosophy* (2008), provides a useful summary of the "quarrel between philosophy and poetry" in Plato's dialogues, while recent studies challenge the traditional arguments about Plato's role in the split between poetry and philosophy in the Western tradition, offering new readings of *Republic*'s critique of poetry. See also Susan Levin, *The Ancient Quarrel between Philosophy and Poetry Revisited: Plato and the Greek Literary Tradition* (2001); Ramona Naddaff, *Exiling the Poets: The Production of Censorship in Plato's Republic* (2002); and David Wolfsdorf, *Trials of Reason: Plato and the Crafting of Philosophy* (2008). In *Between Ecstasy and Truth: Interpretations of Greek Poetics from Homer to Longinus* (2011), Stephen Halliwell contextualizes Plato's seemingly contradictory pronouncements about poetry in *Ion* and *Republic* as a dialectic that runs throughout Greek poetics: it focuses on the tension between ecstasy—emotional, imaginative responses—and truth, which emphasizes poetry's cognitive and ethical value. On *Phaedrus* and Plato's discussions of rhetoric and writing, see Ronna Burger, *Plato's "Phaedrus": A Defense of a Philosophic Art of Writing* (1980), and David A. White, *Rhetoric and Reality in Plato's "Phaedrus"* (1993). For an advanced, close reading of this dialogue, see Seth Benardete's *Rhetoric of Morality and Philosophy: Plato's "Gorgias" and "Phaedrus"* (1994). The most complete and up-to-date bibliography can be found in *The Cambridge Companion to Plato's Republic* (cited above).

Edgar Allan Poe

Poe wrote in a surprising variety of literary genres: poems, fantastic tales designed to explore what Freud would call "the uncanny," detective stories (a genre he seems to have invented), novels, reviews, and literary theory. For a good collection of Poe's literary theory and criticism, see the interesting short collection edited by Leonard Cassuto, *Edgar Allan Poe: Literary Theory and Criticism* (1999). For more extensive collections, see the Library of America volume titled *Edgar Allan Poe:*

Essays and Reviews (1984), with selections, notes, and a useful chronology by G. R. Thompson. *Literary Criticism of Edgar Allan Poe*, edited by Robert L. Hough (1965), and *Selections from the Critical Writings of Edgar Allan Poe*, edited by F. C. Prescott (1981), are also useful. Kenneth Silverman's *Edgar Allan Poe: Mournful and Never-Ending Remembrance* (1991) and Arthur Hobson Quinn's *Edgar Allan Poe* (1941; reprint, 1997) are towering full-length biographies. For a more recent brief life, see Peter Ackroyd's *Poe: A Life Cut Short* (2008). For an appreciation of broader biographical issues, the two essays on the history of Poe biography in *A Companion to Poe Studies*, edited by Eric W. Carlson (1996), are indispensable, as is *A Poe Log: A Documentary Life of Edgar Allan Poe*, edited by Dwight Thomas and David K. Jackson (1987).

For a book-length study of Poe's criticism, see Robert D. Jacobs's *Poe: Journalist and Critic* (1969). For good general collections of essays, see *Critical Essays on Edgar Allan Poe*, edited by Eric W. Carlson (1987), and *The Cambridge Companion to Edgar Allan Poe*, edited by Kevin J. Hayes (2002), as well as Hayes's anthology *Edgar Allan Poe in Context* (2013); *Poe and the Remapping of Antebellum Print Culture*, edited by J. Gerald Kennedy and Jerome McGann (2012) is also a useful source. Recent American work on poetic theory, race, gender, and historical context is found in *The American Face of Edgar Allan Poe*, edited by Shawn Rosenheim and Stephen Rachman (1995), which alludes to the earlier *The French Face of Edgar Allan Poe*, by Patrick Quinn (1954). The texts generated around Jacques Lacan's "Seminar on 'The Purloined Letter'"—authored by Lacan, Jacques Derrida, Barbara Johnson, and others—are collected in *The Purloined Poe* (ed. John P. Muller and William J. Richardson, 1988). And Roman Jakobson's essay on "The Raven" is in his *Language and Literature* (1987). For bibliographies, see J. Lasley Dameron and Irby B. Cauthen Jr., *Edgar Allan Poe: A Bibliography of Criticism, 1827–1967* (1974); Esther Hyneman, *Edgar Allan Poe: An Annotated Bibliography of Books and Articles in English* (1974); Leona Rasmussen, *Edgar Allan Poe: An Annotated Bibliography* (1978); and the *Cambridge Companion*.

Alexander Pope

The standard source for studying Pope is the *Twickenham Edition of the Works of Alexander Pope* (11 vols., 1939–69). Volume 1 (1961), edited by E. Audra and Aubrey Williams, includes a carefully annotated text of *An Essay on Criticism*. Also recommended is Robert M. Schmitz's *"Essay on Criticism," 1709; A Study of the Bodleian Manuscript Text with Facsimiles, Transcripts, and Variants* (1962), which examines the manuscript version of the *Essay*. A good one-volume selection is *Poetry and Prose of Alexander Pope*, edited by Aubrey Williams (1969), which uses the text established for the Twickenham edition. Another good edition, and one more up-to-date, is *Alexander Pope: The Rape of the Lock and Other Major Writings*, edited by Leo Damrosch (2011). Other important primary sources include *The Correspondence of Alexander Pope*, edited by George Sherburn (5 vols., 1956); and two volumes of prose works, the first edited by Norman Ault, *The Prose Works of Alexander Pope* (1936), and the second by Rosemary Cowler, *The Prose Works of Alexander Pope*, vol. 2, *The Major Works, 1725–1744* (1986). For selections from Pope's critical writings, see *Literary Criticism of Alexander Pope*, edited by Bertrand A. Goldgar (1965).

There are two superb biographical treatments: George Sherburn, *The Early Career of Alexander Pope* (1934), which covers the period to 1727; and Maynard Mack, *Alexander Pope: A Life* (1985), which examines the life and the writings in depth and detail. Also recommended: Howard Erskine-Hill, *The Social Milieu of Alexander Pope: Lives, Example, and the Poetic Response* (1975); Maynard Mack, *The Garden and the City: Retirement and Politics in the Later Poetry of Pope, 1731–1743* (1969); and Reginald Berry, *A Pope Chronology* (1988).

Two older studies of Pope's verse remain valuable: Geoffrey Tillotson, *On The Poetry of Pope* (2d ed., 1950), and Reuben A. Brower, *Alexander Pope: The Poetry of Allusion* (1959). These should be supplemented by Laura Brown, *Alexander Pope* (1985), a Marxist study that relates Pope to the culture of empire and capitalism; Ellen Pollak, *The Poetics of Sexual Myth: Gender and Ideology in the Verse of Swift and Pope* (1985), a feminist analysis; G. Douglas Atkins, *Quests of Difference: Reading Pope's Poems* (1986), which draws on Jacques Derrida's and Paul de Man's deconstructive theories and practices; Leopold Damrosch Jr., *The Imaginative World of Alexander Pope* (1987), an exploration of Pope's literary career as the product of his feelings of isolation and sexual, artistic, political, and financial marginality; Valerie Rumbold, *Women's Place in Pope's World* (1989), a cogent treatment of Pope's relationships with women and his poetry about them; and Helen Deutsch, *Resemblance and Disgrace: Alexander Pope and the Deformation of Culture* (1996). For a stimulating account of "philosophical skepticism" in Pope's poetic theory and practice, see James Noggle, *The Skeptical Sublime: Aesthetic Ideology in Pope and the Tory Satirists* (2001). In *Swift and Pope: Satirists in Dialogue* (2010), Dustin H. Griffin compares and contrasts the work of these lifelong friends and fellow satirists, studying their letters, poems, and satires as stages in an ongoing literary dialogue.

Much of the best critical work on Pope has been collected in *Essential Articles for the Study of Pope*, edited by Maynard Mack (1968); *Alexander Pope: A Critical Anthology*, edited by F. W. Bateson and N. A. Joukovsky (1971); *Alexander Pope: Writers and Their Backgrounds*, edited by Peter

Dixon (1972); and *Pope: The Critical Heritage*, edited by James Barnard (1973). More recent collections include *The Enduring Legacy: Alexander Pope Tercentenary Essays*, edited by G. S. Rousseau and Pat Rogers (1988), and *Pope: New Contexts*, edited by David Fairer (1990). See also the special issue of *The New Orleans Review*, vol. 15 (1980), edited by Ronald Schleifer and titled *The Poststructuralist Pope*. Helpful bibliographical works are Reginald H. Griffith, *Alexander Pope: A Bibliography* (2 vols., 1922–27), and Wolfgang Kowalk, *Alexander Pope: An Annotated Bibliography of Twentieth-Century Criticism, 1900–1979* (1981). Also helpful is Paul Baines, *The Complete Critical Guide to Alexander Pope* (2000). A good recent bibliography is included, along with a wide range of biographical, interpretive, and thematic essays, in *The Cambridge Companion to Alexander Pope*, edited by Pat Rogers (2007).

John Crowe Ransom

Ransom's books include *The World's Body* (1938), *The New Criticism* (1941), *Poems and Essays* (1955), and *Beating the Bushes* (1971). See also Ransom's *Selected Essays*, edited by Thomas Daniel Young and John Hindle (1984), and *Selected Letters*, edited by Young and George Core (1985). He also edited *The Kenyon Critics: Studies in Modern Literature from "The Kenyon Review"* (1951). Thomas Daniel Young has written an excellent biography: *Gentleman in a Dustcoat: A Biography of John Crowe Ransom* (1976). See also *John Crowe Ransom: Critical Essays and a Bibliography*, edited by Young (1968).

On the Agrarian movement and its relationship to the New Criticism, see John Lincoln Stewart, *The Burden of Time: The Fugitives and Agrarians* (1965); Alexander Karanikas, *Tillers of a Myth: Southern Agrarians as Social and Literary Critics* (1966); Mark Jancovich, *The Cultural Politics of the New Criticism* (1993); and Charlotte H. Beck, *The Fugitive Legacy: A Critical History* (2001). Detailed information about Ransom and the New Critics can also be found in Marian Janssen, *The Kenyon Review, 1939–1970: A Critical History* (1990). *The New Criticism and Contemporary Literary Theory: Connections and Continuities*, edited by William J. Spurlin and Michael Fischer (1995), examines the history of modern criticism from the New Critics to later poststructuralist theorists. For bibliography of primary and secondary sources, consult Thomas Daniel Young, *John Crowe Ransom: An Annotated Bibliography* (1982).

Adrienne Rich

Rich published nearly two dozen books of poetry. Her prose is collected in *On Lies, Secrets, and Silence: Selected Prose, 1966–1978* (1979), *Blood, Bread, and Poetry: Selected Prose, 1979–1985* (1986), *What Is Found There: Notebooks on Poetry and Politics* (1993), *Arts of the Possible: Essays and Conversations* (2001), *Poetry and Commitment: An Essay* (2007), and *A Human Eye: Essays on Art and Society* (2009). Her book on motherhood, *Of Woman Born: Motherhood as Experience and Institution*, was published in 1976. *Adrienne Rich's Poetry and Prose*, edited by Barbara Charlesworth Gelpi and Albert Gelpi (1993), offers selections from the span of Rich's career, along with critical essays on her work. The best biographical sources are the entry on Rich in *Contemporary Authors*, New Revision Series 53 (ed. Jeff Chapman, John D. Jorgenson, and Pamela S. Dear, 1997), and Philip Hobsbaum, "Adrienne Rich," in *American Writers, Retrospective Supplement II: A Collection of Literary Biographies* (ed. Jay Parini, 2003).

Reading Adrienne Rich: Reviews and ReVisions 1951–1981, edited by Jane Roberta Cooper (1984), is a collection of critical responses to Rich, while Jeannette Riley's *Understanding Adrienne Rich* (2016) is the best overview of Rich's entire career. A book-length treatment of Rich's feminist work is Liz Yorke's *Adrienne Rich: Passion, Politics and the Body* (1997). Alice Templeton's *The Dream and the Dialogue: Adrienne Rich's Feminist Poetics* (1994) focuses primarily on the poetry. Two broader studies that consider Rich's contribution to feminism are noteworthy: Krista Ratcliff's *Anglo-American Feminist Challenges to the Rhetorical Tradition: Virginia Woolf, Mary Daly, Adrienne Rich* (1996) and Sabine Sielke's *Fashioning the Female Subject: The Intertextual Networking of Dickinson, Moore, and Rich* (1997). *From Motherhood to Mothering: The Legacy of Adrienne Rich's "Of Woman Born,"* edited by Andrea O'Reilly (2004), collects feminist responses to and expansions on that work, while Cheri Colby Langdell's *Adrienne Rich: The Moment of Change* (2004) and Amy Sickels's *Adrienne Rich* (2005) offer two comprehensive looks at Rich's whole career. Essays that attend to Rich's feminist work include D. Lynn O'Brien Hallstein, "The Intriguing History and Silences of *Of Woman Born*: Rereading Adrienne Rich Rhetorically to Better Understand the Contemporary Context," *Feminist Formations* 22.2 (2010); Judith Taylor, "Enduring Friendship: Women's Intimacies and the Erotics of Survival," *Frontiers* 34.1 (2013); and Candace Johnson, "Negotiating Maternal Identity: Adrienne Rich's Legacy for Inquiry into the Political Philosophical Dimensions of Pregnancy and Childbirth," *PhiloSOPHIA* 4 (2014). The obituaries for Rich in the *Chicago Tribune* and *New York Times* (both May 29, 2012) and the longer memorial essay by Alice Friman in *Southern Review* 49 (2013) are good places to start to get a sense of Rich's importance and influence. Langdell's book (cited above) provides a good bibliography of Rich's own writings and of critical responses to her work.

Andrew Ross

The first book by Ross, a prolific writer, is a psychoanalytic account of modern poetry, *The Failure of Modernism: Symptoms of American Poetry* (1986). Thereafter, he left literary studies behind, writing on the New York Intellectuals and their fraught relation to popular culture in *No Respect: Intellectuals and Popular Culture* (1989), which gained him wide attention. He also was an active member for more than a decade (1986–2000) of the editorial collective of the journal *Social Text*, from which he drew several edited collections, the first of which was *Universal Abandon? The Politics of Postmodernism* (1988). His next group of books deals with science and technology; they include *Strange Weather: Culture, Science, and Technology in the Age of Limits* (1991), *The Chicago Gangster Theory of Life: Nature's Debt to Society* (1994), and the edited collections *Technoculture* (co-edited with Constance Penley, 1991) and *Science Wars* (1996). On other cultural trends, he collected his essays in *Real Love: In Pursuit of Cultural Justice* (1998) and, with Tricia Rose, co-edited *Microphone Fiends: Youth Music and Youth Culture* (1994). His writing shifted in the late 1990s, as he began conducting ethnographic research on how people work and live, in *The Celebration Chronicles: Life, Liberty, and the Pursuit of Property Value in Disney's New Town* (1999), an account of a year spent living in Celebration, Florida, the town built by the Disney Company; *No-Collar: The Humane Workplace and Its Hidden Costs* (2003), an account of his time observing high-tech companies in New York; *Low Pay, High Profile: The Global Push for Fair Labor* (2004), which includes "The Mental Labor Problem" (a shorter version was first published in *Social Text* 18.2 [2000]); *Fast Boat to China: Corporate Flight and the Consequences of Free Trade—Lessons from Shanghai* (2006), his report on the new economy in China; *Nice Work If You Can Get It: Life and Labor in Precarious Times* (2009), on the global exploitation of workers; *Bird on Fire: Lessons from the World's Least Sustainable City* (2011), reporting on Phoenix; and *Creditocracy: And the Case for Debt Refusal* (2014). He also edited or co-edited *No Sweat: Fashion, Free Trade, and the Rights of Garment Workers* (1997), *Anti-Americanism* (with Kristin Ross, 2005), *The University against Itself: The NYU Strike and the Future of the Academic Workplace* (with Monika Krause et al., 2008), and *The Gulf: High Culture/Hard Labor* (2015). For an account of his shift in method, see "Scholarly Reporter: An Interview with Andrew Ross," conducted by Jeffrey J. Williams, *Minnesota Review*, nos. 73–74 (2009–10).

Ross has been subject to a considerable amount of public attention, including profiles in the *New York Times Magazine*, *GQ*, and *New York* magazine. He was criticized by the philosopher Richard Rorty in "Intellectuals in Politics," *Dissent* (fall 1991); a response by Ross and reply by Rorty appear in *Dissent* (spring 1992). Mark McGurl, "Green Ideas Sleep Furiously: Andrew Ross on Ecocriticism," *Lingua Franca*, November–December 1994, recounts his work on ecology. On Ross's role in the "Science Wars" of the 1990s, see the various charges and defenses in *The Sokal Hoax: The Sham That Shook the Academy*, edited by the editors of *Lingua Franca* (2000). Susan Fraiman, "Andrew Ross, Cultural Studies, and Feminism," *Minnesota Review*, nos. 52–54 (2001), analyzes his relative lack of attention to gender. Melissa Gregg, "Justice and Accountability: Andrew Ross, Intellectual Labour and the New Academic Activism," in her *Cultural Studies' Affective Voices* (2006), surveys his later writing and its connection to activism; on mental labor, see also Gregg's *Work's Intimacy* (2011). Jeffrey J. Williams, "How to Be an Intellectual: The Cases of Richard Rorty and Andrew Ross," *Dissent* (winter 2011), reassesses an attack on Ross's cultural politics and surveys his career. Probably because of the range of his topics, there has been to date no general account of his work, nor a bibliography.

Gayle Rubin

Rubin is a writer of essays, not books. Her landmark essay "The Traffic in Women: Notes on the 'Political Economy' of Sex" first appeared in *Toward an Anthropology of Women* (ed. Rayna Reiter, 1975); it has been frequently anthologized. Rubin's early writings on sexuality include "Sexual Politics, the New Right, and the Sexual Fringe," in *The Age Taboo: Gay Male Sexuality, Power, and Consent* (ed. Daniel Tseng, 1981), and "The Leather Menace," *Body Politic* 82 (1981). "Thinking Sex: Notes for a Radical Theory of the Politics of Sexuality" was published in *Pleasure and Danger: Exploring Female Sexuality* (ed. Carole Vance, 1984), and has subsequently been reprinted in several anthologies. "Of Catamites and Kings: Reflections on Butch, Gender, and Boundaries" was published in *The Persistent Desire: A Femme-Butch Reader* (ed. Joan Nestle, 1992). "Misguided, Dangerous, and Wrong: An Analysis of Anti-pornography Politics" appeared initially in *Bad Girls and Dirty Pictures: The Challenge to Reclaim Feminism* (ed. Alison Assiter and Avedon Carol, 1993) and was reprinted in *Gender, Race, and Class in Media: A Text-Reader* (ed. Gail Dines and Jean M. Humez, 1995). Rubin's later works have focused on the subject of her 1994 dissertation on leather culture among gay men. They include "The Catacombs: A Temple of the Butthole," in *Leatherfolk: Radical Sex, People, Politics, and Practice* (ed. Mark Thompson, 1991; 2d ed., 2001); "Elegy for the Valley of the Kings: AIDS and the Leather Community in San Francisco," in *In Changing Times: Gay Men and Lesbians Encounter HIV/AIDS* (ed. Martin P. Levine, Peter M. Nardi, and John H. Gagnon, 1997); "The Miracle Mile: South of Market and Gay Male Leather in San Francisco, 1962–1996," in *Reclaiming San Francisco: History, Politics, Culture* (ed. James Brook, Chris Carlsson, and Nancy J. Peters, 1998); "Sites, Settlements, and Urban Sex: Archaeology and the Study of Gay Leathermen in San Francisco, 1955–1995," in *Archaeologies of Sexuality* (ed. Robert A. Schmidt and Barbara L. Voss, 2000); and "Studying Sexual Subcultures: The Ethnography of Gay Communities in Urban North America," in *Out in Theory: The Emergence of Lesbian and Gay Anthropology* (ed. Ellen Lewin and William L. Leap, 2002). "A Little Humility," in *Gay Shame* (ed. David M. Halperin and Valerie Traub, 2009), represents a departure from her engagement with gay male culture, as she examines the invention of the silicone dildo, used by lesbian women, by a disabled straight man. Here Rubin discusses female pleasure and the need for humility on the part of queer thinkers and activists with respect to who may contribute to political and sexual progress. "'Anthropologists Are Talking' about Feminist Anthropology," *Ethnos* 72 (2007), an interview of important feminist anthropologists including Rubin, Rayna Rapp, and Louise Lamphere, sketches the genesis of "Traffic in Women" in the early days of feminist activism at the University of Michigan and offers biographical information, as does the collection *Gay & Lesbian Biography* (ed. Michael J. Tyrkus, 1997). Rubin's *Deviations: A Gayle Rubin Reader* (2011) is a collection of previously published canonical and lesser-known works. Its introduction, "Sex, Gender, Politics," which tackles more than forty years of material, makes for a particularly engrossing autobiographical and intellectual read.

Mariane Valverde's "Beyond Gender Dangers and Private Pleasures: Theory and Ethics in the Sex Debates," *Feminist Studies* 15 (1989), contrasts "Thinking Sex" with the work of Catharine MacKinnon, offering critiques of both anti- and pro-sex perspectives. Elizabeth Weed and Naomi Schor's anthology *Feminism Meets Queer Theory* (1997) collects a number of valuable essays published in the journal *differences* in 1994 that expand on the aims of "Thinking Sex" and articulate its relation to queer theory. These pieces include an interview of Rubin by Judith Butler, titled "Sexual Traffic," as well as Butler's essay "Against Proper Objects," Biddy Martin's "Extraordinary Homosexuals and the Fear of Being Ordinary," and Elizabeth Weed's "The More Things Change." Two recent reevaluations of Rubin's first essay—Laura Kipnis, "Response to 'The Traffic in Women'" and Elizabeth A. Povinelli, "Feminism as a Way of Life"—appeared in *Women's Studies Quarterly* 34 (2006). Brooke Meredith Beloso's "Sex, Work, and the Feminist Erasure of Class," *Signs* 38 (2012), rethinks both "Thinking Sex" and "The Traffic in Women" with respect to women, gender, class, capitalism, labor, and sex work.

Edward W. Said

Said's first book, *Joseph Conrad and the Fiction of Autobiography* (1966), an outgrowth of his doctoral dissertation, is a literary study of Conrad's life and fiction. The groundbreaking *Beginnings: Intention and Method* (1975) established Said as a central figure in the leftist poststructuralist literary theory then emerging. *Orientalism* (1978), his most famous book, extended Said's influence to other disciplines and established him as a major contemporary public intellectual. See also his retrospective comments, "Orientalism Reconsidered," in *Literature, Politics and Theory* (ed. Francis Barker et al., 1986), and the afterword to the 1995 edition of *Orientalism*. Said next published three books more directly addressing politics and the Middle East: *Reaction and Counterrevolution in the Contemporary Arab World* (1978), a brief exposé; *The Question of Palestine* (1979), a history of the status of Palestine; and *Covering Islam: How the Media and the Experts Determine How We See the Rest of the World* (1981), an analysis of popular media representations. The latter two, directed at nonacademic audiences, form a trilogy with *Orientalism*. Returning to the field of contemporary theory, *The World, the Text, and the Critic* (1983) gathers many important essays and provides perhaps the best introduction to Said's views on criticism. *After the Last Sky: Palestinian Lives* (1986) offers his personal, poetic reflections on Palestine alongside photographs (by Jean Mohr). Said also co-edited (with Christopher Hitchens) and contributed three essays to the collection *Blaming the Victims: Spurious Scholarship and the Palestinian Question* (1988), which attacks stereotypes of Arabs (as terrorists, for instance).

Said performed as a concert pianist and wrote an occasional column on music for the *Nation*; *Musical Elaborations* (1991) gathers his writings in this area. *Culture and Imperialism* (1993) is a capstone of his investigation into literary and cultural representations of imperialism. *Representations of the Intellectual: The 1993 Reith Lectures* (1994), a succinct and accessible survey of the role of the intellectual, culminates in Said's call for an independent intellectual who "speaks truth to power." Several later collections gather his diverse commentary on politics in the Middle East: *The Politics of Dispossession: The Struggle for Palestinian Self-Determination, 1969–1994* (1994), *The Pen and the Sword: Conversations with David Barsamian* (1994), *Peace and Its Discontents: Essays on Palestine in the Middle East Peace Process* (1998), and *End of the Peace: Oslo and After* (2000). *The Edward Said Reader*, edited by Moustafa Bayoumi and Andrew Rubin (2000), presents a range of selections covering his career. *Reflections on Exile and Other Essays* (2001), a companion to *The World, the Text, and the Critic*, gathers his later critical essays, and *Humanism and Democratic Criticism* (2004) brings together his final considerations of humanism. *Power, Politics, and Culture: Interviews with Edward W. Said*, edited by Gauri Viswanathan (2001), collects twenty-nine informative interviews about his writing, politics, and life. *Out of Place: A Memoir* (1999) is an illuminating biographical account, covering Said's early life in Palestine and Cairo through his college years at Princeton University.

From early in his career, Said attracted a large body of criticism. A special issue of the theory journal *Diacritics* (6.3 [1976]) is devoted to *Beginnings*; it also contains an illuminating interview with Said. In *Intellectuals in Power: A Genealogy of Critical Humanism* (1986), Paul A. Bové analyzes Said's relation to the humanistic tradition. Jim Merod, in *The Political Responsibility of the Critic* (1987), sees Said rather than more academically oriented figures like Fredric Jameson as an exemplary politically engaged critic. *The Predicament of Culture: Twentieth-Century Ethnography, Literature, and Art* (1988), by the anthropologist James Clifford, contains a noted critique of *Orientalism*. In *White Mythologies: Writing History and the West* (1990), Robert Young assigns Said a central role in establishing postcolonial studies. John McGowan, in *Postmodernism and Its Critics* (1991), explores the problem of freedom in Said's concept of exile. *Edward Said: A Critical Reader*, edited by Michael Sprinker (1992), contains an excellent selection of essays examining the range of Said's work, as well as an informative interview with Said.

The Marxist critic Aijaz Ahmad, in his *In Theory: Classes, Nations, Literatures* (1992), criticizes Said's relation to postcolonial studies, taking him to task for his focus on the humanistic Western tradition and for his liberal politics. That attack was followed by a special issue of *Public Culture* 12 (1993) debating Ahmad's and Said's merits. Bruce Robbins, in *Secular Vocations: Intellectuals, Professionalism, Culture* (1993), analyzes Said's ambivalent views toward professionalism. In "Jane Austen and Edward Said: Gender, Culture, and Imperialism," *Critical Inquiry* 21 (1995), Susan Fraiman criticizes Said's lack of attention to gender and to texts by women. Bill Ashcroft and Pal Ahlumwalia's *Edward Said: The Paradox of Identity* (1999) is a useful overview, as is Valerie Kennedy's *Edward Said: A Critical Introduction* (2000). *Edward Said and the Work of the Critic: Speaking Truth to Power*, edited by Paul A. Bové (2000), gathers a range of essays on Said. Timothy Brennan, "The Illusion of a Future: *Orientalism* as Traveling Theory," *Critical Inquiry* 26 (2000), provides a retrospective account of the influence of *Orientalism*, arguing that it critiques rather than follows Foucault. Abdirahman A. Hussein, *Edward Said: Criticism and Society* (2002), argues that *Beginnings* is more important than *Orientalism* in understanding Said's work.

Since his death, the stream of books on Said's work and influence has only grown. Among monographs, see Mustapha Marrouchi, *Edward Said at the Limits* (2004); Conor McCarthy, *The Cambridge Introduction to Edward Said* (2008); and a critical account from a former student, H. Aram Veeser, *Edward Said: The Charisma of Criticism* (2010). Testifying to its influence, several books have devoted themselves to attacking *Orientalism*; see Robert Irwin, *Dangerous Knowledge: Orientalism and Its Discontents* (2006). Many collections of essays assessing Said, in special issues of journals and in books, have appeared; see *Edward Said: Continuing the Conversation*, edited by Homi K. Bhabha and W. J. T. Mitchell (2005); *Counterpoints: Edward Said's Legacy*, edited by May Telmissany and Stephanie Tara Schwartz (2010); *Edward Said: A Legacy of Emancipation and Representation*, edited by Adel Iskandar and Hakem Rustom (2010); and *Edward Said's Translocations: Essays in Secular Criticism*, edited by Tobias Döring and Mark Stein (2012). For a comprehensive bibliography, see "A Bibliographical Guide to Edward Said," by Yasmine Ramadan, *Alif* 25 (2005).

Ferdinand de Saussure

There are two existing English translations of the *Course in General Linguistics*, first edited by Charles Bally and Albert Sechehaye in 1916. The one that has become canonical is by Wade Baskin (1959). Roy Harris's more recent version (1983) solves certain problems but creates as many new ones. A critical edition comparing six different sources was published in French by Rudolf Engler (1967). Saussure's anagram project, edited by Jean Starobinski, has been translated as *Words upon Words* (1979). The leading Saussure scholars Simon Bouquet, Rudolf Engler, Carol Sanders, Matthew Pires, and Peter Figueroa have edited and translated a newly discovered work by Saussure on language, the sign, and performance, *Writings in General Linguistics* (2006). John E. Joseph's *Saussure* (2012) is the first exhaustive biography of the linguist.

Several introductions to Saussure's work are excellent: Jonathan Culler's *Ferdinand de Saussure* (rev. ed., 1986) and David Holdcroft's *Saussure: Signs, System, and Arbitrariness* (1991) are accessible and clear. For an excellent exposition of the theories and limits of Saussure and the Russian formalists, see Fredric Jameson, *The Prison-House of Language: A Critical Account of Structuralism and Russian Formalism* (1972). Roy Harris's *Reading Saussure: A Critical Commentary of the "Cours de linguistique generale"* (1987) and Françoise Gadet's *Saussure and Contemporary Culture* (1987; trans. 1989) offer more information about Saussure in the context of linguistics. The even more detailed *Re-Reading Saussure: The Dynamics of Signs in Social Life* (1997) by Paul J. Thibault updates the discussion of many of the key concepts. For a confusing but detailed history of linguistics leading up to Saussure, see E. F. K. Koerner's *Ferdinand de Saussure: Origin and Development of His Linguistic Thought in Western Studies of Language* (1973). Beata Stawarska's *Saussure's Philosophy of Language as Phenomenology: Undoing the Doctrine of the "Course in General Linguistics"* (2015) offers a phenomenological interpretation of Saussure's conception of language. For a more theoretical discussion of Saussure's place in the history of linguistics, see Hans Aarsleff's insightful but not chronological *From Locke to Saussure: Essays on the*

Study of Language and Intellectual History (1982). A bibliography, *Bibliographia Saussureana*, was compiled by E. F. K. Koerner (1972); more recent items can be found in the bibliographies of the Harris and Thibault volumes cited above. *Writings in General Linguistics* includes a comprehensive bibliography on Saussure from 1970 to 2004. Carol Sanders has also put together a useful collection of scholarly writings and an equally impressive bibliography on Saussure in *The Cambridge Companion to Saussure* (2004). Joseph's biography (see above) also has an updated bibliography.

Friedrich von Schiller

German editions of Schiller's writings include the *Säkular-Ausgabe*, edited by Eduard von der Hellen (16 vols., 1904–05), and the *Horenausgabe*, edited by C. Schüddekopf and C. Hofer (22 vols., 1910–26), which includes many of his letters. German scholars have noted that many English translations of Schiller's texts are unreliable. Coleridge's translation of *Wallenstein* (1800) is important. The translation and edition of *On the Aesthetic Education of Man* by E. M. Wilkinson and L. A. Willoughby (1967) is outstanding. A single-volume edition is *Friedrich Schiller: An Anthology for Our Times* (trans. Jane Bannard Greene et al., 1959). For a selection of Schiller's writings on criticism and aesthetics, see *Essays*, edited by Walter Hinderer and Daniel O. Dahlstrom (1993). *Schiller's Literary Prose Works: New Translations and Critical Essays*, edited by Jeffrey L. High (2008), includes seven tales and novel fragments.

A good biographical point of departure is William Witte, *Schiller* (1949). See also John Simon, *Friedrich Schiller* (1981), and T. J. Reed, *Schiller* (1991). For critical analysis, consult S. S. Kerry, *Schiller's Writings on Aesthetics* (1961); Charles E. Passage, *Friedrich Schiller* (1975); Juliet Sychrava, *Schiller to Derrida: Idealism in Aesthetics* (1989); and Lesley Sharpe, *Friedrich Schiller: Drama, Thought, and Politics* (1991), a well-contextualized treatment of Schiller's work as a dramatist, poet, and literary theorist. Patrick T. Murray, *The Development of German Aesthetic Theory from Kant to Schiller: A Philosophical Commentary on Schiller's "Aesthetic Education of Man," 1795* (1994), places Schiller's aesthetics in their literary and national contexts. See also Linda Marie Brooks, *The Menace of the Sublime to the Individual Self: Kant, Schiller, Coleridge, and the Disintegration of Romantic Identity* (1996), and R. D. Miller, *Schiller and the Ideal of Freedom* (1970). For a study of Schiller's writings on aesthetics and their impact on Coleridge, see Michael John Kooy, *Coleridge, Schiller, and Aesthetic Education* (2002). *Who Is This Schiller Now? Essays on His Reception and Significance*, edited by Jeffrey L. High, Nicholas Martin, and Norbert Oellers (2011), is a wide-ranging collection of essays, some in German but most in English; two (in English) examine Schiller's aesthetic views. D. C. Schindler, *The Perfection of Freedom: Schiller, Schelling, and Hegel between the Ancients and the Moderns* (2012), interprets freedom in terms of aesthetic form (Schiller), organic form (Schelling), and social form (Hegel).

For a concise study of the critical writings, see René Wellek, "Kant and Schiller," in *A History of Modern Criticism, 1750–1950*, vol. 1, *The Later Eighteenth Century* (1955). A more detailed, challenging assessment can be found in Anthony Savile, *Aesthetic Reconstructions: The Seminal Writings of Lessing, Kant, and Schiller* (1987). T. J. Reed, *The Classical Centre: Goethe and Weimar, 1775–1832* (1980), is stimulating on the relationship between Goethe and Schiller. For bibliography, see Wolfgang Vulpius, *Schiller-Bibliographie, 1893–1958* (1959) and *Schiller-Bibliographie, 1959–63* (1967); and R. Pick, "Schiller in England, 1787–1960: A Bibliography," *Publications of the English Goethe Society* 30 (1961). *The Cambridge Companion to German Idealism*, edited by Karl Ameriks (2000), provides a more recent bibliography of primary and secondary sources in both English and German, as well as essays on Kant, Schiller, Hegel, Marx, and other writers and philosophers in this tradition of theory and criticism.

Friedrich Schleiermacher

Schleiermacher's collected works, *Sämtliche Werke* (1835–64), mainly lecture notes, were published after his death in thirty-one volumes, including theological writings, sermons, and philosophical and miscellaneous texts, plus four volumes of letters (1858–63). Starting in the early 1980s his collected writings and correspondence began to appear in a multivolume German edition, *Kritische Gesamtausgabe*, with forty-eight volumes reaching print in the first three and a half decades. His manuscripts on interpretation theory were published posthumously and first translated into English by James Duke and Jack Forstman as *Hermeneutics: The Handwritten Manuscripts* (1977), based on the German edition by Heinz Kimmerle (1959; 2d ed., 1974), and then more fully in a new translation, *Hermeneutics and Criticism and Other Writings*, edited and translated by Andrew Bowie (1998). Several dozen texts by Schleiermacher covering an array of topics aside from hermeneutics are available in English translation.

Biographical information is available in *The Life of Schleiermacher as Unfolded in His Autobiography and Letters* (2 vols., 1860), translated by Frederica Rowan; Wilhelm Dilthey's monumental but unfinished *Das Leben Schleiermachers* (1870); Friedrich Wilhelm Kantzenbach's *Friedrich Daniel Ernst Schleiermacher in Selbstzeugnissen und Bilddokumenten* (1967); and Martin Redeker's spiritually sympathetic intellectual biography, *Schleiermacher: Life and Thought* (1968; trans. 1973).

Informative texts about Schleiermacher's work include Richard B. Brandt's *Philosophy of Schleiermacher: The Development of His Theory of*

Scientific and Religious Knowledge (1941); Richard E. Palmer's valuable introduction, *Hermeneutics: Interpretation Theory in Schleiermacher, Dilthey, Heidegger, and Gadamer* (1969), Manfred Frank's landmark reassessment of Schleiermacher's hermeneutics in *Das individuelle Allgemeine: Textstrukturierung und -interpretation nach Schleiermacher* (1977), Tilottama Rajan's contemporary contextualizing in *The Supplement of Reading: Figures of Understanding in Romantic Theory and Practice* (1990), Julie Ellison's innovative feminist exegesis and critique of Schleiermacher's hermeneutics in *Delicate Subjects: Romanticism, Gender, and the Ethics of Understanding* (1990), the cogent introduction in Jean Grondin's *Introduction to Philosophical Hermeneutics* (1994), Andrew Bowie's chapter factoring in the groundbreaking recent work of Manfred Frank in *From Romanticism to Critical Theory: The Philosophy of German Literary Theory* (1997), and Richard Crouter's engaging and historically nuanced essays in *Friedrich Schleiermacher: Between Enlightenment and Romanticism* (2005). An updated bibliography as well as a collection of scholarly studies on Schleiermacher's contributions to philosophy, Plato scholarship, and theology appears in *The Cambridge Companion to Friedrich Schleiermacher*, edited by Jacqueline Mariña (2005). Significant critical essays on the wide range of contemporary Schleiermacher scholarship, including his hermeneutical theory, can be found in *The State of Schleiermacher Scholarship Today: Selected Essays*, edited by Edwina G. Lawler, Jeffrey Kinlaw, and Ruth Richardson (2006). Terrence Tice's *Schleiermacher Bibliography* (1966) contains almost 2,000 items with annotations, and another 1,250 were added to his *Schleiermacher Bibliography (1784–1984): Updating and Commentary* (1985).

Eve Kosofsky Sedgwick

Sedgwick's books of criticism and theory are *The Coherence of Gothic Conventions* (1980), *Between Men: English Literature and Male Homosocial Desire* (1985), *Epistemology of the Closet* (1990), *Tendencies* (1993), *A Dialogue on Love* (1999), and *Touching Feeling: Affect, Pedagogy, Performativity* (2003). She also published a volume of poetry, *Fat Art, Thin Art* (1994). She edited *Performativity and Performances* (1994), with Andrew Parker; *Shame and Its Sisters: A Silvan Tomkins Reader* (1995); *Gary in Your Pocket: Stories and Notebooks by Gary Fisher* (1996); and *Novel Gazing: Queer Readings in Fiction* (1997), the first collection of queer criticism of the novel. In *The Weather in Proust* (2011), Jonathan Goldberg collected a series of essays written by Sedgwick in the last decade of her life as she worked toward a book on Proust.

One of the earliest critiques of *Between Men* was David Van Leer's "Beast of the Closet: Homosociality and the Pathology of Manhood," *Critical Inquiry* 15 (1989). A number of interviews with Sedgwick appeared in print, including Sarah Chinn, Mario DiGangi, and Patrick Horrigan, "A Talk with Eve Kosofsky Sedgwick," *PreText: A Journal of Rhetoric and Theory* 13 (1992), and Jeffrey Williams, "Sedgwick Unplugged (An Interview with Eve Kosofsky Sedgwick)," *Minnesota Review* 40, n.s. (1993). After her death, several journals published special issues in her honor, including *PMLA* 125.2 (2010); *Criticism: A Quarterly for Literature and the Arts* 52.2 (2010), an issue edited by Erin Murphy and Keith Vincent; and *GLQ: A Journal of Lesbian and Gay Studies* 17.4 (2011), edited by Ann Cvetkovich and Annamarie Jagose. Robyn Wiegman's "Eve's Triangles, or Queer Studies beside Itself," *differences* 26.1 (2015), provides a significant retrospective that explores the power of incoherence and contradiction in Sedgwick's model for queer reading. *Regarding Sedgwick: Essays on Queer Culture and Critical Theory*, edited by Stephen M. Barber and David L. Clark (2002), collects essays about Sedgwick by prominent literary theorists; it includes a bibliography of her works. See also the introductory guide by Jason Edwards, *Eve Kosofsky Sedgwick* (2009), which offers an extensive section of further reading on Sedgwick.

Percy Bysshe Shelley

For Shelley's prose, primary sources include *The Prose Works*, edited by E. B. Murray (1 vol. to date, 1993–), and *The Letters*, edited by Frederick L. Jones (2 vols., 1964). For a single-volume collection that includes critical essays, see *Shelley's Poetry and Prose: Authoritative Texts, Criticism*, edited by Donald H. Reiman and Sharon B. Powers (1977; 2d ed., 2002). Other resources include *Shelley and His Circle, 1773–1822*, edited by Kenneth Neill Cameron (10 vols., 1961–2002), which presents the manuscripts by Shelley, his family, friends, and literary acquaintances held in the New York Public Library; it contains important critical and contextual commentary. The standard biographical work has long been Newman Ivey White, *Shelley* (2 vols., 1940), but a recent contender to replace it is James Bieri, *Percy Bysshe Shelley: A Biography* (2008). Kenneth Neill Cameron, in *The Young Shelley* (1950) and *Shelley: The Golden Years* (1974), is informative on the poet's radical political views. Richard Holmes, *Shelley: The Pursuit* (1974), gives a good sense of the person behind the poetry and prose. See also *The Oxford Handbook of Percy Bysshe Shelley*, edited by Michael O'Neill and Anthony Howe (2013), which provides detailed coverage of the life, work, reputation, and influence. On Shelley's relationship to another great revolutionary poet, see Ian Gilmour, *The Making of the Poets: Byron and Shelley in Their Time* (2002).

On Shelley's literary theory, consult Fanny Delisle, *A Study of Shelley's "A Defence of Poetry": A Textual and Critical Evaluation* (2 vols., 1974). Among the many studies of Shelley's poetic theory and practice are Harold Bloom, *Shelley's Myth-*

making (1959); Earl Wasserman, *Shelley: A Critical Reading* (1971); William Keach, *Shelley's Style* (1984), which deals well with Shelley's complex and contradictory attitudes toward language; and Jerrold E. Hogle, *Shelley's Process: Radical Transference and the Development of His Major Works* (1988). On the relationships between literature and politics in Shelley's life and works, see Timothy Clark, *Embodying Revolution: The Figure of the Poet in Shelley* (1989); Michael O'Neill, *The Human Mind's Imaginings: Conflict and Achievement in Shelley's Poetry* (1989); David Duff, *Romance and Revolution: Shelley and the Politics of a Genre* (1994); and Timothy Morton, *Shelley and the Revolution in Taste: The Body and the Natural World* (1994). Stuart Peterfreund, *Shelley among Others: The Play of the Intertext and the Idea of Language* (2002), explicates Shelley's philosophy of language; and Cian Duffy, *Shelley and the Revolutionary Sublime* (2005), examines Shelley's engagement with British and French discourse on the sublime in an era of radical political change. Among recent studies is Ross Wilson, *Shelley and the Apprehension of Life* (2013), which explores Shelley's fundamental beliefs about life and the significance of poetry.

Helpful on trends in Shelley scholarship are *Shelley: The Critical Heritage*, edited by James E. Barcus (1975); *Deconstruction and Criticism*, by Harold Bloom et al. (1979), which offers a series of exemplary deconstructive readings of "The Triumph of Life"; *Essays on Shelley*, edited by Miriam Allott (1982); *The New Shelley: Later Twentieth-Century Views*, edited by G. Kim Blank (1991); and *Shelley: Poet and Legislator of the World*, edited by Betty T. Bennett and Stuart Curran (1996). For bibliography, look to Clement Dunbar, *Bibliography of Shelley Studies: 1823–1950* (1976) and *Shelley Studies, 1950–1984: An Annotated Bibliography* (1986). *The Cambridge Companion to Shelley*, edited by Timothy Morton (2006), provides a good bibliography on philosophy and politics, poems and poetics, and other important topics in Shelley's life and work.

Sir Philip Sidney

The complete works of Sir Philip Sidney are available in *Complete Works*, edited by Albert Feuillerat (4 vols., 1922–26). The standard edition of *An Apology for Poetry* with copious endnotes may be found in *The Miscellaneous Prose of Sir Philip Sidney*, edited by Katherine Duncan-Jones and Jan Van Dorsten (1973). There are several other editions of the text, including Gavin Alexander's newer edition in *Sidney's "The Defence of Poesy" and Selected Renaissance Literary Criticism* (2004), from which our text is taken. For a seventeenth-century biography, consult *Sir Fulke Greville's Life of Sir Philip Sidney* (1652), available in *The Prose of Fulke Greville*, edited by Mark Caldwell (1987). For a biography, see Katherine Duncan-Jones, *Sir Philip Sidney: Courtier Poet* (1991).

Forrest G. Robinson, *The Shape of Things Known: Sidney's Apology in Its Philosophical Tradition* (1972), is an important book-length study of Sidney's famous essay. For an introduction to Sidney, see Katherine Duncan-Jones's excellent contribution to the Oxford Authors series, *Sir Philip Sidney* (1989). *The Ashgate Research Companion to the Sidneys, 1500–1700*, edited by Margaret P. Hannay, Michael G. Brennan, and Mary Ellen Lamb (2015), assesses the current state of scholarship on Sidney family members and their impact as historical and literary figures between 1500 and 1700. Richard Hillyer's *Sir Philip Sidney, Cultural Icon* (2010) is a valuable study of Sidney's reputation from his day to the present. Critical interest in Sidney's "self-fashioning," his creation of images of himself in both his poetry and criticism, is evidenced by such books as Alan Hager's *Dazzling Images: The Masks of Sir Philip Sidney* (1991) and Edward Berry's *Making of Sir Philip Sidney* (1998). Peter C. Herman's *Squitter-wits and Muse-haters: Sidney, Spenser, Milton, and Renaissance Antipoetic Sentiments* (1996) examines the sixteenth- and seventeenth-century debates about poetry with which Sidney's *Defence* engages. For a full-length study of Sidney's aesthetic theory in *The Defence of Poesy*, see R. W. Maslen's introduction to his edition of *An Apology for Poetry (or The Defence of Poesy)* (2002) and Michael Mack, *Sidney's Poetics: Imitating Creation* (2005). Gavin Alexander's *Writing After Sidney: The Literary Response to Sir Philip Sidney, 1586–1640* (2006) examines Sidney's literary reputation in the years immediately following his death. Kent R. Lehnhof, in "Profeminism in Philip Sidney's *Apologie for Poetrie*," *Studies in English Literature* 48 (2008), argues that Sidney's essay is less a defense of the theater against Stephen Gosson's attack than a critique of his misogyny. In "Sir Philip Sidney's Defense of Prophesying," *Studies in English Literature* 50 (2010), Roger E. Moore argues that Sidney's references to the relationship between poetry and prophecy in the *Defence* point to Sidney's engagement with controversies about inspiration, suggesting that he sees prophecy as a form of moral instruction. William Junker's "'Wonderfully Ravished': Platonic Erotics and the Heroic Genre in Sir Philip Sidney's *Defence of Poesy*," *Ben Jonson Journal* 18 (2011), explores the relationship between the erotic and the ethical in Sidney's *Defence*. Corey McEleney and Jacqueline Wernimont, in "Re-Reading for Forms in Sir Philip Sidney's *Defence of Poesy*," in *New Formalisms and Literary Theory* (ed. Verena Theile and Linda Tredennick, 2013), focus less on what Sidney says in his *Defence* than on how he says it, arguing that the form of the *Defence* has been undertheorized. In "Sidney's Greek Poetics," *Studies in Philology* 112 (2015), Micha Lazarus argues that Sidney's knowledge of Aristotle's *Poetics* was deeper than previously supposed. Catherine Bates, in *On Not Defending Poetry: Defence and Indefensibility in Sidney's* Defence of Poesy (2017), drawing on the new economic criticism, challenges received views of Sidney as an idealist. Against idealist models of poetry as profitable, she argues that Sidney champions poetry as pure expenditure, as gift. Robert E. Stillman, in *Philip Sidney and the Poetics of Renaissance Cosmopolitanism* (2008), argues for placing Sidney's poetics and his defense of fiction in a broader cultural context that includes Continental debates about religion and politics. For a bibliography, consult *Sir Philip Sidney: An Annotated Bibliography of Texts and Criticism (1554–1984)*, edited by Donald V. Stump (1994). Stump updated the bibliography online in the *Sir Philip Sidney World Bibliography* (2001–09).

Susan Sontag

A Susan Sontag Reader (1982), though dated, remains a good point of departure. Arranged chronologically, it includes short stories and selections from two novels, *The Benefactor* (1963) and *Death Kit* (1967); essays from *Against Interpretation: And Other Essays* (1966), *Styles of Radical Will* (1969), and *Under the Sign of Saturn* (1980); and an excerpt from *On Photography* (1977). For a fuller selection of Sontag's critical writings, see *Susan Sontag: Essays of the 1960s and 70s*, edited by David Rieff (2013), which includes the full texts of *Against Interpretation*, *Styles of Radical Will*, *On Photography*, *Illness as Metaphor*, and six previously uncollected essays. The selections are annotated, and there is a detailed chronology. See also the companion volume, *Susan Sontag: Later Essays*, also edited by Rieff (2017). For interviews, see *Conversations with Susan Sontag*, edited by Leland Poague (1995). Also important is Jonathan Cott, *Susan Sontag: The Complete Rolling Stone Interview* (2013); in 1978, he had interviewed Sontag first in Paris and later in New York, but only a third of their conversation was published (for that version, see Poague's volume). This book gives the complete transcript, along with Cott's preface and recollections. Also significant is *Debriefing: Collected Stories*, edited by Benjamin Taylor (2017).

Biographies have been written by Jerome Boyd Maunsell, *Susan Sontag* (2014), in the Reaktion Critical Lives series, and by Daniel Schreiber, *Susan Sontag: A Biography* (2007; trans. 2014). An enlightening film, which includes interviews with Sontag, her sister, her son, and others, is the HBO documentary *Regarding Susan Sontag* (2014), produced and directed by Nancy Kates. Also valuable is Alice Kaplan, *Dreaming in French: The Paris Years of Jacqueline Bouvier Kennedy, Susan Sontag, and Angela Davis* (2012). Sontag's son, David Rieff, has published a perceptive, poignant recollection, *Swimming in a Sea of Death: A Son's Memoir* (2008), which focuses on her final months. He also edited and published excerpts from Sontag's journals: *Reborn: Journals and Notebooks, 1947–1963* (2008) and *As Consciousness Is Harnessed to Flesh: Journals and Notebooks, 1964–1980* (2012).

Carl Rollyson and Lisa Paddock, in *Susan Sontag: The Making of an Icon* (2000; rev. ed., 2016), examine Sontag's life and work in the context of celebrity culture and the mass media. See also Sohnya Sayres, *Susan Sontag: The Elegiac Modernist* (1990), and Liam Kennedy, *Susan Sontag: Mind as Passion* (1995). In *Reading Susan Sontag: A Critical Introduction to Her Work* (2001), Carl Rollyson devotes a chapter to each of Sontag's books and includes a glossary of key terms, references, and allusions. Philip Lopate's *Notes on Sontag* (2009) is shrewd and sympathetic, but also pointed and skeptical in places about Sontag as a personality and as a writer.

The Scandal of Susan Sontag, edited by Barbara Ching and Jennifer A. Wagner-Lawlor (2009), includes essays on Sontag's fiction and nonfiction, reputation, and status as a cultural icon. Carl Rollyson has written *Understanding Susan Sontag* (2016), an introduction to her essays, novels, plays, films, diaries, and uncollected work. Mena Mitrano, in *In the Archive of Longing: Susan Sontag's Critical Modernism* (2016), is insightful about Sontag's intellectual debts to the Frankfurt School of critical theory, to deconstruction, and in particular to Walter Benjamin.

For bibliography, see Sherry Lee Linkon, "Susan Sontag," in *Jewish American Women Writers: A Bio-Bibliographical and Critical Sourcebook* (ed. Ann R. Shapiro et al., 1994), and the 672-page *Susan Sontag: An Annotated Bibliography, 1948–1992*, compiled by Leland Poague and Kathy A. Parsons (2000).

Baruch Spinoza

The standard edition of Spinoza's work in Latin is *Spinoza Opera*, edited by Carl Gebhardt (4 vols., 1925; rpt. 1972 [supplementary vol. 5, 1987]). The best English edition is *Complete Works*, edited by Michael L. Morgan (2002). The most exhaustive biography is Steven Nadler's *Spinoza: A Life* (1999), but the newcomer to Spinoza should start with Richard H. Popkin's *Spinoza* (2004), a superb introduction to his life and work.

The secondary literature is vast; we emphasize here works relevant to *Tractatus Theologico-Politicus* (*Theological-Political Treatise*) and to the engagement with Spinoza's work by literary theorists. Gilles Deleuze's two books specifically on Spinoza are *Expressionism in Philosophy: Spinoza* (1968; trans. 1990) and *Spinoza: Practical Philosophy* (1981; trans. 1988). The best introductory volume on Spinoza for literary theorists is Moira Gatens and Genevieve Lloyd's *Collective Imaginings: Spinoza Past and Present* (1999). It can be supplemented by Rebecca Goldstein's idiosyncratic but engaging *Betraying Spinoza: The Renegade Jew Who Gave Us Modernity* (2006) and Michael Della Rocca's *Spinoza* (2008). *The New Spinoza*, edited by Warren Montag and Ted Stolze (1997), includes essays by Louis Althusser, Deleuze, and Antonio Negri among others. Other useful collections of essays are *Interpreting Spinoza: Critical Essays*, edited by Charlie Huenemann (2008); *Spinoza's "Theological-Political Treatise": A Critical Guide*, edited by Yitzhak Y. Melamed and Michael A. Rosenthal (2010); *Spinoza Now*, edited by Dimitris Vardoulakis (2011); *Spinoza beyond Philosophy*, edited by Beth Lord (2012); *Spinoza: Basic Concepts*, edited by Andre Santos Campos (2015); and *The Oxford Handbook of Spinoza*, edited by Michael Della Rocca (2017). Monographs devoted to the *Tractatus Theologico-Politicus* include J. Samuel Preus's *Spinoza and the Irrelevance of Biblical Authority* (2001), Steven Nadler's *A Book Forged in Hell: Spinoza's Scandalous Treatise and the Birth of the Secular Age* (2011), and Susan James's *Spinoza on Philosophy, Religion, and Politics: The Theological-Political Treatise* (2012). More general treatments of interest include Jonathan I. Israel's very influential *Radical Enlightenment: Philosophy and the Making of Modernity, 1650–1750* (2001), which places Spinoza at the center of radical thought in the period; Antonio Damasio's *Looking for Spinoza: Joy, Sorrow, and the Feeling Brain* (2003), which connects Spinoza to contemporary neuroscience; Antonio Negris *Subversive Spinoza: (Un)contemporary Variations* (2004), which links Spinoza's democratic politics to his metaphysics; and Charles Taylor's *A Secular Age* (2007), which discusses Spinoza in relation to secularization. The Melamed and Rosenthal volume has a good bibliography of secondary literature relevant to the *Tractatus*, while *Spinoza: Basic Concepts* has an excellent bibliography both of the primary texts and of secondary works.

Gayatri Chakravorty Spivak

Spivak's first book was *Myself Must I Remake: The Life and Poetry of W. B. Yeats* (1974). Her later theoretical works include *In Other Worlds: Essays in Cultural Politics* (1987), *Outside in the Teaching Machine* (1993), *A Critique of Postcolonial Reason: Toward a History of the Vanishing Present* (1999), *Death of a Discipline* (2003), *Other Asias* (2008), *Nationalism and the Imagination* (2010), *Harlem* (2012), *An Aesthetic Education in the Era of Globalization* (2012), and, with Judith Butler, *Who Sings the Nation-State? Language, Politics, Belonging* (2007). *The Post-Colonial Critic: Interviews, Strategies, Dialogues*, edited by Sarah Harasym (1990), and *Conversations with Gayatri Chakravorty Spivak*, edited by Swapan Chakravorty, Suzana Milevska, and Tani E. Barlow (2006), both provide useful collections of interviews with Spivak. *The Spivak Reader*, edited by Donna Landry and Gerald MacLean (1995), is a one-volume collection of some of Spivak's most influential essays. Spivak is the translator (with substantial introductions) of Jacques Derrida's *Of Grammatology* (1967, trans. 1976; 40th anniversary ed., trans. 2016), and of several novels and short story collections by the contemporary Bengali writer Mahasweta Devi. She is the co-editor, with Ranajit Guha, of *Selected Subaltern Studies* (1988). The various published interviews with Spivak are a good source of biographical information. *An Aesthetic Education in the Era of Globalization* also includes autobiographical reflections.

The best introduction to Spivak's work is Stephen Morton's *Gayatri Spivak: Ethics, Subalternity and the Critique of Postcolonial Reason* (2007), while Mark Sanders's *Gayatri Spivak: Live Theory* (2006) and Sangeeta Ray's *Gayatri Chakravorty Spivak: In Other Words* (2009) provide more intricately theoretical engagements with her work. Three reviews of *A Critique of Postcolonial Reason* are worth consulting: Terry Eagleton's "In the Gaudy Supermarket," *London Review of Books*, May 13, 1999; Mieke Bal's "Three Ways of Misreading," *Diacritics* 30 (2000); and Isabelle V. Barker's (untitled) in *Signs* 27 (2001). A forum on Spivak's work in *PMLA* 123 (2008) provides an excellent overview of her widespread influence. For responses specific to *A Critique of Postcolonial Reason*, see *Can the Subaltern Speak? Reflections on the History of an Idea*, edited by Rosalind C. Morris (2010), and *Postcolonial Reason and Its Critique: Deliberations on Gayatri Chakravorty Spivak's Thoughts*, edited by Purushottama Bilimoria and Dina Al-Kassim (2014). Both volumes include responses by Spivak, and Morris's invaluably prints the two separate versions of her essay "Can the Subaltern Speak?." Ola Abdalkafor's *Gayatri Spivak: Deconstruction and the Ethics of Postcolonial Literary Interpretation* (2015) offers a more general reflection on the ways that Spivak deploys poststructuralist theory in service of her critique of the West. Morris's volume has a superb bibliography of Spivak's own work and a useful bibliography of secondary sources.

Germaine Necker de Staël

In addition to the literary and cultural works mentioned in the headnote, Mme de Staël's writings include many stories and plays, a tribute to Rousseau (*Letters on Rousseau*, 1788), *Reflections on the Trial of the Queen* (1793), *Reflections on Peace* (1794), *The Influence of the Passions* (1796), *Reflections on Suicide* (1813), and "The Spirit of Translation" (1816). Posthumously published were *Considerations on the Principal Events of the French Revolution* (1818), *Ten Years of Exile* (1820), the *Complete Works* (1820), and many volumes of correspondence, some of which is still being discovered. Mme de Staël's work is not all easy to obtain in English translation. A wide range of selections can be found in *Madame de Staël on Politics, Literature, and National Character*, edited and translated by Monroe Berger (1964), and in *An Extraordinary Woman*, edited and translated by Vivian Folkenflik (1987). The biography by J. Christopher Herold, *Mistress to an Age* (1958; rpt. 2002), is, while somewhat dated, informative and well written. Maria Fairweather's *Madame de Staël* (2005) and Anjelica Goodden's

Madame de Staël: The Dangerous Exile (2008) are equally well-researched and more recent biographies.

In France there is a very active de Staël industry, which publishes a journal, *Cahiers staëliens* (*Staël Notebooks*), and holds many conferences. The most important figure in this enterprise is Simone Ballayé, whose work has not been much translated into English, but who has contributed an essay to the excellent anthology *Germaine de Staël: Crossing the Borders*, edited by Madelyn Gutwirth, Avriel Goldberger, and Karyna Szmurlo (1991). Madelyn Gutwirth's own *Madame de Staël, Novelist: The Emergence of the Artist as Woman* (1978) is also good, especially in its account of the shift in de Staël studies opened up by feminist criticism. Two fine general studies of Mme de Staël's life and works are Charlotte Hogsett, *The Literary Existence of Germaine de Staël* (1987), and Gretchen Rous Besser, *Germaine de Staël Revisited* (1994). For an analysis of the place of *On Germany* in the rise of Romanticism, see John Claiborne Isbell, *The Birth of European Romanticism: Truth and Propaganda in Staël's "De l'Allemagne," 1810–1813* (1994). And for a study of the complexity of gender roles and models in Rousseau and de Staël, see Lori Jo Marso's excellent *(Un)Manly Citizens* (1999). There is an extensive annotated bibliography of criticism on de Staël in French by Pierre H. Dubé, *Bibliographie de la Critique sur Madame de Staël, 1789–1994* (1998). Goodden's *Madame de Staël* also contains a wide-ranging selected bibliography.

Leo Strauss

Leo Strauss published three books in German and twelve in English, and more than 100 essays and reviews. For his contributions to political thought, especially significant are *Natural Right and History* (1953) and *What Is Political Philosophy? and Other Studies* (1959), which in its first three essays outlines Strauss's conception of and approach to political philosophy, history, and classical philosophy. See also his *The Political Philosophy of Hobbes, Its Basis and Its Genesis* (1936) and *Thoughts on Machiavelli* (1958; rpt. 1978). Strauss wrote extensively on writers of the ancient world, too. *The City and Man* (1964) includes essays on Aristotle's *Politics*, Plato's *Republic*, and Thucydides' *History of the Peloponnesian War*. Also noteworthy is *Studies in Platonic Political Philosophy* (1983), with essays on Plato, Thucydides, and Xenophon, supplemented by essays on Maimonides, Machiavelli, and Nietzsche.

Persecution and the Art of Writing (1952; rpt. 1988) features the title essay and other studies. See also *Leo Strauss: The Early Writings (1921–1932)*, translated and edited by Michael Zank (2002), and *Reorientation: Leo Strauss in the 1930s*, edited by Martin D. Yaffe and Richard S. Ruderman (2014), which contains scholarly commentaries on Strauss and seven texts by him, including "Exoteric Teaching" (1939) and "Lecture Notes for 'Persecution and the Art of Writing'" (1939). *On Tyranny*, first published in 1948, revised and expanded in 1963, was further expanded in 1991, in a version (edited by Victor Gourevitch and Michael S. Roth) that includes an exchange between Strauss and the Hegelian philosopher Alexandre Kojève as well as their letters to each other. *The Rebirth of Classical Political Rationalism: An Introduction to the Thought of Leo Strauss: Essays and Lectures*, edited by Thomas L. Pangle (1989), includes an introduction, five of Strauss's previously unpublished lectures, and five published writings that display his major interests.

Very important for the study of work by Strauss and other scholars influenced by him is his *History of Political Philosophy*, first published in 1963, revised in 1972, and now in a third edition (1987), edited by Strauss and Joseph Cropsey. The Leo Strauss Center at the University of Chicago is indispensable, with audio, video, and transcripts of materials by and about Strauss. It offers, for example, a near-complete audio recording and transcript of a course (1971–72) on Nietzsche's *Beyond Good and Evil* that Strauss taught at St. John's College (Annapolis, Maryland).

On Strauss as a teacher, see Allan Bloom, "Leo Strauss: September 20, 1899–October 18, 1973," in his *Giants and Dwarfs: Essays, 1960–1990* (1990), and Harry V. Jaffa, *Crisis of the Strauss Divided: Essays on Leo Strauss and Straussianism, East and West* (2012).

For Strauss's life, work, and legacy, see *The Cambridge Companion to Leo Strauss*, edited by Steven B. Smith (2009). Also helpful is Thomas L. Pangle, *Leo Strauss: An Introduction to His Thought and Intellectual Legacy* (2006), which is very good on Strauss's opposition to "liberal relativism," and Steven B. Smith, *Reading Leo Strauss: Politics, Philosophy, Judaism* (2006), which examines Jewish influences and topics and provides a cogent treatment of Strauss's view of liberal democracy. Daniel Tanguay, *Leo Strauss: An Intellectual Biography* (2003; trans. 2007), is illuminating on the first phase of Strauss's career, 1920–38 (before his immigration to the United States), medieval Jewish and Islamic philosophy, the art of esoteric writing, and Strauss's critique of modernity.

On exoteric/esoteric writing and interpretation, see Laurence Lampert, *The Enduring Importance of Leo Strauss* (2013), and Arthur M. Melzer, *Philosophy between the Lines: The Lost History of Esoteric Writing* (2014), a deeply researched exploration of Strauss and the tradition of philosophic esotericism.

Leo Strauss, the Straussians, and the Study of the American Regime, edited by Kenneth L. Deutsch and John A. Murley (1999), containing essays by both supporters and detractors, is illuminating on the implications of Strauss's thought for the interpretation of the U.S. founders and the Revolutionary period and for the study of contemporary politics. Anne Norton, in *Leo Strauss and the Politics of*

American Empire (2004), scrutinizes Strauss-influenced neoconservatives who argued for the invasion of Iraq. In *The Truth about Leo Strauss: Political Philosophy and American Democracy* (2006), Catherine H. and Michael P. Zuckert challenge misleading and inaccurate views of Strauss's ideas common in both the academy and the media, and survey his work in general. See also Paul Edward Gottfried, *Leo Strauss and the Conservative Movement in America: A Critical Reappraisal* (2012).

Also valuable are Laurence Lampert, *Leo Strauss and Nietzsche* (1996); David N. Myers, *Resisting History: Historicism and Its Discontents in German-Jewish Thought* (2003), which includes an excellent chapter on Strauss's critique of historicism; and Michael R. and Catherine H. Zuckert, *Leo Strauss and the Problem of Political Philosophy* (2014), which examines Strauss in the context of twentieth-century philosophy (e.g., Carl Schmitt, Edmund Husserl, Martin Heidegger). Liisi Keedus, *The Crisis of German Historicism: The Early Political Thought of Hannah Arendt and Leo Strauss* (2015), considers these thinkers' intellectual formation in Weimar Germany and their attitudes toward modernity, freedom, and the political fate of European Jewry. A related study is Jeffrey A. Bernstein, *Leo Strauss on the Borders of Judaism, Philosophy, and History* (2015): making use of published texts, correspondence, archival materials, and seminar transcripts, Bernstein examines the impact of Jewish thought on Strauss's studies in political philosophy and religion. Shadia B. Drury, *The Political Ideas of Leo Strauss* (1988; rev. ed., 2005), is a stimulating, though highly critical, study that includes a good bibliography. Also recommended is the bibliography in Smith's *Cambridge Companion* (see above).

Thomas Aquinas

Not all of Aquinas's works exist in critical editions, but the many volumes of the still-unfinished *Opera Omnia* (1882, *Complete Works*), edited by the Leonine Commission (commissioned by Pope Leo XIII), provide the best available Latin text. The Marietta editions, in several volumes that appeared throughout the twentieth century, reproduce the Leonine Latin text in a more convenient format with useful research aids. Nor have all Aquinas's works been translated into English. The *Summa Theologica* (also known as the *Summa Theologiae*) is available in a twenty-two-volume English edition by the Fathers of the English Dominican Province (1920–31). More recently, the Aquinas Institute has issued an eight-volume edition of the *Summa Theologiae* with Latin and English in parallel columns (2012). The *Summa Contra Gentiles* was translated by the English Dominican Fathers (1923–29). A selection of translations by various hands of Aquinas's biblical commentaries can be found in the Aquinas Scripture Series (1966–). *Thomas Aquinas: Selected Philosophical Writings*, edited by Timothy McDermott (1993; rpt. 2008), offers selections from Aquinas's writings in translation. Denys Turner's *Thomas Aquinas: A Portrait* (2014) is a highly readable biography of the saint.

F. C. Copleston's *Aquinas* (1955) is a useful introduction to both Aquinas's philosophy and its historical background, as is *Thomas Aquinas for Beginners: A Brief Introduction to His Philosophy*, edited by Jeffrey Coleman (2012). M. D. Chenu's *Toward Understanding St. Thomas* (1964) offers a classic interpretation of Aquinas's thought. Umberto Eco's *Aesthetics of Thomas Aquinas* (1988) examines the difficulty of deriving an aesthetics from Aquinas's thought, making connections with issues in contemporary aesthetics. Norman Kretzmann and Eleanore Stump's *Cambridge Companion to Aquinas* (1993) provides ten studies designed to introduce all aspects of Aquinas's thought, including his work on biblical commentary. Jean-Pierre Torrell's two-volume study, *Saint Thomas Aquinas* (1993–96; trans. 1996–2003), offers an indispensable guide to the life and works of the saint by a member of the Leonine Commission; his *Aquinas's Summa: Background, Structure, and Reception* (1998; trans. 2005) provides a more advanced historical background for Aquinas, covering his Christian, Greek, Jewish, and Arabic sources and surveying the *Summa*'s influence up to the twentieth century. In *Philo's Heirs: Moses Maimonides and Thomas Aquinas* (2017), Luis Cortest examines the influence of Philo of Alexandria, the first century Jewish philosopher on the philosophical works of Maimonides and Thomas Aquinas, and in doing so highlights the relationships between the two medieval philosophers. In *On Aquinas* (2008), the prominent British theologian Herbert McCabe elucidates the influence of Aquinas on contemporary thought. Bernard McGinn's *Thomas Aquinas's "Summa Theologiae": A Biography* (2014) tells the story of the *Summa* from the medieval world that shaped it to its subsequent influence over the past seven hundred years, while Brian Davies's *Thomas Aquinas's "Summa Theologiae": A Guide and Commentary* (2014) presents a systematic exposition of the work. *The Oxford Handbook of Aquinas*, edited by Brian Davies and Eleanore Stump (2012), includes a section on Aquinas's theory of language, and Olivier-Thomas Venard, OP, examines the central role Aquinas afforded to language in his philosophy in "Religious Imagination and Poetic Audacity in Thomas Aquinas," in *Poetry and the Religious Imagination: The Power of the Word* (ed. Francesca Bugliani Knox and David Lonsdale, 2015). Pasquale Porro examines Aquinas's complete works in chronological order, attending to Aquinas's philosophical development, influences, manuscript evidence, and historical context, in *Thomas Aquinas: A Historical and Philosophical Profile* (2012; trans. 2016). "Thomas Aquinas" by M. V. Dougherty, in the online *Oxford Bibliographies* (2014), is an up-to-date bibliography.

Tzvetan Todorov

Todorov's work falls into three periods. The first and best-known to English-speaking critics is his structuralist phase; books include *Grammar of the Decameron* (1969); *The Fantastic: A Structural Approach to a Literary Genre* (1970; trans. 1973); *The Poetics of Prose* (1971; trans. 1977), which gathers many important essays on narrative; the *Encyclopedic Dictionary of the Sciences of Language*, coauthored with the philosopher of language Oswald Ducrot (1972; trans. 1979); and *Introduction to Poetics* (1973; trans. 1981), a good starting point in reading Todorov. In addition, he translated into French and edited an influential collection, *Théorie de la littérature: Textes des formalistes russes* (1965, *Theory of Literature: Texts of the Russian Formalists*), which introduced central writings of important Russian formalists to the French scene.

In his second phase, Todorov turned from questions of structure to those of interpretation, publishing *Theories of the Symbol* (1977; trans. 1982), *Symbolism and Interpretation* (1978; trans. 1982), *Genres in Discourse* (1978; abridged trans., 1990), and *Mikhail Bakhtin: The Dialogical Principle* (1981; trans. 1984). He also edited the anthology *French Literary Theory Today: A Reader* (1982) and published the overview *Literature and Its Theorists: A Personal View of Twentieth-Century Criticism* (1984; trans. 1987). Subsequently, Todorov took up broader issues of culture, history, and politics in more than twenty books, including *On Human Diversity: Nationalism, Racism, and Exoticism in French Thought* (1989; trans. 1993), *The Morals of History* (1991; trans. 1995), *Facing the Extreme: Moral Life in the Concentration Camps* (1991; trans. 1996), *Imperfect Garden: The Legacy of Humanism* (1998; trans. 2002), *Hope and Memory: Lessons from the Twentieth Century* (2002; trans. 2003), *The New World Disorder: Reflections of a European* (2003; trans. 2005), *The Fear of Barbarians: Beyond the Clash of Civilizations* (2008; trans. 2010), and *The Inner Enemies of Democracy* (2012; trans. 2014). He also edited two books about Bulgaria during the Holocaust and during Communist rule. The autobiography *L'Homme dépaysé* (1996, *Man without a Country*) gives an account of his life and travels, and *Duties and Delights: The Life of a Go-Between* (2002; trans. 2008) collects interviews with Catherine Portevin about his cross-cultural role.

Todorov's "grammar" of plot remains a touchstone for narrative theory. Gerald Prince's *Narratology: The Form and Functioning of Narrative* (1982) is indebted to Todorov, though it notes the limitations of the grammatical approach. Todorov is a significant actor in François Dosse's *History of Structuralism* (1992; trans. 1997), an excellent account of the major figures and events of the movement. Emma Kafalenos expands on the Propp-Todorov definition of narrative as a disruption of equilibrium; see her contribution to *Narratologies: New Perspectives on Narrative Analysis* (ed. David Herman, 1999). Todorov's seminal work in narrative theory receives comment throughout *What Is Narratology? Questions and Answers Regarding the Status of a Theory*, edited by Tom Kindt and Hans-Harald Müller (2003), and his early concept of literariness was the topic of *What Is Literature Now?*, a special issue of *New Literary History* (38.1 [2007]). For a comprehensive bibliography of Todorov's work, see David Gorman, "Tzvetan Todorov: An Anglo-French Checklist to 1995," *Style* 31 (1997).

Lionel Trilling

For the complete writings, see the Uniform Edition of the Works of Lionel Trilling, edited by Diana Trilling (12 vols., 1977–80). The best place to begin reading Trilling is the excellent 600-page collection *The Moral Obligation to Be Intelligent: Selected Essays*, edited by Leon Wieseltier (2000). *The Liberal Imagination: Essays on Literature and Society* (1950) is Trilling's most influential book. A superb guide to Trilling's life, work, critical reception, and legacy is *Lionel Trilling and the Critics: Opposing Selves*, edited by John Rodden (1999).

An essential biographical source is Diana Trilling, *The Beginning of the Journey: The Marriage of Diana and Lionel Trilling* (1993). Another important related source is Natalie Robins, *The Untold Journey: The Life of Diana Trilling* (2017). Also noteworthy is Geraldine Murphy's introduction to *The Journey Abandoned: The Unfinished Novel* (2009), one-third of a draft for a novel that Trilling did not complete. Important too are "From the Notebooks of Lionel Trilling, part 1," selected by Christopher Zinn, *Partisan Review* 51.4/52.1 (fall 1984–winter 1985); "From the Notebooks of Lionel Trilling, part 2," selected by Christopher Zinn, *Partisan Review* 54.1 (winter 1987); and Jeffrey Meyers, "Lionel Trilling and the Crisis at Columbia," *New Criterion* 21.5 (January 2003), which examines a 75-page interview with Trilling that took place in May 1968. Significant but controversial is James Trilling, "My Father and the Weak-Eyed Devils," *American Scholar* 68.2 (spring 1999), in which the author says that his father suffered from attention deficit disorder (ADD).

It is important to situate Trilling biographically and intellectually within a larger school or movement, the New York Intellectuals. *The New York Intellectuals Reader*, edited by Neil Jumonville (2007), includes major essays by Trilling, Hannah Arendt, Clement Greenberg, Irving Howe, Alfred Kazin, and others. Also illuminating is Joseph Dorman's work of oral history, *Arguing the World: The New York Intellectuals in Their Own Words* (2000), which focuses on Howe, the political essayist Irving Kristol, and the sociologists Daniel Bell and Nathan Glazer. *Prodigal Sons: The New York Intellectuals and Their World* (1986), by Alexander Bloom, is a fascinating account of the New York Intellectuals' careers and literary and cultural communities. See also Terry A. Cooney, *The Rise of the New York Intellectuals: "Partisan Review" and Its Circle* (1986); Alan M. Wald, *The New York Intellectuals: The Rise and Decline of the Anti-Stalinist Left from the 1930s to the 1980s* (1987); and Neil Jumonville, *Critical Crossings: The New York Intellectuals in Postwar America* (1991).

Useful surveys of Trilling's life and career are Edward Joseph Shoben Jr., *Lionel Trilling: Mind and Character* (1981); Stephen L. Tanner, *Lionel Trilling* (1988); and, especially, Adam Kirsch, *Why Trilling Matters* (2011), which presents Trilling as an inspiring writer and thinker who is relevant for literature and criticism today. See also *Art, Politics, and Will: Essays in Honor of Lionel Trilling*, edited by Quentin Anderson, Stephen Donadio, and Steven Marcus (1977), which includes essays on Trilling by Quentin Anderson and Daniel Bell (on his novel *The Middle of the Journey*, 1947).

For more depth and detail, see William M. Chace, *Lionel Trilling: Criticism and Politics* (1980); Mark Krupnick, *Lionel Trilling and the Fate of Cultural Criticism* (1986); and Daniel T. O'Hara, *Lionel Trilling: The Work of Liberation* (1988), which describes Trilling as a "magnanimous" critic capable of "imaginative sympathy" with minds radically different from his own. Somewhat dated but still stimulating is a chapter in Nathan A. Scott Jr., *Three American Moralists: Mailer, Bellow, Trilling* (1973). Michael Kimmage, *The Conservative Turn: Lionel Trilling, Whitaker Chambers, and the Lessons of Anti-Communism* (2009), studies the emergence of neoconservatism by focusing on the relationship between Trilling and the writer and editor Whittaker Chambers, a Communist Party member and Soviet spy who later renounced communism and became an outspoken opponent of Stalinism and the Soviet Union. Trilling used Chambers as the basis for the character Gifford Maxim in *The Middle of the Journey*.

Also recommended are Philip French, *Three Honest Men: Edmund Wilson, F. R. Leavis, and Lionel Trilling: A Critical Mosaic* (1980), the transcripts of BBC programs on these three critics, with commentaries and reminiscences by others; and Carolyn G. Heilbrun, *When Men Were the Only Models We Had: My Teachers Barzun, Fadiman, and Trilling* (2002), recollections of and reflections on three intellectuals and teachers—Trilling, Jacques Barzun, and Clifton Fadiman—by a leading feminist critic and theorist.

For additional primary and secondary sources, consult Thomas M. Leitch, *Lionel Trilling: An Annotated Bibliography* (1993). Also helpful for further reading are the extensive notes in Kimmage's *The Conservative Turn* (see above).

Giambattista Vico

The standard Italian edition of Vico's works is edited by Benedetto Croce and Fausto Nicolini (8 vols. in 11, 1914–42). English translations include *On the Study Methods of Our Time* (1709; trans. 1990); *On the Most Ancient Wisdom of the Italians* (1710; trans. 1988); *Statecraft: The Deeds of Antonio Carafa* (1716; trans. 2004); *Universal Right* (1720–22; trans. 2000); *The First New Science* (1725; trans. 2002); *The Autobiography of Giambattista Vico* (1725–28; trans. 1944); the third edition of *The New Science of Giambattista Vico* (1744; trans. 1968, 2001), to which has been added Vico's "Practic of the New Science"; and *On Humanistic Education* (trans. 1993) and *The Art of Rhetoric* (trans. 1996), both translated and edited by Giorgio A. Pinton and Arthur W. Shippee. *Vico: Selected Writings*, edited and translated by Leon Pompa (1982), includes selections from *On the Most Ancient Wisdom of the Italians*, the 1725 version of the *New Science*, and Vico's orations. For information on Vico's life, see his autobiography cited above; Robert Flint's *Vico* (1901; rpt. 1979); and H. P. Adam's *Life and Writings of Giambattista Vico* (1935). A valuable brief introduction to the life and work is Peter Burke's *Vico* (1985).

Benedetto Croce's *Philosophy of Giambattista Vico* (1911; trans. 1913) is an important critical study that put Vico's work on the map in the early twentieth century. For a sense of the wide range and multidisciplinary nature of Vico studies, see the following three collections: *Giambattista Vico: An International Symposium*, edited by Giorgio Tagliacozzo and Hayden White (1969); *Giambattista Vico's Science of Humanity*, edited by Tagliacozzo and Donald Phillip Verene (1976); and *Vico: Past and Present*, edited by Tagliacozzo (1981). Also helpful in this regard are Max Harold Fisch and Thomas Goddard Bergin's introduction to Vico's autobiography cited above and the annual volumes of *New Vico Studies*, published by the Institute for Vico Studies. Illuminating studies of the *New Science* include Verene's *Vico's Science of the Imagination* (1981), Leon Pompa's *Vico: A Study of the New Science* (2d ed., 1990), Ernesto Grassi's *Vico and Humanism: Essays on Vico, Heidegger, and Rhetoric* (1990), Joseph Mali's *Rehabilitation of Myth: Vico's "New Science"* (1992), Giuseppe Mazzotta's *New Map of the World: The Poetic Philosophy of Giambattista Vico* (1999), Robert C. Miner's *Vico: Genealogist of Modernity* (2002), Sandra Rudnick Luft's *Vico's Uncanny Humanism: Reading the "New Science" between Modern and Postmodern* (2003), Donald Phillip Verene's *Knowledge of Things Human and Divine: Vico's "New Science" and "Finnegans Wake"* (2003), Jürgen Trabant's *Vico's New Science of Ancient Signs: A Study of Sematology* (1994; trans. 2004), *Giambattista Vico: Keys to the "New Science": Translations, Commentaries, and Essays*, edited by Thora Ilin Bayer and Donald Phillip Verene (2009), and Verene's *Vico's "New Science": A Philosophical Commentary* (2015). A philosophical and historically informed study of Vico is available in Isaiah Berlin's *Vico and Herder: Two Studies in the History of*

Ideas (1976). On the subject of Marx and Vico, see *Vico and Marx: Affinities and Contrasts*, edited by Giorgio Tagliacozzo (1983). For discussions of Vico in relationship to rhetoric, see Michael Mooney's *Vico in the Tradition of Rhetoric* (1985), John D. Schaeffer's *Sensus Communis: Vico, Rhetoric, and the Limits of Relativism* (1990), and David L. Marshall's *Vico and the Transformation of Rhetoric in Early Modern Europe* (2010). For an account of Vico's axioms, often mentioned in *New Science*, refer to James Goetsch's *Vico's Axioms: The Geometry of the Human World* (1995). Bibliographies of criticism and primary texts appear in Robert Crease's *Vico in English: A Bibliography of Writings by and about Giambattista Vico* (1978), Molly Black Verene's *Vico: A Bibliography of Works in English from 1884 to 1994* (1994), and the annual volumes of *New Vico Studies* (1983–2009), as well as Timothy Costelloe's "Giambattista Vico," in the online *Stanford Encyclopedia of Philosophy* (2014).

Kenneth W. Warren

Warren's books are *Black and White Strangers: Race and American Literary Realism* (1993), *So Black and Blue: Ralph Ellison and the Occasion of Criticism* (2003), and *What Was African American Literature?* (2011). He is co-editor, with Adolph Reed Jr., of *Renewing Black Intellectual History: The Ideological and Material Foundations of African American Thought* (2010) and, with Tess Chakkalakal, of *Jim Crow, Literature, and the Legacy of Sutton E. Griggs* (2013). An in-depth interview with Warren by Jeffrey Williams can be found in *symplokē* 25.1–2 (2017). An extensive bibliography of Warren's works can be found at his homepage at the University of Chicago. Kenneth Warren's *What Was African American Literature?* is his most widely reviewed and cited work of scholarship. It generated a symposium in the *Los Angeles Review of Books* (2011) that engages his work from three different perspectives. The Modern Language Association hosted a roundtable featuring Warren and five critics, published as "Assessing *What Was African American Literature?*; or, The State of the Field in the New Millennium," *African American Review* 44 (2011). Marlon B. Ross's review essay in *Callaloo* 35 (2012) attacks Warren's thesis for, among other things, arguing that the distinctness of black people producing a particular kind of literature disappeared with the end of Jim Crow in the 1960s. Essays in *Contemporary African American Literature: The Living Canon*, edited by Lovalerie King and Shirley Moody-Turner (2013), provide a nuanced critique of Warren's thesis, while simultaneously recognizing the intentions of his historical methods. The contributions to "What Was African American Literature?," *PMLA* 128 (2013), a forum of seven critics with Warren's response, range from criticizing Warren's periodization to appreciating his call for and praise of certain literary texts that move beyond the past. Avram Alpert's "Epochs, Elephants, and Parts: On the Concept of History in Literary Studies," *Diacritics* 42.4 (2014), uses Warren's work as a starting point for exploring the pitfalls and possible benefits of using history in the study of literature.

Hayden White

White served as the author, editor, or translator of a dozen books on a wide range of topics in history and literature. He was the coauthor, with Wilson H. Coates and J. Selwyn Schapiro, of the two-volume *Emergence of Liberal Humanism: An Intellectual History of Western Europe* (1966–70). He edited *The Uses of History: Essays in Intellectual and Social History* (1968); with Giorgio Tagliacozzo, *Giambattista Vico: An International Symposium* (1969); and with Wilson H. Coates, *The Ordeal of Liberal Humanism* (1970). He next published *The Greco-Roman Tradition* (1973). *Metahistory: The Historical Imagination in Nineteenth-Century Europe* (1973) was the groundbreaking study that first brought him to the attention of literary critics. His interest in historiography led him to translate from the Italian Carlo Antoni's *From History to Sociology: The Tradition in German Historical Thinking* (1976) and to collect his own 1976 Clark Library lectures into a volume titled *Theories of History* (1978). After the late 1970s, White's work became more literary in its focus, including *Tropics of Discourse: Essays in Cultural Criticism* (1978); *Representing Kenneth Burke* (1982), which he edited with Margaret Brose; *The Content of Form: Narrative Discourse and Historical Representation* (1987); and *Figural Realism: Studies in the Mimesis Effect* (1999). In *The Fiction of Narrative: Essays on History, Literature, and Theory, 1957–2007* (2010), Robert Doran has collected twenty-three of White's most important essays, many hard to find, written between 1957 and 2007. In *The Practical Past* (2014), White reaffirmed his commitment to understanding history as narrative about the past, calling on historians to explore the pasts created by artistic works and literary theorists to engage with history. For a biography, see the entry on White in *Twentieth-Century, American Cultural Theorists* (ed. Paul Hansom, 2001).

For an introduction to White's work, see his entry in *Fifty Key Thinkers on History* (3d ed., ed. Marnie Hughes-Warrington, 2015). Herman Paul's *Hayden White: The Historical Imagination* (2011) is an accessible account of the development of White's thought. Two lengthy, thought-provoking reviews of *Metahistory*, Fredric Jameson's "Figural Relativism: or the Poetics of Historiography" and David Carroll's "On Tropology: The Forms of History," appeared in the journal *Diacritics* 6 (1976). The journal *History and Theory* devoted a special issue, *Metahistory: Six Critiques* (19 [1980]), to White's book. Dominick

LaCapra, another historian who has written on the linguistic turn in history, offers a sympathetic evaluation in "A Poetics of Historiography: Hayden White's *Tropics of Discourse*," in his *Rethinking Intellectual History: Texts, Contexts, Language* (1983). James M. Mellard's *Doing Tropology: Analysis of Narrative Discourse* (1989) and Hans Kellner's *Language and Historical Representation: Getting the Story Crooked* (1989) examine, critique, and extend White's approach. Russell Jacoby presents a critique of White's work in his article "A New Intellectual History," *American Historical Review* 97 (1992). By the late 1990s much of the writing on White was dominated by debate over the truth claims of history; for instance, Nancy Partner, "Hayden White (and the content and the form and everyone else) at AHA," *History and Theory* 36 (1997); Chris Lorenz, "Can Histories Be Truth? Narrativism, Positivism, and the 'Metaphorical Turn,'" *History and Theory* 37 (1998); and the cluster of essays published in *History and Theory* in 1998. *Tropes for the Past: Hayden White and the History/Literature Debate*, edited by Kuisma Korhonen (2006), offers a renewed exploration of postmodern debates between literature and historiography, while a 2008 special issue of the journal *Rethinking History* (12.1) is devoted to Hayden White's work. Produced in honor of White's eightieth birthday, *Re-Figuring Hayden White,* edited by Frank Ankersmit, Ewa Domanska, and Hans Kellner (2009), reconsiders the historian's intellectual contributions to history, poststructuralism, and narrative theory, addressing key concepts such as tropes, narrative, figuralism, and the historical sublime. In addition, it contains a bibliography of White's works. Paul's book (cited above) contains a bibliography that includes English works by and about White.

Oscar Wilde

Wilde's *Complete Works* were published in twelve volumes in 1923. *The Complete Works of Oscar Wilde*, edited by Bobby Fong and Karl Beckson, is being published by Oxford University Press (7 vols, to date, 2001–); volume 4 is *Criticism: Historical Criticism, "Intentions," "The Soul of Man,"* edited by Josephine M. Guy (2007). There are a number of one-volume collections, including *Oscar Wilde: Selected Writings*, edited by Richard Ellmann (1961), and *Selected Writings of Oscar Wilde*, edited by Russell Fraser (1969). The best, because it is annotated, is *Oscar Wilde*, edited by Isobel Murray (1989). For the correspondence, see the volumes edited by Rupert Hart-Davis, *Letters* (1962) and *More Letters* (1985), and *The Complete Letters of Oscar Wilde*, edited by Merlin Holland and Rupert Hart-Davis (2000). For his literary criticism, consult *Literary Criticism of Oscar Wilde*, edited by Stanley Weintraub (1968), and *The Artist as Critic: Critical Writings of Oscar Wilde*, edited by Richard Ellmann (1969).

Biographies include Hesketh Pearson, *The Life of Oscar Wilde* (1946), a good overview of Wilde's career that deals well with his shift from poetry to fiction and drama, and Richard Ellmann, *Oscar Wilde* (1988), a major study, especially in its account of Wilde's early life and his response to John Ruskin, Walter Pater, Henry James, and contemporary French writers. Neil McKenna, *The Secret Life of Oscar Wilde* (2005), examines Wilde's life as a gay man and shows the centrality of his homosexuality to his identity, literary work, and politics. Vyvyan Holland, *Oscar Wilde: A Pictorial Biography* (1960), is also valuable. H. Montgomery Hyde has edited *The Trials of Oscar Wilde* (1948); see also Hyde's *The Three Trials of Oscar Wilde* (1956) and *Oscar Wilde in Prison* (1956). Other resources include *Oscar Wilde: Interviews and Recollections*, edited by E. H. Mikhail (2 vols., 1979); *Oscar Wilde's Oxford Notebooks*, edited by Philip E. Smith II and Michael S. Helfand (1989); and Norman Page, *An Oscar Wilde Chronology* (1991). A very good resource is *Oscar Wilde in Context*, edited by Kerry Powell and Peter Raby (2013), with a wide range of essays on many topics, including Wilde's influence and reputation. On the twenty-seven-year-old Wilde's eleven-month speaking tour of the United States, which began in New York City in January 1882, see Roy Morris Jr., *Declaring His Genius: Oscar Wilde in North America* (2013); David M. Friedman, *Wilde in America: Oscar Wilde and the Invention of Modern Celebrity* (2014); and *Oscar Wilde in America: The Interviews*, edited by Matthew Hofer and Gary Scharnhorst (2010). See also *The Reception of Oscar Wilde in Europe*, edited by Stefano Evangelista (2010).

Collections surveying the critical and scholarly response to Wilde include *Oscar Wilde: A Collection of Critical Essays*, edited by Richard Ellmann (1969); *Oscar Wilde: The Critical Heritage*, edited by Karl Beckson (1970); *Critical Essays on Oscar Wilde*, edited by Regenia Gagnier (1991); and *Oscar Wilde: A Collection of Critical Essays*, edited by Jonathan Freedman (1996).

Lawrence Danson, *Wilde's Intentions: The Artist in His Criticism* (1997), is an excellent treatment of Wilde's views on literature and criticism. A number of studies in the 1990s focused on the social, sexual, and cultural issues that Wilde's life and, especially, his trial and imprisonment dramatize. Among these are Eve Kosofsky Sedgwick, *Epistemology of the Closet* (1990); Patricia Flanagan Behrendt, *Oscar Wilde: Eros and Aesthetics* (1991); Ed Cohen, *Talk on the Wilde Side: Toward a Genealogy of a Discourse on Male Sexualities* (1993); Melissa Knox, *Oscar Wilde: A Long and Lovely Suicide* (1994); Gary Schmidgall, *The Stranger Wilde: Interpreting Oscar* (1994); Alan Sinfield, *The Wilde Century: Effeminacy, Oscar Wilde, and the Queer Moment* (1994); and John Stokes, *Oscar Wilde: Myths, Miracles, and Imitations* (1996). Julia Prewitt Brown, *Cosmopolitan Criticism: Oscar Wilde's*

Philosophy of Art (1997), deals succinctly with Wilde's aesthetic theory and its influence on later writers. Michael S. Foldy, *Trials of Oscar Wilde: Deviance, Morality, and Late-Victorian Society* (1998), describes the range of threats (including, but not limited to, deviant sexuality) that English society associated with Wilde. *Wilde the Irishman*, edited by Jerusha McCormack (1998), deals with the Irish dimension of Wilde's work and with the responses to Wilde by poets, playwrights, sculptors, and others. See also Bruce Bashford, *Oscar Wilde: The Critic as Humanist* (1999). Recent work includes Kerry Powell, *Acting Wilde: Victorian Sexuality, Theatre, and Oscar Wilde* (2009), which contends that Wilde's plays, fiction, and critical theory are centered on the idea that reality is a mode of performance; S. I. Salamensky, *The Modern Art of Influence and the Spectacle of Oscar Wilde* (2012), on Wilde as "the first modern man"; and Emer O'Sullivan, *The Fall of the House of Wilde: Oscar Wilde and His Family* (2016), which presents a fascinating, detailed account of Wilde's parents and older brother and their impact on his life and career; Dominic Janes, *Visions of Queer Martyrdom from John Henry Newman to Derek Jarman* (2015), has an excellent chapter on Wilde. Reference works include Stuart Mason, *Bibliography of Oscar Wilde* (1914); Thomas A. Mikolyzk, *Oscar Wilde: An Annotated Bibliography* (1993); Ian Small, *Oscar Wilde Revalued: An Essay on New Materials and Methods of Research* (1993); and Karl Beckson, *The Oscar Wilde Encyclopedia* (1998). A good bibliography is included in Powell and Raby's *Oscar Wilde in Context* (see above).

Raymond Williams

Raymond Williams published more than thirty books and approximately six hundred articles during his lifetime, spanning a wide range, from drama, poetry, and novel criticism to cultural history and media studies to literary theory and political commentary. Williams's early books include *Reading and Criticism* (1950), *Drama from Ibsen to Eliot* (1952; rev. as *Drama from Ibsen to Brecht*, 1968); and *Drama in Performance* (1954; rev. ed., 1968). He also published a textbook, *Preface to Film*, coauthored with Michael Orrom (1954). *Culture and Society, 1780–1950* (1958), a key text for British cultural studies, is a good place to enter his work. Its sequels include *Keywords: A Vocabulary of Culture and Society* (1976; new [3d] ed., 2015), originally planned as an appendix, and *The Long Revolution* (1961).

Williams helped pioneer media studies and the emerging discipline of communications with *Communications* (1962; 3d ed., 1976); *Television: Technology and Cultural Form* (1974) is one of the first significant studies of that medium. *Modern Tragedy* (1966; rev. ed., 1979) continued his work in drama. He co-edited *May Day Manifesto*, a response to the political events of the 1960s (1967; 2d ed., 1968), with his student Stuart Hall. Williams returned to literary criticism with *The English Novel from Dickens to Lawrence* (1970), *George Orwell* (1971), and *The Country and the City* (1973).

His *Marxism and Literature* (1977) is a good introduction to Williams's more theoretical considerations of culture and society. *Problems in Materialism and Culture: Selected Essays* (1980) elaborates his theory of "cultural materialism," and *Culture* (1981; retitled *The Sociology of Culture*, 1982) is a sequel to *Marxism and Literature*. A lengthy collection of interviews, *Politics and Letters: Interviews with New Left Review* (1979; reprint with new intro., 2015), provides an accessible overview of his life and thought. His collections of occasional writings include *Writing in Society* (1984); the posthumous *The Politics of Modernism: Against the New Conformists*, edited by Tony Pinkney (1989); and *Resources of Hope: Culture, Democracy, Socialism*, edited by Robin Gable (1989). *What I Came to Say* (1990) offers a short political summation. *The Raymond Williams Reader*, edited by John Higgins (2001), and *Raymond Williams on Culture and Society: Essential Writings*, edited by Jim McGuigan (2014), present good selections from the range of Williams's work, and the former includes a good bibliography.

Williams edited a number of anthologies on literary figures, drama, and communications, and he regularly published fiction throughout his career, including a trilogy of working-class life in Wales, *Border Country* (1960), *Second Generation* (1964), and *The Fight for Manod* (1979). He also wrote short stories, plays, and television scripts.

The secondary literature on Williams's life and work is considerable. A comprehensive biography, Fred Inglis's *Raymond Williams* (1995) presents a detailed picture of Williams's life. John and Lizzie Eldridge's *Raymond Williams: Making Connections* (1994) is a useful introduction to the many aspects of Williams's work; see also Alan O'Connor, *Raymond Williams* (2006). There are a number of collections: notably, *Raymond Williams: Critical Perspectives*, edited by his student Terry Eagleton (1989), which gathers essays by Stuart Hall, Said, Eagleton, and others, as well as an interview Eagleton conducted with Williams; *Cultural Materialism: On Raymond Williams*, edited by Christopher Prendergast (1995), which presents examinations by contemporary critics; and *About Raymond Williams*, edited by Monika Seidl, Roman Horak, and Lawrence Grossberg (2010). The best single-authored account, John Higgins's *Raymond Williams: Literature, Marxism and Cultural Materialism* (1999), covers all Williams's work, from his early interest in drama to his political interventions. Stephen Woodhams's *History in the Making: Raymond Williams, Edward Thompson and Radical Intellectuals, 1936–1956* (2001) describes his generation's political formation. *Raymond Williams: A Warrior's Tale* (2008), by Dai Smith, draws on new information to recount Williams's biography up to 1962.

Raymond Williams, edited by Eagleton, appends a chronological bibliography of all of Williams's writing, as well as a selected secondary bibliography. Higgins's *Raymond Williams* also includes a chronological bibliography of his writings and a good listing of secondary sources.

William K. Wimsatt Jr. and Monroe C. Beardsley

Wimsatt's books on eighteenth-century literature include *The Prose Style of Samuel Johnson* (1941) and *Philosophic Words: A Study of Style and Meaning in the "Rambler" and "Dictionary" of Samuel Johnson* (1948). He is best known for his literary theory and criticism, notably *The Verbal Icon: Studies in the Meaning of Poetry* (1954), *Hateful Contraries: Studies in Literature and Criticism* (1965), *Day of the Leopards: Essays in Defense of the Poem* (1976), and, with Cleanth Brooks, *Literary Criticism: A Short History* (1957). Beardsley's books include *Aesthetics: Problems in the Philosophy of Criticism* (1958) and *Aesthetics from Classical Greece to the Present* (1966). Secondary sources on Wimsatt include Eliseo Vivas, "Mr. Wimsatt on the Theory of Literature," in *The Artistic Transaction and Essays on Theory of Literature* (1963); *Literary Theory and Structure: Essays in Honor of W. K. Wimsatt*, edited by Frank Brady, John Palmer, and Martin Price (1973); and René Wellek, "The Literary Theory of William K. Wimsatt," *Yale Review* 66 (1977). See also the overview by Robert Moynihan, in *Dictionary of Literary Biography*, vol. 63, *Modern American Critics, 1920–1955* (ed. Gregory S. Jay, 1988), which contains biographical and bibliographical information. In *Literary Intention, Literary Interpretation, and Readers* (2009), John Maynard explores the concepts and theories at the center of debates about intentionality and interpretation, practical criticism, reception theory, and critique of ideology. Other than the two classic essays he coauthored with Wimsatt, Beardsley's work in philosophical aesthetics has had little impact in the field of literary criticism.

Monique Wittig

Wittig is the author of four novels that have been influential for feminist theorists: *The Opoponax* (1964; trans. 1966); *The Guérillères* (1969; trans. 1971); *The Lesbian Body* (1973; trans. 1975); and *Across the Acheron* (1985; trans. 1987). She also published with Sande Zeig *Lesbian Peoples: Material for a Dictionary* (1976; trans. 1987). *The Straight Mind and Other Essays*, a collection of essays (mostly written in English for *Feminist Issues*), was published in 1992. Excerpts of Wittig's early works are included in *The New French Feminisms* (ed. Elaine Marks and Isabelle de Courtivron, 1980). *On Monique Wittig: Theoretical, Political, and Literary Essays*, edited by Namascar Shaktini (2005), includes previously unpublished work by Wittig, as well as several new critical and theoretical essays by French, Francophone, and U.S. writers.

For biographical information on Wittig, see the useful entry by Jeannelle Laillou Savona in *Feminist Writers* (ed. Pamela Kester-Shelton, 1996). Most critical writing on Wittig has focused on her fiction. Alice Jardine's "Pre-Texts for the Transatlantic Feminist," *Yale French Studies* 62 (1981), and Hélène Vivienne Wenzel's "The Text as Body/Politics: An Appreciation of Monique Wittig's Writings in Context," *Feminist Studies* 7 (1981), are two of the earliest theoretical considerations of Wittig's work to appear in English. Teresa de Lauretis examines Wittig's lesbian materialism in "Sexual Indifference and Lesbian Representation," *Theatre Journal* 40 (1988). Diana Fuss's chapter on Monique Wittig in *Essentially Speaking: Feminism, Nature, and Difference* (1989) and Judith Butler's in *Gender Trouble: Feminism and the Subversion of Identity* (1990) include important discussions of Wittig's contribution to the essentialism debate. Erika Ostrovsky's *Constant Journey: The Fiction of Monique Wittig* (1991) charts the relationship between fiction and theory in Wittig's writing. For an analysis of Wittig as a lesbian theorist, see Dianne Chisholm's "Lesbianizing Love's Body: Interventions and Imaginings of Monique Wittig," in *Reimagining Women: Representations of Women in Culture* (ed. Shirley Neuman and Glennis Stephenson, 1993), and Renate Gunther, "Are Lesbians Women? The Relationship between Lesbianism and Feminism in the Works of Luce Irigaray and Monique Wittig," in *Gay Signatures: Gay and Lesbian Theory, Fiction, and Film in France, 1945–1995* (ed. Owen Heathcote, Alex Hughes, and James S. Williams, 1998). *GLQ: A Journal of Lesbian and Gay Studies* published a special issue, *Monique Wittig: At the Crossroads of Criticism*, edited by Brad Epps and Jonathan Katz (13.4 [2007]); it includes essays by Alice Jardine, Diane Griffin Crowder, Robyn Wiegman, Judith Butler, and Wittig herself. For a bibliography of works by and about Wittig, see *French Feminist Thought: Michèle Le Doeuff, Monique Wittig, Catherine Clément: A Bibliography*, edited by Joan Nordquist (1993). An updated biography and bibliography can be found in Shaktini's *On Monique Wittig*.

Mary Wollstonecraft

Mary Wollstonecraft has been well served by modern editors. Her complete works have been edited in seven volumes by Janet Todd and Marilyn Butler (1989), and *A Vindication of the Rights of Woman* is available in several accessible editions. Her two novels *Mary* and *Maria* (along with *Matilda*, an early novel by Mary Wollstonecraft Shelley, her daughter) have been published in a single volume edited by Janet Todd (1991). An excellent edition of the two *Vindications*, with helpful notes and appendixes, has been prepared by D. L. Macdonald and Kathleen Scherf (1997). Following the first modern scholarly biography, Ralph Wardle's *Mary Wollstonecraft* (1951), numerous others have appeared; particularly noteworthy are Claire Tomalin's *Life and Death of Mary Wollstonecraft* (1974), Gary Kelly's *Revolutionary Feminism: The Mind and Career of Mary Wollstonecraft* (1992), Janet Todd's *Mary Wollstonecraft: A Revolutionary Life* (2000), Lyndall Gordon's *Vindication: A Life of Mary Wollstonecraft* (2005), and Charlotte Gordon's biography of mother and daughter, *Romantic Outlaws: The Extraordinary Lives of Mary Wollstonecraft and Her Daughter Mary Shelley* (2015). Many general studies of Wollstonecraft devote substantial space to the intertwining of her life and work: good basic introductions include Moira Ferguson and Janet Todd's *Mary Wollstonecraft* (1984), Jennifer Lorch's *Mary Wollstonecraft: The Making of a Radical Feminist* (1990), and Harriet Jump's *Mary Wollstonecraft: Writer* (1994). For a good selection of essays, see *Feminist Interpretations of Mary Wollstonecraft*, edited by Maria Falco (1996), and *The Cambridge Companion to Mary Wollstonecraft*, edited by Claudia L. Johnson (2002). To contextualize Wollstonecraft within the aesthetics and politics of her day, see Mary Poovey, *The Proper Lady and the Woman Writer: Ideology as Style in the Works of Mary Wollstonecraft, Mary Shelley, and Jane Austen* (1984); the debate about Enlightenment "reason" between Timothy Reiss and Frances Ferguson in *Gender and Theory* (ed. Linda Kauffman, 1989); Syndy Conger, *Mary Wollstonecraft and the Language of Sensibility* (1994); and Claudia Johnson's discussion of politics, gender, and sentimentality in *Equivocal Beings: Politics, Gender, and Sentimentality in the 1790s* (1995). Susan Gubar's examination of current feminist criticism, *Critical Condition: Feminism at the Turn of the Century* (2000), contains an analysis of Wollstonecraft's own misogyny. Janet Todd's *Mary Wollstonecraft: An Annotated Bibliography* (1976) is helpful for the period before the flowering of contemporary feminist criticism, but it needs updating. The *Cambridge Companion* contains a useful bibliography, as does Gordon's *Romantic Outlaws*.

Virginia Woolf

Most of Woolf's works are available in easily accessible editions. *A Room of One's Own* and *Three Guineas*, edited by Hermione Lee, were published together in 1984. Woolf's other essays on women's writing, edited by Michèle Barrett, were published as *Women and Fiction* (1979). In addition to her novels and her feminist essays, Woolf collected some of her articles in two volumes called *The Common Reader* (1925, 1932). Before he died in 1969, Leonard Woolf edited her *Collected Essays* (4 vols., 1967); he also edited *A Writer's Diary* (1953), now superseded by *The Diary of Virginia Woolf*, edited by Anne Olivier Bell (5 vols., 1977–84), and *A Passionate Apprentice: The Early Journals, 1897–1909*, edited by Mitchell Leaska (1990). See also *The Letters of Virginia Woolf*, edited by Nigel Nicolson and Joanne Trautmann (6 vols., 1975–80). *The Platform of Time: Memoirs of Family and Friends*, edited by S. P. Rosenbaum (2007), gives the reader insight into her inner life and writings.

There are more than a dozen biographies of Woolf. The first, *Virginia Woolf*, was written by her nephew, Quentin Bell, in 1973. The most even-handed and well-researched recent biography is Hermione Lee's monumental *Virginia Woolf* (1996). Julia Brigg's *Virginia Woolf: An Inner Life* (2005) is in many respects a biography of Woolf and her process of writing, as is Alexandra Harris's *Virginia Woolf* (2011). Viviane Forrester's *Virginia Woolf: A Portrait* (2009; trans. 2015) introduces new material about Woolf's life and writing from personal interviews and source documents. The flavor of the many "diagnostic" biographical studies can be gleaned from Alma Halbert Bond's *Who Killed Virginia Woolf? A Psychobiography* (1989), the kind of Freudian reading that has given Freudian readings a bad name; Louise de Salvo's *Virginia Woolf: The Impact of Childhood Sexual Abuse on Her Life and Work* (1989); and Mitchell Leaska's *Granite and Rainbow* (1998), which attributes all Woolf's creativity to her repressed relationship with her father.

The history of Woolf criticism mirrors the larger changes in twentieth- and twenty-first-century criticism. An invaluable collection of contemporary reviews was published as *Virginia Woolf: The Critical Heritage*, edited by Robin Majumdar and Allen McLaurin (1975), which includes acerbic reviews in the journal *Scrutiny* (the most memorable may be Q. D. Leavis's review of *Three Guineas*). Woolf's canonization as a modernist is perhaps best illustrated by her inclusion in Erich Auerbach's monumental *Mimesis: The Representation of Reality in Western Literature* (1946). Early feminist criticism was often critical of Woolf: Elaine Showalter's *A Literature of Their Own* (1977), despite its title, dismisses Woolf's experience of femininity. But Jane Marcus's edited collections—*New Feminist Essays on Virginia Woolf* (1981) and *Virginia Woolf: A Feminist Slant* (1983)—began revising that picture; and when, in her groundbreaking *Textual/Sexual Politics* (1985), Toril Moi contrasted Anglo-American feminism's desire for realism with French feminism's interest in textuality, she called for a rereading of Woolf's style that has continued to this day. See, particularly, *Virginia Woolf: A Collection of Critical Essays*, edited by Margaret Homans (1993); Ellen Bayuk Rosenman, *A Room of One's Own: Women Writers and the Politics of Creativity* (1995); and Jane Goldman, *The Feminist Aesthetics of Virginia Woolf: Modernism, Post-Impressionism, and the Politics of the Visual* (1998). The emergence of gay and lesbian studies has focused new attention on the relationship between Virginia Woolf and Vita Sackville-West. Suzanne Raitt's *Vita and Virginia* (1993) gives a good overview of the relationship of the two writers, whose letters were dramatized in 1994 by Eileen Atkins in her play

Vita and Virginia (starring Atkins and Vanessa Redgrave). Other valuable studies include Elizabeth Abel, *Virginia Woolf and the Fictions of Psychoanalysis* (1989); Pamela Caughie, *Virginia Woolf and Postmodernism* (1991); Gillian Beer, *Virginia Woolf: The Common Ground* (1996); and Rachel Bowlby, *Feminist Destinations and Further Essays on Virginia Woolf* (1997). In *Virginia Woolf and the Victorians* (2007), Steve Ellis breaks with the traditional reading of Woolf as the consummate modernist to argue that her oeuvre is post-Victorian. Finally, Justyna Kostkowska's *Ecocriticism and Women Writers: Environmentalist Poetics of Virginia Woolf, Jeanette Winterson, and Ali Smith* (2013) represents growing interests in ecocriticism, while Alice Wood's *Virginia Woolf's Late Cultural Criticism: The Genesis of "The Years," "Three Guineas" and "Between the Acts"* (2013) examines Woolf's social and political commentaries in her later writings.

There are also two useful resources for Woolf studies: Edward Bishop's day-to-day chronicle of Woolf's activities, *A Virginia Woolf Chronology* (1989), and Mark Hussey's dictionary of Woolf information, *Virginia Woolf A to Z* (1995). The proceedings of the annual Virginia Woolf conference are published by Pace University Press (1992–). B. J. Kirkpatrick and Stuart N. Clarke compiled *A Bibliography of Virginia Woolf* (1997); an online bibliographic update, *The Virginia Woolf Miscellany*, initially published by Sonoma State University (1973–2002), is now issued by Southern Connecticut State University. *The Cambridge Companion to Virginia Woolf*, edited by Susan Sellers (2d ed., 2010), offers a useful selective bibliography, as does Alice Wood's *Late Cultural Criticism* (2013) and Forrester's *Virginia Wolf: A Portrait* (2015).

William Wordsworth

A new complete edition, under the general editorship of Stephen Parrish, has been published in 21 volumes by Cornell University Press (1975–2007). For the criticism and related prose writings, see *Prose Works*, edited by W. J. B. Owen and J. M. Smyser (3 vols., 1974). Collections of Wordsworth's critical prose include *The Critical Opinions of William Wordsworth*, edited by Markham L. Peacock (1950), which presents 450 pages of primary source quotations divided into three categories—subjects, authors, and works, plus Wordsworth on his own works; *Literary Criticism of William Wordsworth*, edited by Paul M. Zall (1966); and *Wordsworth's Literary Criticism*, edited by W. J. B. Owen (1974). A good single-volume edition of the poetry and prose is *William Wordsworth*, in the Oxford Authors Series, edited by Stephen Gill (1984). *Wordsworth's Poetry and Prose: Authoritative Texts, Criticism*, edited by Nicholas Halmi (2014), is an excellent collection of primary and secondary sources and has a very good bibliography.

The standard biography, *William Wordsworth: A Biography*, is by Mary Moorman (2 vols., 1957–65), but Stephen Gill's *William Wordsworth: A Life* (1989) and Juliet Barker's *Wordsworth: A Life* (2000) are also valuable. On the poet's early adulthood, see Kenneth R. Johnston, *The Hidden Wordsworth: Poet, Lover, Rebel, Spy* (1998). John Worthen, *The Life of William Wordsworth: A Critical Biography* (2014), is especially good on the poet's early years. See also Mark L. Reed, *Wordsworth: The Chronology of the Early Years, 1770–1799* (1967) and *Wordsworth: The Chronology of the Middle Years, 1800–1815* (1975). For intellectual and literary contexts, consult Duncan Wu, *Wordsworth's Reading, 1770–1799* (1993) and *Wordsworth's Reading, 1800–1815* (1995). *The Cambridge Companion to Wordsworth*, edited by Stephen Gill (2003), includes essays on Wordsworth's life and career and a stimulating piece by Seamus Perry on the Wordsworth–Coleridge relationship.

For an excellent study of Wordsworth's Preface as well as an edition of the text, see *Wordsworth's Preface to "Lyrical Ballads,"* edited by W. J. B. Owen (1957). Also insightful is Owen's *Wordsworth as Critic* (1969). There is an extensive body of scholarship on the relationship between Wordsworth and Coleridge and its importance for literary theory and criticism. Among the best books on this topic are Lucy Newlyn, *Coleridge, Wordsworth, and the Language of Allusion* (1986); Theresa M. Kelley, *Wordsworth's Revisionary Aesthetics* (1988); Paul Magnuson, *Coleridge and Wordsworth: A Lyrical Dialogue* (1988); Nicholas Roe, *Wordsworth and Coleridge: The Radical Years* (1988); and Susan Eilenberg, *Strange Power of Speech: Wordsworth, Coleridge, and Literary Possession* (1992). For commentary on Wordsworth's theory of poetry, epistemology, and philosophy, see the essays in *Wordsworth's Poetic Theory: Knowledge, Language, Experience*, edited by Alexander Regier and Stefan H. Uhlig (2010). Recent books include Stephen Gill, *Wordsworth's Revisitings* (2011), an illuminating study of Wordsworth's revisions of his poems, especially *The Prelude*; Scott Hess, *William Wordsworth and the Ecology of Authorship: The Roots of Environmentalism in Nineteenth-Century Culture* (2012), an account (and critique) of Wordsworth's motives and commitments as laureate, resident, guide, and defender of England's Lake Country; Mary Jacobus, *Romantic Things: A Tree, a Rock, a Cloud* (2012), which examines Wordsworth's lyric poetry through modern and contemporary philosophy and literary theory; and Adam Potkay, *Wordsworth's Ethics* (2013), which argues that Wordsworth rejects the utilitarianism espoused by his contemporaries James Mill and Jeremy Bentham in favor of a view of ethics founded in relationships with particular persons and things. David Rosen, *Power, Plain English, and the Rise of Modern Poetry* (2006), offers a stimulating account of the influence of Wordsworth's poetic theory and practice on the work of William Butler Yeats, T. S. Eliot, and W. H. Auden.

See also three collections of essays: *The Age of William Wordsworth*, edited by Kenneth R. Johnston and Gene W. Ruoff (1987); *Romantic Revolutions: Criticism and Theory*, edited by Kenneth R. Johnston (1990); and *Wordsworth in Context*, edited by Pauline Fletcher and John Murphy (1992). For further background and bibliography, see the relevant entries in *The English Romantic Poets: A Review of Research and Criticism* (ed. Frank Jordan, 1985), and *British Romantic Poets, 1789–1832*, first and second series (ed. John R. Greenfield, 1990). *Literature of the Romantic Period: A Bibliographical Guide*, edited by Michael O'Neill (1998), is valuable for the study of Wordsworth and his contemporaries. See also *An Annotated Critical Bibliography of William Wordsworth* by Keith Hanley and David Barron (1995). The list of primary and secondary sources included in William Wordsworth, *The Major Works*, edited by Stephen Gill (rev. ed., 2000) is also helpful. There is a good bibliography in *The Cambridge Companion to Wordsworth*, as well as cogent essays on Wordsworth's views on language, philosophy, politics, and history and his central place in the Romantic movement.

Slavoj Žižek

Perhaps the best way into Žižek's writing is through *The Žižek Reader*, edited by Elizabeth and Edmond Wright (1999), which offers a selection of key essays written before 1999. Rex Butler and Scott Stephens collected important essays of Žižek's in two volumes, *Interrogating the Real* (2005) and *The Universal Exception* (2006). Žižek first emerged in the West with the publication of *The Sublime Object of Ideology* (1989). Since then, he has written or edited at least one and sometimes two or more books almost every year. *Looking Awry: An Introduction to Jacques Lacan through Popular Culture* (1991) and *For They Know Not What They Do: Enjoyment as a Political Factor* (1991; 2d ed., 2008), which explores the place of Lacan's *jouissance* in political theory, was followed by *Everything You Always Wanted to Know about Lacan (But Were Afraid to Ask Hitchcock)* (1992), a collection of essays on Hitchcock that includes the work of his Slovenian colleagues Mladen Dolar, Renata Salecl, and Alenka Zupančič, and *Enjoy Your Symptom! Lacan in Hollywood and Out* (1992; rev. ed., 2001), an exploration of the Lacanian symptom in popular culture. Žižek returned to the subject of ideology in *Tarrying with the Negative: Kant, Hegel, and the Critique of Ideology* (1993). He then published *Metastases of Enjoyment: Six Essays on Women and Causality* (1994); *Mapping Ideology*, edited by Žižek (1994); *The Indivisible Remainder: An Essay on Schelling and Related Matters* (1996); *Gaze and Voice as Love Objects*, edited by Renata Salecl and Žižek (1996); *The Plague of Fantasies* (1997); *The Abyss of Freedom: Ages of the World* (1997), which pairs an essay by the philosopher Schelling with his commentary; *The Spectre Is Still Roaming Around!* (1998), a commentary on Marx's *Communist Manifesto*; and *Cogito and the Unconscious*, edited by Žižek (1998). Žižek then became more focused on politics and religion, publishing *The Ticklish Subject: The Absent Centre of Political Ontology* (1999), *NATO as the Left Hand of God?* (1999), and *The Fragile Absolute, or Why Is the Christian Legacy Worth Fighting For?* (2000). He also gave a series of lectures at the University of Washington that were published as *The Art of the Ridiculous Sublime: On David Lynch's Lost Highway* (2000) and joined Judith Butler and the Argentinean political theorist Ernesto Laclau in a dialogue on contemporary philosophy and politics in *Contingency, Hegemony, Universality: Contemporary Dialogues on the Left* (2000). In 2001, an extraordinarily productive year even by his standards, Žižek published *Opera's Second Death*, with Mladen Dolar; *The Fright of Real Tears: Krzysztof Kieślowski between Theory and Post-Theory*, a book on film theory; *Did Somebody Say Totalitarianism? Five Essays in the (Mis)Use of a Notion*; *On Belief*; and *Repeating Lenin*. There followed *Welcome to the Desert of the Real* (2002), on the attacks of 9/11; *The Puppet and the Dwarf: The Perverse Core of Christianity* (2003); *Organs without Bodies: On Deleuze and Consequences* (2004); and further reflections on contemporary events, *Iraq: The Borrowed Kettle* (2004). He collaborated with the literary scholars Eric L. Santner and Kenneth Reinhard on *The Neighbor: Three Inquiries in Political Theology* (2005), exploring the meaning of the biblical injunction to "love thy neighbor," and then published the book he considers his most significant work to date, *The Parallax View* (2006), which argues for his revision of the Hegelian dialectic. In 2007, Žižek published *How to Read Lacan* in the Norton "How to Read" series. 2008 saw the publications of *In Defense of Lost Causes* (2008). Žižek explored the post-9/11 world in *Violence: Six Sideways Reflections* (2008), *First as Tragedy, Then as Farce* (2009), *The Year of Dreaming Dangerously* (2012), and *Trouble in Paradise: From the End of History to the End of Capitalism* (2014). Religion and politics came together in *Living in the End Times* (2010). *Less Than Nothing: Hegel and the Shadow of Dialectical Materialism* (2012), *Event* (2014), *Absolute Recoil: Towards a New Foundation of Dialectical Materialism* (2014), and *The Most Sublime Hysteric: Hegel with Lacan* (2014) all investigate challenging problems in contemporary philosophy. With Srećko Horvat, Žižek published *What Does Europe Want? The Union and Its Discontents* (2015). *Against the Double Blackmail: Refugees, Terror and Other Troubles with the Neighbors* and *Disparities* were published in 2016, along with an audacious revision of Sophocles's *Antigone*. In 2017, the centennial of the Russian Revolution, he published *Lenin 2017: Remembering, Repeating, and Working Through*, a monograph reevaluating the political significance of the writing produced by its major architect, Vladimir Lenin, and *Incontinence of the Void: Economico-Philosophical Spandrels* (2017), which brings together philosophy, psychoanalysis, and the critique of political economy. Tony Myers includes a brief but useful biography in his introduction to the theorist, *Slavoj Žižek* (2003).

Žižek publishes so quickly that his critics and admirers are hard-pressed to keep up with him. There are several introductory volumes, the most useful of which are Sarah Kay, *Žižek: A Critical Introduction* (2003), and, more recently, Kelsey Wood, *Žižek: A Reader's Guide* (2012). Christopher Kul-Want and Piero's *Introducing Slavoj Žižek: A Graphic Guide* (2011) offers an introduction through cartoons. Ian Parker, *Slavoj Žižek: A Critical Introduction* (2004), contains a helpful discussion of Slovenia's complex history between World War II and the present. *Slavoj Žižek: Live Theory* (2005), by Rex Butler, and *Žižek and Politics: A Critical Introduction* (2010), by Matthew Sharpe and Geoff Boucher, offer more advanced introductions. Glyn Daly collects his talks with Žižek in a volume titled *Conversations with Žižek* (2004). Matthew Sharpe's *Slavoj Žižek: A Little Piece of the Real* (2004) and Jodi Dean's *Žižek's Politics* (2006) examine his political thinking. Terry Eagleton has a lucid chapter on Žižek in *Figures of Dissent: Critical Essays on Fish, Spivak, Žižek and Others* (2003), as does Geoffrey Galt Harpham in *The Character of Criticism* (2006). In *Žižek's Ontology: A Transcendental Materialist Theory of Subjectivity* (2008), Adrian Johnston offers an account of Žižek's engagement with German idealist philosophy. *Žižek: Beyond Foucault* (2007) by Fabio Vighi and Heiko Feldner stages an encounter between the two contemporary thinkers. Several critical books examine Žižek in relation to other philosophers, including Thomas P. Brockelman, *Žižek and Heidegger: The Question Concerning Techno-capitalism* (2008); Adrian Johnston, *Badiou, Žižek, and Political Transformations: The Cadence of Change* (2009); and Geoff Boucher, *The Charmed Circle of Ideology: A Critique of Laclau and Mouffe, Butler and Žižek* (2009). Fabio Vighi's *On Žižek's Dialectics: Surplus, Subtraction, Sublimation* (2010) attempts to politicize Žižek's critical method. *Žižek Now: Current Perspectives in Žižek Studies*, edited by Jamil Khader and Molly Anne Rothenberg (2012), explores Žižek's contributions to several disciplines. *Žižek and His Contemporaries: On the Emergence of the Slovenian Lacan*, edited by Jones Irwin and Helena Motah (2014), places Žižek's writing within the context of Slovenian politics and intellectual life, tracking the Slovenian interventions in Lacanian psychoanalysis. *The Žižek Dictionary*, edited by Rex Butler (2014), contains a series of brief essays illuminating keywords in the philosopher's work. It also contains a fairly detailed bibliography; the most up-to-date bibliography can be found on the website of the journal *Lacanian Ink*.

Permissions/ Acknowledgments

Chinua Achebe: "An Image of Africa: Racism in Conrad's 'Heart of Darkness'" from *Hopes and Impediments*. Copyright © 1988 by Chinua Achebe. Used by permission of Doubleday, an imprint of the Knopf Doubleday Publishing Group, a division of Penguin Random House LLC. All rights reserved. Any third party use of this material, outside of this publication, is prohibited. Interested parties must apply directly to Penguin Random House LLC for permission. Rights in the British Commonwealth by permission of The Wylie Agency LLC.

Adūnīs: *An Introduction to Arab Poetics*, trans. by Catherine Cobham (Saqi Books, 2003). Originally published in French as "Introduction à la poétique Arabe" (Sindbad, 1985). Reprinted by permission of Saqi Books.

Giorgio Agamben: "What Is a Camp?" from *Means Without End: Notes On Politics*, trans. by Vincenzo Binetti and Cesare Casarino. Copyright © 2000 by the Regents of the University of Minnesota. Originally published in *Mezzi Senza Fine*. Copyright © 1996 by Bollati Boringhieri editore srl. Excerpts from *Homo Sacer: Sovereign Power and Bare Life*, trans. by Daniel Heller-Roazen. Copyright © 1998 by the Board of Trustees of the Leland Stanford Jr. University. All rights reserved. Used with the permission of Stanford University Press, www.sup.org.

Louis Althusser: "Ideology and Ideological State Apparatuses" from *Lenin and Philosophy and Other Essays*, trans. by Ben Brewster (1971). Copyright © 1981 by Monthly Review Press. Reprinted by permission of the Monthly Review Foundation.

Benedict Anderson: *Imagined Communities: Reflections on the Origin and Spread of Nationalism*. Copyright © 1983, 1991 by Benedict Anderson. Reprinted by permission of Verso, the imprint of New Left Books Ltd.

Gloria Anzaldúa: "La conciencia de la mestiza" from *Borderlands*/La Frontera: *The New Mestiza*. Copyright © 1987, 1999, 2007, 2012 by Gloria Anzaldúa. Reprinted by permission of Aunt Lute Books.

Hannah Arendt: "Truth and Politics" from *Between Past and Future*. Copyright © 1954, 1956, 1957, 1958, 1960, 1961, 1963, 1967, 1968 by Hannah Arendt. Used by permission of Viking Books, an imprint of Penguin Publishing Group, a division of Penguin Random House LLC. All rights reserved. Any third party use of this material, outside of this publication, is prohibited. Interested parties must apply directly to Penguin Random House LLC for permission. From *The Human Condition*. Copyright © 1958 by The University of Chicago. Reprinted by permission of the University of Chicago Press.

Aristotle: *Poetics*, trans. by James Hutton. Copyright © 1982 by W. W. Norton & Company, Inc. Used by permission of W. W. Norton & Company, Inc. From *On Rhetoric: A Theory of Civic Discourse* (2006), trans. and ed. by George A. Kennedy (2006), pp. 37–39, 47–50, 112–13, 197–99. Copyright © 2005 by Oxford University Press, Ltd. Used by permission of Oxford University Press USA.

Erich Auerbach: "Odysseus' Scar" from *Mimesis: The Representation of Reality in Western Literature*, trans. by Willard R. Trask. Copyright © 1953 by Princeton University Press. Copyright renewed 1981 by Princeton University Press. Reproduced with permission of Princeton University Press via the Copyright Clearance Center.

Augustine of Hippo: *On Christian Teaching*, trans. by R. P. H. Green (1997), Book 2, excerpts from pp. 30–33, 37–40, 43–46, and excerpts from Book 3, pp. 68–72, 75, 76, 87, 88. Used by permission of Oxford University Press.

J. L. Austin: "Performative Utterances" transcript of an unscripted talk delivered in the Third Programme of the BBC in 1956, reprinted in *Philosophical Papers*, 3rd ed. (Oxford University Press, 1979), pp. 233–52. Reprinted by permission of the Estate of J. L. Austin.

Mikhail M. Bakhtin: *The Dialogic Imagination: Four Essays*, ed. by Michael Holquist, trans. by Caryl Emerson and Michael Holquist. Copyright © 1981. By permission of the University of Texas Press.

Roland Barthes: "Photography and Electoral Appeal" from *Mythologies*, trans. by Annette Lavers. Translation copyright © 1972 by Jonathan Cape Ltd. Reprinted by permission of Hill and Wang, a division of Farrar, Straus and Giroux and Jonathan Cape c/o The Random House Group Limited. "From Work to Text" and "Death of the Author" from *Image/Music/Text*, trans. by Stephen Heath. English translation copyright © 1977 by Stephen Heath. Reprinted by permission of Hill and Wang, a division of Farrar, Straus and Giroux and Harper Collins Publishers Ltd. "The Reality Effect" from *The Rustle of Language*, trans. by Richard Howard. Translation copyright © 1986 by Farrar, Straus and Giroux, Inc. Reprinted by permission of Hill and Wang, a division of Farrar, Straus and Giroux.

Jean Baudrillard: "The Precession of Simulacra," trans. by Paul Foss, Paul Patton, and Phil Beitchman from *Simulations* (1983). Reprinted by permission of Semiotext(e).

Simone de Beauvoir: *The Second Sex*, trans. by Constance Borde and Sheila Malovany-Chevallier. Translation copyright © 2009 by Constance Borde and Sheila Malovany-Chevallier. Used by permission of Alfred A. Knopf, an imprint of the Knopf Doubleday Publishing Group, a division of Penguin Random House LLC. All rights reserved. Any third party use of this material, outside of this publication, is prohibited. Interested parties must apply directly to Penguin Random House LLC for permission. Rights in the British Commonwealth, excluding Canada, by permission of The Random House Group Limited. Published in Great Britain by Jonathan Cape.

Aphra Behn: "Epistle to the Reader" from *The Dutch Lover* from *The Works of Aphra Behn*, Vol. V, and "Preface" to *The Lucky Chance* from *The Works of Aphra Behn*, Vol. VII, ed. by Janet Todd. Copyright © 1996 by Ohio State University Press. Reprinted by permission of Ohio State University Press and Pickering & Chatto (Publishers), Ltd.

Walter Benjamin: "The Work of Art in the Age of Its Technological Reproducibility" from *Walter Benjamin: Selected Writings*, Vol. 4, 1938–40, ed. by Howard Eiland and Michael W. Jennings, trans. by Edmund Jephcott and Others. Cambridge, Mass.: The Belknap Press of Harvard University Press. Copyright © 2003 by The President and Fellows of Harvard College. Based on "The Work of Art in the Age of Mechanical Reproduction" from *Illuminations*, trans. by Harry Zohn. Copyright © 1956 by Suhrkamp Verlag, Frankfurt a. M. English translation copyright © 1968 and renewed 1996 by Houghton Mifflin Harcourt Publishing Company. Reprinted by permission of Harvard University Press, Houghton Mifflin Harcourt Publishing Company, and Writers House LLC, acting as agent for the author. All rights reserved.

Jane Bennett: "The Force of Things" from *Vibrant Matter*. Copyright © 2010 by Duke University Press. All rights reserved. Republished by permission of the copyright holder, www.dukeupress.edu.

Lauren Berlant and Michael Warner: "Sex in Public" from *Critical Inquiry*, vol. 24, no. 2 (Winter 1998), pp. 547–66. Copyright © 1998 by the University of Chicago. Reprinted by permission of the University of Chicago Press via the Copyright Clearance Center.

Stephen Best and Sharon Marcus: "Surface Reading: An Introduction" first published in *Representations*, 108 (Fall 2009). Copyright © 2009 by the Regents of the University of California. Reprinted by permission of the University of California Press via the Copyright Clearance Center.

Homi K. Bhabha: "The Commitment to Theory" from *Location of Culture*, 2nd ed. Copyright © 1994 by Homi K. Bhabha. Published by Routledge. Reproduced by permission of Taylor & Francis Books UK.

Harold Bloom: *The Anxiety of Influence: A Theory of Poetry*, 2nd ed. (1997), excerpts from pp. 5–16, 93–96. Copyright © 1997 by Oxford University Press, Inc. Used by permission of Oxford University Press USA.

Giovanni Boccaccio: "Genealogy of the Gentile Gods" from *Bocaccio on Poetry* (1956), trans. by Charles G. Osgood. Reprinted by permission of the Estate of Charles G. Osgood.

Ian Bogost: "The Rhetoric of Video Games" from *The Ecology of Games: Connecting Youth, Games and Learning*, ed. by Katie Salen Tekinbaş, pp. 117–39. Copyright © 2008 Massachusetts Institute of Technology. Used by permission of The MIT Press.

Susan Bordo: "The Body and the Reproduction of Femininity" from *Unbearable Weight: Feminism, Western Culture, and the Body*. Copyright © 2004 by the Regents of the University of California. Reprinted by permission of the publisher, the University of California Press.

Pierre Bourdieu: *Distinction: A Social Critique of the Judgment of Taste*, trans. by Richard Nice. Cambridge, Mass.: Harvard University Press. Copyright © 1984 by The President and Fellows of Harvard College and Taylor & Francis Books UK. Published in Great Britain by Routledge, Kegan, & Paul. Reprinted by permission of Harvard University Press and Taylor & Francis Books UK. From *The Rules of Art, Genesis and Structure of the Literary Field*, trans. by Susan Emanuel. Copyright © 1996 by Susan Emanuel. Copyright © 1996 by Polity Press. All right reserved. Used with the permission of Stanford University Press, www.sup.org and Polity Press Ltd.

Marc Bousquet: "The Waste Product of Graduate Education: Toward a Dictatorship of the Flexible" from *Social Text*, vol. 20, no.1, pp. 81–104. Copyright © 2002 by Marc Bousquet. All rights reserved. Republished by permission of the publisher, Duke University Press, www.dukeupress.edu.

Rosi Braidotti: *The Posthuman* (2013). Reprinted by permission of Polity Press Ltd.

Cleanth Brooks: "The Heresy of Paraphrase" from *The Well Wrought Urn*. Copyright © 1947 and renewed 1975 by Cleanth Brooks. Reprinted by permission of Houghton Mifflin Harcourt Publishing Company and The Estate of Cleanth Brooks. All rights reserved.

Judith Butler: *Gender Trouble: Feminism and the Subversion of Identity*. Copyright © 1989 by Routledge, Chapman & Hall. Republished by permission of Taylor & Francis Group LLC via the Copyright Clearance Center.

Rey Chow: *Sentimental Fabulations, Contemporary Chinese Films: Attachement in the Age of Global Visibility*. Copyright © 2007 by Columbia University Press. Reprinted with permission of the publisher.

Christine de Pizan: *The Book of the City of Ladies*, trans. by Earl Jeffrey Richards, pp. 3–5, 11–12, 16–18, and 153–55. Copyright © 1982, 1998 by Persea Books, Inc. Reprinted with the permission of Persea Books Inc. (New York), www.perseabooks.com. All rights reserved. "Christine's Reaction to Jean de Montreuil's Treatise on the *Roman de la Rose*" from *Debating the* Roman de la Rose: *A Critical Anthology*, trans. by Earl Jeffrey Richards, ed. by Christine McWebb. Used by permission of Taylor & Francis Group LLC via the Copyright Clearance Center.

Hélène Cixous: "The Laugh of the Medusa," trans. by Keith Cohen and Paula Cohen from *The Signs Reader: Women, Gender, and Scholarship*, ed. by Elizabeth K. Abel and Emily K. Abel. Copyright © 1983 by The University of Chicago. First published in *Signs*, vol. 1, no. 4 (Summer 1976), pp. 875–93. Reprinted by permission of The University of Chicago Press.

Samuel Taylor Coleridge: "Biographia Literaria, or, Biographical Sketches of My Literary Life and Opinions" from *The Collected Works of Samuel Taylor Coleridge*, Vol. 7, ed. by James Engell and W. Jackson Bate. Copyright © 1983 by Princeton University Press. Reproduced with permission of Princeton University Press via the Copyright Clearance Center.

Pierre Corneille: "Of the Three Unities" from *The Continental Model: Selected French Critical Essays of the Seventeenth Century*, trans. by Donald Schier, ed. by Scott Elledge and Donald Schier. Copyright © 1960 by the University of Minnesota. Copyright renewed 1988 by Scott Elledge and Donald Schier. Reprinted by permission of the University of Minnesota Press.

Hamid Dabashi: *The World of Persian Literary Humanism*. Cambridge, Mass.: Harvard University Press. Copyright © 2012 by The President and Fellows of Harvard College. Reprinted by permission of Harvard University Press.

Dante Alighieri: *The Convivio*, trans. by Richard H. Lansing. Copyright © 1990 by Richard H. Lansing. Reprinted by permission of Garland Publishing, Inc. From "The Letter to Can Grande," reprinted from *Literary Criticism of Dante Alighieri*, trans. and ed. by Robert S. Haller, by permission of the University of Nebraska Press. Copyright © 1977 by the University of Nebraska Press.

Lennard Davis: "Visualizing the Disabled Body: The Classical Nude and the Fragmented Torso" from *Enforcing Normalcy: Disability, Deafness, and the Body* (1995). Copyright © 1995 by Lennard J. Davis. Reprinted by permission of the publisher, Verso.

Gilles Deleuze and Félix Guattari: "Introduction: Rhizome" from *A Thousand Plateaus: Capitalism and Schizophrenia*, trans. by Brian Massumi. Copyright © 1987 by the University of Minnesota Press. Originally published in *Mille Plateaux*, Vol. 2 of *Capitalisme et schizophrénie*. Copyright © 1980 by Les Éditions de Minuit, Paris. Reprinted by permission of the University of Minnesota Press and Bloomsbury Academic, an imprint of Bloomsbury Publishing Plc. "What Is a Minor Literature?" from *Kafka: Toward a Minor Literature*, trans. by Dana Polan (1986). Copyright © 1986 by the University of Minnesota. Originally published in *Kafka: Pour une littérature mineure*. Copyright © 1975 by Les Éditions de Minuit, Paris.

Paul de Man: "Semiology and Rhetoric" from *diacritics* 3.3 (1973), 27–33. Copyright © 1973 Diacritics, Inc. Reprinted with permission of Johns Hopkins University Press.

Jacques Derrida: *The Animal That Therefore I Am*, trans. by David Wills, ed. by Marie-Louise Mallet. Copyright © 2008 by Fordham University Press. Reprinted by permission of Fordham University Press. Excerpt from "Plato's Pharmacy" from *Dissemination*, trans. by Barbara Johnson. Copyright © 1981 by The University of Chicago. Reprinted by permission of the University of Chicago Press. From *Specters of Marx: The State of Debt, the Work of Mourning, and the New International*, trans. by Peggy Kamuf. Reprinted with permission of Routledge via the Copyright Clearance Center.

Joachim du Bellay: "The Defense and Enrichment of the French Language" from *The Regrets, with the Antiquities of Rome, Three Latin Elegies, and the Defense and Enrichment of the French*

Language: A Bilingual Edition, trans. and ed. by Richard Helgerson, pp. 332–38; 370–76 [even pages only]. Copyright © 2006 by the University of Pennsylvania Press. Reprinted with permission of the University of Pennsylvania Press.

W. E. B. Du Bois: "Criteria of Negro Art." The publisher wishes to thank the Crisis Publishing Co., Inc., the publisher of the National Association for the Advancement of Colored People, for the use of this material first published in the October 1926 issue of *Crisis Magazine*. From *The Souls of Black Folk*, introduction by Donald B. Gibson, notes by Monica E. Elbert (Penguin Classics, 1989). Copyright © The Estate of W. E. B. Du Bois 1903. Introduction copyright © Viking Penguin, a division of Penguin Books USA Inc., 1989. Reproduced by permission of Penguin Books Ltd.

Terry Eagleton: "The Rise of English" from *Literary Theory: An Introduction*. Copyright © 1983, 1996, 2008 by Terry Eagleton. Reprinted by permission of the publishers, the University of Minnesota Press and John Wiley & Sons Ltd. via PLSclear. From *Culture and the Death of God* (2014). Copyright © 2014 by Terry Eagleton. Reprinted by permission of the publisher, Yale University Press.

T. S. Eliot: "Tradition and the Individual Talent" and "The Metaphysical Poets" from *Selected Essays: 1917–1932*. Reprinted by permission of Faber and Faber Ltd.

Frantz Fanon: *Black Skin, White Masks*, trans. by Charles Lam Markmann. Copyright © 1967 by Grove/Atlantic, Inc. Used by permission of Grove/Atlantic, Inc. Any third party use of this material, outside of this publication, is prohibited. From *The Wretched of the Earth*, trans. by Constance Farrington. English translation copyright © 1963 by Présence Africaine. Used by permission of Grove/Atlantic, Inc. Any third party use of this material, outside of this publication, is prohibited.

Stanley E. Fish: *Is There a Text in This Class? The Authority of Interpretive Communities*. Cambridge, Mass.: Harvard University Press. Copyright © 1980 by The President and Fellows of Harvard College. Reprinted by permission of Harvard University Press.

Michel Foucault: *Discipline and Punish: The Birth of the Prison*. English translation copyright © 1977 by Alan Sheridan (New York: Pantheon). Originally published in French as *Surveiller et punir: Naissance de la prison*. Copyright © 1975 by Éditions Gallimard. Reprinted by permission of Georges Borchardt, Inc., on behalf of Éditions Gallimard and Penguin Books Ltd. "What Is an Author" from *Language, Counter-Memory, Practice: Selected Essays and Interviews*, trans. by Donald F. Bouchard and Sherry Simon, ed. by Donald F. Bouchard. Copyright © 1977 by Cornell University. Used by permission of the publisher, Cornell University Press. From *The History of Sexuality, Vol. 1: An Introduction*, trans. by Robert Hurley. Translation copyright © 1978 by Random House. Originally published in French as *La volonte de savoir*. Copyright © 1976 by Éditions Gallimard. Reprinted by permission of Georges Borchardt, Inc. for Éditions Gallimard and Penguin Books Ltd. From *Society Must Be Defended*, trans. by David Macey. Copyright © 1997 by Éditions de Seuil/Gallimard. Translation copyright © 2003 by David Macey. Introduction copyright © 2003 by Arnold I. Davidson. Copyright © 2003 by Michel Foucault. Reprinted by permission of St. Martin's Press and Penguin Books Ltd. All rights reserved.

Sigmund Freud: "The Interpretation of Dreams" from *The Interpretation of Dreams* (2010), trans. by James Strachey. Reproduced with permission of Basic Books, a member of the Perseus Books Group via the Copyright Clearance Center. "Fetishism," trans. by Joan Rivière, from *Collected Papers*, Vol. 5, ed. by James Strachey, copyright © 1959. Reprinted by permission of Basic Books, an imprint of Perseus Books, LLC, a subsidiary of Hachette Books Group, Inc. "The Uncanny," trans. by Alix Strachey from *Collected Papers*, Vol. 4, ed. by James Strachey, copyright © 1959. Reprinted by permission of Basic Books, an imprint of Perseus Books, LLC, a subsidiary of Hachette Book Group, Inc. All essays are collected in *The Standard Edition of the Complete Psychological Works of Sigmund Freud*, trans. and ed. by James Strachey, published by Hogarth Press. World rights excluding the USA for all essays by permission of The Random House Group Limited.

Northrop Frye: "The Archetypes of Literature" first published in *The Kenyon Review*, vol. 13, no. 1 (Winter 1951), pp. 92–110. Copyright © The Kenyon Review. Reprinted by permission of The Kenyon Review.

Henry Louis Gates Jr.: "Talking Black," originally published in *Loose Cannons: Notes on the Culture Wars*. Copyright © 1992 by Henry Louis Gates Jr. All rights reserved. Reprinted by permission of Oxford University Press USA and the author.

Sandra M. Gilbert and Susan Gubar: *The Madwoman in the Attic: The Woman Writer and the Nineteenth-Century Literary Imagination*, published by Yale University Press. Copyright © 1979 by Yale University. Copyright © 1984 by Sandra M. Gilbert and Susan Gubar. Reprinted by permission of the publisher.

Paul Gilroy: "The Black Atlantic as a Counterculture of Modernity" from *The Black Atlantic* (Verso, 1993). Copyright © 1993 by Paul Gilroy. Reprinted by permission of the author.

Gorgias of Leontini: "Encomium of Helen" from *Early Greek Political Thought*, trans. and ed. by Michael Gagarin and Paul Woodruff. Copyright © 1995 by Cambridge University Press. Reprinted with the permission of Cambridge University Press.

Gerald Graff: "Taking Cover in Coverage" from *Profession* 86, pp. 41–45. Reprinted by permission of the Modern Language Association of America.

Antonio Gramsci: "The Formation of the Intellectuals" from *Selections for the Prison Notebooks*, trans. and ed. by Quintin Hoare and Geoffrey Nowell Smith. Copyright © 1971. Reprinted by permission of International Publishers Company.

Stephen J. Greenblatt: "Resonance and Wonder" from *Learning to Curse: Essays in Early Modern Culture*. Copyright © 1990 by Routledge, Chapman and Hall, Inc. Reprinted by permission of the Taylor & Francis Group LLC via the Copyright Clearance Center.

Jürgen Habermas: "Modernity—An Incomplete Project" was delivered as a James Lecture of the New York Institute for the Humanities at New York University on March 5, 1991. Published as "Modernity versus Postmodernity," trans. by Seyla Ben-Habib, in *New German Critique* 22 (Winter 1981), pp. 3–14. Copyright © 1981 by New German Critique, Inc. All rights reserved. Republished by permission of the copyright holder and the present publisher, Duke University Press, www.dukeupress.edu. "The Public Sphere: An Encyclopedia Article," trans. by Sara Lennox and Frank Lennox, from *New German Critique* 3 (Autumn 1974), pp. 49–55. Copyright © 1974 by New German Critique, Inc. All rights reserved. Republished by permission of the copyright holder and the present publisher, Duke University Press, www.dukeupress.edu.

Judith Jack Halberstam: "An Introduction to Female Sexuality" from *Female Masculinity*, pp. 1–29; 279–82. Copyright © 1998 by Duke University Press. All rights reserved. Republished by permission of the copyright holder and publisher, www.dukeupress.edu.

Stuart Hall: "Cultural Studies and Its Theoretical Legacies" from *Cultural Studies*, ed. by Lawrence Grossberg et al. Copyright ©1992 by Routledge, Taylor & Francis Inc. Published by Routledge. Reproduced by permission of Taylor & Francis Books UK.

Donna Haraway: "A Cyborg Manifesto: Science, Technology, and Socialist-Feminism in the Late Twentieth Century" from *Manifestly Haraway*, published by the University of Minnesota Press. Copyright © 2016 by Donna J. Haraway. Previously published as "A Manifesto for Cyborgs: Science, Technology, and Socialist Feminism in the 1980s" in *Socialist Review*, no. 80 (1985). Reprinted by permission of the University of Minnesota Press. Excerpts from *The Companion Species Manifesto: Dogs, People, and Significant Otherness* (2003) are reprinted by permission of Prickly Paradigm Press.

Michael Hardt and Antonio Negri: *Empire*. Cambridge, Mass.: Harvard University Press. Copyright © 2000 by The President and Fellows of Harvard College. Reprinted by permission of Harvard University Press.

David Harvey: *A Brief History of Neoliberalism*, pp. 1–4; 168–72 (2005). Copyright © 2005 by David Harvey. By permission of Oxford University Press.

Friedrich A. Hayek: "Equality, Value, and Merit" from *The Constitution of Liberty*, ed. by Ronald Hamowy. Copyright © 1960, 2011 by the University of Chicago. Reprinted by permission of the University of Chicago Press and Taylor & Francis Books UK. Published in Great Britain by Routledge.

N. Katherine Hayles: "How We Read: Close, Hyper, Machine" from *ADE Bulletin*, 2010, #150, reprinted by permission of the Association of Departments of English, a subsidiary of the Modern Language Association of America.

Dick Hebdige: "Subculture: The Unnatural Break" from *Subculture: The Meaning of Style*. Copyright © 1979 by Dick Hebdige. Published by Routledge in 1988. Reproduced by permission of Taylor & Francis Books UK.

Georg Wilhelm Friedrich Hegel: *Phenomenology of Spirit*, trans. by A. V. Miller (1997), pp. 111–19. By permission of Oxford University Press. From *Hegel's Aesthetic: Lectures on Fine Art*, Vol. I (1975), trans. and ed. by T. M. Knox, pp. 25–32; 75–81. By permission of Oxford University Press.

Martin Heidegger: *Poetry, Language, Thought*. Translations and Introduction by Albert Hofstadter. Copyright © 1971 by Martin Heidegger. Reprinted by permission of HarperCollins Publishers.

David Herman: "Narrative Theory after the Second Cognitive Revolution" from *Introduction to Cognitive Cultural Studies*, ed. by Lisa Zunshine, pp. 155–75. Copyright © 2010 Johns Hopkins University Press. Reprinted with permission of Johns Hopkins University Press.

bell hooks: "Postmodern Blackness" from *Yearning: Race, Gender and Cultural Politics* (1990) is reprinted by permission of the author.

Horace: "To the Pisos: Horace, De *Arte Poetica*," from *The Poetry of Criticism: Horace*, Epistles II *and* Ars Poetica, trans. and ed. by Ross S. Kilpatrick, pp. 72–83 (Edmonton: The University of Alberta Press, 1990). Reprinted by permission of the publisher.

House Group Limited. This English translation © 1993 by Jonathan Cape Limited. Published in Great Britain by Jonathan Cape.

Li Zehou: *Four Essays on Aesthetics: Toward a Global View* by Li Zehou and Jane Cauvel. Reproduced with permission of Lexington Books via the Copyright Clearance Center.

Longinus: "On Sublimity" from *Ancient Literary Criticism: The Principal Literary Texts in New Translations*, trans. by D. A. Russell, ed. by D. A. Russell and M. Winterbottom (1972), pp. 462–63, 464–68, 472–74, 475–77, 479–80, 481–82. By permission of Oxford University Press.

György Lukács: *The Historical Novel*, trans. by Hannah Mitchell and Stanley Mitchell. Copyright © 1962 by Merlin Press Limited. Reprinted by permission of Merlin Press Ltd.

Jean-François Lyotard: "Defining the Postmodern" from *Postmodernism, ICA Documents 4*, 1986, ed. by Lisa Appignanesi. Reprinted by permission of the Estate of Jean-François Lyotard.

Moses Maimonides: *The Guide of the Perplexed*, Vol. 1, trans. by Shlomo Pines. Copyright © 1963 by The University of Chicago. Reprinted by permission of the University of Chicago Press.

Karl Marx: "Grundrisse" from *Grundrisse: Foundations of the Critique of Political Economy*, trans. by Martin Nicolaus (Penguin Classics, 1993). Reprinted by permission of New Left Review.

Karl Marx and Friedrich Engels: Selections from *The Marx-Engels Reader*, 2nd ed., ed. by Robert C. Tucker. Copyright © 1978, 1972 by W. W. Norton & Company, Inc.

Giacopo Mazzoni: "Introduction" and "Summary" from *On the Defense of the Comedy of Dante*, trans. by Robert Montgomery (Gainesville: University Press of Florida, 1983). Reprinted with permission of the University Press of Florida.

Mark McGurl: "The Program Era: Pluralisms of Postwar American Fiction" from *Critical Inquiry* 32 (Autumn 2005). Copyright © 2005 by the University of Chicago. Reprinted by permission of the publisher the University of Chicago Press via the Copyright Clearance Center.

Franco Moretti: "Graphs" from *Graphs, Maps, Trees: Abstract Models for a Literary History*. Copyright © 2005 by Franco Moretti. Reprinted by permission of Verso, the imprint of New Left Books Ltd.

Toni Morrison: "Unspeakable Things Unspoken: The Afro-American Presence in American Literature" from *Michigan Quarterly Review*, vol. 28, no. 1. Copyright © 1988 by Toni Morrison. Used by permission. All rights reserved.

Timothy Morton: *The Ecological Thought*. Cambridge, Mass.: Harvard University Press. Copyright © 2010 by The President and Fellows of Harvard College.

Laura Mulvey: "Visual Pleasure and Narrative Cinema" published in *Screen* 16.3 (Autumn 1975), pp. 6–18. By permission of Oxford University Press via the Copyright Clearance Center.

C. D. Narasimhaiah: "Towards the Formulation of a Common Poetic for Indian Literatures Today" from *A Common Poetic for Indian Literature* (1984) by C. D. Narasimhaiah and C. N. Srinath. Reprinted by permission of C. N. Srinath.

Alondra Nelson: "AfroFuturism: Past-Future Visions" originally published by Colorlines.com, *Colorlines Magazine*, April 30, 2000. Reprinted by permission of the publisher, Race Forward.

Sianne Ngai: *Ugly Feelings*. Cambridge, Mass.: Harvard University Press. Copyright © 2005 by The President and Fellows of Harvard College. Reprinted by permission of Harvard University Press.

Ngugi wa Thiong'o, Taban Lo Liyong, and Henry Owuor-Anyumba: "On the Abolition of the English Department" from *Homecoming: Essays on African American and Caribbean Literature, Culture and Politics* by Ngugi wa Thiong'o. Copyright © 1972 by Ngugi wa Thiong'o. Reprinted by permission of Pearson Education Ltd.

Friedrich Nietzsche: "On Truth and Lying in a Moral Sense" and "The Birth of Tragedy" from *The Birth of Tragedy and Other Writings*, trans. by Ronald Speirs, ed. by Raymond Geuss. Copyright © 1999 by Cambridge University Press. Reprinted by permission of Cambridge University Press.

Rob Nixon: "The Anthropocene: The Promise and Pitfalls of an Epochal Idea" published in *Edge Effects*, November 6, 2014. Reprinted by permission of Edge Effects c/o the Center for Culture, History, and Environment. From *Slow Violence and the Environmentalism of the Poor*. Cambridge, Mass.: Harvard University Press. Copyright © 2011 by The President and Fellows of Harvard College. Reprinted by permission of Harvard University Press.

Martha C. Nussbaum: *Cultivating Humanity: A Classical Defense of Reform in Liberal Education*. Cambridge, Mass.: Harvard University Press. Copyright © 1997 by The President and Fellows of Harvard College. Reprinted by permission of Harvard University Press.

Richard Ohmann: "The Shaping of a Canon: U.S. Fiction, 1960–1975" from *Politics of Letters*. Copyright © 1987 by Richard Ohmann. Published by Wesleyan University Press. Used by permission.

Kelly Oliver: "Witnessing and Testimony" from *Parallax*, vol. 10, no. 1 (2004). Reprinted by permission of the publisher Taylor & Francis Ltd. via the Copyright Clearance Center, www.tandfonline.com.

Walter Pater: "Preface" and "Conclusion" from *The Renaissance: Studies in Art and Poetry.* Copyright © 1980 by the Regents of the University of California. Reprinted by permission of the publisher, the University of California Press.

Plato: *Plato: Ion and Hippias Major,* trans. by Paul Woodruff. Copyright © 1983 by Hackett Publishing Company. Also published in *Complete Works*, ed. by John Cooper. Reprinted by permission of Hackett Publishing Company, Inc. All rights reserved. From *Phaedrus* (2002), trans. by Robin Waterfield, pp. 67–75, with notes pp. 102–5. By permission of Oxford University Press. From *The Republic*, trans. by Richard W. Sterling and William C. Scott. Copyright © 1985 by Richard W. Sterling and William C. Scott. Used by permission of W. W. Norton & Company, Inc.

John Crowe Ransom: "Criticism, Inc." from *The World's Body* is reprinted with the permission of Scribner, a division of Simon & Schuster, Inc. Copyright © 1938 by Charles Scribner's Sons. Copyright renewed 1966 by John Crowe Ransom. All rights reserved.

Adrienne Rich: "Compulsory Heterosexuality and Lesbian Existence" from *Blood, Bread, and Poetry: Selected Prose 1979–1985.* Copyright © 1986 by Adrienne Rich. Used by permission of W. W. Norton & Company, Inc.

Andrew Ross: "The Mental Labor Problem" from *Low Pay, High Profile: The Global Push for Fair Labor.* Copyright © 2004 by Andrew Ross. Reprinted by permission of The New Press, www.thenewpress.com.

Gayle Rubin: "Thinking Sex: Notes for a Radical Theory of the Politics of Sexuality" from *Deviations*, text excerpts and two figures (pp. 137–81). Copyright © 2012 by Gayle S. Rubin. All rights reserved. Republished by permission of the publisher, Duke University Press, www.dukeupress.edu.

Edward W. Said: "Jane Austen and Empire" and "Consolidated Vision" from *Culture and Imperialism.* Copyright © 1993 by Edward W. Said. Used by permission of Alfred A. Knopf, an imprint of the Knopf Doubleday Publishing Group, a division of Penguin Random House LLC. All rights reserved. Any third party use of this material, outside of this publication, is prohibited. Interested parties must apply directly to Penguin Random House LLC for permission. Rights in the British Commonwealth, excluding Canada, by permission of The Wylie Agency LLC. From *Orientalism.* Copyright © 1978 by Edward W. Said. Used by permission of Pantheon Books, an imprint of the Knopf Doubleday Publishing Group, a division of Penguin Random House LLC. All rights reserved. Any third party use of this material, outside of this publication, is prohibited. Interested parties must apply directly to Penguin Random House LLC for permission.

Ferdinand de Saussure: *Course in General Linguistics*, trans. by Wade Baskin. Copyright © 1966 by The Philosophical Library, Inc. Reprinted by permission of The Philosophical Library, Inc., New York.

Friedrich von Schiller: *On the Aesthetic Education of Man in a Series of Letters* (1967), trans. and ed. by E. M. Wilkinson and L. A. Willoughby, pp. 6–9, 31–43, 54–61. By permission of Oxford University Press.

Friedrich Schleiermacher: "The Hermeneutics: Outline of the 1819 Lectures" from *New Literary History*, vol. 10, no. 1 (1978), pp. 1–16, trans. by Jan Wojcik and Roland Hass. Copyright © 1978 New Literary History, The University of Virginia. Reprinted with permission of Johns Hopkins University Press.

Eve Kosofsky Sedgwick: "Homosocial Desire" and "Introduction" from *Between Men: English Literature and Male Homosocial Desire.* Copyright © 1985 by Columbia University Press. Reprinted with permission of Columbia University Publisher. "Axiom 2" and "Introduction: Axiomatic" from *Epistemology of the Closet.* Copyright © 1990 by the Regents of the University of California. Reprinted by permission of the publisher, the University of California Press.

Percy Bysshe Shelley: "A Defence of Poetry" from *Shelley's Poetry and Prose, Norton Critical Edition*, ed. by Donald Reiman and Sharon Powers. Copyright © 1977 by Donald H. Reiman and Sharon B. Powers. Used by permission of W. W. Norton & Company, Inc.

Susan Sontag: "Against Interpretation" from *Against Interpretation* by Susan Sontag. Copyright © 1964, 1966, renewed 1994 by Susan Sontag. Reprinted by permission of Farrar, Straus and Giroux and Penguin Books Ltd. First published by Penguin Books Ltd. in 1961 and by Penguin Classics in 2009. Copyright © 1961, 1962, 1963, 1964, 1965, 1966 by Susan Sontag.

Baruch Spinoza: "Of the Interpretation of Scripture" from *Theological-Political Treatise*, trans. by Samuel Shirley. Translation copyright © 1991 by E. J. Brill. Reprinted by permission of Brill N. V.

Gayatri Chakravorty Spivak: *A Critique of Postcolonial Reason: Toward a History of the Vanishing Present.* Cambridge, Mass.: Harvard University Press. Copyright © 1999 by The President and Fellows of Harvard College. Reprinted by permission of Harvard University Press.

Germaine Necker de Staël: "Essay on Fictions" and "On Literature Considered in Its Relationship to Social Institutions" from *An Extraordinary Woman: Selected Writings of Germaine de Staël*, trans. and ed. by Vivian Folkenflik. Copyright © 1987 by Columbia University Press.

Author/Title Index